COMICS BUYER'S GUIDE

2010 16th EDITION

COMIC BOOK CHECKLIST & PRICE GUIDE

1961- PRESENT

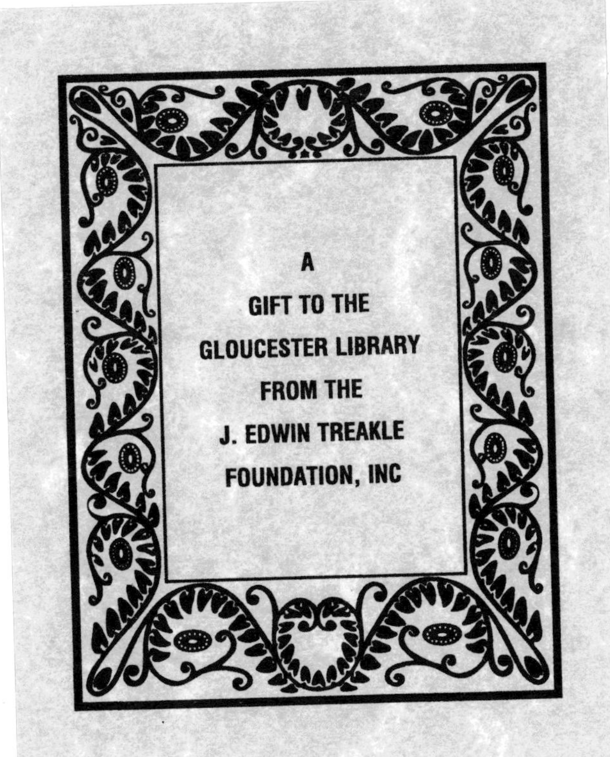
A
GIFT TO THE
GLOUCESTER LIBRARY
FROM THE
J. EDWIN TREAKLE
FOUNDATION, INC

Maggie Thompson • Brent Frankenhoff • Peter Bickford

Published by

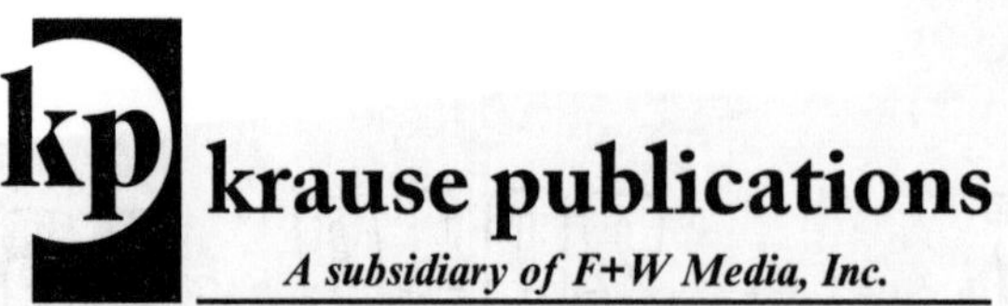

700 East State Street • Iola, WI 54990-0001
715-445-2214 • 888-457-2873
www.krausebooks.com

Our toll-free number to place an order or obtain a free catalog is (800) 258-0929.

ISSN: 1082-5649
ISBN-13: 978-1-4402-0386-2
ISBN-10: 1-4402-0386-5

Edited by:
Brent Frankenhoff
Maggie Thompson

Designed by:
Stacy Bloch
Sandi Morrison
Shawn Williams

Cover image by Marlin Shoop and Jean-Francois Beaulieu. Characters depicted ™ and © DC Comics Used with permission.
Cover art coordination by Marc Patten and Destination Entertainment.

Printed in the United States of America

Contents

Price Guide:

COMICS! COMICS! COMICS!

Thanks, first to **you**, for buying this book — and also to the many people who helped us put this book together. As ever, there are so many of them to thank that we're bound to miss a few. To anyone who should be thanked but isn't (you know who you are): We're sorry, and you know we couldn't have done this without you.

First and foremost, without the copious contributions of ***ComicBase*** developer Peter Bickford, this edition simply wouldn't exist. While his research has often paralleled our own, he has also obtained information to which we didn't have access, just as our information has added many titles to his computerized comics database program. This edition contains a number of fresh updates obtained through various sources, including many of ComicBase's users.

That brings us to the publishers and individual creators who provided copies of their titles, so that we could maintain a database based on actually published material. We thank them all and encourage others to do the same.

Thanks also to the readers of our previous editions who have been providing additional data on their favorite titles. This year again, special thanks go to Carl Tietz, Perry Parsons, and Harold Crump, who provided an ongoing stream of information to make our compendium of information even more detailed and precise. Thanks as well continue to go to Nick Pope, James Jobe, Byron Glass, and Andrew Rathbun, who helped us compile the most complete listing ever of Marvel and DC Whitman variants.

This is the sixth time we've had original art on the cover of this work: Thanks go to DC and artist Dick Giordano for use of it — and to Marc Patten and Destination Entertainment for helping make it all happen.

Thanks go, as well, to our own behind-the-scenes people, including: Tammy Kuhnle and Steve Duberstein, computer services; Sandi Morrison and Stacy Bloch in our book production department; graphic designers Heidi Zastrow and Shawn Williams; book team leader Kristine Manty; and the entire antiques and collectibles division at Krause Publications.

Most of all, we acknowledge the work of Don Thompson, who nursed this project through the last 11 years of his life. We miss you, Don.

And, again, we thank you all.

Maggie Thompson
Brent Frankenhoff
Iola, Wisconsin
September 4, 2009

SAVE YOUR COMICS!

We see it all the time: Rare and valuable comics, going for pennies on the dollar in estate sales. Or rotting away, stuffed in corners in wet basements.

Because most people don't know what they have, whether their comics are rare and valuable — or whether they're plentiful and worth less (though not worth*less*). And because most people don't know how best to take care of the comics they have.

But you won't have that problem — ***The CBG Comic Book Checklist & Price Guide*** is here to help.

We're the people behind ***Comics Buyer's Guide***, the world's longest-running magazine about comics. Started in 1971, it's been published continuously and passed the 1,650-issue mark near the end of 2008. We've maintained a price guide since the early 1980s — and, in the early 1990s, we published the first edition of this ***Checklist*** as both a price guide and a collectors' utility for comics published after 1960.

Since then, we've added to the line with the mammoth ***CBG Standard Catalog of Comic Books***, which includes everything that's in this volume plus story titles, circulation figures, and comics from the 1930s, 1940s, and 1950s. Of course, that's a monster of a book — the latest print edition was 1,624 pages and a DVD-ROM edition is now available with more than 3,500 "virtual" pages in full color — so the ***Checklist*** maintains its value as a quick and handy reference for the comics you're most likely to find. (It's also a lot easier to carry around to conventions and stores!) So the role of the ***Checklist*** has evolved somewhat — but it's still intended to function in a number of fashions.

There's more than one way to use it.

You can use it as a "have" list, in which you maintain an inventory of the comics you're collecting. (Make an "X" in the box for each one you have or use your own symbols indicating what you please, including condition, in the open box. You can then see at a glance what you're still looking for of a title you want to collect.)

You can use it as a guide to show prices you can expect to pay for items, if you look for them in comics shops throughout the country, online, or at conventions. The prices listed are arrived at by surveying comics shops, online sales, convention sales, auctions, and mail-order houses.

With that information, our price guide reflects what a smart person with those choices would be willing to pay for a given issue.

You can use it as a guide for value, when you're buying or trading items.

And you can carry it with you in your comics storage box, because it's sized to fit in a comics box.

NEAR MINT

(Abbreviated **NM**)
This is a nearly perfect comic book.
Its cover shows barely perceptible signs of wear. Its spine is tight, and its cover has only minor loss of luster and only minor printing defects. Some discoloration is acceptable in older comics — as are signs of aging.
Near Mint prices are what are listed in this guide.
[The term for this grade is the same one used for CGC's 9.4 grade.]

Our full-color photo grading guide can be found on Page 417!

Condition is vital.

Whether you're buying or selling comic books, one of the most important factors in setting the price is the condition of the material.

A scuffed, torn "reading copy" (that is, one that is suitable for reading but not for getting high prices at resale) will bring only a fraction of the price of a copy of the same issue which looks as though it has just come off the newsstand.

Picky collectors will even go through all the copies on a newsstand so as to buy the one in best condition. [Even a so-called "newsstand mint" copy of *Fantastic Four* #1 may have what is called "Marvel chipping" (a frayed right edge), since many of those early-'60s issues were badly cut by the printer.]

On the other hand, beat-up copies can provide bargains for collectors whose primary focus is *reading* the comic-book story. The same goes for reprints of comics which would otherwise be hard to find.

In fact, you may find prices on poor-condition copies even lower than the prices in this guide, depending on the attitude of the seller. It's a good time to get into collecting comics for the *fun* of it.

A major change in the comics-collecting world, CGC grading, has meant a huge jump in prices for certain hotly collected issues in almost-perfect condition. The third-party graders of Certified Guaranty Company evaluate the condition of submitted copies and then encapsulate the graded issue in a labeled container. Because of the independent nature of the process and the reliability of the evaluating team, confidence in buying such items has meant a premium over the standard price in that condition.

For example, at press time, a CGC 9.4 (Near Mint) is bringing at auction *four times* our Near Mint price for non-encapsulated comics. More information on the company can be found at its website: *www.cgccomics.com*.

Our price guide is constantly evolving.

For comics, maybe the right word is "mutating."

Each year, the most important changes in this guide from previous editions are, of course, the addition of countless chunks of data that we have compiled from consulting physical copies of the issues in question. (Thanks again to the many who helped.)

We've also provided more than 2,000 cover photos with enough additional information, we hope, to whet a collector's appetite.

We want to provide the most accurate picture of what you, as a customer, can expect to pay for comics when you walk into a shop or comics convention with your want list.

Answers for readers who are NEW TO COMICS!

Readers have been kind enough to ask many questions about our price guide. To help you make the best use of this volume, we're answering many of them here (and we're answering questions you didn't ask, too, in an attempt to provide more information than you can possibly use).

Why do we need a price guide at all?

We've spent nearly 30 years developing a guide so that buyers and sellers of back issues will have help knowing what a consumer with various buying choices can expect to pay, if he's looking — for example — for that issue that will complete his run of the two DC series of *Shade the Changing Man*. The collector will find that even the highest-priced issue in the best condition probably won't cost more than about $4 — and that's the sort of information that can motivate a casual reader to become a collector.

Moreover, we try to provide helpful information to people who purchase it in order to have a (yes) guide to buying comics. Pricing information is just *part* of what we offer. In fact, we are increasingly intrigued by the more detailed information you'll find in this book, including character appearances and publishing anomalies.

Why can't I find a title in your list?

We're working constantly to expand the listings themselves and increase the information on those we already provide. Check out what we have included, and — if you have something we're not listing — please let us know the details!

We need to know the information as given in the indicia of the issue (that's the tiny print, usually on the first few pages, that gives the publishing information): the full title, the number, and the issue month and year — and the U.S. price given on the cover.

If you find work by a creator on our abbreviations list that we haven't noted in this guide, please include that information.

If there's a significant event (especially as given in the abbreviations list), please include that, too.

This is an *annual* volume designed to consolidate our information — but our monthly ***Comics Buyer's Guide*** runs updated information (with commentary on recent sales activity), and we add to the data constantly.

Check, too, on whether you're looking up the title as it appears in the indicia. For example, we list *Vampire Lestat*, not *Anne Rice's The Vampire Lestat*; we list *Mack Bolan: The Executioner*, not *Don Pendleton's Mack Bolan: The Executioner.* Many Marvel titles have adjectives. *Hulk*, for example, is listed as *Incredible Hulk*.

What's in this book?

This Silver Age and more recent price guide began as a quarterly update of activity in comics published since 1961, as reflected in prices comics shops were likely to charge. Moreover, the focus was pretty much limited to Silver Age super-hero titles — in fact, Silver Age super-hero titles *that were being published when the price guide began*. This meant that such titles as *OMAC*, a title that starred a super-hero but was not still being published by 1983, didn't get listed in that earliest edition. It also meant that so-called "funny animal" titles, "war" titles, and the like were not included.

However, once the listings were begun (not by ***Comics Buyer's Guide*** staff, incidentally; the material was started for another publication), Don Thompson took over the compilation. From that point, every effort was made to include every issue of every comic book received in the office. However, since the entries were not on a database and had to be compressed to fit the space available, annotation, dates, and original prices were not usually part of the listing. On the other hand (and because of Don's care, once he took over the project), material which was often overlooked by other reference publishers has been listed from the beginning in the **CBG** listings. *Concrete* and *Teenage Mutant Ninja Turtles*, for example, were first listed in **CBG**'s price listings.

And we continue to fill in remaining information whenever we get it. Our cooperative agreement with *ComicBase* has led to the inclusion of hundreds of new titles and issues, as well as a wealth of variant editions.

What is the "Silver Age?"

Comic-book collectors divide the history of comics into the "Golden Age" and the "Silver Age." "Golden Age" indicates the first era of comic-book production — the '30s and '40s. It was a time of incredible creation in the field, when such characters as Superman and Batman first appeared. It's the era *before* material in this price guide was published.

"Silver Age" is used to indicate a period of comic-book production of slightly less (nostalgic?) luster than that of the Golden Age. It is usually considered to have begun with the publication of the first revival of a '40s super-hero: the appearance of The Flash in *Showcase* #4 (Sep-Oct 1956). However, that was a lone appearance at the time, so this price guide concentrates on titles from the time Marvel reentered the super-hero field with the publication of *Fantastic Four* #1 (1961).

There are additional comics ages, but discussion of those is beyond the scope of this piece.

This guide lists #8 and #10. Where's #9?

We haven't seen a copy and can't verify its existence. There was a time when comics collectors could safely assume that issue numbers would run in normal sequence, when no numbers were skipped and when there were no special numbers to confuse completists. That's not the case any more. What we need from those who want to help add to our information is confirmation that an item has *actually been published.*

This guide *does* include information on published material that was not widely distributed. Eternity's *Uncensored Mouse* #2, for example, was pulled from distribution after legal problems with The Walt Disney Company — but copies *do* exist. So few transactions involve it, however, that retailers have not yet established a standard price for the item.

So do you own all these comics?

No, many publishers and collectors have helped us over the years by sending photocopies of indicia, records of publication, annotations, and the like — all of which has permitted us to provide collectors with more information every year. What *ComicBase* and we cannot do — and *do* not do — is pull information from other price guides or from announcements of what is *scheduled* for publication. The former would not be proper; the latter leads to errors — the sort of errors that have been known to become imbedded in some price guides' information files.

This is also why information sometimes seems varied. Every effort has been made to make the notations consistent, but this list has more than 100,000 individual issues coordinated between *ComicBase* and **CBG**, so this can be an arduous task. Nevertheless, we're whittling away at problems between issues of ***Comics Buyer's Guide*** and assorted other projects.

Why do some of your listings say (first series), (second series), etc., while others have (Vol. 1), (Vol. 2), and so on? Is there a difference?

Although publishers may begin a series again at #1, they often don't update the volume number in the indicia, which leads to the (first series) and (second series) notations. If the volume number changes (and it's a clear change, as in the case of Marvel's "Heroes Reborn" and "Heroes Return" title restarts), that is what differentiates the series.

On the other hand, when the volume number changes each year (as was the case with some early Silver Age material) but the series number is ongoing in sequence (Vol. 2, #21), then we don't note that change.

Marvel's return to original numbering for *Fantastic Four* and *Amazing Spider-Man* in mid-2003 has caused both titles' later listings, beginning with #500 for each, to revert to the respective title's first volume. To help show where the issues from later volumes of those series fall in sequences, we've added parenthetical notations to the original numbers like this: 1 (442).

I've heard some of my squarebound comics referred to variously as "bookshelf format," "prestige format," and "Dark Knight format." What's the difference?

Various formats — usually reserved for special projects (mini-series and one-shots) — have different names, depending on the publisher. We use the term "prestige format" generically to indicate a fancier package than the average comic book. Marvel refers to some titles in upscale formats as "bookshelf format," whereas DC initially solicited some of its titles in the format of *Batman: The Dark Knight* as "Dark Knight format." Details of fancy formats can be widely varied.

I tried to sell my comics to a retailer, but he wouldn't even offer me 10% of the prices you list. Is he trying to cheat me? Are your prices wrong?

Remember, our prices are based on what an informed collector with some choices is willing to pay for a comic book, not necessarily what a shop is charging or paying for that comic book. A shop has huge overhead and needs to tailor its stock to match the interest shown by its customers.

If no one locally is buying comics starring Muggy-Doo, Boy Cat, it doesn't matter that *Muggy-Doo, Boy Cat* is bringing high prices elsewhere in the country.

Comics listed at their original prices may be showing no movement in most comics shops. In such cases, a retailer won't usually be interested in devoting store space to such titles, no matter ***how*** nice they are or ***how*** much you're discounting them. We've seen dealers being more selective than ever in what they will buy in recent months.

I'm a publisher, and I'd be willing to buy a hundred copies of my first issue at the price you list. I get calls from all over America from would-be buyers who would pay 10 times the price you give here for out-of-print issues of my comics. What's going on?

A publisher like you hears from faithful fans across the nation. A comics shop deals with a market of one community or smaller. You're dealing with a narrow, focused market of aficionados of your product who are looking for the specific issues they're missing. And with more and more online offerings, those fans find it easier to seek you out. As a result, a publisher who has back issues for sale may get higher prices than readers will find in this checklist. It doesn't mean you're ripping off fans; it means fans looking to buy that material are competing within a nationwide pool; the Internet may eventually put everyone in the same pool.

Can I just order the back-issue comics I want from Comics Buyer's Guide?

This price guide is just that: a guide to the average back-issue prices comics shops are likely to charge their customers.

We maintain no back-issue stock for sale; we leave that to retailers who specialize in back issues. (Start with your local shops. You'll be able to check out the variety of material available and take a look in advance at what you're buying.)

Comics Buyer's Guide itself is the magazine of the comic-book field. As such, it carries ads from retailers across the country. You can check those ads for specific back issues that you're looking for. You can even take out a "wanted" ad to locate particular items, if that appeals to you. Subscription and advertising information can be found at ***www.cbgxtra.com***.

What are "cover variants"?

These occur when publishers try to increase "collectibility" of and interest in a title by releasing an issue with an assortment of covers. This is in hopes that completists will want to buy multiple copies, instead of just one. (The practice even spread to publications like *TV Guide*.)

So how are these performing as "rare" back issues? So far: poorly. Prices may rise at the time of release, but they usually fall again relatively quickly.

What's the first thing to do when I find a bunch of old comics?

If you've found a box of old comics in the attic and wonder what to do next, the first thing to do is find out what you've got.

The same goes when you're looking for what you want to buy.

Here are some basics: Look at the copyright dates; if there are multiple dates, look at the *last* date. (If they're before 1950, chances are the comics are considered "Golden Age," and they're not covered in this price guide. Comics from the mid-1950s and later are Silver Age or more recent.)

Almost all comics are collected and identified by title and issue number. Look at the indicia, the fine print on the inside front page or inside front cover. That's what you'll use to find a specific issue in this or any other price guide. You'll want to check the issue title as given there — and the issue number.

What's the second thing to look at when I find a bunch of old comics?

Evaluate the condition of the copies. What does the comic book look like? Check the "condition" pages of our price guide to get a feel for the shape your comics are in.

If they're beaten up, enjoy them for reading but don't expect to get a lot of money for them.

For this reason, many beginning collectors focus on exactly such poor issues, getting the pleasure of reading without making a heavy investment.

What's next for comic-book collecting?

The Internet has gained in its importance to collectors, e-mail is connecting collectors around the world, and third-party grading services have led to incredible price variations in some back issues, and computers are permitting collectors, as well as retailers, to monitor what they've got, what condition it's in, and what they want to buy.

One advance we continue to work on is the expansion of the information in our files on as many back issues as possible.

To that end, the assistance of Human Computing's *ComicBase* program has been invaluable. Our combined informational base has grown rapidly, and we look forward to an even greater mutual compilation of data. Collectors who choose to do so will be able to access the information in both electronic and printed form. Both companies have for years been in an aggressive program to improve and increase the data for collectors, and collectors today are already experiencing services not available in the 1900s.

So it'll help my collecting to have a computer?

You bet. If you have a home computer, you'll find it increases your sources for buying and selling. (And *ComicBase* can help in your inventory.)

Some sites of special interest include:

www.cbgxtra.com

www.comicbase.com

www.ebay.com

www.amazon.com

www.diamondcomics.com

But they're not the only spots comics collectors will find fascinating. Surf the Web to find more!

Aaron Strips

Reprints the early Adventures of Aaron
©Image

Abadazad

CrossGen fantasy series
©CrossGen

Abbott & Costello

Stand-up duo's cartoon incarnations
©Charlton

A.B.C. Warriors

"Atomic, Bacterial, Chemical" fighting robots
©Fleetway-Quality

A. Bizarro

Mini-series for the dimwitted Superman foe
©DC

N-MINT

A1 True Life Bikini Confidential
Atomeka

❑1, 1990, b&w; Betty Page pin-ups; Adult 6.95

A1
Atomeka

❑1 1989, BB (c); DaG, BB, AMo, NG (w); DaG, BSz, BB (a); b&w 6.00
❑2 1989, AMo, NG (w); MW, DaG, BT, BB, CV (a); Flipbook format; b&w 10.00
❑3 1990, BB (c); BB, AMo (w); BB (a); b&w 6.00
❑4 1990, JRo, BSz, BB, AMo (w); BSz, KN (a); b&w 6.00
❑5 1991, JKu, JJ, NG (w); JKu, JJ (a); b&w 8.00
❑6 1992, b&w 9.00
❑7 8.00

A1
Marvel / Epic

❑1, ca. 1992; FM, CR (w); CR (a) 6.00
❑2, ca. 1992; FM (w) 6.00
❑3, ca. 1992 6.00
❑4, ca. 1993 6.00

A', A
Viz

❑1, b&w 15.95

Äardwolf
Aardwolf

❑1, Dec 1994; Cover titled "You Gezh Me Now?"; b&w 2.95
❑2, Feb 1995 2.95

Aaron Strips
Image

❑1, Apr 1997 2.95
❑2, Jun 1997 2.95
❑3, Aug 1997 2.95
❑4, Oct 1997; has "Aaron Warner's Year of the Monkey" back-up; goes to Amazing Aaron Productions 2.95
❑5, Jan 1999 2.95
❑6, Mar 1999 2.95

Abadazad
CrossGen

❑1, Feb 2004 5.00
❑1/2nd, Feb 2004, 2nd printing 4.00
❑2, Mar 2004 2.95
❑3, Apr 2004; Final issue; Includes DeMatteis interview 4.00
❑3/2nd, Apr 2004 2.95

Abbott & Costello
Charlton

❑1, Feb 1968 30.00
❑2, Apr 1968 20.00
❑3, Jun 1968 20.00
❑4, Aug 1968 14.00
❑5, Oct 1968 14.00
❑6, Dec 1968 14.00
❑7, Mar 1969 14.00
❑8, Apr 1969 14.00
❑9, Jun 1969 14.00
❑10, Aug 1969 14.00
❑11, Oct 1969 12.00
❑12, Dec 1969, Abbott & Costello, Pie-In-The-Face Maze Page; Hearty Humor (text story); Abbott & Costello Game Page 12.00
❑13, Feb 1970 12.00
❑14, Apr 1970 12.00

N-MINT

❑15, Jun 1970, "Crazy Quiz", Joke Page; Ivan Inventorsky The Inventor "Build Your Private Beach" (text story); Maze Page 12.00
❑16, Aug 1970 12.00
❑17, Oct 1970, Nutty daisy poster; Haunted House Maze 12.00
❑18, Dec 1970 12.00
❑19, Feb 1971 12.00
❑20, Apr 1971 12.00
❑21, Jun 1971 12.00
❑22, Aug 1971, Final Issue 12.00

ABC: A To Z - Greyshirt and Cobweb
DC / America's Best Comics

❑1, Jan 2006 3.99

ABC: A To Z - Terra Obscura and Splash Brannigan
DC / America's Best Comics

❑1, Mar 2006 3.99

ABC: A To Z - Tom Strong and Jack B. Quick
DC / America's Best Comics

❑1 2005 4.00

ABC: A To Z - Top 10 and Teams
DC / America's Best Comics

❑1, Aug 2006 3.99

A.B.C. Warriors
Fleetway-Quality

❑1 1990 2.00
❑2 1990 2.00
❑3 1990 2.00
❑4 1990 2.00
❑5 1990 2.00
❑6 1990 2.00
❑7 1990 2.00
❑8 1990 2.00

ABC Warriors: Khronicles of Khaos
Fleetway-Quality

❑1 2.95
❑2 2.95
❑3 2.95
❑4 2.95

Abe Sapien Drums of the Dead
Dark Horse

❑1, Mar 1998; Hellboy back-up 2.95

Abiding Perdition
APComics

❑1, ca. 2005 0.00
❑1/A, ca. 2005 3.50
❑1/B, ca. 2005 3.50
❑1/C, ca. 2005 3.50
❑1/D, ca. 2005 3.50
❑2, ca. 2005 0.00
❑2/A, ca. 2005 3.50
❑2/B, ca. 2005 3.50

A. Bizarro
DC

❑1, Jul 1999 2.50
❑2, Aug 1999 2.50
❑3, Sep 1999 2.50
❑4, Oct 1999 2.50

A-Bomb
Antarctic / Venus

❑1, Dec 1993; Adult 2.95

N-MINT

❑2, Mar 1994; Adult 2.95
❑3, Jun 1994; Barr Girls story 2.95
❑4, Sep 1994; Barr Girls story 2.95
❑5, Dec 1994; Adult 2.95
❑6, Mar 1995; Adult 2.95
❑7, Jun 1995; Adult 2.95
❑8, Sep 1995; Adult 2.95
❑9, Nov 1995; Adult 2.95
❑10, Jan 1996; Adult 2.95
❑11, Mar 1996; Title page shows Vol. 2 #1 2.95
❑12, May 1996; Adult 2.95
❑13, Jul 1996; Adult 2.95
❑14, Sep 1996; Adult 2.95
❑15, Nov 1996; Adult 2.95
❑16, Jan 1997; Adult 2.95

Abominations
Marvel

❑1, Dec 1996; follows events in Hulk: Future Imperfect 1.50
❑2, Jan 1997 1.50
❑3, Feb 1997; Final Issue 1.50

Abraham Stone (Epic)
Marvel / Epic

❑1, Jul 1995 6.95
❑2, Aug 1995 6.95

Absolute Vertigo
DC / Vertigo

❑1, Win 1995; Previews of The Eaters, Jonah Hex: Riders of the Worm and Such, Preacher, Ghostdancing, Goddess, and a new Invisibles story; Includes two page artists jam; Double sided cover featuring art of all the series in the book 3.50

Absolute Zero
Antarctic

❑1, Feb 1995, b&w; 1: Athena 3.50
❑2, May 1995, b&w 2.95
❑3, Aug 1995, b&w 2.95
❑4, Oct 1995, b&w 2.95
❑5, Dec 1995, b&w 2.95
❑6, Feb 1996, b&w 2.95

Absurd Art of J.J. Grandville
Tome

❑1, b&w; no date of publication 2.50

Abyss
Dark Horse

❑1, Aug 1989 2.50
❑2, Sep 1989 2.50

AC Annual
AC

❑1 3.50
❑2, ca. 1991 5.00
❑3 3.50
❑4, ca. 1993 3.95

Accelerate
DC / Vertigo

❑1, Aug 2000 2.95
❑2, Sep 2000 2.95
❑3, Oct 2000 2.95
❑4, Nov 2000 2.95

Accidental Death, An
Fantagraphics

❑nn, Dec 1993, b&w 3.50

Other grades: Multiply price above by 5/6 for VF/NM • 2/3 for VERY FINE • 1/3 for FINE • 1/5 for VERY GOOD • 1/8 for GOOD

N-MINT

Accident Man
Dark House

❑1, ca. 1993 ... 2.50
❑2, ca. 1993 ... 2.50
❑3, ca. 1993 ... 2.50

Acclaim Adventure Zone
Acclaim

❑1 1997; Ninjak on Cover ... 4.50
❑2 1997; Turok on Cover ... 4.50
❑3 1997; Turok and Dinosaur on Cover ... 4.50

Ace
Harrier

❑1, b&w; no indicia ... 1.95

Ace Comics Presents
Ace

❑1, May 1987; Daredevil (Golden Age) vs. The Claw; Silver Streak ... 2.00
❑2, Jul 1987; Jack Bradbury ... 2.00
❑3, Sep 1987; The Golden Age of Klaus Nordling ... 2.00
❑4, Nov 1987; Lou Fine ... 2.00

Ace McCoy
Avalon

❑1, b&w ... 2.95
❑2, b&w ... 2.95
❑3, b&w ... 2.95

Ace of Spades
ZuZupetal

❑1 ... 2.50

Aces
Eclipse

❑1, Apr 1988 ... 3.00
❑2, ca. 1988 ... 3.00
❑3, ca. 1988 ... 3.00
❑4, ca. 1988 ... 3.00
❑5, ca. 1988 ... 3.00

Aces High (RCP)
RCP

❑1, Apr 1999; Reprints Aces High (E.C.) #1 ... 2.50
❑2, May 1999; Reprints Aces High (E.C.) #2 ... 2.50
❑3, Jun 1999; Reprints Aces High (E.C.) #3 ... 2.50
❑4, Jul 1999; Reprints Aces High (E.C.) #4 ... 2.50
❑5, Aug 1999; Reprints Aces High (E.C.) #5 ... 2.50
❑Ann 1; Collects Aces High #1-5 ... 13.50

ACG Christmas Special
Avalon

❑1, Cover reads "Christmas Horror" ... 2.95

ACG's Civil War
Avalon

❑1 1995 ... 2.50

ACG's Halloween Special
Avalon

❑1; Cover reads "Halloween Horror" ... 2.95

Achilles Storm: Dark Secret
Brainstorm

❑1, Oct 1997; Adult ... 2.95
❑2; Adult ... 2.95

Achilles Storm/Razmataz
Aja Blu

❑1, Oct 1990 ... 2.25
❑2, Jan 1991 ... 2.25
❑3, May 1991 ... 2.25
❑4, Nov 1991 ... 2.25

Acid Bath Case
Kitchen Sink

❑1 ... 4.95

Ack the Barbarian
Innovation

❑1, b&w ... 2.25

Acme
Fandom House

❑1 ... 3.00
❑2 ... 3.00
❑3 ... 3.00
❑4 ... 3.00
❑5 ... 3.00
❑6 ... 3.00
❑7 ... 3.00
❑8, Fal 1987 ... 2.00
❑9, Sum 1989 ... 3.00

N-MINT

Acme Novelty Library
Fantagraphics

❑1, Win 1993 1: Jimmy Corrigan ... 10.00
❑1/2nd, Dec 1995; Jimmy Corrigan ... 3.95
❑2, Sum 1994; Quimby the Mouse ... 7.00
❑2/2nd, Sum 1995; Quimby the Mouse ... 4.95
❑3, Aut 1994; digest-sized; Blind Man ... 5.00
❑4, Win 1994; Sparky's Best Comics and Stories ... 5.00
❑4/2nd ... 4.95
❑5, Apr 1995; digest-sized; Jimmy Corrigan ... 3.95
❑6, Fal 1995; digest-sized; Jimmy Corrigan ... 3.95
❑7, Jul 1996; Oversized; Book of Jokes ... 6.95
❑8, Win 1996; digest-sized; Jimmy Corrigan ... 4.75
❑9, Win 1997; digest-sized; Jimmy Corrigan ... 4.50
❑10, Spr 1998; digest-sized; Jimmy Corrigan ... 4.95
❑11, Fal 1998; digest-sized; Jimmy Corrigan ... 4.50
❑12, Spr 1999; digest-sized; Jimmy Corrigan ... 4.50
❑16, Jan 2006; Hardcover; Rusty Brown ... 15.95
❑14, Aut 1999; Jimmy Corrigan ... 10.95

Acolyte
Mad Monkey

❑1, ca. 1993, b&w ... 3.95

Across the Universe: DC Universe Stories of Alan Moore
DC

❑1, ca. 2003 ... 19.95

Action Comics
DC

❑0, Oct 1994; BG (a); 1: Kenny Braverman. Peer Pressure, Part 4; ▲ 1994-40 ... 3.00
❑1, Jun 1938, FGu (w); FGu (a); O: Superman. 1: Zatara. 1: Superman. 1: Tex Thomson. 1: Lois Lane; 1: Zatara; 1: Congo Bill ... 330000.00
❑1/2nd, ca. 1976, 2nd printing (giveaway, 1976?); FGu (w); FGu (a); O: Superman. 1: Zatara. 1: Superman. 1: Tex Thomson. 1: Lois Lane. 2nd printing (giveaway; 2nd printing; 1976); $0.10 reprint ... 18.00
❑1/3rd, ca. 1983, 3rd printing (giveaway, 1983?); FGu (w); FGu (a); O: Superman. 1: Zatara. 1: Superman. 1: Tex Thomson. 1: Lois Lane. 3rd printing; $0.10 Peanut Butter giveaway; ca. 1983 ... 14.00
❑1/4th, ca. 1987, 4th printing (Nestle Quik 16-page giveaway, 1988); O: Superman. 4th printing; $0.10 Nestle Quik 16-page giveaway; Back cover has ad for Nestle Quik ... 6.00
❑1/5th, ca. 1992; FGu (w); FGu (a); O: Superman. 1: Zatara. 1: Superman. 1: Tex Thomson. 1: Lois Lane. 5th printing (1992) ... 5.00
❑282, Nov 1961, CS (c); JM (a) ... 60.00
❑283, Dec 1961, CS (c); CS, JM (a); Legion of Super-Villains ... 60.00
❑284, Jan 1962, CS (c); CS, JM (a); Mon-El ... 60.00
❑285, Feb 1962, CS (c); NA, JM (a); A: Legion of Super-Heroes. Supergirl goes public ... 100.00
❑286, Mar 1962, CS (c); CS, JM (a); Legion of Super-Villains ... 60.00
❑287, Apr 1962, CS (c); CS, JM (a); A: Legion of Super-Heroes. Jerry Bails L.O.C ... 60.00
❑288, May 1962, CS (c); CS, JM (a); Mon-El ... 60.00
❑289, Jun 1962, CS (c); JM (a); A: Legion of Super-Heroes ... 60.00
❑290, Jul 1962, CS, KS (c); CS, JM (a); A: Legion of Super-Heroes. 1: Supergirl Emergency Squad ... 60.00
❑291, Aug 1962, CS (c); NA, JM (a); Supergirl meets Mr. Mxyzptlk ... 60.00
❑292, Sep 1962, CS (c); JM (a); A: Superhorse (Comet). Superman; Supergirl ... 60.00
❑293, Oct 1962, CS (c); O: Superhorse (Comet) ... 60.00
❑294, Nov 1962, CS (c); CS, JM (a) ... 60.00
❑295, Dec 1962, CS (c); CS, JM (a); Superman; Supergirl ... 90.00
❑296, Jan 1963, CS (c); CS, JM (a); Superman; Supergirl ... 65.00
❑297, Feb 1963, CS (c); CS, JM (a); Superman; Supergirl ... 90.00
❑298, Mar 1963, CS (c); CS, JM (a); Superman; Supergirl ... 60.00
❑299, Apr 1963, CS (c); JM (a); Superman; Supergirl ... 60.00

N-MINT

❑300, May 1963, 300th anniversary issue; CS (c) ... 50.00
❑301, Jun 1963 ... 50.00
❑302, Jul 1963, CS (c); CS, JM (a); Superman; Supergirl ... 50.00
❑303, Aug 1963, CS, JM (a) ... 50.00
❑304, Sep 1963, CS, JM (a); 1: Black Flame ... 50.00
❑305, Oct 1963, Superman; Supergirl; Imaginary Story ... 50.00
❑306, Nov 1963, Superman; Supergirl ... 50.00
❑307, Dec 1963, Superman; Supergirl ... 50.00
❑308, Jan 1964 ... 50.00
❑309, Feb 1964, CS (c); NA, CS, JM (a); A: Supergirl's parents. Legion ... 50.00
❑310, Mar 1964, 1: Jewel Kryptonite ... 50.00
❑311, Apr 1964, Supergirl ... 50.00
❑312, May 1964, Supergirl ... 50.00
❑313, Jun 1964, A: Batman. Superman; Supergirl ... 50.00
❑314, Jul 1964, A: Batman ... 50.00
❑315, Aug 1964, Supergirl ... 50.00
❑316, Sep 1964 ... 50.00
❑317, Oct 1964, Death Nor-Kan of Kandor ... 40.00
❑318, Nov 1964, Supergirl ... 40.00
❑319, Dec 1964 ... 40.00
❑320, Jan 1965 ... 40.00
❑321, Feb 1965, CS, JM (a); Superman; Supergirl ... 40.00
❑322, Mar 1965 ... 40.00
❑323, Apr 1965 ... 40.00
❑324, May 1965 ... 40.00
❑325, Jun 1965 ... 50.00
❑326, Jul 1965 ... 40.00
❑327, Aug 1965, Imaginary Superman story ... 40.00
❑328, Sep 1965 ... 40.00
❑329, Oct 1965 ... 40.00
❑330, Nov 1965 ... 40.00
❑331, Dec 1965 ... 40.00
❑332, Jan 1966, Imaginary Superwoman Story ... 40.00
❑333, Feb 1966, Imaginary Superwoman Story ... 40.00
❑334, Mar 1966; Giant-sized issue; O: Supergirl. aka 80 Page Giant #G-20 ... 60.00
❑335, Mar 1966, Superman; Supergirl; Supergirl backup story ... 40.00
❑336, Apr 1966, O: Akvar. O: Ak-Var (later Flamebird II) ... 40.00
❑337, May 1966 ... 40.00
❑338, Jun 1966, CS, JM (a); 1: Superman of 2966; Supergirl ... 40.00
❑339, Jul 1966, CS, JM (a); Superman of 2966; Supergirl ... 70.00
❑340, Aug 1966, 1: Parasite. 1: Parasite; O: Parasite ... 40.00
❑341, Sep 1966, A: Batman. Superman; Supergirl ... 40.00
❑342, Oct 1966 ... 40.00
❑343, Nov 1966, Marker on front cover; Supergirl reprint ... 40.00
❑344, Dec 1966, A: Batman ... 40.00
❑345, Jan 1967, A: Allen Funt ... 40.00
❑346, Feb 1967, Superman; Supergirl ... 40.00
❑347, Apr 1967; Giant-sized issue; aka 80 Page Giant #G-33; Supergirl; reprints Superman #140 and Action #290 and #293 ... 50.00
❑348, Mar 1967, Superman; Supergirl ... 40.00
❑349, Apr 1967 ... 40.00
❑350, May 1967, JM (a) ... 40.00
❑351, Jun 1967, Superman; Supergirl ... 40.00
❑352, Jul 1967, Superman; Supergirl ... 40.00
❑353, Aug 1967 ... 40.00
❑354, Sep 1967 ... 40.00
❑355, Oct 1967 ... 40.00
❑356, Nov 1967, Superman; Supergirl; V: the Annihilator (Karl Keller); Superman story; Box016; Supergirl story; Palisades Park admission ticket and ride coupons ... 40.00
❑357, Dec 1967, CS (c); CS, JM (a); Superman; Supergirl ... 40.00
❑358, Jan 1968, NA (c); CS, JM (a); Superman; Supergirl ... 40.00
❑359, Feb 1968, NA (c); CS, KS (a); Superman; Supergirl; Martin Pasko L.O.C.; Tony Isabella L.O.C.; Dave Cockrum L.O.C.; Mark Evanier L.O.C. ... 40.00
❑360, Mar 1968; Giant-sized issue; aka 80 Page Giant #G-45; Supergirl ... 40.00
❑361, Apr 1968, NA (c); KS (a); 2: Parasite ... 40.00

Other grades: Multiply price above by 5/6 for VF/NM • 2/3 for VERY FINE • 1/3 for FINE • 1/5 for VERY GOOD • 1/8 for GOOD

Abominations

Mini-series based on Hulk: Future Imperfect

©Marvel

Ace Comics Presents

A tribute series honoring Jack Cole

©Ace

Ace McCoy

Adventures of a stuntman-turned-hero

©Avalon

Aces High

Reprints the E.C. "New Direction" title

©RCP

Achilles Storm: Dark Secret

Costumed martial artist takes to the streets

©Brainstorm

	N-MINT
❑362, May 1968	40.00
❑363, Jun 1968, Irene Vartanoff L.O.C.; Gary Skinner L.O.C.; Palisades Park admission ticket and ride coupons	30.00
❑364, Jul 1968, NA (c); RA, KS (a); D: Superman	30.00
❑365, Aug 1968, D: Superman	30.00
❑366, Sep 1968, D: Superman	30.00
❑367, Oct 1968, NA (c); CS, KS (a)	30.00
❑368, Nov 1968, CI (c); CS, RA, KS, JAb (a); Mr. Mxyzptlk cameo	30.00
❑369, Dec 1968, CS (c); CS, KS, JAb (a)	30.00
❑370, Jan 1969, NA (c); CS, KS, JAb (a)	30.00
❑371, Feb 1969, CS, KS, JAb (a)	30.00
❑372, Mar 1969, NA (c); CS, KS, JAb (a)	30.00
❑373, Apr 1969; Giant-sized issue; NA, CS (a); A: Supergirl. aka Giant #G-57; Supergirl stories; Giants drop to 64 pages	30.00
❑374, Mar 1969, CS, KS, JAb (a); Superman; Supergirl	20.00
❑375, Apr 1969, CS, KS, JAb (a); A: Batman. Cameo of Batman	20.00
❑376, May 1969, CS (c); CS, KS, JAb (a); Last Supergirl solo story	20.00
❑377, Jun 1969, CS (c); CS, JAb (a); Legion; Reprint from Adventure Comics #300	20.00
❑378, Jul 1969, CS (c); CS, JAb (a); Legion	20.00
❑379, Aug 1969, CS (c); CS, JAb (a); Legion	20.00
❑380, Sep 1969, CS (c); CS (a); Legion	20.00
❑381, Oct 1969, CS (c); CS (a); Legion	20.00
❑382, Nov 1969, CS (c); CS (a); Legion	20.00
❑383, Dec 1969, CS (c); CS (a); Legion	20.00
❑384, Jan 1970, CS (c); CS (a); Legion	20.00
❑385, Feb 1970, CS (c); CS (a); Legion	20.00
❑386, Mar 1970, CS (c); CS (a); Legion	20.00
❑387, Apr 1970, CS (c); CS (a); Legion	20.00
❑388, May 1970, CS (c); CS (a); Legion; Reprints Legion story from Adventure Comics #302	25.00
❑389, Jun 1970, CS (c); CS (a); Legion	20.00
❑390, Jul 1970, CS (c); CS (a); Legion	20.00
❑391, Aug 1970, CS (c); CS, RA (a); Legion	20.00
❑392, Sep 1970, CS (c); CS, RA (a); Super-Sons; Last Legion of Super-Heroes	20.00
❑393, Oct 1970, CS (c); CS (a)	20.00
❑394, Nov 1970, CS (a)	20.00
❑395, Dec 1970, CS (a)	20.00
❑396, Jan 1971, MA, CS (a); Tales of the Fortress	20.00
❑397, Feb 1971, CS (a); Tales of the Fortress	20.00
❑398, Mar 1971, CS (a); Untold Tales Of The Fortress	20.00
❑399, Apr 1971, CS (a)	20.00
❑400, May 1971, NA (c); CS (a); Untold Tales of Kandor	40.00
❑401, Jun 1971, CS (a)	17.00
❑402, Jul 1971, NA (c); CS (a); Tales of the Fortress	17.00
❑403, Aug 1971; CI (c); CS (a); Reprints from Adventure #310	17.00
❑404, Sep 1971; GK, CS (a); Aquaman and Atom reprint stories	17.00
❑405, Oct 1971; CS (a); Aquaman and Vigilante reprint stories	17.00
❑406, Nov 1971; CS (c); ATh, CS (a); Atom and Flash story, part 1; reprinted from Brave and the Bold #53	17.00
❑407, Dec 1971; CS (c); ATh, CS (a); Atom and Flash story, part 2; reprinted from Brave and the Bold #53	15.00
❑408, Jan 1972; CS (c); GK, CS (a); reprints The Atom #9	20.00
❑409, Feb 1972; NC (c); GT, CS, NC (a); Teen Titans reprint story	15.00
❑410, Feb 1972; NC (c); CS, NC (a); Teen Titans reprint story	13.00
❑411, Apr 1972; NC (c); CS (a); O: Eclipso. Eclipso reprint story	13.00
❑412, May 1972; NC (c); CS (a); Eclipso reprint story	12.00
❑413, Jun 1972; NC (c); ATh, CS (a); Eclipso and Metamorpho reprint stories	12.00
❑414, Jul 1972, NC (c); CS (a)	12.00
❑415, Aug 1972, NC (c); CS (a)	12.00
❑416, Sep 1972, NC (c); CS (a); David Michelinie L.O.C	11.00
❑417, Oct 1972, NC (c); MA, CS (a); Brainiac appearance; Superman story; Metamorpho story	11.00
❑418, Nov 1972, NC (c); CS (a); Superman story; United Nations; Metamorpho story	11.00
❑419, Dec 1972, NA (c); CI, CS (a); 1&O: Human Target; Superman story; Bob Rozakis L.O.C	14.00
❑420, Jan 1973, NC (c); DG, CS (a); 1: Towbee; Superman story; The minstrel of space; The Human Target story; David Michelinie L.O.C	11.00
❑421, Feb 1973, NC (c); CS (a); Green Arrow begins	11.00
❑422, Mar 1973, NC (c); DG, CS (a); O: Human Target; Part 1; Human Target story; Superman story	11.00
❑423, Apr 1973, NC (c); DG, CS (a); O: Human Target; Part 2; V: Lex Luthor; Human Target story; Superman story	10.00
❑424, Jun 1973, NC (c); MA, DG, DD, CS (a); Green Arrow	10.00
❑425, Jul 1973, NC (c); MA, DG, NA, DD, CS (a); Superman story; The Atom story; The Human Target story	19.00
❑426, Aug 1973, NC (c); DG, DD, CS (a); Green Arrow story; Human Target story	10.00
❑427, Sep 1973, NC (c); DD, CS (a); Atom (Ray Palmer) story	8.00
❑428, Oct 1973, NC (c); DG, CS (a); World Trade Center fire story; Green Arrow back-up feature	8.00
❑429, Nov 1973, NC (c); DG, CS (a)	8.00
❑430, Dec 1973, NC (c); DD, CS (a); Atom back-up	8.00
❑431, Jan 1974, NC (c); DD, CS (a); Green Arrow back-up	8.00
❑432, Feb 1974, NC (c); DG, CS (a); 1: Toyman (Jack Nimball)	8.00
❑433, Mar 1974, NC (c); DD, CS (a)	8.00
❑434, Apr 1974, NC (c); DD, CS (a)	8.00
❑435, May 1974, NC (c); DD, CS (a)	8.00
❑436, Jun 1974, NC (c); DD, CS (a)	8.00
❑437, Jul 1974, Giant-sized issue (100 pages); NC (c); MA, CI, GK, CS, RH, KS (a); Reprints Sea Devils #1, Mystery in Space #85, Western Comics #77, My Greatest Adventure #3, Doll Man #13; Appearance of Flash, Green Arrow, and Green Lantern	29.00
❑438, Aug 1974, NC (c); DD, CS (a)	8.00
❑439, Sep 1974, NC (c); DD, CS (a); Atom back-up	8.00
❑440, Oct 1974, MGr, CS (a); 1st Green Arrow by Mike Grell	25.00
❑441, Nov 1974, NC (c); MGr, CS (a); A: Flash. Green Arrow back-up	12.00
❑442, Dec 1974, NC (c); MGr, CS (a); Atom (Ray Palmer) story	8.00
❑443, Jan 1975, Giant-sized issue (100 pages); NC (c); MA, CI, GK, CS, RH (a); 100-Page Super Spectacular; JLA, Sea Devils, Matt Savage, Adam Strange, Hawkman and Black Pirate; reprints stories from Sea Devils #3, Western Comics #78, Mystery in Space #87 and Sensation Comics #4	26.00
❑444, Feb 1975; NC (c); MGr (w); MGr, CS (a); A: Green Lantern. Green Arrow back-up	7.00
❑445, Mar 1975 NC (c); MGr (w); MGr, CS (a)	7.00
❑446, Apr 1975 MGr, CS (a)	7.00
❑447, May 1975 DG (c); RB, CS (a)	7.00
❑448, Jun 1975 BO (c); DD, CS (a)	7.00
❑449, Jul 1975, BO (c); JK, GK, CS (a); Green Arrow giant	7.00
❑450, Aug 1975 MGr, CS (a)	7.00
❑451, Sep 1975; MGr, CS (a); Green Arrow back-up	7.00
❑452, Oct 1975 MGr, CS (a)	7.00
❑453, Nov 1975; BO (c); CS (a); Atom back-up	7.00
❑454, Dec 1975; BO (c); CS (a); last Atom back-up	7.00
❑455, Jan 1976; BO (c); CS (a); Mel Brooks look-alike	6.00
❑456, Feb 1976; MGr (c); MGr, CS (a); Green Arrow/Black Canary back-up	6.00
❑457, Mar 1976, BO (c); MGr, CS (a); Green Arrow/Black Canary back-up; Superman reveals ID to Pete Ross' son	6.00
❑458, Apr 1976, BO (c); MGr, CS (a); 1: Blackrock. Green Arrow	6.00
❑459, May 1976, CI (c); CS (a); V: Blackrock; The Private Life of Clark Kent	6.00
❑460, Jun 1976, BO (c); CS, KS (a); 1: Karb-Brak. Mxyzptlk back-up	6.00
❑461, Jul 1976, BO (c); CS (a); V: Karb-Brak. Superman in colonial America; Bicentennial #30	6.00
❑462, Aug 1976, CS (a)	6.00
❑463, Sep 1976, CS (a); Bicentennial story	6.00
❑464, Oct 1976, BO (c); CS, KS (a); Superman; The Private Life of Clark Kent	6.00
❑465, Nov 1976, CS (a); V: Lex Luthor	6.00
❑466, Dec 1976, NA (c); CS (a); O: Lex Luthor; V: Lex Luthor	7.00
❑467, Jan 1977, CS (a)	5.00
❑468, Feb 1977, CS (a); Close Up: Morgan Edge	5.00
❑469, Mar 1977, CS (a); The Private Life of Clark Kent	5.00
❑470, Apr 1977, CS (a)	5.00
❑471, May 1977, CS (a); Private Life of Clark Kent	5.00
❑472, Jun 1977, BO (c); CS (a); V: Faora Hu-Ul	5.00
❑473, Jul 1977, CS (a)	5.00
❑474, Aug 1977, CS, KS (a); The Private Life of Clark Kent	5.00
❑475, Sep 1977, CS, KS (a); Lori Lemaris Mermaid of Atlantis	5.00
❑476, Oct 1977, CS, KS (a)	5.00

Other grades: Multiply price above by 5/6 for VF/NM • 2/3 for VERY FINE • 1/3 for FINE • 1/5 for VERY GOOD • 1/8 for GOOD

N-MINT

❑477, Nov 1977, RB (c); DD, CS (a); Private Life of Clark Kent 5.00
❑478, Dec 1977, CS (a) 5.00
❑479, Jan 1978, CS (a) 5.00
❑480, Feb 1978, CS (a); Justice League appears 5.00
❑481, Mar 1978, CS (a); 1: Supermobile. V: Amazo 5.00
❑481/Whitman, Mar 1978, CS (a); 1: Supermobile. V: Amazo. Whitman variant 10.00
❑482, Apr 1978, CS (a) 5.00
❑482/Whitman, Apr 1978, CS (a); Whitman variant 10.00
❑483, May 1978, RB (c); CS (a); V: Amazo 5.00
❑483/Whitman, May 1978, CS (a); V: Amazo. Whitman variant 10.00
❑484, Jun 1978, 40th anniversary; CS (a); Wedding of E-2 Superman and Lois Lane 5.00
❑484/Whitman, Jun 1978, CS (a); Wedding of E-2 Superman and Lois Lane; Whitman variant 10.00
❑485, Jul 1978, NA (c); CS (a); Reprints Superman #233 .... 8.00
❑485/Whitman, Jul 1978, CS (a); Whitman variant 10.00
❑486, Aug 1978, RB (c); GT, CS, KS (a) . 5.00
❑486/Whitman, Aug 1978, CS (a); Whitman variant 10.00
❑487, Sep 1978, CS (a); O: Atom. 1: Microwave Man 5.00
❑487/Whitman, Sep 1978, CS (a); O: Atom. Whitman variant 10.00
❑488, Oct 1978, CS (a); Airwave II back-up feature; Microwave Man apperance 5.00
❑488/Whitman, Oct 1978, CS (a); Whitman variant 10.00
❑489, Nov 1978, RA (c); CS (a); Atom back-up 5.00
❑489/Whitman, Nov 1978, CS (a); Atom back-up; Whitman variant 10.00
❑490, Dec 1978, RA (c); CS (a); V: Brainiac 5.00
❑490/Whitman, Dec 1978, CS (a); Whitman variant 10.00
❑491, Jan 1979, RA (c); CS (a); V: Brainiac 5.00
❑491/Whitman, Jan 1979, CS (a); Whitman variant 10.00
❑492, Feb 1979, RA (c); CS (a) 5.00
❑492/Whitman, Feb 1979, CS (a); Whitman variant 10.00
❑493, Mar 1979, RA (c); CS (a) 5.00
❑493/Whitman, Mar 1979, CS (a); Whitman variant 10.00
❑494, Apr 1979, CS (a) 5.00
❑494/Whitman, Apr 1979, CS (a); Whitman variant 10.00
❑495, May 1979, CS (a); 1: Silver Banshee. 1: Silver Banshee 5.00
❑495/Whitman, May 1979, CS (a); 1: Silver Banshee. Whitman variant.... 10.00
❑496, Jun 1979, RA (c); CS (a) 5.00
❑496/Whitman, Jun 1979, CS (a); Whitman variant 10.00
❑497, Jul 1979, RA (c); CS (a) 5.00
❑497/Whitman, Jul 1979, CS (a); Whitman variant 10.00
❑498, Aug 1979, RA (c); CS (a) 5.00
❑498/Whitman, Aug 1979, CS (a); Whitman variant 10.00
❑499, Sep 1979, RA (c); CS (a) 5.00
❑499/Whitman, Sep 1979, CS (a); Whitman variant 10.00
❑500, Oct 1979; Giant-sized; RA (c); CS (a); O: Superman. Superman's life...... 5.00
❑500/Whitman, Oct 1979; CS (a); O: Superman. Superman's life; Whitman variant 10.00
❑501, Nov 1979, RA (c); CS, KS (a) 5.00
❑501/Whitman, Nov 1979, CS (a); Whitman variant 10.00
❑502, Dec 1979, RA (c); CS (a) 5.00
❑502/Whitman, Dec 1979, CS (a); Whitman variant 10.00
❑503, Jan 1980, RA (c); CS (a) 5.00
❑503/Whitman, Jan 1980, CS (a); Whitman variant 10.00
❑504, Feb 1980, RA (c); CS (a) 4.00
❑504/Whitman, Feb 1980, CS (a); Whitman variant 8.00
❑505, Mar 1980, RA (c); CS (a) 4.00
❑505/Whitman, Mar 1980, CS (a); Whitman variant 8.00
❑506, Apr 1980, RA (c); CS (a) 4.00

N-MINT

❑506/Whitman, Apr 1980, CS (a); Whitman variant 8.00
❑507, May 1980, RA (c); CS (a) 4.00
❑507/Whitman, May 1980, CS (a); Whitman variant 8.00
❑508, Jun 1980, RA (c); CS (a); Crossover with New Adventures of Superboy #5 4.00
❑508/Whitman, Jun 1980, CS (a); Whitman variant 8.00
❑509, Jul 1980, RA (c); JSn, CS, JSt (a); Radio Shack promo insert 4.00
❑510, Aug 1980, RA (c); CS (a); V: Lex Luthor 4.00
❑511, Sep 1980, RA (c); CS (a); V: Terra Man; Airwave back-up feature 4.00
❑512, Oct 1980, RA (c); CS, RT (a); Air Wave back-up 4.00
❑513, Nov 1980, RA (c); CS, RT (a); V: the HIVE; Airwave II back-up feature 4.00
❑514, Dec 1980, RB (c); CS, RT (a); Airwave back-up feature 4.00
❑515, Jan 1981, RB (c); CS (a); V: Vandal Savage. Atom back-up 4.00
❑516, Feb 1981, RB (c); CS (a); V: Vandal Savage. Atom back-up 4.00
❑517, Mar 1981, RA (c); DH, CS (a); Aquaman back-up feature; Aquaman: Brother Rat! storyline continued from Adventure Comics #478 .... 4.00
❑518, Apr 1981, RA (c); DH, CS (a); Aquaman back-up 4.00
❑519, May 1981, RA (c); DH, CS (a); Aquaman back-up feature 4.00
❑520, Jun 1981, RA (c); DH, CS (a); Aquaman back-up feature 4.00
❑521, Jul 1981, RA (c); CS (a); 1: Vixen. Atom, Aquaman back-up 4.00
❑522, Aug 1981, RB (c); CS (a); Atom back-up 4.00
❑523, Sep 1981, RB (c); CS (a); Atom back-up 4.00
❑524, Oct 1981, RA (c); CS (a); Airwave and Atom back-up 4.00
❑525, Nov 1981, RA (c); JSa, CS (a); 1: Neutron. Airwave back-up feature .. 4.00
❑526, Dec 1981, JSa, CS (a); Airwave back-up feature 4.00
❑527, Jan 1982, RA (c); CS (a); 1: Lord Satanis. Airwave, Aquaman back-up .. 4.00
❑528, Feb 1982, RB (c); CS (a); A: Brainiac. Aquaman back-up 4.00
❑529, Mar 1982, GP (c); CS (a); Aquaman back-up feature 4.00
❑530, Apr 1982, RA (c); CS (a); V: Brainiac; Aquaman and The Atom back-up feature 4.00
❑531, May 1982, RA (c); JSa, CS (a); Atom II back-up feature 4.00
❑532, Jun 1982, RA (c); CS (a) 4.00
❑533, Jul 1982, RB (c); CS (a); V: the HIVE 4.00
❑534, Aug 1982, RA (c); CS (a); Airwave back-up feature 4.00
❑535, Sep 1982, GK (c); JSa, CS (a); A: Omega Men. Airwave back-up feature 4.00
❑536, Oct 1982, RB (c); JSa, CS (a); A: Omega Men. Superman story continued into New Teen Titans #24; Aquaman back-up feature 4.00
❑537, Nov 1982, RB (c); CS, IN (a); Aquaman back-up; Masters of the Universe preview 4.00
❑538, Dec 1982, RB (c); CS, IN (a); Jackhammer appearance; Aquaman back-up feature 4.00
❑539, Jan 1983, KG (c); GK, CS (a); Flash, Atom 4.00
❑540, Feb 1983, GK (c); GK, CS (a); Aquaman back-up 4.00
❑541, Mar 1983, GK, CS (a) 4.00
❑542, Apr 1983, CS (a); V: Vandal Savage 4.00
❑543, May 1983, RA (c); CS (a); V: Neutron 4.00
❑544, Jun 1983; 45th anniversary; DG, GK (c); GP, GK, CS (a); O: Brainiac (New). O: Lex Luthor (New). 1: Brainiac (New). 1: Lex Luthor (New). 45th Anniversary issue; Joe Shuster pin-up 4.00
❑545, Jul 1983; GK, CS (a); V: New Brainiac 3.00
❑546, Aug 1983, GK, CS (a); A: JLA, Titans 3.00
❑547, Sep 1983; GK (c); CS (a); O: Planeteer 3.00
❑548, Oct 1983 GK (c); CS (a) 3.00
❑549, Nov 1983 GK (c); CS (a) 3.00
❑550, Dec 1983 GT, CS (a) 3.00
❑551, Jan 1984; GK (c); GK, CS (a) 3.00

N-MINT

❑552, Feb 1984; GK, CS (a); 1: Legion of Forgotten Heroes. A: Animal Man. Cave Carson, Congorilla, Suicide Squad, Animal Man, Rip Hunter, Immortal Man, Sea Devils, Dolphin 3.00
❑553, Mar 1984; GK, CS (a); A: Animal Man. A: Legion of Forgotten Heroes. Cave Carson, Congorilla, Suicide Squad, Animal Man, Rip Hunter, Immortal Man, Sea Devils, Dolphin 3.00
❑554, Apr 1984; GK, CS (a); Jerry and Joey create Superman 3.00
❑555, May 1984; CS (a); A: Supergirl. V: Parasite. Anniversary of Supergirl's debut in Action Comics; Continues in Supergirl #20 .... 3.00
❑556, Jun 1984; CS (a); V: Vandal Savage. Neutron 3.00
❑557, Jul 1984 CS (a) 3.00
❑558, Aug 1984 CS, KS (a) 3.00
❑559, Sep 1984 CS, KS (a) 3.00
❑560, Oct 1984 KG (w); KG, CS (a); A: Ambush Bug 3.00
❑561, Nov 1984 CS, KS (a) 3.00
❑562, Dec 1984 CS, KS (a) 3.00
❑563, Jan 1985; KG (c); KG (w); KG, GP, CS (a); Ambush Bug vs. Mxyzptlk 3.00
❑564, Feb 1985 CS (a) 3.00
❑565, Mar 1985 KG (w); KG, CS, KS (a); A: Ambush Bug 3.00
❑566, Apr 1985; MR (c); CS (a); V: Captain Strong. Marshall Rogers & Jerry Ordway cover 3.00
❑567, May 1985 PB (c); CS, KS (a) 2.00
❑568, Jun 1985 JOy (c); CS (a) 2.00
❑569, Jul 1985 BO (c); CS, IN (a) 2.00
❑570, Aug 1985 CS, KS (a) 2.00
❑571, Sep 1985; BB (c); CS (a); Brian Bolland cover 2.00
❑572, Oct 1985; MWa (w); CS (a); Mark Waid's first major comics work . 2.00
❑573, Nov 1985; CS, KS (a); MASK preview 2.00
❑574, Dec 1985 CS, KS (a) 2.00
❑575, Jan 1986; CS, KS (a); V: Intellex.. 2.00
❑576, Feb 1986 MWa (w); CS, KS (a) 2.00
❑577, Mar 1986; KG (c); KG (w); KG, CS (a); O: Superman 2.00
❑578, Apr 1986 CS, KS (a) 2.00
❑579, May 1986; KG (c); KG, CS (a); Asterix parody 2.00
❑580, Jun 1986; GK (c); CS, KS (a); Kid in Most Dangerous Toy is based on winner of Super Powers contest 2.00
❑581, Jul 1986 CS, KS (a) 2.00
❑582, Aug 1986 CS (a) 2.00
❑583, Sep 1986; MA (c); AMo (w); CS (a); Continued from Superman #423; Last pre-Crisis on Infinite Earths Superman 2.00
❑584, Jan 1987; JBy (c); JBy (w); JBy, DG (a); A: Titans. Post-Crisis Superman begins 2.00
❑585, Feb 1987 JBy (c); JBy (w); JBy, DG (a); A: Phantom Stranger 2.00
❑586, Mar 1987; JBy (c); JBy (w); JBy, DG (a); A: Orion. New Gods; "Legends" Chapter 19 .... 2.00
❑587, Apr 1987; JBy (c); JBy (w); JBy, DG (a); A: Demon. V: Morgaine Le Fey..... 2.00
❑588, May 1987; JBy (c); JBy (w); JBy, DG (a); A: Hawkman. Shadow War; Continued from Hawkman #10, continues in Hawkman #11 and Action #589 .... 2.00
❑589, Jun 1987; JBy (c); JBy (w); JBy, DG (a); A: Green Lantern Corps. Green Lantern Corps 2.00
❑590, Jul 1987; JBy (c); JBy (w); JBy, DG (a); A: Metal Men. new Chemo 2.00
❑591, Aug 1987 JBy (c); JBy (w); JBy, DG (a); A: Superboy 2.00
❑592, Sep 1987 JBy (c); JBy (w); JBy, DG (a); A: Big Barda 2.00
❑593, Oct 1987 JBy (c); JBy (w); JBy, DG (a); A: Mr. Miracle 2.00
❑594, Nov 1987; JBy (c); JBy (w); JBy (a); A: Batman. Continues in Booster Gold #23 2.00
❑595, Dec 1987; JBy (c); JBy (w); JBy (a); A: Batman. J'onn J'onzz 2.00
❑596, Jan 1988; JBy (c); JBy (w); JBy (a); A: Spectre. "Millennium" Week 4 .... 2.00
❑597, Feb 1988; JBy (c); JBy (w); JBy (a); A: Lois Lane and Lana Lang. Lois Lane and Lana Lang 2.00
❑598, Mar 1988; JBy (c); JBy (w); JBy (a); 1: Checkmate 15.00

Other grades: Multiply price above by 5/6 for VF/NM • 2/3 for VERY FINE • 1/3 for FINE • 1/5 for VERY GOOD • 1/8 for GOOD

Ack the Barbarian

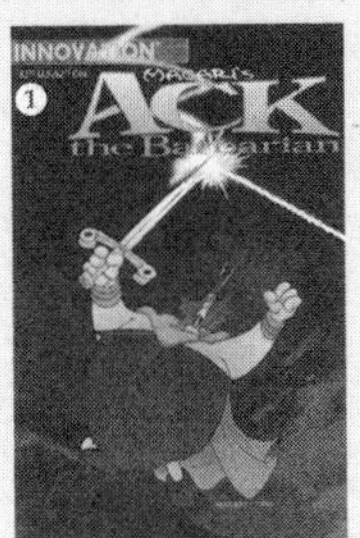

Computer-generated humor comic book

©Innovation

Acme Novelty Library

Chris Ware's award-winning title

©Fantagraphics

Action Comics

The series that gave birth to Superman

©DC

A.C.T.I.O.N. Force (Lightning)

Not related to the Marvel UK series

©Lightning

Action Girl Comics

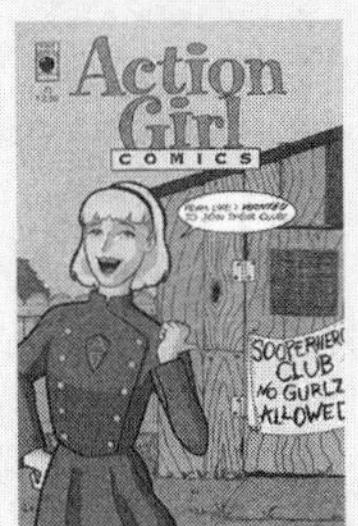

Springboard series for female cartoonists

©Slave Labor

	N-MINT
❑599, Apr 1988; JBy (c); JBy (w); JBy, RA (a); A: Metal Men. Bonus Book #1, Jimmy Olsen	2.00
❑600, May 1988; Giant-sized; JBy, DG, CS, KS (c); JBy (w); GP, JBy, DG, CS, KS (a); 50th Anniversary, 80-page Giant; Wonder Woman; pin-ups; "Genesis" prequel	5.00
❑601, Aug 1988; Superman, Blackhawk, Green Lantern, Deadman, Wild Dog, Secret Six; Action Comics begins weekly issues	2.00
❑602, Aug 1988; Superman, Blackhawk, Green Lantern, Deadman, Wild Dog, Secret Six	1.75
❑603, Aug 1988; Superman, Blackhawk, Green Lantern, Deadman, Wild Dog, Secret Six	1.75
❑604, Aug 1988; Superman, Blackhawk, Green Lantern, Deadman, Wild Dog, Secret Six	1.75
❑605, Aug 1988; Superman, Blackhawk, Green Lantern, Deadman, Wild Dog, Secret Six	1.75
❑606, Sep 1988; Superman, Blackhawk, Green Lantern, Deadman, Wild Dog, Secret Six	1.75
❑607, Sep 1988; Superman, Blackhawk, Green Lantern, Deadman, Wild Dog, Secret Six	1.75
❑608, Sep 1988; Superman, Blackhawk, Green Lantern, Deadman, Wild Dog, Secret Six	1.75
❑609, Sep 1988; BB (c); PD (w); CS, DS (a); Superman, Black Canary, Green Lantern, Deadman, Wild Dog, Secret Six	1.75
❑610, Sep 1988; PD (w); CS, DS (a); Superman, Phantom Stranger, Black Canary, Green Lantern, Deadman, Secret Six	1.75
❑611, Oct 1988; AN (c); PD (w); CS, DS (a); Superman, Catwoman, Black Canary, Green Lantern, Deadman, Secret Six	1.75
❑612, Oct 1988; PG (c); PD (w); CS, DS (a); Superman, Catwoman, Black Canary, Green Lantern, Deadman, Secret Six	1.75
❑613, Oct 1988; Superman, Nightwing/Speedy, Phantom Stranger, Catwoman, Black Canary, Green Lantern	1.75
❑614, Oct 1988; Superman, Nightwing/Speedy, Phantom Stranger, Catwoman, Black Canary, Green Lantern	1.75
❑615, Oct 1988; Superman, Wild Dog, Blackhawk, Nightwing/Speedy, Black Canary, Green Lantern	1.75
❑616, Nov 1988; Superman, Wild Dog, Blackhawk, Nightwing/Speedy, Black Canary, Green Lantern	1.75
❑617, Nov 1988; Superman, Phantom Stranger, Wild Dog, Blackhawk, Nightwing/Speedy, Green Lantern	1.75
❑618, Nov 1988; Superman, Deadman, Wild Dog, Blackhawk, Nightwing/Speedy, Green Lantern	1.75
❑619, Nov 1988; Superman, Secret Six, Deadman, Wild Dog, Blackhawk, Green Lantern	1.75
❑620, Dec 1988; Superman, Secret Six, Deadman, Wild Dog, Blackhawk, Green Lantern	1.75
❑621, Dec 1988; Superman, Secret Six, Deadman, Wild Dog, Blackhawk, Green Lantern	1.75
❑622, Dec 1988; Superman, Starman, Secret Six, Wild Dog, Blackhawk, Green Lantern	1.75
❑623, Dec 1988; BA (c); BA, CS, FS (a); Superman, Deadman, Phantom Stranger, Shazam!, Secret Six, Green Lantern	1.75
❑624, Dec 1988; Superman, Black Canary, Deadman, Shazam!, Secret Six, Green Lantern	1.75
❑625, Dec 1988; Superman, Black Canary, Deadman, Shazam!, Secret Six, Green Lantern	1.75
❑626, Nov 1988; Superman, Black Canary, Deadman, Shazam!, Secret Six, Green Lantern	1.75
❑627, Nov 1988; Superman, Nightwing/Speedy, Black Canary, Secret Six, Green Lantern	1.75
❑628, Nov 1988; Superman, Blackhawk, Nightwing/Speedy, Black Canary, Secret Six, Green Lantern	1.75
❑629, Dec 1988; Superman, Blackhawk, Nightwing/Speedy, Black Canary, Secret Six, Green Lantern	1.75
❑630, Dec 1988; Superman, Blackhawk, Nightwing/Speedy, Black Canary, Secret Six, Green Lantern	1.75
❑631, Dec 1988; Superman, Phantom Stranger, Blackhawk, Nightwing/Speedy, Black Canary, Green Lantern	1.75
❑632, Dec 1988; Superman, Phantom Stranger, Blackhawk, Nightwing/Speedy, Black Canary, Green Lantern	1.75
❑633, Jan 1989; Superman, Phantom Stranger, Blackhawk, Nightwing/Speedy, Black Canary, Green Lantern	1.75
❑634, Jan 1989; Superman, Phantom Stranger, Blackhawk, Nightwing/Speedy, Black Canary, Green Lantern	1.75
❑635, Jan 1989; Superman, Blackhawk, Black Canary, Green Lantern; All characters in first story	1.75
❑636, Jan 1989; 1: new Phantom Lady. Superman, Phantom Lady, Wild Dog, Demon, Speedy, Phantom Stranger	1.75
❑637, Jan 1989; 1: Hero Hotline. Superman, Hero Hotline, Phantom Lady, Wild Dog, Demon, Speedy	1.75
❑638, Feb 1989; JK (c); JK, CS, TD (a); 2: Hero Hotline. Superman, Hero Hotline, Phantom Lady, Wild Dog, Demon, Speedy	1.75
❑639, Feb 1989; A: Hero Hotline. Superman, Hero Hotline, Phantom Lady, Wild Dog, Demon, Speedy	1.75
❑640, Feb 1989; A: Hero Hotline. Superman, Hero Hotline, Phantom Lady, Wild Dog, Demon, Speedy	1.75
❑641, Mar 1989; Superman, Phantom Stranger, Human Target, Phantom Lady, Wild Dog, Demon	1.75
❑642, Mar 1989; Superman, Green Lantern, Nightwing, Deadman, Guy Gardner in one story; Last weekly issue	1.75
❑643, Jul 1989; GP (c); GP (w); GP (a); Cover swipe from Superman #1; Title returns to Action Comics; Monthly issues begin again	1.75
❑644, Aug 1989; GP (c); GP (w); GP (a); O: Matrix	1.75
❑645, Sep 1989; GP (c); GP (w); GP (a); 1: Maxima. V: Maxima. Starman	1.75
❑646, Oct 1989 GP (c); KG, GP (a)	1.75
❑647, Nov 1989; GP (c); GP, KGa (a); O: Brainiac. Braniac Trilogy, Part 1	1.75
❑648, Dec 1989; GP (c); GP, KGa (a); Braniac Trilogy, Part 2	1.75
❑649, Jan 1990; GP (c); GP, KGa (a); Braniac Trilogy, Part 3	1.75
❑650, Feb 1990; GP (c); JO, JOy, GP, CS, KGa (a); A: Lobo. 52 pages; 48 pages	1.75
❑651, Mar 1990; V: Maxima. Day of the Krypton Man, Part 3	1.75
❑652, Apr 1990; Day of the Krypton Man, Part 6	1.75
❑653, May 1990	1.75
❑654, Jun 1990; Batman	1.75
❑655, Jul 1990; 40 pages; Cover logo change	1.75
❑656, Aug 1990	1.75
❑657, Sep 1990; Toyman	1.75
❑658, Oct 1990 KGa (c); CS (a); A: Sinbad.	1.75
❑659, Nov 1990; Krisis of the Krimson Kryptonite, Part 3	1.75
❑660, Dec 1990; D: Lex Luthor (fake death). D: Lex Luthor (fake death)	2.50
❑661, Jan 1991; Plastic Man; ▲1991-3	1.75
❑662, Feb 1991; Clark Kent reveals Superman identity to Lois Lane▲1991-6	4.00
❑662/2nd, Feb 1991; Clark Kent reveals Superman identity to Lois Lane; ▲1991-6, 2nd Printing	1.50
❑663, Mar 1991; Superman in 1940s; JSA; ▲1991-9	1.75
❑664, Apr 1991; A: Chronos. Dinosaurs; ▲1991-12	1.75
❑665, May 1991; ▲1991-15	1.75
❑666, Jun 1991; ▲1991-18	1.75
❑667, Jul 1991; ▲1991-22	2.00
❑668, Aug 1991; ▲1991-26	1.75
❑669, Sep 1991; A: Thorn. ▲1991-30	1.75
❑670, Oct 1991; 1: Lex Luthor II. Armageddon; ▲1991-34	1.75
❑671, Nov 1991; Blackout, Part 2; ▲1991-38	1.75
❑672, Dec 1991; BMc (a); ▲1991-42	1.75
❑673, Jan 1992; BMc (a); V: Hellgrammite. ▲1992-4	1.75
❑674, Feb 1992; BMc (a); Panic in the Sky, Prologue; Supergirl; ▲1992-8	1.75
❑675, Mar 1992; BMc (a); Panic in the Sky, Part 4; ▲1992-12	1.75
❑676, Apr 1992; BG (a); ▲1992-16	1.75
❑677, May 1992; BG (a); ▲1992-20	1.75
❑678, Jun 1992; BG (a); O: Luthor. ▲1992-24	2.00
❑679, Jul 1992; BG (a); ▲1992-28	1.75
❑680, Aug 1992; BG (a); Blaze/Satanus War; ▲1992-32	1.75
❑681, Sep 1992; BG (a); V: Rampage. ▲1992-36	1.75
❑682, Oct 1992; V: Hi-Tech. ▲1992-40	1.75
❑683, Nov 1992; BG (a); Doomsday; ▲1992-44	2.50
❑683/2nd, Nov 1992; BG (a); Doomsday; ▲1992-44, 2nd Printing	1.50
❑684, Dec 1992; BG (a); Doomsday; ▲1992-48	2.50
❑684/2nd, Dec 1992; BG (a); Doomsday; ▲1992-48, 2nd Printing	1.50
❑685, Jan 1993; BG (a); Funeral For a Friend, Part 2; ▲1993-4	2.00
❑685/2nd, Jan 1993; BG (a); Funeral For a Friend, Part 2; ▲1993-4, 2nd Printing	1.25

❑685/3rd, Jan 1993; BG (a); Funeral For a Friend, Part 2; ▲1993-4, 3rd Printing ... 1.25
❑686, Feb 1993; BG (a); Funeral For a Friend, Part 6; ▲1993-8 ... 2.00
❑687, Jun 1993; KGa (c); BG (a); 1: alien Superman. A: ▲1993-12, 1st. Reign of the Supermen; ▲1993-12 ... 1.50
❑687/CS, Jun 1993; KGa (c); BG (a); Reign of the Supermen; Eradicator; ▲1993-12; Die-cut cover ... 2.50
❑688, Jul 1993; BG (a); Reign of the Supermen; Guy Gardner; ▲1993-16 ... 2.00
❑689, Jul 1993; BG (a); Reign of the Supermen; ▲1993-20 ... 2.00
❑690, Aug 1993; KGa (c); BG (a); Reign of the Supermen; ▲1993-24 ... 2.00
❑691, Sep 1993; BG (a); Reign of the Supermen; ▲1993-28 ... 2.00
❑692, Oct 1993; BG (a); Clark Kent returns; ▲1993-32 ... 2.00
❑693, Nov 1993; BG (a); ▲1993-36 ... 2.00
❑694, Dec 1993; BG (a); V: Hi-Tech. ▲1993-40 ... 1.75
❑695, Jan 1994; BG (a); A: Lobo. ▲1994-4 ... 1.75
❑695/Variant, Jan 1994; BG (a); A: Lobo. enhanced cover; ▲1994-4 ... 2.50
❑696, Feb 1994; BG (a); Return of Doomsday; ▲1994-8 ... 1.75
❑697, Mar 1994; BG (a); Bizarro's World, Part 3; ▲1994-12 ... 1.75
❑698, Apr 1994; BG (a); ▲1994-16 ... 1.75
❑699, May 1994; The Battle for Metropolis; ▲1994-20 ... 1.75
❑700, Jun 1994; Giant-size; BG, CS (a); The Fall Of Metropolis; Wedding of Pete Ross and Lana Lang; Destruction of the Daily Planet building; ▲1994-24 ... 3.25
❑700/Platinum, Jun 1994; Giant-size; BG, CS (a); No cover price; The Fall Of Metropolis; Wedding of Pete Ross and Lana Lang; Destruction of the Daily Planet building; ▲1994-24 ... 5.00
❑701, Jul 1994; BG (a); Fall of Metropolis; ▲1994-28 ... 1.75
❑702, Aug 1994; BG (a); V: Bloodsport. ▲1994-32 ... 1.75
❑703, Sep 1994; BG (a); A: Liri Lee. A: Starro. Zero Hour; ▲1994-36 ... 1.75
❑704, Nov 1994; BG (a); V: Eradictor and The Outsiders. Dead Again; ▲1994-44 ... 1.75
❑705, Dec 1994; BG (a); Dead Again; ▲1994-48 ... 1.75
❑706, Jan 1995; BG (a); Supergirl; ▲1995-4 ... 1.75
❑707, Feb 1995; BG (a); V: Shadow-dragon. ▲1995-8 ... 1.75
❑708, Mar 1995; BG (a); A: Mister Miracle. ▲1995-12 ... 1.75
❑709, Apr 1995; V: Guy Gardner. ▲1995-16 ... 1.75
❑710, Jun 1995; D: Clark Kent; ▲1995-20 ... 1.95
❑711, Jul 1995; BG (a); D: Kenny Braverman (Conduit). D: Clark Kent; ▲1995-24 ... 1.95
❑712, Aug 1995; ▲1995-29 ... 1.95
❑713, Sep 1995; ▲1995-33 ... 1.95
❑714, Oct 1995; A: Joker. ▲1995-37 ... 1.95
❑715, Nov 1995; V: Parasite. ▲1995-42 ... 1.95
❑716, Dec 1995; Trial of Superman; ▲1995-46 ... 1.95
❑717, Jan 1996; Trial of Superman; ▲1996-1 ... 1.95
❑718, Feb 1996; 1: Demolitia. ▲1996-5 ... 1.95
❑719, Mar 1996; A: Batman. ▲1996-9 ... 1.95
❑720, Apr 1996; Lois Lane breaks off engagement to Clark Kent; ▲1996-14 ... 2.00
❑720/2nd, Apr 1996; Lois Lane breaks off engagement to Clark Kent; ▲1996-14, 2nd Printing ... 1.95
❑721, May 1996; A: Mxyzptlk. ▲1996-18 ... 1.95
❑722, Jun 1996; ▲1996-22 ... 1.95
❑723, Jul 1996; ▲1996-27 ... 1.95
❑724, Aug 1996; O: Brawl. D: Brawl. ▲1996-31 ... 1.95
❑725, Sep 1996; V: Tolos. The Bottle City, Part 1; ▲1996-35 ... 1.95
❑726, Oct 1996; V: Barrage. ▲1996-40 ... 1.95
❑727, Nov 1996; Final Night; ▲1996-44 ... 1.95
❑728, Dec 1996; Hawaiian Honeymoon; ▲1996-49 ... 1.95
❑729, Jan 1997; A: Mr. Miracle, Big Barda. Power Struggle; ▲1997-3 ... 1.95
❑730, Feb 1997; V: Superman Revenge Squad (Anomaly, Maxima, Misa, Barrage and Riot). ▲1997-8 ... 1.95
❑731, Mar 1997; V: Cauldron. ▲1997-12 ... 1.95

N-MINT

❑732, Apr 1997; V: Atomic Skull. more energy powers manifest; ▲1997-17 ... 1.95
❑733, May 1997; A: Ray. new uniform; ▲1997-21 ... 1.95
❑734, Jun 1997; Scorn vs. Rock; ▲1997-25 ... 1.95
❑735, Jul 1997; V: Saviour. ▲1997-29 ... 1.95
❑736, Aug 1997; ▲1997-33 ... 1.95
❑737, Sep 1997; MWa (w); Jimmy pursued by Intergang; ▲1997-37 ... 1.95
❑738, Oct 1997; 1: Inkling. ▲1997-42 ... 1.95
❑739, Nov 1997; A: Sam Lane. V: Locksmith. Lois captured by Naga; ▲1997-46 ... 1.95
❑740, Dec 1997; V: Ripper. Face cover; ▲1997-50 ... 1.95
❑741, Jan 1998; A: Legion of Super-Heroes. ▲1998-4 ... 1.95
❑742, Mar 1998; Cover forms diptych with Superman: Man of Steel #77; ▲1998-10 ... 1.95
❑743, Apr 1998; O: Inkling; ▲1998-14 ... 1.95
❑744, May 1998; Millennium Giants; ▲1998-18 ... 1.95
❑745, Jun 1998; V: Prankster. Toyman; ▲1998-23 ... 1.95
❑746, Jul 1998; V: Prankster. Toyman; ▲1998-27 ... 1.95
❑747, Aug 1998; A: Dominus. ▲1998-31 ... 1.95
❑748, Sep 1998; A: Waverider. V: Dominus. ▲1998-35 ... 1.95
❑749, Dec 1998; into Kandor; ▲1998-41 ... 2.00
❑750, Jan 1999; Giant-size; 1: Crazytop. ▲1999-1 ... 2.00
❑751, Feb 1999; A: Lex Luthor. A: Geo-Force. A: DEO agents. ▲1999-6 ... 1.99
❑752, Mar 1999; A: Supermen of America. ▲1999-11 ... 1.99
❑753, Apr 1999; A: Justice League of America. A: JLA. ▲1999-15 ... 1.99
❑754, May 1999; V: Dominus. ▲1999-20 ... 1.99
❑755, Jul 1999; ▲1999-25 ... 1.99
❑756, Aug 1999; V: Doomslayers. ▲1999-30 ... 1.99
❑757, Sep 1999; Superman as Hawkman; ▲1999-34 ... 1.99
❑758, Oct 1999; V: Intergang. ▲1999-38 ... 1.99
❑759, Nov 1999; SB (a); A: Strange Visitor. ▲1999-42 ... 1.99
❑760, Dec 1999; ▲1999-49 ... 1.99
❑761, Jan 2000; A: Wonder Woman. ▲2000-4 ... 1.99
❑762, Feb 2000; ▲2000-9 ... 1.99
❑763, Mar 2000; ▲2000-13 ... 1.99
❑764, Apr 2000; ▲2000-17 ... 1.99
❑765, May 2000; Joker, Harley Quinn; ▲2000-21 ... 1.99
❑766, Jun 2000; ▲2000-25 ... 1.99
❑767, Jul 2000; ▲2000-29 ... 1.99
❑768, Aug 2000; A: Captain Marvel Jr.. A: Captain Marvel. A: Mary Marvel. ▲2000-33 ... 1.99
❑769, Sep 2000; ▲2000-37 ... 2.25
❑770, Oct 2000; Giant-size; A: Joker. ▲2000-42 ... 3.50
❑771, Nov 2000; A: Nightwing. ▲2000-46 ... 2.25
❑772, Dec 2000; A: Encantadora. A: Talia. ▲2000-50 ... 2.25
❑773, Jan 2001; ▲2001-5 ... 2.25
❑774, Feb 2001; ▲2001-9 ... 2.25
❑775, Mar 2001; Giant-size; ▲2001-13 ... 5.00
❑775/2nd, Mar 2001; Second Printing ... 3.75
❑776, Apr 2001; ▲2001-17 ... 2.25
❑777, May 2001; ▲2001-21 ... 2.25
❑778, Jun 2001; ▲2001-25 ... 2.25
❑779, Jul 2001; ▲2001-29 ... 2.25
❑780, Aug 2001; ▲2001-33 ... 2.25
❑781, Sep 2001; ▲2001-37 ... 2.25
❑782, Oct 2001; ▲2001-41 ... 2.25
❑783, Nov 2001; ▲2001-45 ... 2.25
❑784, Dec 2001; BSz (c); ▲2001-49 ... 2.25
❑785, Jan 2002; ▲2002-4 ... 2.25
❑786, Feb 2002; V: Kanjar Ro ... 2.25
❑787, Mar 2002; 1: Gunshin; 1: Byakko; 1: Sakki; New cover logo ... 2.25
❑788, Apr 2002; D: Gunshin ... 2.25
❑789, May 2002 ... 2.25
❑790, Jun 2002 ... 2.25
❑791, Jul 2002 ... 2.25
❑792, Aug 2002 ... 2.25
❑793, Sep 2002 ... 2.25
❑794, Oct 2002 ... 2.25
❑795, Nov 2002 KN (c) ... 2.25

N-MINT

❑796, Dec 2002; D: Manchester Black ... 2.25
❑797, Jan 2003; H-E-R-O preview inside ... 2.25
❑798, Feb 2003 ... 2.25
❑799, Mar 2003 ... 2.25
❑800, Apr 2003; ARo, BSz, JLee, KJ (a); O: Superman; Giant-size ... 3.95
❑801, May 2003 ... 2.25
❑802, Jun 2003 ... 2.25
❑803, Jul 2003 ... 2.25
❑804, Jun 2003 ... 2.25
❑805, Jul 2003 ... 2.25
❑806, Aug 2003; 1: Natasha Irons as Steel ... 2.25
❑807, Sep 2003; Supergirls ... 2.25
❑808, Oct 2003; Supergirls ... 2.25
❑809, Jan 2004; Creeper (Jack Ryder) appears ... 2.25
❑810, Feb 2004 ... 2.25
❑811, Mar 2004 ... 5.00
❑812, Apr 2004 ... 8.00
❑812/2nd, Apr 2004 ... 2.25
❑813, May 2004, Storyline continued into Adventures of Superman #626 ... 4.00
❑814, Jun 2004; New cover logo ... 3.00
❑815, Jul 2004 ... 3.00
❑816, Aug 2004 ... 3.00
❑817, Sep 2004; V: Weapon Master ... 3.00
❑818, Oct 2004 ... 4.00
❑819, Nov 2004 ... 2.50
❑820, Dec 2004, V: Silver Banshee ... 2.50
❑821, Jan 2005 ... 2.50
❑822, Feb 2005 ... 2.50
❑823, Mar 2005, Superman ages ... 2.50
❑824, Mar 2005 ... 2.50
❑825, Apr 2005; V: Gog; 40 pages ... 2.99
❑826, May 2005; Storyline continued into Adventures of Superman #639 ... 5.00
❑827, Jun 2005 ... 2.50
❑828, Jul 2005; New DC logo ... 2.50
❑829, Aug 2005; OMAC Project; Green Lantern I cameo; Captain Marvel cameo; V: Darkseid; OMAC Project Tie-In; Storyline continued from Superman (2nd Series) #219 & into Adventures of Superman #642 ... 6.00
❑829/Variant, Aug 2005 ... 2.50
❑830, Sep 2005; V: Dr. Psycho ... 4.00
❑831, Oct 2005; Villains United tie-in ... 2.50
❑832, Dec 2005; V: the Spectre ... 2.50
❑833, Jan 2006; V: Queen of Fables ... 2.50
❑834, Feb 2006 ... 2.50
❑835, Mar 2006, 1: Livewire; Adapted from Superman cartoon ... 2.50
❑836, Apr 2006, Infinite Crisis crossover ... 2.50
❑837, Jun 2006, One Year Later; Storyline continued from Superman (2nd Series) # 650 & into #651 ... 2.50
❑838, Jul 2006; One Year Later; Storyline continued from Superman (2nd Series) #651 & into #652 ... 2.50
❑839, Aug 2006, One Year Later; Storyline continued from Superman (2nd Series) #652 & into #653 ... 2.99
❑840, Sep 2006, Cover by Terry Dodson and Rachel Dodson; Storyline continued from Superman (2nd Series) #653 ... 2.99
❑841, Oct 2006 ... 2.99
❑842, Nov 2006 ... 2.99
❑843, Dec 2006 ... 2.99
❑844, Dec 2006 ... 6.00
❑845, Jan 2007, 1: General Zod; 1: Ursa; 1: Non ... 5.00
❑846, Feb 2007; O: General Zod ... 2.99
❑847, Mar 2007; V: Sun-Eater ... 2.99
❑848, Apr 2007 ... 2.99
❑849, May 2007 ... 2.99
❑850, Jun 2007; O: Superman; V: Blackstar; V: Blackstarr (Rachel Berkowitz) ... 3.99
❑851, Jul 2007 ... 2.99
❑852, Aug 2007; Countdown tie-in ... 2.99
❑853, Sep 2007; Countdown tie-in ... 2.99
❑854, Oct 2007; Countdown tie-in ... 2.99
❑855, Nov 2007; 1: Bizarro Lois Lane; Return of Bizarro ... 2.99
❑856, Dec 2007; Includes Superman Airheads insert story; 1: Bizarro Lex Luthor; 1: Bizarro Mr. Mxyzptlk; 1: Bizarro Doomsday; 1: Bizarro Batman; 1: Bizarro Wonder Woman; 1: Bizarro Flash; 1: Bizarro Green Lantern; 1: Bizarro Hawkgirl ... 2.99

Other grades: Multiply price above by 5/6 for VF/NM • 2/3 for VERY FINE • 1/3 for FINE • 1/5 for VERY GOOD • 1/8 for GOOD

Action Planet Comics

Anthology series starring Monsterman
©Action Planet

Actions Speak

Sergio Aragonès' wordless humor series
©Dark Horse

A.D.A.M.

Scientist discovers the secret to superpowers
©The Toy Man

Adam-12

"One Adam-12!" comes to comics from TV
©Gold Key

Adam and Eve A.D.

Science fiction title from the 1980s b&w boom
©Bam

	N-MINT
❑857, Jan 2008; 1: Bizarro Aquaman; 1: Bizarro Green Arrow; 1: Bizarro Robin; 1: Bizarro Brainiac; D: Bizarro Aquaman; D: Bizarro Robin; D: Bizarro Green Arrow; Includes Adventures of Finn & Friends insert story	2.99
❑858, Feb 2008; Legion of Super-Heroes appearance; Double-sized issue	6.00
❑859, Mar 2008	2.99
❑860, Apr 2008; Six people on cover, center male holding globe in left hand upraised	2.99
❑861, Apr 2008	2.99
❑862, May 2008	2.99
❑863	2.99
❑864	2.99
❑865	2.99
❑866	2.99
❑867	2.99
❑868	2.99
❑869	2.99
❑870	2.99
❑871	2.99
❑872	2.99
❑873	2.99
❑874	2.99
❑1000000, Nov 1998; Story falls between #748 and #749	1.00
❑Ann 1, Dec 1987; JBy (w); DG (a); Batman, female vampire; 1987 Ann	4.00
❑Ann 2, Dec 1989; GP (c); JOy, GP (w); JO, JOy, GP, CS (a); 1: The Eradicator. Matrix and Cat Grant bios; pin-up; 1989 Ann	3.00
❑Ann 3, Dec 1991; Armageddon 2001, Part 8; 1991 Ann	2.50
❑Ann 4, Dec 1992; Eclipso: The Darkness Within, Part 10; 1992 Ann	2.50
❑Ann 5, Jun 1993; MZ (c); JPH (w); 1: Loose Cannon. Bloodlines: Earthplague; 1993 Ann	2.50
❑Ann 6, ca. 1994; JBy (w); JBy (a); Elseworlds; 1994 Ann	2.95
❑Ann 7, ca. 1995; Year One; 1995 Ann	3.95
❑Ann 8, ca. 1996; JOy (c); A: Bizarro. Bizarro; Legends of the Dead Earth; 1996 Ann	2.95
❑Ann 9, ca. 1997; Pulp Heroes #9; 1997 Ann	3.95
❑Ann 10	3.99
❑Ann 11	4.99
❑Ann 12	4.99

A.C.T.I.O.N. Force (Lightning)
Lightning

	N-MINT
❑1, Jan 1987	1.75

Action Girl Comics
Slave Labor

	N-MINT
❑1, Oct 1994	3.50
❑1/2nd, Feb 1996; 2nd printing	2.75
❑2, Jan 1995	3.00
❑2/2nd, Oct 1995; 2nd printing	2.75
❑3, Apr 1995	3.00
❑3/2nd, Feb 1996; 2nd printing	2.75
❑4, Jul 1995	3.00
❑4/2nd, Jul 1996; 2nd printing	3.00
❑4/3rd; 3rd printing	3.00
❑5, Oct 1995	3.00
❑6, Jan 1996	2.75
❑6/2nd; 2nd printing	2.75
❑7, May 1996	2.75
❑8, Jul 1996	2.75
❑9	2.75
❑10, Jan 1997	2.75
❑11, May 1997, b&w	2.75
❑12, Jul 1997	2.75
❑13, Oct 1997	2.75
❑14, Jul 1998	2.75

Action Planet Comics
Action Planet

	N-MINT
❑1, b&w; Black and white	3.95
❑2, Sep 2000, b&w anthology	3.95
❑3, Sep 1997, b&w anthology	3.95
❑Ashcan 1, b&w; preview of series; "Philly Ashcan Ed."	2.00
❑GS 1, Oct 1998; GS; Halloween Special; Anthology; Giant-size	5.95

Actions Speak (Sergio Aragonés)
Dark Horse

	N-MINT
❑1, Jan 2001	2.99
❑2, Feb 2001	2.99
❑3, Mar 2001	2.99
❑4, Apr 2001	2.99
❑5, May 2001	2.99
❑6, Jun 2001	2.99

Ada Lee
NBM

	N-MINT
❑1; Adult	9.95

A.D.A.M.
The Toy Man

	N-MINT
❑1	2.95
❑Ashcan 1; no cover price; preview	1.00

Adam-12
Gold Key

	N-MINT
❑1, Dec 1973, Photo cover	20.00
❑2, Feb 1974	15.00
❑3, May 1974	12.00
❑4, Aug 1974	12.00
❑5, Nov 1974	12.00
❑6, Mar 1975	10.00
❑7, May 1975, Photo cover	10.00
❑8, Aug 1975	10.00
❑9, Nov 1975	10.00
❑10, Feb 1976, Photo cover	10.00

Adam and Eve A.D.
Bam

	N-MINT
❑1, Sep 1985	1.50
❑2, Nov 1985	1.50
❑3, Jan 1986	1.50
❑4, Mar 1986	1.50
❑5, May 1986	1.50
❑6, Jul 1986	1.50
❑7, Oct 1986	1.50
❑8, Nov 1986	1.50
❑9, Jan 1987	1.50
❑10, Mar 1987	1.50

Adam Bomb Comics
Blue Monkey

	N-MINT
❑1, Sum 1999, b&w	2.00

Adam Strange
DC

	N-MINT
❑1, Mar 1990; Wraparound cover art	3.95
❑2, May 1990; Wraparound cover art	3.95
❑3, Jul 1990; Wraparound cover art	3.95

Adam Strange
DC

	N-MINT
❑1, Nov 2004	10.00
❑2, Dec 2004	6.00
❑3, Jan 2005	6.00
❑4, Feb 2005; D: Doc; Harpis; Tigorr; Broot; Seer	5.00
❑5, Mar 2005; Tigorr; Artin; Broot; Harpis; Elu	5.00
❑6, Apr 2005	5.00
❑7, May 2005	7.00
❑8, Jun 2005; D: Ferrin Colos; D: Chaser Bron; D: Munchuk; Leads to Rann/Thanagar War #1	8.00

Addam Omega
Antarctic

	N-MINT
❑1, Jan 1997	2.95
❑2, Apr 1997	2.95
❑3, Jun 1997	2.95
❑4, Aug 1997	2.95

Addams Family
Gold Key

	N-MINT
❑1, Oct 1974	60.00
❑2, ca. 1975	35.00
❑3, Apr 1975	35.00

Addams Family Episode Guide
Comic Chronicles

	N-MINT
❑1, b&w; illustrated episode guide to original TV series	5.95

Adolescent Radioactive Black Belt Hamsters
Eclipse

	N-MINT
❑1, b&w; 1&O: The Adolescent Radioactive Black Belt Hamsters	2.00
❑1/Gold 1993; Gold edition; Published by Parody; 500 copies printed	2.95
❑1/2nd; 2nd printing; 1&O: The Adolescent Radioactive Black Belt Hamsters	1.50
❑2, Spr 1986; Spring 1986	1.50
❑3, Jul 1986	1.50
❑4, Nov 1986	1.50
❑5, Feb 1987	1.50
❑6, May 1987	1.50
❑7, Aug 1987; D: Bruce	1.50
❑8, Oct 1987	2.00
❑9, Jan 1988; Final Issue	2.00

Adolescent Radioactive Black Belt Hamsters Classics
Parody

	N-MINT
❑1, Aug 1992, b&w; Reprints ARBBH in 3-D #1	2.50
❑2, b&w; Reprints ARBBH in 3-D #2	2.50
❑3; Reprints ARBBH (Eclipse) #3	2.50
❑4; Reprints ARBBH: Massacre the Japanese Invasion	2.50
❑5; Reprints ARBBH in 3-D #4; holiday cover	2.50

Adolescent Radioactive Black Belt Hamsters in 3-D
Eclipse

	N-MINT
❑1, Jul 1986	2.50
❑2, Sep 1986	2.50
❑3, Nov 1986, aka Eclipse 3-D #13	2.50
❑4, Dec 1986, aka Eclipse 3-D #14	2.50

Other grades: Multiply price above by 5/6 for VF/NM • 2/3 for VERY FINE • 1/3 for FINE • 1/5 for VERY GOOD • 1/8 for GOOD

N-MINT

Adolescent Radioactive Black Belt Hamsters: Lost and Alone in New York
Parody
- ❑1 ... 2.95

Adolescent Radioactive Black Belt Hamsters Massacre the Japanese Invasion
Eclipse
- ❑1, Aug 1989, b&w ... 2.50

Adolescent Radioactive Black Belt Hamsters: The Lost Treasures
Parody
- ❑1, b&w; Reprints portions of ARBBH (Eclipse) #9; cardstock cover ... 2.95

AD Police
Viz
- ❑1, May 1994, b&w ... 14.95
- ❑1/2nd; 2nd printing with fold-out cover 12.95

Adrenalynn
Image
- ❑1, Aug 1999 ... 2.50
- ❑2, Oct 1999; Tony Daniel cover ... 2.50
- ❑3, Dec 1999; Includes sketchbook pages 2.50
- ❑4, Feb 2000; Pin-up page ... 2.50

Adult Action Fantasy Featuring: Tawny's Tales
Louisiana Leisure
- ❑1; b&w; ca. 1990 ... 2.50
- ❑2; Adult; ca. 1992 ... 2.50

Adults Only! Comic Magazine
Inkwell
- ❑1, Aug 1979; Adult ... 2.50
- ❑2, Fal 1985; Fall 1985; Adult ... 2.50
- ❑3; Adult ... 2.50

Advanced Dungeons & Dragons
DC
- ❑1, Dec 1988 ... 2.00
- ❑2, Jan 1989 ... 1.50
- ❑3, Feb 1989 ... 1.50
- ❑4, Mar 1989 ... 1.50
- ❑5, Apr 1989 ... 1.50
- ❑6, May 1989 ... 1.50
- ❑7, Jun 1989 ... 1.50
- ❑8, Jul 1989 ... 1.50
- ❑9, Aug 1989 ... 1.50
- ❑10, Sep 1989 ... 1.50
- ❑11, Oct 1989 ... 1.50
- ❑12, Nov 1989 ... 1.50
- ❑13, Dec 1989 ... 1.50
- ❑14, Jan 1990 ... 1.50
- ❑15, Feb 1990 ... 1.50
- ❑16, Mar 1990 ... 1.50
- ❑17, Apr 1990 ... 1.50
- ❑18, May 1990 ... 1.50
- ❑19, Jun 1990, Phases of the Moon ... 1.50
- ❑20, Jul 1990 ... 1.50
- ❑21, Aug 1990 ... 1.50
- ❑22, Sep 1990 ... 1.50
- ❑23, Nov 1990 ... 1.50
- ❑24, Dec 1990 ... 1.50
- ❑25, Jan 1991, Scavengers, Part III ... 1.50
- ❑26, Feb 1991 ... 1.50
- ❑27, Mar 1991 ... 1.50
- ❑28, Apr 1991 ... 1.50
- ❑29, May 1991 ... 1.50
- ❑30, Jun 1991 ... 1.50
- ❑31, Jul 1991 ... 1.50
- ❑32, Aug 1991 ... 1.50
- ❑33, Sep 1991 ... 1.50
- ❑34, Oct 1991 ... 1.50
- ❑35, Nov 1991 ... 1.50
- ❑36, Dec 1991, Final Issue ... 1.50
- ❑Ann 1, ca. 1990 ... 3.00

Adventure Comics
DC
- ❑290, Nov 1961, CS (c); O: Sun Boy. A: Legion of Super-Heroes. Sun Boy joins Legion of Super-Heroes ... 100.00
- ❑291, Dec 1961, Superboy cover ... 45.00
- ❑292, Jan 1962, Superboy cover ... 45.00
- ❑293, Feb 1962, CS (c); CS (a); O: Mon-El. 1: Mon-El in Legion. 1: Legion of Super-Pets. Bizarro Luthor ... 100.00
- ❑294, Mar 1962, 1: Bizarro Marilyn Monroe. Superboy cover ... 90.00
- ❑295, Apr 1962, Superboy cover ... 45.00
- ❑296, May 1962, Superboy cover ... 45.00
- ❑297, Jun 1962, Superboy cover ... 45.00
- ❑298, Jul 1962, Superboy cover ... 45.00
- ❑299, Aug 1962, 1: Gold Kryptonite. Superboy; Bizarro world story ... 55.00
- ❑300, Sep 1962, 300th anniversary issue; Legion cover; Mon-El joins team; Legion of Super-Heroes begins as a regular back-up feature ... 200.00
- ❑301, Oct 1962, CS (a); O: Bouncing Boy 70.00
- ❑302, Nov 1962, CS (a); Legion ... 55.00
- ❑303, Dec 1962, 1: Matter-Eater Lad. Matter-Eater Lad joins team; Legion ... 55.00
- ❑304, Jan 1963, D: Lightning Lad. Legion 55.00
- ❑305, Feb 1963, Legion ... 55.00
- ❑306, Mar 1963, 1: Legion of Substitute Heroes. "Teen-age" Mxyzptlk ... 45.00
- ❑307, Apr 1963, 1: Element Lad. 1: Roxxas. Element Lad joins team; Legion ... 45.00
- ❑308, May 1963, 1: Lightning Lass. 1: Proty. Legion; Lightning Lass joins team ... 45.00
- ❑309, Jun 1963, Legion ... 45.00
- ❑310, Jul 1963, Legion ... 45.00
- ❑311, Aug 1963, 1: Legion of Super-Heroes Headquarters. A: Legion of Substitute Heroes. Legion ... 45.00
- ❑312, Sep 1963, D: Proty. Legion; Return of Lightning Lad ... 45.00
- ❑313, Oct 1963, CS (a); Legion ... 45.00
- ❑314, Nov 1963, Legion ... 45.00
- ❑315, Dec 1963, Legion ... 45.00
- ❑316, Jan 1964, CS (a); profile pages; Legion 45.00
- ❑317, Feb 1964, 1: Dream Girl. Dream Girl joins team; Legion ... 45.00
- ❑318, Mar 1964, Legion ... 45.00
- ❑319, Apr 1964, Legion ... 45.00
- ❑320, May 1964, Legion ... 45.00
- ❑321, Jun 1964, 1: Time Trapper. Legion 45.00
- ❑322, Jul 1964, Legion ... 45.00
- ❑323, Aug 1964, Legion ... 45.00
- ❑324, Sep 1964, 1: Duplicate Boy. 1: Heroes of Lallor (later Wanderers). Legion ... 40.00
- ❑325, Oct 1964, Legion ... 40.00
- ❑326, Nov 1964, Legion ... 40.00
- ❑327, Dec 1964, 1: Timber Wolf. Timber Wolf joins team ... 40.00
- ❑328, Jan 1965, Legion ... 40.00
- ❑329, Feb 1965, JM (a); 1: Bizarro Legion of Super-Heroes. Legion ... 40.00
- ❑330, Mar 1965, JM (a); Dynamo Boy joins team; Legion ... 40.00
- ❑331, Apr 1965, JM (a); 1: Saturn Queen. Legion ... 40.00
- ❑332, May 1965, Legion ... 40.00
- ❑333, Jun 1965, Legion ... 40.00
- ❑334, Jul 1965, Legion ... 40.00
- ❑335, Aug 1965, 1: Magnetic Kid. 1: Starfinger. Legion ... 40.00
- ❑336, Sep 1965, Legion ... 40.00
- ❑337, Oct 1965, Legion; Wedding of Lightning Lad and Saturn Girl, Mon-El and Phantom Girl (fake weddings) ... 40.00
- ❑338, Nov 1965, 1: Glorith. V: Time-Trapper, Glorith ... 40.00
- ❑339, Dec 1965, Legion ... 40.00
- ❑340, Jan 1966, CS (a); 1: Computo. D: one of Triplicate Girl's bodies. Legion 45.00
- ❑341, Feb 1966, CS (a); Legion ... 40.00
- ❑342, Mar 1966, CS (a); 1: Color Kid. Legion 40.00
- ❑343, Apr 1966, CS (a); Legion; reprints story from Superboy #90 ... 40.00
- ❑344, May 1966, CS (a); Legion ... 40.00
- ❑345, Jun 1966, CS (a); 1: Khunds. D: Blockade Boy, Weight Wizard. Legion 40.00
- ❑346, Jul 1966, 1: Karate Kid, Princess Projectra, Ferro Lad. Karate Kid, Princess Projecta, Ferro Lad joins team 60.00
- ❑347, Aug 1966, CS (a); Legion ... 40.00
- ❑348, Sep 1966, O: Sunboy. 1: Doctor Regulus. V: Doctor Regulus. Legion ... 40.00
- ❑349, Oct 1966, 1: Rond Vidar ... 40.00
- ❑350, Nov 1966, CS (a); 1: Mysa Nal. 1: Prince Evillo. Legion ... 40.00
- ❑351, Dec 1966, CS (a); 1: White Witch 50.00
- ❑352, Jan 1967, CS (a); 1: The Fatal Five. Legion ... 50.00
- ❑353, Feb 1967, CS (a); D: Ferro Lad ... 35.00
- ❑354, Mar 1967, CS (a); Legion ... 35.00
- ❑355, Apr 1967, CS (a); Adult Legion story 35.00
- ❑356, May 1967, CS (a); Legion ... 30.00
- ❑357, Jun 1967, CS (a); 1: Controllers. Legion ... 60.00
- ❑358, Jul 1967, Legion ... 30.00
- ❑359, Aug 1967, CS (a); Legion ... 30.00
- ❑360, Sep 1967, CS (a); Legion ... 30.00
- ❑361, Oct 1967, JM (a); A: Dominators. V: Unkillables. Legion ... 30.00
- ❑362, Nov 1967, V: Mantis Morlo. Legion 30.00
- ❑363, Dec 1967, V: Mantis Morlo. Legion 30.00
- ❑364, Jan 1968, CS (a); Legion ... 30.00
- ❑365, Feb 1968, NA, CS (a); 1: Shadow Lass 30.00
- ❑366, Mar 1968, NA (c); NA, CS (a); V: Validus. Legion; Shadow Lass joins Legion ... 30.00
- ❑367, Apr 1968, NA (c); CS (a); 1: The Dark Circle. Legion ... 25.00
- ❑368, May 1968, Legion ... 25.00
- ❑369, Jun 1968, 1: Mordru. Legion in Smallville ... 25.00
- ❑370, Jul 1968, Legion ... 25.00
- ❑371, Aug 1968, NA (c); NA, CS (a); 1: Chemical King. 1: Legion Academy. Legion; Colossal Boy leaves team ... 25.00
- ❑372, Sep 1968, NA (c); NA, CS (a); Legion; Chemical King joins Legion; Timber Wolf joins Legion ... 25.00
- ❑373, Oct 1968, Legion ... 22.00
- ❑374, Nov 1968, Legion ... 30.00
- ❑375, Dec 1968, NA (c); NA (a); 1: Wanderers. 1: Quantum Queen. Legion 22.00
- ❑376, Jan 1969, Legion ... 22.00
- ❑377, Feb 1969, NA (c); NA (a); Legion. 22.00
- ❑378, Mar 1969, NA (c); NA (a); Legion 45.00
- ❑379, Apr 1969, NA (c); NA (a); Legion. 22.00
- ❑380, Apr 1969, CS (c); CS (a); Legion; Legion of Super-Heroes stories end ... 22.00
- ❑381, Jun 1969, Supergirl stories begin 60.00
- ❑382, Jul 1969, Supergirl ... 22.00
- ❑383, Aug 1969, Supergirl ... 22.00
- ❑384, Sep 1969, CS (c); KS (a); Supergirl 22.00
- ❑385, Oct 1969, Supergirl ... 22.00
- ❑386, Nov 1969, A: Mxyzptlk. Supergirl 22.00
- ❑387, Dec 1969, V: Lex Luthor. Supergirl 22.00
- ❑388, Jan 1970, V: Lex Luthor. Supergirl 22.00
- ❑389, Feb 1970, Supergirl ... 22.00
- ❑390, Apr 1970, Giant-size issue; aka Giant #G-69; All-Romance issue ... 30.00
- ❑391, Mar 1970, Supergirl ... 22.00
- ❑392, Apr 1970, Supergirl ... 22.00
- ❑393, May 1970, Supergirl ... 22.00
- ❑394, Jun 1970, Supergirl ... 22.00
- ❑395, Jul 1970, Supergirl ... 22.00
- ❑396, Aug 1970, Supergirl ... 22.00
- ❑397, Sep 1970, Supergirl ... 22.00
- ❑398, Oct 1970, Supergirl ... 22.00
- ❑399, Nov 1970, Supergirl; previously unpublished Black Canary story ... 22.00
- ❑400, Dec 1970, 35th anniversary; Supergirl 22.00
- ❑401, Jan 1971, Supergirl ... 21.00
- ❑402, Feb 1971, Supergirl loses powers 21.00
- ❑403, Apr 1971, Giant-size; CS (c); RA (a); aka Giant #G-81; Death and rebirth of Lightning Lad (reprints from Adventure Comics #302, #305, #308, and #312; G-81 ... 50.00
- ❑404, Mar 1971, Supergirl gets exo-skeleton ... 20.00
- ❑405, Apr 1971 ... 20.00
- ❑406, May 1971, Linda graduates from college, takes job at TV station ... 20.00
- ❑407, Jun 1971, Supergirl gets new costume ... 20.00
- ❑408, Jul 1971 ... 20.00
- ❑409, Aug 1971; reprints Legion story from Adventure #313; Supergirl gets new costume ... 20.00
- ❑410, Sep 1971, The Legion of Super-Heroes: Adventure Comics #326 ... 20.00
- ❑411, Oct 1971, BO, CI (a); reprints Legion story from Adventure #337 ... 20.00
- ❑412, Nov 1971, BO, CI (a); 1: Animal Man. Animal Man reprint; reprints Strange Adventures #180 ... 20.00
- ❑413, Dec 1971; BO, GM, JKu (a); Reprints from The Brave and the Bold #44 and Detective Comics #178; Hawkman and Hawkgirl: Brave and Bold #44 Oct-Nov 1962; Robotman: Detective #178 Dec 1951; 48 pages ... 20.00
- ❑414, Jan 1972; BO, GM, GK (a); A: Animal Man. Animal Man: Strange Adventures #184 ... 20.00
- ❑415, Feb 1972; BO (c); BO, GM, CI (a); Animal Man reprint ... 20.00

Other grades: Multiply price above by 5/6 for VF/NM • 2/3 for VERY FINE • 1/3 for FINE • 1/5 for VERY GOOD • 1/8 for GOOD

Adam Strange

Earthborn space hero gets his own miniseries
©DC

Addam Omega

Post-apocalyptic space series
©Antarctic

Addams Family

They're creepy and kooky
©Gold Key

Adolescent Radioactive Black Belt Hamsters

Best-remembered of the Turtles knockoffs
©Eclipse

AD Police

Spinoff from the Bubblegum Crisis series
©Viz

N-MINT

❑416, Mar 1972, Giant-size issue; a.k.a. DC 100-Page Super Spectacular #DC-10; all-women issue; wraparound cover; reprints stories from Flash Comics #86, Wonder Woman #28, Police Comics #17, Star Spangled Comics #90, and Action Comics #324 .... 18.00
❑417, Mar 1972, BO, GM, FF (a); reprints Frazetta Shining Knight story; reprints Enchantress origin 13.00
❑418, Apr 1972, BO, ATh (a); Contains previously unpublished Golden Age Doctor Mid-Nite story 13.00
❑419, May 1972, BO, ATh, DG, TD (a) ... 13.00
❑420, Jun 1972, CS, TD (a); Animal Man reprint 13.00
❑421, Jul 1972, Animal Man reprint 13.00
❑422, Aug 1972, BO (c); BO, GM (a) 13.00
❑423, Sep 1972 .... 13.00
❑424, Oct 1972, Last Supergirl 13.00
❑425, Jan 1973, GK (w); ATh, GK, AN (a); 1&O: Captain Fear. Michael Kaluta cover 13.00
❑426, Mar 1973, Dick Giordano cover ... 13.00
❑427, May 1973 .... 13.00
❑428, Aug 1973, 1: Black Orchid 28.00
❑429, Oct 1973, A: Black Orchid 15.00
❑430, Dec 1973, A: Black Orchid. Adventures' Club 15.00
❑431, Feb 1974, ATh, JA (a); A: Spectre. Spectre stories begin 28.00
❑432, Apr 1974 .... 15.00
❑433, Jun 1974, AN, JA (a); A: Spectre . 15.00
❑434, Aug 1974 .... 12.00
❑435, Oct 1974, MGr, JA (a); A: Spectre. Aquaman back-up 12.00
❑436, Dec 1974, JA (c); MGr, JA (a); A: Spectre. Aquaman back-up 10.00
❑437, Feb 1975; Previously unpublished Seven Soldiers of Victory back-up; Aquaman 10.00
❑438, Apr 1975; Previously unpublished Seven Soldiers of Victory back-up; Aquaman 10.00
❑439, Jun 1975; Previously unpublished Seven Soldiers of Victory back-up; Aquaman 10.00
❑440, Aug 1975, O: Spectre-New. Previously unpublished Seven Soldiers of Victory back-up; Aquaman 10.00
❑441, Oct 1975, Previously unpublished Seven Soldiers of Victory back-up; Aquaman 10.00
❑442, Dec 1975, Previously unpublished Seven Soldiers of Victory back-up; Aquaman 6.00
❑443, Feb 1976, Previously unpublished Seven Soldiers of Victory back-up; Aquaman 6.00
❑444, Apr 1976, Aquaman 6.00
❑445, Jun 1976 .... 6.00
❑446, Aug 1976, Bicentennial #31 .... 6.00
❑447, Oct 1976, Aquaman; Creeper 6.00
❑448, Nov 1976, Aquaman 5.00
❑449, Jan 1977, Aquaman; Martian Manhunter 5.00
❑450, Mar 1977, Aquaman; Martian Manhunter 5.00
❑451, May 1977, Story concludes in World's Finest #245 .... 5.00
❑452, Jul 1977, Aquaman stories end.... 5.00
❑453, Sep 1977, A: Barbara Gordon. Superboy stories begin 5.00
❑454, Nov 1977, O: Kryptonite Kid 5.00
❑455, Jan 1978 .... 5.00
❑456, Mar 1978 .... 5.00
❑457, May 1978 .... 5.00
❑458, Jul 1978 .... 5.00
❑459, Sep 1978; JA (c); DN, JSa, JA, IN, JAb (a); no ads; expands contents and raises price to $1 .... 3.50
❑460, Nov 1978 RA (c); DN, SA, JSa, JA, IN, JAb (a) 3.50
❑461, Jan 1979, Giant-size issue; JSa, JA (c); DN, JSa, JA, IN, JAb (a); incorporates JSA story from unpublished All-Star Comics #75 .... 6.00
❑462, Mar 1979, Giant-size issue; JA (c); DH, DG, JSa, JL, JAb (a); D: E-2 Batman. D: Batman (Earth 2) 7.00
❑463, May 1979, FMc, DH, JSa, JL (a); Wraparound cover 3.50
❑464, Jul 1979; contains previously unpublished Deadman story from Showcase #105 .... 3.50
❑465, Sep 1979 .... 3.50
❑466, Nov 1979, final JSA case before group retired in the '50s; final $1 issue 3.50
❑467, Jan 1980, 1: Starman III (Prince Gavyn) 3.50
❑468, Feb 1980 .... 3.50
❑469, Mar 1980, O: Starman III (Prince Gavyn) 3.50
❑470, Apr 1980, O: Starman III (Prince Gavyn) 3.50
❑471, May 1980 .... 3.50
❑472, Jun 1980 .... 3.50
❑473, Jul 1980 .... 3.50
❑474, Aug 1980 .... 3.50
❑475, Sep 1980 .... 3.50
❑476, Oct 1980 .... 3.50
❑477, Nov 1980 .... 3.50
❑478, Dec 1980, Aquaman: Grand Illus.! storyline continued into Action Comics #517 .... 3.50
❑479, Mar 1981, 1: Victoria Grant. 1: Christopher King. Dial 'H' For Hero 3.50
❑480, Apr 1981, Dial 'H' For Hero 3.00
❑481, May 1981, Dial 'H' For Hero 3.00
❑482, Jun 1981, Dial 'H' For Hero 3.00
❑483, Jul 1981, Dial 'H' For Hero 3.00
❑484, Aug 1981, Dial 'H' For Hero 3.00
❑485, Sep 1981, Dial 'H' For Hero 3.00
❑486, Oct 1981, Dial 'H' For Hero 3.00
❑487, Nov 1981, Dial 'H' For Hero 3.00
❑488, Dec 1981, Dial 'H' For Hero 3.00
❑489, Jan 1982, Dial 'H' For Hero 3.00
❑490, Feb 1982, Dial 'H' For Hero; series goes on hiatus 3.00
❑491, Sep 1982, digest size begins; Returns from hiatus; digests begin; reprints Black Canary story from Adventure #418 .... 3.00
❑492, Oct 1982; reprints Black Canary story from Adventure #419 .... 3.00
❑493, Nov 1982, A: Challengers of the Unknown. Shazam; Aquaman (Aquaman #41); Supergirl (Action #267); Black Canary (Adventures Comics #419); Sandman and Sandy (Adventure Comics #85); Superboy (Superboy #86); Spectre (Showcase #61); Reprints from Aquaman #41, Action #267, Adventures Comics #85, 419, Superboy #86, Showcase #61.... 3.00
❑494, Dec 1982, A: Challengers of the Unknown. Challengers of the Unknown -Origin; Superboy (Adventure Comics #282); Aquaman (Aquaman #42); Zatanna (Adventure Comics #419); Supergirl (Action #276); Captain Marvel (Captain Marvel Adventures #50); Spectre (Showcase #64); Reprints from Adventure Comics #282, 419, Aquaman #42, Action Comics #276, Showcase #64 .... 3.00
❑495, Jan 1983, A: Challengers of the Unknown. Challengers of the Unknown-Origin, Part 2; Superboy/Mon-El (Superboy #89); Aqualad; Captain Marvel; Superman (Superman #147); Spectre; Reprints from Superboy #89, Superman #147 .... 3.00
❑496, Feb 1983, A: Challengers of the Unknown. Challengers of the Unknown-Origin, Part 3; Superboy (Adventure Comics #290); Aquaman; Captain Marvel; Superboy/Legion (Adventure Comics #293); Sandman and Sandy; Spectre 3.00
❑497, Mar 1983, A: Challengers of the Unknown. Challengers of the Unknown; Supergirl/Legion (Action #287); Aquaman; Captain Marvel Jr.; Supergirl (Action #289); Sandman and Sandy; Spectre/Wildcat 3.00
❑498, Apr 1983, Legion; Aquaman; Sandman and Sandy; Mary Marvel 3.00
❑499, May 1983; Legion (Adventure Comics #303); Aquaman; Shazam; Sandman and Sandy; Legion (Adventure Comics #304); Captain Marvel; Spectre; Reprints from Adventure Comics #303, 304 .... 3.00
❑500, Jun 1983, (Adventure Comics #305); (Adventure Comics #306); (Adventure Comics #307); (Adventure Comics #308); (Adventure Comics #309); (Adventure Comics #310); (Adventure Comics #311); (Adventure Comics #312); (Jimmy Olsen #72); (Adventure Comics #313) 3.00
❑501, Jul 1983, Plastic Man (Adventure #469); Legion (Adventure #314); Shazam (Captain Marvel #91); Spectre (Spectre #7); (Smash Comics #17); Aquaman (Aquaman #49); Legion (Adventure #315); Reprints from Adventure #314, 315, 469, Captain Marvel #91, Spectre #7, Smash Comics #17, Aquaman #49 .... 3.00
❑502, Aug 1983; Zatanna appearance (Adventure #413); Plastic Man appearance (Adventure Comics #470); Legion (Adventure #316); Shazam appearance (Captain Marvel #143); Spectre appearance (Spectre 1st Series #8); Aquaman appearance (Aquaman 1st Series #50); Legion (Adventure #317)... 3.00
❑503, Sep 1983, Legion (Adventure #318); (Adventure #471); Aquaman (Aquaman #51); Aquaman (Aquaman #52); Zatanna (Adventure #414); Zatanna (Adventure #415); Guardian (Star Spangled Comics #7); (Jimmy Olsen #76) 3.00

Adventure Comics
DC

❑1, May 1999 .... 1.99
❑GS 1, Oct 1998; GS; Wonder Woman, Captain Marvel, Superboy, Green Arrow, Legion, Supergirl, Bizarro 4.95

Other grades: Multiply price above by 5/6 for VF/NM • 2/3 for VERY FINE • 1/3 for FINE • 1/5 for VERY GOOD • 1/8 for GOOD

Adventure of the Copper Beeches
Tome

- ❑1; Reprints Cases of Sherlock Holmes #9 ... 2.50

Adventurers (Aircel)
Aircel

- ❑1; regular cover ... 2.00
- ❑1/Ltd.; skeleton cover; Limited ed ... 2.00
- ❑2 ... 2.00

Adventurers (Book 1)
Adventure

- ❑0, ca. 1986; b&w ... 1.50
- ❑1, Aug 1986; 1: Argent (sorcerer); 1: Bladehelm; 1: Coron; 1: Dhakab; 1: Nightwind; 1: Shadolok; 1: Sultar; 1: Tirian; D: Tirian ... 1.50
- ❑1/2nd, Aug 1986; published by Adventure ... 1.50
- ❑2, ca. 1986; No indicia ... 1.50
- ❑3, ca. 1986; no indicia ... 1.50
- ❑4, ca. 1986 ... 1.50
- ❑5, ca. 1986 ... 1.50
- ❑6, Jun 1987 ... 1.50
- ❑7, Jul 1987 ... 1.50
- ❑8, Sep 1987 ... 1.50
- ❑9, Oct 1987 ... 1.75
- ❑10, Nov 1987 ... 1.75

Adventurers (Book 2)
Adventure

- ❑0, Jul 1988, b&w ... 1.95
- ❑1, Dec 1987; regular cover ... 1.50
- ❑1/Ltd., Dec 1987; Limited edition cover 1.50
- ❑2, Mar 1988 ... 1.50
- ❑3, Apr 1988 ... 1.50
- ❑4, Jun 1988 ... 1.50
- ❑5, Aug 1988 ... 1.50
- ❑6, Nov 1988 ... 1.50
- ❑7, Mar 1989, b&w ... 1.50
- ❑8, ca. 1989 ... 1.50
- ❑9, ca. 1989 ... 1.50
- ❑10, ca. 1989 ... 1.50

Adventurers (Book 3)
Adventure

- ❑1, Oct 1989; regular cover ... 2.25
- ❑1/Ltd., Oct 1989; Limited edition cover 2.25
- ❑2, Nov 1989 ... 2.25
- ❑3, Dec 1989 ... 2.25
- ❑4, Jan 1990 ... 2.25
- ❑5, Feb 1990 ... 2.25
- ❑6, Mar 1990; Final Issue ... 2.25

Adventures of Bio Boy
Speakeasy Comics

- ❑1, Oct 2005 ... 2.99

Adventures @ eBay
eBay

- ❑1, ca. 2000; eBay employee premium .. 1.00

Adventures in Reading Starring: The Amazing Spider-Man
Marvel

- ❑1, Sep 1990; Giveaway to promote literacy 1.00

Adventures in the DC Universe
DC

- ❑1, Apr 1997, JLA ... 2.50
- ❑2, May 1997, O: The Flash III (Wally West). O: Flash (Wally West) ... 2.00
- ❑3, Jun 1997; Batman vs. Poison Ivy; Wonder Woman vs. Cheetah ... 2.00
- ❑4, Jul 1997, Mr. Miracle;Green Lantern 2.00
- ❑5, Aug 1997, A: Ultra the Multi-Alien. Martian Manhunter ... 2.00
- ❑6, Sep 1997, Power Girl; Aquaman ... 2.00
- ❑7, Oct 1997, A: Clark Kent. A: Lois Lane. Marvel Family ... 2.00
- ❑8, Nov 1997; Question; Blue Beetle; Booster Gold ... 2.00
- ❑9, Dec 1997, Flash vs. Gorilla Grodd ... 2.00
- ❑10, Jan 1998, Legion of Super-Heroes. 2.00
- ❑11, Feb 1998, Wonder Woman, Green Lantern ... 2.00
- ❑12, Mar 1998; JLA vs. Cipher ... 2.00
- ❑13, Apr 1998, Green Arrow; Impulse, Martian Manhunter ... 1.95
- ❑14, May 1998, Nightwing; Superboy, Flash ... 1.95
- ❑15, Jun 1998; Aquaman; Captain Marvel 1.95
- ❑16, Jul 1998; Green Arrow; Green Lantern 1.95
- ❑17, Aug 1998, Creeper; Batman ... 1.95
- ❑18, Sep 1998, JLA vs. Amazo ... 1.95
- ❑19, Oct 1998; Wonder Woman, Catwoman 1.99
- ❑Ann 1, Oct 1998; DG (a); Doctor Fate, Impulse, Superboy, Thorn, Mr. Miracle; events crossover with Superman Adventures Ann #1 and Batman & Robin Adventures Ann #2 ... 3.95

Adventures in the Mystwood
Blackthorne

- ❑1, Aug 1986 ... 2.00

Adventures in the Rifle Brigade
DC / Vertigo

- ❑1, Oct 2000 ... 2.50
- ❑2, Nov 2000 ... 2.50
- ❑3, Dec 2000 ... 2.50

Adventures in the Rifle Brigade: Operation Bollock
DC / Vertigo

- ❑1, Oct 2001 ... 2.50
- ❑2, Nov 2001 ... 2.50
- ❑3, Dec 2001 ... 2.50

Adventures into the Unknown (A+)
A-Plus

- ❑1, ca. 1991, b&w; Reprints ... 2.50
- ❑2, ca. 1990, Reprints ... 2.50
- ❑3, Reprints ... 2.50
- ❑4, Reprints ... 2.50

Adventures Made in America
Rip Off

- ❑0; Preview ... 2.75
- ❑1 ... 2.75
- ❑2 ... 2.75
- ❑3 ... 2.75
- ❑4 ... 2.75
- ❑5 ... 2.75
- ❑6 ... 2.75

Adventures of Aaron
Chiasmus

- ❑1 ... 2.50
- ❑2, Jul 1995 ... 2.50

Adventures of Aaron
Image

- ❑1, Mar 1997 ... 2.95
- ❑2, May 1997 ... 2.95
- ❑3, Sep 1997, "Adventures of Dad" back-up 2.95
- ❑100, Jul 1997, Anthology ... 2.95

Adventures of Adam & Bryon
American Mule

- ❑1, May 1998 ... 2.50

Adventures of a Lesbian College School Girl
NBM

- ❑1; Adult ... 8.95

Adventures of Bagboy and Checkout Girl
Acetelyne

- ❑Ashcan 1, Apr 2002 ... 1.00

Adventures of Baron Munchausen
Now

- ❑1, Jul 1989 ... 2.00
- ❑2, Aug 1989 ... 2.00
- ❑3, Sep 1989 ... 2.00
- ❑4, Oct 1989 ... 2.00

Adventures of Barry Ween, Boy Genius
Image

- ❑1, Mar 1999, b&w; O: Barry Ween ... 2.95
- ❑2, Apr 1999, b&w; Jeremy turned into dinosaur ... 2.95
- ❑3, May 1999, b&w; at museum ... 2.95

Adventures of Barry Ween, Boy Genius 2.0
Oni

- ❑1, Feb 2000, b&w ... 2.95
- ❑2, Mar 2000, b&w; in the old West ... 2.95
- ❑3, Apr 2000, b&w ... 2.95

Adventures of Barry Ween, Boy Genius 3: Monkey Tales
Oni

- ❑1, Feb 2001, b&w ... 2.95
- ❑2, Apr 2001, b&w ... 2.95
- ❑3, Jun 2001, b&w ... 2.95
- ❑4, Aug 2001, b&w ... 2.95
- ❑5, Oct 2001, b&w ... 2.95
- ❑6, Feb 2002, b&w ... 2.95

Adventures of Bayou Billy
Archie

- ❑1, Sep 1989, Archie, Jughead, Betty, and Veronica public service announcement inside back cover ... 1.00
- ❑2, Nov 1989 ... 1.00
- ❑3, Jan 1990 ... 1.00
- ❑4, Apr 1990 ... 1.00
- ❑5, Jun 1990 ... 1.00

Adventures of Bob Hope
DC

- ❑72, Dec 1961 ... 30.00
- ❑73, Feb 1962 ... 30.00
- ❑74, Apr 1962, MD (a) ... 30.00
- ❑75, Jun 1962, MD (a) ... 30.00
- ❑76, Aug 1962, MD (a) ... 30.00
- ❑77, Oct 1962 ... 30.00
- ❑78, Dec 1962 ... 30.00
- ❑79, Feb 1963 ... 30.00
- ❑80, Apr 1963 ... 30.00
- ❑81, Jun 1963 ... 25.00
- ❑82, Aug 1963, MD (a) ... 25.00
- ❑83, Oct 1963 ... 25.00
- ❑84, Dec 1963 ... 25.00
- ❑85, Feb 1964, MD (a) ... 25.00
- ❑86, Apr 1964 ... 25.00
- ❑87, Jun 1964, MD (a) ... 25.00
- ❑88, Aug 1964 ... 25.00
- ❑89, Oct 1964, MD (a) ... 25.00
- ❑90, Dec 1964, MD (a) ... 25.00
- ❑91, Feb 1965, MD (a) ... 15.00
- ❑92, Apr 1965 ... 15.00
- ❑93, Jun 1965 ... 15.00
- ❑94, Aug 1965, A: Aquaman ... 15.00
- ❑95, Oct 1965, 1: Super-Hip and monster faculty ... 15.00
- ❑96, Dec 1965 ... 15.00
- ❑97, Feb 1966 ... 15.00
- ❑98, Apr 1966 ... 15.00
- ❑99, Jun 1966 ... 15.00
- ❑100, Aug 1966, Super-Hip as President 15.00
- ❑101, Oct 1966 ... 15.00
- ❑102, Dec 1966 ... 15.00
- ❑103, Feb 1967, A: Batman, Nancy, Ringo Starr, Frank Sinatra, Stanley and his Monster ... 15.00
- ❑104, May 1967 ... 15.00
- ❑105, Jun 1967, A: David Janssen, Dan Blocker, Ed Sullivan, Don Adams ... 15.00
- ❑106, Aug 1967, NA (c); NA (a); Neal Adams cover ... 25.00
- ❑107, Oct 1967, NA (c); NA (a) ... 25.00
- ❑108, Dec 1967, NA (c); NA (a) ... 25.00
- ❑109, Feb 1968, NA (c); NA (a); Final Issue 25.00

Adventures of B.O.C.
Invasion

- ❑1, Nov 1986 ... 1.50
- ❑2, Jan 1987 ... 1.50
- ❑3, Mar 1987 ... 1.50

Adventures of Browser & Sequoia
SaberCat

- ❑1, Aug 1999 ... 2.95

Adventures of Captain America
Marvel

- ❑1, Sep 1991, Squarebound cardstock cover; O: Captain America ... 4.95
- ❑2, Nov 1991; O: Bucky ... 4.95
- ❑3, Dec 1991, Squarebound cardstock cover 4.95
- ❑4, Jan 1992 ... 4.95

Adventures of Captain Jack
Fantagraphics

- ❑1, Jun 1986 ... 2.00
- ❑2, Sep 1986 ... 2.00
- ❑3, Oct 1986 ... 2.00
- ❑4, Nov 1986 ... 2.00
- ❑5, Dec 1986; no indicia ... 2.00
- ❑6, Jan 1987 ... 2.00
- ❑7, Mar 1987 ... 2.00
- ❑8, Jul 1987 ... 2.00
- ❑9, Oct 1987 ... 2.00
- ❑10, May 1988 ... 2.00
- ❑11, Nov 1988 ... 2.00
- ❑12, Jan 1989 ... 2.00

Adventures of Captain Nemo
Rip Off

- ❑1, b&w ... 2.50

Adrenalynn

A sweet little girl with built-in firepower

©Image

Advanced Dungeons & Dragons

Role-playing game comes to comics

©DC

Adventure Comics

Legion, Superboy all starred in this classic title

©DC

Adventurers

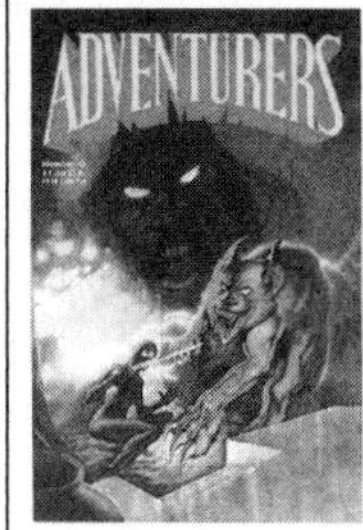

Well-done sword and sorcery title

©Adventure

Adventures in Reading Starring: The Amazing Spider-Man

Spidey Super Stories sequel

©Marvel

N-MINT

Adventures of Chrissie Claus
Hero

❑1, Spr 1991, Spring 1991 .... 2.95
❑2, Jan 1994, w/trading card 2.95

Adventures of Chuk the Barbaric
White Wolf

❑1, Jul 1987 .... 1.50
❑2, Aug 1987, becomes Chuk the Barbaric 1.50

Adventures of Cyclops and Phoenix
Marvel

❑1, May 1994 .... 2.95
❑2, Jun 1994 .... 2.95
❑3, Jul 1994 .... 2.95
❑4, Aug 1994 .... 2.95

Adventures of Dr. Graves
A-Plus

❑1, b&w; Reprints 2.50

Adventures of Dolo Romy
Dôlo Blue

❑1 .... 2.95

Adventures of Doris Nelson, Atomic Housewife
Jake Comics

❑1, Aug 1996, b&w; reprints Doris Nelson, Atomic Housewife 2.95

Adventures of Edgar Mudd and Elaine
Wet Earth

❑1 .... 3.50

Adventures of Evil & Malice
Image

❑1, Jun 1999 .... 3.50
❑2, Aug 1999 .... 3.50
❑3, Nov 1999; cover says Oct, indicia says Nov 3.50

Adventures of Felix the Cat
Harvey

❑1, May 1992 .... 1.50

Adventures of Ford Fairlane
DC

❑1, May 1990; Prequel to the movie 1.50
❑2, Jun 1990 .... 1.50
❑3, Jul 1990 .... 1.50
❑4, Aug 1990 .... 1.50

Adventures of Jerry Lewis
DC

❑67, Nov 1961 .... 28.00
❑68, Jan 1962 .... 28.00
❑69, Mar 1962 .... 28.00
❑70, May 1962 .... 28.00
❑71, Jul 1962 .... 28.00
❑72, Sep 1962, MD (a) 28.00
❑73, Nov 1962 .... 28.00
❑74, Jan 1963, adapts It's Only Money .. 28.00
❑75, Mar 1963 .... 28.00
❑76, May 1963 .... 28.00
❑77, Jul 1963 .... 28.00
❑78, Sep 1963 .... 28.00
❑79, Nov 1963, 1: Mr. Yes 28.00
❑80, Jan 1964 .... 28.00
❑81, Mar 1964 .... 25.00
❑82, May 1964 .... 25.00
❑83, Jul 1964, Frankenstein, Dracula, Werewolf 25.00

N-MINT

❑84, Sep 1964, Jerry becomes The Fearless Tarantula 25.00
❑85, Nov 1964, 1: Renfrew 25.00
❑86, Jan 1965, BO (a) 25.00
❑87, Mar 1965, BO (a); A: Renfrew 25.00
❑88, May 1965, 1: Witch Kraft 25.00
❑89, Jul 1965 .... 25.00
❑90, Sep 1965 .... 25.00
❑91, Nov 1965 .... 25.00
❑92, Jan 1966, A: Superman 30.00
❑93, Mar 1966 .... 25.00
❑94, May 1966 .... 25.00
❑95, Jul 1966 .... 25.00
❑96, Sep 1966 .... 25.00
❑97, Nov 1966, A: Batman, Robin, Penguin, Riddler, Joker 35.00
❑98, Jan 1967, A: Ringo Starr, Ilya Kurakin (on stamps) 25.00
❑99, Mar 1967 .... 25.00
❑100, May 1967, 1: Jerry Mess-terpiece pin-up. Jerry Mess-terpiece pin-up 25.00
❑101, Jul 1967, NA (c); NA (a) 32.00
❑102, Sep 1967, NA (c); NA (a); A: The Beatles 55.00
❑103, Nov 1967, NA (c); NA (a) 32.00
❑104, Jan 1968, NA (c); NA (a) 32.00
❑105, Mar 1968, A: Superman, Lex Luthor 40.00
❑106, May 1968 .... 14.00
❑107, Jul 1968 .... 14.00
❑108, Sep 1968 .... 14.00
❑109, Nov 1968 .... 14.00
❑110, Jan 1969 .... 14.00
❑111, Mar 1969 .... 14.00
❑112, May 1969, A: Flash 14.00
❑113, Jul 1969 .... 14.00
❑114, Sep 1969 .... 14.00
❑115, Nov 1969 .... 14.00
❑116, Jan 1970 .... 14.00
❑117, Mar 1970, A: Wonder Woman 20.00
❑118, May 1970 .... 14.00
❑119, Jul 1970 .... 14.00
❑120, Sep 1970 .... 12.00
❑121, Nov 1970 .... 12.00
❑122, Jan 1971 .... 12.00
❑123, Mar 1971 .... 12.00
❑124, May 1971, Final Issue 12.00

Adventures of Kelly Belle: Peril on the High Seas
Atlantis

❑1 1996, b&w 2.95

Adventures of Kool-Aid Man
Marvel

❑1, ca. 1983, giveaway; JR (c); DDC (a); 60 cent value on cover 1.00
❑5 .... 1.00

Adventures of Liberal Man
Political

❑1 .... 2.95
❑2 .... 2.95
❑3 .... 2.95
❑4, Jul 1996 .... 2.95
❑5, Sep 1996 .... 2.95
❑6, Oct 1996 .... 2.95
❑7, Nov 1996 .... 2.95

N-MINT

Adventures of Luther Arkwright (Valkyrie)
Valkyrie

❑1, Oct 1987 BT (w); BT (a) 2.50
❑2, Dec 1987 BT (w); BT (a) 2.50
❑3, Feb 1988 BT (w); BT (a) 2.50
❑4, Apr 1988 BT (w); BT (a) 2.50
❑5, Jun 1988 BT (w); BT (a) 2.50
❑6, Aug 1988 BT (w); BT (a) 2.50
❑7, Oct 1988 BT (w); BT (a) 2.50
❑8, Dec 1988 BT (w); BT (a) 2.50
❑9, Feb 1989 BT (w); BT (a) 2.50
❑10, Apr 1989; BT (w); BT (a); Essays... 2.50

Adventures of Luther Arkwright
Dark Horse

❑1, Mar 1990; BT (w); BT (a); Reprints Adventures of Luther Arkwright (Valkyrie) #1 .... 2.50
❑2, Apr 1990; BT (w); BT (a); Reprints Adventures of Luther Arkwright (Valkyrie) #2 .... 2.00
❑3, May 1990; BT (w); BT (a); Reprints Adventures of Luther Arkwright (Valkyrie) #3 .... 2.00
❑4, Jun 1990; BT (w); BT (a); Reprints Adventures of Luther Arkwright (Valkyrie) #4 .... 2.00
❑5, Jul 1990; BT (w); BT (a); Reprints Adventures of Luther Arkwright (Valkyrie) #5 .... 2.00
❑6, Aug 1990; BT (w); BT (a); Reprints Adventures of Luther Arkwright (Valkyrie) #6 .... 2.00
❑7, Nov 1990; BT (w); BT (a); Reprints Adventures of Luther Arkwright (Valkyrie) #7 .... 2.00
❑8, Nov 1990; BT (w); BT (a); Reprints Adventures of Luther Arkwright (Valkyrie) #8 .... 2.00
❑9, Feb 1990; BT (w); BT (a); trading cards; Reprints Adventures of Luther Arkwright (Valkyrie) #9 .... 2.00

Adventures of Mark Tyme
John Spencer & Co.

❑1 .... 2.00
❑2 .... 2.00

Adventures of Mighty Mouse
Gold Key

❑166, Mar 1979, Has Spider-Man in Hostess Ad: "...Meets June Jitsui!" 4.00
❑167, May 1979 .... 4.00
❑168, Jul 1979 .... 4.00
❑169, Sep 1979 .... 4.00
❑170, Oct 1979 .... 4.00
❑171, Nov 1979 .... 4.00
❑172, Jan 1980 .... 4.00

Adventures of Mr. Pyridine
Fantagraphics

❑1, b&w 2.50

Adventures of Misty
Forbidden Fruit

❑1, Apr 1991, Adult 2.95
❑2, May 1991, Adult 2.95
❑3, Jun 1991, Adult 2.95
❑4, Jul 1991, Adult 2.95
❑5, Aug 1991, Adult 2.95
❑6, Oct 1991, Adult 2.95

Other grades: Multiply price above by 5/6 for VF/NM • 2/3 for VERY FINE • 1/3 for FINE • 1/5 for VERY GOOD • 1/8 for GOOD

❑7, Dec 1991, Adult 2.95

❑8, Feb 1992, Adult 2.95

❑9, Apr 1992, Adult 2.95

❑10, Jun 1992, Adult 2.95

❑11, Aug 1992, Adult 2.95

❑12, Oct 1992, Adult 2.95

Adventures of Monkey Womp

❑1, Jul 1995 2.00

❑2, Jun 1996 2.00

❑3, Jun 1997 2.00

❑4, Jun 1998; Freshmen back-up 2.00

Adventures of Quik Bunny
Marvel

❑1 1984, giveaway; A: Spider-Man. 60 cent value on cover 3.00

Adventures of Rheumy Peepers & Chunky Highlights
Oni

❑1, Feb 1999; NN 2.95

Adventures of Rick Raygun
Stop Dragon

❑1, Sep 1986 2.00

❑2, Oct 1986 2.00

❑3, Fal 1986 2.00

❑4, Nov 1986 2.00

❑5, Jan 1987 2.00

Adventures of Robin Hood
Gold Key

❑1, Mar 1974 8.00

❑2, May 1974 5.00

❑3, Jul 1974 4.00

❑4, Aug 1974 4.00

❑5, Sep 1974 4.00

❑6, Nov 1974 4.00

❑7, Jan 1975 4.00

Adventures of Roma
Forbidden Fruit

❑1, Jan 1993, b&w; Adult 3.50

Adventures of Snake Plissken
Marvel

❑1, Jan 1997 2.50

Adventures of Spencer Spook
Ace

❑1, Oct 1986; reprints stories from Giggle Comics #77 and Spencer Spook #102 2.00

❑2, Dec 1986; Includes reprint from Giggle Comics #66 2.00

❑3, Jan 1987 2.00

❑4, Mar 1987 2.00

❑5 2.00

❑6 2.00

Adventures of Spider-Man
Marvel

❑1, Apr 1996; A: Punisher. animated series adaptations 2.00

❑2, May 1996; V: Hammerhead 1.50

❑3, Jun 1996; A: X-Men. V: Mr. Sinister 1.50

❑4, Jul 1996; V: Vulture 1.50

❑5, Aug 1996; V: Rhino 1.50

❑6, Sep 1996; A: Thing. Human Torch 1.50

❑7, Oct 1996; V: Enforcers 1.50

❑8, Nov 1996; V: Kingpin 1.50

❑9, Dec 1996; V: Mysterio; V: Vanisher (X-Men) 1.50

❑10, Jan 1997; V: Beetle 1.50

❑11, Feb 1997; A: Venom. V: Doctor Octopus and Venom 1.50

❑12, Mar 1997; A: Venom. V: Doctor Octopus and Venom; Final Issue 1.50

Adventures of Stickboy
Stinky Armadillo

❑1 1.00

Adventures of Superboy
DC

❑19, Sep 1991; Series continued from Superboy (2nd Series) #18 1.50

❑20, Oct 1991; JM (a); O: Knickknack; O: Nicknack 1.50

❑21, Nov 1991 1.50

❑22, Dec 1991; CS (a); Final Issue 1.50

Adventures of Superman
DC

❑0, Oct 1994; ▲1994-39 2.50

❑424, Jan 1987; JOy (c); JOy (a); Series continues from Superman Vol. 1 2.50

❑425, Feb 1987 JOy (c); JOy (a) 4.00

❑426, Mar 1987; JOy (c); JOy, JBy (w); JOy (a); 1: Bibbo. Legends 3.00

❑427, Apr 1987 JOy (c); JOy (a) 2.00

❑428, May 1987; JOy (c); JOy (a); 1: Bibbo 2.00

❑429, Jun 1987 JOy (c); JOy (a) 2.00

❑430, Jul 1987; JOy (c); JOy (a); V: Fearsome Five 2.00

❑431, Aug 1987 JOy (c); JOy, EL (a) 2.00

❑432, Sep 1987; JOy (c); JOy (a); 1: Jose Delgado (Gangbuster) 2.00

❑433, Oct 1987; JOy (c); JOy (a); A: Superman LP: #429 2.00

❑434, Nov 1987; JOy (c); JOy (a); 1: Gangbuster 2.00

❑435, Dec 1987; JOy (c); JOy (w); JOy (a); A: Superman LP: #431 2.00

❑436, Jan 1988; JOy (c); JOy, JBy (w); JOy (a); Millennium 2.00

❑437, Feb 1988; JOy (c); JOy, JBy (w); JOy (a); V: Gangbuster. Millennium 2.00

❑438, Mar 1988; JOy (c); JBy (w); JOy (a); 1&O: Brainiac II (Milton Moses Fine); A: Superman LP: #434 2.00

❑439, Apr 1988 JOy (c); JOy, JBy (w); JOy (a) 2.00

❑440, May 1988; DaG (c); JOy, JBy (w); JOy (a); Continued in Action Comics # 600 2.00

❑441, Jun 1988; JOy (c); JOy, JBy (w); JOy (a); V: Mxyzptlk. A: Superman LP: #437; Publishorial: DC movies 2.00

❑442, Jul 1988; JBy (c); JOy, JBy (w); JOy, JBy (a); A: Superman LP: #438 2.00

❑443, Aug 1988 JOy (c); JOy (w); JOy (a) 2.00

❑444, Sep 1988; JOy (c); JOy, JBy (w); JOy (a); Supergirl 2.00

❑445, Oct 1988 JOy (c); JOy (w); JOy (a) 2.00

❑446, Nov 1988 JOy (c); JOy (w); JOy (a); A: Gangbuster 2.00

❑447, Dec 1988 JOy (c); JOy (w); JOy (a) 2.00

❑448, Dec 1988; JOy (c); JOy (w); JOy (a); Issue has no date; A: Superman LP: Superman #21 and Advs #444 2.00

❑449, Jan 1989; Invasion! 2.00

❑450, Jan 1989; Invasion! 2.00

❑451, Feb 1989 2.00

❑452, Mar 1989; Superman: the Letter Column II: #446 2.00

❑453, Apr 1989 2.00

❑454, May 1989; 1: Draaga 2.00

❑455, Jun 1989; Superman: the Letter Column II: #451 2.00

❑456, Jul 1989 2.00

❑457, Aug 1989 2.00

❑458, Sep 1989; Jimmy as Elastic Lad 2.00

❑459, Oct 1989; Eradicator buried in Antarctic 2.00

❑460, Nov 1989; 1: Fortress of Solitude 2.00

❑461, Dec 1989 2.00

❑462, Jan 1990 2.00

❑463, Feb 1990; A: Flash. Superman/ Flash race 3.00

❑464, Mar 1990; V: Lobo. Krypton Man 2.00

❑465, Apr 1990; Krypton Man 2.00

❑466, May 1990; 1: Hank Henshaw (becomes cyborg Superman); KryptoGrams: #462; 1: Hank Henshaw 3.00

❑467, Jun 1990; Batman 2.00

❑468, Jul 1990; 2: Hank Henshaw 2.00

❑469, Aug 1990; 1: Blaze 2.00

❑470, Sep 1990 2.00

❑471, Oct 1990; A: Sinbad. Story continues from Superman #48 and continues in Action #658 2.00

❑472, Nov 1990; V: Mammoth 2.00

❑473, Dec 1990; A: Green Lantern. Guy Gardner 2.00

❑474, Jan 1991 2.00

❑475, Feb 1991; Wonder Woman; Batman, Flash 2.00

❑476, Mar 1991; 1: The Linear Men. V: Linear Man. ▲1991-8 2.00

❑477, Apr 1991; A: Legion. ▲1991-11 2.00

❑478, May 1991; V: Dev-Em. ▲1991-14 2.00

❑479, Jun 1991; ▲1991-17 2.00

❑480, Jul 1991; Giant-size; ▲1991-21 2.50

❑481, Aug 1991; ▲1991-25 2.00

❑482, Sep 1991; V: Parasite. ▲1991-29 2.00

❑483, Oct 1991; 1: Atomic Skull. ▲1991-33 2.00

❑484, Nov 1991; Blackout 2.00

❑485, Dec 1991; Blackout 2.00

❑486, Jan 1992; ▲1992-3 2.00

❑487, Feb 1992; ▲1992-7 2.00

❑488, Mar 1992; ▲1992-11; V: Brainiac 2.00

❑489, Apr 1992; ▲1992-15; V: Brainiac; Burial of Dragga 2.00

❑490, May 1992; ▲1992-19 2.00

❑491, Jun 1992; V: Metallo. ▲1992-23 2.00

❑492, Jul 1992; JOy (w); V: Agent Liberty. ▲1992-27 2.00

❑493, Aug 1992; 1: Lord Satanus. V: Blaze. ▲1992-31; 1: Lord Satanus (Colin Thornton); The Blaze/Satanus War 2.00

❑494, Sep 1992; 1: Kismet. ▲1992-35 2.00

❑495, Oct 1992; A: Forever People. ▲1992-39 2.00

❑496, Nov 1992; Mxyzptlk 3.00

❑496/2nd, Nov 1992; 2nd printing 2.00

❑497, Dec 1992; JOy (w); Doomsday; ▲1992-47 3.00

❑497/2nd, Dec 1992; JOy (w); 2nd printing, ▲1992-47 2.00

❑498, Jan 1993; JOy (w); ▲1993-3 3.00

❑498/2nd, Jan 1993; JOy (w); ▲1993-3 2.00

❑499, Feb 1993; JOy (w); ▲1993-7 5.00

❑500, Jun 1993; JOy (w); begins return from dead 3.00

❑500/CS, Jun 1993; JOy (w); translucent cover; trading card; begins return from dead 3.50

❑500/Silver, Jun 1993; silver edition JOy (w) 10.00

❑501, Jun 1993; 1: Superboy (clone). ▲1993-15 2.00

❑501/Variant, Jun 1993; 1: Superboy (clone). Die-cut cover; ▲1993-15 2.00

❑502, Jul 1993; A: Supergirl. ▲1993-19 1.75

❑503, Aug 1993; Superboy vs. Cyborg 1.75

❑504, Sep 1993; ▲1993-27; V: Mongul and Cyborg Superman; Reign of the Supermen 1.75

❑505, Oct 1993; ▲1993-31 1.75

❑505/Variant, Oct 1993; ▲1993-31, Special (prism) cover edition 2.50

❑506, Nov 1993; ▲1993-35 1.50

❑507, Dec 1993; V: Bloodsport. ▲1993-39 1.50

❑508, Jan 1994; Challengers 1.50

❑509, Feb 1994; A: Auron. ▲1994-7 1.50

❑510, Mar 1994; Bizarro 1.50

❑511, Apr 1994; A: Guardian. ▲1994-15 1.50

❑512, May 1994; A: Guardian. V: Parasite. ▲1994-19 1.50

❑513, Jun 1994; ▲1994-23 1.50

❑514, Jul 1994; ▲1994-27 1.50

❑515, Aug 1994; V: Massacre. ▲1994-31 1.50

❑516, Sep 1994; A: Alpha Centurion. "Zero Hour" 1.50

❑517, Nov 1994; ▲1994-43 1.50

❑518, Dec 1994; A: Darkseid. ▲1994-47; V: Female Furies; V: Kanto 1.50

❑519, Jan 1995; V: Brainiac. Dead Again; ▲1995-3 1.50

❑520, Feb 1995; A: Thorn. ▲1995-7 1.50

❑521, Mar 1995; A: Thorn. ▲1995-11 1.50

❑522, Apr 1995; Return of Metropolis 1.50

❑523, May 1995; ▲1995-19 1.50

❑524, Jun 1995; ▲1995-23 2.00

❑525, Jul 1995; ▲1995-27 2.00

❑526, Aug 1995; Bloodsport vs. Bloodsport 2.00

❑527, Sep 1995; Alpha-Centurion returns 2.00

❑528, Oct 1995; ▲1995-40 2.00

❑529, Nov 1995; ▲1995-45 2.00

❑530, Dec 1995; SCU vs. Hellgrammite; "Trial of Superman/Underworld Unleashed" 2.00

❑531, Jan 1996; Cyborg Superman sentenced to a black hole; ▲1996-4 2.00

❑532, Feb 1996; Return of Lori Lemaris; ▲1996-8 2.00

❑533, Mar 1996; A: Impulse. ▲1996-12 2.00

❑534, May 1996; ▲1996-17 2.00

❑535, Jun 1996; ▲1996-21 2.00

❑536, Jul 1996; Brainiac takes over Superman's body 2.00

❑537, Aug 1996; ▲1996-30 2.00

❑538, Sep 1996; Clark Kent named acting managing editor; Perry White has cancer 2.00

❑539, Oct 1996; JOy (w); 1&O: Anomaly. ▲1996-39 2.00

❑540, Nov 1996; JOy (w); 1: Ferro. "Final Night"; ▲1996-43 2.00

❑541, Dec 1996; A: Superboy. Clark shot by terrorists 2.00

❑542, Jan 1997; ▲1997-2; Power Struggle 2.00

Adventures in the DC Universe

DC heroes get Batman Adventures treatment
©DC

Adventures in the Rifle Brigade

Bawdy British battle tale
©DC

Adventures of Barry Ween, Boy Genius 3: Monkey Tales

Judd Winick's pint-sized prodigy
©Oni

Adventures of Bob Hope

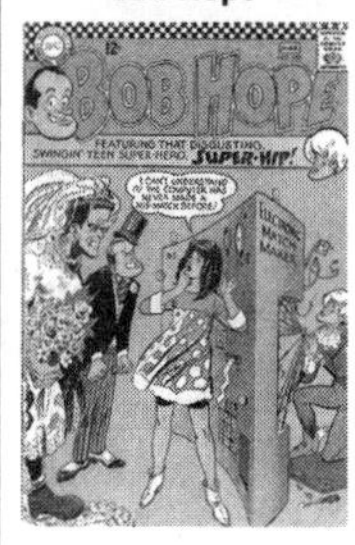

Film, stand-up, and TV star conquers comics
©DC

Adventures of Captain Jack

Funny-animal science fiction series
©Fantagraphics

N-MINT

❑543, Feb 1997; V: Superman Revenge Squad. ▲1997-7 ... 2.00
❑544, Mar 1997; return of Intergang; ▲1997-11 ... 2.00
❑545, Apr 1997; V: Metallo. energy powers begin ... 2.00
❑546, May 1997; V: Metallo. new uniform 2.00
❑547, Jun 1997; A: Atom. ▲1997-24 ... 2.00
❑548, Jul 1997; A: Phantom Stranger. ▲1997-28 ... 2.00
❑549, Aug 1997; A: Newsboy Legion, Dingbats of Danger Street. ▲1997-32 2.00
❑550, Sep 1997; Giant-size; Jimmy's special airs ... 3.50
❑551, Oct 1997; V: Cyborg Superman. ▲1997-41 ... 1.95
❑552, Nov 1997; V: Parasite. ▲1997-45 1.95
❑553, Dec 1997; Face cover ... 1.95
❑554, Dec 1997; V: Ripper. ▲1998-3 ... 1.95
❑555, Feb 1998; Superman Red vs. Superman Blue ... 1.95
❑556, Apr 1998; V: Millennium Guard. ▲1998-13 ... 1.95
❑557, May 1998; Millennium Giants ... 1.95
❑558, Jun 1998; set in Silver Age ... 1.95
❑559, Jul 1998; JOy (w); set in Silver Age 1.95
❑560, Aug 1998; JOy (w); A: Kismet. set in Silver Age ... 1.95
❑561, Sep 1998; V: Dominus. ▲1998-34 2.00
❑562, Oct 1998; D: Machine Gunn, Torcher. D: "Machine" Gunn, Torcher. Daily Planet closed ... 2.00
❑563, Dec 1998; V: Cyborg. in Kandor... 2.00
❑564, Feb 1999; JOy (w); A: Geo-Force. ▲1999-5 ... 2.00
❑565, Mar 1999 JOy (w); A: D.E.O. agents. A: Justice League of America. A: Captain Boomerang. A: Metropolis Special Crimes Unit. A: Captain Cold. . 2.00
❑566, Apr 1999; JOy (w); A: Lex Luthor. ▲1999-14 ... 2.00
❑567, May 1999; JOy (w); Lois' robot guardian returns; ▲1999-19 ... 2.00
❑568, Jun 1999; ▲1999-24 ... 2.00
❑569, Jul 1999; SCU forms meta-unit; ▲1999-28 ... 2.00
❑570, Sep 1999; Superman as protector of Rann ... 2.00
❑571, Oct 1999; V: Atomic Skull. ▲1999-37 2.00
❑572, Nov 1999; SB (a); A: Strange Visitor. V: War. ▲1999-41 ... 2.00
❑573, Dec 1999; ▲1999-47 ... 2.00
❑574, Jan 2000; ▲2000-2 ... 2.00
❑575, Feb 2000; ▲2000-6 ... 2.00
❑576, Mar 2000; ▲2000-11 ... 2.00
❑577, Apr 2000; ▲2000-15 ... 2.00
❑578, May 2000; ▲2000-19 ... 2.00
❑579, Jun 2000; ▲2000-23 ... 2.00
❑580, Jul 2000; ▲2000-27 ... 2.00
❑581, Aug 2000; V: Adversary. ▲2000-31; Lex Luthor announces candidacy for President ... 2.00
❑582, Sep 2000; ▲2000-35 ... 2.00
❑583, Oct 2000; ▲2000-40 ... 2.25
❑584, Nov 2000; 1: Devouris the Conqueror. A: Lord Satanus. ▲2000-44 ... 2.25
❑585, Dec 2000; A: Rampage. A: Adversary. A: Thorn. A: Prankster. ▲2000-48 ... 2.25
❑586, Jan 2001; ▲2000-52 ... 2.25

N-MINT

❑587, Feb 2001; ▲2001-7 ... 2.25
❑588, Mar 2001; ▲2001-11 ... 2.25
❑589, Apr 2001; ▲2001-15 ... 2.25
❑590, May 2001; MG (c); ▲2001-19 ... 2.25
❑591, Jun 2001; ▲2001-23 ... 2.25
❑592, Jul 2001; ▲2001-27 ... 2.25
❑593, Aug 2001; ▲2001-31; Our Worlds At War ... 2.25
❑594, Sep 2001; ▲2001-35; Our Worlds At War ... 2.25
❑595, Oct 2001; BSz (a); ▲2001-39 ... 2.25
❑596, Nov 2001; ▲2001-43 ... 2.25
❑597, Dec 2001; ▲2001-47 ... 2.25
❑598, Jan 2002; ▲2002-6 ... 2.25
❑599, Feb 2002 ... 2.25
❑600, Mar 2002; Giant-size; JPH (w); DaG (a) ... 3.95
❑601, Apr 2002 ... 2.25
❑602, May 2002 ... 2.25
❑603, Jun 2002 A: Super-Baby ... 2.25
❑604, Jul 2002 ... 2.25
❑605, Aug 2002 ... 2.25
❑606, Sep 2002 ... 2.25
❑607, Oct 2002 ... 2.25
❑608, Nov 2002 KN (c) ... 2.25
❑609, Dec 2002 KN (c) ... 2.25
❑610, Jan 2003 ... 2.25
❑611, Feb 2003 ... 2.25
❑612, Mar 2003 ... 2.25
❑613, Apr 2003 ... 2.25
❑614, May 2003 ... 2.25
❑615, Jun 2003 ... 2.25
❑616, Jul 2003 ... 2.25
❑617, Aug 2003 ... 2.25
❑618, Sep 2003 ... 2.25
❑619, Oct 2003 ... 2.25
❑620, Nov 2003 ... 2.25
❑621, Dec 2003; 1: Minuteman ... 2.25
❑622, Jan 2004; V: Anti-Angelica ... 2.25
❑623, Feb 2004 ... 2.25
❑624, Mar 2004 ... 5.00
❑625, Apr 2004 ... 4.00
❑625/2nd, Apr 2004; 2nd printing; Michael Turner sketch cover ... 3.00
❑626, May 2004 ... 2.25
❑627, Jun 2004 ... 2.50
❑628, Jul 2004 ... 2.50
❑629, Aug 2004 ... 2.50
❑630, Sep 2004 ... 2.50
❑631, Oct 2004; Includes Sky Captain and the World of Tomorrow promotional CD 2.50
❑632, Nov 2004 ... 2.50
❑633, Dec 2004 ... 2.50
❑634, Jan 2005 ... 2.50
❑635, Feb 2005, V: Parasites (Alex and Alexandra Allston) ... 2.50
❑636, Mar 2005 ... 5.00
❑637, Apr 2005 ... 4.00
❑638, May 2005; Includes 2 Lord of the Rings Trivial Pursuit cards ... 2.50
❑639, Jun 2005; Continued from Action Comics #826; Credits reversed between colorist and inker ... 5.00
❑640, Jul 2005 ... 4.00
❑641, Aug 2005 ... 4.00
❑642, Sep 2005; Story cont'd Wonder Woman #219 ... 6.00
❑643, Oct 2005 ... 12.00

N-MINT

❑643/2nd, Oct 2005 ... 3.00
❑644, Nov 2005 ... 2.50
❑645, Dec 2005; Infinite Crisis tie-in ... 2.50
❑646, Jan 2006 ... 2.50
❑647, Feb 2006, V: Ruin ... 2.50
❑648, Mar 2006, Infinite Crisis crossover 2.50
❑649, May 2006, Continues in Infinite Crisis #5 ... 10.00
❑1000000, Nov 1998; A: Resurrection Man. Set between issues #562 and #563 ... 2.00
❑Ann 1, Sep 1987 ... 4.00
❑Ann 2, Aug 1990; KGa (c); JBy, CS, KGa, BMc (a); A: Lobo. L.E.G.I.O.N. '90 ... 3.00
❑Ann 3, Oct 1991; Armageddon 2001, part 11 ... 3.00
❑Ann 4, ca. 1992 ... 3.00
❑Ann 5, ca. 1993; 1: Sparx; Bloodlines.. 3.00
❑Ann 6, ca. 1994; concludes in Superboy Ann #1 (1994); Elseworlds ... 2.95
❑Ann 7, ca. 1995; V: Kalibak. Year One.. 3.95
❑Ann 8, ca. 1996; JOy (c); Elseworlds; Legends of the Dead Earth ... 2.95
❑Ann 9, Sep 1997; Pulp Heroes ... 3.95

Adventures of Tad Martin
Caliber

❑1, Adult ... 2.50

Adventures of the Fly
Archie / Radio

❑1, Aug 1959, JK (c); JK (w); JS, GT, JK (a); O: Fly; O: Fly (Tommy Troy) ... 220.00
❑2, Sep 1959, AW, JK (a); Private Strong 140.00
❑3, Nov 1959 ... 100.00
❑4, Jan 1960, The Shield backup story.. 80.00
❑5, Mar 1960 ... 80.00
❑6, May 1960 ... 70.00
❑7, Jul 1960 ... 70.00
❑8, Sep 1960 ... 70.00
❑9, Nov 1960 ... 70.00
❑10, Jan 1961 ... 70.00
❑11, Mar 1961 ... 70.00
❑12, May 1961 ... 70.00
❑13, Jul 1961, Kim Brand appearance before she becomes Fly-Girl; 1: Kim Brand ... 70.00
❑14, Sep 1961, 1: Fly-Girl; 1: Fly-Girl (Kim Brand) ... 70.00
❑15, Oct 1961 ... 70.00
❑16, Nov 1961 ... 70.00
❑17, Jan 1962 ... 70.00
❑18, Mar 1962 ... 40.00
❑19, May 1962, Fly-Girl backup story; Fly-Girl loses the "-" in her name ... 40.00
❑20, Jul 1962, Fly-Girl backup story; Retelling of Fly-Girl origin ... 40.00
❑21, Sep 1962, Fly Girl backup story ... 40.00
❑22, Oct 1962 ... 40.00
❑23, Nov 1962 ... 40.00
❑24, Feb 1963, Fly Girl backup story ... 40.00
❑25, Apr 1963 ... 40.00
❑26, Jun 1963 ... 40.00
❑27, Aug 1963, Fly Girl backup story ... 30.00
❑28, Oct 1963 ... 30.00
❑29, Jan 1964 ... 30.00
❑30, Oct 1964, Fly Girl backup story ... 30.00
❑31, May 1965, Later issues published as Fly Man ... 30.00

Other grades: Multiply price above by 5/6 for VF/NM • 2/3 for VERY FINE • 1/3 for FINE • 1/5 for VERY GOOD • 1/8 for GOOD

Adventures of the Jaguar
Archie / Radio

- ❑1, Sep 1961 ... 125.00
- ❑2, Oct 1961 ... 75.00
- ❑3, Nov 1961, 1: Kree-Nal ... 50.00
- ❑4, Jan 1962 ... 40.00
- ❑5, Mar 1962 ... 40.00
- ❑6, May 1962 ... 30.00
- ❑7, Jul 1962, O: Jaguar Rescue Team ... 30.00
- ❑8, Aug 1962 ... 30.00
- ❑9, Sep 1962 ... 30.00
- ❑10, Nov 1962 ... 30.00
- ❑11, Mar 1963, Cover says Feb. but indicia says Jan ... 22.00
- ❑12, May 1963 ... 22.00
- ❑13, Aug 1963, Cat Girl's new look ... 22.00
- ❑14, Oct 1963 ... 22.00
- ❑15, Nov 1963, Final Issue ... 22.00

Adventures of the Little Green Dinosaur
Last Gasp

- ❑1, b&w; Adult ... 5.00
- ❑2, b&w; Adult ... 5.00

Adventures of the Mad Hunda Day Day
Thaumaturge

- ❑1, Win 1995, b&w ... 2.00

Adventures of the Mask
Dark Horse

- ❑1, Jan 1996 ... 2.50
- ❑2, Feb 1996; V: Walter ... 2.50
- ❑3, Mar 1996 ... 2.50
- ❑4, Apr 1996; 1: Bombshell ... 2.50
- ❑5, May 1996 ... 2.50
- ❑6, Jun 1996 ... 2.50
- ❑7, Jul 1996 ... 2.50
- ❑8, Aug 1996; Milo dons the mask ... 2.50
- ❑9, Sep 1996; James Bond parody ... 2.50
- ❑10, Oct 1996; V: Walter ... 2.50
- ❑11, Nov 1996; Mask as Santa ... 2.50
- ❑12, Dec 1996; Final Issue ... 2.50
- ❑Special 1, Oct 1996; Toys R Us Special Ed. Giveaway; newsprint cover ... 1.00

Adventures of the Outsiders
DC

- ❑33, May 1986; Continued from Batman and the Outsiders #32 ... 1.00
- ❑34, Jun 1986; V: Masters of Disaster ... 1.00
- ❑35, Jul 1986 ... 1.00
- ❑36, Aug 1986 ... 1.00
- ❑37, Sep 1986 ... 1.00
- ❑38, Oct 1986; V: Marine Marauder ... 1.00
- ❑39, Nov 1986; V: Nuclear Family ... 1.00
- ❑40, Dec 1986; TVE (c); JA (a); V: Nuclear Family ... 1.00
- ❑41, Jan 1987; JA (a); V: Force of July .. 1.00
- ❑42, Feb 1987 ... 1.00
- ❑43, Mar 1987 ... 1.00
- ❑44, Apr 1987; V: Duke of Oil ... 1.00
- ❑45, May 1987; V: Duke of Oil ... 1.00
- ❑46, Jun 1987; Final Issue ... 1.00

Adventures of Theown
Pyramid

- ❑1 1986 ... 2.00
- ❑2 1986 ... 2.00
- ❑3 1986 ... 2.00

Adventures of the Screamer Brothers
Superstar

- ❑1, Dec 1990 ... 1.50
- ❑2, Mar 1991 ... 1.50
- ❑3, Jun 1991 ... 1.50

Adventures of the Screamer Brothers
Superstar

- ❑1, Aug 1991 ... 1.95
- ❑2 ... 1.95
- ❑3, Dec 1991 ... 1.95

Adventures of the Super Mario Bros.
Valiant

- ❑1, Feb 1991 ... 4.00
- ❑2, Mar 1991, swimsuit issue ... 3.00
- ❑3, Apr 1991 ... 3.00
- ❑4, May 1991 ... 3.00
- ❑5, Jun 1991 ... 3.00
- ❑6, Jul 1991 ... 2.50
- ❑7, Aug 1991 ... 2.50
- ❑8, Sep 1991 ... 2.50
- ❑9, Oct 1991 ... 2.50

Adventures of the Thing
Marvel

- ❑1, Apr 1992; JBy (w); JBy, JSt (a); Reprints Marvel Two-In-One #50; Thing vs. Thing ... 1.50
- ❑2, May 1992; Rerprints Marvel Two-in-One #80 ... 1.50
- ❑3, Jun 1992; GP, FM (a); Reprints Marvel Two-in-One #51; Pinup ... 1.50
- ❑4, Jul 1992; A: Man-Thing. Reprints Marvel Two-In-One #77 ... 1.50

Adventures of the Vital-Man
Budgie

- ❑1, Jun 1991, b&w ... 2.00
- ❑2 ... 2.00
- ❑3 ... 2.00
- ❑4 ... 2.00

Adventures of the X-Men
Marvel

- ❑1, Apr 1996; Wolverine vs. Hulk ... 2.00
- ❑2, May 1996 ... 1.50
- ❑3, Jun 1996; A: Spider-Man. V: Mr. Sinister 1.50
- ❑4, Jul 1996 ... 1.50
- ❑5, Aug 1996; V: Magneto ... 1.50
- ❑6, Sep 1996; Magneto vs. Apocalypse. 1.50
- ❑7, Oct 1996 ... 1.50
- ❑8, Nov 1996 ... 1.50
- ❑9, Dec 1996; V: Vanisher ... 1.50
- ❑10, Jan 1997; V: Mojo ... 1.50
- ❑11, Feb 1997 A: Man-Thing ... 1.50
- ❑12, Mar 1997; Final Issue ... 1.50

Adventures on Space Station Freedom
Tadcorps

- ❑1; educational giveaway on International Space Station; NN ... 2.50

Adventures on the Fringe
Fantagraphics

- ❑1, Mar 1992 ... 2.25
- ❑2, May 1992 ... 2.25
- ❑3, Jul 1992 ... 2.25
- ❑4, Oct 1992; Photo cover ... 2.25
- ❑5, Feb 1993 ... 2.25

Adventures On the Planet of the Apes
Marvel

- ❑1, Oct 1975; JSn, RB (c); JSn, GT (a); Adapts movie ... 9.00
- ❑2, Nov 1975; Adapts movie ... 4.00
- ❑3, Dec 1976; Adapts movie ... 4.00
- ❑4, Feb 1976 ... 3.50
- ❑5, Apr 1976 ... 3.50
- ❑5/30¢, Apr 1976, 30¢ price variant ... 20.00
- ❑6, Jun 1976 ... 4.00
- ❑6/30¢, Jun 1976, 30¢ price variant ... 20.00
- ❑7, Aug 1976; Adapts movie "Beneath the Planet of the Apes" ... 4.00
- ❑7/30¢, Aug 1976, 30¢ price variant ... 20.00
- ❑8, Sep 1976; Adapts movie "Beneath the Planet of the Apes" ... 4.00
- ❑9, Oct 1976; Adapts Beneath the Planet of the Apes ... 4.00
- ❑10, Nov 1976; AA (a); Adapts Beneath the Planet of the Apes ... 4.00
- ❑11, Dec 1976; AA (a); Adapts Beneath the Planet of the Apes; Destruction of Earth ... 4.00

Adventure Strip Digest
WCG

- ❑1, Aug 1994 ... 2.50
- ❑2, Apr 1995 ... 2.50
- ❑3 ... 2.50
- ❑4, Jun 1996 ... 2.50

Adventurous Uncle Scrooge McDuck
Gladstone

- ❑1, Jan 1998; CB (w); CB (a); reprints Barks' "The Twenty-Four Carat Moon" 2.50
- ❑2, Mar 1998; 50th anniversary of Uncle Scrooge ... 2.50

Aeon Flux
Dark Horse

- ❑1, Sep 2005 ... 2.99
- ❑2, Oct 2005 ... 2.99
- ❑3, Nov 2005 ... 2.99
- ❑4, Dec 2006 ... 2.99

Aeon Focus
Aeon

- ❑1, Mar 1994; Justin Hampton's Twitch 2.95
- ❑2, Jun 1994; Colin Upton's Other Other Even Bigger Than Slightly Smaller That Got Bigger Big Thing ... 2.95
- ❑3, Oct 1994; Filthy Habits ... 2.95
- ❑4, Nov 1994; Ward Sutton's Ink Blot ... 2.95
- ❑5, ca. 1997 ... 2.95

Aertimisan: War of Souls
Almagest

- ❑1, Nov 1997 ... 2.75
- ❑2, Jan 1998 ... 2.75

Aesop's Desecrated Morals
Magnecom

- ❑1, b&w ... 2.95

Aesop's Fables
Fantagraphics

- ❑1, Spr 1991 ... 2.50
- ❑2, Fal 1991 ... 2.50
- ❑3, Win 1991 ... 2.50

Aeternus
Brick

- ❑1, Jun 1997 ... 2.95

Aetos the Eagle
Orphan Underground

- ❑1, Sep 1994, b&w ... 2.50
- ❑2, Oct 1995, b&w ... 2.50

Aetos the Eagle
Ground Zero

- ❑1, Aug 1997 ... 3.00
- ❑2 ... 3.00
- ❑3 ... 3.00

Affable Tales for Your Imaginaton
Lee Roy Brown

- ❑1, Jan 1987, b&w ... 3.00

After Apocalypse
Paragraphics

- ❑1, May 1987 ... 1.95

After Dark
Millennium

- ❑1 ... 2.95

Aftermath
Pinnacle

- ❑1, ca. 1986, b&w; sequel to Messiah ... 1.50

Aftermath
Chaos

- ❑1, ca. 2000 ... 2.95

After/Shock: Bulletins from Ground Zero
Last Gasp

- ❑1, b&w; ca. 1981 ... 2.00

Against Blackshard: 3-D: The Saga of Sketch, the Royal Artist
Sirius

- ❑1 ... 2.25

Agency
Image

- ❑Ashcan 1/Gold; Ashcan preview ... 5.00
- ❑Ashcan 1; Ashcan preview ... 3.00
- ❑1/A, Aug 2001; Several figures standing on cover ... 2.50
- ❑1/B, Aug 2001; Woman sitting on cover 2.50
- ❑1/C, Aug 2001; Woman leaning on gun on cover ... 2.50
- ❑2, ca. 2001 ... 2.50
- ❑3, ca. 2001 ... 2.95
- ❑4, ca. 2001 ... 2.95
- ❑5, Feb 2002 ... 2.95
- ❑6, Mar 2002; Giant-size; Final issue ... 4.95

Agent
Marvel

- ❑1 ... 9.95

Agent "00" Soul
Twist Records

- ❑1; no price ... 5.00

Agent America
Awesome

- ❑Ashcan 1; Preview edition; 1: Coven. Series preempted by Marvel lawsuit ... 5.00

Agent Liberty Special
DC

- ❑1 1991; O: Agent Liberty ... 2.00

Agents
Image

- ❑1, Apr 2003 ... 2.95

Other grades: Multiply price above by 5/6 for VF/NM • 2/3 for VERY FINE • 1/3 for FINE • 1/5 for VERY GOOD • 1/8 for GOOD

Adventures of Felix the Cat

He has a bag of tricks
©Harvey

Adventures of Ford Fairlane

Soundtrack better than film, comic
©DC

Adventures of Jerry Lewis

Series changed names after Martin/Lewis split
©DC

Adventures of Kool-Aid Man

Commercial icon spawned Archie giveaway
©Marvel

Adventures of Liberal Man

Democratic hero serves his political party
©Political

N-MINT

❑2, May 2003 2.95
❑3, Jul 2003 2.95
❑4, Aug 2003 2.95
❑5, Sep 2003 2.95
❑6, Oct 2003 2.95

Agents of Atlas
Marvel

❑1, Oct 2006 2.99
❑2, Nov 2006 2.99
❑3, Dec 2006 2.99
❑4, Jan 2007 2.99
❑5, Feb 2007 2.99

Agents of Law
Dark Horse

❑1, Mar 1995 2.50
❑2, Apr 1995 2.50
❑3, May 1995 2.50
❑4, Jun 1995 2.50
❑5, Jul 1995 2.50
❑6, Sep 1995; V: Predators; Final Issue . 2.50

Agent 13: The Midnight Avenger
TSR

❑1, NN 7.95

Agent Three Zero
Galaxinovels

❑1; Galaxinovels w/Trading Card and Poster 3.95

Agent Three Zero: The Blue Sultan's Quest/Blue Sultan- Galaxi Fact Files
Galaxinovels

❑1; Flip-book; poster; trading card 2.95
❑1/Platinum; Platinum edition 2.95
❑2 2.95
❑3 2.95
❑4 2.95

Agent Unknown
Renegade

❑1, Oct 1987 2.00
❑2, Jan 1988 2.00
❑3, Apr 1988 2.00

Agent X
Marvel

❑1, Sep 2002; 1: Nijo Minamiyori as Agent X (Alex Hayden) 2.25
❑2, Oct 2002 2.25
❑3, Nov 2002 2.25
❑4, Dec 2002 2.25
❑5, Jan 2003 2.25
❑6, Feb 2003 2.25
❑7, Mar 2003 2.99
❑8, Apr 2003 2.99
❑9, May 2003 2.99
❑10, Jun 2003 2.99
❑11, Jul 2003 2.99
❑12, Aug 2003 2.99
❑13, Nov 2003 2.99
❑14, Dec 2003 2.99
❑15, Dec 2003 2.99

Age of Apocalypse: The Chosen
Marvel

❑1 2.50

Age of Bronze
Image

❑1, Nov 1998 3.50
❑2, Jan 1999 3.00
❑3, Mar 1999 3.00
❑4, May 1999 3.00
❑5, Oct 1999 3.00
❑6, Jan 2000; cover says Dec, indicia says Jan 3.00
❑7, Mar 2000; cover says Apr, indicia says Mar 3.00
❑8, Aug 2000, b&w 3.50
❑9, Dec 2000; cover says Nov, indicia says Dec 3.50
❑10, Feb 2001 3.50
❑11, Mar 2001 3.50
❑12, Apr 2001 3.50
❑13, May 2001 3.50
❑14, Aug 2002 3.50
❑15, Nov 2002, Indicia says Nov, cover says Oct 3.50
❑16, Feb 2003 3.50
❑17, Jul 2003 3.50
❑18, Oct 2003 3.50
❑19, Apr 2004 3.50
❑20, Jun 2005 3.50
❑21, Oct 2005 3.50
❑22, Jan 2006 3.50
❑23, Jul 2006 3.50
❑24, Feb 2007 3.50
❑Special 1, Jul 1999; cover says Jun, indicia says Jul 2.95
❑Special 2, May 2002; Behind the Scenes 3.50

Age of Heroes
Halloween

❑1, Oct 1996, b&w 2.95
❑2, Dec 1996, b&w 2.95
❑3, Mar 1997, b&w 2.95
❑4, May 1997, b&w 2.95
❑5, ca. 1999, b&w; Image Comics 3.50
❑Special 1, Jul 1997; reprints Age of Heroes #1 and 2 (Halloween) 4.95
❑Special 2, Nov 1999; Image Comics 6.95

Age of Heroes: Wex
Image

❑1, Nov 1998, b&w 2.95

Age of Innocence: The Rebirth of Iron Man
Marvel

❑1; O: Happy Hogan; O: Iron Man; O: Pepper Potts 2.50

Age of Reptiles
Dark Horse

❑1, Nov 1993 2.50
❑2, Dec 1993 2.50
❑3, Jan 1994 2.50
❑4, Feb 1994 2.50

Age of Reptiles: The Hunt
Dark Horse

❑1, May 1996; Wraparound Cover 2.95
❑2, Jun 1996; Wraparound Cover 2.95
❑3, Jul 1996; Wraparound Cover 2.95
❑4, Aug 1996; Wraparound Cover 2.95
❑5, Sep 1996; Wraparound Cover 2.95

Agony Acres
AA2

❑1, May 1995 2.95
❑1/Ashcan 1996 2.50
❑2, May 1996 2.95
❑3, May 1996, b&w 2.95
❑4, Nov 1996, b&w 2.95
❑5, Jan 1996 2.95

Ahlea
Radio

❑1, Aug 1997 2.95
❑2, Oct 1997 2.95

Aida-Zee
Nate Butler

❑1 1.50

Aiden McKain Chronicles: Battle for Earth
Digital Webbing

❑1, Sep 2005 2.99
❑1/Incentive, Sep 2005 10.00

AIDS Awareness
Chaos City

❑1, ca. 1993, b&w 3.00

Aim
Cryptic

❑1 1.95

Airboy
Eclipse

❑1, Jul 1986, 1&O: Airboy II (modern). D: Airboy I (Golden Age); 1: Airboy (Davy Nelson); D: Airboy (David Nelson); O: Airboy (Davy Nelson) 2.00
❑2, Jul 1986, 1: Skywolf (Golden Age, in modern era). 1: Marisa 1.50
❑3, Aug 1986, A: The Heap 1.50
❑4, Aug 1986 1.50
❑5, Sep 1986, DSt (c); DSt (a); Return of Valkyrie 1.50
❑6, Sep 1986, 1: Iron Ace (in modern age) 1.50
❑7, Oct 1986, PG (c) 1.50
❑8, Oct 1986 1.50
❑9, Nov 1986; Full-size issues begin; O: Airboy (Golden Age). 1: Flying Fool (in modern age); Full-size issues begin; O: Airboy (David Nelson) 1.50
❑10, Nov 1986; 1: Manic 1.25
❑11, Dec 1986; TY (c); O: Airboy (Golden Age). O: Birdie. 1: Ito. Skywolf back-up 1.25
❑12, Dec 1986; 1: Kip Thorne. Iron Ace's identity revealed 1.25
❑13, Jan 1987; 1: Bald Eagle (in modern age). Airfighters back-up 1.25
❑14, Jan 1987 1.25
❑15, Feb 1987 1.25
❑16, Feb 1987; D: Manic 1.25
❑17, Mar 1987; 1: Lacey Lyle. A: Harry Truman 1.25
❑18, Mar 1987; 1: Black Angel (in modern age) 1.25
❑19, Apr 1987; V: Rats 1.25
❑20, Apr 1987; PG (c); 1: The Rats (in modern age). V: Rats 1.25
❑21, May 1987; GE (c); GE (a); 1: Rat Mother 1.25
❑22, May 1987; 1: Lester Mansfield. 1: El Lobo Alado (Skywolf's father). Skywolf back-up story 1.25
❑23, Jun 1987 1.25
❑24, Jun 1987 A: Heap 1.25
❑25, Jul 1987; 1&O: Manure Man. A: Heap 1.25

Other grades: Multiply price above by 5/6 for VF/NM • 2/3 for VERY FINE • 1/3 for FINE • 1/5 for VERY GOOD • 1/8 for GOOD

❑26, Jul 1987; 1: Flying Dutchman (in modern age); 1: Road Rats 1.25
❑27, Aug 1987 .... 1.25
❑28, Aug 1987; 1: Black Axis 1.25
❑29, Sep 1987.......... 1.25
❑30, Sep 1987.......... 1.25
❑31, Oct 1987 .... 1.25
❑32, Oct 1987 .... 1.25
❑33, Nov 1987 .... 1.75
❑34, Dec 1987 DS (a) 1.75
❑35, Jan 1988.......... 1.75
❑36, Feb 1988.......... 1.75
❑37, Mar 1988 .... 1.75
❑38, Apr 1988.......... 1.75
❑39, May 1988.......... 1.75
❑40, Jun 1988.......... 1.75
❑41, Jul 1988.......... 1.75
❑42, Aug 1988 .... 1.95
❑43, Sep 1988.......... 1.95
❑44, Oct 1988 .... 1.95
❑45, Nov 1988 .... 1.95
❑46, Jan 1989; Airboy Diary 1.95
❑47, Mar 1989; Airboy Diary.......... 1.95
❑48, Apr 1989; Airboy Diary 1.95
❑49, Jun 1989; Airboy Diary 1.95
❑50, Oct 1989; Giant-size; JKu (c); JKu (a); Final Issue.......... 4.95

Airboy Meets the Prowler
Eclipse

❑1, Dec 1987.......... 1.95

Airboy-Mr. Monster Special
Eclipse

❑1, Aug 1987 .... 1.75

Airboy V: the Airmaidens
Eclipse

❑1, Jul 1988.......... 1.95

Air Fighters Classics
Eclipse

❑1, Nov 1987; squarebound; cardstock cover; Reprints Air Fighters Comics #1 3.95
❑2, Jan 1988; Reprints Air Fighters Comics #2 .... 3.95
❑3, Mar 1988; Reprints Air Fighters Comics #3 .... 3.95
❑4, May 1988; Reprints Air Fighters Comics#4 .... 3.95
❑5, Jan 1989; Reprints Air Fighters Comics #5 .... 3.95
❑6, May 1989; Reprints Air Fighters Comics #6 .... 3.95
❑7; Reprints Air Fighters Comics #7 .... 3.95

Airfighters Meet Sgt. Strike Special
Eclipse

❑1, Jan 1988 .... 1.95

Airlock
Eclectus

❑1, Jun 1990, b&w 2.50
❑2, Jul 1991.......... 2.50
❑3, Oct 1991 .... 2.50

Airmaidens Special
Eclipse

❑1, Aug 1987; O: La Lupina 1.75

Airman
Malibu

❑1, Jan 1993; 1: Thresher.......... 1.95

Airmen
Mansion

❑1, Feb 1995, b&w.......... 2.50

Air Raiders
Marvel / Star

❑1, Nov 1987 .... 1.00
❑2, Dec 1987.......... 1.00
❑3, Jan 1988 .... 1.00
❑4, Feb 1988 .... 1.00
❑5, Mar 1988 .... 1.00

Airshell
-Ism

❑1, ca. 2005 .... 3.50

Airtight Garage
Marvel / Epic

❑1, Jul 1993.......... 2.50
❑2, Aug 1993 .... 2.50
❑3, Sep 1993.......... 2.50
❑4, Oct 1993 .... 2.50

Air War Stories
Dell

❑1, Nov 1964.......... 22.00
❑2, Feb 1965.......... 14.00
❑3, May 1965.......... 14.00
❑4, Aug 1965.......... 14.00
❑5, Nov 1965.......... 14.00
❑6, Feb 1966.......... 14.00
❑7, May 1966.......... 14.00
❑8, Aug 1966; Final issue?.......... 14.00

Airwaves
Caliber

❑1, Feb 1991.......... 2.50
❑2 1991 .... 2.50
❑3 1991 .... 2.50
❑4 1991 .... 2.50

Ai Yori Aoshi
Tokyopop

❑1, Jan 2004.......... 9.99
❑2, Mar 2004.......... 9.99
❑3, May 2004.......... 9.99
❑4, Jul 2004.......... 9.99
❑5, Sep 2004 .... 9.99
❑6, Nov 2004 .... 9.99
❑7, Jan 2005.......... 9.99
❑8, Mar 2005.......... 9.99
❑9, Jun 2005.......... 9.99
❑10, Sep 2005 .... 9.99
❑11, Dec 2005 .... 9.99

A.K.A. Goldfish
Caliber

❑1, Joker.......... 3.50
❑2, Ace.......... 3.95
❑3, ca. 1995, Jack.......... 3.95
❑4, ca. 1995, Queen.......... 2.95
❑5, Mar 1996, King; cardstock cover.......... 3.95

Akiko
Sirius

❑1, Mar 1996.......... 6.00
❑2, Apr 1996.......... 4.50
❑3, May 1996.......... 4.00
❑4, Jun 1996.......... 4.00
❑5 1996; no indicia 4.00
❑6, Aug 1996.......... 3.50
❑7, Sep 1996 .... 3.50
❑8, Oct 1996 .... 3.50
❑9, Dec 1996 .... 3.50
❑10, Jan 1997.......... 3.50
❑11, Feb 1997.......... 2.50
❑12, Mar 1997 .... 2.50
❑13, Apr 1997.......... 2.50
❑14, May 1997.......... 2.50
❑15, Jul 1997.......... 2.50
❑16, Aug 1997 .... 2.50
❑17, Aug 1997; indicia says "Aug" 2.50
❑18, Sep 1997 .... 2.50
❑19, Oct 1997; Beeba's story.......... 2.50
❑20, Nov 1997; Beeba's story.......... 2.50
❑21, Dec 1997 .... 2.50
❑22, Jan 1998.......... 2.50
❑23, Feb 1998.......... 2.50
❑24, Mar 1998 .... 2.50
❑25, May 1998.......... 2.50
❑26, Jul 1998.......... 2.50
❑27, Aug 1998 .... 2.50
❑28, Oct 1998 .... 2.50
❑29, Nov 1998 .... 2.50
❑30, Dec 1998 .... 2.50
❑31, Feb 1998.......... 2.50
❑32, Mar 1998 .... 2.50
❑33, May 1998.......... 2.50
❑34, Jun 1999.......... 2.50
❑35, Sep 1999, b&w.......... 2.50
❑36, Oct 1999, b&w.......... 2.50
❑37, Dec 1999, b&w.......... 2.50
❑38, Feb 2000, b&w 2.50
❑39, May 2000, b&w.......... 2.50
❑40, Aug 2000, b&w.......... 2.95
❑41, Oct 2000, b&w.......... 2.95
❑42 2001 .... 2.95
❑43 2001 .... 2.95
❑44, May 2001 .... 2.95
❑45 2001 .... 2.95
❑46 2001 .... 2.95
❑47 2002 .... 2.95
❑48 2002 .... 2.95
❑49 2002 .... 2.95
❑50, Jun 2003.......... 3.50
❑51, Nov 2003.......... 2.95

Akiko on the Planet Smoo
Sirius

❑1, Dec 1995, b&w; Fold-out cover 5.00
❑1/HC, b&w; Hardcover edition 19.95
❑1/2nd, May 1998, b&w; cardstock cover 4.00
❑Fan ed. 1/A; free promotional giveaway 3.00

Akiko on the Planet Smoo: The Color Edition
Sirius

❑1, Feb 2000, cardstock cover.......... 4.95

Akira
Marvel / Epic

❑1, Sep 1988 .... 8.00
❑1/2nd 1988; 2nd printing 4.00
❑2, Oct 1988.......... 5.00
❑2/2nd 1988; 2nd printing 4.00
❑3, Nov 1988.......... 5.00
❑4, Dec 1988 .... 4.00
❑5, Jan 1989.......... 4.00
❑6, ca. 1989.......... 4.00
❑7, ca. 1989.......... 4.00
❑8, ca. 1989.......... 4.00
❑9, ca. 1989.......... 4.00
❑10, ca. 1989.......... 4.00
❑11, ca. 1989.......... 4.00
❑12, ca. 1989.......... 4.00
❑13, ca. 1989.......... 4.00
❑14, ca. 1989.......... 4.00
❑15, ca. 1989.......... 4.00
❑16, ca. 1989.......... 4.00
❑17, ca. 1990.......... 4.00
❑18, ca. 1990.......... 4.00
❑19, ca. 1990.......... 4.00
❑20, ca. 1990.......... 4.00
❑21, ca. 1990.......... 4.00
❑22, ca. 1990.......... 4.00
❑23, ca. 1990.......... 4.00
❑24, ca. 1990.......... 4.00
❑25, ca. 1990.......... 4.00
❑26, ca. 1990.......... 4.00
❑27, ca. 1991.......... 4.00
❑28, ca. 1991.......... 4.00
❑29, ca. 1991.......... 4.00
❑30, ca. 1991.......... 4.00
❑31, ca. 1991.......... 4.00
❑32, ca. 1992.......... 4.00
❑33, ca. 1992.......... 4.00
❑34, ca. 1994.......... 6.95
❑35, ca. 1995.......... 6.95
❑36 1995 A: Lady Miyako 6.95
❑37, ca. 1995.......... 6.95
❑38, ca. 1995; Final Issue.......... 6.95

A*K*Q*J
Fantagraphics

❑1, Mar 1991, b&w; Captain Jack.......... 2.75

Aladdin (Conquest)
Conquest

❑0, Feb 1993, b&w.......... 2.95

Aladdin (Disney's...)
Marvel

❑1, Oct 1994.......... 1.50
❑2, Nov 1994.......... 1.50
❑3, Dec 1994 .... 1.50
❑4, Jan 1995.......... 1.50
❑5, Feb 1995.......... 1.50
❑6, Mar 1995.......... 1.50
❑7, Apr 1995.......... 1.50
❑8, May 1995.......... 1.50
❑9, Jun 1995.......... 1.50
❑10, Jul 1995.......... 1.50
❑11, Aug 1995 .... 1.50

Alamo
Antarctic

❑1, Apr 2004.......... 4.95

Alarming Adventures
Harvey

❑1, Oct 1962.......... 40.00
❑2, Dec 1962.......... 25.00
❑3, Feb 1963.......... 20.00

Other grades: Multiply price above by 5/6 for VF/NM • 2/3 for VERY FINE • 1/3 for FINE • 1/5 for VERY GOOD • 1/8 for GOOD

Adventures of Mighty Mouse

Here he comes to save the day
©Gold Key

Adventures of Rick Raygun

Police officer fights crime in outer space
©Stop Dragon

Adventures of Robin Hood

Based on animated Disney adventure
©Gold Key

Adventures of Snake Plissken

He "Escaped from New York" into comics
©Marvel

Adventures of Spencer Spook

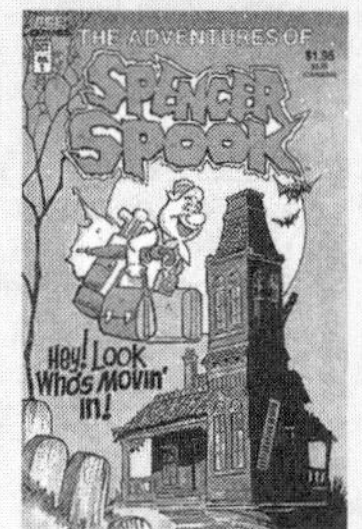

This ghost wasn't as successful as Casper
©Ace

Albedo
Thoughts & Images

	N-MINT
❑0, ca. 1986; Blue cover; 500 printed	8.00
❑0/A, ca. 1986; Only 50 copies printed; White cover (yellow table)	30.00
❑0/B, ca. 1986; Less than 500 copies printed; White cover (no yellow)	15.00
❑0/2nd, ca. 1986; Blue cover	5.00
❑0/3rd, ca. 1986, b&w; Blue cover	3.00
❑0/4th, Dec 1986; Yellow cover front, blue cover back	2.50
❑1, ca. 1984; Dark red cover	14.00
❑1/A, ca. 1984; Bright red cover	10.00
❑1/2nd, ca. 1984; Bright red cover	10.00
❑2, Nov 1984; 1: Usagi Yojimbo. 2: Usagi Yojimbo	250.00
❑3, Apr 1985; Usagi Yojimbo back-up	10.00
❑4, Jul 1985; Usagi Yojimbo back-up	4.00
❑5, Oct 1985	4.00
❑6, Jan 1986	3.00
❑7, Mar 1986	3.00
❑8, Jul 1986	3.00
❑9, May 1987	2.00
❑10, Sep 1987; cardstock cover	2.00
❑11, Dec 1987	2.00
❑12, Mar 1988	2.00
❑13, Jun 1988	2.00
❑14, Spr 1989; Photo cover; Final Issue	2.00

Albedo
Antarctic

	N-MINT
❑1, Jun 1991	4.00
❑2, Sep 1991	3.00
❑3, Dec 1991	3.00
❑4, Mar 1992	3.00
❑5, Jun 1992	2.50
❑6, Sep 1992	2.50
❑7, Dec 1992	2.50
❑8, Mar 1993	2.50
❑9, Jun 1993	2.50
❑10, Oct 1993	2.75
❑Special 1, Jul 1993, Color special	4.00

Albedo
Antarctic

	N-MINT
❑1, Feb 1994, Series name: Albedo Anthropomorphics Vol. 3	2.95
❑2, Oct 1994	2.95
❑3, Feb 1995	2.95
❑4, Jan 1996	2.95

Albedo
Antarctic

	N-MINT
❑1, Dec 1996, Series name: Albedo Anthropomorphics Vol. 4	2.95
❑2, Jan 1999	2.99

Albedo
Antarctic

	N-MINT
❑1, ca. 2002; b&w	4.99

Albino Spider of Dajette
Verotik

	N-MINT
❑1, ca. 1997	2.95
❑2, Jun 1997	2.95
❑0, ca. 1998	2.95

Albion
DC

	N-MINT
❑1, Aug 2005	2.99
❑2, Sep 2005	2.99
❑3, Dec 2005	3.00
❑4, Jun 2006	2.99
❑5, Jul 2006	2.99
❑6, Dec 2006, Final issue	2.99

Alec Dear
Mediocre Concepts

	N-MINT
❑1 1996, b&w; magazine-sized comic book with cardstock cover; no cover price	2.00

Alec: Love and Beerglasses
Escape

	N-MINT
❑1	3.50

Aleister Arcane
Idea & Design Works

	N-MINT
❑1, Apr 2004	3.99
❑2, May 2004	3.99
❑3, Jul 2004	3.99

Alex
Fantagraphics

	N-MINT
❑1	2.95
❑2, Apr 1994	2.95
❑3, Jul 1994	2.95
❑4, Oct 1994	2.95
❑5, Nov 1994	2.95
❑6, Jan 1995, b&w	2.95

Alexis
Fantagraphics / Eros

	N-MINT
❑1 1995; Adult	2.95
❑2, Jul 1995; Adult	2.95
❑3 1995; Adult	2.95
❑4 1995; Adult	2.95
❑5, Mar 1996; Adult	2.95

Alf
Marvel

	N-MINT
❑1, Mar 1988; 1: Alf	2.00
❑2, Apr 1988; 2: Alf	1.25
❑3, May 1988	1.25
❑4, Jun 1988	1.25
❑5, Jul 1988	1.25
❑6, Aug 1988; Photo cover	1.00
❑7, Sep 1988	1.00
❑8, Oct 1988	1.00
❑9, Nov 1988	1.00
❑10, Dec 1988	1.00
❑11, Jan 1989	1.00
❑12, Feb 1989	1.00
❑13, Mar 1989	1.00
❑14, Apr 1989	1.00
❑15, May 1989	1.00
❑16, Jun 1989	1.00
❑17, Jul 1989	1.00
❑18, Aug 1989	1.00
❑19, Sep 1989	1.00
❑20, Oct 1989	1.00
❑21, Nov 1989	1.00
❑22, Nov 1989; X-Men parody	1.00
❑23, Dec 1989	1.00
❑24, Dec 1989	1.00
❑25, Jan 1990	1.00
❑26, Feb 1990	1.00
❑27, Mar 1990	1.00
❑28, Apr 1990	1.00
❑29, May 1990; "3-D" cover	1.00
❑30, Jun 1990	1.00
❑31, Jul 1990	1.00
❑32, Aug 1990	1.00
❑33, Sep 1990	1.00
❑34, Oct 1990	1.00
❑35, Nov 1990	1.00
❑36, Dec 1990	1.00
❑37, Jan 1991	1.00
❑38, Feb 1991	1.00
❑39, Mar 1991	1.00
❑40, Apr 1991	1.00
❑41, May 1991	1.00
❑42, Jun 1991	1.00
❑43, Jul 1991	1.00
❑44, Aug 1991; X-Men parody	1.00
❑45, Sep 1991	1.00
❑46, Oct 1991	1.00
❑47, Nov 1991	1.00
❑48, Dec 1991	1.00
❑49, Jan 1992	1.00
❑50, Feb 1992; Giant-size; Final Issue	1.50
❑Ann 1, ca. 1988; Dynamic Forces edition; Summer Special; Evolutionary War	1.50
❑Ann 2, ca. 1989	1.50
❑Ann 3, ca. 1990; TMNT parody	1.50
❑Holiday 1, Hol 1988; magazine-sized comic book with cardstock cover; Holiday Special #1	1.50
❑Holiday 2, Hol 1989; Dynamic Forces edition; Holiday Special #2	1.50
❑Spring 1; Spring Special	1.75

Alf Comics Magazine
Marvel

	N-MINT
❑1, Nov 1988; digest	2.00
❑2, Jan 1989; digest	2.00

Alias:
Now

	N-MINT
❑1, Jul 1990	1.75
❑2, Aug 1990	1.75
❑3, Sep 1990	1.75
❑4, Oct 1990	1.75
❑5, Nov 1990	1.75

Alias
Marvel / MAX

	N-MINT
❑1, Nov 2001; BMB (w); Has one-night stand with Luke Cage	3.50
❑2, Dec 2001 BMB (w)	3.00
❑3, Jan 2002 BMB (w)	3.00
❑4, Feb 2002 BMB (w)	3.00
❑5, Mar 2002 BMB (w)	3.00
❑6, Apr 2002 BMB (w)	3.00
❑7, May 2002 BMB (w)	3.00
❑8, Jun 2002 BMB (w)	3.00
❑9, Jul 2002; BMB (w); Call of Duty preview inside	3.00
❑10, Aug 2002 BMB (w)	3.00
❑11, Sep 2002 BMB (w)	2.99
❑12, Sep 2002 BMB (w)	2.99
❑13, Oct 2002 BMB (w)	2.99
❑14, Nov 2002 BMB (w)	2.99
❑15, Dec 2002 BMB (w)	2.99
❑16, Jan 2003 BMB (w)	2.99
❑17, Feb 2003; BMB (w); Jessica sleeps with Scott Lang	2.99
❑18, Mar 2003 BMB (w)	2.99
❑19, Apr 2003 BMB (w)	2.99
❑20, May 2003 BMB (w)	2.99
❑21, May 2003 BMB (w)	2.99

Other grades: Multiply price above by 5/6 for VF/NM • 2/3 for VERY FINE • 1/3 for FINE • 1/5 for VERY GOOD • 1/8 for GOOD

❑22, Jul 2003 BMB (w); O: Jessica Jones 2.99
❑23, Aug 2003 BMB (w); O: Jessica Jones 2.99
❑24, Sep 2003, BMB (w) 2.99
❑25, Oct 2003, BMB (w); V: Purple Man 2.99
❑26, Nov 2003, BMB (w) 2.99
❑27, Dec 2003, BMB (w) 2.99
❑28, Jan 2004, BMB (w); Final issue; V: Purple Man 2.99

Ali-Baba: Scourge of the Desert
Gauntlet

❑1 3.50

Alice in Lost World
Radio

❑1; Adult 2.95
❑2, ca. 2001; Adult 2.95
❑3, ca. 2001; Adult 2.95
❑4, ca. 2001; Adult 2.95

Alien 3
Dark Horse

❑1, Jun 1992 2.50
❑2, Jun 1992 2.50
❑3, Jun 1992 2.50

Alien Ducklings
Blackthorne

❑1, Oct 1986 2.00
❑2, Dec 1986 2.00
❑3, Feb 1987 2.00
❑4, Apr 1987 2.00

Alien Encounters (Fantaco)
Fantaco

❑1, Jan 1980 1.50

Alien Encounters (Eclipse)
Eclipse

❑1, Jun 1985 MGu (a) 2.00
❑2, Aug 1965 2.00
❑3, Oct 1985 2.00
❑4, Dec 1985 2.00
❑5, Feb 1986; Dave Dorman cover; Nudity 2.00
❑6, Apr 1986; Story "Nada" used as basis for movie "They Live" 2.00
❑7, Jun 1986 RHo (a) 2.00
❑8, Aug 1986; Marilyn Monroe/Atomic Bomb cover 2.00
❑9, Oct 1986 2.00
❑10, Dec 1986; TS, GM (a); Includes "Exiles" Ray Bradbury adaptation 2.00
❑11, Feb 1987 2.00
❑12, Apr 1987 2.00
❑13, Jun 1987 2.00
❑14, Aug 1987; Final Issue 2.00

Alien Fire
Kitchen Sink

❑1, Jan 1987 2.00
❑2, May 1987 2.00
❑3, May 1987 2.00

Alien Fire: Pass in Thunder
Kitchen Sink

❑1, May 1995, b&w; squarebound 6.95

Alien Hero
Zen

❑1, Feb 1999; illustrated novella featuring Zen 8.95

Alien Legion
Marvel / Epic

❑1, Apr 1984; Giant-size 2.00
❑2, Jun 1984 1.50
❑3, Aug 1984 1.50
❑4, Oct 1984 1.50
❑5, Dec 1984 1.50
❑6, Feb 1985 1.50
❑7, Apr 1985 1.50
❑8, Jun 1985 1.50
❑9, Aug 1985 1.50
❑10, Oct 1985 1.50
❑11, Dec 1985 1.50
❑12, Feb 1986 1.50
❑13, Apr 1986 1.50
❑14, Jun 1986 1.50
❑15, Aug 1986 1.50
❑16, Oct 1986 1.50
❑17, Dec 1986 1.50
❑18, Feb 1987 1.50
❑19, Apr 1987 1.50
❑20, Jun 1987; Final Issue 1.50

Alien Legion
Marvel / Epic

❑1, Oct 1987 1.50
❑2, Dec 1987 1.50
❑3, Feb 1988 1.50
❑4, Apr 1988 1.50
❑5, Jun 1988 1.50
❑6, Aug 1988 1.50
❑7, Oct 1988 1.50
❑8, Dec 1988 1.50
❑9, Feb 1989 1.50
❑10, Apr 1989 1.50
❑11, Jun 1989 1.50
❑12, Aug 1989 1.50
❑13, Oct 1989 1.50
❑14, Dec 1989 1.50
❑15, Feb 1990 1.50
❑16, Apr 1990 1.50
❑17, Jun 1990 1.50
❑18, Aug 1990; Final Issue 1.50

Alien Legion: A Grey Day to Die
Marvel

❑1; Alien Legion; ca. 1986 7.00

Alien Legion: Binary Deep
Marvel / Epic

❑1, Sep 1993; NN 3.50

Alien Legion: Jugger Grimrod
Marvel / Epic

❑1, Aug 1992 5.95

Alien Legion: One Planet at a Time
Marvel / Epic

❑1, ca. 1993 4.95
❑2, ca. 1993 4.95
❑3, ca. 1993; Hoang Nguyen-a 4.95

Alien Legion: On the Edge
Marvel / Epic

❑1, Nov 1990 4.50
❑2, Dec 1990 4.50
❑3, Jan 1991 4.50

Alien Legion: Tenants of Hell
Marvel / Epic

❑1, ca. 1991; cardstock cover 4.50
❑2, ca. 1991; cardstock cover 4.50

Alien Nation
DC

❑1, Dec 1988; Movie adaptation 3.00

Alien Nation: A Breed Apart
Adventure

❑1, Nov 1990 2.50
❑2, Dec 1990 2.50
❑3, Jan 1991 2.50
❑4, Mar 1991 2.50

Alien Nation: The Firstcomers
Adventure

❑1, May 1991 2.50
❑2, Jun 1991 2.50
❑3, Jul 1991 2.50
❑4, Aug 1991 2.50

Alien Nation: The Lost Episode
Malibu

❑1, Jun 1992, b&w; squarebound; adapts second season opener 4.95

Alien Nation: The Public Enemy
Adventure

❑1, Dec 1991 2.50
❑2, Jan 1992 2.50
❑3, Feb 1992 2.50
❑4, Mar 1992 2.50

Alien Nation: The Skin Trade
Adventure

❑1, Mar 1991 2.50
❑2, Apr 1991 2.50
❑3, May 1991 2.50
❑4, Jun 1991 2.50

Alien Nation: The Spartans
Adventure

❑1, Mar 1990; Yellow 2.50
❑1/A, Mar 1990; Green 2.50
❑1/B, Mar 1990; Blue 2.50
❑1/C, Mar 1990; Red 2.50
❑1/Ltd., Mar 1990; Foil logo, numbered edition 3.00
❑2, Sep 1990 2.50
❑3, Nov 1990 2.50
❑4, Feb 1990 2.50

Alien Resurrection
Dark Horse

❑1, Oct 1997 2.50
❑2, Nov 1997 2.50

Aliens
Gold Key

❑1, Reprints The Aliens stories from Magnus, Robot Fighter; Reprints from Magnus, Robot Fighter #1, 3, 4, 6-10 12.00
❑2 1982, Reprints The Aliens stories from Magnus, Robot Fighter; 1982 reprint; Reprints from Magnus, Robot Fighter #1, 3, 4, 6-10; 1972 reprint 5.00

Aliens
Dark Horse

❑1, May 1988 4.50
❑1/2nd; 2nd printing 2.50
❑1/3rd; 3rd printing 2.00
❑1/4th; 4th printing 2.00
❑1/5th; 5th printing 2.00
❑1/6th; 6th printing 2.00
❑2, Sep 1988 3.50
❑2/2nd; 2nd printing 2.50
❑2/3rd; 3rd printing 2.00
❑2/4th, Jul 1989; 4th printing 2.00
❑3, Jan 1989 2.50
❑3/3rd, Sep 1989; 3rd printing 2.00
❑3/2nd; 2nd printing 2.00
❑4, Mar 1989 2.50
❑4/2nd; 2nd printing 2.00
❑5, Jun 1989 2.50
❑5/2nd, Jun 1989; 2nd printing 2.00
❑6, Jul 1989 2.50
❑6/2nd; 2nd printing 2.00

Aliens
Dark Horse

❑1, Aug 1989 3.00
❑2, Dec 1989 2.50
❑3, Mar 1990 2.50
❑4, May 1990 2.50

Aliens: Alchemy
Dark Horse

❑1, Oct 1997 2.95
❑2, Nov 1997 2.95
❑3, Nov 1997 2.95

Aliens: Apocalypse: The Destroying Angels
Dark Horse

❑1, Jan 1999 2.95
❑2, Feb 1999 2.95
❑3, Mar 1999 2.95
❑4, Apr 1999 2.95

Aliens: Berserker
Dark Horse

❑1, Jan 1995 2.50
❑2, Feb 1995 2.50
❑3, Mar 1995 2.50
❑4, Apr 1995 2.50

Aliens: Colonial Marines
Dark Horse

❑1, Jan 1993 2.50
❑2, Feb 1993 2.50
❑3, Mar 1993 2.50
❑4, Apr 1993 2.50
❑5, May 1993; Cover by Joe Phillips 2.50
❑6, Jun 1993 2.50
❑7, Jul 1993 2.50
❑8, Aug 1993 2.50
❑9, Sep 1993 2.50
❑10, Oct 1993; Final Issue 2.50

Aliens: Earth Angel
Dark Horse

❑1, Aug 1994; NN; One-shot, wraparound Cover 2.95

Aliens: Earth War
Dark Horse

❑1, Jun 1990 3.00
❑1/2nd; 2nd printing 2.50
❑2, Jul 1990 2.50
❑3, Sep 1990 2.50
❑4, Oct 1990 2.50

Adventures of Spider-Man

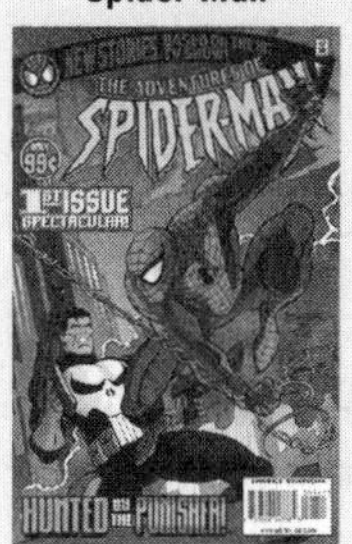

Companion comic book to animated series
©Marvel

Adventures of Superboy

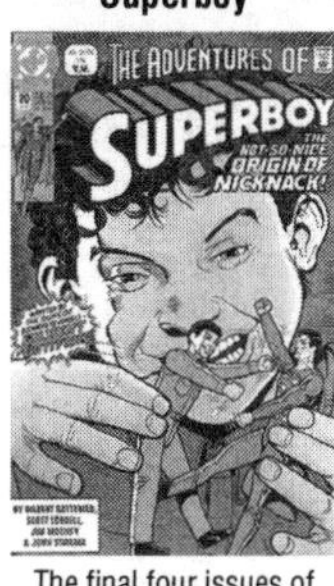

The final four issues of Superboy (2nd Series)
©DC

Adventures of Superman

Picked up where Superman (1st Series) left off
©DC

Adventures of the Big Boy

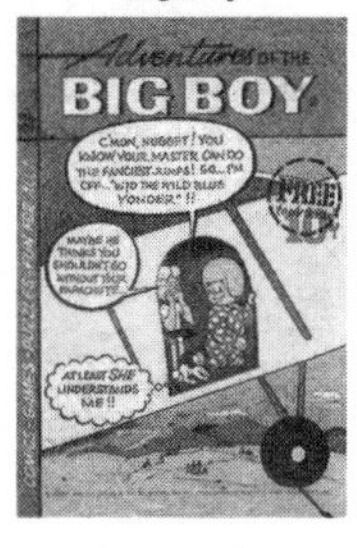

Long-running restaurant chain freebie
©WEBS Group

Adventures of the Big Boy

Shoney's did its own version of Big Boy
©Paragon

N-MINT

Alien Sex/Monster Lust
Fantagraphics / Eros

❑1, Apr 1992, b&w; Adult 2.50

Aliens: Genocide
Dark Horse

❑1, Nov 1991 ...... 2.50
❑2, Dec 1991 ...... 2.50
❑3, Jan 1992 ...... 2.50
❑4, Feb 1992; 2 pin-ups by Arthur Suydam 2.50

Aliens: Glass Corridor
Dark Horse

❑1, Jun 1998; NN; One-shot 2.95

Aliens: Havoc
Dark Horse

❑1, Jun 1997 ...... 2.95
❑2, Jul 1997 SA, CR (a) 3.95

Aliens: Hive
Dark Horse

❑1, Feb 1992 ...... 2.50
❑2, Mar 1992 ...... 2.50
❑3, Apr 1992 ...... 2.50
❑4, May 1992 ...... 2.50

Aliens: Kidnapped
Dark Horse

❑1, Dec 1997 ...... 2.50
❑2, Jan 1998 ...... 2.50
❑3, Feb 1998 ...... 2.50

Aliens: Labyrinth
Dark Horse

❑1, Sep 1993 ...... 2.50
❑2, Oct 1993 ...... 2.50
❑3, Nov 1993 ...... 2.50
❑4, Dec 1993 ...... 2.50

Aliens: Lovesick
Dark Horse

❑1, Dec 1996, One-shot; B&w and color 2.95

Aliens: Mondo Heat
Dark Horse

❑1, Feb 1996; NN; One-shot 2.50

Aliens: Mondo Pest
Dark Horse

❑1; NN; One-shot 2.95

Aliens: Music of the Spears
Dark Horse

❑1, Jan 1994 ...... 2.50
❑2, Feb 1994 ...... 2.50
❑3, Mar 1994 ...... 2.50
❑4, Apr 1994 ...... 2.50

Aliens: Newt's Tale
Dark Horse

❑1, Jun 1992 ...... 4.95
❑2, Aug 1992 ...... 4.95

Aliens: Pig
Dark Horse

❑1, Mar 1997 ...... 2.95

Aliens/Predator: The Deadliest of the Species
Dark Horse

❑1, Jul 1993 ...... 2.50
❑1/Ltd., Jul 1993; no cover price 4.00
❑2, Sep 1993 ...... 2.50

N-MINT

❑3, Nov 1993 ...... 2.50
❑4, Jan 1994 ...... 2.50
❑5, Mar 1994 ...... 2.50
❑6, May 1994 ...... 2.50
❑7, Aug 1994 ...... 2.50
❑8, Oct 1994 ...... 2.50
❑9, Dec 1994 ...... 2.50
❑10, Feb 1995 ...... 2.50
❑11, May 1995 ...... 2.50
❑12, Aug 1995; Final Issue 2.50

Aliens: Purge
Dark Horse

❑1, Aug 1997, NN; One-shot 2.95

Aliens: Rogue
Dark Horse

❑1, Apr 1993 ...... 2.50
❑2, May 1993 ...... 2.50
❑3, Jun 1993 ...... 2.50
❑4, Jul 1993 ...... 2.50

Aliens: Sacrifice
Dark Horse

❑1, ca. 1993; NN 4.95

Aliens: Salvation
Dark Horse

❑1, ca. 1993; NN; One-shot 4.95

Aliens: Salvation and Sacrifice
Dark Horse

❑1, Mar 2001 ...... 12.95

Aliens: Special
Dark Horse

❑1, Jun 1997; NN; One-shot 2.50

Aliens: Stalker
Dark Horse

❑1, Jun 1998; NN; One-shot 2.50

Aliens: Stronghold
Dark Horse

❑1, May 1994 ...... 2.50
❑2, Jun 1994 ...... 2.50
❑3, Jul 1994 ...... 2.50
❑4, Sep 1994 ...... 2.50

Aliens: Survival
Dark Horse

❑1, Feb 1998 ...... 2.95
❑2, Mar 1998 ...... 2.95
❑3, Apr 1998 ...... 2.95

Aliens vs. Predator
Dark Horse

❑0, Jul 1990, b&w; reprints story from Dark Horse Presents #34-36 ...... 5.00
❑1, Jun 1990 ...... 4.00
❑1/2nd, ca. 1990, 2nd printing 2.50
❑2, Aug 1990 ...... 3.50
❑2/2nd, ca. 1990, 2nd printing 2.50
❑3, Oct 1990 ...... 3.00
❑3/2nd, ca. 1990, 2nd printing 2.50
❑4, Dec 1990 ...... 3.00
❑4/2nd, ca. 1990, 2nd printing 2.50
❑Ann 1, Jul 1999; Anthology 4.95

Aliens vs. Predator: Booty
Dark Horse

❑1, Jan 1996; NN; One-shot 2.50

N-MINT

Aliens vs. Predator: Duel
Dark Horse

❑1, Mar 1995 ...... 2.50
❑2, Apr 1995 ...... 2.50

Aliens vs. Predator: Eternal
Dark Horse

❑1, Jun 1998 ...... 2.50
❑2, Jul 1998 ...... 2.50
❑3, Aug 1998 ...... 2.50
❑4, Sep 1998 ...... 2.50

Aliens vs. Predator vs. The Terminator
Dark Horse

❑1, Apr 2000 ...... 2.95
❑2, May 2000 ...... 2.95
❑3, Jun 2000 ...... 2.95
❑4, Jul 2000 ...... 2.95

Aliens vs. Predator: War
Dark Horse

❑0, May 1995; Prologue reprinted from Dark Horse Insider Vol. 2 #1-14 ...... 2.50
❑1, May 1995 ...... 2.50
❑2, Jun 1995 ...... 2.50
❑3, Jul 1995 ...... 2.50
❑4, Aug 1995 ...... 2.50

Aliens vs. Predator: Xenogenesis
Dark Horse

❑1, Dec 1999 ...... 2.95
❑2, Jan 2000 ...... 2.95
❑3, Feb 2000 ...... 2.95
❑4, Mar 2000 ...... 2.95

Aliens: Wraith
Dark Horse

❑1, Jul 1998; NN; One-shot 2.95

Aliens: Xenogenesis
Dark Horse

❑1, Aug 1999 ...... 2.95
❑2, Sep 1999 ...... 2.95
❑3, Oct 1999 ...... 2.95
❑4, Nov 1999 ...... 2.95

Alien: The Illustrated Story
HM Communications

❑1, ca. 1979 ...... 5.00

Alien Worlds
Pacific

❑1, Dec 1982 AW, NR, VM (a) 2.50
❑2, May 1983 DSt (c); DSt (w); DSt (a) . 2.00
❑3, Jul 1983 TY (a) 2.00
❑4, Sep 1983 DSt (c); AW, JJ, DSt (a) ... 2.00
❑5, Dec 1983 TY (a) 2.00
❑6, Feb 1984 FB (c); FB, VM (a) 2.00
❑7, ca. 1984 GM, GP, BA (a) 2.00
❑8, Nov 1984; AW (a); Eclipse Comics begins as publisher 2.00
❑9, Jan 1985; FB (w); FB (a); Final Issue 2.00
❑3D 1, Jul 1984; Full-size issues begin; DSt (a); 3-D Special 2.00

Alien Worlds (Blackthorne)
Blackthorne

❑1, b&w 5.95

Alison Dare, Little Miss Adventures
Oni

❑1, Sep 2000, b&w; 48 pages 4.50

Alister the Slayer
Midnight

❑1, Oct 1995 ... 2.50

Alizarin's Journal
Avatar

❑1, Mar 1999, b&w ... 3.50

Allagash Incident
Tundra

❑1, Jul 1993 ... 2.95

All-American Comics
DC

❑1, May 1999 A: Johnny Thunder. A: Green Lantern ... 2.00

Allegra
Image

❑1, Aug 1996; 1: Allegra ... 2.50
❑1/Variant, Aug 1996; foil cover ... 2.50
❑2, Sep 1996 ... 2.50
❑3, Nov 1996 ... 2.50
❑4, Dec 1996 ... 2.50

Alley Cat
Image

❑1, Jul 1999; Photo cover ... 2.50
❑1/A, Jul 1999; Another Universe Edition; school girl cover ... 3.00
❑1/B, Jul 1999; Wizard World Edition; reclining with claws extended ... 2.50
❑2, Aug 1999; Photo Cover ... 2.50
❑2/A, Aug 1999; Monster Mart Edition; in red dress with stake in hand ... 2.50
❑3, Sep 1999; in front of grave ... 2.50
❑3/A, Sep 1999; Dorian cover ... 2.50
❑4, Oct 1999 ... 2.50
❑5, Dec 1999; Photo cover ... 2.50
❑6, Feb 2000; with headdress ... 2.95
❑Ashcan 1, May 1999; Limited Preview Edition on cover; holding arms over head ... 2.95
❑Ashcan 1/A, May 1999; Dynamic Forces edition; Photo cover; Blue background, holding crystal on cover ... 3.00
❑Ashcan 1/B, May 1999; Dynamic Forces edition; front shot; Wizard World logo at bottom right ... 3.00
❑Ashcan 1/C, May 1999; Dynamic Forces edition; sketch cover ... 3.00
❑Ashcan 1/D, May 1999; Dynamic Forces edition; drawn color cover; kneeling on rooftop ... 3.00
❑Ashcan 1/E; Cover depicts claw outstretched, green background ... 2.50

Alley Cat Lingerie Edition
Image

❑1, Oct 1999; photos and pin-ups; cardstock cover ... 4.95

Alley Cat vs. Lady Pendragon
Image

❑1 2000 ... 3.00
❑1/A 2000; Wizard Mall variant; flipbook with Alley Cat Con Exclusive Preview . 3.00

Alley Oop (Dragon Lady)
Dragon Lady

❑1; O: Oop, Dinny ... 5.95
❑2; time machine ... 6.95
❑3; Hercules ... 7.95

Alley Oop Adventures
Antarctic

❑1, Aug 1998 ... 2.95
❑2, Oct 1998 ... 2.95
❑3, Dec 1998 ... 2.95

Alley Oop Quarterly
Antarctic

❑1, Sep 1999 ... 2.50
❑2, Dec 1999 ... 2.95
❑3, Mar 2000 ... 2.95

All Girls School Meets All Boys School
Angel

❑1 ... 3.00

All Hallow's Eve
Innovation

❑1 ... 4.95

Alliance
Image

❑1, Aug 1995 ... 2.50
❑1/A, Aug 1995; variant cover ... 2.50
❑2, Sep 1995 ... 2.50
❑2/A, Sep 1995; variant cover ... 2.50
❑3, Nov 1995 ... 2.50
❑3/A, Nov 1995; variant cover ... 2.50

All New Adventures of The Mighty Crusaders
Archie / Red Circle

❑1, Mar 1983; O: Shield (Joe Higgins); O: Comet (John Dickering); O: Web (John Raymond); O: Black Hood (Kip Burland); O: Jaguar (Ralph Hardy); O: Fly (Tommy Troy); O: Shield (Lancelot Strong) ... 1.00
❑2, May 1983; Warriors of Omri continued in Galaxia #2 ... 1.00
❑3, Jul 1983, b&w; Title becomes Mighty Crusaders with #4 ... 1.00

All-New Atom
DC

❑1, Sep 2006 ... 2.99
❑2, Oct 2006 ... 2.99
❑3, Nov 2006 ... 2.99
❑4, Dec 2006 ... 2.99
❑5, Jan 2007 ... 2.99
❑6, Feb 2007 ... 2.99
❑7, Mar 2007 ... 2.99

All New Collectors' Edition
DC

❑C-53, Dec 1977; C-53 ... 26.00
❑C-54, Jan 1978; C-54 ... 12.00
❑C-55, Feb 1978; MGr (a); Legion; Wedding of Lightning Lad and Saturn Girl ... 15.00
❑C-56, Apr 1978; NA (w); NA (a); C-56.. 40.00
❑C-56/Whitman, Apr 1978; Whitman variant ... 35.00
❑C-58, Jun 1978; RB, DG (a); Superman vs. Shazam ... 12.00
❑C-60, ca. 1978; C-60; Rudolph's Summer Fun; Includes activity pages and pin-ups ... 20.00
❑C-62, Mar 1979; C-62 ... 12.00

All New Exiles
Malibu / Ultraverse

❑0, Sep 1995; "Black September"; Number infinity ... 1.50
❑0/Variant, Sep 1995; alternate cover; "Black September"; Number infinity... 1.50
❑1, Oct 1995; Juggernaut / Shuriken cover; Contains Ultraforce Vol 2 #1 reprint inside ... 1.50
❑2, Nov 1995; Phoenix Resurrection Flip Book- Chapter 5 ... 1.50
❑3, Dec 1995; The Triumph of One! ... 1.50
❑4, Jan 1996; V: UltraForce ... 1.50
❑5, Feb 1996; "Requiem for a Hero" ... 2.50
❑6, Mar 1996 ... 1.50
❑7, Apr 1996 ... 1.50
❑8, May 1996; Enter Maxis! ... 1.50
❑9, Jun 1996 ... 1.50
❑10, Jul 1996, alternate cover ... 1.50
❑11, Aug 1996, continues in UltraForce #12 ... 1.50

All New Official Handbook of the Marvel Universe A to Z
Marvel

❑1, Mar 2006 ... 3.99
❑2, May 2006 ... 3.99
❑3, Jun 2006 ... 3.99
❑4, Jul 2006 ... 3.99
❑5, Aug 2006 ... 3.99
❑6, Sep 2006 ... 3.99
❑7, Oct 2006 ... 3.99
❑8, Nov 2006 ... 3.99
❑9, Dec 2006 ... 3.99
❑10, Jan 2007 ... 3.99
❑11, Feb 2007 ... 3.99
❑12, Mar 2007 ... 3.99

All-New Tenchi Muyo Part 1
Viz

❑1, May 2002 ... 2.95
❑2, Jun 2002 ... 2.95
❑3, Jul 2002 ... 2.95
❑4, Aug 2002 ... 2.95
❑5, Sep 2002 ... 2.95

All-New Tenchi Muyo Part 2
Viz

❑1, Oct 2002 ... 2.95
❑2, Nov 2002 ... 2.95
❑3, Dec 2002 ... 2.95
❑4, Jan 2003 ... 2.95
❑5, Feb 2003 ... 2.95

All New Underground Comix
Last Gasp

❑1, b&w; Adult ... 5.00
❑2, b&w; Hot Crackers; Adult ... 3.00
❑3, b&w; Flipbook with Mountain on the other side; Adult ... 3.00
❑4, b&w; Adult ... 3.00
❑5, b&w; Two-Fisted Zombies ... 3.00

All-Out War
DC

❑1, Oct 1979; JKu (c); GE, RT (a); O: Viking Commando ... 3.00
❑2, Dec 1979 JKu (c); GE (a) ... 2.50
❑3, Feb 1980 JKu (c); GE (a) ... 2.50
❑4, Apr 1980 JKu (c); GE (a) ... 2.50
❑5, Jun 1980 JKu (c); GE (a) ... 2.50
❑6, Aug 1980 ... 2.50

Alloy
Phenominal Chili

❑Ashcan 1; White Ashcan edition; 1: Alloy ... 1.00
❑Ashcan 1/A; Green ashcan edition; 1: Alloy ... 1.00

All Shook Up
Rip Off

❑1, Jun 1990, b&w; earthquake ... 3.50

All Star Batman and Robin Boy Wonder
DC

❑1/Batman, Aug 2005 ... 5.00
❑1/Robin, Aug 2005 ... 5.00
❑1/Special, Jan 2006 ... 3.99
❑1/RRP, Aug 2005 ... 150.00
❑2/Miller, Sept 2005 ... 4.00
❑2/Lee, Sept 2005 ... 4.00
❑3, Feb 2006 ... 2.99
❑4 ... 2.99
❑5 ... 2.99
❑6 ... 2.99
❑7 ... 2.99
❑8 ... 2.99
❑9 ... 2.99
❑10 ... 2.99

All-Star Comics
DC

❑58, Feb 1976; MGr (c); WW, RE (a); 1: Power Girl. Power Girl joins team; regrouping of JSA; Series begins again after hiatus (1976) ... 12.00
❑59, Apr 1976; V: Brainwave, Per Degaton. V: Brainwave; Per Degaton.. 6.00
❑60, Jun 1976, KG, WW (a); V: Vulcan .. 6.00
❑61, Aug 1976, KG, WW (a); V: Vulcan. Bicentennial #17 ... 6.00
❑62, Oct 1976, KG, WW (a); A: E-2 Superman. V: Zanadu ... 8.00
❑63, Dec 1976, RB (c); KG, WW (a); V: Injustice Gang, Solomon Grundy ... 6.00
❑64, Feb 1977, WW (a); A: Shining Knight. V: Vandal Savage; Star-Spangled Kid creates cosmic converter belt; Power Girl changes costume ... 7.00
❑65, Apr 1977, WW (w); WW (a); V: Vandal Savage ... 7.00
❑66, Jun 1977, RB, JAb (c); BL, JSa (a); V: Icicle, Wizard, Thinker ... 8.00
❑67, Aug 1977, AM (c); BL, JSa (a) ... 6.00
❑68, Oct 1977, AM (c); BL, JSa (a); V: Psycho Pirate ... 6.00
❑69, Dec 1977, AM (c); BL, JSa (a); 1: The Huntress II (Helena Wayne). Original JSA vs. New JSA ... 10.00
❑70, Feb 1978, AM (c); BL, JSa (a); Huntress ... 6.00
❑71, Apr 1978, JSa (c); BL, JSa (a); V: Strike Force ... 6.00
❑72, Jun 1978, V: Thorn, Sportsmaster, original Huntress; V: Thorn (Rose Canton); Sportsmaster; Original Huntress (Paula Brooks) ... 6.00
❑73, Aug 1978, JSa (a); V: Thorn, Sportsmaster, original Huntress ... 6.00
❑74, Oct 1978, JSa (a); V: Master Summoner; Final Issue; 48 pages ... 8.00

All Star Comics
DC

❑1, May 1999; Return of the Justice Society 2.95
❑2, May 1999 ... 2.95
❑GS 1, Sep 1999; 80-Page Giant ... 4.95

Other grades: Multiply price above by 5/6 for VF/NM • 2/3 for VERY FINE • 1/3 for FINE • 1/5 for VERY GOOD • 1/8 for GOOD

Adventures of the Fly

Archie dusted off its own hero for the Silver Age

©Archie

Adventures of the Jaguar

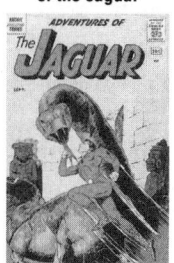

Veterinarian takes on an alter ego

©Archie

Adventures of the Little Green Dinosaur

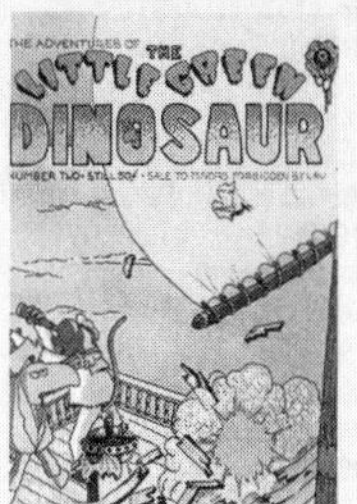

Funny-animal underground title from the 1970s

©Last Gasp

Adventures of the Mask

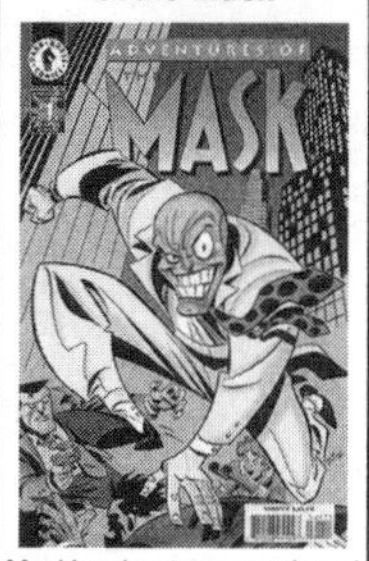

Mask's adventures continued after the movie

©Dark Horse

Adventures of the Outsiders

Continuation of series, without Batman

©DC

N-MINT

All-Star Index
Eclipse / Independent

❑1, Feb 1987; background on members of the JSA and first four issues of All-Star Comics (1st series) and DC Special #29 ... 2.00

All-Star Squadron
DC

❑1, Sep 1981, RB (c); RB, JOy (a); 1: Danette Reilly (later Firebrand II) 4.00
❑2, Oct 1981, JKu (c); RB, JOy (a); O: Hawkman; O: Liberty Belle; O: Plastic Man; O: Robotman; O: Atom; O: Johnny Quick; O: Dr. Mid-Nite; O: Per Degaton ... 2.00
❑3, Nov 1981, RB (c); RB, JOy (a) 2.00
❑4, Dec 1981, RB (c); RB, JOy (a); 1: Dragon King; Last Plastic Man 1.50
❑5, Jan 1982, RB (c); RB, JOy (a); 1: Firebrand II (Danette Reilly)........... 1.50
❑6, Feb 1982 .... 1.50
❑7, Mar 1982, JKu (c); JKu (a) 1.50
❑8, Apr 1982, O: Steel. V: Kung 1.50
❑9, May 1982, JKu (c); JKu (a); O: Baron Blitzkrieg... 1.50
❑10, Jun 1982, JKu (c); JKu (a) 1.50
❑11, Jul 1982, JKu (c); JKu (a) 1.25
❑12, Aug 1982, JKu (c); JKu (a); V: Hastor 1.25
❑13, Sep 1982, JKu (c); JKu (a); Joe Kubert cover; New line-up 1.25
❑14, Oct 1982, JKu (c); JKu (a) 1.25
❑15, Nov 1982, JKu (c); JKu, CS (a); Continued from Justice League of America (1st Series) #208 & in #209 . 1.25
❑16, Dec 1982, JKu (c); JKu (a); V: Nuclear 1.25
❑17, Jan 1983, JKu (c); JKu (a); Trial of Robotman... 1.25
❑18, Feb 1983, JKu (c); JKu (a); V: Villain from Valhalla 1.25
❑19, Mar 1983, V: Brainwave 1.25
❑20, Apr 1983, V: Brainwave 1.25
❑21, May 1983, 1: Deathbolt. 1: Cyclotron. V: Cyclotron... 1.25
❑22, Jun 1983... 1.25
❑23, Jul 1983, 1: Amazing Man; O: Amazing-Man; O: Dr. Fate 1.25
❑24, Aug 1983, 1: Infinity Inc.. 1: Brainwave Jr. 1.25
❑25, Sep 1983, 1: Infinity Inc.; 1: Jade; 1: Nuklon; 1: Silver Scarab; 1: Fury; 1: Northwind; 1: Obsidian.................. 1.25
❑26, Oct 1983, O: Infinity Inc.. 2: Infinity Inc.. 2: Jade. A: Infinity Inc.. 2: Obsidian; 2: Silver Scarab; 2: Nuklon; Continued in All-Star Squadron Ann #2 .... 1.00
❑27, Nov 1983, A: Spectre 1.00
❑28, Dec 1983 A: Spectre 1.00
❑29, Jan 1984 A: Seven Soldiers of Victory 1.00
❑30, Feb 1984; V: Black Dragon Society. V: Black Dragon Society 1.00
❑31, Mar 1984 A: Uncle Sam 1.00
❑32, Apr 1984 .... 1.00
❑33, May 1984; O: Freedom Fighters; V: Baron Blitzkrieg; V: Tsunami........... 1.00
❑34, Jun 1984; V: Tsunami 1.00
❑35, Jul 1984; D: Red Bee. Hourman vs. Baron Blitzkrieg 1.00
❑36, Aug 1984 A: Captain Marvel........... 1.00
❑37, Sep 1984 A: Marvel Family 1.00
❑38, Oct 1984 A: Amazing Man.............. 1.00
❑39, Nov 1984; A: Amazing Man. Junior JSA kit repro....................................... 1.00

N-MINT

❑40, Dec 1984; A: Monitor. Amazing Man vs. Real American 1.00
❑41, Jan 1985; O: Starman.................... 1.00
❑42, Feb 1985... 1.00
❑43, Mar 1985 .... 1.00
❑44, Apr 1985; V: Night and Fog............ 1.00
❑45, May 1985; 1: Zyklon; D: Tom Revere 1.00
❑46, Jun 1985; Liberty Belle gets new powers 1.00
❑47, Jul 1985; TMc (c); TMc (a); O: Doctor Fate; O: Dr. Fate I 3.00
❑48, Aug 1985; A: Shining Knight. Blackhawk... 1.00
❑49, Sep 1985 A: Doctor Occult 1.00
❑50, Oct 1985; Double-size issue; A: Harbinger. Mr. Mind to Earth-2;Crisis; Uncle Sam and others to Earth-X; Steel to Earth-1 .... 1.25
❑51, Nov 1985; V: Monster Society of Evil (Oom, Mr. Who, Ramulus, Nyola, Mr. Mind). V: Monster Society of Evil (Oom, Mr. Who, Ramulus, Nyola, Mr. Mind); Crisis on Infinite Earths crossover 1.00
❑52, Dec 1985; A: Captain Marvel. Crisis 1.00
❑53, Jan 1986; Superman vs. Monster Society;Crisis 1.00
❑54, Feb 1986; V: Monster Society. Crisis 1.00
❑55, Mar 1986; V: Ultra-Humanite in 1980s. Crisis 1.00
❑56, Apr 1986; A: Seven Soldiers of Victory. Crisis..................................... 1.00
❑57, May 1986; Crisis............................ 1.00
❑58, Jun 1986 A: Mekanique 1.00
❑59, Jul 1986; 1: Aquaman in All-Star Squadron 1.00
❑60, Aug 1986; JOy (c); events of Crisis catch up with All-Star Squadron......... 1.00
❑61, Sep 1986; O: Liberty Belle 1.00
❑62, Oct 1986; O: Shining Knight 1.00
❑63, Nov 1986; O: Robotman 1.00
❑64, Dec 1986; retells Golden Age Superman story post-Crisis 1.00
❑65, Jan 1987; O: Johnny Quick............ 1.00
❑66, Feb 1987; O: Tarantula................... 1.00
❑67, Mar 1987; final issue: JSA's first case 1.00
❑Ann 1, Nov 1982; JOy (c); JOy (a); O: Atom, Wildcat, Guardian................ 2.00
❑Ann 2, Nov 1983; JOy (c); JOy (a); A: Infinity Inc.. D: Cyclotron; V: Ultra Humanite; V: Deathbolt; V: Cyclotron; V: Vulcan; V: Mist; V: Ragdoll; V: Monocole; V: Psycho Pirate.............. 1.25
❑Ann 3, Sep 1984; DN, RB, RHo, CI, KG, JOy, GP (a); V: Ian Karkull. V: Ian Karkull; Explanation for JSA's long lifespans 1.25

All-Star Superman
DC

❑1, Jan 2006... 2.99
❑2, Mar 2006... 2.99
❑3, Jun 2006... 2.99
❑4, Sep 2006 .... 2.99
❑5, Nov 2006... 2.99
❑6, Mar 2007, D: Jonathan Kent; W/Superman Squad & Krypto vs. Chronovore; Chronovore comes to Smallville at a time Clark is trying to determine his destiny......................... 2.99
❑7 .... 2.99
❑8 .... 2.99
❑9 .... 2.99
❑10 .... 2.99

N-MINT

All-Star Western
DC

❑1, Sep 1970, (c); CI (a); A: Pow-Wow Smith 30.00
❑2, Nov 1970, NA (c); GM, TD (a); Neal Adams cover 15.00
❑3, Jan 1971, NA (c); GM, GK (a); O: El Diablo. Neal Adams cover 15.00
❑4, Mar 1971, NA (c); GM, GK (a); Neal Adams cover 14.00
❑5, May 1971, NA (c); DG, JA (a); Neal Adams cover 14.00
❑6, Jul 1971, GK (w); GK, TD (a) 9.00
❑7, Sep 1971; DG, JKu, TD (a); expands to 48 pages 9.00
❑8, Nov 1971 CI, JKu, GK, TD (a) 9.00
❑9, Jan 1972; TD (c); SA (w); CI, FF, JKu, NC (a); 48 pages; All reprint issue; Reprints from Western Comics #70, Frontier Fighters #2, Jimmy Wakely #4, 8, Bat Lash #6 .... 9.00
❑10, Mar 1972; TD (c); SA (w); GM, TD, NC (a); 1: Jonah Hex; Reprint from Bat Lash #6 .... 260.00
❑11, May 1972; Giant-size; NR, TD (c); SA (w); GM, CI, TD, NC (a); 2: Jonah Hex. Series continues as Weird Western Tales 75.00

All Suspense
Avalon

❑1 1998, b&w; reprints Nemesis and Mark Midnight stories 2.95

All the Wrong Places
Laszlo / ACG

❑1 .... 2.95

All-Thrill Comics
Mansion

❑845; Actually #1 .... 2.95

Ally
Ally-Winsor

❑1, Fal 1995, b&w; 1&O: Ally................. 2.95
❑2 .... 2.95
❑3, Flip-book... 2.95

Alone in the Dark
Image

❑1, Jul 2002, B&w and color 4.95
❑2, Mar 2003 .... 4.95

Alone in the Shade Special
Alchemy

❑1, b&w; NN 2.00

Alphabet
Dark Visions

❑1, Dec 1993; Pages denoted by letters rather than numbers........................... 2.50

Alpha Centurion Special
DC

❑1, Jun 1996; O: Alpha Centurion; One-shot 2.95

Alpha Flight
Marvel

❑1, Aug 1983; JBy (c); JBy (w); JBy (a); 1: Wildheart (not identified). 1: Diamond Lil (not identified). 1: Puck, Marina. 1: Tundra; 1: Marrina; 1: Box (not identified); 1: Smart Alec (not identified); 1: Flashback (not identified); 1: Madison Jeffries (not identified); 1: Wild Child (not identified).. 5.00

Other grades: Multiply price above by 5/6 for VF/NM • 2/3 for VERY FINE • 1/3 for FINE • 1/5 for VERY GOOD • 1/8 for GOOD

	N-MINT
❑2, Sep 1983, JBy (c); JBy (w); JBy (a); O: Marina. O: Alpha Flight. 1: The Master. 1: Guardian I (James Hudson). Vindicator becomes Guardian I	4.00
❑3, Oct 1983, JBy (c); JBy (w); JBy (a); O: Marina. O: The Master. O: Alpha Flight; O: Marrina; O: Guardian	4.00
❑4, Nov 1983, JBy (w); JBy (a); O: Marina; O: Marrina	4.00
❑5, Dec 1983, JBy (c); JBy (w); JBy (a); O: Elizabeth Twoyoungmen. 1: Elizabeth Twoyoungmen; O: Shaman	4.00
❑6, Jan 1984, JBy (c); JBy (w); JBy (a); O: Shaman. all-white issue	4.00
❑7, Feb 1984, JBy (c); JBy (w); JBy (a); O: Snowbird. 1: Smart Alec (full); 1: Delphine Courtney; 1: Deadly Ernest; O: Snowbird	4.00
❑8, Mar 1984, JBy (c); JBy (w); JBy (a); 1: Nemesis; O: Deadly Ernest	4.00
❑9, Apr 1984, JBy (c); JBy (w); JBy (a); O: Aurora. A: Thing. O: Aurora	4.00
❑10, May 1984, JBy (c); JBy (w); JBy (a); O: Northstar. O: Sasquatch; V: Super-Skrull	4.00
❑11, Jun 1984, JBy (c); JBy (w); JBy (a); O: Sasquatch. 1: Wild Child. 1: Diamond Lil (identified). 1: Diamond Lil (full); 1: Wild Child (full); 1: Box (full); 1: Flashback (full); 1: Omega Flight	3.00
❑12, Jul 1984, Double-size; JBy (c); JBy (w); JBy (a); D: Guardian; V: Omega Flight	3.00
❑13, Aug 1984, JBy (c); JBy (w); JBy (a); A: Wolverine. Heather Hudson becomes team leader	3.00
❑14, Sep 1984, JBy (c); JBy (w); JBy (a)	3.00
❑15, Oct 1984, JBy (c); JBy (w); JBy (a); A: Sub-Mariner	3.00
❑16, Nov 1984, JBy (c); JBy (w); JBy (a); A: Sub-Mariner. Wolverine cameo	3.00
❑17, Dec 1984, JBy (c); JBy (w); JBy (a); X-Men crossover; Wolverine cameo	3.00
❑18, Jan 1985, JBy (c); JBy (w); JBy (a); 1: Ranaq the Devourer	3.00
❑19, Feb 1985, JBy (c); JBy (w); JBy (a); 1&O: Talisman II (Elizabeth Twoyoungmen); V: Ranaq The Devourer	3.00
❑20, Mar 1985, JBy (c); JBy (w); JBy (a); New headquarters	1.50
❑21, Apr 1985, JBy (c); JBy (w); JBy (a); O: Diablo. V: Diablo. O: Gilded Lily	2.00
❑22, May 1985, JBy (c); JBy (w); JBy (a); 1: Pink Pearl	2.00
❑23, Jun 1985, JBy (c); JBy (w); JBy (a); 1: Caliber; O: Sasquatch	2.00
❑24, Jul 1985; Double-size; JBy (c); JBy (w); JBy (a); 1: Somon the Great Artificer; 1: Kariooq the Corruptor; 1: Tolomaq the Fire Beast; V: Great Beasts	1.50
❑25, Aug 1985, JBy (c); JBy (w); JBy (a); V: Caliber	1.00
❑26, Sep 1985, JBy (c); JBy (w); JBy (a); V: Omega Flight	1.00
❑27, Oct 1985, JBy (c); JBy (w); JBy (a); V: Omega Flight	1.00
❑28, Nov 1985, JBy (c); JBy (w); JBy (a); Secret Wars II; Last Byrne issue	3.00
❑29, Dec 1985, A: Hulk	2.00
❑30, Jan 1986, V: Scramble	2.00
❑31, Feb 1986	2.00
❑32, Mar 1986	2.00
❑33, Apr 1986; SB (a); A: X-Men. Wolverine	6.00
❑34, May 1986; SB (a); O: Wolverine. Wolverine	2.50
❑35, Jun 1986; SB (a); Wolverine	1.50
❑36, Jul 1986; SB (a); Wolverine	1.50
❑37, Aug 1986; Wolverine	1.50
❑38, Sep 1986; Wolverine	1.50
❑39, Oct 1986; Wolverine	1.50
❑40, Nov 1986; Wolverine	1.50
❑41, Dec 1986; Wolverine	1.50
❑42, Jan 1987; Wolverine	1.50
❑43, Feb 1987; Wolverine	1.50
❑44, Mar 1987; D: Snowbird. Wolverine	1.50
❑45, Apr 1987; Wolverine	1.50
❑46, May 1987; Wolverine	3.00
❑47, Jun 1987; Wolverine	4.00
❑48, Jul 1987; Wolverine	1.50
❑49, Aug 1987; Wolverine	1.50
❑50, Sep 1987; V: Loki; Double Sized	2.00
❑51, Oct 1987; JLee, JL (a); A: Wolverine. 1st Jim Lee work at Marvel	2.00
❑52, Nov 1987 A: Wolverine	2.00

	N-MINT
❑53, Dec 1987; 1: Laura Dean. A: Wolverine	2.00
❑54, Jan 1988; O: Laura Dean	3.00
❑55, Feb 1988; JLee (a); V: Great Beasts	2.00
❑56, Mar 1988; JLee (c); JLee (a); 1: The Dreamqueen	2.00
❑57, Apr 1988 JLee (c); JLee (a)	1.00
❑58, May 1988 JLee (c); JLee (a)	1.00
❑59, Jun 1988; JLee (c); JLee (a); Puck	1.00
❑60, Jul 1988 JLee (c); JLee (a)	1.25
❑61, Aug 1988 JLee (c); JLee (a)	1.25
❑62, Sep 1988 JLee (c); JLee (a)	1.25
❑63, Oct 1988	1.25
❑64, Nov 1988	1.25
❑65, Dec 1988	1.25
❑66, Jan 1989	1.25
❑67, Feb 1989; O: The Dream Queen	1.25
❑68, Mar 1989	1.25
❑69, Apr 1989	1.25
❑70, May 1989	1.25
❑71, Jun 1989; 1: Llan the Sorcerer	1.25
❑72, Jul 1989	1.25
❑73, Aug 1989	1.25
❑74, Sep 1989; Avengers cameo	1.25
❑75, Oct 1989; Double-size	2.00
❑76, Nov 1989; Gamma Flight	1.50
❑77, Nov 1989; No UPC	1.50
❑78, Dec 1989	1.50
❑79, Dec 1989; Acts of Vengeance	1.50
❑80, Jan 1990; Acts of Vengeance	1.50
❑81, Feb 1990	1.50
❑82, Mar 1990	1.50
❑83, Apr 1990; O: Talisman II (Elizabeth Twoyoungmen)	1.50
❑84, May 1990	1.50
❑85, Jun 1990	1.50
❑86, Jul 1990	1.50
❑87, Aug 1990; JLee (c); JLee (a); 1: Windshear. Wolverine	2.00
❑88, Sep 1990; JLee (c); JLee (a); Wolverine; Guardian I reappears as cyborg	2.00
❑89, Oct 1990; JLee (c); JLee (a); Wolverine; Guardian returns	2.00
❑90, Nov 1990 JLee (c); JLee (a)	2.00
❑91, Dec 1990; Doctor Doom	1.75
❑92, Jan 1991; V: Dr. Doom	1.75
❑93, Feb 1991; Fantastic 4	1.75
❑94, Mar 1991; Fantastic 4	1.75
❑95, Apr 1991; Diamond Lil Reveals She Has Cancer, Aurora Resigns	1.75
❑96, May 1991; Return of Master of the World	1.75
❑97, Jun 1991	1.75
❑98, Jul 1991	1.75
❑99, Aug 1991	1.75
❑100, Sep 1991; A: Galactus. A: Avengers. 52 pages	1.75
❑101, Oct 1991	1.75
❑102, Nov 1991; 1: Weapon Omega; V: Diablo, Whirlwind	1.75
❑103, Dec 1991; V: Diablo	1.75
❑104, Jan 1992	1.75
❑105, Feb 1992; V: Pink Pearl	1.75
❑106, Mar 1992; Northstar admits he's gay	3.00
❑106/2nd, Mar 1992; Northstar admits he's gay	2.00
❑107, Apr 1992 A: X-Factor	1.75
❑108, May 1992; V: Le Peregrine, Shamrock, Micro-Max, Prodigy, Omerta	1.75
❑109, Jun 1992	1.75
❑110, Jul 1992; Infinity War Crossover	1.75
❑111, Aug 1992; PB (c); PB (a); Infinity War Crossover	1.75
❑112, Sep 1992; 1: Beta Flight; Infinity War Crossover	1.75
❑113, Oct 1992	1.75
❑114, Nov 1992; PB (c); PB (a); V: Jackal	1.75
❑115, Dec 1992; 1: Wyre	1.75
❑116, Jan 1993 PB (c); PB (a)	1.75
❑117, Feb 1993 PB (c); PB (a)	1.75
❑118, Mar 1993; PB (c); PB (a); O: Wildheart. 1: Wildheart	1.75
❑119, Apr 1993; PB (c); PB (a); V: Wrecking Crew	1.75
❑120, May 1993; PB (c); PB (a); with poster	2.25
❑121, Jun 1993 PB (c); A: Spider-Man	1.75
❑122, Jul 1993; PB (c); PB (a); Infinity Crusade	1.75

	N-MINT
❑123, Aug 1993; PB (c); PB (a); Infinity Crusade	1.75
❑124, Sep 1993; PB (c); PB (a); Infinity Crusade	1.75
❑125, Oct 1993 PB (c)	1.75
❑126, Nov 1993	1.75
❑127, Dec 1993 KP (a)	1.75
❑128, Jan 1994	1.75
❑129, Feb 1994	1.75
❑130, Mar 1994; Final Issue	2.25
❑Ann 1, Sep 1986	4.00
❑Ann 2, Dec 1987	1.25
❑Special 1, Jun 1992; 1992 Special Edition (Vol. 2); PB (c); PB (a); A: Wolverine. No number on cover	2.50

Alpha Flight
Marvel

❑1, Aug 1997; gatefold summary; wraparound cover	3.00
❑2, Sep 1997; gatefold summary; "Presenting: The Master of Chaos" on cover	2.00
❑2/A, Sep 1997; gatefold summary; alternate cover	2.00
❑3, Oct 1997; gatefold summary	2.00
❑4, Nov 1997; gatefold summary; V: Mesmero	2.00
❑5, Dec 1997; gatefold summary; V: Mesmero	2.00
❑6, Jan 1998; gatefold summary; O: Sasquatch	1.99
❑7, Feb 1998; gatefold summary	1.99
❑8, Mar 1998; gatefold summary; O: Wolverine	1.99
❑9, Apr 1998; gatefold summary; V: Wolverine	1.99
❑10, May 1998; gatefold summary	1.99
❑11, Jun 1998; gatefold summary; Team-up With Micronauts	1.99
❑12, Jul 1998; gatefold summary; D: Sasquatch; V: Zodiac; Double Sized	1.99
❑13, Aug 1998; gatefold summary	1.99
❑14, Sep 1998; gatefold summary; Funeral for Sasquatch	1.99
❑15, Oct 1998; gatefold summary	1.99
❑16, Nov 1998; gatefold summary; V: Brass Bishop	1.99
❑17, Dec 1998; gatefold summary; Team-up With Big Hero 6	1.99
❑18, Jan 1999; gatefold summary; V: Weapon X	1.99
❑19, Feb 1999; Gatefold Summary	1.99
❑20, Mar 1999; Final Issue	1.99
❑Ann 1998, ca. 1998; Alpha Flight/ Inhumans '98; wraparound cover	3.50

Alpha Flight
Marvel

❑1, May 2004	2.99
❑2, Jun 2004, Sasquatch Recruits New Team	2.99
❑3, Jul 2004	2.99
❑4, Aug 2004, V: Mole Man	2.99
❑5, Sep 2004, New Team Rescues Original Team	2.99
❑6, Oct 2004	2.99
❑7, Nov 2004	2.99
❑8, Dec 2004	2.99
❑9, Jan 2005, Big Hero 6 appears	2.99
❑10, Feb 2005	2.99
❑11, Mar 2005	2.99
❑12, Apr 2005, Final Issue	2.99

Alpha Flight: In the Beginning
Marvel

❑-1, Jul 1997, Wedding of James Hudson and Heather McNeil; "Flashback"	2.00

Alpha Flight Special
Marvel

❑1, Jul 1991; Reprints Alpha Flight #97	2.00
❑2, Aug 1991; Reprints Alpha Flight #98	2.00
❑3, Sep 1991; Reprints Alpha Flight #99	2.00
❑4, Oct 1991; Reprints Alpha Flight #100	2.00

Alpha Illustrated
Alpha Productions

❑0, Apr 1994, b&w; free; Preview	1.00
❑1, b&w	3.50

Alpha Korps
Diversity

❑1, Sep 1996	2.50
❑Ashcan 1; Preview issue	1.00

Other grades: Multiply price above by 5/6 for VF/NM • 2/3 for VERY FINE • 1/3 for FINE • 1/5 for VERY GOOD • 1/8 for GOOD

Adventures of the Thing

Reprints Marvel Two-in-One stories

©Marvel

Adventures of the X-Men

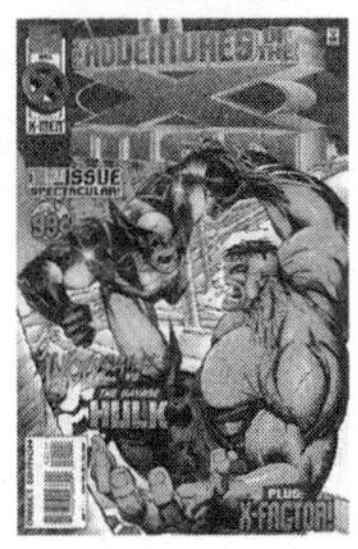

Adapts the fourth season of the cartoon

©Marvel

Adventures On the Planet of the Apes

Marvel adaptation of the movie series

©Marvel

Adventurous Uncle Scrooge McDuck (Walt Disney's...)

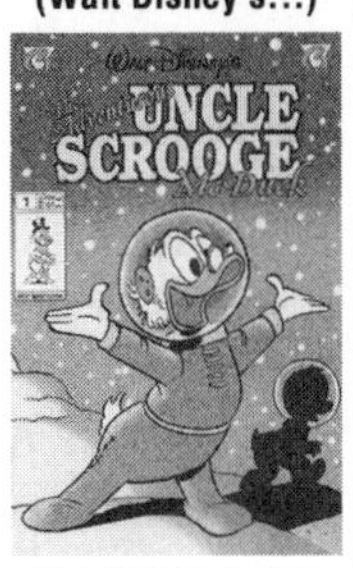

More McDuck mayhem

©Gladstone

Aeon Flux

MTV animated series spawns live-action movie

©Dark Horse

N-MINT

Alpha Team Omega
Fantasy Graphics

❑1, ca. 1983, b&w.... 1.00

Alpha Track
Fantasy General

❑1, Feb 1985.... 1.75
❑2.... 1.75

Alpha Wave
Darkline

❑1.... 1.75

Altered Image
Image

❑1, Apr 1998.... 2.50
❑2, Jun 1998.... 2.50
❑3, Oct 1998; cover says "Sep"; indicia says "Oct".... 2.50

Altered Realities
Altered Reality

❑1; NN.... 2.00

Alter Ego
First

❑1, May 1986; 1: Alter Ego.... 1.50
❑2, Jul 1986.... 1.50
❑3, Sep 1986.... 1.50
❑4, Nov 1986.... 1.50

Alternate Existance
Dragonmaster

❑1, May 1982.... 2.00
❑2, ca 1982.... 2.00

Alternate Heroes
Prelude

❑1, 1: The Crimehater; 1: The Equalizer; 1: The Solar Knight.... 1.95

Alternating Crimes
Alternating Crimes

❑1, Fal 1996.... 2.95
❑2, Fal 1997.... 3.25

Alternation
Image

❑1, Mar 2004.... 2.95
❑2, Mar 2004.... 2.95
❑3, Apr 2004.... 2.95
❑4, Aug 2004.... 2.95

Alternative Comics
Revolutionary

❑1, Jan 1994; Pearl Jam/Cure/REM.... 2.50

Alternity
Navigator

❑1, May 1992.... 2.50

Alvar Mayor: Death and Silver
4Winds

❑1, b&w.... 8.98

Alvin
Dell

❑1, Oct 1962, 12-021-212.... 25.00
❑2, Jan 1963, 12-021-303.... 18.00
❑3, Apr 1963, 12-021-306.... 15.00
❑4, Jul 1963, 12-021-309.... 15.00
❑5, Oct 1963, 12-021-312.... 15.00
❑6, Jan 1964, 12-021-403.... 15.00
❑7, Apr 1964, 12-021-406.... 15.00
❑8, Jul 1964, 12-021-409.... 15.00

N-MINT

❑9, Oct 1964, 12-021-412.... 15.00
❑10, Jan 1965.... 15.00
❑11, Apr 1965.... 12.00
❑12, Jul 1965.... 12.00
❑13, Dec 1965.... 12.00
❑14, Mar 1966.... 12.00
❑15, Jun 1966.... 12.00
❑16, Sep 1966.... 12.00
❑17, Dec 1966.... 12.00
❑18, Mar 1967.... 12.00
❑19, ca. 1968.... 12.00
❑20, Oct 1969.... 12.00
❑21, Oct 1970.... 8.00
❑22, Oct 1971.... 8.00
❑23, Jan 1972, 01-021-201.... 8.00
❑24, Apr 1972, 01-021-204.... 8.00
❑25, Jul 1972.... 8.00
❑26, Oct 1972.... 8.00
❑27, Jul 1973.... 8.00
❑28, Oct 1973.... 8.00

Alvin and the Chipmunks
Harvey

❑1, Jul 1992.... 2.00
❑2, Nov 1993.... 1.50
❑3, Jan 1993.... 1.50
❑4, Mar 1994.... 1.50
❑5, Jun 1994.... 1.50

A Man Called Kev
DC

❑1, Sep 2006.... 2.99
❑2, Oct 2006.... 2.99
❑3, Nov 2006.... 2.99
❑4, Feb 2007.... 2.99
❑5, Mar 2007.... 2.99

Amanda and Gunn
Image

❑1, Apr 1997, b&w.... 2.95
❑2, Jun 1997, b&w.... 2.95
❑3, Aug 1997, b&w.... 2.95
❑4, Oct 1997, b&w.... 2.95

Amazing Adult Fantasy
Marvel

❑7, Dec 1961, SL (w); SD (a); Series continued from Amazing Adventures #6 600.00
❑8, Jan 1962, SL (w); SD (a).... 475.00
❑9, Feb 1962, SL (w); SD (a).... 425.00
❑10, Mar 1962, SL (w); SD (a).... 425.00
❑11, Apr 1962, SL (w); SD (a).... 425.00
❑12, May 1962, SL (w); SD (a).... 425.00
❑13, Jun 1962, SL (w); SD (a).... 425.00
❑13/2nd, SL (w); SD (a); 2nd printing.... 2.50
❑14, Jul 1962, SL (w); SD (a); Professor X prototype; Series continued in Amazing Fantasy #15.... 525.00

Amazing Adventure
Marvel

❑1, Jul 1988; squarebound.... 4.95

Amazing Adventures
Marvel

❑1, Jun 1961, SL (w); SD, JK (a); O: Doctor Droom. A: Doctor Droom. 1:/o: Dr. Droom (first Marvel Silver Age superhero).... 900.00
❑2, Jul 1961, SL (w); SD, JK (a); A: Doctor Droom. Dr. Droom.... 525.00

N-MINT

❑3, Aug 1961, SL (w); SD, JK (a); A: Doctor Droom. Dr. Droom.... 425.00
❑4, Sep 1961, SL (w); SD, JK (a); A: Doctor Droom.... 425.00
❑5, Oct 1961, SL (w); SD, JK (a); A: Doctor Droom.... 425.00
❑6, Nov 1961, SL (w); SD, JK (a); A: Doctor Droom. Series continues as Amazing Adult Fantasy #7.... 425.00

Amazing Adventures
Marvel

❑1, Aug 1970, JK, JR (c); JK (w); JB, JK (a); Inhumans.... 30.00
❑2, Sep 1970, Inhumans.... 20.00
❑3, Nov 1970, JB (c); JK (w); GC, BEv, JK (a); Black Widow; Inhumans.... 20.00
❑4, Jan 1971, JB (c); JK (w); GC, BEv, JK (a); Black Widow; Inhumans.... 14.00
❑5, Mar 1971, JB (c); GC, BEv, NA (a); 1: Astrologer; Paul Levitz L.O.C.... 14.00
❑6, May 1971, NA (c); SB, DH, NA (a); Inhumans, Black Widow.... 20.00
❑7, Jul 1971, NA (c); BEv, DH, NA (a); Inhumans, Black Widow.... 14.00
❑8, Sep 1971, NA (c); BEv, DH, NA (a); Inhumans, Black Widow.... 22.00
❑9, Nov 1971, JB (c); BEv (a); A: Black Bolt 20.00
❑10, Jan 1972, Inhumans; Reprinted from Thor #146.... 20.00
❑11, Mar 1972, GK (c); TS (a); 1&O: Beast (in furry form).... 150.00
❑12, May 1972, GK (c); TS (a); A: Beast. Beast; Iron Man.... 30.00
❑13, Jul 1972, JR (c); TS (a); 1: Robert Buzz Baxter.... 30.00
❑14, Sep 1972, GK (c); TS (a); Beast.... 25.00
❑15, Nov 1972, JSn (c); TS (a); 1&O: Griffin. Beast.... 20.00
❑16, Jan 1973, JSn (c); Beast; Rutland, Vermont story.... 20.00
❑17, Mar 1973, GK (c); JSn (a); Beast; reprinted, with changes, from X-Men (1st series) 49-53.... 20.00
❑18, May 1973, NA (w); HC, NA (a); O: Killraven. 1: Killraven. 1: Killraven; O: Killraven; War of the Worlds.... 14.00
❑19, Jul 1973, Killraven.... 5.00
❑20, Sep 1973, HT (c); HT (a); Killraven 5.00
❑21, Nov 1973, Killraven.... 5.00
❑22, Jan 1974, Killraven.... 5.00
❑23, Mar 1974, Killraven; Marvel Value Stamp #13: Dr. Strange.... 5.00
❑24, May 1974, RB (c); SD, HT (a); V: High Overlord. Killraven; Marvel Value Stamp #58: The Mandarin.... 5.00
❑25, Jul 1974, V: Skar. Killraven.... 5.00
❑26, Sep 1974, JR (c); GC (a); Killraven: Marvel Value Stamp #96: Dr. Octopus 4.00
❑27, Nov 1974, JSn (c); JSn, CR, JSt (a); O: Killraven. Marvel Value Stamp #22: Man-Thing.... 4.00
❑28, Jan 1975, CR (c); CR (a); O: Volcana. Killraven.... 4.00
❑29, Mar 1975, GK (c); CR (a); Killraven 5.00
❑30, May 1975, CR (c); HT, CR (a); Killraven.... 3.00
❑31, Jul 1975, CR (c); CR (a); Killraven. 3.00
❑32, Sep 1975, CR (c); CR (a); Killraven 3.00
❑33, Nov 1975, JR (c); HT, CR (a); Killraven; Marvel Value Stamp #52: Quicksilver.... 3.00

Other grades: Multiply price above by 5/6 for VF/NM • 2/3 for VERY FINE • 1/3 for FINE • 1/5 for VERY GOOD • 1/8 for GOOD

❑34, Jan 1976, CR (c); CR (a); D: Hawk. D: Grok. Killraven;Marvel Value Stamp B/10 3.00
❑35, Mar 1976, CR (c); KG, CR, JAb (a); Killraven 3.00
❑36, May 1976, CR (c); CR (a); Killraven 3.00
❑36/30¢, May 1976, 30¢ regional price variant 20.00
❑37, Jul 1976, CR (c); CR (a); O: Old Skul; Killraven 8.00
❑37/30¢, Jul 1976, CR (a); O: Old Skull. 30¢ regional price variant 8.00
❑38, Sep 1976, KP (c); KG (w); KG, CR (a); Killraven 3.00
❑39, Nov 1976, CR (c); CR (a); Killraven 3.00

Amazing Adventures
Marvel

❑1, Dec 1979; JK (c); SL (w); JK (a); 1: X-Men. Reprints first part of X-Men (1st Series) #1; 2nd story reprinted from X-Men (1st series) #38 3.00
❑2, Jan 1980; SL (w); JK (a); O: Cyclops. Reprints second half of X-Men (1st Series) #1; 2nd story reprinted from X-Men (1st Series) #39 2.00
❑3, Feb 1980; Reprinted from X-Men (first series) #2; 2nd story reprinted from X-Men (1st Series) #40 2.00
❑4, Mar 1980; Reprinted from X-Men (first series) #2, retitled from "No One Can Stop the Vanisher"; 2nd story reprinted from X-Men (1st Series) #41 2.00
❑5, Apr 1980; Reprinted from X-Men (first series) #3; 2nd story reprinted from X-Men (1st Series) #42 2.00
❑6, May 1980; Reprinted from X-Men (first series) #3, retitled from "Beware, the Blob"; 2nd story reprinted from X-Men (1st Series) #43 2.00
❑7, Jun 1980; Reprinted from X-Men (first series) #4; 2nd story reprinted from X-Men (1st Series) #44 2.00
❑8, Jul 1980; Reprinted from X-Men (first series) #4, retitled from "The Brotherhood of Evil Mutants"; 2nd story reprinted from X-Men (1st Series) #45 2.00
❑9, Aug 1980; Reprinted from X-Men (first series) #5, retitled from "Trapped: One X-Man"; 2nd story reprinted from X-Men (1st Series) #46 2.00
❑10, Sep 1980; Reprinted from X-Men (first series) #5; 2nd story reprinted from X-Men (1st Series) #47 2.00
❑11, Oct 1980, Reprinted from X-Men (first series) #6; 2nd story reprinted from X-Men (1st Series) #48 2.00
❑12, Nov 1980, Reprinted from X-Men (first series) #6, retitled from "Search for the Sub-Mariner"; 2nd story reprinted from Strange Tales #168 2.00
❑13, Dec 1980, Reprinted from X-Men (first series) #7 2.00
❑14, Jan 1981, Reprinted from X-Men (first series) #8 2.00

Amazing Adventures of Ace International
Starhead

❑1, Nov 1993, b&w 2.95

Amazing Adventures of Frank and Jolly (Alan Groening's...)
Press This

❑1 1.75
❑2 1.75
❑3 1.75
❑4 1.75
❑5 1.75
❑6 1.75
❑7 1.75
❑8 1.75
❑9 1.75

Amazing Adventures of Professor Jones
Antarctic

❑1, Nov 1996 2.95
❑2, Dec 1996 2.95
❑3 2.95
❑4 2.95

Amazing Adventures of The Escapist (Michael Chabon Presents The)
Dark Horse

❑1, Feb 2004, JSn, HC (w); JSn, HC (a); A: The Escapist. based on Chabon's book The Amazing Adventures of Kavalier and Clay 8.95
❑2, Apr 2004 8.95
❑3, Jun 2004 8.95
❑4, Jul 2004 8.95
❑5, Jan 2005 8.95
❑6, Apr 2005 8.95
❑7, May 2005 10.00
❑8, Nov 2005 8.95

Amazing Adventures of the JLA
DC

❑1, Jun 2006, Collects stories from JLA #77, JLA 80 Page Giant #1, JLA Gallery and, JLA Secret Files #3 3.99

Amazing Chan and the Chan Clan
Gold Key

❑1, May 1973, ME (w); Mark Evanier's first story published in U.S. 14.00
❑2, Aug 1973 9.00
❑3, Nov 1973 9.00
❑4, Feb 1974 9.00

Amazing Comics Premieres
Amazing

❑1, Jan 1987; Ninja Bots 1.95
❑2, Mar 1987 1.95
❑3, May 1987 1.95
❑4, Jul 1987 1.95
❑5, Aug 1987; Stargrazers 1.95

Amazing Cynicalman
Eclipse

❑1, b&w 2.50

Amazing Fantasy
Marvel

❑15, Aug 1962, JK (c); SD, SL (w); SD, JK (a); 1&O: Spider-Man; 1: Peter Parker; 1: Aunt May; 1: Uncle Ben; 1: Flash Thompson; D: Uncle Ben 32000.00
❑15/2nd, Aug 2002; Reprint packaged with Spider-Man movie DVD 5.00
❑16, Dec 1995; KB (w); cardstock cover; fills in gaps between Amazing Fantasy #15 and Amazing Spider-Man #1 4.50
❑17, Jan 1996; KB (w); cardstock cover 4.50
❑18, Mar 1996; KB (w); cardstock cover 4.50

Amazing Fantasy
Marvel

❑1, Aug 2004, Arana; 1: Arana (Anya Corazon) 4.00
❑2, Sep 2004, Arana 2.99
❑3, Oct 2004, Arana 2.99
❑4, Nov 2004, Arana 2.99
❑5, Dec 2004, Arana; 1: Arana (Anya Corazon) 2.99
❑6, Jan 2005, Arana 2.99
❑7, Feb 2005; Scorpion 2.99
❑8, Mar 2005; Scorpion 2.99
❑9, Jun 2005; Scorpion 2.99
❑10, Jul 2005; Scorpion 2.99
❑11, Aug 2005; Scorpion 2.99
❑12, Sep 2005; Scorpion 2.99
❑13, Oct 2005, 1: Vegas 2.99
❑14, Nov 2005 2.99
❑15, Dec 2005, Note price; Mastermind Excello reprinted in World War Hulk Prologue: World Breaker #1 3.99
❑16, Feb 2006 2.99
❑17, Mar 2006 2.99
❑18, May 2006 2.99
❑19, Jun 2006 2.99
❑20, Jul 2006, 1: Steam Rider; Final issue 2.99

Amazing Heroes Swimsuit Special
Fantagraphics

❑Ann 1990, Jun 1990, b&w; Omaha the Cat Dancer cover; 128 pg 6.00
❑Ann 1991, Jun 1991; Wonder Woman cover 8.00
❑Ann 1992, Jun 1992; FT (c); FH, GM, SR, DC (a); Red Sonja and Ghita cover 10.00
❑4, Mar 1993; published by Spoof Comics 3.95
❑5, Aug 1993; GM (a); published by Spoof Comics 4.95

Amazing High Adventure
Marvel

❑1, Aug 1984 JSe (a) 2.50
❑2, Sep 1985 PS (a) 2.50
❑3, Oct 1986 VM, JSe (a) 2.50
❑4, Nov 1986 2.50
❑5, Dec 1986 2.50

Amazing Joy Buzzards
Image

❑1, Feb 2005 2.95
❑2, Mar 2005 2.95
❑3, Apr 2005 2.95
❑4, May 2005 2.95

Amazing Joy Buzzards (Vol. 2)
Image

❑1, Nov 2005 2.99
❑2, Dec 2005 2.99
❑3, Jan 2006 2.99
❑4, Feb 2006 2.99
❑5, Sep 2006 2.99

Amazing Scarlet Spider
Marvel

❑1, Nov 1995; Direct Market Edition 1.95
❑2, Dec 1995 A: Joystick. A: Green Goblin IV 1.95
❑2/Direct ed., Dec 1995; Direct Edition 1.95

Amazing Screw-On Head
Dark Horse

❑1, May 2002, B&w and color 2.99
❑1/2nd, Feb 2004 2.99

Amazing Spider-Girl
Marvel

❑0, Dec 2006, Reprints from What If'? #105, Spider-Girl #0-100, Spider-Girl #1/2, and Spider-Girl Ann 1999 1.99
❑1, Dec 2006 3.00
❑1/Variant, Dec 2006 2.99
❑2, Jan 2007, Includes Incredible Hulk #100 sneak peak and Guiding Light back up story 2.99
❑3, Feb 2007 2.99

Amazing Spider-Man
Marvel

❑-1, Jul 1997, Flashback 2.50
❑1, Mar 1963, SD, JK (c); SD, SL (w); SD, JK (a); O: Spider-Man. 1: John Jameson. 1: J. Jonah Jameson. 1: Chameleon. A: Fantastic Four 27000.00
❑1/Golden, ca. 1966, JK (c); SD, SL (w); SD (a); O: Spider-Man. 1: J. Jonah Jameson. 1: Chameleon. A: Fantastic Four. Golden Records reprint 200.00
❑2, May 1963, SD (c); SD, SL (w); SD (a). 1: Mysterio (as "alien"). 1: Tinkerer. 1: Vulture 3400.00
❑3, Jul 1963, SD (c); SD, SL (w); SD (a); O: Doctor Octopus. 1: Doctor Octopus; First use of the "Spider Signal" light 4600.00
❑4, Sep 1963, SD (c); SD, SL (w); SD (a); O: Sandman (Marvel). 1: Betty Brant; 1: Liz Allen 2300.00
❑5, Oct 1963, SD (c); SD, SL (w); SD (a); V: Doctor Doom 2500.00
❑6, Nov 1963, SD (c); SD, SL (w); SD (a); 1&O: The Lizard 1650.00
❑7, Dec 1963, SD (c); SD, SL (w); SD (a); 2: The Vulture. V: Vulture 1100.00
❑8, Jan 1964, SD (c); SD, SL (w); SD, JK (a); A: Human Torch. V: Flash Thompson. V: Living Brain. 1: The Living Brain 800.00
❑9, Feb 1964, SD (c); SD, SL (w); SD (a); 1&O: Electro. 1: Doctor Bromwell 1025.00
❑10, Mar 1964, SD, JK (c); SD, SL (w); SD, JK (a); 1: Fancy Dan. 1: Big Man. 1: Montana. 1: Enforcers. 1: Ox 990.00
❑11, Apr 1964, SD, JK (c); SD, SL (w); SD (a); 2: Doctor Octopus. V: Doctor Octopus. D: Bennett Brant 1900.00
❑12, May 1964, SD (c); SD, SL (w); SD (a); V: Doctor Octopus. Spider-Man unmasked 825.00
❑13, Jun 1964, SD (c); SD, SL (w); SD (a); O: Mysterio. 1: Mysterio 1200.00
❑14, Jul 1964, SD (c); SD, SL (w); SD (a); 1: Green Goblin I (Norman Osborn). A: Hulk. A: Enforcers 2050.00
❑15, Aug 1964, SD (c); SD, SL (w); SD (a); 1&O: Kraven the Hunter. 1: Anna May Watso. 1: Mary Jane Watson (name mentioned). A: Chameleon 1800.00
❑16, Sep 1964, SD (c); SD, SL (w); SD (a); 1: The Great Gambonnos. 1: Princess Python. A: Daredevil. V: Ringmaster and Circus of Crime 800.00
❑17, Oct 1964, SD (c); SD, SL (w); SD (a); 2: Green Goblin I (Norman Osborn). A: Torch. V: Green Goblin I (Norman Osborn) 800.00
❑18, Nov 1964, SD (c); SD, SL (w); SD (a); V: Sandman (Marvel) 510.00

Age of Bronze	Age of Heroes	Airboy	Airboy Meets the Prowler	Air Raiders

Eric Shanower retells the Trojan War ©Image	Wonders in the land of Xera ©Halloween	Revival of Golden Age aerial hero ©Eclipse	Two popular characters join forces ©Eclipse	No toy license tie-in here ©Marvel

	N-MINT
❑19, Dec 1964, SD (c); SL (w); SD (a); 1: MacDonald Mac Gargan [later becomes the Scorpion]. 1: Rock Gimpy V: Sandman (Marvel). V: Enforcers; 1: Ned Leeds (later becomes Hobgoblin I); V: Sandman	460.00
❑20, Jan 1965, SD (c); SL (w); SD (a); 1&O: The Scorpion	510.00
❑21, Feb 1965, SD (c); SD, SL (w); SD (a); 2: The Beetle. A: Torch. V: Beetle	510.00
❑22, Mar 1965, SD (c); SL (w); SD (a); V: Ringmaster and Circus of Crime. 1: The Masters of Menace (the Clown; The Gambonnos; Cannonball); Princess Python	425.00
❑23, Apr 1965, SD (c); SL (w); SD (a); A: Green Goblin I (Norman Osborn)	510.00
❑24, May 1965, SD (c); SL (w); SD (a); V: Mysterio; Mysterio appearance as Dr. Ludwig Rinehart	500.00
❑25, Jun 1965, SD (c); SD, SL (w); SD (a); 1: Spencer Smythe. 1: Spider-Slayers. 1: Mary Jane Watson (cameo-face not shown)	500.00
❑26, Jul 1965, SD (c); SD, SL (w); SD (a); 1: Crime-Master. 1: Patch. A: Green Goblin I (Norman Osborn). 1: Crime-Master; 1: Crime-Master (Nick Lucky Lewis)	550.00
❑27, Aug 1965, SD (c); SD, SL (w); SD (a); A: Green Goblin I (Norman Osborn). D: Crime-Master; Crime Master apperance; Patch appearance (Frederick Foswell)	500.00
❑28, Sep 1965, SD (c); SD, SL (w); SD (a); O: Molten Man. 1: Molten Man. 2: Spencer Smythe. Peter Parker graduates from high school	450.00
❑29, Oct 1965, SD (c); SD, SL (w); SD (a); 2: The Scorpion. V: The Scorpion	240.00
❑30, Nov 1965, SD (c); SD, SL (w); SD (a); V: Cat Burglar. 1: The Cat	240.00
❑31, Dec 1965, SD (c); SD, SL (w); SD (a); 1: Professor Warren. 1: Gwen Stacy. 1: Harry Osborn; 1: Master Planner (Doctor Octopus)	325.00
❑32, Jan 1966, SD (c); SD, SL (w); SD (a); Master Planner revealed as Doctor Octopus	175.00
❑33, Feb 1966, SD (c); SD, SL (w); SD (a); V: Doctor Octopus (as Master Planner); Guy H. Lillian III L.O.C	140.00
❑34, Mar 1966, SD (c); SD, SL (w); SD (a); A: Green Goblin I (Norman Osborn). V: Kraven the Hunter	240.00
❑35, Apr 1966, SD, JK (c); SD, SL (w); SD (a); 1: Spider Tracer. V: Molten Man	225.00
❑36, May 1966, SD (c); SD, SL (w); SD (a); 1: Looter (later Meteor Man in Marvel Team-Up #33)	225.00
❑37, Jun 1966, SD (c); SD, SL (w); SD (a); 1: Norman Osborn. A: Patch. V: Professor Mendel Stromm	250.00
❑38, Jul 1966, SD (c); SD, SL (w); SD (a); 2: Mary Jane Watson (cameo). 1: Joe Smith; 2: Norman Osborn; Final Steve Ditko issue	195.00
❑39, Aug 1966, JR (c); SL (w); JR (a); V: Green Goblin I (Norman Osborn). Green Goblin revealed as Norman Osborn	350.00
❑40, Sep 1966, JR (c); SL (w); JR (a); O: Green Goblin I (Norman Osborn)	375.00
❑41, Oct 1966, JR (c); SL (w); JR (a); 1: Rhino	300.00

	N-MINT
❑42, Nov 1966, JR (c); SL (w); JR (a); A: Mary Jane Watson (first time her face is shown). A: Rhino; Foggy Nelson cameo	185.00
❑43, Dec 1966, JR (c); SL (w); JR (a) O: Rhino. V: Rhino; Foggy Nelson cameo	120.00
❑44, Jan 1967, JR (c); SL (w); JR (a); V: Lizard. 2: Lizard	175.00
❑45, Feb 1967, JR (c); SL (w); JR (a); V: Lizard	115.00
❑46, Mar 1967, JR (c); SL (w); JR (a); 1&O: Shocker	250.00
❑47, Apr 1967, JR (c); SL (w); JR (a); V: Kraven the Hunter	105.00
❑48, May 1967, JR (c); SL (w); JR (a); 1: Vulture II (Blackie Drago); 2: Professor Miles Warren; V: Vulture II	120.00
❑49, Jun 1967, JR (c); SL (w); JR (a); V: Kraven the Hunter	125.00
❑50, Jul 1967, JR (c); SL (w); JR (a); 1: Kingpin	625.00
❑51, Aug 1967, JR (c); SL (w); JR (a); O: Mysterio. 1: Robbie Robertson. 2: Kingpin. V: Kingpin	200.00
❑52, Sep 1967, JR (c); SL (w); JR (a); 1: Joe Robertson. D: Big Man (Frederick Foswell). V: Kingpin	150.00
❑53, Oct 1967, JR (c); SL (w); JR (a); V: Doctor Octopus	105.00
❑54, Nov 1967, JR (c); SL (w); JR (a); V: Doctor Octopus. 2: Joe Robertson	110.00
❑55, Dec 1967, JR (c); SL (w); JR (a); V: Doctor Octopus	110.00
❑56, Jan 1968, JR (c); SL (w); JR (a); 1: Captain Stacy. V: Doctor Octopus	90.00
❑57, Feb 1968, JR (c); SL (w); DH, JR (a); A: Ka-Zar and Zabu. 2: Captain Stacy; Peter Sanderson L.O.C	80.00
❑58, Mar 1968, JR (c); SL (w); DH, JR (a); A: Ka-Zar and Zabu. V: Spencer Smythe. V: J. Jonah Jameson. 2: Spencer Smythe; 2: Spider-Slayers	100.00
❑59, Apr 1968, JR (c); SL (w); DH, JR (a); 1: Doctor Winkler. 1: Slade. V: Kingpin (as Brainwasher)	70.00
❑60, May 1968, JR (c); JR, SL (w); DH, JR (a); 2: Doctor Winkler. 2: Slade. V: Kingpin	105.00
❑61, Jun 1968, JR (c); JR, SL (w); DH, JR (a); V: Kingpin	72.00
❑62, Jul 1968, JR (c); JR, SL (w); DH, JR (a); A: Medusa	75.00
❑63, Aug 1968, JR (c); JR, SL (w); DH, JR (a); V: both Vultures; Don McGregor L.O.C	160.00
❑64, Sep 1968, JR (c); JR, SL (w); DH, JR (a); V: Vulture	60.00
❑65, Oct 1968, JR (c); JR, SL (w); JR, JM (a)	55.00
❑66, Nov 1968, JR (c); JR, SL (w); DH, JR (a); A: Mysterio. V: Mysterio; Cary Burkett L.O.C.; Tony Isabella L.O.C	80.00
❑67, Dec 1968, JR (c); JR, SL (w); JR, JM (a); 1: Randy Robertson. V: Mysterio	60.00
❑68, Jan 1969, JR (c); JR, SL (w); JR, JM (a); 1: Louis Wilson. V: Kingpin; 2: Randy Robertson	60.00
❑69, Feb 1969, JR (c); JR, SL (w); JR, JM (a); V: Kingpin; Kerry Gammill L.O.C	75.00
❑70, Mar 1969, JR (c); JR, SL (w); JR, JM (a); 1: Vanessa Fisk (Kingpin's wife-face not shown); V: Kingpin	70.00
❑71, Apr 1969, JR (c); JR, SL (w); JR, JM (a); A: Quicksilver. Kingpin; Quicksilver; Scarlet Witch; The Toad	70.00

	N-MINT
❑72, May 1969, JR (c); JR, SL (w); JB, JR, JM (a); V: Shocker	85.00
❑73, Jun 1969, JR (c); SL (w); JB, JR, JM (a); 1: Man-Mountain Marko. 1: Caesar Cicero. 1: Silvermane; Peter Sanderson L.O.C	50.00
❑74, Jul 1969, JR (c); JR, SL (w); JB, JR, JM (a); V: Man-Mountain Marko. V: Caesar Cicero. V: Silvermane	80.00
❑75, Aug 1969, JR (c); JR, SL (w); JB, JR, JM (a); V: Man-Mountain Marko. V: Caesar Cicero. V: Silvermane. D: Silvermane	65.00
❑76, Sep 1969, JR (c); SL (w); JB, JM (a); A: Human Torch. V: Lizard	65.00
❑77, Oct 1969, JR (c); JR, SL (w); JB, JM (a); A: Human Torch. V: Lizard; Don McGregor L.O.C	65.00
❑78, Nov 1969, JB, JR (c); JB, SL (w); JB, JM (a); 1: The Prowler	70.00
❑79, Dec 1969, JB, JR (c); SL (w); JB, JM (a); 2: The Prowler. V: Prowler	60.00
❑80, Jan 1970, JR (c); JR, SL (w); JB, JR, JM (a); V: Chameleon	60.00
❑81, Feb 1970, JR (c); JR, SL (w); JB, JR, JM (a); O: The Kangaroo. 1: The Kangaroo	55.00
❑82, Mar 1970, JR, SL (w); JR, JM (a); O: Electro. V: Electro	50.00
❑83, Apr 1970, JR (c); SL (w); JR (a); 1: Richard Fisk (The Schemer) 1: Vanessa Fisk (Full-Kingpin's wife). V: Kingpin. V: Schemer	50.00
❑84, May 1970, JR (c); JR, SL (w); JB, JR, JM (a); V: Kingpin. V: Schemer	55.00
❑85, Jun 1970, JR (c); JR, SL (w); JB, JR, JM (a); V: Kingpin. V: Schemer	55.00
❑86, Jul 1970, JR (c); JR, SL (w); JR, JM (a); O: Black Widow	60.00
❑87, Aug 1970, JR (c); JR, SL (w); JR, JM (a); Peter reveals his secret identity	75.00
❑88, Sep 1970, JR (c); SL (w); JR, JM (a); A: Doctor Octopus	60.00
❑89, Oct 1970, JR (c); SL (w); GK, JR (a); A: Doctor Octopus	70.00
❑90, Nov 1970, GK, JR (c); SL (w); GK, JR (a); A: Doctor Octopus. D: Captain Stacy	75.00
❑91, Dec 1970, JR (c); SL (w); GK, JR (a); 1: Sam Bullit	50.00
❑92, Jan 1971, JR (c); SL (w); GK, JR (a); A: Sam Bullit. A: Iceman	62.00
❑93, Feb 1971, JR (c); JR, SL (w); JR (a); A: Prowler. 1: Arthur Stacy; Gwen Stacy leaves for England	80.00
❑94, Mar 1971, JR (c); JR, SL (w); SB, JR (a); O: Spider-Man. A: Beetle. Spider-Man's Origin retold	65.00
❑95, Apr 1971, JR (c); JR, SL (w); SB, JR (a); Spider-Man goes to London	52.00
❑96, May 1971, GK (c); SL (w); GK, JR (a); A: Green Goblin I (Norman Osborn). Drug topics not approved by CCA	85.00
❑97, Jun 1971, JR (c); JR, SL (w); GK, JR (a); A: Green Goblin I (Norman Osborn). Drug topics not approved by CCA	72.00
❑98, Jul 1971, GK (c); SL (w); GK (a); A: Green Goblin I (Norman Osborn). Drug topics not approved by CCA	80.00
❑99, Aug 1971, GK (c); SL (w); GK (a); A: Johnny Carson; Ed McMahon	60.00
❑100, Sep 1971, 100th anniversary issue; JR (c); SL (w); GK (a); A: Green Goblin I (Norman Osborn). Peter grows four extra arms	100.00

Other grades: Multiply price above by 5/6 for VF/NM • 2/3 for VERY FINE • 1/3 for FINE • 1/5 for VERY GOOD • 1/8 for GOOD

N-MINT

❑101, Oct 1971, GK (c); GK (w); GK (a); 1: Morbius 130.00
❑101/2nd; GK (a); 1: Morbius. Metallic ink cover 2.50
❑102, Nov 1971, Giant-sized; GK (c); GK, SL (w); GK (a); O: Morbius. A: Lizard. A: Morbius 105.00
❑103, Dec 1971, GK (c); GK (w); GK (a); 1: Gog. V: Kraven the Hunter; Ka-Zar; Zabu 50.00
❑104, Jan 1972, GK (c); GK (w); GK (a). V: Kraven the Hunter; Ka-Zar; Zabu 90.00
❑105, Feb 1972, GK (c); GK, SL (w); GK (a); V: Spider Slayer. V: Spencer Smythe 25.00
❑106, Mar 1972, JR (c); JR, SL (w); JR (a); V: Spider Slayer. V: Spencer Smythe 40.00
❑107, Apr 1972, JR (c); JR, SL (w); JR (a); V: Spider Slayer. V: Spencer Smythe 27.00
❑108, May 1972, JR (c); JR, SL (w); JR (a); 1: Sha Shan. A: Flash Thompson . 27.00
❑109, Jun 1972, JR (c); JR, SL (w); JR (a); A: Doctor Strange 30.00
❑110, Jul 1972, JR (c); JR, SL (w); JR (a); 1&O: The Gibbon 30.00
❑111, Aug 1972, JR (c); JR (w); JR (a); V: The Gibbon, Kraven the Hunter 34.00
❑112, Sep 1972, JR (c); JR (w); JR (a); A: The Gibbon. V: Doctor Octopus 30.00
❑113, Oct 1972, JR (c); JR (w); JSn, JR, JSt (a); 1: Hammerhead. V: Doctor Octopus 35.00
❑114, Nov 1972, JR (c); JR (w); JSn, JR, JSt (a); O: Hammerhead. 1: Doctor Jonas Harrow 50.00
❑115, Dec 1972, JR (c); JR (w); JR (a); V: Hammerhead, Doctor Octopus; Dr. Octopus, Hammerhead 33.00
❑116, Jan 1973, JR (c); JR, SL (w); JR, JM (a); 1: Smasher (was Man Monster). V: Richard Raleigh. Reprints Spectacular Spider-Man #1 ("Lo, This Monster") with some new art and dialogue; Man Monster renamed Smasher 22.00
❑117, Feb 1973, reprints story from Spectacular Spider-Man (magazine) #1 with updates; JR (c); JR, SL (w); HT, JR, JM (a); 1: Disruptor; Man Monster renamed Smasher 25.00
❑118, Mar 1973, JR (c); JR, SL (w); JR, JM (a); V: Disruptor, Smasher. Reprints Spectacular Spider-Man #1 ("Lo, This Monster") with some new art and dialogue; Man Monster renamed Smasher 22.00
❑119, Apr 1973, JR (c); JR (w); JR (a); A: Incredible Hulk. V: Hulk in Canada . 50.00
❑120, May 1973, GK, JR (c); GK, JR (a); A: Incredible Hulk. V: Hulk 50.00
❑121, Jun 1973, GK, JR (c); GK (w); GK, JR (a); D: Gwen Stacy. V: Green Goblin I (Norman Osborn); Green Goblin 150.00
❑122, Jul 1973, GK, JR (c); GK, JR (a); D: Green Goblin I (Norman Osborn); Later revealed as false; D: Green Goblin (Norman Osborn) 150.00
❑123, Aug 1973, GK (c); GK (w); GK, JR (a); A: Luke Cage 35.00
❑124, Sep 1973, GK (c); GK (w); GK, JR (a); 1: Man-Wolf 42.00
❑125, Oct 1973, RA (c); JR, RA (a); O: Man-Wolf 30.00
❑126, Nov 1973, RA (c); JR, RA, JM (a); A: Doctor Jonas Harrow. A: Human Torch. D: Kangaroo. Harry Osborn becomes Green Goblin 18.00
❑127, Dec 1973, RA (c); JR, RA (a); V: third Vulture; Human Torch 25.00
❑128, Jan 1974, RA (c); JR, RA (a); O: third Vulture 20.00
❑129, Feb 1974, GK, RA (c); GK, RA (a); 1: The Punisher. 1: Jackal 225.00
❑129/Ace, Apr 2002, Wizard Ace Edition 6.00
❑130, Mar 1974, GK, RA (c); RA (a); 1: Spider-Mobile. V: Doctor Octopus. V: Hammerhead. V: Jackal. Marvel Value Stamp #2: Hulk 20.00
❑131, Apr 1974, RA (c); GK, RA (a); V: Doctor Octopus. V: Hammerhead. Dr. Octopus, Hammerhead; Marvel Value Stamp #34: Mr. Fantastic 25.00
❑132, May 1974, JR (c); GK, JR (a); V: Molten Man. Marvel Value Stamp #6: Thor 22.00
❑133, Jun 1974, JR, RA (c); RA (a); V: Molten Man. Molten Man's relationship to Liz Allan revealed; Marvel Value Stamp #66: General Ross 16.00

N-MINT

❑134, Jul 1974, RA (c); JR, RA (a); 1: Tarantula I (Anton Rodriguez). A: Punisher. Marvel Value Stamp #3: Conan 28.00
❑135, Aug 1974, JR, RA (c); JR, RA (a); O: Tarantula I (Anton Rodriguez). A: Punisher. Marvel Value Stamp #4: Thing 45.00
❑136, Sep 1974, JR, RA (c); RA (a); 1: Green Goblin II (Harry Osborn). Marvel Value Stamp #95: Mole-Man .. 60.00
❑137, Oct 1974, GK, RA (c); RA (a); V: Green Goblin II (Harry Osborn). Marvel Value Stamp #99: Sandman ... 25.00
❑138, Nov 1974, RA (c); GK, RA (a); O: The Mindworm. 1: The Mindworm. Peter moves in with Flash Thompson; Marvel Value Stamp #41: Gladiator 15.00
❑139, Dec 1974, GK, RA (c); GK, RA (a); 1: Grizzly. A: Jackal. Marvel Value Stamp #42: Man-Wolf 19.00
❑140, Jan 1975, GK (c); GK, RA (a); O: Grizzly. 1: Gloria Grant. V: Jackal. Marvel Value Stamp #75: Morbius 17.00
❑141, Feb 1975, JR (c); JR, RA (a); V: second Mysterio. Spider-Mobile sinks in Hudson; Marvel Value Stamp #35: Killraven 15.00
❑142, Mar 1975, JR (c); JR, RA (a); V: second Mysterio 18.00
❑143, Apr 1975, GK, JR (c); GK, RA (a); 1: Cyclone 15.00
❑144, May 1975, GK, JR (c); GK, RA (a); O: Cyclone. 1: Gwen Stacy clone. V: Cyclone. Marvel Value Stamp #17: Black Bolt 17.00
❑145, Jun 1975, GK, JR (c); RA (a); A: Scorpion. V: Scorpion. Marvel Value Stamp #100: Galactus 15.00
❑146, Jul 1975, JR (c); JR2, JR, RA (a); A: Scorpion. V: Jackal, Scorpion. Marvel Value Stamp #67: Cyclops 15.00
❑147, Aug 1975, JR (c); JR, RA (a); V: Jackal, Tarantula. Marvel Value Stamp #42: Man-Wolf 14.00
❑148, Sep 1975, GK, JR (c); GK, RA (a); V: Jackal, Tarantula. Professor Warren revealed as Jackal 25.00
❑149, Oct 1975, GK, JR (c); RA (a); 1: Ben Reilly. D: Jackal. D: Spider-clone (faked death) 27.00
❑150, Nov 1975, GK (c); GK (a); A: Ben Reilly. Spider-Man attempts to determine if he is the clone or the original 16.00
❑151, Dec 1975, JR (c); JR, RA (a); A: Ben Reilly. V: Shocker. Spider-Man disposes of clone's body (faked) 24.00
❑152, Jan 1976, GK, JR (c); RA (a); V: Shocker; Marvel Value Stamp Series B #6 .... 11.00
❑153, Feb 1976, GK, JR (c); GK, RA (a). 10.00
❑154, Mar 1976, JR (c); SB, JR (a); V: Sandman (Marvel) 10.00
❑155, Apr 1976, JR (c); SB (a); V: Tallon 12.00
❑155/30¢, Apr 1976, JR (c); SB (a); 30¢ regional price variant 20.00
❑156, May 1976, JR (c); JR, RA (a); O: Mirage I (Desmond Charne). 1: Mirage I (Desmond Charne); Wedding of Betty Brant and Ned Leeds 12.00
❑156/30¢, May 1976, JR (c); JR, RA (a); 30¢ regional price variant 20.00
❑157, Jun 1976, JR (c); JR, RA (a); return of Doctor Octopus 12.00
❑157/30¢, Jun 1976, JR (c); JR, RA (a); 30¢ regional price variant; return of Doctor Octopus 40.00
❑158, Jul 1976, GK, JR (c); RA (a); V: Doctor Octopus. Hammerhead regains physical form 10.00
❑158/30¢, Jul 1976, GK, JR (c); RA (a); 30¢ regional price variant; Hammerhead regains physical form ... 20.00
❑159, Aug 1976, GK (c); RA (a); V: Doctor Octopus, Hammerhead 11.00
❑159/30¢, Aug 1976, GK (c); RA (a); 30¢ regional price variant 20.00
❑160, Sep 1976, GK, JR (c); RA (a); V: Tinkerer. return of Spider-Mobile ... 9.00
❑161, Oct 1976, GK, JR (c); RA (a); A: Punisher. A: Nightcrawler. V: Nightcrawler; Wolverine and Colossus cameo 12.00
❑162, Nov 1976, JR, RA (c); RA (a); A: Punisher. A: Nightcrawler 11.00
❑163, Dec 1976, DC, JR (c); RA (a); V: Kingpin 10.00

N-MINT

❑164, Jan 1977, JR (c); RA (a); V: Kingpin 12.00
❑165, Feb 1977, JR (c); RA (a); V: Stegron. Newsstand edition (distributed by Curtis); issue number in box 9.00
❑165/Whitman, Feb 1977, JR (c); RA (a); V: Stegron. Special markets edition (usually sold in Whitman bagged prepacks); price appears in a diamond; UPC barcode appears 9.00
❑166, Mar 1977, JR (c); RA (a); V: Lizard. V: Stegron. Newsstand edition (distributed by Curtis); issue number in box 9.00
❑166/Whitman, Mar 1977, JR (c); RA (a); V: Lizard. V: Stegron. Special markets edition (usually sold in Whitman bagged prepacks); price appears in a diamond; UPC barcode appears 9.00
❑167, Apr 1977, JR (c); RA (a); 1: Will o' the Wisp. Newsstand edition (distributed by Curtis); issue number in box 6.50
❑167/Whitman, Apr 1977, JR (c); RA (a); 1: Will o' the Wisp. Special markets edition (usually sold in Whitman bagged prepacks); price appears in a diamond; UPC barcode appears 6.50
❑168, May 1977, JR (c); RA (a); V: Will o' the Wisp. Newsstand edition (distributed by Curtis); issue number in box 6.50
❑168/Whitman, May 1977, JR (c); RA (a); V: Will o' the Wisp. Special markets edition (usually sold in Whitman bagged prepacks); price appears in a diamond; UPC barcode appears 6.50
❑169, Jun 1977, AM (c); RA (a); Newsstand edition (distributed by Curtis); issue number in box; J. Jonah Jameson acquires photos showing Spider-Man disposing of clone's(?) body 10.00
❑169/Whitman, Jun 1977, AM (c); RA (a); Special markets edition (usually sold in Whitman bagged prepacks); price appears in a diamond; UPC barcode appears; J. Jonah Jameson acquires photos showing Spider-Man disposing of clone's(?) body 10.00
❑169/35¢, Jun 1977, AM (c); RA (a); 35¢ regional price variant; J. Jonah Jameson acquires photos showing Spider-Man disposing of clone's(?) body 15.00
❑170, Jul 1977, RA (c); RA (a); V: Doctor Faustus. Newsstand edition (distributed by Curtis); issue number in box 6.50
❑170/Whitman, Jul 1977, RA (c); RA (a); V: Doctor Faustus. Special markets edition (usually sold in Whitman bagged prepacks); price appears in a diamond; UPC barcode appears 6.50
❑170/35¢, Jul 1977, RA (c); RA (a); V: Doctor Faustus. 35¢ regional price variant 15.00
❑171, Aug 1977, RA (c); RA (a); A: Nova. Newsstand edition (distributed by Curtis); issue number in box 6.50
❑171/Whitman, Aug 1977, RA (c); RA (a); A: Nova. Special markets edition (usually sold in Whitman bagged prepacks); price appears in a diamond; UPC barcode appears 6.50
❑171/35¢, Aug 1977, RA (c); RA (a); 35¢ regional price variant 15.00
❑172, Sep 1977, RA (c); RA (a); 1: Rocket Racer. Newsstand edition (distributed by Curtis); issue number in box 8.00
❑172/Whitman, Sep 1977, RA (c); RA (a); 1: Rocket Racer. Special markets edition (usually sold in Whitman bagged prepacks); price appears in a diamond; UPC barcode appears 8.00
❑172/35¢, Sep 1977, RA (c); RA (a); 1: Rocket Racer. 35¢ regional price variant 15.00
❑173, Oct 1977, JR, RA (c); RA, JM (a); V: Molten Man. Newsstand edition (distributed by Curtis); issue number in box 18.00
❑173/Whitman, Oct 1977, JR, RA (c); RA, JM (a); V: Molten Man. Special markets edition (usually sold in Whitman bagged prepacks); price appears in a diamond; no UPC barcode 18.00
❑173/35¢, Oct 1977, JR, RA (c); RA, JM (a); V: Molten Man. 35¢ regional price variant 25.00
❑174, Nov 1977, RA (c); RA, JM (a); A: Punisher. V: Hitman. Newsstand edition (distributed by Curtis); issue number in box 10.00

Other grades: Multiply price above by 5/6 for VF/NM • 2/3 for VERY FINE • 1/3 for FINE • 1/5 for VERY GOOD • 1/8 for GOOD

Airtight Garage

Moebius makes more magic
©Marvel

Akiko

Charming series follows fourth-grader in space
©Sirius

Akira

Marvel import from before manga was hot
©Marvel

Aladdin (Disney's...)

More adventures of Arabian street thief
©Marvel

Albedo (1st Series)

Funny animal space epic from Steve Gallacci
©Thoughts & Images

	N-MINT
❑174/Whitman, Nov 1977, RA (c); RA, JM (a); A: Punisher. V: Hitman. Special markets edition (usually sold in Whitman bagged prepacks); price appears in a diamond; no UPC barcode	10.00
❑175, Dec 1977, RA (c); RA, JM (a); A: Punisher. V: Hitman. Newsstand edition (distributed by Curtis); issue number in box	10.00
❑175/Whitman, Dec 1977, RA (c); RA, JM (a); A: Punisher. V: Hitman. Special markets edition (usually sold in Whitman bagged prepacks); price appears in a diamond; no UPC barcode	10.00
❑176, Jan 1978, TD, RA (c); TD, RA, JM (a); O: Green Goblin III (Doctor Barton Hamilton). 1: Green Goblin III (Doctor Barton Hamilton)	12.00
❑177, Feb 1978, RA, JSt (c); RA (a); A: Green Goblin III (Doctor Barton Hamilton). V: Silvermane	12.00
❑178, Mar 1978, RA, JSt (c); RA, JM (a); A: Green Goblin III (Doctor Barton Hamilton). V: Silvermane	11.00
❑179, Apr 1978, RA (c); RA (a); A: Green Goblin III (Doctor Barton Hamilton). V: Silvermane. Newsstand edition (distributed by Curtis); issue number in box	11.00
❑179/Whitman, Apr 1978, RA (c); RA (a); A: Green Goblin III (Doctor Barton Hamilton). V: Silvermane. Special markets edition (usually sold in Whitman bagged prepacks); price appears in a diamond; no UPC barcode	11.00
❑180, May 1978, RA (c); RA (a); A: Green Goblin III (Doctor Barton Hamilton). V: Silvermane. Newsstand edition (distributed by Curtis); issue number in box	11.00
❑180/Whitman, May 1978, RA (c); RA (a); A: Green Goblin III (Doctor Barton Hamilton). V: Silvermane. Special markets edition (usually sold in Whitman bagged prepacks); price appears in a diamond; no UPC barcode	11.00
❑181, Jun 1978, GK (c); SB (a); O: Spider-Man. Newsstand edition (distributed by Curtis); issue number in box	9.00
❑181/Whitman, Jun 1978, GK (c); SB (a); O: Spider-Man. Special markets edition (usually sold in Whitman bagged prepacks); price appears in a diamond; no UPC barcode	9.00
❑182, Jul 1978, RA (c); RA (a); V: Rocket Racer	8.00
❑183, Aug 1978, RA (c); RA, BMc (a); O: Big Wheel. 1: Big Wheel. D: Big Wheel. V: Tinkerer. V: Rocket Racer. Newsstand edition (distributed by Curtis); issue number in box	6.50
❑183/Whitman, Aug 1978, RA (c); RA, BMc (a); 1&O: Big Wheel. D: Big Wheel. V: Tinkerer. V: Rocket Racer. Special markets edition (usually sold in Whitman bagged prepacks); price appears in a diamond; UPC barcode appears	6.50
❑184, Sep 1978, RA, BMc (c); RA (a); 1: White Dragon II. Newsstand edition (distributed by Curtis); issue number in box	8.00
❑184/Whitman, Sep 1978, RA, BMc (c); RA (a); 1: White Dragon II. Special markets edition (usually sold in Whitman bagged prepacks); price appears in a diamond; UPC barcode appears	6.00

	N-MINT
❑185, Oct 1978, RA (c); RA (a); V: Dragon Gangs. V: White Dragon II. Newsstand edition (distributed by Curtis); issue number in box; Peter Parker graduates from college	6.50
❑185/Whitman, Oct 1978, RA (c); RA (a); V: Dragon Gangs. V: White Dragon II. Special markets edition (usually sold in Whitman bagged prepacks); price appears in a diamond; UPC barcode appears; Peter Parker graduates from college	6.50
❑186, Nov 1978, KP (c); KP (a); V: Chameleon. Newsstand edition (distributed by Curtis); issue number in box	8.00
❑186/Whitman, Nov 1978, KP (c); KP (a); V: Chameleon. Special markets edition (usually sold in Whitman bagged prepacks); price appears in a diamond; no UPC barcode	8.00
❑187, Dec 1978, KP (c); JSn (w); JSn, BMc (a); A: Shield. A: Captain America. V: Electro. Newsstand edition (distributed by Curtis); issue number in box	8.00
❑187/Whitman, Dec 1978, KP (c); JSn (w); JSn, BMc (a); A: Shield. A: Captain America. V: Electro. Special markets edition (usually sold in Whitman bagged prepacks); price appears in a diamond; no UPC barcode	8.00
❑188, Jan 1979, DC (c); KP (a); O: Jigsaw. 1: Jigsaw. V: Jigsaw. Newsstand edition (distributed by Curtis); issue number in box	6.50
❑188/Whitman, Jan 1979, DC (c); KP (a); O: Jigsaw. 1: Jigsaw. V: Jigsaw. Special markets edition (usually sold in Whitman bagged prepacks); price appears in a diamond; no UPC barcode	6.50
❑189, Feb 1979, JBy, BMc (c); JBy, JM (a); A: Man-Wolf. Newsstand edition (distributed by Curtis); issue number in box	6.00
❑189/Whitman, Feb 1979, JBy, BMc (c); JBy, JM (a); A: Man-Wolf. Special markets edition (usually sold in Whitman bagged prepacks); price appears in a diamond; no UPC barcode	6.00
❑190, Mar 1979, AM, KP (c); JBy, JM (a); A: Man-Wolf	6.50
❑191, Apr 1979, AM (c); KP (a); V: Spider Slayer. V: Spencer Smythe	6.00
❑192, May 1979, KP, BMc (c); KP, JM (a); D: Spencer Smythe. V: The Fly. Newsstand edition (distributed by Curtis); issue number in box	6.00
❑192/Whitman, May 1979, KP, BMc (c); KP, JM (a); D: Spencer Smythe. V: The Fly. Special markets edition (usually sold in Whitman bagged prepacks); price appears in a diamond; no UPC barcode	6.00
❑193, Jun 1979, KP, JM (a); V: The Fly	6.00
❑194, Jul 1979, AM (c); KP (a); 1: Black Cat	21.00
❑195, Aug 1979, AM (c); AM, KP, JM (a); O: Black Cat. Peter Parker informed of Aunt May's death (faked death)	10.00
❑196, Sep 1979, KP (c); AM, JM (a); D: Aunt May (faked death). V: Kingpin. V: Mysterio	6.00
❑197, Oct 1979, KP, JM (a); V: Kingpin	6.00
❑198, Nov 1979, KP (c); SB, JM (a); V: Mysterio	6.00
❑199, Dec 1979, KP (c); SB, JM (a); V: Mysterio	7.00

	N-MINT
❑200, Jan 1980, Giant sized; JR2, JR (c); SL (w); KP, JM (a); O: Spider-Man. D: unnamed burglar that shot Uncle Ben. Aunt May revealed to be alive	10.00
❑201, Feb 1980, JR2, JR, BMc (c); KP, JM (a); A: Punisher	9.00
❑202, Mar 1980, KP (c); KP, JM (a); A: Punisher	7.00
❑203, Apr 1980, FM, JM (c); KP (a); 2: Dazzler. A: Dazzler	6.00
❑204, May 1980, AM, JR2 (c); KP (a); A: Black Cat	8.00
❑205, Jun 1980, AM (c); KP, JM (a); A: Black Cat	6.00
❑206, Jul 1980, AM (c); JBy, GD (a)	6.00
❑207, Aug 1980, JM (a); V: Mesmero.	5.00
❑208, Sep 1980, AM, JR2 (c); AM, JR2 (a); O: Fusion. 1: Lance Bannon. 1: Fusion	6.00
❑209, Oct 1980, KJ (a); O: Calypso. 1: Calypso. V: Kraven the Hunter	6.00
❑210, Nov 1980, AM, JR2 (c); JR2, JSt (a); O: Madame Web. 1: Madame Web	6.00
❑211, Dec 1980, AM, JR2 (c); JR2, JM (a); A: Sub-Mariner	6.00
❑212, Jan 1981, AM, JR2 (c); JR2, JM (a); O: Sandman (Marvel). 1&O: Hydro-Man	5.00
❑213, Feb 1981, AM, JR2 (c); JR2, JM (a); V: Wizard	5.00
❑214, Mar 1981, AM, JR2 (c); JR2, JM (a); A: Sub-Mariner. V: Frightful Four.	5.00
❑215, Apr 1981, AM, JR2 (c); JR2, JM (a)	5.00
❑216, May 1981, AM, JR2 (c); JR2, JM (a)	5.00
❑217, Jun 1981, AM, JR2 (c); JR2, JM (a)	5.00
❑218, Jul 1981, FM (c); AM, JR2, JM (a)	5.00
❑219, Aug 1981, FM (c); LMc, JM (a); V: Grey Gargoyle	6.00
❑220, Sep 1981, BL (c); BMc (a); A: Moon Knight	6.00
❑221, Oct 1981, BWi (c); JM (a); V: Ramrod	4.00
❑222, Nov 1981, BH, JM (a); V: Speed Demon	4.00
❑223, Dec 1981, JR2 (c); AM, JR2 (a); V: Red Ghost	5.00
❑224, Jan 1982, (c); JR2 (a); V: Vulture	4.00
❑225, Feb 1982, (c); JR2, BWi (a); A: Foolkiller II (Greg Salinger)	4.00
❑226, Mar 1982, JR2, (c); JR2, JM (a); A: Black Cat	7.00
❑227, Apr 1982, JR2, (c); JR2, JM (a); A: Black Cat	6.00
❑228, May 1982, MN (c)	4.00
❑229, Jun 1982, AM, JR2 (c); JR2, JM (a); V: Juggernaut	11.00
❑230, Jul 1982, AM, JR2 (c); JR2, JM (a)	6.00
❑231, Aug 1982, AM, JR2 (c); JR2, JM (a); V: Cobra	6.00
❑232, Sep 1982, AM, JR2 (c); JR2, JM (a); V: Mr. Hyde	6.00
❑233, Oct 1982, AM, JR2 (c); JR2, JM (a); V: Tarantula	4.00
❑234, Nov 1982, AM, JR2 (c); DGr, JR2 (a); Free 16 page insert-Marvel Guide to Collecting Comics	6.00
❑235, Dec 1982, AM, JR2 (c); JR2 (a); O: Will o' the Wisp	4.00
❑236, Jan 1983, JR2 (c); JR2 (a); D: Tarantula I (Anton Rodriguez)	5.00
❑237, Feb 1983, (c); BH (a)	5.00

Other grades: Multiply price above by 5/6 for VF/NM • 2/3 for VERY FINE • 1/3 for FINE • 1/5 for VERY GOOD • 1/8 for GOOD

	N-MINT
❑238, Mar 1983, JR2 (c); JR2 (a); 1: Hobgoblin (Ned Leeds). Came with "Tattooz" temporary tattoo decal	22.00
❑239, Apr 1983, AM, JR2 (c); JR2 (a); 2: Hobgoblin	10.00
❑240, May 1983, BL, JR2 (c); BL, JR2 (a)	5.00
❑241, Jun 1983, JR2 (c); JR2 (a); O: Vulture	4.00
❑242, Jul 1983, JR2 (c); JR2 (a); V: Mad Thinker	5.00
❑243, Aug 1983, JR2 (c); JR2 (a)	6.00
❑244, Sep 1983, JR2, BWi (c); JR2, KJ (a); A: Hobgoblin (cameo). A: 3rd. V: Hobgoblin, 3: Hobgoblin (cameo)	5.00
❑245, Oct 1983, PS, JR2 (c); JR2 (a); A: 4th. Lefty Donovan becomes Hobgoblin	5.00
❑246, Nov 1983, DGr, JR2 (c); DGr, JR2 (a)	4.00
❑247, Dec 1983, JR2 (c); JR2 (a); V: Thunderball	4.00
❑248, Jan 1984, JR2 (c); JR2 (a); V: Thunderball	4.00
❑249, Feb 1984, (c); DGr, JR2 (a); V: Hobgoblin	5.00
❑250, Mar 1984, JR2, KJ (c); JR2, KJ (a); A: Hobgoblin	6.00
❑251, Apr 1984, KJ (c); KJ (a); V: Hobgoblin. Last old costume	6.00
❑252, May 1984, KJ (c); new costume	10.00
❑253, Jun 1984, 1: The Rose	5.00
❑254, Jul 1984, V: Jack O'Lantern	5.00
❑255, Aug 1984, V: Red Ghost	4.00
❑256, Sep 1984, 1&O: Puma. V: Puma	4.00
❑257, Oct 1984, 2: Puma. A: Hobgoblin. V: Puma	4.00
❑258, Nov 1984, A: Hobgoblin	4.00
❑259, Dec 1984, O: Mary Jane Watson. A: Hobgoblin. Spider-Man back to old costume	5.00
❑260, Jan 1985, A: Hobgoblin. V: Hobgoblin	5.00
❑261, Feb 1985, CV (c); A: Hobgoblin. V: Hobgoblin	5.00
❑262, Mar 1985, BL (w); BL (a); Spider-man unmasked	5.00
❑263, Apr 1985, 1: Spider-Kid	5.00
❑264, May 1985	4.00
❑265, Jun 1985, 1: Silver Sable	4.00
❑265/2nd, Jun 1985; 1: Silver Sable. 2nd printing	2.00
❑266, Jul 1985, PD (w); SB (a)	3.00
❑267, Aug 1985, (c); PD (w); BMc (a)	3.00
❑268, Sep 1985, JBy (c); A: Kingpin. A: Beyonder. Secret Wars II	4.00
❑269, Oct 1985, (c); V: Firelord	4.00
❑270, Nov 1985, BMc (a); 1: Kate Cushing (Peter Parker's supervisor at the Bugle). A: Avengers. V: Firelord	4.00
❑271, Dec 1985, (c); V: Manslaughter	5.00
❑272, Jan 1986, SB (a); V: Slyde; 1: Slyde	4.00
❑273, Feb 1986, A: Puma. Secret Wars II	4.00
❑274, Mar 1986, A: Zarathos (the spirit of vengeance). V: Beyonder. Secret Wars II	5.00
❑275, Apr 1986, double-sized; SL (w); SD (a); O: Spider-Man. Hobgoblin story	5.00
❑276, May 1986, A: Hobgoblin. D: Fly	5.00
❑277, Jun 1986, CV (c); CV (w); CV (a); V: Kingpin	4.00
❑278, Jul 1986, PD (w); D: Wraith	4.00
❑279, Aug 1986, Jack O' Lantern V: Silver Sable	4.00
❑280, Sep 1986	5.00
❑281, Oct 1986, V: Sinister Syndicate. Jack O' Lantern cover/story	5.00
❑282, Nov 1986	5.00
❑283, Dec 1986, BL (a); V: Absorbing Man. V: Titania	5.00
❑284, Jan 1987, A: Punisher	5.00
❑285, Feb 1987, MZ (c); A: Punisher. A: Hobgoblin	6.00
❑286, Mar 1986	4.00
❑287, Apr 1987, EL (a); A: Hobgoblin. A: Daredevil	5.00
❑288, May 1987, A: Hobgoblin	6.00
❑289, Jun 1987, double-sized issue; PD (w); 1: Hobgoblin II (Jason Macendale). Hobgoblin unmasked; Hobgoblin's identity revealed; Jack O' Lantern becomes Hobgoblin	6.00
❑290, Jul 1987, AM (c); JR2 (a); Peter Parker proposes to Mary Jane	5.00
❑291, Aug 1987, AM (c); JR2 (a); V: Spider-Slayer	5.00
❑292, Sep 1987, AM (c); V: Spider Slayer	5.00
❑293, Oct 1987, MZ (c); MZ (a); V: Kraven the Hunter	5.00
❑294, Nov 1987, MZ, BMc (a); D: Kraven. V: Kraven the Hunter	6.00
❑295, Dec 1987, BSz (c); BSz (a)	6.00
❑296, Jan 1988, JBy (c); V: Doctor Octopus	5.00
❑297, Feb 1988, V: Doctor Octopus	6.00
❑298, Mar 1988, TMc (a); 1: Venom (cameo). V: Chance I (Nicholas Powell). w/o costume	16.00
❑299, Apr 1988, TMc (a); 1: Venom (cameo). V: Chance I (Nicholas Powell)	9.00
❑300, May 1988, 25th anniversary; TMc (a); O: Venom. 1: Venom (Full). Last black costume for Spider-Man	35.00
❑301, Jun 1988, TMc (c); TMc (a)	6.00
❑302, Jul 1988, TMc (a)	4.00
❑303, Aug 1988, TMc (a); A: Silver Sable. A: Sandman	5.00
❑304, Sep 1988, TMc (a); V: The Fox	4.00
❑305, Sep 1988, TMc (a); V: The Prowler. V: The Fox	4.00
❑306, Oct 1988, TMc (a); V: Humbug	4.00
❑307, Oct 1988, TMc (c); TMc (a); O: Chameleon. V: Chameleon	4.00
❑308, Nov 1988, TMc (c); TMc (a); V: Taskmaster	5.00
❑309, Nov 1988, TMc (c); TMc (a)	4.00
❑310, Dec 1988, TMc (c); TMc (a); V: Killer Shrike	5.00
❑311, Jan 1989, TMc (c); TMc (a); V: Mysterio. Inferno	5.00
❑312, Feb 1989, TMc (c); TMc (a); V: Hobgoblin. V: Green Goblin. Inferno; Hobgoblin vs. Green Goblin II (Harry Osborn)	5.00
❑313, Mar 1989, TMc (c); TMc (a); V: Lizard. Inferno	5.00
❑314, Apr 1989, TMc (c); TMc (a)	4.00
❑315, May 1989, TMc (c); TMc (a); A: Venom. V: Venom	5.00
❑316, Jun 1989, TMc (c); TMc (a); A: Venom. V: Venom	5.00
❑317, Jul 1989, TMc (c); TMc (a); A: Venom. V: Venom	6.00
❑318, Aug 1989, TMc (c); TMc (a); A: Venom	6.00
❑319, Sep 1989, TMc (c); TMc (a)	5.00
❑320, Sep 1989, TMc (c); TMc (a); A: Silver Sable. V: Paladin	3.00
❑321, Oct 1989, TMc (c); TMc (a); A: Silver Sable	4.00
❑322, Oct 1989, TMc (c); TMc (a); A: Silver Sable. V: Ultimatum	5.00
❑323, Nov 1989, TMc (c); TMc (a); A: Silver Sable. V: Solo. V: Ultimatum	3.00
❑324, Nov 1989, TMc (c); TMc, EL (a); A: Sabretooth. V: Solo. V: Sabretooth	5.00
❑325, Nov 1989, TMc (c); TMc (a); A: Captain America. V: Red Skull	4.00
❑326, Dec 1989, V: Graviton. Acts of Vengeance	4.00
❑327, Dec 1989, EL (a); V: Magneto. cosmic Spider-Man; Acts of Vengeance	4.00
❑328, Jan 1990, TMc (a); Hulk; Acts of Vengeance; Last McFarlane Issue	5.00
❑329, Feb 1990, EL (a); V: Tri-Sentinel. Acts of Vengeance	4.00
❑330, Mar 1990, EL (a); A: Punisher. V: Punisher	3.00
❑331, Apr 1990, EL (a); A: Punisher. V: Punisher	3.00
❑332, May 1990, EL (a); A: Venom	3.00
❑333, Jun 1990, EL (c); EL (a); A: Venom. V: Venom	3.00
❑334, Jul 1990, EL (c); EL (a); V: Sinister Six (Doctor Octopus, Vulture, Electro, Sandman, Mysterio, Kraven the Hunter); Sinister Six; V: Sinister Six	2.50
❑335, Jul 1990, EL (c); EL (a); Sinister Six	2.50
❑336, Aug 1990, EL (c); EL (a); Sinister Six	2.50
❑337, Aug 1990, EL (c); EL (a); Sinister Six	2.50
❑338, Sep 1990, EL (c); EL (a); Sinister Six	2.50
❑339, Sep 1990, EL (a); Sinister Six	2.50
❑340, Oct 1990, EL (a)	2.50
❑341, Nov 1990, EL (a); V: Tarantula. Powerless; Spider-Man loses powers	2.50
❑342, Dec 1990, EL (a); V: Scorpion. Powerless	2.50
❑343, Jan 1991, EL (a); V: Scorpion. V: Tarantula. Spider-Man gets his powers back	2.50
❑344, Feb 1991, EL (a); 1: Cardiac. 1: Cletus Kassidy (later becomes Carnage)-cameo. V: Rhino	4.00
❑345, Mar 1991, EL (c); O: Cletus Kasady. A: Cletus Kassidy (later becomes Carnage)-full. V: Boomerang	3.00
❑346, Apr 1991, EL (a); A: Venom. V: Venom	3.00
❑347, May 1991, EL (a); A: Venom. V: Venom	3.00
❑348, Jun 1991, EL (a); A: Avengers	2.00
❑349, Jul 1991, EL (a)	2.00
❑350, Aug 1991, EL (c); EL (a); V: Doctor Doom; Giant-Size; Spider-Man vs. Doctor Doom	2.00
❑351, Sep 1991, A: Nova. V: Tri-Sentinel	2.00
❑352, Oct 1991, A: Nova. V: Tri-Sentinel	2.00
❑353, Nov 1991, AM (w); A: Punisher. A: Moon Knight	2.00
❑354, Nov 1991, AM (w); A: Punisher. A: Moon Knight	3.00
❑355, Dec 1991, AM (w); A: Punisher. A: Moon Knight	2.00
❑356, Dec 1991, AM (w); A: Punisher. A: Moon Knight	2.00
❑357, Jan 1992, AM (w); A: Punisher. A: Moon Knight	2.00
❑358, Jan 1992, AM (w); A: Punisher. A: Moon Knight. Gatefold cover	6.00
❑359, Feb 1992	2.00
❑360, Mar 1992, O: Cardiac. 1: Carnage (cameo)	3.00
❑361, Apr 1992, 1: Carnage (full appearance)	6.00
❑361/2nd, ca. 1992, silver cover	1.50
❑362, May 1992, A: Carnage. A: Venom	25.00
❑362/2nd, ca. 1992, 2nd printing	1.50
❑363, Jun 1992, A: Carnage. A: Venom	4.00
❑364, Jul 1992, V: Shocker. Peter Parker's parents (false parents) appear	3.00
❑365, Aug 1992, SL, PD (w); JR (a); 1: Spider-Man 2099. Hologram cover; Peter Parker meets his (false) parents; Gatefold poster with Venom and Carnage; Lizard back-up story	4.00
❑366, Sep 1992, A: Red Skull. V: Red Skull	2.00
❑367, Oct 1992	2.00
❑368, Nov 1992, V: Spider-Slayers	2.00
❑369, Nov 1992, V: Spider-Slayers	2.00
❑370, Dec 1992, V: Spider-Slayers	3.00
❑371, Dec 1992, A: Black Cat. V: Spider-Slayers	2.00
❑372, Jan 1993, V: Spider-Slayers	2.00
❑373, Jan 1993, V: Spider-Slayers	2.00
❑374, Feb 1993, V: Venom	3.00
❑375, Mar 1993, 30th anniversary special; A: Venom. Metallic ink cover; Sets stage for Venom #1	5.00
❑376, Apr 1993, O: Cardiac. V: Cardiac, Styx and Stone	4.00
❑377, May 1993, V: Cardiac	3.00
❑378, Jun 1993, A: Carnage. A: Venom	4.00
❑379, Jul 1993, A: Carnage. A: Venom	5.00
❑380, Aug 1993, A: Carnage. A: Venom. V: Carnage. V: Demogoblin	3.00
❑381, Sep 1993, A: Hulk. V: Hulk	4.00
❑382, Oct 1993, A: Hulk. V: Hulk	3.00
❑383, Nov 1993	3.00
❑384, Dec 1993	3.00
❑385, Jan 1994	3.00
❑386, Feb 1994, V: Vulture	3.00
❑387, Mar 1994, V: Vulture	3.00
❑388, Apr 1994, Double-size; D: Peter Parker's parents (false parents). V: Chameleon. V: Vulture	3.25
❑388/Variant, Apr 1994, Double-size; D: Peter Parker's parents (false parents). V: Vulture. foil cover	2.00
❑389, May 1994, V: Chameleon	3.00
❑390, Jun 1994	3.00
❑390/CS, Jun 1994, Print; Poster; Includes animation cel	3.00
❑391, Jul 1994, V: Shriek. Aunt May suffers stroke	3.00
❑392, Aug 1994, V: Carrion. V: Shriek	3.00
❑393, Sep 1994, V: Carrion. V: Shriek. Carrion	3.00
❑394, Oct 1994, O: Ben Reilly. A: Ben Reilly	3.00
❑394/Variant, Oct 1994, Giant-size; O: Ben Reilly. A: Ben Reilly. enhanced cover	3.50
❑395, Nov 1994, V: Puma. continues in Spectacular Spider-Man #218	3.00
❑396, Dec 1994, A: Daredevil. V: Owl. V: Vulture. continues in Spectacular Spider-Man #219	3.00

Other grades: Multiply price above by 5/6 for VF/NM • 2/3 for VERY FINE • 1/3 for FINE • 1/5 for VERY GOOD • 1/8 for GOOD

Alf

Alien Life Form from NBC cracks comics jokes

©Marvel

Alias (Marvel)

Bendis takes on ex-Avenger private eye

©Marvel

Alien Legion (Vol. 1)

Interplanetary police force from Epic

©Marvel

Alien Nation

Adapts movie that spawned at TV series

©DC

Alien Nation: The Lost Episode

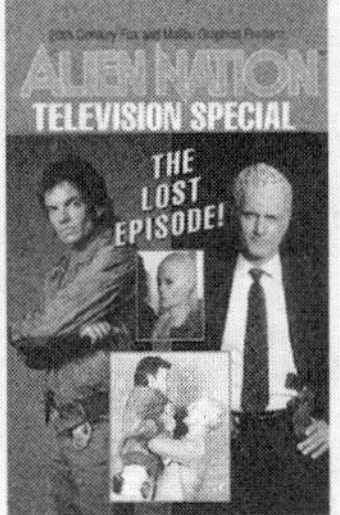

Wraps up TV series after abrupt cancellation

©Malibu

	N-MINT
❑397, Jan 1995, Double-size; V: Lizard. V: Doctor Octopus. flip book with illustrated story from The Ultimate Spider-Man back-up; continues in Spectacular Spider-Man #220	3.00
❑398, Feb 1995, V: Doctor Octopus. continues in Spectacular Spider-Man #221	3.00
❑399, Mar 1995, A: Scarlet Spider. A: Jackal. V: Jackal. continues in Spider-Man #56	3.00
❑400, Apr 1995, SL (w); JR2 (a); D: Aunt May (fake death)	5.00
❑400/Gray, Apr 1995, white cover edition (no ads, back-up story); SL (w); JR2 (a); D: Aunt May (fake death). gray embossed cover	30.00
❑400/White, Apr 1995, SL (w); JR2 (a); D: Aunt May (fake death). Limited edition cover; 10,000 copies	30.00
❑401, May 1995, V: Kaine	1.50
❑402, Jun 1995, V: Traveller	1.50
❑403, Jul 1995, A: Carnage	1.50
❑404, Aug 1995	1.50
❑405, Sep 1995	1.50
❑406, Oct 1995, 1: Doctor Octopus II. OverPower cards inserted; (continues in Amazing Scarlet Spider)	1.50
❑407, Jan 1996, A: Silver Sable. A: Human Torch. A: Sandman	1.50
❑408, Feb 1996, V: Mysterio	1.50
❑409, Mar 1996, V: Rhino	1.50
❑410, Apr 1996, V: Cell 12	1.50
❑411, May 1996	1.50
❑412, Jun 1996	1.50
❑413, Jul 1996	1.50
❑414, Aug 1996, A: Delilah	1.50
❑415, Sep 1996, V: Sentinel. "Onslaught: Impact 2"	1.50
❑416, Oct 1996, post-Onslaught memories	1.50
❑417, Nov 1996	1.50
❑418, Dec 1996, birth of Peter and Mary Jane's baby; Return of Norman Osborn (face shown)	2.00
❑419, Jan 1997, V: Black Tarantula	1.50
❑420, Feb 1997, A: X-Man. D: El Uno	1.50
❑421, Mar 1997, 1&O: The Dragonfly	2.00
❑422, Apr 1997, O: Electro	2.00
❑423, May 1997, V: Electro	2.00
❑424, Jun 1997, A: Elektra. V: Elektra	2.00
❑425, Aug 1997	2.00
❑426, Sep 1997, gatefold summary	2.00
❑427, Oct 1997, gatefold summary; JR2 (a); return of Doctor Octopus	2.00
❑428, Nov 1997, gatefold summary; V: Doctor Octopus	2.00
❑429, Dec 1997, gatefold summary; V: Absorbing Man	2.00
❑430, Jan 1998, gatefold summary; A: Silver Surfer. V: Carnage	2.00
❑431, Feb 1998, gatefold summary; A: Silver Surfer. V: Carnage	2.00
❑432, Mar 1998, gatefold summary	2.00
❑432/Variant, Mar 1998; Variant "Wanted Dead or Alive" cover	5.00
❑433, Apr 1998, gatefold summary; Identity Crisis, Prelude	2.00
❑434, May 1998, gatefold summary; Identity Crisis; 2nd cover as The Amazing Ricochet #1; Outer cover is Amazing Spider-Man	2.00

	N-MINT
❑435, Jun 1998, gatefold summary; A: Ricochet. Identity Crisis	2.00
❑436, Jul 1998, gatefold summary	2.00
❑437, Aug 1998, gatefold summary; A: Synch	2.00
❑438, Sep 1998, gatefold summary; A: Daredevil	2.00
❑439, Sep 1998, gatefold summary; A: Zack and Lana	2.00
❑440, Oct 1998, gatefold summary; V: Molten Man; Continued in Peter Parker: Spider-Man #96; Gatefold summary	2.00
❑441, Nov 1998, gatefold summary; A: Molten Man. D: Madame Web; Final Issue	2.00
❑500, Dec 2003, JR2, JR (a); numbering reverts to original series, adding in issues from Vol. 2	5.00
❑501, Jan 2004, (c); JR2 (a)	4.00
❑502, Feb 2004, JR2 (a)	2.99
❑503, Mar 2004, JR2 (c); JR2 (a)	2.25
❑504, Apr 2004, JR2 (c); JR2 (a)	2.25
❑505, May 2004, JR2 (c); JR2 (a)	2.25
❑506, Jun 2004, JR2 (c); JR2 (a)	2.25
❑507, Jul 2004, JR2, (c); JR2 (a)	2.25
❑508, Jul 2004	2.25
❑509, Aug 2004	2.25
❑509/DirCut, Aug 2004, Director's Cut	7.00
❑510, Sep 2004	4.00
❑511, Oct 2004	3.00
❑512, Nov 2004	5.00
❑513, Dec 2004	3.00
❑514, Jan 2005	2.25
❑515, Feb 2005	2.25
❑516, Mar 2005	2.25
❑517, Apr 2005	2.25
❑518, May 2005	2.25
❑519, Jun 2005	2.25
❑520, Jul 2005	2.25
❑521, Aug 2005; Price increase	2.50
❑522, Sep 2005	2.50
❑523, Oct 2005	2.50
❑524, Nov 2005; Nick Fury's Howling Commandos preview	2.50
❑525, Dec 2005; Has 2005 Statement, filed 8/26/05 [earlier than allowed]; avg print run 150833; avg sales 102,377; avg subs 10,187; avg total paid 112,564 [statement had a one-copy math error]; samples 3,028; max existent 115,592; 23% of run returned	2.50
❑526, Jan 2006	2.50
❑527, Feb 2006	2.50
❑528, Mar 2006	2.50
❑529, May 2006, Cover by Bryan Hitch	20.00
❑529/2nd, May 2006	6.00
❑529/3rd, May 2006	5.00
❑530, Jun 2006, The Road to Civil War	8.00
❑531, Jul 2006, The Road to Civil War	6.00
❑532, Aug 2006, Civil War tie-in	6.00
❑533, Sep 2006, Civil War	4.00
❑534, Oct 2006, V: Captain America; Civil War Tie-In	4.00
❑535, Dec 2006, Civil War Tie-In	4.00
❑536, Jan 2007; Civil War	4.00
❑537, Feb 2007, Civil War tie-in	3.00
❑538, Mar 2007; Civil War Tie-in	6.00
❑539, Apr 2007	10.00

	N-MINT
❑540, May 2007; Back in Black	5.00
❑541, Jun 2007; V: Kingpin	5.00
❑542, Jul 2007	2.99
❑543, Aug 2007; Back in Black	2.99
❑544, Sep 2007; Joe Quesada cover; V: Iron Man; Continued in Friendly Neighborhood Spider-Man #24	2.99
❑545, Dec 2007; Reprints portions of Amazing Spider-Man Ann #21	3.99
❑546, Jan 2008; Cover by Steven McNiven; Brand New Day; Start of 3 issue releases a month	6.00
❑547, Mar 2008; Brand New Day	2.99
❑548, Mar 2008; Brand New Day	2.99
❑549, Mar 2008; Brand New Day	2.99
❑550, Mar 2008; 1: Menace; Brand New Day	2.99
❑551, Mar 2008; Brand New Day	2.99
❑552, May 2008; Brand New Day	2.99
❑553 2008	2.99
❑554 2008	2.99
❑555 2008	2.99
❑556 2008	2.99
❑557 2008	2.99
❑558 2008	2.99
❑559 2008	2.99
❑560 2008	2.99
❑561	2.99
❑562	2.99
❑563	2.99
❑564	2.99
❑565	2.99
❑566	2.99
❑567	2.99
❑568	2.99
❑569	2.99
❑570	2.99
❑571	2.99
❑572	2.99
❑573	2.99
❑574	2.99
❑575	2.99
❑576	2.99
❑577	2.99
❑578	2.99
❑579	2.99
❑580	2.99
❑581	2.99
❑582	2.99
❑583	15.00
❑583/Obama	30.00
❑583/2nd	8.00
❑583/3rd	6.00
❑583/4th	4.00
❑583/5th	4.00
❑583/6th	4.00
❑584	2.99
❑585	2.99
❑586	2.99
❑587	2.99
❑588	2.99
❑589	2.99
❑590	2.99
❑591	2.99
❑Aim Giveaway 1, ca. 1980; Giveaway from Aim Toothpaste; A: Doctor Octopus. Spider-Man vs. Doctor Octopus	4.00

Other grades: Multiply price above by 5/6 for VF/NM • 2/3 for VERY FINE • 1/3 for FINE • 1/5 for VERY GOOD • 1/8 for GOOD

N-MINT N-MINT N-MINT

❑Aim Giveaway 2; Aim toothpaste giveaway A: Green Goblin 2.00
❑Ann 1, ca. 1964; SD (c); SL (w); SD (a); 1: Sinister Six (Doctor Octopus, Vulture, Electro, Sandman, Mysterio, Kraven the Hunter). V: Sinister Six; 72 pages; Cover reads "King-Size Special" 700.00
❑Ann 2, ca. 1965; Cover reads "King-Size Special"; SD (c); SD, SL (w); SD (a); 1: Xandu. A: Doctor Strange; reprints Amazing Spider-Man #1, 2, and 5, plus a new story 550.00
❑Ann 3, Nov 1966; Cover reads "King-Size Special"; JR (c); SL (w); SD, DH, JR (a); A: Daredevil. A: Avengers. V: Hulk; New story; reprints Amazing Spider-Man #11 and 12 .... 140.00
❑Ann 4, Nov 1967; Cover reads "King-Size Special"; SL (w); A: Torch. V: Mysterio. V: Wizard 90.00
❑Ann 5, Nov 1968; Cover reads "King-Size Special"; JR (c); JR, SL (w); 1: Peter Parker's parents. A: Red Skull; fate of Peter Parker's parents revealed 75.00
❑Ann 5/2nd, ca. 1994; Cover reads "King-Size Special"; JR (c); JR, SL (w); JR (a); 1: Peter Parker's parents. A: Red Skull 2.50
❑Ann 6, Nov 1969; Cover reads "King-Size Special"; JR (c); SD, SL (w); SD, JK (a); reprints stories from Amazing Spider-Man #8, Ann #1 and Fantastic Four Ann #1 .... 35.00
❑Ann 7, Dec 1970; Cover reads "King-Size Special"; JR (c); SD, SL (w); SD, JR (a); reprints stories from Amazing Spider-Man #1, 2, and 38 .... 35.00
❑Ann 8, Dec 1971; Cover reads "King-Size Special"; JR (c); SL (w); JR (a); A: Giant Man; reprints stories from Amazing Spider-Man #46 and 50 and Tales to Astonish #57 .... 22.00
❑Ann 9, ca. 1973, reprints Spectacular Spider-Man (magazine) #2; JR, JM (c); JR, SL (w); JR, JM (a); A: Hobgoblin; reprinted with changes from Spectacular Spider-Man #2 .... 22.00
❑Ann 10, Sep 1976, GK, JR (c); GK (a); O: Human Fly. 1: Human Fly 8.00
❑Ann 11, Sep 1977, GK, JSt (c); AM, JR2, GK, DP, JM (a) 8.00
❑Ann 12, Aug 1978, JBy (c); GK, JR (w); JBy, GK, JR (a); Reprints Hulk story from Amazing Spider-Man #119-120 . 8.00
❑Ann 13, Nov 1979; KP, BMc (c); JBy, KP, TD, JM (a); V: Doctor Octopus 7.00
❑Ann 14, Dec 1980; FM, TP (a); A: Doctor Strange. V: Doctor Doom; V: Dormammu 6.00
❑Ann 15, ca. 1981 FM, KJ (c); KP, FM, KJ (a); A: Punisher 7.00
❑Ann 16, ca. 1982; JR2 (c); JR2 (a); 1&O: Captain Marvel II (Monica Rambeau); (1982; 1.00)- 5.00
❑Ann 17, ca. 1983; KJ (c); JM (a) 4.00
❑Ann 18, ca. 1984; BG (c); SL (w); BL, BG (a); Wedding of J. Jonah Jameson 4.00
❑Ann 19, ca. 1985 .... 4.00
❑Ann 20, ca. 1986; D: Blizzard 4.00
❑Ann 21, ca. 1987; newsstand edition; Wedding of Peter Parker and Mary Jane Watson 4.00
❑Ann 21/Direc, ca. 1987; Direct Market edition; Wedding of Peter Parker and Mary Jane Watson 5.00
❑Ann 22, ca. 1988; SD (w); SD (a); O: High Evolutionary. 1: Speedball. A: Daredevil 5.00
❑Ann 23, ca. 1989; JBy (c); FH, RL (a); O: Spider-Man. Atlantis Attacks 3.00
❑Ann 24, ca. 1990; GK (c); SD, GK, MZ (a); A: Ant-Man. Solo story; Sandman story; Ant-Man story 3.00
❑Ann 25, ca. 1991; EL (c); SD, SB (a); O: Spider-Man. Vibranium Vendetta; 1st solo Venom story 3.00
❑Ann 26, ca. 1992; 1: Dreadnought 2000; ca. 1998 .... 4.00
❑Ann 27, ca. 1993; 1: Annex. trading card 3.00
❑Ann 28, ca. 1994; Carnage 3.00
❑Ann 1996, ca. 1996; 2 flashback stories; 64 pages; ca. 1995 .... 4.00
❑Ann 1997, ca. 1997; V: Sundown. wraparound cover 3.00
❑Ashcan 1, b&w; ashcan edition; O: Spider-Man 0.75

Amazing Spider-Man (Vol. 2)
Marvel

❑1/Sunburst, Jan 1999; JR2 (c); JBy (a); sunburst variant cover 18.00
❑2 (443), Feb 1999; gatefold summary; JBy (c); JBy (a); V: Shadrac. new Spider-Man's identity revealed; Skeleton grabbing Spider-Man on cover 2.50
❑2/Kubert, Feb 1999; gatefold summary; JBy (a); V: Shadrac. new Spider-Man's identity revealed 2.50
❑3 (444), Mar 1999; JBy (a); O: Shadrac 2.00
❑4 (445), Apr 1999; JBy (a); A: Fantastic Four. V: Trapster. V: Sandman 2.00
❑5 (446), May 1999 A: new Spider-Woman 2.00
❑6 (447), Jun 1999; V: Spider-Woman .. 2.00
❑7 (448), Jul 1999; Flash Thompson's fantasy 2.00
❑8 (449), Aug 1999; V: Mysterio 2.00
❑9 (450), Sep 1999 A: Doctor Octopus.. 2.00
❑10 (451), Oct 1999; A: Doctor Octopus. V: Captain Power 2.00
❑11 (452), Nov 1999; V: Blob 2.00
❑12 (453), Dec 1999; Giant-size 3.00
❑13 (454), Jan 2000 .... 2.00
❑14 (455), Feb 2000 JBy (c); JBy (w); JBy, DGr (a) 2.00
❑15 (456), Mar 2000 JBy (c); JBy (w); JBy (a) 2.00
❑16 (457), Apr 2000 .... 2.00
❑17 (458), May 2000 .... 2.00
❑18 (459), Jun 2000 .... 2.50
❑19 (460), Jul 2000 EL (a); A: Venom ... 2.50
❑20 (461), Aug 2000; EL (c); SL (w); SD, KP, JR, JM, EL (a); reprints Amazing Spider-Man (Vol. 1) #25, 58, and 192 4.50
❑21 (462), Sep 2000; EL (c); EL (a); V: Spider-Slayers 2.25
❑22 (463), Oct 2000 .... 2.25
❑23 (464), Nov 2000 JR2 (a) 2.25
❑24 (465), Dec 2000; JR2 (a); Maximum Security 2.25
❑25 (466), Jan 2001; regular wraparound cover 3.00
❑25/Speckle, Jan 2001; Speckle foil cover 4.00
❑26 (467), Feb 2001 .... 2.25
❑27 (468), Mar 2001 JR2 (a); A: Mr. Q. A: Mr. P 2.25
❑28 (469), Apr 2001 JR2 (c) 2.25
❑29 (470), May 2001; Return of Mary Jane 2.25
❑30 (471), Jun 2001 .... 5.00
❑31 (472), Jul 2001; Peter Parker becomes high school teacher 3.00
❑32 (473), Aug 2001 .... 4.00
❑33 (474), Sep 2001 .... 4.00
❑34 (475), Oct 2001 .... 5.00
❑35 (476), Nov 2001; JR2 (a); Aunt May learns Peter is Spider-Man 4.00
❑36 (477), Dec 2001; JR2 (a); World Trade Center tribute issue 9.00
❑37 (478), Jan 2002 JR2 (a) 2.50
❑38 (479), Feb 2002 JR2 (a) 2.50
❑39 (480), ca. 2002 JR2 (a) 2.50
❑40 (481), Jun 2002 JR2 (a) 2.25
❑41 (482), Jul 2002 JR2 (a) 4.00
❑42 (483), Aug 2002; JR2 (a) 3.00
❑43 (484), Sep 2002 JR2 (a) 3.00
❑44 (485), Oct 2002; JR2 (a); V: Dr. Octopus 2.25
❑45 (486), Nov 2002; JR2 (a); V: Dr. Octopus 2.25
❑46 (487), Dec 2002; JR2 (a) 2.25
❑47 (488), Jan 2003 JR2 (a) 2.25
❑48 (489), Feb 2003 JR2 (a) 2.25
❑49 (490), Mar 2003 JR2 (c); JR2 (a) ... 2.25
❑50 (491), Apr 2003 JR2 (a) 6.00
❑51 (492), May 2003 JR2 (a) 2.25
❑52 (493), Jun 2003 JR2 (c); JR2 (a).... 2.25
❑53 (494), Jul 2003; JR2 (c); JR2 (a); wraparound cover 2.25
❑54 (495), Aug 2003, JR2 (a) 2.49
❑55 (496), Sep 2003, JR2 (a) 2.49
❑56 (497), Oct 2003, JR2 (a) 2.00
❑57 (498), Oct 2003, (c); JR2 (a); V: Dormammu 2.99
❑58 (499), Nov 2003, (c); JR2 (a); numbering restarts at 500 under Vol. 1 2.99
❑Ann 1999, Jun 1999; V: Trapster. V: Wizard. 1999 Ann 3.50
❑Ann 2000, ca. 2000 .... 3.50
❑Ann 2001, ca. 2001; Cover B 2.99

Amazing Spider-Man 30th Anniversary Poster Magazine
Marvel

❑1; NN 3.95

Amazing Spider-Man Giveaways
Marvel

❑1; (two different, both #1) 4.00
❑2; Managing Materials 4.00
❑3, Feb 1977; Planned Parenthood giveaway; miniature;... vs. The Prodigy! 4.00
❑4, ca. 1979; No issue number; All Detergent giveaway 6.00
❑5, child abuse;with New Mutants 4.00

Amazing Spider-Man (Public Service Series)
Marvel

❑1, ca. 1990; TMc (c); TMc (a); Skating on Thin Ice! 2.50
❑1/2nd, Feb 1993; US Edition; TMc (c); TMc (a); Skating on Thin Ice 2.00
❑2, ca. 1993; TMc (a); Double Trouble! . 2.50
❑2/2nd, Feb 1993; US Edition; TMc (a); Double Trouble 2.00
❑3, ca. 1991; TMc (a); Hit and Run! 2.50
❑3/2nd, Feb 1993; US Edition; TMc (a); A: Ghost Rider. Hit and Run 2.00
❑4, ca. 1992; TMc (a); 1: Turbine. Chaos in Calgary 2.50
❑4/2nd, Feb 1993; US Edition; Chaos in Calgary 2.00

Amazing Spider-Man: Soul of the Hunter
Marvel

❑1, Aug 1992; NN 5.95

Amazing Spider-Man Super Special
Marvel

❑1, ca. 1995; Flip-book; two of the stories continue in Spider-Man Super Special #1;Amazing Scarlet Spider on other side 4.00

Amazing Strip
Antarctic

❑1, Feb 1994; Adult 2.95
❑2, Apr 1994; Indicia says April, cover says March 2.95
❑3, Apr 1994; Adult 2.95
❑4, May 1994; Adult 2.95
❑5, Jun 1994; Adult 2.95
❑6, Jul 1994; Adult 2.95
❑7, Aug 1994; Adult 2.95
❑8, Sep 1994; Adult 2.95
❑9, Nov 1994; Adult 2.95
❑10, Dec 1994; #10 on cover, #4 in indicia (cover correct) 2.95

Amazing Wahzoo
Solson

❑1 1986; 1&O: Amazing Wahzoo; 1: Howard Wasnuski 1.75

Amazing World of Superman
DC

❑1 1973 .... 4.00

Amazing X-Men
Marvel

❑1, Mar 1995; Age of Apocalypse 2.00
❑2, Apr 1995; Cover by Andy Kubert 2.00
❑3, May 1995 .... 2.00
❑4, Jun 1995 .... 2.00

Amazon
DC / Amalgam

❑1, Apr 1996, O: Wonder Woman (Amalgam) 1.95

Amazon Attack 3-D
3-D Zone

❑1, ca. 1990, b&w; NN, glasses included 3.95

Amazons
Fantagraphics

❑1, b&w; ca. 1991 .... 2.95

Amazon Tales
Fantaco

❑1 .... 2.95
❑2 .... 2.95
❑3 .... 2.95

Amazon
Comico

❑1, Mar 1989 .... 1.95
❑2, Apr 1989 .... 1.95
❑3, May 1989 .... 1.95

Amazon Warriors
AC

❑1 1989; b&w Reprint 2.50

Other grades: Multiply price above by 5/6 for VF/NM • 2/3 for VERY FINE • 1/3 for FINE • 1/5 for VERY GOOD • 1/8 for GOOD

Aliens

First issue reprinted back-up story from Magnus

©Gold Key

Aliens (Vol. 1)

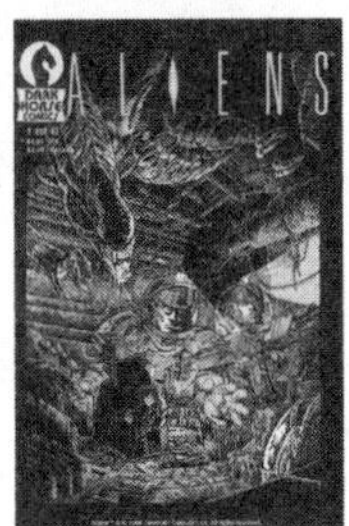

Dark Horse begins its SF adaptation mastery

©Dark Horse

Aliens vs. Predator

Movies spawned comic, which spawned movie

©Dark Horse

Alley Cat

Image gives a Playboy model a comic book

©Image

All-New Atom

Ray Palmer successor not as successful

©DC

N-MINT

Amazon Woman
Fantaco

❑1, ca. 1994 .... 2.95
❑2, ca. 1994 .... 2.95

Amazon Woman
Fantaco

❑1, ca. 1994 .... 2.95
❑2, ca. 1994 .... 2.95
❑3, ca. 1994 .... 2.95
❑4, ca. 1994 .... 2.95

Amber: Nine Princes in Amber (Roger Zelazny's...)
DC

❑1, ca. 1996, prestige format; adapts Zelazny story 6.95
❑2, ca. 1996, prestige format; adapts Zelazny story 6.95
❑3, ca. 1996, prestige format; adapts Zelazny story 6.95

Amber: The Guns of Avalon (Roger Zelazny's...)
DC

❑1, ca. 1996; prestige format; Adaptation of Roger Zelazny novel 6.95
❑2, ca. 1996; prestige format; Adaptation of Roger Zelazny novel 6.95
❑3, ca. 1996; prestige format; Adaptation of Roger Zelazny novel 6.95

Ambush Bug
DC

❑1, Jun 1985 KG (c); KG (w); KG (a) 1.00
❑2, Jul 1985; KG (c); KG (w); KG (a); V: Quantis 1.00
❑3, Aug 1985 KG (c); KG (w); FH, KG (a) 1.00
❑4, Sep 1985; KG (c); KG (w); KG (a); V: Argh Yle 1.00

Ambush Bug Nothing Special
DC

❑1, Sep 1992 .... 2.50

Ambush Bug Stocking Stuffer
DC

❑1, Mar 1986 .... 1.25

Amelia Rules
Renaissance

❑1, ca. 2001 .... 2.95
❑2, ca. 2001 .... 2.95
❑3, ca. 2001 .... 2.95
❑4, ca. 2001 .... 2.95
❑5, ca. 2002 .... 2.95
❑6, ca. 2002 .... 2.95
❑7, ca. 2002 .... 2.95
❑8, ca. 2002 .... 2.95
❑9, ca. 2003 .... 2.95
❑10, ca. 2003 .... 2.95

America's Greatest Comics (AC)
AC

❑1 .... 6.95
❑2 .... 6.95
❑3 .... 6.95
❑4 .... 6.95
❑5 .... 6.95
❑6 .... 6.95
❑7 .... 6.95
❑8 .... 6.95
❑9 .... 6.95
❑10 .... 6.95
❑11, ca. 2005 .... 6.95
❑12, ca. 2005 .... 6.95
❑13, ca. 2005 .... 6.95

American
Dark Horse

❑1, Aug 1987, b&w; 1: The American (modern); 1: The American 1.50
❑2, Oct 1987 .... 1.75
❑3, Dec 1987 .... 1.75
❑4, Apr 1988 .... 1.75
❑5, Jul 1988 .... 1.75
❑6, Sep 1988 .... 1.75
❑7, Oct 1988 .... 1.75
❑8, Feb 1989 .... 1.75
❑Special 1, b&w; Special edition; ca. 1990 2.25

American Book
Dark Horse

❑1, Oct 1988, b&w; O: American 5.95

American Century
DC / Vertigo

❑1, May 2001 .... 2.50
❑2, Jun 2001 .... 2.50
❑3, Jul 2001 .... 2.50
❑4, Aug 2001 .... 2.50
❑5, Aug 2001 .... 2.50
❑6, Sep 2001 .... 2.50
❑7, Oct 2001 .... 2.50
❑8, Nov 2001 .... 2.50
❑9, Dec 2001 .... 2.50
❑10, Jan 2002 .... 2.50
❑11, Feb 2002 .... 2.50
❑12, Mar 2002 .... 2.50
❑13, Apr 2002 .... 2.50
❑14, May 2002 .... 2.50
❑15, Jun 2002 .... 2.50
❑16, Aug 2002 .... 2.50
❑17, Sep 2002 .... 2.50
❑18, Oct 2002 .... 2.75
❑19, Nov 2002 .... 2.75
❑20, Jan 2003 .... 2.75
❑21, Feb 2003 .... 2.75
❑22, Mar 2003 .... 2.75
❑23, Jun 2003; Jun in indicia, Apr on cover 2.75
❑24, Jul 2003 .... 2.75
❑25, Aug 2003 .... 2.75
❑26, Sep 2003 .... 2.75
❑27, Oct 2003 .... 2.75

American Flagg
First

❑1, Oct 1983; HC (w); HC (a); 1: Reuben Flagg 2.50
❑2, Nov 1983 HC (c); HC (w); HC (a) 2.00
❑3, Dec 1983 HC (c); HC (w); HC (a) 2.00
❑4, Jan 1984 HC (w); HC (a) 2.00
❑5, Feb 1984 HC (c); HC (w); HC (a) 2.00
❑6, Mar 1984 HC (w); HC (a) 1.50
❑7, Apr 1984 HC (c); HC (w); HC (a) 1.50
❑8, May 1984 HC (c); HC (w); HC (a) 1.50
❑9, Jun 1984 HC (w); HC (a) 1.50
❑10, Jul 1984 HC (w); HC (a) 1.50
❑11, Aug 1984 HC (w); HC (a) 1.50
❑12, Sep 1984 HC (w); HC (a) 1.50
❑13, Oct 1984 HC (c); HC (w); HC (a) 1.50
❑14, Nov 1984 HC (c); HC (w); PB (a) 1.25
❑15, Dec 1984 HC (c); HC (w); HC (a) 1.25
❑16, Jan 1985 HC (c); HC (w); HC (a) 1.25
❑17, Feb 1985 HC (c); HC (w); HC (a) 1.25
❑18, Mar 1985 HC (c); HC (w); HC (a) 1.25
❑19, Apr 1985 HC (c); HC (w); HC (a) 1.25
❑20, May 1985 HC (c); HC (w); HC (a) 1.25
❑21, Jun 1985 HC (c); HC, AMo (w); HC (a) 1.25
❑22, Jul 1985; HC (c); HC, AMo (w); HC (a); Luther Ironheart backup story 1.25
❑23, Aug 1985; HC (c); HC, AMo (w); HC (a); Raul backup story 1.25
❑24, Sep 1985; HC (c); HC, AMo (w); HC (a); Folquet backup story 1.25
❑25, Oct 1985 HC (c); HC, AMo (w); HC (a) 1.25
❑26, Nov 1985 HC (c); AMo (w); HC (a) 1.25
❑27, Dec 1985 HC (c); AMo (w); HC (a) 1.25
❑28, Apr 1986 HC (c); HC (w); HC, JSa (a) 1.25
❑29, May 1986 HC (c); HC (w); HC, JSa (a) 1.25
❑30, Jun 1986 HC (w); HC, JSa (a) 1.25
❑31, Jul 1986; HC (w); HC (a); O: Bob Violence 1.25
❑32, Aug 1986 HC (w); HC (a) 1.25
❑33, Sep 1986 .... 1.25
❑34, Nov 1986 .... 1.25
❑35, Dec 1986 .... 1.25
❑36, Jan 1987 .... 1.25
❑37, Feb 1987 .... 1.25
❑38, Mar 1987 HC (c); HC (a) 1.25
❑39, Apr 1987 HC (a) 1.25
❑40, May 1987 HC (a) 1.25
❑41, Jun 1987 HC (c); HC (a) 1.25
❑42, Jul 1987 HC (c); HC (a) 1.25
❑43, Aug 1987 HC (c); HC (a) 1.25
❑44, Sep 1987 HC (c); HC (a) 1.25
❑45, Oct 1987 .... 1.25
❑46, Nov 1987; HC (c); HC (w); PS, HC (a); apology 1.75
❑47, Dec 1987 HC (c); HC (w); PS, HC (a) 1.75
❑48, Jan 1988 HC (c); HC (w); PS, HC (a) 1.75
❑49, Feb 1988 HC (c); HC (w); HC (a) 1.75
❑50, Mar 1988 HC (c); HC (w); HC (a) 1.75
❑Special 1, Nov 1986; HC (c); HC (w); HC (a); Special #1 .... 1.75

American Flagg (Howard Chaykin's...)
First

❑1, May 1988 .... 2.00
❑2, Jun 1988 .... 1.75
❑3, Jul 1988 .... 1.75
❑4, Aug 1988 .... 1.75
❑5, Sep 1988 .... 1.75
❑6, Oct 1988 .... 1.95
❑7, Nov 1988 .... 1.95
❑8, Dec 1988 .... 1.95
❑9, Jan 1989 .... 1.95
❑10, Feb 1989 .... 1.95
❑11, Mar 1989 .... 1.95
❑12, Apr 1989 .... 1.95

American Flyer
Last Gasp

❑1, Adult 4.00
❑2, Adult 4.00

American Freak: A Tale of the Un-Men
DC / Vertigo

❑1, Feb 1994 .... 2.00

Other grades: Multiply price above by 5/6 for VF/NM • 2/3 for VERY FINE • 1/3 for FINE • 1/5 for VERY GOOD • 1/8 for GOOD

❑2, Mar 1994 ... 2.00
❑3, Apr 1994 ... 2.00
❑4, May 1994 ... 2.00
❑5, Jun 1994 ... 2.00

American Heroes
Personality

❑1, b&w; ca. 1992 ... 2.95

American: Lost in America
Dark Horse

❑1, Jul 1992 ... 2.50
❑2, Aug 1992 ... 2.50
❑3, Sep 1992 ... 2.50
❑4, Oct 1992 ... 2.50

American Primitive
3-D Zone

❑1, b&w; not 3-D ... 2.50

American Splendor
Pekar

❑1, May 1976; 52 pages; Nudity; Color cover, b&w interiors ... 65.00
❑2, May 1977 ... 30.00
❑3, May 1978 ... 20.00
❑4, Oct 1979 ... 20.00
❑5, ca. 1980 ... 20.00
❑6, ca. 1981 ... 15.00
❑7, ca. 1982 ... 15.00
❑8, ca. 1983 ... 15.00
❑9, ca. 1984; VM (a) ... 15.00
❑10, ca. 1985 VM (a) ... 15.00
❑11, ca. 1986 VM (a) ... 10.00
❑12, ca. 1987; VM (c); VM (a); David Letterman cover/appearance ... 10.00
❑13, ca. 1988 VM (a) ... 10.00
❑14, ca. 1989; David Letterman exploitation issue ... 18.00
❑15, ca. 1990 AMo (a) ... 8.00
❑16, ca. 1991 ... 3.95
❑17, ca. 1993; Published by Dark Horse Comics ... 8.00

American Splendor
DC / Vertigo

❑1, Nov 2006 ... 2.99
❑2, Dec 2006 ... 2.99
❑3, Jan 2007 ... 2.99
❑4, Feb 2007 ... 2.99

American Splendor: Bedtime Stories
Dark Horse

❑1, Jun 2000 ... 3.95

American Splendor: Comic-Con Comics
Dark Horse

❑1, Aug 1996, b&w; NN; B&w anthology 2.95

American Splendor: Music Comics
Dark Horse

❑1, Nov 1997, b&w; collects Pekar's stories about music ... 2.95

American Splendor: Odds & Ends
Dark Horse

❑1, Dec 1997, b&w; collects short pieces 2.95

American Splendor: On the Job
Dark Horse

❑1, May 1997, b&w; NN; One-shot ... 2.95

American Splendor: Portrait of the Author in his Declining Years
Dark Horse

❑1, Apr 2001 ... 3.99

American Splendor: Terminal
Dark Horse

❑1, Sep 1999 ... 2.95

American Splendor: Transatlantic Comics
Dark Horse

❑1, Jul 1998; NN ... 2.95

American Splendor: Unsung Hero
Dark Horse

❑1, Aug 2002; Biography of Robert McNeill 3.99
❑2, Sep 2002; Biography of Robert McNeill 3.99
❑3, Oct 2002; Biography of Robert McNeill 3.99

American Splendor: Windfall
Dark Horse

❑1, Sep 1995, b&w ... 3.95
❑2, Oct 1995, b&w ... 3.95

American Splendor Special: A Step Out of the Nest
Dark Horse

❑1, Aug 1994, b&w ... 2.95

American Tail, An: Fievel Goes West
Marvel

❑1, Jan 1992; Movie adaptation ... 1.25
❑2, Jan 1992; Movie adaptation ... 1.25
❑3, Feb 1992; Movie adaptation ... 1.25

American Virgin
DC / Vertigo

❑1, May 2006 ... 2.99
❑2, Jun 2006 ... 2.99
❑3, Jul 2006 ... 2.99
❑4, Aug 2006 ... 2.99
❑5, Sep 2006 ... 2.99
❑6, Nov 2006, Bondage cover ... 2.99
❑7, Dec 2006 ... 2.99
❑8, Jan 2007 ... 2.99
❑9, Feb 2007 ... 2.99
❑10, Mar 2007 ... 2.99

American Way
DC / Vertigo

❑1, May 2006 ... 2.99
❑2, Jun 2006 ... 2.99
❑3, Jul 2006 ... 2.99
❑4, Aug 2006 ... 2.99
❑5, Sep 2006 ... 2.99
❑6, Oct 2006 ... 2.99
❑7, Nov 2006 ... 2.99
❑8, Dec 2006 ... 2.99

American Woman
Antarctic

❑1, Jun 1998; 1: American Woman ... 2.95
❑2, Oct 1998 ... 2.95

America's Best Comics
America's Best

❑Special 1, Feb 2001; 64 Page Giant ... 6.95

America's Best Comics Preview
America's Best

❑1, Feb 1999, AMo (w); KN (a); Included in Wizard #91 ... 1.50

America's Best Comics Sketchbook
DC / America's Best Comics

❑1 ... 5.95

America's Best Comics TPB
DC

❑1, ca. 2003 ... 17.95

America's Best TV Comics
ABC TV

❑1, ca. 1967; Giant-size; JK (c); SL (w); JK, JR (a); promotional comic published by Marvel for ABC to promote Saturday morning cartoons . 95.00

America vs. the Justice Society
DC

❑1, Jan 1985; Giant-size; O: Justice Society of America; Back cover reprints cover of All-Star Comics #4 ... 1.50
❑2, Feb 1985; O: All-Star Squadron; Back cover reprints cover of All-Star Comics #3 ... 1.00
❑3, Mar 1985; Wizard ... 1.00
❑4, Apr 1985; multiverse (Flash of Two Worlds) ... 1.00

Americomics
AC

❑1, Apr 1983; 1: the Shade (Americomics); O: the Shade (Americomics); 1: the Shade (Roger Brant); O: the Shade (Roger Brant) ... 2.00
❑2, Jun 1983 ... 2.00
❑3, Aug 1983; O: Blue Beetle; O: Blue Beetle (Ted Kord) ... 2.00
❑4, Oct 1983; O: Dragonfly; 1: Dragonfly (Nancy Arazello); O: Dragonfly (Nancy Arazello) ... 2.00
❑5, Dec 1983 ... 2.00
❑6, Mar 1984; O: Scarlet Scorpion ... 2.00
❑Special 1, Jan 1983; Special ... 2.00

Amethyst
DC

❑1, Jan 1985; RE (a); 1: Fire Jade ... 1.00
❑2, Feb 1985 ... 1.00
❑3, Mar 1985 ... 1.00
❑4, Apr 1985 ... 1.00
❑5, May 1985 ... 1.00
❑6, Jun 1985 ... 1.00
❑7, Jul 1985 ... 1.00
❑8, Aug 1985 ... 1.00
❑9, Sep 1985 ... 1.00
❑10, Oct 1985 ... 1.00
❑11, Nov 1985 ... 1.00
❑12, Dec 1985 ... 1.00
❑13, Feb 1986; A: Doctor Fate. Crisis on Infinite Earths ... 1.00
❑14, Apr 1986 ... 1.00
❑15, Jun 1986; 1: Child. 1: Flaw ... 1.00
❑16, Aug 1986; Final Issue ... 1.00
❑Special 1, Oct 1986; Special ... 1.00

Amethyst
DC

❑1, Nov 1987 ... 1.25
❑2, Dec 1987 ... 1.25
❑3, Jan 1988 ... 1.25
❑4, Feb 1988 ... 1.25

Amethyst, Princess of Gemworld
DC

❑1, May 1983, O: Amethyst ... 1.00
❑1/75 cent, May 1983, O: Amethyst. 75 cent regional price variant ... 5.00
❑2, Jun 1983 ... 1.00
❑2/75 cent, Jun 1983, 75 cent regional price variant ... 5.00
❑3, Jul 1983 ... 1.00
❑4, Aug 1983 ... 1.00
❑5, Sep 1983 ... 1.00
❑6, Oct 1983 ... 1.00
❑7, Nov 1983 ... 1.00
❑8, Dec 1983 ... 1.00
❑9, Jan 1984 GP (c) ... 1.00
❑10, Feb 1984 GP (c) ... 1.00
❑11, Mar 1984 GP (c) ... 1.00
❑12, Apr 1984 ... 1.00
❑Ann 1; ca. 1984 ... 1.25

A Midnight Opera
Tokyopop

❑1, Nov 2005 ... 9.99

Ammo Armageddon
Atomeka

❑1 ... 4.95

Amora (Gray Morrow's...)
Fantagraphics / Eros

❑1, Apr 1991, b&w; Adult ... 2.95

Amusing Stories
Renegade

❑1, Mar 1987, b&w ... 2.00

Amy Papuda
Northstar

❑1; Adult ... 2.50
❑2; Adult ... 2.50

Amy Racecar Color Special
El Capitan

❑1, Jul 1997 ... 2.95
❑2, ca. 1999 ... 3.50

Anal Intruders from Uranus
Fantagraphics

❑1 2005 ... 3.95
❑2, Sep 2005 ... 3.95

Anarchy Comics
Last Gasp

❑1; ca. 1978 ... 2.50
❑2; Photo Cover; ca. 1979 ... 2.50
❑3; ca. 1981 ... 2.50
❑4 ... 2.50

Anarky
DC

❑1, May 1997 ... 2.50
❑2, Jun 1997 ... 2.50
❑3, Jul 1997 ... 2.50
❑4, Aug 1997, Final issue ... 2.50

Anarky
DC

❑1, May 1999 ... 2.50
❑2, Jun 1999; V: Aberration; V: Green Lantern (Kyle Rayner); Anarky empowered by Green Lantern ring ... 2.50

Other grades: Multiply price above by 5/6 for VF/NM • 2/3 for VERY FINE • 1/3 for FINE • 1/5 for VERY GOOD • 1/8 for GOOD

All-Out War

Big battle book
©DC

All Star Batman and Robin, The Boy Wonder

One year wait between #4 and #5
©DC

All-Star Comics

1970s revival of classic Golden Age DC series
©DC

All-Star Squadron

Roy Thomas does World War II
©DC

All-Star Western (2nd Series)

Showcase for darker-themed Western tales
©DC

N-MINT

❑3, Jul 1999; V: Green Lantern; V: Aberration; V: Green Lantern (Kyle Rayner); Anarky empowered by Green Lantern ring 2.50
❑4, Aug 1999 ..... 2.50
❑5, Sep 1999 ..... 2.50
❑6, Oct 1999 ..... 2.50
❑7, Nov 1999; Day of Judgment 2.50
❑8, Dec 1999; Final Issue; Joker revealed as Anarky's father 2.50

Ancient Joe
Dark Horse

❑1, ca. 2001 ..... 3.50
❑2, ca. 2001 ..... 3.50
❑3, ca. 2002 ..... 3.50

Andromeda (Andromeda)
Andromeda

❑1, Mar 1995 ..... 2.50
❑2, Apr 1995 ..... 2.50

Andromeda (Silver Snail)
Silver Snail

❑1, Sep 1977 ..... 2.00
❑2 ..... 2.00
❑3, Sep 1978 ..... 2.00
❑4, Dec 1978 ..... 2.00
❑5, Jun 1979 ..... 2.00
❑6 ..... 2.00

Andy Panda
Gold Key / Whitman

❑1, Aug 1973 ..... 4.00
❑2, Nov 1973 ..... 2.50
❑3, Feb 1974 ..... 2.50
❑4, May 1974 ..... 2.50
❑5, Aug 1974 ..... 2.00
❑6, Nov 1974 ..... 2.00
❑7, Feb 1975 ..... 2.00
❑8, May 1975 ..... 2.00
❑9, Aug 1975 ..... 2.00
❑10, Nov 1975 ..... 2.00
❑11, Feb 1976 ..... 2.00
❑12, Apr 1976 ..... 2.00
❑13, May 1976 ..... 2.00
❑14, Jul 1976 ..... 2.00
❑15, Sep 1976 ..... 2.00
❑16, Nov 1976 ..... 2.00
❑17, Jan 1977 ..... 2.00
❑18, Mar 1977 ..... 2.00
❑19, May 1977 ..... 2.00
❑20, Jul 1977 ..... 2.00
❑21, Sep 1977 ..... 2.00
❑22, Nov 1977, Includes Spider-Man Hostess ad "Break the Bank" by Buscema unpublished in Marvel Comics 2.00
❑23, Jan 1978 ..... 2.00

A-Next
Marvel

❑1, Oct 1998; next generation of Avengers 1.99
❑2/A, Nov 1998; Figures busting out of comic page on cover 1.99
❑2/B, Nov 1998; Earth Sentry flying on cover 1.99
❑3, Dec 1998; 1: Doc Magus; V: Defenders 1.99
❑4, Jan 1999; 1: American Dream; 1: Bluestreak; 1: Coal Tiger; 1: Crimson Curse; 1: Freebooter 1.99

N-MINT

❑5, Feb 1999 ..... 1.99
❑6, Mar 1999; 1: Argo 1.99
❑7, Apr 1999; 1: Iron Man (villain) 1.99
❑8, May 1999 ..... 1.99
❑9, Jun 1999 ..... 1.99
❑10, Jul 1999; V: Thunder Guard 1.99
❑11, Aug 1999 ..... 1.99

Angel
Dark Horse

❑1, Nov 1999; Painted cover 3.00
❑1/A, Nov 1999; Dynamic Forces gold logo variant 3.00
❑1/Variant, Nov 1999; Photo cover 3.00
❑2, Dec 1999 ..... 3.00
❑2/Variant, Dec 1999; Photo cover 3.00
❑3, Jan 2000 ..... 3.00
❑3/A, Jan 2000; Valentine's Day Edition; Dynamic Forces purple foil variant (white cover) 3.00
❑3/Variant, Jan 2000; Photo cover 3.00
❑4, Feb 2000; Painted cover 3.00
❑4/Variant, Feb 2000; Photo cover 3.00
❑5, Mar 2000 ..... 3.00
❑5/Variant, Mar 2000; Photo cover 3.00
❑6, Apr 2000 ..... 3.00
❑6/Variant, Apr 2000; Photo cover 3.00
❑7, May 2000 ..... 3.00
❑7/A, May 2000; Dynamic Forces Lucky 7 foil variant (limited to 1500 copies) 3.00
❑7/Variant, May 2000; Photo cover 3.00
❑8, Jun 2000 ..... 3.00
❑8/Variant, Jun 2000; Photo cover 3.00
❑9, Jul 2000 ..... 3.00
❑9/Variant, Jul 2000; Photo cover 3.00
❑10, Aug 2000 ..... 3.00
❑10/Variant, Aug 2000; Photo cover 3.00
❑11, Sep 2000 ..... 2.95
❑11/Variant, Sep 2000; Photo cover 2.95
❑12, Oct 2000 ..... 2.99
❑12/Variant, Oct 2000; Photo cover 2.99
❑13, Nov 2000 ..... 2.99
❑13/Variant, Nov 2000; Photo cover 2.99
❑14, Dec 2000 ..... 2.99
❑14/Variant, Dec 2000; Photo cover 2.99
❑15, Feb 2001; Cover by Christian Zanier 2.99
❑15/Variant, Feb 2001; Photo cover 2.99
❑16, Mar 2001; Final issue 2.99
❑16/Variant, Mar 2001; Photo cover 2.99
❑17, Apr 2001 ..... 2.99
❑17/Variant, Apr 2001; Photo cover 2.99

Angel
Dark Horse

❑1, Sep 2001 ..... 2.99
❑1/Variant, Sep 2001; Photo cover 2.99
❑2, Oct 2001 ..... 2.99
❑2/Variant, Oct 2001; Photo cover 2.99
❑3, Nov 2001 ..... 2.99
❑3/Variant, Nov 2001; Photo cover 2.99
❑4, May 2002 ..... 2.99
❑4/Variant, May 2002; Photo cover 2.99

Angela
Image

❑1, Dec 1994 NG (w); A: Spawn 3.50
❑1/A, Dec 1994; NG (w); A: Spawn. Pirate Spawn cover 3.50

N-MINT

❑2, Jan 1995 NG (w); A: Spawn 3.00
❑3, Feb 1995 NG (w) 3.00

Angel: After the Fall
Idea & Design Works

❑1, Nov 2007 ..... 12.00
❑2, Dec 2007 ..... 5.00

Angela/Glory: Rage of Angels
Image

❑1/A, Mar 1996 ..... 2.50
❑1/B, Mar 1996 ..... 2.50

Angel and the Ape
DC

❑1, Nov 1968 ..... 40.00
❑2, Jan 1969 ..... 20.00
❑3, Mar 1969 ..... 15.00
❑4, May 1969 ..... 15.00
❑5, Jul 1969 ..... 15.00
❑6, Sep 1969 ..... 15.00
❑7, Nov 1969 ..... 15.00

Angel and the Ape
DC

❑1, Mar 1991 PF (c); PF (w); PF (a) 1.25
❑2, Apr 1991 PF (c); PF (w); PF (a) 1.25
❑3, May 1991 PF (w); PF (a) 1.25
❑4, Jun 1991 PF (w); PF (a) 1.25

Angel and the Ape
DC / Vertigo

❑1, Oct 2001 ..... 2.95
❑2, Nov 2001 ..... 2.95
❑3, Dec 2001 ..... 2.95
❑4, Jan 2002 ..... 2.95

Angel: Auld Lang Syne
Idea & Design Works

❑1, Nov 2006 ..... 3.99
❑2, Dec 2006 ..... 3.99

Angel Dust Neo Manga One Shot
ADV Manga

❑1 2007 ..... 10.95

Angel Fire
Crusade

❑1/A, Jun 1997; wraparound photo cover 2.95
❑1/B, Jun 1997; black background cover 2.95
❑1/C, Jun 1997; white background cover 2.95
❑2, Aug 1997 ..... 2.95
❑3, Oct 1997, b&w 2.95

Angel Girl
Angel

❑0; Adult 2.95
❑0/Nude; Nude cover 5.00

Angel Girl: Before the Wings
Angel

❑1, Aug 1997; Adult 2.95

Angel Girl Vs. Vampire Girls
Angel

❑1 ..... 2.95
❑1/Nude; Nude edition 9.95

Angelic Layer
Tokyopop

❑1, Jun 2002, b&w; printed in Japanese format 9.99

Other grades: Multiply price above by 5/6 for VF/NM • 2/3 for VERY FINE • 1/3 for FINE • 1/5 for VERY GOOD • 1/8 for GOOD

N-MINT N-MINT N-MINT

Angel Love
DC

❑1, Aug 1986 .... 1.00
❑2, Sep 1986 .... 1.00
❑3, Oct 1986 .... 1.00
❑4, Nov 1986 .... 1.00
❑5, Dec 1986 .... 1.00
❑6, Jan 1987 .... 1.00
❑7, Feb 1987 .... 1.00
❑8, Mar 1987 .... 1.00
❑Ann 1 .... 1.25
❑Special 1; Special 1.25

Angel: Masks
Idea & Design Works

❑1, Oct 2006 .... 7.49

Angel of Death
Innovation

❑1 .... 2.25
❑2 .... 2.25
❑3 .... 2.25
❑4 .... 2.25

Angel: Old Friends
Idea & Design Works

❑1, Jan 2006 .... 3.99
❑2, Jan 2006 .... 3.99
❑3, Feb 2006 .... 3.99
❑4, Mar 2006 .... 3.99
❑5, Apr 2006 .... 3.99

Angel: Old Friends Cover Gallery
Idea & Design Works

❑1, Dec 2006, Includes Preview of Angel: Auld Lang Syne 3.99

Angels 750
Antarctic

❑1, Apr 2004 .... 2.99
❑2, May 2004 .... 2.99
❑3, Jul 2004 .... 2.99
❑4, Jul 2004 .... 2.99
❑5, Aug 2004 .... 2.99

Angel Sanctuary
Tokyopop

❑1, Apr 2004 .... 9.95
❑2, Jun 2004 .... 9.95
❑3, Aug 2004 .... 9.95
❑4, Nov 2004 .... 9.95
❑5, Dec 2004 .... 9.99
❑6, 2003 2005 .... 9.99
❑7, Apr 2005 .... 9.99
❑8, Jun 2005 .... 9.99
❑9, Aug 2005 .... 9.99
❑10, Oct 2005 .... 9.99

Angel Scriptbook
Idea & Design Works

❑1, Jun 2006 .... 3.99
❑2, May 2006 .... 3.99
❑3, Jun 2006 .... 3.99
❑4, Jul 2006 .... 3.99
❑5, Aug 2006 .... 3.99
❑6, Aug 2006 .... 3.99
❑7, Sep 2006 .... 3.99

Angels of Destruction
Malibu

❑1, Oct 1996; One-shot 2.50

Angel Spotlight: Connor
Idea & Design Works

❑1, Aug 2006 .... 3.99

Angel Spotlight: Doyle
Idea & Design Works

❑1, Aug 2006 .... 3.99

Angel Spotlight: Gunn
Idea & Design Works

❑1, Jun 2006 .... 3.99

Angel Spotlight: Illyria
Idea & Design Works

❑1, May 2006, Zack Howard Cover 3.99

Angel Spotlight: Wesley
Idea & Design Works

❑1, Jun 2006 .... 3.99

Angel Stomp Future
Avatar

❑1 2005 .... 3.50

Angel: The Curse
Idea & Design Works

❑1, Jul 2005 .... 3.99
❑1/Autographed, Jul 2005 .... 19.99
❑2/Byrne, Aug 2005 .... 5.00
❑2/ChrisCross, Aug 2005 .... 4.00
❑2/Messina, Aug 2005 .... 5.00
❑2/Shannon, Aug 2005 .... 4.00
❑2/Photo, Aug 2005 .... 15.00
❑3/Gardner, Sep 2005 .... 5.00
❑3/Kordey, Sep 2005 .... 4.00
❑3/Messina, Sep 2005 .... 5.00
❑3/Wood, Sep 2005 .... 4.00
❑4, Sep 2005 .... 3.99
❑5, Oct 2005 .... 3.99

Angel: The Curse Cover Gallery
Idea & Design Works

❑1, Jul 2006 .... 3.99

Angeltown
DC

❑1, Jan 2005 .... 2.95
❑2, Feb 2005 .... 2.95
❑3, Mar 2005 .... 2.95
❑4, Apr 2005 .... 2.95
❑5, May 2005 .... 2.95

Anger Grrrl
Blatant

❑1, Jun 1999 .... 2.95

Angryman
Caliber

❑1 .... 2.50
❑2 .... 2.50
❑3 .... 2.50

Angryman
Iconografix

❑1 .... 2.50
❑2 .... 2.50
❑3 .... 2.50

Angry Shadows
Innovation

❑1, ca. 1989, b&w; Includes Vampire Lestat preview; Adult 4.95

Anima
DC

❑0, Oct 1994; Series continued in Anima #8 .... 1.75
❑1, Mar 1994 .... 1.75
❑2, Apr 1994; V: Scarecrow 1.75
❑3, May 1994; V: Scarecrow 1.75
❑4, Jun 1994 .... 1.75
❑5, Jul 1994 .... 1.75
❑6, Aug 1994 .... 1.95
❑7, Sep 1994; Zero Hour 1.95
❑8, Nov 1994; Series continued from Anima #0 .... 1.95
❑9, Dec 1994 .... 1.95
❑10, Jan 1995 .... 1.95
❑11, Feb 1995 .... 1.95
❑12, Mar 1995 .... 1.95
❑13, Apr 1995 .... 1.95
❑14, Jun 1995 .... 2.25
❑15, Jul 1995; Final Issue 2.25

Animal Confidential
Dark Horse

❑1, May 1992, b&w; NN; One-shot; B&w anthology 2.25

Animal Man
DC

❑1, Sep 1988 BB (c) 4.00
❑2, Oct 1988 BB (c) 2.50
❑3, Nov 1988 BB (c) 2.00
❑4, Dec 1988 BB (c); A: B'wana Beast 2.00
❑5, Dec 1988; BB (c); Road Runner-Coyote 2.00
❑6, Jan 1989; BB (c); Invasion! 2.00
❑7, Jan 1989 BB (c) 2.00
❑8, Feb 1989; BB (c); V: Mirror Master 2.00
❑9, Mar 1989 BB (c); A: JLA 2.00
❑10, Apr 1989 BB (c); A: Vixen 2.00
❑11, May 1989 BB (c); A: Vixen 2.00
❑12, Jun 1989 BB (c); A: Vixen 2.00
❑13, Jul 1989 BB (c) 2.00
❑14, Aug 1989 BB (c) 2.00
❑15, Sep 1989 BB (c) 2.00
❑16, Oct 1989; BB (c); V: Time Commander 2.00
❑17, Nov 1989 BB (c) 2.00
❑18, Dec 1989 BB (c) 2.00
❑19, Jan 1990 BB (c) 2.00
❑20, Feb 1990 BB (c) 2.00
❑21, Mar 1990 BB (c) 2.00
❑22, Apr 1990 BB (c) 2.00
❑23, May 1990; BB (c); A: Jason Blood. A: Phantom Stranger. Arkham Asylum story 2.00
❑24, Jun 1990 BB (c); A: Inferior Five 2.00
❑25, Jul 1990 BB (c) 2.00
❑26, Aug 1990; BB (c); Morrison puts himself in story 2.00
❑27, Sep 1990 BB (c) 2.00
❑28, Oct 1990; BB (c); 1&o: Nowhere Man; 1: The Notional Man; 1: The Front Page; D:The Front Page 2.00
❑29, Nov 1990; BB (c); D: The Notional Man 2.00
❑30, Dec 1990 BB (c) 2.00
❑31, Jan 1991 BB (c) 2.00
❑32, Feb 1991 BB (c) 2.00
❑33, Mar 1991 BB (c) 2.00
❑34, Apr 1991 BB (c) 2.00
❑35, May 1991 BB (c) 2.00
❑36, Jun 1991 BB (c) 2.00
❑37, Jul 1991 BB (c) 2.00
❑38, Aug 1991; BB (c); Punisher parody 2.00
❑39, Sep 1991 .... 2.00
❑40, Oct 1991; War of the Gods; Part 15 .... 2.00
❑41, Nov 1991 .... 2.00
❑42, Dec 1991 BB (c) 2.00
❑43, Jan 1992 BB (c) 2.00
❑44, Feb 1992 BB (c) 2.00
❑45, Mar 1992; BB (c); Penalizer appears 2.00
❑46, Apr 1992 BB (c) 2.00
❑47, May 1992 .... 2.00
❑48, Jun 1992 BB (c) 2.00
❑49, Jul 1992 BB (c) 2.00
❑50, Aug 1992; Giant-size 3.00
❑51, Sep 1992 BB (c) 2.00
❑52, Oct 1992 BB (c) 2.00
❑53, Nov 1992 BB (c) 2.00
❑54, Dec 1992 .... 2.00
❑55, Jan 1993 BB (c) 2.00
❑56, Feb 1993; Giant-size; BB (c); Double-sized 3.50
❑57, Mar 1993; Begin Vertigo line 2.00
❑58, Apr 1993 BB (c) 2.00
❑59, May 1993 .... 2.00
❑60, Jun 1993 BB (c) 2.00
❑61, Jul 1993 BB (c) 2.00
❑62, Aug 1993 BB (c) 2.00
❑63, Sep 1993 BB (c) 2.00
❑64, Oct 1993 .... 2.00
❑65, Nov 1993 .... 2.00
❑66, Dec 1993 .... 2.00
❑67, Jan 1994 .... 2.00
❑68, Feb 1994 .... 2.00
❑69, Mar 1994 .... 2.00
❑70, Apr 1994 .... 2.00
❑71, May 1994 .... 1.95
❑72, Jun 1994 .... 1.95
❑73, Jul 1994 .... 1.95
❑74, Aug 1994 .... 1.95
❑75, Sep 1994 .... 1.95
❑76, Oct 1994 .... 1.95
❑77, Nov 1994 .... 1.95
❑78, Dec 1994; Includes trading cards 1.95
❑79, Jan 1995 .... 1.95
❑80, Feb 1995 .... 1.95
❑81, Mar 1995 .... 1.95
❑82, Apr 1995 .... 1.95
❑83, May 1995 .... 2.25
❑84, Jun 1995 .... 2.25
❑85, Jul 1995 .... 2.25
❑86, Aug 1995 .... 2.25
❑87, Sep 1995 .... 2.25
❑88, Oct 1995 .... 2.25
❑89, Nov 1995; Final Issue 2.25
❑Ann 1; BB (c); Children's Crusade 4.00

Animal Mystic
Cry for Dawn

❑1; published by Cry For Dawn Productions 10.00
❑1/Ltd.; limited edition with alternate cover and eight additional pages; limited edition with alternate cover and eight additional pages; published by Cry For Dawn Productions 10.00

Other grades: Multiply price above by 5/6 for VF/NM • 2/3 for VERY FINE • 1/3 for FINE • 1/5 for VERY GOOD • 1/8 for GOOD

Alpha Flight

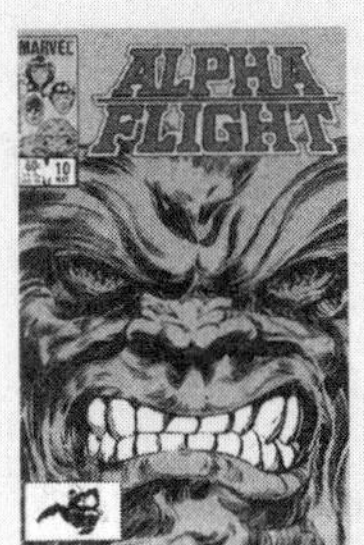

Canada's answer to The Avengers
©Marvel

Alpha Flight

Revival of 1980s hit didn't last as long
©Marvel

Alpha Flight

Second revival in seven years for Canadians
©Marvel

Alter Ego

Fanzine mascot becomes comics hero
©First

Alvin

Annoying chipmunk and siblings
©Dell

	N-MINT
❑1/2nd, May 1995, b&w; new cover; published by Sirius; new cover	5.00
❑2, Jun 1994, b&w 1: Klor	7.00
❑2/2nd, May 1995, b&w; New cover; art re-shot for superior reproduction	4.00
❑3, Oct 1994, b&w	5.00
❑3/2nd; 2nd printing	3.00
❑4, Aug 1995, b&w	5.00
❑4/A, Aug 1995; Alternate centerfold	5.00
❑4/Ltd., Aug 1995; Limited edition with different covers and centerfold; 1500 printed	5.00
❑4/2nd; 2nd printing	4.00

Animal Mystic Water Wars
Sirius

	N-MINT
❑1, Jun 1996	2.95
❑2, Sep 1996	2.95
❑3, Jan 1997	2.95
❑4, Aug 1997	2.95
❑5, May 1998	2.95
❑6, Oct 1998	2.95
❑Ashcan 1, Preview edition	2.50

Animal Rights Comics
Stabur

	N-MINT
❑1, Benefit comic for PETA	2.50

Animaniacs
DC

	N-MINT
❑1, May 1995 A: Pinky & The Brain	2.50
❑2, Jun 1995	2.00
❑3, Jul 1995	2.00
❑4, Aug 1995	2.00
❑5, Sep 1995	2.00
❑6, Oct 1995	2.00
❑7, Nov 1995	2.00
❑8, Dec 1995	2.00
❑9, Jan 1996; Pulp Fiction parody cover	2.00
❑10, Feb 1996; gratuitous pin-up cover	2.00
❑11, Mar 1996; Brain duplicates himself	1.75
❑12, Apr 1996	1.75
❑13, May 1996	1.75
❑14, Jun 1996	1.75
❑15, Jul 1996	1.75
❑16, Aug 1996; Wrestling issue	1.75
❑17, Sep 1996; Animaniacs judge a beauty contest	1.75
❑18, Oct 1996; All France issue	1.75
❑19, Nov 1996; X-Files parody	1.75
❑20, Dec 1996; James Dean tribute	1.75
❑21, Jan 1997; Christmas issue	1.75
❑22, Feb 1997	1.75
❑23, Mar 1997	1.75
❑24, Apr 1997	1.75
❑25, May 1997; Anniversary issue	1.75
❑26, Jun 1997; Tales from the Crypt cover parody	1.75
❑27, Jul 1997; Slappy's plane is hijacked	1.75
❑28, Aug 1997; Star Trek parody; Science issue	1.75
❑29, Sep 1997	1.75
❑30, Oct 1997; "Electra Woman and Dyna Girl" parody	1.75
❑31, Nov 1997; 101 Dalmations parody	1.75
❑32, Dec 1997; Dot hosts a slumber party	1.95
❑33, Jan 1998; 1: Sakko Warner. Lost World cover	1.95
❑34, Feb 1998	1.95
❑35, Mar 1998 A: Freakazoid	1.95
❑36, Apr 1998	1.95
❑37, May 1998	1.95
❑38, Jun 1998; manga-style cover	1.95
❑39, Jul 1998 A: Alfred Nobel	1.95
❑40, Sep 1998; Spice Girls parody	1.95
❑41, Oct 1998; Little Nemo and Little Mermaid parodies	1.95
❑42, Nov 1998; Love Boat parody	1.99
❑43, Dec 1998; Pinky & the Brain	1.99
❑44, Jan 1999; Pinky & the Brain	1.99
❑45, Feb 1999; The Warner Twins; Featuring Pinky and the Brain	1.99
❑46, Mar 1999; Dot the Vampire Slayer; Featuring Pinky and the Brain	1.99
❑47, Apr 1999; Evita parody; Featuring Pinky and the Brain	1.99
❑48, May 1999	1.99
❑49, Jun 1999; literature issue; Featuring Pinky and the Brain; It's the Animaniacal Guide to the Classics!!	1.99
❑50, Jul 1999; Hello Nurse as super-hero; Featuring Pinky and the Brain	1.99
❑51, Aug 1999; Featuring Pinky and the Brain	1.99
❑52, Sep 1999; football; Featuring Pinky and the Brain	1.99
❑53, Oct 1999; Featuring Pinky and the Brain	1.99
❑54, Nov 1999	1.99
❑55, Dec 1999; Featuring Pinky and the Brain	1.99
❑56, Jan 2000; Featuring Pinky and the Brain	1.99
❑57, Feb 2000	1.99
❑58, Mar 2000; Hello Nurse, Agent of H.U.B.B.A	1.99
❑59, Apr 2000; Featuring Pinky and the Brain	1.99
❑Holiday 1, Dec 1994; double-sized; A Christmas Special	3.00

Animation Comics
Viz

	N-MINT
❑1	3.95
❑2	3.95
❑3	3.95
❑4; Pokémon the Movie 2000	3.95

Animax
Marvel / Star

	N-MINT
❑1, Dec 1986	1.00
❑2, Jan 1987	1.00
❑3, Feb 1987	1.00
❑4, Mar 1987	1.00

Animerica Extra
Viz

	N-MINT
❑1, ca. 1998	4.95
❑2, ca. 1998	4.95

Animerica Extra
Viz

	N-MINT
❑1, Jan 1999	4.95
❑2, Feb 1999	4.95
❑3, Mar 1999	4.95
❑4, Apr 1999; Extras include The Videos Of A Video Girl, Previews, Yawara!, Editorial, Art Gallery	4.95
❑5, May 1999; Extras include The Cross-Dressing Girls Of Manga, Previews, Winter Story, Editorial, News Notes, Art Gallery	4.95
❑6, Jun 1999; Extras include Fight Like A Brave, Previews, In Depth: Joker, Editorial, News Notes, A Close-Up On Mamoru Oshii, Art Gallery	4.95
❑7, Jul 1999; Extras include Feature: The Drama Of Food, Previews, In Depth: Kareshi Kanojo No Jijo, Art Gallery	4.95
❑8, Aug 1999; Extras include Feature: Pokemon Manga, Previews, In Depth: Slam Dunk	4.95
❑9, Sep 1999; Extras include Feature: The Words Of Kia Asamiya, Previews, In Depth: F, Extra Art Gallery	4.95
❑10, Oct 1999; Extras include Feature: Anime Convention, Previews, In Depth: Basara, In Depth: Kimagure Orange Road, New Years Contest, Editorial, Extra Art Gallery	4.95
❑11, Nov 1999; Extras include Feature: Stealing Purses And Hearts, In Depth: Seraphic Feather, Previews, Editorial, Extra Art Gallery	4.95
❑12, Dec 1999; Vol. 2 #11 on cover; Extras include Feature: Miyazaki's Manga, In Depth: Akazukin Chacha, Previews, Editorial, Extra Art Gallery	4.95

Animerica Extra
Viz

	N-MINT
❑1, Jan 2000; Extras include: Feature: Maison Ikkoku, In Depth: Crossbone Gundam, Previews, and Extra Art Gallery	4.95
❑2, Feb 2000; Extras Include Feature: Racing Manga, InDepth: Famous Detective Conan, Previews, The Extra New Year's Contest Winner	4.95
❑3, Mar 2000; Extras Include Feature: Haruhiko Mikimoto, In Depth: Yu & Mii, Editorial, Previews, The Extra New Year's Contest Winners!	4.95
❑4, Apr 2000; Extras Include Feature: X/1999, In Depth: Kodomo No Omocha, Previews	4.95
❑5, May 2000; Extras Include Feature: Remakes Of The '90s, Feature: Mizuiro Jidai, In Depth: Kajika, Editorial, Previews, Extra Art Gallery	4.95
❑6, Jun 2000; contains poster	4.95
❑7, Jul 2000; Extras Include Feature: The Worlds Of Rumiko Takahashi, In Depth: Papuwa-Kun, Previews, Extra Art Gallery	4.95
❑8, Aug 2000; Extras Include Feature: Dreams In Manga, A Profile Of The Heart, In Depth: GS Mikami, Previews	4.95
❑9, Sep 2000; Extras Include Feature: Shojo Manga And Science Fiction, Special Preview - Gundam Wing: Ground Zero, Editorial, Extra New Year Contest, Previews, Extra Art Gallery	4.95
❑10, Oct 2000; Extras Include Feature: Otherworldly Manga, Special Preview - El-Hazard, In Depth: Cipher, Editorial, Previews, Extra Art Gallery	4.95
❑11, Nov 2000; Extras Include Feature: Working With Witches, In Depth: Akachan To Boku, In Depth: Tokyo Babylon, Editorial, Previews, Extra Art Gallery, Revolutionary Girl Utena Poster	4.95
❑12, Dec 2000; Extras Include Feature: Kyoko Hikawa, In Depth: Touch, Previews	4.95

Other grades: Multiply price above by 5/6 for VF/NM • 2/3 for VERY FINE • 1/3 for FINE • 1/5 for VERY GOOD • 1/8 for GOOD

Animerica Extra
Viz

❑1, Jan 2001; Extras Include Feature: Chiho Saito, Feature: Interview With Chiho Saito And Kunihiko Ikuhara, In Depth: Kochi-Kame, In Depth: Rose Of Versailles, Previews, Extra Art Gallery 4.95
❑2, Feb 2001; Extras Include Feature: Masakazu Katsura Interview, In Depth: Kamikaze Kaito Jeanne, Previews, Extra's New Year's Design Contest 4.95
❑3, Mar 2001; Extras Include Feature Mysteries in Manga, Previews 4.95
❑4, Apr 2001; Extras Include Feature: Manga By Urusawa, In Depth: Crayon Shin-Chan, In Depth: Jojo's Bizarre Adventure, Editorial, Previews 4.95
❑5, May 2001, Extras Include Feature: Must Read Manga, In Depth: Hanazakari No Kimitachi E, Previews, Editorial, Extra's Art Gallery 4.95
❑6, Jun 2001; Extras Include Feature: Watase's Works, Special Preview - Ceres: Celestial Legend, In Depth: Flame Of Recca, Editorial, Previews, Extra Art Gallery 4.95
❑7, Jul 2001; Extras Include Steam Detectives Poster, Feature: Boys; Bonanza, Previews, In Depth: Hyper Baby 4.95
❑8, Aug 2001; Extras Include Feature: Baseball Manga, In Depth: H2, Editorial, Extra's New Year's Contest, Previews, Extra Art Gallery 4.95
❑9, Sep 2001; Extras Include Feature: Baseball Manga, In Depth: H2, Editorial, Extra's New Year's Contest, Previews, Extra Art Gallery 4.95
❑10, Oct 2001; Extras Include Feature: Monstrous Manga, Special Preview! Bastard!!, In Depth: Yu Yu Hakusho, Previews 4.95
❑11, Nov 2001; Extras Include Feature: Vampire Time, From The Inside Looking Out, In Depth: Mimi O Sumaseba, Editorial, Previews, Extra Art Gallery 4.95
❑12, Dec 2001; Extras Include Feature: Tsukasa Hojo, From The Inside Looking Out, Editorial, In Depth: Wazuka Icchomae, Previews, Extra Art Gallery 4.95

Animerica Extra
Viz

❑1, Jan 2002 4.95
❑2, Feb 2002 4.95
❑3, Mar 2002 4.95
❑4, Apr 2002 4.95
❑5, May 2002 4.95
❑6, Jun 2002 4.95
❑7, Jul 2002 4.95
❑8, Aug 2002 4.95
❑9, Sep 2002 4.95
❑10, Oct 2002 4.95
❑11, Nov 2002 4.95
❑12, Dec 2002 4.95

Animerica Extra (Vol. 6)
Viz

❑1, Jan 2003 4.95

Animism
Centurion

❑1, Jan 1987 1.50

Anita Blake: Vampire Hunter: Guilty Pleasures
Marvel / DB Pro

❑1, Oct 2006 12.00
❑2, Nov 2006 7.00
❑3, Mar 2007 5.00

Aniverse
Weebee

❑1, Oct 1987 1.95
❑2, Dec 1987 1.95

Annex
Marvel

❑1, Aug 1994, O: Annex 1.75
❑2, Sep 1994 1.75
❑3, Oct 1994 1.75
❑4, Nov 1994 1.75

Annex (Chalk Outlines Studios)
Chalk Outlines Studios

❑1, ca. 1999 3.95

Annie
Marvel

❑1, Oct 1982, Official movie adaptation . 1.00
❑1/Special; Tabloid size; Treasury edition 5.00
❑2, Nov 1982, Official movie adaptation 1.00

Annie Oakley and Tagg
Gold Key

❑1, Jul 1965; reuses photo cover from Dell #6 40.00

Annie Sprinkle Is Miss Timed
Rip Off

❑1, Sep 1991 2.50
❑2, Oct 1991 2.50
❑3, Nov 1991 2.50
❑4, Dec 1991 2.50

Annihilation
Marvel

❑1, Oct 2006, Painted cover; Annihilation 2.99
❑2, Nov 2006, Nova Corps database profiles on The Centurions; The Delinquent; Annihilation 2.99
❑4, Jan 2007, D: Thanos 2.99
❑5, Mar 2007 2.99

Annihilation: Nova
Marvel

❑1, Jul 2006, Nova Corps database profiles on Xandarian Worldmind 2.99
❑2, Jul 2006, Nova Corps database profiles on Drax the Destroyer, Moondragon, Quasar 2.99
❑3, Aug 2006, Nova Corps database profile on Phyla 2.99
❑4, Sep 2006, D: Quasar 2.99

Annihilation Prologue
Marvel

❑1, May 2006, Destruction of the Kyln; Destruction of the Nova Corps; Destruction of Xandar; Nova Corps database profiles on Nova Corps; Annihilus; Thanos Annihilation Wave . 3.99

Annihilation: Ronan the Accuser
Marvel

❑1 0.00
❑3, Sep 2006 2.99
❑4, Oct 2006 2.99
❑85, Aug 2006 2.99

Annihilation: Silver Surfer
Marvel

❑1, Jun 2006, D: Air Walker; Nova Corps database profiles on Silver Surfer; Ravenous; Gabriel - the Air Walker 2.99
❑2, Jul 2006, Nova Corps database profiles on Galactus; The Fallen One .. 2.99
❑3, Aug 2006, Nova Corps database profiles on Tenebrous; Aegis 2.99
❑4, Sep 2006, Final Issue; Nova Corps database profiles on Firelord; Stardust 2.99

Annihilation: Super-Skrull
Marvel

❑1, Jun 2006, Nova Corps database profiles on Skrull Empire; Super Skrull 2.99
❑2, Jul 2006 2.99
❑3, Aug 2006, Nova Corps database profiles on Praxagora, R'Kin, Preak 2.99
❑4, Sep 2006, Final Issue 2.99

Annihilation: The Nova Corps Files
Marvel

❑1, Oct 2006, Database Files on all the Marvel characters involved in the Annihilation Storyline 3.99

Anomalies
Abnormal Fun

❑1, Oct 2000 2.95

Anomaly
Bud Plant

❑1, Adult 8.00
❑2, Adult 5.00
❑3, Adult 5.00
❑4, Adult 5.00

Anomaly (Brass Ring)
Brass Ring

❑1 3.95
❑2, Jun 2000 3.95

Another Day
Raised Brow

❑1, Oct 1995, b&w 2.75
❑2, Aug 1997 2.75

Ant
Arcana

❑1, ca. 2004 10.00
❑1/Red foil, ca. 2004, Red foil variant from Diamond 2004 Retailer Summit 35.00
❑2, ca. 2004 5.00
❑3, ca. 2004; Cover A: Mario Gully, Stefani Rennee 5.00
❑3/Variant, ca. 2004 6.00

Ant
Image

❑1, Oct 2005 5.00
❑1/Sketch, Oct 2005 2.95
❑1/RRP, Oct 2005; Distributed at Baltimore 2005 retailer convention; red foil cover; 1 per store 20.00
❑1/Conv, Oct 2005; Wizard World East 2005; 500 created 15.00
❑2, Sep 2005 2.99
❑3, Dec 2005 2.99
❑4, Mar 2006 2.99
❑5, Apr 2006 2.99
❑6, Jul 2006 2.99
❑7, Jul 2006 2.99
❑8, Sep 2006 2.99

Antabuse
High Drive

❑1; Adult 2.50
❑2; Adult 2.50

Antarctic Press Jam 1996
Antarctic

❑1, Dec 1996, B&w and color 2.95

Antares Circle
Antarctic

❑1 1.95
❑2 1.95

Ant Boy
Steeldragon

❑1 1.75
❑2, Oct 1988 1.75

Ant Farm
Gallant

❑1, Jun 1998 2.50
❑2 2.50

Anthro
DC

❑1, Aug 1968, 2: Anthro 50.00
❑2, Oct 1968 20.00
❑3, Dec 1968 20.00
❑4, Feb 1969 20.00
❑5, Apr 1969, Fact File #4 (Vigilante) 20.00
❑6, Aug 1969, WW (a); The Wonderful World of Comics 20.00

Anticipator
Fantasy

❑1, ca. 1996 2.25

Antietam: The Fiery Trail
Heritage Collection

❑1 1997; NN 3.50

Anti-Hitler Comics
New England

❑1 2.75
❑2 2.75

Anti-Social
Helpless Anger

❑1, b&w 2.00
❑2 2.50
❑3 2.50
❑4 2.75

Anti Social for the Disabled
Helpless Anger

❑1, b&w 5.00

Anti Social Jr.
Helpless Anger

❑1, b&w; NN; 20 pages 1.75

Ant-Man's Big Christmas
Marvel

❑1, Feb 2000; prestige format 5.95

Anton's Drekbook
Fantagraphics / Eros

❑1, Mar 1991, b&w; Adult 2.50

Other grades: Multiply price above by 5/6 for VF/NM • 2/3 for VERY FINE • 1/3 for FINE • 1/5 for VERY GOOD • 1/8 for GOOD

Amazing Adult Fantasy

"Middle phase" of Amazing Fantasy title

©Marvel

Amazing Adventures

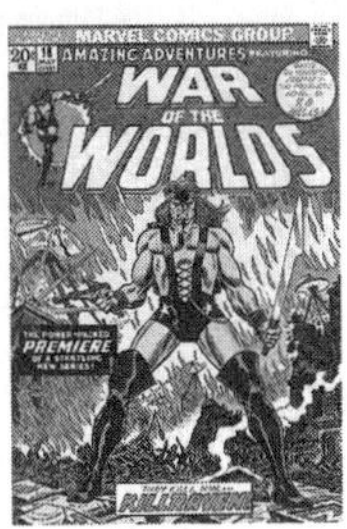

Notable for turning The Beast blue

©Marvel

Amazing Chan and the Chan Clan

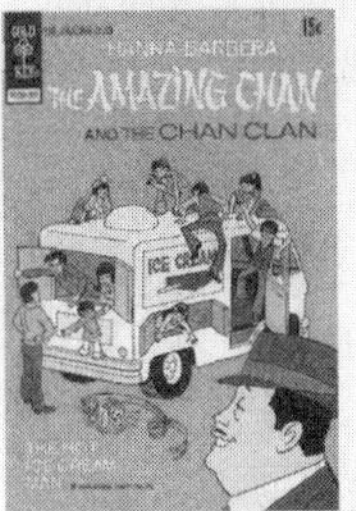

Hanna-Barbera series had Evanier's first work

©Gold Key

Amazing Comics Premieres

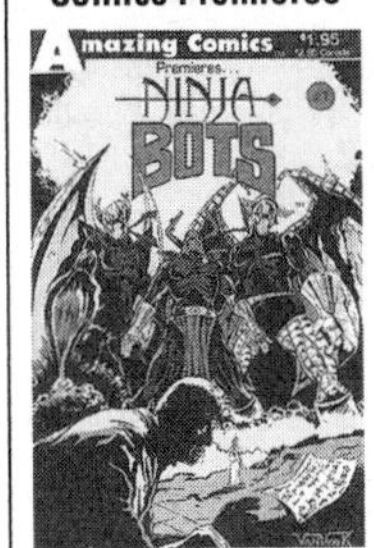

Showcase title for Amazing's new talent

©Amazing

Amazing Cynicalman

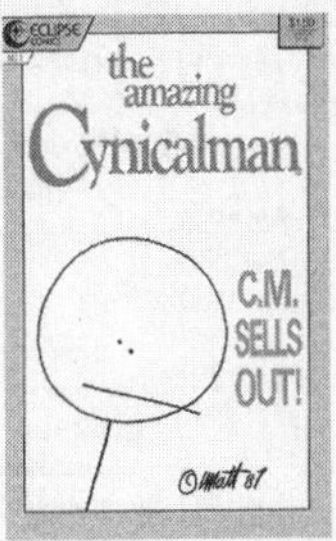

Stick-figure fun from Matt Feazell

©Eclipse

N-MINT

Anubis
Super Crew

❑1 ... 2.50

Anubis
Super Crew

❑1 ... 2.95

Anything but Monday
Anything But Monday

❑1, Dec 1988; Adult ... 2.00
❑2; Adult ... 2.00

Anything Goes!
Fantagraphics

❑1, Oct 1986 ... 2.00
❑2, Dec 1986 ... 2.00
❑3, Mar 1987 ... 2.00
❑4, May 1987 ... 2.00
❑5, Oct 1987; TMNT ... 2.00
❑6, Oct 1987, b&w ... 2.00

A-OK
Antarctic

❑1, Sep 1992 ... 2.50
❑2, Nov 1992 ... 2.50
❑3, Jan 1993 ... 2.50
❑4, Mar 1993 ... 2.50

Apache Dick
Eternity

❑1, Feb 1990 ... 2.25
❑2, Mar 1990 ... 2.25
❑3, Apr 1990 ... 2.25
❑4, May 1990 ... 2.25

Apache Skies
Marvel

❑1, Sep 2002 ... 2.99
❑2, Oct 2002 ... 2.99
❑3, Nov 2002 ... 2.99
❑4, Dec 2002 ... 2.99

Apache Trail
Steinway

❑1, Sep 1957 ... 58.00
❑2, Nov 1957 ... 36.00
❑3, Feb 1958 ... 36.00
❑4, Jun 1958 ... 36.00

Apathy Kat
Express / Entity

❑1, ca. 1995, b&w ... 2.50
❑2, ca. 1996 ... 2.75
❑3, ca. 1996 ... 2.75
❑4, ca. 1996 ... 2.75

Ape City
Adventure

❑1, Aug 1990; Planet of the Apes story ... 2.50
❑2, Sep 1990; Planet of the Apes story ... 2.50
❑3, Oct 1990; Planet of the Apes story ... 2.50
❑4, Nov 1990; Planet of the Apes story ... 2.50

Ape Nation
Adventure

❑1, Feb 1991, Alien Nation/Planet of Apes crossover ... 2.50
❑1/Ltd., limited edition; Alien Nation/Planet of the Apes crossover ... 4.00
❑2, Apr 1991; Alien Nation/Planet of the Apes crossover ... 2.00
❑3, May 1991; Alien Nation/Planet of the Apes crossover ... 2.00
❑4, Jun 1991; Alien Nation/Planet of the Apes crossover ... 2.00

N-MINT

Apex
Aztec

❑1, b&w ... 2.00

Apex Project
Stellar

❑1 ... 1.00
❑2 ... 1.00

Aphrodisia
Fantagraphics / Eros

❑1; Adult ... 2.95
❑2, Mar 1995; Adult ... 2.95

Aphrodite IX
Image

❑0, Mar 2001; Posterior shot on cover ... 2.00
❑0/2nd, Oct 2001; Indicia incorrectly says "Vol 1, Issue 2" ... 5.95
❑0/A, May 2001; Wizard Gold Foil Edition 9.00
❑0/B, May 2001; Wizard Blue Foil Edition 9.00
❑0/C, Mar 2001; Green foil behind logo. 4.00
❑0/D, Mar 2001; Dynamic Forces Gold foil behind title ... 4.00
❑0/E, Mar 2001; Identical cover to #0; Limited to 250 ... 4.00
❑0/F, Mar 2001; Limited to 50 ... 4.00
❑1/A, Sep 2000; Aphrodite reclining against left edge of cover, gun up ... 4.00
❑1/B, Sep 2000; Aphrodite walking on metallic planks ... 2.50
❑1/C, Sep 2000; Red background, Aphrodite shooting on cover ... 2.50
❑1/D, Sep 2000; Green background, standing with guns up ... 2.50
❑1/E, Sep 2000; Tower records exclusive 5.00
❑1/F, Sep 2000; Tower records exclusive w/foil ... 5.00
❑1/G, Sep 2000; Wizard World exclusive 4.00
❑1/H, Sep 2000; Wizard World exclusive w/foil ... 4.00
❑1/I, Sep 2000; Chrome edition of 3,000; Dynamic Forces exclusive ... 5.00
❑2, Mar 2001 ... 2.00
❑2/A, Mar 2001; Graham Crackers comics exclusive ... 2.50
❑2/B, Mar 2001; Blue Foil behind title; connects to Dynamic Forces Exclusive; Graham Crackers Comics/Midwest Comics Co. Exclusive ... 2.50
❑2/C, Mar 2001; connects to Dynamic Forces Exclusive; Graham Crackers Comics/Midwest Comics Co. Exclusive; Green Foil behind title ... 2.50
❑2/D, Mar 2001; Several characters in profile on cover; connects to Graham Crackers Comics/Midwest Comics Co. Exclusive; Dynamic Forces Exclusive. 2.50
❑2/E, Mar 2001; connects to Graham Crackers Comics/Midwest Comics Co. Exclusive; Dynamic Forces Exclusive. 2.50
❑2/F, Mar 2001; connects to Graham Crackers Comics/Midwest Comics Co. Exclusive; Dynamic Forces Exclusive. 2.50
❑2/G, Mar 2001; Blue Foil behind title; connects to Graham Crackers Comics/Midwest Comics Co. Exclusive; Exclusive/Wizard World Authentic ... 2.50

N-MINT

❑2/H, Mar 2001; Blue Foil behind title; connects to Graham Crackers Comics/Midwest Comics Co. Exclusive; Dynamic Forces Exclusive/Wizard Authentic ... 2.50
❑2/I, Mar 2001; connects to Graham Crackers Comics/Midwest Comics Co. Exclusive; Dynamic Forces Exclusive; Green Foil behind title ... 2.50
❑2/J, Mar 2001; connects to Graham Crackers Comics/Midwest Comics Co. Exclusive; Dynamic Forces Exclusive; Green Foil behind title ... 2.50
❑2/K, Mar 2001; connects to Graham Crackers Comics/Midwest Comics Co. Exclusive; Dynamic Forces Exclusive. 2.50
❑3, Dec 2001 ... 2.00
❑4, Mar 2002; Double-size ... 4.00
❑4/A, Mar 2002; sketch cover; Published/solicited by Jay Company Comics ... 4.95
❑Ashcan 1, Dec 2000; Convention Preview 6.00
❑Ashcan 1/Ltd., Dec 2000; Original color sketch and signature by Clarence Lansang; Solicited by Jay Company Comics ... 5.00

Apocalypse
Apocalypse

❑1 ... 3.95
❑2 ... 3.95
❑3, Jun 1991 ... 3.95
❑4, Jul 1991 ... 3.95
❑5 ... 3.95
❑6, Sep 1991 ... 3.95
❑7, Oct 1991; Makabre ... 3.95

Apocalypse Nerd
Dark Horse

❑1, Jan 2005; b&w ... 2.99
❑2, Sep 2005; b&w ... 2.99
❑3, Jul 2006; b&w ... 2.99
❑4, Dec 2007; b&w ... 2.99

Apocalypse: The Eyes of Doom
Kitchen Sink

❑1 ... 14.95

Apollo Smile
Mixx

❑1, Jul 1998 ... 3.50
❑2, Sep 1998; Incicia date 7/1/98 ... 3.00

Apparition
Caliber

❑1 1996, b&w ... 2.95
❑2 1996, b&w ... 2.95
❑3 1996, b&w ... 2.95
❑4 1996, b&w ... 2.95
❑5 1996 ... 2.95

Apparition: Abandoned
Caliber

❑1 1995; prestige format; One-shot ... 3.95

Apparition: Visitations
Caliber

❑1, Aug 1995; One-shot ... 3.95

Apple, P.I.
Parrot Communications

❑1, Sep 1996; pronounced "Apple Pie" ... 1.00

Appleseed Book 1
Eclipse

❑1, Sep 1988 ... 7.00

Other grades: Multiply price above by 5/6 for VF/NM • 2/3 for VERY FINE • 1/3 for FINE • 1/5 for VERY GOOD • 1/8 for GOOD

	N-MINT
❑2, Oct 1988	5.00
❑3, Nov 1988, Squarebound	5.00
❑4, Jan 1989	4.00
❑5, Feb 1989	4.00

Appleseed Book 2
Eclipse

	N-MINT
❑1, Feb 1989	5.00
❑2, Mar 1989	4.00
❑3, Apr 1989	3.50
❑4, May 1989	3.50
❑5, Jun 1989	3.50

Appleseed Book 3
Eclipse

	N-MINT
❑1, Aug 1989; Squarebound	4.00
❑2, Sep 1989	3.50
❑3, Oct 1989	3.50
❑4, Nov 1989	3.50
❑5, Dec 1989	3.50

Appleseed Book 4
Eclipse

	N-MINT
❑1, Jan 1991	3.50
❑2, Mar 1991	3.50
❑3, May 1991	3.50
❑4, Aug 1991	3.50

Appleseed Databook
Dark Horse

	N-MINT
❑1, Apr 1994	3.50
❑2, May 1994; Flip-book; Squarebound	3.50

April Horrors
Rip Off

	N-MINT
❑1, Sep 1993, b&w	2.95

Aquablue
Dark Horse

	N-MINT
❑1, Nov 1989	6.95

Aquablue: The Blue Planet
Dark Horse

	N-MINT
❑1, Aug 1990	8.95

Aqua Knight
Viz

	N-MINT
❑1, ca. 2000	2.95
❑2, ca. 2000	3.50
❑3, ca. 2000	3.50
❑4, ca. 2000	3.50
❑5, ca. 2000	3.50
❑6, ca. 2000	3.50

Aqua Knight Part 2
Viz

	N-MINT
❑1, Oct 2000	3.50
❑2, Nov 2000	3.50
❑3, Dec 2000	3.50
❑4, Jan 2001	3.50
❑5, Feb 2001	3.50

Aqua Knight Part 3
Viz

	N-MINT
❑1, ca. 2001	3.50
❑2, ca. 2001	3.50
❑3, ca. 2001	3.50
❑4, ca. 2001	3.50
❑5, ca. 2001	3.50

Aquaman
DC

	N-MINT
❑1, Feb 1962, 1: Quisp	900.00
❑2, Apr 1962, V: Capt. Sykes	275.00
❑3, Jun 1962	150.00
❑4, Aug 1962	150.00
❑5, Oct 1962	150.00
❑6, Dec 1962	90.00
❑7, Feb 1963	90.00
❑8, Apr 1963	90.00
❑9, Jun 1963	90.00
❑10, Aug 1963	90.00
❑11, Oct 1963, 1: Mera	125.00
❑12, Dec 1963	75.00
❑13, Feb 1964	75.00
❑14, Apr 1964	75.00
❑15, Jun 1964	75.00
❑16, Aug 1964	75.00
❑17, Oct 1964	75.00
❑18, Dec 1964, A: Justice League of America. Aquaman marries Mera	90.00
❑19, Feb 1965	60.00
❑20, Apr 1965	60.00
❑21, Jun 1965, 1: Fisherman	60.00
❑22, Aug 1965	60.00
❑23, Oct 1965, Birth of Aquababy	60.00
❑24, Dec 1965, V: the Terrible Trio	60.00
❑25, Feb 1966	60.00
❑26, Apr 1966	60.00
❑27, Jun 1966	60.00
❑28, Aug 1966	60.00
❑29, Oct 1966, 1: Ocean Master	75.00
❑30, Dec 1966, Flash cameo; Batman cameo; Superman cameo; Hawkman cameo	50.00
❑31, Feb 1967	45.00
❑32, Apr 1967	50.00
❑33, Jun 1967, 1: Aqua-Girl	45.00
❑34, Aug 1967	45.00
❑35, Oct 1967, 1: Black Manta	40.00
❑36, Dec 1967	40.00
❑37, Feb 1968	40.00
❑38, Apr 1968	40.00
❑39, Jun 1968	40.00
❑40, Aug 1968	40.00
❑41, Oct 1968	40.00
❑42, Dec 1968	30.00
❑43, Feb 1969	30.00
❑44, Apr 1969	25.00
❑45, Jun 1969	25.00
❑46, Aug 1969, Quest for Mera ends	25.00
❑47, Oct 1969, Includes The Adventures of Aquaboy, reprinted from Adventure Comics #268	40.00
❑48, Dec 1969, NC (c); JA (a); O: Aquaman; Includes The Adventures of Aquaboy, reprinted from Adventure Comics #260	25.00
❑49, Feb 1970, NC (c); JA (a)	25.00
❑50, Apr 1970, NC (c); NA (w); NA, JA (a); A: Deadman	75.00
❑51, Jun 1970, NC (c); NA (w); NA, JA (a); A: Deadman	50.00
❑52, Aug 1970, NC (c); NA (w); NA, JA (a); A: Deadman	40.00
❑53, Oct 1970, NC (c); JA (a)	20.00
❑54, Dec 1970, NC (c); JA (a)	20.00
❑55, Feb 1971, NC (c); JA (a)	20.00
❑56, Apr 1971, NC (c); JA (a); 1&O: Crusader	20.00
❑57, Aug 1977, JA (c); JA (a); Jim Aparo cover; V: Black Manta	20.00
❑58, Oct 1977, JA (c); JA (a); O: Aquaman; V: Fisherman	20.00
❑59, Dec 1977, V: Fisherman	10.00
❑60, Feb 1978, V: Scavenger	10.00
❑61, Apr 1978, V: Kobra	10.00
❑62, Jun 1978	10.00
❑63, Sep 1978, V: Ocean Master; Final Issue	10.00

Aquaman
DC

	N-MINT
❑1, Feb 1986; New costume	3.00
❑2, Mar 1986	3.00
❑3, Apr 1986; O: Aquaman	3.00
❑4, May 1986	3.00
❑Special 1, Jun 1988	2.00

Aquaman
DC

	N-MINT
❑1, Jun 1989	1.00
❑2, Jul 1989	1.00
❑3, Aug 1989	1.00
❑4, Sep 1989; Mera leaves Aquaman	1.00
❑5, Oct 1989	1.00
❑Special 1, Apr 1989; Legend of Aquaman	2.00

Aquaman
DC

	N-MINT
❑1, Dec 1991	1.50
❑2, Jan 1992	1.00
❑3, Feb 1992	1.00
❑4, Mar 1992	1.00
❑5, Apr 1992; V: Black Manta	1.00
❑6, May 1992	1.25
❑7, Jun 1992	1.25
❑8, Jul 1992; A: Batman. V: Nicodemus	1.25
❑9, Aug 1992	1.25
❑10, Sep 1992	1.25
❑11, Oct 1992	1.25
❑12, Nov 1992	1.25
❑13, Dec 1992; A: Scavanger. Final Issue	1.25

Aquaman
DC

	N-MINT
❑0, Oct 1994; PD (w); Aquaman gets harpoon for arm	3.00
❑1, Aug 1994; PD (w); 1: Charybdis; The Pirhana Man	3.00
❑2, Sep 1994; PD (w); V: Charybdis. Aquaman loses hand	3.00
❑3, Nov 1994; PD (w); V: Superboy. 1: Admiral Strom	2.00
❑4, Dec 1994; PD (w); A: Lobo. V: Lobo	2.00
❑5, Jan 1995; PD (w); 1: Koryak	2.00
❑6, Feb 1995 PD (w)	1.50
❑7, Mar 1995 PD (w)	1.50
❑8, Apr 1995 PD (w)	1.50
❑9, Jun 1995 PD (w)	1.75
❑10, Jul 1995; PD (w); D: King Thesily; V: Green Lantern (Kyle Rayner)	1.75
❑11, Aug 1995; PD (w); Return Mera	1.75
❑12, Sep 1995; PD (w); Mera returns	1.75
❑13, Oct 1995 PD (w)	1.75
❑14, Nov 1995; PD (w); "Underworld Unleashed"	1.75
❑15, Dec 1995; PD (w); Skull ship under Atlantis revealed	1.75
❑16, Jan 1996; PD (w); V: Justice League	1.75
❑17, Feb 1996 PD (w)	1.75
❑18, Mar 1996; PD (w); O: Dolphin	1.75
❑19, Apr 1996; PD (w); Aqualad returns	1.75
❑20, May 1996 PD (w)	1.75
❑21, Jun 1996; MZ (c); PD (w); Aquaman visits Thirna Na Oge	1.75
❑22, Jul 1996 PD (w)	1.75
❑23, Aug 1996; PD (w); A: Sea Devils, Power Girl, Tsunami, Arion. 1: Deep Blue	1.75
❑24, Sep 1996; PD (w); D: Admiral Strom	1.75
❑25, Oct 1996 PD (w)	1.75
❑26, Nov 1996; PD (w); "Final Night"	1.75
❑27, Dec 1996; PD (w); Aquaman declares war on Japan	1.75
❑28, Jan 1997 PD (w); A: Martian Manhunter	1.75
❑29, Feb 1997; PD (w); V: Black Manta	1.75
❑30, Mar 1997 PD (w)	1.75
❑31, Apr 1997; PD (w); V:Shark	1.75
❑32, May 1997 PD (w); A: Swamp Thing	1.75
❑33, Jun 1997 PD (w)	1.75
❑34, Jul 1997; PD (w); V: Triton	1.75
❑35, Aug 1997; PD (w); A: Animal Man. V: Gamesman. Aquaman blind	1.75
❑36, Sep 1997 PD (w)	1.75
❑37, Oct 1997; PD (w); V: Parademons. "Genesis"	1.75
❑38, Nov 1997; PD (w); Poseidonis becomes a tourist attraction	1.75
❑39, Dec 1997; PD (w); A: Neptune Perkins. Face cover	2.00
❑40, Jan 1998; PD (w); V: Doctor Polaris	2.00
❑41, Feb 1998 PD (w); A: Maxima	2.00
❑42, Mar 1998; PD (w); V: Sea Wolf	2.00
❑43, Apr 1998; PD (w); "Millennium Giants"	2.00
❑44, May 1998 A: Golden Age Flash. A: Sentinel	2.00
❑45, Jun 1998; PD (w); Destruction of Poseidonis	2.00
❑46, Jul 1998; PD (w); Two Aquamen return	2.00
❑47, Aug 1998	2.00
❑48, Sep 1998; Mera rejoins cast	2.00
❑49, Oct 1998; Next issue is #1,000,000	2.00
❑50, Dec 1998; EL (c); EL (w); EL (a); 1: Lagoon Boy; 1: Noble	2.00
❑51, Jan 1999 EL (c); EL (w); EL (a); A: King Noble	2.00
❑52, Feb 1999 EL (c); EL (w); BSz, EL, JA (a); A: Fire Trolls. A: Mera. A: Lava Lord. A: Noble	2.00
❑53, Mar 1999 EL (w); EL (a); A: Superman. A: Shrapnel	2.00
❑54, Apr 1999 EL (w); EL (a); A: Sheeva the Mermaid. A: Landlovers. A: Blubber. A: Lagoon Boy	2.00
❑55, May 1999 EL (w); EL (a)	2.00
❑56, Jun 1999 EL (w); EL (a)	2.00
❑57, Jul 1999 EL (w); EL (a)	2.00
❑58, Aug 1999 EL (w); EL (a)	2.00
❑59, Sep 1999 EL (w); EL (a)	2.00
❑60, Oct 1999; EL (w); EL (a); Wedding of Tempest and Dolphin	2.00
❑61, Nov 1999; Day of Judgment	2.00
❑62, Dec 1999 EL (w)	2.00
❑63, Jan 2000	2.00
❑64, Feb 2000	2.00
❑65, Mar 2000	2.00
❑66, Apr 2000	2.00

Other grades: Multiply price above by 5/6 for VF/NM • 2/3 for VERY FINE • 1/3 for FINE • 1/5 for VERY GOOD • 1/8 for GOOD

Amazing Fantasy

The series that spawned Spider-Man
©Marvel

Amazing Fantasy

Revisiting the "unpublished" Fantasy issues
©Marvel

Amazing Heroes Swimsuit Special

Cheesecake ish outlasted parent magazine
©Fantagraphics

Amazing High Adventure

Adventure stories by top-notch creative teams
©Marvel

Amazing Scarlet Spider

"Clone" series replaced Amazing Spider-Man
©Marvel

	N-MINT
❑67, May 2000	2.00
❑68, Jun 2000	2.00
❑69, Jul 2000	2.00
❑70, Aug 2000; Cover incorrectly credits Raimondi and Rapmund	2.00
❑71, Sep 2000 A: Warlord	2.50
❑72, Oct 2000	2.50
❑73, Nov 2000; Cover forms triptych with #74 and #75	2.50
❑74, Dec 2000; Cover forms triptych with #73 and #75	2.50
❑75, Jan 2001; Final Issue; Cover forms triptych with #73 and #74	2.50
❑1000000, Nov 1998; Takes place between #49 and #50; DC One Million Week 3	2.00
❑Ann 1, ca. 1995; PD (w); A: Superman,. A: Wonder Woman, Superman,. A: Wonder Woman. 1995 Ann; Year One	3.50
❑Ann 2, ca. 1996; Legends of the Dead Earth	2.95
❑Ann 3, Jul 1997; Pulp Heroes	3.95
❑Ann 4, Sep 1998; Ghosts	2.95
❑Ann 5, Sep 1999; JLApe	2.95

Aquaman
DC

	N-MINT
❑1, Feb 2003, Aquaman receives water hand	2.50
❑2, Mar 2003	2.50
❑3, Apr 2003	2.50
❑4, May 2003	2.50
❑5, Jun 2003, 1: Thirst	2.50
❑6, Jul 2003	2.50
❑7, Aug 2003	2.50
❑8, Sep 2003	2.50
❑9, Oct 2003, Thirst appearance	2.50
❑10, Nov 2003	2.50
❑11, Dec 2003	2.50
❑12, Jan 2004, Aquaman free to swim the oceans again	2.50
❑13, Feb 2004, Kinetic-DC Focus Preview inside	2.50
❑14, Mar 2004	2.50
❑15, Apr 2004, New cover logo; New costume; San Diego falls into the ocean	12.00
❑16, May 2004; 1: Lorena	6.00
❑17, Jun 2004; 1: Aquagirl	6.00
❑18, Jul 2004	2.50
❑19, Aug 2004	2.50
❑20, Jul 2004; Lorena named as Aquagirl on cover	2.50
❑21, Oct 2004; Sub Diego separates from San Diego	2.50
❑22, Nov 2004	2.50
❑23, Dec 2004; 1: Marauder; Includes Heroscape insert #2 of 2	2.50
❑24, Jan 2005	2.50
❑25, Feb 2005	2.50
❑26, Mar 2005, 1: Aquagirl (in costume); V: Ocean Master; Lorena starts wearing a costume	2.50
❑27, Apr 2005, V: Ocean Master	2.50
❑28, May 2005	2.50
❑29, May 2005	2.50
❑30, Jun 2005	2.50
❑31, Jul 2005; New DC logo	2.50
❑32, Aug 2005	2.50
❑33, Sep 2005	2.50
❑34, Oct 2005	2.50
❑35, Nov 2005; OMAC Project Tie-In	2.50
❑36, Jan 2006	2.50
❑37, Feb 2006, Spectre destroys Atlantis; Infinite Crisis Crossover	2.50
❑38, Mar 2006, D: Koryak confirmed	2.50
❑39, Mar 2006, Continued in Aquaman: Sword of Atlantis #40	2.50
❑40, May 2006, Following the jump-year, this title's name switches to Aquaman: Sword of Atlantis with this issue	2.99
❑41, Jun 2006	2.99
❑43, Sep 2006	2.99
❑44, Nov 2006	2.99
❑46, Feb 2007	2.99
❑47, Mar 2007	2.99

Aquaman Secret Files
DC

	N-MINT
❑1, Dec 1998, O: Aquaman	4.95
❑2, Mar 2003	4.95

Aquaman: Time and Tide
DC

	N-MINT
❑1, Dec 1993; PD (w); O: Aquaman	2.00
❑2, Jan 1994; PD (w); D: Drin	2.00
❑3, Feb 1994 PD (w)	2.00
❑4, Mar 1994; PD (w); O: Ocean Master	2.00

Aquarium
CPM Manga

	N-MINT
❑1/A, Apr 2000, b&w; wraparound cover	2.95
❑1/B, Apr 2000, b&w; alternate wraparound cover	2.95
❑2, ca. 2000, b&w	2.95
❑3, ca. 2000, b&w	2.95
❑4, ca. 2000, b&w	2.95
❑5, ca. 2000, b&w	2.95
❑6, ca. 2000, b&w	2.95

Arabian Nights on the World of Magic: The Gathering
Acclaim / Armada

	N-MINT
❑1, Dec 1995	2.50
❑2	2.50

Arachnophobia
Disney

	N-MINT
❑1	2.95

Aragonés 3-D
3-D Zone

	N-MINT
❑1; paperback	4.95

Araknis
Mushroom

	N-MINT
❑0, Apr 1996; Published by Mystic	2.50
❑1, May 1995	2.50
❑2, ca. 1996	2.50
❑3, ca. 1996; Publisher becomes Morning Star	2.50
❑4, ca. 1996	2.50
❑5, ca. 1996	2.50
❑6, ca. 1996	2.50

Arak Son of Thunder
DC

	N-MINT
❑1, Sep 1981, O: Arak. 1: Angelica	1.00
❑2, Oct 1981, 1: Malagigi	1.00
❑3, Nov 1981, 1: Valda	1.00
❑4, Dec 1981	1.00
❑5, Jan 1982	1.00
❑6, Feb 1982	1.00
❑7, Mar 1982	1.00
❑8, Apr 1982	1.00
❑9, May 1982	1.00
❑10, Jun 1982	1.00
❑11, Jul 1982	1.00
❑12, Aug 1982, O: Valda	1.00
❑13, Sep 1982	1.00
❑14, Oct 1982	1.00
❑15, Nov 1982, 48 pages; 16 page insert of Masters of the Universe; Valda the Iron Maiden story	1.00
❑16, Dec 1982	1.00
❑17, Jan 1983	1.00
❑18, Feb 1983	1.00
❑19, Mar 1983	1.00
❑20, Apr 1983, O: Angelica	1.00
❑21, May 1983	1.00
❑22, Jun 1983	1.00
❑23, Jul 1983	1.00
❑24, Aug 1983; 48 pages	1.00
❑25, Sep 1983	1.00
❑26, Oct 1983	1.00
❑27, Nov 1983	1.00
❑28, Dec 1983	1.00
❑29, Jan 1984	1.00
❑30, Feb 1984	1.00
❑31, Mar 1984	1.00
❑32, Apr 1984	1.00
❑33, May 1984	1.00
❑34, Jun 1984	1.00
❑35, Jul 1984	1.00
❑36, Aug 1984	1.00
❑37, Sep 1984	1.00
❑38, Nov 1984	1.00
❑39, Dec 1984	1.00
❑40, Jan 1985	1.00
❑41, Feb 1985	1.00
❑42, Mar 1985	1.00
❑43, Apr 1985	1.00
❑44, May 1985	1.00
❑45, Jun 1985; Todd McFarlane pin-up of Valda	1.00
❑46, Jul 1985	1.00
❑47, Aug 1985	1.00
❑48, Sep 1985	1.00
❑49, Oct 1985	1.00
❑50, Nov 1985; Giant-size	1.00
❑Ann 1	2.00

Aramis
Comics Interview

	N-MINT
❑1	1.95
❑2	1.95
❑3	1.95

Arana: Heart of the Spider
Marvel

	N-MINT
❑1, Mar 2005	2.99
❑1/Incentive, Mar 2005	7.00
❑2, Apr 2005	2.99
❑3, May 2005	2.99
❑4, Jun 2005	2.99
❑5, Jul 2005	2.99
❑6, Aug 2005	2.99
❑7, Sep 2005	2.99
❑8, Oct 2005	2.99
❑9 2005	2.99
❑10, Dec 2005	2.99

Other grades: Multiply price above by 5/6 for VF/NM • 2/3 for VERY FINE • 1/3 for FINE • 1/5 for VERY GOOD • 1/8 for GOOD

❑11, Jan 2006 ... 2.99
❑12, Feb 2006 ... 2.99

Arc
Arts Industria

❑1, Apr 1994; Adult ... 2.95

Arcade
Print Mint

❑1, Mar 1975; Adult ... 10.00
❑2, Jun 1975; Adult ... 8.00
❑3, Sep 1975; Adult ... 8.00
❑4 1976; Adult ... 7.00
❑5 1976; Adult ... 7.00
❑6, Jun 1976; Adult ... 7.00
❑7 1976; Adult ... 5.00

Arcana
DC / Vertigo

❑Ann 1, ca. 1994; "Children's Crusade" . 4.00

Arcana
Tokyopop

❑1, Jun 2005 ... 9.99
❑2, Sep 2005 ... 9.99
❑3, Dec 2005 ... 9.99

Arcana (Wells & Clark)
Wells & Clark

❑1 1995 ... 3.00
❑2, Mar 1995 ... 3.00
❑3, May 1995 ... 3.00
❑4, Jul 1995 ... 2.25
❑5, Sep 1995 ... 2.25
❑6, Jan 1995 ... 2.25
❑7, Apr 1996 ... 2.25
❑8, Jul 1996 ... 2.25
❑9, Sep 1996 ... 2.25
❑10 1996 ... 2.25

Arcane
Arcane

❑1 ... 2.00
❑2; Fly in My Eye ... 9.95

Arcane
Graphik

❑1, b&w ... 1.25

Arcanum
Image

❑½, Dec 1997; Includes Certificate of Authenticity ... 3.00
❑½/Gold, Dec 1997; Signed by Brandon Peterson ... 5.00
❑1, Apr 1997; Standard Cover (green background) ... 2.50
❑1/A, Apr 1997; variant cover ... 2.50
❑2, May 1997; Standard Cover (red background) ... 2.50
❑2/A, May 1997; variant cover ... 2.50
❑3, Jun 1997; Standard Cover (girl sitting w/back toward front) ... 2.50
❑3/A, Jun 1997; variant cover ... 2.50
❑4, Jul 1997; Standard Cover (man Impalied) ... 2.50
❑4/A, Jul 1997; variant cover ... 2.50
❑5, Sep 1997 ... 2.95
❑6, Nov 1997 ... 2.95
❑7, Jan 1998 ... 2.95
❑8, Feb 1998; Final Issue ... 2.95

Archaic
Fenickx Productions

❑1, ca. 2003, b&w ... 2.99
❑2, ca. 2003, b&w ... 2.99
❑3, ca. 2003, b&w ... 2.99
❑4, ca. 2003, b&w ... 2.99
❑5, ca. 2003, b&w ... 2.99

Archangel
Marvel

❑1, Feb 1996, b&w; wraparound cover .. 2.50

Archangels: The Saga
Eternal

❑1, Mar 1996 ... 2.50
❑1/2nd 1996; 2nd printing ... 2.50
❑2, Aug 1996 ... 2.50
❑3, Aug 1996 ... 2.50
❑4, Nov 1996 ... 2.50
❑5 1996 ... 2.50
❑6 1996 ... 2.50
❑7 1996 ... 2.50
❑8, Oct 1996; Wrap around cover ... 2.50

Archard's Agents
CrossGen

❑1, Jan 2003 ... 2.95

Archenemies
Dark Horse

❑1, May 2006 ... 2.99
❑2, Jun 2006 ... 2.99
❑3, Jul 2006 ... 2.99
❑4, Aug 2006 ... 2.99

Archer & Armstrong
Valiant

❑0, Jul 1992; BL (w); O: Archer & Armstrong 4.00
❑0/Gold, Jul 1992; Gold edition; BL (w); O: Archer & Armstrong ... 25.00
❑1, Aug 1992; FM (c); FM (a); Unity ... 4.00
❑2, Sep 1992; Unity ... 3.00
❑3, Oct 1992 ... 2.00
❑4, Nov 1992 ... 2.00
❑5, Dec 1992 ... 2.00
❑6, Jan 1993 ... 2.00
❑7, Feb 1993 ... 2.00
❑8, Mar 1993; Double-sized: is also "Eternal Warrior #8"; 1: Timewalker (Ivar). Flip-book with Eternal Warrior #8 3.00
❑9, Apr 1993; BL (w); 1: Mademoiselle Noir 2.00
❑10, May 1993 ... 1.00
❑11, Jun 1993 A: Solar ... 1.00
❑12, Jul 1993 ... 1.00
❑13, Aug 1993; Serial number contest .. 1.00
❑14, Sep 1993; Serial number contest... 1.00
❑15, Oct 1993 ... 1.00
❑16, Nov 1993; Serial number contest .. 1.00
❑17, Dec 1993 ... 1.00
❑18, Jan 1994 ... 1.00
❑19, Feb 1994 ... 1.00
❑20, Mar 1994 ... 1.00
❑21, Apr 1994 A: Shadowman ... 1.00
❑22, May 1994; trading card ... 2.00
❑23, Jun 1994 ... 1.00
❑24, Aug 1994 ... 1.00
❑25, Sep 1994 A: Eternal Warrior ... 1.00
❑26, Oct 1994; Flip-book with Eternal Warrior #26;indicia says August ... 5.00

Archie
Archie

❑123, Nov 1961 ... 16.00
❑124, Dec 1961 ... 16.00
❑125, Feb 1962 ... 16.00
❑126, Mar 1962 ... 16.00
❑127, Apr 1962 ... 16.00
❑128, Jun 1962 ... 16.00
❑129, Jul 1962 ... 16.00
❑130, Aug 1962 ... 16.00
❑131, Sep 1962 ... 16.00
❑132, Nov 1962 ... 16.00
❑133, Dec 1962 ... 16.00
❑134, Feb 1963 ... 16.00
❑135, Mar 1963 ... 16.00
❑136, Apr 1963 ... 16.00
❑137, Jun 1963 ... 16.00
❑138, Jul 1963 ... 16.00
❑139, Aug 1963 ... 16.00
❑140, Sep 1963 ... 16.00
❑141, Nov 1963 ... 13.00
❑142, Dec 1963 ... 13.00
❑143, Feb 1964 ... 13.00
❑144, Mar 1964 ... 13.00
❑145, Apr 1964 ... 13.00
❑146, Jun 1964 ... 13.00
❑147, Jul 1964 ... 13.00
❑148, Aug 1964 ... 13.00
❑149, Sep 1964 ... 13.00
❑150, Nov 1964 ... 13.00
❑151, Dec 1964 ... 8.50
❑152, Feb 1965 ... 8.50
❑153, Mar 1965, Caveman Archie story. 8.50
❑154, Apr 1965 ... 8.50
❑155, Jun 1965 ... 8.50
❑156, Jul 1965 ... 8.50
❑157, Aug 1965 ... 8.50
❑158, Sep 1965 ... 8.50
❑159, Nov 1965 ... 8.50
❑160, Dec 1965 ... 8.50
❑161, Feb 1966 ... 8.50
❑162, Mar 1966 ... 8.50
❑163, Apr 1966 ... 8.50
❑164, Jun 1966 ... 8.50
❑165, Jul 1966 ... 8.50
❑166, Aug 1966 ... 8.50
❑167, Sep 1966 ... 8.50
❑168, Nov 1966 ... 8.50
❑169, Dec 1966 ... 8.50
❑170, Feb 1967 ... 8.50
❑171, Mar 1967 ... 8.50
❑172, Apr 1967 ... 8.50
❑173, Jun 1967 ... 8.50
❑174, Jul 1967 ... 8.50
❑175, Aug 1967 ... 8.50
❑176, Sep 1967 ... 8.50
❑177, Nov 1967 ... 8.50
❑178, Dec 1967 ... 8.50
❑179, Feb 1968 ... 8.50
❑180, Mar 1968 ... 8.50
❑181, Apr 1968 ... 5.00
❑182, Jun 1968 ... 5.00
❑183, Jul 1968 ... 5.00
❑184, Aug 1968 ... 5.00
❑185, Sep 1968 ... 5.00
❑186, Nov 1968 ... 5.00
❑187, Dec 1968 ... 5.00
❑188, Feb 1969 ... 5.00
❑189, Mar 1969 ... 5.00
❑190, Apr 1969 ... 5.00
❑191, Jun 1969 ... 5.00
❑192, Jul 1969 ... 5.00
❑193, Aug 1969 ... 5.00
❑194, Sep 1969 ... 5.00
❑195, Nov 1969 ... 5.00
❑196, Dec 1969 ... 5.00
❑197, Feb 1970 ... 5.00
❑198, Mar 1970 ... 5.00
❑199, Apr 1970 ... 5.00
❑200, Jun 1970 ... 5.00
❑201, Jul 1970 ... 3.00
❑202, Aug 1970 ... 3.00
❑203, Sep 1970 ... 3.00
❑204, Nov 1970 ... 3.00
❑205, Dec 1970 ... 3.00
❑206, Feb 1971 ... 3.00
❑207, Mar 1971 ... 3.00
❑208, May 1971 ... 3.00
❑209, Jun 1971 ... 3.00
❑210, Jul 1971 ... 3.00
❑211, Aug 1971 ... 3.00
❑212, Sep 1971 ... 3.00
❑213, Nov 1971 ... 3.00
❑214, Dec 1971 ... 3.00
❑215, Feb 1972 ... 3.00
❑216, Mar 1972 ... 3.00
❑217, Apr 1972 ... 3.00
❑218, Jun 1972 ... 3.00
❑219, Jul 1972 ... 3.00
❑220, Aug 1972 ... 3.00
❑221, Sep 1972 ... 3.00
❑222, Nov 1972 ... 3.00
❑223, Dec 1972 ... 3.00
❑224, Feb 1973 ... 3.00
❑225, Apr 1973 ... 3.00
❑226, Jun 1973 ... 3.00
❑227, Jul 1973 ... 3.00
❑228, Aug 1973 ... 3.00
❑229, Sep 1973 ... 3.00
❑230, Nov 1973 ... 3.00
❑231, Dec 1973 ... 3.00
❑232, Feb 1974 ... 3.00
❑233, Mar 1974 ... 3.00
❑234, Apr 1974 ... 3.00
❑235, Jun 1974 ... 3.00
❑236, Jul 1974 ... 3.00
❑237, Aug 1974 ... 3.00
❑238, Sep 1974 ... 3.00
❑239, Nov 1974 ... 3.00
❑240, Dec 1974 ... 3.00
❑241, Feb 1975 ... 3.00
❑242, Mar 1975 ... 3.00
❑243, Apr 1975 ... 3.00
❑244, Jun 1975 ... 3.00
❑245, Jul 1975 ... 3.00
❑246, Aug 1975 ... 3.00
❑247, Sep 1975 ... 3.00
❑248, Nov 1975 ... 3.00
❑249, Dec 1975 ... 3.00
❑250, Feb 1976 ... 3.00
❑251, Mar 1976 ... 2.00

Other grades: Multiply price above by 5/6 for VF/NM • 2/3 for VERY FINE • 1/3 for FINE • 1/5 for VERY GOOD • 1/8 for GOOD

Amazing Screw-On Head

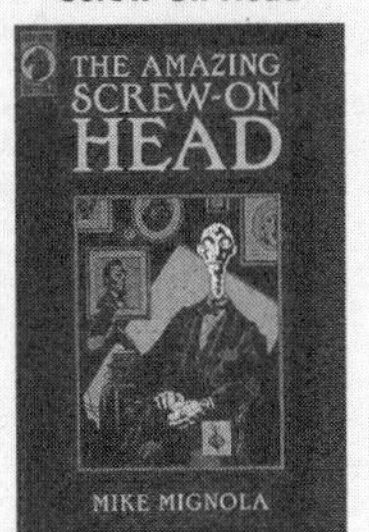

19th-century weirdness from Mike Mignola

©Dark Horse

Amazing Spider-Girl

Peter Parker's progeny in possible future

©Marvel

Amazing Spider-Man

Marvel's flagship series swings high

©Marvel

Amazing Spider-Man

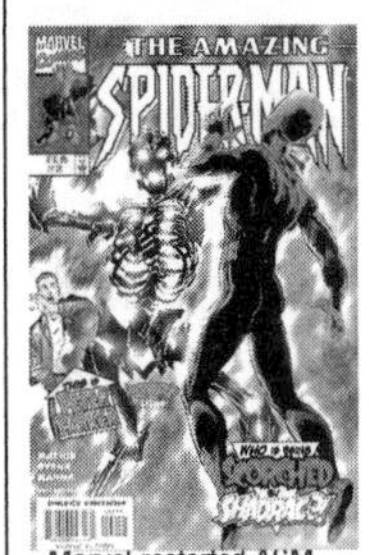

Marvel restarted ASM ... then undid the restart

©Marvel

Amazing Spider-Man Giveaways

Comics giveaway covers child abuse problem

©Marvel

	N-MINT
❑252, Apr 1976	2.00
❑253, Jun 1976	2.00
❑254, Jul 1976	2.00
❑255, Aug 1976	2.00
❑256, Sep 1976	2.00
❑257, Nov 1976	2.00
❑258, Dec 1976	2.00
❑259, Feb 1977	2.00
❑260, Mar 1977	2.00
❑261, Apr 1977	2.00
❑262, Jun 1977	2.00
❑263, Jul 1977	2.00
❑264, Aug 1977	2.00
❑265, Sep 1977	2.00
❑266, Nov 1977	2.00
❑267, Dec 1977	2.00
❑268, Feb 1978	2.00
❑269, Mar 1978	2.00
❑270, Apr 1978	2.00
❑271, Jun 1978	2.00
❑272, Jul 1978	2.00
❑273, Aug 1978	2.00
❑274, Sep 1978	2.00
❑275, Nov 1978	2.00
❑276, Dec 1978	2.00
❑277, Feb 1979	2.00
❑278, Mar 1979	2.00
❑279, Apr 1979	2.00
❑280, May 1979	2.00
❑281, Jun 1979	2.00
❑282, Jul 1979	2.00
❑283, Aug 1979	2.00
❑284, Sep 1979	2.00
❑285, Oct 1979	2.00
❑286, Nov 1979	2.00
❑287, Dec 1979	2.00
❑288, Jan 1980	2.00
❑289, Feb 1980	2.00
❑290, Mar 1980	2.00
❑291, Apr 1980	2.00
❑292, May 1980	2.00
❑293, Jun 1980	2.00
❑294, Jul 1980	2.00
❑295, Aug 1980	2.00
❑296, Sep 1980	2.00
❑297, Oct 1980	2.00
❑298, Nov 1980	2.00
❑299, Dec 1980	2.00
❑300, Jan 1981	2.00
❑301, Feb 1981	1.50
❑302, Mar 1981	1.50
❑303, Apr 1981	1.50
❑304, May 1981	1.50
❑305, Jun 1981	1.50
❑306, Jul 1981	1.50
❑307, Aug 1981	1.50
❑308, Sep 1981	1.50
❑309, Oct 1981	1.50
❑310, Nov 1981	1.50
❑311, Dec 1981	1.50
❑312, Jan 1982	1.50
❑313, Feb 1982	1.50
❑314, Mar 1982	1.50
❑315, Apr 1982	1.50
❑316, May 1982	1.50
❑317, Jun 1982	1.50

	N-MINT
❑318, Jul 1982	1.50
❑319, Sep 1982	1.50
❑320, Nov 1982	1.50
❑321, Jan 1983	1.50
❑322, Mar 1983	1.50
❑323, May 1983	1.50
❑324, Jul 1983	1.50
❑325, Sep 1983	1.50
❑326, Nov 1983	1.50
❑327, Jan 1984	1.50
❑328, Mar 1984	1.50
❑329, May 1984	1.50
❑330, Jul 1984	1.50
❑331, Sep 1984	1.50
❑332, Nov 1984	1.50
❑333, Jan 1985	1.50
❑334, Mar 1985	1.50
❑335, May 1985	1.50
❑336, Jul 1985	1.50
❑337, Sep 1985	1.50
❑338, Nov 1985	1.50
❑339, Jan 1986	1.50
❑340, Mar 1986	1.50
❑341, May 1986	1.50
❑342, Jul 1986	1.50
❑343, Sep 1986	1.50
❑344, Nov 1986	1.50
❑345, Jan 1987	1.50
❑346, Mar 1987	1.50
❑347, May 1987	1.50
❑348, Jun 1987	1.50
❑349, Jul 1987	1.50
❑350, Aug 1987	1.50
❑351, Sep 1987	1.50
❑352, Oct 1987	1.50
❑353, Nov 1987	1.50
❑354, Jan 1988	1.50
❑355, Mar 1988	1.50
❑356, May 1988	1.50
❑357, Jun 1988	1.50
❑358, Jul 1988	1.50
❑359, Aug 1988	1.50
❑360, Sep 1988	1.50
❑361, Oct 1988	1.50
❑362, Nov 1988	1.50
❑363, Jan 1989	1.50
❑364, Feb 1989	1.50
❑365, Mar 1989	1.50
❑366, Apr 1989	1.50
❑367, May 1989	1.50
❑368, Jul 1989	1.50
❑369, Aug 1993	1.50
❑370, Sep 1989	1.50
❑371, Oct 1989	1.50
❑372, Nov 1989	1.50
❑373, Jan 1990	1.50
❑374, Feb 1990	1.50
❑375, Mar 1990	1.50
❑376, Apr 1990	1.50
❑377, May 1990	1.50
❑378, Jul 1990	1.50
❑379, Aug 1990	1.50
❑380, Sep 1990	1.50
❑381, Oct 1990	1.50
❑382, Nov 1990	1.50
❑383, Dec 1990	1.50

	N-MINT
❑384, Feb 1991	1.50
❑385, Mar 1991	1.50
❑386, Apr 1991	1.50
❑387, May 1991	1.50
❑388, Jun 1991	1.50
❑389, Jul 1991	1.50
❑390, Aug 1991	1.50
❑391, Sep 1991	1.50
❑392, Oct 1991	1.50
❑393, Nov 1991	1.50
❑394, Dec 1991	1.50
❑395, Jan 1992	1.50
❑396, Feb 1992	1.50
❑397, Mar 1992	1.50
❑398, Apr 1992	1.50
❑399, May 1992	1.50
❑400, Jun 1992	1.50
❑401, Jul 1992	1.50
❑402, Aug 1992	1.50
❑403, Sep 1992	1.50
❑404, Oct 1992	1.50
❑405, Nov 1992	1.50
❑406, Dec 1992	1.50
❑407, Jan 1993	1.50
❑408, Feb 1993	1.50
❑409, Mar 1993	1.50
❑410, Apr 1993	1.50
❑411, May 1993	1.50
❑412, Jun 1993	1.50
❑413, Jul 1993	1.50
❑414, Aug 1993, prom poster	1.50
❑415, Sep 1993	1.50
❑416, Oct 1993	1.50
❑417, Nov 1993	1.50
❑418, Dec 1993	1.50
❑419, Jan 1994	1.50
❑420, Feb 1994	1.50
❑421, Mar 1994	1.50
❑422, Apr 1994	1.50
❑423, May 1994	1.50
❑424, Jun 1994	1.50
❑425, Jul 1994	1.50
❑426, Aug 1994	1.50
❑427, Sep 1994	1.50
❑428, Oct 1994	1.50
❑429, Nov 1994	1.50
❑430, Dec 1994	1.50
❑431, Jan 1995	1.50
❑432, Feb 1995	1.50
❑433, Mar 1995	1.50
❑434, Apr 1995	1.50
❑435, May 1995	1.50
❑436, Jun 1995	1.50
❑437, Jul 1995	1.50
❑438, Aug 1995	1.50
❑439, Sep 1995	1.50
❑440, Oct 1995	1.50
❑441, Nov 1995	1.50
❑442, Dec 1995, continues in Betty & Veronica #95	1.50
❑443, Jan 1996, Photo cover	1.50
❑444, Feb 1996	1.50
❑445, Mar 1996	1.50
❑446, Apr 1996, Cheryl Blossom Cover.	1.50
❑447, May 1996	1.50
❑448, Jun 1996	1.50

Other grades: Multiply price above by 5/6 for VF/NM • 2/3 for VERY FINE • 1/3 for FINE • 1/5 for VERY GOOD • 1/8 for GOOD

	N-MINT
❑449, Jul 1996	1.50
❑450, Aug 1996	1.50
❑451, Sep 1996	1.50
❑452, Oct 1996	1.50
❑453, Nov 1996	1.50
❑454, Dec 1996	1.50
❑455, Jan 1997	1.50
❑456, Feb 1997	1.50
❑457, Mar 1997	1.50
❑458, Apr 1997	1.50
❑459, May 1997	1.50
❑460, Jun 1997	1.50
❑461, Jul 1997	1.50
❑462, Aug 1997	1.50
❑463, Sep 1997	1.50
❑464, Oct 1997	1.50
❑465, Nov 1997	1.50
❑466, Dec 1997	1.50
❑467, Jan 1998	1.75
❑468, Feb 1998	1.75
❑469, Mar 1998	1.75
❑470, Apr 1998	1.75
❑471, May 1998	1.75
❑472, Jun 1998	1.75
❑473, Jul 1998	1.75
❑474, Aug 1998	1.75
❑475, Sep 1998	1.75
❑476, Oct 1998	1.75
❑477, Nov 1998	1.75
❑478, Dec 1998	1.75
❑479, Jan 1999	1.75
❑480, Feb 1999	1.75
❑481, Mar 1999, DDC (c); DDC (a)	1.75
❑482, Apr 1999	1.79
❑483, May 1999	1.79
❑484, Jun 1999	1.79
❑485, Jul 1999	1.79
❑486, Aug 1999	1.79
❑487, Sep 1999	1.79
❑488, Oct 1999	1.75
❑489, Nov 1999	1.75
❑490, Dec 1999	1.75
❑491, Jan 2000	1.75
❑492, Feb 2000	1.75
❑493, Mar 2000	1.75
❑494, Apr 2000	1.99
❑495, May 2000	1.99
❑496, Jun 2000	1.99
❑497, Jul 2000	1.99
❑498, Aug 2000	1.99
❑499, Sep 2000	1.99
❑500, Oct 2000	1.99
❑501, Nov 2000	1.99
❑502, Dec 2000	1.99
❑503, Jan 2001	1.99
❑504, Feb 2001	1.99
❑505, Mar 2001	1.99
❑506, Apr 2001	1.99
❑507, May 2001	1.99
❑508, Jun 2001	1.99
❑509, Jul 2001	1.99
❑510, Aug 2001	1.99
❑511, Sep 2001	1.99
❑512, Oct 2001	1.99
❑513, Nov 2001	1.99
❑514, Nov 2001	2.19
❑515, Dec 2001	2.19
❑516, Jan 2002	2.19
❑517, Feb 2002	2.19
❑518, Mar 2002	2.19
❑519, Apr 2002	2.19
❑520, May 2002	2.19
❑521, Jun 2002	2.19
❑522, Jul 2002	2.19
❑523, ca. 2002	2.19
❑524, Aug 2002	2.19
❑525, Sep 2002	2.19
❑526, Oct 2002	2.19
❑527, Nov 2002	2.19
❑528, Dec 2002	2.19
❑529, Jan 2003	2.19
❑530, Feb 2003	2.19
❑531, Mar 2003	2.19
❑532, Apr 2003	2.19
❑533, May 2003	2.19
❑534, Jun 2003	2.19
❑535, Jul 2003	2.19

	N-MINT
❑536, Jul 2003	2.19
❑537, Aug 2003	2.19
❑538, Sep 2003, Comic Con Issue	2.19
❑539, Oct 2003	2.19
❑540, Nov 2003	2.19
❑541, Dec 2003	2.19
❑542, Jan 2004	2.19
❑543, Feb 2004	2.19
❑544, Mar 2004	2.19
❑545, Apr 2004, AM (a)	2.19
❑546, May 2004	2.19
❑547, Jun 2004	2.19
❑548, Jul 2004	2.19
❑549, Aug 2004	2.19
❑550, Sep 2004	2.19
❑551, Oct 2004	2.19
❑552, Dec 2004	2.19
❑553, Feb 2005	2.19
❑554, Mar 2005	2.19
❑555, Apr 2005	2.19
❑556, May 2005	2.19
❑557, Jun 2005	2.25
❑558, Jul 2005	2.25
❑559, Aug 2005; Includes Bionicle insert	2.25
❑560, Sep 2005	2.25
❑561, Oct 2005; Includes Bionicle preview	2.25
❑562, Nov 2005	2.25
❑563, Feb 2006	2.25
❑565, Jun 2006	2.25
❑566, Jun 2006	2.25
❑567, Aug 2006	2.25
❑568, Oct 2006	2.25
❑569, Nov 2006	2.25
❑570, Dec 2006	2.25
❑571, Jan 2007	2.25
❑572	2.25
❑573	2.25
❑574	2.25
❑575	2.25
❑576	2.25
❑577	2.25
❑578	2.25
❑579	2.25
❑580	2.25
❑581	2.25
❑582	2.25
❑583	2.25
❑584	2.25
❑585	2.25
❑586	2.25
❑587	2.25
❑588	2.25
❑589	2.25
❑590	2.25
❑591	2.25
❑592	2.25
❑593	2.25
❑594	2.25
❑595	2.50
❑596	2.50
❑597	2.50
❑598	2.50
❑Ann 12, ca. 1961	60.00
❑Ann 13, ca. 1962	58.00
❑Ann 14, ca. 1963	50.00
❑Ann 15, ca. 1964	50.00
❑Ann 16, ca. 1965	26.00
❑Ann 17, ca. 1966	26.00
❑Ann 18, ca. 1967	22.00
❑Ann 19, ca. 1968	22.00
❑Ann 20, ca. 1969	14.00
❑Ann 21, ca. 1970	9.00
❑Ann 22, ca. 1971	9.00
❑Ann 23, ca. 1972	8.00
❑Ann 24, ca. 1973	8.00
❑Ann 25, ca. 1974	8.00
❑Ann 26, ca. 1975	8.00

Archie All Canadian Digest
Archie

	N-MINT
❑1, Aug 1996, digest; reprints Archie stories set in Canada	2.00

Archie and Friends
Archie

	N-MINT
❑1, Dec 1992, A: Great Rondo. A: Hiram Lodge. Great Rondo appearance (Geraldo Rivera parody)	3.00
❑2, Feb 1992	2.00
❑3, Apr 1992	2.00
❑4, Jun 1992	2.00
❑5, Aug 1992	2.00
❑6, Oct 1992, A: Sabrina	2.00
❑7, Mar 1993	2.00
❑8 1993	2.00
❑9, Jun 1994	2.00
❑10, Aug 1994	2.00
❑11, Oct 1994	1.50
❑12, Dec 1994	1.50
❑13, Feb 1995	1.50
❑14, May 1995	1.50
❑15, Aug 1995	1.50
❑16, Nov 1995	1.50
❑17, Feb 1996	1.50
❑18, May 1996	1.50
❑19, Aug 1996, X-Men and E.R. parodies	1.50
❑20, Nov 1996	1.50
❑21, Feb 1997, The class puts on Romeo and Juliet	1.50
❑22, Apr 1997, Friends parody	1.50
❑23, Jun 1997	1.50
❑24, Aug 1997	1.50
❑25, Oct 1997	1.50
❑26, Dec 1997	1.50
❑27, Feb 1998	1.75
❑28, Apr 1998	1.75
❑29, Jun 1998, Pops opens a cyber-cafe	1.75
❑30, Aug 1998	1.75
❑31, Oct 1998	1.75
❑32, Dec 1998	1.75
❑33, Feb 1999	1.75
❑34, Apr 1999	1.75
❑35, Jun 1999	1.79
❑36, Aug 1999	1.79
❑37, Oct 1999	1.79
❑38, Dec 1999	1.79
❑39, Feb 2000	1.79
❑40, Apr 2000	1.79
❑41, Jun 2000	1.79
❑42, Aug 2000	1.99
❑43, Oct 2000	1.99
❑44, Dec 2000	1.99
❑45, Feb 2001	1.99
❑46, Apr 2001	1.99
❑47, Jun 2001	1.99
❑48, Sep 2001,A: Josie & the Pussycats	1.99
❑49, Oct 2001, A: Josie & the Pussycats	1.99
❑50, Nov 2001, A: Josie & the Pussycats	1.99
❑51, ca. 2001, A: Josie & the Pussycats	2.19
❑52, ca. 2001, And The Pussycats	2.19
❑53, Jan 2002, A: Josie & the Pussycats	2.19
❑54, ca. 2002	2.19
❑55, Apr 2002, A: Josie & the Pussycats	2.19
❑56, Jun 2002, A: Josie & the Pussycats	2.19
❑57, Jul 2002	2.19
❑58, Aug 2002, A: Josie & the Pussycats	2.19
❑59, Sep 2002	2.19
❑60, Oct 2002, A: Josie & the Pussycats	2.19
❑61, Oct 2002	2.19
❑62, Nov 2002	2.19
❑63, Dec 2002	2.19
❑64, Jan 2003	2.19
❑65, Feb 2003	2.19
❑66, Mar 2003	2.19
❑67, Apr 2003	2.19
❑68, May 2003	2.19
❑69, Jun 2003	2.19
❑70, Jul 2003	2.19
❑71, Aug 2003	2.19
❑72, Sep 2003, AM (a)	2.19
❑73, Oct 2003	2.19
❑74, Oct 2003	2.19
❑75, Nov 2003	2.19
❑76, Dec 2003	2.19
❑77, Jan 2004	2.19
❑78, Feb 2004	2.19
❑79, Mar 2004	2.19
❑80, Apr 2004	2.19
❑81, Jun 2004	2.19
❑82, Jul 2004, Mr. Weatherbee's past revealed	2.19
❑83, Aug 2004	2.19
❑84, Oct 2004	2.19
❑85, Nov 2004	2.19
❑86, Jan 2005	2.19
❑87, Feb 2005	2.19

Amazing Spider-Man (Public Service Series)

Canadian public-service special issues
©Marvel

Amazing Spider-Man: Soul of the Hunter

Kraven kauses khaos from beyond grave
©Marvel

Amazing Spider-Man Super Special

Venom and Carnage mix it up in special
©Marvel

Amazing X-Men

"Age of Apocalypse" version of The X-Men
©Marvel

Ambush Bug

Corny character started out as a villain
©DC

	N-MINT
❑88, Mar 2005	2.19
❑89, Apr 2005	2.19
❑90, May 2005	2.19
❑91, Jun 2005	2.19
❑92, Jul 2005, Price change	2.25
❑93, Aug 2005	2.25
❑94, Sep 2005	2.25
❑95, Oct 2005, Includes Bionicle comic preview	2.25
❑96, Nov 2006, Includes Heroscape #4 insert	2.25
❑97, Dec 2005	2.25
❑98, Apr 2006	2.25
❑99, May 2006	2.25
❑100, Jul 2006	2.25
❑101, Aug 2006	2.25
❑102, Sep 2006	2.25
❑103, Oct 2006, Archie and Friends: Read Between The Lines; Josie and the Pussycats: Paprazzi Patrol; Katy Keene and Her Sister Mackenzie: Love in Blum	2.25
❑104, Dec 2006	2.25
❑105, Jan 2007, Includes 3-D Heroscape glasses; Includes Teen Titans: Sparktop mini-comic	2.25
❑106, Mar 2007, Includes The Adventures of Finn & Friends backup story	2.25
❑107	2.25
❑108	2.25
❑109	2.25
❑110	2.25
❑111	2.25
❑112	2.25
❑113	2.25
❑114	2.25
❑115	2.25
❑116	2.25
❑117	2.25
❑118	2.25
❑119	2.25
❑120	2.25
❑121	2.25
❑122	2.25
❑123	2.25
❑124	2.25
❑125	2.25
❑126	2.25
❑127	2.25
❑128	2.25
❑129	2.25
❑130	2.25
❑131	2.25
❑132	2.25

Archie and Me
Archie

	N-MINT
❑1, Oct 1964	125.00
❑2, Aug 1965	75.00
❑3, Sep 1965	45.00
❑4, Oct 1965	34.00
❑5, Dec 1965	34.00
❑6, Feb 1966	20.00
❑7, Apr 1966	20.00
❑8, Jun 1966	20.00
❑9, Aug 1966	20.00
❑10, Sep 1966	20.00
❑11, Oct 1966	12.00
❑12, Dec 1966	12.00
❑13, Feb 1967	12.00
❑14, Apr 1967	12.00
❑15, Jun 1967	12.00
❑16, Aug 1967	12.00
❑17, Oct 1967	12.00
❑18, Dec 1967	12.00
❑19, Feb 1968	12.00
❑20, Apr 1968	12.00
❑21, Jun 1968	8.00
❑22, Aug 1968	8.00
❑23, Sep 1968, Summer Camp issue	8.00
❑24, Oct 1968	8.00
❑25, Dec 1968, Election issue	8.00
❑26, Feb 1969, Christmas issue	8.00
❑27, Apr 1969	8.00
❑28, Jun 1969	8.00
❑29, Aug 1969	8.00
❑30, Sep 1969	8.00
❑31, Oct 1969	6.00
❑32, Dec 1969	6.00
❑33, Feb 1970	6.00
❑34, Apr 1970	6.00
❑35, Jun 1970	6.00
❑36, Aug 1970	6.00
❑37, Sep 1970, Japan's Expo 70	6.00
❑38, Oct 1970	6.00
❑39, Dec 1970	6.00
❑40, Feb 1971	6.00
❑41, Apr 1971	4.00
❑42, Jun 1971	4.00
❑43, Aug 1971	4.00
❑44, Sep 1971	4.00
❑45, Oct 1971	4.00
❑46, Dec 1971	4.00
❑47, Feb 1972	4.00
❑48, Apr 1972	4.00
❑49, Jun 1972	4.00
❑50, Aug 1972	4.00
❑51, Sep 1972	3.00
❑52, Oct 1972	3.00
❑53, Dec 1972	3.00
❑54, Feb 1973	3.00
❑55, Apr 1973	3.00
❑56, Jun 1973	3.00
❑57, Jul 1973	3.00
❑58, Aug 1973	3.00
❑59, Sep 1973	3.00
❑60, Oct 1973	3.00
❑61, Dec 1973	3.00
❑62, Jan 1974	3.00
❑63, Feb 1974	3.00
❑64, Apr 1974	3.00
❑65, Jun 1974	3.00
❑66, Jul 1974	3.00
❑67, Aug 1974	3.00
❑68, Sep 1974	3.00
❑69, Oct 1974	3.00
❑70, Dec 1974	3.00
❑71, Jan 1975	2.50
❑72, Feb 1975	2.50
❑73, Apr 1975	2.50
❑74, Jun 1975	2.50
❑75, Jul 1975	2.50
❑76, Aug 1975	2.50
❑77, Sep 1975	2.50
❑78, Oct 1975	2.50
❑79, Dec 1975	2.50
❑80, Jan 1976	2.50
❑81, Feb 1976	1.50
❑82, Apr 1976	1.50
❑83, Jun 1976	1.50
❑84, Jul 1976	1.50
❑85, Aug 1976	1.50
❑86, Sep 1976	1.50
❑87, Oct 1976	1.50
❑88, Dec 1976	1.50
❑89, Jan 1977	1.50
❑90, Feb 1977	1.50
❑91, Apr 1977	1.50
❑92, Jun 1977	1.50
❑93, Jul 1977	1.50
❑94, Aug 1977	1.50
❑95, Sep 1977	1.50
❑96, Oct 1977	1.50
❑97, Dec 1977	1.50
❑98, Jan 1978	1.50
❑99, Feb 1978	1.50
❑100, Apr 1978	1.50
❑101, Jun 1978	1.00
❑102, Jul 1978	1.00
❑103, Aug 1978	1.00
❑104, Sep 1978	1.00
❑105, Oct 1978	1.00
❑106, Dec 1978	1.00
❑107, Jan 1979	1.00
❑108, Feb 1979	1.00
❑109, Apr 1979	1.00
❑110, Jun 1979	1.00
❑111, Jul 1979	1.00
❑112, Aug 1979	1.00
❑113, Sep 1979	1.00
❑114, Oct 1979	1.00
❑115, Dec 1979	1.00
❑116, Jan 1980	1.00
❑117, Feb 1980	1.00
❑118, Apr 1980	1.00
❑119, Jun 1980	1.00
❑120, Jul 1980	1.00
❑121, Aug 1980	1.00
❑122, Sep 1980	1.00
❑123, Oct 1980	1.00
❑124, Dec 1980	1.00
❑125, Feb 1981	1.00
❑126, Apr 1981	1.00
❑127, ca. 1981	1.00
❑128, ca. 1981	1.00
❑129, ca. 1981	1.00
❑130, ca. 1981	1.00
❑131, ca. 1981	1.00
❑132, Feb 1982	1.00
❑133, Apr 1982	1.00
❑134, Jun 1982	1.00
❑135, Aug 1982	1.00
❑136, Oct 1982	1.00
❑137, Dec 1982	1.00
❑138, Feb 1983	1.00
❑139, May 1983	1.00
❑140, ca. 1983	1.00
❑141, ca. 1983	1.00
❑142, ca. 1983	1.00
❑143, Feb 1984, DDC (c)	1.00
❑144, Apr 1984	1.00

Other grades: Multiply price above by 5/6 for VF/NM • 2/3 for VERY FINE • 1/3 for FINE • 1/5 for VERY GOOD • 1/8 for GOOD

N-MINT | N-MINT | N-MINT

❑145, Jun 1984 .... 1.00
❑146, Aug 1984 .... 1.00
❑147, Oct 1984 .... 1.00
❑148, Dec 1984 .... 1.00
❑149, Feb 1985 .... 1.00
❑150, Apr 1985 .... 1.00
❑151, Jun 1985 .... 1.00
❑152, Aug 1985 .... 1.00
❑153, Oct 1985 .... 1.00
❑154, Dec 1985 .... 1.00
❑155, Feb 1986 .... 1.00
❑156, Apr 1986 .... 1.00
❑157, Jun 1986 .... 1.00
❑158, Aug 1986 .... 1.00
❑159, Oct 1986 .... 1.00
❑160, Dec 1986 .... 1.00
❑161, Feb 1987, Final Issue 1.00

Archie... Archie Andrews, Where Are You? Digest Magazine
Archie

❑1, Feb 1977 .... 5.00
❑2, May 1977 .... 3.00
❑3, Aug 1977 .... 3.00
❑4, Nov 1977 .... 3.00
❑5, Feb 1978 .... 3.00
❑6, May 1978 .... 3.00
❑7, Aug 1978 .... 3.00
❑8, Nov 1978, JK (a); reprints story from Adventures of the Fly #1 .... 3.00
❑9, Feb 1979 .... 3.00
❑10, May 1979 .... 3.00
❑11, Aug 1979 .... 2.00
❑12, Nov 1979 .... 2.00
❑13, Feb 1980 .... 2.00
❑14, May 1980 .... 2.00
❑15, Aug 1980 .... 2.00
❑16, Nov 1980 .... 2.00
❑17, Feb 1981 .... 2.00
❑18, May 1981 .... 2.00
❑19, Aug 1981 .... 2.00
❑20, Nov 1981 .... 2.00
❑21, Feb 1982 .... 1.50
❑22, May 1982 .... 1.50
❑23, Aug 1982 .... 1.50
❑24, Nov 1982 .... 1.50
❑25, Feb 1983 .... 1.50
❑26, May 1983 .... 1.50
❑27, Aug 1983 .... 1.50
❑28, Oct 1983 .... 1.50
❑29, Dec 1983 .... 1.50
❑30, Feb 1984 .... 1.50
❑31, Apr 1984 .... 1.50
❑32, Jun 1984 .... 1.50
❑33, Aug 1984 .... 1.50
❑34, Oct 1984 .... 1.50
❑35, Dec 1984 .... 1.50
❑36, Feb 1985 .... 1.50
❑37, Apr 1985 .... 1.50
❑38, Jun 1985 .... 1.50
❑39, Aug 1985 .... 1.50
❑40, Oct 1985 .... 1.50
❑41, Dec 1985 .... 1.50
❑42, Feb 1986 .... 1.50
❑43, Apr 1986 .... 1.50
❑44, Jun 1986 .... 1.50
❑45, Aug 1986 .... 1.50
❑46, Oct 1986 .... 1.50
❑47, Dec 1986 .... 1.50
❑48, Feb 1987 .... 1.50
❑49, Apr 1987 .... 1.50
❑50, Jun 1987 .... 1.50
❑51, Aug 1987 .... 1.50
❑52, Oct 1987 .... 1.50
❑53, Dec 1987 .... 1.50
❑54, Feb 1988 .... 1.50
❑55, Apr 1988 .... 1.50
❑56, Jun 1988 .... 1.50
❑57, Aug 1988 .... 1.50
❑58, Oct 1988 .... 1.50
❑59, Dec 1988 .... 1.50
❑60, Feb 1989 .... 1.50
❑61, Apr 1989 .... 1.50
❑62, Jun 1989 .... 1.50
❑63, Aug 1989 .... 1.50
❑64, Oct 1989 .... 1.50
❑65, Dec 1989 .... 1.50
❑66, Feb 1990 .... 1.50
❑67, Apr 1990 .... 1.50
❑68, Jun 1990 .... 1.50
❑69, Aug 1990 .... 1.50
❑70, Oct 1990 .... 1.50
❑71, Dec 1990 .... 1.50
❑72, Feb 1991 .... 1.50
❑73, Apr 1991 .... 1.50
❑74, Jun 1991 .... 1.50
❑75, Aug 1991 .... 1.50
❑76, Oct 1991 .... 1.50
❑77, Dec 1991 .... 1.50
❑78, Feb 1992 .... 1.50
❑79, Apr 1992 .... 1.50
❑80, Jun 1992 .... 1.50
❑81, Aug 1992 .... 1.50
❑82, Oct 1992 .... 1.50
❑83, Dec 1992 .... 1.50
❑84, Jan 1993 .... 1.50
❑85, Feb 1993 .... 1.50
❑86, Apr 1993 .... 1.50
❑87, Jun 1993 .... 1.50
❑88, Aug 1993 .... 1.50
❑89, Oct 1993 .... 1.50
❑90, Dec 1993 .... 1.50
❑91, Feb 1994 .... 1.75
❑92, Mar 1994 .... 1.75
❑93, May 1994 .... 1.75
❑94, Jul 1994 .... 1.75
❑95, Sep 1994 .... 1.75
❑96, Nov 1994 .... 1.75
❑97, Jan 1995 .... 1.75
❑98, Feb 1995 .... 1.75
❑99, Apr 1995 .... 1.75
❑100, Jun 1995 .... 1.75
❑101, Aug 1995 .... 1.75
❑102, Oct 1995 .... 1.75
❑103, Dec 1995 .... 1.75
❑104, Jan 1996 .... 1.75
❑105, Mar 1996 .... 1.75
❑106, May 1996 .... 1.75
❑107, Aug 1996 .... 1.75
❑108, Nov 1996 .... 1.79
❑109, Feb 1997 .... 1.79
❑110, May 1997 .... 1.79
❑111, Sep 1997 .... 1.79
❑112, Nov 1997 .... 1.79
❑113, Feb 1998 .... 1.95
❑114, May 1998 .... 1.95
❑115, Sep 1998 .... 1.95
❑116, Nov 1998 .... 1.95
❑117, Feb 1999 .... 1.95

Archie As Pureheart the Powerful
Archie

❑1, Sep 1966 .... 55.00
❑2, Nov 1966 .... 35.00
❑3, Jan 1967 .... 25.00
❑4, May 1967, Title changes to Archie as Captain Pureheart 25.00
❑5, Aug 1967 .... 25.00
❑6, Nov 1967 .... 25.00

Archie at Riverdale High
Archie

❑1, Aug 1972 .... 42.00
❑2, Sep 1972 .... 22.00
❑3, Oct 1972 .... 16.00
❑4, Dec 1972 .... 16.00
❑5, Feb 1973 .... 16.00
❑6, Apr 1973 .... 11.00
❑7, Jun 1973 .... 11.00
❑8, Jul 1973 .... 11.00
❑9, Aug 1973 .... 11.00
❑10, Sep 1973 .... 11.00
❑11, Oct 1973 .... 8.00
❑12, Dec 1973 .... 8.00
❑13, Feb 1974 .... 8.00
❑14, Mar 1974 .... 8.00
❑15, Apr 1974 .... 8.00
❑16, Jun 1974 .... 8.00
❑17, Jul 1974 .... 8.00
❑18, Aug 1974 .... 8.00
❑19, Sep 1974 .... 8.00
❑20, ca. 1974 .... 8.00
❑21 .... 5.00
❑22, Feb 1975 .... 5.00
❑23, Mar 1975 .... 5.00
❑24, Apr 1975 .... 5.00
❑25, Jun 1975 .... 5.00
❑26, Jun 1975 .... 5.00
❑27, Aug 1975 .... 5.00
❑28, Sep 1975 .... 5.00
❑29, Oct 1975 .... 5.00
❑30, Nov 1975 .... 5.00
❑31, Dec 1975 .... 4.00
❑32, Jan 1976 .... 4.00
❑33, Feb 1976 .... 4.00
❑34, Mar 1976 .... 4.00
❑35, May 1976 .... 4.00
❑36, Jun 1976 .... 4.00
❑37, Jul 1976 .... 4.00
❑38, Aug 1976 .... 4.00
❑39, Sep 1976 .... 4.00
❑40, Oct 1976 .... 4.00
❑41, Dec 1976 .... 3.00
❑42, ca. 1977 .... 3.00
❑43, Mar 1977 .... 3.00
❑44, May 1977 .... 3.00
❑45, Jun 1977 .... 3.00
❑46, Jul 1977 .... 3.00
❑47, Aug 1977 .... 3.00
❑48, Sep 1977 .... 3.00
❑49, Oct 1977 .... 3.00
❑50, Dec 1977 .... 3.00
❑51, Jan 1978 .... 3.00
❑52, ca. 1978 .... 3.00
❑53, May 1978 .... 3.00
❑54, ca. 1978 .... 3.00
❑55, ca. 1978 .... 3.00
❑56, ca. 1978 .... 3.00
❑57, ca. 1978 .... 3.00
❑58, ca. 1978 .... 3.00
❑59, Dec 1978 .... 3.00
❑60, ca. 1979 .... 3.00
❑61, ca. 1979 .... 2.00
❑62, May 1979 .... 2.00
❑63, ca. 1979 .... 2.00
❑64, ca. 1979 .... 2.00
❑65, ca. 1979 .... 2.00
❑66, ca. 1979 .... 2.00
❑67, ca. 1979 .... 2.00
❑68, Dec 1979 .... 2.00
❑69, ca. 1980 .... 2.00
❑70, ca. 1980 .... 2.00
❑71, May 1980 .... 2.00
❑72, ca. 1980 .... 2.00
❑73, ca. 1980 .... 2.00
❑74, ca. 1980 .... 2.00
❑75, ca. 1980 .... 2.00
❑76, ca. 1980 .... 2.00
❑77, ca. 1980 .... 2.00
❑78, Feb 1981 .... 2.00
❑79, Apr 1981 .... 2.00
❑80, Jun 1981 .... 2.00
❑81, Aug 1981 .... 2.00
❑82, Oct 1981 .... 2.00
❑83, Dec 1981 .... 2.00
❑84, Feb 1982 .... 2.00
❑85, Apr 1982 .... 2.00
❑86, ca. 1982 .... 2.00
❑87 .... 2.00
❑88 .... 2.00
❑89 .... 2.00
❑90 .... 2.00
❑91, May 1983, DDC (c) 2.00
❑92, ca. 1983, DDC (c) 2.00
❑93, ca. 1983 .... 2.00
❑94 .... 2.00
❑95, Feb 1984 .... 2.00
❑96, Apr 1984, Teen smoking issue 2.00
❑97, Jun 1984 .... 2.00
❑98, Aug 1984 .... 2.00
❑99, Oct 1984 .... 2.00
❑100, Dec 1984, 100th anniversary issue 2.00
❑101, Feb 1985 .... 1.00
❑102, Apr 1985 .... 1.00
❑103, Jun 1985 .... 1.00
❑104, Aug 1985 .... 1.00
❑105, Oct 1985 .... 1.00
❑106, Dec 1985 .... 1.00
❑107, Feb 1986 .... 1.00
❑108, Apr 1986 .... 1.00
❑109, Jun 1986 .... 1.00
❑110, Aug 1986, DDC (c) 1.00
❑111, Oct 1986 .... 1.00

Other grades: Multiply price above by 5/6 for VF/NM • 2/3 for VERY FINE • 1/3 for FINE • 1/5 for VERY GOOD • 1/8 for GOOD

Amelia Rules

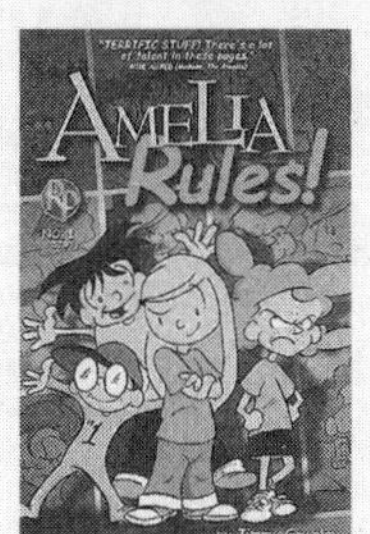

Adventures as pre-teens enter adolescence
©Renaissance

American Century

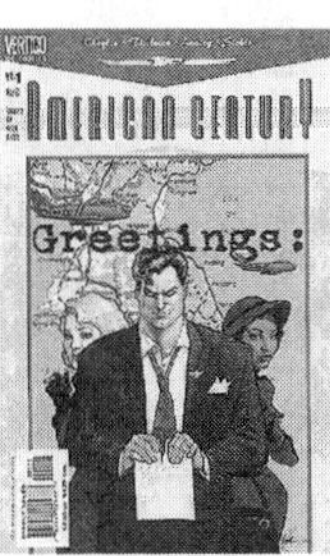

Harry Block travels through America
©DC

American Flagg

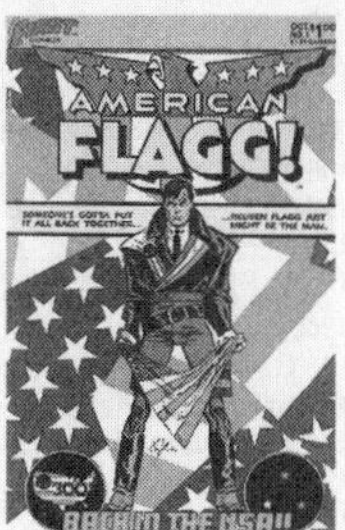

It's 2076, and the world is falling apart...
©First

American Splendor

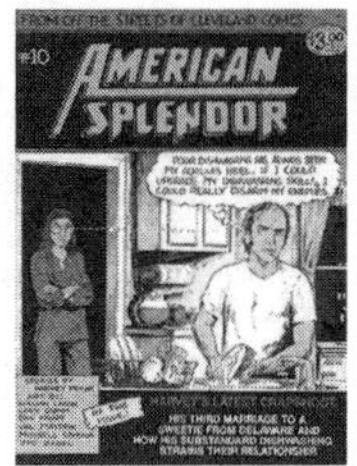

Slice-of-life from gruff Harvey Pekar
©Pekar

America vs. the Justice Society

Reviews All-Star adventures during trial
©DC

	N-MINT
❑112, Dec 1986	1.00
❑113, Feb 1986, DDC (c)	1.00
❑114, ca. 1987, Final Issue	1.00

Archie Digest Magazine
Archie

	N-MINT
❑1, Aug 1973	26.00
❑2, Oct 1973	10.00
❑3, Dec 1973	6.00
❑4, Feb 1974	6.00
❑5, Apr 1974	6.00
❑6, Jun 1974	4.00
❑7, Aug 1974	4.00
❑8, Oct 1974	4.00
❑9, Dec 1974	4.00
❑10, Feb 1975	4.00
❑11, Apr 1975	2.50
❑12, Jun 1975	2.50
❑13, Aug 1975	2.50
❑14, Oct 1975	2.50
❑15, Dec 1975	2.50
❑16, Feb 1976	2.50
❑17, Apr 1976	2.50
❑18, Jun 1976	2.50
❑19, Aug 1976	2.50
❑20, Oct 1976	2.50
❑21, Dec 1976	2.00
❑22, Feb 1977	2.00
❑23, Apr 1977	2.00
❑24, Jun 1977	2.00
❑25, Aug 1977	2.00
❑26, Oct 1977	2.00
❑27, Dec 1977	2.00
❑28, Feb 1978	2.00
❑29, Apr 1978	2.00
❑30, Jun 1978	2.00
❑31, Aug 1978	2.00
❑32, Oct 1978	2.00
❑33, Dec 1978	2.00
❑34, Feb 1979	2.00
❑35, Apr 1979	2.00
❑36, Jun 1979	2.00
❑37, Aug 1979	2.00
❑38, Oct 1979, Reprints Li'l Jinx story featuring comic-book collector paying $1,000 for old Red Circle comics	2.00
❑39, Dec 1979	2.00
❑40, Feb 1980	2.00
❑41, Apr 1980	2.00
❑42, Jun 1980	2.00
❑43, Aug 1980, 75¢ cover	2.00
❑44, Oct 1980	2.00
❑45, Dec 1980	2.00
❑46, Feb 1981	2.00
❑47, Apr 1981	2.00
❑48, Jun 1981	2.00
❑49, Aug 1981	2.00
❑50, Oct 1981	2.00
❑51, Dec 1981	1.50
❑52, Apr 1982	1.50
❑53, Apr 1982	1.50
❑54, Jun 1982	1.50
❑55, Aug 1982	1.50
❑56, Oct 1982	1.50
❑57, Dec 1982	1.50
❑58, Feb 1983	1.50
❑59, Apr 1983	1.50

	N-MINT
❑60, Jun 1983	1.50
❑61, Aug 1983	1.50
❑62, Oct 1983	1.50
❑63, Dec 1983	1.50
❑64, Feb 1984	1.50
❑65, Apr 1984	1.50
❑66, Jun 1984	1.50
❑67, Aug 1984	1.50
❑68, Oct 1984	1.50
❑69, Dec 1984	1.50
❑70, Feb 1985	1.50
❑71, Apr 1985	1.50
❑72, Jun 1985	1.50
❑73, Aug 1985	1.50
❑74, Oct 1985	1.50
❑75, Dec 1985	1.50
❑76, Feb 1986	1.50
❑77, Apr 1986	1.50
❑78, Jun 1986	1.50
❑79, Aug 1986	1.50
❑80, Oct 1986	1.50
❑81, Dec 1986	1.50
❑82, Feb 1987	1.50
❑83, Apr 1987	1.50
❑84, Jun 1987	1.50
❑85, Aug 1987	1.50
❑86, Oct 1987	1.50
❑87, Dec 1987	1.50
❑88, Apr 1988	1.50
❑89, Apr 1988	1.50
❑90, Jun 1988	1.50
❑91, Aug 1988	1.50
❑92, Oct 1988	1.50
❑93, Dec 1988	1.50
❑94, Feb 1989	1.50
❑95, Apr 1989	1.50
❑96	1.50
❑97	1.50
❑98	1.50
❑99	1.50
❑100	1.50
❑101	1.79
❑102	1.79
❑103 1990	1.79
❑104	1.79
❑105	1.79
❑106	1.79
❑107	1.79
❑108	1.79
❑109	1.79
❑110	1.79
❑111	1.79
❑112	1.79
❑113	1.79
❑114	1.79
❑115	1.79
❑116	1.79
❑117	1.79
❑118 1992	1.79
❑119	1.79
❑120	1.79
❑121	1.79
❑122	1.79
❑123	1.79
❑124 1993	1.79
❑125	1.79

	N-MINT
❑126	1.79
❑127	1.79
❑128	1.79
❑129	1.79
❑130	1.79
❑131, Dec 1994, DDC (c)	1.79
❑132, Feb 1995	1.79
❑133, Apr 1995	1.79
❑134, May 1995	1.79
❑135, Jul 1995	1.79
❑136, Sep 1995	1.79
❑137, Nov 1995	1.79
❑138, Jan 1996	1.79
❑139, Mar 1996	1.79
❑140, Apr 1996	1.79
❑141 1996	1.79
❑142 1996	1.79
❑143 1996	1.79
❑144, Dec 1996	1.79
❑145, Jan 1997	1.79
❑146, Mar 1997	1.79
❑147, Apr 1997	1.79
❑148, Jun 1997	1.79
❑149, Aug 1997	1.79
❑150, Sep 1997	1.79
❑151, Nov 1997	1.79
❑152, Jan 1998	1.95
❑153, Mar 1998	1.95
❑154, Apr 1998	1.95
❑155, Jun 1998	1.95
❑156, Jul 1998	1.95
❑157, Sep 1998	1.95
❑158, Oct 1998	1.95
❑159, Dec 1998	1.95
❑160, Jan 1999	1.95
❑161, Mar 1999	1.95
❑162, Apr 1999	1.99
❑163, Jun 1999	1.99
❑164, Jul 1999	1.99
❑165, Sep 1999	1.99
❑166, Oct 1999, DDC (c)	1.99
❑167, Nov 1999	1.99
❑168, Jan 2000	1.99
❑169, Feb 2000	1.99
❑170, Apr 2000	1.99
❑171, Jun 2000	1.99
❑172, Jul 2000	1.99
❑173, Aug 2000	2.19
❑174, Oct 2000	2.19
❑175, Nov 2000	2.19
❑176, Jan 2001	2.19
❑177, Feb 2001	2.19
❑178, Mar 2001	2.19
❑179, Apr 2001	2.19
❑180, Jun 2001	2.19
❑181, Jul 2001	2.19
❑182, Aug 2001	2.19
❑183, Sep 2001	2.19
❑184, Dec 2001	2.39
❑185, Jan 2002	2.39
❑186, Mar 2002	2.39
❑187, Apr 2002	2.39
❑188, May 2002	2.39
❑189, Jul 2002	2.39
❑190, Aug 2002	2.39
❑191, Oct 2002	2.39

Other grades: Multiply price above by 5/6 for VF/NM • 2/3 for VERY FINE • 1/3 for FINE • 1/5 for VERY GOOD • 1/8 for GOOD

	N-MINT
❑192, Nov 2002	2.39
❑193, Dec 2002	2.39
❑194, Feb 2003	2.39
❑195, Mar 2003	2.39
❑196, Apr 2003	2.39
❑197, May 2003	2.39
❑198, Jul 2003	2.39
❑199, Aug 2003	2.39
❑200, Oct 2003	2.39
❑201, Nov 2003	2.39
❑202, Dec 2003	2.39
❑203, Jan 2004	2.39
❑204, Mar 2004	2.39
❑205, Apr 2004	2.39
❑206, Jun 2004	2.39
❑207, Jul 2004	2.39
❑208, Aug 2004	2.39
❑209, Sep 2004	2.39
❑210, Oct 2004	2.39
❑211, Nov 2004	2.39
❑212, Dec 2004	2.39
❑213, Jan 2005	2.39
❑214, Feb 2005	2.39
❑215, Mar 2005	2.39
❑216, Apr 2005	2.39
❑217, May 2005	2.39
❑218, Jun 2005	2.39
❑219, Jul 2005	2.39
❑220, Aug 2005	2.39
❑221, Nov 2005	2.39
❑222, Jan 2006	2.39
❑223, Apr 2006	2.39
❑224, May 2006	2.39
❑225, Jul 2006	2.49
❑226, Aug 2006	2.49
❑227, Sep 2006	2.49
❑228, Oct 2006	2.49
❑229, Dec 2006	2.49
❑230, Jan 2007	2.49
❑231, Feb 2007	2.49
❑232	2.49
❑233	2.49
❑234	2.49
❑235	2.49
❑236	2.49
❑237	2.49
❑238	2.49
❑239	2.49
❑240	2.49
❑241	2.49
❑242	2.49
❑243	2.49
❑244	2.49
❑245	2.49
❑246	2.49
❑247	2.49
❑248	2.49
❑249	2.49
❑250	2.49
❑251	2.49
❑252	2.49
❑253	2.49
❑254	2.49

Archie Giant Series Magazine

Archie

	N-MINT
❑12, ca. 1961, Katy Keene Holiday Fun	125.00
❑13, ca. 1961	140.00
❑14, Dec 1961	110.00
❑15, Mar 1962, Archie's Christmas Stocking (1961)	110.00
❑16, Jun 1962, Betty and Veronica Spectacular	125.00
❑17, Sep 1962, Archie's Jokes	110.00
❑18, ca. 1962	125.00
❑19, ca. 1962	110.00
❑20, Jan 1963, Archie's Christmas Stocking (1962)	100.00
❑21, ca. 1963	85.00
❑22, ca. 1963	60.00
❑23, ca. 1963	80.00
❑24, ca. 1963, The World of Jughead	60.00
❑25, ca. 1964	60.00
❑26, ca. 1964	80.00
❑27, Jun 1964, Archie's Jokes	60.00
❑28, Sep 1964	80.00
❑29, ca. 1964	60.00
❑30, ca. 1964, The World of Jughead	60.00
❑31, ca. 1965	40.00
❑32, ca. 1965	40.00
❑33, ca. 1965	40.00
❑34, ca. 1965, Betty & Veronica Summer Fun	40.00
❑35, ca. 1965, Series continued in #136	40.00
❑136, ca. 1965	40.00
❑137, ca. 1966	40.00
❑138, ca. 1966	40.00
❑139, ca. 1966	40.00
❑140, ca. 1966	40.00
❑141, ca. 1966	40.00
❑142, ca. 1966, O: Captain Pureheart	45.00
❑143, ca. 1967, The World of Jughead	20.00
❑144, ca. 1967	20.00
❑145, ca. 1967	20.00
❑146, ca. 1967, Archie's Jokes	20.00
❑147, ca. 1967, Betty & Veronica Summer Fun	20.00
❑148, ca. 1967	20.00
❑149, ca. 1967, The World of Jughead	20.00
❑150, ca. 1967	20.00
❑151, ca. 1967	20.00
❑152, Feb 1968, The World of Jughead	20.00
❑153, ca. 1968	20.00
❑154, ca. 1968	20.00
❑155, ca. 1968	20.00
❑156, ca. 1968	20.00
❑157, ca. 1968	20.00
❑158, ca. 1969	20.00
❑159, ca. 1969	20.00
❑160, ca. 1969, The World of Archie	20.00
❑161, ca. 1969	12.00
❑162, ca. 1969	12.00
❑163, ca. 1969	12.00
❑164, ca. 1969	12.00
❑165, ca. 1969	12.00
❑166, ca. 1969	12.00
❑167, ca. 1970	12.00
❑168, ca. 1970	12.00
❑169, ca. 1970	12.00
❑170, ca. 1970, Jughead's Eat-Out	12.00
❑171, ca. 1970	12.00
❑172, ca. 1970, The World of Jughead	12.00
❑173, ca. 1970	12.00
❑174, ca. 1970	12.00
❑175, ca. 1970	12.00
❑176, ca. 1970	12.00
❑177, ca. 1970	12.00
❑178, ca. 1970	12.00
❑179, ca. 1971, Archie's Christmas Stocking	12.00
❑180, ca. 1971	12.00
❑181, ca. 1971	10.00
❑182, ca. 1971, The World of Archie	10.00
❑183, ca. 1971, The World of Jughead	10.00
❑184, ca. 1971	10.00
❑185, ca. 1971	10.00
❑186, ca. 1971	10.00
❑187, ca. 1971	10.00
❑188, ca. 1971, The World of Archie	10.00
❑189, ca. 1971	10.00
❑190, ca. 1971	10.00
❑191, ca. 1972	10.00
❑192, ca. 1972	10.00
❑193, ca. 1972	10.00
❑194, ca. 1972	10.00
❑195, ca. 1972	10.00
❑196, ca. 1972	10.00
❑197, Jun 1972	10.00
❑198, ca. 1972, Archie's Jokes	10.00
❑199, ca. 1972	10.00
❑200, ca. 1972, The World of Archie	10.00
❑201, ca. 1972	8.00
❑202, ca. 1972	8.00
❑203, ca. 1972, Archie's Christmas Stocking	8.00
❑204, ca. 1973	8.00
❑205, ca. 1973	8.00
❑206, ca. 1973	8.00
❑207, ca. 1973	8.00
❑208, ca. 1973	8.00
❑209, ca. 1973, The World of Jughead	8.00
❑210, Jun 1973	8.00
❑211, Jul 1973	8.00
❑212, Aug 1973	8.00
❑213, Oct 1973, Archie's Joke Book	8.00
❑214, Nov 1973	8.00
❑215, Nov 1973	8.00
❑216, Dec 1973, Archie's Christmas Stocking (1973)	8.00
❑217, Jan 1974	8.00
❑218, Feb 1974, Archie's Jokebook	8.00
❑219, Mar 1974	8.00
❑220, Apr 1974	8.00
❑221, May 1974	6.00
❑222, Jun 1974, Archie's Jokes	6.00
❑223, Jul 1974	6.00
❑224, Aug 1974	6.00
❑225, Sep 1974	6.00
❑226, Oct 1974	6.00
❑227, Nov 1974	6.00
❑228, Dec 1974, Archie's Christmas Stocking (1974)	6.00
❑229, Jan 1975, Betty & Veronica Christmas Spectacular	6.00
❑230, Feb 1975, Archie's Christmas Love-in	6.00
❑231, Mar 1975, Sabrina's Christmas Magic	6.00
❑232, Apr 1975	6.00
❑233, May 1975	6.00
❑234, Jun 1975	6.00
❑235, ca. 1975	6.00
❑236, ca. 1975, Betty & Veronica Summer Fun	6.00
❑237, ca. 1975	6.00
❑238, ca. 1975, Betty & Veronica Spectacular	6.00
❑239, ca. 1975	6.00
❑240, ca. 1975, Archie's Christmas Stocking (1975)	6.00
❑241, ca. 1975	6.00
❑242, ca. 1976	6.00
❑243, ca. 1976, Sabrina's Christmas Magic	6.00
❑244, ca. 1976	6.00
❑245, ca. 1976, The World of Jughead	6.00
❑246, ca. 1976	6.00
❑247, ca. 1976	6.00
❑248, ca. 1976	6.00
❑249, Sep 1976, The World of Archie	6.00
❑250, Oct 1976, Betty & Veronica Spectacular	6.00
❑251, ca. 1976, Series continued in #452	4.00
❑452, ca. 1976	3.00
❑453, ca. 1976	3.00
❑454, ca. 1976	3.00
❑455, Jan 1977	3.00
❑456, ca. 1977	3.00
❑457, ca. 1977	3.00
❑458, Jun 1977, Betty & Veronica Spectacular	3.00
❑459, Aug 1977, Archie's Jokes	3.00
❑460, Aug 1977	3.00
❑461, Sep 1977, The World of Archie	3.00
❑462, Oct 1977, Betty & Veronica Spectacular	3.00
❑463, Oct 1977, The World of Jughead	3.00
❑464, ca. 1977	3.00
❑465, ca. 1978	3.00
❑466, Jan 1978, Archie's Christmas Love-in	3.00
❑467, ca. 1978	3.00
❑468, Mar 1978, The World of Archie	3.00
❑469, Apr 1978, The World of Jughead	3.00
❑470, Jun 1978	3.00
❑471, Jul 1978	3.00
❑472, Aug 1978	3.00
❑473, Sep 1978	3.00
❑474, Oct 1978	3.00
❑475, Nov 1978	3.00
❑476, Dec 1978	3.00
❑477, Dec 1979, Betty & Veronica Christmas Spectacular	3.00
❑478, Jan 1979, Archie's Christmas Love-in	3.00
❑479, Mar 1979	3.00
❑480, Apr 1979, The World of Archie	3.00
❑481, Apr 1979, The World of Jughead	3.00
❑482, Jun 1979, Betty & Veronica Spectacular	3.00
❑483, Aug 1979, Archie's Jokes	3.00
❑484, Sep 1979, Betty & Veronica Summer Fun	3.00
❑485, Sep 1979, The World of Archie	3.00
❑486, Oct 1979, Betty & Veronica Spectacular	3.00
❑487, Nov 1979, The World of Jughead	3.00
❑488, Dec 1979, Archie's Christmas Stocking (1979)	3.00
❑489, Dec 1980, Betty & Veronica Christmas Spectacular	3.00

Other grades: Multiply price above by 5/6 for VF/NM • 2/3 for VERY FINE • 1/3 for FINE • 1/5 for VERY GOOD • 1/8 for GOOD

Amethyst, Princess of Gemworld

Young girl learns fantasies can come true
©DC

Anarky

Batman troublemaker earns own series
©DC

Angel (2nd Series)

Based on TV Buffy spinoff series
©Dark Horse

Angel and the Ape

Silliness with Angel O'Day and Sam Simeon
©DC

Angel Love

DC's 1980s attempt at romance comic
©DC

	N-MINT
❑490, Jan 1980, Archie's Christmas Love-in	3.00
❑491, Jan 1980, Sabrina's Christmas Magic	3.00
❑492, Mar 1980, The World of Archie	3.00
❑493, Apr 1980, World of Jughead	3.00
❑494, Jun 1980, DDC (c); Betty & Veronica Spectacular	3.00
❑495, Aug 1980, Archie's Jokes	3.00
❑496, Aug 1980, Betty & Veronica Summer Fun	3.00
❑497, Sep 1980, The World of Archie	3.00
❑498, Oct 1980, DDC (c); Betty & Veronica Spectacular	3.00
❑499, Oct 1980, The World of Jughead	3.00
❑500, Dec 1980, DDC (c); Archie's Christmas Stocking (1980)	2.50
❑501, Dec 1981, Betty & Veronica Christmas Spectacular	2.50
❑502, Jan 1981, Archie's Christmas Love-in	2.50
❑503, Jan 1981, Sabrina's Christmas Magic	2.50
❑504, Mar 1981	2.50
❑505, Apr 1981, The World of Jughead	2.50
❑506, ca. 1981	2.50
❑507, ca. 1981, Archie's Jokes	2.50
❑508, ca. 1981	2.50
❑509, ca. 1981	2.50
❑510, ca. 1981, Betty & Veronica Spectacular	2.50
❑511, Oct 1981, The World of Jughead	2.50
❑512, Dec 1981, Archie's Christmas Spectacular (1981)	2.50
❑513, Dec 1981, Betty & Veronica Christmas Spectacular	2.50
❑514, ca. 1982	2.50
❑515, ca. 1982	2.50
❑516, Mar 1982, The World of Archie	2.50
❑517, ca. 1982	2.50
❑518, ca. 1982	2.50
❑519, ca. 1982	2.50
❑520, ca. 1982	2.50
❑521, Sep 1982, The World of Archie	2.50
❑522, ca. 1982	2.50
❑523, ca. 1983	2.50
❑524, ca. 1983	2.50
❑525, ca. 1983	2.50
❑526, ca. 1983	2.50
❑527, ca. 1983	2.50
❑528, ca. 1983	2.50
❑529, ca. 1983	2.50
❑530, ca. 1983	2.50
❑531, ca. 1983	2.50
❑532, ca. 1983	2.50
❑533, ca. 1983	2.50
❑534, ca. 1984	2.50
❑535, ca. 1984	2.50
❑536, ca. 1984	2.50
❑537, ca. 1984	2.50
❑538, ca. 1984	2.50
❑539, ca. 1984	2.50
❑540, ca. 1984	2.50
❑541, Sep 1984, Betty & Veronica Spect.	2.50
❑542, ca. 1984	2.50
❑543, ca. 1984	2.50
❑544, ca. 1984	2.50
❑545, Jan 1984, Little Archie	2.50
❑546, Jan 1984	2.50
❑547, Jan 1984, Betty & Veronica Christmas Spectacular	2.50

	N-MINT
❑548, Jun 1984	2.50
❑549, ca. 1985, Betty & Veronica Spectacular	2.50
❑550, Aug 1985, Betty & Veronica Summer Fun	2.50
❑551, ca. 1985, Josie and the Pussycats	2.00
❑552, ca. 1985	2.00
❑553, ca. 1985	2.00
❑554, ca. 1985	2.00
❑555, Aug 1985, Betty's Diary	2.00
❑556, ca. 1986	2.00
❑557, Jan 1986, Archie's Christmas Stocking (1985)	2.00
❑558, Jan 1986, Betty & Veronica Christmas Spectacular	2.00
❑559, Jun 1986, Betty & Veronica Spectacular	2.00
❑560, Aug 1986, Little Archie	2.00
❑561, ca. 1986	2.00
❑562, ca. 1986	2.00
❑563, ca. 1986	2.00
❑564, ca. 1986	2.00
❑565, ca. 1986	2.00
❑566, ca. 1986	2.00
❑567, ca. 1986	2.00
❑568, ca. 1986	2.00
❑569, ca. 1987	2.00
❑570, Sep 1987, Little Archie	2.00
❑571, ca. 1987	2.00
❑572, ca. 1987	2.00
❑573, ca. 1987	2.00
❑574, ca. 1987	2.00
❑575, ca. 1987	2.00
❑576, ca. 1987	2.00
❑577, ca. 1987	2.00
❑578, ca. 1987	2.00
❑579, ca. 1987	2.00
❑580, Jan 1988, Betty & Veronica Christmas Spectacular	2.00
❑581, ca. 1988	2.00
❑582, ca. 1988	2.00
❑583, ca. 1988	2.00
❑584, ca. 1988	2.00
❑585, ca. 1988	2.00
❑586, ca. 1988	2.00
❑587, ca. 1988	2.00
❑588, ca. 1988	2.00
❑589, ca. 1988	2.00
❑590, Oct 1988, The World of Jughead	2.00
❑591, ca. 1988	2.00
❑592, ca. 1989	2.00
❑593, ca. 1989	2.00
❑594, ca. 1989	2.00
❑595, ca. 1989	2.00
❑596, ca. 1989	2.00
❑597, ca. 1989	2.00
❑598, ca. 1989	2.00
❑599, ca. 1989	2.00
❑600, ca. 1989	2.00
❑601, ca. 1989	1.50
❑602, ca. 1989	1.50
❑603, ca. 1990	1.50
❑604, ca. 1990	1.50
❑605, ca. 1990	1.50
❑606, ca. 1990	1.50

	N-MINT
❑607, ca. 1990, Archie Giant Series Magazine Presents Little Archie; A: Little Sabrina. A: Chester Punkett. A: South-Side Serpents. A: Mad Doctor Doom. A: Sue Stringly. Archie Giant Series Magazine Presents Little Archie	1.50
❑608, ca. 1990	1.50
❑609, ca. 1990	1.50
❑610, ca. 1990	1.50
❑611, ca. 1990	1.50
❑612, ca. 1990	1.50
❑613, ca. 1990	1.50
❑614, Oct 1990, Pep Comics;Archie characters meet Archie Comics staff	1.50
❑615, ca. 1990	1.50
❑616, ca. 1990	1.50
❑617, ca. 1991	1.50
❑618, ca. 1991	1.50
❑619, ca. 1991	1.50
❑620, ca. 1991	1.50
❑621, ca. 1991	1.50
❑622, ca. 1991	1.50
❑623, ca. 1991	1.50
❑624, ca. 1991	1.50
❑625, ca. 1991	1.50
❑626, ca. 1992	1.50
❑627, ca. 1992	1.50
❑628, ca. 1992	1.50
❑629, ca. 1992	1.50
❑630, ca. 1992	1.50
❑631, Jun 1992	1.50
❑632, Jul 1992, Final Issue	1.50

Archie Meets the Punisher
Marvel

	N-MINT
❑1, Aug 1994; JB (a); Archie cover	3.25

Archie's Christmas Stocking
Archie

	N-MINT
❑1, Jan 1994, DDC (a); For 1993 holiday season	2.50
❑2, For 1994 holiday season	2.00
❑3, For 1995 holiday season	2.00
❑4, Apr 1996, For 1996 holiday season	2.00
❑5, For 1997 holiday season	2.25
❑6, Jun 1998, For 1998 holiday season	2.25
❑7, Jul 1999, For 1999 holiday season	2.29

Archie's Date Book
Spire

	N-MINT
❑1, religious	4.00

Archie's Double Digest Magazine
Archie

	N-MINT
❑1, Jan 1982	6.00
❑2, May 1982, DDC (c)	3.50
❑3, Jul 1982, DDC (c)	3.50
❑4, Oct 1982	3.50
❑5, Jan 1983	3.50
❑6, May 1983, DDC (c)	3.50
❑7, Jul 1983, DDC (c)	3.50
❑8, Oct 1983, DDC (c)	3.50
❑9, Jan 1984, DDC (c)	3.50
❑10, May 1984, DDC (c)	3.50
❑11, Jul 1984, DDC (c)	3.00
❑12, Sep 1984, DDC (c)	3.00
❑13, Nov 1984	3.00
❑14, Jan 1985	3.00
❑15, Mar 1985, DDC (c)	3.00

	N-MINT
❑16, May 1985, DDC (c)	3.00
❑17, Jul 1985, DDC (c)	3.00
❑18, Sep 1985, DDC (c)	3.00
❑19, Nov 1985, DDC (c)	3.00
❑20, Jan 1986	3.00
❑21, Mar 1986, DDC (c)	3.00
❑22, May 1986, DDC (c)	3.00
❑23, Jul 1986, DDC (c)	3.00
❑24, Sep 1986, DDC (c)	3.00
❑25, Nov 1986, DDC (c)	3.00
❑26, Jan 1987, DDC (c)	3.00
❑27, Mar 1987, DDC (c)	3.00
❑28, May 1987, DDC (c)	3.00
❑29, Jul 1987, DDC (c)	3.00
❑30, Sep 1987, DDC (c)	3.00
❑31, Nov 1987, DDC (c)	3.00
❑32, Jan 1988, DDC (c)	3.00
❑33, Mar 1988, DDC (c)	3.00
❑34, May 1988, DDC (c)	3.00
❑35, Jul 1988, DDC (c)	3.00
❑36, Sep 1988, DDC (c)	3.00
❑37, Nov 1988, DDC (c)	3.00
❑38, Jan 1989, DDC (c)	3.00
❑39, Mar 1989, DDC (c)	3.00
❑40, May 1989, DDC (c)	3.00
❑41, Jul 1989	3.00
❑42, Sep 1989	3.00
❑43, Nov 1989	3.00
❑44, Jan 1990	3.00
❑45, Mar 1990	3.00
❑46, May 1990	3.00
❑47, Jul 1990	3.00
❑48, Sep 1990	3.00
❑49, Nov 1990	3.00
❑50, Jan 1991	3.00
❑51, Mar 1991	3.00
❑52, May 1991	3.00
❑53, Jul 1991	3.00
❑54, Sep 1991	3.00
❑55, Nov 1991	3.00
❑56, Dec 1991	3.00
❑57, Feb 1992	3.00
❑58, Apr 1992	3.00
❑59, Jun 1992	3.00
❑60, Aug 1992	3.00
❑61, Sep 1992	3.00
❑62, Nov 1992	3.00
❑63, Jan 1993	3.00
❑64, Mar 1993	3.00
❑65, May 1993	3.00
❑66, Jul 1993	3.00
❑67, Sep 1993	3.00
❑68, Oct 1993	3.00
❑69, Dec 1993	3.00
❑70, Feb 1994	3.00
❑71, Apr 1994	3.00
❑72, Jun 1994	3.00
❑73, Aug 1994	3.00
❑74, Oct 1994	3.00
❑75, Nov 1994	3.00
❑76, Jan 1995	3.00
❑77, Mar 1995	3.00
❑78, May 1995	3.00
❑79, Jul 1995	3.00
❑80, Aug 1995	2.75
❑81, Oct 1995	2.75
❑82, Dec 1995	2.75
❑83, Feb 1996	2.75
❑84, Apr 1996	2.75
❑85, May 1996	2.75
❑86, Jul 1996	2.75
❑87, Sep 1996	2.75
❑88, Oct 1996	2.75
❑89, Dec 1996	2.75
❑90, Feb 1997	2.75
❑91, Mar 1997	2.75
❑92, May 1997	2.75
❑93, Jul 1997	2.75
❑94, Aug 1997	2.75
❑95, Oct 1997	2.75
❑96, Dec 1997	2.75
❑97, Feb 1998	2.75
❑98, Mar 1998	2.75
❑99, May 1998	2.75
❑100, Jul 1998	2.75
❑101, Aug 1998	2.75
❑102, Sep 1998	2.75

	N-MINT
❑103, Nov 1998, DDC (w)	2.95
❑104, Dec 1998	2.95
❑105, Feb 1999	2.95
❑106, Apr 1999	2.95
❑107, May 1999	2.99
❑108, Jun 1999	2.99
❑109, Aug 1999	2.99
❑110, Sep 1999	2.99
❑111, Nov 1999	2.95
❑112, Dec 1999	2.99
❑113, Feb 2000	2.95
❑114, Mar 2000	2.99
❑115, May 2000	2.95
❑116, Jul 2000	2.95
❑117, Aug 2000	3.19
❑118, Sep 2000	3.19
❑119, Nov 2000	3.19
❑120, Dec 2000	3.19
❑121, Jan 2001	3.19
❑122, Mar 2001	3.19
❑123, Apr 2001	3.29
❑124, May 2001	3.29
❑125, Jul 2001	3.29
❑126, Aug 2001	3.29
❑127, Sep 2001	3.29
❑128, Nov 2001	3.29
❑129, Dec 2001	3.29
❑130, Jan 2002	3.29
❑131, Mar 2002	3.29
❑132, Apr 2002	3.29
❑133, May 2002	3.29
❑134, Jul 2002	3.29
❑135, Aug 2002	3.29
❑136, Sep 2002	3.29
❑137, Nov 2002	3.29
❑138, Dec 2002	3.29
❑139, Jan 2003	3.59
❑140, Mar 2003	3.59
❑141, Apr 2003	3.59
❑142, May 2003	3.59
❑143, Jul 2003	3.59
❑144, Sep 2003	3.59
❑145, Oct 2003	3.59
❑146, Nov 2003	3.59
❑147, Jan 2004	3.59
❑148, Feb 2004, AM (a)	3.59
❑149, Mar 2004	3.59
❑150, May 2004, AM (a)	3.59
❑151, Jun 2004	3.59
❑152, Jul 2004	3.59
❑153, Aug 2004	3.59
❑154, Sep 2004	3.59
❑155, Oct 2004	3.59
❑156, Nov 2004	3.59
❑157, Dec 2004	3.59
❑158, Jan 2005	3.59
❑159, May 2005	3.59
❑160, May 2005	3.59
❑161, Jun 2005	3.59
❑162, Jul 2005	3.59
❑163, Aug 2005	3.59
❑164, Sep 2005	3.59
❑165, Oct 2005	3.59
❑166, Jan 2006	3.59
❑167, Feb 2006	3.59
❑168, May 2006	3.59
❑169, Jun 2006	3.59
❑170, Jun 2006	3.69
❑171, Aug 2006	3.69
❑172, Oct 2006	3.69
❑173, Oct 2006	3.69
❑174, Nov 2006	3.69
❑175, Jan 2007	3.69
❑176	3.69
❑177	3.69
❑178	3.69
❑179	3.69
❑180	3.69
❑181	3.69
❑182	3.69
❑183	3.69
❑184	3.69
❑185	3.69
❑186	3.69
❑187	3.69
❑188	3.69
❑189	3.69

	N-MINT
❑190	3.69
❑191	3.69
❑192	3.69
❑193	3.69
❑194	3.69
❑195	3.69
❑196	3.69
❑197	3.69
❑198	3.69
❑199	3.69

Archie's Family Album
Spire

	N-MINT
❑1, ca. 1978	4.00

Archie's Girls Betty & Veronica
Archie

	N-MINT
❑71, Nov 1961	32.00
❑72, Dec 1961	32.00
❑73, Jan 1962	32.00
❑74, Feb 1962	32.00
❑75, Mar 1962	32.00
❑76, Apr 1962	32.00
❑77, May 1962	32.00
❑78, Jun 1962	32.00
❑79, Jul 1962	32.00
❑80, Aug 1962	32.00
❑81, Sep 1962	32.00
❑82, Oct 1962	32.00
❑83, Nov 1962	32.00
❑84, Dec 1962	32.00
❑85, Jan 1963	32.00
❑86, Feb 1963	32.00
❑87, Mar 1963	32.00
❑88, Apr 1963	32.00
❑89, May 1963	32.00
❑90, Jun 1963	32.00
❑91, Jul 1963	24.00
❑92, Aug 1963	24.00
❑93, Sep 1963	24.00
❑94, Oct 1963	24.00
❑95, Nov 1963	24.00
❑96, Dec 1963	24.00
❑97, Jan 1964	24.00
❑98, Feb 1964	24.00
❑99, Mar 1964	24.00
❑100, Apr 1964	24.00
❑101, May 1964	24.00
❑102, Jun 1964	24.00
❑103, Jul 1964	24.00
❑104, Aug 1964	24.00
❑105, Sep 1964	24.00
❑106, Oct 1964	24.00
❑107, Nov 1964	24.00
❑108, Dec 1964	24.00
❑109, Jan 1965	24.00
❑110, Feb 1965	24.00
❑111, Mar 1965	16.00
❑112, Apr 1965	16.00
❑113, May 1965	16.00
❑114, Jun 1965	16.00
❑115, Jul 1965	16.00
❑116, Aug 1965	16.00
❑117, Sep 1965	16.00
❑118, Oct 1965	16.00
❑119, Nov 1965	16.00
❑120, Dec 1965	16.00
❑121, Jan 1966	16.00
❑122, Feb 1966	16.00
❑123, Mar 1966	16.00
❑124, Apr 1966	16.00
❑125, May 1966	16.00
❑126, Jun 1966	16.00
❑127, Jul 1966	16.00
❑128, Aug 1966	16.00
❑129, Sep 1966	16.00
❑130, Oct 1966	16.00
❑131, Nov 1966	16.00
❑132, Dec 1966	16.00
❑133, Jan 1967	16.00
❑134, Feb 1967	16.00
❑135, Mar 1967	16.00
❑136, Apr 1967	16.00
❑137, May 1967	16.00
❑138, Jun 1967	16.00
❑139, Jul 1967	16.00
❑140, Aug 1967	16.00
❑141, Sep 1967	13.00

Other grades: Multiply price above by 5/6 for VF/NM • 2/3 for VERY FINE • 1/3 for FINE • 1/5 for VERY GOOD • 1/8 for GOOD

Anima	Animal Man	Animal Mystic	Animaniacs	Animax
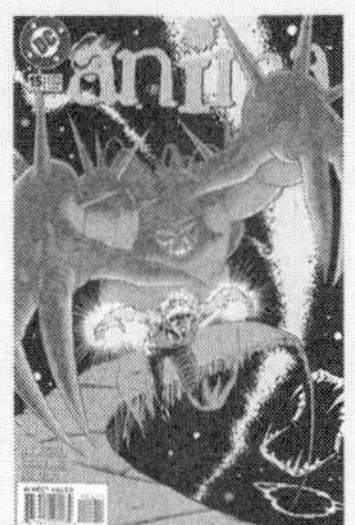				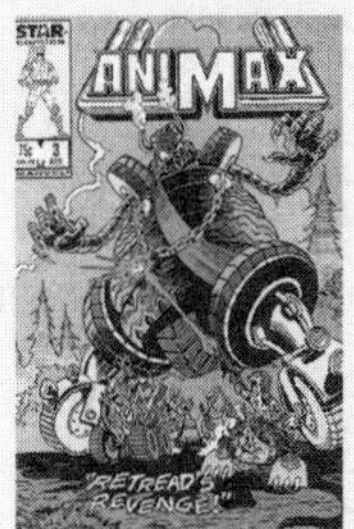
Troubled teen gets super-hero treatment	Series that made a name for Grant Morrison	California girl awakens as a goddess	Based on frenetic Warner Bros. cartoon	Star title inspired by a line of toys
©DC	©DC	©Cry for Dawn	©DC	©Marvel

	N-MINT
❑142, Oct 1967	13.00
❑143, Nov 1967	13.00
❑144, Dec 1967	13.00
❑145, Jan 1968	13.00
❑146, Feb 1968	13.00
❑147, Mar 1968	13.00
❑148, Apr 1968	13.00
❑149, May 1968	13.00
❑150, Jun 1968	13.00
❑151, Jul 1968	13.00
❑152, Aug 1968	13.00
❑153, Sep 1968	13.00
❑154, Oct 1968	13.00
❑155, Nov 1968	13.00
❑156, Dec 1968	13.00
❑157, Jan 1969	13.00
❑158, Feb 1969	13.00
❑159, Mar 1969	13.00
❑160, Apr 1969	13.00
❑161, May 1969	10.00
❑162, Jun 1969	10.00
❑163, Jul 1969	10.00
❑164, Aug 1969	10.00
❑165, Sep 1969	10.00
❑166, Oct 1969	10.00
❑167, Nov 1969	10.00
❑168, Dec 1969	10.00
❑169, Jan 1970	10.00
❑170, Feb 1970	10.00
❑171, Mar 1970	10.00
❑172, Apr 1970	10.00
❑173, May 1970	10.00
❑174, Jun 1970	10.00
❑175, Jul 1970	10.00
❑176, Aug 1970	10.00
❑177, Sep 1970	10.00
❑178, Oct 1970	10.00
❑179, Nov 1970	10.00
❑180, Dec 1970	10.00
❑181, Jan 1971	7.00
❑182, Feb 1971	7.00
❑183, Mar 1971	7.00
❑184, Apr 1971	7.00
❑185, May 1971	7.00
❑186, Jun 1971	7.00
❑187, Jul 1971	7.00
❑188, Aug 1971	7.00
❑189, Sep 1971	7.00
❑190, Oct 1971	7.00
❑191, Nov 1971	7.00
❑192, Dec 1971	7.00
❑193, Jan 1972	7.00
❑194, Feb 1972	7.00
❑195, Mar 1972	7.00
❑196, Apr 1972	7.00
❑197, May 1972	7.00
❑198, Jun 1972	7.00
❑199, Jul 1972	7.00
❑200, Aug 1972	7.00
❑201, Sep 1972	5.00
❑202, Oct 1972	5.00
❑203, Nov 1972	5.00
❑204, Dec 1972	5.00
❑205, Jan 1973	5.00
❑206, Feb 1973	5.00
❑207, Mar 1973	5.00
❑208, Apr 1973	5.00
❑209, May 1973	5.00
❑210, Jun 1973	5.00
❑211, Jul 1973	5.00
❑212, Aug 1973	5.00
❑213, Sep 1973	5.00
❑214, Oct 1973	5.00
❑215, Nov 1973	5.00
❑216, Dec 1973	5.00
❑217, Jan 1974	5.00
❑218, Feb 1974	5.00
❑219, Mar 1974	5.00
❑220, Apr 1974	5.00
❑221, May 1974	5.00
❑222, Jun 1974	5.00
❑223, Jul 1974	5.00
❑224, Aug 1974	5.00
❑225, Sep 1974	5.00
❑226, Oct 1974	5.00
❑227, Nov 1974	5.00
❑228, Dec 1974	5.00
❑229, Jan 1975	5.00
❑230, Feb 1975	5.00
❑231, Mar 1975	5.00
❑232, Apr 1975	5.00
❑233, May 1975	5.00
❑234, Jun 1975	5.00
❑235, Jul 1975	5.00
❑236, Aug 1975	5.00
❑237, Sep 1975	5.00
❑238, Oct 1975	5.00
❑239, Nov 1975	5.00
❑240, Dec 1975	5.00
❑241, Jan 1976	5.00
❑242, Feb 1976	5.00
❑243, Mar 1976	5.00
❑244, Apr 1976	5.00
❑245, May 1976	5.00
❑246, Jun 1976	5.00
❑247, Jul 1976	5.00
❑248, Aug 1976	5.00
❑249, Sep 1976	5.00
❑250, Oct 1976	5.00
❑251, Nov 1976	3.00
❑252, Dec 1976	3.00
❑253, Jan 1977	3.00
❑254, Feb 1977	3.00
❑255, Mar 1977	3.00
❑256, Apr 1977	3.00
❑257, May 1977	3.00
❑258, Jun 1977	3.00
❑259, Jul 1977	3.00
❑260, Aug 1977	3.00
❑261, Sep 1977	3.00
❑262, Oct 1977	3.00
❑263, Nov 1977	3.00
❑264, Dec 1977	3.00
❑265, Jan 1978	3.00
❑266, Feb 1978	3.00
❑267, Mar 1978	3.00
❑268, Apr 1978	3.00
❑269, May 1978	3.00
❑270, Jun 1978	3.00
❑271, Jul 1978	3.00
❑272, Aug 1978	3.00
❑273, Sep 1978	3.00
❑274, Oct 1978	3.00
❑275, Nov 1978	3.00
❑276, Dec 1978	3.00
❑277, Jan 1979	3.00
❑278, Feb 1979	3.00
❑279, Mar 1979	3.00
❑280, Apr 1979	3.00
❑281, May 1979	3.00
❑282, Jun 1979	3.00
❑283, Jul 1979	3.00
❑284, Aug 1979	3.00
❑285, Sep 1979	3.00
❑286, Oct 1979	3.00
❑287, Nov 1979	3.00
❑288, Dec 1979	3.00
❑289, Jan 1980	3.00
❑290, Feb 1980	3.00
❑291, Mar 1980	3.00
❑292, Apr 1980	3.00
❑293, May 1980	3.00
❑294, Jun 1980	3.00
❑295, Jul 1980	3.00
❑296, Aug 1980	3.00
❑297, Sep 1980	3.00
❑298, Oct 1980	3.00
❑299, Nov 1980	3.00
❑300, Dec 1980	3.00
❑301, Jan 1981	2.50
❑302, Feb 1981	2.50
❑303, Mar 1981	2.50
❑304, Apr 1981	2.50
❑305, May 1981	2.50
❑306, Jun 1981	2.50
❑307, Jul 1981	2.50
❑308, Aug 1981	2.50
❑309, Sep 1981	2.50
❑310, Oct 1981	2.50
❑311, Nov 1981	2.50
❑312, Dec 1981	2.50
❑313, Jan 1982	2.50
❑314, Feb 1982	2.50
❑315, Mar 1982	2.50
❑316, Apr 1982	2.50
❑317, May 1982	2.50
❑318, Jun 1982	2.50
❑319, Aug 1982	2.50
❑320, Oct 1982, 1: Cheryl Blossom	8.00
❑321, Dec 1982	4.00
❑322, Feb 1983	3.00
❑323, Apr 1983	3.00
❑324, Jun 1983	2.50
❑325, Aug 1983	2.50
❑326, Oct 1983	2.50
❑327, Dec 1983	2.50
❑328, Feb 1984	2.50
❑329, Apr 1984	2.50
❑330, Jun 1984	2.50
❑331, Aug 1984	2.50
❑332, Oct 1984	2.50
❑333, Dec 1984	2.50
❑334, Feb 1985	2.50
❑335, Apr 1985	2.50
❑336, Jun 1985	2.50
❑337, Aug 1985	2.50
❑338, Oct 1985	2.50
❑339, Dec 1985	2.50

Other grades: Multiply price above by 5/6 for VF/NM • 2/3 for VERY FINE • 1/3 for FINE • 1/5 for VERY GOOD • 1/8 for GOOD

	N-MINT
❑340, Feb 1986	2.50
❑341, Apr 1986	2.50
❑342, Jun 1986	2.50
❑343, Aug 1986	2.50
❑344, Oct 1986	2.50
❑345, Dec 1986	2.50
❑346, Feb 1987	2.50
❑347, Apr 1987	2.50

Archie's Holiday Fun Digest Magazine
Archie

	N-MINT
❑1, Feb 1997	1.95
❑2, Feb 1998	1.95
❑3, Feb 1999	1.95
❑4, Feb 2000	1.99
❑5, Jan 2001	2.19
❑6, Jan 2002	2.19
❑7, Jan 2003	2.19
❑8, Dec 2003	2.39
❑9, Dec 2004	2.39
❑10, Jan 2005	2.39
❑11, Dec 2006	2.50

Archie's Jokebook Magazine
Archie

	N-MINT
❑59, Dec 1961	35.00
❑60, Feb 1962	35.00
❑61, Apr 1962	24.00
❑62, Jun 1962	24.00
❑63, Jul 1962	24.00
❑64, Aug 1962	24.00
❑65, Sep 1962	24.00
❑66, Oct 1962	24.00
❑67, Dec 1962	24.00
❑68, Feb 1963	24.00
❑69, Apr 1963	24.00
❑70, Jun 1963	24.00
❑71, Jul 1963	16.00
❑72, Aug 1963	16.00
❑73, Sep 1963	16.00
❑74, Oct 1963	16.00
❑75, Dec 1963	16.00
❑76, Feb 1964	16.00
❑77, Apr 1964	16.00
❑78, Jun 1964	16.00
❑79, Jul 1964	16.00
❑80, Aug 1964	16.00
❑81, Sep 1964	12.00
❑82, Oct 1964	12.00
❑83, Dec 1964	12.00
❑84, Jan 1965	12.00
❑85, Feb 1965	12.00
❑86, Mar 1965	12.00
❑87, Apr 1965	12.00
❑88, May 1965	12.00
❑89, Jun 1965	12.00
❑90, Jul 1965	12.00
❑91, Aug 1965	8.00
❑92, Sep 1965	8.00
❑93, Oct 1965	8.00
❑94, Nov 1965	8.00
❑95, Dec 1965	8.00
❑96, Jan 1966	8.00
❑97, Feb 1966	8.00
❑98, Mar 1966	8.00
❑99, Apr 1966	8.00
❑100, May 1966	8.00
❑101, Jun 1966	5.00
❑102, Jul 1966	5.00
❑103, Aug 1966	5.00
❑104, Sep 1966	5.00
❑105, Oct 1966	5.00
❑106, Nov 1966	5.00
❑107, Dec 1966	5.00
❑108, Jan 1967	5.00
❑109, Feb 1967	5.00
❑110, Mar 1967	5.00
❑111, Apr 1967	5.00
❑112, May 1967	5.00
❑113, Jun 1967	5.00
❑114, Jul 1967	5.00
❑115, Aug 1967	5.00
❑116, Aug 1967	5.00
❑117, Oct 1967	5.00
❑118, Nov 1967	5.00
❑119, Dec 1967	5.00
❑120, Jan 1968	5.00
❑121, Feb 1968	3.00
❑122, Mar 1968	3.00
❑123, Apr 1968	3.00
❑124, May 1968	3.00
❑125, Jun 1968	3.00
❑126, Jul 1968	3.00
❑127, Aug 1968	3.00
❑128, Sep 1968	3.00
❑129, Oct 1968	3.00
❑130, Nov 1968	3.00
❑131, Dec 1968	3.00
❑132, Jan 1969	3.00
❑133, Feb 1969	3.00
❑134, Mar 1969	3.00
❑135, Apr 1969	3.00
❑136, May 1969	3.00
❑137, Jun 1969	3.00
❑138, Jul 1969	3.00
❑139, Aug 1969	3.00
❑140, Sep 1969	3.00
❑141, Oct 1969	3.00
❑142, Nov 1969	3.00
❑143, Dec 1969	3.00
❑144, Jan 1970	3.00
❑145, Feb 1970	3.00
❑146, Mar 1970	3.00
❑147, Apr 1970	3.00
❑148, May 1970	3.00
❑149, Jun 1970	3.00
❑150, Jul 1970	3.00
❑151, Aug 1970	2.00
❑152, Sep 1970	2.00
❑153, Oct 1970	2.00
❑154, Nov 1970	2.00
❑155, Dec 1970	2.00
❑156, Jan 1971	2.00
❑157, Feb 1971	2.00
❑158, Mar 1971	2.00
❑159, Apr 1971	2.00
❑160, May 1971	2.00
❑161, Jun 1971	2.00
❑162, Jul 1971	2.00
❑163, Aug 1971	2.00
❑164, Sep 1971	2.00
❑165, Oct 1971	2.00
❑166, Nov 1971	2.00
❑167, Dec 1971	2.00
❑168, Jan 1972	2.00
❑169, Feb 1972	2.00
❑170, Mar 1972	2.00
❑171, Apr 1972	2.00
❑172, May 1972	2.00
❑173, Jun 1972	2.00
❑174, Jul 1972	2.00
❑175, Aug 1972	2.00
❑176, Sep 1972	2.00
❑177, Oct 1972	2.00
❑178, Nov 1972	2.00
❑179, Dec 1972	2.00
❑180, Jan 1973	2.00
❑181, Feb 1973	1.50
❑182, Mar 1973	1.50
❑183, Apr 1973	1.50
❑184, May 1973	1.50
❑185, Jun 1973	1.50
❑186, Jul 1973	1.50
❑187, Aug 1973	1.50
❑188, Sep 1973	1.50
❑189, Oct 1973	1.50
❑190, Nov 1973	1.50
❑191, Dec 1973	1.50
❑192, Jan 1974	1.50
❑193, Feb 1974	1.50
❑194, Mar 1974	1.50
❑195, Apr 1974	1.50
❑196, May 1974	1.50
❑197, Jun 1974	1.50
❑198, Jul 1974	1.50
❑199, Aug 1974	1.50
❑200, Sep 1974	1.50
❑201, Oct 1974	1.00
❑202, Nov 1974	1.00
❑203, Dec 1974	1.00
❑204, Jan 1975	1.00
❑205, Feb 1975	1.00
❑206, Mar 1975	1.00
❑207, Apr 1975	1.00
❑208, May 1975	1.00
❑209, Jun 1975	1.00
❑210, Jul 1975	1.00
❑211, Aug 1975	1.00
❑212, Sep 1975	1.00
❑213, Oct 1975	1.00
❑214, Nov 1975	1.00
❑215, Dec 1975	1.00
❑216, Jan 1976	1.00
❑217, Feb 1976	1.00
❑218, Mar 1976	1.00
❑219, Apr 1976	1.00
❑220, May 1976	1.00
❑221, Jun 1976	1.00
❑222, Jul 1976	1.00
❑223, Aug 1976	1.00
❑224, Sep 1976	1.00
❑225, Oct 1976	1.00
❑226, Nov 1976	1.00
❑227, Dec 1976	1.00
❑228, Jan 1977	1.00
❑229, Feb 1977	1.00
❑230, Mar 1977	1.00
❑231, Apr 1977	1.00
❑232, May 1977	1.00
❑233, Jun 1977	1.00
❑234, Jul 1977	1.00
❑235, Aug 1977	1.00
❑236, Sep 1977	1.00
❑237, Oct 1977	1.00
❑238, Nov 1977	1.00
❑239, Dec 1977	1.00
❑240, Jan 1978	1.00
❑241, Feb 1978	1.00
❑242, Mar 1978	1.00
❑243, Apr 1978	1.00
❑244, May 1978	1.00
❑245, Jun 1978	1.00
❑246, Jul 1978	1.00
❑247, Aug 1978	1.00
❑248, Sep 1978	1.00
❑249, Oct 1978	1.00
❑250, Nov 1978	1.00
❑251, Dec 1978	1.00
❑252, Jan 1979	1.00
❑253, Feb 1979	1.00
❑254, Mar 1979	1.00
❑255, Apr 1979	1.00
❑256, May 1979	1.00
❑257, Jun 1979	1.00
❑258, Jul 1979	1.00
❑259, Aug 1979	1.00
❑260, Sep 1979	1.00
❑261, Oct 1979	1.00
❑262, Nov 1979	1.00
❑263, Dec 1979	1.00
❑264, Jan 1980	1.00
❑265, Feb 1980	1.00
❑266, Mar 1980	1.00
❑267, Apr 1980	1.00
❑268, May 1980	1.00
❑269, Jun 1980	1.00
❑270, Jul 1980	1.00
❑271, Aug 1980	1.00
❑272, Sep 1980	1.00
❑273, Nov 1980	1.00
❑274, Jan 1981	1.00
❑275, Mar 1981	1.00
❑276, May 1981	1.00
❑277, Jun 1981	1.00
❑278, Jul 1981	1.00
❑279, Aug 1981	1.00
❑280, Sep 1981	1.00
❑281, Oct 1981	1.00
❑282, Nov 1981	1.00
❑283, Jan 1982	1.00
❑284, Mar 1982	1.00
❑285, May 1982	1.00
❑286, Jul 1982	1.00
❑287, Sep 1982	1.00
❑288, Nov 1982, Final Issue	1.00

Archie's Love Scene
Spire

	N-MINT
❑1, ca. 1973	5.00

Archie's Madhouse
Archie

	N-MINT
❑16, Dec 1961	23.00

Other grades: Multiply price above by 5/6 for VF/NM • 2/3 for VERY FINE • 1/3 for FINE • 1/5 for VERY GOOD • 1/8 for GOOD

Anthro	Apathy Kat	Ape Nation	Aphrodite IX	Aquaman (1st Series)
 Life at the dawn of human history ©DC	 Jazzy cartoon humor from Harold Buchholz ©Express	 Alien Nation meets Planet of the Apes. Really! ©Adventure	 Green-haired killer questions her own existence ©Image	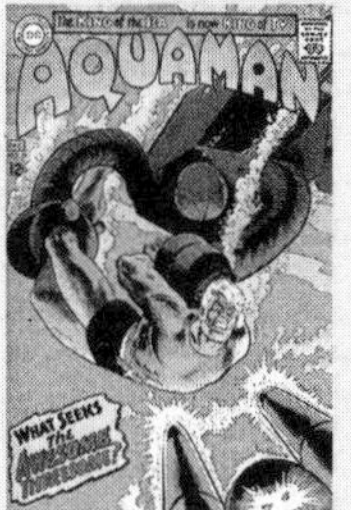 First attempt at a regular Aquaman series ©DC

	N-MINT
❑17, Feb 1962	23.00
❑18, Apr 1962	23.00
❑19, Jun 1962	23.00
❑20, Aug 1962	23.00
❑21, Sep 1962	18.00
❑22, Oct 1962, 1: Sabrina the Teen-age Witch	100.00
❑23, Dec 1962	18.00
❑24, Feb 1963	18.00
❑25, Apr 1963	18.00
❑26, Jun 1963	14.00
❑27, Aug 1963	14.00
❑28, Sep 1963	14.00
❑29, Oct 1963	14.00
❑30, Dec 1963	14.00
❑31, Feb 1963	9.00
❑32, Apr 1964	9.00
❑33, Jun 1964	9.00
❑34, Aug 1964	9.00
❑35, Sep 1964	9.00
❑36, Oct 1964	9.00
❑37, Dec 1964	9.00
❑38, Feb 1965	9.00
❑39, Apr 1965	9.00
❑40, Jun 1965	9.00
❑41, Aug 1965	6.00
❑42, Sep 1965	6.00
❑43, Oct 1965	6.00
❑44, Dec 1965	6.00
❑45, Feb 1966	6.00
❑46, Apr 1966	6.00
❑47, Jun 1966	6.00
❑48, Aug 1966	6.00
❑49, Sep 1966	6.00
❑50, Oct 1966	6.00
❑51, Dec 1966	3.50
❑52, Feb 1967	3.50
❑53, Apr 1967	3.50
❑54, Jun 1967	3.50
❑55, Aug 1967	3.50
❑56, Sep 1967	3.50
❑57, Oct 1967	3.50
❑58, Dec 1967	3.50
❑59, Feb 1968	3.50
❑60, Apr 1968	3.50
❑61, Jun 1968	3.50
❑62, Aug 1968	3.50
❑63, Sep 1968	3.50
❑64, Oct 1968	3.50
❑65, Dec 1968, Series continues as Madhouse Ma-ad Jokes	3.50
❑66, Jan 1969, Final issue	3.50
❑Ann 1, ca. 1962	65.00
❑Ann 2, ca. 1964	25.00
❑Ann 3, ca. 1965	15.00
❑Ann 4, ca. 1966	10.00
❑Ann 5, ca. 1968	10.00
❑Ann 6, ca. 1969	10.00

Archie's Mysteries
Archie

	N-MINT
❑25, Feb 2003, Continues numbering from Archie's Weird Mysteries	2.19
❑26, Apr 2003	2.19
❑27, Jun 2003	2.19
❑28, Aug 2003	2.19
❑29, Sep 2003	2.19
❑30, Oct 2003	2.19
❑31, Nov 2003	2.19
❑32, Jan 2004	2.19
❑33, Mar 2004	2.19
❑34, May 2004	2.19

Archie's Pal Jughead
Archie

	N-MINT
❑78, Nov 1961	16.00
❑79, Dec 1961	16.00
❑80, Jan 1962	16.00
❑81, Feb 1962	10.00
❑82, Mar 1962	10.00
❑83, Apr 1962	10.00
❑84, May 1962	10.00
❑85, Jun 1962	10.00
❑86, Jul 1962	10.00
❑87, Aug 1962	10.00
❑88, Sep 1962	10.00
❑89, Oct 1962	10.00
❑90, Nov 1962	10.00
❑91, Dec 1962	10.00
❑92, Jan 1963	10.00
❑93, Feb 1963	10.00
❑94, Mar 1963	10.00
❑95, Apr 1963	10.00
❑96, May 1963	10.00
❑97, Jun 1963	10.00
❑98, Jul 1963	10.00
❑99, Aug 1963	10.00
❑100, Sep 1963	10.00
❑101, Oct 1963	7.00
❑102, Nov 1963	7.00
❑103, Dec 1963	7.00
❑104, Jan 1964	7.00
❑105, Feb 1964	7.00
❑106, Mar 1964	7.00
❑107, Apr 1964	7.00
❑108, May 1964	7.00
❑109, Jun 1964	7.00
❑110, Jul 1964	7.00
❑111, Aug 1964	7.00
❑112, Sep 1964	7.00
❑113, Oct 1964	7.00
❑114, Nov 1964	7.00
❑115, Dec 1964	7.00
❑116, Jan 1965	7.00
❑117, Feb 1965	7.00
❑118, Mar 1965	7.00
❑119, Apr 1965	7.00
❑120, May 1965	7.00
❑121, Jun 1965	5.00
❑122, Jul 1965	5.00
❑123, Aug 1965	5.00
❑124, Sep 1965	5.00
❑125, Oct 1965	5.00
❑126, Nov 1965, Series continues as Jughead, Vol. 1	5.00

Archie's Pal Jughead Comics
Archie

	N-MINT
❑46, Jun 1993, Series continued from Jughead #45	1.50
❑47, Jul 1993	1.50
❑48, Aug 1993	1.50
❑49, Sep 1993	1.50
❑50, Nov 1993	1.50
❑51, Dec 1993	1.50
❑52, Jan 1994	1.50
❑53, Feb 1994	1.50
❑54, Mar 1994	1.50
❑55, Apr 1994	1.50
❑56, May 1994	1.50
❑57, Jun 1994	1.50
❑58, Jul 1994	1.50
❑59, Aug 1994	1.50
❑60, Sep 1994	1.50
❑61, Oct 1994	1.50
❑62, Nov 1994	1.50
❑63, Dec 1994	1.50
❑64, Jan 1995	1.50
❑65, Feb 1995	1.50
❑66, Mar 1995	1.50
❑67, Apr 1995	1.50
❑68, May 1995	1.50
❑69, Jun 1995	1.50
❑70, Jul 1995	1.50
❑71, Aug 1995	1.50
❑72, Sep 1995, Jellybean's real name revealed	1.50
❑73, Oct 1995	1.50
❑74, Nov 1995	1.50
❑75, Dec 1995	1.50
❑76, Jan 1996	1.50
❑77, Feb 1996	1.50
❑78, Mar 1996	1.50
❑79, Apr 1996	1.50
❑80, May 1996	1.50
❑81, Jun 1996	1.50
❑82, Jul 1996	1.50
❑83, Aug 1996	1.50
❑84, Sep 1996	1.50
❑85, Oct 1996	1.50
❑86, Nov 1996	1.50
❑87, Dec 1996	1.50
❑88, Jan 1997	1.50
❑89, Feb 1997, 1: Trula Twist and J.U.S.T	1.50
❑90, Mar 1997, Jughead asks Trula out.	1.50
❑91, Apr 1997, Trula Twyst's true plan revealed	1.50
❑92, May 1997	1.50
❑93, Jun 1997, A: Trula Twyst	1.50
❑94, Jul 1997, A: Trula Twyst	1.50
❑95, Aug 1997	1.50
❑96, Sep 1997	1.50
❑97, Oct 1997, A: Trula Twyst	1.50
❑98, Nov 1997	1.50
❑99, Dec 1997, A: Trula Twyst	1.50
❑100, Jan 1998, continues in Archie #467	1.50
❑101, Feb 1998, 1: Googie Gilmore	1.50
❑102, Mar 1998	1.50
❑103, Apr 1998	1.50
❑104, May 1998	1.50
❑105, Jun 1998	1.50
❑106, Jul 1998, A: Googie Gilmore	1.50
❑107, Aug 1998	1.50
❑108, Sep 1998	1.75
❑109, Oct 1998	1.75
❑110, Nov 1998	1.75
❑111, Dec 1998	1.75
❑112, Jan 1999, A: Trula Twyst	1.75
❑113, Feb 1999	1.75
❑114, Mar 1999, A: Trula Twyst	1.75

Other grades: Multiply price above by 5/6 for VF/NM • 2/3 for VERY FINE • 1/3 for FINE • 1/5 for VERY GOOD • 1/8 for GOOD

	N-MINT
❑115, Apr 1999	1.75
❑116, May 1999	1.75
❑117, Jun 1999, A: Trula Twyst	1.75
❑118, Jul 1999, A: Trula Twyst	1.75
❑119, Aug 1999, Ethel gets Jughead's baby pictures	1.75
❑120, Sep 1999, A: Trula Twyst	1.75
❑121, Oct 1999	1.75
❑122, Nov 1999	1.75
❑123, Dec 1999	1.75
❑124, Jan 2000	1.75
❑125, Feb 2000	1.75
❑126, Apr 2000	1.75
❑127, May 2000	1.75
❑128, Jul 2000	1.99
❑129, Aug 2000	1.99
❑130, Sep 2000	1.99
❑131, Oct 2000	1.99
❑132, Dec 2000	1.99
❑133, Jan 2001	1.99
❑134, Feb 2001	1.99
❑135, Apr 2001	1.99
❑136, May 2001	1.99
❑137, Jul 2001	1.99
❑138, Aug 2001	1.99
❑139, Sep 2001	1.99
❑140, Dec 2001	2.19
❑141, Feb 2002	2.19
❑142, Apr 2002	2.19
❑143, Jun 2002	2.19
❑144, Aug 2002	2.19
❑145, Sep 2002	2.19
❑146, Oct 2002	2.19
❑147, Dec 2002	2.19
❑148, Feb 2003	2.19
❑149, Apr 2003	2.19
❑150, Jun 2003	2.19
❑151, Jul 2003	2.19
❑152, Sep 2003	2.19
❑153, Oct 2003	2.19
❑154, Dec 2003	2.19
❑155, Feb 2004	2.19
❑156, Apr 2004	2.19
❑157, Jun 2004	2.19
❑158, Aug 2004	2.19
❑159, Sep 2004	2.19
❑160, Oct 2004	2.19
❑161, Dec 2004	2.19
❑162, Jan 2004	2.19
❑163, Feb 2005	2.19
❑164, Jun 2005	2.19
❑165, Jul 2005	2.19
❑166, Aug 2005	2.25
❑167, Sep 2005	2.25
❑168, Oct 2005	2.25
❑169, Nov 2005; Includes Bionicle preview	2.25
❑170, Jan 2006	2.25
❑172, May 2006	2.25
❑173, Jun 2006	2.25
❑174, Aug 2006	2.25
❑175, Sep 2006	2.25
❑176, Nov 2006	2.25
❑177, Dec 2006	2.25
❑178, Feb 2007	2.25
❑179	2.25
❑180	2.25
❑181	2.25
❑182	2.25
❑183	2.25
❑184	2.25
❑185	2.25
❑186	2.25
❑187	2.25
❑188	2.25
❑189	2.25
❑190	2.25
❑191	2.25
❑192	2.25
❑193	2.25
❑194	2.25

Archie's Pals 'n' Gals

Archie

	N-MINT
❑18, Fal 1961	45.00
❑19, Win 1961	45.00
❑20, Spr 1962	45.00
❑21, Sum 1962	22.00
❑22, Fal 1962	22.00
❑23, Win 1962	22.00
❑24, Spr 1963	22.00
❑25, Sum 1963	22.00
❑26, Fal 1963	22.00
❑27, Win 1963	22.00
❑28, Spr 1964	22.00
❑29, Sum 1964, A: The Beatles	45.00
❑30, Fal 1964	22.00
❑31, Win 1964	13.00
❑32, Spr 1965	13.00
❑33, Sum 1965	13.00
❑34, Fal 1965	13.00
❑35, Win 1965	13.00
❑36, Spr 1966	13.00
❑37, Sum 1966	13.00
❑38, Fal 1966	13.00
❑39, Win 1966	13.00
❑40, Spr 1967	13.00
❑41, Aug 1967	9.00
❑42, Oct 1967	9.00
❑43, Dec 1967	9.00
❑44, Feb 1968	9.00
❑45, Apr 1968	9.00
❑46, Jun 1968	9.00
❑47, Aug 1968	9.00
❑48, Oct 1968	9.00
❑49, Dec 1968	9.00
❑50, Feb 1969	9.00
❑51, Apr 1969	7.00
❑52, Jun 1969	7.00
❑53, Aug 1969	7.00
❑54, Oct 1969	7.00
❑55, Dec 1969	7.00
❑56, Feb 1970	7.00
❑57, Apr 1970	7.00
❑58, Jun 1970	7.00
❑59, Aug 1970	7.00
❑60, Oct 1970	7.00
❑61, Dec 1970	7.00
❑62, Feb 1971	7.00
❑63, Apr 1971	7.00
❑64, Jun 1971	7.00
❑65, Aug 1971	7.00
❑66, Oct 1971	7.00
❑67, Dec 1971	7.00
❑68, Feb 1972	7.00
❑69, Apr 1972	7.00
❑70, Jun 1972	7.00
❑71, Aug 1972	5.00
❑72, Sep 1972	5.00
❑73, Oct 1972	5.00
❑74, Dec 1972	5.00
❑75, Feb 1973	5.00
❑76, Apr 1973	5.00
❑77, Jun 1973	5.00
❑78, Jul 1973	5.00
❑79, Aug 1973	5.00
❑80, Sep 1973	5.00
❑81, Nov 1973	5.00
❑82, Dec 1973	4.00
❑83, Jan 1974	4.00
❑84, Apr 1974	4.00
❑85, Jun 1974	4.00
❑86, Jul 1974	4.00
❑87, Aug 1974	4.00
❑88, Sep 1974	4.00
❑89, Oct 1974	4.00
❑90, Nov 1974	4.00
❑91, Dec 1974	4.00
❑92, Mar 1975	4.00
❑93, Apr 1975	4.00
❑94, Jun 1975	4.00
❑95, Jul 1975	4.00
❑96, Aug 1975	4.00
❑97, Sep 1975	4.00
❑98, Oct 1975	4.00
❑99, Nov 1975	4.00
❑100, Dec 1975	4.00
❑101, Jan 1976	2.50
❑102, Feb 1976	2.50
❑103, Mar 1976	2.50
❑104, May 1976	2.50
❑105, Jun 1976	2.50
❑106, Jul 1976	2.50
❑107, Aug 1976	2.50
❑108, Sep 1976	2.50
❑109, Oct 1976	2.50
❑110, Dec 1976	2.50
❑111, Jan 1977	2.50
❑112, Mar 1977	2.50
❑113, May 1977	2.50
❑114, Jun 1977	2.50
❑115, Jul 1977	2.50
❑116, Aug 1977	2.50
❑117, Sep 1977	2.50
❑118, Oct 1977	2.50
❑119, Dec 1977	2.50
❑120, Jan 1978	2.50
❑121, Mar 1978	2.50
❑122, May 1978	2.50
❑123, Jun 1978	2.50
❑124, Jul 1978	2.50
❑125, Aug 1978	2.50
❑126, Sep 1978	2.50
❑127, Oct 1978	2.50
❑128, Dec 1978	2.50
❑129, Jan 1979	2.50
❑130, Mar 1979	2.50
❑131, May 1979	2.50
❑132, Jun 1979	2.50
❑133, Jul 1979	2.50
❑134, Aug 1979	2.50
❑135, Sep 1979	2.50
❑136, Oct 1979	2.50
❑137, Dec 1979	2.50
❑138, Jan 1980	2.50
❑139, Mar 1980	2.50
❑140, May 1980	2.50
❑141, Jun 1980	2.50
❑142, Jul 1980	2.50
❑143, Aug 1980	2.50
❑144, Sep 1980	2.50
❑145, Oct 1980	2.50
❑146, Dec 1980	2.50
❑147, Jan 1981	2.50
❑148, Mar 1981	2.50
❑149, May 1981	2.50
❑150, Jun 1981	2.50
❑151, Jul 1981	2.00
❑152, Aug 1981	2.00
❑153, Sep 1981	2.00
❑154, Oct 1981	2.00
❑155, Dec 1981	2.00
❑156, Jan 1982	2.00
❑157, Mar 1982	2.00
❑158, May 1982	2.00
❑159, Jul 1982	2.00
❑160, Sep 1982	2.00
❑161, Nov 1982	2.00
❑162, Jan 1983	2.00
❑163, May 1983	2.00
❑164, Jul 1983	2.00
❑165, Sep 1983	2.00
❑166, Nov 1983	2.00
❑167, Jan 1984	2.00
❑168, Mar 1984	2.00
❑169, May 1984	2.00
❑170, Jul 1984	2.00
❑171, Sep 1984	2.00
❑172, Nov 1984	2.00
❑173, Jan 1985	2.00
❑174, Mar 1985	2.00
❑175, May 1985	2.00
❑176, Jul 1985	2.00
❑177, Sep 1985	2.00
❑178, Nov 1985	2.00
❑179, Jan 1986	2.00
❑180, Mar 1986	2.00
❑181, May 1986	2.00
❑182, Jul 1986	2.00
❑183, Sep 1986	2.00
❑184, Nov 1986	2.00
❑185, Jan 1987	2.00
❑186, Mar 1987	2.00
❑187, May 1987	2.00
❑188, Jun 1987	2.00
❑189, Jul 1987	2.00
❑190, Aug 1987	2.00
❑191, Sep 1987	2.00
❑192, Oct 1987	2.00
❑193, Nov 1987	2.00
❑194, Jan 1988	2.00
❑195, Mar 1988	2.00
❑196, May 1988	2.00

Other grades: Multiply price above by 5/6 for VF/NM • 2/3 for VERY FINE • 1/3 for FINE • 1/5 for VERY GOOD • 1/8 for GOOD

Aquaman (5th Series)

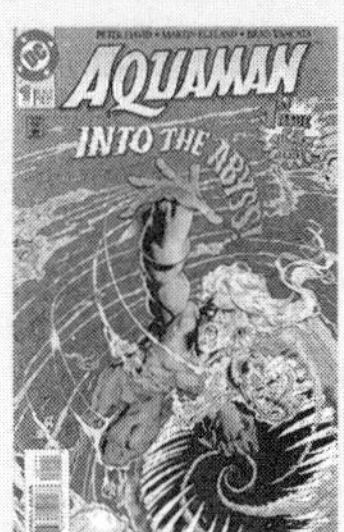

Fifth fishman try, this time from Peter David
©DC

Aquaman: Time and Tide

Peter David at his humorous best
©DC

Arabian Nights on the World of Magic: The Gathering

Game adaptation with ungainly title
©Acclaim

Arak Son of Thunder

Viking sword-and-sorcery tales from DC
©DC

Arcana

Part of the "Children's Crusade" story arc
©DC

	N-MINT
❑197, Jun 1988	2.00
❑198, Jul 1988	2.00
❑199, Aug 1988	2.00
❑200, Sep 1988	2.00
❑201, Oct 1988	1.50
❑202, Nov 1988	1.50
❑203, Jan 1989	1.50
❑204, Mar 1989	1.50
❑205, May 1989	1.50
❑206, Jun 1989	1.50
❑207, Jul 1989	1.50
❑208, Aug 1989	1.50
❑209, Sep 1989	1.50
❑210, Oct 1989	1.50
❑211, Nov 1989	1.50
❑212, Jan 1990	1.50
❑213, Mar 1990	1.50
❑214, May 1990	1.50
❑215, Jun 1990	1.50
❑216, Jul 1990	1.50
❑217, Aug 1990	1.50
❑218, Sep 1990	1.50
❑219, Nov 1990	1.50
❑220, Jan 1991	1.50
❑221, Mar 1991	1.50
❑222, May 1991	1.50
❑223, Jul 1991	1.50
❑224, Sep 1991	1.50

Archie's Pals 'n' Gals Double Digest
Archie

	N-MINT
❑1	4.00
❑2	3.00
❑3	3.00
❑4	3.00
❑5	3.00
❑6	2.75
❑7	2.75
❑8	2.75
❑9, Jan 1995	2.75
❑10, Feb 1995	2.75
❑11, Apr 1995	2.75
❑12, Jun 1995	2.75
❑13, Aug 1995	2.75
❑14, Oct 1995	2.75
❑15, Dec 1995	2.75
❑16, Jan 1996	2.75
❑17, Mar 1996	2.75
❑18, May 1996	2.75
❑19, Jul 1996	2.75
❑20, Aug 1996	2.75
❑21, Oct 1996	2.75
❑22, Dec 1996	2.75
❑23, Jan 1997	2.75
❑24, Mar 1997	2.75
❑25, May 1997	2.75
❑26, Jul 1997	2.75
❑27, Aug 1997	2.75
❑28, Oct 1997	2.75
❑29, Dec 1997	2.75
❑30, Jan 1998	2.95
❑31, Mar 1998	2.95
❑32, May 1998	2.95
❑33, Jun 1998	2.95
❑34, Aug 1998	2.95
❑35, Sep 1998	2.95
❑36, Oct 1998	2.95
❑37, Dec 1998	2.95
❑38, Feb 1999	2.95
❑39, Apr 1999	2.95
❑40, May 1999	2.99
❑41, Jun 1999	2.99
❑42, Aug 1999	2.99
❑43, Sep 1999	2.99
❑44, Oct 1999	2.99
❑45, Dec 1999	2.99
❑46, Feb 2000	2.99
❑47, Mar 2000	2.99
❑48, May 2000	2.99
❑49, Jun 2000	3.19
❑50, Aug 2000	3.19
❑51, Sep 2000	3.19
❑52, Oct 2000	3.19
❑53, Dec 2000	3.19
❑54, Feb 2001	3.19
❑55, Mar 2001	3.19
❑56, May 2001	3.29
❑57, Jun 2001	3.29
❑58, Aug 2001	3.29
❑59, Sep 2001	3.29
❑60, Oct 2001	3.29
❑61, Dec 2001	3.29
❑62, Feb 2002	3.29
❑63, Mar 2002	3.29
❑64, May 2002	3.29
❑65, Jun 2002	3.29
❑66, Aug 2002	3.29
❑67, Sep 2002	3.29
❑68, Oct 2002	3.29
❑69, Dec 2002	3.29
❑70, Feb 2003	3.29
❑71, Mar 2003	3.59
❑72, May 2003	3.59
❑73, Jun 2003	3.59
❑74, Aug 2003	3.59
❑75, Sep 2003	3.59
❑76, Oct 2003	3.59
❑77, Sep 2003	3.59
❑78, Oct 2003	3.59
❑79, Dec 2003	3.59
❑80, Jan 2004	3.59
❑81, Feb 2004	3.59
❑82, Apr 2004	3.59
❑83, May 2004	3.59
❑84, Jun 2004	3.59
❑85, Jul 2004	3.59
❑86, Aug 2004	3.59
❑87, Sep 2004	3.59
❑88, Oct 2004	3.59
❑89, Jan 2005	3.59
❑90, Feb 2005	3.59
❑91, Mar 2005	3.59
❑92, Apr 2005	3.59
❑93, May 2005	3.59
❑94, Aug 2005	3.59
❑95, Sep 2005	3.59
❑96, Oct 2005	3.59
❑97, Nov 2005	3.59
❑98, Jan 2005	3.59
❑99, Feb 2005	3.59
❑100, Mar 2006	3.59
❑101, May 2006	3.59
❑102, Jun 2006	3.69
❑103, Aug 2006	3.69
❑104, Sep 2006	3.69
❑105, Oct 2006	3.69
❑106, Nov 2006	3.69
❑107, Jan 2007	3.69
❑108, Feb 2007	3.69
❑109	3.69
❑110	3.69
❑111	3.69
❑112	3.69
❑113	3.69
❑114	3.69
❑115	3.69
❑116	3.69
❑117	3.69
❑118	3.69
❑119	3.69
❑120	3.69
❑121	3.69
❑122	3.69
❑123	3.69
❑124	3.69
❑125	3.69
❑126	3.69
❑127	3.69
❑128	3.69
❑129	3.69
❑130	3.69

Archie's R/C Racers
Archie

	N-MINT
❑1, Sep 1989; Reggie appearance	2.00
❑2, Nov 1989	1.50
❑3, Jan 1990	1.50
❑4, Mar 1990	1.50
❑5, May 1990; Tennessee tribute corner box	1.50
❑6, Jul 1990; Kentucky tribute corner box	1.50
❑7, Sep 1990; Ohio tribute corner box...	1.50
❑8, Nov 1990; Missouri tribute corner box	1.50
❑9, Jan 1991; Texas tribute cover box ...	1.50
❑10, Mar 1991	1.50

Archie's Spring Break
Archie

	N-MINT
❑1 1996	2.50
❑2 1997	2.50
❑3 1998	2.50
❑4 1999	2.50
❑5 2000	2.50

Archie's Story & Game Digest Magazine
Archie

	N-MINT
❑32, Jul 1995	2.00
❑33, Sep 1995	2.00
❑34, Mar 1996	2.00
❑35, May 1996	2.00
❑36, ca. 1996	2.00
❑37, Jan 1997	2.00
❑38, Aug 1997	2.00
❑39, Jan 1998	2.00

Archie's Super-Hero Special
Archie / Red Circle

	N-MINT
❑1, Jan 1979, GM, JK (a); reprints Adventures of the Fly #2; reprints Double Life of Private Strong #1	3.00

Other grades: Multiply price above by 5/6 for VF/NM • 2/3 for VERY FINE • 1/3 for FINE • 1/5 for VERY GOOD • 1/8 for GOOD

N-MINT

❑2, Aug 1979, GM (w); GM, DG, JK, NA, WW (a); reprints Double Life of Private Strong #1; reprints Double Life of Private Strong #2 ... 3.00

Archie's Super Teens
Archie

❑1 1994, poster ... 2.50
❑2 1995 ... 2.50
❑3 1995 ... 2.50
❑4 1996 ... 2.50

Archie's TV Laugh-Out
Archie

❑1, Dec 1969 ... 42.00
❑2, Mar 1970 ... 24.00
❑3, Jun 1970 ... 16.00
❑4, Sep 1970 ... 16.00
❑5 1971 ... 16.00
❑6 1971 ... 12.00
❑7 1971; Josie and the Pussycats features begin ... 22.00
❑8, Aug 1971 ... 12.00
❑9 1971 ... 12.00
❑10 1971 ... 12.00
❑11, Feb 1972 ... 9.00
❑12, May 1972 ... 9.00
❑13, Aug 1972 ... 9.00
❑14, Sep 1972 ... 9.00
❑15, Oct 1972 ... 9.00
❑16, Dec 1972 ... 9.00
❑17 1973 ... 9.00
❑18 1973 ... 9.00
❑19 1973 ... 9.00
❑20 1973 ... 9.00
❑21 1973 ... 7.00
❑22, Oct 1973 ... 7.00
❑23, Dec 1973 ... 7.00
❑24, May 1974 ... 7.00
❑25, Jul 1974 ... 7.00
❑26, Aug 1974 ... 7.00
❑27, Sep 1974 ... 7.00
❑28, Oct 1974 ... 7.00
❑29, Dec 1974 ... 7.00
❑30, Feb 1975 ... 7.00
❑31, May 1975 ... 6.00
❑32, Jul 1975 ... 6.00
❑33, Aug 1975 ... 6.00
❑34, Sep 1975 ... 6.00
❑35, Oct 1975 ... 6.00
❑36, Dec 1975 ... 6.00
❑37, Feb 1976 ... 6.00
❑38, Mar 1976 ... 6.00
❑39, Apr 1976 ... 6.00
❑40, Jun 1976 ... 6.00
❑41, Jul 1976 ... 4.00
❑42, Aug 1976 ... 4.00
❑43, Sep 1976 ... 4.00
❑44, Nov 1976 ... 4.00
❑45, Dec 1976 ... 4.00
❑46, Feb 1977 ... 4.00
❑47, Mar 1977 ... 4.00
❑48, Apr 1977 ... 4.00
❑49, Jun 1977 ... 4.00
❑50, Jul 1977 ... 4.00
❑51, Aug 1977 ... 4.00
❑52, Sep 1977 ... 4.00
❑53, Nov 1977 ... 4.00
❑54, Dec 1977 ... 4.00
❑55, Feb 1978 ... 4.00
❑56, Mar 1978 ... 4.00
❑57, Apr 1978 ... 4.00
❑58, Jun 1978 ... 4.00
❑59, Jul 1978 ... 4.00
❑60, Aug 1978 ... 4.00
❑61, Sep 1978 ... 3.00
❑62, Nov 1978 ... 3.00
❑63, Dec 1978 ... 3.00
❑64, Feb 1979 ... 3.00
❑65, Mar 1979 ... 3.00
❑66, Apr 1979 ... 3.00
❑67, Jun 1979 ... 3.00
❑68, Jul 1979 ... 3.00
❑69, Aug 1979 ... 3.00
❑70, Sep 1979 ... 3.00
❑71, Nov 1979 ... 3.00
❑72, Dec 1979 ... 3.00
❑73, Feb 1980 ... 3.00
❑74, Mar 1980 ... 3.00

N-MINT

❑75, Apr 1980 ... 3.00
❑76, Jun 1980 ... 3.00
❑77, Jul 1980 ... 3.00
❑78, Aug 1980 ... 3.00
❑79, Oct 1980 ... 3.00
❑80, Feb 1981 ... 3.00
❑81, May 1981 ... 2.50
❑82, Aug 1981 ... 2.50
❑83, Oct 1981 ... 2.50
❑84, Feb 1982 ... 2.50
❑85, May 1982 ... 2.50
❑86, Aug 1982 ... 2.50
❑87, Feb 1983 ... 2.50
❑88, Apr 1983 ... 2.50
❑89, Jun 1983, DDC (c) ... 2.50
❑90, Aug 1983, DDC (c) ... 2.50
❑91, Oct 1983, DDC (c) ... 2.50
❑92, Dec 1983, DDC (c) ... 2.50
❑93, Feb 1984 ... 2.50
❑94, Apr 1984 ... 2.50
❑95, Jun 1984 ... 2.50
❑96, Aug 1984 ... 2.50
❑97, Oct 1984 ... 2.50
❑98, Dec 1984 ... 2.50
❑99, Feb 1985 ... 2.50
❑100, Apr 1985, DDC (a); A: Jackie Maxon. Jackie Maxon appearance (Michael Jackson substitute) ... 2.50
❑101, Jun 1985 ... 2.50
❑102, Aug 1985 ... 2.50
❑103, Oct 1985 ... 2.50
❑104, Dec 1985 ... 2.50
❑105, Feb 1986 ... 2.50
❑106, Apr 1986 ... 2.50

Archie's Vacation Special
Archie

❑1, Sum 1994; DDC (a); Includes poster ... 2.50
❑2, Win 1995 ... 2.50
❑3, Sum 1995 ... 2.50
❑4, Sum 1996 ... 2.50
❑5, Sum 1997 ... 2.50
❑6, Sum 1998 ... 2.50
❑7, Sum 1999 ... 2.50
❑8, Sum 2000 ... 2.50

Archie's Weird Mysteries
Archie

❑1, Feb 2000 ... 2.00
❑2, Mar 2000 ... 2.00
❑3, Apr 2000 ... 2.00
❑4, May 2000 ... 2.00
❑5, Jun 2000 ... 2.00
❑6, Jul 2000 ... 2.00
❑7, Aug 2000 ... 2.00
❑8, Sep 2000 ... 2.00
❑9, Oct 2000 ... 2.00
❑10, Dec 2000 ... 2.00
❑11, Feb 2001 ... 2.00
❑12, Apr 2001 ... 2.00
❑13, ca. 2001 ... 2.00
❑14, ca. 2001 ... 2.00
❑15, ca. 2001 ... 2.00
❑16, ca. 2001 ... 2.00
❑17 ... 2.19
❑18, Feb 2002 ... 2.19
❑19, Apr 2002 ... 2.19
❑20, Jun 2002 ... 2.19
❑21, Aug 2002 ... 2.19
❑22, Sep 2002 ... 2.19
❑23, Oct 2002 ... 2.19
❑24, Dec 2002; Series changes to Archie's Mysteries ... 2.19
❑Ashcan 1; Giveaway from Diamond ... 1.00

Archie 3000
Archie

❑1, May 1989 ... 2.50
❑2, Jul 1989 ... 2.00
❑3, Aug 1989 ... 2.00
❑4, Oct 1989 ... 2.00
❑5, Nov 1989 ... 2.00
❑6, Jan 1990 ... 1.00
❑7, Mar 1990 ... 1.00
❑8, May 1990 ... 1.00
❑9, Jul 1990 ... 1.00
❑10, Aug 1990 ... 1.00
❑11, Oct 1990 ... 1.00
❑12, Nov 1990 ... 1.00
❑13, Jan 1991 ... 1.00

N-MINT

❑14, Mar 1991 ... 1.00
❑15, May 1991 ... 1.00

Arcomics Premiere
Arcomics

❑1, Jul 1993, b&w; lenticular animation cover ... 2.95

Arctic Comics
Nick Burns

❑1; souvenir ... 1.00

Area 52
Image

❑1, Jan 2001 ... 2.95
❑1/A, Jan 2001; Gold Foil Title ... 2.95
❑1/B, Jan 2001; Red Foil Title ... 2.95
❑2, Mar 2001 ... 2.95
❑3, Apr 2001 ... 2.95
❑4, ca. 2001 ... 2.95

Area 88
Eclipse / Viz

❑1, May 1987 ... 3.50
❑1/2nd; 2nd printing ... 2.00
❑2, Jun 1987 ... 2.50
❑2/2nd; 2nd printing ... 2.00
❑3, Jun 1987 ... 2.00
❑4, Jul 1987 ... 2.00
❑5, Jul 1987 ... 2.00
❑6, Aug 1987 ... 2.00
❑7, Aug 1987 ... 2.00
❑8, Sep 1987 ... 2.00
❑9, Sep 1987 ... 2.00
❑10, Oct 1987 ... 2.00
❑11, Oct 1987 ... 2.00
❑12, Nov 1987 ... 2.00
❑13, Nov 1987 ... 2.00
❑14, Dec 1987 ... 2.00
❑15, Dec 1987 ... 2.00
❑16, Jan 1988 ... 2.00
❑17, Jan 1988 ... 2.00
❑18, Feb 1988 ... 2.00
❑19, Feb 1988 ... 2.00
❑20, Mar 1988 ... 2.00
❑21, Mar 1988 ... 2.00
❑22, Apr 1988 ... 2.00
❑23, Apr 1988 ... 2.00
❑24, May 1988 ... 2.00
❑25, May 1988 ... 2.00
❑26, Jun 1988 ... 2.00
❑27, Jun 1988 ... 2.00
❑28, Jul 1988 ... 2.00
❑29, Jul 1988 ... 2.00
❑30, Aug 1988 ... 2.00
❑31, Aug 1988 ... 2.00
❑32, Sep 1988 ... 2.00
❑33, Sep 1988 ... 2.00
❑34, Oct 1988 ... 2.00
❑35, Oct 1988 ... 2.00
❑36, Nov 1988 ... 2.00
❑37, Nov 1988 ... 2.00
❑38, Dec 1988 ... 2.00
❑39, Dec 1988 ... 2.00
❑40, Jan 1989 ... 2.00
❑41, Jan 1989 ... 2.00
❑42, Feb 1989; Final Issue ... 2.00

Areala: Angel of War
Antarctic

❑1, Sep 1998; O: Auria ... 2.95
❑2, Nov 1998 ... 2.95
❑3, Feb 1999 ... 2.95
❑4, Jun 1999 ... 2.99

Arena
Alchemy

❑1, b&w ... 1.50

Ares
Marvel

❑1, Mar 2006 ... 2.99
❑2, Apr 2006 ... 2.99
❑3, Jun 2006 ... 2.99
❑4, Jul 2006 ... 2.99

Argonauts
Eternity

❑1, Jul 1988 ... 1.95
❑2, Sep 1988 ... 1.95
❑3, Dec 1988 ... 1.95
❑4, Jun 1989 ... 1.95

Other grades: Multiply price above by 5/6 for VF/NM • 2/3 for VERY FINE • 1/3 for FINE • 1/5 for VERY GOOD • 1/8 for GOOD

Arcana

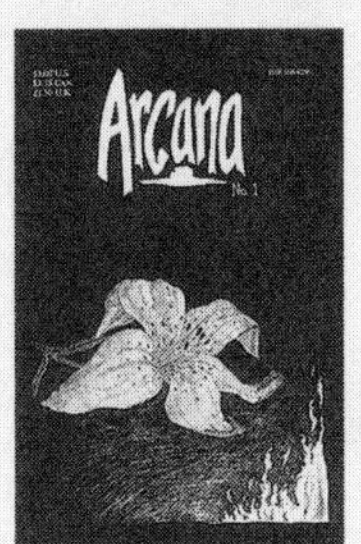

Independent series with magical medieval feel

©Wells & Clark

Arcanum

Short-lived series in the world of Witchblade

©Image

Archangel

Unusual Marvel printed in glossy black and white

©Marvel

Archangels: The Saga

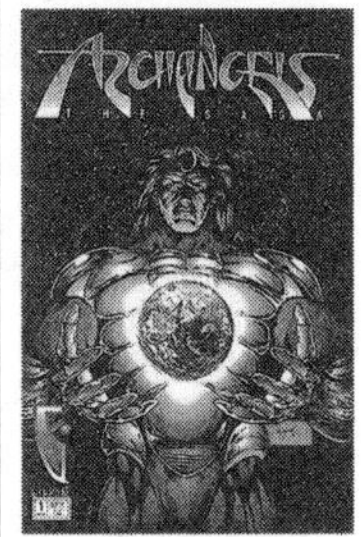

Independent comic with religious feel

©Eternal

Archard's Agents

Spinoff one-shot from CrossGen's Ruse

©CrossGen

N-MINT

Argonauts: System Crash
Alpha Productions

❑1 .... 2.50
❑2 .... 2.50

Argon Zark!
Arclight

❑1 1997; based on on-line comics series 6.95

Argus
DC

❑1, Apr 1995 .... 1.50
❑2, Jun 1995 .... 1.50
❑3, Jul 1995 .... 1.50
❑4, Aug 1995 .... 1.50
❑5, Sep 1995 .... 1.50
❑6, Oct 1995; Final Issue 1.50

Aria
Image

❑1, Jan 1999 .... 3.00
❑1/A, Jan 1999; white background cover 3.00
❑1/B, Jan 1999; Woman looking from balcony on cover 3.00
❑2, Apr 1999 .... 2.50
❑3, May 1999 .... 2.50
❑4/A, Nov 1999; Textured cover stock; Close-up shot of woman in green pointing at chest 2.50
❑4/B, Nov 1999; Variant cover with Angela 2.50
❑5, ca. 1999 .... 2.50
❑6, ca. 1999 .... 2.50
❑7, ca. 1999 .... 2.50
❑Ashcan 1, Nov 1998, b&w; preview issue 3.50

Aria: A Midwinter's Dream
Image

❑1, Jan 2002 .... 4.95

Aria Angela
Image

❑1/A, Feb 2000, Aria and Angela in profile on cover 2.95
❑1/B, Feb 2000, Aria sitting on stairs on cover 2.95
❑1/C, Feb 2000, Close-up on Aria (right half of 1/H cover in close-up) .. 2.95
❑1/D, Feb 2000, Woman walking through astral plane on cover 2.95
❑1/E, Feb 2000, Woman walking through astral plane on cover 2.95
❑1/F, Feb 2000, Two women, hawk on cover 2.95
❑1/G, Feb 2000, Tower records variant; Woman with sword (between legs) on cover 2.95
❑1/H, Feb 2000, Jay Anacleto Gatefold Cover 2.95
❑1/I, Feb 2000, chromium cover 2.95
❑2, Oct 2000 .... 2.95

Aria Angela Blanc & Noir
Image

❑1, Apr 2000, Reprints Aria Angela #1 in black & white 2.95

Aria Blanc & Noir
Image

❑1, Mar 1999; b&w reprint of Aria #1; wraparound cover 2.50
❑2, Sep 1999 .... 2.50

Aria (manga)
ADV Manga

❑1, ca. 2004 .... 9.99

N-MINT

Ariane & Bluebeard
Eclipse

❑1, ca. 1989, Part of Eclipse's Night Music Series 3.95

Arianne
Slave Labor

❑1, May 1991, Adult 4.95
❑2, Oct 1991, Adult 2.95

Arianne (Moonstone)
Moonstone

❑1, Dec 1995, b&w; Reprints Arianne #1-2 by Slave Labor 4.95

Aria Summer's Spell
Image

❑1, Mar 2002 .... 2.95
❑2, Jun 2002 .... 2.95

Aria: The Soul Market
Image

❑1, Mar 2001 .... 2.95
❑2, Apr 2001 .... 2.95
❑3, May 2001 .... 2.95
❑4, Jun 2001 .... 2.95
❑5, Jul 2001 .... 2.95
❑6, Aug 2001 .... 2.95

Aria: The Uses of Enchantment
Image

❑1, Feb 2003 .... 2.95
❑2, Apr 2003 .... 2.95
❑3, Jul 2003 .... 2.95
❑4, Sep 2003 .... 2.95

Arik Khan (A+)
A-Plus

❑1; b&w, reprint 2.50
❑2 .... 2.50

Arik Khan (Andromeda)
Andromeda

❑1, Sep 1977 .... 1.95
❑2 .... 1.95
❑3 .... 1.95

Arion, Lord of Atlantis
DC

❑1, Nov 1982, JDu (c); JDu (a); Story continued from Warlord #62 .... 1.00
❑2, Dec 1982, JDu (a); 1: Mara 1.00
❑3, Jan 1983, JDu (a) 1.00
❑4, Feb 1983, JDu (a); O: Arion, Part 1.. 1.00
❑5, Mar 1983, JDu (a); O: Arion, Part 2. 1.00
❑6, Apr 1983, JDu (a) 1.00
❑7, May 1983, JDu (a) 1.00
❑8, Jun 1983 .... 1.00
❑9, Jul 1983 .... 1.00
❑10, Aug 1983 .... 1.00
❑11, Sep 1983 .... 1.00
❑12, Oct 1983, JDu (a) 1.00
❑13, Nov 1983 .... 1.00
❑14, Dec 1983 .... 1.00
❑15, Jan 1984 .... 1.00
❑16, Feb 1984 .... 1.00
❑17, Mar 1984 .... 1.00
❑18, Apr 1984 .... 1.00
❑19, May 1984 .... 1.00
❑20, Jun 1984 .... 1.00
❑21, Jul 1984 .... 1.00

N-MINT

❑22, Aug 1984 .... 1.00
❑23, Sep 1984 .... 1.00
❑24, Oct 1984 .... 1.00
❑25, Nov 1984 .... 1.00
❑26, Dec 1984 .... 1.00
❑27, Jan 1985 .... 1.00
❑28, Feb 1985 .... 1.00
❑29, Mar 1985 .... 1.00
❑30, Apr 1985 .... 1.00
❑31, May 1985 .... 1.00
❑32, Jun 1985 .... 1.00
❑33, Jul 1985 .... 1.00
❑34, Aug 1985 .... 1.00
❑35, Sep 1985; Final Issue 1.00
❑Special 1, ca. 1985; Special 1.00

Arion the Immortal
DC

❑1, Jul 1992 .... 1.50
❑2, Aug 1992 .... 1.50
❑3, Sep 1992 .... 1.50
❑4, Oct 1992 .... 1.50
❑5, Nov 1992 .... 1.50
❑6, Dec 1992; Final Issue 1.50

Aristocats
Gold Key

❑1, Mar 1971, 30045-103; poster 3.50

Aristocratic X-Traterrestrial Time-Traveling Thieves
Comics Interview

❑1, Feb 1987 .... 2.00
❑2, Apr 1987 .... 2.00
❑3, Jun 1987 .... 2.00
❑4, Aug 1987 .... 2.00
❑5, Oct 1987, Fred sees red 2.00
❑6, Dec 1987 .... 2.00
❑7, Feb 1988 .... 2.00
❑8, Apr 1988, b&w 2.00
❑9, Jun 1988 .... 2.00
❑10, Aug 1988 .... 2.00
❑11, Oct 1988 .... 2.00
❑12, Dec 1988 .... 2.00

Aristocratic X-Traterrestrial Time-Traveling Thieves Micro-Series
Comics Interview

❑1, Aug 1986 .... 2.00
❑1/2nd 2.00

Aristokittens
Gold Key

❑1, Oct 1973 .... 16.00
❑2, Feb 1974 .... 10.00
❑3, Apr 1974 .... 8.00
❑4, Jul 1974 .... 8.00
❑5, Oct 1974 .... 8.00
❑6, Jan 1975 .... 6.00
❑7, Apr 1975 .... 6.00
❑8, Jul 1975 .... 6.00
❑9, Oct 1975 .... 6.00

Arizona: A Simple Horror
London Night

❑1, May 1998; Adult 3.00
❑1/Nude, May 1998 .... 3.00

Other grades: Multiply price above by 5/6 for VF/NM • 2/3 for VERY FINE • 1/3 for FINE • 1/5 for VERY GOOD • 1/8 for GOOD

Arizona: Wild at Heart
London Night

❑1, Feb 1998 .... 3.00

Arkaga
Image

❑1, Sep 1997 .... 2.95
❑2, Nov 1997 .... 2.95

Ark Angels
Tokyopop

❑1, Dec 2005 .... 9.99

Arkanium
Dreamwave

❑1, Sep 2002 .... 2.95
❑2, Nov 2002 .... 2.95
❑3, Jan 2003 .... 2.95
❑4, Feb 2003 .... 2.95
❑5, Mar 2003 .... 2.95

Arkeology
Valkyrie

❑1, Apr 1989; companion one-shot for The Adventures of Luther Arkwright... 2.00

Arkham Asylum Living Hell
DC

❑1, May 2003 .... 2.50
❑2, Jun 2003 .... 2.50
❑3, Jul 2003 .... 2.50
❑4, Aug 2003 .... 2.50
❑5, Sep 2003 .... 2.50
❑6, Oct 2003 .... 2.50

Arlington Hammer in: Get Me to the Church on Time
One Shot

❑1; comic for sale at conventions only... 2.50

A.R.M.
Adventure

❑1, Sep 1990, Introduction by Larry Niven 2.50
❑2, Oct 1990 .... 2.50
❑3, Nov 1990 .... 2.50

Armadillo Comics
Rip Off

❑1 .... 2.50
❑2 .... 2.50

Armageddon
Last Gasp

❑1, Adult 2.50
❑2, Adult 2.50

Armageddon (Chaos)
Chaos

❑1, Oct 1999 .... 2.95
❑2, Nov 1999 .... 2.95
❑3, Dec 1999 .... 2.95
❑4, Jan 2000 .... 2.95

Armageddon 2001
DC

❑1, May 1991; 1: Monarch; 1: Waverider 2.00
❑1/2nd, May 1991; 2nd printing; 1: Waverider; 1: Monarch 2.00
❑1/3rd, May 1991; 3rd printing (silver ink on cover) 2.00
❑2, Oct 1991; Monarch's ID revealed 2.00

Armageddon: Inferno
DC

❑1, Apr 1992 .... 1.00
❑2, May 1992 .... 1.00
❑3, Jun 1992 .... 1.00
❑4, Jul 1992; JSA returns from limbo.... 1.00

Armageddon: The Alien Agenda
DC

❑1, Nov 1991 .... 1.00
❑2, Dec 1991 .... 1.00
❑3, Jan 1992 .... 1.00
❑4, Feb 1992 .... 1.00

Armageddon Factor
AC

❑1, Jun 1987 .... 1.95
❑2, Aug 1987 .... 1.95
❑3 .... 1.95

Armageddon Factor: The Conclusion
AC

❑1 1990, b&w; NN 3.95

Armageddonquest
Starhead

❑1, Apr 1994; Adult; b&w 3.95
❑2, Jun 1994; Adult; b&w 3.95

Armageddon Rising
Millennium

❑1 1997, b&w; special foil edition; features characters from Song of the Sirens 4.95

Armageddon Squad
Haze

❑1, b&w 1.50

Armature
Olyoptics

❑1, Nov 1996 .... 2.95
❑2, ca. 1997 .... 2.95

Armed and Dangerous (Acclaim)
Acclaim / Armada

❑1, Apr 1996, b&w 2.95
❑2, May 1996, b&w 2.95
❑3, Jun 1996, b&w 2.95
❑4, Jul 1996, b&w 2.95
❑Special 1, Aug 1996, b&w; one-shot special; later indicias show this is really issue #5 of series 2.95

Armed & Dangerous: Hell's Slaughterhouse
Acclaim

❑1 .... 2.95
❑2 .... 2.95
❑3, Dec 1996 .... 2.95
❑4, Jan 1997; Armed & Damgerous Vol. 1 No. 9 .... 2.95

Armed & Dangerous
Kitchen Sink

❑1, Jul 1995; magazine-sized graphic novel 9.95

Armen Deep & Bug Boy
Dilemma

❑2 1995, b&w; cardstock cover 2.50

Armitage
Fleetway-Quality

❑1; cardstock cover 2.95
❑2; cardstock cover 2.95

Arm of Kannon
Tokyopop

❑1, May 2004 .... 9.99
❑2, Jul 2004 .... 9.99
❑3, Sep 2004 .... 9.99
❑4, Dec 2004 .... 9.99
❑5, Mar 2005 .... 9.99
❑6, Jun 2005 .... 9.99
❑7, Oct 2005 .... 9.99

Armor
Continuity

❑4, Jul 1988; First three issues published as Revengers Featuring Armor and Silverstreak 2.00
❑5, Dec 1988 .... 2.00
❑6, Apr 1989 .... 2.00
❑7, Jan 1990; Wrap-around cover; O: Armor 2.00
❑8, Apr 1990 .... 2.00
❑9, Apr 1991 .... 2.00
❑10, Aug 1991 .... 2.00
❑11, Nov 1991 .... 2.00
❑12, Mar 1992 .... 2.00
❑13, Apr 1992 .... 2.00

Armor
Continuity

❑1, Apr 1993; wraparound foil cardstock cover; 2 trading cards; indicia calls title "Armor: Deathwatch 2000" 2.50
❑2, May 1993; trading card; diecut outer cover; indicia calls title "Armor: Deathwatch 2000" 2.50
❑3, Aug 1993; Indicia reverts to Armor as title 2.50
❑4, Oct 1993 .... 2.50
❑5, Nov 1993 .... 2.50
❑6, Nov 1993 .... 2.50

Armored Trooper Votoms
CPM

❑1, Jul 1996 .... 2.95

Armorines
Valiant

❑0/Gold, Feb 1993; Gold edition 25.00
❑0, Feb 1993; "Fall Fling Preview Edition"; no cover price 1.00
❑0/StandAlone, Feb 1993 .... 30.00
❑1/VVSS, Jun 1994 .... 40.00
❑1, Jun 1994 .... 1.00
❑2, Aug 1994 .... 1.00
❑3, Sep 1994 .... 1.00
❑4, Oct 1994 .... 1.00
❑5, Nov 1994; Continues from Harbinger #34; Chaos Effect Delta 2 .... 1.00
❑6, Dec 1994 A: X-O 1.00
❑7, Jan 1995; wraparound cover 1.00
❑8, Feb 1995 .... 1.00
❑9, Mar 1995 .... 2.00
❑10, Apr 1995 .... 2.00
❑11, May 1995 .... 2.00
❑12, Jun 1995; Final Issue 4.00

Armorines
Acclaim

❑1, Oct 1999 .... 3.95
❑2, Nov 1999 .... 3.95
❑3, Dec 1999 .... 3.95
❑4, Jan 2000 A: X-O Manowar 3.95

Armorquest
Alias

❑0 2005 .... 2.99
❑1, Sep 2005 .... 2.99
❑2, Dec 2005 .... 2.99

Armor X
Image

❑1, Apr 2005 .... 2.95
❑2, May 2005 .... 2.95
❑3, Jun 2005 .... 2.95
❑4, Jul 2005; Flip cover 2.95

Arm's Length
Third Wind

❑1, Jul 2000, b&w 3.95

Army Ants (Michael T. Desing's...)
Michael T. Desing

❑8, b&w 2.50

Army Attack
Charlton

❑1, Jul 1964 .... 20.00
❑2, Sep 1964 .... 15.00
❑3, Nov 1964 .... 15.00
❑4, Feb 1965 .... 15.00
❑38, Jul 1965; Picks up numbering from U.S. Air Force 15.00
❑39, Aug 1965 .... 15.00
❑40, Oct 1965 .... 15.00
❑41, Dec 1965 .... 15.00
❑42, Feb 1966 .... 15.00
❑43, Jul 1966 .... 15.00
❑44, Aug 1966 .... 15.00
❑45, Oct 1966 .... 15.00
❑46, Dec 1966 .... 15.00
❑47, Feb 1967 .... 15.00

Army at War
DC

❑1, Oct 1978 .... 10.00

Army of Darkness
Dark Horse

❑1, Nov 1992 .... 12.00
❑2, Nov 1992 .... 9.00
❑3, Oct 1993 .... 9.00

Army of Darkness: Ashes 2 Ashes
Devil's Due

❑1, Jul 2004; Cover with green background; Ash with chainsaw above army of the dead 10.00
❑1/Incentive, Jul 2004 .... 5.00
❑1/Photo, Jul 2004 .... 4.00
❑1/Silvestri, Jul 2004 .... 3.00
❑1/Sketch, Jul 2004 .... 11.00
❑1/DirCut, Jul 2004 .... 7.00
❑1/Templesmith, Jul 2004 .... 2.99
❑2, Aug 2004; EC-style cover (brownish background) 4.00
❑2/B&W, Aug 2004 .... 5.00
❑2/Photo, Aug 2004 .... 3.00
❑2/Dynamic, Aug 2004 .... 7.00
❑2/Land, Aug 2004 .... 3.00

Archer & Armstrong

Super-powered adventurers on the run
©Valiant

Archie

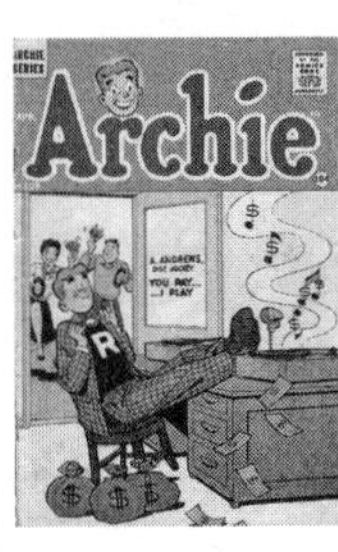

Flagship title for an American icon
©Archie

Archie and Friends

1990s version updates the supporting cast
©Archie

Archie and Me

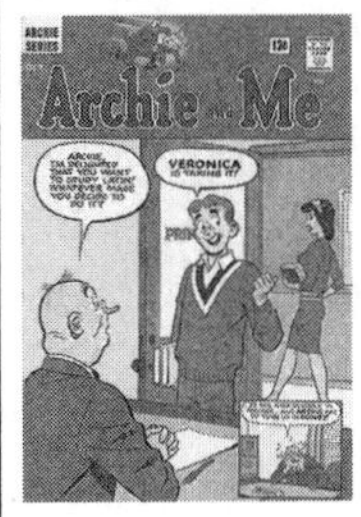

Long-lived Archie spinoff from the 1960s
©Archie

Archie As Pureheart the Powerful

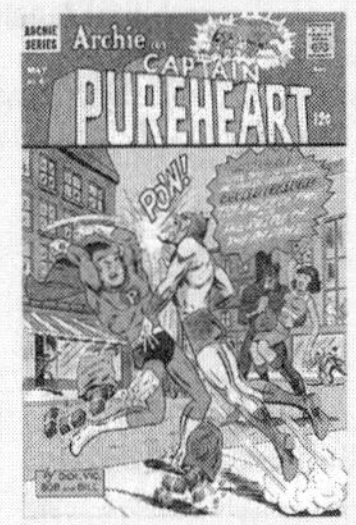

Campy Batman series spawns Archie oddity
©Archie

N-MINT

❑2/Isanove, Aug 2004 ... 4.00
❑3, ca. 2004; Ash slashing soldier with chainsaw ... 3.00
❑4, ca. 2004; NIck Bradshaw cover ... 4.00
❑4/Garza, ca. 2004 ... 3.00

Army of Darkness: Shop Til You Drop (Dead)
Devil's Due

❑1 2005; Bradshaw cover ... 2.99
❑1/Ebas 2005 ... 4.00
❑1/Isanove 2005 ... 3.00
❑1/Lee 2005 ... 4.00
❑1/Rivera 2005 ... 3.00
❑1/Glow 2005; 300 created ... 35.00
❑2 2005 ... 2.99
❑2/Variant 2005 ... 8.00
❑2/DF 2005 ... 15.00
❑3 2005 ... 2.99
❑4 2005 ... 2.99

Army Surplus Komikz Featuring: Cutey Bunny
Quagmire

❑1; Quagmire publishes ... 3.00
❑2 ... 2.50
❑3 ... 2.50
❑4 ... 2.50
❑5 1985, b&w; X-Men parody; Eclipse publishes ... 2.50

Army War Heroes
Charlton

❑1, ca. 1963 ... 20.00
❑2, ca. 1964 ... 10.00
❑3, May 1964 ... 8.00
❑4, Jul 1964 ... 8.00
❑5, Oct 1964 ... 8.00
❑6, Dec 1964 ... 6.00
❑7, ca. 1965 ... 6.00
❑8, May 1965 ... 6.00
❑9, Aug 1965 ... 6.00
❑10, Sep 1965 ... 6.00
❑11, Nov 1965 ... 6.00
❑12, Jan 1966 ... 6.00
❑13, ca. 1966 ... 6.00
❑14, Jun 1966 ... 6.00
❑15, Aug 1966 ... 6.00
❑16, Oct 1966 ... 6.00
❑17, Dec 1966 ... 6.00
❑18, Feb 1967 ... 6.00
❑19, May 1967 ... 6.00
❑20, Jul 1967 ... 4.00
❑21, Sep 1967 ... 4.00
❑22, Nov 1967, 1&O: Iron Corporal ... 6.00
❑23, Jan 1968 ... 4.00
❑24, Mar 1968 ... 4.00
❑25, Jun 1968 ... 4.00
❑26, Aug 1968 ... 4.00
❑27, Oct 1968 ... 4.00
❑28, Nov 1968 ... 4.00
❑29, Jan 1969 ... 4.00
❑30, Feb 1969 ... 4.00
❑31, Apr 1969 ... 4.00
❑32, Jun 1969 ... 4.00
❑33, Aug 1969 ... 4.00
❑34, Oct 1969 ... 4.00
❑35, Dec 1969 ... 4.00

N-MINT

❑36, Feb 1970, A: Iron Corporal ... 4.00
❑37, Apr 1970 ... 4.00
❑38, Jun 1970 ... 4.00

Aromatic Bitters
Tokyopop

❑1, Mar 2004 ... 9.99

Around the World Under the Sea
Dell

❑1, Dec 1966; NN ... 20.00

Arrgh!
Marvel

❑1, Dec 1974, TS (a) ... 15.00
❑2, Feb 1975, TS (w); TS (a) ... 4.00
❑3, May 1975, TS (w); AA (a) ... 3.00
❑4, Jul 1975 ... 3.00
❑5, Sep 1975, RA (a) ... 3.00

Arrow
Malibu

❑1, Oct 1992 ... 1.95

Arrow Anthology
Arrow

❑1, Nov 1997; The Fool, Jabberwocky, Great Scott, Night Streets, Battle Bot . 3.95
❑2, Jan 1998; Simone & Ajax, Battle Bot, Night Streets, Miss Chevious, Dark Oz 3.95
❑3, Mar 1998; The Fool, Dragon Storm, Great Scott, Ninja Duck, Simone & Ajax, Samantha ... 3.95
❑4, Sep 1998; August, Land of Oz, Corhawk, Mr. Nightmare, Simone & Ajax; Flip book, with two front covers 3.95

Arrowman
Parody

❑1, b&w ... 2.50

Arrowsmith
DC / Wildstorm

❑1, Jul 2003 ... 2.95
❑2, Aug 2003 ... 2.95
❑3, Sep 2003 ... 2.95
❑4, Nov 2003 ... 2.95
❑5, Jan 2004 ... 2.95
❑6, May 2004 ... 2.95

Arrowsmith/Astro City
DC / Wildstorm

❑1, Jun 2004 ... 2.95

Arrow Spotlight
Arrow

❑1 1998, b&w; Simone & Ajax ... 2.95

Arsenal
DC

❑1, Oct 1998 ... 2.50
❑2, Nov 1998 ... 2.50
❑3, Dec 1998; V: Vandal Savage ... 2.50
❑4, Jan 1999; V: Vandal Savage ... 2.50

Arsenal Special
DC

❑1 1996; One-shot; ca. 1996 ... 2.95

Arsenic Lullaby
A. Silent

❑1, Dec 1998 ... 5.00
❑2, Mar 1999 ... 2.50
❑3, May 1999 ... 2.50

N-MINT

❑4, Jul 1999 ... 2.50
❑5, Sep 1999 ... 2.50
❑6 2000 ... 2.50
❑7 2000 ... 2.50
❑8 2000 ... 2.50
❑9 2000 ... 2.50
❑10, May 2001 ... 2.50
❑11, Jun 2001 ... 2.50
❑12, Jul 2001 ... 2.50
❑13, Jan 2002, No number on cover; Jan/Feb issue ... 2.50
❑14 ... 2.50
❑15 ... 2.50
❑16 ... 2.65
❑17 ... 2.85
❑18, ca. 2005 ... 2.85
❑19, ca. 2005 ... 2.85
❑20, ca. 2005 ... 2.85

Arsinoe
Fantagraphics

❑1 2005 ... 3.95
❑2 2005 ... 3.95
❑3, Sep 2005 ... 3.95
❑4, Nov 2005 ... 3.95

Art & Beauty Magazine
Kitchen Sink

❑1, b&w; over-sized; cardstock cover ... 4.95
❑2 2003 ... 4.95

Artbabe
Fantagraphics

❑1, May 1997 ... 2.95
❑2, Nov 1997 ... 2.95
❑3, Aug 1998 ... 2.95
❑4, Apr 1999 ... 2.95

Art D'Ecco
Fantagraphics

❑1, Jan 1990, b&w ... 2.50
❑2, Mar 1991, b&w ... 2.50
❑3, Apr 1991 ... 2.75

Artemis: Requiem
DC

❑1, Jun 1996 ... 1.75
❑2, Jul 1996 ... 1.75
❑3, Aug 1996 ... 1.75
❑4, Sep 1996 ... 1.75
❑5, Oct 1996 ... 1.75
❑6, Nov 1996 ... 1.75

Artesia
Sirius

❑1, Jan 1999 ... 2.95
❑2, Feb 1999 ... 2.95
❑3, Mar 1999 ... 2.95
❑4, Apr 1999 ... 2.95
❑5, May 1999 ... 2.95
❑6, Jun 1999 ... 2.95

Artesia Afield
Sirius

❑1, Jul 2000; wraparound cover ... 2.95
❑2, Aug 2000; wraparound cover ... 2.95
❑3, Sep 2000; wraparound cover ... 2.95
❑4, Oct 2000; wraparound cover ... 2.95
❑5, Nov 2000 ... 2.95
❑6, Dec 2000 ... 2.95

Other grades: Multiply price above by 5/6 for VF/NM • 2/3 for VERY FINE • 1/3 for FINE • 1/5 for VERY GOOD • 1/8 for GOOD

	N-MINT

Artesia Afire
Archaia Studios Press

- ❑1, Jun 2003 .... 3.95
- ❑2, Jul 2003; cardstock wraparound cover 3.95
- ❑3, Aug 2003; cardstock wraparound cover 3.95
- ❑4, Oct 2003 .... 3.95
- ❑5, Dec 2003 .... 3.95
- ❑6, Mar 2004; Book of Dooms, Part 3 ... 3.95

Arthur King of Britain
Tome

- ❑1, ca. 1993 .... 2.95
- ❑2, ca. 1993 .... 2.95
- ❑3 .... 2.95
- ❑4 .... 2.95
- ❑5 .... 3.95

Arthur Sex
Aircel

- ❑1, Jun 1991, b&w; Adult 2.50
- ❑2, b&w; Adult 2.50
- ❑3, Jul 1991, b&w; Adult 2.50
- ❑4, Aug 1991, b&w; Adult 2.50
- ❑5, Sep 1991, b&w; Adult 2.50
- ❑6, Oct 1991, b&w; Adult 2.50
- ❑7, Nov 1991, b&w; Adult 2.50
- ❑8, b&w; Adult 2.50

Artillery One-Shot
Red Bullet

- ❑1 1995, b&w 2.50

Artistic Comics
Kitchen Sink

- ❑1, Aug 1995, b&w; adults only; new printing; squarebound 3.00
- ❑1/2nd, Aug 1995; 2nd printing; Adult... 2.50

Artistic Comics
Golden Gate

- ❑0, Mar 1973 .... 10.00

Artistic Licentiousness
Starhead

- ❑1, b&w; Adult 2.50
- ❑2, ca. 1994; Adult 2.95
- ❑3, ca. 1997, b&w; Adult 2.95

Art of Abrams
Lightning

- ❑1, Dec 1996; b&w pin-ups 3.50

Art of Aubrey Beardsley
Tome

- ❑1, b&w 2.95

Art of Heath Robinson
Tome

- ❑1, b&w 2.95

Art of Homage Studios
Image

- ❑1, Dec 1993; JLee (w); JLee (a); 1: Gen13 (pin-ups, sketches) 5.50

Art of Jay Anacleto
Image

- ❑1, Apr 2002 .... 5.95

Art of Mucha
Tome

- ❑1, ca. 1992, b&w 2.95

Art of Pulp Fiction
A-List

- ❑1, Apr 1998 .... 2.95

Art of the Witchblade
Image

- ❑1, Jul 2006 .... 2.99

Art of Usagi Yojimbo
Radio

- ❑1, Apr 1997 .... 3.95
- ❑2, Jan 1998 .... 3.95

Ascension
Image

- ❑0, Jun 1997; Included with Wizard Top Cow Special 3.00
- ❑0/Gold, Jun 1997; Gold edition; Not signed 4.00
- ❑0/Ltd., Jun 1997; Gold cover; Wizard "Certified Authentic" 6.00
- ❑½, May 1998; Wizard Certificate Of Authenticity 4.00
- ❑1, Oct 1997 .... 3.00
- ❑1/A, Oct 1997; Variant cover: Lucien holding head 3.00
- ❑1/B, Oct 1997; Fan club edition; Top Cow Fan Club exclusive 4.00
- ❑1/C, Oct 1997; American Entertainment exclusive 4.00
- ❑1/D, Oct 1997; Sendaway edition; angels on pile of bodies 4.00
- ❑2, Nov 1997 .... 2.50
- ❑2/A, Nov 1997; American Entertainment exclusive 4.00
- ❑2/Gold, Nov 1997; Gold edition 4.00
- ❑3, Dec 1997 .... 2.50
- ❑4, Feb 1998 .... 2.50
- ❑5, Mar 1998 .... 2.50
- ❑6, May 1998 .... 2.50
- ❑7, Jul 1998 .... 2.50
- ❑8, Aug 1998 .... 2.50
- ❑9, Oct 1998 .... 2.50
- ❑10, Nov 1998 .... 2.50
- ❑11, Feb 1999; Painted Cover 2.50
- ❑12, Apr 1999 .... 2.50
- ❑13, May 1999 .... 2.50
- ❑14, Jun 1999 .... 2.50
- ❑15, Jul 1999 .... 2.50
- ❑16, Jul 1999 .... 2.50
- ❑17, Aug 1999 .... 2.50
- ❑18, Sep 1999 .... 2.50
- ❑19, Oct 1999 .... 2.50
- ❑20, Nov 1999 .... 2.50
- ❑21, Dec 1999; cover says Nov, indicia says Dec 2.95
- ❑22, Mar 2000 .... 2.95
- ❑Ashcan 1, Jun 1997; Preview edition; Convention Preview Edition 4.00

Ash
Event

- ❑0, May 1996; "Present" edition; O: Ash. enhanced wraparound cover 3.50
- ❑0/A, May 1996; "Future" edition; O: Ash. alternate enhanced wraparound cover 3.50
- ❑0/B, May 1996; Red foil logo-Present edition 4.00
- ❑0/C, May 1996; Red foil logo-Future edition 4.00
- ❑½, Apr 1997; JRo, MWa (w); Includes Certificate Of Authenticity 2.50
- ❑½/Ltd., Apr 1997; Wizard authentic edition; Signed 4.00
- ❑½/Platinum, Apr 1997; Platinum edition 4.00
- ❑1, Nov 1994; 1: Ash; Wraparound Cover 3.00
- ❑1/A, Nov 1994; 1: Ash. Commemorative Omnichrome cover 4.00
- ❑1/B, Nov 1994; 1: Ash. Dynamic Forces exclusive (DF on cover) 3.00
- ❑2, Jan 1995 .... 3.00
- ❑3, May 1995; Wraparound 3.00
- ❑4, Jul 1995 .... 3.00
- ❑4/A, Jul 1995; Red Edition 3.00
- ❑4/B, Jul 1995; White edition 3.00
- ❑4/Gold, Jul 1995; Gold edition 3.00
- ❑5, Sep 1995 .... 3.00
- ❑6, Dec 1995 .... 2.50
- ❑6/A, Dec 1995; alternate cover 2.50

Ash/22 Brides
Event

- ❑1, Dec 1996 .... 2.95
- ❑2, Apr 1997 .... 2.95

Ash: Cinder & Smoke
Event

- ❑1, May 1997 .... 2.95
- ❑2, Jun 1997, Cover date July 2.95
- ❑2/A, Jun 1997, variant cover 2.95
- ❑3, Jul 1997 .... 2.95
- ❑3/A, Jul 1997, variant cover 2.95
- ❑4, Aug 1997 .... 2.95
- ❑4/A, Aug 1997, variant cover 2.95
- ❑5, Sep 1997 .... 2.95
- ❑5/A, Sep 1997, variant cover 2.95
- ❑6, Oct 1997 .... 2.95
- ❑6/A, Oct 1997, variant cover 2.95

Ashen Victor
Viz

- ❑1, ca. 1997 .... 2.95
- ❑2, ca. 1997 .... 3.25
- ❑3, ca. 1997 .... 2.95
- ❑4, ca. 1997 .... 2.95

Ashes
Caliber

- ❑1 .... 2.50
- ❑2 .... 2.50
- ❑3 .... 2.50
- ❑4 .... 2.50
- ❑5 .... 2.50

Ash Files
Event

- ❑1, Mar 1997; background on series 2.95

Ash: Fire and Crossfire
Event

- ❑1, Jan 1999 JRo (w) 2.95
- ❑1/A, Jan 1999; JRo (w); Signed and numbered 5.00
- ❑2, May 1999; JRo (w); Firemen on cover 2.95

Ashley Dust
Knight

- ❑1, Sep 1994 .... 2.95
- ❑2, Dec 1994 .... 2.95
- ❑3, Mar 1995 .... 2.95

Ashpile
Side Show

- ❑1 .... 8.95

Ash: The Fire Within
Event

- ❑1, Sep 1996 .... 2.95
- ❑2, Jan 1997 .... 2.95

Askani'son
Marvel

- ❑1, Jan 1996, cover says "Feb," indicia says "Jan" 2.95
- ❑2, Apr 1996, cover says "Mar", indicia says "Apr" 2.95
- ❑3, Apr 1996, cardstock wraparound cover 2.95
- ❑4, May 1996, cardstock wraparound cover 2.95

Sort of Homecoming, A
Alternative

- ❑1 .... 3.50
- ❑2, Feb 2004 .... 3.50
- ❑3, May 2004 .... 3.50

Aspen Extended Edition
Aspen

- ❑1, Jun 2004 .... 8.00
- ❑1/Conv, Jun 2004 .... 15.00

Aspen (Michael Turner Presents)
Aspen

- ❑1, Jul 2003 .... 7.00
- ❑1/Variant, Jul 2003 .... 12.00
- ❑1/Conv, Jul 2003 .... 10.00
- ❑2, Jul 2003 .... 4.00
- ❑2/Variant, Jul 2003 .... 6.00
- ❑2/Conv, Jul 2003 .... 10.00
- ❑3, Aug 2003 .... 6.00
- ❑3/Variant, Aug 2003 .... 8.00
- ❑3/Conv, Aug 2003 .... 10.00

Aspen Seasons: Spring 2005
Aspen

- ❑0 2005 .... 2.99

Aspen Sketchbook
Aspen

- ❑1, Feb 2004 .... 2.99

Asrial vs. Cheetah
Antarctic

- ❑1, Mar 1996 .... 2.95
- ❑2, Apr 1996 .... 2.95

Assassin
Arcana

- ❑1, ca. 2005 .... 2.99

Assassination of Malcolm X
Zone

- ❑1 .... 2.95

Assassinette
Pocket Change

- ❑1, ca. 1994; silver foil cover 2.50
- ❑2, ca. 1994 .... 2.50
- ❑3, ca. 1994 .... 2.50
- ❑4, Mar 1995 .... 2.50
- ❑5, ca. 1995 .... 2.50
- ❑6, ca. 1995 .... 2.50
- ❑7, Dec 1995; Shadow Slasher Preview 2.50

Assassinette Hardcore!
Pocket Change

- ❑1, ca. 1995 .... 2.50
- ❑2, ca. 1995 .... 2.50

Archie at Riverdale High

Series spotlights school supporting cast
©Archie

Archie Giant Series Magazine

Ever-changing titles and weird numbering
©Archie

Archie Meets the Punisher

The crossover nobody ever expected
©Marvel

Archie's Christmas Stocking (2nd Series)

A continuing seasonal classic
©Archie

Archie's Date Book

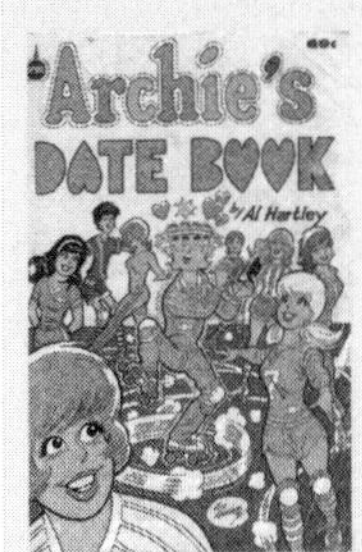

Religious comic preaches against premarital sex
©Spire

N-MINT

Assassins
DC / Amalgam

❑1, Apr 1996, Amalgam of Catwoman/Elektra & Deathstroke/Daredevil 1.95

Assassin School
APComics

❑0, ca. 2003 .... 2.99

Assassin School
APComics

❑1, ca. 2003 .... 5.00
❑2, Apr 2004 .... 4.00
❑3, May 2004 .... 4.00
❑4, Jun 2004 .... 4.00
❑5, Jul 2004 .... 4.00
❑6, Oct 2004 .... 4.00

Assassins Inc.
Silverline

❑1 .... 1.95
❑2 .... 1.95

Assembly
Antarctic

❑1, Nov 2003; b&w 2.99
❑2, Dec 2003; b&w 3.50
❑3, Jan 2004; b&w 2.99

Aster
Express / Entity

❑0, Oct 1994; Gold foil letters 2.95
❑1, Oct 1994, b&w 2.95
❑1/Gold, Oct 1994, b&w; Gold edition ... 3.00
❑2, Nov 1994; enhanced cardstock cover 2.95
❑3, Jan 1995 .... 2.95
❑3/A, Jan 1995; alternate cover 2.95
❑3/B, Jan 1995; enhanced cover 2.95
❑Ashcan 1; no cover price; b&w preview 1.00

Aster: The Last Celestial Knight
Express / Entity

❑1 1995, Chromium cover 3.75

Astonish!
Wehner

❑1, b&w 2.00

Astonishing Excitement
All-Jonh

❑501 .... 2.95
❑502 .... 2.95
❑503 .... 3.50

Astonishing Tales
Marvel

❑1, Aug 1970, SL (w); JK, WW (a); A: Kraven the Hunter. Ka-Zar, Doctor Doom 40.00
❑2, Oct 1970, JB (c); JK, WW (a); A: Kraven the Hunter. Ka-Zar, Doctor Doom 20.00
❑3, Dec 1970, WW (a); 1: Zaladane. Ka-Zar, Doctor Doom 20.00
❑4, Feb 1971, JB (c); WW (a); Ka-Zar, Doctor Doom 20.00
❑5, Apr 1971, A: Red Skull. Ka-Zar, Doctor Doom 20.00
❑6, Jun 1971, 1: Mockingbird (as Bobbi Morse). Ka-Zar, Doctor Doom 12.00
❑7, Aug 1971, Ka-Zar, Doctor Doom 15.00
❑8, Oct 1971, Ka-Zar, Doctor Doom 15.00
❑9, Dec 1971, Ka-Zar 10.00
❑10, Feb 1972, GK (c); SB (a); Ka-Zar ... 20.00
❑11, Apr 1972, O: Ka-Zar. Ka-Zar 10.00
❑12, Jun 1972, JB (c); JB, NA, DA (a); A: Man-Thing. Ka-Zar 30.00
❑13, Aug 1972, RB, JB, DA (a); A: Man-Thing. Ka-Zar 10.00
❑14, Oct 1972, Ka-Zar; reprinted from Savage Tales #1 and Jungle Tales #2 . 10.00
❑15, Dec 1972, Ka-Zar 10.00
❑16, Feb 1973, Ka-Zar 10.00
❑17, Apr 1973, Ka-Zar 10.00
❑18, Jun 1973, Ka-Zar 10.00
❑19, Aug 1973, Ka-Zar 10.00
❑20, Oct 1973, Ka-Zar 10.00
❑21, Dec 1973, Reprinted from Amazing Adult Fantasy #9 .... 25.00
❑22, Feb 1974, Reprinted from Strange Tales #74 .... 10.00
❑23, Apr 1974, Reprinted from Strange Tales #89; Marvel Value Stamp #54: Shanna 15.00
❑24, Jun 1974, Marvel Value Stamp #18: Volstaag 10.00
❑25, Aug 1974, RB (c); RB (w); RB, GP (a); 1&O: Deathlok I (Luther Manning). 1st George Perez work; Marvel Value Stamp #68: Son of Satan 25.00
❑26, Oct 1974, A: Deathlok. Marvel Value Stamp #66: General Ross 10.00
❑27, Dec 1974, A: Deathlok. Marvel Value Stamp #22: Man-Thing 7.00
❑28, Feb 1975, A: Deathlok. Marvel Value Stamp #84: Dr. Doom 7.00
❑29, Apr 1975, 1&O: Guardians of the Galaxy. Reprinted from Marvel Super-Heroes #18 .... 7.00
❑30, Jun 1975, RB (c); RB (w); RB, KP (a); A: Deathlok 5.00
❑31, Aug 1975, RB, SL (w); RB, GC, KP (a); A: Deathlok. Reprinted from Silver Surfer #3 .... 5.00
❑32, Nov 1976, A: Deathlok 5.00
❑33, Jan 1976, A: Deathlok. Marvel Value Stamp Series B #3 .... 10.00
❑34, Mar 1976, A: Deathlok 6.00
❑35, May 1976, A: Deathlok 7.00
❑35/30¢, May 1976, A: Deathlok. 30¢ regional price variant 20.00
❑36, Jul 1976, A: Deathlok. Final Issue; Continued in Marvel Spotlight #33 ..... 10.00
❑36/30¢, Jul 1976, A: Deathlok. 30¢ regional price variant 10.00

Astonishing X-Men
Marvel

❑1, Mar 1995; DGr (a); Age of Apocalypse 6.00
❑2, Apr 1995 DGr (a) 6.00
❑3, May 1995 JPH (w); AM (a) 6.00
❑4, Jun 1995 AM (a) 8.00

Astonishing X-Men
Marvel

❑1, Sep 1999, The Twelve 5.00
❑2, Oct 1999, The Twelve 2.50
❑3, Nov 1999, The Twelve 2.50

Astonishing X-Men
Marvel

❑1, Jul 2004, Black cover with Wolverine's claws; 1: Kavita Rao; 1: Ord 8.00
❑1/Cassaday, Jul 2004; John Cassaday cover 45.00
❑1/Del Otto, Jul 2004; Gabriel Del'Otto cover 45.00
❑1/DirCut, Aug 2004; Director's Cut 45.00
❑1/Dynamic 8.00
❑2, Aug 2004 .... 16.00
❑3, Sep 2004, 1: Wing 4.00
❑4, Oct 2004, John Cassaday Beast picture cover; Return of Colossus; Beast cover; 1: Armor; Colossus returns 8.00
❑4/Variant, Oct 2004, Retailer variant, Colossus cover 25.00
❑5, Nov 2004, Colossus Vs. Ord 8.00
❑6, Dec 2004, Wolverine Vs. Ord; Misprints publish date as Dec. 2005.. 5.00
❑7, Jan 2005; 1: Blindfold; D: Wing 4.00
❑8, Feb 2005; V: Sentinel 2.99
❑9, Mar 2005 .... 2.99
❑10, Apr 2005 .... 2.99
❑10/Variant, Apr 2005 .... 5.00
❑11, Sep 2005 .... 2.99
❑12, Oct 2005 .... 2.99
❑13, May 2006 .... 2.99
❑14, Jul 2006, V: Hellfire Club 2.99
❑15, Sep 2006, V: Hellfire Club 2.99
❑16, Nov 2006, V: Hellfire Club 2.99
❑17, Nov 2006 .... 2.99
❑19, Mar 2007 .... 2.99
❑21 .... 2.99
❑22 .... 2.99
❑23 .... 2.99
❑24 .... 2.99
❑25 .... 2.99
❑26 .... 2.99
❑27 .... 2.99
❑28 .... 2.99
❑29 .... 2.99

Astounding Space Thrills
Day 1

❑1, May 1998, b&w 2.95
❑2, Jul 1998, b&w 2.95
❑3, Jan 1999, b&w 2.95

Astounding Space Thrills: The Comic Book
Image

❑1, Apr 2000 .... 2.95
❑2, Jul 2000 .... 2.95
❑3, Sep 2000 .... 2.95
❑4, Dec 2000 .... 2.95
❑GS 1, Oct 2001 .... 4.95

Astrider Hugo
Radio

❑1, Jul 2000, b&w 3.95

Astro Boy
Gold Key

❑1, Aug 1965 .... 265.00

Astro Boy
Dark Horse

❑1, ca. 2002 .... 9.95
❑2, ca. 2002 .... 9.95
❑3, ca. 2002 .... 9.95
❑4, ca. 2002 .... 9.95
❑5, ca. 2002 .... 9.95
❑6, ca. 2002 .... 9.95
❑7, ca. 2002 .... 9.95
❑8, ca. 2003 .... 9.95

Other grades: Multiply price above by 5/6 for VF/NM • 2/3 for VERY FINE • 1/3 for FINE • 1/5 for VERY GOOD • 1/8 for GOOD

❑9, ca. 2003 9.95
❑10, ca. 2003 9.95
❑11, ca. 2003 9.95
❑12, ca. 2003 9.95
❑13, ca. 2003 9.95
❑14, ca. 2003 9.95
❑15, ca. 2003 9.95
❑16, ca. 2003 9.95
❑17, ca. 2003 9.95
❑18, ca. 2003 9.95
❑19, ca. 2003 9.95
❑20, ca. 2004 9.95
❑21, ca. 2004 9.95
❑22, ca. 2004 9.95
❑23 2004 9.95

Astro City: A Visitor's Guide
DC

❑1 2004 5.95

Astro City Local Heroes
DC

❑1, Apr 2003 2.95
❑2, Jun 2003 2.95
❑3, Aug 2003 2.95
❑4, Dec 2003 2.95
❑5, Feb 2004 2.95

Astro City: Samaritan Special
DC / Wildstorm

❑1, Oct 2006 3.99

Astro City Special
DC / Wildstorm

❑1, Oct 2004 3.95

Astro City: The Dark Age
DC

❑1, Aug 2005 2.99
❑2, Sep 2005 2.99
❑3, Oct 2005 2.99
❑4, Nov 2005 2.99

Astro City (Kurt Busiek's...)
Image

❑1, Aug 1995; ARo (c); KB (w); BA (a); 1: The Honor Guard. 1: The Menagerie Gang. 1: Doctor Saturday. 1: The Samaritan 5.00
❑2, Sep 1995 ARo (c); KB (w); BA (a); A: Silver Agent. A: Honor Guard. 3.00
❑3, Oct 1995 ARo (c); KB (w); BA (a); A: Jack in the Box 3.00
❑4, Nov 1995; ARo (c); KB (w); BA (a); 1: The Hanged Man. A: First Family. A: Winged Victory 3.00
❑5, Dec 1995 ARo (c); KB (w); BA (a); A: Crackerjack. A: Astro City Irregulars 3.00
❑6, Jan 1996; ARo (c); KB (w); BA (a); O: The Samaritan 3.00

Astro City (Kurt Busiek's...)
Image

❑½, Jan 2000, Wizard promotional item 3.00
❑½/Direct ed., Jan 1998, Direct Market edition; reprints "The Nearness of You" and "Clash of Titans" 3.00
❑1, Sep 1996 4.00
❑1/3D, Dec 1997, Signed hardcover edition; 3D Special 5.00
❑2, Oct 1996 3.00
❑3, Nov 1996 3.00
❑4, Dec 1996, 1: Brian Kinney (The Altar Boy) (out of costume) 3.00
❑5, Jan 1997, 1: The Altar Boy (Brian Kinney in costume); O: The Altar Boy. 3.00
❑6, Feb 1997, The Confessor revealed as vampire 3.00
❑7, Mar 1997, O: The Confessor I 2.50
❑8, Apr 1997, D: The Confessor I 2.50
❑9, May 1997, 1: The Confessor II 2.50
❑10, Oct 1997, O: The Junkman 2.50
❑11, Nov 1997, Jack-in-the-Box vs. alternate versions 2.50
❑12, Dec 1997, 1: Jack-in-the-Box II (Roscoe James) 2.50
❑13, Feb 1998, 1&O: Loony Leo 2.50
❑14, Apr 1998, 1: Steeljack; O: Steeljack 2.50
❑15, Dec 1998, 1: new Goldenglove; 2: Steeljack 2.50
❑16, Mar 1999, O: El Hombre 2.50
❑17, May 1999, O: The Mock Turtle 2.50
❑18, Aug 1999 2.50
❑19, Nov 1999 2.50
❑20, Jan 2000 2.50
❑21, Mar 2000 2.50

AstroComics
Harvey

❑1, Giveaway from American Airlines; Reprints Harvey Comics stories 2.50

Astronauts in Trouble: Space 1959
AiT

❑1, Aug 2000 2.95

Astrothrill
Cheeky

❑1, May 1999; cardstock cover; new material and reprints from Nemesister; CD 12.95

Asylum (Maximum)
Maximum

❑1, Dec 1995, Flip-book; Beanworld/ Avengelyne flip covers 2.95
❑1/A, Dec 1995, Warchild/Doubletake flip covers 2.95
❑2, Jan 1996, Flip-book; Pin-Up 2.95
❑3, Apr 1996, Flip-book 2.95
❑4, May 1996, Flip-book 2.95
❑5, Jun 1996, Flipbook 2.95
❑6, Jul 1996, preview of planned Bionix series featuring The Six Million Dollar Man and Bionic Woman; flipbook 2.95
❑7, Sep 1996 2.95
❑8, Sep 1996, Indicia misprint date as September 1996 2.95
❑9, Nov 1996 2.95
❑10, Dec 1996 2.95
❑11, Jan 1997 2.99
❑12, Feb 1997 2.99
❑13, Mar 1997 2.99

Asylum (Millennium)
Millennium

❑1 2.50
❑2 2.50
❑3 4.95

Asylum (NCG)
New Comics

❑1, b&w 1.95
❑2 2.25

Atari Force
DC

❑1, Jan 1984; JL (a); 1: Dark Destroyer. 1: Babe. 1: Atari Force (in standard comics). 1: Dart. 1: Blackjak 1.00
❑2, Feb 1984; 1: Martin Champion 1.00
❑3, Mar 1984 1.00
❑4, Apr 1984 1.00
❑5, May 1984 1.00
❑6, Jun 1984 1.00
❑7, Jul 1984 1.00
❑8, Aug 1984 1.00
❑9, Sep 1984 1.00
❑10, Oct 1984 1.00
❑11, Nov 1984 1.00
❑12, Dec 1984 1.00
❑13, Jan 1985 1.00
❑14, Feb 1985 1.00
❑15, Mar 1985 1.00
❑16, Apr 1985 1.00
❑17, May 1985 1.00
❑18, Jun 1985 1.00
❑19, Jul 1985 1.00
❑20, Aug 1985; Final Issue 1.00
❑Special 1 1986; Giant-size; MR (c); MR (a) 2.00

A-Team
Marvel

❑1, Mar 1984, based on TV series 2.00
❑2, Apr 1984, JR, JM (a) 2.00
❑3, May 1984 2.00

Atheist
Image

❑1, May 2005 3.50
❑2, Sep 2005 3.50
❑3, Apr 206 3.50

Athena
Antarctic

❑0, Dec 1996, Antarctic publishes 2.95
❑1, Nov 1995, A.M. Press publishes 2.95
❑2, Dec 1995 2.95
❑3, Feb 1996 2.95
❑4, Apr 1996 2.95
❑5, Jun 1996 2.95
❑6, Aug 1996 2.95
❑7, Mar 1997, b&w 2.95
❑8, Apr 1997, b&w 2.95
❑9, May 1997, b&w 2.95
❑10, Jun 1997, b&w 2.95
❑11, Aug 1997, b&w 2.95
❑12, Sep 1997, b&w 2.95
❑13, Nov 1997, b&w 2.95
❑14, Dec 1997, b&w 2.95

Athena Inc. Agents Roster
Image

❑1, Nov 2002 5.95

Athena Inc. The Beginning
Image

❑1, Jan 2001, b&w 5.95

Athena Inc. The Manhunter Project
Image

❑1 2002 2.95
❑1/A, Apr 2002 2.95
❑Ashcan 1 2002; Solicited as Megacon 2001 Edition; Limited Edition Ashcan. 1.00
❑2/A, Apr 2002 2.95
❑2/B, Apr 2002 2.95
❑3/A, Aug 2002 2.95
❑3/B, Aug 2002 2.95
❑4/A, Oct 2002 2.95
❑4/B, Oct 2002 2.95
❑5/A, Jan 2003 2.95
❑5/B, Jan 2003 2.95
❑6/A, Apr 2003 4.95
❑6/B, Apr 2003 4.95

Atlantis Chronicles
DC

❑1, Mar 1990, PD (w); The Deluge 3.00
❑2, Apr 1990, PD (w) 3.00
❑3, May 1990, PD (w) 3.00
❑4, Jun 1990, PD (w) 3.00
❑5, Jul 1990, PD (w); 1: Atlan 3.00
❑6, Aug 1990, PD (w) 3.00
❑7, Sep 1990, PD (w); O: Aquaman; Final Issue 3.00

@Large
Tokyopop

❑1, Dec 2003 10.00
❑2, Aug 2004 10.00
❑3, Dec 2005 10.00

Atlas
Dark Horse

❑1, Feb 1994 2.50
❑2, Apr 1994 2.50
❑3, Jun 1994 2.50
❑4, Aug 1994 2.50

Atlas (Avatar)
Avatar

❑1/A, Aug 2002; Gossett cover (Judo Girl and Atlas) 3.50
❑1/B, Aug 2002; Talent Caldwell cover 3.50
❑1/C, Aug 2002; Roger Cruz cover 3.50
❑1/D, Aug 2002; S. Young cover 3.50
❑1/E, Aug 2002; M. Brooks cover 3.50
❑1/F, Aug 2002; Dealer incentive variant of #1/E; Platinum Foil title 3.50
❑1/G, Aug 2002; Judo Girl cover 5.95

Atom
DC

❑1, Jul 1962, MA, GK (a); 1: Plant Master; Dave Cockrum L.O.C 750.00
❑2, Sep 1962, MA, GK (a); Paul Gambaccini L.O.C.; Dave Cockrum L.O.C 300.00
❑3, Nov 1962, MA, GK (a); 1: Chronos; 1: Professor Alpheus V. Hyatt; 1: Time Pool 225.00
❑4, Jan 1963, MA, GK (a); Paul Gambaccini L.O.C; Buddy Saunders L.O.C 175.00
❑5, Mar 1963, MA, GK (a); Mike Sekowsky ghost-pencils pages 4-9 of first story; Paul Gambaccini L.O.C 175.00
❑6, May 1963, MA, GK (a); Buddy Saunders L.O.C 125.00
❑7, Jul 1963, MA, GK (a); A: Hawkman. Paul Gambaccini L.O.C 250.00
❑8, Sep 1963, MA, GK (a); A: Justice League of America. E. Nelson Bridwell L.O.C 125.00
❑9, Nov 1963, MA, GK (a) 90.00
❑10, Jan 1964, MA, GK (a) 85.00

Archie's Family Album

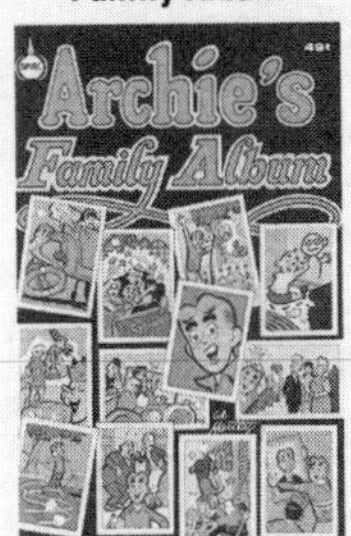

Another religious comic from Al Hartley

©Spire

Archie's Girls Betty & Veronica

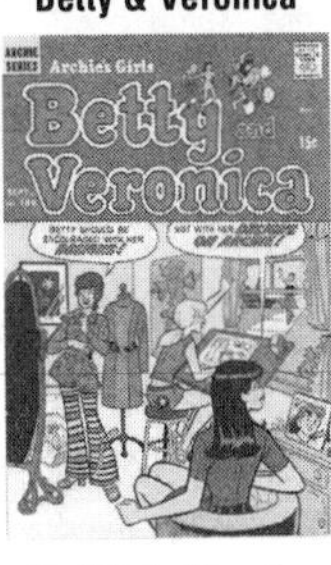

First title by this name; see also "Betty..."

©Archie

Archie's Jokebook Magazine

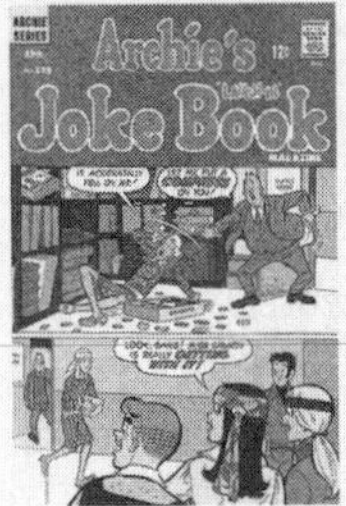

Lots and lots of simple gags with Archie

©Archie

Archie's Madhouse

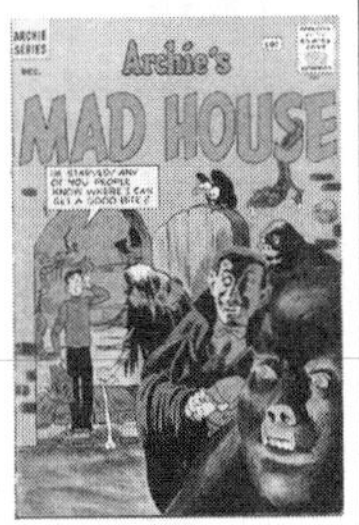

The series that kept changing names

©Archie

Archie's Mysteries

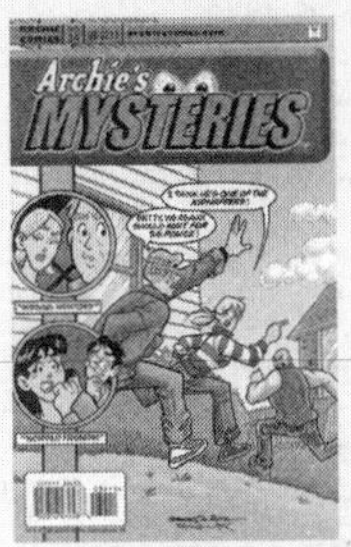

More Scooby-Doo style Archie tales

©Archie

	N-MINT
❑11, Mar 1964, MA, GK (a)	85.00
❑12, May 1964, MA, GK (a)	85.00
❑13, Jul 1964, V: Chronos	85.00
❑14, Sep 1964	95.00
❑15, Nov 1964	85.00
❑16, Jan 1965, MA, GK (a)	45.00
❑17, Mar 1965, MA, GK (a)	45.00
❑18, May 1965, MA, GK (a); Guy H. Lillian L.O.C	50.00
❑19, Jul 1965, GK (c); MA, GK (a); Marv Wolfman L.O.C; Guy H. Lillian L.O.C; Storyline of Zatanna searching for Zatara; Continues from Hawkman (1st Series) #4 & into Green Lantern (2nd Series) #42	45.00
❑20, Sep 1965, MA, GK (a)	60.00
❑21, Nov 1965, Mike Friedrich L.O.C	35.00
❑22, Jan 1966, Guy H. Lillian L.O.C	35.00
❑23, Mar 1966	35.00
❑24, May 1966, V: Plant Master; Guy H. Lillian L.O.C	40.00
❑25, Jul 1966	50.00
❑26, Sep 1966, 1: Bug-Eyed Bandit; Guy H. Lillian L.O.C; Irene Vartanoff L.O.C.	35.00
❑27, Nov 1966, V: Panther	35.00
❑28, Jan 1967, V: Chronos; Irene Vartanoff L.O.C.; Dave Cockrum L.O.C	35.00
❑29, Mar 1967, A: Atom I (Al Pratt). Irene Vartanoff L.O.C	100.00
❑30, May 1967, Guy H. Lillian L.O.C	55.00
❑31, Jul 1967, A: Hawkman. Bill Mantlo L.O.C.; Mike Friedrich L.O.C	48.00
❑32, Sep 1967, Guy H. Lillian L.O.C	35.00
❑33, Nov 1967, V: Bug-Eyed Bandit; Peter Sanderson L.O.C	40.00
❑34, Jan 1968, V: Big Gang; Peter Sanderson L.O.C	35.00
❑35, Mar 1968, GK (a); Gerry Conway L.O.C.; Irene Vartanoff L.O.C.; Last Day on Earth reprinted from Strange Adventures #41	35.00
❑36, May 1968, A: Atom I (Al Pratt)	45.00
❑37, Jul 1968, A: Hawkman. 1: Major Mynah	45.00
❑38, Sep 1968, Series continued in Atom and Hawkman #39	30.00
❑Special 1, Jun 1993; V: Chronos	2.50
❑Special 2, ca. 1995; BB (c); LMc (a)	2.50

Atom and Hawkman
DC

❑39, Oct 1968, JKu (c); MA, JKu (a); Series continued from Atom #38	30.00
❑40, Dec 1968, JKu (c); MA, DD (a)	30.00
❑41, Feb 1969, Peter Sanderson L.O.C	30.00
❑42, Apr 1969, Martin Pasko L.O.C.; Klaus Janson L.O.C	35.00
❑43, Jun 1969, JKu (c); MA, JKu, DD (a); O: Gentlemen Ghost; Martin Pasko L.O.C.; Klaus Janson L.O.C	30.00
❑44, Aug 1969; V: Gentleman Ghost; Bill Mantlo L.O.C.; Martin Pasko L.O.C	30.00
❑45, Oct 1969; Final Issue; Mike Barr L.O.C	30.00

Atom Ant
Gold Key

❑1, Jan 1966	85.00

Atomic Age
Marvel / Epic

	N-MINT
❑1, Nov 1990	4.50
❑2, Dec 1990	4.50
❑3, Jan 1991	4.50
❑4, Feb 1991	4.50

Atomic Age Truckstop Waitress
Fantagraphics / Eros

❑1, Jul 1991, b&w; Adult	2.25

Atomic City Tales
Kitchen Sink

❑1, May 1996	2.95
❑2 1996	2.95
❑3, Sep 1996	2.95
❑Special 1	2.95

Atomic Man
Blackthorne

❑1 1986	1.75
❑2 1986	1.75
❑3 1986	1.75

Atomic Mouse
Charlton

❑10, Sep 1985	5.00
❑11, Nov 1985	3.00
❑12, Jan 1986	3.00
❑13, Mar 1986	3.00

Atomic Mouse (A+)
A+

❑1, ca. 1990	2.50
❑2 1990	2.50
❑3 1990	2.50

Atomicow
Vision

❑1, Aug 1990	2.50

Atomic Rabbit & Friends
Avalon

❑1, b&w; reprints Charlton stories	2.50

Atomics
AAA Pop

❑1, Jan 2000	2.95
❑2, Feb 2000	2.95
❑3, Mar 2000	2.95
❑4, Apr 2000	2.95
❑5, May 2000	2.95
❑6, Jun 2000; O: Zapman	2.95
❑7, Jul 2000	2.95
❑8, Aug 2000	2.95
❑9, Sep 2000	2.95
❑10, Oct 2000	2.95
❑11, Nov 2000	2.95
❑12, Dec 2000	3.50
❑13, Jan 2001	3.50
❑14, Feb 2001	3.50
❑15, Mar 2001	3.50

Atomic Toybox
Image

❑1, Nov 1999; cover says Dec, indicia says Nov	2.95
❑1/A, Nov 1999; Pirate girl cover; Cover says Dec, indicia says Nov; Cavewoman cover	2.95
❑1/B, Nov 1999; Pirate girl cover; Cover says Dec, indicia says Nov	2.95

Atomika
Speakeasy Comics

	N-MINT
❑1, Mar 2005	2.99
❑2, Apr 2005	3.00
❑3, May 2005	2.99
❑4/Turner, Sep 2005	5.00
❑4/Buzz, Sep 2005	2.99
❑4/Jay, Sep 2005	4.00
❑4/Rupps, Sep 2005	2.99

Atomik Angels (William Tucci's...)
Crusade

❑1, May 1996 A: Freefall	2.95
❑1/Variant, May 1996; A: Freefall. variant cover	3.50
❑2, Jul 1996	2.95
❑3, Sep 1996	2.95
❑3/Variant, Sep 1996; alternate cover (orange background with Statue of Liberty)	3.50
❑4, Nov 1996; flipbook with Manga Shi 2000 preview	2.95
❑Special 1, Feb 1996, b&w; "The Intrep-edition"; promotional comic for U.S.S. Intrepid	3.00

Atom the Atomic Cat
Avalon

❑1	2.95

Attack
Charlton

❑54, ca. 1958	24.00
❑55, ca. 1959	10.00
❑56, ca. 1959	10.00
❑57, ca. 1959	10.00
❑58, ca. 1959	10.00
❑59, ca. 1959	10.00
❑60, ca. 1959	10.00
❑1 1962, No number in indicia or cover.	25.00
❑2 1963	15.00
❑3, Oct 1964	12.00
❑4 1964	12.00

Attack
Charlton

❑1, Sep 1971	7.00
❑2, Nov 1971	4.00
❑3, Jan 1972	4.00
❑4, Mar 1972	3.00
❑5, May 1972	3.00
❑6, Jul 1972	2.50
❑7, Sep 1972	2.50
❑8, Nov 1972	2.50
❑9, Dec 1972	2.50
❑10, Feb 1973	2.50
❑11, May 1973	2.50
❑12, Jul 1973	2.50
❑13, Sep 1973	2.50
❑14, Nov 1973	2.50
❑15, Mar 1975	2.50
❑16, Aug 1979	2.50
❑17, Sep 1979	2.50
❑18, Nov 1979	2.50
❑19, Jan 1980	2.50
❑20, Mar 1980	2.50
❑21, May 1980	2.50
❑22, May 1980	2.50
❑23, Aug 1980	2.50
❑24, Oct 1980	2.50
❑25, Dec 1980	2.50
❑26, Feb 1981	2.50
❑27, Apr 1981	2.50

Other grades: Multiply price above by 5/6 for VF/NM • 2/3 for VERY FINE • 1/3 for FINE • 1/5 for VERY GOOD • 1/8 for GOOD

❑28, May 1981 ... 2.50
❑29, Jul 1981 ... 2.50
❑30, Sep 1981 ... 2.50
❑31, Nov 1981 ... 2.00
❑32, Jan 1982 ... 2.00
❑33, Mar 1982 ... 2.00
❑34, May 1982 ... 2.00
❑35, Jul 1982 ... 2.00
❑36, Sep 1982, Reprint from Army War Heroes #38 ... 2.00
❑37, Nov 1982 ... 2.00
❑38, Jan 1983 ... 2.00
❑39, Mar 1983 ... 2.00
❑40, May 1983 ... 2.00
❑41, Jul 1983 ... 2.00
❑42, Sep 1983 ... 2.00
❑43, Nov 1983 ... 2.00
❑44, Jan 1984 ... 2.00
❑45, Mar 1984 ... 2.00
❑46, May 1984 ... 2.00
❑47, Aug 1984 ... 2.00
❑48, Oct 1984, Final Issue ... 2.00

Attack!
Spire

❑1, ca. 1975 ... 5.00

Attack of the Amazon Girls
Fantaco

❑1, NN; Adult ... 4.95

Attack of the Mutant Monsters
A-Plus

❑1, b&w; Reprints ... 2.50

At the Seams
Alternative

❑1, Jun 1997, b&w; NN ... 2.95

Attitude Lad
Slave Labor

❑1 ... 2.95

Attu
4Winds

❑1, Nov 1989, b&w ... 9.95
❑2, b&w ... 9.95

Augie Doggie
Gold Key

❑1, Dec 1963 ... 45.00

August
Arrow

❑1; O: August; V: Blacquon; Pinup galleries ... 2.95
❑2 ... 2.95
❑3 ... 2.95

Aurora Comic Scenes
Aurora

❑181, ca. 1974; NA (a); really 181-140; small comic included in Aurora model kits (Tarzan) ... 30.00
❑182, ca. 1974; JR (a); really 182-140; small comic included in Aurora model kits (Amazing Spider-Man) ... 28.00
❑183, ca. 1974; GK (a); really 183-140; small comic included in Aurora model kits (Tonto) ... 27.00
❑184, ca. 1974; HT (a); really 184-140; small comic included in Aurora model kits (Incredible Hulk) ... 30.00
❑185, ca. 1974; CS (a); really 185-140; small comic included in Aurora model kits (Superman) ... 28.00
❑186, ca. 1974; DC (a); really 186-140; small comic included in Aurora model kits (Superboy) ... 27.00
❑187, ca. 1974; DG (a); really 187-140; small comic included in Aurora model kits (Batman) ... 26.00
❑188, ca. 1974; GK (a); really 188-140; small comic included in Aurora model kits (Lone Ranger) ... 25.00
❑192, ca. 1974; really 192-140; small comic included in Aurora model kits (Captain America) ... 27.00
❑193, ca. 1974; really 193-140; small comic included in Aurora model kits (Robin) ... 30.00

Authority
DC / Wildstorm

❑1, May 1999; wraparound cover ... 5.00
❑2, Jun 1999 ... 4.00
❑3, Jul 1999 ... 4.00
❑4, Aug 1999 ... 3.00
❑5, Oct 1999; cover says "Sep", indicia says "Oct" ... 3.00
❑6, Oct 1999 ... 3.00
❑7, Nov 1999 ... 3.00
❑8, Dec 1999 ... 3.00
❑9, Jan 2000 ... 3.00
❑10, Feb 2000 ... 3.00
❑11, Mar 2000 ... 2.50
❑12, Apr 2000 ... 2.50
❑13, May 2000 ... 2.50
❑14, Jun 2000 ... 2.50
❑15, Jul 2000 ... 2.50
❑16, Aug 2000 ... 2.50
❑17, Sep 2000 ... 2.50
❑18, Sep 2000 ... 2.50
❑19, Nov 2000 ... 2.50
❑20, Jan 2001 ... 2.50
❑21, Feb 2001 ... 2.50
❑22, Mar 2001 ... 2.50
❑23, Apr 2001 ... 2.50
❑24, May 2001 ... 2.50
❑25, Jun 2001 ... 2.50
❑26, Jul 2001 ... 2.50
❑27, Aug 2001 ... 2.50
❑28, Sep 2001 ... 2.50
❑29, Oct 2001 ... 2.50
❑Ann 2000, Dec 2000 ... 3.50

Authority
DC / Wildstorm

❑0, Aug 2003 ... 2.95
❑1, May 2003 ... 2.95
❑2, Jun 2003 ... 2.95
❑3, Jul 2003 ... 2.95
❑4, Aug 2003 ... 2.95
❑5, Sep 2003 ... 2.95
❑6, Oct 2003 ... 2.95
❑7, Nov 2003 ... 2.95
❑8, Dec 2003 ... 2.95
❑9, Jan 2004 ... 2.95
❑10, May 2004 ... 2.95
❑11, Jun 2004 ... 2.95
❑12, Jul 2004 ... 2.95
❑13, Aug 2004 ... 2.95
❑14, Oct 2004 ... 2.95

Authority: Kev
DC / Wildstorm

❑nn, Oct 2002 ... 4.95

Authority/Lobo Christmas Special
DC / Wildstorm

❑1, Dec 2003 ... 4.95

Authority/Lobo: Spring Break Massacre
DC

❑0 2005 ... 4.99

Authority: The Magnificent Kevin
DC

❑1, Oct 2005 ... 2.99
❑2, Nov 2005 ... 2.99
❑3 ... 2.99
❑4, Jan 2006 ... 2.99
❑5, Feb 2006 ... 2.99

Authority: More Kev
DC / Wildstorm

❑1, Jul 2004 ... 2.95
❑2, Aug 2004 ... 2.95
❑3, Oct 2004 ... 2.95
❑4, Nov 2004 ... 2.95

Authority: Revolution
DC / Wildstorm

❑1, Dec 2004 ... 2.95
❑2, Jan 2005 ... 2.95
❑3, Feb 2005 ... 2.95
❑4, Apr 2005 ... 2.95
❑5, May 2005 ... 2.95
❑6, Jun 2005 ... 2.95
❑7, Jun 2005 ... 2.99
❑8, Jul 2005 ... 2.99
❑9, Aug 2005 ... 2.99
❑10, Sep 2005 ... 2.99
❑11, Oct 2005 ... 2.99
❑12, Dec 2005 ... 2.99

Authority: Scorched Earth
DC / Wildstorm

❑1, Feb 2003 ... 4.95

Authority
DC / Wildstorm

❑1, Dec 2006 ... 2.99
❑1/Variant, Dec 2006 ... 2.99
❑1/2nd variant, Dec 2006 ... 2.99

Autobiographix
Dark Horse

❑1, ca. 2004; Shelf ... 14.95

Automatic Kafka
WildStorm

❑1, Sep 2002 ... 2.95
❑2, Oct 2002 ... 2.95
❑3, Nov 2002 ... 2.95
❑4, Dec 2002 ... 2.95
❑5, Jan 2003 ... 2.95
❑6, Feb 2003 ... 2.95
❑7, Mar 2003 ... 2.95
❑8, Apr 2003 ... 2.95
❑9, May 2003 ... 2.95

Automaton
Image

❑1, Sep 1998 ... 2.95
❑2, Oct 1998; no month of publication ... 2.95
❑3, Nov 1998; no month of publication ... 2.95

Autumn
Caliber

❑1, ca. 1995 ... 2.95
❑2, ca. 1995 ... 2.95
❑3 ... 2.95

Autumn Adventures (Walt Disney's)
Disney

❑1 ... 2.95

Autumn...Earth
Acid Rain

❑1 ... 2.50

Avalon
Harrier

❑1, Oct 1986; O: Diana ... 1.95
❑2, ca. 1986 ... 1.95
❑3, ca. 1987 ... 1.95
❑4, ca. 1987 ... 1.95
❑5, ca. 1987 ... 1.95
❑6, ca. 1987 ... 1.95
❑7, ca. 1987 ... 1.95
❑8, ca. 1987 ... 1.95
❑9, ca. 1987 ... 1.95
❑10, ca. 1987 ... 1.95
❑11, ca. 1987 ... 1.95
❑12, ca. 1987 ... 1.95
❑13, ca. 1987 ... 1.95
❑14, ca. 1988 ... 1.95

Avant Guard: Heroes at the Future's Edge
Day One

❑1, Mar 1994, b&w ... 2.50
❑2, Jul 1994, b&w ... 2.50
❑3, Dec 1994, b&w ... 2.50

Avataars: Covenant of the Shield
Marvel

❑1, Sep 2000 ... 2.99
❑2, Oct 2000 ... 2.99
❑3, Nov 2000 ... 2.99

Avatar
DC

❑1 ... 3.50
❑2 ... 3.50
❑3 ... 3.50

Avelon
Drawbridge

❑1 1997 ... 2.95
❑2 ... 2.95
❑3 ... 2.95
❑4 ... 2.95
❑5 ... 2.95
❑6; Giveaway from Wizard Con 8/01 ... 2.95
❑7 ... 2.95
❑8 ... 2.95
❑9; Giveaway at WIzard con 8/01 ... 2.95

Avengeblade
Maximum

❑1, Jul 96 ... 2.99
❑2, Aug 96 ... 2.99

Other grades: Multiply price above by 5/6 for VF/NM • 2/3 for VERY FINE • 1/3 for FINE • 1/5 for VERY GOOD • 1/8 for GOOD

Archie's Pal Jughead Comics

Continuation of Jughead; not the 1950s series

Archie's Pals 'n' Gals

Title began as an annual special in the 1950s

Archie's R/C Racers

Radio-control craze infects Riverdale

Archie's Spring Break

Archie descends on the beach

Archie's TV Laugh-Out

Title inspired by Rowan & Martin's Laugh-in

N-MINT

Avengelyne
Maximum

- ❑1, May 1995; RL (w); RL (a); 1&O: Avengelyne Photo cover; Includes one of 4 posters of Avengelyne ... 3.00
- ❑1/A, May 1995; RL (w); 1&O: Avengelyne. Photo cover ... 3.00
- ❑1/Gold, May 1995; Gold edition; RL (w); 1&O: Avengelyne ... 4.00
- ❑1/Variant, May 1995; RL (w); 1&O: Avengelyne.. chromium cover ... 3.50
- ❑2, Jun 1995; RL (w); polybagged with card ... 2.50
- ❑3/A, Jul 1995; RL (w); Avengelyne striking with sword on cover ... 2.50
- ❑3/B, Jul 1995; RL (w); Avengelyne standing with demons prominent on cover ... 2.50
- ❑Ashcan 1; RL (w); Ashcan edition signed by creators ... 3.50

Avengelyne
Maximum

- ❑0, Oct 1996 ... 3.00
- ❑½ 1996; Wizard promotional mail-in edition; RL (w); Wizard promotional mail-in edition; Includes certificate of authenticity; ca. 1996 ... 3.00
- ❑½/Platinum 1996; Platinum edition with certificate of authenticity (Wizard promo); RL (w) ... 3.50
- ❑1, Apr 1996 ... 3.00
- ❑1/Variant, Apr 1996; alternate cover (photo wraparound) ... 3.00
- ❑2, May 1996; 1: Darkchylde ... 4.00
- ❑2/A, May 1996; RL (w); 1: Darkchylde. Photo cover ... 4.00
- ❑2/B, May 1996; 1: Darkchylde. Nude cover 5.00
- ❑3, Jun 1996; Multiple figures with large demon in background ... 2.50
- ❑4, Jul 1996 A: Cybrid. ... 2.50
- ❑5, Aug 1996; RL (w); A: Cybrid. flipbook with Blindside preview ... 2.99
- ❑6, Sep 1996 RL (w) ... 2.99
- ❑7, Nov 1996 ... 2.99
- ❑8, Dec 1996 RL (w) ... 2.99
- ❑9, Jan 1997 ... 2.99
- ❑10, Feb 1997 RL (w) ... 2.99
- ❑11, Mar 1997 ... 2.99
- ❑11/Variant, Mar 1997; alternate cover (multiple characters behind Avengelyne) 2.99
- ❑12, Mar 1997 ... 2.99
- ❑13, Mar 1997 ... 2.99
- ❑14, Apr 1997 ... 2.99
- ❑15; Final Issue ... 2.99

Avengelyne
Awesome

- ❑1, Mar 1999 ... 2.50

Avengelyne Armageddon
Maximum

- ❑1, Dec 1996 ... 2.99
- ❑2, Jan 1997 ... 2.99
- ❑3, Feb 1997 ... 2.99

Avengelyne Bible
Maximum

- ❑1, Oct 1996 ... 3.50

Avengelyne: Dark Depths
Avatar

- ❑½, Feb 2001; Al Rio cardstock cover... 4.95
- ❑½/A, Feb 2001; Patrick Fillion cover... 4.95
- ❑½/B, Feb 2001; Lloyd painted cover... 4.95
- ❑½/C, Feb 2001; Carrie Hall painted cover; Midnight Terror ... 3.00
- ❑1, Feb 2001; Al Rio wraparound cover; Sunbathing Avengelyne and Coral ... 3.50
- ❑1/A, Feb 2001; Matt Martin cover ... 3.50
- ❑1/B, Feb 2001; Marat Mychaels cover.. 3.50
- ❑1/C, Feb 2001; Heavenly Body cover by Matt Martin ... 3.50
- ❑1/D, Feb 2001; Sean Shaw Connecting cover #1; Diptych ... 3.50
- ❑1/E, Feb 2001; Frenzy edition; Al Rio cover 5.95
- ❑2, Mar 2001; Al Rio cover ... 3.50
- ❑2/A, Mar 2001; Rick Lyon cover ... 3.50
- ❑2/B, Mar 2001; Marat Mychaels cover. 3.50
- ❑2/C, Mar 2001; Sean Shaw Connecting cover #2; Diptych ... 3.50

Avengelyne: Deadly Sins
Maximum

- ❑1, Feb 1996 ... 2.95
- ❑1/Variant, Feb 1996, alternate cover (photo) ... 3.50
- ❑2, Mar 1996, RL (c); Final issue ... 2.95

Avengelyne/Glory
Maximum

- ❑1, Sep 1995; wraparound chromium cover ... 3.95
- ❑1/Variant, Sep 1995; variant cover ... 3.95

Avengelyne/Glory: The Godyssey
Maximum

- ❑1, Sep 1996 ... 2.99
- ❑1/Variant; Photo cover ... 2.99

Avengelyne: Power
Maximum

- ❑1/A, Nov 1995; Red background on cover 2.50
- ❑1/B, Nov 1995; Blue background on cover 2.50
- ❑2, Dec 1995 ... 2.50
- ❑3, Jan 1996 ... 2.50

Avengelyne-Prophet
Maximum

- ❑1/A, May 1996, Close-up of faces on cover 2.95
- ❑1, May 1996 ... 2.95
- ❑2, Jun 1996 ... 2.95

Avengelyne Swimsuit
Maximum

- ❑1/D, Aug 1995; Black suit, wet hair on cover; pin-ups, both drawn and photographed ... 2.95
- ❑1/C, Aug 1995; pin-ups, both drawn and photographed; White suit on cover ... 2.95
- ❑1/B, Aug 1995; Black suit, dry hair, sitting on cliff on cover; pin-ups, both drawn and photographed ... 2.95
- ❑1/A, Aug 1995; Black swimsuit, dry hair, leaning against cliff on cover; pin-ups, both drawn and photographed ... 2.95
- ❑1, Aug 1995; Drawn cover; both drawn and photographed; n-ups ... 2.95

Avengelyne/Warrior Nun Areala
Maximum

- ❑1/A, Nov 1996; Avengelyne in front on cover ... 2.99
- ❑1/B, Nov 1996; Two women back-to-back on cover ... 2.99

Avengers
Marvel

- ❑0, Wizard promotional edition ... 3.00
- ❑1, Sep 1963, JK (c); JK, SL (w); JK (a); O: Avengers. 1:/origin of the Avengers; Team consists of Thor, Ant-Man, Wasp, Hulk, and Iron Man ... 4200.00
- ❑1.5, Dec 1999, Issue #1-1/2 ... 3.00
- ❑2, Nov 1963, JK (c); JK, SL (w); JK (a); 1: Space Phantom. Hulk leaves Avengers; Ant-Man becomes Giant-Man ... 935.00
- ❑3, Jan 1964, JK (c); JK, SL (w); JK (a); Avengers vs. Sub-Mariner and Hulk... 750.00
- ❑4, Mar 1964, JK (c); JK, SL (w); JK (a); 1: Baron Zemo. Captain America returns; Capt. America returns ... 1450.00
- ❑4/Golden, ca. 1966, Golden Records reprint ... 40.00
- ❑5, May 1964, JK (c); JK, SL (w); JK (a); Hulk leaves team ... 350.00
- ❑6, Jul 1964, JK (c); JK, SL (w); JK (a); 1: Masters of Evil (Black Knight; Radioactive Man; Melter; Baron Zemo) 390.00
- ❑7, Aug 1964, JK (c); JK, SL (w); JK (a) 460.00
- ❑8, Sep 1964, JK (c); JK, SL (w); JK (a); 1&O: Kang ... 275.00
- ❑9, Oct 1964, JK (c); SL (w); DH, JK (a); 1&O: Wonder Man. D: Wonder Man... 225.00
- ❑10, Nov 1964, JK (c); SL (w); DH, JK (a); 1: Hercules. 1: Immortus; Gene Day L.O.C 180.00
- ❑11, Dec 1964, JK (c); SL (w); DH, JK (a); A: Spider-Man. Spider-Man ... 275.00
- ❑12, Jan 1965, JK (c); SL (w); DH, JK (a); 1: Monk Keefer (later becomes Ape-Man I). V: Mole Man ... 115.00
- ❑13, Feb 1965, JK (c); SL (w); DH, JK (a); 1: Count Nefaria; 1: Maggia ... 150.00
- ❑14, Mar 1965, JK (c); JK, SL (w); DH, JK (a); 1: Ogor and Kallusians. The Watcher 150.00
- ❑15, Apr 1965, JK (c); JK, SL (w); DH, JK (a); D: Baron Zemo I (Heinrich Zemo) 100.00
- ❑16, May 1965, JK (c); JK, SL (w); JK (a); Cap assembles new team of Hawkeye, Quicksilver, Scarlet Witch ... 125.00
- ❑17, Jun 1965, JK (c); SL (w); DH, JK (a) 115.00
- ❑18, Jul 1965, JK (c); SL (w); DH, JK (a) 100.00
- ❑19, Aug 1965, JK (c); SL (w); DH, JK (a); O: Hawkeye. 1: Swordsman ... 150.00
- ❑20, Sep 1965, JK (c); SL (w); DH, WW (a); V: Swordsman. 2: Swordsman ... 80.00
- ❑21, Oct 1965, JK (c); SL (w); DH, JK (a); 1&O: Power Man I (Erik Josten)... 70.00
- ❑22, Nov 1965, JK (c); SL (w); DH, JK (a) 70.00
- ❑23, Dec 1965, JK (c); SL (w); DH, JK (a); 1: Ravonna ... 75.00
- ❑24, Jan 1966, JK (c); SL (w); DH, JK (a); A: Kang. A: Doctor Doom. A: Princess Ravonna. 1: Baltag ... 70.00
- ❑25, Feb 1966, JK (c); SL (w); DH, JK (a); A: Mr. Fantastic. A: Invisible Girl. A: Thing. A: Human Torch. A: Doctor Doom ... 95.00
- ❑26, Mar 1966, JK (c); SL (w); DH, JK (a); A: Henry Pym. A: Puppet Master. A: Beetle. A: Tony Stark. A: Attuma. A: Sub-Mariner. A: The Wasp ... 65.00
- ❑27, Apr 1966, JK (c); SL (w); DH, JK (a); A: Mr. Fantastic. A: Invisible Girl. A: Collector. A: Henry Pym. A: Beetle. A: Attuma ... 70.00

Other grades: Multiply price above by 5/6 for VF/NM • 2/3 for VERY FINE • 1/3 for FINE • 1/5 for VERY GOOD • 1/8 for GOOD

N-MINT

❑28, May 1966, JK (c); SL (w); DH, JK (a); 1: The Collector. 1: Goliath. A: Beetle. Giant-Man becomes Goliath; Goliath rejoins Avengers; Wasp rejoins Avengers 50.00

❑29, Jun 1966, DH, JK (c); SL (w); DH, JK (a); 1: Hu Chen. 1: Doctor Yen. A: Black Widow. A: S.H.I.E.L.D.. A: Swordsman. Power Man I; Black Widow 50.00

❑30, Jul 1966, DH, JK (c); SL (w); DH, JK (a); 1: Doctor Franz Anton. 1: Keeper of the Flame. 1: Prince Rey. A: Black Widow. A: Power Man I. A: Hu Chen. A: Swordsman. Quicksilver & Scarlet Witch leave Avengers 50.00

❑31, Aug 1966, JK (c); SL (w); DH, JK (a); 2: Doctor Franz Anton; 2: Keeper of the Flame; 2: Prince Rey........................ 43.00

❑32, Sep 1966, DH (c); SL (w); DH (a); 1: Sons of the Serpent. 1: Supreme Serpent I. 1: Bill Foster (Giant-Man II). A: Black Widow. A: Scarlet Witch. A: Quicksilver. A: Nick Fury. A: Tony Stark. Black Widow 37.00

❑33, Oct 1966, DH (c); SL (w); DH (a); A: Black Widow 50.00

❑34, Nov 1966, DH (c); SL (w); DH (a); 1&O: Living Laser-. 1: Lucy Barton..... 55.00

❑35, Dec 1966, DH (c); SL (w); DH (a); 1: Ultrana (off page). 2: Living Laser. 2: Lucy Barton. A: Black Widow. A: Bill Foster; Dave Cockrum L.O.C.............. 50.00

❑36, Jan 1967, DH (c); DH (a); 1: Ultroids. 1: Ultrana (full). 1: Ixar. A: Black Widow. Quicksilver & Scarlet Witch rejoin Avengers 35.00

❑37, Feb 1967, GK (c); DH (a). A: Black Widow. Black Widow........................ 40.00

❑38, Mar 1967, GK (c); DH (a); A: Hercules. A: Black Widow. Hercules; Captain America leaves Avengers 43.00

❑39, Apr 1967, DH (c); DH (a); A: Hercules. A: Black Widow. A: S.H.I.E.L.D.. A: Jasper Sitwell. A: Dum Dum Dugan. A: Nick Fury. A: Mad Thinker. Hercules.................. 40.00

❑40, May 1967, DH, GT (c); DH (a); A: Hercules. A: Black Widow. A: Sub-Mariner. V: Sub-Mariner 40.00

❑41, Jun 1967, JB (c); JB (a); 1: Colonel Ling. A: Hercules. A: Black Widow. A: Dragon Man. A: Bill Foster. A: Diablo. Mr. Fantastic cameo; Human Torch cameo........................ 40.00

❑42, Jul 1967, JB (c); JB (a); V: Diablo, Dragon Man. Captain America rejoins the Avengers........................ 50.00

❑43, Aug 1967, JB (c); JB (a); 1: General Yuri Brushov. 1: Red Guardian I (Alexi Shostakov). A: Hercules. A: Black Widow. A: Edwin Jarvis. A: Colonel Ling; Edwin Jarvis appearance (off screen)........................ 45.00

❑44, Sep 1967, JB (c); JB (a); O: Red Guardian I (Alexi Shostakov). O: Black Widow (part). 2: Red Guardian I (Alexi Shostakov). A: Hercules. A: Black Widow. A: Colonel Ling. D: Red Guardian I (Alexi Shostakov); D: Red Guardian (Alexi Shostakov) 40.00

❑45, Oct 1967, JB (c); DH (w); DH (a); A: Super-Adaptoid. A: Iron Man I. A: Thor. V: Super-Adaptoid. Hercules joins team; Black Widow retires 50.00

❑46, Nov 1967, JB (c); JB (a); 1: Whirlwind. Goliath regains Ant-Man powers 30.00

❑47, Dec 1967, DH (c); JB (a); D: Black Knight II (Nathan Garrett). New Black Knight (Dr. Dane Whitman) origin part 1 37.00

❑48, Jan 1968, JB (c); GT (a); O: Aragorn. 1: Black Knight III (Dane Whitman). 1: Aragorn. New Black Knight (Dr. Dane Whitman) origin part 2 .... 37.00

❑49, Feb 1968, JB (c); JB (a); A: Magneto. Quicksilver & Scarlet Witch leave Avengers; Goliath loses powers.......... 32.00

❑50, Mar 1968, JB (c); JB (a); Hercules leaves the Avengers........................ 30.00

❑51, Apr 1968, JB (c); JB (a); Thor, Iron Man; Goliath regains powers, new costume 40.00

❑52, May 1968, O: Grim Reaper. 1: Grim Reaper. Black Panther joins.............. 41.00

❑53, Jun 1968, JB (c); JB (a); A: X-Men. Tony Isabella L.O.C........................ 60.00

❑54, Jul 1968, JB (c); JB (a); 1: Crimson Cowl; Don & Maggie Thompson L.O.C 30.00

❑55, Aug 1968, JB (c); JB (a); 1: Ultron-5 30.00

❑56, Sep 1968, JB (c); JB (a); Peter Sanderson L.O.C 50.00

N-MINT

❑57, Oct 1968, JB (c); JB (a); 1: The Vision II (android). First Vision 110.00

❑58, Nov 1968, JB (c); JB (a); O: The Vision II (android); The Vision joins the Avengers 65.00

❑59, Dec 1968, JB (c); JB (a); 1: Yellowjacket. Goliath becomes Yellowjacket 40.00

❑60, Jan 1969, JB (c); JB (a); Yellowjacket marries Wasp; Captain America 40.00

❑61, Feb 1969, JB (c); JB (a); Doctor Strange 30.00

❑62, Mar 1969, JB (c); JB (a); 1: W'Kabi. 1: The Man-Ape; 1: N'Gamo 30.00

❑63, Apr 1969, GC (c); GC (a); 1&O: Goliath-New (Hawkeye); Yellowjacket and Wasp rejoin Avengers.................. 30.00

❑64, May 1969, GC (c); GC (a); Black Widow; Hawkeye's identity revealed... 30.00

❑65, Jun 1969, GC (c); GC (a); O: Hawkeye 30.00

❑66, Jul 1969, SB (c); James Van Hise L.O.C 30.00

❑67, Aug 1969, SB (c) 45.00

❑68, Sep 1969, SB (c); SB (a)............... 27.00

❑69, Oct 1969, SB (c); SB (a); 1: Grandmaster. 1: Nighthawk II (Kyle Richmond)-Full. First Nighthawk; Captain America and Black Panther rejoin 30.00

❑70, Nov 1969, SB (c); SB (a) 30.00

❑71, Dec 1969, SB (c); SB (a); 1: Invaders (prototype). Human Torch, Golden Age Captain America and Sub-Mariner; Black Knight joins Avengers 50.00

❑72, Jan 1970, SB (c); SB (a); 1: Zodiac I. 1: Taurus. 1: Pisces I; Keith Pollard L.O.C 30.00

❑73, Feb 1970, HT (a); Quicksilver, Scarlet Witch return; Yellowjacket and Wasp leave 30.00

❑74, Mar 1970, JB (c); JB (a); 2: Monica Lynne 25.00

❑75, Apr 1970, JB (c); JB (a); 1: Arkon; Quicksilver; Scarlet Witch return; Yellowjacket and Wasp leave 25.00

❑76, May 1970, JB (c); JB (a); 2: Arkon; Alan Kupperberg L.O.C.; Peter Sanderson L.O.C 25.00

❑77, Jun 1970, JB (c); JB (a); 1: Split-Second Squad; 1: Cornelius Van Lunt; 1: Kronus 20.00

❑78, Jul 1970, JB (c); JB, SB (a); 1: Lethal Legion; 2:The Man-Ape; 2: N'Gamo; 2: Grim Reaper........................ 25.00

❑79, Aug 1970, JB (c); JB (a); 2: Lethal Legion 23.00

❑80, Sep 1970, JB (c); JB (a); 1&O: Red Wolf; 1: Lobo; 1: Jason Birch; 2: Cornelius Van Lunt........................ 23.00

❑81, Oct 1970, JB (c); JB (a) 23.00

❑82, Nov 1970, JB (c); JB (a); Daredevil 26.00

❑83, Dec 1970, JB (c); JB (a); 1: Valkyrie 36.00

❑84, Jan 1971, SB (c); JB (a); Black Knight's sword destroyed.................. 23.00

❑85, Feb 1971, JB (c); JB (a); 1: Whizzer II (Stanley Stewart). 1: Hawkeye II (Wyatt McDonald). 1: American Eagle II (James Dore Jr.). 1: Tom Thumb. 1: Doctor Spectrum I (Joe Ledger)...... 25.00

❑86, Mar 1971, JB (c); JB, SB (a); 1: Brain-Child 25.00

❑87, Apr 1971, JB (c); O: Black Panther. Black Panther origin retold.............. 40.00

❑88, May 1971, SB (c); SB (a); 1: Psyklop; Continues in Incredible Hulk #140 ..... 25.00

❑88/2nd, SB (c); SB (a); 1: Psyklop. 2nd printing........................ 2.00

❑89, Jun 1971, SB (c); SB (a); Kree/Skrull War part 1; Captain Marvel.............. 20.00

❑90, Jul 1971, SB (c); SB (a); Kree/Skrull War part 2; Captain Marvel origin retold 22.00

❑91, Aug 1971, SB (c); SB (a); Kree/Skrull War part 3; Captain Marvel.............. 22.00

❑92, Sep 1971, NA (c); SB, NA (a); Kree/Skrull War part 4; Captain Marvel....... 26.00

❑93, Nov 1971, Double-size; NA (c); NA (a); Kree/Skrull War part 5; Captain Marvel 120.00

❑94, Dec 1971, NA (c); JB, NA (a); 1: Mandroid armor. Kree/Skrull War part 6; Captain Marvel 35.00

❑95, Jan 1972, JB (c); NA (a); O: Black Bolt. Kree/Skrull War part 7; Inhumans crosover with Amazing Adventures #5-8 .... 38.00

❑96, Feb 1972, NA (c); NA (a); Kree/Skrull War part 8; Captain Marvel.............. 35.00

❑97, Mar 1972, GK (c); NA (w); JB, BEv, SB, GK (a); Kree/Skrull War part 9; Captain Marvel 26.00

N-MINT

❑98, Apr 1972, JB (c); 1: The Warhawks. Goliath becomes Hawkeye again......... 26.00

❑99, May 1972, JB (c); George Olshevsky L.O.C 30.00

❑100, Jun 1972, 100th anniversary issue; Black Knight regains magic sword 55.00

❑101, Jul 1972, RB (c); RB (a); The Watcher 18.00

❑102, Aug 1972, RB, JR (c); RB (a)....... 16.00

❑103, Sep 1972, RB (c); RB (a) 40.00

❑104, Oct 1972, RB (c); RB (a); V: Sentinels; Mike W. Barr L.O.C 20.00

❑105, Nov 1972, JB (c); JB (a); V: Gaza; V: Barbarus; V: Lupo; V: Equilibrius; V: Brainchild; V: Amphibius; V: Lorelei 18.00

❑106, Dec 1972, RB (c); RB, GT (a)....... 17.00

❑107, Jan 1973, RB (c); JSn, GT, DC (a); Wendy Pini L.O.C 20.00

❑108, Feb 1973, RB (c); DH (a); V: Grim Reaper; V: Space Phantom; V: Hydra . 12.00

❑109, Mar 1973, RB (c); DH (a); 1: Imus Champion. Hawkeye leaves Avengers 18.00

❑110, Apr 1973, GK (c); DH (a); A: X-Men. X-Men; crossover with Fantastic Four #132........................ 25.00

❑111, May 1973, RB (c); DH (a); A: X-Men. Daredevil 22.00

❑112, Jun 1973, DH (c); DH (a); 1: Mantis. Black Widow leaves........................ 25.00

❑113, Jul 1973, RB (c); 1: The Living Bombs. D: The Living Bombs. Silver Surfer......... 11.00

❑114, Aug 1973, RB, JR (c); Silver Surfer 15.00

❑115, Sep 1973, JR (c); D: The Living Bombs. Silver Surfer; Avengers and Defenders vs. Loki and Dormammu, part 1 - continues in Defenders #8..... 13.00

❑116, Oct 1973, JR (c); Silver Surfer; Avengers and Defenders vs. Loki and Dormammu, part 3 - continues in Defenders #9........................ 27.00

❑117, Nov 1973, JR (c); Silver Surfer; Avengers and Defenders vs. Loki and Dormammu, part 5 - continues in Defenders #10........................ 20.00

❑118, Dec 1973, Silver Surfer; Avengers and Defenders vs. Loki and Dormammu, part 7 - continues in Defenders #11........................ 24.00

❑119, Jan 1974, Silver Surfer 15.00

❑120, Feb 1974, JSn (c); JSn, DH, JSt (a) 14.00

❑121, Mar 1974, JB (a); Marvel Value Stamp #84: Dr. Doom........................ 10.00

❑122, Apr 1974, GK, JR (c); Marvel Value Stamp #71: Vision........................ 13.00

❑123, May 1974, O: Mantis, part 1; Marvel Value Stamp #4: Thing 9.00

❑124, Jun 1974, JR (c); JB (a); O: Mantis, part 2; Marvel Value Stamp #81: rhino 12.00

❑125, Jul 1974, JB (a); A: Thanos. Thanos; Crossover with Captain Marvel #32 and 33; Marvel Value Stamp #69: Marvel Girl........................ 20.00

❑126, Aug 1974, Marvel Value Stamp #46: Mysterio 18.00

❑127, Sep 1974, GK (c); SB, JSa (a); 1: Ultron-7. A: Fantastic Four. A: Inhumans. continues in Fantastic Four #150 (wedding of Crystal and Quicksilver); Marvel Value Stamp #13: Dr. Strange 12.00

❑128, Oct 1974, GK (c); SB (a); Marvel Value Stamp #70: Super Skrull........... 12.00

❑129, Nov 1974, SB (a); Marvel Value Stamp #88: Leader 12.00

❑130, Dec 1974, GK (c); SB (a); 1: The Slasher. V: Titanium Man, Radioactive Man, Crimson Dynamo, Slasher. Marvel Value Stamp #96: Dr. Octopus 15.00

❑131, Jan 1975, GK (c); SB (a); Immortus; Marvel Value Stamp #70: Super Skrull 12.00

❑132, Feb 1975, SB (a); Iron Man dies (resurrected in Giant-Size Avengers #3); Marvel Value Stamp #78: Owl 10.00

❑133, Mar 1975, GK (c); SB (a); O: the Vision and Golden Age Human Torch, part 1........................ 8.00

❑134, Apr 1975, GK, JR (c); SB (a); O: Vision and Golden Age Human Torch, part 2........................ 10.00

❑135, May 1975, JSn, JR (c); GT (a); O: Moondragon. O: Vision and Golden Age Human Torch, part 3.................. 10.00

❑136, Jun 1975, GK, JR (c); TS (a); reprints with changes Amazing Adventures #12 .... 8.00

❑137, Jul 1975, JR (c); GT (a); membership becomes Beast, Iron Man, Moondragon, Thor, Wasp and Yellowjacket 8.00

Other grades: Multiply price above by 5/6 for VF/NM • 2/3 for VERY FINE • 1/3 for FINE • 1/5 for VERY GOOD • 1/8 for GOOD

Archie's Vacation Special

Deluxe format annuals featuring Archie
©Archie

Archie's Weird Mysteries

More horror-themed comedy from Archie
©Archie

Archie 3000

A look at Archie's life in the future
©Archie

Area 52

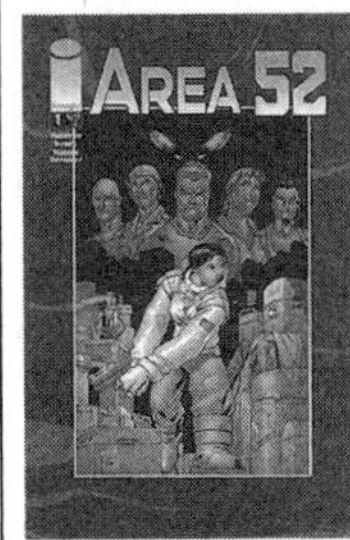

Science-fiction military misfits in action
©Image

Area 88

SF series was one of the earlier manga imports
©Eclipse

	N-MINT
❑138, Aug 1975, GK (c); GT (a); V: Stranger; Toad	7.00
❑139, Sep 1975, GK (c); GT (a)	7.00
❑140, Oct 1975, GK (c); GT (a); Vision and Scarlet Witch return	7.00
❑141, Nov 1975, GK (c); GP (a); 1: Golden Archer II (Wyatt McDonald). Squadron Sinister	10.00
❑142, Dec 1975, GK, JR (c); GP (a); Rawhide Kid, Two-Gun Kid, Kid Colt, Night Rider	8.00
❑143, Jan 1976, GK (c); GP (a); V: Kang	8.00
❑144, Feb 1976, GK (c); GP (a); 1&O: Hellcat; O: The Cat; Marvel Value Stamp Series B #39; Peter B. Gillis L.O.C.; Mary Jo Duffy L.O.C	8.00
❑145, Mar 1976, GK (c); DH (a); V: Assassin	8.00
❑146, Apr 1976, AM (c); KP, DH (a); Falcon	10.00
❑146/30¢, Apr 1976, KP, DH (a); Falcon; 30¢ regional price variant	18.00
❑147, May 1976, RB (c); GP (a); Hellcat	7.00
❑147/30¢, May 1976, Hellcat; 30¢ regional price variant	15.00
❑148, Jun 1976, JK (c); GP (a); 1: Cap'n Hawk; Peter Sanderson L.O.C.; Mary Jo Duffy L.O.C	12.00
❑148/30¢, Jun 1976, JK (c); GP (a); 1: Cap'n Hawk. 30¢ regional price variant	18.00
❑149, Jun 1976, GP (a); V: Orka	5.50
❑149/30¢, Jun 1976, GP (a); 30¢ regional price variant	15.00
❑150, Aug 1976, GP (c); GP (a); New team: Captain America, Iron Man, Yellowjacket, Wasp, Beast, Vision II (android), and Scarlet Witch; Partial Reprint from Avengers #16, retitled from "The Old Order Changeth"	7.00
❑150/30¢, Aug 1976, GP (c); GP (a); New team: Captain America, Iron Man, Yellowjacket, Wasp, Beast, Vision II (android), and Scarlet Witch; Partial Reprint from Avengers #16, retitled from "The Old Order Changeth"	15.00
❑151, Sep 1976, JK (c); GP (a); New Avengers lineup: Beast, Captain America, Iron Man, Scarlet Witch, Vision, Wasp, Yellowjacket; Wonder Man comes back from dead, new costume	7.00
❑152, Oct 1976, JK (c); JB (a); 1: Black Talon II	5.50
❑153, Nov 1976, V: Living Laser; Continued in Giant-Size Avengers #6	5.50
❑154, Dec 1976, V: Attuma	5.50
❑155, Jan 1977	5.50
❑156, Feb 1977, 1: Tyrack. Newsstand edition (distributed by Curtis); issue number in box	9.00
❑156/Whitman, Feb 1977, 1: Tyrack. Special markets edition (usually sold in Whitman bagged prepacks); price appears in a diamond; UPC barcode appears	8.00
❑157, Mar 1977, Newsstand edition (distributed by Curtis); issue number in box	5.50
❑157/Whitman, Mar 1977, Special markets edition (usually sold in Whitman bagged prepacks); price appears in a diamond; UPC barcode appears	5.50
❑158, Apr 1977, JK (c); SB (a); Newsstand edition (distributed by Curtis); issue number in box	8.00

	N-MINT
❑158/Whitman, Apr 1977, JK (c); SB (a); Special markets edition (usually sold in Whitman bagged prepacks); price appears in a diamond; UPC barcode appears	5.50
❑159, May 1977, GK (c); SB (a); Newsstand edition (distributed by Curtis); issue number in box	8.00
❑159/Whitman, May 1977, SB (a); Special markets edition (usually sold in Whitman bagged prepacks); price appears in a diamond; UPC barcode appears	5.50
❑160, Jun 1977, Newsstand edition (distributed by Curtis); issue number in box	5.50
❑160/Whitman, Jun 1977, Special markets edition (usually sold in Whitman bagged prepacks); price appears in a diamond; UPC barcode appears	5.50
❑160/35¢, Jun 1977, 35¢ regional price variant; newsstand edition (distributed by Curtis); issue number in box	15.00
❑161, Jul 1977, GP (c); GP, JBy (a); Newsstand edition (distributed by Curtis); issue number in box	7.00
❑161/Whitman, Jul 1977, GP, JBy (a); Special markets edition (usually sold in Whitman bagged prepacks); price appears in a diamond; UPC barcode appears	5.50
❑161/35¢, Jul 1977, GP (c); GP, JBy (a); 35¢ regional price variant; newsstand edition (distributed by Curtis); issue number in box	15.00
❑162, Aug 1977, GP (c); GP, JBy (a); O: Jocasta. 1: Jocasta. Newsstand edition (distributed by Curtis); issue number in box	8.00
❑162/Whitman, Aug 1977, GP, JBy (a); O: Jocasta. 1: Jocasta. Special markets edition (usually sold in Whitman bagged prepacks); price appears in a diamond; UPC barcode appears	8.00
❑162/35¢, Aug 1977, GP (c); GP, JBy (a); 35¢ regional price variant; newsstand edition (distributed by Curtis); issue number in box	15.00
❑163, Sep 1977, GP, JBy (a); Newsstand edition (distributed by Curtis); issue number in box	7.00
❑163/Whitman, Sep 1977, GP, JBy (a); Special markets edition (usually sold in Whitman bagged prepacks); price appears in a diamond; UPC barcode appears	5.50
❑163/35¢, Sep 1977, GP (c); GP, JBy, GT (a); 35¢ regional price variant; newsstand edition (distributed by Curtis); issue number in box	15.00
❑164, Oct 1977, GP (c); GP, JBy (a); Newsstand edition (distributed by Curtis); issue number in box	15.00
❑164/Whitman, Oct 1977, GP, JBy (a); Special markets edition (usually sold in Whitman bagged prepacks); price appears in a diamond; no UPC barcode	5.50
❑164/35¢, Oct 1977, GP, JBy (a); 35¢ regional price variant; newsstand edition (distributed by Curtis); issue number in box	15.00
❑165, Nov 1977, GP (c); JBy (a); Newsstand edition (distributed by Curtis); issue number in box	5.50

	N-MINT
❑165/Whitman, Nov 1977, JBy (a); Special markets edition (usually sold in Whitman bagged prepacks); price appears in a diamond; no UPC barcode	5.50
❑166, Dec 1977, GP (c); JBy (a); Newsstand edition (distributed by Curtis); issue number in box	5.50
❑166/Whitman, Dec 1977, JBy (a); Special markets edition (usually sold in Whitman bagged prepacks); price appears in a diamond; no UPC barcode	5.50
❑167, Jan 1978, GP (c); GP, JBy (a)	5.00
❑168, Feb 1978, GP (c); GP, JBy (a); Guardians of the Galaxy app	7.00
❑169, Mar 1978, DC (c); SB, JBy (a)	4.00
❑170, Apr 1978, GP (c); GP (w); GP, JBy (a); V: Jocasta; Peter Sanderson L.O.C	4.00
❑171, May 1978, GP (c); GP, JBy (a); Newsstand edition (distributed by Curtis); issue number in box	6.00
❑171/Whitman, May 1978, JBy (a); Special markets edition (usually sold in Whitman bagged prepacks); price appears in a diamond; no UPC barcode	4.00
❑172, Jun 1978, Hawkeye returns	4.00
❑173, Jul 1978	4.00
❑174, Aug 1978, Newsstand edition (distributed by Curtis); issue number in box	4.00
❑174/Whitman, Aug 1978, Special markets edition (usually sold in Whitman bagged prepacks); price appears in a diamond; UPC barcode appears	4.00
❑175, Sep 1978, Newsstand edition (distributed by Curtis); issue number in box	5.00
❑175/Whitman, Sep 1978, Special markets edition (usually sold in Whitman bagged prepacks); price appears in a diamond; no UPC barcode	4.00
❑176, Oct 1978, Newsstand edition (distributed by Curtis); issue number in box	4.00
❑176/Whitman, Oct 1978, Special markets edition (usually sold in Whitman bagged prepacks); price appears in a diamond; no UPC barcode	4.00
❑177, Nov 1978, DC (c); Newsstand edition (distributed by Curtis); issue number in box	4.00
❑177/Whitman, Nov 1978, Special markets edition (usually sold in Whitman bagged prepacks); price appears in a diamond; UPC barcode appears	4.00
❑178, Dec 1978, JB (c); CI, JBy (a); D: Korvac; V: Manipulator	4.00
❑179, Jan 1979, KP (c); JM (a); 1: The Monolith. 1: The Stinger II. Newsstand edition (distributed by Curtis); issue number in box	4.00
❑179/Whitman, Jan 1979, JM (a); 1: The Monolith. 1: The Stinger II. Special markets edition (usually sold in Whitman bagged prepacks); price appears in a diamond; no UPC barcode	4.00
❑180, Feb 1979, DA (c); JM (a); Newsstand edition (distributed by Curtis); issue number in box	4.00
❑180/Whitman, Feb 1979, JM (a); Special markets edition (usually sold in Whitman bagged prepacks); price appears in a diamond; no UPC barcode	4.00

Other grades: Multiply price above by 5/6 for VF/NM • 2/3 for VERY FINE • 1/3 for FINE • 1/5 for VERY GOOD • 1/8 for GOOD

	N-MINT
❑181, Mar 1979, GP (c); GP, JBy, TD (a); New team: Captain America, Falcon, Iron Man, Beast, Vision II (android), and Scarlet Witch	5.00
❑182, Apr 1979, AM (c); JBy (a); Kurt Busiek L.O.C	4.00
❑183, May 1979, GP (c); JBy (a); Newsstand edition (distributed by Curtis); issue number in box	6.00
❑183/Whitman, May 1979, JBy (a); Special markets edition (usually sold in Whitman bagged prepacks); price appears in a diamond; no UPC barcode	5.00
❑184, Jun 1979, GP (c); JBy (a); V: Absorbing Man	6.00
❑185, Jul 1979, GP (c); JBy (a); O: Scarlet Witch. O: Quicksilver. 1: Chthon (in human body)	7.00
❑186, Aug 1979, JBy (c); JBy (a); O: Quicksilver; O: Scarlet Witch	5.00
❑187, Sep 1979, JBy (c); JBy (a); 1: Chthon (in real human form); D: Django Maximoff; O: Chthon; O: Scarlet Witch; O: Darkhold; Cat Yronwode L.O.C	6.00
❑188, Oct 1979, JBy (c); JBy, DGr, FS (a)	6.00
❑189, Nov 1979, JBy (c); JBy (a); V: Deathbird	6.00
❑190, Dec 1979, JBy (c); JBy (a); Daredevil	4.00
❑191, Jan 1980, GP (c); GP, JBy, DGr (a); O: Grey Gargoyle; V: Grey Gargoyle	5.00
❑192, Feb 1980, GP (c); 1: Inferno; V: Inferno; Scarlet Witch takes leave of absence	5.00
❑193, Mar 1980, FM, BMc (c); SB, DGr (a); D: Inferno	5.00
❑194, Apr 1980, GP (c); GP (a); Wonder Man joins team; Falcon resigns from team	5.00
❑195, May 1980, GP (c); GP (a); 1: Taskmaster	5.00
❑196, Jun 1980, GP (c); GP (a); O: Taskmaster; Kurt Busiek L.O.C	7.00
❑197, Jul 1980, GP, BMc (c); Cl (a); Iron Man leaves team	5.00
❑198, Aug 1980, GP (c); GP (a)	5.00
❑199, Sep 1980, GP (c); GP (a)	5.00
❑200, Oct 1980, double-sized; GP (c); GP, BL (w); GP, DGr (a); Ms. Marvel leaves team	9.00
❑201, Nov 1980, GP (c); GP (a)	2.50
❑202, Dec 1980, DC (c); GP (a); V: Ultron	2.50
❑203, Jan 1981, Cl (c); Cl (a)	2.50
❑204, Feb 1981, DN (a); A: Yellow Claw	2.50
❑205, Mar 1981, D: Yellow Claw (according to Vision); V: Yellow Claw	2.50
❑206, Apr 1981, GC (c); GC (a); V: Pyron	2.50
❑207, May 1981, GC (c); GC (a)	2.50
❑208, Jun 1981, GC (c); GC (a); V: Berserker	2.50
❑209, Jul 1981, AM (c)	2.50
❑210, Aug 1981, GC (c); GC, DG (a); V: Weathermen; Samarobryn	2.50
❑211, Sep 1981, GC (c); GC, DG (a); Moon Knight, Dazzler; New team begins	2.50
❑212, Oct 1981, BH (c); Yellowjacket blows it in battle	2.50
❑213, Nov 1981, BH (c); BH (a); Yellowjacket's court martial; Yellowjacket leaves	2.50
❑214, Dec 1981, BH (c); BH (a); A: Ghost Rider	3.00
❑215, Jan 1982, A: Silver Surfer. V: Molecule Man	2.50
❑216, Feb 1982, A: Silver Surfer. V: Molecule Man; Kevin Dooley L.O.C.	2.50
❑217, Mar 1982, BH (c); BH (a); Yellowjacket jailed; Yellowjacket & Wasp return	3.00
❑218, Apr 1982, DP (c); DP (a)	3.00
❑219, May 1982, BH (c); BH (a); A: Drax. V: Moondragon	2.00
❑220, Jun 1982, BH (c); BH (a); A: Drax. D: Drax the Destroyer	2.00
❑221, Jul 1982, BH (c); BH (a); Hawkeye rejoins; She-Hulk joins; Wolverine on cover, not in issue	2.00
❑222, Aug 1982, V: Masters of Evil	2.00
❑223, Sep 1982, A: Ant-Man. V: Taskmaster	2.00
❑224, Oct 1982, Tony Stark/Wasp romance	2.00
❑225, Nov 1982, 1: Balor. A: Black Knight	3.00
❑226, Dec 1982, 1: Valinor. A: Black Knight	2.00
❑227, Jan 1983, SB (a); O: Yellowjacket. O: Ant-Man. O: Goliath. O: Wasp. O: Giant-Man. O: Avengers. Captain Marvel II joins team	2.00
❑228, Feb 1983, AM (c); AM (a); Trial of Yellowjacket	2.00
❑229, Mar 1983, AM (c); AM (a); V: Egghead	2.00
❑230, Apr 1983, AM (c); AM (a); D: Egghead. Yellowjacket leaves	2.00
❑231, May 1983, AM (c); AM (a); Iron Man leaves	2.00
❑232, Jun 1983, AM (c); AM (a); A: Starfox. Starfox (Eros) joins	2.00
❑233, Jul 1983, JBy (c); JBy (w); JBy, JSt (a); V: Annihilus	2.00
❑234, Aug 1983, AM (c); AM (a); O: Scarlet Witch. O: Quicksilver	2.00
❑235, Sep 1983, AM, JSt (c); V: Wizard	2.00
❑236, Oct 1983, AM, JSt (c); AM (a); Spider-Man;New logo	2.00
❑237, Nov 1983, AM, JSt (c); AM, JSt (a); Spider-Man	2.00
❑238, Dec 1983, AM, JSt (c); AM, JSt (a); O: Blackout I (Marcus Daniels)	2.00
❑239, Jan 1984, AM (c); AM (a); A: David Letterman. D: Blackout I (Marcus Daniels); Assistant Editors Month	2.00
❑240, Feb 1984, AM (c); AM, JSt (a); A: Spider-Woman. Spider-Woman revived	2.00
❑241, Mar 1984, AM (c); AM, JSt (a); A: Spider-Woman. V: Morgan Le Fey; New cover logo	2.00
❑242, Apr 1984, AM, JSt (c); AM (a); Thor rejoins team; Leads into Secret Wars.	2.00
❑243, May 1984, AM, JSt (c); AM, JSt (a); Return from Secret Wars	2.00
❑244, Jun 1984, AM, JSt (c); AM, Cl, JSt (a); V: Dire Wraiths	2.00
❑245, Jul 1984, AM, JSt (c); AM, JSt (a); V: Dire Wraiths	2.00
❑246, Aug 1984, AM, JSt (c); AM, JSt (a); A: Sersi	2.00
❑247, Sep 1984, AM, JSt (c); AM, JSt (a); A: Uni-Mind. O: Eternals (both on Earth and on Titan)	2.00
❑248, Oct 1984, AM, JSt (c); AM, JSt (a); A: Eternals. V: Malestrom; Uni-Mind sends chunk of planet with Deviants on it off into space	2.00
❑249, Nov 1984, AM, JSt (c); AM, JSt (a); A: Fantastic Four. V: Hordes of Surtur	2.00
❑250, Dec 1984, AM, JSt (c); AM, JSt (a); Maelstrom	2.50
❑251, Jan 1985, BH, JSt (c); BH, JSt (a); V: Baron Brimstone; Captain America rejoins team	1.75
❑252, Feb 1985, BH (c); BH, JSt (a); V: Blood Brothers	1.75
❑253, Mar 1985, KP (c); BH (a); Wonder Man new costume; Vision takes over the world	1.75
❑254, Apr 1985, BH (c); BH (a); Vision returns world to rightful owners; Removes control crystal from brain	1.75
❑255, May 1985, TP (c); JB, TP (a); Vision; Scarlet Witch leave team; Wasp returns to team	1.75
❑256, Jun 1985, JB, TP (c); JB, TP (a); Savage Land	1.75
❑257, Jul 1985, JB (c); JB (a); 1: Nebula	1.75
❑258, Aug 1985, Spider-Man vs. Firelord	1.75
❑259, Sep 1985, V: Skrulls	1.75
❑260, Oct 1985, JBy (c); JB, TP (a); A: Nebula. Secret Wars II	1.75
❑261, Nov 1985, JB (c); JB (a); Secret Wars II	1.75
❑262, Dec 1985, JB, TP (c); JB, TP (a); A: Sub-Mariner	1.75
❑263, Jan 1986, 1: X-Factor. D: Melter	3.00
❑264, Feb 1986, 1: Yellowjacket II (Rita DeMara)	1.75
❑265, Mar 1986, JB (c); JB (a); Secret Wars II	1.75
❑266, Apr 1986, JB, TP (c); JB, TP (a); Secret Wars II Epilogue	1.50
❑267, May 1986, JB, TP (c); JB, TP (a); V: Kang	1.50
❑268, Jun 1986, JB (c); JB (a); V: Kang	1.50
❑269, Jul 1986, JB, TP (c); JB, TP (a); O: Rama-Tut. V: Kang	1.50
❑270, Aug 1986, JB, TP (c); JB, TP (a); A: Namor. V: Moonstone	1.50
❑271, Sep 1986, JB (c); JB (a); V: Grey Gargoyle; V: Screaming Mimi	1.50
❑272, Oct 1986, JB (c); JB (a); A: Alpha Flight. V: Attuma	1.50
❑273, Nov 1986, JB (c); JB (a); V: Masters of Evil	1.50
❑274, Dec 1986, JB (c); JB (a); V: Masters of Evil	1.50
❑275, Jan 1987, JB (c); JB (a); V: Masters of Evil	1.50
❑276, Feb 1987, JB (c); JB (a); V: Masters of Evil	1.50
❑277, Mar 1987, JB (c); JB (a); D: Blackout; V: Masters of Evil	1.50
❑278, Apr 1987, JB (c); JB (a); V: Tyrak the Treacherous	1.50
❑279, May 1987, Hercules kidnapped; Captain Marvel (Monica Rambeau) elected chairman	1.50
❑280, Jun 1987, BH (c); BH (a)	1.50
❑281, Jul 1987	1.50
❑282, Aug 1987, JB, TP (c); JB, TP (a); V: Neptune	1.50
❑283, Sep 1987, JB, TP (c); JB, TP (a)	1.50
❑284, Oct 1987, JB, TP (c); JB, TP (a); on Olympus	1.50
❑285, Nov 1987, JB, TP (c); JB, TP (a); V: Zeus	1.50
❑286, Dec 1987, JB, TP (c); JB, TP (a); V: Super Adaptoid	1.50
❑287, Jan 1988, JB, TP (c); JB, TP (a); V: Fixer; V: Super-Adaptoid	1.50
❑288, Feb 1988, JB, TP (c); JB, TP (a); V: Sentry Sinister; V: Super-Adaptoid.	1.50
❑289, Mar 1988, JB, TP (c); JB, TP (a); V: Super Adaptoid, Sentry Sinister, Machine Man, Tess-One, Fixer	1.50
❑290, Apr 1988, JB (c); JB (a); V: Super-Adaptoid	1.50
❑291, May 1988, JB (c); JB (a)	1.50
❑292, Jun 1988, JB (c); JB (a); 1: Leviathan III (Marina). D: Leviathan III (Marina)	1.50
❑293, Jul 1988, JB (c); JB (a); 1: Nebula. D: Marina. D: Marrina; D: Leviathan III (Marrina)	1.50
❑294, Aug 1988, JB (c); JB (a); Captain Marvel leaves team	1.50
❑295, Sep 1988, JB (c); JB (a)	1.50
❑296, Oct 1988, JB (c); JB (a)	1.50
❑297, Nov 1988, JB (c); JB (a); D: Doctor Druid. Thor, Black Knight, She-Hulk leaves team	1.50
❑298, Dec 1988, JB (c); JB (a); Inferno	1.50
❑299, Jan 1989, JB (c); JB (a); Inferno	1.50
❑300, Feb 1989, 300th anniversary issue; JB (c); JB (a); Inferno;new team;Thor Joins	2.00
❑301, Mar 1989, BH (c); BH (a); Captain America back in original costume with original name	1.50
❑302, Apr 1989, JB, TP (c); RB, TP (a); V: Super-Nova	1.50
❑303, May 1989, JB, TP (c); RB, TP (a); V: Super-Nova	1.50
❑304, Jun 1989, TP (c); RB, TP (a); 1: Portal. A: Puma. V: U-Foes	1.50
❑305, Jul 1989, JBy (c); JBy (w); JBy (a); V: Lava Men; Reed Richards; Sue Richards leave team; Black Panther joins team	1.50
❑306, Aug 1989, JBy (w)	1.50
❑307, Sep 1989, JBy (w); V: Lava Men	1.50
❑308, Oct 1989, JBy (w)	1.50
❑309, Nov 1989, JBy (w); TP (a); Great Lakes Avengers appear	1.50
❑310, Nov 1989, JBy (w); V: Blastaar	1.50
❑311, Dec 1989, TP (c); JBy (w); TP (a); "Acts of Vengeance"	1.50
❑312, Dec 1989, TP (c); JBy (w); TP (a); "Acts of Vengeance"	1.50
❑313, Jan 1990, TP (c); JBy (w); "Acts of Vengeance"	1.50
❑314, Feb 1990, JBy (w); Spider-Man	1.50
❑315, Mar 1990, JBy (w); TP (a); Spider-Man;Spider-Man x-over	1.50
❑316, Apr 1990, JBy (w); Spider-Man	1.50
❑317, May 1990, JBy (w); Spider-Man	1.50
❑318, Jun 1990, Spider-Man	1.50
❑319, Jul 1990	1.50
❑320, Aug 1990, A: Alpha Flight	1.50
❑321, Aug 1990	1.50
❑322, Sep 1990, A: Alpha Flight	1.50
❑323, Sep 1990, A: Alpha Flight	1.50
❑324, Oct 1990	1.50
❑325, Oct 1990, JBy (c)	1.50
❑326, Nov 1990, 1: Rage	1.50
❑327, Dec 1990	1.50
❑328, Jan 1991, O: Rage. O: Turbo	1.50
❑329, Feb 1991	1.50

Other grades: Multiply price above by 5/6 for VF/NM • 2/3 for VERY FINE • 1/3 for FINE • 1/5 for VERY GOOD • 1/8 for GOOD

Areala: Angel of War

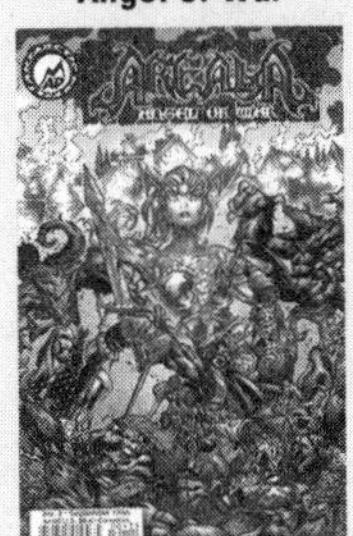

Warrior Nun Areala's Viking origins
©Antarctic

Argus

High-tech agent caught up in intrigue
©DC

Aria

Gods and faeries walk the streets
©Image

Aria: The Soul Market

Mischievous sprite arrives in modern times
©Image

Arion, Lord of Atlantis

Magical series spun off from Warlord #55
©DC

	N-MINT
❑330, Mar 1991	1.50
❑331, Apr 1991, V: Ngh	1.50
❑332, May 1991, V: Doctor Doom	1.50
❑333, Jun 1991, HT (a); V: Doctor Doom	1.50
❑334, Jul 1991, 1: Thane Ector	1.50
❑335, Aug 1991, V: Thane Ector	1.50
❑336, Aug 1991	1.50
❑337, Sep 1991, V: Thane Ector	1.50
❑338, Sep 1991, TP (c); TP (a); numbering of story arc wrong on cover, really Part 5 of story	1.50
❑339, Oct 1991, V: Collector	1.50
❑340, Oct 1991	1.50
❑341, Nov 1991	1.50
❑342, Dec 1991, TP (c); TP (a); A: New Warriors. Rage leaves team	1.50
❑343, Jan 1992, Crystal joins team; Thor (Eric Masterson) joins team; Black Knight switches to energy sword	1.50
❑344, Feb 1992, V: Swordsman	1.50
❑345, Mar 1992, TP (c); TP (a); Operation: Galactic Storm, Part 5; Hawkeye becomes Goliath again	1.50
❑346, Apr 1992, TP (c); TP (a); Operation: Galactic Storm, Part 12	1.50
❑347, May 1992, TP (c); TP (a); D: Supreme Intelligence (apparent death). Conclusion to Operation: Galactic Storm	2.00
❑348, Jun 1992, TP (c); TP (a); Captain America on leave of absence	1.50
❑349, Jul 1992, TP (c); TP (a); 1: Taylor Madison	1.50
❑350, Aug 1992, Dbl. Size; JB (a); Gatefold covers	2.50
❑351, Aug 1992, TP (c)	1.25
❑352, Sep 1992, TP (c); TP (a); V: Grim Reaper	1.25
❑353, Sep 1992, TP (c); V: Grim Reaper	1.25
❑354, Oct 1992, TP (c); V: Grim Reaper.	1.25
❑355, Oct 1992, 1: Coal Tiger	1.25
❑356, Nov 1992, D: Coal Tiger; V: Magdalene	1.25
❑357, Dec 1992	1.25
❑358, Jan 1993, V: Arkon and Thundra..	1.25
❑359, Feb 1993, TP (c); TP (a)	1.25
❑360, Mar 1993, TP (a); foil cover	2.95
❑361, Apr 1993	1.25
❑362, May 1993	1.25
❑363, Jun 1993, Silver embossed cover	2.95
❑364, Jul 1993, V: Sentries	1.25
❑365, Aug 1993, TP (c); TP (a); V: Galen Kor	1.25
❑366, Sep 1993, sculpted foil cover	3.95
❑367, Oct 1993, TP (c); A: Sersi. A: Black Knight. Swordsman comes out of his coma	1.25
❑368, Nov 1993, TP (c); TP (a); UN forbids Avenger interference in Genosha civil war	1.25
❑369, Dec 1993, sculpted foil cover	2.95
❑370, Jan 1994	1.25
❑371, Feb 1994, MGu, TP (a)	1.25
❑372, Mar 1994, TP (c); TP (a)	1.25
❑373, Apr 1994, V: Proctor	1.25
❑374, May 1994, cards	1.25
❑375, Jun 1994, Giant-size; D: Proctor. poster;Dane Whitman and Sersi leave the Avengers	2.00
❑375/Collector's, Jun 1994, Giant-size; D: Proctor. Dane Whitman and Sersi leave the Avengers	2.50
❑376, Jul 1994, (c)	1.50
❑377, Aug 1994	1.50
❑378, Sep 1994, V: The Mephistoid	1.50
❑379, Oct 1994, (c)	1.50
❑379/Double, Oct 1994, GP (w); Double-feature with Giant-Man	2.50
❑380, Nov 1994, TP (c); TP (a); V: High Evolutionary	1.50
❑380/Double, Nov 1994, TP (c); GP (w); TP (a); second indicia gives name as "Marvel Double Feature ... The Avengers/Giant Man"	2.50
❑381, Dec 1994, TP (c); TP (a); V: Exodus	1.50
❑381/Double, Dec 1994, TP (c); GP (w); TP (a); second indicia gives name as "Marvel Double Feature ... The Avengers/Giant Man"	2.50
❑382, Jan 1995, TP (a); V: Exodus	1.50
❑382/Double, Jan 1995, GP (w); TP (a); second indicia gives name as "Marvel Double Feature ... The Avengers/Giant Man"	2.50
❑383, Feb 1995, MGu (c); MGu (a); V: Shatterstar	1.50
❑384, Mar 1995, TP (c); TP (a); V: Hera; Cover date reads 'Mar 94'; Hercules made mortal by Zeus	1.50
❑385, Apr 1995, TP (c); JB, TP (a)	1.50
❑386, May 1995, (c);continues in Captain America #440	1.50
❑387, Jun 1995, TP (a); continues in Captain America #441	1.50
❑388, Jul 1995, TP (c); TP (a); V: Red Skull	1.50
❑389, Aug 1995	1.50
❑390, Sep 1995	1.50
❑391, Oct 1995, The Crossing	1.50
❑392, Nov 1995, Mantis returns	1.50
❑393, Dec 1995, A: Tony Stark. "The Crossing"; Wasp critically injured	1.50
❑394, Jan 1996, 1: New Wasp. "The Crossing"	1.50
❑395, Feb 1996, D: Tony Stark; The Crossing	1.50
❑396, Mar 1996	1.50
❑397, Apr 1996	1.50
❑398, May 1996	1.50
❑399, Jun 1996	1.50
❑400, Jul 1996, MWa (w); wraparound cover	4.00
❑401, Aug 1996, MWa (w); A: Magneto, Rogue. Onslaught Phase 1	2.50
❑402, Sep 1996, TP (c); MWa (w); "Onslaught: Impact 2"; story continues in X-Men #56 and Onslaught: Marvel.	2.50
❑Ann 1, Sep 1967, Cover reads "King-Size Special"; DH (a); A: Hercules. A: Iron Man I. A: Mandarin. A: Black Widow. A: Edwin Jarvis. A: Power Man I. A: Living Laser. A: Thor	125.00
❑Ann 2, Sep 1968, Cover reads "King-Size Special"	120.00
❑Ann 3, Sep 1969, Cover reads "King-Size Special"; Reprinted from Avengers #4 and Tales of Suspense #66, #67, and #68 respectively	22.00
❑Ann 4, Jan 1971, Cover reads "King-Size Special"; SB (c); SL (w); JK (a); O: Moondragon; Reprinted from Avengers #5 & #6 respectively	22.00
❑Ann 5, Jan 1972, Cover reads "King-Size Special"; SL (w); DH, JK (a); Reprinted from Avengers #8 and 11	25.00
❑Ann 6, ca. 1976, JK (c); GP, HT (a); V: Nuklo	7.00
❑Ann 7, ca. 1977, JSn (c); JSn (w); JSn, JSt (a); D: Gamora. D: Warlock	12.00
❑Ann 8, ca. 1978, GP (a); A: Ms. Marvel	8.00
❑Ann 9, ca. 1979, DN (c); DN (a); V: Arsenal	8.00
❑Ann 10, ca. 1981, AM (c); MG (a); 1: Rogue. 1: Destiny. X-Men	9.00
❑Ann 11, ca. 1982, AM (c); AM, JAb (a); D: Nebulon	3.50
❑Ann 12, ca. 1983, AM, JSt (c); BG (a); A: Inhumans	3.50
❑Ann 13, ca. 1984, SD (c); SD, JBy (a); D: Nebulon. V: Fixer; V: Arnim Zola	3.50
❑Ann 14, ca. 1985, KGa (c); JBy (a)	3.50
❑Ann 15, ca. 1986, SD (a)	3.50
❑Ann 16, ca. 1987, BL (c); AW, BSz, KP, BL, BG, JR2, TP, BH, KN, MR, BWi (a)	3.50
❑Ann 17, ca. 1988, SB (c); MGu, TD (a)	3.00
❑Ann 18, ca. 1989, JBy (c); MGu (a); Atlantis Attacks	2.50
❑Ann 19, ca. 1990, KB (w); RHo, HT (a); Terminus	2.50
❑Ann 20, ca. 1991, Subterranean Wars.	2.50
❑Ann 21, ca. 1992, HT (a); O: Terminatrix. 1: Terminatrix. Citizen Kang	2.50
❑Ann 22, ca. 1993, AM, MGu (a); 1: Bloodwraith. Polybagged with trading card	2.95
❑Ann 23, ca. 1994, JB (c); AM (w); AM, JB (a)	2.95

Avengers
Marvel

	N-MINT
❑1 (403), Nov 1996; RL (c); RL (w); RL (a); Thor revived	3.00
❑1/A, Nov 1996; RL (c); RL (w); RL (a); alternate cover; Thor revived	3.00
❑2 (404), Dec 1996; JPH, RL (w); A: Mantis. V: Kang	2.00
❑3 (405), Jan 1997; JPH, RL (w); A: Mantis, Nick Fury. V: Kang	2.00
❑4 (406), Feb 1997; RL (c); JPH, RL (w); V: Hulk	2.00
❑5 (407), Mar 1997; RL (c); JPH, RL (w); RL (a); Thor vs. Hulk	2.00
❑5/A, Mar 1997; RL (c); JPH, RL (w); RL (a); White cover; Thor vs. Hulk	2.00
❑6 (408), Apr 1997; (c); JPH, RL (w); continues in Iron Man #6	1.95
❑7 (409), May 1997; JPH, RL (w); V: Lethal Legion (Enchantress, Wonder Man, Ultron 5, Executioner, Scarlet Witch)	1.95
❑8 (410), Jun 1997; JLee (c); V: Masters of Evil	1.95
❑9 (411), Jul 1997; V: Masters of Evil....	1.95
❑10 (412), Aug 1997; gatefold summary; V: dopplegangers	1.95
❑11 (413), Sep 1997; gatefold summary; D: Thor. V: Loki	1.95
❑12 (414), Oct 1997; cover forms quadtych with Fantastic Four #12, Iron Man #12, and Captain America #12 ...	2.99
❑13 (415), Nov 1997; JRo (w); cover forms quadtych with Fantastic Four #13, Iron Man #13, and Captain America #13	1.95

Avengers
Marvel

	N-MINT
❑0; Promotional edition included with Wizard; KB (w); Supplement to Wizard: The Comics Magazine #95; ca. 1999..	2.00

Other grades: Multiply price above by 5/6 for VF/NM • 2/3 for VERY FINE • 1/3 for FINE • 1/5 for VERY GOOD • 1/8 for GOOD

	N-MINT
❑1 (416), Feb 1998; gatefold summary; GP (c); KB (w); GP (a)	4.00
❑1/Chromium, Feb 1998; GP (c); KB (w); GP (a); chromium cover	6.00
❑1/RoughCut, Jul 1998; GP (c); KB (w); GP (a); Avengers Rough Cut; cardstock cover	4.00
❑1/Variant, Feb 1998; gatefold summary; GP (c); KB (w); GP (a); alternate cover	4.00
❑2 (417), Mar 1998; gatefold summary; GP (c); KB (w); GP (a)	3.00
❑2/Variant, Mar 1998; gatefold summary; KB (w); GP (a); alternate cover	3.00
❑3 (418), Apr 1998; GP (c); KB (w); GP (a); A: Wonder Man gatefold summary	2.50
❑4 (419), May 1998; GP (c); KB (w); GP (a); New team announced gatefold summary	2.50
❑5 (420), Jun 1998; gatefold summary; GP (c); KB (w); GP (a); V: Squadron Supreme	2.50
❑6 (421), Jul 1998; gatefold summary; GP (c); KB (w); GP (a); V: Squadron Supreme; V: Corruptor	2.00
❑7 (422), Aug 1998; gatefold summary; GP (c); KB (w); GP (a); A: Supreme Intelligence. Warbird leaves	2.00
❑8 (423), Sep 1998; gatefold summary; GP (c); KB (w); GP (a); 1: Silverclaw. 1: Triathlon; V: Moses Magnum	2.00
❑9 (424), Oct 1998; gatefold summary; GP (c); KB (w); GP (a); V: Moses Magnum. O: Triathalon	2.00
❑10 (425), Nov 1998; Anniversary issue; GP (c); KB (w); GP (a); V: Grim Reaper. O: Avengers; O: Scarlet Witch; Gatefold summary	2.00
❑11 (426), Dec 1998; gatefold summary; GP (c); KB (w); GP (a); A: Captain Marvel appearance, Thunderstrike. A: Wonder Man. A: Mockingbird. A: Doctor Druid. A: Captain Marvel. A: Hellcat. A: Swordsman. V: Grim Reaper. O: Grim Reaper	2.00
❑12 (427), Jan 1999; double-sized; GP (c); KB (w); GP (a); V: Thunderbolts. Continued from Thunderbolts #22; wraparound cover	3.00
❑12/Dynamic, Jan 1999; GP (c); KB (w); GP (a); Continued from Thunderbolts #22; DFE alternate cover	12.00
❑12/White, Jan 1999; GP (c); KB (w); GP (a); Headshot cover (white background); Continued from Thunderbolts #22	5.00
❑13 (428), Feb 1999; GP (c); KB (w); GP (a); A: New Warriors. 1: Lord Templar	2.00
❑14 (429), Mar 1999; GP (c); KB (w); GP (a); A: Lord Templar. A: George Perez. A: Beast. A: Kurt Busiek. Return of Beast to team	2.00
❑15 (430), Apr 1999; GP (c); KB (w); GP (a); A: Lord Templar. A: Triathalon. V: Pagan	2.00
❑16 (431), May 1999; JOy (c); JOy (w); JOy (a); V: Wrecking Crew	2.00
❑16/A, May 1999; JOy (c); JOy (w); JOy (a); 1 in 4 variant cover (purple background with team charging)	4.00
❑17 (432), Jun 1999; JOy (c); JOy (w); JOy (a); V: Doomsday Man	2.00
❑18 (433), Jul 1999; JOy (c); JOy (w); JOy (a); V: Wrecking Crew	2.00
❑19 (434), Aug 1999; GP (c); KB (w); GP (a); A: Black Panther. V: Ultron; V: Alkhema	2.00
❑20 (435), Sep 1999; GP (c); KB (w); GP (a); V: Ultron	2.00
❑21 (436), Oct 1999; GP (c); KB (w); GP (a); V: Ultron	2.00
❑22 (437), Oct 1999; GP (c); KB (w); GP (a); V: Ultron	2.00
❑23 (438), Dec 1999; GP (c); KB (w); GP (a); Wonder Man V: Vision	2.00
❑24 (439), Jan 2000 GP (c); KB (w); GP (a)	2.00
❑25 (440), Feb 2000; Giant-size; GP (c); KB (w); GP (a); A: Juggernaut	3.00
❑26 (441), Mar 2000; GP (c); KB (w); new team (Warbird, Captain Marvel, Ant-Man, Silverclaw, and Captain America)	2.00
❑27 (442), Apr 2000; GP (c); GP, KB, SL (w); RB, RHo, GP, JK, DA (a); 100 pages; reprints material from Avengers Vol. 1 #16, #101, #150-151, and Ann #19	3.00
❑28 (443), May 2000; GP (c); KB (w); GP (a); V: Kulan Gath	2.00
❑29 (444), Jun 2000; GP (c); KB (w); GP (a); V: Kulan Gath	2.25
❑30 (445), Jul 2000; GP (c); KB (w); GP (a); V: Kulan Gath	2.25

	N-MINT
❑31 (446), Aug 2000 GP (c); KB (w); GP (a); A: Madame Masque. A: Grim Reaper	2.25
❑32 (447), Sep 2000; GP (c); KB (w); GP (a); A: Madame Masque. O: Madame Masque; V: Grim Reaper	2.25
❑33 (448), Oct 2000; GP (c); KB (w); GP (a); A: Madame Masque. A: Thunderbolts. V: Count Nefaria; V: Grim Reaper	2.25
❑34 (449), Nov 2000; double-sized issue; GP (c); KB (w); GP (a); A: Madame Masque. A: Thunderbolts. V: Count Nefaria	2.99
❑35 (450), Dec 2000; JR2 (c); KB (w); JR2 (a); O: Ruul; Maximum Security crossover	2.25
❑36 (451), Jan 2001; KB (w); A: Ten-Thirtifor. Alan Davis poster; Alternate Hank Pym kidnaps and switches with real Henry Pym (Goliath)	2.25
❑37 (452), Feb 2001 KB (w); A: Bloodwraith	2.25
❑38 (453), Mar 2001; KB (w); Slashback issue; price reduced	1.99
❑39 (454), Apr 2001; KB (w); V: Diablo	2.25
❑40 (455), May 2001; KB (w); V: Diablo	2.25
❑41 (456), Jun 2001; KB (w); V: Kang the Conqueror; V: Scarlet Centurion	2.25
❑42 (457), Jul 2001; KB (w); V: Kang the Conqueror; V: Scarlet Centurion	2.25
❑43 (458), Aug 2001; KB (w); V: Deviants; V: Attuma; V: Kang; V: Presence	2.25
❑44 (459), Sep 2001; KB (w); BL (a); V: Deviants; V:Attuma; V: Kang; V: Presence	2.25
❑45 (460), Oct 2001; KB (w); BL (a); O: Scarlet Centurion; V: Scarlet Centurion; V: Kang the Conqueror	2.25
❑46 (461), Nov 2001; KB (w); BL (a); index numbering out of sequence, should be #461, not #463	2.25
❑47 (462), Dec 2001 KB (w); BL (a)	2.25
❑48 (463), Jan 2002; KB (w); TS, SB, JSt, BS (a); 100 pages; reprints Avengers Vol. 1 #98-100	3.50
❑49 (464), Feb 2002; KB (w); silent issue	2.25
❑50 (465), Mar 2002; KB (w); O: 3-D Man; O: Triathlon; Double-sized	2.99
❑51 (466), Apr 2002; KB (w); BA, TP (a); V: Kang the Conqueror	2.25
❑52 (467), May 2002; KB (w); V: Kang the Conqueror; V: Scarlet Centurion	2.25
❑53 (468), Jun 2002; KB (w); V: Kang the Conqueror; V: Scarlet Centurion	2.25
❑54 (469), Jul 2002; KB (w); V: Kang the Conqueror; V: Scarlet Centurion	2.25
❑55 (470), Aug 2002; KB (w); Wraparound cover	2.25
❑56 (471), Sep 2002; KB (w); Wraparound cover	2.25
❑57 (472), Oct 2002; V: Mister Hyde; Wraparound cover	2.25
❑58 (473), Nov 2002; Wraparound cover; Avengers contains voids opening worldwide	2.25
❑59 (474), Dec 2002; Wraparound cover	2.25
❑60 (475), Jan 2003; Wraparound cover	2.25
❑61 (476), Feb 2003; Red Skull appearance (as Dell Rusk), Wraparound cover	2.25
❑62 (477), Feb 2003; Truth about Jack of Hearts revealed	2.25
❑63 (478), Mar 2003; Cont'd from Thor v2 #59; Wraparound cover	2.25
❑64 (479), Apr 2003; V: Scarecrow; Falcon solo	2.25
❑65 (480), May 2003; #480	2.25
❑66 (481), Jun 2003; #481	2.25
❑67 (482), Jul 2003; #482	2.25
❑68 (483), Aug 2003, Dell Rusk revealed as Red Skull	2.25
❑69 (484), Sep 2003, V: Red Skull	2.25
❑70 (485), Oct 2003, V: Red Skull	2.25
❑71 (486), Nov 2003, V: Whirlwind	2.25
❑72 (487), Nov 2003, V: She-Hulk	2.25
❑73 (488), Dec 2003, V: She-Hulk	2.25
❑74 (489), Jan 2004, V: She-Hulk	2.25
❑75 (490), Feb 2004, Quicksilver, Scarlet Witch return; Yellowjacket and Wasp leave; V: She-Hulk; V: Hulk	2.25
❑76 (491), Feb 2004, D: Jack of Hearts	2.25
❑77 (492), Mar 2004, V: Wrecking Crew	2.25
❑78 (493), Apr 2004, V: Wrecking Crew	2.25
❑79 (494), Apr 2004, V: Wrecking Crew	2.25
❑80 (495), May 2004, 1: Captain Britain II; V: Wrecking Crew; Kelsey Leigh becomes Captain Britain II	2.25
❑81 (496), Jun 2004	2.99

	N-MINT
❑82 (497), Jul 2004, #497; Captain America, Iron Man, Yellowjacket, Hawkeye, Wasp	2.99
❑83 (498), Jul 2004, #498; Hawkeye, Wasp, Captain America, Yellowjacket, She-Hulk	2.25
❑84 (499), Aug 2004, concludes in Invaders #0	2.25
❑500, Sep 2004, BMB (w); numbering reverts back to Vol. 1, however, indicia does not	12.00
❑500/DirCut, Oct 2004, BMB (w); Director's Cut	18.00
❑501, Oct 2004, BMB (w)	5.00
❑502, Nov 2004, BMB (w)	7.00
❑503, Dec 2004, BMB (w); events continue in Avengers Finale	3.50
❑Ann 1998, ca. 1998, gatefold summary; GP (c); KB (w); BWi (a); wraparound cover	2.99
❑Ann 1999, Jul 1999, Jarvis' story	3.50
❑Ann 2000, ca. 2000, KB (w); RHo (a); wraparound cover	3.50
❑Ann 2001, ca. 2001, KB (w); 2001 Ann; Wraparound cover; Hank Pym separates into Yellowjacket and Goliath	2.99

Avengers and Power Pack Assemble!
Marvel

❑1, Jul 2006	2.99
❑2, Aug 2006	2.99
❑3, Sep 2006	2.99
❑4, Oct 2006	2.99

Avengers Casebook
Marvel

❑1999, ca. 1999	2.99

Avengers: Celestial Quest
Marvel

❑1, Sep 2001	2.50
❑2, Oct 2001	2.50
❑3, Nov 2001	2.50
❑4, Dec 2001	2.50
❑5, Jan 2002	2.50
❑6, Feb 2002	2.50
❑7, Mar 2002	2.50
❑8, Apr 2002; Final issue	3.50

Avengers: Death Trap, the Vault
Marvel

❑1, Sep 1991; also published as Venom: Deathtrap - The Vault	9.95

Avengers: Earth's Mightiest Heroes
Marvel

❑1, Nov 2004	3.50
❑2, Jan 2005	3.50
❑3, Feb 2005	3.50
❑4, Feb 2005	3.50
❑5, Mar 2005	3.50
❑6, Apr 2005	3.50
❑7, May 2005	3.50
❑8, Jun 2005	3.50

Avengers: Earth's Mightiest Heroes II
Marvel

❑1, Jan 2007	3.99
❑2, Feb 2007	3.99
❑3, Feb 2007	3.99
❑4, Mar 2007	3.99

Avengers Finale
Marvel

❑1, Jan 2005	3.50

Avengers Forever
Marvel

❑1, Dec 1998; Rick Jones on cover	2.99
❑1/WF, Dec 1998; Westfield alternate cover	4.95
❑2, Jan 1999; Team of Captain America, Hawkeye, Wasp, Giant-Man (Henry Pym), Captain Marvel (Genis), Songbird, Yellowjacket (Henry Pym)	2.99
❑3, Feb 1999	2.99
❑4/A, Mar 1999; Avengers of Tomorrow cover	2.99
❑4/B, Mar 1999; Kang in the Old West cover	2.99
❑4/C, Mar 1999; Avengers throughout time cover	2.99
❑4/D, Mar 1999; Avengers of the '50s cover	2.99
❑5, Apr 1999; Wrap-around cover	2.99
❑6, May 1999	2.99
❑7, Jun 1999	2.99
❑8, Jul 1999; True origin of Vision revealed	2.99

Other grades: Multiply price above by 5/6 for VF/NM • 2/3 for VERY FINE • 1/3 for FINE • 1/5 for VERY GOOD • 1/8 for GOOD

Aristocratic X-Traterrestrial Time-Traveling Thieves Micro-Series

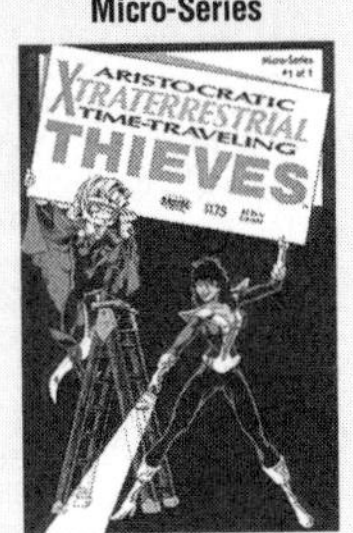

Felon-for-hire title from the black-and-white glut

©Comics Interview

Aristokittens

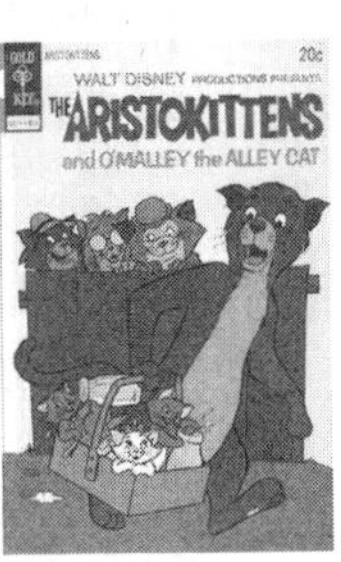

Feauturing the kittens from The Aristocats

©Gold Key

Armorines

Valiant's special strike force of armored marines

©Valiant

Armorines (Vol. 2)

Acclaim reboots series under a new label

©Acclaim

Army of Darkness

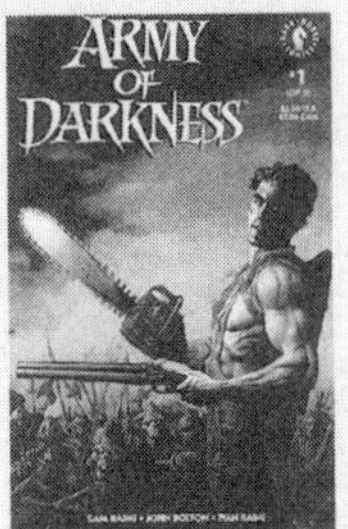

Big-budget sequel to Evil Dead movies

©Dark Horse

N-MINT

❑9, Aug 1999; Origin and history of Kang 2.99
❑10, Oct 1999 2.99
❑11, Jan 2000 2.99
❑12, Feb 2000; Final Issue; Genis bonds with Rick Jones 2.99

Avengers (TV)
Gold Key

❑1, Nov 1968, based on TV series 125.00
❑1/Variant, Nov 1968 200.00

Avengers Icons: The Vision
Marvel

❑1, Oct 2002 2.99
❑2, Nov 2002 2.99
❑3, Dec 2002 2.99
❑4, Jan 2003 2.99

Avengers Infinity
Marvel

❑1, Sep 2000; New team forms 2.99
❑1/Dynamic, Sep 2000; Dynamic Forces variant (Thor brandishing hammer) 4.00
❑2, Oct 2000; V: Servitors 2.99
❑3, Nov 2000; V: Walkers 2.99
❑4, Dec 2000 2.99

Avengers/JLA
DC

❑2, Oct 2003; O: Krona retold; Prestige Format; JLA vs. Avengers 7.00
❑4, Jun 2004; V: Krona & Villains of Marvel & DC Universes; Prestige Format 5.95

Avengers Log
Marvel

❑1, Feb 1994; Listings and brief descriptions of Avengers and villains 1.95

Avengers Next
Marvel

❑1, Jan 2007, Includes Incredible Hulk #100 preview 2.99
❑2, Feb 20007 2.99
❑3, Feb 2007 2.99
❑4, Mar 2007 2.99

Avengers Spotlight
Marvel

❑21, Aug 1989; Starfox; Series continued from Solo Avengers #20 1.00
❑22, Sep 1989; Swordsman 1.00
❑23, Oct 1989; Vision 1.00
❑24, Nov 1989; A: Trickshot. O: Firebird; True origin of Firebird; Hawkeye & Firebird; O: Firebird (Bonita Juarez) 1.00
❑25, Nov 1989 A: Crossfire. A: Mockingbird. A: Trickshot 1.00
❑26, Dec 1989; "Acts of Vengeance" 1.00
❑27, Dec 1989; AM (a); "Acts of Vengeance" 1.00
❑28, Jan 1990; "Acts of Vengeance" 1.00
❑29, Feb 1990; "Acts of Vengeance" 1.00
❑30, Mar 1990; new Hawkeye costume 1.00
❑31, Apr 1990 1.00
❑32, May 1990 1.00
❑33, Jun 1990 1.00
❑34, Jul 1990 1.00
❑35, Aug 1990 A: Gilgamesh 1.00
❑36, Sep 1990 1.00
❑37, Oct 1990; BH (a); Avengers Reborn, Part 1 1.00
❑38, Nov 1990; Avengers Reborn, Part 2 1.00

N-MINT

❑39, Dec 1990; Avengers Reborn, Part 3 1.00
❑40, Jan 1991; Final Issue; Avengers Reborn, Part 4 1.00

Avengers Strike File
Marvel

❑1, Jan 1994; Wraparound cover 1.75

Avengers: The Crossing
Marvel

❑1, Sep 1995, Chromium cover 4.95

Avengers: The Terminatrix Objective
Marvel

❑1, Sep 1993; Holo-grafix cover; U.S.Agent, Thunderstrike, War Machine 2.50
❑2, Oct 1993; New Avengers vs. Old Avengers 1.25
❑3, Nov 1993 1.25
❑4, Dec 1993 1.25

Avengers: The Ultron Imperative
Marvel

❑1, Oct 2001; 1: Antigone; V: Ultron; V: Alkema 5.99

Avengers/Thunderbolts
Marvel

❑1, May 2004 2.99
❑2, Jun 2004 2.99
❑3, Jun 2004 2.99
❑4, Aug 2004 2.99
❑5, Aug 2004 2.99
❑6, Oct 2004 2.99

Avengers: Timeslide
Marvel

❑1, Feb 1996; enhanced wraparound cardstock cover 4.95

Avengers Two: Wonder Man & Beast
Marvel

❑1, May 2000; O: Wonder Man; O: Beast; O: Wonder Man (Simon Williams); O: Beast (Hank McCoy) 2.99
❑2, Jun 2000 2.99
❑3, Jul 2000; V: It the Living Colossus 2.99

Avengers/Ultraforce
Marvel

❑1, Oct 1995, continues in UltraForce/ Avengers #1;Foil logo 3.95

Avengers: Ultron Unleashed
Marvel

❑1, Aug 1999; collects Avengers (1st series) #57-58 and #170-171 3.50

Avengers: United They Stand
Marvel

❑1, Nov 1999 2.99
❑2, Dec 1999 1.99
❑3, Jan 2000 1.99
❑4, Feb 2000 1.99
❑5, Mar 2000 1.99
❑6, Apr 2000 1.99
❑7, May 2000 1.99

Avengers Universe
Marvel

❑1, Aug 2000 2.99
❑2, Sep 2000 2.99
❑3, Oct 2000; Reprints Avengers vol 3 #8-9 and Thor vol 2 #3 2.99

N-MINT

❑4, Nov 2000; reprints Iron Fist: Wolverine #1; indicia is for Iron Fist: Wolverine #1. 2.99
❑5, Dec 2000; reprints Iron Fist: Wolverine #2; indicia is for Iron Fist: Wolverine #2. 2.99
❑6, Jan 2001; reprints Iron Fist: Wolverine #3; indicia is for Iron Fist: Wolverine #3 2.99

Avengers Unplugged
Marvel

❑1, Oct 1995; V: Nefarius and Moonstone 1.25
❑2, Dec 1995; A: Gravitron. Untold Tales of Spider-Man #4 1.00
❑3, Dec 1996; Luna; Black Widow 1.00
❑4, Feb 1996; Wedding of Thunderball and Titania; Peter David appears as reverend in story; Untold Tales of Spider-Man #8 1.00
❑5, Jun 1996; A: Captain Marvel. V: Controller; Captain Marvel becomes Photon; Legacy becomes Captain Marvel 1.00
❑6, Aug 1996; V: the Blood Wraith; Final Issue 1.00

Avengers West Coast
Marvel

❑47, Aug 1989; Series continues as Avengers West Coast; Series continued from West Coast Avengers #46 1.00
❑48, Sep 1989 1.00
❑49, Oct 1989 JBy (c); JBy (w); JBy (a); A: Great Lakes Avengers 1.00
❑50, Nov 1989; JBy (c); JBy (w); JBy (a); A: 1st Silver Age. Golden Age Human Torch returns 1.00
❑51, Nov 1989; JBy (c); JBy (w); JBy (a); A: Iron Man. V: Master Pandemonium; Iron Man rejoins team 1.00
❑52, Dec 1989; V: Master Pandemonium; Scarlet Witch's children revealed to be pieces of Mephisto's soul 1.00
❑53, Dec 1989; JBy (c); JBy (w); JBy (a); V: U-Foes. "Acts of Vengeance" 1.00
❑54, Jan 1990; JBy (c); JBy (w); JBy (a); V: Mole Man. Fantastic Four #1 cover homage; "Acts of Vengeance" 1.00
❑55, Feb 1990; JBy (c); JBy (w); JBy (a); V: Loki. "Acts of Vengeance" 1.00
❑56, Mar 1990; JBy (c); JBy (w); JBy (a); Wanda turns evil 8.00
❑57, Apr 1990 JBy (c); JBy (w); JBy (a); A: Magneto. A: Quicksilver 1.00
❑58, May 1990; V: Vibro 1.00
❑59, Jun 1990; V: Hydro-Man 1.00
❑60, Jul 1990; V: Magneto 1.00
❑61, Aug 1990; V: Immortus 1.00
❑62, Sep 1990 1.00
❑63, Oct 1990; O: Living Lightning. 1: Living Lightning 1.00
❑64, Nov 1990 A: Captain America 1.00
❑65, Dec 1990; V: Grim Reaper 1.00
❑66, Jan 1991; V: Ultron. V: Ultron-13 1.00
❑67, Feb 1991 1.00
❑68, Mar 1991; V: Ultron-13; Wonder Man vs. Grim Reaper 1.00
❑69, Apr 1991; Hawkeye vs. U.S.Agent 1.00
❑70, May 1991; 2: Living Lightning 1.00
❑71, Jun 1991; Sub-Mariner appearance 1.00
❑72, Jul 1991 1.00
❑73, Aug 1991 1.00
❑74, Sep 1991; Tigra leaves team; USAgent; Spider-Woman; Living Lightning join team 1.00

N-MINT

❑75, Oct 1991; Double-size issue; HT (a); A: Fantastic Four, Thundra ... 1.50
❑76, Nov 1991; V: Night Shift ... 1.00
❑77, Dec 1991 ... 1.00
❑78, Jan 1992 ... 1.00
❑79, Feb 1992 ... 1.25
❑80, Mar 1992; Galactic Storm ... 1.25
❑81, Apr 1992; Galactic Storm ... 1.25
❑82, May 1992; Galactic Storm ... 1.25
❑83, Jun 1992; HT (a); V: Hyena ... 1.25
❑84, Jul 1992; O: Spider Woman ... 1.25
❑85, Aug 1992; A: Spider-Man. V: Deathweb 1.25
❑86, Sep 1992; A: Spider-Man. V: Deathweb 1.25
❑87, Oct 1992; A: Wolverine. V: Bogatyri 1.25
❑88, Nov 1992; V: Bogatyri ... 1.25
❑89, Dec 1992; V: Ultron-13 ... 1.25
❑90, Jan 1993; 1: Alkhema; Hawkeye becomes Goliath ... 1.25
❑91, Feb 1993 ... 1.25
❑92, Mar 1993; Wonder Man has quit team; Goliath vs Goliath ... 1.25
❑93, Apr 1993 A: Darkhawk ... 1.25
❑94, May 1993 ... 1.25
❑95, Jun 1993 ... 1.25
❑96, Jul 1993; Infinity Crusade ... 1.25
❑97, Aug 1993; Infinity Crusade ... 1.25
❑98, Sep 1993 ... 1.25
❑99, Oct 1993 A: Lethal Legion. A: Hangman 1.25
❑100, Nov 1993; D: Mockingbird (as Bobbi Morse). sculpted foil cover ... 1.25
❑101, Dec 1993 ... 1.25
❑102, Jan 1994; Final Issue; X-Men x-over 1.25
❑Ann 4, ca. 1989; see West Coast Avengers for previous Anns; "Atlantis Attacks" ... 2.00
❑Ann 5, ca. 1990; "Terminus Factor" ... 2.00
❑Ann 6; Subterranean Wars; ca. 1991 ... 2.00
❑Ann 7, ca. 1992 ... 2.25
❑Ann 8; 1: Raptor. Polybagged with trading card ... 2.95

Avenue D
Fantagraphics

❑1, b&w; Adult ... 3.50

Avenue X
Purple Spiral

❑1, ca. 1992, Innovation publishes; Adult 2.50
❑2, ca. 1992, Adult ... 2.50
❑3, ca. 1992, Adult ... 3.00

Avigon
Image

❑1, Oct 2000 ... 5.95

A-V in 3-D
Aardvark-Vanaheim

❑1, Dec 1984; glasses ... 3.00

Awakening
Image

❑1, Oct 1997 ... 2.95
❑2, Dec 1997 ... 2.95
❑3, Feb 1998 ... 2.95
❑4, Apr 1998 ... 2.95

Awakening Comics
Awakening Comics

❑1 1997 ... 3.50
❑2, Nov 1997 ... 3.50
❑3, Aug 1998; wraparound cover; "The Everwinds Awakening War" ... 2.95
❑4, Nov 1998; 1: Melvin G. Moose; Private Eye ... 2.95

Awakening Comics 1999
Awakening Comics

❑1 1999, b&w anthology ... 3.50

Awesome Adventures
Awesome

❑1/A, Aug 1999, Woman standing (full length) on cover ... 2.50
❑1/B, Aug 1999, Woman standing (3/4 length) on cover ... 2.50

Awesome Holiday Special
Awesome

❑1, Dec 1997; Flip cover; Youngblood side has gold foil logo ... 2.50

Awesome Man
Astonish

❑1, ca. 2002; 1&O: Awesome Man ... 2.95
❑2, Aug 2003 ... 3.50

N-MINT

Awesome Preview
Awesome

❑1 1997; ARo (c); ARo (a); b&w and color previews of upcoming Awesome series given out at Comic-Con International: San Diego '97 ... 1.00

Awkward
Slave Labor

❑1 ... 4.95

Awkward Universe
Slave Labor

❑1, Dec 1995; NN; One-shot ... 9.95

Axa (Eclipse)
Eclipse

❑1, ca. 1987 ... 2.00
❑2, Aug 1987, b&w ... 2.00

Axa (Ken Pierce)
Ken Pierce

❑1, ca. 1981; b&w; ca. 1981; The Beginning reprints strips 1-120; The Chosen reprints strips 121-240 ... 5.95
❑2, ca. 1982; Intro by Catherine Yronwode; b&w; ca. 1982; The Desired reprints strips 241-479 ... 5.95
❑3, ca. 1983 ... 5.95
❑4, ca. 1983; b&w ... 5.95
❑5, ca. 1984; Back cover: photo of Donne Avenell; b&w ... 5.95
❑6, ca. 1984; b&w; The Dwarfed reprints strips 1199-1317; The Untamed reprints strips 1318-1437 ... 5.95
❑7, ca. 1985; b&w ... 5.95
❑8, ca. 1986, b&w ... 5.95
❑GN 1; ca: 1985; Magazine-sized format; 48 pages ... 5.95

Axed Files
Express / Parody

❑1 1995, b&w ... 2.50

Axel Pressbutton
Eclipse

❑1, Nov 1984 ... 2.00
❑2, Jan 1985 ... 2.00
❑3, Mar 1985 ... 2.00
❑4, May 1985 ... 2.00
❑5, Jul 1985; Continues as Pressbutton 2.00
❑6, Jul 1985; Indicia lists as Pressbutton #6 2.00

Axiom
Icon Creations

❑1, Aug 94 ... 2.50

Axis Alpha
Axis

❑1, Feb 1994; Previews of five upcoming titles; only B.E.A.S.T.I.E.S. and Tribe ever published ... 2.50

Axis Mundi
Amaze Ink

❑2, Dec 1996, b&w; no indicia; wraparound cover ... 2.95

Az
Comico

❑1, ca. 1983, b&w ... 1.50
❑2, ca. 1983, b&w ... 1.50

Azrach
Dark Horse / Big Bang

❑nn, ca. 1996 ... 6.95

Azrael
DC

❑1, Feb 1995; 1: Brian Bryan ... 3.00
❑2, Mar 1995 ... 2.00
❑3, Apr 1995 ... 2.00
❑4, May 1995; Sister Lilhy joins cast ... 2.00
❑5, Jun 1995 ... 2.00
❑6, Jul 1995 ... 2.00
❑7, Aug 1995 ... 2.00
❑8, Sep 1995 ... 2.00
❑9, Oct 1995 ... 2.00
❑10, Nov 1995; "Underworld Unleashed" 2.00
❑11, Dec 1995 ... 1.95
❑12, Jan 1996 ... 1.95
❑13, Feb 1996 ... 1.95
❑14, Mar 1996 ... 1.95
❑15, Mar 1996; Marked as Contagion, Part 4 on cover ... 1.95
❑16, Apr 1996; Continued from Catwoman (2nd Series) #32; Continued in Robin #28 ... 1.95

N-MINT

❑17, May 1996 ... 1.95
❑18, Jun 1996 ... 1.95
❑19, Jul 1996 ... 1.95
❑20, Aug 1996 ... 1.95
❑21, Sep 1996; Nomoz joins cast ... 1.95
❑22, Oct 1996 ... 1.95
❑23, Oct 1996 ... 1.95
❑24, Dec 1996 ... 1.95
❑25, Jan 1997 ... 1.95
❑26, Feb 1997 ... 1.95
❑27, Mar 1997; Azrael goes solo ... 1.95
❑28, Apr 1997 ... 1.95
❑29, May 1997 ... 1.95
❑30, Jun 1997 ... 1.95
❑31, Jul 1997 ... 1.95
❑32, Aug 1997 ... 1.95
❑33, Sep 1997 ... 1.95
❑34, Oct 1997; "Genesis" ... 1.95
❑35, Nov 1997 ... 1.95
❑36, Dec 1997; Face cover ... 1.95
❑37, Jan 1998; V: Bane ... 1.95
❑38, Feb 1998; V: Bane ... 1.95
❑39, Mar 1998; V: Bane ... 1.95
❑40, Apr 1998; continues in Detective Comics #720 ... 1.95
❑41, May 1998 ... 1.95
❑42, Jun 1998 ... 1.95
❑43, Jul 1998 ... 1.95
❑44, Aug 1998 ... 1.95
❑45, Sep 1998; V: Deathstroke ... 2.25
❑46, Oct 1998 ... 2.25
❑47, Dec 1998; Signed extra-sized flip-book; Title changes to "Azrael: Agent of the Bat"; "Road to No Man's Land"; flipbook with Batman: Shadow of the Bat #80 (true title) ... 3.95
❑47/Ltd., Dec 1998; Title changes to Azrael: Agent of the Bat; 1: Nicholas Scratch; D: Senator Halivan; Flipbook with Batman: Shadow of the Bat #80 (true title) ... 6.00
❑48, Jan 1999; "Road to No Man's Land"; Batman cameo ... 2.25
❑49, Feb 1999; "Road to No Man's Land" 2.25
❑50, Mar 1999; "No Man's Land" ... 2.25
❑51, Apr 1999; "No Man's Land"; new costume ... 2.25
❑52, May 1999; "No Man's Land" ... 2.25
❑53, Jun 1999; "No Man's Land" ... 2.25
❑54, Jul 1999; "No Man's Land" ... 2.25
❑55, Aug 1999; "No Man's Land" ... 2.25
❑56, Sep 1999; "No Man's Land" ... 2.25
❑57, Oct 1999; "No Man's Land" ... 2.25
❑58, Nov 1999; "No Man's Land"; Day of Judgment ... 2.25
❑59, Dec 1999; No Man's Land ... 2.25
❑60, Jan 2000; No Man's Land ... 2.25
❑61, Feb 2000 ... 2.25
❑62, Mar 2000; Brian Bryan rejoins cast 2.25
❑63, Apr 2000; 'bat books' cover symbol begins; Old costume ... 2.25
❑64, May 2000; Old costume ... 2.25
❑65, Jun 2000; Old costume ... 2.25
❑66, Jul 2000 ... 2.25
❑67, Aug 2000 ... 2.25
❑68, Sep 2000 ... 2.25
❑69, Oct 2000 ... 2.50
❑70, Nov 2000 ... 2.50
❑71, Dec 2000 ... 2.50
❑72, Jan 2001 ... 2.50
❑73, Feb 2001 ... 2.50
❑74, Mar 2001 ... 2.50
❑75, Apr 2001; Giant-size ... 3.95
❑76, May 2001; Azrael relocates to Ossaville; Harold joins cast ... 2.50
❑77, Jun 2001 ... 2.50
❑78, Jul 2001 ... 2.50
❑79, Aug 2001 ... 2.50
❑80, Sep 2001 ... 2.50
❑81, Oct 2001 ... 2.50
❑82, Nov 2001 ... 2.50
❑83, Dec 2001; Joker: Last Laugh crossover 2.50
❑84, Jan 2002 ... 2.50
❑85, Feb 2002 ... 2.50
❑86, Mar 2002 ... 2.50
❑87, Apr 2002 ... 2.50
❑88, May 2002 ... 2.50
❑89, Jun 2002 ... 2.50
❑91, Aug 2002; Continued from Batman: Gotham Knights #30 & into Detective Comics #772 ... 2.50

Other grades: Multiply price above by 5/6 for VF/NM • 2/3 for VERY FINE • 1/3 for FINE • 1/5 for VERY GOOD • 1/8 for GOOD

Army War Heroes

Charlton's tales of military courage

©Charlton

Artesia

Adult sword-and-sorcery with female lead

©Sirius

Ascension

Springboard series took creator Batt to fame

©Image

Ash

Joe Quesada and Jimmy Palmiotti's fireman hero

©Event

Astonishing Tales

Series gave rise to cyborg Deathlok

©Marvel

	N-MINT
❑90, Jul 2002; Nightwing appearanc	2.50
❑92, Sep 2002; Lilhy joins cast	2.50
❑93, Oct 2002	2.95
❑94, Nov 2002	2.95
❑95, Dec 2002	2.95
❑96, Jan 2003; V: Two-Face; Includes preview of Gotham Central #1	2.95
❑97, Feb 2003; New bat cover logo	2.95
❑98, Mar 2003	2.95
❑99, Apr 2003	2.95
❑100, May 2003; D: Azrael; Final issue	2.95
❑Ann 1, ca. 1995; Year One	3.95
❑Ann 2, ca. 1996; Legends of the Dead Earth	2.95
❑Ann 3, ca. 1997; Pulp Heroes	3.95
❑1000000, Nov 1998; becomes Azrael: Agent of the Bat	3.00

Azrael/Ash
DC

	N-MINT
❑1, ca. 1997	4.95

Azrael Plus
DC

	N-MINT
❑1, Dec 1996	2.95

Aztec Ace
Eclipse

	N-MINT
❑1, Mar 1984; Giant-size; 1: Aztec Ace	2.50
❑2, Apr 1984	2.00
❑3, Jun 1984	2.00
❑4, Jul 1984	2.00
❑5, Jul 1984	2.00
❑6, Aug 1984	2.00
❑7, Oct 1984	2.00
❑8, Dec 1984	2.00
❑9, Jan 1985	2.00
❑10, Feb 1985	2.00
❑11, Mar 1985	2.00
❑12, Apr 1985	2.00
❑13, May 1985	2.00
❑14, Jun 1985	2.00
❑15, Sep 1985	2.00

Aztec Anthropomorphic Amazons
Antarctic

	N-MINT
❑1, Mar 1994, b&w	2.75

Aztec of the City
El Salto

	N-MINT
❑1, May 1993; 1: Aztec; O: Aztec	2.25

Aztec of the City
El Salto

	N-MINT
❑1 1996	2.50
❑2, May 1996	2.50

Aztek: The Ultimate Man
DC

	N-MINT
❑1, Aug 1996; 1: Aztek	1.75
❑2, Sep 1996; V: Major Force	1.75
❑3, Oct 1996; 1: Death Doll	1.75
❑4, Nov 1996	1.75
❑5, Dec 1996	1.75
❑6, Jan 1997; V: Joker	1.75
❑7, Feb 1997	1.75
❑8, Mar 1997	1.75
❑9, Apr 1997; V: Parasite	1.75
❑10, May 1997; Final issue; Aztek joins JLA	1.75

Azumanga Daioh
ADV Manga

	N-MINT
❑1, ca. 2003	9.99
❑2, ca. 2003	9.99
❑3, ca. 2004	9.99
❑4, ca. 2004	9.99

Babe
Dark Horse / Legend

	N-MINT
❑1, Jul 1994	2.50
❑2, Aug 1994	2.50
❑3, Sep 1994; 1: The Prototykes	2.50
❑4, Oct 1994	2.50

Babe 2
Dark Horse / Legend

	N-MINT
❑1, Mar 1995	2.50
❑2, Apr 1995	2.50

Babes of Broadway
Broadway

	N-MINT
❑1, May 1996, pin-ups and previews of upcoming Broadway series	2.95

Babewatch
Express / Parody

	N-MINT
❑1 1995, b&w	2.50
❑1/A 1995	2.95

Baby Angel X
Brainstorm

	N-MINT
❑1, b&w; Adult	2.95

Baby Huey Digest
Harvey

	N-MINT
❑1, Jun 1992	1.75

Baby Huey in 3-D
Blackthorne

	N-MINT
❑1, Dec 1998; Blackthorne 3-D series #58; Winter 1988	2.50

Baby Huey The Baby Giant
Harvey

	N-MINT
❑40, Nov 1961	9.00
❑41, Dec 1961	6.00
❑42, Jan 1962	6.00
❑43, Feb 1962	6.00
❑44, Mar 1962	6.00
❑45, Apr 1962	6.00
❑46, Jun 1962	6.00
❑47, Aug 1962	6.00
❑48, Oct 1962	6.00
❑49, Dec 1962	6.00
❑50, Feb 1963	6.00
❑51, Apr 1963	4.00
❑52, Jun 1963	4.00
❑53, Aug 1963	4.00
❑54, Oct 1963	4.00
❑55, Dec 1963	4.00
❑56, Feb 1964	4.00
❑57, Apr 1964	4.00
❑58, Jun 1964	4.00
❑59, Aug 1964	4.00
❑60, Oct 1964	4.00
❑61, Dec 1964	4.00
❑62, Feb 1965	4.00
❑63, Apr 1965	4.00
❑64, Jun 1965	4.00
❑65, Aug 1965	4.00
❑66, Oct 1965	4.00
❑67, Dec 1965	4.00
❑68, Feb 1966	4.00
❑69, Apr 1966	4.00
❑70, Jun 1966	4.00
❑71, Aug 1966	2.50
❑72, Oct 1966	2.50
❑73, Dec 1966	2.50
❑74, Feb 1967	2.50
❑75, Apr 1967	2.50
❑76, Jun 1967	2.50
❑77, Aug 1967	2.50
❑78, Oct 1967	2.50
❑79, Dec 1967	2.50
❑80, Dec 1968, Giant-size	2.50
❑81, Feb 1969, Giant-size	2.50
❑82, Apr 1969, Giant-size	2.50
❑83, Jun 1969, Giant-size	2.50
❑84, Aug 1969, Giant-size	2.50
❑85, Oct 1969, Giant-size	2.50
❑86, Dec 1969, Giant-size	2.50
❑87, Feb 1970, Giant-size	2.50
❑88, Apr 1970, Giant-size	2.50
❑89, Jun 1970, Giant-size	2.50
❑90, Aug 1970, Giant-size	2.50
❑91, Oct 1970, Giant-size	2.50
❑92, Dec 1970, Giant-size	2.50
❑93, Feb 1971, Giant-size	2.50
❑94, Apr 1971, Giant-size	2.50
❑95, Jun 1971, Giant-size	2.50
❑96, Aug 1971, Giant-size	2.50
❑97, Oct 1971, Giant-size	2.50
❑98, Oct 1972	2.50
❑99, Oct 1980, One-shot return from hiatus	2.50
❑100, Oct 1990, Series begins again after hiatus	1.00
❑101, Nov 1990	1.00
❑102	1.00

Baby Huey
Harvey

	N-MINT
❑1, Oct 1991	1.25
❑2, Jan 1992	1.25
❑3, Apr 1992	1.25
❑4, Aug 1992	1.25
❑5, Nov 1992	1.25
❑6, Mar 1993	1.25
❑7, Jun 1993	1.25
❑8, Apr 1994	1.25
❑9, Jun 1994	1.25

Babylon 5
DC

	N-MINT
❑1, Jan 1995	5.00
❑2, Feb 1995	4.00
❑3, Mar 1995	3.50
❑4, Apr 1995; Ann Bruice is Costume Designer for the television show Babylon 5; Babcom: Costumes for a Foreign World	3.50
❑5, Jun 1995	3.00
❑6, Jul 1995	3.00
❑7, Aug 1995	3.00
❑8, Sep 1995	2.50
❑9, Oct 1995	2.50
❑10, Nov 1995	2.50
❑11, Dec 1995; Final Issue	2.50

Babylon 5: In Valen's Name
DC

- ❑1, Mar 1998 ... 3.50
- ❑2, Apr 1998 ... 3.00
- ❑3, May 1998 ... 3.00

Babylon Crush
Boneyard

- ❑1, May 1995; cardstock cover, b&w ... 2.95
- ❑2, Jul 1995; cardstock cover, b&w ... 2.95
- ❑3, Oct 1995, b&w; Adult ... 2.95
- ❑4; Adult ... 2.95
- ❑Xmas 1, Jan 1998; Adult ... 2.95

Baby's First Deadpool Book
Marvel

- ❑1, Dec 1998; children's-book style stories ... 2.99

Baby Snoots
Gold Key

- ❑1, Aug 1970 ... 12.00
- ❑2, Nov 1970 ... 10.00
- ❑3, Feb 1971 ... 8.00
- ❑4, May 1971 ... 6.00
- ❑5, Aug 1971 ... 6.00
- ❑6, Nov 1971 ... 6.00
- ❑7, Feb 1972 ... 6.00
- ❑8, May 1972 ... 6.00
- ❑9, Aug 1972 ... 6.00
- ❑10, Nov 1972 ... 6.00
- ❑11, Feb 1973 ... 6.00
- ❑12, May 1973 ... 6.00
- ❑13, Aug 1973 ... 5.00
- ❑14, Nov 1973 ... 5.00
- ❑15, Feb 1974 ... 5.00
- ❑16, May 1974 ... 5.00
- ❑17, Aug 1974 ... 5.00
- ❑18, Nov 1974 ... 5.00
- ❑19, Feb 1975 ... 5.00
- ❑20, May 1975 ... 5.00
- ❑21, Aug 1975 ... 5.00
- ❑22, Nov 1975 ... 5.00

Baby, You're Really Something!
Fantagraphics / Eros

- ❑1, Sep 1990, b&w; Reprints ... 2.50

Bacchus (Harrier)
Harrier

- ❑1, ca. 1988 ... 5.00
- ❑2, ca. 1988 ... 4.00

Bacchus Color Special
Dark Horse

- ❑1, Apr 1995; NN; One-shot ... 3.25

Bacchus (Eddie Campbell's...)
Eddie Campbell

- ❑1, May 1995 ... 6.00
- ❑1/2nd, May 1999 ... 3.00
- ❑2, Jun 1995 ... 4.00
- ❑3, Jul 1995 ... 4.00
- ❑4, Aug 1995 ... 3.50
- ❑5, Sep 1995 ... 3.50
- ❑6, Oct 1995 ... 3.00
- ❑7, Nov 1995 ... 3.00
- ❑8, Dec 1995 ... 3.00
- ❑9, Jan 1996 ... 3.00
- ❑10, Feb 1996 ... 3.00
- ❑11, Mar 1996 ... 3.00
- ❑12, Apr 1996 ... 3.00
- ❑13, May 1996 ... 3.00
- ❑14, Jun 1996 ... 3.00
- ❑15, Jul 1996 ... 3.00
- ❑16, Aug 1996 ... 3.00
- ❑17, Sep 1996 ... 3.00
- ❑18, Oct 1996, b&w ... 3.00
- ❑19, Nov 1996 ... 3.00
- ❑20, Dec 1996 ... 3.00
- ❑21, Jan 1997 ... 2.95
- ❑22, Feb 1997 ... 2.95
- ❑23, Mar 1997 ... 2.95
- ❑24, ca. 1997 ... 2.95
- ❑25, ca. 1997 ... 2.95
- ❑26, ca. 1997 ... 2.95
- ❑27, Aug 1997 ... 2.95
- ❑28, Sep 1997 ... 2.95
- ❑29, Oct 1997 ... 2.95
- ❑30, Nov 1997 ... 2.95
- ❑31, Dec 1997 ... 2.95
- ❑32, ca. 1998 ... 2.95
- ❑33, Mar 1998 ... 2.95
- ❑34, Apr 1998 ... 2.95
- ❑35, ca. 1998 ... 2.95
- ❑36, ca. 1998 ... 2.95
- ❑37, ca. 1998 ... 2.95
- ❑38, Sep 1998 ... 2.95
- ❑39, Oct 1998 ... 2.95
- ❑40, Dec 1998 ... 2.95
- ❑41, Jan 1999 ... 2.95
- ❑42, Feb 1999 ... 2.95

Bachelor Father
Dell

- ❑2, Nov 1962 ... 50.00

Back Down the Line
Eclipse

- ❑1; NN ... 8.95

Backlash
Image

- ❑1, Nov 1994; Double cover ... 2.50
- ❑2, Dec 1994 ... 2.50
- ❑3, Jan 1995 ... 2.50
- ❑4, Feb 1995 ... 2.50
- ❑5, Feb 1995 ... 2.50
- ❑6, Mar 1995 ... 2.50
- ❑7, Apr 1995; 1: Crimson ... 2.50
- ❑8, May 1995; bound-in trading cards ... 2.50
- ❑9, Jun 1995 ... 2.50
- ❑10, Jul 1995; indicia says Jul, cover says Aug ... 2.50
- ❑11, Aug 1995 ... 2.50
- ❑12, Sep 1995; indicia says Sep, cover says Oct ... 2.50
- ❑13, Nov 1995 ... 2.50
- ❑14, Nov 1995; indicia says Nov, cover says Dec ... 2.50
- ❑15, Dec 1995; indicia says Dec, cover says Jan ... 2.50
- ❑16, Jan 1996; indicia says Jan, cover says Feb ... 2.50
- ❑17, Feb 1996 ... 2.50
- ❑18, Mar 1996 ... 2.50
- ❑19, Apr 1996 ... 2.50
- ❑20, May 1996 ... 2.50
- ❑21, Jun 1996 ... 2.50
- ❑22, Jul 1996 ... 2.50
- ❑23, Aug 1996 ... 2.50
- ❑24, Sep 1996; 1: Omni ... 2.50
- ❑25, Nov 1996; Giant-size; 1: Gramalkin ... 2.50
- ❑26, Nov 1996 ... 2.50
- ❑27, Dec 1996 ... 2.50
- ❑28, Jan 1997 ... 2.50
- ❑29, Feb 1997 ... 2.50
- ❑30, Mar 1997 ... 2.50
- ❑31, Apr 1997 ... 2.50
- ❑32, May 1997; Final Issue ... 2.50

Backlash & Taboo's African Holiday
DC / Wildstorm

- ❑1, Sep 1999 ... 5.95

Backlash/Spider-Man
Image

- ❑1, Aug 1996 ... 2.50
- ❑1/A, Aug 1996; crossover with Marvel, cover says Jul, indicia says Aug ... 2.50
- ❑1/B, Aug 1996; alternate cover, crossover with Marvel, cover says Jul, indicia says Aug ... 2.50
- ❑2, Oct 1996; crossover with Marvel ... 2.50

Backpack Marvels: Avengers
Marvel

- ❑1, Jan 2001; Reprints Avengers (vol. 1) #181-189 ... 6.95

Backpack Marvels: X-Men
Marvel

- ❑1, Nov 2000; Reprints Uncanny X-Men #167-173 ... 6.95
- ❑2, Nov 2000; Reprints Uncanny X-Men #167-173 ... 6.95

Back to the Future
Harvey

- ❑1, Nov 1991, FB, GK (c); GK (a) ... 1.50
- ❑2, Nov 1991, Indicia says January, cover says February ... 1.50
- ❑3, Jan 1992 ... 1.50
- ❑4, Jun 1992 ... 1.50
- ❑Special 1, Universal Studios-Florida giveaway ... 1.00

Back to the Future: Forward to the Future
Harvey

- ❑1, Oct 1992 ... 1.50
- ❑2, Nov 1992 ... 1.50
- ❑3, Jan 1993 ... 1.50

Bad Apples
High Impact

- ❑1, Jan 1997 ... 2.95
- ❑2, ca. 1997 ... 2.95

Bad Art Collection
Slave Labor

- ❑1, Apr 1996; Oversized; NN; Adult ... 1.95

Badaxe
Adventure

- ❑1 ... 1.00
- ❑2 ... 1.00
- ❑3 ... 1.00

Bad Boy
Oni

- ❑1, Dec 1997; oversized one-shot; NN ... 4.95

Bad Comics
Cat-Head

- ❑1, b&w ... 2.75

Bad Company
Fleetway-Quality

- ❑1 ... 1.50
- ❑2 ... 1.50
- ❑3 ... 1.50
- ❑4 ... 1.50
- ❑5 ... 1.50
- ❑6 ... 1.50
- ❑7 ... 1.50
- ❑8 ... 1.50
- ❑9 ... 1.50
- ❑10 ... 1.50
- ❑11 ... 1.50
- ❑12 ... 1.50
- ❑13 ... 1.50
- ❑14 ... 1.50
- ❑15 ... 1.50
- ❑16 ... 1.75
- ❑17 ... 1.75
- ❑18 ... 1.75
- ❑19 ... 1.75

Bade Biker & Orson
Mirage

- ❑1, Nov 1986 ... 1.50
- ❑2, Jan 1987 ... 1.50
- ❑3, Mar 1987 ... 1.50
- ❑4, Jun 1987 ... 1.50

Bad Eggs
Acclaim / Armada

- ❑1, Jun 1996 ... 2.95
- ❑2, Jul 1996 ... 2.95
- ❑3, Aug 1996 ... 2.95
- ❑4, Sep 1996 ... 2.95
- ❑5, Sep 1996; cover says Oct, indicia says Sep ... 2.95
- ❑6, Nov 1996; shoplifting instructions on cover ... 2.95
- ❑7, Dec 1996 ... 2.95
- ❑8, Jan 1997 ... 2.95

Badge
Vanguard

- ❑1 1981 ... 2.95

Badger
Capital

- ❑1, Oct 1983; SR (a); 1: Badger. 1: Ham ... 5.00
- ❑2, Feb 1984 ... 2.50
- ❑3, Mar 1984 ... 2.50
- ❑4, Apr 1984 ... 2.50
- ❑5, May 1985; First Comics begins publishing ... 2.50
- ❑6, Jul 1985 ... 2.00
- ❑7, Sep 1985 ... 2.00
- ❑8, Nov 1985 ... 2.00
- ❑9, Jan 1986 ... 2.00
- ❑10, Mar 1986 ... 2.00
- ❑11, May 1986 ... 2.00
- ❑12, Jun 1986 ... 2.00
- ❑13, Jul 1986 ... 2.00
- ❑14, Aug 1986 ... 2.00
- ❑15, Sep 1986 ... 2.00

Other grades: Multiply price above by 5/6 for VF/NM • 2/3 for VERY FINE • 1/3 for FINE • 1/5 for VERY GOOD • 1/8 for GOOD

Astonishing X-Men (3rd Series)

Buffy's Joss Whedon's spin on mutants

Astro City (Vol. 1) (Kurt Busiek's...)

Critically acclaimed series about city of heroes

Atari Force

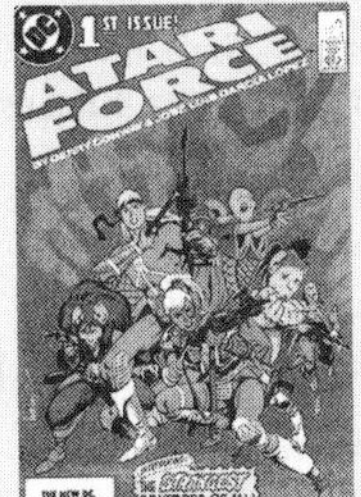

Ancient video game system inspires comics title

A-Team

Adventures of the NBC TV series characters

Atom

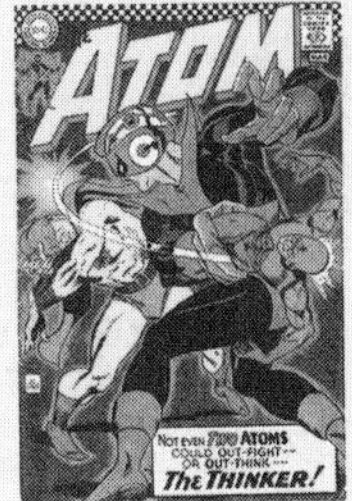

Ray Palmer gets small in Silver Age series

N-MINT

❑16, Oct 1986 ..... 2.00
❑17, Nov 1986 ..... 2.00
❑18, Dec 1986 ..... 2.00
❑19, Jan 1987 ..... 2.00
❑20, Feb 1987 ..... 2.00
❑21, Mar 1987 ..... 2.00
❑22, Apr 1987 ..... 2.00
❑23, May 1987 ..... 2.00
❑24, Jun 1987 ..... 2.00
❑25, Jul 1987 ..... 2.00
❑26, Aug 1987; Roach Wrangler 2.00
❑27, Sep 1987; Roach Wrangler 2.00
❑28, Oct 1987 ..... 2.00
❑29, Nov 1987 ..... 2.00
❑30, Dec 1987 ..... 2.00
❑31, Jan 1988 ..... 2.00
❑32, Feb 1988 ..... 2.00
❑33, Mar 1988 MZ (c) 2.00
❑34, Apr 1988 MZ (c) 2.00
❑35, May 1988 ..... 2.00
❑36, Jun 1988 ..... 2.00
❑37, Jul 1988 ..... 2.00
❑38, Aug 1988 ..... 2.00
❑39, Sep 1988 ..... 2.00
❑40, Oct 1988 ..... 2.00
❑41, Nov 1988 ..... 2.00
❑42, Dec 1988 ..... 2.00
❑43, Jan 1989 ..... 2.00
❑44, Feb 1989; 1: Steve Marmel (The Hilariator-in comics) 2.00
❑45, Mar 1989 ..... 2.00
❑46, Apr 1989 ..... 2.00
❑47, May 1989 ..... 2.00
❑48, Jun 1989 ..... 2.00
❑49, Jul 1989 ..... 2.00
❑50, Aug 1989; Double-size 3.95
❑51, Sep 1989 ..... 2.00
❑52, Oct 1989 ..... 3.00
❑53, Nov 1989 ..... 3.00
❑54, Dec 1989 ..... 3.00
❑55, Jan 1990 ..... 2.00
❑56, Feb 1990 ..... 2.00
❑57, Mar 1990 ..... 2.00
❑58, Apr 1990 ..... 2.00
❑59, May 1990 ..... 2.00
❑60, Jun 1990 ..... 2.00
❑61, Jul 1990 ..... 2.00
❑62, Aug 1990 ..... 2.00
❑63, Sep 1990 ..... 2.00
❑64, Oct 1990 ..... 2.25
❑65, Nov 1990 ..... 2.25
❑66, Dec 1990 ..... 2.25
❑67, Jan 1991 ..... 2.25
❑68, Feb 1991 ..... 2.25
❑69, Mar 1991; O: Badger 2.25
❑70, Apr 1991; Final Issue 2.25

Badger
First

❑1, May 1991; Badger Bedlam 4.95

Badger
Image

❑1, May 1997, b&w; indicia says #78 in series 2.95
❑2, Jun 1997, b&w; indicia says #79 in series 2.95
❑3, Jul 1997, b&w; indicia says #80 in series 2.95

N-MINT

❑4, Aug 1997, b&w; indicia says #81 in series 2.95
❑5, Sep 1997, b&w; indicia says #82 in series 2.95
❑6, Oct 1997, b&w; indicia says #83 in series 2.95
❑7, Nov 1997, b&w; indicia says #84 in series 2.95
❑8, Dec 1997, b&w; indicia says #85 in series 2.95
❑9, Jan 1998, b&w; indicia says #86 in series 2.95
❑10, Feb 1998, b&w; indicia says #87 in series 2.95
❑11, Apr 1998, b&w; indicia says #88 in series 2.95

Badger Goes Berserk
First

❑1, Sep 1989 ..... 2.00
❑2, Oct 1989 ..... 2.00
❑3, Nov 1989 ..... 2.00
❑4, Dec 1989 ..... 2.00

Badger: Shattered Mirror
Dark Horse

❑1, Jul 1994 ..... 2.50
❑2, Aug 1994 ..... 2.50
❑3, Sep 1994 ..... 2.50
❑4, Oct 1994 ..... 2.50

Badger: Zen Pop Funny-Animal Version
Dark Horse

❑1, Jul 1994 ..... 2.50
❑2, Aug 1994 ..... 2.50

Bad Girls
DC

❑1, Aug 2003 ..... 2.50
❑2, Sep 2003; ca. 1992 ..... 2.50
❑3, Oct 2003; ca. 1992 ..... 2.50
❑4, Nov 2003 ..... 2.50
❑5, Dec 2003; Final issue 2.50

Bad Girls (Bill Ward's...)
Forbidden Fruit

❑1 ..... 1.50

Bad Girls of Blackout
Blackout

❑0 1995 ..... 3.50
❑1 1995 ..... 3.50
❑Ann 1, ca. 1995 ..... 3.50

Bad Hair Day
Slab-O-Concrete

❑1; Postcard Comic 1.00

Bad Ideas
Image

❑1, Apr 2004 ..... 5.95
❑2, Sep 2004 ..... 6.00

Bad Kitty
Chaos

❑1, Feb 2001 ..... 2.99
❑1/A, Mar 2001; Alternate cover (nude w/cat) 2.99
❑Ashcan 1; 1,000 copies printed 3.00
❑2, Mar 2001 ..... 2.99
❑3, Apr 2001 ..... 2.99

Bad Kitty: Mischief Night
Chaos

❑1, Nov 2001; Events take place after Lady Death/Bad Kitty #1 ..... 3.00
❑1/A, Nov 2001; Events take place after Lady Death/Bad Kitty #1 ..... 2.99

N-MINT

❑1/B, Nov 2001; Events take place after Lady Death/Bad Kitty #1; Posing next to car on white background 2.99
❑1/C, Nov 2001; Events take place after Lady Death/Bad Kitty #1; Posing next to car on white background 2.99
❑1/D, Nov 2001; Otherwise same as #1 ..... 2.99

Badlands
Dark Horse

❑1, Jul 1991 ..... 2.50
❑2 ..... 2.50
❑3 ..... 2.50
❑4 ..... 2.50
❑5 ..... 2.50
❑6 ..... 2.50

Bad Luck and Rick Dees Sentinel of Justice
King Comics

❑1, Feb 1994 ..... 2.95

Bad Meat
Fantagraphics / Eros

❑1, Jul 1991, b&w; Adult 2.25
❑2; Adult 2.25

Bad News
Fantagraphics

❑3, b&w 3.50

Bad Planet
Image

❑1, Dec 2005 ..... 2.99

Badrock
Image

❑1/A, Mar 1995, Todd McFarlane inks on cover 1.75
❑1/B, Mar 1995, Stephen Platt inks on cover 1.75
❑1/C, Mar 1995, Dan Fraga inks on cover 1.75
❑2 ..... 1.75
❑3 ..... 1.75
❑Ann 1, Jul 1995 ..... 2.95

Badrock & Company
Image

❑1, Sep 1994 ..... 2.50
❑2, Oct 1994 ..... 2.50
❑3, Nov 1994 ..... 2.50
❑4, Dec 1994 ..... 2.50
❑5, Jan 1995 ..... 2.50
❑6, Oct 1995; cover says Feb 95, indicia says Oct 94 ..... 2.50
❑Special 1, Sep 1994; San Diego Comic-Con edition 2.50

Badrock/Wolverine
Image

❑1/A, Jun 1996 ..... 4.95
❑1/B, Jun 1996 ..... 4.95
❑1/C, Jun 1996 ..... 4.95
❑1/D, Jun 1996 ..... 4.95

Bakers
Kyle Baker Publishing

❑1, Oct 2005 ..... 3.00

Bakers Meet Jingle Belle
Dark Horse

❑1, Jan 2007 ..... 2.99

Baker Street
Caliber

❑1, Mar 1989 ..... 2.50

Other grades: Multiply price above by 5/6 for VF/NM • 2/3 for VERY FINE • 1/3 for FINE • 1/5 for VERY GOOD • 1/8 for GOOD

❑2 2.50
❑3 2.50
❑4 2.50
❑5 2.50
❑6 2.50
❑7 2.50
❑8 2.50
❑9 2.50
❑10 2.50

Baker Street Graffiti
Caliber

❑1, b&w 2.50

Baker Street Sketchbook
Caliber

❑1 3.95

Balance of Power
Mu

❑1, b&w 2.50
❑2 2.50
❑3, Mar 1991 2.50
❑4, Jul 1991 2.50

Balder the Brave
Marvel

❑1, Nov 1985 SB (a) 1.00
❑2, Jan 1986 1.00
❑3, Mar 1986 1.00
❑4, May 1986 1.00

Ballad of Halo Jones
Fleetway-Quality

❑1, Sep 1987; AMo (w); 1: Halo Jones. Reprints The Ballad of Halo Jones from 2000 A.D 1.50
❑2, Oct 1987 AMo (w) 1.50
❑3 AMo (w) 1.50
❑4 AMo (w) 1.50
❑5 AMo (w) 1.50
❑6 AMo (w) 1.50
❑7 AMo (w) 1.50
❑8 AMo (w) 1.50
❑9 AMo (w) 1.50
❑10 AMo (w) 1.50
❑11 AMo (w) 1.50
❑12 AMo (w) 1.50

Ballad Of Utopia
Black Daze

❑1, Mar 2000, b&w 2.95
❑2, Apr 2000, b&w 2.95
❑3, May 2000, b&w 2.95
❑4, Feb 2002, b&w; Amryl Entertainment begins publishing 2.95
❑5, Jun 2002, b&w 2.95
❑6, Feb 2003, b&w 2.95
❑7, ca. 2003, b&w 2.95
❑8, Nov 2003, b&w; Antimatter/Hoffman International publishes 2.95

Ball and Chain
DC / Homage

❑1, Nov 1999 2.50
❑2, Dec 1999 2.50
❑3, Jan 2000 2.50
❑4, Feb 2000 2.50

Ballast
Active Images

❑0, Sep 2005 4.00

Ballistic
Image

❑1, Sep 1995 2.50
❑2, Oct 1995 2.50
❑3, Nov 1995 2.50

Ballistic Action
Image

❑1, May 1996; pin-ups 2.95

Ballistic Imagery
Image

❑1, Jan 1996; Anthology 2.50
❑2 2.50

Ballistic Studios Swimsuit Special
Image

❑1, May 1995; pin-ups 2.95

Ballistic/Wolverine
Top Cow

❑1, Feb 1997; crossover with Marvel, continues in Wolverine/Witchblade 3.50

Balloonatiks
Best

❑1, Oct 1991; Includes balloon 2.50

Baloo & Little Britches
Gold Key

❑1, Apr 1968 25.00

Bambeano Boy
Moordam

❑1, May 1998 2.50

Bambi (Walt Disney...)
Whitman

❑1, Reprint of 1942 story 2.50

Bambi and Her Friends
Friendly

❑1, Jan 1991; Adult 2.50
❑2, Feb 1991; Adult 2.50
❑3, Mar 1991; Adult 2.95
❑4, Apr 1991; Adult 2.95
❑5, May 1991; Adult 2.95
❑6, Jun 1991; Adult 2.95
❑7, Jul 1991; Adult 2.95
❑8, Aug 1991; Adult 2.95
❑9, Sep 1991; Adult 2.95

Bambi in Heat
Friendly

❑1; Adult 2.95
❑2; Adult 2.95
❑3; Adult 2.95

Bambi the Hunter
Friendly

❑1 2.95
❑2 2.95
❑3, Mar 1992 2.95
❑4 2.95
❑5 2.95

Bamm-Bamm and Pebbles Flintstone
Gold Key

❑1, ca. 1964 75.00

Banana Fish
Tokyopop

❑1, May 2004 15.95
❑2, Jul 2004 15.95
❑3, Aug 2004 15.95
❑4, Oct 2004 15.95
❑5, Dec 2004 15.95
❑6, Feb 2005 15.95
❑7, Apr 2005 15.95
❑8, Jun 2005 9.95
❑9, Aug 2005 9.95
❑10, Oct 2005 9.99

Banana Splits (Hanna Barbera...)
Gold Key

❑1, Jun 1969, 1: Snorky (in comics). 1: Fleegle (in comics). 1: Drooper (in comics). 1: Bingo (in comics) 30.00
❑2, Apr 1970 18.00
❑3, Jul 1970 14.00
❑4, Oct 1970 14.00
❑5, Jan 1971 14.00
❑6, Apr 1971 12.00
❑7, Jul 1971 12.00
❑8, Oct 1971 12.00

Banana Sundays
Oni

❑1, Aug 2005 2.99
❑2, Sep 2005 2.99
❑3, Oct 2005 2.99
❑4, Nov 2005 2.99

Bandy Man
Caliber

❑1, ca. 1996, b&w 2.95
❑2, ca. 1996, b&w 2.95
❑3, ca. 1997, b&w 2.95

Bang Gang
Fantagraphics / Eros

❑1, b&w; Adult 2.50

Bangs and the Gang
Shhwinng

❑1, Feb 1994, b&w; Adult 2.95

Banished Knights
Image

❑1, Dec 2001; no cover price 6.50
❑1/A, Dec 2001; Group montage cover 3.00
❑1/B, Dec 2001; Sepia-toned montage cover 3.00
❑2/A, Feb 2002; Alvin lee cover 3.00
❑2/B, Feb 2002; Pat Lee cover 3.00

Banzai Girl
Sirius

❑1 2002 2.95
❑2 2002 2.95
❑3, Feb 2003 2.95
❑4, May 2003 2.95
❑Ann 1, Jan 2004 3.50

Baobab
Fantagraphics

❑1, Aug 2005, Part of the Ignatz series; Ignatz collection 7.95

Baoh
Viz

❑1 3.50
❑2 3.00
❑3 3.00
❑4 3.00
❑5 3.00
❑6 3.00
❑7 3.00
❑8 3.00

Barabbas
Slave Labor

❑1, Aug 1986 1.50
❑2, Nov 1985 1.50

Barbarian Comics
California

❑1, ca. 1972, Adult 3.00
❑2, ca. 1973, Adult 2.50

Barbarians
Atlas-Seaboard

❑1, Jun 1975; O: Andrax. 1: Ironjaw 8.00

Barbarians (Avalon)
Avalon

❑1 2.95
❑2 2.95

Barbarians and Beauties
AC

❑1 1990 2.75

Barbaric Tales
Pyramid

❑1 1.70
❑2 1.70

Barbarienne (Fantagraphics)
Fantagraphics / Eros

❑2, b&w; Adult 2.50
❑3, b&w; Adult 2.50
❑4 1992; Adult; b&w 3.50
❑5; Adult; b&w 3.50
❑6 2003; Adult; b&w 3.50
❑7; Adult; b&w 3.50
❑8; Adult; b&w 3.95
❑9; Adult; b&w 3.95
❑10 2004; Adult; b&w 3.95

Barbarienne (Harrier)
Harrier

❑1, Mar 1987; Adult 2.00
❑2; Adult 2.00
❑3; Adult 2.00
❑4, Nov 1987; Adult 2.00
❑5; Adult 2.00
❑6, Apr 1988; V: Cuirass; Adult 2.00
❑7; V: Cuirass; Adult 2.00
❑8; V: Cuirass; Adult 2.00

Barbie
Marvel

❑1, Jan 1991; JR (c); Includes "pink card" 3.00
❑1/A, Jan 1991; Includes door hanger 3.00
❑2, Feb 1991 2.00
❑3, Mar 1991 2.00
❑4, Apr 1991 2.00
❑5, May 1991 2.00
❑6, Jun 1991 1.50
❑7, Jul 1991 1.50
❑8, Aug 1991 1.50
❑9, Sep 1991 1.50
❑10, Oct 1991 1.50
❑11, Nov 1991 1.50
❑12, Dec 1991 1.50

Other grades: Multiply price above by 5/6 for VF/NM • 2/3 for VERY FINE • 1/3 for FINE • 1/5 for VERY GOOD • 1/8 for GOOD

Atom and Hawkman

Continuation of The Atom series
©DC

Atomics

Madman spinoff from Mike Allred
©AAA Pop

Attack (4th Series)

Stand-alone reprints from Charlton's war titles
©Charlton

Authority

Picks up where Stormwatch (Vol. 2) left off
©DC

Automaton

Martian energy creatures travel to Earth
©Image

	N-MINT
❑13, Jan 1992	1.50
❑14, Feb 1992	1.50
❑15, Mar 1992	1.50
❑16, Apr 1992	1.50
❑17, May 1992	1.50
❑18, Jun 1992	1.50
❑19, Jul 1992	1.50
❑20, Aug 1992	1.50
❑21, Sep 1992	1.50
❑22, Oct 1992	1.50
❑23, Nov 1992	1.50
❑24, Dec 1992	1.50
❑25, Jan 1993	1.50
❑26, Feb 1993	1.50
❑27, Mar 1993	1.50
❑28, Apr 1993	1.50
❑29, May 1993	1.50
❑30, Jun 1993	1.50
❑31, Jul 1993	1.50
❑32, Aug 1993 GM (a)	1.50
❑33, Sep 1993	1.50
❑34, Oct 1993 A: Teresa	1.50
❑35, Nov 1993	1.50
❑36, Dec 1993	1.50
❑37, Jan 1994	1.50
❑38, Feb 1994	1.50
❑39, Mar 1994	1.50
❑40, Apr 1994	1.50
❑41, May 1994	1.50
❑42, Jun 1994	1.50
❑43, Jul 1994	1.50
❑44, Aug 1994	1.50
❑45, Sep 1994	1.50
❑46, Oct 1994	1.50
❑47, Nov 1994	1.50
❑48, Dec 1994	1.50
❑49, Jan 1995	1.50
❑50, Feb 1995; Giant-size	2.25
❑51, Mar 1995	1.50
❑52, Apr 1995	1.50
❑53, May 1995	1.50
❑54, Jun 1995	1.50
❑55, Jul 1995	1.50
❑56, Aug 1995	1.50
❑57, Sep 1995	1.50
❑58, Oct 1995	1.50
❑59, Nov 1995	1.50
❑60, Dec 1995	1.50
❑61, Jan 1996	1.50
❑62, Feb 1996; Nutcracker Suite references	1.50
❑63, Mar 1996; Final Issue	1.50

Barbie & Baby Sister Kelly
Marvel

❑1, Oct 1995; Not distributed to comics shops	8.00

Barbie and Ken
Dell

❑1, May 1962	200.00
❑2, Aug 1962	150.00
❑3, May 1963	150.00
❑4, Aug 1963	150.00
❑5, Nov 1963	165.00

Barbie Fashion
Marvel

	N-MINT
❑1, Jan 1991, Includes membership card	3.00
❑1/A, Jan 1991, Includes doorknob hanger	3.00
❑2, Feb 1991	2.00
❑3, Mar 1991	2.00
❑4, Apr 1991	1.50
❑5, May 1991	1.50
❑6, Jun 1991	1.50
❑7, Jul 1991	1.50
❑8, Aug 1991	1.50
❑9, Sep 1991	1.50
❑10, Oct 1991	1.50
❑11, Nov 1991	1.50
❑12, Dec 1991	1.50
❑13, Jan 1992	1.50
❑14, Feb 1992	1.50
❑15, Mar 1992	1.50
❑16, Apr 1992	1.50
❑17, May 1992	1.50
❑18, Jun 1992	1.50
❑19, Jul 1992	1.50
❑20, Aug 1992	1.50
❑21, Sep 1992	1.50
❑22, Oct 1992	1.50
❑23, Nov 1992	1.50
❑24, Dec 1992	1.50
❑25, Jan 1993	1.50
❑26, Feb 1993	1.50
❑27, Mar 1993	1.50
❑28, Apr 1993	1.50
❑29, May 1993	1.50
❑30, Jun 1993	1.50
❑31, Jul 1993, GM (a)	1.50
❑32, Aug 1993	1.50
❑33, Sep 1993	1.50
❑34, Oct 1993	1.50
❑35, Nov 1993	1.50
❑36, Dec 1993	1.50
❑37, Jan 1994	1.50
❑38, Feb 1994	1.50
❑39, Mar 1994	1.50
❑40, Apr 1994	1.50
❑41, May 1994	1.50
❑42, Jun 1994	1.50
❑43, Jul 1994	1.50
❑44, Aug 1994	1.50
❑45, Sep 1994	1.50
❑46, Oct 1994	1.50
❑47, Nov 1994	1.50
❑48, Dec 1994	1.50
❑49, Jan 1995	1.50
❑50, Feb 1995, Giant-size	2.25
❑51, Mar 1995	1.50
❑52, Apr 1995	1.50
❑53, May 1995, Final Issue	1.50
❑54	1.50
❑55	1.50

Barbi Twins Adventures
Topps

❑1, Jul 1995; Flip-book	2.50

Barb Wire
Dark Horse

	N-MINT
❑1, Apr 1994; Foil cover lettering; Silver Foil cover lettering	2.50
❑2, May 1994	2.50
❑3, Jun 1994	2.50
❑4, Aug 1994	2.50
❑5, Sep 1994	2.50
❑6, Oct 1994	2.50
❑7, Nov 1994	2.50
❑8, Jan 1995	2.50
❑9, Feb 1995; Final Issue	2.50

Barb Wire: Ace of Spades
Dark Horse

❑1, May 1996	2.95
❑2, Jun 1996	2.95
❑3, Jul 1996	2.95
❑4, Sep 1996	2.95

Barb Wire Comics Magazine Special
Dark Horse

❑1, May 1996; magazine-sized adaptation of movie, b&w, poster; NN	3.50

Barb Wire Movie Special
Dark Horse

❑1, May 1996; adapts movie	3.95

Bar Crawl of the Damned
Mortco

❑1 1997, b&w	2.50

Barefootz Funnies
Kitchen Sink

❑1, Jul 1975, b&w; Adult	3.00
❑2, Apr 1976, b&w; Adult	2.00
❑3, Dec 1979, b&w; Adult	2.00

Barefootz The Comix Book Stories
Renegade

❑1 A: Dolly. A: Barefootz. A: Headrack	2.50

Barf
Revolutionary

❑1, Apr 1990, b&w	1.95
❑2, Jun 1990, b&w	2.50
❑3, Sep 1990, b&w	2.50

Barney and Betty Rubble
Charlton

❑1, Jan 1973	15.00
❑2, Jan 1973	10.00
❑3, Mar 1973	6.00
❑4, May 1973	6.00
❑5, Jul 1973	6.00
❑6, Sep 1973	6.00
❑7, May 1974	6.00
❑8, Jul 1974	6.00
❑9, Sep 1974	6.00
❑10, Nov 1974	6.00
❑11, Feb 1975	6.00
❑12, Mar 1975	5.00
❑13, May 1975	5.00
❑14, Jun 1975	5.00
❑15, Aug 1975	5.00
❑16, Oct 1975	5.00
❑17, Dec 1975	5.00
❑18, Feb 1976	5.00
❑19, Apr 1976	5.00
❑20, Jun 1976	5.00

Other grades: Multiply price above by 5/6 for VF/NM • 2/3 for VERY FINE • 1/3 for FINE • 1/5 for VERY GOOD • 1/8 for GOOD

N-MINT

❑21, Aug 1976 5.00
❑22, Oct 1976 5.00
❑23, Dec 1976 5.00

Barney the Invisible Turtle
Amazing

❑1 1.95

Barr Girls
Antarctic / Venus

❑1, b&w; Adult 2.95

Barron Storey's Watch Annual
Vanguard

❑1; b&w anthology, squarebound 5.95

Barry Windsor-Smith: Storyteller
Dark Horse

❑1, Oct 1996 4.95
❑1/Variant, Oct 1996, alternate cover (logoless), cover with logos appears as back cover 4.95
❑2, Nov 1996 4.95
❑3, Dec 1996 4.95
❑4, Jan 1997 4.95
❑5, Feb 1997 4.95
❑6, Mar 1997 4.95
❑7, May 1997 4.95
❑8, Jun 1997 4.95
❑9, Jul 1997, Final Issue 4.95

Bar Sinister
Windjammer / Acclaim

❑1, Jun 1995; 1: Bar Sinister 2.50
❑2, Jul 1995 2.50
❑3, Aug 1995 2.50
❑4, Sep 1995 2.50

Bartman
Bongo

❑1, ca. 1993; Silver ink cover 4.00
❑2, ca. 1994 3.00
❑3, ca. 1994; trading card 3.00
❑4, ca. 1995 2.50
❑5, ca. 1995; 1: Lisa the Conjuror. 1: The Great Maggeena 2.50
❑6, ca. 1995; O: Bart Dog. 1: Bart Dog 2.50

Basara
Viz

❑1, Aug 2003 9.95
❑2, Oct 2003 9.95
❑3, Dec 2003 9.95
❑4, Feb 2004 9.95
❑5, Apr 2004 9.95
❑6, Jun 2004 9.95
❑7, Aug 2004 9.95
❑8, Oct 2004 9.95
❑9, Dec 2004 9.95
❑10, Feb 2005 9.95
❑11, Apr 2005 9.99
❑12, Jun 2005 9.99
❑13, Aug 2005 9.99
❑14, Oct 2005 9.99

Baseball Classics
Personality

❑1 2.95
❑2 2.95

Baseball Comics
Kitchen Sink

❑1, May 1991; trading cards 3.95
❑2, ca. 1992; cards on back cover 2.95

Baseball Comics (Personality)
Personality

❑1 2.95
❑2 2.95

Baseball Greats
Dark Horse

❑1, Oct 1992; Jimmy Piersall, with cards 2.95
❑2; Bob Gibson 2.95
❑3; 2 trading cards 2.95

Baseball Hall of Shame in 3-D
Blackthorne

❑1 2.50

Baseball Legends
Revolutionary

❑1, Mar 1992, b&w; Babe Ruth 2.50
❑2, Apr 1992, b&w; Ty Cobb 2.50
❑3, May 1992, b&w; Ted Williams 2.50
❑4, Jun 1992, b&w; Mickey Mantle 2.50

N-MINT

❑5, Jul 1992, b&w; Joe Dimaggio 2.50
❑6, Aug 1992, b&w; Jackie Robinson 2.50
❑7, Sep 1992, b&w; Sandy Koufax 2.50
❑8, Oct 1992, b&w; Willie Mays 2.50
❑9, Nov 1992, b&w; Honus Wagner 2.50
❑10, Dec 1992, Roberto Clemente 2.75
❑11, Jan 1993, Yogi Berra 2.75
❑12, Feb 1993, Billy Martin 2.75
❑13, Mar 1993, Hank Aaron 2.95
❑14, Apr 1993, b&w; Carl Yastrzemski 2.95
❑15, May 1993, b&w; Satchel Paige 2.95
❑16, Jun 1993, b&w; Johnny Bench 2.95
❑17, Jul 1993, b&w; Shoeless Joe Jackson 2.95
❑18, Aug 1993, b&w; Lou Gehrig 2.95
❑19, Sep 1993, b&w; Casey Stengel 2.95

Baseball's Greatest Heroes
Magnum

❑1, Dec 1991; Mickey Mantle 2.50
❑2 2.50

Baseball Sluggers
Personality

❑1 2.95
❑2 2.95
❑3 2.95
❑4 2.95

Baseball Superstars Comics
Revolutionary

❑1, Nov 1991; Nolan Ryan 2.50
❑2, Feb 1992; Bo Jackson 2.50
❑3, Mar 1992; Ken Griffey Jr. 2.50
❑4, Apr 1992; Pete Rose 2.50
❑5, May 1992; Rickey Henderson 2.50
❑6, Jun 1992; Jose Canseco 2.50
❑7, Jul 1992; Cal Ripkin Jr. 2.50
❑8, Aug 1992; Carlton Fisk 2.50
❑9, Sep 1992; George Brett 2.50
❑10, Oct 1992; Darryl Strawberry 2.50
❑11, Nov 1992; Frank Thomas 2.50
❑12, Dec 1992, Ryne Sandberg 2.75
❑13, Jan 1993, Kirby Puckett 2.75
❑14, Feb 1993, Roberto and Sandi Alomar 2.75
❑15, Mar 1993, Roger Clemens 2.95
❑16, Apr 1993, b&w; Mark McGuire 2.95
❑17, May 1993, b&w; Avery/Glavine 2.95
❑18, Jun 1993, b&w; Dennis Eckersley 2.95
❑19, Jul 1993, b&w; Dave Winfield 2.95
❑20, Aug 1993, b&w; Jim Abbott 2.95

Baseball Thrills 3-D
3-D Zone

❑1; NN; Includes glasses 2.95

Basically Strange
John C.

❑1, Nov 1982 WW (w); ATh, FT, WW (a) 4.00

Bastard
Viz

❑1, Dec 2001; Western left to right reading format; B&w series 3.95
❑2, Jan 2002 3.95
❑3, Feb 2002 3.95
❑4, Mar 2002 3.95
❑5, Apr 2002 3.95
❑6, May 2002 3.95
❑7, Jun 2002 3.95
❑8, Jul 2002 3.95
❑9, Aug 2002 3.95
❑10, Sep 2002 3.95
❑11, Oct 2002 3.95
❑12, Nov 2002 3.95
❑13, Dec 2002 3.95
❑14, Jan 2003 3.95
❑15, Feb 2003 3.95

Bastard Samurai
Image

❑1, Apr 2002 2.95
❑2, Jun 2002 2.95
❑3, Aug 2002 2.95

Bastard Tales
Baboon Books

❑1 1998, b&w; Adult 2.95

Bat (Apple)
Apple

❑1, Mar 1994, b&w 2.50

N-MINT

Batbabe
Spoof

❑2 2.50

Batch
Caliber

❑1, b&w 2.95

Batgirl
DC

❑1, Apr 2000 4.00
❑1/2nd, Apr 2000; 2nd printing 3.00
❑2, May 2000 3.50
❑3, Jun 2000 3.50
❑4, Jul 2000 3.50
❑5, Aug 2000 3.50
❑6, Sep 2000 3.00
❑7, Oct 2000; V: Shiva 3.00
❑8, Nov 2000; V: Shiva 3.00
❑9, Dec 2000 3.00
❑10, Jan 2001 3.00
❑11, Feb 2001 2.50
❑12, Mar 2001; Officer Down 2.50
❑13, Apr 2001 2.50
❑14, May 2001 2.50
❑15, Jun 2001 2.50
❑16, Jul 2001 2.50
❑17, Aug 2001 2.50
❑18, Sep 2001; Robin apperance 2.50
❑19, Oct 2001 2.50
❑20, Nov 2001 2.50
❑21, Dec 2001; V: Shadow Thief; Joker: Last Laugh 2.50
❑22, Jan 2002 2.50
❑23, Feb 2002 2.50
❑24, Mar 2002 2.50
❑25, Apr 2002; Giant-size; V: Shiva 3.25
❑26, May 2002 2.50
❑27, Jun 2002; Continued from Detective Comics #769 & into Nightwing #68 2.50
❑28, Jul 2002 2.50
❑29, Aug 2002; Continued from Detective Comics #771 & into Batman: Gotham Knights #30 2.50
❑30, Sep 2002 2.50
❑31, Oct 2002; V: Agrippina 2.50
❑32, Nov 2002; V: Agrippina 2.50
❑33, Dec 2002; Batgirl beats up on Cain 2.50
❑34, Jan 2003; New bat cover logo; Gotham Central preview inside 2.50
❑35, Feb 2003 2.50
❑36, Mar 2003 2.50
❑37, Apr 2003 2.50
❑38, May 2003 2.50
❑39, Jun 2003 2.50
❑40, Jul 2003 2.50
❑41, Aug 2003 2.50
❑42, Sep 2003 2.50
❑43, Oct 2003 2.50
❑44, Nov 2003; V: Dr. Death 2.50
❑45, Dec 2003 2.50
❑46, Jan 2004 2.50
❑47, Feb 2004 2.50
❑48, Mar 2004 2.50
❑49, Apr 2004 2.50
❑50, May 2004; Batgirl vs. Batman 2.50
❑51, Jun 2004 2.50
❑52, Jul 2004, V: Poison Ivy 2.50
❑53, Aug 2004; V: Penguin; Spoiler as Robin 2.50
❑54, Jul 2004 2.50
❑55, Oct 2004; Bagged with promo CD for Sky Captain and the World of Tomorrow 2.50
❑56, Nov 2004, D: Lynx 2.50
❑57, Jan 2005 2.50
❑58, Feb 2005, V: Shrike; Continued from Robin #132 2.50
❑59, Mar 2005; V: Penguin; Continued from Robin #133 2.50
❑60, Apr 2005 2.50
❑61, May 2005; V: Brotherhood of Evil 2.50
❑62, Jun 2005 2.50
❑63, Jun 2005; V: Deathstroke; Heroscape insert 2.50
❑64, Jul 2005 2.50
❑65, Aug 2005; New DC cover logo 2.50
❑66, Sep 2005 2.50
❑67, Oct 2005 2.50
❑68, Nov 2005, V: Lady Shiva and Nyssa 2.50
❑69, Dec 2005; V: Mr. Freeze 2.50

Other grades: Multiply price above by 5/6 for VF/NM • 2/3 for VERY FINE • 1/3 for FINE • 1/5 for VERY GOOD • 1/8 for GOOD

Avalon

Anthology tryout series for new artists
©Harrier

Avengelyne (Mini-Series)

Angel who fell from grace battles demons
©Maximum

Avengers

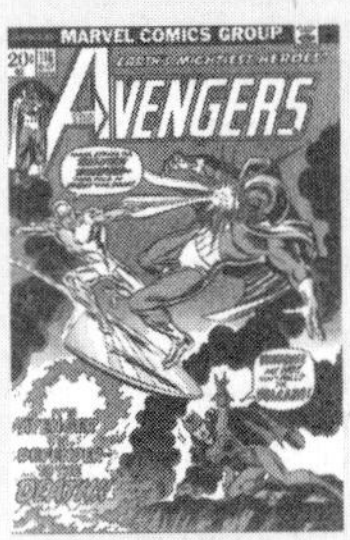

Durable Marvel super-team gets its start
©Marvel

Avengers (Vol. 2)

Ill-fated Rob Liefeld "Heroes Reborn" relaunch
©Marvel

Avengers (Vol. 3)

Undid "Reborn" before being "Disassembled"
©Marvel

N-MINT

❑70, Jan 2006; V: Mr. Freeze, Lady Shiva, Nyssa; Mrs. Freeze becomes Lazara ... 2.50
❑71, Feb 2006, V: League of Assassins .. 2.50
❑72, Mar 2006, V: Mad Dog ... 2.50
❑73, Apr 2006, V: Lady Shiva; True origin of Batgirl; Final issue ... 2.50
❑Ann 1, ca. 2002; 1: Aruna. Planet DC ... 4.00

Batgirl Adventures
DC

❑1, Feb 1998; V: Harley Quinn ... 3.50

Batgirl Secret Files and Origins
DC

❑1, Aug 2002, O: Batgirl ... 4.95

Batgirl Special
DC

❑1, Jul 1988; Batgirl (Barbara Gordon) retires ... 3.00

Batgirl: Year One
DC

❑1, Feb 2003 ... 2.95
❑2, Mar 2003 ... 2.95
❑3, Apr 2003 ... 2.95
❑4, May 2003 ... 2.95
❑5, Jun 2003 ... 2.95
❑6, Jul 2003 ... 2.95
❑7, Aug 2003 ... 2.95
❑8, Sep 2003 ... 2.95
❑9, Oct 2003 ... 2.95

Bathing Machine
C&T

❑1, ca. 1987, b&w ... 2.50
❑2, ca. 1987 ... 1.50
❑3, ca. 1987 ... 1.50

Bathroom Girls
Modern

❑1 1997, b&w; Adult ... 2.95
❑2 1998, b&w; Adult ... 2.95

Bat Lash
DC

❑1, Nov 1968, Sergio Aragones plots ... 25.00
❑2, Jan 1969 ... 15.00
❑3, Mar 1969 ... 15.00
❑4, May 1969 ... 15.00
❑5, Jul 1969, Sergio Aragones plots ... 15.00
❑6, Sep 1969, Sergio Aragones plots ... 15.00
❑7, Nov 1969, SA (w); NC (a); Sergio Aragones plots; Final Issue ... 15.00

Batman
DC

❑0, Oct 1994; O: Batman ... 2.50
❑144, Dec 1961, A: Joker ... 140.00
❑145, Feb 1962, A: Joker ... 140.00
❑146, Mar 1962 ... 110.00
❑147, May 1962 ... 110.00
❑148, Jul 1962, A: Joker ... 140.00
❑149, Aug 1962 ... 110.00
❑150, Oct 1962 ... 110.00
❑151, Nov 1962 ... 90.00
❑152, Dec 1962, A: Joker ... 100.00
❑153, Feb 1963 ... 125.00
❑154, Mar 1963 ... 85.00
❑155, Apr 1963, 1: Penguin (in Silver Age) 300.00
❑156, Jun 1963 ... 85.00
❑157, Aug 1963 ... 85.00

N-MINT

❑158, Sep 1963 ... 85.00
❑159, Nov 1963, A: Joker ... 85.00
❑160, Dec 1963 ... 85.00
❑161, Feb 1964 ... 85.00
❑162, Mar 1964 ... 85.00
❑163, May 1964, A: Joker ... 85.00
❑164, Jun 1964, 1: Mystery Analysts of Gotham City; 1: Kaye Daye; 1: "new look" Batmobile; 1: Batphone ... 85.00
❑165, Aug 1964, 1: Patricia Powell ... 130.00
❑166, Sep 1964, 2: Patricia Powell; Mike Friedirch L.O.C ... 85.00
❑167, Nov 1964 ... 85.00
❑168, Dec 1964, 2: Mystery Analysts of Gotham City; Bob Rozakis L.O.C ... 85.00
❑169, Feb 1965, A: Penguin. Mike Friedirch L.O.C ... 90.00
❑170, Mar 1965, Mike Friedirch L.O.C ... 85.00
❑171, May 1965, CI (c); CI (a); A: Riddler. 1: Riddler (Silver Age); Riddler last appeared Dec 1948 ... 450.00
❑172, Jun 1965 ... 125.00
❑173, Aug 1965 ... 75.00
❑174, Sep 1965 ... 75.00
❑175, Nov 1965, Mike Friedrich L.O.C ... 75.00
❑176, Dec 1965; 80-Page Giant; A: Joker. aka 80 Page Giant #G-17 ... 85.00
❑177, Dec 1965 ... 75.00
❑178, Feb 1966 ... 85.00
❑179, Mar 1966, A: Riddler. Guy Lillian L.O.C ... 120.00
❑180, May 1966, V: Death-Man; Tom Fagan L.O.C ... 60.00
❑181, Jun 1966, 1: Poison Ivy; Batman & Robin pinup; Mike Friedirch L.O.C ... 175.00
❑182, Aug 1966; A: Joker. aka 80 Page Giant #G-24; Reprints ... 60.00
❑183, Aug 1966, TV show reference ... 60.00
❑184, Sep 1966, Irene Vartanoff L.O.C .. 60.00
❑185, Nov 1966; 80-Page Giant; aka 80 Page Giant #G-27 ... 60.00
❑186, Nov 1966, A: Joker. Mike Friedrich L.O.C ... 70.00
❑187, Dec 1966; 80-Page Giant; A: Joker. aka 80 Page Giant #G-30 ... 65.00
❑188, Jan 1967, Irene Vartanoff L.O.C.; Mike Friedrich L.O.C ... 40.00
❑189, Feb 1967, 1: The Scarecrow (in Silver Age) ... 250.00
❑190, Mar 1967, A: Penguin. Guy Lillian L.O.C.; Irene Vartanoff L.O.C ... 45.00
❑191, May 1967, Tom Fagan L.O.C ... 40.00
❑192, Jun 1967 ... 60.00
❑193, Aug 1967; 80-Page Giant; aka 80 Page Giant #G-37 ... 70.00
❑194, Aug 1967, Peter Sanderson L.O.C 80.00
❑195, Sep 1967, 1: Bag O'Bones; O: Bag O'Bones; Tony Isabella L.O.C ... 40.00
❑196, Nov 1967 ... 40.00
❑197, Dec 1967, A: Catwoman. Peter Sanderson L.O.C ... 100.00
❑198, Jan 1968; 80-Page Giant; O: Batman. A: Joker. aka 80 Page Giant #G-43 ... 85.00
❑199, Feb 1968, Operation "Escape"! reprinted from Star-Spangled Comics #124; One-half page omitted ... 40.00
❑200, Mar 1968, NA (c); NA (a); O: Robin I (Dick Grayson). O: Batman. A: Joker ... 100.00
❑201, May 1968, A: Joker ... 35.00
❑202, Jun 1968 ... 35.00

N-MINT

❑203, Aug 1968; 80-Page Giant; aka 80 Page Giant #G-49 ... 30.00
❑204, Aug 1968, Shel Dorf L.O.C ... 30.00
❑205, Sep 1968, Mark Evanier L.O.C.; Irene Vartanoff L.O.C ... 40.00
❑206, Nov 1968, Irene Vartanoff L.O.C .. 30.00
❑207, Dec 1968, Fact File #6 (Tarantula); Fred Hembeck L.O.C ... 50.00
❑208, Jan 1969; 80-Page Giant; O: Batman (new origin). aka 80 Page Giant #G-55 .. 50.00
❑209, Jan 1969, Fact File #2 (Golden Age Green Lantern); Peter Sanderson L.O.C 30.00
❑210, Mar 1969, Mark Evanier L.O.C ... 30.00
❑211, May 1969, Fact File #7 (Detective Comics #27); Irene Vartanoff L.O.C.; Tom Fagan L.O.C ... 30.00
❑212, Jun 1969 ... 30.00
❑213, Aug 1969; Giant-size; O: Robin I (Dick Grayson-new origin). A: Joker. aka Giant #G-61; Joker reprint ... 45.00
❑214, Aug 1969, Peter Sanderson L.O.C 30.00
❑215, Sep 1969 ... 30.00
❑216, Nov 1969, Reprint from Gang Busters #51; Mark Evanier L.O.C ... 30.00
❑217, Dec 1969, Breakup of Batman & Robin team; Dick Grayson goes to college; Bruce and Alfred move from Wayne Manor to the Wayne Foundation 30.00
❑218, Feb 1970; Giant-size; aka Giant #G-67 ... 70.00
❑219, Feb 1970, FR (w); NA, IN (a); Klaus Janson L.O.C ... 50.00
❑220, Mar 1970, NA (c); FR (w); DG, NA, IN (a); Martin Pasko L.O.C ... 30.00
❑221, May 1970, NA (c); FR (w); NA, IN (a) 30.00
❑222, Jun 1970, NA (c); FR (w); NA, IN (a); A: The Beatles. Beatles take-off; L.O.C. from Mike W. Barr ... 75.00
❑223, Aug 1970; Giant-size; MA, CS (c); MA (a); aka Giant #G-73; Reprints stories from Batman #79 & #93, Detective #196 & #248, and Sunday strips from August 8 through September 17, 1944 ... 40.00
❑224, Aug 1970, NA (a) ... 30.00
❑225, Sep 1970, NA (c); NA, IN (a) ... 30.00
❑226, Nov 1970, NA (c); FR (w); NA, IN (a); 1: Man with 10 eyes; A Case-Book Mystery ... 30.00
❑227, Dec 1970, NA (c); NA, IN (a); Robin back-up ... 50.00
❑228, Feb 1971; Giant-size; MA (c); MA (a); aka Giant #G-79 ... 40.00
❑229, Feb 1971, Robin solo story; Mike W. Barr L.O.C ... 30.00
❑230, Mar 1971, Robin solo story; Bob Rozakis L.O.C.; Superman cameo ... 30.00
❑231, May 1971, Robin solo story ... 30.00
❑232, Jun 1971, DG, NA (a); O: Batman. 1: Ra's Al Ghul ... 350.00
❑233, Aug 1971; Giant-size; aka Giant #G-85 ... 30.00
❑234, Aug 1971; NA (c); CI, NA, IN (a); 1: Two-Face (in Silver Age); Bob Rozakis L.O.C.; Robin solo story; 1 reprint story from Detective Comics #335 ... 115.00
❑235, Sep 1971; CI, IN (a); Robin solo story; 1 reprint from Detective Comics #329 ... 17.00
❑236, Nov 1971; NA (c); FR (w); NA, IN (a); Reprints Batman #30 Aug-Sep 1945; Batman #30 Aug-Sep 1945 Batman and Robin ... 25.00

Other grades: Multiply price above by 5/6 for VF/NM • 2/3 for VERY FINE • 1/3 for FINE • 1/5 for VERY GOOD • 1/8 for GOOD

❑237, Dec 1971; NA (c); BWr (w); NA (a); 1: The Reaper; 1 reprint from Detective Comics #37 .... 75.00
❑238, Jan 1972, Giant-size; NA (c); JKu, NA (a); a.k.a. DC 100-Page Super Spectacular #DC-8, wraparound cover 65.00
❑239, Feb 1972; NA (c); RB, NA, IN (a); Robin solo story; Batman #15 Feb-Mar 1943 .... 17.00
❑240, Mar 1972; NA (c); RB, NA, IN (a); Robin solo story; 1 reprint from Batman #164; Bob Rozakis L.O.C 17.00
❑241, May 1972; NA (c); RB, NA, IN (a); Berni Wrightson inks cover; Robin solo story; David Michelinie L.O.C.; 1 reprint from Batman #5; Reprint from Batman #5 .... 30.00
❑242, Jun 1972; RB, IN (a); Michael Kaluna cover; Robin solo story; 1 reprint from Batman #7 .... 17.00
❑243, Aug 1972, DG, NA (a); Ra's al Ghul 70.00
❑244, Sep 1972, DG, NA, IN (a); Ra's al Ghul 65.00
❑245, Oct 1972, FM (c); DG, NA, IN (a); Neal Adams cover; Robin solo story... 70.00
❑246, Dec 1972 .... 15.00
❑247, Feb 1973 .... 15.00
❑248, Apr 1973, Robin solo story 20.00
❑249, Jun 1973, Robin solo story 15.00
❑250, Jul 1973, Mike W. Barr L.O.C.; Bob Rozakis L.O.C.; Robin solo story 15.00
❑251, Sep 1973, NA (c); NA (a); A: Joker 60.00
❑252, Sep 1973, Robin solo story 14.00
❑253, Nov 1973, 100 pages; Bob Rozakis L.O.C 26.00
❑254, Feb 1974, 100 Page giant; FR (w); NA, GK, DD, IN (a); Reprints from World's Best Comics #1; World's Finest Comics #50; Detective Comics #334; And Batman #85; 145; Robin solo story; 100 pages 32.00
❑255, Apr 1974, 100 Page giant; NC (c); CI, DG, NA, GK, JM (a); Reprints from Detective Comics #235; 340; 363; Batman #22; And Star Spangled Comics #123; 100 pages; Mike W. Barr L.O.C.... 32.00
❑256, Jun 1974, 100 Page giant; Reprints from Batman #12; 35; 119; World's Finest Comics #30; And Detective Comics #158; 100 pages 35.00
❑257, Aug 1974, 100 Page giant; Reprints from Detective Comics #374; Batman #22; 30; 32; And Detective Comics #385; 100 pages 35.00
❑258, Oct 1974, 100 Page giant; 100 pages; Detective #61 Mar 1942; Detective #368 Oct 1967; Batman #26 Dec-Jan 1944; Batman #95 Oct 1955; World's Finest #43 Dec-Jan 1949 .... 35.00
❑259, Dec 1974, 100 Page giant; 100 pages; Detective Comics #222 Aug 1955; Detective Comics #165 Nov 1950; Batman #29 Jun-Jul 1945; Batman #177 Dec 1965; Batman #120 Dec 1958 .... 32.00
❑260, Feb 1975, 100 Page giant; A: Joker. 100 Page giant; Batman #16 Apr-May 1943; Mystery Analysts Of Gotham City: Batman #181 Jun 1966; Detective Comics #112 Jun 1946; The Adventures Of Alfred: Batman #27 Feb-Mar 1945; Detective Comics #377 Jul 1968........ 32.00
❑261, Mar 1975, 100 Page giant; 100 Page giant; Detective Comics #92 Oct 1944; Batman #109 Aug 1957; Batman #27 Feb-Mar 1945; Batman #100 Jun 1956; Detective #345 Nov 1965 .... 32.00
❑262, Apr 1975, Giant-size; Reprints from Detective Comics #366 and #367; (68pgs); 68 page Giant 15.00
❑263, May 1975 .... 15.00
❑264, Jun 1975; DG (a); V: Devil Dayre . 9.00
❑265, Jul 1975 .... 9.00
❑266, Aug 1975; A: Catwoman. Catwoman goes back to old costume. 9.00
❑267, Sep 1975 .... 8.00
❑268, Oct 1975 .... 8.00
❑269, Nov 1975 .... 8.00
❑270, Dec 1975 .... 8.00
❑271, Jan 1976 .... 8.00
❑272, Feb 1976 .... 8.00
❑273, Mar 1976 .... 8.00
❑274, Apr 1976 .... 8.00
❑275, May 1976 .... 8.00
❑276, Jun 1976 .... 8.00
❑277, Jul 1976, Bicentennial #11 .... 8.00
❑278, Aug 1976 .... 8.00

N-MINT

❑279, Sep 1976 .... 8.00
❑280, Oct 1976 .... 8.00
❑281, Nov 1976 .... 8.00
❑282, Dec 1976 .... 8.00
❑283, Jan 1977, V: Omega 8.00
❑284, Feb 1977 .... 8.00
❑285, Mar 1977 .... 8.00
❑286, Apr 1977, A: Joker 12.00
❑287, May 1977 .... 9.00
❑288, Jun 1977 .... 9.00
❑289, Jul 1977 .... 9.00
❑290, Aug 1977 .... 9.00
❑291, Sep 1977, A: Joker 12.00
❑292, Oct 1977 .... 9.00
❑293, Nov 1977, A: Lex Luthor. A: Superman 9.00
❑294, Dec 1977, A: Joker 9.00
❑295, Jan 1978, Appearance of Mystery Analysts of Gotham City 8.00
❑296, Feb 1978, V: Scarecrow 8.00
❑297, Mar 1978, V: Mad Hatter 8.00
❑298, Apr 1978 .... 8.00
❑299, May 1978 .... 8.00
❑300, Jun 1978, Double-size; 300th anniversary issue; Imaginary story 15.00
❑301, Jul 1978 .... 7.00
❑302, Aug 1978 .... 7.00
❑303, Sep 1978, Unsolved Cases of the Batman 7.00
❑304, Oct 1978, V: Spook; The Public Life of Bruce Wayne 7.00
❑305, Nov 1978, V: Amos Fortune; Unsolved Cases of the Batman 7.00
❑306, Dec 1978, V: Black Spider; Unsolved Cases of the Batman 7.00
❑306/Whitman, Dec 1978, Whitman variant 14.00
❑307, Jan 1979, 1: Lucius Fox 7.00
❑307/Whitman, Jan 1979, Whitman variant 14.00
❑308, Feb 1979, V: Mr. Freeze 7.00
❑308/Whitman, Feb 1979, Whitman variant 14.00
❑309, Mar 1979, V: Blockbuster 7.00
❑310, Apr 1979, V: Gentleman Ghost 7.00
❑311, May 1979, IN (a); V: Dr. Phosphorus 7.00
❑311/Whitman, May 1979, Whitman variant 20.00
❑312, Jun 1979, V: Calendar Man 7.00
❑312/Whitman, Jun 1979, Whitman variant 14.00
❑313, Jul 1979, V: Two-Face 7.00
❑313/Whitman, Jul 1979, Whitman variant 14.00
❑314, Aug 1979, V: Two-Face 7.00
❑314/Whitman, Aug 1979, Whitman variant 14.00
❑315, Sep 1979, V: Kite-Man 7.00
❑315/Whitman, Sep 1979, Whitman variant 14.00
❑316, Oct 1979, V: Crazy-Quilt 7.00
❑316/Whitman, Oct 1979, Whitman variant 14.00
❑317, Nov 1979, V: the Riddler 7.00
❑317/Whitman, Nov 1979, Whitman variant 17.00
❑318, Dec 1979, 1: Firebug 7.00
❑318/Whitman, Dec 1979, 1: Firebug. Whitman variant 17.00
❑319, Jan 1980, V: Gentleman Ghost 7.00
❑319/Whitman, Jan 1980, Whitman variant 17.00
❑320, Feb 1980 .... 7.00
❑320/Whitman, Feb 1980, Whitman variant 14.00
❑321, Mar 1980, A: Catwoman. A: Joker 7.00
❑322, Apr 1980, V: Captain Boomerang. 7.00
❑323, May 1980, V: Catwoman 7.00
❑323/Whitman, May 1980, Whitman variant 7.00
❑324, Jun 1980, V: Cat-Man 7.00
❑324/Whitman, Jun 1980, Whitman variant 7.00
❑325, Jul 1980 .... 7.00
❑326, Aug 1980, 1: Arkham Asylum 7.00
❑326/Whitman, Aug 1980, 1: Arkham Asylum. Whitman variant 7.00
❑327, Sep 1980, V: Professor Milo 7.00
❑328, Oct 1980 .... 7.00
❑329, Nov 1980, V: Two-Face 7.00
❑330, Dec 1980 .... 7.00
❑331, Jan 1981, 1: Electrocutioner 7.00
❑332, Feb 1981, 1st solo Catwoman story 8.00
❑333, Mar 1981 .... 7.00
❑334, Apr 1981, V: Talia; Tales of Gotham City 7.00
❑335, May 1981, V: Ra's Al Ghul 7.00
❑336, Jun 1981 .... 7.00
❑337, Jul 1981 .... 7.00
❑338, Aug 1981, Robin back up story ... 7.00
❑339, Sep 1981, O: Robin; V: Poison Ivy 7.00

N-MINT

❑340, Oct 1981 .... 7.00
❑341, Nov 1981, Just a Moment Mystery 7.00
❑342, Dec 1981, O: Man-Bat; V: Man-Bat 7.00
❑343, Jan 1982 .... 7.00
❑344, Feb 1982, V: Poison Ivy 7.00
❑345, Mar 1982, V: Doctor Death 7.00
❑346, Apr 1982, V: Two-Face; Batman storyline cont'd in Detective #513 ...... 7.00
❑347, May 1982, Just-A-Moment Mystery 7.00
❑348, Jun 1982, V: Man-Bat 7.00
❑349, Jul 1982 .... 7.00
❑350, Aug 1982, Gene Colan cover 7.00
❑351, Sep 1982 .... 7.00
❑352, Oct 1982, V: Colonel Blimp 7.00
❑353, Nov 1982, A: Joker. V: Joker; Masters of the Universe insert 5.00
❑354, Dec 1982 .... 7.00
❑355, Jan 1983, V: Catwoman 7.00
❑356, Feb 1983, V: Hugo Strange 7.00
❑357, Mar 1983, 1: Killer Croc. 1: Jason Todd 9.00
❑358, Apr 1983, V: Killer Croc 7.00
❑359, May 1983, A: Joker. O: Killer Croc 7.00
❑360, Jun 1983 .... 7.00
❑361, Jul 1983, 1: Harvey Bullock; V: Man-Bat 7.00
❑362, Aug 1983, O: Riddler; V: Riddler.. 7.00
❑363, Sep 1983, V: Night-Thief and Nocturna 7.00
❑364, Oct 1983, V: Chimera 7.00
❑365, Nov 1983 .... 7.00
❑366, Dec 1983; 1: Jason Todd in Robin costume. A: Joker; 1: Robin (Jason Todd) 7.00
❑367, Jan 1984; V: Poison Ivy 7.00
❑368, Feb 1984; DN, AA (a); 1: Robin II (Jason Todd); V: Crazy-Quilt; Continued in Detective Comics #535 .... 8.00
❑369, Mar 1984; V: Deadshot; Continued into Detective Comics #536 .... 6.00
❑370, Apr 1984; V: Dr. Fang; Story cont'd in Detective #537 .... 6.00
❑371, May 1984; V: Catman 5.00
❑372, Jun 1984; Continued into Detective Comics #539 .... 5.00
❑373, Jul 1984; V: Scarecrow; Continued into Detective Comics #540 .... 5.00
❑374, Aug 1984; V: Penguin; Continued into Detective Comics #541 .... 5.00
❑375, Sep 1984; V: Mr. Freeze 5.00
❑376, Oct 1984 .... 5.00
❑377, Nov 1984 .... 5.00
❑378, Dec 1984; V: Mad Hatter 5.00
❑379, Jan 1985; V: Mad Hatter 5.00
❑380, Feb 1985; Story cont'd in Detective #547 .... 5.00
❑381, Mar 1985; Story cont'd from Detective #547 .... 5.00
❑382, Apr 1985 GK (c); A: Catwoman.... 5.00
❑383, May 1985 .... 5.00
❑384, Jun 1985; V: Calendar Man 5.00
❑385, Jul 1985 .... 5.00
❑386, Aug 1985; 1: Black Mask 5.00
❑387, Sep 1985; V: Black Mask; 16 page insert of M.A.S.K.; Mask Preview 5.00
❑388, Oct 1985; V: Mirror Master. V: Capt. Boomerang. V: Captain Boomerang ... 5.00
❑389, Nov 1985; A: Catwoman. Crisis red skies; Storyline cont'd from Detective #556 .... 5.00
❑390, Dec 1985 A: Catwoman 5.00
❑391, Jan 1986 A: Catwoman 5.00
❑392, Feb 1986 .... 5.00
❑393, Mar 1986 PG (c); PG (a) 5.00
❑394, Apr 1986 PG (c); PG (a) 5.00
❑395, May 1986; 1: Film Freak; V: Film Freak; Storyline cont'd in Detective Comics #562 .... 5.00
❑396, Jun 1986 .... 5.00
❑397, Jul 1986; V: Two-Face 5.00
❑398, Aug 1986; A: Catwoman. A: Two-Face. V: Two-Face; Catwoman appearance; UPC box displays: "Abby's in Gotham City in Swamp Thing #51" 5.00
❑399, Sep 1986; UPC box displays: "How will the Dark Knight End?" 5.00
❑400, Oct 1986; Anniversary edition; V: Ra's al Ghul; Introduction by Stephen King; Double-size 10.00
❑401, Nov 1986; V: Magpie. Legends 4.00
❑402, Dec 1986; UPC box displays: "GLC #207 is a Legends crossover" 4.00
❑403, Jan 1987 .... 4.00

Other grades: Multiply price above by 5/6 for VF/NM • 2/3 for VERY FINE • 1/3 for FINE • 1/5 for VERY GOOD • 1/8 for GOOD

Avengers, The: Celestial Quest

Arc from Steve Englehart and Jorge Santamaria

©Marvel

Avengers Forever

Sprawling story spans time and space

©Marvel

Avengers Infinity

Answering a distress call from Jack of Hearts

©Marvel

Avengers Spotlight

Renamed title had been called Solo Avengers

©Marvel

Avengers/Thunderbolts

Crossover title from Kurt Busiek

©Marvel

	N-MINT
❑404, Feb 1987; FM (w); O: Batman. 1: Catwoman (new); Year One	5.00
❑405, Mar 1987; FM (w); Year One	6.00
❑406, Apr 1987; FM (w); Year One	5.00
❑407, May 1987; FM (w); Year One	5.00
❑408, Jun 1987; O: Jason Todd (new origin)	5.00
❑409, Jul 1987	3.00
❑410, Aug 1987; V: Two-Face	3.00
❑411, Sep 1987	3.00
❑412, Oct 1987; 1&O: Mime	3.00
❑413, Nov 1987	3.00
❑414, Dec 1987; JSn (w); JA (a); Millennium	3.00
❑415, Jan 1988; Millennium	3.00
❑416, Feb 1988; JA (c); JSn (w); JA (a); A: Nightwing. O: Jason Todd (new-retold)	3.00
❑417, Mar 1988; MZ (c); JSn (w); JA (a); 1: KGBeast. V: KGBeast	5.00
❑418, Apr 1988; MZ (c); JSn (w); JA (a); V: KGBeast	4.00
❑419, May 1988; MZ (c); JSn (w); JA (a); V: KGBeast	4.00
❑420, Jun 1988; MZ (c); JSn (w); JA (a); V: KGBeast	4.00
❑421, Jul 1988	3.00
❑422, Aug 1988	3.00
❑423, Sep 1988 TMc (c); JSn (w); DC (a)	3.00
❑424, Oct 1988	3.00
❑425, Nov 1988	3.00
❑426, Dec 1988; 52 page giant	6.00
❑427, Dec 1988; D: Robin, newsstand. D: Robin II; 52 pages	6.00
❑427/Direct ed., Dec 1988; D: Robin, direct sale. D: Robin II; Direct sale; 52 pages	4.00
❑428, Jan 1989; D: Robin II (Jason Todd). Robin declared dead	6.00
❑429, Jan 1989 JSn (w); JA (a)	4.00
❑430, Feb 1989	3.00
❑431, Mar 1989	2.00
❑432, Apr 1989	2.00
❑433, May 1989; JBy (c); JBy (w); JBy, JA (a); Almost no dialogue	2.00
❑434, Jun 1989 JBy (c); JBy (w); JBy, JA (a)	2.00
❑435, Jul 1989 JBy (c); JBy (w); JBy, JA (a)	2.00
❑436, Aug 1989; O: Robin	2.50
❑436/2nd; 2nd printing; O: Robin	1.25
❑437, Aug 1989; GP (c); PB (a); O: Robin	2.00
❑438, Sep 1989	2.00
❑439, Sep 1989	2.00
❑440, Oct 1989; GP (c); GP (w); JA (a); 1: Timothy Drake; Part 2 in New Titans #60	2.00
❑441, Nov 1989; V: Two-Face; Continued from New Titans #60; Continues in New Titans #61	2.00
❑442, Dec 1989; 1: Robin III (Timothy Drake); V: Two-Face	2.50
❑443, Jan 1990; Lightning Racers insert	1.50
❑444, Feb 1990; JA (a); V: Crimesmith	1.50
❑445, Mar 1990; BB (c); JA (a); 1: NKVDemon. V: NKVDemon	1.50
❑446, Apr 1990; V: NKVDemon	1.50
❑447, May 1990; V: NKVDemon	1.50
❑448, Jun 1990; V: Penguin. 1: Harold	1.50
❑449, Jun 1990; V: Penguin	1.50
❑450, Jul 1990; V: Joker	1.50

	N-MINT
❑451, Jul 1990; V: Joker	1.50
❑452, Aug 1990; V: Riddler	1.50
❑453, Aug 1990; V: Riddler	1.50
❑454, Sep 1990; V: Riddler	1.50
❑455, Oct 1990; V: Scarecrow	1.50
❑456, Nov 1990; V: Scarecrow	1.50
❑457, Dec 1990; 1: new Robin costume. Timothy Drake as Robin	2.50
❑457/Direct ed., Dec 1990; with #000 on indicia	4.00
❑457/2nd, Dec 1990; Timothy Drake as Robin	2.00
❑458, Jan 1991; 1: Harold	1.50
❑459, Feb 1991	1.50
❑460, Mar 1991 A: Catwoman	1.50
❑461, Apr 1991 A: Catwoman	1.50
❑462, May 1991	1.50
❑463, Jun 1991	1.50
❑464, Jul 1991; !mpact Comics insert	1.50
❑465, Jul 1991; Robin	1.50
❑466, Aug 1991; Robin	1.50
❑467, Aug 1991; A: Robin. covers form triptych	1.50
❑468, Sep 1991; A: Robin. covers form triptych	1.50
❑469, Sep 1991; A: Robin. covers form triptych	1.50
❑470, Oct 1991; War of the Gods	1.50
❑471, Nov 1991; V: Killer Croc	1.50
❑472, Dec 1991; V: Queen of Hearts	1.50
❑473, Jan 1992	1.50
❑474, Feb 1992; Anton Furst's Gotham City	1.50
❑475, Mar 1992; V: Two-Face. V: Scarface. V: Ventriloquist. 1: Renee Montoya	1.50
❑476, Apr 1992	1.50
❑477, May 1992; Photo cover	1.50
❑478, May 1992; Photo cover	1.50
❑479, Jun 1992	1.50
❑480, Jun 1992 JA (a)	1.50
❑481, Jul 1992 JA (a)	1.50
❑482, Jul 1992 JA (a)	1.50
❑483, Aug 1992 JA (a)	1.50
❑484, Sep 1992; V: Black Mask	1.50
❑485, Oct 1992; MG (c); V: Black Mask.	1.50
❑486, Nov 1992; V: Metalhead	1.50
❑487, Dec 1992; V: Headhunter	1.25
❑488, Jan 1993; JA (a); Robin trains Azrael	2.50
❑489, Feb 1993; JA (a); 1: Azrael (as Batman). A: Bane; V: Killer Croc; 1: Batman (Jean Paul Valley)	2.50
❑490, Mar 1993; JA (a); Riddler on Venom	2.50
❑491, Apr 1993; JA (a); Knightfall prequel	2.50
❑492, May 1993; V: Mad Hatter; Continued into Detective Comics #659	2.50
❑492/Silver, May 1993; Silver edition printing; Silver edition printing; Continued into Detective Comics #659	4.50
❑492/2nd, May 1993; 2nd printing; Continued into Detective Comics #659	2.00
❑493, May 1993; V: Mr. Zsasz; Continued from Detective Comics #659 & into #660	3.00
❑494, Jun 1993; JA (a); V: Scarecrow; Continued from Detective Comics #660 & into #661	2.00
❑495, Jun 1993; JA (a); V: Poison Ivy; Continued from Detective Comics #661& into #662	2.00

	N-MINT
❑496, Jul 1993; JA (a); V: Joker; Continued from Detective Comics #662 & into #663; V: Scarecrow; Continued from Detective Comics #662	2.00
❑497, Jul 1993; JA (a); partial overlay outer cover; Bane cripples Batman	3.00
❑497/2nd, Jul 1993; JA (a); 2nd Printing, also has partial overlay; Bane cripples Batman	2.00
❑498, Aug 1993; JA (a); Azrael takes on role of Batman	2.00
❑499, Sep 1993; JA (a); Azrael appearance (as Batman); Continued from Detective Comics #665 & into Batman: Shadow of the Bat #16; Continued from Detective Comics #665	2.00
❑500, Oct 1993; Giant-size; JA (a); Azrael vs. Bane, with poster	2.00
❑500/CS, Oct 1993; Giant-size; JA (a); diecut; two-level cover; Azrael vs. Bane; Collector's set	4.00
❑501, Nov 1993	2.00
❑502, Dec 1993; Azrael appearance (as Batman)	2.00
❑503, Jan 1994 A: Catwoman	2.00
❑504, Feb 1994 A: Catwoman	2.00
❑505, Mar 1994	2.00
❑506, Apr 1994; Azrael appearance (as Batman)	2.00
❑507, May 1994	2.00
❑508, Jun 1994; D: Abattoir; Azrael appearance (as Batman); Continued into Batman: Shadow of Bat #28; D: Abattoir (Arnold Etchison)	2.00
❑509, Jul 1994; Giant-size; Azrael appearance (as Batman); Continued into Batman: Shadow of the Bat #29	2.00
❑510, Aug 1994; Bruce Wayne returns as Batman	2.00
❑511, Sep 1994; A: Batgirl. Zero Hour	2.00
❑512, Nov 1994; MGu, RT (a); V: Killer Croc; Dick Grayson becomes Batman	2.00
❑513, Dec 1994; MGu, RT (a); V: Two-Face	2.00
❑514, Jan 1995	2.00
❑515, Feb 1995; Return of Bruce Wayne as Batman	2.00
❑515/Variant, Feb 1995; Embossed cover; Return of Bruce Wayne as Batman	4.00
❑516, Mar 1995	2.00
❑517, Apr 1995	2.00
❑518, May 1995; V: Black Mask. 1: Black Spider II (Johnny LaMonica); V: Black Spider	2.00
❑519, Jun 1995; V: Black Mask; V: Black Spider	2.00
❑520, Jul 1995	2.00
❑521, Aug 1995; V: Killer Croc	2.00
❑522, Sep 1995; V: Killer Croc, Swamp Thing	2.00
❑523, Oct 1995; V: Scarecrow	2.00
❑524, Nov 1995; V: Scarecrow	2.00
❑525, Dec 1995; V: Mr. Freeze. Underworld Unleashed	2.00
❑526, Jan 1996	2.00
❑527, Feb 1996; V: Two-Face	2.00
❑528, Mar 1996; V: Two-Face	2.00
❑529, Apr 1996; V: Poison Ivy	2.00
❑530, May 1996; Glow-in-the-dark cover	1.95
❑530/Variant, May 1996; Glow-in-the-dark cover	2.50
❑531, Jun 1996; Glow-in-the-dark cover	1.95

Other grades: Multiply price above by 5/6 for VF/NM • 2/3 for VERY FINE • 1/3 for FINE • 1/5 for VERY GOOD • 1/8 for GOOD

BATMAN

	N-MINT
❑531/Variant, Jun 1996; Glow-in-the-dark cover	2.50
❑532, Jul 1996; Glow-in-the-dark cover.	1.95
❑532/Variant, Jul 1996; glow-in-the-dark cardstock cover	2.50
❑533, Aug 1996 JA (a)	2.00
❑534, Sep 1996	2.00
❑535, Oct 1996; self-contained story, V: The Ogre and The Ape	2.00
❑535/Variant, Oct 1996; V: The Ogre and The Ape. Die-cut cover; self-contained story	4.00
❑536, Nov 1996; Final Night	2.00
❑537, Dec 1996; A: Man-Bat	2.00
❑538, Jan 1997 A: Man-Bat	2.00
❑539, Feb 1997	2.00
❑540, Mar 1997; A: Spectre. 1: Vesper Fairchild	2.00
❑541, Apr 1997 A: Spectre	2.00
❑542, May 1997	2.00
❑543, Jun 1997	2.00
❑544, Jul 1997; A: Demon. V: Joker	2.00
❑545, Aug 1997; A: Demon. V: Joker	2.00
❑546, Sep 1997; A: Demon. V: Joker	2.00
❑547, Oct 1997; Genesis	2.00
❑548, Nov 1997; V: Penguin. O: Penguin	2.00
❑549, Dec 1997; V: Penguin. Face cover	2.00
❑550, Jan 1998; O: Clayface	3.00
❑550/Variant, Jan 1998; V: Amygdala; Includes trading cards	3.50
❑551, Feb 1998 A: Ragman	2.00
❑552, Mar 1998 A: Ragman	2.00
❑553, Apr 1998; KJ (a); continues in Azrael #40	2.00
❑554, May 1998; KJ (a); V: Quakemaster, continues in Batman: HuntressSpoiler - Blunt Trauma #1; Continues in Batman: HuntressSpoiler - Blunt Trauma #1	2.00
❑555, Jun 1998; V: Ratcatcher. Aftershock	2.00
❑556, Jul 1998; Aftershock	2.00
❑557, Aug 1998; SB (a); A: Ballistic. Aftershock	2.00
❑558, Sep 1998; Aftershock	2.00
❑559, Oct 1998; Aftershock	2.00
❑560, Dec 1998; Road to No Man's Land, Bruce Wayne testifies	2.00
❑561, Jan 1999; JA (a); Road to No Man's Land, Bruce Wayne testifies	2.00
❑562, Feb 1999; JA (a); A: Mayor Grange. Road to No Man's Land, Gotham City is cut off	2.00
❑563, Mar 1999; A: Oracle. V: Joker. No Man's Land	3.00
❑564, Apr 1999; A: Scarecrow. A: Huntress. No Man's Land	2.50
❑565, May 1999; No Man's Land	2.00
❑566, Jun 1999; A: Superman. No Man's Land	2.00
❑567, Jul 1999; No Man's Land	2.00
❑568, Aug 1999; BSz (a); A: Poison Ivy. No Man's Land	2.00
❑569, Sep 1999; No Man's Land	2.00
❑570, Oct 1999; V: Joker. No Man's Land	2.00
❑571, Nov 1999; V: Bane. No Man's Land	2.00
❑572, Dec 1999; No Man's Land	2.00
❑573, Jan 2000; No Man's Land	2.00
❑574, Feb 2000; No Man's Land	2.00
❑575, Mar 2000; New cover style; March 2000	2.00
❑576, Apr 2000	2.00
❑577, May 2000	2.00
❑578, Jun 2000	2.00
❑579, Jul 2000; 1: Orca	2.00
❑580, Aug 2000; V: Orca	2.25
❑581, Sep 2000; V: Orca	2.25
❑582, Oct 2000; 1: Zeiss	2.25
❑583, Nov 2000	2.25
❑584, Dec 2000	2.25
❑585, Jan 2001; V: the Penguin	2.25
❑586, Feb 2001; V: the Penguin	2.25
❑587, Mar 2001	2.25
❑588, Apr 2001; V: Ventriloquist	2.25
❑589, May 2001; V: Ventriloquist	2.25
❑590, Jun 2001; V: Ventriloquist	2.25
❑591, Jul 2001; V: Deadshot	2.25
❑592, Aug 2001; V: Deadshot	2.25
❑593, Sep 2001; Our Worlds At War	2.25
❑594, Oct 2001; Our Worlds At War	2.25
❑595, Nov 2001	2.25

	N-MINT
❑596, Dec 2001; BSz (c); Joker: Last Laugh crossover	2.25
❑597, Jan 2002; V: Zeiss	2.25
❑598, Feb 2002	2.25
❑599, Mar 2002; Continued from Robin #98 & into Detective Comics #767	2.25
❑600, Apr 2002; Giant-size anniversary issue; SA (a); 64 pages; Continued into Birds of Prey #41	3.95
❑601, May 2002; Bruce Wayne: Fugitive continued from Detective Comics #769; Turning the Town Red continued into Batman #602; Two stories within one	2.25
❑602, Jun 2002	2.25
❑603, Jul 2002; Continued from Birds of Prey #43 & into Detective Comics #771	2.25
❑604, Aug 2002	2.25
❑605, Sep 2002	2.25
❑606, Oct 2002; V: Deadshot	2.25
❑607, Nov 2002; V: Deadshot	2.25
❑608, Dec 2002; JLee (c); JPH (w); JLee (a); V: Killer Croc	5.00
❑608/2nd, Dec 2002; Alternate cover from 1st printing	2.25
❑608/Dynamic, Dec 2002; Dynamic Forces signed edition	25.00
❑608/Retailer ed, Dec 2002; Retailer incentive promo (aka RRP edition); alternate cover with no cover price	500.00
❑608/NYPost 2005, Distributed in July 13, 2005, N.Y. Post newspapers in conjunction with the release of Batman Begins movie. New Jim Lee cover. Included in Sports Extra and Late City Final editions of The Post in the tri-state area.	5.00
❑609, Jan 2003 JLee (c); JPH (w); JLee (a)	4.00
❑610, Feb 2003; JLee (c); JPH (w); JLee (a); V: Killer Croc	3.00
❑611, Mar 2003 JLee (c); JPH (w); JLee (a)	3.00
❑612, Apr 2003; JLee (c); JPH (w); JLee (a); A: Superman. alternate cover with no cover price	3.00
❑612/2nd, Apr 2003; alternate cover with no cover price	3.00
❑613, May 2003; JLee (c); JPH (w); JLee (a); alternate cover with no cover price	3.00
❑614, Jun 2003; V: Joker	3.00
❑615, Jul 2003; V: Riddler, Batman reveals ID to Catwoman	3.00
❑616, Aug 2003, V: Ra's Al Ghul; Catwoman V: Lady Shiva	3.00
❑617, Sep 2003, V: Scarecrow	3.00
❑618, Oct 2003, V: Jason Todd	3.00
❑619, Nov 2003, O: Batman. Heroes cover; Blue background	3.00
❑619/2nd, Nov 2003	3.00
❑620, Dec 2003	2.25
❑621, Jan 2004, V: Killer Croc	2.25
❑622, Feb 2004	2.25
❑623, Mar 2004	2.25
❑624, Apr 2004	2.25
❑625, May 2004	2.25
❑626, Jun 2004; V: Penguin; V: Scarecrow	2.25
❑627, Jul 2004; V: Penguin; V: Scarecrow	2.25
❑628, Jul 2004; V: Penguin; V: Scarecrow	2.25
❑629, Aug 2004; V: Penguin; V: Scarecrow; Jason Todd appearance as hallucination	2.25
❑630, Sep 2004; 1: Fright; V: Scarecrow; V: Penguin	2.50
❑631, Oct 2004; Includes Sky Captain and the World of Tomorrow poster insert.	2.25
❑632, Nov 2004	2.25
❑633, Dec 2004, D: Spoiler; V: Black Mask; $2.95 price	2.95
❑634, Jan 2005	6.00
❑635, Feb 2005, 1: Jason Todd as Red Hood	15.00
❑636, Mar 2005, V: Red Hood	12.00
❑637, Apr 2005, V: Amazo	12.00
❑638, May 2005; V: Red Hood; V: Mr. Freeze; Red Hood revealed as Jason Todd	11.00
❑638/2nd, May 2005	6.00
❑639, Jun 2005	16.00
❑640, Jul 2005	6.00
❑641, Aug 2005	6.00
❑642, Sep 2005	3.00
❑643, Sep 2005; V: Black Mask	3.00
❑644, Oct 2005	2.50
❑645, Nov 2005; O: Jason Todd	2.50
❑646, Dec 2005	2.50

	N-MINT
❑647, Jan 2006, D: Captain Nazi; V: Secret Society	2.50
❑648, Feb 2006, Red Hood V: Black Mask	2.50
❑649, Mar 2006, Joker cover; V: Red Hood; Black Mask and Joker	2.50
❑650, May 2006, V: Joker; V: Jason Todd	2.50
❑651, Jun 2006, D: Magpie; V: Poison Ivy; One Year Later	6.00
❑652, Jul 2006, Robin cover; D: Ventriloquist; One Year Later	2.50
❑653, Aug 2006, One Year Later; Return of Two-Face	2.99
❑654, Sep 2006, Bruce adopts Tim; V: Two-Face; Cover by Simone Bianchi	2.99
❑655, Oct 2006, Andy Kubert cover; V: Joker; 1: Damian Wayne	2.99
❑656, Nov 2006	2.99
❑657, Dec 2006	2.99
❑658, Jan 2007	2.99
❑659, Feb 2007, 1: Grotesk	2.99
❑660, Feb 2007	2.99
❑661, Mar 2007, Late February 2007	2.99
❑662, Mar 2007	2.99
❑663, Apr 2007; V: Joker; V: Harley Quinn	2.99
❑664, May 2007	2.99
❑665, Jun 2007	2.99
❑666, Jul 2007; Damian Wayne as Batman	2.99
❑667, Aug 2007	2.99
❑668, Sep 2007	2.99
❑669, Oct 2007; D: Wingman; V: Wingman	2.99
❑670, Nov 2007; V: Dragon Fly, Tiger Moth, and Silken Spider; Story continues in Robin #168; A Prelude To The Resurrection of Ra's Al Ghul	2.99
❑671, Dec 2007; Story continues from Detective Comics #838; Story continues in Robin #169	2.99
❑672	2.99
❑673	2.99
❑674	2.99
❑675	2.99
❑676	2.99
❑677	2.99
❑678	2.99
❑679	2.99
❑680	2.99
❑681	2.99
❑682	2.99
❑683	2.99
❑684	2.99
❑685	2.99
❑686	2.99
❑687	2.99
❑688	2.99
❑689	2.99
❑1000000, Nov 1998; SB (a); Published between #559 and #560	4.00
❑Ann 1, ca. 1961; CS (a); O: The Batcave	540.00
❑Ann 1/2nd, ca. 1999; CS (a); O: The Batcave. cardstock cover; Reprint	5.50
❑Ann 2, ca. 1961; 80 pages	275.00
❑Ann 3, Sum 1962; 80-Page Giant	215.00
❑Ann 4, Win 1963; 80-Page Giant	110.00
❑Ann 5, Sum 1963; 80-Page Giant	110.00
❑Ann 6, Win 1964; 80-page giant	85.00
❑Ann 7, Sum 1964; 80 pages	85.00
❑Ann 8, Aug 1982; A: Ra's Al Ghul	7.00
❑Ann 9, Jul 1985 JOy, PS, AN (a)	6.00
❑Ann 10 1986; V: Hugo Strange	6.00
❑Ann 11 1987; JBy (c); AMo (w); V: Clayface; V: Penguin	6.00
❑Ann 12 1988 RA (a)	5.00
❑Ann 13 1989; Who's Who entries	5.00
❑Ann 14 1990; O: Two-Face	3.00
❑Ann 15 1991; A: Joker	3.00
❑Ann 15/2nd 1991; 2nd printing	2.00
❑Ann 15/Silver/3 1991	4.00
❑Ann 16 1992; A: Joker. Eclipso	3.00
❑Ann 17 1993; 1: Ballistic. Bloodlines: Earthplague	3.00
❑Ann 18 1994; Elseworlds	3.00
❑Ann 19 1995; O: Scarecrow. Year One.	4.00
❑Ann 20 1996; Legends of the Dead Earth	3.00
❑Ann 21, Jan 1997; Pulp Heroes	3.95
❑Ann 22 1998; Ghosts	2.95
❑Ann 23 1999; JLApe	2.95
❑Ann 24 2000; JA (a); 1: The Boggart; Planet DC	3.50
❑Ann 25 2006	12.00

Other grades: Multiply price above by 5/6 for VF/NM • 2/3 for VERY FINE • 1/3 for FINE • 1/5 for VERY GOOD • 1/8 for GOOD

Avengers: United They Stand

Adaptation of the Avengers cartoon series
©Marvel

Avengers Unplugged

Dollar-comic spinoff for bargain hunters
©Marvel

Avengers West Coast

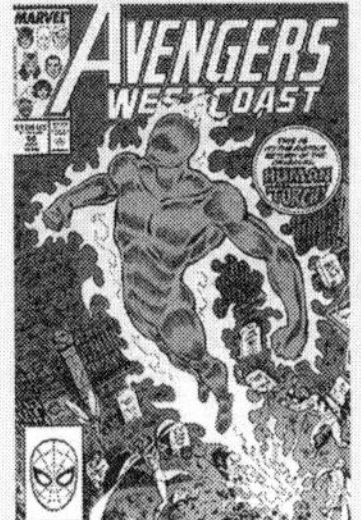

Renamed version of West Coast Avengers
©Marvel

A-V in 3-D

Sampler includes Cerebus, Journey
©Aardvark-Vanaheim

Awesome Preview

San Diego giveaway from Rob Liefeld company
©Awesome

N-MINT

❑GS 1, Aug 1998; KJ, DGry (w); KJ (a); 80 pages 4.95
❑GS 2, Oct 1999; SB (a); V: Two-Face; V: Riddler; V: Poison Ivy; V: Deadshot; 80 pages 4.95
❑GS 3, Jul 2000; BSz, JSa (a); V: Calendar Man; 80 pages 5.95

Batman Adventures
DC

❑1, Oct 1992; A: Penguin. based on animated series, V: Penguin 3.00
❑1/Silver, Oct 1992; silver edition 4.00
❑2, Nov 1992; A: Catwoman. V: Catwoman 2.00
❑3, Dec 1992; A: Joker. V: Joker 2.00
❑4, Jan 1993; Robin 2.00
❑5, Feb 1993; A: Scarecrow. V: Scarecrow 2.00
❑6, Mar 1993 .... 2.00
❑7, Apr 1993; V: Killer Croc; Includes trading card; Trading card missing 2.00
❑7/CS, Apr 1993; trading card, V: Killer Croc 3.00
❑8, May 1993 .... 2.00
❑9, Jun 1993; V: Rupert Thorne 2.00
❑10, Jul 1993; V: Riddler 2.00
❑11, Aug 1993; V: Man-Bat 1.50
❑12, Sep 1993; Batgirl 1.50
❑13, Oct 1993 .... 1.50
❑14, Nov 1993; Robin 1.50
❑15, Dec 1993; V: Rupert Thorne 1.50
❑16, Jan 1994; A: Joker. V: Joker 1.50
❑17, Feb 1994 .... 1.50
❑18, Mar 1994; Batgirl-Robin 1.50
❑19, Apr 1994; V: Scarecrow 1.50
❑20, May 1994; V: Mastermind, Professor, Mr. Nice 1.50
❑21, Jun 1994; Holiday special; A: Catwoman. V: Man-Bat. V: Mr. Freeze. Holiday special 1.50
❑22, Jul 1994; V: Two-Face 1.50
❑23, Aug 1994; V: Poison Ivy 1.50
❑24, Sep 1994 .... 1.50
❑25, Nov 1994; Giant-size; MW, ATh, KN (a); A: Lex Luthor. A: Superman 2.50
❑26, Nov 1994 A: Batgirl 1.50
❑27, Dec 1994 .... 1.50
❑28, Jan 1995 A: Harley Quinn 1.50
❑29, Feb 1995; V: Ra's Al Ghul 1.50
❑30, Mar 1995; O: The Perfesser. O: Mister Nice. O: Mastermind (DC) ... 1.50
❑31, Apr 1995 .... 1.50
❑32, Jun 1995 .... 1.50
❑33, Jul 1995 .... 1.75
❑34, Aug 1995; A: Catwoman. V: Hugo Strange 1.75
❑35, Sep 1995; A: Catwoman. V: Hugo Strange 1.75
❑36, Oct 1995; A: Catwoman. V: Hugo Strange; Final Issue 1.75
❑Ann 1 1994; MW, JBy, DDC, KJ (a); ca. 1994 .... 2.95
❑Ann 2 1995 A: The Demon 3.50
❑Holiday 1, Jan 1995; gatefold summary; V: Mr. Freeze. Holiday special; V: Clayface; V: Poison Ivy; V: Harley Quinn; V: Joker 2.95

Batman Adventures
DC

❑1, Apr 2003 .... 2.25
❑2, May 2003 .... 2.25
❑3, Jun 2003 .... 2.25
❑4, Jul 2003 .... 2.25
❑5, Aug 2003 .... 2.25
❑6, Sep 2003 .... 2.25
❑7, Oct 2003 .... 2.25
❑8, Nov 2003 .... 2.25
❑9, Dec 2003 .... 2.25
❑10, Jan 2004 .... 2.25
❑11, Apr 2004 .... 2.25
❑12, May 2004 .... 2.25
❑13, Jun 2004 .... 2.25
❑14, Jul 2004 .... 2.25
❑15, Aug 2004 .... 2.25
❑16, Sep 2004 .... 2.25
❑17, Oct 2004 .... 2.25

Batman Adventures: Mad Love
DC

❑1, Feb 1994; O: Harley Quinn. A: Joker. NN 7.50
❑1/2nd 1994; prestige format; O: Harley Quinn. A: Joker. NN 5.50

Batman Adventures: The Lost Years
DC

❑1, Jan 1998, fills in time between first and second Batman animated series.. 2.00
❑2, Feb 1998, A: Robin II 2.00
❑3, Mar 1998, V: Two-Face 2.00
❑4, Apr 1998 .... 2.00
❑5, May 1998, A: Nightwing 2.00

Batman/Aliens
Dark Horse

❑1, Mar 1997; prestige format; BWr (a); crossover with DC 5.00
❑2, Apr 1997; prestige format; BWr (a); crossover with DC 5.00

Batman/Aliens II
DC-Dark Horse

❑1, Feb 2003 .... 5.95
❑2, Mar 2003 .... 5.95
❑3, May 2003 .... 5.95

Batman Allies Secret Files 2005
DC

❑0, Jul 2005 .... 4.99

Batman and Other DC Classics
DC

❑1, ca. 1989, GP, BB, FM (c); KG (w); GP, BB, FM (a); O: Batman. Includes guide to collecting comics by Don & Maggie Thompson 2.00

Batman and Robin Adventures
DC

❑1, Nov 1995 .... 3.00
❑2, Dec 1995; V: Two-Face 2.00
❑3, Jan 1996; V: Riddler 2.00
❑4, Feb 1996; V: Penguin 2.00
❑5, Mar 1996; V: Joker 2.00
❑6, May 1996 .... 1.75
❑7, Jun 1996; V: Scarface 1.75
❑8, Jul 1996; Robin is enslaved by Poison Ivy 1.75
❑9, Aug 1996; Batgirl V: Talia 1.75
❑10, Sep 1996; V: Ra's Al Ghul 1.75
❑11, Oct 1996 .... 1.75
❑12, Nov 1996; V: Bane 1.75
❑13, Dec 1996; V: Scarecrow 1.75
❑14, Jan 1997 .... 1.75
❑15, Feb 1997 A: Deadman 1.75
❑16, Mar 1997 A: Catwoman 1.75
❑17, Apr 1997; JSa (a); Multiple villains cover 1.75
❑18, May 1997; V: Joker 1.75
❑19, Jun 1997 .... 1.75
❑20, Jul 1997 .... 1.75
❑21, Aug 1997; JSa (a); Batgirl vs. Riddler 1.75
❑22, Sep 1997; V: Two-Face 1.75
❑23, Oct 1997; V: Killer Croc 1.75
❑24, Nov 1997; V: Poison Ivy 1.75
❑25, Dec 1997; Giant-size; V: Ra's Al Ghul. Face cover 2.95
❑Ann 1, Nov 1996; sequel to Batman: Mask of the Phantasm 4.00
❑Ann 2, Nov 1997; JSa (c); JSa (a); A: Zatara. A: Zatanna. ties in with Adventures in the DC Universe Ann #1 and Superman Adventures Ann #1 ..... 3.95

Batman and Robin Adventures: Sub-Zero
DC

❑1 1998, cover says 98; adapts direct-to-video movie;indicia says 97 .... 3.95

Batman and Robin: The Official Adaptation of the Warner Bros. Motion Picture
DC

❑1, ca. 1997; prestige format; NN; Movie adaptation; Regular format 5.95

Batman & Superman Adventures: World's Finest
DC

❑1 1997; prestige format; adapts 90-minute special 6.95

Batman and Superman: World's Finest
DC

❑1, Apr 1999; prestige format 2.50
❑2, May 1999 .... 2.00
❑3, Jun 1999; V: Joker 2.00
❑4, Jul 1999 .... 2.00
❑5, Aug 1999 A: Batgirl 2.00
❑6, Sep 1999 A: Bat-Mite. A: Mr. Mxyzptlk 2.00
❑7, Oct 1999 .... 2.00
❑8, Nov 1999 .... 2.00
❑9, Dec 1999 .... 2.00
❑10, Jan 2000 .... 2.00

Batman and the Mad Monk
DC

❑1, Nov 2006 .... 3.50
❑2, Dec 2006 .... 3.50
❑3, Dec 2006 .... 3.50
❑4, Jan 2007 .... 3.50
❑5, Mar 2007 .... 3.50

Batman and the Monster Men
DC

❑1, Jan 2006 .... 2.99
❑2, Jan 2006 .... 2.99
❑3, Feb 2006 .... 2.99
❑4, Mar 2006 .... 2.99
❑5, May 2006 .... 2.99
❑6, Jun 2006 .... 3.50

Other grades: Multiply price above by 5/6 for VF/NM • 2/3 for VERY FINE • 1/3 for FINE • 1/5 for VERY GOOD • 1/8 for GOOD

Batman and the Outsiders
DC

- ❑1, Aug 1983, O: Geo-Force. 1: Baron Bedlam 3.00
- ❑2, Sep 1983, JA (c); JA (a); V: Baron Bedlam 2.00
- ❑3, Oct 1983, JA (c); JA (a); V: Agent Orange 2.00
- ❑4, Nov 1983, JA (c); JA (a); V: Meltdown 2.00
- ❑5, Dec 1983; GP, JA (c); JA (a); A: New Teen Titans. Continued from New Teen Titans #37 ..... 2.00
- ❑6, Jan 1984 ..... 1.50
- ❑7, Feb 1984 ..... 1.50
- ❑8, Mar 1984 ..... 1.50
- ❑9, Apr 1984; 1: Masters of Disaster 1.50
- ❑10, May 1984; V: Masters of Disaster .. 1.50
- ❑11, Jun 1984; O: Katana 1.50
- ❑12, Jul 1984; O: Katana 1.50
- ❑13, Aug 1984; O: Batman; Batman, Halo, Geo-Force, Black Lightning, Metamorpho, Katana 1.50
- ❑14, Oct 1984; V: Maxie Zeus; Batman; Halo; Katana; Geo-Force; Metamorpho 1.50
- ❑15, Nov 1984; V: Maxie Zeus; Flash Force 2000 Insert 1.50
- ❑16, Dec 1984 ..... 1.50
- ❑17, Jan 1985 ..... 1.50
- ❑18, Feb 1985; Metamorpho, Batman, Halo, Geo-Force, Katana, Black Lightning 1.50
- ❑19, Mar 1985; Halo, Batman, Geo-Force, Katana, Black Lightning, Metamorpho 1.50
- ❑20, Apr 1985; 1: Syonide II 1.50
- ❑21, May 1985; Katana story; Geo-Force story; Black Lightning story 1.50
- ❑22, Jun 1985; O: Halo 1.50
- ❑23, Jul 1985; Halo, Batman, Geo-Force, Katana, Black Lightning, Metamorpho 1.50
- ❑24, Aug 1985 ..... 1.50
- ❑25, Sep 1985 ..... 1.50
- ❑26, Oct 1985; V: Kobra 1.50
- ❑27, Nov 1985; V: Kobra; MASK insert .. 1.50
- ❑28, Dec 1985; O: Looker 1.50
- ❑29, Jan 1986; O: Looker 1.50
- ❑30, Feb 1986; O: Looker 1.50
- ❑31, Mar 1986; 1: Lia Briggs as Looker; 1: Looker (Lia Briggs) 1.50
- ❑32, Apr 1986; Series continues as Adventures of the Outsiders;Batman leaves 1.50
- ❑Ann 1, ca. 1984; FM (c); JDu, FM (a); 1: Force of July. 1: Major Victory 3.00
- ❑Ann 2, ca. 1985; JA (c); JA (a); Wedding of Metamorpho and Sapphire Stag 2.00

Batman: Arkham Asylum - Tales of Madness
DC

- ❑1, May 1998 ..... 2.95

Batman: A Word to the Wise
DC

- ❑1; (DC giveaway); NN 1.25

Batman: Bane
DC

- ❑1, Jul 1997; prestige format one-shot, cover is part of quadtych 4.95

Batman: Bane of the Demon
DC

- ❑1, Mar 1998; O: Bane 1.95
- ❑2, Apr 1998 ..... 1.95
- ❑3, May 1998 ..... 1.95
- ❑4, Jun 1998; V: Ra's Al Ghul 1.95

Batman: Batgirl
DC

- ❑1, Jul 1997; prestige format one-shot; cover is part of quadtych 4.95

Batman: Batgirl (Girlfrenzy)
DC

- ❑1, Jun 1998; Girlfrenzy;one-shot, V: Mr. Zsasz 1.95

Batman Begins Movie Adaptation
DC

- ❑0 2005 ..... 6.99

Batman Beyond
DC

- ❑1, Mar 1999; O: Batman II (Terry McGuiness). adapts first episode 2.50
- ❑2, Apr 1999; O: Batman II (Terry McGuiness). A: Derek Powers. adapts first episode 2.00
- ❑3, May 1999; V: Blight 2.00
- ❑4, Jun 1999 JSa (a); A: Demon 2.00
- ❑5, Jul 1999 JSa (a) 2.00
- ❑6, Aug 1999 JSa (a) 2.00

Batman Beyond
DC

- ❑1, Nov 1999; adapts first episode 2.50
- ❑2, Dec 1999; adapts first episode 2.00
- ❑3, Jan 2000; V: Blight 2.00
- ❑4, Feb 2000 A: Demon 1.99
- ❑5, Mar 2000 ..... 1.99
- ❑6, Apr 2000 ..... 1.99
- ❑7, May 2000 ..... 1.99
- ❑8, Jun 2000 ..... 1.99
- ❑9, Jul 2000 ..... 1.99
- ❑10, Aug 2000; V: Golem 1.99
- ❑11, Sep 2000 ..... 1.99
- ❑12, Oct 2000; V: Terminal 1.99
- ❑13, Nov 2000 A: Scarecrow. A: Batgirl. 1.99
- ❑14, Dec 2000 A: Demon 1.99
- ❑15, Jan 2001 ..... 1.99
- ❑16, Feb 2001 ..... 1.99
- ❑17, Mar 2001 ..... 1.99
- ❑18, Apr 2001 ..... 1.99
- ❑19, May 2001 ..... 1.99
- ❑20, Jun 2001 ..... 1.99
- ❑21, Jul 2001 ..... 1.99
- ❑22, Aug 2001 ..... 1.99
- ❑23, Sep 2001 ..... 1.99
- ❑24, Oct 2001 ..... 1.99

Batman Beyond: Return of the Joker
DC

- ❑1, Feb 2001 ..... 2.95

Batman Beyond Special Origin Issue
DC

- ❑1, Jun 1999, Free 1.00

Batman: Birth of the Demon
DC

- ❑1, ca. 1992; Embossed cover 12.95
- ❑1/HC, ca. 1992; Hardcover edition 24.95

Batman Black and White
DC

- ❑1, Jun 1996, b&w; JLee (c); HC, JKu (w); HC, JKu (a); B&W anthology 3.50
- ❑2, Jul 1996, b&w; FM (c); NG (w); b&w anthology 3.00
- ❑3, Aug 1996, b&w; MW, BSz, KJ (w); MW, BSz, CR, KJ (a); B&w anthology 3.00
- ❑4, Sep 1996, b&w; ATh (c); BB (w); BB, KN (a); Final Issue; B&w anthology 3.00

Batman: Blackgate
DC

- ❑1, Jan 1997; One-shot 3.95

Batman: Blackgate, Isle of Men
DC

- ❑1, Apr 1998; one-shot, continues in Batman: Shadow of the Bat #74 ..... 2.95

Batman: Book of the Dead
DC

- ❑1, Jun 1999 ..... 4.95
- ❑2, Jul 1999 ..... 4.95

Batman: Bullock's Law
DC

- ❑1, Aug 1999; One-shot 4.95

Batman/Captain America
DC

- ❑1 1996; prestige format crossover with Marvel, Elseworlds 5.95

Batman: Castle of the Bat
DC

- ❑1 1994; prestige format; Elseworlds 5.95

Batman: Catwoman Defiant
DC

- ❑1, ca. 1992; prestige format; cover forms diptych with Batman: Penguin Triumphant 5.00

Batman/Catwoman: Trail of the Gun
DC

- ❑1, Oct 2004 ..... 5.95
- ❑2, Nov 2004 ..... 5.95

Batman Chronicles
DC

- ❑1, Jun 1995; Giant-size; BSz (a) 4.00
- ❑2, Sep 1995; O: Feedback 3.50
- ❑3, Dec 1995; BB (c); BSz (a); O: Mr. Zsasz. A: Riddler. A: Killer Croc; Killer Croc 3.50
- ❑4, Mar 1996; A: Hitman. Contagion cross-over 4.00
- ❑5, Jun 1996; HC (c); HC (w); DG (a); O: Oracle; O: Oracle (Barbara Gordon) 3.50
- ❑6, Sep 1996 CS (a) 3.50
- ❑7, Dec 1996 JO (c); JOy, MGr, DGry (w); JA (a); A: Superman 3.50
- ❑8, Mar 1997; SB (a); V: Ra's Al Ghul; V: Two-Face 3.50
- ❑9, Jun 1997; Movie poster cover 3.50
- ❑10, Sep 1997 BSz (a) 3.50
- ❑11, Dec 1997; Elseworlds 3.50
- ❑12, Mar 1998 KJ, DGry (w); BSz, KJ (a) 3.50
- ❑13, Jun 1998; SB, DG (a); Shiny bat on cover logo 3.00
- ❑14, Sep 1998; Aftershock 3.00
- ❑15, Dec 1998; A: Man-Bat. A: Green Lantern. A: Question. A: Oracle. team-up issue 3.00
- ❑16, Mar 1999; A: Renee Montoya. A: Batgirl. A: Two Face. No Man's Land 3.00
- ❑17, Jun 1999; BSz (a); No Man's Land; Man-Bat's child 3.00
- ❑18, Sep 1999; DGry (w); No Man's Land 3.00
- ❑19, Dec 1999; Cover reads 'Winter '00 3.00
- ❑20, Mar 2000 DGry (w) 3.00
- ❑21, Jun 2000; Cover logo change 2.95
- ❑22, Sep 2000 ..... 2.95
- ❑23, Dec 2000; KN (w); KN (a); Cover reads 'Winter 01' 2.95

Batman Chronicles Gallery
DC

- ❑1, May 1997; pin-ups 3.50

Batman Chronicles: The Gauntlet
DC

- ❑1 1997, prestige format; 1st Robin solo adventure 4.95

Batman: City of Light
DC

- ❑1, Dec 2003 ..... 2.95
- ❑2, Jan 2004 ..... 2.95
- ❑3, Feb 2004 ..... 2.95
- ❑4, Mar 2004 ..... 2.95
- ❑5, Apr 2004 ..... 2.95
- ❑6, May 2004 ..... 2.95
- ❑7, Jun 2004 ..... 2.95
- ❑8, Jul 2004 ..... 2.95

Batman: Collected Legends of the Dark Knight
DC

- ❑199, Mar 2006 ..... 2.50

Batman Confidential
DC

- ❑1, Feb 2007 ..... 2.99
- ❑2, Mar 2007 ..... 2.99

Batman/Danger Girl
DC

- ❑1, Feb 2005, Leinil Yu cover 4.95

Batman/Daredevil
DC

- ❑1 2000 ..... 5.95

Batman: Dark Allegiances
DC

- ❑1 1996 ..... 5.95

Batman: Dark Detective
DC

- ❑1, Jun 2005 ..... 2.99
- ❑2, Jul 2005 ..... 2.99
- ❑3, Aug 2005 ..... 2.99
- ❑4, Aug 2005 ..... 2.99
- ❑5, Sep 2005 ..... 2.99
- ❑6, Sep 2005 ..... 2.99

Batman: Dark Knight Gallery
DC

- ❑1, Jan 1996, pin-ups 3.50

Batman: Dark Knight of the Round Table
DC

- ❑1, ca. 1999; prestige format; Elseworlds story 4.95
- ❑2, ca. 1999; prestige format; Elseworlds story 4.95

Other grades: Multiply price above by 5/6 for VF/NM • 2/3 for VERY FINE • 1/3 for FINE • 1/5 for VERY GOOD • 1/8 for GOOD

Axel Pressbutton

Early Eclipse title reprints from U.K.'s Warrior

©Eclipse

Azrael

Batman's replacement gets his own series

©DC

Aztec Ace

Future warrior who's a defender of time itself

©Eclipse

Aztek: The Ultimate Man

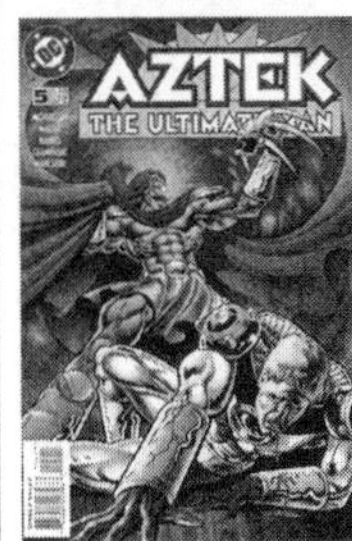

Short-lived Grant Morrison title

©DC

Baby Huey The Baby Giant

Cartoon antics with brain-damaged duck

©Harvey

N-MINT

Batman: Dark Victory
DC

❑0, ca. 1999; Wizard giveaway 1.00
❑1, Dec 1999; prestige format 5.00
❑2, Jan 2000; cardstock cover 3.00
❑3, Feb 2000; cardstock cover 3.00
❑4, Mar 2000; cardstock cover 3.00
❑5, Apr 2000; cardstock cover 3.00
❑6, May 2000; cardstock cover 3.00
❑7, Jun 2000; cardstock cover 3.00
❑8, Jul 2000; cardstock cover 3.00
❑9, Aug 2000; cardstock cover 3.00
❑10, Sep 2000; cardstock cover 3.00
❑11, Oct 2000; cardstock cover 3.00
❑12, Nov 2000; cardstock cover 3.00
❑13, Dec 2000; prestige format 3.00

Batman: Day of Judgment
DC

❑1, Nov 1999 .... 3.95

Batman/Deadman: Death and Glory
DC

❑1 .... 12.95

Batman: Death and the Maidens
DC

❑1, Oct 2003 .... 2.95
❑2, Nov 2003 .... 2.95
❑3, Dec 2003 .... 2.95
❑4, Jan 2004 .... 2.95
❑5, Feb 2004 .... 2.95
❑6, Mar 2004 .... 2.95
❑7, Apr 2004 .... 2.95
❑8, Jun 2004 .... 2.95
❑9, Jun 2004 .... 2.95

Batman/Deathblow: After the Fire
DC

❑1, May 2002 .... 5.95
❑2, Jun 2002 .... 5.95
❑3, Oct 2002 .... 5.95

Batman: D: Innocents
DC

❑1, Dec 1996, one-shot about the dangers of landmines and unexploded ordnance 3.95

Batman/Demon
DC

❑1 1996; prestige format one-shot 4.95

Batman/Demon: A Tragedy
DC

❑1 2000 .... 5.95

Batman: DOA
DC

❑1, Jan 2000 .... 6.95

Batman: Dreamland
DC

❑1, Jul 2000 .... 5.95

Batman: Ego
DC

❑1, Oct 2000 .... 6.95

Batman Family
DC

❑1, Oct 1975, Reprints Batman #28, 186, and Detective Comics #400; Batgirl and Robin 16.00

N-MINT

❑2, Dec 1975, Reprints Detective Comics #369, #245, #351 and Batman #191; Batgirl and Robin 10.00
❑3, Feb 1976, Reprints Batman #105, #133, and #26; Batgirl and Robin 8.00
❑4, Apr 1976, Cl (a); A: Fatman. Reprints from Batman #113, Detective comics #343 .... 8.00
❑5, Jun 1976, Batgirl and Robin; Reprints from Batman #92, 124 .... 8.00
❑6, Aug 1976, 1: Duela Dent; The Bicentennial #5; Reprints from Batman #32; 1: Joker's Daughter (Duela Dent); 161 .... 8.00
❑7, Sep 1976, Reprints Detective Comics #261 and Batman #103; V: Sportsmaster and Huntress; Batgirl and Robin; Reprints from Detective Comics #261, Batman #103 .... 6.00
❑8, Nov 1976, V: Duela Dent; Reprints from Batman #129, Detective Comics #424 .... 6.00
❑9, Jan 1977, A: Duela Dent. Reprints from Batman #26, Detective Comics #349 .... 7.00
❑10, Mar 1977, V: Cavalier; V: Killer Moth; Reprints from Batman #20, 105 .... 7.00
❑11, May 1977, B: New stories; B: Man-Bat 7.00
❑12, Jul 1977 .... 7.00
❑13, Sep 1977, A: Man-Bat. V: Outsider. V: Outsider 5.00
❑14, Oct 1977 .... 5.00
❑15, Dec 1977, V: Cavalier; V: Killer Moth 5.00
❑16, Feb 1978 .... 5.00
❑17, Apr 1978; V: Madame Zodiac; V: Catwoman; V: Poison Ivy 7.00
❑18, Jun 1978; V: Madame Zodiac; V: Snafu; Huntress by Staton 7.00
❑19, Aug 1978; V: Snafu; Huntress by Staton 7.00
❑20, Oct 1978; O: Ragman; Final Issue 8.00

Batman: Family
DC

❑1, Dec 2002; D: Tracker 2.95
❑2, Jan 2003; Includes preview of Aquaman (6th Series) #1; Spotlight on Athena 2.95
❑3, Jan 2003; Spotlight on Dr. Excess and The Bugg 2.95
❑4, Jan 2003; Spotlight on Suicide King 2.95
❑5, Jan 2003; Spotlight on Freeway 2.95
❑6, Feb 2003; Spotlight on The Technician 2.95
❑7, Feb 2003; Spotlight on Mr. Fun 2.95
❑8, Feb 2003 .... 2.95

Batman Forever: The Official Comic Adaptation of the Warner Bros. Motion Picture
DC

❑1 1995; NN; Movie adaptation 3.95
❑1/Prestige; movie adaptation, prestige format 5.95

Batman: Full Circle
DC

❑1, ca. 1991, b&w; prestige format; NN 6.00

Batman Gallery
DC

❑1; Wraparound cover; All pin-ups 2.95

Batman: GCPD
DC

❑1, Aug 1996 .... 2.25
❑2, Sep 1996 .... 2.25

N-MINT

❑3, Oct 1996 .... 2.25
❑4, Nov 1996 .... 2.25

Batman: Ghosts
DC

❑1 1995; prestige format one-shot 4.95

Batman: Gordon of Gotham
DC

❑1, Jun 1998 .... 1.95
❑2, Jul 1998 .... 1.95
❑3, Aug 1998 .... 1.95
❑4, Sep 1998 .... 1.95

Batman: Gordon's Law
DC

❑1, Dec 1996 .... 1.95
❑2, Jan 1997 .... 1.95
❑3, Feb 1997 .... 1.95
❑4, Mar 1997 .... 1.95

Batman: Gotham Adventures
DC

❑1, Jun 1998; based on animated series, Joker has a price on his head 3.00
❑2, Jul 1998; V: Two-Face 2.50
❑3, Aug 1998; cover is toy package mock-up 2.50
❑4, Sep 1998; V: Catwoman 2.50
❑5, Oct 1998 .... 2.50
❑6, Nov 1998 A: Deadman 2.50
❑7, Dec 1998 .... 2.50
❑8, Jan 1999; 1: Hunchback. A: Batgirl 2.50
❑9, Feb 1999; A: League of Assassins. A: Batgirl. V: Sensei 2.50
❑10, Mar 1999 A: Joker. A: Nightwing. A: Harley Quinn. A: Robin III (Timothy Drake) 2.50
❑11, Apr 1999; A: Riddler. V: Riddler 2.00
❑12, May 1999; V: Two-Face 2.00
❑13, Jun 1999; A: final. Final appearance of the Threatening Three 2.00
❑14, Jul 1999; V: Harley Quinn 2.00
❑15, Aug 1999; A: Bane. V: Venom 2.00
❑16, Sep 1999; Alfred is kidnapped 2.00
❑17, Oct 1999 .... 2.00
❑18, Nov 1999 A: Man-Bat 2.00
❑19, Dec 1999 .... 2.00
❑20, Jan 2000 .... 2.00
❑21, Feb 2000 .... 2.00
❑22, Mar 2000 .... 2.00
❑23, Apr 2000 .... 2.00
❑24, May 2000 .... 2.00
❑25, Jun 2000 .... 2.00
❑26, Jul 2000 .... 2.00
❑27, Aug 2000 .... 2.00
❑28, Sep 2000 .... 2.00
❑29, Oct 2000 JSa (a) 2.00
❑30, Nov 2000 .... 2.00
❑31, Dec 2000 A: Joker 2.00
❑32, Jan 2001 .... 2.00
❑33, Feb 2001 .... 2.00
❑34, Mar 2001 .... 2.00
❑35, Apr 2001 .... 2.00
❑36, May 2001 .... 2.00
❑37, Jun 2001 A: Joker 2.00
❑38, Jul 2001 .... 2.00
❑39, Aug 2001 .... 2.00
❑40, Sep 2001 .... 2.00

Other grades: Multiply price above by 5/6 for VF/NM • 2/3 for VERY FINE • 1/3 for FINE • 1/5 for VERY GOOD • 1/8 for GOOD

N-MINT

❑41, Oct 2001 2.00
❑42, Nov 2001 2.00
❑43, Dec 2001 2.00
❑44, Jan 2002 A: Two-Face 2.00
❑45, Feb 2002 2.00
❑46, Mar 2002 2.00
❑47, Apr 2002 2.00
❑48, May 2002 2.00
❑49, Jun 2002 2.00
❑50, Jul 2002 2.00
❑51, Aug 2002 2.00
❑52, Sep 2002 2.00
❑53, Oct 2002 2.25
❑54, Nov 2002 2.25
❑55, Dec 2002 2.25
❑56, Jan 2003; V: Riddler 2.25
❑57, Feb 2003; V: Riddler 2.25
❑58, Mar 2003 2.25
❑59, Apr 2003 2.25
❑60, May 2003; Final Issue 2.25

Batman: Gotham By Gaslight
DC

❑1, ca. 1989; prestige format; CR (a); first Elseworlds story; Victorian-era Batman; Prelude by Robert Bloch 4.00

Batman Gotham City Secret Files
DC

❑1, Apr 2000 4.95

Batman: Gotham County Line
DC

❑1 2005, ca. 2005 5.99
❑2, Jan 2006 5.99
❑3, Feb 2006 5.99

Batman: Gotham Knights
DC

❑1, Mar 2000; Black and White back-up 4.00
❑2, Apr 2000 BB (c); JBy, DGry (w); JBy (a) 2.50
❑3, May 2000 BB (c); DGry (w) 2.50
❑4, Jun 2000 BB (c); DGry (w) 2.50
❑5, Jul 2000; V: Key 2.50
❑6, Aug 2000 BB (c); WK, DGry (w) 2.50
❑7, Sep 2000 BB (c); DGry (w); JB (a) 2.50
❑8, Oct 2000; BB (c); DGry (w); V: Hugo Strange 2.50
❑9, Nov 2000; BB (c); HC, DGry (w); V: Hugo Strange 2.50
❑10, Dec 2000; BB (c); DGry (w); V: Hugo Strange 2.50
❑11, Jan 2001; BB (c); DGry (w); V: Hugo Strange 2.50
❑12, Feb 2001 DaG (w); DaG (a) 2.50
❑13, Mar 2001 2.50
❑14, Apr 2001 BB (c); DGry (w) 2.50
❑15, May 2001 BB (c); DGry (w); GC (a) 2.50
❑16, Jun 2001; BB (c); DGry (w); V: Scarecrow; V: Matatoa 2.50
❑17, Jul 2001; BB (c); DGry (w); V: Matatoa; Bruce adopts Dick 2.50
❑18, Aug 2001 BB (c); DaG, DGry (w) 2.50
❑19, Sep 2001 BB (c); DG (a) 2.50
❑20, Oct 2001 BB (c); DGry (w) 2.50
❑21, Nov 2001; BB (c); DGry (w); DDC (a); Brian Bolland cover 2.50
❑22, Dec 2001; MG, DGry (w); Joker: Last Laugh crossover 2.50
❑23, Jan 2002; BB (c); DGry (w); A: Scarecrow. V: Scarecrow 2.50
❑24, Feb 2002 BB (c); DGry (w) 2.50
❑25, Mar 2002 BB (c); DGry (w) 2.50
❑26, Apr 2002 BB (c); DGry (w) 2.50
❑27, May 2002 BB (c); DGry (w) 2.50
❑28, Jun 2002 2.50
❑29, Jul 2002; BB (c); DGry (w); V: Riddler 2.50
❑30, Aug 2002; BB (c); DGry (w); V: Azrael 2.50
❑31, Sep 2002 DaG (c); DGry (w) 2.50
❑32, Oct 2002 BB (c); DGry (w) 2.75
❑33, Nov 2002; BB (c); V: Kite-Man; V: Signalman; V: Corrosive Man; Bane claims to be Bruce's brother 2.75
❑34, Dec 2002 2.75
❑35, Jan 2003; New cover logo; Superman: Metropolis preview inside 2.75
❑36, Feb 2003; Includes Batman Black, White & Red 2.75
❑37, Mar 2003 2.75
❑38, Apr 2003 2.75

N-MINT

❑39, May 2003 2.75
❑40, Jun 2003; Huntress new costume shown 2.75
❑41, Jul 2003 2.75
❑42, Aug 2003 2.75
❑43, Sep 2003 2.75
❑44, Oct 2003 2.75
❑45, Nov 2003 2.75
❑46, Dec 2003, V: Spook 2.75
❑47, Jan 2004, V: Riddler 2.75
❑48, Feb 2004, O: Bane 2.75
❑49, Mar 2004, V: Scarecrow 2.75
❑50, Apr 2004 2.75
❑51, May 2004 2.75
❑52, Jun 2004; Price increase 2.75
❑52/2nd, Jul 2004, 2nd printing 2.95
❑53, Jul 2004, V: Prometheus 2.95
❑54, Aug 2004; O:Joker 2.95
❑55, Sep 2004; V: Hush; Price increase. 3.75
❑56, Oct 2004 2.50
❑57, Nov 2004 2.95
❑58, Jan 2005 2.50
❑59, Feb 2005, V: Mr. Freeze 2.50
❑60, Mar 2005, V: Hush 2.50
❑61, Apr 2005, V: Hush 2.50
❑62, May 2005; V: Hush 2.50
❑63, Jun 2005; V: Hush 2.50
❑64, Jul 2005; V: Hush 2.50
❑65 2005; V: Hush 2.50
❑66, Aug 2005; O: Prometheus; New DC logo 2.50
❑67, Sep 2005 2.50
❑68, Oct 2005; O: new Clayface 2.50
❑69, Nov 2005, V: Hush; V: Clayface 2.50
❑70, Dec 2005; V: Hush; V: Clayface 2.50
❑71, Jan 2006; V: Hush; V: Clayface 2.50
❑72, Feb 2006 2.50
❑73, Mar 2006 2.50
❑74, Apr 2006, Final issue 2.50

Batman: Gotham Noir
DC

❑1, May 2001; Elseworlds 6.95

Batman/Green Arrow: The Poison Tomorrow
DC

❑1 1992; prestige format; NN 6.00

Batman/Grendel
DC / Comico

❑1, ca. 1993; prestige format; MW (c); MW (w); MW (a) 6.00
❑2, ca. 1993; MW (c); MW (w); MW (a); Index title: Grendel/Batman: Devil's Masque; prestige format, cover indicates Grendel/Batman 6.00

Batman/Grendel
DC / Dark Horse

❑1, Jun 1996; Batman/Grendel: Devil's Bones;prestige format crossover with Dark Horse; concludes in Grendel/ Batman: Devil's Dance 5.00
❑2, Jul 1996; prestige format; MW (w); MW (a); Grendel/Batman: Devil's Dance; continued from Batman/ Grendel: Devil's Bones 5.00

Batman: Harley & Ivy
DC / Wildstorm

❑1, Jun 2004 2.50
❑2, Jul 2004 2.50
❑3, Aug 2004 2.50

Batman: Harley Quinn
DC

❑1, ca. 1999; prestige format; ARo (c); ARo (a); NN; O: Harley Quinn 12.00
❑1/2nd, ca. 1999; ARo (c); ARo (a); 2nd printing 6.00

Batman: Haunted Gotham
DC

❑1 2000; prestige format; Elseworlds 4.95
❑2 2000; prestige format; Elseworlds 4.95
❑3 2000; prestige format; Elseworlds 4.95
❑4 2000; prestige format; Elseworlds 4.95

Batman/Hellboy/Starman
DC / Dark Horse

❑1, Jan 1999; Back cover art 3.00
❑1/Autographed, Jan 1999; Autographed by James Robinson and Mike Mignola 10.00
❑2, Feb 1999; Back cover art 3.00

N-MINT

Batman: Hollywood Knight
DC

❑1, Apr 2001; Elseworlds 2.50
❑2, May 2001; Elseworlds 2.50
❑3, Jun 2001; Elseworlds 2.50

Batman: Holy Terror
DC

❑1, Oct 1991; prestige format; Elseworlds 5.00

Batman/Houdini: The Devil's Workshop
DC

❑1; prestige format; Elseworlds 4.50

Batman/Huntress: Cry for Blood
DC

❑1, Jun 2000 2.50
❑2, Jul 2000 2.50
❑3, Aug 2000 2.50
❑4, Sep 2000; O: The Huntress 2.50
❑5, Oct 2000; O: the Huntress; O: Huntress (Helena Bertinelli) 2.50
❑6, Nov 2000 2.50

Batman: Hush Double Feature
DC

❑1, Apr 2003; Reprints Batman #608-609 4.95

Batman: I, Joker
DC

❑1, Oct 1998; prestige format; Elseworlds 4.95

Batman: In Darkest Knight
DC

❑1, ca. 1994, prestige format; Elseworlds; Bruce Wayne as Green Lantern 4.95

Batman: Jekyll and Hyde
DC

❑1, Jun 2005 2.99
❑2, Jul 2005 2.99
❑3, Aug 2005 2.99
❑4, Sep 2005 2.99
❑5, Oct 2005 2.99

Batman: Joker's Apprentice
DC

❑1, May 1999 3.95

Batman/Joker: Switch
DC

❑1, ca. 2003 12.95

Batman: Joker Time
DC

❑1, ca. 2000; prestige format 4.95
❑2, ca. 2000; prestige format 4.95
❑3, ca. 2000; prestige format 4.95

Batman: Journey into Knight
DC

❑1, Oct 2005 2.50
❑2, Nov 2005; 1: Virus 2.50
❑3, Dec 2005 2.50
❑4, Jan 2006; Virus becomes the Carrier 2.50
❑5, Feb 2006 2.50
❑6, Mar 2006 2.50
❑7, May 2006 2.50
❑8, Jun 2006 2.50
❑9, Jul 2006 2.50
❑10, Aug 2006, Price increase; Cover by Pat Lee 2.99
❑11, Nov 2006 2.99
❑12, Dec 2006 2.99

Batman/Judge Dredd: Die Laughing
DC

❑1; prestige format; Joker in Mega-City One 4.95
❑2; prestige format; Joker in Mega-City One 4.95

Batman/Judge Dredd: Judgment on Gotham
DC

❑1, NN 5.95

Batman/Judge Dredd: The Ultimate Riddle
DC

❑1; prestige format; NN 5.00

Batman/Judge Dredd: Vendetta in Gotham
DC

❑1, Jan 1993; NN 6.00

Babylon 5

Series creator had a hand in comics spinoff

©DC

Babylon 5: In Valen's Name

Babylon 4 station reappears in limited series

©DC

Baby's First Deadpool Book

Silly spoof on children's books

©Marvel

Bacchus (Eddie Campbell's...)

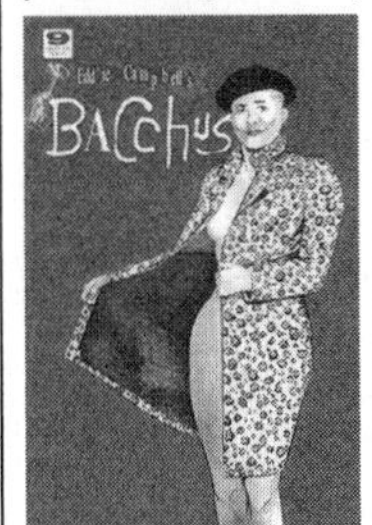

Greek god of wine and poetry hits comics

©Eddie Campbell

Backlash

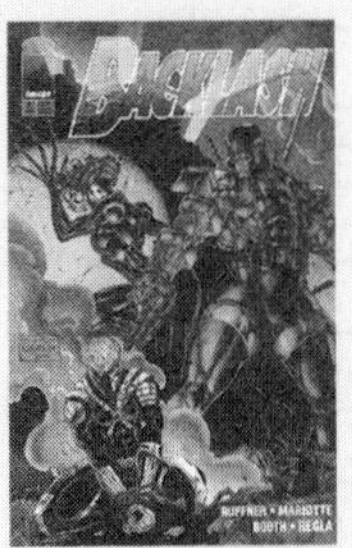

Solo series spinoff from Stormwatch

©Image

	N-MINT
Batman: League of Batmen	
DC	
❑1, Jun 2001	5.95
❑2, Jul 2001	5.95
Batman: Legends of the Dark Knight	
DC	
❑1, Nov 1989; Outer cover comes in four different colors (yellow, blue, orange, pink); poster	3.00
❑2, Dec 1989	2.75
❑3, Jan 1990	2.75
❑4, Feb 1990	2.75
❑5, Mar 1990	2.75
❑6, Apr 1990 KJ (c); KJ (a)	2.50
❑7, May 1990 KJ (c); KJ (a)	2.50
❑8, Jun 1990 KJ (c); KJ (a)	2.50
❑9, Jul 1990 KJ (c); KJ (a)	2.50
❑10, Aug 1990 KJ (c); KJ (a)	2.50
❑11, Sep 1990 PG (c); PG, TD (a)	2.50
❑12, Oct 1990 PG (c); PG, TD (a)	2.50
❑13, Nov 1990 PG (c); PG, TD (a)	2.50
❑14, Dec 1990 PG (c); PG, TD (a)	2.50
❑15, Feb 1991 PG (c); PG, TD (a)	2.50
❑16, Mar 1991; TVE (a); Tie-in to Bane/KnightsEnd	3.50
❑17, Apr 1991; TVE (a); Tie-in to Bane/KnightsEnd	2.50
❑18, May 1991; TVE (a); Tie-in to Bane/KnightsEnd	2.50
❑19, Jun 1991; TVE (a); Tie-in to Bane/KnightsEnd	2.50
❑20, Jul 1991; TVE (a); Tie-in to Bane/KnightsEnd	2.50
❑21, Aug 1991 (a)	2.00
❑22, Sep 1991; (a); Leslie Thompkins learns Batman's identity	2.00
❑23, Oct 1991 (a)	2.00
❑24, Nov 1991 GK (c); HC, GK (w); GK (a)	2.00
❑25, Dec 1991 GK (c); HC, GK (w); GK (a)	2.00
❑26, Jan 1992 GK (c); HC, GK (w); GK (a)	2.00
❑27, Feb 1992; Gotham City Visions by Anton Furst feature	2.50
❑28, Mar 1992; MW (c); MW (w); MW (a); Two-Face	2.00
❑29, Apr 1992; MW (c); MW (w); MW (a); Two-Face	2.00
❑30, May 1992; MW (c); MW (w); MW (a); Two-Face	2.00
❑31, Jun 1992 BA (c); BA (a)	2.00
❑32, Jun 1992; JRo (w); 1: Cavalier	2.00
❑33, Jul 1992 JRo (w)	2.00
❑34, Jul 1992; JRo (w); D: Cavalier	2.00
❑35, Aug 1992	2.00
❑36, Aug 1992	2.00
❑37, Aug 1992; Series continues as Batman: Legends of the Dark Knight	2.00
❑38, Oct 1992 A: Bat-Mite	2.00
❑39, Nov 1992 BT (c); BT (w); BT (a)	2.00
❑40, Dec 1992 BT (c); BT (w); BT (a)	2.00
❑41, Jan 1993	2.00
❑42, Feb 1993 CR (c); CR (a)	2.00
❑43, Mar 1993 CR (c); CR (a)	2.00
❑44, Apr 1993	2.00
❑45, May 1993	2.00
❑46, Jun 1993; RH (a); A: Catwoman. V: Catwoman. V: Catman	2.00
❑47, Jul 1993; RH (a); A: Catwoman. V: Catwoman. V: Catman	2.00

	N-MINT
❑48, Aug 1993; RH (a); A: Catwoman. V: Catwoman. V: Catman	2.00
❑49, Aug 1993; RH (a); A: Catwoman. V: Catwoman. V: Catman	2.00
❑50, Sep 1993; Giant-size; BB (c); HC, CR, MZ, JLee, KN, BWi (a); A: Joker. foil cover	4.00
❑51, Sep 1993 JKu (c)	2.00
❑52, Oct 1993	2.00
❑53, Oct 1993	2.00
❑54, Nov 1993	2.00
❑55, Dec 1993	2.00
❑56, Jan 1994	2.00
❑57, Feb 1994	2.00
❑58, Mar 1994	2.00
❑59, Apr 1994; O: Shondra Kinsolving	2.00
❑60, May 1994	2.00
❑61, Jun 1994; Batman's back healed	2.00
❑62, Jul 1994	2.00
❑63, Aug 1994; Azrael stops being Batman	2.00
❑64, Sep 1994	2.00
❑0, Oct 1994 JRo, JPH (w); JSa, MZ (a)	2.50
❑65, Nov 1994; JSa (c); JSa (a); A: Joker. V: Joker	2.00
❑66, Dec 1994; JSa (c); JSa (a); A: Joker. V: Joker	2.00
❑67, Jan 1995; JSa (c); JSa (a); A: Joker. V: Joker	2.00
❑68, Feb 1995; JSa (c); JSa (a); V: Joker	2.00
❑69, Mar 1995 MZ (c); MZ (a)	2.00
❑70, Apr 1995 MZ (c); MZ (a)	2.00
❑71, May 1995	2.00
❑72, Jun 1995	2.00
❑73, Jul 1995 JRo (w)	2.00
❑74, Aug 1995	2.00
❑75, Sep 1995	2.00
❑76, Oct 1995	2.00
❑77, Nov 1995	2.00
❑78, Dec 1995	2.00
❑79, Jan 1996	2.00
❑80, Feb 1996	2.00
❑81, Mar 1996	2.00
❑82, May 1996	2.00
❑83, Jun 1996	2.00
❑84, Jul 1996	2.00
❑85, Aug 1996; JRo (w); Cover logo change	2.00
❑86, Sep 1996	2.00
❑87, Oct 1996	2.00
❑88, Nov 1996	2.00
❑89, Dec 1996; O: Clayface (Matt Hagen)	2.00
❑90, Jan 1997	2.00
❑91, Feb 1997	2.00
❑92, Mar 1997	2.00
❑93, Apr 1997	2.00
❑94, May 1997; three eras of Batman	2.00
❑95, Jun 1997	2.00
❑96, Jul 1997	2.00
❑97, Aug 1997	2.00
❑98, Sep 1997	2.00
❑99, Oct 1997	2.00
❑100, Nov 1997; Double-size; ARo (c); JRo (w); ARo, FM, CS, KJ (a); O: Robin I and Robin II, pin-up gallery. A: Joker. pin-up gallery	4.50
❑101, Dec 1997; KN (c); Face cover; 100 years in the future	2.00
❑102, Jan 1998 JRo (w)	2.00
❑103, Feb 1998 JRo (w)	2.00

	N-MINT
❑104, Mar 1998 JRo (w)	2.00
❑105, Apr 1998; V: Joker	2.00
❑106, May 1998; Gordon vs. Joker	2.00
❑107, Jun 1998	2.00
❑108, Jul 1998	2.00
❑109, Aug 1998; V: Riddler	2.00
❑110, Sep 1998; V: Riddler	2.00
❑111, Oct 1998; V: Riddler	2.00
❑112, Nov 1998	2.00
❑113, Dec 1998	2.00
❑114, Jan 1999	2.00
❑115, Feb 1999; LMc (a); The Darkness	2.00
❑116, Apr 1999; A: Scarecrow. A: Huntress. No Man's Land	2.00
❑117, May 1999; V: Penguin. No Man's Land	2.00
❑118, Jun 1999; KJ (c); No Man's Land.	2.00
❑119, Jul 1999; BB (c); A: Two-Face. No Man's Land	2.00
❑120, Aug 1999; 1: Batgirl III (in costume). A: Huntress. A: Nightwing. A: Robin. No Man's Land	3.50
❑121, Sep 1999; V: Mr. Freeze. No Man's Land	2.00
❑122, Oct 1999; PG (a); A: Lynx. No Man's Land	2.00
❑123, Nov 1999; BSz (c); No Man's Land	2.00
❑124, Dec 1999; No Man's Land	2.00
❑125, Jan 2000; No Man's Land; Batman attempts to reveal identity to Commissioner Gordon	2.00
❑126, Feb 2000; DGry (w); No Man's Land	2.00
❑127, Mar 2000	2.00
❑128, Apr 2000; Cover logo change; 'bat logo' on bat-books begins	2.00
❑129, May 2000	2.00
❑130, Jun 2000	2.00
❑131, Jul 2000	2.00
❑132, Aug 2000 JRo (c); JRo, MR (a); A: Silver St. Cloud.	2.00
❑133, Sep 2000 MR (c); JRo (w); JRo, MR (a); A: Silver St. Cloud.	2.25
❑134, Oct 2000 MR (c); JRo (w); JRo, MR (a); A: Silver St. Cloud.	2.25
❑135, Nov 2000 MR (c); JRo (w); JRo, MR (a)	2.25
❑136, Dec 2000 MR (c); JRo (w); JRo, MR (a)	2.25
❑137, Jan 2001 PG (c); PG (a)	2.25
❑138, Feb 2001; PG (c); PG (a); O: Scarecrow (Jonathan Crane)	2.25
❑139, Mar 2001; PG (c); PG (a); D: Hugo Strange	2.25
❑140, Apr 2001 PG (c); PG (a)	2.25
❑141, May 2001 PG (c); PG (a)	2.25
❑142, Jun 2001 JA (a)	2.25
❑143, Jul 2001; JA (a); V: Joker; V: Ra's Al Ghul	2.25
❑144, Aug 2001; JA (a); V: Joker; V: Ra's Al Ghul	2.25
❑145, Sep 2001; JA (a); V: Joker; V: Ra's Al Ghul	2.25
❑146, Oct 2001	2.25
❑147, Nov 2001	2.25
❑148, Dec 2001	2.25
❑149, Jan 2002; TVE (a); V: Mother Grimm	2.25
❑150, Feb 2002; TVE (a); V: Mother Grimm	2.25
❑151, Mar 2002 TVE (a)	2.25
❑152, Apr 2002 TVE (a)	2.25
❑153, May 2002 TVE (a)	2.25

Other grades: Multiply price above by 5/6 for VF/NM • 2/3 for VERY FINE • 1/3 for FINE • 1/5 for VERY GOOD • 1/8 for GOOD

❑154, Jun 2002 ... 2.25
❑155, Jul 2002 ... 2.25
❑156, Aug 2002 ... 2.25
❑157, Sep 2002 ... 2.25
❑158, Oct 2002 ... 2.50
❑159, Nov 2002 ... 2.50
❑160, Dec 2002 ... 2.50
❑161, Jan 2003; Gotham Central preview inside ... 2.50
❑162, Feb 2003 ... 2.50
❑163, Mar 2003; V: Joker ... 2.50
❑164, Apr 2003; 'bat logo' no longer appears on cover ... 2.50
❑165, May 2003 ... 2.50
❑166, Jun 2003 ... 2.50
❑167, Jul 2003 ... 2.50
❑168, Aug 2003 ... 2.50
❑169, Sep 2003 ... 2.50
❑170, Oct 2003 ... 2.50
❑171, Nov 2003 ... 2.50
❑172, Dec 2003 ... 2.50
❑173, Jan 2004 ... 2.50
❑174, Feb 2004 ... 2.50
❑175, Mar 2004 ... 2.50
❑176, Apr 2004 ... 2.50
❑177, May 2004, (c); DGry (w) ... 2.50
❑178, Jun 2004 ... 2.50
❑179, Jul 2004 ... 2.50
❑180, Aug 2004 ... 2.50
❑181, Sep 2004 ... 2.50
❑182, Oct 2004; War Games ... 2.50
❑183, Nov 2004, War Games ... 2.50
❑184, Dec 2004, War Games ... 2.50
❑185, Jan 2005, V: Riddler ... 2.50
❑186, Feb 2005, V: Riddler ... 2.50
❑187, Mar 2005, V: Riddler ... 2.50
❑188, Apr 2005, V: Riddler ... 2.50
❑189, May 2005; V: Riddler ... 2.50
❑190, Jun 2005; V: Mr. Freeze ... 2.50
❑191, Jul 2005; V: Mr. Freeze ... 2.50
❑192, Aug 2005; V: Mr. Freeze ... 2.50
❑193, Sep 2005; V: Mr. Freeze ... 2.50
❑194, Oct 2005; V: Mr. Freeze ... 2.50
❑195, Nov 2005; V: Mr. Freeze ... 2.50
❑196, Dec 2005; V: Mr. Freeze ... 2.50
❑197, Jan 2006 ... 2.50
❑198, Feb 2006 ... 2.50
❑200, Apr 2006, Giant-size anniversary issue ... 4.99
❑201, May 2006 ... 2.50
❑202, Jun 2006 ... 2.50
❑203, Jun 2006 ... 2.50
❑204, Jul 2006, 1: Remorse ... 2.50
❑206, Aug 2006 ... 2.99
❑207, Aug 2006, Cover by Ariel Olivetti . 2.99
❑208, Sep 2006 ... 2.99
❑209, Oct 2006 ... 2.99
❑210, Nov 2006 ... 2.99
❑211, Dec 2006 ... 2.99
❑212, Jan 2007 ... 2.99
❑213, Mar 2007 ... 2.99
❑Ann 1, Dec 1991 MG, KG, DS, JA (a) ... 4.50
❑Ann 2, ca. 1992; Wedding of James Gordon ... 3.50
❑Ann 3, ca. 1993; GM, LMc (a); 1: Cardinal Sin; Bloodlines: Earthplague; 1993 Ann 3.50
❑Ann 4, ca. 1994; MWa (w); JSa (a); Elseworlds ... 3.50
❑Ann 5, ca. 1995; O: Man-Bat. Year One 3.95
❑Ann 6, ca. 1996; Legends of the Dead Earth ... 2.95
❑Ann 7, ca. 1997; A: Balloon Buster. Pulp Heroes ... 3.95
❑Special 1, ca. 1993; prestige format; Halloween Special; V: Scarecrow ... 6.95

Batman: Legends of the Dark Knight: Jazz
DC

❑1, Apr 1995; Painted cover ... 2.50
❑2, May 1995 ... 2.50
❑3, Jun 1995 ... 2.50

Batman: Madness a Legends of the Dark Knight Halloween Special
DC

❑1, ca. 1994, prestige format; One-shot 4.95

Batman: Manbat
DC

❑1, prestige format; Elseworlds ... 5.00
❑2, prestige format; Elseworlds ... 5.00
❑3, prestige format; Elseworlds ... 5.00

Batman: Mask of the Phantasm-The Animated Movie
DC

❑1, ca. 1993, newstand ... 2.95
❑1/Prestige, ca. 1993, slick paper ... 4.95
❑1/Video, ca. 1993, Included with video release; smaller than regular comic book 5.00

Batman: Masque
DC

❑1, Jan 1997; prestige format; Elseworlds; Phantom of the Opera theme ... 6.95

Batman: Master of the Future
DC

❑1, ca. 1991, NN ... 5.95

Batman: Mr. Freeze
DC

❑1, May 1997; prestige format; cover is part of quadtych ... 4.95

Batman: Mitefall
DC

❑1, Jan 1995; prestige format; prestige format one-shot ... 4.95

Batman: Nevermore
DC

❑1, Jun 2003; Painted cover; Elseworld story ... 2.50
❑2, Jul 2003; Painted cover; Elseworld story ... 2.50
❑3, Aug 2003 ... 2.50
❑4, Sep 2003 ... 2.50
❑5, Oct 2003 ... 2.50

Batman/Nightwing: Bloodborne
DC

❑1, Mar 2002, prestige format ... 5.95

Batman: No Man's Land
DC

❑0, Dec 1999; Huntress becomes Batgirl 4.95
❑1, Mar 1999 ARo (c); ARo (a) ... 2.95
❑1/Variant, Mar 1999; ARo (c); ARo (a); lenticular animation cover ... 3.95
❑2, ca. 1999 ... 2.95
❑3, ca. 1999 ... 2.95
❑4, ca. 1999 ... 2.95

Batman: No Man's Land Gallery
DC

❑1, Jul 1999; pin-ups ... 3.95

Batman: No Man's Land Secret Files
DC

❑1, Dec 1999 ... 4.95

Batman: Nosferatu
DC

❑1, May 1999; prestige format; Elseworlds 5.95

Batman of Arkham
DC

❑1 ... 5.95

Batman: Order of the Beasts
DC

❑1, Jul 2004 ... 5.95

Batman: Orpheus Rising
DC

❑1, Oct 2001; 1: Orpheus ... 2.50
❑2, Nov 2001 ... 2.50
❑3, Dec 2001 ... 2.50
❑4, Jan 2002 ... 2.50
❑5, Feb 2002 ... 2.50

Batman: Our Worlds at War
DC

❑1, Aug 2001; V: Lex Luthor ... 2.95

Batman: Outlaws
DC

❑1, Sep 2000 ... 4.95
❑2, Oct 2000 ... 4.95
❑3, Nov 2000 ... 4.95

Batman: Penguin Triumphant
DC

❑1, ca. 1992; prestige format; JSa (a); cover forms diptych with Batman: Catwoman Defiant ... 5.00

Batman/Phantom Stranger
DC

❑1, Dec 1997, prestige format; NN ... 5.00

Batman Plus
DC

❑1, Feb 1997, V: KGBeast ... 2.95

Batman: Poison Ivy
DC

❑1, Jul 1997, prestige format; O: Poison Ivy. A: Croc. A: Batman. A: Poison Ivy. cover is part of quadtych ... 5.00

Batman/Poison Ivy: Cast Shadows
DC

❑1, ca. 2004 ... 6.95

Batman/Predator III
DC

❑1, Nov 1997 ... 1.95
❑2, Dec 1997 ... 1.95
❑3, Jan 1998 ... 1.95
❑4, Feb 1998 ... 1.95

Batman/Punisher: Lake of Fire
DC / Marvel

❑1 1994 ... 5.00

Batman: Reign of Terror
DC

❑1, Feb 1999; prestige format; Elseworlds 4.95

Batman Returns: The Official Comic Adaptation of the Warner Bros. Motion Picture
DC

❑1, ca. 1992; Comic adaptation of Warner Bros. Movie ... 4.00
❑1/Prestige, ca. 1992; prestige format; Comic adaptation of Warner Bros. Movie ... 6.00

Batman: Riddler: The Riddle Factory
DC

❑1; prestige format; cover forms diptych with Batman: Two-Face - Crime and Punishment ... 4.95

Batman: Roomful of Strangers
DC

❑1, Apr 2004 ... 5.95

Batman: Run, Riddler, Run
DC

❑1, Jan 1992, prestige format ... 5.00
❑2, Jan 1992, prestige format ... 5.00
❑3 1992, prestige format ... 5.00

Batman/Scarecrow 3-D
DC

❑1, Dec 1998; with glasses ... 3.95
❑1/Variant, Dec 1998; Signed ... 7.50

Batman/Scarface: A Psychodrama
DC

❑1, Mar 2001 ... 5.95

Batman: Scar of the Bat
DC

❑1; prestige format; Elseworlds ... 4.95

Batman: Scottish Connection
DC

❑1, ca. 1998, prestige format; NN; One-shot ... 5.95

Batman Secret Files
DC

❑1, Oct 1997, background information .. 4.95

Batman: Secrets
DC

❑1, May 2006 ... 2.99
❑2, Jun 2006 ... 2.99
❑3, Jul 2006 ... 2.99
❑4, Aug 2006 ... 2.99
❑5, Sep 2006 ... 2.99

Batman: Seduction of the Gun
DC

❑1, Feb 1993, Special edition on gun control; dedicated to John Reisenbach (Son of DC editor slain in gun killing) 3.50

Batman: Shadow of the Bat
DC

❑0, Oct 1994; O: Batman. falls between issues #31 and 32 ... 2.50
❑1, Jun 1992; Last Arkham ... 2.50

Other grades: Multiply price above by 5/6 for VF/NM • 2/3 for VERY FINE • 1/3 for FINE • 1/5 for VERY GOOD • 1/8 for GOOD

Badger

Series gives Madison, Wis., its own hero

©Capital

Badrock/Wolverine

Crossover between Image and Marvel

©Image

Balder the Brave

Thor's friend is Balder, yet has plenty of hair

©Marvel

Ballad Of Utopia

Dark, forbidding Western comics series

©Black Daze

Banana Splits

Awful live-action TV show spins off a comic book

©Gold Key

	N-MINT
❑1/CS, Jun 1992; collector's set	3.50
❑2, Jul 1992; Last Arkham	2.75
❑3, Aug 1992; Last Arkham	2.75
❑4, Sep 1992; Last Arkham	2.75
❑5, Oct 1992; D: Black Spider	2.75
❑6, Nov 1992	2.50
❑7, Dec 1992; V: Chancer, Cat-Man, Calendar Man, Killer Moth; Cover forms triptych with #8 and #9	2.50
❑8, Jan 1993; Misfits	2.50
❑9, Feb 1993; V: Chancer, Cat-Man, Calendar Man, Killer Moth; Cover forms triptych with #7 and #8	2.50
❑10, Mar 1993	2.50
❑11, Apr 1993	2.50
❑12, May 1993	2.50
❑13, Jun 1993	2.50
❑14, Jul 1993; JSa (a); Staton-a (p)	2.50
❑15, Aug 1993; JSa (a); V: Mirage	2.50
❑16, Sep 1993; V: Scarecrow; Knightfall	2.50
❑17, Sep 1993; V: Scarecrow; Knightfall	2.50
❑18, Oct 1993; V: Scarecrow; Knightfall tie-in	2.50
❑19, Oct 1993; V: Tally Man	2.50
❑20, Nov 1993; V: Tally Man	2.50
❑21, Nov 1993	2.50
❑22, Dec 1993; Knightquest tie-ins w/Azrael as Batman	2.50
❑23, Jan 1994; Knightquest tie-ins w/Azrael as Batman	2.50
❑24, Feb 1994; Knightquest tie-ins w/Azrael as Batman	2.50
❑25, Mar 1994; A: Joe Public. V: Corrosive Man; Knightquest tie-ins w/Azrael as Batman; Joe Public app.; Silver inc-c; Anniversary issue	2.50
❑26, Apr 1994; V: Clayface	2.50
❑27, May 1994; V: Clayface	2.50
❑28, Jun 1994	2.50
❑29, Jul 1994; Giant-size	2.50
❑30, Aug 1994; Batman vs Az-Bats	2.50
❑31, Sep 1994; Zero Hour, R: Alfred as detective	2.50
❑32, Nov 1994; V: Ventriloquist; Cover forms diptych with #33	2.50
❑33, Dec 1994; V: Two-Face; Cover forms diptych with #32; Story continues in Detective Comics #680	2.50
❑34, Jan 1995; O: Nightwing; V: Tally Man	2.50
❑35, Feb 1995	4.00
❑35/Variant, Feb 1995; enhanced cover	2.95
❑36, Mar 1995; A: Black Canary. O: Black Canary II (Dinah Lance)	2.00
❑37, Apr 1995; V: Joker	2.00
❑38, May 1995; V: Joker	2.00
❑39, Jun 1995; V: Anarky. V: Solomon Grundy	2.00
❑40, Jul 1995; V: Anarky	2.00
❑41, Aug 1995	2.00
❑42, Sep 1995	2.00
❑43, Oct 1995; V: Cat-Man; V: Ratcatcher; Cover forms diptych with #44	2.00
❑44, Nov 1995; V: Cat-Man; V: Ratcatcher; Cover forms diptych with #43	2.00
❑45, Dec 1995; Wayne Manor history	2.00
❑46, Jan 1996; V: Cornelius Stirk	2.00
❑47, Feb 1996; V: Cornelius Stirk	2.00
❑48, Mar 1996; trading card bound in	2.00
❑49, Apr 1996	2.00
❑50, May 1996; V: Narcosis	2.00
❑51, Jun 1996; V: Narcosis	2.00
❑52, Jul 1996; V: Narcosis	2.00
❑53, Aug 1996 A: Huntress	2.00
❑54, Sep 1996	2.00
❑55, Oct 1996 KJ (a)	2.00
❑56, Nov 1996; V: Poison Ivy; V: Floronic Man	2.00
❑57, Dec 1996; V: Poison Ivy. V: Floronic Man	2.00
❑58, Jan 1997; V: Floronic Man. V: Floronic Man	2.00
❑59, Feb 1997; V: Scarface	2.00
❑60, Mar 1997; V: Scarface	2.00
❑61, Apr 1997 JA (a)	2.00
❑62, May 1997; V: Two-Face. O: Two-Face	2.00
❑63, Jun 1997; V: Two-Face	2.00
❑64, Jul 1997	2.00
❑65, Aug 1997	2.00
❑66, Sep 1997	2.00
❑67, Oct 1997	2.00
❑68, Nov 1997	2.00
❑69, Dec 1997; A: Fate. "face" cover	2.00
❑70, Jan 1998 A: Fate	2.00
❑71, Feb 1998	2.00
❑72, Mar 1998; 1: Drakken	2.00
❑73, Apr 1998; continues in Nightwing #19	2.00
❑74, May 1998; continues in Batman Chronicles #12	2.00
❑75, Jun 1998; V: Clayface. V: Mr. Freeze. Aftershock	2.00
❑76, Jul 1998; Aftershock	2.00
❑77, Aug 1998; Aftershock	2.00
❑78, Sep 1998; Aftershock	2.00
❑79, Oct 1998; Aftershock	2.00
❑80, Dec 1998; Road to No Man's Land; flipbook with Azrael: Agent of the Bat #47	5.00
❑80/Ltd., Dec 1998; Extra-sized flip-book	5.00
❑81, Jan 1999; A: Jeremiah Arkham. Road to No Man's Land	2.00
❑82, Feb 1999; Road to No Man's Land	2.00
❑83, Mar 1999; 1: new Batgirl. No Man's Land	9.00
❑84, Apr 1999; A: Scarecrow. A: Huntress. A: Batgirl. No Man's Land	2.00
❑85, May 1999; A: Batgirl. V: Penguin. No Man's Land	2.00
❑86, Jun 1999; No Man's Land	2.00
❑87, Jul 1999; BB (c); A: Two-Face. No Man's Land	2.00
❑88, Aug 1999; BSz (a); A: Poison Ivy. V: Clayface. No Man's Land; continues in Batman #568	2.00
❑89, Sep 1999; V: Killer Croc. No Man's Land	2.00
❑90, Oct 1999; PG (a); A: Lynx. No Man's Land	2.00
❑91, Nov 1999; No Man's Land	2.00
❑92, Dec 1999; DGry (w); No Man's Land	2.00
❑93, Jan 2000; BSz (a); No Man's Land	2.00
❑94, Feb 2000; Final Issue; No Man's Land	2.00
❑1000000, Nov 1998; Aftershock	3.00
❑Ann 1, ca. 1993; TVE (a); 1: Joe Public; Bloodlines: Earthplague	4.00
❑Ann 2, ca. 1994; JSa (a); Elseworlds	3.95
❑Ann 3, ca. 1995; O: Poison Ivy. Year One	3.95
❑Ann 4, Nov 1996; Legends of the Dead Earth; 1996 Ann	2.95
❑Ann 5, Oct 1997; V: Poison Ivy. 1997 Ann; Pulp Heroes	3.95

Batman-Spawn: War Devil
DC

	N-MINT
❑1, ca. 1994; prestige format; crossover with Image	4.95

Batman Special
DC

	N-MINT
❑1, ca. 1984, MG (c); MG (a)	2.50

Batman/Spider-Man
DC

	N-MINT
❑1, Oct 1997, prestige format; crossover with Marvel	4.95

Batman: Spoiler/Huntress: Blunt Trauma
DC

	N-MINT
❑1, May 1998	2.95
❑2, ca. 1998	2.95
❑3, ca. 1998	2.95
❑4, ca. 1998	2.95

Batman Strikes
DC

	N-MINT
❑1, Nov 2004	2.25
❑2, Dec 2004	2.25
❑3, Jan 2005	2.25
❑4, Feb 2005	2.25
❑5, Mar 2005	2.25
❑6, Apr 2005	2.25
❑7, May 2005	2.25
❑8, Jun 2005	2.25
❑9, Jun 2005	2.25
❑10, Jul 2005	2.25
❑11, Aug 2005	2.25
❑12, Sep 2005	2.25
❑13, Oct 2005	2.25
❑14	2.25
❑15, Jan 2006	2.25
❑16, Feb 2006	2.25
❑17, Mar 2006	2.25
❑18, Apr 2006	2.25
❑19, May 2006	2.25
❑20, Jun 2006	2.25
❑21, Jul 2006	2.25
❑22, Aug 2006	2.25
❑23, Sep 2006	2.25
❑24, Oct 2006	2.25
❑25, Nov 2006	2.25
❑26, Dec 2006	2.25
❑27, Jan 2007	2.25
❑28, Feb 2007	2.25
❑29, Mar 2007	2.25

Batman/Superman/ Wonder Woman Trinity
DC

	N-MINT
❑1, Aug 2003	9.00
❑2, Oct 2003	8.00
❑3, Dec 2003	6.95

Batman: Sword of Azrael
DC

	N-MINT
❑1, Oct 1992, 1: Azrael. Wraparound, gatefold cover	4.00
❑1/Silver, Oct 1992, silver edition	2.00
❑2, Nov 1992	3.00
❑2/Silver, Nov 1992, silver edition	2.00
❑3, Dec 1992	3.00
❑3/Silver, Dec 1992, silver edition	2.00

Other grades: Multiply price above by 5/6 for VF/NM • 2/3 for VERY FINE • 1/3 for FINE • 1/5 for VERY GOOD • 1/8 for GOOD

❑4, Jan 1993 .... 2.50
❑4/Silver, Jan 1993, silver edition 2.00

Batman/Tarzan: Claws Of The Cat-Woman
Dark Horse

❑1, Sep 1999 .... 2.95
❑2, Oct 1999 .... 2.95
❑3, Nov 1999 .... 2.95
❑4, Dec 1999 .... 2.95

Batman: Tenses
DC

❑1, Oct 2003 .... 6.95
❑2 ca. 2004 .... 6.95

Batman: The Abduction
DC

❑1, Jun 1998; prestige format; Batman kidnapped by aliens 5.95

Batman: The Ankh
DC

❑1, Jan 2002 .... 5.95
❑2, Feb 2002 .... 5.95

Batman: The Blue, the Grey, and the Bat
DC

❑1 1992; prestige format; Elseworlds 5.95

Batman: The Book of Shadows
DC

❑1; prestige format; NN 5.95

Batman: The Cult
DC

❑1, Aug 1988; BWr (c); JSn (w); JSn, BWr (a); Painted cover 5.00
❑2, Sep 1988; BWr (c); JSn (w); JSn, BWr (a); Painted cover 4.00
❑3, Oct 1988; BWr (c); JSn (w); JSn, BWr (a); Painted cover 4.00
❑4, Nov 1988; BWr (c); JSn (w); JSn, BWr (a); Painted cover 4.00

Batman: The Dark Knight
DC

❑1, Mar 1986; FM (c); FM (w); FM (a); Squarebound 25.00
❑1/2nd, Mar 1986; FM (c); FM (w); FM (a); 2nd printing 7.00
❑1/3rd, ca. 1986; FM (c); FM (w); FM (a); 3rd printing 5.00
❑2, Mar 1986; FM (c); FM (w); FM (a); Squarebound 9.00
❑2/2nd, ca. 1986; FM (c); FM (w); FM (a); 2nd printing 3.00
❑2/3rd, ca. 1986; FM (c); FM (w); FM (a); 3rd printing 3.00
❑3, ca. 1986; FM (c); FM (w); FM (a); D: Joker (future). D: Joker (future); Squarebound 6.00
❑3/2nd, ca. 1986; FM (c); FM (w); FM (a); D: Joker (future). 2nd printing 3.00
❑4, ca. 1986; FM (c); FM (w); FM (a); D: Alfred (future); Squarebound 5.00

Batman: The Doom that Came to Gotham
DC

❑1, Nov 2000 .... 4.95
❑2, Dec 2000 .... 4.95
❑3, Jan 2001 .... 4.95

Batman: The Hill
DC

❑1, May 2000 .... 2.95

Batman: The Killing Joke
DC

❑1, Jul 1988; prestige format; BB (c); AMo (w); BB (a); O: Joker. V: Joker. first printing; green logo 7.00
❑1/2nd, ca. 1988; prestige format; BB (c); AMo (w); BB (a); O: Joker. V: Joker. second printing; pink logo 5.50
❑1/3rd, ca. 1988; prestige format; BB (c); AMo (w); BB (a); O: Joker. V: Joker. third printing; yellow logo 5.00
❑1/4th, ca. 1988; prestige format; BB (c); AMo (w); BB (a); O: Joker. V: Joker. fourth printing; orange logo 5.00
❑1/5th, ca. 1988; prestige format; BB (c); AMo (w); BB (a); O: Joker. V: Joker. 5th printing; Joker cripples Barbara Gordon 5.00
❑1/6th, ca. 1988; prestige format; BB (c); AMo (w); BB (a); O: Joker. V: Joker. 6th printing; Prestige format; Joker cripples Barbara Gordon 5.00
❑1/7th, ca. 1988; prestige format; BB (c); AMo (w); BB (a); O: Joker. V: Joker. 7th printing; Joker cripples Barbara Gordon 5.00
❑1/8th, ca. 1988; prestige format; BB (c); AMo (w); BB (a); O: Joker. V: Joker. 8th printing; Joker cripples Barbara Gordon 5.00

Batman: The Long Halloween
DC

❑1, Dec 1996; prestige format; JPH (w) 8.50
❑2, Jan 1997; JPH (w); V: Solomon Grundy. cardstock cover 6.50
❑3, Feb 1997; JPH (w); V: Joker. cardstock cover 5.50
❑4, Mar 1997; JPH (w); V: Joker. cardstock cover 5.00
❑5, Apr 1997; JPH (w); A: Catwoman. A: Poison Ivy. cardstock cover 4.50
❑6, May 1997; JPH (w); V: Poison Ivy. cardstock cover 4.50
❑7, Jun 1997; JPH (w); V: Riddler. cardstock cover 3.50
❑8, Jul 1997; JPH (w); V: Scarecrow. cardstock cover 3.50
❑9, Aug 1997; JPH (w); cardstock cover 3.50
❑10, Sep 1997; JPH (w); A: Catwoman. V: Scarecrow. V: Mad Hatter. cardstock cover 3.50
❑11, Oct 1997; JPH (w); O: Two-Face. cardstock cover 3.50
❑12, Nov 1997; JPH (w); D: Maroni. cardstock cover; identity of Holiday revealed 3.50
❑13, Dec 1997; prestige format; JPH (w); 1: Holiday. V: Arkham inmates 5.50

Batman: The Man Who Laughs
DC

❑1, Feb 2005 .... 20.00

Batman: The Official Comic Adaptation of the Warner Bros. Motion Picture
DC

❑1, ca. 1989; regular edition; JOy (a); newsstand format; Comic adaptation of Warner Bros. Movie 3.00
❑1/Prestige, ca. 1989; prestige format; Comic adaptation of Warner Bros. Movie 5.00

Batman/The Spirit
DC

❑1, Feb 2007 .... 4.99

Batman: The 10-Cent Adventure
DC

❑1, Mar 2002, O: Batman; Begins Bruce Wayne: Murderer story; Story continues in Detective Comics #766 .. 1.00

Batman: The Ultimate Evil
DC

❑1; prestige format; adapts Andrew Vachss novel 6.00
❑2; prestige format; adapts Andrew Vachss novel 6.00

Batman: Toyman
DC

❑1, Nov 1998 .... 2.25
❑2, Dec 1998; V: Toyman, Stilleto 2.25
❑3, Jan 1999; Wordless issue 2.25
❑4, Feb 1999 .... 2.25

Batman: Turning Points
DC

❑1, Jan 2001 .... 2.50
❑2, Jan 2001 .... 2.50
❑3, Jan 2001 .... 2.50
❑4, Jan 2001 .... 2.50
❑5, Jan 2001 .... 2.50

Batman: Two-Face: Crime and Punishment
DC

❑1; prestige format; cover forms diptych with Batman: Riddler - The Riddle Factory 4.95

Batman: Two Faces
DC

❑1, Nov 1998; Elseworlds 4.95

Batman: Two-Face Strikes Twice
DC

❑1; JSa (a); Flip book 5.00
❑2; JSa (a); Flip book 5.00

Batman: Vengeance of Bane II
DC

❑1; NN; One-shot 4.00

Batman: Vengeance of Bane Special
DC

❑1, Jan 1993; O: Bane. 1: Bane 4.00

Batman V: Predator
DC / Dark Horse

❑1, ca. 1991; DaG (w); newsstand 2.50
❑1/Prestige Batm, ca. 1991; prestige format; DaG (w); trading cards; Batman on front cover 5.00
❑1/Prestige Pred, ca. 1991; prestige format; DaG (w); trading cards; Predator on front; Batman on back cover 5.00
❑2, ca. 1992; DaG (w); newsstand 2.50
❑2/Prestige, ca. 1992; prestige format; DaG (w); pin-ups 5.00
❑3, ca. 1992; DaG (w); newsstand 2.50
❑3/Prestige, ca. 1992; prestige format; DaG (w) 5.00

Batman V: Predator II: Bloodmatch
DC / Dark Horse

❑1, ca. 1994; Crossover, no year in indicia 2.50
❑2, ca. 1994; Crossover 2.50
❑3, ca. 1995; Crossover 2.50
❑4, ca. 1995; Crossover 2.50

Batman vs. the Incredible Hulk
DC

❑1, Fal 1981; oversized, (DC Special Series #27) 2.50
❑1/2nd; 2nd Printing, comics-sized; Reprinting with gold "canvas" around the original cover. "A Special Collector's Edition of the Crossover Classic"; ca. 1995 .... 3.95

Batman Villains Secret Files
DC

❑1, Oct 1998; Joker profile; Bane profile; Scarecrow profile; Two-Face profile; Clayfaces profile; Charaxes profile; Poison Ivy profile; Ra's Al Ghul profile; The Answer profile; Mr. Freeze profile; Ferak profile; Black Mask profile; Catwoman profile 4.95

Batman Villains Secret Files 2005
DC

❑0, Jul 2005 .... 4.99

Batman/Wildcat
DC

❑1, Apr 1997, V: Lock-Up 2.25
❑2, May 1997, V: Lock-Up; Batman profile; Wildcat profile 2.25
❑3, Jun 1997, V: Lock-Up 2.25

Batman: Year 100
DC

❑1, Apr 2006 .... 5.99
❑2, May 2006 .... 5.99
❑3, Jun 2006 .... 5.99

Bat (Mary Roberts Rinehart's)
Adventure

❑1, Aug 1992, b&w 2.50

Bat Men
Avalon

❑1 .... 2.95

Bats, Cats & Cadillacs
Now

❑1, Oct 1990 .... 2.00
❑2, Nov 1990 .... 2.00

Bat-Thing
DC / Amalgam

❑1, Jun 1997, Amalgam of Man-Bat & Man-Thing 1.95

Battle Angel Alita: Last Order Part 1
Viz

❑1, Sep 2002 .... 2.95
❑2, Oct 2002 .... 2.95
❑3, Nov 2002 .... 2.95
❑4, Dec 2002 .... 2.95
❑5, Jan 2003 .... 2.95
❑6, Feb 2003 .... 2.95

Battle Angel Alita Part 1
Viz

❑1, Jul 1992; 1: Alita 4.00
❑2, Aug 1992 .... 3.50

Other grades: Multiply price above by 5/6 for VF/NM • 2/3 for VERY FINE • 1/3 for FINE • 1/5 for VERY GOOD • 1/8 for GOOD

Barbie

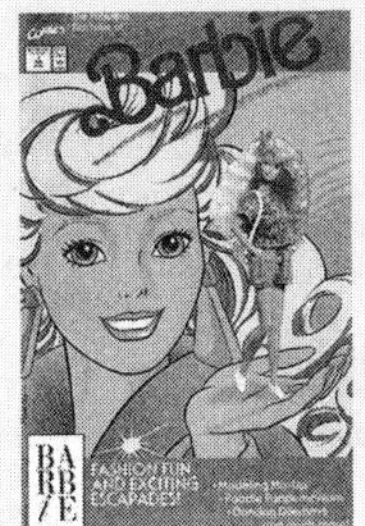

Marvel/Mattel project had many subscribers
©Marvel

Barb Wire

The comic book was better than the movie
©Dark Horse

Barney and Betty Rubble

Flintstone neighbors get their own series
©Charlton

Bartman

Adventures of Bart Simpson's alter ego
©Bongo

Baseball Superstars Comics

Unauthorized bio comics from Revolutionary
©Revolutionary

	N-MINT
❑3, Sep 1992	3.50
❑4, Oct 1992	3.00
❑5, Nov 1992	3.00
❑6, Dec 1992	3.00
❑7, Jan 1993	3.00
❑8, Feb 1993	3.00
❑9, Mar 1993	3.00

Battle Angel Alita Part 2
Viz

	N-MINT
❑1, Apr 1993	3.00
❑2, May 1993	2.75
❑3, Jun 1993	2.75
❑4, Jul 1993	2.75
❑5, Aug 1993	2.75
❑6, Sep 1993	2.75
❑7, Oct 1993	2.75

Battle Angel Alita Part 3
Viz

	N-MINT
❑1, Nov 1993	2.75
❑2, Dec 1993	2.75
❑3, Jan 1994	2.75
❑4, Feb 1994	2.75
❑5, Mar 1994	2.75
❑6, Apr 1994	2.75
❑7, May 1994	2.75
❑8, Jun 1994	2.75
❑9, Jul 1994	2.75
❑10, Aug 1994	2.75
❑11, Sep 1994	2.75
❑12, Oct 1994	2.75
❑13, Nov 1994	2.75

Battle Angel Alita Part 4
Viz

	N-MINT
❑1, Dec 1994	2.75
❑2, Jan 1995	2.75
❑3, Feb 1995	2.75
❑4, Mar 1995	2.75
❑5, Apr 1995	2.75
❑6, May 1995	2.75
❑7, Jun 1995	2.75

Battle Angel Alita Part 5
Viz

	N-MINT
❑1, Jul 1995	2.75
❑2, Aug 1995	2.75
❑3, Sep 1995	2.75
❑4, Oct 1995	2.75
❑5, Nov 1995	2.75
❑6, Dec 1995	2.75
❑7, Jan 1996	2.95

Battle Angel Alita Part 6
Viz

	N-MINT
❑1, Feb 1996	2.95
❑2, Mar 1996	2.95
❑3, Apr 1996	2.95
❑4, May 1996	2.95
❑5, Jun 1996	2.95
❑6, Jul 1996	2.95
❑7, Aug 1996	2.95
❑8, Sep 1996	2.95

Battle Angel Alita Part 7
Viz

	N-MINT
❑1, Oct 1996	2.95
❑2, Nov 1996	2.95
❑3, Dec 1996	2.95
❑4, Jan 1997	2.95
❑5, Feb 1997	2.95
❑6, Mar 1997	2.95
❑7, Apr 1997	2.95
❑8, May 1997	2.95

Battle Angel Alita Part 8
Viz

	N-MINT
❑1, Jun 1997	2.95
❑2, Jul 1997	2.95
❑3, Aug 1997	2.95
❑4, Sep 1997	2.95
❑5, Oct 1997	2.95
❑6, Nov 1997	2.95
❑7, Dec 1997	2.95
❑8, Jan 1998	2.95
❑9, Feb 1998	2.95

Battle Armor
Eternity

	N-MINT
❑1, Oct 1988	1.95
❑2, Jan 1989	1.95
❑3, Jun 1989	1.95

Battle Axe
Comics Interview

	N-MINT
❑1, b&w	2.50

Battleaxes
DC / Vertigo

	N-MINT
❑1, May 2000	2.50
❑2, Jun 2000	2.50
❑3, Jul 2000	2.50
❑4, Aug 2000	2.50

Battle Axis
Intrepid

	N-MINT
❑1, Feb 1993	2.95

Battle Beasts
Blackthorne

	N-MINT
❑1, Feb 1988	1.75
❑2, ca. 1988	1.50
❑3, ca. 1988	1.50
❑4, ca. 1988	1.75

Battle Binder Plus
Antarctic / Venus

	N-MINT
❑1, Nov 1994; Adult	2.95
❑2, Dec 1994; Adult	2.95
❑3, Jan 1995; Adult	2.95
❑4, Feb 1995; Adult	2.95
❑5, Mar 1995; Adult	2.95
❑6, Apr 1995; Final Issue; Adult	2.95

Battle Chasers
Image / Cliffhanger

	N-MINT
❑1, Apr 1998	5.00
❑1/Wraparound, Apr 1998; alternate cover, logo on back side of wraparound cover	5.00
❑1/Holochrome, Apr 1998; Limited holochrome cover (limited to 5,000 copies); Wrap-around	16.50
❑1/Gold, Apr 1998; Gold "Come on, take a peek" cover (Monika)	14.00
❑1/2nd, Apr 1998; 2nd printing	3.00
❑2, May 1998	4.00
❑2/Dynamic, May 1998; Special "omnichrome" cover from Dynamic Forces	5.00
❑2/B, May 1998; Battlechrome edition; Auto.	6.00
❑3, Jul 1998	4.00
❑4/A, Oct 1998; four alternate back covers form quadtych	2.50
❑4/B, Oct 1998; Old man on cover	2.50
❑4/C, Oct 1998; four alternate back covers form quadtych	2.50
❑4/D, Oct 1998; four alternate back covers form quadtych	2.50
❑5, May 1999	2.50
❑6, Aug 1999; Man sitting, red background on cover	2.50
❑7, Jan 2001	2.50
❑8, May 2001	2.50
❑9, Jun 2001; Flip book with bonus story	3.50
❑Ashcan 1, Aug 1998; Preview edition; 1: Battle Chasers	5.00
❑Ashcan 1/Gold, Aug 1998; Preview edition; 1: Battle Chasers. Gold logo	7.00

Battle Classics
DC

	N-MINT
❑1, Oct 1978, Reprints	4.00

Battlefield Action
Charlton

	N-MINT
❑38, Nov 1961	7.00
❑39, Dec 1961	7.00
❑40, Feb 1962	7.00
❑41, May 1962	6.00
❑42, ca. 1962	6.00
❑43, ca. 1962	6.00
❑44, ca. 1962	6.00
❑45, Jan 1963	6.00
❑46, Mar 1963	6.00
❑47, May 1963	6.00
❑48, Jul 1963	6.00
❑49, Sep 1963	6.00
❑50, Nov 1963	6.00
❑51, Jan 1964	5.00
❑52, ca. 1964	5.00
❑53, Jun 1964	5.00
❑54, ca. 1964	5.00
❑55, Nov 1964	5.00
❑56, Jan 1965	5.00
❑57, ca. 1965	5.00
❑58, Jul 1965	5.00
❑59, ca. 1965	5.00
❑60, Oct 1965	5.00
❑61, Mar 1963	5.00
❑62, Feb 1966, Last issue of 1960s run.	5.00
❑63, Jul 1980, Series begins again	2.50
❑64, Sep 1980	2.50
❑65, Nov 1980	2.50
❑66, Jan 1981	2.50
❑67, Mar 1981	2.50
❑68, Apr 1981	2.50
❑69, Jun 1981	2.50
❑70, Aug 1981	2.50
❑71, Oct 1981	2.50
❑72, Dec 1981	2.50
❑73, Feb 1982	2.50
❑74, Apr 1982	2.50
❑75, Jun 1982	2.50
❑76, Aug 1982	2.50
❑77, Oct 1982	2.50
❑78, Dec 1982	2.50
❑79, Feb 1983	2.50
❑80, Apr 1983	2.50

Other grades: Multiply price above by 5/6 for VF/NM • 2/3 for VERY FINE • 1/3 for FINE • 1/5 for VERY GOOD • 1/8 for GOOD

	N-MINT
❑81, Jun 1983	2.50
❑82, Aug 1983	2.50
❑83, Oct 1983	2.50
❑84, Dec 1983, Reprints from Foxhole #6 ("Boidie" & "Steven"), and #5 ("Stiff")	2.50
❑85, Feb 1984	2.50
❑86, May 1984	2.50
❑87, Jul 1984	2.50
❑88, Sep 1984	2.50
❑89, Nov 1984, Final Issue	2.50

Battle for a Three Dimensional World
3-D Cosmic

	N-MINT
❑1, ca. 1982, b&w; no cover price	2.50

Battleforce
Blackthorne

	N-MINT
❑1, Nov 1987	1.75
❑2, Feb 1988, b&w	1.75

Battle Girlz
Antarctic

	N-MINT
❑1, ca. 2002, b&w	2.99

Battle Gods: Warriors of the Chaak
Dark Horse

	N-MINT
❑1, Apr 2000	2.95
❑2, May 2000	2.95
❑3, Jun 2000	2.95

Battleground Earth
Best

	N-MINT
❑1, b&w	2.50
❑2, b&w	2.50

Battle Group Peiper
Tome

	N-MINT
❑1, b&w	2.95

Battle Hymn
Image

	N-MINT
❑1, ca. 2005, Different cover on both sides	2.95
❑2, ca. 2005, Different cover on both sides	2.95
❑3, Jun 2005	2.95
❑4, Sep 2005; Different cover on both sides	2.95
❑5, Jan 2006	2.95

Battle of the Planets
Gold Key / Whitman

	N-MINT
❑1, Jun 1979	20.00
❑2, Aug 1979	15.00
❑3, Oct 1979	12.00
❑4, Dec 1979	12.00
❑5, Feb 1980	12.00
❑6, Apr 1980	12.00
❑7, Oct 1980	30.00
❑8, Nov 1980	20.00
❑9, Dec 1980	20.00
❑10, Feb 1981	20.00

Battle of the Planets Artbook
Image

	N-MINT
❑1, ca. 2003	4.99

Battle of the Planets
Image

	N-MINT
❑½, Jul 2002; Black & white cover	3.00
❑½/Gold, Jul 2002; Black & white cover	5.00
❑1/A, Aug 2002; ARo (c); Alex Ross cover (25% of print run)	3.00
❑1/B, Aug 2002; Marc Silvestri cover (25% of print run)	3.00
❑1/C, Aug 2002; J. Scott Campbell cover (25% of print run)	3.00
❑1/D, Aug 2002; Michael Turner cover (25% of print run)	3.00
❑1/E, Aug 2002; ARo (c); Holofoil cover	5.95
❑1/F, Aug 2002; Wizard World 2002 Convention Edition, limited to 5,000 copies	3.00
❑1/G, Aug 2002; ARo (c); Limited to 7,000 copies; DFE red foil cover	3.00
❑1/H, Aug 2002; ARo (c); Limited to 2,000 copies; DFE blue foil cover	3.00
❑1/I, Aug 2002; ARo (c); Limited to 1,978 copies; DFE gold foil cover	3.00
❑1/J, Aug 2002; "Virgin" cover without price or logo	3.00
❑1/K, Aug 2002; Black & white cover	3.00
❑2, Sep 2002 ARo (c)	2.99
❑2/Variant, Sep 2002; Animation cover; Limited to 5,000 copies	3.00
❑2/A, Sep 2002; 2002 San Diego Convention exclusive; Limited to 1,000 copies	3.00
❑2/B, Sep 2002; "Virgin" cover without price or logo	3.00
❑3, Oct 2002 ARo (c)	2.99
❑4, Nov 2002 ARo (c)	2.99
❑5, Dec 2002	2.99
❑6, Feb 2003	2.99
❑7, Mar 2003; Cover by Alex Ross	2.99
❑7/A, Mar 2003; Retailer incentive; variant cover	5.00
❑8, Apr 2003	2.99
❑9, May 2003	2.99
❑10, Jun 2003	2.99
❑11, Jul 2003	2.99
❑12, Aug 2003	4.99

Battle of the Planets: Jason
Image

	N-MINT
❑1, Jun 2003; Preview of Tomb Raider: Epiphany	4.99

Battle of the Planets: Manga
Image

	N-MINT
❑1, Oct 2003	2.99
❑2, Nov 2003	2.99
❑3, Dec 2003	2.99

Battle of the Planets: Mark
Image

	N-MINT
❑1, May 2003	4.99

Battle of the Planets: Princess
Image

	N-MINT
❑1, Nov 2004; b&w	2.99
❑2, Dec 2004; b&w	2.99
❑3, Jan 2005; b&w	2.99
❑4, Feb 2005	2.99
❑5, Mar 2005	2.99
❑6, Apr 2005	2.99

Battle of the Planets/Thundercats
Image

	N-MINT
❑1, May 2003	4.90
❑1/A, May 2003; Alex Ross variant cover	4.90

Battle of the Planets/Witchblade
Image

	N-MINT
❑1, Feb 2003	5.95

Battle of the Ultra-Brothers
Viz

	N-MINT
❑1	4.95
❑2	4.95
❑3	4.95
❑4	4.95
❑5	4.95

Battle Pope
Funk-O-Tron

	N-MINT
❑1	5.00
❑2	4.00
❑3	4.00
❑5	2.99
❑6	2.99
❑7 2006	2.99
❑8 2006	2.99
❑9, Aug 2006	2.99
❑11, Dec 2006	4.99

BattlePope
Funk-O-Tron

	N-MINT
❑9	2.95
❑8	2.95
❑13, Oct 2002	3.50
❑12, Jun 2002	3.50
❑11, Jun 2002	3.50
❑10	4.95
❑1, Jun 2000, b&w	2.95
❑2, Jul 2000, b&w	2.95
❑3, Aug 2000, b&w	2.95
❑4, Sep 2000, b&w	2.95
❑5, Mar 2001, b&w; A.K.A. Battle Pope Shorts #1	4.95
❑6, Jun 2001, b&w; A.K.A. Battle Pope: Mayhem #1	2.95
❑7, Jul 2001, b&w; A.K.A. Battle Pope: Mayhem #2	2.95

Battle Pope Color
Image

	N-MINT
❑1, Sep 2005	2.95
❑2, Oct 2005	2.95
❑3, Nov 2005	0.00
❑6, Apr 2006	2.99
❑7, May 2006	2.99
❑8, Jul 2006	2.99
❑12, Jan 2007	3.50

Battler Britton
DC

	N-MINT
❑1, Sep 2006	2.99
❑2, Oct 2006	2.99
❑3, Nov 2006	2.99
❑4, Dec 2006	2.99
❑5, Jan 2007	2.99

Battle Royale
Tokyopop

	N-MINT
❑1, May 2003, Text novel	15.95
❑2, Jul 2003	9.99
❑3, Nov 2003	9.99
❑4, Dec 2003	9.99
❑5, Jan 2004	9.99
❑6, Mar 2004	9.99
❑7, Jun 2004	9.99
❑8, Aug 2004	9.99
❑9, Oct 2004	9.99
❑10, Dec 2004	9.99
❑11, Feb 2005	9.99
❑12, Apr 2005	9.99
❑13, Jul 2005	9.99
❑14, Nov 2005	9.99

Battlestar Galactica 1999 Tour Book
Realm

	N-MINT
❑1/A, May 1999	2.99
❑1/B, May 1999; Dynamic Forces Edition, no cover price	3.00
❑1/C, May 1999; cardstock cover version	6.99

Battlestar Galactica: Apollo's Journey
Maximum

	N-MINT
❑1, Apr 1996, Wrong year listed in indicia; came out in 1996, not 1995	2.95
❑2, Jun 1996	2.50
❑3, Jun 1996	2.95

Battlestar Galactica: Eve of Destruction Prelude
Realm

	N-MINT
❑nn, Dec 1999, Matt Busch interview	3.99

Battlestar Galactica: Journey's End
Maximum

	N-MINT
❑1, Aug 1996	2.99
❑2, Sep 1996	2.99
❑3, Oct 1996	2.99
❑4, Nov 1996	2.99

Battlestar Galactica
Marvel

	N-MINT
❑1, Mar 1979, DC (c); Pilot movie adaptation; reformatted from Marvel Super Special #8; newsstand edition (issue number appears in box)	4.00
❑1/Whitman, Mar 1979, Special markets edition (usually sold in Whitman bagged prepacks); price appears in a diamond; no UPC barcode	4.00
❑1/2nd, 20 Yahren reunion edition; DC (c); reprint	5.00
❑2, Apr 1979, DC (c); Pilot movie adaptation; reformatted from Marvel Super Special #8; newsstand edition (issue number appears in box)	3.00
❑2/Whitman, Apr 1979, Special markets edition (usually sold in Whitman bagged prepacks); price appears in a diamond; no UPC barcode	3.00
❑3, May 1979, Pilot movie adaptation; reformatted from Marvel Super Special #8; newsstand edition (issue number appears in box)	3.00
❑3/Whitman, May 1979, Special markets edition (usually sold in Whitman bagged prepacks); price appears in a diamond; no UPC barcode	3.00
❑4, Jun 1979, Adapts first hour-long episode of TV series	3.00
❑5, Jul 1979, Adapts second hour-long episode of TV series	3.00
❑6, Aug 1979, First original comics story	3.00
❑7, Sep 1979, Adama trapped in Memory Machine	3.00
❑8, Oct 1979, Young Adama on Scorpia; fill-in issue	3.00
❑9, Nov 1979	3.00
❑10, Dec 1979, PB (c); PB (a); Flashback story	3.00
❑11, Jan 1980, KJ (a)	2.00
❑12, Feb 1980, Adama leaves Memory Machine	2.00

Bastard Samurai

Character raves and rants about everything
©Image

Batgirl

Batgirl's first solo series was hot seller for a while
©DC

Bat Lash

Humorous Western adventure series from DC
©DC

Batman

Caped Crusader's title spun off from Detective
©DC

Batman Adventures

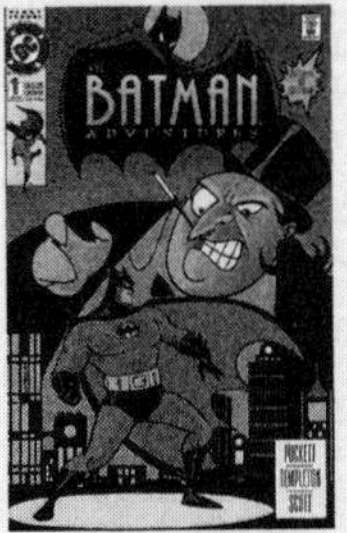

Art has the look of the Fox cartoon series
©DC

N-MINT

❑13, Mar 1980 .... 2.00
❑14, Apr 1980, Muffit Two is melted 2.00
❑15, May 1980, KJ (a); Boomer discovers Adama's wife alive 2.00
❑16, Jun 1980 .... 2.00
❑17, Jul 1980, Red "Hulks" 2.00
❑18, Aug 1980, Red "Hulks" 2.00
❑19, Sep 1980, Starbuck returns 2.00
❑20, Oct 1980 .... 2.00
❑21, Nov 1980, BA, KJ (a) 2.00
❑22, Dec 1980 .... 2.00
❑23, Jan 1981, Last issue 2.00

Battlestar Galactica (Maximum)
Maximum

❑1, Jul 1995 .... 2.50
❑2, Aug 1995 .... 2.50
❑3, Sep 1995 .... 2.50
❑4, Nov 1995 .... 2.50
❑Special 1, Jan 1997, Painted cover 2.99

Battlestar Galactica (Realm)
Realm

❑1/A, Dec 1997; Spaceships cover 2.99
❑1/B, Dec 1997; Cylons cover 2.99
❑2, Jan 1998 .... 2.99
❑3, Mar 1998 .... 2.99
❑3/Variant, Mar 1998; alternate cover (eyes in background) 2.99
❑4, Jun 1998 .... 2.99
❑5, Jul 1998 .... 2.99

Battlestar Galactica: Search for Sanctuary
Realm

❑1, Sep 1998 .... 2.99
❑Special 1, Sep 1998, 10 page Chris Scalf Gallery 3.99

Battlestar Galactica: Season III
Realm

❑1, Jun 1999 .... 2.99
❑1/A, Jun 1999; Special Convention Edition; Cover by Robert Scott and Mark L. Haynes 5.00
❑1/B, Jun 1999; Deluxe Variant; Cover by Jae Lee and Jose Villarubia; Viper Cutout on back 4.99
❑2, Jul 1999 .... 4.99
❑2/Conv, Jul 1999; Convention edition 5.00
❑3/A, Sep 1999; Marked "Special Convention Edition" on cover 5.00
❑3/B, Sep 1999; Alternate cover 2.99
❑3/Conv, Sep 1999; Convention edition 5.00

Battlestar Galactica: Starbuck
Maximum

❑1, Dec 1995 .... 2.50
❑2, Jan 1996 .... 2.50
❑3, Mar 1996 .... 2.50

Battlestar Galactica: The Compendium
Maximum

❑1, Feb 1997, b&w 2.95

Battlestar Galactica: The Enemy Within
Maximum

❑1, Nov 1995 .... 2.50
❑2, Jan 1996 .... 2.50
❑3, Feb 1996 .... 2.95
❑3/Variant, Feb 1996; alternate cover 2.95

N-MINT

Battlestone
Image

❑1 .... 2.50
❑1/A, Nov 1994 .... 2.50
❑1/B, Nov 1994, alternate cover 2.50
❑2, Dec 1994 .... 2.50

BattleTech
Malibu

❑0 .... 2.95

Battletech (Blackthorne)
Blackthorne

❑1, Oct 1997, Based on game 2.00
❑2, Feb 1988, b&w; Based on game 2.00
❑3, Apr 1988, b&w; Based on game 2.00
❑4, Jul 1988, b&w 2.00
❑5, Sep 1988, b&w; Based on game 2.00
❑6, Dec 1988, b&w; Based on game 2.00

BattleTech: Fallout
Malibu

❑1, Dec 1994 .... 2.50
❑2, Jan 1995 .... 2.95
❑3, Feb 1995 .... 2.95
❑4, Mar 1995 .... 2.95

Battletech in 3-D
Blackthorne

❑1, Apr 1988; Battletech in 3-D #1 .... 2.50

Battletide
Marvel

❑1, Dec 1992 .... 1.75
❑2, Jan 1993 .... 1.75
❑3, Feb 1993 .... 1.75
❑4, Mar 1993 .... 1.75

Battletide II
Marvel

❑1, Aug 1993; Embossed cover 2.50
❑2, Sep 1993 .... 1.75
❑3, Oct 1993 .... 1.75
❑4, Nov 1993 .... 1.75

Battle to the Death
Imperial

❑1, b&w 1.50
❑2, Nov 1987 .... 1.50
❑3 .... 1.50

Battle Vixens
Tokyopop

❑1, Apr 2004 .... 9.99

Battlezones: Dream Team 2
Malibu

❑1, Mar 1996; pin-ups of battles between Malibu and Marvel characters 3.95

Battron
NEC

❑1, b&w 2.75
❑2, b&w 2.75

Battron's 4 Queens: Guns, Babes & Intrigue
Commode

❑1 .... 3.50

Bay City Jive
DC / Wildstorm

❑1, Jul 2001 .... 2.95
❑1/A, Jul 2001, alternate cover 2.95

N-MINT

❑2, Aug 2001 .... 2.95
❑3, Sep 2001 .... 2.95

Baywatch Comic Stories
Acclaim / Armada

❑1 .... 4.95
❑2 .... 4.95
❑3 .... 4.95
❑4 .... 4.95

Bazooka Jules
Com.x

❑1, ca. 2001 .... 2.99
❑2, ca. 2001 .... 2.95

Beach High
Big

❑1, Feb 1997, illustrated text story, one-shot 3.25

Beach Party
Eternity

❑1; b&w pin-ups 2.50

Beagle Boys
Gold Key

❑1, Nov 1964 .... 22.00
❑2, Nov 1965 .... 16.00
❑3, Aug 1966 .... 16.00
❑4, Nov 1966 .... 16.00
❑5, Feb 1967 .... 16.00
❑6, May 1967 .... 12.00
❑7, ca. 1968 .... 12.00
❑8, Oct 1968 .... 12.00
❑9, Apr 1970 .... 12.00
❑10, ca. 1970 .... 12.00
❑11, ca. 1971 .... 8.00
❑12, Sep 1971 .... 8.00
❑13, Jul 1972 .... 8.00
❑14, Sep 1972 .... 8.00
❑15, ca. 1973 .... 8.00
❑16, Apr 1973, A: Uncle Scrooge 8.00
❑17, Jul 1973 .... 8.00
❑18, Oct 1973 .... 8.00
❑19, Jan 1974 .... 8.00
❑20, Apr 1974 .... 8.00
❑21, Jul 1974 .... 6.00
❑22, Oct 1974 .... 6.00
❑23, Jan 1975 .... 6.00
❑24, Apr 1975 .... 6.00
❑25, Jul 1975 .... 6.00
❑26, Oct 1975 .... 6.00
❑27, Jan 1976 .... 6.00
❑28, Mar 1976 .... 6.00
❑29, May 1976 .... 6.00
❑30, Jul 1976 .... 6.00
❑31, Sep 1976 .... 4.00
❑32, Nov 1976 .... 4.00
❑33, Jan 1977 .... 4.00
❑34, Apr 1977 .... 4.00
❑35, Jun 1977 .... 4.00
❑36, Aug 1977 .... 4.00
❑37, Sep 1977 .... 4.00
❑38, Oct 1977 .... 4.00
❑39, Dec 1977 .... 4.00
❑40, Jan 1978 .... 4.00
❑41, Apr 1978 .... 3.00
❑42, Jun 1978 .... 3.00
❑43, Aug 1978 .... 3.00

Other grades: Multiply price above by 5/6 for VF/NM • 2/3 for VERY FINE • 1/3 for FINE • 1/5 for VERY GOOD • 1/8 for GOOD

❑44, Sep 1978 3.00
❑45, Oct 1978 3.00
❑46, Dec 1978 3.00
❑47 1979 3.00

Beagle Boys vs. Uncle Scrooge
Whitman

❑1, Mar 1979 6.00
❑2, Apr 1979 5.00
❑3, May 1979 4.00
❑4, Jun 1979 4.00
❑5, Jul 1979 4.00
❑6, Aug 1979 4.00
❑7, Sep 1979 4.00
❑8, Oct 1979 3.00
❑9, Nov 1979 3.00
❑10, Dec 1979 3.00
❑11, Jan 1980 3.00
❑12, Feb 1980 3.00

Beany and Cecil
Dell

❑1, Jul 1962 75.00
❑2, Oct 1962 60.00
❑3, Jan 1963 60.00
❑4, Apr 1963 60.00
❑5, Jul 1963 60.00

Bear
Slave Labor

❑1, ca. 2003 2.95
❑2, ca. 2003 2.95
❑3, ca. 2003 2.95
❑4, ca. 2004 2.95
❑5, ca. 2004 2.95
❑6, ca. 2004 2.95
❑7 2.95
❑8 2.95
❑9, Sep 2005 2.95
❑10, Jan 2006 2.95

Bearers of the Blade Special
Image

❑1, Jul 2006 2.99

Bearfax Funnies
Treasure

❑1 2.75

Bearskin: A Grimm Tale
Thecomic.Com

❑1, b&w; no cover price 1.50

Beast
Marvel

❑1, May 1997 2.50
❑2, Jun 1997; V: Spiral, Viper 2.50
❑3, Jul 1997; V: Spiral, Viper 2.50

Beast Boy
DC

❑1, Jan 2000; O: Beast Boy 2.95
❑2, Feb 2000 2.95
❑3, Mar 2000 2.95
❑4, Apr 2000; V: Gemini 2.95

B.E.A.S.T.I.E.S.
Axis

❑1, Apr 1994 2.00

Beast Warriors of Shaolin
Pied Piper

❑1, Jul 1987 1.95
❑2 1.95
❑3 1.95

Beatles
Dell

❑1, Sep 1964 440.00

Beatles Experience
Revolutionary

❑1, Mar 1991 2.50
❑2, May 1991 2.50
❑3, Jul 1991 2.50
❑4, Sep 1991 2.50
❑5, Nov 1991 2.50
❑6, Jan 1992 2.50
❑7, Mar 1992 2.50
❑8, May 1992 2.50

Beatles (Personality)
Personality

❑1, b&w 5.00
❑1/Ltd.; limited edition, b&w 8.00
❑2, b&w 4.00

Beatles vs. The Rolling Stones
Celebrity

❑1, May 1992 2.95

Beatrix
Vision

❑1 2.95
❑2, Mar 1997 2.95

Beauties & Barbarians
AC

❑1 WW (a) 1.50

Beautiful People
Slave Labor

❑1, Apr 1994; Oversized; NN 4.50

Beautiful Stories for Ugly Children
DC / Piranha

❑1, ca. 1989 2.50
❑2, ca. 1989 2.50
❑3, ca. 1989 2.50
❑4, ca. 1989 2.50
❑5, ca. 1989 2.50
❑6, ca. 1989 2.50
❑7, ca. 1989 2.50
❑8, ca. 1990 2.50
❑9, ca. 1990 2.50
❑10, ca. 1990 2.50
❑11, ca. 1990 2.50
❑12, ca. 1990 2.50
❑13, ca. 1990 2.50
❑14, ca. 1990 2.50
❑15, ca. 1990 2.50
❑16, ca. 1990 2.50
❑17, ca. 1990 2.50
❑18, ca. 1990 2.50
❑19, ca. 1991 2.50
❑20, ca. 1991 2.50
❑21, ca. 1991 2.50
❑22, ca. 1991 2.50
❑23, ca. 1991 2.50
❑24, ca. 1992 2.50
❑25, ca. 1992 2.50
❑26, ca. 1992 2.50
❑27, ca. 1992 2.50
❑28, ca. 1992 2.50
❑29, ca. 1992 2.50
❑30, ca. 1992; Final issue 2.50

Beauty and the Beast
Disney

❑1; NN; Movie adaptation 2.50
❑1/Direct ed.; squarebound 4.95

Beauty and the Beast (Disney's...)
Disney

❑1, Sep 1994 1.50
❑2, Oct 1994 1.50
❑3, Nov 1994 1.50
❑4, Dec 1994 1.50
❑5, Jan 1995 1.50
❑6, Feb 1995 1.50
❑7, Mar 1995 1.50
❑8, Apr 1995 1.50
❑9, May 1995 1.50
❑10, Jun 1995 1.50
❑11, Jul 1995 1.50
❑12, Aug 1995 1.50
❑13, Sep 1995 1.50
❑Holiday 1; digest; based on direct-to-video feature 4.50

Beauty and the Beast
Innovation

❑1, May 1993 2.50
❑1/CS, Includes poster 3.95
❑2, Jun 1993 2.50
❑3, Jul 1993 2.50
❑4, Aug 1993 2.50
❑5, Sep 1993 2.50
❑6, Oct 1993, indicia says Jul, should be Oct 2.50

Beauty and the Beast
Marvel

❑1, Dec 1984; BSz (c); DP (a); Beast and Dazzler 2.50
❑2, Feb 1985; BSz (c); DP (a); Beast and Dazzler 2.00
❑3, Apr 1985; BSz (c); DP (a); Beast and Dazzler 2.00
❑4, Jun 1985; BSz (c); DP (a); Beast and Dazzler 2.00

Beauty and the Beast: Night of Beauty
First

❑1, Mar 1990 5.95

Beauty and the Beast: Portrait of Love
First

❑1, May 1989 5.95

Beauty and the Beast (Stan Shaw's...)
Dark Horse

❑1; NN 4.95

Beauty Is the Beast
Viz

❑1, Dec 2005 8.99

Beauty of the Beasts
Mu

❑1, Nov 1991, b&w 2.50
❑2, May 1992, b&w 2.50
❑3, Jul 1993 2.50

Beavis & Butt-Head
Marvel

❑1, Mar 1994; 1: Beavis & Butt-Head (in comics). A: Punisher 2.50
❑1/2nd, Mar 1994; 2nd printing 1.95
❑2, Apr 1994 2.50
❑3, May 1994 JR (a) 2.50
❑4, Jun 1994 2.50
❑5, Jul 1994 2.50
❑6, Aug 1994 2.00
❑7, Sep 1994 2.00
❑8, Oct 1994 2.00
❑9, Nov 1994 2.00
❑10, Dec 1994 2.00
❑11, Jan 1995 2.00
❑12, Feb 1995 2.00
❑13, Mar 1995 2.00
❑14, Apr 1995 2.00
❑15, May 1995 2.00
❑16, Jun 1995 2.00
❑17, Jul 1995 2.00
❑18, Aug 1995 2.00
❑19, Sep 1995 2.00
❑20, Oct 1995 2.00
❑21, Nov 1995 2.00
❑22, Dec 1995 2.00
❑23, Jan 1996 2.00
❑24, Feb 1996 2.00
❑25, Mar 1996 2.00
❑26, Apr 1996 2.00
❑27, May 1996 2.00
❑28, Jun 1996; Final Issue 2.00

Beck & Caul Investigations
Caliber

❑1, Jan 1994; O: Caul (Mercedes Guillane) 2.95
❑2, Mar 1994 2.95
❑3, May 1994 2.95
❑4, Aug 1994 2.95
❑5 2.95
❑Ann 1, May 1995 3.50

Beck: Mongolian Chop Squad
Tokyopop

❑1, Jul 2005 9.99
❑2, Nov 2005 9.99

Bedlam
Image

❑1, Sep 2006 4.99

Bedlam!
Eclipse

❑1, Aug 1985 1.75
❑2, Sep 1985 1.75

Bedlam (Chaos)
Chaos

❑1, Sep 2000 2.95
❑1/Variant, Sep 2000; Premium cover by David Michael Beck 2.95

Beelzelvis
Slave Labor

❑1, Feb 1994 2.95

Beep Beep Road Runner
Gold Key

❑1, Oct 1966 50.00
❑2, Jan 1967 30.00
❑3, Apr 1967 30.00

Other grades: Multiply price above by 5/6 for VF/NM • 2/3 for VERY FINE • 1/3 for FINE • 1/5 for VERY GOOD • 1/8 for GOOD

Batman Adventures, The: Mad Love

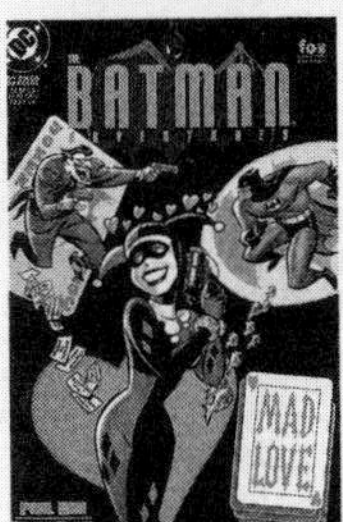

Critically acclaimed Harley Quinn story

©DC

Batman/Aliens II

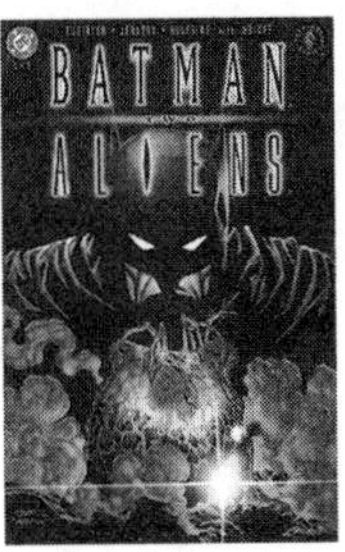

Second crossover for these franchises

©DC-Dark Horse

Batman and Robin Adventures, The

Younger-reader Batman series adds sidekick

©DC

Batman and Superman: World's Finest

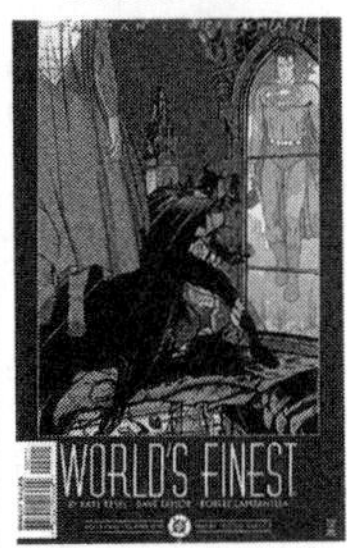

Prestige format series reteaming heroes

©DC

Batman and the Outsiders

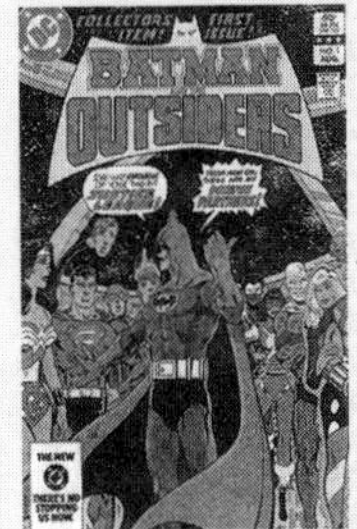

Batman team-up series with hard-luck bunch

©DC

	N-MINT
❑4, Jul 1967	30.00
❑5, Oct 1967	30.00
❑6, Jan 1968	15.00
❑7, Apr 1968	15.00
❑8, Jul 1968	15.00
❑9, Oct 1968	15.00
❑10, Feb 1969	15.00
❑11, Apr 1969	15.00
❑12, Jun 1969	15.00
❑13, Aug 1969	15.00
❑14, Oct 1969	15.00
❑15, Dec 1969	15.00
❑16, Feb 1970	10.00
❑17, Apr 1970	10.00
❑18, Jun 1970, Cover code 10189-006	10.00
❑19, Aug 1970, Poster inserted	10.00
❑20, Oct 1970	10.00
❑21, Dec 1970	10.00
❑22, Feb 1971	10.00
❑23, Apr 1971, Cover code 10189-104	10.00
❑24, Jun 1971	10.00
❑25, Aug 1971	10.00
❑26, Oct 1971	10.00
❑27, Dec 1971	10.00
❑28, Feb 1972	10.00
❑29, Apr 1972	10.00
❑30, Jun 1972	10.00
❑31, Aug 1972	10.00
❑32, Oct 1972	10.00
❑33, Dec 1972	10.00
❑34, Feb 1973	10.00
❑35, Apr 1973, Cover code 90189-304; Wile's triplet nephews appear	10.00
❑36, Jun 1973	10.00
❑37, Aug 1973	10.00
❑38, Sep 1973	10.00
❑39, Oct 1973	10.00
❑40, Dec 1973	10.00
❑41, Feb 1974	8.00
❑42, Apr 1974	8.00
❑43, Jun 1974	8.00
❑44, Aug 1974	8.00
❑45, Sep 1974	8.00
❑46, Oct 1974	8.00
❑47, Dec 1974	8.00
❑48, Feb 1975	8.00
❑49, Apr 1975	8.00
❑50, Jun 1975	8.00
❑51, Jul 1975	8.00
❑52, Aug 1975	8.00
❑53, Oct 1975	8.00
❑54, Dec 1975	8.00
❑55, Jan 1976	8.00
❑56, Mar 1976	8.00
❑57, May 1976	8.00
❑58, Jul 1976	8.00
❑59, Sep 1976	8.00
❑60, Oct 1976	6.00
❑61, Nov 1976	6.00
❑62, Jan 1977	6.00
❑63, Mar 1977	6.00
❑64, May 1977	6.00
❑65, Jul 1977	6.00
❑66, Sep 1977	6.00
❑67, Oct 1977	6.00
❑68, Nov 1977, Includes Spider-Man Hostess ad "Break the Bank" by Buscema unpublished in Marvel Comics	6.00
❑69, Jan 1978	6.00
❑70, Mar 1978	6.00
❑71, May 1978	6.00
❑72, Jul 1978	6.00
❑73, Sep 1978	6.00
❑74, Oct 1978	6.00
❑75, Nov 1978	6.00
❑76, Jan 1979	6.00
❑77, Mar 1979	6.00
❑78, Apr 1979	6.00
❑79, May 1979	6.00
❑80, Jun 1979	3.00
❑81, Jul 1979	3.00
❑82, Aug 1979	3.00
❑83, Sep 1979	3.00
❑84, Oct 1979	3.00
❑85, Nov 1979	3.00
❑86, Dec 1979	3.00
❑87, Jan 1980	3.00
❑88, Feb 1980	3.00
❑89, Apr 1980	3.00
❑90, Jul 1980	3.00
❑91, Aug 1980	12.00
❑92, Sep 1980	12.00
❑93, Oct 1980	17.00
❑94, Feb 1981	3.00
❑95 1981	3.00
❑96 1981	3.00
❑97, Sep 1981	3.00
❑98 1981	3.00
❑99 1981	3.00
❑100 1982	3.00
❑101, Apr 1982	3.00
❑102, Jun 1983	12.00
❑103, Jul 1983	12.00
❑104, ca. 1983	12.00
❑105, Jun 1984	12.00

Beer & Roaming in Las Vegas
Slave Labor

	N-MINT
❑1, ca. 1998, b&w	2.95
❑Ashcan 1	1.00

Beer Nutz
Tundra

	N-MINT
❑1	2.95
❑2	2.00
❑3, b&w	2.25

Beethoven
Harvey

	N-MINT
❑1, Mar 1994	1.50
❑2, May 1994	1.50
❑3, Jul 1994	1.50

Beetle Bailey
Dell

	N-MINT
❑35, Nov 1961	10.00
❑36, Jan 1962	10.00
❑37, Mar 1962	10.00
❑38, May 1962	10.00
❑39, Nov 1962	10.00
❑40, Feb 1963	10.00
❑41, May 1963	8.00
❑42, Aug 1963	8.00
❑43, Nov 1963	8.00
❑44, Feb 1964	8.00
❑45, May 1964	8.00
❑46, Aug 1964	8.00
❑47, Nov 1964	8.00
❑48, Feb 1965	8.00
❑49, May 1965	8.00
❑50, Aug 1965	8.00
❑51, Nov 1965	7.00
❑52, Feb 1966	7.00
❑53, May 1966, Last Dell/Gold Key issue	7.00
❑54, Aug 1966, First King issue	7.00
❑55, Oct 1966	7.00
❑56, Dec 1966	7.00
❑57, Feb 1967	7.00
❑58, Apr 1967	7.00
❑59, Jun 1967	7.00
❑60, Jul 1967	7.00
❑61, Aug 1967	6.00
❑62, Sep 1967	6.00
❑63 1968	6.00
❑64 1968	6.00
❑65 1968	6.00
❑66 1968, Last King issue	6.00
❑67, Feb 1969, First Charlton issue	6.00
❑68, Apr 1969	6.00
❑69, Jun 1969	6.00
❑70, Aug 1969; ca. 1969	6.00
❑71, Oct 1969	4.00
❑72, Nov 1969	4.00
❑73, Jan 1970	4.00
❑74, Mar 1970	4.00
❑75, May 1970	4.00
❑76, Jul 1970	4.00
❑77, Sep 1970	4.00
❑78, Nov 1970	4.00
❑79, Jan 1971	4.00
❑80, Mar 1971	4.00
❑81, May 1971	4.00
❑82, Jul 1971	4.00
❑83, Sep 1971	4.00
❑84, Oct 1971	4.00
❑85, Nov 1971	4.00
❑86, Dec 1971	4.00
❑87, Jan 1972	4.00
❑88, Mar 1972	4.00
❑89, Apr 1972	4.00
❑90, Jun 1972	4.00
❑91, Jul 1972	4.00
❑92, Aug 1972	4.00
❑93, Oct 1972	4.00
❑94, Nov 1972	4.00
❑95, Dec 1972	4.00
❑96, Jan 1973	4.00
❑97, Mar 1973	4.00
❑98, Apr 1973	4.00
❑99, Jun 1973	4.00
❑100, Jul 1973	4.00
❑101, Aug 1973	3.00
❑102, Oct 1973	3.00
❑103, Nov 1973	3.00
❑104, Jan 1974	3.00
❑105, May 1974	3.00
❑106, Jul 1974	3.00
❑107, Oct 1974	3.00
❑108, Dec 1974	3.00

Other grades: Multiply price above by 5/6 for VF/NM • 2/3 for VERY FINE • 1/3 for FINE • 1/5 for VERY GOOD • 1/8 for GOOD

	N-MINT
❑109 1975	3.00
❑110, Apr 1975	3.00
❑111, Jun 1975	3.00
❑112, Sep 1975	3.00
❑113 1975	3.00
❑114 1976	3.00
❑115, Mar 1976	3.00
❑116, May 1976	3.00
❑117, Jul 1976	3.00
❑118, Sep 1976	3.00
❑119, Nov 1976; Last Charlton issue	3.00
❑120, Apr 1978, Returns to Gold Key	3.00
❑121, Jun 1978, Gold Key	3.00
❑122, Aug 1978	3.00
❑123, Oct 1978	3.00
❑124, Dec 1978	3.00
❑125, Feb 1979	3.00
❑126, Apr 1979	3.00
❑127, Jun 1979	3.00
❑128, Aug 1979	3.00
❑129, Oct 1979	3.00
❑130, Dec 1979	3.00
❑131, Feb 1980	3.00
❑132, Apr 1980; Final Issue	3.00

Beetle Bailey
Harvey

❑1, Sep 1992	2.00
❑2, Jan 1993	2.00
❑3, Apr 1993	2.00
❑4, Jul 1993	2.00
❑5, Oct 1993	2.00
❑6, Jan 1994	2.00
❑7, Apr 1994	2.00
❑8, Jun 1994	2.00
❑9, Aug 1994, Final Issue	2.00
❑GS 1, Oct 1992, Giant-size	2.25
❑GS 2, Mar 1993, Giant-size	2.25

Beetle Bailey Big Book
Harvey

❑2, May 1993	2.00

Beetlejuice
Harvey

❑1, Oct 1991	1.50
❑2	1.50

Beetlejuice: Elliot Mess and the Unwashables
Harvey

❑1, Sep 1992, Indicia lists #1 as "Beetlejuice: Crimebusters on the Haunt"	1.50
❑2, Oct 1992	1.50
❑3, Nov 1992	1.50

Beetlejuice Holiday Special
Harvey

❑1, Feb 1992	1.50

Beetlejuice in the Neitherworld
Harvey

❑1, Nov 1991	1.50
❑2	1.50

Beet the Vandel Buster
Viz

❑1, Oct 2004	7.99
❑2, Dec 2004	7.99
❑3, Feb 2005	7.99
❑4, Apr 2005	7.99
❑5, May 2005	7.99
❑6, Aug 2005	7.99
❑7, Oct 2005	7.99

Before the Fantastic Four: Ben Grimm and Logan
Marvel

❑1, Jul 2000	2.99
❑2, Aug 2000	2.99
❑3, Sep 2000	2.99

Before the FF: Reed Richards
Marvel

❑1, Sep 2000	2.99
❑2, Oct 2000	2.99
❑3, Dec 2000, Final issue	2.99

Before the FF: The Storms
Marvel

❑1, Dec 2000	2.99
❑2, Jan 2001	2.99
❑3, Feb 2001	2.99

Behold 3-D
Edge Group

	N-MINT
❑1; 3-D glasses inserted	3.95

Believe in Yourself Productions
Believe in Yourself Productions

❑1/Ashcan; Ashcan Edition. Cardstock cover. Includes 6 page story only available in Ashcan format with 14 pin-u; Cardstock cover	1.00
❑1/B; Sapphire Edition. Only 25 made	1.00
❑1/Ltd.; Limited, signed numbered edition. 1000 made	1.00

Bella Donna
Pinnacle

❑1, b&w	1.75

Belly Button
Fantagraphics

❑1, Oct 2004	4.95
❑2, Dec 2004	4.95

Ben Casey Film Stories
Gold Key

❑1, ca. 1962	55.00

Beneath the Planet of the Apes
Gold Key

❑1, Dec 1970, Photo cover; Includes poster	35.00

Benzango Obscuro
Starhead

❑1	2.75

Benzine
Antarctic

❑1, Oct 2000	4.95
❑2, Nov 2000	4.95
❑3, Dec 2000	4.95
❑4, Jan 2001	4.95
❑5, Feb 2001	4.95
❑6, Mar 2001	4.95
❑7, May 2001	4.95

Beowulf
DC

❑1, May 1975; 1: Grendel (monster). 1: Beowulf	5.00
❑2, Jul 1975	3.00
❑3, Sep 1975	1.50
❑4, Nov 1975	1.50
❑5, Jan 1976	1.50
❑6, Mar 1976; Final Issue	1.50

Beowulf (TheComic.Com)
Comic.Com

❑1, ca. 1999	4.95
❑2 1999	4.95
❑3 1999	4.95

Beowulf (Speakeasy)
Speakeasy Comics

❑1, Apr 2005	2.99
❑2, May 2005	2.99
❑3, Sep 2005	2.99
❑4, Oct 2005	2.99

Berlin
Drawn & Quarterly

❑1, Apr 1996	2.50
❑2, Jul 1996	2.50
❑3, Feb 1997	2.50
❑4, Feb 1998	2.50
❑5, ca. 1998	2.95
❑6, ca. 1999	2.95
❑7, Apr 2000, b&w; smaller than normal comic book	2.95
❑8, b&w	2.95
❑9	0.00
❑10 2003	3.50
❑11 2005	3.95
❑12, Dec 2005	3.95

Bernie Wrightson, Master of the Macabre
Pacific

❑1, Jun 1983; BWr (w); BWr (a); Edgar Allen Poe adaptation ("The Black Cat")	2.50
❑2, Aug 1983 BWr (w); BWr (a)	2.50
❑3, Aug 1983 BWr (w); BWr (a)	2.50
❑4, Aug 1984 BWr (w); BWr (a)	2.50
❑5, Nov 1984; BWr (w); BWr (a); Final Issue	2.50

Berserk
Dark Horse

	N-MINT
❑1, ca. 2003; Reads right to left; b&w; ca. 2004	13.95
❑2, ca. 2004; Graphic novel; Reads right to left; b&w	13.95
❑3, ca. 2004; 0	13.95

Berzerker
Gauntlet

❑1, Feb 1993; Medina	2.95
❑2	2.95
❑3	2.95
❑4	2.95
❑5	2.95

Berzerkers
Image

❑1, Aug 1995	2.50
❑1/Variant, Aug 1995; alternate cover	2.50
❑2, Sep 1995	2.50
❑3, Oct 1995	2.50

Best Cellars
Out of the Cellar

❑1; Adult	2.50

Best of Barron Storey's W.A.T.C.H. Magazine
Vanguard

❑1, Dec 1993	2.95

Best of Dark Horse Presents
Dark Horse

❑1, b&w; Reprints	5.95
❑2, Jan 1989, b&w; Reprints	8.95

Best of DC
DC

❑1, Sep 1979; JO, DG, RA (c); MA, CS, KS (a); Superman	5.00
❑2, Nov 1979; NA (a); Batman	4.00
❑3, Jan 1980; JO, JL (c);Super Friends .	4.00
❑4, Mar 1980	4.00
❑5, May 1980, DG, RA (c); DN, JSa, CS, JL, KS, DA, JAb (a); Year's Best Comics Stories 1979	4.00
❑6, Jul 1980, DG, RA (c); CS, KS (a); Daily Planet	4.00
❑7, Sep 1980, DG, RA (c); FR (w); MA, CS (a); Superboy	4.00
❑8, Nov 1980; DG, RA (c); MA, CS (a); Superman, Other Identities	4.00
❑9, Jan 1981; JA (c); FR (w); DG, JA, IN (a); Batman: Bat-Murderer	4.00
❑10, Mar 1981; DG, RA (c); MA, CI, JKu, GK, NC, RT (a); O: Penguin; O: Ocean-Master; O: Captain Boomerang; O: Shark; O: Shadow-Thief; O: Red Dart; O: Parasite; Secret Origins of Super-Villains	4.00
❑11, Apr 1981 DG, RA (c); DG, CS, TVE, DS, JL (a)	4.00
❑12, May 1981; DG, RA (c); MA, CS (a); Superman	4.00
❑13, Jun 1981; DG, RA (c); DD, CS (a); DC Comics Presents	4.00
❑14, Jul 1981, DG, RA (c); DG, NA, MR, IN (a); Batman's Villains	4.00
❑15, Aug 1981; DG, RA (c); MA, WW (a); Superboy	4.00
❑16, Sep 1981, RB, DG (c); NA, CS (a); Superman Anniversaries	4.00
❑17, Oct 1981 DG (c); BO, TD, JM (a)	4.00
❑18, Nov 1981, GP, RT (c); NA (w); CI, NA, GK, NC, RT (a); New Teen Titans	4.00
❑19, Dec 1981; DG, RA (c); BO, CS, KS, JAb (a); Superman, Imaginary Stories	4.00
❑20, Jan 1982; DG, RA (c); DD (a); World's Finest Comics	4.00
❑21, Feb 1982; GP (c); MA, BL, JSa (a); Justice Society	4.00
❑22, Mar 1982, RB, GP, DG (c); DG, JK, DD, NC, IN (a); Sandman	4.00
❑23, Apr 1982, DG (c); DN, FMc, GP, DG, JSa, CS, DS, DA, RT (a); Year's Best Comics Stories 1981	4.00
❑24, May 1982; EC (c); CI, GP, GT, CS, JAb (a); Legion	4.00
❑25, Jun 1982, RA (c); BO, MA, NA, CS (a)	4.00
❑26, Jul 1982; JA (c); JKu, NA, TVE, RA, RH, JA, IN (a); Brave and the Bold	4.00
❑27, Aug 1982; DG, RA (c); BO, MA, CS, KS, JAb (a); Superman vs. Luthor	4.00
❑28, Sep 1982; BO (c); Binky's Summer Fun	4.00

Other grades: Multiply price above by 5/6 for VF/NM • 2/3 for VERY FINE • 1/3 for FINE • 1/5 for VERY GOOD • 1/8 for GOOD

Batman: Bane of the Demon

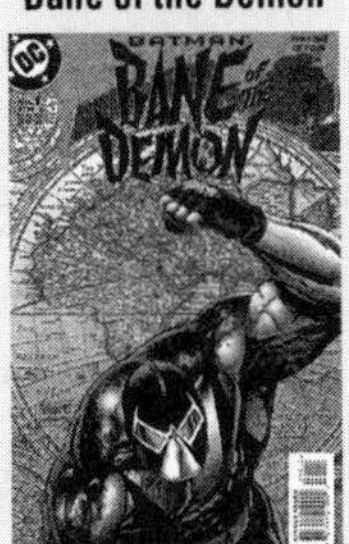

Bane goes on a journey to learn his origins

©DC

Batman Beyond

Another series kicked off by a cartoon

©DC

Batman Black and White

Anthology series published in black and white

©DC

Batman Chronicles

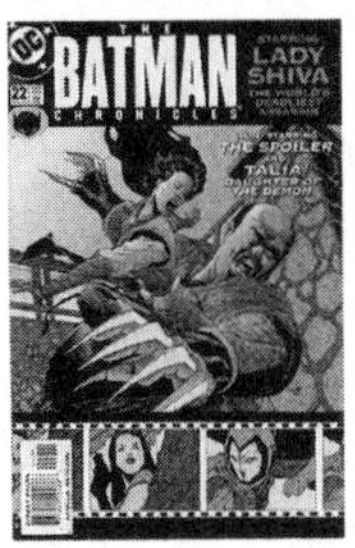

Quarterly filled "13th week" gap in Bat-titles

©DC

Batman: Dark Victory

Sequel to Batman: The Long Halloween

©DC

	N-MINT
❑29, Oct 1982; Sugar & Spike	4.00
❑30, Nov 1982, JA (c); FR (w); CI, FR, DG, GK, IN, RMo (a); Batman	4.00
❑31, Dec 1982, GK (c); DD (a); Justice League	4.00
❑32, Jan 1983, RB (c); CS (a); Superman	4.00
❑33, Feb 1983, KG (c); GT, MGr, DC (a); Origins of the Legion	4.00
❑34, Mar 1983, Metal Men	4.00
❑35, Apr 1983, Year's Best 82	4.00
❑36, May 1983; Superman vs. Kryptonite	4.00
❑37, Jun 1983; Funny Stuff	4.00
❑38, Jul 1983; Superman vs supernatural	4.00
❑39, Aug 1983; Binky and his Buddies	4.00
❑40, Sep 1983; Superman, Krypton	4.00
❑41, Oct 1983; Sugar and Spike	4.00
❑42, Nov 1983; Superman vs aliens	4.00
❑43, Dec 1983; Funny Stuff	4.00
❑44, Jan 1984, GK, KS (c); KG, KS (a); Legion	4.00
❑45, Feb 1984; Binky	4.00
❑46, Mar 1984; Jimmy Olsen	4.00
❑47, Apr 1984; Sugar and Spike	4.00
❑48, May 1984; Superman Team-Up	4.00
❑49, Jun 1984; Reprints stories from Funny Stuff# 67, 74, Funny Stuff, Peter Porkchops #24, Peter Panda #17, Comic Cavalcade #58, Stanley and His Moster #112, Thee Mouseketeers #3; A Place to Sleep, The Wishing Bean, Swap Shop, Art Smart, The Big Fight, and The Frog War all untitled when originally printed (titles added for this reprint collection)	4.00
❑50, Jul 1984; Superman	4.00
❑51, Aug 1984; Reprints Batman Family #11 - 13, #17, #20; Batman Family; Batman #232, #237	4.00
❑52, Sep 1984; Year's Best 83	4.00
❑53, Oct 1984; Reprints storys from Binky #78, 80; Binky's Buddies; Debbi #7, 14-16; Date With Debbi #5; Swing With Scooter #28-29, 34-35	4.00
❑54, Nov 1984; Superman vs. weird villains	4.00
❑55, Dec 1984; Funny Stuff	4.00
❑56, Jan 1985; Superman	4.00
❑57, Feb 1985; Legion	4.00
❑58, Mar 1985; Superman Jrs	4.00
❑59, Apr 1985; Superman	4.00
❑60, May 1985; Plop; (House of Mystery #202)	4.00
❑61, Jun 1985; Year's Best Comics Stories	4.00
❑62, Jul 1985; Batman	4.00
❑63, Aug 1985, WW (c); SA (w); SA, SD, BWr, BW, AA, WW, NC (a); Plop	4.00
❑64, Sep 1985; Legion	4.00
❑65, Oct 1985; Sugar & Spike	4.00
❑66, Nov 1985; Superman	4.00
❑67, Dec 1985; The Legion of Super-Heroes (Adventure #335); Spread throughout book; (Adventure #336); (Superboy #124); (Adventure #337); (Adventure #338); (Superboy #125); (Adventure #339)	4.00
❑68, Jan 1986; Sugar & Spike	4.00
❑69, Feb 1986; Year's Best 85	4.00
❑70, Mar 1986; Binky's Buddies	4.00

Best of Donald Duck and Uncle Scrooge
Gold Key

	N-MINT
❑1, Nov 1964, Reprints stories from Four Color Comics #189 and 408 (Donald Duck)	50.00
❑2, Sep 1967, CB (a); Reprints stories from Four Color Comics #256 (Donald Duck) and Uncle Scrooge #7 and 8	50.00

Best of Dork Tower
Dork Storm

	N-MINT
❑1, ca. 2001, b&w	2.00

Best of Furrlough
Antarctic

	N-MINT
❑1, Jan 1995, b&w	3.95
❑2, Jan 1996	3.95

Best of Gold Digger
Antarctic

	N-MINT
❑Ann 1, May 1999, b&w	2.99

Best of Northstar
Northstar

	N-MINT
❑1, b&w; Adult	1.95

Best of the Brave and the Bold
DC

	N-MINT
❑1, Oct 1988, Batman, Green Arrow	2.50
❑2, Nov 1988, Batman, Flash	2.50
❑3, Dec 1988, Batman, Aquaman	2.50
❑4, Dec 1988, Batman, Creeper	2.50
❑5, Jan 1989, Batman, House of Mystery	2.50
❑6, Jan 1989, Batman, Teen Titans	2.50

Best of the British Invasion
Revolutionary

	N-MINT
❑1, Sep 1993, b&w	2.50
❑2, Jan 1994, b&w	2.50

Best of the West (AC)
AC

	N-MINT
❑1, b&w	6.95
❑2, b&w	4.95
❑3, b&w	4.95
❑4, b&w	5.95
❑5, b&w	5.95
❑6, b&w	5.95
❑7, b&w	5.95
❑8, b&w	5.95
❑9, b&w	5.95
❑10, b&w	5.95
❑11, b&w	5.95
❑12, b&w	5.95
❑13, b&w	5.95
❑14, b&w	5.95
❑15, b&w	5.95
❑16, b&w	5.95
❑17, b&w	5.95
❑18, b&w	5.95
❑19, b&w	5.95
❑20, b&w	5.95
❑21, b&w	5.95
❑22, b&w	5.95
❑23, b&w	5.95
❑24, b&w	5.95
❑25, b&w; ca. 2002	5.95
❑26, b&w	5.95
❑27, b&w	5.95
❑28, b&w	5.95
❑29, b&w	5.95
❑30, b&w	5.95
❑31, b&w	5.95
❑32, b&w	5.95
❑33, b&w	6.95
❑34, b&w	6.95
❑35, b&w	6.95
❑36, b&w	6.95
❑37, b&w	6.95
❑38, b&w	6.95
❑39, b&w	6.95
❑40, b&w	6.95
❑41, b&w	6.95
❑42, b&w	6.95
❑43, b&w	6.95
❑44, b&w	6.95
❑45, Reprints Durango Kid #33; Ghost Rider (Magazine Enterprises) #4; b&w	6.95
❑46, b&w	6.95
❑47, ca. 2005; b&w	6.95
❑48, ca. 2005; b&w	6.95
❑49, ca. 2005; b&w	6.95
❑50, ca. 2005; b&w	6.95
❑51, ca. 2005; b&w	6.95
❑52, ca. 2005	6.95
❑53, ca. 2005; Reprints from Durango Kid #2, Rocky Lane #46, Ghost Rider #14, Whiz Comics	6.95
❑54, Reprints material from Redmast #46, Prize Western, Rocky Lane Western #46, and Black Diamond Western; b&w	6.95
❑55, Collects stories from Tim Holt #27, Ghost Rider #13, Rocky Lane Western, Master Comics #110; ca. 2006	6.95
❑56, ca. 2006	6.95
❑57, Includes reprints from Durango Kid #19, Redmask #50, Latigo Kid #2, and Me's Dan'l Boone #4; ca. 2006	6.95
❑58, ca. 2006	6.95
❑59, Monte Hale tribute issue	6.95
❑60, b&w; ca. 2007	6.95
❑61, b&w; ca. 2007	6.95
❑62, b&w; ca. 2007	6.95
❑63, b&w; ca. 2007	6.95
❑64, b&w; ca. 2007	6.95

Best of Tribune Co.
Dragon Lady

	N-MINT
❑1	2.95
❑2, Oct 1985; Dick Tracy	2.95
❑3	2.95
❑4; (becomes Thrilling Adventure Strips)	2.95

Best of Uncle Scrooge & Donald Duck
Gold Key

	N-MINT
❑1, Nov 1968; reprints parts of Four Color #159 and #456 and Uncle Scrooge #6 and #7	45.00

Best of Walt Disney Comics
Western

	N-MINT
❑1, ca. 1974; 96170; Reprints stories from Four Color Comics #62 (Donald Duck)	15.00
❑2, ca. 1974; 96171	12.00
❑3, ca. 1974; 96172; Reprints stories from Four Color Comics #386 and 495 (Uncle Scrooge) and Uncle Scrooge #7	12.00
❑4, ca. 1974; 96173; Reprints stories from Four Color Comics #159 and 178 (Donald Duck)	12.00

Other grades: Multiply price above by 5/6 for VF/NM • 2/3 for VERY FINE • 1/3 for FINE • 1/5 for VERY GOOD • 1/8 for GOOD

N-MINT N-MINT N-MINT

Beta Sexus
Fantagraphics / Eros

❏1, b&w; Adult 2.75
❏2, Jul 1994, b&w; Adult 2.75

Betta: Time Warrior
Immortal / Eros

❏1 .... 2.95
❏2 .... 2.95
❏3 .... 2.95

Betti Cozmo
Antarctic

❏1, Apr 1999 .... 2.99
❏2, Jun 1999 .... 2.99

Bettie Page Comics
Dark Horse

❏1, Mar 1996; one-shot, cardstock cover 3.95

Bettie Page Comics: Spicy Adventure
Dark Horse

❏1, Jan 1997; NN; One-shot 2.95

Bettie Page: Queen of the Nile
Dark Horse

❏1, Dec 1999 .... 2.95
❏2, Feb 2000 .... 2.95
❏3, Apr 2000 .... 2.95

Betty
Archie

❏1, Sep 1992 .... 4.00
❏2, Oct 1992 .... 2.00
❏3, Dec 1992 .... 2.00
❏4, Feb 1993 .... 2.00
❏5, Apr 1993 .... 2.00
❏6, Jun 1993 .... 1.50
❏7, Aug 1993 .... 1.50
❏8, Sep 1993 .... 1.50
❏9, Oct 1993 .... 1.50
❏10, Nov 1993 .... 1.50
❏11, Dec 1993 .... 1.50
❏12, Feb 1994 .... 1.50
❏13, Apr 1994 .... 1.50
❏14, Jun 1994 .... 1.50
❏15, Jul 1994 .... 1.50
❏16, Aug 1994 .... 1.50
❏17, Sep 1994 .... 1.50
❏18, Oct 1994 .... 1.50
❏19, Nov 1994 .... 1.50
❏20, Dec 1994 .... 1.50
❏21, Jan 1995 .... 1.50
❏22, Feb 1995 .... 1.50
❏23, Mar 1995 .... 1.50
❏24, Apr 1995 .... 1.50
❏25, May 1995 .... 1.50
❏26, Jun 1995 .... 1.50
❏27, Jul 1995 .... 1.50
❏28, Aug 1995 .... 1.50
❏29, Sep 1995 .... 1.50
❏30, Oct 1995 .... 1.50
❏31, Nov 1995 .... 1.50
❏32, Dec 1995 .... 1.50
❏33, Jan 1996 .... 1.50
❏34, Feb 1996 .... 1.50
❏35, Mar 1996 .... 1.50
❏36, Apr 1996 .... 1.50
❏37, May 1996 .... 1.50
❏38, Jun 1996 .... 1.50
❏39, Jul 1996 .... 1.50
❏40, Aug 1996 .... 1.50
❏41, Sep 1996 .... 1.50
❏42, Oct 1996, cover has reader sketches of Betty 1.50
❏43, Nov 1996 .... 1.50
❏44, Dec 1996 .... 1.50
❏45, Jan 1997 .... 1.50
❏46, Feb 1997 .... 1.50
❏47, Mar 1997 .... 1.50
❏48, Apr 1997 .... 1.50
❏49, May 1997 .... 1.50
❏50, Jun 1997 .... 1.50
❏51, Jul 1997 .... 1.50
❏52, Aug 1997 .... 1.50
❏53, Sep 1997 .... 1.50
❏54, Oct 1997 .... 1.50
❏55, Nov 1997 .... 1.50
❏56, Dec 1997, return of Polly Cooper... 1.50
❏57, Jan 1998 .... 1.75
❏58, Feb 1998, Virtual Pets 1.75
❏59, Mar 1998 .... 1.75
❏60, Apr 1998 .... 1.75
❏61, May 1998 .... 1.75
❏62, Jun 1998 .... 1.75
❏63, Jul 1998 .... 1.75
❏64, Aug 1998 .... 1.75
❏65, Sep 1998 .... 1.75
❏66, Oct 1998 .... 1.75
❏67, Nov 1998 .... 1.75
❏68, Dec 1998 .... 1.75
❏69, Jan 1999 .... 1.75
❏70, Feb 1999 .... 1.75
❏71, Mar 1999 .... 1.75
❏72, Apr 1999 .... 1.79
❏73, May 1999 .... 1.79
❏74, Jun 1999 .... 1.79
❏75, Jul 1999 .... 1.79
❏76, Aug 1999 .... 1.79
❏77, Sep 1999 .... 1.79
❏78, Oct 1999 .... 1.79
❏79, Nov 1999 .... 1.79
❏80, Dec 1999 .... 1.79
❏81, Jan 2000 .... 1.79
❏82, Feb 2000 .... 1.79
❏83, Mar 2000 .... 1.79
❏84, Apr 2000 .... 1.79
❏85, May 2000 .... 1.79
❏86, Jun 2000 .... 1.79
❏87, Jul 2000 .... 1.99
❏88, Aug 2000 .... 1.99
❏89, Sep 2000 .... 1.99
❏90, Oct 2000 .... 1.99
❏91, Nov 2000 .... 1.99
❏92, Dec 2000 .... 1.99
❏93, Jan 2001 .... 1.99
❏94, Feb 2001 .... 1.99
❏95, Mar 2001 .... 1.99
❏96, Apr 2001 .... 1.99
❏97, May 2001 .... 1.99
❏98, Jun 2001 .... 1.99
❏99, Jul 2001 .... 1.99
❏100, Aug 2001 .... 1.99
❏101, Sep 2001 .... 1.99
❏102, Oct 2001 .... 1.99
❏103, Oct 2001 .... 2.19
❏104, Nov 2001 .... 2.19
❏105, Dec 2001 .... 2.19
❏106, Jan 2002 .... 2.19
❏107, Feb 2002 .... 2.19
❏108, Mar 2002 .... 2.19
❏109, Apr 2002 .... 2.19
❏110, May 2002 .... 2.19
❏111, Jun 2002 .... 2.19
❏112, Jul 2002 .... 2.19
❏113, Aug 2002 .... 2.19
❏114, Sep 2002 .... 2.19
❏115, Oct 2002 .... 2.19
❏116, Oct 2002 .... 2.19
❏117, Nov 2002 .... 2.19
❏118, Dec 2002 .... 2.19
❏119, Jan 2003 .... 2.19
❏120, Feb 2003 .... 2.19
❏121, Mar 2003 .... 2.19
❏122, Apr 2003 .... 2.19
❏123, May 2003 .... 2.19
❏124, Jun 2003 .... 2.19
❏125, Jul 2003 .... 2.19
❏126, Aug 2003 .... 2.19
❏127, Sep 2003 .... 2.19
❏128, Oct 2003 .... 2.19
❏129, Oct 2003 .... 2.19
❏130, Nov 2003 .... 2.19
❏131, Dec 2003 .... 2.19
❏132, Jan 2004 .... 2.19
❏133, Feb 2004 .... 2.19
❏134, Mar 2004 .... 2.19
❏135, Apr 2004 .... 2.19
❏136, May 2004 .... 2.19
❏137, Jul 2004 .... 2.19
❏138, Aug 2004 .... 2.19
❏139, Sep 2004 .... 2.19
❏140, Oct 2004 .... 2.19
❏141, Nov 2004 .... 2.19
❏142, Jan 2005 .... 2.19
❏143, Feb 2005 AM (a) 2.19
❏144, Mar 2005 .... 2.19
❏145, Apr 2005 .... 2.19
❏146, May 2005 .... 2.19
❏147, Jun 2005 .... 2.25
❏148, Aug 2005 .... 2.25
❏149, Aug 2005 .... 2.25
❏150, Oct 2005 .... 2.25
❏151, Nov 2005 .... 2.25
❏152, Dec 2005 .... 2.25
❏153, Mar 2006, Includes Download Access card 2.25
❏154, May 2006 .... 2.25
❏156, Aug 2006 .... 2.25
❏157, Aug 2006 .... 2.25
❏158, Oct 2006 .... 2.25
❏159, Nov 2006 .... 2.25
❏160, Jan 2007, Includes 3-D Heroscape glasses; Includes Teen Titans: Sparktop mini-comic; Includes Teen Titans: Sparktop giveaway 2.25
❏161, Feb 2007 .... 2.25
❏162 .... 2.25
❏163 .... 2.25
❏164 .... 2.25
❏165 .... 2.25
❏166 .... 2.25
❏167 .... 2.25
❏168 .... 2.25
❏169 .... 2.25
❏170 .... 2.25
❏171 .... 2.25
❏172 .... 2.25
❏173 .... 2.25
❏174 .... 2.25
❏175 .... 2.25
❏176 .... 2.25
❏177 .... 2.25
❏178 .... 2.25
❏179 .... 2.25
❏180 .... 2.25

Betty & Me
Archie

❏1, Aug 1965 .... 65.00
❏2, Nov 1965 .... 40.00
❏3, Aug 1966 .... 24.00
❏4, Oct 1966 .... 24.00
❏5, Dec 1966 .... 24.00
❏6, Feb 1967 .... 15.00
❏7, Apr 1967 .... 15.00
❏8, Jun 1967 .... 15.00
❏9, Aug 1967 .... 15.00
❏10, Oct 1967 .... 15.00
❏11, Dec 1967 .... 10.00
❏12, Feb 1968 .... 10.00
❏13, Apr 1968 .... 10.00
❏14, Jun 1968 .... 10.00
❏15, Aug 1968 .... 10.00
❏16, Sep 1968 .... 10.00
❏17, Oct 1968 .... 10.00
❏18, Dec 1968 .... 10.00
❏19, Feb 1969 .... 10.00
❏20, Apr 1969 .... 10.00
❏21, Jun 1969 .... 7.00
❏22, Aug 1969 .... 7.00
❏23, Sep 1969 .... 7.00
❏24, Oct 1969 .... 7.00
❏25, Dec 1969 .... 7.00
❏26, Feb 1970 .... 7.00
❏27, Apr 1970 .... 7.00
❏28, Jun 1970 .... 7.00
❏29, Aug 1970 .... 7.00
❏30, Sep 1970 .... 7.00
❏31, Oct 1970 .... 6.00
❏32, Dec 1970 .... 6.00
❏33, Feb 1971 .... 6.00
❏34, Apr 1971 .... 6.00
❏35, Jun 1971 .... 6.00
❏36, Aug 1971 .... 6.00
❏37, Sep 1971 .... 6.00
❏38, Oct 1971 .... 6.00
❏39, Dec 1971 .... 6.00
❏40, Feb 1972 .... 6.00
❏41, Apr 1972 .... 5.00
❏42, Jun 1972 .... 5.00
❏43, Aug 1972 .... 5.00
❏44, Sep 1972 .... 5.00
❏45, Oct 1972 .... 5.00
❏46, Dec 1972 .... 5.00
❏47, Feb 1973 .... 5.00

Other grades: Multiply price above by 5/6 for VF/NM • 2/3 for VERY FINE • 1/3 for FINE • 1/5 for VERY GOOD • 1/8 for GOOD

Batman Family

1970s anthology show-cased Batgirl and Robin

©DC

Batman: Gotham Adventures

Another series in the "animated" DC universe

©DC

Batman: Gotham By Gaslight

Notable as the first DC "Elseworlds" story

©DC

Batman: Gotham Knights

Spotlights members of the Batman family

©DC

Batman: Joker Time

Reality TV goes too far with Joker show

©DC

	N-MINT
❑48, Apr 1973	5.00
❑49, Jun 1973	5.00
❑50, Jul 1973	5.00
❑51, Aug 1973	4.00
❑52, Sep 1973	4.00
❑53, Oct 1973	4.00
❑54, Dec 1973	4.00
❑55, Feb 1974	4.00
❑56, Apr 1974	4.00
❑57, Jun 1974	4.00
❑58, Jul 1974	4.00
❑59, Aug 1974	4.00
❑60, Sep 1974	4.00
❑61, Oct 1974	3.00
❑62, Dec 1974	3.00
❑63, Feb 1975	3.00
❑64, Mar 1975	3.00
❑65, Apr 1975	3.00
❑66, May 1975	3.00
❑67, Jul 1975	3.00
❑68, Aug 1975	3.00
❑69, Sep 1975	3.00
❑70, Oct 1975	3.00
❑71, Dec 1975	2.00
❑72, Feb 1976	2.00
❑73, Mar 1976	2.00
❑74, Apr 1976	2.00
❑75, May 1976	2.00
❑76, Jul 1976	2.00
❑77, Aug 1976	2.00
❑78, Sep 1976	2.00
❑79, Oct 1976	2.00
❑80, Dec 1976	2.00
❑81, Feb 1977	2.00
❑82, Mar 1977	2.00
❑83, Apr 1977	2.00
❑84, May 1977	2.00
❑85, Jul 1977	2.00
❑86, Aug 1977	2.00
❑87, Sep 1977	2.00
❑88, Oct 1977	2.00
❑89, Dec 1977	2.00
❑90, Feb 1978	2.00
❑91, Mar 1978	2.00
❑92, Apr 1978	2.00
❑93, May 1978	2.00
❑94, Jul 1978	2.00
❑95, Aug 1978	2.00
❑96, Sep 1978	2.00
❑97, Oct 1978	2.00
❑98, Dec 1978	2.00
❑99, Feb 1979	2.00
❑100, Mar 1979	2.00
❑101, Apr 1979	2.00
❑102, May 1979	2.00
❑103, Jul 1979	2.00
❑104, Aug 1979	2.00
❑105, Sep 1979	2.00
❑106, Oct 1979	2.00
❑107, Dec 1979	2.00
❑108, Feb 1980	2.00
❑109, Mar 1980	2.00
❑110 1980	2.00
❑111 1980	2.00
❑112 1980	2.00
❑113 1980	2.00

	N-MINT
❑114	2.00
❑115	2.00
❑116	2.00
❑117, Feb 1981	2.00
❑118, Mar 1981	2.00
❑119	2.00
❑120	2.00
❑121	2.00
❑122	2.00
❑123	2.00
❑124	2.00
❑125, Dec 1981	2.00
❑126 1982	2.00
❑127 1982	2.00
❑128 1982	2.00
❑129 1982	2.00
❑130 1982	2.00
❑131 1982	2.00
❑132, Jan 1983	2.00
❑133, Apr 1983	2.00
❑134, Jul 1983	2.00
❑135, Sep 1983	2.00
❑136, Nov 1983	2.00
❑137, Jan 1984	2.00
❑138, Mar 1984	2.00
❑139, May 1984	2.00
❑140, Jul 1984	2.00
❑141, Sep 1984	2.00
❑142, Nov 1984	2.00
❑143, Jan 1985	2.00
❑144, Mar 1985	2.00
❑145, May 1985	2.00
❑146, Jul 1985	2.00
❑147, Sep 1985	2.00
❑148, Nov 1985	2.00
❑149, Jan 1986	2.00
❑150, Mar 1986	2.00
❑151, May 1986	1.50
❑152, Jul 1986	1.50
❑153, Sep 1986	1.50
❑154, Nov 1986	1.50
❑155, Jan 1987	1.50
❑156, Mar 1987	1.50
❑157, May 1987	1.50
❑158, Jun 1987	1.50
❑159, Jul 1987	1.50
❑160, Aug 1987	1.50
❑161, Sep 1987	1.50
❑162, Oct 1987	1.50
❑163, Dec 1987	1.50
❑164, Jan 1988	1.50
❑165, Mar 1988	1.50
❑166, May 1988	1.50
❑167, Jun 1988	1.50
❑168, Jul 1988	1.50
❑169, Aug 1988	1.50
❑170, Sep 1988	1.50
❑171, Oct 1988	1.50
❑172, Jan 1989	1.50
❑173, Mar 1989	1.50
❑174, May 1989	1.50
❑175, Jun 1989	1.50
❑176, Jul 1989	1.50
❑177, Aug 1989 DDC (c)	1.50
❑178, Sep 1989 DDC (c); A: Veronica Lodge	1.50

	N-MINT
❑179, Oct 1989	1.50
❑180, Jan 1990	1.50
❑181, Mar 1990	1.50
❑182, May 1990	1.50
❑183, Jun 1990	1.50
❑184, Jul 1990	1.50
❑185, Aug 1990	1.50
❑186, Sep 1990	1.50
❑187, Oct 1990	1.50
❑188, Jan 1991	1.50
❑189, Mar 1991	1.50
❑190, May 1991	1.50
❑191, Jul 1991	1.50
❑192, Aug 1991	1.50
❑193, Sep 1991	1.50
❑194, Oct 1991	1.50
❑195, Nov 1991	1.50
❑196, Jan 1992	1.50
❑197, Mar 1992	1.50
❑198, May 1992	1.50
❑199, Jul 1992	1.50
❑200, Aug 1992	1.50

Betty and Veronica
Archie

	N-MINT
❑1, Jun 1987	6.00
❑2 1987	4.00
❑3 1987	4.00
❑4	3.00
❑5	3.00
❑6, Nov 1987	3.00
❑7	3.00
❑8 1988	3.00
❑9 1988	3.00
❑10 1988	3.00
❑11 1988	2.50
❑12 1988	2.50
❑13 1988	2.50
❑14	2.50
❑15	2.50
❑16	2.50
❑17	2.50
❑18	2.50
❑19	2.50
❑20 1989	2.50
❑21 1989	2.00
❑22 1989	2.00
❑23 1989	2.00
❑24 1989	2.00
❑25 1989	2.00
❑26	2.00
❑27	2.00
❑28 1990	2.00
❑29 1990	2.00
❑30, May 1990	2.00
❑31 1990	2.00
❑32 1990	2.00
❑33 1990	2.00
❑34 1990	2.00
❑35 1990	2.00
❑36	2.00
❑37 1991	2.00
❑38 1991	2.00
❑39 1991	2.00
❑40 1991	2.00
❑41 1991	2.00

Other grades: Multiply price above by 5/6 for VF/NM • 2/3 for VERY FINE • 1/3 for FINE • 1/5 for VERY GOOD • 1/8 for GOOD

	N-MINT
❑42 1991	2.00
❑43 1991	2.00
❑44 1991	2.00
❑45 1991	2.00
❑46 1991	2.00
❑47, Jan 1992	2.00
❑48, Feb 1992	2.00
❑49, Mar 1992	2.00
❑50, Apr 1992	2.00
❑51, May 1992	1.50
❑52, Jun 1992	1.50
❑53, Jul 1992	1.50
❑54, Aug 1992	1.50
❑55, Sep 1992	1.50
❑56, Oct 1992	1.50
❑57, Nov 1992	1.50
❑58, Dec 1992	1.50
❑59, Jan 1993	1.50
❑60, Feb 1993	1.50
❑61, Mar 1993	1.50
❑62, Apr 1993	1.50
❑63, May 1993	1.50
❑64, Jun 1993	1.50
❑65, Jul 1993	1.50
❑66, Aug 1993, DDC (a)	1.50
❑67, Sep 1993	1.50
❑68, Oct 1993	1.50
❑69, Nov 1993	1.50
❑70, Dec 1993	1.50
❑71, Jan 1994	1.50
❑72, Feb 1994	1.50
❑73, Mar 1994	1.50
❑74, Apr 1994	1.50
❑75, May 1994	1.50
❑76, Jun 1994	1.50
❑77, Jul 1994	1.50
❑78, Aug 1994	1.50
❑79, Sep 1994	1.50
❑80, Oct 1994	1.50
❑81, Nov 1994	1.50
❑82, Dec 1994	1.50
❑83, Jan 1995	1.50
❑84, Feb 1995	1.50
❑85, Mar 1995	1.50
❑86, Apr 1995	1.50
❑87, May 1995	1.50
❑88, Jun 1995	1.50
❑89, Jul 1995	1.50
❑90, Aug 1995	1.50
❑91, Sep 1995	1.50
❑92, Oct 1995, DDC (a)	1.50
❑93, Nov 1995	1.50
❑94, Dec 1995	1.50
❑95, Jan 1996, concludes in Archie's Pal Jughead #76	1.50
❑96, Feb 1996	1.50
❑97, Mar 1996	1.50
❑98, Apr 1996	1.50
❑99, May 1996	1.50
❑100, Jun 1996	1.50
❑101, Jul 1996	1.50
❑102, Aug 1996	1.50
❑103, Sep 1996	1.50
❑104, Oct 1996	1.50
❑105, Nov 1996	1.50
❑106, Dec 1996	1.50
❑107, Jan 1997	1.50
❑108, Feb 1997	1.50
❑109, Mar 1997	1.50
❑110, Apr 1997	1.50
❑111, May 1997	1.50
❑112, Jun 1997	1.50
❑113, Jul 1997	1.50
❑114, Aug 1997	1.50
❑115, Sep 1997	1.50
❑116, Oct 1997	1.50
❑117, Nov 1997	1.50
❑118, Dec 1997	1.50
❑119, Jan 1998	1.75
❑120, Feb 1998	1.75
❑121, Mar 1998	1.75
❑122, Apr 1998	1.75
❑123, May 1998	1.75
❑124, Jun 1998	1.75
❑125, Jul 1998	1.75
❑126, Aug 1998	1.75
❑127, Sep 1998, DDC (a)	1.75
❑128, Oct 1998	1.75
❑129, Nov 1998, DDC (a)	1.75
❑130, Dec 1998	1.75
❑131, Jan 1999	1.75
❑132, Feb 1999	1.75
❑133, Mar 1999, DDC (a)	1.75
❑134, Apr 1999	1.79
❑135, May 1999, DDC (a)	1.79
❑136, Jun 1999	1.79
❑137, Jul 1999	1.79
❑138, Aug 1999	1.79
❑139, Sep 1999	1.79
❑140, Oct 1999	1.79
❑141, Nov 1999	1.79
❑142, Dec 1999	1.79
❑143, Jan 2000	1.79
❑144, Feb 2000	1.79
❑145, Mar 2000	1.79
❑146, Apr 2000	1.79
❑147, May 2000	1.79
❑148, Jun 2000	1.79
❑149, Jul 2000	1.99
❑150, Aug 2000	1.99
❑151, Sep 2000	1.99
❑152, Oct 2000	1.99
❑153, Nov 2000	1.99
❑154, Dec 2000	1.99
❑155, Jan 2001	1.99
❑156, Feb 2001	1.99
❑157, Mar 2001	1.99
❑158, Apr 2001	1.99
❑159, May 2001	1.99
❑160, May 2001	1.99
❑161, Jun 2001	1.99
❑162, Jul 2001	1.99
❑163, Aug 2001	1.99
❑164, Sep 2001	1.99
❑165, Oct 2001	1.99
❑166, Nov 2001	2.19
❑167, Dec 2001	2.19
❑168, Jan 2002	2.19
❑169, Feb 2002	2.19
❑170, Mar 2002	2.19
❑171, Apr 2002	2.19
❑172, Apr 2002	2.19
❑173, May 2002	2.19
❑174, Jun 2002	2.19
❑175, Jul 2002	2.19
❑176, Aug 2002	2.19
❑177, Sep 2002	2.19
❑178, Oct 2002	2.19
❑179, Nov 2002	2.19
❑180, Dec 2002	2.19
❑181, Jan 2003	2.19
❑182, Feb 2003	2.19
❑183, Mar 2003	2.19
❑184, Apr 2003	2.19
❑185, Apr 2003	2.19
❑186, May 2003	2.19
❑187, Jun 2003	2.19
❑188, Jul 2003	2.19
❑189, Aug 2003	2.19
❑190, Sep 2003	2.19
❑191, Oct 2003	2.19
❑192, Nov 2003	2.19
❑193, Dec 2003	2.19
❑194, Jan 2004	2.19
❑195, Feb 2004	2.19
❑196, Mar 2004	2.19
❑197, Mar 2004	2.19
❑198, May 2004	2.19
❑199, Jun 2004	2.19
❑200, Jul 2004	2.19
❑201, Aug 2004	2.19
❑202, Sep 2004	2.19
❑203, Oct 2004	2.19
❑204, Nov 2004	2.19
❑205, Dec 2004	2.19
❑206, Apr 2005	2.19
❑207, May 2005	2.19
❑208, Jun 2005	2.19
❑209, Aug 2005	2.25
❑210, Sep 2005	2.25
❑211, Oct 2005	2.25
❑212, Dec 2005	2.25
❑213, Jan 2006	2.25
❑214, Jan 2006	2.25
❑215, Apr 2006	2.25
❑216, May 2006	2.25
❑217, Jun 2006	2.25
❑218, Aug 2006	2.25
❑219, Sep 2006	2.25
❑220, Oct 2006	2.25
❑221, Dec 2006	2.25
❑222, Jan 2007, Includes 3-D Heroscape glasses; Includes Teen Titans: Sparktop mini-comic	2.25
❑223, Feb 2007	2.25
❑224	2.25
❑225	2.25
❑226	2.25
❑227	2.25
❑228	2.25
❑229	2.25
❑230	2.25
❑231	2.25
❑232	2.25
❑233	2.25
❑234	2.25
❑235	2.25
❑236	2.25
❑237	2.25
❑238	2.25
❑239	2.25
❑240	2.25

Betty & Veronica Annual Digest Magazine
Archie

	N-MINT
❑12, Jan 1995	1.75
❑13, Sep 1995	1.75
❑14, Feb 1996	1.75
❑15, Jul 1996	1.75
❑16, Aug 1997	1.79

Betty and Veronica Comics Digest
Archie

	N-MINT
❑1, Aug 1982	9.00
❑2, Nov 1982	5.00
❑3, Feb 1983	5.00
❑4, May 1983	4.00
❑5, Aug 1983	4.00
❑6, Nov 1983	4.00
❑7, Feb 1984	4.00
❑8, May 1984	4.00
❑9, Aug 1984	4.00
❑10, Nov 1984	4.00
❑11, Feb 1985	3.00
❑12, Apr 1985	3.00
❑13, Jun 1985	3.00
❑14, Aug 1985	3.00
❑15, Oct 1985	3.00
❑16, Dec 1985	3.00
❑17, Feb 1986	3.00
❑18, Apr 1986	3.00
❑19, Jun 1986	3.00
❑20, Aug 1986	3.00
❑21, Oct 1986	3.00
❑22, Dec 1986	3.00
❑23, Feb 1987	3.00
❑24, Apr 1987	3.00
❑25, Jun 1987	3.00
❑26, Aug 1987	3.00
❑27, Nov 1987	3.00
❑28, Jan 1988	3.00
❑29, Mar 1988	3.00
❑30, May 1988	3.00
❑31, Jul 1988	2.50
❑32, Sep 1988	2.50
❑33, Nov 1988	2.50
❑34, Jan 1989	2.50
❑35, Mar 1989	2.50
❑36, May 1989	2.50
❑37, Jul 1989	2.50
❑38, Sep 1989	2.50
❑39, Nov 1989	2.50
❑40, Jan 1990	2.50
❑41, Mar 1990	2.50
❑42, May 1990	2.50
❑43, Jul 1990, becomes Betty and Veronica Digest Magazine	2.50

Betty and Veronica Digest Magazine
Archie

	N-MINT
❑44, Sep 1990, Series continued from Betty and Veronica Comics Digest	2.50
❑45, Nov 1990	2.50

Other grades: Multiply price above by 5/6 for VF/NM • 2/3 for VERY FINE • 1/3 for FINE • 1/5 for VERY GOOD • 1/8 for GOOD

Batman: Legends of the Dark Knight

First issue launched the variant cover craze
©DC

Batman: Manbat

Elseworlds story pits bat V: bat
©DC

Batman: Mr. Freeze

Cover forms quadritych with other movie spinoffs
©DC

Batman: No Man's Land

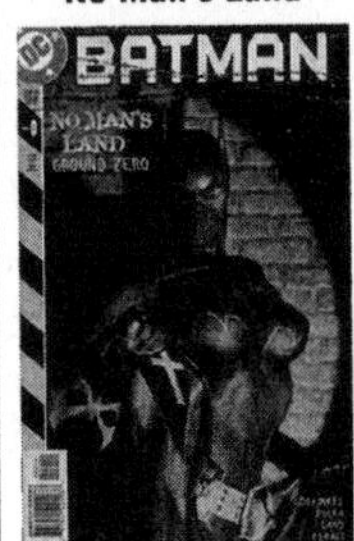

Events after an earthquake levels Gotham
©DC

Batman/Predator III

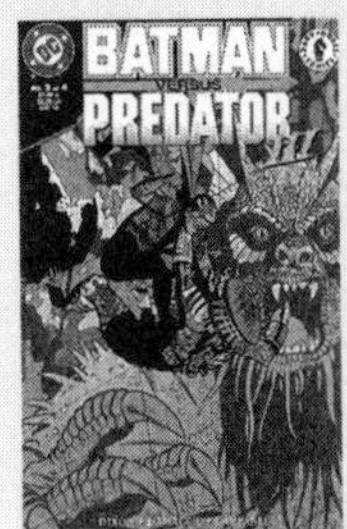

Earlier series called "Batman Vs. Predator"
©DC

	N-MINT
❑46, Jan 1991	2.50
❑47, Mar 1991	2.50
❑48, May 1991	2.50
❑49, Jul 1991	2.50
❑50, Sep 1991	2.50
❑51, Nov 1991	2.00
❑52, ca. 1992	2.00
❑53, ca. 1992	2.00
❑54, ca. 1992	2.00
❑55, ca. 1992	2.00
❑56, ca. 1992	2.00
❑57, ca. 1992	2.00
❑58, ca. 1992	2.00
❑59, ca. 1992	2.00
❑60, Feb 1993	2.00
❑61, Apr 1993	2.00
❑62, Jun 1993	2.00
❑63, Aug 1993	2.00
❑64, Oct 1993	2.00
❑65, Dec 1993	2.00
❑66, Feb 1994	2.00
❑67, Apr 1994	2.00
❑68, ca. 1994	2.00
❑69, Jul 1994	2.00
❑70, ca. 1994	2.00
❑71, ca. 1994	2.00
❑72, Jan 1995	2.00
❑73, Mar 1995	2.00
❑74, Apr 1995	2.00
❑75, Jun 1995	2.00
❑76, Aug 1995	2.00
❑77, Oct 1995	2.00
❑78, Dec 1995	2.00
❑79, Feb 1996	2.00
❑80, Apr 1996	2.00
❑81, Jun 1996	2.00
❑82, Jul 1996	2.00
❑83, Sep 1996	2.00
❑84, Nov 1996	2.00
❑85, Jan 1997	2.00
❑86, Feb 1997	2.00
❑87, Apr 1997	2.00
❑88, Jun 1997	2.00
❑89, Jul 1997	2.00
❑90, Sep 1997	2.00
❑91, Oct 1997	2.00
❑92, Dec 1997	2.00
❑93, Feb 1998	2.00
❑94, Apr 1998	2.00
❑95, May 1998	2.00
❑96, Jul 1998	2.00
❑97, Aug 1998	2.00
❑98, Sep 1998	2.00
❑99, Nov 1998, DDC (a)	2.00
❑100, Dec 1998	2.00
❑101, Feb 1999	2.00
❑102, Apr 1999	2.00
❑103, May 1999	2.00
❑104, Jul 1999	2.00
❑105, Aug 1999	2.00
❑106, Sep 1999	2.00
❑107, Nov 1999	2.00
❑108, Sep 1999	2.00
❑109, Feb 2000	2.00
❑110, Apr 2000	2.00
❑111, May 2000	2.00

	N-MINT
❑112, Jul 2000	2.19
❑113, Aug 2000	2.19
❑114, Oct 2000	2.19
❑115, Nov 2000	2.19
❑116, Dec 2000	2.19
❑117, Feb 2001	2.19
❑118, Apr 2001	2.19
❑119, May 2001	2.19
❑120, Jun 2001	2.19
❑121, Aug 2001	2.19
❑122, Sep 2001	2.19
❑123, Oct 2001	2.19
❑124, Dec 2001	2.19
❑125, Jan 2002	2.19
❑126, Mar 2002	2.19
❑127, Apr 2002	2.19
❑128, May 2002	2.19
❑129, Jul 2002	2.19
❑130, Aug 2002	2.19
❑131, Oct 2002	2.19
❑132, Nov 2002	2.19
❑133, Dec 2002	2.19
❑134, Feb 2003	2.19
❑135, Mar 2003	2.39
❑136, Apr 2003	2.39
❑137, May 2003	2.39
❑138, Jul 2003	2.39
❑139, Aug 2003	2.39
❑140, Sep 2003	2.39
❑141, Oct 2003	2.39
❑142, Dec 2003	2.39
❑143, Jan 2004	2.39
❑144, Mar 2004	2.39
❑145, Apr 2004	2.39
❑146, May 2004	2.39
❑147, Jul 2004	2.39
❑148, Aug 2004	2.39
❑149, Sep 2004	2.39
❑150, Oct 2004	2.39
❑151, Nov 2004	2.39
❑152, Dec 2004	2.39
❑153, Jan 2004	2.39
❑154, Apr 2005	2.39
❑155, May 2005	2.39
❑156, Jun 2005	2.39
❑157, Aug 2005	2.39
❑158, Sep 2005	2.39
❑159, Oct 2005	2.39
❑160, Nov 2005	2.39
❑161, Dec 2005	2.39
❑162, Jan 2006	2.39
❑163, Feb 2006	2.39
❑164, May 2006	2.39
❑165, Jun 2006	2.49
❑166, Aug 2006	2.49
❑167, Aug 2006	2.49
❑168, Oct 2006	2.49
❑169, Nov 2006	2.49
❑170, Jan 2007	2.49
❑171, Feb 2007	2.49
❑172	2.49
❑173	2.49
❑174	2.49
❑175	2.49
❑176	2.49
❑177	2.49

	N-MINT
❑178	2.49
❑179	2.49
❑180	2.49
❑181	2.49
❑182	2.49
❑183	2.49
❑184	2.49
❑185	2.49
❑186	2.49
❑187	2.49
❑188	2.49
❑189	2.49
❑190	2.49
❑191	2.49
❑192	2.49
❑193	2.49
❑194	2.49

Betty and Veronica Double Digest
Archie

	N-MINT
❑1, Jun 1987	8.00
❑2, Aug 1987	5.00
❑3, Oct 1987	5.00
❑4, Dec 1987	4.00
❑5, Feb 1988	4.00
❑6, Apr 1988	4.00
❑7, Jun 1988	4.00
❑8, Aug 1988	4.00
❑9, Oct 1988	4.00
❑10, Dec 1988	4.00
❑11, Feb 1989	3.00
❑12, Apr 1989	3.00
❑13, Jun 1989	3.00
❑14, Aug 1989	3.00
❑15, Oct 1989	3.00
❑16, Dec 1989	3.00
❑17, Feb 1990	3.00
❑18, Apr 1990	3.00
❑19, Jun 1990	3.00
❑20, Aug 1990	3.00
❑21, Oct 1990	3.00
❑22, Dec 1990	3.00
❑23, Feb 1991	3.00
❑24, Apr 1991	3.00
❑25, Jun 1991	3.00
❑26, Aug 1991	3.00
❑27, Oct 1991	3.00
❑28, Nov 1991	3.00
❑29, Jan 1992	3.00
❑30, Mar 1992	3.00
❑31, May 1992	3.00
❑32, Jul 1992	3.00
❑33, Sep 1992	3.00
❑34, Oct 1992	3.00
❑35, Dec 1992	3.00
❑36, Feb 1993	3.00
❑37, Apr 1993	3.00
❑38, Jun 1993	3.00
❑39, Aug 1993	3.00
❑40, Sep 1993	3.00
❑41, Nov 1993	3.00
❑42, Jan 1994	3.00
❑43, Apr 1994	3.00
❑44, May 1994	3.00
❑45, Jul 1994	3.00
❑46, Aug 1994	3.00

Other grades: Multiply price above by 5/6 for VF/NM • 2/3 for VERY FINE • 1/3 for FINE • 1/5 for VERY GOOD • 1/8 for GOOD

	N-MINT
❑47, Oct 1994	3.00
❑48, Dec 1994, DDC (c)	3.00
❑49, Feb 1995	3.00
❑50, Apr 1995	3.00
❑51, Jun 1995	3.00
❑52, Aug 1995	3.00
❑53, Sep 1995	3.00
❑54, Nov 1995	3.00
❑55, Jan 1996	3.00
❑56, Mar 1996	3.00
❑57, Apr 1996	3.00
❑58, Jun 1996	3.00
❑59, Aug 1996	3.00
❑60, Oct 1996	3.00
❑61, Nov 1996	3.00
❑62, Jan 1997	3.00
❑63, Mar 1997	3.00
❑64, Apr 1997	3.00
❑65, Jun 1997	3.00
❑66, Aug 1997	3.00
❑67, Sep 1997	3.00
❑68, Nov 1997	3.00
❑69, Jan 1998	3.00
❑70, Mar 1998	3.00
❑71, Apr 1998	3.00
❑72, Jun 1998	3.00
❑73, Jul 1998	3.00
❑74, Sep 1998	3.00
❑75, Oct 1998	3.00
❑76, Dec 1998	3.00
❑77, Jan 1999	3.00
❑78, Mar 1999	3.00
❑79, Apr 1999	3.00
❑80, Jun 1999	3.00
❑81, Jul 1999	3.00
❑82, Sep 1999	3.00
❑83, Oct 1999	3.00
❑84, Dec 1999	3.00
❑85, Jan 2000	3.00
❑86, Mar 2000	3.00
❑87, Apr 2000	3.00
❑88, Jun 2000	3.00
❑89, Jul 2000	3.00
❑90, Sep 2000	3.19
❑91, Oct 2000	3.19
❑92, Nov 2000	3.19
❑93, Jan 2001	3.19
❑94, Feb 2001	3.19
❑95, Apr 2001	3.29
❑96, Jun 2001	3.29
❑97, Jul 2001	3.29
❑98, Sep 2001	3.29
❑99, Oct 2001	3.29
❑100, Nov 2001	3.29
❑101, Dec 2001	3.29
❑102, Feb 2002	3.29
❑103, Mar 2002	3.29
❑104, Apr 2002	3.29
❑105, Jun 2002	3.29
❑106, Jul 2002	3.29
❑107, Sep 2002	3.29
❑108, Oct 2002	3.29
❑109, Nov 2002	3.59
❑110, Dec 2002	3.59
❑111, Feb 2003	3.59
❑112, Mar 2003	3.59
❑113, Apr 2003	3.59
❑114, Jun 2003	3.59
❑115, Jul 2003	3.59
❑116, Sep 2003	3.59
❑117, Oct 2003	3.59
❑118, Nov 2003	3.59
❑119, Dec 2003	3.59
❑120, Feb 2004	3.59
❑121, Mar 2004	3.59
❑122, Apr 2004	3.59
❑123, May 2004	3.59
❑124, Jun 2004	3.59
❑125, Jul 2004	3.59
❑126, Aug 2004	3.59
❑127, Sep 2004	3.59
❑128, Oct 2004	3.59
❑129, Nov 2004	3.59
❑130, Dec 2004	3.59
❑131, Jan 2005	3.59
❑132, Feb 2005	3.59
❑133, Jul 2005	3.59
❑134, Aug 2005	3.59
❑135, Sep 2005	3.59
❑136, Oct 2005	3.59
❑137, Dec 2005	3.59
❑138, Dec 2005	3.59
❑139, Jan 2006	3.59
❑140, Apr 2006	3.59
❑141, May 2006	3.59
❑142, Jul 2006	3.69
❑143, Aug 2006	3.69
❑144, Sep 2006	3.69
❑145, Oct 2006	3.69
❑146, Nov 2006	3.69
❑147, Jan 2007	3.69
❑148, Mar 2007	3.69
❑149	3.69
❑150	3.69
❑151	3.69
❑152	3.69
❑153	3.69
❑154	3.69
❑155	3.69
❑156	3.69
❑157	3.69
❑158	3.69
❑159	3.69
❑160	3.69
❑161	3.69
❑162	3.69
❑163	3.69
❑164	3.69
❑165	3.69
❑166	3.69
❑167	3.69
❑168	3.69
❑169	3.69
❑171	3.69

Betty and Veronica Spectacular
Archie

	N-MINT
❑1, Oct 1992	4.00
❑2	3.00
❑3, May 1993	3.00
❑4 1993	2.50
❑5, Oct 1993	2.50
❑6, Feb 1994	2.00
❑7, Apr 1994	2.00
❑8, May 1994	2.00
❑9, Jul 1994	2.00
❑10, Sep 1994	2.00
❑11, Nov 1994	2.00
❑12, Jan 1995	2.00
❑13, Feb 1995	2.00
❑14, Apr 1995	2.00
❑15, Jul 1995	2.00
❑16, Oct 1995	2.00
❑17, Jan 1996	2.00
❑18, Apr 1996	2.00
❑19, Jul 1996	2.00
❑20, Oct 1996	2.00
❑21, Jan 1997, Betty becomes a fashion model	2.00
❑22, Mar 1997	2.00
❑23, May 1997	2.00
❑24, Jul 1997, Betty and Veronica set up web pages	2.00
❑25, Sep 1997	2.00
❑26, Nov 1997	2.00
❑27, Feb 1998	2.00
❑28, Mar 1998	2.00
❑29, May 1998	2.00
❑30, Jul 1998	2.00
❑31, Sep 1998	2.00
❑32, Nov 1998, Betty and Veronica are maids for each other	2.00
❑33, Jan 1999, talent competition	2.00
❑34, Mar 1999	2.00
❑35, May 1999, Swing issue	2.00
❑36, Jul 1999	2.00
❑37, Sep 1999	2.00
❑38, Nov 1999	2.00
❑39, Jan 2000	2.00
❑40, Mar 2000	2.00
❑41, May 2000	2.00
❑42, Jul 2000	2.00
❑43, Sep 2000	2.00
❑44, Nov 2000	2.00
❑45, Jan 2001	2.00
❑46, Mar 2001	2.00
❑47, May 2001	2.00
❑48, Jul 2001	2.00
❑49, Sep 2001	2.00
❑50, Nov 2001	2.00
❑51, Jan 2002	2.00
❑52, Mar 2002	2.00
❑53, May 2002	2.00
❑54, Jul 2002	2.00
❑55, Sep 2002	2.00
❑56, Nov 2002	2.00
❑57, Jan 2003	2.00
❑58, Mar 2003	2.20
❑59, May 2003	2.20
❑60, Jul 2003	2.20
❑61, Sep 2003	2.19
❑62, Nov 2003	2.19
❑63, Dec 2003	2.19
❑64, Feb 2004	2.19
❑65, May 2004	2.19
❑66, Jul 2004	2.19
❑67, Aug 2004	2.19
❑68, Jan 2005	2.19
❑69, Mar 2005	2.19
❑72, Dec 2005; Includes Heroscape #4 insert	2.25
❑73, Feb 2006	2.25
❑75, Oct 2006	2.25
❑76, Jan 2007, Includes 3-D Heroscape glasses; Includes Teen Titans: Sparktop mini-comic	2.25
❑77	2.25
❑78	2.25
❑79	2.25
❑80	2.25
❑81	2.25
❑82	2.25
❑83	2.25
❑84	2.25
❑85	2.25
❑86	2.25
❑87	2.25
❑88	2.25

Betty & Veronica Summer Fun
Archie

	N-MINT
❑1, Sum 1994	3.00
❑2, Sum 1995	2.50
❑3, Sum 1996	2.50
❑4, Sum 1997	2.50
❑5, Sum 1998	2.25
❑6, Sum 1999	2.29

Betty Boop 3-D
Blackthorne

❑1, Nov 1986 — 2.50

Betty Boop's Big Break
First

❑1, Oct 1990; NN — 5.95

Betty in Bondage: Betty Mae
Shunga

❑1; Adult — 6.95

Betty in Bondage (Teo Jonelli's...)
Shunga

	N-MINT
❑1, b&w; Adult	3.00
❑2, b&w; Adult	3.00
❑3, b&w; Adult	3.00
❑4, b&w; Adult	3.00
❑5; Adult	3.00
❑6; Adult	3.00
❑7; Adult	3.00
❑8, Apr 1994; Adult; b&w	3.00
❑Ann 1; 1993 Ann	5.95
❑Ann 2, Jan 1994; 1994 Ann	5.95
❑Ann 3; 1995 Ann	5.95

Betty Page 3-D Comics
3-D Zone

❑1 — 3.95

Betty Page 3-D Picture Book
3-D Zone

❑1; photos, adult — 3.95

Betty Page Captured Jungle Girl 3-D
3-D Zone

❑1, Jun 1990; photos — 3.95

Batman: Shadow of the Bat

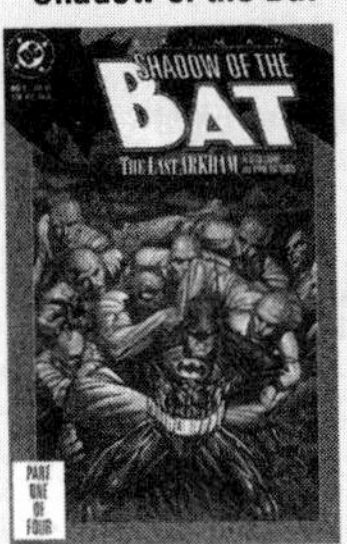

Batman Returns film prompted third Bat-title
©DC

Batman: The Dark Knight

Real name of spectacular "Dark Knight Returns"
©DC

Batman: The Killing Joke

Infamous Alan Moore one-shot crippled Batgirl
©DC

Batman: The Long Halloween

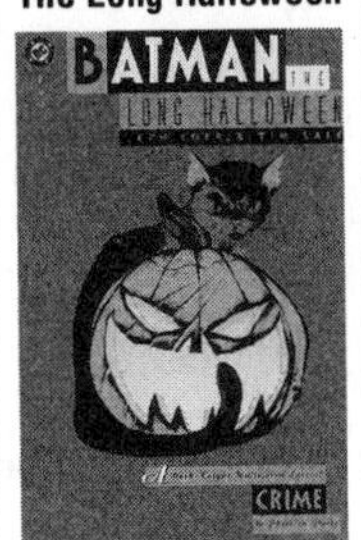

Popular Jeph Loeb/Tim Sale production
©DC

Batman vs. Predator

First of a trio of Bats/Predator crossovers
©DC

N-MINT

Betty Pages
Pure Imagination

❑1; DSt (a); Ward, photos ... 6.00
❑1/2nd; 2nd printing; New cover; Dave Stevens cover; Reprints Betty Pages #1; ca. 1990 ... 5.00
❑2; Bill Wray cover ... 5.00
❑2/2nd; 2nd printing ... 5.00
❑3 ... 5.00
❑4; Spring 1989 ... 5.00
❑5, Win 1989 ... 4.50
❑6 ... 4.50
❑7 ... 4.50
❑8; Photo Cover; Summer Fun!; Summer 1992 ... 4.50
❑9 ... 5.00

Betty Page: The 50's Rage
Illustration

❑1/A, Jan 1993; tame cover ... 3.25
❑1/B, Jan 1993; Adult cover ... 3.25
❑2/A; tame cover ... 3.25
❑2/B; Adult cover ... 3.25

Betty's Diary
Archie

❑1, Apr 1986 ... 4.00
❑2 1986 ... 2.50
❑3 1986 ... 2.50
❑4 1986 ... 2.50
❑5 1986 ... 2.50
❑6 1986 ... 2.00
❑7 1987 ... 2.00
❑8 1987 ... 2.00
❑9 1987 ... 2.00
❑10, Aug 1987 ... 2.00
❑11, Sep 1987 ... 1.50
❑12, Oct 1987 ... 1.50
❑13 1987 ... 1.50
❑14 1987 ... 1.50
❑15 1988 ... 1.50
❑16 1988 ... 1.50
❑17 1988 ... 1.50
❑18 1988 ... 1.50
❑19 1988 ... 1.50
❑20 1988 ... 1.50
❑21 1988 ... 1.50
❑22 1988 ... 1.50
❑23 1989 ... 1.50
❑24 1989 ... 1.50
❑25 1989 ... 1.50
❑26, Jul 1989 ... 1.50
❑27, Aug 1989 ... 1.50
❑28, Sep 1989 ... 1.50
❑29, Oct 1989 ... 1.50
❑30 1989 ... 1.50
❑31 1990 ... 1.50
❑32 1990 ... 1.50
❑33 1990 ... 1.50
❑34 1990 ... 1.50
❑35 1990 ... 1.50
❑36 1990 ... 1.50
❑37 1990 ... 1.50
❑38 1990 ... 1.50
❑39 1991 ... 1.50
❑40 1991 ... 1.50

N-MINT

Betty's Digest Magazine
Archie

❑1, Nov 1996 ... 2.00
❑2, Nov 1997 ... 2.00

Between the Sheets
Tokyopop

❑1, May 2003, b&w; printed in Japanese format ... 9.99

Beverly Hillbillies
Dell

❑1, Apr 1963, Photo cover ... 60.00
❑2, Jul 1963 ... 38.00
❑3, Oct 1963, Black and white publicity photo on inside back cover ... 28.00
❑4, Jan 1964 ... 24.00
❑5, Apr 1964 ... 24.00
❑6, Jul 1964 ... 18.00
❑7, Oct 1964 ... 18.00
❑8, Jan 1965 ... 18.00
❑9, Apr 1965 ... 18.00
❑10, ca. 1965, Not a photo cover; cartoon Clampetts appear on cover, but actors' names still listed with them ... 18.00
❑11, Dec 1965 ... 15.00
❑12, Mar 1966 ... 15.00
❑13, Jun 1966 ... 15.00
❑14, Sep 1966 ... 15.00
❑15, Dec 1966 ... 15.00
❑16, Mar 1967 ... 15.00
❑17, May 1967 ... 15.00
❑18, Aug 1967 ... 12.00
❑19, Oct 1969, Same cover as #1 ... 12.00
❑20, Oct 1970 ... 12.00
❑21, Oct 1971 ... 12.00

Beware
Marvel

❑1, Mar 1973, "Witch" reprinted from Tales of Suspense #27 ... 8.00
❑2, May 1973 ... 5.00
❑3, Jul 1973 ... 5.00
❑4, Sep 1973 ... 5.00
❑5, Nov 1973 ... 5.00
❑6, Jan 1974 ... 5.00
❑7, Mar 1974 ... 5.00
❑8, May 1974; Series continued in Tomb of Darkness #9 ... 5.00

Beware the Creeper
DC

❑1, Jun 1968, SD (c); SD (w); SD (a); 1: Terror (DC); 2: Creeper ... 45.00
❑2, Aug 1968, SD (c); SD (a); 1: Proteus (DC) ... 32.00
❑3, Oct 1968, SD (c); SD (a); 1: Remington Percival "Rip"' Cord ... 32.00
❑4, Dec 1968, SD (c); SD (a); 1: Yogi Bizerk ... 32.00
❑5, Feb 1969, SD (c); SD (a); ID of Proteus revealed ... 32.00
❑6, Apr 1969, GK (c); SD (a); Final Issue ... 55.00

Beware the Creeper
DC

❑1, Jun 2003 ... 2.95
❑2, Jul 2003 ... 2.95
❑3, Aug 2003 ... 2.95
❑4, Sep 2003 ... 2.95
❑5, Oct 2003 ... 2.95

N-MINT

Bewitched
Dell

❑1, Apr 1965 ... 85.00
❑2, Jul 1965 ... 50.00
❑3, Oct 1965 ... 40.00
❑4, Mar 1966 ... 40.00
❑5, Jun 1966 ... 40.00
❑6, Sep 1966 ... 40.00
❑7, Dec 1966 ... 40.00
❑8, Mar 1967 ... 40.00
❑9, Apr 1967 ... 40.00
❑10, Jul 1967 ... 40.00
❑11, Oct 1967 ... 30.00
❑12, Oct 1968 ... 30.00
❑13, Jan 1969 ... 30.00
❑14, Oct 1969 ... 30.00

Beyblade
Viz

❑1, Oct 2004 ... 7.99
❑2, Dec 2004 ... 7.99
❑3, Feb 2005 ... 7.99
❑4, Apr 2005 ... 7.99
❑5, May 2005 ... 7.99
❑6, Aug 2005 ... 7.99
❑7, Oct 2005 ... 7.99

Beyond!
Marvel

❑1, Sep 2006 ... 2.99
❑2, Oct 2006 ... 2.99
❑3, Nov 2006 ... 2.99
❑4, Dec 2006 ... 2.99
❑5, Jan 2007 ... 2.99
❑6, Feb 2007 ... 2.99

Beyond (Blue)
Blue

❑1, Jun 1996 ... 2.95

Beyond Avalon
Image

❑1, Feb 2005 ... 2.95
❑2, May 2005 ... 3.50
❑3, Apr 2006 ... 3.50

Beyond Communion
Caliber

❑1 ... 2.95

Beyond Mars
Blackthorne

❑1, Jan 1989, b&w ... 2.00
❑2, Feb 1989, b&w ... 2.00
❑3, Mar 1989 ... 2.00
❑4, ca. 1989 ... 2.00
❑5, ca. 1989 ... 2.00

Beyond the Grave
Charlton

❑1, Jul 1975 ... 6.50
❑2, Oct 1975 ... 4.00
❑3, Dec 1975 ... 4.00
❑4, Feb 1976 ... 3.00
❑5, Apr 1976 ... 3.00
❑6, Jun 1976 ... 2.50
❑7 ... 2.50
❑8 ... 2.50
❑9 ... 2.50
❑10, Aug 1983 ... 2.50

Other grades: Multiply price above by 5/6 for VF/NM • 2/3 for VERY FINE • 1/3 for FINE • 1/5 for VERY GOOD • 1/8 for GOOD

❑11, Oct 1983 ... 2.50
❑12, Dec 1983 ... 2.50
❑13, Feb 1984 ... 2.50
❑14, Apr 1984 ... 2.50
❑15, Jun 1984 ... 2.50
❑16, Aug 1984 ... 2.50
❑17, Oct 1984, Reprints from Ghostly Haunts #28, Ghostly Tales #80, Ghost Manor #18; Final Issue ... 2.50

Bicentennial Gross-Outs
Yentzer and Gonif

❑1, Jul 1976 ... 3.00

Biff Bang Pow!
Paisano

❑1 ... 2.95
❑2, Feb 1992 ... 2.95

Big
Dark Horse

❑1, Mar 1989; adaptation ... 2.50

Big Ass Comics
Rip Off

❑1, Jun 1969 ... 50.00
❑1/2nd ... 24.00
❑1/3rd ... 10.00
❑1/4th ... 10.00
❑1/5th ... 6.00
❑1/6th ... 6.00
❑2, Aug 1971 ... 25.00
❑2/2nd ... 15.00

Big Bad Blood of Dracula
Apple

❑1; reprints, b&w ... 2.75
❑2 ... 2.95

Big Bang Comics: Round Table of America
Image

❑1, Mar 2004 ... 3.95

Big Bang Comics
Caliber / Big Bang

❑0, May 1995, ARo (c); ARo (a); B&w and color ... 3.50
❑1, Spr 1994, b&w ... 2.50
❑2, Sum 1994, b&w ... 2.50
❑3, Oct 1994, b&w ... 2.50
❑4, Feb 1995, b&w ... 2.50

Big Bang Comics
Image

❑1, May 1996; Mighty Man, Knight Watchman, Doctor Weird ... 3.00
❑2, Jun 1996; Silver Age Shadowhawk, Knight Watchman, The Badge ... 2.75
❑3, Jul 1996; Knight Watchman, Ultiman, Thunder Girl ... 2.75
❑4, Sep 1996; O: The Knights of Justice; Dr. Stellar joins The Knights of Justice ... 2.75
❑5, Oct 1996; origins issue ... 2.95
❑6, Nov 1996 CS (c); CS (a) ... 2.95
❑7, Dec 1996; Mighty Man vs. Mighty Man ... 2.95
❑8, Jan 1997; 1: Mister U.S ... 2.95
❑9, Mar 1997; A: Sphinx. A: Blitz. Showplace ... 2.95
❑10, May 1997 ... 2.95
❑11, Jul 1997; Knight Watchman vs. Faulty Towers ... 2.95
❑12, Sep 1997 A: Savage Dragon ... 2.95
❑13, Aug 1997; cover says Jul, indicia says Aug ... 2.95
❑14, Oct 1997 A: Savage Dragon ... 2.95
❑15, Oct 1997; Doctor Weird vs. Bog Swamp Demon, cover says Dec, indicia says Oct/Nov ... 2.95
❑16, Jan 1998; Thunder Girl ... 2.95
❑17, Feb 1998; Shadow Lady ... 2.95
❑18, Apr 1998 DC (c); DC (a); A: Savage Dragon, Pantheon of Heroes ... 2.95
❑19, Jun 1998; O: The Beacon II (Doctor Julia Gardner). O: The Hummingbird. O: The Beacon I (Scott Martin). cover says Apr, indicia says Jun ... 2.95
❑20, Jul 1998; A: Dimensioneer. A: Knight Watchman. A: The Blitz. A: The Sphinx. photo back cover ... 2.95
❑21, Aug 1998; Shadow Lady ... 2.95
❑22, Sep 1998; Knight Watchman ... 2.95
❑23, Nov 1998; Tales of the Sphinx, Book 2 ... 3.95
❑24, Apr 1999; The Big Bang History of Comics ... 2.95
❑25, Jun 1999 ... 2.95
❑26, Jul 1999 ... 2.95
❑27, Oct 1999; The Big Bang History of Comics, Part 2 ... 3.95
❑28, Dec 1999; Knight Watchman ... 3.95
❑29, Feb 2000 ... 3.95
❑30, Mar 2000 ... 3.95
❑31, Apr 2000 ... 3.95
❑32, Jun 2000 ... 3.95
❑33, Jul 2000 ... 3.95
❑34, Aug 2000 ... 3.95
❑35, Jan 2001 ... 3.95

Big Bang Presents: Ultiman Family
Image

❑1, Mar 2005 ... 3.50

Big Bang (Red Calloway's...)
Zoo Arsonist

❑1; Adult ... 2.95

Big Bang Summer Special
Image

❑1, Aug 2003 ... 4.95

Big Black Kiss
Vortex

❑1, Sep 1989 HC (w); HC (a) ... 3.95
❑2, Oct 1989 HC (w); HC (a) ... 3.95
❑3, Nov 1989 HC (w); HC (a) ... 3.95

Big Black Thing (Colin Upton's...)
Upton

❑1, b&w; Adult ... 3.25

Big Blown Baby
Dark Horse

❑1, Aug 1996 ... 2.95
❑2, Sep 1996 ... 2.95
❑3, Oct 1996 ... 2.95
❑4, Nov 1996 ... 2.95

Big Blue Couch Comix
Couch

❑1, b&w ... 2.00

Big Boob Bondage
Antarctic / Venus

❑1, Jan 1997; b&w pin-ups, adult ... 2.95

Big Bruisers
Image

❑1, Jul 1996 ... 3.50

Big Daddy Danger
DC

❑1, Oct 2002 ... 2.95
❑2, Nov 2002 ... 2.95
❑3, Dec 2002 ... 2.95
❑4, Jan 2003 ... 2.95
❑5, Feb 2003 ... 2.95
❑6, Mar 2003 ... 2.95
❑7, Apr 2003 ... 2.95
❑8, May 2003 ... 2.95
❑9, Jun 2003 ... 2.95

Big Dog Funnies
Rip Off

❑1, Jun 1992; NN ... 2.50

Big Funnies
Radio

❑1, ca. 2001 ... 3.95
❑2, ca. 2001 ... 3.99
❑3, ca. 2001 ... 3.99

Bigger
Free Lunch

❑1, ca. 1998, b&w ... 3.50

Bigger: Will Rison & the Devil's Concubine
Free Lunch

❑1, Dec 1998 ... 2.95
❑2, Feb 1999 ... 2.95
❑3, Apr 1999 ... 2.95
❑4, Jun 1999; Indicia says #3, really #4. ... 2.95

Big Guy and Rusty the Boy Robot
Dark Horse / Legend

❑1, Jul 1995 FM (w) ... 10.00
❑2, Aug 1995 FM (w) ... 10.00

Big Hair Productions
Image

❑1, Mar 2000 ... 3.50
❑2, Apr 2000 ... 3.50

Big Lou
Side Show

❑1 ... 2.95

Big Monster Fight
Kidgang Comics

❑0 ... 2.50
❑1 ... 2.50

Big Mouth
Starhead

❑1, b&w ... 2.95
❑2, b&w ... 2.95
❑3 ... 2.95
❑4 ... 2.95
❑5; no indicia, b&w ... 2.95
❑6, Dec 1996 ... 2.95
❑7, Jan 1998 ... 2.95

Big Numbers
Mad Love

❑1 ... 5.50
❑2, Aug 1990; Final published issue ... 5.50

Big O Part 1
Viz

❑1, Feb 2002 ... 3.50
❑2, Mar 2002 ... 3.50
❑3, Apr 2002 ... 3.50
❑4, May 2002 ... 3.50
❑5, Jun 2002 ... 3.50

Big O Part 2
Viz

❑1, Jul 2002 ... 3.50
❑2, Aug 2002 ... 3.50
❑3, Sep 2002 ... 3.50
❑4, Oct 2002 ... 3.50

Big O Part 3
Viz

❑1, Nov 2002 ... 3.50
❑2, Dec 2002 ... 3.50
❑3, Jan 2003 ... 3.50
❑4, Feb 2003 ... 3.50

Big O Part 4
Viz

❑1, Mar 2003 ... 3.50
❑2, Apr 2003 ... 3.50
❑3, May 2003 ... 3.50
❑4, Jun 2003 ... 3.50

Big Prize
Eternity

❑1, May 1988, b&w ... 1.95
❑2, Aug 1985, b&w ... 1.95

Big Questions
Drawn & Quarterly

❑7 2005, This small-press title moved to Drawn & Quarterly with #7 ... 4.95

Big Time
Delta

❑1, Mar 1996; Adult ... 1.95

Big Top Bondage
Fantagraphics / Eros

❑1, b&w; Adult ... 2.50

Big Town
Marvel

❑1, Jan 2001; A: X-Men. A: Avengers. says Fantastic Four Big Town on cover; alternate Marvel history ... 3.50
❑2, Feb 2001 A: Hulk. A: Avengers. A: Sub-Mariner ... 3.50
❑3, Mar 2001 A: Hulk. A: Avengers. A: Sub-Mariner ... 3.50
❑4, Apr 2001 A: Hulk. A: Avengers. A: Sub-Mariner ... 3.50

Big Valley
Dell

❑1, ca. 1966 ... 40.00
❑2, ca. 1966 ... 25.00
❑3, ca. 1967 ... 25.00
❑4, ca. 1967 ... 25.00
❑5, ca. 1967 ... 25.00
❑6, ca. 1967 ... 25.00

Bijou Funnies
Kitchen Sink

❑1, ca. 1968 ... 85.00
❑1/2nd, May 1968, 2nd printing ... 30.00
❑2, ca. 1969 ... 30.00

Other grades: Multiply price above by 5/6 for VF/NM • 2/3 for VERY FINE • 1/3 for FINE • 1/5 for VERY GOOD • 1/8 for GOOD

Battle Angel Alita Part 1

Scavenger rebuilds robot martial artist

©Viz

Battle Chasers

Infamously late-shipping Cliffhanger title

©Image

Battlefield Action

Restarted in 1980 with nothing but reprints

©Charlton

Battle of the Planets

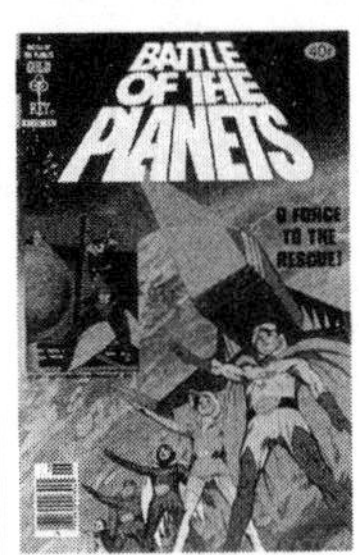

Early anime adaptation from Gold Key

©Gold Key

Battlestar Galactica

TV series launched comics adventures

©Marvel

N-MINT

- ❑3, Oct 1969 ... 25.00
- ❑3/2nd, ca. 1970, 2nd printing ... 15.00
- ❑3/3rd, ca. 1972, 3rd printing ... 10.00
- ❑4, ca. 1970, Inidcia reads Published by The Bijou Publishing Empire ... 25.00
- ❑5, ca. 1970 ... 20.00
- ❑6, Sep 1971 ... 18.00
- ❑7, Apr 1972 ... 18.00
- ❑8, ca. 1973 ... 18.00
- ❑8/2nd, ca. 1974, 2nd printing ... 4.00

Biker Mice from Mars
Marvel

- ❑1, Nov 1993, O: The Biker Mice From Mars ... 2.00
- ❑2, Dec 1993, O: The Biker Mice From Mars ... 2.00
- ❑3, Jan 1994 ... 2.00

Bikini Assassin Team
Catfish

- ❑1 ... 2.50

Bikini Battle 3-D
3-D Zone

- ❑1; NN; Adult ... 3.95

Bill & Ted's Bogus Journey
Marvel

- ❑1, Sep 1991; adapts movie ... 2.95

Bill & Ted's Excellent Adventure Movie Adaptation
DC

- ❑1; adapts movie, wraparound cover, no cover price ... 1.50

Bill & Ted's Excellent Comic Book
Marvel

- ❑1, Dec 1991 ... 1.50
- ❑2, Jan 1992 ... 1.50
- ❑3, Feb 1992 ... 1.50
- ❑4, Mar 1992; 1: Fight Man ... 1.50
- ❑5, Apr 1992 ... 1.50
- ❑6, May 1992 ... 1.50
- ❑7, Jun 1992 ... 1.50
- ❑8, Jul 1992 ... 1.50
- ❑9, Aug 1992 ... 1.50
- ❑10, Sep 1992 ... 1.50
- ❑11, Oct 1992 ... 1.50
- ❑12, Nov 1992; Final issue ... 1.50

Bill, the Galactic Hero
Topps

- ❑1, Jul 1994; prestige format, based on Harry Harrison novel series ... 4.95
- ❑2, Sep 1994 ... 4.95
- ❑3, Nov 1994 ... 4.95

Billi 99
Dark Horse

- ❑1 ... 3.50
- ❑2 ... 3.50
- ❑3 ... 3.50
- ❑4 ... 3.50

Bill the Bull: Burnt Cain
Boneyard

- ❑1, Jul 1992, Includes eulogy for Michelle Davis (Hart Fisher's girlfriend) ... 4.95
- ❑2 ... 4.95
- ❑3 ... 4.95

N-MINT

Bill the Bull: One Shot, One Bourbon, One Beer
Boneyard

- ❑1, Dec 1994; Adult ... 2.95
- ❑2, indicia says Mar 94, a misprint ... 2.95

Bill the Clown
Slave Labor

- ❑1, Feb 1992, b&w; 2nd Printing ... 2.50
- ❑1/2nd, 2nd Printing, b&w ... 2.95

Bill the Clown: Comedy Isn't Pretty
Slave Labor

- ❑1, Nov 1992, b&w ... 2.50

Bill the Clown: Death & Clown White
Slave Labor

- ❑1, Sep 1993, b&w ... 2.95

Billy Boy The Sick Little Fat Kid
Asylum

- ❑1, ca. 2001 ... 2.95

Billy Cole
Cult

- ❑1, Jun 1994, b&w ... 2.75
- ❑2 ... 2.75
- ❑3 ... 2.75
- ❑4 ... 2.75

Billy Dogma
Modern

- ❑1, Apr 1997 ... 2.95
- ❑2, Aug 1997 ... 2.95
- ❑3, Dec 1997 ... 2.95

Billy Joe Van Helsing: Redneck Vampire Hunter
Alpha

- ❑1 ... 2.50

Billy Nguyen, Private Eye
Attitude

- ❑1, Mar 1988 ... 2.00
- ❑2, Jun 1988 ... 2.00
- ❑3, Oct 1988 ... 2.00

Billy Nguyen, Private Eye
Caliber

- ❑1, b&w ... 2.50

Billy Ray Cyrus
Marvel Music

- ❑1; prestige format; NN ... 5.95

Billy the Kid
Charlton

- ❑31, Nov 1961 ... 14.00
- ❑32, Jan 1962 ... 14.00
- ❑33, Apr 1962 ... 14.00
- ❑34 1962 ... 14.00
- ❑35, Aug 1962 ... 14.00
- ❑36, Oct 1962 ... 14.00
- ❑37, Dec 1963 ... 14.00
- ❑38, Feb 1963 ... 14.00
- ❑39, Apr 1963 ... 14.00
- ❑40, Jun 1963 ... 14.00
- ❑41, Aug 1963 ... 8.00
- ❑42 ... 8.00
- ❑43, Jan 1964 ... 8.00
- ❑44, Mar 1964 ... 8.00
- ❑45, May 1964 ... 8.00

N-MINT

- ❑46, Jul 1964 ... 8.00
- ❑47, Sep 1964 ... 8.00
- ❑48, Nov 1964 ... 8.00
- ❑49, Mar 1965 ... 8.00
- ❑50, Jun 1965 ... 8.00
- ❑51 1965 ... 7.00
- ❑52, Oct 1965 ... 7.00
- ❑53, Dec 1965 ... 7.00
- ❑54, Mar 1966 ... 7.00
- ❑55, May 1966 ... 7.00
- ❑56, Jul 1966 ... 7.00
- ❑57, Sep 1966 ... 7.00
- ❑58, Nov 1966 ... 7.00
- ❑59, Jan 1967 ... 7.00
- ❑60, Mar 1967 ... 7.00
- ❑61, Jun 1967 ... 5.00
- ❑62, Aug 1967 ... 5.00
- ❑63, Oct 1967 ... 5.00
- ❑64, Dec 1967 ... 5.00
- ❑65, Feb 1968 ... 5.00
- ❑66, May 1968 ... 5.00
- ❑67, ca. 1968 ... 5.00
- ❑68, Sep 1968 ... 5.00
- ❑69, Nov 1968 ... 5.00
- ❑70, Jan 1969 ... 5.00
- ❑71, Mar 1969 ... 4.00
- ❑72, May 1969 ... 4.00
- ❑73, Jul 1969 ... 4.00
- ❑74, Sep 1969, Bounty Hunter side story ... 4.00
- ❑75, Nov 1969 ... 4.00
- ❑76, Jan 1970, Bounty Hunter side story ... 4.00
- ❑77, Mar 1970 ... 4.00
- ❑78, May 1970 ... 4.00
- ❑79, Jul 1970 ... 4.00
- ❑80, Sep 1970, Bounty Hunter side story ... 4.00
- ❑81, Nov 1970 ... 3.50
- ❑82, Jan 1971 ... 3.50
- ❑83, Mar 1971 ... 3.50
- ❑84, May 1971 ... 3.50
- ❑85, Jul 1971 ... 3.50
- ❑86, Sep 1971 ... 3.50
- ❑87, Nov 1971 ... 3.50
- ❑88, Dec 1971 ... 3.50
- ❑89, Feb 1972 ... 3.50
- ❑90, Mar 1972 ... 3.50
- ❑91, Apr 1972 ... 3.50
- ❑92, May 1972 ... 3.50
- ❑93, Jul 1972 ... 3.50
- ❑94, Aug 1972 ... 3.50
- ❑95, Oct 1972 ... 3.50
- ❑96, Nov 1972 ... 3.50
- ❑97, Dec 1972 ... 3.50
- ❑98, Jan 1973 ... 3.50
- ❑99, Feb 1973 ... 3.50
- ❑100, Mar 1973 ... 3.50
- ❑101, May 1973 ... 3.00
- ❑102, Jun 1973 ... 3.00
- ❑103, Aug 1973, Spanish lesson text piece; no credits listed ... 3.00
- ❑104, Sep 1973 ... 3.00
- ❑105, Nov 1973 ... 3.00
- ❑106, Dec 1973 ... 3.00
- ❑107, May 1974 ... 3.00
- ❑108, Jul 1974 ... 3.00
- ❑109, Oct 1974 ... 3.00
- ❑110, Dec 1974 ... 3.00

Other grades: Multiply price above by 5/6 for VF/NM • 2/3 for VERY FINE • 1/3 for FINE • 1/5 for VERY GOOD • 1/8 for GOOD

	N-MINT
❑111, Feb 1975	3.00
❑112, Apr 1975	3.00
❑113, Jun 1975	3.00
❑114, Oct 1975	3.00
❑115, Dec 1975	3.00
❑116, Feb 1976	3.00
❑117, Apr 1976	3.00
❑118, Jun 1976	3.00
❑119, Aug 1976	3.00
❑120, Oct 1976	3.00
❑121, Dec 1976	3.00
❑122, Sep 1977	3.00
❑123, Nov 1977	3.00
❑124, Feb 1978	3.00
❑125, Oct 1978	3.00
❑126, Jan 1979	3.00
❑127, Feb 1979	3.00
❑128, Apr 1979	3.00
❑129, Jun 1979	3.00
❑130, Aug 1979	3.00
❑131, Sep 1979	3.00
❑132, Oct 1979	3.00
❑133, Dec 1979	3.00
❑134, Feb 1980	3.00
❑135, Apr 1980	3.00
❑136, Jun 1980	3.00
❑137, Aug 1980	3.00
❑138, Oct 1980	3.00
❑139, Dec 1980	3.00
❑140, Feb 1981	3.00
❑141, Apr 1981	3.00
❑142, Jun 1981	3.00
❑143, Aug 1981	3.00
❑144, Oct 1981	3.00
❑145, Nov 1981	3.00
❑146, Jan 1982	3.00
❑147, Mar 1982	3.00
❑148, Jun 1982	3.00
❑149, Aug 1982	3.00
❑150, Oct 1982	3.00
❑151, Dec 1982	3.00
❑152, Feb 1983	3.00
❑153, Mar 1983, Final Issue	3.00

Billy the Kid's Old-Timey Oddities
Dark Horse

❑1, May 2005	2.99
❑2, Jun 2005	2.99
❑3, Jul 2005	2.99
❑4, Aug 2005	2.99

B1N4RY
APComics

❑0, ca. 2004	3.50
❑1, Jul 2004	3.50
❑2, Aug 2004	3.50
❑3, Sep 2004	5.00
❑3/Sketch 2004	6.00
❑4, Oct 2004	3.50

Binky
DC

❑72, May 1970; Series continued from "Leave it to Binky #71"	7.00
❑73, Jul 1970	7.00
❑74, Sep 1970	7.00
❑75, Nov 1970	7.00
❑76, Jan 1971	6.00
❑77, Mar 1971	6.00
❑78, May 1971	6.00
❑79, Jul 1971	6.00
❑80, Sep 1971	6.00
❑81, Nov 1971; Final issue of original series	6.00
❑82, Sum 1977; 1977 one-shot revival	3.00

Binky's Buddies
DC

❑1, Jan 1969	26.00
❑2, Mar 1969	16.00
❑3, May 1969	12.00
❑4, Jul 1969	10.00
❑5, Sep 1969	10.00
❑6, Nov 1969	10.00
❑7, Jan 1970	10.00
❑8, Mar 1970	10.00
❑9, May 1970	10.00
❑10, Jul 1970	10.00
❑11, Sep 1970	10.00
❑12, Nov 1970	10.00

Bio 90
Bullet

	N-MINT
❑1, Aug 1992, b&w	2.50

Bio-Booster Armor Guyver
Viz

❑1	4.00
❑2	3.50
❑3	3.50
❑4	3.50
❑5	3.50
❑6	3.00
❑7	3.00
❑8	3.00
❑9	3.00
❑10	3.00
❑11	3.00
❑12	3.00

Bio-Booster Armor Guyver Part 2
Viz

❑1, Oct 1994	3.00
❑2, Nov 1994	3.00
❑3, Dec 1994	3.00
❑4, Jan 1995	3.00
❑5, Feb 1995	3.00
❑6, Mar 1995	3.00

Bio-Booster Armor Guyver Part 3
Viz

❑1, Apr 1995; b&w	2.75
❑2, May 1995; b&w	2.75
❑3, Jun 1995; b&w	2.75
❑4, Jul 1995; b&w	2.75
❑5, Aug 1995; b&w	2.75
❑6, Sep 1995; b&w	2.75
❑7, Oct 1995; b&w	2.75

Bio-Booster Armor Guyver Part 4
Viz

❑1, Nov 1995; b&w	2.75
❑2, Dec 1995; b&w	2.75
❑3, Jan 1996; b&w	2.95
❑4, Feb 1996; b&w	2.95
❑5, Mar 1996; b&w	2.95
❑6, Apr 1996; b&w	2.95

Bio-Booster Armor Guyver Part 5
Viz

❑1, May 1996; b&w	2.95
❑2, Jun 1996; b&w	2.95
❑3, Jul 1996; b&w	2.95
❑4, Aug 1996; b&w	2.95
❑5, Sep 1996; b&w	2.95
❑6, Oct 1996; b&w	2.95
❑7, Nov 1996; b&w	2.95

Bio-Booster Armor Guyver Part 6
Viz

❑1, Dec 1996; b&w	2.95
❑2, Jan 1997; b&w	2.95
❑3, Feb 1997; b&w	2.95
❑4, Mar 1997; b&w	2.95
❑5, Apr 1997; b&w	2.95
❑6, May 1997; b&w	2.95

Biologic Show
Fantagraphics

❑0, Oct 1994, b&w; magazine; cardstock cover	2.95
❑1, Jan 1995, b&w	2.75

Bioneers
Mirage

❑1, Aug 1994; 1: Bioneers	2.75
❑2	2.75
❑3	2.75

Bionic Dog
Hugo Rex

❑1	3.25

Bionicle
DC

❑1, ca. 2001	2.25
❑2 2001	2.25
❑3, Oct 2001	2.25
❑4 2002	2.25
❑5, Apr 2002	2.25
❑6, May 2002	2.25
❑7 2002	2.25
❑8 2002	2.25
❑9, Dec 2002	2.25

Bionic Woman
Charlton

	N-MINT
❑1, Oct 1977	14.00
❑2, Feb 1978	6.00
❑3, Mar 1978	6.00
❑4, May 1978	6.00
❑5, Jun 1978	6.00

Bionix
Maximum

❑1, ca. 1996	2.99

Birdland
Fantagraphics / Eros

❑1, Oct 1990, b&w; Adult	1.95
❑2, Feb 1991; Adult; b&w	2.25
❑3; Adult	2.25

Birdland
Fantagraphics / Eros

❑1, Jun 1994, b&w; Adult	2.95

Birds of Prey
DC

❑1, Jan 1999 A: Hellhound. A: Oracle	4.00
❑2, Feb 1999 A: Hellhound. A: Black Canary. A: Jackie Pajamas	3.00
❑3, Mar 1999; A: Hellhound. A: Black Canary. V: Hellhound	3.00
❑4, Apr 1999 A: Ravens. A: Kobra	3.00
❑5, May 1999 A: Ravens	3.00
❑6, Jun 1999; V: Ravens; V: Kobra	3.00
❑7, Jul 1999	3.00
❑8, Aug 1999; A: Nightwing. Low print run	12.00
❑9, Sep 1999	3.00
❑10, Oct 1999	3.00
❑11, Nov 1999; DG (a); V: Joe Gardner	3.00
❑12, Dec 1999 DG (a)	3.00
❑13, Jan 2000	3.00
❑14, Feb 2000; V: Lashina	3.00
❑15, Mar 2000; Guice-a begins	3.00
❑16, Apr 2000 BG (a); A: Joker	3.00
❑17, May 2000 BG (a)	3.00
❑18, Jun 2000 BG, DG (a)	3.00
❑19, Jul 2000; BG (a); Continued in Nightwing #45	3.00
❑20, Aug 2000; BG (a); V: Brutale; V: Lady Vic	3.00
❑21, Sep 2000; BG (a); V: Blockbuster; V: Electrocutioner	3.00
❑22, Oct 2000 BSz, BG (a)	3.00
❑23, Nov 2000; BG (a); V: Grodd; V: Deathstroke	3.00
❑24, Dec 2000 BG (a)	3.00
❑25, Jan 2001 BG (a)	3.00
❑26, Feb 2001 BG (a)	3.00
❑27, Mar 2001	3.00
❑28, Apr 2001 BG (a)	3.00
❑29, May 2001 BG (a)	3.00
❑30, Jun 2001 BG (a)	3.00
❑31, Jul 2001	2.50
❑32, Aug 2001	2.50
❑33, Sep 2001; BG (a); V: Ra's Al Ghul and Talia	2.50
❑34, Oct 2001; BG (a); V: Ra's Al Ghul and Talia	2.50
❑35, Nov 2001	2.50
❑36, Dec 2001; Joker: Last Laugh; V: Spellbinder; V: Shadow Thief; V: Joker; V: Charaxes; V: Copperhead; Black Canary investigates riot at Slab penitentiary	2.50
❑37, Jan 2002	2.50
❑38, Feb 2002; Black Canary quarantines nano-technology run amok	2.50
❑39, Mar 2002; Bruce Wayne: Murderer?; Part 5	2.50
❑40, Apr 2002	2.50
❑41, May 2002	2.50
❑42, Jun 2002	2.50
❑43, Jul 2002; Bruce Wayne: Fugitive; Part 10	2.50
❑44, Aug 2002	2.50
❑45, Sep 2002	2.50
❑46, Oct 2002; On Dinosaur Island	2.50
❑47, Nov 2002	2.50
❑48, Dec 2002	2.50
❑49, Jan 2003	2.50
❑50, Feb 2003; Gilbert Hernandez-s begins	2.50
❑51, Mar 2003	2.50

Beagle Boys

Uncle Scrooge's arch-enemies go wild
©Gold Key

Beast Boy

Changeling uses his older, sillier name
©DC

Beatles Experience

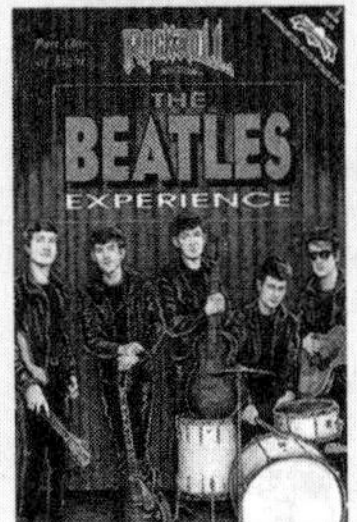

Unauthorized tales of the Fab Four
©Revolutionary

Beautiful Stories for Ugly Children

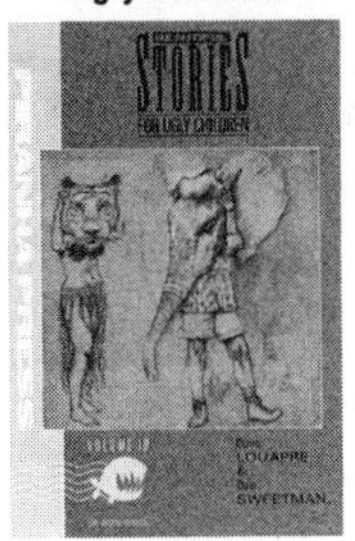

Piranha series ventures into the grotesque
©DC

Beauty and the Beast

Odd romantic pairing of Beast and Dazzler
©Marvel

N-MINT

❑52, Apr 2003; D: Killer Moth; V: Killer Moth; Metamorpho rescues Simon Stagg and Sapphire Stagg ... 2.50
❑53, May 2003 ... 2.50
❑54, Jun 2003 ... 2.50
❑55, Jul 2003 ... 2.50
❑56, Aug 2003 ... 2.50
❑57, Sep 2003 ... 2.50
❑58, Oct 2003 ... 2.50
❑59, Nov 2003 ... 2.50
❑60, Dec 2003 ... 2.50
❑61, Jan 2004 ... 2.50
❑62, Feb 2004 ... 2.50
❑63, Mar 2004; V: Cheshire ... 2.50
❑64, Apr 2004 ... 2.50
❑65, May 2004; V: Cheshire ... 2.50
❑66, Jun 2004 ... 2.50
❑67, Jul 2004, V: Cheshire ... 2.50
❑68, Aug 2004 ... 2.50
❑69, Sep 2004 ... 2.50
❑70, Sep 2004 ... 2.50
❑71, Oct 2004 ... 2.50
❑72, Oct 2004, V: Brainiac; Bagged with promo CD for Sky Captain and the World of Tomorrow ... 2.50
❑73, Nov 2004, V: Brainiac ... 2.50
❑74, Dec 2004 ... 2.50
❑75, Jan 2005, Heroscape insert ... 2.95
❑76, Feb 2005, 1: Black Alice ... 15.00
❑77, Mar 2005, 1: Harvest ... 2.50
❑78, Apr 2005, V: Harvest ... 2.50
❑79, May 2005 ... 2.50
❑80, Jun 2005, Advent Rising insert ... 2.50
❑81, Jun 2005 ... 2.50
❑82, Jul 2005 ... 2.50
❑83, Aug 2005; Omac Project tie-in ... 2.50
❑84, Sep 2005 ... 2.50
❑85, Oct 2005 ... 2.50
❑86, Nov 2005 ... 2.50
❑87, Dec 2005 ... 2.50
❑88, Jan 2006 ... 2.50
❑89, Feb 2006, V: Calculator ... 2.50
❑90, Mar 2006, There is no Part 4 ... 2.50
❑91, Apr 2006 ... 2.50
❑92, May 2006, V: Clayface; V: Ventriloquist; V: Killer Croc; One Year Later; Lady Shiva joins; Gypsy joins ... 2.50
❑93, Jun 2006, V: HIVE; One Year Later ... 2.50
❑94, Aug 2006, V: Prometheus; One Year Later ... 2.99
❑95, Sep 2006, V: Prometheus ... 2.99
❑96, Oct 2006, V: Cheetah; V: Talia; V: Dr. Psycho ... 2.99
❑97, Nov 2006, V: Cheetah; V: Talia; V: Dr. Psycho ... 2.99
❑98, Nov 2006 ... 2.99
❑99, Dec 2006, Black Canary; Huntress; Oracle; Lady Blackhawk ... 2.99
❑100, Jan 2007, 1: Judomaster (Sonia Sato); Double-sized issue ... 3.99
❑101, Mar 2007, Oracle; Lady Blackhawk; Big Barda; Judo Master; Huntress; Manhunter; Spy Smasher; Lois Lane; Misfit; Judomaster ... 2.99
❑102 ... 2.99
❑103 ... 2.99
❑104 ... 2.99
❑105 ... 2.99

N-MINT

❑106 ... 2.99
❑107 ... 2.99
❑108 ... 2.99
❑109 ... 2.99
❑110 ... 2.99
❑111 ... 2.99
❑112 ... 2.99
❑113 ... 2.99
❑114 ... 2.99
❑115 ... 2.99
❑116 ... 2.99
❑117 ... 2.99
❑118 ... 2.99
❑119 ... 2.99
❑120 ... 2.99
❑121 ... 2.99
❑122 ... 2.99
❑123 ... 2.99
❑124 ... 2.99

Birds of Prey: Batgirl
DC

❑1, Feb 1998; V: Spellbinder ... 3.00

Birds of Prey: Catwoman
DC

❑1, Feb 2003 ... 5.95
❑2, Mar 2003 ... 5.95

Birds of Prey: Manhunt
DC

❑1, Sep 1996 ... 2.25
❑2, Oct 1996 ... 2.00
❑3, Nov 1996 ... 2.00
❑4, Dec 1996; SB (a); V: Lady Shiva; Final Issue ... 2.00

Birds of Prey: Revolution
DC

❑1, Apr 1997; One-shot ... 2.95

Birds of Prey: Secret Files 2003
DC

❑1, Jun 2003 ... 4.95

Birds of Prey: The Ravens
DC

❑1, Jun 1998; Girlfrenzy ... 1.95

Birds of Prey: Wolves
DC

❑1, Oct 1997; One-shot ... 2.95

Birth Caul
Eddie Campbell

❑1, Jun 1999; NN ... 5.95

Birthright
Fantagraphics

❑1; A.K.A. Critters #47 ... 2.50
❑2, Apr 1990; A.K.A. Critters #48 ... 2.50
❑3, May 1990; A.K.A. Critters #49 ... 2.50

Birthright (TSR)
TSR

❑1 ... 1.50

Birth Rite
Congress

❑1 ... 2.50
❑2 ... 2.50
❑3 ... 2.50
❑4 ... 2.50

N-MINT

Bishop
Marvel

❑1, Dec 1994; 1: Mountjoy. foil cover ... 4.00
❑2, Jan 1995; Foil cover; V: Mountjoy ... 2.95
❑3, Feb 1995; Foil cover; V: Mountjoy ... 2.95
❑4, Mar 1995; Foil cover; V: Mountjoy ... 2.95

Bishop The Last X-Man
Marvel

❑1, Oct 1999 ... 2.99
❑2, Nov 1999 ... 1.99
❑3, Dec 1999 ... 1.99
❑4, Jan 2000 ... 1.99
❑5, Feb 2000 ... 1.99
❑6, Mar 2000 ... 1.99
❑7, Apr 2000 ... 1.99
❑8, May 2000 ... 1.99
❑9, Jun 2000 ... 2.25
❑10, Jul 2000 ... 2.25
❑11, Aug 2000 ... 2.25
❑12, Sep 2000; double-sized ... 2.99
❑13, Oct 2000 ... 2.25
❑14, Nov 2000 ... 2.25
❑15, Dec 2000 ... 2.25
❑16, Jan 2001; Final Issue ... 2.25

Bishop: Xse
Marvel

❑1, Jan 1998; gatefold summary ... 2.50
❑2, Feb 1998; gatefold summary ... 2.50
❑3, Mar 1998; Gatefold summary ... 2.50

Bisley's Scrapbook
Atomeka

❑1, NN ... 2.50

Bitch in Heat
Fantagraphics / Eros

❑1, Mar 1997; Adult ... 2.95
❑2; Adult ... 2.95
❑3; Adult ... 2.95
❑4; Adult ... 2.95
❑5, Jul 1998; Adult ... 2.95
❑6, Sep 1998; Adult ... 2.95
❑7, Jan 1999; Adult ... 2.95
❑8, Apr 1999; Adult ... 2.95
❑9, ca. 1999; Adult ... 2.95
❑10, ca. 2000; Adult ... 2.95

Bite Club
DC / Vertigo

❑1, May 2004 ... 2.95
❑2, Jun 2004 ... 4.00
❑3, Aug 2004 ... 2.95
❑4, Sep 2004 ... 2.95
❑5, Oct 2004 ... 2.95
❑6, Nov 2004 ... 2.95

Bite Club: Vampire Crime Unit
DC / Vertigo

❑1, Jun 2006 ... 2.99
❑3, Sep 2006 ... 2.99
❑4, Sep 2006 ... 2.99
❑5, Dec 2006 ... 2.99

Bits and Pieces
Mortified

❑1, Nov 1994 ... 3.00

Other grades: Multiply price above by 5/6 for VF/NM • 2/3 for VERY FINE • 1/3 for FINE • 1/5 for VERY GOOD • 1/8 for GOOD

Bitter Cake
Tin Cup

❑1, b&w 2.00

Bizarre 3-D Zone
Blackthorne

❑1, Jul 1986; Blackthorne 3-D Series #5 .... 2.25
❑2 .... 2.25
❑3 .... 2.25
❑4 .... 2.25
❑5, Jul 1986; #1 on cover 2.25

Bizarre Adventures
Marvel

❑25, Mar 1981, A: Black Widow. Lethal Ladies; Was Marvel Preview 2.50
❑26, May 1981, King Kull 2.50
❑27, Jul 1981, X-Men 4.00
❑28, Oct 1981, FM, NA (w); WP, FM, NA (a); A: Elektra. Unlikely Heroes 5.00
❑29, Dec 1981, Stephen King; Horror 2.50
❑30, Feb 1982, Paradox; Tomorrow 2.50
❑31, Apr 1982, FM (w); BSz, HT, FM (a); After the Violence Stops 2.50
❑32, Aug 1982, AM, VM (a); Thor and other Gods 2.50
❑33, ca. 1982, BH (a); 1: Varnae. Dracula; Zombie; Horror 2.50
❑34, Feb 1983, gatefold summary; AM (w); AM, PS (a); A: Howard the Duck. Format changes to comic book 2.50

Bizarre Fantasy
Flashback

❑0, Jan 1995 .... 2.50
❑0/Autographed; 1500 copies printed 9.95
❑1, Apr 1995; 1: The Evolver; 1: Morguu 2.50
❑2 .... 2.50

Bizarre Heroes
Kitchen Sink

❑1, May 1990; parody, b&w 2.50

Bizarre Heroes (Don Simpson's...)
Fiasco

❑0, Dec 1994, b&w; Originally Published by Kitchen Sink as Bizarre Heroes #1 (1990) 2.95
❑1, May 1994, b&w 3.25
❑2, Jun 1994, b&w 2.95
❑3, Jul 1994, b&w 2.95
❑4, Aug 1994, b&w 2.95
❑5, Sep 1994, b&w 2.95
❑6, Oct 1994, b&w 2.95
❑7, Nov 1994, b&w 2.95
❑8, Dec 1994, b&w 2.95
❑9, Feb 1995, b&w 2.95
❑10, Mar 1995, b&w 2.95
❑11, May 1995, b&w 2.95
❑12, b&w 2.95
❑13, Sep 1995, b&w 2.95
❑14, Oct 1995, b&w; Title changes to Bizarre Heroes 2.95
❑15, Jan 1996, b&w; O: The Slick 2.95
❑16, Apr 1996, aka Megaton Man vs. Forbidden Frankenstein 2.95

Bizarre Sex
Kitchen Sink

❑1, May 1972; Adult 15.00
❑2, Nov 1972; Adult 9.00
❑3, Jun 1973; White "remove this outer cover at your own risk" cover 7.00
❑4, Oct 1975; White "remove this outer cover at your own risk" cover 5.00
❑4/2nd, Sep 1976; White "remove this outer cover at your own risk" cover 4.00
❑4/3rd, Jul 1977; Adult 4.00
❑5, Oct 1976; Adult 5.00
❑6, Oct 1977; Adult 5.00
❑7, Jan 1979; Adult 5.00
❑8, Mar 1980; Adult 5.00
❑9, Aug 1981, b&w; 1: Omaha; Adult 18.00

Bizzarian
Ironcat

❑1, ca. 2000 .... 2.95
❑2, ca. 2000 .... 2.95
❑3, ca. 2000 .... 2.95
❑4, ca. 2000 .... 2.95
❑5, ca. 2001 .... 2.95
❑6, ca. 2001 .... 2.95
❑7, ca. 2001 .... 2.95
❑8, ca. 2001 .... 2.95

B. Krigstein Sampler, A
Independent

❑1 BK (c); BK (w); BK (a) 2.50

Blab!
Kitchen Sink

❑8, Sum 1995; odd-sized anthology 16.95
❑9, Fal 1997; odd-sized anthology 18.95
❑10, Fal 1998; odd-sized anthology 19.95

Black & White
Image

❑1, Oct 1994 .... 1.95
❑2, Nov 1994 .... 1.95
❑3, Jan 1995 .... 1.95

Black & White
Image

❑1, Feb 1996 .... 2.50
❑Ashcan 1; No cover price; ashcan preview of series 1.00

Black & White (Viz)
Viz

❑1, Aug 1999 .... 3.25
❑2 1999 .... 3.25
❑3 1999 .... 3.25

Black and White Bondage
Verotik

❑1; Adult 4.95

Black and White Comics
Apex Novelties

❑1; Adult 4.00

Black and White Theater
Double M

❑1, Jun 1996, b&w 2.95
❑2, b&w 2.95

Black Axe
Marvel

❑1, Apr 1993 .... 1.75
❑2, May 1993 .... 1.75
❑3, Jun 1993 .... 1.75
❑4, Jul 1993 .... 1.75
❑5, Aug 1993 .... 1.75
❑6, Sep 1993 .... 1.75
❑7, Oct 1993 .... 1.75

Blackball Comics
Blackball

❑1, Mar 1994 .... 3.00

Black Book (Brian Bolland's...)
Eclipse

❑1, Jul 1985 BB (a) 2.00

Black Bow
Artline

❑1 .... 2.50

Blackburne Covenant
Dark Horse

❑1, Jun 2003 .... 2.99
❑2, Jul 2003 .... 2.99
❑3, Aug 2003 .... 2.99
❑4, Sep 2003 .... 2.99

Black Canary
DC

❑1, Nov 1991 DG, TVE (a) 2.50
❑2, Dec 1991 DG (c); TVE (a) 2.50
❑3, Jan 1992 DG (c); TVE (a) 2.50
❑4, Feb 1992 DG, TVE (a) 2.50

Black Canary
DC

❑1, Jan 1993, TVE (a) 2.00
❑2, Feb 1993, TVE (a) 2.00
❑3, Mar 1993, TVE (a) 2.00
❑4, Apr 1993, TVE (a) 2.00
❑5, May 1993, TVE (a) 2.00
❑6, Jun 1993, TVE (a) 2.00
❑7, Jul 1993, TVE (a) 2.00
❑8, Aug 1993, A: The Ray 2.00
❑9, Sep 1993, TVE (a) 2.00
❑10, Oct 1993, TVE (a) 2.00
❑11, Nov 1993, JA (c); TVE (a) 2.00
❑12, Dec 1993, Final Issue 2.00

Black Canary/Oracle: Birds of Prey
DC

❑1, Jun 1996; One-shot; Published 1996; Black Canary and Oracle history text pages 3.95

Black Cat (The Origins)
Lorne-Harvey

❑1, color and b&w; reprints Black Cat and Sad Sack strips; text feature on Alfred Harvey 3.50

Black Cat The War Years
Recollections

❑1; Golden Age reprints, b&w 1.00

Black Condor
DC

❑1, Jun 1992; 1&O: Black Condor II 1.50
❑2, Jul 1992 .... 1.25
❑3, Aug 1992 .... 1.25
❑4, Sep 1992; V: Shark 1.25
❑5, Oct 1992 .... 1.25
❑6, Nov 1992 .... 1.25
❑7, Dec 1992 .... 1.25
❑8, Jan 1993 MGu (a) 1.25
❑9, Feb 1993 .... 1.25
❑10, Mar 1993 A: The Ray 1.25
❑11, Apr 1993 .... 1.25
❑12, May 1993; A: Batman. Final Issue 1.25

Black Cross: Dirty Work
Dark Horse

❑1, Apr 1997; NN 2.95

Black Cross Special
Dark Horse

❑1, Jan 1988, b&w 2.50
❑1/2nd, Dec 1988; 2nd printing 1.75

Black Diamond
AC

❑1, May 1983; 1: Black Diamond; 1: Colt; 1: Darkfire 2.00
❑2, Jul 1983 .... 2.00
❑3, Dec 1983 .... 2.00
❑4, Feb 1984 .... 2.00
❑5, May 1984 .... 2.00

Black Diamond Effect
Black Diamond Effect

❑1, Sep 1991 .... 3.00
❑2, Oct 1991 .... 3.10
❑3 .... 3.10
❑4 .... 3.10
❑5 .... 3.10
❑6, Dec 1992 .... 3.00
❑7 .... 3.10

Black Dragon
Marvel / Epic

❑1, May 1985 .... 3.00
❑2, Jun 1985 .... 2.50
❑3, Jul 1985 .... 2.50
❑4, Aug 1985 .... 2.50
❑5, Sep 1985 .... 2.00
❑6, Oct 1985 .... 2.00

Black Flag
Image

❑1, Jun 1994, b&w; Fold-out cover 1.95
❑Ashcan 1; Preview edition; 1: Geisha; 1: Sniper; 1: Black Rain 1.95

Black Flag (Maximum)
Maximum

❑0, Jul 1995 .... 2.50
❑1, Jan 1995 .... 2.50
❑2/A, Feb 1995; Woman on cover 2.50
❑2/B, Feb 1995; Variant cover with man 2.50
❑3, Mar 1995 .... 2.50
❑4/A, Apr 1995; cover has black background 2.50
❑4/B, Apr 1995; cover has white background 2.50

Black Forest
Image

❑1, ca. 2003 .... 9.95

Black Goliath
Marvel

❑1, Feb 1976, RB (c); GT (a); O: Black Goliath. 1: Atom-Smasher; 1: Herbert Bell; 1: Dale West; 1: Talia Kruma 11.00
❑2, Apr 1976, RB (c); GT (a); 1: Celia 'Ceil' Jackson; 2: Atom-Smasher 5.00
❑2/30¢, Apr 1976, RB (c); GT (a); 30-cent regional price variant 20.00
❑3, Jun 1976, GT (a); 1: Vulcan; D: Atom-Smasher; Kurt Busiek L.O.C 4.00
❑3/30¢, Jun 1976, GT (a); 30-cent regional price variant 20.00

Other grades: Multiply price above by 5/6 for VF/NM • 2/3 for VERY FINE • 1/3 for FINE • 1/5 for VERY GOOD • 1/8 for GOOD

Beavis & Butt-Head

Dim duo goes from MTV to Marvel

©Marvel

Beep Beep

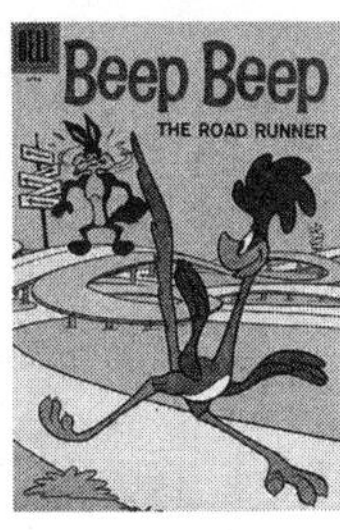

First series starring pesky running fowl

©Dell

Beetle Bailey

Misadventures with comic strip soldier

©Dell

Beowulf

Medieval tale updated for 1970s DC series

©DC

Berzerkers

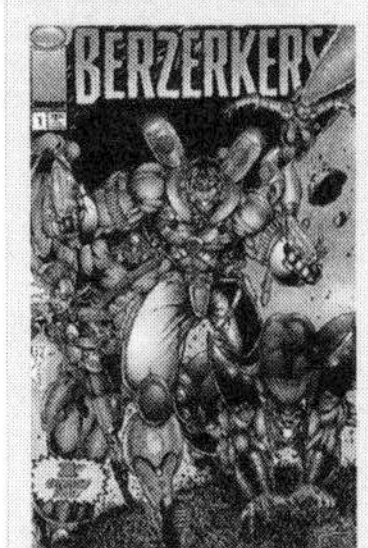

Prison escapees live a life of violence

©Image

N-MINT

❑4, Aug 1976, JK (c); RB, DH (a); V: Stilt Man ... 4.00
❑4/30¢, Aug 1976, JK (c); RB, DH (a); 30-cent regional price variant ... 20.00
❑5, Nov 1976, AM, GK (c); KP (a); Final Issue; Story continues in Champions #11; Gil Kane cover ... 4.00

Black Harvest
Devil's Due

❑1, Nov 2005 ... 3.25
❑2, Jan 2006 ... 3.25
❑3, Feb 2006 ... 3.25
❑4, Mar 2006 ... 3.25
❑5, Apr 2006 ... 3.25
❑6, Aug 2006 ... 3.25

Blackhawk
DC

❑164, Sep 1961, O: Blackhawks ... 60.00
❑165, Oct 1961 ... 48.00
❑166, Nov 1961 ... 48.00
❑167, Dec 1961 ... 22.00
❑168, Jan 1962 ... 22.00
❑169, Feb 1962 ... 22.00
❑170, Mar 1962 ... 22.00
❑171, Apr 1962 ... 22.00
❑172, May 1962 ... 22.00
❑173, Jun 1962 ... 22.00
❑174, Jul 1962 ... 22.00
❑175, Aug 1962 ... 22.00
❑176, Sep 1962 ... 22.00
❑177, Oct 1962 ... 22.00
❑178, Nov 1962 ... 22.00
❑179, Dec 1962 ... 22.00
❑180, Jan 1963 ... 22.00
❑181, Feb 1963 ... 16.00
❑182, Mar 1963 ... 16.00
❑183, Apr 1963 ... 16.00
❑184, May 1963 ... 16.00
❑185, Jun 1963 ... 16.00
❑186, Jul 1963 ... 16.00
❑187, Aug 1963 ... 16.00
❑188, Sep 1963 ... 16.00
❑189, Oct 1963, O: Blackhawks ... 16.00
❑190, Nov 1963 ... 16.00
❑191, Dec 1963 ... 16.00
❑192, Jan 1964 ... 16.00
❑193, Feb 1964 ... 16.00
❑194, Mar 1964 ... 16.00
❑195, Apr 1964 ... 16.00
❑196, May 1964, Biographies of Dick Dillon and Chuck Cuidera (Blackhawk artists) ... 16.00
❑197, Jun 1964, new look ... 16.00
❑198, Jul 1964, O: Blackhawks ... 16.00
❑199, Aug 1964 ... 16.00
❑200, Sep 1964 ... 16.00
❑201, Oct 1964 ... 15.00
❑202, Nov 1964 ... 15.00
❑203, Dec 1964, O: Chop-Chop ... 15.00
❑204, Jan 1965 ... 15.00
❑205, Feb 1965 ... 15.00
❑206, Mar 1965 ... 15.00
❑207, Apr 1965 ... 15.00
❑208, May 1965 ... 15.00
❑209, Jun 1965 ... 15.00
❑210, Jul 1965 ... 15.00

N-MINT

❑211, Aug 1965 ... 15.00
❑212, Sep 1965 ... 15.00
❑213, Oct 1965 ... 15.00
❑214, Nov 1965 ... 15.00
❑215, Dec 1965 ... 15.00
❑216, Jan 1966 ... 15.00
❑217, Feb 1966 ... 15.00
❑218, Mar 1966 ... 15.00
❑219, Apr 1966 ... 15.00
❑220, May 1966 ... 15.00
❑221, Jun 1966 ... 15.00
❑222, Jul 1966 ... 15.00
❑223, Aug 1966 ... 15.00
❑224, Sep 1966 ... 15.00
❑225, Oct 1966 ... 15.00
❑226, Nov 1966 ... 15.00
❑227, Dec 1966 ... 15.00
❑228, Jan 1967 ... 30.00
❑229, Feb 1967 ... 15.00
❑230, Mar 1967, Blackhawks become super-heroes; New costumes ... 15.00
❑231, Apr 1967, Blackhawks as super-heroes ... 15.00
❑232, May 1967, Blackhawks as super-heroes ... 15.00
❑233, Jun 1967, Blackhawks as super-heroes ... 15.00
❑234, Jul 1967, Blackhawks as super-heroes ... 15.00
❑235, Aug 1967, Blackhawks as super-heroes ... 15.00
❑236, Sep 1967, Blackhawks as super-heroes ... 15.00
❑237, Nov 1967, Blackhawks as super-heroes ... 15.00
❑238, Jan 1968, Blackhawks as super-heroes ... 15.00
❑239, Mar 1968, Blackhawks as super-heroes ... 15.00
❑240, May 1968, Blackhawks as super-heroes ... 15.00
❑241, Jul 1968, Blackhawks as super-heroes ... 15.00
❑242, Sep 1968, Blackhawks back to old costumes ... 15.00
❑243, Nov 1968, Last issue of 1960s run ... 15.00
❑244, Feb 1976; JKu (c); GE (a); New issues begin with old # sequence ... 4.00
❑245, Apr 1976 ... 4.00
❑246, Jun 1976 ... 4.00
❑247, Aug 1976, Bicentennial #25 ... 4.00
❑248, Sep 1976 ... 4.00
❑249, Nov 1976 ... 4.00
❑250, Jan 1977, D: Chuck ... 4.00
❑251, Oct 1982 ... 4.00
❑252, Nov 1982, ME (w); DS (a); V: War Wheel ... 4.00
❑253, Dec 1982 ... 4.00
❑254, Jan 1983, V: Agent Domino; Back Up Story ... 4.00
❑255, Feb 1983 ... 4.00
❑256, Mar 1983 ... 4.00
❑257, Apr 1983, HC (c); ME (w); DS (a) ... 4.00
❑258, May 1983, HC (c); ME (w); DS (a) ... 4.00
❑259, Jun 1983, HC (c); ME (w); DS (a) ... 4.00
❑260, Jul 1983, HC (c); ME (w); HC, DS (a) ... 4.00
❑261, Aug 1983 ... 3.00
❑262, Sep 1983, HC (c); ME (w); DS (a) ... 3.00

N-MINT

❑263, Oct 1983, GK (c); ME (w); DS (a); V: War Wheel ... 3.00
❑264, Nov 1983 ... 3.00
❑265, Dec 1983 ... 3.00
❑266, Jan 1984 ... 3.00
❑267, Feb 1984 ... 3.00
❑268, Mar 1984 ... 3.00
❑269, Apr 1984; 1: Killer Shark I (General Haifisch) ... 3.00
❑270, May 1984 ... 3.00
❑271, Jul 1984 ... 3.00
❑272, Sep 1984 ... 3.00
❑273, Nov 1984; HC, GK (c); ME (w); DS (a); Final Issue ... 3.00

Blackhawk
DC

❑1, Mar 1988; HC (w); HC (a); no mature readers advisory ... 3.50
❑2, Apr 1988 HC (w); HC (a) ... 3.50
❑3, May 1988 HC (w); HC (a) ... 3.50

Blackhawk
DC

❑1, Mar 1989 ... 2.00
❑2, Apr 1989 ... 1.75
❑3, May 1989 ... 1.75
❑4, Jun 1989 ... 1.75
❑5, Aug 1989 ... 1.75
❑6, Sep 1989 ... 1.50
❑7, Oct 1989; Double-size; WE (w); Reprints ... 2.50
❑8, Nov 1989 ... 1.50
❑9, Dec 1989 ... 1.50
❑10, Jan 1990 ... 1.50
❑11, Feb 1990 ... 1.50
❑12, Mar 1990 ... 1.50
❑13, Apr 1990 ... 1.50
❑14, May 1990 ... 1.50
❑15, Jul 1990 ... 1.50
❑16, Aug 1990 ... 1.50
❑Ann 1, ca. 1989 ... 2.95
❑Special 1, ca. 1992; Special edition (1992) ... 3.50

Black Heart: Assassin
Iguana

❑1; 1: Black Heart ... 2.95

Black Heart Billy
Slave Labor

❑1, Mar 2000, b&w ... 2.95

Black Hole
Kitchen Sink

❑1 ... 3.50
❑2, Nov 1995 ... 3.50
❑3, Jul 1996 ... 3.50
❑4, Jun 1997 ... 3.50
❑5, Mar 1998 ... 3.95
❑6, Dec 1998 ... 4.50
❑7, ca. 1999 ... 4.50
❑8, ca. 2000 ... 4.50
❑9, ca. 2001 ... 4.50

Black Hole (Walt Disney...)
Whitman

❑1, Mar 1980, Movie adaptation ... 2.00
❑2, May 1980, Movie adaptation ... 2.00
❑3, Jul 1980 ... 2.00
❑4, Sep 1980, Final Issue ... 2.00

Other grades: Multiply price above by 5/6 for VF/NM • 2/3 for VERY FINE • 1/3 for FINE • 1/5 for VERY GOOD • 1/8 for GOOD

Black Hood
DC / Impact

- ❑1, Dec 1991, 1: Pirate Blue; 1: The Black Hood (Giles Hit Coffee); 1: The Black Hood (Nathan Cray); O: The Black Hood ... 1.00
- ❑2, Jan 1992 ... 1.00
- ❑3, Feb 1992, 1: The Creeptures; 1: Tom Sickler ... 1.00
- ❑4, Mar 1992, 1: Ozone ... 1.00
- ❑5, Apr 1992 ... 1.00
- ❑6, May 1992 ... 1.00
- ❑7, Jun 1992 ... 1.00
- ❑8, Aug 1992 ... 1.00
- ❑9, Sep 1992 ... 1.00
- ❑10, Oct 1992 ... 1.00
- ❑11, Nov 1992, 1: The Fox ... 1.00
- ❑12, Dec 1992, O: Black Hood; Final Issue ... 1.00
- ❑Ann 1, trading card ... 1.50

Black Hood (Red Circle)
Archie / Red Circle

- ❑1, Jun 1983, ATh, GM (a) ... 3.00
- ❑2, Aug 1983, ATh, GM (a) ... 2.00
- ❑3, Oct 1983, ATh, GM (a) ... 2.00

Blackjack
Dark Angel

- ❑1, Sep 1996 ... 2.95
- ❑2, Oct 1996 ... 2.95
- ❑3, Jan 1997 ... 2.95
- ❑4 1997 ... 2.95
- ❑Special 1, Sep 1998 ... 3.50

Blackjack
Dark Angel

- ❑1, Apr 1997; Blood and Honor ... 2.95
- ❑2, Feb 1998 ... 2.95

Black Jack (Viz)
Viz

- ❑Special 1 ... 3.25

Black Kiss
Vortex

- ❑1, Jun 1988 HC (w); HC (a) ... 2.50
- ❑1/2nd, Jun 1988 HC (w); HC (a) ... 2.00
- ❑1/3rd HC (w); HC (a) ... 2.00
- ❑2, Jul 1988 HC (w); HC (a) ... 2.50
- ❑2/2nd HC (w); HC (a) ... 2.00
- ❑3, Aug 1988 HC (w); HC (a) ... 2.00
- ❑4, Sep 1988; HC (w); HC (a); polybagged w/black insert card covering actual cover ... 2.00
- ❑5, Oct 1988 HC (w); HC (a) ... 2.00
- ❑6, Nov 1988 HC (w); HC (a) ... 2.00
- ❑7, Dec 1988 HC (w); HC (a) ... 2.00
- ❑8, Jan 1989; HC (w); HC (a); indicia says 88 (misprint) ... 2.00
- ❑9, Feb 1989; HC (w); HC (a); indicia says 88 (misprint) ... 2.00
- ❑10, Mar 1989; HC (w); HC (a); indicia says 88 (misprint) ... 2.00
- ❑11, May 1989 HC (w); HC (a) ... 2.00
- ❑12, Jul 1989 HC (w); HC (a) ... 2.00

Black Knight
Marvel

- ❑1, Jun 1990; RB (c); TD (a); O: Black Knight III (Dane Whitman). O: Black Knight I (Sir Percy). O: Black Knight II (Nathan Garrett); O: Black Knight (Sir Percy); O: Black Knight (Nathan Garrett); O: Black Knight (Dane Whitman) ... 2.00
- ❑2, Jul 1990; A: Captain Britain. V: Dreadknight ... 1.50
- ❑3, Aug 1990; RB (a); 1: new Valkyrie. A: Doctor Strange ... 1.50
- ❑4, Sep 1990 A: Doctor Strange. A: Valkyrie ... 1.50

Black Knight: Exodus
Marvel

- ❑1, Dec 1996; One-shot ... 2.50

Black Lamb
DC / Helix

- ❑1, Nov 1996 ... 2.50
- ❑2, Dec 1996 ... 2.50
- ❑3, Jan 1997 ... 2.50
- ❑4, Feb 1997 ... 2.50
- ❑5, Mar 1997 ... 2.50
- ❑6, Apr 1997 ... 2.50

Blacklight
Image

- ❑1, Jul 2005 ... 2.99
- ❑2, Dec 2005 ... 2.99

Black Lightning
DC

- ❑1, Apr 1977, RB (c); TVE, FS (a); O: Black Lightning. 1: Black Lightning; 1st Tobias Whale (in shadows) ... 10.00
- ❑2, May 1977, V: Merlyn ... 5.00
- ❑3, Jul 1977, 1st Tobias Whale (full) ... 5.00
- ❑4, Sep 1977, V: Cyclotronic Man ... 5.00
- ❑5, Nov 1977, V: Cyclotronic Man ... 5.00
- ❑6, Jan 1978, 1: Syonide I ... 5.00
- ❑7, Mar 1978, V: Syonide; V: Tobias Whale ... 5.00
- ❑8, Apr 1978, V: Tobias Whale ... 5.00
- ❑9, May 1978, V: Annihilist ... 5.00
- ❑10, Jul 1978, V: Trickster ... 5.00
- ❑11, Sep 1978, A: The Ray. Final Issue ... 5.00

Black Lightning
DC

- ❑1, Feb 1995 ... 2.50
- ❑2, Mar 1995; 1: Painkiller ... 2.00
- ❑3, Apr 1995 ... 2.00
- ❑4, May 1995 ... 2.00
- ❑5, Jun 1995 ... 2.00
- ❑6, Jul 1995 A: Gangbuster ... 2.75
- ❑7, Aug 1995 A: Gangbuster ... 2.25
- ❑8, Sep 1995; V: Tobias Whale; V: Ishmael; V: Queequeq ... 2.25
- ❑9, Oct 1995 ... 2.25
- ❑10, Nov 1995 ... 2.25
- ❑11, Dec 1995 ... 2.25
- ❑12, Jan 1996 ... 2.25
- ❑13, Feb 1996; Final Issue ... 2.25

Black Lion The Bantu Warrior
Heroes from the Hood

- ❑1, ca. 1997, b&w ... 2.95

Black Magic
DC

- ❑1, Nov 1973 ... 15.00
- ❑2, Dec 1973, Reprints from Black Magic (Prize) #2, 3, 18, 20, 23 ... 7.00
- ❑3, Apr 1974, Reprints from Black Magic (Prize) #13-15, 18 ... 7.00
- ❑4, Jun 1974, MM, JK (a); Reprints from Black Magic (Prize) #1, 6 ... 7.00
- ❑5, Aug 1974, Reprints from Black Magic (Prize) #12, 13, 17, 25 ... 7.00
- ❑6, Oct 1974, Reprints from Black Magic (Prize) #3, 5, 11, 17 ... 7.00
- ❑7, Dec 1974 ... 7.00
- ❑8, Feb 1975 ... 7.00
- ❑9, Apr 1975 ... 7.00

Black Magic (Eclipse)
Eclipse

- ❑1, Apr 1990; Japanese, b&w ... 3.50
- ❑2, Jun 1990 ... 2.75
- ❑3, Aug 1990 ... 2.75
- ❑4, Oct 1990 ... 2.75

Blackmask
DC

- ❑1, ca. 2000 ... 4.95
- ❑2, ca. 2000 ... 4.95
- ❑3, ca. 2000 ... 4.95

Blackmask (Eastern)
Eastern

- ❑1, ca. 1988, Translated by Franz Hankel ... 1.75
- ❑2, ca. 1988 ... 1.75
- ❑3, ca. 1988 ... 1.75

Black Mist
Caliber

- ❑1, ca. 1994 ... 2.95
- ❑2, ca. 1994 ... 2.95
- ❑3, ca. 1994 ... 2.95
- ❑4, ca. 1994 ... 2.95

Black Mist: Blood of Kali
Caliber

- ❑1, Jan 1998 ... 2.95
- ❑2, ca. 1998 ... 2.95
- ❑3, ca. 1998 ... 2.95

Blackmoon
U.S.Comics

- ❑1 1985; O: Blackmoon ... 2.00
- ❑2 ... 2.00
- ❑3 ... 2.00

Black Ops
Image

- ❑1, Jan 1996; 1: Geek & H.E.R.B.; 1: Redbird; 1: Shire ... 2.50
- ❑2, Feb 1996; 1: Crane ... 2.50
- ❑3, Mar 1996 ... 2.50
- ❑4, Apr 1996 ... 2.50
- ❑5/A, Jun 1996 ... 2.50
- ❑5/B, Jun 1996; alternate cover ... 2.50

Black Orchid
DC / Vertigo

- ❑1, Sep 1993 ... 2.50
- ❑1/Platinum, Sep 1993, Platinum edition ... 5.00
- ❑2, Oct 1993 ... 2.25
- ❑3, Nov 1993 ... 2.25
- ❑4, Dec 1993 ... 2.25
- ❑5, Jan 1994, Continued in Swamp Thing (2nd Series) #139 ... 2.25
- ❑6, Feb 1994 ... 2.00
- ❑7, Mar 1994 ... 2.00
- ❑8, Apr 1994 ... 2.00
- ❑9, May 1994 ... 2.00
- ❑10, Jun 1994 ... 2.00
- ❑11, Jul 1994 ... 2.00
- ❑12, Aug 1994 ... 2.00
- ❑13, Sep 1994 ... 2.00
- ❑14, Oct 1994 ... 2.00
- ❑15, Nov 1994 ... 2.00
- ❑16, Dec 1994 ... 2.00
- ❑17, Jan 1995 ... 1.95
- ❑18, Feb 1995 ... 1.95
- ❑19, Mar 1995 ... 1.95
- ❑20, Apr 1995 ... 1.95
- ❑21, May 1995 ... 2.25
- ❑22, Jun 1995, Final Issue ... 2.25
- ❑Ann 1, Children's Crusade ... 4.00

Black Orchid
DC

- ❑1 1988, NG (w); 1st Neil Gaiman U.S. comics work ... 6.00
- ❑2 1989, NG (w); A: Batman ... 5.00
- ❑3 1989, NG (w) ... 5.00

Black Panther
Marvel

- ❑1, Jan 1977, JK (c); JK (w); JK (a); 1: Abner Little; 1: Princess Zanda ... 12.00
- ❑2, Mar 1977, JK (c); JK (w); JK (a); 2: Abner Little; 2: Princess Zanda ... 7.00
- ❑3, May 1977, JK (c); JK (w); JK (a) ... 5.00
- ❑4, Jul 1977, JK (c); JK (w); JK (a) ... 5.00
- ❑4/35¢, Jul 1977, JK (c); JK (w); JK (a); 35¢ regional price variant ... 5.00
- ❑5, Sep 1977, JK (c); JK (w); JK (a); 2: Count Zorba; 2: Colonel Pigman; 2: Silas Mourner ... 5.00
- ❑5/35¢, Sep 1977, JK (c); JK (w); JK (a); 35¢ regional price variant ... 15.00
- ❑6, Nov 1977, JK (c); JK (w); JK (a); 1: Jakarra; 1: N'Gassi ... 5.00
- ❑7, Jan 1978, JK (c); JK (w); JK (a); 1: Joshua Itobo; 2: N'Gassi; 2: Jakarra; O: Jakarra ... 5.00
- ❑8, Mar 1978, JK (c); JK (w); JK (a); 1: Nick Scarpa; 1: Khanata; 1: Zuni; 1: Ishanta; 2: Joshua Itobo ... 5.00
- ❑9, May 1978, JK (c); JK (w); JK (a); 1: Black Musketeers; 2: Nick Scarpa; 2: Khanata; 2: Zuni; 2: Ishanta ... 5.00
- ❑10, Jul 1978, JK, JSt (c); JK (w); JK (a); 2: Black Musketeers ... 5.00
- ❑11, Sep 1978, JK, JSt (c); JK (w); JK (a); 1: Kiber the Cruel ... 4.00
- ❑12, Nov 1978, JK, TP (c); JK (w); JK (a); 2: Kiber the Cruel ... 4.00
- ❑13, Jan 1979, BL (c); GD (a) ... 4.00
- ❑14, Mar 1979, BSz, TP (c); GD (a); 2: Windeagle ... 4.00
- ❑15, May 1979, AM, JB (c); GD (a); A: Klaw. Final Issue ... 4.00

Black Panther
Marvel

- ❑1, Nov 1998; gatefold summary; 1: Everett K. Ross; 1: Dora Milaje ... 5.00
- ❑1/Variant, Nov 1998; DFE alternate cover ... 7.00
- ❑2/A, Dec 1998; gatefold summary; Facing huge demon on cover ... 4.00
- ❑2/B, Dec 1998; gatefold summary; Bruce Timm variant ... 4.00
- ❑3, Jan 1999; gatefold summary; A: Fantastic Four ... 3.00
- ❑4, Feb 1999 A: Mephisto ... 3.00
- ❑5, Mar 1999 A: Mephisto ... 3.00
- ❑6, Apr 1999; V: Kraven the Hunter ... 3.00
- ❑7, May 1999 ... 3.00

Other grades: Multiply price above by 5/6 for VF/NM • 2/3 for VERY FINE • 1/3 for FINE • 1/5 for VERY GOOD • 1/8 for GOOD

Best of Furrlough

Reprinting adventures from anthropomorphic title
©Antarctic

Bettie Page: Queen of the Nile

Jim Silke's risquè Bettie Page adventures
©Dark Horse

Betty

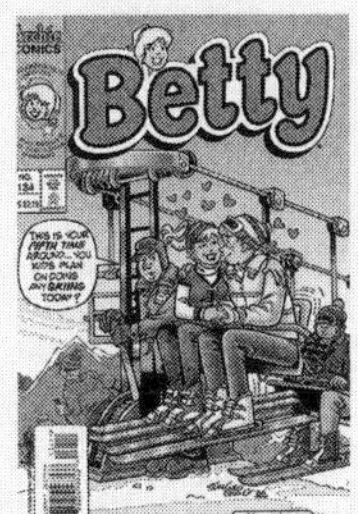

Nice-girl Archie character gets own series
©Archie

Betty & Me

But there was no "Veronica & Me." Hmmm...
©Archie

Betty and Veronica

Mid-1980s restart for Archie's girls
©Archie

	N-MINT
❑8, Jun 1999	3.00
❑9, Jul 1999	3.00
❑10, Aug 1999	3.00
❑11, Sep 1999	3.00
❑12, Oct 1999	3.00
❑13, Dec 1999	3.00
❑14, Jan 2000	3.00
❑15, Feb 2000	3.00
❑16, Mar 2000; V: Nightshade	3.00
❑17, Apr 2000	3.00
❑18, May 2000	3.00
❑19, Jun 2000; V: Killmonger	3.00
❑20, Jul 2000; V: Killmonger	3.00
❑21, Aug 2000; V: Nightmare	2.50
❑22, Sep 2000; V: Nightmare	2.50
❑23, Oct 2000; Avengers appearance	2.50
❑24, Nov 2000	2.50
❑25, Dec 2000	2.50
❑26, Jan 2001 A: Storm	2.50
❑27, Feb 2001; Klaw attacks US warships; Doctor Doom and Namor enter Lemurian/Wakanda conflict	2.50
❑28, Mar 2001	2.50
❑29, Apr 2001	2.50
❑30, May 2001; A: Captain America. World War II story	2.50
❑31, Jun 2001	2.50
❑32, Jul 2001	2.50
❑33, Aug 2001; V: Malice	2.50
❑34, Sep 2001	2.50
❑35, Oct 2001	2.50
❑36, Nov 2001	2.50
❑37, Dec 2001	2.50
❑38, Jan 2002	2.50
❑39, Feb 2002; Nuff Said	2.50
❑40, Mar 2002	2.50
❑41, Apr 2002	2.50
❑42, May 2002	2.50
❑43, Jun 2002	2.50
❑44, Jul 2002; wraparound cover	2.50
❑45, Aug 2002; wraparound cover	2.50
❑46, Aug 2002; wraparound cover	2.50
❑47, Sep 2002; wraparound cover	2.50
❑48, Oct 2002; wraparound cover	2.50
❑49, Nov 2002; wraparound cover	2.50
❑50, Dec 2002; wraparound cover	2.50
❑51, Jan 2003; wraparound cover	2.50
❑52, Feb 2003; wraparound cover	2.50
❑53, Mar 2003; wraparound cover	2.50
❑54, Apr 2003	2.99
❑55, May 2003	2.99
❑56, May 2003	2.99
❑57, Jun 2003	2.99
❑58, Jun 2003	2.99
❑59, Jul 2003	2.99
❑60, Jul 2003	2.99
❑61, Sep 2003, V: Killmonger	2.99
❑62, Sep 2003, Kasper becomes new White Tiger	2.99

Black Panther
Marvel

❑1, Jul 1988	2.00
❑2, Aug 1988; 1: Supremacists; V: Supremacists	2.00
❑3, Sep 1988	2.00
❑4, Oct 1988	2.00

Black Panther: Panther's Prey
Marvel

	N-MINT
❑1, May 1991	4.95
❑2, Jun 1991	4.95
❑3, Aug 1991	4.95
❑4, Oct 1991	4.95

Black Panther
Marvel

❑1, Mar 2005	6.00
❑1/2nd, Mar 2005	4.00
❑1/Ribic, Mar 2005	20.00
❑2, Apr 2005	2.99
❑3, May 2005	2.99
❑4, Jun 2005	2.99
❑5, Jul 2005; V: Klaw	2.99
❑6, Aug 2005	2.99
❑7, Sep 2005; House of M	2.99
❑8, Nov 2005; V: Super-Apes; Howling Commandos preview	2.99
❑9, Dec 2005; V: Super-Apes	2.99
❑10, Jan 2006	2.99
❑11, Feb 2006	2.99
❑12, Mar 2006	2.99
❑13, May 2006	2.99
❑14, Jun 2006	2.99
❑15, Jul 2006, 1: Arabian Knight II	2.99
❑16, Aug 2006	2.99
❑17, Sep 2006	2.99
❑18, Oct 2006, Frank Cho cover; Wedding of Storm & Black Panther; Civil War; Wraparound cover; 48 pages	3.99
❑19, Nov 2006	2.99
❑20, Dec 2006	2.99
❑21, Jan 2007; Gary Frank cover; Civil War tie in	14.00
❑22, Feb 2007; Civil War tie in	6.00
❑23, Mar 2007; Civil War tie in	5.00
❑24	2.99
❑25	2.99
❑26	2.99
❑27	2.99
❑28	2.99
❑29	2.99
❑30	2.99
❑31	2.99
❑32	2.99
❑33	2.99
❑34	2.99
❑35	2.99
❑36	2.99
❑37	2.99
❑38	2.99
❑39	2.99
❑40	2.99
❑41	2.99

Black Pearl
Dark Horse

❑1, Sep 1996	3.50
❑2, Oct 1996	3.00
❑3, Nov 1996	3.00
❑4, Dec 1996	3.00
❑5, Jan 1997	3.00

Black Phantom
AC

❑1, b&w	2.50

	N-MINT
❑2	2.50
❑3, b&w	2.75

Black Raven
ArtEffect Entertainment

❑1, ca. 1998	2.95

Black Sabbath
Rock-It / Malibu

❑1, Feb 1994	3.95

Black Scorpion
Special Studio

❑1, b&w	2.75
❑2, b&w	2.75
❑3, b&w	2.75

Black September
Malibu / Ultraverse

❑Infinity, Sep 1993; events affect the Infinity issues of the other Ultraverse titles	2.00

Blackstar
Imperial

❑1	2.00
❑2, Feb 1987	2.00

Black Sun
WildStorm

❑1, Nov 2002; Woman sitting on cover	2.95
❑2, Dec 2002	2.95
❑3, Jan 2003	2.95
❑4, Feb 2003	2.95
❑5, Mar 2003	2.95
❑6	2.95

Black Sun: X-Men
Marvel

❑1, Nov 2000	2.99
❑1/A, Nov 2000; Dynamic Forces cover	6.00
❑2, Nov 2000; Painted cover; Reads Black Sun: Storm in indica	2.99
❑3, Nov 2000; Painted cover; Reads Black Sun: Banshee and Sunfire in indica	2.99
❑4, Nov 2000; Painted cover; Reads Black Sun: Colossus and Nightcrawler in indica	2.99
❑5, Nov 2000; Painted cover; Final issue; Reads Black Sun: Wolverine and Thunderbird in indica	2.99

Black Terror (Eclipse)
Eclipse

❑1, Oct 1989	4.95
❑1/Autographed, Oct 1989; Autographed by Beau Smith	3.50
❑2, Mar 1990	4.95
❑2/Autographed, Mar 1990; Autographed by Beau Smith	3.50
❑3, Jun 1990	4.95
❑3/Autographed, Jun 1990; Autographed by Beau Smith	3.50

Blackthorne's 3 in 1
Blackthorne

❑1, Nov 1986	1.75
❑2, Feb 1987	1.75

Blackthorne's Harvey Flip Book
Blackthorne

❑1, b&w	2.00

Black Tide
Image

❑1/A, Nov 2001; Grey background; 3 figures standing on cover	2.95

Other grades: Multiply price above by 5/6 for VF/NM • 2/3 for VERY FINE • 1/3 for FINE • 1/5 for VERY GOOD • 1/8 for GOOD

❑1/B, Nov 2001; 2 figures charging on cover ... 2.95
❑1/C, Nov 2001; Sun in background; 3 figures posing on cover ... 2.95
❑2, Jan 2002 ... 2.95
❑3, Mar 2002 ... 2.95
❑4, May 2002; Yellow/orange background 2.95

Black Tide
Avatar

❑1 ... 2.95
❑1/A ... 2.95
❑1/C, Wrap-Around cover ... 2.95
❑2 ... 2.95
❑2/A ... 2.95
❑3 ... 2.95
❑3/A ... 2.95
❑4 ... 2.95
❑4/A ... 2.95
❑5, May 2003 ... 2.95
❑5/A, May 2003 ... 2.95
❑6, Jun 2003 ... 2.95
❑6/A, Jun 2003 ... 2.95
❑7, Sep 2003 ... 2.95
❑7/A, Sep 2003 ... 2.95
❑8, Nov 2003 ... 2.95
❑8/A, Nov 2003 ... 2.95
❑9, Feb 2004 ... 2.95
❑9/A, Feb 2004 ... 2.95
❑10 2004 ... 2.95

Black Web
Inks

❑1; 1&O: Black Web ... 2.95

Black Widow
Marvel

❑1, Jun 1999 ... 3.50
❑2, Jul 1999 ... 3.00
❑3, Aug 1999 ... 3.00

Black Widow
Marvel

❑1, Jan 2001 ... 2.99
❑2, Feb 2001 ... 2.99
❑3, May 2001 ... 2.99

Black Widow
Marvel

❑1, Nov 2004 ... 2.99
❑2, Dec 2004 ... 2.99
❑3, Jan 2005 ... 2.99
❑4, Feb 2005 ... 2.99
❑5, Mar 2005 ... 2.99
❑6, Apr 2005 ... 2.99

Black Widow: Pale Little Spider
Marvel

❑1, Jun 2002 ... 2.99
❑2, Jul 2002 ... 2.99
❑3, Aug 2002 ... 2.99

Black Widow: Things They Say About Her
Marvel

❑1, Nov 2005 ... 2.99
❑2, Dec 2005 ... 2.99

Black Widow 2
Marvel

❑1, Nov 2005; Nick Fury's Howling Commandoes preview ... 2.99
❑3, Jan 2006 ... 2.99
❑4, Feb 2006 ... 2.99
❑5, Apr 2006 ... 2.99
❑6, May 2006 ... 2.99

Black Widow: Web of Intrigue
Marvel

❑1, Jun 1999; collects Marvel Fanfare #10-13 ... 3.50

Blackwulf
Marvel

❑1, Jun 1994; Embossed cover ... 2.50
❑2, Jul 1994 ... 1.50
❑3, Aug 1994 ... 1.50
❑4, Sep 1994 ... 1.50
❑5, Oct 1994 ... 1.50
❑6, Nov 1994 ... 1.50
❑7, Dec 1994 ... 1.50
❑8, Jan 1995 ... 1.50
❑9, Feb 1995 ... 1.50
❑10, Mar 1995; Final Issue ... 1.50

Black Zeppelin (Gene Day's...)
Renegade

❑1, Apr 1985, GD (w); GD (a) ... 2.00
❑2, Jun 1985 ... 2.00
❑3, Aug 1985 ... 2.00
❑4 ... 2.00
❑5, Oct 1986 ... 2.00

Blade (Buccaneer)
Buccaneer

❑1, Dec 1989 ... 2.00
❑2 ... 2.00

Blade
Marvel

❑1, May 1997; giveaway; GC, TP (a); O: Blade. Reprints ... 1.50

Blade
Marvel

❑1, Mar 1998 ... 3.50

Blade
Marvel

❑1, Oct 1998; gatefold summary; NN; One-shot; Movie adaptation ... 2.99

Blade
Marvel

❑1, Nov 1998; gatefold summary ... 3.50
❑2/A, Dec 1998; gatefold summary; cover says Nov, indicia says Dec ... 2.99
❑2/B, Dec 1998 ... 2.99
❑3, Jan 1999; gatefold summary; cover says Dec, indicia says Jan ... 2.99

Blade
Marvel

❑1, Nov 2006 ... 2.99
❑2, Dec 2006 ... 2.99
❑3, Jan 2007 ... 2.99
❑4, Feb 2007 ... 2.99

Blade of Heaven
Tokyopop

❑1, Mar 2005 ... 9.99
❑2, May 2005 ... 9.99
❑3, Jul 2005 ... 9.99
❑4, Sep 2005 ... 9.99
❑5, Nov 2005 ... 9.99
❑6, Jan 2006 ... 9.99

Blade of Kumori
Devil's Due

❑1, Jan 2005 ... 2.95
❑2, Feb 2005 ... 2.95
❑3, Mar 2005 ... 2.95
❑4, Apr 2005 ... 2.95
❑5, May 2005 ... 2.95

Blade of Shuriken
Eternity

❑1, May 1987 ... 1.95
❑2, Jul 1987 ... 1.95
❑3, Sep 1987 ... 1.95
❑4, Nov 1987 ... 1.95
❑5, Jan 1988 ... 1.95

Blade of the Immortal
Dark Horse

❑1, Jun 1996 ... 3.50
❑2, Jul 1996 ... 3.00
❑3, Aug 1996 ... 3.00
❑4, Sep 1996 ... 3.00
❑5, Oct 1996 ... 3.00
❑6, Nov 1996 ... 2.95
❑7, Dec 1996 ... 2.95
❑8, Jan 1997 ... 2.95
❑9, Apr 1997, Giant-size; SA (a) ... 3.95
❑10, May 1997, Giant-size; DG (a) ... 3.95
❑11, Jun 1997, Giant-size; GK (a) ... 3.95
❑12, Jul 1997 ... 2.95
❑13, Aug 1997 ... 2.95
❑14, Sep 1997 ... 2.95
❑15, Oct 1997 ... 2.95
❑16, Nov 1997 ... 2.95
❑17, Dec 1997 ... 2.95
❑18, Jan 1998 ... 2.95
❑19, Mar 1998 ... 2.95
❑20, Apr 1998 ... 2.95
❑21, May 1998 ... 2.95
❑22, Jun 1998 ... 2.95
❑23, Jul 1998 ... 2.95
❑24, Aug 1998 ... 2.95
❑25, Sep 1998 ... 2.95
❑26, Oct 1998 ... 2.95
❑27, Nov 1998 ... 2.95
❑28, Dec 1998 ... 2.95
❑29, Jan 1999 ... 2.95
❑30, Feb 1999 ... 2.95
❑31, Mar 1999 ... 2.95
❑32, Apr 1999 ... 2.95
❑33, May 1999 ... 2.95
❑34, Jun 1999, 48 pages ... 3.95
❑35, Jul 1999 ... 2.95
❑36, Aug 1999 ... 3.95
❑37, Sep 1999 ... 3.95
❑38, Oct 1999 ... 3.95
❑39, Nov 1999 ... 2.99
❑40, Dec 1999 ... 2.99
❑41, Jan 2000 ... 2.99
❑42, Feb 2000 ... 2.99
❑43, Mar 2000 ... 2.99
❑44, Apr 2000 ... 2.99
❑45, May 2000 ... 2.99
❑46, Jun 2000 ... 2.99
❑47, Jul 2000 ... 2.99
❑48, Aug 2000 ... 2.99
❑49, Sep 2000 ... 2.99
❑50, Oct 2000 ... 2.99
❑51, Nov 2000 ... 2.99
❑52, Dec 2000 ... 2.99
❑53, Jan 2001 ... 2.99
❑54, Feb 2001 ... 2.99
❑55, Mar 2001 ... 2.99
❑56, Apr 2001 ... 2.99
❑57, May 2001 ... 2.99
❑58, Jun 2001 ... 2.99
❑59, Jul 2001 ... 2.99
❑60, Aug 2001 ... 2.99
❑61, Sep 2001 ... 2.99
❑62, Oct 2001 ... 2.99
❑63, Nov 2001 ... 2.99
❑64, Dec 2001 ... 2.99
❑65, Feb 2002 ... 2.99
❑66, Mar 2002 ... 2.99
❑67, Apr 2002 ... 2.99
❑68, May 2002 ... 2.99
❑69, Jun 2002 ... 2.99
❑70, Jul 2002 ... 2.99
❑71, Aug 2002 ... 2.99
❑72, Sep 2002 ... 2.99
❑73, Nov 2002 ... 2.99
❑74, Dec 2002 ... 2.99
❑75, Jan 2003 ... 2.99
❑76, Feb 2003 ... 2.99
❑77, Mar 2003 ... 2.99
❑78, Apr 2003 ... 2.99
❑79, Jun 2003 ... 2.99
❑80, Jul 2003 ... 2.99
❑81, Aug 2003 ... 2.99
❑82, Sep 2003 ... 2.99
❑83, Oct 2003 ... 2.99
❑84, Nov 2003 ... 2.99
❑85, Dec 2003 ... 2.99
❑86, Jan 2004 ... 2.99
❑87, Feb 2004 ... 2.99
❑88, Apr 2004 ... 2.99
❑89, Jul 2004 ... 2.99
❑90, Aug 2004 ... 2.99
❑91, Sep 2004 ... 2.99
❑92, Oct 2004 ... 2.99
❑93, Nov 2004 ... 2.99
❑94, Dec 2004 ... 2.99
❑95, Jan 2005, b&w ... 2.99
❑96, Feb 2005, b&w ... 2.99
❑97, Mar 2005 ... 2.99
❑98, Apr 2005 ... 2.99
❑99, May 2005 ... 2.99
❑100, Jun 2005 ... 5.99
❑101, Jul 2005, b&w ... 2.99
❑102, Aug 2005 ... 2.99
❑103, Sep 2005 ... 2.99
❑104, Oct 2005 ... 2.99
❑105, Nov 2005 ... 2.99
❑106, Dec 2005 ... 2.99
❑107, Nov 2005 ... 2.99
❑108, Dec 2005, b&w ... 2.99
❑109, Feb 2006, b&w ... 2.99
❑110, Mar 2006, b&w ... 2.99
❑111, Apr 2006 ... 2.99

Betty and Veronica Spectacular

More comics focusing on the competitive girls
©Archie

Betty & Veronica Summer Fun

Giant annual specials take girls to the beach
©Archie

Betty Boop 3-D

One of many 3-D specials from Blackthorne
©Blackthorne

Betty Boop's Big Break

Success finds the wide-eyed animation star
©First

Betty's Diary

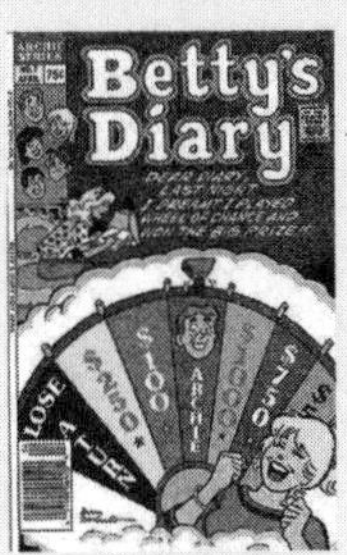

Another title for the smiling tomboy
©Archie

	N-MINT
❑112, May 2006	2.99
❑113, Jun 2006, Color Pinup by Becky Cloonan	2.99
❑114, Jul 2006	2.99
❑115, Sep 2006; b&w	2.99
❑116, Oct 2006	2.99
❑117, Nov 2006	2.99
❑118, Nov 2006, b&w	2.99
❑119, Dec 2006; b&w	2.99
❑120, Jan 2007, b&w	2.99
❑121, Feb 2007, b&w	2.99

Blade Runner
Marvel

❑1, Oct 1982, AW (a); Movie adaptation 1.50
❑2, Nov 1982, BA (c); AW, BA (a); Movie adaptation 1.00

Blade: Sins of the Father
Marvel

❑1, Oct 1998 5.99

Bladesmen
Blue Comet

❑0, b&w 2.00
❑1, b&w 2.00
❑2 2.00

Blade: The Vampire-Hunter
Marvel

❑1, Jul 1994; foil cover 2.95
❑2, Aug 1994 1.95
❑3, Sep 1994 1.95
❑4, Oct 1994 1.95
❑5, Nov 1994 1.95
❑6, Dec 1994 1.95
❑7, Jan 1995 1.95
❑8, Feb 1995 1.95
❑9, Mar 1995 1.95
❑10, Apr 1995; Final Issue 1.95

Blade: Vampire Hunter
Marvel

❑1, Dec 1999 3.50
❑2, Jan 2000; Art cover 2.50
❑2/Photo, Jan 2000; Photo variant 2.50
❑3, Feb 2000 2.50
❑4, Mar 2000 2.50
❑5, Apr 2000 2.50
❑6, May 2000; V: vampire blood-god 2.50

Blade 2: Movie Adaptation
Marvel

❑1, May 2002, b&w 5.95

Blair Which? (Sergio Aragonés')
Dark Horse

❑1, Dec 1999 2.95

Blair Witch Chronicles
Oni

❑1, Mar 2000, b&w 2.95
❑2, Apr 2000 2.95
❑3, Jun 2000 2.95
❑4, Jul 2000 2.95

Blair Witch: Dark Testaments
Image

❑1, Oct 2000 2.95

N-MINT

Blair Witch Project
Oni

❑1, Aug 1999; prequel to movie 10.00
❑1/2nd; 2nd printing; Red title lettering 3.00

Blame!
Tokyopop

❑1, Aug 2005 9.99
❑2, Nov 2005 9.99

Blanche Goes to Hollywood
Dark Horse

❑1, b&w; NN 2.95

Blanche Goes to New York
Dark Horse

❑1, Nov 1992, b&w; NN 2.95

Blarney
Discovery

❑1; cardstock cover, b&w 2.95

Blast Corps
Dark Horse

❑1, Oct 1998; based on Nintendo 64 games 2.50

Blasters Special
DC

❑1, May 1989 2.00

Blast-Off
Harvey

❑1, Oct 1965, AW, JK (w); AW, JK (a); A: The Three Rocketeers 28.00

Blaze
Marvel

❑1, Aug 1994; silver enhanced cover 2.95
❑2, Sep 1994 1.95
❑3, Oct 1994 1.95
❑4, Nov 1994 1.95
❑5, Dec 1994 1.95
❑6, Jan 1995 1.95
❑7, Feb 1995 1.95
❑8, Mar 1995 1.95
❑9, Apr 1995 1.95
❑10, May 1995 1.95
❑11, Jun 1995 1.95
❑12, Jul 1995; Final Issue 1.95

Blaze: Legacy of Blood
Marvel

❑1, Dec 1993 1.75
❑2, Jan 1994 1.75
❑3, Feb 1994 1.75
❑4, Mar 1994 1.75

Blaze of Glory
Marvel

❑1, Feb 2000, biweekly mini-series 2.95
❑2, Feb 2000 2.95
❑3, Mar 2000 2.95
❑4, Mar 2000 2.99

Blazin' Barrels
Tokyopop

❑1, Jun 2005 9.99
❑2, Sep 2005 9.99
❑3, Dec 2005 9.99

Blazing Battle Tales
Seaboard / Atlas

❑1, Jul 1975 2.50

N-MINT

Blazing Combat
Warren

❑1, Oct 1965, FF (c); GE, JO, GM, FF, AT (a); scarcer 90.00
❑2, Jan 1965, FF (c); AW, ATh, JO, FF, JSe, AT (a) 30.00
❑3, Apr 1966, FF (c); ATh, JO, GM, GC, FF, JSe, WW (a) 30.00
❑4, Jul 1966, FF (c); ATh, GC, FF, JSe, WW, AT, RH, DA (a) 40.00
❑Ann 1 45.00

Blazing Combat (Apple)
Apple

❑1, Aug 1993 4.50
❑2, Nov 1993, b&w; Reprints 4.50

Blazing Combat: World War I and World War II
Apple

❑1, Mar 1994; Reprints 3.75
❑2, Jun 1994; Reprints 3.75

Blazing Foxholes
Fantagraphics / Eros

❑1, Sep 1994; 24 pages; Adult 2.95
❑2; Adult 2.95
❑3, Jan 1995; Adult 2.95

Blazing Western (AC)
AC

❑1, b&w 2.50

Blazing Western (Avalon)
Avalon

❑1, ca. 1997 2.75

Bleach
Viz

❑1, Jun 2004 7.95
❑2, Aug 2004 7.95
❑3, Oct 2004 7.95
❑4, Dec 2004 7.95
❑5, Feb 2005 7.95
❑6, Apr 2005 7.95
❑7, May 2005 7.95
❑8, Aug 2005 7.95
❑9, Oct 2005 7.95

Bleat
Slave Labor

❑1, Aug 1995; Adult 2.95

Bleeding Heart
Fantagraphics

❑1, Dec 1991 2.50
❑2, Spr 1992 2.50
❑3 2.50
❑4 2.50
❑5, Aug 1993 2.50

Blindside
Image

❑1, Feb 1998; video game magazine in comic-book format; 1: Donkey Kong; 1: Mario; Video game magazine in comic-book format 1.00
❑1/A, Aug 1996; Wraparound cover 2.50
❑1/B, Aug 1996; white background cover 2.50
❑2, Sep 1996 1.00
❑3, Dec 1996 1.00
❑4 1997 1.00

N-MINT

❑5 1997 ... 1.00
❑6 1997 ... 1.00
❑7 1997 ... 1.00

Blink
Marvel

❑1, Mar 2001 ... 2.99
❑2, Apr 2001 ... 2.99
❑3, May 2001 ... 2.99
❑4, Jun 2001 ... 2.99

Blip
Marvel

❑1, Feb 1983; video game magazine in comic-book format; 1: Donkey Kong; 1: Mario; Video game magazine in comic-book format ... 1.00
❑2, Mar 1983 ... 1.00
❑3, Apr 1983 ... 1.00
❑4, May 1983 ... 1.00
❑5, Jun 1983 ... 1.00
❑6, Jul 1983 ... 1.00
❑7, Aug 1983 ... 1.00

Blip (Bardic)
Bardic

❑1, Feb 1998 ... 1.25

Blip and the C.C.A.D.S.
Amazing

❑1 ... 2.00
❑2 ... 2.00

Bliss Alley
Image

❑1, Jul 1997 ... 2.95
❑2, Sep 1997 ... 2.95

Blite
Fantagraphics

❑1, b&w ... 2.25

Blitz
Nightwynd

❑1 ... 2.50
❑2 ... 2.50
❑3 ... 2.50
❑4 ... 2.50

Blitzkrieg
DC

❑1, Jan 1976 JKu (c); RE (a) ... 16.00
❑2, Mar 1976 ... 8.00
❑3, May 1976, JKu (c); RE (a) ... 6.00
❑4, Jul 1976, Bicentennial #20 ... 6.00
❑5, Sep 1976, Final Issue ... 6.00

Blokhedz
Image

❑1, Dec 2003 ... 2.95
❑2 2004 ... 2.95

Blonde
Fantagraphics / Eros

❑1; Adult ... 2.50
❑2; Adult ... 2.50
❑3; Adult ... 2.50

Blonde Addiction
Blitzweasel

❑1 ... 2.95
❑2 ... 2.95
❑3 ... 2.95
❑4; flip-book with Blonde Avenger's Subplots ... 2.95

Blonde Avenger
Blitz Weasel

❑27/A ... 3.95
❑27/B; Photo cover ... 3.95

Blonde Avenger: Crossover Crazzeee
Blitzweasel

❑1; NN; One-shot ... 3.95

Blonde Avenger
Fantagraphics / Eros

❑1, Mar 1993; Adult ... 2.75
❑2, ca. 1993; Adult ... 2.75
❑3; Adult ... 2.75
❑4, Apr 1994; Adult ... 2.75

Blonde Avenger Monthly
Blitzweasel

❑1, Mar 1996, b&w ... 4.00
❑2, Apr 1996 ... 3.00
❑3, May 1996 ... 2.95
❑4, Jun 1996 ... 2.95
❑5 ... 2.95
❑6 ... 2.95

Blonde Avenger One-Shot Special: The Spying Game
Blitzweasel

❑1, Mar 1996, b&w; Adult ... 2.95

Blonde: Bondage Palace
Fantagraphics / Eros

❑1; Adult ... 2.95
❑2; Adult ... 2.95
❑3; Adult ... 2.95
❑5, May 1994; Adult ... 2.95

Blondie Comics
David McKay

❑148, Nov 1961 ... 8.00
❑149 1961 ... 8.00
❑150 1962 ... 8.00
❑151 1962 ... 8.00
❑152 1962 ... 8.00
❑153 1962 ... 8.00
❑154, Oct 1962 ... 8.00
❑155, Nov 1963 ... 8.00
❑156 1963 ... 8.00
❑157, May 1963 ... 8.00
❑158 1963 ... 8.00
❑159, Nov 1963 ... 8.00
❑160, Mar 1965 ... 8.00
❑161 1965 ... 8.00
❑162, Sep 1965 ... 8.00
❑163, Nov 1965 ... 8.00
❑164, Aug 1966, King Features Syndicate begins publishing ... 8.00
❑165, Oct 1966 ... 8.00
❑166, Dec 1966 ... 8.00
❑167, Feb 1967 ... 8.00
❑168, Apr 1967 ... 5.00
❑169, Jun 1967 ... 5.00
❑170, Jul 1967 ... 5.00
❑171, Aug 1967 ... 5.00
❑172, Sep 1967 ... 5.00
❑173, Oct 1967 ... 5.00
❑174, Nov 1967 ... 5.00
❑175, Dec 1967 ... 5.00
❑177, Feb 1969, #176 appears not to have been published ... 5.00
❑178, Apr 1969 ... 5.00
❑179, Jun 1969 ... 5.00
❑180, Aug 1969 ... 5.00
❑181, Oct 1969 ... 4.00
❑182, Nov 1969 ... 4.00
❑183, Jan 1970 ... 4.00
❑184, Mar 1970 ... 4.00
❑185, May 1970 ... 4.00
❑186, Jul 1970 ... 4.00
❑187, Sep 1970 ... 4.00
❑188, Nov 1970 ... 4.00
❑189, Jan 1971 ... 4.00
❑190, Mar 1971 ... 4.00
❑191, May 1971 ... 4.00
❑192, Jul 1971 ... 4.00
❑193, Sep 1971 ... 4.00
❑194, Nov 1971 ... 4.00
❑195, Jan 1971 ... 4.00
❑196, Mar 1972 ... 4.00
❑197, Apr 1972 ... 4.00
❑198, May 1972 ... 4.00
❑199, Jul 1972 ... 4.00
❑200, Oct 1972, Anniversary issue ... 4.00
❑201, Dec 1972 ... 3.00
❑202, Jan 1973 ... 3.00
❑203, Mar 1973 ... 3.00
❑204, May 1973 ... 3.00
❑205, Jul 1973 ... 3.00
❑206, Sep 1973 ... 3.00
❑207, Nov 1973 ... 3.00
❑208, May 1974 ... 3.00
❑209, Jul 1974 ... 3.00
❑210, Oct 1974 ... 3.00
❑211, Dec 1974 ... 3.00
❑212, Feb 1975 ... 3.00
❑213, Apr 1975 ... 3.00
❑214, Jun 1975 ... 3.00
❑215, Sep 1975 ... 3.00
❑216, Nov 1975 ... 3.00
❑217, Jan 1976 ... 3.00
❑218, Mar 1976 ... 3.00
❑219, May 1976 ... 3.00
❑220, Jul 1976 ... 3.00
❑221 1976 ... 3.00
❑222, Nov 1976, Final Issue ... 3.00

Blood
Fantaco

❑1, b&w ... 3.95

Blood and Glory
Marvel

❑1; Embossed cover ... 5.95
❑2; ca. 1992 ... 5.95
❑3; ca. 1992 ... 5.95

Blood & Kisses
Fantaco

❑1; Adult ... 2.95
❑2; Adult ... 3.95

Blood & Roses Adventures
Knight

❑1, May 1995, b&w ... 2.95

Blood & Roses: Future Past Tense
Sky

❑1, Dec 1993; Silver logo regular edition ... 2.25
❑1/Ashcan; ashcan edition ... 3.00
❑1/Gold; Gold logo promotional edition ... 3.00
❑2 ... 2.25

Blood & Roses: Search for the Time-Stone
Sky

❑1, Apr 1994 ... 2.50
❑1/Ashcan, Apr 1994 ... 3.00
❑2, Jan 1995; Indicia has incorrect initial date, really Jan 1995 ... 2.50

Blood & Roses Special
Knight

❑1, Mar 1996, b&w ... 2.95

Blood and Shadows
DC / Vertigo

❑1 ... 5.95
❑2 ... 5.95
❑3 ... 5.95
❑4 ... 5.95

Blood and Thunder
Conquest

❑1, b&w ... 2.95

Blood & Water
Slave Labor

❑1, Oct 1991, b&w ... 2.95

Blood and Water
DC / Vertigo

❑1, May 2003 ... 2.95
❑2, Jun 2003 ... 2.95
❑3, Jul 2003 ... 2.95
❑4, Aug 2003 ... 2.95
❑5, Sep 2003 ... 2.95

Blood: A Tale
Marvel / Epic

❑1 1987 ... 3.25
❑2 1987 ... 3.25
❑3 1987 ... 3.25
❑4 1987 ... 3.25

Blood: A Tale
DC / Vertigo

❑1, Nov 1996; Reprints Blood: A Tale #1; Adult ... 2.95
❑2, Dec 1996; Reprints Blood: A Tale #2; Adult ... 2.95
❑3, Jan 1997; Reprints Blood: A Tale #3; Adult ... 2.95
❑4, Feb 1997; Reprints Blood: A Tale #4; Adult ... 2.95

Bloodbath
DC

❑1, Dec 1993; Most DC Heroes appear ... 3.50
❑2, Dec 1993 ... 3.50

Blood Bounty
Highland

❑1 ... 2.00

Bloodbrothers
Eternity

❑1 ... 1.95
❑2 ... 1.95
❑3 ... 1.95
❑4 ... 1.95

Beverly Hillbillies

Load up the truck and head for comics-land

©Dell

Beware (Marvel)

Part of Marvel's return to horror comics

©Marvel

Beware the Creeper

More with the character from Showcase #73

©DC

Bewitched

Does the comics version count as a third Darren?

©Dell

Beyond the Grave

Ghosts, witches, and demons from Charlton

©Charlton

N-MINT

Bloodchilde
Millennium

❑1, Dec 1994; Adult ... 2.50
❑2, Feb 1995; Adult ... 2.50
❑3, May 1995; Adult ... 2.50
❑4, Jul 1995; Adult ... 2.95

Blood Club
Kitchen Sink

❑2; Cover says "Blood Club Featuring Big Baby" ... 5.95

Bloodfang
Epitaph

❑0, Mar 1996 ... 2.50
❑1 ... 2.50

Blood Feast
Eternity

❑1, b&w; tame cover ... 2.50
❑1/Variant, b&w; Explicit cover ... 2.50
❑2, b&w; Adult ... 2.50
❑2/Variant, b&w; Explicit cover ... 2.50

Blood Feast: The Screenplay
Eternity

❑1, b&w; not comics ... 4.95

Bloodfire
Lightning

❑0, Jun 1994; Giant-size; O: Bloodfire ... 3.50
❑0/A, Jun 1994; Giant-size; Yellow logo on cover ... 3.50
❑1, Mar 1993, b&w; promotional copy ... 3.50
❑1/Platinum, Jun 1993; platinum ... 3.50
❑1/Variant, Jun 1993; red foil ... 3.50
❑2, Jul 1993 ... 2.95
❑8, Jan 1994; O: Prodigal ... 2.95
❑3, Aug 1993 ... 2.95
❑4, Sep 1993 ... 2.95
❑5, Oct 1993; trading card ... 2.95
❑6, Nov 1993 ... 2.95
❑7, Dec 1993 ... 2.95
❑9, Feb 1994 ... 2.95
❑10, Mar 1994 ... 2.95
❑11, Apr 1994 ... 2.95
❑12, May 1994 ... 2.95

Bloodfire/Hellina
Lightning

❑1, Aug 1995; O: Hellina ... 3.00
❑1/Nude, Aug 1995; Nude edition; O: Hellina ... 4.00
❑1/Platinum; Platinum edition ... 3.00

Blood Gothic
Fantaco

❑1 ... 4.95
❑2 ... 4.95

Bloodhound
DC

❑1, Sep 2004 ... 2.95
❑2, Oct 2004 ... 2.95
❑3, Nov 2004 ... 2.95
❑4, Dec 2004 ... 2.95
❑5, Jan 2005 ... 2.95
❑6, Feb 2005 ... 2.95
❑7, Mar 2005 ... 2.95
❑8, Apr 2005 ... 2.95
❑9, May 2005 ... 2.95
❑10, Jun 2005; Final issue ... 2.95

N-MINT

Bloodhunter
Brainstorm

❑1, Oct 1996, b&w; cardstock cover ... 2.95

Blood Is the Harvest (Eclipse)
Eclipse

❑1, Jul 1992 ... 2.50
❑2, Aug 1992 ... 2.50
❑3 ... 2.50
❑4, Dec 1992 ... 2.50

Blood Junkies
Eternity

❑1 ... 2.50
❑2 ... 2.50

Blood Legacy: The Story of Ryan
Image

❑1, Jul 2000 ... 2.50
❑2, Aug 2000 ... 2.50
❑3, Sep 2000 ... 2.50
❑4, Nov 2000 ... 2.50

Blood Legacy/ Young Ones One Shot
Image

❑1, Apr 2003 ... 4.99

Bloodletting
Fantaco

❑1 ... 2.95

Bloodletting
Fantaco

❑1 ... 3.95
❑2 ... 3.95

Bloodlines
Aircel

❑1; Aircel publishes ... 2.50
❑2 ... 2.50
❑3; Blackburn begins as publisher ... 2.50
❑4 ... 2.50
❑5 ... 2.50
❑6 ... 2.50

Bloodlines: A Tale from the Heart of Africa
Marvel / Epic

❑1, ca. 1992 ... 5.95

Bloodlust
Slave Labor

❑1, Dec 1990; For Mature Readers; b&w ... 2.25

Blood 'n' Guts
Aircel

❑1, Nov 1990, b&w; 1: Blood & Guts ... 2.50
❑2 ... 2.50
❑3 ... 2.50
❑4 ... 2.50

Blood of Dracula
Apple

❑1, Nov 1987 ... 2.00
❑2, Dec 1987 ... 2.00
❑3, Jun 1988 ... 2.00
❑4, Jul 1988 ... 2.00
❑5, Aug 1988 ... 2.00
❑6, Sep 1988 ... 2.00
❑7, Oct 1988 ... 2.00
❑8, Nov 1988 ... 2.00
❑9, Jan 1989 ... 2.00
❑10, Mar 1989 ... 2.00

N-MINT

❑11, May 1989 ... 2.00
❑12, Jun 1989 ... 2.00
❑13, Jul 1989 BWr (a) ... 2.00
❑14, Sep 1989 BWr (a) ... 2.25
❑15, Nov 1989; flexidisc ... 3.75
❑16, May 1990 BWr (a) ... 2.25
❑17, Jul 1990 BWr (a) ... 2.25
❑18, Sep 1990 BWr (a) ... 2.25
❑19, Mar 1991 BWr (a) ... 2.25

Blood of the Demon
DC

❑1, Apr 2005 ... 4.00
❑2, May 2005 ... 2.50
❑3, Jun 2005 ... 2.50
❑4, Jul 2005; New DC logo ... 2.50
❑5, Aug 2005 ... 2.50
❑6, Sep 2005; Day of Vengeance tie-in ... 2.50
❑7, Oct 2005; Day of Vengeance tie-in ... 2.50
❑8, Nov 2005 ... 2.50
❑9, Dec 2005 ... 2.50
❑10, Jan 2006 ... 2.50
❑11, Mar 2006 ... 2.50
❑12, Mar 2006 ... 2.50
❑13, May 2006, One Year Later ... 2.50
❑14, Jun 2006, One Year Later ... 2.50
❑15, Jul 2006, One Year Later; Price increase ... 2.99
❑16, Aug 2006 ... 2.99
❑17, Sep 2006, Final issue; Cover by Byrne 2.99

Blood of the Innocent
Warp

❑1, Jan 1986; Mature ... 2.00
❑2, Jan 1986; Mature; Includes essay about Bram Stoker's Dracula ... 2.00
❑3, Jan 1986; Mature; Includes essay about Jack the Ripper; Adult ... 2.00
❑4, Jan 1986; Mature; Includes essay about London's Whitechapel section; Adult ... 2.00

Blood Pack
DC

❑1, Mar 1995 ... 1.50
❑2, Apr 1995 ... 1.50
❑3, May 1995 ... 1.50
❑4, Jun 1995 ... 1.50

Bloodpool
Image

❑1, Aug 1995 ... 2.50
❑1/Variant, Aug 1995, alternate cover ... 2.50
❑2, Sep 1995 ... 2.50
❑3, Oct 1995 ... 2.50
❑4, Nov 1995 ... 2.50
❑Special 1, Mar 1996, Special ... 4.00

Blood Reign
Fathom

❑1 ... 2.95
❑2, Sep 1991 ... 2.95
❑3, Oct 1991 ... 2.95

Bloodscent
Comico

❑1, Oct 1988 ... 2.00

Bloodseed
Marvel

❑1, Oct 1993 ... 1.95

Other grades: Multiply price above by 5/6 for VF/NM • 2/3 for VERY FINE • 1/3 for FINE • 1/5 for VERY GOOD • 1/8 for GOOD

❑2, Nov 1993; Gold cover; nudity; Final issue (series was rescheduled as 2-issue series) 1.95

Bloodshed
Damage!

❑1; Adult; b&w; ca. Fall 1994 2.95
❑1/Ltd.; no cover price, b&w 2.95
❑2; Adult; b&w; ca. 1994 2.95
❑3, ca. 1994; no cover price; cardstock cover 2.95
❑Ashcan 1, ca. 1997; no cover price; "Promo Edition" on cover; retailer promotional item 2.00

Bloodshot
Valiant

❑0/VVSS 25.00
❑0/PlatError, Mar 1994 750.00
❑0, Mar 1994; O: Bloodshot. A: Eternal Warrior. chromium cover 3.00
❑0/Gold, Mar 1994; Gold edition; O: Bloodshot. A: Eternal Warrior. no cover price 25.00
❑1, Feb 1993; DP, BWi (a); Metallic embossed foil cover 2.00
❑2, Mar 1993; DP (c); DP, BWi (a); V: X-O Manowar 1.00
❑3, Apr 1993 DP (c); DP, BWi (a) 1.00
❑4, May 1993 DP (c); DP, BWi (a); A: Eternal Warrior 1.00
❑5, Jun 1993 DP (c); DP, BWi (a); A: Rai. A: Eternal Warrior 1.00
❑6, Jul 1993; DP (c); DP, BWi (a); 1: Ninjak 1.00
❑6/VVSS, Jul 1993, DP, BWi (a) 50.00
❑7, Aug 1993 DP (c); DP (a); A: Ninjak 1.00
❑8, Sep 1993; DP (c); Serial Number Contest coupon 1.00
❑9, Oct 1993 DP (c); DP (a) 1.00
❑10, Nov 1993 DP (c); DP (a) 1.00
❑11, Dec 1993 DP (c); DP (a) 1.00
❑12, Jan 1994 DP (c); DP (a) 1.00
❑13, Feb 1994 1.00
❑14, Mar 1994 1.00
❑15, Apr 1994 1.00
❑16, May 1994; trading card 2.00
❑17, Jun 1994 A: H.A.R.D.Corps 1.00
❑18, Aug 1994 1.00
❑19, Sep 1994; 1: Uzzi the Clown 1.00
❑20, Oct 1994; Chaos Effect Gamma 1 1.00
❑21, Nov 1994; V: Ax 1.00
❑22, Dec 1994 1.00
❑23, Jan 1995; 1: Phaze 1.00
❑24, Feb 1995 1.00
❑25, Mar 1995; 1: Monkey Boy 2.00
❑26, Apr 1995 2.00
❑27, May 1995 2.00
❑28, May 1995; V: Ninjak 2.00
❑29, Jun 1995; Valiant becomes Acclaim imprint 2.00
❑30, Jul 1995; Birthquake 2.00
❑31, Jul 1995; Birthquake 2.00
❑32, Aug 1995; Birthquake 2.00
❑33, Aug 1995; Birthquake 2.00
❑34, Sep 1995; 1: Rampage; O: Rampage 2.00
❑35, Sep 1995; V: Rampage 2.00
❑36, Oct 1995; BA (c); MGr (w); MGr, BA (a); 1: Papa Juju 2.00
❑37, Oct 1995 BA (c); MGr (w); BA (a) 2.00
❑38, Nov 1995 3.00
❑39, Nov 1995; D: Rampage 3.00
❑40, Dec 1995 3.00
❑41, Dec 1995 PG (a) 3.00
❑42, Jan 1996 3.00
❑43, Jan 1996 3.00
❑44, Feb 1996 4.00
❑45, Mar 1996; O: Proteus 4.00
❑46, Apr 1996 4.00
❑47, May 1996 4.00
❑48, May 1996 5.00
❑49, Jun 1996 5.00
❑50, Jul 1996 6.00
❑51, Aug 1996; Final Issue 10.00
❑YB 1, ca. 1994; YB (annual) #1; YB (annual) #1 5.00

Bloodshot: Last Stand
Valiant

❑0, Mar 1996 10.00

Bloodshot
Acclaim

❑1, Jul 1997 2.50
❑1/Variant, Jul 1997; alternate painted cover 2.50
❑2, Aug 1997 2.50
❑3, Sep 1997 2.50
❑4, Oct 1997 2.50
❑5, Nov 1997; Steranko tribute cover 2.50
❑6, Dec 1997 2.50
❑7, Jan 1998; V: X-O Manowar 2.50
❑8, Feb 1998; V: X-O Manowar 2.50
❑9, Mar 1998 2.50
❑10, Apr 1998; in Area 51 2.50
❑11, May 1998; No cover date 2.50
❑12, Jun 1998; No cover date; indicia says Feb 2.50
❑13, Jul 1998; No cover date; indicia says Mar 2.50
❑14, Aug 1998; No cover date; indicia says Apr 2.50
❑15, Sep 1998; No cover date; indicia says May 2.50
❑16, Oct 1998; No cover date; indicia says Jun 2.50
❑Ashcan 1, Mar 1997; No cover price; b&w preview of upcoming series 1.00

Bloodstone
Marvel

❑1, Dec 2001 2.99
❑2, Jan 2002 2.99
❑3, Feb 2002 2.99
❑4, Mar 2002 2.99

Bloodstream
Image

❑1, Jan 2004 2.95
❑2, Mar 2004 2.95
❑3, Jul 2004 2.95
❑4, Nov 2004 2.95

Bloodstrike
Image

❑1, Apr 1993; RL (w); RL (a); 1: Tag. 1: Deadlock. 1: Shogun. 1: Col. Cabbot. 1: Fourplay. fading blood cover 3.00
❑2, Jun 1993; 1: Lethal 2.00
❑3, Jul 1993 2.00
❑4, Oct 1993 KG (w) 2.00
❑5, Nov 1993; 1: Noble. A: Supreme. 1: Noble 2.00
❑6, Dec 1993; Chapel becomes team leader 2.00
❑7, Jan 1994 A: Chapel 2.00
❑8, Feb 1994 2.00
❑9, Mar 1994 2.00
❑10, Apr 1994 2.00
❑11, Jul 1994 2.00
❑12, Aug 1994 2.00
❑13, Aug 1994 2.50
❑14, Sep 1994 2.50
❑15, Oct 1994 2.50
❑16, Nov 1994 2.50
❑17, Dec 1994 2.50
❑18, Jan 1995; polybagged with trading card 2.50
❑19, Feb 1995; polybagged 2.50
❑20, Mar 1995 2.50
❑21, Apr 1995 2.50
❑22, May 1995 2.50
❑23 2.50
❑24 2.50
❑25, May 1994; Images of Tomorrow; Published out of sequence as a preview of the future 1.95

Bloodstrike Assassin
Image

❑0, Oct 1995 2.50
❑1/A, Jun 1995 2.50
❑1/B, Jun 1995, alternate cover 2.50
❑2, Jul 1995 2.50
❑3, Aug 1995 2.50
❑4 2.50

Bloodsucker
Fantagraphics / Eros

❑1, b&w; Adult 2.50

Blood Sword
Jademan

❑1, Aug 1988 1.95
❑2, Sep 1988 1.95
❑3, Oct 1988 1.95
❑4, Nov 1988 1.95
❑5, Dec 1988 1.95
❑6, Jan 1989 1.95
❑7, Feb 1989 1.95
❑8, Mar 1989 1.95
❑9, Apr 1989 1.95
❑10, May 1989 1.95
❑11, Jun 1989 1.95
❑12, Jul 1989 1.95
❑13, Aug 1989 1.95
❑14, Sep 1989 1.95
❑15, Oct 1989 1.95
❑16, Nov 1989 1.95
❑17, Dec 1989 1.95
❑18, Jan 1990 1.95
❑19, Feb 1990 1.95
❑20, Mar 1990 1.95
❑21, Apr 1990 1.95
❑22, May 1990 1.95
❑23, Jun 1990 1.95
❑24, Jul 1990 1.95
❑25, Aug 1990 1.95
❑26, Sep 1990 1.95
❑27, Oct 1990 1.95
❑28, Nov 1990 1.95
❑29, Dec 1990 1.95
❑30, Jan 1991 1.95
❑31, Feb 1991 1.95
❑32, Mar 1991 1.95
❑33, Apr 1991 1.95
❑34, May 1991 1.95
❑35, Jun 1991 1.95
❑36, Jul 1991 1.95
❑37, Aug 1991 1.95
❑38, Sep 1991 1.95
❑39, Oct 1991 1.95
❑40, Nov 1991 1.95
❑41, Dec 1991 1.95
❑42, Jan 1992 1.95

Blood Sword Dynasty
Jademan

❑1, Sep 1989 1.25
❑2, Oct 1989 1.25
❑3, Nov 1989 1.25
❑4, Dec 1989 1.25
❑5, Jan 1990 1.25
❑6, Feb 1990 1.25
❑7, Mar 1990 1.25
❑8, Apr 1990 1.25
❑9, May 1990 1.25
❑10, Jun 1990 1.25
❑11, Jul 1990 1.25
❑12, Aug 1990 1.25
❑13, Sep 1990 1.25
❑14, Oct 1990 1.25
❑15, Nov 1990 1.25
❑16, Dec 1990 1.25
❑17, Jan 1991 1.25
❑18, Feb 1991 1.25
❑19, Mar 1991 1.25
❑20, Apr 1991 1.25
❑21, May 1991 1.25
❑22, Jun 1991 1.25
❑23, Jul 1991 1.25
❑24, Aug 1991 1.25
❑25, Sep 1991 1.25
❑26, Oct 1991 1.25
❑27, Nov 1991 1.25
❑28, Dec 1991 1.25
❑29, Jan 1992 1.25

Blood Syndicate
DC / Milestone

❑1, Apr 1993, TVE (a); 1: Blood Syndicate. 1: Rob Chaplik 1.50
❑1/CS, Apr 1993, TVE (a); 1: Blood Syndicate. 1: Rob Chaplik. poster, trading card 2.95
❑2, May 1993, 1: Boogieman. V: Holocaust 1.50
❑3, Jun 1993, 1: MOM. A: Boogieman. 1: MOM 1.50
❑4, Jul 1993, D: Tech-9 1.50
❑5, Aug 1993, 1: Demon Fox. 1: John Wing. 1: Kwai 1.50
❑6, Sep 1993 1.50
❑7, Oct 1993, 1: Edmund. 1: Cornelia 1.50
❑8, Nov 1993, 1: Kwai 1.50

Big Bang Comics (Vol. 1)

Silver Age tributes abound in this series
©Caliber

Big Bang Comics (Vol. 2)

Image takes on the Silver Age here
©Image

Bill & Ted's Excellent Comic Book

Marvel's take on the future Wild Stallyns
©Marvel

Bill, the Galactic Hero

Based on the Harry Harrison novel series
©Topps

Billy the Kid

William Bonney gets the hero treatment
©Charlton

N-MINT

❑9, Dec 1993, O: Blood Syndicate. 1: Templo ... 1.50
❑10, Jan 1994, Giant-size; 1: Bubbasaur. Metallic ink cover ... 2.50
❑11, Feb 1994, Aquamaria joins Blood Syndicate ... 1.50
❑12, Mar 1994, 1: The Rat Congress ... 1.50
❑13, Apr 1994, 1: The White Roaches ... 1.50
❑14, May 1994 ... 1.50
❑15, Jun 1994, JBy (c) ... 1.50
❑16, Jul 1994, A: Superman. Continued from Steel #6 & into Worlds Collide #1 ... 1.50
❑17, Aug 1994, Continued from Steel #7; Continues into Static #14 ... 1.75
❑18, Sep 1994 ... 1.75
❑19, Oct 1994 ... 1.75
❑20, Nov 1994, A: Shadow Cabinet ... 1.75
❑21, Dec 1994 ... 1.75
❑22, Jan 1995 ... 1.75
❑23, Feb 1995 ... 1.75
❑24, Mar 1995 ... 1.75
❑25, Apr 1995, Giant-size; Tech-9 returns ... 2.95
❑26, May 1995 ... 1.75
❑27, Jun 1995 ... 1.75
❑28, Jul 1995 ... 2.50
❑29, Aug 1995, Long Hot Summer ... 1.00
❑30, Sep 1995, Long Hot Summer ... 2.50
❑31, Oct 1995 ... 2.50
❑32, Nov 1995 ... 2.50
❑33, Dec 1995 ... 0.99
❑34, Jan 1996 ... 2.50
❑35, Feb 1996, Final Issue ... 3.50

Bloodthirst: Terminus Option
Alpha Productions

❑1, b&w ... 2.50
❑2 ... 2.50

Bloodthirst: The Nightfall Conspiracy
Alpha

❑1 ... 2.50
❑2 ... 2.50

Bloodthirsty Pirate Tales
Black Swan

❑1 ... 2.50
❑2 ... 2.50
❑3, Win 1995 ... 2.50
❑4, Fal 1996 ... 2.50
❑5, Spr 1997 ... 2.50
❑6, Win 1997 ... 2.50
❑7 ... 2.50
❑8 ... 2.50

Blood Ties
Full Moon

❑1, ca. 1991 ... 2.25

Bloodwing
Eternity

❑1, Jan 1988 ... 1.95
❑2, Feb 1988 ... 1.95
❑3, Mar 1988 ... 1.95
❑4, Apr 1988 ... 1.95
❑5, May 1988 ... 1.95
❑6 ... 1.95

Bloodwulf
Image

❑1, Feb 1995; five different covers ... 2.50
❑2, Mar 1995 ... 2.50

N-MINT

❑3, Apr 1995 ... 2.50
❑4, May 1995 ... 2.50
❑Summer 1, Aug 1995; Summer Special ... 2.50

Bloody Bones & Blackeyed Peas
Galaxy

❑1 ... 1.00

Bloodyhot
Parody

❑1 ... 2.95

Bloody Mary
DC / Helix

❑1, Oct 1996 ... 2.25
❑2, Nov 1996 ... 2.25
❑3, Dec 1996 ... 2.25
❑4, Jan 1997; Final Issue ... 2.25

Bloody Mary: Lady Liberty
DC / Helix

❑1, Sep 1997 ... 2.50
❑2, Oct 1997 ... 2.50
❑3, Nov 1997 ... 2.50
❑4, Dec 1997 ... 2.50

Bloody School
Curtis Comic

❑1 ... 2.95

Blue
Image

❑1, Aug 1999 ... 2.50
❑2, Apr 2000 ... 2.50

Bluebeard
Slave Labor

❑1, Nov 1993, b&w ... 2.95
❑2, Dec 1993, b&w ... 2.95
❑3, Mar 1994, b&w ... 2.95

Blue Beetle
Charlton

❑1, Jun 1964, SD (a) ... 45.00
❑2, Sep 1964, SD (a) ... 30.00
❑3, Nov 1964, SD (a) ... 20.00
❑4, Jan 1965, SD (a) ... 20.00
❑5, Apr 1965, SD (a) ... 20.00

Blue Beetle
Charlton

❑50, Jul 1965 ... 27.00
❑51, Aug 1965 ... 27.00
❑52, Oct 1965, SD (a) ... 27.00
❑53, Dec 1965, SD (a) ... 27.00
❑54, Feb 1966 ... 27.00
❑1, Jun 1967, SD (c); SD (a) ... 60.00
❑2, Aug 1967, SD (c); SD (w); SD (a); O: Blue Beetle ... 40.00
❑3, Oct 1967, SD (c); SD (w); SD (a) ... 27.00
❑4, Dec 1967, SD (c); SD (w); SD (a) ... 27.00
❑5, Nov 1968, SD (c); SD (w); SD (a) ... 27.00

Blue Beetle
DC

❑1, Jun 1986 O: Blue Beetle. V: Firefist ... 1.00
❑2, Jul 1986 O: Firefist. V: Firefist ... 1.00
❑3, Aug 1986 V: Madmen ... 1.00
❑4, Sep 1986 V: Doctor Alchemy ... 1.00
❑5, Oct 1986 A: The Question ... 1.00
❑6, Nov 1986 A: The Question ... 1.00
❑7, Dec 1986 A: The Question. D: Muse ... 1.00

N-MINT

❑8, Jan 1987 V: Calculator ... 1.00
❑9, Feb 1987; A: Chronos. Legends tie-in ... 1.00
❑10, Mar 1987; V: Chronos. Legends tie-in ... 1.00
❑11, Apr 1987 A: Teen Titans ... 1.00
❑12, May 1987 A: Teen Titans ... 1.00
❑13, Jun 1987 A: Teen Titans ... 1.00
❑14, Jul 1987 1: Carapax ... 1.00
❑15, Aug 1987 RA (c); RA (a); A: Carapax ... 1.00
❑16, Sep 1987 RA (c); RA (a) ... 1.00
❑17, Oct 1987 A: Blue Beetle (Dan Garrett) ... 1.00
❑18, Nov 1987 V: Blue Beetle (Dan Garrett) ... 1.00
❑19, Dec 1987 DG (c); RA (a) ... 1.00
❑20, Jan 1988; DG (c); RA (a); Millennium tie-in ... 1.00
❑21, Feb 1988; RA (a); A: Mister Miracle. Millennium tie-in ... 1.00
❑22, Mar 1988 RA (a); A: Chronos ... 1.00
❑23, Apr 1988 DH (a); V: Madmen ... 1.00
❑24, May 1988 DH (a); V: Carapax ... 1.00

Blue Beetle (Modern)
Modern

❑1, ca. 1977; SD (c); SD (a); reprints Charlton's Blue Beetle (Vol. 3) #1; no #2 ... 5.00
❑3, ca. 1977; SD (c); SD (a); reprints Charlton's Blue Beetle (Vol. 3) #3 ... 5.00

Blue Beetle
DC

❑1, Jun 2006 ... 6.00
❑1/2nd, Jun 2006 ... 4.00
❑2, Jul 2006 ... 2.99
❑3, Aug 2006 ... 2.99
❑4, Sep 2006 ... 2.99
❑5, Oct 2006 ... 2.99
❑6, Nov 2006 ... 2.99
❑7, Dec 2006 ... 2.99
❑8, Jan 2007 ... 2.99
❑9, Feb 2007 ... 2.99
❑10, Mar 2007 ... 2.99
❑11 ... 2.99
❑12 ... 2.99
❑13 ... 2.99
❑14 ... 2.99
❑15 ... 2.99
❑16 ... 2.99
❑17 ... 2.99
❑18 ... 2.99
❑19 ... 2.99
❑20 ... 2.99
❑21 ... 2.99
❑22 ... 2.99
❑23 ... 2.99
❑24 ... 2.99
❑25 ... 2.99
❑26 ... 2.99
❑27 ... 2.99
❑28 ... 2.99
❑29 ... 2.99
❑30 ... 2.99
❑31 ... 2.99
❑32 ... 2.99
❑33 ... 2.99
❑34 ... 2.99
❑35 ... 2.99
❑36 ... 2.99

Blue Block
Kitchen Sink

❑1 ... 2.95

Blue Bulleteer
AC

❑1, Jan 1989, b&w; O: Blue Bulleteer ... 2.50

Blue Devil
DC

❑1, Jun 1984; O: Blue Devil. 1: Nebiros ... 1.00
❑2, Jul 1984; V: Shockwave ... 1.00
❑3, Aug 1984; V: Metallo ... 1.00
❑4, Sep 1984; A: Zatanna. V: Nebiros ... 1.00
❑5, Oct 1984; A: Zatanna. V: Nebiros ... 1.00
❑6, Nov 1984; 1: Bolt; Flash Force 2000 insert ... 1.00
❑7, Dec 1984; V: Bolt; V: Trickster ... 1.00
❑8, Jan 1985; V: Bolt. V: Trickster ... 1.00
❑9, Feb 1985; V: Bolt. V: Trickster ... 1.00
❑10, Mar 1985 ... 1.00
❑11, Apr 1985 ... 1.00
❑12, May 1985; A: Demon. V: Shockwave ... 1.00
❑13, Jun 1985 A: Green Lantern. A: Zatanna ... 1.00
❑14, Jul 1985; 1: Kid Devil ... 1.00
❑15, Aug 1985 ... 1.00
❑16, Sep 1985; MASK insert ... 1.00
❑17, Oct 1985; Crisis ... 1.00
❑18, Nov 1985; Crisis ... 1.00
❑19, Dec 1985; V: Captain Cold; V: Trickster ... 1.00
❑20, Jan 1986 ... 1.00
❑21, Feb 1986 ... 1.00
❑22, Mar 1986 ... 1.00
❑23, Apr 1986; A: Firestorm. V: Mindboggler; V: Bolt; V: Hyena; V: Slipknot; V: Multiplex ... 1.00
❑24, May 1986; V: Toyman ... 1.00
❑25, Jun 1986 ... 1.00
❑26, Jul 1986; V: Green Gargoyle ... 1.00
❑27, Aug 1986 ... 1.00
❑28, Sep 1986; Featuring real-life contest winner Bryan Buck ... 1.00
❑29, Oct 1986 ... 1.00
❑30, Nov 1986; Double-size; V: Flash's Rogues' Gallery ... 1.25
❑31, Dec 1986; Giant-size; Final Issue ... 1.25
❑Ann 1, Nov 1985; V: Felix Faust ... 2.00

Blue Hole
Christine Shields

❑1 ... 2.95

Blue Ice
Martyr

❑1, ca. 1992 ... 2.50
❑2, ca. 1992 ... 2.50

Blue Lily
Dark Horse

❑1, Mar 1993 ... 3.95
❑2, Apr 1993 ... 3.95
❑3 ... 3.95
❑4 ... 3.95

Blue Loco
Kitchen Sink

❑1, Feb 1997; cardstock cover ... 5.95

Blue Monday: Absolute Beginners
Oni

❑1, ca. 2001 ... 2.95
❑2, ca. 2001 ... 2.95
❑3, ca. 2001 ... 2.95
❑4, ca. 2001 ... 2.95

Blue Monday: Lovecats
Oni

❑1, ca. 2002 ... 2.95

Blue Monday: Painted Moon
Oni

❑1, Feb 2004; b&w ... 2.99
❑2, Jun 2004; b&w ... 2.99
❑3, Sep 2004; b&w ... 2.99
❑4, Mar 2004; b&w ... 2.99

Blue Monday: The Kids Are Alright
Oni

❑1, ca. 2000 ... 2.95
❑2, ca. 2000 ... 2.95
❑3, ca. 2000 ... 2.95

Blue Moon
Mu

❑1, Sep 1992 ... 2.50
❑2, Nov 1992 ... 2.50
❑3, Feb 1993 ... 2.50
❑4, May 1993 ... 2.50
❑5, Dec 1993 ... 2.50

Blue Moon
Aeon

❑1, Aug 1994, b&w ... 2.95

Blue Ribbon Comics
Archie / Red Circle

❑1, Nov 1983, SD (c); AW, JK (a); Red Circle publishes ... 2.50
❑2, Nov 1983, RB (c); AN (a) ... 1.50
❑3, Dec 1983 ... 1.50
❑4, Jan 1984, Wraparound cover ... 1.50
❑5, Feb 1984, A: Steel Sterling. All reprinted from "The Double Life of Private Strong" #1 ... 1.50
❑6, Mar 1984 ... 1.50
❑7, Apr 1984, RB (w); TD (a) ... 1.50
❑8, May 1984 ... 1.50
❑9, Jun 1984 ... 1.50
❑10, Jul 1984 ... 1.50
❑11, Aug 1984 ... 1.50
❑12, Sep 1984 ... 1.50
❑13, Oct 1984 ... 1.50
❑14, Dec 1984 ... 1.50

Bluesman

❑1, ca. 2005 ... 6.95

B-Movie Presents
B-Movie

❑1 ... 1.70
❑2 ... 1.70
❑3 ... 1.70
❑4 ... 1.70

BMW Films: The Hire
Dark Horse

❑1 2004 ... 2.99
❑2 2005 ... 2.99
❑3, Oct 2005 ... 2.99
❑4, Jan 2006 ... 2.99

Board of Superheros
Not Available

❑1 ... 1.00

Bobby Benson's B-Bar-B Riders (AC)
AC

❑1, ca. 1990, b&w ... 2.75

Bobby Ruckers
Art

❑1 ... 2.95

Bobby Sherman
Charlton

❑1, Feb 1972 ... 15.00
❑2, Mar 1972 ... 10.00
❑3, May 1972 ... 10.00
❑4, Jun 1972 ... 10.00
❑5, Jul 1972 ... 10.00
❑6, Sep 1972 ... 10.00
❑7, Oct 1972 ... 10.00

Bob, the Galactic Bum
DC

❑1, Feb 1995 ... 2.00
❑2, Mar 1995 ... 2.00
❑3, Apr 1995 ... 2.00
❑4, Jun 1995 ... 2.00

Bob Marley, Tale of the Tuff Gong
Marvel

❑1 ... 5.95
❑2 ... 5.95
❑3 ... 5.95

Bobobo-bo Bo-bobo
Viz

❑1, Dec 2005 ... 7.99

"Bob's" Favorite Comics
Rip Off

❑1, b&w ... 2.50
❑1/2nd, b&w ... 2.50
❑1/3rd, b&w ... 2.50

Bob Steele Western (AC)
AC

❑1 1990, b&w; Reprints ... 2.75

Body Bags
Dark Horse / Blanc Noir

❑1, Sep 1996 ... 3.50
❑2, Oct 1996 ... 3.00
❑3, Nov 1996 ... 3.00
❑4, Jan 1997 ... 3.00
❑Ashcan 1 ... 3.00

Body Bags: Father's Day
Image

❑1, Aug 2005 ... 5.99
❑2, Oct 2005 ... 5.99

Body Count (Aircel)
Aircel

❑1; TMNT storyline ... 2.25
❑2; TMNT storyline ... 2.25
❑3; TMNT storyline ... 2.25
❑4; TMNT storyline ... 2.25

Bodycount
Image

❑1, Mar 1996; Painted Cover; (Cover says Feb) ... 2.50
❑2, Apr 1996; Painted Cover ... 2.50
❑3, May 1996; Painted Cover ... 2.50
❑4, Final Issue ... 2.50

Body Doubles
DC

❑1, Oct 1999 ... 2.50
❑2, Nov 1999 ... 2.50
❑3, Dec 1999 ... 2.50
❑4, Jan 2000 ... 2.50

Body Doubles (Villains)
DC

❑1, Feb 1998; New Year's Evil ... 2.00

Bodyguard
Aircel

❑1, Sep 1990, b&w; intro by Todd McFarlane ... 2.50
❑2, Oct 1990, b&w; Adult ... 2.50
❑3, Nov 1990, b&w; Polybagged; Adult ... 2.50

Body Heat
NBM

❑1; Adult ... 11.95

Body Paint
Fantagraphics / Eros

❑1; Adult ... 2.95
❑2, Jun 1995; Adult ... 2.95

Body Swap
Roger Mason

❑1 ... 2.95

Boffo in Hell
Neatly Chiseled Features

❑1 ... 2.50

Boffo Laffs
Paragraphics

❑1; first hologram cover ... 2.50
❑2 ... 1.95
❑3 ... 1.95
❑4 ... 1.95
❑5 ... 1.95

Boffy the Vampire Layer
Fantagraphics / Eros

❑1, ca. 2000 ... 2.95
❑2, ca. 2000 ... 2.95
❑3, ca. 2001 ... 2.95

Bogie Man
Fat Man

❑1, Sep 1989 ... 2.50
❑2, Feb 1990 ... 2.50
❑3, Aug 1990 ... 2.50
❑4, Sep 1990 ... 2.50

Bogie Man: Chinatoon
Atomeka

❑1 ... 2.95
❑2 ... 2.95
❑3 ... 2.95
❑4 ... 2.95

Bogie Man: The Manhattan Project
Tundra

❑1, Jul 1992 ... 4.95

Bog Swamp Demon
Hall of Heroes

❑1, Aug 1996 ... 2.50

Other grades: Multiply price above by 5/6 for VF/NM • 2/3 for VERY FINE • 1/3 for FINE • 1/5 for VERY GOOD • 1/8 for GOOD

Binky

Continuation of "Leave It to Binky" series

©DC

Birds of Prey

Oracle and Black Canary fight crime

©DC

Bishop

Mutant from the future returns to star in comic

©Marvel

Bishop: Xse

It stands for "Xavier Security Enforcers"

©Marvel

Black Axe

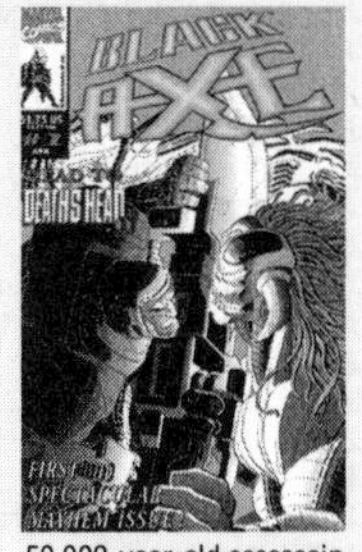

50,000-year-old asssassin in Marvel UK import

©Marvel

N-MINT

- ❑1/Variant, Aug 1996; alternate cover 2.50
- ❑1/Commem, Aug 1996; Commemorative Edition; limited to 500 copies 5.00
- ❑2, Oct 1996; no indicia 2.50
- ❑2/Variant, Oct 1996; alternate cover 2.50
- ❑3, Dec 1996 .... 2.50
- ❑4, Mar 1997 .... 2.50

Bohos
Image

- ❑1, May 1998; cover says Jun, indicia says May 2.95
- ❑2, Jun 1998 .... 2.95
- ❑3, Jul 1998; no month of publication 2.95

Bo Jackson vs. Michael Jordan
Celebrity

- ❑1 .... 2.95
- ❑2 .... 2.95

Bold Adventure
Pacific

- ❑1, Nov 1983 TVE, BMc (a) 2.00
- ❑2, Mar 1984 .... 2.00
- ❑3, Jun 1984; Final Issue 2.00

Bolt and Starforce Six
AC

- ❑1, Jul 1984 .... 1.75

Bolt Special
AC

- ❑1 .... 2.00

Bomarc
Nightwynd

- ❑1 .... 2.50
- ❑2 .... 2.50
- ❑3 .... 2.50

Bomba The Jungle Boy
DC

- ❑1, Sep 1967, 1: Bomba 16.00
- ❑2, Nov 1967 .... 8.00
- ❑3, Jan 1968, Throw to Part 3 at the end of Part 2 has a "Part 2" typo 8.00
- ❑4, Mar 1968 .... 8.00
- ❑5, May 1968 .... 8.00
- ❑6, Jul 1968 .... 8.00
- ❑7, Sep 1968, Final Issue 8.00

Bombast
Topps

- ❑1, Apr 1993; Savage Dragon, #1 - Factory bagged 2.95

Bombastic
Screaming Dodo

- ❑1, Nov 1996 .... 2.50
- ❑2, Feb 1997 .... 2.50
- ❑3, May 1997 .... 2.50
- ❑4, Aug 1997 .... 2.50
- ❑5, Dec 1997; cardstock cover 2.50

Bomb Queen
Image

- ❑1, Mar 2006 .... 3.50
- ❑2, Apr 2006 .... 3.50
- ❑3, May 2006 .... 3.50

Bomb Queen
Image

- ❑1, Nov 2006 .... 3.50
- ❑2, Dec 2006 .... 3.50
- ❑3, Jan 2007 .... 3.50

Bomb Queen vs. Blacklight
Image

- ❑1, Sep 2006, One-shot 3.50

Bonafide
Bonafide

- ❑0/2nd, Mar 1994; 2nd printing 3.95
- ❑0 .... 3.95

Bonanza
Gold Key

- ❑1, Dec 1962, Series continued from appearances in Four Color Comics 110.00
- ❑2, Mar 1963 .... 75.00
- ❑3, Jun 1963 .... 50.00
- ❑4, Sep 1963 .... 50.00
- ❑5, Dec 1963 .... 50.00
- ❑6, Feb 1964 .... 32.00
- ❑7, Apr 1964 .... 32.00
- ❑8, Jun 1964 .... 32.00
- ❑9, Aug 1964 .... 32.00
- ❑10, Oct 1964 .... 32.00
- ❑11, Dec 1964 .... 22.00
- ❑12, Feb 1965 .... 22.00
- ❑13, Apr 1965 .... 22.00
- ❑14, Jun 1965 .... 22.00
- ❑15, Aug 1965 .... 22.00
- ❑16, Oct 1965 .... 22.00
- ❑17, Dec 1965 .... 22.00
- ❑18, Feb 1966 .... 22.00
- ❑19, Apr 1966 .... 22.00
- ❑20, Jun 1966 .... 22.00
- ❑21, Aug 1966 .... 15.00
- ❑22, Oct 1966 .... 15.00
- ❑23, Feb 1967 .... 15.00
- ❑24, May 1967 .... 15.00
- ❑25, Aug 1967, Includes reprints 15.00
- ❑26, Nov 1967 .... 15.00
- ❑27, Feb 1968 .... 15.00
- ❑28, May 1968 .... 15.00
- ❑29, Aug 1968 .... 15.00
- ❑30, Nov 1968, Price increase 15.00
- ❑31, Feb 1969 .... 12.00
- ❑32, May 1969 .... 12.00
- ❑33, Aug 1969 .... 12.00
- ❑34, Nov 1969 .... 12.00
- ❑35, Feb 1970 .... 12.00
- ❑36, May 1970 .... 12.00
- ❑37, Aug 1970, Final Issue 12.00

Bondage Confessions
Fantagraphics / Eros

- ❑1; Adult 2.95
- ❑2; Adult 2.95
- ❑3; Adult 2.95
- ❑4, Nov 1998; Adult 2.95

Bondage Fairies
Antarctic / Venus

- ❑1, Mar 1994; Adult 4.00
- ❑1/2nd, May 1994; 2nd printing; Adult 2.95
- ❑1/3rd, Aug 1994; 3rd printing; Adult 2.95
- ❑1/4th, Jan 1995; 4th printing; Adult 2.95
- ❑2, Apr 1994; Adult 4.00
- ❑2/2nd, Jun 1994; 2nd printing; Adult 2.95
- ❑2/3rd, Oct 1994; 3rd printing; Adult 2.95
- ❑2/4th, Apr 1995; 4th printing; Adult 2.95
- ❑3, May 1994; Adult 3.25
- ❑3/2nd, Sep 1994; 2nd printing; Adult 2.95
- ❑3/3rd, Dec 1994; 3rd printing; Adult 2.95
- ❑4, Jun 1994; Adult 3.25
- ❑4/2nd, Nov 1994; 2nd printing; Adult 2.95
- ❑4/3rd, Jan 1995; 3rd printing; Adult 2.95
- ❑5, Jul 1994; Adult 3.25
- ❑5/2nd, Nov 1994; 2nd printing; Adult 2.95
- ❑5/3rd, Feb 1995; 3rd printing; Adult 2.95
- ❑6, Aug 1994; Adult 2.95
- ❑6/2nd, Feb 1995; 2nd printing; Adult 2.95

Bondage Fairies Extreme
Fantagraphics / Eros

- ❑1, Oct 1999 .... 3.50
- ❑2, Nov 1999 .... 3.50
- ❑3, Dec 1999 .... 3.50
- ❑4, Jan 2000 .... 3.50
- ❑5, Feb 2000 .... 3.50
- ❑6, Mar 2000 .... 3.50
- ❑7, Apr 2000 .... 3.50
- ❑8, May 2000 .... 3.95
- ❑9, Jun 2000 .... 3.50
- ❑10, Jul 2000 .... 3.50
- ❑11, Sep 2000 .... 3.50
- ❑12, Oct 2000 .... 3.50
- ❑13, Nov 2000 .... 3.95
- ❑14, ca. 2000 .... 3.50

Bondage Girls at War
Fantagraphics / Eros

- ❑1 1996 .... 2.95
- ❑2 1996 .... 2.95
- ❑3 1996 .... 2.95
- ❑4 1996 .... 2.95
- ❑5, Feb 1997 .... 2.95
- ❑6, ca. 1997 .... 2.95

Bone
Cartoon Books

- ❑1, Jul 1991, b&w; 1: Phoney Bone. 1: Smiley Bone. 1: Fone Bone. 3000 printed 80.00
- ❑1/2nd, Mar 1992; 1: Phoney Bone. 1: Fone Bone. 2nd printing 8.00
- ❑1/3rd; 1: Phoney Bone. 1: Fone Bone. 3rd printing 3.00
- ❑1/4th, Jan 1993; 1: Phoney Bone. 1: Fone Bone. 4th printing 3.00
- ❑1/5th; 1: Phoney Bone. 1: Fone Bone. fifth printing 3.00
- ❑1/6th, Nov 1993; 1: Phoney Bone. 1: Fone Bone. sixth printing 3.00
- ❑1/7th; 1: Phoney Bone. 1: Fone Bone. seventh printing 3.00
- ❑1/8th; 1: Phoney Bone. 1: Fone Bone. eighth printing 3.00
- ❑1/9th, 1: Phoney Bone. 1: Fone Bone. Image reprint 3.00
- ❑2, Sep 1991, b&w; 1: Thorn 45.00
- ❑2/2nd; 1: Thorn. 2nd printing 6.00
- ❑2/3rd, Jan 1993; 1: Thorn. 3rd printing 3.00
- ❑2/4th, Jun 1993; 1: Thorn. 4th printing 3.00
- ❑2/5th; 1: Thorn. fifth printing 3.00
- ❑2/6th; 1: Thorn. sixth printing 3.00
- ❑2/7th; 1: Thorn. seventh printing 3.00
- ❑2/8th, Image reprint 3.00
- ❑3, Dec 1991, b&w 25.00

❑3/2nd; 2nd printing 3.00
❑3/3rd, Jan 1993; 3rd printing 3.00
❑3/4th, Jun 1993; 4th printing 3.00
❑3/5th; fifth printing 3.00
❑3/6th; sixth printing 3.00
❑3/7th; seventh printing 3.00
❑3/8th, Image reprint 3.00
❑4, Mar 1992, b&w 16.00
❑4/2nd, Sep 1992; 2nd printing 3.00
❑4/3rd, Apr 1993; Image reprint 3.00
❑4/4th; 4th printing 3.00
❑4/5th; 5th printing 3.00
❑4/6th; 6th printing 3.00
❑5, Jun 1992, b&w 12.00
❑5/2nd, Sep 1992; Image reprint 3.00
❑5/3rd, Image reprint 3.00
❑5/4th; 4th printing 3.00
❑5/5th; 5th printing 3.00
❑5/6th; 6th printing 3.00
❑5/7th; 7th printing 3.00
❑6, Nov 1992, b&w 7.00
❑6/2nd; 2nd printing 3.00
❑6/3rd, Image reprint 3.00
❑6/4th; 4th printing 3.00
❑6/5th; 5th printing 3.00
❑6/6th; 6th printing 3.00
❑7, Dec 1992, b&w 7.00
❑7/2nd; 2nd printing 3.00
❑7/3rd, Aug 1993; Image reprint 3.00
❑7/4th; 4th printing 3.00
❑7/5th; 5th printing 3.00
❑8, Feb 1993, b&w; Eisner award-winning story (1994) 7.00
❑8/2nd; second printing; Eisner award-winning story (1994) 3.00
❑8/3rd; third printing; Eisner award-winning story (1994) 3.00
❑8/4th; fourth printing; Eisner award-winning story (1994) 3.00
❑8/5th; fifth printing; Eisner award-winning story (1994) 3.00
❑8/6th; sixth printing; Eisner award-winning story (1994) 3.00
❑8/7th, Image reprint 3.00
❑9, Jul 1993, b&w; Eisner award-winning story (1994) 4.00
❑9/2nd; second printing; Eisner award-winning story (1994) 3.00
❑9/3rd, Image reprint; Eisner award-winning story (1994) 3.00
❑9/4th; fourth printing; Eisner award-winning story (1994) 3.00
❑10, Sep 1993, b&w; Eisner award-winning story (1994) 3.50
❑10/2nd; second printing; Eisner award-winning story (1994) 2.95
❑10/3rd, Image reprint; Eisner award-winning story (1994) 2.95
❑11, Dec 1993, b&w 3.50
❑11/2nd, Image reprint 2.95
❑12, Feb 1994, b&w 3.50
❑12/2nd, Dec 1994; Image reprint 2.95
❑12/3rd; 3rd printing 2.95
❑13, Mar 1994, b&w 3.50
❑13/2nd, Image reprint 2.95
❑13.5; Wizard promotional edition 3.50
❑13.5/Gold; Gold edition 3.50
❑14, May 1994, b&w 2.95
❑14/2nd, Feb 1994; Image reprint 2.95
❑15, Aug 1994, b&w 2.95
❑15/2nd, Image reprint 2.95
❑16, Oct 1994, b&w 2.95
❑16/2nd, Image reprint 2.95
❑17, Jan 1995, b&w 2.95
❑17/2nd, May 1995; Image reprint 2.95
❑18, Apr 1995, b&w 2.95
❑18/2nd, Jun 1995; Image reprint 2.95
❑19, Jun 1995, b&w 2.95
❑19/2nd, Jul 1995; Image reprint 2.95
❑20, Oct 1995, b&w; moves to Image 2.95
❑20/2nd, Aug 1995; Image reprint 2.95
❑21, Dec 1995, b&w; Image begins as publisher 2.95
❑22, Feb 1996, b&w 2.95
❑23, May 1996, b&w; 1: Baby Rat Creature; Includes two pin-ups by Dave Sim and Gerhard set in the Bone world 2.95
❑24, Jun 1996, b&w 2.95
❑25, Aug 1996, b&w 2.95
❑26, Dec 1996, b&w 2.95
❑27, Apr 1997, b&w; Phoney captures Red Dragon; series returns to Cartoon Books 2.95
❑28, Aug 1997, b&w; Cartoon Books begins as publisher 2.95
❑29, Nov 1997, b&w 2.95
❑30, Jan 1998, b&w 2.95
❑31, Apr 1998, b&w 2.95
❑32, Jun 1998, b&w 2.95
❑33, Aug 1998, b&w 2.95
❑34, Dec 1998, b&w 2.95
❑35, Mar 1999, b&w 2.95
❑36, May 1999, b&w 2.95
❑37, Aug 1999, b&w; cover says Sep, indicia says Aug 2.95
❑38/A, Aug 2000, b&w; FM (c); Frank Miller cover; Pin-up gallery 2.95
❑38/B, Aug 2000, b&w; ARo, FM (c); FM (a); alternate cover 2.95
❑38/C, Aug 2000, b&w; ARo (c); ARo (a); alternate cover 2.95
❑39, Oct 2000, b&w 2.95
❑40, Jan 2001, b&w 2.95
❑41, Mar 2001, b&w 2.95
❑42, May 2001, b&w 2.95
❑43, Jul 2001, b&w 2.95
❑44, Sep 2001, b&w 2.95
❑45, Nov 2001 2.95
❑46, Jan 2001 2.95
❑47, May 2002 2.95
❑48, Jul 2002 2.95
❑49, Oct 2002 2.95
❑50, Dec 2002 2.95
❑51, Mar 2002 2.95
❑52, Oct 2003 3.00
❑53, Nov 2003 3.00
❑54, Apr 2003 3.00
❑55, Jun 2004 3.00
❑Special 1, ca. 1993; Special edition; Holiday Special polybagged with Hero Illustrated 2.00

Bone Sourcebook
Image

❑1/A, Nov 1995, b&w; No cover price; promotional handout 2.00
❑1/B, Nov 1995; San Diego Comic-Con edition 2.00

Bonerest
Image

❑1, Aug 2005 2.95
❑2, Sep 2005 2.95
❑8, Mar 2006 2.99

Bone Rest

❑1, Jul 2005 5.00
❑1/Variant, Jul 2005 4.00
❑2, Sep 2005 2.99
❑3, Oct 2005 2.99
❑4, Nov 2005 2.99
❑5, Dec 2005 2.99
❑6, Jan 2006 2.99
❑7, Jan 2006 2.99

Bones
Malibu

❑1 1.95
❑2 1.95
❑3, Oct 1987 1.95
❑4, Nov 1987 1.95

Boneshaker
Caliber

❑1, ca. 1994, b&w; Collects serial from Negative Burn 3.50

Boneyard
NBM

❑1, ca. 2001; B&w series 2.95
❑2, ca. 2001 2.95
❑3, ca. 2001 2.95
❑4, ca. 2002 2.95
❑5, ca. 2002 2.95
❑6 2.95
❑7 2.95
❑8 2.95
❑9 2003 2.95
❑10, ca. 2003 2.95
❑11 2003 2.95
❑12 2003 2.95
❑13 2004 2.95
❑14 2004 2.95
❑15 2004 2.95
❑16 2004; ca. 2004 2.95
❑17 2005; ca. 2005 2.95
❑18 2005; b&w; ca. 2005 2.95
❑19 2005; ca. 2005 2.95
❑20, Jan 2006 2.95
❑21 2.95
❑22 2.95
❑23 2.95
❑24 2.95
❑25 2.95
❑26 2.95
❑27 2.95

Boneyard Press 1993 Tourbook
Boneyard

❑1; Distributor giveaway previewing Boneyard Press books; Distributor giveaway previewing Boneyard Press books; Adult 1.50

Boof (Iconografix)
Iconografix

❑1, b&w 2.50

Boof
Image

❑1, Jul 1994; Boof alone on cover; 1: Boof 1.95
❑1/A, Jul 1994; alternate cover 1.95
❑2, Aug 1994 1.95
❑2/A, Aug 1994; alternate cover 1.95
❑3, Sep 1994 1.95
❑3/A, Sep 1994; alternate cover 1.95
❑4, Oct 1994 1.95
❑5, Nov 1994 1.95
❑6, Dec 1994 1.95

Boof and the Bruise Crew
Image

❑1, Jul 1994 1.95
❑1/A, Jul 1994, alternate cover 1.95
❑2, Aug 1994 1.95
❑2/A, Aug 1994, alternate cover 1.95
❑3, Sep 1994 1.95
❑3/A, Sep 1994, alternate cover 1.95
❑4, Oct 1994 1.95
❑5, Nov 1994 1.95
❑6, Dec 1994 1.95

Boogeyman (Sergio Aragonés')
Dark Horse

❑1, Jun 1998 2.95
❑2, Jul 1998 2.95
❑3, Aug 1998 2.95
❑4, Sep 1998 2.95

Boogieman
Rion

❑1, b&w 1.50

Book
Dreamsmith

❑1, May 1998, b&w; Anthology 3.50
❑2, Aug 1998; b&w 3.50

Book of Angels
Caliber

❑1, ca. 1997, b&w; cardstock cover 3.95

Book of Ballads and Sagas
Green Man

❑1 1996, b&w 2.95
❑2 1996, b&w 2.95
❑3, Jun 1996, b&w 3.50
❑4, Dec 1996, b&w; Wraparound cover; Includes preview of Castle Waiting by Linda Medley 3.50

Book of Fate
DC

❑1, Feb 1997; KG (w); O: Fate. O: Jared Stevens 2.25
❑2, Mar 1997 KG (w); A: Sentinel 2.25
❑3, Apr 1997 KG (w) 2.25
❑4, May 1997; V: Two-Face 2.25
❑5, Jun 1997 KG (w) 2.25
❑6, Jul 1997; KG (w); continues in Night Force #8 2.25
❑7, Aug 1997; V: Rats 2.25
❑8, Sep 1997 KG (w) 2.25
❑9, Oct 1997 KG (w); KG (a) 2.25
❑10, Nov 1997; Price increase 2.50
❑11, Dec 1997; KG (w); Face cover 2.50
❑12, Jan 1998; KG (c); KG (w); KG (a); A: Lobo. Final issue; Lobo appearance 2.50

Black Canary (Mini-Series)

Sonic-screaming heroine gets own title
©DC

Black Condor

Reuses name from an old Quality character
©DC

Black Goliath

Short-lived 1970s African-American superhero title
©Marvel

Blackhawk (1st Series)

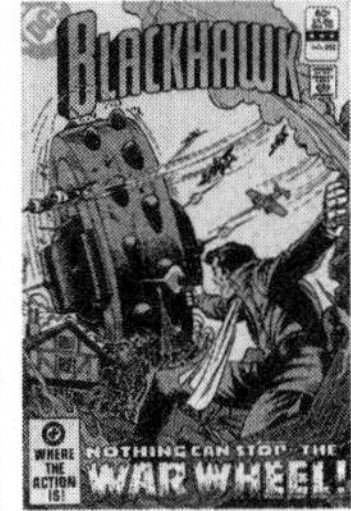

Allied ace fighters star in aerial series
©DC

Blackhawk (2nd Series)

Racy Chaykin version angered retailers
©DC

N-MINT

Book of Lost Souls
Marvel

❑1, Dec 2005 .... 2.99
❑2, Jan 2006 .... 2.99
❑3, Feb 2006 .... 2.99
❑4, Mar 2006 .... 2.99
❑5, May 2006 .... 2.99
❑6, Jun 2006 .... 2.99

Book of Night
Dark Horse

❑1, Jul 1987 CV (c); CV (w); CV (a) 2.50
❑2, Aug 1987 CV (c); CV (w); CV (a) 2.00
❑3, Sep 1987 CV (c); CV (w); CV (a) 2.00

Book of Shadows
Image

❑1, May 2006 .... 3.50
❑2, Jun 2006 .... 3.50

Book of Spells
Double Edge

❑1 .... 2.00
❑2, Sep 1994 .... 2.00
❑3 .... 2.00
❑4 .... 2.00

Book of the Damned: A Hellraiser Companion (Clive Barker's...)
Marvel / Epic

❑1, Oct 1991 .... 4.95
❑2, Apr 1992 .... 4.95
❑3, Nov 1992 .... 4.95
❑4, Sep 1993 .... 4.95

Book of the Dead
Marvel

❑1, Dec 1993, MP (a) 2.00
❑2, Jan 1994, GM, HC, MP (a); Reprints from Frankenstein (The Monster of...) 2.00
❑3, Feb 1994, MP (a); Reprints from Frankenstein (The Monster of...); The Walking Dead 2.00
❑4, Mar 1994, MP (a) 2.00

Book of the Tarot
Caliber / Tome

❑1, b&w; NN 3.95

Book of Thoth
Circle

❑1, Jun 1995 .... 2.50

Books of Doom
Marvel

❑1, Jan 2006 .... 2.99
❑2, Feb 2006 .... 2.99
❑3, Mar 2006 .... 2.99
❑4, May 2006 .... 2.99
❑5, Jun 2006 .... 2.99
❑6, Aug 2006, Final issue 2.99

Books of Faerie
DC / Vertigo

❑1, Mar 1997; O: Titania 2.50
❑2, Apr 1997 .... 2.50
❑3, May 1997 .... 2.50

Books of Faerie: Auberon's Tale
DC / Vertigo

❑1, Aug 1998 .... 2.50
❑2, Sep 1998 .... 2.50
❑3, Oct 1998 .... 2.50

N-MINT

Books of Faerie: Molly's Story
DC / Vertigo

❑1, Sep 1999 .... 2.50
❑2, Oct 1999 .... 2.50
❑3, Nov 1999 .... 2.50
❑4, Dec 1999 .... 2.50

Books of Lore: Special Edition
Peregrine Entertainment

❑1, Sep 1997, b&w; cardstock cover 2.95
❑1/Ltd., Collector's Edition, bagged with poster and limited and regular editions of #1 .... 5.00
❑2, Nov 1997 .... 2.95

Books of Lore: Storyteller
Peregrine Entertainment

❑1 .... 2.95

Books of Lore: The Kaynin Gambit
Peregrine Entertainment

❑0, Dec 1998 .... 2.95
❑1, Nov 1998 .... 2.95
❑1/Variant, Nov 1998; alternate cover 2.95
❑2, Jan 1999 .... 2.95
❑3, Mar 1999 .... 2.95
❑Ashcan 1, Jul 1998; b&w preview of Books Of Lore: The Kaynin Gambit 3.00

Books of Magic
DC

❑1, Dec 1990; NG (w); 1: Timothy Hunter 4.00
❑2, Jan 1991 NG (w) 4.00
❑3, Feb 1991 NG (w); CV (a) 4.00
❑4, Mar 1991; NG (w); Paul Johnson 4.00

Books of Magic
DC / Vertigo

❑1, May 1994 .... 3.00
❑1/Silver, May 1994; Silver (limited promotional) edition; no cover price 4.00
❑2, Jun 1994 .... 2.50
❑3, Jul 1994 .... 2.50
❑4, Aug 1994 .... 2.50
❑5, Sep 1994 .... 2.50
❑6, Oct 1994 .... 2.50
❑7, Nov 1994 CV (c) 2.50
❑8, Dec 1994 .... 2.50
❑9, Jan 1995 CV (c) 2.50
❑10, Feb 1995 CV (c) 2.50
❑11, Mar 1995 CV (c) 2.50
❑12, Apr 1995 CV (c) 2.50
❑13, May 1995 CV (c) 2.50
❑14, Jul 1995 .... 2.50
❑15, Aug 1995 .... 2.50
❑16, Sep 1995 .... 2.50
❑17, Oct 1995 .... 2.50
❑18, Nov 1995 .... 2.50
❑19, Dec 1995 .... 2.50
❑20, Jan 1996 .... 2.50
❑21, Feb 1996 .... 2.50
❑22, Mar 1996 .... 2.50
❑23, Apr 1996 .... 2.50
❑24, May 1996 .... 2.50
❑25, Jun 1996; A: Death (Sandman). Death (from The Endless) appearance 2.50
❑26, Jul 1996 .... 2.50
❑27, Aug 1996 .... 2.50
❑28, Sep 1996 .... 2.50
❑29, Oct 1996 .... 2.50

N-MINT

❑30, Nov 1996 .... 2.50
❑31, Dec 1996; D: elemental in Mojave Desert 2.50
❑32, Jan 1997 .... 2.50
❑33, Feb 1997 .... 2.50
❑34, Mar 1997 .... 2.50
❑35, Apr 1997 .... 2.50
❑36, May 1997 .... 2.50
❑37, Jun 1997 .... 2.50
❑38, Jul 1997 .... 2.50
❑39, Aug 1997; Encounters the aging, yet immortal, Tannarak 2.50
❑40, Sep 1997 .... 2.50
❑41, Oct 1997 .... 2.50
❑42, Nov 1997 .... 2.50
❑43, Dec 1997 .... 2.50
❑44, Jan 1998 .... 2.50
❑45, Feb 1998 .... 2.50
❑46, Mar 1998 .... 2.50
❑47, Apr 1998 .... 2.50
❑48, May 1998 .... 2.50
❑49, Jun 1998 .... 2.50
❑50, Jul 1998; preview of issue #51 .... 2.50
❑51, Aug 1998 .... 2.50
❑52, Sep 1998 .... 2.50
❑53, Oct 1998 .... 2.50
❑54, Nov 1998 .... 2.50
❑55, Dec 1998 .... 2.50
❑56, Jan 1999 A: Cain 2.50
❑57, Feb 1999; Books of Faerie back-up 2.50
❑58, Mar 1999; Books of Faerie back-up 2.50
❑59, Apr 1999; Books of Faerie back-up 2.50
❑60, May 1999 .... 2.50
❑61, Jun 1999 .... 2.50
❑62, Jul 1999; Books of Faerie back-up 2.50
❑63, Aug 1999; V: goblin posing as British mobster 2.50
❑64, Sep 1999 .... 2.50
❑65, Oct 1999 .... 2.50
❑66, Nov 1999 .... 2.50
❑67, Dec 1999 .... 2.50
❑68, Jan 2000 .... 2.50
❑69, Feb 2000 .... 2.50
❑70, Mar 2000 .... 2.50
❑71, Apr 2000 .... 2.50
❑72, May 2000 .... 2.50
❑74, Jul 2000 .... 2.50
❑73, Jun 2000 .... 2.50
❑75, Aug 2000; Final issue 2.50
❑Ann 1, Feb 1997; 1997 Ann 3.95
❑Ann 2, Feb 1998; 1998 Ann 3.95
❑Ann 3, Jun 1999; CV (c);1999 Ann 3.95

Books of Magick: Life During Wartime
DC / Vertigo

❑1, Sep 2004 .... 2.50
❑2, Oct 2004; Bagged with promo CD for Sky Captain and the World of Tomorrow 2.50
❑3, Nov 2004 .... 2.50
❑4, Dec 2004 .... 2.50
❑5, Jan 2005 .... 2.50
❑6, Feb 2005 .... 2.50
❑7, Mar 2005 .... 2.50
❑8, Apr 2005 .... 2.50
❑9, May 2005 .... 2.50
❑10, Jun 2005 .... 2.50
❑11, Jul 2005 .... 2.50

Other grades: Multiply price above by 5/6 for VF/NM • 2/3 for VERY FINE • 1/3 for FINE • 1/5 for VERY GOOD • 1/8 for GOOD

❑12, Aug 2005 ..... 2.75
❑13, Sep 2005 ..... 2.75
❑14, Oct 2005 ..... 2.75
❑15, Dec 2005; Final issue 2.75

Boom Boom
Aeon

❑1, b&w 2.50
❑2, Sep 1994, b&w 2.50
❑3 ..... 2.50
❑4, ca. 1995 ..... 2.50

Boondoggle
Knight

❑1, Mar 1995 ..... 2.95
❑2, Jul 1995, b&w 2.95
❑3, Nov 1995 ..... 2.95
❑4, Jan 1996, b&w 2.95
❑Special 1, Nov 1996, b&w 2.95

Boondoggle
Caliber / Tapestry

❑1, Jan 1997 ..... 2.95
❑2, Apr 1997 ..... 2.95

Booster Gold
DC

❑1, Feb 1986; 1: Booster Gold. V: Blackguard 2.50
❑2, Mar 1986; 1: Mindancer 1.00
❑3, Apr 1986 ..... 1.00
❑4, May 1986 ..... 1.00
❑5, Jun 1986; V: Mister Twister 1.00
❑6, Jul 1986 A: Superman 1.00
❑7, Aug 1986 A: Superman 1.00
❑8, Sep 1986; A: Legion. O: Booster Gold; V: Chiller 1.00
❑9, Oct 1986; A: Legion. O: Booster Gold; V: Chiller 1.00
❑10, Nov 1986 ..... 1.00
❑11, Dec 1986; V: Shockwave 1.00
❑12, Jan 1987 ..... 1.00
❑13, Feb 1987; 1: Goldstar (Trixie Collins); 1: Rip Hunter post Crisis 1.00
❑14, Mar 1987; back to future 1.00
❑15, Apr 1987 ..... 1.00
❑16, May 1987; 1: Booster Gold International 1.00
❑17, Jun 1987 A: CheshireHawk 1.00
❑18, Jul 1987; Killer returns from future to kill Booster 1.00
❑19, Aug 1987; V: Rainbow Raider 1.00
❑20, Sep 1987; blind 1.00
❑21, Oct 1987; V: Aliens of Dimension X 1.00
❑22, Nov 1987; A: Justice League International. D: Michelle Carter 1.00
❑23, Dec 1987 A: Superman 1.00
❑24, Jan 1988; Millennium 1.00
❑25, Feb 1988; Millennium; final issue 1.00

Booster Gold
DC

❑0, May 2008 ..... 2.99
❑1, Nov 2007 ..... 6.00
❑2, Dec 2007 ..... 2.99
❑3, Jan 2008 ..... 2.99
❑4, Feb 2008 ..... 2.99
❑5, Mar 2008 ..... 2.99
❑6, Apr 2008 ..... 2.99
❑7, Jun 2008 ..... 2.99
❑8 ..... 2.99
❑9 ..... 2.99
❑10 ..... 2.99
❑11 ..... 2.99
❑12 ..... 2.99
❑13 ..... 2.99
❑14 ..... 2.99
❑15 ..... 2.99
❑16 ..... 2.99
❑17 ..... 2.99
❑18 ..... 2.99
❑19 ..... 2.99
❑20 ..... 2.99
❑21 ..... 2.99

Boots of the Oppressor
Northstar

❑1, Apr 1993; Adult 2.95

Borderguard
Eternity

❑1, Nov 1987 ..... 1.95
❑2, Dec 1987 ..... 1.95

Borderline
Kardia

❑1, Jun 1992 ..... 2.25

Border Worlds
Kitchen Sink

❑1, Jul 1986; Reprinted from Megaton Man 1.95
❑2, Sep 1986 ..... 1.95
❑3, Nov 1986 ..... 1.95
❑4, Jan 1987 ..... 1.95
❑5, Apr 1987 ..... 1.95
❑6, Jun 1987 ..... 1.95
❑7, Aug 1987; pages 4-5 transposed 2.00
❑7/A; Corrected edition; corrected 2.00

Border Worlds
Kitchen Sink

❑1, b&w; Adult 2.00

Boris' Adventure Magazine
Nicotat

❑1, Aug 1988, b&w; Rocketeer Adventure Magazine parody 2.00
❑2, Punishbear 2.95
❑3, Sep 1996 ..... 2.95
❑4, BlackBear 2.95

Boris Karloff Tales of Mystery
Gold Key

❑3, Apr 1963 ..... 27.00
❑4, Jul 1963 ..... 25.00
❑5, Oct 1963 ..... 25.00
❑6, Jan 1964 ..... 20.00
❑7, Sep 1964 ..... 20.00
❑8, Dec 1965 ..... 20.00
❑9, Mar 1965, WW (a) 25.00
❑10, Jun 1965 ..... 15.00
❑11, Sep 1965 ..... 22.00
❑12, Dec 1965, back cover pin-up 15.00
❑13, Mar 1966 ..... 12.00
❑14, Jun 1966 ..... 12.00
❑15, Sep 1966 ..... 15.00
❑16, Dec 1966 ..... 12.00
❑17, Mar 1967 ..... 12.00
❑18, Jun 1967 ..... 12.00
❑19, Sep 1967 ..... 12.00
❑20, Dec 1967 ..... 12.00
❑21, Mar 1968, JO, JJ (a) 18.00
❑22, Jun 1968 ..... 10.00
❑23, Sep 1968, 10053-809 ..... 10.00
❑24, Dec 1968 ..... 10.00
❑25, Mar 1969 ..... 10.00
❑26, Jun 1969, 10053-906 ..... 10.00
❑27, Sep 1969 ..... 10.00
❑28, Dec 1969 ..... 10.00
❑29, Feb 1970 ..... 10.00
❑30, May 1970 ..... 10.00
❑31, Aug 1970 ..... 8.50
❑32, Nov 1970 ..... 8.50
❑33, Feb 1971, 10053-102 ..... 8.50
❑34, Apr 1971 ..... 8.50
❑35, Jun 1971 ..... 8.50
❑36, Aug 1971 ..... 8.50
❑37, Oct 1971 ..... 8.50
❑38, Dec 1971 ..... 8.50
❑39, Feb 1972 ..... 8.50
❑40, Apr 1972 ..... 8.50
❑41, Jun 1972 ..... 7.50
❑42, Oct 1972 ..... 7.50
❑43, Dec 1972 ..... 7.50
❑44, Feb 1973 ..... 7.50
❑45, Apr 1973 ..... 7.50
❑46, May 1973 ..... 7.50
❑47, Jun 1973 ..... 7.50
❑48, Jul 1973 ..... 7.50
❑49, Aug 1973, 90053-308 ..... 7.50
❑50, Oct 1973 ..... 7.50
❑51, Dec 1973 ..... 6.00
❑52, Feb 1974 ..... 6.00
❑53, Apr 1974 ..... 6.00
❑54, Jun 1974 ..... 6.00
❑55, Jul 1974 ..... 6.00
❑56, Aug 1974 ..... 6.00
❑57, Oct 1974 ..... 6.00
❑58, Dec 1974 ..... 6.00
❑59, Feb 1975 ..... 6.00
❑60, Apr 1975 ..... 5.00
❑61, ca. 1975 ..... 5.00
❑62, ca. 1975 ..... 5.00
❑63, Aug 1975 ..... 5.00
❑64, Oct 1975 ..... 5.00
❑65, Dec 1975 ..... 5.00
❑66, Feb 1976 ..... 5.00
❑67, Apr 1976 ..... 5.00
❑68, Jun 1976 ..... 5.00
❑69, ca. 1976 ..... 5.00
❑70, Sep 1976 ..... 5.00
❑71, ca. 1976 ..... 5.00
❑72, Dec 1976 ..... 5.00
❑73, ca. 1977 ..... 5.00
❑74, Apr 1977 ..... 5.00
❑75, ca. 1977 ..... 3.00
❑76, ca. 1977 ..... 3.00
❑77, ca. 1977 ..... 3.00
❑78, Oct 1977 ..... 3.00
❑79, ca. 1977 ..... 3.00
❑80, Feb 1978 ..... 7.00
❑81, Apr 1978 ..... 6.00
❑82, ca. 1978 ..... 5.00
❑83, Aug 1978 ..... 6.00
❑84, Sep 1978 ..... 5.00
❑85, Oct 1978 ..... 6.00
❑86, Nov 1978 ..... 3.00
❑87, Dec 1978 ..... 3.00
❑88, Jan 1979 ..... 3.00
❑89, Feb 1979 ..... 3.00
❑90, ca. 1979 ..... 3.00
❑91, May 1979 ..... 3.00
❑92, Jul 1979 ..... 3.00
❑93, Aug 1979 ..... 3.00
❑94, Sep 1979 ..... 3.00
❑95, Oct 1979 ..... 3.00
❑96, Nov 1979 ..... 3.00
❑97, Feb 1980, Final Issue; Reprints from oris Karloff Tales of Mystery #34 ..... 3.00

Boris Karloff Thriller
Gold Key

❑1, Oct 1962, Photo cover 75.00
❑2, Jan 1963 ..... 55.00

Boris the Bear
Dark Horse

❑1, ca. 1986, b&w 3.00
❑1/2nd, ca. 1986, b&w; 2nd printing 1.75
❑2, ca. 1986, b&w; V: Transformers 2.25
❑3, ca. 1986, b&w; Boris takes on Marvel Comics for Jack Kirby 2.50
❑4, ca. 1986, b&w; O: Boris the Bear. two different covers; Man of Steel parody cover (far shot) 2.50
❑4/A, ca. 1986; Man of Steel parody cover (close-up) 2.50
❑5, ca. 1986, b&w; Swamp Thing parody 2.50
❑6, ca. 1987, b&w; Batman parody 2.50
❑7, ca. 1987, b&w; Elfquest parody 2.25
❑8, ca. 1987, b&w; 40 pages 2.25
❑9, ca. 1987, b&w; G.I. Joe parody; Wacky Squirrel backup 2.25
❑10, May 1987, b&w; G.I. Joe parody continues; Wacky Squirrel backup 2.25
❑11, Jun 1987, b&w; DA (a); T.H.U.N.D.E.R. Agents 2.25
❑12, Jul 1987, b&w; PG (a); Boris' Birthday; Last Dark Horse issue 2.25
❑13, Nov 1987, b&w; 1: Punishbear. Drug abuse issue; First Nicotat issue, remaining issues scarce 2.25
❑14, Dec 1987, b&w; V: Number Two 2.25
❑15, ca. 1988, b&w 2.25
❑16, Mar 1988, b&w; Indiana Jones parody 2.25
❑17, ca. 1988, b&w; BlackHawk parody; Sininju Coneys back-up 2.25
❑18, ca. 1988, b&w; Spider-Slayer (Spider-Man) parody 2.25
❑19, Sep 1988, b&w; PG (c); The Old Swap Shop back-up 2.25
❑20, Nov 1988, b&w; The Old Swap Shop back-up 2.25
❑21, Feb 1989, b&w; The Old Swap Shop back-up 2.00
❑22, Apr 1989, b&w; Kraven the Hunter/ Sonny and Cher parody 2.00
❑23, May 1989, b&w 2.00
❑24, Jul 1989, b&w; Bingo Glumm back-up 2.00
❑25, ca. 1989, b&w; A: Southern Squadron 2.00
❑26, Jul 1990, b&w; A: Beardevil. Tom & Jerry parody 2.00
❑27, Oct 1990, b&w 2.00
❑28, Dec 1990, b&w 2.00
❑29, Jan 1991, b&w 2.00

Black Hole

Adaptation of film about a bathtub drain in space
©Whitman

Black Lightning

Teacher turns vigilante in Isabella series
©DC

Black Panther

Jack Kirby handled the 1977 return of T'Challa
©Marvel

Black Pearl

Series from actor and comics fan Mark Hamill
©Dark Horse

Blackwulf

One of 3 Marvel 1994 titles starting with "Bla"
©Marvel

	N-MINT
❑30, Apr 1991, b&w; Gulf War issue/ parody	2.50
❑31, Jun 1991, b&w	2.50
❑32, Jul 1991, b&w; Dinosaurs; very scarce	2.50
❑33, Sep 1991, b&w; very scarce	2.50
❑34, Nov 1991, b&w; A: BlackBear. #1 of 4, but series cancelled; very scarce	2.50

Boris the Bear Instant Color Classics
Dark Horse

❑1, Jul 1987; 1: Boris the Bear. Reprints Boris the Bear #1 in color	2.00
❑2, Aug 1987	2.00
❑3, Dec 1987	2.00

Born
Marvel / MAX

❑1, Aug 2003, cardstock cover; Vietnam	5.00
❑2, Sep 2003, cardstock cover; Vietnam	3.50
❑3, Oct 2003, cardstock cover; Vietnam	3.50
❑4, Nov 2003, cardstock cover; Vietnam	3.50

Born Again
Spire

❑1; Chuck Colson	3.50

Born to Kill
Aircel

❑1, May 1991, b&w	2.50
❑2	2.50
❑3	2.50

Boston Bombers
Caliber

❑1, ca. 1990	2.50
❑2, ca. 1990	2.50
❑3, ca. 1990	2.50
❑4	2.50
❑5	2.50
❑6	2.50
❑Special 1, ca. 1997	3.95

Boulevard of Broken Dreams
Fantagraphics

❑1; NN	3.95

Bound and Gagged
Iconografix

❑1; Adult	2.50

Bound in Darkness: Infinity Issue
CFD

❑1, b&w	2.50

Bounty
Caliber

❑1, ca. 1991; Adult	2.50
❑2, ca. 1991; Adult	2.50
❑3, ca. 1991; Adult	2.50

Bounty of Zone-Z
Sunset Strips

❑1; NN	2.50

Bowie Butane
Mike Murdock

❑1, ca. 1995, b&w	1.95

Box
Fantagraphics / Eros

	N-MINT
❑1, Apr 1991; Adult	2.25
❑2; Adult; b&w	2.25
❑3; Adult; b&w	2.25
❑4, Aug 1991; Adult; b&w	2.25
❑5, Nov 1991; Adult; b&w	2.25
❑6; Adult; b&w	2.25

Boxboy
Slave Labor

❑1, Aug 1993	1.00
❑1/2nd, May 1995; 2nd printing	1.25
❑2, Jul 1995	1.25

Box Office Poison
Antarctic

❑0; Collects stories from mini-comics	4.00
❑1, Oct 1996; b&w	8.00
❑2, Dec 1996; b&w	5.00
❑3, Feb 1997; b&w	4.00
❑4, Mar 1997; b&w	4.00
❑5, ca. 1997; b&w	3.00
❑6, ca. 1997; b&w	3.00
❑7, Nov 1997; b&w	3.00
❑8, Feb 1998; cover says Feb 97, indicia says Feb 98	2.95
❑9, Apr 1998; cover says May, indicia says Apr	2.95
❑10, Jul 1998; b&w	2.95
❑11, Oct 1998; b&w	2.95
❑12, Dec 1998; wraparound cover	2.95
❑13, Feb 1999; b&w	2.99
❑14, Jun 1999; b&w	2.99
❑15, Aug 1999; b&w	2.99
❑16 1999; b&w	2.99
❑17 2000; b&w	2.99
❑18, ca. 2000; b&w	2.99
❑20, Aug 2000, b&w	2.99
❑SS 1, May 1997; Super Special	4.95

Box Office Poison: Kolor Karnival
Antarctic

❑1, May 1999; cover says Apr, indicia says May; Kolor Karnival	3.50

Boy and His 'Bot, A
Now

❑1, Jan 1987; digest-sized; Holiday special	1.95

Boy Commandos
DC

❑1, Oct 1973, JK (a); Reprinted from Detective Comics #66 ("Sphinx") and Boy Commandos #1 ("Heroes")	8.00
❑2, Dec 1973, JK (a); Reprinted from Boy Commandos #2 & #6 respectively	5.00

Boys
DC

❑1, Oct 2006	2.99
❑2, Nov 2006	2.99
❑3, Dec 2006	2.99
❑4, Jan 2006	2.99
❑5, Feb 2007	2.99
❑6, Mar 2007	2.99

Boys Dynamite

	N-MINT
❑7	2.99
❑8	2.99
❑9	2.99
❑10	2.99
❑11	2.99
❑12	2.99
❑13	2.99
❑14	2.99
❑15	2.99
❑16	2.99
❑17	2.99
❑18	2.99
❑19	2.99
❑20	2.99
❑21	2.99
❑22	2.99
❑23	2.99
❑24	2.99
❑25	2.99
❑26	2.99
❑27	2.99
❑28	2.99
❑29	2.99
❑30	2.99

Boys Be ...
Tokyopop

❑1, Nov 2004	9.99
❑2, Jan 2005	9.99
❑3, Mar 2005	9.99
❑4, May 2005	9.99
❑5, Jul 2005	9.99
❑6, Sep 2005	9.99
❑7, Nov 2005	9.99

Boys Over Flowers
Viz

❑1, Aug 2003	9.95
❑2, Oct 2003	9.95
❑3, Dec 2003	9.95
❑4, Feb 2004	9.95
❑5, Apr 2004	9.95
❑6, Jun 2004	9.95
❑7, Aug 2004	9.95
❑8, Oct 2004	9.95
❑9, Dec 2004	9.95
❑10, Feb 2005	9.95
❑11, Apr 2005	9.99
❑12, Jun 2005	9.99
❑13, Aug 2005	9.99
❑14, Oct 2005	9.99

Bozo
Dell

❑1, May 1962, 01-073-207	60.00
❑2, Apr 1963	35.00
❑3, Jul 1963	35.00
❑4, Oct 1963	28.00

Bozo: The World's Most Famous Clown (Larry Harmon's...)
Innovation

❑1; some reprint; Reprints Four Color Comics #285	6.00

Bozz Chronicles
Marvel / Epic

❑1, Dec 1985, 1&O: Bozz.	2.00
❑2, Feb 1986	2.00
❑3, Apr 1986	2.00
❑4, Jun 1986	2.00
❑5, Aug 1986	2.00
❑6, Oct 1986, Final Issue	2.00

BPRD: A Plague of Frogs
Dark Horse

❑1, Mar 2004	2.99
❑2, Apr 2004	2.99
❑3, May 2004	2.99

Other grades: Multiply price above by 5/6 for VF/NM • 2/3 for VERY FINE • 1/3 for FINE • 1/5 for VERY GOOD • 1/8 for GOOD

- ❑4, Aug 2004 ... 2.99
- ❑5, Sep 2004 ... 3.00

BPRD: Dark Waters
Dark Horse

- ❑1, Jul 2003 ... 2.99

BPRD: Hollow Earth
Dark Horse

- ❑1, Jan 2002 ... 2.99
- ❑2, Apr 2002 ... 2.99
- ❑3, Jun 2002 ... 2.99

BPRD: Night Train
Dark Horse

- ❑1, Sep 2003 ... 2.99

BPRD: Soul of Venice
Dark Horse

- ❑1, May 2003 ... 2.99

BPRD: The Black Flame
Dark Horse

- ❑1, Aug 2005 ... 2.99
- ❑2, Sep 2005 ... 2.99
- ❑3, Oct 2005 ... 2.99
- ❑4, Nov 2005 ... 2.99
- ❑5, Dec 2005 ... 2.99
- ❑6, Jan 2006 ... 2.99

BPRD: The Dead
Dark Horse

- ❑1, Nov 2004 ... 2.99
- ❑2, Dec 2004 ... 2.99
- ❑3, Jan 2005 ... 2.99
- ❑4, Feb 2005 ... 2.99
- ❑5, Mar 2005 ... 2.99

BPRD: There's Something Under my Bed
Dark Horse

- ❑1, Nov 2003 ... 2.99

BPRD: The Universal Machine
Dark Horse

- ❑1, May 2006, #24 in series ... 3.00
- ❑2, Jun 2006 ... 2.99
- ❑3, Jul 2006 ... 2.99
- ❑4, Aug 2006 ... 2.99
- ❑5, Sep 2006 ... 2.99

Bradleys
Fantagraphics

- ❑1, Apr 1999 ... 2.95
- ❑2, May 1999 ... 2.95
- ❑3, Jul 1999 ... 2.95

Brady Bunch
Dell

- ❑1, ca. 1970 ... 45.00
- ❑2, ca. 1970 ... 30.00

Bragade
Parody

- ❑1, Mar 1993 ... 2.50

Brainbanx
DC / Helix

- ❑1, Mar 1997 ... 2.50
- ❑2, Apr 1997 ... 2.50
- ❑3, May 1997 ... 2.50
- ❑4, Jun 1997 ... 2.50
- ❑5, Jul 1997 ... 2.50
- ❑6, Aug 1997 ... 2.50

Brain Bat 3-D
3-D Zone

- ❑1, ca. 1992, b&w; No cover price; Oversized ... 3.95

Brain Boy
Dell

- ❑2, Jul 1962, Series numbering continued from appearance in Four Color Comics ... 65.00
- ❑3, Dec 1962 ... 50.00
- ❑4, Mar 1963 ... 45.00
- ❑5, Jun 1963 ... 45.00
- ❑6, Sep 1963, Final Issue ... 45.00

Brain Capers
Fantagraphics

- ❑1 ... 3.95

Brain Fantasy
Last Gasp

- ❑1 ... 3.00

Brain (I.W.)
I.W.

- ❑1, Sep 1958 ... 12.00
- ❑2 ... 9.00
- ❑3 ... 9.00
- ❑4 ... 9.00
- ❑5, Exists? ... 9.00
- ❑6; Exists? ... 9.00
- ❑7, Exists? ... 9.00
- ❑8 ... 9.00
- ❑9 ... 9.00
- ❑10, ca. 1963 ... 9.00
- ❑11; Exists? ... 8.00
- ❑12; Exists? ... 8.00
- ❑13; Exists? ... 8.00
- ❑14, Exists? ... 8.00
- ❑15; Exists? ... 8.00
- ❑16; Exists? ... 8.00
- ❑17 ... 8.00
- ❑18 ... 8.00

Braintrust Komicks
Spoon

- ❑1, Mar 1993 ... 2.75

Brand New York
Mean

- ❑1, Jul 1997, cardstock cover ... 3.95
- ❑2; Adult ... 3.95

Brass
Image

- ❑1, Aug 1996, 1&O: Brass ... 2.50
- ❑1/Deluxe, Aug 1996, Folio edition ... 4.50
- ❑2, Sep 1996 ... 2.50
- ❑3, May 1997 ... 2.50

Brass
DC / Wildstorm

- ❑1, Aug 2000 ... 2.50
- ❑2, Sep 2000 ... 2.50
- ❑3, Oct 2000 ... 2.50
- ❑4, Nov 2000 ... 2.50
- ❑5, Dec 2000 ... 2.50
- ❑6, Jan 2001 ... 2.50

Brath
CrossGen

- ❑1, Mar 2003 ... 2.95
- ❑2, Apr 2003 ... 2.95
- ❑3, May 2003 ... 2.95
- ❑4, Jun 2003 ... 2.95
- ❑5, Jul 2003 ... 2.95
- ❑6, Aug 2003 ... 2.95
- ❑7, Sep 2003 ... 2.95
- ❑8, Oct 2003 ... 2.95
- ❑9, Nov 2003 ... 2.95
- ❑10, Dec 2003 ... 2.95
- ❑11, Jan 2004; Kiss Kiss, Bang Bang preview ... 2.95
- ❑12, Feb 2004 ... 2.95
- ❑13, Apr 2004; Negaton War Preview Inside! ... 2.95
- ❑14, May 2004 ... 2.95

Bratpack
King Hell

- ❑1, Aug 1990, b&w; 1: Doctor Blasphemy. 1: Luna. 1: Kid Vicious. 1: Wild Boy ... 3.00
- ❑1/2nd, 1: Doctor Blasphemy. 1: Luna. 1: Kid Vicious. 1: Wild Boy. 2nd printing ... 3.00
- ❑1/3rd, 1: Doctor Blasphemy. 1: Luna. 1: Kid Vicious. 1: Wild Boy. 3rd printing ... 3.00
- ❑2, Nov 1990 ... 2.95
- ❑3, Jan 1991 ... 2.95
- ❑4, Mar 1991 ... 2.95
- ❑5, May 1991 ... 2.95

Brat Pack/Maximortal Super Special
King Hell

- ❑1, Sep 1996 ... 2.95

Brats Bizarre
Marvel / Epic

- ❑1, May 1994 ... 2.50
- ❑2, Jun 1994 ... 2.50
- ❑3, Jul 1994; trading card ... 2.50
- ❑4, Aug 1994 ... 2.50

Brave and the Bold
DC

- ❑1, Aug 1955; JKu, RA, RH, IN (a); Viking Prince, Golden Gladiator, Silent Knight ... 3000.00
- ❑2, Oct 1955; Viking Prince, Golden Gladiator, Silent Knight ... 1500.00
- ❑3, Dec 1955, Viking Prince, Golden Gladiator, Silent Knight ... 700.00
- ❑4, Feb 1956; Viking Prince, Golden Gladiator, Silent Knight ... 650.00
- ❑5, Apr 1956; Robin Hood, Silent Knight, Viking Prince ... 650.00
- ❑6, Jun 1956; JKu, RH, IN (a); Robin Hood, Silent Knight, Golden Gladiator ... 500.00
- ❑7, Aug 1956; JKu, RH, IN (a); Robin Hood, Silent Knight, Viking Prince ... 500.00
- ❑8, Oct 1956; JKu, RH, IN (a); Robin Hood, Silent Knight, Golden Gladiator ... 500.00
- ❑9, Dec 1956; JKu, RH, IN (a); Robin Hood, Silent Knight, Viking Prince ... 500.00
- ❑10, Feb 1957, JKu, RH, IN (a); Robin Hood, Silent Knight, Viking Prince ... 500.00
- ❑11, Apr 1957; JKu, RH, IN (a); Robin Hood, Silent Knight, Viking Prince ... 400.00
- ❑12, Jun 1957; JKu, RH, IN (a); Robin Hood, Silent Knight, Viking Prince ... 400.00
- ❑13, Sep 1957; JKu, RH, IN (a); Robin Hood, Silent Knight, Viking Prince ... 400.00
- ❑14, Nov 1957; JKu, RH, IN (a); Robin Hood, Silent Knight, Viking Prince ... 400.00
- ❑15, Jan 1958; JKu, RH, IN (a); Robin Hood, Silent Knight, Viking Prince ... 400.00
- ❑16, Mar 1958; JKu, IN (a); Silent Knight, Viking Prince ... 400.00
- ❑17, May 1958; JKu, IN (a); Silent Knight, Viking Prince ... 400.00
- ❑18, Jul 1958; JKu, IN (a); Silent Knight, Viking Prince ... 400.00
- ❑19, Sep 1958; JKu, IN (a); Silent Knight, Viking Prince ... 400.00
- ❑20, Nov 1958; JKu, IN (a); Silent Knight, Viking Prince ... 400.00
- ❑21, Jan 1959; JKu, IN (a); Silent Knight, Viking Prince ... 400.00
- ❑22, Mar 1959; JKu, RH (a); Silent Knight, Viking Prince ... 400.00
- ❑23, May 1959; JKu (a); O: Viking Prince. Viking Prince ... 500.00
- ❑24, Jul 1959; JKu (a); Viking Prince ... 350.00
- ❑25, Sep 1959; 1: The Suicide Squad (Golden Age) ... 500.00
- ❑26, Nov 1959; 2: Suicide Squad ... 325.00
- ❑27, Jan 1960; A: Suicide Squad. 3: Suicide Squad ... 330.00
- ❑28, Mar 1960; 1: Justice League of America. 1: Starro the Conqueror. 1: Snapper Carra; 1: Snapper Carr ... 5000.00
- ❑29, May 1960, 2: Justice League of America ... 2000.00
- ❑30, Jul 1960; 1: Amazo. 1: Professor Ivo. A: Justice League of America; 3: Justice League of America ... 1750.00
- ❑31, Sep 1960, 1: Cave Carson ... 350.00
- ❑32, Nov 1960; Cave Carson ... 200.00
- ❑33, Jan 1961; Cave Carson ... 200.00
- ❑34, Mar 1961; JKu (c); JK, JKu (a); 1: Thanagar. 1: Byth. 1: Hawkwoman II (Shayera Thal). 1: Hawkman II (Katar Hol). 1: Byth; 1: Hawkman II (Katar Hol); 1: Hawkwoman II (Shayera Thal); 1: Thanagar; 1: Hawkman (Katar Hol); 1: Hawkgirl (Shayera Hol) ... 1750.00
- ❑35, May 1961; JK, JKu (a); 1: Matter Master. Hawkman ... 400.00
- ❑36, Jul 1961; JK, JKu (a); 1: Shadow-Thief. Hawkman ... 400.00
- ❑37, Sep 1961; Suicide Squad ... 250.00
- ❑38, Nov 1961, Suicide Squad ... 225.00
- ❑39, Jan 1962; Suicide Squad ... 225.00
- ❑40, Mar 1962, Cave Carson ... 140.00
- ❑41, May 1962, Cave Carson ... 140.00
- ❑42, Jul 1962, JK, JKu (a); A: Hawkman ... 300.00
- ❑43, Sep 1962, JKu (c); JK, JKu (a); O: Hawkman (Silver Age). 1: Manhawks; O: Hawkman (Katar Hol) ... 350.00
- ❑44, Nov 1962, JK, JKu (a); A: Hawkman ... 260.00
- ❑45, Jan 1963, CI (a); Strange Sports Stories ... 60.00
- ❑46, Mar 1963, CI (a); Strange Sports Stories ... 60.00
- ❑47, May 1963, MA, CI (a); Strange Sports Stories ... 60.00
- ❑48, Jul 1963, CI (a); Strange Sports Stories ... 60.00
- ❑49, Sep 1963, CI (a); Strange Sports Stories ... 60.00
- ❑50, Nov 1963, Green Arrow; Team-ups begin ... 175.00
- ❑51, Jan 1964, Aquaman, Hawkman; Early Hawkman/Aquaman team-up ... 225.00

Other grades: Multiply price above by 5/6 for VF/NM • 2/3 for VERY FINE • 1/3 for FINE • 1/5 for VERY GOOD • 1/8 for GOOD

Blade of the Immortal

Hiroaki Samura's manga, faithfully reprinted

©Dark Horse

Blade: The Vampire-Hunter

Tomb of Dracula character returns

©Marvel

Blair Witch Project

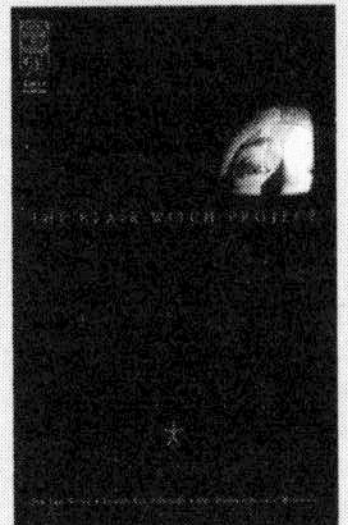

Oni struck oil with cult movie comic

©Oni

Blaze

Relic from the short-lived Ghost Rider craze

©Marvel

Blip

Marvel's comic-book-sized video game entry

©Marvel

	N-MINT
❑52, Mar 1964, JK, JKu (a); Sgt. Rock...	125.00
❑53, May 1964, ATh (a); Atom & Flash..	75.00
❑54, Jul 1964, 1&O: Teen Titans	350.00
❑55, Sep 1964, Metal Men, Atom...........	45.00
❑56, Nov 1964, 1: Wynde. Flash	45.00
❑57, Jan 1965, 1&O: Metamorpho.........	150.00
❑58, Mar 1965, 2: Metamorpho	65.00
❑59, May 1965, Batman; Batman/Green Lantern team-up............	80.00
❑60, Jul 1965, NC (c); 1: Wonder Girl (Donna Troy). Teen Titans..................	100.00
❑61, Sep 1965, MA (a); O: Starman I (Ted Knight). O: Black Canary. Starman, Black Canary..	125.00
❑62, Nov 1965, MA (a); Starman, Black Canary	100.00
❑63, Jan 1966, Supergirl.........................	40.00
❑64, Mar 1966, A: Eclipso. Batman........	60.00
❑65, May 1966, Doom Patrol	22.00
❑66, Jul 1966, Metamorpho, Metal Men	22.00
❑67, Sep 1966, CI (a); Batman, Flash; Batman in all remaining issues...........	65.00
❑68, Nov 1966, A: Joker. Metamorpho...	80.00
❑69, Jan 1967, Green Lantern................	50.00
❑70, Mar 1967, CI (c); JCr (a); Hawkman	50.00
❑71, May 1967, Green Arrow	50.00
❑72, Jul 1967, CI (a); Spectre	50.00
❑73, Sep 1967, Aquaman, Atom	50.00
❑74, Nov 1967, Metal Men.....................	40.00
❑75, Jan 1968, Spectre........................	60.00
❑76, Mar 1968, Plastic Man..................	50.00
❑77, May 1968, Batman and the Atom...	40.00
❑78, Jul 1968, 1: Copperhead. Wonder Woman..	40.00
❑79, Sep 1968, NA (a); A: Deadman	75.00
❑80, Nov 1968, NA (a); A: Creeper........	50.00
❑81, Jan 1969, NA (a); A: Deadman. Flash	50.00
❑82, Mar 1969, NA (a); O: Ocean Master. A: Deadman.......................................	50.00
❑83, May 1969, IN (c); NA (a); Titans	60.00
❑84, Jul 1969, NA (a); Sgt. Rock	50.00
❑85, Sep 1969, NA (a); Green Arrow gets new costume	60.00
❑86, Nov 1969, NA (w); NA (a); Deadman	50.00
❑87, Jan 1970, Wonder Woman	26.00
❑88, Mar 1970, Wildcat.........................	20.00
❑89, May 1970, Phantom Stranger	20.00
❑90, Jul 1970, Adam Strange................	20.00
❑91, Sep 1970, Black Canary	18.00
❑92, Nov 1970, Bat Squad	18.00
❑93, Jan 1971, NA (a); House of Mystery	30.00
❑94, Mar 1971, Titans...........................	18.00
❑95, May 1971, Plastic Man..................	24.00
❑96, Jul 1971, Sgt. Rock.......................	15.00
❑97, Sep 1971; Wildcat.........................	15.00
❑98, Nov 1971; Phantom Stranger.........	15.00
❑99, Jan 1972; NA (c); JKu, NC (a); Flash	22.00
❑100, Mar 1972; Double-size; NC (c); NA, JA (a); Green Arrow...........................	30.00
❑101, May 1972; Metamorpho...............	15.00
❑102, Jul 1972; NC (c); NA, JA (a); Titans	15.00
❑103, Oct 1972, Metal Men....................	12.00
❑104, Dec 1972, NC (c); JA (a); Deadman	12.00
❑105, Feb 1973, JA (a); Wonder Woman	12.00
❑106, Apr 1973, JA (a); Green Arrow.....	12.00
❑107, Jul 1973, Black Canary	12.00
❑108, Sep 1973, JA (a); Sgt. Rock.........	12.00
❑109, Nov 1973, JA (a); Demon.............	12.00

	N-MINT
❑110, Jan 1974, NC (c); JA (a); Wildcat	12.00
❑111, Mar 1974, JA (a); Joker..............	18.00
❑112, May 1974, 100 Page giant; Mr. Miracle	18.00
❑113, Jul 1974, 100 Page giant; JKu, JA (a); Metal Men....................................	18.00
❑114, Sep 1974, 100 Page giant; JM, NC, JA (a); Aquaman	18.00
❑115, Nov 1974, 100 Page giant; MA, JKu, GK, JA (a); O: Viking Prince. O: Viking Prince (reprint); 100 pages	22.00
❑116, Jan 1975, 100 Page giant; NC, JA, IN (a); Spectre................................	18.00
❑117, Mar 1975, 100 Page giant; JA (c); JKu, DD, FS, JA (a); Sgt. Rock; reprints Secret Six #1	18.00
❑118, Apr 1975; JA (a); Wildcat, Joker..	18.00
❑119, Jun 1975; JA (a); Man-Bat...........	7.00
❑120, Jul 1975, JA (c); FS, JA (a); Kamandi, 68 pgs., reprints Secret Six #2..............	7.00
❑121, Sep 1975; JA (a); Metal Men	7.00
❑122, Oct 1975; Swamp Thing	7.00
❑123, Dec 1975; JA (a); Plastic Man, Metamorpho..	7.00
❑124, Jan 1976; JA (a); Sgt. Rock.........	7.00
❑125, Mar 1976; JA (a); Flash	7.00
❑126, Apr 1976, JA (a); Aquaman	7.00
❑127, Jun 1976, JA (a); Wildcat............	6.00
❑128, Jul 1976, JA (a); Mr. Miracle; Bicentennial #19................................	6.00
❑129, Sep 1976, Green Arrow/Joker......	11.00
❑130, Oct 1976, Green Arrow/Joker	11.00
❑131, Dec 1976, JA (a); A: Catwoman. Wonder Woman	6.00
❑132, Feb 1977, JA (a); Kung Fu Fighter	4.00
❑133, Apr 1977, JA (a); Deadman	5.00
❑134, May 1977, JA (a); Green Lantern.	4.00
❑135, Jul 1977, JA (a); Metal Men.........	4.00
❑136, Sep 1977, Green Arrow, Metal Men	4.00
❑137, Oct 1977, Demon........................	4.00
❑138, Nov 1977, JA (a); Mr. Miracle......	4.00
❑139, Jan 1978, JA (a); Hawkman.........	4.00
❑140, Mar 1978, JA (a); Wonder Woman	4.00
❑141, May 1978, Black Canary, Joker....	10.00
❑142, Jul 1978, JA (a); Aquaman	4.00
❑143, Sep 1978, DG, JA (a); O: Human Target; Batman and Creeper	4.00
❑144, Nov 1978, DG, JA (a); Green Arrow	4.00
❑145, Dec 1978, JA (a); Phantom Stranger	4.00
❑145/Whitman, Dec 1978, JA (a); Phantom Stranger; Whitman variant ..	8.00
❑146, Jan 1979, JA, RT (a); E-2 Batman/ Unknown Soldier...............................	4.00
❑146/Whitman, Jan 1979, JA (a); E-2 Batman/Unknown Soldier; Whitman variant..	8.00
❑147, Feb 1979, JA (a); A: Doctor Light. V: Doctor Light; Batman and Supergirl	4.00
❑147/Whitman, Feb 1979, JA (a); A: Doctor Light. Whitman variant	8.00
❑148, Mar 1979, Plastic Man...............	4.00
❑149, Apr 1979, JA (a); Teen Titans.......	4.00
❑149/Whitman, Apr 1979, JA (a); Teen Titans; Whitman variant	8.00
❑150, May 1979, JA (a); Superman.......	4.00
❑150/Whitman, May 1979, JA (a); Superman; Whitman variant...............	12.00
❑151, Jun 1979, JA (a); Flash...............	4.00
❑151/Whitman, Jun 1979, JA (a); Flash; Whitman variant..................................	8.00

	N-MINT
❑152, Jul 1979, JA (a); Atom	4.00
❑152/Whitman, Jul 1979, JA (a); Atom; Whitman variant................................	8.00
❑153, Aug 1979, JA (c); DN (a); Red Tornado..	4.00
❑153/Whitman, Aug 1979, DN (a); Red Tornado; Whitman variant	20.00
❑154, Sep 1979, JA (c); JA (a); Metamorpho..	4.00
❑154/Whitman, Sep 1979, JA (a); Metamorpho; Whitman variant...........	8.00
❑155, Oct 1979, JA (a); Green Lantern ..	4.00
❑155/Whitman, Oct 1979, JA (a); Green Lantern; Whitman variant...................	8.00
❑156, Nov 1979, JA (c); DN (a); Doctor Fate	4.00
❑156/Whitman, Nov 1979, DN (a); Doctor Fate; Whitman variant	8.00
❑157, Dec 1979, JA (c); JA (a); Kamandi, continues story from Kamandi #59....	4.00
❑157/Whitman, Dec 1979, JA (a); Kamandi, continues story from Kamandi #59; Whitman variant..........	8.00
❑158, Jan 1980, JA (c); JA (a); Wonder Woman..	4.00
❑158/Whitman, Jan 1980, JA (a); Wonder Woman; Whitman variant...................	8.00
❑159, Feb 1980, JA (c); JA (a); Ra's al Ghul	4.00
❑159/Whitman, Feb 1980, JA (a); Ra's al Ghul; Whitman variant.......................	8.00
❑160, Mar 1980, JA (a); Supergirl	4.00
❑160/Whitman, Mar 1980, JA (a); Supergirl; Whitman variant	8.00
❑161, Apr 1980, JA (a); Adam Strange..	4.00
❑161/Whitman, Apr 1980, JA (a); Adam Strange; Whitman variant...................	8.00
❑162, May 1980, JA (a); Sgt. Rock........	4.00
❑162/Whitman, May 1980, JA (a); Sgt. Rock; Whitman variant......................	8.00
❑163, Jun 1980, JA (c); DG (a); Black Lightning..	4.00
❑163/Whitman, Jun 1980, DG (a); Black Lightning; Whitman variant	8.00
❑164, Jul 1980, JL (a); A: Hawkgirl. A: Hawkman. Hawkman	4.00
❑164/Whitman, Jul 1980, JL (a); A: Hawkgirl. A: Hawkman. Hawkman; Whitman variant................................	8.00
❑165, Aug 1980, JA (c); DN (a); Man-Bat	4.00
❑165/Whitman, Aug 1980, DN (a); Man-Bat; Whitman variant.................	8.00
❑166, Sep 1980, JA (c); DG, DS, TD (a); 1: Nemesis. Black Canary....................	4.00
❑167, Oct 1980, JA (c); DC, DS, DA (a); Blackhawk	4.00
❑168, Nov 1980, JA (c); DS, JA (a); Green Arrow	4.00
❑169, Dec 1980, DS, JA (a); Zatanna.....	4.00
❑170, Jan 1981, JA (a); Nemesis...........	4.00
❑171, Feb 1981, JA (c); GC, DS, JL (a); Scalphunter...	4.00
❑172, Mar 1981, JA (c); CI, DS (a); Firestorm..	4.00
❑173, Apr 1981, DS, JA (a); Guardians..	4.00
❑174, May 1981, DS, JA (a); Green Lantern..	4.00
❑175, Jun 1981, JA (c); DS, JA (a); Lois Lane	4.00
❑176, Jul 1981, JA (a); Swamp Thing....	4.00
❑177, Aug 1981, DS, JA (a); Elongated Man..	4.00

	N-MINT
❑178, Sep 1981, RB (c); DS, JA (a); Creeper	4.00
❑179, Oct 1981, RA (c); Legion	4.00
❑180, Nov 1981, DS, JA (a); Spectre, Nemesis	3.00
❑181, Dec 1981, JA (c); DS, JA (a); Hawk & Dove, Nemesis	3.00
❑182, Jan 1982, DS, JA (a); E-2 Robin	3.00
❑183, Feb 1982, JA (c); CI, DS (a); Riddler, Nemesis	3.00
❑184, Mar 1982, DS, JA (a); Huntress	3.00
❑185, Apr 1982, Green Lantern	3.00
❑186, May 1982, DS, JA (a); Hawkman, Nemesis	3.00
❑187, Jun 1982, JA (c); DS, JA (a); Metal Men, Nemesis	3.00
❑188, Jul 1982, DS, JA (a); Rose & Thorn	3.00
❑189, Aug 1982, DS, JA (a); Thorn, Nemesis	3.00
❑190, Sep 1982, JA (c); CI, DS, JA (a); Adam Strange, Nemesis	3.00
❑191, Oct 1982, DS, JA (a); A: Penguin. A: Nemesis. Joker	8.00
❑192, Nov 1982, DS, JA (a); V: Mr. IQ. Superboy	3.00
❑193, Dec 1982, JA (a); D: Nemesis; Batman and Nemesis	3.00
❑194, Jan 1983, CI (a); V: Double-X. V: Rainbow Raider. Flash, Double-X	3.00
❑195, Feb 1983, JA (a); I...Vampire	3.00
❑196, Mar 1983, JA (a); Ragman	3.00
❑197, Apr 1983, JA (a); JSa (a); Catwoman; Wedding of Earth-2 Batman & Earth-2 Catwoman	4.00
❑198, May 1983, Karate Kid	3.00
❑199, Jun 1983, JA (c); RA (a); Spectre	3.00
❑200, Jul 1983; Giant-size; DaG, JA (a); 1: Halo. 1: Katana. 1: Geo-Force. 1: Outsiders. E-1 and E-2 Batman	7.00
❑Ann 1, ca. 2001; JK (w); SD, CI (a); Revival issue (2001)	5.95

Brave and the Bold
DC

❑1, Dec 1991 MGr (w)	2.50
❑2, Jan 1992 MGr (w)	2.00
❑3, Feb 1992 MGr (c); MGr (w)	2.00
❑4, Mar 1992 MGr (c); MGr (w)	2.00
❑5, May 1992 MGr (c); MGr (w)	2.00
❑6, Jun 1992 MGr (c); MGr (w)	2.00

Brave Old World
DC / Vertigo

❑1, Feb 2000	2.50
❑2, Mar 2000	2.50
❑3, Apr 2000	2.50
❑4, May 2000	2.50

Bravestarr in 3-D
Blackthorne

❑1	2.50
❑2; Blackthorne 3-D series #40	2.50

Bravo for Adventure
Dragon Lady

❑1	5.95

Bravura Preview Book
Malibu / Bravura

❑0, Jan 1995, JSn, HC (w); JSn, HC, GK (a); Coupon redemption promotion	3.00
❑1, Nov 1993, No cover price; 1994 Preview book	1.50
❑2, Aug 1994, 1995 Preview book (#1 on cover)	1.50

Breach
DC

❑1, Mar 2005; O: Breach	2.95
❑2, Mar 2005	2.50
❑3, Apr 2005	5.00
❑4, May 2005	2.50
❑5, Jun 2005	2.50
❑6, Jul 2005; New DC logo	2.50
❑7, Aug 2005; Villains United tie-in	2.50
❑8, Sep 2005	2.50
❑9, Oct 2005	2.50
❑10, Dec 2005	2.50
❑11, Jan 2006; Final issue	2.50

Breakdown
Devil's Due

	N-MINT
❑1, Oct 2004	4.00
❑1/Variant, Oct 2004	5.00
❑2, Nov 2004	4.00
❑2/Variant, Nov 2004	5.00
❑3, Dec 2004	3.00
❑4, Feb 2005	3.00
❑5, Mar 2005	2.95
❑6, Apr 2005	2.95

Breakdowns
Infinity

❑1, Oct 1986, b&w	1.70

Breakfast After Noon
Oni

❑1, May 2000, b&w	2.95
❑2, Aug 2000, b&w	2.95
❑3, Sep 2000, b&w	2.95
❑4, Nov 2000, b&w	2.95
❑5, Dec 2000, b&w	2.95
❑6, Jan 2001, b&w	2.95

Breakneck Blvd. (Motion)
Motion

❑0, Feb 1994, b&w; Reprints from Hazard! #1	2.50
❑1, Jul 1994, b&w; 1: Blu-J	2.50
❑2, Sep 1994, b&w	2.50

Breakneck Blvd. (Slave Labor)
Slave Labor

❑1, Jul 1995	2.95
❑2, Oct 1995	2.95
❑3, Jan 1996	2.95
❑4, May 1996	2.95
❑5, Aug 1996	2.95
❑6, Dec 1996	2.95

Break the Chain
Marvel Music

❑1; polybagged with KRS-1 cassette tape	6.95

Break-Thru
Malibu

❑1, Dec 1993 GP (c); JRo, GP (w); GP (a)	2.50
❑1/Ltd., Dec 1993; Ultra Limited; foil logo	4.00
❑2, Jan 1994 GP (c); GP (a)	2.50

Breathtaker
DC

❑1, Jul 1990; 1: The Man. 1: Breathtaker	5.00
❑2, Aug 1990	5.00
❑3, Sep 1990; O: Breathtaker	5.00
❑4, Oct 1990	5.00

'Breed
Malibu / Bravura

❑1, Jan 1994, JSn (w); JSn (a); Includes coupon	2.50
❑1/Gold, Jan 1994; sendaway with gold ink on the cover	3.00
❑2, Feb 1994, JSn (w); JSn (a); Includes coupon	2.50
❑3, Mar 1994, JSn (w); JSn (a); Includes coupon	2.50
❑4, Apr 1994, JSn (w); JSn (a); Includes coupon	2.50
❑5, May 1994, JSn (c); JSn (w); JSn (a); Includes coupon	2.50
❑6, Jun 1994, JSn (w); JSn (a); Includes coupon	2.50

'Breed II
Malibu / Bravura

❑1, Nov 1994	2.95
❑2, Dec 1994	2.95
❑3, Jan 1995	2.95
❑4, Feb 1995	2.95
❑5, Mar 1995	2.95
❑6, Apr 1995	2.95

Brenda Lee's Life Story
Dell

❑1, Sep 1962	50.00

Brenda Starr (Avalon)
Avalon

❑1	2.95
❑2	2.95

Brenda Starr Cut-Outs and Coloring Book
Blackthorne

❑1	6.95

Brickman
Harrier

❑1	1.95

Bridgman's Constructive Anatomy
A-List

❑1, Apr 1998, b&w	2.95

Brigade
Image

	N-MINT
❑1, Aug 1992; 1: Brigade; 1: Genocide; Includes trading cards	2.00
❑1/Gold, Aug 1992; Gold edition; 1: Genocide; 1: Brigade	2.00
❑2, Oct 1992; Includes trading cards; Includes coupon for Image Comics #0; Continued in Shadowhawk #2	3.50
❑2/Gold, Oct 1992; Gold edition	3.50
❑3, Feb 1993; 1: Birds of Prey	2.00
❑4, Jul 1993; flip side of Youngblood #5	2.00

Brigade
Image

❑0, Sep 1993; RL (w); 1: Warcry. gatefold cover	2.00
❑1, May 1993; RL (w); 1: Boone; 1: Hacker; Foldout wraparound cover	2.00
❑2, Jun 1993; RL (w); Foil cover	2.95
❑2/A, Jun 1993; foil alternate cover	2.00
❑3, Sep 1993; RL (w); 1: Roman. Indicia says Volume 1 instead of Volume 2	2.00
❑4, Oct 1993	2.00
❑5, Nov 1993	2.00
❑6, Dec 1993; 1: Worlok. 1: Coral	1.95
❑7, Feb 1994	1.95
❑8, Mar 1994	1.95
❑9, Apr 1994	1.95
❑10, Jun 1994	1.95
❑11, Aug 1994 A: WildC.A.T.s	1.95
❑12, Sep 1994 A: WildC.A.T.s	2.50
❑13, Oct 1994	2.50
❑14, Nov 1994	2.50
❑15, Dec 1994	2.50
❑16, Jan 1995; Includes trading card	2.50
❑17, Feb 1995	2.50
❑18, Mar 1995	2.50
❑18/Variant, Mar 1995; alternate cover	2.50
❑19, Apr 1995 A: Glory	2.50
❑20/A, May 1995 A: Glory	2.50
❑20/B, May 1995; A: Glory. alternate cover	2.50
❑21, Jun 1995; Funeral of Shadowhawk	2.50
❑22, Jul 1995	2.50
❑25, May 1994; Images of Tomorrow; Published out of sequence as a preview of the future	1.95
❑26, Jun 1994; Published out of sequence as a preview of the future	1.95
❑27, Jul 1994	2.50

Brigade (Awesome)
Awesome

❑1, Jul 2000; White logo	2.99

Brigade Sourcebook
Image

❑1, Aug 1994	2.95

Brik Hauss
Blackthorne

❑1, Jul 1987	1.75

Brilliant Boy
Circus

❑1, Jan 1997	2.95
❑2, Mar 1997	2.50
❑3, May 1997	2.50
❑4	2.50
❑5	2.50

Brinke of Destruction
High-Top

❑1, Dec 1995; Vol I of III	2.95
❑1/CS, Dec 1995; packaged with audio tape	6.99
❑2, Feb 1996; Includes phot section and art pin-ups; Julie Bell Cover	2.95
❑3, Jan 1997	2.95
❑Special 1; Includes audio tape	6.95

Brinke of Disaster
High-Top

❑1, Sep 1996; San Diego Edition; Photo cover	2.25

Brinke of Eternity
Chaos

❑1, Apr 1994; Adult	2.75

Brit
Image

❑1, Jul 2003	4.95

Blitzkrieg

A unusual twist on the war comics genre

©DC

Blondie Comics

King and Charlton later published this title

©David McKay

Bloodfire

Yet another "super-soldier serum" story

©Lightning

Blood of Dracula

Serial anthology had three stories per issue

©Apple

Bloodshot

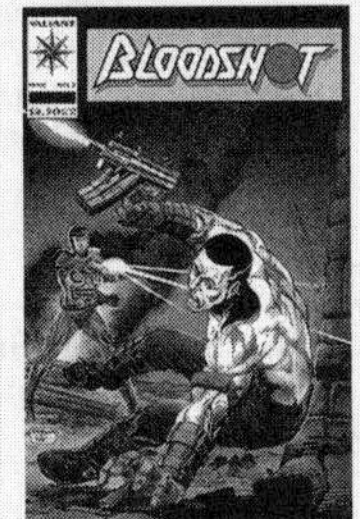

Valiant title about an enhanced warrior

©Valiant

N-MINT

Brit-Cit Babes
Fleetway-Quality

❑1 ... 5.95

Brit/Cold Death One Shot
Image

❑1, Jan 2004 ... 4.95

Brit: Red, White, Black & Blue One-Shot
Image

❑1 2004 ... 5.00

Broadway Babes
Avalon

❑1, reprints Moronica stories, b&w ... 2.95

Broadway Video Special Collectors Edition
Broadway

❑1, Dec 1995; Promotional giveaway; 1150 copies printed; cardstock cover. ... 1.00

Broid
Eternity

❑1, May 1990, b&w ... 2.75
❑2, Jun 1990 ... 2.25
❑3, Jul 1990 ... 2.25
❑4 ... 2.25

Broken Axis
Antarctic

❑1, b&w ... 2.95

Broken Fender
Top Shelf Productions

❑1, ca. 1997, b&w ... 2.95
❑2, b&w ... 2.95

Broken Halo: Is There Nothing Sacred?
Broken Halos

❑2, Oct 1998, b&w ... 2.95
❑2/Nude, Oct 1998, b&w; nude cover edition ... 4.95

Broken Heroes
Sirius

❑1, Mar 1998 ... 2.50
❑2, Apr 1998 ... 2.50
❑3, May 1998 ... 2.50
❑4, Jun 1998 ... 2.50
❑5, Jul 1998 ... 2.50
❑6, Aug 1998 ... 2.50
❑7, Sep 1998 ... 2.50
❑8, Oct 1998 ... 2.50
❑9, Nov 1998 ... 2.50
❑10, Dec 1998 ... 2.50
❑11, Jan 1999 ... 2.50
❑12, Feb 1999 ... 2.50

Bronte's Infernal Angria
Headless Shakespeare Press

❑1, Aug 2005 ... 4.00

Bronx
Eternity

❑1 ... 2.50
❑2 ... 2.50
❑3 ... 2.50

Brooklyn Dreams
DC / Paradox

❑1 1994, b&w ... 4.95
❑2 1994, b&w ... 4.95
❑3 1994, b&w ... 4.95
❑4 1994, b&w ... 4.95

Brother Billy The Pain From Plains
Marvel

❑1, Jun 1979; Billy Carter parody ... 20.00

Brother Destiny
Mecca

❑1 2004 ... 2.99
❑2, Nov 2004; Cover says July, indicia says November ... 2.99
❑3 2004 ... 2.99

Brotherhood
Marvel

❑1, Jul 2001 ... 2.25
❑2, Aug 2001 ... 2.25
❑3, Sep 2001 ... 2.25
❑4, Oct 2001 ... 2.25
❑5, Nov 2001 ... 2.25
❑6, Dec 2001 ... 2.25
❑7, Jan 2002 ... 2.25
❑8, Feb 2002 ... 2.25
❑9, Mar 2002 ... 2.25

Brotherman
Big City

❑1 ... 2.00
❑2 ... 2.00
❑3 ... 2.00
❑4 ... 2.00
❑5 ... 2.00
❑6 ... 2.00
❑7 ... 2.00
❑8 ... 2.00

Brother Man: Dictator of Discipline
Big City

❑11, Jul 1996; magazine-sized ... 2.95

Brother Power, the Geek
DC

❑1, Sep 1968, 1: Brother Power, the Geek ... 45.00
❑2, Nov 1968, 1: Lord Sliderule ... 20.00

Brothers of the Spear
Gold Key

❑1, Jun 1972 ... 20.00
❑2, Sep 1972 ... 10.00
❑3, Dec 1972 ... 6.00
❑4, Mar 1973 ... 6.00
❑5, Jun 1973 ... 6.00
❑6, Sep 1973 ... 4.00
❑7, Dec 1973 ... 4.00
❑8, Mar 1974 ... 4.00
❑9, Jun 1974 ... 4.00
❑10, Sep 1974 ... 4.00
❑11, Dec 1974 ... 4.00
❑12, Mar 1975 ... 4.00
❑13, May 1975 ... 4.00
❑14, Jul 1975, 90277-506 ... 4.00
❑15, Aug 1975 ... 4.00
❑16, Nov 1975 ... 4.00
❑17, Feb 1976, Original series ends (1976) ... 4.00
❑18, ca. 1982, One-shot continuation of series (1982) ... 2.50

Bruce Lee
Malibu

❑1, Jul 1994 ... 2.95
❑2, Aug 1994 ... 2.95
❑3, Sep 1994 ... 2.95
❑4, Oct 1994 ... 2.95
❑5, Nov 1994 ... 2.95
❑6, Dec 1994 ... 2.95

Bruce Wayne: Agent of S.H.I.E.L.D.
Marvel / Amalgam

❑1, Apr 1996, O: Bruce Wayne, Agent of S.H.I.E.L.D.; One-shot ... 1.95

Bru-Hed
Schism

❑1, Mar 1994; 1: Bru-Hed. 1: Grrim & Grritty ... 3.00
❑1/Ashcan, ca. 1993; Test-Market Ashcan edition 1: Bru-Hed. 1: Grrim & Grritty ... 3.00
❑1/Variant, Mar 1994; metallic foil logo on cover ... 2.50
❑2, Jul 1994, b&w ... 2.50
❑3, ca. 1995, b&w; D: Grrim & Grritty. Pete Bickford thanked on letters page ... 2.50
❑4, ca. 1996; Final Issue ... 2.50

Bru-Hed's Breathtaking Beauties
Schism

❑1, Jun 1995, b&w pin-ups, cardstock cover ... 2.50

Bru-Hed's Bunnies, Baddies & Buddies
Schism

❑1 ... 2.50

Bru-Hed's Guide to Gettin' Girls Now!
Schism

❑1 ... 2.95
❑2 ... 2.50

Bruiser
Anthem

❑1, Feb 1994 ... 2.45

Bruiser
Mythic

❑1, No cover price ... 2.50

Brunner's Beauties
Fantagraphics / Eros

❑1; pin-ups, adult, b&w ... 4.95

Brusel
NBM

❑1 ... 19.95

Brute
Atlas-Seaboard

❑1, Feb 1975; 1&O: Brute ... 7.00
❑2, Apr 1975 ... 5.00
❑3, Jul 1975 ... 5.00

Brute Force
Marvel

❑1, Aug 1990; 1&O: Brute Force ... 1.00
❑2, Sep 1990 ... 1.00
❑3, Oct 1990 ... 1.00
❑4, Nov 1990 ... 1.00

B-Sides
Marvel

❑1, Nov 2002, b&w ... 3.50
❑2, Dec 2002; No indicia inside ... 2.99
❑3, Jan 2003 ... 2.99

B'Tx
Tokyopop

❑1, Jan 2006 .... 9.99

Bubblegum Crisis: Grand Mal
Dark Horse

❑1, Mar 1994 .... 2.50
❑2, Apr 1994 .... 2.50
❑3, May 1994 .... 2.50
❑4, Jun 1994 .... 2.50

Buckaroo Banzai
Marvel

❑1, Dec 1984; Movie adaptation 1.00
❑2, Feb 1985; Movie adaptation 1.00

Buck Godot, Zap Gun For Hire
Palliard

❑1, Jul 1993, PF (w); PF (a) 3.50
❑2, Nov 1993, PF (w); PF (a) 3.00
❑3, Apr 1994, PF (w); PF (a) 2.95
❑4, Aug 1994, PF (w); PF (a) 2.95
❑5, Sep 1995, PF (w); PF (a) 2.95
❑6, Oct 1995, PF (w); PF (a) 2.95
❑7, Aug 1997, PF (w); PF (a) 2.95
❑8, Mar 1998, PF (w); PF (a); Final Issue 2.95

Buck Rogers (Gold Key/Whitman)
Gold Key / Whitman

❑1, Oct 1964, Gold Key publishes 36.00
❑2, Aug 1979, Movie adaptation 5.00
❑3, Sep 1979, Movie adaptation 4.00
❑4, Oct 1979, Movie adaptation 4.00
❑5, Dec 1979 .... 3.00
❑6, Feb 1980 .... 3.00
❑7, Apr 1980, Series begins under Whitman imprint 3.00
❑8, ca. 1980, ca. 1980 .... 3.00
❑9, ca. 1980, ca. 1980 .... 3.00
❑11, Feb 1981, #10 never printed 3.00
❑12, Jul 1981 .... 3.00
❑13, Oct 1981 .... 3.00
❑14, Feb 1982 .... 3.00
❑15, ca. 1982 .... 3.00
❑16, May 1982, Final Issue 3.00

Buck Rogers Comics Module
TSR

❑1; Listed as 1 of 3 .... 2.95
❑2 .... 2.95
❑3 .... 2.95
❑4 .... 2.95
❑5; Black Barney (#5, misnumbered #6) 2.95
❑6 .... 2.95
❑7 .... 2.95
❑8 .... 2.95
❑9 .... 2.95

Bucky O'Hare
Continuity

❑1, Jan 1991 .... 2.50
❑2, May 1991 .... 2.00
❑3, Jul 1991 .... 2.00
❑4, Dec 1991 .... 2.00
❑5, Mar 1992 .... 2.00

Buddha on the Road
Aeon

❑1, Aug 1996 .... 2.95
❑2, Nov 1996 .... 2.95
❑3, Feb 1997 .... 2.95
❑4, May 1997 .... 2.95
❑5, Sep 1997 .... 2.95
❑6, Mar 1997, Indicia says 1997, should be 1998 .... 2.95

Buffalo Bill Jr.
Gold Key

❑1, Jun 1965, reprints Four-Color #798. 30.00

Buffalo Wings
Antarctic

❑1, Sep 1993, b&w 2.50
❑2, Nov 1993, b&w 2.75

Buffy the Vampire Slayer
Dark Horse

❑½, Wizard promotional edition; Buffy Reading spellbook on cover 4.00
❑½/Gold, Wizard promotional edition; Gold logo 8.00
❑½/Platinum, Wizard promotional edition; Platinum logo 10.00
❑1, Sep 1998, no month of publication.. 5.00
❑1/A, Sep 1998, Another Universe foil logo variant 10.00
❑1/B, Sep 1998, Another Universe edition; depicts Buffy holding gate without foil logo 5.00
❑1/Gold, Sep 1998, Gold art cover with gold foil logooil logo 10.00
❑1/Variant, Sep 1998, Photo cover 10.00
❑1/2nd, Feb 1999, 2nd printing 4.00
❑2, Oct 1998, Liquid!-c 4.00
❑2/Variant, Oct 1998, Photo cover 5.00
❑3, Nov 1998, no month of publication . 5.00
❑3/Variant, Nov 1998, Photo cover 5.00
❑4, Dec 1998 .... 4.00
❑4/Variant, Dec 1998, Photo cover 4.00
❑5, Jan 1999, Randy Green cover 4.00
❑5/Variant, Jan 1999, Photo cover 4.00
❑6, Feb 1999 .... 3.50
❑6/Variant, Feb 1999, Photo cover 3.50
❑7, Mar 1999 .... 3.50
❑7/Variant, Mar 1999, Photo cover 3.50
❑8, Apr 1999 .... 3.50
❑8/Variant, Apr 1999, Photo cover 3.50
❑9, May 1999 .... 3.50
❑9/Variant, May 1999, Photo cover 3.50
❑10, Jun 1999, teen magazine-style cover 3.50
❑10/Variant, Jun 1999, Photo cover 3.50
❑11, Jul 1999 .... 3.50
❑11/Variant, Jul 1999, Photo cover 3.50
❑12, Aug 1999 .... 3.50
❑12/Variant, Aug 1999, Photo cover 3.50
❑13, Sep 1999 .... 3.50
❑13/Variant, Sep 1999, Photo cover 3.50
❑14, Oct 1999 .... 3.50
❑14/Variant, Oct 1999, Photo cover 3.50
❑15, Nov 1999 .... 3.50
❑15/Variant, Nov 1999, Photo cover 3.50
❑16, Dec 1999 .... 3.50
❑16/Variant, Dec 1999, Photo cover 3.50
❑17, Jan 2000 .... 3.50
❑17/Variant, Jan 2000, Photo cover 3.50
❑18, Feb 2000 .... 3.50
❑18/Variant, Feb 2000, Photo cover 3.50
❑19, Mar 2000 .... 3.50
❑19/Variant, Mar 2000, Photo cover 3.50
❑20, Apr 2000 .... 3.50
❑20/Variant, Apr 2000, Photo cover 3.00
❑21, May 2000 .... 3.00
❑21/Variant, May 2000, Photo cover 3.00
❑22, Jun 2000 .... 3.00
❑22/Variant, Jun 2000, Photo cover 3.00
❑23, Jul 2000 .... 3.00
❑23/Variant, Jul 2000, Photo cover 3.00
❑24, Aug 2000 .... 3.00
❑24/Variant, Aug 2000, Photo cover 3.00
❑25, Sep 2000 .... 3.00
❑25/Variant, Sep 2000, Photo cover 3.00
❑26, Oct 2000 .... 3.00
❑26/Variant, Oct 2000, Photo cover 3.00
❑27, Nov 2000, Cover by John Totleben 3.00
❑27/Variant, Nov 2000, Photo cover 3.00
❑28, Dec 2000, Cover by Ryan Sook, Galen Showman 3.00
❑28/Variant, Dec 2000, Photo cover 3.00
❑29, Jan 2001 .... 3.00
❑29/Variant, Jan 2001, Photo cover 3.00
❑30, Feb 2001 .... 3.00
❑30/Variant, Feb 2001, Photo cover 3.00
❑31, Mar 2001 .... 3.00
❑31/Variant, Mar 2001, Photo cover 3.00
❑32, Apr 2001 .... 3.00
❑32/Variant, Apr 2001, Photo cover 3.00
❑33, May 2001 .... 3.00
❑33/Variant, May 2001, Photo cover 3.00
❑34, Jun 2001 .... 3.00
❑34/Variant, Jun 2001, Photo cover 3.00
❑35, Jul 2001 .... 3.00
❑35/Variant, Jul 2001, Photo cover 3.00
❑36, Aug 2001 .... 3.00
❑36/Variant, Aug 2001, Photo cover 3.00
❑37, Sep 2001 .... 3.00
❑37/Variant, Sep 2001, Photo cover 3.00
❑38, Oct 2001 .... 3.00
❑38/Variant, Oct 2001, Photo cover 3.00
❑39, Nov 2001 .... 3.00
❑39/Variant, Nov 2001, Photo cover 3.00
❑40, Dec 2001, Cover by Jeff Matsuda.. 3.00
❑40/Variant, Dec 2001, Photo cover 3.00
❑41, Jan 2002 .... 3.00
❑41/Variant, Jan 2002, Photo cover 3.00
❑42, Feb 2002 .... 3.00
❑42/Variant, Feb 2002, Photo cover 3.00
❑43, Mar 2002 .... 3.00
❑43/Variant, Mar 2002, Photo cover 3.00
❑44, Apr 2002 .... 3.00
❑44/Variant, Apr 2002, Photo cover 3.00
❑45, May 2002 .... 3.00
❑45/Variant, May 2002, Photo cover 3.00
❑46, Jun 2002 .... 3.00
❑46/Variant, Jun 2002, Photo cover 3.00
❑47, Jul 2002 .... 3.00
❑47/Variant, Jul 2002, Photo cover 3.00
❑48, Aug 2002 .... 3.00
❑48/Variant, Aug 2002, Photo cover 3.00
❑49, Sep 2002 .... 3.00
❑49/Variant, Sep 2002, Photo cover 3.00
❑50, Oct 2002 .... 3.50
❑50/Variant, Oct 2002, Photo cover 3.50
❑51, Nov 2002 .... 3.00
❑51/Variant, Nov 2002, Photo cover 3.00
❑52, Dec 2002 .... 3.00
❑52/Variant, Dec 2002, Photo cover 3.00
❑53, Jan 2003 .... 3.00
❑53/Variant, Jan 2003, Photo cover 3.00
❑54, Feb 2003 .... 3.00
❑55, Mar 2003 .... 3.00
❑56, Apr 2003 .... 3.00
❑57, May 2003 .... 3.00
❑58, Jun 2003 .... 2.99
❑59, Jul 2003 .... 2.99
❑60, Aug 2003 .... 2.99
❑61, Sep 2003 .... 2.99
❑62, Oct 2003 .... 2.99
❑63, Nov 2003 .... 2.99
❑Ann 1999, Aug 1999, squarebound; 1999 Ann 5.50

Buffy the Vampire Slayer: Angel
Dark Horse

❑1, May 1999 .... 4.00
❑1/Variant, May 1999; Photo cover 4.00
❑2, Jun 1999 .... 3.00
❑2/Variant, Jun 1999; Photo cover 3.00
❑3, Jul 1999 .... 3.00
❑3/Variant, Jul 1999; Photo cover 3.00

Buffy the Vampire Slayer: Chaos Bleeds
Dark Horse

❑1, Jun 2003; Photo cover 2.99

Buffy the Vampire Slayer: Giles
Dark Horse

❑1, Oct 2000 .... 3.00
❑1/Variant, Oct 2000; Photo cover 3.00

Buffy the Vampire Slayer: Haunted
Dark Horse

❑1, Dec 2001 .... 3.00
❑2, Jan 2002 .... 3.00
❑3, Feb 2002 .... 3.00
❑4, Mar 2002 .... 3.00

Buffy the Vampire Slayer: Jonathan
Dark Horse

❑1, Jan 2001 .... 3.00
❑1/Variant, Jan 2001, Photo cover 3.00
❑1/Gold, Jan 2001 .... 10.00
❑1/Platinum, Jan 2001 .... 20.00

Buffy The Vampire Slayer: Lost and Found
Dark Horse

❑1, Mar 2002, b&w 3.00

Buffy the Vampire Slayer: Lover's Walk
Dark Horse

❑1, Feb 2001 .... 3.00
❑1/Variant, Feb 2001, Photo cover 3.00
❑1/Dynamic, Feb 2001 .... 10.00

Buffy The Vampire Slayer: Oz
Dark Horse

❑1, Jul 2001 .... 3.00
❑1/Variant, Jul 2001; Photo cover 3.00
❑2, Aug 2001 .... 3.00
❑2/Variant, Aug 2001; Photo cover 3.00
❑3, Sep 2001 .... 3.00
❑3/Variant, Sep 2001; Photo cover 3.00

Other grades: Multiply price above by 5/6 for VF/NM • 2/3 for VERY FINE • 1/3 for FINE • 1/5 for VERY GOOD • 1/8 for GOOD

Bloodstrike

Rob Liefeld's elite strike force

©Image

Blood Sword

One of many Jademan imports from Hong Kong

©Jademan

Blue Beetle (DC)

Good-natured import into the DC universe

©DC

Blue Devil

Stuntman becomes supernatural super-hero

©DC

Blue Ribbon Comics (Vol. 2)

Archie dusts off its old super-heroes again

©Archie

N-MINT

Buffy the Vampire Slayer: Reunion
Dark Horse

❑1, Jun 2002, b&w ... 3.50

Buffy the Vampire Slayer: Ring of Fire
Dark Horse

❑1, Aug 2000; Photo cover ... 9.95

Buffy the Vampire Slayer: Season Eight
Dark Horse

❑1, Mar 2007 ... 15.00
❑1/Variant, Mar 2007; 1:4 variant cover. 15.00
❑2, Apr 2007 ... 6.00
❑3, May 2007 ... 4.00
❑4, Jun 2007 ... 2.99
❑5, Jul 2007 ... 2.99
❑6, Aug 2007 ... 2.99
❑7, Sep 2007 ... 2.99
❑8, Oct 2007 ... 2.99
❑9, Nov 2007 ... 2.99
❑10, Dec 2007 ... 2.99
❑11, Jan 2008 ... 2.99
❑12 ... 2.99
❑13 ... 2.99
❑14 ... 2.99
❑15 ... 2.99
❑16 ... 2.99
❑17 ... 2.99
❑18 ... 2.99
❑19 ... 2.99
❑20 ... 2.99
❑21 ... 2.99
❑22 ... 2.99
❑23 ... 2.99
❑24 ... 2.99
❑25 ... 2.99

Buffy the Vampire Slayer: Spike and Dru
Dark Horse

❑1, Apr 1999; Photo cover ... 2.95
❑2, May 1999; Photo cover ... 2.95
❑3, Jun 1999 ... 2.95
❑3/Variant, Dec 2000; Photo cover ... 2.95

Buffy the Vampire Slayer, Tales of the Slayers
Dark Horse

❑1/Variant, Oct 2002; Photo cover ... 3.50
❑1, Oct 2002 ... 3.50

Buffy The Vampire Slayer: The Dust Waltz
Dark Horse

❑1, Oct 1998 ... 9.95

Buffy the Vampire Slayer: The Origin
Dark Horse

❑1, Jan 1999 ... 3.50
❑1/Ltd., Jan 1999; Limited edition foil cover ... 15.00
❑1/Variant, Jan 1999; Photo cover; Dynamic Forces Issue; CoA run of 5,000 Issues ... 4.00
❑2, Feb 1999; Cover by Joe Bennett, Rene' Micheletti ... 2.95
❑2/Variant, Feb 1999; Photo cover ... 2.95
❑3, Mar 1999 ... 2.95
❑3/Variant, Mar 1999; Photo cover ... 2.95

N-MINT

Buffy the Vampire Slayer: Willow & Tara
Dark Horse

❑1, Apr 2001 ... 5.00
❑1/Variant, Apr 2001 ... 5.00

Buffy the Vampire Slayer: Willow & Tara: Wilderness
Dark Horse

❑1, Aug 2002 ... 2.99
❑2, Sep 2002 ... 2.99

Bug
Marvel

❑1, Mar 1997; V: Annihilus; One-shot.... 2.99

Bug (Planet-X)
Planet-X

❑1 ... 1.50

Bug & Stump
Aaargh!

❑1, Aut 1993, b&w; Australian, distributed in U.S ... 2.95
❑2, Spr 1994, b&w; Australian, distributed in U.S ... 2.95

Bugboy
Image

❑1, Jun 1998, b&w ... 3.95

B.U.G.G.'s
Acetylene Comics

❑Ashcan 1, ca. 2001 ... 2.25
❑1, ca. 2001 ... 2.25
❑2, ca. 2001 ... 2.25

B.U.G.G.'s
Acetylene Comics

❑1/A, ca. 2001 ... 2.50
❑1, ca. 2001 ... 2.25
❑2, ca. 2001 ... 2.25
❑3/A, ca. 2001; Fighting on cover, orange stripe down center ... 2.50
❑3, ca. 2001; Woman posing on cover .. 2.50
❑4, ca. 2001 ... 2.50

Bughouse (Cat-Head)
Cat-Head

❑1, ca. 1994, b&w ... 2.95
❑2, Nov 1994, b&w ... 2.95
❑3, Jun 1995, b&w ... 2.95
❑4, ca. 1996, b&w; cardstock cover ... 2.95
❑5, Spr 1997, b&w; Spring 1997 ... 2.95

Bug-Hunters
Trident

❑1, b&w; NN ... 5.95

Bugnut
Comicosley

❑1, Jul 1999 ... 2.95

Bugs Bunny
Gold Key

❑86, Oct 1962 ... 7.00
❑87, Dec 1962, Says "Bugs Bunny Showtime" on cover and in indicia; back cover pin-up; production code 30000-212 ... 7.00
❑88, Mar 1963, Says "Bugs Bunny Showtime" on cover and in indicia; back cover pin-up; productioon code 30000-303 ... 7.00

N-MINT

❑89, Jun 1963 ... 7.00
❑90, Sep 1963 ... 7.00
❑91, Dec 1963 ... 7.00
❑92, Mar 1964 ... 7.00
❑93, May 1964 ... 7.00
❑94, Jul 1964 ... 7.00
❑95, Sep 1964 ... 7.00
❑96, Nov 1964 ... 7.00
❑97, Jan 1965 ... 7.00
❑98, Mar 1965 ... 7.00
❑99, May 1965 ... 7.00
❑100, Jul 1965 ... 7.00
❑101, Sep 1965 ... 7.00
❑102, Nov 1965 ... 6.00
❑103, Jan 1966 ... 6.00
❑104, Mar 1966 ... 6.00
❑105, May 1966 ... 6.00
❑106, Jul 1966 ... 6.00
❑107, Sep 1966 ... 6.00
❑108, Nov 1966 ... 6.00
❑109, Jan 1967 ... 6.00
❑110, Mar 1967 ... 6.00
❑111, May 1967 ... 6.00
❑112, Jul 1967 ... 6.00
❑113, Sep 1967 ... 6.00
❑114, Nov 1967 ... 6.00
❑115, Jan 1968 ... 6.00
❑116, Mar 1968 ... 6.00
❑117, May 1968 ... 6.00
❑118, Jul 1968 ... 6.00
❑119, Sep 1968 ... 6.00
❑120, Nov 1968 ... 6.00
❑121, Jan 1969 ... 6.00
❑122, Mar 1969 ... 6.00
❑123, May 1969 ... 6.00
❑124, Jul 1969 ... 6.00
❑125, Sep 1969 ... 6.00
❑126, Nov 1969 ... 6.00
❑127, Jan 1970 ... 6.00
❑128, Mar 1970 ... 6.00
❑129, May 1970 ... 6.00
❑130, Jul 1970 ... 6.00
❑131, Sep 1970 ... 6.00
❑132, Nov 1970 ... 6.00
❑133, Jan 1971 ... 6.00
❑134, Mar 1971 ... 6.00
❑135, May 1971 ... 6.00
❑136, Jul 1971 ... 6.00
❑137, Sep 1971 ... 6.00
❑138, Oct 1971 ... 6.00
❑139, Dec 1971 ... 6.00
❑140, Jan 1971 ... 6.00
❑141, Mar 1972 ... 6.00
❑142, May 1972 ... 6.00
❑143, Jul 1972 ... 6.00
❑144, Sep 1972 ... 6.00
❑145, Oct 1972 ... 6.00
❑146, Dec 1972 ... 6.00
❑147, Jan 1973 ... 6.00
❑148, Mar 1973 ... 6.00
❑149, May 1973 ... 6.00
❑150, Jul 1973 ... 6.00
❑151, Aug 1973 ... 5.00
❑152, Sep 1973 ... 5.00
❑153, Nov 1973 ... 5.00
❑154, Jan 1974 ... 5.00

❑155, Mar 1974 5.00
❑156, May 1974 5.00
❑157, Jul 1974 5.00
❑158, Aug 1974, Bugs becomes a telekinetic 5.00
❑159, Sep 1974 5.00
❑160, Nov 1974 5.00
❑161, Jan 1975 5.00
❑162, Mar 1975 5.00
❑163, May 1975 5.00
❑164, Jul 1975 5.00
❑165, Aug 1975 5.00
❑166, Sep 1975 5.00
❑167, Oct 1975 5.00
❑168, Nov 1975 5.00
❑169, Jan 1976 5.00
❑170, Mar 1976 5.00
❑171, Apr 1976 5.00
❑172, May 1976 5.00
❑173, Jun 1976 5.00
❑174, Jul 1976 5.00
❑175, Aug 1976 5.00
❑176, Sep 1976 5.00
❑177, Oct 1976 5.00
❑178, Nov 1976 5.00
❑179, Dec 1976 5.00
❑180, Jan 1977 5.00
❑181, Feb 1977 5.00
❑182, Mar 1977 5.00
❑183, Apr 1977 5.00
❑184, May 1977 5.00
❑185, Jun 1977 5.00
❑186, Jul 1977 5.00
❑187, Aug 1977 5.00
❑188, Sep 1977 5.00
❑189, Oct 1977 5.00
❑190, Nov 1977 5.00
❑191, Dec 1977 5.00
❑192, Jan 1978 5.00
❑193, Feb 1978 5.00
❑194, Mar 1978, Includes "Spider-Man vs. the Chairman" Hostess ad by Buscema never published in Marvel Comics 5.00
❑195, Apr 1978 5.00
❑196, May 1978, Includes "Captain America vs. the Aliens" Hostess ad (never printed in Marvel Comics) by Buscema 5.00
❑197, Jun 1978 5.00
❑198, Jul 1978 5.00
❑199, Aug 1978 5.00
❑200, Sep 1978 5.00
❑201, Oct 1978 3.00
❑202, Nov 1978 3.00
❑203, Dec 1978 3.00
❑204, Jan 1979 3.00
❑205, Feb 1979 3.00
❑206, Mar 1979 3.00
❑207, Apr 1979 3.00
❑208, May 1979 3.00
❑209, Jun 1979 3.00
❑210, Jul 1979 3.00
❑211, Aug 1979 3.00
❑212, Sep 1979 3.00
❑213, Oct 1979 2.00
❑214, Nov 1979 2.00
❑215, Dec 1979 2.00
❑216, Jan 1980 2.00
❑217, Feb 1980 2.00
❑218, Mar 1980 2.00
❑219, ca. 1980 2.00
❑220, ca. 1980 2.00
❑221, Sep 1980 2.00
❑222, Nov 1980 2.00
❑223, Jan 1981 2.00
❑224, Mar 1981 2.00
❑225, Jun 1981 2.00
❑226, Jul 1981 2.00
❑227, Aug 1981 2.00
❑228, Sep 1981 2.00
❑229, Oct 1981 2.00
❑230, Nov 1981 2.00
❑231, Dec 1981 2.00
❑232, ca. 1982 2.00
❑233, ca. 1982 2.00
❑234, ca. 1982 2.00
❑235, ca. 1982 2.00
❑236, ca. 1982 2.00
❑237, ca. 1982 2.00
❑238, ca. 1982 2.00
❑239, ca. 1982 2.00
❑240, ca. 1982 2.00
❑241, ca. 1982 2.00
❑242, ca. 1983 2.00
❑243, Aug 1983 2.00
❑244, ca. 1983 2.00
❑245, Final Issue 2.00

Bugs Bunny
DC

❑1, Jun 1990 2.00
❑2, Jul 1990 1.50
❑3, Aug 1990 1.50

Bugs Bunny and Porky Pig
Dell

❑1, ca. 1965 26.00

Bugs Bunny Monthly
DC

❑1 1.95
❑2 1.95
❑3 1.95

Bugs Bunny Winter Fun
Gold Key

❑1, Dec 1967 30.00

Bug's Gift, A
Discovery

❑1 1.95

Bugtown
Aeon

❑1, ca. 2004 2.95
❑2, ca. 2005 2.95
❑3, ca. 2005 2.95
❑4, ca. 2005 2.95
❑5, ca. 2005 2.95
❑6, ca. 2005; MUPubs #448 2.95

Bug Wars
Avalon Communications / ACG

❑1, ca. 1998 2.95

Buja's Diary
NBM

❑1, Oct 2005, Graphic novel 19.95

Bulldog
Five Star

❑1 2.95

Bullet Crow, Fowl of Fortune
Eclipse

❑1 2.00
❑2 2.00

Bullet Points
Marvel

❑1, Jan 2007 2.99
❑2, Feb 2007 2.99
❑3, Mar 2007 2.99

Bulletproof
Known Associates

❑1, b&w 3.95

Bulletproof Comics
Wet Paint Graphics

❑1 2.25
❑2, May 1999 2.25
❑3, Sep 1999 2.25

Bulletproof Monk
Image

❑1, Nov 1998 3.00
❑2, Dec 1998 3.00
❑3, Jan 1999 3.00

Bulletproof Monk: Tales of the Bulletproof Monk
Image

❑1, Mar 2003 2.95

Bullets and Bracelets
Marvel / Amalgam

❑1, Apr 1996; Diana Prince and Trevor Castle 1.95

Bullseye Greatest Hits
Marvel

❑1, Nov 2004 2.99
❑2, Dec 2004 2.99
❑3, Jan 2005 2.99
❑4, Feb 2005 2.99
❑5, Mar 2005 2.99

Bullwinkle
Dell

❑1, Jul 1962, 01-090-209 100.00

Bullwinkle and Rocky
Gold Key

❑1, Nov 1962 90.00
❑2, Feb 1963 68.00
❑3, Apr 1972 45.00
❑4, Jul 1972 40.00
❑5, Sep 1972 40.00
❑6, Jan 1973, Reprints 28.00
❑7, Apr 1973, Reprints 28.00
❑8, Jul 1973 28.00
❑9, Oct 1973 28.00
❑10, Jan 1974 28.00
❑11, Apr 1974, Last issue of original run 28.00
❑12, Jun 1976, Series picks up after hiatus 14.00
❑13, Sep 1976 20.00
❑14, Dec 1976 16.00
❑15, Mar 1977 10.00
❑16, Jun 1977 10.00
❑17, Sep 1977 10.00
❑18, Dec 1977 10.00
❑19 10.00
❑20 10.00
❑21 8.00
❑22 8.00
❑23, Oct 1979 8.00
❑24, Dec 1979 8.00
❑25, Final Issue 8.00

Bullwinkle and Rocky
Charlton

❑1, Jul 1970, poster 30.00
❑2, Sep 1970 18.00
❑3, Nov 1970 15.00
❑4, Jan 1971 12.00
❑5, Mar 1971 12.00
❑6, May 1971 12.00
❑7, Jul 1971 12.00

Bullwinkle and Rocky (Star)
Marvel / Star

❑1, Nov 1987 2.00
❑2, Jan 1988 1.50
❑3, Mar 1988 1.50
❑4, May 1988 1.50
❑5, Jul 1988 1.50
❑6, Sep 1988 1.50
❑7, Nov 1988 1.50
❑8, Jan 1989; Marvel publishes 1.50
❑9, Mar 1989; Final Issue 1.50

Bullwinkle & Rocky (Blackthorne)
Blackthorne

❑1 2.50
❑2 2.50
❑3 2.50
❑3D 1, Mar 1987 2.50

Bullwinkle for President in 3-D
Blackthorne

❑1, Mar 1987, b&w; no cover price 2.50

Bullwinkle Mother Moose Nursery Pomes
Dell

❑1, May 1962 85.00

Bumbercomix
Starhead

❑1; Giveaway from arts festival; Adult 1.00

Bumperboy Loses His Marbles
Adhouse Books

❑1, ca. 2005; Duotone 7.95

Bunny Town
Radio

❑1, Jan 2002, b&w 2.95

Burger Bomb
Funny Book Institute

❑1, Nov 1999 2.95
❑½, Mar 2000, b&w 2.95

Burglar Bill
Image

❑1 3.00
❑2 2005 3.00
❑3, Jul 2005 2.95
❑4 2005 2.95

Other grades: Multiply price above by 5/6 for VF/NM • 2/3 for VERY FINE • 1/3 for FINE • 1/5 for VERY GOOD • 1/8 for GOOD

Boffo Laffs

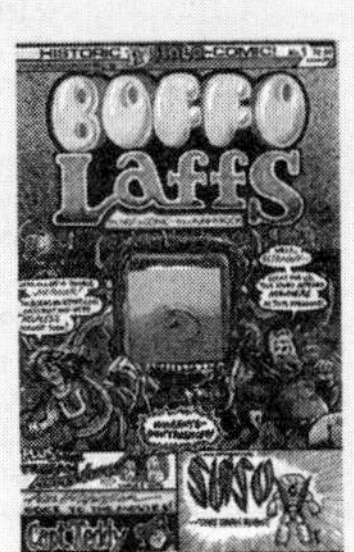
Humor title had the first holographic cover
©Paragraphics

Bomba The Jungle Boy

Based on children's adventure novels
©DC

Bonanza

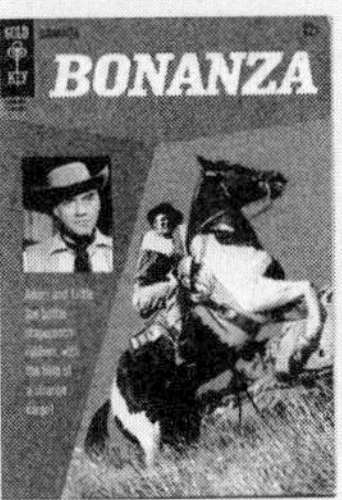
Saddle up for the Ponderosa
©Gold Key

Bone

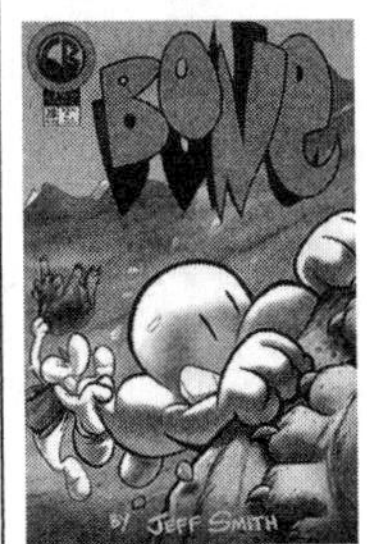
Jeff Smith's 1990s classic series
©Cartoon Books

Bone (2nd Series)

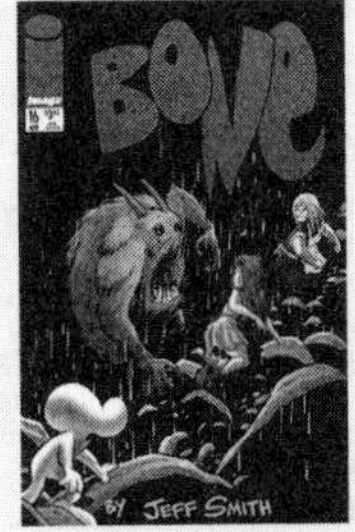
Image reprints of Cartoon Books issues
©Image

N-MINT

Burial of the Rats (Bram Stoker's...)
Roger Corman's Cosmic Comics

❑1 ... 2.50
❑2, May 1995 ... 2.50

Buried Terror
NEC

❑1, Mar 1995 ... 2.75

Buried Treasure
Pure Imagination

❑1 ... 5.95
❑2 ... 5.95
❑3; moves to Caliber ... 5.95

Buried Treasure
Caliber

❑1; reprints, b&w ... 2.50
❑2; Reprints ... 2.50
❑3; reprints Frankenstein ... 2.50
❑4; Reprints Heroic Comics; ca. 1991 ... 2.50

Burke's Law
Dell

❑1, Jan 1964, Photo cover ... 24.00
❑2, ca. 1964, Photo cover ... 20.00
❑3, Mar 1965, Photo cover ... 20.00

Burrito
Accent!

❑1, Jan 1995 ... 2.75
❑2, Apr 1995 ... 2.75
❑3, Jul 1995 ... 2.75
❑4, Nov 1995 ... 2.75
❑5, Jul 1996 ... 2.75

Bushido
Eternity

❑1, Jul 1988 ... 1.95
❑2 ... 1.95
❑3 ... 1.95
❑4 ... 1.95

Bushido Blade of Zatoichi Walrus
Solson

❑1 ... 2.00
❑2, ca. 1987, b&w ... 2.00

Bushwhacked
Fantagraphics / Eros

❑1; Adult ... 2.95

Buster
Crisis

❑1 ... 2.50
❑2 ... 2.50

Buster the Amazing Bear
Ursus

❑1, Aug 1992; says Aug 93 on cover, Aug 92 in indicia; Surprise Poster Insert ... 2.50
❑2, Oct 1993 ... 2.50
❑2/2nd, Oct 1994; 2nd printing ... 2.50
❑3, Jan 1994 ... 2.50
❑4, May 1994 ... 2.50
❑5, Nov 1994 ... 2.50

Bustline Combat
Fantagraphics / Eros

❑1, May 1999; Adult ... 2.95

Butcher
DC

❑1, May 1990; 1: John Butcher ... 2.50
❑2, Jun 1990 ... 2.00
❑3, Jul 1990 ... 2.00
❑4, Aug 1990 ... 2.00
❑5, Sep 1990 ... 2.00

Butcher Knight
Image

❑1/A, Dec 2000; Demon's teeth cover ... 2.50
❑1/B, Dec 2000; Woman standing next to demon on cover ... 2.50
❑1/C, Dec 2000; Woman posing on demon on cover ... 2.50
❑1/D, Dec 2000; White cover ... 2.50
❑2, Jan 2001 ... 2.50
❑3, Apr 2001 ... 2.95
❑4, May 2001 ... 2.95

Butt Biscuit
Fantagraphics

❑1; Adult ... 2.25
❑2; Adult ... 2.25
❑3, Sep 1992; Adult ... 2.25

Butterscotch
Fantagraphics / Eros

❑1; Adult ... 2.50
❑2; Adult ... 2.50
❑3; Adult ... 2.50

Button Man: The Killing Game
Kitchen Sink

❑1, Aug 1995; oversized graphic novel ... 15.95

Buz Sawyer Quarterly
Dragon Lady

❑1, Nov 1986 ... 5.95
❑2, Apr 1987 ... 5.95
❑3, Apr 1987 ... 5.95

Buzz
Kitchen Sink

❑1, Sep 1990; Adult ... 6.00
❑2; Adult ... 2.95
❑3; Adult ... 2.95

Buzz
Marvel

❑1, Jul 2000 ... 2.99
❑2, Aug 2000 ... 2.99
❑3, Sep 2000 ... 2.99

Buzz and Colonel Toad
Belmont

❑1 ... 2.50
❑2 ... 2.50
❑3, Jan 1998 ... 2.50

Buzzard
Cat-Head

❑1 ... 3.00
❑2, Oct 1990 ... 3.00
❑3 ... 3.00
❑4 ... 3.00
❑5 ... 3.00
❑6, Aug 1992 ... 3.00
❑7, Feb 1993 ... 3.00
❑8 ... 3.00
❑9 ... 3.00
❑10 ... 3.00
❑11 ... 3.25
❑12 ... 3.50
❑13 ... 3.50
❑14 ... 3.50
❑15 ... 3.50
❑16 ... 3.50
❑17 ... 3.50
❑18 ... 3.75
❑19 ... 3.75
❑20 ... 3.75

Buzzboy
Skydog

❑1, May 1998 ... 2.95
❑2, Aug 1998 ... 2.95
❑3, Oct 1998; Flip cover (Buzzy Babies) ... 2.95
❑4, Win 1998 ... 2.95

By Bizarre Hands
Dark Horse

❑1, Apr 1994 ... 2.50
❑2, May 1994 ... 2.50
❑3, Jun 1994 ... 2.50

By Bizarre Hands (Joe Lansdale's)
Avatar

❑1, Apr 2004 ... 3.50
❑1/Red foil ... 10.00
❑1/Wraparound ... 5.00
❑2, May 2004 ... 3.50
❑2/Red foil ... 8.00
❑2/Wraparound ... 5.00
❑3 ... 3.50
❑3/Red foil ... 8.00
❑3/Wraparound ... 5.00
❑4 ... 3.50
❑4/Red foil ... 8.00
❑4/Wraparound ... 5.00
❑5 ... 3.50
❑5/Red foil ... 8.00
❑5/Wraparound ... 5.00
❑6 ... 3.50
❑6/Red foil ... 8.00
❑6/Wraparound ... 5.00

By the Time I Get to Wagga Wagga
Harrier

❑1 ... 1.50

C•23
Image

❑1, Apr 1998; 1: Fluxus. 1: Zum. 1: A-Mortal. 1: The Hyperclan. 1: Armek. 1: Tronix. 1: Primaid. 1: Zenturion. 1: Protex ... 5.00
❑1/Ashcan, Apr 1998 ... 4.00
❑2, May 1998 ... 2.50
❑2/Variant, May 1998 ... 2.00
❑3, Jun 1998; bound-in card ... 2.50
❑4, Jul 1998 ... 2.50
❑5, Aug 1998 ... 2.50
❑6, Sep 1998; Includes Planetary preview ... 2.50
❑7, Oct 1998 ... 2.50
❑8, Nov 1998 ... 2.50
❑8/Variant, Nov 1998; alternate cover (group) ... 4.00

Cabbot: Bloodhunter
Maximum

❑1, Jan 1997 ... 2.50

Cabinet of Dr. Caligari
Monster

❑1, Apr 1992 ... 2.25

Other grades: Multiply price above by 5/6 for VF/NM • 2/3 for VERY FINE • 1/3 for FINE • 1/5 for VERY GOOD • 1/8 for GOOD

N-MINT | N-MINT | N-MINT

- ❑2, Jun 1992 .... 2.25
- ❑3, Sep 1992 .... 2.25

Cable
Marvel

- ❑-1, Jul 1997; JRo (w); Flashback; Alpha Flight, Vol. 2 preview 2.25
- ❑1, May 1993; Embossed cover 4.00
- ❑2, Jun 1993 .... 2.50
- ❑3, Jul 1993 AM, PS, TP, KGa, KJ, BWi (a) 2.50
- ❑4, Aug 1993 RL (a) 2.50
- ❑5, Nov 1993; O: Sinsear; V: Sinsear; Tolliver revealed as temporal agent 2.50
- ❑6, Dec 1993 A: Other. A: Sinsear 2.50
- ❑7, Jan 1994 .... 2.50
- ❑8, Feb 1994 .... 2.50
- ❑9, Mar 1994 A: Omega Red 2.50
- ❑10, Apr 1994; Cable hunts Omega Red; Cable trapped by Alcoytes 2.50
- ❑11, May 1994 A: Colossus 2.25
- ❑12, Jun 1994 .... 2.25
- ❑13, Jul 1994; V: D'spayre 2.25
- ❑14, Aug 1994 .... 2.25
- ❑15, Sep 1994 JPH (w) 2.25
- ❑16, Oct 1994 .... 2.50
- ❑16/Variant, Oct 1994; Prismatic foil cover 4.00
- ❑17, Nov 1994; JPH (w); V: Lifeforce; V: Hurricane; V: Deadbolt; V: Spyne; V: Gauntlet 1.50
- ❑17/Deluxe, Nov 1994; Deluxe edition; JPH (w) 2.00
- ❑18, Dec 1994 JPH (w) 1.50
- ❑18/Deluxe, Dec 1994; Deluxe edition; JPH (w) 2.00
- ❑19, Jan 1995; JPH (w); V: Genesis 1.50
- ❑19/Deluxe, Jan 1995; Deluxe edition; JPH (w) 2.00
- ❑20, Feb 1995; JPH (w); A: X-Men. Legion Quest Addendum 1.50
- ❑20/Deluxe, Feb 1995; Deluxe edition; JPH (w); A: X-Men. Legion Quest Addendum 2.00
- ❑21, Jul 1995 .... 2.00
- ❑22, Aug 1995 .... 2.00
- ❑23, Sep 1995 .... 2.00
- ❑24, Oct 1995; no issue number on cover 2.00
- ❑25, Nov 1995; Giant-size; JPH (w); enhanced wraparound fold-out cardstock cover; 25th Issue Extravaganza 4.00
- ❑26, Dec 1995 A: Weapon X 2.00
- ❑27, Jan 1996; V: Sugar Man 2.00
- ❑28, Feb 1996; V: Sugar Man 2.00
- ❑29, Mar 1996 JPH (w) 2.00
- ❑30, Apr 1996; JPH (w); A: X-Man. Cable meets X-Man 2.00
- ❑31, May 1996; V: X-Man 2.00
- ❑32, Jun 1996; V: Post 2.00
- ❑33, Jul 1996 .... 2.00
- ❑34, Aug 1996; V: Hulk; Onslaught Phase 1 .... 2.00
- ❑35, Sep 1996; V: Apocalypse; Onslaught Phase 2 .... 2.00
- ❑36, Oct 1996 .... 2.00
- ❑37, Nov 1996 A: Weapon X 2.00
- ❑38, Dec 1996 JPH (w); A: Micronauts .. 2.00
- ❑39, Jan 1997 JPH (w); A: Micronauts .. 2.00
- ❑40, Feb 1997; 1: Nils Styger (Abyss) in 616 Universe 2.00
- ❑41, Mar 1997 A: Bishop 2.00
- ❑42, Apr 1997 .... 2.00
- ❑43, May 1997 .... 2.00
- ❑44, Jun 1997; JRo (w); V: Madelyne Pryor 2.00
- ❑45, Aug 1997; gatefold summary; JRo (w); Operation Zero Tolerance 2.00
- ❑46, Sep 1997; gatefold summary; JRo (w); Operation Zero Tolerance 2.00
- ❑47, Oct 1997; gatefold summary; JRo (w); Operation Zero Tolerance 2.00
- ❑48, Nov 1997; gatefold summary; JRo (w) 2.00
- ❑49, Dec 1997; gatefold summary; JRo (w) 2.00
- ❑50, Jan 1998; Giant-size; Gatefold summary 2.95
- ❑51, Feb 1998; gatefold summary 1.99
- ❑52, Mar 1998; gatefold summary 1.99
- ❑53, Apr 1998; gatefold summary 1.99
- ❑54, May 1998; gatefold summary; A: Black Panther. V: Klaw. V: Klaw 1.99
- ❑55, Jun 1998; gatefold summary; A: Domino 1.99
- ❑56, Jul 1998; gatefold summary 1.99
- ❑57, Aug 1998; gatefold summary 1.99
- ❑58, Sep 1998; gatefold summary 1.99
- ❑59, Oct 1998; gatefold summary; V: Zzzax 1.99
- ❑60, Nov 1998; gatefold summary; 1: Agent 18 .... 1.99
- ❑61, Nov 1998; gatefold summary; captured by S.H.I.E.L.D 1.99
- ❑62, Dec 1998; gatefold summary; A: Nick Fury 1.99
- ❑63, Jan 1999; gatefold summary; A: Stryfe. V: Stryfe 1.99
- ❑64, Feb 1999; gatefold summary; O: Cable. A: Ozymandias 1.99
- ❑65, Mar 1999; 1: Acidroid. A: Rachel Summers 1.99
- ❑66, Apr 1999 .... 1.99
- ❑67, May 1999 A: Avengers 1.99
- ❑68, Jun 1999 A: Avengers 1.99
- ❑69, Jul 1999 .... 1.99
- ❑70, Aug 1999 .... 1.99
- ❑71, Sep 1999; V: Hound Master 1.99
- ❑72, Oct 1999 .... 1.99
- ❑73, Nov 1999 .... 1.99
- ❑74, Dec 1999 .... 1.99
- ❑75, Jan 2000; Giant sized Anniversary issue 5.00
- ❑76, Feb 2000 .... 2.25
- ❑77, Mar 2000 .... 2.25
- ❑78, Apr 2000 .... 2.25
- ❑79, May 2000 .... 2.25
- ❑80, Jun 2000; Price increase 2.25
- ❑81, Jul 2000 .... 2.25
- ❑82, Aug 2000 .... 2.25
- ❑83, Sep 2000 .... 2.25
- ❑84, Oct 2000 .... 2.25
- ❑85, Nov 2000 .... 2.25
- ❑86, Dec 2000; V: Guant 2.25
- ❑87, Jan 2001 .... 2.25
- ❑88, Feb 2001 A: Nightcrawler 2.25
- ❑89, Mar 2001 .... 2.25
- ❑90, Apr 2001 .... 2.25
- ❑91, May 2001 .... 2.25
- ❑92, Jun 2001 .... 2.25
- ❑93, Jul 2001; V: Dark Sisterhood 2.25
- ❑94, Aug 2001; V: Dark Sisterhood; History of Dark Sisterhood 2.25
- ❑95, Sep 2001; V: Dark Sisterhood 2.25
- ❑96, Oct 2001 .... 2.25
- ❑97, Nov 2001; V: Shining Path (Peruvian guerillas) 2.25
- ❑98, Dec 2001 .... 2.25
- ❑99, Jan 2002 .... 2.25
- ❑100, Feb 2002; Giant-size; Includes silent story 3.99
- ❑101, Mar 2002 .... 2.25
- ❑102, Apr 2002 .... 2.25
- ❑103, May 2002 .... 2.25
- ❑104, Jun 2002 .... 2.25
- ❑105, Jul 2002 .... 2.25
- ❑106, Aug 2002 .... 2.25
- ❑107, Sep 2002; Final issue 2.25
- ❑Ann 1998, Sep 1998; Cable/Machine Man '98; continues in Machine Man/ Bastion '98; wraparound cover 2.99
- ❑Ann 1999, Sep 1999; V: Sinister 3.50

Cable: Blood and Metal
Marvel

- ❑1, Oct 1992; JR2 (a); V: Mutant Liberation Front; Wraparound cover... 3.50
- ❑2, Nov 1992; JR2 (c); JR2 (a); V: Stryfe; Wraparound cover; No ads; 48 pages 3.00

Cable/Deadpool
Marvel

- ❑1, May 2004, RL (c) 4.00
- ❑2, Jun 2004, RL, (c) 2.99
- ❑3, Jul 2004, RL, (c) 2.99
- ❑4, Aug 2004 .... 2.99
- ❑5, Sep 2004 .... 2.99
- ❑6, Oct 2004 .... 2.99
- ❑7, Nov 2004 .... 2.99
- ❑8, Dec 2004 .... 2.99
- ❑9, Jan 2005 .... 2.99
- ❑10, Feb 2005 .... 2.99
- ❑11, Mar 2005 .... 2.99
- ❑12, Apr 2005 .... 2.99
- ❑13, May 2005 .... 2.99
- ❑14, Jun 2005 .... 2.99
- ❑15, Jul 2005 .... 2.99
- ❑16, Aug 2005 .... 2.99
- ❑17, Sep 2005 .... 2.99
- ❑18, Oct 2005 .... 2.99
- ❑19, Nov 2005 .... 2.99
- ❑20, Dec 2005 .... 2.99
- ❑21, Dec 2005 .... 2.99
- ❑22, Jan 2006 .... 2.99
- ❑23, Feb 2006 .... 2.99
- ❑24, Mar 2006 .... 2.99
- ❑25, Apr 2006 .... 2.99
- ❑26, May 2006 .... 2.99
- ❑27, Jun 2006 .... 2.99
- ❑28, Jul 2006 .... 2.99
- ❑29, Aug 2006 .... 2.99
- ❑30, Sep 2006, Civil War tie-in 2.99
- ❑31, Nov 2006, Civil War tie-in 2.99
- ❑32, Dec 2006, Appearances by Black Box and President Bush., Civil War tie-in .. 2.99
- ❑33, Dec 2006, Six Pack 2.99
- ❑34, Jan 2007 .... 2.99
- ❑35, Mar 2007 .... 2.99

Cable: Second Genesis
Marvel

- ❑1, Sep 1999; collects New Mutants #1-2 and X-Force #1 .... 3.99

Cable TV
Parody

- ❑1, b&w 2.50

Cadavera
Monster

- ❑1, b&w 1.95
- ❑2, b&w 1.95

Cadillacs & Dinosaurs
Marvel / Epic

- ❑1, Nov 1990; Reprints Xenozoic Tales #1 in color 2.50
- ❑2, Dec 1990; Reprints Xenozoic Tales #2 in color 2.50
- ❑3, Jan 1991; Reprints Xenozoic Tales #3 in color 2.50
- ❑4, Feb 1991; Reprints Xenozoic Tales #4 in color 2.50
- ❑5, Mar 1991; Reprints Xenozoic Tales #5 in color 2.50
- ❑6, Apr 1991; Reprints Xenozoic Tales #6 in color 2.50
- ❑3D 1, Jul 1992; 100 Page giant; 3D Special; Includes glasses; 100 Page giant; Reprint from Xenozoic Tales #6; Reprint from Xenozoic Tales #7 .... 3.95

Cadillacs & Dinosaurs
Kitchen Sink

- ❑1, Dec 1993, One-shot 4.00

Cadillacs & Dinosaurs
Topps

- ❑1, Feb 1994; Blood and Bones, Part 1 .. 2.50
- ❑1/Variant, Feb 1994; foil cover 2.95
- ❑2, Mar 1994 .... 2.50
- ❑2/Deluxe, Mar 1994; poster by Moebius 2.50
- ❑3, Apr 1994 .... 2.50
- ❑3/Deluxe, Apr 1994; poster 2.50
- ❑4, Jun 1994; Newsstand edition; Man Eater, Part 1 .... 2.50
- ❑4/Variant, Jun 1994 .... 2.50
- ❑5, Aug 1994; Newsstand shop edition; Man Eater, Part 2 .... 2.50
- ❑6, Oct 1994; Newsstand edition; Man Eater, Part 3 .... 2.50
- ❑7, Dec 1994 .... 2.50
- ❑8, Feb 1995 .... 2.50
- ❑9, Apr 1995; The Wild Ones, Part 3; Poster of Big Red 2.50
- ❑10, Jun 1995 .... 2.50

Caffeine
Slave Labor

- ❑1, Jan 1996 .... 2.95
- ❑2, Apr 1996 .... 2.95
- ❑3, Jul 1996 .... 2.95
- ❑4, Nov 1996 .... 2.95
- ❑5, Jan 1997 .... 2.95
- ❑6, Apr 1997 .... 2.95
- ❑7, Jul 1997; flip book 2.95
- ❑8, Nov 1997 .... 2.95
- ❑9, Jan 1998 .... 2.95
- ❑10, Apr 1998; Final Issue 2.95

Cage
Marvel

- ❑1, Apr 1992; O: Cage; V: Hardcore 3.00

Other grades: Multiply price above by 5/6 for VF/NM • 2/3 for VERY FINE • 1/3 for FINE • 1/5 for VERY GOOD • 1/8 for GOOD

Boof (Image)

Short, fat warrior from planet Smashmouth
©Image

Book of Fate

Keith Giffen's relaunch of Doctor Fate
©DC

Books of Faerie

Mini-series explores the origins of Titania
©DC

Books of Magic

All-powerful boy magician learns tricks
©DC

Booster Gold

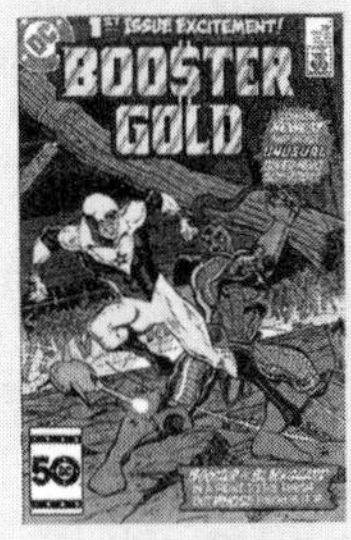

Super-hero is only in it for the money
©DC

N-MINT

❑2, May 1992 1.00
❑3, Jun 1992; V: Tombstone; V: Nitro; V: Hardcore; V: Kickback, Cameo of the Punisher 1.00
❑4, Jul 1992; V: Tombstone; V: Nitro; V: Hardcore; V: Kickback 1.00
❑5, Aug 1992 1.00
❑6, Sep 1992 1.00
❑7, Oct 1992; V: Hardcore 1.00
❑8, Nov 1992 1.00
❑9, Dec 1992; V: Rhino 1.00
❑10, Jan 1993; V: Rhino 1.00
❑11, Feb 1993 1.00
❑12, Mar 1993; Giant-size; Iron Fist 1.00
❑13, Apr 1993; V: Tinkerer 1.00
❑14, May 1993; V: Coldfire 1.00
❑15, Jun 1993 1.00
❑16, Jul 1993 1.00
❑17, Aug 1993; V: Crusader; Infinity Crusade crossover 1.00
❑18, Sep 1993 1.00
❑19, Oct 1993 1.00
❑20, Nov 1993; Final Issue 1.00

Cage
Marvel / MAX

❑1, Mar 2002 4.00
❑2, May 2002 2.99
❑3, Jul 2002 2.99
❑4, Aug 2002 2.99
❑5, Sep 2002 2.99

Caged Heat 3000
Roger Corman's Cosmic Comics

❑1 2.50
❑2 2.50

Cages
Tundra

❑1, b&w 5.00
❑2, b&w 4.00
❑3, b&w 4.00
❑4 4.00
❑5 4.00
❑6 4.00
❑7 4.00
❑8, Aug 1993, Published by Kitchen Sink; b&w with 8 color pages 4.00
❑9 4.00
❑10, May 1996, Final Issue; Published by Kitchen Sink 5.00

Cain
Harris

❑1; trading card 2.95
❑2, Oct 1993; two alternate covers 2.95

Calculated Risk
Genesis

❑1, Mar 1990, b&w 2.00

Caliber Christmas, A
Caliber

❑1, Crow; Sampler 3.95

Caliber Christmas, A
Caliber

❑1, Dec 1998; Crow; sampler 5.95

Caliber Core
Caliber

❑0, b&w; intro to imprint 2.95
❑Ashcan 1, b&w; No cover price; intro to imprint 1.00

Caliber Presents
Caliber

❑1, Jan 1989, b&w; Crow 15.00
❑2 1989, b&w; Cuda by Tim Vigil; Deadworld by Vince Locke; Cover by James O'Barr 2.50
❑3 1989, b&w 2.50
❑4 1989, b&w 2.50
❑5 1989, b&w 2.50
❑6, Aug 1989 2.50
❑7, Nov 1989, b&w 2.50
❑8 2.00
❑9 2.50
❑10 2.95
❑11; Misnumbered #12; b&w 2.95
❑12 2.50
❑13; b&w 2.95
❑14; b&w 2.50
❑15, Sep 1990; 64 pages 3.00
❑16; 64 pages 3.00
❑17; 64 pages 3.00
❑18; 64 pages 3.00
❑19; 64 pages 3.00
❑20; 64 pages 3.00
❑21; 64 pages 3.00
❑22; 64 pages 3.00
❑23; 64 pages 3.00
❑24; 64 pages 3.00

Caliber Presents: Cinderella on Fire
Caliber

❑1, ca. 1994, b&w; NN 2.95

Caliber Presents: Generator Comics
Caliber

❑1, b&w; NN 2.95

Caliber Presents: Hybrid Stories
Caliber

❑1, b&w; NN 2.95

Caliber Presents: Petit Mal
Caliber

❑1, b&w; NN 2.95

Caliber Presents: Romantic Tales
Caliber

❑1, ca. 1995, b&w; NN 2.95

Caliber Presents: Sepulcher Opus
Caliber

❑1, ca. 1993, b&w; NN 2.95

Caliber Presents: Something Inside
Caliber

❑1, b&w; NN 3.50

Caliber Presents: Sub-Atomic Shock
Caliber

❑1, b&w; NN 2.95

Caliber Spotlight
Caliber

❑1, May 1995; b&w anthology with A.K.A. Goldfish, Kabuki, Kilroy is Here, Oz, and previews 2.95

Calibrations
Caliber

❑1, b&w 1.00
❑2 1.00
❑3 1.00
❑4 1.00
❑5 1.00

Calibrations
Caliber

❑1, Jun 1996; preview of The Lost and Atmospherics 1.00
❑2, Jul 1996 1.00
❑3, Aug 1996 1.00
❑4, Sep 1996; b&w 1.00
❑5, Oct 1996 1.00

California Comics
California

❑1; Adult 5.00
❑2; Adult 4.00

California Girls
Eclipse

❑1, Jun 1987 2.00
❑2, Jul 1987 2.00
❑3, Aug 1987 2.00
❑4, Sep 1987 2.00
❑5, Oct 1987 2.00
❑6, Nov 1987 2.00
❑7, Dec 1987 2.00
❑8, Jan 1988 2.00

California Raisins in 3-D
Blackthorne

❑1, Dec 1987; a.k.a. Blackthorne in 3-D #31 2.50
❑1/2nd 2.50
❑1/3rd 2.50
❑2 2.50
❑3; Blackthorne 3-D series #46 2.50
❑4; Blackthorne 3-D series #63 2.50
❑5; Blackthorne 3-D series #69 2.50

Caligari 2050
Monster

❑1, Apr 1992 2.25
❑2 2.25
❑3 2.25

Caligari 2050: Another Sleepless Night
Caliber

❑1, ca. 1993 3.95

Call
Marvel

❑1, Jun 2003 2.25
❑2, Jul 2003 2.25
❑3, Aug 2003 2.25
❑4, Sep 2003, cardstock cover 2.25

Called From Darkness
Anarchy

❑1/2nd; "Uncut" edition 2.95
❑1 2.95

Call Me Princess
CPM

❑1, May 1999, b&w series 2.95
❑1/A, May 1999, b&w 2.95
❑2, Jun 1999, b&w 2.95
❑3 1999, b&w 2.95
❑4 1999, b&w 2.95

N-MINT

❑5 1999, b&w 2.95
❑6 1999, b&w 2.95

Call of Duty: The Brotherhood
Marvel

❑1, Aug 2002 .... 2.25
❑2, Sep 2002 .... 2.25
❑3, Oct 2002 .... 2.25
❑4, Nov 2002 .... 2.25
❑5, Dec 2002 .... 2.25
❑6, Jan 2003 .... 2.25

Call of Duty: The Precinct
Marvel

❑1, Sep 2002 .... 2.25
❑2, Oct 2002 .... 2.25
❑3, Nov 2002 .... 2.25
❑4, Dec 2002 .... 2.25
❑5, Jan 2003 .... 2.25

Call of Duty: The Wagon
Marvel

❑1, Oct 2002 .... 2.25
❑2, Nov 2002 .... 2.25
❑3, Dec 2002 .... 2.25
❑4, Jan 2003 .... 2.25

Calvin and the Colonel
Dell

❑2, Sep 1962; See Four Color #1354 for #1 .... 25.00

Cambion
Slave Labor

❑1, Dec 1995 .... 2.95
❑2, Feb 1996 .... 2.95
❑3, Feb 1997, b&w; Published by Moonstone 2.95

Camelot Eternal
Caliber

❑1 .... 2.50
❑2 .... 2.50
❑3 .... 2.50
❑4 .... 2.50
❑5 .... 2.50
❑6 .... 2.50
❑7 .... 2.50
❑8 .... 2.50

Camelot 3000
DC

❑1, Dec 1982; BB (c); BB (a); O: Merlin. O: Arthur 2.50
❑2, Jan 1983 BB (c); BB (a) 2.00
❑3, Feb 1983 BB (c); BB (a) 2.00
❑4, Mar 1983 BB (c); BB (a) 2.00
❑5, Apr 1983 BB (c); BB (a) 2.00
❑6, Jul 1983 BB (c); BB (a) 2.00
❑7, Aug 1983 BB (c); BB (a) 2.00
❑8, Sep 1983 BB (c); BB (a) 2.00
❑9, Dec 1983 BB (c); BB (a) 2.00
❑10, Mar 1984 BB (c); BB (a) 2.00
❑11, Jul 1984 BB (c); BB (a) 2.00
❑12, Apr 1985 BB (c); BB (a) 2.00

Camp Candy
Marvel

❑1, May 1990 .... 1.00
❑2, Jun 1990 .... 1.00
❑3, Jul 1990 .... 1.00
❑4, Aug 1990 .... 1.00
❑5, Sep 1990 .... 1.00
❑6, Oct 1990 .... 1.00
❑7, Nov 1990 .... 1.00

Campfire Stories
Global

❑1, ca. 1992 .... 2.25

Camping with Bigfoot
Slave Labor

❑1, Sep 1995 .... 2.95

Camp Runamuck
Dell

❑1, Apr 1966, Based on 1965-66 NBC TV show 40.00

Canadian Rock Special
Revolutionary

❑1, Apr 1994, b&w; Rush 2.50

Cancer: The Crab Boy
Sabre's Edge

❑1 .... 2.95
❑2 .... 2.95

N-MINT

❑3 .... 2.95
❑4 .... 2.95
❑5 .... 2.95

Candidate Goddess
Tokyopop

❑5, Dec 2004; Graphic novel; Read right to left; Ends series 9.99
❑4, Oct 2004; Graphic novel; Read right to left 9.99
❑3; Graphic novel; Read right to left 9.99
❑2; Graphic novel; Read right to left 9.99
❑1, Apr 2004; Graphic novel; Read right to left 9.99

Candide Revealed
Fantagraphics / Eros

❑1, b&w; Adult 2.25

Candyappleblack
Good Intentions Paving

❑1 2004; b&w 3.50
❑2 2004; b&w 3.50
❑3 2004; b&w 3.50
❑4 2004; b&w 3.50
❑5 2004; b&w 3.50

Cannibalis
Raging Rhino

❑1, b&w; Adult 2.95

Cannon
Fantagraphics / Eros

❑1, Feb 1991, b&w; WW (w); WW (a) 2.75
❑1/2nd, WW (w); WW (a); 2nd printing 2.95
❑2, Mar 1991, b&w; WW (w); WW (a) 2.95
❑2/2nd, WW (w); WW (a); 2nd printing 2.95
❑3, Apr 1991, WW (w); WW (a); O: Madame Toy. O: Sue Stevens 2.95
❑3/2nd, WW (w); WW (a); O: Madame Toy. O: Sue Stevens. 2nd printing 2.95
❑4, May 1991, WW (w); WW (a) 2.95
❑5, Jun 1991, WW (w); WW (a) 2.95
❑6, Jul 1991, WW (w); WW (a) 2.95
❑7, Aug 1991, WW (w); WW (a) 2.95
❑8, Sep 1991, WW (w); WW (a) 2.95

Cannon Busters
Devil's Due

❑0, Jun 2004; Available at 2004 San Diego Comic Con 15.00
❑1 2004 .... 2.95
❑1/Variant 2004 .... 4.00
❑2 2004 .... 2.95
❑2/Variant 2004 .... 4.00

Cannon God Exaxxion
Dark Horse

❑1, Nov 2001; Stage 1.1 .... 2.99
❑2, Dec 2001; Stage 1.2 .... 2.99
❑3, Jan 2002; Stage 1.3 .... 2.99
❑4, Feb 2002; Stage 1.4 .... 2.99
❑5, Mar 2002; Stage 1.5 .... 2.99
❑6, Apr 2002; Stage 1.6 .... 2.99
❑7, May 2002; Stage 1.7 .... 2.99
❑8, Jun 2002; Stage 1.8 .... 2.99
❑9, Sep 2002; 48 pages; Stage 2.1 .... 3.99
❑10, Oct 2002; Stage 2.2 .... 3.50
❑11, Nov 2002; Stage 2.3 .... 3.50
❑12, Dec 2002; Stage 2.4 .... 3.50
❑13, Jan 2003; Stage 2.5 .... 3.50
❑14, Jun 2003; Stage 3.1 .... 3.50
❑15, Jul 2003; Stage 3.2; Price drop 2.99
❑16, Aug 2003; Stage 3.3 .... 2.99
❑17, Sep 2003; Stage 3.4 .... 2.99
❑18, Oct 2003; Stage 3.5 .... 2.99
❑19, Nov 2003; Stage 3.6 .... 2.99
❑20, Dec 2003; Stage 3.7 .... 2.99

Cannon Hawke: Dawn of War (Michael Turner's)
Aspen

❑1, Jun 2004 .... 6.00

Canyon Comics Presents
Grand Canyon Association

❑1, Fal 1995, Sold at Grand Canyon Information Center 1.95
❑2, Sum 1996; Sold at Grand Canyon Information Center 1.95

Cape City
Dimension X

❑1, b&w 2.75
❑2, b&w 2.75

N-MINT

Caper
DC

❑1, Dec 2003 .... 2.95
❑2, Jan 2004 .... 2.95
❑3, Feb 2004 .... 2.95
❑4, Mar 2004 .... 2.95
❑5, Apr 2004 .... 2.95
❑6, May 2004 .... 2.95
❑7, Jun 2004 .... 2.95
❑8, Jul 2004 .... 2.95
❑9, Aug 2004 .... 2.95
❑10, Sep 2004 .... 2.95
❑11, Oct 2004 .... 2.95
❑12, Nov 2004, Final issue 2.95

Capes
Image

❑1, Oct 2003 .... 3.50
❑2, Nov 2003 .... 3.50
❑3, Dec 2003 .... 3.50

Capital Capers Presents
BLT

❑1, Oct 1994, b&w 2.95

Cap'n Oatmeal
All American

❑1, b&w 2.25

Cap'n Quick & a Foozle
Eclipse

❑1, Jul 1984 .... 1.50
❑2, Mar 1985 .... 1.50
❑3; Title changes to The Foozle 1.50

Captain Action
Karl Art

❑0; preview of ongoing series;Insert in Space Bananas #1 .... 1.95

Captain Action
DC

❑1, Nov 1968, CI, IN (c); WW (a); O: Captain Action; 1: Captain Action (in comics); 1: Clive Arno; 1: Carl Arno; 1: Krellik; 1: Khem the panther; 1: The Elders of Aspu; Chernobog; Based on toy 45.00
❑2, Jan 1969, GK (c); GK, WW (a); 1: Action Boy (in comics) 35.00
❑3, Mar 1969, GK (c); GK (w); GK, WW (a); 1: Dr. Evil; O: Dr. Evil 35.00
❑4, May 1969, GK (c); GK (w); GK (a); 1: Kathryn Arno 35.00
❑5, Jul 1969, GK (c); GK (w); GK, WW (a); 1: Matthew Blackwell; 1: Eugene Johnson; 1: Johnny Johnson; Final issue 20.00

Captain Africa
African Prince Productions

❑1, Jun 1992, b&w 2.50

Captain America
Marvel

❑100, Apr 1968, JK (c); SL (w); JK (a); A: Avengers. Series continued from Tales of Suspense #99 .... 210.00
❑101, May 1968, JK (c); SL (w); JK (a); 1: 4th Sleeper 55.00
❑102, Jun 1968, JK (c); SL (w); JK (a); 1: Exiles; 2: 4th Sleeper; The; Doug Moench L.O.C 35.00
❑103, Jul 1968, JK (c); SL (w); JK (a); A: Red Skull. Agent 13's identity revealed as Sharon Carter 35.00
❑104, Aug 1968, JK (c); SL (w); JK (a); V: Red Skull 35.00
❑105, Sep 1968, JK (c); SL (w); JK (a); V: Batroc; Peter Sanderson L.O.C 35.00
❑106, Oct 1968, JK (c); SL (w); JK (a) 35.00
❑107, Nov 1968, JK (c); SL (w); JK (a); 1: Doctor Faustus. A: Red Skull; 1: Ferret; Peter Sanderson L.O.C 35.00
❑108, Dec 1968, JK (c); SL (w); JK (a) 35.00
❑109, Jan 1969, JK (c); SL (w); JK (a); O: Captain America 45.00
❑109/2nd, ca. 1994, JK (c); SL (w); JK (a); O: Captain America. Reprint 2.50
❑110, Feb 1969, JSo (c); JSo (w); JSo (a); 1: Viper II (as Madame Hydra). 1: Viper. A: Hulk. A: Rick Jones. Rick Jones dons Bucky costume 75.00
❑111, Mar 1969, JSo (c); JSo (w); JSo (a); 2: Viper II (as Madame Hydra) 65.00
❑112, Apr 1969, JK (c); SL (w); GT, JK (a); O: Viper II (as Madame Hydra). O: Captain America. album 50.00

Other grades: Multiply price above by 5/6 for VF/NM • 2/3 for VERY FINE • 1/3 for FINE • 1/5 for VERY GOOD • 1/8 for GOOD

Boris Karloff Tales of Mystery

Horror star "introduces" horror tales

©Gold Key

Boris the Bear

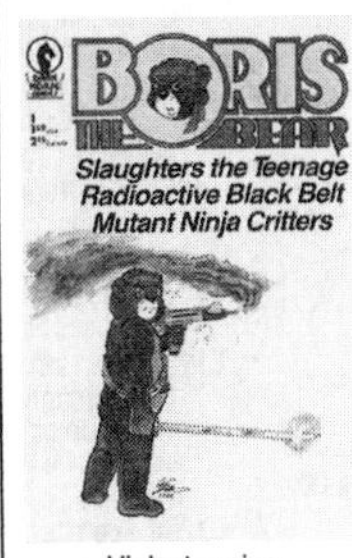

Violent ursine parodies many in series

©Dark Horse

Box Office Poison

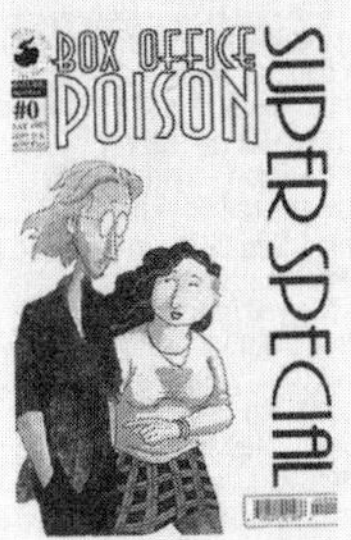

Relationship humor from Alex Robinson

©Antarctic

Bradleys

Peter Bagge's take on a dysfunctional family

©Fantagraphics

Brain Boy

Matt Price's mental magic adventures

©Dell

	N-MINT
❑113, May 1969, JSo (c); JSo (w); JSo (a); Avengers	60.00
❑114, Jun 1969, JR (c); SL (w); JR (a)	30.00
❑115, Jul 1969	30.00
❑116, Aug 1969	30.00
❑117, Sep 1969, GC (c); SL (w); GC, JSt (a); 1: Falcon; 1: Redwing; James Van Hise L.O.C	95.00
❑118, Oct 1969, GC (c); SL (w); GC, JSt (a); A: Falcon. 2: Falcon; 2: Redwing; Exiles apperance; Steve Gerber L.O.C.	25.00
❑119, Nov 1969, GC (c); SL (w); GC, JSt (a); A: Falcon. 2: M.O.D.O.K	25.00
❑120, Dec 1969, GC (c); SL (w); GC, JSt (a); A: Falcon	25.00
❑121, Jan 1970, GC (c); SL (w); GC (a); O: Captain America. 1: Man-Brute; 1: Silas X. Cragg; D: Silas X. Cragg	25.00
❑122, Feb 1970, GC (c); SL (w); GC (a); Don McGregor L.O.C	25.00
❑123, Mar 1970, GC (c); SL (w); GC, JSt (a); 1: Suprema (later becomes Mother Night); 1: Scarbo	25.00
❑124, Apr 1970, SL (w); GC (a); 1: Cyborg	25.00
❑125, May 1970, SL (w); GC (a)	20.00
❑126, Jun 1970, SL (w); GC (a); 1: Diamond Head. A: Falcon	20.00
❑127, Jul 1970, SL (w); GC (a)	20.00
❑128, Aug 1970, SL (w); GC (a)	15.00
❑129, Sep 1970, SL (w); GC (a)	15.00
❑130, Oct 1970, SL (w); GC (a); 1: Hood; 1: Batroc's Brigade	15.00
❑131, Nov 1970, SL (w); GC (a); 1: Hood	18.00
❑132, Dec 1970, SL (w); GC (a); 2: Bucky Barnes android; M.O.D.O.K. appearence	18.00
❑133, Jan 1971, SL (w); GC (a); O: Modok. Falcon becomes Captain America's partner	15.00
❑134, Feb 1971, HT (c); SL (w); GC (a); 1: Stone-Face; 1: Jody Casper (Falcon's nephew); 1: Sarah Wilson Casper; 1: Jody Casper	18.00
❑135, Mar 1971, JR (c); SL (w); GC (a); 1: Monster Ape	18.00
❑136, Apr 1971, JB (c); SL (w); GC (a); D: Monster Ape; 2: Monster Ape	18.00
❑137, May 1971, SB (c); SL (w); GC, BEv (a); A: Spider-Man. 2: Stone-Face	35.00
❑138, Jun 1971, SL (w); JR (a); A: Spider-Man. 2: Jody Casper	30.00
❑139, Jul 1971, SL (w); GC, JR (a); 1: Leila Taylor; 1: Sgt. Brian Muldoon	25.00
❑140, Aug 1971, SL (w); JR (a); O: Grey Gargoyle. 2: Leila Taylor; 2: Sgt. Brian Muldoon; O: Grey Gargoyle	25.00
❑141, Sep 1971, SL (w); JR (a)	25.00
❑142, Oct 1971, JR (a); V: Grey Gargoyle	25.00
❑143, Nov 1971, Giant-size; JR (a); 1: Rafe Michel	25.00
❑144, Dec 1971, JR (a)	25.00
❑145, Jan 1972, JR (c); GK (a)	25.00
❑146, Feb 1972, SB (a)	25.00
❑147, Mar 1972	18.00
❑148, Apr 1972, Steve Englehart wrote all letters on letters page	16.00
❑149, May 1972, GK (c); SB (a)	15.00
❑150, Jun 1972	25.00
❑151, Jul 1972	15.00
❑152, Aug 1972, SB (a)	15.00
❑153, Sep 1972, 1: Bucky III (Jack Monroe). 1: Captain America IV. V: Red Skull	15.00
❑154, Oct 1972	25.00
❑155, Nov 1972, SB (a); O: Captain America II (Jack Monroe). O: Captain America	25.00
❑156, Dec 1972	20.00
❑157, Jan 1973, SB (a)	10.00
❑158, Feb 1973	10.00
❑159, Mar 1973, SB (a)	10.00
❑160, Apr 1973, 1: Solarr	10.00
❑161, May 1973, SB (a)	10.00
❑162, Jun 1973, SB (a); O: Sharon Carter	10.00
❑163, Jul 1973, SB (a); 1: Dave Cox	12.00
❑164, Aug 1973, 1: Nightshade	12.00
❑165, Sep 1973, SB (a)	10.00
❑166, Oct 1973, SB (a)	10.00
❑167, Nov 1973, SB (a)	10.00
❑168, Dec 1973, SB (a); 1: Phoenix I (Helmut Zemo). A: Baron Zemo (Helmut). D: Phoenix I (Helmut Zemo)	15.00
❑169, Jan 1974, 1: Moonstone I (Lloyd Bloch)-cameo	10.00
❑170, Feb 1974, SB (a); 1: Moonstone I (Lloyd Bloch)-full	12.00
❑171, Mar 1974, SB (a); Marvel Value Stamp #50: Black Panther	10.00
❑172, Apr 1974, SB (a); A: X-Men. A: Banshee. Marvel Value Stamp #43: Enchantress	10.00
❑173, May 1974, GK (c); SB (a); A: X-Men. Marvel Value Stamp #61: Red Ghost	15.00
❑174, Jun 1974, SB (a); A: X-Men. Marvel Value Stamp #48: Kraven	12.00
❑175, Jul 1974, SB (a); A: X-Men. Marvel Value Stamp #77: Swordsman	10.00
❑176, Aug 1974, JR (c); SB (a); Marvel Value Stamp #15: Iron Man	10.00
❑177, Sep 1974, JR (c); SB (a); recalls origin and quits; Marvel Value Stamp #26: Mephisto	8.00
❑178, Oct 1974, JR (c); SB (a); Marvel Value Stamp #89: Hammerhead	8.00
❑179, Nov 1974, SB (a); Marvel Value Stamp #52: Quicksilver	8.00
❑180, Dec 1974, SB, GK (a); O: Nomad. 1: Nomad (Steve Rogers). 1: Viper II. Marvel Value Stamp #61: Red Ghost	8.00
❑181, Jan 1975, GK (c); SB (a); O: Captain America (new). 1: Captain America (new). Marvel Value Stamp #46 Mysterio	8.00
❑182, Feb 1975, JR (c); FR (a); Marvel Value Stamp #36: Ancient One	8.00
❑183, Mar 1975, JSt (c); FR, GK (a); D: Captain America (new). Steve Rogers becomes Captain America again	8.00
❑184, Apr 1975, JR (c); HT, GK (a); Marvel Value Stamp #94: Electro	5.00
❑185, May 1975, SB, FR, GK (a); V: the Red Skull	5.00
❑186, Jun 1975, GK (c); FR (a); O: Falcon (real origin)	5.00
❑187, Jul 1975	5.00
❑188, Aug 1975, SB, GK (a)	8.00
❑189, Sep 1975, FR, GK (a)	6.00
❑190, Oct 1975, JSt (c); FR, GK (a)	6.00
❑191, Nov 1975, SB, FR (a)	6.00
❑192, Dec 1975, FR, JR (a); 1: Karla Sofen (becomes Moonstone). Marvel Value Stamp #56: Rawhide Kid	6.00
❑193, Jan 1976, JK (w); JK (a)	6.00
❑194, Feb 1976, JK (c); JK (w); JK (a); Marvel Value Stamp Series B #27	6.00
❑195, Mar 1976, JK (c); JK (w); JK (a)	6.00
❑196, Apr 1976, JK (c); JK (w); JK (a)	6.00
❑196/30¢, Apr 1976, JK (c); JK (w); JK (a); 30¢ regional price variant	20.00
❑197, May 1976, JK (c); JK (w); JK (a); Marvel Value Stamp Series B #78; Ralph Macchio L.O.C	5.00
❑197/30¢, May 1976, JK (c); JK (w); JK (a); 30¢ regional price variant	20.00
❑198, Jun 1976, JK (c); JK (w); JK (a); Marvel Value Stamp Series B #91	6.00
❑198/30¢, Jun 1976, JK (c); JK (w); JK (a); 30¢ regional price variant	20.00
❑199, Jul 1976, JK (c); JK (w); JK (a)	5.00
❑199/30¢, Jul 1976, JK (c); JK (w); JK (a); 30¢ regional price variant	20.00
❑200, Aug 1976, 200th anniversary issue; JK (c); JK (w); JK (a)	6.00
❑200/30¢, Aug 1976, JK (c); JK (w); JK (a); 30¢ regional price variant	20.00
❑201, Sep 1976, JK (c); JK (w); JK (a)	6.00
❑202, Oct 1976, JK (c); JK (w); JK (a)	4.00
❑203, Nov 1976, JK (c); JK (w); JK (a)	5.00
❑204, Dec 1976, JK (c); JK (w); JK (a); 1: Agron	4.00
❑205, Jan 1977, JK (c); JK (w); JK (a)	4.00
❑206, Feb 1977, JK (c); JK (w); JK (a); 1: Donna Maria Puentes. Newsstand edition (distributed by Curtis); issue number in box	5.00
❑206/Whitman, Feb 1977, JK (w); JK (a); 1: Donna Maria Puentes. Special markets edition (usually sold in Whitman bagged prepacks); price appears in a diamond; UPC barcode appears	5.00
❑207, Mar 1977, JK (c); JK (w); JK (a); Newsstand edition (distributed by Curtis); issue number in box	4.00
❑207/Whitman, Mar 1977, JK (w); JK (a); Special markets edition (usually sold in Whitman bagged prepacks); price appears in a diamond; UPC barcode appears	4.00
❑208, Apr 1977, JK (c); JK (w); JK (a); 1: Arnim Zola. Newsstand edition (distributed by Curtis); issue number in box	5.00
❑208/Whitman, Apr 1977, JK (w); JK (a); 1: Arnim Zola. Special markets edition (usually sold in Whitman bagged prepacks); price appears in a diamond; UPC barcode appears	5.00
❑209, May 1977, JK (c); JK (w); JK (a); 1: Arnim Zola. 1: Doughboy. Newsstand edition (distributed by Curtis); issue number in box	5.00
❑209/Whitman, May 1977, JK (w); JK (a); 1: Arnim Zola. 1: Doughboy. Special markets edition (usually sold in Whitman bagged prepacks); price appears in a diamond; UPC barcode appears	5.00
❑210, Jun 1977, JK (c); JK (w); JK (a); Newsstand edition (distributed by Curtis); issue number in box	4.00
❑210/Whitman, Jun 1977, JK (w); JK (a); Special markets edition (usually sold in Whitman bagged prepacks); price appears in a diamond; UPC barcode appears	4.00

Other grades: Multiply price above by 5/6 for VF/NM • 2/3 for VERY FINE • 1/3 for FINE • 1/5 for VERY GOOD • 1/8 for GOOD

N-MINT N-MINT N-MINT

❑210/35¢, Jun 1977, JK (c); JK (w); JK (a); 35¢ regional price variant; newsstand edition (distributed by Curtis); issue number in box 15.00

❑211, Jul 1977, JK (c); JK (w); JK (a); Newsstand edition (distributed by Curtis); issue number in box 4.00

❑211/Whitman, Jul 1977, JK (w); JK (a); Special markets edition (usually sold in Whitman bagged prepacks); price appears in a diamond; UPC barcode appears.. 4.00

❑211/35¢, Jul 1977, JK (c); JK (w); JK (a); 35¢ regional price variant; newsstand edition (distributed by Curtis); issue number in box.. 15.00

❑212, Aug 1977, JK (c); JK (w); JK (a); Newsstand edition (distributed by Curtis); issue number in box 4.00

❑212/Whitman, Aug 1977, JK (w); JK (a); Special markets edition (usually sold in Whitman bagged prepacks); price appears in a diamond; UPC barcode appears.. 4.00

❑212/35¢, Aug 1977, JK (c); JK (w); JK (a); 35¢ regional price variant; newsstand edition (distributed by Curtis); issue number in box 15.00

❑213, Sep 1977, JK (c); JK (w); JK (a); Newsstand edition (distributed by Curtis); issue number in box 4.00

❑213/Whitman, Sep 1977, JK (w); JK (a); Special markets edition (usually sold in Whitman bagged prepacks); price appears in a diamond; UPC barcode appears.. 4.00

❑213/35¢, Sep 1977, JK (c); JK (w); JK (a); 35¢ regional price variant; newsstand edition (distributed by Curtis); issue number in box 15.00

❑214, Oct 1977, JK (c); JK (w); JK (a); Newsstand edition (distributed by Curtis); issue number in box 4.00

❑214/Whitman, Oct 1977, JK (w); JK (a); Special markets edition (usually sold in Whitman bagged prepacks); price appears in a diamond; no UPC barcode 4.00

❑214/35¢, Oct 1977, JK (c); JK (w); JK (a); 35¢ regional price variant; newsstand edition (distributed by Curtis); issue number in box 15.00

❑215, Nov 1977, GK (c); GK (a); Newsstand edition (distributed by Curtis); issue number in box 4.00

❑215/Whitman, Nov 1977, GK (a); Special markets edition (usually sold in Whitman bagged prepacks); price appears in a diamond; no UPC barcode 4.00

❑216, Dec 1977, GK (c); SL (w); GK (a); Reprinted from Strange Tales #114; newsstand edition (distributed by Curtis); issue number in box 4.00

❑216/Whitman, Dec 1977, GK (a); Reprinted from Strange Tales #114; special markets edition (usually sold in Whitman bagged prepacks); price appears in a diamond; no UPC barcode 4.00

❑217, Jan 1978, JB (a); 1: Quasar (Marvel Man). 1: Blue Streak; 1: Vamp (Animus) 4.00

❑218, Feb 1978, SB (a); O: Captain America 4.00

❑219, Mar 1978, SB (a); Based on 1940's Captain America serial 4.00

❑220, Apr 1978, GK (c); SB, GK (a); Newsstand edition (distributed by Curtis); issue number in box 4.00

❑220/Whitman, Apr 1978, SB, GK (a); Special markets edition (usually sold in Whitman bagged prepacks); price appears in a diamond; no UPC barcode 4.00

❑221, May 1978, GK (c); SB, GK (a); Newsstand edition (distributed by Curtis); issue number in box 4.00

❑221/Whitman, May 1978, SB, GK (a); Special markets edition (usually sold in Whitman bagged prepacks); price appears in a diamond; no UPC barcode 4.00

❑222, Jun 1978, SB (a); Newsstand edition (distributed by Curtis); issue number in box.. 4.00

❑222/Whitman, Jun 1978, SB (a); Special markets edition (usually sold in Whitman bagged prepacks); price appears in a diamond; no UPC barcode 4.00

❑223, Jul 1978, SB, JK (a); V: Animus. 4.00

❑224, Aug 1978, MZ (a); 1: Se-or Muerte II (Philip Garcia). Newsstand edition (distributed by Curtis); issue number in box.. 4.00

❑224/Whitman, Aug 1978, MZ (a); 1: Se-or Muerte II (Philip Garcia). Special markets edition (usually sold in Whitman bagged prepacks); price appears in a diamond; no UPC barcode 4.00

❑225, Sep 1978, FR (c); SB (a); Newsstand edition (distributed by Curtis); issue number in box 4.00

❑225/Whitman, Sep 1978, SB (a); Special markets edition (usually sold in Whitman bagged prepacks); price appears in a diamond; UPC barcode appears.. 4.00

❑226, Oct 1978, SB (a); Newsstand edition (distributed by Curtis); issue number in box.. 4.00

❑226/Whitman, Oct 1978, SB (a); Special markets edition (usually sold in Whitman bagged prepacks); price appears in a diamond; no UPC barcode 4.00

❑227, Nov 1978, SB (a); Newsstand edition (distributed by Curtis); issue number in box.. 4.00

❑227/Whitman, Nov 1978, SB (a); Special markets edition (usually sold in Whitman bagged prepacks); price appears in a diamond; no UPC barcode 4.00

❑228, Dec 1978, SB (a); Newsstand edition (distributed by Curtis); issue number in box.. 4.00

❑228/Whitman, Dec 1978, SB (a); Special markets edition (usually sold in Whitman bagged prepacks); price appears in a diamond; no UPC barcode 4.00

❑229, Jan 1979, KP (c); SB (a); A: Marvel Man (Quasar). Newsstand edition (distributed by Curtis); issue number in box.. 4.00

❑229/Whitman, Jan 1979, SB (a); A: Marvel Man (Quasar). Special markets edition (usually sold in Whitman bagged prepacks); price appears in a diamond; no UPC barcode 4.00

❑230, Feb 1979, SB, DP (a); A: Hulk. V: Hulk. Newsstand edition (distributed by Curtis); issue number in box 4.00

❑230/Whitman, Feb 1979, SB, DP (a); A: Hulk. V: Hulk. Special markets edition (usually sold in Whitman bagged prepacks); price appears in a diamond; no UPC barcode 4.00

❑231, Mar 1979, KP (c); SB, DP (a); V: Grand Director 4.00

❑232, Apr 1979, KP (c); SB, DP (a) 4.00

❑233, May 1979, SB, DP (a); D: Sharon Carter. Newsstand edition (distributed by Curtis); issue number in box 4.00

❑233/Whitman, May 1979, SB, DP (a); D: Sharon Carter. Special markets edition (usually sold in Whitman bagged prepacks); price appears in a diamond; no UPC barcode 4.00

❑234, Jun 1979, A: Daredevil.................. 6.00

❑235, Jul 1979, SB, FM, JAb (a); A: Daredevil 4.00

❑236, Aug 1979, KP (c); SB, DP (a); D: Captain America IV. D: Captain America IV.. 4.00

❑237, Sep 1979, SB, DP (a); 1: Anna Kappelbaum. 1: Joshua Cooper. 1: Copperhead. 1: Mike Farrel. Steve moves to Brooklyn 4.00

❑238, Oct 1979, JBy (c); JBy (a).......... 4.00

❑239, Nov 1979, JBy (c); JBy (a).......... 4.00

❑240, Dec 1979, JBy (c) 4.00

❑241, Jan 1980, FM (c); FM, FS (a); A: Punisher. Human Torch in Hostess ad ("The Icemaster Cometh")............. 8.00

❑242, Feb 1980, FM (c); DP, JSt (a); Mr. Fantastic in Hostess ad ("A Passion for Gold") 4.00

❑243, Mar 1980, GP (c); RB, GP, DP (a); Iron Man in Hostess ad ("The Hungry Battleaxe").. 4.00

❑244, Apr 1980, FM (c); FM, DP (a); Human Torch in Hostess ad ("A Hot Time in the Old Town").. 4.00

❑245, May 1980, FM (c); CI, FM (a); Thor in Hostess ad ("Meets the Ricochet Monster!") 4.00

❑246, Jun 1980, GP (c); GP (a); Spider-Man in Hostess ad ("The Trap") 4.00

❑247, Jul 1980, JBy (c); JBy (w); JBy (a); 1: Machinesmith. Thing in Hostess ad ("Sunday Punch!") 4.00

❑248, Aug 1980, JBy (c); JBy (w); JBy (a); 1: Bernie Rosenthal. Hulk in Hostess ad ("vs. the Roller Disco Devils!") 4.00

❑249, Sep 1980, JBy (c); JBy (w); JBy (a); O: Machinesmith. Captain Marvel in Hostess ad ("Defends the Earth!") 4.00

❑250, Oct 1980, JBy (c); JBy (w); JBy (a); Human Torch in Hostess ad ("Saves the Valley!") 4.00

❑251, Nov 1980, JBy (c); JBy (a); Mr. Fantastic in Hostess ad ("The Power of Gold") 4.00

❑252, Dec 1980, JBy (c); JBy (a); Iron Man in Hostess ad ("vs. The Bank Robbers") 4.00

❑253, Jan 1981, JBy (c); JBy (w); JBy (a); 1: Joe Chapman (becomes Union Jack III). D: Union Jack II (Brian Falsworth). Iron Man in Hostess ad ("vs. The Bank Robbers").. 4.00

❑254, Feb 1981, JBy (c); JBy (w); JBy (a); 1&O: Union Jack III (Joe Chapman). D: Baron Blood. D: Union Jack I (Lord Falsworth). Daredevil in Hostess ad ("vs. Johnny Punk!") 4.00

❑255, Mar 1981, 40th anniversary; FM (c); JBy, FM (a); O: Captain America. 1: Sarah Rogers (Steve's mother). Human Torch in Hostess ad ("Blown About") 4.00

❑256, Apr 1981, JSe (c); GC (a); Spider-Man in Hostess ad ("The Rescue") 2.00

❑257, May 1981, AM (c); A: Hulk. Has Not Brand Ecch reprints; Thing in Hostess ad ("Earthly Delights") 2.00

❑258, Jun 1981, MZ (c); MZ (a) 2.00

❑259, Jul 1981, MZ (c); MZ (a); V: Doctor Octopus. Spider-Man in Hostess ad ("V: The Human Computer") 2.00

❑260, Aug 1981, AM (w); AM (a)........... 2.00

❑261, Sep 1981, MZ (c); MZ (a); A: Avengers. Human Torch in Hostess ad ("Hot-Tempered Heroes!") 2.00

❑262, Oct 1981, MZ (c); MZ (a); Hulk in Hostess ad ("vs. The Phoomie Goonies") 2.00

❑263, Nov 1981, MZ (a); Thing in Hostess ad ("A Lesson to Be Learned"); D&D ad comic #2 .... 2.00

❑264, Dec 1981, MZ (a); A: X-Men. X-Men cameo; Spider-Man in Hostess ad ("Dream Girl") 2.00

❑265, Jan 1982, MZ (a); A: Nick Fury & Spider-Man. Captain Marvel in Hostess ad ("Flea Bargaining") 2.00

❑266, Feb 1982, MZ (a); Daredevil in Hostess ad ("Daredevil's Longest Fight"); D&D ad comic #3 .... 2.00

❑267, Mar 1982, MZ (a); 1: Everyman. Daredevil in Hostess ad ("Daredevil's Longest Fight"); D&D ad comic #4..... 2.00

❑268, Apr 1982, MZ (a); Daredevil in Hostess ad ("Daredevil's Longest Fight") 2.00

❑269, May 1982, MZ (a); 1: Team America. D&D ad comic #5............... 2.00

❑270, Jun 1982, MZ (a); T.M. Maple L.O.C 2.00

❑271, Jul 1982, D&D ad comic #6......... 2.00

❑272, Aug 1982, MZ (a); 1: Vermin. D&D ad comic #7 .... 3.00

❑273, Sep 1982, MZ (a); D&D ad comic #8 2.00

❑274, Oct 1982, MZ (a); D: General Samuel "Happy Sam" Sawyer; V: Baron Strucker; V: Hydra 2.00

❑275, Nov 1982, MZ (a); Bernie Rosenthal learns Cap's identity 2.00

❑276, Dec 1982, MZ (a); 1: Baron Zemo II (Helmut Zemo). Later becomes Citizen V 4.00

❑277, Jan 1983, MZ (a); V: Baron Zemo; V: Primus 2.00

❑278, Feb 1983, MZ (a); V: Baron Zemo; Falcon backup story 2.00

❑279, Mar 1983, MZ (c); MZ (a); V: Primus 2.00

❑280, Apr 1983, MZ (a); V: Scarecrow .. 2.00

❑281, May 1983, MZ (c); MZ (a); A: Jack Monroe. V: Constrictor; V: Viper......... 2.00

❑282, Jun 1983, MZ (c); MZ (a); 1: Joseph Rogers (Steve's father). 1: Nomad II (Jack Monroe). 1: Joseph Rogers (Steve's father); V: Viper; V: Constrictor 3.00

❑282/2nd, Jun 1983, MZ (c); MZ (a); 1: Nomad II (Jack Monroe). silver ink 2.00

❑283, Jul 1983, MZ (a); 2: Nomad (Jack Monroe); V: Viper 2.00

❑284, Aug 1983, MZ (c); SB, MZ (a); A: Patriot (Jeffrey Mace). 3.00

❑285, Sep 1983, MZ (c); SB, MZ (a); D: Patriot (Jeffrey Mace). V: Porcupine 2.00

❑286, Oct 1983, MZ (a); A: Deathlok 3.00

❑287, Nov 1983, MZ (a); A: Deathlok..... 3.00

❑288, Dec 1983, MZ (a); A: Deathlok..... 3.00

Other grades: Multiply price above by 5/6 for VF/NM • 2/3 for VERY FINE • 1/3 for FINE • 1/5 for VERY GOOD • 1/8 for GOOD

Brass (WildStorm)

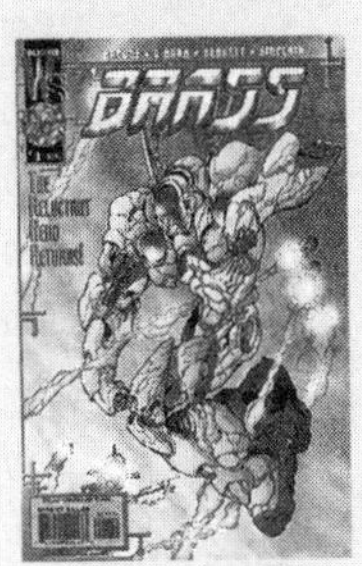

Soldiers prepare for alien invasion

©DC

Brave and the Bold

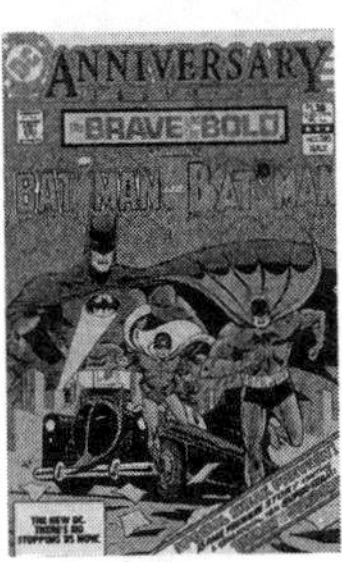

Batman team-ups in the Haney-verse

©DC

Brave and the Bold

Green Arrow, Question team up

©DC

Brave Old World

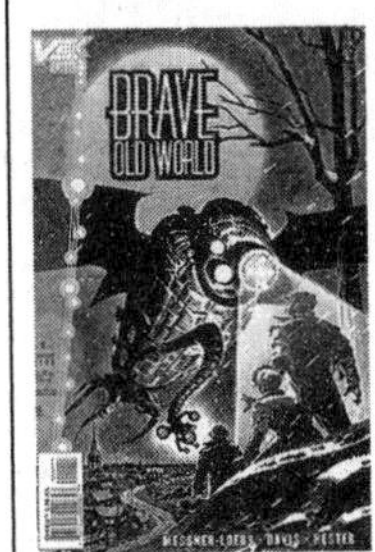

It's "1900 House" for the entire planet

©DC

Brigade

Rob Liefeld published this super-hero team

©Image

	N-MINT
❑289, Jan 1984, MZ (a); A: Bernie America. Assistant Editors' Month	2.00
❑290, Feb 1984, JBy (c); JBy (a); 1: Black Crow (in crow form). A: Mother Night. Zemo	2.00
❑291, Mar 1984, JBy (c); HT (a); 1: Tumbler II	2.00
❑292, Apr 1984, O: Black Crow. 1: Black Crow (in human form)	2.00
❑293, May 1984	2.00
❑294, Jun 1984, V: Slayer	2.00
❑295, Jul 1984	2.00
❑296, Aug 1984	2.00
❑297, Sep 1984, V: Baron Zemo; V: Red Skull	2.00
❑298, Oct 1984, O: Red Skull	3.00
❑299, Nov 1984, O: Red Skull; V: Red Skull	2.00
❑300, Dec 1984, MZ (c); MZ (a); V: Red Skull	2.00
❑301, Jan 1985, MZ (c); O: Captain America	2.00
❑302, Feb 1985, 1: Machete; V: Zaran; T.M. Maple L.O.C	2.00
❑303, Mar 1985, V: Batroc; V: Machete; V: Zaran	2.00
❑304, Apr 1985	2.00
❑305, May 1985, A: Captain Britain. V: Modred	2.00
❑306, Jun 1985, A: Captain Britain. V: Modred	2.00
❑307, Jul 1985, 1: Madcap	2.00
❑308, Aug 1985, JBy (c); JBy (a); Secret Wars II	2.00
❑309, Sep 1985, O: Madcap. V: Madcap. Nomad leaves team	2.00
❑310, Oct 1985, 1: Diamondback. 1: Rattler. 1: Cottonmouth II. 1: Serpent Society. 1: Bushmaster. 1: Asp II (Cleo). 1: Asp II (Cleo); 1: Bushmaster; V: Anaconda; Cobra & Rattler	2.00
❑311, Nov 1985, V: Super-Adaptoid	2.00
❑312, Dec 1985, 1&O: Flag-Smasher	2.00
❑313, Jan 1986, JBy (c); JBy (a); V: Serpent Society	2.00
❑314, Feb 1986, V: Pinball; V: Remnant; V: Mink; Squadron Supreme crossover	2.00
❑315, Mar 1986, D: Porcupine. V: Serpent Society	2.00
❑316, Apr 1986, V: Armadillo	2.00
❑317, May 1986, V: Crossfire and Death-Throws	2.00
❑318, Jun 1986, D: The Blue Streak. D: Death-Adder; V: Scourge	2.00
❑319, Jul 1986, D: Bird-Man II. D: Bird-Man II Achil; D: Steeplejack II; D: Turner D. Century; D: Vamp; D: Cheetah; D: Jaguar; D: Shellshock; D: Cyclone; D: Commander Krakken; D: Letha; D:Hijacker; D: Mirage; D: Mind-Wave; D: Ringer; D:Grappler; D: Hell-Zazor; D: Rapier; D: Firebrand; V: Blacklash; D: Steeplejack (Maxwell Plumm); D: Cheetah (Esteban Carracus); D: Bird-Man (A	2.00
❑320, Aug 1986, V: Scourge	2.00
❑321, Sep 1986, MZ (c); MZ (a); 1: Ultimatum; 1: Flag-Smasher	2.00
❑322, Oct 1986, 1: Super-Patriot; V: Flag-Smasher	2.00
❑323, Nov 1986, MZ (c); MZ (a); 1: Super-Patriot II (later becomes USAgent)	2.00
❑324, Dec 1986, MZ (c); V: Tinkerer; V: Whirlwind; V: Trapster	2.00
❑325, Jan 1987, MZ (c); MZ (a); 1: Slug	2.00
❑326, Feb 1987, MZ (c); MZ (a); V: Dr. Faustus	2.00
❑327, Mar 1987, MZ (c); MZ (a); V: Super-Patriot	2.00
❑328, Apr 1987, MZ (c); MZ (a); O: Demolition-Man. 1: Demolition-Man; 1: Dennis Dunphy as Demolition-Man; V: Dr. Malus	2.00
❑329, May 1987, MZ (a)	2.00
❑330, Jun 1987, MZ (c); MZ (a); A: Demolition-Man. 1: Night Shift	2.00
❑331, Jul 1987, MZ (c); MZ (a); V: Power Broker; V: G.I. Max	2.00
❑332, Aug 1987, MZ (c); MZ (a); Steve Rogers quits as Captain America	3.00
❑333, Sep 1987, MZ (c); MZ (a); 1: Captain America VI (John Walker). John Walker (Super-Patriot II) becomes Captain America	2.00
❑334, Oct 1987, MZ (c); MZ (a); 1: Bucky IV (Lemar Hoskins)	2.00
❑335, Nov 1987, 1: Watchdogs	2.00
❑336, Dec 1987, MZ (c); MZ (a)	2.00
❑337, Jan 1988, MZ (c); MZ (a); 1: Fer-de-Lance. 1: The Captain. 1: Puff Adder	2.00
❑338, Feb 1988, D: Professor Power; V: Leviathan	2.00
❑339, Mar 1988, Fall of Mutants	2.00
❑340, Apr 1988, V: Vibro; V: Griffin; V: Mr. Hyde; V: Armadillo; V: Titania	2.00
❑341, May 1988, 1: Left-Winger. 1: Rock Python (cameo). 1: Battle Star. A: Iron Man. 1: Battle Star; 1: Left-Winger; 1: Rock Python (cameo); 1: Left-Winger and Right-Winger; Cap's ID revealed..	2.00
❑342, Jun 1988, 1: Rock Python (full appearance); V: Serpent Society; 1: Rock Python (M'Gula)	2.00
❑343, Jul 1988, 1: Quill; V: Resistants; V: Viper	2.00
❑344, Aug 1988, Giant-size	2.00
❑345, Sep 1988, D: Captain America's parents	2.00
❑346, Oct 1988, V: Resistants	2.00
❑347, Nov 1988, D: Left-Winger; D: Right-Winger; D: Red Skull II	2.00
❑348, Dec 1988, V: Flag Smasher	2.00
❑349, Jan 1989, D: Demolition Man	2.00
❑350, Feb 1989, Giant-size; The Captain and Super-Patriot fight for title of Captain America	3.00
❑351, Mar 1989, A: Nick Fury. D: Watchdog; D: John Walker	2.00
❑352, Apr 1989, 1: Machete. A: Soviet Super Soldiers	2.00
❑353, May 1989, A: Soviet Super Soldiers	2.00
❑354, Jun 1989, 1: U.S. Agent. A: Fabian Stankowitz. Super-Patriot becomes USAgent	2.00
❑355, Jul 1989, RB (a); V: Serpent Society	2.00
❑356, Aug 1989, AM (a); 1: Mother Night	2.00
❑357, Sep 1989, CBG Fan Awards parody ballot	2.00
❑358, Sep 1989, A: John Jameson. V: Scourge	2.00
❑359, Oct 1989, 1: Crossbones (cameo). 1: Crossbones (cameo); V: Baron Zemo; V: Zaran; V: Batroc; V: Machete; V: Scourge; 1: Crossbones (Brock Rumlow) - cameo	2.00
❑360, Oct 1989, 1: Crossbones (full appearance); V: Baron Zemo; V: Batroc; V: Scourge; 1: Crossbones (Brock Rumlow)	2.00
❑361, Nov 1989, V: Baron Zemo	2.00
❑362, Nov 1989, V: Baron Zemo; V: Batroc; V: Crossbones; V: Scourge	2.00
❑363, Nov 1989, V: Crossbones	2.00
❑364, Dec 1989, V: Crossbones	2.00
❑365, Dec 1989, Acts of Vengeance	2.00
❑366, Jan 1990, Acts of Vengeance	2.00
❑367, Feb 1990, Acts of Vengeance; Red Skull vs. Magneto	2.00
❑368, Mar 1990, O: Machinesmith; V: Magneto robot	2.00
❑369, Apr 1990, 1: Skeleton Crew	2.00
❑370, May 1990	2.00
❑371, Jun 1990, Black Mamba appearanace	2.00
❑372, Jul 1990, D: Boomslang; Streets of Poison	2.00
❑373, Jul 1990, V: Bullseye; Streets of Poison	2.00
❑374, Aug 1990, V: Bullseye; V: Power Tools; Streets of Poison	2.00
❑375, Aug 1990, Cap battles Daredevil; Streets of Poison	2.00
❑376, Sep 1990, V: Crossbones; Streets of Poison	2.00
❑377, Sep 1990, V: Bullseye; Streets of Poison	2.00
❑378, Oct 1990, V: Crossbones; Streets of Poison	2.00
❑379, Nov 1990, O: Nefarius. 1: Nefarius. A: Quasar. V: Nefarius	2.00
❑380, Dec 1990, O: U.S. Agent	2.00
❑381, Jan 1991, O: U.S. Agent; V: Serpent Society	2.00
❑382, Feb 1991, V: Serpent Society	2.00
❑383, Mar 1991, 50th anniversary issue; JLee (c); JLee (a); O: Crossbones; Double-size	3.00
❑384, Apr 1991, A: Jack Frost	2.00
❑385, May 1991, V: Watchdogs; V: Serpent Society	2.00
❑386, Jun 1991, A: U.S. Agent. V: Watchdogs; V: Serpent Society	2.00
❑387, Jul 1991, Red Skull back-up stories	2.00
❑388, Jul 1991, 1: Impala. Red Skull back-up stories	2.00
❑389, Aug 1991, Red Skull back-up stories	2.00
❑390, Aug 1991, V: Superia	2.00
❑391, Sep 1991, V: Superia	2.00
❑392, Sep 1991, V: Superia	2.00
❑393, Oct 1991, V: Red Skull; V: Hauptmann Deutschland; Avengers appear	2.00
❑394, Nov 1991	2.00
❑395, Dec 1991	2.00
❑396, Jan 1992, 1: Jack O'Lantern II; V: Arnim Zola; V: Blackwing	2.00
❑397, Feb 1992, D: Jack O'Lantern; D: Blackwing; V: Jack O'Lantern; V: Blackwing	2.00
❑398, Mar 1992, Galactic Storm	2.00
❑399, Apr 1992, Galactic Storm	2.00
❑400, May 1992, SL (w); JK (a); O: Cutthroat. O: Diamondback. Double-gatefold cover; Galactic Storm; reprints Avengers #4	3.00
❑401, Jun 1992, Operation: Galactic Storm Aftermath	2.00

Other grades: Multiply price above by 5/6 for VF/NM • 2/3 for VERY FINE • 1/3 for FINE • 1/5 for VERY GOOD • 1/8 for GOOD

N-MINT

❑402, Jul 1992, 1: Dredmund Druid. A: Wolverine; V: Crossbones 2.00
❑403, Jul 1992, 2: Dredmund Druid. A: Wolverine; O: Diamondback; V: Moonhunter; Diamonback backup story 2.00
❑404, Aug 1992, A: Wolverine. V: Nightshade; V: Moonhunter............ 2.00
❑405, Aug 1992, A: Wolverine. V: Nightshade; V: Moonhunter............ 2.00
❑406, Sep 1992, A: Wolverine. V: Nightshade; V: Moonhunter; V: Cutthroat 2.00
❑407, Sep 1992, FM (a); A: Wolverine. A: Cable. V: Starwolf............ 2.00
❑408, Oct 1992, D: Cutthroat; Infinity War 2.00
❑409, Nov 1992, V: Red Skull; V: Skeleton Crew 2.00
❑410, Dec 1992, V: Skeleton Crew......... 2.00
❑411, Jan 1993, V: Mad Dog; V: Ramrod 2.00
❑412, Feb 1993, V: General Wo; V: Razorfist; V: Batroc 2.00
❑413, Mar 1993, V: Modam; V: Snapdragon............ 2.00
❑414, Apr 1993, Savage Land............ 2.00
❑415, May 1993............ 2.00
❑416, Jun 1993............ 2.00
❑417, Jul 1993, V: Terminus............ 2.00
❑418, Aug 1993 .... 2.00
❑419, Sep 1993, A: Silver Sable. V: Viper; V: Iron Monger 2.00
❑420, Oct 1993, A: Nomad. A: Blazing Skull. A: Viper. V: Night Shift............ 2.00
❑420/CS, Oct 1993, Includes copy of Dirt Magazine; A: Nomad. A: Blazing Skull. A: Viper. V: Night Shift; Includes copy of Dirt Magazine 3.00
❑421, Nov 1993, A: Nomad............ 2.00
❑422, Dec 1993, V: Blistik............ 2.00
❑423, Jan 1994, V: Namor 2.00
❑424, Feb 1994 .... 2.00
❑425, Mar 1994, Giant-size; V: Super-Patriot II 3.00
❑425/Variant, Mar 1994, Giant-size; Foil-embossed cover 4.00
❑426, Apr 1994............ 2.00
❑427, May 1994, Includes Marvel Masterworks cards............ 2.00
❑428, Jun 1994, 1: Americop; V: Americop............ 2.00
❑429, Jul 1994, 1: Kono the Sumo 2.00
❑430, Aug 1994, V: Damon Dran 2.00
❑431, Sep 1994, 1: Free Spirit; V: Baron Zemo 2.00
❑432, Oct 1994, V: Baron Zemo; Quarterback Club Insert............ 2.00
❑433, Nov 1994, V: Superia; V: Baron Zemo 2.00
❑434, Dec 1994, 1: Jack Flag; V: Mr. Hyde 2.00
❑435, Jan 1995, V: new Cobra; V: Serpent Society; V: Mr. Hyde............ 2.00
❑436, Feb 1995, V: Mr. Hyde; V: Serpent Society 2.00
❑437, Mar 1995, V: Serpent Society 2.00
❑438, Apr 1995, 1: Cap-Armor; V: Flag-Smasher 2.00
❑439, May 1995, V: Death-Stalker. D: Super-Patriot II; V: Dead Ringer..... 2.00
❑440, Jun 1995, V: AIM 2.00
❑441, Jul 1995, V: Super-Adaptoid; V: Red Skull 2.00
❑442, Aug 1995, V: Madcap; V: Everyman 2.00
❑443, Sep 1995, D: Captain America; Captain America Disappears............ 2.00
❑444, Oct 1995, MWa (w); Title changes to Steve Rogers, Captain America; Red Skull brings Cap back to life;Return of Sharon Carter 3.00
❑445, Nov 1995, MWa (w); Return of Sharon Carter; Cap revived............ 2.00
❑446, Dec 1995, MWa (w); A: Red Skull 2.00
❑447, Jan 1996, MWa (w)............ 2.00
❑448, Feb 1996, Giant-size; MWa (w).... 3.00
❑449, Mar 1996, MWa (w)............ 2.00
❑450, Apr 1996, MWa (w); Title returns to Captain America; Cap's American citizenship is revoked 2.00
❑450/A, Apr 1996, MWa (w); alternate cover 2.00
❑451, May 1996, MWa (w); V: Machinesmith............ 2.00
❑452, Jun 1996, MWa (w); V: Machinesmith............ 2.00
❑453, Jul 1996, MWa (w); Cap's citizenship restored 2.00
❑454, Aug 1996, MWa (w); Final Issue.. 2.00
❑Ann 1, ca. 1971, Cover reads "King-Size Special"; Cover reads King Size Special; Reprints from Tales of Suspense #63, 69-71, 75 .... 35.00
❑Ann 2, Jan 1972, Cover reads "King-Size Special"; SL (w); GC, GT, JK (a); Cover reads King Size Special; Reprints from Tales of Suspense #72-74; Not Brand Ecch #3 .... 20.00
❑Ann 3, ca. 1976, JK (c); JK (w); JK (a); ca. 1976 .... 8.00
❑Ann 4, ca. 1977, JK (w); JK (a); 1: Slither. 1: Crucible (Marvel) 8.00
❑Ann 5, ca. 1981, FM (c); GC, FM (a); V: Constrictor............ 3.00
❑Ann 6, ca. 1982, Four Caps............ 3.00
❑Ann 7, ca. 1983, O: Kubik (Cosmic Cube); Cosmic Cube............ 3.00
❑Ann 8, ca. 1986, A: Wolverine............ 12.00
❑Ann 9, ca. 1990, A: Iron Man. V: Terminus; V: Red Skull; Main story continues in Iron Man Ann #11; Nomad story continues in Nomad #1 .... 3.00
❑Ann 10, ca. 1991, DH (a); O: Captain America. O: Bushmaster; 68 pages; Von Strucker Gambit story continues from Punisher Ann #4; ca. 1991 .... 3.00
❑Ann 11, ca. 1992, V: Kang; Nebula; Stone Men from Saturn; Citizen Kang story continued in Thor Ann #17; ca. 1992 . 3.00
❑Ann 12, ca. 1993, 1: Battling Bantam. Polybagged with trading card............ 3.00
❑Ann 13, ca. 1994, V: Red Skull 3.00
❑Ashcan 1, May 1995, ashcan edition; no indicia; Mini "Ashcan" preview............ 1.00
❑Special 1, Feb 1984, Special Edition #1; JSo (c); JSo (w); JSo, JSt (a); reprint of Steranko issues............ 4.00
❑Special 2, Mar 1984, Special Edition #2; JSo (c); JSo, SL (w); TS, JSo, JSt, FS (a); reprint of Steranko issues; Double-gatefold cover 4.00

Captain America
Marvel

❑1, Nov 1996; RL (c); JPH, RL (w); RL (a); Steve Rogers regains memories of WW II action; Captain America jumping forward on cover............ 3.00
❑1/Flag, Nov 1996; RL (c); JPH, RL (w); RL (a); Variant cover (flag background) 4.00
❑1/Conv, Nov 1996; RL (c); JPH, RL (w); RL (a); variant cover............ 25.00
❑2, Dec 1996 RL (c); JPH, RL (w); RL (a); A: Nick Fury, Red Skull 2.00
❑3, Jan 1997; RL (c); JPH, RL (w); RL (a); V: Crossbones. V: Crossbones 2.00
❑4, Feb 1997; RL (c); JPH, RL (w); RL (a); V: Master Man. V: Master Man; V: Red Skull; V: Crossbones 2.00
❑5, Mar 1997; RL (c); JPH, RL (w); RL (a); Green background on cover; Four figures (Cap, Bucky, Nick Fury, one other)......... 2.00
❑6, Apr 1997; RL (c); JPH, RL (w); RL (a); A: Cable. V: Modok; V: Baron Zemo ... 2.00
❑7, May 1997; JLee (c); JRo (w); O: Captain America (Heroes Reborn version); O: Captain America............ 2.00
❑8, Jun 1997; JLee (c); JRo (w); Jim Lee cover; V: Sons of the Serpent; Cap's letter "A" returns to his costume........ 2.00
❑9, Jul 1997; JRo (w); V: Sons of the Serpent............ 2.00
❑10, Aug 1997; gatefold summary; JRo (w); A: Falcon. V: Sons of the Serpent; Gatefold summary 2.00
❑11, Sep 1997; gatefold summary; JRo (w); V: Nick Fury 2.00
❑12, Oct 1997; gatefold summary; JPH (w); cover forms quadtych with Avengers #12, Iron Man #12;and Fantastic Four #12............ 2.00
❑13, Nov 1997; gatefold summary; JRo (w); Crossover with Wildstorm universe 2.00
❑Ashcan 1, Mar 1995; Collector's Preview 1.00
❑Ashcan 1/A; Special Comicon Edition; No cover price; preview of Vol. 2......... 1.00

Captain America
Marvel

❑1, Jan 1998; gatefold summary; follows events in Heroes Return;Cap in Japan; wraparound cover 3.50
❑1/Sunburst, Jan 1998; gatefold summary; alternate cover; follows events in Heroes Return;Cap in Japan 5.00
❑2, Feb 1998; gatefold summary; Cap loses his shield............ 2.50
❑2/Variant, Feb 1998; variant cover 4.00
❑3, Mar 1998; gatefold summary............ 2.00
❑4, Apr 1998; gatefold summary; true identity of Sensational Hydra revealed 2.00
❑5, May 1998; gatefold summary; Cap replaced by Skrull............ 2.00
❑6, Jun 1998; gatefold summary; Skrulls revealed............ 2.00
❑7, Jul 1998; gatefold summary; V: Skrulls 2.00
❑8, Aug 1998; gatefold summary; Cap's shield destroyed;continues in Quicksilver #10 .... 2.00
❑9, Sep 1998; gatefold summary; Cap gets new virtual shield............ 2.00
❑10, Oct 1998; gatefold summary; Nightmare 2.00
❑11, Nov 1998; gatefold summary; V: Nightmare............ 2.00
❑12, Dec 1998; double-sized; wraparound cover 2.00
❑12/Ltd., Dec 1998; V: Nightmare; Signed; Wraparound cover; Gatefold summary; Double-sized 6.00
❑13, Jan 1999; gatefold summary; V: A.I.M 2.00
❑14, Feb 1999; gatefold summary 2.00
❑15, Mar 1999; V: Red Skull; V: Mr. Hyde 2.00
❑16, Apr 1999; V: Red Skull............ 2.00
❑17, May 1999; D: Red Skull 2.00
❑18, Jun 1999; V: Korvac 2.99
❑19, Jul 1999; V: Red Skull............ 2.00
❑20, Aug 1999; Sgt. Fury back-up (b&w) 2.00
❑21, Sep 1999; Sgt. Fury back-up (b&w) 2.00
❑22, Oct 1999; Cap's shield restored 2.00
❑23, Nov 1999; Captain America infiltrates abusive privately run prison 2.00
❑24, Dec 2000; V: Crossbones; V: Absorbing Man............ 2.00
❑25, Jan 2000; Giant-size; O: Captain America; V: Hate Monger 3.00
❑26, Feb 2000; V: Hate Monger 2.25
❑27, Mar 2000; V: Hate Monger............ 2.25
❑28, Apr 2000; 1: Protocide............ 2.25
❑29, May 2000; 2: Protocide; V: Count Nefaria............ 2.25
❑30, Jun 2000; V: Count Nefaria............ 2.25
❑31, Jul 2000............ 2.25
❑32, Aug 2000; World War II story........ 2.25
❑33, Sep 2000 .... 2.25
❑34, Oct 2000; V: Cache 2.25
❑35, Nov 2000; V: Protocide; Continued in Captain America Ann 2000............ 2.25
❑36, Dec 2000; V: Mercurio; Maximum Security............ 2.25
❑37, Jan 2001; V: Protocide............ 2.25
❑38, Feb 2001; V: Protocide............ 2.25
❑39, Mar 2001; V: AIM............ 2.25
❑40, Apr 2001 .... 2.25
❑41, May 2001; V: Batroc; V: Red Skull . 2.25
❑42, Jun 2001; V: Crimson Dynamo...... 2.25
❑43, Jul 2001; V: Crimson Dynamo....... 2.25
❑44, Aug 2001; V: Taskmaster............ 2.25
❑45, Sep 2001; V: Red Skull 2.25
❑46, Oct 2001; V: Red Skull............ 2.25
❑47, Nov 2001; V: Red Skull; V: Hate-Monger............ 2.25
❑48, Dec 2001; V: Red Skull; V: Hate-Monger............ 2.25
❑49, Jan 2002............ 2.25
❑50, Feb 2002; Giant-size; Includes silent story............ 5.95
❑Ann 1998, ca. 1998; wraparound cover 3.50
❑Ann 1999, ca. 1999; V: Flag-Smasher.. 3.50
❑Ann 2000, ca. 2000; continued from Captain America #35............ 3.50
❑Ann 2001, ca. 2001; V: Red Skull 2.99

Captain America
Marvel

❑1, Jun 2002; 48 pages 4.00
❑2, Jul 2002; Call of Duty insert............ 3.00
❑3, Aug 2002............ 3.00
❑4, Sep 2002............ 3.00
❑5, Oct 2002............ 3.00
❑6, Dec 2002............ 3.00
❑7, Feb 2003; Incorrectly labeled as a four part series 3.00
❑8, Mar 2003; Incorrectly labeled as a four part series 3.00
❑9, Apr 2003............ 3.00

Other grades: Multiply price above by 5/6 for VF/NM • 2/3 for VERY FINE • 1/3 for FINE • 1/5 for VERY GOOD • 1/8 for GOOD

Brilliant Boy

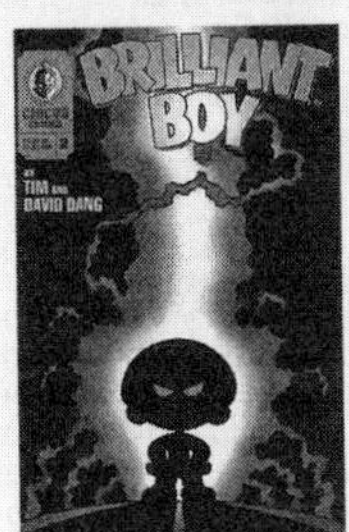

The new kid has some strange habits
©Circus

Brother Power, the Geek

Joe Simon's take on hippie culture
©DC

Brothers of the Spear

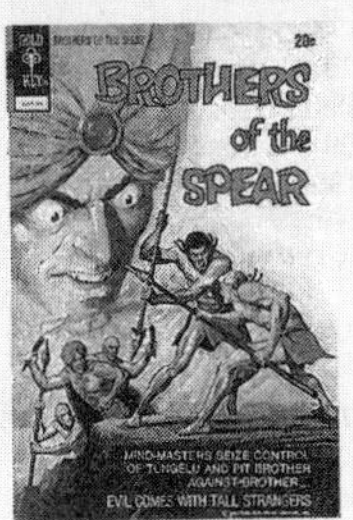

Originally appeared as back-ups in Tarzan
©Gold Key

Bru-Hed

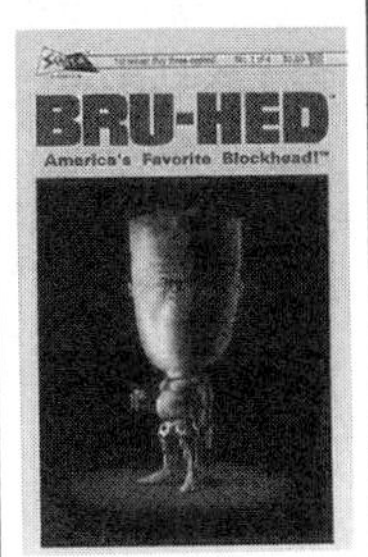

Lovable loser has no tact at all
©Schism

Buckaroo Banzai

Cult-movie adventures adapted for comics
©Marvel

N-MINT

❑10, May 2003; Red Skull, Baron Blood, Baron Zemo, Baron Strucker, Bucky, MODOK, and Sharon Carter appear as hallucinations 3.00
❑11, Jun 2003 3.00
❑12, Jun 2003 3.00
❑13, Jul 2003 3.00
❑14, Aug 2003, Cardstock cover 3.00
❑15, Sep 2003, Cardstock cover 3.00
❑16, Oct 2003, Cardstock cover 3.00
❑17, Nov 2003, DaG (w); JK, JR, TP (a); Title assumed from next issue; Cardstock cover 3.00
❑18, Nov 2003, DaG (w); TP (a); Cardstock cover 3.00
❑19, Dec 2003, DaG (w); TP (a); Cardstock cover 3.00
❑20, Jan 2004, DaG (w); TP (a); Cardstock cover 3.00
❑21, Feb 2004, Marvel Knights branding on cover begins; New cover logo 3.00
❑22, Mar 2004 3.00
❑23, Apr 2004 3.00
❑24, May 2004 3.00
❑25, Jun 2004 3.00
❑26, Jul 2004 2.99
❑27, Aug 2004 2.99
❑28, Aug 2004; Aids Isaiah Bradley from parallel Earth 2.99
❑29, Sep 2004; V: Mr. Hyde; Avengers Disassembled 2.99
❑30, Oct 2004; V: Batroc; V: Red Skull; V: Serpent Society; Avengers Disassembled 2.99
❑31, Nov 2004, V: Serpent Society; V: Red Skull; Avengers Disassembled 2.99
❑32, Dec 2004, V: Red Skull; Avengers Disassembled 2.99

Captain America
Marvel

❑1, Jan 2005, 1: General Lukin; D: Red Skull 8.00
❑2, Feb 2005 5.00
❑3, Mar 2005, D: Nomad 5.00
❑4, Apr 2005; V: Crossbones 2.99
❑5, May 2005 2.99
❑6, Jun 2005; 1: Winter Soldier (Bucky Barnes) 7.00
❑6/Variant, Jun 2005 5.00
❑7, Jul 2005; History of Jack Monroe 2.99
❑8, Aug 2005 5.00
❑9, Sep 2005 2.99
❑10, Oct 2005, House of M tie-in 2.99
❑11, Nov 2005; O:Winter Soldier 2.99
❑12, Jan 2006 2.99
❑13, Feb 2006, V: Winter Soldier 2.99
❑14, Mar 2006 2.99
❑15, May 2006 2.99
❑16, Jun 2006, V: Crossbones; V: Sin 2.99
❑17, Jul 2006, V: Crossbones; V: Sin 2.99
❑19, Sep 2006, V: Master Man 2.99
❑20, Oct 2006 2.99
❑21, Nov 2006, V: Deathbot; V: Master Man 2.99
❑22, Dec 2006, Civil War 5.00
❑23, Jan 2007, Civil War tie-in 5.00
❑24, Feb 2007, Civil War 5.00
❑25, Mar 2007; D: Captain America; D: Captain America (Steve Rogers) 15.00

N-MINT

❑25/Variant, Mar 2007; Cap running on cover 15.00
❑25/2nd, Mar 2007; Cap sprawled on courthouse steps on cover 5.00
❑26, May 2007 3.00
❑27, Jun 2007 3.00
❑28, Jul 2007 3.00
❑29, Aug 2007 3.00
❑30, Sep 2007 3.00
❑31, Oct 2007 3.00
❑32, Nov 2007 3.00
❑33, Dec 2007 3.00
❑34, Jan 2008 6.00
❑35, Feb 2008 5.00
❑36, Mar 2008 3.00
❑37, Apr 2008 3.00
❑38, May 2008 3.00
❑39 3.00
❑40 3.00
❑41 3.00
❑42 3.00
❑43 3.00
❑44 3.00
❑45 3.00
❑46 3.00
❑47 3.00
❑48 3.00
❑49 3.00
❑50 3.00

Captain America and the Campbell Kids
Marvel

❑1, ca. 1980; giveaway; NN 3.00

Captain America & The Falcon
Marvel

❑1, May 2004, 1: Anti-Cap 2.99
❑2, Jun 2004, 2: Anti-Cap 2.99
❑3, Jul 2004, V: Anti-Cap 2.99
❑4, Aug 2004, O: Anti-Cap 2.99
❑5, Sep 2004, Avengers Disassembled 2.99
❑6, Oct 2004, Avengers Disassembled 4.00
❑7, Nov 2004 2.99
❑8, Dec 2004 2.99
❑9, Jan 2005 2.99
❑10, Feb 2005, V: Modok 2.99
❑11, Mar 2005, V: Modok 2.99
❑12, Apr 2005, V: Modok 2.99
❑13, May 2005; V: Anti-Cap 2.99
❑14, Jun 2005; D: Anti-Cap; V: Anti-Cap; Final Issue 2.99

Captain America: Dead Man Running
Marvel

❑1, Mar 2002 2.99
❑2, Apr 2002 2.99
❑3, May 2002 2.99

Captain America: Deathlok Lives!
Marvel

❑1; Reprints from Captain America #286-288 4.95

Captain America: Drug War
Marvel

❑1, Apr 1993 2.00

N-MINT

Captain America Goes to War Against Drugs
Marvel

❑1, ca. 1990; Anti-drug giveaway; PD (w); NN 1.00

Captain America: Medusa Effect
Marvel

❑1, Mar 1994 2.95

Captain America/Nick Fury: Blood Truce
Marvel

❑1, Feb 1995; prestige format one-shot. 5.95

Captain America/Nick Fury: The Otherworld War
Marvel

❑1, Oct 2001 6.95

Captain America: Sentinel of Liberty
Marvel

❑1, Sep 1998; gatefold summary; wraparound cover 1.99
❑1/Variant, Sep 1988; Roughcut edition; Roughcut edition 2.99
❑2, Oct 1998; gatefold summary; Invaders 1.99
❑2/Variant, Oct 1998 1.99
❑3, Nov 1998; gatefold summary; Invaders 1.99
❑4, Dec 1998; gatefold summary; Invaders 1.99
❑5, Jan 1999; gatefold summary; Tales of Suspense tribute 1.99
❑6, Feb 1999; double-sized; Tales of Suspense tribute 2.99
❑7, Mar 1999; Bicentennial story 1.99
❑8, Apr 1999 1.99
❑9, May 1999 1.99
❑10, Jun 1999; V: M.O.D.O.K 1.99
❑11, Jul 1999; V: Human Torch; V: Acrobat 1.99
❑12, Aug 1999; V: Baron Zemo; Final Issue 2.99

Captain Universe/Silver Surfer
Marvel

❑1, Jan 2006, Final part of series 2.99

Captain America 65th Anniversary Special
Marvel

❑1, Jun 2006 3.99

Captain America: The Legend
Marvel

❑1, Sep 1996; background on Cap and his supporting cast; wraparound cover 4.00

Captain America: The Movie Special
Marvel

❑1, May 1992; NN 3.50

Captain America: What Price Glory
Marvel

❑1, May 2003 2.99
❑2, May 2003 2.99
❑3, May 2003 2.99
❑4, May 2003 2.99

Captain Armadillo: The Adventure Begins
Staton Graphics

❑1, ca. 1989, b&w 2.00

N-MINT N-MINT N-MINT

Captain Atom
Charlton

❑78, Dec 1965, SD (c); SD (w); SD (a); O: Captain Atom. Series continued from Strange Suspense Stories #77 .... 40.00
❑79, Mar 1966, SD (c); SD (w); SD (a); 1: Doctor Spectro 25.00
❑80, May 1966, SD (c); SD (w); SD (a).. 25.00
❑81, Jul 1966, SD (c); FMc, SD (w); FMc, SD (a) 25.00
❑82, Sep 1966, SD (c); FMc (w); FMc, SD (a) 25.00
❑83, Nov 1966, SD (c); SD (w); SD (a); 1: Ted Kord (Blue Beetle) 25.00
❑84, Jan 1967, SD (c); SD (w); SD (a); 1: Captain Atom (new) 25.00
❑85, Mar 1967, SD (c); SD (w); SD (a); 1: Punch and Jewelee; "Jewelee" misspelled in story title 25.00
❑86, Jun 1967, SD (c); SD (w); SD (a)... 20.00
❑87, Aug 1967, SD (c); SD (w); SD, JA (a); Nightshade back-up story 20.00
❑88, Oct 1967, FMc, SD (c); SD (w); FMc, SD, JA (a) 20.00
❑89, Dec 1967, FMc, SD (c); SD (w); FMc, SD, JA (a); Final Issue; Nightshade V: Jewelee 20.00

Captain Atom
DC

❑1, Mar 1987; PB (c); PB (a); O: Captain Atom. New costume 1.00
❑2, Apr 1987; V: Plastique 1.00
❑3, May 1987; O: Captain Atom (fake origin) 1.00
❑4, Jun 1987 .... 1.00
❑5, Jul 1987; A: Firestorm. 1: Dr. Spectro (DC) 1.00
❑6, Aug 1987; V: Doctor Spectro 1.00
❑7, Sep 1987 .... 1.00
❑8, Oct 1987 A: Plastique 1.00
❑9, Nov 1987; V: Bolt 1.00
❑10, Dec 1987 .... 1.00
❑11, Jan 1988; A: Firestorm. Millennium 1.00
❑12, Feb 1988; 1: Major Force 1.00
❑13, Mar 1988 .... 1.00
❑14, Apr 1988; V: The Ghost 1.00
❑15, May 1988; V: Major Force; V: Dr. Spectro 1.00
❑16, Jun 1988; A: JLI. V: Red Tornado .. 1.00
❑17, Jul 1988; A: Swamp Thing. V: Red Tornado 1.00
❑18, Aug 1988 .... 1.00
❑19, Sep 1988 .... 1.00
❑20, Oct 1988; A: Blue Beetle. V: Doctor Spectro 1.00
❑21, Nov 1988; V: Plastique 1.00
❑22, Dec 1988; Plastique vs. Nightshade 1.00
❑23, ca. 1988; V: Ghost. no month of publication 1.00
❑24, ca. 1989; Invasion!; no month of publication 1.00
❑25, Jan 1989; Invasion! 1.00
❑26, Feb 1989; O: Captain Atom. A: JLA 1.00
❑27, Mar 1989; PB (a); O: Captain Atom 1.00
❑28, Apr 1989; O: Captain Atom. V: Ghost; V: Bolt 1.00
❑29, May 1989 PB (c) 1.00
❑30, Jun 1989; V: Black Manta; The Janus Directive; Part 11 .... 1.00
❑31, Jul 1989; V: Rocket Red 1.00
❑32, Aug 1989 .... 1.00
❑33, Sep 1989; Batman;new costume 1.00
❑34, Oct 1989; V: Doctor Spectro 1.00
❑35, Nov 1989; A: Major Force. back to old costume 1.00
❑36, Dec 1989; O: Captain Atom; O: Major Force 1.00
❑37, Jan 1990; V: Atomic Skull 1.00
❑38, Feb 1990; V: Black Racer. V: Black Racer 1.00
❑39, Mar 1990 .... 1.00
❑40, Apr 1990; V: Kobra; V: Ghost 1.00
❑41, May 1990; O: Captain Atom 1.00
❑42, Jun 1990 .... 1.00
❑43, Jul 1990; V: Nekron 1.00
❑44, Aug 1990 A: Plastique 1.00
❑45, Sep 1990 .... 1.00
❑46, Oct 1990; Superman 1.00
❑47, Nov 1990 .... 1.00
❑48, Dec 1990 .... 1.00
❑49, Jan 1991; Trial of Plastique 1.00
❑50, Feb 1991; Giant-size; D: Megala; V: Ghost; V: Ironfire; V: Doctor Spectro 2.00
❑51, Mar 1991 .... 1.00
❑52, Apr 1991 .... 1.00
❑53, May 1991 .... 1.00
❑54, Jun 1991; V: Shadowstorm 1.00
❑55, Jul 1991; V: Shadowstorm 1.00
❑56, Aug 1991 .... 1.00
❑57, Sep 1991; V: Shadowstorm; War of the Gods; Part 18; Final Issue 1.00
❑Ann 1, ca. 1988; 1: Major Force. V: Major Force. says 88 on cover, 87 in indicia. 2.00
❑Ann 2, ca. 1989; V: Queen Bee 1.50

Captain Atom: Armageddon
DC

❑1, Dec 2005, Jim Lee cover 2.99
❑2, Jan 2006 .... 2.99
❑3, Feb 2006 .... 2.99
❑4, Mar 2006 .... 2.99
❑5, Apr 2006 .... 2.99
❑6, May 2006 .... 2.99
❑7, Jun 2006, V: Engineer 2.99
❑8, Jul 2006, D: Grifter; V: Midnighter; V: Apollo 2.99
❑9, Aug 2006, D: Apollo; D: Midnighter; D: Jenny Quantum; Void recreates Wildstorm universe; Captain Atom returns to DC universe 2.99

Captain Atom
Modern

❑83, ca. 1977; reprints Charlton series #83 5.00
❑84, ca. 1977; reprints Charlton series #84 5.00
❑85, ca. 1977; SD (c); SD (a); reprints Charlton series #85 .... 5.00

Captain Britain
Marvel UK

❑1, Jan 1985, O: Free-Fall Warriors 2.50
❑2, Feb 1985, b&w; No logo, Gold cover 2.00
❑3, Mar 1985, b&w; No logo, Gold cover 2.00
❑4, Apr 1985, b&w; No logo, Gold cover 2.00
❑5, May 1985, b&w; No logo, Gold cover 2.00
❑6, Jun 1985, b&w; No logo, Gold cover 2.00
❑7, Jul 1985, b&w; No logo, Gold cover 2.00
❑8, Aug 1985, b&w; No logo, Gold cover 2.00
❑9, Sep 1985, b&w; No logo, Gold cover 2.00
❑10, Oct 1985, b&w; No logo, Gold cover 2.00
❑11, Nov 1985, b&w; No logo, Gold cover 2.00
❑12, Dec 1985, b&w; No logo, Gold cover 2.00
❑13, Jan 1986, b&w; No logo, Gold cover 2.00
❑14, Feb 1986 .... 2.00

Captain Canuck
Comely

❑1, Jul 1975 .... 3.00
❑2, ca. 1975, no month of publication ... 2.00
❑3, ca. 1976, no month of publication ... 2.00
❑4, Aug 1979, New publisher 1.50
❑5, Sep 1979 .... 1.50
❑6, Nov 1979 .... 1.50
❑7, Jan 1980 .... 1.50
❑8, Mar 1980 .... 1.50
❑9, May 1980, says Jun on cover; May in indicia 1.50
❑10, Aug 1980 .... 1.50
❑11, Oct 1980 .... 1.50
❑12, Dec 1980 .... 1.50
❑13, Feb 1981 .... 1.50
❑14, Apr 1981 .... 1.50

Captain Canuck First Summer Special
Comely

❑1, Sep 1980 .... 1.50

Captain Canuck Reborn
Semple

❑0, Sep 1993 .... 1.50
❑1, Jan 1994 .... 2.50
❑1/Gold; Gold polybagged edition with trading cards 2.95
❑2, Jul 1994 .... 2.50
❑3, b&w; strip reprints; cardstock cover 2.50

Captain Carrot and His Amazing Zoo Crew
DC

❑1, Mar 1982, RA (c); RA (a); A: Superman. A: Starro 1.50
❑2, Apr 1982, AA (a); A: Superman 1.00
❑3, May 1982 .... 1.00
❑4, Jun 1982 .... 1.00
❑5, Jul 1982, A: Oklahoma Bones 1.00
❑6, Aug 1982, V: Bunny from Beyond. Back-up stories begin 1.00
❑7, Sep 1982, A: Bow-zar the Barbarian 1.00
❑8, Oct 1982, 1: Z-Building (Zoo Crew's Headquarters) 1.00
❑9, Nov 1982, CS (a); A: Terrific Whatzie. A: Three Mouseketeers. Masters of the Universe preview 1.00
❑10, Dec 1982 .... 1.00
❑11, Jan 1983 .... 1.00
❑12, Feb 1983, 1: Little Cheese. 1st Art Adams art (pin-up of Fara Foxette) 1.00
❑13, Mar 1983 .... 1.00
❑14, Apr 1983, Justa Lotta Animals 1.00
❑15, May 1983, JOy (a); Justa Lotta Animals 1.00
❑16, Jun 1983 .... 1.00
❑17, Jul 1983 .... 1.00
❑18, Aug 1983 .... 1.00
❑19, Sep 1983, V: Frogzilla. Superman III movie contest 1.00
❑20, Nov 1983, A: Changeling. V: Gorilla Grodd; Final Issue; Little Cheese joins 1.00

Captain Confederacy (Steeldragon)
Steeldragon

❑1 .... 1.50
❑2 .... 1.50
❑3 .... 1.50
❑4 .... 1.50
❑5 .... 1.50
❑6, Sum 1987 .... 1.50
❑7, Aut 1987 .... 1.75
❑8, Win 1987 .... 1.75
❑9, Spr 1988 .... 1.75
❑10, Jun 1988 .... 1.75
❑11, Jun 1988 .... 1.75
❑12, Oct 1988 .... 1.75
❑Special 1, Sum 1987; O: Captain Confederacy 1.75
❑Special 2, Sum 1987; O: Captain Confederacy 1.75

Captain Confederacy (Epic)
Marvel / Epic

❑1, Nov 1991 .... 2.00
❑2, Dec 1991 .... 2.00
❑3, Jan 1992 .... 2.00
❑4, Feb 1992 .... 2.00

Captain Cosmos, the Last Starveyor
Ybor City

❑1 .... 2.95

Captain Crafty
Conception

❑1, Jun 1994, b&w; wraparound cover.. 2.50
❑2, Win 1994, b&w; wraparound cover . 2.50
❑2.5, Apr 1998 .... 1.00

Captain Crafty Color Spectacular
Conception

❑1, Aug 1996; wraparound cover 2.50
❑2, Dec 1996; wraparound cover 2.50

Captain Crusader
TPI

❑1, Aug 1990 .... 1.25

Captain Cult
Hammac

❑1, b&w; 1: Captain Cult 2.00

Captain Dingleberry
Slave Labor

❑1, Aug 1998 .... 2.95
❑2, Sep 1998 .... 2.95
❑3, Oct 1998 .... 2.95
❑4 1998 .... 2.95
❑5, Jan 1999 .... 2.95
❑6, Feb 1999; Includes sticker 2.95

Captain D's Adventure Magazine
Paragon

❑1, ca. 1983, Promotional comic book for Shoney's Captain D's seafood restaurants in the Southeast 1.00
❑2, ca. 1983 .... 1.00
❑3, ca. 1984 .... 1.00
❑4, ca. 1984 .... 1.00
❑5, ca. 1984 .... 1.00
❑6, ca. 1984 .... 1.00

Captain Eo 3-D
Eclipse

❑1, Aug 1987; oversized (11x17); NN 5.00

Other grades: Multiply price above by 5/6 for VF/NM • 2/3 for VERY FINE • 1/3 for FINE • 1/5 for VERY GOOD • 1/8 for GOOD

Buck Rogers (Gold Key/Whitman)

Series resurfaced following TV show launch

Bucky O'Hare

Kid is trapped in dimension of funny animals

Buffy the Vampire Slayer

Lots and lots of Sarah Michelle Gellar photos

Bugs Bunny (Gold Key)

Wascally wabbit wreaks woe, wegulawly

Bulletproof Monk

Ancient legends meet modern gang wars

Captain Fortune
Rip Off

	N-MINT
❑1	2.95
❑2	3.25
❑3	3.25
❑4	3.25

Captain Glory
Topps

	N-MINT
❑0, Apr 1993; trading card	2.95
❑1, Apr 1993; Includes trading card	2.95

Captain Gravity
Penny-Farthing

	N-MINT
❑1, Dec 1998	2.75
❑2, Jan 1999	2.75
❑3, Feb 1999	2.75
❑4, Mar 1999	2.75

Captain Gravity: One True Hero
Penny-Farthing

	N-MINT
❑1, Aug 1999; One-shot	2.95

Captain Harlock
Eternity

	N-MINT
❑1, b&w; Character created by Leiji Matsumoto	2.50
❑2	2.50
❑3	2.50
❑4	2.50
❑5	2.50
❑6	2.50
❑7	2.50
❑8	2.50
❑9	2.50
❑10	2.50
❑11	2.50
❑12	2.50
❑13	2.50
❑Holiday 1, b&w; prestige format; Christmas Special	2.50

Captain Harlock: Deathshadow Rising
Eternity

	N-MINT
❑1	2.25
❑2	2.25
❑3	2.25
❑4	2.25
❑5	2.25
❑6	2.25

Captain Harlock: The Fall of the Empire
Eternity

	N-MINT
❑1	2.50
❑2, Aug 1992	2.50
❑3; Created by Leiji Matsumoto	2.50
❑4	2.50

Captain Harlock: The Machine People
Eternity

	N-MINT
❑1	2.50
❑2	2.50
❑3	2.50
❑4	2.50

Captain Johner & the Aliens
Valiant

	N-MINT
❑1, May 1995, PS (c); RM (w); PS, RM (a); reprints back-ups from Magnus, Robot Fighter (Gold Key) #1-7; cardstock cover	6.00
❑2, May 1995, PS (c); RM (w); RM (a); reprints back-ups from Magnus, Robot Fighter (Gold Key); cardstock cover	6.00

Captain Justice
Marvel

	N-MINT
❑1, ca. 1988; TV show	1.25
❑2, Apr 1988; TV show	1.25

Captain Marvel
M.F.

	N-MINT
❑1, Apr 1966	40.00
❑2, Jun 1966	25.00
❑3, Sep 1966	25.00
❑4, Nov 1966	25.00

Captain Marvel
Marvel

	N-MINT
❑1, May 1968, GC (c); GC (a); Indicia: Marvel's Space-Born Superhero: Captain Marvel	60.00
❑2, Jun 1968, GC (c); GC (a); A: Sub-Mariner. V: Skrull	18.00
❑3, Jul 1968, GC (c); GC (a); V: Skrull; Guy H. Lillian III L.O.C	18.00
❑4, Aug 1968, GC (a); A: Sub-Mariner. V: Sub-Mariner	24.00
❑5, Sep 1968, GC (c); DH (a); 1: Metazoid; D: Metazoid; O: Metazoid; Peter Sanderson L.O.C	15.00
❑6, Oct 1968, DH (a); 1: Solam; Tony Isabella L.O.C	30.00
❑7, Nov 1968, JR (c); DH (a); V: Quasimodo; Richard Howell L.O.C.	15.00
❑8, Dec 1968, GC (c); DH (a); 1: Aakon (alien race); 1: Cyberex	15.00
❑9, Jan 1969, GC (c); DH (a); 2: Aakon (alien race); 2: Cyberex	25.00
❑10, Feb 1969, DH (a)	15.00
❑11, Mar 1969, D: Una. 1: Zo; D: Una	15.00
❑12, Apr 1969, GK (c);1: Man-Slayer; 2: Zo; Black Widow apperance; Carol Danvers apperance; Black Widow appearance; Carol Danvers appearance	15.00
❑13, May 1969, 2: Man-Slayer; Carol Danvers appearance; 2: Man-Slayer: Carol Danvers appearance	15.00
❑14, Jun 1969, A: Iron Man	15.00
❑15, Aug 1969	15.00
❑16, Sep 1969	25.00
❑17, Oct 1969, GK, DA (c); GK, DA (a); O: Rick Jones retold. new costume; crossover with Captain America #114-116	22.00
❑18, Nov 1969, 1: Mordecai P. Boggs; D: Col. Yon-Rogg	22.00
❑19, Dec 1969, GK, DA (a); series goes on hiatus	22.00
❑20, Jun 1970, GK, DA (c); GK, DA (a); 2: Mordecai P. Boggs; Alan Kupperberg L.O.C	22.00
❑21, Aug 1970, A: Hulk. series goes on hiatus	22.00
❑22, Sep 1972, V: Megaton. Title changes to Captain Marvel after hiatus	22.00
❑23, Nov 1972, V: Megaton	22.00
❑24, Jan 1973	22.00
❑25, Mar 1973, JSn (a); Thanos War begins	25.00
❑26, May 1973, JSn (w); JSn, DC (a); A: Thanos. Thing; Masterlord revealed as Thanos	25.00
❑27, Jul 1973, JSn (w); JSn (a); 1: Death (Marvel). A: Thanos. D: Super Skrull	25.00
❑28, Sep 1973, JSn (w); AM, JSn (a); A: Thanos. Avengers	30.00
❑29, Nov 1973, JSn (w); AM, JSn (a); O: Kronos. A: Thanos. Captain Marvel gets new powers	16.00
❑30, Jan 1974, JSn (w); AM, JSn (a); A: Thanos. V: Controller	12.00
❑31, Mar 1974, JSn (w); JSn, DGr (a); 1: ISAAC. A: Thanos. Avengers	16.00
❑32, May 1974, JSn (w); JSn, DGr (a); O: Moondragon. O: Drax. A: Thanos. Rick Jones vs. Thanos; continued in Avengers #125; Marvel Value Stamp #19: Balder, Hogun, Fandral	12.00
❑33, Jul 1974, JSn (w); JSn, KJ (a); O: Thanos. Thanos War ends; continued from Avengers #125; Marvel Value Stamp #6: Thor	12.00
❑34, Sep 1974, JSn (w); JSn, JAb (a); 1: Nitro; Marvel Value Stamp #25: Torch	6.00
❑35, Nov 1974, AA (a); V: Living Laser. Ant-Man, Wasp; Marvel Value Stamp #1: Spider-Man	3.00
❑36, Jan 1975, AM (c); SL (w); AM, JSn, GC (a); A: Thanos. Watcher; Marvel Value Stamp #25: Torch	3.00
❑37, Mar 1975, GK (c); AM (w); AM (a); Watcher	3.00
❑38, May 1975, AM (w); AM, KJ (a); Trial of the Watcher	5.00
❑39, Jul 1975, AM (w); AM, KJ (a); 1: Aron the Rogue Watcher. Watcher (Uatu)	3.00
❑40, Sep 1975, AM (w); AM (a); Watcher	3.00
❑41, Nov 1975, AM (c); AM (w); AM (a); A: Supreme Intelligence. V: Ronan. Marvel Value Stamp #2: Hulk	3.00
❑42, Jan 1976, AM (w); AM (a); V: Stranger	3.00
❑43, Mar 1976, AM (c); AM (w); AM (a); V: Drax	3.00
❑44, May 1976, AM (w); AM (a); V: Drax	3.00
❑44/30¢, May 1976, AM (w); V: Drax. 30¢ regional price variant	20.00
❑45, Jul 1976, AM (w); AM (a)	3.00
❑45/30¢, Jul 1976, AM (w); AM (a); 30¢ regional price variant	20.00
❑46, Sep 1976, 1: Supremor. 1: Supremor	3.00
❑47, Nov 1976, A: Human Torch. V: Sentry Sinister	3.00
❑48, Jan 1977, 1: Cheetah (Esteban Carracus). V: Cheetah. V: Sentry Sinister	9.00
❑49, Mar 1977, V: Ronan	3.00
❑50, May 1977, AM (a); 1: Doctor Minerva. A: Avengers. A: Adaptoid	10.00
❑51, Jul 1977, V: Mercurio	4.00
❑52, Sep 1977, 35¢ regional price variant	4.00
❑52/35¢, Sep 1977, 35¢ regional price variant	15.00
❑53, Nov 1977	3.00
❑54, Jan 1978, V: Nitro	3.00
❑55, Mar 1978, V: Death-Grip	5.00
❑56, May 1978, GK (c); PB (a); V: Death-Grip	3.00
❑57, Jul 1978, PB (c); PB, BWi (a); A: Thanos. V: Thor. Flashback	6.00
❑58, Sep 1978, V: Drax	3.00
❑59, Nov 1978, 1: Elysius. V: Drax	3.00
❑60, Jan 1979	3.00
❑61, Mar 1979, PB (a)	3.00
❑62, May 1979, Final Issue	3.00

Other grades: Multiply price above by 5/6 for VF/NM • 2/3 for VERY FINE • 1/3 for FINE • 1/5 for VERY GOOD • 1/8 for GOOD

Captain Marvel
Marvel

❑1, Nov 1989; New Captain Marvel (Monica Rambeau) gets her powers back 2.00

Captain Marvel
Marvel

❑1, Feb 1994 2.00

Captain Marvel
Marvel

❑1, Dec 1995; enhanced cardstock cover 2.95
❑2, Jan 1996 1.95
❑3, Feb 1996 1.95
❑4, Mar 1996 1.95
❑5, Apr 1996 1.95
❑6, May 1996 1.95

Captain Marvel
Marvel

❑0, Nov 1999; Wizard promotional edition; Inserted in Wizard: The Comics Magazine #2000 3.00
❑1, Jan 2000; PD (w); Regular cover (space background w/rocks) 3.00
❑1/A, Jan 2000; PD (w); 1: 10 ratio. Variant cover (Marvel against white background) 4.00
❑2, Feb 2000; PD (w); A: Wendigo. A: Moondragon. A: Hulk. D: Lorraine.. 2.50
❑3, Mar 2000 PD (w); A: Wendigo. A: Moondragon. A: Hulk. A: Drax. D: Lorraine 2.50
❑4, Apr 2000 PD (w); A: Moondragon. A: Drax 2.50
❑5, May 2000; PD (w); A: Moondragon. A: Drax. in microverse 2.50
❑6, Jun 2000 PD (w) 2.50
❑7, Jul 2000 2.50
❑8, Aug 2000; V: Super-Skrull 2.50
❑9, Sep 2000; JSn (c); PD (w); A: Super Skrull. A: Silver Surfer. V: Super Skrull 2.50
❑10, Oct 2000 2.50
❑11, Nov 2000 JSn (c); PD (w); JSn (a); A: Moondragon. A: Silver Surfer. A: Mar-Vell 2.50
❑12, Dec 2000; PD (w); Maximum Security 2.50
❑13, Jan 2001 JSn (c); PD (w) 2.50
❑14, Feb 2001; O: Captain Marvel III 2.50
❑15, Mar 2001; PD (w); V: Psycho-Man 2.50
❑16, Apr 2001; PD (w); V: Psycho-Man . 2.50
❑17, May 2001 PD (w); JSn (a); A: Thor 2.50
❑18, Jun 2001 2.50
❑19, Jul 2001 2.50
❑20, Aug 2001 2.50
❑21, Sep 2001; V: Merlin 2.50
❑22, Oct 2001 2.50
❑23, Nov 2001 2.50
❑24, Dec 2001; V: Blastarr 2.50
❑25, Jan 2002; V: Blastarr 2.50
❑26, Feb 2002; 'Nuff Said 2.50
❑27, Mar 2002; Covers of #27-30 form image 2.50
❑29, Apr 2002; Covers of #27-30 form image 2.50
❑28, Mar 2002; Covers of #27-30 form image 2.50
❑30, May 2002; Covers of #27-30 form image 2.50
❑31, Jun 2002; Background on Marlo 2.50
❑32, Jul 2002 2.50
❑33, Aug 2002; V: Magus 2.50
❑34, Sep 2002 2.50
❑35, Oct 2002; Final issue 2.50

Captain Marvel
Marvel

❑1, Nov 2002 2.25
❑2, Dec 2002; Punisher app 2.25
❑3, Jan 2003; New costume debutes 2.25
❑4, Feb 2003; Cover by Phil Noto 2.25
❑5, Mar 2003 2.99
❑6, Apr 2003; Rick Jones convinces Entropy to recreate universe; Entropy becomes Eternity 2.99
❑7, May 2003 2.99
❑8, Jun 2003 2.99
❑9, Jul 2003 2.99
❑10, Jul 2003 2.99
❑11, Aug 2003, Cardstock cover 2.99
❑12, Sep 2003, Cardstock cover 2.99
❑13, Oct 2003, V: Burstaar; Cardstock cover 2.99
❑14, Oct 2003, Cardstock cover 2.99
❑15, Nov 2003, Cardstock cover 2.99
❑16, Jan 2004, 1: Phyla; Cardstock cover 2.99
❑17, Feb 2004, 2: Phyla 2.99
❑18, Mar 2004 2.99
❑19, Apr 2004 2.99
❑20, May 2004 2.99
❑21, May 2004 2.99
❑22, Jun 2004, Moondragon V: Magus . 2.99
❑23, Jul 2004 2.99
❑24, Aug 2004 2.99
❑25, Sep 2004; Final issue 2.99

Captain Nauticus & the Ocean Force
Express / Entity

❑1, May 1994; 1: Captain Nauticus 2.95
❑1/Ltd., Oct 1994; limited promotional edition 2.95
❑2, Dec 1994; for The National Maritime Center Authority 2.95

Captain Nice
Gold Key

❑1, Nov 1967, One-shot 35.00

Captain N: the Game Master
Valiant

❑1, ca. 1990 1.95
❑2, ca. 1990 1.95
❑3, ca. 1990 1.95
❑4, ca. 1990 1.95
❑5, ca. 1990 1.95
❑6, ca. 1990 1.95

Captain Oblivion
Harrier

❑1, Aug 1987 1.95

Captain Paragon
AC

❑1, Dec 1983 1.50
❑2 1.50
❑3 1.50
❑4 1.50

Captain Paragon and the Sentinels of Justice
AC

❑1; O: Commando D; ca. 1985 1.75
❑2; ca. 1985 1.75
❑3; ca. 1985 1.75
❑4; ca. 1985 1.75
❑5; O: Captain Paragon. Title changes to Sentinels of Justice 1.75
❑6 1.75

Captain Phil
Steeldragon

❑1 1.50

Captain Planet and the Planeteers
Marvel

❑1, Oct 1991; TV 1.00
❑2, Nov 1991 1.00
❑3, Dec 1991 1.00
❑4, Jan 1992 1.00
❑5, Feb 1992 1.00
❑6, Mar 1992 1.00
❑7, Apr 1992 1.00
❑8, Jun 1992 1.00
❑9, Jul 1992 1.00
❑10, Aug 1992 1.00
❑11, Sep 1992 1.00
❑12, Oct 1992; Final Issue 1.00

Captain Power and the Soldiers of the Future
Continuity

❑1, Aug 1988; newsstand cover: Captain Power standing 2.00
❑1/Direct ed., Aug 1988; direct-sale cover: Captain Power kneeling 2.00
❑2, Jan 1989 2.00

Captain Salvation
Streetlight

❑1 1.95

Captain Satan
Millennium

❑1; Flip-book format 2.95
❑2; Flip-book format 2.95

Capt. Savage and His Leatherneck Raiders
Marvel

❑1, Jan 1968, O: Captain Savage and his Leatherneck Raiders. A: Sgt. Fury 35.00
❑2, Mar 1968, O: Hydra. V: Baron Strucker 25.00
❑3, May 1968, V: Baron Strucker, Hydra 15.00
❑4, Jul 1968, V: Baron Strucker 15.00
❑5, Aug 1968 15.00
❑6, Sep 1968, A: Izzy Cohen 15.00
❑7, Oct 1968, A: Ben Grimm. Tony Isabella L.O.C 15.00
❑8, Nov 1968, (becomes Captain Savage) 15.00
❑9, Dec 1968, Title changes to Captain Savage (and his Battlefield Raiders) 15.00
❑10, Jan 1969, JSe (c); JSe (a) 15.00
❑11, Feb 1969, A: Sgt. Fury. D: Baker. Story continued in Sgt. Fury #64 15.00
❑12, Mar 1969, DH (c); DH (a) 10.00
❑13, Apr 1969, DH (c); DH (a) 10.00
❑14, May 1969, DH (c); DH (a) 10.00
❑15, Jul 1969, JSe (c); DH (a); Title changes to Capt. Savage 10.00
❑16, Sep 1969, JSe (c); DH, JSe (a) 10.00
❑17, Nov 1969, JSe (c); JSe (a); 1: Gweny Lee 10.00
❑18, Jan 1970, JSe (c); JSe (a); 2: Gweny Lee 10.00
❑19, Mar 1970, JSe (c); JSe (a); Final Issue 10.00

Captain's Jolting Tales
One Shot

❑1, Aug 1991 2.95
❑2, Oct 1991 3.50
❑3; trading card 3.50
❑3/Deluxe, Dec 1992; Signed special collector addition [sic] 3.50
❑4 3.50

Captain Sternn: Running Out of Time
Kitchen Sink

❑1, Sep 1993, b&w; BWr (w); BWr (a) .. 5.50
❑2, Dec 1993, b&w; BWr (w); BWr (a) .. 5.00
❑3, Mar 1994 BWr (w); BWr (a) 5.00
❑4, May 1994 BWr (w); BWr (a) 5.00
❑5, Sep 1994 BWr (w); BWr (a) 5.00

Capt. Storm
DC

❑1, Jun 1964, O: Captain Storm 28.00
❑2, Aug 1964 18.00
❑3, Oct 1964 18.00
❑4, Dec 1964 18.00
❑5, Feb 1965 18.00
❑6, Apr 1965 14.00
❑7, Jun 1965 12.00
❑8, Aug 1965 12.00
❑9, Oct 1965 12.00
❑10, Dec 1965 12.00
❑11, Feb 1966 12.00
❑12, Apr 1966 12.00
❑13, Jun 1966 12.00
❑14, Aug 1966 12.00
❑15, Oct 1966 12.00
❑16, Dec 1966 9.00
❑17, Feb 1967 9.00
❑18, Apr 1967, Final Issue 9.00

Captain Tax Time
Paul Haynes Comics

❑1 4.00

Captain Thunder and Blue Bolt
Hero

❑1 1987, O: Blue Bolt 1.95
❑2, Oct 1987 1.95
❑3 1988, O: Captain Thunder 1.95
❑4 1988 1.95
❑5 1988 1.95
❑6 1.95
❑7 1989 1.95
❑8, 1: King's Gambit 1.95
❑9 1.95
❑10 1.95

Captain Thunder and Blue Bolt
Hero

❑1, Aug 1992 3.50
❑2 3.50

Bullwinkle and Rocky (Gold Key)

"Now here's something you'll really like!"
©Gold Key

Burke's Law

TV police drama spawns comics spinoff
©Dell

Burrito

Humor comic book from Carlos Saldaòa
©Accent!

Butcher

Native American adventure from Mike Baron
©DC

Cadillacs & Dinosaurs

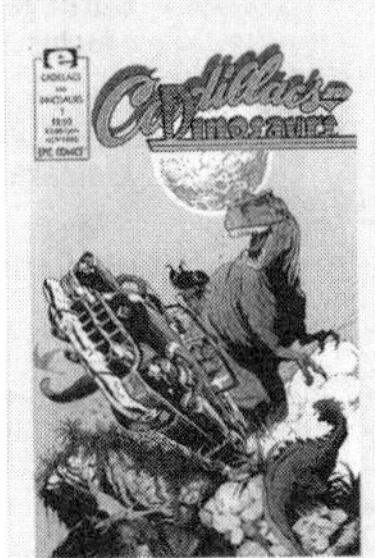

Renamed version of Xenozoic Tales
©Marvel

N-MINT

Captain Universe/Daredevil
Marvel

❑1, Jan 2006, b&w; Story continued in Captain Universe/X-23 #1 ... 2.99

Captain Universe/Invisible Woman
Marvel

❑1, Jan 2006 ... 2.99

Captain Universe/The Incredible Hulk
Marvel

❑1, Jan 2006 ... 2.99

Captain Universe/X-23
Marvel

❑1, Jan 2006, Part 3 of saga ... 2.99

Captain Venture and the Land Beneath the Sea
Gold Key

❑1, Oct 1968 ... 26.00
❑2, Oct 1969, DS (a) ... 18.00

Captain Victory and the Galactic Rangers
Pacific

❑1, Nov 1981; 1: Mr. Mind ... 1.00
❑2, Jan 1982 ... 1.00
❑3, Mar 1982; 1: Ms. Mystic ... 1.00
❑4, May 1982; Goozlebobber ... 1.00
❑5, Jul 1982; Goozlebobber ... 1.00
❑6, Sep 1982; Goozlebobber ... 1.00
❑7, Oct 1982; Martius Klavus ... 1.00
❑8, Dec 1982; Martius Klavus ... 1.00
❑9, Feb 1983; Martius Klavus ... 1.00
❑10, Apr 1983 ... 1.00
❑11, Jun 1983; O: Captain Victory ... 1.00
❑12, Oct 1983 ... 1.00
❑13, Jan 1984; indicia lists title as Captain Victory ... 1.50
❑Special 1, Oct 1983 ... 1.50

Captain Victory and the Galactic Rangers
Jack Kirby

❑1, Jul 2000, b&w; no cover price ... 2.95
❑2, Sep 2000 ... 2.95
❑3, Nov 2000 ... 2.95

Captain Wings Compact Comics
AC

❑1; Reprints ... 3.95
❑2; Reprints ... 3.95

Caravan Kidd
Dark Horse

❑1, Jul 1992 ... 2.50
❑2, Aug 1992 ... 2.50
❑3, Sep 1992 ... 2.50
❑4, Oct 1992 ... 2.50
❑5, Nov 1992 ... 2.50
❑6, Dec 1992 ... 2.50
❑7, Jan 1993 ... 2.50
❑8, Feb 1993 ... 2.50
❑9, Mar 1993 ... 2.50
❑10, Apr 1993 ... 2.50

Caravan Kidd Part 2
Dark Horse

❑1, May 1993 ... 2.50
❑2, Jun 1993 ... 2.50
❑3, Jul 1993 ... 2.95
❑4, Aug 1993 ... 2.50
❑5, Sep 1993 ... 2.50
❑6, Oct 1993 ... 2.50
❑7 ... 2.50
❑8 ... 2.50
❑9, Mar 1994 ... 2.50
❑10, Apr 1994 ... 2.50

Caravan Kidd Part 3
Dark Horse

❑1, May 1994 ... 2.50
❑2, Jun 1994 ... 2.50
❑3, Jul 1994 ... 2.50
❑4, Aug 1994 ... 2.50
❑5, Sep 1994 ... 2.50
❑6, Oct 1994 ... 2.50
❑7, Nov 1994 ... 2.95
❑8, Dec 1994 ... 2.50

Carbon Knight
Lunar

❑1, b&w ... 2.95
❑2, b&w ... 2.95
❑3, ca. 1997, b&w ... 2.95
❑4, ca. 1998, b&w ... 2.95

Cardcaptor Sakura Comic
Mixx

❑1, ca. 2000 ... 2.95
❑2, ca. 2000 ... 2.95
❑3 2000 ... 2.95
❑4 2000 ... 2.95
❑5 2000 ... 2.95
❑6 2000 ... 2.95
❑7 2000 ... 2.95
❑8 2000 ... 2.95
❑9 2000 ... 2.95
❑10 2000 ... 2.95
❑11 2000 ... 2.95
❑12 2000 ... 2.95
❑13, ca. 2001 ... 2.95
❑14 2001 ... 2.95
❑15 2001 ... 2.95
❑16 2001 ... 2.95
❑17 2001 ... 2.95
❑18 2001 ... 2.95
❑19 2001 ... 2.95
❑20 2001 ... 2.95
❑21 2001 ... 2.95
❑22 2001 ... 2.95
❑23 2001 ... 2.95
❑24, Jan 2002 ... 2.95
❑25, Feb 2002 ... 2.95
❑26, Mar 2002 ... 2.95
❑27, Apr 2002 ... 2.95
❑28, May 2002 ... 2.99
❑29, Jun 2002 ... 2.99
❑30, Jul 2002 ... 2.99
❑31, Aug 2002 ... 2.99
❑32, Sep 2002 ... 2.99
❑33, Oct 2002 ... 2.99
❑34, Nov 2002 ... 2.99

Cardcaptor Sakura: Master of the Clow
Tokyopop

❑1, Aug 2002, b&w; printed in Japanese format ... 9.99

Care Bears
Marvel / Star

❑1, Nov 1985 ... 1.00
❑2, Jan 1986 ... 1.00
❑3, Mar 1986 ... 1.00
❑4, May 1986 ... 1.00
❑5, Jul 1986 ... 1.00
❑6, Sep 1986 ... 1.00
❑7, Nov 1986 ... 1.00
❑8, Jan 1987 ... 1.00
❑9, Mar 1987 ... 1.00
❑10, May 1987 ... 1.00
❑11, Jul 1987 ... 1.00
❑12, Sep 1987 ... 1.00
❑13, Nov 1987 A: Madballs ... 1.00
❑14, Jan 1988 ... 1.00
❑15, Mar 1988 ... 1.00
❑16, May 1988 ... 1.00
❑17, Jul 1988 ... 1.00
❑18, Sep 1988 ... 1.00
❑19, Nov 1988 ... 1.00
❑20, Jan 1989; Final Issue ... 1.00

Car 54 Where Are You?
Dell

❑2, Aug 1962 ... 75.00
❑3, Oct 1962 ... 45.00
❑4, Dec 1962 ... 40.00
❑5, Mar 1963 ... 40.00
❑6, Jun 1963 ... 35.00
❑7, Sep 1963 ... 35.00

Carl and Larry Christmas Special
Comics Interview

❑1, b&w ... 2.25

Carmen
NBM

❑1; Adult ... 10.95

Carmilla
Aircel

❑1, Feb 1991, b&w; outer paper wrapper to cover nude cover ... 2.50
❑2, Mar 1991, b&w; Adult ... 2.50
❑3, Apr 1991, b&w; Adult ... 2.50
❑4, b&w; Adult ... 2.50
❑5, b&w; Adult ... 2.50
❑6, b&w; Adult ... 2.50

Carnage
Eternity

❑1 ... 1.95

Carnage: It's a Wonderful Life
Marvel

❑1, Oct 1996 ... 1.95

Carnage: Mindbomb
Marvel

❑1, Feb 1996; foil cover ... 2.95

Carnal Comics Presents Demi's Wild Kingdom Adventure
Revisionary

❑1, Sep 1999, b&w; no cover price ... 3.50

Carnal Comics Presents Ginger Lynn is Torn
Revisionary

❑1, Sep 1999, b&w; Drawn cover ... 3.50
❑1/A, Sep 1999, b&w; adult ... 3.50

Other grades: Multiply price above by 5/6 for VF/NM • 2/3 for VERY FINE • 1/3 for FINE • 1/5 for VERY GOOD • 1/8 for GOOD

Carneys
Archie

❑1, Sum 1994 ... 2.00

Carnosaur Carnage
Atomeka

❑1; ca. 1993 ... 4.95

Cartoon Cartoons
DC

❑1, Mar 2001 ... 2.25
❑2, Apr 2001 ... 2.00
❑3, May 2001 ... 2.00
❑4, Jun 2001 ... 2.00
❑5, Jul 2001 ... 2.00
❑6, Aug 2001 ... 2.00
❑7, Sep 2001 ... 2.00
❑8, Jan 2002 ... 2.00
❑9, Mar 2002 ... 2.00
❑10, May 2002 ... 2.00
❑11, Jun 2002 ... 2.00
❑12, Sep 2002 ... 2.00
❑13, Nov 2002 ... 2.25
❑14, Jan 2003 ... 2.25
❑15, Mar 2003; Space Ghost ... 2.25
❑16, May 2003 ... 2.25
❑17, Jun 2003 ... 2.25
❑18, Jul 2003 ... 2.25
❑19, Jul 2003 ... 2.25
❑20, Aug 2003 ... 2.25
❑21, Sep 2003 ... 2.25
❑22, Oct 2003 ... 2.25
❑23, Nov 2003 ... 2.25
❑24, Dec 2003 ... 2.25
❑25, Jan 2004 ... 2.25
❑26, Feb 2004 ... 2.25
❑27, Apr 2004 ... 2.25
❑28, May 2004 ... 2.25
❑29, Jun 2005 ... 2.25
❑30, Jul 2004 ... 2.25
❑31, Aug 2004 ... 2.25
❑32, Sep 2004 ... 2.25
❑33, Oct 2004 ... 2.25

Cartoon History of the Universe
Rip Off

❑1, b&w; cardstock cover ... 4.50
❑2, b&w; cardstock cover ... 3.50
❑3, b&w; cardstock cover ... 3.50
❑4, b&w; cardstock cover ... 3.50
❑5, b&w; cardstock cover ... 3.50
❑6, b&w; cardstock cover ... 2.50
❑7, b&w; cardstock cover ... 2.50
❑8, b&w ... 2.95
❑9, b&w ... 2.95

Cartoonist
Sirius / Dog Star

❑1, Nov 1997, b&w; collects strips ... 2.95

Cartoon Network
DC

❑1, Giveaway from DC Comics to promote comics; Reprints stories from Cartoon Networks Presents #6 ... 1.00

Cartoon Network Action Pack
DC

❑1, Jul 2006 ... 2.25
❑2, Aug 2006 ... 2.25
❑3, Sep 2006 ... 2.25
❑4, Oct 2006 ... 2.25
❑5, Nov 2006 ... 2.25
❑6, Dec 2006 ... 2.25
❑7, Jan 2007, Includes 3-D Heroscape glasses; Includes Teen Titans: Sparktop mini-comic ... 2.25
❑8, Feb 2007 ... 2.25
❑9, Mar 2007, Includes the Adventures of Finn & Friends insert comic ... 2.25
❑10 ... 2.25
❑11 ... 2.25
❑12 ... 2.25
❑13 ... 2.25
❑14 ... 2.25
❑15 ... 2.25
❑16 ... 2.25
❑17 ... 2.25
❑18 ... 2.25
❑19 ... 2.25
❑20 ... 2.25
❑21 ... 2.25
❑22 ... 2.25
❑23 ... 2.25
❑24 ... 2.25
❑25 ... 2.25
❑26 ... 2.25
❑27 ... 2.25
❑28 ... 2.25
❑29 ... 2.25
❑30 ... 2.25
❑31 ... 2.25
❑32 ... 2.25
❑33 ... 2.25
❑34 ... 2.25
❑35 ... 2.25
❑36 ... 2.25
❑37 ... 2.25
❑38 ... 2.25
❑39 ... 2.25
❑40 ... 2.25

Cartoon Network Block Party
DC

❑1, Dec 2004 ... 2.25
❑2, Jan 2005 ... 2.25
❑3, Feb 2005 ... 2.95
❑4, Mar 2005 ... 2.25
❑5, Apr 2005 ... 2.25
❑6, May 2005 ... 2.25
❑7, Jun 2005 ... 2.25
❑8, Jun 2005 ... 2.25
❑9, Jul 2005 ... 2.25
❑10, Aug 2005 ... 2.25
❑11, Sep 2005 ... 2.25
❑13, Nov 2005 ... 2.25
❑14, Dec 2005; Includes Bionicle preview 2.25
❑15, Jan 2006; Includes Heroscape #4 insert ... 2.25
❑16, Feb 2006 ... 2.25
❑17, Mar 2006 ... 2.25
❑18, May 2006 ... 2.25
❑19, Jun 2006 ... 2.25
❑20, Jul 2006 ... 2.25
❑21, Aug 2006 ... 2.25
❑22, Sep 2006 ... 2.25
❑23, Oct 2006, Includes Heroscape ad insert ... 2.25
❑24, Nov 2006 ... 2.25
❑25, Dec 2006 ... 2.25
❑26, Jan 2007 ... 2.25
❑27, Feb 2007, Includes 3-D Heroscape glasses; Includes Teen Titans: Sparktop mini-comic ... 2.25
❑28, Mar 2007 ... 2.25
❑29 ... 2.50
❑30 ... 2.50
❑31 ... 2.50
❑32 ... 2.50
❑33 ... 2.50
❑34 ... 2.50
❑35 ... 2.50
❑36 ... 2.50
❑37 ... 2.50
❑38 ... 2.50
❑39 ... 2.50
❑40 ... 2.50
❑41 ... 2.50
❑42 ... 2.50
❑43 ... 2.50
❑44 ... 2.50
❑45 ... 2.50
❑46 ... 2.50
❑47 ... 2.50
❑48 ... 2.50
❑49 ... 2.50
❑50 ... 2.50
❑51 ... 2.50
❑52 ... 2.50
❑53 ... 2.50
❑54 ... 2.50
❑55 ... 2.50
❑56 ... 2.50
❑57 ... 2.50

Cartoon Network Christmas Spectacular
Archie

❑1 ... 2.00

Cartoon Network Presents
DC

❑1, Aug 1997; Dexter's Laboratory, Top Cat 2.00
❑2, Sep 1997; Space Ghost, Yogi Bear .. 2.00
❑3, Oct 1997; Hanna-Barbera crossover with Mr. Peebles, Ranger Smith, Officer Dibble, Mr. Twiddle, and Colonel Fusby; Wally Gator back-up;Cartoon All-Stars 2.00
❑4, Nov 1997; Dial M for Monkey ... 2.00
❑5, Dec 1997; A: Birdman, Herculoids. Toonami ... 2.00
❑6, Jan 1998; Cow and Chicken ... 2.00
❑7, Feb 1998; Wacky Races ... 2.00
❑8, Mar 1998; Fighting Monkies; Johnny Bravo ... 2.00
❑9, Apr 1998; A: Herculoids, Birdman. Toonami ... 2.00
❑10, May 1998; Cow & Chicken ... 2.00
❑11, Jun 1998; Wacky Races ... 2.00
❑12, Aug 1998; Cartoon All-Stars; Peter Potamus ... 2.00
❑13, Sep 1998; Toonami, Birdman, Herculoids ... 2.00
❑14, Oct 1998; Cow and Chicken ... 2.00
❑15, Nov 1998; Wacky Races ... 1.99
❑16, Dec 1998; Cartoon All-Stars;Top Cat 1.99
❑17, Jan 1999; Toonami, Herculoids, Galaxy Trio ... 1.99
❑18, Feb 1999; Cartoon All-Stars; Funtastic Treasure Hunt ... 1.99
❑19, Mar 1999; Cow and Chicken ... 1.99
❑20, Apr 1999; Cartoon All-Stars; Hong Kong Phooey, Atom Ant, Secret Squirrel 1.99
❑21, May 1999; Toonami, Blue Falcon and Dyno-Mutt, Galtar and the Golden Lance 1.99
❑22, Jun 1999; A: Yogi Bear. A: Quick Draw McGraw. A: Magilla Gorilla. A: Boo Boo Bear. A: El Kabonng. A: Ranger Jones. A: Ranger Smith. Cartoon All-Stars; Baba Looey ... 1.99
❑23, Jul 1999; Jabberjaw, Speed Buggy, Captain Caveman; Jabberjaw; Speed Buggy; Captain Caveman ... 1.99
❑24, Aug 1999; Scrappy-Doo ... 1.99

Cartoon Network Presents Space Ghost
Archie

❑1, Mar 1997 ... 2.00

Cartoon Network Starring
DC

❑1, Sep 1999; The Powerpuff Girls ... 3.00
❑2, Oct 1999; 1: Johnny Bravo (in comics) 3.00
❑3, Nov 1999 ... 2.00
❑4, Dec 1999; Space Ghost ... 2.00
❑5, Jan 2000; The Powerpuff Girls ... 2.00
❑6, Feb 2000 ... 2.00
❑7, Mar 2000 ... 2.00
❑8, Apr 2000 ... 2.00
❑9, May 2000; Space Ghost ... 2.00
❑10, Jun 2000 ... 2.00
❑11, Jul 2000 ... 2.00
❑12, Aug 2000 ... 2.00
❑13, Sep 2000 ... 2.00
❑14, Oct 2000; Johnny Bravo ... 2.00
❑15, Nov 2000; Space Ghost ... 2.00
❑16, Dec 2000; Cow and Chicken ... 2.00
❑17, Jan 2001; Johnny Bravo ... 2.00
❑18, Feb 2001; Space Ghost ... 2.00

Cartoon Quarterly
Gladstone

❑1; Mickey Mouse ... 5.00

Cartoon Tales (Disney's...)
Disney

❑1, ca. 1992 ... 2.95
❑2, ca. 1992; 21809; Darkwing Duck ... 2.95
❑3, ca. 1992; 21810;Tale Spin: Surprise in the Skies; Reprints stories from Disney's Tale Spin #4, 6 ... 2.95
❑4; Beauty and the Beast ... 2.95

Cartune Land
Magic Carpet

❑1, b&w ... 1.50
❑2, Jul 1987, b&w ... 1.50

Carvers
Image

❑1, Oct 1998 ... 2.95
❑2, Nov 1998 ... 2.95
❑3, Dec 1998 ... 2.95

Other grades: Multiply price above by 5/6 for VF/NM • 2/3 for VERY FINE • 1/3 for FINE • 1/5 for VERY GOOD • 1/8 for GOOD

Cage

Power Man becomes a not-very-nice guy
©Marvel

Cage

A not-very-nice guy gets worse in "mature" title
©Marvel

Caliber Presents

Series had early appearance of The Crow
©Caliber

California Raisins in 3-D

This fad was left out in the sun too long
©Blackthorne

Camelot 3000

Even Merlin couldn't keep it from shipping late
©DC

N-MINT

Car Warriors
Marvel / Epic

❑1, Jun 1991 ... 2.25
❑2, Jul 1991 ... 2.25
❑3, Aug 1991 ... 2.25
❑4, Sep 1991 ... 2.25

Casa Howhard
NBM

❑1; Adult; ca. 2001 ... 10.95

Casanova
Aircel

❑1, b&w ... 2.50
❑2, b&w ... 2.50
❑3, b&w ... 2.50
❑4, Oct 2006, b&w; Adult ... 2.50
❑5, b&w ... 2.50
❑6, b&w ... 2.50
❑7, b&w; Adult ... 2.50
❑8, b&w; Adult ... 2.50
❑9, Nov 1991, b&w; Adult ... 2.95
❑10, Dec 1991, b&w; Adult ... 2.95

Casanova
Image

❑1, Jul 2006, Adult; b&w ... 2.50
❑2, Jul 2006; Adult; b&w ... 2.50
❑3, Sep 2006, Adult; b&w ... 2.50
❑4, Oct 2006 ... 1.99
❑5, Nov 2006; Adult; b&w ... 2.50
❑6, Nov 2006, b&w; Adult ... 2.50

Casefiles: Sam & Twitch
Image

❑1, Jun 2003 ... 2.50
❑2, Aug 2003 ... 2.50
❑3, Sep 2003 ... 2.50
❑4, Oct 2003 ... 2.50
❑5, Nov 2003 ... 2.50
❑6, Dec 2003 ... 2.50
❑7, Mar 2004 ... 2.50
❑8, Apr 2004 ... 2.50
❑9, ca. 2004 ... 2.50
❑10, ca. 2004 ... 2.50
❑11, Dec 2004 ... 2.50
❑12, Jan 2005 ... 2.50
❑13, Feb 2005 ... 2.95
❑14, ca. 2005 ... 2.50
❑15, May 2005 ... 2.50
❑16, Jun 2005 ... 2.50
❑17, Jul 2005 ... 2.50
❑18, Aug 2005 ... 2.50
❑19 2005 ... 2.50
❑20, Dec 2005 ... 2.50
❑21, Jan 2006 ... 2.50
❑22, Mar 2006 ... 2.95
❑23, May 2006 ... 2.95
❑24, Jun 2006 ... 2.95
❑25, Jul 2006 ... 2.95

Case Morgan, Gumshoe Private Eye
Forbidden Fruit

❑1, Apr 1991, b&w; Adult ... 2.95
❑2, May 1991, b&w; All reprints from Gent; Adult ... 2.95
❑3, b&w; Adult ... 2.95
❑4, Jul 1991, b&w; All reprints from Gent; Adult ... 2.95
❑5, Aug 1991, b&w; Reprints from Gent + new story; Adult ... 2.95
❑6, Oct 1991, b&w; Reprints from Gent + new material; Adult ... 2.95
❑7, b&w; Reprints from Gent + new material; Adult ... 2.95
❑8, b&w; Adult ... 2.95
❑9, b&w; Adult ... 2.95
❑10, b&w; Adult ... 2.95
❑11, b&w; Adult ... 3.50

Case of Blind Fear, A
Eternity

❑1, Jan 1989, b&w; Sherlock Holmes, Invisible Man ... 1.95
❑2, Apr 1989, b&w; Sherlock Holmes, Invisible Man ... 1.95
❑3, b&w; Sherlock Holmes, Invisible Man ... 1.95
❑4, b&w; Sherlock Holmes, Invisible Man ... 1.95

Cases of Sherlock Holmes
Renegade

❑1, May 1986, b&w; Renegade publishes ... 2.00
❑2, Jul 1986, b&w ... 2.00
❑3, Sep 1986 ... 2.00
❑4, Nov 1986 ... 2.00
❑5, Jan 1987 ... 2.00
❑6, Mar 1987 ... 2.00
❑7, May 1987 ... 2.00
❑8, Jul 1987 ... 2.00
❑9, Sep 1987 ... 2.00
❑10, Nov 1987 ... 2.00
❑11, Jan 1988 ... 2.00
❑12, Mar 1988 ... 2.00
❑13, May 1988 ... 2.00
❑14, Jul 1988 ... 2.00
❑15, Sep 1988 ... 2.00
❑16, Nov 1988, b&w; Northstar begins as publisher ... 2.25
❑17, Jan 1989, b&w ... 2.25
❑18, Mar 1989, b&w ... 2.25
❑19, May 1989 ... 2.25
❑20, Jul 1989 ... 2.25
❑21, Sep 1989 ... 2.25
❑22, Nov 1989 ... 2.25
❑23, Jan 1990 ... 2.25
❑24, Mar 1990 ... 2.25

Casey Jones & Raphael
Mirage

❑1, Oct 1994 ... 2.75

Casey Jones: North By Downeast
Mirage

❑1, May 1994 ... 2.75
❑2, Jul 1994; Final Issue ... 2.75

Casper Adventure Digest
Harvey

❑1, Oct 1992 ... 2.00
❑2, Dec 1992 ... 1.75
❑3, Jan 1993 ... 1.75
❑4, Apr 1993 ... 1.75
❑5, Jul 1993 ... 1.75
❑6, Oct 1993 ... 1.75
❑7 ... 1.75
❑8 ... 1.75

Casper and Friends
Harvey

❑1, ca. 1991 ... 1.50
❑2, ca. 1991 ... 1.50
❑3, ca. 1992 ... 1.50
❑4, ca. 1992 ... 1.50
❑5, ca. 1992 ... 1.50

Casper and Friends Magazine
Marvel

❑1, Mar 1997, magazine ... 3.99
❑2, May 1997, magazine ... 3.99
❑3, Jul 1997, magazine ... 3.99

Casper and Nightmare
Harvey

❑6, Nov 1964; was Nightmare & Casper ... 35.00
❑7, Feb 1965 ... 24.00
❑8, May 1965 ... 24.00
❑9, Aug 1965 ... 24.00
❑10, Nov 1965 ... 24.00
❑11, Feb 1966 ... 16.00
❑12, May 1966 ... 16.00
❑13, Aug 1966 ... 16.00
❑14, Oct 1966 ... 16.00
❑15, Dec 1966 ... 16.00
❑16, Feb 1967 ... 16.00
❑17, May 1967 ... 16.00
❑18, Aug 1967 ... 16.00
❑19, ca. 1968 ... 16.00
❑20, ca. 1968 ... 16.00
❑21, ca. 1968 ... 14.00
❑22, ca. 1968 ... 14.00
❑23, Apr 1969 ... 14.00
❑24, ca. 1969 ... 14.00
❑25, ca. 1969; Giant-Size ... 14.00
❑26, ca. 1969; Giant-Size ... 14.00
❑27, ca. 1970; Giant-Size ... 14.00
❑28, ca. 1970 ... 14.00
❑29, Sep 1970 ... 14.00
❑30, ca. 1970 ... 14.00
❑31, ca. 1971 ... 14.00
❑32, ca. 1971 ... 14.00
❑33, ca. 1971 ... 14.00
❑34, Nov 1971 ... 14.00
❑35, Feb 1972; Spooky apearance ... 14.00
❑36, May 1972 ... 10.00
❑37, Aug 1972 ... 10.00
❑38, Nov 1972 ... 10.00
❑39, ca. 1973 ... 10.00
❑40, ca. 1973 ... 10.00
❑41, ca. 1973 ... 10.00
❑42, Jun 1973 ... 10.00
❑43, Aug 1973 ... 10.00
❑44, Oct 1973 ... 10.00
❑45, Jun 1974 ... 10.00
❑46, Aug 1974 ... 10.00

Casper and the Ghostly Trio
Harvey

❑1, Nov 1972 ... 20.00
❑2, Jan 1973 ... 15.00
❑3, Mar 1973 ... 15.00
❑4, May 1973 ... 15.00
❑5, Jul 1973 ... 12.00
❑6, Sep 1973 ... 12.00
❑7, Nov 1973 ... 12.00
❑8, Aug 1990 ... 1.50
❑9, Oct 1990 ... 1.50
❑10, Dec 1990 ... 1.50

Other grades: Multiply price above by 5/6 for VF/NM • 2/3 for VERY FINE • 1/3 for FINE • 1/5 for VERY GOOD • 1/8 for GOOD

Casper & Wendy
Harvey

❑1, Sep 1972, Alice in Wonderland 9.00
❑2, Nov 1972 .... 5.00
❑3, Jan 1973 .... 4.00
❑4, Mar 1973 .... 4.00
❑5, May 1973 .... 4.00
❑6, Jul 1973 .... 3.00
❑7, Sep 1973 .... 3.00
❑8, Nov 1973 .... 3.00

Casper Digest Magazine
Harvey

❑1, Oct 1986 .... 2.50
❑2, Dec 1986 .... 2.00
❑3, Feb 1987 .... 2.00
❑4, Apr 1987 .... 2.00
❑9, Sep 1989 .... 2.00
❑10, Feb 1990, Casper Thanksgiving Parade Special on cover 2.00
❑11, May 1990 .... 2.00
❑12, Jul 1990 .... 2.00
❑13, Aug 1990 .... 2.00

Casper Digest Magazine
Harvey

❑1, Sep 1991 .... 2.00
❑2, Jan 1992, Nightmare apearance; Indicia indicates issue #5 .... 1.75
❑3, Apr 1992 .... 1.75
❑4, Jul 1992, indicia says Casper Digest 1.75
❑5, Nov 1992 .... 1.75
❑6, Feb 1993 .... 1.75
❑7, May 1993 .... 1.75
❑8, Aug 1993 .... 1.75
❑9, Nov 1993 .... 1.75
❑10, Feb 1994 .... 1.75
❑11, May 1994 .... 1.75
❑12, Jul 1994 .... 1.75
❑13, Aug 1994 .... 1.75
❑14, Nov 1994 .... 1.75

Casper Enchanted Tales Digest
Harvey

❑1, May 1992 .... 2.00
❑2, Sep 1992 .... 1.75
❑3, Mar 1993 .... 1.75
❑4, Jun 1993 .... 1.75
❑5, Sep 1993 .... 1.75
❑6, Dec 1993 .... 1.75
❑7, Mar 1994 .... 1.75
❑8, Jun 1994 .... 1.75
❑9, Aug 1994 .... 1.75
❑10, Oct 1994 .... 1.75

Casper Ghostland
Harvey

❑1, ca. 1992 .... 1.50

Casper Giant Size
Harvey

❑1 .... 2.25
❑2 .... 2.25
❑3 .... 2.25
❑4 .... 2.25

Casper in 3-D
Blackthorne

❑1, Win 1988; Blackthorne 3-D Series #57 2.50

Casper's Ghostland
Harvey

❑1, Win 1958 .... 175.00
❑2, Spr 1959 .... 75.00
❑3, Sum 1959 .... 50.00
❑4, Fal 1959 .... 50.00
❑5, Apr 1960 .... 50.00
❑6, Jul 1960 .... 40.00
❑7, Oct 1960 .... 40.00
❑8, Jan 1961, Halloween cover 40.00
❑9, Apr 1961 .... 40.00
❑10, Jul 1961 .... 40.00
❑11, Oct 1961 .... 25.00
❑12, Jan 1962 .... 25.00
❑13, Apr 1962 .... 25.00
❑14, Jul 1962 .... 25.00
❑15, Oct 1962 .... 25.00
❑16, Jan 1963, Halloween cover 25.00
❑17, Apr 1963 .... 25.00
❑18, Jul 1963 .... 25.00
❑19, Oct 1963 .... 25.00
❑20, Jan 1964 .... 25.00
❑21, Apr 1964 .... 20.00
❑22, Jul 1964 .... 20.00
❑23, Oct 1964 .... 20.00
❑24, Jan 1965 .... 20.00
❑25, Apr 1965 .... 20.00
❑26, Jul 1965 .... 20.00
❑27, Oct 1965 .... 20.00
❑28, Jan 1966 .... 20.00
❑29, Apr 1966 .... 20.00
❑30, Jun 1966 .... 20.00
❑31, Aug 1966 .... 15.00
❑32, Oct 1966 .... 15.00
❑33, Dec 1966 .... 15.00
❑34, Feb 1967 .... 15.00
❑35, Apr 1967 .... 15.00
❑36, Jun 1967 .... 15.00
❑37, Aug 1967 .... 15.00
❑38, Oct 1967 .... 15.00
❑39, Dec 1967 .... 15.00
❑40, Feb 1968 .... 15.00
❑41, Apr 1968 .... 10.00
❑42, Jun 1968 .... 10.00
❑43, Aug 1968 .... 10.00
❑44, Oct 1968 .... 10.00
❑45, Dec 1968 .... 10.00
❑46, Jan 1969 .... 10.00
❑47, Mar 1969 .... 10.00
❑48, May 1969 .... 10.00
❑49, Jul 1969 .... 10.00
❑50, Sep 1969 .... 10.00
❑51, Nov 1969 .... 10.00
❑52, Jan 1970, Wendy appearance 10.00
❑53, Mar 1970, Wendy appearance 10.00
❑54, May 1970, Wendy appearance 10.00
❑55, Jul 1970 .... 10.00
❑56, Sep 1970 .... 10.00
❑57, Nov 1970 .... 10.00
❑58, Jan 1971 .... 10.00
❑59, Mar 1971 .... 10.00
❑60, May 1971 .... 10.00
❑61, Jul 1971 .... 5.00
❑62, Sep 1971 .... 5.00
❑63, Nov 1971 .... 5.00
❑64, Jan 1972 .... 5.00
❑65, Mar 1972 .... 5.00
❑66, May 1972 .... 5.00
❑67, Jul 1972 .... 5.00
❑68, Sep 1972 .... 5.00
❑69, Nov 1972 .... 5.00
❑70, Jan 1973 .... 5.00
❑71, Mar 1973 .... 5.00
❑72, May 1973 .... 5.00
❑73, Jul 1973 .... 5.00
❑74, Sep 1973 .... 5.00
❑75, Nov 1973 .... 5.00
❑76, Jan 1974 .... 5.00
❑77, Mar 1974 .... 5.00
❑78, May 1974 .... 5.00
❑79, Jul 1974 .... 5.00
❑80, Sep 1974 .... 5.00
❑81, Nov 1974 .... 5.00
❑82, Jan 1975 .... 4.00
❑83, Mar 1975 .... 4.00
❑84, May 1975 .... 4.00
❑85, Jul 1975 .... 4.00
❑86, Sep 1975 .... 4.00
❑87, Nov 1975 .... 4.00
❑88, Feb 1976 .... 4.00
❑89, Apr 1976 .... 4.00
❑90, Jun 1976 .... 4.00
❑91, Aug 1976 .... 4.00
❑92, Oct 1976 .... 4.00
❑93, Dec 1976 .... 4.00
❑94, Feb 1977, Richie Rich in Hostess Ad ("Aunt Chatter Bucks") 4.00
❑95, May 1977 .... 4.00
❑96, Jul 1977 .... 4.00
❑97, Dec 1977 .... 4.00
❑98, Dec 1978 .... 4.00

Casper Space Ship
Harvey

❑1, Aug 1972 .... 16.00
❑2, Oct 1972 .... 13.00
❑3, Dec 1972 .... 13.00
❑4, Feb 1973 .... 10.00
❑5, Apr 1973 .... 10.00

Casper The Friendly Ghost
Harvey

❑254, Jul 1990; was Friendly Ghost, Casper, The 2.00
❑255, Aug 1990 .... 2.00
❑256, Sep 1990 .... 2.00
❑257, Oct 1990 .... 2.00
❑258, Nov 1990 .... 2.00
❑259, Dec 1990 .... 2.00
❑260, Jan 1991 .... 2.00

Casper the Friendly Ghost
Harvey

❑1, Mar 1991 .... 2.00
❑2, May 1991 .... 1.50
❑3, Jul 1991 .... 1.50
❑4, Sep 1991 .... 1.50
❑5, Nov 1991 .... 1.50
❑6, Jan 1992 .... 1.50
❑7, Mar 1992 .... 1.50
❑8, Jun 1992 .... 1.50
❑9, Sep 1992 .... 1.50
❑10 1992 .... 1.50
❑11, Dec 1992 .... 1.50
❑12, Apr 1993 .... 1.50
❑13 1993 .... 1.50
❑14, Sep 1993 .... 1.50
❑15, Oct 1993 .... 1.50
❑16, Nov 1993 .... 1.50
❑17, Dec 1993 .... 1.50
❑18, Jan 1994 .... 1.50
❑19, Feb 1994 .... 1.50
❑20, Mar 1994 .... 1.50
❑21, Apr 1994 .... 1.50
❑22, May 1994 .... 1.50
❑23, Jun 1994, Wendy appearance 1.50
❑24, Jul 1994 .... 1.50
❑25, Aug 1994 .... 1.50
❑26, Sep 1994 .... 1.50
❑27, Oct 1994 .... 1.50
❑28, Nov 1994, (c) 1.50
❑GS 1, Oct 1992 .... 2.25
❑GS 2, Mar 1993, Christmas Cover 2.25
❑GS 3, Jun 1993 .... 2.25
❑GS 4, Nov 1993 .... 2.25

Casper The Friendly Ghost Big Book
Harvey

❑1, Aug 1992 .... 2.00
❑2, Jan 1993 .... 2.00
❑3, May 1993 .... 2.00

Cast
Nautilus Comics

❑1 2005 .... 2.99
❑2, Sep 2005 .... 2.99

Castlevania: The Belmont Legacy
Idea & Design Works

❑1, ca. 2005 .... 3.99
❑2, ca. 2005 .... 3.99
❑3, May 2005 .... 3.99
❑4, Jun 2005 .... 3.99
❑5, Sep 2005 .... 3.99

Castle Waiting
Olio

❑1, b&w 4.50
❑1/2nd; 2nd printing 3.50
❑1/3rd; 3rd printing 3.50
❑2, b&w 3.00
❑2/2nd; 2nd printing 3.00
❑3, ca. 1997, b&w; Akiko pin-up 3.00
❑3/2nd; 2nd printing 3.00
❑4, b&w; Scott Roberts pin-up 3.00
❑4/2nd; 2nd printing 3.00
❑5, Mar 1998, b&w 3.00
❑5/2nd; 2nd printing 3.00
❑6, May 1998, b&w; profiles of 12 Witches begins 3.00
❑7, Oct 1998, b&w; Series moves to Cartoon Books, where there are four issues; returns to Olio for #12 .... 3.00
❑12, ca. 2001, b&w; Also known as Vol. 2 #5 after the Cartoon Books numbering 3.00
❑13, ca. 2001; Also known as Vol. 2 #6 after the Cartoon Books numbering ... 3.00
❑14, ca. 2002; Also known as Vol. 2 #7 after the Cartoon Books numbering ... 3.00
❑15, ca. 2002 .... 3.00
❑16, ca. 2003 .... 3.00

Camp Candy

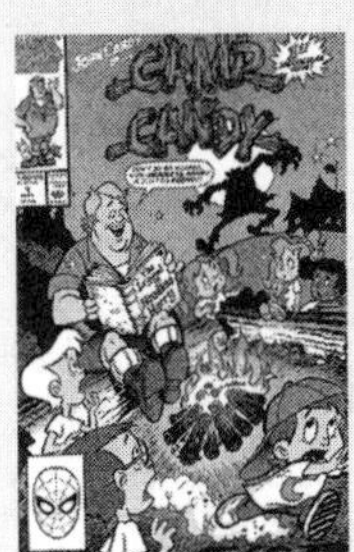

Humor title based on John Candy cartoon
©Marvel

Cap'n Quick & a Foozle

Lighthearted fare from Marshall Rogers
©Eclipse

Captain Action

Early toy tie-in from 1960s
©DC

Captain America

Title picked up from Tales of Suspense
©Marvel

Captain America

Liefeld rewrote Cap's Origin for restart
©Marvel

N-MINT

❑Ashcan 1, Jan 1999; Limited ashcan edition given away (20 printed); Hiatus issue 10.00

Castle Waiting
Cartoon Books

❑1, Jul 2000, b&w; follows events of Olio series; also considered #8 in the Olio numbering 3.00
❑2, Oct 2000; follows events of Olio series; also considered #9 in the Olio numberingfollows events of Olio series; also considered #8 in the Olio numbering 3.00
❑3, Dec 2000; follows events of Olio series; also considered #10 in the Olio numbering 3.00
❑4, Mar 2001; follows events of Olio series; also considered #11 in the Olio numbering 3.00

Casual Heroes
Image

❑1, Apr 1996 .... 2.25

Cat
Marvel

❑1, Nov 1972, WW (a); O: Cat. 1: Cat. Cat later becomes Tigra 35.00
❑2, Jan 1973, JR (c); JM (a); V: Owl 15.00
❑3, Apr 1973, BEv (a); A: Contains letter by Frank Miller. V: Commander Kraken 12.00
❑4, Jun 1973, JR (c); JSn (w); FMc (a); V: Man-Bull; Includes The Female of the Species, reprinted from X-Men (1st Series) #57 .... 10.00

Cat (Aircel)
Aircel

❑1, Nov 1991, b&w; Adult 2.50
❑2, b&w; Adult 2.50

Catalyst: Agents of Change
Dark Horse

❑1, Feb 1994; cardstock cover with foil logo 2.00
❑2, Mar 1994 .... 2.00
❑3, Apr 1994 .... 2.00
❑4, May 1994 .... 2.00
❑5; No Date given 2.00
❑6, Aug 1994 .... 2.00
❑7, Sep 1994 .... 2.00

Cat & Mouse
EF Graphics

❑1, Jan 1989, part color 2.00
❑1/2nd; 2nd printing 1.75

Cat & Mouse (Aircel)
Aircel

❑1, Mar 1990, b&w 2.25
❑2, Apr 1990, b&w 2.25
❑3, May 1990, b&w 2.25
❑4, Jun 1990, b&w 2.25
❑5, Jul 1990, b&w 2.25
❑6, Aug 1990, b&w 2.25
❑7, Sep 1990, b&w 2.25
❑8, Oct 1990, b&w 2.25
❑9, Nov 1990, b&w 2.25
❑10, Dec 1990, b&w 2.25
❑11, Jan 1991, b&w 2.25
❑12, Feb 1991, b&w; D: Nail 2.25
❑13, Mar 1991, b&w 2.25
❑14, Apr 1991, b&w 2.25

N-MINT

❑15, May 1991, b&w 2.25
❑16, Jun 1991, b&w 2.25
❑17, Aug 1991, b&w 2.25
❑18, Sep 1991, b&w; Final Issue 2.25

Cat Claw
Eternity

❑1, Sep 1990, b&w; O: Cat Claw 2.50
❑1/2nd; 2nd printing; O: Cat Claw 2.50
❑2, Nov 1990 .... 2.50
❑3, Jan 1991 .... 2.50
❑4, Feb 1991 .... 2.50
❑5, Apr 1991 .... 2.50
❑6, Jun 1991 .... 2.50
❑7, Aug 1991 .... 2.50
❑8 .... 2.50
❑9 .... 2.50

Catfight
Insomnia

❑1, Mar 1995, b&w; 1: Catfight; 1: Lolli-pop Man 2.75
❑1/Gold; Gold edition; 1: Lolli-pop Man; 1: Catfight 3.00

Catfight: Dream into Action
Lightning

❑1, Mar 1996, b&w; Creed Guest Star 2.75

Catfight: Dream Warrior
Lightning

❑1 .... 2.75

Catfight: Escape from Limbo
Lightning

❑1, Nov 1996 .... 2.75

Catfight: Sweet Revenge
Lightning

❑1, Apr 1997, b&w; alternate cover B 2.95

Catharsis
Being

❑1, Oct 1994 .... 2.50

Cathexis
NBM

❑1; Adult 13.95

Catnip
Side Show

❑1 .... 2.95

Catseye
Manic

❑1, Dec 1998 .... 2.95
❑2 1999 .... 2.95
❑3 1999 .... 2.95
❑4 1999 .... 2.95
❑5 1999 .... 2.50
❑6 1999 .... 2.50
❑7 1999 .... 2.50
❑8 1999 .... 2.50

Catseye Agency
Rip Off

❑1, Sep 1992, b&w 2.50
❑2, Oct 1992, b&w 2.50

Cat, T.H.E.
Dell

❑1, ca. 1967, Photo cover 18.00
❑2, ca. 1967, Photo cover 12.00

N-MINT

❑3, ca. 1967, Photo cover 12.00
❑4, Oct 1967, Photo cover 12.00

Cattle Brain
Itchy Eyeball

❑1, b&w 2.75
❑2, b&w 2.75
❑3, b&w 2.75

Catwoman
DC

❑1, Feb 1989; O: Catwoman (new origin) 3.00
❑2, Mar 1989 .... 2.50
❑3, Apr 1989 .... 2.00
❑4, May 1989 .... 2.00

Catwoman
DC

❑0, Oct 1994; O: Catwoman 2.00
❑1, Aug 1993; O: Catwoman, Raised cover 3.00
❑2, Sep 1993 .... 3.00
❑3, Oct 1993 .... 2.50
❑4, Nov 1993 .... 2.50
❑5, Dec 1993 .... 2.50
❑6, Jan 1994; Knightquest: The Search 2.50
❑7, Feb 1994; Knightquest: The Crusade 2.50
❑8, Mar 1994 .... 2.50
❑9, Apr 1994; V: Zephyr 2.50
❑10, May 1994 .... 2.50
❑11, Jun 1994 .... 2.00
❑12, Jul 1994 .... 2.00
❑13, Aug 1994; KnightsEnd Aftermath 2.00
❑14, Sep 1994; Zero Hour 2.00
❑15, Nov 1994 .... 2.00
❑16, Dec 1994 .... 2.00
❑17, Jan 1995 .... 2.00
❑18, Feb 1995 .... 2.00
❑19, Mar 1995 .... 2.00
❑20, Apr 1995 .... 2.00
❑21, May 1995 .... 2.00
❑22, Jul 1995 .... 2.00
❑23, Aug 1995 .... 2.00
❑24, Sep 1995 .... 2.00
❑25, Oct 1995; Giant-size; A: Psyba-Rats. A: Robin 2.00
❑26, Nov 1995; Story continues in Shadow Of The Bat #44 .... 2.00
❑27, Dec 1995 .... 2.00
❑28, Jan 1996 .... 2.00
❑29, Feb 1996 .... 2.00
❑30, Mar 1996 .... 2.00
❑31, Mar 1996 DG (a) 2.00
❑32, Apr 1996 .... 2.00
❑33, May 1996 .... 2.00
❑34, Jun 1996 .... 2.00
❑35, Jul 1996 .... 2.00
❑36, Aug 1996 .... 2.00
❑37, Sep 1996 .... 2.00
❑38, Oct 1996; Penguin appearance 2.00
❑39, Nov 1996; Penguin appearance 2.00
❑40, Dec 1996; V: Two-Face, Penguin 2.00
❑41, Jan 1997 .... 2.00
❑42, Feb 1997; 1: Cybercat 2.00
❑43, Mar 1997 A: She-Cat 2.00
❑44, Apr 1997 .... 2.00
❑45, May 1997; McCarthy (inks) incorrectly listed on cover 2.00
❑46, Jun 1997; V: Two-Face 2.00

Other grades: Multiply price above by 5/6 for VF/NM • 2/3 for VERY FINE • 1/3 for FINE • 1/5 for VERY GOOD • 1/8 for GOOD

❑47, Jul 1997; V: Two-Face 2.00
❑48, Aug 1997 2.00
❑49, Sep 1997; V: Spider 2.00
❑50, Oct 1997 2.00
❑50/A, Oct 1997; yellow logo 2.95
❑50/B, Oct 1997; purple logo 2.95
❑51, Nov 1997; V: Huntress 2.00
❑52, Dec 1997; Face cover 2.00
❑53, Jan 1998 2.00
❑54, Feb 1998; DGry (w); self-contained story; 1st Devin Grayson script 2.00
❑55, Mar 1998; DGry (w); self-contained story 2.00
❑56, Apr 1998; DGry (w); continues in Robin #52 2.00
❑57, May 1998; V: Poison Ivy. continues in Batman: Arkham Asylum - Tales of Madness #1 2.00
❑58, Jun 1998; DGry (w); V: Scarecrow. 2.00
❑59, Jul 1998; DGry (w); V: Scarecrow.. 2.00
❑60, Aug 1998; V: Scarecrow 2.00
❑61, Sep 1998 2.00
❑62, Oct 1998 A: Nemesis 2.00
❑63, Dec 1998; V: Joker 2.00
❑64, Jan 1999; DGry (w); A: Joker. A: Batman. V: Joker 2.00
❑65, Feb 1999; DGry (w); A: Scarecrow. A: Joker. A: Batman. V: Joker 2.00
❑66, Mar 1999; DGry (w); Mona Lisa/ Catwoman cover 2.00
❑67, Apr 1999 DGry (w) 2.00
❑68, May 1999; DGry (w); V: Body Doubles. Lady Vic 2.00
❑69, Jun 1999 DGry (w); A: Trickster 2.00
❑70, Jul 1999 DGry (w) 2.00
❑71, Aug 1999 DGry (w) 2.00
❑72, Sep 1999; DGry (w); No Man's Land 2.00
❑73, Oct 1999; No Man's Land 2.00
❑74, Nov 1999; No Man's Land 2.00
❑75, Dec 1999; No Man's Land 2.00
❑76, Jan 2000; No Man's Land 2.00
❑77, Feb 2000 2.00
❑78, Mar 2000 2.00
❑79, Apr 2000 2.00
❑80, May 2000 2.00
❑81, Jun 2000 2.00
❑82, Jul 2000 2.00
❑83, Aug 2000 2.25
❑84, Sep 2000 2.25
❑85, Oct 2000 2.25
❑86, Nov 2000 2.25
❑87, Dec 2000 2.25
❑88, Jan 2001 2.25
❑89, Feb 2001 2.25
❑90, Mar 2001 2.25
❑91, Apr 2001 2.25
❑92, May 2001 2.25
❑93, Jun 2001 2.25
❑94, Jul 2001; V: Batman; Final issue 2.25
❑1000000, Nov 1998 DGry (w) 3.00
❑Ann 1, ca. 1994; Elseworlds 3.50
❑Ann 2, ca. 1995; Year One 3.95
❑Ann 3, ca. 1996; Legends of the Dead Earth 2.95
❑Ann 4, ca. 1997; Pulp Heroes 3.95

Catwoman
DC

❑1, Jan 2002; V: serial killer targetting Gotham City prostitutes 4.00
❑2, Feb 2002 2.50
❑3, Mar 2002 2.50
❑4, Apr 2002 2.50
❑5, May 2002 2.50
❑6, Jun 2002 2.50
❑7, Jul 2002 2.50
❑8, Aug 2002 2.50
❑9, Sep 2002 2.50
❑10, Oct 2002 2.50
❑11, Nov 2002 2.50
❑12, Dec 2002 2.50
❑13, Jan 2003 2.50
❑14, Feb 2003 2.50
❑15, Mar 2003 2.50
❑16, Apr 2003; D: Sylvia Sinclair; V: Black Mask 2.50
❑17, May 2003 2.50
❑18, Jun 2003 2.50
❑19, Jul 2003 2.50
❑20, Aug 2003 2.50
❑21, Sep 2003 2.50
❑22, Oct 2003 2.50
❑23, Nov 2003; Opal City 2.50
❑24, Dec 2003; Hawkgirl; St. Roch 2.50
❑25, Jan 2004 2.50
❑26, Feb 2004 PG (c); PG (a) 2.50
❑27, Mar 2004 PG (c); PG (a) 2.50
❑28, Apr 2004, PG (c); PG (a) 2.50
❑29, May 2004 PG (c); PG (a) 2.50
❑30, Jun 2004; PG (c); PG (a); V: Mr. Zeiss 2.50
❑31, Jul 2004 2.50
❑32, Aug 2004 2.50
❑33, Jul 2004 2.50
❑34, Oct 2004 2.50
❑35, Nov 2004, V: Ravens 2.50
❑36, Dec 2004, V: Mr. Zeiss 2.50
❑37, Jan 2005 2.50
❑38, Feb 2005 2.50
❑39, Mar 2005 2.50
❑40, Apr 2005; V: Wooden Nickel 2.50
❑41, May 2005 2.50
❑42, Jun 2005 2.50
❑43, Jul 2005 2.50
❑44, Aug 2005 2.50
❑45, Sep 2005 2.50
❑46, Oct 2005 2.50
❑47, Nov 2005, V: Hammer and Sickle 2.50
❑48, Dec 2005 2.50
❑49, Jan 2006 2.50
❑50, Feb 2006 2.50
❑51, Mar 2006, Batman; Slam Bradley 2.50
❑52, May 2006 2.50
❑53, Jun 2006 2.50
❑54, Jul 2006, One Year Later story 2.50
❑55, Aug 2006, One Year Later; Wildcat; Angle Man; Slam Bradley 2.99
❑56, Sep 2006 2.99
❑57, Sep 2006, Cover art homage to Frank Miller's Lone Wolf and Cub #5 2.99
❑58, Oct 2006, Indicia page misprint: reprints issue #57's indicia page 2.99
❑59, Nov 2006 2.99
❑60, Dec 2006 2.99
❑61, Jan 2007 2.99
❑62, Mar 2007, D: Sam Bradley 2.99
❑64 2.99
❑65 2.99
❑66 2.99
❑67 2.99
❑68 2.99
❑69 2.99
❑70 2.99
❑71 2.99
❑72 2.99
❑73 2.99
❑74 2.99
❑75 2.99
❑76 2.99
❑77 2.99
❑78 2.99
❑79 2.99
❑80 2.99
❑81 2.99
❑82 2.99

Catwoman: Guardian of Gotham
DC

❑1, ca. 1999 5.95
❑2, ca. 1999 5.95

Catwoman Plus
DC

❑1, Nov 1997; continues in Robin Plus #2 2.95

Catwoman Secret Files and Origins
DC

❑1, Nov 2002 4.95

Catwoman The Movie
DC / Vertigo

❑1, Sep 2004 4.95

Catwoman/Vampirella: The Furies
DC

❑1, Feb 1997, prestige format; crossover with Harris 4.95

Catwoman: When in Rome
DC

❑1, Nov 2004 3.50
❑2, Dec 2004 3.50
❑3, Jan 2005 3.50
❑4, Feb 2005 3.50
❑5, Jun 2005 3.50

Catwoman/Wildcat
DC

❑1, Aug 1998 2.50
❑2, Sep 1998 2.50
❑3, Oct 1998; V: Red Blade; V: Claw Hammer 2.50
❑4, Nov 1998; D: Luciano; D: Red Blade; V: Luciano psychotic mob boss; V: Red Blade; V: Luciano 2.50

Cave Bang
Fantagraphics / Eros

❑1, Oct 1996; Adult 2.95
❑2, Jul 2000; Adult 2.95

Cave Girl
AC

❑1; O: Cave Girl; Reprint 2.95

Cave Kids
Gold Key

❑1, Feb 1963 35.00
❑2, ca. 1963 18.00
❑3, Nov 1963 15.00
❑4, Mar 1964 15.00
❑5, Jun 1964 15.00
❑6, Sep 1964 12.00
❑7, Dec 1964 12.00
❑8, Mar 1965 12.00
❑9, Jun 1965 12.00
❑10, Sep 1965 12.00
❑11, Dec 1965 12.00
❑12, Mar 1966 12.00
❑13, Jun 1966 9.00
❑14, Sep 1966 9.00
❑15, Dec 1966 9.00
❑16, Mar 1967 9.00

Caveman
Caveman

❑1, Apr 1998 3.50
❑2, Jun 1998 3.50
❑3, Aug 1998 3.50
❑4, Oct 1998 3.50
❑GN 1, b&w; graphic novel 9.95

Cavewoman
Basement

❑1, Jan 1994, b&w 26.00
❑2, ca. 1994, b&w 20.00
❑3, Jul 1994, b&w 15.00
❑4, Nov 1994, b&w 12.00
❑5, b&w 10.00
❑6, b&w 10.00

Cavewoman Color Special
Avatar

❑1, Nov 1999; Includes nudity 3.50

Cavewoman: Missing Link
Basement

❑1, Sep 1997, b&w 2.95
❑2, Nov 1997, b&w 2.95

Cavewoman: Odyssey
Caliber

❑1; ca. 1999 2.95

Cavewoman One-Shot
Basement

❑1, Apr 2001, Klyde & Meriem 4.00

Cavewoman: Pangaean Sea
Avatar

❑Ashcan 1, Oct 1999; Preview edition 4.95

Cavewoman: Rain
Basement

❑1, ca. 1996; Includes trading card 3.00
❑1/2nd; 2nd printing 2.95
❑1/3rd; 3rd printing 2.95
❑2 3.50
❑2/2nd; 2nd printing 2.95
❑2/3rd; 3rd printing 2.95
❑3, ca. 1997 3.50
❑3/2nd; 2nd printing 2.95
❑4 3.00
❑4/2nd; 2nd printing 2.95
❑5, Nov 1996 3.00
❑5/2nd; 2nd printing 2.95
❑6, Feb 1997 3.00
❑7, May 1997 3.00
❑8, Sep 1997 3.00

Captain America

Second restart after "Heroes Reborn"
©Marvel

Captain America

Third restart didn't outlast the second one
©Marvel

Captain America

Fourth restart features "return" of Bucky
©Marvel

Captain America & The Falcon

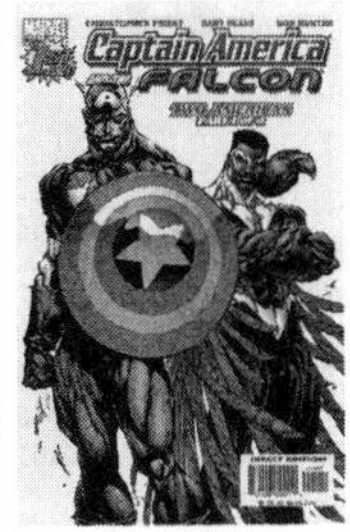

Team-up title revives old partnership
©Marvel

Captain America: Dead Man Running

Series interlude between 3rd and 4th series
©Marvel

N-MINT

Cavewoman: Raptor
Basement

❑1, Jul 2002 .... 3.25

Cecil Kunkle
Darkline

❑1 .... 3.50
❑2 .... 3.50
❑3, b&w; Santa cover 2.00

Cecil Kunkle
Renegade

❑1, May 1986, b&w 2.00

Celestial Mechanics: The Adventures of Widget Wilhelmina Jones
Innovation

❑1, Dec 1990, b&w 2.25
❑2, Feb 1991, b&w 2.25
❑3, b&w 2.25

Celestine
Image

❑1, May 1996 .... 2.50
❑1/Variant, May 1996; alternate cover 2.50
❑2, Jun 1996 .... 2.50

Cell
Antarctic

❑1, Sep 1996, b&w 2.95
❑2, Nov 1996, b&w 2.95
❑3, Jan 1997, b&w 2.95

Cement Shooz
Horse Feathers

❑1, Sep 1991 .... 2.50

Cenotaph
Northstar

❑1; Adult 3.95

Centerfield
Alternative

❑1, ca. 2005; b&w; ca. 2004 .... 3.50

Centrifugal Bumble-Puppy
Fantagraphics

❑1, b&w 2.25
❑2, b&w 2.25
❑3, b&w 2.25
❑4, b&w 2.25
❑5, b&w 2.25
❑6, b&w 2.25
❑7 .... 2.25
❑8 .... 2.50

Centurions
DC

❑1, Jun 1987; O: Centurions 1.00
❑2, Jul 1987; DH (a); O: Centurions 1.00
❑3, Aug 1987 .... 1.00
❑4, Sep 1987 .... 1.00

Century: Distant Sons
Marvel

❑1, Feb 1996; D: The Broker 2.95

Cereal Killings
Fantagraphics

❑1, Mar 1992, b&w 2.50
❑2, ca. 1992, b&w 2.50
❑3, ca. 1992, b&w 2.50
❑4, Mar 1993, b&w 2.50
❑5, ca. 1993, b&w 2.50

N-MINT

Cerebus Bi-Weekly
Aardvark-Vanaheim

❑1, Dec 1988, b&w; A: Reprints Cerebus the Aardvark #1, 1: Reprints Cerebus the Aardvark #1 .... 1.50
❑2, Dec 1988, b&w; Reprints Cerebus the Aardvark #2 .... 1.50
❑3, Dec 1988, b&w; Reprints Cerebus the Aardvark #3 .... 1.50
❑4, Jan 1989, b&w; Reprints Cerebus the Aardvark #4 .... 1.50
❑5, Jan 1989, b&w; Reprints Cerebus the Aardvark #5 .... 1.50
❑6, Feb 1989, b&w; Reprints Cerebus the Aardvark #6 .... 1.50
❑7, Feb 1989, b&w; Reprints Cerebus the Aardvark #7 .... 1.50
❑8, Mar 1989, b&w; Reprints Cerebus the Aardvark #8 .... 1.50
❑9, Mar 1989, b&w; Reprints Cerebus the Aardvark #9 .... 1.50
❑10, Apr 1989, b&w; Reprints Cerebus the Aardvark #10 .... 1.50
❑11, Apr 1989, b&w; Reprints Cerebus the Aardvark #11 .... 1.50
❑12, May 1989, b&w; Reprints Cerebus the Aardvark #12 .... 1.50
❑13, May 1989, b&w; Reprints Cerebus the Aardvark #13 .... 1.50
❑14, May 1989, b&w; Reprints Cerebus the Aardvark #14 .... 1.50
❑15, Jun 1989, b&w; Reprints Cerebus the Aardvark #15 .... 1.50
❑16, Jun 1989, b&w; Reprints Cerebus the Aardvark #16 .... 1.50
❑17, Jul 1989, b&w; 1: Hepcats. Reprints Cerebus the Aardvark #17 with new material 4.00
❑18, Jul 1989, b&w; Reprints Cerebus the Aardvark #18 .... 1.50
❑19, Aug 1989, b&w; Reprints Cerebus the Aardvark #19 .... 1.50
❑20, Aug 1989, b&w; 1: Milk & Cheese. Reprints Cerebus the Aardvark #20 with new material 6.00
❑21, Sep 1989, b&w; Reprints Cerebus the Aardvark #21 .... 1.50
❑22, Sep 1989, b&w; Reprints Cerebus the Aardvark #22 .... 1.50
❑23, Oct 1989, b&w; Reprints Cerebus the Aardvark #23 .... 1.50
❑24, Oct 1989, b&w; Reprints Cerebus the Aardvark #24 .... 1.50
❑25, Nov 1989, b&w; Reprints Cerebus the Aardvark #25 .... 1.50
❑26, Nov 1989, b&w; Reprints Cerebus the Aardvark "Prince Silverspoon" strips from The Buyer's Guide for Comic Fandom no indicia or cover number 1.50

Cerebus: Church & State
Aardvark-Vanaheim

❑1, Feb 1991, b&w; Reprints Cerebus the Aardvark #51 .... 2.00
❑2, Feb 1991, b&w; Reprints Cerebus the Aardvark #52 .... 2.00
❑3, Mar 1991, b&w; Reprints Cerebus the Aardvark #53 .... 2.00
❑4, Mar 1991, b&w; Reprints Cerebus the Aardvark #54 .... 2.00
❑5, Apr 1991, b&w; Reprints Cerebus the Aardvark #55 .... 2.00

N-MINT

❑6, Apr 1991, b&w; Reprints Cerebus the Aardvark #56 .... 2.00
❑7, May 1991, b&w; Reprints Cerebus the Aardvark #57 .... 2.00
❑8, May 1991, b&w; Reprints Cerebus the Aardvark #58 .... 2.00
❑9, Jun 1991, b&w; Reprints Cerebus the Aardvark #59 .... 2.00
❑10, Jun 1991, b&w; Reprints Cerebus the Aardvark #60 .... 2.00
❑11, Jul 1991, b&w; Reprints Cerebus the Aardvark #61 .... 2.00
❑12, Jul 1991, b&w; Reprints Cerebus the Aardvark #62 .... 2.00
❑13, Aug 1991, b&w; Reprints Cerebus the Aardvark #63 .... 2.00
❑14, Aug 1991, b&w; Reprints Cerebus the Aardvark #64 .... 2.00
❑15, Sep 1991, b&w; Reprints Cerebus the Aardvark #65 .... 2.00
❑16, Sep 1991, b&w; Reprints Cerebus the Aardvark #66 .... 2.00
❑17, Oct 1991, b&w; Reprints Cerebus the Aardvark #67 .... 2.00
❑18, Oct 1991, b&w; Reprints Cerebus the Aardvark #68 .... 2.00
❑19, Nov 1991, b&w; Reprints Cerebus the Aardvark #69 .... 2.00
❑20, Nov 1991, b&w; Reprints Cerebus the Aardvark #70 .... 2.00
❑21, Dec 1991, b&w; Reprints Cerebus the Aardvark #71 .... 2.00
❑22, Dec 1991, b&w; Reprints Cerebus the Aardvark #72 .... 2.00
❑23, Jan 1992, b&w; Reprints Cerebus the Aardvark #73 .... 2.00
❑24, Jan 1992, b&w; Reprints Cerebus the Aardvark #74 .... 2.00
❑25, Feb 1992, b&w; Reprints Cerebus the Aardvark #75 .... 2.00
❑26, Feb 1992, b&w; Reprints Cerebus the Aardvark #76 .... 2.00
❑27, Mar 1992, b&w; Reprints Cerebus the Aardvark #77 .... 2.00
❑28, Mar 1992, b&w; Reprints Cerebus the Aardvark #78 .... 2.00
❑29, Apr 1992, b&w; Reprints Cerebus the Aardvark #79 .... 2.00
❑30, Apr 1992, b&w; Reprints Cerebus the Aardvark #80 .... 2.00

Cerebus Companion
Win-Mill

❑1, Dec 1993, b&w 3.95
❑2, Dec 1994, b&w 3.95

Cerebus Guide to Self Publishing
Aardvark-Vanaheim

❑1, Nov 1997, b&w; collects Sim text pieces on the subject from Cerebus ... 3.95

Cerebus: Guys Party Pack
Aardvark-Vanaheim

❑1, b&w; Reprints Cerebus the Aardvark #201-204 .... 3.95

Cerebus High Society
Aardvark-Vanaheim

❑1, Feb 1990, b&w 2.00
❑2, Feb 1990, b&w 2.00
❑3, Mar 1990, b&w 2.00
❑4, Mar 1990, b&w 2.00
❑5, Apr 1990, b&w 2.00

Other grades: Multiply price above by 5/6 for VF/NM • 2/3 for VERY FINE • 1/3 for FINE • 1/5 for VERY GOOD • 1/8 for GOOD

	N-MINT
❑6, Apr 1990, b&w	2.00
❑7, May 1990, b&w	2.00
❑8, May 1990, b&w	2.00
❑9, Jun 1990, b&w	2.00
❑10, Jun 1990, b&w	2.00
❑11, Jul 1990, b&w	2.00
❑12, Jul 1990, b&w	2.00
❑13, Aug 1990, b&w	2.00
❑14, Aug 1990, b&w	2.00
❑15, Sep 1990, b&w	2.00
❑16, Sep 1990, b&w	2.00
❑17, Oct 1990, b&w	2.00
❑18, Oct 1990, b&w	2.00
❑19, Nov 1990, b&w	2.00
❑20, Nov 1990, b&w	2.00
❑21, Dec 1990, b&w	2.00
❑22, Dec 1990, b&w	2.00
❑23, Jan 1991, b&w	2.00
❑24, Jan 1991, b&w	2.00
❑25, Feb 1991, b&w	2.00

Cerebus Jam
Aardvark-Vanaheim

	N-MINT
❑1, Apr 1985, b&w	3.00

Cerebus the Aardvark
Aardvark-Vanaheim

	N-MINT
❑0, Jun 1993, b&w; Reprints Cerebus the Aardvark #51, 112/113, 137/138	4.00
❑0/Gold, b&w; Reprints Cerebus the Aardvark #51, 112/113, 137/138; Gold logo on cover	6.00
❑1, Dec 1977, b&w; 1: Cerebus. genuine; Low circulation	700.00
❑1/Counterfeit, b&w; Counterfeit edition (glossy cover stock on inside cover); 1: Cerebus. Counterfeit edition (glossy cover stock on inside cover); Low circulation	60.00
❑2 1978, b&w	150.00
❑3 1978, b&w 1: Red Sophia	90.00
❑4 1978, b&w 1: Elrod the Albino	75.00
❑5, Aug 1978, b&w	50.00
❑6, Oct 1978, b&w 1: Jaka	35.00
❑7, Dec 1978, b&w	20.00
❑8, Feb 1979, b&w	15.00
❑9, Apr 1979, b&w	15.00
❑10, Jun 1979, b&w	15.00
❑11, Aug 1979, b&w 1: Captain Cockroach	12.00
❑12, Oct 1979, b&w	10.00
❑13, Dec 1979, b&w	10.00
❑14, Mar 1980, b&w 1: Lord Julius	10.00
❑15, Apr 1980, b&w	10.00
❑16, May 1980, b&w	10.00
❑17, Jun 1980, b&w	10.00
❑18, Jul 1980, b&w	10.00
❑19, Aug 1980, b&w	10.00
❑20, Sep 1980, b&w	10.00
❑21, Oct 1980, b&w; 1: Weisshaupt. Low circulation	10.00
❑22, Nov 1980, b&w; no cover price	10.00
❑23, Dec 1980, b&w	6.00
❑24, Jan 1981, b&w	6.00
❑25, Mar 1981, b&w	6.00
❑26, May 1981, b&w	6.00
❑27, Jun 1981, b&w	6.00
❑28, Jul 1981, b&w	6.00
❑29, Aug 1981, b&w 1: Elf f	6.00
❑30, Sep 1981, b&w	6.00
❑31, Oct 1981, b&w 1: Astoria	6.00
❑32, Nov 1981, b&w; First "Unique Story" backup	5.00
❑33, Dec 1981, b&w	5.00
❑34, Jan 1982, b&w	5.00
❑35, Feb 1982, b&w	5.00
❑36, Mar 1982, b&w	5.00
❑37, Apr 1982, b&w	5.00
❑38, May 1982, b&w	5.00
❑39, Jun 1982, b&w	5.00
❑40, Jul 1982, b&w	5.00
❑41, Aug 1982, b&w	4.00
❑42, Sep 1982, b&w	4.00
❑43, Oct 1982, b&w	4.00
❑44, Nov 1982, b&w; sideways	4.00
❑45, Dec 1982, b&w; sideways	4.00
❑46, Jan 1983, b&w; sideways	4.00
❑47, Feb 1983, b&w; sideways	4.00
❑48, Mar 1983, b&w; sideways	4.00
❑49, Apr 1983, b&w; rotating issue	4.00
❑50, May 1983, b&w	4.00
❑51, Jun 1983, b&w; Low circulation	6.00
❑52, Jul 1983, b&w	4.00
❑53, Aug 1983, b&w 1: Wolveroach (cameo)	4.00
❑54, Sep 1983, b&w 1: Wolveroach (full story). A: Wolveroach	4.00
❑55, Oct 1983, b&w A: Wolveroach	4.00
❑56, Nov 1983, b&w 1: Normalman. A: Wolveroach	4.00
❑57, Dec 1983, b&w 2: Normalman	4.00
❑58, Jan 1984, b&w	3.00
❑59, Feb 1984, b&w	3.00
❑60, Mar 1984, b&w	3.00
❑61, Apr 1984, b&w; A: Flaming Carrot. Flaming Carrot	4.00
❑62, May 1984, b&w; A: Flaming Carrot. Flaming Carrot	4.00
❑63, Jun 1984, b&w	2.50
❑64, Jul 1984, b&w	2.50
❑65, Aug 1984, b&w; Gerhard begins as background artist	2.50
❑66, Sep 1984, b&w	2.50
❑67, Oct 1984, b&w	2.50
❑68, Nov 1984, b&w	2.50
❑69, Dec 1984, b&w	2.50
❑70, Jan 1985, b&w	2.50
❑71, Feb 1985, b&w; Last "Unique Story" backup	2.50
❑72, Mar 1985, b&w	2.50
❑73, Apr 1985, b&w	2.50
❑74, May 1985, b&w	2.50
❑75, Jun 1985, b&w	2.50
❑76, Jul 1985, b&w	2.50
❑77, Aug 1985, b&w	2.50
❑78, Sep 1985, b&w	2.50
❑79, Oct 1985, b&w	2.50
❑80, Nov 1985, b&w	2.50
❑81, Dec 1985, b&w	2.50
❑82, Jan 1986, b&w	2.50
❑83, Feb 1986, b&w	2.50
❑84, Mar 1986, b&w	2.50
❑85, Apr 1986, b&w	2.50
❑86, May 1986, b&w	2.50
❑87, Jun 1986, b&w	2.50
❑88, Jul 1986, b&w	2.50
❑89, Aug 1986, b&w	2.50
❑90, Sep 1986, b&w	2.50
❑91, Oct 1986, b&w	2.50
❑92, Nov 1986, b&w	2.50
❑93, Dec 1986, b&w	2.50
❑94, Jan 1987, b&w	2.50
❑95, Feb 1987, b&w	2.50
❑96, Mar 1987, b&w	2.50
❑97, Apr 1987, b&w	2.50
❑98, May 1987, b&w	2.50
❑99, Jun 1987, b&w 1: Cirin	2.50
❑100, Jul 1987, b&w	2.50
❑101, Aug 1987, b&w	2.00
❑102, Sep 1987, b&w	2.00
❑103, Oct 1987, b&w	2.00
❑104, Nov 1987, b&w A: Flaming Carrot	2.00
❑105, Dec 1987, b&w	2.00
❑106, Jan 1988, b&w	2.00
❑107, Feb 1988, b&w	2.00
❑108, Mar 1988, b&w	2.00
❑109, Apr 1988, b&w	2.00
❑110, May 1988, b&w	2.00
❑111, Jun 1988, b&w	2.00
❑112, Jul 1988, b&w; Double-issue #112 and #113	2.00
❑114, Sep 1988, b&w	2.00
❑115, Oct 1988, b&w	2.00
❑116, Nov 1988, b&w	2.00
❑117, Dec 1988, b&w	2.00
❑118, Jan 1989, b&w	2.00
❑119, Feb 1989, b&w	2.00
❑120, Mar 1989, b&w	2.00
❑121, Apr 1989, b&w	2.00
❑122, May 1989, b&w	2.00
❑123, Jun 1989, b&w	2.00
❑124, Jul 1989, b&w	2.00
❑125, Aug 1989, b&w	2.00
❑126, Sep 1989, b&w	2.00
❑127, Oct 1989, b&w	2.00
❑128, Nov 1989, b&w	2.00
❑129, Dec 1989, b&w	2.00
❑130, Jan 1990, b&w	2.00
❑131, Feb 1990, b&w	2.00
❑132, Mar 1990, b&w	2.00
❑133, Apr 1990, b&w	2.00
❑134, May 1990, b&w	2.00
❑135, Jun 1990, b&w	2.00
❑136, Jul 1990, b&w	2.00
❑137, Aug 1990, b&w	2.25
❑138, Sep 1990, b&w	2.25
❑139, Oct 1990, b&w	2.25
❑140, Nov 1990, b&w	2.25
❑141, Dec 1990, b&w	2.25
❑142, Jan 1991, b&w	2.25
❑143, Feb 1991, b&w	2.25
❑144, Mar 1991, b&w	2.25
❑145, Apr 1991, b&w	2.25
❑146, May 1991, b&w	2.25
❑147, Jun 1991, b&w	2.25
❑148, Jul 1991, b&w	2.25
❑149, Aug 1991, b&w	2.25
❑150, Sep 1991, b&w	2.25
❑151, Oct 1991, b&w	2.25
❑152, Nov 1991, b&w	2.25
❑153, Dec 1991, b&w	2.25
❑154, Jan 1992, b&w	2.25
❑155, Feb 1992, b&w	2.25
❑156, Mar 1992, b&w	2.25
❑157, Apr 1992, b&w	2.25
❑158, May 1992, b&w	2.25
❑159, Jun 1992, b&w	2.25
❑160, Jul 1992, b&w	2.25
❑161, Aug 1992, b&w; Bone back-up	2.25
❑162, Sep 1992, b&w	2.25
❑163, Oct 1992, b&w	2.25
❑164, Nov 1992, b&w	2.25
❑165, Dec 1992, b&w	2.25
❑165/2nd, Dec 1992, b&w	2.25
❑166, Jan 1993, b&w	2.25
❑167, Feb 1993, b&w	2.25
❑168, Mar 1993, b&w	2.25
❑169, Apr 1993, b&w	2.25
❑170, May 1993, b&w	2.25
❑171, Jun 1993, b&w	2.25
❑172, Jul 1993, b&w	2.25
❑173, Aug 1993, b&w	2.25
❑174, Sep 1993, b&w	2.25
❑175, Oct 1993, b&w	2.25
❑176, Nov 1993, b&w	2.25
❑177, Dec 1993, b&w	2.25
❑178, Jan 1994, b&w	2.25
❑179, Feb 1994, b&w	2.25
❑180, Mar 1994, b&w	2.25
❑181, Apr 1994, b&w	2.25
❑182, May 1994, b&w	2.25
❑183, Jun 1994, b&w	2.25
❑184, Jul 1994, b&w	2.25
❑185, Aug 1994, b&w	2.25
❑186, Sep 1994, b&w	2.25
❑187, Oct 1994, b&w	2.25
❑188, Nov 1994, b&w	2.25
❑189, Dec 1994, b&w	2.25
❑190, Jan 1994, b&w	2.25
❑191, Feb 1994, b&w	2.25
❑192, Mar 1994, b&w	2.25
❑193, Apr 1994, b&w	2.25
❑194, May 1995, b&w	2.25
❑195, Jun 1995, b&w	2.25
❑196, Jul 1995, b&w	2.25
❑197, Aug 1995, b&w	2.25
❑198, Sep 1995, b&w	2.25
❑199, Oct 1995, b&w	2.25
❑200, Nov 1995, b&w; Patty Cake back-up	2.25
❑201, Dec 1995, b&w	2.25
❑202, Jan 1996, b&w	2.25
❑203, Feb 1996, b&w	2.25
❑204, Mar 1996, b&w	2.25
❑205, Apr 1996, b&w	2.25
❑206, May 1996, b&w	2.25
❑207, Jun 1996, b&w	2.25
❑208, Jul 1996, b&w	2.25
❑209, Aug 1996, b&w	2.25
❑210, Sep 1996, b&w	2.25
❑211, Oct 1996, b&w	2.25
❑212, Nov 1996, b&w	2.25
❑213, Dec 1996, b&w	2.25
❑214, Jan 1997, b&w	2.25
❑215, Feb 1997, b&w	2.25
❑216, Mar 1997, b&w	2.25
❑217, Apr 1997, b&w	2.25
❑218, May 1997, b&w	2.25

Other grades: Multiply price above by 5/6 for VF/NM • 2/3 for VERY FINE • 1/3 for FINE • 1/5 for VERY GOOD • 1/8 for GOOD

Captain America: The Movie Special

And it's the only thing special about the movie

©Marvel

Captain Atom

Title picked up from Strange Suspense Stories

©Charlton

Captain Atom

Learn how to cope with disintegration

©DC

Captain Carrot and His Amazing Zoo Crew

Very funny funny-animal super-hero title

©DC

Captain Marvel

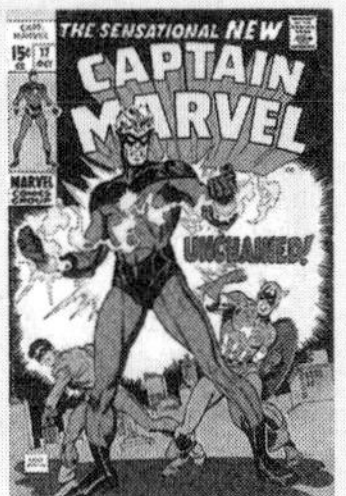

Adventures of Mar-Vell of the Kree

©Marvel

N-MINT

❑219, Jun 1997, b&w 2.25
❑220, Jul 1997, b&w 2.25
❑221, Aug 1997, b&w 2.25
❑222, Sep 1997, b&w 2.25
❑223, Oct 1997, b&w 2.25
❑224, Nov 1997, b&w 2.25
❑225, Dec 1997, b&w 2.25
❑226, Jan 1998, b&w 2.25
❑227, Feb 1998, b&w 2.25
❑228, Mar 1998, b&w 2.25
❑229, Apr 1998, b&w 2.25
❑230, May 1998, b&w A: Jaka 2.25
❑231, Jun 1998, b&w 2.25
❑232, Jul 1998, b&w 2.25
❑233, Aug 1998, b&w 2.25
❑234, Sep 1998, b&w 2.25
❑235, Oct 1998, b&w 2.25
❑236, Nov 1998, b&w 2.25
❑237, Dec 1998, b&w 2.25
❑238, Jan 1999, b&w 2.25
❑239, Feb 1999, b&w 2.25
❑240, Mar 1999, b&w 2.25
❑241, Apr 1999, b&w 2.25
❑242, May 1999, b&w 2.25
❑243, Jun 1999, b&w 2.25
❑244, Jul 1999, b&w 2.25
❑245, Aug 1999, b&w 2.25
❑246, Sep 1999, b&w 2.25
❑247, Oct 1999, b&w 2.25
❑248, Nov 1999, b&w 2.25
❑249, Dec 1999, b&w 2.25
❑250, Jan 2000, b&w 2.25
❑251, Feb 2000, b&w 2.25
❑252, Mar 2000, b&w 2.25
❑253, Apr 2000, b&w 2.25
❑254, May 2000, b&w 2.25
❑255, Jun 2000, b&w 2.25
❑256, Jul 2000, b&w 2.25
❑257, Aug 2000, b&w 2.25
❑258, Sep 2000, b&w 2.25
❑259, Oct 2000, b&w 2.25
❑260, Nov 2000, b&w 2.25
❑261, Dec 2000, b&w 2.25
❑262, Jan 2001, b&w 2.25
❑263, Feb 2001, b&w 2.25
❑264, Mar 2001, b&w 2.25
❑265, Apr 2001, b&w 2.25
❑266, May 2001, b&w 2.25
❑267, Jun 2001, b&w 2.25
❑268, Jul 2001, b&w 1: The Three Wise Fellows 2.25
❑269, Aug 2001, b&w 2.25
❑270, Sep 2001, b&w 2.25
❑271, Oct 2001, b&w 2.25
❑272, Nov 2001, b&w 1: Rabbi 2.25
❑273, Dec 2001, b&w 2.25
❑274, Jan 2002, b&w 2.25
❑275, Feb 2002, b&w 2.25
❑276, Mar 2002, b&w 2.25
❑277, Apr 2002, b&w 2.25
❑278, May 2002, b&w 2.25
❑279, Jun 2002, b&w 2.25
❑280, Jul 2002, b&w 2.25
❑281, Aug 2002, b&w 2.25
❑282, Sep 2002, b&w 2.25
❑283, Oct 2002, b&w 2.25
❑284, Nov 2002, b&w 2.25
❑285, Dec 2002, b&w 2.25
❑286, Jan 2003, b&w 2.25
❑287, Feb 2003, b&w 2.25
❑288, Mar 2003, b&w 2.25
❑289, Apr 2003, b&w 2.25
❑290, May 2003, b&w 2.25
❑291, Jun 2003, b&w 2.25
❑292, Jul 2003, b&w 2.25
❑293, Aug 2003, b&w 2.25
❑294, Sep 2003, b&w 2.25
❑295, Oct 2003, b&w 2.25
❑296, Nov 2003, b&w 2.25
❑297, Dec 2003, b&w 2.25
❑298, Jan 2004, b&w 2.25
❑299, Feb 2004, b&w 2.25
❑300, Mar 2004, b&w D: Cerebus 4.00

Cerebus World Tour Book
Aardvark-Vanaheim

❑1, b&w 3.00

Ceres Celestial Legend Part 1
Viz

❑1, Jun 2001 3.25
❑2, Jul 2001 2.95
❑3, Aug 2001 2.95
❑4, Sep 2001 2.95
❑5, Oct 2001 2.95
❑6, Nov 2001 2.95

Ceres Celestial Legend Part 2
Viz

❑1, Dec 2001 2.95
❑2, Jan 2002 2.95
❑3, Feb 2002 2.95
❑4, Mar 2002 2.95
❑5, Apr 2002 2.95
❑6, May 2002 2.95

Ceres Celestial Legend Part 3
Viz

❑1, Jun 2002 2.95
❑2, Jul 2002 3.50
❑3, Aug 2002 3.50
❑4, Sep 2002 3.50

Ceres Celestial Legend Part 4
Viz

❑1, Oct 2002 3.50
❑2, Nov 2002 3.50
❑3, Dec 2002 3.50
❑4, Jan 2003 3.50

Ceres Celestial Legend Part 5
Viz

❑1, Feb 2003 3.50

Chadz Frendz
Smiling Face

❑1, Jan 1998 1.50

Chaingang
Northstar

❑1, b&w 2.50
❑2 2.50

Chain Gang War
DC

❑1, Jul 1993; Foil embossed cover 2.50
❑1/Silver, Jul 1993; Silver promotional ed. 2.50
❑2, Aug 1993 1.75
❑3, Sep 1993 1.75
❑4, Oct 1993 1.75
❑5, Nov 1993; Embossed cover 2.50
❑6, Dec 1993 1.75
❑7, Jan 1994 1.75
❑8, Feb 1994 1.75
❑9, Mar 1994 1.75
❑10, Apr 1994 1.75
❑11, May 1994 1.75
❑12, Jun 1994; End of Chain Gang 1.75

Chainsaw Vigilante
NEC

❑1 3.50
❑1/A; Orange cover 5.00
❑1/B; Gold foil cover 6.00
❑1/C; Pseudo-3D "platinum" foil cover 6.00
❑2 2.75
❑3 2.75

Chains of Chaos
Harris

❑1, Nov 1994 2.95
❑2, Dec 1994 2.95
❑3, Jan 1995 2.95

Chakan
Rak

❑1, Aug 1994, b&w 5.00

Challengers of the Fantastic
Marvel / Amalgam

❑1, Jun 1997 2.00

Challengers of the Unknown
DC

❑22, Nov 1961 52.00
❑23, Jan 1962 52.00
❑24, Mar 1962 25.00
❑25, May 1962 25.00
❑26, Jul 1962 25.00
❑27, Sep 1962 25.00
❑28, Nov 1962 25.00
❑29, Jan 1963 25.00
❑30, Mar 1963 25.00
❑31, May 1963, O: Challengers of the Unknown 25.00
❑32, Jul 1963 20.00
❑33, Sep 1963 20.00
❑34, Nov 1963, O: Multi-Woman. 1: Multi-Woman 20.00
❑35, Jan 1964 20.00
❑36, Mar 1964 20.00
❑37, May 1964 20.00
❑38, Jul 1964 20.00
❑39, Sep 1964 20.00
❑40, Nov 1964 20.00
❑41, Jan 1965 20.00
❑42, Mar 1965 20.00
❑43, May 1965, Challengers of the Unknown get new uniforms 20.00
❑44, Jul 1965 20.00
❑45, Sep 1965 20.00
❑46, Nov 1965 20.00
❑47, Jan 1966 20.00
❑48, Mar 1966, A: The Doom Patrol. Story continues in Doom Patrol #102 20.00
❑49, May 1966 20.00

❑50, Jul 1966, 1: Villo. 1: Villo 15.00
❑51, Sep 1966, A: Sea Devils. V: Sponge Man 15.00
❑52, Nov 1966 15.00
❑53, Jan 1967 15.00
❑54, Mar 1967 15.00
❑55, May 1967, 1: Tino Manarry. D: Red Ryan 15.00
❑56, Jul 1967 15.00
❑57, Sep 1967 11.00
❑58, Nov 1967, V: Neutro 11.00
❑59, Jan 1968 11.00
❑60, Mar 1968, Red Ryan returns 11.00
❑61, May 1968 11.00
❑62, Jul 1968 11.00
❑63, Sep 1968 11.00
❑64, Nov 1968, JKu (c); JK (a); O: Challengers of the Unknown. reprints Showcase #6 11.00
❑65, Jan 1969, JK (a); O: Challengers of the Unknown. reprints Showcase #6 11.00
❑66, Mar 1969 11.00
❑67, May 1969 11.00
❑68, Jul 1969, NA (c) 11.00
❑69, Sep 1969, 1: Corinna. Stark 11.00
❑70, Nov 1969 7.00
❑71, Jan 1970 7.00
❑72, Mar 1970 7.00
❑73, May 1970 7.00
❑74, Jul 1970, BWr, GT, NA (a); A: Deadman 14.00
❑75, Sep 1970, GT, JK (a); V: Ultivac. reprints Showcase #7 7.00
❑76, Nov 1970, Reprints stories from Challengers of the Unknown #2 & #3. 7.00
❑77, Jan 1971, reprints Showcase #12 7.00
❑78, Feb 1973, Reprints stories from Challengers of the Unknown #6 & #7. 7.00
❑79, Apr 1973, JKu (c); JK (a); reprints stories from Challengers of the Unknown #1 and 2 7.00
❑80, Jul 1973, reprints Showcase #11; series goes on hiatus for four years 7.00
❑81, Jul 1977, V: Multi-Man 6.00
❑82, Aug 1977, A: Swamp Thing 5.00
❑83, Oct 1977 5.00
❑84, Dec 1977 5.00
❑85, Feb 1978, A: Deadman, Swamp Thing 5.00
❑86, Apr 1978, A: Deadman, Swamp Thing 5.00
❑87, Jul 1978, KG (a); A: Deadman, Swamp Thing, Rip Hunter. Final Issue 5.00

Challengers of the Unknown
DC

❑1, Mar 1991; O: Challengers of the Unknown (new origin) 1.75
❑2, Apr 1991 1.75
❑3, May 1991 1.75
❑4, Jun 1991 1.75
❑5, Jul 1991 1.75
❑6, Aug 1991 1.75
❑7, Sep 1991; Cover based on Jim Steranko's cover to Captain America 113 1.75
❑8, Oct 1991 1.75

Challengers of the Unknown
DC

❑1, Feb 1997; new team 2.25
❑2, Mar 1997 2.25
❑3, Apr 1997 2.25
❑4, May 1997; O: Challengers 2.25
❑5, Jun 1997 2.25
❑6, Jul 1997; concludes in Scare Tactics #8 2.25
❑7, Aug 1997; return of original Challengers 2.25
❑8, Sep 1997; O: Both Challenger teams 2.25
❑9, Oct 1997 2.25
❑10, Nov 1997 2.25
❑11, Dec 1997; Face cover 2.25
❑12, Jan 1998 2.25
❑13, Feb 1998 2.25
❑14, Mar 1998 2.25
❑15, Apr 1998; Millennium Giants; continues in Superman #134 2.25
❑16, May 1998; tales of the original Challengers 2.25
❑17, Jun 1998 2.25
❑18, Jul 1998; Final Issue 2.50

Challengers of the Unknown
DC

❑1, Aug 2004 2.95
❑2, Sep 2004 2.95
❑3, Oct 2004 2.95
❑4, Nov 2004 2.95
❑5, Dec 2004 2.95
❑6, Jan 2005 2.95

Chamber
Marvel

❑1, Oct 2002 3.00
❑2, Nov 2002 3.00
❑3, Dec 2002 3.00
❑4, Jan 2003 3.00

Chamber of Chills
Marvel

❑1, Nov 1972, GK (c); SL (w); CR, RH, DA (a); "Delusion for a Dragon Slayer!" based on Harlan Ellison story 25.00
❑2, Jan 1973, GK (c); DA (w); FB, VM, CR, JSt, DA (a) 15.00
❑3, Mar 1973, FB, BEv, DH (a) 15.00
❑4, May 1973, FB (c); FB, HC, JSt (a) 15.00
❑5, Jul 1973, Reprint from Journey into Mystery #1 15.00
❑6, Sep 1973, JR (c); FMc (a); Reprint from Spellbound #13 15.00
❑7, Nov 1973, All reprints except "Prey for Keeps" 15.00
❑8, Jan 1974 15.00
❑9, Mar 1974, "Man Who Changed" reprinted from Uncanny Tales #11; "Running" reprinted from Mystical Tales #11; "Dared" reprinted from Mystic #41; "The Test" reprinted from Mystic #44 15.00
❑10, May 1974, "Lost City" and "Harry's Hideout" reprinted from Unknown Worlds #17; "Man Who Melted" reprinted from Astonishing #36; "Gold" reprinted from Marvel Tales #117; "Mother" reprinted from Mystic #23 15.00
❑11, Jul 1974, JK (c); SL (w); BEv, JK (a); Reprints stories from Tales of Suspense #18, Weird Worlds #10, Adventures in Terror #4, and Menace #3 12.00
❑12, Sep 1974, GC (a); Reprints stories from Unknown Worlds #17, Weird Worlds #6, and Mystic #7 and #25 12.00
❑13, Nov 1974 12.00
❑14, Jan 1975 12.00
❑15, Mar 1975, SL (w); RH (a); Reprints stories from Weird Worlds #2, Uncanny Tales #7, and Menace #3 12.00
❑16, May 1975, "Room" reprinted from Strange Tales #7; "Do Not Feed" reprinted from Weird Worlds #9; "Masquerade" Party reprinted from Strange Tales #83 12.00
❑17, Jul 1975 12.00
❑18, Sep 1975, Reprints story from Tales to Astonish #11 12.00
❑19, Nov 1975, Reprints story from Tales to Astonish #26 12.00
❑20, Jan 1976, Reprints stories from Men's Adventure #24 and Mystic #57 12.00
❑21, Mar 1976, BEv (a); Reprints stories from Venus #18 and Astonishing Tales #63 12.00
❑22, May 1976, Reprints story from Tales to Astonish #26 12.00
❑22/30¢, May 1976, Reprints story from Tales to Astonish #26; 30¢ regional price variant 20.00
❑23, Jul 1976 12.00
❑23/30¢, Jul 1976, 30¢ cover 20.00
❑24, Sep 1976, "Underground Gambit" reprinted from Creatures on the Loose #11; "Man Who Isn't there" reprinted from Marvel Tales #113; "Monster Waits Outside" reprinted from Tales to Astonish #12 12.00
❑25, Nov 1976 12.00

Chamber of Darkness
Marvel

❑1, Oct 1968, JR (c); SL (w); TS, JB, DH (a) 60.00
❑2, Dec 1968 35.00
❑3, Feb 1969 30.00
❑4, Apr 1969, JK (w); TS, JK (a); Conan try-out 60.00
❑5, Jun 1969, Alan Kupperberg L.O.C. 30.00
❑6, Aug 1969 30.00
❑7, Oct 1969, TS, BWr (w); TS, SD, BWr, JK (a); 1: Bernie Wrightson work; reprints story from Tales to Astonish #13 30.00
❑8, Dec 1969, Title switches to Monsters on the Prowl 20.00
❑1/Special 1972; Special Edition 20.00

Chamber of Evil
Comax

❑1; Adult 2.95

Champion
Special Studio

❑1, b&w 2.50

Champion of Katara
Mu

❑1, Jan 1992, b&w 2.50
❑2, Apr 1992 2.50

Champion of Katara: Dum-Dums & Dragons
Mu

❑1, Jun 1995, b&w 2.95
❑2, Jul 1995, b&w 2.95
❑3, Aug 1995, b&w 2.95

Champions Classics
Hero

❑1; Reprints 1.00
❑13, Oct 1993; b&w reprint 3.95
❑14, Jan 1994; b&w reprint 3.95

Champions Classics/Flare Adventures
Hero

❑2; flip-format 2.95
❑3; flip-format 2.95
❑4; flip-format 3.50
❑5; flip-format 3.50
❑6; flip-format 3.50
❑7; flip-format 3.50

Champions (Eclipse)
Eclipse

❑1, Jun 1986; 1: Flare; 1: Foxbat; 1: Giant; 1: Icestar; 1: Marksman; 1: Rose; 1: The Champions (game characters) 1.25
❑2, Sep 1986 1.25
❑3, Oct 1986 1.25
❑4, Nov 1986 1.25
❑5, Feb 1987; O: Flare 1.25
❑6, Feb 1987 1.25

Champions (Hero)
Hero

❑1, Sep 1987; 1: The Galloping Galooper. 1: Madame Synn 1.95
❑2, Oct 1987; 1: Black Enchantress. 1: The Fat Man 1.95
❑3, Nov 1987; O: Flare. 1: Icicle. 1: Sparkplug 1.95
❑4, Dec 1987; 1: Pulsar. 1: Exo-Skeleton Man 1.95
❑5, Jan 1988 1.95
❑6, Feb 1988; 1: Mechanon 1.95
❑7, Mar 1988 1.95
❑8, May 1988; O: Foxbat 1.95
❑9, Jun 1988; (also was Flare #0) 1.95
❑10, Jul 1988 1.95
❑11, Sep 1988 1.95
❑12, Oct 1988 1.95
❑13 1.95
❑14 1.95
❑15, b&w 3.95
❑Ann 1, Dec 1988; O: Giant. O: Dark Malice 2.75
❑Ann 2 3.95

Champions
Marvel

❑1, Oct 1975, GK (c); DH (a); 1&O: The Champions. A: Venus; V: Pluto 15.00
❑2, Jan 1976, V: Pluto 6.00
❑3, Feb 1976, V: Pluto 6.00
❑4, Mar 1976, Marvel Value Stamp Series B #57 5.00
❑5, Apr 1976, DH (a); 1&O: Rampage (Marvel). A: Ghost Rider 5.00
❑5/30¢, Apr 1976, DH (a); 30¢ regional price variant 20.00
❑6, Jun 1976, 2: Rampage (Marvel); V: Rampage 4.00
❑6/30¢, Jun 1976, 30¢ regional price variant 20.00
❑7, Aug 1976, 1: Darkstar; 1: Commisar; 1: Yuri Ivanovitch Petrovich; V: Griffin; V: Darkstar; V: Rampage; Black Widow origin; Griffin apperance 4.00

Other grades: Multiply price above by 5/6 for VF/NM • 2/3 for VERY FINE • 1/3 for FINE • 1/5 for VERY GOOD • 1/8 for GOOD

Captain Planet and the Planeteers

Spinoff from environmentalist TV cartoon

©Marvel

Capt. Savage and His Leatherneck Raiders

One of the more action-packed war comics

©Marvel

Captain Sternn: Running Out of Time

Bernie Wrightson's SF satire goes glossy

©Kitchen Sink

Capt. Storm

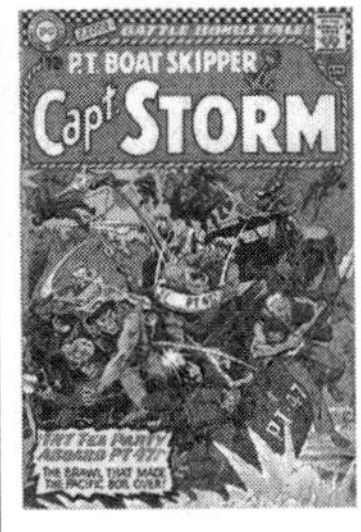

One-legged captain commands PT boat

©DC

Captain Victory and the Galactic Rangers

Independent space-spanning Kirby work

©Pacific

	N-MINT
❑7/30¢, Aug 1976, 30¢ regional price variant	20.00
❑8, Oct 1976, GK (c); GK, BH (a); V: Rampage; V: Darkstar; V: Griffin; V: Titanium Man; V: Crimson Dynamo	4.00
❑9, Dec 1976, GK (c); GK, BH (a); V: Darkstar, Titanium Man, Crimson Dynamo; V: Griffin	4.00
❑10, Jan 1977, DC (c); DC, BH (a); V: Griffin; V: Titanium Man; V: Crimson Dynamo	4.00
❑11, Feb 1977, GK (c); JBy (a)	4.00
❑12, Mar 1977, DC (c); JBy (a); Kurt Busiek L.O.C	4.00
❑13, May 1977, DC (c); JBy (a); 1: Mechanoids	4.00
❑14, Jul 1977, GK (c); JBy (w); JBy (a); 1: Swarm	4.00
❑14/35¢, Jul 1977, GK (c); JBy (w); JBy (a); 1: Swarm. 35¢ regional price variant	15.00
❑15, Sep 1977, GK (c); JBy (a); 2: Swarm; (Regular.30 edition)	4.00
❑15/35¢, Sep 1977, JBy (a); 35¢ regional price variant	15.00
❑16, Nov 1977, GK (c); JBy, BH (a); A: Doctor Doom	4.00
❑17, Jan 1978, JBy, GT (a); V: Sentinels; Final Issue	4.00

Champion Sports
DC

❑1, Nov 1973	5.00
❑2, Jan 1974	3.50
❑3, Mar 1974	3.50

Change Commander Goku
Antarctic

❑1, Oct 1993; 1&O: Change Commander Goku; Adult	2.95
❑2, Nov 1993; Adult	2.95
❑3, Dec 1993; Adult	2.95
❑4, Jan 1994; 1: The True-Brewing Magnetic Man; Adult	2.95
❑5, Feb 1994; Adult	2.95

Change Commander Goku 2
Antarctic

❑1, Sep 1996	2.95
❑2, Nov 1996	2.95
❑3, Jan 1997	2.95
❑4, Mar 1997	2.95

Changes
Tundra

❑1	7.95

Channel Zero
Image

❑1, Feb 1998	2.95
❑2, Apr 1998	2.95
❑3, Jun 1998	2.95
❑4, Aug 1998	2.95
❑5, Nov 1998	2.95
❑6, Feb 1999	2.95

Channel Zero: Dupe
Image

❑1, Jan 1999, b&w; NN	2.95

Chaos! Bible
Chaos

❑1, Nov 1995	3.50

Chaos! Chronicles
Chaos

	N-MINT
❑1, Feb 2000	3.50

Chaos Effect: Alpha
Valiant

❑1, ca. 1994; giveaway; BL (w); A: Timewalker. no cover price	3.00
❑1/Red foil, ca. 1994; Approx. 2,500 printed; retailers needed to order 100 Chaos Effect comics to receive one copy of the Red variant. Copies also given away for completing a Valiant survey in 1995	90.00

Chaos Effect: Epilogue
Valiant

❑1, Dec 1994; Magnus in 20th century; cardstock cover	2.00
❑2, Jan 1995; Magnus in 20th century; cardstock cover	2.00

Chaos Effect: Omega
Valiant

❑1, Nov 1994; Magnus in 20th century; cardstock cover	2.00
❑1/Gold, Nov 1994; Gold edition; Magnus in 20th century; cardstock cover	20.00

Chaos Effect: Beta
Valiant

❑1	2.25

Chaos! Gallery
Chaos!

❑1, Aug 1997; pin-ups	2.95

Chaos! Presents Jade
Chaos

❑1, May 2001; Adult	2.99
❑2, Jun 2001; Adult	2.99
❑3, Jul 2001; Adult	2.99
❑4, Aug 2001; Adult	2.99

Chaos! Quarterly
Chaos

❑1, Oct 1995	4.95
❑2, Jan 1996	4.95
❑3, May 1996	3.95

Chapel
Image

❑1, Feb 1995	2.50
❑2, Mar 1995	2.50
❑2/Variant, Mar 1995, Alternate cover; Chapel firing right, white lettering in logo	4.00

Chapel
Image

❑1	2.50
❑2, Mar 1995	2.50

Chapel
Image

❑1, Aug 1995	2.50
❑1/Variant, Aug 1995, alternate cover	2.50
❑2, Sep 1995	2.50
❑3, Oct 1995	2.50
❑4, Nov 1995, Babewatch	2.50
❑5, Dec 1995, V: Spawn	2.50
❑6, Feb 1996	2.50
❑7, Apr 1996, V: Shadowhawk	2.50

Chapel
Awesome

	N-MINT
❑1, Sep 1997; Says "Vol. 1" in indicia	2.99

Charlemagne
Defiant

❑0, Feb 1994, giveaway; Giveaway	1.00
❑1, Mar 1994, 1&O: Charlemagne; Special 48 page issue	3.25
❑2, Apr 1994	2.50
❑3, May 1994	2.50
❑4, Jun 1994, Special 48 page issue	2.50
❑5, Jul 1994	2.50
❑6	2.50
❑7	2.50
❑8, Final Issue	2.50

Charles Burns' Modern Horror Sketchbook
Kitchen Sink

❑1; NN	6.95

Charlie Chan
Eternity

❑1, Mar 1989; b&w strip reprint	1.95
❑2, Mar 1989; b&w strip reprint	1.95
❑3, Apr 1989; b&w strip reprint	1.95
❑4, May 1989; b&w strip reprint	1.95
❑5, Jul 1989	2.25
❑6, Aug 1989	2.25

Charlie the Caveman
Fantasy General

❑1, b&w; Ca 1985	2.00

Charlton Action Featuring Static
Charlton

❑11, Oct 1985	1.50
❑12, Dec 1985	1.50

Charlton Bullseye
Charlton

❑1, Jun 1981, SD (c); Labeled as Volume 1	7.00
❑2, Jul 1981	2.00
❑3, Sep 1981	2.00
❑4, Nov 1981, Vanguards	2.00
❑5, Jan 1982	2.00
❑6, Mar 1982	2.00
❑7, May 1982, A: Captain Atom	2.00
❑8, Jul 1982	2.00
❑9, Sep 1982, GD (w); GD (a)	2.00
❑10, Dec 1982	2.00

Charlton Classics
Charlton

❑1, Apr 1980	3.00
❑2, Jun 1980	2.00
❑3, Aug 1980	2.00
❑4, Oct 1980	2.00
❑5, Dec 1980	2.00
❑6, Feb 1981	2.00
❑7, Apr 1981	2.00
❑8, Jun 1981, Hercules; Joe Gill story, Sam Glanzman art credits; Tom Sutton script and art	2.00
❑9, Aug 1981	2.00

Charlton Premiere
Charlton

❑19, Jul 1967	20.00

Other grades: Multiply price above by 5/6 for VF/NM • 2/3 for VERY FINE • 1/3 for FINE • 1/5 for VERY GOOD • 1/8 for GOOD

N-MINT | N-MINT | N-MINT

Charlton Premiere
Charlton

- ❑1, Sep 1967, Restarted; Vol. 1, #19 was the end of Marine War Heroes 6.00
- ❑2, Nov 1967 .... 4.00
- ❑3, Jan 1968 .... 4.00
- ❑4, May 1968 .... 4.00

Charlton Sport Library: Professional Football
Charlton

- ❑1, Win 1969 .... 35.00

Charm School
Slave Labor

- ❑1, Apr 2000, b&w 2.95
- ❑2, Jul 2000, b&w 2.95
- ❑3, Dec 2000, b&w 2.95

Chase
DC

- ❑1, Feb 1998; bound-in trading cards 2.50
- ❑2, Mar 1998 .... 2.50
- ❑3, Apr 1998 .... 2.50
- ❑4, May 1998 .... 2.50
- ❑5, Jun 1998 .... 2.50
- ❑6, Jul 1998 .... 2.50
- ❑7, Aug 1998 .... 2.50
- ❑8, Sep 1998 .... 2.50
- ❑9, Oct 1998 .... 2.50
- ❑1000000, Nov 1998; Final Issue 2.00

Chase
APComics

- ❑1 2004 .... 3.50
- ❑1/Sketch 2004 .... 5.00
- ❑2 2004 .... 3.50
- ❑3, ca 2005 .... 3.50
- ❑4, ca. 2005 .... 3.50

Chaser Platoon
Aircel

- ❑1, Feb 1991, b&w 2.25
- ❑2, Mar 1991, b&w 2.25
- ❑3, Apr 1991, b&w 2.25
- ❑4, May 1991, b&w 2.25
- ❑5, b&w 2.25
- ❑6, b&w 2.25

Chasing Dogma
Image

- ❑1; Silent Bob holding video on cover 14.95

Chassis
Millennium / Expand

- ❑1, May 1996; foil logo 2.95
- ❑1/2nd, May 1997; 2nd printing 2.95
- ❑2 .... 2.95
- ❑3, Apr 1998 .... 2.95

Chassis
Hurricane

- ❑0, Apr 1999, biographical information on Chassis characters 2.95
- ❑1, Jun 1998 .... 2.95
- ❑2, Sep 1998 .... 2.95
- ❑3, Jan 1999 .... 2.95

Chassis
Image

- ❑0, Apr 1999; background information .. 2.95
- ❑1, Nov 1999 .... 2.95
- ❑1/A, Nov 1999; Alternate cover with Chassis standing against blueprint background 2.95
- ❑2, Dec 1999 .... 2.95
- ❑3, Mar 2000 .... 2.95
- ❑4, Mar 2000 .... 2.95

Chastity
Chaos!

- ❑½, Jan 2001 .... 2.95

Chastity: Lust for Life
Chaos!

- ❑1/Dynamic, May 1999; Dynamic Forces cover (falling with two outstretched swords) 5.00
- ❑1/Ltd., May 1999; Premium Edition; Chastity sitting down in pool of blood 20.00
- ❑1, May 1999 .... 3.50
- ❑2, Jun 1999 .... 2.95

Chastity: Reign of Terror
Chaos!

- ❑1, Oct 2000 .... 2.95

Chastity: Rocked
Chaos!

- ❑1, Nov 1998; Glaring against sword-wielding demons, lady with outstretched claw-hand in background 2.95
- ❑2, Dec 1998 .... 2.95
- ❑3, Jan 1999 .... 2.95
- ❑4, Feb 1999 .... 2.95

Chastity: Theatre of Pain
Chaos!

- ❑1, Feb 1997 .... 2.95
- ❑1/Variant, Feb 1997; Onyx Premium Edition; cardstock cover 4.00
- ❑2, Apr 1997 .... 2.95
- ❑3, Jun 1997; back cover pin-up 2.95
- ❑3/Variant, Jun 1997; Final Curtain Edition; No cover price; Limited Engagement 4.00

Cheapskin
Fantagraphics / Eros

- ❑1, b&w; Featuring Betty Page; Adult 2.95

Checkmate
DC

- ❑1, Jul 2006, O: Checkmate 2.99
- ❑2, Aug 2006 .... 2.99
- ❑3, Aug 2006, Cover by Lee Bermejo 2.99
- ❑4, Sep 2006, Lee Bermejo & Patricia Mulvihill cover, Green Lantern (Alan Scott) cover/appearance; Lee Bermejo & Patricia Mulvihill cover 2.99
- ❑5, Oct 2006 .... 2.99
- ❑6, Nov 2006, Suicide Squad returns 2.99
- ❑7, Dec 2006 .... 2.99
- ❑8, Jan 2007 .... 2.99
- ❑9, Mar 2007 .... 2.99

Checkmate
Gold Key

- ❑1, Oct 1962 .... 30.00
- ❑2, Dec 1962 .... 20.00

Checkmate
DC

- ❑1, Apr 1988 .... 1.25
- ❑2, May 1988 .... 1.25
- ❑3, Jun 1988 .... 1.25
- ❑4, Jul 1988 .... 1.25
- ❑5, Aug 1988 .... 1.25
- ❑6, Sep 1988 .... 1.25
- ❑7, Oct 1988 .... 1.25
- ❑8, Nov 1988 .... 1.25
- ❑9, Dec 1988 .... 1.25
- ❑10, Win 1988 .... 1.25
- ❑11, Hol 1988; Invasion! First Strike 1.25
- ❑12, Feb 1989; Invasion! Aftermath 1.25
- ❑13, Mar 1989 .... 1.50
- ❑14, Apr 1989 .... 1.50
- ❑15, May 1989; continues in Suicide Squad #27 .... 1.50
- ❑16, May 1989; continues in Suicide Squad #28 .... 1.50
- ❑17, Jun 1989; continues in Manhunter #14 .... 1.50
- ❑18, Jun 1989; continues in Suicide Squad #30 .... 1.50
- ❑19, Jul 1989 .... 1.50
- ❑20, Aug 1989 .... 1.50
- ❑21, Oct 1989 .... 1.50
- ❑22, Nov 1989 .... 1.50
- ❑23, Dec 1989 .... 1.50
- ❑24, Jan 1990 .... 1.50
- ❑25, Feb 1990 .... 1.50
- ❑26, Mar 1990 .... 1.50
- ❑27, May 1990 .... 1.50
- ❑28, Jun 1990 .... 1.50
- ❑29, Jul 1990 .... 1.50
- ❑30, Aug 1990 .... 1.50
- ❑31, Oct 1990 .... 1.50
- ❑32, Dec 1990 .... 1.50
- ❑33, Jan 1991; Final Issue 1.50

Checkmate
DC

- ❑1 .... 2.99
- ❑2 .... 2.99
- ❑3 .... 2.99
- ❑4 .... 2.99
- ❑5 .... 2.99
- ❑6 .... 2.99
- ❑7 .... 2.99
- ❑8 .... 2.99
- ❑9 .... 2.99
- ❑10 .... 2.99
- ❑11 .... 2.99
- ❑12 .... 2.99
- ❑13 .... 2.99
- ❑14 .... 2.99
- ❑15 .... 2.99
- ❑16 .... 2.99
- ❑17 .... 2.99
- ❑18 .... 2.99
- ❑19 .... 2.99
- ❑20 .... 2.99
- ❑21 .... 2.99
- ❑22 .... 2.99
- ❑23 .... 2.99
- ❑24 .... 2.99
- ❑25 .... 2.99
- ❑26 .... 2.99
- ❑27 .... 2.99
- ❑28 .... 2.99
- ❑29 .... 2.99
- ❑30 .... 2.99
- ❑31 .... 2.99

Check-Up
Fantagraphics

- ❑1, b&w 2.75

Cheech Wizard
Last Gasp

- ❑1; Adult 3.00

Cheeky Angel
Viz

- ❑1, Jul 2004, b&w 9.95
- ❑2, Sep 2004; b&w 9.95
- ❑3, Nov 2004; b&w 9.95
- ❑4, Jan 2005; b&w 9.95
- ❑5, Mar 2005; b&w 9.95
- ❑6, May 2005; b&w 9.95
- ❑7, Jul 2005; Read right to left; b&w 9.95
- ❑8, Sep 2005 .... 9.99

Cheerleaders from Hell
Caliber

- ❑1, Jan 1988, b&w 2.50

Cheese Heads
Tragedy Strikes

- ❑1, b&w; second edition 2.50
- ❑1/2nd, b&w; second edition 2.95
- ❑2, b&w 2.50
- ❑3 .... 2.95
- ❑4 .... 2.95
- ❑5 .... 2.95

Cheese Weasel
Side Show

- ❑1; Color cover 2.95
- ❑2; Black & white covers begin 2.95
- ❑3 .... 2.95
- ❑4 .... 2.95
- ❑5 .... 2.95
- ❑6 .... 2.95
- ❑7 .... 2.95

Cheese Weasel: Innocent Until Proven Guilty
Side Show

- ❑1 .... 9.95

Cheeta Pop Scream Queen
Antarctic / Venus

- ❑1, May 1994; Adult 2.95
- ❑2, Nov 1994; Adult 2.95
- ❑3, Jan 1995; Adult 2.95
- ❑4, Mar 1995; Adult 2.95
- ❑5, May 1995; Adult 2.95

Cheeta Pop
Fantagraphics / Eros

- ❑1 .... 2.95
- ❑2 .... 2.95
- ❑3, Jan 1996 .... 2.95

Chemical Warfare
Checker Comics

- ❑1, b&w 2.95
- ❑2, Sum 1998, b&w 2.95
- ❑3; b&w; CA. 1998 .... 2.95

Other grades: Multiply price above by 5/6 for VF/NM • 2/3 for VERY FINE • 1/3 for FINE • 1/5 for VERY GOOD • 1/8 for GOOD

Care Bears

Cavity-causing cartoon spreads to comics
©Marvel

Cartoon Cartoons

DC's catchall for other Cartoon Network titles
©DC

Cartoon Network Presents

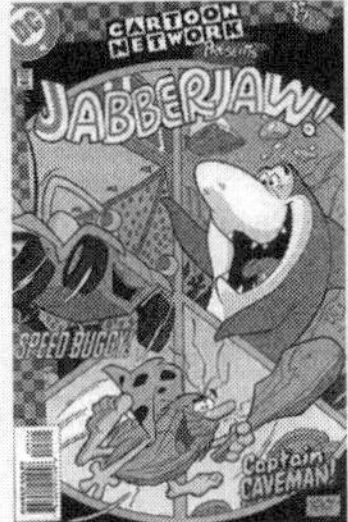

DC's first Cartoon Network anthology
©DC

Cartoon Network Starring

Anthology evolved into Cartoon Cartoons
©DC

Cases of Sherlock Holmes

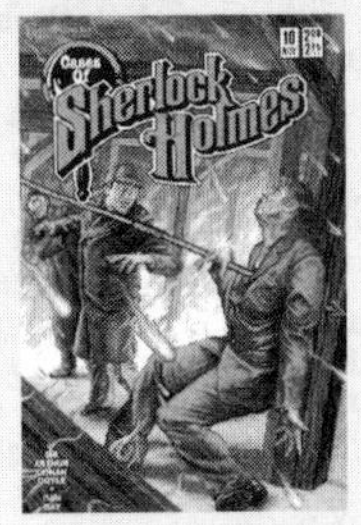

Reprinted actual stories with illustrations
©Renegade

N-MINT

Cheque, Mate
Fantagraphics

❑1, b&w; NN ... 3.50

Cherry
Last Gasp

❑1, ca. 1977; 1: Cherry Poptart ... 8.00
❑1/2nd; 1: Cherry Poptart. 1982 ... 4.00
❑2; Adult ... 4.00
❑3; Title changes to Cherry; indicia says Cherry (nee Poptart) ... 4.00
❑4; Adult ... 3.50
❑5; Adult ... 3.50
❑6; Adult ... 3.50
❑7; Star Trek:TNG-Star Wars parody, Gilligan's Island parody; Adult ... 3.50
❑8; Oz parody Land of Woz ... 3.50
❑9; ca. 1990; Adult ... 3.50
❑10; ca. 1990; Adult ... 3.50
❑11; 3-D issue ... 4.00
❑11/2nd; Kitchen Sink reprint ... 4.00
❑12, Sum 1991; Cherry goes to Iraq ... 3.00
❑13; Last Cherry issue from Last Gasp .. 3.00
❑14, Feb 1993; O: Cherry. moves to Kitchen Sink; 1st issue at Kitchen Sink 3.00
❑15, Nov 1993; Adult ... 3.00
❑16, Nov 1994; Adult ... 3.00
❑17, Apr 1995; TMNT parody ... 3.00
❑18, Oct 1995; Adult ... 3.00
❑19, Sep 1996; moves to Cherry Comics 3.00
❑20, Mar 1999; was Kitchen Sink ... 3.00

Cherry Deluxe
Cherry

❑1, Aug 1998, b&w; Adult ... 4.00

Cherry's Jubilee
Tundra

❑1; ca. 1992; Adult ... 2.95
❑2; ca. 1992; Adult ... 2.95
❑3; ca. 1993; Adult ... 2.95
❑4, Apr 1994; Adult ... 2.95

Cheryl Blossom
Archie

❑1, Sep 1995 ... 2.50
❑2, Oct 1995 ... 2.00
❑3, Nov 1995 ... 2.00

Cheryl Blossom
Archie

❑1, Jul 1996, DDC (a) ... 2.00
❑2, Aug 1996 ... 1.50
❑3, Sep 1996 ... 1.50

Cheryl Blossom
Archie

❑1, Apr 1997 ... 2.00
❑2, May 1997 ... 1.50
❑3, Jun 1997 ... 1.50
❑4, Aug 1997 ... 1.50
❑5, Sep 1997 ... 1.50
❑6, Oct 1997 ... 1.50
❑7, Nov 1997 ... 1.50
❑8, Jan 1998 ... 1.75
❑9, Feb 1998 ... 1.75
❑10, Mar 1998 ... 1.75
❑11, Apr 1998 ... 1.75
❑12, May 1998 ... 1.75
❑13, Jun 1998 ... 1.75

N-MINT

❑14, Aug 1998 ... 1.75
❑15, Sep 1998, cover forms triptych with issue #16 and #17 ... 1.75
❑16, Oct 1998 ... 1.75
❑17, Nov 1998, DDC (c) ... 1.75
❑18, Jan 1999, Cheryl as super-model with readers' fashions ... 1.75
❑19, Feb 1999 ... 1.75
❑20, Mar 1999, DDC (c) ... 1.75
❑21, Apr 1999 ... 1.79
❑22, May 1999 ... 1.79
❑23, Jun 1999 ... 1.79
❑24, Aug 1999 ... 1.79
❑25, Sep 1999 ... 1.79
❑26, Oct 1999 ... 1.79
❑27, Nov 1999 ... 1.79
❑28, Jan 2000 ... 1.79
❑29, Feb 2000 ... 1.79
❑30, Mar 2000 ... 1.79
❑31, May 2000 ... 1.79
❑32, Jul 2000, Indicia says May, cover says Jul ... 1.79
❑33, Aug 2000 ... 1.99
❑34, Sep 2000 ... 1.99
❑35, Oct 2000 ... 1.99
❑36, Jan 2001 ... 1.99
❑37, Mar 2001 ... 1.99

Cheryl Blossom Goes Hollywood
Archie

❑1, Dec 1996 ... 1.50
❑2, Jan 1997 ... 1.50
❑3, Feb 1997 ... 1.50

Cheryl Blossom Special
Archie

❑1 ... 2.00
❑2 ... 2.00
❑3 ... 2.00
❑4 ... 2.00

Chesty Sanchez
Antarctic

❑1, Nov 1995, b&w ... 2.95
❑2, Mar 1996, b&w ... 2.95
❑3 ... 2.95
❑Special 1, Feb 1999, b&w; Super Special Edition; collects two-issue series; cardstock cover ... 5.99

Cheval Noir
Dark Horse

❑1, Aug 1989, b&w; DSt (c) ... 3.50
❑2, Oct 1989, b&w; DSt (c) ... 3.50
❑3 ... 3.50
❑4 1990 ... 3.50
❑5, Mar 1990, BB (a) ... 3.50
❑6 1990, BB (w); BB (a) ... 3.50
❑7 1990, DSt (c) ... 3.50
❑8 1990 ... 3.50
❑9 1990 ... 3.50
❑10 1990 ... 3.50
❑11 1990 ... 3.50
❑12 1990 ... 3.50
❑13 1990 ... 3.50
❑14 ... 3.50
❑15 1991 ... 3.50
❑16 1991, trading cards ... 3.75
❑17 1991, trading cards ... 3.50

N-MINT

❑18 1991, trading cards ... 3.50
❑19 1991, trading cards ... 3.50
❑20 1991 ... 4.50
❑21 1991 ... 3.95
❑22 1991 ... 4.50
❑23 1991 ... 3.95
❑24 1991 ... 3.50
❑25 1991 ... 3.50
❑26, Jan 1992 ... 3.50
❑27, Feb 1992 ... 2.95
❑28, Mar 1992 ... 2.95
❑29, Apr 1992 ... 2.95
❑30, May 1992 ... 2.95
❑31, Jun 1992 ... 2.95
❑32, Jul 1992 ... 2.95
❑33, Aug 1992 ... 2.95
❑34, Sep 1992 ... 2.95
❑35, Oct 1992 ... 2.95
❑36, Nov 1992 ... 2.95
❑37, Dec 1992 ... 2.95
❑38, Jan 1993 ... 2.95
❑39, Feb 1993 ... 2.95
❑40, Mar 1993 ... 2.95
❑41, Apr 1993 ... 2.95
❑42, May 1993 ... 2.95
❑43, Jun 1993 ... 2.95
❑44, Jul 1993 ... 2.95
❑45, Aug 1993 ... 2.95
❑46, Sep 1993 ... 2.95
❑47, Oct 1993 ... 2.95
❑48, Nov 1993 ... 2.95
❑49, Dec 1993 ... 2.95
❑50, Jan 1994, Final Issue ... 2.95

Chiaroscuro
DC / Vertigo

❑1, Jul 1995 ... 2.50
❑2, Aug 1995 ... 2.50
❑3, Sep 1995 ... 2.50
❑4, Oct 1995 ... 2.50
❑5, Nov 1995 ... 2.50
❑6, Dec 1995 ... 2.50
❑7, Jan 1996 ... 2.50
❑8, Feb 1996 ... 2.50
❑9, Mar 1996 ... 2.95
❑10, Apr 1996; Final Issue ... 2.95

Chicanos
Idea & Design Works

❑1, Dec 2005, b&w ... 3.99
❑2, Jan 2006, b&w ... 3.99
❑3, Jan 2006; b&w ... 3.99
❑4, Feb 2006; b&w ... 3.99
❑5, Apr 2006; b&w ... 3.99
❑6, Apr 2006, b&w ... 3.99
❑7, May 2006; b&w ... 3.99
❑8, Jun 2006; b&w ... 3.99

Chi Chian
Sirius

❑1, Oct 1997 ... 2.95
❑2, Dec 1997, b&w; Rough & Pulpy cover 2.95
❑2/2nd; 2nd printing ... 2.95
❑2/3rd, b&w; Rough & Pulpy cover ... 2.95
❑3, Feb 1998 ... 2.95
❑4, Apr 1998 ... 2.95
❑5, Jun 1998 ... 2.95
❑6, Aug 1998 ... 2.95

Other grades: Multiply price above by 5/6 for VF/NM • 2/3 for VERY FINE • 1/3 for FINE • 1/5 for VERY GOOD • 1/8 for GOOD

N-MINT

Chick Magnet
Voluptuous

❑1 ..... 2.95

Childhood's End
Image

❑1, Oct 1997, b&w 2.95

Children of Fire
Fantagor

❑1 ..... 2.00
❑2 ..... 2.00
❑3 ..... 2.00

Children of the Fallen Angel
Ace

❑1, Feb 1997 ..... 2.95

Children of the Night
Nightwynd

❑1, b&w 2.50
❑2, b&w 2.50
❑3, b&w 2.50
❑4, b&w 2.50

Children of the Voyager
Marvel

❑1, Sep 1993; Embossed cover 2.95
❑2, Oct 1993 ..... 1.95
❑3, Nov 1993 ..... 1.95
❑4, Dec 1993 ..... 1.95

Children's Crusade
DC / Vertigo

❑1, Dec 1993 NG (w) 4.50
❑2, Jan 1994 NG (w) 4.00

Child's Play 2: The Official Movie Adaptation
Innovation

❑1; Adapted from the screenplay by Don Mancini 2.50
❑2; Movie adaptation 2.50
❑3; Movie adaptation 2.50

Child's Play 3
Innovation

❑1; Movie adaptation 2.50
❑2; Movie adaptation 2.50
❑3, Mar 1992; Movie adaptation 2.50
❑4; Movie adaptation 2.50

Child's Play: The Series
Innovation

❑1 ..... 2.50
❑2 ..... 2.50
❑3 ..... 2.50
❑4 ..... 2.50
❑5 ..... 2.50

Chiller
Marvel / Epic

❑1 ..... 3.00
❑2, Dec 1993 ..... 3.00

Chilling Tales of Horror
Stanley

❑1 ..... 12.00
❑2, Aug 1969 ..... 10.00
❑3 ..... 10.00
❑4, Jun 1970 ..... 10.00
❑5 ..... 10.00
❑6 ..... 10.00
❑7 ..... 10.00

Chilling Tales of Horror
Stanley

❑1 ..... 9.00
❑2/A, Feb 1971 ..... 8.00
❑2/B 8.00
❑3 ..... 6.00
❑4 ..... 6.00
❑5 ..... 6.00

Chimera
CrossGen

❑1, Mar 2003 ..... 2.95
❑2, Apr 2003 ..... 2.95
❑3, May 2003 ..... 2.95
❑4, Jul 2003 ..... 2.95

Chinago and Other Stories
Tome

❑1, b&w 2.50

China Sea
Nightwynd

❑1, b&w 2.50

N-MINT

❑2, b&w 2.50
❑3, b&w 2.50
❑4, b&w 2.50

Chipmunks & Squirrels
Original Syndicate

❑1, Dec 1994; Adult 5.95

Chip 'n' Dale
Gold Key

❑1, May 1967 ..... 20.00
❑2, Aug 1968 ..... 12.00
❑3, Apr 1969 ..... 8.00
❑4, Aug 1969 ..... 8.00
❑5, Dec 1969 ..... 8.00
❑6, Mar 1970 ..... 5.00
❑7, Jun 1970 ..... 5.00
❑8, Sep 1970 ..... 5.00
❑9, Dec 1970 ..... 5.00
❑10, Mar 1971 ..... 5.00
❑11, Jun 1971 ..... 5.00
❑12, Sep 1971 ..... 5.00
❑13, Dec 1971 ..... 5.00
❑14, Mar 1972 ..... 5.00
❑15, May 1972 ..... 5.00
❑16, Jul 1972 ..... 5.00
❑17, Sep 1972 ..... 5.00
❑18, Nov 1972 ..... 5.00
❑19, Jan 1973 ..... 5.00
❑20, Mar 1973 ..... 5.00
❑21, May 1973 ..... 3.00
❑22, Jul 1973 ..... 3.00
❑23, Sep 1973 ..... 3.00
❑24, Nov 1973 ..... 3.00
❑25, Jan 1974 ..... 3.00
❑26, Mar 1974 ..... 3.00
❑27, May 1974 ..... 3.00
❑28, Jul 1974, Reprints stories from Chip 'n' Dale (1st series) #24 and 25 ..... 3.00
❑29, Sep 1974, Reprints Chip 'n' Dale stories from Walt Disney's Comics & Stores #213, 246, 251, 260, and 263. ..... 3.00
❑30, Nov 1974 ..... 3.00
❑31, Jan 1975 ..... 3.00
❑32, Mar 1975 ..... 3.00
❑33, May 1975 ..... 3.00
❑34, Jul 1975 ..... 3.00
❑35, Sep 1975 ..... 3.00
❑36, Nov 1975 ..... 3.00
❑37, Jan 1976 ..... 3.00
❑38, Mar 1976 ..... 3.00
❑39, May 1976 ..... 3.00
❑40, Jul 1976 ..... 3.00
❑41, Aug 1976 ..... 2.50
❑42, Sep 1976 ..... 2.50
❑43, Nov 1976 ..... 2.50
❑44, Jan 1977 ..... 2.50
❑45, Mar 1977 ..... 2.50
❑46, May 1977 ..... 2.50
❑47, Jul 1977 ..... 2.50
❑48, Aug 1977 ..... 2.50
❑49, Nov 1977 ..... 2.50
❑50, Jan 1978 ..... 2.50
❑51, Mar 1978 ..... 2.50
❑52, May 1978 ..... 2.50
❑53, Jul 1978 ..... 2.50
❑54, Sep 1978 ..... 2.50
❑55, Nov 1978 ..... 2.50
❑56, Jan 1979 ..... 2.50
❑57, Mar 1979 ..... 2.50
❑58, May 1979 ..... 2.50
❑59, Jul 1979 ..... 2.50
❑60, Aug 1979 ..... 2.50
❑61, Sep 1979 ..... 2.50
❑62, Oct 1979 ..... 2.50
❑63, Nov 1979 ..... 2.50
❑64, Feb 1980 ..... 2.50
❑65, Apr 1980 ..... 5.00
❑66, Jun 1980 ..... 5.00
❑67, Aug 1980 ..... 20.00
❑68, Oct 1980 ..... 17.00
❑69, ca. 1980 ..... 17.00
❑70 1981 ..... 2.50
❑71, Jun 1981 ..... 2.50
❑72, Aug 1982 ..... 2.50
❑73, Oct 1982 ..... 2.50
❑74, Dec 1982 ..... 2.50
❑75, Feb 1982 ..... 2.50
❑76 1982 ..... 2.50

N-MINT

❑77, Mar 1982 ..... 2.50
❑78 1982 ..... 10.00
❑79 1982 ..... 10.00
❑80, Jul 1983 ..... 10.00
❑81 1983 ..... 10.00
❑82 1983 ..... 10.00
❑83, Jul 1984 ..... 10.00

Chip 'n' Dale (one-shot)
Disney

❑1 ..... 3.50

Chip 'n' Dale Rescue Rangers (Disney's...)
Disney

❑1, Jun 1990 ..... 1.50
❑2, Jul 1990 ..... 1.50
❑3, Aug 1990 ..... 1.50
❑4, Sep 1990 ..... 1.50
❑5, Oct 1990 ..... 1.50
❑6, Nov 1990 ..... 1.50
❑7, Dec 1990 ..... 1.50
❑8, Jan 1991 ..... 1.50
❑9, Feb 1991 ..... 1.50
❑10, Mar 1991 ..... 1.50
❑11, Apr 1991 ..... 1.50
❑12, May 1991 ..... 1.50
❑13, Jun 1991 ..... 1.50
❑14, Jul 1991 ..... 1.50
❑15, Aug 1991 ..... 1.50
❑16, Sep 1991 ..... 1.50
❑17, Oct 1991 ..... 1.50
❑18, Nov 1991 ..... 1.50
❑19, Dec 1991 ..... 1.50

Chips and Vanilla
Kitchen Sink

❑1, Jun 1988, b&w 1.75

Chirality
CPM

❑1, Mar 1997; 1: Carol; 1: Shiori; 1: Shizuma; 1: Vic; Wraparound cover; Adult 2.95
❑2, Apr 1997; Carol reveals morph power 2.95
❑3, May 1997; 1: Patty; Adult 2.95
❑4, Jun 1997; Adult 2.95
❑5, Jul 1997; Adult 2.95
❑6, Aug 1997; 1: Adam; Adult 2.95
❑7, Sep 1997; Adult 2.95
❑8, Oct 1997; Adult 2.95
❑9, Nov 1997; Adult 2.95
❑10, Dec 1997; Adult 2.95
❑11, Jan 1998; Adult 2.95
❑12, Feb 1998; Adult 2.95
❑13, Mar 1998; Adult 2.95
❑14, Apr 1998; Adult 2.95
❑15, May 1998; Adult 2.95
❑16, Jun 1998; Adult 2.95
❑17, Jul 1998; Adult 2.95
❑18, Aug 1998; Final Issue; Adult 2.95

Chirön
Hammac

❑1, b&w; Hammac Publications 2.00
❑2, b&w; Hammac Publications 2.00
❑3, b&w; Alpha Productions takes over 2.00

Chisuji
Antarctic

❑1, ca. 2004 ..... 2.99
❑2, ca. 2004 ..... 2.99
❑3, ca. 2004 ..... 2.99
❑4, ca. 2005 ..... 2.99

Chitty Chitty Bang Bang
Gold Key

❑1, Feb 1969 ..... 35.00

C.H.I.X.
Image

❑1, Jan 1998; Bad Girl parody comic book 2.50
❑1/Variant, Jan 1998; X-Ray edition; Bad Girl parody comic book; Comic Cavalcade alternate 2.50

C.H.I.X. that Time Forgot
Image

❑1, Aug 1998; 2: Good Girl 2.95

Chobits
Tokyopop

❑1, Apr 2003, b&w; printed in Japanese format 9.99

Other grades: Multiply price above by 5/6 for VF/NM • 2/3 for VERY FINE • 1/3 for FINE • 1/5 for VERY GOOD • 1/8 for GOOD

Casper the Friendly Ghost (3rd Series)

Earlier title was called "Friendly Ghost, Casper"
©Harvey

Castle Waiting

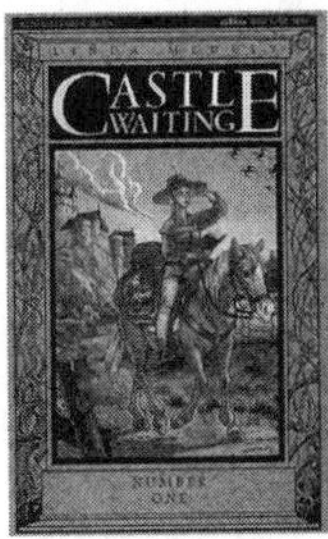

Linda Medley's medieval fantasyland
©Cartoon Books

Cat

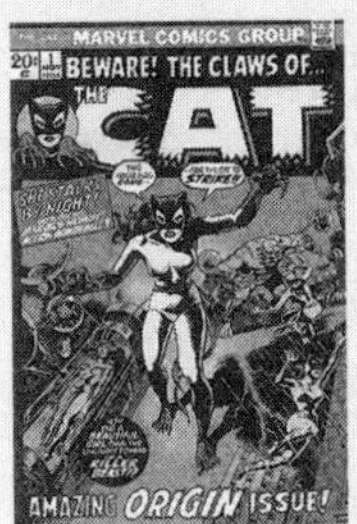

She got cattier when she became Tigra
©Marvel

Catwoman

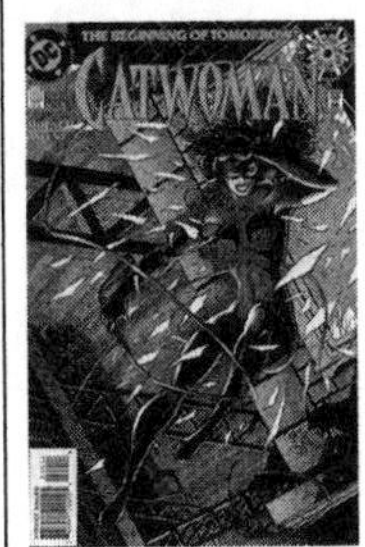

Long-running Catwoman series from 1990s
©DC

Catwoman

Restarted series somehow survived movie
©DC

N-MINT

❑2, Jul 2002, b&w; printed in Japanese format ... 9.99
❑3, Oct 2002, b&w; printed in Japanese format ... 9.99

Choices
Angry Isis

❑1; NN ... 4.00

Choke
Anubis

❑1, Mar 1993 ... 2.95
❑2 ... 2.95
❑2/Ltd., Centaur cover ... 2.95
❑Ann 1, Jul 1994 ... 2.75

Cholly & Flytrap
Image

❑1, ca. 2004 ... 4.95
❑2, May 2005 ... 4.95
❑3, ca. 2005 ... 4.95
❑4, Aug 2005 ... 4.95

Choo-Choo Charlie
Gold Key

❑1, Dec 1969 ... 60.00

Chopper: Earth, Wind & Fire
Fleetway-Quality

❑1; cardstock cover ... 2.95
❑2 ... 2.95

Chopper: Song of the Surfer
Fleetway-Quality

❑1 ... 9.95

Chosen
Martinez

❑1, Jul 1995; cover indicates Premiere Issue ... 2.50

Chosen
Dark Horse

❑1, Feb 2004 ... 2.99
❑1/2nd, Feb 2004; Reprints ... 2.99
❑2, Apr 2004 ... 2.99
❑3, Aug 2004 ... 3.00

Christian Comics & Games Magazine
Aida-Zee

❑0, b&w ... 3.50
❑1, b&w ... 3.50

Christina Winters: Agent of Death
Fantagraphics / Eros

❑1; 24 pages; Adult ... 2.95
❑2, Mar 1995; Adult ... 2.95

Christmas Classics (Walt Kelly's...)
Eclipse

❑1, Dec 1987; Peter Wheat ... 1.75

Christmas with Superswine
Fantagraphics

❑1, b&w ... 2.00

Christmas with the Super-Heroes
DC

❑1, Dec 1988; JBy (c); MA, DG, FM, NA, DD, CS, NC, JL (a); Reprints stories from DC Special Series #21, Justice League of America #110; Teen Titans #13; DC Comics Presents #67, and Batman #219; Mark Waid editorial ... 3.00
❑2, Dec 1989; DaG, JBy, ES (w); GM, JBy, DG, ES (a); New stories; Mark Waid editorial; Cover says 1989, indicia says 1988 ... 3.00

Chroma-Tick
New England

❑1, Feb 1992, trading cards;Reprints The Tick #1 in color ... 3.95
❑2, Jun 1992, "Special Edition #2"; trading cards ... 3.95
❑3, Aug 1992, Reprints ... 3.50
❑4, Oct 1992, Bush cover ... 3.50
❑4/A, Oct 1992; Perot cover ... 3.50
❑4/B, Oct 1992; Clinton cover ... 3.50
❑5 ... 3.50
❑6, Jun 1993, Includes trading card ... 3.50
❑7 ... 3.50
❑8 ... 3.50
❑9 ... 3.50

Chrome
Hot Comics

❑1, Oct 1986 ... 1.50
❑2, Oct 1986; Reprints indicia from issue #1 ... 1.50
❑3, Mar 1987 ... 1.50

Chromium Man
Triumphant

❑0, Apr 1994 ... 2.50
❑1, Jan 1994 ... 2.50
❑1/Ashcan 1994; ashcan edition ... 2.50
❑2, Sep 1994; indicia not updated through issue #7;says Jan 94; Violent Past ... 2.50
❑3, Oct 1994 ... 2.50
❑4, Nov 1994; Unleashed! ... 2.50
❑5, Nov 1994; Unleashed! ... 2.50
❑6, Jun 1994 ... 2.50
❑7, Feb 1994 ... 2.50
❑8, Mar 1994 ... 2.50
❑9, Mar 1994 ... 2.50
❑10, May 1994 ... 2.50
❑11 ... 2.50
❑12 ... 2.50
❑13 ... 2.50
❑14 ... 2.50
❑15 ... 2.50

Chromium Man: Violent Past
Triumphant

❑1 ... 2.50
❑2 ... 2.50

Chronic Apathy
Illiterature

❑1, Aug 1995, b&w ... 2.95
❑2, Sep 1995, b&w ... 2.95
❑3, Oct 1995, b&w ... 2.95
❑4, Dec 1995, b&w ... 2.95

Chronic Idiocy
Caliber

❑1, b&w; Adult ... 2.50
❑2, b&w; Adult ... 2.50
❑3, b&w; Adult ... 2.50

Chronicles of Corum
First

❑1, Jan 1987 ... 2.00
❑2, Mar 1987 ... 2.00
❑3, May 1987 ... 2.00
❑4, Jul 1987 ... 2.00
❑5, Sep 1987 ... 2.00
❑6, Nov 1987 ... 2.00
❑7, Jan 1988 ... 2.00
❑8, Mar 1988 ... 2.00
❑9, May 1988 ... 2.00
❑10, Jul 1988 ... 2.00
❑11, Sep 1988 ... 2.00
❑12, Nov 1988 ... 2.00

Chronicles of Crime and Mystery: Sherlock Holmes
Northstar

❑1, b&w ... 2.25

Chronicles of Panda Khan
Abacus

❑1 ... 1.50
❑2 ... 1.50
❑3, Apr 1988 ... 1.50
❑4 ... 1.50

Chronicles of the Cursed Sword
Tokyopop

❑1, Jul 2003 ... 9.99
❑2, Sep 2003 ... 9.99
❑3, Nov 2003 ... 9.99
❑4, Jan 2004 ... 9.99
❑5, Mar 2004 ... 9.99
❑6, May 2004 ... 9.99
❑7, Jul 2004 ... 9.99
❑8, Sep 2004 ... 9.99
❑9, Nov 2004 ... 9.99
❑10, Jan 2005 ... 9.99
❑11, Mar 2005 ... 9.99
❑12, Jun 2005 ... 9.99
❑13, Oct 2005 ... 9.99
❑14, Jan 2006 ... 9.99

Chrono Code
Tokyopop

❑1, Jul 2005, Graphic novel; b&w ... 9.99
❑2, Oct 2005 ... 9.99

Chrono Crusade
ADV Manga

❑1, ca. 2004; Graphic novel; Right to left Japanese format; b&w ... 9.99
❑2, ca. 2004; Graphic novel; Right to left Japanese format; b&w ... 9.99
❑3, ca. 2004; Graphic novel; Right to left Japanese format; b&w ... 9.99
❑4, ca. 2004; Graphic novel; Right to left Japanese format; b&w ... 9.99
❑5, ca. 2004; Graphic novel; Right to left Japanese format; b&w ... 9.99
❑6, ca. 2004; Graphic novel; Right to left Japanese format; b&w ... 9.99

Chronos
DC

❑1, Mar 1998 ... 2.50
❑2, Apr 1998 ... 2.50
❑3, May 1998 ... 2.50
❑4, Jun 1998; D: original Chronos ... 2.50
❑5, Jul 1998; O: Lucas Goodfellow Traveling Theatrical Troupe ... 2.50
❑6, Aug 1998; A: Tattooed Man. funeral of original Chronos ... 2.50
❑7, Sep 1998 ... 2.50

N-MINT | N-MINT | N-MINT

❑8, Oct 1998 .... 2.50
❑9, Dec 1998 A: Destiny 2.50
❑10, Jan 1999 A: Azrael 2.50
❑11, Feb 1999; Final Issue 2.50
❑1000000, Nov 1998 A: Hourman 3.50

Chronowar
Dark Horse / Manga

❑1, Aug 1996, b&w 2.95
❑2, Sep 1996, b&w 2.95
❑3, Oct 1996, b&w 2.95
❑4, Nov 1996, b&w 2.95
❑5, Dec 1996, b&w 2.95
❑6, Jan 1997, b&w 2.95
❑7, Feb 1997, b&w 2.95
❑8, Mar 1997, b&w 2.95
❑9, Apr 1997, b&w 2.95

Chuck Norris
Marvel / Star

❑1, Jan 1987 SD (a) 1.50
❑2, Mar 1987 SD (a) 1.25
❑3, May 1987 SD (a) 1.25
❑4, Jul 1987 .... 1.25
❑5, Sep 1987 .... 1.25

Chuk the Barbaric
Avatar

❑3; no color cover 1.25

Chyna
Chaos!

❑1, Sep 2000 .... 2.95
❑1/Variant, Sep 2000; Special cover 2.95

Cinderalla
Viz

❑1, Jun 2002; Adult 15.95

Cinder and Ashe
DC

❑1, May 1988 .... 1.75
❑2, Jun 1988 .... 1.75
❑3, Jul 1988 .... 1.75
❑4, Aug 1988 .... 1.75

Cinderella
Gold Key

❑1, Aug 1965, reprints Four-Color #786 .... 24.00

Cinnamon El Ciclo
DC

❑1, Oct 2003 .... 2.50
❑2, Nov 2003 .... 2.50
❑3, Dec 2003 .... 2.50
❑4, Jan 2004 .... 2.50
❑5, Feb 2004 .... 2.50

Circle Unleashed
Epoch

❑1, May 1995 .... 3.00

Circle Weave: Apprentice to a God
Abalone

❑1, b&w 2.00
❑2, b&w 2.00

Circus World
Hammac

❑1, b&w 2.50
❑2 .... 2.50
❑3 .... 2.50

Citizen V and the V-Battalion
Marvel

❑1, Jun 2001 .... 2.99
❑2, Jul 2001 .... 2.99
❑3, Aug 2001 .... 2.99

Citizen V and the V Battalion: The Everlasting
Marvel

❑1, Apr 2002 .... 2.99
❑2, May 2002 .... 2.99
❑3, Jun 2002 .... 2.99
❑4, Jul 2002 .... 2.99

City of Heroes
Blue King Studios

❑1, Jun 2004, based on online videogame; player's guide in back 2.95
❑2, Jul 2004 .... 2.95
❑3, Aug 2004 .... 2.95
❑4, Sep 2004 .... 2.95
❑5, Oct 2004 .... 2.95
❑6, Nov 2004 .... 2.95
❑7, Dec 2004 .... 2.95
❑8, Jan 2005 .... 2.95
❑9, Feb 2005 .... 2.95
❑10, Mar 2005 .... 2.95
❑11, Apr 2005 .... 2.95
❑12, May 2005 .... 2.95

City of Heroes
Image

❑1, Jun 2005 MWa (w) 2.99
❑1/Keown, Jun 2005 MWa (w) 5.00
❑1/Perez, Jun 2005 GP (c); MWa (w) 4.00
❑2, Jul 2005 MWa (w) 2.99
❑3, Aug 2005 MWa (w) 2.99
❑4, Sep 2005 .... 2.99
❑5, Oct 2005 .... 2.99
❑6, Nov 2005 .... 2.99
❑7, Dec 2005 .... 2.99
❑8, Jan 2006 .... 2.99
❑9, Jan 2006 .... 2.99
❑10, Feb 2006 .... 2.99
❑11, Mar 2006 .... 2.99
❑12, May 2006 .... 2.99
❑13, Jun 2006 .... 2.99
❑14, Jul 2006 .... 2.99
❑15, Oct 2006 .... 2.99
❑16, Nov 2006 .... 2.99
❑17, Feb 2007 .... 2.99

City of Silence
Image

❑1, May 2000 .... 2.50
❑2, Jun 2000 .... 2.50
❑3, Jul 2000 .... 2.50

City of Tomorrow
DC

❑1, Jun 2005 .... 5.00
❑2, Jul 2005 .... 2.99
❑3, Aug 2005 .... 2.99
❑4, Sep 2005 .... 2.99
❑5, Oct 2005 .... 2.99
❑6, Nov 2005 .... 2.99

City Surgeon
Gold Key

❑1, Aug 1963 .... 18.00

Civil War
Marvel

❑1, Jul 2006, D: Namorita; D: Night Thrasher; D: Microbe 5.00
❑2, Aug 2006, Spider-Man reveals his identity to the world 7.00
❑2/Variant, Aug 2006 .... 8.00
❑3, Oct 2006 .... 5.00
❑3/2nd, Oct 2006 .... 2.99
❑4, Nov 2006, D: Goliath 5.00
❑4/Variant, Nov 2006 .... 2.99
❑5/Variant, Dec 2006 .... 2.99
❑5, Dec 2006 .... 4.00
❑6, Jan 2007 .... 4.00

Civil War: Choosing Sides
Marvel

❑1, Jan 2007 .... 3.99

Civil War Files
Marvel

❑1, Nov 2006, Arachne thru Young Avengers; Civil War Files Appendix; Arachne through Young Avengers 3.99

Civil War: Front Line
Marvel

❑1, Aug 2006 .... 2.99
❑2, Sep 2006 .... 2.99
❑3, Sep 2006; D: Bantam 2.99
❑4, Oct 2006 .... 2.99
❑5, Oct 2006 .... 2.99
❑6, Dec 2006 .... 2.99
❑7, Dec 2006 .... 2.99
❑8, Feb 2007 .... 2.99
❑9, Mar 2007 .... 2.99
❑10, Mar 2007, 1: Penance 2.99

Civil War: The Confession
Marvel

❑1, Mar 2007 .... 8.00

Civil War: The Initiative
Marvel

❑1, Apr 2007; 1: Omega Flight; Civil War Epilogue 6.00

Civil War: War Crimes One-Shot
Marvel

❑1, Mar 2007 .... 3.99

Civil War: X-Men
Marvel

❑1, Oct 2006 .... 2.99
❑2, Oct 2006 .... 2.99
❑3, Nov 2006 .... 2.99
❑4, Dec 2006, Shatterstar; Domino; Bishop; Iceman; Cyclops; Emma Frost; Angel; Beast 2.99

Civil War: Young Avengers & Runaways
Marvel

❑1, Oct 2006, Civil War 2.99
❑2, Nov 2006, Civil War 2.99
❑3, Dec 2006, Civil War 2.99
❑4, Jan 2007, Civil War tie-in 2.99

Clair Voyant
Lightning

❑1, Jun 1996, b&w 3.50

Clan Apis
Active Synapse

❑1, b&w; educational comic about bees 2.95
❑2, Dec 1998 .... 2.95
❑3, Feb 1999 .... 2.95
❑4, Apr 1999 .... 2.95
❑5, Apr 1999, b&w 3.95

Clandestine
Marvel

❑1, Oct 1994; foil cover 2.95
❑2, Nov 1994; Wraparound cover 2.50
❑3, Dec 1994 .... 2.50
❑4, Jan 1995 .... 2.50
❑5, Feb 1995 .... 2.50
❑6, Mar 1995 .... 2.50
❑7, Apr 1995 .... 2.50
❑8, May 1995 .... 2.50
❑9, Jun 1995 .... 2.50
❑10, Jul 1995 .... 2.50
❑11, Aug 1995 .... 2.50
❑12, Sep 1995; Final Issue 2.50
❑Ashcan 1, Oct 1994; Preview 1.50

Claritin Syrup Presents Looney Tunes
DC

❑1, ca. 1998; Promotional giveaway about allergies and Claritin Syrup 3.00

Clash
DC

❑1, ca. 1991 .... 4.95
❑2, ca. 1991 .... 4.95
❑3, ca. 1991 .... 4.95

Classic Adventure Strips
Dragon Lady

❑1, May 1985; King of the Royal Mounted 4.00
❑2, Jul 1985; Red Ryder 4.00
❑3, Sep 1985; Dickie Dare, Flash Gordon 4.00
❑4, Nov 1985; FR (w); FR (a); Buz Sawyer; Johnny Hazard; Steve Canyon 4.00
❑5, Jan 1986; Wash Tubbs 4.00
❑6, Mar 1986; Mandrake the Magician, Johnny Hazard, Rip Kirby 4.00
❑7, Jul 1986; Buz Sawyer 4.00
❑8, Oct 1986 .... 4.00
❑9, Jan 1987 .... 4.00
❑10, Apr 1987 MA (w); MA (a) 4.00

Classic Girls
Eternity

❑1, b&w; Reprints 2.50
❑2, Jan 1991, b&w; Reprints 2.50
❑3, b&w; Reprints 2.50
❑4, b&w; Reprints 2.50

Classic Jonny Quest: Skull & Double Crossbones
Illustrated Productions

❑1, Mar 1996; smaller than normal size comic book; No cover price; inserted with Jonny Quest videos 1.00

Classic Jonny Quest: The Quetong Missile Mystery
Illustrated Productions

❑1, Mar 1996; smaller than normal size comic book; No cover price; inserted with Jonny Quest videos 1.00

Other grades: Multiply price above by 5/6 for VF/NM • 2/3 for VERY FINE • 1/3 for FINE • 1/5 for VERY GOOD • 1/8 for GOOD

Cave Kids

Pebbles and Bamm Bamm dropped in

©Gold Key

Cavewoman Color Special

Jungle titillation with overendowed heroine

©Avatar

Centurions

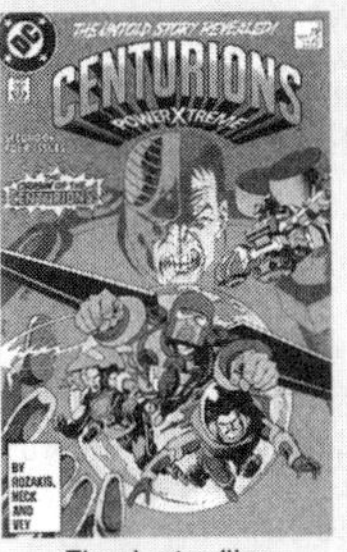

They kept yelling "Power Xtreme!"

©DC

Cerebus Bi-Weekly

Faithful reprinting of Cerebus the Aardvark

©Aardvark-Vanaheim

Cerebus Guide to Self Publishing

Excellent primer from Dave Sim

©Aardvark-Vanaheim

N-MINT

Classic Punisher
Marvel

❑1, Dec 1989, b&w; prestige format; Reprints Punisher stories from Marvel Preview #2, Marvel Super Action #1... 4.95

Classics Illustrated (First)
First

❑1, Feb 1990; Raven ... 4.00
❑2, Feb 1990 ... 4.00
❑3, Feb 1990 ... 4.00
❑4, Feb 1990 BSz (c); BSz (a) ... 4.00
❑5, Mar 1990 ... 4.00
❑6, Mar 1990; CR (w); CR (a); Scarlet Letter 4.00
❑7, Apr 1990; DS (a); Count of Monte Cristo 4.00
❑8, Apr 1990; JK (a); Doctor Jekyll & Mr. Hyde ... 4.00
❑9, May 1990; MP (c); MP (a); Adventures of Tom Sawyer ... 4.00
❑10, Jun 1990 ... 4.00
❑11, Jul 1990 ... 4.00
❑12, Aug 1990; Island of Doctor Moreau 4.00
❑13, Oct 1990 ... 4.00
❑14, Sep 1990 CR (a) ... 4.00
❑15, Nov 1990; Gift of Magi ... 4.00
❑16, Dec 1990; JSa (w); JSa (a); Christmas Carol ... 4.00
❑17 1991 ... 4.00
❑18 1991; Jungle ... 4.00
❑19, Feb 1991 ... 4.00
❑20, Mar 1991; Invisible Man ... 4.00
❑21 1991 ... 4.00
❑22 1991; Jungle Books; The Jungle Books ... 4.00
❑23, Apr 1991; Robinson Crusoe ... 4.00
❑24, May 1991 ... 4.00
❑25, May 1991 ... 4.00
❑26, Jun 1991 ... 4.00
❑27, Jun 1991 ... 4.00

Classics Illustrated Study Guide
Acclaim

❑1, Jan 1997; All Quiet on the Western Front 4.99
❑2, Jan 1997; Around the World in 80 Days 4.99
❑3, Sep 1997; The Call of the Wild ... 4.99
❑4, Nov 1997; Captains Courageous ... 4.99
❑5, Dec 1997; A Christmas Carol ... 4.99
❑6, Jan 1997; The Count of Monte Cristo 4.99
❑7, Aug 1997; David Copperfield ... 4.99
❑8, Oct 1997; Doctor Jekyll and Mr. Hyde 4.99
❑9, Dec 1997; Don Quixote ... 5.25
❑10, Feb 1997; Faust ... 4.99
❑11, Oct 1997; Frankenstein ... 4.99
❑12, Apr 1997; Great Expectations ... 4.99
❑13, Sep 1997; The Hunchback of Notre Dame ... 4.99
❑14, Dec 1997; The Iliad ... 4.99
❑15, Oct 1997; The Invisible Man ... 4.99
❑16, Aug 1997; Julius Caesar ... 4.99
❑17, Aug 1997; The Jungle Book ... 4.99
❑18, Jan 1997; Kidnapped ... 4.99
❑19, Feb 1997; Kim ... 4.99
❑20, Dec 1997; The Last of the Mohicans 4.99
❑21, Sep 1997; Lord Jim ... 4.99
❑22, Aug 1997; The Man in the Iron Mask 4.99
❑23, Nov 1997; The Master of Ballantrae 4.99
❑24, Apr 1997; A Midsummer Night's Dream ... 4.99

N-MINT

❑25, Apr 1997; Moby Dick ... 4.99
❑26 1997; new adaptation of Narrative of the Life of Frederick Douglass ... 4.99
❑27, Apr 1997; The Prince and the Pauper 4.99
❑28, Aug 1997; Pudd'nhead Wilson ... 4.99
❑29, Sep 1997; Robinson Crusoe ... 4.99
❑30 1997; new adaptation of The Scarlet Pimpernel ... 4.99
❑31, Nov 1997; Silas Marner ... 4.99
❑32, Feb 1997; War of the Worlds ... 4.99
❑33, Nov 1997; Wuthering Heights ... 4.99
❑34, Feb 1997; NN ... 4.99
❑35, Feb 1997; NN ... 4.99
❑36, Feb 1997; NN ... 4.99
❑37, Jul 1997; NN ... 4.99
❑38, Feb 1997; NN ... 4.99

Classic Star Wars
Dark Horse

❑1, Aug 1992, AW (c); AW (a) ... 4.00
❑2, Sep 1992, AW (c); AW (a) ... 3.50
❑3, Oct 1992, AW (c); AW (a) ... 3.50
❑4, Nov 1992, AW (c); AW (a) ... 3.25
❑5, Dec 1992, AW (c); AW (a) ... 3.25
❑6, Jan 1993, AW (c); AW (a) ... 3.00
❑7, Feb 1993, AW (c); AW (a) ... 3.00
❑8, Apr 1993, AW (c); AW (a); trading card 3.00
❑9, May 1993, AW (c); AW (a) ... 3.00
❑10, Jun 1993, AW (c); AW (a) ... 3.00
❑11, Aug 1993, AW (a) ... 3.00
❑12, Sep 1993, AW (a) ... 3.00
❑13, Oct 1993, TY (c); AW (a) ... 3.00
❑14, Nov 1993, AW (c); AW (a) ... 3.00
❑15, Jan 1994, AW (c); AW (a) ... 3.00
❑16, Feb 1994, TY (c); AW (a) ... 3.00
❑17, Mar 1994, AW (a) ... 3.00
❑18, Apr 1994, AW (a) ... 3.00
❑19, May 1994, GE (c); AW (a) ... 3.00
❑20, Jun 1994, Giant-size; AW (c); AW (a); Final Issue; Includes trading card ... 3.50

Classic Star Wars: A Long Time Ago
Dark Horse

❑1, Mar 1999 ... 12.95
❑2, Apr 1999 ... 12.95
❑3, May 1999; no cover price ... 12.95
❑4, Jun 1999; no cover price ... 12.95
❑5, Jul 1999; no cover price ... 12.95
❑6, Aug 1999 ... 12.95

Classic Star Wars: A New Hope
Dark Horse

❑1, Jun 1994; prestige format; Collects Star Wars (Marvel) #1-3 ... 3.95
❑2, Jul 1994; prestige format; Collects Star Wars (Marvel) #4-6 ... 3.95

Classic Star Wars: Devilworlds
Dark Horse

❑1, Aug 1996, Reprints from Star Wars: The Empire Strikes Back Weekly #153, 155, 157, 159 ... 2.50
❑2, Sep 1996, Reprints from Star Wars: The Empire Strikes Back Weekly #151, 154, 156 ... 2.50

Classic Star Wars: Han Solo at Stars' End
Dark Horse

❑1, Mar 1997; adapts Brian Daley novel; cardstock cover ... 2.95

N-MINT

❑2, Apr 1997; adapts Brian Daley novel; cardstock cover ... 2.95
❑3, May 1997; adapts Brian Daley novel; cardstock cover ... 2.95

Classic Star Wars: Return of the Jedi
Dark Horse

❑1, Oct 1994, AW (a); polybagged with trading card ... 3.50
❑2, Nov 1994, AW (a); Cardstock cover. 3.95

Classic Star Wars: The Early Adventures
Dark Horse

❑1, Aug 1994 ... 2.50
❑2, Sep 1994 ... 2.50
❑3, Oct 1994 ... 2.50
❑4, Nov 1994 ... 2.50
❑5, Dec 1994 ... 2.50
❑6, Jan 1995 ... 2.50
❑7, Feb 1995 ... 2.50
❑8, Mar 1995 ... 2.50
❑9, Apr 1995 ... 2.50

Classic Star Wars: The Empire Strikes Back
Dark Horse

❑1, Aug 1994; prestige format ... 3.95
❑2, Sep 1994; prestige format ... 3.95

Classic Star Wars: The Vandelhelm Mission
Dark Horse

❑1, Mar 1995; Reprint from Star Wars (Marvel) Vol.1, No.89, "Supply And Demand" ... 2.50

Classic X-Men
Marvel

❑1, Sep 1986 DC (a) ... 6.00
❑2, Oct 1986; DC (a); Reprints X-Men (1st Series) #94 ... 4.00
❑3, Nov 1986; DC (a); Reprints X-Men (1st Series) #95; Front cover by Arthur Adams; Back Cover by John Bolton ... 3.00
❑4, Dec 1986; DC (a); Reprints X-Men (1st Series) #96; Front cover by Arthur Adams and Craig Russell; Back Cover by John Bolton ... 3.00
❑5, Jan 1987; DC (a); Reprints X-Men (1st Series) #97 ... 3.00
❑6, Feb 1987; DC (a); Reprints X-Men (1st Series) #98 ... 2.50
❑7, Mar 1987; DC (a); Reprints X-Men (1st Series) #99; D: Lourdes Chantel; D: Ned Buckman ... 2.50
❑8, Apr 1987; DC (a); Reprints X-Men (1st Series) #100; Front cover by Arthur Adams; Back Cover by John Bolton ... 2.50
❑9, May 1987; DC (a); Reprints X-Men (1st Series) #101; Front cover by Arthur Adams; Back Cover by John Bolton ... 2.50
❑10, Jun 1987; DC, JR (a); Reprints X-Men (1st Series) #102 ... 2.50
❑11, Jul 1987; Reprints X-Men (1st Series) #103 ... 2.50
❑12, Aug 1987; DC (a); Reprints X-Men (1st Series) #104 ... 2.50
❑13, Sep 1987; BL, DC (a); Reprints X-Men (1st Series) #105 ... 2.50
❑14, Oct 1987; DC (a); Reprints X-Men (1st Series) #106 ... 2.50

❑15, Nov 1987; JBy (a); Reprints X-Men (1st Series) #108; O: Starjammers 2.50
❑16, Dec 1987; JBy (a); Reprints X-Men (1st Series) #109 ..... 2.50
❑17, Jan 1988; Reprints X-Men (1st Series) #111; V: Mesmero 2.50
❑18, Feb 1988; JBy (a); Reprints X-Men (1st Series) #112 ..... 2.50
❑19, Mar 1988; JBy (w); JBy (a); Reprints X-Men (1st Series) #113 ..... 2.50
❑20, Apr 1988; JBy (w); JBy (a); Reprints X-Men (1st Series) #114 ..... 2.50
❑21, May 1988; JBy (w); JBy (a); Reprints X-Men (1st Series) #115 ..... 2.50
❑22, Jun 1988; JBy (w); JBy, FM (a); Reprints X-Men (1st Series) #116 ..... 2.50
❑23, Jul 1988; JBy (w); JBy (a); Reprints X-Men (1st Series) #117 ..... 2.50
❑24, Aug 1988; Reprints X-Men (1st Series) #118 ..... 2.50
❑25, Sep 1988; Reprints X-Men (1st Series) #119 ..... 2.50
❑26, Oct 1988; Reprints X-Men (1st Series) #120 ..... 2.50
❑27, Nov 1988; Reprints X-Men (1st Series) #121 ..... 2.50
❑28, Dec 1988; Reprints X-Men (1st Series) #122 ..... 2.50
❑29, Jan 1989; Reprints X-Men (1st Series) #123 ..... 2.50
❑30, Feb 1989; Reprints X-Men (1st Series) #124 ..... 2.00
❑31, Mar 1989; JBy (a); Reprints X-Men (1st Series) #125 ..... 2.00
❑32, Apr 1989; Reprints X-Men (1st Series) #126 ..... 2.00
❑33, May 1989; Reprints X-Men (1st Series) #127 ..... 2.00
❑34, Jun 1989; Reprints X-Men (1st Series) #128 ..... 2.00
❑35, Jul 1989; Reprints X-Men (1st Series) #129 ..... 2.00
❑36, Aug 1989; Reprints X-Men (1st Series) #130 ..... 2.00
❑37, Sep 1989; Reprints X-Men (1st Series) #131 ..... 2.00
❑38, Oct 1989; Reprints X-Men (1st Series) #132 ..... 2.00
❑39, Nov 1989; Reprints X-Men (1st Series) #133 ..... 2.00
❑40, Nov 1989; Reprints X-Men (1st Series) #134 ..... 2.00
❑41, Dec 1989; Reprints X-Men (1st Series) #135 ..... 2.00
❑42, Dec 1989; Reprints X-Men (1st Series) #136 ..... 2.00
❑43, Jan 1990; Reprints X-Men (1st Series) #137 ..... 2.00
❑44, Feb 1990; Reprints X-Men (1st Series) #138 ..... 2.00
❑45, Mar 1990; Series continued in X-Men Classic #46 ..... 2.00

Claus
Draco

❑1, Dec 1997 ..... 2.95
❑2, Feb 1998 ..... 2.95

Claws
Conquest

❑1, b&w 2.95

Claws
Marvel

❑1, Oct 2006, b&w 3.99
❑2, Nov 2006 ..... 3.99
❑3, Dec 2006 ..... 3.99

Claw the Unconquered
DC

❑1, Jun 1975, 1: Claw the Unconquered. 7.00
❑2, Aug 1975 ..... 4.00
❑3, Oct 1975 ..... 3.00
❑4, Dec 1975 ..... 2.00
❑5, Feb 1976 ..... 2.00
❑6, Apr 1976 ..... 2.00
❑7, Jun 1976 ..... 4.00
❑8, Aug 1976, Bicentennial #18 ..... 2.00
❑9, Oct 1976, O: Claw the Unconquered 2.00
❑10, May 1978 ..... 2.00
❑11, Jul 1978 ..... 2.00
❑12, Sep 1978, Final Issue 2.00

Claw the Unconquered
DC

❑1, Sep 2006, 1: Claw the Unconquered; 1: King Occulas 7.00
❑2, Sep 2006 ..... 2.99
❑3, Nov 2006 ..... 2.99
❑4, Nov 2006 ..... 2.99
❑5, Dec 2006 ..... 2.99
❑6, Jan 2007 ..... 2.99

Clem: Mall Security
Spit Take

❑0, ca. 1997, b&w 2.00

Cleopatra
Rip Off

❑1, Feb 1992, b&w; NN; Adult 2.50

Clerks: The Comic Book
Oni

❑1, Feb 1998 KSm (w) 5.00
❑1/2nd; KSm (w); 2nd printing 3.00
❑1/3rd; KSm (w); 3rd printing 3.00
❑1/4th, May 1998; KSm (w); 4th printing 3.00
❑2, Dec 1999; KSm (w); The Lost Scene 3.00
❑Holiday 1, Dec 1998, b&w; Double-size KSm (w) 4.00

Cletus and Floyd Show
Asylum

❑1, Mar 2002 ..... 2.95

CLF: Cybernetic Liberation Front
Anubis

❑1 ..... 2.75

Click!
NBM

❑1; Adult 10.95
❑2; Adult 12.95
❑3; ca. 1998; Adult 12.95
❑4; ca. 2002; Adult 10.95

Cliffhanger!
Image

❑1, ca. 1997 ..... 3.00

Cliffhanger Comics
AC

❑1, ca. 1989, b&w; Tom Mix Western; Don Winslow serial (photo-text) 2.50
❑2, ca. 1989, b&w; Tom Mix Western 2.50

Cliffhanger Comics
AC

❑1/A 1990, b&w; new and reprint 2.75
❑2/A, Aug 1990, b&w; new and reprint.. 2.75

Climaxxx
Aircel

❑1, Apr 1991, Adult 3.50
❑2, May 1991, Adult 3.50
❑3, Jun 1991, Adult 3.50
❑4, Jul 1991, Adult 3.50

Clint
Trigon

❑1, Sep 1986 ..... 1.50
❑2, Jan 1987 ..... 1.50

Clint: The Hamster Triumphant
Eclipse

❑1, b&w 1.50
❑2, b&w 1.50

Clive Barker's The Great and Secret Show
Idea & Design Works

❑1, Apr 2006 ..... 3.99
❑2, May 2006 ..... 3.99
❑3, Jun 2006 ..... 3.99
❑4, Jul 2006 ..... 3.99
❑5, Aug 2006 ..... 3.99
❑6, Sep 2006 ..... 3.99
❑7, Nov 2006 ..... 3.99
❑8, Jan 2007 ..... 3.99

Cloak & Dagger
Marvel

❑1, Oct 1983, TD (a); 1: Brigid O'Reilly.. 2.95
❑2, Nov 1983, TD (a) 2.95
❑3, Dec 1983, TD (a) 2.00
❑4, Jan 1984, TD (a); O: Cloak & Dagger 2.00

Cloak & Dagger
Marvel

❑1, Jul 1985 ..... 2.00
❑2, Sep 1985, TD (a) 1.50
❑3, Nov 1985, TD (a); A: Spider-Man 1.50
❑4, Jan 1986, Secret Wars II 1.50
❑5, Mar 1985; TD (a); 1&O: Mayhem 1.25
❑6, May 1985 TD (a) 1.25
❑7, Jul 1985 TD (a) 1.25
❑8, Sep 1985 TD (a) 1.25
❑9, Nov 1985 TD (a) 1.25
❑10, Jan 1986; TD (a); V: Dr. Doom 1.25
❑11, Mar 1986; Giant-size; TD (a); Final Issue 1.50

Cloak and Dagger in Predator and Prey
Marvel

❑1; prestige format; Cloak & Dagger; ca. 1988 ..... 6.95

Clock!
Top Shelf

❑3, b&w 2.95

Clockmaker
Image

❑1, Feb 2003 ..... 2.50
❑2, Mar 2003 ..... 2.50
❑3, May 2003 ..... 2.50
❑4, Jun 2003 ..... 2.50

Clockmaker Act 2
Image

❑1 2003 ..... 4.95
❑2, Aug 2004 ..... 4.95

Clockwork Angels
Image

❑1, b&w; digest-sized 10.95

Clonezone Special
Dark Horse

❑1, b&w 2.00

Close Shaves of Pauline Peril
Gold Key

❑1, Jun 1970 ..... 20.00
❑2, Sep 1970 ..... 14.00
❑3, Dec 1970 ..... 14.00
❑4, Mar 1971 ..... 14.00

Cloudfall
Image

❑1, Dec 2003 ..... 4.95

Clown Figure
Image

❑1, ca. 1994; packaged with Todd Toys' Clown action figure 1.00

Clown: Nobody's Laughing Now
Fleetway-Quality

❑1 ..... 4.95

Clowns
Yahoo Pro

❑1, Adult 3.00

Clowns
Dark Horse

❑1, Apr 1998, b&w; adapts Leoncavallo opera 2.95

Clyde Crashcup
Dell

❑1, Aug 1963 ..... 90.00
❑2 1963 ..... 65.00
❑3, May 1964 ..... 48.00
❑4, Jun 1964 ..... 48.00
❑5, Sep 1964 ..... 48.00

Cobalt 60
Tundra

❑1 ..... 4.95
❑2 ..... 4.95

Cobalt Blue
Power

❑1, Jan 1978, MGu (c); MGu (a) 2.00

Cobalt Blue
Innovation

❑1, Sep 1989 MGu (a) 2.00
❑2, Oct 1989 MGu (a) 2.00
❑GN 1; KP (a); Graphic novel 5.95

Cobbler's Monster
Image

❑1, Jul 2006 ..... 14.99

Cobb: Off the Leash
Idea & Design Works

❑1, Jun 2006 ..... 3.99
❑2, Jul 2006 ..... 3.99
❑3, Sep 2006 ..... 3.99

Other grades: Multiply price above by 5/6 for VF/NM • 2/3 for VERY FINE • 1/3 for FINE • 1/5 for VERY GOOD • 1/8 for GOOD

Cerebus High Society

Reprinting the second Cerebus story arc

Cerebus Jam

Will Eisner and more contributed

Cerebus the Aardvark

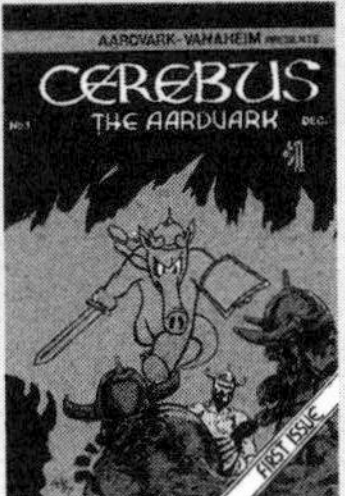

Amazing "6,000-page graphic novel"

Chain Gang War

Vigilantes seek to make villains serve time

Challengers of the Unknown

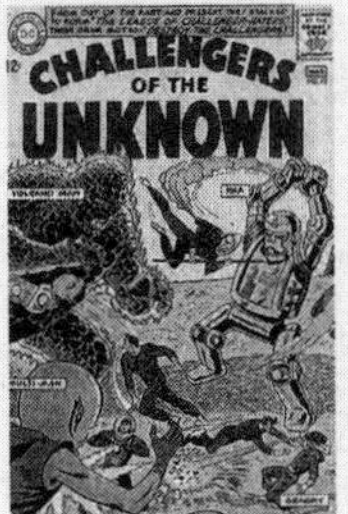

Team of adventurers goes exploring

N-MINT

Cobra
Viz

❑1 2.95
❑2 2.95
❑3 2.95
❑4 2.95
❑5 2.95
❑6 2.95
❑7 3.25
❑8 3.25
❑9 3.25
❑10 3.25
❑11 3.25
❑12 3.25

Cocopiazo
Slave Labor

❑1, Dec 2004 2.95
❑2, Dec 2005 2.95
❑3, Apr 2005 2.95
❑4, Sep 2005 2.95

Coda
Coda

❑1 2.00
❑2 2.00
❑3 2.00
❑4 2.00

Code Blue
Image

❑1, Apr 1998 2.95

Codename: Danger
Lodestone

❑1, Aug 1985 RB (a) 2.00
❑2, Oct 1985 1.75
❑3, Jan 1986 PS (a) 1.75
❑4, May 1986 1.75

Codename: Firearm
Malibu

❑0, Jun 1995, b&w 2.95
❑1, Jun 1995, b&w 2.95
❑2, Jul 1995, b&w 2.95
❑3, Jul 1995, b&w 2.95
❑4, Aug 1995, b&w 2.95
❑5, Aug 1995, b&w 2.95

Codename: Genetix
Marvel

❑1, Feb 1993 1.75
❑2, Mar 1993 1.75
❑3, Apr 1993 1.75
❑4, May 1993 1.75

Codename: Knockout
DC / Vertigo

❑0, Jun 2001 2.50
❑1, Jul 2001 2.50
❑2, Aug 2001 2.50
❑3, Sep 2001 2.50
❑4, Oct 2001 2.50
❑5, Nov 2001 2.50
❑6, Dec 2001 2.50
❑7, Jan 2002 2.50
❑8, Feb 2002 2.50
❑9, Mar 2002 2.50
❑10, Apr 2002 2.50
❑11, May 2002 2.50

N-MINT

❑12, Jun 2002 2.50
❑13, Jul 2002 2.50
❑14, Aug 2002; 1: Divinita Beastly; 1: Ravish Kinkimanboi 2.50
❑15, Sep 2002 2.50
❑16, Oct 2002 2.75
❑17, Nov 2002 2.75
❑18, Dec 2002 2.75
❑19, Feb 2003 2.75
❑20, Mar 2003 2.75
❑21, Apr 2003 2.75
❑22, May 2003 2.75
❑23, Jun 2003; Final issue 2.75

Code Name Ninja
Solson

❑1, b&w 2.00

Codename: Scorpio
Antarctic

❑1, Oct 1996, b&w 2.95
❑2, Apr 1997, b&w 2.95
❑3, Jul 1997, b&w 2.95
❑4, Sep 1997, b&w 2.95

Codename: Spitfire
Marvel

❑10, Jul 1987; Series continued from Spitfire and the Troubleshooters #9 1.00
❑11, Aug 1987 1.00
❑12, Sep 1987 1.00
❑13, Oct 1987 1.00

Codename: Strikeforce
Spectrum

❑1, Jun 1984 1.50

Codename: Stryke Force
Image

❑0, Jun 1995, indicia says Jun, cover says Jul 2.50
❑1, Jan 1994 2.50
❑1/Gold, Jan 1994, Gold promotional ed. 3.00
❑1/Variant, Jan 1994, blue embossed ed. 2.50
❑2, Mar 1994 1.95
❑3, Apr 1994 1.95
❑4, Jun 1994 1.95
❑5, Jul 1994 1.95
❑6, Aug 1994 1.95
❑7, Oct 1994 1.95
❑8/A, Nov 1994, same cover, different poster 1.95
❑8/B, Nov 1994, same cover, different poster 1.95
❑8/C, Nov 1994, same cover, different poster 1.95
❑9, Dec 1994 1.95
❑10, Jan 1995 1.95
❑11, Mar 1995 1.95
❑12, Apr 1995 1.95
❑13, May 1995 2.25
❑14, Aug 1995 2.25

Code of Honor
Marvel

❑1, Jan 1997 5.95
❑2, Mar 1997 5.95
❑3, Apr 1997 5.95
❑4, May 1997 5.95

N-MINT

Cody Starbuck
Star*Reach

❑1, Jul 1978 2.00

Co-Ed Sexxtasy
Fantagraphics / Eros

❑1, Dec 1999; Adult 3.50
❑2, Jan 2000; Adult 3.50
❑3, Feb 2000; Adult 3.50
❑4, Mar 2000; Adult 3.50
❑5, Apr 2000; Adult 3.50
❑6, May 2000; Adult 3.50
❑7, Jun 2000; Adult 3.50
❑8, Jul 2000; Adult 3.50
❑9, Aug 2000; Adult 3.50
❑10, Sep 2000; Adult 3.50
❑11, Oct 2000; Adult 3.50

Coexisting
Alternative

❑1, ca. 2005 2.99

Coffin
Oni

❑1, Sep 2000, b&w 6.00
❑2, Nov 2000; b&w 4.00

Coffin Blood
Monster

❑1, b&w 3.95

Cold Blooded
Northstar

❑1, b&w; Adult 2.95
❑2, Sep 1993, b&w; Adult 2.95
❑3, Dec 1993, b&w; Adult 4.95

Cold-Blooded Chameleon Commandos
Blackthorne

❑1; 1&O: The Cold-Blooded Chameleon Commandos 1.50
❑2 1.50
❑3 1.50
❑4 1.50
❑5 1.50

Cold Blooded: The Burning Kiss
Northstar

❑1, Nov 1993, b&w; cardstock cover 4.95

Cold Eden
Legacy

❑4, Nov 1995, b&w; cover says Feb 96, indicia says Nov 95 2.35

Collection
Eternity

❑1 2.95

Collector's Dracula
Millennium

❑1; 48 pgs; ca. 1994 3.95
❑2 3.95

Collectors Guide to the Ultraverse
Malibu / Ultraverse

❑1, Aug 1994 1.00

Collier's
Fantagraphics

❑1, b&w 2.75
❑2, b&w 3.25

Colonia
Colonia

❑1, Oct 1998, b&w ... 2.95
❑1/2nd, ca. 1998, b&w; 2nd printing ... 2.95
❑2, ca. 1999, b&w ... 2.95
❑3, ca. 1999, b&w ... 2.95
❑4, ca. 2000, b&w ... 2.95
❑5, ca. 2001, b&w ... 2.95
❑6, ca. 2002, b&w ... 2.95
❑7, ca. 2002, b&w ... 2.95
❑8, ca. 2003, b&w ... 2.95
❑9, ca. 2004, b&w ... 2.95
❑10, ca. 2004, b&w ... 2.95
❑11, Nov 2004; b&w ... 3.50

Colors in Black
Dark Horse

❑1, Mar 1995 ... 2.95
❑2 1995 ... 2.95
❑3 1995 ... 2.95
❑4 1995 ... 2.95

Colossal Show
Gold Key

❑1, Oct 1969 ... 25.00

Colossus
Marvel

❑1, Oct 1997; gatefold summary; gatefold cover ... 2.99

Colossus: God's Country
Marvel

❑1; prestige format; One-shot ... 6.95

Colour of Magic
Innovation

❑1 ... 2.50
❑2 ... 2.50
❑3 ... 2.50
❑4 ... 2.50

Colt Special
AC

❑1, Aug 1985; 1: The Specialists ... 1.50

Columbus
Dark Horse

❑1, b&w ... 2.50

Colville
King Ink

❑1, Sep 1997, b&w; NN ... 3.00

Combat
Image

❑1, Jan 1996 ... 2.50
❑2, Jan 1996 ... 2.50

Combat Kelly
Marvel

❑1, Jun 1972, JSe (c); JM (a); O: Combat Kelly. Combat Kelly becomes leader of Dum-Dum Dugan's Deadly Dozen (from Sgt. Fury #98) ... 10.00
❑2, Aug 1972, JSe (c) ... 6.00
❑3, Oct 1972, (c); O: Combat Kelly ... 6.00
❑4, Dec 1972, (c); A: Sgt. Fury and his Howling Commandos ... 4.00
❑5, Feb 1973, (c) ... 4.00
❑6, Apr 1973, (c) ... 4.00
❑7, Jun 1973, (c) ... 4.00
❑8, Aug 1973, (c) ... 4.00
❑9, Oct 1973, D: Deadly Dozen. Combat Kelly leaves team ... 4.00

Combat Zone
Avalon

❑1, b&w; Reprints ... 2.95

Come Again
Fantagraphics / Eros

❑1, Feb 1997 ... 2.95
❑2, May 1997 ... 2.95

Comet
Archie / Red Circle

❑1, Oct 1983, O: Comet ... 1.00
❑2, Dec 1983, O: Comet continued ... 1.00

Comet
DC / Impact

❑1, Jul 1991; O: Comet ... 1.00
❑2, Aug 1991; 1: Applejack; 1: Lance Perry ... 1.00
❑3, Sep 1991 ... 1.00
❑4, Oct 1991; 1: Inferno; V: Black Hood ... 1.00
❑5, Nov 1991; 1: The Hangman (as Roger Adams) ... 1.00
❑6, Dec 1991; 1: The Hangman (in costume); 1: Hangman ... 1.00
❑7, Jan 1992; 1: Bob Phantom; 1: The Wolf ... 1.00
❑8, Feb 1992; 1: The Black Witch; V: Web ... 1.00
❑9, Mar 1992 ... 1.00
❑10, Apr 1992; trading card ... 1.00
❑11, May 1992 ... 1.00
❑12, Jun 1992 ... 1.00
❑13, Jul 1992 ... 1.00
❑14, Aug 1992; O: The Comet ... 1.00
❑15, Sep 1992 ... 1.00
❑16, Oct 1992 ... 1.00
❑17, Nov 1992 ... 1.00
❑18, Dec 1992; Final Issue ... 1.00
❑Ann 1; trading card ... 2.00

Comet Man
Marvel

❑1, Feb 1987; 1: Comet Man; O: Comet Man ... 1.00
❑2, Mar 1987 ... 1.00
❑3, Apr 1987 ... 1.00
❑4, May 1987 ... 1.00
❑5, Jun 1987 ... 1.00
❑6, Jul 1987; Final Issue ... 1.00

Comet Tales
Rocket

❑1, Apr 1983 ... 1.00
❑2 ... 1.00
❑3 ... 1.00

Comicana
-Ism

❑1, ca. 2005 ... 3.50
❑2, ca. 2005 ... 3.50
❑3, ca. 2005 ... 3.50

Comic Book
Marvel / Spumco

❑1, ca. 1996; oversized anthology ... 6.95
❑2, ca. 1997; oversized anthology ... 6.95

Comic Book Confidential
Sphinx

❑1, ca. 1988, b&w; giveaway promo for documentary film of same name; No cover price; Film promo ... 2.00

Comic Book Heaven
Slave Labor

❑1 ... 2.00
❑2 ... 2.00

Comic Book Talent Search
Silverwolf

❑1, Feb 1987 ... 1.50

Comico Black Book
Comico

❑1, ca. 1987 ... 2.00

Comico Christmas Special
Comico

❑1, Dec 1988 ... 2.50

Comico Collection
Comico

❑1; 10 comics & Grendel: Devil's Vagary ... 9.95

Comic Party
Tokyopop

❑1, Jun 2004, Right to left reading format; b&w ... 9.99
❑2, Aug 2004; b&w ... 9.99
❑3, Oct 2004; Last Call; b&w ... 9.99
❑4, Dec 2004 ... 9.99
❑5, Jan 2006 ... 9.99

Comics and Stories
Dark Horse

❑1, Apr 1996; Wolf & Red ... 2.95
❑2, May 1996 ... 2.95
❑3, Jun 1996; Bad Luck Blackie ... 2.95
❑4, Jan 1997; Screwball Squirrel ... 2.95

Comics Are Dead
Slap Happy

❑1, Mar 1999, b&w anthology ... 4.95

Comics Artist Showcase
Showcase

❑1 ... 1.00

Comics for Stoners
Jason Neuman

❑1 ... 1.00

Comics' Greatest World
Dark Horse

❑1, Jun 1993; preview copy of Comics' Greatest World: X; 1500 printed ... 1.00

Comics' Greatest World: Arcadia
Dark Horse

❑1, Jun 1993; FM (c); FM (a); 1: X. X; Arcadia, Week 1 ... 2.00
❑1/Ltd., Jun 1993; limited edition for Heroes World Distribution; FM (c); FM (a); enhanced cardstock cover; X ... 2.50
❑2, Jun 1993; Pit Bulls; Arcadia, Week 2 ... 1.00
❑3, Jun 1993; 1: Ghost. Ghost; Arcadia, Week 3 ... 3.00
❑4; Monster; continues in Comics' Greatest World - Golden City; Arcadia, Week 4 ... 1.00

Comics' Greatest World: Cinnabar Flats
Dark Horse

❑1, Jun 1993; Division 13; Vortex, Week 1 ... 1.00
❑1/A, Aug 1993; limited edition for American Distribution; Division 13; Vortex, Week 1; cardstock cover ... 2.50
❑1/Ltd., Aug 1993; limited edition; Division 13; cardstock cover ... 2.50
❑2, Jun 1993; Hero Zero; Vortex, Week 2 ... 1.00
❑3, Jun 1993; King Tiger; Vortex, Week 3 ... 1.00
❑4, Jun 1993; Out of the Vortex; continues in Out of the Vortex (Comics' Greatest World...), Week 4 ... 1.00

Comics' Greatest World: Golden City
Dark Horse

❑1, Jul 1993; JO (c); Rebel; Golden City, Week 1 ... 1.00
❑1/Ltd.; limited edition for Heroes World Distribution; JO (c); enhanced cardstock cover; Rebel; Golden City, Week 1 ... 2.50
❑2, Jul 1993; Mecha; Golden City, Week 2 ... 1.00
❑3, Jul 1993; Titan; Golden City, Week 3 ... 1.00
❑4, Aug 1993; JDu (a); continues in Comics' Greatest World - Steel Harbor; Catalyst: Agents of Change; Golden City, Week 4 ... 1.00

Comics' Greatest World: Out of the Vortex
Dark Horse

❑1, Oct 1993, Foil embossed cover ... 2.00
❑2, Nov 1993 ... 2.00
❑3, Dec 1993 ... 2.00
❑4, Jan 1994, becomes Out of the Vortex ... 2.00

Comics' Greatest World Sourcebook
Dark Horse

❑1, Mar 1993; Free with Advance Comics ... 1.00

Comics' Greatest World: Steel Harbor
Dark Horse

❑1, Aug 1993; PG (a); 1: Barb Wire. Barb Wire; Steel Harbor, Week 1 ... 2.50
❑2; The Machine;Steel Harbor, Week 2 ... 1.00
❑3, Aug 1993; Wolf Gang; Steel Harbor, Week 3 ... 1.00
❑4, Aug 1993; Motorhead; continues in Comics' Greatest World - Cinnabar Flats; Steel Harbor, Week 4 ... 1.00

Comics 101 Presents
Cheap Thrills

❑1, Aug 1994, b&w; two covers, one inside the other ... 1.50

Coming of Aphrodite
Hero

❑1, b&w ... 3.95

Comix Book
Marvel

❑1, ca. 1974; 1974 ... 10.00
❑2, ca. 1974; Adult ... 8.00
❑3, ca. 1975; Adult ... 8.00
❑4, ca. 1975; Adult ... 5.00
❑5, ca. 1975; Adult ... 5.00

Comix International
Warren

❑1, Jul 1974 ... 125.00
❑2; Edgar Allen Poe adaptation ... 90.00
❑3 ... 75.00
❑4 ... 75.00
❑5, Spr 1977 ... 75.00

Other grades: Multiply price above by 5/6 for VF/NM • 2/3 for VERY FINE • 1/3 for FINE • 1/5 for VERY GOOD • 1/8 for GOOD

Chamber of Chills

Dungeons, werewolves, and dragons abound
©Marvel

Chamber of Darkness

Marvel's horror and suspense anthology
©Marvel

Champions (Marvel)

Hard-luck heroes form forgettable super-team
©Marvel

Champion Sports

Some inspirational stories, some unbelievable
©DC

Charlton Bullseye

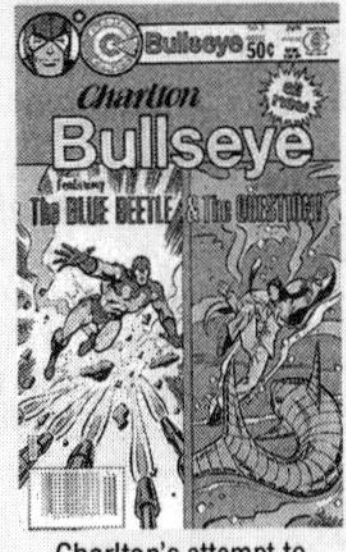

Charlton's attempt to revitalize its line
©Charlton

N-MINT

Command Review
Thoughts & Images

❑1, Jul 1986, b&w; collects stories from Albedo #1-4 .... 4.00
❑2, Aug 1987, b&w; collects stories from Albedo #5-8 .... 4.00
❑3, b&w 5.00
❑4, Jan 1994; (former Thoughts & Imagess title) 4.95

Commies From Mars
Last Gasp

❑1 .... 2.00
❑2 .... 2.00
❑3 .... 2.00
❑4 .... 2.00
❑5 .... 2.00
❑6 .... 2.50

Common Foe
Image

❑1, Aug 2005 .... 3.50
❑2, Sep 2005 .... 3.50
❑3, Nov 2005 .... 3.50
❑4, Dec 2006 .... 3.99

Common Grounds
Image

❑1, Jan 2004 .... 2.99
❑2, Feb 2004 .... 2.99
❑3, Mar 2004 .... 2.99
❑4, Apr 2004 .... 2.99
❑5, Jun 2004 .... 2.99
❑6, Aug 2004 .... 2.99

Communion
Fantagraphics / Eros

❑1, Dec 1991, b&w; Adult 2.75

Complete Cheech Wizard
Rip Off

❑1, Oct 1986, b&w 2.25
❑2, Jan 1987, b&w 2.25
❑3, May 1987 .... 2.50
❑4, Nov 1987 .... 2.50

Completely Bad Boys
Fantagraphics

❑1, b&w 2.50

Complex City
Better

❑1, Oct 2000 .... 2.50
❑2, Dec 2000 .... 2.50
❑3, Mar 2001 .... 2.50
❑4, May 2001 .... 2.50

Compu-M.E.C.H.
Monolith

❑1, Oct 1999 .... 2.75
❑2, Jul 2000 .... 2.75
❑3, ca. 2004; squarebound 7.95
❑4, ca. 2004; squarebound 7.95
❑5, ca. 2004; squarebound 7.95
❑6, ca. 2004; squarebound 7.95
❑7, ca. 2004; squarebound 7.95
❑8, ca. 2004; squarebound 7.95
❑9, ca. 2004; squarebound 7.95
❑10, ca. 2004; squarebound 7.95

N-MINT

Conan
Marvel

❑1, Aug 1995, cardstock cover 2.95
❑2, Sep 1995, cardstock cover 2.95
❑3, Oct 1995, cardstock cover 2.95
❑4, Nov 1995, A: Rune. cardstock cover 2.95
❑5, Dec 1995, A: yeti. cardstock cover 2.95
❑6, Jan 1996, cardstock cover 2.95
❑7, Feb 1996, V: Man of Iron 2.95
❑8, Mar 1996, cardstock cover 2.95
❑9, Apr 1996, cardstock cover 2.95
❑10, May 1996, cardstock cover 2.95
❑11, Jun 1996, cardstock cover 2.95
❑12, Jul 1996, Final Issue 2.95
❑32, Oct 2006 .... 2.99

Conan
Dark Horse

❑0 2004 .... 4.00
❑1, Feb 2004, Cover by Joseph Michael Linsner 10.00
❑1/2nd, Aug 2004, re-print 3.00
❑2, Mar 2004, Cover by Joseph Michael Linsner 5.00
❑2/2nd, Aug 2004, re-print 2.99
❑3, Apr 2004, Cover by Joseph Michael Linsner 2.99
❑4, Jun 2004, Cover by Joseph Michael Linsner 2.99
❑5, Aug 2004, Cover by Joseph Michael Linsner 2.99
❑6, Sep 2004, Cover by Joseph Michael Linsner 2.99
❑7, Oct 2004, Cover by Joseph Michael Linsner 2.99
❑8, Nov 2004 .... 2.99
❑9, Dec 2004 .... 2.99
❑10, Jan 2005 .... 2.99
❑11, Feb 2005 .... 2.99
❑12, Mar 2005, Cover by Leinil Francis Yu 2.99
❑13, Apr 2005 .... 2.99
❑14, May 2005 .... 2.99
❑15, May 2005 .... 2.99
❑16, Jun 2005 .... 2.99
❑17, Jul 2005 .... 2.99
❑18, Aug 2005 .... 2.99
❑19, Sept 2005 .... 2.99
❑20, Oct 2005 .... 2.99
❑21, Nov 2005 .... 2.99
❑22, Dec 2005 .... 2.99
❑23, Jan 2006 .... 2.99
❑24, Feb 2006 .... 2.99
❑25, Mar 2006 .... 2.99
❑26, Apr 2006 .... 2.99
❑27, Apr 2006 .... 2.99
❑28, May 2006 .... 2.99
❑29, Jun 2006, Mike Mignola cover 2.99
❑30, Aug 2006, Mike Mignola cover 2.99
❑31, Sep 2006, Tony Harris Cover 2.99
❑32, Oct 2006 .... 2.99
❑33, Nov 2006 .... 2.99
❑34, Dec 2006 .... 2.99
❑35, Jan 2007 .... 2.99
❑36 .... 2.99
❑37 .... 2.99
❑38 .... 2.99
❑39 .... 2.99
❑40 .... 2.99

N-MINT

❑41 .... 2.99
❑42 .... 2.99
❑43 .... 2.99
❑44 .... 2.99
❑45 .... 2.99
❑46 .... 2.99
❑47 .... 2.99
❑48 .... 2.99
❑49 .... 2.99
❑50 .... 2.99

Conan Classic
Marvel

❑1, Jun 1994; Reprints Conan the Barbarian #1 .... 1.50
❑2, Jul 1994; Reprints Conan the Barbarian #2 .... 1.50
❑3, Aug 1994; Reprints Conan the Barbarian #3 .... 1.50
❑4, Sep 1994; Reprints Conan the Barbarian #4 .... 1.50
❑5, Oct 1994; Reprints Conan the Barbarian #5 .... 1.50
❑6, Nov 1994; Reprints Conan the Barbarian #6 .... 1.50
❑7, Dec 1994; Reprints Conan the Barbarian #7 .... 1.50
❑8, Jan 1995; Reprints Conan the Barbarian #8 .... 1.50
❑9, Feb 1995; Reprints Conan the Barbarian #9 .... 1.50
❑10, Mar 1995; Reprints Conan the Barbarian #10 .... 1.50
❑11, Apr 1995; Reprints Conan the Barbarian #11; Final Issue 1.50

Conan and the Daughters of Midora
Dark Horse

❑1, Nov 2004, One-shot 5.00

Conan and the Demons of Khitai
Dark Horse

❑1, Sep 2005 .... 2.99
❑2, Oct 2005 .... 2.99
❑3, Nov 2005, Nude preview of Conan #24 (back page) 2.99
❑4, Dec 2005, King Conan 2.99

Conan and the Songs of the Dead
Dark Horse

❑1, Aug 2006 .... 2.99
❑2, Oct 2006 .... 2.99
❑3, Oct 2006 .... 2.99
❑4, Nov 2006 .... 2.99
❑5, Dec 2006 .... 2.99

Conan: Book of Thoth
Dark Horse

❑1, Apr 2006 .... 4.99
❑2, Apr 2006 .... 4.99
❑3, May 2006 .... 4.99
❑4, Jun 2006 .... 4.99

Conan and the Jewels of Gwahlur
Dark Horse

❑1, Apr 2005 .... 2.99
❑2, Jun 2005 .... 2.99
❑3, Jul 2005 .... 2.99

Conan: Death Covered In Gold
Marvel

❑1, Sep 1999 .... 2.99
❑3, Nov 1999 .... 2.99

Other grades: Multiply price above by 5/6 for VF/NM • 2/3 for VERY FINE • 1/3 for FINE • 1/5 for VERY GOOD • 1/8 for GOOD

Conan: Flame and the Fiend
Marvel

	N-MINT
❑1, Aug 2000	2.99
❑2, Sep 2000	2.99
❑3, Oct 2000	2.99

Conan: Return of Styrm
Marvel

	N-MINT
❑1, Sep 1998; gatefold summary	2.99
❑2, Oct 1998; gatefold summary	2.99
❑3, Nov 1998; gatefold summary	2.99

Conan: River of Blood
Marvel

	N-MINT
❑1, Jun 1998	2.50
❑2, Jul 1998	2.50
❑3, Aug 1998	2.50

Conan Saga
Marvel

	N-MINT
❑1, May 1987, b&w; Reprints	3.00
❑2, Jun 1987; Reprints Conan the Barbarian #4-6; b&w	2.50
❑3, Jul 1987; Reprints Conan the Barbarian #7-9; b&w	2.50
❑4, Aug 1987; Reprints Conan the Barbarian #10-11; b&w	2.50
❑5, Sep 1987; Reprints Conan the Barbarian #12-14; b&w	2.50
❑6, Oct 1987; Reprints Conan the Barbarian #15-16 & 19; b&w	2.50
❑7, Nov 1987; Reprints Conan the Barbarian #20-21 & 23; b&w	2.50
❑8, Dec 1987; Reprints Conan the Barbarian #24-25 & 37; b&w	2.50
❑9, Jan 1988; Reprints Conan the Barbarian special	2.50
❑10, Feb 1988	2.50
❑11, Mar 1988	2.50
❑12, Apr 1988	2.50
❑13, May 1988	2.50
❑14, Jun 1988	2.50
❑15, Jul 1988	2.50
❑16, Aug 1988	2.50
❑17, Sep 1988	2.50
❑18, Oct 1988	2.50
❑19, Nov 1988	2.50
❑20, Dec 1988	2.50
❑21, Jan 1989	2.50
❑22, Feb 1989	2.50
❑23, Mar 1989	2.50
❑24, Apr 1989	2.50
❑25, May 1989	2.50
❑26, Jun 1989	2.50
❑27, Jul 1989	2.50
❑28, Aug 1989, b&w; Reprints	2.50
❑29, Sep 1989, b&w; Reprints	2.50
❑30, Oct 1989, b&w; Reprints	2.50
❑31, Nov 1989, b&w; Reprints	2.50
❑32, Dec 1989, b&w; Reprints	2.50
❑33, Dec 1989, b&w; Reprints	2.50
❑34, Jan 1990, b&w; Reprints	2.50
❑35, Feb 1990, b&w; Reprints	2.50
❑36, Mar 1990, b&w; Reprints	2.50
❑37, Apr 1990, b&w; Reprints	2.50
❑38, May 1990, b&w; Reprints	2.50
❑39, Jun 1990, b&w; Reprints	2.50
❑40, Jul 1990, b&w; Reprints	2.50
❑41, Aug 1990, b&w; Reprints	2.50
❑42, Sep 1990, b&w; Reprints	2.50
❑43, Oct 1990, b&w; Reprints	2.50
❑44, Nov 1990, b&w; Reprints	2.50
❑45, Dec 1990, b&w; Reprints	2.50
❑46, Jan 1991, b&w; Reprints	2.50
❑47, Feb 1991, b&w; Reprints	2.50
❑48, Mar 1991, b&w; Reprints	2.50
❑49, Apr 1991, b&w; Reprints	2.50
❑50, May 1991, b&w; Reprints	2.50
❑51, Jun 1991, b&w; Reprints	2.50
❑52, Jul 1991, b&w; Reprints	2.50
❑53, Aug 1991, b&w; Reprints	2.50
❑54, Sep 1991, b&w; JB (a); Reprints	2.50
❑55, Oct 1991, b&w; JB (a); Reprints	2.50
❑56, Nov 1991, b&w; JB (a); Reprints	2.50
❑57, Dec 1991, b&w; FB (a); Reprints	2.50
❑58, Jan 1992, b&w; Reprints	2.50
❑59, Feb 1992, b&w; Reprints	2.50
❑60, Mar 1992, b&w; JB (a); Reprints	2.50
❑61, Apr 1992, b&w; JB (a); Reprints	2.50
❑62, May 1992, b&w; JB (a); Reprints	2.50
❑63, Jun 1992, b&w; JB (a); Reprints	2.50
❑64, Jul 1992, b&w; Reprints	2.50
❑65, Aug 1992, b&w; JB (a); Reprints	2.50
❑66, Sep 1992, b&w; Reprints	2.50
❑67, Oct 1992, b&w; JB (a); Reprints	2.50
❑68, Nov 1992, b&w; JB (a); Reprints	2.50
❑69, Dec 1992, b&w; Reprints	2.50
❑70, Jan 1993, b&w; Reprints	2.50
❑71, Feb 1993, b&w; JB (a); Reprints	2.50
❑72, Mar 1993, b&w; JB, MP (a); Reprints	2.50
❑73, Apr 1993, b&w; JB (a); Reprints	2.50
❑74, May 1993, b&w; JB (a); Reprints	2.50
❑75, Jun 1993; poster, handbook	4.00
❑76, Jul 1993, b&w; Reprints	2.25
❑77, Aug 1993, b&w; Reprints	2.25
❑78, Sep 1993, b&w; Reprints	2.25
❑79, Oct 1993, b&w; JB, FT, NA (a); A: Red Sonja. Reprints Conan the Barbarian #43-45	2.25
❑80, Nov 1993, b&w; JB (a); Reprints	2.25
❑81, Dec 1993, b&w; JB (a); Reprints	2.25
❑82, Jan 1994, b&w; JB (a); Reprints	2.25
❑83, Feb 1994, b&w; Reprints	2.25
❑84, Mar 1994, b&w; Reprints	2.25
❑85, Apr 1994, b&w; Reprints	2.25
❑86, May 1994, b&w; JB (a); Reprints	2.25
❑87, Jun 1994, b&w; JB (a); Reprints	2.25
❑88, Jul 1994, b&w; JB (a); Reprints	2.25
❑89, Aug 1994, b&w; JB (a); Reprints	2.25
❑90, Sep 1994, b&w; Reprints	2.25
❑91, Oct 1994, b&w; HC (a); Reprints	2.25
❑92, Nov 1994, b&w; JB (a); Reprints	2.25
❑93, Dec 1994, b&w; JB (a); Reprints	2.25
❑94, Jan 1995, b&w; JB (a); Reprints	2.25
❑95, Feb 1995, b&w; JB (a); Reprints	2.25
❑96, Mar 1995, b&w; JB (a); Reprints Conan the Barbarian #101-103 in black and white	2.25
❑97, Apr 1995, b&w; JB (a); Reprints	2.25

Conan: Scarlet Sword
Marvel

	N-MINT
❑1, Dec 1998, gatefold summary	2.99
❑2, Jan 1999, gatefold summary	2.99
❑3, Feb 1999	2.99

Conan the Adventurer
Marvel

	N-MINT
❑1, Jun 1994; Embossed foil cover	2.00
❑2, Jul 1994	1.50
❑3, Aug 1994	1.50
❑4, Sep 1994	1.50
❑5, Oct 1994	1.50
❑6, Nov 1994	1.50
❑7, Dec 1994	1.50
❑8, Jan 1995; Adapting The Weird of Avoosl Wuthoqquan by Clark Ashton Smith	1.50
❑9, Feb 1995	1.50
❑10, Mar 1995	1.50
❑11, Apr 1995	1.50
❑12, May 1995	1.50
❑13, Jun 1995	1.50
❑14, Jul 1995; Final Issue	1.50

Conan the Barbarian
Marvel

	N-MINT
❑1, Oct 1970, DA (a); 1&O: Conan. A: Kull. Hyborian Age map	160.00
❑2, Dec 1970, Howard story' Harlan Ellison L.O.C.; Maggie Thompson L.O.C.; Don Thompson L.O.C	55.00
❑3, Feb 1971, TS (a); low dist	72.00
❑4, Apr 1971, TS, SB (a); Adapts The Tower of the Elephant by Robert E. Howard	26.00
❑5, May 1971, TS (a); Adapts Zukala's Hour by Robert E. Howard	30.00
❑6, Jun 1971	26.00
❑7, Jul 1971, 1: Thoth Amon. Howard story	26.00
❑8, Aug 1971, Hidden Message in Panel 2, page 14	30.00
❑9, Aug 1971, Adapts the Garden of Fear by Robert E. Howard	20.00
❑10, Oct 1971, Giant-size; A: King Kull	35.00
❑11, Nov 1971, Giant-size; Adapting Rogues in the House by Robert E. Howard	35.00
❑12, Dec 1971, GK (c)	15.00
❑13, Jan 1972	20.00
❑14, Mar 1972, 1: Elric. Michael Moorcock characters	20.00
❑15, May 1972, A: Elric. Michael Moorcock characters	17.00
❑16, Jul 1972, TS (a); reprinted from Savage Tales #1 and Chamber of Darkness #4	20.00
❑17, Aug 1972, GK (c); GK (a); J.M. DeMatties L.O.C	17.00
❑18, Aug 1972, GK (c); GK (a); Adapts The Gods of Bal-Sagoth by Robert E. Howard	20.00
❑19, Oct 1972	17.00
❑20, Nov 1972	27.00
❑21, Dec 1972	20.00
❑22, Jan 1973, reprinted from Conan the Barbarian #1	20.00
❑23, Feb 1973, GK (c); TS, GK (a); 1: Red Sonja. 1: Red Sonj	20.00
❑24, Mar 1973, A: Red Sonja. 1st full Red Sonja story	20.00
❑25, Apr 1973, GK (c); TS, JB, SB, GK (a); Adapts "The Mirrors of Tuzun Thune" by Robert E. Howard	10.00
❑26, May 1973, JB (c); JB (a)	8.00
❑27, Jun 1973, GK (c); JB (a); Adapts "The Blood of Belshazzar" by Robert E. Howard	8.00
❑28, Jul 1973, GK (c); TS, JB, GK (a); Adapts "Moon of Zimbabwei" by Robert E. Howard	8.00
❑29, Aug 1973, TS, JB, GK (a); Adapts "Two Against Tyre" by Robert E. Howard	8.00
❑30, Sep 1973, GK (c); TS, JB, GK (a); Adapts "The Hand of Nergal" by Lin Carter and Robert E. Howard	8.00
❑31, Oct 1973, JB (a)	7.00
❑32, Nov 1973, JB (a); Adapts "Flame Winds" by Norvell W. Page	7.00
❑33, Dec 1973, JR (c); JB (a)	7.00
❑34, Jan 1974, GK (c); JB (a); Adapts "Flame Winds" by Norvell W. Page	7.00
❑35, Feb 1974, GK (c); JB (a); Adapts "The Fire of Asshurbanipal" by Robert E. Howard	7.00
❑36, Mar 1974, JR (c); JB (a); Marvel Value Stamp #10: Power Man	9.00
❑37, Apr 1974, NA (c); TS, NA (a); Marvel Value Stamp #8: Captain America	9.00
❑38, May 1974, GK (c); JB (a); Marvel Value Stamp #30: Grey Gargoyle	9.00
❑39, Jun 1974, GK (c); JB (a); Marvel Value Stamp #72: Lizard	7.00
❑40, Jul 1974, RB (c); RB (a); Marvel Value Stamp #31: Modok	7.00
❑41, Aug 1974, GK (c); JB, GK (a); Marvel Value Stamp #91: Hela	7.00
❑42, Sep 1974, GK (c); JB, GK (a); Marvel Value Stamp #24: Falcon	7.00
❑43, Oct 1974, GK (c); JB, GK (a); Red Sonja; Marvel Value Stamp #55: Medusa	7.00
❑44, Nov 1974, JB (c); JB (a); Red Sonja; Marvel Value Stamp #71: Vision	7.00
❑45, Dec 1974, NA (c); NA (a)	7.00
❑46, Jan 1975, JB (a)	7.00
❑47, Feb 1975, WW (w); JB, WW (a)	7.00
❑48, Mar 1975, GK (c); JB (a); O: Conan	6.00
❑49, Apr 1975, GK (c); JB (a); Marvel Value Stamp #80: Ghost Rider	6.00
❑50, May 1975, GK (c); JB, DG (a); Adapting Kothar and the Conjurer's Curse by Gardner F. Fox	6.00
❑51, Jun 1975, GK (c); JB (a); V: Unos	5.00
❑52, Jul 1975, JB (c); JB, TP (a); Adapts "The Altar and the Scorpion" by Robert E. Howard	5.00
❑53, Aug 1975, JR (c); JB (a)	5.00
❑54, Sep 1975, GK (c); JB (a)	5.00
❑55, Oct 1975, GK (c); JB (a)	5.00
❑56, Nov 1975, JB (c); JB (a)	5.00
❑57, Dec 1975, GK (c); MP (a)	5.00
❑58, Jan 1976, JB (c); JB (a); 2: of Bélit. 2: BÉlit; Adapts "Queen of the Black Coast" by Robert E. Howard	5.00
❑59, Feb 1976, JB (c); JB (a); O: Bélit	5.00
❑60, Mar 1976, JB (c); JB (a)	5.00
❑61, Apr 1976, JB (c); JB (a)	5.00
❑61/30¢, Apr 1976, 30¢ regional price variant	20.00
❑62, May 1976, GK (c); JB (a)	5.00
❑62/30¢, May 1976, 30¢ regional price variant	20.00
❑63, Jun 1976, GK (c); JB (a)	5.00
❑63/30¢, Jun 1976, 30¢ regional price variant	20.00
❑64, Jul 1976, JB (c); AM, JSn (a); Reprinting Savage Tales #3	5.00
❑64/30¢, Jul 1976, 30¢ regional price variant	20.00

Other grades: Multiply price above by 5/6 for VF/NM • 2/3 for VERY FINE • 1/3 for FINE • 1/5 for VERY GOOD • 1/8 for GOOD

Checkmate (Gold Key)

TV private detective series from 1960-62

©Gold Key

Checkmate

Secret organization for dealing with criminals

©DC

Cheryl Blossom (2nd Series)

Redhead competitor to Betty and Veronica

©Archie

Cheyenne

Western ran on TV from 1955-63

©Dell

Chiaroscuro

The life of Leonardo da Vinci

©DC

	N-MINT
❑65, Aug 1976, GK (c); JB, GK (a); Adapted from The Thunder Rider by Robert E. Howard	5.00
❑65/30¢, Aug 1976, 30¢ regional price variant	20.00
❑66, Sep 1976, GK (c); JB, GK (a); V: Dagon	5.00
❑67, Oct 1976, GK (c); JB, GK (a); A: Red Sonja. Red Sonja	5.00
❑68, Nov 1976, GK (c); JB, GK (a); A: Red Sonja. (continued from Marvel Feature #7)	5.00
❑69, Dec 1976, GK (c); VM (a)	5.00
❑70, Jan 1977, GK (c); JB (a)	5.00
❑71, Feb 1977, GK (c); JB (a); Newsstand edition (distributed by Curtis); issue number in box	5.00
❑71/Whitman, Feb 1977, JB (a); Special markets edition (usually sold in Whitman bagged prepacks); price appears in a diamond; UPC barcode appears	5.00
❑72, Mar 1977, GK (c); JB (a); Newsstand edition (distributed by Curtis); issue number in box	5.00
❑72/Whitman, Mar 1977, JB (a); Special markets edition (usually sold in Whitman bagged prepacks); price appears in a diamond; UPC barcode appears	5.00
❑73, Apr 1977, GK (c); JB (a)	5.00
❑74, May 1977, GK (c); JB (a); Newsstand edition (distributed by Curtis); issue number in box	5.00
❑74/Whitman, May 1977, JB (a); Special markets edition (usually sold in Whitman bagged prepacks); price appears in a diamond; UPC barcode appears	5.00
❑75, Jun 1977, JB (a); Newsstand edition (distributed by Curtis); issue number in box	5.00
❑75/Whitman, Jun 1977, JB (a); Special markets edition (usually sold in Whitman bagged prepacks); price appears in a diamond; UPC barcode appears	5.00
❑75/35¢, Jun 1977, 35¢ regional price variant; newsstand edition (distributed by Curtis); issue number in box	15.00
❑76, Jul 1977, GK (c); JB (a); Newsstand edition (distributed by Curtis); issue number in box	5.00
❑76/Whitman, Jul 1977, JB (a); Special markets edition (usually sold in Whitman bagged prepacks); price appears in a diamond; UPC barcode appears	5.00
❑76/35¢, Jul 1977, GK (c); JB (a); 35¢ regional price variant; newsstand edition (distributed by Curtis); issue number in box	15.00
❑77, Aug 1977, GK (c); JB (a); Newsstand edition (distributed by Curtis); issue number in box	5.00
❑77/Whitman, Aug 1977, JB (a); Special markets edition (usually sold in Whitman bagged prepacks); price appears in a diamond; UPC barcode appears	5.00
❑77/35¢, Aug 1977, 35¢ regional price variant; newsstand edition (distributed by Curtis); issue number in box	15.00
❑78, Sep 1977, JB (c); JB (a); Newsstand edition (distributed by Curtis); issue number in box	5.00
❑78/Whitman, Sep 1977, JB (a); Special markets edition (usually sold in Whitman bagged prepacks); price appears in a diamond; UPC barcode appears	5.00

	N-MINT
❑78/35¢, Sep 1977, JB (c); JB (a); 35¢ regional price variant; newsstand edition (distributed by Curtis); issue number in box	15.00
❑79, Oct 1977, HC (a); Newsstand edition (distributed by Curtis); issue number in box	5.00
❑79/Whitman, Oct 1977, HC (a); Special markets edition (usually sold in Whitman bagged prepacks); price appears in a diamond; no UPC barcode	5.00
❑79/35¢, Oct 1977, JB (c); HC (a); 35¢ regional price variant; newsstand edition (distributed by Curtis); issue number in box	15.00
❑80, Nov 1977, JB (c); HC (a); Newsstand edition (distributed by Curtis); issue number in box	5.00
❑80/Whitman, Nov 1977, HC (a); Special markets edition (usually sold in Whitman bagged prepacks); price appears in a diamond; no UPC barcode	5.00
❑81, Dec 1977, JB (c); HC (a); Newsstand edition (distributed by Curtis); issue number in box	5.00
❑81/Whitman, Dec 1977, HC (a); Special markets edition (usually sold in Whitman bagged prepacks); price appears in a diamond; no UPC barcode	5.00
❑82, Jan 1978, JB (c); HC (a)	5.00
❑83, Feb 1978, JB (c); HC (a)	5.00
❑84, Mar 1978, JB (c); JB (a); 1: Zula	5.00
❑85, Apr 1978, JB (c); JB (a); O: Zula	5.00
❑86, May 1978, JB (c); JB (a); Newsstand edition (distributed by Curtis); issue number in box	5.00
❑86/Whitman, May 1978, JB (a); Special markets edition (usually sold in Whitman bagged prepacks); price appears in a diamond; no UPC barcode	5.00
❑87, Jun 1978, JB (c); JB (a); Reprints Savage Sword of Conan #3 in color	5.00
❑88, Jul 1978, JB (c); JB (a); Return of Belit	5.00
❑89, Aug 1978, JB (c); JB (a); V: Thoth-Amon. Newsstand edition (distributed by Curtis); issue number in box	5.00
❑89/Whitman, Aug 1978, JB (a); V: Thoth-Amon. Special markets edition (usually sold in Whitman bagged prepacks); price appears in a diamond; no UPC barcode	5.00
❑90, Sep 1978, JB (c); JB (a); Newsstand edition (distributed by Curtis); issue number in box	5.00
❑90/Whitman, Sep 1978, JB (a); Special markets edition (usually sold in Whitman bagged prepacks); price appears in a diamond; no UPC barcode	5.00
❑91, Oct 1978, JB (c); JB (a); Newsstand edition (distributed by Curtis); issue number in box	5.00
❑91/Whitman, Oct 1978, JB (a); Special markets edition (usually sold in Whitman bagged prepacks); price appears in a diamond; no UPC barcode	5.00
❑92, Nov 1978, SB (c); JB, SB (a); Newsstand edition (distributed by Curtis); issue number in box	5.00
❑92/Whitman, Nov 1978, JB (a); Special markets edition (usually sold in Whitman bagged prepacks); price appears in a diamond; UPC barcode appears	5.00

	N-MINT
❑93, Dec 1978, JB (c); JB (a); Belit regains throne; newsstand edition (distributed by Curtis); issue number in box	5.00
❑93/Whitman, Dec 1978, JB (a); Belit regains throne; special markets edition (usually sold in Whitman bagged prepacks); price appears in a diamond; no UPC barcode	5.00
❑94, Jan 1979, JB (c); JB (a); Newsstand edition (distributed by Curtis); issue number in box	4.00
❑94/Whitman, Jan 1979, JB (a); Special markets edition (usually sold in Whitman bagged prepacks); price appears in a diamond; no UPC barcode	4.00
❑95, Feb 1979, JB (c); JB (a); Newsstand edition (distributed by Curtis); issue number in box	4.00
❑95/Whitman, Feb 1979, JB (a); Special markets edition (usually sold in Whitman bagged prepacks); price appears in a diamond; no UPC barcode	4.00
❑96, Mar 1979, JB (c); JB (a)	4.00
❑97, Apr 1979, JB (c); JB (a)	4.00
❑98, May 1979, JB (c); JB (a); Newsstand edition (distributed by Curtis); issue number in box	4.00
❑98/Whitman, May 1979, JB (a); Special markets edition (usually sold in Whitman bagged prepacks); price appears in a diamond; no UPC barcode	4.00
❑99, Jun 1979, JB (c); JB (a); Adapting The People of the Black Coast by Robert E. Howard	4.00
❑100, Jul 1979, Double-size issue; JB (c); TS, JB (a); D: Bélit. D: BÊlit; Double-size issue; Adapts "The People of the Black Coast" by Robert E. Howard	6.00
❑101, Aug 1979, JB (c); JB (a)	2.00
❑102, Sep 1979, JB (c); JB (a)	2.00
❑103, Oct 1979, JB (c); JB (a)	2.00
❑104, Nov 1979, JB (a); Ernie Chan cover; Adapting The Vale of Lost Women by Robert E. Howard	2.00
❑105, Dec 1979, JB (c); JB (a); Adapting Castle of Terror by L. Sprague De Camp & Lin Carter	2.00
❑106, Jan 1980, JB (c); JB (a); Adapting The Snout in the Dark by L. Sprague De Camp & Lin Carter	2.00
❑107, Feb 1980, JB (c); JB (a); Adapting The Snout in the Dark by L. Sprague De Camp & Lin Carter	2.00
❑108, Mar 1980, JB (c); JB (a)	2.00
❑109, Apr 1980, JB (c); JB (a); Adapting Sons of the Bear God by Norvell W. Page	2.00
❑110, May 1980, JB (c); JB (a); Adapting Sons of the Bear God by Norvell W. Page	2.00
❑111, Jun 1980, JB (c); JB (a); Adapts Sons of the Bear God by Norvell W. Page	2.00
❑112, Jul 1980, JB (c); JB (a); Adapts Sons of the Bear God by Norvell W. Page	2.00
❑113, Aug 1980, JB (c); JB (a)	2.00
❑114, Sep 1980, JB (a); Adapts The Shadow of the Beast by Robert E. Howard	2.00
❑115, Oct 1980, double-sized; JB (c); JB (a); 10th anniversary	2.00
❑116, Nov 1980, JB, NA (a); Reprints	2.00
❑117, Dec 1980, JB (c); JB (a)	2.00
❑118, Jan 1981, JB (c); JB (a)	2.00
❑119, Feb 1981, JB (c); JB (a)	2.00
❑120, Mar 1981, JB (c); JB (a)	2.00
❑121, Apr 1981, JB (c); JB (a)	2.00

	N-MINT
❑122, May 1981, JB (c); JB (a)	2.00
❑123, Jun 1981, JB (c); JB (a)	2.00
❑124, Jul 1981, JB (c); JB (a)	2.00
❑125, Aug 1981, JB (c); JB (a)	2.00
❑126, Sep 1981, JB (c); JB (a)	2.00
❑127, Oct 1981, GK (c); JB, GK (a)	2.00
❑128, Nov 1981, GK (c); GK (a)	2.00
❑129, Dec 1981	2.00
❑130, Jan 1982, GK (c); GK (a)	2.00
❑131, Feb 1982, GK (c); GK (a)	2.00
❑132, Mar 1982, GK (c); GK (a)	2.00
❑133, Apr 1982, GK (c); GK (a)	2.00
❑134, May 1982, GK (c); GK (a)	2.00
❑135, Jun 1982	2.00
❑136, Jul 1982, JB (c); JB (a)	2.00
❑137, Aug 1982, JB (c); AA (a)	2.00
❑138, Sep 1982, JB (c); VM (a)	2.00
❑139, Oct 1982, JB (c); VM (a)	2.00
❑140, Nov 1982, JB (c); JB (a)	2.00
❑141, Dec 1982, JB (c); JB (a)	2.00
❑142, Jan 1983, JB (c); JB (a)	2.00
❑143, Feb 1983, JB (c); JB (a)	2.00
❑144, Mar 1983, JB (c); JB (a)	2.00
❑145, Apr 1983, JB (c); RHo, JB (a)	2.00
❑146, May 1983, JB (c); JB (a)	2.00
❑147, Jun 1983, JB (c); JB (a)	2.00
❑148, Jul 1983, JB (c); JB (a)	2.00
❑149, Aug 1983, JB (c); JB (a)	2.00
❑150, Sep 1983, JB (c); JB (a)	2.00
❑151, Oct 1983, JB (c); JB (a)	2.00
❑152, Nov 1983, MG (c); JB (a)	2.00
❑153, Dec 1983, JB (a)	2.00
❑154, Jan 1984, Assistant Editors' Month	2.00
❑155, Feb 1984, JB (c); JB (w); JB (a)	2.00
❑156, Mar 1984, JB (c); JB (w); JB (a)	2.00
❑157, Apr 1984, JB (c); JB (w); JB (a)	2.00
❑158, May 1984, JB (c); JB (w); JB (a)	2.00
❑159, Jun 1984, JB (c); JB (w); JB (a)	2.00
❑160, Jul 1984	2.00
❑161, Aug 1984, JB (c); JB (a)	2.00
❑162, Sep 1984, JB (c); JB (a)	2.00
❑163, Oct 1984, JB (a)	2.00
❑164, Nov 1984	2.00
❑165, Dec 1984, JB (a)	2.00
❑166, Jan 1985, JB (c); JB (a)	2.00
❑167, Feb 1985, JB (a)	2.00
❑168, Mar 1985, JB (a)	2.00
❑169, Apr 1985, JB (c); JB (a)	2.00
❑170, May 1985, JB (a)	2.00
❑171, Jun 1985, JB (c); JB (a)	2.00
❑172, Jul 1985, JB (c); JB (a)	2.00
❑173, Aug 1985, JB (a)	2.00
❑174, Sep 1985, JB (c); JB (a)	2.00
❑175, Oct 1985, JB (c); JB (a)	2.00
❑176, Nov 1985, JB (a)	2.00
❑177, Dec 1985, JB (a)	2.00
❑178, Jan 1986, JB (c); JB (a)	2.00
❑179, Feb 1986, JB (c); JB (a)	2.00
❑180, Mar 1986, JB (c); JB (a)	2.00
❑181, Apr 1986, JB (c); JB (a)	2.00
❑182, May 1986, JB (c); JB (a)	2.00
❑183, Jun 1986, JB (c); JB (a)	2.00
❑184, Jul 1986	2.00
❑185, Aug 1986	2.00
❑186, Sep 1986	2.00
❑187, Oct 1986, JB (a)	2.00
❑188, Nov 1986	2.00
❑189, Dec 1986	2.00
❑190, Jan 1987	2.00
❑191, Feb 1987	2.00
❑192, Mar 1987	2.00
❑193, Apr 1987	2.00
❑194, May 1987	2.00
❑195, Jun 1987	2.00
❑196, Jul 1987	2.00
❑197, Aug 1987	2.00
❑198, Sep 1987	2.00
❑199, Oct 1987	2.00
❑200, Nov 1987, 200th issue anniversary; Double-size	2.00
❑201, Dec 1987	2.00
❑202, Jan 1988	2.00
❑203, Feb 1988	2.00
❑204, Mar 1988	2.00
❑205, Apr 1988	2.00
❑206, May 1988	2.00
❑207, Jun 1988	2.00

	N-MINT
❑208, Jul 1988	2.00
❑209, Aug 1988	2.00
❑210, Sep 1988	2.00
❑211, Oct 1988	2.00
❑212, Nov 1988	2.00
❑213, Dec 1988	2.00
❑214, Jan 1989	2.00
❑215, Feb 1989	2.00
❑216, Mar 1989	2.00
❑217, Apr 1989	2.00
❑218, May 1989	2.00
❑219, Jun 1989	2.00
❑220, Jul 1989	2.00
❑221, Aug 1989	2.00
❑222, Sep 1989	2.00
❑223, Oct 1989	2.00
❑224, Nov 1989	2.00
❑225, Nov 1989	2.00
❑226, Dec 1989	2.00
❑227, Dec 1989	2.00
❑228, Jan 1990	2.00
❑229, Feb 1990	2.00
❑230, Mar 1990	2.00
❑231, Apr 1990	2.00
❑232, May 1990, JLee (c); starts over	2.00
❑233, Jun 1990	2.00
❑234, Jul 1990	2.00
❑235, Aug 1990	2.00
❑236, Sep 1990	2.00
❑237, Oct 1990	2.00
❑238, Nov 1990	2.00
❑239, Dec 1990	2.00
❑240, Jan 1991	2.00
❑241, Feb 1991, TMc (c); TMc (a)	2.00
❑242, Mar 1991, JLee (c); JLee (a)	2.00
❑243, Apr 1991, Red Sonja	2.00
❑244, May 1991, Red Sonja	2.00
❑245, Jun 1991, Red Sonja	2.00
❑246, Jul 1991, Red Sonja	2.00
❑247, Aug 1991, Red Sonja	2.00
❑248, Sep 1991, Red Sonja	2.00
❑249, Oct 1991, Red Sonja	2.00
❑250, Nov 1991, 250th issue anniversary; Double-size; Adapts Gates of Empire by Robert E. Howard	2.00
❑251, Dec 1991, TD (a)	2.00
❑252, Jan 1992	2.00
❑253, Feb 1992	2.00
❑254, Mar 1992	2.00
❑255, Apr 1992	2.00
❑256, May 1992	2.00
❑257, Jun 1992, V: Thoth-Amon	2.00
❑258, Jul 1992, returns to Cimmeria	2.00
❑259, Aug 1992	2.00
❑260, Sep 1992	2.00
❑261, Oct 1992	2.00
❑262, Nov 1992, Adapts Guns of Khartum by Robert E. Howard	2.00
❑263, Dec 1992, Adapts The Voice of El-Lil by Robert E. Howard	2.00
❑264, Jan 1993	2.00
❑265, Feb 1993, Adapts The Thief of Forthe by Clifford Ball	2.00
❑266, Mar 1993, Adapts Conan the Renegade by Leonard Carpenter	2.00
❑267, Apr 1993, Adapts Conan the Renegade by Leonard Carpenter	2.00
❑268, May 1993, Adapts Conan the Renegade by Leonard Carpenter	2.00
❑269, Jun 1993, Adapts Conan the Renegade by Leonard Carpenter	2.00
❑270, Jul 1993	2.00
❑271, Aug 1993	2.00
❑272, Sep 1993	2.00
❑273, Oct 1993, A: Lord of the Purple Lotus	2.00
❑274, Nov 1993	2.00
❑275, Dec 1993, Final Issue; 64 pages	2.50
❑Ann 1, ca. 1973, Cover reads "King-Size Special"; Reprints Conan the Barbarian #2 and 4	10.00
❑Ann 2, Jan 1976, JB (a); Adapting The Phoenix On the Sword by Robert E. Howard	6.00
❑Ann 3, ca. 1977, JB, HC, NA (a); A: King Kull. Reprints Savage Sword of Conan #2	6.00
❑Ann 4, ca. 1978, JB (a); King Conan story	2.00
❑Ann 5, ca. 1979, JB (a)	2.00
❑Ann 6, ca. 1981, JB (a)	2.00

	N-MINT
❑Ann 7, ca. 1982, JB (a)	1.50
❑Ann 8, ca. 1983, VM (a)	1.50
❑Ann 9, ca. 1984	1.50
❑Ann 10, ca. 1985	1.50
❑Ann 11, ca. 1986	1.50
❑Ann 12, ca. 1987	1.50
❑Special 1; Reprints	2.50

Conan the Barbarian
Marvel

❑1, Jul 1997	2.50
❑2, Aug 1997	2.50
❑3, Oct 1997	2.50

Conan the Barbarian Movie Special
Marvel

❑1, Oct 1982, JB (c); JB (w); JB (a); Movie adaptation	1.00
❑2, Nov 1982, JB (c); JB (w); JB (a); Movie adaptation	1.00

Conan the Barbarian: The Usurper
Marvel

❑1, Dec 1997; gatefold summary; gatefold cover	2.50
❑2, Jan 1998; gatefold summary	2.50
❑3, Feb 1998	2.50

Conan the Destroyer
Marvel

❑1, Jan 1985; Movie adaptation	1.00
❑2, Mar 1985; Movie adaptation	1.00

Conan the King
Marvel

❑20, Jan 1984; Continued from King Conan #19	1.50
❑21, Mar 1984	1.50
❑22, May 1984; T.M. Maple L.O.C.	1.50
❑23, Jul 1984	1.50
❑24, Sep 1984	1.50
❑25, Nov 1984; T.M. Maple L.O.C	1.50
❑26, Jan 1985	1.50
❑27, Mar 1985	1.50
❑28, May 1985	1.50
❑29, Jul 1985	1.50
❑30, Sep 1985	1.50
❑31, Nov 1985	1.50
❑32, Jan 1986	1.50
❑33, Mar 1986	1.50
❑34, May 1986	1.50
❑35, Jul 1986	1.50
❑36, Sep 1986	1.50
❑37, Nov 1986; Assistant Editor Month	1.50
❑38, Jan 1987	1.50
❑39, Mar 1987	1.50
❑40, May 1987	1.50
❑41, Jul 1987	1.50
❑42, Sep 1987	1.50
❑43, Nov 1987	1.50
❑44, Jan 1988	1.50
❑45, Mar 1988	1.50
❑46, May 1988	1.50
❑47, Jul 1988	1.50
❑48, Sep 1988	1.50
❑49, Nov 1988	1.50
❑50, Jan 1989	1.50
❑51, Mar 1989	1.50
❑52, May 1989	1.50
❑53, Jul 1989	1.50
❑54, Sep 1989	1.50
❑55, Nov 1989; Final Issue	1.50

Conan: The Lord of the Spiders
Marvel

❑1, Mar 1998; gatefold summary; gatefold cover	2.50
❑2, Apr 1998; gatefold summary	2.50
❑3, May 1998; gatefold summary	2.50

Conan the Savage
Marvel

❑1, Aug 1995; b&w magazine; Oversized	2.95
❑2, Sep 1995; b&w magazine	2.95
❑3, Oct 1995; b&w magazine	2.95
❑4, Nov 1995; b&w magazine; indicia gives title as Conan	2.95
❑5, Dec 1995; b&w magazine	2.95
❑6, Jan 1996; b&w magazine	2.95
❑7, Feb 1996; b&w magazine	2.95
❑8, Mar 1996; b&w magazine	2.95
❑9, Apr 1996; b&w magazine	2.95

Chip 'n' Dale (2nd series)

Less annoying when you can't hear their voices

©Gold Key

Choo-Choo Charlie

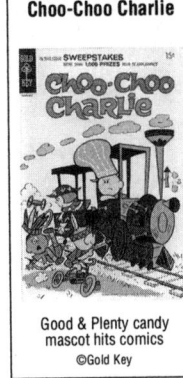

Good & Plenty candy mascot hits comics

©Gold Key

Chroma-Tick

Color! Color! Color! Color! Color! Color! Color!

©New England

Chromium Man

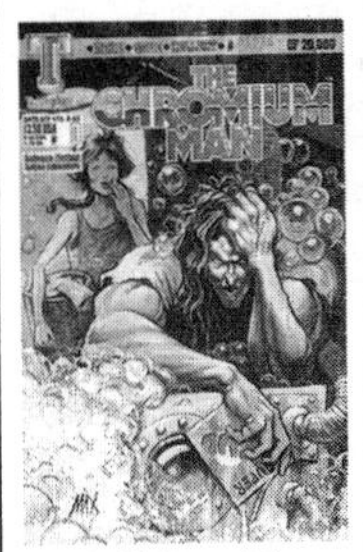

Publisher serially numbered all copies

©Triumphant

Chronos

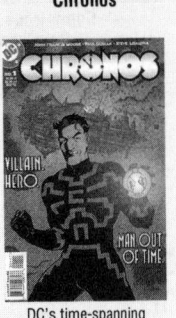

DC's time-spanning super-hero

©DC

N-MINT

❑10, May 1996; b&w magazine 2.95
❑11, Jun 1996 2.95
❑12, Jul 1996 2.95

Conan vs. Rune
Marvel

❑1, Nov 1995; One-shot 2.95

Concrete
Dark Horse

❑1, Mar 1987 2.50
❑1/2nd; 2nd printing 1.50
❑2, Jun 1987 2.00
❑3, Aug 1987; O: Concrete 2.00
❑4, Oct 1987; O: Concrete 2.00
❑5, Dec 1987 2.00
❑6, Feb 1988 2.00
❑7, Apr 1988 2.00
❑8, Jun 1988 2.00
❑9, Sep 1988 2.00
❑10; Final Issue 2.00
❑Hero ed. 1, Apr 1985; Hero Special edition; Included with Hero Illustrated #23 1.00

Concrete: A New Life
Dark Horse

❑1, Oct 1989; b&w reprint 2.95

Concrete Celebrates Earth Day
Dark Horse

❑1, Apr 1990; Moebius 3.50

Concrete Color Special
Dark Horse

❑1, Feb 1989; reprint in color 2.95

Concrete: Eclectica
Dark Horse

❑1, Apr 1993; wraparound cover from 1992 WonderCon program book 2.95
❑2, May 1993; wraparound cover 2.95

Concrete: Fragile Creature
Dark Horse

❑1, Jun 1991, wraparound cover 2.50
❑2, Jul 1991, wraparound cover 2.50
❑3, Aug 1991, wraparound cover 2.50
❑4, Feb 1992, wraparound cover 2.50

Concrete Jungle: The Legend of the Black Lion
Acclaim

❑1, Apr 1998 2.50

Concrete: Killer Smile
Dark Horse / Legend

❑1, Jul 1994 2.95
❑2, Aug 1994 2.95
❑3, Sep 1994 2.95
❑4, Oct 1994 2.95

Concrete: Land & Sea
Dark Horse

❑1, Feb 1989, b&w; reprints first two Concrete stories with additional material; wraparound cardstock cover 2.95

Concrete: Odd Jobs
Dark Horse

❑1, Jul 1990; b&w reprint;Collects Concrete #5-6 3.50

N-MINT

Concrete: Strange Armor
Dark Horse

❑1, Dec 1997, O: Concrete 2.95
❑2, Jan 1998, O: Concrete 2.95
❑3, Mar 1998, O: Concrete 2.95
❑4, Apr 1998, O: Concrete 2.95
❑5, May 1998, O: Concrete 2.95

Concrete: The Human Dilemma
Dark Horse

❑1 2005 3.50
❑2, Jan 2005 3.50
❑3, Feb 2005 3.50
❑4, Mar 2005 3.50
❑5, May 2005 3.50
❑6, May 2005 3.50

Concrete: Think Like a Mountain
Dark Horse / Legend

❑1, Mar 1996 2.95
❑2, Apr 1996 2.95
❑3, May 1996 2.95
❑4, Jun 1996 2.95
❑5, Jul 1996 2.95
❑6, Aug 1996 2.95
❑Ashcan 1, b&w; promotional giveaway for mini-series 1.00

Condom-Man
Aaaahh!!

❑1; Gold ink limited edition; Gold ink limited edition; 5,000 printed 3.95

Condorman (Walt Disney)
Whitman

❑1, Nov 1981, Adapts Disney film; sold only in bagged three-packs 2.00
❑2, Dec 1981, Adapts Disney film; sold only in bagged three-packs 2.00
❑3, Jan 1982, Original material; sold only in bagged three-packs 2.00

Coneheads
Marvel

❑1, Jun 1994 1.75
❑2, Jul 1994 1.75
❑3, Aug 1994 1.75
❑4, Sep 1994 1.75

Confessions of a Cereal Eater
NBM

❑1, ca. 2000, b&w 2.95
❑2, ca. 2000, b&w 2.95
❑3, ca. 2000, b&w 2.95
❑4, ca. 2001 2.95

Confessions of a Teenage Vampire: The Turning
Scholastic

❑1, Jul 1997; digest; NN 4.99

Confessions of a Teenage Vampire: Zombie Saturday Night
Scholastic

❑1, Jul 1997; digest; NN 4.99

Confessor (Demonicus Ex Deo)
Dark Matter

❑1, b&w; Mature readers; 1996 2.95

N-MINT

Confidential Confessions
Tokyopop

❑1, Jul 2003, b&w; printed in Japanese format 9.99

Confrontation
Sacred Origin

❑1, Jul 1997 2.95
❑2, Oct 1997 2.95
❑3 1997 2.95
❑4 1998 2.95
❑Special 1; Convention exclusive edition 5.00

Congo Bill
DC / Vertigo

❑1, Oct 1999 2.95
❑2, Nov 1999 2.95
❑3, Dec 1999 2.95
❑4, Jan 2000 2.95

Congorilla
DC

❑1, Nov 1992, BB (c) 2.00
❑2, Dec 1992, BB (c) 1.75
❑3, Jan 1993 1.75
❑4, Feb 1993 1.75

Conjurors
DC

❑1, Apr 1999; Elseworlds story 2.95
❑2, May 1999; Elseworlds story 2.95
❑3, Jun 1999; Elseworlds story 2.95

Connor Hawke: Dragon's Blood
DC

❑1, Feb 2007 2.99
❑2, Mar 2007 2.99

Conqueror
Harrier

❑1, Aug 1984 1.75
❑2, Oct 1984 1.75
❑3, Dec 1984 1.75
❑4, Feb 1985 1.75
❑5, Apr 1985 1.75
❑6, Jun 1985 1.75
❑7, Aug 1985 1.75
❑8, Oct 1985 1.75
❑9, Dec 1985 1.75
❑Special 1; Special edition (1987) 1.95

Conqueror of the Barren Earth
DC

❑1, Feb 1983 1.00
❑2, Mar 1983 1.00
❑3, Apr 1983 1.00
❑4, May 1983 1.00

Conqueror Universe
Harrier

❑1 2.75

Conservation Corps
Archie

❑1, Aug 1993 1.25
❑2, Sep 1993 1.25
❑3, Nov 1993 1.25

Conspiracy
Marvel

❑1, Feb 1998 2.99
❑2, Mar 1998 2.99

N-MINT

Conspiracy Comics
Revolutionary
❑1, Oct 1991; Marilyn Monroe ... 2.50
❑2, Feb 1992, b&w; John F. Kennedy ... 2.50
❑3, Jul 1992, b&w; Robert F. Kennedy ... 2.50

Constellation Graphics
Stages
❑1 ... 1.50
❑2 ... 1.50

Construct
Caliber
❑1 ... 2.95
❑2 ... 2.95
❑3 ... 2.95
❑4 ... 2.95
❑5 ... 2.95
❑6 ... 2.95

Containment (Eric Red's)
Idea & Design Works
❑1, ca. 2004 ... 3.99
❑2, ca. 2005 ... 3.99
❑3, ca. 2005 ... 3.99
❑4, ca. 2005 ... 3.99

Contaminated Zone
Brave New Words
❑1, Apr 1991, b&w ... 2.50
❑2 1991, b&w ... 2.50
❑3 1991, b&w ... 2.50

Contemporary Bio-Graphics
Revolutionary
❑1, Dec 1991, b&w; Stan Lee ... 2.50
❑2, Apr 1992, b&w; Boris Yeltsin ... 2.50
❑3, May 1992, b&w; Gene Roddenberry 2.50
❑4, Jun 1992; Pee Wee Herman ... 2.50
❑5, Sep 1992, b&w; David Lynch ... 2.50
❑6, Oct 1992; Ross Perot ... 2.50
❑7, Dec 1992, b&w; Spike Lee ... 2.50
❑8, Jun 1993, b&w; Image story ... 2.50

Contender Comics Special
Contender
❑1, b&w ... 1.00

Contest of Champions II
Marvel
❑1, Sep 1999; Iron Man vs. Psylocke; Iron Man vs. X-Force ... 2.50
❑2, Sep 1999; Human Torch vs. Spider-Girl, Storm, She-Hulk; Mr. Fantastic vs. Hulk ... 2.50
❑3, Oct 1999; Thor vs. Storm; Cable vs. Scarlet Witch; New Warriors vs. Slingers 2.50
❑4, Nov 1999; Black Panther vs Captain America ... 2.50
❑5, Nov 1999; Rogue vs Warbird ... 2.50

Continüm Presents
Continüm
❑1, Oct 1988 ... 1.75
❑2, Fal 1989 ... 1.75

Contractors
Eclipse
❑1, Jun 1987, b&w; Summer Special ... 2.00

Convent of Hell
NBM
❑1; Adult ... 12.95

Convocations: A Magic: The Gathering Gallery
Acclaim / Armada
❑1, Jan 1995; pin-ups; reproduces covers from several Magic mini-series ... 2.50

Cool World
DC
❑1, Apr 1992; Base upon characters in Paramount Pictures' Cool World ... 1.75
❑2, May 1992 ... 1.75
❑3, Jun 1992 ... 1.75
❑4, Sep 1992 ... 1.75

Cool World Movie Adaptation
DC
❑1; NN ... 3.50

Cop Called Tracy, A
Avalon
❑1 ... 2.95
❑2 ... 2.95
❑3 ... 2.95
❑4 ... 2.95
❑5 ... 2.95
❑6 ... 2.95
❑7 ... 2.95
❑8 ... 2.95
❑9 ... 2.95
❑10 ... 2.95
❑11 ... 2.95
❑12 ... 2.95
❑13 ... 2.95
❑14 ... 2.95
❑15 ... 2.95
❑16 ... 2.95
❑17 ... 2.95
❑18 ... 2.95
❑19 ... 2.95
❑20 ... 2.95
❑21 ... 2.95
❑22 ... 2.95

COPS
DC
❑1, Aug 1988; Giant-size; 1&O: COPS ... 1.00
❑2, Sep 1988 ... 1.00
❑3, Oct 1988 ... 1.00
❑4, Nov 1988 ... 1.00
❑5, Dec 1988 ... 1.00
❑6, Win 1988 ... 1.00
❑7, Hol 1988 ... 1.00
❑8, Jan 1989 ... 1.00
❑9, Feb 1989 ... 1.00
❑10, Mar 1989 ... 1.00
❑11, Apr 1989 ... 1.00
❑12, May 1989 ... 1.00
❑13, Jun 1989 ... 1.00
❑14, Jul 1989 ... 1.00
❑15, Aug 1989; Final Issue ... 1.00

Cops: The Job
Marvel
❑1, Jun 1992 ... 1.25
❑2, Jul 1992 ... 1.25
❑3, Aug 1992 ... 1.25
❑4, Sep 1992 ... 1.25

Copybook Tales
Slave Labor
❑1, Jul 1996, b&w ... 2.95
❑2, Oct 1996, b&w ... 2.95
❑3, Jan 1997, b&w ... 2.95
❑4, Apr 1997, b&w ... 2.95
❑5, Jul 1997, b&w ... 2.95
❑6, Aug 1997; Cover swipe of X-Men (1st Series) #141 ... 2.95

Corben Special, A
Pacific
❑1, May 1984, Adapted From Edgar Allan Poe ... 1.50

Corbo
Sword in Stone
❑1 ... 1.75

Cormac Mac Art
Dark Horse
❑1, Jul 1989, b&w ... 1.95
❑2, Aug 1989, b&w ... 1.95
❑3, Mar 1990, b&w ... 1.95
❑4, Apr 1990, b&w ... 1.95

Corny's Fetish
Dark Horse
❑1, Apr 1998, b&w; NN; One-shot ... 4.95

Corporate Crime Comics
Kitchen Sink
❑1, Jul 1977 ... 2.50
❑2 ... 2.50

Corporate Ninja
Slave Labor
❑1, Nov 2005 ... 2.95

Cortez and the Fall of the Aztecs
Tome
❑1, b&w ... 2.95
❑2, b&w ... 2.95

Corto Maltese: Ballad of the Salt Sea
NBM
❑1 ... 2.95
❑2 ... 2.95
❑3 ... 2.95
❑4 ... 2.95

Corum: The Bull and the Spear
First
❑1 ... 1.50
❑2 ... 1.50
❑3 ... 1.50
❑4 ... 1.50

Corvus Rex: A Legacy of Shadows
Crow
❑1, Feb 1996, b&w; Prologue ... 1.95

Cosmic Book
Ace
❑1 ... 1.95

Cosmic Boy
DC
❑1, Dec 1986; KG (a); Legends Spin-Off, Part 4 ... 1.00
❑2, Jan 1987; Legends Spin-Off, Part 8 . 1.00
❑3, Feb 1987; Legends Spin-Off, Part 13 1.00
❑4, Mar 1987; V: Time Trapper. Legends Spin-Off, Part 20 ... 1.00

Cosmic Guard
Devil's Due
❑1, Nov 2004 ... 5.00
❑2, Dec 2004 ... 4.00
❑3, Jan 2005 ... 2.99
❑4, Feb 2005 ... 2.99
❑5, Mar 2005 ... 2.99
❑6, Apr 2005 ... 2.99

Cosmic Heroes
Eternity
❑1, b&w; Buck Rogers ... 1.95
❑2, b&w; Buck Rogers ... 1.95
❑3, b&w; Buck Rogers ... 1.95
❑4, b&w; Buck Rogers ... 1.95
❑5, b&w; Buck Rogers ... 1.95
❑6, b&w; Buck Rogers ... 1.95
❑7 ... 2.25
❑8 ... 2.25
❑9 ... 2.95
❑10 ... 3.50
❑11 ... 3.95

Cosmic Kliti
Fantagraphics / Eros
❑1, Jul 1991, b&w; Adult ... 2.25

Cosmic Odyssey
DC
❑1, Nov 1988; V: Darkseid ... 3.50
❑2, Dec 1988; John Stewart fails to save planet from destruction ... 3.50
❑3, Dec 1988 ... 3.50
❑4, Jan 1989; D: Forager ... 3.50

Cosmic Powers
Marvel
❑1, Mar 1994; Thanos ... 2.50
❑2, Apr 1994; Terrax ... 2.50
❑3, May 1994; Jack of Hearts & Ganymede 2.50
❑4, Jun 1994 ... 2.50
❑5, Jul 1994; Morg ... 2.50
❑6, Aug 1994; Tyrant ... 2.50

Cosmic Powers Unlimited
Marvel
❑1, May 1995; Wraparound cover ... 3.95
❑2, Aug 1995; indicia says Aug; cover says Sep ... 3.95
❑3, Dec 1995 ... 3.95
❑4, Feb 1996; Wrap around cover; Starring Silver Surfer ... 3.95
❑5, May 1996; Wrap around cover; Starring Silver Surfer ... 3.95

Cosmic Ray
Image
❑1/A, Jun 1999; green sunglasses cover 2.95
❑1/B, Jun 1999; Murderer or Hero cover 2.95
❑2, Aug 1999 ... 2.95
❑3, Oct 1999 ... 2.95

Cosmic Steller Rebellers
Hammac
❑1 ... 1.50
❑2 ... 1.50

Cosmic Waves
AmF
❑1, Aug 1994, Science-fiction anthology 2.50

Other grades: Multiply price above by 5/6 for VF/NM • 2/3 for VERY FINE • 1/3 for FINE • 1/5 for VERY GOOD • 1/8 for GOOD

Chuck Norris

Fighter beats people up for Marvel's kids' line
©Marvel

Clan Apis

Educational independent comic about bees
©Active Synapse

Classics Illustrated (First)

Outstanding adaptations of classic fiction
©First

Classic X-Men

Retold new X-Men tales plus new material
©Marvel

Clerks: The Comic Book

Kevin Smith book was hot at inception
©Oni

N-MINT

Cougar
Atlas-Seaboard
❑1, Apr 1975 FS, DA (a) 5.00
❑2, Jul 1975; O: Cougar 3.00

Countdown
DC / Wildstorm
❑1, Jun 2000 2.95
❑2, Jul 2000 2.95
❑3, Aug 2000 2.95
❑4, Sep 2000 2.95
❑5, Oct 2000 2.95
❑6, Nov 2000 2.95
❑7, Dec 2000 2.95
❑8, Jan 2001 2.95

Count Duckula
Marvel
❑1, Jan 1989, O: Count Duckula 1.00
❑2, Feb 1989 1.00
❑3, Mar 1989, 1: Danger Mouse 1.00
❑4, Apr 1989, Danger Mouse 1.00
❑5, May 1989, Danger Mouse 1.00
❑6, Jun 1989, Danger Mouse 1.00
❑7, Jul 1989, Danger Mouse 1.00
❑8, Aug 1989, Geraldo Rivera 1.00
❑9, Sep 1989 1.00
❑10, Oct 1989 1.00
❑11, Nov 1989 1.00
❑12, Dec 1989 1.00
❑13, Jan 1990 1.00
❑14, Feb 1990 1.00
❑15, Mar 1990 1.00

Counter Ops
Antarctic
❑1, Mar 2003 3.95
❑2, Apr 2003 3.95
❑3, May 2003 3.95
❑4, Jun 2003 3.95

Counterparts
Tundra
❑1, Jan 1993, b&w 2.95
❑2, Mar 1993, b&w 2.95
❑3 2.95

Coup D'Etat: Afterword
DC / Wildstorm
❑1, May 2004; follows other Coup D'Etat issues; Wetworks Vol. 2 and Sleeper Season Two preludes 2.95

Coup D'Etat: The Authority
DC / Wildstorm
❑1, Apr 2004; Says "Four of Four" on cover 4.00

Coup D'Etat: Sleeper
DC / Wildstorm
❑1, Apr 2004; Says "One of Four" on cover; story continues in Coup D'Etat: Stormwatch 6.00
❑1/Variant, Apr 2004; Says "One of Four" on cover; story continues in Coup D'Etat: Stormwatch 10.00

Coup D'Etat: Stormwatch
DC / Wildstorm
❑1, Apr 2004; Says "Two of Four" on cover; story continues in Coup D'Etat: Wildcats Version 3.0 5.00

N-MINT

❑1/Variant, Apr 2004; Says "Two of Four" on cover; story continues in Coup D'Etat: Wildcats Version 3.0 7.00

Coup D'Etat: Wildcats Version 3.0
DC / Wildstorm
❑1, Apr 2004; Says "Three of Four" on cover; story concludes in Coup D'Etat: Authority 5.00
❑1/Variant, Apr 2004; Says "Three of Four" on cover; story concludes in Coup D'Etat: Authority 6.00

Couple of Winos, A
Fantagraphics
❑1, ca. 1991, b&w 2.25

Courageous Man Adventures
Moordam
❑1, b&w; Mr. Beat back-up 2.95
❑2, b&w 2.95
❑3, Oct 1998 2.95

Courageous Princess
Antarctic
❑1, Apr 2000; Trade paperback; Graphic novel 11.95

Courtney Crumrin & The Night Things
Oni
❑1, Mar 2002 2.95
❑2, Apr 2002 2.95
❑3, May 2002 2.95
❑4, Jun 2002 2.95

Courtney Crumrin Tales
Oni
❑1, Sep 2005 5.95

Courtship of Eddie's Father
Dell
❑1, Jan 1970 30.00
❑2, May 1970 24.00

Courtyard (Alan Moore's)
Avatar
❑1, Feb 2003, b&w 3.50
❑1/A, Feb 2003, b&w; Wraparound art cover 3.95
❑2, Mar 2003, b&w 3.50
❑2/A, Mar 2003, b&w; Wraparound art cover 3.95

Coutoo
Dark Horse
❑1, b&w; NN; One-shot 3.50

Coven
Awesome
❑1/A, Aug 1997; RL (c); JPH (w); RL (a); "Butt" cover 5.00
❑1/B, Aug 1997; JPH (w); Man with flaming hands on cover; Red border 2.50
❑1/C, Aug 1997; JPH (w); "Wizard Authentic" cover 4.00
❑1/D, Aug 1997; JPH (w); Team on cover; White border 2.50
❑1/E, Aug 1997; Dynamic Forces edition; RL (c); JPH (w); RL (a); Chromium cover otherwise same as 1/A 2.50
❑1/F, Aug 1997; 1st Edition; JPH (w); Flip book with Kaboom 1+ 2.50
❑1/G, Aug 1997; JPH (w); "Flame Hands" cover 2.50
❑1/2nd 1997; "Fan Appreciation Edition"; JPH (w); Is really 2nd Printing 2.50
❑2, Sep 1997 JPH (w) 2.50

N-MINT

❑2/Gold, Sep 1997; Gold edition limited to 5000 copies; JPH (w) 2.50
❑3, Oct 1997 JPH (w) 2.50
❑3/A, Oct 1997; JPH (w); Red foil logo on cover 2.50
❑4, Nov 1998 JPH (w) 2.50
❑5, Jan 1998 JPH (w) 2.50
❑5/A, Jan 1998; JPH (w); Variant cover, woman, ghouls standing in water 2.50
❑6, Feb 1998 JPH (w) 2.50

Coven
Awesome
❑1, Jan 1999; regular cover: Woman with glowing gloves facing forward 2.50
❑1/A, Jan 1999; Chrome ("Covenchrome") edition with certificate of authenticity; Two team-members flying on cover with white Coven logo 2.50
❑1/B, Jan 1999; Variant "scratch" cover by Ian Churchill 2.50
❑1/C, Jan 1999; Gold edition; Gold edition 2.50
❑1/D, Jan 1999; "Spellcaster" cover by Rob Liefeld 2.50
❑1/E, Jan 1999; "Black Mass" cover 2.50
❑1/F, Jan 1999; Dynamic Forces exclusive cover with two women surfing 2.50
❑2, Feb 1999; Team Cover 2.50
❑3, Mar 1999 2.50
❑4, Apr 1999; Flipbook with Lionheart #2 2.50

Coven Black and White
Awesome
❑1, Sep 1998 2.95

Coven: Dark Origins
Awesome
❑1, Jun 1999 2.50

Coven: Fantom
Awesome
❑1, Feb 1998 JPH (w) 3.00
❑1/Gold, Feb 1998; JPH (w); Gold logo 3.00

Coven of Angels
Jitterbug
❑1, Nov 1995 4.00
❑2 4.00
❑Ashcan 1; Ashcan edition with Linsner cover 8.00

Coven 13
No Mercy
❑1, Aug 1997 2.50

Coven: Tooth and Nail
Avatar
❑1, Mar 2002; Matt Martin cover 2.95
❑1/Ltd., Mar 2002; White foil-embossed leatherette cover; No indicia 29.95

Coventry
Fantagraphics
❑1, Nov 1996, b&w; cardstock cover 3.95
❑2, Mar 1997, b&w; cardstock cover 3.95
❑3, Jul 1997, b&w; cardstock cover 3.95

Covert Vampiric Operations
Idea & Design Works
❑1, ca. 2003 5.99

Covert Vampiric Operations: Artifact
Idea & Design Works
❑1, Oct 2003 3.99

Other grades: Multiply price above by 5/6 for VF/NM • 2/3 for VERY FINE • 1/3 for FINE • 1/5 for VERY GOOD • 1/8 for GOOD

	N-MINT
❑2, Nov 2003	3.99
❑3, Jan 2004	3.99

Cow
MonsterPants

❑1	1.99
❑2	1.99
❑3	1.99

Cow-Boy
Ogre

❑1, ca. 1997, b&w; O: Cow-Boy	4.00

Cowboy in Africa
Gold Key

❑1, Mar 1968, based on 1967-68 TV series; Chuck Connors back cover pin-up	40.00

Cowboy Love (Avalon)
Avalon

❑1, b&w; Reprints	2.95

Cow Special
Image

❑1, Jun 2001, b&w; Spring/Summer issue	2.95

Coyote
Marvel / Epic

❑1, Apr 1983; O: Coyote	2.50
❑2, Jun 1983	2.00
❑3, Sep 1983 BWi (a)	2.00
❑4, Jan 1984 BWi (a)	1.50
❑5, Apr 1984 BWi (a)	1.50
❑6, Jun 1984 BWi (a)	1.50
❑7, Jul 1984 SD (a)	1.50
❑8, Oct 1984 SD (a)	1.50
❑9, Dec 1984 SD (a)	1.50
❑10, Jan 1985 SD (a)	1.50
❑11, Mar 1985; TMc, FS (a); 1st Todd McFarlane art	2.50
❑12, May 1985 TMc, FS (a)	2.00
❑13, Jul 1985 TMc, FS (a)	2.00
❑14, Sep 1985 TMc, FS (a); A: Badger	1.50
❑15, Nov 1985 FS (a)	1.50
❑16, Jan 1986; Last issue	1.50

Crabbs
Cat-Head

❑1, b&w; Adult	3.75

Crack Busters
Showcase

❑1, Nov 1986	1.95
❑2	1.95

Cracked
Globe

	N-MINT
❑20, ca. 1961, b&w JSe (a)	12.00
❑21, b&w JSe (c); JSe (a)	10.00
❑22, ca. 1962, b&w JSe (c); JSe (a)	10.00
❑23, ca. 1962, b&w BWa, BEv, JSe (a)	10.00
❑24, ca. 1962, b&w BWa, BEv, JSe (a)	10.00
❑25, Jul 1962, b&w BEv, JSe (a)	10.00
❑26, b&w JSe (a)	10.00
❑27, Feb 1962, b&w BWa, JSe, WW (a)	10.00
❑28, ca. 1963, b&w JSe (a)	10.00
❑29, ca. 1963, b&w JSe (a)	10.00
❑30, ca. 1963, b&w JSe (a)	10.00
❑31, Sep 1963, b&w JSe (a)	8.00
❑32 1963, b&w JSe (a)	8.00
❑33, Dec 1963, b&w JSe (c); JSe (a)	8.00
❑34, b&w JSe (a)	8.00
❑35, ca. 1964, b&w JSe (c); JSe (a)	8.00
❑36, ca. 1964, b&w JSe (a)	8.00
❑37, ca. 1964, b&w; JSe (c); JSe (a); Comic strip parody feature includes cameos, by Beetle Bailey, Mutt & Jeff, Popeye, Dick Tracy, Peanuts, Henry, Nancy, Pogo, Mickey Mouse, Donald Duck, Blondie, Alley Oop, Tarzan, Superman, Mandrake the Magician, Prince Valiant, the Lone Ranger, Archie, Little Orphan Annie, Dennis the Menace	8.00
❑38, ca. 1964, b&w JSe (c); JSe (a)	8.00
❑39, b&w JSe (c); JSe (a)	8.00
❑40, b&w JSe (c); JSe (a)	8.00
❑41, b&w JSe (c); JSe (a)	8.00
❑42, b&w JSe (a)	8.00
❑43, May 1965, b&w JSe (a)	8.00
❑44, ca. 1965, b&w JSe (c); DP, JSe (a)	8.00
❑45, ca. 1965, b&w JSe (c); JSe (a)	8.00
❑46 1965, b&w JSe (a)	8.00
❑47, b&w JSe (c); JSe (a)	8.00
❑48, b&w JSe (c); JSe (a)	8.00
❑49, b&w JSe (c); JSe (a)	8.00
❑50, b&w JSe (c); JSe (a)	8.00
❑51, ca. 1966, b&w JSe (a)	5.00
❑52, ca. 1966, b&w JSe (a)	5.00
❑53, ca. 1966, b&w JSe (c); JSe (a)	5.00
❑54 1966, b&w JSe (a)	5.00
❑55, Sep 1966, b&w JSe (a)	5.00
❑56, b&w JSe (a)	5.00
❑57, b&w JSe (a)	5.00
❑58, b&w JSe (a)	5.00
❑59 1967, b&w JSe (a)	5.00
❑60 1967, b&w JSe (a)	5.00
❑61, Jul 1967, b&w BEv, JSe (a)	5.00
❑62, Aug 1967, b&w JSe (a)	5.00
❑63, Sep 1967, b&w JSe (a)	5.00
❑64, Oct 1967, b&w JSe (a)	5.00
❑65, Nov 1967, b&w JSe (a)	5.00
❑66, b&w JSe (a)	5.00
❑67 1968, b&w JSe (a)	5.00
❑68 1968, b&w JSe (c); JSe (a)	5.00
❑69 1968, b&w JSe (a)	5.00
❑70 1968, b&w JSe (a)	5.00
❑71 1968, b&w JSe (c); JSe (a)	5.00
❑72 1968, b&w JSe (a)	5.00
❑73 1968, b&w JSe (a)	5.00
❑74, Jan 1969, b&w JSe (a)	5.00
❑75 1969, b&w JSe (a)	5.00
❑76, May 1969, b&w JSe (a)	5.00
❑77 1969, b&w JSe (a)	5.00
❑78 1969, b&w JSe (a)	5.00
❑79 1969, b&w JSe (a)	5.00
❑80 1969, b&w JSe (a)	5.00
❑81 1969, b&w JSe (a)	5.00
❑82, Jan 1970, b&w JSe (a)	5.00
❑83 1970, b&w JSe (a)	5.00
❑84 1970, b&w JSe (a)	5.00
❑85 1970, b&w JSe (a)	5.00
❑86 1970, b&w JSe (a)	5.00
❑87, Sep 1970, b&w JSe (a)	5.00
❑88, Oct 1970, b&w JSe (a)	5.00
❑89, Nov 1970, b&w JSe (a)	5.00
❑90, Jan 1971, b&w JSe (a)	5.00
❑91, Mar 1971, b&w JSe (a)	5.00
❑92, May 1971, b&w JSe (a)	5.00
❑93, Jul 1971, b&w JSe (a)	5.00
❑94, Aug 1971, b&w JSe (a)	5.00
❑95, Sep 1971, b&w JSe (a)	5.00
❑96, Oct 1971, b&w JSe (a)	5.00
❑97, Nov 1971, b&w JSe (a)	5.00
❑98, Jan 1972, b&w JSe (a)	5.00
❑99, Mar 1972, b&w JSe (a)	5.00
❑100, May 1972, b&w JSe (a)	5.00
❑101, Jul 1972, b&w JSe (a)	4.00
❑102, Aug 1972, b&w JSe (a)	4.00
❑103, Sep 1972, b&w JSe (a)	4.00
❑104, Oct 1972, b&w JSe (a)	4.00
❑105, Nov 1972, b&w JSe (a)	4.00
❑106, Jan 1973, b&w JSe (a)	4.00
❑107, Mar 1973, b&w JSe (a)	4.00
❑108, May 1973, b&w JSe (a)	4.00
❑109, Jul 1973, b&w JSe (a)	4.00
❑110, Aug 1973, b&w JSe (a)	4.00
❑111, Sep 1973, b&w; JSe (a); Poseidon Adventure, McCloud parodies	4.00
❑112, Oct 1973, b&w; JSe (c); JSe (a); Kung Fu parody	4.00
❑113, Nov 1973, b&w JSe (a)	4.00
❑114, Jan 1974, b&w JSe (a)	4.00
❑115, Mar 1974, b&w JSe (a)	4.00
❑116, May 1974, b&w JSe (a)	4.00
❑117, Jul 1974, b&w JSe (a)	4.00
❑118, Aug 1974, b&w; JSe (c); JSe (a); Sting parody	4.00
❑119, Sep 1974, b&w JSe (a)	4.00
❑120, Oct 1974, b&w JSe (a)	4.00
❑121, Nov 1974, b&w JSe (a)	4.00
❑122, Jan 1975, b&w; JSe (c); JSe (a); Kojak	4.00
❑123, Mar 1975, b&w JSe (a)	4.00
❑124, May 1975, b&w JSe (a)	4.00
❑125, Jul 1975, b&w; JSe (c); JSe (a); Earthquake parody	4.00
❑126, Aug 1975, b&w JSe (a)	4.00
❑127, Sep 1975, b&w JSe (a)	4.00
❑128, Oct 1975, b&w; JSe (c); JSe (a); Capone parody	4.00
❑129, Nov 1975, b&w; JSe (c); JSe (a); Jaws parody	4.00
❑130, Jan 1976, b&w JSe (c); BWa, JSe (a)	4.00
❑131, Mar 1976, b&w; JSe (c); BWa, JSe (a); Godfather, Jaws parodies	4.00
❑132, May 1976, b&w; JSe (c); JSe (a); Baretta parody	4.00
❑133, Jul 1976, b&w JSe (c); BWa, JSe (a)	4.00
❑134, Aug 1976, b&w JSe (a)	4.00
❑135, Sep 1976, b&w; JSe (c); BWa, JSe (a); The Bionic Woman	4.00
❑136, Oct 1976, b&w JSe (c); BWa, JSe (a)	4.00
❑137, Nov 1976, b&w; JSe (a); Welcome Back Kotter parody	4.00
❑138, Dec 1976, b&w JSe (a)	4.00
❑139, Jan 1977, b&w JSe (a)	4.00
❑140, Mar 1977, b&w JSe (c); BWa, JSe (a)	4.00
❑141, May 1977, b&w JSe (a)	4.00
❑142, Jul 1977, b&w JSe (a)	4.00
❑143, Aug 1977, b&w; JSe (a); Rocky parody	4.00
❑144, Sep 1977, b&w JSe (a)	4.00
❑145, Oct 1977, b&w JSe (a)	4.00
❑146, Nov 1977, b&w; JSe (c); JSe (a); Star Wars parody; Cracked cover stickers	8.00
❑147, Dec 1977, b&w; JSe (a); Star Wars II, What's Happening parodies; postcards	5.00
❑148, Jan 1978, b&w; JSe (a); Star Wars Cantina parody	5.00
❑149, Mar 1978, b&w; JSe (c); JSe (a); Star Wars, Bionic Man parodies; poster inside	5.00
❑150, May 1978, b&w; JSe (a); Close Encounters parody	4.00
❑151, Jul 1978, b&w JSe (a)	3.00
❑152, Aug 1978, b&w JSe (c); BWa, JSe (a)	3.00
❑153, Sep 1978, b&w JSe (a)	3.00
❑154, Oct 1978, b&w; JSe (c); JSe (a); Jaws 2 parody; T-shirt iron-on inside	3.00
❑155, Nov 1978, b&w JSe (a)	3.00
❑156, Dec 1978, b&w; JSe (c); JSe (a); Grease parody; poster inside	3.00
❑157, Jan 1979, b&w; JSe (a); Battlestar Galactica parody	6.00
❑158, Mar 1979, b&w JSe (c); JSe (a)	3.00
❑159, May 1979, b&w JSe (a)	3.00
❑160, Jul 1979, b&w; JSe (c); JSe (a); Superman parody; poster inside	3.00
❑161, Aug 1979, b&w JSe (c); BWa, JSe (a)	3.00
❑162, Sep 1979, b&w JSe (c); BWa, JSe (a)	3.00
❑163, Oct 1979, b&w; JSe (c); JSe (a); Mork and Mindy parody; postcards inside	3.00
❑164, Nov 1979, b&w; JSe (c); BWa, JSe (a); Alien parody	4.00
❑165, Dec 1979, b&w JSe (a)	3.00
❑166, Jan 1980, b&w JSe (a)	3.00
❑167, Mar 1980, b&w; JSe (c); JSe (a); Mork and Mindy parody; infinity cover; poster inside	3.00
❑168, May 1980, b&w; JSe (c); JSe (a); M*A*S*H parody	3.00
❑169, Jul 1980, b&w; JSe (c); JSe (a); Star Trek: The Motion Picture parody; poster inside	4.00
❑170, Aug 1980, b&w JSe (a)	3.00
❑171, Sep 1980, b&w JSe (a)	3.00
❑172, Oct 1980, b&w; JSe (c); JSe (a); ChiPs/Dukes of Hazzard cross-over; iron-ons	3.00
❑173, Nov 1980, b&w JSe (a)	3.00
❑174, Dec 1980, b&w JSe (a)	3.00
❑175, Jan 1981, b&w JSe (a)	3.00
❑176, Mar 1981, b&w JSe (a)	3.00
❑177, May 1981, b&w JSe (a)	3.00
❑178, Jul 1981, b&w JSe (a)	3.00
❑179, Aug 1981, b&w JSe (a)	3.00
❑180, Sep 1981, b&w JSe (a)	3.00
❑181, Oct 1981, b&w JSe (a)	3.00
❑182, Nov 1981, b&w; JSe (c); JSe (a); Hulk parody; Alfred E. Neuman on cover	4.00
❑183, Dec 1981, b&w JSe (a)	3.00
❑184, Jan 1982, b&w JSe (a)	3.00
❑185, Mar 1982, b&w JSe (a)	3.00
❑186, May 1982, b&w; JSe (a); Barney Miller, Three's Company parodies	3.00
❑187, Jul 1982, b&w JSe (a)	3.00
❑188, Aug 1982, b&w JSe (a)	3.00
❑189, Sep 1982, b&w JSe (a)	3.00
❑190, Oct 1982, b&w JSe (a)	3.00
❑191, Nov 1982, b&w JSe (c); BWa, JSe (a)	3.00
❑192, Jan 1983, b&w JSe (a)	3.00

Other grades: Multiply price above by 5/6 for VF/NM • 2/3 for VERY FINE • 1/3 for FINE • 1/5 for VERY GOOD • 1/8 for GOOD

Cloak & Dagger

Limited series about drug-induced mutants

©Marvel

Cold-Blooded Chameleon Commandos

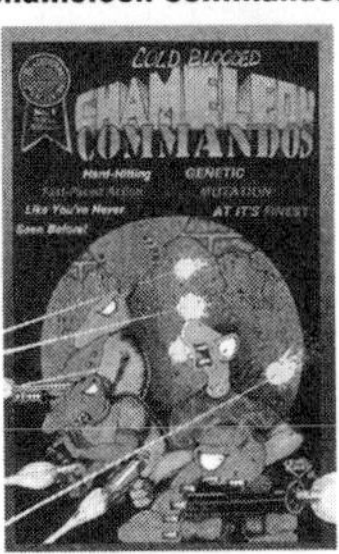

Lesser-known series from the Turtles age

©Blackthorne

Colonia

Jeff Nicholson's fantasy about a strange island

©Colonia

Combat Kelly (2nd Series)

Most of cast run over by a tank in last issue

©Marvel

Comet Man

Obscure Marvel mini-series from 1987

©Marvel

	N-MINT
❑193, Mar 1983, b&w JSe (a)	3.00
❑194, May 1983, b&w; JSe (a); M.A.S.H. parody	3.00
❑195, Jul 1983, b&w JSe (a)	3.00
❑196, Aug 1983, b&w JSe (a)	3.00
❑197, Sep 1983, b&w JSe (a)	3.00
❑198, Oct 1983, b&w; JSe (c); JSe (a); Jaws 3-D, Fall Guy parodies; poster inside	3.00
❑199, Nov 1983, b&w JSe (a)	3.00
❑200, Dec 1983, b&w JSe (a)	3.00
❑201, Jan 1984, b&w JSe (a)	2.50
❑202, Mar 1984, b&w; JSe (a); Alfred E. Neuman/Smythe cover	3.00
❑203, May 1984, b&w JSe (a)	2.50
❑204, Jul 1984, b&w JSe (a)	2.50
❑205, Aug 1984, b&w JSe (a)	2.50
❑206, Sep 1984, b&w JSe (a)	2.50
❑207, Oct 1984, b&w JSe (a)	2.50
❑208, Nov 1984, b&w JSe (a)	2.50
❑209, Jan 1985, b&w JSe (a)	2.50
❑210, Mar 1985, b&w JSe (a)	2.50
❑211, May 1985, b&w JSe (a)	2.50
❑212, Jul 1985, b&w JSe (a)	2.50
❑213, Aug 1985, b&w; JSe (a); Boy George, Transformer parodies	2.50
❑214, Sep 1985, b&w JSe (a)	2.50
❑215, Oct 1985, b&w JSe (a)	2.50
❑216, Nov 1985, b&w JSe (a)	2.50
❑217, Dec 1985, b&w JSe (a)	2.50
❑218, Jan 1986, b&w; JSe (a); G.I. Joe, Back to the Future parodies	2.50
❑219, Mar 1986, b&w; JSe (a); Sylvester P. Smythe as Rambo	2.50
❑220, May 1986, b&w JSe (a)	2.50
❑221, Jul 1986, b&w JSe (a)	2.50
❑222, Aug 1986, b&w JSe (a)	2.50
❑223, Sep 1986, b&w JSe (a)	2.50
❑224, Nov 1986, b&w; JSe (a); Music-themed issue	2.50
❑225, Jan 1987, b&w JSe (a)	2.50
❑226, Mar 1987, b&w JSe (a)	2.50
❑227, Apr 1987, b&w; JSe (c); SD, JSe (a); Soviet-themed issue	2.50
❑228, Jul 1987, b&w JSe (a)	2.50
❑229, Aug 1987, b&w JSe (a)	2.50
❑230, Sep 1987, b&w; JSe (a); Monkees, Growing Pains, Murder She Wrote, Gumby parodies	2.50
❑231, Oct 1987, b&w JSe (a)	2.50
❑232, Nov 1987, b&w; JSe (c); JSe (a); Cheers, Max Headroom, others parodied	2.50
❑233, Jan 1988, b&w JSe (a)	2.50
❑234, Mar 1988, b&w JSe (a)	2.50
❑235, May 1988, b&w JSe (a)	2.50
❑236, Jul 1988, b&w JSe (a)	2.50
❑237, Aug 1988, b&w JSe (a)	2.50
❑238, Sep 1988, b&w JSe (a)	2.50
❑239, Oct 1988, b&w JSe (a)	2.50
❑240, Nov 1988, b&w JSe (a)	2.50
❑241, Dec 1988, b&w JSe (a)	2.50
❑242, Jan 1989, b&w JSe (a)	2.50
❑243, Mar 1989, b&w JSe (a)	2.50
❑244, May 1989, b&w JSe (a)	2.50
❑245, Jul 1989, b&w JSe (a)	2.50
❑246, Aug 1989, b&w JSe (a)	2.50
❑247, Sep 1989, b&w JSe (a)	2.50
❑248, Oct 1989, b&w JSe (a)	2.50
❑249, Nov 1989, b&w JSe (a)	2.50

	N-MINT
❑250, Dec 1989, b&w JSe (a)	2.50
❑251, Jan 1990, b&w JSe (a)	2.00
❑252, Mar 1990, b&w JSe (a)	2.00
❑253, May 1990, b&w JSe (a)	2.00
❑254, Jul 1990, b&w JSe (a)	2.00
❑255, Aug 1990, b&w JSe (a)	2.00
❑256, Sep 1990, b&w JSe (a)	2.00
❑257, Oct 1990, b&w JSe (a)	2.00
❑258, Nov 1990, b&w JSe (a)	2.00
❑259, Dec 1990, b&w JSe (a)	2.00
❑260, Jan 1991, b&w	2.00
❑261, Mar 1991, b&w JSe (a)	2.00
❑262, May 1991, b&w JSe (a)	2.00
❑263, Jul 1991, b&w JSe (a)	2.00
❑264, Aug 1991, b&w JSe (a)	2.00
❑265, Sep 1991, b&w JSe (a)	2.00
❑266, Oct 1991, b&w JSe (a)	2.00
❑267, Nov 1991, b&w JSe (a)	2.00
❑268, Dec 1991, b&w JSe (a)	2.00
❑269, Jan 1992, b&w JSe (a)	2.00
❑270, Mar 1992, b&w JSe (a)	2.00
❑271, May 1992, b&w JSe (a)	2.00
❑272, Jul 1992, b&w JSe (a)	2.00
❑273, Aug 1992, b&w JSe (a)	2.00
❑274, Sep 1992, b&w JSe (a)	2.00
❑275, Oct 1992, b&w JSe (a)	2.00
❑276, Nov 1992, b&w JSe (a)	2.00
❑277, Dec 1992, b&w JSe (a)	2.00
❑278, Jan 1993, b&w JSe (a)	2.00
❑279, Mar 1993, b&w JSe (a)	2.00
❑280, May 1993, b&w JSe (a)	2.00
❑281, Jul 1993, b&w JSe (a)	2.00
❑282, Aug 1993, b&w JSe (a)	2.00
❑283, Sep 1993, b&w JSe (a)	2.00
❑284, Oct 1993, b&w JSe (a)	2.00
❑285, Nov 1993, b&w JSe (a)	2.00
❑286, Dec 1993, b&w JSe (a)	2.00
❑287, Jan 1994, b&w JSe (a)	2.00
❑288, Mar 1994, b&w JSe (a)	2.00
❑289, May 1994, b&w JSe (a)	2.00
❑290, Jul 1994, b&w JSe (a)	2.00
❑291, Aug 1994, b&w magazine; JSe (c); JSe (a)	2.00
❑292, Sep 1994, b&w magazine; JSe (a)	2.00
❑293, Oct 1994, b&w JSe (a)	2.00
❑294, Nov 1994, b&w magazine; JSe (a)	2.00
❑295, Dec 1994, b&w magazine; JSe (a)	2.00
❑296, Jan 1995, b&w magazine; JSe (a)	2.00
❑297, Mar 1995, b&w magazine; JSe (a)	2.00
❑298, May 1995, b&w JSe (a)	2.00
❑299, Jul 1995, b&w JSe (a)	2.00
❑300, Aug 1995, b&w JSe (a)	2.00
❑301, Sep 1995, b&w JSe (a)	2.00
❑302, Oct 1995, b&w magazine; JSe (a)	2.00
❑303, Nov 1995, b&w JSe (a)	2.00
❑304, Dec 1995, b&w JSe (a)	2.00
❑305, Jan 1996, b&w JSe (a)	2.00
❑306, Mar 1996, b&w magazine; JSe (a)	2.00
❑307, ca. 1996, b&w JSe (a)	2.00
❑308, ca. 1996, b&w JSe (a)	2.00
❑309, Aug 1996, b&w JSe (a)	2.00
❑310, Sep 1996, b&w JSe (a)	2.00
❑311, Oct 1996, b&w JSe (a)	2.00
❑312, Nov 1996, b&w JSe (a)	2.00
❑313 1997, b&w JSe (a)	2.00
❑314 1997, b&w JSe (a)	2.00

	N-MINT
❑315, Mar 1997, b&w JSe (a)	2.00
❑316 1997, b&w JSe (a)	2.00
❑317 1997, b&w JSe (a)	2.00
❑318, Aug 1997, b&w JSe (a)	2.00
❑319 1997, b&w JSe (a)	2.00
❑320, b&w JSe (a)	2.00
❑321, b&w JSe (a)	2.00
❑322, b&w JSe (a)	2.00
❑323, b&w JSe (a)	2.00
❑324, b&w JSe (a)	2.00
❑325, May 1998, b&w; JSe (a); 40th anniversary issue; Titanic parody	2.00
❑326, Jul 1998, b&w; JSe (a); King of the Hill, Flubber parodies	2.00
❑327, b&w JSe (a)	2.00
❑328, b&w; JSe (a); Simpsons, South Park, King of the Hill parody	2.00
❑329, b&w JSe (a)	2.00
❑330, b&w JSe (a)	2.00
❑331, b&w JSe (a)	2.00
❑332, Jan 1999, b&w; JSe (a); Armageddon, Saving Private Ryan parodies	2.00
❑333, b&w JSe (a)	2.00
❑334, b&w JSe (a)	2.00
❑335, b&w JSe (a)	2.00
❑336, b&w JSe (a)	2.00
❑337, b&w JSe (a)	2.00
❑338, Oct 1999, b&w; JSe (a); Star Wars, Mystery Men, Inspector Gadget parodies	2.00
❑339, Nov 1999, b&w; JSe (a); Tarzan, Animorphs, American Pie parodies	2.00
❑340 2000, b&w JSe (a)	2.00
❑341 2000, b&w JSe (a)	2.00
❑342 2000, b&w JSe (a)	2.00
❑343 2000, b&w JSe (a)	2.00
❑344, Jun 2000 JSe (a)	2.00
❑345 2000 JSe (a)	2.00
❑346, Aug 2000 JSe (a)	2.00
❑347 2000 JSe (a)	2.00
❑348 2000 JSe (a)	2.00
❑349 2000 JSe (a)	2.00
❑350, Dec 2000 JSe (a)	2.00
❑351, Jan 2001, First issue without John Severin	2.95
❑352, Feb 2001	2.95
❑353, Mar 2001; Pokemon, X-Men movie parodies	2.95
❑354 2001; Eminem parody; super-hero issue	2.95
❑Ann 1, b&w JSe (a)	7.00
❑Ann 2, b&w JSe (a)	5.00
❑Ann 3, b&w JSe (a)	5.00
❑Ann 4, b&w JSe (a)	4.00
❑Ann 5, b&w JSe (a)	4.00
❑Ann 6, b&w JSe (a)	4.00
❑Ann 7, b&w JSe (a)	4.00
❑Ann 8, b&w JSe (a)	4.00
❑Ann 9 1975, b&w; JSe (c); JSe (a); 1975 Ann.	4.00
❑Ann 10 1976 JSe (a)	4.00
❑Ann 11 1977 JSe (a)	4.00
❑Ann 12 1978 JSe (a)	4.00
❑Ann 13 1979 JSe (a)	4.00
❑Ann 14 1980 JSe (a)	4.00
❑Ann 15 1981 JSe (a)	4.00
❑Ann 16 1982 JSe (a)	4.00
❑Ann 17 1983 JSe (a)	4.00

Other grades: Multiply price above by 5/6 for VF/NM • 2/3 for VERY FINE • 1/3 for FINE • 1/5 for VERY GOOD • 1/8 for GOOD

❑Ann 18 1984 JSe (a) 4.00
❑Ann 19, Sum 1985; JSe (a); Knight Rider, Raiders of the Lost Ark, Too Close for Comfort parodies 4.00

Cracked Collectors' Edition
Globe

❑4, ca. 1973, JSe (a); No #1-3 10.00
❑5 1973, JSe (a) 8.00
❑6 1974, JSe (a); Gangster issue 6.00
❑7 1974, JSe (c); JSe (a); TV issue 6.00
❑8 1975, JSe (a) 6.00
❑9 1975, JSe (a) 6.00
❑10 1975, JSe (a) 6.00
❑11 1975, JSe (c); JSe (a); World of Advertising 5.00
❑12 1975, JSe (a) 5.00
❑13 1976, JSe (a) 5.00
❑14 1976, BWa, JSe (a); More From the Cracked TV Screen 5.00
❑15 1976, JSe (a) 5.00
❑16 1976, JSe (c); JSe (a); Fonz for President cover 5.00
❑17 1976 JSe (a) 5.00
❑18 1976 JSe (a) 5.00
❑19 1977; JSe (a); TV issue 5.00
❑20 1977 JSe (a) 5.00
❑21 1977; BWa, JSe (a); Cracked's Big Pictures; January cover date, no year. 5.00
❑22 1978 JSe (a) 5.00
❑23, May 1978; JSe (a); Cracked Visits Outer Space 5.00
❑nn (24), Jul 1978; JSe (a); No number 5.00
❑nn (25), Sep 1978; JSe (a); No number 5.00
❑nn (26), Nov 1978; JSe (c); JSe (a); Sharks special; no number 5.00
❑nn (27), Dec 1978; JSe (a); No number 5.00
❑nn (28), Feb 1979; JSe (a); No number 5.00
❑nn (29), May 1979; JSe (c); JSe (a); Mork issue; No number 10.00
❑nn (30), Jul 1979; JSe (a); No number 5.00
❑nn (31), Sep 1979; JSe (a); No number 4.00
❑nn (32), Nov 1979; JSe (c); JSe (a); Summer Fun; No number 4.00
❑nn (33), Dec 1979; JSe (a); No number 4.00
❑nn (34), Feb 1980; JSe (a); No number 4.00
❑nn (35), May 1980; JSe (a); No number 4.00
❑nn (36), Jul 1980; JSe (a); No number 4.00
❑nn (37), Sep 1980; JSe (a); No number 4.00
❑nn (38), Nov 1980; JSe (a); No number 4.00
❑nn (39), Dec 1980; JSe (a); No number 4.00
❑nn (40), Feb 1981; JSe (c); JSe (a); TV special; No number 4.00
❑41, May 1981 JSe (a) 4.00
❑nn (42), Jul 1981; JSe (a); No number 4.00
❑nn (43), Sep 1981; JSe (a); No number 4.00
❑nn (44), Nov 1981; JSe (a); No number 4.00
❑nn (45), Dec 1981; JSe (a); No number 4.00
❑nn (46), Feb 1982; JSe (a); No number 4.00
❑nn (47), May 1982; JSe (a); No number 4.00
❑nn (48), Jul 1982; JSe (a); No number 4.00
❑nn (49), Sep 1982; JSe (a); No number 4.00
❑nn (50), Nov 1982; JSe (a); No number 4.00
❑nn (51), Dec 1982; JSe (a); No number 3.00
❑nn (52), Feb 1983; JSe (a); No number 3.00
❑nn (53), May 1983; JSe (a); No number 3.00
❑nn (54), Sep 1983; JSe (a); No number 3.00
❑nn (55), Nov 1983; JSe (a); No number 3.00
❑nn (56), Dec 1983; JSe (a); No number 3.00
❑nn (57), Feb 1984; JSe (a); No number 3.00
❑nn (58), May 1984; JSe (a); No number 3.00
❑nn (59), Jul 1984; JSe (a); No number 3.00
❑nn (60), Nov 1984; JSe (a); No number 3.00
❑nn (61), Feb 1985; JSe (a); No number 3.00
❑nn (62), Sep 1985; JSe (a); No number 3.00
❑nn (63), Nov 1985; JSe (a); No number 3.00
❑64, Dec 1985 JSe (a) 3.00
❑65 1986 JSe (a) 3.00
❑66 1986 JSe (a) 3.00
❑67 1986 JSe (a) 3.00
❑68 1986 JSe (a) 3.00
❑69 1987 JSe (a) 3.00
❑70 1987 JSe (a) 3.00
❑71 1987 JSe (a) 3.00
❑72, Sep 1987 JSe (a) 3.00
❑73, Jan 1988 JSe (a) 3.00
❑74 1988 JSe (a) 3.00
❑75 1988 JSe (a) 3.00
❑76 1988 JSe (a) 3.00
❑77 1989 JSe (a) 3.00

❑78 1989 JSe (a) 3.00
❑79 1989 JSe (a) 3.00
❑80 1989 JSe (a) 3.00
❑81 1990 JSe (a) 3.00
❑82 1990 JSe (a) 3.00
❑83 1990 JSe (a) 3.00
❑84 1990 JSe (a) 3.00
❑85 1991 JSe (a) 3.00
❑86 1991 JSe (a) 3.00
❑87 1991 JSe (a) 3.00
❑88 1991 JSe (a) 3.00
❑89 1992 JSe (a) 3.00
❑90 1992 JSe (a) 3.00
❑91 1992 JSe (a) 3.00
❑92, Sep 1992; JSe (a); Family Matters, Robin Hood, Funniest Home Videos parodies 3.00
❑93 1993 JSe (a) 3.00
❑94 1993 JSe (a) 3.00
❑95 1993 JSe (a) 3.00
❑96 1993 JSe (a) 3.00
❑97, Jan 1994; JSe (a); 35th Anniversary issue; polybagged with reprint of #1 3.00
❑98, Apr 1994 JSe (a) 3.00
❑99, Jul 1994 JSe (a) 3.00
❑100, Oct 1994 JSe (a) 3.00
❑101, Jan 1995; b&w magazine; JSe (a) 3.00
❑102, Apr 1995 JSe (a) 3.00
❑103, Jul 1995 JSe (a) 3.00
❑104, Oct 1995 JSe (a) 3.00
❑105, Jan 1996 JSe (a) 3.00
❑106, Apr 1996 JSe (a) 3.00
❑107, Jul 1996 JSe (a) 3.00
❑108, Oct 1996; JSe (a); Year's Best 3.00
❑109, Jan 1997 JSe (a) 3.00
❑110, Apr 1997 JSe (a) 3.00
❑111 1997 JSe (a) 3.00
❑112 1997 JSe (a) 3.00
❑113 1998 JSe (a) 3.00
❑114 1998 JSe (a) 3.00
❑115 1998 JSe (a) 3.00
❑116 1998 JSe (a) 3.00
❑117 1998 JSe (a) 3.00
❑118 1999 JSe (a) 3.00
❑119 1999 JSe (a) 3.00
❑120 1999 JSe (a) 3.00
❑121 1999 JSe (a) 3.00
❑122 1999 JSe (a) 3.00
❑123 2000 JSe (a) 3.00
❑124 2000 JSe (a) 3.00
❑125, Fal 2000 JSe (a) 3.00

Cracked Guide to the Movies
NBM

❑1 8.95

Crap
Fantagraphics

❑1, Aug 1993 2.50
❑2, Oct 1993 2.50
❑3, Feb 1994 2.50
❑4, May 1994 2.50
❑5, Aug 1994 2.50

Crash Dummies
Harvey

❑1, Nov 1994 1.50
❑2, Dec 1994 1.50
❑3, Jun 1994 1.50

Crash Metro & the Star Squad
Oni

❑1, May 1999, b&w 2.95

Crash Ryan
Marvel / Epic

❑1, Oct 1984 1.50
❑2, Nov 1984 1.50
❑3, Dec 1984 1.50
❑4, Jan 1985 1.50

Cray Baby Adventures Special
Electric Milk

❑1; Adult 2.95

Cray-Baby Adventures: Wrath of the Pediddlers
Destination Entertainment

❑1, b&w 2.95
❑2, ca. 1998 2.95
❑3, ca. 1998 2.95

Crazy
Marvel

❑1, Feb 1973, reprints Not Brand Ecch 16.00
❑2, Apr 1973, reprints Not Brand Ecch #6 10.00
❑3, Jun 1973, reprints Not Brand Ecch #7 10.00

Crazy
Marvel

❑1, Oct 1973, b&w 16.00
❑2 1973, b&w; Neal Adams art 10.00
❑3, Mar 1974, b&w 10.00
❑4, May 1974, b&w 5.00
❑5, Jul 1974, b&w 5.00
❑6, Aug 1974, b&w 3.00
❑7, Oct 1974, b&w 3.00
❑8, Dec 1974, b&w 3.00
❑9, Feb 1975, b&w 3.00
❑10, Apr 1975, b&w 3.00
❑11, Jun 1975, b&w 3.00
❑12, Aug 1975, b&w 3.00
❑13, Oct 1975, b&w 3.00
❑14, Nov 1975, b&w 3.00
❑15, Jan 1976, b&w 3.00
❑16, Mar 1976, b&w 2.00
❑17, May 1976, b&w 2.00
❑18, Jul 1976, b&w 2.00
❑19, Aug 1976, b&w 2.00
❑20, Oct 1976, b&w 2.00
❑21, Nov 1976, b&w 2.00
❑22, Jan 1977, b&w 2.00
❑23 1977, b&w 2.00
❑24 1977, b&w 2.00
❑25 1977, b&w 2.00
❑26, Jun 1977, b&w 2.00
❑27, Jul 1977, b&w 2.00
❑28, Aug 1977, b&w 2.00
❑29, Sep 1977, b&w 2.00
❑30, Oct 1977, b&w 2.00
❑31, Nov 1977, b&w 2.00
❑32, Dec 1977, b&w 2.00
❑33, Jan 1978, b&w 2.00
❑34, Feb 1978, b&w 2.00
❑35, Mar 1978, b&w 2.00
❑36, Apr 1978, b&w 2.00
❑37, May 1978, b&w 2.00
❑38, Jun 1978, b&w 2.00
❑39, Jul 1978, b&w 2.00
❑40, Aug 1978, b&w 2.00
❑41, Sep 1978, b&w 2.00
❑42, Sep 1978, b&w 2.00
❑43, Oct 1978, b&w 2.00
❑44, Nov 1978, b&w 2.00
❑45, Dec 1978, b&w 2.00
❑46, Jan 1979, b&w 2.00
❑47, Feb 1979, b&w 2.00
❑48, Mar 1979, b&w 2.00
❑49, Apr 1979, b&w 2.00
❑50, May 1979, b&w 2.00
❑51, Jun 1979, b&w 2.00
❑52, Jul 1979, b&w 2.00
❑53, Aug 1979, b&w 2.00
❑54, Sep 1979, b&w 2.00
❑55, Oct 1979, b&w 2.00
❑56, Nov 1979, b&w 2.00
❑57, Dec 1979, b&w 2.00
❑58, Jan 1980, b&w 2.00
❑59, Feb 1980, b&w 2.00
❑60, Mar 1980, b&w 2.00
❑61, Apr 1980, b&w 2.00
❑62, May 1980, b&w 2.00
❑63, Jun 1980, b&w 2.00
❑64, Jul 1980, b&w 2.00
❑65, Aug 1980, b&w 2.00
❑66, Sep 1980, b&w; "Creatures" parodies Journey into Mystery #51 2.00
❑67, Oct 1980, b&w 2.00
❑68, Nov 1980, b&w 2.00
❑69, Dec 1980, b&w 2.00
❑70, Jan 1981, b&w 2.00
❑71, Feb 1981, b&w 2.00
❑72, Mar 1981, b&w 2.00
❑73, Apr 1981, b&w 2.00
❑74, May 1981, b&w 2.00
❑75, Jun 1981, b&w 2.00
❑76, Jul 1981, b&w 2.00
❑77, Aug 1981, b&w 2.00
❑78, Sep 1981, b&w 2.00
❑79, Oct 1981, b&w 2.00

Other grades: Multiply price above by 5/6 for VF/NM • 2/3 for VERY FINE • 1/3 for FINE • 1/5 for VERY GOOD • 1/8 for GOOD

Command Review

Features reprints from Albedo

©Thoughts & Images

Conan

Marvel's "adjective-less" series relaunch

©Marvel

Conan

Dark Horse version was red hot in 2004

©Dark Horse

Conan Saga

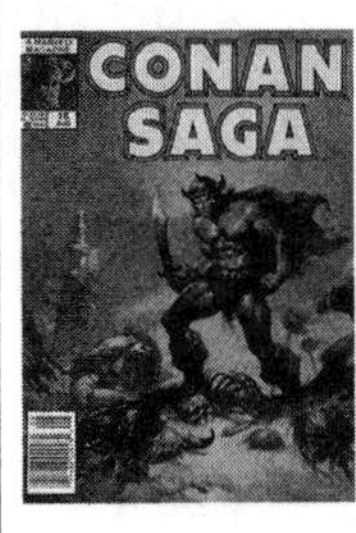

Black-and-white reprint magazine

©Marvel

Conan the Adventurer

Relaunch followed 275-issue series

©Marvel

N-MINT

❑80, Nov 1981, b&w 2.00
❑81, Dec 1981, b&w 2.00
❑82, Jan 1982, b&w; parodies Amazing Spider-Man #8 .... 2.00
❑83, Feb 1982, b&w; Raiders of the Lost Ark parody 2.00
❑84, Mar 1982, b&w 2.00
❑85, Apr 1982, b&w 2.00
❑86, May 1982, b&w 2.00
❑87, Jun 1982, b&w 2.00
❑88, Jul 1982, b&w 2.00
❑89, Aug 1982, b&w 2.00
❑90, Sep 1982, b&w 2.00
❑91, Oct 1982, b&w; Blade Runner parody 2.00
❑92, Dec 1982, b&w; Star Trek II parody 2.00
❑93, Feb 1983, b&w 2.00
❑94, Apr 1983, b&w 2.00

Crazy Bob
Blackbird

❑1, b&w 2.75
❑2, b&w; Final Issue; ca. 1991 .... 2.00

Crazyfish Preview
Crazyfish

❑1 .... 0.50
❑2 .... 0.50

Crazy Love Story
Tokyopop

❑1, Oct 2004, Red foil cover lettering 9.99
❑2, Jan 2005; Blue foil cover lettering 9.99
❑3, Apr 2005; Blue foil cover lettering 9.99
❑4, Sep 2005; Blue foil cover lettering ... 9.99
❑5, Jan 2006 .... 9.99

Crazyman
Continuity

❑1, Apr 1992; enhanced cover 3.95
❑2, May 1992 .... 2.50
❑3, Jul 1992 .... 2.50

Crazyman
Continuity

❑1, May 1993; Die-cut comic book 3.95
❑2, Dec 1993; Wrap-around cover 2.50
❑3, Dec 1993 .... 2.50
❑4, Jan 1994; indicia says #3 .... 2.50

Creature
Antarctic

❑1, Oct 1997, b&w 2.95
❑2, Dec 1997, b&w 2.95

Creature Commandos
DC

❑1, May 2000 .... 2.50
❑2, Jun 2000 .... 2.50
❑3, Jul 2000 .... 2.50
❑4, Aug 2000 .... 2.50
❑5, Sep 2000 .... 2.50
❑6, Oct 2000 .... 2.50
❑7, Nov 2000 .... 2.50
❑8, Dec 2000; Final Issue 2.50

Creature Features
Mojo

❑1, b&w; prestige format one-shot 4.95

Creature Features (Art Adams'...)
Dark Horse

❑1, Aug 1996; Trade Paperback; NN 13.95

N-MINT

Creatures of the Id
Caliber

❑1, Jan 1990, b&w; 1: Madman (Frank Einstein) 11.00

Creatures on the Loose
Marvel

❑10, Mar 1971, SL (w); BWr, JK (a); Title changes to Creatures on the Loose; first King Kull story; Series continued from Tower of Shadows #9; "Trull" reprints story from Tales to Astonish #21 .... 50.00
❑11, May 1971, reprints story from Tales to Astonish #23 .... 15.00
❑12, Jul 1971, reprints story from Journey into Mystery #69 .... 15.00
❑13, Sep 1971, reprints stories from Tales to Astonish #25 & #28 .... 15.00
❑14, Nov 1971, reprints story from Tales to Astonish #33 .... 15.00
❑15, Jan 1972, Reprints 15.00
❑16, Mar 1972, JK, GK (a); O: Gullivar Jones, Warrior of Mars 10.00
❑17, May 1972, JK, GK (a); A: Gullivar Jones, Warrior of Mars 10.00
❑18, Jul 1972, SD, RA (a); A: Gullivar Jones, Warrior of Mars 10.00
❑19, Sep 1972, JK, GK, JM (a); A: Gullivar Jones, Warrior of Mars 10.00
❑20, Nov 1972, GK (c); SD, GM (a); A: Gullivar Jones, Warrior of Mars 10.00
❑21, Jan 1973, JSo (c); SL (w); GM, JSo, JSt (a); A: Gullivar Jones, Warrior of Mars 10.00
❑22, Mar 1973, JSo (c); SL (w); SD, VM (a); A: Thongor. Adaptation of "Thieves of Zangabal" 10.00
❑23, May 1973, JR (c); VM, DH (a); A: Thongor 6.00
❑24, Jul 1973, SD, VM (a); A: Thongor.. 6.00
❑25, Sep 1973, VM (a); A: Thongor 6.00
❑26, Nov 1973, VM (a); A: Thongor 6.00
❑27, Jan 1974, VM (a); A: Thongor 5.00
❑28, Mar 1974, JR (c); A: Thongor. Marvel Value Stamp #15: Iron Man 5.00
❑29, May 1974; A: Thongor. Marvel Value Stamp #37: Watcher 5.00
❑30, Jul 1974; A: Man-Wolf. Marvel Value Stamp #65: Iceman 25.00
❑31, Sep 1974; GK (c); GT (a); A: Man-Wolf. Marvel Value Stamp #30: Grey Gargoyle 12.00
❑32, Nov 1974; A: Man-Wolf. Marvel Value Stamp #34: Mr. Fantastic 8.00
❑33, Jan 1975; A: Man-Wolf. Marvel Value Stamp #24: Falcon 8.00
❑34, Mar 1975 A: Man-Wolf 8.00
❑35, May 1975; A: Man-Wolf. Ralph Macchio L.O.C. 8.00
❑36, Jul 1975; A: Man-Wolf. Marvel Value Stamp #73: Kingpin 8.00
❑37, Sep 1975; A: Man-Wolf. Final issue 12.00
❑King Size 1; King-size special 10.00

Creech
Image

❑1, Oct 1997; O: Creech 1.95
❑1/A, Oct 1997; alternate cover 1.95
❑2, Nov 1997 .... 2.50
❑3, Dec 1997 .... 2.50

N-MINT

Creech: Out for Blood
Image

❑1, Jul 2001 .... 4.95
❑2, Sep 2001 .... 4.95

CreeD
Hall of Heroes

❑1, Dec 1994 .... 4.00
❑2, Dec 1994 .... 3.00

CreeD
Lightning

❑1, Sep 1995, b&w; reprints Hall of Heroes #1 and #2 with corrections; Black and white 3.00
❑1/A, Sep 1995, Lightning Variant Edition 3.00
❑1/B, Sep 1995; Purple edition; Includes Certificate of Authenticity 3.00
❑1/Platinum, Sep 1995; Collector's edition; enhanced cover 3.00
❑2, Jan 1996 .... 3.00
❑2/Platinum, Jan 1996; Platinum edition; alternate cover 4.00
❑3, Jul 1996; bagged with trading card . 3.00
❑3/Platinum; Platinum edition 3.00

CreeD: Apple Tree
Gearbox

❑1, Dec 2000, b&w 2.95

CreeD: Cranial Disorder
Lightning

❑1, Nov 1996 .... 3.00
❑2, Nov 1996; alternate cover, cover says Dec, indicia says Nov 3.00
❑3, Apr 1997; alternate cover 3.00

CreeD: Mechanical Evolution
Gearbox

❑1, Sep 2000 .... 2.95
❑1/Variant, Sep 2000 .... 2.95
❑2, Oct 2000 .... 2.95

CreeD/Teenage Mutant Ninja Turtles
Lightning

❑1, May 1996 .... 3.00

CreeD: The Good Ship and the New Journey Home
Lightning

❑1, Jul 1997, b&w 2.95

CreeD Use Your Delusion
Avatar

❑1, Jan 1998 .... 3.00
❑2, Feb 1998 .... 3.00

CreeD: Utopiate
Image

❑1, Jan 2002 .... 2.95
❑2/A, Mar 2002; Indicia is from #1 .... 2.95
❑2/B, Mar 2002; Indicia is from #1 .... 2.95
❑3, Aug 2002 .... 2.95
❑4 2002 .... 2.95

Creeper
DC

❑1, Dec 1997; O: Creeper 2.50
❑2, Jan 1998; V: Proteus 2.50
❑3, Feb 1998; V: Proteus 2.50
❑4, Mar 1998 .... 2.50
❑5, Apr 1998; V: disgruntled ex-employee targetting Jack Ryder 2.50

Other grades: Multiply price above by 5/6 for VF/NM • 2/3 for VERY FINE • 1/3 for FINE • 1/5 for VERY GOOD • 1/8 for GOOD

	N-MINT
❑6, May 1998	2.50
❑7, Jun 1998 V: Joker	2.50
❑8, Jul 1998; SB (a); A: Batman. V: Joker	2.50
❑9, Aug 1998	2.50
❑10, Sep 1998	2.50
❑11, Oct 1998	2.50
❑1000000, Nov 1998; Final Issue	3.00

Creeper
DC

❑1, Oct 2006	2.99
❑2, Nov 2006	2.99
❑3, Dec 2006	2.99
❑4, Feb 2007	2.99
❑5, Mar 2007	2.99

Creeps
Image

❑1, Oct 2001	2.95
❑2	2.95
❑3, Feb 2002	2.95
❑4, May 2002	2.95

Creepsville
Go-Go

❑1, b&w; trading cards	2.95
❑2, b&w; trading cards	2.95
❑3	2.95
❑4	2.95
❑5	2.95

Creepy Tales
Pinnacle

❑1 1975	1.75

Creepy: The Limited Series
Dark Horse

❑1, ca. 1992, b&w; prestige format	4.00
❑2, ca. 1992, b&w; prestige format; KB, PD (w)	4.00
❑3, ca. 1992, b&w; prestige format; RHo, PD (w); BG, JM (a)	4.00
❑4, ca. 1992, b&w; prestige format	4.00
❑FB 1993, ca. 1993; RHo, KB, PD (w); A: Vampirella. 1993 "Fearbook"; Relaunch of Vampirella for '90s	12.00

Cremator
Chaos

❑1, Dec 1998	2.95
❑2, Dec 1999; Wraparound cover	2.95
❑3, Jan 1999	2.95
❑4, Feb 1999	2.95
❑5, Apr 1999	2.95

Crescent
B-Line

❑0, May 1996	1.00

Crescent Moon
Tokyopop

❑1, May 2004	9.99

Crew
Marvel

❑1, Jul 2003	2.50
❑2, Aug 2003, Cardstock cover	2.50
❑3, Sep 2003, Cardstock cover	2.50
❑4, Oct 2003, Cardstock cover	2.99
❑5, Nov 2003, Cardstock cover; O: Josiah X	2.99
❑6, Dec 2003, Cardstock cover	2.99
❑7, Jan 2004, Cardstock cover	2.99

Crime & Justice
Avalon

❑1, Mar 1998, b&w	2.95

Crime and Punishment Marshal Law Takes Manhattan
Marvel / Epic

❑1, ca. 1989, prestige format; NN; One-shot	4.95

Crimebuster
AC

❑0	2.95

Crimebuster Classics
AC

❑1	3.50

Crime Classics
Eternity

❑1, Jul 1988, The Shadow	1.95
❑2, Jul 1988, The Shadow	1.95
❑3, Aug 1988, The Shadow	1.95
❑4, Sep 1989, The Shadow	1.95
❑5, Jan 1989, The Shadow	1.95
❑6, Feb 1989, The Shadow	1.95
❑7, Mar 1989, The Shadow	1.95
❑8, Apr 1989, The Shadow	1.95
❑9, May 1989, The Shadow	1.95
❑10, Jun 1989, The Shadow	1.95
❑11, Aug 1989, The Shadow	1.95
❑12, Sep 1989, The Shadow	1.95
❑13, Oct 1989, The Shadow	1.95

Crime Clinic
Slave Labor

❑1, Nov 1995	2.95
❑2, May 1995	2.95

Crime Patrol
Gemstone

❑1, Apr 2000; Reprints Crime Patrol #1 (#7)	2.50
❑2, May 2000; Reprints Crime Patrol #2 (#8)	2.50
❑3, Jun 2000; Reprints Crime Patrol #3 (#9)	2.50
❑4, Jul 2000; Reprints Crime Patrol #4	2.50
❑5, Aug 2000; Reprints Crime Patrol #5	2.50
❑Ann 1, ca. 2000; Collects issues #1-5	13.50

Crime Pays
Boneyard

❑1, Oct 1996, b&w; Adult; B&w anthology	2.95
❑2, Sep 1997; Adult	2.95

Crime-Smasher (Blue Comet)
Blue Comet

❑Special 1, Jul 1987	2.00

Crime SuspenStories (RCP)
Gemstone

❑1, Nov 1992; HK, JCr, WW, GI (w); HK, JCr, WW, GI (a); Reprints Crime SuspenStories (EC) #1	2.00
❑2, Nov 1992; Reprints Crime SuspenStories (EC) #2	2.00
❑3, Feb 1993; Reprints Crime SuspenStories (EC) #3	2.00
❑4, May 1993; JCr, JKa, GI (w); JCr, JKa, GI (a); Reprints Crime SuspenStories (EC) #4	2.00
❑5, Aug 1993; Reprints Crime SuspenStories (EC) #5	2.00
❑6, Nov 1993; Reprints Crime SuspenStories (EC) #6	2.00
❑7, Feb 1994; Reprints Crime SuspenStories (EC) #7	2.00
❑8, May 1994; Reprints Crime SuspenStories (EC) #8	2.00
❑9, Aug 1994; Reprints Crime SuspenStories (EC) #9	2.00
❑10, Nov 1994; Reprints Crime SuspenStories (EC) #10	2.00
❑11, Feb 1995; Reprints Crime SuspenStories (EC) #11	2.00
❑12, May 1995; Reprints Crime SuspenStories (EC) #12	2.00
❑13, Aug 1995; Reprints Crime SuspenStories (EC) #13	2.00
❑14, Nov 1995; Reprints Crime SuspenStories (EC) #14	2.00
❑15, Feb 1996; Ray Bradbury story; Reprints Crime SuspenStories (EC) #15	2.00
❑16, May 1996; AW, JO, JCr, JKa (w); AW, JO, JCr, JKa (a); Reprints Crime SuspenStories (EC) #16	2.50
❑17, Aug 1996; AW, JCr, FF, BE, JKa (w); AW, JCr, FF, BE, JKa (a); Ray Bradbury story; Reprints Crime SuspenStories (EC) #17	2.50
❑18, Nov 1996; JCr, BE, JKa (w); JCr, BE, JKa (a); Reprints Crime SuspenStories (EC) #18	2.50
❑19, Feb 1997; GE, JCr (w); GE, JCr (a); Reprints Crime SuspenStories (EC) #19	2.50
❑20, May 1997; Reprints Crime SuspenStories (EC) #20	2.50
❑21, Aug 1997; Reprints Crime SuspenStories (EC) #21	2.50
❑22, Nov 1997; Reprints Crime SuspenStories (EC) #22	2.50
❑23, Feb 1998; Reprints Crime SuspenStories (EC) #23	2.50
❑24, May 1998; JO, BK, JKa (a); Reprints Crime SuspenStories (EC) #24	2.50
❑25, Aug 1998; GE, BK, JKa (a); Reprints Crime SuspenStories (EC) #25	2.50
❑26, Nov 1998; JO, JKa (a); Reprints Crime SuspenStories (EC) #26	2.50
❑27, Feb 1999; GE, BK, JKa, GI (a); Reprints Crime SuspenStories (EC) #27	2.50
❑Ann 1; Reprints Crime SuspenStories (EC) #1-5	8.95
❑Ann 2; Reprints Crime SuspenStories (EC) #6-10	9.95
❑Ann 3; Reprints Crime SuspenStories (EC) #11-15	9.95
❑Ann 4; Reprints Crime SuspenStories (EC) #15-19	10.50
❑Ann 5; Reprints Crime SuspenStories (EC) #20-23	10.95
❑Ann 6; Reprints Crime SuspenStories (EC) #24-27	10.95

Criminal
Marvel

❑1, Dec 2006, Caught in the Undertow is a 2 page text story	2.99
❑2, Jan 2007	2.99
❑3, Mar 2007	2.99

Criminal Macabre
Dark Horse

❑1, May 2003	2.99
❑2, Jun 2003	2.99
❑3, Jul 2003	2.99
❑4, Aug 2003	2.99
❑5, Sep 2003	2.99

Criminal Macabre: Feat of Clay
Dark Horse

❑1, Jun 2006, #16 in continuing Cal McDonald series	2.99

Criminal Macabre: Two Red Eyes
Dark Horse

❑1, Jan 2007, Indicia notes as Criminal Macabre #17: Two Red Eyes	2.99

Crimson
Image / Cliffhanger

❑1, May 1998, Several figures on cover, one in cowboy hat smoking	3.50
❑1/A, May 1998, Boy covered in blood/ rain	3.50
❑1/B, May 1998, chromium cover; Three figures on ledge	6.00
❑1/C, May 1998, Dynamic Forces chromium edition with certificate of authenticity; Boy in graveyard; chromium cover	6.00
❑2, May 1998	3.00
❑2/A, Jun 1998, alternate cover (vampire)	6.00
❑2/B, Jun 1998, Crimson chrome edition; Crimson chrome edition; Autographed	6.00
❑3, Jun 1998	3.00
❑3/A, Jul 1998, alternate cover (red background)	3.50
❑4, Jul 1998	2.50
❑5, Aug 1998	2.50
❑6, Sep 1998	2.50
❑7, Dec 1998, Last published by Image	2.50
❑7/A, Nov 1998, DFE Hard-to-Get Foil covers pack	15.00
❑7/B, Dec 1998, alternate cover (angels)	3.00
❑7/C, Dec 1998, alternate cover (archway)	3.00
❑8, Dec 1999, First published by DC	2.50
❑9, Mar 1999	2.50
❑10, May 1999	2.50
❑11, Jun 1999	2.50
❑12, Aug 1999	2.50
❑13, Dec 1999	2.50
❑14, Jan 2000	2.50
❑15, Feb 2000	2.50
❑16, Mar 2000	2.50
❑17, Apr 2000	2.50
❑18, Jul 2000	2.50
❑19, Sep 2000	2.50
❑20, Oct 2000	2.50
❑21, Nov 2000	2.50
❑22, Dec 2000	2.50
❑23, Jan 2001	2.50
❑24, Apr 2001	2.50
❑Special 1	6.95
❑Special 1/A, European cover	8.00
❑Special 1/Varia, DFE alternate cover	7.00

Crimson Avenger
DC

❑1, Jun 1988	1.50
❑2, Jul 1988	1.50
❑3, Aug 1988 MGu (a)	1.50
❑4, Sep 1988 MGu (a)	1.50

Other grades: Multiply price above by 5/6 for VF/NM • 2/3 for VERY FINE • 1/3 for FINE • 1/5 for VERY GOOD • 1/8 for GOOD

Conan the Barbarian

Most important title of the early 1970s
©Marvel

Conan the Barbarian

Volume 1: 275 issues. Volume 2: Three.
©Marvel

Conan the Destroyer

Adaptation of second Conan film
©Marvel

Conan the King

Series continued from King Conan
©Marvel

Concrete

Interesting series with environmentalist themes
©Dark Horse

N-MINT

Crimson Dreams
Crimson

❑1 .... 2.00
❑2 .... 2.00
❑3 .... 2.00
❑4 .... 2.00
❑5 .... 2.00
❑6 .... 2.00
❑7, ca. 1985 .... 2.00
❑8, ca. 1986 .... 2.00
❑9, Sum 1986 .... 2.00
❑10, ca. 1986 .... 2.00
❑11, ca. 1986 .... 2.00

Crimson Dynamo
Marvel / Epic

❑1, Oct 2003 .... 2.50
❑2, Nov 2003 .... 2.50
❑3, Dec 2003 .... 2.50
❑4, Jan 2004, Going Up! 2.50
❑5, Jan 2004, Retells origin of Crimson Dynamo; price erroneously printed as $2.99, retailers charged $2.50 .... 2.99
❑6, May 2004 .... 2.50

Crimson Letters
Adventure

❑1, Jul 1990; Adventurers b&w 2.25

Crimson Nun
Antarctic

❑1, May 1997 .... 2.95
❑2, Jul 1997 .... 2.95
❑3, Sep 1997 .... 2.95
❑4, Nov 1997 .... 2.95

Crimson Plague
Event

❑1, Jun 1997 .... 2.95
❑1/Ltd., Jun 1997; alternate limited edition only sold at 1997 Heroes Con 5.00

Crimson Plague
Image

❑1, Jun 2000 .... 2.95
❑2, Aug 2000 .... 2.50

Crimson: Scarlet X Blood on the Moon
DC / Cliffhanger

❑1, Oct 1999; One-shot 3.95

Crimson Sourcebook
WildStorm

❑1, Nov 1999 .... 2.95

Crisis Aftermath: The Battle for Bludhaven

❑1, Jun 2006 .... 2.99
❑2, Jul 2006 .... 2.99
❑3, Jul 2006 .... 2.99
❑4, Aug 2006 .... 2.99
❑5, Aug 2006 .... 2.99
❑6, Sep 2006 .... 2.99

Crisis Aftermath: The Spectre
DC

❑1, Aug 2006 .... 2.99
❑2, Sep 2006 .... 2.99
❑3, Oct 2006 .... 2.99

Crisis on Infinite Earths
DC

❑1, Apr 1985; wraparound cover 5.00
❑2, May 1985; 1: Anti-Monitor (as shadow; Voice) 4.00
❑3, Jun 1985; 1: Nighthawk (modern); D: Gunner; D: Johnny Cloud; D: Kid Psycho; D: Losers; D: Nighthawk; D: Sarge; D: Captain Storm 4.00
❑4, Jul 1985; 1: Doctor Light II; 1: Lady Quark; D: The Monitor; D: Liana; D: Lord Volt 3.00
❑5, Aug 1985; 1: Anti-Monitor (fully shown) 5.00
❑6, Sep 1985; 1: New Wildcat 3.00
❑7, Oct 1985; Double-size; D: Supergirl; O: Anti-Monitor; O: DC Multiverse; O: Monitor 5.00
❑8, Nov 1985; D: Flash II (Barry Allen) 5.00
❑9, Dec 1985; 1: Doctor Spectro in DC universe; D: Lex Luthor (Earth-2); D: five of six renegade Guardians 3.00
❑10, Jan 1986; D: Aquagirl; D: Chemo; D: Icicle; D: Immortal Man; D: Maaldor; D: Mirror Master; D: Psimon; D: Shaggy Man; D: Starman 3 .... 3.00
❑11, Feb 1986; 1: Ghost (at DC); D: Angle-Man 3.00
❑12, Mar 1986; Final issue 3.00

Crisp
Crisp Biscuit

❑1, Apr 1997 .... 3.00
❑2, Apr 1998 .... 3.00

Crisp Biscuit
Crisp Biscuit

❑1, Jul 1991 .... 2.00

Cristian Dark
Darque

❑1 1993 .... 2.50
❑2 1993 .... 2.50
❑3, Dec 1993 .... 2.50

Critical Error
Dark Horse

❑1, Jul 1992; color reprint of silent story from The Art of John Byrne 2.50

Critical Mass
Marvel / Epic

❑1, Jan 1989 .... 4.95
❑2, Feb 1989 .... 4.95
❑3, Mar 1989 .... 4.95
❑4, Apr 1989 .... 4.95
❑5, May 1989 .... 4.95
❑6, Jun 1989 .... 4.95
❑7, Jul 1989; Final Issue 4.95

Critters
Fantagraphics

❑1, Jun 1986, b&w; A: Usagi Yojimbo 10.00
❑2, Jul 1986; Captain Jack debut 3.00
❑3, Aug 1986 A: Usagi Yojimbo 8.00
❑4, Sep 1986 .... 3.00
❑5, Oct 1986 .... 3.00
❑6, Nov 1986 A: Usagi Yojimbo 5.00
❑7, Dec 1986 A: Usagi Yojimbo 5.00
❑8, Jan 1987 .... 3.00
❑9, Feb 1987 .... 3.00
❑10, Mar 1987 A: Usagi Yojimbo 4.00
❑11, Apr 1987 .... 3.00
❑12, May 1987 .... 3.00
❑13, Jun 1987; Gnuff story; Birthright II story 3.00
❑14, Jul 1987 A: Usagi Yojimbo 3.00
❑15, Aug 1987 .... 3.00
❑16, Sep 1987 .... 3.00
❑17, Oct 1987 .... 3.00
❑18, Nov 1987; indicia says Sep 87 .... 3.00
❑19, Dec 1987 .... 3.00
❑20, Jan 1988 .... 3.00
❑21, Feb 1988 .... 2.50
❑22, Mar 1988; Watchmen parody cover; indicia repeated from issue #21 .... 2.50
❑23, Apr 1988; AMo (w); Includes flexi-disc 3.95
❑24, May 1988 .... 2.50
❑25, Jun 1988 .... 2.50
❑26, Jul 1988 .... 2.50
❑27, Aug 1988 .... 2.50
❑28, Sep 1988 .... 2.50
❑29, Oct 1988 .... 2.50
❑30, Nov 1988 .... 2.50
❑31, Dec 1988 .... 2.50
❑32, Jan 1989 .... 2.50
❑33, Feb 1989 .... 2.50
❑34, Mar 1989 .... 2.50
❑35, Apr 1989 .... 2.50
❑36, May 1989 .... 2.50
❑37, Jun 1989 .... 2.50
❑38, Jul 1989; 1: Stinz. Usagi Yojimbo 2.50
❑39, Aug 1989; Fission Chicken 2.50
❑40, Aug 1989 .... 2.50
❑41, Sep 1989; Platypus 2.00
❑42, Sep 1989; Captain Jack 2.00
❑43 1989 .... 2.00
❑44 1989 .... 2.00
❑45 1989; Ambrose 2.00
❑46 1989 .... 2.00
❑47, Mar 1990 .... 2.00
❑48, Apr 1990 .... 2.00
❑49, May 1990 .... 2.00
❑50 1990; Final Issue 4.95
❑Special 1, Jan 1988; A: Usagi Yojimbo 2.00

Critturs
Mu

❑0, Nov 1992 .... 2.50

Cromartie High School
ADV Manga

❑1, ca. 2005 .... 9.99
❑2, ca. 2005 .... 10.95
❑3, ca. 2005 .... 10.95
❑4, ca. 2005 .... 10.95

Cromwell Stone
Dark Horse

❑1, b&w; NN 3.50

Cross
Dark Horse

❑0, Oct 1995 .... 2.95
❑1, Nov 1995 .... 2.95
❑2, Dec 1995 .... 9.99
❑3, Jan 1996 .... 2.95
❑4, Feb 1996 .... 2.95
❑5, Mar 1996 .... 9.99
❑6, Apr 1996 .... 2.95

Cross
Tokyopop

❑1, Nov 2004 .... 9.99

Other grades: Multiply price above by 5/6 for VF/NM • 2/3 for VERY FINE • 1/3 for FINE • 1/5 for VERY GOOD • 1/8 for GOOD

	N-MINT
❑2, Feb 2005	9.99
❑3, May 2005	9.99
❑4, Aug 2005	9.99
❑5, Jan 2006	9.99

Cross and the Switchblade
Spire

❑1, Based on the book, The Cross and the Switchblade	3.00
❑1/2nd, ca. 1972	2.00
❑1/Barbour, ca. 1993, Barbour Christian Comics reprint with newsprint covers	1.00

Cross Bronx
Image

❑1, Oct 2006	2.99
❑2, Nov 2006	2.99
❑3, Nov 2006	2.99
❑4, Jan 2007	2.99

Crossed Swords
K-Z

❑1, Dec 1986	1.00

Crossfire
Eclipse

❑1, May 1984, DS, ME (w); DS (a)	5.00
❑2, Jun 1984, DS (a)	1.75
❑3, Jul 1984, DS (a)	1.75
❑4, Aug 1984, DS (a)	1.75
❑5, Sep 1984, DS (a)	1.75
❑6, Nov 1984, DS (a)	1.75
❑7, Dec 1984, DS (a)	1.75
❑8, Jan 1985, DS (a)	1.75
❑9, Mar 1985, DS (a)	1.75
❑10, Apr 1985, DS (a)	1.75
❑11, May 1985, DS (a)	1.75
❑12, Jun 1985, DSt (c); DS (a); Marilyn Monroe story, cover	1.75
❑13, Jul 1985, DS (a)	1.75
❑14, Aug 1985, DS (a)	1.75
❑15, Oct 1985, DS (a)	1.75
❑16, Jan 1986, BA (c); BA, DS (a)	1.75
❑17, Mar 1986, DS (a)	1.75
❑18, Jan 1987, Black & white issues begin	1.75
❑19, Feb 1987	1.75
❑20, Mar 1987	1.75
❑21, Apr 1987	1.75
❑22, Jun 1987	1.75
❑23, Jul 1987	1.75
❑24, Aug 1987	1.75
❑25, Oct 1987	1.75
❑26, Feb 1988	1.75

Crossfire and Rainbow
Eclipse

❑1, Jun 1986	1.25
❑2, Jul 1986	1.25
❑3, Aug 1986	1.25
❑4, Sep 1986	1.25

CrossGen Chronicles
CrossGen

❑1, Jun 2000; lead-in to ongoing CrossGen series; background info on creators and series	3.95
❑2, Mar 2001	3.95
❑3, Jun 2001	3.95
❑4, Sep 2001	3.95
❑5, Dec 2001	3.95
❑6, Mar 2002; The First	3.95
❑7, May 2002; Negation	3.95

Crossgenesis
CrossGen

❑1, Jan 2000; No cover price; serves as basis for first four CrossGen titles: Mystic, Sigil, Scion, and Meridian	4.95

CrossGen Sampler
CrossGen

❑1, Feb 2000; No cover price; previews of upcoming series	1.00

Crossing Midnight
DC / Vertigo

❑1, Feb 2007	2.99
❑2, Mar 2007	2.99
❑3	2.99
❑4	2.99
❑5	2.99
❑6	2.99
❑7	2.99
❑8	2.99
❑9	2.99
❑10	2.99
❑11	2.99
❑12	2.99
❑13	2.99
❑14	2.99
❑15	2.99
❑16	2.99
❑17	2.99
❑18	2.99
❑19	2.99

Crossovers
CrossGen

❑1, Feb 2003	2.95
❑2, Mar 2003	2.95
❑3, Apr 2003	2.95
❑4, May 2003	2.95
❑5, Jun 2003	2.95
❑6, Jul 2003	2.95
❑7, Oct 2003	2.95
❑8, Nov 2003	2.95
❑9, Dec 2003	2.95

Crossroads
First

❑1, Jul 1988; Sable, Whisper	3.50
❑2, Aug 1988; Sable, Badger	3.50
❑3, Sep 1988; Badger, Luther Ironheart.	3.50
❑4, Oct 1988; Grimjack, Judah	3.50
❑5, Nov 1988; Grimjack, Nexus, Dreadstar	3.50

Crow
Caliber

❑1, Feb 1989; O: The Crow. b&w (10, 000 print run)	22.00
❑1/2nd; O: The Crow. 2nd Printing (5, 000 print run)	3.50
❑1/3rd, Jun 1990; O: The Crow. 3rd printing (5, 000 print run)	3.00
❑2, Mar 1989; (7000 print run)	12.00
❑2/2nd, Dec 1989; 2nd Printing (5, 000 print run)	3.50
❑2/3rd, Jun 1990; 3rd printing (5, 000 print run)	3.00
❑3, Aug 1989; (5000 print run)	10.00
❑3/2nd, Jun 1990; 2nd Printing (5, 000 print run)	3.50
❑4, ca. 1989; only printing (12, 000 print run)	10.00

Crow
Tundra

❑1, Jan 1992, b&w; prestige format	4.95
❑2, Mar 1992, b&w; prestige format	4.95
❑3, May 1992, b&w; prestige format	4.95
❑4	4.95

Crow
Image

❑1, Feb 1999; Cover - rising from graves	3.00
❑1/A, Feb 1999; TMc (c); gravestones	3.00
❑2, Mar 1999	2.50
❑3, Apr 1999	2.50
❑4, May 1999	2.50
❑5, Jun 1999	2.50
❑6, Jul 1999	2.50
❑7, Aug 1999	2.50
❑8, Sep 1999	2.50
❑9, Oct 1999	2.50
❑10, Nov 1999	2.50

Crow: City of Angels
Kitchen Sink

❑1, Jul 1996; adapts movie	2.95
❑1/Variant, Jul 1996; adapts movie	2.95
❑2, Aug 1996; adapts movie	2.95
❑2/Variant, Aug 1996; adapts movie	2.95
❑3, Sep 1996; Final Issue	2.95
❑3/Variant, Sep 1996; Final Issue; Photo cover (head shot of Crow)	2.95

Crow: Dead Time
Kitchen Sink

❑1, Jan 1996, b&w	2.95
❑2, Feb 1996	2.95
❑3, Mar 1996	2.95

Crow: Flesh & Blood
Kitchen Sink

❑1, May 1996, b&w	2.95
❑2, Jun 1996, b&w	2.95
❑3, Jul 1996, b&w	2.95

Crow of the Bearclan
Blackthorne

❑1, Oct 1986	1.50
❑2 1987	1.50
❑3 1987	1.50
❑4 1987	1.50
❑5 1987	1.50
❑6, Mar 1988	1.50

Crow: Waking Nightmares
Kitchen Sink

❑1, Jan 1997, b&w	2.95
❑2, Jan 1998, b&w	2.95
❑3, Feb 1998, b&w	2.95
❑4, May 1998, b&w	2.95

Crow: Wild Justice
Kitchen Sink

❑1, Oct 1996, b&w	2.95
❑2, Nov 1996, b&w	2.95
❑3, Dec 1996, b&w	2.95

Crozonia
Image

❑1	2.95

Crucial Fiction
Fantagraphics

❑1, Mar 1992, b&w	2.50
❑2, b&w	2.25
❑3, b&w	2.25

Crucible
DC / Impact

❑1, Feb 1993 MWa (w)	1.50
❑2, Mar 1993 MWa (w)	1.25
❑3, Apr 1993 DG (c); MWa (w)	1.25
❑4, May 1993 DG (c); MWa (w)	1.25
❑5, Jun 1993 DG (c); MWa (w)	1.25
❑6, Jul 1993; DG (c); MWa (w); Final issue	1.25

Cruel and Unusual
DC / Vertigo

❑1, Jun 1999	2.95
❑2, Jul 1999	2.95
❑3, Aug 1999	2.95
❑4, Sep 1999	2.95

Cruel & Unusual Punishment
Starhead

❑1, Nov 1993, b&w; Adult	2.50
❑2, Oct 1994, b&w; Adult	2.95

Cruel World
Fantagraphics

❑1, b&w	3.50

Crusaders
Guild

❑1; Title continued in Southern Nights #2	1.00

Crusaders
DC / Impact

❑1, May 1992; 1: Captain Commando; 1: Kalathar; 1: The American Crusaders; 1: The Crusaders (Impact); Includes trading cards	1.00
❑2, Jun 1992	1.00
❑3, Jul 1992	1.00
❑4, Aug 1992	1.00
❑5, Sep 1992	1.00
❑6, Oct 1992	1.00
❑7, Nov 1992	1.00
❑8, Dec 1992; Final Issue	1.00

Crusades
DC / Vertigo

❑1, May 2001	2.50
❑2, Jun 2001	2.50
❑3, Jul 2001	2.50
❑4, Aug 2001	2.50
❑5, Sep 2001	2.50
❑6, Oct 2001	2.50
❑7, Nov 2001	2.50
❑8, Dec 2001	2.50
❑9, Jan 2002	2.50
❑10, Feb 2002	2.50
❑11, Mar 2002	2.50
❑12, Apr 2002	2.50
❑13, May 2002	2.50
❑14, Jun 2002	2.50
❑15, Jul 2002	2.50
❑16, Aug 2002	2.50
❑17, Sep 2002	2.50
❑18, Oct 2002	2.95

Other grades: Multiply price above by 5/6 for VF/NM • 2/3 for VERY FINE • 1/3 for FINE • 1/5 for VERY GOOD • 1/8 for GOOD

Condorman (Walt Disney)

Adaptation of Disney film almost nobody saw
©Whitman

Contest of Champions II

Sequel had little of the original's charm
©Marvel

Cop Called Tracy

Avalon reprinting of early comic strips
©Avalon

COPS

"Central Organization of Police Specialists"
©DC

Cosmic Boy

Legionnaires spin-off limited series
©DC

N-MINT

❑19, Nov 2002 ... 2.95
❑20, Dec 2002 ... 2.95

Crusades: Urban Decree
DC / Vertigo

❑1, Apr 2001 ... 3.95

Crush
Aeon

❑1, Nov 1995, b&w; cardstock cover ... 2.95
❑2, Dec 1995, b&w; cardstock cover ... 2.95
❑3, Jan 1996, b&w; cardstock cover ... 2.95
❑4, Feb 1996, b&w; cardstock cover ... 2.95

Crush
Dark Horse

❑1, Oct 2003 ... 2.99
❑2, Dec 2003 ... 2.99
❑3, Feb 2004 ... 2.99
❑4, Mar 2004 ... 2.99

Crush
Image

❑1, Jan 1996; cover says Mar, indicia says Jan ... 2.25
❑2, Apr 1996 ... 2.25
❑3, May 1996 ... 2.25
❑4, Jun 1996 ... 2.25
❑5, Jul 1996 ... 2.25

Crusher Joe
Ironcat

❑1 1999 ... 2.25
❑2 1999 ... 2.25
❑3, Mar 1999 ... 2.25

Crust
Top Shelf

❑1, b&w; no cover date ... 3.00

Crux
CrossGen

❑1, May 2001 ... 2.95
❑2, Jun 2001 ... 2.95
❑3, Jul 2001 ... 2.95
❑4, Aug 2001 ... 2.95
❑5, Sep 2001 ... 2.95
❑6, Oct 2001 ... 2.95
❑7, Nov 2001 ... 2.95
❑8, Dec 2001 ... 2.95
❑9, Jan 2002 ... 2.95
❑10, Feb 2002 ... 2.95
❑11, Mar 2002 ... 2.95
❑12, Apr 2002 ... 2.95
❑13, May 2002 ... 2.95
❑14, Jun 2002 ... 2.95
❑15, Jul 2002 ... 2.95
❑16, Aug 2002 ... 2.95
❑17, Sep 2002 ... 2.95
❑18, Oct 2002 ... 2.95
❑19, Nov 2002 ... 2.95
❑20, Dec 2002 ... 2.95
❑21, Jan 2003 ... 2.95
❑22, Feb 2003; Key issue ... 2.95
❑23, Mar 2003 ... 2.95
❑24, Apr 2003 ... 2.95
❑25, May 2003; Deliberate creases on cover ... 2.95
❑26, Jun 2003 ... 2.95
❑27, Jul 2003 ... 2.95
❑28, Aug 2003 ... 2.95

N-MINT

❑29, Nov 2003 ... 2.95
❑30, Nov 2003 ... 2.95
❑31, Dec 2003 ... 2.95
❑32, Dec 2003 ... 2.95
❑33, Feb 2004 ... 2.95

Cry for Dawn
Cry for Dawn

❑1, Apr 1989, b&w; 1: Dawn; Adult ... 45.00
❑1/A; Black light edition ... 15.00
❑1/Counterfeit; Counterfeit version of #1; Has blotchy tones on cover ... 2.25
❑1/2nd; 2nd printing; Adult ... 20.00
❑1/3rd; 3rd printing; Adult ... 18.00
❑2, ca. 1990; Adult ... 30.00
❑2/2nd; 2nd printing; Adult ... 15.00
❑3; Adult; ca. 1990 ... 25.00
❑4, Win 1991; Adult ... 15.00
❑5, b&w; Adult, Spring 1991 ... 15.00
❑5/2nd; 2nd printing; Adult, Spring 1991 ... 8.00
❑6, Fal 1991, b&w; Adult ... 15.00
❑7, b&w; Adult, Winter 1992 ... 15.00
❑8, Win 1992, b&w; Adult ... 10.00
❑9, Spr 1992, b&w; Adult ... 10.00

Crying Freeman Part 1
Viz

❑1 1989 ... 4.00
❑2 ... 4.00
❑3 ... 4.00
❑4 1990 ... 4.00
❑5 1990 ... 4.00
❑6 1990 ... 4.00
❑7 1990 ... 4.00
❑8 1990 ... 4.00

Crying Freeman Part 2
Viz

❑1 1990 ... 4.00
❑2 ... 4.00
❑3 ... 4.00
❑4 ... 4.00
❑5 ... 4.00
❑6 ... 4.00
❑7 ... 4.00
❑8 ... 4.00
❑9 1991 ... 4.00

Crying Freeman Part 3
Viz

❑1 1991 ... 5.50
❑2 ... 5.00
❑3 ... 5.00
❑4 ... 5.00
❑5 ... 5.00
❑6 ... 5.00
❑7 ... 5.00
❑8 ... 5.00
❑9 ... 5.00
❑10 1992 ... 5.00

Crying Freeman Part 4
Viz

❑1 ... 5.00
❑2 ... 5.00
❑3 ... 5.00
❑4 ... 3.00
❑5 ... 3.00
❑6 ... 3.00

N-MINT

❑7 ... 3.00
❑8 ... 3.00

Crying Freeman Part 5
Viz

❑1 ... 2.75
❑2 ... 2.75
❑3 ... 2.75
❑4 ... 2.75
❑5 ... 2.75
❑6 ... 2.75
❑7 ... 2.75
❑8 ... 2.75
❑9 ... 2.75
❑10 ... 2.75
❑11 ... 2.75

Crypt
Image

❑1, Aug 1995 ... 2.50
❑2, Oct 1995 ... 2.50

Cryptics
Image

❑1, Jul 2006 ... 3.50

Cryptic Tales
Showcase

❑1 ... 1.95

Cryptic Writings of Megadeth
Chaos!

❑1, Sep 1997; Necro Limited Premium Edition; comics adaptation of Megadeath songs; alternate cardstock cover ... 2.95
❑2, Dec 1997; comics adaptation of Megadeath songs ... 2.95

Crypt of C*m
Fantagraphics / Eros

❑1, Feb 1999; Adult ... 2.95

Crypt of Dawn
Sirius

❑1, Oct 1996, Adult ... 3.50
❑1/Ltd., Oct 1996, Adult ... 6.00
❑2, Apr 1997, Volume II; Adult ... 3.00
❑3, Feb 1998, Adult ... 3.00
❑4, Jun 1998, color story ... 2.95
❑5, Nov 1998, Adult ... 2.95
❑6, Mar 1999, Adult ... 2.95

Crypt of Shadows
Marvel

❑1, Jan 1973, GK (c); BW, RH (a); Reprints Adventures into Terror #7 ... 35.00
❑2, Mar 1973, All reprints plus new cover ... 16.00
❑3, May 1973 ... 15.00
❑4, Jul 1973 ... 12.00
❑5, Sep 1973 ... 12.00
❑6, Oct 1973 ... 10.00
❑7, Nov 1973 ... 10.00
❑8, Jan 1974 ... 10.00
❑9, Mar 1974 ... 10.00
❑10, May 1974, "Man in the Tank" reprinted from Mystery Tales #15; "Can't Touch Bottom" reprinted from Marvel Tales #129; "Scream" reprinted from Mystic #16; "Devil's Island" reprinted from Uncany Tales #12 ... 10.00
❑11, Jul 1974 ... 10.00
❑12, Sep 1974 ... 10.00
❑13, Oct 1974 ... 10.00

Other grades: Multiply price above by 5/6 for VF/NM • 2/3 for VERY FINE • 1/3 for FINE • 1/5 for VERY GOOD • 1/8 for GOOD

❑14, Nov 1974 .... 10.00
❑15, Jan 1975 .... 8.00
❑16, Mar 1975, "Shadows" reprinted from Uncanny Tales #6; "Little Man" reprinted from Strange Tales #5; "Love Affair" reprinted from Mystical Tales #11; "Screaming" reprinted from Uncanny Tales #3 .... 8.00
❑17, May 1975 .... 8.00
❑18, Jul 1975, Reprints Tales to Astonish #11 .... 8.00
❑19, Sep 1975 .... 8.00
❑20, Oct 1975, Reprints Tales of Suspense #29 .... 8.00
❑21, Nov 1975 .... 8.00

Crystal Balls
Fantagraphics / Eros

❑1; Adult 2.95
❑2, Sep 1995; Adult 2.95

Crystal Breeze Unleashed
High Impact

❑1, Oct 1996, b&w; no cover price 3.00

Crystal War
Atlantis

❑1 .... 3.50

CSI: Bad Rap
Idea & Design Works

❑1, ca. 2003 .... 6.00
❑2, ca. 2003 .... 4.00
❑3, ca. 2003 .... 4.00
❑4, ca. 2004 .... 4.00
❑5, ca. 2004 .... 4.00

CSI: Crime Scene Investigation
Idea & Design Works

❑1, Jan 2003; Painted cover 3.00
❑1/A, Jan 2003; Variant cover (man holding flashlight) 3.00
❑2, Feb 2003 .... 3.00
❑2/A, Feb 2003 .... 3.00
❑3, Mar 2003 .... 3.00
❑3/A, Mar 2003 .... 3.00
❑4, Apr 2003 .... 3.00
❑4/A, Apr 2003 .... 3.00
❑5, May 2003 .... 3.00
❑5/A, May 2003 .... 3.00

CSI: Demon House
Idea & Design Works

❑1, ca. 2004 .... 5.00
❑2, ca. 2004 .... 4.00
❑3, ca. 2004 .... 4.00
❑4, Jun 2004 .... 3.99
❑5, Jul 2004 .... 3.99

CSI: Dying in the Gutters
Idea & Design Works

❑1, Sep 2006, CVO: Covert Vampiric Operations—African Blood preview ... 3.99
❑2, Sep 2006; Cover by Jim Mahfood 3.99
❑3, Oct 2006 .... 3.99
❑4, Nov 2006, Photo cover 3.99
❑5, Jan 2007 .... 3.99

CSI Miami: Smoking Gun
Idea & Design Works

❑1, ca. 2003 .... 6.99

CSI Miami: Thou Shalt Not
Idea & Design Works

❑1, ca. 2004 .... 6.99

CSI: New York Bloody Murder
Idea & Design Works

❑1, Sep 2005 .... 3.99
❑2, Oct 2005 .... 3.99
❑3, Nov 2005 .... 3.99
❑4, Dec 2005 .... 3.99
❑5, Jan 2006 .... 3.99

CSI: Secret Identity
Idea & Design Works

❑1, ca. 2005 .... 3.99
❑2, ca. 2005 .... 3.99
❑3, ca. 2005 .... 3.99
❑4 2005 .... 3.99
❑5 2005 .... 3.99

CSI: Serial
Idea & Design Works

❑1, ca. 2003 .... 19.99

CSI: Thicker Than Blood
Idea & Design Works

❑1, ca. 2003 .... 6.99

Cthulhu (H.P. Lovecraft's...)
Millennium

❑1; Adult 2.50
❑1/CS; trading cards 3.50
❑2; trading cards 2.50
❑3; Adult 2.50

Cuckoo
Green Door

❑1, b&w; cardstock cover 2.75
❑2, Win 1996, b&w; cardstock cover 2.75
❑3, Spr 1997, b&w; cardstock cover 2.75
❑4, Sum 1997, b&w; cardstock cover 2.75
❑5, Fal 1997, b&w; cardstock cover 2.75

Cud
Fantagraphics

❑1, b&w 3.00
❑2, b&w 2.50
❑3, Apr 1993, b&w 2.50
❑4, b&w 2.50
❑5, b&w 2.50
❑6, b&w 2.50
❑7, Aug 1994, b&w 2.50

Cuda
Avatar

❑1/C, Oct 1998; Woman bathing on cover 3.50
❑1/B, Oct 1998; Nude cover 6.00
❑1/A, Oct 1998; Woman battling man on cover 3.50
❑1, Oct 1998; wraparound cover 3.50

Cuda B.C.
Rebel

❑1 .... 2.00

Cud Comics
Dark Horse

❑1, Nov 1995, b&w 2.95
❑2, Jan 1996, b&w 2.95
❑3, Mar 1996, b&w 2.95
❑4, Jun 1996 .... 2.95
❑5, Sep 1996, b&w 2.95
❑6, Dec 1996, b&w 2.95
❑7, Apr 1997, b&w 2.95
❑8, Sep 1997, b&w 2.95
❑Ashcan 1, Ashcan promotional giveaway from comic con appearances 1.00

Cuirass
Harrier

❑1, b&w 1.95

Cult Television
Zone

❑1, Nov 1992 .... 2.95

Cultural Jet Lag
Fantagraphics

❑1, Jul 1991, b&w; Indicia lists as #2 .... 2.50

Culture Vultures
Iconografix

❑1 .... 2.95

Cupid's Revenge
Fantagraphics / Eros

❑1; Adult 2.95
❑2; Adult 2.95

Curio Shoppe
Phoenix

❑1, Mar 1995, b&w 2.50

Cursed
Image

❑1, Oct 2003 .... 2.99
❑2, Nov 2003 .... 2.99
❑3, Dec 2003 .... 2.99
❑4, Jan 2004 .... 2.99

Cursed Worlds Source Book
Blue Comet

❑1 .... 2.95

Curse of Dracula
Dark Horse

❑1, Jul 1998 .... 2.95
❑2, Aug 1998 .... 2.95
❑3, Sep 1998 .... 2.95

Curse of Dreadwolf
Lightning

❑1, Sep 1994, b&w 2.75

Curse of Rune
Malibu

❑1, May 1995 .... 2.50
❑2, Jun 1995, b&w; no indicia 2.50
❑3, Jul 1995, b&w 2.50
❑4, Aug 1995, b&w 2.50

Curse of the Molemen
Kitchen Sink

❑1 .... 4.95

Curse of the She-Cat
AC

❑1, Feb 1989, b&w; O: She-Cat 2.50

Curse of the Spawn
Image

❑1, Sep 1996; b&w promo 3.00
❑1/A, Sep 1996, b&w; softcover; promo 4.00
❑2, Oct 1996 .... 3.00
❑3, Nov 1996 .... 3.00
❑4, Dec 1996 .... 2.50
❑5, Dec 1996 .... 2.50
❑6, Feb 1997 .... 2.50
❑7, Mar 1997 .... 2.50
❑8, Apr 1997 .... 2.50
❑9, May 1997 A: Angela 2.50
❑10, Jun 1997 A: Angela 2.50
❑11, Aug 1997 A: Angela 2.50
❑12, Sep 1997; Photo cover 2.50
❑13, Oct 1997 .... 2.50
❑14, Nov 1997 .... 2.50
❑15, Dec 1997 .... 2.50
❑16, Jan 1998 .... 2.00
❑17, Feb 1998 .... 2.00
❑18, Mar 1998 .... 2.00
❑19, Apr 1998 .... 2.00
❑20, May 1998 .... 2.00
❑21, Jun 1998 .... 2.00
❑22, Jul 1998 .... 2.00
❑23, Aug 1998 .... 2.00
❑24, Sep 1998 .... 1.95
❑25, Oct 1998 .... 1.95
❑26, Nov 1998 .... 1.95
❑27, Dec 1998 .... 1.95
❑28, Feb 1999 TMc (a) 1.95
❑29, Mar 1999 TMc (a) 1.95

Curse of the Weird
Marvel

❑1, Dec 1993; RH (a); Reprints stories from Adventures in Terror #4, Astonishing Tales #10, others 1.50
❑2, Jan 1994; Reprints 1.50
❑3, Feb 1994; BW, RH (a); Reprints 1.50
❑4, Mar 1994; Reprints 1.50

Curse of the Zombie
Marvel

❑4; Reprints 1.25

CuteGirl
Not Available

❑1 .... 0.50
❑2 .... 0.50

Cutting Class
B Comics

❑1, Sep 1995 .... 2.00

Cutting Edge
Marvel

❑1, Dec 1995; continued from The Incredible Hulk #436; continues in The Incredible Hulk #437 .... 2.95

CVO: African Blood
Idea & Design Works

❑1, Sep 2006 .... 3.99

CVO: Covert Vampiric Operations Rogue State
Idea & Design Works

❑1 2004 .... 3.99
❑2 2004 .... 3.99
❑3 2004 .... 3.99
❑4 2005 .... 3.99
❑5 2005 .... 3.99

Cosmic Powers

Marvel's stellar characters are showcased
©Marvel

Courtship of Eddie's Father

"People, let me tell you 'bout my best friend..."
©Dell

Cow-Boy

Comics Buyer's Guide strip gets a comic book
©Ogre

Coyote

American Indian lore with modern mystery
©Marvel

Cracked

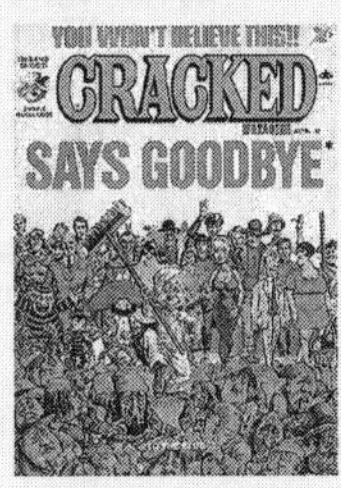

Mad copycat had great John Severin art
©Globe

N-MINT

Cyber 7
Eclipse

❑1, Mar 1989, b&w; Japanese 2.00
❑2, Apr 1989, b&w; Japanese 2.00
❑3, May 1989, b&w; Japanese 2.00
❑4, Jun 1989, b&w; Japanese 2.00
❑5, Jul 1989, b&w; Japanese 2.00
❑6, Aug 1989, b&w; Japanese 2.00
❑7, Sep 1989, b&w; Japanese 2.00

Cyber 7 Book Two
Eclipse

❑1, Oct 1989, b&w; Japanese 2.00
❑2, Nov 1989, b&w; Japanese 2.00
❑3, Dec 1989, b&w; Japanese 2.00
❑4, Jan 1990, b&w; Japanese 2.00
❑5, Mar 1990, b&w; Japanese 2.00
❑6, Apr 1990, b&w; Japanese 2.00
❑7, May 1990, b&w; Japanese 2.00
❑8, Jun 1990, b&w; Japanese 2.00
❑9, Sep 1990, b&w; Japanese 2.00
❑10, Nov 1990, b&w; Japanese 2.00

Cyber City: Part 1
CPM

❑1, Sep 1995, adapts anime 2.95
❑2, Sep 1995, adapts anime 2.95

Cyber City: Part 2
CPM

❑1, Oct 1995; adapts anime 2.95
❑2, Nov 1995; adapts anime 2.95

Cyber City: Part 3
CPM

❑1, Dec 1995; adapts anime 2.95
❑2, Jan 1996; adapts anime 2.95

Cybercom, Heart of the Blue Mesa
Matrix

❑1, Dec 1987, b&w 2.00

Cyber Crush: Robots in Revolt
Fleetway-Quality

❑1, Sep 1991 .... 1.95
❑2, Oct 1991 .... 1.95
❑3, Nov 1991 .... 1.95
❑4, Dec 1991 .... 1.95
❑5, Feb 1992 .... 1.95
❑6, Mar 1992 .... 1.95
❑7, Apr 1992 .... 1.95
❑8, May 1992 .... 1.95
❑9, Jun 1992 .... 1.95
❑10, Jul 1992 .... 1.95
❑11, Aug 1992 .... 1.95
❑12, Sep 1992 .... 1.95
❑13, Oct 1992 .... 1.95
❑14, Nov 1992 .... 1.95

Cyberella
DC / Helix

❑1, Sep 1996 .... 2.25
❑2, Oct 1996 .... 2.25
❑3, Nov 1996 .... 2.25
❑4, Dec 1996 .... 2.25
❑5, Jan 1997 .... 2.25
❑6, Feb 1997 .... 2.25
❑7, Mar 1997 .... 2.50
❑8, Apr 1997 .... 2.50
❑9, May 1997 .... 2.50

N-MINT

❑10, Jun 1997 .... 2.50
❑11, Jul 1997 .... 2.50
❑12, Aug 1997; Final Issue 2.50

Cyberfarce
Parody

❑1, b&w 2.50

Cyber Femmes
Spoof

❑1, Jan 1992; Cover by Sven O 2.95

Cyberforce
Image

❑1, Oct 1992; 1: Cyberforce; Includes coupon for Image Comics #0 .... 3.00
❑2, Mar 1993; V: Shocs 2.50
❑3, May 1993 A: Pitt 2.00
❑4, Jul 1993; foil cover 2.00

Cyberforce
Image

❑0, Sep 1993; O: Cyberforce; Wraparound cover 2.50
❑1, Nov 1993 .... 2.50
❑1/Gold, Gold edition 3.00
❑1/2nd, Nov 1993; 2nd printing 1.25
❑2, Feb 1994 .... 2.50
❑2/Platinum, Feb 1994; Platinum edition; foil-embossed outer wrap 3.00
❑3, Mar 1994 .... 2.50
❑3/Gold, Mar 1994; Gold edition 2.50
❑4, Apr 1994; V: SHOC 2.50
❑5, Jun 1994 .... 2.50
❑6, Jul 1994 .... 2.00
❑7, Sep 1994 .... 2.00
❑8, Oct 1994; TMc (a); Image X-Month 2.50
❑9, Dec 1994 .... 2.50
❑10, Feb 1995 .... 2.50
❑10/Gold, Feb 1995; Gold edition 2.50
❑10/Platinum, Feb 1995; Platinum edition 2.50
❑10/Variant, Feb 1995; alternate cover 2.50
❑11, Mar 1995 .... 2.00
❑12, Apr 1995 .... 2.00
❑13, Jun 1995 .... 2.50
❑14, Jul 1995 .... 2.50
❑15, Aug 1995 .... 2.50
❑16, Nov 1995 .... 2.50
❑17, Dec 1995 .... 2.25
❑18, Jan 1996 .... 2.50
❑18/A, Jan 1996; alternate cover 2.50
❑19, Feb 1996 .... 2.50
❑20, Mar 1996 .... 2.50
❑21, May 1996 .... 2.50
❑22, May 1996 .... 2.50
❑23, Jun 1996 .... 2.50
❑24, Jun 1996 .... 2.50
❑25, Aug 1996; enhanced wraparound cardstock cover 3.95
❑26, Sep 1996 .... 2.50
❑27, Oct 1996 .... 2.50
❑27/Variant, Oct 1996; A: Ash. alternate cover 2.50
❑28, Nov 1996 A: Gabriel (from Ash) 2.50
❑29, Dec 1996 .... 2.50
❑30, Feb 1997 .... 2.50
❑31, Mar 1997 .... 2.50
❑32, Apr 1997 .... 2.50
❑33, May 1997 .... 2.50

N-MINT

❑34, Jul 1997 .... 2.50
❑35, Sep 1997 .... 2.50
❑Ann 1, Mar 1995 .... 4.00
❑Ann 2, Aug 1996 .... 2.95

Cyberforce Origins
Image

❑1, Jan 1995; O: Cyblade 2.50
❑1/Gold, Jan 1995; Gold edition; O: Cyblade 3.00
❑1/2nd, Mar 1996; O: Cyblade. 2nd printing 1.25
❑2, Feb 1995; O: Stryker 2.50
❑3, Nov 1995; O: Impact 2.50

Cyberforce, Stryke Force: Opposing Forces
Image

❑1, Sep 1995 .... 2.50
❑2, Oct 1995 .... 2.50

Cyberforce Universe Sourcebook
Image

❑1, Aug 1994 .... 2.50
❑2, Feb 1995 .... 2.50

Cyberforce
Image

❑0, ca. 2006 .... 2.99
❑1, Apr 2006 .... 2.99
❑1/Variant, Apr 2006 .... 2.99
❑2, May 2006 .... 2.99
❑4, Jul 2006 .... 2.99
❑5, Oct 2006 .... 2.99
❑5/Variant, Oct 2006 .... 2.99
❑6, Nov 2006 .... 2.99

Cyberforce/X-Men
Image

❑1, Feb 2007, Pat Lee cover 3.99
❑1/Variant, Feb 2007 .... 3.99

CyberFrog (Harris)
Harris

❑1/A, Feb 1996; Alternate cover (titles along left side) 2.95
❑0, Mar 1997 .... 3.00
❑0/A, Mar 1997; Arthur Adams cover 3.00
❑2/A; Alternate cover ("Wax the Kutyack!") 2.95
❑1, Feb 1996 .... 3.00
❑3/A; Alternate cover (rendered) 2.95
❑4/A; Alternate cover (holding man's face against wall) 2.95
❑2 1996 .... 3.00
❑3 1996 .... 3.00
❑4 1996 .... 3.00

Cyberfrog: Reservoir Frog
Harris

❑1, Sep 1996; Eric Larsen/Ethan Van Sciver cover art 2.95
❑1/A; Ethan Van Sciver Cover Art 2.95
❑2, Oct 1996; Ethan Van Sciver Cover Art 2.95
❑2/A, Oct 1996; Ethan Van Sciver Cover Art 2.95

CyberFrog: 3rd Anniversary Special
Harris

❑1, Jan 1997, b&w; Reprints from Hall of Heroes 2.50
❑2, Feb 1997, b&w; Reprints from Hall of Heroes 2.50

Other grades: Multiply price above by 5/6 for VF/NM • 2/3 for VERY FINE • 1/3 for FINE • 1/5 for VERY GOOD • 1/8 for GOOD

Cyberfrog vs CreeD
Harris

❑1, Jul 1997 ... 2.95

Cybergen
CFD

❑1, Jan 1996 ... 2.50

Cyberhawks
Pyramid

❑1, Jul 1987, b&w ... 1.80
❑2, b&w ... 1.80

Cyberlust
Aircel

❑1, Jun 1991, b&w; Adult ... 2.95
❑2, b&w; Adult ... 2.95
❑3, Oct 1991, b&w; Adult ... 2.95

Cybernary
Image

❑1, Nov 1995 ... 2.50
❑2, Dec 1995 ... 2.50
❑3, Jan 1996 ... 2.50
❑4, Feb 1996 ... 2.50
❑5, Mar 1996 ... 2.50

Cybernary 2.0
DC / Wildstorm

❑1, Sep 2001 ... 2.95
❑2, Oct 2001 ... 2.95
❑3, Nov 2001 ... 2.95
❑4, Dec 2001 ... 2.95
❑5, Jan 2002 ... 2.95
❑6, Apr 2002 ... 2.95

Cyberpunk (Book 1)
Innovation

❑1 ... 1.95
❑2 ... 1.95

Cyberpunk (Book 2)
Innovation

❑1 ... 2.25
❑2 ... 2.25

Cyberpunk Graphic Novel
Innovation

❑1 ... 6.95

Cyberpunk: The Seraphim Files
Innovation

❑1 ... 2.50
❑2 ... 2.50

Cyberpunx
Image

❑1/A, Mar 1996; Woman with purple/ white costume at bottom of cover ... 2.50
❑1/B, Mar 1996; Man with green hair at bottom of cover ... 2.50
❑1/C, Mar 1996; variant cover ... 2.50
❑1/D, Mar 1996; variant cover ... 2.50

CyberRad
Continuity

❑1, Jan 1991 ... 2.00
❑2, Apr 1991 ... 2.00
❑3, May 1991 ... 2.00
❑4, Jun 1991 ... 2.00
❑5, glow cover ... 2.00
❑6, Nov 1991, foldout poster ... 2.00
❑7, Mar 1992 ... 2.00

Cyberrad
Continuity

❑1, Nov 1992; Hologram cover ... 2.95
❑1/A, Nov 1992; With regular cover ... 2.00

CyberRad Deathwatch 2000
Continuity

❑1, Apr 1993; trading card ... 2.50
❑2, Jul 1993; trading card; indicia drops Deathwatch 2000 ... 2.50

Cyber Reality Comix
Wonder Comix

❑1, Fal 1994 ... 3.95
❑2, Win 1995 ... 3.95

Cybersexation
Antarctic / Venus

❑1, Mar 1997, b&w; Adult ... 2.95

Cyberspace 3000
Marvel

❑1, Jul 1993; Glow-in-the-dark cover ... 2.95
❑2, Aug 1993 ... 1.75
❑3, Sep 1993 ... 1.75
❑4, Oct 1993 ... 1.75
❑5, Nov 1993 ... 1.75
❑6, Dec 1993 ... 1.75
❑7, Jan 1994 ... 1.75
❑8, Feb 1994 ... 1.75

Cybersuit Arkadyne
Ianus

❑1, b&w ... 2.50
❑2, b&w ... 2.50
❑3, Jun 1992, b&w ... 2.50
❑4 ... 2.50
❑5 ... 2.50
❑6 ... 2.50

Cybertrash and the Dog
Silverline

❑1, May 1998 ... 2.95

Cyberzone
Jet-Black Grafiks

❑1, Jul 1994 ... 2.50
❑2, Sep 1994 ... 2.50
❑3, Dec 1994 ... 2.50
❑4, Mar 1995 ... 2.50
❑5, May 1995 ... 2.50
❑6, Sep 1995 ... 2.50
❑7, Feb 1996 ... 2.50
❑8; Final Issue ... 2.50

Cyblade/Ghost Rider
Marvel

❑1, Jan 1997; crossover with Top Cow; continues in Ghost Rider/Ballistic ... 2.95

Cyblade/Shi: The Battle for Independents
Image

❑1; 1: Witchblade ... 6.00
❑1/A; 1: Witchblade. alternate cover; crossover; concludes in Shi/Cyblade: The Battle for Independents #2 ... 6.00
❑1/B; crossover;concludes in Shi/ Cyblade: The Battle for Independents #2; San Diego Preview ... 6.00
❑1/CS; boxed set;crossover with Crusade;also contains Shi/Cyblade: The Battle for Independents #2 ... 10.00
❑Ashcan 1, ca. 1995; preview of crossover with Crusade ... 3.00

Cyboars
Vintage

❑1, Aug 1996 ... 1.95
❑1/A, Aug 1996, alternate cover ... 1.95

Cyborg, the Comic Book
Cannon

❑1, Jun 1989 ... 1.00

Cybrid
Maximum

❑1, Jul 1995; Indicia states June 1995 .. 2.95

Cyclops
Marvel

❑1, Oct 2000 ... 2.50
❑2, Nov 2000 ... 2.50
❑3, Dec 2000, Cover says Nov 2001 ... 2.50
❑4, Jan 2001, Cover says Dec 2001 ... 2.50

Cycops
Comics Interview

❑1, Jun 1988, b&w ... 1.95
❑2, Sum 1988, b&w ... 1.95
❑3, b&w ... 1.95

Cygnus X-1
Twisted Pearl Press

❑1, ca. 1994 ... 2.50
❑2, ca. 1995, 1: Johnny Raygun ... 2.50

Cy-Gor
Image

❑1, Jul 1999 ... 2.50
❑2, Aug 1999 ... 2.50
❑3, Sep 1999 ... 2.50
❑4, Oct 1999 ... 2.50
❑5, Nov 1999 ... 2.50

Cylinderhead
Slave Labor

❑1, Feb 1989, b&w ... 1.95

Cynder
Immortelle

❑1; 1&O: Cynder ... 2.50
❑2 ... 2.50
❑3 ... 2.50
❑Ann 1, Nov 1996 ... 2.95

Cynder/Hellina Special
Immortelle

❑1, Nov 1996 ... 2.95

Cynosure
Cynosure

❑1, Nov 1994 ... 1.95

Cyntherita
Side Show

❑1 ... 2.95

Czar Chasm
C&T

❑1, b&w ... 2.00
❑2, b&w ... 2.00

Dadaville
Caliber

❑1, b&w ... 2.95

Daemonifuge: The Screaming Cage
Black Library

❑1, Mar 2002 ... 2.50
❑2 ... 2.50
❑3 ... 2.50

Daemon Mask
Amazing

❑1 ... 1.95

Daemonstorm
Caliber

❑1 1997, b&w; TMc (c); Partial color ... 3.95
❑Ashcan 1, b&w; preview of upcoming series ... 1.00

Daffy Duck
Dell / Gold Key/Whitman

❑27, Dec 1961 ... 7.00
❑28 1962 ... 7.00
❑29 1962 ... 7.00
❑30, Jul 1962, Last Dell issue; cover code 01-154-209 ... 7.00
❑31, Dec 1962, Back cover pin-up; Gold Key begins publishing; cover code 10029-212 ... 7.00
❑32 1963 ... 7.00
❑33, Jun 1963 ... 7.00
❑34, Sep 1963 ... 7.00
❑35, Nov 1963 ... 7.00
❑36, Mar 1964 ... 7.00
❑37, Jun 1964 ... 7.00
❑38, Sep 1964 ... 7.00
❑39, Dec 1964, Cover code 10029-412 . 7.00
❑40, Mar 1965 ... 7.00
❑41, Jun 1965 ... 5.00
❑42, Sep 1965 ... 5.00
❑43, Dec 1965 ... 5.00
❑44, Mar 1966 ... 5.00
❑45, Jun 1966 ... 5.00
❑46, Sep 1966 ... 5.00
❑47, Dec 1966 ... 5.00
❑48, Mar 1967 ... 5.00
❑49, Jun 1967 ... 5.00
❑50, Sep 1967, Cover code 10029-709 . 5.00
❑51, Dec 1967 ... 5.00
❑52, Mar 1968 ... 5.00
❑53, Jun 1968 ... 5.00
❑54, Sep 1968 ... 5.00
❑55, Dec 1968 ... 5.00
❑56, Mar 1969 ... 5.00
❑57, May 1969, Cover code 10029-905. 5.00
❑58, Jul 1969 ... 5.00
❑59, Sep 1969 ... 5.00
❑60, Nov 1969 ... 5.00
❑61, Jan 1970 ... 4.00
❑62, Mar 1970 ... 4.00
❑63, May 1970 ... 4.00
❑64, Jul 1970 ... 4.00
❑65, Sep 1970 ... 4.00
❑66, Nov 1970 ... 4.00
❑67, Jan 1971, Cover code 10029-101.. 4.00
❑68, Mar 1971 ... 4.00
❑69, May 1971, Cover code 10029-105. 4.00
❑70, Jul 1971 ... 4.00
❑71, Sep 1971, Cover code 10029-109 . 4.00
❑72, Nov 1971 ... 4.00
❑73, Jan 1972 ... 4.00
❑74, Mar 1972 ... 4.00

Other grades: Multiply price above by 5/6 for VF/NM • 2/3 for VERY FINE • 1/3 for FINE • 1/5 for VERY GOOD • 1/8 for GOOD

Cracked Collectors' Edition	Crash Dummies	Crash Ryan	Craz	Crazy

Issues #24-63 have no numbers ©Globe	Comic based on cartoon based on commercial ©Harvey	Pilot becomes involved in adventure ©Marvel	Reprints from Marvel's Not Brand Ecch ©Marvel	Marvel joins satire magazine crowd ©Marvel

	N-MINT
❑75, May 1972	4.00
❑76, Jul 1972, Cover code 90029-207; cover reads ...and the Road Runner ...	4.00
❑77, Aug 1972	4.00
❑78, Oct 1972	4.00
❑79, Dec 1972	4.00
❑80, Feb 1973	4.00
❑81, Apr 1973	2.50
❑82, Jun 1973	2.50
❑83, Aug 1973	2.50
❑84, Oct 1973	2.50
❑85, Dec 1973, Cover code 90029-312; contains 16-page run-of-press Kenner catalog, reprinting many Kenner ads	2.50
❑86, Feb 1974	2.50
❑87, Apr 1974	2.50
❑88, Jun 1974	2.50
❑89, Aug 1974	2.50
❑90, Oct 1974	2.50
❑91, Dec 1974	2.50
❑92, Feb 1975	2.50
❑93, Apr 1975	2.50
❑94, Jun 1975	2.50
❑95, Aug 1975	2.50
❑96, Sep 1975	2.50
❑97, Oct 1975	2.50
❑98, Dec 1975	2.50
❑99, Feb 1976	2.50
❑100, Apr 1976	2.50
❑101, Jun 1976	2.00
❑102, Jul 1976	2.00
❑103, Aug 1976	2.00
❑104, Oct 1976	2.00
❑105, Dec 1976	2.00
❑106, Feb 1977	2.00
❑107, Apr 1977	2.00
❑108, Jun 1977	2.00
❑109, Jul 1977	2.00
❑110, Aug 1977	2.00
❑111, Oct 1977	2.00
❑112, Dec 1977	2.00
❑113, Feb 1978	2.00
❑114, Apr 1978	2.00
❑115, Jun 1978	2.00
❑116, Jul 1978	2.00
❑117, Aug 1978	2.00
❑118, Oct 1978	2.00
❑119, Dec 1978	2.00
❑120, Feb 1979	2.00
❑121, Apr 1979	2.00
❑122, Jun 1979, Whitman	2.00
❑123, Aug 1979	2.00
❑124, Oct 1979	2.00
❑125, Dec 1979	2.00
❑126, Feb 1980	2.00
❑127, Apr 1980	2.00
❑128, Jun 1980	2.00
❑129, Aug 1980	18.00
❑130, Oct 1980	25.00
❑131, Dec 1980	15.00
❑134, Mar 1981; #132 and #133 never printed	15.00
❑135, Jul 1981	5.00
❑136, Nov 1981	5.00
❑137, Dec 1981	5.00
❑138, Jan 1982	2.00
❑139, Feb 1982	5.00
❑140, Mar 1982	5.00
❑141, Apr 1982	5.00
❑142 1982	15.00
❑143 1982	15.00
❑144 1983	15.00
❑145 1983; Final Issue	7.00

Daffy Qaddafi
Comics Unlimited

	N-MINT
❑1 1986, b&w; A: Oliver North. A: Moammar Qaddafi. A: Daffy Duck. A: Ronald Reagan. Nancy Reagan cameo	2.00

Dagar the Invincible
Gold Key

	N-MINT
❑1, Oct 1972, O: Dagar. 1: Scorpio. 1: Ostellon	16.00
❑2, Jan 1973	11.00
❑3, Apr 1973, 1: Graylin	7.00
❑4, Jul 1973	7.00
❑5, Oct 1973	7.00
❑6, Jan 1974, Dark Gods story	7.00
❑7, Apr 1974	7.00
❑8, Jul 1974	7.00
❑9, Oct 1974	7.00
❑10, Jan 1975, 90279-412	7.00
❑11, Apr 1975	7.00
❑12, Jul 1975	5.00
❑13, Oct 1975	5.00
❑14, Jan 1976	5.00
❑15, Apr 1976	3.00
❑16, Jul 1976	3.00
❑17, Oct 1976	3.00
❑18, Dec 1976, Final issue of original run (1976)	3.00
❑19, Apr 1982, O: Dagar. One-shot revival: 1982;Reprints Dagar #1	2.00

Dahmer's Zombie Squad
Boneyard

	N-MINT
❑1, Feb 1993; Adult	3.95

Dai Kamikaze!
Now

	N-MINT
❑1, Jun 1987; Preview of Speed Racer	1.50
❑1/2nd, Sep 1987; 2nd printing	1.75
❑2, Jul 1987	1.50
❑3, Aug 1987	1.50
❑4, Oct 1987	1.50
❑5, Nov 1987	1.75
❑6, Dec 1987	1.75
❑7, Jan 1988	1.75
❑8, Feb 1988	1.75
❑9, Mar 1988	1.75
❑10, Apr 1988	1.75
❑11, Jun 1988	1.75
❑12, Jul 1988	1.75

Daikazu
Ground Zero

	N-MINT
❑1, b&w	1.50
❑1/2nd, b&w; 2nd printing	1.50
❑2, b&w	1.50
❑2/2nd, b&w; 2nd printing	1.50
❑3, Jul 1988, b&w	1.50
❑4, b&w	1.50
❑5, b&w	1.50
❑6, b&w	1.50
❑7, b&w	1.50
❑8, b&w	1.75

Daily Bugle
Marvel

	N-MINT
❑1, Dec 1996, b&w	2.50
❑2, Jan 1997, b&w	2.50
❑3, Feb 1997, b&w; Final Issue	2.50

Daily Bugle: Civil War Special Edition
Marvel

	N-MINT
❑1, Oct 2006	0.50

Daily Planet Invasion! Extra
DC

	N-MINT
❑1; newspaper	2.00

Daimons
Cry for Dawn

	N-MINT
❑1; Adult	2.50

Daisy and Donald
Gold Key

	N-MINT
❑1, May 1973, CB (w); CB (a); A: June. A: May. A: April. Reprints story from Walt Disney's Comics #308	25.00
❑2, Aug 1973	15.00
❑3, Nov 1973	15.00
❑4, Jan 1974, CB (w); CB (a); Reprints story from Walt Disney's Comics #224	15.00
❑5, May 1974	10.00
❑6, Aug 1974	10.00
❑7, Nov 1974	10.00
❑8, Jan 1975	4.00
❑9, Mar 1975	4.00
❑10, May 1975	4.00
❑11, Jul 1975	3.00
❑12, Sep 1975, Hostess Twinkies ad: Bugs Bunny in "Scatter Shot"; cover code 90284-509	3.00
❑13, Nov 1975	3.00
❑14, Jan 1976	3.00
❑15, Mar 1976	3.00
❑16, May 1976, Road Runner in Hostess ad ("Phony Express")	3.00
❑17, Jul 1976	3.00
❑18, Aug 1976	3.00
❑19, Sep 1976	3.00
❑20, Nov 1976	3.00
❑21, Jan 1977	3.00
❑22, Mar 1977, Casper in Hostess ad ("The Boogy-Woogy Man")	3.00
❑23, May 1977	3.00
❑24, Jul 1977	3.00
❑25, Aug 1977	3.00
❑26, Sep 1977	3.00
❑27, Nov 1977	3.00
❑28, Jan 1978	3.00
❑29, Mar 1978	3.00
❑30, May 1978	3.00
❑31, Jul 1978	2.50
❑32, Aug 1978, CB (w); CB (a); Reprints stories from Walt Disney Comics & Stories #280 and #308	2.50
❑33, Sep 1978, Captain America in Hostess ad ("Vs. The Aliens")	2.50
❑34, Nov 1978	2.50
❑35, Jan 1979, Thor in Hostess ad ("The Storm Meets Its Master")	2.50
❑36, Mar 1979	2.50
❑37, May 1979	2.50

Other grades: Multiply price above by 5/6 for VF/NM • 2/3 for VERY FINE • 1/3 for FINE • 1/5 for VERY GOOD • 1/8 for GOOD

❑38, Jul 1979 .... 2.50
❑39, Aug 1979 .... 2.50
❑40, Sep 1979 .... 2.50
❑41, Nov 1979 .... 2.50
❑42, Mar 1980, Spider-Man in Hostess ad ("Puts Himself in the Picture") 2.50
❑43, Apr 1980 .... 2.50
❑44, May 1980 .... 2.50
❑45, Jun 1980 .... 25.00
❑46, Oct 1980 .... 25.00
❑47, Dec 1980 .... 60.00
❑49 1981, #48 never printed 10.00
❑50, Aug 1981 .... 10.00
❑51, Oct 1981 .... 10.00
❑52, Dec 1981 .... 10.00
❑53, Feb 1982 .... 10.00
❑54 1982 .... 10.00
❑55 1982 .... 15.00
❑56 1982 .... 15.00
❑57 1983 .... 15.00
❑58, Aug 1983 .... 15.00
❑59, Jul 1984 .... 15.00

Daisy Kutter: The Last Train
Viper

❑1 2004 .... 5.00
❑1/Conv 2004, 2004 San Diego Con premium 6.00
❑2, Sep 2004 .... 4.00
❑3, Oct 2004 .... 4.00
❑4, Dec 2004 .... 3.99

Dakota North
Marvel

❑1, Jun 1986 .... 1.50
❑2, Aug 1986 .... 1.50
❑3, Oct 1986 .... 1.50
❑4, Dec 1986 .... 1.50
❑5, Feb 1987 .... 1.50

Daktari
Dell

❑1, Jul 1967 .... 35.00
❑2, Nov 1967, Yale Summers' name misspelled on cover 30.00
❑3, Oct 1968, Yale Summers' name misspelled again on cover, a different way; same for Hedley Mattingly; no interior ads 30.00
❑4, Oct 1969, Cover from #1 reused 30.00

Dalgoda
Fantagraphics

❑1, Aug 1984, b&w 2.25
❑2, Dec 1984, b&w 1.50
❑3, Feb 1985, b&w 1.50
❑4, Apr 1985, b&w 1.50
❑5, Jun 1985, b&w 2.00
❑6, Oct 1985, b&w 2.00
❑7, Jan 1986, b&w; Wolverine MacAlistaire backup story 2.00
❑8, Apr 1986, b&w 2.00

Dalkiel: The Prophecy
Verotik

❑1, Aug 1998; cardstock cover 3.95

Dam
Dam

❑1 .... 2.95

Damage
DC

❑0, Oct 1994, Follows Damage #6 .... 1.95
❑1, Apr 1994, 1: Damage; V: Metallo 1.75
❑2, May 1994 .... 1.75
❑3, Jun 1994, 1: Wyldheart 1.75
❑4, Jul 1994 .... 1.75
❑5, Aug 1994, Iron Munro 1.95
❑6, Sep 1994, A: New Titans. Zero Hour 1.95
❑7, Nov 1994 .... 1.95
❑8, Dec 1994, V: Steppenwolf 1.95
❑9, Jan 1995, A: Iron Munro. V: Dr. Polaris 1.95
❑10, Feb 1995, A: Iron Munro 1.95
❑11, Mar 1995 .... 1.95
❑12, Apr 1995, O: Damage 1.95
❑13, Jun 1995 .... 2.25
❑14, Jul 1995, A: Ray 2.25
❑15, Aug 1995 .... 2.25
❑16, Sep 1995 .... 2.25
❑17, Oct 1995 .... 2.25
❑18, Nov 1995, Underworld Unleashed 2.25
❑19, Dec 1995 .... 2.25
❑20, Jan 1996, Final Issue 2.25

Damage Control
Marvel

❑1, May 1989, A: Spider-Man. A: Thor 1.50
❑2, Jun 1989, A: Doctor Doom. Doctor Doom app 1.00
❑3, Jul 1989, A: Iron Man 1.00
❑4, Aug 1989, A: Wolverine. Inferno 1.00

Damage Control
Marvel

❑1, Dec 1989, A: Captain America. A: Thor. Acts of Vengeance 1.50
❑2, Dec 1989, A: Punisher. Acts of Vengeance 1.00
❑3, Jan 1990, A: She-Hulk. Acts of Vengeance 1.00
❑4, Feb 1990, A: Punisher. A: Shield. A: Captain America. A: Thor. Acts of Vengeance 1.00

Damage Control
Marvel

❑1, Jun 1991 .... 1.50
❑2, Jul 1991 .... 1.00
❑3, Aug 1991 .... 1.00
❑4, Sep 1991, Cosmic entities confront Edifice Rex 1.00

Dame Patrol
Spoof

❑1, b&w 2.95

Damlog
Pyramid

❑1, b&w 2.00

Damnation
Fantagraphics

❑1, Sum 1994, b&w; magazine 2.95

Damned
Image

❑1, Jun 1997 .... 2.50
❑2, Jul 1997 .... 2.50
❑3, Aug 1997 .... 2.50
❑4, Sep 1997; Final Issue 2.50

Damn Nation
Dark Horse

❑1 2005 .... 2.99
❑2 2005 .... 2.99
❑3, Jun 2005 .... 3.00

Dampyr
Idea & Design Works

❑1, ca. 2005, b&w 7.99
❑2, May 2005, b&w 7.99
❑3, Jun 2005 .... 7.99
❑4, Aug 2005, Nocturne in Red 7.99
❑5, Sep 2005, Under the Stone Bridge 7.99
❑6, Sep 2005; b&w 7.99
❑7, Dec 2005 .... 7.99
❑8, Jan 2006 .... 7.99

Dance of Lifey Death
Dark Horse

❑1, Jan 1994; NN 3.95

Dance Party DOA
Slave Labor

❑1, Nov 1993; Adult 3.95

Dances with Demons
Marvel

❑1, Sep 1993; Embossed foil cover 2.95
❑2, Oct 1993 .... 1.95
❑3, Nov 1993 .... 1.95
❑4, Dec 1993 .... 1.95

Danger Girl
Image / Cliffhanger

❑1, Mar 1998 .... 5.00
❑1/Chromium, Mar 1998; chromium cover 8.00
❑1/Mag sized, Mar 1998; magazine-sized; Deluxe oversized 20.00
❑1/Toured, Mar 1998; Tour Edition; Woman holding rifle, white background Tour Ed. 8.00
❑1/Go-go cover, Mar 1988; Chromium a-go-go cover 31.00
❑2, May 1998 .... 3.00
❑2/Chrome, May 1998; Special holochrome cover 8.00
❑2/Dynamic, May 1988; Dynamic Forces cover, later recalled 45.00
❑2/Gold, May 1998; Gold logo 6.00
❑3, Aug 1998; White background, 3 girls on cover 3.00
❑3/A, Aug 1998; Girls surrounding guy, knife cover 5.00
❑3/B, Aug 1998; "Filled to the Brim with Danger" cover 3.00
❑4, Dec 1998; Knife to nose cover 3.00
❑4/A, Dec 1998; alternate cover (purple background) 7.00
❑5, Jul 1999; Woman in green bikini & 2 heads behind her with sunset background 2.50
❑5/Dynamic red, Jul 1999; Dynamic Forces variant; Woman in red bikini 6.00
❑5/Dynamic blue, Jul 1999; Dynamic Forces variant; Woman in blue bikini 6.00
❑6, Dec 1999; Woman with hands on hips center front on cover 2.50
❑6/Dynamic, Dec 1999; DFE gold foil edition; Autographed 15.00
❑6/Gold, Dec 1999; DFE gold foil edition 5.00
❑7, Feb 2001 .... 5.95
❑Ashcan 1; Preview edition 5.00
❑Ashcan 1/Gold; Preview edition; Gold logo 6.00
❑SP 1, Feb 2000 .... 3.50

Danger Girl 3-D
DC

❑1, Apr 2003 .... 4.95

Danger Girl: Back in Black
DC

❑1, Jan 2006 .... 2.99
❑2, Jan 2006 .... 2.99
❑3, Mar 2006 .... 2.99
❑4, Apr 2006 .... 2.99

Danger Girl: Hawaiian Punch
DC

❑1, May 2003 .... 4.95

Danger Girl Kamikaze
DC / Wildstorm

❑1, Nov 2001 .... 2.95
❑2, Dec 2001 .... 2.95

Danger Girl Sketchbook
DC / Wildstorm

❑1 .... 6.95

Danger Girl: Viva Las Danger
DC

❑1, Jan 2004 .... 4.95

Dangerous Times
Evolution

❑1 .... 1.75
❑1/2nd; 2nd printing 1.75
❑2 .... 1.75
❑2/2nd; 2nd printing 1.75
❑3 .... 1.95
❑3/2nd; 2nd printing 1.95
❑4 .... 1.95
❑4/2nd; 2nd printing 1.95
❑5 .... 1.95
❑5/2nd; 2nd printing 1.95
❑6 .... 1.95
❑6/2nd; 2nd printing 2.25

Danger Ranger
Checker

❑1, Sum 1998 .... 1.95
❑2, Fal 1998 .... 1.95

Danger Trail
DC

❑1, Apr 1993 .... 1.50
❑2, May 1993 .... 1.50
❑3, Jun 1993 .... 1.50
❑4, Jul 1993 .... 1.50

Danger Unlimited
Dark Horse / Legend

❑1, Feb 1994; JBy (w); JBy (a); 1: Miss Mirage. 1: Torch of Liberty. 1: Hunk. 1: Thermal. 1: Doc Danger. 1: Danger Unlimited 2.50
❑2, Mar 1994; JBy (w); JBy (a); Painted Cover 2.50
❑3, Apr 1994; JBy (w); JBy (a); 1&O: Caucus 2.50
❑4, May 1994 JBy (w); JBy (a) 2.50

Daniel Boone
Gold Key

❑1, Jan 1965 .... 45.00
❑2, May 1965 .... 28.00
❑3, Nov 1965 .... 24.00

Creature Commandos

Monsters team up in short-lived DC book

©DC

Creatures on the Loose

Later incarnation of Tower of Shadows

©Marvel

Creeper

Journalist is haunted by other self

©DC

Crime Patrol

Gemstone reprinting of E.C. series

©Gemstone

Crime SuspenStories

Russ Cochran reprinting of the E.C. classic

©Gemstone

N-MINT

❑4, Feb 1966 .... 24.00
❑5, May 1966 .... 24.00
❑6, Aug 1966 .... 18.00
❑7, Nov 1966 .... 18.00
❑8, Feb 1967 .... 18.00
❑9, May 1967 .... 18.00
❑10, Aug 1967 .... 18.00
❑11, Nov 1967 .... 18.00
❑12, Feb 1968 .... 18.00
❑13, Oct 1968 .... 18.00
❑14, Jan 1969 .... 18.00
❑15, Apr 1969, Final Issue 18.00

Dan Turner: Ace in the Hole
Eternity

❑1, b&w 2.50

Dan Turner: Dark Star of Death
Eternity

❑1, b&w 2.50

Dan Turner: Homicide Hunch
Eternity

❑1, Jul 1991, b&w 2.50

Dan Turner: Star Chamber
Eternity

❑1, Sep 1991, b&w 2.50

Darby O'Gill and the Little People
Gold Key

❑1, Jan 1970, Reprints Four Color Comics (2nd Series) #1024 .... 20.00

D'arc Tangent
Ffantasy Ffactory

❑1, Aug 1982 .... 2.00

Daredevil
Marvel

❑-1, Jul 1997, GC (c); GC (a); Flashback 2.25
❑1, Apr 1964, BEv, JK (c); SL (w); SD, BEv (a); 1&O: Daredevil. 1: Karen Page. 1: Battling Jack Murdock. 1: Foggy Nelson. D: Battling Jack Murdock 3000.00
❑2, Jun 1964, JK (c); SL (w); JO (a); A: Fantastic Four. V: Electro 750.00
❑3, Aug 1964, JK (c); SL (w); JO (a); 1&O: Owl 550.00
❑4, Oct 1964, JK (c); SL (w); JO (a); 1&O: The Purple Man 400.00
❑5, Dec 1964, JK, WW (c); SL (w); WW (a); V: Masked Matador 300.00
❑6, Feb 1965, WW (c); SL (w); WW (a); 1: Mister Fear I (Zoltan Drago). V: Fellowship of Fear 225.00
❑7, Apr 1965, WW (c); SL (w); WW (a); 1: red costume. A: Sub-Mariner 675.00
❑8, Jun 1965, WW (c); SL (w); WW (a); 1&O: Stilt Man 135.00
❑9, Aug 1965, WW (c); SL (w); WW (a). 135.00
❑10, Oct 1965, WW (c); WW (w); WW (a); 1: Ape-Man I (Gordon Monk Keefer). 1: Frog-Man I (Francois LeBlanc). 1: Ani-Men. 1: Cat-Man I (Townshend Horgan). 1: Bird-Man I (Henry Hawk). 135.00
❑11, Dec 1965, WW (c); SL (w); WW (a) 85.00
❑12, Jan 1966, JR (c); SL (w); JK, JR (a); 2: Ka-Zar 85.00
❑13, Feb 1966, JK (c); SL (w); JK, JR (a); O: Ka-Zar 85.00
❑14, Mar 1966, JR (c); SL (w); JR (a); A: Ka-Zar 85.00
❑15, Apr 1966, JR (c); SL (w); JR (a) 85.00
❑16, May 1966, JR (c); SL (w); JR (a); 1: Masked Marauder. A: Spider-Man .. 120.00
❑17, Jun 1966, JR (c); SL (w); JR (a); A: Spider-Man 120.00
❑18, Jul 1966, JR (c); SL (w); JR (a); 1&O: Gladiator I (Melvin Potter) 70.00
❑19, Aug 1966, JR (c); SL (w); JR (a); A: Gladiator I (Melvin Potter) 60.00
❑20, Sep 1966, JR (c); SL (w); GC (a); V: Owl 55.00
❑21, Oct 1966, GC (c); SL (w); GC, BEv (a); V: Owl 50.00
❑22, Nov 1966, GC (c); SL (w); GC (a) .. 50.00
❑23, Dec 1966, GC (c); SL (w); GC (a)... 50.00
❑24, Jan 1967, GC (c); SL (w); GC (a); A: Ka-Zar 50.00
❑25, Feb 1967, GC (c); SL (w); GC (a); V: The Leap-Frog 50.00
❑26, Mar 1967, GC (c); SL (w); GC (a); V: Stilt-Man; Identity of Masked Marauder revealed 50.00
❑27, Apr 1967, GC (c); SL (w); GC (a); A: Spider-Man 50.00
❑28, May 1967, GC (c); SL (w); GC (a).. 45.00
❑29, Jun 1967, GC (c); SL (w); GC (a)... 45.00
❑30, Jul 1967, GC (c); SL (w); GC (a); A: Thor 45.00
❑31, Aug 1967, GC (c); SL (w); GC (a); Cobra 40.00
❑32, Sep 1967, GC (c); SL (w); GC (a)... 40.00
❑33, Oct 1967, GC (c); SL (w); GC (a) ... 40.00
❑34, Nov 1967, GC (c); GC (a) 40.00
❑35, Dec 1967, GC (c); SL (w); GC (a); A: Invisible Girl. V: Trapster 40.00
❑36, Jan 1968, GC (c); SL (w); GC (a); A: Fantastic Four. A: Doctor Doom 40.00
❑37, Feb 1968, GC (c); SL (w); GC (a); A: Doctor Doom. V: Doctor Doom 40.00
❑38, Mar 1968, GC (c); SL (w); GC (a); A: Fantastic Four. A: Doctor Doom 40.00
❑39, Apr 1968, GC (c); SL (w); GC (a); 1: Exterminator (later Death-Stalker).. 40.00
❑40, May 1968, GC (c); SL (w); GC (a); 2: Exterminator (later Death-Stalker); Mark Gruenwald L.O.C 40.00
❑41, Jun 1968, GC (c); SL (w); GC (a); D: Mike Murdock (Daredevil's "twin brother") 40.00
❑42, Jul 1968, GC (c); SL (w); GC (a); 1: Jester; 2: Richard Raleigh; Mark Gruenwald L.O.C 40.00
❑43, Aug 1968, JK, JSt (c); SL (w); GC (a); O: Daredevil. V: Captain America . 45.00
❑44, Sep 1968, GC (c); SL (w); GC (a)... 30.00
❑45, Oct 1968, GC (c); SL (w); GC (a); Characters drawn on Statue of Liberty photo 30.00
❑46, Nov 1968, GC (c); SL (w); GC (a) .. 30.00
❑47, Dec 1968, GC (c); SL (w); GC (a); 1: Willie Lincoln; 1: Biggie Benson 30.00
❑48, Jan 1969, GC (c); SL (w); GC (a) ... 30.00
❑49, Feb 1969, GC (c); SL (w); GC (a); 1: Samuel Starr Saxon 30.00
❑50, Mar 1969, GC (c); SL (w); 2: Samuel Starr Saxon; Carl Gafford L.O.C 33.00
❑51, Apr 1969, A: Captain America 33.00
❑52, May 1969, A: Black Panther 33.00
❑53, Jun 1969, GC (c); SL (w); GC (a); O: Daredevil 20.00
❑54, Jul 1969, GC (c); GC (a); 1: Mister Fear II (Samuel Starr Saxon). A: Spider-Man 20.00
❑55, Aug 1969, GC (c); GC (a); Martin Pasko L.O.C 20.00
❑56, Sep 1969, GC (c); GC (a); 1: Death's Head (Dr. Paxton Page); 1: Mrs. Page; 1: Garth 20.00
❑57, Oct 1969, GC (c); GC (a); Daredevil reveals identity to Karen Page 20.00
❑58, Nov 1969, GC (c); GC (a); 1: Stunt-Master 20.00
❑59, Dec 1969, GC (c); GC (a); 1: Crime-Wave; 1: Torpedo; D: Torpedo 20.00
❑60, Jan 1970, GC (c); GC (a) 20.00
❑61, Feb 1970, GC (a) 20.00
❑62, Mar 1970, GC (a); O: Nighthawk II (Kyle Richmond) 20.00
❑63, Apr 1970, GC (a); Martin Pasko L.O.C 20.00
❑64, May 1970, GC (a) 20.00
❑65, Jun 1970, GC (a); Alan Kupperberg L.O.C 20.00
❑66, Jul 1970, GC (a) 20.00
❑67, Aug 1970, GC (a) 20.00
❑68, Sep 1970, GC (a); 1: Kid Gawaine; 1: Pop Fenton 20.00
❑69, Oct 1970, SB (c); GC (a); 1: William Carver (Thunderbolt) 20.00
❑70, Nov 1970, HT (c); GC (a); 1: Tribune 20.00
❑71, Dec 1970, GC (a); 2: Tribune 20.00
❑72, Jan 1971, GC (a); 1: Tagak the Leopard Lord; 1: Quothar 17.00
❑73, Feb 1971, GC (a); 1: Brotherhood of the Ankh; 1: Lawholder; 2: Capricorn; 2: Aquarius; 2: Sagittarius; Alan Kupperberg L.O.C 17.00
❑74, Mar 1971, GC (a); 1: Smasher 17.00
❑75, Apr 1971, GC (a); 1: El Condor 17.00
❑76, May 1971, GC (a); D: El Condor; 2: El Condor 17.00
❑77, Jun 1971, SB (c); GC (a); 1: Lady Tuvia; 1: Phil Hichock 17.00
❑78, Jul 1971, HT (c); GC (a); 1: Man-Bull; 2: Phil Hichock 17.00
❑79, Aug 1971, SB (c); GC (a); 1: Mr. Kline; 2: Man-Bull 17.00
❑80, Sep 1971, GK (c); GC (a) 17.00
❑81, Nov 1971, GK (c); GC (a); A: Human Torch. giant; reprints story from Strange Tales #132 .... 25.00
❑82, Dec 1971, GK (c); GC (a) 17.00
❑83, Jan 1972, JR (c); V: Mr. Hyde 17.00
❑84, Feb 1972, GK (c); GC (a) 14.00
❑85, Mar 1972, Mark Gruenwald L.O.C.. 14.00
❑86, Apr 1972 .... 14.00
❑87, May 1972 .... 14.00
❑88, Jun 1972, GK (c); GC (a); O: Black Widow 14.00
❑89, Jul 1972 .... 14.00
❑90, Aug 1972 .... 14.00
❑91, Sep 1972, 1: Mister Fear III (Larry Cranston) 14.00
❑92, Oct 1972, GK (c); GC (a) 14.00
❑93, Nov 1972 .... 14.00
❑94, Dec 1972 .... 14.00
❑95, Jan 1973 .... 14.00
❑96, Feb 1973 .... 14.00
❑97, Mar 1973, GK (c); GC (a); 1: Dark Messiah. 1: Disciples of Doom 14.00
❑98, Apr 1973 .... 14.00
❑99, May 1973, story continues in Avengers #110 .... 14.00

Other grades: Multiply price above by 5/6 for VF/NM • 2/3 for VERY FINE • 1/3 for FINE • 1/5 for VERY GOOD • 1/8 for GOOD

Issue	N-MINT
❑100, Jun 1973, 100th anniversary issue; RB (c); GC (a); 1: Angar the Screamer	30.00
❑101, Jul 1973	8.00
❑102, Aug 1973, RB (c)	8.00
❑103, Sep 1973, DH (c); DH (a); 1&O: Ramrod I	8.00
❑104, Oct 1973	8.00
❑105, Nov 1973, 1&O: Moondragon. A: Thanos; V: Kraven the Hunter	8.00
❑106, Dec 1973, RB (c); DH (a); 1: Black Spectre (female group). A: Black Widow	8.00
❑107, Jan 1974, JSn (c); SB (a); A: Captain Marvel	8.00
❑108, Mar 1974, JR (c); Marvel Value Stamp #22: Man-Thing	8.00
❑109, May 1974, Story continues in Marvel Two-In-One #3; Marvel Value Stamp #52: Quicksilver	8.00
❑110, Jun 1974, GC (a); Marvel Value Stamp #51: Bucky Barnes	8.00
❑111, Jul 1974, 1: Silver Samurai. Marvel Value Stamp #70: Super Skrull	8.00
❑112, Aug 1974, Marvel Value Stamp #63: Sub-Mariner	8.00
❑113, Sep 1974, Marvel Value Stamp #85: Lilith	8.00
❑114, Oct 1974, GK (c); 1: Death-Stalker. Marvel Value Stamp #7: Werewolf	8.00
❑115, Nov 1974, RA (c); Marvel Value Stamp #35: Killraven	8.00
❑116, Dec 1974, Marvel Value Stamp #95: Mole-Man	8.00
❑117, Jan 1975, JR (c); Marvel Value Stamp #88: Leader	8.00
❑118, Feb 1975, JR (c); DH (a); 1: Blackwing. Marvel Value Stamp #28: Hawkeye	8.00
❑119, Mar 1975	8.00
❑120, Apr 1975, GK (c); Marvel Value Stamp #99: Sandman	8.00
❑121, May 1975, GK (c)	8.00
❑122, Jun 1975, GK (c)	8.00
❑123, Jul 1975, SB (c)	8.00
❑124, Aug 1975, GK (c); GC, KJ (a); 1: Blake Towe; 1: Copperhead	8.00
❑125, Sep 1975, GK (c); KJ (a)	8.00
❑126, Oct 1975, GK (c); KJ (a); 1: Torpedo	8.00
❑127, Nov 1975, GK (c); KJ (a); Marvel Value Stamp #80: Ghost Rider	8.00
❑128, Dec 1975, GK (c); KJ (a)	8.00
❑129, Jan 1976, RB (c); KJ (a); V: Man-Bull	8.00
❑130, Feb 1976, RB (c); KJ (a)	8.00
❑131, Mar 1976, RB (c); KJ (a); 1&O: Bullseye	75.00
❑132, Apr 1976, 2: Bullseye	15.00
❑132/30¢, Apr 1976, 30¢ regional variant	20.00
❑133, May 1976, 1: Mind-Wave	6.00
❑133/30¢, May 1976, 30¢ regional variant	20.00
❑134, Jun 1976, V: Chameleon	6.00
❑134/30¢, Jun 1976, 30¢ regional variant	20.00
❑135, Jul 1976, RB (c)	6.00
❑135/30¢, Jul 1976, RB (c); 30¢ regional variant	20.00
❑136, Aug 1976, JB (c); JB (a)	6.00
❑136/30¢, Aug 1976, JB (c); JB (a); 30¢ regional variant	20.00
❑137, Sep 1976, JB (c); JB (a); V: the Jester	6.00
❑138, Oct 1976, GC (c); JBy (a); A: Ghost Rider. A: Death's Head (monster)	6.00
❑139, Nov 1976, GK (c); SB (a)	6.00
❑140, Dec 1976, DC (c); SB (a); V: Gladiator; V: Beetle	6.00
❑141, Jan 1977, DC (c); GK (a)	6.00
❑142, Feb 1977, JB (c); JM (a); V: Cobra, Mr. Hyde	6.00
❑143, Mar 1977, DC (c)	6.00
❑144, Apr 1977	6.00
❑145, May 1977, AM (c); GT, JM (a)	6.00
❑146, Jun 1977, GK (c); GK (a); V: Bullseye. Newsstand edition (distributed by Curtis); issue number in box	6.00
❑146/Whitman, Jun 1977, GK (a); V: Bullseye. Special markets edition (usually sold in Whitman bagged prepacks); price appears in a diamond; UPC barcode appears	6.00
❑146/35¢, Jun 1977, GK (c); GK (a); V: Bullseye. 35¢ regional price variant; newsstand edition (distributed by Curtis); issue number in box	15.00
❑147, Jul 1977, GK (c); GK, KJ (a)	6.00
❑147/35¢, Jul 1977, GK (c); GK, KJ (a); 35¢ regional price variant	15.00
❑148, Sep 1977, GK (w); GK, KJ (a)	6.00
❑148/35¢, Sep 1977, GK (w); GK, KJ (a); 35¢ regional variant	15.00
❑149, Nov 1977, CI, KJ (a)	6.00
❑150, Jan 1978, GK (c); CI, KJ (a); 1: Paladin	6.00
❑151, Mar 1978, DC (c); GK (w); GK, KJ (a); Daredevil reveals identity to Heather Glenn	6.00
❑152, May 1978, GK (c); CI, KJ (a); A: Paladin	6.00
❑153, Jul 1978, 1: Ben Urich	6.00
❑154, Sep 1978, GC (c); GC (a)	6.00
❑155, Nov 1978, GC (c); FR (a); Black Widow returns	6.00
❑156, Jan 1979, GC (c); GC (a); A: 1960's Daredevil. Newsstand edition (distributed by Curtis); issue number in box	6.00
❑156/Whitman, Jan 1979, GC (a); A: 1960's Daredevil. Special markets edition (usually sold in Whitman bagged prepacks); price appears in a diamond; no UPC barcode	6.00
❑157, Mar 1979, GC (c); GC, KJ (a); 1: Bird-Man II (Achille DiBacco). 1: Cat-Man II (Sebastian Patane). 1: Ape-Man II (Roy McVey)	6.00
❑158, May 1979, FM (c); FM (w); FM (a); O: Death-Stalker. D: Cat-Man II (Sebastian Patane). D: Ape-Man II (Roy McVey). D: Death-Stalker. V: Deathstalker. First Miller Daredevil	50.00
❑159, Jul 1979, FM, KJ (c); FM, KJ (a); V: Bullseye	22.00
❑160, Sep 1979, FM, KJ (c); FM, KJ (a); V: Bullseye	17.00
❑161, Nov 1979, FM (c); FM, KJ (a); V: Bullseye	17.00
❑162, Jan 1980, SD (c); SD (a)	9.00
❑163, Mar 1980, FM (c); FM, KJ (a)	18.00
❑164, May 1980, FM (c); FM, KJ (a); O: Daredevil	11.00
❑165, Jul 1980, FM (c); FM (w); FM (a)	11.00
❑166, Sep 1980, FM (c); FM (w); FM (a)	11.00
❑167, Nov 1980, FM (c); FM (a)	11.00
❑168, Jan 1981, FM (c); FM (w); FM (a); O: Elektra. 1: Elektra	75.00
❑169, Mar 1981, FM (c); FM (w); FM (a); A: Elektra. V: Bullseye	16.00
❑170, May 1981, FM (c); FM (w); FM (a); V: Bullseye	10.00
❑171, Jun 1981, FM (c); FM (w); FM (a)	12.00
❑172, Jul 1981, FM (c); FM (w); FM (a)	7.00
❑173, Aug 1981, FM (c); FM (w); FM (a)	7.00
❑174, Sep 1981, FM (c); FM (w); FM (a)	7.00
❑175, Oct 1981, FM (c); FM (w); FM (a)	7.00
❑176, Nov 1981, FM (c); FM (w); FM (a); 1: Stick. A: Elektra	7.00
❑177, Dec 1981, FM (c); FM (w); FM (a); A: Elektra	7.00
❑178, Jan 1982, FM (c); FM (w); FM (a); A: Elektra	6.00
❑179, Feb 1982, FM (c); FM (w); FM (a); A: Elektra	6.00
❑180, Mar 1982, FM (c); FM (w); FM (a); A: Elektra	6.00
❑181, Apr 1982, double-sized; FM (c); FM (w); FM (a); D: Elektra. V: Bullseye. Punisher cameo out of costume	15.00
❑182, May 1982, FM (c); FM (w); FM (a); A: Punisher. V: Punisher	7.00
❑183, Jun 1982, FM (c); FM (w); FM (a); A: Punisher. V: Punisher	7.00
❑184, Jul 1982, FM (c); FM (w); FM, KJ (a); A: Punisher. V: Punisher	6.00
❑185, Aug 1982, FM (c); FM (w); FM, KJ (a)	5.00
❑186, Sep 1982, FM (c); FM (w); FM, KJ (a); V: Stilt-Man	6.00
❑187, Oct 1982, FM (c); FM (w); FM, KJ (a); A: Black Widow	5.00
❑188, Nov 1982, FM (c); FM (w); FM, KJ (a)	5.00
❑189, Dec 1982, FM (c); FM (w); FM, KJ (a); D: Stick	5.00
❑190, Jan 1983, Double-size; FM (c); FM (w); FM, KJ (a); O: Elektra. A: Elektra	5.00
❑191, Feb 1983, FM (c); FM (w); FM (a)	6.00
❑192, Mar 1983, KJ (c); KJ (a)	3.00
❑193, Apr 1983, KJ (c); KJ (a)	3.00
❑194, May 1983, KJ (a)	3.00
❑195, Jun 1983, KJ (c); KJ (a)	3.00
❑196, Jun 1983, KJ (c); KJ (a); A: Wolverine	6.00
❑197, Aug 1983, BSz (c); KJ (a); V: Bullseye	3.00
❑198, Sep 1983	3.00
❑199, Oct 1983, KJ (c)	3.00
❑200, Nov 1983, JBy (c); V: Bullseye	3.00
❑201, Dec 1983, JBy (c); A: Black Widow	3.00
❑202, Jan 1984, BL (c); LMc (a)	3.00
❑203, Feb 1984, JBy (c); 1: Trump	3.00
❑204, Mar 1984, BSz (c); LMc (a)	3.00
❑205, Apr 1984	4.00
❑206, May 1984	3.00
❑207, Jun 1984	3.00
❑208, Jul 1984	3.00
❑209, Aug 1984	3.00
❑210, Sep 1984, MZ, BWi (c)	3.00
❑211, Oct 1984	3.00
❑212, Nov 1984	3.00
❑213, Dec 1984	3.00
❑214, Jan 1985	3.00
❑215, Feb 1985, A: Two-Gun Kid.	3.00
❑216, Mar 1985	3.00
❑217, Apr 1985, FM (c)	3.00
❑218, May 1985, KP (c); SB (a); V: Jester	3.00
❑219, Jun 1985, FM (c); FM (w); JB, FM (a)	3.00
❑220, Jul 1985	3.00
❑221, Aug 1985	3.00
❑222, Sep 1985, KP (c); A: Black Widow	3.00
❑223, Oct 1985, JBy (c);Secret Wars II .	3.00
❑224, Nov 1985, BL (c); V: Sunturion	3.00
❑225, Dec 1985, (c); V: Vulture	3.00
❑226, Jan 1986, FM (w); FM (a)	3.00
❑227, Feb 1986, FM (w); A: Kingpin	4.00
❑228, Mar 1986, FM (w)	3.00
❑229, Apr 1986, FM (w); FM (a); 1: Sister Maggie; O: Daredevil	3.00
❑230, May 1986, FM (w)	3.00
❑231, Jun 1986, FM (w)	3.00
❑232, Jul 1986, FM (w)	3.00
❑233, Aug 1986, FM (w)	3.00
❑234, Sep 1986, KJ (c); SD (a); V: Madcap	3.00
❑235, Oct 1986, KJ (c); SD (a); V: Mr. Hyde	3.00
❑236, Nov 1986	3.00
❑237, Dec 1986, MZ (c);V: Klaw	3.00
❑238, Jan 1987, SB (a); A: Sabretooth. V: Sabretooth; Mutant Massacre	3.00
❑239, Feb 1987	3.00
❑240, Mar 1987, MZ (c)	3.00
❑241, Apr 1987, MZ (c); TMc (a)	3.00
❑242, May 1987, KP (c); KP (a)	3.00
❑243, Jun 1987	3.00
❑244, Jul 1987	3.00
❑245, Aug 1987, AM (c); A: Black Panther	3.00
❑246, Sep 1987	3.00
❑247, Oct 1987, CV (c); KG, KP (a)	3.00
❑248, Nov 1987, A: Wolverine. V: Bushwacker	4.00
❑249, Dec 1987, A: Wolverine. V: Bushwacker	4.00
❑250, Jan 1988, JR2 (a); 1: Bullet	3.00
❑251, Feb 1988, JR2 (c); JR2 (a); V: Bullet	5.00
❑252, Mar 1988, double-sized; JR2 (a); Fall of Mutants	4.00
❑253, Apr 1988, JR2 (c); JR2 (a)	3.00
❑254, May 1988, JR2 (c); JR2 (a); 1&O: Typhoid Mary	6.00
❑255, Jun 1988, JR2 (a); 2: Typhoid Mary	2.50
❑256, Jul 1988, JR2 (a); A: Typhoid Mar	2.50
❑257, Aug 1988, JR2 (a); A: Punisher	2.50
❑258, Sep 1988, 1&O: Bengal	4.00
❑259, Oct 1988, JR2 (a); A: Typhoid Mary	3.00
❑260, Nov 1988, double-sized; JR2 (a) .	3.00
❑261, Dec 1988, JR2 (a); A: Human Torch	3.00
❑262, Jan 1989, JR2 (a); Inferno	3.00
❑263, Feb 1989, JR2 (a); Inferno	3.00
❑264, Mar 1989, SD (a)	3.00
❑265, Apr 1989, JR2 (w); JR2 (a); Inferno	3.00
❑266, May 1989, JR2 (w); JR2 (a)	3.00
❑267, Jun 1989, JR2 (a)	3.00
❑268, Jul 1989, JR2 (a)	3.00
❑269, Aug 1989, JR2 (a)	3.00
❑270, Sep 1989, JR2 (a); 1&O: Blackheart. A: Spider-Man	3.00
❑271, Oct 1989, JR2 (a); 1: Number Nine; Daredevil aids animal activist	3.00
❑272, Nov 1989, JR2 (a); 1: Shotgun II.	3.00
❑273, Nov 1989, JR2 (a)	3.00
❑274, Dec 1989, JR2 (a)	3.00
❑275, Dec 1989, JR2 (c); JR2 (a); Acts of Vengeance	3.00

Crimson	Crimson Dynamo	Crisis on Infinite Earths	Crow	Crusaders

Contemporary spin on vampire legends ©Image	Only completed series in Epic's second run ©Marvel	Maxi-series pared DC universe mightily ©DC	Series that spawned a successful movie ©Caliber	Super-team combining Archie super-heroes ©DC

N-MINT

❑276, Jan 1990, JR2 (a); Acts of Vengeance 3.00
❑277, Feb 1990 .... 3.00
❑278, Mar 1990, JR2 (a) 3.00
❑279, Apr 1990, JR2 (a) 3.00
❑280, May 1990, JR2 (a) 3.00
❑281, Jun 1990, JR2 (a); Silver Surfer cameo 3.00
❑282, Jul 1990, A: Silver Surfer 3.00
❑283, Aug 1990, A: Captain America 3.00
❑284, Sep 1990 .... 3.00
❑285, Oct 1990 .... 3.00
❑286, Nov 1990, AW (c) 3.00
❑287, Dec 1990 .... 3.00
❑288, Jan 1991 .... 3.00
❑289, Feb 1991 .... 3.00
❑290, Mar 1991 .... 3.00
❑291, Apr 1991 .... 3.00
❑292, May 1991, A: Punisher 3.00
❑293, Jun 1991, A: Punisher 3.00
❑294, Jul 1991 .... 3.00
❑295, Aug 1991, A: Ghost Rider 3.00
❑296, Sep 1991 .... 1.50
❑297, Oct 1991, AW (a); A: Typhoid Mary. V: Typhoid Mary 1.50
❑298, Nov 1991, AW (a) 1.50
❑299, Dec 1991, AW (a) 1.50
❑300, Jan 1992, double-sized; AW (a); Kingpin deposed 3.00
❑301, Feb 1992, V: Owl 1.50
❑302, Mar 1992, V: Owl 1.50
❑303, Apr 1992, V: Owl 1.50
❑304, May 1992 .... 3.00
❑305, Jun 1992, 1: Surgeon General 1.50
❑306, Jul 1992 .... 1.50
❑307, Aug 1992 .... 1.50
❑308, Sep 1992, (c) 1.50
❑309, Oct 1992 .... 1.50
❑310, Nov 1992 .... 1.50
❑311, Dec 1992 .... 1.50
❑312, Jan 1993 .... 3.00
❑313, Feb 1993 .... 1.50
❑314, Mar 1993 .... 1.50
❑315, Apr 1993, V: Mr. Fear 1.50
❑316, May 1993 .... 1.50
❑317, Jun 1993, (c); V: Stiltman 1.50
❑318, Jul 1993, V: Stiltman. V: Devil-Man 1.50
❑319, Aug 1993, first printing (white); Elektra returns 5.00
❑319/2nd, Aug 1993, 2nd Printing (black); Elektra returns 2.00
❑320, Sep 1993, A: Silver Sable. red costume destroyed;New costume 2.00
❑321, Oct 1993 .... 2.00
❑321/Variant, Oct 1993, Special glow-in-the-dark cover 3.00
❑322, Nov 1993 .... 2.00
❑323, Dec 1993, V: Venom 2.00
❑324, Jan 1994 .... 2.00
❑325, Feb 1994, Double-size; D: Hellspawn. poster 3.00
❑326, Mar 1994 .... 1.50
❑327, Apr 1994 .... 1.50
❑328, May 1994 .... 1.50
❑329, Jun 1994 .... 1.50
❑330, Jul 1994, Gambit 1.50
❑331, Aug 1994 .... 1.50

N-MINT

❑332, Sep 1994 .... 1.50
❑333, Oct 1994 .... 1.50
❑334, Nov 1994 .... 1.50
❑335, Dec 1994, (c) 1.50
❑336, Jan 1995 .... 1.50
❑337, Feb 1995 .... 1.50
❑338, Mar 1995, BSz (c) 1.50
❑339, Apr 1995, (c) 1.50
❑340, May 1995 .... 1.50
❑341, Jun 1995, (c); KP (a) 1.50
❑342, Jul 1995 .... 1.50
❑343, Aug 1995 .... 1.50
❑344, Sep 1995, Yellow and red-costumed Daredevil returns 2.00
❑345, Oct 1995, Red-costumed Daredevil returns;OverPower card inserted 2.00
❑346, Nov 1995 .... 2.00
❑347, Dec 1995, Identity of both Daredevils revealed 2.00
❑348, Jan 1996, A: Sister Maggie. A: Stick. cover says Dec, indicia says Jan 2.00
❑349, Feb 1996, AW (c); AW (a); A: Sister Maggie. A: Stick 2.00
❑350, Mar 1996, Giant-size; Daredevil switches back to red costume 2.95
❑350/Variant, Mar 1996, Giant-size; gold ink on cover; Daredevil switches back to red costume 3.50
❑351, Apr 1996, 1: The Vice Cop 2.00
❑352, May 1996, A: Bullseye. V: Bullseye 2.00
❑353, Jun 1996, V: Mr. Hyde 2.00
❑354, Jul 1996, A: Spider-Man 1.50
❑355, Aug 1996, V: Pyro 1.50
❑356, Sep 1996, V: Enforcers 1.50
❑357, Oct 1996, V: Enforcers 1.50
❑358, Nov 1996, V: Mysterio 1.50
❑359, Dec 1996 .... 1.50
❑360, Jan 1997, V: Absorbing Man 1.50
❑361, Feb 1997, A: Black Widow 1.50
❑362, Mar 1997 .... 1.99
❑363, Apr 1997, GC (c); GC (a); 1: Insomnia. V: Insomnia 1.95
❑364, May 1997, (c) 1.95
❑365, Jun 1997, V: Molten Man 1.99
❑366, Aug 1997, gatefold summary; AW, GC (a) 1.99
❑367, Sep 1997, gatefold summary; GC GC (a) 1.99
❑368, Oct 1997, gatefold summary; GC; (a); V: Omega Red 1.99
❑369, Nov 1997, gatefold summary 1.99
❑370, Dec 1997, gatefold summary; GC (a); A: Black Widow 1.99
❑371, Jan 1998, gatefold summary; Ghost Rider 1.99
❑372, Feb 1998, gatefold summary; A: Ghost Rider 1.99
❑373, Mar 1998, gatefold summary 1.99
❑374, Apr 1998, gatefold summary 1.99
❑375, May 1998, Giant-size; V: Mr. Fear; Gatefold summary; 2.95
❑376, Jun 1998, gatefold summary; Matt sent deep undercover, regains eyesight 1.99
❑377, Jul 1998, gatefold summary; Matt as Laurent Levasseur with new costume 1.99
❑378, Aug 1998, gatefold summary 1.99
❑379, Sep 1998, gatefold summary; Matt regains his identity and loses sight 1.99

N-MINT

❑380, Oct 1998, Giant-size; A: Kingpin. Final Issue; Gatefold summary; Last issue 2.99
❑Ann 1, Sep 1967, Cover reads "King-Size Special"; SL (w); GC (a) 50.00
❑Ann 2, Feb 1971, Cover reads "King-Size Special" 9.00
❑Ann 3, Jan 1972, Cover reads "King-Size Special"; SL (w); JR (a)l; Reprints Daredevil #16-17 .... 9.00
❑Ann 4, ca. 1976, JSt, KJ (c); AM, JR2, GT, JLee, KJ (a); Reprints 8.00
❑Ann 5, JR2, JLee (a); Cover issue number reads #4, seems to be a mistake; Atlantis Attacks; 1989 annual 4.00
❑Ann 6, TS (a); Lifeform 3.00
❑Ann 7, ca. 1991, BG (a); O: Crippler. 1: Crippler. Von Strucker Gambit 2.50
❑Ann 8, ca. 1992, AW (c) 2.50
❑Ann 9, ca. 1993, 1&O: Devourer. trading card 2.95
❑Ann 10, 1994 Ann 2.95
❑Ann 1997, Sep 1997, gatefold summary; Daredevil/Deadpool '97; combined annuals for Daredevil and Deadpool 4.00

Daredevil
Marvel

❑½, Nov 1998; gatefold summary; KSm (w); JR, KN (a) 5.00
❑1, Nov 1998; gatefold summary; KSm (w) 7.00
❑1/Ltd., Nov 1998; KSm (w); DFE alternate cover signed 50.00
❑1/Variant, Nov 1998; KSm (w); DFE alternate cover 9.00
❑2/A, Dec 1998; gatefold summary; KSm (w); Daredevil swinging with Black Widow on cover 5.00
❑2/B, Dec 1998 KSm (w) 5.00
❑3, Jan 1999; gatefold summary; KSm (w); A: Karen Page. A: Foggy Nelson. Matt quits law firm 4.00
❑4, Feb 1999 KSm (w) 4.00
❑5, Mar 1999; KSm (w); A: Mephisto. A: Doctor Strange. D: Karen Page. V: Bullseye. Bullseye cover 4.00
❑5/A, Mar 1999; KSm (w); Black/white/ red cover 5.00
❑6, Apr 1999; KSm (w); V: Mysterio 3.00
❑7, May 1999; KSm (w); D: Karen Page. D: Mysterio 4.00
❑8, Jun 1999; KSm (w); A: Spider-Man. Karen's funeral 3.00
❑9, Dec 1999; A: Echo. 1: Echo; Includes Marvel Comics Fast Lane #1 insert 3.00
❑10, Mar 2000 A: Echo 3.00
❑11, May 2000; A: Echo. Includes Marvel Comics Fast Lane #4 insert 3.00
❑12, Jun 2000 A: Echo 3.00
❑13, Oct 2000; A: Echo. Trial of Kingpin 3.00
❑14, Mar 2001 A: Echo 3.00
❑15, Apr 2001; A: Echo. O: Kingpin 3.00
❑16, May 2001 BMB (w) 5.00
❑16/Unlimited, May 2001 .... 6.00
❑17, Jun 2001 BMB (w) 3.00
❑17/Unlimited, Jun 2001; Marvel Unlimited newsstand variant 5.00
❑18, Jul 2001 BMB (w) 3.00
❑19, Aug 2001 BMB (w) 3.00
❑20, Sep 2001 SL (w); GC (a) 3.00

Other grades: Multiply price above by 5/6 for VF/NM • 2/3 for VERY FINE • 1/3 for FINE • 1/5 for VERY GOOD • 1/8 for GOOD

	N-MINT
❑20/Unlimited, Sep 2001	5.00
❑21, Oct 2001; V: Jester; Dardevil served with subpeona	2.99
❑21/Unlimited, Oct 2001	5.00
❑22, Oct 2001; Daredevil hires attorney	2.99
❑22/Unlimited, Oct 2001	5.00
❑23, Nov 2001; Black Panther appearances	2.99
❑23/Unlimited, Nov 2001	5.00
❑24, Nov 2001	2.99
❑25, Dec 2001	2.99
❑26, Jan 2002; BMB (w); Kingpin overthrown by underboss	2.99
❑27, Feb 2002 BMB (w)	2.99
❑28, Mar 2002; BMB (w); Silent issue	2.99
❑29, Apr 2002 BMB (w)	2.99
❑30, May 2002 BMB (w)	2.99
❑31, Jun 2002 BMB (w)	2.99
❑32, Jul 2002; BMB (w); Aka #412	2.99
❑33, Aug 2002; BMB (w); Has part 3 of Spider-Man/Jay Leno team-up	2.99
❑34, Sep 2002 BMB (w)	2.99
❑35, Oct 2002 BMB (w); A: Spider-Man	2.99
❑36, Nov 2002 BMB (w)	2.99
❑36/No #, Nov 2002	5.00
❑37, Dec 2002 BMB (w); A: Elektra	2.99
❑37/Unlimited, Dec 2002	5.00
❑37/No #, Dec 2002	4.00
❑38, Dec 2002 BMB (w)	2.99
❑39, Jan 2003 BMB (w)	2.99
❑40, Feb 2003; BMB (w); D: White Tiger	2.99
❑41, Mar 2003 BMB (w)	2.99
❑42, Apr 2003 BMB (w)	2.99
❑43, Apr 2003 BMB (w)	2.99
❑44, Apr 2003 BMB (w)	2.99
❑45, May 2003; BMB (w); V: Owl	2.99
❑46, Jun 2003 BMB (w)	2.99
❑47, Jul 2003 BMB (w)	2.99
❑48, Aug 2003, BMB (w); V: Typhoid Mary	2.99
❑49, Sep 2003, BMB (w); V: Bullseye	2.99
❑50, Oct 2003, BMB (w); GC, JR, KJ (a); Cardstock cover; V: Kingpin	2.99
❑51, Nov 2003, Cardstock cover	2.99
❑52, Nov 2003, Cardstock cover	2.99
❑53, Dec 2003, Cardstock cover	2.99
❑54, Jan 2004, Cardstock cover	2.99
❑55, Feb 2004	2.99
❑56, Mar 2004, BMB (w)	2.99
❑57, Apr 2004, BMB (w)	4.00
❑58, May 2004, BMB (w)	2.99
❑59, Jun 2004, BMB (w); Inside cover says "The King of Hell's Kitchen, Part 3"	2.99
❑60, Jul 2004, BMB (w); Daredevil's Identity Revealed	2.99
❑61, Aug 2004, BMB (w)	2.99
❑62, Sep 2004, BMB (w)	2.99
❑63, Oct 2004, BMB (w)	2.99
❑64, Nov 2004	2.99
❑65, Dec 2004, 40th Anniversary Special	3.99
❑66, Jan 2005	2.99
❑67, Feb 2005	2.99
❑68, Feb 2005	2.99
❑69, Mar 2005	2.99
❑70, Apr 2005	2.99
❑71, May 2005	2.99
❑72, Jun 2005	2.99
❑73, Jul 2005	2.99
❑74, Aug 2005	2.99
❑75, Sep 2005; A.k.a. #455	2.99
❑76, Oct 2005	2.99
❑77, Nov 2005	2.99
❑78, Dec 2005	2.99
❑79, Jan 2006	2.99
❑80, Feb 2006	2.99
❑81, Mar 2006	2.99
❑82, Apr 2006	2.99
❑83, Jun 2006	2.99
❑84, Jul 2006, V: Hammerhead; Daredevil in Rykers Island Prison	2.99
❑85, Aug 2006	2.99
❑86, Sep 2006	2.99
❑87, Oct 2006	2.99
❑88, Nov 2006	2.99
❑89, Dec 2006	2.99
❑89/Sketch, Nov 2006; Sketch cover	6.00
❑90, Jan 2007	2.99
❑91, Feb 2007	2.99
❑92, Mar 2007	2.99
❑93	2.99
❑94	2.99
❑95	2.99
❑96	2.99
❑97	2.99
❑98	2.99
❑99	2.99
❑100	2.99
❑101	2.99
❑102	2.99
❑103	2.99
❑105	2.99
❑106	2.99
❑107	2.99
❑108	2.99
❑109	2.99
❑110	2.99
❑111	2.99
❑112	2.99
❑113	2.99
❑114	2.99
❑115	2.99

Daredevil/Batman
Marvel

	N-MINT
❑1, ca. 1997; prestige format; crossover with DC	5.99

Daredevil: Father
Marvel

	N-MINT
❑1, Jun 2004	5.00
❑1/DirCut, Sep 2005	4.00
❑2, Oct 2005	2.99
❑3, Nov 2005	2.99
❑4, Jan 2006	2.99
❑5, Feb 2006	2.99

Daredevil: Ninja
Marvel

	N-MINT
❑1, Dec 2000	2.99
❑1/A, Dec 2000; Dynamic Forces Exclusive Signed by Brian Michael Bendis and Rob Haynes	2.99
❑2, Jan 2001	2.99
❑3, May 2001	2.99

Daredevil: Redemption
Marvel

	N-MINT
❑1, Mar 2005	2.99
❑2, Apr 2005	2.99
❑3, May 2005	2.99
❑4, Jun 2005	2.99
❑5, Jul 2005	2.99
❑6, Aug 2005	2.99

Daredevil/Shi
Marvel

	N-MINT
❑1, Feb 1997, AW (a); crossover with Crusade	3.00

Daredevil/Spider-Man
Marvel

	N-MINT
❑1, Jan 2001	2.99
❑1/A, Jan 2000; Dynamic Forces Exclusive cover	2.99
❑2, Feb 2001	2.99
❑3, Mar 2001	2.99
❑4, Apr 2001	2.99

Daredevil The Man without Fear
Marvel

	N-MINT
❑1, Oct 1993; JR2 (c); FM (w); AW, JR2 (a); O: Daredevil. Partial foil cover	3.50
❑2, Nov 1993; JR2 (c); FM (w); AW, JR2 (a); Partial foil cover	3.50
❑3, Dec 1993; JR2 (c); FM (w); AW, JR2 (a); cardstock cover	3.50
❑4, Jan 1994; JR2 (c); FM (w); AW, JR2 (a); Partial foil cover	3.00
❑5, Feb 1994; JR2 (c); FM (w); AW, JR2 (a); cardstock cover	3.00

Daredevil: The Target
Marvel

	N-MINT
❑1, Jan 2003, Collects issues #4-5, plus variant covers and sketches	3.50

Daredevil vs. Vapora
Marvel

	N-MINT
❑nn, ca. 1996, Fire-prevention comic; giveaway	1.25

Daredevil vs. Punisher
Marvel

	N-MINT
❑1, Aug 2005	2.99
❑2, Sep 2005	2.99
❑3, Oct 2005	2.99
❑4, Nov 2005	2.99
❑5, Dec 2005	2.99
❑6, Jan 2006	2.99

Daredevil: Yellow
Marvel

	N-MINT
❑1, Aug 2001	3.50
❑2, Sep 2001; V: Fixer (murderer of Matt Murdock's father); Matt Murdock hires Karen Page	3.50
❑3, Oct 2001; V: Owl	3.50
❑4, Nov 2001; V: Electro	3.50
❑5, Dec 2001; V: Owl; Owl kidnaps Karen Page	3.50
❑6, Jan 2002; V: Purple Man	3.50

Darerat/Tadpole
Mighty Pumpkin

	N-MINT
❑1, Feb 1987, b&w; parody of Frank Miller's Daredevil work; flip book with Tadpole: Prankster back-up; color poster	1.95

Daria Jontak
JMJ

	N-MINT
❑1, Jan 2001; Adult; Covers shows girl crouching with beast behind her	3.99

Daring Adventures
I.W.

	N-MINT
❑9, ca. 1963	20.00
❑10, ca. 1963	20.00
❑11, ca. 1964	20.00
❑12, ca. 1964	40.00
❑13, ca. 1964	20.00
❑14, ca. 1964	20.00
❑15, ca. 1964	20.00
❑16, ca. 1964	20.00
❑17, ca. 1964	20.00
❑18, ca. 1964	20.00

Daring Adventures
B Comics

	N-MINT
❑1 1993	2.00
❑2, Jul 1993	2.00
❑3 1993	2.00

Daring Escapes
Image

	N-MINT
❑1, Sep 1998; Featuring Houdini	2.50
❑1/Variant, Sep 1998; alternate cover	2.50
❑2, Oct 1998	2.50
❑3, Nov 1998	2.50
❑4, Dec 1998	2.50

Daring New Adventures of Supergirl
DC

	N-MINT
❑1, Nov 1982, RB (c); CI, CS (a); O: Supergirl. 1: Psi; Masters of the Universe insert	2.50
❑2, Dec 1982, V: Psi	2.00
❑3, Jan 1983, 1: The Council; V: Decay	2.00
❑4, Feb 1983, 1: The Gang	1.50
❑5, Mar 1983, V: the Gang	1.50
❑6, Apr 1983, 1: Matrix-Prime	1.50
❑7, May 1983, Lois Lane story	1.50
❑8, Jun 1983, 1: Reactron. A: The Doom Patrol	1.50
❑9, Jul 1983, A: The Doom Patrol. O: Tempest; V: Reactron; The Doom Patrol appearance	1.50
❑10, Aug 1983, Lois Lane story	1.50
❑11, Sep 1983, Lois Lane story	1.50
❑12, Oct 1983, Lois Lane story	1.50
❑13, Nov 1983, 1: Blackstarr. New costume; Series continues as Supergirl	1.50

Dark
Continuüm

	N-MINT
❑1, Jun 1993, blue foil cover	2.00
❑1/Variant, Jun 1993; red foil cover	2.00
❑1/2nd, Jun 1993; blue foil cover	2.00
❑1/3rd, Oct 1993, blue foil cover	2.00
❑2, Jul 1993	2.00
❑3, Aug 1993; GP (c); GP (a); foil cover	2.00
❑3/Autographed, Aug 1993; GP (a); foil cover	2.00
❑4, Sep 1993	2.00
❑5, Feb 1994	2.00
❑6, Mar 1994	2.00
❑7, Jul 1994	2.00
❑7/2nd, Jul 1994; blue foil cover	2.00

Dark
Continuüm

	N-MINT
❑1, Jan 1995	2.00
❑1/A, Jan 1995; enhanced cover	2.50

Crux

Six Atlantean survivors rudely awaken

©CrossGen

Cry for Dawn

Linsner's shapely horror-comics character

©Cry for Dawn

Crying Freeman Part 1

Chinese mafia changes painter's life

©Viz

CSI: Crime Scene Investigation

First TV cop series-turned-comic in years

©Idea & Design Works

Curse of the Spawn

Spinoff from Todd McFarlane's series

©Image

	N-MINT
❑2, Feb 1995	2.25
❑3, Mar 1995	2.50
❑4, Apr 1995	2.50

Dark (August House)
August House

❑1, May 1995; enhanced cover	2.50
❑2, Jun 1995	2.50

Dark Adventures
Darkline

❑1	1.25
❑2	1.75
❑3	1.50
❑4; 1: Terror Knight	1.25

Dark Angel
Boneyard

❑1, May 1997, b&w	2.25
❑2, Sep 1991	2.25
❑3, Oct 1991	2.25

Dark Angel
Marvel

❑6, Dec 1992, Title changes to Dark Angel; Series continued from Hell's Angel #5	1.75
❑7, Jan 1993	1.75
❑8, Feb 1993	1.75
❑9, Apr 1993	1.75
❑10, May 1993	1.75
❑11, Jun 1993	1.75
❑12, Jul 1993	1.75
❑13, Aug 1993	1.75
❑14, Sep 1993	1.75
❑15, Oct 1993	1.75
❑16, Nov 1993	1.75
❑17, Dec 1993	1.75

Dark Angel
Boneyard

❑1 1997	4.95
❑2, Aug 1997	1.95
❑3, Sep 1997	1.95

Dark Angel
CPM Manga

❑1, May 1999, Wraparound cover; Portrait of Dark	2.95
❑2, Jun 1999	2.95
❑3, Jul 1999, Wraparound cover	2.95
❑4, Aug 1999, Kyo in foreground	2.95
❑5, Sep 1999, Sepia cover of Sou	2.95
❑6, Oct 1999, Wraparound cover	2.95
❑7, Nov 1999	2.95
❑8, Dec 1999, Wraparound cover	2.95
❑9, Jan 2000, Wraparound cover	2.95
❑10, Feb 2000, Wraparound cover	2.95
❑11, Mar 2000, Wraparound cover	2.95
❑12, Apr 2000, Wraparound cover	2.95
❑13, May 2000	2.95
❑14, Jun 2000	2.95
❑15, Jul 2000	2.95
❑16, Aug 2000, Wraparound cover	2.95
❑17, Sep 2000, Wraparound cover	2.95
❑18, Oct 2000	2.95
❑19, Nov 2000, Wraparound cover	2.95
❑20, Dec 2000	2.95
❑21, Jan 2001	2.95
❑22, Feb 2001, Wraparound cover	2.95
❑23, Mar 2001, Wraparound cover	2.95

	N-MINT
❑24, Apr 2001, Wraparound cover	2.95
❑25, May 2001, Wraparound cover	2.95
❑26, Jun 2001, Wraparound cover	2.95
❑27, Jul 2001, Wraparound cover	2.95
❑28, Aug 2001, Wraparound cover	2.95
❑29, Sep 2001	2.95

Dark Angel: Phoenix Resurrection
Image

❑1, May 2000	2.95
❑2, Aug 2000	2.95
❑3, Mar 2001	2.95
❑4, Oct 2001	2.95

Dark Assassin
Silverwolf

❑1, Feb 1987, b&w; cardstock cover	1.50

Dark Assassin
Greater Mercury

❑1, Jul 1989	2.00
❑2, Aug 1989	2.00
❑3, Sep 1989; Cover says Sep, indicia says Aug	2.00
❑4, Jul 1990	2.00
❑5, Sep 1990	2.00
❑6, ca. 1990	2.00
❑7, Dec 1990; Title changes to Dark Assassin and Chance	2.00
❑8, Mar 1991	2.00
❑9, May 1991	2.00

Darkchylde (Maximum)
Maximum

❑1, Jun 1996	3.00
❑2, Jul 1996	2.50
❑3, Sep 1996	2.50

Darkchylde
Image

❑0/A, Mar 1998; Ariel posed in close-up w/blue tank	2.50
❑0/B, Mar 1998, b&w; Variant Cover Another Universe	2.50
❑0/C, Mar 1998; Ariel sitting	2.50
❑½, Aug 1997; Wizard 1/2 edition; purple background, girl sitting on skull	3.00
❑½/Variant, Aug 1997; Wizard 1/2 edition; Black background, demoness	3.00
❑1, Jun 1996; Standing with wings outstretched, purplish background, green foreground	5.00
❑1/AmEnt; American Entertainment variant	5.00
❑1/B; Magazine-style variant; Magazine-style variant	2.95
❑1/Conv; San Diego Comic-Con variant (Darkchylde with wings standing on front); Flip-book with Glory/Angela #1	5.00
❑2, Jul 1996	5.00
❑2/A, Jul 1996; Spider-Web/Moon variant cover	5.00
❑3, Sep 1996	5.00
❑3/A, Sep 1996; All-white variant	2.50
❑4/A, Mar 1997; was Maximum Press title; Image begins as publisher	2.50
❑4/B, Mar 1997; "Fear" Edition; alternate cover; Image begins as publisher	2.50
❑5/A, Sep 1997; variant cover	2.50
❑5/B, Sep 1997; alternate cover	2.50
❑5/C, Sep 1997; alternate cover	2.50
❑Ashcan 1, Jan 1998; Preview edition	2.00

	N-MINT
❑Ashcan 1/Gold; Preview edition; Gold logo	3.00
❑Ashcan 1/Ltd.; Autographed by Randy Queen	5.00

Darkchylde Remastered
Image

❑0, Mar 1998	2.50
❑1/A, May 1997; reprints Darkchylde #1 with corrections	2.50
❑1/B, May 1997; alternate cover; reprints Darkchylde #1 with corrections	2.50
❑2, Sep 1998; reprints Darkchylde #2 with corrections	2.50
❑3, Nov 1998; reprints Darkchylde #3 with corrections	2.50

Darkchylde Sketchbook
Image

❑1, ca. 1998	3.00

Darkchylde Summer Swimsuit Spectacular
DC / Wildstorm

❑1, Aug 1999; pin-ups	3.95

Darkchylde Swimsuit Illustrated
Image

❑1, ca. 1998; JLee (a); pin-ups	3.50
❑1/Gold; JLee (a); Gold logo	4.50

Darkchylde the Diary
Image

❑1/A, Jun 1997; pin-ups with diary entries	2.50
❑1/B, Jun 1997; alternate cover; pin-ups with diary entries	2.50
❑1/C, Jun 1997; alternate cover; pin-ups with diary entries	2.50
❑1/D, Jun 1997; alternate cover; pin-ups with diary entries	2.50

Darkchylde: The Legacy
Image

❑1, Aug 1998; cardstock cover	2.50
❑1/A, Aug 1998; DFE alternate chrome cover	4.00
❑1/Variant, Aug 1998; DFE alternate chrome cover	4.00
❑2, Dec 1998; Darkchylde and Blue Monster on cover	2.50
❑2/Variant, Dec 1998; alternate cover	2.50
❑3, Jun 1999	2.50

Dark Claw Adventures
DC / Amalgam

❑1, Jun 1997	1.95

Dark Convention Book
Continuüm

❑1	1.95

Dark Crossings: Dark Cloud Rising
Image

❑1, Sep 2003	5.95

Dark Crossings
Image

❑1, Jun 2000	5.95
❑2, Oct 2000	5.95

Dark Crossings: Dark Clouds Overhead
Image

❑1, Jun 2000; prestige format; cover says Dark Crossings: Dark Clouds Rising	5.95

Other grades: Multiply price above by 5/6 for VF/NM • 2/3 for VERY FINE • 1/3 for FINE • 1/5 for VERY GOOD • 1/8 for GOOD

Dark Crystal
Marvel

❑1, Apr 1983, Movie adaptation 1.25
❑2, May 1983, Movie adaptation 1.25

Dark Destiny
Alpha

❑1, Oct 1994, b&w; cardstock cover 3.50

Darkdevil
Marvel

❑1, Nov 2000 .... 2.99
❑2, Dec 2000 .... 2.99
❑3, Jan 2001 .... 2.99

Dark Dominion
Defiant

❑1, Oct 1993, 1: Chasm; 1: Doctor Michael Alexander 2.50
❑2, Nov 1993 .... 2.50
❑3, Dec 1993 .... 2.50
❑4, Jan 1994 .... 2.50
❑5, Feb 1994 .... 2.50
❑6, Mar 1994 .... 2.50
❑7, Apr 1994 .... 2.50
❑8, May 1994 .... 2.50
❑9, Jun 1994 .... 2.50
❑10, Jul 1994, Final Issue 2.50
❑11, Aug 1994 .... 2.50
❑12, Sep 1994 .... 2.50
❑13, Oct 1994, Final Issue 2.50

Darker Image
Image

❑1, Mar 1993; RL, JLee (w); RL, JLee (a); 1: Maxx. 1: Deathblow; Includes trading card 2.50
❑1/Gold, Mar 1993; RL, JLee (w); RL, JLee (a); 1: Maxx. 1: Deathblow. Gold logo 4.00
❑1/Ltd., Mar 1993; White limited edition cover; RL, JLee (w); RL, JLee (a); 1: Maxx. 1: Deathblow. White cover ... 4.00

Dark Fantasy
Apple

❑1, Sep 1992, b&w 2.75

Dark Fringe
Brainstorm

❑2, Dec 1996, b&w 2.95

Dark Guard
Marvel

❑1, Oct 1993; 1: The Time Guardian. Prism cover 2.95
❑2, Nov 1993 .... 1.75
❑3, Dec 1993 .... 1.75
❑4, Jan 1994 .... 1.75
❑5 .... 1.75

Darkhawk
Marvel

❑1, Mar 1991; O: Darkhawk. 1: Darkhawk. A: Hobgoblin 2.00
❑2, Apr 1991 A: Hobgoblin. A: Spider-Man 1.50
❑3, May 1991 A: Hobgoblin. A: Spider-Man 1.50
❑4, Jun 1991 .... 1.50
❑5, Jul 1991 .... 1.50
❑6, Aug 1991; A: Daredevil. A: Captain America. V: U-Foes 1.50
❑7, Sep 1991; V: Lodestone 1.50
❑8, Oct 1991; V: Lodestone 1.50
❑9, Nov 1991 A: Punisher 1.50
❑10, Dec 1991 .... 1.50
❑11, Jan 1992; V: Tombstone 1.50
❑12, Feb 1992; V: Tombstone 1.50
❑13, Mar 1992 A: Venom 1.50
❑14, Apr 1992 A: Venom 1.50
❑15, May 1992; V: Tombstone 1.25
❑16, Jun 1992; V: Peristrike Force 1.25
❑17, Jul 1992; V: Peristrike Force 1.25
❑18, Aug 1992; V: Psi-Wolf 1.25
❑19, Sep 1992; A: Spider-Man. V: Brotherhood of Evil Mutants 1.25
❑20, Oct 1992; A: Sleepwalker. A: Spider-Man. V: Brotherhood of Evil Mutants; Cont'd Sleepwalker #17 .... 1.25
❑21, Nov 1992; O: Darkhawk 1.25
❑22, Dec 1992 A: Ghost Rider 1.25
❑23, Jan 1993 .... 1.25
❑24, Feb 1993; V: Evilhawk 1.25
❑25, Mar 1993; Double-size; O: Darkhawk armor. foil cover 2.95
❑26, Apr 1993 A: New Warriors 1.25
❑27, May 1993 .... 1.25
❑28, Jun 1993; V: Zarrko the Tomorrow Man 1.25
❑29, Jul 1993; V: Zarrko the Tomorrow Man 1.25
❑30, Aug 1993; Infinity Crusade crossover 1.25
❑31, Sep 1993; Infinity Crusade crossover 1.25
❑32, Oct 1993 .... 1.25
❑33, Nov 1993 .... 1.25
❑34, Dec 1993 .... 1.25
❑35, Jan 1994 A: Venom 1.25
❑36, Feb 1994 A: Venom 1.25
❑37, Mar 1994 A: Venom 1.25
❑38, Apr 1994; New costume 1.25
❑39, May 1994 .... 1.50
❑40, Jun 1994 .... 1.50
❑41, Jul 1994 .... 1.50
❑42, Aug 1994 .... 1.50
❑43, Sep 1994 .... 1.50
❑44, Oct 1994; NFL insert 1.50
❑45, Nov 1994 .... 1.50
❑46, Dec 1994 .... 1.50
❑47, Jan 1995 .... 1.50
❑48, Feb 1995 .... 1.50
❑49, Mar 1995; V: Overhawk 1.50
❑50, Apr 1995; Giant-size; Final Issue ... 2.50
❑Ann 1 .... 2.50
❑Ann 2; 1: Dreamkiller; Includes trading card; Polybagged 2.95
❑Ann 3; ca. 1994 .... 2.95

Darkhold
Marvel

❑1/CS, Oct 1992; Midnight Sons 2.75
❑2, Nov 1992 .... 1.75
❑3, Dec 1992 .... 1.75
❑4, Jan 1993 .... 1.75
❑5, Feb 1993 .... 1.75
❑6, Mar 1993 .... 1.75
❑7, Mar 1993 .... 1.75
❑8, Apr 1993 .... 1.75
❑9, May 1993 .... 1.75
❑10, Jun 1993 .... 1.75
❑11, Jul 1993; Double-cover 1.75
❑12, Aug 1993 .... 1.75
❑13, Sep 1993; Missing CCA approval stamp 1.75
❑14, Oct 1993 .... 1.75
❑15, Nov 1993 .... 1.75
❑16, Dec 1993; Final Issue 1.75

Dark Horse Classics: Aliens V: Predator
Dark Horse

❑1, Feb 1997; Reprints Aliens Vs. Predator #1 with new cover 2.95
❑2, Mar 1997; Reprints Aliens Vs. Predator #2 with new cover 2.95
❑3, Apr 1997; Reprints Aliens Vs. Predator #3 with new cover 2.95
❑4, May 1997; Reprints Aliens Vs. Predator #4 with new cover 2.95
❑5, Jun 1997; Reprints Aliens Vs. Predator #5 with new cover 2.95
❑6, Jul 1997; Reprints Aliens Vs. Predator #6 with new cover 2.95

Dark Horse Classics: Godzilla
Dark Horse

❑1, Apr 1998 .... 2.95

Dark Horse Classics: Godzilla: King of the Monsters
Dark Horse

❑1, Jul 1998 .... 2.95
❑2, Aug 1998; Can G-Force Survive? In the Grip of Godzilla! 2.95
❑3, Sep 1998; No Blast from the Past-Godzilla Rules! 2.95
❑4, Oct 1998 .... 2.95
❑5, Nov 1998 .... 2.95
❑6, Dec 1998 .... 2.95

Dark Horse Classics: Star Wars: Dark Empire
Dark Horse

❑1, Mar 1997 .... 2.95
❑2, Apr 1997 .... 2.95
❑3, May 1997 .... 2.95
❑4, Jun 1997 .... 2.95
❑5, Jul 1997 .... 2.95
❑6, Aug 1997 .... 2.95

Dark Horse Classics: Terror of Godzilla
Dark Horse

❑1, Aug 1998; Translation by Mike Richardson and Randy Stradley of Viz Communications 2.95
❑2, Sep 1998; Translation by Mike Richardson and Randy Stradley of Viz Communications 2.95
❑3, Oct 1998; Translation by Mike Richardson and Randy Stradley of Viz Communications 2.95
❑4, Nov 1998 .... 2.95
❑5, Dec 1998 .... 2.95
❑6, Jan 1999 .... 2.95

Dark Horse Comics
Dark Horse

❑1, Aug 1992; 1: Time Cop. wraparound gatefold cover; Predator, RoboCop, Time Cop, Renegade 3.50
❑2, Sep 1992; RoboCop, Renegade, Time Cop, Predator 2.50
❑3, Oct 1992; Aliens: Horror Show, RoboCop, Indiana Jones, Time Cop; RoboCop, Indiana Jones, Time Cop, Aliens: Horror Show 2.50
❑4, Nov 1992; Aliens, Predator, Indiana Jones, Mad Dogs 2.50
❑5, Dec 1992; Aliens, Predator, Indiana Jones, Mad Dogs 2.50
❑6, Jan 1993; RoboCop, Predator, Indiana Jones, Mad Dogs 2.50
❑7, Feb 1993; RoboCop, Star Wars, Mad Dogs, Predator 5.00
❑8, Mar 1993; 1: X. RoboCop, James Bond, Star Wars 5.00
❑9, Apr 1993; 2: X. 2: X. James Bond, Star Wars, RoboCop 4.00
❑10, May 1993; X, Predator, Godzilla, James Bond 3.00
❑11, Jul 1993; Predator, Godzilla, James Bond, Aliens 2.50
❑12, Aug 1993; Aliens, Predator 2.50
❑13, Sep 1993; Aliens, Predator, Thing from Another World 2.50
❑14, Oct 1993; Predator, The Mark, Thing from Another World 2.50
❑15, Nov 1993 .... 2.50
❑16, Dec 1993 .... 2.50
❑17, Jan 1994 .... 2.50
❑18, Feb 1994; Aliens, Star Wars: Droids, Predator 2.50
❑19, Mar 1994; X, Aliens, Star Wars: Droids 2.50
❑20, Apr 1994 .... 2.50
❑21, May 1994; Mecha; Predator 2.50
❑22, Jun 1994 .... 2.50
❑23, Jul 1994; Aliens, The Machine 2.50
❑24, Aug 1994 .... 2.50
❑25, Sep 1994; Flip-book; Final Issue 2.50

Dark Horse Down Under
Dark Horse

❑1, Jun 1994, b&w 2.50
❑2, Aug 1994, b&w 2.50
❑3, Oct 1994, b&w 2.50

Dark Horse Maverick: Happy Endings
Dark Horse / Maverick

❑1, Sep 2002; Smaller-size anthology 9.95

Dark Horse Maverick 2000
Dark Horse

❑0, Jul 2000 .... 3.95

Dark Horse Maverick 2001
Dark Horse / Maverick

❑1, Jul 2001 .... 4.99

Dark Horse Monsters
Dark Horse

❑1, Feb 1997; Reprinted from Dark Horse Presents #33 & #47 .... 2.95

Dark Horse Presents
Dark Horse

❑1, Jul 1986; 1: Concrete. A: Black Cross 4.00
❑1/2nd Green, ca. 1992; Commemorative edition; 1: Concrete. A: Black Cross. Green border 2.25
❑1/2nd Silver, ca. 1992; Silver border 2.25
❑2, ca. 1986, b&w; 2: Concrete 2.50
❑3, Nov 1986; A: Concrete. b&w 2.50
❑4, Jan 1987 A: Concrete 2.50
❑5, Feb 1987 PG (c); A: Concrete 2.00
❑6, Apr 1987 A: Concrete 2.00
❑7, May 1987 .... 2.00

Cyberella

Howard Chaykin's addition to DC's SF line

©DC

Cyberforce

One of the first titles from the Image line

©Image

CyberFrog

Big armored amphibian causes trouble

©Harris

Cyberspace 3000

Galactus pays a call to a space station

©Marvel

Daffy Duck

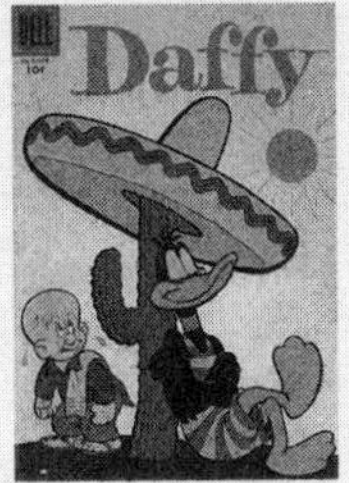

Waterfowl is less hyperactive in comics

©Dell

	N-MINT
❑8, Jun 1987 A: Concrete	2.00
❑9, Jul 1987 PG (c)	2.00
❑10, Sep 1987; 1: The Mask. A: Concrete	3.00
❑11, Oct 1987; 2: The Mask	2.50
❑12, Nov 1987 A: Concrete. A: The Mask	2.50
❑13, Dec 1987 A: The Mask	2.50
❑14, Jan 1987 A: Concrete. A: The Mask	2.50
❑15, Feb 1988 A: The Mask	2.50
❑16, Mar 1988 A: Concrete. A: The Mask	2.50
❑17, Apr 1988; Spume, Muzzi & Woim, Roachmill	2.00
❑18, Jun 1988 A: Concrete. A: The Mask	2.50
❑19, Jul 1988 A: The Mask	2.00
❑20, Aug 1988; Double Size; A: Flaming Carrot. A: Concrete. A: The Mask. 64 page Ann	2.00
❑21, Aug 1988 A: The Mask	2.00
❑22, Sep 1988; 1: Duckman	2.00
❑23, Oct 1988	2.00
❑24, Nov 1988; 1&O: Aliens	6.00
❑25, Dec 1988	2.00
❑26, Jan 1989	2.00
❑27, Feb 1989	2.00
❑28, Mar 1989; Double Size; 48 pages; Concrete, Mr. Monster	3.00
❑29, Apr 1989	2.00
❑30, May 1989	2.00
❑31, Jul 1989; Duckman	2.00
❑32, Aug 1989; Giant-size; A: Concrete	3.50
❑33, Sep 1989; Giant-size	2.50
❑34, Nov 1989; Aliens story	3.00
❑35, Dec 1989; Predator, Heartbreakers, A Tough Nut To Crack, Aliens	3.00
❑36, Feb 1990; regular cover; Predator pin-up on back cover	4.00
❑36/A, Feb 1990; painted cover; Predator pin-up on back cover	3.00
❑37, Mar 1990; Delia & Celia pin-up on back cover	2.00
❑38, Apr 1990 A: Concrete	2.00
❑39, May 1990	2.00
❑40, May 1990; Giant-size; MW (a); Wacky Squirrel fold-in on back cover	3.00
❑41, Jun 1990	2.00
❑42, Jul 1990; Aliens	2.00
❑43, Aug 1990; Aliens; b&w	2.00
❑44, Sep 1990; b&w	2.00
❑45, Nov 1990; MW (w); MW (a); B&W	2.00
❑46, Nov 1990; Predator, Bacchus, Crash Ryan; b&w	2.00
❑47, Jan 1991; Monsters; b&w	2.00
❑48, Feb 1991; contains Aliens: Earth Wars and Starstruck trading cards	2.00
❑49, Mar 1991; contains The Mask and checklist trading cards	2.00
❑50, Apr 1991; contains Bob the Alien and Black Cross trading cards	3.00
❑51, Jun 1991; FM (w); FM (a); Sin City story continued from Dark Horse Presents Fifth Anniversary Special	4.00
❑52, Jul 1991; FM (w); FM (a); B&W	3.00
❑53, Aug 1991; FM (w); GM, FM (a); B&W	3.00
❑54, Sep 1991; JBy, FM (w); GM, JBy, FM (a); 1: Next Men. 1: Next Men; b&w	4.00
❑55, Oct 1991; JBy, FM (w); GM, JBy, FM (a); 2: Next Men; b&w	2.25
❑56, Nov 1991; Double-size; JBy, FM (w); JBy, FM (a); "Silverware Anniversary Issue"; cover homage to DC silver anniversary issues	3.95
❑57, Dec 1991; Giant-size; JBy, FM (w); JBy, FM (a); 48-page "Post-Ann"; cover homage to Daredevil #1	3.50
❑58, Jan 1992; FM (w); FM (a); B&W	2.00
❑59, Feb 1992; FM (w); FM (a); B&W	2.50
❑60, Mar 1992; FM (w); FM (a); B&W	2.50
❑61, Apr 1992; FM (w); FM (a); B&W	2.50
❑62, May 1992; FM (w); FM (a); all Sin City issue	4.00
❑63, Jun 1992; FM (w); b&w	2.50
❑64, Jul 1992; b&w	2.50
❑65, Aug 1992; Interact-o-Rama is a scriptwriting contest	2.50
❑66, Sep 1992; ES (a); Concrete, Dr. Giggles, An Accidental Death; b&w	2.50
❑67, Nov 1992; Double-size issue; CR, ES (a); A: Zoo-Lou. Flash #123 homage cover	3.95
❑68, Dec 1992; Predator: Race War; b&w	2.50
❑69, Feb 1993; Predator: Race War; b&w	2.50
❑70, Feb 1993; b&w	2.50
❑71, Mar 1993; b&w	2.50
❑72, Apr 1993; b&w	2.50
❑73, Jun 1993; Begins Mature Readers label; b&w	2.50
❑74, Jun 1993; b&w	2.50
❑75, Jul 1993; CV (a); B&W	2.50
❑76, Aug 1993; b&w	2.50
❑77, Sep 1993; b&w	2.50
❑78, Oct 1993; b&w	2.50
❑79, Nov 1993; b&w	2.50
❑80, Dec 1993; b&w	3.00
❑81, Jan 1994; b&w	2.50
❑82, Feb 1994; b&w	2.50
❑83, Mar 1994; b&w	2.50
❑84, Apr 1994; b&w	2.50
❑85, May 1994; b&w	2.50
❑86, Jun 1994; b&w	2.50
❑87, Jul 1994; b&w	2.50
❑88, Aug 1994; Hellboy	2.50
❑89, Sep 1994; Hellboy	2.50
❑90, Oct 1994; b&w	2.50
❑91, Nov 1994; b&w	2.50
❑92, Dec 1994; A: Too Much Coffee Man. b&w	2.50
❑93, Jan 1995; A: Too Much Coffee Man. b&w	2.50
❑94, Feb 1995; b&w	2.50
❑95, Mar 1995; A: Too Much Coffee Man. b&w	2.50
❑96, Apr 1995; b&w	2.50
❑97, May 1995; b&w	2.50
❑98, Jun 1995; b&w	2.50
❑99, Jul 1995; b&w	2.50
❑100.1, Aug 1995; FM, DSt (c); FM, DSt (w); FM, DSt (a); Issue 100 #1	2.50
❑100.2, Aug 1995; Issue 100 #2: Hellboy cover and story	2.50
❑100.3, Aug 1995; Issue 100 #3; Concrete cover and story	2.50
❑100.4, Aug 1995; DaG (c); FM (w); DaG (a); Martha Washington story;Issue 100 #4	2.50
❑100½, Aug 1995; Issue 100 #5	2.50
❑101, Sep 1995; BWr (a); A: Aliens. b&w	2.50
❑102, Oct 1995; BWr (a); Aliens story; b&w	2.50
❑103, Nov 1995; JK (a); Kirby centerfold; Mr. Painter, One-Trick Rip-Off, The Pink Tornado, Hairball	2.95
❑104, Dec 1995; b&w	2.95
❑105, Jan 1996	2.95
❑106, Feb 1996	2.95
❑107, Mar 1996	2.95
❑108, Apr 1996	2.95
❑109, May 1996	2.95
❑110, Jun 1996	2.95
❑111, Jul 1996; b&w	2.95
❑112, Aug 1996; Wraparound cover; b&w	2.95
❑113, Sep 1996; b&w	2.95
❑114, Oct 1996; FM (c); FM (w); FM (a); Star Slammers, Lance Blastoff, Lowlife, Trypto the Acid Dog	2.95
❑115, Nov 1996; FM (c);Doctor Spin, The Creep, Lowlife, Trypto the Acid Dog	2.95
❑116, Dec 1996; Fat Dog Mendoza, Trypto the Acid Dog, Doctor Spin	2.95
❑117, Jan 1997; GC (a); Aliens, Trypto the Acid Dog, Doctor Spin	2.95
❑118, Feb 1997; Monkeyman & O'Brien, Hectic Planet, Trypto the Acid Dog, Doctor Spin	2.95
❑119, Mar 1997; Monkeyman & O'Brien, Hectic Planet, Trout, Predator	2.95
❑120, Apr 1997; One Last Job, The Lords of Misrule, Trout, Hectic Planet	2.95
❑121, May 1997; Jack Zero, Aliens, The Lords of Misrule, Trout	2.95
❑122, Jun 1997; Jack Zero, Imago, Trout, The Lords of Misrule	2.95
❑123, Jul 1997; Imago, Jack Zero, Trout	2.95
❑124, Aug 1997; Predator, Jack Zero, Outside, Inside	2.95
❑125, Sep 1997; b&w	2.95
❑126, Oct 1997; 48 pg.; Flipbook; b&w	2.95
❑127, Nov 1997; Nocturnals, Metalfer, Stiltskin, Blue Monday	2.95
❑128, Jan 1998; Dan & Larry, Metalfer, Stiltskin	2.95
❑129, Feb 1998; b&w	2.95
❑130, Mar 1998; Dan & Larry, Wanted Man, Mary Walker: The Woman	2.95
❑131, Apr 1998; Girl Crazy, The Fall, Dan & Larry, Boogie Picker	2.95
❑132, Apr 1998; The Fall, Dan & Larry, Dirty Pair	2.95
❑133, May 1998; Carson of Venus, The Fall, Dirty Pair, Blue Monday	2.95
❑134, Jul 1998; Flipbook; b&w	2.95
❑135, Sep 1998; Carson of Venus, The Mark, The Fall, The Ark	3.50
❑136, Oct 1998; The Ark, Spirit of the Badlander	2.95
❑137, Nov 1998; Predator, The Ark, My Vagabond Days	2.95
❑138, Dec 1998; Terminator, The Moth, My Vagabond Days	2.95
❑139, Jan 1999; Roachmill, Saint Slayer	2.95
❑140, Feb 1999; Aliens, Usagi Yojimbo, Saint Slayer	2.95
❑141, Mar 1999; Buffy the Vampire Slayer	2.95
❑142, Apr 1999; 1: Doctor Gosburo Coffin. Codex Arcana	2.95
❑143, May 1999; TY (w); TY (a); Tarzan: Tales of Pellucidar	2.95
❑144, Jun 1999; The Vortex, Burglar Girls, Galactic Jack	2.95
❑145, Jul 1999; Burglar Girls	2.95
❑146, Sep 1999; Aliens vs Predator	2.95
❑147, Oct 1999; Ragnok	2.95

Other grades: Multiply price above by 5/6 for VF/NM • 2/3 for VERY FINE • 1/3 for FINE • 1/5 for VERY GOOD • 1/8 for GOOD

❑148, Oct 1999; b&w 2.95
❑149, Dec 1999 .... 2.95
❑150, Jan 2000; Giant-size 4.50
❑151, Feb 2000, b&w; Hellboy; Doc Thunder 2.95
❑152, Mar 2000, b&w 2.95
❑153, Apr 2000, b&w; Flipbook 2.95
❑154, May 2000, b&w; Angel; Full Throttle; Iron Reich 3000 .... 2.95
❑155, Jul 2000, b&w; Flip Book; Angel; Full Throttle; Iron Reich 3000 .... 2.95
❑156, Aug 2000, b&w 2.95
❑157, Sep 2000, b&w; Last issue of the series 2.95
❑Ann 1997, Feb 1998, b&w; GM (a); cover says 1997, indicia says 1998 .... 4.95
❑Ann 1998, Sep 1998, b&w; Hellboy, Buffy, Skeleton Key, The Ark, My Vagabond Days, Infirmary 4.95
❑Ann 1999, Aug 1999; SA, ME (w); SA (a); Dark Horse Jr 4.95
❑Ann 2000, Jun 2000; Flip-book; PD (w); Flip-book; Girls Rule! 4.95

Dark Horse Presents: Aliens
Dark Horse

❑1, ca. 1992; color reprints;Reprints Aliens stories from Dark Horse Presents 4.95
❑1/A, ca. 1992; Promotion only 4.95

Dark Horse Twenty Years
Dark Horse

❑1, Aug 2006, Artbook, appearances by Hellboy, Ghost, Monkeyman & O'Brien, The Mask, Go Boy 7, Aliens, Conan, Groo, Concrete, Black Cross, Star Wars, The Goon, Grendel, The Escapist, Tarzan, Sock Monkey, Emily The Strange, Fray, Sin City, Usagi Yojimbo, Jam Cover 1.00

Dark Island
Davdez

❑1, May 1998, b&w 2.95
❑2, Jun 1998, b&w 2.95
❑3, Jul 1998, b&w 2.50

Dark Knight Strikes Again
DC

❑1, ca. 2001; Only DK2 on cover 3.00
❑1/A, ca. 2001; Full title on cover; Variant cover edition 5.00
❑2, ca. 2002; Only DK2 on cover 3.00
❑2/A, ca. 2002; Full title on cover; Variant cover edition 4.00
❑3, ca. 2002; Only DK2 on cover 3.00
❑3/A, ca. 2002; Full title on cover; Variant cover edition 4.00

Darklight: Prelude
Sirius

❑1, Jan 1994, b&w 2.95
❑2, b&w 2.95
❑3, b&w 2.95

Darklon the Mystic
Pacific

❑1, Nov 1983; "The Price" story here is not to be confused with Starlin's Dreadstar story of the same name 2.00

Darkman
Marvel

❑1, Oct 1990 BH (c); BH (a) 2.00
❑2, Nov 1990 BH (c); BH (a) 1.50
❑3, Dec 1990 BH (c); BH (a) 1.50

Darkman
Marvel

❑1, Apr 1993 .... 3.95
❑2, May 1993 .... 2.95
❑3, Jun 1993 .... 2.95
❑4, Jul 1993 .... 2.95
❑5, Aug 1993 .... 2.95
❑6, Sep 1993, Final Issue 2.95

Darkman
Marvel

❑1, Sep 1990, b&w; Magazine size; Movie Adaptation 2.25

Dark Mansion of Forbidden Love
DC

❑1, Sep 1971 TD (a) 125.00
❑2, Nov 1971 .... 50.00
❑3, Jan 1972 DH (a) 50.00
❑4, Mar 1972; Series continued in Forbidden Tales of Dark Mansion #5 .... 50.00

Darkminds
Image

❑½, May 1999 .... 2.50
❑1, Jul 1998 .... 3.50
❑1/Gold, Aug 1998; DFE gold foil edition; DFE gold foil edition 4.00
❑1/Variant, Jul 1998; alternate cover (solo figure) 3.50
❑1/2nd; 2nd printing 2.50
❑2, Aug 1998 .... 3.00
❑2/Variant, Aug 1998; alternate cover 3.00
❑3, Sep 1998 .... 3.00
❑3/Variant, Sep 1998; alternate cover 3.00
❑4, Oct 1998; cover says Dec, indicia says Oct 3.00
❑5, Nov 1998 .... 2.50
❑6, Dec 1998 .... 2.50
❑7, Feb 1999 .... 2.50
❑8, Apr 1999 .... 2.50

Darkminds
Image

❑0, Jul 2000 .... 2.50
❑1, Feb 2000; Joe Quesada Cover 2.50
❑2, Mar 2000; Woman gesturing, man firing on cover; Michael Turner Cover 2.50
❑3, Apr 2000; Yellow-green cover with naked woman seeming to fly 2.50
❑4, May 2000 .... 2.50
❑5, Jun 2000 .... 2.50
❑6, Sep 2000 .... 2.50
❑7, Oct 2000 .... 2.50
❑8, Nov 2000 .... 2.50
❑9, Feb 2001 .... 2.50
❑10, Apr 2001 .... 2.50

Darkminds: Macropolis
Image

❑1/A, Jan 2002; Knife-wielding man stalking prostitutes on cover 2.95
❑1/B, Jan 2002 .... 2.95
❑2/A, Mar 2002 .... 2.95
❑2/B, Mar 2002 .... 2.95

Darkminds: Macropolis
Dreamwave

❑1, Sep 2003 .... 2.95
❑2, Oct 2003 .... 2.95
❑3, Dec 2003 .... 2.95
❑4, Sep 2004 .... 2.95

Darkminds/Witchblade
Image

❑1, Aug 2000 .... 5.95

Dark Mists
APComics

❑1, Jul 2005 .... 3.50
❑2, Sep 2005 .... 3.50

Dark Moon Prophesy
Dark Moon Productions

❑1, May 1995; free color and b&w preview of Dark Moon line 1.00

Dark Nemesis (Villains)
DC

❑1, Feb 1998; New Year's Evil 1.95

Darkness
Top Cow

❑0, Jul 2000 .... 3.00
❑½, ca. 1996; Wizard mail-away promotion 3.00
❑½/Variant, ca. 1996; Christmas cover; Wizard mail-away promotion 3.00
❑½/2nd, Mar 2001 .... 2.95
❑1, Dec 1996 .... 3.00
❑1/A, Dec 1996; Dark cover variant 3.00
❑1/B, Dec 1996; Wizard Ace edition; Variant 3.00
❑1/C, Dec 1996; Fan club edition; Fan club edition with logo on cover; Cover by Marc Silvestri 3.00
❑1/Gold, Dec 1996; Gold edition 3.00
❑1/Platinum, Dec 1996; Platinum edition; Platinum cover 8.00
❑2, Jan 1997 .... 3.00
❑3, Mar 1997 .... 3.00
❑4, May 1997 .... 3.00
❑5, Jun 1997 .... 3.00
❑6, Jul 1997 .... 3.00
❑7, Aug 1997; Standard Cover - (green background) 2.50
❑7/A, Aug 1997; Variant cover with Michael Turner and babes 2.50
❑8, Oct 1997; Joe Benitez Cover 2.50
❑8/A, Oct 1997; alternate cover 2.50
❑8/B, Oct 1997; alternate cover 2.50
❑8/C, Oct 1997; alternate cover 2.50
❑9, Nov 1997 .... 2.50
❑9/A, Nov 1997; alternate cover 2.50
❑10, Dec 1997 .... 2.50
❑10/A, Dec 1997; alternate cover (gold) 2.50
❑10/B, Dec 1997; alternate cover (gold) 2.50
❑11/A, Jan 1998; chromium cover 8.00
❑11/B, Jan 1998; Dale Keown cover 2.50
❑11/C, Jan 1998; David Finch cover 2.50
❑11/D, Jan 1998; Nathan Cabrera cover 2.50
❑11/E, Jan 1998; Greg and Tim Hildebrandt cover 2.50
❑11/F, Jan 1998; Billy Tan cover 2.50
❑11/G, Jan 1998; Whilce Portacio cover 2.50
❑11/H, Jan 1998; Joe Benitez cover 2.50
❑11/I, Jan 1998; Michael Turner cover 2.50
❑11/J, Jan 1998; Museum Edition 2.50
❑12, Feb 1998 .... 2.50
❑13, Mar 1998 .... 2.50
❑14, Apr 1998 .... 2.50
❑15, Jun 1998 .... 2.50
❑16, Jul 1998 .... 2.50
❑17, Sep 1998; O: Magdalena 2.50
❑18, Nov 1998 .... 2.50
❑19, Jan 1999 .... 2.50
❑20/A, Apr 1999; Regular Cover (with Darklings) 2.50
❑20/B, Apr 1999; Museum Edition 2.50
❑20/C, Apr 1999; Alternate Cover (With Darklings) 2.50
❑21, May 1999 .... 2.50
❑22, Jun 1999 .... 2.50
❑23, Jul 1999 .... 2.50
❑24, Aug 1999 .... 2.50
❑25, Sep 1999 .... 3.99
❑25/A, Sep 1999; Chrome Holofoil variant 20.00
❑26, Oct 1999 .... 2.50
❑27, Oct 1999 .... 2.50
❑28, Jan 2000 .... 2.50
❑28/Graham, Jan 2000, Exclusive for Graham Crackers Comics (Naperville, Ill.). Features Keu Cha cover 5.00
❑29 2000 .... 2.50
❑30, Apr 2000 .... 2.50
❑31, May 2000 .... 2.50
❑32, Jul 2000 .... 2.50
❑33, Aug 2000 .... 2.50
❑34, Oct 2000 .... 2.50
❑35, Nov 2000 .... 2.50
❑36, Dec 2000 .... 2.50
❑37, Feb 2001 .... 2.50
❑38, Apr 2001 .... 2.50
❑39, May 2001 .... 2.50
❑40, Aug 2001 .... 2.50
❑Ashcan 1, Jul 1996; No cover price; preview of upcoming series 3.00
❑Ashcan 1/A; Prelude; "Wizard Authentic" variant 3.00

Darkness
Image

❑1, Dec 2002 .... 4.00
❑1/A, Dec 2002; Black and White 2.99
❑1/B, Dec 2002; DF Cover 2.99
❑1/C, Dec 2002; Holofoil Cover 2.99
❑1/D, Dec 2002; Sketch Cover 2.99
❑2, Feb 2003 .... 2.99
❑3, Apr 2003 .... 2.99
❑4, Jun 2003 .... 2.99
❑5, Sep 2003 .... 2.99
❑6, Nov 2003 .... 2.99
❑7, Apr 2004 .... 2.99
❑8, Apr 2004 .... 2.99
❑9, May 2004 .... 2.99
❑10, May 2004 .... 2.99
❑11, Jun 2004 .... 2.99
❑12, Aug 2004 .... 2.99
❑13, Sep 2004 .... 2.99
❑14, Oct 2004 .... 2.99
❑15, Nov 2004 .... 2.99
❑16, Dec 2004 .... 2.99
❑17, Jan 2005 .... 2.99
❑18, Feb 2005 .... 2.99
❑19, Mar 2005 .... 2.99

Daffy Qaddafi

Dated artifact spoofing Libyan dictator

©Comics Unlimited

Dagar the Invincible

Sword-wielding barbarian swears revenge

©Gold Key

Dagwood Comics

Sandwich-chomper loses series in 1965

©Harvey

Daisy and Donald

Fairly clever tales of social-climber Daisy

©Gold Key

Damage Control

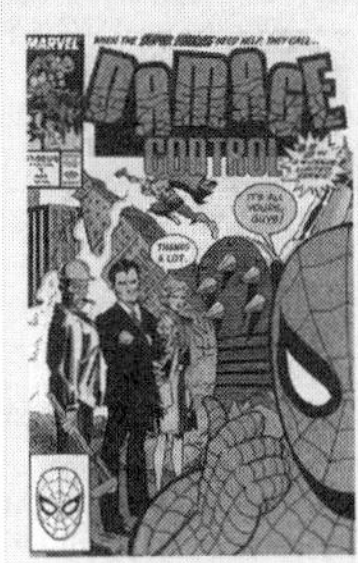

Team cleans up after super-hero fights

©Marvel

	N-MINT
❑20, Apr 2005	2.99
❑21 2005	2.99
❑22, Sep 2005	2.99
❑23, Oct 2005	2.99
❑24, Nov 2005	2.99

Darkness & Tomb Raider
Top Cow

❑1 2005 ... 2.99

Darkness/Batman
Image

❑1, Aug 1999; Squarebound ... 5.95

Darkness Collected Edition
Image

❑1, Oct 2003 ... 4.95

Darkness Falls: The Tragic Life of Matilda Dixon
Dark Horse

❑1, Dec 2002; Movie-based one-shot ... 2.99

Darkness/Hulk
Image

❑1, Jul 2004 ... 5.00

Darkness Infinity
Image

❑1, Aug 1999 ... 3.50

Darkness: Level 0
Image

❑1, Jan 2007 ... 2.99

Darkness: Level 1
Image

❑1, Feb 2007 ... 2.99
❑1/Variant, Feb 2007 ... 2.99
❑1/2nd variant, Feb 2007 ... 2.99

Darkness: Megacon Issue
Image

❑1, Aug 2003 ... 0.00

Darkness/Painkiller Jane
Image

❑Ashcan 1 ... 3.00
❑Ashcan 1/A; variant cover ... 3.00

Darkness Prelude
Image

❑0, Jan 2003, Dynamic Foces Exclusive ... 4.00
❑0/Dynamic ... 10.00
❑0/A, Jan 2003 ... 4.00

Darkness/Superman
Image

❑1, Feb 2005 ... 2.99
❑2, Mar 2005 ... 2.99

Darkness: Wanted Dead One Shot
Image

❑1, Aug 2003 ... 2.99

Darkness/Witchblade Special
Image

❑1, Dec 1999 ... 3.95

Darkness/Wolverine
Image

❑1, Oct 2006 ... 2.99

Dark Oz
Arrow

❑1 1997 ... 2.75
❑2 1997 ... 2.75
❑3 1998 ... 2.75
❑4 1998 ... 2.75
❑5 1998; indicia says 97, a misprint ... 2.75

Dark Rat
Maverick Pulp Comix

❑1, Sep 1997, b&w ... 2.50

Dark Realm
Image

❑1, Oct 2000 ... 2.95
❑2, Dec 2000 ... 2.95
❑3, Feb 2001; Mech Destroyer Prequel flip book ... 2.95
❑4, Jun 2001 ... 2.95

Dark Regions
White Wolf

❑1, Feb 1987 ... 1.75
❑2, Apr 1987 ... 1.75
❑3, May 1987 ... 1.75

Darkseid (Villains)
DC

❑1, Feb 1998; New Year's Evil ... 1.95

Dark Shadows
Gold Key

❑1, Mar 1969, based on TV series ... 175.00
❑1/A, based on TV series; without poster ... 25.00
❑2, Aug 1969, Photo cover ... 48.00
❑3, Nov 1969, Includes poster; Photo cover ... 48.00
❑4, Feb 1970, Photo cover ... 25.00
❑5, May 1970, Photo cover ... 25.00
❑6, Aug 1970, Photo cover ... 25.00
❑7, Nov 1970, Photo cover ... 25.00
❑8, Feb 1971 ... 20.00
❑9, May 1971 ... 20.00
❑10, Aug 1971 ... 20.00
❑11, Nov 1971 ... 20.00
❑12, Feb 1972 ... 20.00
❑13, Apr 1972 ... 20.00
❑14, Jun 1972, Painted cover ... 20.00
❑15, Aug 1972 ... 20.00
❑16, Oct 1972 ... 20.00
❑17, Dec 1972 ... 12.00
❑18, Feb 1973 ... 12.00
❑19, Apr 1973 ... 12.00
❑20, Jun 1973 ... 12.00
❑21, Aug 1973 ... 10.00
❑22, Oct 1973 ... 10.00
❑23, Dec 1973 ... 10.00
❑24, Feb 1974 ... 10.00
❑25, Apr 1974 ... 10.00
❑26, Jun 1974 ... 10.00
❑27, Aug 1974 ... 10.00
❑28, Oct 1974 ... 10.00
❑29, Nov 1974 ... 10.00
❑30, Dec 1974 ... 10.00
❑31, Apr 1975 ... 10.00
❑32, Jun 1975 ... 10.00
❑33, Aug 1975 ... 10.00
❑34, Nov 1975 ... 10.00
❑35, Feb 1976 ... 10.00

Dark Shadows
Innovation

❑1, Jun 1992, TV series ... 3.00
❑2, Aug 1992, TV series ... 2.50
❑3, Nov 1992, TV series ... 2.50
❑4, Spr 1993, TV series ... 2.50
❑5, Jun 1993, Book 2, #1 ... 2.50
❑6, Jun 1993, Book 2, #2 ... 2.50
❑7, Jun 1993, Book 2, #3 ... 2.50

Dark Shrine
Antarctic

❑1, May 1999; Solo cover ... 2.99
❑2, Jun 1999 ... 2.50

Dark Shrine Gallery
Basement

❑1 ... 3.25

Darkside Blues
ADV Manga

❑1, Mar 2004 ... 14.98

Darkstalkers
Devil's Due

❑1 2004 ... 3.00
❑1/Variant 2004 ... 4.00
❑2 2004 ... 3.00
❑2/Variant 2004 ... 4.00
❑3 2005 ... 3.00
❑3/Variant 2005 ... 4.00
❑4 2005 ... 3.00
❑4/Variant 2005 ... 4.00
❑4/Foil 2005 ... 3.00
❑5 2005 ... 4.00
❑5/Variant 2005 ... 3.00
❑5/Foil 2005 ... 4.00

Darkstars
DC

❑0, Oct 1994; Series continued in Darkstars #24 ... 2.00
❑1, Oct 1992; 1: Darkstars ... 1.75
❑2, Nov 1992 ... 1.75
❑3, Dec 1992; V: Evil Star; Includes letters page from Hawkworld ... 1.75
❑4, Jan 1993; V: Evil Star ... 1.75
❑5, Feb 1993 ... 1.75
❑6, Mar 1993 ... 1.75
❑7, Apr 1993 ... 1.75
❑8, May 1993 ... 1.75
❑9, Jun 1993 ... 1.75
❑10, Jun 1993 ... 1.75
❑11, Aug 1993 ... 1.75
❑12, Sep 1993 ... 1.75
❑13, Oct 1993 ... 1.75
❑14, Nov 1993 ... 1.75
❑15, Dec 1993 ... 1.75
❑16, Jan 1994 ... 1.75
❑17, Feb 1994 ... 1.75
❑18, Mar 1994 ... 1.75
❑19, Apr 1994; Flash ... 1.75
❑20, May 1994; Flash ... 1.75
❑21, Jun 1994 ... 1.75
❑22, Jul 1994 ... 1.75
❑23, Aug 1994; Series continued in Darkstars #0, Donna Troy joins Darkstars ... 1.95
❑24, Sep 1994; Zero Hour ... 1.95
❑25, Nov 1994 ... 1.95
❑26, Dec 1994; V: Bolt; V: Sudden Death; V: Deadline; V: Powerhouse ... 1.95

❑27, Jan 1995; V: Bolt; V: Sudden Death; V: Deadline; V: Powerhouse 1.95
❑28, Feb 1995 1.95
❑29, Mar 1995 1.95
❑30, Apr 1995 1.95
❑31, Jun 1995 2.25
❑32, Jul 1995 2.25
❑33, Aug 1995 2.25
❑34, Sep 1995 2.25
❑35, Oct 1995 2.25
❑36, Nov 1995 2.25
❑37, Dec 1995; V: Guy Gardner 2.25
❑38, Jan 1996; Final Issue 2.25

Dark Tales of Daily Horror
Antarctic

❑1, Feb 1994, b&w 2.95

Dark Tower: The Gun slinger Born
Marvel

❑1, Apr 2007 5.00
❑2, May 2007; Open Letter from Stephen King; Maerlyn's Rainbow prose story by Robin Furth; Map of the Barony of Mejis; Jae Lee Sketchbook 3.99
❑3, Jun 2007; Jae Lee cover 3.99

Dark Visions
Pyramid

❑1, Nov 1986 2.00
❑2 2.00

Darkwing Duck
Disney

❑1, Nov 1991 1.50
❑2, Dec 1991 1.50
❑3, Jan 1992 1.50
❑4, Feb 1992 1.50

Dark Wolf
Eternity

❑1 1988, b&w 1.95
❑2 1988, b&w 1.95
❑3 1988, b&w 1.95
❑4 1988, b&w 1.95
❑5, Jun 1988, b&w 1.95
❑6 1988, b&w 1.95
❑7 1988, b&w 1.95
❑8 1988, b&w 1.95
❑9, b&w 1.95
❑10, b&w 1.95
❑11, b&w 1.95
❑12, b&w 1.95
❑13, b&w 1.95
❑14, b&w 1.95
❑Ann 1, b&w 2.25

Dark Wolf
Malibu

❑1 1.95
❑2, Aug 1987 1.95
❑3, Sep 1987 1.95
❑4, Oct 1987 1.95

Darque Passages
Valiant

❑1, Jan 1994; Was included with the Shadowman Trade Paperback 2.00

Darque Passages
Acclaim

❑1, Apr 1998 2.50
❑2, Jan 1998; No cover date; indicia says Jan 2.50
❑3, Feb 1998; No cover date; indicia says Feb 2.50
❑4, Mar 1998; No cover date; indicia says Mar 2.50

Darque Razor
London Night

❑1, Oct 1997; Adult 3.00

Dart
Image

❑1, Feb 1996 2.50
❑1/A, Feb 1996; alternate cover 2.50
❑2, Apr 1996 2.50
❑3, May 1996 2.50

Date with Debbi
DC

❑1, Feb 1969 16.00
❑2, Apr 1969 12.00
❑3, Jun 1969 10.00
❑4, Aug 1969 10.00
❑5, Oct 1969 10.00
❑6, Dec 1969 10.00
❑7, Feb 1970, Includes note from Dawn Giordano in "Debbi Makes the Teen Scene" 10.00
❑8, Apr 1970 10.00
❑9, Jun 1970 10.00
❑10, Aug 1970 10.00
❑11, Oct 1970 10.00
❑12, Dec 1970 10.00
❑13, Feb 1971 12.00
❑14, Apr 1971 12.00
❑15, Jun 1971 12.00
❑16, Aug 1971 12.00
❑17, Oct 1971 12.00
❑18, ca. 1972 10.00

Daughters of the Dragon
Marvel

❑1, Mar 2006 2.99
❑2, May 2006 2.99
❑3, Jun 2006 2.99
❑4, Jul 2006 2.99
❑5, Aug 2006 2.99
❑6, Sep 2006 2.99

Daughters of the Dragon: Deadly Hands
Marvel

❑1, Feb 2006 3.99

Daughters of Time 3-D
3-D Zone

❑1; NN 3.95

David & Goliath
Image

❑1, Sep 2003 2.95
❑2, Dec 2003 2.95
❑3, Jun 2004 2.95

David Cassidy
Charlton

❑1, Feb 1972, Photo cover 25.00
❑2, Mar 1972 16.00
❑3, May 1972 16.00
❑4, Jun 1972 16.00
❑5, Aug 1972 16.00
❑6, Sep 1972 14.00
❑7, Oct 1972 14.00
❑8, Nov 1972 14.00
❑9, Dec 1972 14.00
❑10, Feb 1973 12.00
❑11, Mar 1973 12.00
❑12, May 1973 12.00
❑13, Jul 1973 12.00
❑14, Sep 1973, Final Issue 12.00

David Chelsea in Love
Eclipse

❑1, b&w 3.50
❑2, b&w 3.50
❑3, b&w 3.50
❑4, b&w 3.50

David Shepherd's Song
Alias

❑1, Nov 2005 2.99
❑2, ca. 2005 2.99

David's Mighty Men
Alias

❑1, ca. 2005 4.99

Davy Crockett
Gold Key

❑1, Dec 1963 115.00
❑2, Nov 1969 30.00

Dawn
Sirius Entertainment

❑½, ca. 1996, Wizard mail-away 3.00
❑½/Variant, ca. 1996, Wizard mail-away; "Hey Kids" Variant cover 5.00
❑1, Jul 1995 3.00
❑1/Black, Jul 1995, blacklight edition; "Black light" cover 8.00
❑1/Sharp, Jul 1995, "White Trash" edition; Look Sharp Edition 6.00
❑1/Kids, Jul 1995, "Look Sharp" edition; Kids 5.00
❑2, Sep 1995 3.00
❑2/Mystery, Sep 1995, Signed, limited edition; Mystery Book 6.00
❑3, ca. 1996 3.00
❑4, ca. 1996 3.00
❑5, Sep 1996 3.00
❑6, Oct 1996 3.00

Dawn 15th anniversary Poster Book
Image

❑1, Dec 2004 4.95

Dawn 2004 Con Sketchbook One-Shot
Image

❑1, May 2004 2.95

Dawn Convention Sketch Book
Image

❑1, Apr 2003 2.95

Dawn: Convention Sketchbook
Image

❑1, Mar 2002 2.95

Dawn of the Dead (George Romero's)
Idea & Design Works

❑1, Apr 2004 3.99
❑2, May 2004 3.99
❑3, Jun 2004 3.99

Dawn Tenth Anniversary Special
Sirius Entertainment

❑1, Sep 1999 2.95

Dawn: The Return of the Goddess
Sirius Entertainment

❑1, Apr 1999 2.95
❑1/Ltd., Apr 1999; Limited edition 8.00
❑2, May 1999 2.95
❑3, Nov 1999 2.95
❑4, Jul 2000 2.95

Dawn: Three Tiers
Image

❑1, Jul 2003 2.95
❑2, Sep 2003 2.95
❑3, Feb 2004 2.95
❑4, Jul 2004 2.95
❑5, Feb 2005 2.95
❑6, Oct 2005 2.95

Daydreamers
Marvel

❑1, Aug 1997; gatefold summary; teams Howard the Duck, Man-Thing, Franklin Richards, Leech, Artie, and Tana 2.50
❑2, Sep 1997; gatefold summary 2.50
❑3, Oct 1997; gatefold summary 2.50

Day of Judgment
DC

❑1, Nov 1999 2.50
❑2, Nov 1999 2.50
❑3, Nov 1999, Purgatory 2.50
❑4, Nov 1999, D: Enchantress 2.50
❑5, Nov 1999, Hal Jordan becomes Spectre 2.50

Day of Judgment Secret Files
DC

❑1, Nov 1999; background on participants in event 4.95

Day of the Defenders
Marvel

❑1, Mar 2001; Reprints 3.50

Day of Vengeance
DC

❑1, Jun 2005, 1: Shadowpact; D: Black Bison II 10.00
❑1/Variant, Jun 2005 5.00
❑1/3rd variant, Jul 2005 6.00
❑2, Jul 2005 5.00
❑2/2nd variant, Jul 2005 4.00
❑3, Aug 2005 2.50
❑4, Sep 2005; O: Detective Chimp 2.50
❑5, Oct 2005 2.50
❑6, Nov 2005; D: Shazam 2.50

Day of Vengeance: Infinite Crisis Special
DC

❑1, Feb 206, Infinite Crisis Special; D: Nabu 3.99

Days of Wrath
Apple

❑1, Aug 1993, b&w 2.75
❑2, Oct 1993, b&w 2.75
❑3, Dec 1993, b&w 2.75
❑4, Jun 1994, b&w 2.75

Danger Girl

First Cliffhanger title was popular for a while

©Image

Daniel Boone

Fess Parker follows trail from TV to comics

©Gold Key

Darby O'Gill and the Little People

Sean Connery sings, but you can't hear him here

©Gold Key

Daredevil

Blind super-hero gets popular under Frank Miller

©Marvel

Daredevil (Vol. 2)

Kevin Smith relaunch got hot quickly

©Marvel

N-MINT

Dazzle
Tokyopop

❑1, Jan 2006 ..... 9.99

Dazzler
Marvel

❑1, Mar 1981, JR2 (a); O: Dazzler. A: X-Men. First Marvel direct market-only comic 5.00
❑2, Apr 1981, JR2 (c); JR2, AA (a); A: X-Men. V: Enchantress 1.50
❑3, May 1981, BA (c); JR2, BA (a); A: Doctor Doom. V: Doctor Doom 1.00
❑4, Jun 1981, FS (c); FS (a); V: Doctor Doom. V: Nightmare 1.00
❑5, Jul 1981, 1: Blue Shield 1.00
❑6, Aug 1981 ..... 1.00
❑7, Sep 1981 ..... 1.00
❑8, Oct 1981, V: Enforcers 1.00
❑9, Nov 1981, V: Klaw 1.00
❑10, Dec 1981, A: Galactus. V: Terrax 1.00
❑11, Jan 1982, A: Galactus. V: Terrax 1.00
❑12, Feb 1982 ..... 1.00
❑13, Mar 1982 ..... 1.00
❑14, Apr 1982 ..... 1.00
❑15, May 1982, BSz (c); FS (a) 1.00
❑16, Jun 1982, BSz (c); FS (a); V: Enchantress 1.00
❑17, Jul 1982, FS (c); FS (a); Angel 1.00
❑18, Aug 1982, BSz (c); FS (a); V: Absorbing Man 1.00
❑19, Sep 1982, V: Absorbing Man 1.00
❑20, Oct 1982, 1: Johnny Guitar 1.00
❑21, Nov 1982; Double-size; FS (a); Photo cover; ; O: Dazzler (Alison Blaire) 1.00
❑22, Dec 1982, A: Rogue. V: Rogue; V: Mystique; V: Destiny 1.00
❑23, Jan 1983 ..... 1.00
❑24, Feb 1983, V: Rogue 1.00
❑25, Mar 1983 ..... 1.00
❑26, May 1983, FS (a) 1.00
❑27, Jul 1983, BSz (c); FS (w); FS (a); V: Rogue 1.00
❑28, Sep 1983, BSz (c); FS (w); FS (a); A: Rogue. V: Rogue 1.00
❑29, Nov 1983, BSz (c); FS (w); FS (a) 1.00
❑30, Jan 1984, BSz (c); FS (a); Assistant Editor's Month 1.00
❑31, Mar 1984, BSz (c); FS (a) 1.00
❑32, Jun 1984, BSz (c); A: Inhumans. V: Moonstone; V: Blackout 1.00
❑33, Aug 1984, BSz (c) 1.00
❑34, Oct 1984, BSz (c) 1.00
❑35, Jan 1985, BSz (c); FS (a) 1.00
❑36, Mar 1985, JBy (c); V: Tatterdemalion 1.00
❑37, May 1985 ..... 1.00
❑38, Jul 1985, A: X-Men. 1: O.Z. Chase 1.00
❑39, Sep 1985 ..... 1.00
❑40, Nov 1985, Secret Wars II 1.00
❑41, Jan 1986 ..... 1.00
❑42, Mar 1986; Final Issue 1.00

DC 100-Page Super Spectacular: World's Greatest Super-Heroes
DC / Wildstorm

❑1, Jul 2004 ..... 6.95

DC Challenge
DC

❑1, Nov 1985 JOy (c); ME (w); GC (a) 1.50
❑2, Dec 1985 ..... 1.50
❑3, Jan 1986 CI (a) 1.50
❑4, Feb 1986 GK, KJ (a) 1.50
❑5, Mar 1986 DaG (a) 1.50
❑6, Apr 1986 ..... 1.50
❑7, May 1986 JSa (a) 1.50
❑8, Jun 1986 DG (a) 1.50
❑9, Jul 1986 DH (a) 1.50
❑10, Aug 1986 CS (a) 1.50
❑11, Sep 1986 KG, RT (a) 1.50
❑12, Oct 1986; JOy (c); ME (w); GP, LMc, RA (a); 48 pg 2.00

DC Comics Presents
DC

❑1, Jul 1978, JL, DA (a); Flash 9.00
❑1/Whitman, Jul 1978, JL, DA (a); Flash; Whitman variant 14.00
❑2, Sep 1978, JL, DA (a); Flash 7.00
❑2/Whitman, Sep 1978, JL, DA (a); Flash; Whitman variant 12.00
❑3, Oct 1978, JL (a); Adam Strange 4.00
❑3/Whitman, Oct 1978, JL (a); Adam Strange; Whitman variant 8.00
❑4, Dec 1978, JL (a); Metal Men 2.00
❑4/Whitman, Dec 1978, JL (a); Metal Men; Whitman variant 4.00
❑5, Jan 1979, MA (a); Aquaman 2.00
❑6, Feb 1979, RA (c); CS (a); Green Lantern 6.00
❑7, Mar 1979, DD (a); Red Tornado 2.00
❑8, Apr 1979, MA (a); Swamp Thing 2.00
❑9, May 1979, RA (c); JSa (a); Wonder Woman 2.00
❑9/Whitman, May 1979 ..... 6.00
❑10, Jun 1979, RA (c); JSa (a); Sgt. Rock 2.00
❑10/Whitman, Jun 1979, JSa (a); Sgt. Rock; Whitman variant 4.00
❑11, Jul 1979, RA (c); JSa (a); Hawkman 2.00
❑11/Whitman, Jul 1979, JSa (a); Hawkman; Whitman variant 4.00
❑12, Aug 1979, RA (c); RB, DG (a); Mr. Miracle 2.00
❑12/Whitman, Aug 1979, RB, DG (a); Mr. Miracle; Whitman variant 4.00
❑13, Sep 1979, DG, DD (a); Legion of Super-Heroes 2.00
❑14, Oct 1979, DG, DD (a); Superboy 1.50
❑14/Whitman, Oct 1979, DG, DD (a); Superboy; Whitman variant 3.00
❑15, Nov 1979, JSa (c); JSa (a); Atom 1.50
❑15/Whitman, Nov 1979, JSa (a); Atom; Whitman variant 3.00
❑16, Dec 1979, Black Lightning 1.50
❑16/Whitman, Dec 1979, Black Lightning; Whitman variant 3.00
❑17, Jan 1980, JL (a); Firestorm 1.50
❑18, Feb 1980, RA (c); DD (a); Zatanna 1.50
❑19, Mar 1980, RA (c); JSa (a); Batgirl 1.50
❑19/Whitman, Mar 1980, JSa (a); Batgirl; Whitman variant 3.00
❑20, Apr 1980, RA (c); JL (a); Green Arrow 1.50
❑20/Whitman, Apr 1980, JL (a); Green Arrow; Whitman variant 3.00
❑21, May 1980, RA (c); JSa (a); Elongated Man 1.50
❑21/Whitman, May 1980, JSa (a); Elongated Man; Whitman variant 3.00
❑22, Jun 1980, Captain Comet 1.50
❑22/Whitman, Jun 1980, Whitman variant 3.00
❑23, Jul 1980, RA (c); JSa (a); Doctor Fate 1.50
❑24, Aug 1980, JL (a); Deadman 1.50
❑25, Sep 1980, Phantom Stranger 1.50
❑26, Oct 1980, JSn (c); JSn (w); JSn, GP (a); 1: New Teen Titans. 1: Raven. 1: Starfire II (Koriand'r). 1: Cyborg. Green Lantern 14.00
❑27, Nov 1980, JSn, RT (a); 1: Mongul. Martian Manhunter; Congorilla back-up 2.50
❑28, Dec 1980, JSn, GK (a); V: Mongul. Supergirl; Johnny Thunder Lawman back-up 1.50
❑29, Jan 1981, JSn, RT (a); Spectre 1.50
❑30, Feb 1981, RB (c); CS (a); Black Canary 1.50
❑31, Mar 1981, RA (c); DG, JL (a); Robin; Robotman back-up 1.50
❑32, Apr 1981, Wonder Woman 1.50
❑33, May 1981, Captain Marvel 1.50
❑34, Jun 1981, Marvel Family 1.50
❑35, Jul 1981, RA (c); GK, CS (a); Man-Bat 1.50
❑36, Aug 1981, JSn (a); Starman 1.50
❑37, Sep 1981, JSn (w); JSn, RT (a); Hawkgirl; Rip Hunter back-up 1.50
❑38, Oct 1981, D: Crimson Avenger. Flash 1.50
❑39, Nov 1981, RA (c); JSn, JSa (a); A: Toyman. V: Toyman 1.50
❑40, Dec 1981, Metamorpho 1.50
❑41, Jan 1982, 1: new Wonder Woman. A: Joker. V: Prankster; Wonder Woman insert; Contains untitled Wonder Woman 16-page insert 2.25
❑42, Feb 1982, Unknown Soldier; Golden Age Sandman back-up 1.25
❑43, Mar 1982, BB (c); CS (a); Legion 1.25
❑44, Apr 1982, A: Joker. Dial 'H' for Hero 2.25
❑45, May 1982, RA (c); RB (a); Firestorm 1.25
❑46, Jun 1982, 1: Global Guardians 1.25
❑47, Jul 1982, 1: Masters of Universe 17.00
❑48, Aug 1982, Aquaman; Black Pirate back-up 1.25
❑49, Sep 1982, RB (a); Captain Marvel 1.25
❑50, Oct 1982, RB (c); CS (a); Clark Kent 1.25
❑51, Nov 1982, FMc, CS (a); Atom 6.00
❑52, Dec 1982, KG (a); 1: Ambush Bug. Doom Patrol 2.50
❑53, Jan 1983, 1: Atari Force. House of Mystery 1.00
❑54, Feb 1983, DN (c); DN (a); Green Arrow, Black Canary 1.00
❑55, Mar 1983, A: Superboy. V: Parasite. Air Wave 1.00
❑56, Apr 1983, GK (c); CS (a); 1: Maaldor the Darklord. Power Girl 1.00
❑57, May 1983, Atomic Knights 1.00
❑58, Jun 1983, GK (c); CS (a); 1: The Untouchables (DC). Robin, Elongated Man 1.00
❑59, Jul 1983, KG (w); KG (a); Legion of Super-Heroes, Ambush Bug 1.00
❑60, Aug 1983, Guardians of the Universe 1.00
❑61, Sep 1983, OMAC 1.00
❑62, Oct 1983, Freedom Fighters 1.00
❑63, Nov 1983, Amethyst 1.00
❑64, Dec 1983; Kamandi 1.00
❑65, Jan 1984; Madame Xanadu 1.00
❑66, Feb 1984; JKu (c); JK, JKu (a); 1: Blackbriar Thorn. Demon 1.00
❑67, Mar 1984; V: Toyman. Santa Claus 1.00
❑68, Apr 1984; GK (c); MA, CS (a); Vixen 1.00

N-MINT | N-MINT | N-MINT

❑69, May 1984; IN (c); ME (w); IN (a); Blackhawk ... 1.00
❑70, Jun 1984; Metal Men ... 1.00
❑71, Jul 1984; CS (a); Bizarro ... 1.00
❑72, Aug 1984; Phantom Stranger, Joker 1.50
❑73, Sep 1984; CI (a); Flash ... 1.00
❑74, Oct 1984; Hawkman ... 1.00
❑75, Nov 1984; Arion ... 1.00
❑76, Dec 1984; A: Monitor. Wonder Woman ... 1.00
❑77, Jan 1985; 1: The Forgotten Villains. Animal Man, Dolphin, Congorilla, Cave Carson, Immortal Man, Rip Hunter, Rick Flagg ... 3.00
❑78, Feb 1985; Animal Man, Dolphin, Congorilla, Cave Carson, Immortal Man, Rip Hunter, Rick Flagg ... 3.00
❑79, Mar 1985; Clark Kent ... 1.00
❑80, Apr 1985; Legion ... 1.00
❑81, May 1985; V: Kobra. Ambush Bug . 1.00
❑82, Jun 1985; Adam Strange ... 1.00
❑83, Jul 1985; Outsiders ... 1.00
❑84, Aug 1985; Challengers of the Unknown ... 1.00
❑85, Sep 1985; AMo (w); Swamp Thing 6.00
❑86, Oct 1985; V: Blackstarr. Crisis; Supergirl ... 4.00
❑87, Nov 1985; 1: Superboy of Earth-Prime. Crisis ... 1.25
❑88, Dec 1985; KG (a); Crisis ... 1.00
❑89, Jan 1986; Omega Men ... 1.00
❑90, Feb 1986; O: Captain Atom. Firestorm ... 1.00
❑91, Mar 1986; Captain Comet ... 1.00
❑92, Apr 1986; Vigilante ... 1.00
❑93, May 1986; Plastic Man, Elongated Man, Elastic Lad ... 2.00
❑94, Jun 1986; Harbinger, Lady Quark, Pariah ... 1.00
❑95, Jul 1986; Hawkman ... 1.00
❑96, Aug 1986; Blue Devil ... 1.00
❑97, Sep 1986; Double-size; A: Bizarro. A: Mxyzptlk. V: Phantom Zone Criminals; Final Issue ... 1.25
❑Ann 1, ca. 1982; RB (c); RB (a); Superman & E-2 Superman ... 3.00
❑Ann 2, ca. 1983; O: Superwoman. 1: Superwoman ... 3.00
❑Ann 3, ca. 1984; Doctor Sivana gains the Shazam! powers ... 3.00
❑Ann 4, ca. 1985; A: Superwoman. ca. 1985 ... 3.00

DC Comics Presents: Batman
DC

❑1, Sep 2004; V: Clayface; V: Scarecrow; V: Two-Face; Julie Schwartz tribute issue, Batman #183 ... 2.50

DC Comics Presents: Green Lantern
DC

❑1, Sep 2004; V: Grodd ... 2.50

DC Comics Presents: Hawkman
DC

❑1, Sep 2004; Julie Schwartz tribute issue, Hawkman #6 Tribute ... 2.50

DC Comics Presents: JLA
DC

❑1, Oct 2004 ... 2.50

DC Comics Presents: Mystery in Space
DC

❑1, Sep 2004; Julie Schwartz tribute issue, Mystery in Space #82 ... 2.50

DC Comics Presents: Superman
DC

❑1, Oct 2004 ... 2.50

DC Comics Presents: The Atom
DC

❑1, Oct 2004; V: Chronos; Julie Schwartz tribute issue, Atom #10 ... 2.50

DC Comics Presents: The Flash
DC

❑1, Oct 2004 ... 2.50

DC Countdown
DC

❑1, May 2005; D: Blue Beetle. D: Blue Beetle II (Ted Kord); V: Maxwell Lord; D: Blue Beetle (Ted Kord) ... 6.00
❑1/2nd, May 2005; Second print ... 3.00

DC First: Batgirl/Joker
DC

❑1, Jul 2002 ... 3.50

DC First: Flash/Superman
DC

❑1, Jul 2002, V: Abra Kadabra ... 3.50

DC First: Green Lantern/Green Lantern
DC

❑1, Jul 2002 ... 3.50

DC First: Superman/Lobo
DC

❑1, Jul 2002 ... 3.50

DC Graphic Novel
DC

❑1; Star Raiders ... 5.95
❑2; Warlords ... 5.95
❑3; Medusa Chain ... 5.95
❑4, Jan 1985; Hunger Dogs ... 5.95
❑5; Me and Joe Priest ... 5.95
❑6; Metalzoic ... 6.95
❑7; Space Clusters ... 5.95

DC/Marvel: All Access
DC

❑1, Dec 1996; BG (a); A: Superman, Spider-Man, Venom. crossover with Marvel ... 2.95
❑2, Jan 1997; BG (a); A: Jubilee, Robin, Two-Face, Scorpion. crossover with Marvel ... 2.95
❑3, Jan 1997; BG (a); A: Jubilee, Robin, Batman, Doctor Strange, Scorpion, JLA, X-Men. crossover with Marvel ... 2.95
❑4, Feb 1997; BG (a); A: JLA, X-Men, Doctor Strangefate, Amalgam universe. crossover with Marvel ... 2.95

DC/Marvel Crossover Classics IV
DC

❑1, ca. 2003 ... 14.95

DC 100 Page Super Spectacular
DC

❑4, ca. 1971, BWr (c); MM, SA, BWr, MD, CI, JM, NC (a); Weird Mystery Tales; reprints; back cover pin-up ... 175.00
❑5, ca. 1971, BO, MD, RE (a); Love Stories; back cover pin-up ... 350.00
❑5/2nd; Replica edition; BO, MD, RE (a); Love Stories ... 7.00
❑6, ca. 1971, World's Greatest Super-Heroes; reprints JLA #21-22; wraparound cover ... 150.00
❑7, Dec 1971, really DC-7; a.k.a. Superman #245; back cover pin-up ... 60.00
❑8, Jan 1972, really DC-8;a.k.a. Batman #238; wraparound cover ... 75.00
❑9, Feb 1972, really DC-9; a.k.a. Our Army at War #242; Sgt. Rock, wraparound cover ... 75.00
❑10, Mar 1972, really DC-10; a.k.a. Adventure Comics #416; Supergirl; wraparound cover ... 60.00
❑11, Apr 1972, really DC-11; a.k.a. Flash #214; wraparound cover ... 60.00
❑12, May 1972, really DC-12; a.k.a. Superboy #185; wraparound cover ... 60.00
❑13, Jun 1972, really DC-13; a.k.a. Superman #252; wraparound cover ... 60.00
❑14, Feb 1973, really DC-14; Batman; wraparound cover ... 45.00
❑15, Mar 1973, really DC-15; Superboy; back cover pin-up ... 45.00
❑16, Apr 1973, really DC-16; Sgt. Rock; back cover cover gallery ... 45.00
❑17, Jun 1973, NC (c); CI, JKu (a); really DC-17; JLA; back cover cover gallery. 45.00
❑18, Jul 1973, Superman's 35th anniversary; NC (c); MA, GK, CS, KS (a); really DC-18; back cover cover gallery; Superman cast, Golden Age Atom, TNT, Hourman, Captain Triumph; Reprints from Superman #25, #97, & #162, Flash Comics #90, Atom #8, World's Finest Comics #5, Adventure #57, and Crack Comics #42 ... 30.00
❑19, Aug 1973, JKu (c); RM, (w); RM (a); really DC-19; Tarzan; back cover pin-up 24.00
❑20, Sep 1973, O: Two-Face. really DC-20; Batman; back cover cover gallery. 35.00
❑21, Oct 1973, really DC-21; Superboy; back cover cover gallery ... 22.00
❑22, Nov 1973, really DC-22; Flash; Super Specs become part of individual series beginning with Shazam! #8 ... 22.00

DC One Million
DC

❑1, Nov 1998; V: Solaris; V: Vandal Savage 2.95
❑2, Nov 1998; V: Vandal Savage ... 2.00
❑3, Nov 1998; V: Vandal Savage ... 2.00
❑4, Nov 1998; V: Solaris; V: Vandal Savage 2.00
❑GS 1, Aug 1999; 80-Page Giant ... 4.95

DC Sampler
DC

❑1, Sep 1983; Promotional giveaway; CI, KG, JDu, JOy, GP, PB, DH, JKu, GK, JA (a); no cover price ... 1.50
❑2, Sep 1984; Promotional giveaway; AMo (w); TS, FH, GC, KG, JOy, GP, TVE, RA, JA, JL (a); No cover price; Atari Force, etc. ... 1.00
❑3, Jan 1985; Promotional giveaway; FH (c); AMo (w); DaG, FH, JOy, DG, JK, CS, JA, RE (a); No cover price; The Saga of the Swamp Thing, etc. ... 1.00

DC Science Fiction Graphic Novel
DC

❑1; Hell on Earth ... 5.95
❑2; Nightwings ... 5.95
❑3; ca. 1985 ... 5.95
❑4; Merchants Venus ... 6.00
❑5; Adaptation of 1960s Outer Limits TV episode; ca. 1986 ... 5.95
❑6; Magic Goes Away ... 5.95
❑7; Sand Kings ... 5.95

DC Silver Age Classics Action Comics
DC

❑252; reprints Action Comics #252 ... 1.00

DC Silver Age Classics Adventure Comics
DC

❑247; reprints Adventure Comics #247 . 1.00

DC Silver Age Classics Detective Comics
DC

❑225; reprints Detective Comics #225 ... 1.00
❑327; reprints Detective Comics #327 ... 1.00

DC Silver Age Classics Green Lantern
DC

❑76; reprints Green Lantern #76 ... 1.00

DC Silver Age Classics House of Secrets
DC

❑92; reprints House of Secrets #92 ... 1.00

DC Silver Age Classics Showcase
DC

❑4; reprints Showcase #4 ... 1.00
❑22; reprints Showcase #22 ... 1.00

DC Silver Age Classics Sugar & Spike
DC

❑99; DG (w); not a reprint;first publication of Sugar and Spike #99 ... 2.00

DC Silver Age Classics The Brave and the Bold
DC

❑28; 1: JLA. 1: The Justice League of America. reprints The Braveand the Bold #28 ... 1.25

DC Special
DC

❑1, Dec 1968; CI (a); Flash, Batman, Adam Strange ... 60.00
❑2, Mar 1969; teen ... 50.00
❑3, Jun 1969; ATh, CI, GK, JM (a); All female issue; Wonder Woman, Green Lantern/Star Sapphire, Green Arrow/Black Canary, Supergirl/Black Flame; Reprints stories from Green Lantern (2nd series) #16 and Action #304 ... 35.00
❑4, Sep 1969; NA (c); GC, CI, JK (a); Partial reprint from Tales of the Unexpected #16 ... 25.00
❑5, Dec 1969; Sgt. Rock: Our Army at War #113; Showcase #2; Hawkman: Brave and the Bold #35; Viking Prince: Brave and the Bold #18; The Secret Lives of Joe Kubert ... 20.00

Other grades: Multiply price above by 5/6 for VF/NM • 2/3 for VERY FINE • 1/3 for FINE • 1/5 for VERY GOOD • 1/8 for GOOD

Daredevil/Black Widow: Abattoir

Terrifying 1993 graphic novel reunion

©Marvel

Daredevil: Father

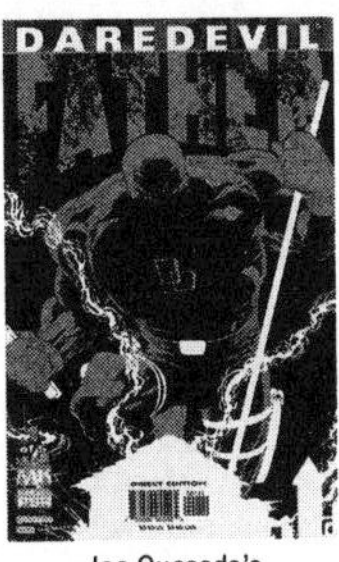

Joe Quesada's take on Daredevil

©Marvel

Daredevil: Ninja

Ninja steals from under Daredevil's nose

©Marvel

Daredevil: Yellow

Jeph Loeb and Tim Sale "color" mini-series

©Marvel

Daring New Adventures of Supergirl

Series continues as simply "Supergirl"

©DC

N-MINT

❑6, Mar 1970; Daniel Boone: Legends of Daniel Boone #1; Tomahawk: World's Finest Comics #69; Davy Crockett: Frontier Fighters #4; Kit Carson: Frontier Fighters #4; Buffalo Bill: Frontier Fighters #1; Pow Wow Smith: Detective Comics #178; The Wild Frontier 20.00
❑7, Jun 1970; Strange Sports 20.00
❑8, Sep 1970; Wanted 20.00
❑9, Dec 1970; CI (a); Brave and the Bold #45; Brave and the Bold #46; Brave and the Bold #47; Brave and the Bold #48; Strangest Sports Stories Ever Told 20.00
❑10, Feb 1971; Gang Busters #61; Gang Busters #58; Showcase #5; Gang Busters #40; Showcase #1; Gang Busters #65; StopÖYou Can't Beat the Law 20.00
❑11, Apr 1971; Monsters 20.00
❑12, Jun 1971; JKu, RH, IN (a); Viking Prince 20.00
❑13, Aug 1971; Strange Sports 20.00
❑14, Oct 1971; Giant-size; Wanted: The World's Most Dangerous Villains 20.00
❑15, Dec 1971; Giant-size; O: Woozy Winks. O: Plastic Man (Golden Age). Plastic Man reprints 16.00
❑16, Spr 1975, CI, RA (a); Gorillas 10.00
❑17, Sum 1975, Reprints Green Lantern (2nd Series) #2; 26; Summer 1975 .... 10.00
❑18, Nov 1975, Earth-Shaking Stories 10.00
❑19, Jan 1976, Superman: Action Comics #343; Green Lantern: Green Lantern (2nd Series) #53; Strange Adventures #28; Wonder Woman: Wonder Woman #106; War Against the Giants 10.00
❑20, Mar 1976, Green Lantern 10.00
❑21, May 1976, Monsters, War That Time Forgot 10.00
❑22, Jul 1976, Three Musketeers, Robin Hood 10.00
❑23, Sep 1976, Three Musketeers, Robin Hood 10.00
❑24, Oct 1976, Robin Hood, Viking Prince 10.00
❑25, Dec 1976, Robin Hood, Viking Prince 10.00
❑26, Feb 1977, Enemy Ace 10.00
❑27, Apr 1977, Captain Comet 10.00
❑28, Jun 1977, Batman; new Legion of Super-Heroes story 10.00
❑29, Sep 1977, NA (c); BL, JSa (a); O: Justice Society of America (Secret Origin); Hawkman I appearnce 12.00

DC Special Blue Ribbon Digest
DC

❑1, Apr 1980; Legion of Super Heroes 5.00
❑2, Jun 1980; Flash 4.00
❑3, Aug 1980; Justice Society 4.00
❑4, Oct 1980; Green Lantern 4.00
❑5, Dec 1980; Secret Origins 4.00
❑6, Jan 1981; DG, NC (c); AA, TD, JA (a); House of Mystery 3.00
❑7, Mar 1981; Flying Tigers, Haunted Tank, War That Time Forgot, Enemy Ace 3.00
❑8, Apr 1981; Legion 3.00
❑9, May 1981; The Atom 3.00
❑10, Jun 1981; Warlord 3.00
❑11, Jul 1981; Justice League, Justice Society, Seven Soldiers 3.00
❑12, Aug 1981; Haunted Tank 3.00
❑13, Sep 1981; Strange Sports 3.00
❑14, Oct 1981; Science Fiction 3.00
❑15, Nov 1981; Superboy, Green Lantern, Batman 3.00
❑16, Dec 1981; Green Lantern/Green Arrow 3.00
❑17, Jan 1982; Mystery 3.00
❑18, Feb 1982; Sgt. Rock 4.00
❑19, Mar 1982; Reprints My Greatest Adventure #80 and Doom Patrol #86, 90 and 91 .... 3.00
❑20, Apr 1982; Mystery 7.00
❑21, May 1982; ATh, JK, JKu, RA, RH, RE (a); War 3.00
❑22, Jun 1982; Secret Origins 3.00
❑23, Jul 1982; Green Arrow 3.00

DC Special Series
DC

❑1, Sep 1977; NA (c); FMc, MN, JSa, DD, JR, JA, IN (a); 5-Star Super-Hero Spectacular 10.00
❑2, Sep 1977, BWr (a); Swamp Thing reprint;Swamp Thing 7.00
❑3, Oct 1977, JK (a); Sgt. Rock 7.00
❑4, Oct 1977; Unexpected Ann 7.00
❑5, Nov 1977; A: Superman. A: Luthor. A: Brainiac. a.k.a. Superman Spectacular; first DC Dollar Comic; Superman, Luthor 7.00
❑6, Nov 1977, JLA 6.00
❑7, Dec 1977, AN (a); Ghosts 6.00
❑8, Feb 1978, JA (c); DG, RE (a); Brave & Bold 6.00
❑9, Mar 1978; SD, RH (a); Wonder Woman vs. Hitler 16.00
❑10, Apr 1978, DN, MN, JSa (a); Super-Heroes 6.00
❑11, May 1978; MA, WW, KS, IN (a); A: Johnny Quick. Flash; a.k.a. Flash Spectacular 6.00
❑12, Jun 1978; Secrets of Haunted House 6.00
❑13, Jul 1978; Sgt. Rock 6.00
❑14, Jul 1978, Swamp Thing reprint 6.00
❑15, Aug 1978; Batman, Ra's al Ghul 8.00
❑16, Sep 1978; RH (a); D: Jonah Hex; Bat Lash; Scalphunter 20.00
❑17, Sep 1979; Swamp Thing reprint 5.00
❑18, Oct 1979; digest Sgt. Rock; Sgt. Rock's Prize Battle Tales Digest 5.00
❑19, Oct 1979; digest; O: Wonder Woman. Secret Origins 6.00
❑20, Jan 1980; BWr (w); BWr (a); Swamp Thing reprint; a.k.a. Original Swamp Thing Saga 6.00
❑21, Mar 1980; FM, RT (a); Batman; Legion; 1st Frank Miller Batman 12.00
❑22, Sep 1980; G.I. Combat 6.00
❑23, Feb 1981; digest; Flash 6.00
❑24, Feb 1981; Flash 6.00
❑25, Sum 1981; treasury-sized; Superman II movie adaptation 6.00
❑26, Sum 1981; treasury-sized; RA, RT (a); Superman's Fortress 6.00
❑27, Dec 1981; treasury-sized; Batman vs. The Incredible Hulk 18.00

DC Special: The Return of Donna Troy
DC

❑1, Aug 2005 .... 8.00
❑2, Sep 2005 .... 5.00
❑3, Oct 2005 .... 2.99
❑4, Oct 2005; Prelude to Infinite Crisis 2.99

DC Spotlight
DC

❑1, Sep 1985; JL (c); Previews of Crisis on Infinite Earths, Who's Who, DC Challenge, Mask, Nathaniel Dusk, Outsiders, Hex, Legion of Super-Heroes, New Teen Titans, Swamp Thing, Omega Men, Super Powers, Batman: The Dark Knight, Watchmen, and others 1.00

DC Super-Stars
DC

❑1, Mar 1976, Double-size; GK, NC (a); Teen Titans reprint 10.00
❑2, Apr 1976, Double-size; Space 5.00
❑3, May 1976, CS (a); A: Legion of Super-Heroes. Superman; Reprints Legion of Super-Heroes story from Adventure Comics #354 and #355 .... 5.00
❑4, Jun 1976, Super-Stars of Space; Adam Strange reprint from Mystery in Space #91; Space Ranger reprint from Tales of the Unexpected #45; Captain Comet reprint from Strange Adventures #14 .... 2.00
❑5, Jul 1976, Flash;Bicentennial #33 .... 10.00
❑6, Aug 1976, Reprints from Mystery In Space #45, 88, World's Finest Comics #113, Strange Adventures #17; Super Stars of Space 2.00
❑7, Sep 1976, Reprints from Aquaman #37, Teen Titans #30; Aquaman 2.00
❑8, Oct 1976, Reprints Showcase #15 .... 4.00
❑9, Nov 1976, Man Behind the Gun 2.00
❑10, Dec 1976, A: Joker. Sports stories and Batman story 5.00
❑11, Jan 1977, Reprints from Adventure Comics #413-415; Flash #128; Super-Stars of Magic 7.00
❑12, Feb 1977, Reprints Adventure Comics #240; Superboy; Lead story new; Back-up reprints Adventure Comics #240 .... 2.00
❑13, Mar 1977, SA (w); SA (a); Spotlight on Sergio Aragones 2.00
❑14, May 1977, O: Doctor Light. O: Braniac. O: Two-Face. O: Gorilla Grodd. O: Shark. O: Brainiac (text); O: Doctor Light; O: Grodd; O: Shark (text); Secret Origins of Super-Villains; First all-new issue; 68 pages 4.00
❑15, Jul 1977, war stories 4.00
❑16, Sep 1977, DN (c); DN, BL (a); 1: Star Hunters 3.00
❑17, Nov 1977, JSa (c); BL, JSa (w); BL, MGr, JSa (a); O: Green Arrow. O: The Huntress II (Helena Wayne). Secret Origins; Legion story 16.00
❑18, Jan 1978, Deadman, Phantom Stranger 2.00

DC: The New Frontier
DC

❑1, Jan 2004 .... 6.95
❑2, Apr 2004 .... 6.95
❑3, May 2004 .... 6.95
❑4, Jul 2004 .... 6.95
❑5, Sep 2004 .... 6.95
❑6, Oct 2004 .... 6.95

DC 2000
DC

❑1 2000 .... 6.95
❑2 2000 .... 6.95

N-MINT

DCU: Brave New World
DC

❑1, Sep 2006, Introduces new series OMAC 1.00

DCU Heroes Secret Files
DC

❑1, Feb 1999 4.95

DCU Infinite Christmas Special
DC

❑1, Feb 2007 4.99

DC Universe Holiday Bash
DC

❑1, Jan 1997; Preview edition; JA, MWa (w); SB, KN, JA (a); Holiday special for 1996 season 3.95
❑2, Jan 1998; prestige format; Holiday special for 1997 season 4.95
❑3, Jan 1999; Signed edition; Holiday special for 1998 season 4.95

DC Universe: Trinity
DC

❑1, Aug 1993; foil cover 2.95
❑2, Sep 1993; foil cover 2.95

DCU Villains Secret Files
DC

❑1, Apr 1999 4.95

D-Day
Avalon

❑1 2.95

DDP Quarterly
Devil's Due

❑1, Sep 2006, Fall 2006 Sneak Peeks 1.00

Dead
Arrow

❑1, Jan 1993 2.95
❑1/A; alternate cover 2.95
❑2 2.95
❑3 2.95

Dead
Arrow

❑1 2.95

Dead Air
Slave Labor

❑1 5.95

Dead@17
Viper

❑0 2003 27.00
❑1, Nov 2003 35.00
❑2, Dec 2003 22.00
❑3, Jan 2004 10.00
❑4, Feb 2004 7.00

Dead@17: Blood of Saints
Viper

❑1, Apr 2004 2.95
❑2, May 2004 2.95
❑3, Jun 2004 2.95
❑4, Jul 2004 2.95

Dead@17: Protectorate
Viper

❑1, Oct 2005 2.95
❑2, Nov 2005 2.95
❑3, Dec 2005 2.95

Dead@17: Revolution
Viper

❑1, Nov 2004 4.00
❑2, Dec 2004 2.95
❑3, Jan 2005 2.95
❑4, Mar 2005 2.95

Dead@17: Rough Cut
Viper

❑1, Jan 2004 2.95

Deadbeats
Claypool

❑1, Jun 1992, b&w RHo (w); RHo (a) 4.00
❑2, Jul 1992, b&w RHo (w); RHo (a) 3.00
❑3, Sep 1992, b&w RHo (w); RHo (a) 3.00
❑4, Oct 1992, b&w RHo (w); RHo (a) 3.00
❑5, Sep 1993, b&w RHo (w); RHo (a) 3.00
❑6, Mar 1994, b&w RHo (w); RHo (a) 2.50
❑7, Jun 1994, b&w RHo (w); RHo (a) 2.50
❑8, Aug 1994, b&w RHo (w); RHo (a) 2.50
❑9, Nov 1994, b&w 2.50
❑10, Jan 1995, b&w 2.50
❑11, Mar 1995, b&w 2.50
❑12, May 1995, b&w 2.50
❑13, Jul 1995, b&w 2.50
❑14, Sep 1995, b&w 2.50
❑15, Nov 1995, b&w 2.50
❑16, Jan 1996, b&w 2.50
❑17, Mar 1996, b&w 2.50
❑18, May 1996, b&w 2.50
❑19, Jul 1996, b&w 2.50
❑20, Sep 1996, b&w 2.50
❑21, Nov 1996, b&w 2.50
❑22, Jan 1997, b&w 2.50
❑23, Mar 1997, b&w 2.50
❑24, May 1997, b&w 2.50
❑25, Jul 1997, b&w 2.50
❑26, Sep 1997, b&w RHo (w) 2.50
❑27, Nov 1997, b&w RHo (w) 2.50
❑28, Jan 1998, b&w RHo (w); RHo (a) 2.50
❑29, Mar 1998, b&w 2.50
❑30, May 1998, b&w 2.50
❑31, Jul 1998, b&w 2.50
❑32, Oct 1998, b&w 2.50
❑33, Dec 1998, b&w 2.50
❑34, Feb 1999, b&w 2.50
❑35, Apr 1999, b&w 2.50
❑36, Jun 1999, b&w 2.50
❑37, Aug 1999, b&w 2.50
❑38, Oct 1999, b&w 2.50
❑39, Dec 1999, b&w 2.50
❑40, Feb 2000, b&w 2.50
❑41, Apr 2000, b&w 2.50
❑42, Jun 2000, b&w 2.50
❑43, Aug 2000, b&w RHo (w); RHo (a) 2.50
❑44, Oct 2000, b&w 2.50
❑45, Dec 2000, b&w 2.50
❑46, Feb 2001, b&w 2.50
❑47, Apr 2001, b&w 2.50
❑48, Jun 2001, b&w 2.50
❑49, Aug 2001, b&w 2.50
❑50, Oct 2001, b&w 2.50
❑51, Dec 2001, b&w 2.50
❑52, Feb 2002, b&w 2.50
❑53, Apr 2002, b&w 2.50
❑54, Jun 2002, b&w 2.50
❑55, Aug 2002, b&w 2.50
❑56, Oct 2002, b&w 2.50
❑57, Dec 2002, b&w 2.50
❑58, Feb 2003, b&w 2.50
❑59, Apr 2003, b&w 2.50
❑60, Jun 2003, b&w 2.50
❑61, Aug 2003, b&w 2.50
❑62, Oct 2003, b&w 2.50
❑63, Dec 2003, b&w 2.50
❑64, Feb 2004, b&w 2.50
❑65, Apr 2004, b&w 2.50
❑66, Jun 2004, b&w 2.50
❑67, Aug 2004, b&w 2.50
❑68, Oct 2004 2.50

Dead Clown
Malibu

❑1, Oct 1996 2.50
❑2, Nov 1993 2.50
❑3, Feb 1994 2.50

Dead Corps(E)
DC / Helix

❑1, Sep 1998 2.50
❑2, Oct 1998 2.50
❑3, Nov 1998 2.50
❑4, Dec 1998 2.50

Deadenders
DC / Vertigo

❑1, Mar 2000 2.50
❑2, Apr 2000 2.50
❑3, May 2000 2.50
❑4, Jun 2000 2.50
❑5, Jul 2000 2.50
❑6, Aug 2000 2.50
❑7, Sep 2000 2.50
❑8, Oct 2000 2.50
❑9, Nov 2000 2.50
❑10, Dec 2000 2.50
❑11, Jan 2001 2.50
❑12, Feb 2001 2.50
❑13, Mar 2001 2.50
❑14, Apr 2001 2.50
❑15, May 2001 2.50
❑16, Jun 2001 2.50

Dead Eyes Open
Slave Labor

❑1 2005, b&w 2.95
❑2, Oct 2005, b&w 2.95

Deadface
Harrier

❑1, ca. 1987 5.00
❑2, ca. 1987 4.00
❑3, ca. 1987 3.00
❑4, ca. 1987 3.00
❑5, ca. 1987 3.00
❑6, ca. 1987 2.50
❑7, ca. 1987 2.50
❑8, ca. 1987 2.50

Deadface: Doing the Islands with Bacchus
Dark Horse

❑1, Jul 1991, b&w 2.95
❑2, Aug 1991, b&w 2.95
❑3, Sep 1991, b&w 2.95

Deadface: Earth, Water, Air, and Fire
Dark Horse

❑1 1992, b&w 2.50
❑2 1992, b&w 2.50
❑3 1992, b&w 2.50
❑4 1992, b&w 2.50

Dead Folks
Avatar

❑1, Mar 2003 3.50
❑1/A, Mar 2003; Wrap Cover 3.95
❑2, May 2003 3.50
❑2/A, May 2003; Wrap Cover 3.95
❑3, Jul 2003 3.50

Deadforce
Studio Noir

❑1, Jul 1996, b&w; Adult 2.50

Deadforce
Antarctic

❑1, May 1999, b&w 2.50
❑2, Jun 1999 2.50
❑Ashcan 1 1.00

Dead Grrrl: Dead at 21
Boneyard

❑1, Apr 1998 2.95

Dead in the West
Dark Horse

❑1, Oct 1993, b&w; Adult 3.95
❑2, Mar 1994, b&w; Adult 3.95

Dead Kid Adventures
Knight

❑1, Jul 1998 2.95

Dead Killer
Caliber

❑1; Includes material from Deadworld #19-21 2.95

Dead King: Burnt
Chaos

❑1, May 1998 2.95
❑2, Jun 1998 2.95
❑3, Jul 1998 2.95
❑4, Aug 1998 2.95

Deadline
Marvel

❑1, Jun 2002 2.99
❑2, Jul 2002 2.99
❑3, Aug 2002 2.99
❑4, Sep 2002 2.99

Deadline USA
Dark Horse

❑1, Sep 1991, b&w; Reprints 3.95
❑2, b&w; Reprints 3.95
❑3, b&w; Reprints 3.95
❑4 3.95
❑5 A: Gwar 3.95
❑6 3.95
❑7 3.95
❑8; Final Issue 3.95

Deadly Duo
Image

❑1, Nov 1994 2.50

Other grades: Multiply price above by 5/6 for VF/NM • 2/3 for VERY FINE • 1/3 for FINE • 1/5 for VERY GOOD • 1/8 for GOOD

Darkchylde

Troubled girl's nightmares become reality
©Image

Dark Crystal

Henson movie spawns two-issue adaptation
©Marvel

Darker Image

The shadowy reaches of the Image universe
©Image

Darkhawk

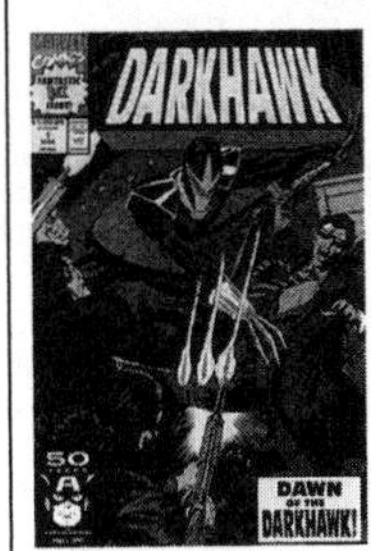

Ebony amulet changes teen's life
©Marvel

Darkhold

Pages of ancient book cause chaos
©Marvel

N-MINT

❑2, Dec 1994 ... 2.50
❑3, Jan 1995; Deadly Duo observing alien woman in glass tube ... 2.50

Deadly Duo
Image

❑1, Jul 1995 ... 2.50
❑2, Aug 1995 ... 2.50
❑3, Sep 1995 ... 2.50
❑4, Oct 1995 ... 2.50

Deadly Foes of Spider-Man
Marvel

❑1, May 1991; AM (c); AM, KGa (a); Punisher, Rhino, Kingpin, others appear ... 1.50
❑2, Jun 1991 AM (c); AM, KGa (a) ... 1.50
❑3, Jul 1991 AM (c); AM (a) ... 1.50
❑4, Aug 1991 AM (c); AM (a) ... 1.50

Deadly Hands of Kung Fu
Marvel

❑1, Apr 1974; JSn (w); AM, JSn, DG (a); 1: Abraham Brown ... 30.00
❑2, Jun 1974 JSn (a) ... 8.00
❑3, Aug 1974 ... 6.00
❑4, Sep 1974 ... 6.00
❑5, Oct 1974; Captain America story; Reprint from Tales of Suspense #85 ... 6.00
❑6, Nov 1974 ... 5.00
❑7, Dec 1974 ... 5.00
❑8, Jan 1975 ... 5.00
❑9, Feb 1975 ... 5.00
❑10, Mar 1975 ... 5.00
❑11, Apr 1975 ... 4.00
❑12, May 1975 ... 4.00
❑13, Jun 1975 ... 4.00
❑14, Jul 1975 ... 4.00
❑15, Aug 1975 ... 4.00
❑16, Sep 1975 ... 4.00
❑17, Oct 1975 ... 4.00
❑18, Nov 1975 ... 4.00
❑19, Dec 1975 ... 4.00
❑20, Jan 1976; Iron Fist story ... 7.00
❑21, Feb 1976 ... 3.00
❑22, Mar 1976 ... 3.00
❑23, Apr 1976; Iron Fist story; Sons Of The Tiger story ... 3.00
❑24, May 1976 ... 3.00
❑25, Jun 1976 ... 3.00
❑26, Jul 1976 ... 3.00
❑27, Aug 1976 ... 3.00
❑28, Sep 1976 ... 3.00
❑29, Oct 1976 ... 3.00
❑30, Nov 1976 ... 3.00
❑31, Dec 1976 ... 6.00
❑32, Jan 1977 ... 3.00
❑33, Feb 1977 ... 3.00
❑Special 1 1974; ca. 1974 ... 4.00

Deadman
DC

❑1, May 1985; NA (c); CI, NA (w); CI, NA (a); Reprints Strange Adventures #205-206 ... 2.50
❑2, Jun 1985; NA (c); CI (w); NA, GK (a); Reprints Strange Adventures #207-208 ... 2.50
❑3, Jul 1985; NA (c); NA, GK (a); Reprints Strange Adventures #209-210 ... 2.50
❑4, Aug 1985; NA (c); SA, NA (w); NA (a); Reprints Strange Adventures #211-212 ... 2.50

N-MINT

❑5, Sep 1985; NA (c); NA (w); NA (a); Reprints Strange Adventures #213 and Brave and The Bold #79 ... 2.50
❑6, Oct 1985; NA (c); NA (w); NA (a); Reprints Strange Adventures #214-215 ... 2.50
❑7, Nov 1985 NA (c); NA (w); NA (a) ... 2.50

Deadman
DC

❑1, Mar 1986 JL (a) ... 2.00
❑2, Apr 1986 JL (a) ... 2.00
❑3, May 1986 JL (a) ... 2.00
❑4, Jun 1986 JBy (c); JL (a) ... 2.00

Deadman
DC

❑1, Feb 2002 ... 2.50
❑2, Mar 2002 ... 2.50
❑3, Apr 2002 ... 2.50
❑4, May 2002 ... 2.50
❑5, Jun 2002 ... 2.50
❑6, Jul 2002 ... 2.50
❑7, Aug 2002 ... 2.50
❑8, Sep 2002 ... 2.50
❑9, Oct 2002; Final Issue ... 2.50

Deadman: Dead Again
DC

❑1, Oct 2001 ... 2.50
❑2, Oct 2001 ... 2.50
❑3, Oct 2001 ... 2.50
❑4, Oct 2001 ... 2.50
❑5, Oct 2001 ... 2.50

Deadman: Exorcism
DC

❑1; prestige format ... 4.95
❑2; prestige format ... 4.95

Deadman
DC

❑1, Oct 2006, Indicia misprint- issue credited as DMZ #10 ... 2.99
❑2, Nov 2006 ... 2.99
❑3, Dec 2006 ... 2.99
❑4, Jan 2007 ... 2.99
❑5, Mar 2007 ... 2.99

Deadman: Love After Death
DC

❑1, Dec 1989; prestige format ... 3.95
❑2, Jan 1990; prestige format ... 3.95

Dead Men Tell No Tales
Arcana

❑1, ca. 2005 ... 3.95
❑2, ca. 2005 ... 3.95
❑3, ca. 2005 ... 3.95

Dead of Night
Marvel

❑1, Dec 1973, JSt (w); JSt (a); Reprints ... 35.00
❑2, Feb 1974, Reprints ... 12.00
❑3, Apr 1974, Reprints ... 8.00
❑4, Jun 1974, Reprints ... 8.00
❑5, Aug 1974, Reprints ... 8.00
❑6, Oct 1974, Reprints ... 8.00
❑7, Dec 1974, Reprints ... 8.00
❑8, Feb 1975, Reprints ... 8.00
❑9, Apr 1975, Reprints ... 8.00
❑10, Jun 1975, Reprints ... 8.00

N-MINT

❑11, Aug 1975; BWr, GK (c); 1: Scarecrow; Final Issue ... 16.00

Dead or Alive: A Cyberpunk Western
Dark Horse

❑1, Apr 1998 ... 2.50
❑2, May 1998 ... 2.50
❑3, Jun 1998 ... 2.50
❑4, Jul 1998 ... 2.50

Deadpan
Ichor

❑1, Mar 1995 ... 3.95

Deadpan
Slave Labor

❑1, Jan 2006 ... 5.95

Deadpool
Marvel

❑1, Aug 1994 MWa (w) ... 3.00
❑2, Sep 1994 MWa (w) ... 2.50
❑3, Oct 1994 MWa (w) ... 2.50
❑4, Nov 1994 MWa (w) ... 2.50

Deadpool
Marvel

❑-1, Jul 1997; O: Deadpool. Flashback ... 2.25
❑0, ca. 1998; Included as giveaway with Wizard Magazine; Wizard giveaway ... 1.50
❑1, Jan 1997; wraparound cover ... 4.00
❑2, Feb 1997 ... 3.00
❑3, Mar 1997; A: Siryn. Siryn ... 2.50
❑4, Apr 1997; A: Hulk. V: Hulk ... 2.50
❑5, May 1997 ... 2.00
❑6, Jun 1997 ... 2.00
❑7, Aug 1997; gatefold summary ... 2.00
❑8, Sep 1997; gatefold summary ... 2.00
❑9, Oct 1997; gatefold summary ... 2.00
❑10, Nov 1997; gatefold summary; A: Great Lakes Avengers. back-up feature on making of Deadpool #11 ... 2.00
❑11, Dec 1997; gatefold summary; A: Great Lakes Avengers. Deadpool and Blind Al interact with Amazing Spider-Man #47 ... 3.99
❑12, Jan 1998; gatefold summary; parody of Faces of the DC Universe month ... 2.00
❑13, Feb 1998; gatefold summary ... 2.00
❑14, Mar 1998; gatefold summary ... 2.00
❑15, Apr 1998; gatefold summary ... 2.00
❑16, May 1998; gatefold summary ... 2.00
❑17, Jun 1998; gatefold summary ... 2.00
❑18, Jul 1998; gatefold summary; V: Ajax ... 2.00
❑19, Aug 1998; gatefold summary; V: Ajax ... 2.00
❑20, Sep 1998; gatefold summary ... 2.00
❑21, Oct 1998; gatefold summary ... 2.00
❑22, Nov 1998; gatefold summary; A: Cable ... 2.00
❑23, Dec 1998; gatefold summary; wraparound cover ... 2.99
❑24, Jan 1999; gatefold summary; A: Tiamat. A: Cosmic Messiah ... 1.99
❑25, Feb 1999 A: Tiamat. A: Captain America ... 2.99
❑26, Mar 1999 ... 1.99
❑27, Apr 1999; A: Wolverine. V: Doc Bong. V: Doc Bong ... 1.99
❑28, May 1999 ... 1.99
❑29, Jun 1999 ... 1.99
❑30, Jul 1999 ... 1.99

Other grades: Multiply price above by 5/6 for VF/NM • 2/3 for VERY FINE • 1/3 for FINE • 1/5 for VERY GOOD • 1/8 for GOOD

❑31, Aug 1999 1.99
❑32, Sep 1999 1.99
❑33, Oct 1999 1.99
❑34, Nov 1999 1.99
❑35, Dec 1999 2.25
❑36, Jan 2000 2.25
❑37, Feb 2000; Thor apperance 2.25
❑38, Mar 2000 2.25
❑39, Apr 2000 2.25
❑40, May 2000 2.25
❑41, Jun 2000 2.25
❑42, Jul 2000 2.25
❑43, Aug 2000; Wolff (Lobo parody) aids Deadpool's return to Earth; Constrictor V: Absorbing Man 2.25
❑44, Sep 2000; Black Panther apperance; Avengers appearance; V: Black Panther; V: Avengers; Hired by Achebe to steal Black Panther's pet leopard 2.25
❑45, Oct 2000; V: Copycat; Titania revealed as Copycat working for Taskmaster and Wizard; Loki's curse removed 2.25
❑46, Nov 2000 2.25
❑47, Dec 2000 2.25
❑48, Jan 2001; V: police officer 2.25
❑49, Feb 2001; Deadpool is romanced by Copycat 2.25
❑50, Mar 2001; Deadpool hires sidekick Poolboy 2.25
❑51, Apr 2001; A: Kid Deadpool. Detective Comics #39 cover homage 2.25
❑52, May 2001 2.25
❑53, Jun 2001 2.25
❑54, Jul 2001; Punisher apperance 2.25
❑55, Aug 2001; Punisher apperance 2.25
❑56, Sep 2001; Copycat impersonates Deadpool and attacks Siren 2.25
❑57, Oct 2001 2.25
❑58, Nov 2001 2.25
❑59, Dec 2001; D: Copycat; V: Weapon X (Garrison Kane) 2.25
❑60, Jan 2002; V: Sauron; V: Sabretooth; V: Wild Child; Temporary death of Deadpool 2.25
❑61, Feb 2002 2.25
❑62, Mar 2002 2.25
❑63, Apr 2002 2.25
❑64, May 2002 2.25
❑65, Jun 2002; 1: Nijo Minamiyori (Agent X) 2.25
❑66, Jul 2002 2.25
❑67, Aug 2002 2.25
❑68, Sep 2002 2.25
❑69, Oct 2002; Final issue 2.25
❑Ann 1998, ca. 1988; gatefold summary; Deadpool/Death '98; wraparound cover 2.99

Deadpool Team-Up
Marvel

❑1, Dec 1998; gatefold summary; Secret Wars II tie-in 2.99

Deadpool: The Circle Chase
Marvel

❑1, Aug 1993; Embossed cover 2.50
❑2, Sep 1993 2.00
❑3, Oct 1993 2.00
❑4, Nov 1993 2.00

Deadshot
DC

❑1, Nov 1988, LMc (c); LMc (a); O: Deadshot 1.50
❑2, Dec 1988, LMc (c); LMc (a) 1.50
❑3, Win 1988, LMc (c); LMc (a) 1.50
❑4, Hol 1988, LMc (c); LMc (a) 1.50

Deadshot
DC

❑1, Feb 2005; 1: Firebug II 2.95
❑2, Mar 2005 2.95
❑3, Apr 2005 2.95
❑4, May 2005 2.99
❑5, Jun 2005; D: Firebug II; D: Metamorpheus; D: Sidewinder; D: Schreck 2.99

Deadtime Stories
New Comics

❑1, Oct 1987, b&w; Pin-ups only by Mignola, Starlin, Milgrom, Adams, Gulacy, Simonson 1.75

Deadwalkers
Aircel

❑1/A, Jan 1991, "gross" cover 2.50
❑1/B, Jan 1991, "not-so-gross" cover 2.50
❑2, Feb 1991 2.50
❑3, Mar 1991 2.50
❑4, Apr 1991 2.50

Deadworld
Arrow

❑1, ca. 1986, b&w; Arrow publishes 6.00
❑2 2.50
❑3 2.50
❑4 2.50
❑5 2.50
❑6 2.50
❑7 2.50
❑8 2.50
❑9 2.50
❑10, b&w; Caliber begins as publisher 2.50
❑11, b&w 2.50
❑12, b&w 2.50
❑13, b&w 2.50
❑14, b&w 2.50
❑15, b&w 2.50
❑16, b&w 2.50
❑17, b&w 2.50
❑18, b&w 2.50
❑19, b&w 2.50
❑20, b&w 2.50
❑21, b&w 2.50
❑22, b&w 2.50
❑23, b&w 2.50
❑24, b&w 2.50
❑25, b&w 2.50
❑26, b&w; Final Issue 2.50

Deadworld
Caliber

❑1, ca. 1993, b&w; Giant-size; Adult 3.50
❑2, b&w; Adult 3.00
❑3, b&w; Adult 3.00
❑4, b&w; Adult 3.00
❑5, b&w; Adult 3.00
❑6, b&w; Adult 3.00
❑7, b&w; Adult 2.95
❑8, b&w; Adult 2.95
❑9, b&w; Adult 2.95
❑10, b&w; Adult 2.95
❑11, b&w; Adult 2.95
❑12, b&w; Adult 2.95
❑13, b&w; Adult 2.95
❑14, b&w; Adult 2.95
❑15, b&w; Adult 2.95

Deadworld
Image

❑1, Apr 2005 3.50
❑2 2005 3.50
❑3, May 2006 3.50
❑4, Jul 2006 3.50
❑6, Dec 2006 3.50

Deadworld Archives
Caliber

❑1, b&w 2.50
❑2, b&w 2.50
❑3, b&w 2.50

Deadworld: Bits and Pieces
Caliber

❑1, b&w; Reprints 2.95

Deadworld Chronicles: Plague
Caliber

❑1 2.95

Deadworld: Daemonstorm
Caliber

❑1 3.95

Deadworld: Necropolis
Caliber

❑1 3.95

Deadworld: To Kill a King
Caliber

❑1; Sinergy as flip-book 2.95
❑1/Ltd.; limited edition; Adult 5.95
❑2; Adult 2.95
❑3; Adult 2.95

Deal with the Devil
Alias

❑1, Apr 2005 2.99
❑2, May 2005 2.99
❑3, Jul 2005 2.99
❑4, Sep 2005; Includes preview of Sixgun Samurai 2.99
❑5, Nov 2005 2.99

Dear Julia
Black Eye

❑1 3.50
❑2 3.50
❑3, Feb 1997 3.50
❑4 3.50

DearS
Tokyopop

❑1, Jan 2005 9.99
❑2, Apr 2005; Includes pin-up poster insert 9.99
❑3, Jul 2005 9.99
❑4, Oct 2005 9.99
❑5, Jan 2006 9.99

Death3
Marvel

❑1, Sep 1993, Embossed cover 2.95
❑2, Oct 1993 1.75
❑3, Nov 1993 1.75
❑4, Dec 1993 1.75

Death & Candy
Fantagraphics

❑1, Win 1999 3.95
❑2 3.95
❑3 3.95
❑4, Mar 2005; b&w 4.95

Death & Taxes: The Real Costs of Living
Parody

❑1, b&w 2.50

Deathangel
Lightning

❑1/A, Dec 1997 2.95
❑1/B, Dec 1997; alternate cover 2.95

Death: At Death's Door
DC / Vertigo

❑1, ca. 2003 9.95

Deathblow
Image

❑0, Aug 1996 JLee (w); JLee (a) 2.50
❑1, Apr 1993; JLee (w); JLee (a); 1: Cybernary. Black varnish cover; Cybernary #1 as flip-book 3.00
❑2, Aug 1993; JLee (c); JLee (w); JLee (a); Cybernary #2 as flip-book 2.50
❑3, Feb 1994; 1: Cisco. Cybernary #3 as flip-book 3.00
❑4, Apr 1994; Cybernary #4 as flip-book 2.00
❑5, May 1994 2.00
❑5/A, May 1994; Variant cover edition; alternate cover 2.00
❑6, Jun 1994 1.95
❑7, Jul 1994 1.95
❑8, Aug 1994 1.95
❑9, Oct 1994 1.95
❑10, Nov 1994; wraparound cover 2.50
❑11, Dec 1994; Wraparound cover 2.50
❑12, Jan 1995; Pinup by Brett Booth 2.50
❑13, Feb 1995 2.50
❑14, Mar 1995 2.50
❑15, Apr 1995 2.50
❑16, May 1995; bound-in trading cards 1.95
❑16/Variant, May 1995 4.00
❑17, Jun 1995 2.50
❑17/A, Jun 1995; Chicago Comicon limited edition 4.00
❑18, Jul 1995 2.50
❑19, Sep 1995 2.50
❑20, Oct 1995; Pinup by Jeff Rebner 2.50
❑21, Nov 1995 A: Gen13 2.50
❑22, Dec 1995 2.50
❑23, Jan 1996 2.50
❑24, Feb 1996 A: Grifter 2.50
❑25, Mar 1996; Wraparound cover 2.50
❑26, Mar 1996 2.50
❑27, Apr 1996 2.50
❑28, Jul 1996 2.50

Dark Horse Comics

Companion series to Dark Horse Presents
©Dark Horse

Dark Horse Presents

Long-running anthology spawned many titles
©Dark Horse

Dark Horse Presents: Aliens

Color reprints of Dark Horse Presents stories
©Dark Horse

Dark Knight Strikes Again

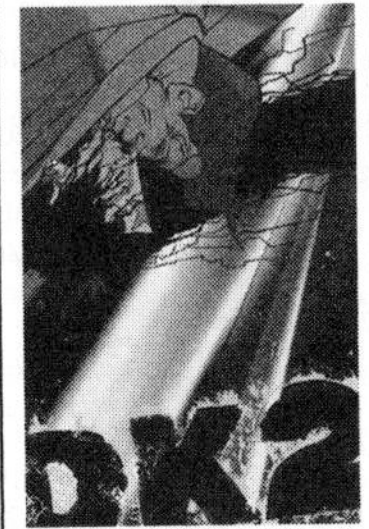

Less-beloved sequel to Miller's blockbuster
©DC

Darkman

Rare case of movie super-hero coming to comics
©Marvel

N-MINT

❑28/Variant, Jul 1996; alternate cover.... 4.00
❑29, Aug 1996; Final Issue.................... 2.50

Deathblow: Byblows
WildStorm

❑1, Nov 1999 .... 2.95
❑2, Dec 1999.......... 2.95
❑3, Jan 2000.......... 2.95

Deathblow (WildStorm)
DC / Wildstorm

❑1, Jan 2007 .... 2.99
❑1/Variant, Jan 2007.......... 2.99
❑1/2nd variant, Jan 2007 .... 2.99
❑2, Feb 2007 .... 2.99
❑2/Variant, Feb 2007.......... 2.99

Deathblow/Wolverine
Image

❑1, Sep 1996, crossover with Marvel..... 2.50
❑2, Feb 1997, crossover with Marvel 2.50

Death By Chocolate
Sleeping Giant

❑1, Mar 1996, b&w; NN 2.50

Death By Chocolate: Sir Geoffrey and the Chocolate Car
Sleeping Giant

❑1, b&w; NN 2.50

Death By Chocolate: The Metabolators
Sleeping Giant

❑1, b&w; NN 2.50

Death Crazed Teenage Superheroes
Arf! Arf!

❑1.......... 1.50
❑2.......... 1.50

Death Dealer
Verotik

❑1, Jul 1995, Embossed cover.......... 5.95
❑2, May 1996.......... 6.95
❑3, Apr 1997 .... 6.95
❑4, Jul 1997.......... 6.95

Death Dreams of Dracula
Apple

❑1, b&w 2.50
❑2, b&w 2.50
❑3, b&w 2.50
❑4, b&w 2.50

Death Gallery, A
DC / Vertigo

❑1; portraits 3.00

Death Hawk
Adventure

❑1, May 1988, b&w.......... 1.95
❑2, Jul 1988, b&w.......... 1.95
❑3, Nov 1988, b&w.......... 1.95

Death Hunt
Eternity

❑1, b&w 1.95

Death Jr.
Image

❑1, May 2005.......... 4.99
❑2 2005.......... 4.99
❑3, Oct 2005 .... 4.99

N-MINT

Death Jr.
Image

❑1, Jul 2006.......... 4.99
❑2, Dec 2006 .... 4.99

Deathlok
Marvel

❑1, Jul 1990; 1: Deathlok II (Mike Collins); O: Deathlok II (Mike Collins); Squarebound.......... 3.95
❑2, Aug 1990; Squarebound.......... 3.95
❑3, Sep 1990; Squarebound 3.95
❑4, Oct 1990; Squarebound.......... 3.95

Deathlok
Marvel

❑1, Jul 1991; Silver ink cover 2.50
❑2, Aug 1991 A: Forge.......... 2.00
❑3, Sep 1991; V: Doctor Doom.......... 2.00
❑4, Oct 1991 .... 2.00
❑5, Nov 1991; X-Men & Fantastic Four crossover 2.00
❑6, Dec 1991; Punisher crossover.......... 2.00
❑7, Jan 1992; Punisher crossover 2.00
❑8, Feb 1992; Punisher crossover 2.00
❑9, Mar 1992; A: Ghost Rider. V: Ghost Rider 2.00
❑10, Apr 1992; A: Ghost Rider. V: Ghost Rider 2.00
❑11, May 1992; 1: High-Tech.......... 1.75
❑12, Jun 1992.......... 1.75
❑13, Jul 1992.......... 1.75
❑14, Aug 1992; O: Deathlok III (Luther Manning) 1.75
❑15, Sep 1992 .... 1.75
❑16, Oct 1992.......... 1.75
❑17, Nov 1992 .... 1.75
❑18, Dec 1992 .... 1.75
❑19, Jan 1993; O: Siege. 1: Siege. foil cover 2.25
❑20, Feb 1993.......... 1.75
❑21, Mar 1993 .... 1.75
❑22, Apr 1993.......... 1.75
❑23, May 1993.......... 1.75
❑24, Jun 1993.......... 1.75
❑25, Jul 1993; A: Black Panther. foil cover 1.75
❑26, Aug 1993 A: Hobgoblin.......... 1.75
❑27, Sep 1993 .... 1.75
❑28, Oct 1993; A: Timestream. A: Goddess. Infinity Crusade crossover 1.75
❑29, Nov 1993; Infinity Crusade crossover 1.75
❑30, Dec 1993 .... 1.75
❑31, Jan 1994.......... 1.75
❑32, Feb 1994.......... 1.75
❑33, Mar 1994 .... 1.75
❑34, Apr 1994; Final Issue.......... 1.75
❑Ann 1, ca. 1992; BG (a) 2.50
❑Ann 2, ca. 1993; O: Tracer. 1: Tracer. Polybagged 2.95
❑Special 1, May 1991; BG (a); reprints Deathlok (1st series) #1 .... 2.00
❑Special 2, Jun 1991; BG (a); reprints Deathlok (1st series) #2 .... 2.00
❑Special 3, Jun 1991; reprints Deathlok (1st series) #3.......... 2.00
❑Special 4, Jun 1991; reprints Deathlok (1st series) #4.......... 2.00

N-MINT

Deathlok
Marvel

❑1, Sep 1999 .... 2.00
❑2, Oct 1999.......... 1.99
❑3, Nov 1999 .... 1.99
❑4, Nov 1999; V: Clown (Circus of Crime) 1.99
❑5, Dec 1999 .... 1.99

Deathmark
Lightning

❑1, Dec 1994, b&w.......... 2.95

Deathmask
Future

❑1, Apr 2003.......... 2.99
❑2, Jun 2003.......... 2.99
❑3, Jul 2003.......... 2.99

Deathmate
Image / Valiant

❑1, Sep 1993; JLee (c); BL (w); RL (a); crossover; prologue; silver cover 2.95
❑1/Gold, Sep 1993; Gold cover (limited promotional edition); JLee (c); BL (w); RL (a); Prologue.......... 4.00
❑2, Sep 1993; JLee (a); 1: Fairchild. 1: Burn-Out. 1: Gen13 (full). 1: Freefall. Black 3.00
❑2/Gold, Sep 1993; Gold edition; 1: Gen13 (full); 1: Fairchild; 1: Freefall; 1: Burn-Out 6.00
❑3, Sep 1993; BL, BH (w); DP (a); Yellow; cover says Oct, indicia says Sep 4.95
❑3/Gold, Sep 1993; Gold edition; BL, BH (w); DP (a); Yellow 6.00
❑4, Oct 1993; Blue 4.95
❑4/Gold, Oct 1993; Gold edition; Blue.... 6.00
❑5, Nov 1993; Red 4.95
❑5/Gold, Nov 1993; Gold edition; Red ... 6.00
❑6, Feb 1994; BL (w); Epilogue; silver cover 2.95
❑6/Gold, Feb 1994; Gold edition 4.00
❑Ashcan 1, Aug 1993; ashcan edition; Green; Included in Advance Comics... 1.00

Death Metal
Marvel

❑1, Jan 1994.......... 1.95
❑2, Feb 1994.......... 1.95
❑3, Mar 1994 .... 1.95
❑4, Apr 1994.......... 1.95

Death Metal vs. Genetix
Marvel

❑1, Dec 1993 .... 2.95
❑2, Jan 1994.......... 2.95

Death Note
Viz

❑1, Oct 2005.......... 7.99
❑2, Dec 2005 .... 7.99

Death of Angel Girl
Angel

❑1; Adult.......... 2.95

Death of Antisocialman
Not Available

❑1 .... 0.50
❑2 .... 0.50
❑3 .... 0.50
❑4 .... 0.50
❑5 .... 0.50

Other grades: Multiply price above by 5/6 for VF/NM • 2/3 for VERY FINE • 1/3 for FINE • 1/5 for VERY GOOD • 1/8 for GOOD

❑6 ... 0.50
❑7 ... 0.50
❑8 ... 0.50
❑9 ... 0.50
❑10 ... 0.50

Death of Lady Vampré
Blackout

❑1, O: Lady Vampré ... 2.95

Death of Stupidman
Parody

❑1 ... 3.50

Death of Superbabe
Spoof

❑1, Feb 1993, b&w ... 3.95

Death of Vampirella
Harris

❑1, Feb 1997; Memorial Edition; Chromium cover; Green logo ... 15.00
❑1/Variant, Feb 1997; Holofoil chromium edition; 750 copies printed; Yellow logo ... 15.00

Death Race 2020
Cosmic

❑1, Apr 1995; sequel to Corman film ... 2.50
❑2, May 1995 ... 2.50
❑5, Aug 1995 ... 2.50

Death Rattle
Kitchen Sink

❑1, Oct 1985 ... 2.00
❑2, Dec 1985, Includes Spirit story (previously unpublished) ... 2.00
❑3, Feb 1986 ... 2.00
❑4 ... 2.00
❑5 ... 2.00
❑6, b&w; Black and white; Listed as #5 in indicia ... 2.00
❑7, b&w ... 2.00
❑8, Dec 1986; 1: Xenozoic ... 2.00
❑9, Jan 1987 ... 2.00
❑10, Mar 1987 ... 2.00
❑11, May 1987 ... 2.00
❑12, Jul 1987 ... 2.00
❑13, Nov 1987 ... 2.00
❑14, Jan 1988 ... 2.00
❑15, Mar 1988 ... 2.00
❑16, May 1988 ... 2.00
❑17, Jul 1988 ... 2.00
❑18, Oct 1988 ... 2.00

Death Rattle
Kitchen Sink

❑½, Nov 1995, b&w ... 2.95
❑1, Oct 1995, b&w ... 2.95
❑2, Dec 1995, b&w ... 2.95
❑3, Feb 1996 ... 2.95
❑4, Apr 1996 ... 2.95
❑5, Jun 1996, b&w ... 2.95
❑6 ... 2.95

Deathrow
Heroic / Blue Comet

❑1, Sep 1993, b&w; 1: X-187; Includes trading card; Adult ... 2.50

Death's Head
Marvel

❑1, Dec 1988 ... 1.75
❑2, Jan 1989 ... 1.75
❑3, Feb 1989 ... 1.75
❑4, Mar 1989 ... 1.75
❑5, Apr 1989 ... 1.75
❑6, May 1989 ... 1.75
❑7, Jun 1989 ... 1.75
❑8, Jul 1989 ... 1.75
❑9, Aug 1989 ... 1.75
❑10, Sep 1989 ... 1.75

Death's Head II
Marvel

❑1, Mar 1992 1: Death's Head II. D: Death's Head. ... 2.50
❑1/2nd, Mar 1992; 1: Death's Head II. D: Death's Head. Silver ink cover ... 1.75
❑2, Apr 1992 ... 2.00
❑2/2nd, Apr 1992; Silver ink cover ... 1.75
❑3, May 1992 1: Tuck ... 2.00
❑4, Jun 1992 A: Wolverine. A: Captain America ... 2.00

Death's Head II
Marvel

❑1, Dec 1992; A: X-Men. gatefold cover ... 2.00
❑2, Jan 1993 A: X-Men ... 2.00
❑3, Feb 1993 A: X-Men ... 2.00
❑4, Mar 1993 A: X-Men ... 2.00
❑5, Apr 1993 ... 1.75
❑6, May 1993 ... 1.95
❑7, Jun 1993 ... 1.95
❑8, Jul 1993 ... 1.95
❑9, Aug 1993 ... 1.95
❑10, Sep 1993 ... 1.95
❑11, Oct 1993 1: Death's Head III. A: Doctor Necker. A: Charnel ... 1.95
❑12, Nov 1993 ... 1.95
❑13, Dec 1993 ... 1.95
❑14, Jan 1994; Prelude to Death's Head Gold #1; foil cover ... 2.95
❑15, Feb 1994 ... 1.95
❑16, Mar 1994 ... 1.95

Death's Head II & the O: Die-Cut
Marvel

❑1, Aug 1993, foil cover ... 2.95
❑2, Sep 1993 ... 1.75

Death's Head II Gold
Marvel

❑1; foil cover ... 3.95

Death Shrike
Brainstorm

❑1, Jul 1993, b&w ... 2.95

Deathsnake
Fantagraphics / Eros

❑1, Aug 1994; Adult ... 2.95
❑2, Oct 1994, b&w; Adult ... 2.95

Deathstroke the Terminator
DC

❑0, Oct 1994; published between #40 and #41; Title changes to Deathstroke the Hunted ... 2.00
❑1, Aug 1991; MZ (c); O: Deathstroke the Terminator ... 3.00
❑1/2nd; O: Deathstroke the Terminator. 2nd printing ... 1.75
❑2, Sep 1991 ... 2.00
❑3, Oct 1991 ... 2.00
❑4, Nov 1991; V: Ravager ... 2.00
❑5, Dec 1991 MZ (c) ... 2.00
❑6, Jan 1992 MZ (c) ... 2.00
❑7, Feb 1992; MZ (c); Batman ... 2.00
❑8, Mar 1992; MZ (c); Batman ... 2.00
❑9, Apr 1992; MZ (c); 1: Vigilante III (Pat Trayce). Batman ... 2.00
❑10, Jun 1992 MZ (c) ... 2.00
❑11, Jun 1992; Vigilante ... 2.00
❑12, Jul 1992 MZ (c); MG (a) ... 2.00
❑13, Aug 1992 MZ (c) ... 2.00
❑14, Sep 1992; MZ (c); Continued into New Titans #90 ... 2.00
❑15, Oct 1992; MZ (c); Continued from Team Titans #1 & into New Titans #91 ... 2.00
❑16, Nov 1992; MZ (c); D: Deathstroke the Terminator; Continued from Team Titans #2 & into New Titans #92 ... 2.00
❑17, Dec 1992; MZ (c); Deathstroke the Terminator revived ... 2.00
❑18, Jan 1993; MZ (c); V: Cheshire ... 2.00
❑19, Feb 1993; MZ (c); Quarac destroyed ... 2.00
❑20, Mar 1993 MZ (c) ... 1.75
❑21, Apr 1993 MZ (c) ... 1.75
❑22, May 1993 MZ (c) ... 1.75
❑23, May 1993 MZ (c) ... 1.75
❑24, Jun 1993 MZ (c) ... 1.75
❑25, Jun 1993 MZ (c) ... 1.75
❑26, Jul 1993 MZ (c) ... 1.75
❑27, Aug 1993 MZ (c) ... 1.75
❑28, Sep 1993 MZ (c) ... 1.75
❑29, Oct 1993 ... 1.75
❑30, Nov 1993 ... 1.75
❑31, Dec 1993 ... 1.75
❑32, Jan 1994 ... 1.75
❑33, Feb 1994 ... 1.75
❑34, Mar 1994 ... 1.75
❑35, Apr 1994 ... 1.75
❑36, May 1994 ... 1.75
❑37, Jun 1994 ... 1.75
❑38, Jul 1994 A: Vigilante III (Pat Trayce). A: Vigilante ... 1.95
❑39, Aug 1994; A: Green Arrow. Title becomes "Deathstroke the Hunted" ... 1.95
❑40, Sep 1994 ... 1.95
❑41, Nov 1994 ... 1.95
❑42, Dec 1994 ... 1.95
❑43, Jan 1995 ... 1.95
❑44, Feb 1995 ... 1.95
❑45, Mar 1995 ... 1.95
❑46, Apr 1995 ... 1.95
❑47, May 1995 ... 1.95
❑48, Jun 1995 ... 2.25
❑49, Jul 1995 ... 2.25
❑50, Aug 1995; Giant-size; Title changes to Deathstroke ... 3.50
❑51, Sep 1995 ... 2.25
❑52, Oct 1995 GP (a); A: Hawkman ... 2.25
❑53, Nov 1995 ... 2.25
❑54, Dec 1995 ... 2.25
❑55, Jan 1996 ... 2.25
❑56, Feb 1996 ... 2.25
❑57, Mar 1996 ... 2.25
❑58, Apr 1996; V: Joker ... 2.25
❑59, May 1996 ... 2.25
❑60, Jun 1996; Final Issue ... 2.25
❑Ann 1, ca. 1992; MZ (c); A: Vigilante. Eclipso; 1992 Ann; Continued from Robin (mini series) Ann #1 & into New Titans Ann #8 ... 3.50
❑Ann 2, ca. 1993; 1: Gunfire; Bloodlines ... 3.50
❑Ann 3, ca. 1994; Elseworlds ... 3.95
❑Ann 4 1995; Year One ... 3.95

Death Talks About Life
DC / Vertigo

❑1; NG (w); 16-page booklet about AIDS; b&w; ca. 1994 ... 1.50

Death: The High Cost of Living
DC / Vertigo

❑1, Mar 1993 NG (w) ... 3.00
❑1/Platinum, Jun 1993; Platinum edition; NG (w) ... 6.00
❑2, Apr 1993 NG (w) ... 3.00
❑3, May 1993; regular edition; NG (w); Error editions with reversed pages exist-no difference in value; Corrected edition has no cover price ... 3.00
❑3/A, May 1993; with error ... 4.00

Death: The Time of Your Life
DC / Vertigo

❑1, Apr 1996 NG (w) ... 3.50
❑2, May 1996 NG (w) ... 3.00
❑3, Jun 1996; NG (w); Cover date shows June, indicia shows July; Final issue ... 3.00

Deathwatch
Harrier

❑1, Jul 1987 ... 1.95

Deathwish
Milestone / DC

❑1, Dec 1994 ... 2.50
❑2, Jan 1995 ... 2.50
❑3, Feb 1995 ... 2.50
❑4, Mar 1995 ... 2.50

Deathworld
Adventure

❑1, Nov 1990, b&w ... 2.50
❑2, Dec 1990, b&w ... 2.50
❑3, Jan 1991, b&w ... 2.50
❑4, Feb 1991, b&w ... 2.50

Deathworld Book II
Adventure

❑1, Apr 1991, b&w ... 2.50
❑2, May 1991, b&w ... 2.50
❑3, Jun 1991, b&w ... 2.50
❑4, Jul 1991, b&w ... 2.50

Deathworld Book III
Adventure

❑1, Aug 1991, b&w ... 2.50
❑2, Sep 1991, b&w ... 2.50
❑3, Nov 1991, b&w ... 2.50
❑4, Dec 1991, b&w ... 2.50

Death Wreck
Marvel

❑1, Jan 1994 ... 1.95
❑2, Feb 1994 ... 1.95
❑3, Mar 1994 ... 1.95
❑4, Apr 1994 ... 1.95

Dark Mansion of Forbidden Love

Horror meets romance in hotly collected series
©DC

Darkness

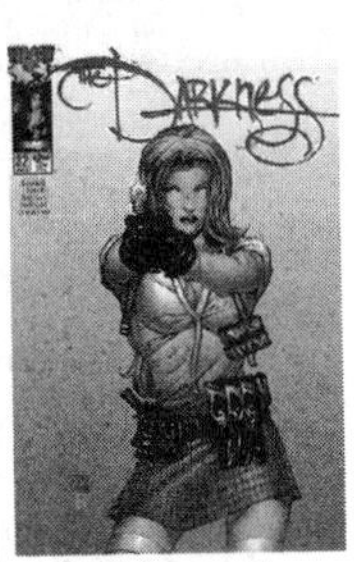

Mob hit man makes deal with devil
©Top Cow

Dark Shadows (Gold Key)

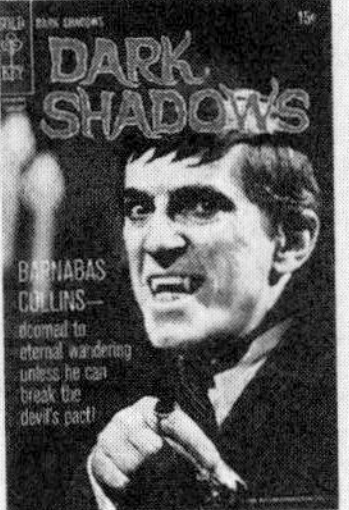

Creepy Gothic soap opera comes to comics
©Gold Key

Darkstars

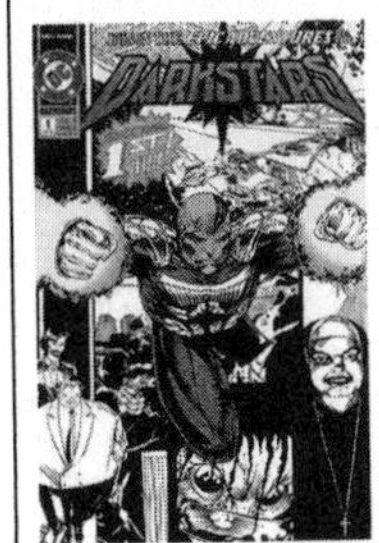

Intergalactic security-for-hire force
©DC

Date with Debbi

Late 1960s DC teen romance title
©DC

N-MINT

Debbie Does Comics
Aircel

- ❑1, b&w; Adult ... 2.95

Debbie Does Dallas
Aircel

- ❑1, Mar 1991; Adult ... 2.50
- ❑1/3D; Adult ... 3.95
- ❑1/2nd; 2nd printing; Adult ... 2.50
- ❑2, Apr 1991; Adult ... 2.50
- ❑3, May 1991; Adult ... 2.50
- ❑4, Jun 1991; Adult ... 2.50
- ❑5, Jul 1991; Adult ... 2.50
- ❑6 1991; Adult ... 2.50
- ❑7, Oct 1991; Adult ... 2.50
- ❑8, Nov 1991; Adult ... 2.50
- ❑9, Dec 1991; Adult ... 2.95
- ❑10, Jan 1992; Adult ... 2.95
- ❑11, Mar 1992; Adult ... 2.95
- ❑12 1992; Adult ... 2.95
- ❑13 1992; Adult ... 2.95
- ❑14 1992; Adult ... 2.95
- ❑15; Adult ... 2.95
- ❑16; Adult ... 2.95
- ❑17; Adult ... 2.95
- ❑18, Mar 1993; Adult ... 2.95

Debbi's Dates
DC

- ❑1, May 1969 ... 30.00
- ❑2, Jul 1969 ... 18.00
- ❑3, Sep 1969 ... 18.00
- ❑4, Nov 1969 ... 18.00
- ❑5, Jan 1970 ... 18.00
- ❑6, Mar 1970 ... 30.00
- ❑7, May 1970 ... 18.00
- ❑8, Jul 1970 ... 18.00
- ❑9, Sep 1970 ... 18.00
- ❑10, Nov 1970 ... 18.00
- ❑11, Jan 1971 ... 18.00

Decade
Dark Horse

- ❑1 ... 12.95

Decade of Dark Horse, A
Dark Horse

- ❑1, Jul 1996, Sin City, Predator, Grendel stories ... 2.95
- ❑2, Aug 1996; Star Wars, Ghost, Trekker stories ... 2.95
- ❑3, Sep 1996, Aliens, Outlanders, Nexus, The Mask stories ... 2.95
- ❑4, Oct 1996; b&w and color, Concrete, Black Cross, Exon Depot, Godzilla stories, final issue ... 2.95

Decapitator
Dark Horse

- ❑1, Jun 1998 ... 2.95
- ❑2, Jul 1998 ... 2.95
- ❑3, Aug 1998 ... 2.95
- ❑4, Sep 1998 ... 2.95

Deception
Image

- ❑1, ca. 1999 ... 2.95
- ❑2, ca. 1999 ... 2.95
- ❑3, ca. 1999 ... 2.95

N-MINT

Decimation: House of M - The Day After
Marvel

- ❑1, Jan 2006, b&w ... 3.99

Decorator
Fantagraphics / Eros

- ❑1, b&w; Adult ... 2.50

Decoy
Penny-Farthing

- ❑1, Mar 1999 ... 2.75
- ❑1/Autographed, Mar 1999; Auographed edition ... 3.25
- ❑2, Apr 1999 ... 2.75
- ❑3, May 1999 ... 2.75
- ❑4, Jun 1999 ... 2.75

Herobear and the Kid and Decoy
Astonish

- ❑1, Jul 2002 ... 2.95
- ❑2, ca. 2002, Title changes to Decoy and Herobear and the Kid ... 2.95

Decoy: Storm of the Century
Penny-Farthing

- ❑1, Jul 2002 ... 2.95
- ❑2, Aug 2002 ... 2.95
- ❑3, Sep 2002 ... 2.95
- ❑4, Oct 2002; Indicia lists as Vol. 2 #4 ... 2.95

Dee Dee
Fantagraphics / Eros

- ❑1, Jul 1996, b&w; Adult ... 2.95

Deep
Marvel

- ❑1, Nov 1977, Cl (c); Cl (a); Movie adaptation ... 1.50

Deep Black
Chaos!

- ❑1/A, Aug 1997; No cover price; b&w pencilled pin-ups ... 2.00
- ❑1/B, Aug 1997; b&w pencilled pin-ups; all-white cardstock cover ... 2.00

Deepest Dimension
Revolutionary

- ❑1, Jun 1993 ... 2.50
- ❑2, Aug 1993 ... 2.50

Deep Girl
Ariel Bordeaux

- ❑1; Adult ... 2.50
- ❑2; Adult ... 2.50
- ❑3; Mini-comic; Adult ... 1.50
- ❑4; Adult ... 2.50
- ❑5; Adult ... 2.50

Deep Sleeper
Oni

- ❑1, Feb 2004 ... 3.50
- ❑2, Apr 2004, Moves to Image with #3 ... 3.50

Deep Sleeper
Image

- ❑3, Aug 2004 ... 2.95
- ❑4, Sep 2004 ... 2.95

Deep Terror
Avalon

- ❑1, b&w ... 2.95

N-MINT

Dee Vee
Dee Vee

- ❑1, Feb 1997 ... 2.95
- ❑5, Feb 1998, b&w; wraparound cover ... 2.95
- ❑6, Apr 1998, b&w; wraparound cover ... 2.95
- ❑7, Jun 1998, b&w; wraparound cover ... 2.95

DefCon 4
Image

- ❑1/A, Feb 1996; wraparound cover ... 2.50
- ❑1/B, Feb 1996; alternate wraparound cover ... 2.50
- ❑2, Mar 1996 ... 2.50
- ❑3, Jun 1996; cover says May, indicia says Jun ... 2.50
- ❑4, Sep 1996 ... 2.50
- ❑5 1996 ... 2.50

Defenders
Dell

- ❑1, Sep 1962 ... 26.00
- ❑2, Feb 1963 ... 16.00

Defenders
Marvel

- ❑1, Aug 1972, SB (c); SB (a); Team consists of Doctor Strange, Hulk, and Sub-Mariner ... 90.00
- ❑2, Oct 1972, SB (c); SB (a); A: Silver Surfer. Silver Surfer joins Defenders ... 35.00
- ❑3, Dec 1972, GK (c); SB, JM (a); A: . A: Black Knight. A: Silver Surfer. Black Knight ... 30.00
- ❑4, Feb 1973, SB (c); FMc, SB (a); Valkyrie joins Defenders ... 26.00
- ❑5, Apr 1973, SB (c); FMc, SB (a); D: Omegatron ... 26.00
- ❑6, Jun 1973, SB (c); FMc, SB (a) ... 16.00
- ❑7, Aug 1973, SB, (c); SB (a); A: Hawkeye. Hawkeye ... 16.00
- ❑8, Sep 1973, SB (c); FMc, SB (a); A: Avengers. Avengers and Defenders vs. Loki and Dormammu, part 2 - continues in Avengers #116 (continued from Avengers #115) ... 25.00
- ❑9, Oct 1973, SB (c); FMc, SB (a); A: Avengers. Avengers and Defenders vs. Loki and Dormammu, part 4 - continues in Avengers #117 ... 16.00
- ❑10, Nov 1973, SB, JR (c); SB (a); A: Avengers. Avengers and Defenders vs. Loki and Dormammu, part 6 - continues in Avengers #118 ... 55.00
- ❑11, Dec 1973, SB (c); SB (a); A: Avengers. Avengers and Defenders vs. Loki and Dormammu, part 8, continued from Avengers #118; Hawkeye, Silver Surfer and Sub-Mariner leave Defenders ... 15.00
- ❑12, Feb 1974, SB, (c); SB, JAb (a); Hulk fights Xemnu the Titan ... 9.00
- ❑13, May 1974, SB, GK, KJ (c); SB, KJ (a); 1: Nebulon. A: . A: Nighthawk. Marvel Value Stamp #86: Zemo ... 9.00
- ❑14, Jul 1974, SB, (c); SB, DGr (a); Nighthawk joins Defenders ... 10.00
- ❑15, Sep 1974, SB (c); SB, KJ (a); A: Professor X. A: Magneto. V: Magneto. Nighthawk gets new costume; Marvel Value Stamp #8: Captain America ... 10.00
- ❑16, Oct 1974, GK (c); SB (a); A: Professor X. A: Magneto. Marvel Value Stamp #44: Absorbing Man ... 10.00

Other grades: Multiply price above by 5/6 for VF/NM • 2/3 for VERY FINE • 1/3 for FINE • 1/5 for VERY GOOD • 1/8 for GOOD

	N-MINT
❑17, Nov 1974, (c); SB, DGr (a); 1: Bulldozer. A: Luke Cage. Marvel Value Stamp #20: Brother Voodoo	6.50
❑18, Dec 1974, SB, GK (c); SB, DGr (a); O: Bulldozer. A: Luke Cage. V: Wrecking Crew. Luke Cage	6.50
❑19, Jan 1975, GK, (c); SB, KJ (a); A: Luke Cage. Marvel Value Stamp #98: Puppet Master	6.50
❑20, Feb 1975, SB, GK (c); SB (a); O: Valkyrie. A: Thing. Marvel Value Stamp #31: Mordo	7.00
❑21, Mar 1975, SB, KJ (c); SB (a); 1: The Headmen. The Headmen introduced	6.00
❑22, Apr 1975, GK (c); SB (a); A: Sons of the Serpent. The Sons of the Serpent	6.00
❑23, May 1975, GK, KJ (c); SB (a); A: Yellowjacket. Marvel Value Stamp #78: Owl	6.00
❑24, Jun 1975, GK, KJ (c); SB, BMc (a); A: Yellowjacket. A: Daredevil. A: Luke Cage. A: Son of Satan. Luke Cage, Daredevil, Daimon Hellstorm, Yellowjacket	6.00
❑25, Jul 1975, SB, (c); SB, JAb (a); A: Yellowjacket. A: Yellowjacket. A: Daredevil. A: Luke Cage. A: Son of Satan. Luke Cage, Daredevil, Daimon Hellstorm, Yellowjacket	6.50
❑26, Aug 1975, SB, GK (c); SB (a); A: Guardians of the Galaxy. Continued from Giant-Size Defenders #5	7.00
❑27, Sep 1975, SB, GK (c); SB (a); 1: Starhawk II (Aleta)-cameo. A: Guardians of the Galaxy. Guardians of the Galaxy	7.00
❑28, Oct 1975, GK, (c); SB (a); 1: Starhawk II (Aleta)-full. A: Guardians of the Galaxy. Guardians of the Galaxy, Starhawk	7.00
❑29, Nov 1975, GK, (c); SB (a); A: Guardians of the Galaxy. Guardians of the Galaxy, Starhawk; Ralph Macchio L.O.C	7.00
❑30, Dec 1975, SB, (c); JAb (a)	4.00
❑31, Jan 1976, GK (c); SB, JM (a); V: Headmen	4.00
❑32, Feb 1976, GK, KJ (c); SB, JM (a); O: Nighthawk II (Kyle Richmond); V: Headmen; Marvel Value Stamp Series B #26; Jo Duffy L.O.C	4.00
❑33, Mar 1976, GK (c); SB, JM (a); V: Headmen	4.00
❑34, Apr 1976, RB, DA (c); SB, JM (a); V: Nebulon	5.00
❑34/30¢, Apr 1976, RB, DA (c); SB, JM (a); V: Nebulon. 30¢ regional price variant	20.00
❑35, May 1976, GK (c); SB, KJ (a); 1: Red Guardian II (Doctor Tanja Belinskya). 1: Red Guardian II (Doctor Tanja Belinskya)	5.00
❑35/30¢, May 1976, GK (c); SB, KJ (a); 1: Red Guardian II (Doctor Tanja Belinskya). 30¢ regional price variant	20.00
❑36, Jun 1976, GK (c); SB, KJ (a); V: Plant Man	5.00
❑36/30¢, Jun 1976, GK (c); SB, KJ (a); 30¢ regional price variant	20.00
❑37, Jul 1976, GK (c); SB, KJ (a); V: Plant Man	5.00
❑37/30¢, Jul 1976, GK (c); SB, KJ (a); 30¢ regional price variant	20.00
❑38, Aug 1976, SB (c); SB, KJ (a); V: Nebulon; V: Eel; V: Porcupine	5.00
❑38/30¢, Aug 1976, SB (c); SB, KJ (a); 30¢ regional price variant	20.00
❑39, Sep 1976, SB, (c); SB, KJ (a)	4.00
❑40, Oct 1976, SB, GK, KJ (c); SB, KJ (a); Continued Defenders Ann #1	4.00
❑41, Nov 1976, GK, KJ (c); SB, KJ (a)	4.00
❑42, Dec 1976, JK, (c); KG, KJ (a)	4.00
❑43, Jan 1977, AM, JK (c); KG, KJ (a)	4.00
❑44, Feb 1977, JK, (c); KG, KJ (a); Newsstand edition (distributed by Curtis); issue number in box; Hellcat joins Defenders	4.00
❑44/Whitman, Feb 1977, (c); KG, KJ (a); Special markets edition (usually sold in Whitman bagged prepacks); price appears in a diamond; UPC barcode appears; Hellcat joins Defenders	4.00
❑45, Mar 1977, JK (c); KG, KJ (a); Newsstand edition (distributed by Curtis); issue number in box	4.00
❑45/Whitman, Mar 1977, JK (c); KG, KJ (a); Special markets edition (usually sold in Whitman bagged prepacks); price appears in a diamond; UPC barcode appears	4.00

	N-MINT
❑46, Apr 1977, (c); KG, KJ (a)	4.00
❑47, May 1977, (c); KG, KJ (a); A: Moon Knight. Newsstand edition (distributed by Curtis); issue number in box	4.00
❑47/Whitman, May 1977, (c); KG, KJ (a); A: Moon Knight. Special markets edition (usually sold in Whitman bagged prepacks); price appears in a diamond; UPC barcode appears	4.00
❑48, Jun 1977, (c); KG, DGr (a); O: Zodiac II. Newsstand edition (distributed by Curtis); issue number in box	5.00
❑48/Whitman, Jun 1977, (c); KG, DGr (a); O: Zodiac II. Special markets edition (usually sold in Whitman bagged prepacks); price appears in a diamond; UPC barcode appears	5.00
❑48/35¢, Jun 1977, (c); KG, DGr (a); O: Zodiac II. Newsstand edition (distributed by Curtis); issue number in box; 35¢ regional price variant	4.00
❑49, Jul 1977, (c); KG (a); O: Zodiac II.	4.00
❑49/35¢, Jul 1977, AM, (c); KG (a); O: Zodiac II. 35¢ regional price variant	4.00
❑50, Aug 1977, AM (c); KG (a); O: Zodiac II. Newsstand edition (distributed by Curtis); issue number in box	4.00
❑50/Whitman, Aug 1977, KG (a); O: Zodiac II. Special markets edition (usually sold in Whitman bagged prepacks); price appears in a diamond; UPC barcode appears	4.00
❑50/35¢, Aug 1977, Newsstand edition (distributed by Curtis); issue number in box; 35¢ regional price variant	15.00
❑51, Sep 1977, GP (c); KG, KJ (a); 1: Ringer I (Anthony Davis). A: Moon Knight. Newsstand edition (distributed by Curtis); issue number in box; Moon Knight	4.00
❑51/Whitman, Sep 1977, GP (c); KG, KJ (a); 1: Ringer I (Anthony Davis). A: Moon Knight. Special markets edition (usually sold in Whitman bagged prepacks); price appears in a diamond; UPC barcode appears	4.00
❑51/35¢, Sep 1977, GP (c); KG, KJ (a); 1: Ringer I (Anthony Davis). A: Moon Knight. Newsstand edition (distributed by Curtis); issue number in box; Moon Knight; 35¢ regional price variant	15.00
❑52, Oct 1977, GK (c); KG (a); O: Presence. 1: Presence. A: Hulk. V: Sub-Mariner. Newsstand edition (distributed by Curtis); issue number in box	4.00
❑52/Whitman, Oct 1977, GK (c); KG (a); O: Presence. 1: Presence. A: Hulk. V: Sub-Mariner. Special markets edition (usually sold in Whitman bagged prepacks); price appears in a diamond; no UPC barcode	4.00
❑52/35¢, Oct 1977, GK (c); KG (a); O: Presence. 1: Presence. A: Hulk. V: Sub-Mariner. Newsstand edition (distributed by Curtis); issue number in box; 35¢ regional price variant	15.00
❑53, Nov 1977, GP, BWi (c); MG, KG, DC (a); 1: Lunatik. Newsstand edition (distributed by Curtis); issue number in box	4.00
❑53/Whitman, Nov 1977, GP, BWi (c); MG, KG, DC (a); 1: Lunatik. Special markets edition (usually sold in Whitman bagged prepacks); price appears in a diamond; no UPC barcode	4.00
❑54, Dec 1977, GP, (c); MG, KG, BMc (a)	4.00
❑55, Jan 1978, GK (c); Cl, KJ (a); O: Red Guardian II (Doctor Tanja Belinskya). O: Red Guardian II (Doctor Tanja Belinskya); V: the Presence	4.00
❑56, Feb 1978, (c); Cl, KJ (a); V: Lunatik	4.00
❑57, Mar 1978, (c); DGr, GT, DC (a)	4.00
❑58, Apr 1978, (c); DGr, KJ (a)	4.00
❑59, May 1978, (c); DGr (a)	4.00
❑60, Jun 1978, (c); DGr (a)	4.00
❑61, Jul 1978, (c); V: Lunatik; Guest Starring Spider-Man. Vs. Lunatik	4.00
❑62, Aug 1978, BL, JR2 (c); SB, JM (a); Newsstand edition (distributed by Curtis); issue number in box	4.00
❑62/Whitman, Aug 1978, BL, JR2 (c); SB, JM (a); Special markets edition (usually sold in Whitman bagged prepacks); price appears in a diamond; no UPC barcode	4.00
❑63, Sep 1978, JSt (c); SB, JM (a); Newsstand edition (distributed by Curtis); issue number in box	5.00

	N-MINT
❑63/Whitman, Sep 1978, JSt (c); SB, JM (a); Special markets edition (usually sold in Whitman bagged prepacks); price appears in a diamond; UPC barcode appears	5.00
❑64, Oct 1978, SB (c); SB, DP (a); Newsstand edition (distributed by Curtis); issue number in box	4.00
❑64/Whitman, Oct 1978, SB (c); SB, DP (a); Special markets edition (usually sold in Whitman bagged prepacks); price appears in a diamond; no UPC barcode	4.00
❑65, Nov 1978, KP (c); DP (a)	4.00
❑66, Dec 1978, JB, SB (c);Valkerie goes to Asgard	4.00
❑67, Jan 1979, HT, (c); Newsstand edition (distributed by Curtis); issue number in box	4.00
❑67/Whitman, Jan 1979, (c); Special markets edition (usually sold in Whitman bagged prepacks); price appears in a diamond; no UPC barcode	4.00
❑68, Feb 1979, (c); HT (a); Newsstand edition (distributed by Curtis); issue number in box	4.00
❑68/Whitman, Feb 1979, (c); HT (a); Special markets edition (usually sold in Whitman bagged prepacks); price appears in a diamond; no UPC barcode	4.00
❑69, Mar 1979, (c); AM, HT (a)	4.00
❑70, Apr 1979, (c); HT (a); A: Lunatik. V: Lunatik	4.00
❑71, May 1979, HT (c); HT, JAb (a); O: Lunatik	4.00
❑72, Jun 1979, HT (c); HT (a); A: Lunatik	4.00
❑73, Jul 1979, HT (c); HT (a); A: Foolkiller II (Greg Salinger).	4.00
❑74, Aug 1979, HT (c); HT (a); A: Foolkiller II (Greg Salinger). Nighthawk II resigns from Defenders	4.00
❑75, Sep 1979, HT (c); HT (a); A: Foolkiller II (Greg Salinger). V: Foolkiller II (Greg Salinger)	4.00
❑76, Oct 1979, RB (c); HT (a); O: Omega. O: Omega the Unknown	4.00
❑77, Nov 1979, RB (c); AM, HT (a); D: James-Michael Starling (Omega the Unknown's counterpart)	4.00
❑78, Dec 1979, HT (a); Original Defenders return	4.00
❑79, Jan 1980, RB (c); HT (a)	4.00
❑80, Feb 1980, RB (c); DGr, HT (a)	4.00
❑81, Mar 1980, RB (c); HT, JAb (a)	4.00
❑82, Apr 1980, RB (c); DP, JSt (a)	4.00
❑83, May 1980, RB (c); DP (a)	4.00
❑84, Jun 1980, RB (c); DP (a)	4.00
❑85, Jul 1980, RB (c); DP, JM (a)	4.00
❑86, Aug 1980, RB (c); DP (a)	4.00
❑87, Sep 1980, (c); DP (a)	4.00
❑88, Oct 1980, MN (c); DP (a)	4.00
❑89, Nov 1980, MN (c); DP (a)	4.00
❑90, Dec 1980, RB (c); DP (a); A: Daredevil. V: Mandrill	4.00
❑91, Jan 1981, RB (c); DP (a); A: Daredevil. V: Mandrill	4.00
❑92, Feb 1981, DP (a)	4.00
❑93, Mar 1981, DP, JSt (a); V: Nebulon.	2.50
❑94, Apr 1981, MG (c); DP, JSt (a); 1: Gargoyle	2.50
❑95, May 1981, PB (c); DP, JSt (a); O: Gargoyle. A: Dracula	2.50
❑96, Jun 1981, MG (c); DP, JSt (a); A: Ghost Rider	2.50
❑97, Jul 1981, AM (c); DP, JSt (a)	2.50
❑98, Aug 1981, MR (c); DP, JSt (a)	2.50
❑99, Sep 1981, AM (c); DP, JSt (a); V: Mephisto	2.50
❑100, Oct 1981, Giant-size; AM (c); DP, JSt (a)	2.50
❑101, Nov 1981, AM (c); DP, JSt (a); A: Silver Surfer	2.00
❑102, Dec 1981, AM (c); DP, JSt, JAb (a)	2.00
❑103, Jan 1982, AM (c); DP, JSt (a); O: Null the Living Darkness. 1: Null the Living Darkness; O: Gargoyle	2.00
❑104, Feb 1982, AM (c); DP, JSt (a)	2.00
❑105, Mar 1982, AM (c); DP, JSt (a)	2.00
❑106, Apr 1982, AM (c); AM, DP, JAb (a); A: Daredevil. D: Nighthawk II (Kyle Richmond)	2.00
❑107, May 1982, AM (c); AM, DP (a); A: Enchantress	2.00
❑108, Jun 1982, AM, DP (c); AM, DP, JSt (a); V: Enchantress	2.00

Other grades: Multiply price above by 5/6 for VF/NM • 2/3 for VERY FINE • 1/3 for FINE • 1/5 for VERY GOOD • 1/8 for GOOD

David Cassidy

Partridge Family heartthrob in action
©Charlton

Dazzler

Disco darling turns sound into light
©Marvel

DC Challenge

Different writer/artist team each issue
©DC

DC Comics Presents

It's a Superman team-up series
©DC

DC One Million

Comics from the 853rd Century
©DC

N-MINT

❑109, Jul 1982, AM (c); DP, JSt (a); V: The Enchantress 2.00
❑110, Aug 1982, AM, JSn (c); DP (a) 2.00
❑111, Sep 1982, AM (c); DP (a) 2.00
❑112, Oct 1982, BA (c); DP, MGu (a); 1: Power Princess. 1: Nuke I (Albert Gaines) 2.00
❑113, Nov 1982, DP (c); DP (w); DP, MGu (a); V: Over-Mind 2.00
❑114, Dec 1982, AM, DP (c); DP (w); DP, MGu (a) 2.00
❑115, Jan 1983, DP (c); DP (a); Dr. Seuss homage 2.00
❑116, Feb 1983, DP (c); DP (a) 2.00
❑117, Mar 1983, DP, JAb (c); DP, JAb (a) 2.00
❑118, Apr 1983, AM, DP (c); DP (a) 2.00
❑119, May 1983, SB, JAb (a); 1: Yandroth II 2.00
❑120, Jun 1983, DP, JAb (c); DP, JAb (a); V: Miracle Man 2.00
❑121, Jul 1983, DP (c); DP (w); DP, JAb (a); V: Miracle Man 2.00
❑122, Aug 1983, BA, DP (c); DP (a)....... 2.00
❑123, Sep 1983, BSz (c); DP (a); 1: Cloud. 2.00
❑124, Oct 1983, DP (a); Angel appearance (cover only) 2.00
❑125, Nov 1983, double-sized; BSz (c); DP (a); 1: Mad-Dog. New team begins: Valkyrie, Beast, Iceman, Angel, Gargoyle, and Moondragon 2.00
❑126, Dec 1983, MZ (c); 1&O: Leviathan I (Edward Cobert) 2.00
❑127, Jan 1984, MZ (c); SB (a); V: Professor Power; Assistant Editors' Month 2.00
❑128, Feb 1984, KN (c); V: Professor Power 2.00
❑129, Mar 1984, BG (c); DP (a); A: New Mutants. V: New Mutants; V: Mad-Dog; V: Mutant Force 2.00
❑130, Apr 1984, MZ (a); V: Mad-Dog; V: Mutant Force; V: Professor Power.. 2.00
❑131, May 1984, BSz (c); V: Walrus 1.50
❑132, Jun 1984, DP (a) 1.50
❑133, Jul 1984, KN (c); 1: Manslaughter (cameo) 1.50
❑134, Aug 1984, KN (c); DP (a); 1: Manslaughter (full appearance)...... 1.50
❑135, Sep 1984, BSz (c); DP (a); Michael Eury L.O.C 1.50
❑136, Oct 1984, DP (a) 1.50
❑137, Nov 1984, KN (c); DP (a) 1.50
❑138, Dec 1984, DP (a); O: Moondragon 1.50
❑139, Jan 1985, DP (a); Series continues as The New Defenders 1.50
❑140, Feb 1985, DP (a); Title changes to New Defenders in indicia 1.50
❑141, Mar 1985, DP (a) 1.50
❑142, Apr 1985, DP (a) 1.50
❑143, May 1985, BA (c); DP (a); O: Moondragon. 1: Runner. 1: Dragon of the Moon. 1: Andromeda 1.50
❑144, Jun 1985, DP (a) 1.50
❑145, Jul 1985, DP (a); A: Johnny Blaze 1.50
❑146, Aug 1985, LMc (a) 1.50
❑147, Sep 1985, CV (c); DP (a); Sgt. Fury and His Howling Defenders on both cover and in indicia 1.50
❑148, Oct 1985, SB (a) 1.50
❑149, Nov 1985, KN (c); DP (a); O: Andromeda 1.50
❑150, Dec 1985, double-sized; DP (a); O: Cloud 1.50

N-MINT

❑151, Jan 1986, KN (c); DP (a); V: Manslaughter 1.50
❑152, Feb 1986, double-sized; DP (a); O: Manslaughter. Secret Wars II........ 1.50
❑Ann 1, Nov 1976, (c); SB, KJ (a); O: Hulk. V: Headmen; V: Nebulon 12.00

Defenders
Marvel

❑1, Mar 2001, V: Toad Men; V: Quasimodo; V: Yandroth; Double-Size Issue 2.99
❑2, Apr 2001, Hulk/Sub-Mariner cover; V: Attuma; V: Pluto 2.25
❑2/Variant, Apr 2001 .... 2.25
❑3, May 2001, V: Pluto; V: Lorelei 2.25
❑4, Jun 2001, V: Pluto; V: Lorelei 2.25
❑5, Jul 2001, V: Headmen; V: Attuma.... 2.25
❑6, Aug 2001, V: Bi-Beast 2.25
❑7, Sep 2001, V: Attuma; V: Orka; V: Sea Urchin; V: Tiger Shark; V: Piranha; V: Nagala 2.25
❑8, Oct 2001, Cover quotes Comics International review: "Worst Comic Ever Published" 2.25
❑9, Nov 2001, V: Headmen; V: Modok; V: Orrgo the Unconquerable 2.25
❑10, Dec 2001, V: Headmen; V: Modok; V: Orrgo the Unconquerable 2.25
❑11, Jan 2002, V: Attuma; V: Orka; V: Sea Urchin; V: Tiger Shark; V: Piranha; V: Nagala 2.25
❑12, Feb 2002, Final issue; Story continues in The Order 3.50

Defenders
Marvel

❑1, Sep 2005 .... 5.00
❑2, Oct 2005 .... 2.99
❑3 2005 .... 2.99
❑4 2005 .... 2.99
❑5, Mar 2006 .... 2.99

Defenders of Dynatron City
Marvel

❑1, Feb 1992 .... 1.25
❑2, Mar 1992; O: Defenders of Dynatron City 1.25
❑3, Apr 1992 .... 1.25
❑4, May 1992 .... 1.25
❑5, Jun 1992 .... 1.25
❑6, Jul 1992 .... 1.25

Defenders of the Earth
Marvel / Star

❑1, Jan 1987; Flash Gordon, Mandrake, Phantom 1.00
❑2, Mar 1987; Flash Gordon, Mandrake, Phantom 1.00
❑3, May 1987; Flash Gordon, Mandrake, Phantom 1.00
❑4, Jul 1987; Final Issue 1.00

Defenseless Dead
Adventure

❑1, Feb 1991, b&w; based on Larry Niven story 2.50
❑2, ca. 1991, b&w; based on Larry Niven story 2.50
❑3, ca. 1991, b&w; based on Larry Niven story 2.50

N-MINT

Defex
Devil's Due

❑1, Oct 2004 .... 5.00
❑1/Variant 2004 .... 1.48
❑2, Nov 2004 .... 2.95
❑3, Dec 2004 .... 2.95
❑4, Jan 2005 .... 2.95
❑5, Mar 2005 .... 2.95
❑6, Jun 2005 .... 2.95

Defiance
Image

❑1, Feb 2002 .... 3.50
❑2, Apr 2002 .... 2.95
❑3, Jun 2002 .... 2.95
❑4, Sep 2002 .... 2.95
❑5, Nov 2002; variant cover 2.95
❑6, Mar 2003; variant cover 2.95
❑7, Apr 2003; variant cover 2.95
❑8, Jul 2003 .... 2.95

Defiant Genesis
Defiant

❑1, Oct 1993; no cover price 1.00

Definition
Slave Labor

❑1, Aug 1997, b&w; Oversized; NN........ 12.95

Deicide
DC

❑1, ca. 2004 .... 14.95

Deity
Image

❑0, May 1998; exclusive New Dimension Comics edition; Flip cover 6.00
❑0/A, May 1998 .... 3.00
❑1, Sep 1997; White background on cover 3.00
❑1/A, Sep 1997; variant cover 3.00
❑2, Oct 1997; Regular cover (power blasts) 3.00
❑2/A, Oct 1997; variant cover; Brandishing gun, sword 3.00
❑3, Nov 1997; Regular cover (brown background, bandages on face) 2.95
❑3/A, Nov 1997; variant cover; Cyborg girl 3.50
❑4, Dec 1997 .... 2.95
❑4/A, Dec 1997; variant cover 3.00
❑5, Feb 1998 .... 2.95
❑5/A, Feb 1998; variant cover 3.00
❑6, Apr 1998; Girl with backpack on cover 2.95
❑6/A, Apr 1998; variant cover 3.00

Deity
Image

❑1, Sep 1998; Flipbook preview of Catseye 2.95
❑1/A, Sep 1998; Variant cover with blue background, wielding sword 2.95
❑1/B, Sep 1998; Variant cover with monster threatening 2.95
❑1/C, Sep 1998; Variant cover with gratuitous bathing suit, cleavage........ 2.95
❑2, Nov 1998; Wrapped in bath towel cover 2.95
❑3, Jan 1999 .... 2.95
❑4, Jan 1999; Group montage cover...... 2.95
❑5, May 1999; Green background on cover 2.95
❑Ashcan 1, Jun 1998; Special Preview edition 2.95

Other grades: Multiply price above by 5/6 for VF/NM • 2/3 for VERY FINE • 1/3 for FINE • 1/5 for VERY GOOD • 1/8 for GOOD

Deity: Requiem
Image

❑1, May 2005; Gatefold summary.......... 6.95

Deity: Revelations
Image

❑1, Jul 1999; Woman on floating skateboard, figures in background..... 2.95
❑1/A, Jul 1999; variant cover: woman holding her face on cover.................. 2.95
❑1/B, Jul 1999; variant cover................ 2.95
❑2, Sep 1999; variant cover.................. 2.95
❑3, Nov 1999.. 2.95
❑4, Jan 2000... 2.95

Deja Vu
Fantaco

❑1, ca. 2000, Flip cover........................ 2.95

Deja Vu
Radio

❑1, Nov 2000, Flip cover....................... 2.95

Delia Charm
Red Menace

❑1.. 2.95
❑2.. 2.95

Delicate Creatures
Image

❑1/HC, Dec 2001.................................. 16.95

Delirium
Metro

❑1.. 2.00

Deliverer
Zion

❑1, Oct 1994... 2.50

Delta Squadron
Anderpol

❑1.. 2.00

Delta Tenn
Entertainment

❑1, Jul 1987.. 1.50
❑2, Sep 1987.. 1.50
❑3, Nov 1987.. 1.50
❑4, Jan 1988.. 1.50
❑5, Mar 1988.. 1.50
❑6, May 1988... 1.50
❑7, Jul 1988.. 1.50
❑8, Sep 1988.. 1.50
❑9, b&w... 1.50
❑10, b&w... 1.50

Delta, the Ultimate Difference
Apex One

❑1, Oct 1997, b&w; no cover price........ 2.00
❑2, Fal 1998, b&w; cardstock cover...... 2.95

Delta-Wave
Miller

❑1, ca. 1992.. 2.50

Demented: Scorpion Child
DMF

❑1, Nov 2000.. 2.95
❑2, Dec 2000.. 2.95
❑3, Jan 2001... 2.95
❑4, Feb 2001... 2.95
❑5, Mar 2001... 2.95

Demi's Wild Kingdom Adventure
Opus

❑1, Mar 2000, b&w; squarebound......... 9.95

Demi the Demoness
Rip Off

❑1, Mar 1993, Carnal Comics publishes 2.50
❑1/2nd, Rip-Off publishes..................... 2.95
❑2, Nov 1993... 2.95
❑3, Mar 1995, flip-book with Kit-Ra back-up.. 2.95
❑4, 1: Imed the Angelic.......................... 3.25
❑5.. 2.95
❑6, Jun 2002, Carnal Comics publishes. 5.95
❑Special 1, "Choose your own adventure"- style special.................. 5.95

Demolition Man
DC

❑1, Nov 1993... 1.75
❑2, Dec 1993... 1.75
❑3, Jan 1994.. 1.75
❑4, Feb 1994.. 1.75

Demon
DC

❑1, Aug 1972, JK (c); JK (w); JK (a); O: Etrigan. 1: Jason Blood. 1: Etrigan. 1: Randu Singh. 1st Demon.............. 30.00
❑2, Oct 1972, JK (c); JK (w); JK (a)....... 12.00
❑3, Nov 1972, JK (c); JK (w); JK (a); A: Batman. Batman............................. 10.00
❑4, Dec 1972, JK (c); JK (w); JK (a)...... 10.00
❑5, Jan 1973, JK (c); JK (w); JK (a)....... 9.00
❑6, Feb 1973, JK (c); JK (w); JK (a)....... 9.00
❑7, Mar 1973, JK (c); JK (w); JK (a); 1: Klarion the Witch Boy....................... 9.00
❑8, Apr 1973, JK (c); JK (w); JK (a)....... 9.00
❑9, Jun 1973, JK (c); JK (w); JK (a)...... 9.00
❑10, Jul 1973, JK (c); JK (w); JK (a)..... 7.00
❑11, Aug 1973, JK (c); JK (w); JK (a).... 7.00
❑12, Sep 1973, JK (c); JK (w); JK (a).... 10.00
❑13, Oct 1973, JK (c); JK (w); JK (a)..... 10.00
❑14, Nov 1973, JK (c); JK (w); JK (a); 2: Klarion the Witch Boy.................... 7.00
❑15, Dec 1973, JK (c); JK (w); JK (a).... 7.00
❑16, Jan 1974, JK (c); JK (w); JK (a).... 7.00

Demon
DC

❑1, Jan 1987 MW (c); MW (w); MW (a) 2.00
❑2, Feb 1987 MW (c); MW (w); MW (a) 2.00
❑3, Mar 1987 MW (c); MW (w); MW (a) 2.00
❑4, Apr 1987 MW (c); MW (w); MW (a) 2.00

Demon
DC

❑0, Oct 1994; O: Jason Blood. O: Etrigan 2.00
❑1, Jul 1990... 4.00
❑2, Aug 1990... 2.50
❑3, Sep 1990; Batman........................... 2.50
❑4, Oct 1990.. 2.25
❑5, Nov 1990... 2.25
❑6, Dec 1990... 2.25
❑7, Jan 1991.. 2.25
❑8, Feb 1991; Batman........................... 2.25
❑9, Mar 1991.. 2.25
❑10, Apr 1991.. 2.25
❑11, May 1991....................................... 3.00
❑12, Jun 1991 A: Lobo........................... 2.00
❑13, Jul 1991 A: Lobo............................ 2.00
❑14, Aug 1991 A: Lobo........................... 2.00
❑15, Sep 1991 A: Lobo........................... 2.00
❑16, Oct 1991.. 2.00
❑17, Nov 1991; War of the Gods........... 2.00
❑18, Dec 1991.. 2.00
❑19, Jan 1992; Double-size; Lobo poster 2.50
❑20, Feb 1992.. 2.00
❑21, Mar 1992.. 2.00
❑22, Apr 1992 MW (w); MW (a)............ 2.00
❑23, May 1992; Robin........................... 2.00
❑24, Jun 1992; Robin............................ 2.00
❑25, Jul 1992 KG (w); KG (a)................ 1.50
❑26, Aug 1992....................................... 1.50
❑27, Sep 1992.. 1.50
❑28, Oct 1992; Superman...................... 1.50
❑29, Nov 1992....................................... 1.75
❑30, Dec 1992....................................... 1.75
❑31, Jan 1993.. 1.75
❑32, Feb 1993.. 1.75
❑33, Mar 1993....................................... 1.75
❑34, Apr 1993; Lobo.............................. 1.75
❑35, May 1993; Lobo............................. 1.75
❑36, Jun 1993.. 1.75
❑37, Jul 1993... 1.75
❑38, Aug 1993....................................... 1.75
❑39, Sep 1993.. 1.75
❑40, Oct 1993.. 1.75
❑41, Nov 1993....................................... 1.75
❑42, Dec 1993....................................... 1.75
❑43, Jan 1994; A: Hitman. 1: Baytor...... 3.50
❑44, Feb 1994 A: Hitman...................... 3.00
❑45, Mar 1994 A: Hitman...................... 3.00
❑46, Apr 1994 A: Haunted Tank............ 1.75
❑47, May 1994 A: Haunted Tank........... 1.75
❑48, Jun 1994.. 1.95
❑49, Jul 1994... 1.95
❑50, Aug 1994; Giant-size; 50th anniversary issue................................. 2.95
❑51, Sep 1994.. 1.95
❑52, Nov 1994 A: Hitman...................... 3.00
❑53, Dec 1994 A: Hitman...................... 3.00
❑54, Jan 1995 A: Hitman....................... 3.00
❑55, Feb 1995; Cover after Joe Kubert's classic cover to "The Losers"............. 1.95
❑56, Mar 1995....................................... 1.95
❑57, Apr 1995.. 1.95
❑58, May 1995; Final Issue.................... 1.95
❑Ann 1, ca. 1992; V: Klarion.................. 3.00
❑Ann 2, ca. 1993; 1: Hitman.................. 12.00

Demon Beast Invasion
CPM / Bare Bear

❑1, Oct 1996, b&w; wraparound cover.. 2.95

Demon Beast Invasion: The Fallen
CPM / Bare Bear

❑1, Sep 1998, b&w; Adult..................... 2.95
❑2, Oct 1998, b&w; Adult..................... 2.95

Demonblade
New Comics

❑1, b&w.. 1.95

Demon Dreams
Pacific

❑1, Feb 1984... 1.50
❑2, May 1984... 1.50

Demon Driven Out
DC / Vertigo

❑1, Nov 2003... 2.50
❑2, Dec 2003... 2.50
❑3, Jan 2004.. 2.50
❑4, Feb 2004... 2.50
❑5, Mar 2004... 2.50
❑6, Apr 2004.. 2.50

Demongate
Sirius

❑1, May 1996.. 2.50
❑2, Jun 1996... 2.50
❑3, Jul 1996.. 2.50
❑4 1996... 2.50
❑5, Oct 1996... 2.50
❑6, Nov 1996.. 2.50
❑7, Dec 1996... 2.50
❑8, Jan 1997.. 2.50
❑9, Feb 1997, b&w................................. 2.50

Demon Gun
Crusade

❑1, Jun 1996, b&w................................ 2.95
❑2, Sep 1996, b&w................................ 2.95
❑3, Jan 1997, b&w................................. 2.95

Demon-Hunter
Atlas-Seaboard

❑1, Sep 1975; RB (c); RB (w); RB (a); 1: Gideon Cross.................................. 2.00

Demon Hunter
Aircel

❑1, Mar 1989, b&w................................ 1.95
❑2, Apr 1989, b&w................................ 1.95
❑3, May 1989, b&w............................... 1.95
❑4, Jun 1989, b&w................................ 1.95

Demon Hunter
Davdez

❑1, Aug 1998; Adult............................... 2.50

Demonic Toys
Eternity

❑1, Jan 1992.. 2.50
❑2.. 2.50
❑3.. 2.50
❑4.. 2.50

Demonique
London Night

❑1, Oct 1994, b&w................................. 3.00
❑2 1995... 3.00
❑3 1995... 3.00
❑4 1995... 3.00

Demonique: Angel of Night
London Night

❑1, Jul 1997... 3.00

Demon Ororon
Tokyopop

❑1, Apr 2004.. 9.99

Demon Realm
Medeia

❑0.. 2.50

Demons & Dark Elves
Weirdworx

❑1, b&w.. 2.95

DC Special

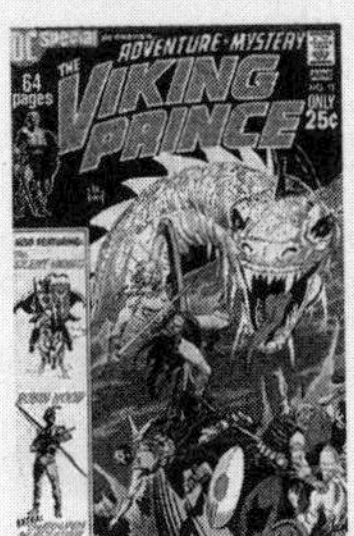

Double-sized issues spotlighting the DC world
©DC

DC Super-Stars

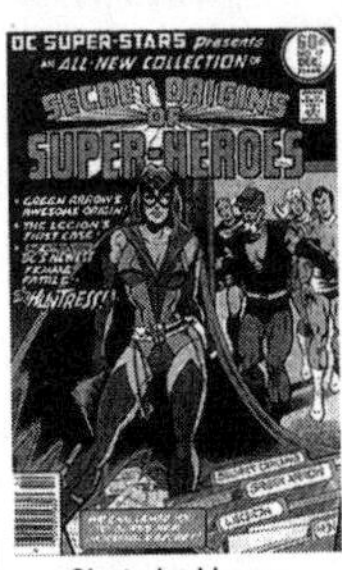

Giant-sized issues reprinting classic DC stories
©DC

Dead, The

Blood and gore from Arrow Comics
©Arrow

Deadbeats

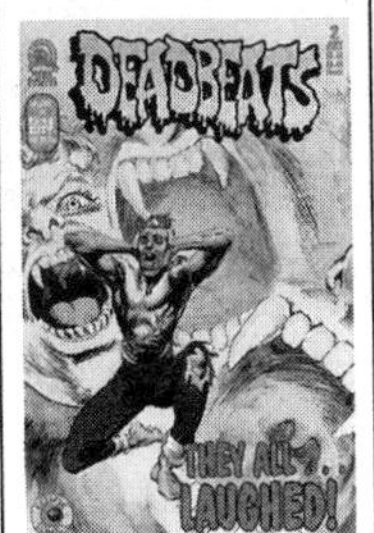

Black-and-white vampire soap opera
©Claypool

Deadenders

Haves and have-nots in post-apocalyptic future
©DC

Demon's Blood
Odyssey

	N-MINT
❑1	2.00

Demonslayer
Image

	N-MINT
❑1, Nov 1999	2.95
❑2, Dec 1999	2.95
❑3, Jan 2000	2.95

Demonslayer
Next

	N-MINT
❑0; Tower Records cover	2.95

Demonslayer
Image

	N-MINT
❑1, Jun 2000	2.95
❑2, Jul 2000	2.95
❑3, Aug 2000	2.95

Demon's Tails
Adventure

	N-MINT
❑1, Jan 1993, b&w	2.50
❑2, Feb 1993, b&w	2.50
❑3, Mar 1993, b&w	2.50
❑4, Apr 1993, b&w	2.50

Demon Warrior
Eastern

	N-MINT
❑1, Aug 1987, b&w	1.50
❑2 1987, b&w	1.50
❑3 1987, b&w	1.50
❑4 1988, b&w	1.50
❑5, b&w	1.50
❑6, b&w	1.50

DemonWars: Eye for an Eye
CrossGen

	N-MINT
❑1, Jun 2003	2.95
❑2, Jul 2003	2.95
❑3, Aug 2003	2.95
❑4, Sep 2003	2.95
❑5, Oct 2003	2.95

DemonWars: Trial by Fire
CrossGen

	N-MINT
❑1, Jan 2003	2.95
❑2, Feb 2003	2.95
❑3, Mar 2003	2.95
❑4, Apr 2003	2.95
❑5, May 2003	2.95

Demonwish
Pocket Change

	N-MINT
❑1, ca. 1995, b&w; Indicia gives title as one word; copy on inside front cover gives it as two	2.50

Den
Fantagor

	N-MINT
❑1	3.00
❑2	3.00
❑3	3.00
❑4	3.00
❑5	3.00
❑6	2.50
❑7	2.50
❑8	2.50
❑9 AN (a)	2.50
❑10	2.50

Denizens of Deep City
Kitchen Sink

	N-MINT
❑1, ca. 1988, b&w	2.00
❑2, ca. 1988, b&w	2.00
❑3, ca. 1988, b&w	2.00
❑4, ca. 1988, b&w	2.00
❑5, ca. 1988, b&w	2.00
❑6, ca. 1988, b&w	2.00
❑7, ca. 1988, b&w	2.00
❑8, ca. 1988, b&w	2.00
❑9, ca. 1988	2.00

Dennis the Menace
Fawcett

	N-MINT
❑55 1961	14.00
❑56 1962	14.00
❑57 1962	14.00
❑58 1962	14.00
❑59 1962	14.00
❑60, Jul 1962	14.00
❑61 1962	14.00
❑62 1962	14.00
❑63 1963	14.00
❑64, Jan 1963	14.00
❑65, Mar 1963	14.00
❑66, May 1963	14.00
❑67, Jul 1963	14.00
❑68, Sep 1963	14.00
❑69, Nov 1963	14.00
❑70, Jan 1964	14.00
❑71, Mar 1964	10.00
❑72, May 1964	10.00
❑73, Jul 1964	10.00
❑74, Sep 1964	10.00
❑75, Nov 1964	10.00
❑76, Jan 1965	10.00
❑77, Mar 1965	10.00
❑78, May 1965	10.00
❑79, Jul 1965	10.00
❑80, Sep 1965	10.00
❑81, Nov 1965	10.00
❑82, Jan 1966	10.00
❑83, Mar 1966	10.00
❑84, May 1966	10.00
❑85, Jul 1966	10.00
❑86, Sep 1966	10.00
❑87, Nov 1966	10.00
❑88, Jan 1967	10.00
❑89, Mar 1967	10.00
❑90, May 1967	10.00
❑91, Jul 1967	6.00
❑92, Sep 1967	6.00
❑93, Nov 1967	6.00
❑94, Jan 1968	6.00
❑95, Mar 1968	6.00
❑96, May 1968	6.00
❑97, Jul 1968	6.00
❑98, Sep 1968	6.00
❑99, Nov 1968	6.00
❑100, Jan 1969	6.00
❑101, Mar 1969	4.00
❑102, May 1969	4.00
❑103, Jul 1969	4.00
❑104, Sep 1969	4.00
❑105, Nov 1969	4.00
❑106, Jan 1970	4.00
❑107, Mar 1970	4.00
❑108, May 1970	4.00
❑109, Jul 1970	4.00
❑110, Sep 1970	4.00
❑111, Nov 1970	4.00
❑112, Jan 1971	4.00
❑113, Mar 1971	4.00
❑114, May 1971	4.00
❑115, Jul 1971	4.00
❑116, Sep 1971, anti-pollution issue	4.00
❑117, Nov 1971	4.00
❑118, Jan 1972	4.00
❑119, Mar 1972	4.00
❑120, May 1972	4.00
❑121, Jul 1972	3.00
❑122, Sep 1972, Spirit of '72	3.00
❑123, Nov 1972	3.00
❑124, Jan 1973	3.00
❑125, Mar 1973	3.00
❑126, May 1973, A: Gina	3.00
❑127, Jul 1973	3.00
❑128, Sep 1973	3.00
❑129, Nov 1973	3.00
❑130, Jan 1974	3.00
❑131, Mar 1974	3.00
❑132, May 1974	3.00
❑133, Jul 1974	3.00
❑134, Sep 1974	3.00
❑135, Nov 1974, Dennis visits The Exploratorium at The Palace of Fine Arts in San Francisco	3.00
❑136, Jan 1975	3.00
❑137, Mar 1975	3.00
❑138, May 1975	3.00
❑139, Jul 1975	3.00
❑140, Sep 1975, at Winchester mansion	3.00
❑141, Nov 1975	2.00
❑142, Jan 1976	2.00
❑143, Mar 1976	2.00
❑144, May 1976	2.00
❑145, Jun 1976	2.00
❑146, Jul 1976	2.00
❑147, Sep 1976	2.00
❑148, Nov 1976	2.00
❑149, Jan 1977	2.00
❑150, Mar 1977	2.00
❑151, May 1977, Dennis visits Solvang	2.00
❑152, Jul 1977	2.00
❑153, Sep 1977, Dennis the Menace visits the Lawrence Hall of Science	2.00
❑154, Nov 1977	2.00
❑155, Jan 1978	2.00
❑156, Mar 1978	2.00
❑157, May 1978	2.00
❑158, Jul 1978	2.00
❑159, Sep 1978	2.00
❑160, Nov 1978	2.00
❑161, Jan 1979	2.00
❑162, Mar 1979	2.00
❑163, May 1979	2.00
❑164, Jul 1979	2.00
❑165, Sep 1979	2.00
❑166, Nov 1979, Final Issue	2.00

Dennis the Menace (Giants)
Fawcett

	N-MINT
❑10, Win 1961, Giant Christmas issue	50.00

Other grades: Multiply price above by 5/6 for VF/NM • 2/3 for VERY FINE • 1/3 for FINE • 1/5 for VERY GOOD • 1/8 for GOOD

N-MINT

❑11, Win 1962, Giant Christmas issue... 50.00
❑12, Win 1962, Three Books in One: ...and his Pal Joey; ...and Margaret; ...and Mr. Wilson... 50.00
❑13, Spr 1963, The Best of Dennis the Menace... 35.00
❑14, Sum 1963, ...and His Dog Ruff... 35.00
❑15, Sum 1963, ...in Washington, D.C.; flag cover... 35.00
❑16, Sum 1963, Vacation Special; reprints #9... 35.00
❑17, Win 1963, ...and His Pal Joey; one date stamp has been seen on this issue for Oct. 17, 1963... 35.00
❑18, Sum 1963, ...in Hawaii; reprints #6; cover says it's the sixth printing... 35.00
❑19, Win 1963, ...in Christmas City... 35.00
❑20, Spr 1964, Spring Special... 35.00
❑21, Spr 1964, The Very Best of Dennis the Menace... 22.00
❑22, Spr 1964, Television Special... 22.00
❑23, Sum 1964, ...in Hollywood; reprints #7... 22.00
❑24, Sum 1964, ...Goes to Camp; reprints #9... 22.00
❑25, Sum 1964, ...in Mexico; reprints #8 22.00
❑26, Sum 1964, ...in Washington, D.C.; reprints #15... 22.00
❑27, Win 1964, ...Christmas Special... 22.00
❑28, Spr 1965, Triple Feature... 22.00
❑29, Spr 1965, Best of Dennis the Menace (reprints)... 22.00
❑30, Sum 1965, ...in Hawaii; reprints #6 18.00
❑31, Sum 1965, ...All Year ëRound... 18.00
❑32, Sum 1965, ...and His Pal Joey; reprints #17... 18.00
❑33, Sum 1965, ...in California... 18.00
❑34, Sum 1965, ...and His Dog Ruff; reprints #14... 18.00
❑35, Win 1965, gatefold summary; Christmas Special... 18.00
❑36, Spr 1966, Spring Special... 18.00
❑37, Spr 1966, Television Special; reprints #22... 18.00
❑38, Sum 1966, ...in Mexico; reprints #8 18.00
❑39, Sum 1966, ...Goes to Camp; reprints #9... 18.00
❑40, Sum 1966, ...Visits Washington D.C.; reprints #15... 18.00
❑41, Sum 1966, ...From A to Z... 15.00
❑42, Sum 1966, ...In Hollywood; reprints #7... 15.00
❑43, Win 1966, Christmas Special... 15.00
❑44, Spr 1967, ...Around the Clock... 15.00
❑45, Spr 1967, ...and His Pal Joey; reprints #17... 15.00
❑46, Sum 1967, ...Triple Feature; reprints #28... 15.00
❑47, Sum 1967, ...in California; reprints #33... 15.00
❑48, Sum 1967, ...Way Out Stories... 15.00
❑49, Fal 1967, ...All Year ëRound; reprints #31... 15.00
❑50, Sum 1967, ...at the Circus... 15.00
❑51, Win 1967, Christmas Special... 12.00
❑52, Spr 1968, Sports Special... 12.00
❑53, Spr 1968, Spring Special; reprints part of #36... 12.00
❑54, Sum 1968, ...and His Dog Ruff; reprints #14... 12.00
❑55, Spr 1968, Television Special; reprints #22... 12.00
❑56, Spr 1968, ...Tall Stories... 12.00
❑57, Sum 1968, ...Pet Parade... 12.00
❑58, Sum 1968, Best of Dennis the Menace (reprints from regular series) 12.00
❑59, Sum 1968, ...Day By Day... 12.00
❑60, Fal 1968, ...in Hollywood; reprints #7 12.00
❑61, Win 1968, Christmas Favorites... 10.00
❑62, Win 1968, ...Fun Book; partially reprints Dennis the Menace Fun Book #1... 10.00
❑63, Win 1969, ...and His I-Wish-I-Was Book; retail incentive program announcement on last page... 10.00
❑64, Spr 1969, ...in Mexico; reprints #8. 10.00
❑65, Spr 1969, ...Around the Clock; reprints #44... 10.00
❑66, Sum 1969, ...Gags and Games... 10.00
❑67, Sum 1969, ...Goes to Camp; reprints #9 10.00
❑68, Sum 1969, ...in Hawaii; reprints #6 10.00
❑69, Aug 1969, The Best of Dennis the Menace (reprints from regular series) 10.00

N-MINT

❑70, Aug 1969, ...Tangled Tales... 10.00
❑71, Sep 1969, ...Highlights... 10.00
❑72, Aug 1969, ...in Washington D.C.; reprints #15; date really is earlier than #71... 10.00
❑73, Sep 1969, ...Way Out Stories; reprints #48... 10.00
❑74, Dec 1969, ... and Mr. Wilson and His Gang at Christmas... 10.00
❑75, Dec 1969, Christmas Special; numbering continues as Dennis the Menace Bonus Magazine Series... 10.00

Dennis the Menace
Marvel

❑1, Nov 1981... 2.00
❑2, Dec 1981... 1.50
❑3, Jan 1982... 1.50
❑4, Feb 1982... 1.50
❑5, Mar 1982... 1.50
❑6, Apr 1982, Reuses dragon image on cover from Thor #277... 1.50
❑7, May 1982... 1.50
❑8, Jun 1982... 1.50
❑9, Jul 1982... 1.50
❑10, Aug 1982... 1.50
❑11, Sep 1982... 1.50
❑12, Oct 1982... 1.50
❑13, Nov 1982... 1.50

Dennis the Menace and his Friends
Fawcett

❑1, ca. 1969, ...and Joey (#2 on cover). 12.00
❑2, ca. 1969, ...and Ruff (#2 on cover).. 12.00
❑3, Oct 1969, ...and Mr. Wilson (#1 on cover)... 12.00
❑4, ca. 1969, ...and Margaret (#1 on cover)... 12.00
❑5, Jan 1970, ...and Margaret (#5 on cover)... 8.00
❑6, Jun 1970, Joey... 5.00
❑7, Aug 1970... 5.00
❑8, Oct 1970... 5.00
❑9, Jan 1971... 5.00
❑10, Jun 1971... 5.00
❑11, Aug 1971... 4.00
❑12, Oct 1971, Mr. Wilson... 4.00
❑13, Jan 1972, Margaret... 4.00
❑14, Jun 1972... 4.00
❑15, Aug 1972, Ruff... 4.00
❑16, Oct 1972, Mr. Wilson... 4.00
❑17, Jan 1973... 4.00
❑18, Jun 1973, Joey... 4.00
❑19, Aug 1973... 4.00
❑20, Oct 1973... 4.00
❑21, Jan 1974... 3.00
❑22, Jun 1974, Joey... 3.00
❑23, Aug 1974... 3.00
❑24, Oct 1974... 3.00
❑25, Jan 1975... 3.00
❑26, Jun 1975... 3.00
❑27, Aug 1975... 3.00
❑28, Oct 1975... 3.00
❑29, Jan 1976, ...and Margaret (#29)... 3.00
❑30, Jun 1976... 3.00
❑31, Aug 1976... 3.00
❑32, Oct 1976... 3.00
❑33, Jan 1977... 3.00
❑34, Jun 1977... 3.00
❑35, Aug 1977, Ruff... 3.00
❑36, Oct 1977... 3.00
❑37, Oct 1977... 3.00
❑38, Apr 1978, digest size begins; Digest size begins... 2.50
❑39, Jun 1978... 2.50
❑40, Aug 1978... 2.50
❑41, Oct 1978, Reprints first Margaret story; Screamy Mimi story; Chub story 2.50
❑42, Apr 1979... 2.50
❑43, Jun 1979, Reprints 24 of 26 Dennis Alphabet stories, omitting A and B... 2.50
❑44, Jul 1979... 2.50
❑45, Oct 1979... 2.50
❑46, Apr 1980, Final Issue... 2.50

Dennis the Menace Big Bonus Series
Fawcett

❑10, Feb 1980... 3.00
❑11, Apr 1980... 3.00

N-MINT

Dennis the Menace Bonus Magazine Series
Fawcett

❑76, Jan 1970, ...in the Caribbean, Jamaica, and Puerto Rico; series continued from Dennis the Menace (Giants) #75... 8.00
❑77, Feb 1970, ...Sports Special... 8.00
❑78, Mar 1970, Spring Special... 8.00
❑79, Apr 1970, ...Tall Stories; reprints Dennis the Menace Giant #56... 8.00
❑80, May 1970, ...Day by Day; reprints Dennis the Menace Giant #59... 8.00
❑81, Jun 1970, ...Summer Funner... 8.00
❑82, Jun 1970, ...In California; reprints Dennis the Menace Giant #33... 8.00
❑83, Jul 1970, ...Mama Goose... 8.00
❑84, Jul 1970, ...At the Circus; reprints Dennis the Menace Giant #50... 8.00
❑85, Aug 1970, ...Fall-Ball... 8.00
❑86, Oct 1970, ...and Mr. Wilson and His Gang at Christmas; reprints Dennis the Menace Giant #74... 8.00
❑87, Oct 1970, Christmas Special... 8.00
❑88, Jan 1971, ...in London... 8.00
❑89, Feb 1971, Spring Fling... 8.00
❑90, Mar 1971, ...Here's How... 8.00
❑91, Apr 1971, ...Fun Book; reprints part of Dennis the Menace Fun Book #1... 7.00
❑92, May 1971, ...in Hollywood; reprints Dennis the Menace Giant #7... 7.00
❑93, Jun 1971, ...Visits Paris... 7.00
❑94, Jun 1971, ...Jackpot... 7.00
❑95, Jul 1971, ...That's Our Boy; there are two #95s and no #96... 7.00
❑95/A, Jul 1971, ...Summer Games; there are two #95s and no #96... 7.00
❑97, Aug 1971, ...Comicapers... 7.00
❑98, Oct 1971, Mr. Wilson and His Gang at Christmas; reprints Dennis the Menace Giant #74... 7.00
❑99, Oct 1971, ...Fiesta... 7.00
❑100, Jan 1972, Christmas Special... 7.00
❑101, Feb 1972, ...Up in the Air... 7.00
❑102, Mar 1972, ...Rise and Shine... 7.00
❑103, Apr 1972, ...and His I-Wish-I-Was Book; reprints Dennis the Menace Giant #63... 7.00
❑104, May 1972, ...Short Stuff Special.. 7.00
❑105, Jun 1972, ...in Mexico; reprints Dennis the Menace Giant #8... 7.00
❑106, Jun 1972, ...Birthday Special... 7.00
❑107, Jul 1972, ...Fast & Funny... 7.00
❑108, Jul 1972, ...Around the Clock; reprints Dennis the Menace Giant #44 7.00
❑109, Aug 1972, ...Goes to Camp; reprints Dennis the Menace Giant #9... 7.00
❑110, Oct 1972, ...Gags and Games; reprints Dennis the Menace Giant #66 7.00
❑111, Oct 1972, Christmas Special... 7.00
❑112, Jan 1973, ...Go-Go Special... 7.00
❑113, Feb 1973... 7.00
❑114, Mar 1973... 7.00
❑115, Apr 1973, Ting-a-Ling Special... 7.00
❑116, May 1973... 7.00
❑117, Jun 1973... 7.00
❑118, Jun 1973, Here's How!... 7.00
❑119, Jul 1973, Summer Number and state flags... 7.00
❑120, Jul 1973... 7.00
❑121, Aug 1973... 6.00
❑122, Oct 1973... 6.00
❑123, Oct 1973... 6.00
❑124, Jan 1974, Happy Holidays!... 6.00
❑125, Feb 1974... 6.00
❑126, Mar 1974... 6.00
❑127, Apr 1974... 6.00
❑128, May 1974... 6.00
❑129, Jun 1974... 6.00
❑130, Jun 1974... 6.00
❑131, Jul 1974... 6.00
❑132, Jul 1974... 6.00
❑133, Aug 1974, That's the Spirit!; The Mitchells take a cruise... 6.00
❑134, Oct 1974, Christmas... 6.00
❑135, Oct 1974... 6.00
❑136, Jan 1975... 6.00
❑137, Feb 1975... 6.00
❑138, Mar 1975... 6.00
❑139, Apr 1975... 6.00
❑140, May 1975... 6.00

Other grades: Multiply price above by 5/6 for VF/NM • 2/3 for VERY FINE • 1/3 for FINE • 1/5 for VERY GOOD • 1/8 for GOOD

Deadman

You can't keep a good man down

©DC

Dead of Night

Deservedly obscure horror series from Marvel

©Marvel

Deadpool

Wise-cracking mercenary gets own series

©Marvel

Deadworld

Zombies and worse walk the Earth

©Arrow

Deathblow

Human killing machine does dirty work

©Image

	N-MINT
❑141, Jun 1975	6.00
❑142, Jun 1975	6.00
❑143, Jul 1975	6.00
❑144, Jul 1975	6.00
❑145, Aug 1975	6.00
❑146, Oct 1975, Christmas	6.00
❑147, Oct 1975, ... and Mr. Wilson and His Gang at Christmas	6.00
❑148, Jan 1976, ... In Florida	6.00
❑149, Feb 1976	6.00
❑150, Mar 1976	6.00
❑151, Apr 1976	4.00
❑152, May 1976	4.00
❑153, Jun 1976	4.00
❑154, Jun 1976	4.00
❑155, Jul 1976	4.00
❑156, Jul 1976	4.00
❑157, Aug 1976	4.00
❑158, Oct 1976	4.00
❑159, Oct 1976	4.00
❑160, Jan 1977	4.00
❑161, Feb 1977	4.00
❑162, Mar 1977, ... At Marriott's Great America	4.00
❑163, Apr 1977	4.00
❑164, May 1977	4.00
❑165, Jun 1977	4.00
❑166, Jun 1977	4.00
❑167, Jun 1977	4.00
❑168, Jul 1977	4.00
❑169, Aug 1977	4.00
❑170, Oct 1977, A Special Christmas; contains paper dolls and 1978 calendar	4.00
❑171, Oct 1977	3.00
❑172, Jan 1978	3.00
❑173, Feb 1978	3.00
❑174, Mar 1978	3.00
❑175, Apr 1978	3.00
❑176, May 1978	3.00
❑177, Jun 1978	3.00
❑178, Jun 1978	3.00
❑179, Jul 1978	3.00
❑180, Jul 1978	3.00
❑181, Aug 1978, San Diego tour	3.00
❑182, Oct 1978	3.00
❑183, Oct 1978	3.00
❑184, Jan 1979	3.00
❑185, Feb 1979	3.00
❑186, Mar 1979	3.00
❑187, Apr 1979	3.00
❑188, May 1979	3.00
❑189, Jun 1979	3.00
❑190, Jun 1979	3.00
❑191, Jul 1979	3.00
❑192, Jul 1979	3.00
❑193, Oct 1979, Christmas Special	3.00
❑194, Oct 1979, Final Issue	3.00

Dennis the Menace Comics Digest
Marvel

	N-MINT
❑1; DC logo placed on cover in error by World Color Press; reprints	20.00
❑2; reprints	1.25
❑3; reprints	1.25

Dennis the Menace Pocket Full of Fun
Fawcett

	N-MINT
❑1, Spr 1969	25.00
❑2, Win 1969; Christmas cover	20.00
❑3, Jan 1970	20.00
❑4, Apr 1970	20.00
❑5 1970	20.00
❑6 1970	20.00
❑7 1971	20.00
❑8 1971	20.00
❑9 1971	20.00
❑10 1971	20.00
❑11 1972	15.00
❑12 1972	15.00
❑13 1972	15.00
❑14 1972	15.00
❑15 1973	15.00
❑16 1973	15.00
❑17 1973	10.00
❑18 1973, Holiday cover	10.00
❑19 1974	10.00
❑20 1974	10.00
❑21, Jul 1974	10.00
❑22 1974	10.00
❑23, Jan 1975	10.00
❑24, Mar 1975	10.00
❑25 1975	10.00
❑26 1975	10.00
❑27 1976	10.00
❑28, Jun 1976	10.00
❑29 1976	10.00
❑30 1976	10.00
❑31, Jan 1977	10.00
❑32, Apr 1977	10.00
❑33 1977	10.00
❑34, Apr 1977	10.00
❑35, Jul 1977	10.00
❑36 1977	10.00
❑37, Jan 1978	10.00
❑38, Apr 1978	10.00
❑39, May 1978	10.00
❑40, Jun 1978	10.00
❑41, Aug 1978	10.00
❑42, Sep 1978	10.00
❑43, Jan 1979	10.00
❑44 1979	10.00
❑45, Oct 1979	10.00
❑46 1979	10.00
❑47, Jul 1979	10.00
❑48 1979	10.00
❑49, Jan 1980; Winter cover	10.00
❑50, Mar 1980	10.00

Deputy Dawg
Gold Key

	N-MINT
❑1, Aug 1965	55.00

Deputy Dawg Presents Dinky Duck and Hashimoto-San
Gold Key

	N-MINT
❑1, Aug 1965	30.00

Der Countess
Avalon Communications / ACG

	N-MINT
❑1, ca. 1996; reprints Scary Tales #1	2.75

Der Vandale
Innervision

	N-MINT
❑1, b&w	2.50
❑1/Variant, b&w; alternate cover	2.50
❑2	2.50
❑3	2.50

Descendants of Toshin
Arrow

	N-MINT
❑1, Apr 1999, b&w; NN	2.95

Descending Angels
Millennium

	N-MINT
❑1	2.95

Desert Peach
Thoughts & Images

	N-MINT
❑1, Jul 1988, b&w; Thoughts & Images publishes	10.00
❑2, Feb 1989, b&w	6.00
❑3, Jan 1990, b&w; Goes to Mu Press	4.00
❑4, Mar 1990, b&w; First Mu Issue	4.00
❑5, Jun 1990, b&w; MU Press begins publishing	4.00
❑6, Aug 1990, b&w	4.00
❑7, Sep 1990	3.00
❑8, Nov 1990	3.00
❑9, Dec 1990	3.00
❑10, Feb 1991	3.00
❑11, Jun 1991	3.00
❑12, Aug 1991	2.50
❑13, Oct 1991	2.50
❑14, Dec 1991	2.50
❑15, Feb 1992	2.50
❑16, Apr 1992	2.50
❑17, Aug 1992, b&w; Giant-size	3.95
❑18, Aug 1992, b&w; Last Mu Press issue	2.50
❑19, ca. 1993, b&w; aka Desert Peach: Self-Propelled Target; Aeon begins publishing	4.95
❑20, ca. 1993, b&w; aka Desert Peach: Fever Dream	4.95
❑21, Jun 1994, b&w	4.95
❑22, Nov 1994, b&w	4.95
❑23, Jun 1995, b&w; a.k.a. The Desert Peach: Visions	2.95
❑24, Sep 1995, b&w; a.k.a. The Desert Peach: Ups and Downs	2.95
❑25, ca. 1996; Last Aeon issue; moves to A Fine Line	2.95
❑26, ca. 1997, b&w; a.k.a. The Desert Peach: Miki; first issue from A Fine Line; cardstock cover	2.95
❑27, ca. 1997	2.95
❑28, Aug 1998	2.95
❑29, Apr 2000	2.95
❑30, Jun 2001	2.95

Desert Storm Journal
Apple

	N-MINT
❑1, Sep 1991; Saddam Hussein on cover	2.75
❑1/A, Sep 1991; Gen. Norman Schwartzkopf on cover	2.75
❑2, Dec 1991, b&w	2.75
❑3, Feb 1992, b&w	2.75
❑4, Apr 1992, b&w	2.75
❑5, Jun 1992, b&w	2.75
❑6, Aug 1992, b&w	2.75
❑7, Oct 1992, b&w	2.75
❑8, Dec 1992, b&w	2.75

Desert Storm: Send Hussein to Hell!
Innovation

	N-MINT
❑1, ca. 1991	2.95

Desert Streams
DC / Piranha

	N-MINT
❑1	5.95

Other grades: Multiply price above by 5/6 for VF/NM • 2/3 for VERY FINE • 1/3 for FINE • 1/5 for VERY GOOD • 1/8 for GOOD

Desolation Jones
DC

- ❑1, Jun 2005 — 2.99
- ❑2, Jul 2005 — 2.99
- ❑3, Oct 2005 — 2.99
- ❑4, Jan 2006 — 2.99
- ❑5, Mar 2006 — 2.99
- ❑6, Jun 2006 — 2.99
- ❑7, Dec 2006 — 2.99
- ❑8, Feb 2007 — 2.99

Despair
Print Mint

- ❑1, ca. 1969 — 10.00

Desperadoes
Image

- ❑1, Sep 1997 — 2.50
- ❑1/2nd, Sep 1997; 2nd printing — 2.50
- ❑2, Oct 1997 — 2.95
- ❑3, Nov 1997 — 2.95
- ❑4, Dec 1997 — 2.95
- ❑5, Jun 1998 — 2.95

Desperadoes: Banners of Gold
Idea & Design Works

- ❑1, ca. 2004 — 3.99
- ❑2, ca. 2004 — 3.99
- ❑3, ca. 2005 — 3.99
- ❑4, ca. 2005 — 3.99
- ❑5, ca. 2005 — 3.99

Desperadoes: Epidemic!
DC / Wildstorm

- ❑1, Nov 1999; prestige format; NN — 5.95

Desperadoes: Quiet of the Grave
DC / Homage

- ❑1, Jul 2001 — 2.95
- ❑2, Aug 2001 — 2.95
- ❑3, Sep 2001 — 2.95
- ❑4, Oct 2001 — 2.95
- ❑5, Nov 2001 — 2.95

Desperate Times
Image

- ❑0, Jan 2004 — 3.50
- ❑1, Jun 1998 — 2.95
- ❑2, Aug 1998 — 2.95
- ❑3, Oct 1998 — 2.95
- ❑4, Dec 1998 — 2.95

Desperate Times
Image

- ❑1, Apr 2004 — 2.95

Desperate Times
Aaargh / Wildstorm

- ❑1, Oct 2000, b&w — 2.95
- ❑2, Jan 2001, b&w — 2.95
- ❑3, Mar 2001, b&w — 2.95
- ❑4, May 2001, b&w — 2.35

Desso-Lette
Follis Brothers

- ❑1, Jul 1997 — 2.95

Destiny: A Chronicle of Deaths Foretold
DC / Vertigo

- ❑1, ca. 1997, prestige format — 5.95
- ❑2, ca. 1997, prestige format — 5.95
- ❑3, ca. 1997, prestige format — 5.95

Destiny Angel
Dark Fantasy

- ❑1 — 3.95

Destroy!!
Eclipse

- ❑1, Nov 1986, b&w; oversize — 4.95
- ❑1/3D, 3-D — 3.00

Destroy All Comics
Slave Labor

- ❑1, Nov 1994; Oversized — 3.50
- ❑2, Feb 1995; Oversized — 3.50
- ❑3, Aug 1995; Oversized — 3.50
- ❑4, Jan 1996; Oversized — 3.50
- ❑5, Apr 1996; Oversized — 3.50

Destroyer Duck
Eclipse

- ❑1, Feb 1982; JK (c); ME (w); SA, VM, JK (a); O: Destroyer Duck. 1: Groo. 1: Destroyer Duck — 4.00
- ❑2, Jan 1983 JK (c); VM, JK (a) — 1.50
- ❑3, Jun 1983 JK (c); VM, JK (a) — 1.50
- ❑4, Oct 1983 JK (c); VM, JK (a) — 1.50
- ❑5, Dec 1983 JK (c); VM, JK (a) — 1.50
- ❑6, Mar 1984 VM (a) — 1.50
- ❑7, May 1984; FM (c); VM (a); Final Issue — 1.50

Destroyer
Marvel

- ❑1, Nov 1989, b&w; O: Remo Williams — 3.00
- ❑2, Dec 1989, b&w — 2.50
- ❑3, Dec 1989, b&w — 2.50
- ❑4, Jan 1990, b&w SD (a) — 2.50
- ❑5, Feb 1990, b&w — 2.50
- ❑6, Mar 1990, b&w — 2.50
- ❑7, Apr 1990, b&w — 2.50
- ❑8, May 1990, b&w — 2.50

Destroyer
Marvel

- ❑1, Mar 1991 — 1.95

Destroyer
Marvel

- ❑1, Dec 1991 — 1.95
- ❑2, Jan 1992 — 1.95
- ❑3, Feb 1992 — 1.95
- ❑4, Mar 1992 — 1.95

Destroyer
Valiant

- ❑0, Apr 1995 — 4.00
- ❑0/$2.50, Apr 1995 — 10.00

Destructor
Atlas-Seaboard

- ❑1, Feb 1975, SD, WW (a); O: Destructor — 10.00
- ❑2, Apr 1975, SD, WW (a) — 7.00
- ❑3, Jun 1975, SD (a) — 5.00
- ❑4, Aug 1975 — 5.00

Detective: Chronicles of Max Faccioni
Caliber

- ❑1 — 2.95

Detective Comics
DC

- ❑0, Oct 1994; O: Batarangs. O: Batmobile. O: Batman — 2.50
- ❑297, Nov 1961; John Jones Manhunter from Mars — 125.00
- ❑298, Dec 1961, 1: Clayface II (Matt Hagen) — 200.00
- ❑299, Jan 1962 — 100.00
- ❑300, Feb 1962 — 100.00
- ❑301, Mar 1962 — 100.00
- ❑302, Apr 1962, A: Batwoman — 100.00
- ❑303, May 1962 — 100.00
- ❑304, Jun 1962 — 100.00
- ❑305, Jul 1962 — 100.00
- ❑306, Aug 1962 — 100.00
- ❑307, Sep 1962, A: Batwoman — 100.00
- ❑308, Oct 1962 — 100.00
- ❑309, Nov 1962, A: Batwoman — 100.00
- ❑310, Dec 1962 — 100.00
- ❑311, Jan 1963, 1: Cat-Man (DC). A: Batwoman — 200.00
- ❑312, Feb 1963 — 100.00
- ❑313, Mar 1963 — 100.00
- ❑314, Apr 1963 — 100.00
- ❑315, May 1963 — 100.00
- ❑316, Jun 1963 — 100.00
- ❑317, Jul 1963 — 100.00
- ❑318, Aug 1963, A: Batwoman — 100.00
- ❑319, Sep 1963 — 100.00
- ❑320, Oct 1963 — 100.00
- ❑321, Nov 1963, A: Batwoman — 100.00
- ❑322, Dec 1963, John Jones Manhunter From Mars — 100.00
- ❑323, Jan 1964 — 100.00
- ❑324, Feb 1964 — 100.00
- ❑325, Mar 1964, A: Batwoman — 100.00
- ❑326, Apr 1964, 1: Idol Head of Diablo — 100.00
- ❑327, May 1964, 25th anniversary; CI (c); CI (a); symbol change; 300th Batman in Detective Comics — 225.00
- ❑328, Jun 1964, D: Alfred. 1: Aunt Harriet — 175.00
- ❑329, Jul 1964 — 75.00
- ❑330, Aug 1964 — 75.00
- ❑331, Sep 1964 — 65.00
- ❑332, Oct 1964, A: Joker — 115.00
- ❑333, Nov 1964, Mike Friedrich L.O.C — 60.00
- ❑334, Dec 1964, A: Joker. 1: Outsider; 1: Grasshopper; Elongated Man back-up — 60.00
- ❑335, Jan 1965, Elongated Man back-up; Guy Lillian L.O.C — 60.00
- ❑336, Feb 1965, 2: Outsider; Elongated Man back-up; Mike Friedrich L.O.C — 60.00
- ❑337, Mar 1965, Elongated Man back-up; Guy Lillian L.O.C.; MIke Friedcirh L.O.C — 60.00
- ❑338, Apr 1965, Mike Friedrich L.O.C — 60.00
- ❑339, May 1965, Elongated Man back-up; Mike Friedrich L.O.C — 60.00
- ❑340, Jun 1965, Elongated Man back-up; Cary Bates L.O.C — 60.00
- ❑341, Jul 1965, A: Joker. Elongated Man back-up — 75.00
- ❑342, Aug 1965, Elongated Man back-up; Guy H. Lillian III L.O.C — 60.00
- ❑343, Sep 1965, Elongated Man back-up — 60.00
- ❑344, Oct 1965, Elongated Man back-up — 60.00
- ❑345, Nov 1965, 1: Blockbuster; Elongated Man back-up — 60.00
- ❑346, Dec 1965, Elongated Man back-up; Mike Friedrich L.O.C — 60.00
- ❑347, Jan 1966, Elongated Man back-up; Guy H. Lillian L.O.C.; Mike Friedrich L.O.C — 60.00
- ❑348, Feb 1966, Elongated Man back-up — 60.00
- ❑349, Mar 1966, Elongated Man back-up — 60.00
- ❑350, Apr 1966, Elongated Man back-up; New costume for Elongated Man — 60.00
- ❑351, May 1966, 1: Cluemaster; Elongated Man back-up — 60.00
- ❑352, Jun 1966, Elongated Man back-up — 60.00
- ❑353, Jul 1966, V: Weather Wizard — 75.00
- ❑354, Aug 1966, 1: Doctor Tzin-Tzin; Mike Friedrich L.O.C — 75.00
- ❑355, Sep 1966, Guy Lillian L.O.C — 75.00
- ❑356, Oct 1966, Alfred returns — 75.00
- ❑357, Nov 1966, Elongated Man back-up — 75.00
- ❑358, Dec 1966, 1: Spellbinder; Guy Lillian L.O.C — 75.00
- ❑359, Jan 1967, 1: Batgirl (Barbara Gordon); Elongated Man back-up; Mark Evanier L.O.C — 350.00
- ❑360, Feb 1967 — 65.00
- ❑361, Mar 1967 — 65.00
- ❑362, Apr 1967, A: Riddler. Elongated Man back-up; Guy Lillian L.O.C — 65.00
- ❑363, May 1967, A: Batgirl (Barbara Gordon). Elongated Man back-up; Irene Vartanoff L.O.C.; Guy Lillian L.O.C.; Mike Friedrich L.O.C — 100.00
- ❑364, Jun 1967, A: Batgirl (Barbara Gordon). Elongated Man back-up; Peter Sanderson L.O.C.; Jack C. Harris L.O.C — 60.00
- ❑365, Jul 1967, A: Joker. Mark Evanier L.O.C.; Mike Friedrich L.O.C — 90.00
- ❑366, Aug 1967, Elongated Man back-up; Peter Sanderson L.O.C — 60.00
- ❑367, Sep 1967, Elongated Man back-up; Guy Lillian L.O.C — 60.00
- ❑368, Oct 1967, Peter Sanderson L.O.C.; Elongated Man back-up — 60.00
- ❑369, Nov 1967, GK (c); CI, NA (a); Robin teams with Batgirl; Elongated Man back-up — 75.00
- ❑370, Dec 1967, CI (c); GK, BK (a); Elongated Man — 45.00
- ❑371, Jan 1968, A: Batgirl (Barbara Gordon). Elongated Man back-up — 80.00
- ❑372, Feb 1968, Guy Lillian L.O.C.; Peter Sanderson L.O.C — 50.00
- ❑373, Mar 1968, A: Riddler. 1: Mr. Freeze; Irene Vartanoff L.O.C.; Elongated Man back-up — 50.00
- ❑374, Apr 1968, Elongated Man back-up; Peter Sanderson L.O.C — 50.00
- ❑375, May 1968, Elongated Man back-up; Peter Sanderson L.O.C.; Guy Lillian L.O.C — 50.00
- ❑376, Jun 1968, Elongated Man back-up — 50.00
- ❑377, Jul 1968, Guy Lillian L.O.C — 65.00
- ❑378, Aug 1968, Elongated Man back-up — 50.00
- ❑379, Sep 1968, Elongated Man back-up — 50.00
- ❑380, Oct 1968, Harlan Ellison L.O.C.; Elongated Man back-up — 50.00
- ❑381, Nov 1968, Peter Sanderson L.O.C.; Elongated Man back-up — 40.00
- ❑382, Dec 1968, Elongated Man back-up — 40.00
- ❑383, Jan 1969, Mike Barr L.O.C.; Martin Pasko L.O.C — 40.00
- ❑384, Feb 1969, Carl Gafford L.O.C.; Elongated Man back-up — 40.00
- ❑385, Mar 1969, Peter Sanderson L.O.C.; Mark Evanier L.O.C — 40.00

Deathlok (1st Series)

First mini-series for troubled cyborg soldier

©Marvel

Deathlok (2nd Series)

Cyborg finally lands ongoing series in 1991

©Marvel

Deathmate

Image/Valiant crossover plagued by delays

©Image

Deathstroke the Terminator

Bad-guy Slade Wilson gets own series

©DC

Death Talks About Life

AIDS-prevention giveaway comic

©DC

	N-MINT
❑386, Apr 1969, Mark Evanier L.O.C.	40.00
❑387, May 1969, 1: Batman. Reprints Detective Comics #27	75.00
❑388, Jun 1969, A: Joker. Tony Isabella L.O.C	50.00
❑389, Jul 1969, Guy Lillian L.O.C.; Martin Pasko L.O.C	35.00
❑390, Aug 1969, Martin Pasko L.O.C	35.00
❑391, Sep 1969	25.00
❑392, Oct 1969, NA (c); FR (w); MA, GK (a); 1: Jason Bard	25.00
❑393, Nov 1969, 2: Jason Bard	25.00
❑394, Dec 1969, Martin Pasko L.O.C	35.00
❑395, Jan 1970, FR (w); MA, DG, NA, GK (a)	125.00
❑396, Feb 1970, NA (c); FR (w); GK (a); A: Batgirl	35.00
❑397, Mar 1970, FR (w); NA, GK (a)	35.00
❑398, Apr 1970, Mike Barr L.O.C	30.00
❑399, May 1970	30.00
❑400, Jun 1970, FR (w); GC, NA, GK (a); O: Man-Bat. 1: Man-Bat	175.00
❑401, Jul 1970, Doug Moench L.O.C.; Martin Pasko L.O.C	30.00
❑402, Aug 1970, FR (w); NA, GK (a); 2: Man-Bat; Martin Pasko L.O.C	55.00
❑403, Sep 1970, NA (c); FR (w); GK (a); Robin	35.00
❑404, Oct 1970, FR (w); DG, NA, GK (a); Batgirl	35.00
❑405, Nov 1970	30.00
❑406, Dec 1970	30.00
❑407, Jan 1971, FR (w); NA, GK (a); A: Man-Bat	30.00
❑408, Feb 1971, FR (w); DH, NA (a); Martin Pasko L.O.C	40.00
❑409, Mar 1971, NA (c); FR (w); DG, IN (a)	40.00
❑410, Apr 1971, FR (w); DH, DG, NA (a); Batgirl	40.00
❑411, May 1971, 1: Talia	30.00
❑412, Jun 1971	25.00
❑413, Jul 1971, NA (c); FR (w); DH, DG (a)	25.00
❑414, Aug 1971, Giant-size; Reprints from World's Finest Comics #66 & Strange Adventures #83; Guy Lillian L.O.C.; 48 pages begin	25.00
❑415, Sep 1971; Giant-size; Reprints from Detective #211 and Gangbusters #54; 48 pages; Mike Barr L.O.C	25.00
❑416, Oct 1971; Giant-size; 48 pages; Adventures of Rex the Wonder Dog #3 and Gangbusters #30	25.00
❑417, Nov 1971; Giant-size; Reprints from Batman #31 & Gangbusters #49; 48 pages	25.00
❑418, Dec 1971; Giant-size; Reprints from Gangbusters #40 & Dale Evans' Comics #1; Fred Hembeck L.O.C.; Bob Rozakis L.O.C.; 48 pages	25.00
❑419, Jan 1972; Giant-size; Reprints from Detective Comics #213 & Gangbusters #61; Mike Barr L.O.C.; Bob Rozakis L.O.C.; 48 pages (52 pages with covers)	25.00
❑420, Feb 1972; Giant-size; Reprints from Detective Comics #215 & Gangbusters #57; Bob Rozakis L.O.C.; 48 pages (52 pages with cover)	25.00
❑421, Mar 1972; Giant-size; FR (w); FR, DH (a); Batgirl story	25.00
❑422, Apr 1972; Giant-size; Reprints from World's Finest Comics #59 & Gangbusters #54	25.00
❑423, May 1972; Giant-size; Reprints from Gangbusters #26 & Big Town #15	25.00
❑424, Jun 1972; Giant-size; Reprints from Dave Evans Comics #7 & Gangbusters #47; Bob Rozakis L.O.C	25.00
❑425, Jul 1972	20.00
❑426, Aug 1972	20.00
❑427, Sep 1972, Jason Bard cover	20.00
❑428, Oct 1972, FR (w); DD (a); Bob Rozakis L.O.C	15.00
❑429, Nov 1972	15.00
❑430, Dec 1972, Guy Lillian L.O.C	15.00
❑431, Jan 1973, Jason Bard cover	15.00
❑432, Feb 1973, Mike Barr L.O.C	15.00
❑433, Mar 1973, Mike Barr L.O.C	15.00
❑434, Apr 1973, FR (w); RB, IN (a); 1: The Spook; Mike Barr L.O.C	15.00
❑435, Jul 1973, Mike Barr L.O.C	15.00
❑436, Sep 1973	15.00
❑437, Nov 1973, JA (a); 1: Manhunter	20.00
❑438, Jan 1974, JKu, GK, JA (a); Manhunter	28.00
❑439, Mar 1974, NA (c); CI, JKu, GK (a); O: Manhunter. Manhunter	28.00
❑440, May 1974, JA (c); JK (w); MA, JK (a); Manhunter	28.00
❑441, Jul 1974, JA (c); HC, JM, KS (a); Manhunter	28.00
❑442, Sep 1974, JA (c); JK (w); MA, CI, JK (a); Manhunter	28.00
❑443, Nov 1974, JA (c); SD (w); SD (a); D: Manhunter. Reprints from More Fun Comics #65; Showcase #73; Batman #18; All-American Comics #98; 100 pages	28.00
❑444, Jan 1975, Reprints from Strange Adventures #114; Detective Comics #285; Star-Spangled Comics #109 & #111; Davle Evans Comics #9; Gangbusters #48; 100 pages (s)	28.00
❑445, Mar 1975, Reprints from Strange Adventures #116; Detective Comics #327 & #222; Star-Spangled Comics #105; Gangbusters #5 & 25; Big Town #2; 100 pages	28.00
❑446, Apr 1975; RB, JA (a); 1: Sterling Silversmith. Hawkman back-up	12.00
❑447, May 1975	8.00
❑448, Jun 1975	8.00
❑449, Jul 1975	8.00
❑450, Aug 1975	8.00
❑451, Sep 1975; Robin The Teen Wonder	6.00
❑452, Oct 1975; JL (a); Hawkman back-up	6.00
❑453, Nov 1975	6.00
❑454, Dec 1975 JL (a)	6.00
❑455, Jan 1976 MGr, JL (a)	6.00
❑456, Feb 1976	9.00
❑457, Mar 1976, O: Batman. Elongated Man back-up	9.00
❑458, Apr 1976	6.00
❑459, May 1976	6.00
❑460, Jun 1976, 1st appearance Captain Stingaree; V: Captain Stingaree	6.00
❑461, Jul 1976, Bicentennial #29	6.00
❑462, Aug 1976, V: Captain Stingaree	6.00
❑463, Sep 1976, 1: Black Spider. 1: Calculator; 1: Calculator (Noah Kutter)	45.00
❑464, Oct 1976, V: Black Spider; V: Calculator	6.00
❑465, Nov 1976, TD (a); A: Elongated Man	9.00
❑466, Dec 1976, TD, MR (a)	9.00
❑467, Jan 1977, RB (c); TD, MR (a)	9.00
❑468, Mar 1977, JA (c); TD, MR (a)	9.00
❑469, May 1977, JA (c); AM, MR (a); 1: Doctor Phosphorus. Jim Aparo cover; O: Doctor Phosphorus	5.00
❑470, Jun 1977, AM, MR (a); A: Hugo Strange. 1: Silver St. Cloud	5.00
❑471, Aug 1977, MR (a); A: Hugo Strange. V: Hugo Strange	8.00
❑472, Sep 1977, MR (a); D: Hugo Strange; V: Hugo Strange	8.00
❑473, Oct 1977, MR (a); V: Penguin	8.00
❑474, Dec 1977, MR (a)	15.00
❑475, Feb 1978, MR (a); A: Joker	15.00
❑476, Mar 1978, MR (a); A: Joker. V: Joker	15.00
❑477, May 1978, NA, MR (a); V: Dr. Tzin-Tzin; Reprinted from issue #408 with new three-page framing sequence; The House that Haunted Batman! reprinted from issue #408 with new three-page framing sequence	8.00
❑478, Jul 1978, MR (a); 1: Clayface III (Preston Payne)	8.00
❑479, Sep 1978, RB, MR (a); 1: The Fadeaway Man	8.00
❑480, Nov 1978, JA (c); DN, MA (a); V: Pied Piper	5.00
❑481, Dec 1978; Double-size; JSn (w); DN, JSn, DH, CR, MR, DA (a); Double-size; Batman Family format; Wraparound cover	7.00
❑482, Feb 1979; Double-size; RB (c); JSn (w); JSn, MG, DH, HC, DG, CR (a); Double-size; Batman Family format; Wraparound cover	5.00
❑483, Apr 1979; Double-size; BO, DN, SD, MG, HC, DG, DD, KS, DA (a); 1: Maxie Zeus; The Human Target; Robin The Teen Wonder; Batman; Double-size 40th Anniversary Issue	8.00
❑484, Jun 1979; Double-size; O: Robin I (Dick Grayson); Wraparound cover; Batman Family format; The Human Target; The Demon apeparance	5.00
❑485, Aug 1979; Double-size; Double-sized; Batman Family format; Wraparound cover	4.00
❑486, Oct 1979; Double-size; The Human Target; Double-sized	4.00
❑487, Dec 1979; Double-size; Reprints content from Cancelled Comics Cavalcade #2; 68 pages	4.00
❑488, Feb 1980; Double-size; V: Spook; Batman Family format; Tales of Gotham City	4.00
❑489, Apr 1980; Double-size; Batgirl forgets Batman and Robin's secret identities	4.00
❑490, May 1980; Double-size; V: Ra's Al Ghul; Batman Family format; Green Arrow appearance	4.00
❑491, Jun 1980; Double-size; V: Maxie Zeus; Batman Family format	4.00
❑492, Jul 1980; Double-size; V: Penguin; Batman Family formate	4.00
❑493, Aug 1980; Double-size; 1: Swashbuckler; V: Riddler; Batman Family format	4.00
❑494, Sep 1980; Double-size; 1: Crime Doctor; Batman Family format	4.00
❑495, Oct 1980; Double-size; 68 pages; Tales of Gotham City	4.00
❑496, Nov 1980, V: Clayface	4.00
❑497, Dec 1980, V: Squid	4.00

Other grades: Multiply price above by 5/6 for VF/NM • 2/3 for VERY FINE • 1/3 for FINE • 1/5 for VERY GOOD • 1/8 for GOOD

	N-MINT
❑498, Jan 1981, V: Blockbuster	4.00
❑499, Feb 1981	4.00
❑500, Mar 1981; 500th anniversary issue; CI, DG, TY, JKu, JA (a); A: Deadman, Slam Bradley, Hawkman, Robin. Double-size.	5.00
❑501, Apr 1981	4.00
❑502, May 1981	4.00
❑503, Jun 1981, JSn (c); DN, JSn (a); V: Scarecrow	4.00
❑504, Jul 1981, JSn (c); DN, JSn (a); A: Joker. V: Joker; Tales of Gotham City	6.00
❑505, Aug 1981	4.00
❑506, Sep 1981, 1: Manikin	4.00
❑507, Oct 1981, V: Manikin; Tales of Gotham City	4.00
❑508, Nov 1981	4.00
❑509, Dec 1981, V: Cat-Man	4.00
❑510, Jan 1982, V: Mad Hatter	4.00
❑511, Feb 1982, 1: Mirage (DC)	4.00
❑512, Mar 1982, 45th Anniversary Special; V: Dr. Death; Batman cont'd from Batman #345	4.00
❑513, Apr 1982, V: Two-Face; Continued from Batman #346	4.00
❑514, May 1982, V: Maxie Zeus	4.00
❑515, Jun 1982	4.00
❑516, Jul 1982	4.00
❑517, Aug 1982, Batman cont'd Batman #351	4.00
❑518, Sep 1982, 1: Velvet Tiger; V: Deadshot	4.00
❑519, Oct 1982, Batman cont'd from Batman #352	4.00
❑520, Nov 1982, Masters of the Universe Preview; Story continues in Batman #354	4.00
❑521, Dec 1982, V: Catwoman; Green Arrow back-up begins; Batman cont'd in Batman #355	4.00
❑522, Jan 1983	4.00
❑523, Feb 1983, V: Solomon Grundy; Green Arrow back-up	4.00
❑524, Mar 1983, 2: Jason Todd; V: Squid; Batman cont'd from Batman #357	5.00
❑525, Apr 1983, V: Killer Croc; Batman cont'd from Batman #358	4.00
❑526, May 1983; DN, AA (a); V: Riddler; V: Cavalier; V: Mad Hatter; V: Scarecrow; V: Signalman; V: Spook; V: Mr. Freeze; V: Black Spider; V: Killer Croc; V: Joker; V: Two-Face; V: Killer Moth; V: Clayface; V: Gentleman Ghost; Batman's 500th appearance issue; Batman cont'd from Batman #359	4.00
❑527, Jun 1983, Batman continued in Batman #361	4.00
❑528, Jul 1983, Green Arrow back-up	4.00
❑529, Aug 1983, Batman cont'd Batman #363	4.00
❑530, Sep 1983, V: Nocturna; Batman cont'd from Batman #363; Green Arrow back-up	4.00
❑531, Oct 1983, Batman cont'd from Batman #364	4.00
❑532, Nov 1983, A: Joker. V: Joker; Continued in Batman #366; Green Arrow back-up	4.00
❑533, Dec 1983	4.00
❑534, Jan 1984; V: Poison Ivy; Green Arrow back-up	4.00
❑535, Feb 1984; 2: Robin II (Jason Todd). V: Crazy Quilt; Batman cont'd from Batman #368	5.00
❑536, Mar 1984; V: Deadshot	4.00
❑537, Apr 1984	4.00
❑538, May 1984; V: Catman. V: Cat-Man; Batman cont'd from Batman #371; Green Arrow back-up	4.00
❑539, Jun 1984; V: Catman. V: Dr. Fang; Batman cont'd from Batman #372	4.00
❑540, Jul 1984; V: Scarecrow; Batman cont'd from Batman #373; Green Arrow back-up	4.00
❑541, Aug 1984; V: Penguin; Batman cont'd from Batman #374; Green Arrow back-up	4.00
❑542, Sep 1984; V: Nocturna; Green Arrow back-up	4.00
❑543, Oct 1984; Green Arrow back-up	4.00
❑544, Nov 1984; Flash Force 2000 Insert; Batman cont'd from Batman #377	4.00
❑545, Dec 1984	4.00
❑546, Jan 1985; 1: Onyx	4.00
❑547, Feb 1985; V: Night-Slayer; Batman cont'd in Batman #381; Batman cont'd from Batman #380	4.00
❑548, Mar 1985; V: Darkwolf	4.00
❑549, Apr 1985 AMo (w); PB, KJ (a)	4.00
❑550, May 1985; AMo (w); PB, KJ (a); Green Arrow back-up	4.00
❑551, Jun 1985; V: Calendar Man; Batman cont'd from Batman #384; Batman cont'd in Batman #385	4.00
❑552, Jul 1985	4.00
❑553, Aug 1985; V: Black Mask; Batman cont'd from Batman #386; Batman cont'd in Batman #387	4.00
❑554, Sep 1985; New costume Black Canary	4.00
❑555, Oct 1985; V: Mirror Master. V: Captain Boomerang. V: Captain Boomerang; Batman cont'd from Batman #388; Green Arrow backup feature	4.00
❑556, Nov 1985; V: Night-Slayer; Crisis on Infinite Earths red skies; Batman cont'd from Batman #389; Batman cont'd in Batman #390	4.00
❑557, Dec 1985; Batman cont'd from Batman #390; Batman cont'd in Batman #391; Crisis on Infinite Earths red skies; Green Arrow back-up	4.00
❑558, Jan 1986; Batman cont'd from Batman #391; Crisis on Infinite Earths red skies	4.00
❑559, Feb 1986 A: Catwoman. A: Green Arrow. A: Black Canary	4.00
❑560, Mar 1986; 1: Steelclaw	4.00
❑561, Apr 1986; Robin solo	4.00
❑562, May 1986; V: Film Freak; Batman cont'd from Batman #395; Batman cont'd in Batman #396	4.00
❑563, Jun 1986; V: Two-Face. O: Two-Face; Batman cont'd in Batman #397.	4.00
❑564, Jul 1986; D: Steelclaw. V: Two-Face; Green Arrow back-up	4.00
❑565, Aug 1986; D: Steelclaw; Batman cont'd in Batman #399	3.00
❑566, Sep 1986; A: Joker. Batman cont'd in Batman #400	3.00
❑567, Oct 1986 KJ (c); JSn, GC (a)	3.00
❑568, Nov 1986; Legends	3.00
❑569, Dec 1986; A: Catwoman. A: Joker. V: Joker	4.00
❑570, Jan 1987; A: Joker. V: Joker; V: Catwoman	4.00
❑571, Feb 1987; V: Scarecrow. O: Scarecrow	3.00
❑572, Mar 1987; Giant-size; A: Slam Bradley. 50th anniversary issue	4.00
❑573, Apr 1987; V: Mad Hatter	2.50
❑574, May 1987; O: Batman	3.00
❑575, Jun 1987; 1: The Reaper	3.50
❑576, Jul 1987; TMc (a); V: Reaper	3.00
❑577, Aug 1987; TMc (a); V: Reaper	3.00
❑578, Sep 1987; TMc (a); V: Reaper	4.00
❑579, Oct 1987; V: Two-Face	4.00
❑580, Nov 1987; V: Two-Face	4.00
❑581, Dec 1987; V: Two-Face	4.00
❑582, Jan 1988; Millennium	4.00
❑583, Feb 1988; 1: Ventriloquist	4.00
❑584, Mar 1988; V: Ventriloquist	4.00
❑585, Apr 1988; 1: Rat-Catcher	4.00
❑586, May 1988; V: Rat-catcher	3.00
❑587, Jun 1988	3.00
❑588, Jul 1988	4.00
❑589, Aug 1988; Bonus Book #5	4.00
❑590, Sep 1988	4.00
❑591, Oct 1988; V: Australian Aboriginal	3.00
❑592, Nov 1988	3.00
❑593, Dec 1988	3.00
❑594, Dec 1988; 1: Joe Potato	3.00
❑595, Jan 1989; Bonus Book; Invasion!	3.00
❑596, Jan 1989	3.00
❑597, Feb 1989	3.00
❑598, Mar 1989; Double-size; ME (w); CI, TMc, HC, GD, JA (a)	3.00
❑599, Apr 1989	3.00
❑600, May 1989; Double-size; SL (w); SA, BWr, KG, WE, FM, NA, MZ (a); 50th anniversary issue of Batman	3.00
❑601, Jun 1989 A: Demon	3.00
❑602, Jul 1989 A: Demon	3.00
❑603, Aug 1989 A: Demon	3.00
❑604, Sep 1989; poster	3.00
❑605, Sep 1989; V: Clayface	3.00
❑606, Oct 1989; V: Clayface	3.00
❑607, Oct 1989; V: Clayface	3.00
❑608, Nov 1989; 1: Anarky	3.00
❑609, Dec 1989; 2: Anarky	3.00
❑610, Jan 1990; Penguin	3.00
❑611, Feb 1990; Penguin	3.00
❑612, Mar 1990; Catman, Catwoman	3.00
❑613, Apr 1990	3.00
❑614, May 1990	3.00
❑615, Jun 1990; Penguin	3.00
❑616, Jun 1990	3.00
❑617, Jul 1990; A: Joker. V: Joker	3.00
❑618, Jul 1990	3.00
❑619, Aug 1990	3.00
❑620, Aug 1990	3.00
❑621, Sep 1990; D: Tim Drake's mother	3.00
❑622, Oct 1990	3.00
❑623, Nov 1990; V: Joker	3.00
❑624, Dec 1990; V: Catwoman	3.00
❑625, Jan 1991; V: Abattoir	3.00
❑626, Feb 1991; V: Electrocutioner	3.00
❑627, Mar 1991; A: Batman's 600th. giant	3.00
❑628, Apr 1991; V: Abattoir	3.00
❑629, May 1991	3.00
❑630, Jun 1991	3.00
❑631, Jul 1991	3.00
❑632, Jul 1991	3.00
❑633, Aug 1991	3.00
❑634, Aug 1991	3.00
❑635, Sep 1991	3.00
❑636, Sep 1991	3.00
❑637, Oct 1991	3.00
❑638, Nov 1991 JA (a)	3.00
❑639, Dec 1991; JA (a); Story cont'd from Batman #472; Story cont'd in Batman #473; Sonic The Hedgehog Insert	3.00
❑640, Jan 1992; JA (a); Story cont'd from Batman #473	3.00
❑641, Feb 1992; JA (a); Anton Furst's Gotham City designs	3.00
❑642, Mar 1992; JA (a); V: Scarface. V: Ventriloquist; Story cont'd from Batman #475	3.00
❑643, Apr 1992 JA (a)	3.00
❑644, May 1992; MG (c); V: Galvan; V: Electrocutioner	3.00
❑645, Jun 1992; MG (c); V: Galvan; V: Electrocutioner	3.00
❑646, Jul 1992; MG (c); V: Galvan; V: Electrocutioner	3.00
❑647, Aug 1992; MW (c); 1: Spoiler; V: Cluemaster	3.00
❑648, Aug 1992; MW (c); 2: Spoiler; V: Cluemaster	3.00
❑649, Sep 1992; MW (c); V: Cluemaster	3.00
❑650, Sep 1992; Robin solo	3.00
❑651, Oct 1992	3.00
❑652, Oct 1992 A: The Huntress III (Helena Bertinelli)	3.00
❑653, Nov 1992 A: The Huntress III (Helena Bertinelli)	3.00
❑654, Dec 1992; 1: The General; V: the General	3.00
❑655, Jan 1993; V: Ulysses. V: The General	3.00
❑656, Feb 1993; A: Bane. V: The General	3.00
❑657, Mar 1993	3.00
❑658, Apr 1993	3.00
❑659, May 1993; V: Ventriloquist; V: Amygdala; Cont'd in Batman #493.	3.00
❑659/2nd, May 1993; 2nd printing; V: Ventriloquist; V: Amygdala; Cont'd in Batman #493	3.00
❑660, May 1993; V: Bane; V: Killer Croc; Cont'd Batman #494; Knightfall; Part 4	3.00
❑661, Jun 1993; V: Firefly; V: Cavalier; Cont'd Batman #495	3.00
❑662, Jun 1993; V: Riddler; V: Firefly; Cont'd Batman #496	3.00
❑663, Jul 1993; V: Bane; Cont'd Batman #497	3.00
❑664, Aug 1993; V: Bane; Cont'd Showcase ë93 #7	3.00
❑665, Aug 1993; Story cont'd Batman #499	3.00
❑666, Sep 1993; V: Bane; Cont'd Batman #500	3.00
❑667, Oct 1993; Knightquest: The Crusade	3.00
❑668, Nov 1993; Cont'd Robin #1	3.00
❑669, Dec 1993; V: Trigger Twins	3.00
❑670, Jan 1994; V: Mr. Freeze	3.00
❑671, Feb 1994	3.00
❑672, Mar 1994	3.00
❑673, Apr 1994; V: Joker	3.00
❑674, May 1994	3.00

Other grades: Multiply price above by 5/6 for VF/NM • 2/3 for VERY FINE • 1/3 for FINE • 1/5 for VERY GOOD • 1/8 for GOOD

Death: The High Cost of Living	Decade of Dark Horse	Decoy	Defenders	Defenders
				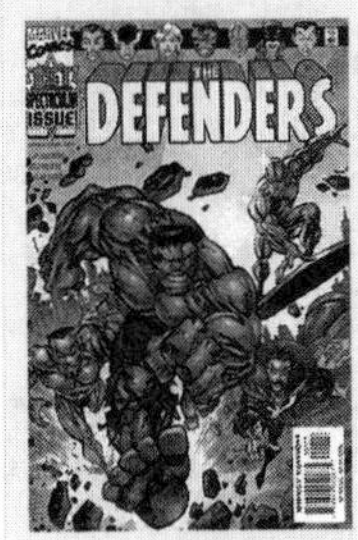
Acclaimed Neil Gaiman limited series	All-new stories from Dark Horse creators	Pudgy green alien helps policeman	Often occult-themed super-hero "non-team"	Short-lived series return from Kurt Busiek
©DC	©Dark Horse	©Penny-Farthing	©Marvel	©Marvel

	N-MINT
❑675, Jun 1994; V: Gunhawk	3.00
❑675/Platinum, Jun 1994; Platinum edition; no cover price	5.00
❑675/Variant, Jun 1994; premium edition; Special cover	4.00
❑676, Jul 1994; Giant-size	2.50
❑677, Aug 1994; V: Nightwing	1.50
❑678, Sep 1994; O: Batman. Zero Hour	1.50
❑679, Nov 1994; V: Ratcatcher	1.50
❑680, Dec 1994; V: Two-Face	1.50
❑681, Jan 1995	1.50
❑682, Feb 1995; V: KGBeast	1.50
❑682/Variant, Feb 1995; enhanced cover	2.50
❑683, Mar 1995; V: Penguin	1.50
❑684, Apr 1995; V: Penguin	1.50
❑685, May 1995; V: King Snake	1.50
❑686, Jun 1995; A: Huntress. A: Nightwing. V: King Snake	2.00
❑687, Jul 1995	2.00
❑688, Aug 1995; V: Cap'N Fear	2.00
❑689, Sep 1995; V: Firefly	2.00
❑690, Oct 1995; V: Firefly. D: Firebug	2.00
❑691, Nov 1995; V: Spellbinder. Underworld Unleashed	2.00
❑692, Dec 1995; Underworld Unleashed	2.00
❑693, Jan 1996; 1: Allergent. A: Poison Ivy	2.00
❑694, Feb 1996; A: Poison Ivy. V: Allergent	2.00
❑695, Mar 1996; Contagion Tie-in	2.00
❑696, Apr 1996	2.00
❑697, Jun 1996; V: Two-Face	2.00
❑698, Jul 1996; V: Two-Face. V: Lock-Up	2.00
❑699, Jul 1996; V: Lock-Up	2.00
❑700, Aug 1996; Anniversary issue; V: Ra's Al Ghul	3.50
❑700/Variant, Aug 1996; Anniversary issue; cardstock outer wrapper	5.00
❑701, Sep 1996; V: Bane	2.00
❑702, Oct 1996; Bagged with On the Edge insert	2.00
❑703, Nov 1996; Final Night	2.00
❑704, Dec 1996; self-contained story	2.00
❑705, Jan 1997; V: Riddler. V: Cluemaster	2.00
❑706, Feb 1997; A: Riddler. V: Riddler	2.00
❑707, Mar 1997; V: Riddler	2.00
❑708, Apr 1997; BSz (a); V: Gunhawk	2.00
❑709, May 1997; BSz (a); V: Gunhawk	2.00
❑710, Jun 1997; BSz (a); V: Gunhawk; V: Deathstroke	2.00
❑711, Jul 1997	2.00
❑712, Aug 1997; 1: Gearhead (Nathan Finch); V: Gearhead	2.00
❑713, Sep 1997; V: Gearhead	2.00
❑714, Oct 1997; V: Firefly. V: Firefly	2.00
❑715, Nov 1997; A: J'onn J'onzz. V: Firefly	2.00
❑716, Dec 1997; JA (a); Face cover	2.00
❑717, Jan 1998; V: Gearhead	2.00
❑718, Feb 1998; BMc (a); V: Finch. V: Gearhead	2.00
❑719, Mar 1998 BSz (c); JA (a)	2.50
❑720, Apr 1998; continues in Catwoman #56	3.50
❑721, May 1998; continues in Catwoman #57	3.00
❑722, Jun 1998; JA (a); Aftershock	2.50
❑723, Jul 1998; continues in Robin #55	2.00
❑724, Aug 1998; Aftershock	2.00
❑725, Sep 1998; Aftershock	2.00
❑726, Oct 1998; A: Joker. Aftershock	1.95
❑727, Dec 1998; A: Nightwing. A: Robin. Road to No Man's Land	1.99
❑728, Jan 1999; A: Nightwing. A: Robin. Road to No Man's Land	1.99
❑729, Feb 1999; A: Nightwing. A: Robin. A: Commissioner Gordan. Road to No Man's Land	1.99
❑730, Mar 1999; A: Scarface. No Man's Land	1.99
❑731, Apr 1999; A: Scarecrow. A: Huntress. No Man's Land	1.99
❑732, May 1999; A: Batgirl. No Man's Land	1.99
❑733, Jun 1999; No Man's Land	1.99
❑734, Jul 1999; A: Batgirl. No Man's Land	1.99
❑735, Aug 1999; BSz (a); A: Poison Ivy. V: Clayface. No Man's Land	1.99
❑736, Sep 1999; No Man's Land	1.99
❑737, Oct 1999; V: Joker. V: Harley Quinn. No Man's Land	1.99
❑738, Nov 1999; No Man's Land	1.99
❑739, Dec 1999; No Man's Land	1.99
❑740, Jan 2000; No Man's Land	1.99
❑741, Feb 2000; DGry (w); D: Sarah. D: Sarah Essen Gordon; V: Joker; Includes preview of No Man's Land—The Novel; No Man's Land; Continued from Batman #574	2.50
❑742, Mar 2000	1.99
❑743, Apr 2000	1.99
❑744, May 2000	1.99
❑745, Jun 2000	1.99
❑746, Jul 2000	1.99
❑747, Aug 2000	2.50
❑748, Sep 2000	2.50
❑749, Oct 2000	2.50
❑750, Nov 2000; Giant-size; V: Ra's Al Ghul	4.95
❑751, Dec 2000; 1: Sasha Bordeaux; V: Poison Ivy	12.00
❑752, Jan 2001; 2: Sasha Bordeaux; V: Poison Ivy	2.50
❑753, Feb 2001	2.50
❑754, Mar 2001; 40 pages; Continued from Nightwing #53; Story continued in Batman: Gotham Knights #13	2.50
❑755, Apr 2001	2.50
❑756, May 2001; Story continued from Superman #168	2.50
❑757, Jun 2001	2.50
❑758, Jul 2001; V: Mad Hatter	2.50
❑759, Aug 2001; V: Mad Hatter	2.50
❑760, Sep 2001; V: Mad Hatter	2.50
❑761, Oct 2001	2.50
❑762, Nov 2001	2.50
❑763, Dec 2001; Joker: Last Laugh crossover	2.50
❑764, Jan 2002; Josie Mac story	2.50
❑765, Feb 2002; Josie Mac story	2.50
❑766, Mar 2002; Batman cont'd in Batgirl #24; Josie Mac story	2.50
❑767, Apr 2002; Story continued in Nightwing #66; Josie Mac story	2.50
❑768, May 2002; Josie Mac story	2.50
❑769, Jun 2002; Josie Mac story	2.50
❑770, Jul 2002; Josie Mac story	2.50
❑771, Aug 2002; Josie Mac story	2.50
❑772, Sep 2002; Josie Mac story	2.50
❑773, Oct 2002 BSz (c)	2.75
❑774, Nov 2002 BSz (c)	2.75
❑775, Dec 2002 BSz (c)	3.50
❑776, Jan 2003; Includes preview of Aquaman (6th Series) #1	2.75
❑777, Feb 2003	2.75
❑778, Mar 2003	2.75
❑779, Apr 2003	2.75
❑780, May 2003	2.75
❑781, Jun 2003	2.75
❑782, Jul 2003	2.75
❑783, Aug 2003	2.75
❑784, Sep 2003	2.75
❑785, Oct 2003	2.75
❑786, Nov 2003	2.75
❑787, Dec 2003, V: Mad Hatter	2.75
❑788, Jan 2004	2.75
❑789, Feb 2004	2.75
❑790, Mar 2004, The Tailor back-up	2.75
❑791, Apr 2004	2.75
❑792, May 2004	2.75
❑793, Jun 2004; V: Mr. Freeze	2.75
❑794, Jul 2004	2.75
❑795, Aug 2004	2.95
❑796, Sep 2004; V: Mr. Zsasz	2.95
❑797, Oct 2004; War Games continued in Legends of the Dark Knight #182	2.95
❑798, Nov 2004, Tim Drake returns as Robin; War Games cont'd in Legends of the Dark Knight #183; Includes Sky Captain and the World of Tomorrow Poster insert	2.95
❑799, Dec 2004, V: Black Mask; Heroscape Insert #2; War Games continued in Legends of the Dark Knight #184	2.95
❑800, Jan 2005, V: Mad Hatter; V: Killer Croc	3.50
❑801, Feb 2005	2.95
❑802, Mar 2005	2.95
❑803, Apr 2005, The Talons of Crimes	2.95
❑804, May 2005; Advent Rising insert	2.99
❑805, Jun 2005; V: Clayface	2.99
❑806, Jun 2005	2.99
❑807, Jul 2005	2.99
❑808, Aug 2005	2.99
❑809, Sep 2005; War Crimes cont'd in Batman #643	2.99
❑810, Oct 2005; V: Black Mask; V: Joker; War Crimes cont'd in Batman #644	2.99
❑811, Nov 2005	2.50
❑812, Dec 2005	2.50
❑813, Jan 2006	2.50
❑814, Jan 206	2.50
❑815, Mar 2006	2.50
❑816, Mar 2006	2.50
❑817, May 2006, 1 Year Later; Face the Face cont'd in Batman #651	12.00
❑818, Jun 2006, D: Magpie; 1 Year Later; Cont'd in Batman #652	2.50
❑819, Jul 2006, D: Orka; Price increase; 1 Year Later	2.99
❑820, Aug 2006, One Year Later; Cover by Simone Bianchi	2.99
❑821, Sep 2006	2.99
❑822, Oct 2006	2.99
❑823, Nov 2006, O: Harvest	2.99
❑824, Dec 2006, V: Penguin	2.99
❑825, Jan 2007, Dr. Phosphorus	2.99
❑826, Feb 2007	2.99

Other grades: Multiply price above by 5/6 for VF/NM • 2/3 for VERY FINE • 1/3 for FINE • 1/5 for VERY GOOD • 1/8 for GOOD

	N-MINT
❑827, Mar 2007, V: Two-Face with new female Ventriloquist	2.99
❑828, Apr 2007	2.99
❑829, May 2007	2.99
❑830, Jun 2007	2.99
❑831, Jul 2007; V: Ventriloquist	2.99
❑832, Aug 2007; V: Terrible Trio	2.99
❑833, Sep 2007	2.99
❑834, Oct 2007	2.99
❑835, Oct 2007; V: Scarecrow	2.99
❑836, Nov 2007	2.99
❑837, Nov 2007; Countdown Tie-In	2.99
❑838, Dec 2007; Story continued from Nightwing #138; Story continues in Batman #671	2.99
❑839, Jan 2008	2.99
❑840	2.99
❑841	2.99
❑842	2.99
❑843	2.99
❑844	2.99
❑845	2.99
❑846	2.99
❑847	2.99
❑848	2.99
❑849	2.99
❑850	2.99
❑851	2.99
❑852	2.99
❑1000000, ca. 1998; V: Firefly	4.00
❑1000000/Variant, ca. 1998; Signed	14.99
❑Ann 1, ca. 1988; KJ (c); TD, KJ (a); V: Penguin; Fables	5.00
❑Ann 2, ca. 1989; Who's Who entries	4.00
❑Ann 3, ca. 1990	2.50
❑Ann 4, ca. 1991; Armageddon 2001	2.50
❑Ann 5, ca. 1992; V: Joker. Eclipso	2.75
❑Ann 6, ca. 1993; 1: Geist. 1993 Ann; Bloodlines	2.50
❑Ann 7, ca. 1994; Elseworlds	2.95
❑Ann 8, ca. 1995; O: Riddler. Year One	3.95
❑Ann 9, ca. 1996; Legends of the Dead Earth; 1996 annual	2.95
❑Ann 10, ca. 1997; SB (a); Pulp Heroes	3.95

Detectives
Alpha Productions

❑1, Apr 1993, b&w; Celebrating Seventy Years of The American Private Eye; Introduction by Ed Gorman; Johnny Dynamite story reprinted from an unnamed Charlton Comic	4.95

Detectives, Inc.: A Terror of Dying Dreams
Eclipse

❑1, Jun 1987; GC (a); sepia	2.00
❑2, Sep 1987; GC (a); sepia	2.00
❑3, Dec 1987; GC (a); sepia	2.00

Detectives Inc. (Micro-Series)
Eclipse

❑1, Apr 1985 MR (a)	2.00
❑2, Apr 1985 MR (a)	2.00

Detention Comics
DC

❑1, Oct 1996; Robin, Superboy, and Warrior stories	3.50

Detonator
Chaos!

❑1, Dec 1994	2.75
❑2, Jan 1994	2.75

Detonator
Image

❑1, Jan 2005	2.50
❑2, Feb 2005	2.50
❑3, Mar 2005	2.50

Detour
Alternative

❑1, Oct 1997, b&w	2.95

Detroit! Murder City Comix
Kent Myers

❑1 1993, b&w	3.00
❑2 1994, b&w	2.50
❑3 1994, b&w	2.50
❑4, Jun 1994, b&w	2.95
❑5, Aug 1994, b&w	2.95
❑6, Jan 1995, b&w; A: Iggy Pop	2.95
❑7, May 1995, b&w	2.95

Devastator
Image

❑1, ca. 1998, b&w	2.95
❑2, ca. 1998, b&w	2.95
❑3, ca. 1998	2.95

Deviant
Antarctic / Venus

❑1, Mar 1999, b&w; Adult	2.99

Devil Chef
Dark Horse

❑1, Jul 1994, b&w	2.50

Devil Dinosaur
Marvel

❑1, Apr 1978, JK (c); JK (w); JK (a); O: Devil Dinosaur. 1: Devil Dinosaur. 1: Moon Boy	5.00
❑2, May 1978, JK (c); JK (w); JK (a)	3.50
❑3, Jun 1978, JK (c); JK (w); JK (a)	4.00
❑4, Jul 1978, JK (c); JK (w); JK (a)	5.00
❑5, Aug 1978, JK (c); JK (w); JK (a)	4.00
❑6, Sep 1978, JK (c); JK (w); JK (a); Newsstand edition (distributed by Curtis); issue number in box	2.50
❑6/Whitman, Sep 1978, JK (a); Special markets edition (usually sold in Whitman bagged prepacks); price appears in a diamond; no UPC barcode	2.50
❑7, Oct 1978, JK (c); JK (w); JK (a)	2.50
❑8, Nov 1978, JK (c); JK (w); JK (a)	2.50
❑9, Dec 1978, JK (c); JK (w); JK (a); Final Issue	2.50

Devil Dinosaur Spring Fling
Marvel

❑1, Jun 1997; One-shot	2.99

Devilina
Atlas-Seaboard

❑1, Jan 1975, b&w; magazine	9.00
❑2, May 1975, b&w; magazine	12.00

Devil Jack
Doom Theater

❑1, Jul 1995	2.95
❑2	2.95

Devil Kids
Harvey

❑1, Jul 1962	150.00
❑2, Sep 1962	75.00
❑3, Nov 1962	50.00
❑4, Jan 1963	25.00
❑5, Mar 1963, Portions of this issue reprinted in Hot Stuff #106 (Sep 71)	25.00
❑6, May 1963	20.00
❑7, Jul 1963	20.00
❑8, Sep 1963	20.00
❑9, Nov 1963	20.00
❑10, Jan 1964	20.00
❑11, Mar 1964	15.00
❑12, May 1964	15.00
❑13, Jul 1964	15.00
❑14, Sep 1964	15.00
❑15, Nov 1964	15.00
❑16, Jan 1965	15.00
❑17, Mar 1965	15.00
❑18, May 1965	10.00
❑19, Jul 1965	10.00
❑20, Sep 1965	10.00
❑21, Nov 1965	8.00
❑22, Jan 1966	8.00
❑23, Mar 1966	8.00
❑24, May 1966	8.00
❑25, Jul 1966	8.00
❑26, Sep 1966	8.00
❑27, Nov 1966	8.00
❑28, Jan 1967	8.00
❑29, Mar 1967	8.00
❑30, May 1967	8.00
❑31, Jul 1967	5.00
❑32, Sep 1967	5.00
❑33, Nov 1967	5.00
❑34, Jan 1968	5.00
❑35, Sep 1968	5.00
❑36, Nov 1968	5.00
❑37 1969	5.00
❑38 1969	5.00
❑39 1969	5.00
❑40, Jun 1969	5.00
❑41 1969	4.00
❑42 1969	4.00
❑43 1970	4.00
❑44 1970	4.00
❑45, Jul 1970	4.00
❑46 1970	4.00
❑47, Dec 1970	4.00
❑48 1971	4.00
❑49 1971	4.00
❑50 1971	4.00
❑51, Sep 1971	4.00
❑52, Dec 1971	4.00
❑53, Mar 1972	4.00
❑54 1972	4.00
❑55 1972	4.00
❑56 1972	4.00
❑57, Dec 1972	4.00
❑58, Feb 1973	4.00
❑59, Apr 1973	4.00
❑60, Jun 1973	4.00
❑61, Aug 1973	3.00
❑62, Oct 1973	3.00
❑63, Dec 1973	3.00
❑64 1974	3.00
❑65 1974	3.00
❑66 1974	3.00
❑67, Dec 1974	3.00
❑68 1974	3.00
❑69, Apr 1975	3.00
❑70, Jun 1975	3.00
❑71, Aug 1975	3.00
❑72, Oct 1975	3.00
❑73, Dec 1975	3.00
❑74, Feb 1976	3.00
❑75, Apr 1976	3.00
❑76, Jun 1976	3.00
❑77, Aug 1976	3.00
❑78, Oct 1976	3.00
❑79, Dec 1976	3.00
❑80, Feb 1977	2.00
❑81, Apr 1977	2.00
❑82, Jun 1977	2.00
❑83, Aug 1977	2.00
❑84 1977	2.00
❑85 1977	2.00
❑86, Jan 1978	2.00
❑87, Mar 1978	2.00
❑88, May 1978	2.00
❑89, Jul 1978	2.00
❑90 1978	2.00
❑91, Dec 1978	2.00
❑92, Feb 1979	2.00
❑93, May 1979	2.00
❑94 1979	2.00
❑95, Sep 1979	2.00
❑96, Nov 1979	2.00
❑97, Feb 1980	2.00
❑98, Apr 1980	2.00
❑99, Jun 1980	2.00
❑100, Aug 1980	2.00
❑101, Oct 1980	2.00
❑102, Dec 1980	2.00
❑103, Feb 1981	2.00
❑104, Apr 1981	2.00
❑105, Jun 1981	2.00
❑106, Aug 1981	2.00
❑107, Oct 1981	2.00

Devilman
Verotik

❑1, Jun 1995	3.50
❑2	3.00
❑3	3.00
❑4	2.95
❑5	2.95
❑6	3.50

Devil May Cry
Dreamwave

❑1, Mar 2004	3.95
❑1/2nd, Mar 2004; Reprints	3.95
❑2, Sep 2004	3.95
❑3, Apr 2004	3.95

Devil May Cry 3
Tokyopop

❑1, Oct 2005	9.99

Devil's Angel
Fantagraphics / Eros

❑1	2.95

Other grades: Multiply price above by 5/6 for VF/NM • 2/3 for VERY FINE • 1/3 for FINE • 1/5 for VERY GOOD • 1/8 for GOOD

Defenders of Dynatron City

Lucasarts' foray into all-ages comics
©Marvel

Delta Tenn

1980s glutcomic set in the scary world of 1997
©Entertainment

Demolition Man

Adaptation of Sly Stallone/ Wesley Snipes film
©DC

Demon (1st Series)

The demon Etrigan is set free
©DC

Demon Hunter (Aircel)

Former cultist runs from assassins
©Aircel

N-MINT

Devil's Bite
Boneyard

❑1..... 2.95
❑2; Indicia lists as #1..... 2.95

Devil's Due Studios Previews 2003
Image

❑1, Mar 2003..... 1.00

Devil's Footprints
Dark Horse

❑1, Mar 2003..... 2.99
❑2, Apr 2003..... 2.99
❑3, May 2003..... 2.99
❑4, Jul 2003..... 2.99

Devil's Keeper
Alias

❑1, Aug 2005..... 1.00
❑2, Dec 2005..... 2.99

Devil's Reign
Image

❑½, ca. 1996; Wizard mail-in..... 3.00
❑½/Autographed, ca. 1996; Signed, limited edition; Signed..... 3.00
❑½/Platinum, ca. 1996; Platinum edition 3.00

Devil's Rejects
Idea & Design Works

❑0/Baby, Jul 2005; Based on 2005 Rob Zombie movie; given away with "Wanted" cards and pins at San Diego Comic-Con International 2005..... 5.00
❑0/Otis, Jul 2005; Based on 2005 Rob Zombie movie; given away with "Wanted" cards and pins at San Diego Comic-Con International 2005..... 6.00
❑0/Spaulding, Jul 2005..... 5.00
❑1, Aug 2005..... 3.99

Devlin
Maximum

❑1, Apr 1996..... 2.50

Devlin Demon: Not for Normal Children
Dublin

❑1; ca. 1993..... 2.95

Dewey DeSade
Item

❑1..... 3.50
❑2..... 3.50
❑Ashcan 1; Promotional, mini-ashcan (4 x 2)..... 1.00

Dexter's Laboratory
DC

❑1, Sep 1999..... 2.50
❑2, Oct 1999 A: Mandark..... 2.00
❑3, Nov 1999; Dexter's robot takes his place..... 2.00
❑4, Dec 1999..... 2.00
❑5, Jan 2000..... 2.00
❑6, Feb 2000..... 2.00
❑7, Mar 2000..... 2.00
❑8, Apr 2000..... 2.00
❑9, May 2000..... 2.00
❑10, Jun 2000..... 2.00
❑11, Jul 2000..... 1.99
❑12, Aug 2000..... 1.99
❑13, Sep 2000..... 1.99
❑14, Oct 2000..... 1.99
❑15, Nov 2000..... 1.99
❑16, Dec 2000..... 1.99
❑17, Jan 2001..... 1.99
❑18, Feb 2001..... 1.99
❑19, Mar 2001..... 1.99
❑20, Apr 2001..... 1.99
❑21, May 2001..... 1.99
❑22, Jun 2001..... 1.99
❑23, Jul 2001..... 1.99
❑24, Aug 2001..... 1.99
❑25, Sep 2001..... 0.50
❑26, Oct 2001..... 1.99
❑27, Nov 2001..... 1.99
❑28, Dec 2001..... 1.99
❑29, Jan 2002..... 1.99
❑30, Aug 2002..... 1.99
❑31, Oct 2002..... 2.25
❑32, Dec 2002..... 2.25
❑33, Feb 2004..... 2.25
❑34, Apr 2004..... 2.25

Dhampire: Stillborn
DC / Vertigo

❑1, Sep 1996; prestige format; Adult..... 5.95

Diablo: Tales of Sanctuary
Dark Horse

❑1, Nov 2001; Several characters in profile on cover..... 5.95

Dia de los Muertos (Sergio Aragonés')
Dark Horse

❑nn, Oct 1998; Day of the Dead stories. 2.95

Diatom
Photographics

❑1, Apr 1995, b&w; prestige format; fumetti..... 4.95
❑2..... 4.95
❑3..... 4.95

Dick Danger
Olsen

❑1, Jan 1998..... 2.95
❑2..... 2.95
❑3..... 2.95
❑4..... 2.95
❑5..... 2.95

Dick Tracy
Blackthorne

❑1, Jun 1986..... 5.95
❑2, Jun 1986..... 5.95
❑3, Jul 1986..... 6.95
❑4, Aug 1986..... 6.95
❑5, Oct 1986..... 6.95
❑6, Oct 1986..... 6.95
❑7, Dec 1986..... 6.95
❑8, Jan 1987..... 6.95
❑9, Jan 1987..... 6.95
❑10, Feb 1987..... 6.95
❑11, Mar 1987..... 6.95
❑12, Apr 1987; 1/14/1949-4/5/1949..... 6.95
❑13, May 1987..... 6.95
❑14, Jun 1987..... 6.95
❑15, Jul 1987..... 6.95
❑16, Aug 1987..... 6.95
❑17, Sep 1987..... 6.95
❑18, Sep 1987; V: Pruneface..... 6.95
❑19, Oct 1987; V: Pruneface..... 6.95
❑20, Oct 1987; V: Pruneface..... 6.95
❑21, Nov 1987; Story is famous as one of the best deathtraps devised in comics..... 6.95
❑22, Nov 1987..... 6.95
❑23, Nov 1987..... 6.95
❑24, Dec 1987; V: Flattop..... 6.95

Dick Tracy (Disney)
Disney

❑1; newsstand format..... 2.95
❑1/Direct ed.; prestige format; ca. 1990 4.95
❑2; newsstand format..... 2.95
❑2/Direct ed.; prestige format..... 5.95
❑3; newsstand format..... 2.95
❑3/Direct ed.; prestige format; Movie adaptation..... 5.95

Dick Tracy 3-D
Blackthorne

❑1, Jul 1986; Includes 3-D glasses..... 2.50

Dick Tracy Adventures
Gladstone

❑1, Sep 1991; V: B.B. Eyes..... 4.95

Dick Tracy Adventures
Hamilton

❑1, b&w..... 3.95

Dick Tracy Crimebuster
Avalon

❑1..... 2.95
❑2..... 2.95
❑3..... 2.95
❑4..... 2.95

Dick Tracy Detective
Avalon

❑1..... 2.95
❑2..... 2.95
❑3..... 2.95
❑4..... 2.95

Dick Tracy Monthly
Blackthorne

❑1, May 1986..... 2.50
❑2, Jun 1986..... 2.00
❑3, Jul 1986..... 2.00
❑4, Aug 1986..... 2.00
❑5, Sep 1986..... 2.00
❑6, Oct 1986..... 2.00
❑7, Nov 1986..... 2.00
❑8, Dec 1986..... 2.00
❑9, Jan 1987..... 2.00
❑10, Feb 1987..... 2.00
❑11, Mar 1987..... 2.00
❑12, Apr 1987; no month in indicia..... 2.00
❑13, May 1987..... 2.00
❑14, Jun 1987..... 2.00
❑15, Jul 1987..... 2.00
❑16 1988..... 2.00
❑17 1988..... 2.00
❑18 1988..... 2.00
❑19 1988..... 2.00
❑20 1988..... 2.00
❑21 1988..... 2.00
❑22 1988..... 2.00
❑23 1988..... 2.00

Other grades: Multiply price above by 5/6 for VF/NM • 2/3 for VERY FINE • 1/3 for FINE • 1/5 for VERY GOOD • 1/8 for GOOD

❑24 1988 ... 2.00
❑25 1988; Series continues as Dick Tracy Weekly ... 2.00

Dick Tracy Special
Blackthorne

❑1, Jan 1988; O: Tracy ... 2.95
❑2, Mar 1988; O: Tracy ... 2.95
❑3, May 1988; O: Tracy ... 2.95

Dick Tracy: The Early Years
Blackthorne

❑1, Aug 1987 ... 6.95
❑2, Oct 1987 ... 6.95
❑3, Apr 1988 ... 6.95
❑4 ... 2.95

Dick Tracy "Unprinted Stories"
Blackthorne

❑1, Sep 1987 ... 2.95
❑2, Nov 1987 ... 2.95
❑3, Jan 1988 ... 2.95
❑4, Jun 1988 ... 2.95

Dick Tracy Weekly
Blackthorne

❑26, Jan 1988 ... 2.00
❑27, Jan 1988 ... 2.00
❑28, Jan 1988 ... 2.00
❑29, Jan 1988 ... 2.00
❑30, Feb 1988 ... 2.00
❑31, Feb 1988 ... 2.00
❑32, Feb 1988 ... 2.00
❑33, Feb 1988 ... 2.00
❑34, Mar 1988 ... 2.00
❑35, Mar 1988 ... 2.00
❑36, Mar 1988 ... 2.00
❑37, Mar 1988 ... 2.00
❑38, Jun 1988 ... 2.00
❑39, Jun 1988 ... 2.00
❑40, Jun 1988 ... 2.00
❑41, Jun 1988 ... 2.00
❑42, Jul 1988 ... 2.00
❑43, Jul 1988 ... 2.00
❑44, Jul 1988 ... 2.00
❑45, Jul 1988 ... 2.00
❑46, Aug 1988 ... 2.00
❑47, Aug 1988 ... 2.00
❑48, Aug 1988 ... 2.00
❑49, Aug 1988 ... 2.00
❑50, Sep 1988 ... 2.00
❑51, Sep 1988 ... 2.00
❑52, Sep 1988 ... 2.00
❑53, Sep 1988 ... 2.00
❑54, Oct 1988 ... 2.00
❑55, Oct 1988 ... 2.00
❑56, Oct 1988 ... 2.00
❑57, Oct 1988 ... 2.00
❑58, Oct 1988 ... 2.00
❑59, Oct 1988 ... 2.00
❑60, Nov 1988 ... 2.00
❑61, Nov 1988 ... 2.00
❑62, Nov 1988 ... 2.00
❑63, Nov 1988 ... 2.00
❑64, Nov 1988 ... 2.00
❑65, Nov 1988 ... 2.00
❑66, Dec 1988 ... 2.00
❑67, Dec 1988 ... 2.00
❑68, Dec 1988 ... 2.00
❑69, Dec 1988 ... 2.00
❑70, Jan 1989 ... 2.00
❑71, Jan 1989 ... 2.00
❑72, Jan 1989 ... 2.00
❑73, Jan 1989 ... 2.00
❑74, Feb 1989 ... 2.00
❑75, Feb 1989 ... 2.00
❑76, Feb 1989 ... 2.00
❑77, Feb 1989 ... 2.00
❑78, Mar 1989 ... 2.00
❑79, Mar 1989 ... 2.00
❑80, Mar 1989 ... 2.00
❑81, Mar 1989 ... 2.00
❑82, Apr 1989 ... 2.00
❑83, Apr 1989 ... 2.00
❑84, Apr 1989 ... 2.00
❑85, Apr 1989 ... 2.00
❑86, May 1989 ... 2.00
❑87, May 1989 ... 2.00
❑88, May 1989 ... 2.00
❑89, May 1989 ... 2.00
❑90, Jun 1989 ... 2.00
❑91, Jun 1989 ... 2.00
❑92, Jun 1989 ... 2.00
❑93, Jun 1989 ... 2.00
❑94, Aug 1989 ... 2.00
❑95, Aug 1989 ... 2.00
❑96, Aug 1989 ... 2.00
❑97, Aug 1989; 1: Moon Maid ... 2.00
❑98, Sep 1989 ... 2.00
❑99, Sep 1989 ... 2.00

Dick Wad
Slave Labor

❑1, Sep 1993, b&w; Adult ... 2.50

Dictators of the Twentieth Century: Hitler
Antarctic

❑1, Apr 2004 ... 2.99
❑2, May 2004 ... 2.99
❑3, Jun 2004 ... 2.99
❑4, Jul 2004 ... 2.99

Dictators of the Twentieth Century: Saddam Hussein
Antarctic

❑1, Aug 2004 ... 3.95
❑2, Sep 2004 ... 3.95

Didymous: The Night and Day Worlds
Ironhorse

❑1, Jun 1999, b&w ... 2.50
❑2, ca. 1999, b&w; Repeats indicia from #1 2.50

Diebold
Silent Partners

❑1 1996, b&w; ca. 1994 ... 2.95
❑2 1996, b&w ... 2.95

Die-Cut
Marvel

❑1, Nov 1993; diecut cover ... 2.50
❑2, Dec 1993 ... 1.75
❑3, Jan 1994 ... 1.75
❑4, Feb 1994 ... 1.75

Die-Cut vs. G-Force
Marvel

❑1, Nov 1993; Holo-Grafx cover ... 2.75
❑2, Dec 1993; foil cover ... 2.75

Diesel
Antarctic

❑1, Apr 1997 ... 2.95

Digimon Digital Monsters
Dark Horse

❑1, May 2000 ... 2.95
❑2, May 2000 ... 2.95
❑3, May 2000 ... 2.95
❑4, May 2000 ... 2.95
❑5, Aug 2000 ... 2.95
❑6, Sep 2000 ... 2.95
❑7, Sep 2000 ... 2.95
❑8, Sep 2000 ... 2.95
❑9, Sep 2000 ... 2.99
❑10, Oct 2000 ... 2.99
❑11, Nov 2000 ... 2.99
❑12, Nov 2000 ... 2.99

Digimon Tamers
Tokyopop

❑1, Apr 2004; Graphic novel; Reads right to left; b&w ... 9.99

Digital Dragon
Peregrine Entertainment

❑1, Jan 1999, b&w ... 2.95
❑2, Apr 1999, b&w ... 2.95

Digital Webbing Presents
Digital Webbing

❑1 2001, b&w ... 2.95
❑2 2001, b&w ... 2.95
❑3 2001, b&w ... 2.95
❑4, Aug 2001, b&w (c) ... 2.95
❑5, Oct 2001, b&w ... 2.95
❑6, Dec 2001, b&w ... 2.95
❑7, Feb 2002, b&w ... 2.95
❑8, Apr 2002, b&w ... 2.95
❑9, Jun 2002, b&w ... 2.95
❑10, Aug 2002, b&w ... 2.95
❑11, Oct 2002, b&w ... 2.95
❑12, Nov 2003, b&w ... 2.95
❑13 2003, b&w ... 2.95
❑14 2003, b&w ... 2.95
❑15, Jun 2003, b&w ... 2.95
❑16, Jul 2004, b&w ... 2.95
❑17, Aug 2004, b&w ... 2.95
❑18, Sep 2004, b&w ... 2.95
❑19, ca. 2004, b&w; Price increase ... 3.50
❑20, ca. 2005, b&w ... 3.50

Digitek
Marvel

❑1, Dec 1992 ... 2.00
❑2, Jan 1993 ... 2.00
❑3, Feb 1993 ... 2.00
❑4, Mar 1993 ... 2.00

Dik Skycap
Rip Off

❑1, Dec 1991, b&w ... 2.50
❑2, May 1992, b&w ... 2.50

Dilemma Presents
Dilemma

❑1, Oct 1994, b&w ... 2.50
❑2, b&w; Flip-book ... 2.50
❑3, Apr 1995, b&w; Flip-book ... 2.50
❑4, b&w; Flip-book ... 2.50

Dilton's Strange Science
Archie

❑1, May 1989 ... 2.00
❑2, Aug 1989 ... 1.50
❑3, Nov 1989 ... 1.50
❑4, Feb 1990 ... 1.50
❑5, May 1990 ... 1.50

Dimension 5
Edge

❑1, Oct 1995, b&w; Adult ... 3.95

Dimension X
Karl Art

❑1, b&w; ca. 1992 ... 3.50

Dimension Z
Pyramid

❑1 ... 2.00
❑2 ... 2.00

Dimm Comics Presents
Dimm

❑Ashcan 0, Jan 1996, b&w; ashcan promotional comic ... 1.00
❑Ashcan 1, May 1996, b&w; ashcan promotional comic ... 1.00

Dim-Witted Darryl
Slave Labor

❑1, Jun 1998, b&w ... 2.95
❑2 ... 2.95
❑3 ... 2.95

Dingledorfs
Skylight

❑1, b&w ... 2.75

Dinky on the Road
Blind Bat

❑1, Jun 1994, b&w ... 1.95

Dino Island
Mirage

❑1, Feb 1993; covers form diptych ... 2.75
❑2, Mar 1993; covers form diptych ... 2.75

Dino-Riders
Marvel

❑1, Mar 1989 ... 1.50
❑2, Apr 1989 ... 1.50
❑3, May 1989 ... 1.50

Dinosaur Bop
Monster

❑1, b&w ... 2.50
❑2, b&w ... 2.50

Dinosaur Island
Monster

❑1, b&w ... 2.50

Dinosaur Mansion
Edge

❑1, b&w; no indicia ... 2.95

Dinosaur Rex
Upshot

❑1 ... 2.00
❑2, b&w ... 2.00
❑3, b&w ... 2.00

Den

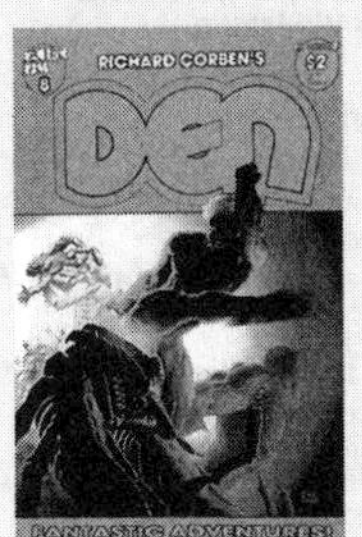

Richard Corben's fantasy continues
©Fantagor

Denizens of Deep City

Odd series about mundane urban travails
©Kitchen Sink

Dennis the Menace

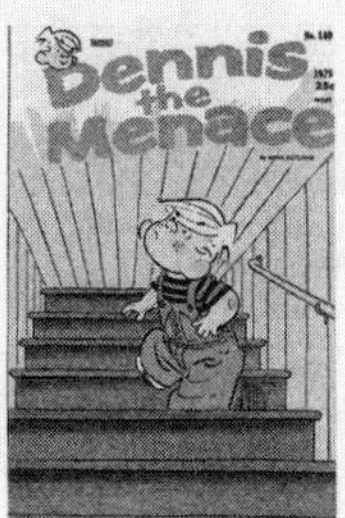

Long-running series adapts Ketcham terror
©Fawcett

Dennis the Menace and his Friends

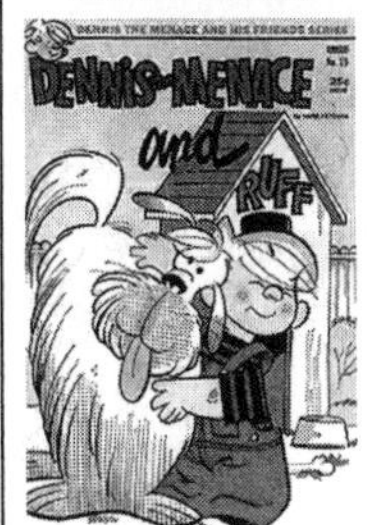

Reprint series later goes digest-size
©Fawcett

Desert Peach

Follows Rommel's grave-digging division
©Thoughts & Images

N-MINT

Dinosaurs
Hollywood

❑1, Dec 1991; TV based 3.00
❑2, Apr 1991; TV based 3.00

Dinosaurs: An Illustrated Guide
Caliber / Tome

❑1, Win 1991, b&w; Carnivores 2.50

Dinosaurs Attack!
Eclipse

❑1, trading cards 3.95
❑2 3.95
❑3 3.95

Dinosaurs, A Celebration
Marvel / Epic

❑1, ca. 1992; Horns and Heavy Armor 4.95
❑2, ca. 1992; Bone heads and Duck-bills 4.95
❑3, ca. 1992; Egg stealers and Earth shakers 4.95
❑4, ca. 1992; Terrible Claws and Tyrants 4.95

Dinosaurs For Hire
Eternity

❑1, Mar 1988, b&w 2.00
❑1/3D, Oct 1988; 3-D; 3-D 2.95
❑1/2nd, Mar 1988; 2nd printing 1.95
❑2, Jun 1988 1.95
❑3, Aug 1988 1.95
❑4 1.95
❑5 1.95
❑6 1.95
❑7 1.95
❑8 1.95
❑9 1.95

Dinosaurs For Hire
Malibu

❑1, Feb 1993 1.95
❑2, Mar 1993 1.95
❑3, Apr 1993 1.95
❑4, May 1993 1.95
❑5, Jun 1993; V: Poacher 2.50
❑6, Jul 1993; Jurassic Park parody cover 2.50
❑7, Aug 1993; V: Turret, Hunter of Dinosaurs 2.50
❑8, Sep 1993 2.50
❑9, Oct 1993 2.50
❑10, Nov 1993; Comics' Greatest World parody cover 2.50
❑11, Dec 1993 2.50
❑12, Feb 1994; Ultraverse parody cover 2.50

Dinosaurs for Hire: Dinosaurs Rule!
Eternity

❑1; Dinosaurs Rule! 5.95

Dinosaurs For Hire Fall Classic
Eternity

❑1, Nov 1988, b&w; Fall Classic; Elvis 2.25

Dinosaurs for Hire: Guns 'n' Lizards
Eternity

❑1; Guns 'n' Lizards 5.95

Dioramas: Love Story
Image

❑1, ca. 2004 12.95

Directory to a Nonexistent Universe
Eclipse

❑1, Dec 1987 2.00

N-MINT

Dire Wolves: A Chronicle of the Deadworld
Caliber

❑1, b&w 3.95

Dirtbag
Twist N Shout

❑1, ca. 1993 2.95
❑2, ca. 1993 2.95
❑3, Nov 1993 2.95
❑4, Dec 1993 2.95
❑5, ca. 1994 2.95
❑6 2.95
❑7 2.95

Dirty Dozen
Dell

❑1, Oct 1967, 12-180-710 25.00

Dirty Pair
Eclipse

❑1, Dec 1988, b&w 4.00
❑2, Jan 1989, b&w 3.00
❑3, Feb 1989, b&w 3.00
❑4, Mar 1989, b&w 3.00

Dirty Pair II
Eclipse

❑1, May 1989, b&w 2.50
❑2, Aug 1989, b&w 2.50
❑3, Nov 1989; Misnumbered #1 2.50
❑4, Feb 1990 2.50
❑5, May 1990 2.50

Dirty Pair III
Eclipse

❑1, Aug 1990, b&w; A Plague of Angels 2.25
❑2, Nov 1990, b&w 2.25
❑3, Feb 1991 2.25
❑4, May 1991 2.25
❑5, Aug 1991 2.25

Dirty Pair
Viz

❑1; Animation adapted into comic form. 4.95
❑2; Animation adapted into comic form. 4.95
❑3; Animation adapted into comic form. 4.95
❑4; Animation adapted into comic form. 4.95
❑5; Animation adapted into comic form. 4.95

Dirty Pair: Dangerous Acquaintances
Dark Horse / Manga

❑1, b&w 2.95
❑2, b&w 2.95
❑3, b&w 2.95
❑4, b&w 2.95
❑5, b&w 2.95

Dirty Pair: Fatal but Not Serious
Dark Horse / Manga

❑1, Jul 1995 2.95
❑2, Aug 1995 2.95
❑3, Sep 1995 2.95
❑4, Oct 1995 2.95
❑5, Nov 1995 2.95

Dirty Pair: Run from the Future
Dark Horse / Manga

❑1, Jan 2000; Cover by Adam Hughes 2.95
❑1/A, Jan 2000; alternate cover 2.95
❑2, Feb 2000; Warren Cover 2.95

N-MINT

❑3, Mar 2000 2.95
❑4, Apr 2000; Kei Bound, Yuri marked for Butchering Warren cover 2.95

Dirty Pair: Sim Hell
Dark Horse / Manga

❑1 1993, b&w 2.95
❑2 1993, b&w 2.95
❑3 1993, b&w 2.95
❑4 1993, b&w 2.95
❑5 1993 2.95

Dirty Pair: Sim Hell Remastered
Dark Horse / Manga

❑1, May 2001 2.99
❑2, Jun 2001 2.99
❑3, Jul 2001 2.99
❑4, Aug 2001 2.99

Dirty Pair: Start The Violence
Dark Horse

❑1/A, Sep 1999; Jason Pearson cover 2.95
❑1/B, Sep 1999; variant cover 2.95

Dirty Pictures
Aircel

❑1, Apr 1991, b&w; Adult 2.50
❑2, b&w; Adult 2.50
❑3, b&w; Adult 2.50

Dirty Plotte
Drawn and Quarterly

❑1 2.50
❑2 2.50
❑3 2.50
❑4 2.50
❑5 2.50
❑6 2.50
❑7 2.95
❑8 2.95
❑9 2.95
❑10, Nov 1996 3.50

Disavowed
DC / Wildstorm

❑1, Mar 2000 2.50
❑2, Apr 2000 2.50
❑3, May 2000 2.50
❑4, Jun 2000 2.50
❑5, Jul 2000 2.50
❑6, Aug 2000 2.50

Disciples
Image

❑1, Apr 2001 2.95
❑2, Jun 2001 2.95

Dishman
Eclipse

❑1, Sep 1988, b&w; 1: Dishman; O: Dishman 2.50

Disney Afternoon
Marvel

❑1, Nov 1994; Darkwing Duck, Bonkers, Goof Troop, Tailspin 2.00
❑2, Dec 1994 1.50
❑3, Jan 1995 1.50
❑4, Feb 1995 1.50
❑5, Mar 1995 1.50
❑6, Apr 1995 1.50
❑7, May 1995 1.50

❑8, Jun 1995 .... 1.50
❑9, Jul 1995 .... 1.50
❑10, Aug 1995; Final Issue 1.50

Disney Comic Hits
Marvel

❑1, Oct 1995, Pocahontas 2.00
❑2, Nov 1995, Timon and Pumbaa 2.00
❑3, Dec 1995, A: Pocahontas. A: Captain John Smith. Pocahontas 2.00
❑4, Jan 1996, Adapts Toy Story 2.00
❑5, Feb 1996, Winter Wonderland 2.00
❑6, Mar 1996 .... 2.00
❑7, Apr 1996 .... 2.00
❑8, May 1996, Timon and Pumbaa 2.00
❑9, Jun 1996 .... 2.00
❑10, Jul 1996, adapts Hunchback of Notre Dame 2.00
❑11, Aug 1996, Hunchback of Notre Dame 2.00
❑12, Sep 1996, The Little Mermaid 2.00
❑13, Oct 1996, adapts Aladdin and the King of Thieves 2.00
❑14, Nov 1996, Timon & Pumbaa 2.00
❑15, Dec 1996, Toy Story adventures 2.00
❑16, Jan 1997, adapts 101 Dalmations .. 2.00

Disneyland Birthday Party
Gladstone

❑1, ca. 1985, CB (a); Reprints Disneyland Birthday Party (Giant), Uncle Scrooge Goes to Disneyland 10.00
❑1/A, digest 10.00

Disney Movie Book
Disney

❑1; Roger Rabbit in Tummy Trouble 7.95

Disney's Action Club
Acclaim

❑1; digest; Hercules, Hunchback, Lion King, Aladdin, Toy Story, Mighty Ducks 4.50
❑2 .... 4.50
❑3 .... 4.50
❑4; digest; Mighty Ducks, Toy Story, Aladdin, Hercules stories 4.50
❑5 .... 4.50
❑6 .... 4.50
❑7, Jun 1997 .... 4.50

Disney's Colossal Comics
Disney

❑1 .... 2.00

Disney's Colossal Comics Collection
Disney

❑1; digest 2.00
❑2; digest 2.00
❑3; digest 2.00
❑4; digest 2.00
❑5; digest 2.00
❑6; digest 2.00
❑7; digest 2.00
❑8; digest 2.00
❑9; digest 2.00
❑10; digest 2.00

Disney's Comics in 3-D
Disney

❑1 .... 2.95

Disney's Enchanting Stories
Acclaim

❑1 .... 4.50
❑2; Pocahontas 4.50
❑3; Beauty & The Beast 4.50
❑4; 101 Dalmations 4.50

Disobedient Daisy
Fantagraphics / Eros

❑1, Aug 1995, b&w; Adult 2.95
❑2, Oct 1995, b&w; Adult 2.95

Distant Soil, A
Warp

❑1 1983 .... 8.00
❑2 1984 .... 5.00
❑3 1984 .... 4.00
❑4 1984 .... 4.00
❑5 1985 .... 4.00
❑6, Jun 1985; Standard comic size; 1: Panda Khan; Standard comic size .. 3.00
❑7, Sep 1985 .... 3.00
❑8, Dec 1985 .... 3.00
❑9, Mar 1986 .... 3.00

Distant Soil, A
Aria

❑1 1991 .... 5.00
❑1/2nd; 2nd printing 3.00
❑1/3rd; 3rd printing 2.00
❑1/4th; 4th printing 1.75
❑2 .... 3.00
❑2/2nd; 2nd printing 1.75
❑3 1992 .... 3.00
❑3/2nd; 2nd printing 1.75
❑4 1993 .... 2.00
❑4/2nd; 2nd printing 1.75
❑5 1993 .... 1.75
❑6 .... 1.75
❑7 1994 .... 1.75
❑8, Jun 1994 .... 1.75
❑9, Aug 1994 .... 2.50
❑10 .... 2.50
❑11, Apr 1995 .... 2.50
❑12, Nov 1995 .... 2.50
❑13, Jun 1996 .... 2.95
❑14, Aug 1996 .... 2.95
❑15, Aug 1996; Image begins as publisher 2.95
❑16, Oct 1996; b&w 2.95
❑17, Dec 1996; b&w 2.95
❑18, Feb 1997 .... 2.95
❑19, Apr 1997 .... 2.95
❑20, Jun 1997 .... 2.95
❑21, Sep 1997; Includes sketchbook pages 2.95
❑22, Dec 1997 .... 2.95
❑23, Feb 1998 .... 2.95
❑24, Apr 1998 .... 2.95
❑25, Jun 1998; double-sized; NG (w); 15th anniversary issue 3.95
❑25/Ltd., Jun 1998; 15th anniversary issue; NG (w); Autographed by Colleen Doran and Neil Gaiman 8.00
❑26, Nov 1998; Christmas cover; not Christmas story 2.95
❑27, Apr 1999 .... 2.95
❑28, Jul 1999 .... 3.95
❑29, Dec 1999 .... 3.95
❑30, Aug 2000 .... 3.95
❑31, Jan 2001 .... 3.95
❑38, Feb 2007 .... 4.50
❑32, May 2001 .... 3.95
❑33, Aug 2001; Includes sketchbook pages, data file 3.95
❑34, Sep 2001; Giant-size; Includes data file, sketchbook pages 4.95
❑35, Sep 2002 .... 3.95
❑36, Oct 2003 .... 4.50

District X
Marvel

❑1, Jul 2004 .... 4.00
❑2, Aug 2004, 1: Arturo Falcones 2.99
❑3, Sep 2004 .... 2.99
❑4, Oct 2004 .... 2.99
❑5, Nov 2004 .... 2.99
❑6, Dec 2004 .... 2.99
❑7, Jan 2005 .... 2.99
❑8, Feb 2005 .... 2.99
❑9, Mar 2005 .... 2.99
❑10, Apr 2005 .... 2.99
❑11, May 2005 .... 2.99
❑12, May 2005 .... 2.99
❑13, Jun 2005 .... 2.99

Ditko Package
Ditko

❑1; squarebound 8.95

Diva Grafix & Stories
Starhead

❑1, Nov 1993, b&w; Adult 3.95
❑2, b&w; Adult 3.95

Divas
Caliber

❑1, b&w 2.50
❑2, b&w 2.50
❑3, b&w 2.50
❑4, b&w 2.50

Divine Intervention/Gen13
DC / Wildstorm

❑1, Nov 1999 .... 2.50

Divine Intervention/Wildcats
DC / Wildstorm

❑1, Nov 1999 .... 2.50

Divine Right
Image

❑1, Sep 1997 JLee (w); JLee (a) 3.00
❑1/A, Sep 1997; JLee (w); JLee (a); variant cover 3.00
❑1/B, Sep 1997; JLee (c); JLee (w); JLee (a); American Entertainment variant; Christy Blaze with flag in background 3.00
❑1/C, Sep 1997; Bagged edition; JLee (c); JLee (w); JLee (a); Bagged edition; Voyager pack with preview of Stormwatch 3.00
❑1/D, Sep 1997; Spanish edition; alternate cover 2.50
❑1/E, Sep 1997; Voyager pack with preview of Stormwatch 2.50
❑2, Oct 1997; JLee (w); JLee (a); Sword battle scene on cover 3.00
❑2/Variant, Oct 1997; alternate cover; fight scene 2.50
❑3, Nov 1997 JLee (w); JLee (a); A: Fairchild. 2.50
❑3/Variant, Nov 1997; no cover price on outer cover 2.50
❑4, Dec 1997; JLee (w); JLee (a); White cover w/blue figure (no Fairchild) 2.50
❑4/Variant, Dec 1997; JLee (w); JLee (a); Variant cover (Fairchild) 2.50
❑5, Feb 1998 JLee (w); JLee (a) 2.50
❑5/Variant, Feb 1998; Pacific Comicon variant cover edition; JLee (w); JLee (a); Pacific Comicon variant cover edition 2.50
❑6, Aug 1998 JLee (w); JLee (a) 2.50
❑7, Dec 1998 JLee (w); JLee (a) 2.50
❑8, Jan 1999 JLee (w); JLee (a) 2.50
❑8/Variant, Jan 1999; alternate cover 2.50
❑9, Jul 1999 JLee (w); JLee (a) 2.50
❑10, Oct 1999 JLee (w); JLee (a) 2.50
❑11, Nov 1999 JLee (w); JLee (a) 2.50
❑Ashcan 1, Jul 1997; JLee (w); JLee (a); 1: Divine Right. Team on cover 3.00
❑Ashcan 1/A, Jul 1997; JLee (w); JLee (a); 1: Divine Right. variant cover: Faraday typing, woman's leg in foreground 3.00

Division 13
Dark Horse

❑1, Sep 1994 .... 2.50
❑2, Oct 1994 .... 2.50
❑3, Dec 1994 .... 2.50
❑4, Jan 1995, b&w 2.50

Dixie Road
NBM

❑1 .... 10.95
❑2 .... 10.95

Django and Angel
Caliber

❑1, b&w 2.50
❑2, b&w 2.50
❑3, b&w 2.50
❑4, b&w 2.50
❑5, b&w 2.50

DMZ
DC / Vertigo

❑1, Jan 2006 .... 2.99
❑2, Feb 2006 .... 2.99
❑3, Mar 2006 .... 2.99
❑4, Apr 2006 .... 2.99
❑5, May 2006 .... 2.99
❑6, Jun 2006 .... 2.99
❑8, Aug 2006 .... 2.99
❑9, Sep 2006 .... 2.99
❑10, Nov 2006 .... 2.99
❑11, Nov 2006 .... 2.99
❑12, Dec 2006 .... 2.99
❑13, Jan 2007 .... 2.99
❑14, Feb 2007, Includes preview of Scalped #1 .... 2.99
❑15 .... 2.99
❑16 .... 2.99
❑17 .... 2.99
❑18 .... 2.99
❑19 .... 2.99
❑20 .... 2.99
❑21 .... 2.99
❑22 .... 2.99
❑23 .... 2.99

Desert Storm Journal

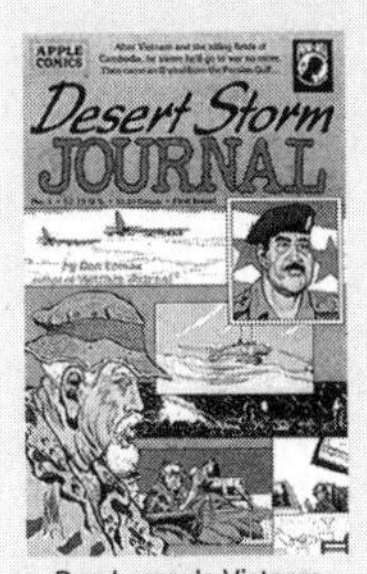

Don Lomax's Vietnam Journal follow-up
©Apple

Desperate Times

Humor series from Chris Eliopoulos
©Image

Destroyer Duck

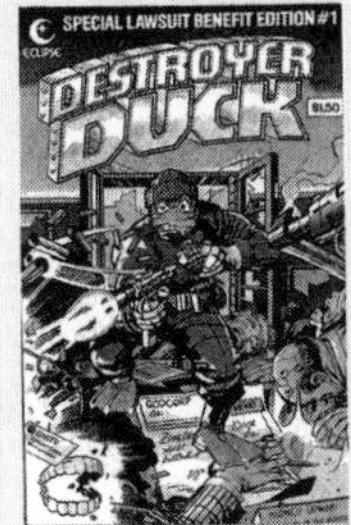

Gerber's duck in exile during Howard fight
©Eclipse

Detective Comics

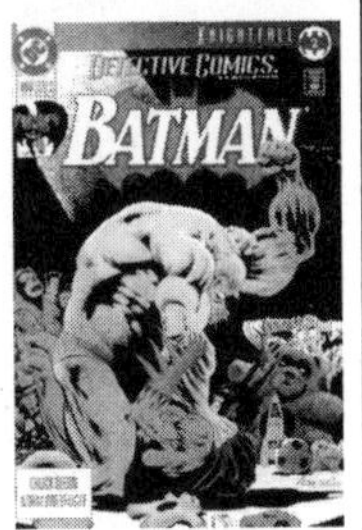

Batman series is world's longest-published comic
©DC

Detectives, Inc.: A Terror of Dying Dreams

Detective story drawn with sepia tones
©Eclipse

	N-MINT
❑24	2.99
❑25	2.99
❑26	2.99
❑27	2.99
❑28	2.99
❑29	2.99
❑30	2.99
❑31	2.99
❑32	2.99
❑33	2.99
❑34	2.99
❑35	2.99
❑36	2.99
❑37	2.99
❑38	2.99
❑39	2.99
❑40	2.99
❑41	2.99
❑42	2.99

DNAgents
Eclipse

	N-MINT
❑1, Mar 1983; 1: Surge; 1: Rainbow; 1: Sham; 1: Tank; 1: Amber	2.50
❑2, Apr 1983 ME (w)	2.00
❑3, May 1983 ME (w)	2.00
❑4, Jul 1983	2.00
❑5, Aug 1983	2.00
❑6, Oct 1983	1.75
❑7, Nov 1983	1.75
❑8, Jan 1984	1.75
❑9, Feb 1984; 1: Crossfire	1.75
❑10, Mar 1984; 2: Crossfire	1.75
❑11, May 1984	1.75
❑12, May 1984	1.75
❑13, Jun 1984	1.75
❑14, Jul 1984	1.75
❑15, Aug 1984 ME (w); RHo, EL (a)	1.75
❑16, Sep 1984	1.75
❑17, Dec 1984	1.75
❑18, Jan 1985; Infinity cover	1.75
❑19, Feb 1985	1.75
❑20, Mar 1985	1.75
❑21, Apr 1985	1.75
❑22, May 1985	1.75
❑23, Jun 1985	1.75
❑24, Jul 1985; DSt (c); ME (w); DS (a); Story continued in Crossfire #14	1.75
❑3D 1, Jan 1986; 3-Dminensional DNAgents	2.50

DNAgents Super Special
Antarctic

	N-MINT
❑1, Apr 1994, b&w; Flipbook format; B&w and color	3.50

D-N-Angel
Tokyopop

	N-MINT
❑1, Apr 2004	9.99
❑2, May 2004	9.99
❑3, Jul 2004	9.99
❑4, Oct 2004	9.99
❑5, Nov 2004	9.99
❑6, Feb 2005	9.99
❑7, Mar 2005	9.99
❑8, Jun 2005	9.99
❑9, Sep 2005	9.99
❑10, Dec 2005	9.99

D.O.A.
Saving Grace

	N-MINT
❑1; Adult	1.00

Doc Chaos: The Strange Attractor
Vortex

	N-MINT
❑1, Apr 1990	3.00
❑2 1990	3.00
❑3 1990	3.00

Doc Frankenstein
Burlyman

	N-MINT
❑1, Nov 2004; Painted cover; Cardstock cover; Includes 2 cut pages of pencils	7.00
❑1/Darrow	10.00
❑2	3.50
❑2/Sketch 2004	5.00
❑3, May 2005; Painted cover	3.50
❑3/Variant 2005	5.00

Doc Samson
Marvel

	N-MINT
❑1, Jan 1996	1.95
❑2, Feb 1996	1.95
❑3, Mar 1996; V: Punisher	1.95
❑4, Apr 1996	1.95

Doc Samson
Marvel

	N-MINT
❑1, Feb 2006	2.99
❑2, Mar 2006	2.99
❑3, May 2006	2.99
❑4, Jun 2006	2.99
❑5, Jul 2006	2.99

Doc Savage
Gold Key

	N-MINT
❑1, Nov 1966, 10192-611	38.00

Doc Savage
Marvel

	N-MINT
❑1, Oct 1972, JB (c); RA, JM (a); adapts Man of Bronze	20.00
❑2, Dec 1972, JSo (c); RA (a); adapts Man of Bronze	5.00
❑3, Feb 1973, JSo (c); RA (a); adapts Death in Silver	3.00
❑4, Apr 1973, GK (c); RA (a); adapts Death in Silver	3.00
❑5, Jun 1973, GK (c); RA (a); adapts The Monsters	3.00
❑6, Aug 1973, GK (c); RA (a); adapts The Monsters	3.00
❑7, Oct 1973, adapts Brand of the Werewolf	3.00
❑8, Jan 1974, adapts Brand of the Werewolf	3.00

Doc Savage
Marvel

	N-MINT
❑1, Aug 1975	9.00
❑2, Oct 1975	4.00
❑3, Jan 1976	4.00
❑4, Apr 1976	4.00
❑5, Jul 1976	4.00
❑6, Oct 1976	3.00
❑7, Jan 1977	3.00
❑8, Spr 1977	3.00

Doc Savage
DC

	N-MINT
❑1, Nov 1987	2.00
❑2, Dec 1987	2.00
❑3, Jan 1988	2.00
❑4, Feb 1988	2.00

Doc Savage
DC

	N-MINT
❑1, Nov 1988	2.00
❑2, Dec 1988	2.00
❑3, Dec 1988	2.00
❑4, Jan 1989	2.00
❑5, Jan 1989	2.00
❑6, Mar 1989	2.00
❑7, Apr 1989	2.00
❑8, May 1989	2.00
❑9, Jun 1989	2.00
❑10, Jul 1989	2.00
❑11, Aug 1989; V: John Sunlight	2.00
❑12, Sep 1989; V: John Sunlight	2.00
❑13, Oct 1989; V: John Sunlight	2.00
❑14, Nov 1989; V: John Sunlight	2.00
❑15, Dec 1989	2.00
❑16, Jan 1990	2.00
❑17, Feb 1990; Shadow	2.00
❑18, Mar 1990; Shadow	2.00
❑19, May 1990	2.00
❑20, Jun 1990	2.00
❑21, Jul 1990	2.00
❑22, Aug 1990	2.00
❑23, Sep 1990	2.00
❑24, Oct 1990; Final Issue	2.00
❑Ann 1, ca. 1989	3.50

Doc Savage: Curse of the Fire God
Dark Horse

	N-MINT
❑1, Sep 1995	2.95
❑2, Oct 1995	2.95
❑3, Nov 1995	2.95
❑4, Dec 1995	2.95

Doc Savage: Devil's Thoughts
Millennium

	N-MINT
❑1	2.50
❑2	2.50
❑3	2.50

Doc Savage: Doom Dynasty
Millennium

	N-MINT
❑1	2.00
❑2	2.00

Doc Savage: Manual of Bronze
Millennium

	N-MINT
❑1, Aug 1992	2.50

Doc Savage: Repel
Millennium

	N-MINT
❑1; only issue ever released	2.50

Doc Savage: The Man of Bronze
Millennium

	N-MINT
❑1	2.50
❑2	2.50
❑3	2.50
❑4	2.50

Doctor Fate
DC

	N-MINT
❑1, Oct 2003	2.50
❑2, Nov 2003	2.50
❑3, Dec 2003	2.50
❑4, Jan 2004	2.50
❑5, Feb 2004	2.50

Other grades: Multiply price above by 5/6 for VF/NM • 2/3 for VERY FINE • 1/3 for FINE • 1/5 for VERY GOOD • 1/8 for GOOD

Dr. Andy
Alliance

❑1, Aug 1994, b&w ... 2.50

Dr. Atomic
Last Gasp

❑1, Adult ... 5.00
❑2, Adult ... 4.00
❑3, Adult ... 4.00
❑4, Adult ... 3.00
❑5, Adult ... 3.00
❑6, Adult ... 3.00

Doctor Bang
Rip Off

❑1, Feb 1992, b&w ... 2.50

Doctor Boogie
Media Arts

❑1 ... 1.75

Doctor Chaos
Triumphant

❑1; Unleashed! ... 2.50
❑2; Unleashed! ... 2.50
❑3, Jan 1994 ... 2.50
❑4, Feb 1994 ... 2.50
❑5, Mar 1994 ... 2.50
❑6, Mar 1994 ... 2.50
❑7 1994 ... 2.50
❑8 1994 ... 2.50
❑9 1994 ... 2.50
❑10 1994 ... 2.50
❑11 1994 ... 2.50
❑12 1994 ... 2.50

Doctor Cyborg
Attention!

❑1, b&w; 1: Doctor Cyborg ... 2.95
❑1/Ashcan, b&w; Preview edition of Doctor Cyborg #1; 1: Doctor Cyborg. preview of series ... 1.00
❑2, b&w ... 2.95
❑3, b&w ... 2.95

Doctor Doom's Revenge
Marvel

❑1, ca. 1989, giveaway comic included with computer game from Paragon Software; Came with computer game by Paragon Software ... 1.00

Doctor Fate (1st Mini-Series)
DC

❑1, Jul 1987 KG (a) ... 2.00
❑2, Aug 1987 KG (a) ... 2.00
❑3, Sep 1987 KG (a) ... 2.00
❑4, Oct 1987 KG (a); 1: Doctor Fate II (Eric Strauss & Linda Strauss). D: Doctor Fate I (Kent Nelson) ... 2.00

Doctor Fate
DC

❑1, Dec 1988 ... 2.00
❑2, Jan 1989 ... 1.25
❑3, Jan 1989 ... 1.25
❑4, Feb 1989 ... 1.25
❑5, Apr 1989 ... 1.25
❑6, May 1989 ... 1.75
❑7, Jun 1989 ... 1.75
❑8, Jul 1989 ... 1.75
❑9, Aug 1989 ... 1.75
❑10, Sep 1989 ... 1.75
❑11, Nov 1989 ... 1.50
❑12, Dec 1989 ... 1.50
❑13, Jan 1990 ... 1.50
❑14, Feb 1990 ... 1.50
❑15, Mar 1990 ... 1.50
❑16, Apr 1990 ... 1.50
❑17, May 1990 ... 1.50
❑18, Jun 1990 ... 1.50
❑19, Jul 1990 ... 1.50
❑20, Aug 1990 ... 1.50
❑21, Oct 1990 ... 1.50
❑22, Nov 1990 ... 1.50
❑23, Dec 1990 ... 1.50
❑24, Jan 1991 ... 1.50
❑25, Feb 1991 ... 1.50
❑26, Mar 1991 ... 1.50
❑27, Apr 1991 ... 1.50
❑28, May 1991 ... 1.50
❑29, Jun 1991 ... 1.50
❑30, Jul 1991 ... 1.50
❑31, Aug 1991 ... 1.50
❑32, Sep 1991; War of the Gods ... 1.75
❑33, Oct 1991; War of the Gods ... 1.75
❑34, Nov 1991 ... 1.75
❑35, Dec 1991 ... 1.75
❑36, Jan 1992 ... 1.75
❑37, Feb 1992 ... 1.75
❑38, Mar 1992 ... 1.75
❑39, Apr 1992 ... 1.75
❑40, May 1992 ... 1.75
❑41, Jun 1992 ... 1.75
❑Ann 1, Nov 1989 ... 2.95

Doctor Faustus
Anarchy

❑1, b&w; Adult ... 2.95
❑2 1994, b&w; Adult ... 2.95
❑Ashcan 1; ashcan, b&w ... 2.00

Doctor Frankenstein's House of 3-D
3-D Zone

❑1, ca. 1992, Oversized ... 4.00

Dr. Fu Manchu
I.W.

❑1, ca. 1964 ... 45.00

Dr. Giggles
Dark Horse

❑1, Oct 1992, Movie adaptation ... 2.50
❑2 1992, Movie adaptation ... 2.50

Doctor Gorpon
Eternity

❑1, b&w ... 2.50
❑2, b&w ... 2.50
❑3, Aug 1991, b&w ... 2.50

Dr. Goyle Special
Arrow

❑1, b&w ... 2.95

Doctor! I'm Too Big!
NBM

❑1; Adult ... 10.95

Dr. Jekyll and Mr. Hyde
NBM

❑1 ... 15.95

Dr. Kildare
Dell

❑2 1962 ... 50.00
❑3, Oct 1962 ... 40.00
❑4, Dec 1962 ... 40.00
❑5, Mar 1963 ... 40.00
❑6, Jun 1963 ... 40.00
❑7, Sep 1963 ... 40.00
❑8, Oct 1964 ... 40.00
❑9, Apr 1965 ... 40.00

Doctor Mid-Nite
DC

❑1, ca. 1999; D.O.A. ... 5.95
❑2, ca. 1999 ... 5.95
❑3, ca. 1999 ... 5.95

Dr. Radium and the Gizmos of Boola-Boola
Slave Labor

❑1, Jan 1992, b&w; NN ... 4.95

Dr. Radium, Man of Science
Slave Labor

❑1, Oct 1992, b&w ... 2.50
❑2, Jan 1993, b&w ... 2.50
❑3, Jul 1993 ... 2.95
❑4, Jan 1994 ... 2.95
❑5, Jan 1995, b&w ... 2.95

Dr. Robot Special
Dark Horse

❑1, Apr 2000 ... 2.95

Dr. Slump
Viz

❑1, May 2005 ... 7.99
❑2, Jul 2005 ... 7.99
❑3, Sep 2005 ... 7.99
❑4, Nov 2005 ... 7.99

Doctor Solar, Man of the Atom
Gold Key

❑1, Oct 1962, 1&O: Doctor Solar. 1st Gold Key comic ... 150.00
❑2, Dec 1962, 1: Professor Harbinger ... 80.00
❑3, Mar 1963 ... 50.00
❑4, Jun 1963 ... 60.00
❑5, Sep 1963, 1: Doctor Solar (in costume) ... 30.00
❑6, Nov 1963 ... 25.00
❑7, Mar 1964, Painted cover ... 25.00
❑8, Jul 1964 ... 25.00
❑9, Oct 1964 ... 25.00
❑10, Jan 1965 ... 25.00
❑11, Mar 1965 ... 16.00
❑12, May 1965, makes multiple versions of self ... 16.00
❑13, Jul 1965 ... 16.00
❑14, Sep 1965, Painted cover ... 16.00
❑15, Dec 1965, O: Doctor Solar ... 20.00
❑16, Jun 1966, Painted cover ... 16.00
❑17, Sep 1966 ... 16.00
❑18, Dec 1966 ... 16.00
❑19, Apr 1967 ... 16.00
❑20, Jul 1967 ... 16.00
❑21, Oct 1967 ... 12.00
❑22, Jan 1968 ... 12.00
❑23, Apr 1968 ... 12.00
❑24, Jul 1968 ... 12.00
❑25, Oct 1968 ... 12.00
❑26, Jan 1969 ... 12.00
❑27, Apr 1969, End of original series ... 12.00
❑28, Apr 1981, Series begins again (1981) 3.50
❑29, Oct 1981 ... 3.50
❑30, Feb 1982, A: Magnus, Robot Fighter (Gold Key). ... 3.50
❑31, Mar 1982, A: Magnus, Robot Fighter (Gold Key). Final Issue ... 3.50

Dr. Speck
Bug Books

❑1, b&w ... 2.95
❑2, b&w ... 2.95
❑3, b&w ... 2.95
❑4, b&w ... 2.95

Doctor Spectrum
Marvel

❑1, Oct 2004 ... 2.99
❑2, Nov 2004 ... 2.99
❑3, Dec 2004 ... 2.99
❑4, Jan 2005 ... 2.99
❑5, Feb 2005 ... 2.99
❑6, Mar 2005 ... 2.99

Doctor Strange
Marvel

❑169, Jun 1968, DA (c); DA (a); O: Doctor Strange. Series continued from Strange Tales #168 ... 75.00
❑170, Jul 1968, DA (a); V: Nightmare ... 30.00
❑171, Aug 1968, TP, DA (a) ... 30.00
❑172, Sep 1968, GC (c); GC (a); V: Dormammu ... 27.00
❑173, Oct 1968, DA (c); GC (a); V: Dormammu ... 27.00
❑174, Nov 1968, GC (c); GC (a); 1: Satannish ... 20.00
❑175, Dec 1968, GC (c); GC (a); 1: Asmodeus; 1: Marduk; 2: Superme Satannish ... 35.00
❑176, Jan 1969, GC (c); GC (a); 2: Asmodeus; 2: Marduk ... 27.00
❑177, Feb 1969, GC (c); GC (a); 1: new costume ... 27.00
❑178, Mar 1969, GC (c); GC (a); A: Black Knight. Don McGregor L.O.C. ... 27.00
❑179, Apr 1969, SD, SL (w); SD (a); A: Spider-Man. reprints Amazing Spider-Man Ann #2 ... 27.00
❑180, May 1969, GC (a); A: Eternity. Photo cover ... 27.00
❑181, Jun 1969, GC (c); GC (a); Scott Shaw L.O.C ... 27.00
❑182, Sep 1969, GC (c); GC (a); V: Juggernaut ... 27.00
❑183, Nov 1969, GC (a); J.M. DeMatteis L.O.C ... 27.00

Doctor Strange
Marvel

❑1, Jun 1974, FB (c); FB, DG (a); Marvel Value Stamp #23: Sgt. Fury ... 25.00
❑2, Aug 1974, FB (c); FB (w); FB, DG (a); 1: Silver Dagger. A: Defenders. Marvel Value Stamp #5: Dracula ... 18.00
❑3, Sep 1974, SL (w); SD, FB, DG (a); V: Dormammu. reprints with changes Strange Tales #126 and 127; Marvel Value Stamp #14: Living Mummy ... 10.00

Other grades: Multiply price above by 5/6 for VF/NM • 2/3 for VERY FINE • 1/3 for FINE • 1/5 for VERY GOOD • 1/8 for GOOD

Detectives Inc. (Micro-Series)

Writer Don McGregor's modern noir series

©Eclipse

Detention Comics

One-shot with Superboy, Robin, Guy Gardner

©DC

Detonator

Human becomes explosive figure

©Chaos!

Detroit! Murder City Comix

Post-apocalyptic paean to rusted cars

©Kent Myers

Devil Dinosaur

Silly Jack Kirby return trip to Marvel

©Marvel

N-MINT

☐4, Oct 1974, FB (c); FB, DG (a); Marvel Value Stamp #33: Invisible Girl........... 10.00
☐5, Nov 1974, FB (c); FB, DG (a); O: Silver Dagger. Marvel Value Stamp #76: Dormammu 8.00
☐6, Dec 1974, FB (c); GC (a); Marvel Value Stamp #37: Watcher.......................... 8.00
☐7, Apr 1975, GC (a); V: Umar and Orini 7.00
☐8, Jun 1975, GC (a); O: Clea................ 4.00
☐9, Aug 1975, GC (a); O: Clea 4.00
☐10, Oct 1975, GC (a) 7.00
☐11, Dec 1975, GC (a) 6.00
☐12, Feb 1976, GC (a); V: Baron Mordo. 4.00
☐13, Apr 1976, GC (a)............................ 4.00
☐13/30¢, Apr 1976, 30¢ regional price variant 20.00
☐14, May 1976, GC (c); GC (a); V: Dracula; Cont'd from Tomb from Dracula #44; Leads to Tomb of Dracula #44............ 3.00
☐14/30¢, May 1976, 30¢ regional price variant 20.00
☐15, Jun 1976, GC (a)............................ 3.00
☐15/30¢, Jun 1976, 30¢ regional price variant 20.00
☐16, Jul 1976, GC (a)............................. 3.00
☐16/30¢, Jul 1976, 30¢ regional price variant 20.00
☐17, Aug 1976, GC (c); GC (a); Ralph Macchio L.O.C 3.00
☐17/30¢, Aug 1976, 30¢ regional price variant 20.00
☐18, Sep 1976, GC (a) 3.00
☐19, Oct 1976, GC (c); GC, AA (a); 1: Xander.. 3.00
☐20, Dec 1976... 3.00
☐21, Feb 1977, O: Doctor Strange. reprinted from Doctor Strange (1st series) #169 .... 2.50
☐22, Apr 1977 .... 2.50
☐23, Jun 1977.. 2.50
☐23/35¢, Jun 1977, 35¢ regional price variant 15.00
☐24, Aug 1977 .... 2.50
☐24/35¢, Aug 1977, 35¢ regional price variant 15.00
☐25, Oct 1977 .... 2.50
☐25/35¢, Oct 1977, 35¢ regional price variant 15.00
☐26, Dec 1977.. 2.00
☐27, Feb 1978 .... 2.00
☐28, Apr 1978 .... 2.00
☐29, Jun 1978, TS (a) 2.00
☐30, Aug 1978, TS (a)............................. 2.00
☐31, Oct 1978, TS (a)............................. 2.00
☐32, Dec 1978.. 2.00
☐33, Feb 1979, TS (a); Newsstand edition (distributed by Curtis); issue number in box 2.00
☐33/Whitman, Feb 1979, Special markets edition (usually sold in Whitman bagged prepacks); price appears in a diamond; no UPC barcode.................. 2.00
☐34, Apr 1979 .... 2.00
☐35, Jun 1979.. 2.00
☐36, Aug 1979, GC, DGr (a).................... 2.00
☐37, Oct 1979 .... 2.00
☐38, Dec 1979, BH (c); GC, DGr (a) 2.00
☐39, Feb 1980 .... 2.00
☐40, Apr 1980 .... 2.00
☐41, Jun 1980.. 2.00

N-MINT

☐42, Aug 1980 .... 2.00
☐43, Oct 1980.. 2.00
☐44, Dec 1980 .... 2.00
☐45, Feb 1981, Ink credits from #47 letterpage 2.00
☐46, Apr 1981, FM (c); MG, FM, KGa (a) 2.00
☐47, Jun 1981.. 2.00
☐48, Aug 1981, A: Brother Voodoo. 1: Morgana Blessing; O: Brother Voodoo... 2.00
☐49, Oct 1981, A: Baron Mordo............. 2.00
☐50, Dec 1981, A: Baron Mordo 2.00
☐51, Feb 1982, MR (c); MR (a).............. 2.00
☐52, Apr 1982, MR (c); MR (a).............. 2.00
☐53, Jun 1982.. 2.00
☐54, Aug 1982, PS, BA (a)...................... 2.00
☐55, Oct 1982, MG (c); MG (a) 2.00
☐56, Dec 1982, PS (c); PS (a); O: Dr. Strange... 2.00
☐57, Feb 1983, KN (a); V: Margali.......... 2.00
☐58, Apr 1983, DGr (c); DGr (a) 2.00
☐59, Jun 1983, DGr (c); DGr (a) 2.00
☐60, Aug 1983, DGr (c); DGr (a); A: Dracula. V: Dracula 2.00
☐61, Oct 1983, DGr (a); A: Dracula. O: Dracula; V: Dracula 2.00
☐62, Dec 1983, A: Dracula..................... 2.00
☐63, Feb 1984.. 2.00
☐64, Apr 1984.. 2.00
☐65, Jun 1984, PS (c); PS (a).................. 2.00
☐66, Aug 1984, PS (c); PS (a) 2.00
☐67, Oct 1984.. 2.00
☐68, Dec 1984, PS (c); PS (a)................ 2.00
☐69, Feb 1985, PS (a)........................... 2.00
☐70, Apr 1985.. 2.00
☐71, Jun 1985, PS (a); O: Umar............. 2.00
☐72, Aug 1985, PS (a); V: Umar 2.00
☐73, Oct 1985, PS (a); V: Umar.............. 2.00
☐74, Dec 1985, 1: Ecstasy. Secret Wars II 2.00
☐75, Feb 1986, SB (a); O: Wong (Doctor Strange's manservant); V: Mephisto; Crossover with FF #277...................... 2.00
☐76, Apr 1986.. 2.00
☐77, Jun 1986.. 2.00
☐78, Aug 1986, New costume................ 2.00
☐79, Oct 1986.. 2.00
☐80, Dec 1986 .... 2.00
☐81, Feb 1987, KN (c);1 : Rintrah; Final Issue 2.00
☐Ann 1, ca. 1976.................................... 6.00
☐Special 1, Mar 1983, BWr (c); FB (w); FB (a); Reprints Dr. Strange #1-2; V: Silver Dagger; #4-5 .... 3.00

Doctor Strange
Marvel

☐1, Feb 1999.. 2.99
☐2, Mar 1999.. 2.99
☐3, Apr 1999.. 2.99
☐4, May 1999.. 2.99

Doctor Strange and Doctor Doom: Triumph and Torment
Marvel

☐1, Oct 1989, softcover 9.95
☐1/HC, Oct 1989; hardcover 17.95

N-MINT

Doctor Strange Classics
Marvel

☐1, Mar 1984; AM, JBy (c); SL (w); SD, KN (a); Reprints 2.00
☐2, Apr 1984; JBy (c); SL (w); AM, SD, DGr (a); Reprints................................ 2.00
☐3, May 1984; JBy (c); SD, SL (w); SD, BSz, CR (a); Reprint; Collects stories from Stange Tales #136-138; Pin-ups by Bill Sienkiewicz, Arthur Adams, P. Craig Russell 2.00
☐4, Jun 1984; Reprint; Collects stories from Strange Tales #139-141 (141 edited to remove cliffhanger ending); Pin-ups by Golden, Adams, Leialoha; Wraparound cover............................ 2.00

Doctor Strange/Ghost Rider Special
Marvel

☐1, Apr 1991; reprints Doctor Strange #28;Continued from Ghost Rider # 12 1.50

Dr. Strange: Oath
Marvel

☐1, Dec 2006 .... 2.99
☐2, Jan 2007.. 2.99
☐3, Feb 2007.. 2.99

Doctor Strange: Shamballa
Marvel

☐1, ca. 1986; Doctor Strange................. 7.00

Doctor Strange: Sorcerer Supreme
Marvel

☐1, Nov 1988 .... 3.00
☐2, Jan 1989; Inferno 2.00
☐3, Mar 1989 .... 2.00
☐4, May 1989.. 1.50
☐5, Jul 1989; V: Baron Mordo................ 1.50
☐6, Aug 1989; O: Baron Mordo; V: Mephista; V: Satannish; V: Mephisto 1.50
☐7, Sep 1989; O: Baron Mordo; V: Satannish 1.50
☐8, Oct 1989; O: Satannish. O: Mephisto; O: Baron Mordo................................. 1.50
☐9, Nov 1989 .... 1.50
☐10, Dec 1989; A: Morbius. Mid-Nov cover date; Re-intro Morbius with new costume 1.50
☐11, Dec 1989; A: Hobgoblin. Acts of Vengeance.. 1.50
☐12, Dec 1989; Acts of Vengeance 1.50
☐13, Jan 1990; Acts of Vengeance......... 1.50
☐14, Feb 1990; vampires 1.50
☐15, Mar 1990; Amy Grant cover (unauthorized, caused Marvel to be sued); vampires 3.00
☐16, Apr 1990; BG (a); vampires 1.50
☐17, May 1990; vampires 1.50
☐18, Jun 1990; vampires........................ 1.50
☐19, Jul 1990 GC (a)............................. 1.50
☐20, Aug 1990... 1.50
☐21, Sep 1990 .... 1.50
☐22, Oct 1990; O: Umar......................... 1.50
☐23, Nov 1990... 1.50
☐24, Dec 1990 .... 1.50
☐25, Jan 1991 .... 1.50
☐26, Feb 1991; werewolf........................ 1.50
☐27, Mar 1991; werewolf........................ 1.50
☐28, Apr 1991; Ghost Rider x-over 1.50
☐29, May 1991.. 1.50

❑30, Jun 1991; V: Mephista; V: Satannish; V: Mephisto 1.50
❑31, Jul 1991; Infinity Gauntlet 1.50
❑32, Aug 1991; Infinity Gauntlet 1.50
❑33, Sep 1991; Infinity Gauntlet 1.50
❑34, Oct 1991; Infinity Gauntlet 1.50
❑35, Nov 1991; Infinity Gauntlet 1.50
❑36, Dec 1991; Infinity Gauntlet;Prelude to Warlock & the Infinity Watch #1 1.50
❑37, Jan 1992 A: Silver Surfer 1.50
❑38, Feb 1992 1.75
❑39, Mar 1992 1.75
❑40, Apr 1992; V: Nightmare; V: D'Spayre; V: Dweller In Darkness 1.75
❑41, May 1992; Wolverine 1.75
❑42, Jun 1992; Galactus 1.75
❑43, Jul 1992; Infinity War 1.75
❑44, Aug 1992; Infinity War 1.75
❑45, Sep 1992; Infinity War 1.75
❑46, Oct 1992; Infinity War 1.75
❑47, Nov 1992; Infinity War 1.75
❑48, Dec 1992; V: Umar; V: Baron Zemo 1.75
❑49, Jan 1993 1.75
❑50, Feb 1993; Prelude to Secret Defenders #1; Prism cover 2.95
❑51, Mar 1993 1.75
❑52, Apr 1993; A: Morbius. V: Nightmare; Story cont'd from Morbius #8 1.75
❑53, May 1993 1.75
❑54, Jun 1993; Infinity Crusade 1.75
❑55, Jul 1993; Infinity Crusade 1.75
❑56, Aug 1993; V: Baron Blood; Infinity Crusade Crossover 1.75
❑57, Sep 1993 1.75
❑58, Oct 1993 A: Urthona 1.75
❑59, Nov 1993; Dr. Strange cont'd in Spirits of Vengeance #16 1.75
❑60, Dec 1993; Spot varnish cover 1.75
❑61, Jan 1994; V: Salome 1.75
❑62, Feb 1994 1.75
❑63, Mar 1994 1.75
❑64, Apr 1994 1.75
❑65, May 1994; V: Salome; Includes trading cards 1.75
❑66, Jun 1994 1.95
❑67, Jul 1994; Return of Clea 1.95
❑68, Aug 1994 1.95
❑69, Sep 1994 1.95
❑70, Oct 1994 A: Hulk 1.95
❑71, Nov 1994 A: Hulk 1.95
❑72, Dec 1994 1.95
❑73, Jan 1995 1.95
❑74, Feb 1995 1.95
❑75, Mar 1995; Giant-size 2.50
❑75/Holo-grafix, Mar 1995; Giant-size; Holo-grafix cover 3.50
❑76, Apr 1995 1.95
❑77, May 1995 1.95
❑78, Jun 1995 1.95
❑79, Jul 1995 1.95
❑80, Aug 1995; indicia changes to Doctor Strange, Sorcerer Supreme for remainder of run 1.95
❑81, Sep 1995 1.95
❑82, Oct 1995 1.95
❑83, Nov 1995 1.95
❑84, Dec 1995 A: Mordo 1.95
❑85, Jan 1996 O: Mordo 1.95
❑86, Feb 1996 1.95
❑87, Mar 1996 D: Mordo 1.95
❑88, Apr 1996 1.95
❑89, May 1996 1.95
❑90, Jun 1996; Final Issue 1.95
❑Ann 1 2.50
❑Ann 2, ca. 1992 2.25
❑Ann 3, ca. 1993; trading card 2.95
❑Ann 4, ca. 1994 2.95
❑Ashcan 1, ca. 1995, b&w; no indicia 0.75

Dr. Strange Vs. Dracula
Marvel

❑1, Mar 1994, Reprints 1.75

Doctor Strange: What is it That Disturbs You Stephen?
Marvel

❑1, Oct 1997; squarebound 5.99

Doctor Strangefate
DC / Amalgam

❑1, Apr 1996 1.95

Doctor Tom Brent, Young Intern
Charlton

❑1, Feb 1963 15.00
❑2, Apr 1963 10.00
❑3, Jun 1963 10.00
❑4, Aug 1963 10.00
❑5, Oct 1963 10.00

Dr. Tomorrow
Acclaim

❑1, Sep 1997 2.50
❑2, Oct 1997; V: Teutonic Knight 2.50
❑3, Nov 1997; V: Nazi X-O 2.50
❑4, Dec 1997 2.50
❑5, Jan 1998; D: Cappy 2.50
❑6, Feb 1998; 1: Mushroom Cloud 2.50
❑7, Mar 1998; Tomorrow and Mushroom Cloud go to Vietnam 2.50
❑8, Apr 1998; V: Warmaster 2.50
❑9, May 1998; No cover date; indicia says Jan 98 2.50
❑10, Jun 1998; No cover date; indicia says Jan 98 2.50
❑11, Jul 1998; No cover date; Indicia says March 98 2.50
❑12, Aug 1998; No cover date; Indicia says April 98, Final Issue 2.50

Doctor Weird
Caliber / Big Bang

❑1, Oct 1994, b&w 2.95
❑2, May 1995, b&w 2.95
❑Special 1, Feb 1994, b&w 3.95

Dr. Weird
October

❑1, Oct 1997 2.95
❑2, Jul 1998 2.95

Doctor Who
Marvel

❑1, Oct 1984; DaG (a); BBC TV series; Reprint from Doctor Who Monthly (British) 3.00
❑2, Nov 1984; DaG, DC (a); Reprint from Doctor Who Monthly (British) 2.00
❑3, Dec 1984; DaG (a); Reprint from Doctor Who Monthly (British) 2.00
❑4, Jan 1985; Reprint from Doctor Who Monthly (British) 2.00
❑5, Feb 1985; Reprint from Doctor Who Monthly (British) 2.00
❑6, Mar 1985; Reprint from Doctor Who Monthly (British) 2.00
❑7, Apr 1985; Reprint from Doctor Who Monthly (British) 2.00
❑8, May 1985; Reprint from Doctor Who Monthly (British) 2.00
❑9, Jun 1985; Reprint from Doctor Who Monthly (British) 2.00
❑10, Jul 1985; Reprint from Doctor Who Monthly (British) 2.00
❑11, Aug 1985; Reprint from Doctor Who Monthly (British) 1.50
❑12, Sep 1985; Reprint from Doctor Who Monthly (British) 1.50
❑13, Oct 1985; Reprint from Doctor Who Monthly (British) 1.50
❑14, Nov 1985; Reprint from Doctor Who Monthly (British) 1.50
❑15, Dec 1985; Reprint from Doctor Who Monthly (British) 1.50
❑16, Jan 1986; Reprint from Doctor Who Monthly (British) 1.50
❑17, Feb 1986; Reprint from Doctor Who Monthly (British) 1.50
❑18, Mar 1986; Reprint from Doctor Who Monthly (British) 1.50
❑19, Apr 1986; Reprint from Doctor Who Monthly (British) 1.50
❑20, May 1986; Reprint from Doctor Who Monthly (British) 1.50
❑21, Jun 1986; Reprint from Doctor Who Monthly (British) 1.50
❑22, Jul 1986; Reprint from Doctor Who Monthly (British) 1.50
❑23, Aug 1986; Reprint from Doctor Who Monthly (British) 1.50

Dr. Wonder
Old Town

❑1, Jun 1996, b&w; O: Doctor Wonder 2.95
❑2, Jul 1996, b&w 2.95
❑3, Aug 1996, b&w 2.95
❑4, Oct 1996, b&w 2.95
❑5, Fal 1997, b&w; magazine-sized 2.95

Doctor Zero
Marvel / Epic

❑1, Apr 1988, BSz (c); BSz (a) 1.50
❑2, Jun 1988, BSz (c) 1.50
❑3, Aug 1988 1.50
❑4, Oct 1988 1.50
❑5, Dec 1988 1.50
❑6, Feb 1989 1.50
❑7, Apr 1989, DS (a) 1.50
❑8, Jun 1989, Final Issue 1.50

Doc Weird's Thrill Book
Pure Imagination

❑1 AW, ATh, FF (a) 2.00
❑2; WW (a); Jack Cole 2.00
❑3 WW (a) 2.00

Dodekain
Antarctic

❑1, Nov 1994, b&w 2.95
❑2, Dec 1994, b&w 2.95
❑3, Jan 1995, b&w 2.95
❑4, Feb 1995, b&w 2.95
❑5, Mar 1995, b&w 2.95
❑6, Apr 1995, b&w 2.95
❑7, May 1995, b&w 2.95
❑8, Jun 1995, b&w; Final Issue 2.95

Dodges Bullets
Image

❑1, ca. 2004 9.95

Do-Do Man
Edge

❑1 2.99

Dog Boy
Fantagraphics

❑1 2.00
❑2, Apr 1987 1.75
❑3, May 1987 1.75
❑4 1.75
❑5 1.75
❑6 1.75
❑7, Sep 1987 1.75
❑8 1.75
❑9 1.75

Dog Moon
DC / Vertigo

❑1, NN; One-shot 6.95

Dogs of War
Defiant

❑1, Apr 1994 2.50
❑2, May 1994 2.50
❑3, Jun 1994 2.50
❑4, Jul 1994 2.50
❑5, Aug 1994 2.50
❑6, Sep 1994 2.50
❑7, Oct 1994 2.50
❑8, Nov 1994, Final Issue 2.50

Dog Soup
Dog Soup

❑1, b&w 2.50

Dogs-O-War
Crusade

❑1, Jun 1996, b&w 2.95
❑2, Jul 1996, b&w 2.95
❑3, Jan 1997, b&w; Final Issue 2.95

Dog T.A.G.S.: Trained Animal Gun Squadron
Bugged Out

❑1, Jun 1993, b&w 1.95

Dogwitch
Sirius

❑1 6.00
❑2 4.00
❑3 4.00
❑4, Feb 2003 4.00
❑5, May 2003 4.00
❑6, Jul 2003 4.00
❑7, Oct 2003 2.95
❑8, Nov 2003 2.95
❑9, Jan 2004 2.95
❑10, Mar 2004 2.95
❑11, May 2004 2.95
❑12 2004 2.95
❑13 2004 2.95
❑14 2004 2.95

Other grades: Multiply price above by 5/6 for VF/NM • 2/3 for VERY FINE • 1/3 for FINE • 1/5 for VERY GOOD • 1/8 for GOOD

Dexter's Laboratory

Based on the Cartoon Network series

©DC

Diablo: Tales of Sanctuary

Based on the computer game fantasy

©Dark Horse

Dia de los Muertos (Sergio Aragonès')

Sergio's take on Mexico's "Day of the Dead"

©Dark Horse

Dick Tracy (Blackthorne)

Reprinted stories from the classic comic strip

©Blackthorne

Digitek

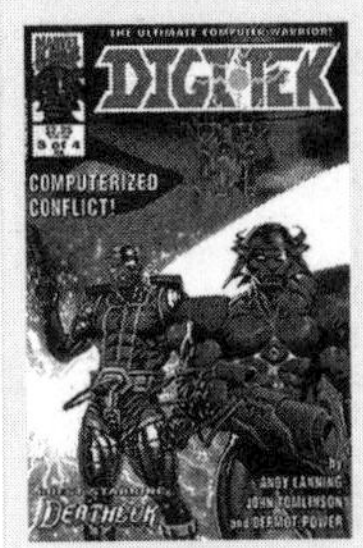

Series spinoff from Mys-TECH

©Marvel

N-MINT

❏15 2005 ... 2.95
❏16 2005 ... 2.95
❏17 2005 ... 2.95

Doin' Time with OJ
Boneyard

❏1, Dec 1994, b&w; Adult ... 3.50

Dojinshi
Antarctic

❏1, Oct 1992, b&w ... 2.95
❏2, Dec 1992, b&w ... 2.95
❏3, Feb 1993, b&w ... 2.95
❏4, Apr 1993, b&w ... 2.95

Doll
Rip Off

❏1, Feb 1989, b&w; Adult ... 3.00
❏2, Mar 1989, b&w; Adult ... 2.50
❏3, May 1989, b&w; Adult ... 2.50
❏4, Feb 1990, b&w; Adult ... 2.50
❏5, Mar 1991, b&w; Adult ... 2.50
❏6, May 1991, b&w; Adult ... 2.50
❏7, Jun 1991, b&w; Adult ... 2.50
❏8, Sep 1992, b&w; Adult ... 2.95

Doll and Creature
Image

❏1, Apr 2006 ... 12.95
❏2, Jun 2006 ... 2.99
❏3, Jul 2006 ... 2.99
❏4, Sep 2006 ... 2.99

Dollman
Eternity

❏1, Nov 1991, movie tie-in ... 2.50
❏2, Dec 1992, movie tie-in ... 2.50
❏3, Feb 1992, movie tie-in ... 2.50
❏4, Mar 1992, movie tie-in ... 2.50

Doll Parts
Sirius

❏1, Oct 2000, b&w; Adult ... 2.95

Dolls
Sirius

❏1, Jun 1996 ... 2.95

Doll
Tokyopop

❏1, Aug 2004, Graphic novel; Reads right to left; Adult; b&w ... 9.99
❏2, Oct 2004; Graphic novel; Reads right to left; Adult; b&w ... 9.99
❏3, Jan 2005; Graphic novel; Reads right to left; Adult; b&w ... 9.99
❏4, Apr 2005; Graphic novel; Reads right to left; Adult; b&w ... 9.99
❏5, Jul 2005; Graphic novel; Reads right to left; Adult; b&w ... 9.99
❏6, Oct 2005; Graphic novel; Reads right to left; Adult; b&w ... 9.99

Dollz
Image

❏1/A, Apr 2001; Two girls facing monster on cover ... 2.95
❏1/B, Apr 2001; Dynamic Forces cover: Girl posing with bunny, gun ... 2.95
❏1/C, Apr 2001; Alternate cover (figures include girl holding bunny) ... 2.95
❏1/D, Apr 2001; Girls posing with large face in background ... 2.95

N-MINT

❏1/E, Apr 2001; Nighttime fight scene on cover ... 2.95
❏2, Jun 2001 ... 2.95

Dome: Ground Zero
DC / Helix

❏1; prestige format; computer-generated 7.95

Domination Factor: Avengers
Marvel

❏1, Nov 1999; says 1.2 on cover, 1 in indicia ... 2.50
❏2, Nov 1999; says 2.4 on cover, 2 in indicia ... 2.50

Domination Factor: Fantastic Four
Marvel

❏1, Dec 1999; cover forms diptych with Domination Factor: Avengers #1 ... 2.50
❏2, Dec 1999; says 2.3 on cover, 2 in indicia ... 2.50

Dominion
Eclipse

❏1, ca. 1990, b&w; Japanese ... 3.00
❏2, ca. 1990, b&w; Japanese ... 2.50
❏3, ca. 1991, b&w; Japanese ... 2.50
❏4, ca. 1991, b&w; Japanese ... 2.00
❏5, ca. 1991, b&w; Japanese ... 2.00
❏6, ca. 1991, b&w; Japanese ... 2.00

Dominion
Image

❏1, Feb 2003 ... 2.95
❏2, May 2003 ... 2.95

Dominion: Conflict 1
Dark Horse / Manga

❏1, Mar 1996, b&w ... 2.95
❏2, Apr 1996, b&w ... 2.95
❏3, May 1996, b&w ... 2.95
❏4, Jun 1996, b&w ... 2.95
❏5, Jul 1996, b&w ... 2.95
❏6, Aug 1996, b&w; Final Issue ... 2.95

Dominion: Phantom of the Audience
Dark Horse

❏1; NN ... 2.50

Dominique: Family Matters
Caliber

❏1, b&w ... 2.95

Dominique: Killzone
Caliber

❏1, ca. 1995, b&w; One-shot ... 2.95

Dominique: Protect and Serve
Caliber

❏1, ca. 1995, b&w; One-shot ... 2.95

Dominique: White Knuckle Drive
Caliber

❏1, b&w; One-shot ... 2.95

Domino
Marvel

❏1, Jan 1997; V: Pico ... 2.00
❏2, Feb 1997; V: Deathstrike. V: Lady Deathstrike ... 2.00
❏3, Mar 1997; V: Donald Pierce; V: Lady Deathstrike ... 2.00

Domino
Marvel

❏1, Jun 2003 ... 2.50

N-MINT

❏2, Jun 2003, Cardstock cover ... 2.50
❏3, Jul 2003, Cardstock cover ... 2.50
❏4, Aug 2003, Cardstock cover ... 2.50

Domino Chance
Chance

❏1, May 1982, b&w ... 2.50
❏1/2nd, b&w; 2nd printing ... 1.50
❏2, Jul 1982, b&w ... 2.00
❏3, Sep 1982, b&w ... 2.00
❏4 1983, b&w ... 2.00
❏5, Jul 1983, b&w ... 2.00
❏6 1984, b&w ... 2.00
❏7 1984, b&w; 1: Gizmo ... 2.00
❏8 1985, b&w; 2: Gizmo ... 2.00
❏9 1985, b&w ... 2.00

Domino Chance: Roach Extraordinaire
Amazing

❏1 ... 1.95

Domino Lady
Fantagraphics / Eros

❏1, Dec 1990, b&w; Adult ... 1.95
❏2, Jan 1991, b&w; Adult ... 1.95
❏3, Mar 1991, b&w; Adult ... 1.95

Domino Lady's Jungle Adventure
Fantagraphics / Eros

❏1, b&w; Adult ... 2.75
❏2, b&w; Adult ... 2.75
❏3, Nov 1992, b&w; Adult ... 2.75

Domu: A Child's Dream
Dark Horse / Manga

❏1, Mar 1995 ... 5.95
❏2, Apr 1995 ... 5.95
❏3, May 1995 ... 5.95

Donald and Mickey
Gladstone

❏19, Sep 1993; Reprints ... 1.50
❏20, Nov 1993; 64 pages ... 2.95
❏21, Jan 1994; Reprints ... 1.50
❏22, Mar 1994; Reprints ... 1.50
❏23, May 1994; Reprints ... 1.50
❏24, Jul 1994; Reprints ... 1.50
❏25, Sep 1994; 64 pages ... 2.95
❏26, Nov 1994; newsstand distribution by Marvel ... 1.50
❏27, Jan 1995 ... 1.50
❏28, Mar 1995 ... 1.50
❏29, May 1995 ... 1.50
❏30, Jul 1995 ... 1.50

Donald and Scrooge
Disney

❏1, ca. 1992 ... 1.75
❏2, ca. 1992 ... 1.75
❏3, ca. 1992 ... 1.75

Donald Duck
Dell / Gold Key

❏80, Nov 1961 ... 30.00
❏81, Jan 1962 ... 30.00
❏82, Mar 1962 ... 30.00
❏83, May 1962 ... 30.00
❏84, Jul 1962 ... 30.00
❏85, Sep 1962, Gold Key imprints begin 25.00
❏86, Nov 1962 ... 25.00
❏87, Jan 1963 ... 25.00

	N-MINT
❑88, Mar 1963	25.00
❑89, May 1963	25.00
❑90, Jul 1963	25.00
❑91, Sep 1963	25.00
❑92, Nov 1963	25.00
❑93, Jan 1964	25.00
❑94, Mar 1964	25.00
❑95, May 1964	25.00
❑96, Jul 1964	25.00
❑97, Sep 1964	25.00
❑98, Nov 1964	25.00
❑99, Jan 1965, Reprints story from Donald Duck #46	25.00
❑100, Mar 1965	25.00
❑101, May 1965	25.00
❑102, Jul 1965	25.00
❑103, Sep 1965	25.00
❑104, Nov 1965	25.00
❑105, Jan 1966	25.00
❑106, Mar 1966	25.00
❑107, May 1966	25.00
❑108, Jul 1966	25.00
❑109, Sep 1966	25.00
❑110, Nov 1966	25.00
❑111, Jan 1967	25.00
❑112, Mar 1967	25.00
❑113, May 1967	25.00
❑114, Jul 1967	25.00
❑115, Sep 1967	25.00
❑116, Nov 1967	25.00
❑117, Jan 1968	25.00
❑118, Mar 1968	25.00
❑119, May 1968	25.00
❑120, Jul 1968	25.00
❑121, Sep 1968	20.00
❑122, Nov 1968	20.00
❑123, Jan 1969	20.00
❑124, Mar 1969	20.00
❑125, May 1969	20.00
❑126, Jul 1969	20.00
❑127, Sep 1969	20.00
❑128, Nov 1969	20.00
❑129, Jan 1970	20.00
❑130, Mar 1970	20.00
❑131, May 1970	20.00
❑132, Jul 1970	20.00
❑133, Sep 1970	20.00
❑134, Nov 1970, Reprints stories from Donald Duck #52 and Walt Disney's Comics #194	20.00
❑135, Jan 1971, Reprints stories from Uncle Scrooge #27 and Walt Disney's Comics #198	20.00
❑136, Mar 1971	15.00
❑137, May 1971	15.00
❑138, Jul 1971	15.00
❑139, Sep 1971	15.00
❑140, Nov 1971	15.00
❑141, Jan 1972	15.00
❑142, Mar 1972	15.00
❑143, May 1972	15.00
❑144, Jul 1972	15.00
❑145, Sep 1972	15.00
❑146, Nov 1972	15.00
❑147, Jan 1973	15.00
❑148, Mar 1973	15.00
❑149, May 1973	15.00
❑150, Jul 1973	15.00
❑151, Sep 1973	10.00
❑152, Oct 1973	10.00
❑153, Nov 1973	10.00
❑154, Jan 1974, Reprints story from Donald Duck #46	10.00
❑155, Mar 1974	10.00
❑156, May 1974	10.00
❑157, Jul 1974, Reprints story from Donald Duck #45	10.00
❑158, Sep 1974	10.00
❑159, Oct 1974, Reprints story from Walt Disney's Comics #192	10.00
❑160, Nov 1974, Reprints story from Donald Duck #26	10.00
❑161, Jan 1975	10.00
❑162, Mar 1975	10.00
❑163, May 1975	10.00
❑164, Jul 1975	10.00
❑165, Sep 1975	10.00
❑166, Oct 1975	10.00
❑167, Nov 1975	10.00

	N-MINT
❑168, Jan 1976	10.00
❑169, Mar 1976	10.00
❑170, Apr 1976	10.00
❑171, May 1976	10.00
❑172, Jun 1976	10.00
❑173, Jul 1976	10.00
❑174, Aug 1976	10.00
❑175, Sep 1976	10.00
❑176, Oct 1976	10.00
❑177, Nov 1976	10.00
❑178, Dec 1976	10.00
❑179, Jan 1977	10.00
❑180, Feb 1977	10.00
❑181, Mar 1977	10.00
❑182, Apr 1977	10.00
❑183, May 1977, Reprints story from Donald Duck #138	10.00
❑184, Jun 1977	10.00
❑185, Jul 1977	10.00
❑186, Aug 1977	10.00
❑187, Sep 1977	10.00
❑188, Oct 1977, Reprints story from Donald Duck #68	10.00
❑189, Nov 1977	10.00
❑190, Dec 1977	10.00
❑191, Jan 1978	5.00
❑192, Feb 1978, Reprints stories from Donald Duck #60 and Walt Disney's Comics #226 and 234	5.00
❑193, Mar 1978	5.00
❑194, Apr 1978	5.00
❑195, May 1978	5.00
❑196, Jun 1978	5.00
❑197, Jul 1978	5.00
❑198, Aug 1978	5.00
❑199, Sep 1978	5.00
❑200, Oct 1978	5.00
❑201, Nov 1978, Reprints story from Christmas Parade (Dell) #26	5.00
❑202, Dec 1978	5.00
❑203, Jan 1979	5.00
❑204, Feb 1979	5.00
❑205, Mar 1979	5.00
❑206, Apr 1979	5.00
❑207, May 1979	5.00
❑208, Jun 1979	5.00
❑209, Jul 1979	5.00
❑210, Aug 1979	5.00
❑211, Sep 1979	3.00
❑212, Oct 1979	3.00
❑213, Nov 1979	3.00
❑214, Dec 1979	3.00
❑215, Jan 1980	3.00
❑216, Feb 1980	3.00
❑217, Mar 1980, Whitman begins as publisher	5.00
❑218, Apr 1980	10.00
❑219, May 1980	10.00
❑220, Jun 1980	15.00
❑221, Aug 1980	15.00
❑222, Oct 1980	15.00
❑223, Nov 1980	15.00
❑224, Dec 1980	15.00
❑225, Feb 1981	15.00
❑226, Mar 1981	15.00
❑227, Apr 1981	15.00
❑228, May 1981	15.00
❑229, Jun 1981	8.00
❑230, Jul 1981, "The Lost Peg Leg Mine" reprinted from Donald Duck #52; "Scientific Lifesaving" reprinted from Donald Duck #134; "Smoke Writer in the Sky" reprinted fromWDC&S #194; "Vacation at Grandma's" reprinted from Walt Disney's Vacation Parade #6	8.00
❑231, Aug 1981	8.00
❑232, Sep 1981	8.00
❑233, Oct 1981	8.00
❑234, Nov 1981	8.00
❑235, Dec 1981	8.00
❑236, Jan 1982	8.00
❑237, Feb 1982	8.00
❑238, Mar 1982	8.00
❑239, Apr 1982	8.00
❑240, May 1982	8.00
❑241, Mar 1983	15.00
❑242, May 1983	15.00
❑243, Mar 1984	15.00
❑244, Apr 1984	15.00

	N-MINT
❑245, Jul 1984, Last issue of original run	15.00
❑246, Oct 1986, CB (w); CB (a); Series begins again (1986); Gladstone publishes	17.00
❑247, Nov 1986, CB (w); CB (a)	5.00
❑248, Dec 1986, CB (w); CB (a)	5.00
❑249, Jan 1987, CB (a)	5.00
❑250, Feb 1987, CB (w); CB (a); reprints 1st Barks comic	8.00
❑251, Mar 1987, CB (a)	4.00
❑252, Apr 1987, CB (a)	4.00
❑253, May 1987, CB (w); CB (a)	4.00
❑254, Jun 1987	4.00
❑255, Jul 1987	4.00
❑256, Aug 1987	4.00
❑257, Sep 1987, CB (w); CB (a); forest fire	4.00
❑258, Oct 1987, CB (w); CB (a)	4.00
❑259, Nov 1987, CB (w); CB (a)	4.00
❑260, Dec 1987, CB (w); CB (a)	4.00
❑261, Jan 1988, CB (w); CB (a)	3.00
❑262, Mar 1988, CB (w); CB (a)	3.00
❑263, Jun 1988, CB (w); CB (a)	3.00
❑264, Jul 1988, CB (w); CB (a)	3.00
❑265, Aug 1988	3.00
❑266, Sep 1988	3.00
❑267, Oct 1988, South Pole Summer Special!	3.00
❑268, Nov 1988	3.00
❑269, Jan 1989	3.00
❑270, Mar 1989	3.00
❑271, Apr 1989, says Jun on cover, Apr in indicia	2.50
❑272, Jul 1989	2.50
❑273, Aug 1989, CB (w); CB (a)	2.50
❑274, Sep 1989	2.50
❑275, Oct 1989, CB (c); CB, WK (w); CB, WK (a); Donocchio story reprinted from Four Color #92	2.50
❑276, Nov 1989, CB (w); CB (a)	2.50
❑277, Jan 1990, CB (w); CB (a)	2.50
❑278, Mar 1990, CB (c); CB, DR (w); CB, DR (a); Special Double-Sized Issue	2.50
❑279, May 1990, DR (c); CB (w); CB (a); Series ends again (1990)	2.50
❑280, Sep 1993, Series begins again (1993)	1.50
❑281, Nov 1993	1.50
❑282, Jan 1994, CB (w); CB (a); Reprints	1.50
❑283, Mar 1994, DR (w); DR (a)	1.50
❑284, May 1994, CB (w); CB (a); Reprints	1.50
❑285, Jul 1994, CB (w); CB (a); Reprints	1.50
❑286, Sep 1994, Giant-size; Donald Duck's 60th	3.00
❑287, Nov 1994	1.50
❑288, Jan 1995, CB (w); CB (a)	1.50
❑289, Mar 1995	1.50
❑290, May 1995	1.50
❑291, Jul 1995	1.50
❑292, Sep 1995	1.50
❑293, Nov 1995	1.50
❑294, Jan 1996, CB (c); CB (w); CB (a); Reprints	1.50
❑295, Mar 1996, newsprint covers begin	1.50
❑296, May 1996	1.50
❑297, Jul 1996	1.50
❑298, Sep 1996, Newsprint paper cover; "Knight In Shining Armor" reprinted from Walt Disney Comics and Stories #198; Daily Newspaper Strips reprinted	1.50
❑299, Nov 1996, CB (w); CB (a); Newsprint paper cover; "Life Guard Dazer" reprinted from Walt Disney Comics and Stories #33; "The Dog Watcher" reprinted from Donald Duck #94; "The Stander-Uppers" reprinted from Chip 'N' Dale #6	1.50
❑300, Jan 1997, Big 48-Page Celebration Issue!	1.50
❑301, Mar 1997, newsprint covers end	1.50
❑302, May 1997, CB (c); CB (w); CB (a); Reprints	1.95
❑303, Jul 1997	1.95
❑304, Sep 1997, CB (w); CB (a); Reprints	1.95
❑305, Nov 1997, CB (c); CB (w); CB (a); Reprints	1.95
❑306, Jan 1998	1.95
❑307, Mar 1998, Series continues as Donald Duck and Friends #308; Final Issue	1.95

Donald Duck and Friends
Gemstone

❑308, Sep 2003	2.95

Other grades: Multiply price above by 5/6 for VF/NM • 2/3 for VERY FINE • 1/3 for FINE • 1/5 for VERY GOOD • 1/8 for GOOD

Dim-Witted Darryl

Short stories from Michael Bresnahan
©Slave Labor

Dinosaurs For Hire (Eternity)

Series just missed Turtles popularity wave
©Eternity

Dirty Dozen

Adaptation of beloved 1967 war film
©Dell

Disney Afternoon

Characters from TV syndicated package
©Marvel

Distant Soil (1st Series)

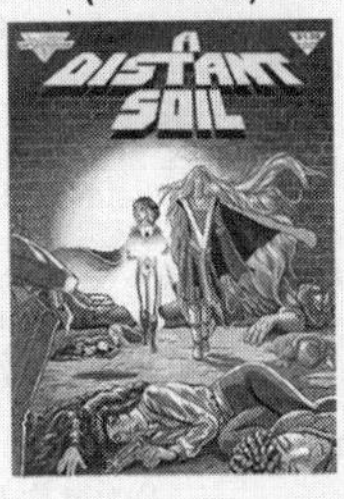

Colleen Doran's long-running fantasy series
©Warp

	N-MINT
❑309, Oct 2003	2.95
❑310, Nov 2003	2.95
❑311, Dec 2003	2.95
❑312, Jan 2004	2.95
❑313, Feb 2004	2.95
❑314, Mar 2004	2.95
❑315, Apr 2004	2.95
❑316, May 2004	2.95
❑317, Jun 2004	2.95
❑318, Jul 2004	2.95
❑319, Aug 2004	2.95
❑320, Sep 2004	2.95
❑321, Oct 2004	2.95
❑322, Nov 2004	2.95
❑323, Dec 2004	2.95
❑324, Jan 2005	2.95
❑325, Feb 2005	2.95
❑326, Mar 2005	2.95
❑327, Apr 2005	2.95
❑328, May 2005	2.95
❑329, Jun 2005	2.95
❑330, Jul 2005	2.95
❑331, Aug 2005	2.95
❑332, Sep 2005	2.95
❑333, Oct 2005	2.95
❑334, Nov 2005	2.95
❑335, Dec 2005	2.95

Donald Duck Adventures
Gemstone

❑1, Jul 2003	7.95
❑2, Oct 2003	7.95
❑3, Dec 2003	7.95
❑4, Feb 2004	7.95
❑5, Mar 2004	7.95
❑6, Jun 2004	7.95
❑7, Jul 2004	7.95
❑8, Oct 2004	7.95
❑9, Dec 2004	7.95
❑10, Feb 2005	7.95
❑11, Mar 2005	7.95
❑12, Jun 2005	7.95
❑13, Jul 2005	7.95
❑14, Oct 2005	7.95

Donald Duck Adventures (Disney)
Disney

❑1, Jun 1990, DR (c); DR (w); DR (a)	2.50
❑2, Jul 1990, CB (w); CB (a)	2.00
❑3, Aug 1990	2.00
❑4, Sep 1990, CB (w); CB (a)	2.00
❑5, Oct 1990	2.00
❑6, Nov 1990	2.00
❑7, Dec 1990	2.00
❑8, Jan 1991	2.00
❑9, Feb 1991, CB (w); CB (a); reprint of 1: Uncle Scrooge	2.00
❑10, Mar 1991	2.00
❑11, Apr 1991, Mad #1 cover parody	2.00
❑12, May 1991	2.00
❑13, Jun 1991	2.00
❑14, Jul 1991, CB (w); CB (a)	2.00
❑15, Aug 1991	2.00
❑16, Sep 1991	2.00
❑17, Oct 1991	2.00
❑18, Nov 1991, CB (w); CB (a)	2.00
❑19, Dec 1991	2.00
❑20, Jan 1992	2.00
❑21, Feb 1992, CB (c); CB (w); CB (a); golden Christmas tree	1.50
❑22, Mar 1992, DR (w); DR (a)	1.50
❑23, Apr 1992, CB (w); CB (a)	1.50
❑24, May 1992, DR (w); DR (a)	1.50
❑25, Jun 1992, map piece	1.50
❑26, Jul 1992, CB (w); CB (a); map piece	1.50
❑27, Aug 1992, CB (w); CB (a); map piece	1.50
❑28, Sep 1992, Olympics	1.50
❑29, Oct 1992	1.50
❑30, Nov 1992	1.50
❑31, Dec 1992	1.50
❑32, Jan 1993	1.50
❑33, Feb 1993	1.50
❑34, Mar 1993, DR (c); DR (w); DR (a); Return of Super-Duck	1.50
❑35, Apr 1993, CB (w); CB (a); Reprints	1.50
❑36, May 1993, CB (w); CB (a); Reprints	1.50
❑37, Jun 1993, DR (c); CB, DR (w); CB, DR (a); Reprints	1.50
❑38, Jul 1993, Gladstone resumes publishing its series	1.50

Donald Duck Adventures
Gladstone

❑1, Nov 1987 CB (w); CB (a)	2.50
❑2, Jan 1988 CB (c); CB (w); CB (a)	2.00
❑3, Mar 1988 CB (c); CB (w); CB (a)	2.00
❑4, May 1988 CB (w); CB (a)	2.00
❑5, Jul 1988 CB (w); CB, DR (a)	2.00
❑6, Aug 1988 CB (w); CB (a)	1.50
❑7, Sep 1988 CB (w); CB (a)	1.50
❑8, Oct 1988 CB (c); CB, DR (w); CB, DR (a)	1.50
❑9, Nov 1988 CB (w); CB (a)	1.50
❑10, Dec 1988 CB (c); CB (w); CB (a)	1.50
❑11, Feb 1989 CB (w); CB (a)	1.50
❑12, May 1989; DR (c); CB, DR (w); CB, DR (a); Giant-Sized Issue, Free Poster Inside	1.50
❑13, Jul 1989 DR (c); CB (w); CB (a)	1.50
❑14, Aug 1989 CB (c); CB (w); CB (a)	1.50
❑15, Sep 1989 CB (w); CB (a)	1.50
❑16, Oct 1989 DR (c); CB (w); CB (a)	1.50
❑17, Nov 1989 CB (w); CB (a)	1.50
❑18, Dec 1989 DR (c); CB (w); CB (a)	1.50
❑19, Feb 1990; CB (w); CB (a); Special Double-Sized Issue	1.95
❑20, Apr 1990; CB (c); CB (w); CB (a); series goes on hiatus during Disney run	1.95
❑21, Aug 1993; DR (c); CB (w); CB (a); Reprints	1.50
❑22, Oct 1993; CB (c); CB (w); CB (a); Reprints	1.50
❑23, Dec 1993 DR (c)	1.50
❑24, Feb 1994	1.50
❑25, Apr 1994	1.50
❑26, Jun 1994; CB (c); CB (w); CB (a); 64 pages	2.95
❑27, Aug 1994	1.50
❑28, Oct 1994; CB (c); CB (w); CB (a); cover uses portion of Barks painting	1.50
❑29, Dec 1994; newsstand distribution by Marvel	1.50
❑30, Feb 1995; CB (w); CB (a); Reprints	2.95
❑31, Apr 1995	1.50
❑32, Jun 1995	1.50
❑33, Aug 1995; CB (w); CB (a); Reprints	1.95
❑34, Oct 1995; newsprint covers begin	1.50
❑35, Dec 1995	1.50
❑36, Feb 1996	1.50
❑37, Apr 1996	1.50
❑38, Jun 1996	1.50
❑39, Aug 1996	1.50
❑40, Oct 1996	1.50
❑41, Dec 1996	1.50
❑42, Feb 1997	1.50
❑43, Apr 1997; newsprint covers end	1.50
❑44, Jun 1997	1.95
❑45, Aug 1997	1.95
❑46, Oct 1997	1.95
❑47, Dec 1997; CB (w); CB (a); Reprints	1.95
❑48, Feb 1998; Final Issue	1.95

Donald Duck Album
Gold Key

❑1, Aug 1963	50.00
❑2, Oct 1963	40.00

Donald Duck & Mickey Mouse
Gladstone

❑1, Sep 1995; Newsprint cover	1.50
❑2, Nov 1995; Newsprint cover	1.50
❑3, Jan 1996; Newsprint cover	1.50
❑4, Mar 1996; Newsprint cover	1.50
❑5, May 1996; Newsprint cover	1.50
❑6, Jul 1996; Newsprint cover	1.50
❑7, Sep 1996; Newsprint cover	1.50

Donald Duck Beach Party
Gold Key

❑1, Sep 1965; reprints Walt Disney's Comics & Stories #45	40.00

Donatello Teenage Mutant Ninja Turtle
Mirage

❑1, Aug 1986, b&w	2.00

Donielle: Enslaved at Sea
Raging Rhino

❑1, b&w; Adult	2.95
❑2, b&w; Adult	2.95
❑3, b&w; Adult	2.95
❑4, b&w; Adult	2.95
❑5 1993, Adult	2.95
❑6, Adult	2.95
❑7, Adult	2.95
❑8, Adult	2.95
❑9, Adult	2.95

Donna Matrix
Reactor

❑1, Aug 1993; O: Donna Matrix. 1: Donna Matrix. computer-generated	3.50

Donna Mia
Avatar

❑1, Dec 1996; Adult	3.00
❑2, Jan 1997; Adult	3.00
❑3, Feb 1997; Adult	3.00

Donna's Day
Slab-O-Concrete

❑1; Postcard comic book	1.00

Doofer
Fantagraphics

❑1, b&w	2.75

N-MINT | N-MINT | N-MINT

Doofus
Fantagraphics

❑1, Dec 1994, b&w 2.75
❑2, Spr 1997, b&w 2.75

Doom
Marvel

❑1, Oct 2000 ..... 2.99
❑2, Nov 2000 ..... 2.99
❑3, Dec 2000 ..... 2.99

Doom Force Special
DC

❑1, Jul 1992; X-Force parody 2.95

Doom Patrol
DC

❑86, Mar 1964, 1: Monsieur Mallah. 1: The Brain. 1: Madame Rouge. Series continued from My Greatest Adventure #85 ..... 135.00
❑87, May 1964, O: Negative Man (new details); "Secret" reprinted in Super-Team Family #8 ..... 70.00
❑88, Jun 1964, O: The Chief; O: General Immortus 50.00
❑89, Aug 1964, 1: Animal-Mineral-Vegetable Man 50.00
❑90, Sep 1964, V: Brotherhood of Evil ... 50.00
❑91, Nov 1964, 1: Mento; 1: Garguax 40.00
❑92, Dec 1964, 1: Dr. Tyme 40.00
❑93, Feb 1965, V: Brotherhood of Evil; V: Rog 40.00
❑94, Mar 1965 ..... 40.00
❑95, May 1965, V: Animal-Mineral-Vegetable Man 40.00
❑96, Jun 1965, V: Brotherhood of Evil ... 40.00
❑97, Aug 1965, 1: Garguax; V: Garguax; V: General Immortus 40.00
❑98, Sep 1965, 1: Mr. 103 ..... 40.00
❑99, Nov 1965, 1: Changeling a.k.a. Beast Boy 60.00
❑100, Dec 1965, O: Changeling; O: Beast Boy; Begins O: Robotman backup serial 75.00
❑101, Feb 1966, V: The Brain; V: Kranus; V: Mr. Z 25.00
❑102, Mar 1966, A: Challengers of the Unknown. V: League of Challenger-Haters 25.00
❑103, May 1966, V: Meteor Man 25.00
❑104, Jun 1966, V: Garguax, V: Brotherhood of Evil, Wedding of Elasti-Girl and Mento, Cameo appearance of Superman, Batman, Wonder Woman, Flash, Robin, Kid Flash, Wonder Girl, Super-Hip 25.00
❑105, Aug 1966, Concludes O: Robotman serial 25.00
❑106, Sep 1966, O: Negative Man; V: Mr. 103; Begins O: Negative Man serial 25.00
❑107, Nov 1966, 1: Dr. Death (Dr. Drew); V: Ultimax 25.00
❑108, Dec 1966, V: Brotherhood of Evil . 25.00
❑109, Feb 1967, V: Dr. Death; V: Mandred; V: Brotherhood of Evil 25.00
❑110, Mar 1967, V: Brotherhood of Evil . 25.00
❑111, May 1967, V: Zarox-13; V: Brotherhood of Evil; V: Dr. Death; Concludes O: Negative Man serial 25.00
❑112, Jun 1967, V: Zarox-13; V: Brotherhood of Evil; Beast-Boy origin serial begins 25.00
❑113, Aug 1967, 1: The Arsenal 25.00
❑114, Sep 1967, 1: Kor 25.00
❑115, Nov 1967, V: Brotherhood of Evil; Beast Boy origin serial concludes 25.00
❑116, Dec 1967 ..... 25.00
❑117, Feb 1968, reprints story from Tales of the Unexpected #3 ..... 25.00
❑118, Mar 1968, V: Videx; V: The Brain; V: Monsieur Mallah 25.00
❑119, May 1968, V: Great Guru 25.00
❑120, Jun 1968, V: Wrecker 25.00
❑121, Aug 1968, JO (c); JO (a); D: The Doom Patrol. 1: Captain Zahl 45.00
❑122, Feb 1973, Reprints begin (1973); From DP #76 and 89 ..... 2.00
❑123, Apr 1973, From DP #95; Premiani biography 2.00
❑124, Jul 1973, From DP #90 ..... 2.00

Doom Patrol
DC

❑1, Oct 1987; JBy, JSa (a); The Doom Patrol returns from their supposed deaths 2.50
❑2, Nov 1987; V: Kali 1.50
❑3, Dec 1987; 1: Rhea Jones. 1: Lodestone 1.50
❑4, Jan 1988; O: Lodestone. 1: Karma; O: Negative Man 1.50
❑5, Feb 1988; V: Hellbender; V: Goldstar 1.50
❑6, Mar 1988; EL (c); EL (a); Doom Patrol cont'd in Doom Patrol/Suicide Squad Special; 1st appearance Scott Fischer 1.50
❑7, Apr 1988; 1: Shrapnel 1.50
❑8, May 1988; EL (c); EL (a); V: Shrapnel 1.50
❑9, Jun 1988; Bonus Book 1.50
❑10, Jul 1988; A: Superman. V: Metallo; Story cont'd in Superman #20 ..... 1.50
❑11, Aug 1988; O: Tempest; V: Garguax; V: Reactron 1.50
❑12, Sep 1988; V: Garguax 1.50
❑13, Oct 1988; V: Pythia 1.50
❑14, Nov 1988; 1: Dorothy Spinner. A: Power Girl. 1: Dorothy Spinner 1.50
❑15, Dec 1988; V: Animal-Vegetable-Mineral Man; V: General Immortus; The Chief returns 1.50
❑16, Dec 1988; The Return of General Immortus 1.50
❑17, Jan 1989; D: Celsius. Invasion! 1.50
❑18, Jan 1989; Invasion! 1.50
❑19, Feb 1989; 1: Crazy Jane. 1st Grant Morrison;New, very strange direction for The Doom Patrol 3.00
❑20, Mar 1989; 1: The Scissormen 2.00
❑21, Apr 1989; V: Scissormen 2.00
❑22, May 1989; V: Scissormen 2.00
❑23, Jun 1989; V: Red Jack 2.00
❑24, Jul 1989; V: Red Jack 2.00
❑25, Aug 1989 ..... 2.00
❑26, Sep 1989; 1: The Brotherhood of Dada 2.00
❑27, Nov 1989; V: Brotherhood of Dada 2.00
❑28, Dec 1989; V: Brotherhood of Dada 2.00
❑29, Jan 1990; JL (a); Superman cover. 2.00
❑30, Feb 1990 ..... 2.00
❑31, Apr 1990 ..... 2.00
❑32, May 1990 ..... 2.00
❑33, Jun 1990 ..... 2.00
❑34, Jul 1990; V: Brain and Mallah; V: Brain; V: Monsieur Mallah 2.00
❑35, Aug 1990; 1: Danny the Street. 1: Flex Mentallo; 1: Men From N.O.W.H.E.R.E 2.00
❑36, Sep 1990; V: Men from N.O.W.H.E.R.E 2.00
❑37, Oct 1990 ..... 2.00
❑38, Nov 1990 ..... 2.00
❑39, Dec 1990 ..... 2.00
❑40, Jan 1991 ..... 2.00
❑41, Feb 1991 ..... 2.00
❑42, Mar 1991; O: Flex Mentallo. 1: The Fact 2.00
❑43, Apr 1991 ..... 2.00
❑44, May 1991; 1: The Candlemaker 2.00
❑45, Jul 1991 ..... 2.00
❑46, Aug 1991 ..... 2.00
❑47, Sep 1991 ..... 2.00
❑48, Oct 1991 ..... 2.00
❑49, Nov 1991 ..... 2.00
❑50, Dec 1991; Giant-size; BB (a) 2.50
❑51, Jan 1992; 1: Yankee Doodle Dandy 2.00
❑52, Feb 1992 ..... 1.75
❑53, Mar 1992; Fantastic Four parody ... 1.75
❑54, Apr 1992; Photo cover 1.75
❑55, May 1992 ..... 1.75
❑56, Jun 1992 ..... 1.75
❑57, Jul 1992; Giant-size 2.50
❑58, Aug 1992 ..... 1.75
❑59, Sep 1992 ..... 1.75
❑60, Oct 1992 ..... 1.75
❑61, Nov 1992 ..... 1.75
❑62, Dec 1992 ..... 1.75
❑63, Jan 1993 ..... 1.75
❑64, Mar 1993; BB (c); Begins Vertigo line 1.75
❑65, Apr 1993 ..... 1.75
❑66, May 1993 ..... 1.95
❑67, Jun 1993; Photo cover; 1: Inner Child; 1: Bandage People 1.95
❑68, Jul 1993 ..... 1.95
❑69, Aug 1993 ..... 1.95
❑70, Sep 1993; Partial photo cover 1.95
❑71, Oct 1993 ..... 1.95
❑72, Nov 1993 ..... 1.95
❑73, Dec 1993 ..... 1.95
❑74, Jan 1994 ..... 1.95
❑75, Feb 1994 BB (c) 1.95
❑76, Mar 1994 ..... 1.95
❑77, Apr 1994 ..... 1.95
❑78, May 1994 ..... 1.95
❑79, Jun 1994 ..... 1.95
❑80, Jul 1994 ..... 1.95
❑81, Aug 1994 ..... 1.95
❑82, Sep 1994 ..... 1.95
❑83, Oct 1994 ..... 1.95
❑84, Nov 1994 ..... 1.95
❑85, Dec 1994 ..... 1.95
❑86, Jan 1995 ..... 1.95
❑87, Feb 1995; Final Issue 1.95
❑Ann 1, ca. 1988 ..... 1.00
❑Ann 2, ca. 1994; Children's Crusade 3.95

Doom Patrol
DC

❑1, Dec 2001; 1: Robotman IV; 1: Fever; 1: Freak; 1: Fast Forward; 1: Kid Slick 3.00
❑2, Jan 2002 ..... 2.50
❑3, Feb 2002 ..... 2.50
❑4, Mar 2002; 1: New Doom Patrol (Elongated Man; Beast Boy; Metamorpho; Dr. Light IV) 2.50
❑5, Apr 2002; V: supernatural creature; Robotman IV fades from existence 2.50
❑6, May 2002 ..... 2.50
❑7, Jun 2002; Return Robotman II 2.50
❑8, Jul 2002 ..... 2.50
❑9, Aug 2002; Robotman IV revealed as mental construct of Dorothy Spinner . 2.50
❑10, Sep 2002 ..... 2.50
❑11, Oct 2002; V: Raum 2.50
❑12, Nov 2002; V: Raum 2.50
❑13, Dec 2002; O: Elasti-Girl; O: Negative Man 2.50
❑14, Jan 2003; Includes preview of Aquaman (6th Series) #1 ..... 2.50
❑15, Feb 2003 ..... 2.50
❑16, Mar 2003 ..... 2.50
❑17, Apr 2003 ..... 2.50
❑18, May 2003 ..... 2.50
❑19, Jun 2003 ..... 2.50
❑20, Jul 2003 ..... 2.50
❑21, Aug 2003 ..... 2.50
❑22, Sep 2003, Final issue 2.50

Doom Patrol
DC

❑1, Aug 2004 ..... 2.95
❑2, Sep 2004; O: Negative Man 2.50
❑3, Oct 2004 ..... 2.50
❑4, Nov 2004 ..... 2.50
❑5, Dec 2004 ..... 2.50
❑6, Jan 2005 ..... 2.50
❑7, Feb 2005 ..... 2.50
❑8, Mar 2005 ..... 2.50
❑9, Apr 2005 ..... 2.50
❑10, May 2005; O: Grunt; O: Nudge 2.50
❑11, Jun 2005; O: Grunt; Heroscape Insert #3 ..... 2.50
❑12, Jul 2005; O: Chief 2.50
❑13, Aug 2005 ..... 2.50
❑14, Sep 2005 ..... 2.50
❑15, Oct 2005 ..... 2.50
❑16, Nov 2005 ..... 2.50
❑17, Dec 2005 ..... 2.50
❑18, Jan 2006; Final issue 2.50

Doom Patrol and Suicide Squad Special
DC

❑1, Feb 1988; EL (a); Wrap-around cover; D: Thinker; D: Weasel; D: Psi; D: Mr. 104 2.00

Doomsday + 1
Charlton

❑1, Jul 1975, JBy (c); JBy (a) 8.00
❑2, Sep 1975, JBy (a) 5.00
❑3, Nov 1975, JBy (c); JBy (a) 4.00
❑4, Jan 1976, JBy (c); JBy (a) 4.00
❑5, Mar 1976, JBy (c); JBy (a) 4.00
❑6, May 1976, JBy (c); JBy (a) 4.00
❑7, Jun 1978, JBy (c); JBy (a); Reprints Doomsday + 1 #1 ..... 3.00
❑8, Sep 1978, JBy (c); JBy (a); Reprints Doomsday + 1 #2 ..... 3.00
❑9, Nov 1978, JBy (c); JBy (a); Reprints Doomsday + 1 #3 ..... 3.00
❑10, Jan 1979, JBy (c); JBy (a); Reprints Doomsday + 1 #4 ..... 3.00

Other grades: Multiply price above by 5/6 for VF/NM • 2/3 for VERY FINE • 1/3 for FINE • 1/5 for VERY GOOD • 1/8 for GOOD

Divine Right	DNAgents	Doc Samson	Doc Savage	Doctor Fate
				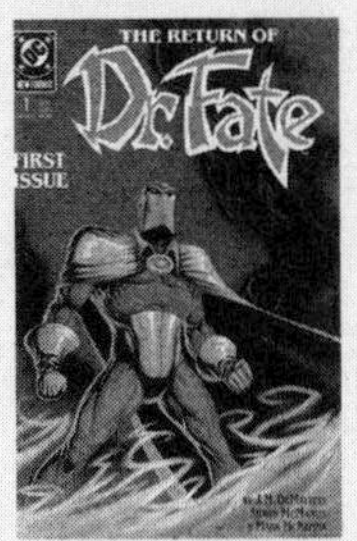
Physics undergrad becomes powerful ©Image	More mutants, this time from Eclipse ©Eclipse	Adventures of the super-hero psychiatrist ©Marvel	Adapts "The Man of Bronze" and other tales ©Marvel	DC mystic uses Egyptian powers ©DC

N-MINT

❑11, Mar 1979, JBy (c); JBy (a); Reprints Doomsday + 1 #5 — 3.00
❑12, May 1979, JBy (a); Reprints Doomsday + 1 #6 — 3.00

Doomsday + 1 (Avalon)
Avalon

❑1 — 2.95
❑2 — 2.95

Doomsday Annual
DC

❑1, ca. 1995 — 3.95

Doomsday Squad
Fantagraphics

❑1, Aug 1986; JBy (a); Dalgoda Backup Story — 2.00
❑2 JBy (a) — 2.00
❑3, Oct 1986 JBy (a); A: Usagi Yojimbo — 3.00
❑4, Nov 1986 JBy (a) — 2.00
❑5; GK (c); JBy (a); Gill Kane Cover — 2.00
❑6 JBy (a) — 2.00
❑7 JBy (a) — 2.00

Doom's IV
Image

❑½, Dec 1994; Preview promotional ed. — 2.50
❑1, Jul 1994 RL (w) — 2.50
❑1/A, Jul 1994; RL (w); Alternate cover with left half of yellow two-part picture — 2.50
❑1/B, Jul 1994; RL (w); Alternate cover with right half of yellow two-part picture — 2.50
❑2, Aug 1994 — 2.50
❑2/A, Aug 1994 — 2.50
❑3, Sep 1994 — 2.50
❑4, Oct 1994 — 2.50

Doom: The Emperor Returns
Marvel

❑1, Jan 2002 — 2.50
❑2, Feb 2002 — 2.50
❑3, Mar 2002 — 2.50

Doom 2099
Marvel

❑1, Jan 1993; PB (c); PB (a); 1: Doom 2099. Metallic ink cover — 2.50
❑2, Feb 1993 PB (c); PB (a) — 1.75
❑3, Mar 1993 PB (c); PB (a) — 1.75
❑4, Apr 1993 PB (c); PB (a) — 1.75
❑5, May 1993; 1: Fever. 1: Fever — 1.75
❑6, Jun 1993 PB (c); PB (a) — 1.50
❑7, Jul 1993 PB (c); PB (a) — 1.50
❑8, Aug 1993 PB (c); PB (a) — 1.50
❑9, Sep 1993 — 1.50
❑10, Oct 1993; PB (c); PB (a); A: Xandra. Covers of #10-12 combine to form triptych — 1.50
❑11, Nov 1993; PB (c); PB (a); Covers of Doom 2099 10-12 combine to form triptych — 1.25
❑12, Dec 1993; PB (c); PB (a); Covers of Doom 2099 10-12 combine to form triptych — 1.25
❑13, Jan 1994 PB (c) — 1.25
❑14, Feb 1994 PB (a) — 1.25
❑15, Mar 1994 PB (c); PB (a) — 1.25
❑16, Apr 1994 — 1.25
❑17, May 1994 PB (c); PD (w); PB (a) — 1.25
❑18, May 1994; PB (c); PB (a); D: Radian. poster — 1.50
❑19, Jul 1994 PB (c); PB (a) — 1.50
❑20, Aug 1994; PB (c); PB (a); V: Christian L'Argent (Alchemax operative); In Savage Land — 1.50
❑21, Sep 1994 PB (c); PB (a) — 1.50
❑22, Oct 1994 PB (c); PB (a) — 1.50
❑23, Nov 1994; PB (c); PB (a); V: Tiger Wylde — 1.50
❑24, Dec 1994 PB (c); PB (a) — 1.50
❑25, Jan 1995; Giant-size; PB (c); PB (a); regular cover — 2.25
❑25/Variant, Jan 1995; Giant-size; PB (c); PB (a); Embossed foil cover — 2.95
❑26, Feb 1995 PB (c); PB (a) — 1.50
❑27, Mar 1995 PB (c); PB (a) — 1.50
❑28, Apr 1995; One Nation under Doom crossover — 1.95
❑29, May 1995; One Nation under Doom crossover — 1.95
❑29/Variant, May 1995; enhanced acetate overlay cover — 3.50
❑30, Jun 1995; One Nation under Doom crossover — 1.95
❑31, Jul 1995; One Nation under Doom crossover — 1.95
❑32, Aug 1995; One Nation under Doom crossover — 1.95
❑33, Sep 1995; One Nation under Doom crossover — 1.95
❑34, Oct 1995; One Nation under Doom crossover — 1.95
❑35, Nov 1995; One Nation under Doom crossover — 1.95
❑36, Dec 1995; X-Nation crossover — 1.95
❑37, Jan 1996; X-Nation crossover — 1.95
❑38, Feb 1996; X-Nation crossover — 1.95
❑39, Mar 1996 JB (c); JB (a) — 1.95
❑39/Variant, Mar 1996; Special cover — 3.50
❑40, Apr 1996; JB (c); JB (a); Doom 2099 comes to present — 1.95
❑41, May 1996; V: Namor. V: Daredevil. — 1.95
❑42, Jun 1996; V: Fantastic Four — 1.95
❑43, Jul 1996; story continues in Fantastic Four 2099 #7 — 1.95
❑44, Aug 1996; continues in 2099: World of Tomorrow — 1.95

Doorman
Caliber

❑1 — 2.95

DoorMan
Cult

❑1, Aug 1993, b&w; Double-cover — 2.95
❑2, b&w — 2.50
❑3, b&w — 2.50
❑4, b&w — 2.95
❑Ashcan 1; Ashcan — 1.00

Doorman: Family Secrets
Caliber

❑1; ca. 1995 — 2.95

Doorway to Nightmare
DC

❑1, Feb 1978, VM (a); 1: Madame Xanadu — 7.00
❑2, Apr 1978 — 3.00
❑3, Jun 1978 — 3.00
❑4, Aug 1978 — 3.00
❑5, Oct 1978, Final Issue — 3.00

Dope Comix
Kitchen Sink

❑1; Adult — 5.00
❑2; Adult — 3.00
❑3; Adult — 3.00
❑4; Adult — 3.00
❑5; Adult — 3.00

Dopin' Dan
Last Gasp

❑1, Apr 1972, Adult — 5.00
❑2; Adult — 3.00
❑3; Adult — 3.00

Doris Nelson: Atomic Housewife
Jake Comics

❑1, Dec 1995, b&w — 2.75

Dork
Slave Labor

❑1, Jun 1993, b&w — 3.00
❑1/2nd, Aug 1995, b&w; 2nd printing; b&w — 2.75
❑1/3rd, Mar 1997, b&w; 3rd printing — 2.75
❑2, May 1994, b&w — 2.50
❑2/2nd, Jan 1996, b&w; 2nd printing — 2.75
❑3, Aug 1995, b&w — 2.75
❑3/2nd, Sep 1996, b&w; 2nd printing — 2.75
❑4, Mar 1997, b&w — 2.75
❑5, Jan 1998, b&w — 2.95
❑6, May 1998, b&w — 2.95
❑7, Aug 1999, b&w — 2.95
❑8, Sep 2000, b&w — 3.50
❑9, Aug 2001; b&w — 2.95

Dork House Comics
Parody

❑1 — 2.50

Dorkier Images
Parody

❑1, Mar 1993; Standard edition — 2.50
❑1/Variant; gold, silver, blue edition — 3.00

Dork Tower
Dork Storm

❑1, Jul 1998 — 4.00
❑2, Oct 1998 — 3.00
❑3, Jan 1999 — 3.00
❑4, May 1999; Star Wars — 3.00
❑5, Jul 1999; Babylon 5 — 2.95
❑6 1999 — 2.95
❑7, Jan 2000 — 2.95
❑8, Mar 2000 — 2.95
❑9, Aug 2000, b&w; switches to Dork Storm — 2.95
❑10, Aug 2000 — 2.95
❑11, Sep 2000 — 2.95
❑12, Nov 2000 — 2.95
❑13, Feb 2001 — 2.95
❑14 2001 — 2.95
❑15 2001 — 2.95
❑16 2001 — 2.99
❑17 2002 — 2.99
❑18 2002 — 2.99
❑19 2002 — 2.99
❑20 2002 — 2.99
❑21 2002 — 2.99
❑22 2002 — 2.99
❑23 2003 — 2.99
❑24 2003 — 2.99

Other grades: Multiply price above by 5/6 for VF/NM • 2/3 for VERY FINE • 1/3 for FINE • 1/5 for VERY GOOD • 1/8 for GOOD

	N-MINT
❑25 2003	2.99
❑26 2004	2.99
❑27, Apr 2004	2.99
❑28 2004	2.99
❑29, Mar 2005	2.99
❑30, Jan 2005	2.99
❑31, May 2005	2.99

Double Dragon
Marvel

❑1, Jul 1991; 1&O: Double Dragon (Billy & Jimmy Lee)	1.00
❑2, Aug 1991	1.00
❑3, Sep 1991	1.00
❑4, Oct 1991	1.00
❑5, Nov 1991	1.00
❑6, Dec 1991; Final Issue	1.00

Double Edge: Alpha
Marvel

❑1, Aug 1995; Chromium cover; Punisher	4.95

Double Edge: Omega
Marvel

❑1, Oct 1995; enhanced wraparound cover; Punisher	4.95

Double Image
Image

❑1, Feb 2001; Flip-book	2.95
❑2, Mar 2001; Had two different front covers and was NOT a flipbook	2.95
❑3, Apr 2001; Flip-book	2.95
❑4, May 2001; Flip-book	2.95
❑5, Jun 2001; Flip-book	2.95

Double Impact
High Impact

❑1, Mar 1995, No cover price; no indicia; gray polybag; preview of Double Impact #3 and 4; San Diego Comic-Con ed	3.95
❑1/Ltd., Mar 1995, No cover price; no indicia; black polybag; letters pages and pin-ups;limited to 5000	3.95
❑2, May 1995	3.00
❑3, Jul 1995	3.00
❑5, Nov 1995	3.00
❑4, Sep 1995	3.00

Double Impact
High Impact

❑0, Dec 1996	2.95
❑1 1997; Chromium cover	4.00
❑2 1997	3.00
❑3 1997	3.00
❑4 1997	3.00
❑5 1997	3.00
❑6 1997	3.00
❑7, May 1996	3.00

Double Impact: Art Attack
ABC

❑1	3.00
❑1/A; China & Jazz Nude Edition	4.00
❑1/B; Nude Jazz Edition	4.00

Double Impact: Assassins for Hire
High Impact

❑1, Apr 1997, b&w; Hard Core! Edition; cardstock cover	2.95

Double Impact Bikini Special
High Impact

❑1, Sep 1998, b&w; pin-ups	3.00

Double Impact: From the Ashes
High Impact

❑1, b&w; Adult	3.00
❑2, b&w; says Swedish Erotika Vol. 5 on cover	5.95

Double Impact/Hellina
ABC

❑1, Jan 1998, b&w; crossover with Lightning	3.00
❑1/Autographed, Mar 1996, b&w; Signed, limited edition nude cover	4.00
❑1/Gold, Mar 1996, Gold nude cover	5.00
❑1/Nude, Jan 1998, Nude cover	3.00
❑1/Variant, Mar 1996, Nude cover	3.00

Double Impact: One Step Beyond
High Impact

❑1, Sep 1998	3.00
❑1/Variant; Leather cover	20.00

Double Impact: Raising Hell
ABC

	N-MINT
❑1, Sep 1997, b&w; Adult	2.95
❑1/Nude, Sep 1997, b&w; nude cover	3.50

Double Impact: Raw
ABC

❑1, Nov 1997; cardstock cover	2.95
❑1/A, Nov 1997; Eurotika Edition; no cover price	4.00
❑1/Nude, Nov 1997; Eurotika Edition; nude cover	4.00
❑1/2nd; 2nd printing	3.50
❑2, ca. 1998	3.00
❑2/Nude, ca. 1998; nude cover	3.00
❑3, ca. 1998	3.00

Double Impact: Raw
ABC

❑1/Nude, Sep 1998; Nude cover	3.00

Double Impact: Suicide Run
High Impact

❑1, Jun 1997	3.00
❑1/A, Jun 1997	4.00
❑1/Leather, Jun 1997; no cover price	4.00
❑1/Nude, Jun 1997	4.00

Double Impact: Trigger Happy
High Impact

❑1, ca. 1997	3.00
❑1/B, ca. 1997; Jazz Edition	3.00
❑1/Ltd., ca. 1997; Gold edition; No cover price; limited to 300 copies	4.00

Down
Image

❑1, Jan 2006	2.99
❑2, Jan 2006	2.99
❑3, Jan 2006	2.99
❑4, Apr 2006	2.99

D.P.7
Marvel

❑1, Nov 1986, O: D.P.7	1.00
❑2, Dec 1986	1.00
❑3, Jan 1987	1.00
❑4, Feb 1987	1.00
❑5, Mar 1987	1.00
❑6, Apr 1987	1.00
❑7, May 1987	1.00
❑8, Jun 1987	1.00
❑9, Jul 1987	1.00
❑10, Aug 1987, 1: Evan Huebner (Shadowman)	1.00
❑11, Sep 1987	1.00
❑12, Oct 1987, V: Overshadow	1.00
❑13, Nov 1987	1.00
❑14, Dec 1987	1.00
❑15, Jan 1988	1.00
❑16, Feb 1988	1.00
❑17, Mar 1988, 1: Mutator; 1: Sponge	1.00
❑18, Apr 1988, Crossover with The Pitt	1.00
❑19, May 1988	1.00
❑20, Jun 1988, 1: Pit Bull	1.00
❑21, Jul 1988	1.00
❑22, Aug 1988, Handbook entry for Mastodon	1.00
❑23, Sep 1988	1.00
❑24, Oct 1988, Viva becomes Glitter; Handbook entries for Glitter; Scuzz; Twilight	1.00
❑25, Nov 1988, D: Shadowman	1.00
❑26, Dec 1988, D: Twilight; Handbook entries for Mutator, Pit Bull	1.00
❑27, Jan 1989, V: Dirtbag	1.00
❑28, Feb 1989, V: Overshadow	1.00
❑29, Mar 1989, V: Deadweight	1.00
❑30, Apr 1989, 1: Captain Manhattan	1.00
❑31, May 1989	1.00
❑32, Jun 1989, Final Issue	1.00
❑Ann 1, Nov 1987, 1: Witness; O: D.P.7.	1.00

Dracula
Eternity

❑1	2.50
❑1/2nd; 2nd printing	2.50
❑2, b&w	2.50
❑3, b&w	2.50
❑4, b&w	2.50

Dracula
Topps

	N-MINT
❑1, Oct 1992; Includes trading cards	2.95
❑1/Variant, Oct 1992; no cover price	3.50
❑2, Nov 1992; Includes trading cards, poster enclosed	2.95
❑3, Dec 1992; Includes trading cards	2.95
❑4, Jan 1993; Includes trading cards	2.95

Dracula 3-D
3-D Zone

❑1; NN	3.95

Dracula Chronicles
Topps

❑1	2.50
❑2	2.50
❑3	2.50

Dracula in Hell
Apple

❑1, Jan 1992, b&w; Adult	2.50
❑2, b&w; Adult	2.50

Dracula Lives!
Marvel

❑1, Jun 1973, b&w	5.00
❑2, Aug 1973, b&w O: Dracula	4.00
❑3, Oct 1973, b&w A: Soloman Kane	3.00
❑4, Jan 1974, b&w; title changes to Dracula Lives!	3.00
❑5, Mar 1974, b&w; adapts Bram Stoker novel	3.00
❑6, May 1974, b&w	3.00
❑7, Jul 1974, b&w	3.00
❑8, Sep 1974, b&w	3.00
❑9, Nov 1974, b&w	3.00
❑10, Jan 1975, b&w	3.00
❑11, Mar 1975, b&w	3.00
❑12, May 1975, b&w	3.00
❑13, Jul 1975, b&w	3.00
❑Ann 1, ca. 1975, b&w; magazine	25.00

Dracula: Lord of the Undead
Marvel

❑1, Dec 1998; gatefold summary	2.99
❑2, Dec 1998; gatefold summary	2.99
❑3, Dec 1998; gatefold summary	2.99

Dracula: Return of the Impaler
Slave Labor

❑1, Jul 1993; b&w	2.95
❑2, Jan 1994; b&w	2.95
❑3, Mar 1994; b&w	2.95
❑4, Oct 1994; b&w	2.95

Dracula's Daughter
Fantagraphics / Eros

❑1, Sep 1991, b&w; Adult	2.50

Dracula's Revenge
Idea & Design Works

❑1, May 2004	3.99
❑2, Jun 2004	3.99

Dracula: The Lady in the Tomb
Eternity

❑1, b&w	2.50

Dracula: The Suicide Club
Adventure

❑1, Aug 1992	2.50
❑2, Sep 1992	2.50
❑3, Oct 1992	2.50
❑4, Nov 1992	2.50

Dracula vs. Zorro
Topps

❑1, Oct 1993 TY (a)	4.00
❑2, Nov 1993; TY (c); TY (a); Polybagged with #0 Special Collectors Edition	3.50

Dracula vs. Zorro
Topps

❑1, Apr 1994	5.95

Dracula vs. Zorro
Image

❑1, Sep 1998	2.95
❑2, Oct 1998	2.95

Dracula: Vlad the Impaler
Topps

❑1, Feb 1993; trading cards	2.95
❑2, Mar 1993; trading cards	2.95
❑3, Apr 1993; trading cards	2.95

Draculina
Draculina

❑1; O: Draculina	2.50

Other grades: Multiply price above by 5/6 for VF/NM • 2/3 for VERY FINE • 1/3 for FINE • 1/5 for VERY GOOD • 1/8 for GOOD

Doctor Solar, Man of the Atom

Radioactivity turned researcher green
©Gold Key

Doctor Strange

Picks up numbering from Strange Tales
©Marvel

Doctor Strange

Second longest-running Dr. Strange series
©Marvel

Doctor Strange: Sorcerer Supreme

1990s version updated Doc's look
©Marvel

Dr. Tomorrow

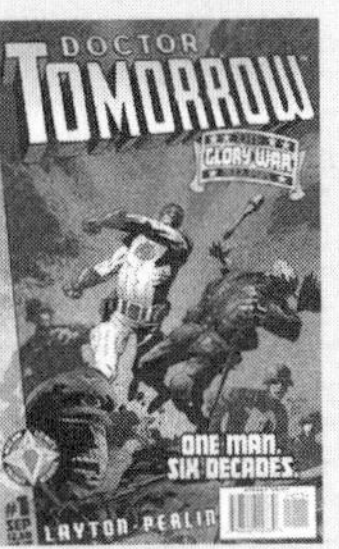

Super-hero gets help from future
©Acclaim

N-MINT

Draculina's Cozy Coffin
Draculina

❑1, b&w; no indicia 2.50
❑2, Jan 1994, b&w; no indicia 2.50

Draft
Marvel

❑1, Jul 1988; D.P.7, Nightmask 2.00

Drag 'n' Wheels
Charlton

❑30, Sep 1968, Previous issues published as Top Eliminator 12.00
❑31, Nov 1968 .... 12.00
❑32, Jan 1969 .... 12.00
❑33, Mar 1969 .... 12.00
❑34, May 1969 .... 12.00
❑35, Jul 1969 .... 12.00
❑36, Sep 1969 .... 10.00
❑37, Nov 1969 .... 10.00
❑38, Jan 1970 .... 10.00
❑39, Feb 1970 .... 10.00
❑40, Apr 1970 .... 10.00
❑41, Jun 1970 .... 10.00
❑42, Aug 1970 .... 10.00
❑43, Oct 1970 .... 10.00
❑44, Dec 1970 .... 10.00
❑45, Feb 1971 .... 10.00
❑46, Apr 1971 .... 10.00
❑47, Jun 1971 .... 10.00
❑48, Aug 1971 .... 10.00
❑49, Oct 1971 .... 10.00
❑50, Dec 1971 .... 10.00
❑51, Feb 1972 .... 10.00
❑52, Mar 1972 .... 10.00
❑53 1972 .... 10.00
❑54, Jul 1972 .... 10.00
❑55, Sep 1972 .... 10.00
❑56, Nov 1972 .... 10.00
❑57, Jan 1973 .... 10.00
❑58, Mar 1973 .... 10.00
❑58/2nd, ca. 1978, Modern Comics reprint 10.00
❑59, May 1973 .... 10.00

Dragon
Comics Interview

❑1, Aug 1987; weekly 1.75
❑2, Aug 1987; weekly 1.75
❑3, Aug 1987; weekly 1.75
❑4, Aug 1987; weekly 1.75

Dragon
Image

❑1, Mar 1996 .... 2.00
❑2, Apr 1996 .... 2.00
❑3, May 1996 .... 2.00
❑4, Jun 1996 .... 2.00
❑5, Jul 1996; A: Badrock. Final Issue 2.00

Dragon Arms
Antarctic

❑1, Dec 2002 .... 3.50
❑2, Jan 2003 .... 3.50
❑3, Feb 2003 .... 3.50
❑4, Mar 2003 .... 3.50
❑5, Apr 2003 .... 3.50
❑6, May 2003 .... 3.50

N-MINT

Dragon Arms: Chaos Blade
Antarctic

❑1, Jan 2004 .... 2.99
❑2, Feb 2004 .... 2.99
❑3, May 2004 .... 2.99
❑4, Apr 2004 .... 2.99
❑5, May 2004 .... 2.99
❑6, Jun 2004 .... 2.99

Dragon Arms Stand Alone
Antarctic

❑1, ca. 2005 .... 2.99

Dragonball
Viz

❑1, Mar 1998; 'Manga Style' Edition; 'Manga Style ' Edition 4.00
❑2, Apr 1998; 'Manga Style' Edition; 'Manga Style ' Edition 3.50
❑3, May 1998; 'Manga Style' Edition; 'Manga Style ' Edition 3.50
❑4, Jun 1998; 'Manga Style' Edition; 'Manga Style' Edition 3.50
❑5, Jul 1998; 'Manga Style' Edition; 'Manga Style' Edition 3.50
❑6, Aug 1998; 'Manga Style' Edition; 'Manga Style' Edition 3.50
❑7, Sep 1998; 'Manga Style' Edition; 'Manga Style' Edition 3.50
❑8, Oct 1998 .... 3.00
❑9, Nov 1998 .... 3.00
❑10, Dec 1998 .... 3.00
❑11, Jan 1999 .... 3.00
❑12, Feb 1999 .... 3.00

Dragonball Part 2
Viz

❑1, Mar 1999 .... 4.00
❑2, Apr 1999 .... 3.00
❑3, May 1999 .... 3.00
❑4, Jun 1999 .... 3.00
❑5, Jul 1999 .... 3.00
❑6, Aug 1999 .... 3.00
❑7, Sep 1999 .... 3.00
❑8, Oct 1999 .... 3.00
❑9, Nov 1999 .... 2.95
❑10, Dec 1999 .... 2.95
❑11, Jan 2000 .... 2.95
❑12, Feb 2000 .... 2.95
❑13, Mar 2000 .... 2.95
❑14, Apr 2000 .... 2.95
❑15, May 2000 .... 2.95

Dragonball Part 3
Viz

❑1, Jun 2000 .... 2.95
❑2, Jul 2000 .... 2.95
❑3, Aug 2000 .... 2.95
❑4, Sep 2000 .... 2.95
❑5, Oct 2000 .... 2.95
❑6, Nov 2000 .... 2.95
❑7, Dec 2000 .... 2.95
❑8, Jan 2001 .... 2.95
❑9, Feb 2001 .... 2.95
❑10, Mar 2001 .... 2.95
❑11, Apr 2001 .... 2.95
❑12, May 2001 .... 2.95
❑13, Jun 2001 .... 2.95
❑14, Jul 2001 .... 2.95

N-MINT

Dragonball Part 4
Viz

❑1, Aug 2001 .... 2.95
❑2, Sep 2001 .... 2.95
❑3, Oct 2001 .... 2.95
❑4, Nov 2001 .... 2.95
❑5, Dec 2001 .... 2.95
❑6, Jan 2002 .... 2.95
❑7, Feb 2002 .... 2.95
❑8, Mar 2002 .... 2.95
❑9, Apr 2002 .... 2.95
❑10, May 2002 .... 2.95

Dragonball Part 5
Viz

❑1, Jun 2002 .... 2.95
❑2, Jul 2002 .... 2.95
❑3, Aug 2002 .... 2.95
❑4, Sep 2002 .... 2.95
❑5, Oct 2002 .... 2.95
❑6, Nov 2002 .... 2.95
❑7, Dec 2002 .... 2.95

Dragonball Part 6
Viz

❑1, Jan 2003 .... 3.50
❑2, Feb 2003 .... 3.50

Dragonball Z
Viz

❑1, Mar 1998 .... 4.00
❑2, Apr 1998 .... 3.50
❑3, May 1998 .... 3.50
❑4, Jun 1998 .... 3.50
❑5, Jul 1998 .... 3.50
❑6, Aug 1998 .... 3.00
❑7, Sep 1998 .... 3.00
❑8, Oct 1998 .... 3.00
❑9, Nov 1998 .... 3.00
❑10, ca. 1998 .... 3.00

Dragonball Z Part 2
Viz

❑1, Dec 1998; 'Manga Style' Edition 3.50
❑2, Jan 1999; 'Manga Style' Edition 3.00
❑3, Feb 1999; 'Manga Style' Edition 3.00
❑4, Mar 1999; 'Manga Style' Edition 3.00
❑5, Apr 1999; 'Manga Style' Edition 3.00
❑6, May 1999; 'Manga Style' Edition 2.95
❑7, Jun 1999; 'Manga Style' Edition 2.95
❑8, Jul 1999 .... 2.95
❑9, Aug 1999 .... 2.95
❑10, Sep 1999 .... 2.95
❑11, Oct 1999 .... 2.95
❑12, Nov 1999 .... 2.95
❑13, Dec 1999 .... 2.95
❑14, Jan 2000 .... 2.95

Dragonball Z Part 3
Viz

❑1, Feb 2000 .... 2.95
❑2, Mar 2000 .... 2.95
❑3, Apr 2000 .... 2.95
❑4, May 2000 .... 2.95
❑5, Jun 2000 .... 2.95
❑6, Jul 2000 .... 2.95
❑7, Aug 2000 .... 2.95
❑8, Sep 2000 .... 2.95
❑9, Oct 2000 .... 2.95
❑10, Nov 2000 .... 2.95

Other grades: Multiply price above by 5/6 for VF/NM • 2/3 for VERY FINE • 1/3 for FINE • 1/5 for VERY GOOD • 1/8 for GOOD

N-MINT | N-MINT | N-MINT

Dragonball Z Part 4
Viz

❑1, Dec 2000 .... 2.95
❑2, Jan 2001 .... 2.95
❑3, Feb 2001 .... 2.95
❑4, Mar 2001 .... 2.95
❑5, Apr 2001 .... 2.95
❑6, May 2001 .... 2.95
❑7, Jun 2001 .... 2.95
❑8, Jul 2001 .... 2.95
❑9, Aug 2001 .... 2.95
❑10, Sep 2001 .... 2.95
❑11, Oct 2001 .... 2.95
❑12, Nov 2001 .... 2.95
❑13, Dec 2001 .... 2.95

Dragonball Z Part 5
Viz

❑1, Jan 2002 .... 2.95
❑2, Feb 2002 .... 2.95
❑3, Mar 2002 .... 2.95
❑4, Apr 2002 .... 2.95
❑5, May 2002 .... 2.95
❑6, Jun 2002 .... 2.95
❑7, Jul 2002 .... 2.95
❑8, Aug 2002 .... 2.95
❑9, Sep 2002 .... 2.95
❑10, Oct 2002 .... 2.95
❑11, Nov 2002 .... 2.95
❑12, Dec 2002 .... 2.95

Dragon: Blood & Guts
Image

❑1, Mar 1995 .... 2.50
❑2, Apr 1995 .... 2.50
❑3, May 1995 .... 2.50

Dragon Chiang
Eclipse

❑1, ca. 1991, b&w; nn; cardstock cover; no indicia 3.95

Dragonfire
Nightwynd

❑1, b&w 2.50
❑2, b&w 2.50
❑3, b&w 2.50
❑4, b&w 2.50

Dragonfire
Nightwynd

❑1, Mar 1992, b&w 2.50
❑2, Apr 1992, b&w 2.50
❑3, May 1992, b&w 2.50
❑4, Jun 1992, b&w 2.50

Dragonfire: The Classified Files
Nightwynd

❑1, b&w 2.50
❑2, b&w 2.50
❑3, b&w 2.50
❑4, b&w 2.50

Dragonfire: The Early Years
Night Wynd

❑1, b&w 2.50
❑2, b&w 2.50
❑3, b&w 2.50
❑4, b&w 2.50
❑5, b&w 2.50
❑6, b&w 2.50
❑7, b&w 2.50
❑8, b&w 2.50

Dragonfire: UFO Wars
Nightwynd

❑1, b&w 2.50
❑2, b&w 2.50
❑3, b&w 2.50

Dragonflight
Eclipse

❑1, Feb 1991; Anne McCaffrey 4.95
❑2 1991; Anne McCaffrey 4.95
❑3 1991; Anne McCaffrey 4.95

Dragon Flux
Antarctic

❑2, Jun 1996, b&w 2.95
❑3, Nov 1996, b&w 2.95

Dragonfly
AC

❑1, Aug 1985 .... 1.75
❑2 .... 1.75
❑3 .... 1.75
❑4 .... 1.75
❑5 .... 1.75
❑6, Feb 1987 .... 1.75
❑7, Jul 1987 .... 1.75
❑8; Final Issue 1.95

Dragonforce
Aircel

❑1, ca. 1988, b&w; 1&O: Dragonforce. O: Alloy. 1: Kohl. 1: Maire. 1: Alloy. 1: Kamikaze. 1: Sental 2.00
❑2, ca. 1988, b&w 2.00
❑3, ca. 1988, b&w 2.00
❑4, ca. 1988, b&w 2.00
❑5, ca. 1988, b&w 2.00
❑6, ca. 1988, b&w 2.00
❑7, ca. 1989, b&w 2.00
❑8, ca. 1989, b&w 2.00
❑9, ca. 1989, b&w 2.00
❑10, ca. 1989, b&w 2.00
❑11, ca. 1989, b&w 2.00
❑12, ca. 1989, b&w 2.00
❑13, ca. 1989, b&w 2.00

Dragonforce Chronicles
Aircel

❑1, ca. 1989, b&w; Reprints 2.95
❑2, ca. 1989, b&w; Reprints 2.95
❑3, ca. 1989, b&w; Reprints 2.95
❑4, ca. 1989, b&w; Reprints 2.95
❑5, ca. 1989, b&w; Reprints 2.95

Dragon Head
Tokyopop

❑1, Jan 2006 .... 9.99

Dragonheart
Topps

❑1, May 1996; Movie adaptation 2.95
❑2, Jun 1996; 64 pages; Movie adaptation 4.95

Dragon Hunter
Tokyopop

❑1, Jun 2003 .... 9.99
❑2, Aug 2005 .... 9.99
❑3, Oct 2003 .... 9.99
❑4, Jan 2004 .... 9.99
❑5, Mar 2004 .... 9.99
❑6, May 2004 .... 9.99
❑7, Jul 2004 .... 9.99
❑8, Sep 2004 .... 9.99
❑9, Nov 2004 .... 9.99
❑10, Jan 2005 .... 9.99
❑11, Mar 2005 .... 9.99
❑12, May 2005 .... 9.99
❑13, Nov 2005 .... 9.99

Dragon Knights
Slave Labor / Amaze Ink

❑1, Aug 1998, b&w 1.75
❑2 .... 1.75
❑3 .... 1.75

Dragon Knights
Tokyopop

❑1, Apr 2002, b&w; printed in Japanese format 9.99
❑2, Jun 2006 .... 9.99
❑3, Aug 2002 .... 9.99
❑4, Oct 2002 .... 9.99
❑5, Dec 2002 .... 9.99
❑6, Feb 2003 .... 9.99
❑7, Apr 2003 .... 9.99
❑8, Jun 2003 .... 9.99
❑9, Aug 2003 .... 9.99
❑10, Oct 2003 .... 9.99
❑11, Dec 2003 .... 9.99
❑12, Feb 2004 .... 9.99
❑13, Apr 2004 .... 9.99
❑14, Jun 2004 .... 9.99
❑15, Aug 2004 .... 9.99
❑16, Oct 2004 .... 9.99
❑17, Dec 2004 .... 9.99
❑18, Feb 2005 .... 9.99
❑19, May 2005 .... 9.99
❑20, Aug 2005 .... 9.99
❑21, Nov 2005 .... 9.99

Dragon Lady
Dragon Lady

❑1, Aug 1985; King of Mounted 6.95
❑2, Oct 1985; Red Ryder 6.95
❑3, Jan 1986; Captain Easy 5.95
❑4, Apr 1986; Secret Agent X-9 .... 5.95
❑5, Feb 1987; Brick Bradford 5.95
❑6; Secret Agent X-9 .... 5.95
❑7, Jul 1987; Captain Easy 5.95
❑8, Jan 1988; Terry 5.95

Dragonlance
DC

❑1, Dec 1988 .... 2.00
❑2, Win 1988 .... 1.50
❑3, Hol 1988 .... 1.25
❑4, Jan 1989 .... 1.25
❑5, Feb 1989 .... 1.25
❑6, Mar 1989 .... 1.50
❑7, Apr 1989 .... 1.50
❑8, Jun 1989 .... 1.50
❑9, Jul 1989 .... 1.50
❑10, Aug 1989 .... 1.50
❑11, Sep 1989 .... 1.50
❑12, Oct 1989 .... 1.50
❑13, Nov 1989 .... 1.50
❑14, Dec 1989 .... 1.50
❑15, Jan 1990 .... 1.50
❑16, Feb 1990 .... 1.50
❑17, Mar 1990 .... 1.50
❑18, Apr 1990 .... 1.50
❑19, May 1990 .... 1.50
❑20, Jun 1990 .... 1.50
❑21, Jul 1990 .... 1.50
❑22, Aug 1990 .... 1.50
❑23, Oct 1990 .... 1.50
❑24, Nov 1990 .... 1.75
❑25, Dec 1990 .... 1.75
❑26, Jan 1991 .... 1.75
❑27, Feb 1991 .... 1.75
❑28, Mar 1991 .... 1.75
❑29, Apr 1991 .... 1.75
❑30, May 1991 .... 1.75
❑31, Jun 1991 .... 1.75
❑32, Jul 1991 .... 1.75
❑33, Aug 1991 .... 1.75
❑34, Sep 1991; Final Issue 1.75

Dragonlance Chronicles: Dragons of Autumn Twilight
Devil's Due

❑1, Sep 2005 .... 2.95
❑2 2005 .... 3.00
❑2/Special 2005 .... 6.00
❑3, Dec 2005 .... 2.95
❑3/Special, Dec 2005 .... 5.95
❑4, Nov 2005 .... 2.95
❑4/Special, Nov 2005 .... 5.95
❑5, Jan 2006 .... 2.95
❑5/Special, Jan 2006 .... 5.95
❑6, Feb 2006 .... 2.95
❑6/Special, Feb 2006 .... 5.95
❑7, Mar 2006 .... 2.95
❑7/Special, Mar 2006 .... 5.95
❑8, Apr 2006 .... 2.95
❑8/Variant, Apr 2006 .... 5.95

Dragonlance Chronicles: Dragons of Winter Night
Devil's Due

❑1, Jun 2006 .... 4.95
❑1/Special, Jun 2006 .... 8.95
❑2, Sep 2006 .... 4.95
❑2/Special, Sep 2006 .... 8.95
❑3, Nov 2006 .... 4.95
❑3/Special, Nov 2006 .... 8.95

Dragonlance Comic Book
TSR

❑1; ca. 1996 .... 1.00

Dragonlance Saga
TSR

❑1, Nov 1987; Adapted from Dragons of Autumn Twilight 9.95
❑2; Adapted from Dragons of Autumn Twilight 9.95
❑3; Adapted from Dragons of Winter Night 9.95
❑4 .... 9.95
❑5 .... 9.95

Dragon Lines
Marvel / Epic

❑1, May 1993; Embossed cover 2.50

Other grades: Multiply price above by 5/6 for VF/NM • 2/3 for VERY FINE • 1/3 for FINE • 1/5 for VERY GOOD • 1/8 for GOOD

Doctor Who

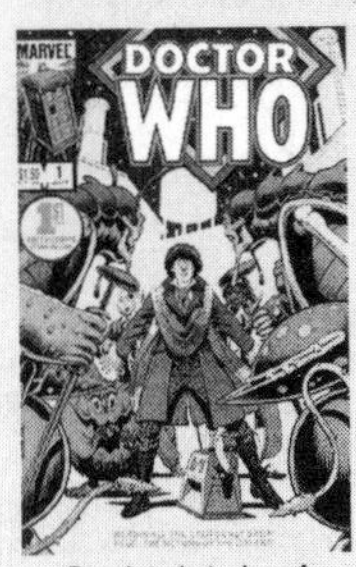

Reprinted stories of time-traveling meddler
©Marvel

Domination Factor: Avengers

Weird numbering scheme caused confusion
©Marvel

Donald and Mickey

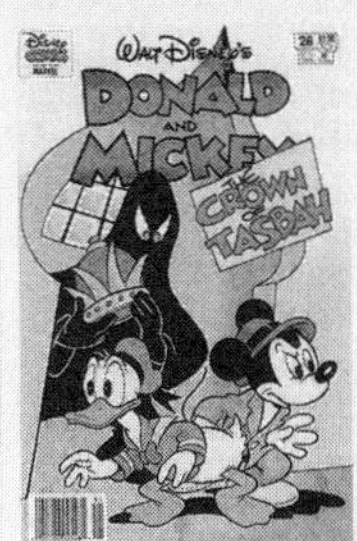

Was Mickey and Donald through #18
©Gladstone

Donald Duck (Walt Disney's...)

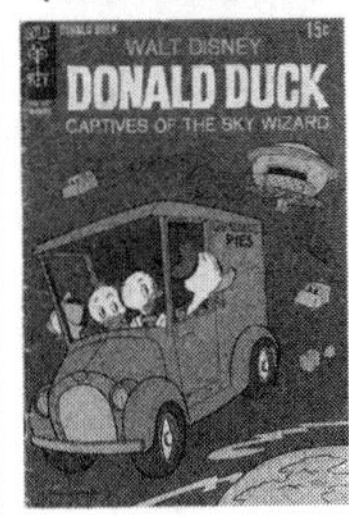

Includes many Carl Barks stories
©Dell

Donald Duck Adventures (Gladstone)

Don Rosa sent Ducks on more outings
©Gladstone

	N-MINT
❑2, Jun 1993	1.95
❑3, Jul 1993	1.95
❑4, Aug 1993	1.95

Dragon Lines: Way of the Warrior
Marvel / Epic

❑1, Nov 1993	2.25
❑2, Jan 1994	2.25

Dragon of the Valkyr
Rak

❑1, b&w	1.75
❑2	1.75
❑3	1.75

Dragon Quest
Silverwolf

❑1, Dec 1986, b&w	2.00
❑2, Feb 1987	2.00

Dragonring
Aircel

❑1 1986, b&w; ca. 1986	2.00
❑2 1986, b&w	2.00
❑3 1986, b&w	2.00
❑4 1986, b&w	2.00
❑5 1986, b&w	2.00
❑6 1986, b&w	2.00

Dragonring
Aircel

❑1 1986; ca. 1986	2.00
❑2 1987; ca. 1986	2.00
❑3 1987; ca. 1987	2.00
❑4 1987; ca. 1987	2.00
❑5 1987; ca. 1987	2.00
❑6 1987; ca. 1987	2.00
❑7 1987; ca. 1987	2.00
❑8 1987; ca. 1987	2.00
❑9 1987; ca. 1987	2.00
❑10 1987	2.00
❑11 1987	2.00
❑12 1987	2.00
❑13 1987	2.00
❑14 1988; ca. 1988	2.00
❑15 1988; ca. 1988	2.00

Dragonrok Saga
Hanthercraft

❑1	2.50
❑2	2.50
❑3	2.50
❑4	2.50
❑5	2.50
❑6	2.50
❑7	2.50
❑8	2.50
❑9	2.50
❑10	2.50

Dragon's Bane
Hall of Heroes

❑1	2.50
❑Ashcan 1, Chicago Comic Con Ashcan limited to 100 copies	4.95

Dragon's Claws
Marvel

❑1, Jul 1988, 1: Dragon's Claws	1.50
❑2, Aug 1988	1.50
❑3, Sep 1988	1.50
❑4, Oct 1988	1.50
❑5, Nov 1988, 1: Death's Head I	2.00
❑6, Dec 1988	1.75
❑7, Jan 1989	1.75
❑8, Feb 1989	1.75
❑9, Mar 1989	1.75
❑10, Apr 1989	1.75

Dragons in the Moon
Aircel

❑1, Oct 1990, b&w	2.50
❑2, Oct 1990, b&w	2.50
❑3, Oct 1990, b&w	2.50
❑4, Oct 1990, b&w	2.50

Dragon's Lair: Singe's Revenge
CrossGen

❑1, Sep 2003	2.95
❑2, Nov 2003	2.95
❑3, Nov 2003	2.95

Dragonslayer
Marvel

❑1, Oct 1981, Movie adaptation	1.50
❑2, Nov 1981, Movie adaptation	1.50

Dragon's Star
Matrix

❑1, Dec 1986	2.00
❑2, Feb 1987	2.00
❑3 1987	2.00

Dragon's Star 2
Caliber

❑1 1994	2.95
❑2 1994	2.95
❑3	2.95

Dragon's Teeth
Dragon's Teeth

❑1, b&w	2.95

Dragon Strike
Marvel

❑1, Feb 1994	1.50

Dragonstrike Prime
Illusion

❑2, Dec 1996, b&w	1.95

Dragon Voice
Tokyopop

❑1, Oct 2004	9.99
❑2, Dec 2004	9.99
❑3, Feb 2005	9.99
❑4, May 2005	9.99
❑5, Oct 2005	9.99
❑6, Apr 2006	9.99

Dragon Wars
Ironcat

❑1, Apr 1998	2.95
❑2, May 1998	2.95
❑3, Jun 1998	2.95
❑4, Jul 1998	2.95
❑5, Aug 1998	2.95
❑6, Sep 1998	2.95
❑7, Oct 1998	2.95

Drag-Strip Hotrodders
Charlton

❑1, Sum 1963	40.00
❑2, ca. 1964	25.00
❑3, ca. 1964	25.00
❑4, Jun 1965	25.00
❑5, Aug 1965	25.00
❑6, Oct 1965	25.00
❑7, Dec 1965	25.00
❑8, Feb 1966	25.00
❑9, Apr 1966	25.00
❑10, Jun 1966	25.00
❑11, Aug 1966	25.00
❑12, Oct 1966	25.00
❑13, Dec 1966	25.00
❑14, Mar 1967	25.00
❑15, Jun 1967	25.00
❑16, Aug 1967, Later issues published as World of Wheels	25.00

Drain
Image

❑1, Nov 2006, b&w	2.99
❑1/Variant, Nov 2006	2.99

Drake: Demon Box
Image

❑1, Dec 2003	2.50

Drakkon Wars
Realm

❑0, Jul 1997; Battlestar Galactica story written by Richard Hatch	2.99

Drakuun
Dark Horse / Manga

❑1, Feb 1997	2.95
❑2, Mar 1997	2.95
❑3, Apr 1997	2.95
❑4, May 1997	2.95
❑5, Jun 1997	2.95
❑6, Jul 1997	2.95
❑7, Aug 1997	2.95
❑8, Sep 1997	2.95
❑9, Oct 1997	2.95
❑10, Nov 1997	2.95
❑11, Dec 1997	2.95
❑12, Jan 1998	2.95
❑13, Feb 1998	2.95
❑14, Mar 1998	2.95
❑15, Apr 1998	2.95
❑16, May 1998	2.95
❑17, Jun 1998	2.95
❑18, Jul 1998	2.95
❑19, Oct 1998	2.95
❑20, Nov 1998	2.95
❑21, Dec 1998	2.95
❑22, Jan 1999	2.95
❑23, Feb 1999	2.95
❑24, Mar 1999	2.95

Drama
Sirius Entertainment

❑1, Jun 1994, Chronium Cover	4.00
❑1/Ltd., Chronium Cover; limited to 1400 copies; signed by Linsner; w/trading cards & Art Plate of Authenticity in an illustrated envelope	12.00

Dramacon
Tokyopop

❑1, Oct 2005	9.99

Other grades: Multiply price above by 5/6 for VF/NM • 2/3 for VERY FINE • 1/3 for FINE • 1/5 for VERY GOOD • 1/8 for GOOD

Drawing on your Nightmares: Halloween 2003 Special
Dark Horse

❑1, Oct 2003 ... 2.99

Drawn & Quarterly
Drawn & Quarterly

❑1 1990, b&w ... 3.00
❑2 1990 ... 3.00
❑3, Jan 1991 ... 3.50
❑4, Mar 1991 ... 3.75
❑5 1991 ... 3.75
❑6 1991 ... 3.75
❑7 1992 ... 3.75
❑8, Apr 1992, b&w ... 3.75

Drax the Destroyer
Marvel

❑1, Nov 2005 ... 2.99
❑2, Dec 2005 ... 2.99
❑3, Jan 2006 ... 2.99
❑4, Feb 2006 ... 2.99

Dr. Blink, Super-Hero Shrink
Dork Storm

❑1 2005 ... 3.49
❑2 2005 ... 3.49

Dreadlands
Marvel / Epic

❑1, ca. 1992 ... 3.95
❑2, ca. 1992 ... 3.95
❑3, ca. 1992 ... 3.95
❑4, ca. 1992 ... 3.95

Dread of Night
Hamilton

❑1, Nov 1991, b&w ... 3.95
❑2, b&w ... 3.95

Dreadstar
Marvel / Epic

❑1, Nov 1982; JSn (c); JSn (w); JSn (a); Story continued from Epic Illustrated #15 ... 2.50
❑2, Jan 1983; JSn (c); JSn (w); JSn (a); O: Willow. Willow ... 2.00
❑3, Mar 1983; JSn (c); JSn (w); JSn (a); Lord Papal ... 2.00
❑4, May 1983 JSn (c); JSn (w); JSn (a). 2.00
❑5, Jul 1983 JSn (c); JSn (w); JSn (a)... 2.00
❑6, Sep 1983 JSn (c); JSn, BWr (w); JSn, BWr (a) ... 1.75
❑7, Nov 1983 JSn (c); JSn (w); JSn (a). 1.75
❑8, Jan 1984 JSn (c); JSn (w); JSn (a).. 1.75
❑9, Mar 1984; JSn (c); JSn (w); JSn (a); O: Z ... 1.75
❑10, Apr 1984 JSn (c); JSn (w); JSn (a) 1.75
❑11, Jun 1984 JSn (c); JSn (w); JSn (a) 1.75
❑12, Jul 1984; JSn (c); JSn (w); JSn (a); New costume ... 1.75
❑13, Aug 1984 JSn (c); JSn (w); JSn (a) 1.75
❑14, Oct 1984; JSn (c); JSn (w); JSn (a); Fights Lord Papal ... 1.75
❑15, Nov 1984 JSn (c); JSn (w); JSn (a) 1.75
❑16, Dec 1984 JSn (c); JSn (w); JSn (a) 1.50
❑17, Feb 1985 JSn (c); JSn (w); JSn (a) 1.50
❑18, Apr 1985 JSn (c); JSn (w); JSn (a) 1.50
❑19, Jun 1985 JSn (c); JSn (w); JSn (a) 1.50
❑20, Aug 1985 JSn (c); JSn (w); JSn (a) 1.50
❑21, Oct 1985 JSn (c); JSn (w); JSn (a) 1.50
❑22, Dec 1985 JSn (c); JSn (w); JSn (a) 1.50
❑23, Feb 1986 JSn (c); JSn (w); JSn (a) 1.50
❑24, Apr 1986 JSn (c); JSn (w); JSn (a) 1.50
❑25, Jun 1986 JSn (c); JSn (w); JSn (a) 1.50
❑26, Aug 1986 JSn (c); JSn (w); JSn (a) 1.50
❑27, Nov 1986; JSn (c); JSn (w); JSn (a); First Comics begins publishing ... 1.75
❑28, Jan 1987 JSn (c); JSn (w); JSn (a) 1.75
❑29, Mar 1987 JSn (c); JSn (w); JSn (a) 1.75
❑30, May 1987 JSn (c); JSn (w); JSn (a) 1.75
❑31, Jul 1987 JSn (c); JSn (w); JSn (a). 1.75
❑32, Sep 1987 JSn (c); JSn (w); JSn (a) 1.75
❑33, Nov 1987 JSn (c); JSn (w); JSn, LMc (a) ... 1.75
❑34, Jan 1988 JSn (c); JSn (w); JSn, LMc (a) ... 1.75
❑35, Mar 1988 JSn (c); JSn (w); JSn, LMc (a) ... 1.75
❑36, May 1988 JSn (c); JSn (w); JSn, LMc (a) ... 1.75
❑37, Jul 1988 JSn (c); JSn (w); JSn, LMc (a) ... 1.75
❑38, Sep 1988 JSn (c); JSn (w); JSn, LMc (a) ... 1.75
❑39, Nov 1988; JSn (c); JSn (w); JSn (a); Crossroads ... 1.95
❑40, Jan 1989 JSn (c); JSn (w); JSn, LMc (a) ... 1.95
❑41, Mar 1989; PD (w); Peter David writing starts ... 1.95
❑42, May 1989 JSn, PD (w) ... 1.95
❑43, Jun 1989 JSn, PD (w) ... 1.95
❑44, Jul 1989 JSn, PD (w) ... 1.95
❑45, Aug 1989 JSn, PD (w) ... 1.95
❑46, Sep 1989 JSn, PD (w) ... 1.95
❑47, Oct 1989 JSn, PD (w) ... 1.95
❑48, Nov 1989 JSn, PD (w) ... 1.95
❑49, Dec 1989 JSn, PD (w) ... 1.95
❑50, Jan 1990; Double-size; JSn, PD (w); Embossed cover ... 2.75
❑51, Feb 1990 JSn, PD (w) ... 1.95
❑52, Mar 1990 JSn, PD (w) ... 1.95
❑53, Apr 1990 JSn, PD (w) ... 1.95
❑54, May 1990 JSn, PD (w) ... 1.95
❑55, Jun 1990 PD (w) ... 2.25
❑56, Jul 1990 PD (w) ... 2.25
❑57, Aug 1990 PD (w) ... 2.25
❑58, Sep 1990 PD (w) ... 2.25
❑59, Oct 1990 PD (w) ... 2.25
❑60, Nov 1990 PD (w) ... 2.25
❑61, Dec 1990 PD (w) ... 2.25
❑62, Jan 1991 PD (w) ... 2.25
❑63, Feb 1991 PD (w) ... 2.25
❑64, Mar 1991; PD (w); Final Issue ... 2.25
❑Ann 1, ca. 1983; JSn (w); JSn (a); ca. 1983 ... 3.00

Dreadstar
Malibu / Bravura

❑½, Mar 1994, Promotional edition included in Hero Illustrated; Promotional edition included in Hero Illustrated ... 2.00
❑1/Gold, Mar 1994; sendaway with gold ink on cover ... 3.00
❑1, Apr 1994, PD (w); Includes coupon. 2.50
❑2, May 1994, PD (w); Includes coupon 2.50
❑3, Jun 1994, PD (w); Includes coupon 2.50
❑4, Sep 1994, PD (w); Includes coupon 2.50
❑5, Oct 1994, PD (w); D: Dreadstar (Vanth); Includes coupon ... 2.50
❑6, Jan 1995, PD (w); Final Issue; Includes coupon ... 2.50

Dreadstar & Co.
Marvel / Epic

❑1, Jul 1985; JSn (c); JSn (w); JSn (a); Reprints ... 1.00
❑2, Aug 1985; JSn (c); JSn (w); JSn (a); Reprints ... 1.00
❑3, Sep 1985; JSn (c); JSn (w); JSn (a); Reprints ... 1.00
❑4, Oct 1985; JSn (c); JSn (w); JSn (a); Reprints ... 1.00
❑5, Nov 1985; JSn (c); JSn (w); JSn (a); Reprints ... 1.00
❑6, Dec 1985; JSn (c); JSn (w); JSn (a); Reprints ... 1.00

Dream Angel
Angel Entertainment

❑0, Fal 1996, b&w; Regular cover; Fall 1996 ... 2.95

Dream Angel and Angel Girl
Angel

❑1 ... 3.00

Dream Angel: The Quantum Dreamer
Angel

❑0 ... 2.95
❑1 ... 2.95
❑2 ... 2.95

Dream Corridor
Dark Horse

❑1, Mar 1995 JBy, ES (a) ... 3.50
❑2, Apr 1995 TS, JBy, ES (a) ... 3.25
❑3, May 1995 JBy, ES (a) ... 3.00
❑4, Jun 1995 JBy, ES (a) ... 3.00
❑5, Aug 1995 ES (a) ... 3.00
❑Special 1, Jan 1995; prestige format; PB, ES, PF (a) ... 5.00
❑Special 1/2nd, Sep 1995; prestige format; 2nd printing ... 4.95

Dream Corridor Quarterly
Dark Horse

❑1, Aug 1996; prestige format; Reprints Creepy (Magazine) #32 (in color) ... 5.95

Dreamer
DC

❑1, Jun 2000 ... 7.95

Dreamery
Eclipse

❑1, Dec 1986, b&w; Councilman Stinz story ... 2.00
❑2, Feb 1987, b&w; Lela Dowling bio ... 2.00
❑3, Apr 1987, b&w; Councilman Stinz story; Donna Barr bio ... 2.00
❑4, Jun 1987, b&w; 1: Cheshire Cat ... 2.00
❑5, Aug 1987, b&w; Councilman Stinz story; Time Release entirely done on a Macintosh computer ... 2.00
❑6, Oct 1987, b&w; 2: Cheshire Cat; 2: White Rabbit; O: Chicken; O: Feuerbach family; Councilman Stinz story ... 2.00
❑7, Dec 1987, b&w; Last installment Alice; Young Stinz story ... 2.00
❑8, Feb 1988, b&w; 1: Prince Iv ... 2.00
❑9, Apr 1988, b&w; Young Stinz story... 2.00
❑10, Jun 1988, b&w; Young Stinz story 2.00
❑11, Aug 1988, b&w; Young Stinz story 2.00
❑12, Oct 1988, b&w; Councilman Stinz story ... 2.00
❑13, Dec 1988, b&w; Councilman Stinz story ... 2.00
❑14, Feb 1989, b&w; Cover reads "The Ninjery" ... 2.00

Dreaming
DC / Vertigo

❑1, Jun 1996 ... 3.00
❑2, Jul 1996 ... 2.50
❑3, Aug 1996 ... 2.50
❑4, Sep 1996 ... 2.50
❑5, Oct 1996; Photo cover; Destiny cameo 2.50
❑6, Nov 1996 ... 2.50
❑7, Dec 1996 ... 2.50
❑8, Jan 1997; self-contained story; cover says Nov 96, indicia says Jan 97 ... 2.50
❑9, Feb 1997 ... 2.50
❑10, Mar 1997 ... 2.50
❑11, Apr 1997 ... 2.50
❑12, May 1997 ... 2.50
❑13, Jun 1997 ... 2.50
❑14, Jul 1997 ... 2.50
❑15, Aug 1997 ... 2.50
❑16, Sep 1997 ... 2.50
❑17, Oct 1997 ... 2.50
❑18, Nov 1997 ... 2.50
❑19, Dec 1997 ... 2.50
❑20, Jan 1998 ... 2.50
❑21, Feb 1998 ... 2.50
❑22, Mar 1998 ... 2.50
❑23, Apr 1998 ... 2.50
❑24, May 1998 ... 2.50
❑25, Jun 1998 ... 2.50
❑26, Jul 1998 ... 2.50
❑27, Aug 1998 ... 2.50
❑28, Sep 1998; House of Mystery burns down ... 2.50
❑29, Oct 1998 ... 2.50
❑30, Nov 1998; Many Mansions: Temporary OverFlow ... 2.50
❑31, Dec 1998; Anthology; Many Mansions: November Eve ... 2.50
❑32, Jan 1999; London Pride ... 2.50
❑33, Feb 1999 ... 2.50
❑34, Mar 1999; Many Mansions: Ruin... 2.50
❑35, Apr 1999 ... 2.50
❑36, May 1999 ... 2.50
❑37, Jun 1999 ... 2.50
❑38, Jul 1999 ... 2.50
❑39, Aug 1999 ... 2.50
❑40, Sep 1999 ... 2.50
❑41, Oct 1999 ... 2.50
❑42, Nov 1999 ... 2.50
❑43, Dec 1999 ... 2.50
❑44, Jan 2000 ... 2.50
❑45, Feb 2000 ... 2.50
❑46, Mar 2000 ... 2.50
❑47, Apr 2000 ... 2.50
❑48, May 2000 ... 2.50
❑49, Jun 2000 ... 2.50

Donna Matrix

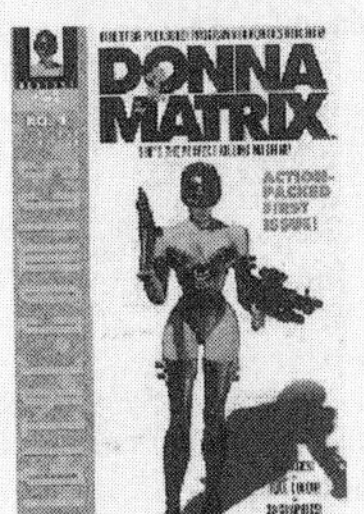

Only issue of computer-generated series
©Reactor

Doom

Latverian tyrant takes over Counter-Earth
©Marvel

Doom Patrol (1st Series)

Continues from My Greatest Adventure
©DC

Doom Patrol (2nd Series)

Revived team takes strange twist
©DC

Doomsday + 1 (Charlton)

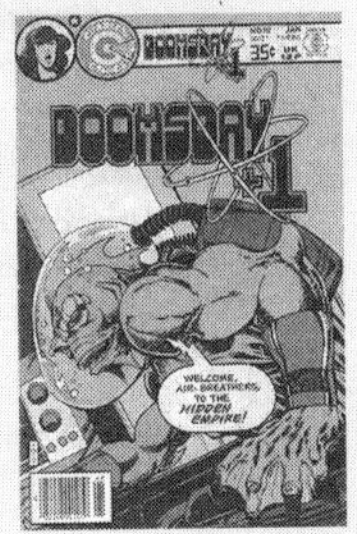

Early John Byrne work appears
©Charlton

N-MINT

❑50, Jul 2000 ... 2.50
❑51, Aug 2000 ... 2.50
❑52, Sep 2000 ... 2.50
❑53, Oct 2000 ... 2.50
❑54, Nov 2000 ... 2.50
❑55, Dec 2000 ... 2.50
❑56, Jan 2001 ... 2.50
❑57, Feb 2001 ... 2.50
❑58, Mar 2001 ... 2.50
❑59, Apr 2001 ... 2.50
❑60, May 2001 ... 2.50
❑Special 1, Jul 1998; wraparound cover 5.95

Dreaming
Tokyopop

❑1, Dec 2005 ... 9.99

Dreamland Chronicles
Astonish

❑1/Kunkel, Mar 2004 ... 3.50
❑1/Sava, Mar 2004 ... 3.50
❑1/Wieringo, Mar 2004 ... 3.50
❑1/Yeagle, Mar 2004 ... 3.50
❑2, Sep 2005; Published by Alias Comics 4.50
❑3, Oct 2005 ... 4.50

Dream Police
Marvel / Icon

❑1, Jul 2005 ... 3.99

Dream-Quest of Unknown Kadath
Mock Man

❑1 ... 2.95
❑1/2nd, Mar 1998 ... 2.95
❑2 ... 2.95
❑3 ... 2.95
❑4 ... 2.95
❑5, Final Issue ... 2.95

Dreams Cannot Die!
Mark's Giant Economy Size

❑1, Jun 1996; Trade Paperback; Collects Radical Dreamer Vol. 1 #0-4, Vol. 2 #1-6, and tug & Buster #2 ... 17.95

Dreams 'n' Schemes of Col. Kilgore
Special Studio

❑1, Mar 1991, b&w ... 2.50
❑2, May 1991, b&w ... 2.50

Dreams of a Dog
Rip Off

❑1, May 1990, b&w ... 2.00
❑2, Jun 1992, b&w ... 2.50

Dreams of Everyman
Rip Off

❑1, Jun 1992; NN ... 2.50

Dreams of the Darkchylde
Darkchylde

❑1, Oct 2000 ... 3.50
❑1/A, Oct 2000, variant cover ... 3.50
❑1/B, Oct 2000, chromium cover ... 10.00
❑1/C, Oct 2000, Dynamic Forces cover .. 6.00
❑1/D, Oct 2000, DFE blue foil cover ... 10.00
❑1/E, Oct 2000, DFE chrome cover ... 14.95
❑1/F, Oct 2000, Tower Records cover ... 5.00
❑2, Nov 2000 ... 3.00
❑3, Dec 2000 ... 3.00
❑4, Mar 2001 ... 2.95

N-MINT

❑5, ca. 2001 ... 2.95
❑6, Sep 2001 ... 2.95

Dream Team
Malibu

❑1, Jul 1995; Malibu/Marvel Pin-ups ... 4.95

Dreamtime
Blind Bat

❑1, May 1995, b&w ... 2.50
❑2, b&w; no indicia ... 2.50

Dreamwalker
Dreamwalker

❑1, ca. 1996, b&w ... 2.95
❑2, ca. 1996, b&w ... 2.95
❑3, ca. 1996, b&w ... 2.95
❑4, ca. 1996, b&w ... 2.95
❑5, ca. 1996, b&w ... 2.95

Dreamwalker
Caliber / Tapestry

❑1, Dec 1996, b&w ... 2.95
❑2, Feb 1997, b&w ... 2.95
❑3 1997, b&w ... 2.95
❑4, Jul 1997, b&w ... 2.95
❑5, Sep 1997, b&w ... 2.95
❑6, Jul 1998, b&w ... 2.95

Dreamwalker
Avatar

❑0, Nov 1998, b&w; One-shot; Adult ... 3.00

Dreamwalker
Marvel

❑1 ... 6.95

Dreamwalker: Autumn Leaves
Avatar

❑1, Sep 1999, b&w; Adult ... 3.00
❑2, Oct 1999, b&w; Adult ... 3.00

Dreamwalker: Carousel
Avatar

❑1, Mar 1999, b&w; Adult ... 3.00
❑2, Apr 1999, b&w; Adult ... 3.00

Dreamwalker: Summer Rain
Avatar

❑1, Jul 1999, b&w; One-shot; Adult ... 3.00

Dream Weaver
Robert Lankford

❑1, Aug 1987 ... 1.95

Dream Weavers
Golden Realm Unlimited

❑1 ... 1.50
❑2 ... 1.50

Dream Wolves
Dramenon

❑1, b&w ... 3.00
❑2, Dec 1994, b&w; cardstock cover ... 3.00
❑3, Jan 1995, b&w; cardstock cover ... 3.00
❑4, Feb 1995, b&w ... 3.00

Dream Wolves Swimsuit Bizarre
Gothic

❑0, Dec 1995 ... 3.00

Dredd By Bisley
Fleetway-Quality

❑1 ... 5.95

N-MINT

Dredd Rules!
Fleetway-Quality

❑1 ... 3.50
❑2 ... 3.00
❑3 ... 3.00
❑4 ... 3.00
❑5 ... 3.00
❑6 ... 2.95
❑7 ... 2.95
❑8 ... 2.95
❑9 ... 2.95
❑10 ... 2.95
❑11 ... 2.95
❑12 ... 2.95
❑13 ... 2.95
❑14 V: Santa ... 2.95
❑15 ... 2.95
❑16 ... 2.95
❑17 ... 2.95
❑18 ... 2.95
❑19 ... 2.95
❑20 ... 2.95

Drifter
Brainstorm

❑1, b&w ... 2.95

Drifters
Infinity

❑1, Oct 1986 ... 2.00

Drifters
Cornerstone

❑1, b&w ... 2.00

Drive-In
Avatar

❑1, Nov 2003 ... 3.50
❑1/A, Nov 2003; Wrap Cover ... 3.95
❑2, Dec 2003 ... 3.50
❑3, Jan 2004 ... 3.95
❑3/A, Jan 2004; Wrap Cover ... 3.50
❑4, Mar 2004 ... 3.50

Droids
Marvel / Star

❑1, Apr 1986 ... 3.00
❑2, Jun 1986 JR (a) ... 2.00
❑3, Aug 1986 ... 2.00
❑4, Oct 1986 ... 2.00
❑5, Dec 1986 ... 2.00
❑6, Feb 1987; A New Hope told from droids' p.o.v ... 2.00
❑7, Apr 1987; A New Hope told from droids' p.o.v ... 2.00
❑8, Jun 1987; A New Hope told from droids' p.o.v ... 2.00

Drool Magazine
Co. & Sons

❑1 ... 3.00

Droopy
Dark Horse

❑1, Oct 1995; Screwball Squirrel back-up 2.50
❑2, Nov 1995; Wolf and Red back-up ... 2.50
❑3, Dec 1995; Screwball Squirrel back-up 2.50

Dropsie Avenue: The Neighborhood
Kitchen Sink

❑1, Jun 1995, b&w ... 15.95

Druid
Marvel

❑1, May 1995; O: Doctor Druid ... 2.50
❑2, Jun 1995 ... 1.95
❑3, Jul 1995 ... 1.95
❑4, Aug 1995; Final Issue ... 1.95

Drunken Fist
Jademan

❑1, Aug 1988 ... 1.95
❑2, Sep 1988 ... 1.95
❑3, Oct 1988 ... 1.95
❑4, Nov 1988 ... 1.95
❑5, Dec 1988 ... 1.95
❑6, Jan 1989 ... 1.95
❑7, Feb 1989 ... 1.95
❑8, Mar 1989 ... 1.95
❑9, Apr 1989 ... 1.95
❑10, May 1989 ... 1.95
❑11, Jun 1989 ... 1.95
❑12, Jul 1989 ... 1.95
❑13, Aug 1989 ... 1.95
❑14, Sep 1989 ... 1.95
❑15, Oct 1989 ... 1.95
❑16, Nov 1989 ... 1.95
❑17, Dec 1989 ... 1.95
❑18, Jan 1990 ... 1.95
❑19, Feb 1990 ... 1.95
❑20, Mar 1990 ... 1.95
❑21, Apr 1990 ... 1.95
❑22, May 1990 ... 1.95
❑23, Jun 1990 ... 1.95
❑24, Jul 1990 ... 1.95
❑25, Aug 1990 ... 1.95
❑26, Sep 1990 ... 1.95
❑27, Oct 1990 ... 1.95
❑28, Nov 1990 ... 1.95
❑29, Dec 1990 ... 1.95
❑30, Jan 1991 ... 1.95
❑31, Feb 1991 ... 1.95
❑32, Mar 1991 ... 1.95
❑33, Apr 1991 ... 1.95
❑34, May 1991 ... 1.95
❑35, Jun 1991 ... 1.95
❑36, Jul 1991 ... 1.95
❑37, Aug 1991 ... 1.95
❑38, Sep 1991 ... 1.95
❑39, Oct 1991 ... 1.95
❑40, Nov 1991 ... 1.95
❑41, Dec 1991 ... 1.95
❑42, Jan 1992 ... 1.95
❑43, Feb 1992 ... 1.95
❑44, Mar 1992 ... 1.95
❑45, Apr 1992 ... 1.95
❑46, May 1992 ... 1.95
❑47, Jun 1992 ... 1.95
❑48, Jul 1992 ... 1.95
❑49, Aug 1992 ... 1.95
❑50, Sep 1992 ... 1.95
❑51, Oct 1992 ... 1.95
❑52, Nov 1992 ... 1.95
❑53, Dec 1992 ... 1.95
❑54, Jan 1993; Final issue ... 1.95

Dry Rot
Zolton

❑1, b&w ... 2.95

Duck and Cover
Cat-Head

❑1, b&w ... 2.00
❑2, b&w ... 2.00

Duckbots
Blackthorne

❑1, Feb 1987 ... 2.00
❑2 ... 2.00

Duckman
Dark Horse

❑1, Sep 1990, b&w; 1: Duckman ... 2.00
❑2, b&w ... 2.00
❑Special 1, Apr 1990, b&w; NN; One-shot 2.00

Duckman
Topps

❑1, Nov 1994; Includes coupon for trading card ... 2.50
❑2, Dec 1994; 1: King Chicken; V: King Chicken ... 2.50
❑3, Mar 1995 ... 2.50
❑4, Mar 1995 ... 2.50
❑5, May 1995 ... 2.50
❑6 ... 2.50

Duckman: The Mob Frog Saga
Topps

❑1, Nov 1994; Includes coupon for Duckman trading card ... 2.50
❑2, Dec 1994 ... 2.50
❑3, Feb 1995 ... 2.50

DuckTales
Gladstone

❑1, Oct 1988 CB (w); CB (a) ... 2.00
❑2, Nov 1988 ... 1.50
❑3, Jan 1989 ... 1.50
❑4, Feb 1989 ... 1.50
❑5, Apr 1989 ... 1.50
❑6, May 1989 ... 1.50
❑7, Jul 1989 ... 1.50
❑8, Aug 1989 ... 1.50
❑9, Oct 1989 CB (w); CB (a) ... 1.50
❑10, Nov 1989 CB (a) ... 1.50
❑11, Jan 1990; CB (w); CB (a); Reprints stories from Four Color #1047 [Gyro Gearloose] and Uncle Scrooge #37 ... 1.50
❑12, Mar 1990; CB (w); CB (a); "Mythtic Mystery" reprinted from US #34 ... 1.50
❑13, May 1990; CB (w); CB (a); Reprints stories from Four Color #1047 and #1184 [Gyro Gearloose] and Uncle Scrooge #39 ... 1.50

DuckTales
Disney

❑1, Jun 1990 ... 2.00
❑2, Jul 1990 ... 1.50
❑3, Aug 1990; V: Magica de Spell ... 1.50
❑4, Sep 1990 ... 1.50
❑5, Oct 1990 ... 1.50
❑6, Nov 1990 ... 1.50
❑7, Dec 1990 ... 1.50
❑8, Jan 1991 ... 1.50
❑9, Feb 1991 ... 1.50
❑10, Mar 1991 ... 1.50
❑11, Apr 1991 ... 1.50
❑12, May 1991 ... 1.50
❑13, Jun 1991 ... 1.50
❑14, Jul 1991 ... 1.50
❑15, Aug 1991 ... 1.50
❑16, Sep 1991 ... 1.50
❑17, Oct 1991 ... 1.50
❑18, Nov 1991 ... 1.50

Ducktales: The Movie
Disney

❑1; adaptation ... 5.95

Dudley Do-Right
Charlton

❑1, Aug 1970 ... 45.00
❑2, Oct 1970 ... 18.00
❑3, Dec 1970 ... 12.00
❑4, Feb 1971 ... 10.00
❑5, Apr 1971 ... 10.00
❑6, Jun 1971 ... 10.00
❑7, Aug 1971 ... 10.00

Duel
Antarctic

❑0, ca. 2005 ... 2.99
❑1, ca. 2005 ... 2.99

Duel Masters
Dreamwave

❑1, Nov 2003; Polybagged with trading card; Fire Cover (Yellow w/ Orange Fuzzy Creatures) ... 2.95
❑1/Dynamic, Nov 2003; Holofoil Cover ... 5.95
❑1/A, Dec 2003; Polybagged with trading card; Face in background (green hair), monster-like figures in foreground ... 2.95
❑1/B, Nov 2003, no holo-foil on cover; packaged with cards ... 5.95
❑2, Dec 2003 ... 2.95
❑3, Jan 2004 ... 2.95
❑3/2nd, Mar 2004 ... 2.95
❑4, Apr 2004 ... 2.95
❑5, May 2004 ... 3.95
❑6, Jun 2004 ... 2.95
❑7, Aug 2004 ... 2.95
❑8, Sep 2004 ... 2.95

Dumb-Ass Express
McMann & Tate

❑1; slightly oversized ... 2.95

Dumm $2099
Parody

❑1; Cover forms triptych with Rummage $2099, Pummeler $2099 ... 2.95

Dune
Marvel

❑1, Apr 1985; BSz (a); Movie adaptation 1.50
❑2, May 1985; BSz (a); Movie adaptation 1.50
❑3, Jun 1985; BSz (a); Movie adaptation 1.50

Dung Boys
Kitchen Sink

❑1, Apr 1996, b&w; Adult ... 2.95
❑2, May 1996; nude cover with black bars 2.95
❑3, Jun 1996; Final Issue; Adult ... 2.95

Dungeon
NBM

❑1, ca. 2002, Several characters in profile on cover ... 2.95

Dungeoneers
Silverwolf

❑1 ... 1.50
❑2, Oct 1986 ... 1.50
❑3, Nov 1986 ... 1.50
❑4 ... 1.50

Dungeons & Dragons: Where Shadows Fall
Kenzer and Company

❑1, Aug 2003 ... 3.50
❑2, Oct 2003 ... 3.50
❑3, Dec 2003 ... 3.50
❑4, Feb 2004 ... 3.50
❑5, Jul 2004 ... 3.50

Duplex Planet Illustrated
Fantagraphics

❑1, Jan 1993, b&w; Includes record ... 2.95
❑2 1993 ... 2.50
❑3 1993 ... 2.50
❑4 1993 ... 2.50
❑5 1993 ... 2.95
❑6 1994 ... 2.95
❑7 1994, b&w ... 2.50
❑8, May 1994, b&w ... 2.50
❑9, Jul 1994, b&w ... 2.50
❑10, Sep 1994, b&w ... 2.50
❑11, Dec 1994 ... 2.50
❑12 1995 ... 2.50
❑13 1995 ... 2.50
❑14 1995 ... 2.50
❑15, Apr 1996, b&w ... 4.95

Durango Kid
AC

❑1; some color ... 2.50
❑2, b&w ... 2.75
❑3 ... 4.95

Dusk
Deadwood

❑1, b&w; cardstock cover ... 3.00

Dusty Star
Image

❑0, Apr 1997, b&w; collects stories from Negative Burn #28 and #37 ... 2.95
❑2, Sep 2006 ... 3.50
❑1, Jun 1997, b&w ... 2.95

DV8
DC / Wildstorm

❑0, Dec 1998 ... 3.00
❑½, Jan 1997, Wizard 1/2 Promotional edition; Wine bottle in foreground; Mail-away comic from promotion in Wizard #68; Includes certificate of authenticity ... 3.00
❑½/A, Jan 1997, Wizard 1/2 Promotional edition; variant cover ... 3.00
❑½/Gold, Jan 1997, Wizard 1/2 "Authentic Gold" promotional edition; Wizard 1/2 Authentic Gold promotional edition; Signed by Warren Ellis ... 3.00
❑½/Platinum, Jan 1997, Wizard 1/2 Platinum promotional edition; Wizard promotional item;platinum version ... 3.00
❑1/A, Aug 1996, cover says Sep, indicia says Aug ... 3.00

Doom's IV

Series optioned for film in mid-1990s

©Image

Dork

Evan Dorkin's humor anthology

©Slave Labor

Dork Tower

Gamer and cartoonist laughs with gamers

©Dork Storm

Double Dragon

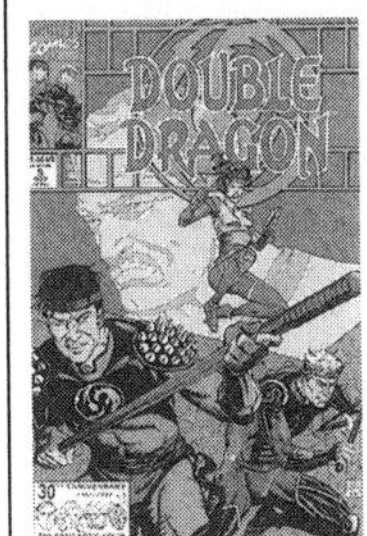

Fighting videogame features two brothers

©Marvel

D.P.7

New Universe title featuring EMT

©Marvel

N-MINT

❑1/B, Aug 1996, cover says Sep, indicia says Aug 3.00
❑1/C, Aug 1996, cover says Sep, indicia says Aug 3.00
❑1/D, Aug 1996, cover says Sep, indicia says Aug 3.00
❑1/E, Aug 1996, cover says Sep, indicia says Aug 3.00
❑1/F, Aug 1996, cover says Sep, indicia says Aug 3.00
❑1/G, Aug 1996, cover says Sep, indicia says Aug 3.00
❑1/H, Aug 1996, cover says Sep, indicia says Aug 3.00
❑2, Nov 1996 ..... 2.50
❑3, Dec 1996 ..... 2.50
❑4, Jan 1997 ..... 2.50
❑5, Feb 1997 ..... 2.50
❑6, Mar 1997 ..... 2.50
❑7, Apr 1997, cover says May, indicia says Apr 2.50
❑8, May 1997, cover says Jun, indicia says May 2.50
❑9, Jun 1997 ..... 2.50
❑10, Jul 1997 ..... 2.50
❑11, Sep 1997 ..... 2.50
❑12, Oct 1997 ..... 2.50
❑13, Nov 1997 ..... 2.50
❑14/A, Dec 1997, Has woman on cover 2.50
❑14/B, Dec 1997, Whole group on cover; white background 2.50
❑14/C, Dec 1997, Voyager pack with preview of Danger Girl 5.00
❑15, Jan 1998 ..... 2.50
❑16, Feb 1998 ..... 2.50
❑17, Apr 1998 ..... 2.50
❑18, May 1998 ..... 2.50
❑19, Jun 1998 ..... 2.50
❑20, Jul 1998 ..... 2.50
❑21, Aug 1998 ..... 2.50
❑22, Sep 1998 ..... 2.50
❑22/A, Sep 1998, alternate cover (white background) 2.50
❑23, Oct 1998 ..... 2.50
❑24, Nov 1998 ..... 2.50
❑25, Dec 1998 ..... 2.50
❑26, May 1999 ..... 2.50
❑27, Jun 1999 ..... 2.50
❑28, Jul 1999 ..... 2.50
❑29, Aug 1999 ..... 2.50
❑30, Sep 1999 ..... 2.50
❑31, Oct 1999 ..... 2.50
❑32, Nov 1999 ..... 2.50
❑Ann 1, Jan 1998 ..... 2.95
❑Ann 1999, Mar 1999, continued from Gen13 Ann 1999; wraparound cover 3.50

DV8 Rave
Image

❑1, Jul 1996 ..... 2.00

DV8 vs. Black Ops
Image

❑1, Oct 1997 ..... 2.50
❑2, Nov 1997 ..... 2.50
❑3, Dec 1997 ..... 2.50

N-MINT

Dyke's Delight
Fanny

❑1 ..... 2.95
❑2 ..... 2.95

Dylan Dog
Dark Horse

❑1, Mar 1999 ..... 4.95
❑2, Apr 1999 ..... 4.95
❑3, May 1999 ..... 4.95
❑4, Jun 1999 ..... 4.95
❑5, Jul 1999 ..... 4.95
❑6, Aug 1999 ..... 4.95

Dynamic Classics
DC

❑1, Sep 1978 ..... 4.00

Dynamo
Tower

❑1, Aug 1966 WW, DA (a) 35.00
❑2, Oct 1966 WW (c); GT, WW, DA (a) 25.00
❑3, Mar 1967 WW (c); GT, WW, DA (a) 25.00
❑4, Jun 1967 WW (a) 40.00

Dynamo Joe
First

❑1, May 1986 ..... 1.50
❑2, Jun 1986 ..... 1.25
❑3, Jul 1986 ..... 1.25
❑4, Feb 1987 ..... 1.25
❑5, Mar 1987 ..... 1.25
❑6, Apr 1987 ..... 1.25
❑7, May 1987 ..... 1.25
❑8, Jun 1987 ..... 1.25
❑9, Jul 1987 ..... 1.25
❑10, Aug 1987 ..... 1.25
❑11, Sep 1987 ..... 1.25
❑12, Oct 1987 ..... 1.75
❑13, Nov 1987 ..... 1.75
❑14, Dec 1987 ..... 1.75
❑15, Jan 1988; Final issue 1.75
❑Special 1, Jan 1987 ..... 1.25

Dynomutt
Marvel

❑1, Nov 1977, Scooby Doo 10.00
❑2, Jan 1978, Scooby Doo 5.00
❑3, Mar 1978, Scooby Doo 3.00
❑4, May 1978, Scooby Doo 3.00
❑5, Jul 1978, Scooby Doo 3.00
❑6, Sep 1978, Scooby Doo 3.00

Dystopik Snomen
Slave Labor

❑1, Oct 1994; was college newspaper strip 4.95

Dystopik Snomen
Slave Labor

❑1, Sep 1995 ..... 1.50
❑2, Dec 1995 ..... 1.75

Eagle
Crystal

❑1, Sep 1986; Matt Wagner Pin-Up 1.50
❑1/Ltd., Sep 1986; Limited edition of 2500 ..... 1.50
❑2, Dec 1986; Tim Truman Pin-Up 1.50
❑3, Feb 1987; b&w 1.50
❑4, Apr 1987; b&w 1.50
❑5, May 1987; Erik Larsen Pin-Up 1.50

N-MINT

❑6, Jun 1987; Adam Hughes pin-up (his first major comics work) 1.50
❑7, Jul 1987; b&w 1.50
❑8, Aug 1987; b&w 1.50
❑9, Sep 1987; b&w 1.50
❑10, Oct 1987; Adam Hughes credit Background Pencils 1.50
❑11, Nov 1987; Adam Hughes credit Background Pencils 1.50
❑12, Dec 1987; 48 Page Origin Issue, Pin-Ups Matt Wagner, Ron Lim 1.50
❑13, Jan 1988; b&w 1.50
❑14, Feb 1988; b&w 1.50
❑15, Mar 1988; b&w 1.50
❑16, May 1988; b&w 1.50
❑17, Aug 1988, b&w; Publisher changes to Apple Comics 1.95
❑18, Sep 1988, b&w 1.95
❑19, Oct 1988, b&w 1.95
❑20, Nov 1988, b&w; Death's-Head Back-Up Story: Toccata 1.95
❑21, Dec 1989, b&w; Death's-Head Back-Up Story 1.95
❑22, Feb 1989, b&w; Due to a Marvel Comics Cease and Desist Order Death's-Head becomes Death's Dark Angel; Death's Dark Angel Back-Up Story 1.95
❑23 1989 ..... 2.25

Eagle
Comic Zone

❑1, Jan 1992, b&w; Reprints story from Eagle (Crystal) issues 20,21,22, & 23 with new material 2.75
❑2, Feb 1992, b&w; Reprints story from Eagle (Crystal) issues 20,21,22, & 23 with new material 2.75
❑3, Apr 1992, b&w; Reprints story from Eagle (Crystal) issues 20,21,22, & 23 with new material, Adam Hughes Cover Art 2.75

Eagles Dare
Aager

❑1 ..... 1.95
❑2, Sep 1994 ..... 1.95

Eagle: The Dark Mirror Saga
Comic Zone

❑1, Jan 1992 ..... 2.75
❑2 ..... 2.75
❑3 ..... 2.75

Early Days of the Southern Knights
Comics Interview

❑1 1986 ..... 4.95
❑1/2nd; 2nd printing 4.95
❑2, Feb 1987; Reprints Southern Knights #3-5 plus new story 4.95
❑3, Jul 1987; Reprints Southern Knights #6-7 plus new story 4.95
❑4 1987; Reprints Southern Knights #8 ..... 4.95
❑5 1988 ..... 5.95
❑6, Nov 1988 ..... 6.50
❑7, Jan 1989 ..... 6.95
❑8, Mar 1989 ..... 6.95

Earth C.O.R.E.
Independent

❑1 ..... 1.95

Other grades: Multiply price above by 5/6 for VF/NM • 2/3 for VERY FINE • 1/3 for FINE • 1/5 for VERY GOOD • 1/8 for GOOD

Earth 4
Continuity

❑1, Dec 1993; Previous series was spelled "Urth 4" 2.50
❑2, Dec 1993 .... 2.50
❑3, Dec 1993 .... 2.50
❑4, Jan 1994 .... 2.50

Earth 4 Deathwatch 2000
Continuity

❑0, Apr 1993; Trading Cards 2.50
❑1, Apr 1993; trading cards; indicia says #0, a misprint 2.50
❑2, May 1993; trading card 2.50
❑3, Aug 1993; trading card; Deathwatch 2000 dropped from indicia 2.50

Earthlore
Eternity

❑1 .... 2.00
❑2 .... 2.00

Earthworm Jim
Marvel

❑1, Dec 1995; based on video game 2.25
❑2, Jan 1996 .... 2.25
❑3, Feb 1996 .... 2.25
❑4, Mar 1996 .... 2.25

Earth X
Marvel

❑0, Mar 1999; ARo (c); ARo (w); ARo (a); Red "X" cover 4.00
❑0/A, Mar 1999; ARo (c); ARo (w); ARo (a); A: X-51. A: Watcher. Covers of series form giant picture 5.00
❑0/B, Mar 1999; ARo (c); ARo (w); ARo (a); A: X-51. A: Watcher. Covers of series form giant picture 4.00
❑0/C, Mar 1999; ARo (c); ARo (w); ARo (a); A: X-51. A: Watcher. DFE alternate cover 5.00
❑1, Apr 1999; ARo (c); ARo (w); ARo (a); A: Inhumans. A: Hydra. Covers of series form giant picture 3.00
❑1/A, Apr 1999; ARo (c); ARo (w); ARo (a); A: Inhumans. A: Hydra. Covers of series form giant picture 5.00
❑1/B, Apr 1999; ARo (w); A: Inhumans. A: Hydra. DFE alternate cover 29.99
❑1/C, Apr 1999; ARo (w); A: Inhumans. A: Hydra. DFE alternate cover 69.99
❑2, May 1999 ARo (c); ARo (w); ARo (a) 2.99
❑3, Jun 1999 ARo (c); ARo (w); ARo (a) 2.99
❑4, Jul 1999 ARo (c); ARo (w); ARo (a). 2.99
❑5, Aug 1999 ARo (c); ARo (w); ARo (a) 2.99
❑6, Sep 1999 ARo (c); ARo (w); ARo (a) 2.99
❑7, Oct 1999 ARo (c); ARo (w); ARo (a) 2.99
❑8, Nov 1999 ARo (c); ARo (w); ARo (a) 2.99
❑9, Dec 1999 ARo (c); ARo (w); ARo (a) 2.99
❑10, Jan 2000 ARo (c); ARo (w); ARo (a) 2.99
❑11, Mar 2000 ARo (c); ARo (w); ARo (a) 2.99
❑12, Apr 2000 ARo (c); ARo (w); ARo (a) 2.99
❑13, Jun 2000; ARo (c); ARo (w); ARo (a); "X" issue 3.99

Earth X Sketchbook
Marvel

❑1, Mar 1999 .... 4.50

East Meets West
Innovation

❑1, Apr 1990 .... 2.50

Easy Way
Idea & Design Works

❑1, ca. 2005 .... 3.99
❑2, May 2005 .... 3.99
❑3, Jun 2005 .... 3.99
❑4, Sep 2005; Embossed bullet holes in cover 3.99

Eating Raoul
Kim Deitch

❑1, ca. 1982, b&w; Adapts movie 2.00

Eat-Man
Viz

❑1, Aug 1997, b&w 2.95
❑2, Sep 1997, b&w 2.95
❑3, Oct 1997, b&w 2.95
❑4, Nov 1997, b&w 2.95
❑5, Dec 1997, b&w 2.95
❑6, Jan 1997, b&w 2.95

Eat-Man Second Course
Viz

❑1, Feb 1998, b&w 2.95
❑2, Mar 1998, b&w 3.50
❑3, Apr 1998, b&w 3.50
❑4, May 1998, b&w 3.25
❑5, b&w 2.95

Eberron: Eye of the Wolf
Devil's Due

❑1, Aug 2006 .... 4.95
❑1/Special, Aug 2006 .... 8.95

Eb'nn
Now

❑3, Jun 1986 .... 1.50
❑4, Aug 1986 .... 1.50
❑5, Nov 1986 .... 1.50
❑6, Jan 1987 .... 1.50

Eb'nn the Raven
Crowquill

❑1 .... 3.00
❑2 .... 3.00

Ebony Warrior
Africa Rising

❑1, Apr 1993 .... 1.95

E.C. Classic Reprints
East Coast Comix

❑1, May 1973; AF (w); GE, JO, GI (a); Reprints Crypt of Terror #1 (a series meant to have been launched when EC ceased publishing horror) 4.00
❑2; AF (w); AW, JO, WW, JKa (a); Reprints Weird Science #15 .... 3.00
❑3; Reprints Shock SuspenStories #12 . 3.00
❑4; Reprints Haunt of Fear #12 .... 3.00
❑5; Reprints Weird Fantasy #13 .... 3.00
❑6; AF (w); GE, BK (a); Reprints Crime SuspenStories #25 .... 3.00
❑7; Reprints Vault of Horror #26 .... 3.00
❑8; Reprints Shock SuspenStories #6 ... 3.00
❑9; Reprints Two-Fisted Tales #34 .... 3.00
❑10; Reprints Haunt of Fear #23 .... 3.00
❑11; Reprints Weird Science #12 .... 3.00
❑12, ca. 1976; Reprints Shock SuspenStories #2 .... 3.00

EC Classics
Cochran

❑1 .... 5.00
❑2 .... 5.00
❑3 .... 5.00
❑4 .... 5.00
❑5; AW (a); Reprints from Weird Fantasy #14, 15, 16, 17 .... 5.00
❑6 .... 5.00

Echo
Image

❑0, Jul 2000; Boy with basketball on cover 2.50
❑1, Mar 2000 .... 2.95
❑2, Apr 2000 .... 2.50
❑3, May 2000 .... 2.50
❑4, Jun 2000 .... 2.50
❑5, Sep 2000 .... 2.50

Echo of Futurepast
Continuity

❑1, May 1984 .... 2.95
❑2 1984 .... 2.95
❑3, Nov 1984; Nudity 2.95
❑4, Feb 1985 .... 2.95
❑5, Apr 1985 .... 2.95
❑6, Jul 1985 .... 2.95
❑7, Aug 1985 .... 2.95
❑8, Dec 1985 .... 2.95
❑9, Jan 1986 .... 2.95

Eclipse Graphic Album Series
Eclipse

❑1, Oct 1978; PG (a); Sabre 7.00
❑1/2nd, Feb 1979; PG (a); Sabre 6.00
❑1/3rd; Sabre: 10th anniversary; PG (a); Sabre 5.95
❑2, Nov 1979; CR (w); CR (a); Night Music 5.00
❑3, May 1980; MR (a); Detectives, Inc... 6.95
❑4; GC (a); Stewart the Rat 5.95
❑5; JSn (w); JSn (a); The Price 7.00
❑6; MR (a); I am Coyote 6.00
❑7; DSt (c); DSt (w); DSt (a); The Rocketeer 7.95
❑7/HC; Hardcover edition; DSt (w); DSt (a); Hardcover; The Rocketeer 19.95
❑7/2nd; DSt (c); DSt (w); DSt (a); The Rocketeer 8.00
❑7/3rd; DSt (w); DSt (a); The Rocketeer 9.00
❑8; Zorro 6.00
❑9, Feb 1987; Somerset Holmes; The Sacred and the Profane 14.00
❑10, Mar 1987; BA (a); Sacred & Profane; Somerset Holmes 14.00
❑10/HC, Mar 1987; Hardcover edition; BA (a); Hardcover; Somerset Holmes 24.95
❑11 1987; Floyd Farland 25.00
❑12, Jul 1987; Silverheels 7.95
❑12/HC, Jul 1987, b&w; Hardcover edition; Silverheels 14.95
❑12/Ltd., Jul 1987; Signed hardcover; Silverheels 24.95
❑13; The Sisterhood of Steel 9.00
❑14; Samurai, Son of Death 5.00
❑15; DSt (c);Twisted Tales 3.95
❑16; Air Fighters Classics #1 .... 4.50
❑17; PG (a); Valkyrie: Prisoner of the Past 6.95
❑18; Air Fighters Classics #2 .... 4.50
❑19; Scout: Four Monsters; Collects Scout #1-7 .... 14.95
❑20; Air Fighters Classics #3 .... 4.50
❑21; XYR "choose your own adventure" game 3.95
❑22; Alien Worlds 5.00
❑23; Air Fighters Classics #4 .... 4.50
❑24; Heartbreak Comics 5.00
❑25; ATh (w); ATh (a); Alex Toth's Zorro #1 9.00
❑26; ATh (w); ATh (a); Alex Toth's Zorro #2 9.00
❑27; She; Fast Fiction 6.00
❑28; AMo (w); DaG, BSz, TY (a); Brought to Light 8.95
❑29; JK (w); JK (a); Miracleman Book One 15.00
❑30; AMo (w); BSz, JK (a); Real Love: The Best of Simon & Kirby Romance Comics 9.00
❑30/HC, b&w; Hardcover edition; AMo (w); BSz (a) 30.00
❑31; Pigeons from Hell 7.00
❑31/Ltd.; Limited hardcover edition 30.00
❑32; HK, JK (w); HK, JK (a); Teenaged Dope Slaves & Reform School Girls... 9.95
❑33; Bogie 9.95
❑34; Air Fighters Classics #5 .... 3.95
❑35; Into the Shadow of the Sun; Rael .. 7.95
❑36; CR (a); Ariane & Bluebeard 4.95
❑37; Air Fighters Classics #6 .... 3.95
❑38; Doctor Watchstop 8.95
❑39; MGr (a); James Bond 007: Permission to Die 1 .... 4.95
❑40; MGr (a); James Bond 007: Permission to Die 2 .... 4.95
❑41; MGr (a); James Bond 007: Permission to Die 3 .... 4.95
❑42; MGr (a); James Bond 007: Licence to Kill 8.95
❑43; Tapping the Vein #1 .... 7.95
❑44; Hobbit #1 .... 5.95
❑45; Toadswart 10.95
❑46; Tapping the Vein #2 .... 7.95
❑47; Scout: Mount Fire 14.95
❑48; Moderne Man Comics 9.95
❑49; Tapping the Vein #3 .... 6.95
❑50; Miracleman Book Two 12.95
❑51; Tapping the Vein 4 .... 7.95
❑52; James Bond 007: Permission to Die #3 .... 4.95

Eclipse Magazine
Eclipse

❑1, May 1981, b&w; 1: Ms. Tree; Foozle 2.95
❑2, Jul 1981; 1: Coyote 2.95
❑3, Nov 1981; 1: Ragamuffins 2.95
❑4, Jan 1982 .... 2.95
❑5, Mar 1982 .... 2.95
❑6, Jul 1982 .... 2.95
❑7, Nov 1982; 1: Masked Man 2.95
❑8, Jan 1983 .... 2.95

Eclipse Monthly
Eclipse

❑1, Aug 1983 .... 2.00
❑2, Sep 1983 .... 2.00
❑3, Oct 1983 .... 2.00
❑4, Jan 1984 .... 1.50
❑5, Feb 1984 .... 1.50
❑6, Mar 1984 .... 1.50

Other grades: Multiply price above by 5/6 for VF/NM • 2/3 for VERY FINE • 1/3 for FINE • 1/5 for VERY GOOD • 1/8 for GOOD

Dragonball

Midget mystic quests for seven spheres

©Viz

Dragonball Z

Goku fights alien race for Dragonballs

©Viz

Dragonflight

Based on Anne McCaffrey fantasy series

©Eclipse

Dragonforce

Mercenaries in fantasy world join forces

©Aircel

Dragonheart

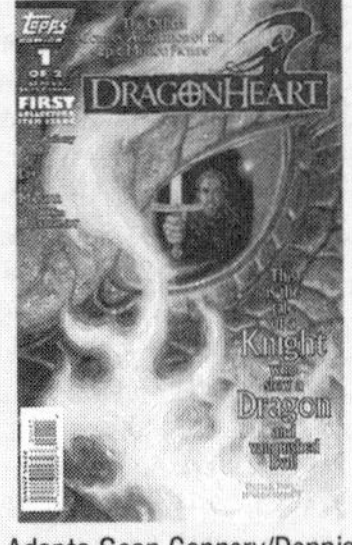

Adapts Sean Connery/Dennis Quaid film

©Topps

N-MINT

❑7, Apr 1984 .... 1.50
❑8, May 1984 .... 1.50
❑9, Jun 1984 .... 1.50
❑10, Jul 1984 .... 1.50

Eclipso
DC

❑1, Nov 1992 .... 2.00
❑2, Dec 1992 KG (w); KG (a) 1.75
❑3, Jan 1993 KG (w); KG (a) 1.75
❑4, Feb 1993 KG (w); KG, LMc (a) 1.50
❑5, Mar 1993 KG (w); KG, LMc (a) 1.50
❑6, Apr 1993 KG (w); KG, LMc (a) 1.25
❑7, May 1993 KG (w); KG (a) 1.25
❑8, Jun 1993 .... 1.25
❑9, Jul 1993 .... 1.25
❑10, Aug 1993; D: Heggra (Darkseid's mother); O: Desaad 1.25
❑11, Sep 1993 .... 1.25
❑12, Oct 1993 .... 1.25
❑13, Nov 1993; D: Creeper; D: Doctor Midnight; D: Commander Steel; D: Major Victory; D:Peacemaker; D: Manhunter III (later revealed alive); D: Wildcat II; D: Creeper (later revealed alive) 1.25
❑14, Dec 1993 .... 1.25
❑15, Jan 1994 .... 1.50
❑16, Feb 1994 .... 1.50
❑17, Mar 1994 .... 1.50
❑18, Apr 1994; A: Spectre. Final Issue ... 1.50
❑Ann 1, ca. 1993; 1: Prism; Bloodlines: Earthplague 2.50

Eclipso: The Darkness Within
DC

❑1, Jul 1992; KG (w); KG (a); Without plastic gem (newsstand version) 2.50
❑1/Direct ed., Jul 1992; Direct Market edition; KG (w); KG (a); plastic diamond glued to cover 3.00
❑2, Jul 1992; D: Starman Will Payton (later revealed alive) 2.50

Ectokid
Marvel

❑1, Sep 1993; JRo (w); Foil embossed cover 2.50
❑2, Oct 1993; JRo (w); O: Ectokid 1.75
❑3, Nov 1993 .... 1.75
❑4, Dec 1993 JRo (w) 1.75
❑5, Jan 1994 .... 1.75
❑6, Feb 1994 .... 1.75
❑7, Mar 1994 .... 1.75
❑8, Apr 1994 .... 1.75
❑9, May 1994; Final issue 1.95

Ectokid Unleashed!
Marvel

❑1, Oct 1994 .... 2.95

Ed
3CG Comics

❑1, Mar 1997, b&w 2.95

Eddy Current
Mad Dog

❑1, Jul 1987 .... 2.50
❑2, Sep 1987 .... 2.50
❑3, Oct 1987 .... 2.50
❑4, Nov 1987 .... 2.50
❑5, Jan 1988 .... 2.50

N-MINT

❑6, Feb 1988 .... 2.50
❑7, Apr 1988 A: Amazing Broccoli 2.50
❑8, Jun 1988 .... 2.50
❑9, Jul 1988 .... 2.50
❑10, Sep 1988 .... 2.50
❑11, Nov 1988 .... 2.50
❑12, Dec 1988 .... 2.50

Eden Descendants
Quester Entertainment

❑1, b&w; cardstock cover 3.95

Eden Matrix
Adhesive

❑1/A 2.95
❑1/B 2.95

Eden's Trail
Marvel

❑1, Jan 2003 .... 2.99
❑2, Feb 2003 .... 2.99
❑3, Mar 2003 .... 2.99
❑4, Apr 2003 .... 2.99
❑5, May 2003 .... 2.99

Edgar Allan Poe
Eternity

❑1 1988, b&w; Black Cat 1.95
❑2 1988, b&w; Pit & Pendulum 1.95
❑3, Dec 1988, b&w; Red Death 1.95
❑4 1989, b&w; Rue Morgue 1.95
❑5 1989, b&w; Tell-Tale Heart 1.95

Edge
Silverwolf

❑1, Feb 1987, b&w 1.50
❑2, Mar 1987, b&w 1.50

Edge
Greater Mercury

❑1, Jun 1989; Continues Silverwolf series 2.00
❑2, Jul 1989 .... 2.00
❑3, Aug 1989 .... 2.00
❑4, Sep 1989 .... 2.00
❑5, Apr 1990 .... 2.00
❑6, Jul 1990 .... 2.00
❑7, Sep 1990 .... 2.00
❑8, Oct 1990 .... 2.00
❑9, Dec 1990 .... 2.00
❑10, Mar 1991 .... 2.00
❑11, Mar 1991 .... 2.00

Edge
Malibu / Bravura

❑1, Jul 1994, GK (c); GK (a); 1: The Ultimates. 1: Intruder. 1: Edge. 1: Will Power. 1: Barricade. 1: Free Agent. 1: Winged Victory. 1: Phaseshifter; Includes coupon 2.50
❑1/Gold, Jul 1994, sendaway with gold ink on cover 3.00
❑2, Aug 1994, GK (c); GK (a); Includes coupon 2.50
❑3, Apr 1995, GK (a); story concludes in 'Books' The Last Heroes 2.95

Edge of Chaos
Pacific

❑1, Jul 1983 .... 1.00
❑2, Oct 1984, Adam Kubert's first major comics work 1.00
❑3, Jan 1983, Last issue 1.00

N-MINT

Eek! the Cat
Hamilton

❑1, Feb 1994; TV show 1.95
❑2, Mar 1994; TV show 1.95
❑3, Apr 1994; TV show 1.95

Eerie
I.W.

❑1 .... 24.00
❑2 .... 17.00

Eerie Queerie!
Tokyopop

❑1, Mar 2004; Graphic novel; Reads right to left; b&w 9.99
❑2 2004 .... 9.99
❑3, Jun 2004 .... 9.99
❑4, Sep 2004 .... 9.99

Eerie Tales
Super

❑12, Reprints(?) 15.00

Egon
Dark Horse

❑1, Jan 1998 .... 2.95
❑2 .... 2.95

Egypt
DC / Vertigo

❑1, Aug 1995; Adult 2.50
❑2, Sep 1995; Adult 2.50
❑3, Oct 1995; Adult 2.50
❑4, Nov 1995; Adult 2.50
❑5, Dec 1995; Adult 2.50
❑6, Jan 1996; Adult 2.50
❑7, Feb 1996; Final Issue; Adult 2.50

Ehlissa
Highland Graphics

❑1, Nov 1992; Color on cover 2.00
❑1/2nd; Black & white cover 2.00
❑1/3rd; Black & white cover 2.00
❑2, Dec 1992; Color on cover 2.00
❑2/2nd; Black & white cover 2.00
❑3, Jan 1993; Color on cover 2.00
❑3/2nd; Black & white cover 2.00
❑4, Mar 1993; Color on cover 2.00
❑4/2nd; Black & white cover 2.00
❑5, Mar 1993; Color on cover 2.00
❑5/2nd; Black & white cover 2.00
❑6; Color on cover 2.00
❑6/2nd; Black & white cover 2.00
❑7; Color on cover 2.00
❑7/2nd; Black & white cover 2.00
❑8, May 1993; Color on cover 2.00
❑8/2nd; Black & white cover 2.00
❑9, Jul 1993; Color on cover 2.00
❑9/2nd; Black & white cover 2.00
❑10 1993; Color on cover 2.00
❑10/2nd; Black & white cover 2.00
❑11 1993; Color on cover 2.00
❑11/2nd; Black & white cover 2.00
❑12 1993; Color on cover 2.00
❑12/2nd; Black & white cover 2.00
❑13 1993; Color on cover 2.00
❑13/2nd; Black & white cover 2.00
❑14, Jan 1994; Color on cover 2.00
❑14/2nd; Black & white cover 2.00
❑15, Feb 1994; Color cover 2.00

Other grades: Multiply price above by 5/6 for VF/NM • 2/3 for VERY FINE • 1/3 for FINE • 1/5 for VERY GOOD • 1/8 for GOOD

- ❑15/2nd; Black & white cover 2.00
- ❑16, Mar 1994; Color on cover 2.00
- ❑16/2nd; Black & white cover 2.00
- ❑17, Apr 1994; Color on cover.............. 2.00
- ❑17/2nd; Black & white cover 2.00
- ❑18, May 1994; Color on cover............. 2.00
- ❑18/2nd; Black & white cover 2.00
- ❑19, Jun 1994; Color on cover.............. 2.00
- ❑19/2nd; Black & white cover 2.00
- ❑20, Jul 1994; Color on cover............... 2.00
- ❑20/2nd; Black & white cover 2.00
- ❑21, Aug 1994; Adult 2.00
- ❑22, Sep 1994; Adult 2.00
- ❑23, Oct 1994; Adult............................ 2.00
- ❑24, Nov 1994; Adult 2.00
- ❑25, Dec 1994; Adult 2.00
- ❑26, Jan 1995; Adult............................ 2.00
- ❑27, Feb 1995; Adult............................ 2.00
- ❑28, Mar 1995; Adult 2.00
- ❑29, Apr 1995; Adult............................ 2.00
- ❑30, May 1995; 1: Nathan; Adult............. 2.00
- ❑31, Jun 1995; has #27's indicia........... 2.00
- ❑32; 1: Lanith; Adult............................ 2.00
- ❑33; Adult 2.00

Eightball
Fantagraphics

- ❑1... 10.00
- ❑1/2nd; 2nd printing 5.00
- ❑1/3rd; 3rd printing............................. 3.50
- ❑1/4th; 4th printing 3.00
- ❑2... 6.00
- ❑3... 5.00
- ❑4... 5.00
- ❑5... 4.00
- ❑6... 4.00
- ❑7... 4.00
- ❑8... 4.00
- ❑9... 3.00
- ❑10... 3.00
- ❑11... 3.00
- ❑12, Nov 1993 .... 3.00
- ❑13... 3.00
- ❑14... 3.00
- ❑15... 3.00
- ❑16, Nov 1995; cardstock cover 4.00
- ❑17... 2.95
- ❑18, Mar 1997 .... 2.95
- ❑19, May 1998...................................... 3.95
- ❑20, Feb 1999; cardstock cover 4.50
- ❑21, Feb 2000 .... 4.95
- ❑22, Aug 2001 .... 2.95
- ❑23, Jul 2004.. 2.95

Eighth Wonder
Dark Horse

- ❑1, Nov 1997, b&w; cover says The 8th Wonder, indicia says The Eighth Wonder.. 2.95

Eight Legged Freaks
WildStorm

- ❑1, Sep 2002, Several characters in profile on cover 6.95

80 Page Giant Magazine
DC

- ❑1, Aug 1964, Superman; Imaginary stories 295.00
- ❑2, Sep 1964, Jimmy Olsen.................. 150.00
- ❑3, Sep 1964, Lois Lane 125.00
- ❑4, Oct 1964, Cl (a); Flash 125.00
- ❑5, Nov 1964, Batman 125.00
- ❑6, Jan 1965, Superman....................... 125.00
- ❑7, Feb 1965, Sgt. Rock........................ 150.00
- ❑8, Mar 1965, Secret Origins 265.00
- ❑9, Apr 1965, Cl (c); MA, Cl (a); Flash; reprints stories from Showcase #14, and Flash #106, 108, 117, and 123.... 125.00
- ❑10, May 1965, Superboy..................... 125.00
- ❑11, Jun 1965, Superman..................... 125.00
- ❑12, Jul 1965, Batman........................... 80.00
- ❑13, Aug 1965, Jimmy Olsen.................. 80.00
- ❑14, Sep 1965, Lois Lane 80.00
- ❑15, Oct 1965, Batman/Superman; reprints stories from World's Finest Comics #74, #81, #82, #88, #95, and #97 .... 80.00

86 Voltz: Dead Girl One-Shot
Image

- ❑1, ca. 2005 .... 5.95

Ekos Preview
Aspen

- ❑1, Jan 2004.. 8.00

El Arsenal Unknown Enemy
Arcana

- ❑1, Sep 2005 .... 2.95
- ❑2, Oct 2005... 2.95

El Cazador
CrossGen

- ❑1, Oct 2003... 2.95
- ❑1/2nd, Nov 2003................................. 2.95
- ❑2, Nov 2003... 2.95
- ❑3, Dec 2003 .... 2.95
- ❑4, Jan 2004... 2.95
- ❑4/2nd, Feb 2004.................................. 2.95
- ❑5, Mar 2004... 2.95
- ❑6, May 2004... 2.95

El Cazador: Blackjack Tom
CrossGen

- ❑1, Apr 2004... 2.95

El Diablo
DC

- ❑1, Aug 1989 .... 2.50
- ❑2, Sep 1989 .... 1.50
- ❑3, Oct 1989... 1.50
- ❑4, Dec 1989 .... 1.50
- ❑5, Jan 1990... 1.50
- ❑6, Feb 1990... 1.50
- ❑7, Mar 1990... 1.75
- ❑8, Apr 1990... 1.75
- ❑9, May 1990... 1.75
- ❑10, Jun 1990....................................... 1.75
- ❑11, Jul 1990.. 1.75
- ❑12, Aug 1990; Golden Age Vigilante 2.00
- ❑13, Sep 1990 .... 2.00
- ❑14, Oct 1990....................................... 2.00
- ❑15, Dec 1990 .... 2.00
- ❑16, Jan 1991; Final Issue.................... 2.00

El Diablo
DC / Vertigo

- ❑1, Mar 2001 .... 2.50
- ❑2, Apr 2001... 2.50
- ❑3, May 2001... 2.50
- ❑4, Jun 2001... 2.50

Electric Fear
Sparks

- ❑1, Win 1984... 1.50
- ❑2, Spr 1986... 1.50

Electric Girl
Mighty Gremlin

- ❑1, May 1998... 3.50
- ❑2, Spr 1999... 2.95
- ❑3, Sum 1999... 2.95

Electric Warrior
DC

- ❑1, May 1986... 1.50
- ❑2, Jun 1986... 1.50
- ❑3, Jul 1986.. 1.50
- ❑4, Aug 1986... 1.50
- ❑5, Sep 1986... 1.50
- ❑6, Oct 1986... 1.50
- ❑7, Nov 1986... 1.50
- ❑8, Dec 1986... 1.50
- ❑9, Jan 1987... 1.50
- ❑10, Feb 1987....................................... 1.50
- ❑11, Mar 1987....................................... 1.50
- ❑12, Apr 1987....................................... 1.50
- ❑13, May 1987....................................... 1.50
- ❑14, Jun 1987....................................... 1.50
- ❑15, Jul 1987.. 1.50
- ❑16, Aug 1987....................................... 1.50
- ❑17, Sep 1987 .... 1.50
- ❑18, Oct 1987....................................... 1.50

Electropolis
Image

- ❑1, May 2001... 2.95
- ❑2, Jun 2001... 2.95
- ❑3, Dec 2001 .... 2.95

Elektra
Marvel

- ❑1, Mar 1995; enhanced cover 4.00
- ❑2, Apr 1995; enhanced cover.............. 3.25
- ❑3, May 1995; enhanced cover............. 3.25
- ❑4, Jun 1995; enhanced cover.............. 3.25

Elektra
Marvel

- ❑-1, Jul 1997, A: Daredevil. Flashback... 2.25
- ❑1, Nov 1996 .... 4.00
- ❑1/A, Nov 1996, variant cover 3.00
- ❑2, Dec 1996, V: Bullseye..................... 2.50
- ❑3, Jan 1997... 2.50
- ❑4, Feb 1997... 2.00
- ❑5, Mar 1997 .... 2.00
- ❑6, Apr 1997, V: Razorfist..................... 2.00
- ❑7, May 1997... 2.00
- ❑8, Jun 1997... 2.00
- ❑9, Aug 1997, gatefold summary 2.00
- ❑10, Sep 1997, gatefold summary......... 2.00
- ❑11, Oct 1997, gatefold summary; A: Daredevil.. 2.00
- ❑12, Nov 1997, gatefold summary; A: Daredevil.. 2.00
- ❑13, Dec 1997, gatefold summary; A: Daredevil.. 2.00
- ❑14, Jan 1998, gatefold summary 2.00
- ❑15, Feb 1998, gatefold summary 2.00
- ❑16, Mar 1998, gatefold summary; A: Shang-Chi 2.00
- ❑17, Apr 1998, gatefold summary 2.00
- ❑18, May 1998, gatefold summary 2.00
- ❑19, Jun 1998, gatefold summary; Final Issue 2.00

Elektra
Marvel / MAX

- ❑1, Sep 2001, BMB (w) 3.50
- ❑2, Oct 2001, BMB (w) 2.99
- ❑2/A, Oct 2001 .... 2.99
- ❑3, Nov 2001, BMB (w) 4.00
- ❑3/Nude, Nov 2001, b&w; Recalled due to interior nudity................................ 10.00
- ❑4, Dec 2001, BMB (w) 2.99
- ❑5, Jan 2002, BMB (w) 2.99
- ❑6, Feb 2002, BMB (w); Silent issue...... 2.99
- ❑7, Mar 2002 .... 2.99
- ❑8, Apr 2002... 2.99
- ❑9, May 2002... 2.99
- ❑10, Jun 2002....................................... 2.99
- ❑11, Aug 2002 .... 2.99
- ❑12, Sep 2002 .... 2.99
- ❑13, Oct 2002....................................... 2.99
- ❑14, Nov 2002 .... 2.99
- ❑15, Dec 2002 .... 2.99
- ❑16, Jan 2003....................................... 2.99
- ❑17, Jan 2003....................................... 2.99
- ❑18, Feb 2003....................................... 2.99
- ❑19, Feb 2003....................................... 2.99
- ❑20, Mar 2003....................................... 2.99
- ❑21, Jun 2003....................................... 2.99
- ❑22, Jun 2003....................................... 2.99
- ❑23, Jul 2003, BSz (c); TP (a)............... 2.99
- ❑24, Aug 2003, BSz (c); TP (a) 2.99
- ❑25, Sep 2003, BSz (c);cardstock cover 2.99
- ❑26, Oct 2003....................................... 2.99
- ❑27, Nov 2003, color (c)........................ 2.99
- ❑28, Dec 2003 .... 2.99
- ❑29, Jan 2004....................................... 2.99
- ❑30, Feb 2004, V: rebel insurgents in Naou (SE Asia) 2.99
- ❑31, Mar 2004....................................... 2.99
- ❑32, Apr 2004....................................... 2.99
- ❑33, May 2004....................................... 2.99
- ❑34, May 2004....................................... 2.99
- ❑35, Jun 2004....................................... 2.99

Elektra & Wolverine: The Redeemer
Marvel

- ❑1, Jan 2002... 5.95
- ❑2, Feb 2002... 5.95
- ❑3, Mar 2002 .... 5.95

Elektra: Assassin
Marvel / Epic

- ❑1, Aug 1986; BSz (c); FM (w); BSz (a); Inside cover subtitled The Lost Years. 3.00
- ❑2, Sep 1986 BSz (c); FM (w); BSz (a) .. 2.50
- ❑3, Oct 1986 BSz (c); FM (w); BSz (a)... 2.50
- ❑4, Nov 1986 BSz (c); FM (w); BSz (a).. 2.50
- ❑5, Dec 1986 BSz (c); FM (w); BSz (a) .. 2.50
- ❑6, Jan 1987 BSz (c); FM (w); BSz (a)... 2.50
- ❑7, Feb 1987 BSz (c); FM (w); BSz (a)... 2.50
- ❑8, Mar 1987; BSz (c); FM (w); BSz (a); Relatively scarce................................ 3.00

Other grades: Multiply price above by 5/6 for VF/NM • 2/3 for VERY FINE • 1/3 for FINE • 1/5 for VERY GOOD • 1/8 for GOOD

Dragonlance

Based on Dungeons & Dragons setting
©DC

Dragonslayer

Adapts early 1980s fantasy film
©Marvel

Dreadstar

Jim Starlin's excellent space opera
©Marvel

Dream Corridor (Harlan Ellison's...)

Adaptation anthology of Ellison stories
©Dark Horse

Dreaming

Uses characters from Neil Gaiman's Sandman
©DC

N-MINT

Elektra/Cyblade
Image

❑1, Mar 1997; crossover with Marvel; concludes in Silver Surfer/Weapon Zero 2.95
❑1/A, Mar 1997; Alternate cover; crossover with Marvel; concludes in Silver Surfer/Weapon Zero 2.95

Elektra: Glimpse & Echo
Marvel

❑1, Sep 2002, Several characters in profile on cover 2.99
❑2, Oct 2002 ..... 2.99
❑3, Nov 2002 ..... 2.99
❑4, Dec 2002 ..... 2.99

Elektra Lives Again
Marvel / Epic

❑1, Mar 1991; hardcover 24.95

Elektra Megazine
Marvel

❑1, Nov 1996, Reprints Elektra stories from Daredevil 3.95
❑2, Nov 1996, Reprints Elektra stories from Daredevil 3.95

Elektra Saga
Marvel

❑1, Feb 1984; FM (w); FM (a); Daredevil reprint 4.00
❑2, Mar 1984; FM (w); FM (a); Daredevil reprint 3.50
❑3, Apr 1984; FM (w); FM (a); Daredevil reprint 3.50
❑4, May 1984; FM (w); FM (a); Daredevil reprint 3.50

Elektra: The Hand
Marvel

❑1, Sep 2004 ..... 2.99
❑2, Oct 2004 ..... 2.99
❑3, Nov 2004 ..... 2.99
❑4, Dec 2004 ..... 2.99
❑5, Jan 2005 ..... 2.99

Elektra: The Movie
Marvel

❑1, Jan 2005, Includes b&w Elektra short story by Frank Miller 5.99

Elementals
Comico

❑1 1984; 2: Elementals; V: Destroyers; ca. 1984 ..... 2.50
❑2 1985; V: Saker; V: Destroyers; ca. 1984 ..... 2.00
❑3 1985; V: Saker; V: Destroyers; ca. 1984 ..... 2.00
❑4, Jun 1985; O: Saker; V: Saker; V: Destroyers 2.00
❑5, Dec 1985; V: Saker; V: Destroyers 2.00
❑6, Feb 1986 ..... 1.50
❑7, Apr 1986 ..... 1.50
❑8, Jun 1986; V: Ratman 1.50
❑9, Aug 1986 ..... 1.50
❑10, Oct 1986 ..... 1.50
❑11, Dec 1986 ..... 1.50
❑12, Feb 1987 ..... 1.50
❑13, Apr 1987 ..... 1.50
❑14, Jun 1987; O: Captain Cadaver 1.50
❑15, Jul 1987 ..... 1.50
❑16, Aug 1987; V: Captain Cadaver 1.50
❑17, Sep 1987; 1: Crysalis II; V: Captain Cadaver 1.50
❑18, Oct 1987; V: Behemoth 1.50
❑19, Nov 1987; 1: Ambrose 1.50
❑20, Dec 1987; 2: Ambrose 1.50
❑21, Jan 1988; V: Destroyers 1.50
❑22, Feb 1988; 1: The Rapture; V: Chrysalis 1.50
❑23, Mar 1988; V: Thor 1.75
❑24, Apr 1988 ..... 1.75
❑25, May 1988 ..... 1.75
❑26, Jun 1988 ..... 1.75
❑27, Jul 1988 ..... 1.75
❑28, Aug 1988 ..... 1.75
❑29, Sep 1988; Final Issue 1.75
❑Special 1, Mar 1986; Child abuse special 3.00
❑Special 2, Jan 1989; V: Fantasia Faust. 1.95

Elementals
Comico

❑1, Mar 1989 ..... 2.50
❑2, Apr 1989 ..... 2.00
❑3, May 1989, V: Rapture 2.00
❑4, Jun 1989, V: Rapture 2.50
❑5, Jul 1989, V: Rapture 2.50
❑6, Aug 1989 ..... 2.50
❑7, Sep 1989 ..... 2.50
❑8, Oct 1989 ..... 2.50
❑9, Nov 1989 ..... 2.50
❑10, Dec 1989, V: Holocaust; V: Floater. 2.50
❑11, Jan 1990, V: Holocaust; V: Floater. 2.50
❑12, Feb 1990, 1: Lord Oblivion; V: Holocaust 2.50
❑13, Mar 1990, 1: Walker 2.50
❑14, May 1990 ..... 2.50
❑15, Jul 1990 ..... 2.50
❑16, May 1991, 1st Strikeforce America 2.50
❑17, May 1991 ..... 2.50
❑18, Jun 1991, 1: Dave Dragavon 2.50
❑19, Aug 1991 ..... 2.50
❑20, Oct 1991 ..... 2.50
❑21, Nov 1991 ..... 2.50
❑22, Mar 1992 ..... 2.50
❑23, May 1992, 1: New Monolith 2.50
❑24, Aug 1992, V: Lord Oblivion 2.50
❑25, Nov 1992 ..... 2.50
❑26, Apr 1993, Wraparound cover 2.50

Elementals
Comico

❑1, Dec 1995, Bagged with card 2.95
❑2, ca. 1996 ..... 2.95
❑3, May 1996 ..... 2.95

Elementals: Ghost of a Chance
Comico

❑1, Dec 1995 ..... 5.95

Elementals: How the War Was Won
Comico

❑1, Jun 1996 ..... 2.95
❑2, Aug 1996 ..... 2.95

Elementals Lingerie
Comico

❑1, May 1996; pin-ups 2.95

Elementals Sex Special
Comico

❑1/Gold, Oct 1991; Gold edition; Gold edition (Gold Comico logo); Adult 4.95
❑1, Oct 1991; Adult 2.95
❑2, Jun 1992; Adult 2.95
❑3, Sep 1992; Adult 2.95
❑4, Feb 1993; Adult 2.95

Elementals Sex Special
Comico

❑1, Dec 1997, Adult; B&w and color 2.95

Elemental's Sexy Lingerie Special
Comico

❑1/A, Jan 1993; without poster 2.95
❑1/B, Jan 1993; Includes poster 5.95

Elementals Swimsuit Spectacular 1996
Comico

❑1/Gold, Jun 1996; Gold edition; pin-ups 3.50
❑1, Jun 1996; pin-ups 2.95

Elementals: The Vampires' Revenge
Comico

❑1, Jun 1996 ..... 2.95
❑2, Jun 1996; Gold edition 3.00

Elephantmen
Image

❑0, Nov 2006 ..... 2.99
❑1, Jul 2006 ..... 2.99
❑2, Oct 2006, Flipbook with two storylines 2.99
❑3, Nov 2006 ..... 2.99
❑4, Nov 2006 ..... 2.99
❑5, Jan 2007 ..... 2.99

Eleven or One
Sirius Entertainment

❑1, Apr 1995, reprints new story from Angry Christ Comics tpb 4.00
❑1/2nd, 2nd printing 3.00

Elfheim
Nightwynd

❑1 1991, b&w 2.50
❑2, b&w 2.50
❑3, b&w 2.50
❑4, b&w 2.50

Elfheim
Nightwynd

❑1, b&w 2.50
❑2, b&w 2.50
❑3, b&w 2.50
❑4, b&w 2.50

Elfheim
Nightwynd

❑1, b&w 2.50
❑2, b&w 2.50
❑3, b&w 2.50
❑4, b&w 2.50

Elfheim
Nightwynd

❑1, b&w 2.50
❑2, b&w 2.50

Elfheim: Dragon Dream
Night Wynd

❑1 ..... 2.50
❑2, Apr 1993; Backup story, Foxfire/Stardusters #19; b&w 2.50
❑3 ..... 2.50
❑4 ..... 2.50

N-MINT

Elfin Romance
Mt. Wilson

❑1, Feb 1994, b&w 1.50
❑2, Apr 1994, b&w 1.50
❑3, Apr 1994, b&w 1.50
❑4, Jun 1994, b&w 2.00
❑5, Aug 1994, b&w 2.00
❑6, Oct 1994, b&w 1.75
❑7, Dec 1996, b&w 3.25

Elflord
Aircel

❑1, Feb 1986, b&w 2.00
❑1/2nd; 2nd printing 2.00
❑2, Mar 1986 2.00
❑2/2nd; 2nd printing 2.00
❑3, Apr 1986 2.00
❑4, May 1986 2.00
❑5, Jun 1986 2.00
❑6, Jul 1986 2.00
❑7, Aug 1986; Never published? 2.00
❑8, Sep 1986; Never published? 2.00

Elflord
Aircel

❑1, Oct 1986 2.00
❑2, Nov 1986 2.00
❑3, Dec 1986 2.00
❑4, Jan 1987 2.00
❑5, Feb 1987 2.00
❑6, Mar 1987 2.00
❑7, Apr 1987 2.00
❑8, May 1987 2.00
❑9, Jun 1987 2.00
❑10, Jul 1987 2.00
❑11, Aug 1987 2.00
❑12, Sep 1987 2.00
❑13, Oct 1987 2.00
❑14, Nov 1987 2.00
❑15, Dec 1987; Jake Thrash preview 2.00
❑15.5, Jan 1988; The Falcon Special 2.00
❑16, Jan 1988 2.00
❑17, Feb 1988 2.00
❑18, Mar 1988 2.00
❑19 1988 2.00
❑20 1988 2.00
❑21 1988; double-sized 4.95
❑22 1988 1.95
❑23, Oct 1988; b&w 1.95
❑24, Nov 1988; Aircel Crossword puzzle; b&w 1.95
❑25, Dec 1988; b&w 1.95
❑26, Dec 1988; b&w 1.95
❑27, Jan 1989; b&w 1.95
❑28, May 1989 1.95
❑29, Jun 1989; b&w 1.95
❑30, Jul 1989 1.95
❑31, Oct 1989 1.95

Elflord
Night Wynd

❑1, b&w 2.50
❑2, b&w 2.50
❑3, b&w 2.50
❑4, b&w 2.50

Elflord
Warp

❑1, Jan 1997, b&w 2.95
❑2, Feb 1997, b&w 2.95
❑3, Mar 1997, b&w; Continued from Elflore: High Seas #2 2.95
❑4, Apr 1997, b&w 2.95

Elflord
Warp

❑1, Sep 1997, b&w 2.95
❑2, Oct 1997, b&w 2.95
❑3, Nov 1997, b&w 2.95
❑4, Dec 1997, b&w 2.95
❑5, Jan 1997 2.95
❑6, Feb 1997 2.95
❑7, Mar 1997 2.95

Elflord Chronicles
Aircel

❑1, Oct 1990, b&w; Reprints 2.50
❑2, Oct 1990, b&w; Reprints 2.50
❑3, Nov 1990, b&w; Reprints 2.50
❑4, Dec 1990, b&w; Reprints 2.50
❑5, Jan 1991, b&w; Reprints 2.50

N-MINT

❑6, Feb 1991, b&w; Reprints 2.50
❑7, Mar 1991, b&w; Reprints 2.75
❑8, Apr 1991 2.75
❑9 2.75
❑10 2.75
❑11 2.75
❑12 2.75

Elflord: Dragon's Eye
Night Wynd

❑1, ca. 1993 2.50
❑2, ca. 1993 2.50
❑3, ca. 1993 2.50

Elflord the Return
Mad Monkey

❑1, ca. 1996 6.96

Elflord: The Return of the King
Night Wynd

❑1 2.50
❑2 2.50
❑3 2.50
❑4 2.50

Elflore
Nightwynd

❑1, b&w; ca. 1992 2.50
❑2, b&w; ca. 1992 2.50
❑3, b&w; ca. 1992 2.50
❑4, b&w; ca. 1992 2.50

Elflore
Nightwynd

❑1, b&w; ca. 1992 2.50
❑2, b&w; ca. 1992 2.50
❑3, b&w; ca. 1992 2.50
❑4, b&w; ca. 1992 2.50

Elflore: High Seas
Night Wynd

❑1; b&w; ca. 1993 2.50
❑2, Apr 1993; b&w 2.50
❑3; Friends and Foes, Part 2 continued in Elfheim; b&w; ca. 1993 2.50

Elflore
Nightwynd

❑1, b&w; ca. 1992 2.50
❑2, b&w; ca. 1993 2.50
❑3, b&w; Foxfire: Waifs At War continued from Elfheim #3; ca. 1993 2.50
❑4, b&w; ca. 1993 2.50

Elfquest
Warp

❑1, Apr 1979 WP (w); WP (a) 32.00
❑1/2nd; WP (w); WP (a); 2nd printing 12.00
❑1/3rd; WP (w); WP (a); 3rd printing 8.00
❑1/4th; WP (w); WP (a); 4th printing 5.00
❑2, Aug 1978 WP (w); WP (a) 18.00
❑2/2nd; WP (w); WP (a); 2nd printing 6.00
❑2/3rd; WP (w); WP (a); 3rd printing 4.00
❑2/4th; WP (w); WP (a); 4th printing 3.00
❑3, Dec 1978 WP (w); WP (a) 18.00
❑3/2nd; WP (w); WP (a); 2nd printing 3.00
❑3/3rd; WP (w); WP (a); 3rd printing 3.00
❑3/4th; WP (w); WP (a); 4th printing 3.00
❑4, Apr 1979 WP (w); WP (a) 16.00
❑4/2nd; WP (w); WP (a); 2nd printing 5.00
❑4/3rd; WP (w); WP (a); 3rd printing 4.00
❑4/4th; WP (w); WP (a); 4th printing 2.50
❑5, Aug 1979 WP (w); WP (a) 16.00
❑5/2nd; WP (w); WP (a); 2nd printing 3.00
❑5/3rd; WP (w); WP (a); 3rd printing 3.00
❑6, Jan 1980 WP (w); WP (a) 13.00
❑6/2nd; WP (w); WP (a); 2nd printing 4.00
❑6/3rd; WP (w); WP (a); 3rd printing 3.00
❑7, May 1980 WP (w); WP (a) 10.00
❑7/2nd; WP (w); WP (a); 2nd printing 4.00
❑7/3rd; WP (w); WP (a); 3rd printing 3.00
❑8, Sep 1980 WP (w); WP (a) 10.00
❑8/2nd; WP (w); WP (a); 2nd printing 4.00
❑8/3rd; WP (w); WP (a); 3rd printing 3.00
❑9, Feb 1981 WP (w); WP (a) 10.00
❑9/2nd; WP (w); WP (a); 2nd printing 4.00
❑9/3rd; WP (w); WP (a); 3rd printing 3.00
❑10, Jun 1981 WP (w); WP (a) 7.50
❑11, Oct 1981 WP (w); WP (a) 7.50
❑12, Feb 1982 WP (w); WP (a) 7.50
❑13, Jun 1982 WP (w); WP (a) 7.50
❑14, Oct 1982 WP (w); WP (a) 7.50

N-MINT

❑15, Feb 1983 WP (w); WP (a) 7.50
❑16, Jun 1983; WP (w); WP (a); Includes preview of "A Distant Soil" 10.00
❑17, Oct 1983; WP (w); WP (a); Elf orgy 7.00
❑18, Feb 1984 WP (w); WP (a) 7.00
❑19, Jun 1984 WP (w); WP (a) 7.00
❑20, Oct 1984 WP (w); WP (a) 7.00
❑21, Feb 1985; WP (w); WP (a); all letters issue 7.00

Elfquest
Warp

❑1, May 1996; b&w 6.00
❑2, Jun 1996 5.00
❑3, Jul 1996 5.00
❑4, Aug 1996 5.00
❑5, Sep 1996; b&w 5.00
❑6, Nov 1996; b&w 5.00
❑7, Dec 1996; Wavedancer Gallery; Includes Elflord preview; b&w 5.00
❑8, Jan 1997; b&w 5.00
❑9, Feb 1997; A: Mr. Beat. b&w 5.00
❑10, Mar 1997; b&w 5.00
❑11, Apr 1997; b&w 4.95
❑12, May 1997; b&w 4.95
❑13, Jun 1997; b&w 4.95
❑14, Jul 1997 4.95
❑15, Aug 1997; b&w 4.95
❑16, Sep 1997; b&w 4.95
❑17, Oct 1997; Kings Cross storyline continued in Kings Cross #1; b&w 4.95
❑18, Nov 1997; b&w 4.95
❑19, Dec 1997; Return to Centaur continued in Elfquest (Vol. 2) #23; b&w 4.95
❑20, Jan 1998 4.95
❑21, Feb 1998 4.95
❑22, Mar 1998 4.95
❑23, Apr 1998; b&w 4.95
❑24, May 1998; Return to Centaur continued in Elfquest (Vol. 2) #28; b&w 4.95
❑25, Jun 1998; needlepoint style cover 4.95
❑26, Jul 1998; b&w 4.95
❑27, Aug 1998; A: Mr. Beat. b&w 4.95
❑28, Sep 1998; Return to Centaur continued in Elfquest (Vol. 2) #30; b&w 4.95
❑29, Oct 1998 4.95
❑30, Nov 1998; b&w 4.95
❑31, Dec 1998; Christmas cover 4.95
❑32, Jan 1999; b&w 2.95
❑33, Feb 1999; Final Issue; Wolfrider continued in Elfquest Reader's Collection #9A; b&w 2.95

Elfquest (Epic)
Marvel / Epic

❑1, Aug 1985 WP (w); WP (a) 3.50
❑2, Sep 1985 WP (w); WP (a) 2.50
❑3, Oct 1985 WP (w); WP (a) 2.50
❑4, Nov 1985 WP (w); WP (a) 2.50
❑5, Dec 1985 WP (w); WP (a) 2.50
❑6, Jan 1986 WP (w); WP (a) 2.25
❑7, Feb 1986 WP (w); WP (a) 2.25
❑8, Mar 1986 WP (w); WP (a) 2.25
❑9, Apr 1986 WP (w); WP (a) 2.25
❑10, May 1986 WP (w); WP (a) 2.25
❑11, Jun 1986 WP (w); WP (a) 2.00
❑12, Jul 1986 WP (w); WP (a) 2.00
❑13, Aug 1986 WP (w); WP (a) 2.00
❑14, Sep 1986 WP (w); WP (a) 2.00
❑15, Oct 1986 WP (w); WP (a) 2.00
❑16, Nov 1986 WP (w); WP (a) 2.00
❑17, Dec 1986 WP (w); WP (a) 2.00
❑18, Jan 1987 WP (w); WP (a) 2.00
❑19, Feb 1987 WP (w); WP (a) 2.00
❑20, Mar 1987 WP (w); WP (a) 2.00
❑21, Apr 1987 WP (w); WP (a) 1.50
❑22, May 1987 WP (w); WP (a) 1.50
❑23, Jun 1987 WP (w); WP (a) 1.50
❑24, Jul 1987 WP (w); WP (a) 1.50
❑25, Aug 1987 WP (w); WP (a) 1.50
❑26, Sep 1987 WP (w); WP (a) 1.50
❑27, Oct 1987 WP (w); WP (a) 1.50
❑28, Nov 1987 WP (w); WP (a) 1.50
❑29, Dec 1987 WP (w); WP (a) 1.50
❑30, Jan 1988 WP (w); WP (a) 1.50
❑31, Feb 1988 WP (w); WP (a) 1.50
❑32, Mar 1988; WP (w); WP (a); Final Issue 1.50

Dredd Rules!

More adventures of Mega City One lawman

©Fleetway-Quality

Droids

Solo outings of Star Wars favorites

©Marvel

Droopy

Tex Avery creation's misadventures

©Dark Horse

Duckman

Animated series aired on USA

©Dark Horse

Dumm $2099

One of trio of Marvel 2099 parodies

©Parody

N-MINT

Elfquest
Warp

- ❑1, May 1989 .... 2.00
- ❑2, Jun 1989 .... 2.00
- ❑3, Jul 1989 .... 2.00
- ❑4, Aug 1989 .... 2.00

Elfquest 25th Anniversary Edition
DC

- ❑1, Sep 2003 .... 2.95

Elfquest: Blood of Ten Chiefs
Warp

- ❑1, Aug 1993 .... 2.50
- ❑2, Sep 1993 .... 2.50
- ❑3, Nov 1993 .... 2.50
- ❑4, Jan 1994; Backup Story "Hunters" by Drew Hayes (Poison Elves) 2.50
- ❑5, Mar 1994 .... 2.50
- ❑6, May 1994 .... 2.50
- ❑7, Jun 1994 .... 2.50
- ❑8, Jul 1994 .... 2.50
- ❑9, Aug 1994 .... 2.50
- ❑10, Sep 1994 .... 2.50
- ❑11, Oct 1994 .... 2.50
- ❑12, Nov 1994 .... 2.50
- ❑13, Dec 1994 .... 2.50
- ❑14, Jan 1995 .... 2.50
- ❑15, Feb 1995 .... 2.50
- ❑16, Apr 1995 .... 2.50
- ❑17, May 1995 .... 2.50
- ❑18, Jun 1995 .... 2.50
- ❑19, Aug 1995; contains Elfquest timeline 2.50
- ❑20, Sep 1995; Final Issue 2.50

Elfquest: Hidden Years
Warp

- ❑1, May 1992 .... 3.00
- ❑2, Jul 1992 .... 2.50
- ❑3, Sep 1992; This story was previewed in Harbinger #11 (character reads it as in a comic book) 2.50
- ❑4, Nov 1992 .... 2.50
- ❑5, Jan 1993 .... 2.50
- ❑6, Mar 1993 .... 2.50
- ❑7, May 1993 .... 2.50
- ❑8, Jul 1993; Contains Elfquest Universie Centerspread (#2 in a series) The Wolfriders Then 2.50
- ❑9, Sep 1993; Contains Elfquest Universe Centerspread (#6 in a series) The Sun Folk 2.50
- ❑9.5, Nov 1993; double-sized; WP (w); JBy (a); Holiday special; Contains Elfquest Universe Centerspread (#10 in a Series) Rats, Wildcards & Loners; Double-sized 2.95
- ❑10, Jan 1994 .... 2.50
- ❑11, Mar 1994 .... 2.50
- ❑12, Apr 1994 .... 2.50
- ❑13, May 1994 .... 2.50
- ❑14, Jun 1994 WP (w) 2.50
- ❑15, Jul 1994; Continued in Elfquest: Shards #1 .... 2.50
- ❑16, Aug 1994 .... 2.50
- ❑17, Oct 1994 .... 2.50
- ❑18, Dec 1994 .... 2.50
- ❑19, Jan 1995 .... 2.50
- ❑20, Apr 1995 .... 2.50
- ❑21, May 1995 .... 2.50
- ❑22, Jul 1995; Contains World Map 2.50
- ❑23, Aug 1995; contains Elfquest timeline 2.50
- ❑24, Sep 1995 .... 2.50
- ❑25, Oct 1995, b&w 2.50
- ❑26, Dec 1995, b&w 2.50
- ❑27, Jan 1996, b&w 2.50
- ❑28, Feb 1996, b&w 2.50
- ❑29, Mar 1996, b&w; Final issue 2.50

Elfquest: Jink
Warp

- ❑1, Nov 1994 .... 2.50
- ❑2, Dec 1994 .... 2.50
- ❑3, Jan 1995 WP (w) 2.50
- ❑4, Apr 1995 .... 2.50
- ❑5, May 1995 .... 2.50
- ❑6, Jul 1995; contains Elfquest world map 2.50
- ❑7, Aug 1995; contains Elfquest timeline 2.50
- ❑8, Oct 1995; b&w for remainder of series 2.50
- ❑9, Nov 1995 .... 2.50
- ❑10, Dec 1995 .... 2.50
- ❑11, Jan 1996 .... 2.50
- ❑12, Feb 1996 .... 2.50

Elfquest: Kahvi
Warp

- ❑1, Oct 1995 .... 2.25
- ❑2, Nov 1995 .... 2.25
- ❑3, Dec 1995 .... 2.25
- ❑4, Jan 1996 .... 2.25
- ❑5, Feb 1996 .... 2.25
- ❑6, Mar 1996 .... 2.25

Elfquest: Kings Cross
Warp

- ❑1, Nov 1997, b&w 2.95
- ❑2, Dec 1997, b&w 2.95

Elfquest: Kings of the Broken Wheel
Warp

- ❑1, Jun 1990 WP (a) 2.50
- ❑2, Aug 1990 WP (a) 2.00
- ❑3, Sep 1990 WP (a) 2.00
- ❑4, Dec 1990 WP (a) 2.00
- ❑5, Feb 1991 WP (a) 2.00
- ❑6, May 1991 WP (a) 2.00
- ❑7, Aug 1991 WP (a) 2.00
- ❑8, Nov 1991 WP (a) 2.00
- ❑9, Feb 1992 WP (a) 2.00

Elfquest: Metamorphosis
Warp

- ❑1, Apr 1996 .... 2.95

Elfquest: New Blood
Warp

- ❑1, Aug 1992, gatefold summary; JBy (w); WP, JBy (a); "Elfquest Summer Special" 5.00
- ❑2, Oct 1992; Continued from Elfquest: New Blood #1 .... 2.50
- ❑3, Dec 1992; Continued from Elfquest: New Blood #2 .... 2.50
- ❑4, Feb 1993; Continued from Elfquest: New Blood #1 .... 2.50
- ❑5, Apr 1993 .... 2.50
- ❑6, Jun 1993 .... 2.50
- ❑7, Jul 1993; Contains Elfquest Universe Centerspread (#1 in a Series) The Wolfriders - Now 2.50
- ❑8, Aug 1993; Contains Elfquest Universe Centerspread (#4 in a series) The Preservers 2.50
- ❑9, Sep 1993; Contains Elfquest Universe Centerspread (#5 in a series) The Firstcomers 2.50
- ❑10, Oct 1993; Contains Elfquest Universe Centerspread (#8 in a series) The Humans 2.50
- ❑11, Nov 1993; Contains Elfquest Universe Centerspread (#11 in a series) The Go-Backs 2.25
- ❑12, Dec 1993; Contains Elfquest Universe Centerspread (#11 in a series) The Gliders 2.25
- ❑13, Jan 1994 .... 2.25
- ❑14, Feb 1994 .... 2.25
- ❑15, Mar 1994 .... 2.25
- ❑16, Apr 1994 .... 2.25
- ❑17, May 1994 .... 2.25
- ❑18, Jun 1994 .... 2.25
- ❑19, Jul 1994 .... 2.25
- ❑20, Aug 1994 .... 2.25
- ❑21, Sep 1994 .... 2.25
- ❑22, Oct 1994 .... 2.25
- ❑23, Nov 1994 .... 2.25
- ❑24, Dec 1994 .... 2.25
- ❑25, Jan 1995; Prelude to Doorwar 1 .... 2.25
- ❑26, Feb 1995; Prelude to Doorwar 2 .... 2.25
- ❑27, Apr 1995 .... 2.50
- ❑28, May 1995 .... 2.50
- ❑29, Jul 1995; Contains World Map 2.50
- ❑30, Aug 1995; contains Elfquest timeline 2.50
- ❑31, Sep 1995 .... 2.50
- ❑32, Oct 1995; b&w 2.50
- ❑33, Nov 1995; b&w 2.50
- ❑34, Dec 1995; b&w 2.25
- ❑35, Jan 1996; b&w 2.25
- ❑Special 1, Jul 1993; KB (w); JBy, RE (a); '93 Summer Special 3.95

Elfquest: Recognition Summer 2001 Special
Warp

- ❑2, Jul 2001, b&w; Previous issue was Elfquest: Wolfshadow 2.95

Elfquest: Shards
Warp

- ❑1, Aug 1994 WP (w) 2.50
- ❑2, Sep 1994 WP (w) 2.50
- ❑3, Oct 1994 WP (w) 2.50
- ❑4, Nov 1994 WP (w) 2.50
- ❑5, Dec 1994 WP (w) 2.50
- ❑6, Jan 1995 WP (w) 2.25
- ❑7, Mar 1995 WP (w) 2.25
- ❑8, May 1995 WP (w) 2.25
- ❑9, Jun 1995 WP (w) 2.50
- ❑10, Aug 1995; WP (w); contains Elfquest timeline 2.50
- ❑11, Sep 1995 WP (w) 2.50
- ❑12, Oct 1995 WP (w) 2.50
- ❑13, Dec 1995 .... 2.25
- ❑14, Feb 1996 .... 2.25
- ❑15, Apr 1996 .... 2.25
- ❑16, Jun 1996 .... 2.25
- ❑Ashcan 1, ashcan preview/San Diego Comic-Con premium 1.00

Other grades: Multiply price above by 5/6 for VF/NM • 2/3 for VERY FINE • 1/3 for FINE • 1/5 for VERY GOOD • 1/8 for GOOD

Elfquest: Siege at Blue Mountain
Warp / Apple

❑1, Mar 1987, b&w; WP (c); WP (w); WP, JSa (a); B&W 3.00
❑1/2nd, WP (c); WP (w); WP (a); 2nd printing; b&w 2.50
❑2, May 1987, WP (c); WP (w); WP, JSa (a); B&W 3.00
❑2/2nd, May 1987, WP (c); WP (w); WP (a); 2nd printing; b&w 2.25
❑2/3rd, b&w; 3rd printing; b&w 3.00
❑3, Jul 1987, WP (c); WP (w); WP, JSa (a); B&W 2.50
❑3/2nd, WP (c); WP (w); WP (a); 2nd printing; b&w 2.00
❑4, Sep 1987, WP (c); WP (w); WP, JSa (a); B&W 2.50
❑5, Nov 1987, WP (c); WP (w); WP, JSa (a); B&W 2.50
❑6, Aug 1988, WP (c); WP (w); WP, JSa (a); B&W 2.50
❑7, Oct 1988, WP (c); WP (w); WP, JSa (a); B&W 2.50
❑8, Dec 1988, WP (c); WP (w); WP, JSa (a); B&W 2.50

Elfquest: The Discovery
DC

❑1, Mar 2006 3.99
❑2, May 2006 3.99
❑3, Jul 2006 3.99
❑4, Sep 2006 3.99

Elfquest: The Rebels
Warp

❑1, Nov 1994 2.50
❑2, Dec 1994 2.25
❑3, Jan 1995 2.25
❑4, Mar 1995 2.25
❑5, Apr 1995 2.25
❑6, Jun 1995 2.25
❑7, Jul 1995, contains Elfquest world map 2.25
❑8, Sep 1995 2.25
❑9, Oct 1995, b&w 2.25
❑10, Nov 1995, b&w 2.25
❑11, Jan 1996, b&w 2.25
❑12, Feb 1996, Final issue; b&w 2.25

Elfquest: Two-Spear
Warp

❑1, Oct 1995 2.25
❑2, Nov 1995 2.25
❑3, Dec 1995 2.25
❑4, Jan 1996 2.25
❑5, Feb 1996 2.25

Elfquest: Wavedancers
Warp

❑1, Dec 1993; O: The Wavedancers 2.25
❑2, Feb 1994 2.25
❑3, Apr 1994 2.25
❑4, Jun 1994 2.25
❑5, Aug 1994 2.25
❑6, Oct 1994 2.25
❑Special 1 2.25

Elfquest: Wolfshadow Summer 2001 Special
Warp

❑1, Jul 2001, b&w; Continued as Elfquest: Recognition 3.95

Elfquest: Worldpool
Warp

❑1, Jul 1997, b&w 2.95

Elf-Thing
Eclipse

❑1, Mar 1987, b&w 1.50

Elftrek
Dimension

❑1, Jul 1986; parody of Star Trek, Elfquest 1.75
❑2, Oct 1986; parody of Star Trek, Elfquest 1.75

Elf Warrior
Adventure

❑1, Feb 1987 1.95
❑2 1.95
❑3 1.95
❑4; Published by Quadrant 1.95

El Gato Negro
Azteca

❑1, Oct 1993, b&w 2.00
❑2, Sum 1994, b&w 2.00
❑3, Fal 1995, b&w 2.00
❑4 2.50

El Gaucho
NBM

❑1; Adult 20.95

El-Hazard
Viz

❑1, Apr 1997 2.95

El Hazard: The Magnificent World Part 1
Viz

❑1, Sep 2000 2.95
❑2, Oct 2000 2.95
❑3, Nov 2000 2.95
❑4, Dec 2000 2.95
❑5, Jan 2001 2.95

El Hazard: The Magnificent World Part 2
Viz

❑1, Feb 2001 2.95
❑2, Mar 2001 2.95
❑3, Apr 2001 2.95
❑4, May 2001 2.95
❑5, Jun 2001 2.95

El Hazard: The Magnificent World Part 3
Viz

❑1, Jul 2001 2.95
❑2, Aug 2001 2.95
❑3, Sep 2001 2.95
❑4, Oct 2001 2.95
❑5, Nov 2001 2.95
❑6, Dec 2001 2.95

Eliminator
Malibu / Ultraverse

❑0, Apr 1995; Collects Eliminator appearances from Ultraverse Premiere 2.95
❑1, May 1995; 7th Infinity Gem revealed 2.50
❑1/Variant, May 1995; Black cover edition; Black cover edition; 7th Infinity Gem revealed 3.95
❑2, Jun 1995 2.50
❑3, Jul 1995 2.50

Eliminator
Eternity

❑1, b&w 2.50
❑2, b&w 2.50
❑3, b&w 2.50

Eliminator Full Color Special
Eternity

❑1, Oct 1991 2.95

Elongated Man
DC

❑1, Jan 1992 1.25
❑2, Feb 1992 1.00
❑3, Mar 1992 1.00
❑4, Apr 1992 1.00

Elric
Pacific

❑1, Apr 1983 CR (c); CR (a) 2.00
❑2, Aug 1983 CR (c); CR (a) 1.75
❑3, Oct 1983 CR (a) 1.75
❑4, Dec 1983 CR (a) 1.75
❑5, Feb 1984 CR (a) 1.75
❑6, Apr 1984 CR (a) 1.75

Elric (Topps)
Topps

❑0, ca. 1996; CR (c); NG (w); CR (a); Noted as "Elric #0 — One Life" in indicia 3.50
❑1, ca. 1996 2.95
❑2, ca. 1996 2.95
❑3, ca. 1996 2.95
❑4, ca. 1996 CR (w); CR (a) 2.95

Elric: Sailor on the Seas of Fate
First

❑1, Jun 1985 2.00
❑2, Aug 1985 1.75
❑3, Oct 1985 1.75
❑4, Dec 1985 1.75
❑5, Feb 1986 1.75
❑6, Apr 1986 1.75
❑7, Jun 1986 1.75

Elric: Stormbringer
Dark Horse / Topps

❑1, ca. 1997 2.95
❑2, ca. 1997 2.95
❑3, ca. 1997 2.95
❑4, ca. 1997 2.95
❑5, ca. 1997 2.95
❑6, ca. 1997 2.95
❑7, ca. 1997 2.95

Elric: The Bane of the Black Sword
First

❑1, Aug 1988 2.00
❑2, Oct 1988 2.00
❑3, Dec 1988 2.00
❑4, Feb 1989 2.00
❑5, Apr 1989 2.00
❑6, Jun 1989 2.00

Elric: The Making of a Sorcerer
DC

❑1 2004 5.95
❑2 2005 5.95
❑3, Aug 2006 5.99
❑4, Oct 2006 5.99

Elric: The Vanishing Tower
First

❑1, Aug 1987 1.75
❑2, Oct 1987 1.75
❑3, Dec 1987 1.75
❑4, Feb 1988 1.75
❑5, Apr 1988 1.75
❑6, Jun 1988 1.75

Elric: Weird of the White Wolf
First

❑1, Oct 1986; A five issue adaptation of Michael Moorcock's Weird of the White Wolf 1.75
❑2, Dec 1986 1.75
❑3, Feb 1987 1.75
❑4, Apr 1987 1.75
❑5, Jun 1987 1.75

Elsewhere Prince
Marvel / Epic

❑1, May 1990 1.95
❑2, Jun 1990 1.95
❑3, Jul 1990 1.95
❑4, Aug 1990 1.95
❑5, Sep 1990 1.95
❑6, Oct 1990 1.95

Elseworlds 80-Page Giant
DC

❑1, Aug 1999; U.S. copies destroyed, only released in England; less than 700 copies estimated to exist 110.00

Elseworld's Finest
DC

❑1, ca. 1997, prestige format; Superman and Batman in the 1920s; Elseworlds story 4.95
❑2, ca. 1997, prestige format; Superman and Batman in the 1920s 4.95

Elseworld's Finest: Supergirl & Batgirl
DC

❑1, ca. 1998; prestige format; NN; One-shot 5.95

Elsinore
Devil's Due

❑4, Mar 2006, Indicia lists as 2/1/05; Price increase 3.25
❑5, May 2006 3.25

Elsinore
Alias

❑1, Apr 2005, $0.75 cover price 2.99
❑2, Jul 2005 2.99
❑3, Oct 2005 2.99
❑4, ca. 2005 2.99
❑5, ca. 2005 3.25
❑6, ca. 2005 2.99
❑7, ca. 2005 2.99

Elven
Malibu / Ultraverse

❑0, Oct 1994; 1: Elven 2.95
❑1, Feb 1995 A: Prime 2.25
❑1/Ltd., Feb 1995; Limited foil edition; A: Prime 2.50
❑2, Mar 1995 2.25

Other grades: Multiply price above by 5/6 for VF/NM • 2/3 for VERY FINE • 1/3 for FINE • 1/5 for VERY GOOD • 1/8 for GOOD

Dynamo

Super-belt powers T.H.U.N.D.E.R. agent
©Tower

Dynomutt

Blue Falcon sidekick's solo adventures
©Marvel

Earth X

Alex Ross covers form one large image
©Marvel

E.C. Classic Reprints

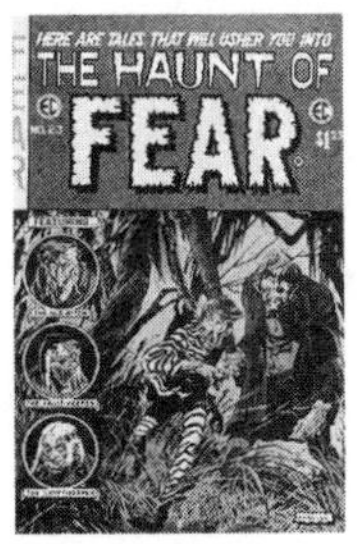

Early 1970s reprints from East Coast Comix
©East Coast Comix

Eclipso: The Darkness Within

First issue had plastic gem attached to cover
©DC

N-MINT

❑3, Apr 1995 .... 2.25
❑4, May 1995 .... 2.25

Elvira, Mistress of the Dark
Claypool

❑1, May 1993, b&w; DS (a); Photo cover 4.00
❑2, Jun 1993, b&w; KB (w); DS (a); Photo cover 3.00
❑3, Jul 1993, b&w; KB (w); DS (a); Photo cover 3.00
❑4, Aug 1993, b&w; RHo (w); DS (a); Photo cover 3.00
❑5, Sep 1993, b&w; KB (w); DS, JM (a); Photo cover 3.00
❑6, Oct 1993, b&w; FH (w); DS (a); Photo cover 3.00
❑7, Nov 1993, b&w; RHo, KB (w); DC (a); Photo cover 3.00
❑8, Dec 1993, b&w RHo (w); RHo (a) 3.00
❑9, Jan 1994, b&w RHo, KB (w) 3.00
❑10, Feb 1994, b&w RHo, KB (w) 3.00
❑11, Mar 1994, b&w RHo, KB (w) 2.75
❑12, Apr 1994, b&w RHo, KB (w) 2.75
❑13, May 1994, b&w RHo, KB (w); JM (a) 2.75
❑14, Jun 1994, b&w RHo (w); JM (a) 2.75
❑15, Jul 1994, b&w; RHo (w); JM (a); Photo cover 2.75
❑16, Aug 1994, b&w RHo (w) 2.75
❑17, Sep 1994, b&w RHo (w); DC (a) 2.75
❑18, Oct 1994, b&w RHo (w) 2.75
❑19, Nov 1994, b&w RHo (w) 2.75
❑20, Dec 1994, b&w RHo (w) 2.75
❑21, Jan 1995, b&w RHo (w) 2.50
❑22, Feb 1995, b&w RHo (w) 2.50
❑23, Mar 1995, b&w RHo (w) 2.50
❑24, Apr 1995, b&w RHo (w) 2.50
❑25, May 1995, b&w RHo, KB (w) 2.50
❑26, Jun 1995, b&w RHo, KB (w) 2.50
❑27, Jul 1995, b&w DC (a) 2.50
❑28, Aug 1995, b&w DC (a) 2.50
❑29, Sep 1995, b&w DC (a) 2.50
❑30, Oct 1995, b&w RHo (w) 2.50
❑31, Nov 1995, b&w RHo (w); RHo (a) . 2.50
❑32, Dec 1995, b&w RHo (w) 2.50
❑33, Jan 1996, b&w RHo (w) 2.50
❑34, Feb 1996, b&w 2.50
❑35, Mar 1996, b&w RHo (w); RHo (a) . 2.50
❑36, Apr 1996, b&w RHo (w) 2.50
❑37, May 1996, b&w RHo (w) 2.50
❑38, Jun 1996, b&w RHo (w) 2.50
❑39, Jul 1996, b&w RHo (w); DC (a); A: Portia Prinz 2.50
❑40, Aug 1996, b&w RHo (w); DC (a) 2.50
❑41, Sep 1996, b&w DC (a) 2.50
❑42, Oct 1996, b&w; RHo (w); DC (a); House of Misery 2.50
❑43, Nov 1996, b&w RHo (w); DC (a) 2.50
❑44, Dec 1996, b&w 2.50
❑45, Jan 1997, b&w 2.50
❑46, Feb 1997, b&w 2.50
❑47, Mar 1997, b&w 2.50
❑48, Apr 1997, b&w 2.50
❑49, May 1997, b&w 2.50
❑50, Jun 1997, b&w KB (w); RHo (a) 2.50
❑51, Jul 1997, b&w 2.50
❑52, Aug 1997, b&w RHo (w) 2.50
❑53, Sep 1997, b&w RHo (w) 2.50
❑54, Oct 1997, b&w 2.50

N-MINT

❑55, Nov 1997, b&w RHo (w) 2.50
❑56, Dec 1997, b&w 2.50
❑57, Jan 1998, b&w RHo (w) 2.50
❑58, Feb 1998, b&w 2.50
❑59, Mar 1998, b&w RHo (w) 2.50
❑60, Apr 1998, b&w RHo (w) 2.50
❑61, May 1998, b&w 2.50
❑62, Jun 1998, b&w 2.50
❑63, Jul 1998, b&w 2.50
❑64, Aug 1998, b&w 2.50
❑65, Sep 1998, b&w 2.50
❑66, Oct 1998, b&w 2.50
❑67, Nov 1998, b&w 2.50
❑68, Dec 1998, b&w 2.50
❑69, Jan 1999, b&w BWi (w) 2.50
❑70, Feb 1999, b&w 2.50
❑71, Mar 1999, b&w 2.50
❑72, Apr 1999, b&w RHo (w) 2.50
❑73, May 1999, b&w 2.50
❑74, Jun 1999, b&w 2.50
❑75, Jul 1999, b&w JM (a) 2.50
❑76, Aug 1999, b&w 2.50
❑77, Sep 1999, b&w 2.50
❑78, Oct 1999, b&w JM (a) 2.50
❑79, Nov 1999, b&w 2.50
❑80, Dec 1999, b&w 2.50
❑81, Jan 2000, b&w RHo (a) 2.50
❑82, Feb 2000, b&w RHo (w) 2.50
❑83, Mar 2000, b&w JM (a) 2.50
❑84, Apr 2000, b&w 2.50
❑85, May 2000, b&w 2.50
❑86, Jun 2000, b&w 2.50
❑87, Jul 2000, b&w RHo (w) 2.50
❑88, Aug 2000, b&w RHo (w) 2.50
❑89, Sep 2000, b&w 2.50
❑90, Oct 2000, b&w RHo (w) 2.50
❑91, Nov 2000, b&w 2.50
❑92, Dec 2000, b&w 2.50
❑93, Jan 2001, b&w RHo (w) 2.50
❑94, Feb 2001, b&w RHo (w) 2.50
❑95, Mar 2001, b&w 2.50
❑96, Apr 2001, b&w 2.50
❑97, May 2001, b&w RHo (w) 2.50
❑98, Jun 2001, b&w JM (a) 2.50
❑99, Jul 2001, b&w RHo (a) 2.50
❑100, Aug 2001, b&w RHo, KB (w); DDC (a) 2.50
❑101, Sep 2001, b&w RHo (w) 2.50
❑102, Oct 2001, b&w RHo (w) 2.50
❑103, Nov 2001, b&w RHo (w) 2.50
❑104, Dec 2001, b&w 2.50
❑105, Jan 2002, b&w RHo (w) 2.50
❑106, Feb 2002, b&w 2.50
❑107, Mar 2002, b&w 2.50
❑108, Apr 2002, b&w 2.50
❑109, May 2002, b&w 2.50
❑110, Jun 2002, b&w 2.50
❑111, Jul 2002, b&w 2.50
❑112, Aug 2002, b&w BMc (a) 2.50
❑113, Sep 2002, b&w RHo (w) 2.50
❑114, Oct 2002, b&w RHo (w) 2.50
❑115, Nov 2002, b&w 2.50
❑116, Dec 2002, b&w 2.50
❑117, Jan 2003, b&w 2.50
❑118, Feb 2003, b&w 2.50
❑119, Mar 2003, b&w RHo (w) 2.50

N-MINT

❑120, Apr 2003, b&w RHo (w) 2.50
❑121, May 2003, b&w; RHo (a); Crossover with Deadbeats and Soulsearchers & Company 2.50
❑122, Jun 2003, b&w 2.50
❑123, Jul 2003, b&w 2.50
❑124, Aug 2003, b&w 2.50
❑125, Sep 2003, b&w 2.50
❑126, Oct 2003, b&w 2.50
❑127, Nov 2003, b&w 2.50
❑128, Dec 2003, b&w 2.50
❑129, Jan 2004, b&w 2.50
❑130, Feb 2004, b&w 2.50
❑131, Mar 2004, b&w 2.50
❑132, Apr 2004, b&w 2.50
❑133, May 2004, b&w 2.50
❑134, Jun 2004, b&w 2.50
❑135, Jul 2004, b&w 2.50
❑136, Aug 2004, b&w 2.50
❑137, Sep 2004, b&w 2.50
❑138, Oct 2004, b&w 2.50
❑139, Nov 2004 .... 2.50
❑140, Dec 2004 .... 2.50
❑141, Feb 2005; Jump in issue 2.50

Elvira's House of Mystery
DC

❑1, Jan 1986; Double-size; BB (c); DS (a) 2.50
❑2, Apr 1986 .... 2.00
❑3, May 1986 .... 2.00
❑4, Jun 1986 .... 2.00
❑5, Jul 1986 .... 2.00
❑6, Aug 1986; sideways issue 2.00
❑7, Sep 1986; science-fiction issue 2.00
❑8, Oct 1986 .... 2.00
❑9, Nov 1986 .... 2.00
❑10, Dec 1986 A: Cain 2.00
❑11, Jan 1987; Double-size; DSt (c); GC, DS (a); Final Issue 2.50
❑Special 1, ca. 1987; Christmas stories. 2.00

Elvis Mandible
DC / Piranha

❑1, ca. 1990, b&w; NN; One-shot 3.50

Elvis Presley Experience
Revolutionary

❑1, Aug 1992, b&w 2.50
❑2, Oct 1992, b&w 2.50
❑3, Jan 1993, b&w 2.50
❑4, Feb 1993, b&w 2.50
❑5, Jul 1993, b&w 2.50
❑6, Aug 1993, b&w 2.50
❑7, Apr 1994, b&w 2.50

Elvis Shrugged
Revolutionary

❑1, Feb 1992, b&w 2.50
❑2, Aug 1992, b&w 2.50
❑3, Apr 1992, b&w 3.95

El Zombo
Dark Horse

❑1, Apr 2004 .... 2.99
❑2, May 2004 .... 2.99
❑3, Aug 2004 .... 3.00

E-Man
Charlton

❑1, Oct 1973, O: E-Man 4.00

Other grades: Multiply price above by 5/6 for VF/NM • 2/3 for VERY FINE • 1/3 for FINE • 1/5 for VERY GOOD • 1/8 for GOOD

N-MINT

❑2, Dec 1973 .... 2.50
❑3, Jun 1974 .... 2.50
❑4, Aug 1974 .... 2.50
❑5, Nov 1974 .... 2.50
❑6, Jan 1975, JBy (a) 2.50
❑7, Mar 1975, JBy (a) 2.50
❑8, May 1975, JBy (a); Nova becomes E-Man's partner 2.50
❑9, Jul 1975, JBy (a) 2.50
❑10, Sep 1975, JBy (a) 2.50

E-Man
First

❑1, Apr 1983; JSa (a); O: E-Man 2.00
❑2, Jun 1983; JSa (a); A: F-Men. X-Men parody 1.50
❑3, Jun 1983; JSa (a); X-Men Parody 1.50
❑4, Jul 1983 JSa (a) 1.50
❑5, Aug 1983 JSa (a) 1.50
❑6, Sep 1983; JSa (a); O: E-Man 1.25
❑7, Oct 1983 JSa (a) 1.25
❑8, Nov 1983 JSa (a) 1.25
❑9, Dec 1983 JSa (a) 1.25
❑10, Jan 1984; JSa (a); O: Nova Kane 1.25
❑11, Feb 1984 JSa (a) 1.25
❑12, Mar 1984 JSa (a) 1.25
❑13, Apr 1984 JSa (a) 1.25
❑14, May 1984 JSa (a) 1.25
❑15, Jun 1984 JSa (a) 1.25
❑16, Jul 1984 JSa (a) 1.25
❑17, Aug 1984 JSa (a) 1.25
❑18, Sep 1984 JSa (a) 1.25
❑19, Oct 1984 JSa (a) 1.25
❑20, Nov 1984 JSa (a) 1.25
❑21, Dec 1984 JSa (a) 1.25
❑22, Feb 1985 JSa (a) 1.25
❑23, Apr 1985 JSa (a) 1.25
❑24, Jun 1985; JSa (a); O: Michael Mauser 1.25
❑25, Aug 1985; JSa (a); Final Issue 1.25

E-Man
Comico

❑1, Sep 1989, O: E-Man; O: Nova Kane; O: Vamfire 2.75

E-Man
Comico

❑1, Jan 1990 .... 2.50
❑2, Feb 1990 .... 2.50
❑3, Mar 1990 .... 2.50

E-Man
Alpha

❑1, Oct 1993, 1&O: Eco-Man 2.75

E-Man Returns
Alpha Productions

❑1, Mar 1994, b&w 2.75

Emblem
Antarctic / Venus

❑1, May 1994, b&w; Adult 3.50
❑2, Jun 1994, b&w; Adult 2.95
❑3, Jul 1994, b&w; Adult 2.95
❑5, Oct 1994, b&w; Adult 2.95
❑6, Nov 1994, b&w; Adult 2.95
❑7, Dec 1994, b&w; Adult 2.95
❑8, Feb 1995, b&w; Adult 2.95

Embrace
London Night

❑1, Jun 1997; Carmen Electra cover aka NC-17 Edition; Adult 5.00

Emeraldas
Eternity

❑1, Nov 1990, b&w 2.25
❑2, b&w 2.25
❑3, b&w 2.25
❑4, b&w 2.25

Emergency!
Charlton

❑1, Jun 1976, JBy (a) 20.00
❑2, Aug 1976 .... 16.00
❑3, Oct 1976 .... 14.00
❑4, Dec 1976, Scarce 16.00

Emergency!
Charlton

❑1, Jun 1976, NA (c); NA (a) 30.00
❑2, Aug 1976 .... 25.00
❑3, Oct 1976 .... 22.00
❑4, Dec 1976 .... 22.00

N-MINT

Emil and the Detectives
Gold Key

❑1, Nov 1964; adapts Disney movie 25.00

Emily the Strange
Dark Horse

❑1, Oct 2005; Boring Issue 7.95
❑2, Jan 2006; Lost Issue 7.95
❑3, Nov 2006, Stickers included 7.95

Emissary
Image

❑1, Jul 2006 .... 3.50
❑2, Sep 2006 .... 3.50
❑3, Sep 2006 .... 3.50
❑4, Oct 2006 .... 3.50
❑5, Nov 2006 .... 3.50
❑6, Jan 2007 .... 3.50

Emissary
Strateia

❑1, Jul 1998 .... 2.50

Emma Davenport
Lohman Hills

❑1, Apr 1995, b&w 3.00
❑2, Jun 1995, b&w 2.75
❑3, Aug 1995, b&w 2.75
❑4, Oct 1995, b&w 2.75
❑5, Dec 1995, b&w 2.75
❑6, Feb 1996, b&w 2.75
❑7, Apr 1996, b&w 2.75
❑8, Feb 1996, b&w; crossover with Femforce 2.75

Emma Frost
Marvel

❑1, Aug 2003 .... 4.00
❑2, Sep 2003, Emma in High School 2.50
❑3, Oct 2003 .... 2.50
❑4, Dec 2003 .... 2.50
❑5, Jan 2004 .... 2.50
❑6, Feb 2004 .... 2.50
❑7, Mar 2004 .... 2.50
❑8, Apr 2004 .... 2.99
❑9, May 2004 .... 2.99
❑10, Jun 2004 .... 2.99
❑11, Jul 2004 .... 2.99
❑12, Aug 2004 .... 2.99
❑13, Sep 2004 .... 2.99
❑14, Oct 2004 .... 2.99
❑15, Nov 2004 .... 2.99
❑16, Dec 2004 .... 2.99
❑17, Jan 2005 .... 2.99
❑18, Feb 2005, Final issue 2.99

Emo Boy
Slave Labor

❑1, Jun 2005 .... 2.95
❑2, Sep 2005 .... 2.95
❑3, Oct 2005 .... 2.95
❑4, Jan 2006 .... 2.95

Empire
Eternity

❑1, Mar 1988 .... 1.95
❑2, Apr 1988 .... 1.95
❑3, May 1988 .... 1.95
❑4, Jun 1988 .... 1.95

Empire
Image

❑1, May 2000 .... 2.50
❑2, Sep 2000 .... 2.50

Empire
DC

❑0, Jul 2003 .... 4.95
❑1, Sep 2003 .... 2.50
❑2, Sep 2003 .... 2.50
❑3, Oct 2003 .... 2.50
❑4, Dec 2003 .... 2.50
❑5, Dec 2003 .... 2.50
❑6, Jan 2004 .... 2.50

Empire Lanes
Northern Lights

❑1, Dec 1986 .... 1.75
❑2 .... 1.75
❑3 .... 1.75
❑4 .... 1.75

Empire Lanes
Keyline

❑1 .... 1.75

N-MINT

Empire Lanes
Keyline

❑1, Dec 1989 .... 2.95

Empires of Night
Rebel

❑1, Dec 1993, b&w 2.25
❑2 .... 2.25
❑3 .... 2.25
❑4 .... 2.25

Empty Love Stories
Slave Labor

❑1, Nov 1994, b&w 2.95
❑2, Aug 1996, b&w 2.95

Empty Love Stories
Funny Valentine

❑1, Jul 1998, b&w; reprints Slave Labor issue 2.95
❑Special 1, Jan 1998, b&w; NN; Anthology 2.95

Empty Love Stories: 1999
Funny Valentine

❑1, Feb 1999 .... 2.95

Empty Skull Comics
Fantagraphics

❑1, Apr 1996, b&w; Oversized; cardstock cover 4.95

Empty Zone
Sirius

❑1 .... 2.50
❑2 .... 2.50
❑3 .... 2.50
❑4 .... 2.50

Empty Zone
Sirius

❑1, ca. 1998 .... 2.95
❑2, ca. 1998 .... 2.95
❑3, ca. 1998 .... 2.95
❑4, ca. 1998 .... 2.95
❑5, ca. 1998 .... 2.95
❑6, ca. 1998 .... 2.95
❑7, ca. 1998 .... 2.95
❑8, ca. 1998 .... 2.95

Empty Zone: Trancemissions
Sirius

❑1 .... 2.95

Enchanted
Sirius

❑1, ca. 1997 .... 2.95
❑2, ca. 1997 .... 2.95
❑3, ca. 1997 .... 2.95

Enchanted
Sirius

❑1 .... 2.95
❑2 .... 2.95
❑3 .... 2.95

Enchanted Valley
Blackthorne

❑1, May 1997 .... 1.75
❑2, Jun 1987 .... 1.75

Enchanted Worlds
Blackmore

❑1, b&w 2.75

Enchanter
Eclipse

❑1, Oct 1985; Circulation reported in Comics Buyer's Guide #726 pg. 65 .... 2.00
❑2, Nov 1985 .... 2.00
❑3, Dec 1985 .... 2.00
❑4, Jan 1986 .... 2.00
❑5, Feb 1986 .... 2.00
❑6, Mar 1986 .... 2.00
❑7, Apr 1986 .... 2.00
❑8, May 1986 .... 2.00

Enchanter: Apocalypse Moon
Express / Entity

❑1, b&w; illustrated novella 2.95

Enchanter: Prelude to Apocalypse
Express

❑1, b&w 2.50
❑2, b&w 2.50
❑3, b&w 2.50

Other grades: Multiply price above by 5/6 for VF/NM • 2/3 for VERY FINE • 1/3 for FINE • 1/5 for VERY GOOD • 1/8 for GOOD

Ectokid

Part of the ill-fated Clive Barker Marvel line
©Marvel

Ehlissa

Fantasy had black-and-white cover variants
©Highland Graphics

80 Page Giant Magazine

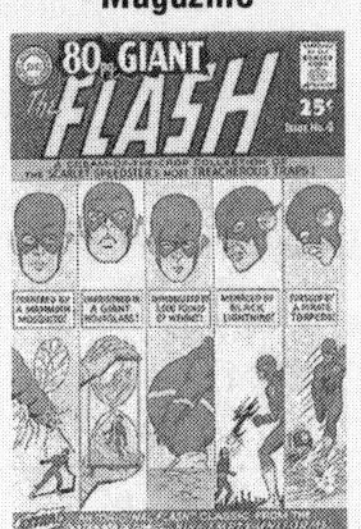

Beloved giant-sized series from Silver Age
©DC

Elektra

Limited series for back-from-dead character
©Marvel

Elektra: Assassin

Clever Frank Miller series for Epic imprint
©Marvel

N-MINT

Enchanters
Hidden Poet
❑1, Jun 1996 .... 2.50

Encyclopædia Deadpoolica
Marvel
❑1, Dec 1998; Deadpool reference 2.99

End: In the Beginning
AFC
❑1, Jun 2000, b&w; Adult 2.95

Endless Gallery
DC / Vertigo
❑1; pin-ups; Introduction by Neil Gaiman 3.50

Enemy
Dark Horse
❑1, May 1994 .... 2.50
❑2, Jun 1994 .... 2.50
❑3, Jul 1994 .... 2.50
❑4, Aug 1994, O: The Enemy 2.50
❑5, Sep 1994 .... 2.50

Enemy Ace Special
DC
❑1, Oct 1990; JKu (a); reprints Showcase and Our Army at War 3.00

Enemy Ace: War in Heaven
DC
❑1, May 2001 .... 5.95
❑2, Jun 2001 .... 5.95

EnForce
Reoccurring Images
❑1; 1: EnForce; O: EnForce 2.95

Enginehead
DC
❑1, May 2004 .... 2.50
❑2, Jun 2004 .... 2.50
❑3, Aug 2004 .... 2.50
❑4, Oct 2004 .... 2.50
❑5, Nov 2004 .... 2.50
❑6, Jan 2005 .... 2.50

Enigma
DC / Vertigo
❑1, Mar 1993 .... 2.50
❑2, Apr 1993 .... 2.50
❑3, May 1993 .... 2.50
❑4, Jun 1993 .... 2.50
❑5, Jul 1993 .... 2.50
❑6, Aug 1993 .... 2.50
❑7, Sep 1993 .... 2.50
❑8, Oct 1993 .... 2.50

Eno & Plum
Oni
❑1, Mar 1998, b&w 2.95

Ensign O'Toole
Dell
❑1, Oct 1963 .... 30.00

Entropy Tales
Entropy
❑1 .... 1.50
❑2 .... 1.50
❑3 .... 1.50
❑4 .... 1.50

N-MINT

Ents
Manic
❑1, b&w 2.50
❑2, b&w 2.50
❑3, b&w 2.50

Eo
Rebel
❑1; Adult 3.00
❑1/Ltd.; Limited "Premier" edition, Adult 3.00
❑2; Adult 3.00
❑2/Ltd.; limited edition; Adult 3.00
❑3; Adult 3.00
❑4; Adult 3.00

Epic Anthology
Marvel / Epic
❑1, Apr 2004, Sleepwalker, Young Ancient One, and Strange Magic stories 5.99

Epic Illustrated
Marvel / Epic
❑1, Spr 1980, FF (c); WP, JSn, SL (w); WP, JSn, JB, FF (a); 1: Dreadstar. A: Silver Surfer 6.00
❑2, Sum 1980 .... 4.00
❑3, Aut 1980, Fall 1980 .... 4.00
❑4, Win 1980 .... 4.00
❑5, Apr 1981 .... 3.00
❑6, Jun 1981 .... 3.00
❑7, Aug 1981 .... 3.00
❑8, Oct 1981 .... 3.00
❑9, Dec 1981 .... 3.00
❑10, Feb 1982 .... 3.00
❑11, Apr 1982 .... 3.00
❑12, Jun 1982 .... 3.00
❑13, Aug 1982 .... 3.00
❑14, Oct 1982 .... 3.00
❑15, Dec 1982 .... 3.00
❑16, Feb 1983 .... 3.00
❑17, Apr 1983 .... 3.00
❑18, Jun 1983 .... 3.00
❑19, Aug 1983 .... 3.00
❑20, Oct 1983 .... 3.00
❑21, Dec 1983 .... 3.00
❑22, Feb 1984 .... 3.00
❑23, Apr 1984 .... 3.00
❑24, Jun 1984 .... 3.00
❑25, Aug 1984 .... 3.00
❑26, Oct 1984 .... 3.00
❑27, Dec 1984 .... 3.00
❑28, Feb 1985 .... 3.00
❑29, Apr 1985 .... 3.00
❑30, Jun 1985, JSn, JBy (w); JSn, JBy, CV (a) 3.00
❑31, Aug 1985 .... 3.00
❑32, Oct 1985 .... 3.00
❑33, Dec 1985 .... 3.00
❑34, Feb 1986, Final Issue 3.00

Epic Lite
Marvel / Epic
❑1, Sep 1991 .... 4.50

Epsilon Wave
Independent
❑1, Oct 1985; Independent Comics publishes 1.50
❑2, Dec 1985 .... 1.50
❑3, Feb 1986 .... 1.50
❑4, Apr 1986 .... 1.50
❑5, May 1986; Elite begins as publisher 1.75
❑6, Jun 1986 .... 1.75
❑7, Aug 1986 .... 1.75
❑8 1986 .... 1.75

N-MINT

Equine the Uncivilized
Graphxpress
❑1, b&w 2.00
❑2 .... 2.00
❑3 .... 2.00
❑4 .... 2.00
❑5 .... 2.00
❑6 .... 2.00

Equinox Chronicles
Innovation
❑1, b&w 2.25
❑2, b&w 2.25

Eradicator
DC
❑1, Aug 1996 .... 1.75
❑2, Sep 1996 .... 1.75
❑3, Oct 1996 .... 1.75

Eradicators
Silverwolf
❑1, May 1986 .... 1.50
❑2, Jul 1986 .... 1.50
❑3, Aug 1986 .... 1.50
❑4, Sep 1986 .... 1.50

Eradicators
Silverwolf
❑1, Aug 1989, b&w; Cover says September 2.00
❑2, Apr 1990, b&w 2.00

Eric Basaldua Sketchbook
Image
❑1, Nov 2006, b&w 2.99

Eric Preston Is the Flame
B-Movie
❑1 .... 1.00

Erika Telekinetika
Fantagraphics
❑1, Aug 2004; Adult; b&w 3.95
❑2, Nov 2004; Adult; b&w 3.95
❑3, Apr 2005; Adult; b&w 3.95

Ernie
Kitchen Sink
❑1; comics 2.00

Eros Forum
Fantagraphics / Eros
❑1, b&w; Adult 2.50
❑3, Apr 1993, b&w; Adult; B&w, internal notes say #2 .... 2.95

Eros Graphic Album
Fantagraphics / Eros
❑1 .... 9.95
❑2 .... 12.95
❑3 .... 10.95
❑4 .... 10.95
❑5 .... 14.95
❑6 .... 16.95
❑7 .... 12.95
❑8 .... 12.95
❑9 .... 9.95

Other grades: Multiply price above by 5/6 for VF/NM • 2/3 for VERY FINE • 1/3 for FINE • 1/5 for VERY GOOD • 1/8 for GOOD

N-MINT

- ❑10 12.95
- ❑11, Feb 1994 11.95
- ❑12, Jul 1994 12.95
- ❑13, Aug 1994; b&w 12.95
- ❑14 14.95
- ❑15 14.95
- ❑16 14.95
- ❑17 15.95
- ❑18 12.95
- ❑19 14.95
- ❑20 12.95
- ❑21 14.95
- ❑22 14.95
- ❑23 12.95
- ❑24 12.95
- ❑25 16.95
- ❑26 13.95
- ❑27 11.95
- ❑28 16.95
- ❑29 16.95
- ❑30 13.95
- ❑31 19.95
- ❑32 16.95
- ❑33 16.95
- ❑34; Buffy Collection 14.95
- ❑35 14.95
- ❑36 19.95
- ❑37 19.95
- ❑38, Mar 1998; Adult; b&w 19.95
- ❑39, Mar 1999; Adult; b&w 19.95
- ❑40 19.95
- ❑41 19.95
- ❑42 19.95
- ❑43 16.95
- ❑44 16.95

Eros Hawk
Fantagraphics / Eros

- ❑1 2.75
- ❑2 2.75
- ❑3 2.75
- ❑4 2.75

Eros Hawk III
Fantagraphics / Eros

- ❑1, Jul 1994, b&w 2.75

Erotic Fables & Faerie Tales
Fantagraphics / Eros

- ❑1, b&w; Adult 2.50
- ❑2, b&w; Adult 2.50

Eroticom
Caliber

- ❑1; Adult; ca. 1991 2.50

Eroticom II
Caliber

- ❑1, ca. 1994, b&w; pin-ups, many swiped from Playboy's Book of Lingerie 2.95

Erotic Orbits
Comax

- ❑1, b&w; Adult 2.95

Erotic Tales
Aircel

- ❑1, Sep 1991, b&w; Adult 2.95
- ❑2, b&w; Adult 2.95
- ❑3, b&w; Adult 2.95

Erotic Worlds of Frank Thorne
Fantagraphics / Eros

- ❑1, Oct 1990; FT (w); FT (a); sexy cover. 2.95
- ❑1/A, Oct 1990; FT (w); FT (a); Violent cover 2.95
- ❑2, Nov 1990; FT (w); FT (a); Adult 2.95
- ❑3, Dec 1990; FT (w); FT (a); Adult 2.95
- ❑4, Jan 1991; FT (w); FT (a); Adult 2.95
- ❑5, Apr 1991; FT (w); FT (a); Danger Rangerette cover/story; Adult 2.95
- ❑6; FT (w); FT (a); Adult 2.95

Erotique
Aircel

- ❑1, May 1991, b&w; Adult 2.50

Ersatz Peach
Aeon

- ❑1, Jul 1995; see also The Desert Peach; Charity fund-raiser; Desert Peach stories by various artists and writers 7.95

N-MINT

Esc
Comico

- ❑1 1996 2.95
- ❑2, Sep 1996 2.95
- ❑3 1996 2.95
- ❑4 1997 2.95

Escapade in Florence
Gold Key

- ❑1, Jan 1963, Photo cover 40.00

Escape to the Stars
Solson

- ❑1 1.75

Escapists
Dark Horse

- ❑1, Jul 2006 1.00
- ❑2, Oct 2006 2.99
- ❑3, Nov 2006, Cover by John Cassaday 2.99
- ❑4, Nov 2006 2.99
- ❑5, Dec 2006 2.99
- ❑6, Jan 2007 2.99

Espers
Eclipse

- ❑1, Jul 1986 3.00
- ❑2, Sep 1986 2.00
- ❑3, Nov 1986 BB (c); BB (a) 2.00
- ❑4, Feb 1987 2.00
- ❑5, Apr 1987; Story continued in Interface #1 2.00

Espers
Halloween

- ❑1, ca. 1996, b&w 2.95
- ❑2, ca. 1996, b&w 2.95
- ❑3, ca. 1997, b&w 2.95
- ❑4, ca. 1997, b&w 2.95
- ❑5, ca. 1997, b&w; Features David Lloyd's original Espers Designs (Pt. 1) 2.95
- ❑6, ca. 1997; b&w 2.95

Espers
Image

- ❑1 1997, b&w 3.50
- ❑2 1997, b&w 3.00
- ❑3, Aug 1997, b&w 3.00
- ❑4 1997, b&w 3.00
- ❑5 1997, b&w 3.00
- ❑6 1997, b&w 3.00
- ❑7 1998, b&w 3.00
- ❑8 1998 3.00
- ❑9 3.00

Espionage
Dell

- ❑1 18.00
- ❑2 15.00

Essential Elfquest
Warp

- ❑1, Apr 1995; giveaway; WP (w); Free Preview 1.50

Essential Vertigo: Swamp Thing
DC / Vertigo

- ❑1, Nov 1996; AMo (w); Reprints Saga of the Swamp Thing #21 3.00
- ❑2, Dec 1996; AMo (w); Reprints Saga of the Swamp Thing #22 2.50
- ❑3, Jan 1997; AMo (w); Reprints Saga of the Swamp Thing #23 2.50
- ❑4, Feb 1997; AMo (w); Reprints Saga of the Swamp Thing #24 2.50
- ❑5, Mar 1997; AMo (w); Reprints Saga of the Swamp Thing #25 2.50
- ❑6, Apr 1997; AMo (w); Reprints Saga of the Swamp Thing #26 2.00
- ❑7, May 1997; Reprints Saga of the Swamp Thing #27 2.00
- ❑8, Jun 1997; AMo (w); Reprints Saga of the Swamp Thing #28 2.00
- ❑9, Jul 1997; Reprints Saga of the Swamp Thing #29 2.00
- ❑10, Aug 1997; AMo (w); AA (a); Reprints Saga of the Swamp Thing #30 2.00
- ❑11, Sep 1997; AMo (w); Reprints Saga of the Swamp Thing #31 2.00
- ❑12, Oct 1997; Reprints Saga of the Swamp Thing #32 2.00
- ❑13, Nov 1997; AMo (w); Reprints Saga of the Swamp Thing #32 2.00
- ❑14, Dec 1997; AMo (w); Reprints Saga of the Swamp Thing #34 2.00
- ❑15, Jan 1998; AMo (w); Reprints Saga of the Swamp Thing #34 2.00

N-MINT

- ❑16, Feb 1998; AMo (w); Reprints Saga of the Swamp Thing #35 2.00
- ❑17, Mar 1998; AMo (w); Reprints Saga of the Swamp Thing #36 2.00
- ❑18, Apr 1998; AMo (w); Reprints Saga of the Swamp Thing #37 2.00
- ❑19, May 1998; AMo (w); Reprints Saga of the Swamp Thing #38 2.00
- ❑20, Jun 1998; Reprints Saga of the Swamp Thing #39 2.00
- ❑21, Jul 1998; AMo (w); Reprints Saga of the Swamp Thing #40 2.00
- ❑22, Aug 1998; AMo (w); AA (a); Reprints Saga of the Swamp Thing #41 2.00
- ❑23, Sep 1998; Reprints Saga of the Swamp Thing #42 2.25
- ❑24, Oct 1998; Final Issue 2.25

Essential Vertigo: The Sandman
DC / Vertigo

- ❑1, Aug 1996, NG (w); Reprints Sandman #1 3.00
- ❑2, Sep 1996, NG (w); Reprints Sandman #2 2.50
- ❑3, Oct 1996, NG (w); Reprints Sandman #3 2.50
- ❑4, Oct 1996, NG (w); Reprints Sandman #4 2.50
- ❑5, Dec 1996, NG (w); Reprints Sandman #5 2.50
- ❑6, Jan 1997, NG (w); Reprints Sandman #6 2.00
- ❑7, Feb 1997, NG (w); Reprints Sandman #7 2.00
- ❑8, Mar 1997, NG (w); 1: Death (Sandman). Reprints Sandman #8 2.00
- ❑9, Apr 1997, NG (w); Reprints Sandman #9 2.00
- ❑10, May 1997, NG (w); Reprints Sandman #10 2.00
- ❑11, Jun 1997, NG (w); Reprints Sandman #11 2.00
- ❑12, Jul 1997, NG (w); Reprints Sandman #12 2.00
- ❑13, Aug 1997, NG (w); Reprints Sandman #13 2.00
- ❑14, Sep 1997, NG (w); Reprints Sandman #14 2.00
- ❑15, Oct 1997, NG (w); Reprints Sandman #15 2.00
- ❑16, Nov 1997, NG (w); Reprints Sandman #16 2.00
- ❑17, Dec 1997, NG (w); Reprints Sandman #17 2.00
- ❑18, Jan 1998, NG (w); Reprints Sandman #18 2.00
- ❑19, Feb 1998, NG (w); CV (a); Reprints Sandman #19 2.00
- ❑20, Mar 1998, NG (w); Reprints Sandman #20 2.00
- ❑21, Apr 1998, NG (w); Reprints Sandman #21 1.95
- ❑22, May 1998, NG (w); Reprints Sandman #22 1.95
- ❑23, Jun 1998, NG (w); Reprints Sandman #23 1.95
- ❑24, Jul 1998, NG (w); Reprints Sandman #24 1.95
- ❑25, Aug 1998, NG (w); MW (a); Reprints Sandman #25 1.95
- ❑26, Sep 1998, NG (w); Reprints Sandman #26 2.25
- ❑27, Oct 1998, NG (w); Reprints Sandman #27 2.25
- ❑28, Nov 1998, NG (w); Reprints Sandman #28 2.25
- ❑29, Dec 1998, NG (w); Reprints Sandman #29 2.25
- ❑30, Jan 1999, NG (w); BT (a); Reprints Sandman #30 2.25
- ❑31, Feb 1999, NG (w); Reprints Sandman #31 2.25
- ❑32, Mar 1999, NG (w); BT (a); Reprints Sandman Special #1 4.50

Establishment
DC / Wildstorm

- ❑1, Nov 2001 3.00
- ❑2, Dec 2001 2.50
- ❑3, Jan 2002 2.50
- ❑4, Feb 2002 2.50
- ❑5, Mar 2002 2.50
- ❑6, Apr 2002 2.50
- ❑7, May 2002 2.50
- ❑8, Jun 2002 2.50
- ❑9, Jul 2002 2.50
- ❑10, Aug 2002 2.50
- ❑11, Sep 2002 2.50
- ❑12, Oct 2002 2.50
- ❑13, Nov 2002 2.50

Elektra Saga

Reformatted reprint of Daredevil Elektra stories
©Marvel

Elementals

Band of super-heroes from Bill Willingham
©Comico

Elflord

Elvish heroes in action from Barry Blair
©Aircel

Elfquest

Comics cultural phenomenon in 1980s
©Warp

Elfquest

Marvel reprints of the famous Warp series
©Marvel

N-MINT

Etc
DC / Piranha

❑1, ca. 1989 .... 4.50
❑2, ca. 1989 .... 4.50
❑3, ca. 1989 .... 4.50
❑4, ca. 1990 .... 4.50
❑5, ca. 1990 .... 4.50

Et Cetera
Tokyopop

❑1, Aug 2004, Graphic novel; b&w 9.99
❑2, Oct 2004; Graphic novel; b&w 9.99
❑3, Dec 2004; Graphic novel; b&w 9.99
❑4, Feb 2005; Graphic novel; b&w 9.99
❑5, May 2005; Graphic novel; b&w 9.99
❑6, Oct 2005; Graphic novel; b&w 9.99

Eternal
Marvel / MAX

❑1, Aug 2003 .... 2.99
❑2, Sep 2003 .... 2.99
❑3, Oct 2003 .... 2.99
❑4, Nov 2003 .... 2.99
❑5, Dec 2003 .... 2.99
❑6, Jan 2004 .... 2.99

Eternal Romance
Best Destiny

❑1, Feb 1997, b&w 3.00
❑2, May 1997, b&w 2.50
❑3, Dec 1997 .... 2.50
❑4, Jul 1998 .... 2.50

Eternal Romance Labor of Love Sketchbook
Best Destiny

❑1; Labor of Love sketchbook. 250 printed 2.50

Eternals
Marvel

❑1, Jul 1976, JK (c); JK (w); JK (a); O: Eternals. 1: Kro. 1: Margo Damian. 1: Brother Tode. 1: Ikaris 10.00
❑1/30¢, Jul 1976, JK (c); JK (w); JK (a); O: Eternals. 1: Kro. 1: Margo Damian. 1: Brother Tode. 1: Ikaris. 30¢ regional price variant 25.00
❑2, Aug 1976, JK (c); JK (w); JK (a); 1: Ajak. 1: Arishem the Judge 5.00
❑2/30¢, Aug 1976, JK (w); JK (a); 1: Ajak. 1: Arishem the Judge. 30¢ regional price variant 15.00
❑3, Sep 1976, JK (c); JK (w); JK (a); 1: Sersi; Ralph Macchio L.O.C. 2.50
❑4, Oct 1976, JK (c); JK (w); JK (a); 1: Gammenon the Gatherer 2.50
❑5, Nov 1976, JK (c); JK (w); JK (a); 1: Makkari. 1: Zuras (Thena) 2.50
❑6, Dec 1976, JK (c); JK (w); JK (a) 2.00
❑7, Jan 1977, JK (c); JK (w); JK (a); 1: Nezarr 2.00
❑8, Feb 1977, JK (c); JK (w); JK (a); 1: Karkas. Newsstand edition (distributed by Curtis); issue number in box 2.00
❑8/Whitman, Feb 1977, JK (w); JK (a); 1: Karkas. Special markets edition (usually sold in Whitman bagged prepacks); price appears in a diamond; UPC barcode appears 2.00
❑9, Mar 1977, JK (c); JK (w); JK (a); 1: Sprite I. Newsstand edition (distributed by Curtis); issue number in box 2.00
❑9/Whitman, Mar 1977, JK (w); JK (a); 1: Sprite I. Special markets edition (usually sold in Whitman bagged prepacks); price appears in a diamond; UPC barcode appears 2.00
❑10, Apr 1977, JK (c); JK (w); JK (a); Newsstand edition (distributed by Curtis); issue number in box 2.00
❑10/Whitman, Apr 1977, JK (w); JK (a); Special markets edition (usually sold in Whitman bagged prepacks); price appears in a diamond; UPC barcode appears 2.00
❑11, May 1977, JK (c); JK (w); JK (a); 1: Aginar; Mike W. Barr L.O.C. 2.00
❑12, Jun 1977, JK (c); JK (w); JK (a); 1: Uni-Mind. Newsstand edition (distributed by Curtis); issue number in box 2.00
❑12/Whitman, Jun 1977, JK (w); JK (a); 1: Uni-Mind. Special markets edition (usually sold in Whitman bagged prepacks); price appears in a diamond; UPC barcode appears 2.00
❑12/35¢, Jun 1977, JK (c); JK (w); JK (a); 1: Uni-Mind. 35¢ regional price variant; newsstand edition (distributed by Curtis); issue number in box 15.00
❑13, Jul 1977, JK (c); JK (w); JK (a); 1: Gilgamesh. 1: One Above All. Newsstand edition (distributed by Curtis); issue number in box 2.00
❑13/Whitman, Jul 1977, JK (w); JK (a); 1: Gilgamesh. 1: One Above All. Special markets edition (usually sold in Whitman bagged prepacks); price appears in a diamond; UPC barcode appears 2.00
❑13/35¢, Jul 1977, JK (c); JK (w); JK (a); 1: Gilgamesh. 1: One Above All. 35¢ regional price variant; newsstand edition (distributed by Curtis); issue number in box 15.00
❑14, Aug 1977, JK (c); JK (w); JK (a); A: Hulk. Newsstand edition (distributed by Curtis); issue number in box 2.00
❑14/Whitman, Aug 1977, JK (w); JK (a); A: Hulk. Special markets edition (usually sold in Whitman bagged prepacks); price appears in a diamond; UPC barcode appears 2.00
❑14/35¢, Aug 1977, JK (c); JK (w); JK (a); A: Hulk. 35¢ regional price variant; newsstand edition (distributed by Curtis); issue number in box 15.00
❑15, Sep 1977, JK (c); JK (w); JK (a); A: Hulk. Newsstand edition (distributed by Curtis); issue number in box 2.00
❑15/Whitman, Sep 1977, JK (w); JK (a); A: Hulk. Special markets edition (usually sold in Whitman bagged prepacks); price appears in a diamond; UPC barcode appears 2.00
❑15/35¢, Sep 1977, JK (c); JK (w); JK (a); A: Hulk. 35¢ regional price variant; newsstand edition (distributed by Curtis); issue number in box 15.00
❑16, Oct 1977, JK (c); JK (w); JK (a); Newsstand edition (distributed by Curtis); issue number in box 2.00
❑16/Whitman, Oct 1977, JK (w); JK (a); Special markets edition (usually sold in Whitman bagged prepacks); price appears in a diamond; no UPC barcode 2.00
❑16/35¢, Oct 1977, JK (c); JK (w); JK (a); 35¢ regional price variant; newsstand edition (distributed by Curtis); issue number in box 15.00
❑17, Nov 1977, JK (c); JK (w); JK (a); Newsstand edition (distributed by Curtis); issue number in box 2.00
❑17/Whitman, Nov 1977, JK (w); JK (a); Special markets edition (usually sold in Whitman bagged prepacks); price appears in a diamond; no UPC barcode 2.00
❑18, Dec 1977, JK (c); JK (w); JK (a) 2.00
❑19, Jan 1978, JK (c); JK (w); JK (a); 1: Ziran 2.00
❑Ann 1, Oct 1977, JK (c); JK (w); JK (a); Squarebound 7.00

Eternals
Marvel

❑1, Oct 1985; Giant-size; 1: Khoryphos. 1.50
❑2, Nov 1985; 1: Ghaur 1.00
❑3, Dec 1985 .... 1.00
❑4, Jan 1986 .... 1.00
❑5, Feb 1986 .... 1.00
❑6, Mar 1986 .... 1.00
❑7, Apr 1986 .... 1.00
❑8, May 1986 .... 1.00
❑9, Jun 1986 .... 1.00
❑10, Jul 1986; O: Ghaur. D: Margo Damian 1.00
❑11, Aug 1986 .... 1.00
❑12, Sep 1986; Giant-size; final issue 1.25

Eternals
Marvel

❑1, Sep 2006 .... 3.99
❑1/Variant, Sep 2006 .... 4.99
❑1/2nd variant, Sep 2006 .... 4.99
❑2, Sep 2006 .... 3.99
❑3, Nov 2006 .... 3.99
❑4, Dec 2006 .... 3.99
❑4/Variant, Dec 2006 .... 3.99
❑5, Jan 2007 .... 3.99
❑5/Variant, Jan 2007 .... 3.99

Eternals Sketchbook
Marvel

❑1, Aug 2006, b&w 1.99

Eternals: The Herod Factor
Marvel

❑1, Nov 1991; D: Ajak; D: Doctor Damian 2.50

Eternal Thirst
Alpha Productions

❑3, b&w 1.95
❑4, b&w 1.95
❑5, b&w 1.95

Eternal Warrior
Valiant

❑1, Aug 1992; FM (c);Unity 4.00
❑1/GoldEmboss, Aug 1992, FM (c) 25.00
❑1/Gold, Aug 1992; FM (c); Gold logo (dealer promotion) 10.00
❑2, Sep 1992; Unity 3.00
❑3, Oct 1992 A: Armstrong 2.00
❑4, Nov 1992; 1: Bloodshot (cameo); 1: Bloodshot (Angelo Moretti); 1: Immortal Enemy 5.00
❑5, Dec 1992 A: Bloodshot 2.00
❑6, Jan 1993; V: Master Darque 2.00
❑7, Feb 1993 .... 2.00

Other grades: Multiply price above by 5/6 for VF/NM • 2/3 for VERY FINE • 1/3 for FINE • 1/5 for VERY GOOD • 1/8 for GOOD

❑8, Mar 1993; Double-size; combined with Archer & Armstrong #8 .... 3.00
❑9, Apr 1993 .... 1.00
❑10, May 1993 .... 1.00
❑11, Jun 1993 .... 1.00
❑12, Jul 1993 .... 1.00
❑13, Aug 1993; V: Eternal Enemy 1.00
❑14, Sep 1993 A: Bloodshot 1.00
❑15, Oct 1993 A: Bloodshot 1.00
❑16, Nov 1993 .... 1.00
❑17, Dec 1993 .... 1.00
❑18, Jan 1994 .... 1.00
❑19, Feb 1994 A: Doctor Mirage 1.00
❑20, Mar 1994 .... 1.00
❑21, Apr 1994 .... 1.00
❑22, May 1994; trading card 2.00
❑23, Jun 1994 .... 1.00
❑24, Aug 1994; V: Immortal Enemy 1.00
❑25, Sep 1994; A: Archer & Armstrong. Contiuned from Archer and Armstrong #25 .... 1.00
❑26, Oct 1994; indicia says August; Flip-book with Archer & Armstrong #26; Chaos Effect Gamma 4 .... 4.00
❑27, Nov 1994 .... 1.00
❑27/VVSS, Nov 1994 .... 125.00
❑28, Dec 1994 .... 1.00
❑29, Jan 1995 .... 1.00
❑30, Feb 1995 .... 2.00
❑31, Mar 1995 .... 2.00
❑32, Apr 1995 JDu (c); JDu (a) 2.00
❑33, May 1995 PG (c) 2.00
❑34, Jun 1995 PG (c) 2.00
❑35, Jul 1995; PG (c); Birthquake; outer white cover with warning 2.00
❑36, Jul 1995; PG (c); PG (a); Birthquake 2.00
❑37, Aug 1995 .... 2.00
❑38, Aug 1995; V: Spider Queen 2.00
❑39, Sep 1995 PG (c) 2.00
❑40, Sep 1995 PG (c) 2.00
❑41, Oct 1995 .... 3.00
❑42, Oct 1995 .... 3.00
❑43, Nov 1995 .... 3.00
❑44, Nov 1995 .... 3.00
❑45, Dec 1995 .... 3.00
❑46, Dec 1995 .... 4.00
❑47, Jan 1996 .... 4.00
❑48, Jan 1996 .... 4.00
❑49, Feb 1996 .... 4.00
❑50, Mar 1996; A: Geomancer. Final Issue 7.00
❑Special 1, Feb 1996; Eternal Warrior in WW II 4.00
❑YB 1, ca. 1993; cardstock cover 5.00
❑YB 2, ca. 1994; PG (c); cardstock cover 5.00

Eternal Warrior: Fist and Steel
Acclaim / Valiant
❑1, May 1996, A: Geomancer 5.00
❑2, Jun 1996, A: Geomancer. Includes introduction comic for Resurrection Rise 2 video game 6.00

Eternal Warriors
Acclaim / Valiant
❑1, Jun 1997 .... 3.95
❑1/Variant, Jun 1997; alternate painted cover 3.95
❑Ashcan 1, Feb 1997, b&w; No cover price; preview of Time and Treachery one-shot 1.00

Eternal Warriors: Archer & Armstrong
Acclaim / Valiant
❑1, Dec 1997; price stickered on cover .. 3.95

Eternal Warriors Blackworks
Acclaim / Valiant
❑1, Mar 1998 .... 3.95

Eternal Warriors: Digital Alchemy
Acclaim / Valiant
❑1, Sep 1997; One-shot 3.95

Eternal Warriors: Mog
Acclaim / Valiant
❑1, Mar 1998; One-shot 3.95

Eternal Warrior Special
Acclaim / Valiant
❑1, Feb 1996; Eternal Warrior in WW II . 2.50

Eternal Warriors: The Immortal Enemy
Acclaim / Valiant
❑1, Jun 1998; Final issue of VH-2 universe 3.95

Eternal Warriors: Time and Treachery
Acclaim / Valiant
❑1, ca. 1997 .... 3.95

Eternity Smith
Renegade
❑1, Sep 1986, 1: Eternity Smith; 1: Skylark Smith 1.50
❑2, Nov 1986 .... 1.50
❑3, Jan 1987 .... 1.50
❑4, Mar 1987 .... 1.50
❑5, May 1987; Final issue at Renegade Press 1.50

Eternity Smith
Hero
❑1, Sep 1987 .... 1.95
❑2, Oct 1987 .... 1.95
❑3, Nov 1987 .... 1.95
❑4, Dec 1987 .... 1.95
❑5, Jan 1988 .... 1.95
❑6, Feb 1988 .... 1.95
❑7, Apr 1988 .... 1.95
❑8, Jun 1988 .... 1.95
❑9, Aug 1988; Final Issue 1.95

Eternity Triple Action
Eternity
❑1, b&w 2.50
❑2, b&w 2.50
❑3, b&w 2.50
❑4, b&w 2.50

Eudaemon
Dark Horse
❑1, Aug 1993 .... 2.50
❑2 .... 2.50
❑3 .... 2.50

Eugenus
Eugenus
❑1, b&w 3.50
❑2, b&w 3.50
❑3 .... 2.50

Eureka
Radio
❑1, Apr 2000, b&w 2.95
❑2, Jul 2000, b&w 2.95
❑3, Sep 2000, b&w 2.95

Europa and the Pirate Twins
Powder Monkey
❑1, Oct 1996, b&w 2.95
❑1/A, Oct 1996, b&w; no cover price 2.95
❑Ashcan 1, Mar 1996, b&w; No cover price; smaller than normal comic 1.00

Evangeline Special
Lodestone
❑1, May 1986; Wraparound cover; Collects Comico issues #1 and #2 with added pages 2.00

Evangeline
Comico
❑1, ca. 1984, 1: Evangeline 2.50
❑2, ca. 1984 .... 2.00

Evangeline
First
❑1, May 1987; Continued From Evangeline #2 Published by Comico... 2.50
❑2, Jul 1987 .... 2.00
❑3, Sep 1987 .... 2.00
❑4, Nov 1987 .... 2.00
❑5, Jan 1988 .... 2.00
❑6, Mar 1988 .... 2.00
❑7, May 1988 .... 2.00
❑8, Jul 1988 .... 2.00
❑9, Sep 1988 .... 2.00
❑10, Nov 1988 .... 2.00
❑11, Jan 1989 .... 2.00
❑12, Mar 1989; Final Issue 2.00

Evel Knievel
Marvel
❑1; giveaway; Giveaway 10.00

Evenfall
Slave Labor
❑1, Mar 2003, b&w; Title is actually The Fallen: Evenfall 2.95
❑2, May 2003, b&w 2.95
❑3, ca. 2003, b&w 2.95
❑4, ca. 2004, b&w 2.95
❑5, ca. 2004, b&w 2.95
❑6, ca. 2004, b&w 2.95
❑7, Feb 2005, b&w 2.95

Even More Secret Origins 80-Page Giant
DC
❑1, ca. 2003 .... 6.95

E.V.E. Protomecha
Image
❑1, Mar 2000; Blue background on cover 2.50
❑1/A, Mar 2000, Alternate Cover Finch .. 2.50
❑1/Gold; Gold Cover 2.50
❑1/Hologram; Holofield 2.50
❑2, Apr 2000; Woman on cover 2.50
❑3, May 2000 .... 2.50
❑4, Nov 2000 .... 2.50
❑5 .... 2.50
❑6, Sep 2000 .... 2.50

Everquest: The Ruins of Kunark
DC / Wildstorm
❑1, Feb 2002, Several characters in profile on cover 5.95

Everquest: Transformation
DC
❑1, Aug 2002, Several characters in profile on cover 5.95

Everwinds
Slave Labor / Amaze Ink
❑1, Aug 1997, b&w 2.95
❑2, Oct 1997, b&w 2.95
❑3, Dec 1997, b&w 2.95
❑4, Mar 1998 .... 2.95

Every Dog Has His Day
Shiga
❑1 .... 2.00

Everyman
Marvel / Epic
❑1, Nov 1991; NN 4.50

Everything's Archie
Archie
❑1, May 1969, Giant-size 48.00
❑2 1969 .... 26.00
❑3 1969 .... 20.00
❑4 1969 .... 20.00
❑5 .... 20.00
❑6 1970 .... 12.00
❑7 1970 .... 12.00
❑8 1970 .... 12.00
❑9 .... 12.00
❑10 1971 .... 12.00
❑11 1971 .... 7.00
❑12 1971 .... 7.00
❑13 1971 .... 7.00
❑14 1971 .... 7.00
❑15 1971 .... 7.00
❑16 .... 7.00
❑17 1972 .... 7.00
❑18 1972 .... 7.00
❑19 1972 .... 7.00
❑20 1972 .... 7.00
❑21, Aug 1972 .... 4.00
❑22, Oct 1972 .... 4.00
❑23, Dec 1972 .... 4.00
❑24, Feb 1973 .... 4.00
❑25, Apr 1973 .... 4.00
❑26, Jun 1973 .... 4.00
❑27, Aug 1973 .... 4.00
❑28, Sep 1973 .... 4.00
❑29, Oct 1973 .... 4.00
❑30, Dec 1973 .... 4.00
❑31, Feb 1974 .... 4.00
❑32, Apr 1974 .... 4.00
❑33, Jun 1974 .... 4.00
❑34, Aug 1974 .... 4.00
❑35, Sep 1974 .... 4.00
❑36, Oct 1974 .... 4.00
❑37, Dec 1974 .... 4.00
❑38, Feb 1975 .... 4.00
❑39, Apr 1975 .... 4.00
❑40, Jun 1975 .... 4.00
❑41, Aug 1975 .... 3.00
❑42, Sep 1975 .... 3.00
❑43, Oct 1975 .... 3.00
❑44, Dec 1975 .... 3.00

Other grades: Multiply price above by 5/6 for VF/NM • 2/3 for VERY FINE • 1/3 for FINE • 1/5 for VERY GOOD • 1/8 for GOOD

Elfquest: Blood of Ten Chiefs

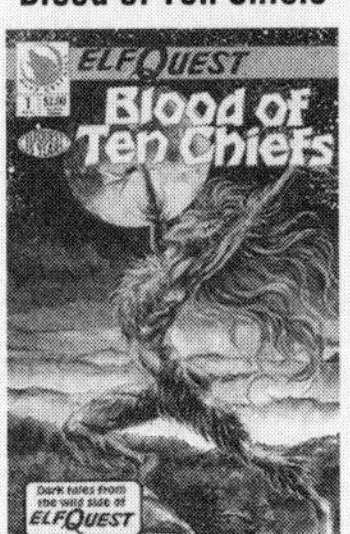

Tales from the wild side of Elfquest
©Warp

Elfquest: New Blood

Rotating teams of creators write the elves
©Warp

Elftrek

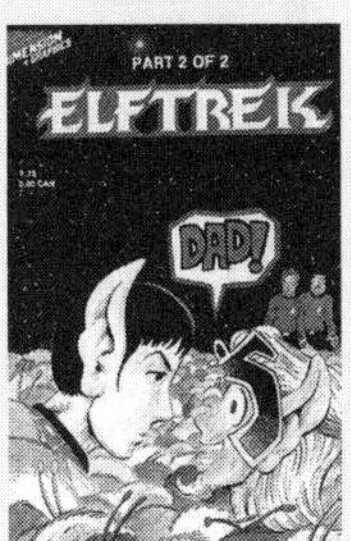

Simultaneous parody of Star Trek and Elfquest
©Dimension

Eliminator

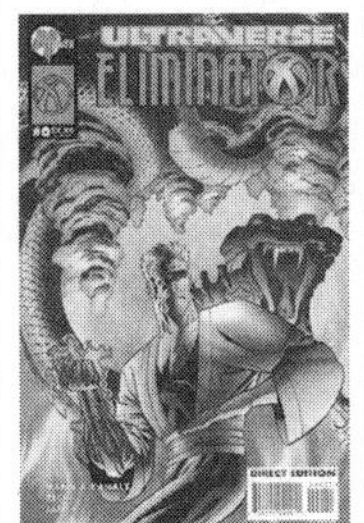

Ultraverse resident with cybernetic arm
©Malibu

Elvira, Mistress of the Dark

Horror hostess has satiric adventures
©Claypool

	N-MINT
❑45, Feb 1976	3.00
❑46, Apr 1976	3.00
❑47, May 1976	3.00
❑48, Jun 1976	3.00
❑49, Jul 1976	3.00
❑50, Aug 1976	3.00
❑51, Sep 1976	3.00
❑52, Oct 1976	3.00
❑53, Dec 1976	3.00
❑54, Feb 1977	3.00
❑55, Apr 1977	3.00
❑56, May 1977	3.00
❑57, Jun 1977	3.00
❑58, Jul 1977	3.00
❑59, Aug 1977	3.00
❑60, Sep 1977	3.00
❑61, Oct 1977	2.00
❑62, Dec 1977	2.00
❑63, Feb 1978	2.00
❑64, Apr 1978	2.00
❑65, May 1978	2.00
❑66, Jun 1978	2.00
❑67, Jul 1978	2.00
❑68, Aug 1978	2.00
❑69, Sep 1978	2.00
❑70, Oct 1978	2.00
❑71, Dec 1978	2.00
❑72, Feb 1979	2.00
❑73, Apr 1979	2.00
❑74, May 1979	2.00
❑75, Jun 1979	2.00
❑76, Jul 1979	2.00
❑77, Aug 1979	2.00
❑78, Sep 1979	2.00
❑79, Oct 1979	2.00
❑80, Dec 1979	2.00
❑81, Feb 1980	2.00
❑82, Apr 1980	2.00
❑83, May 1980	2.00
❑84, Jun 1980	2.00
❑85, Jul 1980	2.00
❑86, Aug 1980	2.00
❑87, Sep 1980	2.00
❑88, Oct 1980	2.00
❑89, Dec 1980	2.00
❑90, Feb 1981	2.00
❑91, Apr 1981, (c)	2.00
❑92, May 1981	2.00
❑93, Jun 1981	2.00
❑94, Jul 1981	2.00
❑95, Aug 1981, DDC (c)	2.00
❑96, Sep 1981	2.00
❑97, Oct 1981	2.00
❑98, Dec 1981, DDC (c)	2.00
❑99, Feb 1982	2.00
❑100, Apr 1982	2.00
❑101, Jun 1982	1.50
❑102, Aug 1982	1.50
❑103, Oct 1982	1.50
❑104, Dec 1982	1.50
❑105, Mar 1983	1.50
❑106, Jun 1983, DDC (c)	1.50
❑107, Sep 1983, DDC (c)	1.50
❑108, Nov 1983, DDC (c)	1.50
❑109, Jan 1984, DDC (c)	1.50
❑110, Mar 1984, DDC (c)	1.50
❑111, May 1984	1.50
❑112, Jul 1984	1.50
❑113, Sep 1984, DDC (c)	1.50
❑114, Nov 1984, DDC (c); A: Reggie the Ruthless. A: Archie the Barbarian. A: Betty. A: Jughead. Veronica	1.50
❑115, Jan 1985, DDC (c)	1.50
❑116, Mar 1985, DDC (c)	1.50
❑117, May 1985, DDC (c)	1.50
❑118, Jul 1985, DDC (c)	1.50
❑119, Sep 1985, DDC (c)	1.50
❑120, Nov 1985, DDC (c)	1.50
❑121, Jan 1986, DDC (c)	1.50
❑122, Mar 1986, DDC (c)	1.50
❑123, May 1986, DDC (c)	1.50
❑124, Jul 1986, DDC (c)	1.50
❑125, Sep 1986, DDC (c); DDC (a)	1.50
❑126, Nov 1986, DDC (c)	1.50
❑127, Jan 1987, DDC (c)	1.50
❑128, Mar 1987, DDC (c)	1.50
❑129, May 1987, DDC (c)	1.50
❑130, Jul 1987, DDC (c)	1.50
❑131, Sep 1987, DDC (c)	1.50
❑132, Nov 1987, DDC (c)	1.50
❑133, Jan 1988, DDC (c)	1.50
❑134, Mar 1988, DDC (c)	1.50
❑135, May 1988, DDC (c)	1.50
❑136, Jul 1988, DDC (c)	1.50
❑137, Aug 1988, DDC (c)	1.50
❑138, Oct 1988, DDC (c)	1.50
❑139, Nov 1988, DDC (c)	1.50
❑140, Jan 1989	1.50
❑141, Mar 1989, DDC (c)	1.50
❑142, May 1989, DDC (c)	1.50
❑143, Jul 1989, DDC (c)	1.50
❑144, Aug 1989, DDC (c)	1.50
❑145, Oct 1989, DDC (c)	1.50
❑146, Nov 1989, DDC (c)	1.50
❑147, Jan 1990, DDC (c)	1.50
❑148, Mar 1990, DDC (c)	1.50
❑149, May 1990, DDC (c)	1.50
❑150, Jul 1990, DDC (c)	1.50
❑151, Sep 1990, DDC (c)	1.50
❑152, Nov 1990, DDC (c)	1.50
❑153, Jan 1991, DDC (c)	1.50
❑154, Mar 1991, DDC (c)	1.50
❑155, May 1991, DDC (c)	1.50
❑156, Jul 1991, DDC (c)	1.50
❑157, Sep 1991, DDC (c)	1.50

Evil Ernie
Eternity

	N-MINT
❑1, ca. 1991, b&w; O: Evil Ernie. 1: Evil Ernie. 1: Lady Death	35.00
❑1/Ltd.; Limited edition reprint (1992); O: Evil Ernie. 1: Evil Ernie. 1: Lady Death; Includes new material	6.00
❑2, ca. 1992, b&w	5.00
❑3, ca. 1992, b&w	4.00
❑4, ca. 1992, b&w	4.00
❑5, ca. 1992, b&w	4.00

Evil Ernie (Chaos!)
Chaos!

	N-MINT
❑0	3.00
❑0/Platinum, Platinum edition	5.00
❑1, Jul 1998	3.00
❑2, Aug 1998	3.00
❑3, Sep 1998	3.00
❑4, Oct 1998	3.00
❑5, Nov 1998	2.95
❑6, Dec 1998	2.95
❑7, Jan 1999	2.95
❑8, Feb 1999	2.95
❑9, Mar 1999	2.95
❑10, Apr 1999	2.95

Evil Ernie: Baddest Battles
Chaos

	N-MINT
❑1, Jan 1997; 16 different pin-ups	1.50
❑1/Variant, Jan 1997; Splatterfest Premium Edition cover	1.50

Evil Ernie: Depraved
Chaos!

	N-MINT
❑1, Jul 1999	2.95
❑2, Aug 1999	2.95
❑3, Sep 1999	2.95

Evil Ernie: Destroyer
Chaos!

	N-MINT
❑1, Oct 1997	2.95
❑2, Nov 1997	2.95
❑3, Dec 1997	2.95
❑4, Jan 1998	2.95
❑5, Feb 1998	2.95
❑6, Mar 1998	2.95
❑7, Apr 1998	2.95
❑8, May 1998	2.95
❑9, Jun 1998	2.95
❑Ashcan 1, Sep 1997, Preview ashcan	2.50

Evil Ernie in Santa Fe
Devil's Due / Chaos

	N-MINT
❑1, Oct 2005	2.95
❑2, Jan 2006	2.95
❑2/Variant, Jan 2006	2.95
❑3, Dec 2005	2.95
❑4, Mar 2006	2.95

Evil Ernie: New Year's Evil
Chaos!

	N-MINT
❑1; NN	5.00

Evil Ernie: Pieces of Me
Chaos!

	N-MINT
❑1, Nov 2000, b&w; Adult	2.95
❑1/Variant, Nov 2000; Chromium Mega-Premium Edition; Limited to 2,500	2.95

Evil Ernie: Revenge
Chaos!

	N-MINT
❑0, Dec 1993; New Years Evil	2.50
❑1, Oct 1994; Evil Ernie and Lady Death regular cover	3.00
❑1/Deluxe, Oct 1994; Master of Annihilation premium edition	4.00
❑1/Ltd., Oct 1994; Glow-in-the-dark limited edition	4.00
❑2 1994	3.00
❑3, Jan 1995	2.50
❑4, Feb 1995	2.50

Evil Ernie: Straight to Hell
Chaos!

	N-MINT
❑1, Oct 1995; Coffin fold-out cover	3.00
❑1/A, Oct 1995; chromium cover	4.00
❑2, Dec 1995	3.00
❑3, Feb 1996	3.00

Other grades: Multiply price above by 5/6 for VF/NM • 2/3 for VERY FINE • 1/3 for FINE • 1/5 for VERY GOOD • 1/8 for GOOD

❑4, Apr 1996 3.00
❑5, Jun 1996; Final Issue 3.00

Evil Ernie: The Lost Sketches
Chaos

❑Ashcan 1, Jul 2001 1.00

Evil Ernie: The Resurrection
Chaos!

❑1, ca. 1993, O: Evil Ernie 4.00
❑1/Gold, ca. 1993, Gold promotional edition; O: Evil Ernie 5.00
❑2, ca. 1994, Silver foil cover 3.50
❑3, ca. 1994, Cover by Tom Morgan, Mark McKenna, Tom Smith; Centerfold by George Perez, Mark McKenna, Tom Smith 3.50
❑4, ca. 1994, A: Lady Death. Cover by Steven Hughes & Allyn Conley 3.00
❑Ashcan 1, ca. 1993, Previews Evil Ernie #1, 2, 3; Signed and numbered; Includes embossed Chaos! card, Krome Production's Evil Ernie trading card, Evil Ernie foil sticker 5.00

Evil Ernie vs. the Movie Monsters
Chaos!

❑1/A, ca. 1997; TerrorVision cover 2.95
❑1, ca. 1997; One-shot 3.00

Evil Ernie vs. the Super Heroes
Chaos!

❑1, Aug 1995; O: Evil Ernie 3.00
❑1/Variant, Aug 1995; premium edition (10,000 copies); O: Evil Ernie. no cover price 3.00
❑2, Sep 1998 2.95

Evil Ernie: War Of The Dead
Chaos!

❑1, Nov 1999 2.95
❑2, Dec 1999 2.95
❑3, Jan 2000 2.95

Evil Ernie: Youth Gone Wild
Chaos!

❑1, Nov 1996, b&w; reprints Eternity's Evil Ernie 1.95
❑2, Dec 1996, b&w; reprints Eternity's Evil Ernie 1.95
❑3, Jan 1997, b&w; reprints Eternity's Evil Ernie 1.95
❑4, Feb 1997, b&w; reprints Eternity's Evil Ernie 1.95
❑5, Mar 1997, b&w; reprints Eternity's Evil Ernie 1.95
❑Special 1; "Director's Cut" #1 4.95

Evil Eye
Fantagraphics

❑1, Jun 1998 2.95
❑2, Oct 1998 2.95
❑3, Apr 1999 2.95

Evilman Saves the World
Moonstone

❑1, Jul 1996, b&w; NN 2.95

Evil's Return
Tokyopop

❑1, Jul 2004 9.99
❑2, Oct 2004 9.99
❑3, Jan 2005 9.99
❑4, Dec 2005 9.99

Evo
Image

❑1, Feb 2003 2.99

Ewoks
Marvel / Star

❑1, May 1985 3.00
❑2, Jul 1985 2.00
❑3, Sep 1985 2.00
❑4, Nov 1985 2.00
❑5, Jan 1986 2.00
❑6, Mar 1986 2.00
❑7, May 1986 2.00
❑8, Jul 1986 2.00
❑9, Sep 1986 4.00
❑10, Nov 1986 2.00
❑11, Jan 1987 2.00
❑12, Mar 1987 2.00
❑13, May 1987 2.00
❑14, Jul 1987 2.00

Excalibur
Marvel

❑-1, Jul 1997; Flashback 2.00
❑1, Oct 1988; 1: Tweedledope (in America); 1: Widget 2.50
❑2, Nov 1988; 1: Tweedledope (in America). 1: Kylun 2.00
❑3, Dec 1988; V: Juggernaut 2.00
❑4, Jan 1989; 1: Jester (in America). 1: Red Queen (in America). 1: The Crazy Gang (in America). 1: Executioner (in America). 1: Knave (in America). 1: Crazy Gang (in America) 2.00
❑5, Feb 1989; V: Crazy Gang; V: Arcade. 2.00
❑6, Mar 1989; Inferno 1.75
❑7, Apr 1989; Inferno 1.75
❑8, May 1989; Wrap around cover 1.75
❑9, Jun 1989; 1: Hauptmann Englande; 1: Lightning Force 1.75
❑10, Jul 1989; V: Lightning Force 1.75
❑11, Aug 1989 1.75
❑12, Sep 1989 1.75
❑13, Oct 1989 1.75
❑14, Nov 1989 1.75
❑15, Nov 1989; V: Doctor Crocodile 1.75
❑16, Dec 1989 1.75
❑17, Dec 1989 1.75
❑18, Jan 1990 1.75
❑19, Feb 1990; V: Jamie Braddock 1.75
❑20, Mar 1990; V: Demon Druid 1.75
❑21, Apr 1990; 1: Crusader X 1.75
❑22, May 1990 1.75
❑23, Jun 1990 1.75
❑24, Jul 1990 1.75
❑25, Aug 1990 1.75
❑26, Aug 1990 1.75
❑27, Aug 1990 A: Nth Man 1.75
❑28, Sep 1990 1.75
❑29, Sep 1990 1.75
❑30, Oct 1990 1.75
❑31, Nov 1990 1.75
❑32, Dec 1990; with $1.75 price 1.75
❑32/A, Dec 1990; with $1.50 price 1.75
❑33, Jan 1991 1.75
❑34, Feb 1991 1.75
❑35, Mar 1991 1.75
❑36, Apr 1991; Outlaws 1.75
❑37, May 1991 1.75
❑38, Jun 1991 1.75
❑39, Jul 1991 1.75
❑40, Aug 1991 1.75
❑41, Sep 1991 1.75
❑42, Oct 1991 1.75
❑43, Nov 1991 1.75
❑44, Nov 1991; 1: Micromax 1.75
❑45, Dec 1991; 1: Necrom 1.75
❑46, Jan 1992 1.75
❑47, Feb 1992; 1: Cerise. 1: Cerise 1.75
❑48, Mar 1992; 1: Feron 1.75
❑49, Apr 1992 1.75
❑50, May 1992; Double-size; O: Feron. glow in the dark cover 2.75
❑51, Jun 1992 1.75
❑52, Jul 1992; O: Phoenix III (Rachel Summers). A: X-Men 1.75
❑53, Aug 1992 A: Spider-Man 1.75
❑54, Sep 1992 1.75
❑55, Oct 1992 1.75
❑56, Nov 1992 A: X-Men 1.75
❑57, Nov 1992 1.75
❑58, Dec 1992 1.75
❑59, Dec 1992 1.75
❑60, Jan 1993 1.75
❑61, Jan 1993 1.75
❑62, Feb 1993 1.75
❑63, Mar 1993 1.75
❑64, Apr 1993 1.75
❑65, May 1993 1.75
❑66, Jun 1993 1.75
❑67, Jul 1993 1.75
❑68, Aug 1993 A: Starjammers 1.75
❑69, Sep 1993 1.75
❑70, Oct 1993; O: Cerise. A: Starjammers. A: Shi'Ar 1.75
❑71, Nov 1993; Hologram cover; Fatal Attractions, Finale 3.95
❑72, Dec 1993 1.75
❑73, Jan 1994 1.75
❑74, Feb 1994 1.75
❑75, Mar 1994; Giant-size; 1: Britannic; First Tim Sale work at Marvel 2.25
❑75/Variant, Mar 1994; Giant-size; 1: Britannic. Holo-grafix cover 3.50
❑76, Apr 1994 1.75
❑77, May 1994 1.95
❑78, Jun 1994 1.95
❑79, Jul 1994 1.95
❑80, Aug 1994 1.95
❑81, Sep 1994 1.95
❑82, Oct 1994; Giant-size 2.50
❑82/Variant, Oct 1994; Giant-size; foil cover 3.50
❑83, Nov 1994 1.50
❑83/Deluxe, Nov 1994; Deluxe edition 1.95
❑84, Dec 1994 1.50
❑84/Deluxe, Dec 1994; Deluxe edition 1.95
❑85, Jan 1995 1.50
❑85/Deluxe, Jan 1995; Deluxe edition 1.95
❑86, Feb 1995; (1.50)-Standard Edition. 1.95
❑86/Deluxe, Feb 1995; Deluxe edition 1.95
❑87, Jul 1995 1.95
❑88, Aug 1995 1.95
❑89, Sep 1995 1.95
❑90, Oct 1995; OverPower cards inserted 1.95
❑91, Nov 1995 1.95
❑92, Dec 1995 A: Colossus. A: Pete Wisdom 1.95
❑93, Jan 1996; Rahne's past 1.95
❑94, Feb 1996 1.95
❑95, Mar 1996 A: X-Man 1.95
❑96, Apr 1996 1.95
❑97, May 1996 1.95
❑98, Jun 1996 1.95
❑99, Jul 1996 1.95
❑100, Aug 1996; Giant-size; wraparound cover 2.95
❑101, Sep 1996 1.95
❑102, Oct 1996; bound-in trading cards 1.95
❑103, Nov 1996 1.95
❑104, Dec 1996 1.95
❑105, Jan 1997 KG (w) 1.95
❑106, Feb 1997 1.95
❑107, Mar 1997 1.95
❑108, Apr 1997 1.95
❑109, May 1997; V: Spiral. V: Spiral 1.95
❑110, Jun 1997 1.99
❑111, Aug 1997; gatefold summary 1.99
❑112, Sep 1997; gatefold summary 1.99
❑113, Oct 1997; gatefold summary; A: High Evolutionary 1.99
❑114, Nov 1997; gatefold summary 1.99
❑115, Dec 1997; gatefold summary 1.99
❑116, Jan 1998; gatefold summary 1.99
❑117, Feb 1998; gatefold summary 1.99
❑118, Mar 1998; gatefold summary; V: Bamfs 1.99
❑119, Apr 1998; gatefold summary; V: Nightmare 1.99
❑120, May 1998; gatefold summary 1.99
❑121, Jun 1998; gatefold summary; V: Legion 1.99
❑122, Jul 1998; gatefold summary; V: Prime Sentinels 1.99
❑123, Aug 1998; gatefold summary; V: Mimic 1.99
❑124, Sep 1998; gatefold summary; Captain Britain's bachelor party 1.99
❑125, Oct 1998; Giant-size; Wedding of Captain Britain, Meggan 3.00
❑Ann 1, ca. 1993; 1: Ghath. trading card 4.00
❑Ann 2, ca. 1994; 1994 Ann 2.95

Excalibur
Marvel

❑1, Feb 2001 2.99
❑2, Mar 2001 2.99
❑3, Apr 2001 2.99
❑4, May 2001 2.99

Excalibur
Marvel

❑1, Jul 2004, 1: Wicked; 1: Freakshow; 1: Hub; 1: Hack 2.99
❑2, Aug 2004, Cover art by Andy Park 2.99
❑3, Sep 2004, 1: Purge; 1: Karima Shapandar (Omega Sentinel); 1: Shola 2.99
❑4, Oct 2004, Cover art by Andy Park 2.99
❑5, Nov 2004, 1: Stripmine 2.99
❑6, Dec 2004, Cover art by Andy Park 2.99
❑7, Jan 2005, Cover art by Andy Park 2.99

Other grades: Multiply price above by 5/6 for VF/NM • 2/3 for VERY FINE • 1/3 for FINE • 1/5 for VERY GOOD • 1/8 for GOOD

Elvira's House of Mystery

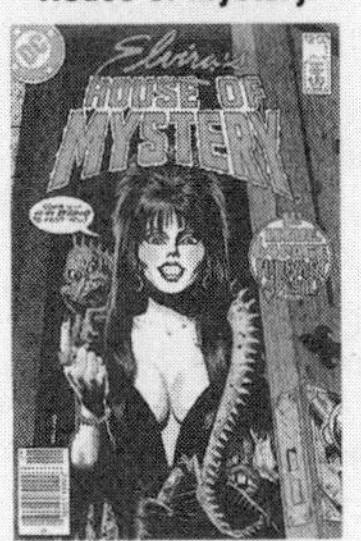

DC horror anthology gets new hostess
©DC

E-Man

Joe Staton, Nicola Cuti super-hero series
©Charlton

Emma Davenport

Series began as strips in CBG
©Lohman Hills

Empire

Tyrant takes over Earth
©Image

Encyclopèdia Deadpoolica

Reveals background on Marvel mercenary
©Marvel

N-MINT

❑8, Feb 2005; Avengers Disassembled crossover ... 2.99
❑9, Mar 2005 ... 2.99
❑10, Apr 2005; V: Sugar Man; V: Rastus 2.99
❑11, May 2005; 1: Askari; V: Viper ... 2.99
❑12, Jun 2005 ... 2.99
❑13, Jul 2005 ... 2.99

Excalibur: Air Apparent
Marvel

❑1, Dec 1991; Air Apparent Special Edition; NN ... 4.95

Excalibur: Mojo Mayhem
Marvel

❑1, Dec 1989; NN ... 4.50

Excalibur: Sword of Power
Marvel

❑1, Feb 2002 ... 2.99
❑2, Mar 2002 ... 2.99
❑3, Apr 2002 ... 2.99
❑4, May 2002 ... 2.99

Excalibur: The Possession
Marvel

❑1, Jul 1991; 48 pages, no ads ... 2.95

Excalibur: The Sword Is Drawn
Marvel

❑1, ca. 1987; prestige format; O: Excalibur. 1: Excalibur. Indicia reads Excalibur Special Edition; V: Technet .. 4.00
❑1/2nd; 1: Excalibur. 2nd printing ... 3.50
❑1/3rd; 1: Excalibur. 3rd printing ... 3.50

Excalibur: XX Crossing
Marvel

❑1, May 1992; indicia says May, cover says Jul ... 2.50

Exciting X-Patrol
Marvel / Amalgam

❑1, Jun 1997 ... 1.95

Exec
Comics Conspiracy

❑1, Feb 2001, Several characters in profile on cover ... 3.95

Exhibitionist
Fantagraphics / Eros

❑1; Adult ... 2.75
❑2, Aug 1994; Adult ... 2.75

Exile
Eyeball Soup Designs

❑1, May 1996, b&w; cardstock cover ... 2.95
❑2, Jul 1996, b&w; cardstock cover ... 2.95

Exiled
Exiled

❑1, Jan 1998 ... 2.75
❑2, Apr 1998 ... 2.75
❑3, Jun 1998; cover says 98, indicia says 97 2.75

Exile Earth
River City

❑1, ca. 1994 ... 1.95
❑2, ca. 1994 ... 1.95

Exiles
Malibu

❑1, Aug 1993, b&w 1: The Exiles ... 2.00
❑1/Variant, Aug 1993, b&w; 1: The Exiles. Hologram cover ... 5.00
❑2, Sep 1993 ... 2.00
❑3, Oct 1993; Rune ... 2.50
❑4, Nov 1993 D: Exiles ... 2.00

Exiles
Marvel

❑1, Aug 2001; 1: Magnus; 1: Noctourne 4.00
❑2, Sep 2001; 1: Sunfire (Mariko Yashida); D: Magnus; V: Domino; V: Chamber; V: Spider-Woman; V: Juggernaut; V: Professor X; V: Human Torch ... 2.25
❑3, Oct 2001 ... 2.25
❑4, Nov 2001 ... 2.25
❑5, Dec 2001; V: Hulk ... 2.25
❑6, Jan 2002; V: Hulk ... 2.25
❑7, Feb 2002; Silent issue ... 2.25
❑8, Mar 2002; V: Galactus ... 2.25
❑9, Apr 2002; V: Galactus ... 2.25
❑10, Apr 2002; 1: Sasquatch (Heather Hudson); V: Galactus ... 2.25
❑11, May 2002 ... 2.25
❑12, Jun 2002 ... 2.25
❑13, Jul 2002; Call of Duty preview ... 2.25
❑14, Aug 2002 ... 2.25
❑15, Sep 2002 ... 2.25
❑16, Oct 2002; Spotlight on Thunderbird 2.25
❑17, Nov 2002 ... 2.25
❑18, Dec 2002; V: Mojo; V: Spiral ... 2.25
❑19, Jan 2003; V: Mojo; V: Spiral; Uncanny X-Men preview ... 2.25
❑20, Feb 2003; Preview of Incredible Hulk 2.25
❑21, Mar 2003; Preview of Avengers ... 2.25
❑22, Apr 2003; Blink leaves ... 2.25
❑23, May 2003; Iron Man conquers Earth; Iron Man attempts to conquer Inhumans ... 2.25
❑24, Jun 2003; Weapon X aids Iron Man; Colossus joins Weapon X ... 2.25
❑25, Jun 2003; Price Increase ... 2.99
❑26, Jul 2003; Ultimate X-Men preview. 2.99
❑27, Jul 2003; Ultimate X-Men preview. 2.99
❑28, Aug 2003; V: Maximus Lobo ... 2.99
❑29, Sep 2003, V: Maximus Lobo ... 2.99
❑30, Sep 2003, V: Maximus Lobo ... 2.99
❑31, Oct 2003, Avengers turned into vampires ... 2.99
❑32, Oct 2003 ... 2.99
❑33, Nov 2003 ... 2.99
❑34, Nov 2003 ... 2.99
❑35, Dec 2003 ... 2.99
❑36, Dec 2003 ... 2.99
❑37, Jan 2004, D: Sunfire; Blink returns 2.99
❑38, Feb 2004 ... 2.99
❑39, Feb 2004 ... 2.99
❑40, Mar 2004 ... 2.99
❑41, Apr 2004 ... 2.99
❑42, May 2004 ... 2.99
❑43, May 2004, V: Hyperion ... 2.99
❑44, May 2004, V: Hyperion ... 2.99
❑45, Jun 2004, V: Hyperion ... 2.99
❑46, Jul 2004 ... 2.99
❑47, Jul 2004 ... 2.99
❑48, Aug 2004 ... 2.99
❑49, Sep 2004 ... 2.99
❑50, Oct 2004 ... 2.99
❑51, Oct 2004 ... 2.99
❑52, Nov 2004 ... 2.99
❑53, Dec 2004 ... 2.99
❑54, Jan 2005 ... 2.99
❑55, Jan 2005 ... 2.99
❑56, Feb 2005 ... 2.99
❑57, Mar 2005 ... 2.99
❑58, Mar 2005 ... 2.99
❑59, Apr 2005 ... 2.99
❑60, May 2005; V: Holocaust ... 5.00
❑61, May 2005; V: Holocaust ... 4.00
❑62, Jun 2005; V: Hyperion ... 2.99
❑63, Jun 2005; V: Hyperion ... 2.99
❑64, Jun 2005; V: Hyperion ... 2.99
❑65, Jul 2005; V: Hyperion ... 2.99
❑66, Aug 2005 ... 2.99
❑67, Sep 2005; V: Krakoa ... 2.99
❑68, Oct 2005; V: Fin Fang Foom ... 2.99
❑69, Nov 2005; House of M ... 2.99
❑70, Nov 2005; House of M ... 2.99
❑71, Dec 2005; V: Proteus; House of M. 2.99
❑72, Jan 2006; V: Proteus; Beak leaves. 2.99
❑73, Jan 2006, D: Mimic; V: Proteus; X-Men and Power Pack preview ... 2.99
❑74, Feb 2006, V: Proteus; Longshot joins 2.99
❑75, Mar 2006, V: Proteus ... 2.99
❑76, Mar 2006, V: Proteus; Spider-Man 2099 joins ... 2.99
❑77, May 2006, V: Proteus ... 2.99
❑78, Jun 2006, Power Princess joins ... 2.99
❑79, Jun 2006 ... 2.99
❑80, Jul 2006 ... 2.99
❑81, Aug 2006 ... 2.99
❑82, Aug 2006 ... 2.99
❑83, Sep 2006 ... 2.99
❑84, Oct 2006 ... 2.99
❑85, Nov 2006 ... 2.99
❑86, Nov 2006 ... 2.99
❑87, Jan 2007 ... 2.99
❑88, Feb 2007 ... 2.99
❑89, Mar 2007 ... 2.99
❑90 ... 2.99
❑91 ... 2.99
❑92 ... 2.99
❑93 ... 2.99
❑94 ... 2.99
❑95 ... 2.99
❑96 ... 2.99
❑97 ... 2.99
❑98 ... 2.99
❑99 ... 2.99
❑100 ... 2.99
❑Ann 1, Feb 2007 ... 3.99

Exiles (Alpha)
Alpha Productions

❑1, b&w ... 1.95

Existing Earth
Windwolf Graphics

❑1, Nov 1987, b&w ... 1.75

Exit
Caliber

❑1 ... 2.95
❑2 ... 2.95
❑3 ... 2.95
❑4 ... 2.95
❑5; Continues as Exit: Epilogue ... 2.95

Exit 6
Plastic Spoon
- ❑1, Aug 1998, b&w 2.95
- ❑2/Ashcan, Aug 1998; preview of upcoming issue 2.95
- ❑3, Jan 1999 2.95
- ❑3/Ashcan, Aug 1998; preview of upcoming issue 2.95

Exit from Shadow
Bronze Man
- ❑4; indicia has name change, cover doesn't; was Secret Killers 2.95

Ex-Libris Eroticis
NBM
- ❑1 9.95

Ex Machina
DC
- ❑1, Aug 2004; 1&O: Great Machine 8.00
- ❑2, Sep 2004 4.00
- ❑3, Oct 2004 2.95
- ❑4, Nov 2004 2.95
- ❑5, Dec 2004 2.95
- ❑6, Jan 2005 2.95
- ❑7, Feb 2005 2.95
- ❑8, Mar 2005 2.95
- ❑9, Apr 2005; Price increase 2.95
- ❑10, Jun 2005 2.99
- ❑11, Jul 2005 2.99
- ❑12, Aug 2005 2.99
- ❑13, Sep 2005 2.99
- ❑14, Oct 2005 2.99
- ❑15, Dec 2005 2.99
- ❑16, Jan 2006 2.99
- ❑17, Mar 2006 2.99
- ❑18, May 2006 2.99
- ❑19, Jun 2006 2.99
- ❑20, Jul 2006 2.99
- ❑21, Sep 2006, Cover by Tony Harris 2.99
- ❑22, Oct 2006 2.99
- ❑23, Nov 2006 2.99
- ❑24, Jan 2007 2.99
- ❑25, Feb 2007 2.99
- ❑26 2.99
- ❑27 2.99
- ❑28 2.99
- ❑29 2.99
- ❑30 2.99
- ❑31 2.99
- ❑32 2.99
- ❑33 2.99
- ❑34 2.99
- ❑35 2.99
- ❑36 2.99
- ❑37 2.99
- ❑38 2.99
- ❑39 2.99
- ❑40 2.99
- ❑41 2.99
- ❑42 2.99

Ex Machina Special
DC
- ❑1, Jun 2006 2.99
- ❑2, Aug 2006 2.99

Ex-Mutants
Pied Piper / Amazing
- ❑1; ca. 1986; b&w; Moves to Amazing 2.00
- ❑2; ca. 1987 2.00
- ❑3; b&w; ca. 1986 2.00
- ❑4; b&w; ca. 1987 2.00
- ❑5; ca. 1987; A: New Humans. b&w 2.00
- ❑6, Jul 1987; Moves to Pied Piper from Amazing; b&w; Reprint from Ex-Mutants #6 2.00
- ❑7; ca. 1987; b&w 2.00
- ❑8; ca. 1987; b&w 2.00
- ❑Special 1, Spr 1987, b&w 2.00

Ex-Mutants
Eternity
- ❑1 2.00
- ❑2 2.00
- ❑3 2.00
- ❑4, Oct 1988, RL (c) 2.00
- ❑5 1988 2.00
- ❑6, Dec 1988, Reprints Ex-Mutants (Amazing) #6; b&w 2.00
- ❑7 1988, Series continues as Ex-Mutants: The Shattered Earth Chronicles; Reprints Ex-Mutants (Amazing) #7; b&w 2.00
- ❑8, Jan 1989 2.00
- ❑9, Feb 1989 2.00
- ❑10 2.00
- ❑11 2.00
- ❑12 2.00
- ❑13, Series continued from Ex-Mutants: The Shattered Earth Chronicles #12; b&w 2.00
- ❑14, b&w 2.00
- ❑15, b&w 1.95
- ❑Ann 1, Mar 1998, b&w 1.95

Ex-Mutants
Malibu
- ❑1, Nov 1992; O: Ex-Mutants 2.00
- ❑1/Variant, Nov 1992; O: Ex-Mutants. shiny cover 2.50
- ❑2, Dec 1992 1.95
- ❑3, Jan 1993 1.95
- ❑4, Feb 1993 1.95
- ❑5, Mar 1993 1.95
- ❑6, Apr 1993 1.95
- ❑7, May 1993 1.95
- ❑8, Jun 1993 1.95
- ❑9, Jul 1993 1.95
- ❑10, Aug 1993 1.95
- ❑11, Sep 1993; Crossover with Dinosaurs for Hire and Protectors 1.95
- ❑12, Oct 1993; Crossover with Dinosaurs for Hire and Protectors 2.25
- ❑13, Nov 1993; Genesis begins publishing 2.25
- ❑14, Dec 1993; Genesis 2.25
- ❑15, Jan 1994; Genesis 2.25
- ❑16, Feb 1994; Genesis 2.25
- ❑17, Mar 1994; Genesis 2.50
- ❑18, Apr 1994; Genesis 2.50

Ex-Mutants Microseries: Erin
Pied Piper
- ❑1, b&w; ca. 1987 1.95

Ex-Mutants Pin-Up Book
Eternity
- ❑1, Mar 1988 1.95

Ex-Mutants Special Consumer Electronics Show Edition
Malibu
- ❑1, ca. 1992; Reprints part of Ex-Mutants (Malibu) #1 plus previews Ex-Mutants Sega videogame 2.50

Exodus Revelation
Exodus
- ❑1, Nov 1994, b&w; no cover price 1.00

Exosquad
Topps
- ❑0, Jan 1994; cardstock cover 1.00

Exotica
Cry for Dawn
- ❑1, b&w; Adult; ca. 1992 4.00
- ❑2, Nov 1993, Adult 3.00

Exotic Fantasy
Fantagraphics / Eros
- ❑1, Nov 1992, b&w; sketches 4.95
- ❑2, May 1993, b&w; sketches 4.95
- ❑3, Jul 1993, b&w; sketches 4.95

Expatriate
Image
- ❑1, May 2005 2.95
- ❑2 2005 2.95
- ❑3, Oct 2005 2.95
- ❑4, Jan 2006 2.99

Experience
Aircel
- ❑1, b&w; Adult 3.25

Explorers
Explorer
- ❑1, ca. 1996, b&w 2.95
- ❑2, ca. 1996, b&w 2.95
- ❑3, ca. 1996, b&w 2.95

Explorers of the Unknown
Archie
- ❑1, Jun 1990 1.00
- ❑2, Aug 1990 1.00
- ❑3, Oct 1990 1.00
- ❑4, Dec 1990 1.00
- ❑5, Feb 1991 1.00
- ❑6, Apr 1991 1.00

Explorers
Caliber / Tapestry
- ❑1, ca. 1996, b&w 2.95
- ❑2, ca. 1996, b&w 2.95
- ❑3, ca. 1997, b&w 2.95

Expose
Cracked Pepper
- ❑1, Dec 1993, b&w 2.50

Exposure
Image
- ❑1, Nov 1999 2.50
- ❑2, Dec 1999 2.50
- ❑2/A, Dec 1999; Photo cover 2.50
- ❑3, Jan 2000 2.50
- ❑4, Feb 2000; Digital Photo Alternative Cover 2.50
- ❑5, Mar 2000; Vol. 2 #1 3.50
- ❑6, Apr 2000; Vol. 2 #2 3.50

Exquisite Corpse
Dark Horse
- ❑1; Yellow issue 2.50
- ❑2; Red Issue 2.50
- ❑3; Green Issue 2.50

Exterminators
DC / Vertigo
- ❑1, Feb 2006 2.99
- ❑2, Mar 2006 2.99
- ❑3, May 2006 2.99
- ❑4, Jun 2006 2.99
- ❑5, Jul 2006 2.99
- ❑6, Aug 2006 2.99
- ❑7, Sep 2006 2.99
- ❑8, Oct 2006 2.99
- ❑9, Nov 2006 2.99
- ❑10, Dec 2006 2.99
- ❑11, Jan 2007 2.99
- ❑12, Feb 2007 2.99
- ❑13, Mar 2007 2.99
- ❑14 2.99
- ❑15 2.99
- ❑16 2.99
- ❑17 2.99
- ❑18 2.99
- ❑19 2.99
- ❑20 2.99
- ❑21 2.99
- ❑22 2.99
- ❑23 2.99
- ❑24 2.99
- ❑25 2.99
- ❑26 2.99
- ❑27 2.99
- ❑28 2.99
- ❑29 2.99
- ❑30 2.99

Extinct!
New England
- ❑1, b&w; Reprints 3.50
- ❑2, b&w; Reprints 3.50

Extinctioners
Shanda Fantasy Arts
- ❑1, Apr 1999, b&w 2.95
- ❑2, Sep 1999; b&w 2.95

Extinction Event
DC / Wildstorm
- ❑1, Sep 2003 2.50
- ❑2, Oct 2003 2.50
- ❑3, Nov 2003 2.50
- ❑4, Dec 2003 2.50
- ❑5, Jan 2004 2.50

Extra!
Gemstone
- ❑1, Jan 2000 2.50
- ❑2, Feb 2000 2.50
- ❑3, Mar 2000 2.50
- ❑4, Apr 2000 2.50
- ❑5, May 2000 2.50
- ❑Ann 1 13.50

Extra Terrestrial Trio
Smiling Face
- ❑1, ca. 1995, b&w 2.95

Endless Gallery

Pin-ups of Sandman and relatives

©DC

Enemy Ace Special

Reprints Showcase and Our Army at War

©DC

Ernie

Newspaper strip reprints

©Kitchen Sink

Espers

James Robinson's series about psychics

©Halloween

Essential Vertigo: Swamp Thing

Black and white Alan Moore story reprints

©DC

N-MINT

Extreme
Image

- ❑0, Aug 1993 RL (w); RL (a) 2.50
- ❑0/A, Aug 1993 RL (w); RL (a) 2.50
- ❑0/B, Aug 1993; San Diego Con edition RL (w); RL (a) 2.50
- ❑0/Gold, Aug 1993; Gold edition RL (w); RL (a) 3.00
- ❑Holiday 1; "Extreme Hero" promotional edition from Hero Magazine; RL (w); RL (a); no cover price 1.00

Extreme (Curtis)
Curtis

- ❑1 .... 2.95

Extreme Destroyer Epilogue
Image

- ❑1, Jan 1996 .... 2.50

Extreme Destroyer Prologue
Image

- ❑1, Jan 1996; bagged with card 2.50

Extreme Hero
Image / Extreme Studios

- ❑1, ca. 1994, RL (w); RL (a); No number; no cover price; previews of Extreme Studio properties; Hero Illustrated giveaway...... 1.00

Extreme Justice
DC

- ❑0, Jan 1995 .... 2.00
- ❑1, Feb 1995 .... 1.75
- ❑2, Mar 1995 .... 1.75
- ❑3, Apr 1995 .... 1.75
- ❑4, May 1995 .... 1.75
- ❑5, Jun 1995; Firestorm joins 1.75
- ❑6, Jul 1995 .... 1.75
- ❑7, Aug 1995 .... 1.75
- ❑8, Sep 1995 .... 1.75
- ❑9, Oct 1995; 1: Zan and Jayna 1.75
- ❑10, Nov 1995; Undeworld Unleashed... 1.75
- ❑11, Dec 1995; Undeworld Unleashed tie-in 1.75
- ❑12, Jan 1996; V: Monarch 1.75
- ❑13, Feb 1996; V: Monarch; True origin of Captain Atom 1.75
- ❑14, Mar 1996; V: Monarch 1.75
- ❑15, Apr 1996 .... 1.75
- ❑16, May 1996 .... 1.75
- ❑17, Jun 1996; V: Legion of Doom 1.75
- ❑18, Jul 1996; V: Legion of Doom; Final Issue 1.75

Extremely Silly
Antarctic

- ❑1 .... 3.00

Extremely Silly
Antarctic

- ❑1, Nov 1996, b&w; Star Trek parody 1.25

Extremely Youngblood
Image

- ❑1, Sep 1996, One-shot 3.50

Extreme Prejudice
Image

- ❑0, Nov 1994 .... 2.50

Extreme Previews
Image

- ❑1, Mar 1996 .... 1.00

N-MINT

Extreme Previews 1997
Image

- ❑1; No cover price; pin-ups 1.00

Extreme Sacrifice
Image

- ❑1, Jan 1995, Prelude, polybagged with trading card 2.50
- ❑2, Jan 1995, Epilogue 2.50

Extremes of Violet
Blackout

- ❑0 .... 2.95
- ❑1 .... 2.95
- ❑2, Mar 1995 .... 2.95

Extreme Super Christmas Special
Image

- ❑1, Dec 1994 .... 2.95

Extreme Super Tour Book
Image

- ❑1 .... 1.00
- ❑1/Gold; Gold edition 2.00

Extreme Tour Book
Image

- ❑1; no cover price 2.50
- ❑1/Gold; Gold edition 2.50

Extremist
DC / Vertigo

- ❑1, Sep 1993; 1: The Extremist; Adult ... 2.50
- ❑1/Platinum, Sep 1993; Platinum edition; 1: The Extremist; Adult 4.00
- ❑2, Oct 1993; Adult 2.50
- ❑3, Nov 1993; Adult 2.50
- ❑4, Dec 1993; Adult 2.50

Eye
Hamster

- ❑Special 1, Jun 1999; Special edition 2.95

Eyeball Kid
Dark Horse

- ❑1, b&w; 1: Eyeball Kid (in comic books) 2.50
- ❑2, b&w 2.50
- ❑3, b&w; Final Issue 2.50

Eyebeam
Adhesive

- ❑1, b&w; strip reprints 2.50
- ❑2, ca. 1994, b&w; strip reprints 2.50
- ❑3, ca. 1994, b&w; strip reprints 2.50
- ❑4, b&w; strip reprints 2.50
- ❑5, b&w; strip reprints 2.50

Eye of Mongombo
Fantagraphics

- ❑1, b&w; Adult 2.00
- ❑2, b&w; Adult 2.00
- ❑3, b&w; Adult 2.00
- ❑4, b&w; Adult 2.00
- ❑5, b&w; Adult 2.00
- ❑6 1991, b&w; Adult 2.00
- ❑7, Dec 1991, b&w; Adult 2.25

Eye of the Beholder
NBM

- ❑1 .... 10.95

Eye of the Storm
Rival

- ❑1, Dec 1994 .... 2.95

N-MINT

Eye of the Storm Annual
DC / Wildstorm

- ❑1, Sep 2003 .... 4.95

Eyeshield 21
Viz

- ❑1, Apr 2005 .... 7.99
- ❑2, May 2005 .... 7.99
- ❑3, Aug 2005 .... 7.99
- ❑4, Oct 2005 .... 7.99

Eyes of Asia
Digital Webbing

- ❑1, Oct 2004, b&w 3.50
- ❑2, Dec 2004, b&w 3.50

Faans
Six Handed

- ❑1, b&w 2.95

Fables
DC / Vertigo

- ❑1, Jul 2002; Pencil cover 3.50
- ❑2, Aug 2002 .... 3.00
- ❑3, Sep 2002 .... 3.00
- ❑4, Oct 2002 .... 2.75
- ❑5, Nov 2002 .... 2.50
- ❑6/Retailer ed., Dec 2002; Retailer Representative Program variant 15.00
- ❑6, Dec 2002 .... 2.50
- ❑7, Jan 2003 .... 2.50
- ❑8, Feb 2003 .... 2.50
- ❑9, Mar 2003 .... 2.50
- ❑10, Apr 2003 .... 2.50
- ❑11, May 2003 BT (a) 2.50
- ❑12, Jun 2003 .... 2.50
- ❑13, Jul 2003 .... 2.50
- ❑14, Aug 2003 .... 2.50
- ❑15, Sep 2003 .... 2.50
- ❑16, Oct 2003 .... 2.50
- ❑17, Nov 2003 .... 2.50
- ❑18, Dec 2003 .... 2.50
- ❑19, Jan 2004; 1: Red Riding Hood 2.50
- ❑20, Feb 2004 .... 2.50
- ❑21, Mar 2004 .... 2.50
- ❑22, Apr 2004 .... 2.50
- ❑23, May 2004 .... 2.50
- ❑24, Jun 2004 .... 2.50
- ❑25, Jul 2004 .... 2.50
- ❑26, Aug 2004 .... 2.50
- ❑27, Sep 2004 .... 2.50
- ❑28, Oct 2004 .... 2.50
- ❑29, Nov 2004 .... 2.50
- ❑30, Dec 2004 .... 2.50
- ❑31, Jan 2005 .... 2.50
- ❑32, Feb 2005 .... 2.50
- ❑33, Mar 2005 .... 2.50
- ❑34, Apr 2005 .... 2.50
- ❑35, May 2005 .... 2.50
- ❑36, Jun 2005; Sneak Preview of Neil Gaiman's Neverwhere! 2.50
- ❑37, Jun 2005 .... 2.50
- ❑38, Jul 2005 .... 2.75
- ❑39, Aug 2005 .... 2.75
- ❑40, Sep 2005 .... 2.75
- ❑41, Oct 2005 .... 2.75
- ❑42, Jul 2005, b&w; Sneak Preview of Testament 2.75
- ❑43, Jan 2006 .... 2.75

Other grades: Multiply price above by 5/6 for VF/NM • 2/3 for VERY FINE • 1/3 for FINE • 1/5 for VERY GOOD • 1/8 for GOOD

❑44, Feb 2006 2.75
❑45, Mar 2006 2.75
❑46, Apr 2006 2.75
❑47, May 2006 2.75
❑48, Jun 2006 2.75
❑49, Jul 2006 2.99
❑50, Aug 2006, Sneak Preview of Jack Fables; Wedding of Snow White and Bigby Wolf 3.99
❑51, Sep 2006 2.99
❑52, Oct 2006 2.99
❑53, Nov 2006 2.99
❑54, Dec 2006 2.99
❑55, Jan 2007, Free preview of Crossing Midnight 2.99
❑56, Mar 2007, Santa Claus 3.50
❑57 3.50
❑58 3.50
❑59 3.50
❑60 3.50
❑61 3.50
❑62 3.50
❑63 3.50
❑64 3.50
❑65 3.50
❑66 3.50
❑67 3.50
❑68 3.50
❑69 3.50
❑70 3.50
❑71 3.50
❑72 3.50
❑73 3.50
❑74 3.50
❑75 3.50
❑76 3.50
❑77 3.50
❑78 3.50
❑79 3.50
❑80 3.50
❑81 3.50
❑82 3.50
❑83 3.50
❑84 3.50

Fables By the Brothers Dimm
Dimm

❑1, Apr 1995, b&w 1.50

Fables: Last Castle
DC / Vertigo

❑1, ca. 2003 5.00

Fables Special Edition
DC / Vertigo

❑1, Dec 2006 0.25

Fabulous Furry Freak Brothers
Rip Off

❑0; 1985 Compilation 6.00
❑1, b&w; Collected Adventures of the...; 1971 55.00
❑1/2nd; Collected Adventures of the...; 1980 30.00
❑1/3rd 2002; Collected Adventures of the.. 28.00
❑2, b&w; Further Adventures of the.. 35.00
❑2/2nd; Further Adventures of the...; 1989 25.00
❑3, b&w; A Year Passes Like Nothing With.. 15.00
❑4, ca. 1975, b&w; Brother Can You Spare 75¢ For.. 13.00
❑5, ca. 1977, b&w; Fabulous Furry Freak Brothers 10.00
❑6, b&w; Six Snappy Sockeroos From the Archives Of.. 7.00
❑7, b&w; Several Short Stories From The Fabulous Furry Freak Brothers; ca. 1982 5.00
❑8, The Idiots Abroad, Part 1 5.00
❑9, ca. 1985; The Idiots Abroad, Part 2 5.00
❑10, The Idiots Abroad, Part 3 2.25
❑11, The Freak Brothers Bus Line and Other Tales 4.00
❑12, b&w 4.00
❑13, b&w; reprints stories from High Times 3.25

Face
DC / Vertigo

❑1, Jan 1995 4.95

Faction Paradox
Image

❑1, Aug 2003 2.95
❑2, Nov 2003 3.50

Factor-X
Marvel

❑1, Mar 1995, AM (a); Age of Apocalypse 2.00
❑2, Apr 1995 2.00
❑3, May 1995 2.00
❑4, Jun 1995 2.00

Faculty Funnies
Archie

❑1, Jun 1989 4.00
❑2, Sep 1989 2.50
❑3, Dec 1989 2.50
❑4, Mar 1990 2.50
❑5, May 1990 2.50

Faerie Codex
Raven

❑1, b&w 2.95
❑2, b&w 2.95
❑3, Dec 1997, b&w 2.95

Faeries' Landing
Tokyopop

❑1, Jan 2004 9.99
❑2, Mar 2004 9.99
❑3, May 2004 9.99
❑4, Jul 2004 9.99
❑5, Sep 2004 9.99
❑6, Nov 2004 9.99
❑7, Jan 2005 9.99
❑8, Mar 2005 9.99
❑9, Jun 2005 9.99
❑10, Sep 2005 9.99
❑11, Dec 2005 9.99

Fafhrd and the Gray Mouser
Marvel / Epic

❑1, Oct 1990 4.50
❑2, Nov 1990 4.50
❑3, Dec 1990 4.50
❑4, Jan 1991 4.50

Failed Universe
Blackthorne

❑1, Dec 1986 1.75

Fairy Tales of the Brothers Grimm
NBM

❑1 15.95

Faith (Lightning)
Lightning

❑1/A, Jul 1997, b&w 2.95

Faith
DC / Vertigo

❑1, Nov 1999; Adult 2.50
❑2, Dec 1999; Adult 2.50
❑3, Jan 2000; Adult 2.50
❑4, Feb 2000; Adult 2.50
❑5, Mar 2000; Adult 2.50

Faith: A Fable
Carbon-Based Books

❑1, Jan 2000, b&w; Trade Paperback; smaller than normal comic book 8.95

Fake
Tokyopop

❑1, May 2003, b&w; printed in Japanese format 9.99

Falcon
Marvel

❑1, Nov 1983, PS (c); PS (a) 2.00
❑2, Dec 1983, PS (c); PS (a); V: Sentinel 2.00
❑3, Jan 1984, O: Falcon; V: Electro 2.00
❑4, Feb 1984, V: Electro 2.00

Fall
Big Bad World

❑1, b&w 3.00

Fall
Caliber

❑1, b&w 2.95

Fallen
NBM

❑1 8.95

Fallen Angel
DC

❑1, Sep 2003 2.50
❑2, Oct 2003 2.50
❑3, Nov 2003 2.50
❑4, Dec 2003 2.50
❑5, Jan 2004 2.50
❑6, Feb 2004 2.50
❑7, Mar 2004 2.50
❑8, Apr 2004 2.50
❑9, May 2004 2.50
❑10, Jun 2004 2.50
❑11, Jul 2004 2.95
❑12, Aug 2004 2.95
❑13, Sep 2004 2.95
❑14, Oct 2004; Bagged with promo CD for Sky Captain and the World of Tomorrow 2.95
❑15, Nov 2004 2.95
❑16, Dec 2004 2.95
❑17, Jan 2005 2.95
❑18, Feb 2005 2.95
❑19, Mar 2005; Price increase 2.99
❑20, Jun 2005; Final Issue 2.99

Fallen Angel (IDW)
Idea & Design Works

❑1, Jan 2006 3.99
❑2, Feb 2006 3.99
❑3, Mar 2006 3.99
❑4, Apr 2006 3.99
❑6, Jul 2006 3.99
❑7, Aug 2006 3.99
❑8, Sep 2006 3.99
❑9, Oct 2006 3.99
❑10, Nov 2006 3.99
❑11, Dec 2006 3.99
❑12 3.99
❑13 3.99
❑14 3.99
❑15 3.99
❑16 3.99
❑17 3.99
❑18 3.99
❑19 3.99
❑20 3.99
❑21 3.99
❑22 3.99
❑23 3.99
❑24 3.99
❑25 3.99
❑26 3.99
❑27 3.99
❑28 3.99
❑29 3.99
❑30 3.99

Fallen Angel on the World of Magic: The Gathering
Acclaim / Armada

❑1, May 1996; prestige format; polybagged with Fallen Angel card 5.95

Fallen Angels
Marvel

❑1, Apr 1987; 1: Chance 2.00
❑2, May 1987; 1: Ariel; 1: Gomi; 1: Bill the Lobster; 1: Don the Lobster 1.50
❑3, Jun 1987; 1: Chance II 1.50
❑4, Jul 1987 1.50
❑5, Aug 1987; D: Don the Lobster 1.50
❑6, Sep 1987 1.50
❑7, Oct 1987 1.50
❑8, Nov 1987 1.50

Fallen Empires on the World of Magic: The Gathering
Acclaim / Armada

❑1, Sep 1995; polybagged with pack of Fallen Empires cards 2.75
❑2, Oct 1995; polybagged with sheet of creature tokens 2.75

Falling Man
Image

❑1, Feb 1998, b&w 2.95

Fall of the Roman Empire
Gold Key

❑1, Jul 1964 25.00

Fallout 3000
Caliber

❑1, ca. 1996; reprints Brazilian comic book 2.95

Falls The Gotham Rain
Comico

❑1 4.95

Other grades: Multiply price above by 5/6 for VF/NM • 2/3 for VERY FINE • 1/3 for FINE • 1/5 for VERY GOOD • 1/8 for GOOD

Eternals

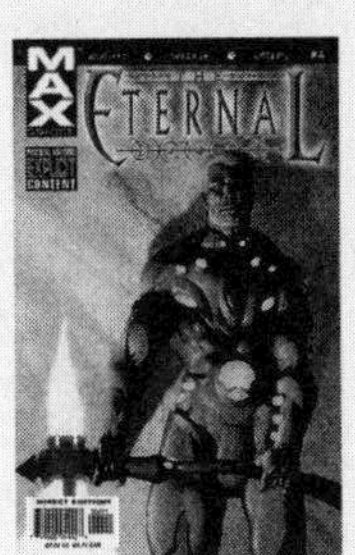

Jack Kirby's celestial series

©Marvel

Eternal Warrior

Armstrong's mercenary brother's adventures

©Valiant

Eternity Smith

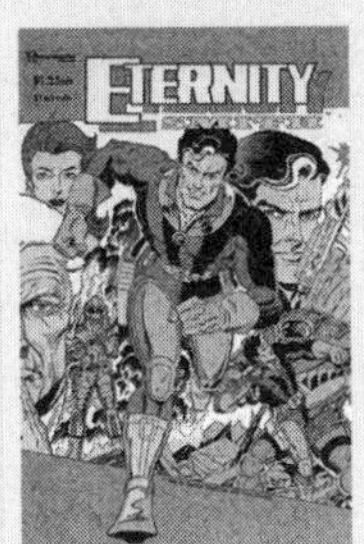

Super-powered companions thwart evil plots

©Renegade

Eudaemon

Friendly demon passes powers to son

©Dark Horse

Evel Knievel

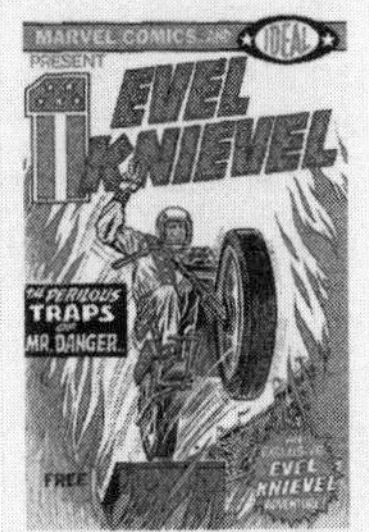

Tie-in for Ideal toy line

©Marvel

Family Affair
Gold Key

	N-MINT
❑1, Jan 1970, Includes poster	24.00
❑2, Apr 1970	20.00
❑3, Jul 1970	14.00
❑4, Oct 1970, Final Issue	14.00

Family Guy
Devil's Due

	N-MINT
❑1, Aug 2006	6.95
❑2, Aug 2006	6.95

Family Man
DC / Paradox

	N-MINT
❑1, ca. 1995; b&w; digest	4.95
❑2, ca. 1995; b&w; digest	4.95
❑3, ca. 1995; b&w; digest	4.95

Famous Features
Pacific

	N-MINT
❑1, Jul 1984; Flamingo	2.50

Famous First Edition
DC

	N-MINT
❑F-4, Nov 1974; reprints Whiz Comics #2	15.00
❑F-5, Jan 1975; reprints Batman #1	13.00
❑F-6, May 1975; reprints Wonder Woman #1	10.00
❑F-7, Jul 1975; reprints All-Star #3	12.00
❑F-8, Sep 1975; reprints Flash Comics #1	9.00
❑C-26; 1: Superman. reprints Action Comics #1	10.00
❑C-28; reprints Detective Comics #27	9.00
❑C-30; 1: Wonder Woman. reprints Sensation Comics #1	10.00
❑C-61, Mar 1979; reprints Superman #1	9.00
❑C-61/Whitman, Mar 1979; Whitman variant; reprints Superman #1	18.00

Fana
Comax

	N-MINT
❑1, b&w; Adult	2.95

Fana the Jungle Girl
Comax

	N-MINT
❑1, b&w	2.95

Fanboy
DC

	N-MINT
❑1, Mar 1999	2.50
❑2, Apr 1999	2.50
❑3, May 1999	2.50
❑4, Jun 1999, Our Army at War take-off	2.50
❑5, Jul 1999	2.50
❑6, Aug 1999	2.50

Fandom Confidential
Kitchen Sink

	N-MINT
❑1	2.95

Fang
Sirius Entertainment

	N-MINT
❑1, Feb 1995	2.95
❑2, Apr 1995	2.95
❑3, Jun 1995	2.95

Fang
Conquest

	N-MINT
❑1, b&w	2.95

Fang
Tangram

	N-MINT
❑1, b&w; NN	2.95

Fang: Testament
Sirius Entertainment

	N-MINT
❑1	2.50
❑2	2.50
❑3	2.50
❑4	2.50

Fangraphix
Fangraphix

	N-MINT
❑1	1.95
❑2	1.95
❑3	1.95

Fangs of the Cobra
Mythic

	N-MINT
❑1, Win 1996; color and b&w	2.95

Fanny
Fanny

	N-MINT
❑1	3.00
❑2	3.00
❑3, b&w	3.95

Fanny Hill
Shunga

	N-MINT
❑1, b&w; Adult	2.50

Fantaescape
Zinzinnati

	N-MINT
❑1, Jun 1988	1.75

Fantagor
Last Gasp

	N-MINT
❑1	3.00
❑2	3.00
❑3	3.00

FantaSci
Apple

	N-MINT
❑1, b&w	2.00
❑2, b&w	2.00
❑3, b&w; Apple Comics publisher Begins	2.00
❑4	2.00
❑5	1.75
❑6	1.75
❑7	1.75
❑8, Jul 1988	1.75
❑9	1.95

Fantastic Adventures
Ace

	N-MINT
❑1, Mar 1987; b&w	1.75
❑2, Jun 1987	1.75
❑3, Oct 1987	1.75

Fantastic Fables
Dark Horse

	N-MINT
❑1, Oct 1993, b&w; Reprints	2.50
❑2	2.50

Fantastic Fanzine
Arrow

	N-MINT
❑1	1.50
❑2	1.50
❑3	1.50

Fantastic Five
Marvel

	N-MINT
❑1, Oct 1999	1.99
❑2, Nov 1999	1.99
❑2/A, Nov 1999; variant cover	1.99
❑3, Dec 1999	1.99

Fantastic Force
Marvel

	N-MINT
❑1, Nov 1994; O: Fantastic Force. 1: Fantastic Force. foil cover	2.50
❑2, Dec 1994; V: Zarathustra	2.00
❑3, Jan 1995; V: the Seeker	2.00
❑4, Feb 1995; V: Adaptoid	1.75
❑5, Mar 1995; V: Dreadface	1.75
❑6, Apr 1995; V: Gray Gargoyle; V: Go-Devil	1.75
❑7, May 1995; Continues in Fantastic Four #400	1.75
❑8, Jun 1995; V: Inhumans; Atlantis Rising; Continued from Fantastic Four	1.75
❑9, Jul 1995	1.75
❑10, Aug 1995; V: Lord Moses	1.75
❑11, Sep 1995; V: Lord Moses	1.75
❑12, Oct 1995; V: Vanguard	1.75
❑13, Nov 1995; She-Hulk joins team	1.75
❑14, Dec 1995; A: She-Hulk. A: Black Panther. A: Human Torch. A: Wakanda. O: Vibraxas	1.75
❑15, Jan 1996; Team disbands; cover says Jan 95, indicia says Jan 96	1.75
❑16, Feb 1996	1.75
❑17, Mar 1996	1.75
❑18, Apr 1996	1.75

Fantastic Four
Marvel

	N-MINT
❑1, Nov 1961, JK (c); JK, SL (w); JK (a); 1&O: Fantastic Four. 1&O: Mole Man. Artie Simek credited with the inks in Fantastic Four #281's letters page by Jack and Roz Kirby	20000.00
❑1/Golden 1966, JK (c); JK, SL (w); JK (a); Golden Record reprint	70.00
❑2, Jan 1962, JK (c); JK, SL (w); JK (a); O: Fantastic Four. 1: Skrulls	4500.00
❑3, Mar 1962, JK (c); JK, SL (w); JK (a); 1: Fantasti-Copter. 1: The Miracle Man (Marvel). 1: Fantasti-Car. 1: Pogo Plane. 1: Baxter Building. Fantastic Four wear uniforms for first time	3000.00
❑4, May 1962, JK (c); JK, SL (w); JK (a); 1: Sub-Mariner (in Silver Age). 1: Giganto. D: Giganto	3500.00
❑5, Jul 1962, JK (c); JK, SL (w); JK (a); 1&O: Doctor Doom	5000.00
❑6, Sep 1962, JK (c); JK, SL (w); JK (a); 1: The Yancy Street Gang (name only). A: Doctor Doom. Doctor Doom & Sub-Mariner vs. Fantastic Four	2000.00
❑7, Oct 1962, JK (c); JK, SL (w); JK (a); 1: Kurrgo. 1: The Xantha	1250.00
❑8, Nov 1962, JK (c); JK, SL (w); JK (a); 1: Puppet Master. 1: Alicia Mastersr...	1200.00
❑9, Dec 1962, JK (c); JK, SL (w); JK (a); A: Sub-Mariner	1150.00
❑10, Jan 1963, JK (c); JK, SL (w); JK (a); 1: The Ovoids. 1: Jack Kirby (as character in story). 1: Stan Lee (as character in story). A: Doctor Doom. V: Doctor Doom; 1: Stan Lee	1150.00
❑11, Feb 1963, JK (c); JK, SL (w); JK (a); O: Fantastic Four. 1&O: Impossible Man. 1: Willie Lumpkin (Fantastic Four's mailman)-Silver Age. 1: The Popuppians	1000.00
❑12, Mar 1963, JK (c); JK, SL (w); JK (a); 1: The Wrecker I (Dr. Karl Kort). V: Hulk. Thing fights Hulk for first time	2700.00
❑13, Apr 1963, JK (c); JK, SL (w); JK (a); 1&O: Red Ghost. 1: The Watcher	600.00

Other grades: Multiply price above by 5/6 for VF/NM • 2/3 for VERY FINE • 1/3 for FINE • 1/5 for VERY GOOD • 1/8 for GOOD

N-MINT

❑14, May 1963, JK (c); JK, SL (w); JK (a); A: Sub-Mariner. V: Puppet Master; V: Sub-Mariner ... 500.00
❑15, Jun 1963, JK (c); JK, SL (w); JK (a); 1: Awesome Android. 1: Mad Thinker. 700.00
❑16, Jul 1963, JK (c); SL (w); JK (a); A: Ant Man. A: Doctor Doom. A: The Wasp. V: Doctor Doom. 1: Princess Perla and the King of the Micro World; 1: Lizard Men of Tok; V: Doctor Doom 500.00
❑17, Aug 1963, JK (c); SL (w); JK (a); A: Ant Man. A: Doctor Doom. V: Doctor Doom ... 500.00
❑18, Sep 1963, JK (c); SL (w); JK (a); 1&O: Super-Skrull ... 500.00
❑19, Oct 1963, JK (c); SL (w); JK (a); 1&O: Rama-Tut ... 500.00
❑20, Nov 1963, JK (c); SL (w); JK (a); 1&O: Molecule Man. A: Watcher ... 600.00
❑21, Dec 1963, JK (c); SL (w); JK (a); 1&O: Hate-Monger. A: Nick Fury ... 450.00
❑22, Jan 1964, JK (c); SL (w); JK (a); V: Mole Man ... 250.00
❑23, Feb 1964, JK (c); SL (w); JK (a); V: Doctor Doom ... 250.00
❑24, Mar 1964, JK (c); SL (w); JK (a); 1: Moloids; 1: Infant Terrible ... 240.00
❑25, Apr 1964, JK (c); SL (w); JK (a); A: Rick Jones. A: Avengers. V: Hulk. first mention of Thing's Aunt Petunia; Hulk Battles Thing ... 550.00
❑26, May 1964, JK (c); SL (w); JK (a); A: Rick Jones. A: Avengers. V: Hulk ... 600.00
❑27, Jun 1964, JK (c); SL (w); JK (a); A: Doctor Strange. V: Sub-Mariner ... 300.00
❑28, Jul 1964, JK (c); SL (w); JK (a); A: X-Men. V: Puppet Master. V: Mad Thinker ... 500.00
❑29, Aug 1964, JK (c); SL (w); JK (a); A: Watcher. V: Red Ghost ... 260.00
❑30, Sep 1964, JK (c); SL (w); JK (a); 1&O: Diablo ... 260.00
❑31, Oct 1964, JK (c); SL (w); JK (a); A: Avengers. V: Mole Man. 1: Franklin Storm ... 260.00
❑32, Nov 1964, JK (c); SL (w); JK (a); 1: Sue and Johnny's parents (Franklin and Mary). V: Super-Skrull; 1: The Invincible Man (the Super Skrull disguised as Franklin Storm); D: Franklin Storm; V: Super-Skrull ... 250.00
❑33, Dec 1964, JK (c); SL (w); JK (a); 1: Attuma. A: Sub-Mariner ... 250.00
❑34, Jan 1965, JK (c); SL (w); JK (a); 1: Thomas Gideon (later becomes Glorian) ... 250.00
❑35, Feb 1965, JK (c); SL (w); JK (a); 1&O: Dragon Man. V: Diablo ... 165.00
❑36, Mar 1965, JK (c); SL (w); JK (a); 1&O: Frightful Four. 1: Medusa ... 165.00
❑37, Apr 1965, JK (c); SL (w); JK (a); 1: Morrat (Skrull Warlord); 1: Annelle (daughter of Skrull King); D: Morratt; 1: Anelle (Skrull) ... 165.00
❑38, May 1965, JK (c); SL (w); JK (a); 1: Trapster I (Peter Petruski). A: Frightful Four. Paste-Pot Pete becomes Trapster I 165.00
❑39, Jun 1965, JK (c); SL (w); JK (a); A: Daredevil. A: Doctor Doom. V: Doctor Doom ... 165.00
❑40, Jul 1965, JK (c); SL (w); JK (a); A: Daredevil. V: Doctor Doom ... 165.00
❑41, Aug 1965, JK (c); SL (w); JK (a); V: Frightful Four ... 110.00
❑42, Sep 1965, JK (c); SL (w); JK (a); V: Frightful Four ... 110.00
❑43, Oct 1965, JK (c); SL (w); JK (a); V: Frightful Four. V: Doctor Doom ... 110.00
❑44, Nov 1965, JK (c); SL (w); JK (a); 1: Gorgon. A: Dragon Man. A: Medusa 85.00
❑45, Dec 1965, JK (c); SL (w); JK (a); 1: Karnak. 1: Inhumans. 1: Crystal. 1: Triton. 1: Lockjaw. 1: Black Bolt. A: Trapster I. A: Sandman. V: Maximus. V: Dragon Man ... 325.00
❑46, Jan 1966, JK (c); JK, SL (w); JK (a); A: Inhumans. 1: The Seeker ... 150.00
❑47, Feb 1966, JK (c); JK, SL (w); JK (a); 1: Maximus. A: Inhumans. V: Maximus; 1: Alpha primitives; 1: Aireo (later Skybreaker) ... 100.00
❑48, Mar 1966, JK (c); JK, SL (w); JK (a); 1: Galactus. 1: Silver Surfer. A: Inhumans; 2: Maximus ... 460.00
❑49, Apr 1966, JK (c); JK, SL (w); JK (a); A: Galactus. A: Silver Surfer. A: Watcher. V: Galactus. 1: The Punisher (Galactus' robot); Silver Surfer ... 350.00

N-MINT

❑50, May 1966, JK (c); JK, SL (w); JK (a); 1: Wyatt Wingfoot. A: Galactus. A: Silver Surfer. A: Watcher. V: Galactus. Silver Surfer vs. Galactus 400.00
❑51, Jun 1966, JK (c); JK, SL (w); JK (a); 1: Negative Zone; D: 'Ben Grimm imposter'; 2: Wyatt Wingfoot ... 150.00
❑52, Jul 1966, JK (c); JK, SL (w); JK (a); 1: Black Panther ... 300.00
❑53, Aug 1966, JK (c); JK, SL (w); JK (a); O: Black Panther. 1&O: Klaw ... 140.00
❑54, Sep 1966, JK (c); JK, SL (w); JK (a); 1&O: Prester John. A: Inhumans. A: Black Panther ... 105.00
❑55, Oct 1966, JK (c); JK, SL (w); JK, JSt (a). Thing vs. Silver Surfer ... 210.00
❑56, Nov 1966, JK (c); JK, SL (w); JK (a). V: Klaw; Black Panther cameo; Doctor Doom cameo; Silver Surfer cameo ... 100.00
❑57, Dec 1966, JK (c); JK, SL (w); JK, JSt (a); A: Inhumans. A: Doctor Doom. V: Doctor Doom. V: Wizard. V: Sandman ... 115.00
❑58, Jan 1967, JK (c); JK, SL (w); JK, JSt (a); A: Doctor Doom. A: Lockjaw. A: Silver Surfer. V: Doctor Doom ... 90.00
❑59, Feb 1967, JK (c); JK, SL (w); JK, JSt (a); A: Inhumans. A: Silver Surfer. V: Doctor Doom ... 60.00
❑60, Mar 1967, JK (c); JK, SL (w); JK, JSt (a); A: Inhumans. A: Black Panther. A: Doctor Doom. A: Silver Surfer. A: Watcher. V: Doctor Doom ... 65.00
❑61, Apr 1967, JK (c); JK, SL (w); JK (a); A: Inhumans. A: Silver Surfer. V: Sandman. 70.00
❑62, May 1967, JK (c); JK, SL (w); JK (a); 1: Blastaar. A: Sandman ... 60.00
❑63, Jun 1967, JK (c); JK, SL (w); JK (a); V: Blastaar. V: Sandman ... 60.00
❑64, Jul 1967, JK (c); JK, SL (w); JK (a); 1: Supreme Intelligence; 1: Kree Sentry #459 ... 50.00
❑65, Aug 1967, JK (c); JK, SL (w); JK (a); 1: Kree. 1: Ronan the Accuser ... 55.00
❑66, Sep 1967, JK (c); JK, SL (w); JK (a); O: The Enclave. 1&O: Him (later Warlock). 115.00
❑66/2nd, Sep 1967, JK (c); JK, SL (w); JK (a) 2.00
❑67, Oct 1967, JK (c); JK, SL (w); JK (a); O: Him (later Warlock); 2: The Enclave 105.00
❑67/2nd, Oct 1967, JK (c); JK, SL (w); JK (a); 2nd printing ... 2.00
❑68, Nov 1967, JK (c); JK, SL (w); JK (a); V: Mad Thinker. 1: Dr. Santini ... 60.00
❑69, Dec 1967, JK (c); JK, SL (w); JK (a); V: Mad Thinker. 2: Dr. Santini ... 60.00
❑70, Jan 1968, JK (c); JK, SL (w); JK (a); V: Mad Thinker ... 55.00
❑71, Feb 1968, JK, SL (w); JK (a); V: Mad Thinker ... 45.00
❑72, Mar 1968, JK, SL (w); JK (a); A: Silver Surfer ... 100.00
❑73, Apr 1968, JK (c); JK, SL (w); JK (a); A: Daredevil. A: Spider-Man. A: Thor. V: Doctor Doom ... 80.00
❑74, May 1968, JK (c); JK, SL (w); JK (a); A: Galactus. A: Silver Surfer. V: Galactus; Don McGregor L.O.C.; Tony Isabella L.O.C ... 85.00
❑75, Jun 1968, JK (c); JK, SL (w); JK (a); A: Galactus. A: Silver Surfer. V: Galactus 55.00
❑76, Jul 1968, JK (c); JK, SL (w); JK (a); A: Silver Surfer. V: Galactus. V: Psycho-Man ... 45.00
❑77, Aug 1968, JK (c); JK, SL (w); JK (a); A: Silver Surfer. V: Galactus. V: Psycho-Man ... 50.00
❑78, Sep 1968, JK, SL (w); JK (a); V: Wizard ... 35.00
❑79, Oct 1968, JK, SL (w); JK (a); V: Mad Thinker ... 50.00
❑80, Nov 1968, JK, SL (w); JK (a) ... 40.00
❑81, Dec 1968, JK, SL (w); JK (a); V: Wizard. Crystal joins Fantastic Four ... 40.00
❑82, Jan 1969, JK (c); JK, SL (w); JK (a); A: Inhumans. V: Maximus ... 40.00
❑83, Feb 1969, JK (c); JK, SL (w); JK (a); A: Inhumans. V: Maximus ... 40.00
❑84, Mar 1969, JK (c); JK, SL (w); JK (a); A: Doctor Doom. V: Doctor Doom ... 40.00
❑85, Apr 1969, JK (c); JK, SL (w); JK (a); A: Doctor Doom. V: Doctor Doom ... 40.00
❑86, May 1969, JK (c); JK, SL (w); JK (a); A: Doctor Doom. V: Doctor Doom. 2: Hauptmann; Don McGregor L.O.C.. 50.00
❑87, Jun 1969, JK (c); JK, SL (w); JK (a); A: Doctor Doom. V: Doctor Doom. D: Hauptmann ... 40.00

N-MINT

❑88, Jul 1969, JK (c); JK, SL (w); JK (a); V: Mole Man ... 35.00
❑89, Aug 1969, JK (c); JK, SL (w); JK (a); V: Mole Man. 1: Skrull Slave-Master .. 35.00
❑90, Sep 1969, JK (c); JK, SL (w); JK (a); V: Mole Man. 2: Skrull Slave-Master .. 30.00
❑91, Oct 1969, JK (c); JK, SL (w); JK (a); 1: Torgo ... 30.00
❑92, Nov 1969, JK (c); JK, SL (w); JK (a); 2: Torgo. V: Torgo ... 30.00
❑93, Dec 1969, JK (c); JK, SL (w); JK (a); A: Torgo. V: Torgo ... 30.00
❑94, Jan 1970, JK (c); JK, SL (w); JK (a); 1: Agatha Harkness. V: Trapster. V: Wizard. V: Sandman ... 40.00
❑95, Feb 1970, JK (c); JK, SL (w); JK (a); 1: The Monocle; Crystal returns to the Inhumans ... 30.00
❑96, Mar 1970, JK (c); JK, SL (w); JK (a); V: Mad Thinker ... 30.00
❑97, Apr 1970, JK (c); JK, SL (w); JK (a) 25.00
❑98, May 1970, JK (c); JK, SL (w); JK (a); A: Neil Armstrong ... 25.00
❑99, Jun 1970, JK (c); JK, SL (w); JK (a); A: Inhumans ... 30.00
❑100, Jul 1970, anniversary; JK (c); JK, SL (w); JK (a); A: Puppet Master. A: Sandman (Marvel). A: Doctor Doom. A: Sub-Mariner. A: Mad Thinker. V: Lots of villains; 100th anniversary issue ... 70.00
❑101, Aug 1970, JK (c); JK, SL (w); JK (a); 1: Gimlet. 1: Top Man; Alan Kupperberg L.O.C ... 30.00
❑102, Sep 1970, JR (c); JK, SL (w); JK (a); A: Magneto. A: Sub-Mariner. V: Magneto ... 30.00
❑103, Oct 1970, JR (c); JR, SL (w); JR (a); 2: Agatha Harkness. A: Richard M. Nixon. A: Magneto. A: Sub-Mariner. V: Magneto ... 30.00
❑104, Nov 1970, SL (w); JR (a); A: Richard M. Nixon. A: Magneto. A: Sub-Mariner. V: Magneto ... 30.00
❑105, Dec 1970, SL (w); JR (a); 1: The "monster" (Larry Rambow) ... 30.00
❑106, Jan 1971, JR, SL (w); JR (a); 2: The "monster" (Larry Rambow) ... 22.00
❑107, Feb 1971, SL (w); JB (a); 1: Janus (the scientist) ... 30.00
❑108, Mar 1971, JB (c); JK, JR, SL (w); JB, JK, JR (a); 2: Janus (the scientist). 1: Nega-Man (Janus' evil other self)... 22.00
❑109, Apr 1971, SL (w); JB (a); A: Captain Marvel. D: Janus (the scientist). V: Annihilus ... 20.00
❑110, May 1971, SL (w); JB (a); A: Joe Robertson. A: J. Jonah Jameson. V: Annihilus ... 20.00
❑111, Jun 1971, SL (w); JB (a); 1: Collins (landlord of Baxter building). A: Joe Robertson. A: Peter Parker. A: Hulk. A: J. Jonah Jameson ... 20.00
❑112, Jul 1971, SL (w); JB (a); 2: Collins. A: Bruce Banner. A: Hulk. A: J. Jonah Jameson. Thing vs. Hulk ... 175.00
❑113, Aug 1971, SL (w); JB (a); 1: Overmind. A: Bruce Banner. A: The Watcher ... 25.00
❑114, Sep 1971, SL (w); JB (a); 2: Overmind. A: The Watcher. V: Overmind ... 27.00
❑115, Oct 1971, SL (w); JB (a); O: Overmind. 1: The Eternals (a.k.a. Eternians). A: The Watcher ... 25.00
❑116, Nov 1971, Giant-size; JB (a); O: Stranger. A: The Stranger. A: The Watcher. A: Edwin Jarvis. A: Doctor Doom 65.00
❑117, Dec 1971, JB (a); 1: Chiron. 1: Asmodeus. A: Crystal. A: Diablo. A: Kaliban. V: Diablo; 1: Kaliban ... 15.00
❑118, Jan 1972, JB (a); 1: Reed Richards of Earth-A. 1: Ben Grimm of Earth-A. 1: Sue Storm Grimm of Earth-A. A: Crystal. A: Diablo. A: Lockjaw. V: Diablo 15.00
❑119, Feb 1972, JB (a); A: Black Panther. A: Klaw. V: Klaw ... 15.00
❑120, Mar 1972, JB, SL (w); JB (a); 1: Air-Walker (robot form). A: General T. E. "Thunderbolt" Ross. V: Air-Walker Automaton ... 15.00
❑121, Apr 1972, JB, SL (w); JB (a); 2: Air-Walker (robot form). A: Galactus. A: Silver Surfer. V: Air-Walker Automaton 30.00
❑122, May 1972, SL (w); JB (a); A: Galactus. A: Silver Surfer. V: Galactus 45.00
❑123, Jun 1972, SL (w); JB (a); A: General T. E. "Thunderbold" Ross. A: Galactus. A: Richard M. Nixon. A: Silver Surfer. V: Galactus ... 27.00

Other grades: Multiply price above by 5/6 for VF/NM • 2/3 for VERY FINE • 1/3 for FINE • 1/5 for VERY GOOD • 1/8 for GOOD

Evil Ernie (Eternity)

Lust for Lady Death sends Ernie on spree

©Eternity

Evil Ernie vs. the Super Heroes

Hellion takes out heroes

©Chaos!

Ewoks

Adventures of inhabitants of Endor moon

©Marvel

Excalibur

U.S. and British mutants join forces

©Marvel

Ex Machina

Tech controller becomes NYC mayor

©DC

	N-MINT
❑124, Jul 1972, SL (w); JB (a)	20.00
❑125, Aug 1972, SL (w); JB (a)	20.00
❑126, Sep 1972, JB (a); O: Fantastic Four	30.00
❑127, Oct 1972, JB (a); V: Mole Man	35.00
❑128, Nov 1972, JB (a); V: Tyrannus. V: Mole Man	30.00
❑129, Dec 1972, JB (a); 1: Thundra. A: Medusa	25.00
❑130, Jan 1973, JSo (c); JB (a); 2: Thundra. A: Inhumans. V: Trapster. V: Thundra. V: Wizard. V: Sandman	15.00
❑131, Feb 1973, JB, JSo (c); RA (a); 1: Omega (the ultimate Alpha Primitive). A: Inhumans. V: Maximus.	15.00
❑132, Mar 1973, JSo (c); JB (a); V: Maximus. Medusa Joins	15.00
❑133, Apr 1973, JB (c); V: Trapster. V: Thundra. V: Wizard. V: Sandman	12.00
❑134, May 1973, JB (a); V: Dragon Man	12.00
❑135, Jun 1973, JB (a); V: Dragon Man.	12.00
❑136, Jul 1973, JB (a); V: Shaper of Worlds	12.00
❑137, Aug 1973, JB (a); V: Shaper of Worlds	12.00
❑138, Sep 1973, JB (a); V: Miracle Man.	12.00
❑139, Oct 1973, JB (a); V: Miracle Man.	12.00
❑140, Nov 1973, RB (c); JB (a); O: Annihilus. V: Annihilus	12.00
❑141, Dec 1973, JR (c); JB (a); V: Annihilus	12.00
❑142, Jan 1974, RB (c); RB (a); 1: Darkoth the Death-Demon. V: Doctor Doom	12.00
❑143, Feb 1974, GK (c); RB (a); V: Doctor Doom	12.00
❑144, Mar 1974, RB (c); RB (a); A: Doctor Doom. V: Doctor Doom. Marvel Value Stamp #39: Iron Fist	12.00
❑145, Apr 1974, GK (c); RA (a); A: Doctor Doom. Marvel Value Stamp #9: Captain Marvel	12.00
❑146, May 1974, GK (c); RA (a); Marvel Value Stamp #91: Hela	10.00
❑147, Jun 1974, RB (c); RB (a); A: Sub-Mariner. Marvel Value Stamp #82: Mary Jane	15.00
❑148, Jul 1974, RB (c); RB (a); V: Frightful Four	10.00
❑149, Aug 1974, RB (c); RB (a); Marvel Value Stamp #78: Owl	10.00
❑150, Sep 1974, GK (c); RB (a); A: Inhumans. A: Avengers. Wedding of Crystal and Quicksilver; Marvel Value Stamp #27: Black Widow	10.00
❑151, Oct 1974, RB (a); O: Thundra. 1: Mahkizmo. Marvel Value Stamp #21: Kull	10.00
❑152, Nov 1974, RB, JM (a); Marvel Value Stamp #23: Sgt. Fury	10.00
❑153, Dec 1974, GK (c); RB, JSt (a); V: Mahkizmo. Marvel Value Stamp #62: Plunderer	10.00
❑154, Jan 1975, GK (c); partial reprint of Strange Tales #127; Marvel Value Stamp #100: Galactus	10.00
❑155, Feb 1975, RB (a); A: Silver Surfer. V: Doctor Doom. Marvel Value Stamp #16: Shang-Chi	15.00
❑156, Mar 1975, RB (a); A: Doctor Doom. A: Silver Surfer. V: Doctor Doom	12.00
❑157, Apr 1975, RB (c); RB (a); A: Doctor Doom. A: Silver Surfer. V: Doctor Doom	12.00
❑158, May 1975, RB (a); V: Xemu	12.00
❑159, Jun 1975, RB (c); RB (a); A: Inhumans. V: Xemu. Marvel Value Stamp #84: Dr. Doom	10.00

	N-MINT
❑160, Jul 1975, GK (c); JB (a); V: Arkon. Marvel Value Stamp #32: Red Skull	10.00
❑161, Aug 1975, RB (a); A: Valeria. A: Reed Richards of Earth-A. A: Sue Grimm of Earth-A. A: Ben Grimm of Earth-A. A: Lockjaw. A: Phineas	10.00
❑162, Sep 1975, RB (a); A: Albert E. DeVoor. A: The "Old One". A: Valeria. A: Reed Richards of Earth-A. A: Gaard (Johnny Storm of Earth-A, reconstructed). A: Arkon. A: Ben Grimm of Earth-A. A: Phineas	10.00
❑163, Oct 1975, RB (a); A: Albert E. DeVoor. A: Reed Richards of Earth-A. A: Gaard (Johnny Storm of Earth-A, reconstructed). A: Arkon	10.00
❑164, Nov 1975, JK (c); GP (a); 1: Crusader (a.k.a. Marvel Boy). 1: Frankie Raye; 1: Crusader (Marvely)	9.00
❑165, Dec 1975, GP (a); O: Crusader (a.k.a. Marvel Boy). D: Crusader	7.00
❑166, Jan 1976, RB (c); GP (a); A: Hulk. A: Puppet Master. V: Hulk	10.00
❑167, Feb 1976, JK (c); GP (a); A: Hulk. A: Puppet Master. V: Hulk	15.00
❑168, Mar 1976, RB (a); A: Wreaker. Thing replaced by Luke Cage (Power Man)	10.00
❑169, Apr 1976, RB (c); RB (a); A: Luke Cage	10.00
❑169/30¢, Apr 1976, RB (c); RB (a); A: Luke Cage. 30¢ regional price variant	20.00
❑170, May 1976, GP (a); A: Luke Cage. V: Puppet Master	10.00
❑170/30¢, May 1976, GP (a); A: Luke Cage. 30¢ regional price variant	20.00
❑171, Jun 1976, JK (c); RB, GP (a); 1: Gorr. V: Galactus	6.00
❑171/30¢, Jun 1976, JK (c); RB, GP (a); 1: Gorr. V: Galactus. 30¢ regional price variant	20.00
❑172, Jul 1976, JK (c); GP (a); 2: Gorr. A: Galactus. A: The High Evolutionary. A: The Destroyer. V: Galactus	6.00
❑172/30¢, Jul 1976, JK (c); GP (a); 2: Gorr. A: Galactus. A: The High Evolutionary. A: The Destroyer. V: Galactus. 30¢ regional price variant	20.00
❑173, Aug 1976, JK (c); JB (a); A: Galactus. A: Gorr. A: The High Evolutionary. A: Torgo. V: Galactus	6.00
❑173/30¢, Aug 1976, JK (c); JB (a); A: Galactus. A: Gorr. A: The High Evolutionary. A: Torgo. V: Galactus. 30¢ regional price variant	20.00
❑174, Sep 1976, JK (c); JB (a); A: Galactus. A: Gorr. A: The High Evolutionary. A: Torgo. V: Galactus	6.00
❑175, Oct 1976, JK (c); JB (a); A: Galactus. A: The Impossible Man. A: Gorr. A: The High Evolutionary. V: Galactus	6.00
❑176, Nov 1976, JK (c); GP (a); A: The Impossible Man. A: Roy Thomas. A: Stan Lee. A: Jack Kirby. V: Trapster. V: Wizard. V: Sandman	6.00
❑177, Dec 1976, JK (c); GP (a); O: Texas Twister. 1: Texas Twister. 1: Captain Ultra. A: Tigra. A: Impossible Man. V: Trapster. V: Brute. V: Wizard. V: Sandman	6.00
❑178, Jan 1977, JR (c); GP (a); A: The Impossible Man. A: Brute. V: Trapster. V: Brute. V: Wizard. V: Sandman	6.00

	N-MINT
❑179, Feb 1977, AM (c); 1: Metalloid. A: Tigra. A: Thundra. A: Reed Richards of Counter-Earth. A: Impossible Man. A: Annihilus. A: Mad Thinker. V: Annihilus. V: Mad Thinker. Newsstand edition (distributed by Curtis); issue number in box	6.00
❑179/Whitman, Feb 1977, AM (c); 1: Metalloid. A: Tigra. A: Thundra. A: Reed Richards of Counter-Earth. A: Impossible Man. A: Annihilus. A: Mad Thinker. V: Annihilus. V: Mad Thinker. Special markets edition (usually sold in Whitman bagged prepacks); price appears in a diamond; UPC barcode appears	6.00
❑180, Mar 1977, JK (c); JK, SL (w); JK (a); Reprints FF #101; newsstand edition (distributed by Curtis); issue number in box	6.00
❑180/Whitman, Mar 1977, JK (c); JK, SL (w); JK (a); Special markets edition (usually sold in Whitman bagged prepacks); price appears in a diamond; UPC barcode appears	6.00
❑181, Apr 1977, JK (c); A: Reed Richards of Counter-Earth. A: Annihilus. V: Reed Richards of Counter-Earth. V: Annihilus. V: Mad Thinker. Newsstand edition (distributed by Curtis); issue number in box	6.00
❑181/Whitman, Apr 1977, JK (c); A: Reed Richards of Counter-Earth. A: Annihilus. V: Reed Richards of Counter-Earth. V: Annihilus. V: Mad Thinker. Special markets edition (usually sold in Whitman bagged prepacks); price appears in a diamond; UPC barcode appears	6.00
❑182, May 1977, V: Reed Richards of Counter-Earth. V: Annihilus. V: Mad Thinker. Newsstand edition (distributed by Curtis); issue number in box	6.00
❑182/Whitman, May 1977, V: Reed Richards of Counter-Earth. V: Annihilus. V: Mad Thinker. Special markets edition (usually sold in Whitman bagged prepacks); price appears in a diamond; UPC barcode appears	6.00
❑183, Jun 1977, GP (c); SB (a); A: Tigra. A: Thundra. A: Impossible Man. A: Brute. A: Annihilus. A: Mad Thinker. V: Brute. V: Annihilus. V: Mad Thinker. Newsstand edition (distributed by Curtis); issue number in box	6.00
❑183/Whitman, Jun 1977, GP (c); SB (a); A: Tigra. A: Thundra. A: Impossible Man. A: Brute. A: Annihilus. A: Mad Thinker. V: Brute. V: Annihilus. V: Mad Thinker. Special markets edition (usually sold in Whitman bagged prepacks); price appears in a diamond; UPC barcode appears	6.00
❑183/35¢, Jun 1977, 35¢ regional price variant; newsstand edition (distributed by Curtis); issue number in box	15.00
❑184, Jul 1977, GP (c); GP (a); A: Tigra. A: Thundra. A: Impossible Man. Newsstand edition (distributed by Curtis); issue number in box	6.00
❑184/Whitman, Jul 1977, GP (a); A: Tigra. A: Thundra. A: Impossible Man. Special markets edition (usually sold in Whitman bagged prepacks); price appears in a diamond; UPC barcode appears	6.00

Other grades: Multiply price above by 5/6 for VF/NM • 2/3 for VERY FINE • 1/3 for FINE • 1/5 for VERY GOOD • 1/8 for GOOD

N-MINT

❑184/35¢, Jul 1977, 35¢ regional price variant; newsstand edition (distributed by Curtis); issue number in box 15.00
❑185, Aug 1977, GP (a); 1: Nicholas Scratch. 2: New Salem's Witches. A: Impossible Man. Newsstand edition (distributed by Curtis); issue number in box 5.00
❑185/Whitman, Aug 1977, GP (a); 1: Nicholas Scratch. 2: New Salem's Witches. A: Impossible Man. Special markets edition (usually sold in Whitman bagged prepacks); price appears in a diamond; UPC barcode appears............. 5.00
❑185/35¢, Aug 1977, 35¢ regional price variant; newsstand edition (distributed by Curtis); issue number in box 15.00
❑186, Sep 1977, GP (a); O: New Salem's Witches. 2: Nicholas Scratch. A: Impossible Man. Newsstand edition (distributed by Curtis); issue number in box 5.00
❑186/Whitman, Sep 1977, GP (a); O: New Salem's Witches. 2: Nicholas Scratch. A: Impossible Man. Special markets edition (usually sold in Whitman bagged prepacks); price appears in a diamond; no UPC barcode................. 5.00
❑186/35¢, Sep 1977, GP (a); O: New Salem's Witches. 2: Nicholas Scratch. A: Impossible Man. 35¢ regional price variant; newsstand edition (distributed by Curtis); issue number in box 15.00
❑187, Oct 1977, GP (a); A: Molecule Man. A: Klaw. A: Impossible Man. V: Molecule Man. V: Klaw. Newsstand edition (distributed by Curtis); issue number in box. 5.00
❑187/Whitman, Oct 1977, GP (a); A: Molecule Man. A: Klaw. A: Impossible Man. V: Molecule Man. V: Klaw. Special markets edition (usually sold in Whitman bagged prepacks); price appears in a diamond; no UPC barcode................................ 5.00
❑187/35¢, Oct 1977, GP (a); A: Molecule Man. A: Klaw. A: Impossible Man. V: Molecule Man. V: Klaw. 35¢ regional price variant; newsstand edition (distributed by Curtis); issue number in box 15.00
❑188, Nov 1977, GP (c); GP (a); A: The Watcher. A: Molecule Man. A: Impossible Man. V: Molecule Man. V: Klaw. Newsstand edition (distributed by Curtis); issue number in box 5.00
❑188/Whitman, Nov 1977, GP (a); A: The Watcher. A: Molecule Man. A: Impossible Man. V: Molecule Man. V: Klaw. Special markets ed. (usually sold in Whitman bagged prepacks); price appears in a diamond; no UPC barcode. 5.00
❑189, Dec 1977, KP (c); JK, SL (w); JK (a); Reprints FF Ann #4; newsstand edition (distributed by Curtis); issue number in box 5.00
❑189/Whitman, Dec 1977, KP (c); JK, SL (w); JK (a); Special markets edition (usually sold in Whitman bagged prepacks); price appears in a diamond; no UPC barcode................................ 5.00
❑190, Jan 1978, JK (c); SB (a); Thing recounts FF's career 5.00
❑191, Feb 1978, GP (c); GP (a); A: Plunderer. A: Thundra. V: Plunderer. Fantastic Four resign 5.00
❑192, Mar 1978, GP (c); GP (a); A: Texas Twister.. 5.00
❑193, Apr 1978, KP (c); KP (w); KP (a); O: Darketh the Death-Demon. 1: Victor Von Doom II (not face). A: Diablo. A: Impossible Man. V: Diablo. Newsstand edition (distributed by Curtis); issue number in box 5.00
❑193/Whitman, Apr 1978, KP (w); KP (a); O: Darketh the Death-Demon. 1: Victor Von Doom II (not face). A: Diablo. A: Impossible Man. V: Diablo. Special markets edition (usually sold in Whitman bagged prepacks); price appears in a diamond; no UPC barcode 5.00
❑194, May 1978, GP (c); KP (w); KP (a); A: Darketh. A: Diablo. A: Impossible Man. A: Sub-Mariner. V: Diablo. Newsstand edition (distributed by Curtis); issue number in box 5.00
❑194/Whitman, May 1978, GP (c); KP (w); KP (a); A: Darketh. A: Diablo. A: Impossible Man. A: Sub-Mariner. V: Diablo. Special markets edition (usually sold in Whitman bagged prepacks); price appears in a diamond; no UPC barcode................................ 5.00

N-MINT

❑195, Jun 1978, GP (c); KP (a); 2: Victor Von Doom II (not face). A: Lord Vashti. A: Impossible Man. A: Sub-Mariner. Newsstand edition (distributed by Curtis); issue number in box 5.00
❑195/Whitman, Jun 1978, GP (c); KP (a); 2: Victor Von Doom II (not face). A: Lord Vashti. A: Impossible Man. A: Sub-Mariner. Special markets edition (usually sold in Whitman bagged prepacks); price appears in a diamond; no UPC barcode 5.00
❑196, Jul 1978, GP (c); KP (a); A: Victor Von Doom II. A: Doctor Doom. Doctor Doom appearance (face revealed); Victor Von Doom II appearance (face revealed)................................... 5.00
❑197, Aug 1978, GP (c); KP (a); A: Red Ghost. A: Victor Von Doom II. A: Dr. Doom. A: Nick Fury. V: Red Ghost. V: Doctor Doom. Reed Richards gets powers back; newsstand edition (distributed by Curtis); issue number in box 5.00
❑197/Whitman, Aug 1978, GP (c); KP (a); A: Red Ghost. A: Victor Von Doom II. A: Dr. Doom. A: Nick Fury. V: Red Ghost. V: Doctor Doom. Special markets edition (usually sold in Whitman bagged prepacks); price appears in a diamond; UPC barcode appears 5.00
❑198, Sep 1978, JB (c); KP, JSt (a); A: Prince Zorba. A: Victor Von Doom II. A: Doctor Doom. V: Doctor Doom. Team gets together to fight Doctor Doom; newsstand edition (distributed by Curtis); issue number in box 5.00
❑198/Whitman, Sep 1978, JB (c); KP (a); A: Prince Zorba. A: Victor Von Doom II. A: Doctor Doom. V: Doctor Doom. Special markets edition (usually sold in Whitman bagged prepacks); price appears in a diamond; no UPC barcode 5.00
❑199, Oct 1978, KP (c); KP (a); O: Victor Von Doom II. A: Prince Zorba. A: Doctor Doom. D: Victor Von Doom II. Newsstand edition (distributed by Curtis); issue number in box 5.00
❑199/Whitman, Oct 1978, KP (a); O: Victor Von Doom II. A: Prince Zorba. A: Doctor Doom. D: Victor Von Doom II. Special markets edition (usually sold in Whitman bagged prepacks); price appears in a diamond; no UPC barcode 5.00
❑200, Nov 1978, KP (a); A: Doctor Doom. V: Doctor Doom; Prince Zorba 5.00
❑201, Dec 1978, KP (c); KP, JSt (a); A: Prince Zorba. A: Quasimodo. Newsstand edition (distributed by Curtis); issue number in box 4.00
❑201/Whitman, Dec 1978, KP (a); A: Prince Zorba. A: Quasimodo. Special markets edition (usually sold in Whitman bagged prepacks); price appears in a diamond; no UPC barcode 4.00
❑202, Jan 1979, JB (c); JB, KP, DC, JSt (a); A: Iron Man. A: Quasimodo. A: Tony Stark. Newsstand edition (distributed by Curtis); issue number in box 4.00
❑202/Whitman, Jan 1979, JB, KP (a); A: Iron Man. A: Quasimodo. A: Tony Stark. Special markets edition (usually sold in Whitman bagged prepacks); price appears in a diamond; no UPC barcode. 4.00
❑203, Feb 1979, DC (c); KP, JSt (a); Newsstand edition (distributed by Curtis); issue number in box 4.00
❑203/Whitman, Feb 1979, KP (a); Special markets edition (usually sold in Whitman bagged prepacks); price appears in a diamond; no UPC barcode 4.00
❑204, Mar 1979, AM (c); KP, JSt (a); 1: Queen Adora (of Xandar). 1: Skrull X. A: Man-Wolf. A: The Watcher. A: Monocle. A: Edwin Jarvis. A: Spider-Man 4.00
❑205, Apr 1979, KP, JSt (a); 1: Thoran Rul (Protector). 2: Queen Adora (of Xandar). A: The Watcher. A: Monocle. A: Emperor Dorrek.......... 4.00
❑206, May 1979, KP (c); KP, JSt (a); Newsstand edition (distributed by Curtis); issue number in box 4.00
❑206/Whitman, May 1979, KP (a); Special markets edition (usually sold in Whitman bagged prepacks); price appears in a diamond; no UPC barcode 4.00
❑207, Jun 1979, KP (c); SB, JSt (a); 1: The Enclave (identified). A: Barney Bushkin. A: Medusa. A: Monocle. A: Spider-Man 4.00

N-MINT

❑208, Jul 1979, KP, DC (c); AM, SB, FS (a); O: Protector. A: Nova. A: Sphinx. A: Queen Adora. A: Comet. A: Diamondhead. A: Thoran Rul (Protector). A: Crimebuster. A: Doctor Sun. A: Powerhouse. 1: Protector 4.00
❑209, Aug 1979, KP (c); JBy, JSt (a); 1: Herbie.. 4.00
❑210, Sep 1979, JBy, JSt (a); 2: Herbie. A: Galactus 4.00
❑211, Oct 1979, JBy (a); 1: Terrax the Tamer. A: Galactus. A: The Watcher.... 4.00
❑212, Nov 1979, JBy, JSt (a); A: Galactus. A: Sphinx. A: The Watcher. A: Sayge. A: Skrull X 4.00
❑213, Dec 1979, color JBy, JSt (a); A: Galactus. A: Sphinx. A: The Watcher. A: Sayge 4.00
❑214, Jan 1980, JBy (c); JBy, JSt (a); A: Queen Adora. A: Dum Dum Dugan. D: Skrull X... 4.00
❑215, Feb 1980, JBy, JSt (a).................. 4.00
❑216, Mar 1980, RB (c); JBy (a) 4.00
❑217, Apr 1980, JBy, JSt (a); A: Dazzler 4.00
❑218, May 1980, AM (c); JBy, JSt (a); Continued from Peter Parker, the Spectacular Spider-Man #42 .... 4.00
❑219, Jun 1980...................................... 4.00
❑220, Jul 1980, JBy (c); JBy (w); JBy, JSt (a); O: Fantastic Four......................... 4.00
❑221, Aug 1980, JSt (c); JBy (w); BSz, JBy, JSt (a)... 4.00
❑222, Sep 1980, BSz, JSt (a)................ 4.00
❑223, Oct 1980, BSz, JSt (a); V: The Salem Seven 4.00
❑224, Nov 1980, JSt (c); BSz (a) 4.00
❑225, Dec 1980, BSz (c); BSz (a); A: Thor 4.00
❑226, Jan 1981, BSz (a) 4.00
❑227, Feb 1981, BSz (a) 4.00
❑228, Mar 1981, BSz, JSt (a)................. 4.00
❑229, Apr 1981, BSz, JSt (a) 4.00
❑230, May 1981, BSz, JSt (a) 4.00
❑231, Jun 1981, BSz, JSt (a) 4.00
❑232, Jul 1981, JBy (c); JBy (w); JBy (a); V: Diablo... 4.00
❑233, Aug 1981, JBy (c); JBy (w); JBy (a); V: Hammerhead...................................... 4.00
❑234, Sep 1981, JBy (c); JBy (w); JBy (a) 4.00
❑235, Oct 1981, JBy (c); JBy (w); JBy (a); V: Ego. O: Ego the Living Planet......... 4.00
❑236, Nov 1981, 20th Anniversary Issue; JBy (c); JBy, SL (w); JBy, JK (a); O: Fantastic Four. V: Doctor Doom; Giant-size 4.00
❑237, Dec 1981, JBy (c); JBy (w); JBy (a); 1: Julie Angel...................................... 4.00
❑238, Jan 1982, JBy (c); JBy (w); JBy (a); O: Frankie Raye. A: Aunt Petunia. 1: Aunt Petunia.................................. 4.00
❑239, Feb 1982, JBy (c); JBy (w); JBy (a) 4.00
❑240, Mar 1982, JBy (c); JBy (w); JBy (a); 1: Luna... 2.50
❑241, Apr 1982, JBy (c); JBy (w); JBy (a); A: Black Panther 2.50
❑242, May 1982, JBy (c); JBy (w); JBy (a); A: Daredevil. V: Terrax................. 2.50
❑243, Jun 1982, JBy (c); JBy (w); JBy (a); V: Galactus 2.50
❑244, Jul 1982, JBy (c); JBy (w); JBy (a); 1: Nova II (Frankie Raye). Frankie Raye becomes herald of Galactus 2.50
❑245, Aug 1982, JBy (c); JBy (w); JBy (a); V: Franklin 2.50
❑246, Sep 1982, JBy (c); JBy (w); JBy (a); V: Doctor Doom 2.50
❑247, Oct 1982, JBy (c); JBy (w); JBy (a); 1: Kristoff Vernard; D: Zorba 2.50
❑248, Nov 1982, JBy (c); JBy (w); JBy (a) 2.50
❑249, Dec 1982, JBy (c); JBy (w); JBy (a); V: Gladiator 4.00
❑250, Jan 1983, Double-size; JBy (c); JBy (w); JBy (a); A: X-Men. A: Captain America. A: Spider-Man. V: Gladiator; X-Men appearance (Skrulls impersonating)..................... 5.00
❑252, Mar 1983, JBy (c); JBy (w); JBy (a); sideways format 2.50
❑251, Feb 1983, JBy (c); JBy (w); JBy (a); Negative Zone 4.00
❑253, Apr 1983, JBy (c); JBy (w); JBy (a) 2.50
❑254, May 1983, JBy (c); JBy (w); JBy (a); A: She-Hulk.. 2.50
❑255, Jun 1983, JBy (c); JBy (w); JBy (a) 2.50
❑256, Jul 1983, JBy (c); JBy (w); JBy (a); V: Annihilus 4.00

Other grades: Multiply price above by 5/6 for VF/NM • 2/3 for VERY FINE • 1/3 for FINE • 1/5 for VERY GOOD • 1/8 for GOOD

Ex-Mutants

Post-apocalyptic heroes fight to survive

©Malibu

Extra!

Reprints short-lived E.C. New Direction title

©Gemstone

Extreme Justice

Darker version of Justice League

©DC

Fables

Fairy tale folks hide and survive in real world

©DC

Fabulous Furry Freak Brothers

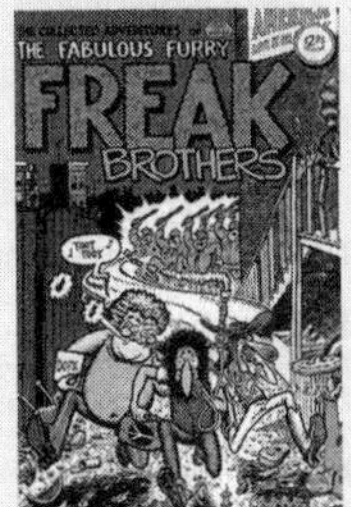

Underground comic featuring hippie high jinks

©Rip Off

	N-MINT
❑257, Aug 1983, JBy (c); JBy (w); JBy (a); D: Anelle; Skrull throne-world destroyed by Galactus	2.50
❑258, Sep 1983, JBy (c); JBy (w); JBy (a); O: Terrax the Tamer; Fantastic Four do not appear in story	2.50
❑259, Oct 1983, JBy (c); JBy (w); JBy (a); V: Doctor Doom; V: Tyros the Terrible	2.50
❑260, Nov 1983, JBy (c); JBy (w); JBy (a); A: Doctor Doom. A: Silver Surfer. D: Terrax. Silver Surfer, Doctor Doom	5.00
❑261, Dec 1983, color JBy (c); JBy (w); JBy (a); A: Silver Surfer. A: Watcher	4.00
❑262, Jan 1984, JBy (c); JBy (w); JBy (a); O: Galactus. Trial of Reed Richards; John Byrne appears in story	2.50
❑263, Feb 1984, JBy (c); JBy (w); JBy (a)	2.50
❑264, Mar 1984, JBy (c); JBy (w); JBy (a); V: Karisma. Cover swipe of Fantastic Four #1	2.50
❑265, Apr 1984, JBy (c); JBy (w); JBy (a); 1: Lyja (as Alicia Masters). 1: Roberta the Receptionist. She-Hulk joins Fantastic Four (replaces Thing, who left in Secret Wars)	2.50
❑266, May 1984, JBy (c); JBy (w); JBy, KGa (a); 1: Karisma; V: Karisma	2.50
❑267, Jun 1984, JBy (c); JBy (w); JBy (a); Sue has a miscarriage	2.50
❑268, Jul 1984, JBy (w); JBy (a); A: Hulk. A: Doctor Octopus. O: She-Hulk	2.50
❑269, Aug 1984, JBy (c); JBy (w); JBy (a); 1: Terminus	4.00
❑270, Sep 1984, JBy (c); JBy (w); JBy (a); V: Terminus	2.50
❑271, Oct 1984, JBy (c); JBy (w); JBy (a); V: Gormuu	4.00
❑272, Nov 1984, JBy (c); JBy (w); JBy (a); 1: Nathaniel Richards (Reed's father)	5.00
❑273, Dec 1984, JBy (c); JBy (w); JBy (a); O: Kang	2.50
❑274, Jan 1985, JBy (c); JBy (w); JBy (a); Thing solo story; alien costume freed	2.50
❑275, Feb 1985, JBy (c); JBy (w); JBy (a)	2.50
❑276, Mar 1985, JBy (c); JBy (w); JBy (a); B&W Cover	2.50
❑277, Apr 1985, JBy (c); JBy (w); JBy (a); V: Mephisto; V: Dire Wraiths; Thing returns from Battleworld	2.50
❑278, May 1985, JBy (c); JBy (w); JBy (a); O: Doctor Doom. Kristoff becomes second Doctor Doom	2.50
❑279, Jun 1985, JBy (c); JBy (w); JBy (a); 1: Hate-Monger III (H.M. Unger); V: Doctor Doom	2.50
❑280, Jul 1985, JBy (c); JBy (w); JBy (a); 1: Hate-Monger III ("H.M. Unger"). Sue becomes Malice	2.50
❑281, Aug 1985, JBy (c); JBy (w); JBy (a); V: Malice	2.50
❑282, Sep 1985, JBy (c); JBy (w); JBy (a); Secret Wars II	2.50
❑283, Oct 1985, JBy (c); JBy (w); JBy (a); V: Psycho-Man	2.50
❑284, Nov 1985, JBy (c); JBy (w); JBy (a); Invisible Girl becomes Invisible Woman	2.50
❑285, Dec 1985, JBy (c); JBy (w); JBy (a); Secret Wars II	2.50
❑286, Jan 1986, JBy (c); JBy (w); JBy (a); 2: X-Factor. A: X-Men. return of Jean Grey	3.00
❑287, Feb 1986, JBy (c); JBy (w); JBy (a); A: Doctor Doom	2.00
❑288, Mar 1986, JBy (c); JBy (w); JBy, JSt (a); A: Doctor Doom. Secret Wars II; Doctor Doom vs. Beyonder	2.00
❑289, Apr 1986, JBy (c); JBy (w); JBy (a); D: Basilisk I (Basil Elks); V: Blastaar	2.00
❑290, May 1986, JBy (c); JBy (w); JBy (a); V: Annihilus; V: Blastaar	2.00
❑291, Jun 1986, JBy (c); JBy (w); JBy (a)	2.00
❑292, Jul 1986, JBy (c); JBy (w); JBy (a); A: Nick Fury	2.00
❑293, Aug 1986, JBy (w); JBy (a)	2.00
❑294, Sep 1986, JOy (c); JBy (w); JOy (a)	2.00
❑295, Nov 1986, JOy (c); JOy (a)	2.00
❑296, Nov 1986, Double-size; Thing comes back	2.50
❑297, Dec 1986, JB, SB (a)	2.00
❑298, Jan 1987, JB, SB (a)	2.00
❑299, Feb 1987	2.00
❑300, Mar 1987, JB, SB (a); Wedding of Johnny Storm and Alicia; "Alicia" later revealed to be Lyja (a Skrull)	2.50
❑301, Apr 1987, JB (a)	2.00
❑302, May 1987, JB, SB (a)	2.00
❑303, Jun 1987, JB (a)	2.00
❑304, Jul 1987, JB, JSt (a); Reed and Sue take leave of absence	2.00
❑305, Aug 1987, JB, JSt (a)	2.00
❑306, Sep 1987, JB, JSt (a); A: Ms. Marvel (Sharon Ventura). V: Diablo and the Elementals; Thing asks Ms. Marvel to join FF	2.00
❑307, Oct 1987, JB, JSt (a); Crystal and new Ms. Marvel joins team	2.00
❑308, Nov 1987, JB, JSt (a); 1: Fasaud	2.00
❑309, Dec 1987, JB, JSt (a)	2.00
❑310, Jan 1988, KP (a); Ms. Marvel becomes She-Thing	2.00
❑311, Feb 1988, color KP (a)	2.00
❑312, Mar 1988, KP (a); A: Doctor Doom. Fall of Mutants	2.00
❑313, Apr 1988, SB, JSt (a)	2.00
❑314, May 1988, KP, JSt (a); V: Belasco	2.00
❑315, Jun 1988, KP, JSt (a); V: Master Pandemonium	2.00
❑316, Jul 1988, KP, JSt (a); O: Savage Land	2.00
❑317, Aug 1988, KP (a); Continued in Fantastic Four Ann #21	2.00
❑318, Sep 1988, KP (a); V: Blastaar	2.00
❑319, Oct 1988, Giant-size; KP (a); Doctor Doom vs. Beyonder; Beyonder returns, merges with Molecule Man	2.50
❑320, Nov 1988, KP (a); Thing vs. Hulk	2.00
❑321, Dec 1988, 1: Aron the Rogue Watcher. Ms. Marvel vs. She-Hulk	1.50
❑322, Jan 1989, KP (a); Inferno	1.50
❑323, Feb 1989, KP (a); Inferno	1.50
❑324, Mar 1989, KP (a); Inferno	1.50
❑325, Apr 1989, RB (a)	1.50
❑326, May 1989, KP (a); Reed and Sue return to team	1.50
❑327, Jun 1989, KP (a); Thing reverts to human form	1.50
❑328, Jul 1989, KP (a); V: Frightful Four; V: Dragon Man	1.50
❑329, Aug 1989, RB (a)	1.50
❑330, Sep 1989, RB (a); V: Doom	1.50
❑331, Oct 1989, RB (a); V: Ultron	1.50
❑332, Nov 1989, RB (a)	1.50
❑333, Nov 1989, RB (a)	1.50
❑334, Dec 1989, RB (a); Acts of Vengeance	1.50
❑335, Dec 1989, RB (a); Acts of Vengeance	1.50
❑336, Jan 1990, Acts of Vengeance	1.50
❑337, Feb 1990	2.00
❑338, Mar 1990	2.00
❑339, Apr 1990, Thor vs. Gladiator	2.00
❑340, May 1990	2.00
❑341, Jun 1990	2.00
❑342, Jul 1990, A: Spider-Man. V: Seekers	2.00
❑343, Aug 1990	2.00
❑344, Sep 1990	2.00
❑345, Oct 1990	2.00
❑346, Nov 1990	2.00
❑347, Dec 1990, A: Hulk. A: Ghost Rider. A: Wolverine. A: Spider-Man	2.50
❑347/2nd, Dec 1990, A: Hulk. A: Ghost Rider. A: Wolverine. 2nd printing	1.50
❑348, Jan 1991, A: Hulk. A: Ghost Rider. A: Wolverine. A: Spider-Man	2.50
❑348/2nd, Jan 1991, 2nd printing	1.50
❑349, Feb 1991, A: Punisher. A: Hulk. A: Ghost Rider. A: Wolverine. A: Spider-Man	2.50
❑350, Mar 1991, Giant-size; A: Doctor Doom. Return of Thing	2.50
❑351, Apr 1991	2.00
❑352, May 1991, Reed and Doctor Doom battle through time	2.00
❑353, Jun 1991	2.00
❑354, Jul 1991	2.00
❑355, Aug 1991, AM (a)	2.00
❑356, Sep 1991, Alicia is Skrull; Fantastic Four vs. New Warriors	2.00
❑357, Oct 1991, 1: Lyja (in true form). Skrull's identity revealed as Lyja	2.00
❑358, Nov 1991, 30th Anniversary Issue; JBy (w); JBy (a); O: Paibok the Power Skrull. 1: Paibok the Power Skrull. Die-cut cover	2.50
❑359, Dec 1991, 1: Devos the Devastator. The real Alicia returns	1.50
❑360, Jan 1992, V: Dreadface	1.50
❑361, Feb 1992, V: Doctor Doom	1.50
❑362, Mar 1992, 1: Wild Blood	1.50
❑363, Apr 1992, O: Occulus. 1: Occulus	1.50
❑364, May 1992, V: Occulus	1.50
❑365, Jun 1992, V: Occulus	1.50
❑366, Jul 1992, Infinity War tie-in	1.50
❑367, Aug 1992, Infinity War tie-in	1.50
❑368, Sep 1992, V: Magus; V: Thanos; Infinity War tie-in	1.50
❑369, Oct 1992, V: Thanos; Infinity War tie-in	1.50
❑370, Nov 1992, 1: Lyja the Lazerfist; V: Magus; Infinity War tie-in	1.50
❑371, Dec 1992, All-white embossed cover	3.00
❑371/2nd, Dec 1992, red embossed cover	2.50
❑372, Jan 1993, V: Paibok	1.25
❑373, Feb 1993, A: Silver Sable	1.25
❑374, Mar 1993, Spider-Man, Hulk, Ghost Rider, Wolverine team up again; Secret Defenders crossover	1.25
❑375, Apr 1993, Prism cover	3.00
❑376, May 1993, Franklin returns from future as a young man	1.25
❑377, Jun 1993, 1: Huntara. Secret Defenders crossover	1.25

Other grades: Multiply price above by 5/6 for VF/NM • 2/3 for VERY FINE • 1/3 for FINE • 1/5 for VERY GOOD • 1/8 for GOOD

N-MINT

❑378, Jul 1993, V: Huntara; V: Klaw; V: Devos; V: Paibok 1.25
❑379, Aug 1993 1.50
❑380, Sep 1993, V: Doctor Doom 1.50
❑381, Oct 1993, A: Hunger. D: Mister Fantastic (apparent death). D: Doctor Doom; D: Mister Fantastic (apparent death) 3.00
❑382, Nov 1993, V: Devos; V: Huntara; V: Klaw; V: Paibok 2.00
❑383, Dec 1993, V: Paibok 1.25
❑384, Jan 1994, A: Ant-Man (Scott Lang). 1.25
❑385, Feb 1994, Continued from Namor the Sub-Mariner #46-47 1.25
❑386, Mar 1994, 1: Egg (Lyja's baby). Birth of Lyja's baby 1.25
❑387, Apr 1994 1.25
❑387/Variant, Apr 1994, diecut cover 3.00
❑388, May 1994, A: Avengers. cards 1.50
❑389, Jun 1994, V: Collector 1.50
❑390, Jun 1994, A: Galactus 1.50
❑391, Aug 1994, A: Galactus 1.50
❑392, Sep 1994, 1: Devlor; V: Dark Raider; Lyja leaves 1.50
❑393, Oct 1994, A: Puppet Master. Nathaniel Richards takes over Latveria 1.50
❑394, Nov 1994, V: Raptor the Renegade 1.50
❑394/CS, Nov 1994, polybagged with 16-page Marvel Action Hour preview, acetate print, and other items 2.95
❑395, Dec 1994, A: Wolverine. V: Super-Adaptoid 1.50
❑396, Jan 1995 1.50
❑397, Feb 1995, V: Aron 1.50
❑398, Mar 1995, V: Aron 1.50
❑398/Variant, Mar 1995, foil cover 2.50
❑399, Apr 1995, V: Aron; V: Dark Raider 1.50
❑399/Variant, Apr 1995, enhanced cardstock cover 2.50
❑400, May 1995, Giant-size; foil cover 3.95
❑401, Jun 1995, V: Maximus; V: Morgan Le Fey; Atlantis Rising; Continued in Fantastic Force #9 1.50
❑402, Jul 1995, A: Thor. Atlantis Rising 1.50
❑403, Aug 1995 1.50
❑404, Sep 1995 1.50
❑405, Oct 1995, A: Iron Man 2020. A: Conan. A: Red Raven. A: Young Allies. A: Zarko. A: Green Goblin. The Thing becomes human 1.50
❑406, Nov 1995, 1: Hyperstorm. Return of Doctor Doom 1.50
❑407, Dec 1995, Return of Reed Richards 1.50
❑408, Jan 1996, V: Hyperstorm 1.50
❑409, Feb 1996, The Thing's face is healed 1.50
❑410, Mar 1996, O: Kristoff 1.50
❑411, Apr 1996, A: Inhumans. V: Black Bolt 1.50
❑412, May 1996 1.50
❑413, Jun 1996, Franklin Richards becomes a child again 1.50
❑414, Jul 1996, O: Hyperstorm. Franklin Richards becomes a child again 1.50
❑415, Aug 1996, Franklin captured by Onslaught 2.00
❑416, Sep 1996, Giant-size; Series continues in Fantastic Four Vol. 2; wraparound cover 3.50
❑500, Sep 2003, numbering restarts at 500 adding in issues from Vol. 2 and Vol. 3 45.00
❑500/CS, Sep 2003 3.50
❑501, Oct 2003, JK (c); JK, SL, MWa (w); JK (a) 100.00
❑502, Oct 2003, MWa (w) 5.00
❑503, Nov 2003, MWa (w) 2.99
❑504, Nov 2003, MWa (w) 2.99
❑505, Dec 2003, MWa (w) 2.99
❑506, Jan 2003, MWa (w) 2.99
❑507, Jan 2004, JK (c); SL, MWa (w); JK (a); V: Wizard 35.00
❑508, Feb 2004, JK (c); JK, SL, MWa (w); JK (a); 1: The Android Man; V: Mad Thinker 50.00
❑509, Mar 2004, 1: Silent Fox; Don McGregor L.O.C. 40.00
❑510, Apr 2004, JK (c); SL, MWa (w); JK (a); V: Wizard; Crystal joins Fantastic Four 40.00
❑511, May 2004, MWa (w); Reprints 2.25
❑512, Jun 2004, MWa (w); PS (a); V: Hydro-Man 2.99
❑513, Jul 2004, MWa (w); PS (a); V: Hydro-Man 2.99

N-MINT

❑514, Aug 2004, 1: Salamandra; V: Frightful Four 2.25
❑515, Aug 2004, V: Frightful Four 2.25
❑516, Sep 2004, V: Frightful Four 2.25
❑517, Oct 2004, Avengers Dissassembled tie-in 2.99
❑518, Nov 2004, Avengers Dissassembled tie-in 2.99
❑519, Dec 2004, Avengers Dissassembled tie-in 2.99
❑520, Jan 2005 2.99
❑521, Feb 2005 2.99
❑522, Mar 2005, O: Fantastic Four 2.99
❑523, Apr 2005 2.99
❑524, May 2005 2.99
❑525, Jun 2005, O: Diablo; V: Diablo 2.99
❑526, Jul 2005, V: Diablo 2.99
❑527, Aug 2005; Team charging fotward out of wreckage; Cover has team charging forward out of wreckage 7.00
❑527/Variant, Aug 2005 4.00
❑527/DirCut, Aug 2005 5.00
❑527/Conv, Aug 2005, Wizard World Philadelphia 7.00
❑528, Sep 2005 2.99
❑529, Oct 2005 2.99
❑530, Oct 2005 2.99
❑531, Nov 2005 2.99
❑532, Jan 2006 2.99
❑533, Feb 2006 2.99
❑534, Mar 2006, O: Hulk 2.99
❑535, May 2006 2.99
❑536, Jun 2006, Road to Civil War; Thor's Hammer appears 10.00
❑537, Jul 2006, Road to Civil War; Thor's Hammer appears 7.00
❑537/2nd, Jul 2006; Black and white cover 3.00
❑538, Sep 2006, Civil War; Civil War Tie-in 2.99
❑539, Oct 2006, V: Thinker; V: Puppet Master; Civil War; V: Thinker and the Puppet Master 2.99
❑540, Dec 2006, Civil War; Civil War Tie-in 2.99
❑541, Mar 2007, Civil War Cross-Over 2.99
❑542 2.99
❑543 2.99
❑544 2.99
❑545 2.99
❑546 2.99
❑547 2.99
❑548 2.99
❑549 2.99
❑550 2.99
❑551 2.99
❑552 2.99
❑553 2.99
❑554 2.99
❑555 2.99
❑556 2.99
❑557 2.99
❑558 2.99
❑559 2.99
❑560 2.99
❑561 2.99
❑562 2.99
❑563 2.99
❑564 2.99
❑565 2.99
❑566 2.99
❑567 2.99
❑Ann 1, ca. 1963, SL (w); JK (a); O: Fantastic Four. O: Sub-Mariner. 1: Krang. A: Spider-Man. A: Doctor Doom. A: Sub-Mariner. V: Sub-Mariner. Spider-Man; reprints FF #1 900.00
❑Ann 2, ca. 1964, O: Doctor Doom. 1: Boris. reprints FF #5 500.00
❑Ann 3, ca. 1965, Wedding of Reed Richards and Susan Storm; Virtually all Marvel super-heroes appear; reprints FF #6 and 11 175.00
❑Ann 4, Nov 1966, JK (c); JK, SL (w); JK (a); 1: Quasimodo. Return of Golden Age Human Torch; reprints FF #25 and 26 90.00
❑Ann 5, Nov 1967, JK, SL (w); JK (a); 1: Psycho-Man. A: Inhumans, Black Panther 60.00
❑Ann 6, Nov 1968, JK (c); JK, SL (w); JK (a); 1: Franklin Richards. 1: Annihilus 40.00
❑Ann 7, Nov 1969, JK, SL (w); JK (a); reprints FF #1, FF Ann #2 18.00

N-MINT

❑Ann 8, Dec 1970, JK, SL (w); JK (a); reprints FF Ann #1 18.00
❑Ann 9, Dec 1971, JK, SL (w); JK (a); reprints stories from FF #43, Ann #3, and Strange Tales #131 10.00
❑Ann 10, ca. 1973, JK, SL (w); JK (a); reprints stories from FF Ann #3 and 4; Reprints wedding of Reed and Sue Richards 8.00
❑Ann 11, ca. 1976, JK (c); JB (a); A: The Watcher. A: Invaders. V: Invaders 8.00
❑Ann 12, ca. 1977, KP, BH (a); A: Karnak. A: Sphinx. A: Medusa. A: Crystal. A: Triton. A: Quicksilver. A: Lockjaw. A: Gorgon. A: Black Bolt 5.00
❑Ann 13, ca. 1978, SB (a); A: Daredevil. A: Mole Man 5.00
❑Ann 14, ca. 1979, JSt (c); GP (a) 5.00
❑Ann 15, ca. 1980, GP (c); TS, GP (a); Skrulls 3.00
❑Ann 16, ca. 1982, SD (c); SD, JBy (a); 1: Dragon Lord 3.00
❑Ann 17, ca. 1983, JBy (c); JBy (w); JBy (a); ca. 1983 3.00
❑Ann 18, ca. 1984, JBy (c); JBy (w); Kree-Skrull War 3.00
❑Ann 19, ca. 1985, KGa (c); JBy (w); JBy (a); A: Avengers. Cont'd FF #286 3.00
❑Ann 20, ca. 1986, V: Doctor Doom; V: Mephisto; Cont'd FF #306; ca. 1987 3.00
❑Ann 21, ca. 1988, KP (a); V: High Evolutionary 3.00
❑Ann 22, ca. 1989, RB (a); Atlantis Attacks 3.00
❑Ann 23, ca. 1990, 1: Kosmos; V: Moonstone; 1: Ahab (Rory Campbell) 3.00
❑Ann 24, ca. 1991, AM (w); AM (a); O: Fantastic Four. A: Guardians of Galaxy. Korvac Quest 2.50
❑Ann 25, ca. 1992, HT (a); 1: Temptress. Citizen Kang 2.50
❑Ann 26, ca. 1993, HT (a); 1: Wildstreak. Polybagged with trading card 3.00
❑Ann 27, ca. 1994, MGu (c); MGu (a); 1994 Ann 3.00
❑Special 1, JBy (a); Reprints Sub-Mariner vs. Fantastic Four from Ann #1 with added material 2.00
❑Ashcan 1, ashcan edition; O: Fantastic Four; Wraparound cover, no credits 1.00

Fantastic Four
Marvel

❑1 (417), Nov 1996; JLee (c); JLee (w); JLee (a); O: Fantastic Four (new origin). AKA Fantastic Four Vol. 1, #417 4.00
❑1/Variant, Nov 1996; JLee (c); JLee (w); JLee (a); O: Fantastic Four (new origin). AKA Fantastic Four Vol. 1, #417; alternate cover 50.00
❑1/Gold, Nov 1996; JLee (w); JLee (a); AKA Fantastic Four Vol. 1, #417; Gold Signature Edition 3.50
❑2 (418), Dec 1996; JLee (c); JLee (w); JLee (a); V: Namor. AKA Fantastic Four Vol. 1, #418 2.00
❑3 (419), Jan 1997; JLee (c); JLee (w); JLee (a); A: Avengers. V: Namor. AKA Fantastic Four Vol. 1, #419 2.00
❑4 (420), Feb 1997; JLee (c); JLee (w); JLee (a); A: Black Panther. A: Doctor Doom. V: Doctor Doom. AKA Fantastic Four Vol. 1, #420 2.00
❑4/Variant, Feb 1997; JLee (w); JLee (a); AKA Fantastic Four Vol. 1, #420 2.00
❑5 (421), Mar 1997; JLee (c); JLee (w); JLee (a); V: Doctor Doom. AKA Fantastic Four Vol. 1, #421 2.00
❑6 (422), Apr 1997; JLee (w); JLee (a); A: Silver Surfer. V: Super Skrull. AKA Fantastic Four Vol. 1, #422; continues in Avengers #6 2.00
❑7 (423), May 1997; JLee (w); A: Galactus. A: Wolverine. A: Blastaar. AKA Fantastic Four Vol. 1, #423 2.00
❑8 (424), Jun 1997; JLee (w); A: Inhumans. AKA Fantastic Four Vol. 1, #424 2.00
❑9 (425), Jul 1997; A: Inhumans. A: Firelord. AKA Fantastic Four Vol. 1, #425 2.00
❑10 (426), Aug 1997; gatefold summary; JLee (c); JLee (w); A: Inhumans. AKA Fantastic Four Vol. 1, #426 2.00
❑11 (427), Sep 1997; gatefold summary; V: Terrax. AKA Fantastic Four Vol. 1, #427 2.00

Other grades: Multiply price above by 5/6 for VF/NM • 2/3 for VERY FINE • 1/3 for FINE • 1/5 for VERY GOOD • 1/8 for GOOD

Fafhrd and the Gray Mouser

Adapts Fritz Leiber fantasy series
©Marvel

Fallen Angel

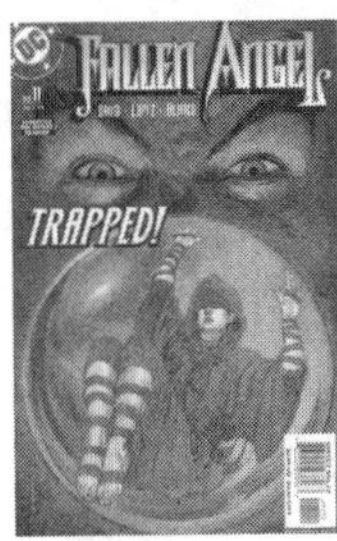

Peter David series with reluctant heroine
©DC

Fantastic Five

Potential future Richards' family super-team
©Marvel

Fantastic Four

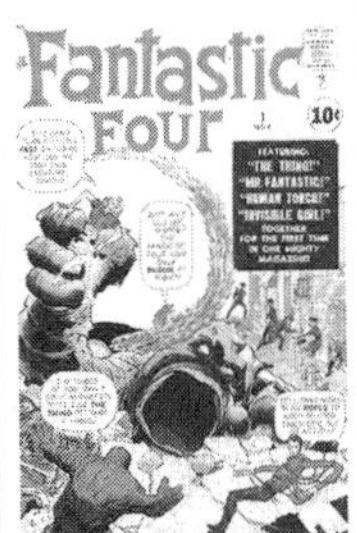

Super-team launches Marvel Age of Comics
©Marvel

Fantastic Four

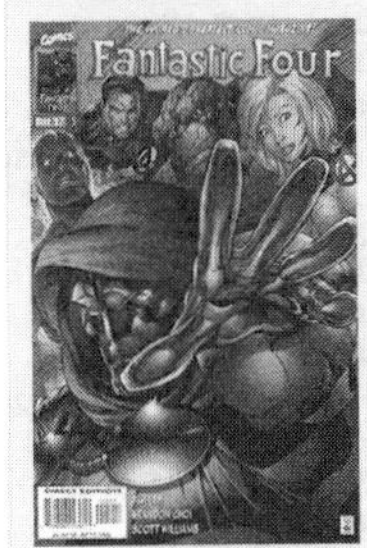

Jim Lee takes over during "Heroes Reborn"
©Marvel

N-MINT

❑12 (428), Oct 1997; gatefold summary; JLee (w); AKA Fantastic Four Vol. 1, #428; covers forms quadtych with Avengers #12, Iron Man #12, and Captain America #12 .... 2.99
❑13 (429), Nov 1997; gatefold summary; JRo (w); A: StormWatch. A: Wetworks. A: WildC.A.T.s. AKA Fantastic Four Vol. 1, #429; covers forms quadtych with Avengers #13, Iron Man #13, and Captain America #13 .... 2.00

Fantastic Four
Marvel

❑1 (430), Jan 1998; Giant-size; AKA Fantastic Four Vol. 1, #430; Cover has green background with team facing forward 3.00
❑1/A, Jan 1998; gatefold summary; AKA Fantastic Four Vol. 1, #430; alternate cover 4.00
❑2 (431), Feb 1998; gatefold summary; AKA Fantastic Four Vol. 1, #431 .... 3.00
❑2/A, Feb 1998; gatefold summary; AKA Fantastic Four Vol. 1, #431; alternate cover 3.00
❑3 (432), Mar 1998; gatefold summary; 1: Crucible. AKA Fantastic Four Vol. 1, #432 .... 3.00
❑4 (433), Apr 1998; gatefold summary; 1: Billie the Postman. A: Silver Surfer. V: Terminus. AKA Fantastic Four Vol. 1, #433 .... 2.50
❑5 (434), May 1998; gatefold summary; V: Crucible. AKA Fantastic Four Vol. 1, #434 .... 2.50
❑6 (435), Jun 1998; gatefold summary; A: Iron Fist. AKA Fantastic Four Vol. 1, #435; Thing vs. Technet 2.25
❑7 (436), Jul 1998; gatefold summary; V: Warwolves. AKA Fantastic Four Vol. 1, #436 .... 2.25
❑8 (437), Aug 1998; gatefold summary; AKA Fantastic Four Vol. 1, #437 .... 2.25
❑9 (438), Sep 1998; gatefold summary; A: Spider-Man. AKA Fantastic Four Vol. 1, #438 .... 2.25
❑10 (439), Oct 1998; gatefold summary; V: Trapster. AKA Fantastic Four Vol. 1, #439 .... 2.25
❑11 (440), Nov 1998; gatefold summary; A: Her. AKA Fantastic Four Vol. 1, #440 .... 2.25
❑12 (441), Dec 1998; gatefold summary; V: Her. V: Crucible. AKA Fantastic Four Vol. 1, #441; wraparound cover 2.25
❑13 (442), Jan 1999; gatefold summary; V: Ronan. AKA Fantastic Four Vol. 1, #442 .... 2.25
❑14 (443), Feb 1999; gatefold summary; A: Ronan the Accuser. V: Ronan. AKA Fantastic Four Vol. 1, #443 .... 2.25
❑15 (444), Mar 1999; A: Kree. A: S.H.I.E.L.D.. A: Shi'Ar. A: Iron Man. A: Ronan the Accuser. A: Watcher. V: Ronan. AKA Fantastic Four Vol. 1, #444; Iron Man crossover, Part 1 .... 2.25
❑16 (445), Apr 1999; A: Kree. V: Kree. AKA Fantastic Four Vol. 1, #445 .... 2.25
❑17 (446), May 1999; AKA Fantastic Four Vol. 1, #446 .... 2.25
❑18 (447), Jun 1999; AKA Fantastic Four Vol. 1, #447 .... 2.25
❑19 (448), Jul 1999; V: Annihilus. AKA Fantastic Four Vol. 1, #448 .... 2.25

N-MINT

❑20 (449), Aug 1999; AKA Fantastic Four Vol. 1, #449 .... 2.25
❑21 (450), Sep 1999; AKA Fantastic Four Vol. 1, #450 .... 2.00
❑22 (451), Oct 1999; AKA Fantastic Four Vol. 1, #451 .... 2.00
❑23 (452), Nov 1999; AKA Fantastic Four Vol. 1, #452 .... 2.00
❑24 (453), Dec 1999; AKA Fantastic Four Vol. 1, #453 .... 2.00
❑25 (454), Jan 2000; Giant-size; AKA Fantastic Four Vol. 1, #454 .... 3.00
❑26 (455), Feb 2000; AKA Fantastic Four Vol. 1, #455 .... 2.25
❑27 (456), Mar 2000; AKA Fantastic Four Vol. 1, #456 .... 2.25
❑28 (457), Apr 2000; AKA Fantastic Four Vol. 1, #457 .... 2.25
❑29 (458), May 2000; AKA Fantastic Four Vol. 1, #458 .... 2.25
❑30 (459), Jun 2000; AKA Fantastic Four Vol. 1, #459 .... 2.25
❑31 (460), Jul 2000; AKA Fantastic Four Vol. 1, #460 .... 2.25
❑32 (461), Aug 2000; AKA Fantastic Four Vol. 1, #461 .... 2.25
❑33 (462), Sep 2000; AKA Fantastic Four Vol. 1, #462 .... 2.25
❑34 (463), Oct 2000; AKA Fantastic Four Vol. 1, #463 .... 2.25
❑35 (464), Nov 2000; AKA Fantastic Four Vol. 1, #464 .... 3.25
❑36 (465), Dec 2000; A: Daredevil. A: Spider-Man. A: Diablo. AKA Fantastic Four Vol. 1, #465 .... 2.25
❑37 (466), Jan 2001; AKA Fantastic Four Vol. 1, #466 .... 2.25
❑38 (467), Feb 2001; JPH (w); AKA Fantastic Four Vol. 1, #467 .... 2.25
❑39 (468), Mar 2001; JPH (w); A: Grey Gargoyle. A: Avengers. AKA Fantastic Four Vol. 1, #468; Thing can switch from rock form to human and back.... 2.25
❑40 (469), Apr 2001; JPH (w); AKA Fantastic Four Vol. 1, #469; Baxter Building reopens 2.25
❑41 (470), May 2001; JPH (w); A: First. AKA Fantastic Four Vol. 1, #470; First appearance of Hellscout 2.25
❑42 (471), Jun 2001; AKA Fantastic Four Vol. 1, #471 .... 2.25
❑43 (472), Jul 2001; AKA Fantastic Four Vol. 1, #472 .... 2.25
❑44 (473), Aug 2001; AKA Fantastic Four Vol. 1, #473 .... 2.25
❑45 (474), Sep 2001; AKA Fantastic Four Vol. 1, #474 .... 2.25
❑46 (475), Oct 2001; AKA Fantastic Four Vol. 1, #475 .... 2.25
❑47 (476), Nov 2001; AKA Fantastic Four Vol. 1, #476 .... 2.25
❑48 (477), Dec 2001; AKA Fantastic Four Vol. 1, #477 .... 2.25
❑49 (478), Jan 2002; AKA Fantastic Four Vol. 1, #478 .... 2.25
❑50 (479), Feb 2002; AKA Fantastic Four Vol. 1, #479 .... 3.99
❑51 (480), Mar 2002; AKA Fantastic Four Vol. 1, #480 .... 3.50
❑52 (481), Apr 2002; AKA Fantastic Four Vol. 1, #481 .... 2.25
❑53 (482), May 2002; AKA Fantastic Four Vol. 1, #482 .... 3.25

N-MINT

❑54 (483), Jun 2002; AKA Fantastic Four Vol. 1, #483 .... 3.50
❑55 (484), Jul 2002; AKA Fantastic Four Vol. 1, #484 .... 2.25
❑56 (485), Aug 2002; AKA Fantastic Four Vol. 1, #485 .... 2.25
❑57 (486), Aug 2002; AKA Fantastic Four Vol. 1, #486 .... 2.25
❑58 (487), Sep 2002; AKA Fantastic Four Vol. 1, #487 .... 2.25
❑59 (488), Oct 2002; AKA Fantastic Four Vol. 1, #488 .... 2.25
❑60 (489), Oct 2002; MWa (w); AKA Fantastic Four Vol. 1, #489 .... 1.00
❑61 (490), Nov 2002; AKA Fantastic Four Vol. 1, #490 .... 2.25
❑62 (491), Dec 2002; AKA Fantastic Four Vol. 1, #491 .... 2.25
❑63 (492), Jan 2003; AKA Fantastic Four Vol. 1, #492 .... 2.25
❑64 (493), Feb 2003; AKA Fantastic Four Vol. 1, #493 .... 2.25
❑65 (494), Mar 2003; AKA Fantastic Four Vol. 1, #494 .... 2.25
❑66 (495), Apr 2003; AKA Fantastic Four Vol. 1, #495 .... 2.25
❑67 (496), May 2003; AKA Fantastic Four Vol. 1, #496 .... 2.25
❑68 (497), Jun 2003; MWa (w); AKA Fantastic Four Vol. 1, #497 .... 2.25
❑69 (498), Jul 2003; MWa (w); AKA Fantastic Four Vol. 1, #498 .... 2.25
❑70 (499), Aug 2003, MWa (w); Numbering restarts at 500 under Vol. 1 .... 2.25
❑Ann 1998, ca. 1998; Fantastic Four/Fantastic 4 '98; alternate universe FF . 5.00
❑Ann 1999, ca. 1999; Fantastic Four/Fantastic 4 '99 .... 3.50
❑Ann 2001, ca. 2001; Dragon Man appearn; Continued Fantastic Four #46; 1: Abraxas (Dark Man); Continued in Fantastic Four (Vol. 3) #46 .... 2.99

Fantastic Four: A Death in the Family
Marvel

❑1, Aug 2006 .... 3.99

Fantastic Four: Atlantis Rising
Marvel

❑1, Jun 1995; Atlantis rises from sea; acetate outer cover 3.95
❑2, Jul 1995; acetate outer cover 3.95
❑Ashcan 1, May 1995; Collector's Preview 2.25

Fantastic Four: Fireworks
Marvel

❑1, Jan 1999; Marvel Remix 2.99
❑2, Feb 1999; Marvel Remix 2.99
❑3, Mar 1999; Marvel Remix 2.99

Fantastic Four: First Family
Marvel

❑1, May 2006, Reprints; 1: The Fantastic Four; O: The Fantastic Four 2.99
❑2, Jun 2006 .... 2.99
❑3, Jul 2006 .... 2.99
❑4, Aug 2006 .... 2.99
❑5, Sep 2006 .... 2.99
❑6, Oct 2006 .... 2.99

Fantastic Four: Foes
Marvel

❑1, Jan 2005 .... 2.99
❑2, Apr 2005 .... 2.99

Other grades: Multiply price above by 5/6 for VF/NM • 2/3 for VERY FINE • 1/3 for FINE • 1/5 for VERY GOOD • 1/8 for GOOD

❑3, May 2005 .... 2.99
❑4, Jun 2005 .... 2.99
❑5, Jul 2005 .... 2.99
❑6, Aug 2005 .... 2.99

Fantastic Four: House of M
Marvel

❑1, Aug 2005 .... 5.00
❑1/Variant, Aug 2005 .... 4.00
❑2, Sep 2005 .... 2.99
❑3, Oct 2005 .... 2.99

Fantastic Four/Iron Man: Big in Japan
Marvel

❑1 .... 3.50
❑2, Jan 2006 .... 3.50
❑3, Feb 2006 .... 3.50
❑4, Mar 2006 .... 3.50

Fantastic Four: 1 2 3 4
Marvel

❑1, Oct 2001 .... 2.99
❑2, Nov 2001 .... 2.99
❑3, Dec 2001 .... 2.99
❑4, Jan 2002 .... 2.99

Fantastic Four Roast
Marvel

❑1, May 1982; Celebrates 20th Anniversary of Fantastic Four; FH (w); MA, FH, MG, JB, FM, TD (a); Wraparound cover 2.00

Fantastic Four Special
Marvel

❑1, May 1984; JBy (c); reprints FF Ann #1 .... 3.00

Fantastic Four Special
Marvel

❑1, Feb 2006, Wraparound cover 3.00

Fantastic Four: The End
Marvel

❑1, Jan 2007 .... 2.99
❑1/RoughCut, Jan 2007 .... 3.99
❑2, Feb 2007 .... 2.99
❑3, Feb 2007 .... 2.99
❑4, Mar 2007 .... 2.99

Fantastic Four: The Legend
Marvel

❑1, Oct 1996; highlights of group's history 3.95

Fantastic Four: The Movie
Marvel

❑1, Jul 2005; Photo cover; Origin story; V: Dr. Doom; Includes movie adaptation plus Fantastic Four #358 story; Jack Kirby FF double page pin up; Stuart Immonen Dr. Doom pin up; Essay - "Marvel's First Family Hits the Big Screen!" by Michael Ruscoe 4.99

Fantastic Four: The Wedding Special
Marvel

❑1, Jan 2006, b&w; Includes story from Fantastic Four Ann #3 .... 4.99

Fantastic Four: The World's Greatest Comics Magazine
Marvel

❑1, Feb 2001; EL (c); EL (w); KG, EL (a); set after events of Fantastic Four (Vol. 1) #100 .... 3.00
❑2, Mar 2001 MG (c); EL (w); KG, EL (a) 2.99
❑3, Apr 2001 EL (w); KG, EL, ES (a) 2.99
❑4, May 2001 .... 2.99
❑5, Jun 2001 .... 2.99
❑6, Jul 2001 .... 2.99
❑7, Aug 2001 .... 2.99
❑8, Sep 2001 .... 2.99
❑9, Oct 2001 .... 2.99
❑10, Nov 2001 .... 2.99
❑11, Dec 2001 .... 2.99
❑12, Jan 2002 .... 2.99

Fantastic Four 2099
Marvel

❑1, Jan 1996; enhanced wraparound cover 3.95
❑2, Feb 1996; JB (a); Fantastic Four hunted by Total Recall 2.00
❑3, Mar 1996; AW (a); V: Total Recall; V: Runaway; V: Hipshot; V: Black Stone; V: Squeeze 2.00
❑4, Apr 1996; AW (a); A: Spider-Man 2099. Fantastic Four enlists aid of Spiderman 2099 .... 2.00
❑5, May 1996; A: Doctor Strange. Joe Kelly's first major comics work 2.00
❑6, Jun 1996; A: Spider-Man 2099. A: Doctor Strange. Doomsday planetoid approaches Earth 2.00
❑7, Jul 1996; A: Doom 2099. V: Attuma. V: Attuma 2.00
❑8, Aug 1996; A: Doom 2099. Humanity flees to Savage Land 2.00

Fantastic Four Unlimited
Marvel

❑1, Mar 1993 HT (a) 4.50
❑2, Jun 1993 HT (a) 4.00
❑3, Sep 1993 HT (a) 4.00
❑4, Dec 1993; HT (a); Thing vs. Hulk 3.95
❑5, Mar 1994 HT (a) 3.95
❑6, Jun 1994; HT (a); V: Namor 3.95
❑7, Sep 1994; HT (a); V: early Marvel monsters. wraparound cover 3.95
❑8, Dec 1994; V: Doom; Wraparound Cover 3.95
❑9, Mar 1995; HT (a); Wraparound Cover 3.95
❑10, Jul 1995; Wraparound Cover 3.95
❑11, Sep 1995; A: Inhumans. Inhumans appearance, Wraparound Cover 4.00
❑12, Dec 1995; HT (a); A: Hyperstorm. A: Doctor Doom. how Reed and Doom vanished; wraparound cover 3.95

Fantastic Four Unplugged
Marvel

❑1, Sep 1995 .... 1.25
❑2, Nov 1995; reading of Reed Richards' will 1.00
❑3, Jan 1996 .... 1.00
❑4, Mar 1996; Flip book with Untold Tales of Spider-Man #7 .... 1.00
❑5, May 1996; V: Blastaar. V: Blastaar 1.00
❑6, Jul 1996; Final Issue 1.00

Fantastic Four: Unstable Molecules
Marvel

❑1, Mar 2003 .... 2.99
❑2, Apr 2003 .... 2.99
❑3, May 2003 .... 2.99
❑4, Jun 2003 .... 2.99

Fantastic Four vs. X-Men
Marvel

❑1, Feb 1987 .... 2.50
❑2, Mar 1987 .... 2.50
❑3, Apr 1987 .... 2.50
❑4, May 1987 .... 2.50

Fantastic Panic
Antarctic

❑1, Aug 1993 .... 3.00
❑2, Oct 1993 .... 3.00
❑3, Dec 1993 .... 3.00
❑4, Feb 1994 .... 3.00
❑5, Apr 1994 .... 3.00
❑6, Jun 1994 .... 3.00
❑7, Aug 1994 .... 3.00
❑8, Oct 1994 .... 3.00

Fantastic Panic
Antarctic

❑1, Nov 1995 .... 2.95
❑2, Jan 1996 .... 2.95
❑3, Mar 1996 .... 2.95
❑4, May 1996 .... 2.95
❑5, Jul 1996 .... 2.95
❑6, Sep 1996 .... 2.95
❑7, Nov 1996 .... 2.95
❑8, Dec 1996 .... 2.95

Fantastic Voyage
Gold Key

❑1, Feb 1967 .... 40.00

Fantastic Voyage
Gold Key

❑1, Aug 1969 .... 25.00
❑2, Dec 1969 .... 16.00

Fantastic Voyages of Sindbad
Gold Key

❑1, Oct 1965, pin-up on back cover 18.00
❑2, Jun 1967 .... 12.00

Fantasy Features
AC

❑1 1987; 1: Eric the Dragon Slayer 1.75
❑2 1987 .... 1.95

Fantasy Girls
Comax

❑1, b&w; Adult 2.50

Fantasy Masterpieces
Marvel

❑1, Feb 1966, SD, DH, JK (c); SL (w); SD, DH, JK, JSt (a); Golden Age reprints 75.00
❑2, Apr 1966, SD, DH, JK (c); SL (w); SD, DH, JK (a); Golden Age reprints; Fin Fang Foom reprinted from Strange Tales #89 .... 35.00
❑3, Jun 1966; Golden Age reprints; Captain America, other Golden Age super-heroes appear 30.00
❑4, Aug 1966; Golden Age reprints; Captain America, other Golden Age super-heroes appear 18.00
❑5, Oct 1966; Golden Age reprints; Captain America, other Golden Age super-heroes appear 18.00
❑6, Dec 1966; Golden Age reprints; Captain America, other Golden Age super-heroes appear 18.00
❑7, Feb 1967; Golden Age reprints; Captain America, other Golden Age super-heroes appear 18.00
❑8, Apr 1967; Golden Age reprints; Sub-Mariner vs. Human Torch (original) 18.00
❑9, Jun 1967; O: Human Torch (original). Golden Age reprints; Reprints from Marvel Comics #1 .... 30.00
❑10, Aug 1967; O: All Winners Squad. 1: All Winners Squad. Golden Age reprints; Reprints from All Winners #19 .... 10.00
❑11, Oct 1967; O: Toro. Series continues as Marvel Super-Heroes; Reprinted from Human Torch #1 .... 15.00

Fantasy Masterpieces
Marvel

❑1, Dec 1979; SL (w); JB (a); Reprints Silver Surfer (Vol. 1) #1 .... 6.00
❑2, Jan 1980; SL (w); JB (a); Reprints Silver Surfer (Vol. 1) #2 .... 3.50
❑3, Feb 1980; SL (w); JB (a); Reprints Silver Surfer (Vol. 1) #3 .... 3.00
❑4, Mar 1980; SL (w); JB (a); Reprints Silver Surfer (Vol. 1) #4 .... 3.00
❑5, Apr 1980; SL (w); JB (a); Reprints Silver Surfer (Vol. 1) #5 .... 3.00
❑6, May 1980; SL (w); JB (a); Reprints Silver Surfer (Vol. 1) #6 .... 2.50
❑7, Jun 1980; SL (w); JB (a); Reprints Silver Surfer (Vol. 1) #7 .... 2.50
❑8, Jul 1980; SL (w); JB (a); Reprints Silver Surfer (Vol. 1) #8 .... 2.50
❑9, Aug 1980; SL (w); JB (a); Reprints Silver Surfer (Vol. 1) #9 .... 2.50
❑10, Sep 1980; SL (w); JB (a); Reprints Silver Surfer (Vol. 1) #10 .... 2.50
❑11, Oct 1980; Reprints Silver Surfer (Vol. 1) #11 .... 2.00
❑12, Nov 1980; Reprints Silver Surfer (Vol. 1) #12 .... 2.00
❑13, Dec 1980; Reprints Silver Surfer (Vol. 1) #13 .... 2.00
❑14, Jan 1981, Reprints Silver Surfer (Vol. 1) #14 .... 2.00

Fantasy Quarterly
Independent Pub. Synd.

❑1, Spr 1978, b&w; WP (w); WP (a); 1: Elfquest. back-up story with art by Sim 55.00

Faraway Looks
Faraway Press

❑nn, Fal 2002, b&w; "Fall Preview Edition" 9.95

Farewell, Moonshadow
DC / Vertigo

❑1, Jan 1997; prestige format; NN; One-shot 7.95

Farewell to Weapons
Marvel / Epic

❑1; NN 2.25

Farscape: War Torn
DC / Wildstorm

❑1, Apr 2002 .... 4.95
❑2, May 2002 .... 4.95

Far West
Antarctic

❑1, Nov 1998; 1: Meg 2.95
❑2, Jan 1999 .... 2.95
❑3, Mar 1999 .... 2.95
❑4, May 1999 .... 2.95

Fantastic Four

Third series reverts to Volume 1 at end
©Marvel

Fantastic Four: Atlantis Rising

Giant-sized special kicked off summer event
©Marvel

Fantastic Four: Fireworks

Modernized retelling of classic stories
©Marvel

Fantastic Four: 1 2 3 4

Marvel Knights series from Grant Morrison
©Marvel

Fantastic Four Roast

Hembeck book is one of funniest comics ever
©Marvel

N-MINT

Fashion in Action
Eclipse

	N-MINT
❑Summer 1, Aug 1986; gatefold summary; Summer Special	2.00
❑WS 1; anniversary; Winter Special	2.00

Fashion Police
Bryce Alan

❑1	2.50

Fast Forward
DC / Piranha

❑1, phobias	4.95
❑2, family	4.95
❑3, Storytellers	4.95

Fastlane Illustrated
Fastlane

❑½; Giveaway at 1994 San Diego Comicon	1.50
❑1, Sep 1994, b&w	2.50
❑2, Jun 1995, b&w	2.50
❑3, Jul 1996, b&w; wraparound cover	2.50

Fast Willie Jackson
Fitzgerald Periodicals

❑1, Oct 1976	24.00
❑2, Dec 1976	16.00
❑3, Feb 1977	16.00
❑4, Apr 1977	16.00
❑5, Jun 1977	16.00
❑6, Aug 1977	16.00
❑7, Sep 1977, Last issue	16.00

Fatal Beauty
Illustration

❑Ashcan 1/A, Jun 1996; Adult cover	3.95

Fat Albert
Gold Key

❑1, Mar 1974	12.00
❑2, Jun 1974	8.00
❑3, Sep 1974	7.00
❑4, Dec 1974	7.00
❑5, Feb 1975, 90290-503	7.00
❑6, Apr 1975	6.00
❑7, Jun 1975	6.00
❑8, Aug 1975	6.00
❑9, Oct 1975	6.00
❑10, Dec 1975	6.00
❑11, Feb 1976	4.00
❑12, Apr 1976	4.00
❑13, Jun 1976	4.00
❑14, Aug 1976	4.00
❑15, Oct 1976	4.00
❑16, Dec 1976	4.00
❑17, Feb 1977	4.00
❑18, Apr 1977	4.00
❑19, Jun 1977	4.00
❑20, Aug 1977	4.00
❑21, Oct 1977	4.00
❑22, Dec 1977	4.00
❑23, Feb 1978	4.00
❑24, Apr 1978	4.00
❑25, Jun 1978	4.00
❑26, Aug 1978	4.00
❑27, Oct 1978	4.00
❑28, Dec 1978	4.00
❑29, Feb 1979	4.00

N-MINT

Fatale
Broadway

	N-MINT
❑1, Jan 1996; Embossed cover	2.50
❑2, Feb 1996	2.50
❑3, Mar 1996	2.50
❑4, May 1996	2.50
❑5, Jul 1996	2.95
❑6, Oct 1996; Final Issue	2.95
❑Ashcan 1, Sep 1995, b&w; giveaway preview edition	1.00

Fat Dog Mendoza
Dark Horse

❑1, Dec 1992, b&w	2.50

Fate
DC

❑0, Oct 1994; 1&O: Doctor Fate IV (Jared Stevens). D: Doctor Fate III (Kent & Inza Nelson)	2.50
❑1, Nov 1994; O: Doctor Fate IV (Jared Stevens)	2.50
❑2, Dec 1994	2.00
❑3, Jan 1995	2.00
❑4, Feb 1995	2.00
❑5, Mar 1995	2.00
❑6, Apr 1995	2.00
❑7, May 1995	2.00
❑8, Jun 1995	2.25
❑9, Jul 1995	2.25
❑10, Aug 1995	2.25
❑11, Sep 1995	2.25
❑12, Oct 1995 A: Sentinel	2.25
❑13, Nov 1995; Underworld Unleashed	2.25
❑14, Dec 1995	2.25
❑15, Jan 1996	2.25
❑16, Feb 1996	2.25
❑17, Mar 1996	2.25
❑18, May 1996	2.25
❑19, Jun 1996	2.25
❑20, Jul 1996	2.25
❑21, Aug 1996	2.25
❑22, Sep 1996; Kent and Inza Nelson go to heaven	2.25

Fate of the Blade
Dreamwave

❑1, Aug 2002	2.95
❑2, Oct 2002	2.95
❑3, Nov 2002	2.95
❑4, Jan 2003	2.95
❑5, Feb 2003	2.95

Fate's Five
Innervision

❑1, b&w	2.50
❑2	2.50
❑3	2.50
❑4	2.50

Fat Freddy's Comics & Stories
Rip Off

❑1, Dec 1983; Adult	3.00
❑2, Dec 1985; Adult	2.50

Fat Fury Special
Avalon

❑1, b&w; reprints Herbie stories	2.95

N-MINT

Father & Son
Kitchen Sink

	N-MINT
❑1, Jul 1995, b&w	2.75
❑2, Sep 1995, b&w	2.75
❑3, Dec 1995, b&w	2.75
❑4, Jan 1996, b&w	2.75
❑Ashcan 1, Jul 1995; ashcan edition limited to 200, b&w	2.00
❑Special 1, b&w; "Like, Special #1"	3.95

Fathom
Aspen

❑1 2005	5.00
❑1/A cover 2005	4.00
❑1/B cover 2005	5.00
❑2 2005	2.99
❑3, Aug 2005	2.99

Fathom
Comico

❑1, May 1987	1.50
❑2, Jun 1987	1.50
❑3, Jul 1987; wraparound cover	1.50

Fathom
Comico

❑1, Nov 1992	2.50
❑2, Apr 1993	2.50
❑3, Jun 1993	2.50

Fathom
Image

❑0/Dynamic	15.00
❑0/Conv, 2003 2003	10.00
❑0, Jan 2000; Wizard Promotional Edition: Given away with subsrciption to Wizard; Issue #0, with gold logo, had Jan. '00 in the indicia and Feb. on the cover	5.00
❑0/A, Jan 2000; Green holografix cover.	5.00
❑0/B, Jan 2000; Wizard authentic edition; Www.JayCompanyComics.Com	5.00
❑½, Feb 2003	3.00
❑½/A, Feb 2003; Gold foil variant	4.00
❑1/A, Aug 1998; Variant covers, some pages	6.00
❑1/B, Aug 1998, b&w; Fathom standing underwater; Variant covers, some pages, bubbles	3.00
❑1/C, Aug 1998; Fathom, dolphins on cover w/inset close-up	3.00
❑1/D, Aug 1998; Museum edition; Limited to 50 copies	115.00
❑2, Sep 1998	3.00
❑2/A, Sep 1998; Museum edition	100.00
❑3, Oct 1998	3.00
❑3/Variant, Oct 1998; Monster Edition: No cover price	3.00
❑4, Mar 1999	2.50
❑5, May 1999	2.50
❑6, Jun 1999	2.50
❑7, Aug 1999	2.50
❑8, Sep 1999	2.50
❑9, Oct 1999	5.00
❑9/A, Oct 1999; Holofoil edition	8.00
❑9/B, Oct 1999; Platinum Holofoil edition	7.00
❑9/C, Oct 1999; Aspen on outcropping	5.00
❑9/D, Oct 1999; Green logo variant w/Aspen on rock outcropping	8.50
❑10, Jan 2000	2.50
❑10/A, Jan 2000; Perfect 10 DFE Alternate cover	4.00

Other grades: Multiply price above by 5/6 for VF/NM • 2/3 for VERY FINE • 1/3 for FINE • 1/5 for VERY GOOD • 1/8 for GOOD

N-MINT N-MINT N-MINT

❑10/B, Jan 2000; Perfect 10 DFE Alternate cover with Gold Stamp and certificate of authenticity 5.00
❑11, Apr 2000 .... 2.50
❑12, Jul 2000; Witchblade in background, Fathom crawling on cover 6.00
❑12/A, Jul 2000 .... 6.00
❑12/B, Jul 2000; Holofoil edition; Fathom crawling on cover; Witchblade in background 6.00
❑12/C, Jul 2000; DF Alternate edition; DF Alternate edition 5.00
❑12/D, Jul 2000; DF Alternate edition with certificate of authenticity; Gold logo ... 8.00
❑13, Feb 2002 .... 2.50
❑13/A 2002; Dynamic Forces variant with Certificate of Authenticity 5.00
❑13/B 2002; Dynamic Forces gold foil variant;Limited to 999 copies 15.00
❑13/C 2002; Dynamic Forces blue foil variant;Limited to 999 copies 15.00
❑14, May 2002; Final issue 2.50
❑14/A, May 2002; Pittsburgh Convention exclusive 6.00

Fathom: Beginnings
Aspen

❑1, Jun 2003 .... 5.00
❑1/Conv, Jun 2003 .... 6.00

Fathom: Cannon Hawke
Aspen

❑0, Jun 2004 .... 6.00
❑0/Dynamic, Jun 2004 .... 15.00
❑0/Conv, Jun 2004 .... 10.00

Fathom: Cannon Hawke: Beginnings
Aspen

❑1, Jun 2004 .... 5.00
❑1/Conv, Jun 2004 .... 10.00

Fathom: Dawn of War
Aspen

❑0 2004 .... 5.00
❑1 2004 .... 7.00
❑1/Jay 10.00
❑2 2004 .... 4.00
❑2/Conv 10.00
❑3 2005 .... 4.00

Fathom: East & West Coast Tour Books
Image

❑1, Jan 2004 .... 3.00

Fathom: Killian's Tide
Image

❑1, Apr 2001 .... 3.00
❑2, Jun 2001 .... 3.00
❑3/A, Sep 2001; Blue background on cover 3.00
❑3/B, Sep 2001; Dark background on cover, skull reflected in water 3.00
❑4/A, Nov 2001 .... 3.00
❑4/B, Nov 2001 .... 3.00

Fathom Preview Special
Image

❑1, ca. 1998; Fathom Preview 3.00

Fathom Swimsuit Special
Image

❑1, May 1999 .... 2.95
❑2000, Dec 2000 .... 2.95
❑2002; 2002 San Diego giveaway; Sketch cover; 500 produced 8.00

Fatman, the Human Flying Saucer
Lightning

❑1, Apr 1967 .... 35.00
❑2, Jun 1967 .... 25.00
❑3, Sep 1967 .... 25.00

Fat Ninja
Silverwolf

❑1, Aug 1986, b&w 1.50
❑2, Sep 1986, b&w 1.50
❑3, Oct 1986, b&w 1.50
❑4, Nov 1986, b&w 1.50
❑5, Dec 1986, b&w 1.50

Fatt Family
Side Show

❑1, b&w; 1: The Fatt Family 2.95

Faultlines
DC / Vertigo

❑1, May 1997 .... 2.50
❑2, Jun 1997 .... 2.50
❑3, Jul 1997 .... 2.50
❑4, Aug 1997 .... 2.50
❑5, Sep 1997 .... 2.50
❑6, Oct 1997 .... 2.50

Fauna Rebellion
Fantagraphics

❑1, Mar 1990, b&w 2.00
❑2, Apr 1990, b&w 2.00
❑3, b&w 2.00

Faust
Northstar

❑1, ca. 1989; Published by Northstar; Includes a backup story "Fritz Whistle"; Signed by David Quinn and Tim Vigil on page 1; Adult 8.00
❑1/2nd; 2nd printing 4.00
❑1/3rd; ca. 1991; 3rd printing 3.00
❑2, ca. 1989 .... 6.00
❑2/2nd; 2nd printing 4.00
❑2/3rd; 3rd printing 3.00
❑3, ca. 1989; Adult 5.00
❑3/2nd; ca. 1992; 2nd printing; Adult 3.00
❑4; Adult; b&w 4.00
❑4/2nd; 2nd printing; Adult 3.00
❑5, Aug 1989; Adult 4.00
❑5/2nd; 2nd printing; Adult 3.00
❑6, Nov 1989; becomes Rebel title 3.50
❑6/2nd; 2nd printing; Adult 2.50
❑7; ca. 1991; Adult 3.50
❑7/2nd; gatefold cover 2.50
❑8; Adult 3.50
❑8/2nd; ca. 1991; 2nd printing 2.50
❑9 .... 3.00
❑9/2nd; ca. 1992; 2nd printing 2.50
❑10; Adult 3.00
❑10/2nd; 2nd printing; Adult 2.50
❑11 .... 2.50
❑Special 1, ca. 1988; Adult 10.00

Faust 777: The Wrath
Avatar

❑0, Dec 1998 .... 3.00
❑1, ca. 1998; Regular 3.00
❑1/A, ca. 1998; wraparound cover 3.50
❑2, ca. 1998; Regular 3.00
❑3, ca. 1998; Regular 3.00

Faust: The Book of M
Avatar

❑1, Aug 1999; Regular 3.00

F.B.I.
Dell

❑1, Apr 1965 .... 60.00

Fear
Marvel

❑1, Nov 1970; I Found Monstrom! The Dweller in the Black Swamp! reprinted from Tales to Astonish #11; I Am the Man Who Will—Destroy Your World! reprinted from Strange Tales #71; I-Am-the-Genie! reprinted from Tales to Astonish #8; I Was Face-to-Face With the Forbidden Robot! reprinted from Tales to Astonish #11; What Was the Strange Power of Simon Drudd!! reprinted from Tales to Astonish #10; Something Lurks Inside! reprinted from Tales to Astonish #10; Only I Know When the World Will End!!! reprinted from Ta 95.00
❑2, Jan 1971 .... 30.00
❑3, Mar 1971 .... 15.00
❑4, Jul 1971 SD (c); SD, DH, JK, JSt (a) 15.00
❑5, Nov 1971 JK (c); SL (w); SD, DH, JK (a) 20.00
❑6, Feb 1972 GK (c); SL (w); SD, DH, JK, JSt (a) 15.00
❑7, May 1972, I Dream of Doom! reprinted from Strange Tales #96; The Curse of M'Gumbu! reprinted from Journey into Mystery #61; The Thing Behind the Wall! reprinted from Journey into Mystery #66; The Martian Who Stole My Body! reprinted from Journey into Mystery #57 .... 15.00
❑8, Jun 1972, It Crawls By Night! reprinted from Tales of Suspense #26; Never Trust a Martian! reprinted from Tales of Suspense #26; I Can't Escape From the Creeping Things! reprinted from Journey into Mystery #62; The Face! reprinted from Tales of Suspense #26 .... 15.00
❑9, Aug 1972, I Entered the Dimension of Doom! reprinted from Tales of Suspense #23; Dead Man's Escape! reprinted from Adventures into Terror #11 .... 15.00
❑10, Oct 1972, GM (c); SL (w); GM, DH, HC (a); Man-Thing stories begin ("Adventures into Fear") 35.00
❑11, Dec 1972, Man-Thing 18.00
❑12, Feb 1973, Man-Thing 12.00
❑13, Apr 1973, Man-Thing 9.00
❑14, Jun 1973, Man-Thing 9.00
❑15, Aug 1973, Man-Thing 12.00
❑16, Sep 1973, Man-Thing 12.00
❑17, Oct 1973, V: Wundarr. Man-Thing . 12.00
❑18, Nov 1973, Man-Thing 9.00
❑19, Dec 1973, 1: Howard the Duck. Man-Thing 25.00
❑20, Feb 1974, GK (c); SD, PG (a); Morbius stories begin; first Gulacy color work 20.00
❑21, Apr 1974, Morbius; Marvel Value Stamp #77: Swordsman 9.00
❑22, Jun 1974; Morbius; Marvel Value Stamp #49: Odin 7.00
❑23, Aug 1974; GK (c); GC, CR (a); A: Morbius. 1st Russell art; Marvel Value Stamp #86: Zemo 8.00
❑24, Oct 1974; A: Blade the Vampire Slayer. V: Blade. Morbius; Marvel Value Stamp #38: Red Sonja 12.00
❑25, Dec 1974; Morbius 8.00
❑26, Feb 1975; Morbius; Marvel Value Stamp #75: Morbius 7.00
❑27, Apr 1975; V: Simon Stroud. Morbius 7.00
❑28, Jun 1975; GK (c); FR (a); Morbius. 7.00
❑29, Aug 1975 DH (c); DH (a); A: Helleyes. A: Simon Stroud. A: Morbius 7.00
❑30, Oct 1975; Morbius 12.00
❑31, Dec 1975; Morbius; Marvel Value Stamp #75: Morbius 7.00

Fear Agent
Image

❑1, Oct 2005 .... 2.99
❑2, Jan 2006 .... 2.99
❑3, Mar 2006 .... 2.99
❑5, Jul 2006 .... 2.99
❑6, Aug 2006 .... 2.99
❑7, Oct 2006 .... 2.99
❑8, Nov 2006 .... 2.99
❑9, Jan 2007 .... 2.99
❑10, Feb 2007 .... 2.99

Fear Effect: Retro Helix
Image

❑1, Mar 2002 .... 2.95
❑1/Gold, Mar 2002; Gold logo edition 3.00

Fear Effect Special
Image

❑1, May 2000 .... 2.95

Feather
Image

❑1, Aug 2003 .... 2.95
❑2, Oct 2003 .... 2.95
❑3, Dec 2003 .... 2.95
❑4, Feb 2004 .... 2.95
❑5, Jun 2004 .... 5.95

Feds 'n' Heads
Print Mint

❑1 .... 8.00

Feeders
Dark Horse

❑1, Oct 1999 .... 2.95

Feelgood Funnies
Rip Off

❑1 .... 3.00

Felicia Hardy: The Black Cat
Marvel

❑1, Jul 1994; Spider-Man 1.50
❑2, Aug 1994 .... 1.50
❑3, Sep 1994 .... 1.50
❑4, Oct 1994; Final Issue 1.50

Felix the Cat Silly Stories
Felix

❑1, Aug 2005 .... 2.50

Felix the Cat
Dell

❑1, ca. 1962 .... 35.00
❑2, Jan 1963 .... 24.00

Other grades: Multiply price above by 5/6 for VF/NM • 2/3 for VERY FINE • 1/3 for FINE • 1/5 for VERY GOOD • 1/8 for GOOD

Fantastic Four: The Legend

One-shot wraps up history before "Reborn"
©Marvel

Fantastic Four: The World's Greatest Comics Magazine

Series takes place between FF #100 and #101
©Marvel

Fantastic Four 2099

Future-universe variation of Fantastic Four
©Marvel

Fantastic Four Unlimited

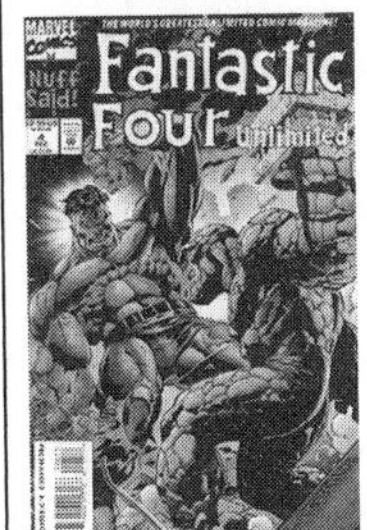

Quarterly anthology series with short stories
©Marvel

Fantastic Four Unplugged

Part of a low-price budget comics experiment
©Marvel

N-MINT

❑3, Apr 1963 .... 24.00
❑4, Jul 1963 .... 24.00
❑5, Oct 1963 .... 24.00
❑6, Jan 1964 .... 24.00
❑7, Apr 1964 .... 24.00
❑8, Jul 1964 .... 24.00
❑9, Oct 1964 .... 24.00
❑10, Jan 1965 .... 24.00
❑11, Apr 1965 .... 24.00
❑12, Jul 1965 .... 24.00

Felix the Cat
Harvey

❑1, Sep 1991 .... 2.00
❑2, Nov 1991 .... 1.25
❑3, Jan 1992 .... 1.25
❑4, Mar 1992 .... 1.25
❑5, Jun 1992 .... 1.25
❑6, Sep 1992 .... 1.25
❑7, Jan 1993 .... 1.25

Felix the Cat and Friends
Felix

❑1, ca. 1994 .... 1.95
❑2, ca. 1994 .... 1.95
❑3, ca. 1994 .... 1.95
❑4, ca. 1994 .... 1.95
❑5, ca. 1994 .... 1.95

Felix the Cat Big Book
Harvey

❑1, Sep 1992 .... 1.95

Felix the Cat Black & White
Felix

❑1 .... 1.95
❑2 .... 1.95
❑3 .... 1.95
❑4 .... 1.95
❑5 .... 1.95
❑6 .... 1.95
❑7 .... 2.25
❑8 .... 2.25

Felix the Cat Digest Magazine
Harvey

❑1, Jul 1992 .... 1.75

Fell
Image

❑1, Oct 2005 .... 3.99
❑2, Oct 2005 .... 1.99
❑3, Jan 2006 .... 1.99
❑4, Apr 2006 .... 1.99

Felon
Image

❑1, Nov 2001 .... 2.95
❑2, Jan 2002 .... 2.95
❑3, Feb 2002 .... 2.95
❑4, Apr 2002 .... 2.95

Felt: True Tales of Underground Hip Hop
Image

❑1, Apr 2005; b&w 2.95

Fem 5
Express / Parody

❑1/A; variant cover 2.95
❑1/B; variant cover 2.95

N-MINT

❑1/C; variant cover 2.95
❑1/D; variant cover 2.95
❑2 .... 2.95

Female Sex Pirates
Friendly

❑1; Adult 2.95

Fem Fantastique
AC

❑1, Jul 1988, b&w 1.95

Femforce
AC

❑1, ca. 1985, O: Femforce 4.00
❑2 1986 .... 3.50
❑3 1986 .... 3.00
❑4 1986 .... 3.00
❑5 1986 .... 3.00
❑6, Feb 1987 .... 2.50
❑7, May 1987 .... 2.50
❑8, Jul 1987 .... 2.50
❑9, Aug 1987 .... 2.50
❑10 1987 .... 2.50
❑11, Mar 1988 .... 2.50
❑12, May 1988 .... 2.50
❑13, May 1988 .... 2.50
❑14 1988 .... 2.50
❑15, Aug 1988 .... 2.50
❑16 1988 .... 2.50
❑17, Jan 1989 .... 2.50
❑18 1989 .... 2.50
❑19, Apr 1989 .... 2.50
❑20 1989, b&w 2.50
❑21 1989, b&w 2.50
❑22 1989, b&w; Reprint from Cave Girl #11; ca. 1989 .... 2.50
❑23 1990, b&w 2.50
❑24, Apr 1990, b&w 2.50
❑25, May 1990, b&w 2.50
❑26, Jun 1990, b&w 2.50
❑27, Jul 1990, b&w 2.50
❑28, Aug 1990, b&w 2.50
❑29, Sep 1990, b&w 2.50
❑30, Oct 1990, b&w 2.50
❑31, Nov 1990; b&w 2.75
❑32, Dec 1990 .... 2.75
❑33, Jan 1991 .... 2.75
❑34, Feb 1991 .... 2.75
❑35, Mar 1991 .... 2.75
❑36, Apr 1991 .... 2.75
❑37, May 1991 .... 2.75
❑38, Jun 1991 .... 2.75
❑39, Jul 1991 .... 2.75
❑40, Aug 1991 .... 2.75
❑41, Sep 1991 .... 2.75
❑42, Oct 1991 .... 2.75
❑43, Nov 1991; Includes pull-out comic, Rocketman and Jet Girl #0 .... 2.75
❑44, Dec 1991 .... 2.75
❑45, Jan 1992 .... 2.75
❑46, Feb 1992 .... 2.75
❑47, Mar 1992 .... 2.75
❑48, Apr 1992 .... 2.75
❑49, May 1992 .... 2.75
❑50, Jun 1992; Includes flexi-disc 2.95
❑51, Jul 1992; Photo cover 2.75
❑52, Aug 1992; b&w 2.75

N-MINT

❑53, ca. 1992 .... 2.75
❑54, ca. 1992 .... 2.75
❑55, ca. 1992 .... 2.75
❑56, ca. 1993 .... 2.75
❑57, ca. 1993 .... 2.75
❑58, ca. 1993; O: Microman 2.75
❑59, ca. 1993 .... 2.75
❑60, ca. 1993 .... 2.75
❑61, ca. 1993 .... 2.75
❑62, ca. 1993 .... 2.75
❑63, ca. 1993 .... 2.95
❑64, ca. 1993 .... 2.95
❑65, ca. 1993 .... 2.95
❑66, ca. 1993 .... 2.95
❑67, ca. 1994 .... 2.95
❑68, ca. 1994 .... 2.95
❑69, ca. 1994 .... 2.95
❑70, ca. 1994 .... 2.95
❑71, ca. 1994 .... 2.95
❑72, ca. 1994 .... 2.95
❑73, ca. 1994 .... 2.95
❑74, ca. 1994 .... 2.95
❑75, ca. 1994 .... 2.95
❑76, ca. 1994 .... 2.95
❑77, ca. 1994 .... 2.95
❑78, ca. 1994 .... 2.95
❑79, ca. 1994 .... 2.95
❑80, ca. 1994; V: Iron Jaw 2.95
❑81, ca. 1994 .... 2.95
❑82, ca. 1995 .... 2.95
❑83, ca. 1995 .... 2.95
❑84, ca. 1995 .... 2.95
❑85, ca. 1995 .... 2.95
❑86, ca. 1995 .... 2.95
❑87, ca. 1995; 10th anniversary issue; A: AC staff 3.50
❑88, ca. 1995 .... 2.95
❑89, ca. 1995 .... 2.95
❑90, ca. 1995 .... 2.95
❑91, ca. 1995 .... 2.95
❑92, ca. 1995 .... 2.95
❑93, ca. 1995 .... 2.95
❑94, ca. 1996 .... 2.95
❑95, ca. 1996 .... 2.95
❑96, ca. 1996 .... 2.95
❑97, ca. 1996, b&w 2.95
❑98, ca. 1996, b&w; subtitled in Spanish 2.95
❑99, ca. 1996, b&w 2.95
❑100, ca. 1996, b&w; photo back cover 3.95
❑100/CS, ca. 1996, b&w; Includes poster; Signed by Black, Gorby and Mark 6.90
❑101, ca. 1997, b&w 4.95
❑102, ca. 1997, b&w 4.95
❑103, ca. 1997, b&w 4.95
❑104, ca. 1997, b&w 4.95
❑105, ca. 1997, b&w 4.95
❑106, ca. 1997, b&w 4.95
❑107, ca. 1997, b&w 4.95
❑108, ca. 1998, b&w 4.95
❑109, ca. 2000, b&w 4.95
❑110/A, ca. 2000, b&w; Rayda on cover 2.95
❑110/B, ca. 2000, b&w; Femforce on cover 2.95
❑111, ca. 2001, b&w 2.95
❑112, ca. 2001, b&w 2.95
❑113, ca. 2001, b&w 2.95

Other grades: Multiply price above by 5/6 for VF/NM • 2/3 for VERY FINE • 1/3 for FINE • 1/5 for VERY GOOD • 1/8 for GOOD

Issue	N-MINT
❑114, ca. 2001, b&w	2.95
❑115, ca. 2002, b&w	5.95
❑116, ca. 2002, b&w; Photo Cover	5.95
❑117, ca. 2002, b&w	5.95
❑118, ca. 2002, b&w; 20th anniversary special	5.95
❑119, ca. 2003, b&w	5.95
❑120, ca. 2003, b&w	5.95
❑121, ca. 2003, b&w	5.95
❑123, ca. 2003, b&w	5.95
❑122, Jan 2004, b&w	6.95
❑124, ca. 2003, b&w	6.95
❑125, ca. 2004, b&w	6.95
❑126, ca. 2004, b&w	6.95
❑127, ca. 2004, b&w	6.95
❑128, ca. 2004, b&w; Halloween special	6.95
❑130, ca. 2005; 20th Anniversary Special	6.95
❑131, ca. 2005	6.95
❑132, ca. 2005	6.95
❑133, ca. 2005; Listed as #132 on cover and indicia; A sticker on the front gives the proper issue number	6.95
❑Special 1, Nov 1984; b&w	1.50

Femforce Frightbook
AC

Issue	N-MINT
❑1, b&w	2.95

Femforce in the House of Horror
AC

Issue	N-MINT
❑1, b&w	2.50

Femforce: Night of the Demon
AC

Issue	N-MINT
❑1, b&w; NN; ca. 1990	2.75

Femforce: Out of the Asylum Special
AC

Issue	N-MINT
❑1, Aug 1987, b&w	2.50

Femforce Pin Up Portfolio
AC

Issue	N-MINT
❑1	2.50
❑2; ca. 1991	2.95
❑3	2.95
❑4, Dec 1991	5.00
❑5	5.00

Femforce: To Die For
AC

Issue	N-MINT
❑1, ca. 2005; Graphic novel; b&w	15.95

Femforce Uncut
AC

Issue	N-MINT
❑1; Reprint Synnwatch #2	9.95

Femforce Up Close
AC

Issue	N-MINT
❑1, Apr 1992, Nightveil	3.00
❑2, Jul 1992; Stardust	3.00
❑3; Dragonfly	3.00
❑4, Dec 1992; O: She Cat	2.95
❑5; Blue Bulleteer	2.95
❑6; Ms. Victory	2.95
❑7; Ms. Victory	2.95
❑8; Tara, Garganta	2.95
❑9; Synn	2.95
❑10, b&w; Yankee Girl	2.95
❑11, b&w; Nightveil	2.95

Femforce Victory Reborn
AC

Issue	N-MINT
❑1, ca. 2005	15.95

Femme Macabre
London Night

Issue	N-MINT
❑1; Adult	2.95

Femme Noire
Cat-Head

Issue	N-MINT
❑1; Adult	1.75
❑2; Adult	1.75

Fenry
Raven

Issue	N-MINT
❑1	6.95

Ferret
Malibu

Issue	N-MINT
❑1, ca. 1992	1.95

Ferret
Malibu

Issue	N-MINT
❑1, May 1993	2.50
❑1/Variant, May 1993; die-cut	2.50
❑2, Jun 1993; Includes poster	2.50
❑3, Jul 1993	2.50
❑4, Aug 1993; Includes poster	2.50
❑5, Sep 1993	2.25
❑6, Oct 1993	2.25
❑7, Nov 1993	2.25
❑8, Dec 1993	2.25
❑9, Jan 1994	2.25
❑10, Feb 1994	2.25

Ferro City
Image

Issue	N-MINT
❑1, Sep 2005	2.99
❑2, Oct 2005	2.99
❑3, Nov 2005	2.99
❑4, Jan 2006	2.99

Feud
Marvel / Epic

Issue	N-MINT
❑1, Jul 1993; embossed cardstock cover	2.50
❑2, Aug 1993	1.95
❑3, Sep 1993	1.95
❑4, Oct 1993	1.95

Fever
Wonder Comix

Issue	N-MINT
❑1, b&w; Anthology	1.95

Fever Dreams
Kitchen Sink

Issue	N-MINT
❑1, Adult	3.00

Fever in Urbicand
NBM

Issue	N-MINT
❑1	12.95

F5
Image

Issue	N-MINT
❑1, Apr 2000; Giant-size	2.95
❑2, Jun 2000	2.50
❑3, Aug 2000	2.50
❑4, Oct 2000	2.50
❑Ashcan 1, Jan 2000; Preview issue	2.50

F5 Origin
Dark Horse

Issue	N-MINT
❑1, Nov 2001, Several characters in profile on cover	2.99

15 Minutes
Slave Labor

Issue	N-MINT
❑1, Aug 2004	3.95
❑2, Dec 2004	3.95
❑3, Jun 2005	3.95

Fifth Force Featuring Hawk and Animal
Antarctic

Issue	N-MINT
❑1, Apr 1999; 1: Hawk and Animal (in comics)	1.99
❑2, Jul 1999	2.50

Fifties Terror
Eternity

Issue	N-MINT
❑1, Oct 1988, b&w; Reprints	2.00
❑2, Nov 1988, b&w; Reprints	2.00
❑3, Dec 1988, b&w; Reprints	2.00
❑4, Jan 1989, b&w; Reprints	2.00
❑5, Feb 1989, b&w; Reprints	2.00
❑6, Mar 1989, b&w; Reprints	2.00

52
DC

Issue	N-MINT
❑1, Jul 2006, DC Comics 52: Week One	4.00
❑2, Jul 2006	2.50
❑3, Jul 2006, D: Terra-Man	2.50
❑4, Aug 2006	2.50
❑5, Aug 2006, Cover by J.G. Jones	2.50
❑6, Aug 2006, Cover by J.G. Jones	2.50
❑7, Sep 2006, 1: Katherine Kane	4.00
❑8, Sep 2006, Cover credits Norm Rapmund but interior credits Andy Lanning	2.50
❑9, Sep 2006, 1: Batwoman (cameo); 1: Batwoman (Kathy Kane)	2.50
❑10, Sep 2006	2.50
❑11, Oct 2006	2.50
❑12, Oct 2006, 1: Isis; O: Wonder Woman; 1: Isis (Adrianna Tomaz)	2.50
❑13, Oct 2006, O: Elongated Man	2.50
❑14, Oct 2006, O: Metamorpho	2.50
❑15, Oct 2006, D: Booster Gold; O: Steel; D: Booster Gold (Michael Carter); O: Steel (John Henry Iron)	2.50
❑16, Nov 2006, O: Black Adam; Wedding of Black Adam & Isis; O: Black Adam (Teth-Adam)	2.50
❑17, Nov 2006, D: Devilance the Pursuer; O: Lobo	2.50
❑19, Nov 2006, O: Animal Man; O: Animal Man (Buddy Baker)	2.50
❑20, Nov 2006, O: Adam Strange	2.50
❑21, Dec 2006, 1: Infinity Inc.; D: Trajectory; D:Trajectory (Eliza Harmon)	2.50
❑22, Dec 2006, 1: Jon Standing Bear; O: Green Lantern	2.50
❑23, Dec 2006, 1: Osiris; O: Wildcat; 1: Osiris (Amon Tomaz); O: Wildcat (Ted Grant); Doctor Magnus; Renee Montoya; Question; Black Adam; Isis	2.50
❑24, Dec 2006, D: Super-Chief; The O: Booster Gold; O: Booster Gold (Michael Carter)	2.50
❑25, Jan 2007, D: Mirage; O: Nightwing; O: Nightwing (Dick Grayson); Captain Marvel Jr.; Mary Marvel; Isis; Black Adam; Osiris; Ralph Dibny; Infinity Inc.; Fury; Skyman; Starlight; Matrix; Alan Scott; Mr. Terrific; Doctor Magnus	2.50
❑26, Jan 2007, 1: Sobek; O: Hawkman; O: Hawkgirl; O: Hawkman (Carter Hall); O: Hawkgirl (Kendra Saunders); Black Adam; Isis; Osiris; Renee Montoya; Question; Richard Dragon; Steel; Starlight; Doctor Magnus	2.50
❑27, Jan 2007, O: Black Canary; O: Black Canary (Dinah Laurel Lance)	2.50
❑28, Jan 2007, O: Catman; O: Catman (Thomas Blake); Renee Montoya; Question; Batwoman; Red Tornado; Lobo; Starfire; Adam Strange; Animal Man	2.50
❑29, Feb 2007, 1: new Jade; 1: Jade (Nicki Jones); Alan Scott; Wildcat; Jay Garrick; Infinity Inc.; Skyman; Starlight; Matrix; Nuklon; Everyman; Fury; Obsidian; Doctor Magnus; Beast Boy; Steel	2.50
❑30, Feb 2007, O: Metal Men	2.50
❑31, Feb 2007, D: Captain Comet; O: Robin; D: Captain Comet (Adam Blake); Jade; Starlight; Everyman; Ralph Dibny; Wonder Girl; Supernova; Lobo	2.50
❑32, Feb 2007, 1: Talon; 1: Riddler's Daughter; 1: Son of Frankenstein; O: Blue Beetle; O: Blue Beetle (Jaime Reyes); Raven; Beast Boy; Osiris; Sobek; Captain Marvel Jr.; Kid Devil; Adam Strange; Animal Man; Starfire; Lobo; Ralph Dibny	2.50
❑33, Mar 2007, O: Martian Manhunter; O: Martian Manhunter (J'onn J'onnz); Ralph Dibny; Batwoman; Nightwing; Infinity Inc.; Renee Montoya; Question; Black Adam; Isis; Osiris; Sobek	2.50
❑34, Jan 2007, D: Persuader; O: Zatanna; D: Persuader (Cole Parker)	2.50
❑35, Mar 2007	2.50
❑35/Variant, Mar 2007	2.50
❑36, Mar 2007, D: Buddy Baker (Animal Man); O: Power Girl; D: Animal Man (Buddy Baker); O: Power Girl (Karen Starr)	2.50
❑37	2.50
❑38	2.50
❑39	2.50
❑40	2.50
❑41	2.50
❑42	2.50
❑43	2.50
❑44	2.50
❑45	2.50
❑46	2.50
❑47	2.50
❑48	2.50
❑49	2.50
❑50	2.50
❑51	2.50
❑52	2.50

Fight for Tomorrow
DC / Vertigo

Issue	N-MINT
❑1, Nov 2002; Several characters in profile on cover	2.50
❑2, Dec 2002	2.50
❑3, Jan 2003	2.50
❑4, Feb 2003	2.50
❑5, Mar 2003	2.50
❑6, Apr 2003	2.50

Fightin' 5
Charlton

Issue	N-MINT
❑28, Jul 1964, Continued from Space War (Vol. 2) #27	20.00
❑29, Oct 1964	10.00
❑30, Dec 1964	10.00
❑31, Feb 1965	9.00
❑32, May 1965	9.00

Fantastic Four vs. X-Men

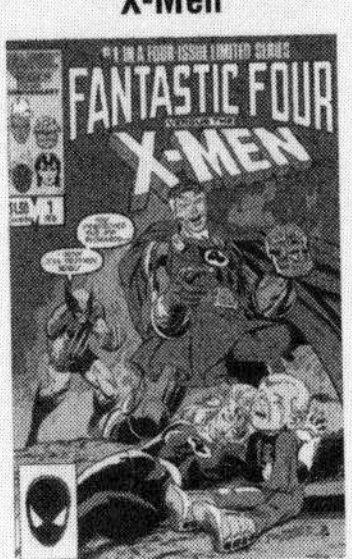

Mutants tangle with super-hero family

©Marvel

Fantastic Voyage

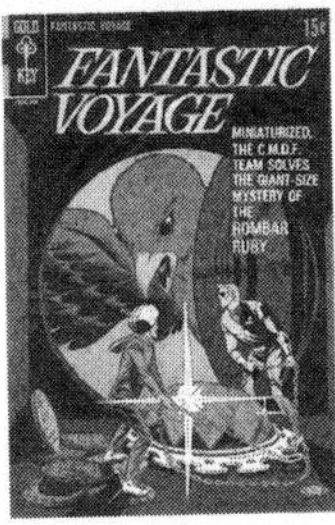

Based on animated TV version of SF film

©Gold Key

Fantastic Voyages of Sindbad

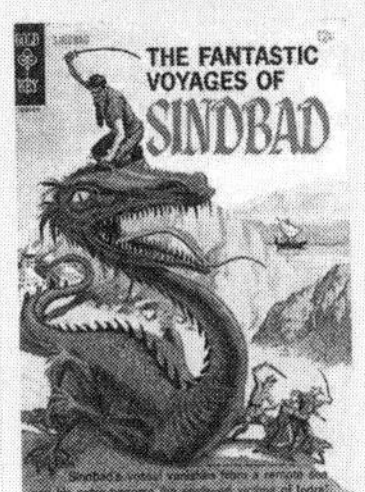

Gold Key mythological adventures

©Gold Key

Fantasy Masterpieces

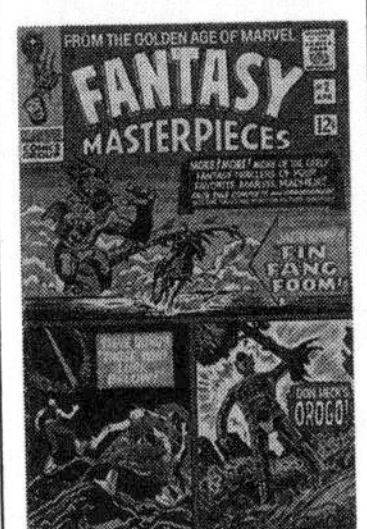

Series reprints Golden Age Marvel comics

©Marvel

Fantasy Masterpieces

Reprints the original Silver Surfer series

©Marvel

	N-MINT
❑33, Jul 1965	9.00
❑34, Sep 1965	9.00
❑35, Nov 1965	9.00
❑36, Jan 1966	9.00
❑37, May 1966	9.00
❑38, Jul 1966	9.00
❑39, Sep 1966	9.00
❑40, Nov 1966, 1: The Peacemaker	18.00
❑41, Jan 1967	10.00
❑42, Oct 1981, Reprints	3.00
❑43, Dec 1981, Reprints	3.00
❑44, Feb 1982, Reprints	3.00
❑45, Apr 1982, Reprints	3.00
❑46, Jun 1982, Reprints	3.00
❑47, Aug 1982, Reprints	3.00
❑48, Oct 1982, Reprints	3.00
❑49, Dec 1982, Reprints	3.00

Fightin' Air Force
Charlton

	N-MINT
❑30, Dec 1961	8.00
❑31, Mar 1962	8.00
❑32, May 1962	8.00
❑33, Jul 1962	8.00
❑34, Sep 1962	8.00
❑35, Nov 1962, DG (c)	8.00
❑36, Jan 1963	8.00
❑37, Mar 1963	8.00
❑38, May 1963	8.00
❑39, Jul 1963	8.00
❑40, Sep 1963	8.00
❑41, Nov 1963	8.00
❑42, Jan 1964	8.00
❑43, Mar 1964	8.00
❑44, Jun 1964	8.00
❑45, Sep 1964	8.00
❑46, Nov 1964	8.00
❑47, Jan 1965	8.00
❑48, ca. 1965	8.00
❑49, Jul 1965	8.00
❑50, Aug 1965, A: American Eagle	8.00
❑51, Oct 1965, A: American Eagle	8.00
❑52, Dec 1965, A: American Eagle	8.00
❑53, Mar 1966, A: American Eagle. Series continues as War and Attack with #54	8.00

Fightin' Army
Charlton

	N-MINT
❑44, Dec 1961	10.00
❑45, ca. 1962	10.00
❑46, May 1962	10.00
❑47, ca. 1962	10.00
❑48, ca. 1962	10.00
❑49, Nov 1962	10.00
❑50, Jan 1963	10.00
❑51, ca. 1963	8.00
❑52, ca. 1963	8.00
❑53, Jul 1963	8.00
❑54, Sep 1963	8.00
❑55, Nov 1963	8.00
❑56, Jan 1964	8.00
❑57, Mar 1964	8.00
❑58, Jun 1964	8.00
❑59, ca. 1964	8.00
❑60, Nov 1964	8.00
❑61, Jan 1965	8.00
❑62, Mar 1965	8.00
❑63, Jun 1965	8.00
❑64, Aug 1965	8.00
❑65, Oct 1965	8.00
❑66, Dec 1965	8.00
❑67, Mar 1966	8.00
❑68, May 1966	8.00
❑69, Jul 1966	8.00
❑70, Sep 1966	8.00
❑71, Nov 1966	8.00
❑72, Jan 1967	8.00
❑73, Mar 1967	8.00
❑74, ca. 1967	8.00
❑75, Aug 1967	8.00
❑76, Oct 1967, Lonely War of Capt. Willy Schultz begins	10.00
❑77, Dec 1967	6.00
❑78, Feb 1968	6.00
❑79, May 1968	6.00
❑80, Jul 1968	6.00
❑81, Sep 1968	6.00
❑82, Nov 1968	6.00
❑83, Jan 1969	6.00
❑84, Mar 1969	6.00
❑85, May 1969	6.00
❑86, Jul 1969	6.00
❑87, Sep 1969	6.00
❑88, Nov 1969	6.00
❑89, Jan 1970	6.00
❑90, Mar 1970	6.00
❑91, May 1970	6.00
❑92, Jul 1970	6.00
❑93, Sep 1970	6.00
❑94, Nov 1970	6.00
❑95, Jan 1971	6.00
❑96, Mar 1971	6.00
❑97, May 1971	6.00
❑98, Jul 1971	6.00
❑99, Sep 1971	6.00
❑100, Nov 1971	6.00
❑101, Jan 1972	5.00
❑102, Mar 1972	5.00
❑103, May 1972	5.00
❑104, Jul 1972	5.00
❑105, Sep 1972	5.00
❑106, Nov 1972	5.00
❑107, Jan 1973	5.00
❑108, Mar 1973	5.00
❑109, May 1973	5.00
❑110, Jul 1973	5.00
❑111, Sep 1973	5.00
❑112, Nov 1973	5.00
❑113, May 1974	5.00
❑114, Jul 1974	5.00
❑115, Sep 1974	5.00
❑116, Nov 1974	5.00
❑117, Feb 1975	5.00
❑118, ca. 1975	5.00
❑119, Jun 1975	5.00
❑120, Sep 1975	5.00
❑121, Nov 1975	4.00
❑122, Jan 1976	4.00
❑123, ca. 1976	4.00
❑124, May 1976	4.00
❑125, ca. 1976	4.00
❑126, Oct 1976	4.00
❑127, Dec 1976	4.00
❑128, Sep 1977	4.00
❑129, Nov 1977	4.00
❑130, Feb 1978	4.00
❑131, Mar 1978	4.00
❑132, Apr 1978	4.00
❑133, Jun 1978	4.00
❑134, Sep 1978, has Iron Corporal story	4.00
❑135, Nov 1978	4.00
❑136, Jan 1979	4.00
❑137, ca. 1979	4.00
❑138, May 1979	4.00
❑139, Jul 1979	4.00
❑140, Aug 1979	4.00
❑141, ca. 1979	4.00
❑142, Nov 1979	4.00
❑143, Jan 1980	4.00
❑144, Feb 1980	4.00
❑145, Apr 1980	4.00
❑146, Jul 1980	4.00
❑147, Sep 1980	4.00
❑148, Nov 1980	4.00
❑149, Jan 1981	4.00
❑150, Mar 1981	4.00
❑151, Apr 1981	4.00
❑152, Jun 1981	4.00
❑153, Aug 1981	4.00
❑154, Oct 1981	4.00
❑155, Dec 1981	4.00
❑156, Feb 1982	4.00
❑157, Apr 1982	4.00
❑158, Jun 1982	4.00
❑159, Aug 1982	4.00
❑160, Oct 1982	4.00
❑161, Dec 1982	4.00
❑162, Feb 1983	4.00
❑163, Apr 1983	4.00
❑164, Jun 1983	4.00
❑165, Aug 1983	4.00
❑166, Oct 1983	4.00
❑167, Dec 1983	4.00
❑168, Feb 1984	4.00
❑169, May 1984	4.00
❑170, Jul 1984	4.00
❑171, Sep 1984	4.00
❑172, Nov 1984	4.00

Fighting American
DC

	N-MINT
❑1, Feb 1994; O: Fighting American	2.00
❑2, Mar 1994; 1: The Media Circus	2.00
❑3, Apr 1994; 1: Gross National Product	2.00
❑4, May 1994	2.00
❑5, Jun 1994	2.00
❑6, Jul 1994; Final issue	2.00

Fighting American
Awesome

	N-MINT
❑1/A, Aug 1997; Diving at guns, bayonets on cover	2.50
❑1/B, Aug 1997; Holding flag on cover	2.50
❑1/C, Aug 1997; Comics Cavalcade regular edition (two heroes diving toward a gun at lower left corner); Cover by Rob Liefeld	2.50
❑1/D, Aug 1997; Comics Cavalcade Liberty Gold Foil Edition; Same as #1/C without background; Cover by Rob Liefeld	15.95

N-MINT

❑2, Oct 1997 .... 2.50
❑3, Dec 1997 .... 2.50

Fighting American: Dogs of War
Awesome

❑1, Sep 1998, JSn (w); 1: Scarlet Dragon; Cover by Stephen Platt; 3rd Awesome Fighting American series 2.50
❑1/A, Sep 1998, 98 Tour Edition cover; RL (c); JSn (w) 3.00

Fighting American: Rules of the Game
Awesome

❑1, Nov 1997 .... 2.50
❑1/A, Nov 1997, Fighting American standing on cover 2.50
❑1/B, Nov 1997, Woman pointing gun on cover 2.50

Fighting American Special Comicon Edition
Awesome

❑1, ca. 1997; No cover price; b&w preview of upcoming series given out at Comic-Con International: San Diego 1997 .... 1.00

Fighting Fem Classics
Forbidden Fruit

❑1, b&w; Adult 3.50

Fighting Fems
Forbidden Fruit

❑1, b&w; Adult 3.50
❑2, b&w; Adult 3.50

Fightin' Marines
Charlton

❑44, Nov 1961 .... 10.00
❑45, Feb 1962 .... 10.00
❑46, Apr 1962 .... 10.00
❑47, Jun 1962 .... 10.00
❑48, Aug 1962 .... 10.00
❑49, Oct 1962 .... 10.00
❑50, Dec 1962 .... 10.00
❑51, Feb 1963 .... 7.00
❑52, Apr 1963 .... 7.00
❑53, Jun 1963 .... 7.00
❑54, Aug 1963 .... 7.00
❑55 1963 .... 7.00
❑56, Dec 1963 .... 7.00
❑57, Feb 1964 .... 7.00
❑58, May 1964 .... 7.00
❑59, Jul 1964 .... 7.00
❑60, Oct 1964 .... 7.00
❑61, Dec 1964 .... 7.00
❑62, Feb 1965 .... 7.00
❑63, May 1965 .... 7.00
❑64, Jul 1965 .... 7.00
❑65, Sep 1965 .... 7.00
❑66, Nov 1965 .... 7.00
❑67, Jan 1966 .... 7.00
❑68, Mar 1966 .... 7.00
❑69, ca. 1966 .... 7.00
❑70, Aug 1966 .... 7.00
❑71 1966 .... 6.00
❑72 1966 .... 6.00
❑73 1967 .... 6.00
❑74 1967 .... 6.00
❑75, Jul 1967 .... 4.00
❑76, Sep 1967 .... 4.00
❑77, Nov 1967 .... 4.00
❑78, Jan 1968, 1: Shotgun Harker. 1: The Chicken. 1: Shotgun Harker (Sgt. Arkie Harker) 4.00
❑79, ca. 1968, ca. 1968 .... 4.00
❑80, Jul 1968 .... 4.00
❑81, Sep 1968 .... 4.00
❑82, Nov 1968, Giant-size 6.00
❑83, Jan 1969 .... 4.00
❑84, Mar 1969 .... 4.00
❑85, May 1969 .... 4.00
❑86, Jul 1969 .... 4.00
❑87, Sep 1969 .... 4.00
❑88, Nov 1969 .... 4.00
❑89, Jan 1970 .... 4.00
❑90, Mar 1970 .... 4.00
❑91, May 1970 .... 3.50
❑92, Jul 1970 .... 3.50
❑93, Sep 1970 .... 3.50
❑94, Nov 1970 .... 3.50
❑95, Jan 1971 .... 3.50
❑96, Mar 1971 .... 3.50
❑97, May 1971 .... 3.50
❑98, Jul 1971 .... 3.50
❑99, Sep 1971 .... 3.50
❑100, Nov 1971 .... 3.50
❑101, Jan 1972 .... 3.00
❑102, Mar 1972 .... 3.00
❑103, Apr 1972 .... 3.00
❑104, Jun 1972 .... 3.00
❑105, Aug 1972, Don Perlin cover 3.00
❑106, Oct 1972 .... 3.00
❑107, Dec 1972, Nicolas A. Lascia cover 3.00
❑108, Jan 1973 .... 3.00
❑109, Mar 1973 .... 3.00
❑110, Apr 1973 .... 3.00
❑111, Jun 1973 .... 3.00
❑112, ca. 1973 .... 3.00
❑113, ca. 1973 .... 3.00
❑114, Oct 1973 .... 3.00
❑115, Dec 1973 .... 3.00
❑116, Jan 1974 .... 3.00
❑117, Jun 1974 .... 3.00
❑118, ca. 1974 .... 3.00
❑119, Nov 1974 .... 3.00
❑120, Jan 1975, General Douglas MacArthur text biography 3.00
❑120/2nd, ca. 1975, reprints Charlton #120 .... 1.50
❑121, Mar 1975 .... 3.00
❑122, ca. 1975 .... 3.00
❑123, May 1975 .... 3.00
❑124, ca. 1975 .... 3.00
❑125, Sep 1975 .... 3.00
❑126, ca. 1975 .... 2.50
❑127, Jan 1976 .... 2.50
❑128, Mar 1976 .... 2.50
❑129, May 1976 .... 2.50
❑130, Jul 1976 .... 2.50
❑131, Sep 1976 .... 2.50
❑132, Nov 1976 .... 2.50
❑133, Oct 1977 .... 2.50
❑134, Dec 1977 .... 2.50
❑135, Feb 1978 .... 2.50
❑136, Apr 1978 .... 2.50
❑137, Jun 1978 .... 2.50
❑138, Aug 1978 .... 2.50
❑139, Oct 1978 .... 2.50
❑140, Dec 1978 .... 2.50
❑141, Feb 1979 .... 2.50
❑142, ca. 1979 .... 2.50
❑143, ca. 1979 .... 2.50
❑144, Jul 1979 .... 2.50
❑145, ca. 1979 .... 2.50
❑146, ca. 1979 .... 2.50
❑147, Dec 1979 .... 2.50
❑148, Jan 1980 .... 2.50
❑149, Mar 1980 .... 2.50
❑150, May 1980 .... 2.50
❑151, ca. 1980 .... 2.00
❑152, Oct 1980 .... 2.00
❑153, Dec 1980 .... 2.00
❑154, Jan 1981 .... 2.00
❑155, Mar 1981 .... 2.00
❑156, May 1981 .... 2.00
❑157, Jul 1981 .... 2.00
❑158, Sep 1981 .... 2.00
❑159, Oct 1981 .... 2.00
❑160, Dec 1981 .... 2.00
❑161, Feb 1982 .... 2.00
❑162, Apr 1982 .... 2.00
❑163, Jul 1982 .... 2.00
❑164, Sep 1982 .... 2.00
❑165, Nov 1982 .... 2.00
❑166, Jan 1983 .... 2.00
❑167, Mar 1983 .... 2.00
❑168, May 1983 .... 2.00
❑169, Jul 1983 .... 2.00
❑170, Sep 1983 .... 2.00
❑171, Nov 1983 .... 2.00
❑172, Jan 1984 .... 2.00
❑173, Mar 1984 .... 2.00
❑174, May 1984 .... 2.00
❑175, Jul 1984 .... 2.00
❑176, Sep 1984, Final Issue 2.00

Fightin' Navy
Charlton

❑101, Nov 1961 .... 8.00
❑102, Jan 1962 .... 8.00
❑103, Apr 1962 .... 8.00
❑104, ca. 1962 .... 8.00
❑105, Aug 1962 .... 8.00
❑106, ca. 1962 .... 8.00
❑107, ca. 1962 .... 8.00
❑108, ca. 1963 .... 8.00
❑109, ca. 1963 .... 8.00
❑110, ca. 1963 .... 8.00
❑111, Aug 1963 .... 8.00
❑112, ca. 1963 .... 8.00
❑113, ca. 1963 .... 8.00
❑114, Feb 1964 .... 8.00
❑115, May 1964 .... 8.00
❑116, Jul 1964 .... 8.00
❑117, Sep 1964 .... 8.00
❑118, Nov 1964 .... 8.00
❑119, Feb 1965 .... 8.00
❑120, May 1965 .... 8.00
❑121, ca. 1965 .... 5.00
❑122, ca. 1965 .... 5.00
❑123, Dec 1965 .... 5.00
❑124, Jan 1966 .... 5.00
❑125, ca. 1966, Last issue of original run 5.00
❑126, Aug 1983, Series begins again 2.00
❑127, Oct 1983 .... 2.00
❑128, Dec 1983 .... 2.00
❑129, Feb 1984 .... 2.00
❑130, Apr 1984 .... 2.00
❑131, Jun 1984 .... 2.00
❑132, Aug 1984 .... 2.00
❑133, Oct 1984, Final Issue 2.00

Fight Man
Marvel

❑1, Jun 1993 .... 2.00

Fight the Enemy
Tower

❑1, Aug 1966 .... 22.00
❑2, Oct 1966 .... 16.00
❑3, Mar 1967 .... 16.00

Figments
Blackthorne

❑1 .... 1.75
❑2 .... 1.75

Figments Unlimited
Graphik

❑1 .... 1.25
❑2 .... 1.25
❑3 .... 1.25

Files of Ms. Tree
Renegade

❑1, Jun 1984, b&w 6.00
❑2, Sep 1985, b&w 6.00
❑3, b&w 6.00

Filibusting Comics
Fantagraphics

❑1, Jan 1995, b&w; Parody of Understanding Comics; b&w pin-ups, cardstock cover 2.75

Filth
DC / Vertigo

❑1, Aug 2002 .... 2.95
❑2, Sep 2002 .... 2.95
❑3, Oct 2002 .... 2.95
❑4, Nov 2002 .... 2.95
❑5, Dec 2002 .... 2.95
❑6, Jan 2003 .... 2.95
❑7, Feb 2003 .... 2.95
❑8, Mar 2003 .... 2.95
❑9, Apr 2003 .... 2.95
❑10, Jun 2003 .... 2.95
❑11, Jul 2003 .... 2.95
❑12, Aug 2003 .... 2.95
❑13, Sep 2003 .... 2.95

Filthy Animals
Radio

❑1, Aug 1997; Adult 2.95
❑2 1998; Adult 2.95
❑3, Aug 1998; Adult 2.95
❑4; Adult 2.95

Filthy Habits
Aeon

❑1, Jul 1996, b&w; Adult 2.95
❑2, Nov 1996, b&w; Adult 2.95
❑3, Feb 1997, b&w; Adult 2.95

Fat Albert

Fun with Bill Cosby's animated characters
©Gold Key

Fatale

Over-endowed heroine absorbs energy
©Broadway

Fathom (3rd Series)

First issue had variant story pages
©Image

Fatman, the Human Flying Saucer

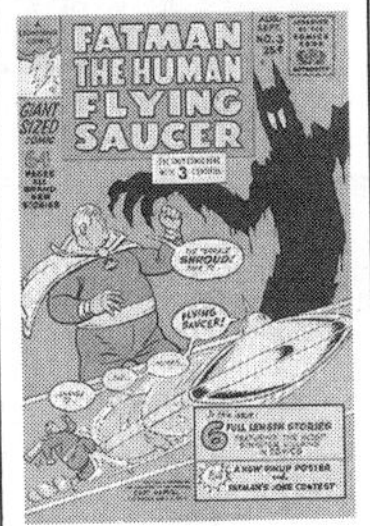

Parody of Silver Age comic stories
©Lightning

Fear

Anthology reprinted Marvel monster tales
©Marvel

N-MINT

Final Cycle
Dragon's Teeth

❑1, Jul 1987, b&w ... 1.75
❑2, b&w ... 1.75
❑3, b&w ... 1.75
❑4, b&w ... 1.75

Final Man
C&T

❑1, b&w ... 1.50

Final Night
DC

❑1, Nov 1996; Week One: Armageddon; Suneater begins consumption of sun ... 6.00
❑2, Nov 1996; DC comics crossover ... 4.00
❑3, Nov 1996 ... 4.00
❑4, Nov 1996; D: Hal Jordan. Parallax reignites sun; Week Four: Emerald Dawn ... 4.00

Final Taboo
Aircel

❑1, Oct 1991, b&w; Adult ... 2.50
❑2, b&w; Adult ... 2.50

Finals
DC / Vertigo

❑1, Sep 1999 ... 2.95
❑2, Oct 1999 ... 2.95
❑3, Nov 1999 ... 2.95
❑4, Dec 1999 ... 2.95

Finder
Lightspeed

❑1, Nov 1996, b&w; wraparound cover ... 4.00
❑2, Jan 1997, b&w ... 3.50
❑3, Mar 1997, b&w ... 3.50
❑4, May 1997, b&w ... 3.50
❑5, Jul 1997, b&w ... 3.50
❑6, Sep 1997, b&w ... 3.50
❑7, Nov 1997, b&w ... 3.50
❑8 1998 ... 3.50
❑9 1998 ... 3.50
❑10 1998 ... 3.50
❑11 1998 ... 3.50
❑12 1999 ... 3.50
❑13 1999 ... 3.50
❑14 1999 ... 3.50
❑15, Dec 1999 ... 2.95
❑16, Feb 2000 ... 2.95
❑17, May 2000 ... 2.95
❑18 2000 ... 2.95
❑19, Sep 2000 ... 2.95
❑20 2000 ... 2.95
❑21 2001 ... 2.95
❑22, May 2001; Fight Scene ... 2.95
❑23, Jul 2001 ... 2.95
❑24, Nov 2001 ... 2.95
❑25, Jan 2002 ... 2.95
❑26, Mar 2002 ... 2.95
❑27, Jul 2002 ... 2.95
❑28, Sep 2002 ... 2.95
❑29, Nov 2002 ... 2.95
❑30, Jan 2003 ... 2.95
❑31 2003 ... 2.95
❑32 2003 ... 2.95
❑33 2004 ... 2.95
❑34 2004 ... 2.95
❑35, Sep 2004 ... 2.95
❑Ashcan 1 ... 1.00

Finder Footnotes
Lightspeed

❑1 ... 6.00

Finieous Treasury
TSR

❑1; magazine-sized; NN; Collects Finieous Fingers strips from Dragon magazine ... 3.00

Fink, Inc.
Fink, Inc.

❑1 ... 3.50

Fire
Caliber

❑1, b&w ... 2.95
❑2, b&w ... 2.95

Firearm
Malibu / Ultraverse

❑0, Aug 1993, with videotape ... 14.95
❑1, Sep 1993, 1: Firearm ... 2.25
❑1/Ltd., limited promotional edition; foil cover ... 3.00
❑2, Oct 1993, Rune ... 2.50
❑3, Nov 1993, 1: The Sportsmen ... 1.95
❑4, Dec 1993, Break-Thru ... 1.95
❑5, Jan 1994, O: Prime ... 1.95
❑6, Feb 1994, Search for Prime ... 1.95
❑7, Mar 1994 ... 1.95
❑8, May 1994 ... 1.95
❑9, Jun 1994, 1: Ms. Rule; 1: Willy Manila ... 1.95
❑10, Jul 1994, 1: Aeon; 1: Faulkner; 1: Iron Clad; Flip book with Ultraverse Premiere #5 ... 3.50
❑11, Aug 1994, Flipbook with Ultraverse Premiere #5 ... 1.95
❑12, Sep 1994, 1: Rafferty; D: Last; D: Lukasz; D: Doctor Z ... 1.95
❑13, Oct 1994 ... 1.95
❑14, Nov 1994, D: Organism 0.9B; D: Vinaigrette ... 1.95
❑15, Dec 1994 ... 1.95
❑16, Jan 1995, 1: Sigma; D: Sigma ... 1.95
❑17, Feb 1995, 1: The Silence; D: The Silence ... 1.95
❑18, Mar 1995, D: Rafferty ... 1.95
❑19, Apr 1995 ... 1.95

Firebirds One Shot
Image

❑1 ... 6.00

Firebrand
DC

❑1, Feb 1996, O: Firebrand III (Alex Sanchez). 1: Firebrand III (Alex Sanchez) ... 2.00
❑2, Mar 1996 ... 1.75
❑3, Apr 1996 ... 1.75
❑4, May 1996 ... 1.75
❑5, Jun 1996 ... 1.75
❑6, Jul 1996 ... 1.75
❑7, Aug 1996 ... 1.75
❑8, Sep 1996 ... 1.75
❑9, Oct 1996, Final Issue ... 1.75

Firebreather
Image

❑1, Jan 2003; Miniseries ... 2.95
❑2, Feb 2003 ... 2.95
❑3, Mar 2003 ... 2.95
❑4, Apr 2003 ... 2.95

Firebreather: Iron Saint One-Shot
Image

❑1 2005 ... 6.95

Fire from Heaven
Image

❑½; Promotional edition from Wizard #57; Includes certificate of authenticity; ca. 1996 ... 1.00
❑1, Mar 1996; wraparound cover ... 2.50
❑2, Jul 1996 ... 2.50

Fire Sale
Rip Off

❑1, Dec 1989, b&w; benefit ... 2.50

Firestar
Marvel

❑1, Mar 1986; O: Firestar. A: X-Men. A: New Mutants ... 1.50
❑2, Apr 1986 A: Wolverine ... 1.50
❑3, May 1986 ... 1.00
❑4, Jun 1986 ... 1.00

Firestorm
DC

❑1, Mar 1978, AM, JR (a); 1&O: Firestorm ... 8.00
❑2, Apr 1978, AM (a) ... 2.00
❑3, Jun 1978, AM (a); 1: Killer Frost ... 2.50
❑4, Aug 1978, AM (a) ... 2.00
❑5, Oct 1978, AM (a) ... 2.00

Firestorm
DC

❑1, Jul 2004 ... 8.00
❑2, Aug 2004 ... 2.50
❑3, Sep 2004 ... 2.50
❑4, Oct 2004 ... 2.50
❑5, Nov 2004 ... 2.50
❑6, Dec 2004, Identity Crisis tie-in ... 5.00
❑7, Jan 2005 ... 2.50
❑8, Feb 2005 ... 2.50
❑9, Mar 2005 ... 2.50
❑10, Apr 2005 ... 2.50
❑11, May 2005; Advent Rising #1 Included ... 2.50
❑12, Jun 2005 ... 2.50
❑13, Jun 2005; D: Ron Raymond ... 2.50
❑14, Jul 2005 ... 2.50
❑15, Aug 2005 ... 2.50
❑16, Sep 2005 ... 2.50
❑17, Oct 2005; Villians United tie-in ... 2.50
❑18, Dec 2005; Omac Project tie-in ... 2.50
❑19, Jan 2006; Infinite Crisis crossover ... 2.50
❑20, Feb 2006, Infinite Crisis crossover ... 2.50
❑21, Mar 2006, Infinite Crisis crossover ... 2.50
❑22, Apr 2006, Infinite Crisis crossover ... 2.50
❑23, May 2006, One Year Later ... 2.99
❑24, Jun 2006, One Year Later ... 2.50
❑25, Jul 2006, One Year Later; Price increase ... 2.99
❑26, Aug 2006, Cover by Brian Stelfreeze ... 2.99
❑27, Sep 2006 ... 2.99
❑28, Oct 2006 ... 2.99
❑29, Nov 2006 ... 2.99
❑30 ... 2.99

N-MINT

❑31 .... 2.99
❑32 .... 2.99
❑33 .... 2.99
❑34 .... 2.99
❑35 .... 2.99

Firestorm, the Nuclear Man
DC

❑65, Nov 1987; A: Green Lantern. A: new Firestorm. Series continued from Fury of Firestorm #64 .... 1.00
❑66, Dec 1987 A: Green Lantern 1.00
❑67, Jan 1988; Millennium 1.00
❑68, Feb 1988; Millennium 1.00
❑69, Mar 1988; V: Zuggernaut 1.00
❑70, Apr 1988 .... 1.00
❑71, May 1988; V: Stalnoivolk 1.00
❑72, Jun 1988; V: Zuggernaut 1.00
❑73, Jul 1988; A: Soyuz. V: Stalnoivolk 1.00
❑74, Aug 1988 .... 1.00
❑75, Sep 1988 .... 1.00
❑76, Oct 1988; A: Firehawk. V: Brimstone 1.00
❑77, Nov 1988 .... 1.00
❑78, Dec 1988 .... 1.00
❑79; no cover date 1.00
❑80; A: Firehawk, Power Girl. No cover date; Invasion! 1.00
❑81, Jan 1989; A: Soyuz. Invasion! Aftermath 1.00
❑82, Feb 1989; V: Killer Frost 1.00
❑83, Mar 1989; 1: Svarozhich 1.00
❑84, Apr 1989; O: Firestorm; V: Svarozhich 1.00
❑85, May 1989; new Firestorm 1.00
❑86, Jun 1989; V: Parasite; The Janus Directive; Part 7; Janus Directive continued Suicide Squad #28 .... 1.00
❑87, Jul 1989 .... 1.00
❑88, Aug 1989 .... 1.00
❑89, Sep 1989 .... 1.00
❑90, Oct 1989; 1: Naiad 1.00
❑91, Nov 1989; V: Naiad 1.00
❑92, Dec 1989; V: Red Tornado; V: Naiad 1.00
❑93, Jan 1990; V: Red Tornado; V: Naiad 1.00
❑94, Feb 1990 .... 1.00
❑30, Dec 2006 .... 2.99
❑31, Jan 2007 .... 2.99
❑95, Mar 1990 .... 1.00
❑96, Apr 1990 .... 1.00
❑32, Feb 2007 .... 2.99
❑97, May 1990 .... 1.00
❑98, Jun 1990 .... 1.00
❑99, Jul 1990; V: Parasite 1.00
❑100, Aug 1990; Giant-size; O: Firestorm; V: Brimstone; Martin Stein becomes Firestorm; Final Issue 2.95
❑Ann 5 .... 1.25

Fire Team
Aircel

❑1, Dec 1990, b&w 2.50
❑2, Jan 1991, b&w 2.50
❑3, Feb 1991, b&w 2.50
❑4, Mar 1991, b&w 2.50
❑5, May 1991, b&w 2.50
❑6, b&w 2.50

Firkin
Knockabout

❑1; Adult 2.50
❑2; Adult 2.50
❑6, b&w; Adult 2.50

First
CrossGen

❑1, Dec 2000 .... 4.00
❑2, Jan 2001 .... 3.00
❑3, Feb 2001 .... 3.00
❑4, Mar 2001 .... 3.00
❑5, Apr 2001, Wraparound cover 3.00
❑6, May 2001 .... 2.95
❑7, Jun 2001 .... 2.95
❑8, Jul 2001 .... 2.95
❑9, Aug 2001 .... 2.95
❑10, Sep 2001 .... 2.95
❑11, Oct 2001 .... 2.95
❑12, Nov 2001 .... 2.95
❑13, Dec 2001 .... 2.95
❑14, Jan 2002 .... 2.95
❑15, Feb 2002 .... 2.95
❑16, Mar 2002 .... 2.95
❑17, Apr 2002 .... 2.95

N-MINT

❑18, May 2002 .... 2.95
❑19, Jun 2002 .... 2.95
❑20, Jul 2002 .... 2.95
❑21, Aug 2002 .... 2.95
❑22, Sep 2002 .... 2.95
❑23, Oct 2002 .... 2.95
❑24, Nov 2002 .... 2.95
❑25, Dec 2002 .... 2.95
❑26, Jan 2003 .... 2.95
❑27, Feb 2003 .... 2.95
❑28, Mar 2003 .... 2.95
❑29, Apr 2003 .... 2.95
❑30, May 2003 .... 2.95
❑31, Jun 2003 .... 2.95
❑32, Jul 2003 .... 2.95
❑33, Aug 2003 .... 2.95
❑34, Sep 2003 .... 2.95
❑35, Nov 2003 .... 2.95
❑36, Dec 2003 .... 2.95
❑37, Dec 2003 .... 2.95

First Adventures
First

❑1, Dec 1985 .... 1.25
❑2, Jan 1986 .... 1.25
❑3, Feb 1986 .... 1.25
❑4, Mar 1986 .... 1.25
❑5, Apr 1986 .... 1.25

First Deterrent
Devious Drawings

❑1, Jul 1996, b&w 2.75

1st Folio
Pacific

❑1, Mar 1984; Joe Kubert School 1.50

1st Issue Special
DC

❑1, Apr 1975; JK (c); JK (w); JK (a); 1: Atlas 7.00
❑2, May 1975; Green Team 5.00
❑3, Jun 1975; Metamorpho 4.00
❑4, Jul 1975; DG, (c); Lady Cop 4.00
❑5, Aug 1975; JK (c); JK (w); JK (a); 1: Manhunters. 1: Manhunter II (Mark Shaw; 1: Manhunters as a group; Manhunter 4.00
❑6, Sep 1975; JK (c); JK (w); JK (a); Dingbats 4.00
❑7, Oct 1975; (c); SD (a); A: Creeper. V: the Firefly 5.00
❑8, Nov 1975; MGr (c); MGr (w); MGr (a); O: Warlord. 1: Deimos. 1: Skartaris. 1: Warlord 15.00
❑9, Dec 1975 JKu (c); A: Doctor Fate 4.00
❑10, Jan 1976; (c); Outsiders 4.00
❑11, Feb 1976; MGr (c); AM (a); Code Name: Assassin 4.00
❑12, Mar 1976, JKu (c); 1&O: Starman II (Mikaal Tomas) 4.00
❑13, Apr 1976, DG, (c); Return of the New Gods 5.00

First King Adventure
ADV Manga

❑1, ca. 2005 .... 9.99
❑2, ca. 2005 .... 9.99

First Kingdom
Bud Plant

❑1; ca. 1974 .... 3.00
❑2; ca. 1975 .... 2.50
❑3; ca. 1975 .... 2.50
❑4 .... 2.50
❑5; ca. 1976 .... 2.50
❑6 .... 2.00
❑7; ca. 1977 .... 2.00
❑8 .... 2.00
❑9 .... 2.00
❑10 .... 2.00
❑11 .... 2.00
❑12 .... 2.00
❑13 .... 2.00
❑14 .... 2.00
❑15 .... 2.00
❑16 .... 2.00
❑17 .... 2.00
❑18 .... 2.00
❑19; ca. 1983 .... 2.00
❑20 .... 2.00
❑21 .... 2.00
❑22 .... 2.00

N-MINT

❑23 .... 2.00
❑24; Final Issue 2.00

First Man
Image

❑1, Jun 1997; cover says 1st Man, indicia says First Man 2.50

First Six Pack
First

❑1, Jul 1987, Nexus, Badger, Jon, etc 1.00
❑2, JSn, HC, MGr (w); PS, LMc (a); Psychoblast, Shatter, American Flagg, Jon Sable, Dreadstar, Whisper 1.00

First Trip to the Moon
Avalon

❑1, b&w; reprints Charlton story 2.50

First Wave
Andromeda

❑1, Dec 2000 .... 2.99

Fishmasters
Slave Labor

❑1, May 1994; adapts TV show 2.95

Fish Police
Fishwrap

❑1, Dec 1985; Indicia title: Inspector Gill of the Fish Police 1.25
❑1/2nd; Indicia changed to "Fish Police" 1.25
❑2, Feb 1986 .... 1.25
❑3, Apr 1986 .... 1.25
❑4, Jun 1986 .... 1.50
❑5, Aug 1986; Indicia says Aug 1986 .... 1.50
❑6, Dec 1986; Indicia says Oct 1986 .... 1.50
❑7, Feb 1987; indicia says Feb 86 .... 1.50
❑8, May 1987 .... 1.50
❑9, Jul 1987 .... 1.50
❑10, Sep 1987 .... 1.50
❑11 1987 .... 1.50

Fish Police
Comico

❑5 1987 .... 1.75
❑6 1987 .... 1.75
❑7 .... 1.75
❑8 .... 1.75
❑9 .... 1.75
❑10 1988 .... 1.75
❑11 1988 .... 1.75
❑12 1988 .... 1.75
❑13 1988 .... 1.75
❑14, Dec 1988 .... 1.75
❑15 .... 1.75
❑16 .... 1.75
❑17, Jun 1989; Wrapaound cover; Last Comico issue 2.50
❑18, Aug 1989, b&w; Black & white format begins, Apple Comics 2.25
❑19, Oct 1989, b&w 2.25
❑20, Mar 1990, b&w 2.25
❑21 1990, b&w 2.25
❑22 1990, b&w 2.25
❑23 1990, b&w 2.25
❑24 1990, b&w 2.25
❑25, Nov 1990, b&w 2.25
❑26, b&w 2.25
❑Special 1, ca. 1987 .... 2.25

Fish Police
Marvel

❑1, Oct 1992, b&w 1.25
❑2, Nov 1992, b&w 1.25
❑3, Dec 1992, b&w 1.25
❑4, Jan 1993, b&w 1.25
❑5, Feb 1993, b&w 1.25
❑6, Mar 1993 .... 1.25

Fish Shticks
Apple

❑1, Nov 1991, b&w 2.00
❑2, b&w 2.00
❑3, May 1992, b&w 2.00
❑4, b&w 2.00
❑5, b&w 2.00
❑6, b&w 2.00

Fission Chicken
Fantagraphics

❑1, ca. 1990, b&w 2.00
❑2, b&w 2.00
❑3, b&w 2.00
❑4, b&w 2.00

Other grades: Multiply price above by 5/6 for VF/NM • 2/3 for VERY FINE • 1/3 for FINE • 1/5 for VERY GOOD • 1/8 for GOOD

Felicia Hardy: The Black Cat

Teams with Spidey to fight Cardiac
©Marvel

Felix the Cat

Early animation icon returns in 1990s title
©Harvey

Femforce

Ms. Victory leads team of heroines
©AC

Ferret

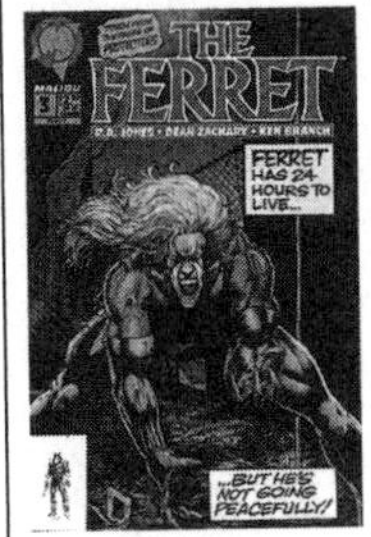

Protectors member gets solo series
©Malibu

Fightin' Air Force

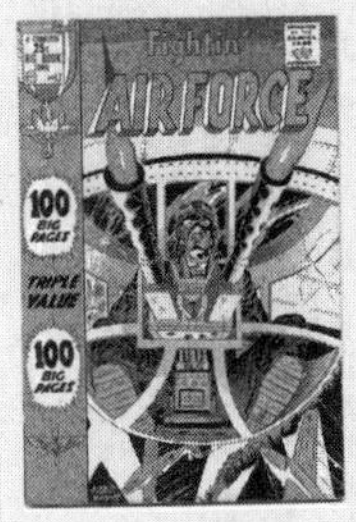

Charlton title featured specific military branch
©Charlton

Fission Chicken: Plan Nine from Vortox
Mu

	N-MINT
❑1, Jul 1994	3.95

Fist of God
Eternity

	N-MINT
❑1, May 1988	2.25
❑2, Jul 1988	1.95
❑3, Sep 1988	1.95
❑4, Nov 1988	1.95

Fist of the North Star
Viz

	N-MINT
❑1, Apr 1989; b&w	2.95
❑2, May 1989; b&w	2.95
❑3, Jun 1989; b&w	2.95
❑4, Jul 1989; b&w	2.95
❑5, Aug 1989; O: Fist; b&w	2.95
❑6, Sep 1989; b&w	2.95
❑7, Oct 1989; b&w	2.95
❑8, Nov 1989; b&w	2.95

Fist of the North Star Part 2
Viz

	N-MINT
❑1	2.75
❑2	2.75
❑3	2.95
❑4	2.95
❑5	2.95
❑6	2.95
❑7	2.95
❑8	2.95

Fist of the North Star Part 3
Viz

	N-MINT
❑1	2.95
❑2	2.95
❑3, Sep 1996	2.95
❑4, Oct 1996	2.95
❑5, Nov 1996	2.95

Fist of the North Star Part 4
Viz

	N-MINT
❑1, Dec 1996	2.95
❑2, Jan 1997	2.95
❑3, Feb 1997	2.95
❑4, Mar 1997	2.95
❑5	2.95
❑6	2.95
❑7	2.95

Five Fists of Science
Image

	N-MINT
❑1, Jul 2006	12.99

Five Years of Pain
Boneyard

	N-MINT
❑1, Jan 1997; Adult	3.95

Flag Fighters
Ironcat

	N-MINT
❑1, Sep 1997, b&w	2.95
❑2 1997, b&w	2.95
❑3, Nov 1997, b&w	2.95
❑4	2.95
❑5	2.95

Flamehead
JNCO

	N-MINT
❑0, Jul 1998; 4.25" x 6.25"; Faerytails backup story	1.00

Flame of Recca
Viz

	N-MINT
❑1, Aug 2003	9.95
❑2, Oct 2003	9.95
❑3, Dec 2003	9.95
❑4, Feb 2004	9.95
❑5, Apr 2004	9.95
❑6, Jun 2004	9.95
❑7, Aug 2004	9.95
❑8, Oct 2004	9.95
❑9, Dec 2004	9.95
❑10, Feb 2005	9.95
❑11, Apr 2005	9.99
❑12, Jun 2005	9.99
❑13, Aug 2005	9.99
❑14, Oct 2005	9.99

Flame (Ajax)
Ajax

	N-MINT
❑1; 1: Flame II	285.00
❑2	165.00
❑3	150.00

Flame Twisters
Brown Study

	N-MINT
❑1, Oct 1994, b&w	2.50
❑2, Mar 1995, b&w	2.50

Flaming Carrot (Kilian)
Kilian

	N-MINT
❑1, Sum 1981, magazine; One-shot	35.00

Flaming Carrot
Image

	N-MINT
❑1, Dec 2004	2.95
❑2, Apr 2005	3.50
❑3, Jul 2005	3.50
❑4, Dec 2005	3.50

Flaming Carrot Comics
Aardvark-Vanaheim

	N-MINT
❑1, May 1984, b&w; 1: Flaming Carrot. Aardvark-Vanaheim publishes	26.00
❑2, Jul 1984, b&w	15.00
❑3, Sep 1984, b&w	12.00
❑4, Nov 1984, b&w	10.00
❑5, Jan 1985, b&w	8.00
❑6, Mar 1985, b&w; becomes Flaming Carrot Comics	8.00
❑7, May 1985, b&w; Renegade begins publishing	7.00
❑8, Aug 1985, b&w	5.00
❑9, Oct 1985, b&w	5.00
❑10, Dec 1985, b&w	4.00
❑11, Mar 1986, b&w	4.00
❑12, May 1986, b&w	4.00
❑13, Jul 1986, b&w	3.00
❑14, Oct 1986, b&w	3.00
❑15, Jan 1987, b&w	3.00
❑15/A, Jan 1987, b&w; no cover price	4.00
❑16, Jun 1987, b&w; 1: Mystery Men	4.00
❑17, Jul 1987, b&w A: Mystery Men	3.00
❑18, Jun 2001, b&w; Dark Horse begins publishing	3.00
❑19, Jun 2001, b&w	3.00
❑20, Nov 1988, b&w	3.00
❑21, Spr 1989, b&w	3.00
❑22, Jun 1989, b&w	3.00
❑23, Nov 1989, b&w	3.00
❑24, Apr 1990, b&w; 48 pages	3.00
❑25, Apr 1991, b&w; A: Teenage Mutant Ninja Turtles. Includes trading cards	3.50
❑26, Jun 1991, b&w A: Teenage Mutant Ninja Turtles	2.50
❑27, b&w; TMc (c); A: Mystery Men. A: Teenage Mutant Ninja Turtles. no indicia	2.50
❑28, Aug 1992, b&w	2.50
❑29, Oct 1992, b&w	2.50
❑30, Dec 1992, b&w; brown background	2.50
❑30/A, Dec 1992, b&w; blue background	2.50
❑32, Dec 2002, b&w; Reid Fleming guest appearance	3.95
❑31, Oct 1994, b&w; A: Herbie. Story originally scheduled for Herbie (Dark Horse) #3	2.50
❑Ann 1, Jan 1997, b&w; A: Mystery Men. 1997 Ann; cardstock cover	5.00

Flaming Carrot Stories
Dark Horse

	N-MINT
❑1; "Version A"	5.00

Flare
Hero

	N-MINT
❑1, Nov 1988; 52 pages	2.75
❑2, Dec 1988; 52 pages	2.75
❑3, Jan 1989; 52 pages	2.75

Flare
Hero

	N-MINT
❑1	3.00
❑2	3.00
❑3, Jan 1989	3.00
❑4, Sum 1991	2.75
❑5; Eternity Smith	2.75
❑6, Sep 1991	2.75
❑7, Nov 1991	2.75
❑8, b&w	2.75
❑9, b&w	2.75
❑10, b&w	2.75
❑11, Apr 1993, b&w	2.75
❑12, Jun 1993, b&w	2.75
❑13, Aug 1993, b&w	2.75
❑14, Oct 1993, b&w	2.75
❑15, Jan 1994	2.75
❑16	2.75
❑Ann 1, b&w	4.50

Flare
Heroic

	N-MINT
❑1	2.99
❑2	2.99
❑3	2.99
❑4	2.99
❑5	2.99
❑25; Goes to whole numbering counting issues from first two Flare series	2.99
❑26	2.99
❑27	2.99
❑28	2.99
❑29	2.99

Flare Adventures
Heroic

	N-MINT
❑1, Feb 1992, Reprints	1.25
❑2, Flip-book format with Champions Classics #2	2.95
❑3, Flip-book format with Champions Classics #3	2.95

Other grades: Multiply price above by 5/6 for VF/NM • 2/3 for VERY FINE • 1/3 for FINE • 1/5 for VERY GOOD • 1/8 for GOOD

N-MINT

❑4, b&w; Flip-book format with Champions Classics #4 ..... 3.95
❑5, b&w; Flip-book format with Champions Classics #5 ..... 3.95
❑6, b&w; Flip-book format with Champions Classics #6 ..... 3.95
❑7, b&w; Flip-book format with Champions Classics #7 ..... 3.95
❑8, b&w; Flip-book format with Champions Classics #8 ..... 3.95
❑9, b&w; Flip-book format 3.95
❑10, b&w; Flip-book format 3.95
❑11, b&w; Flip-book format 3.95
❑12, b&w; Flip-book format 3.95
❑13, b&w; Flip-book format 3.95
❑14, Oct 2005, returns from hiatus; contains League of Champions story . 3.95

Flare First Edition
Hero

❑1; contents will vary 3.50
❑2; contents will vary 3.50
❑3, b&w 3.50
❑4, b&w 4.50
❑5, b&w 4.50
❑6, b&w 3.95
❑7, b&w 3.95
❑8, b&w 3.95
❑9; Sparkplug 3.95
❑10 ..... 3.95
❑11, Oct 1993, b&w 3.95

Flash
DC

❑105, Feb 1959, CI (a); O: Flash II (Barry Allen). 1: Mirror Master. numbering continued from Flash Comics 6500.00
❑106, May 1959; CI (a); 1&O: Pied Piper. 1&O: Gorilla Grodd. 1: Gorilla City 2000.00
❑107, Jul 1959; CI (a); 2: Gorilla Grodd . 1000.00
❑108, Sep 1959 CI (a); A: Gorilla Grodd. 850.00
❑109, Nov 1959, CI (a); 1: Pale People; 2: Mirror Master 650.00
❑110, Jan 1960, MA, CI (a); O: Kid Flash. 1: Weather Wizard. 1: Kid Flash 1500.00
❑111, Mar 1960, CI (a); 2: Kid Flash 450.00
❑112, May 1960, CI (a); O: Elongated Man. 1: Elongated Man 600.00
❑113, Jul 1960, CI (a); 1&O: Trickster 550.00
❑114, Aug 1960; CI (a); O: Captain Cold. 2: Captain Cold 275.00
❑115, Sep 1960, MA, CI (a); 2: Elongated Man 350.00
❑116, Nov 1960, CI (a); Roy Thomas L.O.C 250.00
❑117, Dec 1960, MA, CI (a); 1&O: Captain Boomerang 300.00
❑118, Feb 1961, CI (a) 250.00
❑119, Mar 1961, CI (a); Wedding of Elongated Man and Sue Dearborn 250.00
❑120, May 1961, CI (a) 250.00
❑121, Jun 1961, CI (a); 2: Trickster; Tom Batiuk L.O.C 200.00
❑122, Aug 1961, CI (a); 1&O: Top 200.00
❑123, Sep 1961, CI (a); O: Flash I (Jay Garrick). O: Flash II (Barry Allen). 1: Earth-2 (as an alternate Earth). A: Flash I (Jay Garrick). First Alley Award winner: Best Cover, Best Single Issue of a Comic Book, Best Story 1500.00
❑124, Nov 1961, CI (a); 2: Captain Boomerang; Carmine Infantino L.O.C . 150.00
❑125, Dec 1961, CI (a); 1: cosmic treadmill 150.00
❑126, Feb 1962, CI (a); 1: Daphne Dean; Don Thompson L.O.C 150.00
❑127, Mar 1962, CI (a) 150.00
❑128, May 1962, CI (a); O: Abra Kadabra. 1: Abra Kadabra 150.00
❑129, Jun 1962, CI (a); A: Flash I (Jay Garrick). Don McGregor L.O.C ... 325.00
❑130, Aug 1962, CI (a) 150.00
❑131, Sep 1962, CI (a); A: Green Lantern 125.00
❑132, Nov 1962, CI (a); 2: Daphne Dean 125.00
❑133, Dec 1962, CI (a); Guy H. Lillian L.O.C 125.00
❑134, Feb 1963, CI (a); 1: Ira West; Jerry Bails L.O.C 125.00
❑135, Mar 1963, CI (a); Kid Flash gets new costume; Buddy Saunders L.O.C 125.00
❑136, May 1963, CI (a); 1: Dexter Mles . 125.00
❑137, Jun 1963, CI (a); A: Flash I (Jay Garrick). Vandal Savage 475.00
❑138, Sep 1963, CI (a); 2: Dexter Miles; Jeyy Bails L.O.C 125.00
❑139, Sep 1963, CI (a); O: Professor Zoom; (AKA Reverse-Flash) 125.00
❑140, Nov 1963, CI (a); 1&O: Heat Wave 125.00
❑141, Dec 1963, CI (a); 1: Paul Gambi; 2: Ira West 150.00
❑142, Feb 1964, CI (a) 150.00
❑143, Mar 1964, CI (a); 1: T.O. Morrow. 125.00
❑144, May 1964, CI (a) 100.00
❑145, Jun 1964, CI (a) 100.00
❑146, Aug 1964, CI (a) 100.00
❑147, Sep 1964, CI (a); 2: Mr. Element; 2: Professor Zoom 100.00
❑148, Nov 1964, CI (a); V: Captain Boomerang 100.00
❑149, Dec 1964, CI (a) 100.00
❑150, Feb 1965, CI (a) 100.00
❑151, Mar 1965, CI (a); A: Flash I (Jay Garrick). Guy Lillian L.O.C 80.00
❑152, May 1965, CI (a) 65.00
❑153, Jun 1965, CI (a) 65.00
❑154, Aug 1965, CI (a) 60.00
❑155, Sep 1965, CI (a); 2: Heat Wave 60.00
❑156, Nov 1965, CI (a) 60.00
❑157, Dec 1965, CI (a) 60.00
❑158, Feb 1966, CI (a); Mike Friedrich L.O.C.; Guy Lillian L.O.C 60.00
❑159, Mar 1966, CI (a) 75.00
❑160, Apr 1966; Giant-size; MA, CI (c); MM, CI (a); aka 80 Page Giant #G-21; reprints stories from Flash (1st series) #107, All-Flash #32, Flash (1st series) #113, Flash (1st series) #114, Flash (1st series) #124), and Adventure Comics #123 ..... 90.00
❑161, May 1966, CI (a) 50.00
❑162, Jun 1966, CI (a); Guy Lillian L.O.C 50.00
❑163, Aug 1966, CI (a) 50.00
❑164, Sep 1966, CI (a); Irene Vartanoff L.O.C.; Mike Friedrich L.O.C 50.00
❑165, Nov 1966, CI (a); Wedding of Flash II (Barry Allen) and Iris West 70.00
❑166, Dec 1966, CI (a); Marv Wolfman L.O.C.; Steve Leialoha L.O.C.; "Tempting" reprinted in Super-Team Family #1 ..... 50.00
❑167, Feb 1967, CI (a); O: Flash II (Barry Allen). 1: Mopee 50.00
❑168, Mar 1967, Guy Lillian L.O.C.; Irene Vartanoff L.O.C 95.00
❑169, May 1967; Giant-size; O: Flash II (Barry Allen). aka 80 Page Giant #G-34 70.00
❑170, Jun 1967 ..... 50.00
❑171, Jun 1967, V: Doctor Light; Mark Evanier L.O.C.; Cary Bates L.O.C 50.00
❑172, Aug 1967 ..... 50.00
❑173, Sep 1967 ..... 50.00
❑174, Nov 1967, V: Rogue's Gallery. Flash II reveals identity to wife 50.00
❑175, Dec 1967, Flash II races Superman 175.00
❑176, Feb 1968, Flash II; Mystery in Space #34 ..... 40.00
❑177, Mar 1968 ..... 40.00
❑178, May 1968; Giant-size; aka 80 Page Giant #G-46 ..... 40.00
❑179, May 1968, Flash visits DC Comics 40.00
❑180, Jun 1968 ..... 50.00
❑181, Aug 1968 ..... 35.00
❑182, Sep 1968 ..... 35.00
❑183, Nov 1968 ..... 35.00
❑184, Dec 1968 ..... 50.00
❑185, Feb 1969 ..... 35.00
❑186, Mar 1969 ..... 35.00
❑187, May 1969; Giant-size; aka Giant #G-58 ..... 65.00
❑188, May 1969 ..... 35.00
❑189, Jun 1969, JKu (c); RA (a) 35.00
❑190, Aug 1969 ..... 35.00
❑191, Sep 1969 ..... 35.00
❑192, Nov 1969 ..... 25.00
❑193, Dec 1969 ..... 25.00
❑194, Feb 1970, The Flash II (Barry Allen); Strange Adventures #13 ..... 40.00
❑195, Mar 1970 ..... 25.00
❑196, May 1970; Giant-size; aka Giant #G-70 ..... 40.00
❑197, May 1970 ..... 25.00
❑198, Jun 1970 ..... 25.00
❑199, Aug 1970, 1: Colonel K 25.00
❑200, Sep 1970 ..... 25.00
❑201, Nov 1970, Flash II (Barry Allen); Flash I (Jay Garrick); Strange Adventures #73 ..... 20.00
❑202, Dec 1970 ..... 20.00
❑203, Feb 1971 ..... 25.00
❑204, Mar 1971, Kid Flash 20.00
❑205, May 1971; Giant-size; aka Giant #G-82 ..... 35.00
❑206, May 1971, Flash; Elongated Man . 20.00
❑207, Jun 1971, Flash II (Barry Allen); Kid Flash 17.00
❑208, Aug 1971; Giant-size; Elongated Man back-up 17.00
❑209, Sep 1971; Giant-size; V: Captain Boomerang. V: Trickster. V: Captain Boomerang; V: Trickster; Elongated Man: The Flash (1st Series) #119; Flash II (Barry Allen); Kid Flash 17.00
❑210, Dec 1971; Giant-size; in future 17.00
❑211, Dec 1971; Giant-size; Golden Age Flash back-up 17.00
❑212, Feb 1972; Elongated Man backup 17.00
❑213, Mar 1972; Flash II (Barry Allen): The Flash (1st Series) #137; Flash II (Barry Allen): The Flash (1st Series) #146; Giant-size 25.00
❑214, Apr 1972, CI (a); a.k.a. DC 100-Page Super Spectacular #DC-11; wraparound cover; reprints O: Metal Men; Reprints Showcase #37 ..... 40.00
❑215, May 1972; A: Golden Age Flash. V: Vandal Savage. giant 35.00
❑216, Jun 1972; Flash II (Barry Allen); Kid Flash; Flash I (Jay Garrick): All-Flash #30 17.00
❑217, Sep 1972, FMc, DG, NA, IN (a); Green Lantern/Green Arrow back-up; Green Arrow back-up 17.00
❑218, Nov 1972, FMc, NA, IN (a) 17.00
❑219, Jan 1973, NA (a); last Green Arrow back-up 17.00
❑220, Mar 1973, Flash II (Barry Allen); Green Lantern II (Hal Jordan) 15.00
❑221, May 1973 ..... 15.00
❑222, Aug 1973 ..... 15.00
❑223, Oct 1973, NA (a); Green Lantern back-up 15.00
❑224, Dec 1973, Flash II (Barry Allen); Green Lantern II (Hal Jordan) 15.00
❑225, Feb 1974 ..... 15.00
❑226, Apr 1974, NA (a); V: Captain Cold. Flash II (Barry Allen); Green Lantern II (Hal Jordan) 15.00
❑227, Jun 1974, Flash II (Barry Allen); Green Lantern II (Hal Jordan) 15.00
❑228, Aug 1974, Flash II (Barry Allen); Green Lantern II (Hal Jordan) 15.00
❑229, Oct 1974, 100 Page giant; V: Rag Doll. V: Rag Doll; Green Lantern: Green Lantern (2nd Series) #29; Kid Flash: The Flash (1st Series) #133; Johnny Quick: Adventure Comics #117; Flash I (Jay Garrick): All-Flash #31; Flash II (Barry Allen): The Flash (1st Series) #145; Flash II (Barry Allen) and Flash I (Jay Garrick) 30.00
❑230, Dec 1974, V: Doctor Alchemy; Green Lantern 15.00
❑231, Feb 1975; V: Doctor Alchemy 15.00
❑232, Apr 1975, 100 Page giant; Flash II (Barry Allen) and Kid Flash; Green Lantern II and Flash II: Green Lantern #13; Flash I (Jay Garrick): Flash Comics #94; Johnny Quick: Adventure Comics #121; Flash II (Barry Allen): The Flash (1st Series) #124 ..... 30.00
❑233, May 1975; 100 Page giant; Green Lantern 10.00
❑234, Jun 1975; Green Lantern 10.00
❑235, Aug 1975; A: Green Lantern. A: Golden Age Flash. V: Vandal Savage 10.00
❑236, Sep 1975 A: Doctor Fate. A: Golden Age Flash 10.00
❑237, Nov 1975 A: Green Lantern 10.00
❑238, Dec 1975 ..... 7.00
❑239, Feb 1976; V: Mirror Master; V: Pied Piper; V: Trickster; V: Top 7.00
❑240, Mar 1976, 1: Itty 7.00
❑241, May 1976, V: Mirror Master; V: Heat Wave; Flash II (Barry Allen); Green Lantern II (Hal Jordan) 7.00
❑242, Jun 1976 ..... 7.00
❑243, Aug 1976, D: The Top 7.00
❑244, Sep 1976 ..... 7.00
❑245, Nov 1976, V: Plant-Master; Jason Woodrue transforms into Floronic Man 7.00
❑246, Jan 1977 ..... 12.00
❑247, Mar 1977 ..... 7.00
❑248, Apr 1977, 1: Master Villain 7.00
❑249, May 1977, 1: Super-Hero (Flash in disguise) 7.00

Fightin' Army

Lonely War of Capt. Willy Schultz highlight

©Charlton

Fighting American

Attempted revival by Rob Liefeld

©Awesome

Fightin' Marines

Leatherneck adventures in various theaters

©Charlton

Fightin' Navy

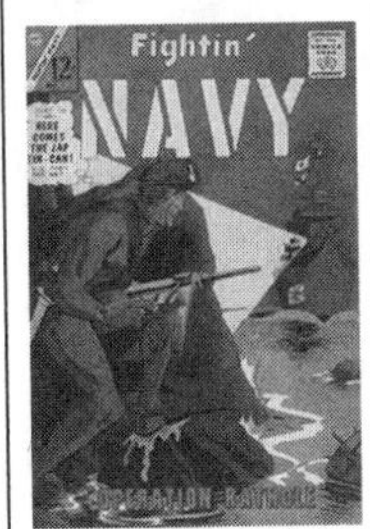

Battles above and beneath the waves

©Charlton

Finals

Series delayed after Columbine, Colo., shooting

©DC

	N-MINT
❑250, Jun 1977, 1: Golden Glider. V: Golden Glider	7.00
❑251, Aug 1977	7.00
❑252, Sep 1977	7.00
❑253, Sep 1977	7.00
❑254, Oct 1977, V: Rogue's Gallery	7.00
❑255, Nov 1977	7.00
❑256, Dec 1977, V: Rogue's Gallery	7.00
❑257, Jan 1978	7.00
❑258, Feb 1978	7.00
❑259, Mar 1978	7.00
❑260, Apr 1978	7.00
❑261, May 1978, 1: Ringmaster; V: Golden Glider	7.00
❑262, Jun 1978, V: Golden Glider	7.00
❑263, Jul 1978, V: Golden Glider	4.00
❑264, Aug 1978, V: Golden Glider	4.00
❑265, Sep 1978	4.00
❑266, Oct 1978, V: Heat Wave	4.00
❑267, Nov 1978, V: Heat Wave	4.00
❑268, Dec 1978	4.00
❑268/Whitman, Dec 1978, Whitman variant	12.00
❑269, Jan 1979	4.00
❑270, Mar 1979, 1: Clown; V: the Clown	4.00
❑271, Mar 1979, RB (a); V: the Clown	3.50
❑272, Apr 1979, RB (a); V: the Clown	3.50
❑273, May 1979, RA (c); RB (a)	3.50
❑273/Whitman, May 1979, RB (a); Whitman variant	7.00
❑274, Jun 1979, RA (c); RB (a)	5.00
❑274/Whitman, Jun 1979, RB (a); Whitman variant	7.00
❑275, Jul 1979, D: Iris West Allen (Flash II's wife)	7.00
❑275/Whitman, Jul 1979, D: Iris West Allen (Flash II's wife). Whitman variant	7.00
❑276, Aug 1979, A: JLa.	3.50
❑276/Whitman, Aug 1979, A: JLA. Whitman variant	7.00
❑277, Sep 1979, A: JLA. V: Mirror Master	3.50
❑278, Oct 1979, V: Captain Boomerang; V: Heat Wave; V: Yorkin	3.50
❑278/Whitman, Oct 1979, Whitman variant	7.00
❑279, Nov 1979, V: Yorkin	3.50
❑280, Dec 1979, V: Yorkin	3.50
❑281, Jan 1980, V: Professor Zoom	3.50
❑282, Feb 1980, V: Professor Zoom	3.50
❑283, Mar 1980, V: Professor Zoom	3.50
❑283/Whitman, Mar 1980, Whitman variant	7.00
❑284, Apr 1980, V: Limbo Lord	3.50
❑285, May 1980, V: Trickster	3.50
❑286, Jun 1980, 1: Rainbow Raider; V: Rainbow Raider	3.50
❑286/Whitman, Jun 1980, 1: Rainbow Raider. Whitman variant	7.00
❑287, Jul 1980, V: Dr. Alchemy	3.50
❑288, Aug 1980, V: Dr. Alchemy	3.50
❑289, Sep 1980, DH (c); GP, DH (a); O: Firestorm. George Perez's first work at DC	5.00
❑290, Oct 1980, DH (c); GP, DH (a); A: Firestorm. O: Firestorm	3.00
❑291, Nov 1980, V: Sabre-Tooth	3.00
❑292, Dec 1980, V: Mirror Master; V: Hyena	3.00
❑293, Jan 1981, A: Firestorm. V: Pied Piper, V: Atomic Skull, Flash appearance in Firestorm	3.00
❑294, Feb 1981, O: Typhoon	3.00
❑295, Mar 1981, V: Gorilla Grodd. O: Typhoon; V: Grodd	3.00
❑296, Apr 1981, V: Typhoon	3.00
❑297, May 1981, V: Captain Cold; V: Multiplex	3.00
❑298, Jun 1981, V: Shade; V: Multiplex.	3.00
❑299, Jul 1981, V: Rainbow Raider; V: Shade	3.00
❑300, Aug 1981; Giant-size; CI (c); FH, CI (a); O: Flash. A: New Teen Titans. wraparound cover	5.00
❑301, Sep 1981, CI, DG (c); CI (a); V: Hyena	3.00
❑302, Oct 1981, V: Golden Glider; V: Hyena; Firestorm	3.00
❑303, Nov 1981, V: Top; V: Golden Glider; V: Hyena	3.00
❑304, Dec 1981, 1: Colonel Computron; V: Colonel Computron	3.00
❑305, Jan 1982, V: Limbo Lord	3.50
❑306, Feb 1982, CI (c); CI, KG (a); O: Doctor Fate; V: Mirror Master; Mirror Master appearane	3.50
❑307, Mar 1982, CI (c); CI, KG (a); Doctor Fate back-up	2.50
❑308, Apr 1982, CI (c); CI, KG (a)	2.50
❑309, May 1982, CI (c); CI, KG (a); O: Flash	2.50
❑310, Jun 1982, KG (c); CI, KG (a); V: Colonel Computron; V: Captain Boomerang	2.50
❑311, Jul 1982, JA (c); CI, KG (a); V: Colonel Computron; V: Captain Boomerang	2.50
❑312, Aug 1982, GK (c); CI, KG (a); 1: Creed Phillips	2.50
❑313, Sep 1982, CI (c); CI, KG (a); V: Grodd	2.50
❑314, Oct 1982, 1: The Eradicator	2.50
❑315, Nov 1982, V: Goldface	2.50
❑316, Dec 1982, V: Goldface	2.50
❑317, Jan 1983, V: Goldface	2.50
❑318, Feb 1983, CI (c); DaG, CI (a); 1: Big Sir. 1: Big Sir	2.50
❑319, Mar 1983, V: Eradicator	2.50
❑320, Apr 1983, V: Eradicator	2.50
❑321, May 1983	2.50
❑322, Jun 1983, V: Reverse Flash. Flash Vs. Reverse Flash	2.50
❑323, Jul 1983, V: Reverse Flash. Flash Vs. Reverse Flash	2.50
❑324, Aug 1983, D: Reverse-Flash; V: Reverse-Flash; Kid Flash appearance (as Wally West)	2.50
❑325, Sep 1983	2.50
❑326, Oct 1983	2.50
❑327, Nov 1983, V: Grodd	2.50
❑328, Dec 1983, V: Reverse-Flash; Reprinted from Flash #165	2.50
❑329, Jan 1984; V: Gorilla Grodd. V: Grodd	2.50
❑330, Feb 1984; V: Grodd	2.50
❑331, Mar 1984; CI (c); CI (a); A: Gorilla Grodd. V: Grodd	2.50
❑332, Apr 1984; A: Green Lantern. V: Rainbow Raider	2.50
❑333, May 1984	2.50
❑334, Jun 1984	2.50
❑335, Jul 1984; V: Pied Piper	2.50
❑336, Aug 1984	2.50
❑337, Sep 1984; V: Pied Piper	2.50
❑338, Oct 1984; V: Big Sir. 1: Big Sir; V: Pied Piper;	2.50
❑339, Nov 1984; V: Big Sir	2.50
❑340, Dec 1984; Trial begins	2.50
❑341, Jan 1985; V: Big Sir	2.50
❑342, Feb 1985	2.50
❑343, Mar 1985	2.50
❑344, Apr 1985; O: Kid Flash. Reprints from Flash #110 and #149	2.50
❑345, May 1985	2.50
❑346, Jun 1985	2.50
❑347, Jul 1985	2.50
❑348, Aug 1985	2.50
❑349, Sep 1985 CI (c); FMc, CI (a)	2.50
❑350, Oct 1985; Double-size; Final Issue; 48 pages	6.50
❑Ann 1, Dec 1963; O: Elongated Man. O: Kid Flash. Golden-Age Flash story.	400.00
❑Ann 1/2nd, Nov 2001; Replica edition; O: Elongated Man. O: Kid Flash. 80 pages; Golden-Age Flash story	6.95

Flash
DC

	N-MINT
❑0, Oct 1994; O: Flash III (Wally West)..	4.00
❑1, Jun 1987; BG (a); Wally West as Flash	5.00
❑2, Jul 1987; BG (a); V: Vandal Savage.	3.00
❑3, Aug 1987; 1: Tina McGee. V: Kilg%re	2.50
❑4, Sep 1987; V: Kilg%re	2.50
❑5, Oct 1987; 1: Speed Demon	2.50
❑6, Nov 1987	2.50
❑7, Dec 1987; 1: Red Trinity; 1: Blue Trinity; T.M. Maple L.O.C	2.50
❑8, Jan 1988; Millennium	2.50
❑9, Feb 1988; 1: Chunk. Millennium	2.50
❑10, Mar 1988; V: Chunk	2.50
❑11, Apr 1988	2.50
❑12, May 1988; Bonus Book #2	2.50
❑13, Jun 1988; V: Vandal Savage	2.50
❑14, Jul 1988; V: Vandal Savage	2.50
❑15, Aug 1988; GP (c); 1: Mason Trollbridge	2.50
❑16, Sep 1988; GP (c); V: Blue Trinity	2.50
❑17, Oct 1988 GP (c)	2.50
❑18, Nov 1988	2.50
❑19, Dec 1988; Bonus Book #9	2.50
❑20, Dec 1988	2.50
❑21, Jan 1989; Invasion!	2.00
❑22, Jan 1989; A: Manhunter. Invasion!	2.00
❑23, Feb 1989; V: Abra Kadabra	2.00
❑24, Mar 1989	2.00
❑25, Apr 1989; 1: Porcupine Man	2.00
❑26, May 1989	2.00
❑27, Jun 1989; V: Captain Cold; V: Golden Glider	2.00
❑28, Jul 1989; 1: Linda Park; V: Captain Cold; V: Golden Glider	2.00
❑29, Aug 1989; A: Phantom Lady. V: Merlyn; V: Syonide	2.00
❑30, Sep 1989	2.00
❑31, Oct 1989; 2: Linda Park; V: Comfort	1.50
❑32, Nov 1989; V: Mr. Sprynt; V: Turtle.	1.50
❑33, Dec 1989	1.50
❑34, Jan 1990; V: Turtle	1.50
❑35, Feb 1990; V: Turtle; V: Sloe and Steddy	1.50
❑36, Mar 1990	1.50
❑37, Apr 1990	1.50
❑38, May 1990	1.50
❑39, Jun 1990	1.50
❑40, Jul 1990; V: Doctor Alchemy	1.50

Other grades: Multiply price above by 5/6 for VF/NM • 2/3 for VERY FINE • 1/3 for FINE • 1/5 for VERY GOOD • 1/8 for GOOD

N-MINT

❑41, Aug 1990; V: Doctor Alchemy; D: Doctor Alchemy II 1.50
❑42, Sep 1990; V: Kilg%re 1.50
❑43, Oct 1990; V: Kilg%re 1.50
❑44, Nov 1990 V: Gorilla Grodd 1.50
❑45, Dec 1990; V: Gorilla Grodd 1.50
❑46, Jan 1991; A: Vixen. V: Grodd 1.50
❑47, Feb 1991; A: Vixen. V: Gorilla Grodd 1.50
❑48, Mar 1991 .... 1.50
❑49, Apr 1991; V: Vandal Savage 1.50
❑50, May 1991; GS; V: Vandal Savage; Giant-Size; Christina from Blue Trinity becomes Lady Flash 2.50
❑51, Jun 1991; V: Proletariat 1.50
❑52, Jul 1991; V: Pyranis; V: Dr. Pain; V: Pgrunt 1.50
❑53, Aug 1991; Superman 1.50
❑54, Sep 1991; V: meta-human terrorist group, Altered Strain 1.50
❑55, Oct 1991; War of the Gods 1.50
❑56, Nov 1991; Icicle 1.50
❑57, Dec 1991; Icicle 1.50
❑58, Jan 1992 .... 1.50
❑59, Feb 1992; A: Power Girl. V: Last Resort 1.50
❑60, Mar 1992; FMc (a); V: Last Resort. 1.50
❑61, Apr 1992 .... 1.50
❑62, May 1992; MWa (w); O: Flash 2.00
❑63, May 1992; MWa (w); O: Flash 2.00
❑64, Jun 1992; O: Flash; V: Mirror Master 1.50
❑65, Jun 1992; MWa (w); O: Flash 1.50
❑66, Jul 1992; MWa (w); Aquaman 1.50
❑67, Aug 1992; MWa (w); V: Abra Kadabra 1.50
❑68, Sep 1992; MWa (w); V: Abra Kadabra 1.50
❑69, Oct 1992; MWa (w); A: Green Lantern. V: Hector Hammond. V: Gorilla Grodd; V: Grood 1.50
❑70, Nov 1992; MWa (w); A: Green Lantern. V: Hector Hammond. V: Gorilla Grodd; V: Grodd; Contiuned from Green Lantern #31 .... 1.50
❑71, Dec 1992; MWa (w); V: Doctor Alchemy. V: Doctor Alchemy 1.50
❑72, Jan 1993; MWa (w); V: Doctor Alchemy 1.50
❑73, Feb 1993 MWa (w); A: Jay Garrick. 1.50
❑74, Mar 1993 MWa (w) 1.50
❑75, Apr 1993 MWa (w) 1.50
❑76, May 1993; MWa (w); 1: Max Mercury (Quicksilver) 1.50
❑77, Jun 1993 MWa (w) 1.50
❑78, Jul 1993; MWa (w); V: Reverse Flash 1.50
❑79, Jul 1993; Giant-size; MWa (w); O: Reverse Flash; V: Reverse Flash 2.50
❑80, Aug 1993; MWa (w); regular cover 1.50
❑80/Variant, Aug 1993; MWa (w); foil cover 2.50
❑81, Sep 1993 MWa (w); A: Nightwing. A: Starfire 1.50
❑82, Oct 1993 MWa (w); A: Nightwing. A: Starfire 1.50
❑83, Oct 1993 MWa (w) 1.50
❑84, Nov 1993; MWa (w); V: Razer 1.50
❑85, Dec 1993; MWa (w); V: Razer 1.50
❑86, Jan 1994 MWa (w) 1.50
❑87, Feb 1994 MWa (w) 1.50
❑88, Mar 1994; MWa (w); 1: Chillblaine; V: Chillblaine 2.00
❑89, Apr 1994 MWa (w) 2.00
❑90, May 1994; MWa (w); V: Abra Kadabra; Flash cleared of charges 2.00
❑91, Jun 1994; MWa (w); Flash uses Jesse Quick's formula to enhance speed 4.00
❑92, Jul 1994; MWa (w); 1: Impulse 8.00
❑93, Aug 1994; MWa (w); 2: Impulse; V: Kobra 5.00
❑94, Sep 1994; MWa (w); Zero Hour 3.00
❑95, Nov 1994; V: Kobra 3.00
❑96, Dec 1994; MWa (w); V: Kobra 2.00
❑97, Jan 1995; MWa (w); 1: Chillblaine II 2.00
❑98, Feb 1995; MWa (w); V: Kobra 2.00
❑99, Mar 1995; MWa (w); V: Kobra 2.00
❑100, Apr 1995; Giant-size; MWa (w); V: Kobra 3.00
❑100/Variant, Apr 1995; Giant-size; MWa (w); Holo-grafix cover 4.00
❑101, May 1995 .... 2.00
❑102, Jun 1995; V: Mongul 2.00
❑103, Jul 1995; V: Demons 2.00
❑104, Aug 1995; MWa (w); V: Demons.. 2.00
❑105, Sep 1995; V: Mirror Master 2.00

N-MINT

❑106, Oct 1995; MWa (w); return of Frances Kane 2.00
❑107, Nov 1995; A: Captain Marvel. Underworld Unleashed 2.00
❑108, Dec 1995; 1: Savitar; V: Savitar; Continued Impulse #9 .... 2.00
❑109, Jan 1996; continues in Impulse #10 2.00
❑110, Feb 1996; MWa (w); continues in Impulse #11 .... 2.00
❑111, Mar 1996; MWa (w); V: Savitar 2.00
❑112, Apr 1996; MWa (w); A: John Fox. V: Chillblaine 2.00
❑113, May 1996 MWa (w) 2.00
❑114, Jun 1996; MWa (w); A: Don and Dawn Allen. V: Chillblaine 2.00
❑115, Jul 1996 .... 2.00
❑116, Aug 1996; MWa (w); V: Abra Kadabra; V: Doctor Polaris; Doctor Polaris and Abra Kadabra cause new ice age 2.00
❑117, Sep 1996; Flash returns to present 2.00
❑118, Oct 1996 MWa (w) 2.00
❑119, Nov 1996; MWa (w); Final Night.. 2.00
❑120, Dec 1996; MWa (w); A: Trickster. Wally West asked to leave Keystone... 2.00
❑121, Jan 1997; MWa (w); V: Top 2.00
❑122, Feb 1997; MWa (w); Flash becomes a commuting super-hero 2.00
❑123, Mar 1997; MWa (w); Cover tribute to Flash (1st series) #123 .... 2.00
❑124, Apr 1997; MWa (w); V: Major Disaster 2.00
❑125, May 1997; V: Major Disaster 2.00
❑126, Jun 1997; MWa (w); V: Major Disaster. return of Rogues Gallery 2.00
❑127, Jul 1997; MWa (w); A: Neron. A: Jay Garrick. V: Soulless Rogues Gallery. V: Captain Boomerang; V: Weather Wizard; V: Heat Wave; V: Captain Cold; V: Mirror Master 2.00
❑128, Aug 1997; MWa (w); A: Wonder Woman. A: Superman. A: Martian Manhunter. A: Green Lantern. V: Soulless Rogues Gallery; V: Neron. 2.00
❑129, Sep 1997; MWa (w); V: Neron; V: Soulless Rogues Gallery 2.00
❑130, Oct 1997; Wally has his legs broken 2.00
❑131, Nov 1997; Wally gets new costume 2.00
❑132, Dec 1997; A: Mirror Master. Face cover 1.95
❑133, Jan 1998; V: Mirror Master 1.95
❑134, Feb 1998; A: Thinker. A: Wildcat. A: Johnny Thunder. A: Ted Knight. A: Sentinel. A: Jay Garrick. V: Captain Boomerang; V: Captain Cold 1.95
❑135, Mar 1998; cover forms triptych with Green Arrow #130 and Green Lantern #96 .... 1.95
❑136, Apr 1998 A: Krakkl 1.95
❑137, May 1998 .... 1.95
❑138, Jun 1998; 1: Black Flash; D: Krakkl 1.95
❑139, Jul 1998; D: Linda Park. D: Linda Park; V: Weather Wizard 1.95
❑140, Aug 1998; Linda's funeral 1.95
❑141, Sep 1998; V: Black Flash; Linda Park returns 1.95
❑142, Oct 1998; Wedding of Wally and Linda 1.95
❑143, Dec 1998; V: Cobalt Blue 1.99
❑144, Jan 1999; O: Cobalt Blue 1.99
❑145, Feb 1999 MWa (w); A: Cobalt Blue 1.99
❑146, Mar 1999 MWa (w); A: Cobalt Blue 1.99
❑147, Apr 1999 MWa (w); A: Reverse Flash. A: Cobalt Blue 1.99
❑148, May 1999; MWa (w); A: Barry Allen. V: Cobalt Blue; V: Reverse Flash 1.99
❑149, Jun 1999; MWa (w); Crisis ending changed 1.99
❑150, Jul 1999; MWa (w); Wally vs. Anti-Monitor 2.95
❑151, Aug 1999; MWa (w); Teen Titans adventure 1.99
❑152, Sep 1999; MWa (w); V: Dr. Alchemy 1.99
❑153, Oct 1999; MWa (w); V: Folded Man 1.99
❑154, Nov 1999; new Flash reveals identity 1.99
❑155, Dec 1999; MWa (w); V: Replicant 1.99
❑156, Jan 2000; MWa (w); V: Abra Kadabra; V: Replicant 1.99
❑157, Feb 2000; V: Replicant; V: Abra Kadabra; V: Reverse Flash 1.99
❑158, Mar 2000; V: Abra Kadabra; V: Replicant; V: Reverse Flash 1.99
❑159, Apr 2000 MWa (w) 1.99
❑160, May 2000; V: Kobra 1.99

N-MINT

❑161, Jun 2000 A: JSA. A: Flash I (Jay Garrick) 1.99
❑162, Jul 2000; V: Felix Faust 1.99
❑163, Aug 2000; V: Turtle 2.25
❑164, Sep 2000; BB (c); O: Flash (Jay Garrick); O: (Barry Allen) 2.25
❑165, Oct 2000; BB (c); 1: Plunder 2.25
❑166, Nov 2000; BB (c); V: Plunder 2.25
❑167, Dec 2000 BB (c) 2.25
❑168, Jan 2001; BB (c); V: Brother Grimm 2.25
❑169, Feb 2001; BB (c); V: Brother Grimm 2.25
❑170, Mar 2001; BB (c); 1: Cicada (in shadow); V: Typhoon 2.25
❑171, Apr 2001; BB (c); 1: Cicada; 1: Jared Morillo; V: Magenta 2.25
❑172, May 2001; BB (c); V: Magenta; V: Cicada 2.25
❑173, Jun 2001; BB (c); V: Magenta; V: Cicada 2.25
❑174, Jul 2001; BB (c); 1: Tar Pit 2.25
❑175, Aug 2001; BB (c); V: Weather Wizard 2.25
❑176, Sep 2001; BB (c); V: Weather Wizard 2.25
❑177, Oct 2001; BB (c); V: Plunder 2.25
❑178, Nov 2001; BB (c); V: Grodd 2.25
❑179, Dec 2001; JLee (c); Joker: Last Laugh crossover 2.25
❑180, Jan 2002; BB (c); 1: Peek-a-Boo.. 2.25
❑181, Feb 2002; D: Morillo; O: Fallout; V: Fallout 2.25
❑182, Mar 2002; BB (c); D: Chillblaine; O: Captain Cold; O: Golden Glider; V: Chillblaine 2.25
❑183, Apr 2002; BB (c); 1: Trickster II (Axel Walker); D: Rainbow Raider; V: Trickster (Axel Walker) 2.25
❑184, May 2002; BB (c); V: Thinker; V: Network; V: Rogues 2.25
❑185, Jun 2002; BB (c); O: Thinker; V: Rogues; V: Thinker; V: Network 2.25
❑186, Jul 2002; BB (c); O: Blacksmith; O: Goldface; V: Network; V: Thinker; V: Rogues 2.25
❑187, Aug 2002; BB (c); V: Thinker; V: Rogues; V: Network 2.25
❑188, Sep 2002; V: Network; V: Rogues 2.95
❑189, Oct 2002 .... 2.25
❑190, Nov 2002; O: Pied Piper; Pied Piper spotlight 2.25
❑191, Dec 2002; V: Brother Grimm 2.25
❑192, Jan 2003; V: Gorilla Grodd; V: Murmur; V: Girder; V: Tar Pit; V: Cicada; V: Double Down; V: Blacksmith 2.25
❑193, Feb 2003; V: Gorilla Grodd 2.25
❑194, Mar 2003; V: Gorilla Grodd 2.25
❑195, Apr 2003; V: Top 2.25
❑196, May 2003; O: Zoom; V: Peek-A-Boo 2.25
❑197, Jun 2003; 1: Zoom; 1: Ashley Zolomon; 1: Professor Zoom II 2.25
❑198, Jul 2003; O: Flash; V: Zoom 2.25
❑199, Aug 2003, V: Zoom 2.25
❑200, Sep 2003, V: Zoom; Wraparound cover; Giant-size 3.50
❑201, Oct 2003 .... 2.25
❑202, Nov 2003, 1: Mr. Element II 2.25
❑203, Dec 2003, 1: Mr. Element II 2.25
❑204, Jan 2004 .... 2.25
❑205, Feb 2004, Wally West regains his memories 2.25
❑206, Mar 2004, D: Mr. Element II 6.00
❑207, Apr 2004 .... 6.00
❑208, May 2004 .... 5.00
❑209, Jun 2004 .... 4.00
❑210, Jul 2004 .... 3.00
❑210/2nd, Aug 2004 .... 2.25
❑211, Aug 2004, V: Grodd; V: Gorilla Grodd 4.00
❑212, Sep 2004, O: Mirror Master II (Evan McCulloch) 2.25
❑213, Oct 2004 .... 2.25
❑214, Nov 2004, Identity Crisis cross-over; Identity Crisis tie-in 6.00
❑215, Dec 2004, Identity Crisis tie-in 5.00
❑216, Jan 2005, Identity Crisis crossover 6.00
❑217, Feb 2005; Identity Crisis tie-in 5.00
❑218, Mar 2005, O: Heat Wave; V: Murmur; Trickster apperarance 4.00
❑219, Apr 2005, V: Cheetah; V: Zoom 9.00
❑220, May 2005, V: Captain Cold; V: Mirror Master; V: Weather Wizard; V: Trickster 6.00
❑221, Jun 2005 .... 5.00

Other grades: Multiply price above by 5/6 for VF/NM • 2/3 for VERY FINE • 1/3 for FINE • 1/5 for VERY GOOD • 1/8 for GOOD

Firestorm

Short-lived first series led to later success
©DC

Firestorm, the Nuclear Man

Was Fury of Firestorm
©DC

1st Folio

Showcase of new artists' potential
©Pacific

1st Issue Special

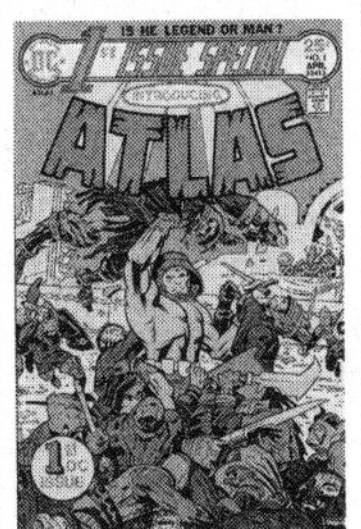

Tryout title yielded Warlord
©DC

First Kiss

Romance title features early loves
©Charlton

N-MINT

❑222, Jul 2005; D: Top 4.00
❑223, Aug 2005 4.00
❑224, Sep 2005; V: Zoom; V: Professor Zoom 2.50
❑225, Oct 2005; V: Zoom; V: Professor Zoom; Last Geoff Johns 2.50
❑226, Nov 2005 2.50
❑227, Dec 2005 2.50
❑228, Jan 2006 2.50
❑229, Feb 2006 2.50
❑230, Mar 2006, Final issue; Series goes on hiatus 2.50
❑1000000, Nov 1998 MWa (w) 3.00
❑Ann 1, ca. 1987; BG (a) 5.00
❑Ann 2; Private Lives 2.00
❑Ann 3; Who's Who entries 2.25
❑Ann 4; V: Paradox; V: Rainbow Raider; V: Golden Glider; V: Chillblaine; Armageddon 2001; ca. 1991 2.25
❑Ann 5; MWa (w); V: Trickster; V: Weather Wizard; V: Captain Boomerang; V: Golden Glider; V: Chillblaine; ca. 1992; 1992 Ann; Eclipso: The Darkness Within 2.75
❑Ann 6; MWa (w); 1: Argus; Bloodlines: Earthplague; ca. 1993 2.50
❑Ann 7; Elseworlds 2.95
❑Ann 8, ca. 1995; MWa (w); Year One 3.50
❑Ann 9, ca. 1996; Legends of the Dead Earth 2.95
❑Ann 10, ca. 1997; DG (a); Pulp Heroes; 1997 Ann 3.95
❑Ann 11, ca. 1998; A: Johnny Quick. Ghosts; 1998 Ann 3.95
❑Ann 12, Oct 1999; JLApe; 1999 Ann 2.95
❑Ann 13, Sep 2000; 2000 Ann;Planet DC 3.50
❑GS 1, Aug 1998; JBy, MWa (w); JBy (a); A: Flash II (Barry Allen). A: Lightning. A: Flash III (Wally West). A: Jesse Quick. A: Impulse. A: Flash I (Jay Garrick). A: Captain Boomerang. A: Flash IV (John Fox). 80-Page Giant 4.95
❑GS 2, Apr 1999; 80-Page Giant 4.95
❑Special 1; 50th anniversary issue; JKu (c); MWa (w); CI, IN (a); 1: John Fox. 3 Flashes 3.50
❑TV 1 1991; JBy, MWa (w); JKu (a); A: Kid Flash. TV Special; Stories about TV show Flash 3.95

Flash & Green Lantern: The Brave and the Bold
DC

❑1, Oct 1999 2.50
❑2, Nov 1999 2.50
❑3, Dec 1999 2.50
❑4, Jan 2000 2.50
❑5, Feb 2000; Flash (Barry Allen) enlisted as temporary Green Lantern 2.50
❑6, Mar 2000; Star Sapphire 2.50

Flashback
Special

❑1 3.00
❑2 3.00
❑3, ca. 1974 3.00
❑4 1974 3.00
❑5 1974 3.00
❑6 1974 3.00
❑7 1974 3.00
❑8 1974 3.00
❑9 1974 3.00
❑10, ca. 1974 3.00
❑11 1974 3.00
❑12 1974 3.00
❑13 1974 3.00
❑14, ca. 1974 3.00
❑15 3.00
❑16 3.00
❑17 3.00
❑18 3.00
❑19 3.00
❑20 3.00
❑21 3.00
❑22 3.00
❑23 3.00
❑24 3.00
❑25 3.00
❑26 3.00
❑27 3.00

Flash Gordon
Gold Key

❑1, Jun 1965, Dinosaur cover 26.00

Flash Gordon
King

❑1, Sep 1966, King begins publishing 25.00
❑2, Nov 1966 20.00
❑3, Jan 1967 20.00
❑4, Mar 1967 20.00
❑5, May 1967 20.00
❑6, Jul 1967 20.00
❑7, Aug 1967 20.00
❑8, Sep 1967 10.00
❑9, Oct 1967, AR (a) 10.00
❑10, Nov 1967, AR (a) 10.00
❑11, Dec 1967 10.00
❑12, Feb 1969, Charlton begins publishing 10.00
❑13, Apr 1969 10.00
❑14, Jun 1969 10.00
❑15, Aug 1969 8.00
❑16, Oct 1969 8.00
❑17, Nov 1969 8.00
❑18, Jan 1969 8.00
❑19, Sep 1978, Gold Key begins publishing 8.00
❑20, Nov 1978 6.00
❑21, Jan 1979 6.00
❑22, Mar 1979, Gold Key cover 6.00
❑23, May 1979 6.00
❑24, Jul 1979, Whitman begins publishing 5.00
❑25, Sep 1979 4.00
❑26, Nov 1979, Hostess ad: The Human Torch in "Sparks Fly" 4.00
❑27, Jan 1980 4.00
❑28, Mar 1980 4.00
❑29, May 1980 4.00
❑30, Oct 1980, Released outside U.S. market 8.00
❑30/50¢, ca. 1981; Later printing for U.S. market 4.00
❑31, Mar 1981, AW (a); The Movie Adaptation 3.00
❑32, Apr 1981, AW (a); The Movie Adaptation 3.00
❑33, May 1981, AW (a); The Movie Adaptation 3.00
❑34, Oct 1981 3.00
❑35, Dec 1981 3.00
❑36, Feb 1982 3.00
❑37, ca. 1982 3.00

Flash Gordon
DC

❑1, Jun 1988 2.00
❑2, Jul 1988 1.50
❑3, Aug 1988 1.50
❑4, Sep 1988 1.50
❑5, Oct 1988 1.50
❑6, Nov 1988 1.50
❑7, Dec 1988 1.50
❑8, Win 1988 1.50
❑9, Hol 1988 1.50

Flash Gordon
Marvel

❑1, Jun 1995; wraparound cardstock cover 2.95
❑2, Jul 1995; wraparound cardstock cover 2.95

Flash Gordon: The Movie
Golden Press

❑1 AW (a) 2.50

Flash/Green Lantern: Faster Friends
DC

❑1; prestige format; continued from Green Lantern/Flash: Faster Friends 4.95

Flash: Our Worlds at War
DC

❑1, Oct 2001 2.95

Flash Plus
DC

❑1, Jan 1997 2.95

Flash Secret Files
DC

❑1, Nov 1997; bios on major cast members and villains; timeline 4.95
❑2, Nov 1999; updates on cast 4.95
❑3, Nov 2001; V: Murmur; V: Girder; V: Magenta 4.95

Flash: The Fastest Man Alive
DC

❑1, Sep 2006 6.00
❑2, Sep 2006 2.99
❑3, Nov 2006 2.99
❑4, Nov 2006 2.99
❑5, Dec 2006, Velluto credited on cover; But no work by him in issue; Velluto credited on cover, but no work by him in issue 2.99
❑6, Feb 2007, D: Griffin 2.99
❑7, Mar 2007 2.99
❑8 2.99
❑9 2.99
❑10 2.99
❑11 2.99
❑12 2.99
❑13 2.99

Flash: Iron Heights
DC

❑1, Oct 2001; 1: Murmur; 1: Girder; 1: Blacksmith; 1: Double Down; 1: Iron Heights 5.95

Flash: Time Flies
DC

❑nn, ca. 2002 5.95

Flashmarks
Fantagraphics
❑1, b&w 2.95

Flashpoint
DC
❑1, Dec 1999; Elseworlds 2.95
❑2, Jan 2000 2.95
❑3, Feb 2000 2.95

Flatline Comics Presents...
Flatline
❑1, Dec 1993 2.50

Flaxen
Dark Horse
❑1; photo back cover 2.95

Flaxen: Alter Ego
Caliber
❑1, Mar 1995 2.95

Fleener
Zongo
❑1, b&w 2.95
❑2, Dec 1996, b&w 2.95
❑3, b&w 2.95

Flesh
Fleetway-Quality
❑1 2.95
❑2 2.95
❑3 2.95
❑4 2.95

Flesh & Blood
Brainstorm
❑1; Partial foil cover 2.95
❑1/Ashcan; Ashcan preview from 1995 Philadelphia Comic Con 1.00

Flesh & Blood: Pre-Existing Conditions
Blindwolf
❑1 2.95

Flesh and Bones
Upshot
❑1 2.00
❑2 2.00
❑3 2.00
❑4 2.00

Flesh Crawlers
Kitchen Sink
❑1, ca. 1994 2.50
❑2, Jan 1995 2.50
❑3, Feb 1995 2.50

Flesh Gordon
Aircel
❑1, Mar 1992; Adult 2.95
❑2, Apr 1992; Adult 2.95
❑3, May 1992; Adult 2.95
❑4, Jun 1992; Adult 2.95

Fleshpot
Fantagraphics / Eros
❑1, Oct 1997; Adult 2.95

Flex Mentallo
DC / Vertigo
❑1, Jun 1996 10.00
❑2, Jul 1996; EC parody cover 8.00
❑3, Aug 1996; Dark Knight parody cover 8.00
❑4, Sep 1996; Final Issue 8.00

Flickering Flesh
Boneyard
❑1, Mar 1993 2.50

Flicker's Fleas
Fifth Wheel
❑1 3.00

Flinch
DC / Vertigo
❑1, Jun 1999 JLee (a) 3.00
❑2, Jul 1999 BSz (a) 2.50
❑3, Aug 1999 2.50
❑4, Sep 1999 PG (a) 2.50
❑5, Oct 1999 2.50
❑6, Nov 1999 2.50
❑7, Dec 1999 DGry (w) 2.50
❑8, Jan 2000 2.50
❑9, Feb 2000 2.50
❑10, Mar 2000 2.50
❑11, Apr 2000 2.50
❑12, May 2000 2.50
❑13, Jul 2000 2.50
❑14, Sep 2000 BWr (a) 2.50
❑15, Nov 2000 2.50
❑16, Jan 2001; Final Issue 2.50

Flint Armbuster Jr. Special
Alchemy
❑1, b&w; NN 2.95

Flintstone Kids
Marvel / Star
❑1, Aug 1987 2.00
❑2, Oct 1987 1.50
❑3, Dec 1987 1.50
❑4, Feb 1988 1.50
❑5, Apr 1988 1.50
❑6, Jun 1988 1.50
❑7, Aug 1988 1.50
❑8, Oct 1988 1.50
❑9, Dec 1988 1.50
❑10, Feb 1989 1.50
❑11, Apr 1989 1.50

Flintstones
Dell / Gold Key
❑1, a.k.a. Dell Giant #48 55.00
❑2, Dec 1961 38.00
❑3, Jan 1962 30.00
❑4, Mar 1962 30.00
❑5, May 1962 30.00
❑6, Jul 1962 24.00
❑7, Oct 1962, First Gold Key issue 24.00
❑8 20.00
❑9, Feb 1963 20.00
❑10, Apr 1963 20.00
❑11, Jun 1963 18.00
❑12, Jul 1963 18.00
❑13, Sep 1963 18.00
❑14, Oct 1963 18.00
❑15, Nov 1963 18.00
❑16, Jan 1964 18.00
❑17, Mar 1964 18.00
❑18, May 1964 18.00
❑19, Jul 1964 18.00
❑20, Aug 1964 18.00
❑21, Sep 1964 15.00
❑22, Oct 1964 15.00
❑23, Nov 1964 15.00
❑24, Jan 1965 15.00
❑25, Mar 1965 15.00
❑26, May 1965 15.00
❑27, Jul 1965 15.00
❑28, Aug 1965 15.00
❑29, Sep 1965 15.00
❑30, Oct 1965 15.00
❑31, Dec 1965 12.00
❑32, Feb 1966 12.00
❑33, Apr 1966 12.00
❑34, Jun 1966 12.00
❑35, Aug 1966 12.00
❑36, Oct 1966 12.00
❑37, Dec 1966 12.00
❑38, Feb 1967 12.00
❑39, Apr 1967 12.00
❑40, Jun 1967 12.00
❑41, Aug 1967 9.00
❑42, Oct 1967 9.00
❑43, Dec 1967 9.00
❑44, Feb 1968 9.00
❑45, Apr 1968 9.00
❑46, Jun 1968 9.00
❑47, Aug 1968 9.00
❑48, Oct 1968 9.00
❑49, Dec 1968 9.00
❑50, Feb 1969 9.00
❑51, Apr 1969 9.00
❑52, Jun 1969 9.00
❑53, Aug 1969 9.00
❑54, Oct 1969 9.00
❑55, Dec 1969 9.00
❑56, Feb 1970 9.00
❑57, Apr 1970 9.00
❑58, May 1970 9.00
❑59, Jul 1970 9.00
❑60, Sep 1970 9.00

Flintstones
Charlton
❑1, Nov 1970 36.00
❑2, Jan 1971 22.00
❑3, Mar 1971 14.00
❑4, May 1971 14.00
❑5, Jul 1971 14.00
❑6, Sep 1971 9.00
❑7, Oct 1971 9.00
❑8, Nov 1971 9.00
❑9, Dec 1971 9.00
❑10, Jan 1972 9.00
❑11, Feb 1972 7.00
❑12, Mar 1972 7.00
❑13, May 1972 7.00
❑14, Jun 1972 7.00
❑15, Jul 1972 7.00
❑16, Aug 1972 7.00
❑17, Sep 1972 7.00
❑18, Nov 1972 7.00
❑19, Dec 1972 7.00
❑20, Jan 1973 7.00
❑21, Mar 1973 5.00
❑22, Apr 1973 5.00
❑23, ca. 1973 5.00
❑24, ca. 1973 5.00
❑25, ca. 1973 5.00
❑26, Oct 1973 5.00
❑27 1973 5.00
❑28, Jan 1974 5.00
❑29, May 1974 5.00
❑30, ca. 1974 5.00
❑31, ca. 1974 4.00
❑32, ca. 1974 4.00
❑33, Oct 1974 4.00
❑34, Nov 1974 4.00
❑35, Feb 1975 4.00
❑36, Mar 1975 4.00
❑37, May 1975 4.00
❑38, Jun 1975 4.00
❑39, ca. 1975 4.00
❑40, ca. 1975 4.00
❑41, ca. 1975 4.00
❑42, Dec 1975 4.00
❑43, Feb 1976 4.00
❑44, Mar 1976, Ray Dirgo, Jay Gill credits 4.00
❑45, ca. 1976 4.00
❑46, ca. 1976 4.00
❑47, Aug 1976, Ray Dirgo, Jay Gill credits 4.00
❑48, Oct 1976, Ray Dirgo credits 4.00
❑49, Dec 1976 4.00
❑50, Feb 1977 4.00

Flintstones 3-D
Blackthorne
❑1, Apr 1987; a.k.a. Blackthorne 3-D #19 2.50
❑2, Fal 1987; a.k.a. Blackthorne 3-D #22 2.50
❑3 2.50
❑4 2.50

Flintstones
Marvel
❑1, Oct 1977 5.00
❑2, Dec 1977 3.00
❑3, Feb 1978 3.00
❑4, Apr 1978 3.00
❑5, Jun 1978 3.00
❑6, Aug 1978 3.00
❑7, Oct 1978 3.00
❑8, Dec 1978 3.00
❑9, Feb 1979 3.00

Flintstones
Harvey
❑1, Sep 1992 2.50
❑2, Jan 1993, Dino talks 2.00
❑3, ca. 1993 2.00
❑4, Sep 1993 2.00
❑5, Oct 1993 2.00
❑6, Nov 1993 2.00
❑7, Dec 1993 2.00
❑8, Jan 1994 2.00
❑9, Feb 1994 2.00
❑10, Mar 1994 2.00
❑11, Apr 1994 2.00
❑12, May 1994 2.00
❑13, Jun 1994 2.00

Flintstones
Archie
❑1, Sep 1995 2.00
❑2, Oct 1995 1.50
❑3, Nov 1995 1.50

Fish Police

Spawned poor animated TV effort

©Fishwrap

Flaming Carrot Comics

Mystery Men first appeared in Bob Burden title

©Aardvark-Vanaheim

Flare

Female heroine fights crime in leather jacket

©Hero

Flash

Picks up numbering of Flash Comics

©DC

Flash

Wally West takes over as the new Flash

©DC

N-MINT

❑4, Dec 1995 — 1.50
❑5, Jan 1996 — 1.50
❑6, Feb 1996 — 1.50
❑7, Mar 1996 — 1.50
❑8, Apr 1996 — 1.50
❑9, May 1996 — 1.50
❑10, Jun 1996 — 1.50
❑12, Aug 1996 — 1.50
❑13, Sep 1996 — 1.50
❑14, Oct 1996 — 1.50
❑15, Nov 1996 — 1.50
❑16, Dec 1996 — 1.50
❑17, Jan 1997 — 1.50
❑18, Feb 1997, Fred becomes a cartoonist — 1.50
❑19, Mar 1997, A: Great Gazoo — 1.50
❑20, Apr 1997 — 1.50
❑21, May 1997 — 1.50
❑22, Jun 1997, A: Gruesomes — 1.50

Flintstones and the Jetsons
DC

❑1, Aug 1997 — 2.00
❑2, Sep 1997 — 2.00
❑3, Oct 1997, Spacely turned into baby — 2.00
❑4, Nov 1997, Gazoo turns Fred and Barney into women — 2.00
❑5, Dec 1997, Judy and Elroy throw a party — 2.00
❑6, Jan 1998 — 2.00
❑7, Feb 1998, Spies issue — 2.00
❑8, Mar 1998, Kung Fu issue — 2.00
❑9, Apr 1998 — 2.00
❑10, May 1998 — 2.00
❑11, Jun 1998, Time travel — 2.00
❑12, Jul 1998 — 2.00
❑13, Aug 1998 — 2.00
❑14, Oct 1998 — 2.00
❑15, Nov 1998, Super-Fred — 2.00
❑16, Dec 1998 — 2.00
❑17, Jan 1999 — 2.00
❑18, Feb 1999, A: Great Gazoo. It's A Wonderful Life homage — 2.00
❑19, Mar 1999, Jetsons Bizarro story — 2.00
❑20, Apr 1999 — 2.00
❑21, May 1999, Fred and George switch places — 1.99

Flintstones at the New York World's Fair
Dell

❑1, ca. 1964 — 48.00

Flintstones Big Book
Harvey

❑1, Nov 1992 — 1.95
❑2, Mar 1993 — 1.95

Flintstones Bigger and Boulder
Gold Key

❑1, Nov 1962 — 65.00
❑2, Jun 1966 — 45.00

Flintstones Doublevision
Harvey

❑1, Sep 1994, polybagged with double vision glasses, adaptation of movie — 2.95

Flintstones Giant Size
Harvey

❑2, ca. 1992 — 2.50
❑3, ca. 1993 — 2.50

N-MINT

Flintstones with Pebbles and Bamm-Bamm
Gold Key

❑1, Nov 1965, Regular paper (non-glossy) cover — 50.00

Flipper
Gold Key

❑1, Apr 1966 — 25.00
❑2, Nov 1966 — 18.00
❑3, Nov 1967 — 18.00

Floaters
Dark Horse

❑1, Sep 1993, b&w — 2.50
❑2, Oct 1993, b&w — 2.50
❑3, Nov 1993, b&w — 2.50
❑4, Dec 1993, b&w — 2.50
❑5, Jan 1994 — 2.50

Flock of Dreamers
Kitchen Sink

❑1, Nov 1997, b&w; NN; Anthology — 12.95

Flood Relief
Malibu

❑1; Ultraverse Red Cross giveaway — 5.00

Flowers
Drawn and Quarterly

❑1 — 2.95

Flowers on the Razorwire
Boneyard

❑1, b&w; Adult — 2.95
❑2, b&w; Adult — 2.95
❑3, b&w; Adult — 2.95
❑4, Nov 1994, b&w; Adult — 2.95
❑5, May 1995, b&w; Adult — 2.95
❑6, May 1995, b&w; Adult — 2.95
❑7, Oct 1995, b&w; Adult — 2.95
❑8, b&w; Adult — 2.95
❑9, b&w; Adult — 2.95
❑10, Apr 1997, b&w; Adult — 2.95

Fly
Archie / Red Circle

❑1, May 1983, O: Shield — 3.00
❑2, Jul 1983 — 1.50
❑3, Oct 1983 — 1.50
❑4, Dec 1983, RB (w); SD (a) — 1.50
❑5, Feb 1984 — 1.50
❑6, Apr 1984 — 1.50
❑7, Jun 1984 — 1.50
❑8, Aug 1984 — 1.50
❑9, Oct 1984 — 1.50

Fly
DC / Impact

❑1, Aug 1991; O: The Fly — 1.25
❑2, Sep 1991; V: Chromium — 1.00
❑3, Oct 1991; 1: Lt. Walker Odell — 1.00
❑4, Nov 1991; V: Black Hood — 1.00
❑5, Dec 1991; V: Arachnus — 1.00
❑6, Jan 1992; 1: Blackjack; 1: Dolphus; 1: General Mechanix — 1.00
❑7, Feb 1992; 1: Jason Troy Sr — 1.00
❑8, Mar 1992 — 1.00
❑9, Apr 1992; 1: Fireball; Includes trading cards; Continued from Comet (Impact) #10 & into Web #9 — 1.00

N-MINT

❑10, May 1992 — 1.00
❑11, Jun 1992 — 1.25
❑12, Jul 1992; 1: Domino (Impact) — 1.25
❑13, Aug 1992; 1: Tremor — 1.25
❑14, Sep 1992; 1: Domino (Impact) — 1.25
❑15, Oct 1992 — 1.25
❑16, Nov 1992 — 1.25
❑17, Dec 1992; Final Issue — 1.25
❑Ann 1; trading card — 2.00

Fly Man
Archie / Radio

❑32, Jul 1965, Series continued from Adventures of the Fly #31 — 32.00
❑33, Sep 1965 — 20.00
❑34, Nov 1965 — 20.00
❑35, Jan 1966, O: The Black Hood (back-up story); The Shield backup story — 16.00
❑36, Mar 1966, O: The Web (back-up story), Shield back-up story — 16.00
❑37, May 1966, The Shield back-up story — 16.00
❑38, Jul 1966, The Web backup story — 16.00
❑39, Sep 1966, Series continued in Mighty Comics #40 — 16.00

Flying Colors 10th Anniversary Special
Flying Colors

❑1, Sep 1998 — 2.95

Flying Nun
Dell

❑1, Feb 1968 — 32.00
❑2, May 1968 — 20.00
❑3, Aug 1968 — 20.00
❑4, Nov 1968, Sally Fields photo cover — 20.00

Flying Saucers
Dell

❑1, Apr 1967, FS (a) — 26.00
❑2, Jul 1967 — 15.00
❑3, Oct 1967, FS (a) — 15.00
❑4, Nov 1967 — 15.00
❑5, Oct 1969, Final Issue — 15.00

Focus
DC

❑1, Sum 1987; MWa (w); BSz, GP (a); no cover price — 1.00

Foes
Ram

❑1 — 1.95

Fog City Comics
Stampart

❑1; Adult — 1.00

Foodang
Continuüm

❑1, Jul 1994, b&w; foil cover — 1.95
❑Ashcan 1; Ashcan promotional edition; 1: Foodang. Previews Foodang #1; Flip Book with The Dark Ashcan #1 — 1.00

Foodang
August House

❑1, Jan 1995, oversized trading card; enhanced cover — 2.50
❑2, Mar 1995 — 2.50

Food First Comics
IFDP

❑1 — 3.00

Other grades: Multiply price above by 5/6 for VF/NM • 2/3 for VERY FINE • 1/3 for FINE • 1/5 for VERY GOOD • 1/8 for GOOD

- ❑1/2nd, b&w; 2nd printing 3.00
- ❑1/3rd, b&w; 3rd printing 3.00

Foofur
Marvel / Star

- ❑1, Aug 1987 1.00
- ❑2, Oct 1987 1.00
- ❑3, Dec 1987 1.00
- ❑4, Feb 1988 1.00
- ❑5, Apr 1988 1.00
- ❑6, Jun 1988 1.00

Foolkiller
Marvel

- ❑1, Oct 1990; 1&O: FoolKiller III. A: Greg Salinger (FoolKiller II) 2.00
- ❑2, Nov 1990 2.00
- ❑3, Dec 1990; cover says Nov, indicia says Dec 2.00
- ❑4, Jan 1991 2.00
- ❑5, Feb 1991 TD (a) 2.00
- ❑6, Apr 1991; TD (a); Indicia says March 2001 2.00
- ❑7, Apr 1991; Indicia says April 2001 2.00
- ❑8, Jul 1991; A: Spider-Man. Wrong date on cover; Indicia says June 1991 2.00
- ❑9, Sep 1991 2.00
- ❑10, Oct 1991 2.00

FOOM Magazine
Marvel

- ❑1, Feb 1973; Fantastic Four article and index; Stan Lee, Roy Thomas, and Gerry Conway biographies 45.00
- ❑2, Sum 1973; New Steranko cove, Bullpen photos, Article profiling the Hulk's Silver Age appearances 30.00
- ❑3, Fal 1973; Spider-Man issue; Interview with Stan Lee 25.00
- ❑4, Win 1973; Jim Steranko biography; Dr. Doom article and quotations 25.00
- ❑5, Spr 1974; Thing article; Deathlok article; Steve Gerber profile; Rich Buckler profile 20.00
- ❑6, Sum 1974; Neal Adams design sketches for Marvel Preview #1 20.00
- ❑7, Fal 1974; Bullpen photos 20.00
- ❑8, Dec 1974 20.00
- ❑9, Mar 1975; "Special Cosmic Issue"; Silver Surfer article; Captain Marvel article; Watcher article; Warlock article 20.00
- ❑10, Jun 1975 20.00
- ❑11, Sep 1975 20.00
- ❑12, Dec 1975; Vision article; Scarlet Witch article 20.00
- ❑13, Mar 1976; Daredevil articles and checklist; Wally Wood character designs for Daredevil characters 20.00
- ❑14, Jun 1976; Roy Thomas interview; Robert E. Howard article and chronology; Conan checklist; Red Sonja and King Kull articles 20.00
- ❑15, Sep 1976; Howard the Duck Presidential Campaign issue; Steve Gerber interview 20.00
- ❑16, Dec 1976; Unpublished Captain America #125 cover; Bullpen photos, articles; Marie Severin interview 20.00
- ❑17, Mar 1977; Cardstock cover; Kiss back cover; Stan Lee interview, including stills from razor TV commercial starring Stan Lee; Reprint of Lee/Romita New York Times Magazine page from 4/16/1972; Preview of Howard the Duck newspaper strip 20.00
- ❑18, Jun 1977; John Romita article; Photos of Wendy Pini in Red Sonja costume 20.00
- ❑19, Fal 1977; Special Defenders Issue . 20.00
- ❑20, Win 1977; Edgar Rice Burroughs issue 20.00
- ❑21, Spr 1978; Science Fiction Special 25.00
- ❑22, Aut 1978; Mighty Marvel Media Special 40.00

Foot Soldiers
Dark Horse

- ❑1, Jan 1996 2.95
- ❑2, Feb 1996 2.95
- ❑3, Mar 1996 2.95
- ❑4, Apr 1996 2.95

Foot Soldiers
Image

- ❑1, Sep 1997, b&w 2.95
- ❑2, Nov 1997, b&w 2.95
- ❑3, Jan 1998, b&w 2.95
- ❑4, Mar 1998, b&w 2.95
- ❑5, May 1998, b&w 2.95

Foozle
Eclipse

- ❑1 1985 1.75
- ❑2 1985 1.75
- ❑3, Aug 1985; Reprints original Foozle Story in color 1.75

Forbidden Frankenstein
Fantagraphics / Eros

- ❑1, May 1991, b&w; Adult 2.25
- ❑2, Sep 1991, b&w; Adult 2.50

Forbidden Kingdom
Eastern

- ❑1, Nov 1987, b&w 1.95
- ❑2, Jan 1988, b&w 1.95
- ❑3, Mar 1988, b&w 1.95
- ❑4, May 1988, b&w 1.95
- ❑5, Jul 1988, b&w 1.95
- ❑6, b&w 1.95
- ❑7, b&w 1.95
- ❑8, b&w 1.95

Forbidden Knowledge
Last Gasp

- ❑1, May 1975 4.00

Forbidden Knowledge: Adventure Beyond the Doorway to Souls with Radical Dreamer
Mark's Giant Economy Size

- ❑1, b&w; infinity cover 3.50

Forbidden Planet
Innovation

- ❑1, May 1992, Movie adaptation 2.50
- ❑2, Jul 1992, Movie adaptation 2.50
- ❑3, Sep 1992, Movie adaptation 2.50
- ❑4, Spr 1993, Spring 1993; Movie adaptation 2.50

Forbidden Subjects
Angel

- ❑0; Adult 2.95
- ❑0/A; Nude edition A; Adult 3.95
- ❑0/B; Nude edition B; Adult 3.95

Forbidden Subjects: Candy Kisses
Angel

- ❑1; Censored cover 3.00
- ❑1/B; Adult cover 3.00

Forbidden Tales of Dark Mansion
DC

- ❑5, Jun 1972; Series continued from The Dark Mansion of Forbidden Love #4 .. 35.00
- ❑6, Aug 1972 17.00
- ❑7, Oct 1972, JO (w); HC, TD (a) 17.00
- ❑8, Dec 1972 12.00
- ❑9, Feb 1973 12.00
- ❑10, Apr 1973 10.00
- ❑11, Jul 1973 10.00
- ❑12, Sep 1973 10.00
- ❑13, Nov 1973 10.00
- ❑14, Jan 1974 10.00
- ❑15, Mar 1974, Final Issue 15.00

Forbidden Vampire
Angel

- ❑0, Adult 2.95

Forbidden Worlds
ACG

- ❑100, Nov 1961, CCB (a) 20.00
- ❑101, Jan 1962 16.00
- ❑102, Mar 1962 16.00
- ❑103, May 1962 16.00
- ❑104, Jul 1962 16.00
- ❑105, Aug 1962 16.00
- ❑106, Sep 1962 16.00
- ❑107, Oct 1962 16.00
- ❑108, Nov 1962 16.00
- ❑109, Jan 1963 16.00
- ❑110, Mar 1963, A: Herbie 35.00
- ❑111, May 1963 16.00
- ❑112, Jul 1963 16.00
- ❑113, Aug 1963 16.00
- ❑114, Sep 1963, A: Herbie 35.00
- ❑115, Oct 1963 16.00
- ❑116, Nov 1963, A: Herbie 30.00
- ❑117, Jan 1964 16.00
- ❑118, Mar 1964 16.00
- ❑119, May 1964 16.00
- ❑120, Jul 1964 16.00
- ❑121, Aug 1964 12.00
- ❑122, Sep 1964 12.00
- ❑123, Oct 1964 12.00
- ❑124, Nov 1964 12.00
- ❑125, Jan 1965, 1&O: Magicman 25.00
- ❑126, Mar 1965 12.00
- ❑127, May 1965 12.00
- ❑128, Jul 1965, A: Magicman 14.00
- ❑129, Aug 1965, Magicman story 12.00
- ❑130, Sep 1965, A: Magicman 14.00
- ❑131, Oct 1965 12.00
- ❑132, Nov 1965 12.00
- ❑133, Jan 1966 12.00
- ❑134, Mar 1966 12.00
- ❑135, May 1966 12.00
- ❑136, Jul 1966 12.00
- ❑137, Aug 1966 12.00
- ❑138, Sep 1966 12.00
- ❑139, Oct 1966 12.00
- ❑140, Nov 1966 12.00
- ❑141, Jan 1967 10.00
- ❑142, Mar 1967 10.00
- ❑143, May 1967 10.00
- ❑144, Jul 1967 10.00
- ❑145, Aug 1967, Final Issue 10.00

Forbidden Worlds
A-Plus

- ❑1, b&w; Reprints 2.50

Forbidden Worlds
Avalon

- ❑1 2.95

Forbidden X Angel
Angel

- ❑1; Adult 2.95

Forbidden Zone
Galaxy Entertainment

- ❑1, Adult 5.95

Force 10
Crow

- ❑1; 1: Impel 2.50
- ❑1/Ashcan; Ashcan preview edition; 1: Flux. 1: Armadillos. 1: Spook. 1: Rukh. 1: Lodestar. 1: Teknik. 1: Leprechaun. 1: Force 10 3.00

Force of Buddha's Palm
Jademan

- ❑1, ca. 1988 2.00
- ❑2, ca. 1988 1.95
- ❑3, ca. 1988 1.95
- ❑4, ca. 1988 1.95
- ❑5, ca. 1988 1.95
- ❑6, ca. 1989 1.95
- ❑7, ca. 1989 1.95
- ❑8, ca. 1989 1.95
- ❑9, ca. 1989 1.95
- ❑10, ca. 1989 1.95
- ❑11, ca. 1989 1.95
- ❑12, ca. 1989 1.95
- ❑13, ca. 1989 1.95
- ❑14, ca. 1989 1.95
- ❑15, ca. 1989 1.95
- ❑16, ca. 1989 1.95
- ❑17, ca. 1989 1.95
- ❑18, ca. 1990 1.95
- ❑19, ca. 1990 1.95
- ❑20, ca. 1990 1.95
- ❑21, ca. 1990 1.95
- ❑22, ca. 1990 1.95
- ❑23, ca. 1990 1.95
- ❑24, ca. 1990 1.95
- ❑25, ca. 1990 1.95
- ❑26, ca. 1990 1.95
- ❑27, ca. 1990 1.95
- ❑28, ca. 1990 1.95
- ❑29, ca. 1990 1.95
- ❑30, ca. 1991 1.95
- ❑31, ca. 1991 1.95
- ❑32, ca. 1991 1.95
- ❑33, ca. 1991 1.95
- ❑34, ca. 1991 1.95
- ❑35, ca. 1991 1.95
- ❑36, ca. 1991 1.95
- ❑37, ca. 1991 1.95
- ❑38, ca. 1991 1.95

Flash & Green Lantern: The Brave and the Bold

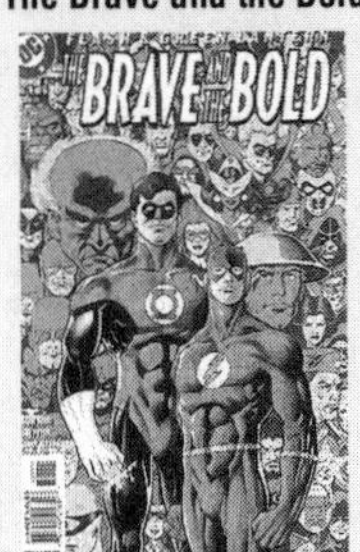

Mark Waid and Tom Peyer power team-up
©DC

Flash/Green Lantern: Faster Friends

Continues from Green Lantern/Flash
©DC

Flash Plus

Flash and Nightwing take a road trip
©DC

Flash Secret Files

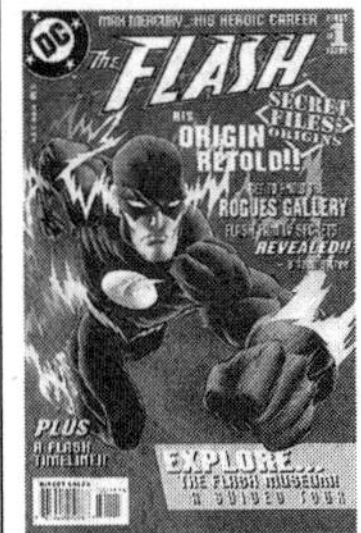

Encyclopedic info bout the Flash's world
©DC

Flash, The: Iron Heights

Viral outbreak hits Keystone City prison
©DC

	N-MINT
❑39, ca. 1991	1.95
❑40, ca. 1991	1.95
❑41, ca. 1991	1.95
❑42, ca. 1992	1.95
❑43, Feb 1992	1.95
❑44, Mar 1992	1.95
❑45	1.95
❑46, Apr 1992	1.95
❑47, May 1992	1.95
❑48, Jun 1992	1.95
❑49, Jul 1992	1.95
❑50, Sep 1992	1.95
❑51, Oct 1992	1.95
❑52, Nov 1992	1.95
❑53, Dec 1992	1.95
❑54, Jan 1993	1.95
❑55, Feb 1993	1.95

Force Seven
Lone Star

❑1, Aug 1999	2.95
❑2, Sep 1999	2.95
❑3, Mar 2000	2.95

Force Works
Marvel

❑1, Jul 1994; Giant-size; Pop-up cover	3.95
❑2, Aug 1994	1.50
❑3, Sep 1994	1.50
❑4, Oct 1994	1.50
❑5, Nov 1994; V: Black Brigade; V: Ember	1.50
❑5/CS, Nov 1994; with sericel	2.95
❑6, Dec 1994; V: Mandarin; Continued in War Machine #9	1.50
❑7, Jan 1995; Hands of the Mandarin	1.50
❑8, Feb 1995	1.50
❑9, Mar 1995; 1: Dreamguard	1.50
❑10, Apr 1995	1.50
❑11, May 1995	1.50
❑12, Jun 1995; 48 page flipbook; War Machine continued War Machine #15 then Iron Man #317	2.50
❑13, Jul 1995	1.50
❑14, Aug 1995	1.50
❑15, Sep 1995	1.50
❑16, Oct 1995	1.50
❑17, Nov 1995; 1: Cybermancer	1.50
❑18, Dec 1995	1.50
❑19, Jan 1996; V: Mantis; V: Kang; Continued from Avengers #393; Continued in War Machine #22	1.50
❑20, Feb 1996; Continued War Machine #23	1.50
❑21, Mar 1996; V: Ultron	1.50
❑22, Apr 1996; V: Ultron; Final Issue	1.50
❑Ashcan 1; ashcan edition	0.75

Foreplay
NBM

❑1; Adult	18.95

Fore/Punk
Parody

❑1/A; punk cover	2.50
❑1/B; fore cover	2.50

Foreternity
Antarctic

❑1, Jul 1997, b&w	2.95
❑2, Sep 1997, b&w	2.95
❑3, Nov 1997, b&w	2.95
❑4, Jan 1998, b&w	2.95

Forever Amber
Image

	N-MINT
❑1/A, Jul 1999	2.95
❑1/B, Jul 1999, alternate cover has white background	2.95
❑2, Aug 1999	2.95
❑3, Sep 1999	2.95
❑4, Oct 1999	2.95

Forever Eve
Shadow Song

❑1, Jul 1997, b&w	2.95
❑2, Dec 1997, b&w	2.95
❑3, Jun 1998, b&w	2.95
❑4, Sep 1998, b&w	2.95

Forever Maelstrom
DC

❑1, Jan 2003; Includes preview of Superman: Metropolis #1	2.95
❑2, Feb 2003	2.95
❑3, Mar 2003	2.95
❑4, Apr 2003	2.95
❑5, May 2003	2.95
❑6, Jun 2003	2.95

Forever Now
Entertainment

❑1	1.50
❑2	1.50

Forever People
DC

❑1, Mar 1971, JK (c); JK (w); JK (a); O: Forever People. Darkseid	35.00
❑2, May 1971, JK (c); JK (w); JK (a); 1: Desaad. 1: Mantis (DC). Darkseid	20.00
❑3, Jul 1971, JK (c); JK (w); JK (a); 1: Glorious Godfrey. Darkseid	18.00
❑4, Sep 1971; JK (c); JK (w); JK (a); Darkseid	18.00
❑5, Nov 1971; Giant-size; JK (c); JK (w); JK (a)	18.00
❑6, Jan 1972; Giant-size; JK (c); JK (w); JK (a); A: Sandy. A: Sandman. Darkseid	14.00
❑7, Mar 1972 JK (c); JK (w); JK (a)	14.00
❑8, May 1972; JK (c); JK (w); JK (a); Darkseid	14.00
❑9, Jul 1972 JK (c); JK (w); JK (a)	14.00
❑10, Jul 1972, JK (c); JK (w); JK (a)	14.00
❑11, Nov 1972, JK (c); JK (w); JK (a); 1: The Pursuer	14.00

Forever People
DC

❑1, Feb 1988; V: Dark; Return of the Forever People	2.00
❑2, Mar 1988	2.00
❑3, Apr 1988	2.00
❑4, May 1988	2.00
❑5, Jun 1988; Return Infinity Man	2.00
❑6, Jul 1988; O: Forever People	2.00

Forever Warriors
CFD

❑1, May 1997	2.95

Forge
CrossGen

❑1, May 2002; Includes Soujourn Prequel, #1, Negation Prequel, Merdian #15, Crux #1-3, The Path preview	9.95

	N-MINT
❑2, Jun 2002	9.95
❑3, Jul 2002	9.95
❑4, Aug 2002	11.95
❑5, Sep 2002	11.95
❑6, Oct 2002	11.95
❑7, Nov 2002	11.95
❑8, Dec 2002	7.95
❑9, Jan 2003	7.95
❑10, Feb 2003	7.95
❑11, Mar 2003	7.95
❑12, Apr 2003	7.95
❑13, May 2003	7.95

Forgotten Realms
DC

❑1, Sep 1989	1.50
❑2, Oct 1989	1.00
❑3, Nov 1989	1.00
❑4, Dec 1989	1.00
❑5, Jan 1990	1.00
❑6, Feb 1990	1.00
❑7, Mar 1990; The Dragonreach Saga	1.00
❑8, Apr 1990	1.00
❑9, May 1990	1.00
❑10, Jun 1990	1.00
❑11, Jul 1990	1.00
❑12, Aug 1990	1.00
❑13, Sep 1990	1.00
❑14, Oct 1990	1.00
❑15, Nov 1990	1.00
❑16, Dec 1990	1.00
❑17, Jan 1991	1.00
❑18, Feb 1991	1.00
❑19, Mar 1991	1.00
❑20, Apr 1991	1.00
❑21, May 1991	1.00
❑22, Jun 1991	1.00
❑23, Jul 1991	1.00
❑24, Aug 1991	1.00
❑25, Sep 1991; Final Issue	1.00
❑Ann 1, ca. 1990	1.50

Forgotten Realms: Exile
Devil's Due

❑1, Nov 2005	4.95
❑1/Special, Nov 2005	8.95
❑2, Jan 2006	4.95
❑2/Special, Jan 2006	8.95
❑3, Feb 2006	4.95
❑3/Special, Feb 2006	8.95

Forgotten Realms: Homeland
Devil's Due

❑1, Aug 2005	5.00
❑1/Variant, Aug 2005	9.00
❑1/Conv, Aug 2005, Available at San Diego 2005 ($10); 500 produced; Tyler Walpole cover	10.00
❑2, Sep 2005	4.95
❑2/Variant, Sep 2005	8.95
❑3, Oct 2005	4.95
❑3/Variant, Oct 2005	8.95

Forgotten Realms: Sojourn
Devil's Due

❑1, Apr 2006	4.95
❑1/Variant, Apr 2006	8.95
❑2, May 2006	4.95
❑2/Special, May 2006	8.95

Other grades: Multiply price above by 5/6 for VF/NM • 2/3 for VERY FINE • 1/3 for FINE • 1/5 for VERY GOOD • 1/8 for GOOD

N-MINT

❑3, Jun 2006 ... 4.95
❑3/Special, Jun 2006 ... 8.95

Forgotten Realms: The Crystal Shard
Devil's Due

❑1, Aug 2006 ... 4.95
❑1/Special, Aug 2006 ... 8.95
❑2, Oct 2006 ... 4.95
❑2/Variant, Oct 2006 ... 8.95
❑3, Dec 2006 ... 4.95
❑3/Silver, Dec 2006 ... 8.95

Forgotten Realms: The Grand Tour
TSR

❑1; no cover price ... 1.00

For Lovers Only
Charlton

❑60, Aug 1971 ... 20.00
❑61, Oct 1971 ... 10.00
❑62, Dec 1971 ... 10.00
❑63, Feb 1972 ... 10.00
❑64, Apr 1972, Shirley Jones pin-up ... 10.00
❑65, Jun 1972 ... 10.00
❑66, Aug 1972 ... 10.00
❑67, Oct 1972, Bobby Sherman pictures ... 10.00
❑68, Dec 1972 ... 10.00
❑69, Feb 1973 ... 10.00
❑70, Apr 1973 ... 10.00
❑71, Jun 1973 ... 10.00
❑72, Aug 1973 ... 10.00
❑73, Oct 1973 ... 10.00
❑74, Dec 1973 ... 10.00
❑75, Sep 1974 ... 10.00
❑76, Nov 1974 ... 10.00
❑77, ca. 1975 ... 10.00
❑78, ca. 1975 ... 10.00
❑79, Jun 1975 ... 10.00
❑80, ca. 1975 ... 10.00
❑81, Oct 1975 ... 10.00
❑82, Dec 1975 ... 10.00
❑83, ca. 1976 ... 10.00
❑84, ca. 1976 ... 10.00
❑85, ca. 1976 ... 10.00
❑86, ca. 1976 ... 10.00
❑87, Nov 1976 ... 10.00

Formerly Known as the Justice League
DC

❑1, Sep 2003 KG (w) ... 2.50
❑2, Oct 2003 KG (w) ... 2.50
❑3, Nov 2003 KG (w) ... 2.50
❑4, Dec 2003 KG (w) ... 2.50
❑5, Jan 2004 KG (w) ... 2.50
❑6, Feb 2004 KG (w) ... 2.50

Forsaken
Image

❑1, Aug 2004 ... 2.95
❑2, Sep 2004 ... 2.95
❑3, Oct 2004 ... 2.95

Fort: Prophet of the Unexplained
Dark Horse

❑1, Jun 2002 ... 2.99
❑2, Jul 2002 ... 2.99
❑3, Aug 2002 ... 2.99
❑4, Sep 2002 ... 2.99

Fortune and Glory
Oni

❑1, Dec 1999, b&w ... 4.95
❑2, Feb 2000, b&w ... 4.95
❑3, Apr 2000, b&w ... 4.95

Fortune's Fool Story of Jinxer
Cranium

❑0, Jul 1999 ... 2.95

Fortune's Friends: Hell Week
Aria

❑1; graphic novel ... 6.95

Forty Winks
Odd Jobs Limited

❑1, Nov 1997 ... 2.95
❑2, Dec 1997 ... 2.95
❑3, Mar 1998 ... 2.95
❑4, Jun 1998 ... 2.95

Forty Winks Christmas Special
Peregrine Entertainment

❑1, Aug 1998, b&w ... 2.95

N-MINT

Forty Winks Super Special Edition: TV Party Tonite!
Peregrine Entertainment

❑1, Apr 1999, b&w ... 2.95

Foton Effect
Aced

❑1, Oct 1986 ... 1.50
❑2 ... 1.50
❑3 ... 1.50

Foul!
Traitors Gait

❑1 ... 3.00

4
Marvel

❑1, Oct 2000; Universe X tie-in; Sue Richards restored to life ... 3.99

4-D Monkey
Dr. Leung's

❑1 1988 ... 2.00
❑2 1988 ... 2.00
❑3 1988 ... 2.00
❑4 1989 ... 2.00
❑5 1989 ... 2.00
❑6 1989 ... 2.00
❑7 1989 ... 2.00
❑8 1989 ... 2.00
❑9 1990 ... 2.00
❑10 1990 ... 2.00
❑11 1990 ... 2.00
❑12 1990 ... 2.00

Four Horsemen
DC / Vertigo

❑1, Feb 2000 ... 2.50
❑2, Mar 2000 ... 2.50
❑3, Apr 2000 ... 2.50
❑4, May 2000 ... 2.50

Four Kunoichi: Bloodlust
Lightning

❑1, Dec 1996, b&w; Standard edition ... 2.75
❑1/Nude; Nude cover ... 9.95
❑1/Platinum; Platinum edition ... 9.95
❑1/Platinum Nude; Platinum Nude edition ... 4.00

Four Kunoichi: Enter the Sinja
Lightning

❑1, Feb 1997, b&w ... 2.95

411
Marvel

❑1, Jun 2003, cardstock cover ... 3.50
❑2, Jul 2003, cardstock cover ... 3.50

Four-Star Battle Tales
DC

❑1, Feb 1973, Reprints ... 20.00
❑2, May 1973, Reprints ... 7.00
❑3, Aug 1973, Reprints ... 6.00
❑4, Oct 1973, Reprints ... 6.00
❑5, Nov 1973, Reprints ... 6.00

Four Star Spectacular
DC

❑1, Apr 1976, Giant-size; Reprints Adventure Comics #270; Sensation Comics #17; Hawkman #7; And All-Flash Comics #22 (new art) ... 12.00
❑2, Jun 1976, Giant-size; Superboy #102, Wonder Woman #107, and Flash #130 ... 7.00
❑3, Aug 1976, Giant-size; Bicentennial #15 ... 7.00
❑4, Oct 1976, Giant-size; Reprints Sensation Comics #19, Superboy #62, and Hawkman #7 ... 7.00
❑5, Dec 1976, Giant-size; Reprints Adventure Comics #303, Wonder Woman #7, Adventure Comics #246 and Action Comics #194 ... 7.00
❑6, Feb 1977, Giant-size; Reprints Wonder Woman #5; 103; Superboy #118; Blackhawk #11; Final Issue ... 7.00

Fourth World (Jack Kirby's...)
DC

❑1, Mar 1997 JBy (w); JBy (a) ... 2.50
❑2, Apr 1997; JBy (w); JBy (a); O: Darkseid; Tales of the New Gods back-up by Byrne ... 2.00
❑3, May 1997; JBy (w); JBy (a); O: Darkseid; Tales of the New Gods back-up by Byrne ... 2.00
❑4, Jun 1997; JBy (w); JBy (a); O: Darkseid; Tales of the New Gods back-up by Byrne ... 2.00

N-MINT

❑5, Jul 1997; JBy (w); JBy (a); O: Darkseid; Tales of the New Gods back-up by Byrne ... 2.00
❑6, Aug 1997; JBy (w); JBy (a); Tales of the New Gods back-up by Byrne; Mister Miracle in old west ... 2.00
❑7, Sep 1997; JBy (w); JBy (a); Tales of the New Gods back-up by Byrne; Mister Miracle in old west ... 2.00
❑8, Oct 1997; JBy (w); JBy (a); Genesis ... 2.00
❑9, Nov 1997; JBy (w); JBy (a); O: Kanto; Tales of the New Gods back-up by Simonson ... 2.00
❑10, Dec 1997; JBy (w); JBy (a); Face cover ... 2.00
❑11, Jan 1998 JBy (w); JBy (a) ... 2.00
❑12, Feb 1998 JBy (w); JBy (a) ... 2.00
❑13, Mar 1998 JBy (w); JBy (a) ... 2.00
❑14, Apr 1998; JBy (w); JBy (a); Darkseid and Ares escape Source Wall ... 2.00
❑15, May 1998; JBy (w); JBy (a); O: Moebius Chair; Tales of the New Gods back-up by Byrne & Ron Wagner ... 2.00
❑16, Jun 1998; JBy (w); JBy (a); O: Moebius Chair; Tales of the New Gods back-up by Byrne & Ron Wagner; Tales of the New Gods back-up by Byrne and Ron Wagner ... 2.00
❑17, Jul 1998; JBy (w); JBy (a); D: Valkyra; O: Infinity Man; Tales of the New Gods back-up by Byrne ... 2.00
❑18, Aug 1998; JBy (w); JBy (a); O: Infinity Man; Tales of the New Gods back-up by Byrne ... 2.00
❑19, Sep 1998; JBy (w); JBy (a); Return of Supertown ... 2.25
❑20, Oct 1998; JBy (w); JBy (a); A: Superman. Post-Crisis re-telling of Supermans first encounter with the New Gods ... 2.25

Fourth World Gallery
DC

❑1 1996; pin-ups based on Jack Kirby creations ... 3.50

Four Women
DC / Homage

❑1, Dec 2001 ... 2.95
❑2, Jan 2002 ... 2.95
❑3, Feb 2002 ... 2.95
❑4, Mar 2002 ... 2.95
❑5, Apr 2002 ... 2.95

Fox and the Crow
DC

❑70, Nov 1961 ... 42.00
❑71, Jan 1962 ... 42.00
❑72, Mar 1962 ... 42.00
❑73, May 1962 ... 42.00
❑74, Jul 1962 ... 42.00
❑75, Sep 1962 ... 42.00
❑76, Nov 1962 ... 42.00
❑77, Jan 1963 ... 42.00
❑78, Mar 1963 ... 42.00
❑79, May 1963 ... 42.00
❑80, Jul 1963 ... 42.00
❑81, Sep 1963 ... 26.00
❑82, Nov 1963 ... 26.00
❑83, Jan 1964 ... 26.00
❑84, Mar 1964 ... 26.00
❑85, May 1964 ... 26.00
❑86, Jul 1964 ... 26.00
❑87, Sep 1964 ... 26.00
❑88, Nov 1964 ... 26.00
❑89, Jan 1965 ... 26.00
❑90, Feb 1965 ... 26.00
❑91, May 1965 ... 26.00
❑92, Jul 1965 ... 26.00
❑93, Sep 1965 ... 26.00
❑94, Nov 1965 ... 26.00
❑95, Dec 1965, 1&O: Stanley and His Monster ... 50.00
❑96, Mar 1966, Stanley and his Monster; Brat Finks ... 22.00
❑97, May 1966, Stanley and his Monster ... 22.00
❑98, Jul 1966, Stanley and his Monster; Brat Finks ... 22.00
❑99, Sep 1966, Stanley and his Monster; The Hounds and the Hare ... 22.00
❑100, Nov 1966 ... 22.00
❑101, Jan 1967, Stanley and his Monster ... 18.00
❑102, Mar 1967 ... 18.00
❑103, May 1967 ... 18.00

Other grades: Multiply price above by 5/6 for VF/NM • 2/3 for VERY FINE • 1/3 for FINE • 1/5 for VERY GOOD • 1/8 for GOOD

Flashpoint

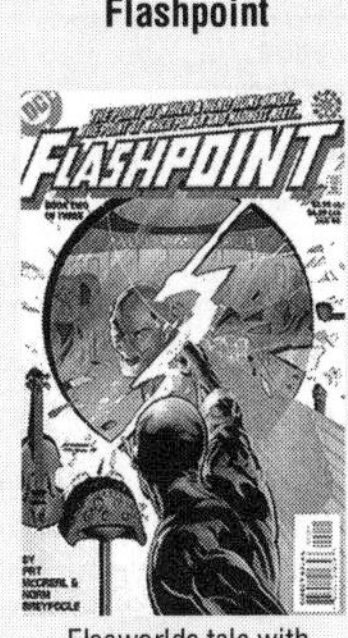

Elseworlds tale with Vandal Savage villainy

©DC

Flinch

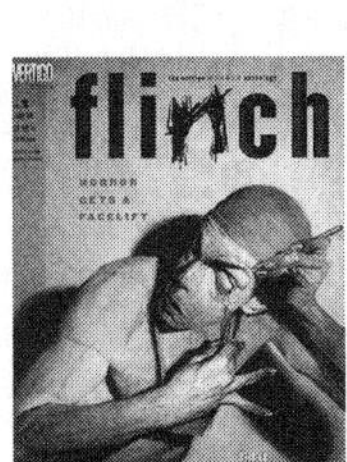

DC tries another horror anthology

©DC

Flintstones

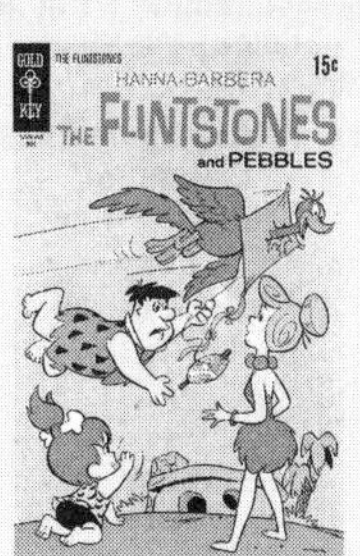

Prehistoric family hits comics early on

©Dell

Flintstones

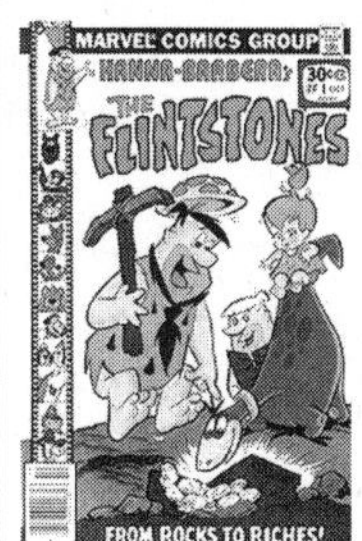

Part of Marvel's short Hanna-Barbera phase

©Marvel

Flipper

Beloved TV dolphin flopped in comics

©Gold Key

	N-MINT
❑104, Jul 1967	18.00
❑105, Sep 1967, A: Stanley and His Monster	18.00
❑106, Nov 1967, Stanley and his Monster	18.00
❑107, Jan 1968	18.00
❑108, Mar 1968, Series continued in Stanley and His Monster	18.00

Fox Comics
Fantagraphics

❑24, b&w	2.95
❑25, b&w	2.95
❑26, b&w	2.95
❑Special 1, b&w; Australian; Special	2.95

Fox Comics Legends Series
Fantagraphics

❑1, Jul 1992, b&w; Three Stooges	2.50
❑2, b&w; Elvis	2.50

Foxfire
Malibu / Ultraverse

❑1, Feb 1996, Glen Fabry cover	1.50
❑2, Mar 1996, V: UltraForce	1.50
❑3, Apr 1996	1.50
❑4, May 1996	1.50

Foxfire
Nightwynd

❑1, b&w	2.50
❑2, b&w	2.50
❑3, b&w	2.50

Fox Kids Funhouse
Acclaim

❑1, digest; The Tick, Life with Louie, Bobby's World	4.50
❑2	4.50

Fraction
DC / Focus

❑1, Jun 2004	2.50
❑2, Jul 2004	2.50
❑3, Aug 2004	2.50
❑4, Sep 2004	2.50
❑5, Oct 2004	2.50
❑6, Nov 2004	2.50

Fractured Fairy Tales
Gold Key

❑1, Oct 1962	75.00

Fraggle Rock
Marvel / Star

❑1, Apr 1985	1.50
❑2, Jun 1985	1.25
❑3, Aug 1985	1.25
❑4, Oct 1985	1.25
❑5, Dec 1985	1.25
❑6, Feb 1986	1.25
❑7, Apr 1986	1.25
❑8, Jun 1986	1.25

Fraggle Rock
Marvel

❑1, Apr 1988, Reprints	1.50
❑2, Jun 1988, Reprints	1.00
❑3, Jun 1988, Reprints	1.00
❑4, Jul 1988, Reprints	1.00
❑5, Aug 1988, Reprints	1.00

Fragile Prophet
Lost in the Dark

	N-MINT
❑1, Sep 2005	2.95

Fragments
Screaming Cat

❑1	2.50

Francis, Brother of the Universe
Marvel

❑1; JB (a); Life of St. Francis of Assisi; ca. 1980	1.50

Frank (Nemesis)
Nemesis

❑1, Apr 1994; newsstand	1.75
❑1/Direct ed., Apr 1994; variant cover: direct sale	2.50
❑2, May 1994; newsstand	1.75
❑2/Direct ed., May 1994; direct sale	2.50
❑3, Jun 1994; newsstand	1.75
❑3/Direct ed., Jun 1994; direct sale	2.50
❑4, Jul 1994; newsstand	1.75
❑4/Direct ed., Jul 1994; direct sale	2.50

Frank (Fantagraphics)
Fantagraphics

❑1, Sep 1996, b&w	2.95
❑2, Dec 1997, b&w	3.95

Frank Frazetta Fantasy Illustrated
Frank Frazetta Fantasy Illustrated

❑1, Spr 1998; Spring 1998	7.00
❑1/Variant, Spr 1998; alternate cover	7.00
❑2, Sum 1998; Battle Chasers story	6.00
❑2/Variant, Sum 1998; alternate cover	6.00
❑3, Fal 1998	6.00
❑3/Variant, Fal 1998; alternate cover	6.00
❑4, Win 1998	5.99
❑4/Variant, Win 1998; alternate cover	6.00
❑5, Mar 1999	5.99
❑5/Variant, Mar 1999; alternate cover	7.50
❑6, May 1999	6.00
❑6/Variant, May 1999; alternate cover	6.00
❑7, Jul 1999	5.99
❑7/Variant, Jul 1999; alternate cover	5.99

Frank in the River
Tundra

❑1; "Tantalizing Stories Presents Frank in the River"	2.95

Frank the Unicorn
Fragments West

❑1, Sep 1986	2.00
❑2, Nov 1986	2.00
❑3, Jan 1987	2.00
❑4	2.00
❑5	2.00
❑6	2.00
❑7	2.00
❑8	2.00
❑9	2.00

Frank Zappa: Viva La Bizarre
Revolutionary

❑1, Feb 1994, b&w	3.00

Frankenstein
Dell

	N-MINT
❑1, Mar 1963	35.00
❑2, Sep 1966	25.00
❑3, Dec 1966	15.00
❑4, Mar 1967	15.00

Frankenstein (The Monster of...)
Marvel

❑1, Jan 1973, MP (c); MP (a); O: Frankenstein's Monster	40.00
❑2, Mar 1973, MP (c); MP (w); MP (a); O: Bride of Frankenstein	15.00
❑3, May 1973, MP (c); MP (a)	9.00
❑4, Jul 1973	9.00
❑5, Sep 1973	9.00
❑6, Oct 1973, Cover changes titles to "The Frankenstein Monster"	7.00
❑7, Nov 1973	7.00
❑8, Jan 1974, A: Dracula. Meets Dracula	18.00
❑9, Mar 1974, A: Dracula. Marvel Value Stamp #68: Son of Satan	20.00
❑10, May 1974, Marvel Value Stamp #69: Marvel Girl	6.00
❑11, Jul 1974, V: Ivan. Marvel Value Stamp #12: Daredevil	5.00
❑12, Sep 1974, The monster comes to the modern day; Marvel Value Stamp #59: Golem	5.00
❑13, Nov 1974, Marvel Value Stamp #60: Ka-Zar	5.00
❑14, Jan 1975, Marvel Value Stamp #90: Hercules	5.00
❑15, Mar 1975, GK (c); VM, KJ (a); Back-up story reprinted from Tales of Suspense #10	5.00
❑16, May 1975, 1: Veronica Frankenstein. 1: Berserker. Marvel Value Stamp #8: Captain America	5.00
❑17, Jul 1975, V: Berserker. Monster regains speech	5.00
❑18, Sep 1975, Final Issue	5.00

Frankenstein
Eternity

❑1, b&w	2.00
❑2, b&w	2.00
❑3, Aug 1989, b&w	2.00

Frankenstein
Topps

❑1, Oct 1994	2.95
❑2	2.95
❑3, Includes trading cards	2.95
❑4	2.95

Frankenstein/Dracula War
Topps

❑1, Feb 1995	2.50
❑2	2.50
❑3	2.50

Frankenstein Jr.
Gold Key

❑1, Jan 1967	55.00

Frankenstein Mobster
Image

❑0, Oct 2003	2.95
❑1, Dec 2003	2.95
❑2, Feb 2004	2.95
❑3, May 2004	2.95
❑4 2004	3.00
❑5 2004	3.00
❑6 2004	3.00
❑7/A, Dec 2004	2.95
❑7/B, Dec 2004	2.95

Frankenstein: Or the Modern Prometheus
Caliber

❑1 ... 2.95

Frank Ironwine
Avatar

❑1 ... 3.50
❑1/Foil ... 20.00

Franklin Richards: Happy Franksgiving
Marvel

❑1, Jan 2007, Included Guiding Light backup story ... 2.99

Franklin Richards, Son of a Genius - Everybody Loves Franklin
Marvel

❑1, Apr 2006 ... 2.99

Franklin Richards: Son of a Genius Super Summer Spectacular
Marvel

❑1, Sep 2006 ... 2.99

Fray
Dark Horse

❑1, Jun 2001 ... 3.00
❑2, Jul 2001 ... 2.99
❑3, Aug 2001 ... 2.99
❑4, Sep 2001 ... 2.99
❑5, Oct 2001 ... 2.99
❑6, Nov 2001 ... 2.99
❑7, Apr 2003 ... 2.99
❑8, ca. 2003 ... 2.99

Freak Force
Image

❑1, Dec 1993; KG, EL (w); 1: Freak Force ... 2.00
❑2, Jan 1994 ... 1.95
❑3, Feb 1994 ... 1.95
❑4, Mar 1994 A: Vanguard. ... 1.95
❑5, Apr 1994 ... 1.95
❑6, Jun 1994; Identity of Mighty Man revealed ... 1.95
❑7, Jul 1994 ... 1.95
❑8, Aug 1994 ... 2.50
❑9, Sep 1994 A: Cyber Force ... 2.50
❑10, Oct 1994 ... 2.50
❑11, Nov 1994 ... 2.50
❑12, Dec 1994 ... 2.50
❑13, Jan 1995; Jerry Ordway pin-up ... 2.50
❑13/A, Jan 1995; alternate cover ... 2.50
❑14, Feb 1995 ... 2.50
❑15, Mar 1995 A: Maxx ... 2.50
❑16, Apr 1995 ... 2.50
❑17, Jun 1995 ... 2.50
❑18, Jul 1995; Final Issue ... 2.50

Freak Force
Image

❑1, Apr 1997 ... 2.95
❑2, May 1997 ... 2.95
❑3, Jul 1997 ... 2.95

Freak Out on Infant Earths
Blackthorne

❑1, Jan 1987 ... 2.00
❑2 ... 2.00

Freaks
Fantagraphics / Eros

❑1; Movie adaptation ... 2.25
❑2; Movie adaptation ... 2.25
❑3; Movie adaptation ... 2.25

Freaks' Amour
Dark Horse

❑1, Jul 1992; Adult ... 3.95
❑2, Sep 1992; Adult ... 3.95
❑3; Doctor Giggles Bound-In Poster; Adult ... 3.95

Freaks of the Heartland
Dark Horse

❑1, Jan 2004 ... 2.99
❑2, Mar 2004 ... 2.99
❑3, May 2004 ... 2.99
❑4, Jul 2004 ... 2.99
❑5, Sep 2004 ... 2.99
❑6, Nov 2004 ... 3.00

Fred & Bianca Censorship Sucks Special
Comics Interview

❑1, b&w; Reprints ... 2.25

Fred & Bianca Mother's Day Massacre
Comics Interview

❑1, b&w; Reprints ... 2.25

Fred & Bianca Valentine's Day Massacre
Comics Interview

❑1, b&w; Reprints ... 2.25

Fred the Clown
Hotel Fred

❑1, Sep 2001 ... 2.95
❑2, Jan 2002 ... 2.95

Freddy
Dell

❑1, Jul 1964 ... 26.00
❑2, Sep 1964 ... 18.00
❑3, Dec 1964 ... 18.00

Freddy Krueger's Nightmare on Elm Street
Marvel

❑1, Oct 1989, b&w; magazine; RB, AA, TD (a); O: Freddy Krueger ... 4.50
❑2, Nov 1989, b&w; magazine; AA, TD (a) ... 4.00

Freddy's Dead: The Final Nightmare
Innovation

❑1; Movie adaptation ... 2.50
❑1/3D; part 3-D ... 2.50
❑2; Movie adaptation ... 2.50
❑3; Movie adaptation ... 2.50
❑3/3D; 3-D version of #3; Requires glasses provided at movie showings.. ... 2.50

Freddy vs. Jason vs. Ash
DC / Wildstorm

❑1, Dec 2007 ... 12.00
❑2, Jan 2008 ... 6.00
❑3, Feb 2008 ... 4.00
❑4, Mar 2008 ... 4.00

Frederic Remington: The Man Who Painted the West
Tome

❑1, b&w ... 2.95

Fred Hembeck Destroys the Marvel Universe
Marvel

❑1, Jul 1989; D: Everyone ... 1.50

Fred Hembeck Sells the Marvel Universe
Marvel

❑1, Oct 1990, FH (w); FH (a) ... 1.50

Fred the Possessed Flower
Happy Predator

❑1, b&w ... 2.95
❑2, b&w ... 2.95
❑3, b&w ... 2.95
❑4, b&w ... 2.95
❑5, b&w ... 2.95
❑6, b&w ... 2.95

Free Cerebus
Aardvark-Vanaheim

❑1, b&w; giveaway ... 1.00

Free Laughs
Deschaine

❑1, b&w ... 1.00

Free Speeches
Oni

❑1, Aug 1998; collects Nadine Strossen, Dave Sim, Neil Gaiman, and Frank Miller speeches; Fundraiser for Comic Book Legal Defense Fund ... 2.95

Free-View
Acclaim

❑1, Mar 1993 VM (a) ... 1.00

Freebooters/Young Gods/Paradoxman Preview
Dark Horse

❑1 ... 1.00

Freedom Agent
Gold Key

❑1, Apr 1963 ... 24.00

Freedom Fighters
DC

❑1, Apr 1976, RE (a); 1: Silver Ghost. V: Silver Ghost. Freedom Fighters arrive on Earth-1 ... 12.00
❑2, Jun 1976, V: Silver Ghost ... 5.00
❑3, Aug 1976, A: Wonder Woman. Bicentennial #8 ... 5.00
❑4, Oct 1976, A: Wonder Woman ... 4.00
❑5, Dec 1976, V: King Samson; V: Silver Ghost ... 4.00
❑6, Feb 1977 ... 4.00
❑7, Apr 1977, 1: The Crusaders (DC) ... 4.00
❑8, Jun 1977, V: Crusaders; Crusaders are parallel to Marvel's Invaders ... 4.00
❑9, Aug 1977, V: Crusaders. O: Crusaders ... 4.00
❑10, Oct 1977, RB (c); O: Doll Man. V: Cat-Man; V: Silver Ghost ... 4.00
❑11, Dec 1977, O: Ray ... 4.00
❑12, Feb 1978, O: Firebrand I (Rod Reilly) ... 4.00
❑13, Apr 1978, O: Black Condor ... 4.00
❑14, Jun 1978, A: Batwoman. A: Batgirl ... 4.00
❑15, Aug 1978, O: Phantom Lady. events continue in Secret Society of Super Villains #16 ... 4.00

Freedom Force
Image

❑1, Mar 2005 ... 2.95
❑2, Apr 2005 ... 2.95
❑3, May 2005 ... 2.95
❑4, Jun 2005 ... 2.95
❑5, Jul 2005 ... 2.95
❑6, Aug 2005 ... 2.95

Freeflight
Thinkblots

❑1, Apr 1994 ... 2.95

Freejack
Now

❑1, Apr 1992, newsstand ... 1.95
❑1/Direct ed., Apr 1992, direct-sale edition; Movie adaptation ... 2.50
❑2, May 1992, newsstand ... 1.95
❑2/Direct ed., May 1992, direct-sale ... 2.50
❑3, Jun 1992, newsstand ... 1.95
❑3/Direct ed., Jun 1992, direct-sale ... 2.50

Freemind
Future

❑1, Nov 2002; No cover price ... 3.50
❑2, Dec 2002 ... 3.50
❑3, Jan 2003 ... 3.50
❑4, Feb 2003 ... 3.50
❑5, Apr 2003 ... 3.50
❑6, May 2003 ... 3.50
❑7, Jul 2003 ... 2.99

Freeway Ninja Hanzo
SleepyHouse

❑1; Heavyweight premiere issue ... 3.50

Freex
Malibu / Ultraverse

❑1, Jul 1993; 1: Freex. 1: Pressure; Includes coupon for Ultraverse #0 ... 2.00
❑1/Hologram, Jul 1993; 1: Freex. 1: Pressure. Hologram cover; "Ultra Limited" ... 5.00
❑2, Aug 1993; 1: Rush ... 2.00
❑3, Sep 1993; 1: Bloodhounds ... 2.00
❑4, Oct 1993; SR (c); Rune ... 2.50
❑5, Nov 1993 ... 1.95
❑6, Dec 1993; Break-Thru ... 1.95
❑7, Jan 1994; MZ (a); O: Pressure. O: Hardcase; O: Pressure (Valerie Sharp) ... 1.95
❑8, Feb 1994 ... 1.95
❑9, Mar 1994; O: Sweetface. 1: Contrary; O: Sweetface (Angela Salazar) ... 1.95
❑10, Apr 1994; O: Boomboy ... 1.95
❑11, May 1994; O: Plug; O: Plug (Michael Rafani) ... 1.95
❑12, Aug 1994; 1: The Guardian ... 1.95
❑13, Sep 1994; 1: Prometheus ... 1.95
❑14, Oct 1994; 1: The Savior ... 1.95
❑15, Jan 1995; 1: Eliminator. 1: Manic. 1: Oyabun. Flip-book with Ultraverse Premiere #9 ... 3.50
❑16, Jan 1995 ... 1.95
❑17, Feb 1995 A: Rune ... 2.50
❑18, Feb 1995; 1: A.J. Analla. 1: Tulath; Final Issue ... 2.50
❑GS 1; Giant-Size Freex #1; 1: Pixx ... 2.50

French Ice
Renegade

❑1, b&w ... 2.00
❑2, Apr 1987, b&w ... 2.00

Other grades: Multiply price above by 5/6 for VF/NM • 2/3 for VERY FINE • 1/3 for FINE • 1/5 for VERY GOOD • 1/8 for GOOD

Forbidden Tales of Dark Mansion

Dark Mansion of Forbidden Love continues
©DC

Forbidden Worlds

ACG's horror title spawned Herbie
©ACG

Force of Buddha's Palm

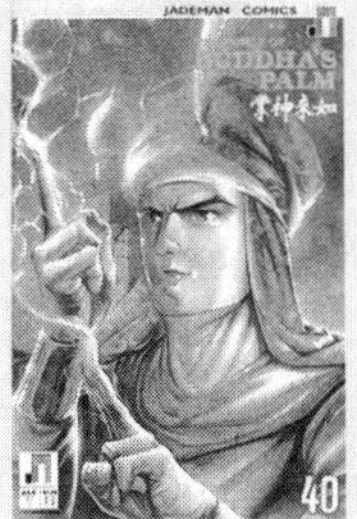

Hong Kong publisher tried American market
©Jademan

Force Works

Avengers task force featured Iron Man
©Marvel

Forever People

Fourth World youngsters flee Darkseid
©DC

N-MINT

❑3, May 1987, b&w 2.00
❑4, Jun 1987, b&w 2.00
❑5, Jul 1987, b&w 2.00
❑6, Sep 1987, b&w 2.00
❑7, Oct 1987, b&w 2.00
❑8, Nov 1987, b&w 2.00
❑9, Dec 1987, b&w 2.00
❑10, Jan 1988, b&w 2.00
❑11, Feb 1988, b&w 2.00
❑12, Mar 1988, b&w 2.00
❑13, Apr 1988, b&w 2.00

French Ticklers
Kitchen Sink

❑1, Oct 1989, b&w 2.00
❑2, Oct 1989, b&w 2.00
❑3, Oct 1989, b&w 2.00

Frenzy
Independent

❑1 1.00
❑1/A 1.00

Frescazizis
Last Gasp

❑1; Adult 1.00

Fresh Blood Funny Book
Last Gasp

❑1; Adult 1.25

Freshmen
Image

❑1/Preview, Jun 2005; Distributed at Wizard World Philadelphia 2005; 1,000 produced 7.00
❑1/Linsner, Aug 2005 4.00
❑1/Migliari, Aug 2005 2.99
❑1/Perez, Aug 2005 4.00
❑2, Sep 2005 2.99
❑3, Nov 2005 2.99
❑4, Jan 2005 2.99
❑5, Jan 2006 2.99
❑6, Mar 2006 2.99

Freshmen II
Image

❑1, Dec 2006 2.99
❑1/Variant, Dec 2006 2.99
❑2, Jan 2007 2.99

Freshmen Yearbook One Shot
Image

❑1, Jan 2006 2.99

Friday the 13th
DC

❑1, Feb 2007 2.99
❑2, Mar 2007 2.99

Friendly Ghost, Casper
Harvey

❑39, Nov 1961 18.00
❑40, Dec 1961 18.00
❑41, Jan 1962 15.00
❑42, Feb 1962 15.00
❑43, Mar 1962 15.00
❑44, Apr 1962 15.00
❑45, May 1962 15.00
❑46, Jun 1962 15.00
❑47, Jul 1962 15.00
❑48, Aug 1962 15.00

N-MINT

❑49, Sep 1962 15.00
❑50, Oct 1962 15.00
❑51, Nov 1962 12.00
❑52, Dec 1962 12.00
❑53, Jan 1963 12.00
❑54, Feb 1963 12.00
❑55, Mar 1963 12.00
❑56, Apr 1963 12.00
❑57, May 1963 12.00
❑58, Jun 1963 12.00
❑59, Jul 1963 12.00
❑60, Aug 1963 12.00
❑61, Sep 1963 10.00
❑62, Oct 1963 10.00
❑63, Nov 1963 10.00
❑64, Dec 1963 10.00
❑65, Jan 1964 10.00
❑66, Feb 1964 10.00
❑67, Mar 1964 10.00
❑68, Apr 1964 10.00
❑69, May 1964 10.00
❑70, Jun 1964 10.00
❑71, Jul 1964 8.00
❑72, Aug 1964 8.00
❑73, Sep 1964 8.00
❑74, Oct 1964 8.00
❑75, Nov 1964 8.00
❑76, Dec 1964 8.00
❑77, Jan 1965 8.00
❑78, Feb 1965 8.00
❑79, Mar 1965 8.00
❑80, Apr 1965 8.00
❑81, May 1965 7.00
❑82, Jun 1965 7.00
❑83, Jul 1965 7.00
❑84, Aug 1965 7.00
❑85, Sep 1965 7.00
❑86, Oct 1965 7.00
❑87, Nov 1965 7.00
❑88, Dec 1965 7.00
❑89, Jan 1966 7.00
❑90, Feb 1966 6.00
❑91, Mar 1966 6.00
❑92, Apr 1966 6.00
❑93, May 1966 6.00
❑94, Jun 1966 6.00
❑95, Jul 1966 6.00
❑96, Aug 1966 6.00
❑97, Sep 1966 6.00
❑98, Oct 1966 6.00
❑99, Nov 1966 6.00
❑100, Dec 1966 6.00
❑101, Jan 1967; Halloween cover 5.00
❑102, Feb 1967 5.00
❑103, Mar 1967 5.00
❑104, Apr 1967 5.00
❑105, May 1967 5.00
❑106, Jun 1967 5.00
❑107, Jul 1967 5.00
❑108, Aug 1967 5.00
❑109, Sep 1967 5.00
❑110, Oct 1967 5.00
❑111, Nov 1967 5.00
❑112, Dec 1967 5.00
❑113, Jan 1968 5.00
❑114, Feb 1968 5.00

N-MINT

❑115, Mar 1968 5.00
❑116, Apr 1968 5.00
❑117, May 1968 5.00
❑118, Jun 1968 5.00
❑119, Jul 1968 5.00
❑120, Aug 1968 5.00
❑121, Sep 1968 4.00
❑122, Oct 1968 4.00
❑123, Nov 1968 4.00
❑124, Dec 1968 4.00
❑125, Jan 1969 4.00
❑126, Feb 1969 4.00
❑127, Mar 1969 4.00
❑128, Apr 1969 4.00
❑129, May 1969 4.00
❑130, Jun 1969 4.00
❑131, Jul 1969 4.00
❑132, Aug 1969 4.00
❑133, Sep 1969 4.00
❑134, Oct 1969 4.00
❑135, Nov 1969 4.00
❑136, Dec 1969 4.00
❑137, Jan 1970 4.00
❑138, Feb 1970 4.00
❑139, Mar 1970 4.00
❑140, Apr 1970 4.00
❑141, May 1970 3.00
❑142, Jun 1970 3.00
❑143, Jul 1970 3.00
❑144, Aug 1970 3.00
❑145, Sep 1970 3.00
❑146, Oct 1970 3.00
❑147, Nov 1970 3.00
❑148, Dec 1970 3.00
❑149, Jan 1971; Halloween cover 3.00
❑150, Feb 1971 3.00
❑151, Mar 1971 3.00
❑152, Apr 1971 3.00
❑153, May 1971 3.00
❑154, Jun 1971 3.00
❑155, Jul 1971 3.00
❑156, Aug 1971 3.00
❑157, Sep 1971 3.00
❑158, Oct 1971 3.00
❑159, Nov 1971 3.00
❑160, Mar 1972 3.00
❑161, May 1972 3.00
❑162, Jul 1972 3.00
❑163, Sep 1972 3.00
❑164, Nov 1972 3.00
❑165, Jan 1973 3.00
❑166, Mar 1973 3.00
❑167, May 1973 3.00
❑168, Jul 1973 3.00
❑169, Sep 1973 3.00
❑170, Nov 1973 2.00
❑171, Jan 1974 2.00
❑172, Mar 1974 2.00
❑173, May 1974; Cub Scout issue 2.00
❑174, Jul 1974 2.00
❑175, Sep 1974 2.00
❑176, Nov 1974 2.00
❑177, Jan 1975 2.00
❑178, Mar 1975; Switches to current comic book size 2.00
❑179, May 1975; Cub Scout issue 2.00

Other grades: Multiply price above by 5/6 for VF/NM • 2/3 for VERY FINE • 1/3 for FINE • 1/5 for VERY GOOD • 1/8 for GOOD

❑180, Jul 1975 2.00
❑181, Sep 1975 2.00
❑182, Nov 1975 2.00
❑183, Jan 1976 2.00
❑184, Mar 1976 2.00
❑185, Apr 1976; Cub Scout issue 2.00
❑186, Jun 1976 2.00
❑187, Aug 1976 2.00
❑188, Oct 1976; Richie Rich in Hostess ad ("Around the World") 2.00
❑189, Dec 1976 2.00
❑190, Feb 1977 2.00
❑191, Apr 1977 2.00
❑192, Jun 1977 2.00
❑193, Aug 1977 2.00
❑194, Oct 1977 2.00
❑195, Dec 1977; Ghostly Trio on cover 2.00
❑196, Feb 1978 2.00
❑197, Apr 1978 2.00
❑198, Jun 1978 2.00
❑199, Aug 1978 2.00
❑200, Oct 1978 2.00
❑201, Dec 1978 2.00
❑202, Feb 1979 2.00
❑203, Apr 1979 2.00
❑204, Jun 1979 2.00
❑205, Aug 1979 2.00
❑206, Oct 1979 2.00
❑207, Dec 1979 2.00
❑208, Feb 1980 2.00
❑209, Apr 1980 2.00
❑210, Jun 1980 2.00
❑211, Aug 1980 2.00
❑212, Oct 1980 2.00
❑213, Dec 1980 2.00
❑214, Feb 1981 2.00
❑215, Apr 1981 2.00
❑216, Jun 1981 2.00
❑217, Aug 1981 2.00
❑218, Oct 1981 2.00
❑219, Dec 1981 2.00
❑220, Feb 1982 2.00
❑221, Apr 1982 2.00
❑222, Jun 1982 2.00
❑223, Aug 1982 2.00
❑224, Oct 1982 2.00
❑225, Oct 1986 2.00
❑226, Nov 1986 2.00
❑227, Dec 1986 2.00
❑228, Jan 1987 2.00
❑229, Feb 1987 2.00
❑230, Mar 1987 2.00
❑231, Apr 1987 2.00
❑232, May 1987 2.00
❑233, Jun 1987 2.00
❑234, Jul 1987 2.00
❑235, Aug 1987 2.00
❑236, Sep 1987 2.00
❑237, Oct 1987 2.00
❑238, Jan 1988 2.00
❑239, Mar 1988 2.00
❑240, May 1988 2.00
❑241, Jul 1988 2.00
❑242, Sep 1988 2.00
❑243, Nov 1988 2.00
❑244, Jan 1989 2.00
❑245, Mar 1989 2.00
❑246, Jul 1989 2.00
❑247, Sep 1989 2.00
❑248, Oct 1989 2.00
❑249, Jan 1990 2.00
❑250, Mar 1990; Christmas Cover 2.00
❑251, Apr 1990 2.00
❑252, May 1990 2.00
❑253, Jun 1990; Series continued in Casper the Friendly Ghost (2nd series) #254 2.00

Friendly Neighborhood Spider-Man
Marvel

❑1, Dec 2005 10.00
❑2, Jan 2006 6.00
❑3, Feb 2006 6.00
❑4, Mar 2006 2.99
❑5, May 2006 2.99
❑6, May 2006 2.99
❑7, Jun 2006 2.99
❑8, Jul 2006 2.99
❑9, Aug 2006 2.99
❑10, Sep 2006 2.99
❑11, Oct 2006, Spider-Man Unmasked; Mysterio's return 2.99
❑12, Nov 2006, Spider-Man Unmasked 2.99
❑13, Dec 2006, Spider-Man Unmasked 2.99
❑14, Feb 2007, Spider-Man Unmasked 2.99
❑15, Mar 2007, Spider-Man Unmasked 2.99
❑16, Apr 2007 2.99
❑17, May 2007; Back In Black; Mini-Marvels back up story inlcuded; Franklin Richards back up story included 6.00
❑18, Jun 2007; Back In Black; Sandman 4.00
❑19, Jul 2007; Back in Black 2.99
❑20, Aug 2007; Back in Black 2.99
❑21, Sep 2007; Back in Black 2.99
❑22, Oct 2007; Back in Black 2.99
❑23, Nov 2007; Back in Black 2.99
❑24, Dec 2007; Includes back-up storyl originally from Amazing Spider-Man #259; Includes layout art by Joe Quesada 3.99

Friends
Renegade

❑1, May 1987, b&w 2.00
❑2, b&w 2.00
❑3, b&w 2.00

Friends of Maxx
Image

❑1, Apr 1996; Dude Japan 2.95
❑2, Nov 1996; Broadminded 2.95
❑3, Mar 1997 2.95

Fright
Atlas-Seaboard

❑1, Jun 1975; O: Son of Dracula 6.00

Fright
Eternity

❑1 2.00
❑2 2.00
❑3 2.00
❑4 2.00
❑5 2.00
❑6 2.00
❑7 2.00
❑8 2.00
❑9, Apr 1989 2.00
❑10, May 1989 2.00
❑11, Jun 1989 2.00
❑12, Jul 1989 2.00

Fright Night
Now

❑1, Oct 1988; Adapts movie 2.50
❑2, Nov 1988; Adapts movie 2.00
❑3, Dec 1988 2.00
❑4, Feb 1989 2.00
❑5, Mar 1989 2.00
❑6, Apr 1989 2.00
❑7, May 1989 2.00
❑8, Jun 1989 2.00
❑9, Jul 1989 2.00
❑10, Aug 1989 2.00
❑11, Sep 1989 2.00
❑12, Oct 1989 2.00
❑13, Nov 1989 2.00
❑14, Dec 1989 2.00
❑15, Jan 1990 2.00
❑16, Feb 1990 2.00
❑17, Mar 1990 2.00
❑18, Apr 1990 2.00
❑19, May 1990 2.00
❑20, Jun 1990 2.00
❑21, Jul 1990 2.00
❑22, Aug 1990 2.00

Fright Night 1993 Halloween Annual
Now

❑1, Oct 1993; 3-D; NN 2.95

Fright Night 3-D
Now

❑1, Jun 1992; with glasses 2.95
❑2, Fal 1992; Dracula 2.95

Fright Night 3-D Winter Special
Now

❑1, Win 1993; Brainbats 2.95

Fright Night II Graphic Novel
Now

❑1; Movie adaptation 3.95

Fringe
Caliber

❑1, b&w 2.50
❑2, b&w 2.50
❑3, b&w 2.50
❑4, b&w 2.50
❑5, b&w 2.50
❑6, b&w 2.50
❑7, b&w 2.50
❑8, b&w 2.50

Frogmen
Dell

❑2, May 1962, Continued from Four Color Comics #1258 34.00
❑3, Sep 1962 26.00
❑4, Feb 1963 20.00
❑5, May 1963, ATh (a) 22.00
❑6, Aug 1963 20.00
❑7, Nov 1963 18.00
❑8, Feb 1964 18.00
❑9, May 1964 18.00
❑10, Aug 1964 18.00
❑11, Nov 1964, Final Issue 18.00

From Beyonde
Studio Insidio

❑1, b&w 2.25

From Beyond the Unknown
DC

❑1, Nov 1969 45.00
❑2, Jan 1970 20.00
❑3, Mar 1970, Martin Pasko L.O.C 15.00
❑4, May 1970 15.00
❑5, Jul 1970 15.00
❑6, Sep 1970 15.00
❑7, Nov 1970 JKu (c) 12.00
❑8, Jan 1971; 64 pages 12.00
❑9, Mar 1971 12.00
❑10, May 1971 CS (c) 12.00
❑11, Jul 1971 10.00
❑12, Sep 1971 JKu (c) 10.00
❑13, Nov 1971; 64 pages 10.00
❑14, Jan 1972 JKu (c) 10.00
❑15, Mar 1972; 52 pages; 64 pages 10.00
❑16, May 1972 MA, CI (a) 10.00
❑17, Jul 1972; Reprints from Mystery in Space #11, 30, 56, Strange Adventures #31, 162 10.00
❑18, Sep 1972 8.00
❑19, Nov 1972, CI, GK (a) 8.00
❑20, Jan 1973 8.00
❑21, Mar 1973, reprints from Strange Adventures #23, #149, and #159 8.00
❑22, May 1973, Combo artwork/photograph cover; Reprints from Tales of the Unexpected #20, Strange Adventures #24, and Strange Adventures #163 8.00
❑23, Aug 1973 8.00
❑24, Oct 1973 8.00
❑25, Dec 1973, Final Issue 8.00

From Dusk Till Dawn
Big

❑1/Deluxe, Deluxe Edition 9.95
❑1 4.95

From Far Away
Viz

❑1, Nov 2004 9.99
❑2, Jan 2005 9.99
❑3, Mar 2005 9.99
❑4, May 2005 9.99
❑5, Jul 2005 9.99
❑6, Sep 2005 9.99
❑7, Nov 2005 9.99

From Hell
Tundra

❑1, Mar 1991 AMo (w) 6.00
❑1/2nd, Feb 1992; AMo (w); 2nd printing 5.00
❑1/3rd, Jun 1994; AMo (w); 3rd printing (Kitchen Sink) 5.00
❑1/4th; 4th printing (Kitchen Sink) 4.95
❑2, Jun 1993 AMo (w) 5.00
❑2/2nd; AMo (w); 2nd printing (Kitchen Sink) 5.00
❑2/3rd; AMo (w); 3rd printing 5.00
❑3, Dec 1993 AMo (w) 5.00
❑3/2nd; AMo (w); 2nd printing 5.00
❑3/3rd; AMo (w); 3rd printing 5.00

Four-Star Battle Tales

Reprints DC war stories

©DC

Fox and the Crow

Stanley and His Monster took over title

©DC

Fractured Fairy Tales

Bullwinkle feature spawned one-shot

©Gold Key

Fraggle Rock

Muppet-like characters frolic underground

©Marvel

Frankenstein Mobster

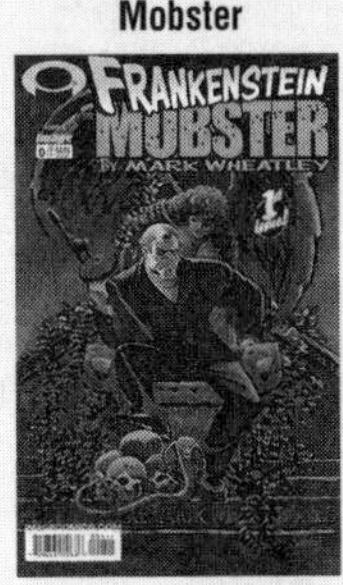

Lawman merges with gangsters he killed

©Image

	N-MINT
❑4, Mar 1994 AMo (w)	5.00
❑4/2nd; AMo (w); 2nd printing	5.00
❑4/3rd; AMo (w); 3rd printing	5.00
❑5, Jun 1994 AMo (w)	4.95
❑6, Nov 1994 AMo (w)	4.95
❑7, Apr 1995 AMo (w)	4.95
❑8, Jul 1995 AMo (w)	4.95
❑9, Apr 1996 AMo (w)	4.95
❑10, Aug 1996; AMo (w); Eleventh issue published as From Hell: Dance of the Gull Catchers	4.95

From Hell: Dance of the Gull Catchers
Kitchen Sink

❑1, Sep 1998, sequel to From Hell; #11 on spine	7.00

From the Darkness
Adventure

❑1, Oct 1990	3.00
❑2, Nov 1990	2.50
❑3, Dec 1990, b&w	2.50
❑4, Jan 1991, b&w	2.50

From the Darkness Book II: Blood Vows
Cry for Dawn

❑1; Adult; b&w; ca. 1992	2.50
❑2; Adult; b&w; ca. 1992	2.50
❑3; Adult	2.50

Frontier
Slave Labor

❑1, Jul 1994	2.95

Frontiers '86 Presents
Frontiers

❑1; Crusaders	1.50
❑2; Crusaders	1.50

Frontline Combat (RCP)
Gemstone

❑1, Aug 1995; Reprints Frontline Combat (EC) #1	2.00
❑2, Nov 1995; Reprints Frontline Combat (EC) #2	2.00
❑3, Feb 1996; Reprints Frontline Combat (EC) #3	2.00
❑4, May 1996; Reprints Frontline Combat (EC) #4	2.00
❑5, Aug 1996; Reprints Frontline Combat (EC) #5	2.50
❑6, Nov 1996; Reprints Frontline Combat (EC) #6	2.50
❑7, Feb 1997; Reprints Frontline Combat (EC) #7	2.50
❑8, May 1997; Reprints Frontline Combat (EC) #8	2.50
❑9, Aug 1997; Reprints Frontline Combat (EC) #9	2.50
❑10, Nov 1997; Reprints Frontline Combat (EC) #10	2.50
❑11, Feb 1998; Reprints Frontline Combat (EC) #11	2.50
❑12, May 1998; Reprints Frontline Combat (EC) #12	2.50
❑13, Aug 1998; Reprints Frontline Combat (EC) #13	2.50
❑14, Nov 1998; Reprints Frontline Combat (EC) #14	2.50
❑15, Feb 1999; Reprints Frontline Combat (EC) #15	2.50

	N-MINT
❑Ann 1; Collects Frontline Combat #1-5	10.95
❑Ann 2; Collects Frontline Combat #6-10	12.95

Frost
Caliber

❑1, b&w	1.95

Frostbiter: Wrath of the Wendigo
Caliber

❑1	2.95
❑2	2.95
❑3	2.95

Frost: The Dying Breed
Caliber

❑1, b&w	2.50
❑2, b&w	2.50
❑3, b&w	2.50

Frozen Embryo
Slave Labor

❑1, Dec 1992	2.95

Fruits Basket
Tokyopop

❑1, Feb 2004	9.99
❑2, Apr 2004	9.99
❑3, Jun 2004	9.99
❑4, Aug 2004	9.99
❑5, Oct 2004	9.99
❑6, Dec 2004	9.99
❑7, Feb 2005	9.99
❑8, Apr 2005	9.99
❑9, Jun 2005	9.99
❑10, Jul 2005	9.99
❑11, Aug 2005	9.99
❑12, Dec 2005	9.99

F-3 Bandit
Antarctic

❑1, Jan 1995; mini-poster	2.95
❑2, Mar 1995; trading card	2.95
❑3, May 1995; trading card	2.95
❑4, Jul 1995; trading card	2.95
❑5, Sep 1995; trading card	2.95
❑6, Nov 1995	2.95
❑7, Jan 1996	2.95
❑8, Mar 1996	2.95
❑9, May 1996, b&w	2.95
❑10, Jul 1996, b&w; trading card	2.95

F-Troop
Gold Key

❑1, Aug 1966, Photo cover	50.00
❑2, Nov 1966	40.00
❑3, Feb 1967	36.00
❑4, Apr 1967	36.00
❑5, May 1967	36.00
❑6, Jun 1967	32.00
❑7, Aug 1967, Final Issue	32.00

Fugitive
Caliber

❑1, ca. 1989, b&w; No indicia	2.50

Fugitoid
Mirage

❑1 1985; Teenage Mutant Ninja Turtles tie-in; Continued from TMNT #4; continued in TMNT #5	3.00

	N-MINT

Full Frontal Nerdity
Dork Storm

❑Ann 1, Jan 2005	2.99

Full Metal Fiction
London Night

❑1, Mar 1997; Adult; b&w	3.95

Full Metal Panic
ADV Manga

❑1, ca. 2003; Reads right to left; Graphic novel; b&w	9.99
❑2, ca. 2003; Reads right to left; Graphic novel; b&w	9.99

Full Metal Panic!
ADV Manga

❑1, ca. 2005	9.99
❑2, ca. 2005	9.99
❑3, ca. 2005	9.99
❑4, ca. 2005	9.99
❑5, ca. 2005	9.99
❑6, ca. 2005	9.99
❑7, ca. 2005	9.99
❑8, ca. 2005	9.99

Full Metal Panic: Overload
ADV Manga

❑1, ca. 2005	9.99
❑2, ca. 2005	9.99

Full Moon
Viz

❑1, Jul 2005	8.99
❑2, Aug 2005	8.99
❑3, Oct 2005	8.99

Full Throttle
Aircel

❑1, b&w; Adult	2.95
❑2, b&w; Adult	2.95

Fun Boys Spring Special
Tundra

❑1, b&w; NN	1.95

Fun Comics
AC

❑1, b&w magazine format	2.00
❑2, b&w magazine format	2.00
❑3; b&w magazine format	2.00
❑4, Mar 1983; Captain Paragon, Nightfall	2.00

Fun House
MN Design

❑1, photos	6.50

Fun House (J.R. Williams'...)
Starhead

❑1, Nov 1993, b&w; Collections of Comics, Strips	3.95

Fun-In
Gold Key

❑1, Feb 1970	16.00
❑2, May 1970	10.00
❑3 1970	9.00
❑4, Nov 1970	9.00
❑5, Jan 1971, Motormouse and Autocat, Dastardly and Muttley	8.00
❑6, Mar 1971, Dastardly and Muttley, It's the Wolf	8.00
❑7, May 1971, Motormouse and Autocat, Dastardly and Muttley, It's the Wolf	6.00

Other grades: Multiply price above by 5/6 for VF/NM • 2/3 for VERY FINE • 1/3 for FINE • 1/5 for VERY GOOD • 1/8 for GOOD

❑8, Jul 1971 .... 6.00
❑9, Oct 1971 .... 6.00
❑10, Jan 1972 .... 6.00
❑11, Apr 1974 .... 5.00
❑12, Jun 1974 .... 5.00
❑13, Aug 1974 .... 5.00
❑14, Oct 1974 .... 5.00
❑15 .... 5.00

Funky Phantom
Gold Key

❑1, Mar 1972 .... 24.00
❑2, Jun 1972 .... 15.00
❑3, Sep 1972 .... 10.00
❑4, Dec 1972 .... 10.00
❑5, Mar 1973 .... 10.00
❑6, Jun 1973 .... 8.00
❑7, Sep 1973 .... 8.00
❑8, Dec 1973, A: April. A: Skip. A: Augie. A: Elmo. A: Prissy Atwater 8.00
❑9, Mar 1974 .... 8.00
❑10, Jun 1974 .... 8.00
❑11, Sep 1974 .... 6.00
❑12, Dec 1974 .... 6.00
❑13, Mar 1975 .... 6.00

Funny Stuff Stocking Stuffer
DC

❑1, Mar 1985 .... 1.25

Funnytime Features
Eenieweenie

❑1, Jul 1994, b&w 2.50
❑1/2nd, ca. 1994, b&w; 2nd printing 2.50
❑2, ca. 1994, b&w 2.50
❑3, ca. 1994, b&w 2.50
❑4, ca. 1995, b&w 2.50
❑5, ca. 1995, b&w 2.50
❑6, ca. 1995, b&w 2.50
❑7/Variant, ca. 1995 .... 2.50
❑7, ca. 1995 .... 2.50
❑8, ca. 1995, b&w 2.50

Funtastic World of Hanna-Barbera
Marvel

❑1, Dec 1977 .... 13.00
❑2, Mar 1978 .... 9.00
❑3, Jun 1978 .... 6.00

Fun with Milk & Cheese
Slave Labor

❑1, Apr 1994, b&w; collects stories; has pages 59 and 62 switched 9.95

Furies (Avatar)
Avatar

❑0, Feb 1997 .... 3.00
❑0/Nude, Mar 1997; Nude cover 3.00

Furies (Carbon-Based)
Carbon-Based

❑1, May 1996, b&w 2.75
❑2, Jul 1996, b&w 2.75
❑3, Sep 1996, b&w 2.75
❑4, Nov 1996, b&w 2.75
❑5, Jan 1997, b&w 2.75
❑6, Mar 1997, b&w 2.75
❑7, ca. 1997 .... 2.75
❑8, Sep 1997 .... 2.75

Furkindred
Mu

❑1, Jan 1992, b&w 6.95
❑2, Nov 1992, b&w 7.95

Furrlough
Antarctic

❑1, Nov 1991 .... 4.00
❑2, Feb 1992 .... 3.50
❑3, May 1992 .... 3.50
❑4, Jul 1992 .... 3.00
❑5, Nov 1992 .... 3.00
❑6, Jan 1993 .... 3.00
❑7, Mar 1993 .... 3.00
❑8, May 1993 .... 3.00
❑9, Jul 1993 .... 3.00
❑10, Sep 1993 .... 3.00
❑11, Nov 1993 .... 2.75
❑12, Dec 1993 .... 2.75
❑13, Jan 1994 .... 2.75
❑14, Feb 1994 .... 2.75
❑15, Mar 1994 .... 2.75
❑16, Apr 1994 .... 2.75
❑17, May 1994 .... 2.75
❑18, Jun 1994 .... 2.75
❑19, Jul 1994 .... 2.75
❑20, Aug 1994 .... 2.75
❑21, Sep 1994 .... 2.75
❑22, Oct 1994 .... 2.75
❑23, Nov 1994; Giant-size 3.50
❑24, Dec 1994 .... 2.75
❑25, Jan 1995 .... 2.75
❑26, Feb 1995 .... 2.75
❑27, Mar 1995 .... 2.75
❑28, Apr 1995 .... 2.75
❑29, May 1995 .... 2.75
❑30, Jun 1995 .... 2.75
❑31, Jul 1995 .... 2.75
❑32, Aug 1995 .... 2.75
❑33, Sep 1995 .... 2.75
❑34, Oct 1995 .... 2.75
❑35, Nov 1995; fourth anniversary special; Giant-size 3.50
❑36, Dec 1995 .... 2.95
❑37, Jan 1996 .... 2.95
❑38, Feb 1996 .... 2.95
❑39, Mar 1996 .... 2.95
❑40, Apr 1996 .... 2.95
❑41, May 1996 .... 2.95
❑42, Jun 1996 .... 2.95
❑43, Jul 1996 .... 2.95
❑44, Aug 1996 .... 2.95
❑45, Sep 1996 .... 2.95
❑46, Oct 1996 .... 2.95
❑47, Nov 1996; 48 pages 2.95
❑48, Dec 1996 .... 2.95
❑49, Jan 1997 .... 2.95
❑50, Feb 1997; Giant-size; Includes Furrlough index 3.95
❑51, Mar 1997 .... 2.95
❑52, Apr 1997 .... 2.95
❑53, May 1997 .... 2.95
❑54, Jun 1997 .... 2.95
❑55, Jul 1997 .... 2.95
❑56, Aug 1997 .... 2.95
❑57, Sep 1997 .... 2.95
❑58, Oct 1997 .... 2.95
❑59, Nov 1997 .... 2.95
❑60, Dec 1997 .... 2.95
❑61, Jan 1998 .... 2.95
❑62, Feb 1998 .... 2.95
❑63, Mar 1998 .... 2.95
❑64, Apr 1998 .... 2.95
❑65, May 1998 .... 2.95
❑66, Jun 1998 .... 2.95
❑67, Jul 1998 .... 2.95
❑68, Aug 1998 .... 2.95
❑69, Sep 1998 .... 2.95
❑70, Oct 1998 .... 2.95
❑71, Nov 1998 .... 2.95
❑72, Dec 1998 .... 2.95
❑73, Jan 1999 .... 2.95
❑79, Jul 1999 .... 2.95
❑80, Aug 1999 .... 2.95
❑81, Sep 1999 .... 2.95
❑82, Oct 1999 .... 2.95
❑83, Nov 1999 .... 2.95
❑84, Dec 1999 .... 2.95
❑85, Jan 2000 .... 2.95
❑86, Feb 2000 .... 2.95
❑87, Mar 2000 .... 2.95
❑88, Apr 2000 .... 2.95
❑89, May 2000 .... 2.95
❑90, Jun 2000 .... 2.95
❑91, Jul 2000 .... 2.95
❑92, Aug 2000 .... 2.95
❑93, Sep 2000 .... 2.95
❑94, Oct 2000 .... 2.95
❑95, Nov 2000 .... 2.95
❑96, Dec 2000 .... 2.95
❑97, Jan 2001 .... 2.95
❑98, Feb 2001 .... 2.95
❑99, Mar 2001 .... 2.95
❑100, Apr 2001 .... 2.95
❑101, May 2001 .... 2.95
❑102, Jun 2001 .... 2.95
❑103, Jul 2001 .... 2.99
❑104, Aug 2001 .... 2.99
❑105, Sep 2001 .... 2.99
❑106, Oct 2001 .... 2.99
❑107, Nov 2001 .... 2.99
❑108, Dec 2001 .... 2.99
❑109, Jan 2002 .... 2.99
❑110, Feb 2002 .... 2.99
❑111, Mar 2002 .... 2.99
❑112, Apr 2002 .... 2.99
❑113, May 2002 .... 2.99
❑114, Jun 2002 .... 2.99
❑115, Jul 2002 .... 2.99
❑116, Aug 2002 .... 2.99
❑117, Sep 2002 .... 2.99
❑118, Oct 2002 .... 2.99
❑119, Nov 2002 .... 2.99
❑120, Dec 2002 .... 2.99
❑121, Jan 2003 .... 2.99
❑122, Feb 2003 .... 2.99
❑123, Mar 2003 .... 2.99
❑124, Apr 2003 .... 2.99
❑125 2003 .... 2.99
❑126 2003 .... 2.99
❑127 2003 .... 2.99
❑128 2003 .... 2.99
❑129 2003 .... 2.99
❑130 2003 .... 2.99
❑131 2003 .... 2.99
❑132 2004 .... 2.99
❑133 2004 .... 2.99
❑134 2004 .... 2.99
❑135 2004 .... 2.99
❑136, Apr 2004 .... 2.99
❑137, May 2004 .... 2.99
❑138, Jun 2004 .... 2.99
❑139, Jul 2004 .... 2.99
❑140, Aug 2004; Price increase 3.50
❑141, Sep 2004 .... 3.50
❑142, Oct 2004 .... 3.50
❑143, Nov 2005; Typo in contents 3.50
❑144, Dec 2005 .... 3.50

Further Adventures of Cyclops and Phoenix
Marvel

❑1, Jun 1996; O: Mr. Sinister 1.95
❑2, Jul 1996 .... 1.95
❑3, Aug 1996 .... 1.95
❑4, Sep 1996; Conclusion 1.95

Further Adventures of Indiana Jones
Marvel

❑1, Jan 1983, JBy (w); JBy, TD (a) 2.50
❑2, Feb 1983, JBy (c); JBy, TD (a) 2.00
❑3, Mar 1983 .... 2.00
❑4, Apr 1983 .... 2.00
❑5, May 1983 .... 2.00
❑6, Jun 1983 .... 2.00
❑7, Jul 1983 .... 2.00
❑8, Aug 1983 .... 2.00
❑9, Sep 1983 .... 2.00
❑10, Oct 1983 .... 2.00
❑11, Nov 1983 .... 2.00
❑12, Dec 1983 .... 2.00
❑13, Jan 1984 .... 2.00
❑14, Feb 1984 .... 2.00
❑15, Mar 1984 .... 2.00
❑16, Apr 1984 .... 2.00
❑17, May 1984 .... 2.00
❑18, Jun 1984 .... 2.00
❑19, Jul 1984 .... 2.00
❑20, Aug 1984 .... 2.00
❑21, Sep 1984 .... 2.00
❑22, Oct 1984 .... 2.00
❑23, Nov 1984 .... 2.00
❑24, Dec 1984 .... 2.00
❑25, Jan 1985, MG (c); SD (a) 2.00
❑26, Feb 1985, SD (a) 2.00
❑27, Mar 1985, KP (c); SD (a) 2.00
❑28, Apr 1985, KP (c); SD (a) 2.00
❑29, May 1985, KP (c); SD (a) 2.00
❑30, Jul 1985, KP (c); SD (a) 2.00
❑31, Sep 1985, KP (c); SD (a) 2.00
❑32, Nov 1985, KP (c); SD (a) 2.00
❑33, Jan 1986 .... 2.00
❑34, Mar 1986; Final Issue 2.00

Further Adventures of Nyoka the Jungle Girl
AC

❑1 .... 2.25
❑2; Photo cover 2.25

Other grades: Multiply price above by 5/6 for VF/NM • 2/3 for VERY FINE • 1/3 for FINE • 1/5 for VERY GOOD • 1/8 for GOOD

Fred Hembeck Destroys the Marvel Universe

Every Marvel character dies

©Marvel

Free Speeches

Comic Book Legal Defense Fund fundraiser

©Oni

French Ice

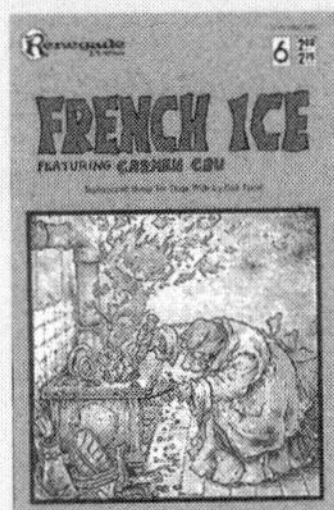

Crotchety old woman's tangles with authority

©Renegade

Friendly Ghost, Casper

Dyslexic title still confuses collectors

©Harvey

Friends of Maxx

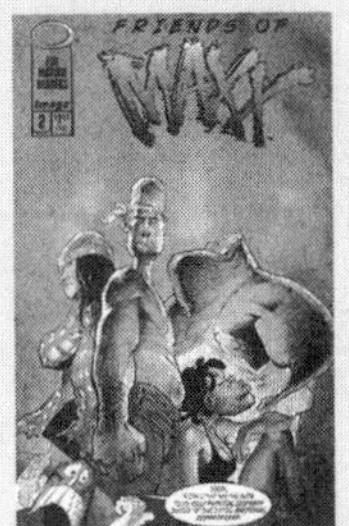

Sam Kieth's purple monster hosts anthology

©Image

N-MINT

❑3, b&w; Photo cover; b&w 2.25
❑4, b&w 2.25
❑5 .... 2.50
❑6, ca. 2005; Reprints from Master Comics #126, 108, 102 .... 6.95
❑7, ca. 2005; Reprints from Nyoka #17, Master Comics #124, Don Winslow, Master Comics #100, Jungle Comics; ca. 2005 .... 6.95

Further Adventures of Young Jeffy Dahmer
Boneyard

❑1, b&w; Adult 3.00

Further Fattening Adventures of Pudge, Girl Blimp
Star*Reach

❑1; Comic size 4.00
❑1/A; large size 5.00
❑2; Comic size 4.00
❑3; Comic size 4.00

Fury
Dell

❑1, Aug 1962 .... 25.00

Fury
Marvel

❑1, May 1994; O: S.H.I.E.L.D.. O: Hydra. O: Nick Fury 3.00

Fury
Marvel / MAX

❑1, Nov 2001 BSz (c) 4.00
❑2, Dec 2001 BSz (c) 2.99
❑3, Jan 2002 BSz (c) 2.99
❑4, Feb 2002 BSz (c) 2.99
❑5, Mar 2002 BSz (c) 2.99
❑6, Apr 2002 BSz (c) 2.99

Fury/Agent 13
Marvel

❑1, Jun 1998; gatefold summary 2.99
❑2, Jul 1998; gatefold summary; Fury returns to Marvel universe 2.99

Fury/Black Widow: Death Duty
Marvel

❑1, Feb 1995; prestige format 5.95

Fury of Firestorm
DC

❑1, Jun 1982, PB (c); PB (a); O: Firestorm. 1: Lorraine Reilly. 1: Black Bison 6.00
❑2, Jul 1982, PB (c); PB (a) 1.75
❑3, Aug 1982, PB (c); PB (a); A: Killer Frost 1.75
❑4, Sep 1982, PB (c); PB (a); A: Justice League of America. A: Killer Frost. Superman apperance; V: Killer Frost; V: Justice League of America 1.75
❑5, Oct 1982, PB (c); PB (a); A: Pied Piper 1.75
❑6, Nov 1982, PB (c); PB, CS (a); Master of the Universe preview insert 1.50
❑7, Dec 1982, PB (c); PB (a); 1: Plastique 1.50
❑8, Jan 1983, PB (c); A: Typhoon 1.50
❑9, Feb 1983, PB (c); A: Typhoon 1.50
❑10, Mar 1983, PB (c); PB (a); A: Hyena 1.50
❑11, Apr 1983, PB (c); PB (a) 1.25
❑12, May 1983, PB (c); PB (a) 1.25
❑13, Jun 1983, PB (c); PB (a) 1.25
❑14, Jul 1983, PB (c); PB (a); 1: Mica (Enforcer II). 1: Enforcer I (Leroy Merkyn) 1.25

N-MINT

❑15, Aug 1983, PB (c); PB (a); A: Multiplex 1.25
❑16, Sep 1983, PB (c); PB (a) 1.25
❑17, Oct 1983, PB (c); PB, GT (a); 1: Firehawk 1.25
❑18, Nov 1983, PB (c); GT (a); 1: Enforcer II (Mica) 1.25
❑19, Jan 1984; GC (a); V: Goldenrod 1.25
❑20, Feb 1984; 1: Louise Lincoln. A: Firehawk. V: Killer Frost 1.25
❑21, Mar 1984; D: Killer Frost I (Crystal Frost). V: Killer Frost 1.00
❑22, Apr 1984; PB (a); O: Firestorm 1.00
❑23, May 1984; V: Byte 1.00
❑24, Jun 1984; 1: Bug. 1: Blue Devil. 1: Byte; 16 page insert 1.00
❑25, Jul 1984; 1: Silver Deer. V: Black Bison 1.00
❑26, Aug 1984; V: Black Bison 1.00
❑27, Sep 1984; V: Silver Deer 1.00
❑28, Oct 1984; 1: Slipknot. V: Slipknot 1.00
❑29, Nov 1984; 1: Mindboggler. 1: Breathtaker (villain). V: Stratos 1.00
❑30, Dec 1984; GK (c); V: Mindboggler 1.00
❑31, Jan 1985; V: Mindboggler 1.00
❑32, Feb 1985 A: Phantom Stranger 1.00
❑33, Mar 1985 .... 1.00
❑34, Apr 1985; 1: Killer Frost II (Louise Lincoln). V: Killer Frost 1.00
❑35, May 1985; V: Killer Frost. V: Plastique 1.00
❑36, Jun 1985; V: Killer Frost. V: Plastique 1.00
❑37, Jul 1985 .... 1.00
❑38, Aug 1985; V: Weasel 1.00
❑39, Sep 1985; V: Weasel 1.00
❑40, Oct 1985; Ronnie Graduates 1.00
❑41, Nov 1985; Crisis 1.00
❑42, Dec 1985; Crisis 1.00
❑43, Jan 1986; V: Typhoon 1.00
❑44, Feb 1986; V: Typhoon 1.00
❑45, Mar 1986 .... 1.00
❑46, Apr 1986 A: Blue Devil 1.00
❑47, May 1986; A: Blue Devil. V: Multiplex 1.00
❑48, Jun 1986; 1: Moonbow 1.00
❑49, Jul 1986 .... 1.00
❑50, Aug 1986 .... 1.00
❑51, Sep 1986 .... 1.00
❑52, Oct 1986 .... 1.00
❑53, Nov 1986 .... 1.00
❑54, Dec 1986 .... 1.00
❑55, Jan 1987; A: Cosmic Boy. V: Brimstone. Legends 1.00
❑56, Feb 1987; A: Hawk. Legends 1.00
❑57, Mar 1987 .... 1.00
❑58, Apr 1987; 1: Parasite II. V: Parasite 1.00
❑59, May 1987; A: Firehawk. V: Parasite 1.00
❑60, Jun 1987 .... 1.00
❑61, Jul 1987; V: Typhoon. regular cover 1.00
❑61/A, Jul 1987; V: Typhoon. Alternate cover (test cover) 10.00
❑62, Aug 1987 .... 1.00
❑63, Sep 1987 A: Captain Atom 1.00
❑64, Oct 1987; A: Suicide Squad. series continues as Firestorm, the Nuclear Man 1.00
❑Ann 1, ca. 1983 .... 2.00
❑Ann 2, ca. 1984; text story 1.50
❑Ann 3, ca. 1985 .... 1.50
❑Ann 4, ca. 1986 .... 1.50

N-MINT

Fury of Hellina
Lightning

❑1, Jan 1995, b&w 2.75

Fury of S.H.I.E.L.D.
Marvel

❑1, Apr 1995; HC (w); chromium cover 2.50
❑2, May 1995 HC (w); A: Iron Man 2.00
❑3, Jun 1995 HC (w); A: Iron Man 2.00
❑4, Jul 1995; HC (w); polybagged with decoder 2.50

Fused
Image

❑1, Mar 2002; Dark background on cover 2.95
❑2, Jul 2002 .... 2.95
❑3, Oct 2002 .... 2.95
❑4, Jan 2003 .... 2.95

Fused
Dark Horse

❑1, Jan 2004 .... 2.99
❑2, Feb 2004 .... 2.99
❑3, Feb 2004 .... 2.99
❑4, Mar 2004 .... 2.99

Fushigi Yugi
Viz

❑1, Dec 2002 .... 9.95
❑2, Feb 2003 .... 9.95
❑3, Apr 2003 .... 9.95
❑4, Jun 2003 .... 9.95
❑5, Aug 2003 .... 9.95
❑6, Oct 2003 .... 9.95
❑7, Dec 2003 .... 9.95
❑8, Feb 2004 .... 9.95
❑9, Apr 2004 .... 9.95
❑10, Jun 2004 .... 9.95
❑11, Aug 2004 .... 9.95
❑12, Oct 2004 .... 9.95
❑13, Jan 2005 .... 9.95
❑14, Apr 2005 .... 9.95
❑15, Aug 2005 .... 9.95
❑16, Oct 2005 .... 9.95

Fusion
Eclipse

❑1, Jan 1987, b&w 2.00
❑2, Mar 1987, b&w 2.00
❑3, May 1987, b&w 2.00
❑4, Jul 1987, b&w 2.00
❑5, Sep 1987, b&w 2.00
❑6, Nov 1987, b&w 2.00
❑7, Jan 1988, b&w 2.00
❑8, Mar 1988, b&w 2.00
❑9, May 1988, b&w 2.00
❑10, Jul 1988, b&w 2.00
❑11, Sep 1988, b&w 2.00
❑12, Nov 1988, b&w 2.00
❑13, Jan 1989, b&w 2.00
❑14, Mar 1989, b&w 2.00
❑15, May 1989, b&w 2.00
❑16, Jul 1989, b&w 2.00
❑17, Sep 1989, b&w 2.00

Futaba-kun Change
Ironcat

❑1 .... 2.95
❑2 .... 2.95
❑3 .... 2.95

Other grades: Multiply price above by 5/6 for VF/NM • 2/3 for VERY FINE • 1/3 for FINE • 1/5 for VERY GOOD • 1/8 for GOOD

Futaba-kun Change
Ironcat

- ❑1, Jul 1999 ... 2.95
- ❑2 ... 2.95
- ❑3 ... 2.95
- ❑4 ... 2.95

Futurama
Slave Labor

- ❑1, Apr 1989, b&w ... 2.00
- ❑2, Jun 1989, b&w ... 2.00
- ❑3, Aug 1989, b&w ... 2.00

Futurama
Bongo

- ❑1, ca. 2000; ca. 2000 ... 7.00
- ❑1/2nd, ca. 2000 ... 2.50
- ❑2 2001 ... 2.50
- ❑3 2001 ... 2.50
- ❑4 2001 ... 2.50
- ❑5 2001; ca. 2001 ... 2.50
- ❑6 2001; ca. 2001 ... 2.50
- ❑7 2002 ... 2.50
- ❑8 2002; Fake CGC cover ... 2.50
- ❑9 2002 ... 2.50
- ❑10 2002 ... 2.50
- ❑11 2003 ... 2.50
- ❑12 2003 ... 2.50
- ❑13 2003 ... 2.50
- ❑14, Jul 2003 ... 2.50
- ❑15, Oct 2003 ... 2.99
- ❑16, Feb 2004 ... 2.99
- ❑17, May 2004 ... 2.99
- ❑18 ... 2.99
- ❑19 ... 2.99

Futurama/Simpsons Infinitely Secret Crossover Crisis
Bongo

- ❑1, ca. 2002 ... 2.50
- ❑2, ca. 2002 ... 2.50

Future Beat
Oasis

- ❑1, Jul 1986 ... 1.50
- ❑2 ... 1.50

Future Cop: L.A.P.D.
DC / Wildstorm

- ❑1, Jan 1999; magazine-sized ... 4.95
- ❑Ashcan 1 1998; Supplement to Wizard: The Comics Magazine #89; ca. 1998 .. 1.00

Future Course
Reoccurring Images

- ❑1, Dec 1993; Fold-out cover ... 2.95

Futuretech
Mushroom

- ❑1, Feb 1995, b&w; 2nd Printing (first printing published by BlackLine Studios, Oct 94) ... 3.50

Future World Comix
Warren

- ❑1, Sep 1978 ... 7.00

Futurians by Dave Cockrum
Lodestone

- ❑1, Oct 1985, DC (w); DC (a); 1: Doctor Zeus. 1: Hammerhand. 2: The Futurians. Story continued from Marvel Graphic Novel #9 ... 2.00
- ❑2, Dec 1985, DC (w); DC (a) ... 2.00
- ❑3, Apr 1986, DC (w); DC (a); Final Issue 2.00

Futurians
Aardwolf

- ❑1, Aug 1995, b&w ... 2.95

Fuzzy Buzzard and Friends
Hall of Heroes

- ❑1, Apr 1995 ... 2.50

G-8 and His Battle Aces
Blazing

- ❑1, Oct 1966, Tim Truman cover; Flip book with Spider's Web # 1 ... 1.50

Gabriel
Caliber

- ❑1, ca. 1995, b&w; prestige format; One-shot ... 3.95

!Gag!
Harrier

- ❑1 1987 ... 3.50
- ❑2, Jul 1987 ... 3.00
- ❑3 1987 ... 3.00
- ❑4 1987; magazine ... 3.00
- ❑5 1988; magazine ... 3.00
- ❑6 1988; magazine ... 3.00
- ❑7 1988; magazine ... 3.00

Gag Reflex (Skip Williamson's...)
Williamson

- ❑1, Jan 1994, b&w ... 2.95

Gaijin (Matrix)
Matrix

- ❑1, Feb 1987 ... 1.75

Gaijin
Caliber

- ❑1, b&w ... 3.50

Gajit Gang
Amazing

- ❑1 ... 1.95

Galactic
Dark Horse

- ❑1, Aug 2003 ... 2.99
- ❑2, Oct 2003 ... 2.99
- ❑3, Oct 2003 ... 2.99

Galactica: The New Millennium
Realm

- ❑1, Sep 1999; Agroship cover ... 2.99
- ❑1/Conv, Sep 1999; Convention edition. 5.00

Galactic Gladiators
Playdigm

- ❑1 2001 ... 2.95
- ❑2 2001 ... 2.95
- ❑3 2002 ... 2.95
- ❑4 2002 ... 2.95

Galactic Guardians
Marvel

- ❑1, Jul 1994 ... 1.50
- ❑2, Aug 1994 ... 1.50
- ❑3, Sep 1994 ... 1.50
- ❑4, Oct 1994 ... 1.50

Galactic Patrol
Eternity

- ❑1, Jul 1990, b&w ... 2.25
- ❑2, b&w ... 2.25
- ❑3, b&w ... 2.25
- ❑4, b&w ... 2.25
- ❑5, b&w ... 2.25

Galactus the Devourer
Marvel

- ❑1, Sep 1999 JB (c); BSz (a) ... 3.50
- ❑2, Oct 1999 ... 3.50
- ❑3, Nov 1999 ... 3.50
- ❑4, Dec 1999 JB (c); JB (a) ... 3.50
- ❑5, Jan 2000 ... 3.50
- ❑6, Feb 2000 ... 3.50

Galaxina
Aircel

- ❑1, Dec 1991, b&w; Adult ... 2.95
- ❑2, Jan 1991, b&w; Adult ... 2.95
- ❑3, Feb 1991, b&w; Adult ... 2.95
- ❑4, Mar 1991; Adult ... 2.95

Galaxion
Helikon

- ❑1, May 1997, b&w ... 2.75
- ❑2, Jul 1997, b&w ... 2.75
- ❑3, Sep 1997, b&w ... 2.75
- ❑4, Nov 1997, b&w ... 2.75
- ❑5, Jan 1998, b&w ... 2.75
- ❑6, Mar 1998, b&w ... 2.75
- ❑7 1998 ... 2.75
- ❑8 1998 ... 2.75
- ❑9 1999 ... 2.75
- ❑10 1999 ... 2.75
- ❑11, Nov 1999 ... 2.75
- ❑Special 1, May 1998, b&w ... 1.00

Galaxy Girl
Dynamic

- ❑1, b&w ... 2.50

Gallegher Boy Reporter
Gold Key

- ❑1, May 1965 ... 15.00

Gall Force: Eternal Story
CPM

- ❑1, Mar 1995 ... 2.95
- ❑2, May 1995 ... 2.95
- ❑3, Jul 1995 ... 2.95
- ❑4, Sep 1995 ... 2.95

Gambit
Eternity

- ❑1, Sep 1988, b&w ... 4.00

Gambit
Oracle

- ❑1, Sep 1986 ... 1.50
- ❑2, Nov 1986 ... 1.50

Gambit
Marvel

- ❑1, Dec 1993, foil cover ... 3.00
- ❑1/Gold, Dec 1993, Gold promotion edition 4.00
- ❑2, Jan 1994 ... 2.50
- ❑3, Feb 1994, Gambit steals elixir from Chandra (External) ... 2.50
- ❑4, Mar 1994, Gambit utilizes elixir to revive Bella Donna; Gambit exiled from New Orleans ... 2.50

Gambit
Marvel

- ❑1, Sep 1997, gatefold summary ... 2.50
- ❑2, Oct 1997, gatefold summary ... 2.50
- ❑3, Nov 1997 ... 2.50
- ❑4, Dec 1997 ... 2.50

Gambit
Marvel

- ❑1, Feb 1999, A: X-Men. A: X-Cutioner.. 3.00
- ❑1/A, Feb 1999, A: X-Men. A: X-Cutioner. DFE alternate cover ... 4.00
- ❑1/B, Feb 1999, A: X-Men. A: X-Cutioner. DFE alternate cover ... 4.00
- ❑1/C, Feb 1999, A: X-Men. A: X-Cutioner. Marvel Authentix printed sketch cover; 600 printed ... 6.00
- ❑1/D, Feb 1999, White cover with sepiatone sketch art ... 4.00
- ❑2, Mar 1999, A: Storm ... 2.50
- ❑3, Apr 1999, A: Courier. A: Mengo Brothers 2.50
- ❑4, May 1999, V: vampires in New Orleans 2.50
- ❑5, Jun 1999, V: X-Cutioner ... 1.99
- ❑6, Jul 1999, early adventure ... 1.99
- ❑7, Aug 1999, V: Pig ... 1.99
- ❑8, Sep 1999 ... 1.99
- ❑9, Oct 1999 ... 1.99
- ❑10, Nov 1999 ... 1.99
- ❑11, Dec 1999 ... 1.99
- ❑12, Jan 2000, Giant- Sized Special ... 2.25
- ❑13, Feb 2000 ... 2.25
- ❑14, Mar 2000 ... 2.25
- ❑15, Apr 2000 ... 2.25
- ❑16, May 2000, Kissing Rogue on cover 2.25
- ❑17, Jun 2000, V: Bullseye; V: Constrictor; V: Fireballs; V: X-Cutioner; New Son issues contract on Gambit's life ... 2.25
- ❑18, Jul 2000, V: Fireballs; V: X-Cutioner; V: Batroc; V: Zaran; V: Crossbones..... 2.25
- ❑19, Aug 2000, V: Zaran; V: Batroc; V: Crossbones; Contract on Gambit's life expires; Assassin's Guild and Thieves' Guild unite ... 2.25
- ❑20, Sep 2000 ... 2.25
- ❑21, Oct 2000, V: Mystique; Gambit attempts to steal government files concerning Black Womb ... 2.25
- ❑22, Nov 2000, V: Rax of the Neo ... 2.25
- ❑23, Dec 2000, V: Ego ... 2.25
- ❑24, Jan 2001, D: New Son; O: New Son; V: New Son ... 2.25
- ❑25, Feb 2001, double-sized; Final Issue 2.99
- ❑Ann 1999, Sep 1999 ... 3.50
- ❑Ann 2000, ca. 2000 ... 3.50
- ❑GS 1, Dec 1998, Giant sized; Cover says Feb 99, indicia says Dec 98; Reprints material from X-Men #33 and #41 and Uncanny X-Men #323 and #326 ... 5.00

Gambit
Marvel

- ❑1, Nov 2004 ... 2.99
- ❑2, Nov 2004 ... 2.99
- ❑3, Dec 2004 ... 2.99
- ❑4, Jan 2005 ... 2.99
- ❑5, Feb 2005 ... 2.99
- ❑6, Mar 2005 ... 2.99
- ❑7, Apr 2005 ... 2.99
- ❑8, May 2005 ... 2.99
- ❑9, May 2005 ... 2.99
- ❑10, Jun 2005 ... 2.99

Fright Night

Based on 1985 horror host homage

©Now

Frogmen

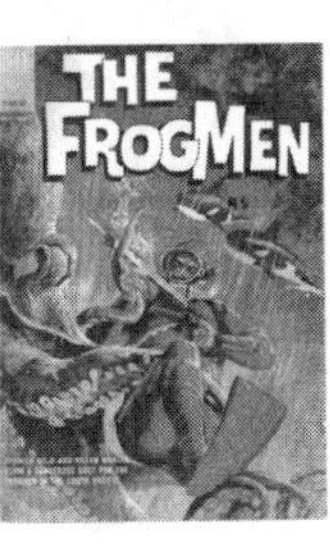

Underwater investigations began in Four Color

©Dell

From Beyond the Unknown

Science fiction anthology reprinted classics

©DC

From Hell

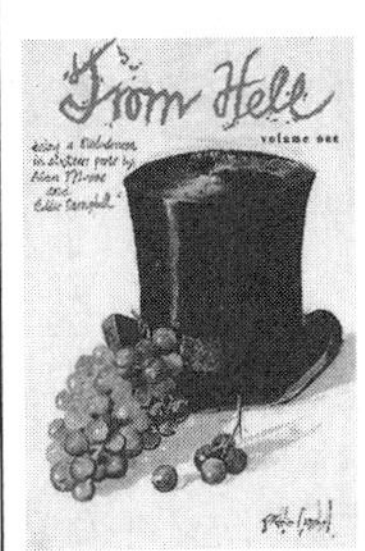

Jack the Ripper revelations from Alan Moore

©Tundra

F-Troop

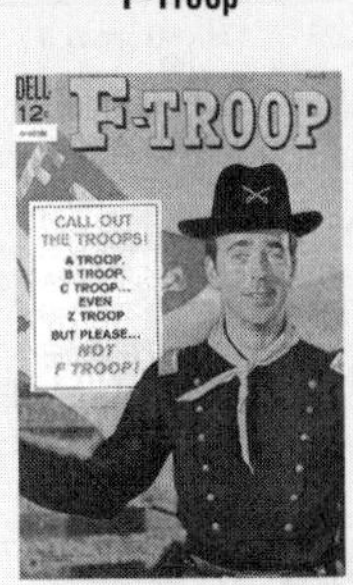

Ken Barry leads inept cavalry unit

©Gold Key

N-MINT

❑11, Jul 2005 ... 2.99
❑12, Aug 2005 ... 2.99

Gambit and Bishop
Marvel

❑1, Mar 2001; Bishop discovered infected by parasitic energy being ... 2.25
❑2, Apr 2001 ... 2.25
❑3, May 2001 ... 2.25
❑4, Jun 2001; V: Cable; Cable kidnaps Stryfe ... 2.25
❑5, May 2001; Stryfe reveals that parasitic entity as Bete Noir ... 2.25
❑6, Jun 2001; D: Stryfe; Stryfe absorbs parasitic energy being ... 2.25

Gambit and Bishop Alpha
Marvel

❑1, Feb 2001 ... 2.25

Gambit and Bishop Genesis
Marvel

❑1, Mar 2001; reprints Uncanny X-Men #266, Uncanny X-Men #283, and X-Men (2nd series) #8 ... 3.50

Gambit & the X-Ternals
Marvel

❑1, Mar 1995 ... 2.00
❑2, Apr 1995; The Age of Apocalypse ... 2.00
❑3, May 1995; The Age of Apocalypse ... 2.00
❑4, Jun 1995; AM (a); The Age of Apocalypse ... 2.00

Game Boy
Valiant

❑1, Jun 1990 ... 1.95
❑2, Jul 1990 ... 1.95
❑3, Aug 1990 ... 1.95
❑4, Sep 1990 ... 1.95

Game Guys!
Wonder

❑1 ... 2.50

Gamera
Dark Horse

❑1, Aug 1996, V: Gyaos ... 2.95
❑2, Sep 1996 ... 2.95
❑3, Oct 1996, V: Zigra and Viras ... 2.95
❑4, Nov 1996, Final Issue ... 2.95

Gammarauders
DC

❑1, Jan 1989 ... 1.25
❑2, Mar 1989 ... 1.25
❑3, Apr 1989 ... 1.25
❑4, May 1989 ... 1.25
❑5, Jul 1989 ... 1.25
❑6, Aug 1989 ... 1.25
❑7, Sep 1989 ... 2.00
❑8, Oct 1989 ... 2.00
❑9, Nov 1989 ... 2.00
❑10, Dec 1989, Final Issue ... 2.00

Gamorra Swimsuit Special
Image

❑1, Jun 1996; pin-ups ... 2.50

Gangland
DC / Vertigo

❑1, Jun 1998; cover overlay ... 2.95
❑2, Jul 1998 ... 2.95

N-MINT

❑3, Aug 1998 ... 2.95
❑4, Sep 1998 ... 2.95

Gantar: The Last Nabu
Target

❑1, Dec 1986 ... 1.75
❑2, Feb 1987 ... 1.75
❑3, Apr 1987, b&w ... 1.75
❑4 ... 1.75
❑5 ... 1.75
❑6 ... 1.75
❑7 ... 1.75

Gargoyle
Marvel

❑1, Jun 1985 BWr (c); BWr (a) ... 1.50
❑2, Jul 1985 ... 1.50
❑3, Aug 1985 ... 1.50
❑4, Sep 1985 ... 1.50

Gargoyles
Marvel

❑1, Feb 1995; enhanced cover ... 2.50
❑2, Mar 1995 ... 1.50
❑3, Apr 1995 ... 1.50
❑4, May 1995 ... 1.50
❑5, Jun 1995 ... 1.50
❑6, Jul 1995 ... 1.50
❑7, Aug 1995 ... 1.50
❑8, Sep 1995 ... 1.50
❑9, Oct 1995 ... 1.50
❑10, Nov 1995 ... 1.50
❑11, Dec 1995; Final Issue ... 1.50

Garou: The Lone Wolf
Bare Bones

❑1, Jul 1999 ... 2.00

Garrison's Gorillas
Dell

❑1, Jan 1968, Photo cover ... 21.00
❑2, Apr 1968, Photo cover ... 14.00
❑3, Jul 1968 ... 14.00
❑4, Oct 1968 ... 14.00
❑5, Oct 1969, Reprints #1 ... 12.00

Gasp!
Quebecor

❑1 1994; PF (w); PF (a); Previews Tyrant, Rare Bit Fiends, Wandering Star, and more. Contains new Buck Godot, Zap Gun for Hire story ... 1.00

Gatecrasher: Ring of Fire
Black Bull

❑1, Mar 2000; Yellow cover with five figures ... 2.50
❑1/A, Mar 2000; Green cover with two figures ... 2.50
❑2, Apr 2000 ... 2.50
❑3, May 2000 ... 2.50
❑3/A, May 2000; variant cover ... 2.50
❑4, Jun 2000 ... 2.50
❑4/A, Jun 2000; Variant (woman in lingerie, shipped 1:4) ... 2.50

Gatekeeper
Gatekeeper

❑1, b&w ... 2.50

Gate Manga
ADV Manga

❑1, ca. 2005 ... 9.99

N-MINT

Gates of Eden
Fantaco

❑1, ca. 1982, b&w ... 3.50

Gates of Pandragon
Ianus

❑1, b&w ... 2.25

Gatesville Company
Speakeasy Comics

❑1, Sep 2005 ... 2.99

Gateway to Horror
Dark Horse

❑1, Aug 1987, b&w ... 1.75

Gathering of Tribes
KC Arts

❑1; giveaway; no cover price ... 1.00

Gauntlet
Aircel

❑1, Jul 1992; Adult ... 3.00
❑2, Aug 1992; Adult ... 3.00
❑3, Sep 1992; Adult ... 3.00
❑4, Oct 1992; Adult ... 3.00
❑5, Nov 1992; Adult ... 3.00
❑6, Dec 1992; Adult ... 3.00
❑7, Jan 1993; Adult ... 3.00
❑8, Feb 1993; Adult ... 3.00

Gay Comics
Bob Ross

❑1, Sep 1980, "Gay Comix"; Published by Kitchen Sink ... 12.50
❑2, ca. 1981; "Gay Comix"; Published by Kitchen Sink ... 8.00
❑3, Dec 1982; "Gay Comix"; Published by Kitchen Sink ... 6.00
❑4, Nov 1983; "Gay Comix"; Published by Kitchen Sink ... 6.00
❑5; "Gay Comix"; Published by Kitchen Sink ... 6.00
❑6, Dec 1985; Bob Ross begins as publisher ... 4.50
❑7, Mar 1986; Spring 1986 ... 4.50
❑8, Jun 1986; Summer 1986; Flip Book; Flip cover is Superman Bizarro Tribute ... 4.50
❑9, Win 1986; Winter 1986-87; All Poppers Issue ... 4.50
❑10, Mar 1987; Spring 1987 ... 3.50
❑11, ca. 1987; Wee-Wee's Gayhouse ... 3.50
❑12, Spr 1988; Spring-Summer 1988 ... 3.50
❑13, Sum 1991; Summer1991; Indicia says Summer/Autumn 1988, Corrected on inside page 1; Flip Book ... 3.50
❑14, ca. 1991; Winter 1991 ... 3.50
❑15, Mar 1992; Title changes to "Gay Comics" ... 3.50
❑16, Sum 1992; Desert Peach story ... 3.50
❑17, ca. 1992; Early 1993 ... 3.00
❑18; Spring 1993 ... 3.00
❑19, Sum 1993; Alison Bechdel Special ... 3.00
❑20; super-heroes ... 3.00
❑21 ... 3.00
❑22, Sum 1994; Funny Animals Special with Omaha the Cat Dancer story ... 5.00
❑23, Sum 1996; Funny Animals Special ... 5.00
❑24, Fal 1996; A: The Maxx. Fall 1996; Indicia says Spring 1997; Crossover with The Maxx ... 5.00

Other grades: Multiply price above by 5/6 for VF/NM • 2/3 for VERY FINE • 1/3 for FINE • 1/5 for VERY GOOD • 1/8 for GOOD

❑25, ca. 1997; 80 pages, 71 creators; b&w; ca. 1998 .... 3.50
❑Special 1, Mar 1992, Spring 1992 .... 3.00

Gazillion
Image

❑1, Nov 1998 .... 2.50
❑1/Variant, Nov 1998; alternate cover; framed 2.50

GD Minus 18
Antarctic

❑1, Feb 1998, b&w; Gold Digger Special 2.95

Gear
Fireman

❑1, Nov 1998 .... 2.95
❑2, Dec 1998 .... 2.95
❑3, Jan 1999 .... 2.95
❑4, Feb 1999 .... 2.95
❑5, ca. 1999 .... 2.95
❑6, Apr 1999 .... 2.95

Gear Station
Image

❑1, Mar 2000 .... 2.50
❑2, Apr 2000; Cover say April, indicia states May 2000 .... 2.50
❑3, Jun 2000 .... 2.50
❑4, Jul 2000 .... 2.50
❑5, Nov 2000 .... 2.95

Geeksville
3 Finger Prints

❑1, Aug 1999, b&w 3.00
❑2, Oct 1999, b&w 3.00
❑3, Dec 1999, b&w 2.75

Geeksville
Image

❑0, Mar 2000, b&w 3.00
❑1, May 2000, b&w 3.00
❑2, Jul 2000, b&w 2.95
❑3, Sep 2000, b&w 2.95
❑4, Nov 2000, b&w 2.95
❑5, Jan 2001 .... 2.95
❑6, Mar 2001, Final Issue 2.95

Geisha
Oni

❑1, Sep 1998 .... 2.95
❑2, Oct 1998 .... 2.95
❑3, Nov 1998 .... 2.95
❑4, Dec 1998 .... 2.95

Geminar
Image

❑Special 1, Jul 2000 .... 4.95

Gemini Blood
DC / Helix

❑1, Sep 1996 .... 2.25
❑2, Oct 1996 .... 2.25
❑3, Nov 1996 .... 2.25
❑4, Dec 1996 .... 2.25
❑5, Jan 1997 .... 2.25
❑6, Feb 1997 .... 2.25
❑7, Mar 1997 .... 2.25
❑8, Apr 1997 .... 2.25
❑9, May 1997 .... 2.25

Gen-Active
WildStorm

❑1, May 2000, Superchick Smackdown cover 3.95
❑1/A, May 2000, Woman with knife on cover 3.95
❑2, Aug 2000, Group cover 3.95
❑2/A, Aug 2000, Woman kicking on cover 3.95
❑3, Nov 2000 .... 3.95
❑4, Feb 2001 .... 3.95
❑5, May 2001 .... 3.95
❑6, Aug 2001 .... 3.95

Gene Dogs
Marvel

❑1, Oct 1993, four trading cards; Polybagged 2.75
❑2, Nov 1993 .... 1.75
❑3, Dec 1993 .... 1.75
❑4, Jan 1994 .... 1.75

Gene Pool
Idea & Design Works

❑1, ca. 2003 .... 6.99

Generation Hex
DC / Amalgam

❑1, Jun 1997, Amalgam DC Western Heroes/Generation X 1.95

Generation M
Marvel

❑1, Jan 2006 .... 2.99
❑2, Feb 2006 .... 2.99
❑3, Mar 2006 .... 2.99
❑4, Apr 2006 .... 2.99
❑5, May 2006 .... 2.99

Generation Next
Marvel

❑1, Mar 1995 .... 1.95
❑2, Apr 1995 .... 1.95
❑3, May 1995, Age of Apocalypse 1.95
❑4, Jun 1995 .... 1.95

Generation X
Marvel

❑-1, Jul 1997, JRo (w); A: Stan Lee. Flashback 2.00
❑½, ca. 1998; Wizard 1/2. This Generation X #1/2 was available only through a special offer in Wizard: The Comic Magazine #81. Each copy is part of a limited edition which was distributed in a special protective holder with a copy of a certificate 2.50
❑1, Nov 1994, enhanced cover 4.00
❑2, Dec 1994 .... 1.75
❑2/Deluxe, Dec 1994; Deluxe edition 2.00
❑3, Jan 1995, Standard Edition 1.75
❑3/Deluxe, Jan 1995; Deluxe edition 2.00
❑4, Feb 1995, Holiday Spectacular 1.75
❑4/Deluxe, Feb 1995, Deluxe edition; Holiday Spectacular 2.00
❑5, Jul 1995 .... 2.00
❑6, Aug 1995 .... 2.00
❑7, Sep 1995 .... 2.00
❑8, Oct 1995 .... 2.00
❑9, Nov 1995, AM (a) 2.00
❑10, Dec 1995; AM (a); A: Wolverine. A: Omega Red. A: Banshee. V: Omega Red 2.00
❑11, Jan 1996, AM (a) 2.00
❑12, Feb 1996; AM (a); V: Emplate 2.00
❑13, Mar 1996; V: Emplate 2.00
❑14, Apr 1996 .... 2.00
❑15, May 1996, AM (a); V: Emplate-controlled Synch 2.00
❑16, Jun 1996, V: Emplate-controlled Synch 2.00
❑17, Jul 1996 .... 2.00
❑18, Aug 1996 .... 2.00
❑19, Sep 1996 .... 2.00
❑20, Oct 1996, A: Howard the Duck 2.00
❑21, Nov 1996, A: Howard the Duck 2.00
❑22, Dec 1996 A: Nightmare 2.00
❑23, Jan 1997 .... 2.00
❑24, Feb 1997 .... 2.00
❑25, Mar 1997, Giant-size; wraparound cover 3.00
❑26, Apr 1997 .... 2.00
❑27, May 1997 .... 2.00
❑28, Jun 1997 .... 2.00
❑29, Aug 1997, gatefold summary; JRo (w); AM (a); Operation Zero Tolerance 2.00
❑30, Sep 1997, gatefold summary; JRo (w); Operation Zero Tolerance 2.00
❑31, Oct 1997, gatefold summary; JRo (w); Operation Zero Tolerance 2.00
❑32, Nov 1997, gatefold summary; V: Circus of Crime 2.00
❑33, Dec 1997; gatefold summary 2.00
❑34, Jan 1998, gatefold summary; V: White Queen 2.00
❑35, Feb 1998, gatefold summary 2.00
❑36, Mar 1998; gatefold summary 2.00
❑37, Apr 1998, gatefold summary 2.00
❑38, May 1998, gatefold summary 2.00
❑39, Jun 1998, gatefold summary 2.00
❑40, Jul 1998, gatefold summary 2.00
❑41, Aug 1998, gatefold summary 2.00
❑42, Sep 1998; gatefold summary 2.00
❑43, Oct 1998; gatefold summary; White Queen powerless 2.00
❑44, Nov 1998, gatefold summary 2.00
❑45, Dec 1998, gatefold summary; White Queen regains powers 2.00
❑46, Dec 1998, gatefold summary 2.00
❑47, Jan 1999, gatefold summary; A: Forge 2.00
❑48, Feb 1999 A: Jubilee 2.00
❑49, Mar 1999, A: Maggott 2.00
❑50, Apr 1999, A: Dark Beast 3.00
❑51, May 1999 .... 2.00
❑52, Jun 1999; Paladin arrives at X-Mansion 2.00
❑53, Jul 1999, V: Rising Suns; Paladin enlists Gen X for Mandripoor mission 2.00
❑54, Aug 1999, V: Rising Suns 2.00
❑55, Sep 1999, V: Adrienne Frost; Gen X trapped in reenactment of Hellions' death 2.00
❑56, Oct 1999 .... 2.00
❑57, Nov 1999 .... 2.99
❑58, Dec 1999, V: sasquatch (not Alpha Flight Sasquatch); Monet withdrawn from Xavier's 1.99
❑59, Jan 2000 .... 1.99
❑60, Feb 2000 .... 2.25
❑61, Mar 2000 .... 2.25
❑62, Apr 2000 .... 2.25
❑63, May 2000, Red revolutions band on right, blue face in background 2.25
❑64, Jun 2000 .... 2.25
❑65, Jul 2000 .... 2.25
❑66, Aug 2000 .... 2.25
❑67, Sep 2000 .... 2.25
❑68, Oct 2000 .... 2.25
❑69, Nov 2000 .... 2.25
❑70, Dec 2000, D: Synch 2.25
❑71, Jan 2001 .... 2.25
❑72, Feb 2001 .... 2.25
❑73, Mar 2001 .... 2.25
❑74, Apr 2001 .... 2.25
❑75, May 2001, Final issue 2.99
❑Ann 1995, ca. 1995, wraparound cover 3.95
❑Ann 1996, ca. 1996; MG (w); Generation X '96; wraparound cover 2.99
❑Ann 1997, ca. 1997; gatefold summary; Generation X '97; wraparound cover .. 2.99
❑Ann 1998, ca. 1998, gatefold summary; Generation X/Dracula '98; wraparound cover 3.50
❑Ann 1999, ca. 1999 .... 3.50
❑Ashcan 1, Oct 1994; ashcan edition; "Collector's Preview" 1.75
❑Holiday 1, Feb 1998; Giant-size; Holiday Special 3.50

Generation X/Gen13
Marvel

❑1, ca. 1997; crossover with Image; wraparound cover 4.00
❑1/A, ca. 1997; variant cover 3.99

Generation X Underground
Marvel

❑1, May 1998, b&w; cardstock cover 2.50

Generic Comic
Marvel

❑1, Apr 1984 .... 2.50

Generic Comic (Comics Conspiracy)
Comics Conspiracy

❑1, Jan 2001 .... 1.95
❑2, May 2001 .... 1.95
❑3, ca. 2001 .... 1.95
❑4, ca. 2001 .... 1.95
❑5 .... 1.95
❑5/Variant; Special cover 5.95
❑6, Feb 2002 .... 1.95
❑7, Apr 2002 .... 1.95
❑8, Jun 2002 .... 1.95
❑9 .... 1.95

Genesis
Malibu

❑0, Oct 1993; foil cover 3.50

Genesis
DC

❑1, Oct 1997 .... 1.95
❑2, Oct 1997 .... 1.95
❑3, Oct 1997 .... 1.95
❑4, Oct 1997 .... 1.95

Genesis: The #1 Collection
Image

❑1; Reprints Backlash #1, DV8 #1, Deathblow #1, Gen13 #1, Grifter #1, StormWatch #1, Union #1, Wetworks #1, WildC.A.T.s #1, Urban Storm 9.99

Other grades: Multiply price above by 5/6 for VF/NM • 2/3 for VERY FINE • 1/3 for FINE • 1/5 for VERY GOOD • 1/8 for GOOD

Fun-In

Hanna-Barbera character anthology
©Gold Key

Furrlough

Long-running anthropomorphic anthology
©Antarctic

Further Adventures of Indiana Jones

Follows Raiders of the Lost Ark adaptation
©Marvel

Fury

Nick Fury gets naughty while doing nasty job
©Marvel

Futurama

Science fiction send-ups from Bongo
©Bongo

N-MINT

Genetix
Marvel

❑1, Oct 1993, wraparound cover 2.75
❑2, Nov 1993 .... 1.75
❑3, Dec 1993 .... 1.75
❑4, Jan 1994 .... 1.75
❑5, Feb 1994 .... 1.75
❑6, Mar 1994 .... 1.75

Genie
Fc9 Publishing

❑1, Aug 2005 .... 2.95
❑2, Sep 2005 .... 2.95

Genocide
Renegade Tribe

❑1, Aug 1994 .... 2.95
❑1/2nd, Aug 1994; 2nd printing 2.95

Genocyber
Viz

❑1 1993, b&w; Japanese 2.75
❑2 1993, b&w; Japanese 2.75
❑3, b&w; Japanese 2.75
❑4, b&w; Japanese 2.75
❑5, b&w; Japanese 2.75

Gen of Hiroshima
Educomics

❑1, Jan 1980 .... 2.00
❑2, ca. 1981 .... 2.00

Gensaga
Express / Entity

❑1 .... 2.50

Gen12
Image

❑1, Feb 1998 .... 2.50
❑2, Mar 1998 .... 2.50
❑3, Apr 1998 .... 2.50
❑4, May 1998 .... 2.50
❑5, Jun 1998 .... 2.50

Gen13
Image

❑0, Sep 1994 .... 3.50
❑½, Mar 1994; Wizard promotional edition 2.00
❑½/A, Mar 1994; Autographed by Jim Lee 5.00
❑1, Feb 1994; 1: Grunge (full appearance). 1: Burnout (full appearance). 1: Freefall (full appearance). first printing 4.00
❑1/A, Oct 1997; 3-D; 1: Grunge (full appearance). 1: Burnout (full appearance). 1: Freefall (full appearance). alternate cover; with glasses 4.95
❑1/B, Oct 1997; 3-D; 1: Grunge (full appearance). 1: Burnout (full appearance). 1: Freefall (full appearance). with glasses 5.00
❑1/C; 1: Grunge (full appearance). 1: Burnout (full appearance). 1: Freefall (full appearance). Fairchild flexing on cover 4.00
❑1/2nd, Jun 1994; 1: Grunge (full appearance). 1: Burnout (full appearance). 2nd printing; 1: Grunge (full appearance); 1: Burnout (full appearance); Includes coupon for Gen 13 Ashcan 3.00
❑2, Mar 1994; JLee (w); Includes coupon for Gen 13 Ashcan 3.00
❑3, Apr 1994; A: Pitt. Includes coupon for Gen 13 Ashcan 3.00

N-MINT

❑4, May 1994, b&w; A: Pitt. wraparound cover 2.50
❑5, Jul 1994 .... 3.00
❑5/A, Jul 1994; JLee (w); alternate cover 2.50
❑Ashcan 1; ashcan edition 4.00

Gen13
Image

❑-1, Jan 1997, American Entertainment exclusive 3.00
❑0, Sep 1994, JLee (a) 3.00
❑1/3D, Feb 1998, 3D Edition; 1: Trance. 1: The Bounty Hunters. 1: Alex Fairchild. with glasses 4.95
❑1/A, Mar 1995, 1: Trance. 1: The Bounty Hunters. 1: Alex Fairchild. Cover 1 of 13: Charge!; ommon 3.00
❑1/B, Mar 1995, 1: Trance. 1: The Bounty Hunters. 1: Alex Fairchild. Cover 2 of 13: Thumbs Up; common 3.00
❑1/C, Mar 1995, 1: Trance. 1: The Bounty Hunters. 1: Alex Fairchild. Cover 3 of 13: Li'l GEN13 .... 3.00
❑1/D, Mar 1995, 1: Trance. 1: The Bounty Hunters. 1: Alex Fairchild. Cover 4 of 13: Barbari-GEN 3.00
❑1/E, Mar 1995, 1: Trance. 1: The Bounty Hunters. 1: Alex Fairchild. Cover 5 of 13: Your Friendly Neighborhood Grunge 3.00
❑1/F, Mar 1995, 1: Trance. 1: The Bounty Hunters. 1: Alex Fairchild. Cover 6 of 13: Gen13 Goes Madison Avenue 3.00
❑1/G, Mar 1995, 1: Trance. 1: The Bounty Hunters. 1: Alex Fairchild. Cover 7 of 13: Lin-GEN-re 3.50
❑1/H, Mar 1995, 1: Trance. 1: The Bounty Hunters. 1: Alex Fairchild. Cover 8 of 13: GEN-et Jackson 3.50
❑1/I, Mar 1995, 1: Trance. 1: The Bounty Hunters. 1: Alex Fairchild. Cover 9 of 13: That's the Way We Became the GEN13 .... 3.00
❑1/J, Mar 1995, 1: Trance. 1: The Bounty Hunters. 1: Alex Fairchild. Cover 10 of 13: All Dolled Up 3.00
❑1/K, Mar 1995, 1: Trance. 1: The Bounty Hunters. 1: Alex Fairchild. Cover 11 of 13: Verti-GEN 3.00
❑1/L, Mar 1995, 1: Trance. 1: The Bounty Hunters. 1: Alex Fairchild. Cover 12 of 13: Picto-Fiction 3.00
❑1/M, Mar 1995, 1: Trance. 1: The Bounty Hunters. 1: Alex Fairchild. Cover 13 of 13: Do-It-Yourself-Cover 3.00
❑1/N, 1: Trance. 1: The Bounty Hunters. 1: Alex Fairchild. Included all variant covers, plus new puzzle cover 39.95
❑1/2nd, Encore edition; Fairchild in French maid outfit on cover 2.50
❑2, May 1995, 1: Helmut. Flip cover 2.50
❑3, Jul 1995 .... 2.50
❑4, Jul 1995, 1: Lucius. indicia says Jul, cover says Aug 2.50
❑5, Oct 1995 .... 2.50
❑6, Nov 1995, 1: Frostbite. 1: The Order of the Cross 2.50
❑7, Jan 1996, 1: Copycat. 1: Evo. indicia says Jan, cover says Dec 2.50
❑8, Feb 1996, 1: Powerhaus. 1: Sublime 2.50
❑9, Mar 1996, 1: Absolom 2.50
❑10, Apr 1996, 1: Sigma 2.50
❑11, May 1996 .... 5.00

N-MINT

❑11/A, May 1996, European Tour Edition 5.00
❑12, Aug 1996 .... 2.50
❑13/A, Nov 1996, JLee (w); A: Archie, Jughead, Betty, Veronica, Reggie 1.50
❑13/B, Nov 1996, JLee (w); A: TMNTs, Bone, Beanworld, Spawn, Madman. cover says Oct, indicia says Sep 1.50
❑13/C, Nov 1996, JLee (w); A: Madman, Maxx, Shi, Francine, Katchoo, Monkeyman, O'Brien, Hellboy 1.50
❑13/CS, Nov 1996, Collected Edition of #13A, B, and C; A: Maxx. A: Madman. A: Hellboy. A: Bone. A: Shi. A: Teenage Mutant Ninja Turtles. A: Spawn. Collected Edition of #13A; B; And C ... 6.95
❑13/D, Nov 1996, Collected Edition of #13A, B, and C; A: Maxx. A: Madman. A: Hellboy. A: Bone. A: Shi. A: Teenage Mutant Ninja Turtles. A: Spawn. Variant cover collected edition 6.95
❑14, Nov 1996 .... 2.50
❑15, Dec 1996, JLee (w) 2.50
❑16, Jan 1997, JLee (w) 2.50
❑17, Feb 1997 .... 2.50
❑18, Apr 1997 .... 2.50
❑19, May 1997 .... 2.50
❑20, Jun 1997 .... 2.50
❑21, Aug 1997, in space 2.50
❑22, Sep 1997 .... 2.50
❑23, Oct 1997 .... 2.50
❑24, Nov 1997 .... 2.50
❑25, Dec 1997 .... 3.50
❑25/A, Dec 1997, Alternate cover; white background 3.50
❑25/B, Dec 1997, chromium cover 3.50
❑25/CS, Dec 1997, Voyager pack 4.00
❑26, Feb 1998 .... 2.50
❑26/A, Feb 1998, Alternate cover; fight scene 2.50
❑27, Mar 1998 .... 2.50
❑28, Apr 1998 .... 2.50
❑29, May 1998 .... 2.50
❑30, Jun 1998, Cover by Steve Skroce; Woman holding man over her head ... 2.50
❑30/A, Jun 1998, alternate swimsuit cover 2.50
❑31, Jul 1998 .... 2.50
❑32, Aug 1998 .... 2.50
❑33, Sep 1998, Planetary preview 2.50
❑34, Oct 1998 .... 2.50
❑34/A, Oct 1998, Variant cover depicts Fairchild posing black background 2.50
❑35, Nov 1998 .... 2.50
❑36, Dec 1998 .... 2.50
❑36/A, Dec 1998, KN (c); KN (a); Variant cover depicts corn dogs 2.50
❑37, Mar 1999 .... 2.50
❑38, Apr 1999, Team Cover 2.50
❑38/Variant, Apr 1999, Variant cover depicts Grunge w/popcorn 2.50
❑39, May 1999 .... 2.50
❑40, Jun 1999 .... 2.50
❑40/Variant, Jun 1999, Variant cover depicts Roxy in shower 2.50
❑41, Jul 1999 .... 2.50
❑42, Aug 1999 .... 2.50
❑43, Sep 1999 .... 2.50
❑44, Oct 1999, A: Mr. Majestic 2.50
❑45, Nov 1999 .... 2.50

Other grades: Multiply price above by 5/6 for VF/NM • 2/3 for VERY FINE • 1/3 for FINE • 1/5 for VERY GOOD • 1/8 for GOOD

N-MINT N-MINT N-MINT

❑46, Dec 2000 2.50
❑47, Jan 2000 2.50
❑48, Feb 2000 2.50
❑49, Mar 2000 2.50
❑50, Apr 2000, Giant-size 3.95
❑51, May 2000 2.50
❑52, Jun 2000 2.50
❑53, Jul 2000 2.50
❑54, Aug 2000 2.50
❑55, Sep 2000 2.50
❑56, Oct 2000 2.50
❑57, Nov 2000 2.50
❑58, Dec 2000 2.50
❑59, Jan 2001 2.50
❑60, Feb 2001 2.50
❑61, Mar 2001 2.50
❑62, Apr 2001 2.50
❑63, May 2001 2.50
❑64, Jun 2001 2.50
❑65, Jul 2001 2.50
❑66, Aug 2001, JLee (a) 2.50
❑67, Sep 2001 2.50
❑68, Oct 2001 2.50
❑69, Nov 2001 2.50
❑70, Dec 2001 2.50
❑71, Jan 2002 2.50
❑72, Feb 2002 2.50
❑73, Mar 2002 2.50
❑74, Apr 2002 2.50
❑75, May 2002 2.50
❑76, Jun 2002 2.50
❑77, Jul 2002 2.50
❑3D 1, European Tour Edition; 3-D Special 6.00
❑3D 1/A, double-sized; Fairchild holding open dinosaur mouth on cover 5.00
❑Ann 1, May 1997, 1997 Ann 2.95
❑Ann 1999, Mar 1999, wraparound cover; continues in DV8 Ann 1999 3.50
❑Ann 2000, Dec 2000 3.50

Gen13 (WildStorm)
WildStorm

❑0, Sep 2002 1.00
❑0/Variant, Sep 2002, b&w; Alternate art on cover 1.00
❑1, Nov 2002 2.95
❑2, Dec 2002 2.95
❑3, Jan 2003 2.95
❑4, Feb 2003 2.95
❑5, Mar 2003 JLee (c) 2.95
❑6, Apr 2003 2.95
❑7, May 2003 2.95
❑8, Jun 2003 2.95
❑9, Jul 2003 2.95
❑10, Aug 2003 2.95
❑11, Sep 2003 2.95
❑12, Oct 2003 2.95
❑13, Nov 2003 2.95
❑14, Dec 2003 2.95
❑15, Jan 2004 2.95
❑16, Feb 2004 2.95

Gen13: A Christmas Caper
WildStorm

❑1, Jan 2000 5.95

Gen13: Backlist
Image

❑1, Nov 1996; collects Gen13 #1/2, Gen13 #0, Gen13 #1, Gen13: The Unreal World, and WildStorm! #1 2.50

Gen13 Bikini Pin-Up Special
Image

❑1, American Entertainment Exclusive 5.00

Gen13 Bootleg
Image

❑1/A, Nov 1996, Team standing, Fairchild front on cover 3.00
❑1/B, Nov 1996; Team falling 3.00
❑2, Dec 1996 2.50
❑3, Jan 1997 2.50
❑4, Feb 1997 2.50
❑5, Mar 1997 2.50
❑6, Apr 1997 2.50
❑7, May 1997, JRo (w) 2.50
❑8, Jun 1997, manga-style story 2.50
❑9, Jul 1997, manga-style story; action movie references 2.50
❑10, Aug 1997; manga-style story; video game references 2.50
❑11, Sep 1997 2.50
❑12, Oct 1997 2.50
❑13, Nov 1997 2.50
❑14, Dec 1997 2.50
❑15, Jan 1998 2.50
❑16, Feb 1998 2.50
❑17/A, Mar 1998, alternate cover; videogame 2.50
❑17/B, Mar 1998, alternate cover; videogame 2.50
❑18/A, May 1998, Surfing cover 2.50
❑18/B, May 1998; Beach cover 2.50
❑19, Jun 1998 2.50
❑20, Jul 1998, Final Issue 2.50
❑Ann 1, Feb 1998 2.95

Gen13: Carny Folk
WildStorm

❑1, Jan 2000 3.50

Gen13/Fantastic Four
WildStorm

❑1, Mar 2001 5.95

Gen13/Generation X
Image

❑1/A, Jul 1997, crossover with Marvel 2.95
❑1/B, Jul 1997; alternate cover; crossover with Marvel 2.95
❑1/C, Jul 1997; 3D Edition; Limited cover 5.00
❑1/D, Jul 1997, 3D Edition; alternate cover; crossover with Marvel; with glasses 5.00
❑1/E, Jul 1997, San Diego Comic-Con edition 4.00

Gen13: Going West
DC / Wildstorm

❑1, Jun 1999, NN; One-shot 2.50

Gen13: Grunge Saves the World
DC / Wildstorm

❑1, May 1999, prestige format 5.95

Gen13 Interactive
Image

❑1, Oct 1997 2.50
❑2, Nov 1997 2.50
❑3, Jan 1998, cover says Dec, indicia says Jan 2.50

Gen13: London, New York, Hell
DC / Wildstorm

❑1, Aug 2001, Collects Gen13 Anl #1, Gen13: Bootleg Anl #1 6.95

Gen13: Magical Drama Queen Roxy
Image

❑1, Oct 1998 3.50
❑1/A, Oct 1998; alternate cover 4.00
❑1/B, Oct 1998, DFE alternate cover 4.00
❑2, Nov 1998 3.50
❑2/A, Nov 1998, alternate cover 3.50
❑3, Dec 1998 3.50
❑3/A, Dec 1998; alternate cover 3.50

Gen13/Maxx
Image

❑1, Dec 1995 3.50

Gen13: Medicine Song
WildStorm

❑1 5.95

Gen13/Monkeyman & O'Brien
Image

❑1, Jun 1998 2.50
❑1/A, Jun 1998, alternate cover 3.00
❑1/B, Jun 1998, Variant chromium cover 3.00
❑1/C, Jun 1998, Monkeyman holding team on cover, blue/gold background 3.00
❑2, Aug 1998 2.50
❑2/A, Aug 1998; alternate cover 2.50

Gen13: Ordinary Heroes
Image

❑1, Feb 1996 2.50
❑2, Jul 1996 2.50

Gen13 Rave
Image

❑1, Mar 1995, wraparound cover 3.00

Gen13: Science Friction
WildStorm

❑1, Jun 2001 5.95

Gen13: The Unreal World
Image

❑1, Jul 1996, 1: Cull; One-shot 2.50

Gen13 (WildStorm, 2006)
DC / Wildstorm

❑1, Dec 2006 2.99
❑1/Variant, Dec 2006 2.99
❑1/2nd variant, Dec 2006 2.99
❑2, Jan 2007 2.99
❑2/Variant, Jan 2007 2.99
❑3, Feb 2007 2.99
❑3/Variant, Feb 2007 2.99
❑4, Mar 2007 2.99
❑4/Variant, Mar 2007 2.99

Gen13: Wired
DC / Wildstorm

❑1, Apr 1999 2.50

Gen13 Yearbook '97
Image

❑1, Jun 1997, YB-style info on team 2.50

Gen13 'Zine
Image

❑1, Dec 1996, b&w; digest 2.00

Gentle Ben
Dell

❑1, Feb 1968 30.00
❑2, May 1968 20.00
❑3, Aug 1968 20.00
❑4, Nov 1968 20.00
❑5, Oct 1969, Same cover as #1 20.00

Genus
Antarctic / Venus

❑1, May 1993; Antarctic publishes 3.50
❑2, Sep 1993 3.00
❑3, Nov 1993 3.00
❑4, Jan 1994 3.00
❑5, Mar 1994 3.00
❑6, May 1994 3.00
❑7, Jul 1994 3.00
❑8, Sep 1994 3.00
❑9, Nov 1994 3.00
❑10, Jan 1995 3.00
❑11, Mar 1995 2.95
❑12, May 1995 2.95
❑13, Jul 1995 2.95
❑14, Sep 1995 2.95
❑15, Nov 1995 2.95
❑16, Jan 1996 2.95
❑17, Mar 1996 2.95
❑18, May 1996 2.95
❑19, Jul 1996 2.95
❑20, Sep 1996 2.95
❑21, Nov 1996 2.95
❑22, Jan 1997 2.95
❑23, Apr 1997; all-skunk issue; Radio Comix publishes 2.95
❑24, Jun 1997 2.95
❑25, Aug 1997 2.95
❑26, Oct 1997 2.95
❑27, Dec 1997 2.95
❑28, Feb 1998 2.95
❑29, Apr 1998 2.95
❑30, Jun 1998 2.95
❑31, Aug 1998 2.95
❑32, Oct 1998 2.95
❑33, Dec 1998 2.95
❑34, Feb 1999 2.95
❑35, Apr 1999 2.95
❑36, Jun 1999 2.95
❑37, Aug 1999 2.95
❑38, Oct 1999 2.95
❑39, Dec 1999 2.95
❑40, Feb 2000 2.95
❑41, Apr 2000 2.95
❑42, Jun 2000 2.95
❑43, Aug 2000 2.95
❑44, Oct 2000 2.95
❑45, Dec 2000 2.95
❑46, Feb 2001 2.95
❑47, Apr 2001 2.95
❑48, Jun 2001 2.99
❑49, Aug 2001 2.99
❑50, Oct 2001 2.99
❑51, Dec 2001 2.99
❑52, Feb 2002 2.99

Other grades: Multiply price above by 5/6 for VF/NM • 2/3 for VERY FINE • 1/3 for FINE • 1/5 for VERY GOOD • 1/8 for GOOD

Galactic Guardians

Guardians of the Galaxy spin-off
©Marvel

Gambit (5th Series)

Reveals backstory of Cajun mutant
©Marvel

Game Boy

Pre-heroes Valiant comic book
©Valiant

Gargoyles

Based on Disney animated series
©Marvel

Geeksville

Fuses "3 Geeks" with "Innocent Bystander"
©3 Finger Prints

N-MINT

- ❑53, Apr 2002 2.99
- ❑54, Jun 2002 2.99
- ❑55, Aug 2002 2.99
- ❑56, Oct 2002 2.99
- ❑57, Dec 2002 2.99
- ❑58, Feb 2003 3.50

Genus Greatest Hits
Antarctic

- ❑1, Apr 1996; Adult 4.50
- ❑2, May 1997; Adult 4.95

Genus Spotlight
Radio

- ❑1, Jul 1998; Skunkworks 2.95
- ❑2, Nov 1998; Skunkworks 2.95

Geobreeders
CPM Manga

- ❑1, Mar 1999 2.95
- ❑2, Apr 1999 2.95
- ❑3, May 1999 2.95
- ❑4, Jun 1999 2.95
- ❑5, Jul 1999 2.95
- ❑6, Aug 1999 2.95
- ❑7, Sep 1999 2.95
- ❑8, Oct 1999 2.95
- ❑9, Nov 1999 2.95
- ❑10, Dec 1999 2.95
- ❑11, Jan 2000 2.95
- ❑12, Feb 2000 2.95
- ❑13, Mar 2000 2.95
- ❑14, Apr 2000 2.95
- ❑15, May 2000 2.95
- ❑16, Jun 2000 2.95
- ❑17, Jul 2000 2.95
- ❑18, Aug 2000 2.95
- ❑19, Sep 2000 2.95
- ❑20, Oct 2000 2.95
- ❑21, Nov 2000 2.95
- ❑22, Dec 2000 2.95
- ❑23, Jan 2001 2.95
- ❑24, Feb 2001 2.95
- ❑25, Mar 2001 2.95
- ❑26, Apr 2001 2.95
- ❑27, May 2001 2.95
- ❑28, Jun 2001 2.95
- ❑29, Jul 2001 2.95
- ❑30, Aug 2001 2.95
- ❑31, Sep 2001 2.95

Geomancer
Valiant

- ❑1, Nov 1994; 1: Clay McHenry. A: Eternal Warrior. Chromium wraparound cover 2.00
- ❑1/VVSS, Nov 1994 40.00
- ❑2, Dec 1994 A: Eternal Warrior 1.00
- ❑3, Jan 1995 1.00
- ❑4, Feb 1995 2.00
- ❑5, Mar 1995 A: Turok 2.00
- ❑6, Apr 1995 A: Turok 2.00
- ❑7, May 1995 2.00
- ❑8, Jun 1995; Final Issue 4.00

George of the Jungle
Gold Key

- ❑1, Feb 1969, George, Tom Slick, and Super Chicken stories 35.00
- ❑2, Oct 1969, George, Tom Slick, and Super Chicken stories 24.00

N-MINT

George Romero's Land of the Dead
Idea & Design Works

- ❑1 3.99
- ❑2 2005 3.99
- ❑3, Nov 2005 3.99
- ❑4, Dec 2005 3.99
- ❑5, Feb 2006 3.99

Gepetto Files
Quick to Fly

- ❑1, Sep 1998 3.00

Geriatric Gangrene Jujitsu Gerbils
Planet-X

- ❑1, b&w 1.50
- ❑2 1.50

Geriatricman
C&T

- ❑1, b&w 1.75

ge rouge
Verotik

- ❑½, Oct 1998; Adult 2.95
- ❑1, Feb 1997; Adult 2.95
- ❑2, Apr 1997; Adult 2.95
- ❑3, Jul 1997; Adult 2.95

Gertie the Dinosaur Comics
Gertie the Dinosaur

- ❑1, Jul 2000 2.95

Gestalt (NEC)
New England

- ❑1, Apr 1993, b&w 1.95
- ❑2 1.95

Gestalt
Caliber

- ❑0 2.95

Get Along Gang
Marvel / Star

- ❑1, May 1985 1.00
- ❑2, Jul 1985 1.00
- ❑3, Sep 1985 1.00
- ❑4, Nov 1985 1.00
- ❑5, Jan 1986 1.00
- ❑6, Mar 1986 1.00

GetBackers
Tokyopop

- ❑1, Feb 2004 9.99
- ❑2, Apr 2004 9.99
- ❑3, Jun 2004 9.99
- ❑4, Aug 2004 9.99
- ❑5, Oct 2004 9.99
- ❑6, Dec 2004 9.99
- ❑7, Feb 2005 9.99
- ❑8, Apr 2005 9.99
- ❑9, Jun 2005 9.99
- ❑10, Jul 2005 9.99
- ❑11, Aug 2005 9.99
- ❑12, Nov 2005 9.99

Get Bent!
Ben T. Steckler

- ❑1 2.50
- ❑2, Dec 1998 2.50
- ❑3 2.50
- ❑4 2.50
- ❑5 2.50

N-MINT

- ❑6 2.50
- ❑7; Mini-comic 2.00
- ❑8 2.50
- ❑9 2.50

Get Lost
New Comics

- ❑1, Oct 1987, b&w; Reprints 1.95
- ❑2, ca. 1988, b&w; Reprints 1.95
- ❑3, ca. 1988, b&w; Reprints 1.95

Get Real Comics
Tides Center

- ❑1 1.95

Get Smart
Dell

- ❑1, Jun 1966 45.00
- ❑2, Sep 1966 30.00
- ❑3, Nov 1966 22.00
- ❑4, Jan 1967 22.00
- ❑5, Mar 1967 22.00
- ❑6, Apr 1967 20.00
- ❑7, Jun 1967 20.00
- ❑8, Sep 1967, Cover from #1 reprinted 20.00

Ghetto Bitch
Fantagraphics / Eros

- ❑1, b&w; Adult 2.75

Ghetto Blasters
Whiplash

- ❑1, Sep 1997, b&w 2.50

Ghost
Dark Horse

- ❑1, Apr 1995 3.00
- ❑2, May 1995 2.50
- ❑3, Jun 1995 2.50
- ❑4, Jul 1995 2.50
- ❑5, Aug 1995, V: Predator 2.50
- ❑6, Sep 1995 2.50
- ❑7, Oct 1995 2.50
- ❑8, Nov 1995 2.50
- ❑9, Dec 1995 2.50
- ❑10, Jan 1996 2.50
- ❑11, Feb 1996 2.50
- ❑12, Mar 1996, preview of Ghost/Hellboy crossover 2.50
- ❑13, Apr 1996 2.50
- ❑14, May 1996 2.50
- ❑15, Jun 1996 2.50
- ❑16, Jul 1996 2.50
- ❑17, Aug 1996, Cover credits Randy Emberlin instead of Barbara Kaalberg 2.50
- ❑18, Sep 1996 2.50
- ❑19, Nov 1996 2.50
- ❑20, Dec 1996, Cover by John Cassaday, Randy Emberlin 2.50
- ❑21, Jan 1997 2.50
- ❑22, Feb 1997 2.50
- ❑23, Mar 1997 2.50
- ❑24, Apr 1997 2.50
- ❑25, May 1997, Giant-size; 48-page special; photo front and back covers 3.95
- ❑26, Jun 1997 2.95
- ❑27, Jul 1997 2.95
- ❑28, Aug 1997 2.95
- ❑29, Sep 1997, flip-book with Timecop story 2.95
- ❑30, Oct 1997 2.95

Other grades: Multiply price above by 5/6 for VF/NM • 2/3 for VERY FINE • 1/3 for FINE • 1/5 for VERY GOOD • 1/8 for GOOD

	N-MINT
❑31, Nov 1997	2.95
❑32, Dec 1997	2.95
❑33, Jan 1998	2.95
❑34, Feb 1998	2.95
❑35, Mar 1998	2.95
❑36, Apr 1998, Final issue	2.95
❑Special 1, Jul 1994, Ghost Special	3.95
❑Special 2, Jun 1998, Immortal Coil	3.95
❑Special 3, Dec 1998, Scary Monsters	3.95

Ghost
Dark Horse

❑1, Sep 1998	3.50
❑2, Oct 1998	3.00
❑3, Nov 1998	3.00
❑4, Dec 1998	3.00
❑5, Jan 1999	3.00
❑6, Feb 1999	2.95
❑7, Mar 1999	2.95
❑8, Apr 1999	2.95
❑9, May 1999	2.95
❑10, Jun 1999, A: Vortex	2.95
❑11, Jul 1999	2.95
❑12, Sep 1999	2.95
❑13, Oct 1999	2.95
❑14, Nov 1999	2.95
❑15, Dec 1999	2.95
❑16, Jan 2000	2.95
❑17, Feb 2000	2.95
❑18, Mar 2000	2.95
❑19, Apr 2000	2.95
❑20, Jun 2000	2.95
❑21, Jul 2000, A: X	2.95
❑22, Aug 2000	2.95

Ghost and the Shadow
Dark Horse

❑1, Dec 1995; NN; One-shot	2.95

Ghost/Batgirl
Dark Horse

❑1, Aug 2000	2.95
❑2, Oct 2000	2.99
❑3, Nov 2000; Cover by Ryan Benjamin	2.95
❑4, Dec 2000; Cover by Ryan Benjamin	2.95

Ghostbusters
First

❑1, Feb 1986	1.50
❑2, Mar 1986	1.50
❑3, May 1986	1.50
❑4, Jun 1986	1.50
❑5, Aug 1986	1.50
❑6, Sep 1986	1.50

Ghostbusters II
Now

❑1, Oct 1989; Movie adaptation	2.00
❑2, Nov 1989; Movie adaptation	2.00
❑3, Dec 1989; Movie adaptation	2.00

Ghostdancing
DC / Vertigo

❑1, Mar 1995	1.95
❑2, Apr 1995	1.95
❑3, Jun 1995	2.50
❑4, Jul 1995	2.50
❑5, Aug 1995	2.50
❑6, Sep 1995	2.50

Ghost Handbook
Dark Horse

❑1, Aug 1999; background on characters	2.95

Ghost/Hellboy Special
Dark Horse

❑1, May 1996	2.50
❑2, Jun 1996; Final Issue	2.50

Ghost in the Shell
Dark Horse / Manga

❑1, Mar 1995	4.00
❑2, Apr 1995	4.00
❑3, Apr 1995	4.00
❑4, Jun 1995	4.00
❑5, Jul 1995	4.00
❑6, Aug 1995	4.00
❑7, Sep 1995	4.00
❑8, Oct 1995, Final Issue	4.00

Ghost in the Shell 2: Man/Machine Interface
Dark Horse

	N-MINT
❑1, Feb 2003	3.99
❑1/Hologram, Feb 2003, Holo cover	10.00
❑2, Feb 2003	3.50
❑2/A, Apr 2003, New cover painting	3.50
❑3, Apr 2003	3.50
❑4, May 2003	3.50
❑5, Jul 2003	3.50
❑6, Aug 2003	3.50
❑7, Sep 2003	3.50
❑8, Oct 2003	3.50
❑9, Nov 2003	3.50
❑10, Dec 2003	3.50
❑11, Dec 2003	3.50

Ghost in the Shell 1.5: Human Error Processor
Dark Horse

❑1, Dec 2006	2.99
❑2, Dec 2006	2.99
❑3, Jan 2007	2.99
❑4	2.99
❑5	2.99
❑6	2.99
❑7	2.99
❑8	2.99

Ghostly Haunts
Charlton

❑20, Sep 1971, SD (a); Series continued from Ghost Manor (1st Series) #19	6.00
❑21, Nov 1971	5.00
❑22, Jan 1972	5.00
❑23, Mar 1972	5.00
❑24, Apr 1972	5.00
❑25, Jun 1972	5.00
❑26, Aug 1972	5.00
❑27, Nov 1972	5.00
❑28, Dec 1972	5.00
❑29, Jan 1972	5.00
❑30, Mar 1973	5.00
❑31, Apr 1973	4.00
❑32, May 1973	4.00
❑33, Jul 1973	4.00
❑34, Aug 1973	4.00
❑35, Oct 1973	4.00
❑36, Nov 1973	4.00
❑37, Jan 1974	4.00
❑38, May 1974	4.00
❑39, Jul 1974	4.00
❑40, Sep 1974	4.00
❑41, Nov 1974	3.00
❑42, Jan 1975	3.00
❑43, Mar 1975	3.00
❑44, May 1975, SD (a)	3.00
❑45, Jul 1975	3.00
❑46, Oct 1975	3.00
❑47, Dec 1975	3.00
❑48, Feb 1976	3.00
❑49, Apr 1976	3.00
❑50, Jun 1976	3.00
❑51, Aug 1976	3.00
❑52, Oct 1976	3.00
❑53, Dec 1976	3.00
❑54, Sep 1977	3.00
❑55, Oct 1977	3.00
❑56, Jan 1978	3.00
❑57, Mar 1978	3.00
❑58, Apr 1978, Final Issue	3.00

Ghost Manor
Charlton

❑1, Jul 1968	12.00
❑2, Sep 1968	7.00
❑3, Nov 1968	7.00
❑4, Jan 1969	7.00
❑5, Mar 1969	7.00
❑6, May 1969	6.00
❑7, Jul 1969	6.00
❑8, Sep 1969	6.00
❑9, Nov 1969	6.00
❑10, Jan 1970	6.00
❑11, Mar 1970	5.00
❑12, May 1970	5.00
❑13, Jul 1970	5.00
❑14, Sep 1970	5.00
❑15, Nov 1970	5.00
❑16, Jan 1971	5.00
❑17, Mar 1971	5.00
❑18, May 1971	5.00
❑19, Jul 1971, Series continued in Ghostly Haunts #20	5.00

Ghost Manor
Charlton

	N-MINT
❑1, Oct 1971, O: Ghost Manor	10.00
❑2, Dec 1971	6.00
❑3, Feb 1972	6.00
❑4, Apr 1972	6.00
❑5, Jun 1972	6.00
❑6, Aug 1972	6.00
❑7, Oct 1972	6.00
❑8, Nov 1972, WW (a)	7.50
❑9, Feb 1973	5.00
❑10, Mar 1973	5.00
❑11, Apr 1973	4.00
❑12, Jun 1973	4.00
❑13, Jul 1973	4.00
❑14, Sep 1973	4.00
❑15, Oct 1973	4.00
❑16, Dec 1973	4.00
❑17, Jan 1974	4.00
❑18, May 1974	4.00
❑19, Jul 1974	4.00
❑20, Sep 1974	4.00
❑21, Nov 1974	4.00
❑22, Mar 1975	4.00
❑23, May 1975	4.00
❑24, Jul 1975	4.00
❑25, Sep 1975	4.00
❑26, Nov 1975	4.00
❑27, Jan 1976	4.00
❑28, Mar 1976	4.00
❑29, Jun 1976	4.00
❑30, Aug 1976	4.00
❑31, Oct 1976	3.00
❑32, Dec 1976	3.00
❑33, Sep 1977	3.00
❑34, Nov 1977	3.00
❑35, Feb 1978	3.00
❑36, Mar 1978	3.00
❑37, May 1978	3.00
❑38, Jun 1978	3.00
❑39, Oct 1978	3.00
❑40, Dec 1978, Warren Sattler credits	3.00
❑41, Feb 1979	3.00
❑42, Mar 1979	3.00
❑43, Jun 1979	3.00
❑44, Jul 1979	3.00
❑45, Sep 1979	3.00
❑46, Oct 1979	3.00
❑47, Nov 1979	3.00
❑48, Jan 1979	3.00
❑49, Mar 1980	3.00
❑50, May 1980	3.00
❑51, Jul 1980	3.00
❑52, Sep 1980	3.00
❑53, Nov 1980	3.00
❑54, Jan 1981	3.00
❑55, Mar 1981	3.00
❑56, May 1981	3.00
❑57, Jul 1981	3.00
❑58, Aug 1981	3.00
❑59, Oct 1981	3.00
❑60, Dec 1981	3.00
❑61, Feb 1982	3.00
❑62, Apr 1982	3.00
❑63, Jun 1982	3.00
❑64, Aug 1982	3.00
❑65, Oct 1982	3.00
❑66, Dec 1982	3.00
❑67, Feb 1983	3.00
❑68, Apr 1983	3.00
❑69, Jul 1983	3.00
❑70, Sep 1983	3.00
❑71, Nov 1983	3.00
❑72, Jan 1984	3.00
❑73, Mar 1984	3.00
❑74, May 1984	3.00
❑75, Jul 1984	3.00
❑76, Sep 1984	3.00
❑77, Nov 1984	3.00

Ghost Rider
Marvel

❑1, Feb 1967, O: Ghost Rider. 1: Ghost Rider. Western; back-up reprints story from Kid Colt Outlaw #105	28.00
❑2, Apr 1967, V: Tarantula. Western; back-up reprints story from Kid Colt Outlaw #99	20.00

Other grades: Multiply price above by 5/6 for VF/NM • 2/3 for VERY FINE • 1/3 for FINE • 1/5 for VERY GOOD • 1/8 for GOOD

Gemini Blood

Twins raised from birth to hunt humans

©DC

Generation X

The "new" new mutants, sort of...

©Marvel

Generic Comic

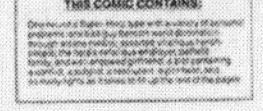

Contains one hero, one villain, and one plot

©Marvel

Gen13

Jim Lee's super-team starts at Image

©Image

Gen13 Bootleg

Features creators new to the series

©Image

	N-MINT
❑3, Jun 1967, Western; back-up reprints story from Kid Colt Outlaw #116	20.00
❑4, Aug 1967, A: Tarantula. V: Sting-Ray a.k.a. Scorpion. Western; back-up reprints story from Two-Gun Kid #69	12.50
❑5, Sep 1967, V: Tarantula. Western	12.50
❑6, Oct 1967, V: Towering Oak. Western	12.50
❑7, Nov 1967, Western	12.50

Ghost Rider
Marvel

	N-MINT
❑1, Aug 1973, TS, GK (a); 1: Son of Satan (partially shown)	130.00
❑2, Oct 1973	37.00
❑3, Dec 1973, JM (a)	25.00
❑4, Feb 1974, JM (a)	25.00
❑5, Apr 1974, Marvel Value Stamp #24: Falcon	23.00
❑6, Jun 1974, Marvel Value Stamp #74: Stranger	15.00
❑7, Aug 1974, Marvel Value Stamp #20: Brother Voodoo	15.00
❑8, Oct 1974, JM (a); 1: Inferno. A: Roxanne. Marvel Value Stamp #48: Kraven	15.00
❑9, Dec 1974, Marvel Value Stamp #81: Rhino	15.00
❑10, Feb 1975, A: Hulk. Reprints Marvel Spotlight #5	15.00
❑11, Apr 1975, SB, GK, KJ (a); A: Hulk. Marvel Value Stamp #66: General Ross	15.00
❑12, Jun 1975, D: Phantom Eagle	15.00
❑13, Aug 1975	15.00
❑14, Oct 1975, V: The Orb	15.00
❑15, Dec 1975	12.00
❑16, Feb 1976	12.00
❑17, Apr 1976	10.00
❑17/30¢, Apr 1976, 30¢ regional price variant	20.00
❑18, Jun 1976, A: Spider-Man	10.00
❑18/30¢, Jun 1976, A: Spider-Man. 30¢ regional price variant	20.00
❑19, Aug 1976	10.00
❑19/30¢, Aug 1976, 30¢ regional price variant	20.00
❑20, Oct 1976, JBy, GK, KJ (a); A: Daredevil. Story continued from Daredevil #138	10.00
❑21, Dec 1976, D: Eel I (Leopold Stryke)	7.00
❑22, Feb 1977, 1: Enforcer (Marvel)	7.00
❑23, Apr 1977, O: Water Wizard. 1: Water Wizard	7.00
❑24, Jun 1977, 35¢ regional price variant	15.00
❑24/35¢, Jun 1977, 35¢ regional price variant	15.00
❑25, Aug 1977	7.00
❑25/35¢, Aug 1977, 35¢ regional price variant	15.00
❑26, Oct 1977, 35¢ regional price variant	15.00
❑26/35¢, Oct 1977, 35¢ regional price variant	15.00
❑27, Dec 1977	7.00
❑28, Feb 1978	7.00
❑29, Apr 1978	7.00
❑30, Jun 1978	7.00
❑31, Aug 1978	6.00
❑32, Oct 1978, O: Bounty Hunter	6.00
❑33, Dec 1978	6.00
❑34, Feb 1979	6.00
❑35, Apr 1979	6.00
❑36, Jun 1979	6.00
❑37, Aug 1979	6.00
❑38, Oct 1979	6.00
❑39, Dec 1979	6.00
❑40, Jan 1980	6.00
❑41, Feb 1980	6.00
❑42, Mar 1980	6.00
❑43, Apr 1980	6.00
❑44, May 1980	6.00
❑45, Jun 1980	6.00
❑46, Jul 1980	6.00
❑47, Aug 1980	6.00
❑48, Sep 1980	6.00
❑49, Oct 1980	6.00
❑50, Nov 1980, Giant-size; DP (a); A: Night Rider	12.00
❑51, Dec 1980	5.00
❑52, Jan 1981	5.00
❑53, Feb 1981, 1: Asmodeus	5.00
❑54, Mar 1981	5.00
❑55, Apr 1981	5.00
❑56, May 1981, 1: Night Rider II (Hamilton Slade)	5.00
❑57, Jun 1981	5.00
❑58, Jul 1981	5.00
❑59, Aug 1981	5.00
❑60, Sep 1981	5.00
❑61, Oct 1981	5.00
❑62, Nov 1981	5.00
❑63, Dec 1981	5.00
❑64, Jan 1982	5.00
❑65, Feb 1982	5.00
❑66, Mar 1982	5.00
❑67, Apr 1982	5.00
❑68, May 1982, O: Ghost Rider (Johnny Blaze)	5.00
❑69, Jun 1982	4.00
❑70, Jul 1982	4.00
❑71, Aug 1982	4.00
❑72, Sep 1982, 1: Fire-Eater	4.00
❑73, Oct 1982	4.00
❑74, Nov 1982, 1: Centurius	4.00
❑75, Dec 1982	4.00
❑76, Jan 1983	4.00
❑77, Feb 1983, O: Zarathos. O: Centurius	4.00
❑78, Mar 1983	4.00
❑79, Apr 1983	4.00
❑80, May 1983, O: Centurius	4.00
❑81, Jun 1983, D: Ghost Rider. Zarathos leaves Johnny Blaze-end of Ghost Rider I	10.00

Ghost Rider
Marvel

	N-MINT
❑-1, Jul 1997; Flashback	1.95
❑1, May 1990; 1&O: Ghost Rider II (Dan Ketch). 1: Deathwatch	4.00
❑1/2nd, Sep 1990; 1&O: Ghost Rider II (Dan Ketch). 1: Deathwatch. 2nd Printing (gold)	2.25
❑2, Jun 1990; 1: Blackout II	3.00
❑3, Jul 1990; V: Blackout. V: Kingpin. V: Deathwatch	3.00
❑4, Aug 1990; V: Mr. Hyde. Scarecrow	3.00
❑5, Sep 1990 JLee (c); JLee (a); A: Punisher	3.00
❑5/Variant, Jun 1994; JLee (c); JLee (a); A: Punisher. Die-cut cover	3.00
❑5/2nd, Sep 1990; JLee (c); JLee (a); A: Punisher. 2nd printing (gold)	1.50
❑6, Oct 1990 A: Punisher	2.50
❑7, Nov 1990; V: Scarecrow	2.00
❑8, Dec 1990; 1: Alex	2.00
❑9, Jan 1991 A: X-Factor	2.00
❑10, Feb 1991	2.00
❑11, Mar 1991	1.50
❑12, Apr 1991 A: Doctor Strange	1.50
❑13, May 1991; 1: Snowblind. A: Doctor Strange	1.50
❑14, Jun 1991; Johnny Blaze; Ghost Rider vs. Johnny Blaze	1.50
❑15, Jul 1991; glow in the dark cover	5.00
❑15/2nd, Jul 1991; 2nd Printing (gold); glow in the dark cover	2.00
❑16, Aug 1991 A: Hobgoblin. A: Spider-Man. A: Johnny Blaze	1.75
❑17, Sep 1991 A: Hobgoblin. A: Spider-Man	1.75
❑18, Oct 1991; Painted cover	1.75
❑19, Nov 1991	1.75
❑20, Dec 1991	1.75
❑21, Jan 1992	1.75
❑22, Feb 1992	1.75
❑23, Mar 1992; V: Deathwatch	1.75
❑24, Apr 1992; D: Snowblind. V: Deathwatch	1.75
❑25, May 1992; Pop-up centerfold, double-sized	2.00
❑26, Jun 1992 JLee (c); A: X-Men	1.75
❑27, Jul 1992 JLee (c); A: X-Men	1.75
❑28, Aug 1992; 1: Lilith II; Includes poster	2.50
❑29, Sep 1992 JKu (a); A: Wolverine. A: Beast	1.75
❑30, Oct 1992; JKu (a); V: Nightmare	1.75
❑31, Nov 1992; JKu (a); Includes Poster	2.50
❑32, Dec 1992; V: Firm; Doctor Strange attempts to save Ghost Rider	1.75
❑33, Jan 1993 AW (a)	1.75
❑34, Feb 1993	1.75
❑35, Mar 1993; AW (a); V: Heart Attack	1.75
❑36, Apr 1993	1.75
❑37, May 1993	1.75
❑38, Jun 1993	1.75
❑39, Jul 1993	1.75
❑40, Aug 1993; black cover	2.25
❑41, Sep 1993; V: Blackout; V: Lilith	1.75
❑42, Oct 1993; A: Deathwatch. A: Centurius. A: Ghostie. A: John Blaze. Neon cover	1.75
❑43, Nov 1993	1.75
❑44, Dec 1993; Neon cover	1.75
❑45, Jan 1994; Spot-varnished cover	1.75
❑46, Feb 1994	1.75
❑47, Mar 1994; V: Dread	1.75
❑48, Apr 1994 A: Spider-Man	1.75
❑49, May 1994	1.75
❑50, Jun 1994; Giant-size; foil cover	2.50
❑50/Variant, Jun 1994; Giant-size; Die-cut cover	4.00
❑51, Jul 1994; V: Slaughterboy	1.95
❑52, Aug 1994	1.95
❑53, Sep 1994	1.95
❑54, Oct 1994	1.95
❑55, Nov 1994	1.95
❑56, Dec 1994	1.95
❑57, Jan 1995 A: Wolverine	1.95

Other grades: Multiply price above by 5/6 for VF/NM • 2/3 for VERY FINE • 1/3 for FINE • 1/5 for VERY GOOD • 1/8 for GOOD

N-MINT

❑58, Feb 1995 1.95
❑59, Mar 1995 1.95
❑60, Apr 1995 1.95
❑61, May 1995; Giant-size 2.50
❑62, Jun 1995 1.95
❑63, Jul 1995 1.95
❑64, Aug 1995 1.95
❑65, Sep 1995 1.95
❑66, Oct 1995; D: Blackout 1.95
❑67, Nov 1995 A: Gambit 1.95
❑68, Dec 1995 A: Gambit. A: Wolverine 1.95
❑69, Jan 1996 1.95
❑70, Feb 1996 1.95
❑71, Mar 1996 1.95
❑72, Apr 1996; V: Snowblind 1.95
❑73, May 1996; V: Snowblind 1.95
❑74, Jun 1996 1.95
❑75, Jul 1996 1.50
❑76, Aug 1996 1.50
❑77, Sep 1996 A: Doctor Strange 1.50
❑78, Oct 1996 1.50
❑79, Nov 1996 1.50
❑80, Dec 1996; V: Furies (Dark Lady, Lady Ash & Ember) 1.50
❑81, Jan 1997 A: Howard the Duck 1.50
❑82, Feb 1997 A: Devil Dinosaur. A: Howard the Duck. A: Moonboy 1.50
❑83, Mar 1997 1.95
❑84, Apr 1997 1.95
❑85, May 1997 A: Scarecrow 1.95
❑86, Jun 1997; Damage Control researches Ghost Rider 1.95
❑87, Aug 1997; gatefold summary 1.95
❑88, Sep 1997; gatefold summary 1.95
❑89, Oct 1997; gatefold summary 1.95
❑90, Nov 1997; gatefold summary 1.95
❑91, Dec 1997; gatefold summary 1.95
❑92, Jan 1998; gatefold summary 1.95
❑93, Feb 1998; Giant-size; Final Issue; Gatefold summary 2.99
❑Ann 1, ca. 1993; trading card 4.00
❑Ann 2, ca. 1994; V: Scarecrow 2.95

Ghost Rider
Marvel

❑½, ca. 2001; Wizard promo 3.50
❑1, Aug 2001 2.99
❑2, Sep 2001 2.99
❑3, Oct 2001 2.99
❑4, Nov 2001 2.99
❑5, Dec 2001 2.99
❑6, Jan 2002 2.99

Ghost Rider
Marvel

❑1, Oct 2005 6.00
❑1/Ribic, Oct 2005; Incentive distributed one for every 20 copies ordered 18.00
❑1/DirCut, Oct 2005 3.99
❑1/RRP, Oct 2005, Distributed one per retail attendee at the 2005 Diamond seminar as part of the Retailer Rewards Program (RRP) 45.00
❑2, Nov 2005 2.99
❑3, Jan 2006 2.99
❑4, Feb 2006 2.99
❑5, Mar 2006 2.99
❑6, Apr 2006 2.99

Ghost Rider & Cable: Servants of the Dead
Marvel

❑1, Sep 1991; cardstock cover; no indicia; Reprints Ghost Rider/Cable series from Marvel Comics Presents 3.95

Ghost Rider and the Midnight Sons Magazine
Marvel

❑1 3.95

Ghost Rider/Ballistic
Marvel

❑1, Feb 1997; crossover with Top Cow; continues in Ballistic/Wolverine 2.95

Ghost Rider/Blaze: Spirits of Vengeance
Marvel

❑1, Aug 1992; without poster 1.50
❑1/CS, Aug 1992; Includes poster 2.75
❑2, Sep 1992 1.75
❑3, Oct 1992 1.75

N-MINT

❑4, Nov 1992 1.75
❑5, Dec 1992; Venom 1.75
❑6, Jan 1993 1.75
❑7, Feb 1993 1.75
❑8, Mar 1993 1.75
❑9, Apr 1993 1.75
❑10, May 1993 1.75
❑11, Jun 1993 1.75
❑12, Jul 1993; Glow-in-the-dark cover 2.75
❑13, Aug 1993; black cover 2.25
❑14, Sep 1993 1.75
❑15, Oct 1993; Neon ink cover; Blaze's new costume and powers 1.75
❑16, Nov 1993 1.75
❑17, Dec 1993; Neon inks on cover 1.75
❑18, Jan 1994; Spot-varnished cover 1.75
❑19, Feb 1994 1.75
❑20, Mar 1994 1.75
❑21, Apr 1994 1.75
❑22, May 1994 1.75
❑23, Jun 1994; Final Issue 1.95

Ghost Rider/Captain America: Fear
Marvel

❑1, Oct 1992; Fold-out cover 5.95

Ghost Rider: Crossroads
Marvel

❑1, Dec 1995; enhanced wraparound cardstock cover 3.95

Ghost Rider: Highway to Hell
Marvel

❑1, Aug 2001 3.50

Ghost Rider Poster Magazine
Marvel

❑1, Jul 1992 4.95

Ghost Rider: The Hammer Lane
Marvel

❑1, Aug 2001 2.99
❑2, Sep 2001 2.99
❑3, Oct 2001 2.99
❑4, Nov 2001 2.99
❑5, Dec 2001 2.99
❑6, Jan 2002 2.99

Ghost Rider 2099
Marvel

❑1, May 1994; 1&O: Ghost Rider 2099 2.00
❑1/CS, May 1994; Polybagged with trading card 2.50
❑2, Jun 1994; Polybagged with poster 1.50
❑3, Jul 1994 1.50
❑4, Aug 1994 1.50
❑5, Sep 1994 1.50
❑6, Oct 1994 1.50
❑7, Nov 1994 A: Spider-Man 2099 1.50
❑8, Dec 1994 1.50
❑9, Jan 1995 1.50
❑10, Feb 1995 1.50
❑11, Mar 1995 1.50
❑12, Apr 1995 1.50
❑13, May 1995; One Nation of Doom; Ghost Rider reassembles himself 1.95
❑14, Jun 1995 1.95
❑15, Jul 1995; 1: Heartbreaker 1.95
❑16, Aug 1995 1.95
❑17, Sep 1995 1.95
❑18, Oct 1995 1.95
❑19, Nov 1995 1.95
❑20, Dec 1995 A: L-Cypher. A: Heartbreaker. A: Archfiends. A: Zero Cochrane 1.95
❑21, Jan 1996; V: Vengeance 1.95
❑22, Feb 1996; V: Vengeance; Ghost Rider resigns as federal marshal 1.95
❑23, Mar 1996 1.95
❑24, Apr 1996 1.95
❑25, May 1996; double-sized; wraparound cover 2.50

Ghost Rider
Marvel

❑1, Sep 2006 2.99
❑2, Oct 2006 2.99
❑3, Nov 2006 2.99
❑4, Dec 2006 2.99
❑5, Jan 2007 2.99
❑6, Feb 2007 2.99

N-MINT

Ghost Rider; Wolverine; Punisher: The Dark Design
Marvel

❑1, Dec 1991, squarebound; Double fold-out cover 5.95

Ghosts
DC

❑1, Oct 1971 NC (c); TD, JA (a) 100.00
❑2, Dec 1971 TD (a) 35.00
❑3, Feb 1972 TD (w) 17.00
❑4, Apr 1972 17.00
❑5, Jun 1972 17.00
❑6, Aug 1972 12.00
❑7, Sep 1972 12.00
❑8, Oct 1972 12.00
❑9, Nov 1972 12.00
❑10, Jan 1973 12.00
❑11, Feb 1973 10.00
❑12, Mar 1973 10.00
❑13, Apr 1973 10.00
❑14, May 1973 10.00
❑15, Jun 1973 10.00
❑16, Jul 1973 10.00
❑17, Aug 1973 10.00
❑18, Sep 1973 10.00
❑19, Oct 1973 10.00
❑20, Nov 1973 10.00
❑21, Dec 1973 6.00
❑22, Jan 1974 6.00
❑23, Feb 1974 6.00
❑24, Mar 1974 6.00
❑25, Apr 1974 6.00
❑26, May 1974 6.00
❑27, Jun 1974 6.00
❑28, Jul 1974 6.00
❑29, Aug 1974 6.00
❑30, Sep 1974 6.00
❑31, Oct 1974 5.00
❑32, Nov 1974 5.00
❑33, Dec 1974 5.00
❑34, Jan 1975 5.00
❑35, Feb 1975 5.00
❑36, Mar 1975 5.00
❑37, Apr 1975 5.00
❑38, May 1975 5.00
❑39, Jun 1975 5.00
❑40, Jul 1975, giant 6.00
❑41, Aug 1975 5.00
❑42, Sep 1975 5.00
❑43, Oct 1975 5.00
❑44, Nov 1975 5.00
❑45, Jan 1976 5.00
❑46, Mar 1976 5.00
❑47, Jun 1976 5.00
❑48, Aug 1976, Bicentennial #2 5.00
❑49, Oct 1976 5.00
❑50, Nov 1976 5.00
❑51, Jan 1977 4.00
❑52, Mar 1977 4.00
❑53, Apr 1977 4.00
❑54, May 1977 4.00
❑55, Jul 1977 4.00
❑56, Sep 1977 4.00
❑57, Oct 1977 4.00
❑58, Nov 1977 4.00
❑59, Dec 1977 4.00
❑60, Jan 1978 4.00
❑61, Feb 1978 4.00
❑62, Mar 1978 4.00
❑63, Apr 1978 4.00
❑64, May 1978 4.00
❑65, Jun 1978 4.00
❑66, Jul 1978 4.00
❑67, Aug 1978 4.00
❑68, Sep 1978 4.00
❑69, Oct 1978 4.00
❑70, Nov 1978 4.00
❑71, Dec 1978 3.00
❑72, Jan 1979 3.00
❑73, Feb 1979 3.00
❑74, Mar 1979 3.00
❑75, Apr 1979 3.00
❑76, May 1979 3.00
❑77, Jun 1979 3.00
❑78, Jul 1979 3.00
❑79, Aug 1979 3.00
❑80, Sep 1979 3.00

Gen13: Magical Drama Queen Roxy

Manga-ized version of familiar heroes
©Image

Gen13/Monkeyman & O'Brien

Good old-fashioned dimension-hopping
©Image

Genus

Long-running adults-only anthropomorphic title
©Antarctic

Geomancer

Magic-users who speak for Earth
©Valiant

George of the Jungle

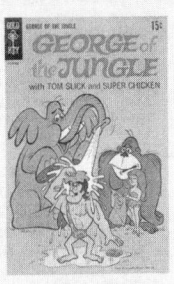

With Tom Slick and Super Chicken, no less
©Gold Key

	N-MINT
❑81, Oct 1979	3.00
❑82, Nov 1979	3.00
❑83, Dec 1979	3.00
❑84, Jan 1980	3.00
❑85, Feb 1980	3.00
❑86, Mar 1980	3.00
❑87, Apr 1980	3.00
❑88, May 1980	3.00
❑89, Jun 1980	3.00
❑90, Jul 1980	3.00
❑91, Aug 1980	3.00
❑92, Sep 1980	3.00
❑93, Oct 1980	3.00
❑94, Nov 1980	3.00
❑95, Dec 1980	3.00
❑96, Jan 1981	3.00
❑97, Feb 1981, A: Spectre	3.00
❑98, Mar 1981, JA (c); A: Spectre	3.00
❑99, Apr 1981, TD (a); A: Spectre	3.00
❑100, May 1981	3.00
❑101, Jun 1981	3.00
❑102, Jul 1981	3.00
❑103, Aug 1981	3.00
❑104, Sep 1981	3.00
❑105, Oct 1981	3.00
❑106, Nov 1981	3.00
❑107, Dec 1981	3.00
❑108, Jan 1982	3.00
❑109, Feb 1982	3.00
❑110, Mar 1982	3.00
❑111, Apr 1982	3.00
❑112, May 1982, Final Issue	3.00

Ghost Ship
Slave Labor

❑1, Mar 1996, b&w; cardstock cover	3.50
❑2, Jun 1996, b&w; cardstock cover	2.95
❑3, Oct 1996, b&w; cardstock cover	2.95

Ghosts of Dracula
Eternity

❑1, Sep 1991, b&w	2.50
❑2, b&w	2.50
❑3, b&w	2.50
❑4, b&w	2.50
❑5, b&w	2.50

Ghost Spy
Image

❑1, Aug 2004	2.95
❑2, Sep 2004	2.95
❑3, Oct 2004	2.95
❑4, Nov 2004	2.95
❑5, Dec 2004	2.95

Ghost Stories
Dell

❑1, Sep 1962	36.00
❑2, Apr 1963	20.00
❑3, Jul 1963	14.00
❑4, Oct 1963	14.00
❑5, Jan 1964	14.00
❑6, Apr 1964	10.00
❑7, Jul 1964	10.00
❑8, Oct 1964	10.00
❑9, Jan 1965	10.00
❑10, Apr 1965	10.00
❑11, Aug 1965, FS (c); FS (a)	7.00

	N-MINT
❑12, Dec 1965	7.00
❑13, Mar 1966	7.00
❑14, Jun 1966	7.00
❑15, Sep 1966	7.00
❑16, Dec 1966	7.00
❑17, Mar 1967	6.00
❑18, May 1967	6.00
❑19, Aug 1967	6.00
❑20, Nov 1967	6.00
❑21, Oct 1968	5.00
❑22, Oct 1969	5.00
❑23, Jan 1970	5.00
❑24, May 1970	5.00
❑25, Jul 1970	5.00
❑26, Oct 1970	5.00
❑27, Jan 1971	5.00
❑28, Apr 1971	5.00
❑29, Jul 1971, Reprints issue #9	5.00
❑30, Oct 1971	5.00
❑31, Jan 1972	5.00
❑32, Apr 1972	5.00
❑33, Jul 1972	5.00
❑34, Oct 1972	5.00
❑35, Jan 1973	5.00
❑36, Jul 1973	5.00
❑37, Oct 1973, Final Issue	5.00

Ghost Stories
Dark Horse

❑1; Collects Comics' Greatest World, Arcadia Week 3: Ghost;Ghost Special;X #8	8.95

Ghouls
Eternity

❑1, b&w; Reprints	2.25

Giantkiller
DC

❑1, Aug 1999	2.50
❑2, Sep 1999	2.50
❑3, Oct 1999	2.50
❑4, Nov 1999	2.50
❑5, Dec 1999	2.50
❑6, Jan 2000	2.50

Giantkiller A to Z
DC

❑1, Aug 1999; no indicia; biographical monster information	2.50

Giant-Size Amazing Spider-Man
Marvel

❑1, Aug 1999; cardstock cover; reprints stories from Spider-Man Adventures #6, #11, #12, and Marvel Tales #205	4.50

Giant-Size Avengers
Marvel

❑1, Aug 1974, SL (w); RB (a); 1: Whizzer I (Robert Frank). D: Miss America. Reprints	30.00
❑2, Nov 1974, DC (a); O: Rama-Tut. D: Swordsman. reprints Fantastic Four #19 (Rama-Tut)	25.00
❑3, Feb 1975, GK (c); SL (w); JK, DC (a); O: Immortus. O: Kang. A: Wonder Man. A: Zemo. A: Human Torch. A: Frankenstein's Monster. continued from Avengers #132; reprints Avengers #2; Marvel Value Stamp #41: Gladiator	20.00
❑4, Jun 1975, GK (c); SL (w); JB, DH (a); Wedding of Vision and Scarlet Witch	20.00
❑5, Dec 1975, Reprints	15.00

Giant-Size Captain America
Marvel

	N-MINT
❑1, O: Captain America. Reprints from Tales of Suspense; Reprints from Tales of Suspense #59-63	20.00

Giant-Size Captain Marvel
Marvel

❑1, A: Hulk. A: Captain America. Reprints	16.00

Giant-Size Chillers
Marvel

❑1, Jun 1974, JR (c); SL (w); GC, JR, RH (a); 1: Lilith. Dracula; reprints stories from Mystic #25 and Weird Worlds #4	25.00

Giant-Size Chillers
Marvel

❑1, Feb 1975, "The Girl Who Couldn't Die!" reprinted from Adventure In Terror #6; "From Out of the Past!" reprinted from Astonishing Tales #49; "Next Stop Eternity" reprinted from Adventure into Mystery #3	20.00
❑2, Aug 1975, "Let's Face It!" reprinted from Astonishing Tales #36; "The Couple Next Door!" reprinted from Mystic #25; "Pit" reprinted from Weird Worlds #10; "The Watchers!" reprinted from Amazing Adventures #5; "Fight for Life" reprinted from World of Suspense #3; "The Next World!" reprinted from Marvel Tales #130; "I Love a Mermaid!" reprinted from Tales to Astonish #4	15.00
❑3, Aug 1975, "Gargoyle Every Night" reprinted from Chamber of Darkness #7; "The Warlock Tree" reprinted from Chamber of Darkness #3; "Desert Scream" reprinted from Monsters on the Prowl #9; "The Moving Finger Writhes" reprinted from Tower of Shadows #3; "The Monster" reprinted from Chamber of Darkness #4; "To Sneak, Perchance to Scream" and "One Little Indian" reprinted from Tower of Shadows #4; Tigra preview panel	15.00

Giant-Size Conan
Marvel

❑1, Sep 1974, GK (c); TS, BB, GK (a); 1: Belit	16.00
❑2, Dec 1974, JB (c); TS, GK (a); Reprints Conan the Barbarian #5; Adapts "The Hour of the Dragon by Robert E. Howard"	10.00
❑3, Apr 1975, GK (c); GK (a); Reprints Conan the Barbarian #6; Adapts "The Hour of the Dragon" by Robert E. Howard	7.00
❑4, Jun 1975, GK (c); GK (a); Reprints Conan the Barbarian #7; Adapts "The Hour of the Dragon" by Robert E. Howard	6.00
❑5, Jun 1975, JK (c); Reprints Conan the Barbarian #12, 14 and 15	6.00

Giant-Size Creatures
Marvel

❑1, Jul 1974, DP (a); O: Tigra. 1: Tigra. Marvel Value Stamp A-34 (Mr. Fantastic)	25.00

Giant-Size Daredevil
Marvel

❑1, ca. 1975, Reprints Daredevil Ann #1	15.00

Giant-Size Defenders
Marvel

❑1, Jul 1974, GK (c); JSn (a); A: Silver Surfer. Silver Surfer	20.00

N-MINT

❑2, Oct 1974, GK (c); BEv, SL (w); GK, KJ (a); Son of Satan ... 10.00
❑3, Jan 1975, JSn, SL (w); DN, JSn, SD, JM, DA (a); 1: Korvac. Marvel Value Stamp #48: Kraven ... 10.00
❑4, Apr 1975, GK (c); DH (a); V: Squadron Sinister; Original material with reprints from Human Torch #4 and Strange Tales #121 ... 7.00
❑5, Jul 1975, GC, DH (a); A: Guardians of the Galaxy. Original material with partial reprint of Daredevil #62 ... 7.00

Giant-Size Doc Savage
Marvel

❑1, Jan 1975, RA, JM (a); reprints Doc Savage (Marvel) #1 and 2; adapts Man of Bronze ... 10.00

Giant-Size Doctor Strange
Marvel

❑1, ca. 1975, GT, DA (a); Reprints stories from Strange Tales #164, 165, 166, 167, 168 ... 15.00

Giant-Size Dracula
Marvel

❑2, Sep 1974, Series continued from Giant-Size Chillers (1st Series) #1; SL (w); FMc, DH, RH (a); Series continued from Giant-Size Chillers (1st Series) #1; reprints stories from Tales to Astonish #32, Menace #2, and Astonishing Tales #17 and #18 ... 22.00
❑3, Dec 1974, SL (w); DH, FS (a); Reprints stories from Uncanny Tales #6 and Spellbound #22 ... 15.00
❑4, Mar 1975, SL (w); SD, DH (a); Reprints stories from Adventure in Terror #4 and #6 and Tales of Suspense #15 and #46 ... 15.00
❑5, Jun 1975, GK (c); JBy (a); Marvel Value Stamp #55: Medusa ... 20.00

Giant-Size Fantastic Four
Marvel

❑1, May 1974, published as Giant-Size Super-Stars; SL (w); RB, JK (a); A: Fantastic Four. A: Hulk. Thing battles Hulk ... 20.00
❑2, Aug 1974, Title changes to Giant-Size Fantastic Four; GK (c); SL (w); JB, JK (a); A: Willie Lumpkin. V: Tempus. also reprints Fantastic Four #13 ... 12.00
❑3, Nov 1974, RB (c); SL (w); RB, JK (a); also reprints Fantastic Four #21 ... 10.00
❑4, Feb 1975, RB (c); JK, SL (w); JB, JK (a); O: Madrox the Multiple Man. 1: Madrox the Multiple Man. A: Professor X. A: Medusa. Marvel Value Stamp #2: Hulk ... 12.00
❑5, May 1975, reprints Fantastic Four Ann #5 and Fantastic Four #15 ... 10.00
❑6, Oct 1975, reprints Fantastic Four Ann #6 ... 10.00

Giant-Size Hulk
Marvel

❑1, Jan 1975, reprints Hulk Ann #1 ... 23.00

Giant-Size Hulk
Marvel

❑1, Sep 2006, Reprint Hulk: The End ... 8.00

Giant-Size Invaders
Marvel

❑1, Jun 1975, O: Sub-Mariner. O: Invaders. 1: Invaders. Reprints ... 15.00

Giant-Size Iron Man
Marvel

❑1, ca. 1975, Reprints ... 17.00

Giant-Size Kid Colt
Marvel

❑1, A: Rawhide Kid ... 27.00
❑2, GK (c) ... 20.00
❑3, Jul 1975, GK (c); A: Night Rider ("Ghost Rider") ... 20.00

Giant-Size Man-Thing
Marvel

❑1, Aug 1974, MP (c); SL (w); SD, JK, MP (a); V: Glob. Reprints from Amazing Adventures #11, Strange Tales Ann #2, Tales of Suspense #15; V: Glob ... 15.00
❑2, Reprints from Tales to Astonish (1st series) #15 & Tales to Astound You #7 ... 9.00
❑3, Feb 1975, Marvel Value Stamp #77: Swordsman ... 12.00
❑4, May 1975, FB (c); SD, FB (a); Howard the Duck; Marvel Value Stamp #36: Ancient One ... 10.00

N-MINT

❑5, Aug 1975, GK (c); TS, FB, JB (a); Howard the Duck ... 12.00

Giant-Size Marvel Triple Action
Marvel

❑1, May 1975, Reprints ... 15.00
❑2, Jul 1975, Reprints ... 12.00

Giant-Size Master of Kung Fu
Marvel

❑1, Sep 1974, FMc, PG, CR (a) ... 17.00
❑2, Dec 1974, AM (c); PG (a) ... 12.00
❑3, Mar 1975, PG (a); Marvel Value Stamp #71: Vision ... 10.00
❑4, Jun 1975, JK (a); Yellow Claw ... 10.00

Giant-Size Mini Comics
Eclipse

❑1, Aug 1986, b&w ... 2.00
❑2, Oct 1986, b&w ... 2.00
❑3, Dec 1986, b&w ... 2.00
❑4, Feb 1987, b&w ... 2.00

Giant Size Mini-Marvels: Starring Spidey
Marvel

❑1, Feb 2002 ... 3.50

Giant-Size Ms. Marvel
Marvel

❑1, Apr 2006, Includes material from Captain Marvel #18, Ms. Marvel #1, 2, and 20 ... 4.99

Giant Size Official Prince Valiant
Pioneer

❑1, b&w; Hal Foster ... 3.95

Giant-Size Power Man
Marvel

❑1, ca. 1975 ... 20.00

Giant-Size Spider-Man
Marvel

❑1, Jul 1974, JR (c); SL (w); JK, RA (a); A: Dracula. reprints story from Strange Tales Ann #2 ... 35.00
❑2, Oct 1974, GK, JR (c); SL (w); DH, GK, JR, RA (a); A: Shang-Chi. reprints story from Amazing Spider-Man Ann #3 ... 12.00
❑3, Jan 1975, GK (c); SL (w); SD, RA (a); A: Doc Savage. also reprints story from Amazing Spider-Man #16 ... 12.00
❑4, Apr 1975, GK (c); SL (w); SD, RA (a); 1: Moses Magnum (Magnum Force). A: Punisher; Last story reprinted from Amazing Spider-Man Ann #2 but recorded as Strange Tales #179 ... 45.00
❑5, Jul 1975, GK (c); SL (w); SD, RA (a); A: Man-Thing. V: Lizard. V: Lizard; Reprint from Amazing Spider-Man #21; Last story reprinted with changes from Amazing Spider-Man #21 ... 12.00
❑6, Sep 1975, reprints Amazing Spider-Man Ann #4 ... 15.00

Giant Size Spider-Man
Marvel

❑1, Dec 1998; reprints stories from Marvel Team-Up ... 4.00

Giant-Size Spider-Woman
Marvel

❑1, Sep 2005; Collects stories from Marvel Spotlight #32, 37, 38, Spider-Woman #1, plus new story ... 4.99

Giant-Size Super-Heroes
Marvel

❑1, Jun 1974, GK, JR (c); SL (w); SD, GK (a); A: Man-Wolf. A: Spider-Man. A: Morbius. "How Stan..." reprinted from Amazing Spider-Man Ann #1 ... 25.00

Giant-Size Super-Stars
Marvel

❑1, May 1974 RB, JSt (c); RB, JK, JSt (a) ... 20.00

Giant-Size Super-Villain Team-Up
Marvel

❑1, Mar 1975, Reprinted from Sub-Mariner #20 and Marvel Super-Heroes #20 ... 17.00
❑2, Jun 1975, Doctor Doom, Sub-Mariner ... 10.00

Giant-Size Thor
Marvel

❑1, Jul 1975, GK (c); SL (w); JK, GK (a); Reprints ... 20.00

N-MINT

Giant-Size Werewolf By Night
Marvel

❑2, Oct 1974, Title changes to GS Werewolf by Night; SD (a); Frankenstein reprint ... 20.00
❑3, Jan 1975, GK (a) ... 15.00
❑4, Apr 1975, GK (a) ... 15.00
❑5, GK (a) ... 15.00

Giant Size Wolverine
Marvel

❑1, Dec 2006 ... 4.99

Giant-Size X-Men
Marvel

❑1, Sum 1975, GK (c); GK, DC (a); O: Storm. O: Nightcrawler. 1: X-Men (new). 1: Thunderbird. 1: Colossus. 1: Storm. 1: Nightcrawler. 1: Illyana Rasputin ... 800.00
❑2, Nov 1975, GK, KJ (a); reprints X-Men #57-59 ... 80.00
❑3, Jul 2005; Reprints Fantastic Four #28, X-Men #9, 27, 35 ... 4.99
❑4 2005; Reprints X-Men #94-95, Classic X-Men #3, and Uncanny X-Men #193; ca. 2005 ... 5.00

Giant THB Parade
Horse

❑1, b&w; over-sized ... 5.00

G.I. Combat
DC

❑87, May 1961, 1: Haunted Tank ... 300.00
❑88, Jul 1961 ... 55.00
❑89, Sep 1961 ... 55.00
❑90, Nov 1961 ... 55.00
❑91, Jan 1962, RH (a) ... 55.00
❑92, Mar 1962 ... 55.00
❑93, May 1962 ... 55.00
❑94, Jul 1962 ... 55.00
❑95, Sep 1962 ... 55.00
❑96, Nov 1962 ... 55.00
❑97, Jan 1963 ... 55.00
❑98, Mar 1963 ... 55.00
❑99, May 1963 ... 55.00
❑100, Jul 1963 ... 55.00
❑101, Sep 1963 ... 45.00
❑102, Nov 1963 ... 45.00
❑103, Jan 1964, RH (c); JKu (a); Painted cover ... 45.00
❑104, Mar 1964, Sgt. Mule back-up ... 45.00
❑105, May 1964, JKu (c); JKu (a) ... 45.00
❑106, Jul 1964, JKu (c); JKu (a) ... 45.00
❑107, Sep 1964, JKu (c); JKu (a) ... 45.00
❑108, Nov 1964, JKu (c); JKu (a) ... 45.00
❑109, Jan 1965, JKu (c); JKu (a) ... 45.00
❑110, Mar 1965, JKu (c); JKu (a) ... 45.00
❑111, May 1965, JKu (c); JKu (a) ... 38.00
❑112, Jul 1965, JKu (c); JKu (a) ... 38.00
❑113, Sep 1965, (c); JKu (a) ... 38.00
❑114, Nov 1965, RH (c); RH (a); O: Haunted Tank ... 75.00
❑115, Jan 1966, (c); RH (a) ... 28.00
❑116, Mar 1966, JKu (c); IN (a); A: Johnny Cloud ... 28.00
❑117, May 1966, JKu (c); RH (a) ... 28.00
❑118, Jul 1966, (c); IN (a) ... 28.00
❑119, Sep 1966 ... 28.00
❑120, Nov 1966, (c); A: Johnny Cloud. A: Sgt. Rock ... 28.00
❑121, Jan 1967, (c) ... 22.00
❑122, Mar 1967, JKu (c); JAb (a) ... 22.00
❑123, May 1967, (c) ... 22.00
❑124, Jul 1967, RH (c); RH (a) ... 22.00
❑125, Sep 1967, RH (c) ... 22.00
❑126, Nov 1967, RH (c); RH, JAb (a) ... 22.00
❑127, Jan 1968, JKu (c); IN, JAb (a) ... 22.00
❑128, Mar 1968, (c) ... 22.00
❑129, May 1968, RH (c) ... 22.00
❑130, Jul 1968, RH (c); A: Attila the Hun's ghost ... 22.00
❑131, Sep 1968 ... 22.00
❑132, Nov 1968, JKu (c); JAb (a) ... 22.00
❑133, Jan 1969, JKu (c) ... 22.00
❑134, Mar 1969, JKu (c) ... 22.00
❑135, May 1969, JKu (c) ... 22.00
❑136, Jul 1969 ... 22.00
❑137, Sep 1969, JKu (c) ... 22.00
❑138, Nov 1969, 1: Losers ... 22.00
❑139, Jan 1970, JKu (c); RH (a) ... 22.00
❑140, Mar 1970 ... 22.00

Other grades: Multiply price above by 5/6 for VF/NM • 2/3 for VERY FINE • 1/3 for FINE • 1/5 for VERY GOOD • 1/8 for GOOD

Ghost Manor

More horror comics from Charlton

©Charlton

Ghost Manor

With your horrible host, Mr. Bones

©Charlton

Ghost Rider

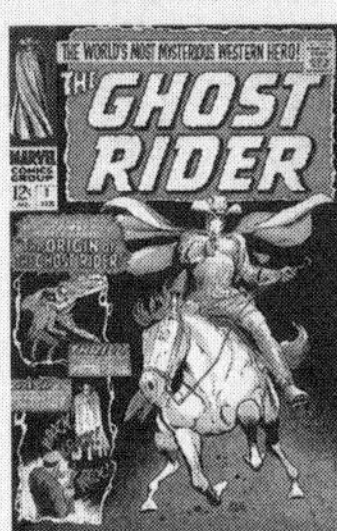

The Western version predated the biker

©Marvel

Ghost Rider

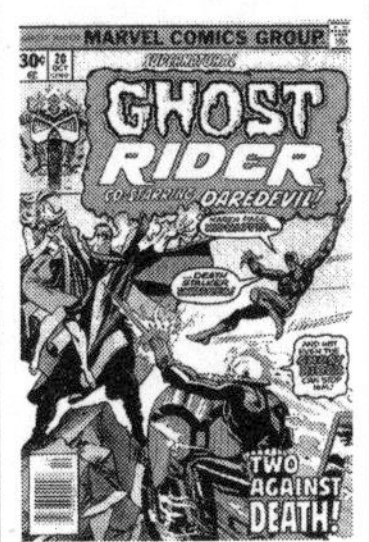

He's a Hell's Angel -- literally

©Marvel

Ghost Rider

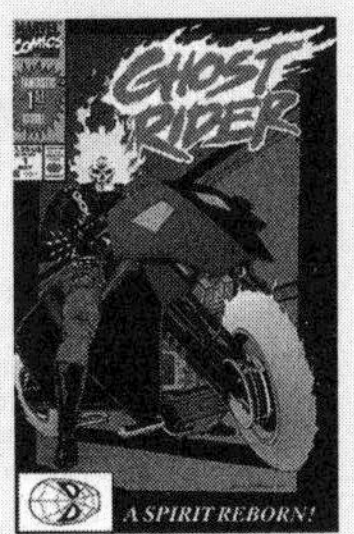

Spirit of Vengeance reborn for the 1990s

©Marvel

	N-MINT
❑141, May 1970, JKu (c)	8.00
❑142, Jul 1970	8.00
❑143, Sep 1970, JKu (c)	8.00
❑144, Nov 1970, JKu (c)	8.00
❑145, Jan 1971	8.00
❑146, Mar 1971, Giant-size	10.00
❑147, May 1971, Giant-size; (c)	10.00
❑148, Jul 1971, Giant-size	10.00
❑149, Sep 1971, JKu (c); Sgt. Rock back-up	10.00
❑150, Nov 1971, JKu (c); JKu, RH (a); 1: New Haunted Tank; 1: The Ice Cream Soldier; Reprinted from Our Army at War #85; The Two-Legged Mine reprinted from All-American Men of War #66	10.00
❑151, Jan 1972, JKu (c); Reprints Capt. Storm #8	8.00
❑152, Mar 1972, JKu (c)	8.00
❑153, May 1972, JKu (c)	8.00
❑154, Jul 1972, JKu (c)	8.00
❑155, Sep 1972	8.00
❑156, Nov 1972	8.00
❑157, Jan 1973, JKu (c)	8.00
❑158, Feb 1973, (c)	8.00
❑159, Mar 1973, JKu (c); GM, RE (a)	8.00
❑160, May 1973	8.00
❑161, Jun 1973, JKu (c)	7.00
❑162, Jul 1973, JKu (c)	7.00
❑163, Aug 1973	7.00
❑164, Sep 1973, (c)	7.00
❑165, Oct 1973	7.00
❑166, Nov 1973, (c)	7.00
❑167, Dec 1973, (c)	7.00
❑168, Jan 1974, (c)	7.00
❑169, Feb 1974, Reprints	7.00
❑170, Mar 1974, (c)	7.00
❑171, Jun 1974, JKu (c)	7.00
❑172, Aug 1974, (c); DGr (a)	7.00
❑173, Oct 1974, JKu (c)	7.00
❑174, Dec 1974, JKu (c); RE (a)	7.00
❑175, Feb 1975, JKu (c)	7.00
❑176, Mar 1975, JKu (c)	7.00
❑177, Apr 1975	7.00
❑178, May 1975, JKu (c)	7.00
❑179, Jun 1975, JKu (c)	7.00
❑180, Jul 1975, JKu (c)	7.00
❑181, Aug 1975	5.00
❑182, Sep 1975	5.00
❑183, Oct 1975, JKu (c)	5.00
❑184, Nov 1975, JKu (c)	5.00
❑185, Dec 1975	5.00
❑186, Jan 1976	5.00
❑187, Feb 1976, JKu (c)	5.00
❑188, Mar 1976, (c)	5.00
❑189, Apr 1976, (c)	5.00
❑190, May 1976	5.00
❑191, Jun 1976	5.00
❑192, Jul 1976, Bicentennial #27; O.S.S. stories begin	5.00
❑193, Aug 1976, JKu (c)	5.00
❑194, Sep 1976	5.00
❑195, Oct 1976, JKu (c)	5.00
❑196, Nov 1976, JKu (c)	5.00
❑197, Dec 1976, JKu (c)	5.00
❑198, Jan 1977, JKu (c)	5.00
❑199, Feb 1977, JKu (c)	5.00
❑200, Mar 1977, JKu (c)	5.00
❑201, Apr 1977, JKu (c)	3.50

	N-MINT
❑202, Jun 1977, JKu, NA (c); GE (a); Haunted Tank, O.S.S., Battling Belle	3.50
❑203, Aug 1977, JKu (c)	3.50
❑204, Oct 1977, JKu (c)	3.50
❑205, Dec 1977, JKu (c)	3.50
❑206, Feb 1978	3.50
❑207, Apr 1978	3.50
❑208, Jun 1978	3.50
❑209, Aug 1978, JKu (c)	3.50
❑210, Oct 1978	3.50
❑211, Dec 1978, JKu (c)	3.50
❑212, Feb 1979, JKu (c)	3.50
❑213, Apr 1979, JKu (c)	3.50
❑214, Jun 1979	3.50
❑215, Aug 1979	3.50
❑216, Oct 1979	3.50
❑217, Dec 1979	3.50
❑218, Feb 1980	3.50
❑219, Apr 1980, JKu (c)	3.50
❑220, Jun 1980, JKu (c)	3.50
❑221, Aug 1980	3.50
❑222, Oct 1980, JKu (c)	3.50
❑223, Nov 1980, JKu (c)	3.50
❑224, Dec 1980, JKu (c)	3.50
❑225, Jan 1981	3.50
❑226, Feb 1981, JKu (c)	3.50
❑227, Mar 1981, JKu (c)	3.50
❑228, Apr 1981, JKu (c)	3.50
❑229, May 1981, JKu (c)	3.50
❑230, Jun 1981, JKu (c)	3.50
❑231, Jul 1981, JKu (c)	3.50
❑232, Aug 1981, JKu (c); 1: Kana	3.50
❑233, Sep 1981, JKu (c)	3.50
❑234, Oct 1981, JKu (c)	3.50
❑235, Nov 1981, JKu (c)	3.50
❑236, Dec 1981, JKu (c)	3.50
❑237, Jan 1982, JKu (c)	3.50
❑238, Feb 1982, JKu (c)	3.50
❑239, Mar 1982, JKu (c)	3.50
❑240, Apr 1982, JKu (c)	3.50
❑241, May 1982, JKu (c)	3.50
❑242, Jun 1982, JKu (c); 1: The Mercenaries	3.50
❑243, Jul 1982, JKu (c)	3.50
❑244, Aug 1982, JKu (c); A: Mercenaries	3.50
❑245, Sep 1982, JKu (c)	3.50
❑246, Oct 1982, 30th anniversary; JKu (c); A: Ninja. A: Johnny Cloud. A: Gunner & Sarge. A: Sgt. Rock. A: Captain Storm. A: Falcon. A: Haunted Tank. Double-size	3.50
❑247, Nov 1982, JKu (c)	3.50
❑248, Dec 1982, JKu (c)	3.50
❑249, Jan 1983, JKu (c)	3.50
❑250, Feb 1983, JKu (c)	3.50
❑251, Mar 1983, JKu (c)	2.50
❑252, Apr 1983, JKu (c)	2.50
❑253, May 1983, JKu (c)	2.50
❑254, Jun 1983, JKu (c)	2.50
❑255, Jul 1983, JKu (c)	2.50
❑256, Aug 1983, JKu (c)	2.50
❑257, Sep 1983, JKu (c)	2.50
❑258, Oct 1983, JKu (c)	2.50
❑259, Nov 1983, JKu (c)	2.50
❑260, Dec 1983, JKu (c)	2.50
❑261, Jan 1984, JKu (c)	2.50
❑262, Feb 1984, JKu (c)	2.50

	N-MINT
❑263, Mar 1984, JKu (c)	2.50
❑264, Apr 1984, JKu (c)	2.50
❑265, May 1984, JKu (c)	2.50
❑266, Jun 1984, JKu (c)	2.50
❑267, Jul 1984, JKu (c); KG (a)	2.50
❑268, Aug 1984, JKu (c)	2.50
❑269, Sep 1984, JKu (c)	2.50
❑270, Oct 1984, JKu (c)	2.50
❑271, Nov 1984, JKu (c)	2.50
❑272, Dec 1984, JKu (c)	2.50
❑273, Jan 1985, JKu (c)	2.50
❑274, Feb 1985, JKu (c); A: Monitor. A: Attila	2.50
❑275, Mar 1985, JKu (c)	2.50
❑276, Apr 1985, JKu (c)	2.50
❑277, May 1985, JKu (c)	2.50
❑278, Jul 1985, JKu (c)	2.50
❑279, Sep 1985, JKu (c)	2.50
❑280, Nov 1985, JKu (c)	2.50
❑281, Jan 1986, JKu (c)	2.50
❑282, Mar 1986, JKu (c); Mercenaries	2.50
❑283, May 1986, JKu (c); Mercenaries	2.50
❑284, Jul 1986, JKu (c); Mercenaries	2.50
❑285, Sep 1986, JKu (c); Mercenaries	2.50
❑286, Nov 1986, JKu (c); Mercenaries	2.50
❑287, Jan 1987, JKu (c); Haunted Tank	2.50
❑288, Mar 1987, JKu (c); JKu (a); Haunted Tank	2.50

Gideon Hawk
Big Shot

❑1, Jan 1995, b&w	2.00
❑2, Mar 1995, b&w	2.00
❑3, Jun 1995, b&w	2.00

Gidget
Dell

❑1, Apr 1966	100.00

Gift
Image

❑1, ca. 2004	2.99
❑1/DirCut, Apr 2005	3.99
❑2, ca. 2004	2.99
❑3, ca. 2004	2.99
❑4, ca. 2004	2.99
❑5, ca. 2004	2.99
❑6, ca. 2004	2.99
❑7, ca. 2004	2.99
❑8 2004	2.99
❑9, Nov 2004	2.99
❑10, Mar 2005	2.99
❑11, ca. 2005	2.99
❑12, May 2005	2.99
❑13, Aug 2005	2.99
❑14, Mar 2006	2.99

Gift: A First Publishing Holiday Special
First

❑1, Nov 1990; NN	5.95

Gifts of the Night
DC / Vertigo

❑1, Feb 1999	2.95
❑2, Mar 1999	2.95
❑3, Apr 1999	2.95
❑4, May 1999	2.95

Other grades: Multiply price above by 5/6 for VF/NM • 2/3 for VERY FINE • 1/3 for FINE • 1/5 for VERY GOOD • 1/8 for GOOD

Gigantor
Antarctic / Vertigo

❑1, Jan 2000 .... 2.50

Gigolo
Fantagraphics / Eros

❑1 .... 2.95
❑2, Nov 1995 .... 2.95

G.I. Government Issued
Paranoid

❑1, Aug 1994, Contains publisher's note that series was solicited in color, but sales limited it to black and white 2.00
❑2, Aug 1994, Has some cover date as #1 in indicia 2.00

G.I. Jackrabbits
Excalibur

❑1, Dec 1986 .... 1.50

GI Joe
Dark Horse

❑1, Dec 1995; FM (c); FM (a); 1: Tall Sally. 1: Short Fuse; Red; White; And Blue logo 2.00
❑2, Jan 1996 .... 2.00
❑3, Mar 1996 .... 2.00
❑4, Apr 1996; Final Issue 2.00

GI Joe
Dark Horse

❑1, Jun 1996 .... 2.50
❑2, Jul 1996 .... 2.50
❑3, Aug 1996 .... 2.50
❑4, Sep 1996; Final Issue 2.50

G.I. Joe
Image

❑1, Sep 2001 .... 3.00
❑1/2nd, Sep 2001 .... 2.95
❑2, ca. 2001 .... 2.95
❑3, ca. 2002 .... 2.95
❑4, ca. 2002 .... 3.50
❑5, ca. 2002; Duke vs. Major Bludd 2.95
❑6, ca. 2002 .... 2.95
❑7, ca. 2002 .... 2.95
❑8, ca. 2002 .... 2.95
❑9, ca. 2002 .... 2.95
❑10, ca. 2002 .... 2.95
❑11, ca. 2002 .... 2.95
❑12, Nov 2002 .... 2.95
❑13, Dec 2002 .... 2.95
❑14, Jan 2003 .... 2.95
❑15, Feb 2003 .... 2.95
❑16, Mar 2003 .... 2.95
❑17, Apr 2003 .... 2.95
❑18, Jun 2003 .... 2.95
❑19, Jul 2003; D: Lt. Gorky 2.95
❑20, Aug 2003; Dyptch cover; Leftside cover; Cover connects to issue #21 .... 2.95
❑21, Aug 2003; Dyptch cover; Rightside cover; Cover connects to issue #20; Silent issue 2.95
❑22, Nov 2003; D: Daemon 2.95
❑22/Graham, Nov 2003; Michael Turner cover art. Produced exclusively for Graham Crackers Comics, Naperville, Ill 12.00
❑23, Nov 2003 .... 2.95
❑24, Nov 2003 .... 2.95
❑25, Dec 2003 .... 2.95

G.I. Joe
Devil's Due

❑26, Mar 2004 .... 2.95
❑27, Apr 2004 .... 2.95
❑28, May 2004 .... 2.95
❑29, Jun 2004 .... 2.95
❑30, Jul 2004 .... 2.95
❑31, Aug 2004 .... 2.95
❑32, Sep 2004 .... 2.95
❑33, Oct 2004 .... 2.95
❑34, Nov 2004 .... 2.95
❑35, Dec 2004 .... 2.95
❑35/Variant, Dec 2004 .... 3.95
❑36, Jan 2005 .... 2.95
❑37, Feb 2005 .... 2.95
❑38, Mar 2005 .... 2.95
❑39, Apr 2005 .... 2.95
❑40, May 2005 .... 2.95
❑41, Jun 2005 .... 2.95
❑42, Jul 2005 .... 2.95

G.I. Joe: America's Elite
Devil's Due

❑0, Jun 2005 .... 1.00
❑1, Jul 2005 .... 2.95
❑1/Conv, Jul 2005; San Diego Con exclusive; sold for $10; 500 produced. Cover by Sunder Raj 10.00
❑2, Aug 2005 .... 2.95
❑3, Sep 2005 .... 2.95
❑4, Oct 2005 .... 2.95
❑5, Nov 2005 .... 4.50
❑6, Dec 2005 .... 4.50
❑7, Jan 2006 .... 2.95
❑9, Mar 2006 .... 2.95
❑10, Apr 2006 .... 2.95
❑11, May 2006 .... 2.95
❑12, Jun 2006 .... 2.95
❑13, Jul 2006 .... 2.95
❑13/Special, Jul 2006 .... 5.95
❑14, Aug 2006 .... 2.95
❑15, Sep 2006 .... 2.95
❑16, Oct 2006 .... 2.95
❑17, Nov 2006 .... 2.95
❑18, Dec 2006 .... 2.95

G.I. Joe: America's Elite Data Desk Handbook
Devil's Due

❑1, Dec 2005 .... 2.95

G.I. Joe: America's Elite - The Hunt for Cobra Commander
Devil's Due

❑1, May 2006 .... 0.25

G.I. Joe and the Transformers
Marvel

❑1, Jan 1987 HT (a) 1.00
❑2, Feb 1987 .... 1.00
❑3, Mar 1987 .... 1.00
❑4, Apr 1987 .... 1.00

G.I. Joe: Battle Files
Image

❑1 2002 .... 5.95
❑2, Jan 2002; COBRA 5.95
❑3, Jan 2002; Weapons and Tech; Cover by David Michael Beck 5.95

G.I. Joe Comics Magazine
Marvel

❑1, Dec 1986; digest 3.00
❑2, Feb 1987; digest 2.00
❑3, Apr 1987; digest 2.00
❑4, Jun 1987; digest 2.00
❑5, Aug 1987; digest 2.00
❑6, Oct 1987; digest 2.00
❑7, Dec 1987; digest 2.00
❑8, Feb 1988; digest 2.00
❑9, Apr 1988; digest 2.00
❑10, Jun 1988; digest 2.00
❑11, Aug 1988; digest 2.00
❑12, Oct 1988; digest 2.00
❑13, Dec 1988; digest 2.00

G.I. Joe: Declassified
Devil's Due

❑1, Jun 2006 .... 4.95
❑1/Spaulding, Jun 2006 .... 8.95
❑2, Aug 2006 .... 4.95
❑2/Special, Aug 2006 .... 8.95
❑3, Oct 2006 .... 4.95
❑3/Special, Oct 2006 .... 8.95

G.I. Joe: Dreadnoks Declassified
Devil's Due

❑1, Jan 2007 .... 4.95
❑1/Special, Nov 2006 .... 8.95

G.I. Joe European Missions
Marvel

❑1, Jun 1988; Includes mini-poster 1.50
❑2, Jul 1988; Includes mini-poster 1.50
❑3, Aug 1988; Includes mini-poster 1.50
❑4, Sep 1988; Includes mini-poster 1.50
❑5, Oct 1988 .... 1.50
❑6, Nov 1988 .... 1.50
❑7, Dec 1988 .... 1.50
❑8, Jan 1989 .... 1.50
❑9, Feb 1989 .... 1.50
❑10, Mar 1989 .... 1.50
❑11, Apr 1989 .... 1.50
❑12, May 1989 .... 1.75
❑13, Jun 1989 .... 1.75
❑14, Jul 1989 .... 1.75
❑15, Aug 1989; Cover by Stewart Johnson, John Burns 1.75

G.I. Joe: Frontline
Image

❑1, Oct 2002; Dave Dorman-c 2.95
❑1/Platinum, Oct 2002 .... 5.00
❑2, Nov 2002 .... 2.95
❑3, Dec 2002 .... 2.95
❑4, Jan 2003 .... 2.95
❑5, Feb 2003; 1: A Da; Preview of Kore . 2.95
❑6, Mar 2003 .... 2.95
❑7, Apr 2003 .... 2.95
❑8, Jul 2003 .... 2.95
❑9, Jul 2003; O: Zanya 2.95
❑10, Jul 2003; O: Zanya 2.95
❑11, Aug 2003; Featuring Chuckles 2.95
❑12, Aug 2003; Featuring Chuckles 2.95
❑13, Aug 2003; Featuring Chuckles 2.95
❑14, Sep 2003; Featuring Chuckles 2.95
❑15, Oct 2003; Featuring Stalker 2.95
❑16, Nov 2003 .... 2.95
❑17, Nov 2003 .... 2.95
❑18, Dec 2003 .... 2.95

G.I. Joe in 3-D
Blackthorne

❑1, Jul 1987; Blackthorne 3-D Series #20 .... 3.00
❑2, Oct 1987 .... 2.50
❑3, Jan 1988 .... 2.50
❑4, Apr 1988 .... 2.50
❑5, Jul 1988 .... 2.50
❑6, Oct 1988; Blackthorne 3-D Series #71 .... 2.50

G.I. Joe: Master & Apprentice
Devil's Due

❑1, Jun 2004 .... 2.95
❑2, Jul 2004 .... 2.95
❑3, Sep 2004 .... 2.95
❑4, Oct 2004 .... 2.95

G.I. Joe: Master & Apprentice Vol. II
Devil's Due

❑1 2005 .... 3.00
❑1/Variant 2005 .... 4.00
❑2 2005 .... 3.00
❑2/Variant 2005 .... 4.00
❑3 2005 .... 3.00
❑3/Variant 2005 .... 4.00

G.I. Joe Order of Battle
Marvel

❑1, Dec 1986; The Official G.I. Joe Handbook 1.25
❑2, Jan 1987; Rocky Balboa 1.25
❑3, Feb 1987; Wraparound cover 1.25
❑4, Mar 1987 .... 1.25

G.I. Joe, A Real American Hero
Marvel

❑1, Jun 1982; Giant-size; HT (c); HT (a); 1: G.I. Joe team; 1: Snake Eyes; 1: Scarlett; 1: Hawk; 1: Cobra Commander; 1: Baroness; 1: Grunt; 1: Breaker; 1: Short-Fuze; 1: Rock-n-Roll; 1: Stalker; Zap; Flash 14.00
❑2, Aug 1982, HT (c); DP (a); 1: Kwinn . 8.00
❑2/2nd, Aug 1982; 2nd printing 2.00
❑3, Sep 1982, AM (c); HT, JAb (a) 4.00
❑3/2nd, Sep 1982; 2nd printing 2.00
❑4, Oct 1982, BH (c); HT, JAb (a); 1: Vance Wingfield; 1: Tyler Wingfield; 1: Shary Wingfield 4.00
❑4/2nd, Oct 1982; 2nd printing 2.00
❑5, Nov 1982, DP (c); HT, JAb (a); 1: General Flagg 4.00
❑5/2nd, Nov 1982; 2nd printing 2.00
❑6, Dec 1982, HT (a); 1: Oktober Guard 4.00
❑6/2nd, Dec 1982; 2nd printing 1.00
❑7, Jan 1983, HT (c); HT (w); HT (a) 4.00
❑7/2nd, Jan 1983; 2nd printing 1.00
❑8, Feb 1983, HT (w); HT (a) 4.00
❑8/2nd, Feb 1983; 2nd printing 1.00
❑9, Mar 1983 .... 4.00
❑9/2nd, Mar 1983; 2nd printing 1.00
❑10, Apr 1983, 1: Billy; 1: Dr. Venom; 1: Springfield 6.00
❑10/2nd, Apr 1983; 2nd printing 1.00
❑11, May 1983, 1: Doc; 1: Snow Job; 1: Destro; 1: Gung-Ho; 1: Airborne; 1: Wild Bill 4.00

Ghost Rider 2099

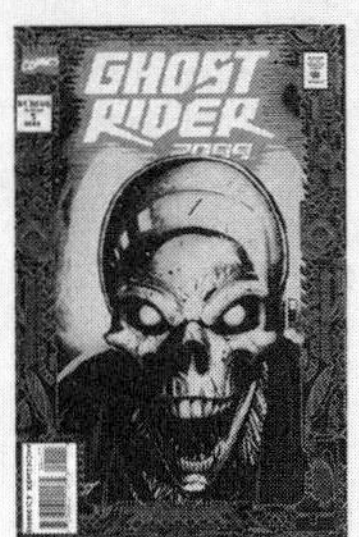

Depressing character in depressing future
©Marvel

Ghosts

True tales of the supernatural, or so they say
©DC

Ghost Stories

So much for the Dell "Pledge to Parents!"
©Dell

Giantkiller

Volcano plus monsters in Southern California
©DC

Giant-Size Creatures

Origin and first appearance of Tigra
©Marvel

	N-MINT
❑11/2nd, May 1983; 2nd printing	1.00
❑12, Jun 1983	4.00
❑12/2nd, Jun 1983; 2nd printing	1.00
❑13, Jul 1983, 1: Torpedo	4.00
❑13/2nd, Jul 1983; 2nd printing	1.00
❑14, Aug 1983, HT (c); 1: Destro	5.00
❑14/2nd, Aug 1983; 2nd printing	1.00
❑15, Sep 1983, 1st Major Bludd	4.00
❑15/2nd, Sep 1983; 2nd printing	1.00
❑16, Oct 1983, 1: Tripwire; 1: Cover Girl	4.00
❑16/2nd, Oct 1983; 2nd printing	1.00
❑17, Nov 1983, 1: Ace	4.00
❑17/2nd, Nov 1983; 2nd printing	1.00
❑18, Dec 1983	4.00
❑18/2nd, Dec 1983; 2nd printing	1.00
❑19, Jan 1984, D: Kwinn; D: General Flagg; D: Dr. Venom; D: Scar-Face	6.00
❑19/2nd, Jan 1984; 2nd printing	1.00
❑20, Feb 1984	4.00
❑20/2nd, Feb 1984; 2nd printing	1.00
❑21, Mar 1984, "silent" issue	15.00
❑21/2nd, Mar 1984; 2nd printing	1.00
❑22, Apr 1984, KJ (c); 1: Duke; 1: Roadblock	4.00
❑22/2nd, Apr 1984; 2nd printing	1.00
❑23, May 1984, MG (c)	4.00
❑23/2nd, May 1984; 2nd printing	1.00
❑24, Jun 1984, MZ (c); RH (a); 1: Firefly; 1: Wild Weasel; 1: Zartan	4.00
❑24/2nd, Jun 1984; 2nd printing	1.00
❑25, Jul 1984, MZ (c); FS (a); 1: Deep Six; 1: Mutt; 1: Dreadnoks; 1: Cutter; 1: Buzzer; 1: Ripper; 1: Torch	4.00
❑25/2nd, Jul 1984; 2nd printing	1.00
❑26, Aug 1984, O: Snake Eyes	4.00
❑26/2nd, Aug 1984, O: Snake Eyes. 2nd printing	1.00
❑27, Sep 1984, MG (c); FS (a); O: Snake Eyes	4.00
❑27/2nd, Sep 1984, O: Snake Eyes. 2nd printing	1.00
❑28, Oct 1984, MZ (c)	4.00
❑28/2nd, Oct 1984, 2nd printing	1.00
❑29, Nov 1984, MG (c); FS (a)	4.00
❑29/2nd, Nov 1984, 2nd printing	1.00
❑30, Dec 1984, MZ (c); FS (a)	4.00
❑30/2nd, Dec 1984, 2nd printing	1.00
❑31, Jan 1985, KJ (c); 1: Spirit	4.00
❑31/2nd, Jan 1985, 2nd printing	1.00
❑32, Feb 1985, FS (c); FS (a); 1: Lady Jaye; 1: Blowtorch; 1: Recondo; 1: Ripcord.	4.00
❑32/2nd, Feb 1985, 2nd printing	1.00
❑33, Mar 1985, MZ (c); FS (a); 1: Bongo the Balloon Bear	4.00
❑33/2nd, Mar 1985, 2nd printing	1.00
❑34, Apr 1985 MZ (c)	4.00
❑34/2nd, Apr 1985; 2nd printing	1.00
❑35, May 1985 JBy (c)	4.00
❑35/2nd, May 1985; 2nd printing	1.00
❑36, Jun 1985 MG (c)	4.00
❑36/2nd, Jun 1985; 2nd printing	1.00
❑37, Jul 1985; MZ (c); FS (a); 1: Flint; 1: Tomax & Xamot; 1: Footloose	4.00
❑38, Aug 1985 MZ (c)	4.00
❑39, Sep 1985 MZ (c)	4.00
❑40, Oct 1985; MZ (c); 1: Shipwreck; 1: Barbecue	4.00
❑41, Nov 1985 MZ (c)	4.00
❑42, Dec 1985 MZ (c)	4.00
❑43, Jan 1986; MZ (c); 1: Scrap-Iron; D: Soft Master; D: Candy (Bongo)	4.00
❑44, Feb 1986; MZ (c); 1: Airtight; 1: Bazooka; 1: Dr. Mindbender; 1: B.A.T.S.; 1: Crankcase; 1: Heavy Metal	4.00
❑45, Mar 1986; MZ (c); 1: Alpine; 1: Quick Kick	4.00
❑46, Apr 1986; MZ (c);1: Terror-Drome; D: Professor Appel	4.00
❑47, May 1986; MZ (c); 1: Beach Head & Wet Suit	4.00
❑48, Jun 1986; MZ (c); 1: Sgt. Slaughter	4.00
❑49, Jul 1986; MZ (c); 1: Leatherneck; 1: Lift-Ticket; 1: Slip Stream; 1: Serpentor; O: Serpentor	4.00
❑50, Aug 1986; Double-size; MZ (c); HT (a)	4.00
❑51, Sep 1986; JBy (c); 1: Thunder; 1: Cross Country; 1: Toll Booth; 1: Zandar; 1: Zarana; 1: Thrasher	4.00
❑52, Oct 1986 MZ (c)	4.00
❑53, Nov 1986; MZ (c); 1: General Hollingsworth	4.00
❑54, Dec 1986; MZ (c); 1: Slip Stream ..	4.00
❑55, Jan 1987; MZ (c); Snake Eyes, Cobra Commander, & Destro unmasked	4.00
❑56, Feb 1987 MZ (c)	5.00
❑57, Mar 1987; MZ (c); 1: Sergeant Major	3.00
❑58, Apr 1987; MZ (c); 1: Dusty; 1: Cobar Commanders battle armor; 1: Fred VII	4.00
❑59, May 1987; MZ (c); 1: Outback; 1: Tunnel rat; 1: Jinx; 1: Raptor; 1: Blind Master	3.00
❑60, Jun 1987; MZ (c); TMc (a); 1: Lt. Falcon; 1: Law & Order; 1: Chuckles; 1: Fast draw; 1: Monkeywrench; 1: Zanzibar; Todd McFarlane art	3.00
❑61, Jul 1987; MZ (c); MR (a); 1: Colonel Ratinkov	3.00
❑62, Aug 1987 MZ (c)	3.00
❑63, Sep 1987; MZ (c);1: Captain Minh; 1: Corporal Olga; 1: Sgt. Moshev	3.00
❑64, Oct 1987; MZ (c);1: Sci-Fi; 1: Psyche Out; 1: Hard Top; 1: Frostbite; 1: Payload; 1: Backstop; 1: Fred VII as Cobra Commander	3.00
❑65, Nov 1987 MZ (c)	3.00
❑66, Dec 1987 MZ (c)	3.00
❑67, Jan 1988; 1: Tyronne	3.00
❑68, Feb 1988; 1: Battle Force 2000	3.00
❑69, Mar 1988	3.00
❑70, Apr 1988	3.00
❑71, May 1988	3.00
❑72, Jun 1988; 1: Croc-Master; 1: Wild Card; 1: Skidmark; 1: Windmill; 1: Star Viper	3.00
❑73, Jul 1988; 1: Sneak Peek I; 1: Iron Grenadiers	3.00
❑74, Aug 1988	3.00
❑75, Sep 1988 MR (a)	3.00
❑76, Sep 1988; 1: Rumbler; 1: Ghost Rider; D: Serpentor	3.00
❑77, Oct 1988 MR (c); MR (a)	3.00
❑78, Oct 1988	3.00
❑79, Nov 1988 MR (a)	3.00
❑80, Nov 1988	3.00
❑81, Dec 1988; MR (c); MR (a); 1: Battle Force 2000; 1: Dodger; 1: Blocker; 1: Blaster; 1: Avalanche; 1: Knockdown; 1: Maverick	3.00
❑82, Jan 1989; MR (a); 1: Repeater; 1: Budo; 1: Charbroil	3.00
❑83, Feb 1989; 1: Roadkill	3.00
❑84, Mar 1989 MR (a)	3.00
❑85, Apr 1989; Silent issue	3.00
❑86, May 1989; MR (a); 1: Joe Colton; 1: Shockwave; 25th anniversaary issue	3.00
❑87, Jun 1989; 1: Darklon	3.00
❑88, Jul 1989; 1: Hardball	3.00
❑89, Aug 1989	3.00
❑90, Sep 1989	3.00
❑91, Oct 1989	3.00
❑92, Nov 1989; 1: Long Range	3.00
❑93, Nov 1989; Snake-Eyes' face is finally revealed	3.00
❑94, Dec 1989	3.00
❑95, Dec 1989	3.00
❑96, Jan 1990	3.00
❑97, Feb 1990	3.00
❑98, Mar 1990; Death Dr. Mindbender; Death Croc Master; Death Raptor	3.00
❑99, Apr 1990 HT (a)	3.00
❑100, May 1990; Giant size, Return of Cobra Commander I	3.00
❑101, Jun 1990; 1: Lt. Gorky; 1: Sgt. Misha; 1: Oktober Guard II	3.00
❑102, Jul 1990	3.00
❑103, Aug 1990	3.00
❑104, Sep 1990	3.00
❑105, Oct 1990	3.00
❑106, Nov 1990	3.00
❑107, Dec 1990	3.00
❑108, Jan 1991; Dossiers begin	3.00
❑109, Feb 1991; D: Doc; D: Breaker; D: Quick Kick; D: Thunder; D: Crazy Legs; D: Heavy Metal; D: Crankcase	3.00
❑110, Mar 1991	3.00
❑111, Apr 1991	3.00
❑112, May 1991	3.00
❑113, Jun 1991	3.00
❑114, Jul 1991; 1: Metal-Head	3.00
❑115, Aug 1991	3.00
❑116, Sep 1991	3.00
❑117, Oct 1991; 1: Ninja Force; 1: Nunchuk; 1: T'Jbang; 1: Dojo	3.00
❑118, Nov 1991	3.00
❑119, Dec 1991 HT (w); HT (a)	3.00
❑120, Jan 1992	3.00
❑121, Feb 1992	3.00
❑122, Mar 1992	3.00
❑123, Apr 1992	3.00
❑124, May 1992	3.00
❑125, Jun 1992	3.00
❑126, Jul 1992	3.00
❑127, Sep 1992; Baroness Pin-Up by George Perez	3.00
❑128, Sep 1992	3.00
❑129, Oct 1992	3.00
❑130, Nov 1992	3.00
❑131, Dec 1992	3.00
❑132, Jan 1993	3.00
❑133, Feb 1993	3.00
❑134, Mar 1993 A: Snake Eyes	3.00
❑135, Apr 1993; Polybagged with trading card; Team members are regrouped into three strike teams	3.00
❑136, May 1993; trading card	3.00
❑137, Jun 1993; trading card	3.00
❑138, Jul 1993; bagged with trading card	3.00
❑139, Aug 1993; Transformers	3.00

Other grades: Multiply price above by 5/6 for VF/NM • 2/3 for VERY FINE • 1/3 for FINE • 1/5 for VERY GOOD • 1/8 for GOOD

❑140, Sep 1993; Transformers 3.00
❑141, Oct 1993; A: Transformers: Generation 2. A: Megatron. A: Cobra Commander. Transformers Gen 2; New Transformers app 3.00
❑142, Nov 1993; Transformers 3.00
❑143, Dec 1993; Flashback issue 3.00
❑144, Jan 1994; O: Snake-Eyes; Flashback issue 3.00
❑145, Feb 1994 3.00
❑146, Mar 1994 3.00
❑147, Apr 1994 3.00
❑148, May 1994 3.00
❑149, Jun 1994 3.00
❑150, Jul 1994; Giant-size 3.00
❑151, Aug 1994 3.00
❑152, Sep 1994 7.00
❑153, Oct 1994 7.00
❑154, Nov 1994 7.00
❑155, Dec 1994; Final Issue 16.00
❑YB 1, Mar 1985; YB (annual) #1; YB (annual) #1 2.50
❑YB 2, Mar 1986; YB (annual) #2; 1: Dragonsky; YB (annual) #2 2.00
❑YB 3, Mar 1987; YB (annual) #3; MZ (a); YB (annual) #3 2.00
❑YB 4, Feb 1988; YB (annual) #4; HT, MZ (a); YB (annual) #4 1.50
❑Special 1, Feb 1995 TMc (c) 20.00

G.I. Joe: Reloaded
Devil's Due

❑1, May 2004 5.00
❑2, Jun 2004 3.00
❑3, Jul 2004 3.00
❑4, Aug 2004 2.95
❑5, Sep 2004 2.95
❑6, Oct 2004 2.95
❑7, Nov 2004 2.95
❑8, Dec 2004 2.95
❑9, Jan 2005 2.95
❑10, Feb 2005 2.95
❑11, Mar 2005 2.95
❑12, Apr 2005 2.95
❑13, May 2005 2.95
❑14, Jun 2005 2.95

G.I. Joe: Scarlett Declassified
Devil's Due

❑1, Aug 2006 4.95

G.I. Joe: Sigma 6
Devil's Due

❑1, Jan 2006 2.95
❑2, Jan 2006 2.95
❑3, Mar 2006 2.95
❑4, Mar 2006, Indicia says February; Cover says March 2.95
❑5, Apr 2006, Indicia says March, Cover says April 2.95
❑6, May 2006 2.95

G.I. Joe: Snake Eyes Declassified
Devil's Due

❑1, Sep 2005 2.95
❑2 2005 2.95
❑3, Dec 2005 2.95
❑4, Jan 2006 2.95
❑5, Jan 2006 2.95
❑6, Feb 2006 2.95

G.I. Joe Special Missions
Marvel

❑1, Oct 1986 MZ (c); HT (a) 1.50
❑2, Dec 1986 MZ (c); HT (a) 1.00
❑3, Feb 1987 MZ (c); HT (a) 1.00
❑4, Apr 1987 MZ (c); HT (a) 1.00
❑5, Jun 1987 MZ (c); HT (a) 1.00
❑6, Aug 1987 MZ (c); HT (a) 1.00
❑7, Oct 1987 MZ (c); HT (a) 1.00
❑8, Dec 1987 MZ (c); HT (a) 1.00
❑9, Feb 1988 DC (c); HT (a) 1.00
❑10, Apr 1988 HT (a) 1.00
❑11, Jun 1988 HT (a) 1.00
❑12, Aug 1988 HT (c); HT (a) 1.00
❑13, Sep 1988 HT (a) 1.00
❑14, Oct 1988 BMc (c); HT (a) 1.00
❑15, Nov 1988 HT (a) 1.00
❑16, Dec 1988 BMc (c); HT (a) 1.00
❑17, Jan 1989 HT (a) 1.00
❑18, Feb 1989 HT (a) 1.00
❑19, Mar 1989 HT (a) 1.00
❑20, Apr 1989 BMc (c); HT (a) 1.00
❑21, May 1989 HT (a) 1.00
❑22, Jun 1989 DC (a) 1.00
❑23, Jul 1989 HT (a) 1.00
❑24, Aug 1989 DC (c); DC (a) 1.00
❑25, Sep 1989 HT (a) 1.00
❑26, Oct 1989 HT (a) 1.00
❑27, Nov 1989 1.00
❑28, Nov 1989; HT (a); Mid Nov. on covers and Dec inside 1.00

G.I. Joe Special Missions: Antarctica
Devil's Due

❑1, Dec 2006 4.95

G.I. Joe Special Missions: Manhattan
Devil's Due

❑1, Apr 2006 4.95

G.I. Joe: Special Missions - Manhattan
Devil's Due

❑1, Feb 2006 4.95

G.I. Joe: Special Missions - Tokyo
Devil's Due

❑1, Sep 2006 4.95

G.I. Joe vs. Transformers: The Art of War
Devil's Due

❑1, Mar 2006 2.95
❑1/Variant, Mar 2006 2.95
❑2, Apr 206 2.95
❑2/Variant, Apr 2006 2.95
❑3, May 2006 2.95
❑3/Variant, May 2006 2.95
❑4, Jun 2006 2.95
❑4/Variant, Jun 2006 2.95

G.I. Joe/Transformers
Image

❑1, Jul 2003 4.00
❑1/Campbell, Jul 2003 3.00
❑1/Foil, Jul 2003 9.00
❑1/Graham, Jul 2003 4.00
❑1/Graham foil, Jul 2003 6.00
❑1/Miller, Jul 2003 3.00
❑2, Aug 2003 2.95
❑2/Sketch, Aug 2003 12.00
❑3, Sep 2003 2.95
❑3/Conv, Sep 2003 4.00
❑3/Variant, Sep 2003 3.00
❑4, Oct 2003 2.00
❑4/Variant, Oct 2003 3.00
❑5, Dec 2003 2.00
❑5/Variant, Dec 2003 3.00
❑6, Dec 2003 2.00

G.I. Joe vs. The Transformers
Devil's Due

❑1 2004 4.00
❑1/Variant 2004 4.00
❑2 2004 2.95
❑2/Variant 2004 2.95
❑3 2004 2.95
❑3/Variant 2004 2.95
❑4 2004 2.95
❑4/Variant 2004 2.95

Gilgamesh II
DC

❑1 1989; prestige format; O: Gilgamesh 3.95
❑2 1989; prestige format 3.95
❑3 1989; prestige format 3.95
❑4 1989; prestige format 3.95

Gimme
Head Imports

❑1 3.00

Gimoles
Alias

❑1, ca. 2005 0.75
❑2, ca. 2005 2.99
❑3, ca 2005 2.99
❑4, ca. 2005 2.99

G.I. Mutants
Eternity

❑1, ca. 1987 1.95
❑2, ca. 1987 1.95
❑3, ca. 1987 1.95
❑4, ca. 1987 1.95

Ginger Fox
Comico

❑1, Sep 1988; Yellow 1.75
❑2, Oct 1988 1.75
❑3, Nov 1988 1.75
❑4, Dec 1988 1.75

Gin-Ryu
Believe in Yourself

❑1, Mar 1995 2.75
❑2, May 1995 2.75
❑3 2.75
❑3/Ashcan 1.00
❑4, Oct 1995 2.75

Gipsy
NBM

❑1; ca. 2000 10.95
❑2; ca. 2002 10.95

G.I. R.A.M.B.O.T.
Wonder Color

❑1, Apr 1987 1.95

Girl
Rip Off

❑1, Feb 1991, b&w; Adult 2.50
❑1/2nd, Oct 1992, b&w; 2nd printing; Adult 2.50
❑2, May 1991, b&w; Adult 2.50
❑3, Aug 1991, b&w; Adult 2.50
❑4, Dec 1991, b&w; Adult 2.50

Girl
NBM

❑1; Adult 15.95

Girl
DC / Vertigo

❑1, Jul 1996 2.50
❑2, Aug 1996 2.50
❑3, Sep 1996 2.50

Girl Called...Willow!, A
Angel

❑1, Fal 1996, b&w; Adult 2.95

Girl Called...Willow! Sketchbook, A
Angel

❑1, b&w; pin-ups and rough pencil sketches; wraparound cover 2.95

Girl Crazy
Dark Horse

❑1, May 1996, b&w 2.95
❑2, Jul 1996, b&w 2.95
❑3, Jul 1996, b&w 2.95

Girl from U.N.C.L.E.
Gold Key

❑1, Jan 1967, 10197-701; pin-up on back cover 36.00
❑2, Apr 1967, Photo cover 24.00
❑3, Jun 1967, Photo cover 20.00
❑4, Aug 1967, Photo cover 15.00
❑5, Oct 1967, Photo cover; Final Issue 15.00

Girl Genius
Studio Foglio

❑Ashcan 1, Oct 2000, b&w; PF (c); PF (w); PF (a); No cover price; preview of upcoming series; smaller than normal comic book 1.00
❑1, Feb 2001, b&w; PF (c); PF (w); PF (a); cardstock cover 2.95
❑2, Apr 2001 PF (c); PF (w); PF (a) 2.95
❑3, Jun 2001 PF (c); PF (w); PF (a) 2.95
❑4, Aug 2001 PF (c); PF (w); PF (a) 3.95
❑5, Nov 2001 PF (c); PF (w); PF (a) 3.95
❑6, May 2002; PF (c); PF (w); PF (a); Publisher name changes to Airship 3.95
❑7, Jul 2002 PF (c); PF (w); PF (a) 3.95
❑8, Nov 2002 PF (c); PF (w); PF (a) 3.95
❑9, ca. 2003 3.95
❑10, ca. 2004 3.95
❑11, Apr 2004; cardstock cover 3.95
❑12, Jul 2004; cardstock cover 3.95

Girlhero
High Drive

❑1, Aug 1993, b&w 3.00
❑2, Feb 1994, b&w 3.00
❑3, Jul 1994, b&w 3.00

Girl on Girl College Kink: New Year's Babes
Angel

❑1; Adult 3.00

Other grades: Multiply price above by 5/6 for VF/NM • 2/3 for VERY FINE • 1/3 for FINE • 1/5 for VERY GOOD • 1/8 for GOOD

Giant-Size Doc Savage

Reprints the first two regular Marvel issues
©Marvel

Giant-Size Fantastic Four

First issue was "Giant-Size Super Stars"
©Marvel

Giant-Size X-Men

#1 's X-Men relaunch helped reinvent comics
©Marvel

G.I. Combat

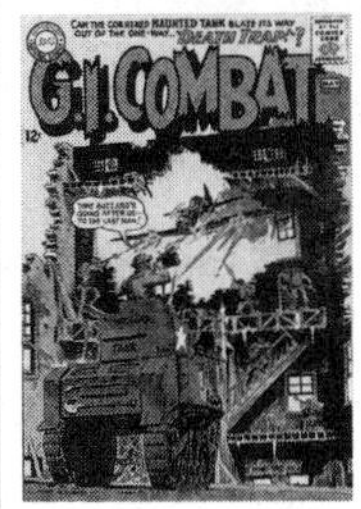

Long-running war comic with Joe Kubert art
©DC

Gideon Hawk

High-tech bounty hunter in outer space
©Big Shot

N-MINT

Girl on Girl: Feedin' Time
Angel

❑1; Adult ... 3.00

Girl on Girl: Ticklish
Angel

❑1; Adult ... 3.00

Girl + Girl
Fantagraphics / Eros

❑1, Dec 2004, Adult; b&w ... 3.95

Girls
Image

❑1, Jun 2005 ... 7.00
❑1/Variant, Jun 2005, 2nd printing ... 5.00
❑1/Sketch, Jun 2005, Sketch version of 2nd print cover ... 6.00
❑2, Jul 2005 ... 4.00
❑2/Variant, Jul 2005, 2nd printing ... 5.00
❑3, Aug 2005 ... 2.99
❑4, Sep 2005 ... 2.99
❑5, Oct 2005 ... 2.99
❑6, Nov 2005 ... 2.99
❑7, Dec 2006 ... 2.99
❑8, Jan 2006 ... 2.99
❑9, Jan 2006 ... 2.99
❑10, Feb 2006 ... 2.99
❑11, Apr 2006 ... 2.99
❑12, May 2006 ... 2.99
❑13, Jun 2006 ... 2.99
❑14, Jul 2006 ... 2.99
❑15, Jul 2006 ... 2.99
❑16, Sep 2006 ... 2.99
❑17, Oct 2006 ... 2.99
❑18, Nov 2006 ... 2.99
❑19, Dec 2006 ... 2.99
❑20, Jan 2007 ... 2.99

Girls Bravo
Tokyopop

❑1, Sep 2005 ... 9.99
❑2, Dec 2005 ... 9.99

Girls' Love Stories
DC

❑83, Nov 1961 ... 25.00
❑84, Jan 1962 ... 25.00
❑85, Feb 1962 ... 25.00
❑86, Apr 1962 ... 25.00
❑87, May 1962 ... 25.00
❑88, Jul 1962 ... 25.00
❑89, Sep 1962 ... 25.00
❑90, Oct 1962 ... 25.00
❑91, Nov 1962 ... 25.00
❑92, Jan 1963 ... 25.00
❑93, Feb 1963 ... 25.00
❑94, Apr 1963 ... 25.00
❑95, May 1963 ... 20.00
❑96, Jul 1963 ... 20.00
❑97, Sep 1963 ... 20.00
❑98, Oct 1963 ... 20.00
❑99, Nov 1963 ... 20.00
❑100, Jan 1964 ... 20.00
❑101, Feb 1964 ... 20.00
❑102, Apr 1964 ... 20.00
❑103, May 1964 ... 20.00
❑104, Jul 1964 ... 20.00
❑105, Sep 1964 ... 20.00
❑106, Oct 1964 ... 17.00

N-MINT

❑107, Nov 1964 ... 17.00
❑108, Jan 1965 ... 17.00
❑109, Feb 1965 ... 17.00
❑110, Apr 1965 ... 17.00
❑111, May 1965 ... 17.00
❑112, Jul 1965 ... 15.00
❑113, Sep 1965 ... 15.00
❑114, Oct 1965 ... 15.00
❑115, Nov 1965 ... 15.00
❑116, Jan 1966 ... 15.00
❑117, Feb 1966 ... 15.00
❑118, Apr 1966 ... 15.00
❑119, May 1966 ... 15.00
❑120, Jul 1966 ... 15.00
❑121, Sep 1966 ... 15.00
❑122, Oct 1966 ... 15.00
❑123, Nov 1966 ... 15.00
❑124, Jan 1967 ... 14.00
❑125, Feb 1967 ... 14.00
❑126, Apr 1967 ... 14.00
❑127, May 1967 ... 14.00
❑128, Jul 1967 ... 14.00
❑129, Sep 1967 ... 14.00
❑130, Oct 1967 ... 14.00
❑131, Nov 1967 ... 14.00
❑132, Jan 1968 ... 14.00
❑133, Feb 1968 ... 14.00
❑134, Apr 1968 ... 14.00
❑135, May 1968 ... 14.00
❑136, Jul 1968 ... 14.00
❑137, Sep 1968 ... 14.00
❑138, Oct 1968 ... 14.00
❑139, Nov 1968 ... 14.00
❑140, Jan 1969 ... 14.00
❑141, Feb 1969 ... 14.00
❑142, Apr 1969 ... 14.00
❑143, May 1969 ... 14.00
❑144, Jul 1969 ... 9.00
❑145, Sep 1969 ... 9.00
❑146, Oct 1969 ... 9.00
❑147, Nov 1969 ... 9.00
❑148, Jan 1970 ... 9.00
❑149, Feb 1970 ... 9.00
❑150, Apr 1970 ... 9.00
❑151, May 1970 ... 9.00
❑152, Jul 1970 ... 9.00
❑153, Sep 1970 ... 9.00
❑154, Oct 1970 ... 9.00
❑155, Nov 1970 ... 9.00
❑156, Jan 1971 ... 9.00
❑157, May 1971 ... 9.00
❑158, Jun 1971 ... 9.00
❑159, Jul 1971 ... 9.00
❑160, Aug 1971 ... 9.00
❑161, Sep 1971 ... 9.00
❑162, Oct 1971 ... 9.00
❑163, Nov 1971 ... 9.00
❑164, Dec 1971 ... 9.00
❑165, Jan 1972 ... 7.00
❑166, Feb 1972 ... 7.00
❑167, Mar 1972 ... 7.00
❑168, Apr 1972 ... 7.00
❑169, May 1972 ... 7.00
❑170, Jun 1972 ... 7.00
❑171, Jul 1972 ... 7.00
❑172, Aug 1972 ... 7.00

N-MINT

❑173, Sep 1972 ... 7.00
❑174, Oct 1972 ... 7.00
❑175, Dec 1972 ... 7.00
❑176, Feb 1973 ... 7.00
❑177, May 1973 ... 7.00
❑178, Aug 1973 ... 7.00
❑179, Oct 1973 ... 7.00
❑180, Dec 1973 ... 7.00

Girls of '95: Good, Bad & Deadly
Lost Cause

❑1, Feb 1996 ... 3.95

Girls of Ninja High School
Antarctic

❑1, Jun 1991, b&w ... 3.75
❑2, May 1992, b&w ... 3.75
❑3, Apr 1993, b&w ... 3.75
❑4, Apr 1994, b&w; 1994 Ann ... 3.95
❑5, Apr 1995; 1995 Ann ... 4.50
❑6, ca. 1996; 1996 Ann ... 3.95
❑7, May 1997; 1997 Ann ... 3.95
❑8/A, May 1998; 1998 Ann ... 3.95
❑8/B, May 1998; 1998 Ann; alternate cover (manga-style) ... 3.95
❑9, Apr 1999; Nylon Menaces: Dandelion; Minerva: Blind Spot; back cover pin-up ... 2.99

Girl Squad X
Fantaco

❑1, b&w ... 2.95

Girl Talk
Fantagraphics

❑4, Sum 1996, b&w; Anthology ... 3.50

Girl: The Rule of Darkness
Cry for Dawn

❑1, ca. 1992; b&w ... 2.50

Girl: The Second Coming
NBM

❑1; Adult ... 10.95

Girl Who Would Be Death
DC / Vertigo

❑1, Dec 1998 ... 2.50
❑2, Jan 1999 ... 2.50
❑3, Feb 1999 ... 2.50
❑4, Mar 1999 ... 2.50

Give It Up! and Other Short Stories
NBM

❑1, Jul 1995, b&w; Hardcover; Peter Kuper adaptations of Kafka stories ... 14.95

Give Me Liberty! (Rip Off)
Rip Off

❑1, Jan 1976 ... 4.00

Give Me Liberty
Dark Horse

❑1, Jun 1990; prestige format; 1: Martha Washington ... 5.00
❑2, Sep 1990; prestige format ... 5.00
❑3, Dec 1990; prestige format ... 5.00
❑4, Apr 1991; prestige format ... 5.00

G.I. War Tales
DC

❑1, Mar 1973 ... 12.00
❑2, Jun 1973, Reprints stories from Star Spangled War Stories #134, G.I. Combat #133 ... 7.00

Other grades: Multiply price above by 5/6 for VF/NM • 2/3 for VERY FINE • 1/3 for FINE • 1/5 for VERY GOOD • 1/8 for GOOD

❑3, Aug 1973, JKu, RH (a); Reprints stories from All American Men of War #55, 38 .... 6.00
❑4, Oct 1973, Reprints from Star-Spangled War Stories #36 & #78, and Our Army at War #10.......... 6.00

Gizmo
Mirage

❑1, Feb 1986, b&w.......... 1.50
❑2, Mar 1986, b&w.......... 1.50
❑3, Apr 1986, b&w.......... 1.50
❑4, May 1986, b&w.......... 1.50
❑5, Mar 1987, b&w.......... 1.50
❑6, Jul 1987, b&w.......... 1.50

Gizmo
Chance

❑1.......... 2.50

Gizmo and the Fugitoid
Mirage

❑1, Jun 1989, b&w 2.00
❑2, Jun 1989, b&w 2.00

GLA
Marvel

❑1, Jun 2005.......... 5.00
❑2, Jul 2005.......... 2.99
❑3, Aug 2005.......... 2.99
❑4, Sep 2005.......... 2.99

Gladiator/Supreme
Marvel

❑1, Mar 1997 .... 4.99

Glamorous Graphix Presents
Glamorous Graphix

❑1, Jan 1996, b&w; Becky Sunshine; pin-ups.......... 3.95

Glass Jaw
Clay Heeled

❑1/AUT; Autographed edition; ca. 1999.. 2.95
❑1; no date.......... 2.95

Global Force
Silverline

❑1.......... 1.95
❑2.......... 1.95

Global Frequency
DC / Wildstorm

❑1, Dec 2002.......... 2.95
❑2, Jan 2003.......... 2.95
❑3, Feb 2003.......... 2.95
❑4, Mar 2003.......... 2.95
❑5, Apr 2003.......... 2.95
❑6, May 2003.......... 2.95
❑7, Jun 2003.......... 2.95
❑8, Jul 2003.......... 2.95
❑9, Sep 2003.......... 2.95
❑10, Sep 2003.......... 2.95
❑11, Mar 2004 .... 2.95
❑12, Aug 2004 .... 2.95

GloomCookie
Slave Labor

❑1, Jun 1999.......... 4.00
❑2, Sep 1999.......... 3.50
❑3, Dec 1999.......... 3.00
❑4, Mar 2000 .... 2.95
❑5, Jun 2000.......... 2.95
❑6, Oct 2000 .... 2.95
❑7, Apr 2001 .... 2.95
❑8, Jun 2001 .... 2.95
❑9, Sep 2001.......... 2.95
❑10, Dec 2001.......... 2.95
❑11, Feb 2002.......... 2.95
❑12, Apr 2002.......... 2.95
❑13 2002.......... 2.95
❑14, Oct 2003.......... 2.95
❑15, Mar 2003.......... 2.95
❑16, Jun 2003.......... 2.95
❑17, Sep 2003.......... 2.95
❑18, Dec 2003.......... 2.95
❑19 2004.......... 2.95
❑20, Jun 2004.......... 2.95
❑21 2004.......... 2.95
❑22, Sep 2004.......... 2.95
❑23, Mar 2005.......... 2.95
❑24, Sep 2005.......... 2.95
❑25, Nov 2005 .... 2.95

Gloom
APComics

❑1, Jun 2005.......... 3.50
❑2, Sep 2005; Indicia indicates May, 2005 as cover date.......... 3.50

Glorianna
Press This

❑1, b&w; NN; One-shot.......... 3.95

Glory
Image

❑0, Feb 1996.......... 2.50
❑1, Mar 1995.......... 2.50
❑1/A, Mar 1995; Image publishes; alternate cover.......... 2.50
❑2, Apr 1995.......... 2.50
❑3, May 1995.......... 2.50
❑4, Jun 1995.......... 2.50
❑4/A, Jun 1995; Variant cover 2.50
❑5, Aug 1995; polybagged with trading card.......... 2.50
❑6, Sep 1995 .... 2.50
❑7, Oct 1995.......... 2.50
❑8, Nov 1995; Babewatch.......... 2.50
❑9, Jan 1996; polybagged with Glory card 2.50
❑10, Mar 1996 A: Angela 2.50
❑11, Apr 1996.......... 2.50
❑12, May 1996; double-sized anniversary issue; Giant-size.......... 3.50
❑12/A, May 1996; double-sized anniversary issue; alternate cover...... 5.00
❑13, Jun 1996.......... 2.50
❑14, Jul 1996.......... 2.50
❑15, Sep 1996 .... 2.50
❑16, Oct 1996; Maximum begins as publisher 2.50
❑17, Nov 1996.......... 2.50
❑18, Dec 1996.......... 2.50
❑19, Jan 1997.......... 2.50
❑20, Feb 1997.......... 2.50
❑21, Mar 1997.......... 2.50
❑22, ca. 1997.......... 2.50
❑23, ca. 1997; Final Issue.......... 2.50

Glory & Friends Bikini Fest
Image

❑1, Sep 1995; pin-ups 2.50
❑1/Variant, Sep 1995; alternate cover; pin-ups.......... 2.50

Glory & Friends Christmas Special
Image

❑1, Dec 1995 .... 2.50

Glory & Friends Lingerie Special
Image

❑1, Sep 1995; pin-ups 2.95
❑1/Variant, Sep 1995; alternate cover; pin-ups.......... 2.95

Glory/Angela: Angels in Hell
Image

❑1, Apr 1996; flipbook with Darkchylde preview.......... 2.50

Glory/Avengelyne
Image

❑1/A, Oct 1995; no title information on cover 3.95
❑1/B, Oct 1995; no title information on cover 3.95

Glory/Celestine: Dark Angel
Image

❑1, Sep 1996 .... 2.50
❑2, Oct 1996.......... 2.50

GLX-Mas Special
Marvel

❑1, Feb 2006.......... 3.99

Glyph
Labor of Love

❑1, b&w; magazine; NN; Anthology...... 4.95
❑2, b&w; magazine; Anthology.......... 4.95
❑3, b&w; magazine; Anthology.......... 4.95

G-Man
Image

❑1 2005; One-shot.......... 5.95

G-Men
Caliber

❑1, b&w.......... 2.50

Gnatrat: The Dark Gnat Returns
Prelude

❑1 1986, b&w; Batman parody; continues in Darerat/Tadpole 1.95

Gnatrat: The Movie
Innovation

❑1, b&w; Batman parody 2.25

Gnome-Mobile
Gold Key

❑1, Oct 1967 .... 25.00

Gnomes, Fairies, and Sex Kittens
Fantagraphics

❑1, Jan 2006.......... 3.95

G'n'R's Greatest Hits
Revolutionary

❑1, Oct 1993, b&w.......... 2.50

Go-Go
Charlton

❑1, Jun 1966, Photos of The Rolling Stones and Herman Hermits; Jim Aparo's 1st published work.......... 40.00
❑2, Aug 1966 .... 30.00
❑3, Oct 1966 .... 30.00
❑4, Dec 1966 .... 30.00
❑5, Feb 1967, Includes Sonny & Cher photos; Justice League of America parody 30.00
❑7, Jun 1967.......... 30.00
❑8, Jun 1967, Photos (2) of The Monkees 30.00
❑9, Oct 1967, A: Miss Bikini Luv.......... 30.00

Gobbledygook
Mirage

❑1; 1: The Teenage Mutant Ninja Turtles 110.00
❑2 .... 70.00

Gobbledygook
Mirage

❑1, Dec 1986, b&w 5.00

Goblin Lord
Goblin

❑1, Oct 1996.......... 2.50
❑2, Dec 1996 .... 2.50
❑3, Feb 1997.......... 2.50
❑4, Apr 1997.......... 2.50
❑5, Jun 1997.......... 2.99
❑6, Sep 1997 .... 2.99

Goblin Magazine
Warren

❑1, Jun 1982.......... 8.50
❑2 .... 5.00
❑3, Nov 1982 AN (a) 5.00
❑4 .... 5.00

Goblin Market
Tome

❑1, b&w; poem 2.50

Goblin Studios
Goblin

❑1 .... 2.25
❑2 .... 2.25
❑3 .... 2.25
❑4 .... 2.25
❑5, Aug 1995 .... 2.25

Go Boy 7 Human Action Machine
Dark Horse

❑1, Jul 2003.......... 2.99
❑2, Aug 2003 .... 2.99
❑3, Oct 2003.......... 2.99
❑4, Nov 2003 .... 2.99
❑5, Mar 2004 .... 2.99

Goddess
DC / Vertigo

❑1, Jun 1995.......... 2.95
❑2, Jul 1995.......... 2.95
❑3, Aug 1995 .... 2.95
❑4, Sep 1995 .... 2.95
❑5, Oct 1995.......... 2.95
❑6, Nov 1995 .... 2.95
❑7, Dec 1995 .... 2.95
❑8, Jan 1996, Final Issue 2.95

Goddess (Twilight Twins)
Twilight Twins

❑1, b&w; Zolastraya.......... 2.00

Other grades: Multiply price above by 5/6 for VF/NM • 2/3 for VERY FINE • 1/3 for FINE • 1/5 for VERY GOOD • 1/8 for GOOD

Gifts of the Night

Paul Chadwick and John Bolton get medieval
©DC

G.I. Joe (Image)

Image relaunced the oes for a new era
©Image

G.I. Joe European Missions

Reprints Action Force comics from Britain
©Marvel

G.I. Joe, A Real American Hero

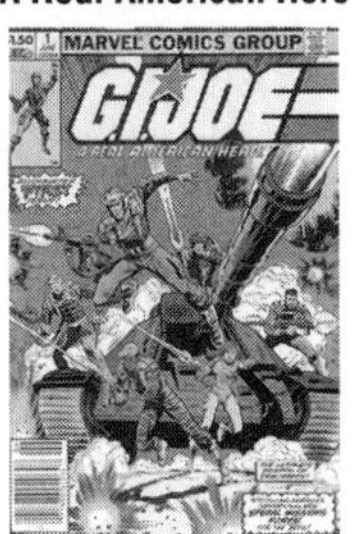

First series advertised on national TV
©Marvel

G.I. Joe Special Missions

Spin-off title from the main Marvel series
©Marvel

N-MINT

Godhead
Anubis

❑1 .... 4.00
❑1/Ltd.; limited edition; 1: Jhatori 4.00
❑2 .... 6.00
❑2/Ltd.; Numbered, Limited edition (1500 printed) 6.00
❑3 .... 6.00

Godland
Image

❑1, Sep 2005 .... 2.99
❑2, Oct 2005 .... 2.99
❑3, Sep 2005 .... 2.99
❑4, Oct 2005 .... 2.99
❑5, Jan 2006 .... 2.99
❑6, Jan 2006 .... 2.99
❑7, Jan 2006 .... 2.99
❑8, Mar 2006 .... 2.99
❑9, May 2006 .... 2.99
❑10, Jun 2006 .... 2.99
❑11, Jul 2006 .... 2.99
❑12, Aug 2006 .... 2.99
❑13, Dec 2006 .... 2.99
❑13/Variant, Dec 2006 .... 2.99
❑14, Nov 2006 .... 2.99

Gods & Tulips
Westhampton

❑1 .... 3.00

Godsent
Lock Graphic Publications

❑1, Jul 1994, b&w 1.75

Gods for Hire
Hot

❑1, Dec 1986 .... 2.00
❑2, Jan 1987 .... 2.00

God's Hammer
Caliber

❑1, b&w 2.50
❑2, b&w 2.50
❑3, May 1990, b&w 2.50

God's Smuggler
Spire

❑1; Based on the book "God's Smuggler" by Brother Andrew 6.00

Godwheel
Malibu / Ultraverse

❑0, Jan 1995, Flip cover 2.50
❑1, Jan 1995, Flip cover 2.50
❑1/Ashcan, Wizard ashcan edition; Flip cover; 1: Primevil 2.50
❑2, Feb 1995, Flip cover 2.50
❑3, Feb 1995, Flip cover; Marvel, Malibu universes cross 2.50

Godzilla
Marvel

❑1, Aug 1977, HT, JM (a) 12.00
❑1/35¢, Aug 1977, HT, JM (a); 35¢ regional price variant 15.00
❑2, Sep 1977 .... 6.00
❑2/35¢, Sep 1977, 35¢ regional price variant 15.00
❑3, Oct 1977, A: Champions. Newsstand edition (distributed by Curtis); issue number in box 5.00
❑3/Whitman, Oct 1977, A: Champions. Special markets edition (usually sold in Whitman bagged prepacks); price appears in a diamond; no UPC barcode 5.00
❑3/35¢, Oct 1977, A: Champions. 35¢ regional price variant; newsstand edition (distributed by Curtis); issue number in box 15.00
❑4, Nov 1977, 1: Doctor Demonicus. V: Batragon 5.00
❑5, Dec 1977, O: Doctor Demonicus 5.00
❑6, Jan 1978 .... 4.00
❑7, Feb 1978, V: Red Ronin 4.00
❑8, Mar 1978, V: Red Ronin 4.00
❑9, Apr 1978 .... 4.00
❑10, May 1978 .... 4.00
❑11, Jun 1978, V: Red Ronin, Yetrigar... 3.00
❑12, Jul 1978 .... 3.00
❑13, Aug 1978 .... 3.00
❑14, Sep 1978 .... 3.00
❑15, Oct 1978 .... 3.00
❑16, Nov 1978 .... 3.00
❑17, Dec 1978, Godzilla shrunk by Henry Pym's gas 3.00
❑18, Jan 1979 .... 3.00
❑19, Feb 1979, HT (a) 3.00
❑20, Mar 1979, A: Fantastic Four 3.00
❑21, Apr 1979, A: Devil Dinosaur 3.00
❑22, May 1979, A: Devil Dinosaur. Newsstand edition (distributed by Curtis); issue number in box 3.00
❑22/Whitman, May 1979, A: Devil Dinosaur. Special markets edition (usually sold in Whitman bagged prepacks); price appears in a diamond; no UPC barcode 3.00
❑23, Jun 1979, A: Avengers 3.00
❑24, Jul 1979, A: Spider-Man. V: Fantastic Four. V: Avengers; Final Issue 3.00

Godzilla
Dark Horse

❑1, Jul 1987, b&w; manga 4.00
❑2, Aug 1987, b&w; manga 3.00
❑3, Sep 1987, b&w; manga 3.00
❑4, Oct 1987, b&w; manga 3.00
❑5, Nov 1987, b&w; manga 3.00
❑6, Dec 1987, b&w; manga 3.00

Godzilla
Dark Horse

❑0, May 1995, reprints and expands story from Dark Horse Comics #10 and 11 . 4.00
❑1, Jun 1995 .... 3.00
❑2, Jul 1995 .... 3.00
❑3, Aug 1995, V: Bagorah, the Bat Monster 3.00
❑4, Sep 1995, V: Bagorah, the Bat Monster 3.00
❑5, Oct 1995 .... 3.00
❑6, Nov 1995 .... 2.95
❑7, Dec 1995 .... 2.95
❑8, Jan 1996 .... 2.95
❑9, Mar 1996 .... 2.95
❑10, Apr 1996, Godzilla vs. Spanish Armada 2.95
❑11, May 1996, Godzilla travels through time to sink the Titanic 2.95
❑12, Jun 1996 .... 2.95
❑13, Jun 1996, V: Burtannus 2.95
❑14, Jul 1996 .... 2.95
❑15, Aug 1996, V: Lord Howe Monster.. 2.95
❑16, Sep 1996, Final Issue 2.95

Godzilla Color Special
Dark Horse

❑1, Aug 1992 .... 4.00

Godzilla, King of the Monsters Special
Dark Horse

❑1/A, Aug 1987; KG, CV, AMo (a); 30 years of Godzilla; b&w 3.00
❑1/B; KG, CV, AMo (a); misprinted cover; fewer than 100 .... 3.00

Godzilla vs. Barkley
Dark Horse

❑1, Dec 1993, NN 3.00

Godzilla vs. Hero Zero
Dark Horse

❑1, Jul 1995 .... 2.50

Go Girl!
Image

❑1, Aug 2000 .... 3.50
❑2, Nov 2000 .... 3.50
❑3, Nov 2001 .... 3.50
❑4, Aug 2001 .... 3.50
❑5, Dec 2001 .... 3.50

Gog (Villains)
DC

❑1, Feb 1998; New Year's Evil 1.95

Going Home
Aardvark-Vanaheim

❑1, b&w; no date 2.00

Gojin
Antarctic

❑1, Apr 1995 .... 2.95
❑2, Jun 1995 .... 2.95
❑3, Aug 1995 .... 2.95
❑3/A, Aug 1995; alternate cover 2.95
❑4, b&w 2.95
❑5, b&w 2.95
❑6, b&w 2.95
❑7, b&w 2.95
❑8, Jun 1996, b&w 2.95

Gold Digger
Antarctic

❑1, Sep 1992; V1#1; Cover says July, 1993, Indicia says June, 1993 .... 35.00
❑2, Nov 1992; V1#2 .... 20.00
❑3, Jan 1993; V1#3 .... 15.00
❑4, Mar 1993; V1#4; Continues in Gold Digger (2nd Series) 13.00
❑5, ca. 2000 .... 2.99
❑6, ca. 2000 .... 2.99
❑7, ca. 2000 .... 2.99
❑8, ca. 2000 .... 2.99
❑9, ca. 2000 .... 2.99
❑10, ca. 2000 .... 2.99
❑11, ca. 2001 .... 2.99
❑12, ca. 2001 .... 2.99
❑13, ca. 2001 .... 2.99
❑14, ca. 2001 .... 2.99
❑15, ca. 2001 .... 2.99
❑16, ca. 2001 .... 2.99
❑17, ca. 2001 .... 2.99
❑18, ca. 2001 .... 2.99
❑19, ca. 2001 .... 2.99
❑20, ca. 2001 .... 2.99

Other grades: Multiply price above by 5/6 for VF/NM • 2/3 for VERY FINE • 1/3 for FINE • 1/5 for VERY GOOD • 1/8 for GOOD

❑21, ca. 2001 ... 2.99
❑22, ca. 2001 ... 2.99
❑23, ca. 2002 ... 0.00
❑24, ca. 2002 ... 2.99
❑25, ca. 2002 ... 2.99
❑26, ca. 2002 ... 2.99
❑27, ca. 2002 ... 2.99
❑28, ca. 2002 ... 2.99
❑29, ca. 2002 ... 2.99
❑30, ca. 2002 ... 2.99
❑31, ca. 2002 ... 2.99
❑32, ca. 2002 ... 2.99
❑33, ca. 2002 ... 2.99
❑34, ca. 2002 ... 2.99
❑35, ca. 2003 ... 2.99
❑36, ca. 2003 ... 2.99
❑37, ca. 2003 ... 2.99
❑38, ca. 2003 ... 2.99
❑39, ca. 2003 ... 2.99
❑40, ca. 2003 ... 2.99
❑41, ca. 2003 ... 2.99
❑42, ca. 2003 ... 2.99
❑43, ca. 2003 ... 2.99
❑44, ca. 2003 ... 2.99
❑45, ca. 2003 ... 2.99
❑46, ca. 2003 ... 2.99
❑47, ca. 2004 ... 2.99
❑48, ca. 2004 ... 2.99
❑49, ca. 2004 ... 2.99
❑50, ca. 2004 ... 2.99
❑51, ca. 2004 ... 2.99
❑52, ca. 2004 ... 2.99
❑53, ca. 2004 ... 2.99
❑54, ca. 2004 ... 2.99
❑55, ca. 2004 ... 2.99
❑56, ca. 2004 ... 2.99
❑57, ca. 2004 ... 2.99
❑58, ca. 2004 ... 2.99
❑59, ca. 2005 ... 2.99
❑60, ca. 2005 ... 2.99
❑61, ca. 2005 ... 2.99
❑62, ca. 2005 ... 2.99
❑63, ca. 2005 ... 2.99
❑64, ca. 2005 ... 2.99
❑65, ca. 2005 ... 2.99
❑66, ca. 2005 ... 2.99
❑67, ca. 2005 ... 2.99
❑68, ca. 2005 ... 2.99
❑69, ca. 2005 ... 2.99
❑70, ca. 2005 ... 2.99

Gold Digger
Antarctic

❑1, Jul 1993 ... 5.00
❑2, Aug 1993 ... 4.00
❑3, Sep 1993 ... 4.00
❑4, Oct 1993 ... 4.00
❑5, Nov 1993; has issue #0 on cover; production mistake ... 4.00
❑6, Dec 1993 ... 4.00
❑7, Jan 1994 ... 4.00
❑8, Feb 1994 ... 4.00
❑9, Mar 1994 ... 4.00
❑10, Apr 1994 ... 4.00
❑11, May 1994; V1#11 ... 4.00
❑12, Jun 1994 ... 4.00
❑13, Jul 1994 ... 4.00
❑14, Aug 1994 ... 4.00
❑15, Sep 1994 ... 4.00
❑16, Oct 1994 ... 4.00
❑17, Nov 1994 ... 4.00
❑18, Dec 1994 ... 4.00
❑19, Feb 1995 ... 4.00
❑20, Apr 1995 ... 4.00
❑21, May 1995 ... 3.50
❑22, Jun 1995 ... 3.50
❑23, Jul 1995 ... 3.50
❑24, Aug 1995 ... 3.50
❑25, Oct 1995 ... 3.50
❑26, Nov 1995 ... 3.50
❑27, Dec 1995 ... 3.50
❑28, Feb 1996 ... 3.50
❑29, Apr 1996 ... 3.50
❑30, Jul 1996 ... 3.50
❑31, Aug 1996; V1#31 ... 3.50
❑32, Oct 1996 ... 3.50
❑33, Dec 1996 ... 3.50
❑34, Feb 1997; V1#34 ... 3.50
❑35, Apr 1997; V1#35 ... 3.50
❑36, Jul 1997; V1#36 ... 3.50
❑37, Aug 1997; V1#37 ... 3.50
❑38, Jan 1998; cover says Nov 97, indicia says Jan 98 ... 3.50
❑39, Mar 1998 ... 3.50
❑40, May 1998 ... 3.50
❑41, Jun 1998 ... 3.50
❑42, Jul 1998 ... 3.50
❑43, Aug 1998 ... 3.50
❑44, Sep 1998 ... 3.50
❑45, Oct 1998 ... 3.50
❑46, Dec 1998 ... 3.50
❑47, Jan 1999 ... 3.50
❑48, Feb 1999 ... 3.50
❑49, Apr 1999 ... 3.50
❑50, Jun 1999 ... 3.50
❑50/CS, Jun 1999; poster edition; Includes poster ... 5.99
❑Ann 1, Sep 1995 ... 3.95
❑Ann 2, Sep 1996, b&w ... 3.95
❑Ann 3, Sep 1997, b&w; 1997 Ann. ... 3.95
❑Ann 4, Sep 1998, b&w; 1998 Ann. ... 3.95
❑GN 1; Graphic Novel ... 10.95
❑Special 1; Special edition; Reprints Gold Digger Vol. 1 #1 ... 3.00

Gold Digger
Antarctic

❑1, Jul 1999; new color series ... 4.00
❑2, Aug 1999 ... 3.00
❑3, Sep 1999 ... 3.00
❑4, Oct 1999 ... 3.00
❑5, Nov 1999 ... 3.00
❑6, Dec 1999 ... 3.00
❑7, Jan 2000 ... 3.00
❑8, Feb 2000 ... 3.00
❑9, Mar 2000 ... 3.00
❑10, Apr 2000 ... 3.00
❑11, May 2000 ... 3.00
❑12, Jun 2000; V2#12 ... 3.00
❑13, Jul 2000; V2#13 ... 3.00
❑14, Aug 2000 ... 3.00
❑15, Oct 2000 ... 3.00
❑16, Nov 2000 ... 3.00
❑17, Dec 2000; V2#17 ... 3.00
❑18, Jan 2000 ... 3.00
❑19, Feb 2001 ... 3.00
❑20, Mar 2001 ... 3.00
❑21, Apr 2001 ... 2.95
❑22, May 2001 ... 2.95
❑23, Jun 2001 ... 2.95
❑24, Jul 2001 ... 2.95
❑25, Aug 2001 ... 2.95
❑26, Nov 2001 ... 2.99
❑27, Dec 2001 ... 2.99
❑28, Jan 2002 ... 2.99
❑29, Feb 2002 ... 2.99
❑30, Mar 2002 ... 2.99
❑31, Apr 2002 ... 2.99
❑32, May 2002 ... 2.99
❑33, Jun 2002 ... 2.99
❑34, Jul 2002; V2#34 ... 2.99
❑35, Aug 2002; V3#35 ... 2.99
❑36, Oct 2002 ... 2.99
❑37, Nov 2002; V3#37 ... 2.99
❑38, Dec 2002; V2#38 ... 2.99
❑39, Jan 2003 ... 3.50
❑40, Feb 2003; V2#40 ... 3.50
❑41, Mar 2003; V2#41 ... 3.50
❑42, Apr 2003; V2#42 ... 3.50
❑43, May 2003; V2#43 ... 2.99
❑44, Jun 2003; Vol. 2; #44 ... 2.99
❑45, Oct 2003; V3#45 ... 2.99
❑46, Oct 2003 ... 2.99
❑47, Nov 2003 ... 2.99
❑48, Dec 2003 ... 2.99
❑49, Jan 2004 ... 2.99
❑50, Feb 2004 ... 2.99
❑51, Mar 2004 ... 2.99
❑52, May 2004 ... 2.99
❑53, Jun 2004 ... 2.99
❑54, Jul 2004 ... 2.99
❑55, Aug 2004 ... 2.99
❑56, Sep 2004 ... 2.99
❑57, Oct 2004 ... 2.99
❑58, Nov 2004 ... 2.99
❑59, Dec 2004 ... 2.99
❑60, Jan 2005 ... 2.99
❑61, Feb 2005 ... 2.99
❑62, Mar 2005 ... 2.99
❑63, Apr 2005 ... 2.99
❑64, May 2005 ... 2.99
❑65, Jun 2005 ... 2.99
❑Ann 4, Sep 2003 ... 4.95
❑Ann 2004 ... 4.95

Gold Digger Annual 2005
Antarctic

❑1, ca. 2005 ... 4.50

Gold Digger: Beta
Antarctic

❑1, Feb 1998; Civ-Alpha; Civ-Beta ... 2.95

Gold Digger: Edge Guard
Radio

❑1, Aug 2000 ... 2.95
❑2, Sep 2000 ... 2.95
❑3, Oct 2000 ... 2.95
❑4, Nov 2000 ... 2.95
❑5, Dec 2000 ... 2.95

Gold Digger Halloween Special
Antarctic

❑1, ca. 2005 ... 2.99

Gold Digger Mangazine
Antarctic

❑1, Mar 1994 ... 2.99
❑1/2nd, Apr 1999; 2nd printing; Collects Mangazine, Vol. 2, Issues 11-14 ... 2.99

Gold Digger Perfect Memory
Antarctic

❑1, Jul 1996, b&w; story synopses, character profiles, and other material ... 4.50
❑2, Sep 2001 ... 6.95
❑3, Sep 2003 ... 6.95
❑4, Sep 2004 ... 6.95

Gold Digger Swimsuit End of Summer Special
Antarctic

❑1, Jul 2003 ... 4.50

Gold Digger Swimsuit Special
Antarctic

❑1, May 2000 ... 4.50
❑2, May 2003; 2003 Swimsuit special ... 4.50
❑3, May 2004; 2004 Swimsuit special ... 4.50
❑4, ca. 2005; Front Cover by Rod Espinosa; Back Cover by Joseph Wight; Aug,2002 ... 4.50

Golden Age
DC

❑1, ca. 1993; PS (c); JRo (w); PS (a); Elseworlds ... 5.50
❑2, Jan 1993; PS (c); JRo (w); PS (a); O: Dynaman. Elseworlds ... 5.50
❑3, ca. 1993; PS (c); JRo (w); PS (a); Elseworlds ... 5.50
❑4, ca. 1993; PS (c); JRo (w); PS (a); D: Dynaman. D: Ultra-Humanite. D: Hawkman. D: Doll Man. D: Miss America. Elseworlds ... 5.50

Golden Age Of Triple-X
Revisionary

❑1, b&w; Adult ... 3.50

Golden Age of Triple-X: John Holmes Special "Johnny Does Paris"
Re-Visionary

❑1 ... 2.95

Golden Age Secret Files
DC

❑1, Feb 2001 ... 4.95

Golden Age Sheena
AC

❑1 ... 9.95

Golden Comics Digest
Gold Key

❑1, May 1969, Looney Tunes/Woody Woodpecker/Tom and Jerry ... 20.00
❑2, Jun 1969, Hanna-Barbera TV Fun Favorites ... 20.00
❑3, Jul 1969, Looney Tunes/Woody Woodpecker/Tom and Jerry ... 20.00
❑4, Aug 1970, Tarzan ... 20.00
❑5, Sep 1969, Looney Tunes/Woody Woodpecker/Tom and Jerry ... 20.00

Gilgamesh II

Fun tale of aliens from Jim Starlin

©DC

Girl from U.N.C.L.E.

Stephanie Powers swings in TV spinoff

©Gold Key

Girls' Love Stories

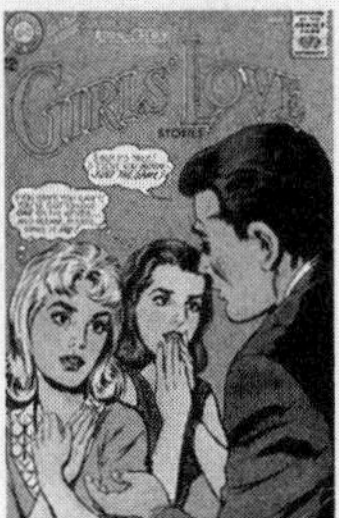

Long-running romance title survived to 1973

©DC

Give Me Liberty

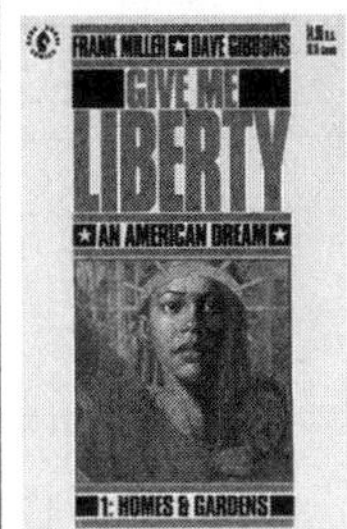

Frank Miller's tale of a future civil war

©Dark Horse

Global Frequency

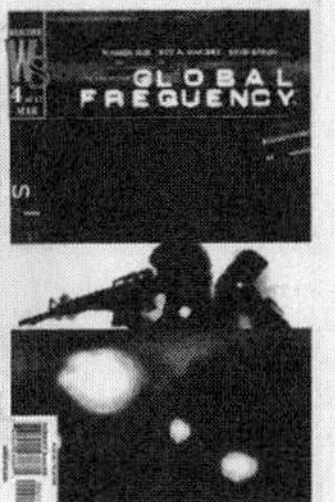

World-wide network of experts solves crises

©DC

	N-MINT
❑6, Oct 1969, Looney Tunes/Woody Woodpecker/Tom and Jerry	20.00
❑7, Nov 1969, Hanna-Barbera TV Fun Favorites	20.00
❑8, Jan 1970, Looney Tunes/Woody Woodpecker/Tom and Jerry	20.00
❑9, Mar 1970, Tarzan	20.00
❑10, May 1970, Looney Tunes	20.00
❑11, Jun 1970, Hanna-Barbera TV Fun Favorites	20.00
❑12, Aug 1970, Looney Tunes/Woody Woodpecker/Tom and Jerry	20.00
❑13 1970, Tom and Jerry	20.00
❑14, Oct 1970, Looney Tunes	20.00
❑15, Jan 1971, Looney Tunes/Woody Woodpecker/Tom and Jerry	20.00
❑16, Mar 1971, Woody Woodpecker	20.00
❑17, May 1971, Looney Tunes	20.00
❑18, Jul 1971, Tom and Jerry	20.00
❑19, Sep 1971, Little Lulu	20.00
❑20, Nov 1971, Woody Woodpecker	20.00
❑21, Jan 1972, Looney Tunes	20.00
❑22, Mar 1972, Tom and Jerry	20.00
❑23, May 1972, Little Lulu	20.00
❑24, Jul 1972, Woody Woodpecker	20.00
❑25, Sep 1972, Tom and Jerry	20.00
❑26, Nov 1972, Looney Tunes	20.00
❑27, Jan 1973, Little Lulu	20.00
❑28, Mar 1973, Tom and Jerry	20.00
❑29, May 1973, Little Lulu	20.00
❑30, Jul 1973, Looney Tunes	20.00
❑31, Aug 1973, Turok	15.00
❑32, Sep 1973, Woody Woodpecker	15.00
❑33, Nov 1973, Little Lulu	15.00
❑34, Jan 1974, Looney Tunes	15.00
❑35, Mar 1974, Tom and Jerry	15.00
❑36, May 1974, Little Lulu	15.00
❑37, Jul 1974, Woody Woodpecker	15.00
❑38, Aug 1974, The Pink Panther	15.00
❑39, Sep 1974, Looney Tunes	15.00
❑40, Nov 1974, Little Lulu	15.00
❑41, Jan 1975, Tom and Jerry	15.00
❑42, Mar 1975, Looney Tunes	15.00
❑43, May 1975, Little Lulu	15.00
❑44, Jul 1975, Woody Woodpecker	15.00
❑45, Aug 1975, The Pink Panther	15.00
❑46, Sep 1975, Little Lulu	15.00
❑47, Nov 1975, Looney Tunes	15.00
❑48, Jan 1976, Lone Ranger	15.00

Golden Dragon
Synchronicity

	N-MINT
❑1, Nov 1987	1.50

Golden Features
Blackthorne

	N-MINT
❑1	2.00
❑2	2.00
❑3, Jun 1986	2.00
❑4, Aug 1986	2.00
❑5, Oct 1986	2.00
❑6	2.00

Golden Plates
AAA Pop

	N-MINT
❑1, ca. 2004	7.99
❑2, ca. 2005	7.99
❑3, ca. 2005	7.99

Golden Warrior
Industrial Design

	N-MINT
❑1, Mar 1997, b&w	2.95

Golden Warrior Iczer One
Antarctic

	N-MINT
❑1, Apr 1994, b&w	2.95
❑2, May 1994, b&w	2.95
❑3, Jun 1994, b&w	2.95
❑4, Jul 1994, b&w	2.95
❑5, Aug 1994, b&w; Final Issue	2.95

Gold Key Spotlight
Gold Key

	N-MINT
❑1, May 1976, Tom, Dick, and Harriet	6.00
❑2 1976	4.00
❑3 1976, Wacky Witch	4.00
❑4 1977	4.00
❑5 1977	4.00
❑6, Jun 1977, Dagar	4.00
❑7 1977	4.00
❑8, Aug 1977, Dr. Spektor	4.00
❑9, Sep 1977, Tragg	4.00
❑10 1977	4.00
❑11, Feb 1978, Tom, Dick and Harriet	4.00

Goldyn 3-D
Blackthorne

	N-MINT
❑1	2.00

Golgothika
Caliber

	N-MINT
❑1, ca. 1996, b&w	2.95
❑2, ca. 1996, b&w	2.95
❑3, ca. 1996, b&w	2.95
❑4, b&w	2.95

Golgo 13
Lead

	N-MINT
❑1, b&w	1.00
❑2	1.50

Golgo 13
Viz

	N-MINT
❑1, b&w	4.95
❑2, b&w	4.95
❑3, b&w	4.95

Go-Man!
Caliber

	N-MINT
❑1, Nov 1989, b&w	2.50
❑2, b&w	2.50
❑3, b&w	2.50
❑4, b&w	2.50

Gomer Pyle
Gold Key

	N-MINT
❑1, Jul 1966	40.00
❑2, Oct 1966	25.00
❑3, Oct 1967	25.00

Gon
DC / Paradox Press

	N-MINT
❑1, Sep 1996, b&w; digest; Introduction by Andy Helfer	5.95
❑2, Sep 1996, b&w; digest; Gon Again!.	5.95
❑3, b&w; digest	5.95
❑4, b&w; digest	5.95
❑5, Oct 1997, b&w; digest; Introduction by Andy Helfer; Gon Swimmin'	6.95

Gonad the Barbarian
Eternity

	N-MINT
❑1	2.25

Gon Color Spectacular
DC / Paradox Press

	N-MINT
❑1; prestige format; NN; Comic-book-sized one-shot	5.95

Gon Underground
DC / Paradox Press

	N-MINT
❑1	7.95

Good-Bye, Chunky Rice
Top Shelf

	N-MINT
❑1, Oct 1999, b&w; graphic novel	14.95

Good Girl Art Quarterly
AC

	N-MINT
❑1, Jul 1990; new & reprints	3.95
❑2, Fal 1990	3.95
❑3, Win 1991	3.95
❑4, Spr 1991	3.95
❑5, Sum 1991	3.95
❑6, Fal 1991	3.95
❑7, Win 1992	3.95
❑8, Spr 1992	3.95
❑9, Sum 1992	3.95
❑10, Fal 1992	3.95
❑11, Win 1993; Winter 1992	3.95
❑12, Spr 1993	3.95
❑13, Sum 1993	3.95
❑14, Fal 1993	3.95
❑15, Win 1994; Winter 1993	3.95
❑16, Spr 1994	3.95
❑17, Sum 1994	3.95
❑18, Fal 1994	3.95
❑19, Win 1995; Winter 1994	6.95

Good Girls
Fantagraphics

	N-MINT
❑1, Apr 1987, b&w; Adult	2.00
❑2, Oct 1987; Adult	2.00
❑3 1988; Adult	2.00
❑4, Feb 1989; Adult	2.00
❑5, Jan 1991; Last Fantagraphics issue.	2.00
❑6, Jun 1991, b&w; Published by Rip Off Press	2.00

Good Guys
Defiant

	N-MINT
❑1, Nov 1993; Giant-size; 1: Master Ridgely Gatesman; 1&O: The Good Guys	2.50
❑2, Dec 1993	2.50
❑3, Jan 1994	2.50
❑4, Feb 1994	2.50
❑5, Mar 1994	2.50
❑6, Apr 1994	2.50
❑7, May 1994	2.50
❑8, Jun 1994	2.50
❑9, Jul 1994; Final Issue; Defiant ceases publication	2.50
❑10, Aug 1994	2.50
❑11, Sep 1994	2.50
❑12, Oct 1994	2.50

Goody Good Comics
Fantagraphics

	N-MINT
❑1, Jun 2000	2.95

Other grades: Multiply price above by 5/6 for VF/NM • 2/3 for VERY FINE • 1/3 for FINE • 1/5 for VERY GOOD • 1/8 for GOOD

Goofy
Dell

❑-211, Nov 1962, (c); Cover code 12-308-211 .... 40.00

Goofy Adventures
Disney

❑1, Jun 1990 .... 2.50
❑2, Jul 1990 .... 1.50
❑3, Aug 1990 .... 1.50
❑4, Sep 1990 .... 1.50
❑5, Oct 1990 .... 1.50
❑6, Nov 1990 .... 1.50
❑7, Dec 1990; Three Musketeers 1.50
❑8, Jan 1991 .... 1.50
❑9, Feb 1991; FG (a); James Bond parody 1.50
❑10, Mar 1991 .... 1.50
❑11, Apr 1991 .... 1.50
❑12, May 1991 .... 1.50
❑13, Jun 1991 .... 1.50
❑14, Jul 1991 .... 1.50
❑15, Aug 1991; Super-Goof 1.50
❑16, Sep 1991; Sherlock Holmes parody 1.50
❑17, Oct 1991; GC (a); Final Issue 1.50

Goon
Avatar

❑1, Mar 1999 .... 15.00
❑2, May 1999 .... 10.00
❑3, Jul 1999 .... 10.00

Goon
Albatross Exploding

❑1, ca. 2002 .... 10.00
❑1/Variant, ca. 2002, Sketch cover, limited convention edition 10.00
❑2, ca. 2002 .... 5.00
❑3, ca. 2002, Norman Rockwell tribute cover 5.00
❑4, ca. 2002, Says Vol. 2, #3 in indicia .. 5.00

Goon
Dark Horse

❑1, Jun 2003 .... 2.99
❑2, Aug 2003 .... 2.99
❑3, Oct 2003 .... 2.99
❑4, Dec 2003 .... 2.99
❑5, Feb 2004 .... 2.99
❑6, Apr 2004 .... 2.99
❑7, Aug 2004 .... 2.99
❑8 .... 3.00
❑9 .... 2.99
❑10 2005 .... 2.99
❑11 2005 .... 2.99
❑12 2005 .... 2.99
❑13, Aug 2005 .... 2.99
❑14 2005 .... 2.99
❑15, Jan 2006 .... 2.99
❑16, Mar 2006 .... 2.99
❑17, Apr 2006 .... 2.99
❑18, Aug 2006 .... 2.99
❑19 .... 2.99
❑20 .... 2.99
❑21 .... 2.99
❑22 .... 2.99
❑23 .... 2.99
❑24 .... 2.99
❑25 .... 2.99
❑26 .... 2.99
❑27 .... 2.99
❑28 .... 2.99
❑29 .... 2.99
❑30 .... 2.99
❑31 .... 2.99
❑32 .... 2.99

Goon Noir
Dark Horse

❑1, Oct 2006 .... 2.99
❑2, Dec 2006, b&w 2.99

Goon Patrol
Pinnacle

❑1 .... 1.75

Goon: 25 Cent Issue
Dark Horse

❑1 .... 0.25

Gordon Yamamoto and the King of the Geeks
Humble

❑1, Oct 1997, b&w 2.95

Gore Shriek
Fantaco

❑1, ca. 1986, b&w; 1: Greg Capullo story 3.00
❑2, b&w; Adult 3.00
❑3, b&w; Adult 3.00
❑4, b&w; Adult 3.00
❑5; Adult 3.50
❑6; Adult 3.50
❑Ann 1, b&w; Adult 4.95

Gore Shriek
Fantaco

❑1, b&w 2.50
❑2, b&w 2.50
❑3, b&w 2.50

Gore Shriek Delectus
Fantaco

❑1; NN 8.95

Gorgana's Ghoul Gallery
AC

❑1, b&w; Reprints 2.95
❑2; Reprints 2.95

Gorgo
Charlton

❑1, May 1961, SD (a) 200.00
❑2, Aug 1961 .... 100.00
❑3, Sep 1961, SD (a) 100.00
❑4, Nov 1961, SD (c) 75.00
❑5, Jan 1962 .... 50.00
❑6, Apr 1962 .... 40.00
❑7, Jun 1962 .... 40.00
❑8, Aug 1962 .... 40.00
❑9, Oct 1962 .... 40.00
❑10, Dec 1962 .... 40.00
❑11, Feb 1963 .... 30.00
❑12, Apr 1963 .... 30.00
❑13, Jun 1963, SD (a) 30.00
❑14, Aug 1963, SD (a) 30.00
❑15, Oct 1963, SD (a) 30.00
❑16, Dec 1963, SD (a) 30.00
❑17, Feb 1964 .... 20.00
❑18, May 1964 .... 20.00
❑19, Jul 1964 .... 20.00
❑20, Oct 1965 .... 20.00
❑21, Dec 1964 .... 20.00
❑22, Feb 1965 .... 20.00
❑23, Sep 1965 .... 20.00

Gorgon
Venus

❑1, Jun 1996; Adult 2.95
❑2, Jun 1996; Adult 2.95
❑3, Jun 1996; Adult 2.95
❑4, Jun 1996; Adult 2.95
❑5, Aug 1996; Adult 2.95

Gorilla Gunslinger
Mojo

❑0, Sampler 1.00

Gotcha!
Rip Off

❑1, Sep 1991, b&w; Adult 2.50

G.O.T.H.
Verotik

❑1; Adult 3.00
❑2, Mar 1996; Adult 3.00
❑3, Jun 1996; Adult 3.00

Gotham Central
DC

❑1, Jan 2003 .... 2.50
❑2, Feb 2003 .... 2.50
❑3, Mar 2003 .... 2.50
❑4, Apr 2003 .... 2.50
❑5, May 2003 .... 2.50
❑6, Jun 2003 .... 2.50
❑7, Jul 2003 .... 2.50
❑8, Aug 2003 .... 2.50
❑9, Sep 2003 .... 2.50
❑10, Oct 2003 .... 2.50
❑11, Nov 2003 .... 2.50
❑12, Dec 2003 .... 2.50
❑13, Jan 2004 .... 2.50
❑14, Feb 2004 .... 2.50
❑15, Mar 2004 .... 2.50
❑16, Apr 2004 .... 2.50
❑17, May 2004 .... 2.50
❑18, Jun 2004 .... 2.50
❑19, Jul 2004 .... 2.50
❑20, Aug 2004 .... 2.50
❑21, Sep 2004 .... 2.50
❑22, Oct 2004 .... 2.50
❑23, Nov 2004 .... 2.50
❑24, Dec 2004 .... 2.50
❑25, Jan 2005 .... 2.50
❑26, Feb 2005 .... 2.50
❑27, Mar 2005 .... 2.50
❑28, Apr 2005 .... 2.50
❑29, May 2005 .... 2.50
❑30, Jun 2005 .... 2.50
❑31, Jun 2005 .... 2.50
❑32, Jul 2005 .... 2.50
❑33, Aug 2005 .... 2.50
❑34, Sep 2005 .... 2.50
❑35, Oct 2005 .... 2.50
❑36, Nov 2005 .... 2.50
❑37, Jan 2006, D: Fisherman; Infinite Crisis tie-in 2.50
❑38, Jan 2006 .... 2.50
❑39, Mar 2006 .... 2.50
❑40, Mar 2006, Final issue 2.50

Gotham Girls
DC

❑1, Oct 2002 .... 2.25
❑2, Nov 2002 .... 2.25
❑3, Dec 2002 .... 2.25
❑4, Jan 2003 .... 2.25
❑5, Feb 2003 .... 2.25

Gotham Nights
DC

❑1, Mar 1992 .... 2.00
❑2, Apr 1992 .... 2.00
❑3, May 1992 .... 2.00
❑4, Jun 1992 .... 2.00

Gotham Nights II
DC

❑1, Mar 1995 .... 2.00
❑2, Apr 1995 .... 2.00
❑3, May 1995 .... 2.00
❑4, Jun 1995 .... 2.00

Gothic
5th Panel

❑1, Apr 1997, b&w 2.50
❑2 .... 2.50

Gothic Moon
Anarchy Bridgeworks

❑1; Adult 5.95

Gothic Nights
Rebel

❑1, b&w; Adult 2.00
❑2; Adult; b&w; ca. 1996 .... 2.00

Gothic Red
Boneyard

❑1; Adult 2.95
❑3, Mar 1997, b&w; Adult 2.95

Gothic Scrolls: Drayven
Davdez

❑1, Dec 1997 .... 2.95
❑2, Feb 1998 .... 2.50
❑3, Mar 1998 .... 2.50
❑Ashcan 1, Aug 1997; Preview edition; cover says Sep, indicia says Aug 1.50

Grackle
Acclaim

❑1, Jan 1997, b&w 2.95
❑2, Feb 1997, b&w 2.95
❑3, Mar 1997, b&w 2.95
❑4, Apr 1997, b&w 2.95

Graffiti Kitchen
Tundra

❑1; NN 2.95

Grafik Muzik
Caliber

❑1, Nov 1990, b&w; A: Madman 15.00
❑2, ca. 1991 .... 10.00
❑3 .... 6.00
❑4 .... 6.00

Grammar Patrol
Castel

❑1 .... 2.00

Other grades: Multiply price above by 5/6 for VF/NM • 2/3 for VERY FINE • 1/3 for FINE • 1/5 for VERY GOOD • 1/8 for GOOD

Glory

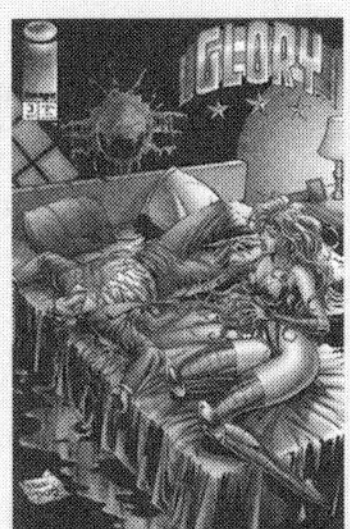

Amazon warrior fights crime and injustice

©Image

God's Smuggler

Bibles penetrate The Iron Curtain

©Spire

Godzilla

Fire-breathing monster faces S.H.I.E.L.D.

©Marvel

Gold Digger

Female archaelogist and werecat seek artifacts

©Antarctic

Golden Age

Elseworlds post-World War II story

©DC

N-MINT

Grand Prix
Charlton

- ❑16, Sep 1967, Previous issues published as Hot Rod Racers 14.00
- ❑17, Nov 1967 .... 8.00
- ❑18, Jan 1968 .... 8.00
- ❑19, May 1968 .... 8.00
- ❑20, Jul 1968 .... 8.00
- ❑21, Sep 1968 .... 5.00
- ❑22, Nov 1968 .... 5.00
- ❑23, Jan 1969 .... 5.00
- ❑24, Mar 1969 .... 5.00
- ❑25, May 1969, DP (a) 5.00
- ❑26, Jul 1969 .... 5.00
- ❑27, Sep 1969 .... 5.00
- ❑28, Nov 1969 .... 5.00
- ❑29, Jan 1970 .... 5.00
- ❑30, Mar 1970 .... 5.00
- ❑31, May 1970 .... 5.00

Graphic
Fantaco

- ❑1 .... 3.95

Graphic Heroes in House of Cards
Graphic Staffing

- ❑1; personalized promotional piece for temporary graphics employees 1.00

Graphic Story Monthly
Fantagraphics

- ❑1, b&w 4.00
- ❑2, b&w 3.50
- ❑3, b&w 3.50
- ❑4, b&w 3.50
- ❑5, b&w 3.50
- ❑6, b&w 3.50
- ❑7 .... 3.50

Graphique Musique
Slave Labor

- ❑1, Dec 1989, b&w 8.00
- ❑2, Mar 1990, b&w 8.00
- ❑3, May 1990, b&w 8.00

Grateful Dead Comix
Kitchen Sink

- ❑1 .... 6.00
- ❑2 .... 5.00
- ❑3 .... 5.00
- ❑4 .... 5.00
- ❑5 .... 5.00
- ❑6 .... 5.00
- ❑7 .... 5.00

Grateful Dead Comix
Kitchen Sink

- ❑1; comic-book size 3.95
- ❑2, Apr 1994 .... 3.95

Gravediggers
Acclaim

- ❑1, Nov 1996, b&w 2.95
- ❑2, Dec 1996, b&w 2.95
- ❑3, Jan 1997, b&w 2.95
- ❑4, Feb 1997, b&w; Final Issue 2.95

Gravedigger Tales
Avalon

- ❑1, b&w 2.95

N-MINT

Grave Grrrls: Destroyers of the Dead
Moonstone

- ❑1, Mar 2005 .... 3.50

Gravestone
Malibu

- ❑1, Jul 1993; 1: Charon 2.25
- ❑2, Aug 1993; Includes poster 2.25
- ❑3, Sep 1993; Genesis 2.25
- ❑4, Oct 1993; Kelley Jones cover 2.25
- ❑5, Nov 1993; Genesis 2.25
- ❑6, Dec 1993; Genesis 2.25
- ❑7, Feb 1994; Genesis; last issue 2.25

Gravestown
Ariel

- ❑1, Oct 1997 .... 2.95

Grave Tales
Hamilton

- ❑1, Oct 1991, b&w 3.95
- ❑2, Dec 1991, b&w 3.95
- ❑3, Feb 1992, b&w 3.95

Gravity
Marvel

- ❑1, Jul 2005 .... 2.99
- ❑2, Aug 2005 .... 2.99
- ❑3, Sep 2005 .... 2.99
- ❑4, Oct 2005 .... 2.99
- ❑5, Dec 2005 .... 2.99

Gray Area
Image

- ❑1, Aug 2004 .... 7.00
- ❑1/Incentive, Aug 2004 .... 8.00
- ❑1/SigSeries, Aug 2004 .... 20.00
- ❑1/Conv, Aug 2004 .... 15.00
- ❑2 2004 .... 5.95
- ❑3 2004 .... 5.95

Grease Monkey
Kitchen Sink

- ❑1, Oct 1995 .... 3.50
- ❑2, Oct 1995 .... 3.50

Grease Monkey
Image

- ❑1, Jan 1998 .... 2.95
- ❑2, Mar 1998 .... 2.95

Great Action Comics
I.W.

- ❑8, Reprints 70.00
- ❑9, Reprints 70.00

Great American Western
AC

- ❑1, ca. 1988 .... 2.00
- ❑2, Sep 1988; Durango Kid. Reprints: Tribute to Magazine Enterprises Comics of 1940's-50's 2.95
- ❑3, Nov 1988; Tom Mix 2.95
- ❑4 .... 3.50
- ❑5 .... 5.00

Great Big Beef
ERR

- ❑97, Jun 1996, b&w 2.00
- ❑98, Jan 1997, b&w; cover says Apr, indicia says Jan 2.00
- ❑99, Sep 1997, b&w 2.00

N-MINT

Greater Mercury Comics Action
Greater Mercury

- ❑5, Sep 1990, b&w; Picks up numbering from Silver Wolf's Grips series 2.00
- ❑6, Oct 1990, b&w 2.00
- ❑7, b&w 2.00
- ❑8, Mar 1991, b&w 2.00
- ❑9, ca. 1991, b&w 2.00

Greatest American Comic Book
Ocean

- ❑1, Nov 1992; Spider-Man parody; Batman 2.55

Greatest Diggs of All Time!
Rip Off

- ❑1, Feb 1991, b&w; NN 2.00

Greatest Stars of the NBA: Allen Iverson
Tokyopop

- ❑1, Nov 2005, b&w 7.99

Greatest Stars of the NBA: Future Greats
Tokyopop

- ❑1, Nov 2005, b&w 7.99

Great Galaxies
Zub

- ❑0, b&w; 1: The Warp Patrol 2.95
- ❑1, b&w; O: Captain Dean 2.50
- ❑2, b&w 2.50
- ❑3, b&w 2.50
- ❑4, b&w 2.50
- ❑5, b&w 2.50
- ❑6/Ashcan; Flip book with Telluria Ashcan #6 .... 0.50

Great Gazoo
Charlton

- ❑1, Aug 1973 .... 20.00
- ❑2, Oct 1973 .... 12.00
- ❑3, Dec 1974 .... 10.00
- ❑4, Jun 1974 .... 10.00
- ❑5, Aug 1974 .... 10.00
- ❑6, Oct 1974 .... 10.00
- ❑7, Dec 1974 .... 10.00
- ❑8, Feb 1975 .... 10.00
- ❑9, Apr 1975 .... 10.00
- ❑10, Jun 1975 .... 10.00
- ❑11, Jul 1975 .... 10.00
- ❑12, Sep 1975 .... 10.00
- ❑13, Nov 1975 .... 10.00
- ❑14, Jan 1976 .... 10.00
- ❑15, Mar 1976 .... 10.00
- ❑16, May 1976 .... 10.00
- ❑17, Jul 1976 .... 10.00
- ❑18, Sep 1976 .... 10.00
- ❑19, Nov 1976 .... 10.00
- ❑20, Jan 1977 .... 10.00

Great Morons in History
Revolutionary

- ❑1, Oct 1993, b&w; Dan Quayle 2.50

Great Society Comic Book
Parallax

- ❑1 .... 16.00
- ❑2 .... 12.00

	N-MINT

Greeenlock
Aircel

❑1, b&w 2.50

Green Arrow
DC

❑0, Oct 1994; 1: Connor Hawke (as adult) 3.00
❑1, Feb 1988; MGr (c); MGr (w); DG (a); Painted cover 4.00
❑2, Mar 1988; MGr (c); MGr (w); DG (a); Painted cover 2.00
❑3, Apr 1988; MGr (c); MGr (w); FMc, DG (a); Painted cover 2.00
❑4, May 1988 MGr (c); MGr (w) 2.00
❑5, Jun 1988 2.00
❑6, Jul 1988 2.00
❑7, Aug 1988 2.00
❑8, Sep 1988 2.00
❑9, Oct 1988 2.00
❑10, Nov 1988 MGr (c); MGr (w) 2.00
❑11, Dec 1988 MGr (c); MGr (w) 1.50
❑12, Dec 1988 MGr (c); MGr (w) 1.50
❑13, Jan 1989 1.50
❑14, Jan 1989 1.50
❑15, Feb 1989 1.50
❑16, Mar 1989 1.50
❑17, Apr 1989 1.50
❑18, May 1989 1.50
❑19, Jun 1989 1.50
❑20, Jul 1989 1.50
❑21, Aug 1989; 1: Connor Hawke (baby) 2.50
❑22, Aug 1989 1.50
❑23, Sep 1989 1.50
❑24, Sep 1989 1.50
❑25, Oct 1989 1.50
❑26, Nov 1989 1.50
❑27, Dec 1989 A: Warlord 1.50
❑28, Jan 1990 A: Warlord 1.50
❑29, Feb 1990; Story inspired by Alaska oil spill 1.50
❑30, Mar 1990 1.50
❑31, Apr 1990 1.50
❑32, May 1990 1.50
❑33, Jun 1990 1.50
❑34, Jul 1990 1.50
❑35, Aug 1990; Black Arrow 1.50
❑36, Sep 1990; Black Arrow 1.50
❑37, Sep 1990; Black Arrow 1.50
❑38, Oct 1990; Black Arrow 1.50
❑39, Nov 1990 1.50
❑40, Dec 1990 MGr (c); MGr (w); MGr (a) 1.50
❑41, Dec 1990 1.50
❑42, Jan 1991 1.50
❑43, Feb 1991 1.50
❑44, Mar 1991 1.50
❑45, Apr 1991 1.50
❑46, May 1991 1.50
❑47, Jun 1991 1.50
❑48, Jun 1991 1.50
❑49, Jul 1991 1.50
❑50, Aug 1991; Giant-size; V: The American Jihad; 50th Anniversary issue 2.50
❑51, Aug 1991 1.50
❑52, Sep 1991 1.50
❑53, Oct 1991 1.50
❑54, Nov 1991 1.50
❑55, Dec 1991 MGr (c); MGr (w) 1.50
❑56, Jan 1992 MGr (c); MGr (w) 1.50
❑57, Feb 1992 MGr (c); MGr (w) 1.50
❑58, Mar 1992 MGr (c); MGr (w) 1.50
❑59, Apr 1992 MGr (c); MGr (w) 1.50
❑60, May 1992 1.50
❑61, May 1992 MGr (c); MGr (w); FS (a) 1.50
❑62, Jun 1992 MGr (c); MGr (w); FS (a) 1.50
❑63, Jun 1992 MGr (c); MGr (w) 1.50
❑64, Jul 1992 MGr (c); MGr (w) 1.50
❑65, Aug 1992 MGr (c); MGr (w) 1.50
❑66, Sep 1992 MGr (c); MGr (w) 1.50
❑67, Oct 1992 MGr (c); MGr (w); FS (a) 1.50
❑68, Nov 1992 MGr (c); MGr (w); FS (a) 1.50
❑69, Dec 1992 MGr (c); MGr (w) 1.75
❑70, Jan 1993 MGr (c); MGr (w) 1.75
❑71, Feb 1993 MGr (c); MGr (w) 1.75
❑72, Mar 1993 MGr (c); MGr (w) 1.75
❑73, Apr 1993 MGr (c); MGr (w) 1.75
❑74, May 1993 MGr (c); MGr (w) 1.75
❑75, Jun 1993; Giant-size; MGr (c); MGr (w) 2.50
❑76, Jul 1993; MGr (c); MGr (w); O: Green Lantern and Green Arrow 1.75
❑77, Aug 1993 MGr (c); MGr (w) 1.75
❑78, Sep 1993 MGr (c); MGr (w) 1.75
❑79, Oct 1993 MGr (c); MGr (w) 1.75
❑80, Nov 1993 MGr (c); MGr (w) 1.75
❑81, Dec 1993 JA (c); JA (a) 1.75
❑82, Jan 1994 JA (a) 1.75
❑83, Feb 1994 JA (a) 1.75
❑84, Mar 1994 JA (a) 1.75
❑85, Apr 1994 JA (a); A: Deathstroke 1.75
❑86, May 1994; JA (a); Catwoman 1.75
❑87, Jun 1994 JA (a) 1.95
❑88, Jul 1994 JA (a); A: JLa 1.95
❑89, Aug 1994 1.95
❑90, Sep 1994; Zero Hour 2.25
❑91, Nov 1994 JA (a) 1.95
❑92, Dec 1994 JA (a) 1.95
❑93, Jan 1995 JA (a) 1.95
❑94, Feb 1995 JA (a) 1.95
❑95, Mar 1995; JA (a); Hal Jordan appearance on last page 1.95
❑96, Apr 1995; Ollie finds out that Connor is his son 3.00
❑97, Jun 1995 3.00
❑98, Jul 1995; JA (a); Arsenal (Roy Harper) cover/appearance 3.00
❑99, Aug 1995 JA (a) 3.00
❑100, Sep 1995; Giant-size; enhanced cover 7.00
❑101, Oct 1995; D: Green Arrow I (Oliver Queen). Later disproved 18.00
❑102, Nov 1995; Underworld Unleashed 2.25
❑103, Dec 1995 A: Green Lantern 2.25
❑104, Jan 1996 2.25
❑105, Feb 1996 A: Robin 2.25
❑106, Mar 1996 2.25
❑107, Apr 1996 2.25
❑108, May 1996 A: Thorn 2.25
❑109, Jun 1996 JA (a) 2.25
❑110, Jul 1996; Cover homage to Green Lantern #87 (2nd series) 2.25
❑111, Aug 1996; Crackshot apperance, Green Lantern (Kyle Rayner) cover/appearance 2.25
❑112, Sep 1996 2.25
❑113, Oct 1996 2.25
❑114, Nov 1996; Final Night 2.25
❑115, Dec 1996 A: Shado, Black Canary 2.25
❑116, Jan 1997 A: Black Canary, Oracle, Shado 2.25
❑117, Feb 1997 A: Black Canary 2.25
❑118, Mar 1997 2.25
❑119, Apr 1997 A: Warlord 2.25
❑120, May 1997 A: Warlord 2.25
❑121, Jun 1997 2.25
❑122, Jul 1997 2.25
❑123, Aug 1997 JA (a) 2.25
❑124, Sep 1997 2.25
❑125, Oct 1997; Giant-size; continues in Green Lantern #92 3.50
❑126, Nov 1997; Concluding the 3-part crossover with Green Lantern continued from Green Lantern #92 2.50
❑127, Dec 1997; Face cover 2.50
❑128, Jan 1998 2.50
❑129, Feb 1998 2.50
❑130, Mar 1998; cover forms triptych with Flash #135 and Green Lantern #96 2.50
❑131, Apr 1998; Team-up with Crackshot 2.50
❑132, May 1998; Return of Eddie Fyers 2.50
❑133, Jun 1998; A: JLA. Return of Eddie Fyers 2.50
❑134, Jul 1998; A: Batman. continues in Detective Comics #723 2.50
❑135, Aug 1998; V: Lady Shiva 2.50
❑136, Sep 1998 A: Hal Jordan 2.50
❑137, Oct 1998; A: Superman. Final Issue 4.00
❑1000000, Nov 1998; Final Issue 3.00
❑Ann 1, Sep 1988 A: Batman 3.50
❑Ann 2, Aug 1989; A: Question. 6 Who's Who bio pages 3.00
❑Ann 3, Dec 1990 A: Question 3.00
❑Ann 4, Jun 1991; 50th Anniversary; Robin Hood 3.00
❑Ann 5, ca. 1994; MGr (c); TVE, FS (a); A: Batman. V: Eclipso, Batman cover/appearance, Black Canary cover/appearance, Story continues into Eclipso: The Darkness Within #2, ca. 1992 3.00
❑Ann 6, ca. 1994; MGr (w); 1: Hook 3.50
❑Ann 7, ca. 1994; Year One 3.95

Green Arrow
DC

❑1, May 1983, TVE (c); DG, TVE (a); O: Green Arrow 3.00
❑2, Jun 1983, TVE (c); DG, TVE (a); V: Count Vertigo 2.50
❑3, Jul 1983, TVE (c); DG, TVE (a) 2.00
❑4, Aug 1983, TVE (c); DG, TVE (a); V: Cap'n Lash; Team-up with Black Canary 2.00

Green Arrow
DC

❑1, Apr 2001; MW (c); KSm (w); Return of Oliver Queen 6.00
❑2, May 2001; MW (c); KSm (w); 1: Mia Ardeen (Speedy II) 6.00
❑3, Jun 2001 MW (c); KSm (w) 3.00
❑4, Jul 2001 MW (c); KSm (w) 3.00
❑5, Aug 2001 MW (c); KSm (w) 3.00
❑6, Sep 2001 MW (c); KSm (w) 3.00
❑7, Oct 2001 MW (c); KSm (w) 2.50
❑8, Nov 2001 MW (c); KSm (w) 2.50
❑9, Dec 2001 MW (c); KSm (w) 2.50
❑10, Jan 2002 MW (c); KSm (w) 2.50
❑11, Feb 2002 MW (c); KSm (w) 2.50
❑12, Mar 2002 MW (c); KSm (w) 2.50
❑13, Apr 2002 MW (c); KSm (w) 2.50
❑14, Aug 2002 MW (c); KSm (w) 2.50
❑15, Sep 2002 MW (c); KSm (w) 2.50
❑16, Oct 2002; MW (c);V: Catman 2.50
❑17, Nov 2002 MW (c) 2.50
❑18, Dec 2002 MW (c) 2.50
❑19, Jan 2003 MW (c) 2.50
❑20, Mar 2003 MW (c) 2.50
❑21, Apr 2003 MW (c) 2.50
❑22, May 2003 MW (c) 2.50
❑23, Jun 2003; MW (c); Continues in Green Lantern #162 2.50
❑24, Jun 2003; MW (c); Continues in Green Lantern #163 2.50
❑25, Jul 2003; MW (c); Continues in Green Lantern #164 2.50
❑26, Jul 2003 MW (c) 2.50
❑27, Aug 2003 MW (c) 2.50
❑28, Sep 2003 MW (c) 2.50
❑29, Oct 2003 MW (c) 2.50
❑30, Nov 2003 MW (c) 2.50
❑31, Dec 2003 MW (c) 2.50
❑32, Jan 2004 BB (c) 2.50
❑33, Feb 2004 2.50
❑34, Mar 2004 2.50
❑35, Apr 2004 2.50
❑36, May 2004 2.50
❑37, Jun 2004 2.50
❑38, Jul 2004 2.50
❑39, Aug 2004 2.50
❑40, Sep 2004; 1: Brick 2.50
❑41, Oct 2004 2.50
❑42, Nov 2004 2.50
❑43, Dec 2004, Mia revealed to be H.I.V. positive 7.00
❑44, Jan 2005 4.00
❑45, Feb 2005; 1: Speedy II 2.50
❑46, Mar 2005 2.50
❑47, Apr 2005 2.50
❑48, May 2005; V: Duke of Oil 2.50
❑49, Jun 2005 2.50
❑50, Jun 2005 3.50
❑51, Jul 2005; New DC cover logo 2.50
❑52, Aug 2005; Identity Crisis fallout 2.50
❑53, Sep 2005 2.50
❑54, Oct 2005; Identity Crisis fallout 2.50
❑55, Dec 2005; Identity Crisis fallout 2.50
❑56, Jan 2006; Identity Crisis fallout 2.50
❑57, Feb 2006, Identity Crisis fallout 2.50
❑58, Mar 2006, Identity Crisis fallout 2.50
❑59, Apr 2006, Identity Crisis fallout 2.50
❑60, May 2006, New cover logo; One Year Later; Ollie is Mayor of Star City 2.50
❑61, Jun 2006, One Year Later 2.50
❑63, Aug 2006, Cover by Scott McDaniel and Andy Owens 2.99
❑64, Sep 2006 2.99
❑65, Oct 2006 2.99
❑66, Nov 2006 2.99
❑67, Dec 2006 2.99
❑68, Jan 2007 2.99
❑69, Feb 2007 2.99
❑70, Mar 2007 2.99
❑71 2.99

Other grades: Multiply price above by 5/6 for VF/NM • 2/3 for VERY FINE • 1/3 for FINE • 1/5 for VERY GOOD • 1/8 for GOOD

Golden-Age Greats	Gold Key Spotlight	Gomer Pyle	Goofy Adventures	Gotham Central

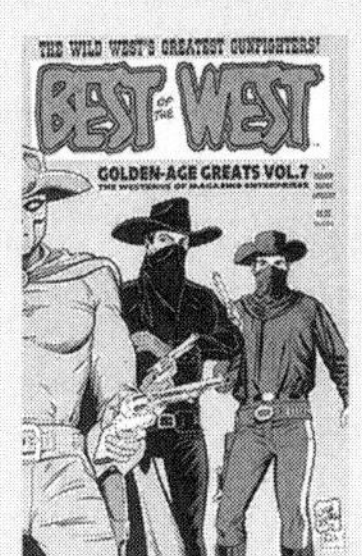
Reprints popular 1940s stories
©AC

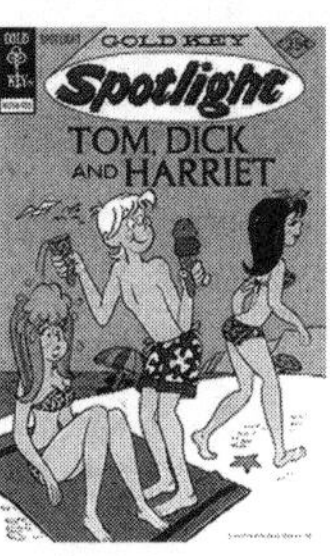
Anthology covered Gold Key genre gamut
©Gold Key

Usage of Shazam didn't produce hero
©Gold Key

Goofy in more serious mode
©Disney

Police procedurals with hero cameos
©DC

N-MINT

❑72 .... 2.99
❑73 .... 2.99
❑74 .... 2.99
❑75 .... 2.99

Green Arrow by Jack Kirby
DC

❑nn, ca. 2001; Prestige one-shot reprinting stories from Adventure Comics and World's Finest 5.95

Green Arrow: The Longbow Hunters
DC

❑1, Aug 1987; MGr (c); MGr (w); MGr (a); 1: Shado 3.50
❑1/2nd, Aug 1987; MGr (c); MGr (w); MGr (a); 1: Shado. 2nd printing 3.00
❑1/3rd, Aug 1987; MGr (c); MGr (w); MGr (a); 1: Shado. 3rd printing 3.00
❑2, Sep 1987 MGr (c); MGr (w); MGr (a) 3.00
❑3, Oct 1987 MGr (c); MGr (w); MGr (a) 3.00

Green Arrow: The Wonder Year
DC

❑1, Feb 1993 MGr (w); GM, MGr (a) 2.00
❑2, Mar 1993 MGr (w); GM, MGr (a) 2.00
❑3, Apr 1993 MGr (w); GM, MGr (a) 2.00
❑4, May 1993 MGr (c); MGr (w); GM, MGr (a) 2.00

Green Candles
DC / Paradox

❑1, ca. 1995, b&w; digest 5.95
❑2, ca. 1995, b&w; digest 5.95
❑3, ca. 1995, b&w; digest 5.95

Greener Pastures
Kronos

❑1 .... 2.50
❑1/2nd, Jan 1997; 2nd printing 2.50
❑2, Oct 1994 .... 2.50
❑3, Feb 1995 .... 2.50
❑4, Dec 1995 .... 2.50
❑4.5, Feb 1996 .... 1.95
❑5, Aug 1996 .... 2.95
❑6, Nov 1996 .... 2.95
❑7, Feb 1997 .... 2.95

Green Goblin
Marvel

❑1, Oct 1995; enhanced cardstock cover 2.95
❑2, Nov 1995; V: Rhino 1.95
❑3, Dec 1995; Story continued from Amazing Scarlet Spider #2 .... 1.95
❑4, Jan 1996; V: Hobgoblin 1.95
❑5, Feb 1996 .... 1.95
❑6, Mar 1996 .... 1.95
❑7, Apr 1996 .... 1.95
❑8, May 1996 .... 1.95
❑9, Jun 1996 .... 1.95
❑10, Jul 1996 .... 1.95
❑11, Aug 1996 .... 1.95
❑12, Sep 1996 .... 1.95
❑13, Oct 1996; Final Issue 1.95

Green-Grey Sponge-Suit Sushi Turtles
Mirage

❑1, parody; cardstock cover 3.50

Greenhaven
Aircel

❑1 .... 2.00

N-MINT

❑2 .... 2.00
❑3, Continued in Elflord #21 .... 2.00

Green Hornet
Gold Key

❑1, Feb 1967 .... 120.00
❑2, May 1967 .... 80.00
❑3, Aug 1967 .... 80.00

Green Hornet
Now

❑1, Nov 1989; JSo (c); JSo (a); O: Green Hornet I. O: 1940s Green Hornet. Jim Steranko cover 3.50
❑1/2nd, Apr 1990; prestige format; O: The Green Hornet. perfect bound 3.95
❑2, Dec 1989 .... 2.50
❑3, Jan 1990 .... 2.00
❑4, Feb 1990; SR (c); Steve Rude cover 2.00
❑5, Mar 1990 .... 2.00
❑6, Apr 1990 .... 2.00
❑7, May 1990; BSz (c); 1: new Kato. Mishi becomes new Kato 2.00
❑8, Jun 1990 .... 2.00
❑9, Jul 1990 .... 2.00
❑10, Aug 1990 .... 2.00
❑11, Sep 1990 .... 2.00
❑12, Oct 1990 .... 2.00
❑13, Nov 1990 .... 2.00
❑14, Feb 1991; Final Issue 2.00

Green Hornet
Now

❑1, Sep 1991 .... 2.00
❑2, Oct 1991 .... 2.00
❑3, Nov 1991; Painted cover 2.00
❑4, Dec 1991; Painted cover 2.00
❑5, Jan 1992 .... 2.00
❑6, Feb 1992; Painted cover 2.00
❑7, Mar 1992; Painted cover 2.00
❑8, Apr 1992; Painted cover 2.00
❑9, May 1992; Val Mayerik 2.00
❑10, Jun 1992; Painted cover 2.00
❑11, Jul 1992; V: Crimson Wasp 2.00
❑12, Aug 1992; bagged; with button 2.50
❑13, Sep 1992; Painted cover; Anniversary Special on cover 1.95
❑14, Oct 1992; Anniversary Special on cover 1.95
❑15, Nov 1992 .... 1.95
❑16, Dec 1992 .... 1.95
❑17, Jan 1993 .... 1.95
❑18, Feb 1993 .... 1.95
❑19, Mar 1993 .... 1.95
❑20, Apr 1993 .... 1.95
❑21, May 1993; V: Mr. Death 1.95
❑22, Jun 1993; newsstand, trading card; newsstand; Has UPC, Comics Code seal 2.95
❑22/Directed., Jun 1993; alternate cover; direct sale; trading card; No Comics Code seal 2.95
❑23, Jul 1993 .... 2.95
❑24, Aug 1993; Pin-ups 1.95
❑25, Sep 1993 .... 1.95
❑26, Oct 1993 .... 1.95
❑27, Nov 1993; Includes trading card 2.95
❑28, Dec 1993 .... 1.95
❑29, Jan 1994 .... 1.95
❑30, Feb 1994 .... 1.95

N-MINT

❑31, Mar 1994 .... 1.95
❑32, Apr 1994 .... 1.95
❑33, May 1994 .... 1.95
❑34, Jun 1994 .... 1.95
❑35, Jul 1994 .... 1.95
❑36, Aug 1994 .... 1.95
❑37, Sep 1994 .... 1.95
❑38, Nov 1994 .... 2.50
❑39, Dec 1994 .... 1.95
❑40, Jan 1995 .... 2.50
❑Ann 1, Dec 1992 .... 2.50
❑Ann 1994, Oct 1994 .... 2.95

Green Hornet Anniversary Special
Now

❑1, Aug 1992; bagged; with button 2.50
❑2, Sep 1992 .... 1.95
❑3, Oct 1992 .... 1.95

Green Hornet: Dark Tomorrow
Now

❑1, Jun 1993 .... 2.50
❑2, Jul 1993 .... 2.50
❑3, Aug 1993 .... 2.50

Green Hornet: Solitary Sentinel
Now

❑1, Dec 1992 .... 2.50
❑2, Jan 1993 .... 2.50
❑3, Feb 1993 .... 2.50

Green Lantern
DC

❑1, Aug 1960; GK (a); O: Green Lantern II (Hal Jordan). 1: Guardians; Roy Thomas L.O.C 4500.00
❑2, Oct 1960; GK (a); 1: Qward. 1: Pieface 1000.00
❑3, Dec 1960, GK (a); 2: of Qward 600.00
❑4, Feb 1961 GK (a) 450.00
❑5, Apr 1961; GK (a); 1: Hector Hammond; Roy Thomas L.O.C 450.00
❑6, Jun 1961; GK (a); 1: Tomar. 1: Tomar-Re 400.00
❑7, Aug 1961; GK (a); 1&O: Sinestro; 1: Terga 300.00
❑8, Oct 1961, GK (a); 1: Pol Manning 300.00
❑9, Dec 1961; GK (a); 1: Jack Jordan; 1: James Jordan; 1: Sue Jordan; 2: Sinestro; Don McGregor L.O.C.; Roy Thomas L.O.C 300.00
❑10, Jan 1962, GK (a); O: Green Lantern's oath; E. Nelson Bridwell L.O.C 300.00
❑11, Mar 1962, GK (a); 1: The Green Lantern Corps; 2: Tomar-Re; Joe Staton L.O.C ... 200.00
❑12, Apr 1962, GK (a); 1: Doctor Polaris; 2: Solar Director 5700 AD 200.00
❑13, Jun 1962, GK (a); A: Flash II (Barry Allen) 250.00
❑14, Jul 1962, GK (a); 1: Sonar 175.00
❑15, Sep 1962, GK (a) 175.00
❑16, Oct 1962, GK (a); 1&O: Star Sapphire. 1: Zamarons 175.00
❑17, Dec 1962, GK (a) 150.00
❑18, Jan 1963, GK (a); Paul Gambaccini L.O.C 150.00
❑19, Mar 1963, GK (a); 2: Sonar 150.00
❑20, Apr 1963, GK (a); A: Flash II (Barry Allen) 150.00
❑21, Jun 1963, GK (a); O: Doctor Polaris 125.00
❑22, Jul 1963, GK (a); 1: Jeremiah Jordan; 2: Hector Hammond 125.00

Other grades: Multiply price above by 5/6 for VF/NM • 2/3 for VERY FINE • 1/3 for FINE • 1/5 for VERY GOOD • 1/8 for GOOD

❑23, Sep 1963, GK (a); 1: Tattooed Man 125.00
❑24, Oct 1963, GK (a); 1&O: The Shark . 125.00
❑25, Dec 1963, GK (a) 125.00
❑26, Jan 1964, GK (a) 125.00
❑27, Mar 1964, GK (a) 125.00
❑28, Apr 1964, GK (a); 1: Goldface; 2: The Shark 100.00
❑29, Jun 1964, GK (a); 1: Black Hand. A: Justice League of America 100.00
❑30, Jul 1964, GK (a); 1: Katma Tui 100.00
❑31, Sep 1964, GK (a); Guy H. Lillian L.O.C 75.00
❑32, Oct 1964, GK (a); Mike Friedrich L.O.C 75.00
❑33, Dec 1964, GK (a) 75.00
❑34, Jan 1965, GK (a) 75.00
❑35, Mar 1965, GK (a); 1: Aerialist 75.00
❑36, Apr 1965, GK (a) 75.00
❑37, Jun 1965, GK (a); 1: Evil Star; Guy H. Lillian L.O.C 75.00
❑38, Jul 1965, GK (a); 2: Goldface; Tomar-Re apearance 75.00
❑39, Sep 1965, GK (a); 2: Black Hand 75.00
❑40, Oct 1965, O: Guardians. 1: Krona. A: Green Lantern I (Alan Scott) 350.00
❑41, Dec 1965, GK (a); A: Star Sapphire. Cary Bates L.O.C 75.00
❑42, Jan 1966, GK (a); 1: Warlock 75.00
❑43, Mar 1966, GK (a); 1: Major Disaster. A: Flash II (Barry Allen) 75.00
❑44, Apr 1966, GK (a); 1: Titus Jordan; 2: Evil Star; Mike Friedrich L.O.C 75.00
❑45, Jun 1966, GK (a); 1: Prince Peril. A: Green Lantern I (Alan Scott) 75.00
❑46, Jul 1966, GK (a); 2: Katma Tui 75.00
❑47, Sep 1966, GK (a) 75.00
❑48, Oct 1966, GK (a); Guy H. Lillian L.O.C 75.00
❑49, Dec 1966, GK (a); 1: Dazzler; Dave Cockrum L.O.C 75.00
❑50, Jan 1967, GK (a); Irene Vartanoff L.O.C 60.00
❑51, Mar 1967 60.00
❑52, Apr 1967, A: Green Lantern I (Alan Scott). 80.00
❑53, Jun 1967, Carl Gafford L.O.C.; Mark Evanier L.O.C 55.00
❑54, Jul 1967, Marv Wolfman L.O.C 55.00
❑55, Sep 1967, 1: Charles Vicker 55.00
❑56, Oct 1967, 2: Charles Vicker 55.00
❑57, Dec 1967, 2: Major Disaster; Guy H. Lillian L.O.C.; Peter Sanderson L.O.C . 55.00
❑58, Jan 1968 55.00
❑59, Mar 1968, 1: Guy Gardner 125.00
❑60, Apr 1968 50.00
❑61, Jun 1968, A: Green Lantern I (Alan Scott). 50.00
❑62, Jul 1968 50.00
❑63, Sep 1968, Neal Adams cover; Marv Wolfman L.O.C 50.00
❑64, Oct 1968, Irene Vartanoff L.O.C.; Don McGregor L.O.C 50.00
❑65, Dec 1968 50.00
❑66, Jan 1969, Don McGregor L.O.C.; Martin Pasko L.O.C.; Mark Evanier L.O.C.; Peter Sanderson L.O.C 50.00
❑67, Mar 1969, Guy H. Lillian L.O.C.; Carl Gafford L.O.C 50.00
❑68, Apr 1969, Fact File #6 (Sargon the Sorcerer) 50.00
❑69, Jun 1969, Peter Sanderson L.O.C.; Martin Pasko L.O.C 50.00
❑70, Jul 1969, GK (a) 50.00
❑71, Sep 1969, GK, DD (a); T.T. Jordan appearance; Irene Vartanoff L.O.C.; Don McGregor L.O.C 50.00
❑72, Oct 1969, GK (a); Irene Vartanoff L.O.C 50.00
❑73, Dec 1969, GK (a); Martin Pasko L.O.C 50.00
❑74, Jan 1970, GK (a); Guy H. Lillian (L.O.C) 50.00
❑75, Mar 1970, GK (a); 50.00
❑76, Apr 1970, NA (a); A: Green Arrow. Green Lantern/Green Arrow series 375.00
❑77, Jun 1970, NA (a); A: Green Arrow. Green Lantern/Green Arrow series 75.00
❑78, Jul 1970, NA (a); A: Green Arrow. Green Lantern/Green Arrow series 75.00
❑79, Sep 1970, NA (a); A: Green Arrow. Green Lantern/Green Arrow series 60.00
❑80, Oct 1970, NA (a); A: Green Arrow. Green Lantern/Green Arrow series 60.00
❑81, Dec 1970, NA (a); A: Green Arrow. Green Lantern/Green Arrow series 60.00
❑82, Mar 1971, NA (a); A: Green Arrow. Green Lantern/Green Arrow series 60.00
❑83, May 1971, NA (a); A: Green Arrow. Green Lantern/Green Arrow series; Anti-drug issue 60.00
❑84, Jul 1971, BWr, NA (a); Green Arrow; Green Lantern/Green Arrow series 60.00
❑85, Sep 1971; NA (c); NA, GK (a); Green Arrow; Anti-drug issue; Green Lantern/ Green Arrow series 50.00
❑86, Nov 1971; ATh, NA (a); Green Lantern/Green Arrow series; Green Arrow; Anti-drug issue 60.00
❑87, Jan 1972; NA, GK (a); 1: John Stewart. A: Green Arrow. Guy Gardner cameo; Green Lantern/Green Arrow series 50.00
❑88, Mar 1972; NA (c); MA, CI, GK (a); A: Green Arrow. fill-in issue; reprints stories from Showcase #23 and Green Lantern (2nd series) #10; also publishes previously unpublished Golden Age Green Lantern story 30.00
❑89, May 1972; NA (a); A: Green Arrow. Green Lantern/Green Arrow series 45.00
❑90, Sep 1976, MGr (w); MGr (a); A: Green Arrow. Green Lantern/Green Arrow series 10.00
❑91, Nov 1976, MGr (a); V: Sinestro 10.00
❑92, Dec 1976, MGr (a); Green Lantern/ Green Arrow series 10.00
❑93, Feb 1977, MGr (a); Green Lantern/ Green Arrow series; Black Canary appearance (as Dinah Lance) 9.00
❑94, Apr 1977, MGr (a); Green Lantern/ Green Arrow series 9.00
❑95, Jun 1977, MGr (a); Green Lantern/ Green Arrow series 9.00
❑96, Aug 1977, MGr (c); MGr (a); Green Lantern/Green Arrow series 9.00
❑97, Oct 1977, MGr (c); MGr (a); Green Lantern/Green Arrow series 9.00
❑98, Nov 1977, MGr (c); MGr (a); Green Lantern/ Green Arrow series; Green Lantern/Green Arrow series 9.00
❑99, Dec 1977, MGr (c); MGr (a); Green Lantern/Green Arrow series 9.00
❑100, Jan 1978, 100th anniversary issue; MGr (c); MGr (a); 1: Air Wave II (Harry "Hal" Jordan); 1: Air Wave (Harold Jordan) 10.00
❑101, Feb 1978, McGinty 9.00
❑102, Mar 1978, MGr (c); MGr (a); A: Green Arrow. Green Lantern/Green Arrow series 4.00
❑103, Apr 1978, MGr (c); MGr (a); A: Green Arrow. Green Lantern/Green Arrow series 4.00
❑104, May 1978, MGr (c); MGr (a); A: Green Arrow. Green Lantern/Green Arrow series 4.00
❑105, Jun 1978, MGr (c); MGr (a); A: Green Arrow. Green Lantern/Green Arrow series 4.00
❑106, Jul 1978, MGr (c); MGr (a); A: Green Arrow. Green Lantern/Green Arrow series 4.00
❑107, Aug 1978, MGr (a); A: Green Arrow. Green Lantern/Green Arrow series; Tales of the Green Lantern Corps 4.00
❑108, Sep 1978, MGr (c); MGr (a); A: Green Arrow. Golden Age Green Lantern back-up 4.00
❑109, Oct 1978, MGr (a); A: Green Arrow. Golden Age Green Lantern back-up 4.00
❑110, Nov 1978, MGr (c); MGr (a); A: Green Arrow. 44 pages; Green Lantern/Green Arrow series 4.00
❑111, Dec 1978, MGr (c); MGr (a); A: Green Arrow. Green Lantern/Green Arrow series 4.00
❑112, Jan 1979, O: Green Lantern I (Alan Scott); Green Lantern/Green Arrow series 8.00
❑113, Feb 1979, Green Lantern/Green Arrow series 3.00
❑114, Mar 1979, Green Lantern/Green Arrow series 3.00
❑115, Apr 1979, Green Lantern/Green Arrow series 3.00
❑116, May 1979, Guy Gardner becomes a Green Lantern 8.00
❑116/Whitman, May 1979, Guy Gardner becomes a Green Lantern; Whitman variant 16.00
❑117, Jun 1979, Green Lantern/ Green Arrow series 3.00
❑117/Whitman, Jun 1979, Whitman variant 6.00
❑118, Jul 1979, Green Lantern/Green Arrow series 3.00
❑118/Whitman, Jul 1979, Whitman variant 6.00
❑119, Aug 1979, Green Lantern/ Green Arrow series 2.50
❑119/Whitman, Aug 1979, Whitman variant 5.00
❑120, Sep 1979, Green Lantern/Green Arrow series 2.50
❑120/Whitman, Sep 1979, Whitman variant 5.00
❑121, Oct 1979, Green Lantern/Green Arrow series 2.50
❑121/Whitman, Oct 1979, Whitman variant 5.00
❑122, Nov 1979, A: Guy Gardner. Green Lantern/ Green Arrow series ends 3.50
❑123, Dec 1979, Guy Gardner as Green Lantern 6.00
❑124, Jan 1980 2.50
❑125, Feb 1980 2.50
❑126, Mar 1980 2.50
❑127, Apr 1980, BB (c); JSa (a) 2.50
❑128, May 1980, DG (c); DC, JSa (a) 2.50
❑129, Jun 1980, JSn (c); JSa (a) 2.50
❑130, Jun 1980, BB (c); JSa (a); Tales of the Green Lantern Corps 2.50
❑131, Aug 1980, BB (c); JSa (a); Tales of the Green Lantern Corps 2.25
❑132, Sep 1980, GP (c); JSa (a); Adam Strange backup stories begin; Tales of the Green Lantern Corps 2.25
❑133, Oct 1980, JSa (a); A: Doctor Polaris 2.25
❑134, Nov 1980, DG (c); JSa (a); A: Doctor Polaris 2.25
❑135, Dec 1980, JSa (c); JSa (a); A: Doctor Polaris 2.25
❑136, Jan 1981, RB, DC (c); JSa (a) 2.50
❑137, Feb 1981, DG (c); CI, JSa (a); 1: Citadel 2.50
❑138, Mar 1981, DG (c); JSa (a) 2.50
❑139, Apr 1981, DG (c); JSa (a) 2.50
❑140, May 1981, DG (c); JSa (a) 2.00
❑141, Jun 1981, GP (c); JSa (a); 1: Broot. 1: Harpis. 1: Omega Men. 1: Auron. 1: Kalista. 1: Demonia. 1: Primus 5.00
❑142, Jul 1981, GP (c); JSa (a); 1: The Gordanians. A: Omega Men; 2: Omega Men 2.50
❑143, Aug 1981, cGP (c); JSa (a); A: Omega Men 2.50
❑144, Sep 1981, GP (c); JSa (a); A: Omega Men 2.50
❑145, Oct 1981, JSa (c); CI, JSa (a) 2.00
❑146, Nov 1981, JSa (c); CI, JSa (a) 2.00
❑147, Dec 1981, CI, JSa (a); Last Adam Strange back-up 2.00
❑148, Jan 1982, DN, JSa (a); Tales of the Green Lantern Coprs series back-up begins; Green Lantern Corps 2.00
❑149, Feb 1982, DN, JSa (a); Tales of the Green Lantern Corps backup 2.00
❑150, Mar 1982; 150th anniversary issue; JSa (c); JSa (a) 5.00
❑151, Apr 1982, Tales of the Green Lantern Corps backup 2.00
❑152, May 1982, Tales of the Green Lantern Corps back-up; Green Lantern Corps 2.00
❑153, Jun 1982, Tales of the Green Lantern Corps backup 2.00
❑154, Jul 1982, Tales of the Green Lantern Corps backup 2.00
❑155, Aug 1982, Tales of the Green Lantern Corps backup 2.00
❑156, Sep 1982, Tales of the Green Lantern Corps backup 2.00
❑157, Oct 1982, Tales of the Green Lantern Corps backup 2.00
❑158, Nov 1982, Tales of the Green Lantern Corps backup 2.00
❑159, Dec 1982, Tales of the Green Lantern Corps backup 2.00
❑160, Jan 1983, Omega Men 2.00
❑161, Feb 1983, Omega Men 1.50
❑162, Mar 1983, KP (c); KB (w); DaG, RHo, KP (a); Back-up story is Kurt Busiek's first major comics work 1.50
❑163, Apr 1983, KP, GK (a); Tales of the Green Lantern Corps backup 1.50
❑164, May 1983, DaG (w); DaG, KP (a); 1: The Green Man; Tales of the Green Lantern Corps backup 1.50
❑165, Jun 1983, GK (c); DaG, KP (a); Tales of the Green Lantern Corps backup; Tales of the Green Lantern Corps 1.50
❑166, Jul 1983, GK (c); DaG, GT (a); Tales of the Green Lantern Corps backup 1.50
❑167, Aug 1983, GK (c); DaG, GT (a); 1: Spider Guild; Tales of the Green Lantern Corps backup 1.50

Gotham Nights

Batman vignette focuses on common man

©DC

Grateful Dead Comix (Vol. 2)

Adapts songs fans already know by heart

©Kitchen Sink

Great Society Comic Book

Political satire starring LBJ

©Parallax

Green Arrow

Character introduced in 1941, series in 1988

©DC

Green Arrow (2nd Series)

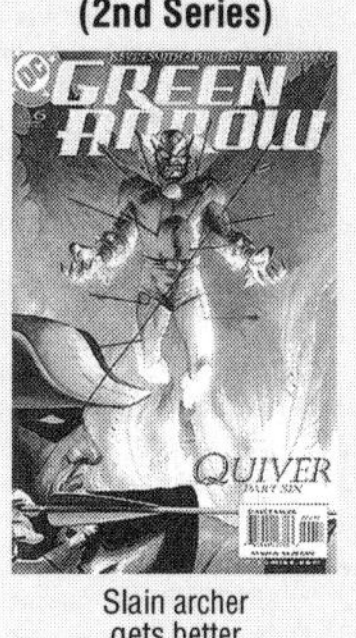

Slain archer gets better

©DC

	N-MINT
❑168, Sep 1983, Tales of the Green Lantern Corps story	1.50
❑169, Oct 1983, Tales of the Green Lantern Corps story	1.50
❑170, Nov 1983, GK (c); GT (a)	1.50
❑171, Dec 1983; GK (c); DaG (a); Noel Naive pen-name a Joey Cavalieri rewrite of a Robin Snyder script; Tales of the Green Lantern Corps backup	1.50
❑172, Jan 1984; DaG (a); Tales of the Green Lantern Corps backup	1.50
❑173, Feb 1984; DaG, DG (a); 1: Javelin. A: Monitor. V: Javelin; Tales of the Green Lantern Corps backup	1.50
❑174, Mar 1984 DaG, DG (a)	3.00
❑175, Apr 1984; DaG, DG (a); A: Flash. V: Shark	1.50
❑176, May 1984; DaG, DG (a); 1: Demolition Team. V: Shark	1.50
❑177, Jun 1984; GK (c); GK, DC (a); V: Hector Hammond; Tales of the Green Lantern Corps backup	1.50
❑178, Jul 1984; DaG, DG (a); 1: The Predator (Carol Ferris). A: Monitor. V: Demolition Team	1.50
❑179, Aug 1984; DaG, DG (a); A: Predator. V: Demolition Team; Tales of the Green Lantern Corps backup	3.00
❑180, Sep 1984; DaG, DG (a); A: Superman. A: Green Arrow. A: Flash. Tales of the Green Lantern Corps backup	1.50
❑181, Oct 1984; DN, DaG, DG (a); Hal Jordan quits as Green Lantern	1.50
❑182, Nov 1984; DaG, DG (a); John Stewart becomes new Green Lantern; retells origin	1.50
❑183, Dec 1984; Tales of the Green Lantern Corps backup	1.50
❑184, Jan 1985; GK (a); reprints origin of Guy Gardner	1.50
❑185, Feb 1985; DaG (c); KB (w); DaG, DH, DG (a); Green Lantern (John Stewart) appeaarance; Tales of the Green Lantern Corps back-up	1.50
❑186, Mar 1985; DaG, DG (a); V: Eclipso	1.50
❑187, Apr 1985; MR (a); Tales of the Green Lantern Corps backup	1.50
❑188, May 1985; AMo (w); DaG, JSa (a); John Stewart reveals ID to public	1.50
❑189, Jun 1985; JSa (a); V: Sonar; Tales of the Green Lantern Corps backup	1.50
❑190, Jul 1985; JSa (a); V: Predator; Tales of the Green Lantern Corps backup	1.50
❑191, Aug 1985 JSa (a)	1.50
❑192, Sep 1985; JSa (a); O: Star Sapphire; V: Star Sapphire!; 16 pages insert; M.A.S.K. preview	1.50
❑193, Oct 1985 JSa (a)	1.50
❑194, Nov 1985; JSa (a); Crisis; Guy Gardner returns; Guy Gardner vs. Hal Jordan	2.50
❑195, Dec 1985; JSa (a); Crisis; Guy Gardner becomes new Green Lantern of Earth	4.00
❑196, Jan 1986; JSa (a); Crisis	1.50
❑197, Feb 1986; JSa (a); Crisis; Guy Gardner vs. John Stewart	1.50
❑198, Mar 1986; JSa (a); Crisis; giant; Hal Jordan returns as Green Lantern	1.50
❑199, Apr 1986; JSa (a); Crisis; Hal Jordan returns as GL	1.50
❑200, May 1986; JSa (a); Crisis; Guardians join Zamarons	2.00
❑201, Jun 1986; JSa (a); Crisis aftermath	1.50
❑202, Jul 1986; JSa (a); Green Lantern Corps	1.50
❑203, Aug 1986; JSa (a); O: Ch'p	1.50
❑204, Sep 1986 JSa (a)	1.50
❑205, Oct 1986; JSa (a); Series continues as Green Lantern Corps	1.50
❑Special 1, Dec 1988	2.50
❑Special 2, ca. 1989	2.50

Green Lantern
DC

	N-MINT
❑0, Oct 1994; O: Green Lantern (Kyle Rayner). V: Hal Jordan. Oa destroyed	3.50
❑1, Jun 1990 PB (c); PB (a)	7.00
❑2, Jul 1990 PB (c); PB (a)	2.50
❑3, Aug 1990; Hal vs. Guy	2.00
❑4, Sep 1990; Cover inccorrectly credits Mark A. Nelson instead of Bruce Patterson	2.00
❑5, Oct 1990	2.00
❑6, Nov 1990	1.50
❑7, Dec 1990	1.50
❑8, Jan 1991	1.50
❑9, Feb 1991 A: G'Nort	1.50
❑10, Mar 1991 A: G'Nort	1.50
❑11, Apr 1991 A: G'Nort	1.50
❑12, May 1991 A: G'Nort	1.50
❑13, Jun 1991; Giant-size	2.25
❑14, Jul 1991	1.50
❑15, Aug 1991	1.50
❑16, Sep 1991	1.50
❑17, Oct 1991	1.50
❑18, Nov 1991	1.50
❑19, Dec 1991; Giant-size; GK (c); PB, JSa, RT (a); 50th anniversary issue	2.00
❑20, Jan 1992 PB (c); PB (a)	1.50
❑21, Feb 1992 PB (c); PB (a)	1.50
❑22, Mar 1992 PB (c); PB (a)	1.50
❑23, Apr 1992 PB (c); PB (a)	1.50
❑24, May 1992; PB (c); PB (a); D: Star Sapphire	1.50
❑25, Jun 1992; Giant size; JSa (a); Hal Jordan vs. Guy Gardner	2.25
❑26, Jul 1992	1.50
❑27, Aug 1992	1.25
❑28, Sep 1992	1.25
❑29, Sep 1992	1.25
❑30, Oct 1992; MWa (w); A: Flash. V: Gorilla Grodd	1.25
❑31, Oct 1992; MWa (w); A: Flash. V: Hector Hammond. V: Gorilla Grodd. V: Grodd	1.25
❑32, Nov 1992	1.25
❑33, Nov 1992	1.25
❑34, Dec 1992	1.25
❑35, Jan 1993	1.25
❑36, Feb 1993; V: Dr. Light	1.25
❑37, Mar 1993	1.25
❑38, Apr 1993; A: Adam Strange	1.25
❑39, May 1993 A: Adam Strange	1.25
❑40, May 1993 A: Darkstar	1.25
❑41, Jun 1993	1.25
❑42, Jun 1993	1.25
❑43, Jul 1993	1.25
❑44, Aug 1993 RT (c); RT (a)	1.25
❑45, Sep 1993	1.25
❑46, Oct 1993; A: Superman. V: Mongul	4.00
❑47, Nov 1993 A: Green Arrow	2.00
❑48, Jan 1994 RT (a)	5.00
❑49, Feb 1994	5.00
❑50, Mar 1994; Double-size; 1: Green Lantern IV (Kyle Rayner). D: Sinestro. D: Kilowog. Glow-in-the-dark cover	5.00
❑51, May 1994; New costume	3.00
❑52, Jun 1994; V: Mongul	2.00
❑53, Jul 1994 A: Superman	2.00
❑54, Aug 1994; V: Major Force	2.00
❑55, Sep 1994; A: Green Lantern I. A: Alan Scott. Zero Hour	2.00
❑56, Nov 1994; Continued in Rebels '94 #1	2.00
❑57, Dec 1994; A: New Titans. continues in New Titans #116	2.00
❑58, Jan 1995	2.00
❑59, Feb 1995; V: Doctor Polaris	2.00
❑60, Mar 1995; A: Guy Gardner. V: Major Force	2.00
❑61, Apr 1995; A: Darkstar. V: Kalibak	2.00
❑62, May 1995	2.00
❑63, Jun 1995	2.00
❑64, Jul 1995	2.00
❑65, Aug 1995; continues in Darkstars #34	2.00
❑66, Sep 1995; teams with Flash	2.00
❑67, Oct 1995	2.00
❑68, Nov 1995; A: Donna Troy. Underworld Unleashed	2.00
❑69, Dec 1995; Underworld Unleashed	2.00
❑70, Jan 1996 A: John Stewart	2.00
❑71, Feb 1996 A: Robin. A: Sentinel. A: Batman	2.00
❑72, Mar 1996 A: Captain Marvel	2.00
❑73, Apr 1996 A: Wonder Woman	2.00
❑74, Jun 1996	2.00
❑75, Jul 1996	2.00
❑76, Jul 1996; Cover homage to Green Lantern #76 (2nd series)	2.00
❑77, Aug 1996	2.00
❑78, Sep 1996	2.00
❑79, Oct 1996; V: Sonar	2.00
❑80, Nov 1996; V: Doctor Light. Final Night	2.00
❑81, Dec 1996; Funeral of Hal Jordan; Memorial for Hal Jordan	3.00
❑81/Variant, Dec 1996; Embossed cover; Funeral of Hal Jordan; Kane back-up story; reprints origin; Memorial for Hal Jordan	4.00
❑82, Jan 1997	1.75
❑83, Feb 1997; 1: Fatality	1.75
❑84, Mar 1997	1.75
❑85, Apr 1997	1.75
❑86, May 1997 A: Jade. A: Obsidian	1.75
❑87, Jun 1997 A: Martian Manhunter. A: Access	1.75
❑88, Jul 1997	1.75
❑89, Aug 1997	1.75
❑90, Sep 1997	1.75
❑91, Oct 1997; V: Desaad. Genesis	1.75
❑92, Nov 1997; concludes in Green Arrow #126	1.75
❑93, Dec 1997; A: Deadman. Face cover	1.95
❑94, Jan 1998 A: Superboy	1.95
❑95, Feb 1998 JSn (c); JSn (a)	1.95
❑96, Mar 1998; cover forms triptych with Flash #135 and Green Arrow #130	1.95
❑97, Apr 1998; V: Grayven	1.95

Other grades: Multiply price above by 5/6 for VF/NM • 2/3 for VERY FINE • 1/3 for FINE • 1/5 for VERY GOOD • 1/8 for GOOD

❑98, May 1998; 1: Cary Wren as Green Lantern. A: Legion of Super-Heroes ... 1.95
❑99, Jun 1998; V: Green Lantern descendants in 30th century; Timetravels to Green Lantern (Hal Jordan)/Sinestro battle 1.95
❑100/A, Jul 1998; Hal Jordan cover (Kyle Rayner cover inside).................. 5.00
❑100/Autographed, Jul 1998.................. 4.00
❑100/B, Jul 1998; Kyle Rayner cover (Hal Jordan cover inside) 2.95
❑101, Aug 1998 .... 1.95
❑102, Aug 1998; V: Kalibak.................... 1.95
❑103, Sep 1998 A: JLa.......................... 1.95
❑104, Sep 1998 A: Green Arrow 1.95
❑105, Oct 1998; V: Parallax.................... 1.95
❑106, Oct 1998; Hal returned to past 1.95
❑107, Dec 1998; Kyle gives a ring to Jade 1.99
❑108, Jan 1999; Wonder Woman 1.99
❑109, Feb 1999; Green Lantern IV (Jade) 1.99
❑110, Mar 1999 A: Green Lantern (Alan Scott). A: Green Arrow. A: Conner Hawke.. 1.99
❑111, Apr 1999; A: Fatality. A: John Stewart. V: Fatality............................. 1.99
❑112, May 1999; Kyle returns................ 1.99
❑113, Jun 1999...................................... 1.99
❑114, Jul 1999.. 1.99
❑115, Aug 1999 A: Plastic Man. A: Booster Gold.. 1.99
❑116, Sep 1999 A: Plastic Man. A: Booster Gold.. 1.99
❑117, Oct 1999; V: Manhunter................ 1.99
❑118, Nov 1999; A: Enchantress. Day of Judgment 1.99
❑119, Dec 1999 A: new Spectre 1.99
❑120, Jan 2000....................................... 1.99
❑121, Feb 2000 .... 1.99
❑122, Mar 2000 .... 1.99
❑123, Apr 2000 .... 1.99
❑124, May 2000; V: Controllers; V: Destroyers.. 1.99
❑125, Jun 2000; V: alien criminal entombed within Earth's moon........... 1.99
❑126, Jul 2000; Infiltrates Slab to investigate location of kidnapping victim 1.99
❑127, Aug 2000 .... 1.99
❑128, Sep 2000...................................... 2.25
❑129, Oct 2000; V: Manhunters; Manhunters kidnap Green Lantern (Kyle Rayner)..................................... 2.25
❑130, Nov 2000; V: Manhunters; Manhunters obtain Green Lantern's ring 2.25
❑131, Dec 2000; V: Manhunters; Qwardians give Sinestro's ring to Fatality.. 2.25
❑132, Jan 2001; 1: Nero; V: Fatality; Qwardians give Sinestro's ring to Nero 2.25
❑133, Feb 2001 MW (c) 2.25
❑134, Mar 2001 .... 2.25
❑135, Apr 2001; V: Nero 2.25
❑136, May 2001; V: Nero; Green Lantern (Kyle Rayner) proposes to Jade 2.25
❑137, Jun 2001; Jade turns down marriage proposal; Jade accepts Green Lantern ring.. 2.25
❑138, Jul 2001.. 2.25
❑139, Aug 2001 .... 2.25
❑140, Sep 2001....................................... 2.25
❑141, Oct 2001 .... 2.25
❑142, Nov 2001 .... 2.25
❑143, Dec 2001; JLee (c); Joker: Last Laugh crossover.................................. 2.25
❑144, Jan 2002....................................... 2.25
❑145, Feb 2002 .... 2.25
❑146, Mar 2002 .... 2.25
❑147, Apr 2002....................................... 2.25
❑148, May 2002...................................... 2.25
❑149, Jun 2002....................................... 2.25
❑150, Jul 2002; JLee (c); 48 pages; Rebirth of the Guardians 3.50
❑151, Aug 2002 JLee (c)......................... 2.25
❑152, Sep 2002 JLee (c)......................... 2.25
❑153, Oct 2002 JLee (c) 2.25
❑154, Nov 2002 JLee (c).......................... 2.25
❑155, Dec 2002 JLee (c).......................... 2.25
❑156, Jan 2003....................................... 2.25
❑157, Feb 2003 .... 2.25
❑158, Mar 2003 .... 2.25
❑159, Apr 2003....................................... 2.25
❑160, May 2003...................................... 2.25
❑161, May 2003...................................... 2.25
❑162, Jun 2003; Continued from Green Arrow #23 .... 2.25
❑163, Jun 2003; Continued from Green Arrow #24 .... 2.25
❑164, Jul 2003; Continued from Green Arrow #25 .... 2.25
❑165, Jul 2003.. 2.25
❑166, Aug 2003...................................... 2.25
❑167, Sep 2003 .... 2.25
❑168, Oct 2003....................................... 2.25
❑169, Nov 2003...................................... 2.25
❑170, Dec 2003 .... 2.25
❑171, Jan 2004....................................... 2.25
❑172, Feb 2004....................................... 2.25
❑173, Mar 2004 .... 2.25
❑174, Apr 2004....................................... 2.25
❑175, May 2004...................................... 4.00
❑176, Jun 2004....................................... 8.00
❑177, Jul 2004.. 4.00
❑178, Aug 2004...................................... 2.25
❑179, Sep 2004 .... 2.25
❑180, Oct 2004....................................... 2.25
❑181, Nov 2004, Final Issue 2.25
❑1000000, Nov 1998; One Million 3.00
❑Ann 1, ca. 1992; Eclipso: The Darkness Within... 4.00
❑Ann 2, ca. 1993; O: Nightblade. 1: Nightblade; Bloodlines: Outbreak; 1993 Ann.. 2.50
❑Ann 3, ca. 1994; Elseworlds 3.00
❑Ann 4, ca. 1995; GK (a); Year One; Kyle and Hal switch places.................... 3.50
❑Ann 5, ca. 1996; Legends of the Dead Earth... 2.95
❑Ann 6, Oct 1997; Pulp Heroes; John Carter of Mars theme 3.95
❑Ann 7, Oct 1998; Ghosts....................... 2.95
❑Ann 8, Oct 1999; KG (w); JLApe.......... 2.95
❑Ann 9, Oct 2000; 1: Sala. Planet DC..... 3.50
❑Ann 1963; MA, ATh, GK (a); published in 1998 in style of 1963 annuals; cardstock cover.................................. 6.00
❑GS 1, Dec 1998; 80-Page Giant; JRo (w); A: G'Nort. 80-Page Giant.................... 4.95
❑GS 2, Jun 1999; 80-Page Giant; MWa (w); A: Plastic Man. A: Guy Gardner. A: Deadman. A: Impulse. A: Zatanna. A: Big Barda. A: Aquaman. 80-Page Giant 4.95
❑GS 3, Aug 2000; 80-Page Giant; Tale of Raker Qarrigat (Green Lantern of Apokolips)... 5.95
❑3D 1, Dec 1998; V: Doctor Light.......... 4.50

Green Lantern
DC

❑1, Jul 2005.. 6.00
❑2, Aug 2005... 4.00
❑3, Sep 2005; V: Manhunters 2.99
❑4, Oct 2005; V: Hector Hammond........ 2.99
❑5, Jan 2006.. 2.99
❑7, Feb 2006, Infinite Crisis crossover .. 2.99
❑8, Mar 2006, Bianchi cover................. 2.99
❑9, May 2006, 1: Tattooed Man II; Bianchi cover (Green Lantern and Batman faceoff) 2.99
❑10, Jun 2006, One Year Later 2.99
❑11, Aug 2006, V: Manhunters; New Global Guardians forcibly recruit Crimson Fox; One Year Later............. 2.99
❑12, Sep 2006, V: Manhunters; V: Cyborg Superman; One Year Later; Cover by Simone Bianchi; Arisia revealed alive . 2.99
❑13, Nov 2006, V: Manhunters; V: Cyborg Superman (Hank Henshaw); Return of Arisa; Superboy-Prime cameo........... 2.99
❑14, Jan 2007, O: flashbacks................. 2.99
❑15, Feb 2007, V: Global Guardians; V: Rocket Red Brigade; V: Faceless hunters.. 2.99
❑16, Mar 2007 .... 2.99
❑17, Apr 2007... 2.99
❑18, May 2007; V: Star Sapphire; Tales of the Sinestro Corps back-up feature begins... 2.99
❑19, Jun 2007; Tales of the Sinestro corps back-up feature 2.99
❑20, Jul 2007; Tale of the Sinestro Corps back-up.. 2.99
❑21, Aug 2007; Story continues in Green Lantern Corps #14 .... 2.99
❑22, Sep 2007; Sinestro Corps............... 2.99
❑23, Oct 2007; D: Ke'Hann; V: Sinestro Corps; Part 6; Book of Oa rewritten so that Green Lantern Corps can use lethal force; The Sinestro Corps War 2.99
❑24, Nov 2007; V: Sinestro Corps; V: Parallax; Return of Kyle Rayner as Green Lantern 2.99
❑25, Dec 2007; 1: Black Lanterns; First mention of the seven Lantern Corps; The Sinestro Corps War Part 11; Double-sized issue 4.99
❑26, Jan 2008; D: Amon Sur; Sinestro Corps Epilogue.................................. 2.99
❑27, Feb 2008; Sinestro Corps Epilogue 2.99
❑28 .... 2.99
❑29 .... 2.99
❑30 .... 2.99
❑31 .... 2.99
❑32 .... 2.99
❑33 .... 2.99
❑34 .... 2.99
❑35 .... 2.99
❑36 .... 2.99
❑37 .... 2.99
❑38 .... 2.99
❑39 .... 2.99
❑40 .... 2.99

Green Lantern/Adam Strange
DC

❑1, Oct 2000; Green Lantern Circle of Fire cross-over; V: Oblivion on Rann......... 2.50

Green Lantern/Atom
DC

❑1, Oct 2000; Green Lantern Circle of Fire cross-over; V: Scarecrow; V: Doctor Psycho; V: Professor Ivo.................... 2.50

Green Lantern: Brightest Day, Blackest Night
DC

❑1, Aug 2002 .... 5.95

Green Lantern: Circle of Fire
DC

❑1, Oct 2000; V: Oblivion....................... 4.95
❑2, Oct 2000; V: Oblivion; Oblivion revealed as Green Lantern creation and reabsorbed by Green Lantern ring...... 4.95

Green Lantern Corps
DC

❑206, Nov 1986; JSa (c); JSa (a); Series continued from Green Lantern (2nd Series) #205 .... 1.50
❑207, Dec 1986; JSa (c); JSa (a); Legends 1.50
❑208, Jan 1987 JSa (c); JSa (a) 1.50
❑209, Feb 1987 JSa (c); JSa (a) 1.50
❑210, Mar 1987 JSa (c); JSa (a)............. 1.50
❑211, Apr 1987 JSa (c); JSa (a) 1.50
❑212, May 1987 JSa (c); JSa (a) 1.50
❑213, Jun 1987 JSa (c); JSa (a) 1.50
❑214, Jul 1987.. 1.50
❑215, Aug 1987 .... 1.50
❑216, Sep 1987 .... 1.50
❑217, Oct 1987 JSa (c); JSa (a).............. 1.50
❑218, Nov 1987 .... 1.50
❑219, Dec 1987 .... 1.50
❑220, Jan 1988; Millennium 1.50
❑221, Feb 1988; JSa (c); JSa (a); Millennium 1.50
❑222, Mar 1988 JSa (c); JSa (a)............. 1.50
❑223, Apr 1988 GK (c); GK (a)............... 1.50
❑224, May 1988; Giant-size; GK (c); GK (a); Final Issue.................................... 1.50
❑Ann 1 1985... 2.50
❑Ann 2 1986; GK (c); AMo (w); TVE (a). 2.25
❑Ann 3 1987; JBy, KB, AMo (w); JBy, JSa, KN, KS (a); Indicia title: Green Lantern Ann #3... 2.00

Green Lantern Corps Quarterly
DC

❑1, Sum 1992 .... 2.50
❑2, Aut 1992; Hector Hammond vs. Alan Scott.. 2.50
❑3, Win 1992; D: Black Canary I 2.50
❑4, Spr 1993; Alan Scott vs. Solomon Grundy 2.50
❑5, Sum 1993; 1&O: Adam.................... 2.50
❑6, Aut 1993; Alan Scott vs. New Harlequin 2.95
❑7, Win 1993 .... 2.95
❑8, Spr 1994; Jack Chance vs. Lobo...... 2.95

Green Lantern Corps: Recharge
DC

❑1, Nov 2005 .... 3.50
❑2, Dec 2005 .... 2.99

Other grades: Multiply price above by 5/6 for VF/NM • 2/3 for VERY FINE • 1/3 for FINE • 1/5 for VERY GOOD • 1/8 for GOOD

Green Arrow: The Longbow Hunters

Mike Grell makes GA grow up

©DC

Green Goblin

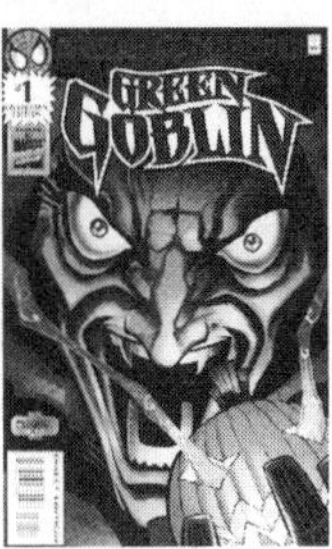

Not the villain, but a new hero

©Marvel

Green Hornet

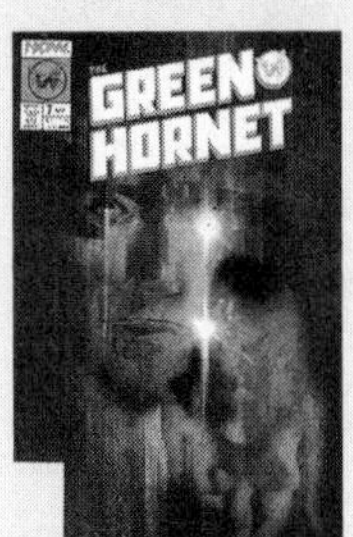

Descendants of original take up mantle

©Now

Green Lantern

Adventures of intergalactic lawman

©DC

Green Lantern

Hal goes crazy, Kyle takes over

©DC

N-MINT

❑3, Feb 2006 ... 2.99
❑4, Mar 2006 ... 2.99
❑5, May 2006 ... 2.99

Green Lantern Corps
DC

❑1, Aug 2006, Cover by Patrick Gleason and Prentis Rollins ... 2.99
❑2, Sep 2006 ... 2.99
❑3, Oct 2006, Cover by Patrick Gleason & Prentis Rollins; Iolande (of Betrassus; Sector 1417) appointed Green Lantern ... 2.99
❑4, Nov 2006, V: Bolphunga ... 2.99
❑5, Dec 2006 ... 2.99
❑6, Jan 2007, O: Ranx (The Sentient City) ... 2.99
❑7, Feb 2007 ... 2.99
❑8, Mar 2007 ... 2.99
❑9, Apr 2007 ... 2.99
❑10, May 2007 ... 2.99
❑11, Jun 2007 ... 2.99
❑12, Jul 2007 ... 2.99
❑13, Aug 2007 ... 2.99
❑14, Sep 2007 ... 2.99
❑15, Oct 2007; The Sinestro Corps War Part 5 ... 2.99
❑16, Nov 2007; Sinestro Corps War, Part 7 ... 2.99
❑17, Dec 2007; 1: Sodam Yat as Ion II; The Sinestro Corps War, Part 9 ... 2.99
❑18, Jan 2008; O: Ion (Sodam Yat); Ion (Sodam Yat) V: Superman Prime; The Sinestro Corps War, Part 10 ... 2.99
❑19, Feb 2008; The Sinestro Corps War Epilogue; Return of Mongul; Mongul obtains a Sinestro Ring ... 2.99
❑20, Mar 2008 ... 2.99
❑21, Apr 2008 ... 2.99
❑22, May 2008 ... 2.99
❑23 ... 2.99
❑24 ... 2.99
❑25 ... 2.99
❑26 ... 2.99
❑27 ... 2.99
❑28 ... 2.99
❑29 ... 2.99
❑30 ... 2.99
❑31 ... 2.99
❑32 ... 2.99
❑33 ... 2.99
❑34 ... 2.99
❑35 ... 2.99
❑36 ... 2.99

Green Lantern: Dragon Lord
DC

❑1, Jun 2001 ... 4.95
❑2, Jul 2001 ... 4.95
❑3, Aug 2001 ... 4.95

Green Lantern: Emerald Dawn
DC

❑1, Dec 1989; KJ (c); RT (a); O: Green Lantern II (Hal Jordan). O:Green Lantern ... 2.00
❑2, Jan 1990; KJ (c); KG (w); KG, RT (a); V: Legion; Green Lantern (Hal Jordan) turns himself in for DWI ... 1.50
❑3, Feb 1990 KJ (c); KG (w); KG, RT (a) 1.50
❑4, Mar 1990 KJ (c); KG (w); RT (a) ... 1.50
❑5, Apr 1990 KJ (c); KG (w); RT (a) ... 1.50
❑6, May 1990 KJ (c); KG (w); RT (a) ... 1.50

N-MINT

Green Lantern: Emerald Dawn II
DC

❑1, Apr 1991 (c); KG (w); RT (a) ... 1.50
❑2, May 1991 (c); KG (w); RT (a) ... 1.00
❑3, Jun 1991 (c); KG (w); RT (a) ... 1.00
❑4, Jul 1991 (c); KG (w); RT (a) ... 1.00
❑5, Aug 1991 (c); KG (w); RT (a) ... 1.00
❑6, Sep 1991 (c); KG (w); RT (a) ... 1.00

Green Lantern: Emerald Twilight New Dawn
DC

❑1, ca. 2003 ... 19.95

Green Lantern: Evil's Might
DC

❑1, Oct 2002 ... 5.95
❑2, Nov 2002 ... 5.95
❑3, Dec 2002 ... 5.95

Green Lantern/Firestorm
DC

❑1, Oct 2000; Green Lantern Circle of Fire cross-over ... 2.50

Green Lantern/Flash: Faster Friends
DC

❑1; prestige format; concludes in Flash/ Green Lantern: Faster Friends ... 4.95

Green Lantern Gallery
DC

❑1, Dec 1996; pin-ups ... 3.50

Green Lantern: Ganthet's Tale
DC

❑1 1992; prestige format; enhanced cover; Larry Niven ... 5.95

Green Lantern/Green Arrow
DC

❑1, Oct 1983; DG, NA (a); Reprints ... 4.00
❑2, Nov 1983; DG, NA, DA (a); Reprints 3.50
❑3, Dec 1983; DG, NA (a); Reprints ... 3.50
❑4, Jan 1984; DG, NA (a); Reprints ... 3.50
❑5, Feb 1984; BWr, DG, NA (a); Reprints 3.50
❑6, Mar 1984; DG, NA (a); Reprints ... 3.50
❑7, Apr 1984; DG, NA (a); Reprints ... 3.50

Green Lantern/Green Lantern
DC

❑1, Oct 2000; Green Lantern Circle of Fire cross-over ... 2.50

Green Lantern: Mosaic
DC

❑1, Jun 1992 ... 1.25
❑2, Jul 1992; D: Ch'p (Green Lantern squirrel) ... 1.25
❑3, Aug 1992 ... 1.25
❑4, Sep 1992 ... 1.25
❑5, Oct 1992 ... 1.25
❑6, Nov 1992 ... 1.25
❑7, Dec 1992 ... 1.25
❑8, Jan 1993 ... 1.25
❑9, Feb 1993 ... 1.25
❑10, Mar 1993 ... 1.25
❑11, Apr 1993 ... 1.25
❑12, May 1993 ... 1.25
❑13, Jun 1993 ... 1.25
❑14, Jul 1993 ... 1.25
❑15, Aug 1993 ... 1.25

N-MINT

❑16, Sep 1993 ... 1.25
❑17, Oct 1993 ... 1.25
❑18, Nov 1993; Final Issue ... 1.25

Green Lantern: 1001 Emerald Nights
DC

❑1, May 2001, Elseworlds ... 6.95

Green Lantern: Our Worlds At War
DC

❑1, Aug 2001; hardcover ... 2.95

Green Lantern Plus
DC

❑1, Dec 1996; 1: Arashi ... 2.95

Green Lantern/Power Girl
DC

❑1, Oct 2000; Green Lantern Circle of Fire cross-over ... 2.50

Green Lantern: Rebirth
DC

❑1, Dec 2004 ... 10.00
❑1/2nd, Dec 2004; 2nd printing ... 12.00
❑1/3rd, Dec 2004; 3rd printing ... 5.00
❑2, Jan 2005 ... 6.00
❑2/2nd, Jan 2005, 2nd printing ... 3.00
❑3, Feb 2005 ... 4.00
❑4, Mar 2005 ... 2.95
❑5, Apr 2005 ... 2.95
❑6, Jun 2005 ... 2.99

Green Lantern Secret Files
DC

❑1, Jul 1998; background on all Green Lanterns ... 4.95
❑2, Sep 1999; background on all Green Lanterns ... 4.95
❑3, Jul 2002 ... 4.95

Green Lantern/Sentinel: Heart of Darkness
DC

❑1, Mar 1998; covers form triptych ... 1.95
❑2, Apr 1998; covers form triptych ... 1.95
❑3, May 1998; covers form triptych ... 1.95

Green Lantern/Silver Surfer: Unholy Alliances
DC

❑1 1995; prestige format; crossover with Marvel ... 4.95

Green Lantern Sinestro Corps Special
DC

❑1, Oct 2007 ... 4.99

Green Lantern/Superman: Legend of the Green Flame
DC

❑1 2000 ... 5.95

Green Lantern: The New Corps
DC

❑1, ca. 1999; prestige format ... 4.95
❑2, ca. 1999; prestige format ... 4.95

Green Lantern vs. Aliens
DC

❑1, Sep 2000 ... 3.00
❑2, Oct 2000 ... 3.00
❑3, Nov 2000 ... 3.00
❑4, Dec 2000 ... 3.00

Green Lantern: Willworld
DC

❑1, Jul 2001; hardcover 24.95
❑2, ca. 2003 .... 17.95

Greenleaf in Exile
Cat's Paw

❑1 .... 2.95
❑2 .... 2.95
❑3 .... 2.95
❑4 .... 2.95
❑5 .... 2.95
❑6 .... 2.95

Greenlock
Aircel

❑1, Mar 1991, b&w; One-shot 2.50

Green Planet
Charlton

❑1, ca. 1962, Vol. 2 #8 .... 26.00

Green Skull
Known Associates

❑1; NN; One-shot 2.50

Gregory
DC / Piranha

❑1, b&w 7.95
❑1/2nd; 2nd printing 7.95
❑2; Herman Vermin's Very Own Best-selling & Critically Acclaimed Book with Gregory 4.95
❑3; b&w 7.95
❑3/Gold; Gold logo edition (limited printing) 9.00
❑4, b&w; Fat Boy 4.95

Gremlin Trouble
Anti-Ballistic

❑1, b&w; 1: Cypher; 1: Remi-el; 1: Xynophylyen; The Chief Imp 3.50
❑2, b&w; 2: Cypher; 2: High Commi 3.00
❑3, b&w 3.00
❑4, b&w; 1: Prince Frothbar of the Mountain Fairies; 2: Dr. Candy Tsai; 2: Grommet 3.00
❑5, b&w; 2: Prince 3.00
❑6, b&w 2.95
❑7, b&w; 2: King of the Mountain Fai 2.95
❑8, b&w; Instigation of the Gremlin-Goblin War 2.95
❑9, b&w; 1: Candy Tsai and the Moist Towelettes; 1: Dr. Brandy Schwarzchild; 1: Dr. Pi Yukawa 2.95
❑10, b&w 2.95
❑11, b&w; Grommet cameo;Mr. Wingnut cameo; Xynophylyen 2.95
❑12, b&w; 1: Ballpoint P. Greml 2.95
❑13, b&w; Dr. Brandy Schwarzchild 2.95
❑14, b&w; 2: The Moist Towel; 2: Tuberians 2.95
❑15, b&w 2.95
❑16, b&w 2.95
❑17, b&w 2.95
❑18, b&w 2.95
❑19, b&w 2.95
❑20, ca. 1999, b&w 2.95
❑21, ca. 2000, b&w 2.95
❑22, ca. 2000, b&w 2.95
❑23, ca. 2000, b&w 2.95
❑24, ca. 2000, b&w 2.95
❑25, ca. 2000, b&w 2.95
❑26, ca. 2001, b&w 2.95
❑27, ca. 2001, b&w 2.95
❑28, ca. 2001, b&w 2.95
❑29, ca. 2002, b&w 2.95
❑30, ca. 2002, b&w 4.95
❑Special 1, ca. 2003, b&w 2.95
❑Special 2, ca. 2004, b&w 3.25

Grendel
Comico

❑1, Mar 1983, b&w; MW (c); MW (w); MW (a) 45.00
❑2, ca. 1983, b&w; MW (c); MW (w); MW (a) 35.00
❑3, Feb 1984, b&w; MW (c); MW (w); MW (a) 26.00

Grendel
Comico

❑1, Oct 1986, MW (w); MW (a) 5.00
❑1/2nd, MW (w); MW (a); 2nd printing 2.50
❑2, Nov 1986, MW (w); MW (a); Wraparound cover 4.00
❑3, Dec 1986, MW (w); MW (a); Wraparound cover 3.50
❑4, Jan 1987, MW, DSt (c); MW (w); Wraparound cover 3.50
❑5, Feb 1987, MW (c); MW (w); MW (a); Wraparound cover 3.50
❑6, Mar 1987, MW (w); MW (a) 3.00
❑7, Apr 1987, MW (w); MW (a); Wraparound cover 3.00
❑8, May 1987, MW (w); MW (a); Wraparound cover 3.00
❑9, Jun 1987, MW (w); MW (a) 3.00
❑10, Jul 1987, MW (w); MW (a); Wraparound cover 3.00
❑11, Aug 1987, MW (w); MW (a); Wraparound cover 3.00
❑12, Sep 1987, MW (w); MW (a); D: Grendel; Wraparound cover 3.00
❑13, Oct 1987, MW (w); MW (a); new Grendel 3.00
❑14, Nov 1987, MW (w); MW (a); new Grendel 3.00
❑15, Dec 1987, MW (w); MW (a); new Grendel 3.00
❑16, Jan 1988, MW (w); MW (a); Mage begins 4.00
❑17, Feb 1988, MW (c); MW (w); MW (a); Wraparound cover; Mage backup 2.50
❑18, Apr 1988, MW (c); MW (w); MW (a); Wraparound cover; Mage backup 3.00
❑19, May 1988, MW (c); MW (w); MW (a); Wraparound cover; Mage Backup 2.50
❑20, Jun 1988, MW (w); MW (a); Wraparound cover 2.50
❑21, Jul 1988, MW (w); MW (a); Wraparound cover 2.50
❑22, Aug 1988, MW (w); MW (a); Wraparound cover 2.50
❑23, Sep 1988, MW (w); MW (a); Wraparound cover 2.50
❑24, Oct 1988, MW (w); MW (a); Wraparound cover 2.50
❑25, Nov 1988, MW (w); MW (a); Wraparound cover 2.50
❑26, Dec 1988, MW (w); MW (a); Wraparound cover 2.50
❑27, Jan 1989, MW (w); MW (a); Wraparound cover 2.50
❑28, Feb 1989, MW (w); MW (a); Wraparound cover 2.50
❑29, Mar 1989, MW (w); MW (a); Wraparound cover 2.50
❑30, Apr 1989, MW (w); MW (a); Wraparound cover 2.50
❑31, May 1989, MW (w); MW (a); Wraparound cover 2.50
❑32, Jun 1989, MW (w); MW (a) 2.50
❑33, Jul 1989, Giant-size; MW (w); MW (a); Giant-size 3.75
❑34, Aug 1989, MW (w); MW (a); Wraparound cover 2.50
❑35, Sep 1989, MW (w); MW (a); Wraparound cover 2.50
❑36, Oct 1989, MW (w); MW (a); Wraparound cover 2.50
❑37, Nov 1989, MW (w); MW (a); Wraparound cover 2.50
❑38, Dec 1989, MW (w); MW (a); Wraparound cover 2.50
❑39, Jan 1990, MW (w); MW (a); Wraparound cover 2.50
❑40, Feb 1990, MW (w); MW (a); flip book with Grendel Tales Special Preview 3.50

Grendel: Black, White, & Red
Dark Horse

❑1, Nov 1998; MW (c); MW (w); Matt Wagner painted cover 4.00
❑2, Dec 1998; MW (c); MW (w); Matt Wagner painted cover 4.00
❑3, Jan 1999; MW (c); MW (w); Matt Wagner painted cover 4.00
❑4, Feb 1999; MW (c); MW (w); Matt Wagner painted cover 4.00

Grendel Classics
Dark Horse

❑1, Jul 1995; cardstock cover 3.95
❑2, Aug 1995; cardstock cover 3.95

Grendel Cycle
Dark Horse

❑1, Oct 1995; prestige format; background information on the various series including a timeline 5.95

Grendel: Devil By the Deed
Comico

❑1, Jul 1993; MW (a); graphic novel; reprints Comico one-shot; cardstock cover 4.00
❑1/Ltd.; MW (w); MW (a); Limited to 2000 .... 8.00
❑1/2nd, Jul 1993; MW (w); MW (a); reprints Comico one-shot; cardstock cover 3.95

Grendel: Devil Child
Dark Horse

❑1, Jun 1999; cardstock cover 2.95
❑2, Aug 1999; cardstock cover 2.95

Grendel: Devil Quest
Dark Horse

❑1, Nov 1995; prestige format; NN; Matt Wagner painted cover; Reprints backups from various Grendel Tales Series; One-shot 4.95

Grendel: Devil's Legacy
Comico

❑1, Mar 2000, Matt Wagner painted cover; Reprints Grendel (2nd Series) #1 .... 2.95
❑2, Apr 2000, Matt Wagner painted cover; Reprints Grendel (2nd Series) #2 .... 2.95
❑3, Apr 2000, Matt Wagner painted cover; Reprints Grendel (2nd Series) #3 .... 2.95
❑4, Jun 2000, Matt Wagner painted cover; Reprints Grendel (2nd Series) #4 .... 2.95
❑5, Jul 2000, Matt Wagner painted cover; Reprints Grendel (2nd Series) #5 .... 2.95
❑6, Aug 2000, Matt Wagner painted cover; Reprints Grendel (2nd Series) #6 .... 2.95
❑7, Sep 2000, Matt Wagner painted cover; Reprints Grendel (2nd Series) #7 .... 2.95
❑8, Oct 2000, Matt Wagner painted cover; Reprints Grendel (2nd Series) #8 .... 2.99
❑9, Nov 2000, Matt Wagner painted cover; Reprints Grendel (2nd Series) #9 .... 2.99
❑10, Dec 2000, Matt Wagner painted cover; Reprints Grendel (2nd Series) #10 .... 2.99
❑11, Jan 2001, Matt Wagner painted cover; Reprints Grendel (2nd Series) #11 .... 2.99
❑12, Feb 2001, Matt Wagner painted cover; Reprints Grendel (2nd Series) #12 .... 2.99

Grendel: Devil's Reign
Dark Horse

❑1, May 2004 .... 3.50
❑2, Aug 2004 .... 3.50
❑3 2004 .... 3.50
❑4 2004 .... 3.50
❑5 2004 .... 3.50
❑6 .... 3.50
❑7 2005 .... 3.50

Grendel: Devil's Vagary
Comico

❑1, 16 pages; B&w and red 8.00

Grendel: God & the Devil
Dark Horse

❑1, Feb 2003 .... 3.50
❑2, Mar 2003 .... 3.50
❑3, Apr 2003 .... 3.50
❑4, May 2003 .... 3.50
❑5, Jun 2003 .... 3.50
❑6, Jul 2003 .... 3.50
❑7, Aug 2003 .... 3.50
❑8, Sep 2003 .... 3.50
❑9, Nov 2003 .... 3.50
❑10, Dec 2003 .... 4.99

Grendel: Past Prime
Dark Horse

❑1, Jul 2000; Matt Wagner painted cover; Text novel 14.95

Grendel: Red, White & Black
Dark Horse

❑1, Sep 2002; Matt wagner painted cover 4.99
❑2, Oct 2002; Matt Wagner painted cover 4.99
❑3, Nov 2002; Matt Wagner painted cover 4.99
❑4, Dec 2002; Matt Wagner painted cover 4.99

Grendel Tales: Devils and Deaths
Dark Horse

❑1, Oct 1994; Matt Wagner painted cover; Batman/Grendel (2nd Series) prequel Devil Quest installment 2.95

Green Lantern/Atom

Part of GL: Circle of Fire mini-series
©DC

Green Lantern: Circle of Fire

Kyle's big crossover with galactic heroes
©DC

Green Lantern Corps

Picks up numbering from GL (2nd series)
©DC

Green Lantern Corps Quarterly

Anthology of intergalactic adventures
©DC

Green Lantern: Emerald Dawn

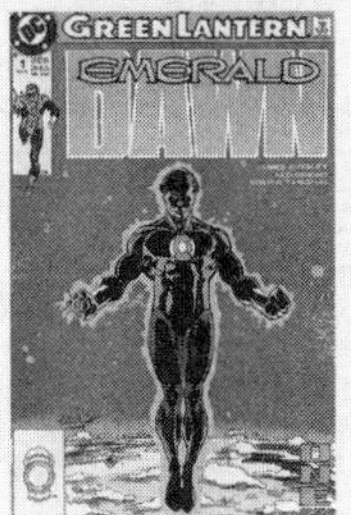

New origin gives Hal Jordan feet of clay
©DC

N-MINT

❑2, Nov 1994; Matt Wagner painted cover; Batman/Grendel (2nd Series) prequel Devil Quest installment ... 2.95

Grendel Tales: Devil's Choices
Dark Horse

❑1, Mar 1995 ... 2.95
❑2, Apr 1995 ... 2.95
❑3, May 1995 ... 2.95
❑4, Jun 1995 ... 2.95

Grendel Tales: Devil's Hammer
Dark Horse

❑1, Feb 1994, Matt Wagner and Rob Walton painted cover; Batman/Grendel (2nd Series) prequel ... 2.95
❑2, Mar 1994, Matt Wanger and Rob Walton painted cover; Batman/Grendel (2nd Series) prequel ... 2.95
❑3, Apr 1994, Matt Wagner painted cover; Batman/Grendel (2nd Series) prequel ... 2.95

Grendel Tales: Four Devils, One Hell
Dark Horse

❑1, Aug 1993, MW (c); JRo (w); cardstock cover ... 3.00
❑2, Sep 1993, MW (c); JRo (w); cardstock cover ... 3.00
❑3, Oct 1993, MW (c); JRo (w); cardstock cover ... 3.00
❑4, Oct 1993, MW (c); JRo (w); cardstock cover ... 3.00
❑5, Dec 1993, MW (c); JRo (w); cardstock cover ... 3.00
❑6, Jan 1994, MW (c); JRo (w); cardstock cover; Grendel-Prime returns ... 3.00

Grendel Tales: Homecoming
Dark Horse

❑1, Dec 1994; cardstock cover ... 2.95
❑2, Jan 1995; cardstock cover ... 2.95
❑3, Feb 1995; cardstock cover ... 2.95

Grendel Tales: The Devil in Our Midst
Dark Horse

❑1, May 1994 ... 2.95
❑2, Jun 1994; Matt Wagner painted cover; Batman/Grendel (2nd Series) prequel Devil's Quest installment ... 2.95
❑3, Jul 1994; Matt Wagner painted cover; Batman/Grendel (2nd Series) prequel Devil's Quest installment ... 2.95
❑4, Aug 1994; Matt Wagner painted cover; Batman/Grendel (2nd Series) prequel Devil's Quest installment ... 2.95
❑5, Sep 1994; Matt Wagner painted cover; Batman/Grendel (2nd Series) prequel Devil's Quest installment ... 2.95

Grendel Tales: The Devil May Care
Dark Horse

❑1, Dec 1995; cardstock cover ... 2.95
❑2, Jan 1996; cardstock cover ... 2.95
❑3, Feb 1996; cardstock cover ... 2.95
❑4, Mar 1996; cardstock cover ... 2.95
❑5, Apr 1996; cardstock cover ... 2.95
❑6, May 1996; cardstock cover ... 2.95

Grendel Tales: The Devil's Apprentice
Dark Horse

❑1, Sep 1997 ... 2.95
❑2, Oct 1997; Matt Wagner painted cover ... 2.95
❑3, Nov 1997; Matt Wagner painted cover ... 2.95

N-MINT

Grendel: The Devil Inside
Comico

❑1, Sep 2001; Dark Horse publishes; reprints of Comico Grendel issues #13-15 ... 2.99
❑2, Oct 2001 ... 2.99
❑3, Nov 2001 ... 2.99

Grendel: War Child
Dark Horse

❑1, Aug 1992; MW (w); MW (a); Part 41 of Grendel total series ... 3.50
❑2, Sep 1992; MW (w); Part 42 of Grendel total series ... 3.00
❑3, Oct 1992; MW (w); Part 43 of Grendel total series ... 3.00
❑4, Nov 1992; MW (w); Part 44 of Grendel total series ... 3.00
❑5, Dec 1992; MW (c); MW (w); Part 45 of Grendel total series ... 3.00
❑6, Jan 1993; MW (c); MW (w); Part 46 of Grendel total series ... 2.50
❑7, Jan 1993; MW (c); MW (w); Part 47 of Grendel total series ... 2.50
❑8, Mar 1993; MW (c); MW (w); Part 48 of Grendel total series ... 2.50
❑9, Apr 1993; MW (c); MW (w); Part 49 of Grendel total series ... 2.50
❑10, Jun 1993; Double-size; MW (c); MW (w); Part 50 of Grendel total series ... 3.75

Grenuord
Fantagraphics

❑1, Sep 2005 ... 5.95

Grey
Viz

❑1, Oct 1989; Introduction by Harlan Ellison ... 4.00
❑2, Nov 1989 ... 3.50
❑3, Dec 1989 ... 3.50
❑4, Jan 1989 ... 3.50
❑5, Feb 1989 ... 3.50
❑6, Mar 1989 ... 3.25
❑7, Apr 1989 ... 3.25
❑8, May 1989 ... 3.25
❑9, Jun 1989 ... 3.25

Grey Legacy
Fragile Elite

❑1, b&w ... 2.75

Greylore
Sirius Comics

❑1, Dec 1985 ... 1.50
❑2, Jan 1986 ... 1.50
❑3, Jan 1986 ... 1.50
❑4, Jan 1986 ... 1.50
❑5, Jan 1986 ... 1.50

Greymatter
Alaffinity

❑1, Oct 1993 ... 2.95
❑2, Nov 1993; b&w ... 2.95
❑3, Dec 1993 ... 2.95
❑4, Jan 1994, b&w ... 2.95
❑5, Apr 1994, b&w ... 2.95
❑6, Sep 1994, b&w; cover forms diptych with #7 ... 2.95
❑7, Oct 1994, b&w; cover forms diptych with #6 ... 2.95
❑8, Mar 1995 ... 2.95
❑9, Dec 1995 ... 2.95

N-MINT

❑10, Mar 1996 ... 2.95
❑11, Jun 1996; Wraparound cover ... 2.95

Greyshirt: Indigo Sunset
DC / America's Best Comics

❑1, Dec 2001 ... 3.50
❑2, Jan 2002 ... 3.50
❑3, Feb 2002 ... 3.50
❑4, Apr 2002 ... 3.50
❑5, Jun 2002 ... 3.50
❑6, Aug 2002 ... 3.50

Griffi
Slave Labor

❑1, Jul 1988, b&w ... 1.75
❑1/2nd, Apr 1989, b&w; 2nd printing ... 1.75
❑2, Dec 1988 ... 1.75
❑3, Apr 1989 ... 1.75

Griffin
DC

❑1, Nov 1991; O: The Griffin ... 4.95
❑2, Dec 1991 ... 4.95
❑3, Jan 1991 ... 4.95
❑4, Feb 1991 ... 4.95
❑5, Mar 1991 ... 4.95
❑6, Apr 1991 ... 4.95

Griffin (Amaze Ink)
Slave Labor

❑1, May 1997 ... 2.95

Griffith Observatory
Fantagraphics

❑1; NN; b&w ... 4.95

Grifter and the Mask
Dark Horse

❑1, Sep 1996; crossover with Image ... 2.50
❑2, Oct 1996; crossover with Image ... 2.50

Grifter/Badrock
Image

❑1/A, Oct 1995 ... 2.50
❑1/B, Oct 1995; alternate cover ... 2.50
❑2/A, Nov 1995; flipbook with Badrock #2A ... 2.50
❑2/B, Nov 1995; flipbook with Badrock #2A ... 2.50

Grifter: One Shot
Image

❑1, Jan 1995 ... 4.95

Grifter/Shi
Image

❑1, Apr 1996; cover says Mar, indicia says Apr; crossover with Crusade ... 2.95
❑2, May 1996; crossover with Crusade ... 2.95

Grifter
Image

❑1, May 1995; bound-in trading cards ... 2.50
❑1/Direct ed., May 1995; Direct Market edition; Direct Market edition; Includes trading card ... 4.00
❑2, Jun 1995 ... 2.00
❑3, Jul 1995; indicia says Jul, cover says Aug ... 2.00
❑4, Aug 1995 ... 2.00
❑5, Oct 1995; indicia says Oct, cover says Jun ... 2.00
❑6, Nov 1995 ... 2.00
❑7, Dec 1995 ... 2.00
❑8, Jan 1996 ... 2.00

Other grades: Multiply price above by 5/6 for VF/NM • 2/3 for VERY FINE • 1/3 for FINE • 1/5 for VERY GOOD • 1/8 for GOOD

❑9, Feb 1996 ... 2.00
❑10, Mar 1996; Final Issue ... 2.00

Grifter
Image

❑1, Jul 1996 ... 2.50
❑2, Aug 1996 ... 2.50
❑3, Sep 1996 ... 2.50
❑4, Oct 1996 ... 2.50
❑5, Nov 1996 ... 2.50
❑6, Dec 1996, cover says Nov, indicia says Dec ... 2.50
❑7, Jan 1997 ... 2.50
❑8, Feb 1997 ... 2.50
❑9, Mar 1997 ... 2.50
❑10, Apr 1997 ... 2.50
❑11, May 1997 ... 2.50
❑12, Jun 1997 ... 2.50
❑13, Jul 1997 ... 2.50
❑14, Aug 1997, Final Issue ... 2.50

Grim Ghost
Atlas-Seaboard

❑1, Jan 1975; O: Grim Ghost. 1: Grim Ghost ... 10.00
❑2, Mar 1975 ... 5.00
❑3, Jul 1975 ... 5.00

Grimjack
First

❑1, Aug 1984 ... 2.50
❑2, Sep 1984 ... 2.00
❑3, Oct 1984 ... 2.00
❑4, Nov 1984; Munden's Bar backup ... 2.00
❑5, Dec 1984; Munden's Bar backup story 2.00
❑6, Jan 1985; Munden's Bar backup story 2.00
❑7, Feb 1985 ... 2.00
❑8, Mar 1985 ... 2.00
❑9, Apr 1985 ... 2.00
❑10, May 1985 ... 2.00
❑11, Jun 1985 ... 2.00
❑12, Jul 1985 ... 2.00
❑13, Aug 1985 ... 2.00
❑14, Sep 1985 ... 2.00
❑15, Oct 1985 ... 2.00
❑16, Nov 1985 ... 2.00
❑17, Dec 1985 ... 2.00
❑18, Jan 1986 ... 2.00
❑19, Feb 1986 ... 2.00
❑20, Mar 1986 ... 2.00
❑21, Apr 1986 ... 1.50
❑22, May 1986 ... 1.50
❑23, Jun 1986 ... 1.50
❑24, Jul 1986 ... 1.50
❑25, Aug 1986 ... 1.50
❑26, Sep 1986 TS (a); A: Teenage Mutant Ninja Turtles ... 3.00
❑27, Oct 1986 ... 1.50
❑28, Nov 1986 ... 1.50
❑29, Dec 1986 ... 1.50
❑30, Jan 1987; Dynamo Joe ... 1.50
❑31, Feb 1987 ... 1.50
❑32, Mar 1987 ... 1.50
❑33, Apr 1987 ... 1.50
❑34, May 1987 ... 1.50
❑35, Jun 1987 ... 1.50
❑36, Jul 1987; D: Grimjack ... 1.50
❑37, Aug 1987 ... 1.50
❑38, Sep 1987 ... 1.50
❑39, Oct 1987 ... 1.50
❑40, Nov 1987 ... 1.95
❑41, Dec 1987 ... 1.95
❑42, Jan 1988 ... 1.95
❑43, Feb 1988 ... 1.95
❑44, Mar 1988 ... 1.95
❑45, Apr 1988 ... 1.95
❑46, May 1988 ... 1.95
❑47, Jun 1988 ... 1.95
❑48, Jul 1988 ... 1.95
❑49, Aug 1988 ... 1.95
❑50, Sep 1988 ... 1.95
❑51, Oct 1988 ... 1.95
❑52, Nov 1988 ... 1.95
❑53, Dec 1988 ... 1.95
❑54, Jan 1989 ... 1.95
❑55, Feb 1989; new Grimjack ... 1.95
❑56, Mar 1989 ... 1.95
❑57, Apr 1989 ... 1.95
❑58, May 1989 ... 1.95
❑59, Jun 1989 ... 1.95
❑60, Jul 1989 ... 1.95
❑61, Aug 1989 ... 1.95
❑62, Sep 1989 ... 1.95
❑63, Oct 1989 ... 1.95
❑64, Nov 1989 ... 1.95
❑65, Dec 1989 ... 1.95
❑66, Jan 1990 ... 1.95
❑67, Feb 1990 ... 1.95
❑68, Mar 1990 ... 1.95
❑69, Apr 1990 ... 1.95
❑70, May 1990 ... 1.95
❑71, Jun 1990 ... 2.00
❑72, Jul 1990 ... 2.00
❑73, Aug 1990 ... 2.00
❑74, Sep 1990 ... 2.00
❑75, Oct 1990; Giant 75th issue ... 3.50
❑76, Nov 1990 ... 2.00
❑77, Dec 1990 ... 2.00
❑78, Jan 1991 ... 2.00
❑79, Feb 1991 ... 2.00
❑80, Mar 1991 ... 2.00
❑81, Apr 1991; Final Issue ... 2.00

Grimjack Casefiles
First

❑1, Nov 1990; Reprints ... 1.95
❑2, Dec 1990; Reprints ... 1.95
❑3, Jan 1991; Reprints ... 1.95
❑4, Feb 1991; Reprints ... 1.95
❑5, Mar 1991; Reprints ... 1.95

Grimjack: Killer Instinct
Idea & Design Works

❑1, ca. 2005 ... 3.99
❑2, ca. 2005 ... 3.99
❑3, ca. 2005 ... 3.99
❑4, ca. 2005 ... 3.99
❑5, May 2005 ... 3.99
❑6, Sep 2005 ... 3.99

Grimlock
Asylum

❑1, Jan 1996, b&w ... 2.95
❑2, ca. 1996, b&w; no cover date ... 2.95
❑3, ca. 1996, b&w ... 2.95

Grimmax
Defiant

❑0, Aug 1994; DC (a); no cover price ... 1.00

Grimm's Ghost Stories
Gold Key

❑1, Jan 1972 ... 14.00
❑2, Mar 1972 ... 8.00
❑3, May 1972 ... 8.00
❑4, Jul 1972 ... 8.00
❑5, Sep 1972, AW (a) ... 8.00
❑6, Nov 1972, Misprinted editions duplicated stories; Misprinted editions duplicated stories ... 6.00
❑7, Jan 1973 ... 6.00
❑8, Mar 1973, AW (a) ... 6.00
❑9, May 1973 ... 6.00
❑10, Jul 1973 ... 6.00
❑11, Aug 1973 ... 4.00
❑12, Sep 1973 ... 4.00
❑13, Nov 1973 ... 4.00
❑14, Jan 1974 ... 4.00
❑15, Mar 1974 ... 4.00
❑16, May 1974 ... 4.00
❑17, Jul 1974 ... 4.00
❑18, Aug 1974 ... 4.00
❑19, Sep 1974 ... 4.00
❑20, Nov 1974 ... 4.00
❑21, Jan 1975 ... 4.00
❑22, Mar 1975 ... 4.00
❑23, May 1975, (c) ... 4.00
❑24, Jul 1975 ... 4.00
❑25, Aug 1975, (c) ... 4.00
❑26, Sep 1975 ... 4.00
❑27, Nov 1975 ... 4.00
❑28, Jan 1976 ... 4.00
❑29, Mar 1976 ... 4.00
❑30, May 1976, (c) ... 4.00
❑31, Jul 1976 ... 3.00
❑32, Aug 1976 ... 3.00
❑33, Sep 1976 ... 3.00
❑34, Oct 1976 ... 3.00
❑35, Nov 1976 ... 3.00
❑36, Mar 1977 ... 3.00
❑37, May 1977, (c); GK (a); Captain Marvel "Killer Bee and Son!" Hostess ad by Kane never published in Marvel Comics ... 3.00
❑38, Jul 1977 ... 3.00
❑39, Aug 1977 ... 3.00
❑40, Sep 1977, (c) ... 3.00
❑41, Oct 1977, (c); BMc (a) ... 3.00
❑42, Nov 1977, (c); DS (a) ... 3.00
❑43, Mar 1978 ... 4.00
❑44, May 1978 ... 4.00
❑45, Jul 1978 ... 3.00
❑46, Sep 1978 ... 3.00
❑47, Oct 1978 ... 3.00
❑48, Nov 1978, (c) ... 3.00
❑49, Mar 1979, (c) ... 3.00
❑50, May 1979 ... 3.00
❑51, Jul 1979 ... 3.00
❑52, Sep 1979 ... 3.00
❑53, Oct 1979 ... 3.00
❑54, Nov 1979, Goes on hiatus ... 3.00
❑55, Apr 1981, Returns as Whitman ... 5.00
❑56, Oct 1981 ... 5.00
❑57, Dec 1981, (c) ... 5.00
❑58, Feb 1982, (c) ... 5.00
❑59, May 1982, (c) ... 5.00
❑60, Jun 1982, Final Issue ... 5.00

Grimoire
Speakeasy Comics

❑1, Mar 2005 ... 2.99
❑2, Apr 2005 ... 2.99
❑3, May 2005 ... 2.99
❑4, Jul 2005 ... 2.99
❑5, Oct 2005 ... 2.99

Gringo
Caliber

❑1, b&w ... 1.95

Grips
Silverwolf

❑1, Sep 1986 ... 3.00
❑1/Ltd.; Signed, Numbered edition (limited to 350) ... 9.95
❑2, Oct 1986 ... 2.50
❑3, Nov 1986 ... 2.50
❑4, Dec 1986 ... 2.50

Grips Adventures
Greater Mercury

❑1, May 1989, b&w; Reprints Legion X-I #1 ... 2.50
❑2, Aug 1989, b&w ... 2.50
❑3, Nov 1989, b&w ... 2.50
❑4, Feb 1990, b&w ... 2.50
❑5, May 1990, b&w ... 2.50
❑6, Sep 1990, b&w ... 2.50
❑7, Dec 1990, b&w ... 2.50
❑8, Mar 1991, b&w ... 2.50

Grips
Greater Mercury

❑1 ... 2.00
❑2, Apr 1990, b&w ... 2.00
❑3, Jul 1990 ... 2.00
❑4, Aug 1990 ... 2.00
❑5, Oct 1990, b&w ... 2.00
❑6, Nov 1990 ... 2.00
❑7, Mar 1991, b&w ... 2.00
❑8, ca. 1991 ... 1.95
❑9, ca. 1991 ... 1.95
❑10, Dec 1991, b&w ... 2.50
❑11, ca. 1992 ... 2.50
❑12, ca. 1992 ... 2.50

Grip: The Strange World of Men
DC / Vertigo

❑1, Jan 2002 ... 2.50
❑2, Feb 2002 ... 2.50
❑3, Mar 2002 ... 2.50
❑4, Apr 2002 ... 2.50
❑5, May 2002 ... 2.50

Grit Bath
Fantagraphics

❑1, Jul 1993, b&w ... 2.50
❑2; no cover price ... 2.50
❑3, Aug 1994; no cover price ... 2.50

Groo
Image

❑1, Dec 1994 SA (c); ME (w); SA (a) ... 4.00

Other grades: Multiply price above by 5/6 for VF/NM • 2/3 for VERY FINE • 1/3 for FINE • 1/5 for VERY GOOD • 1/8 for GOOD

Green Lantern: Ganthet's Tale

Larry Niven writes wandering Guardian tale
©DC

Grendel

Matt Wagner's generation-spanning vigilante
©Comico

Grendel: Black, White, & Red

Other artists' takes on Wagner's creation
©Dark Horse

Grendel: The Devil Inside

Reprints of Comico issues
©Comico

Greyshirt: Indigo Sunset

Rick Veitch spin-off from Tomorrow Stories
©DC

N-MINT

❑2, Jan 1995; SA (c); ME (w); SA (a); indicia says issue #1 ... 2.50
❑3, Feb 1995 SA (c); ME (w); SA (a) ... 2.50
❑4, Mar 1995 SA (c); ME (w); SA (a) ... 2.00
❑5, Apr 1995 SA (c); ME (w); SA (a) ... 2.00
❑6, May 1995 SA (c); ME (w); SA (a) ... 2.00
❑7, Jun 1995 SA (c); ME (w); SA (a) ... 2.00
❑8, Jul 1995 SA (c); ME (w); SA (a) ... 2.00
❑9, Aug 1995 SA (c); ME (w); SA (a) ... 2.25
❑10, Sep 1995 SA (c); ME (w); SA (a) ... 2.25
❑11, Oct 1995 SA (c); ME (w); SA (a) ... 2.25
❑12, Nov 1995; SA (c); ME (w); SA (a); Final Issue ... 2.25

Groo
Dark Horse

❑1, Jan 1998 ... 2.95
❑2, Feb 1998 ... 2.95
❑3, Mar 1998 ... 2.95
❑4, Apr 1998 ... 2.95

Groo and Rufferto
Dark Horse

❑1, Dec 1998; Rufferto sent through time ... 2.95
❑2, Jan 1999 ... 2.95
❑3, Feb 1999 ... 2.95
❑4, Mar 1999 ... 2.95

Groo Chronicles
Marvel / Epic

❑1, Jun 1989; squarebound ... 3.50
❑2 1989; squarebound ... 3.50
❑3 1989; squarebound ... 3.50
❑4; squarebound ... 3.50
❑5; squarebound ... 3.50
❑6, Feb 1990; squarebound ... 3.50

Groo: Death & Taxes
Dark Horse

❑1, Dec 2001 ... 2.99
❑2, Jan 2002 ... 2.99
❑3, Feb 2002 ... 2.99
❑4, Mar 2002 ... 2.99

Groo: Mightier than the Sword
Dark Horse

❑1, Jan 2000 ... 2.95
❑2, Feb 2000 ... 2.95
❑3, Mar 2000 ... 2.95
❑4, Apr 2000 ... 2.95

Groo Special
Eclipse

❑Special 1, Oct 1984; SA (c); ME (w); SA (a); Reprints; 1: Groo; Eclipse publishes; Includes reprints ... 3.00

Groo The Wanderer
Pacific

❑1, Dec 1982; SA (c); ME (w); SA (a); 1: Groo. 1: Minstrel. 1: Sage ... 6.50
❑2, Feb 1983 SA (c); ME (w); SA (a) ... 4.50
❑3, Apr 1983 SA (c); ME (w); SA (a) ... 3.75
❑4, Sep 1983 SA (c); ME (w); SA (a) ... 3.50
❑5, Oct 1983 SA (c); ME (w); SA (a) ... 3.00
❑6, Dec 1983 SA (c); ME (w); SA (a) ... 3.00
❑7, Feb 1984 SA (c); ME (w); SA (a) ... 3.00
❑8, Apr 1984 SA (c); ME (w); SA (a) ... 3.00

Groo the Wanderer
Marvel / Epic

❑1, Mar 1985, SA (c); ME (w); SA (a); 1: Minstrel ... 5.00

N-MINT

❑2, Apr 1985, SA (c); ME (w); SA (a) ... 4.00
❑3, May 1985, SA (c); ME (w); SA (a) ... 3.50
❑4, Jun 1985, SA (c); ME (w); SA (a) ... 3.00
❑5, Jul 1985, SA (c); ME (w); SA (a) ... 3.00
❑6, Aug 1985, SA (c); ME (w); SA (a) ... 3.00
❑7, Sep 1985, SA (c); ME (w); SA (a) ... 3.00
❑8, Oct 1985, SA (c); ME (w); SA (a) ... 3.00
❑9, Nov 1985, SA (c); ME (w); SA (a) ... 3.00
❑10, Dec 1985, SA (c); ME (w); SA (a) ... 3.00
❑11, Jan 1986, SA (c); ME (w); SA (a) ... 2.50
❑12, Feb 1986, SA (c); ME (w); SA (a) ... 2.50
❑13, Mar 1986, SA (c); ME (w); SA (a) ... 2.50
❑14, Apr 1986, SA (c); ME (w); SA (a) ... 2.50
❑15, May 1986, SA (c); ME (w); SA (a) ... 2.50
❑16, Jun 1986, SA (c); ME (w); SA (a) ... 2.50
❑17, Jul 1986, SA (c); ME (w); SA (a) ... 2.50
❑18, Aug 1986, SA (c); ME (w); SA (a) ... 2.50
❑19, Sep 1986, SA (c); ME (w); SA (a) ... 2.50
❑20, Oct 1986, SA (c); ME (w); SA (a) ... 2.50
❑21, Nov 1986, SA (c); ME (w); SA (a) ... 2.50
❑22, Dec 1986, SA (c); ME (w); SA (a) ... 2.50
❑23, Jan 1987, SA (c); ME (w); SA (a) ... 2.50
❑24, Feb 1987, SA (c); ME (w); SA (a) ... 2.50
❑25, Mar 1987, SA (c); ME (w); SA (a) ... 2.50
❑26, Apr 1987, SA (c); ME (w); SA (a) ... 2.50
❑27, May 1987, SA (c); ME (w); SA (a) ... 2.50
❑28, Jun 1987, SA (c); ME (w); SA (a) ... 2.50
❑29, Jul 1987, SA (c); ME (w); SA (a) ... 2.50
❑30, Aug 1987, SA (c); ME (w); SA (a) ... 2.50
❑31, Sep 1987, SA (c); ME (w); SA (a) ... 2.00
❑32, Oct 1987, SA (c); ME (w); SA (a) ... 2.00
❑33, Nov 1987, SA (c); ME (w); SA (a) ... 2.00
❑34, Dec 1987, SA (c); ME (w); SA (a) ... 2.00
❑35, Jan 1988, SA (c); ME (w); SA (a) ... 2.00
❑36, Feb 1988, SA (c); ME (w); SA (a) ... 2.00
❑37, Mar 1988, SA (c); ME (w); SA (a) ... 2.00
❑38, Apr 1988, SA (c); ME (w); SA (a) ... 2.00
❑39, May 1988, SA (c); ME (w); SA (a) ... 2.00
❑40, Jun 1988, SA (c); ME (w); SA (a) ... 2.00
❑41, Jul 1988, SA (c); ME (w); SA (a) ... 2.00
❑42, Aug 1988, SA (c); ME (w); SA (a) ... 2.00
❑43, Sep 1988, SA (c); ME (w); SA (a) ... 2.00
❑44, Oct 1988, SA (c); ME (w); SA (a) ... 2.00
❑45, Nov 1988, SA (c); ME (w); SA (a) ... 2.00
❑46, Dec 1988, SA (c); ME (w); SA (a) ... 2.00
❑47, Jan 1989, SA (c); ME (w); SA (a) ... 2.00
❑48, Feb 1989, SA (c); ME (w); SA (a) ... 2.00
❑49, Mar 1989, SA (c); ME (w); SA (a); A: Chakaal ... 2.00
❑50, Apr 1989, Giant-size SA (c); ME (w); SA (a); A: Chakaal ... 3.00
❑51, May 1989, SA (c); ME (w); SA (a); A: Chakaal ... 2.00
❑52, Jun 1989, SA (c); ME (w); SA (a); A: Chakaal ... 2.00
❑53, Jul 1989, SA (c); ME (w); SA (a); A: Chakaal ... 2.00
❑54, Aug 1989, SA (c); ME (w); SA (a) ... 2.00
❑55, Sep 1989, SA (c); ME (w); SA (a) ... 2.00
❑56, Oct 1989, SA (c); ME (w); SA (a) ... 2.00
❑57, Nov 1989, SA (c); ME (w); SA (a) ... 2.00
❑58, Nov 1989, SA (c); ME (w); SA (a) ... 2.00
❑59, Dec 1989, SA (c); ME (w); SA (a) ... 2.00
❑60, Dec 1989, SA (c); ME (w); SA (a) ... 2.00
❑61, Jan 1990, SA (c); ME (w); SA (a) ... 2.00
❑62, Feb 1990, SA (c); ME (w); SA (a) ... 2.00
❑63, Mar 1990, SA (c); ME (w); SA (a) ... 2.00

N-MINT

❑64, Apr 1990, SA (c); ME (w); SA (a) ... 2.00
❑65, May 1990, SA (c); ME (w); SA (a) ... 2.00
❑66, Jun 1990, SA (c); ME (w); SA (a) ... 2.00
❑67, Jul 1990, SA (c); ME (w); SA (a) ... 2.00
❑68, Aug 1990, SA (c); ME (w); SA (a) ... 2.00
❑69, Sep 1990, SA (c); ME (w); SA (a) ... 2.00
❑70, Oct 1990, SA (c); ME (w); SA (a) ... 2.00
❑71, Nov 1990, SA (c); ME (w); SA (a) ... 1.50
❑72, Dec 1990, SA (c); ME (w); SA (a) ... 1.50
❑73, Jan 1991, SA (c); ME (w); SA (a) ... 1.50
❑74, Feb 1991, SA (c); ME (w); SA (a) ... 1.50
❑75, Mar 1991, SA (c); ME (w); SA (a) ... 1.50
❑76, Apr 1991, SA (c); ME (w); SA (a) ... 1.50
❑77, May 1991, SA (c); ME (w); SA (a) ... 1.50
❑78, Jun 1991, SA (c); ME (w); SA (a); bookburners ... 1.50
❑79, Jul 1991, SA (c); ME (w); SA (a) ... 1.50
❑80, Aug 1991, SA (c); ME (w); SA (a) ... 1.50
❑81, Sep 1991, SA (c); ME (w); SA (a) ... 1.50
❑82, Oct 1991, SA (c); ME (w); SA (a) ... 1.50
❑83, Nov 1991, SA (c); ME (w); SA (a) ... 1.50
❑84, Dec 1991, SA (c); ME (w); SA (a) ... 1.50
❑85, Jan 1992, SA (c); ME (w); SA (a) ... 1.50
❑86, Feb 1992, SA (c); ME (w); SA (a) ... 1.50
❑87, Mar 1992, SA (c); ME (w); SA (a) ... 2.25
❑88, Apr 1992, SA (c); ME (w); SA (a) ... 2.25
❑89, May 1992, SA (c); ME (w); SA (a) ... 2.25
❑90, Jun 1992, SA (c); ME (w); SA (a) ... 2.25
❑91, Jul 1992, SA (c); ME (w); SA (a) ... 2.25
❑92, Aug 1992, SA (c); ME (w); SA (a); Groo finds fountain of youth ... 2.25
❑93, Sep 1992, SA (c); ME (w); SA (a); Groo finds fountain of youth ... 2.25
❑94, Oct 1992, SA (c); ME (w); SA (a) ... 2.25
❑95, Nov 1992, SA (c); ME (w); SA (a) ... 2.25
❑96, Dec 1992, SA (c); ME (w); SA (a) ... 2.25
❑97, Jan 1993, SA (c); ME (w); SA (a) ... 2.25
❑98, Feb 1993, SA (c); ME (w); SA (a) ... 2.25
❑99, Mar 1993, SA (c); ME (w); SA (a) ... 2.25
❑100, Apr 1993, 100th anniversary issue; SA (c); ME (w); SA (a); Groo learns to read ... 2.95
❑101, May 1993, SA (c); ME (w); SA (a) 2.25
❑102, Jun 1993, SA (c); ME (w); SA (a) 2.25
❑103, Aug 1993, SA (c); ME (w); SA (a) 2.25
❑104, Sep 1993, SA (c); ME (w); SA (a); O: Rufferto (Groo's Dog). ... 2.25
❑105, Oct 1993, SA (c); ME (w); SA (a). 2.25
❑106, Nov 1993, SA (c); ME (w); SA (a) 2.25
❑107, Dec 1993, SA (c); ME (w); SA (a) 2.25
❑108, Jan 1994, SA (c); ME (w); SA (a). 2.25
❑109, Feb 1994, SA (c); ME (w); SA (a). 2.25
❑110, Mar 1994, SA (c); ME (w); SA (a) 2.25
❑111, Apr 1994, SA (c); ME (w); SA (a) 2.25
❑112, May 1994, SA (c); ME (w); SA (a) 2.25
❑113, Jun 1994, SA (c); ME (w); SA (a) 2.25
❑114, Jul 1994, SA (c); ME (w); SA (a). 2.25
❑115, Aug 1994, SA (c); ME (w); SA (a) 2.25
❑116, Sep 1994, SA (c); ME (w); SA (a) 2.25
❑117, Oct 1994, SA (c); ME (w); SA (a). 2.25
❑118, Nov 1994, SA (c); ME (w); SA (a) 2.25
❑119, Dec 1994, SA (c); ME (w); SA (a) 2.25
❑120, Jan 1995, SA (c); ME (w); SA (a). 2.25

Grootlore
Fantagraphics

❑1, b&w ... 2.00
❑2, b&w ... 2.00

Other grades: Multiply price above by 5/6 for VF/NM • 2/3 for VERY FINE • 1/3 for FINE • 1/5 for VERY GOOD • 1/8 for GOOD

Grootlore
Fantagraphics

- ❑1, May 1991, b&w ... 2.00
- ❑2, b&w ... 2.00
- ❑3 ... 2.25

Groovy
Marvel

- ❑1, Mar 1968, A: Monkees ... 25.00
- ❑2, May 1968 ... 16.00
- ❑3, Jul 1968, Marvel Comics Group Publisher ... 16.00

Gross Point
DC

- ❑1, Aug 1997 ... 2.50
- ❑2, Sep 1997 ... 2.50
- ❑3, Oct 1997 ... 2.50
- ❑4, Nov 1997 ... 2.50
- ❑5, Dec 1997 ... 2.50
- ❑6, Dec 1997 ... 2.50
- ❑7, Jan 1998 ... 2.50
- ❑8, Feb 1998 ... 2.50
- ❑9, Mar 1998 ... 2.50
- ❑10, Apr 1998 ... 2.50
- ❑11, May 1998 ... 2.50
- ❑12, Jun 1998 ... 2.50
- ❑13, Jul 1998 ... 2.50
- ❑14, Aug 1998, Final Issue ... 2.50

Grounded
Image

- ❑1, Sep 2005 ... 5.00
- ❑1/Variant, Sep 2005 ... 4.00
- ❑2, Oct 2005 ... 2.95
- ❑3, Sep 2005 ... 2.99
- ❑4, Dec 2005 ... 2.99
- ❑5, Apr 2006 ... 2.99
- ❑16, Sep 2006 ... 3.50

Ground Pound! Comix
Blackthorne

- ❑1, Jan 1987 ... 2.00

Ground Zero
Eternity

- ❑1, Oct 1991, b&w ... 2.50
- ❑2, b&w ... 2.50

Group LaRue
Innovation

- ❑1, Aug 1989 ... 1.95
- ❑2, Oct 1989 ... 1.95
- ❑3 ... 1.95
- ❑4 ... 1.95

Growing Up Enchanted
Too Hip Gotta Go

- ❑1, Jul 2002, b&w ... 2.95
- ❑2, Oct 2002, b&w ... 2.95
- ❑3, Mar 2003, b&w ... 2.95

Grrl Scouts
Oni

- ❑1, Mar 1999, b&w ... 2.95
- ❑2, Jun 1999, b&w ... 2.95
- ❑3, Sep 1999, b&w ... 2.95

Grrl Scouts: Work Sucks
Image

- ❑1, Feb 2003 ... 2.95
- ❑2, Mar 2003 ... 2.95
- ❑3, Apr 2003 ... 2.95
- ❑4, Jun 2003 ... 2.95

Grrrl Squad
Amazing Aaron

- ❑1, Mar 1999, b&w; One-shot ... 2.95

Grumpy Old Monsters
Idea & Design Works

- ❑1, Nov 2003 ... 3.99
- ❑2, Jan 2004 ... 3.99
- ❑3, Feb 2004 ... 3.99

Grun
Harrier

- ❑1, Jun 1987 ... 1.95
- ❑2, Aug 1987 ... 1.95
- ❑3, Oct 1987 ... 1.95
- ❑4 ... 1.95

Grunts
Mirage

- ❑1, Nov 1987, b&w ... 2.00

Guardian
Spectrum

- ❑1, Mar 1984 ... 1.00
- ❑2, Jun 1984 ... 1.00

Guardian Angel
Image

- ❑1, May 2002 ... 2.95
- ❑2, Jul 2002 ... 2.95

Guardian Knights: Demon's Knight
Limelight

- ❑1, b&w; no indicia ... 2.95
- ❑2, b&w; no indicia ... 2.95

Guardians
Marvel

- ❑1, Sep 2004; Miniseries ... 2.99
- ❑2, Oct 2004 ... 2.99
- ❑3, Oct 2004 ... 2.99
- ❑4, Nov 2004 ... 2.99
- ❑5, Dec 2004 ... 2.99

Guardians of Metropolis
DC

- ❑1, Nov 1994 ... 1.50
- ❑2, Dec 1994 ... 1.50
- ❑3, Jan 1995 ... 1.50
- ❑4, Feb 1995; V: Female Furies ... 1.50

Guardians of the Galaxy
Marvel

- ❑1, Jun 1990 ... 2.00
- ❑2, Jul 1990; V: The Stark ... 2.00
- ❑3, Aug 1990 ... 2.00
- ❑4, Sep 1990 A: Firelord. ... 2.00
- ❑5, Oct 1990; TMc (c); TMc (a); V: Force ... 2.00
- ❑6, Nov 1990; A: Captain America's shield. No Comics Code stamp on covr ... 1.50
- ❑7, Dec 1990; 1: Malevolence. V: Malevolence ... 1.50
- ❑8, Jan 1991; 1: Rancor ... 1.50
- ❑9, Feb 1991; RL (c); RL (a); O: Rancor. 1: Replica. V: Rancor ... 1.50
- ❑10, Mar 1991 JLee (c); JLee (a) ... 1.50
- ❑11, Apr 1991; 1: Phoenix ... 1.50
- ❑12, May 1991; V: Overkill ... 1.50
- ❑13, Jun 1991; 1: Spirit of Vengeance ... 2.00
- ❑14, Jul 1991 A: Spirit of Vengeance ... 2.00
- ❑15, Aug 1991; JSn (c); JSn (a); 1: Protege ... 1.50
- ❑16, Sep 1991; Giant-size ... 1.75
- ❑17, Oct 1991; 1: Talon (Cameo) ... 1.50
- ❑18, Nov 1991; 1: Talon (Full appearance) ... 1.50
- ❑19, Dec 1991; 1: Talon ... 1.50
- ❑20, Jan 1992; A: Captain America's shield. Vance Astro becomes Major Victory ... 1.50
- ❑21, Feb 1992; V: Rancor ... 1.50
- ❑22, Mar 1992 ... 1.50
- ❑23, Apr 1992 ... 1.50
- ❑24, May 1992 A: Silver Surfer ... 1.50
- ❑25, Jun 1992; V: Galactus. regular cover ... 2.50
- ❑25/Variant, Jun 1992; V: Galactus. foil cover ... 2.50
- ❑26, Jul 1992; O: Guardians of the Galaxy ... 1.50
- ❑27, Aug 1992; O: Talon ... 1.50
- ❑28, Sep 1992; V: Doctor Octopus. Infinity War ... 1.50
- ❑29, Oct 1992; Infinity War ... 1.50
- ❑30, Nov 1992 ... 1.25
- ❑31, Dec 1992 ... 1.25
- ❑32, Jan 1993 A: Dr. Strange ... 1.25
- ❑33, Feb 1993 ... 1.25
- ❑34, Mar 1993; Yellowjacket joins team ... 1.25
- ❑35, Apr 1993; 1: Galactic Guardians. regular cover ... 1.25
- ❑35/Variant, Apr 1993; 1: Galactic Guardians. sculpted cover ... 2.95
- ❑36, May 1993; V: Dormammu ... 1.25
- ❑37, Jun 1993; D: Doctor Strange ... 1.25
- ❑38, Jul 1993 A: Beyonder ... 1.25
- ❑39, Aug 1993; Holo-grafix cover; Rancor vs. Doom ... 2.95
- ❑40, Sep 1993; V: Composite ... 1.25
- ❑41, Oct 1993; A: Inhumans. A: Starhawk. A: Composite. A: Loki. V: Loki ... 1.25
- ❑42, Nov 1993 ... 1.25
- ❑43, Dec 1993; 1: Woden ... 1.25
- ❑44, Jan 1994 ... 1.25
- ❑45, Feb 1994 ... 1.25
- ❑46, Mar 1994 ... 1.25
- ❑47, Apr 1994; Protege vs. Beyonder ... 1.25
- ❑48, May 1994; V: Overkill; With three Marvel Masterpiece cards bound inside ... 1.50
- ❑49, Jun 1994 A: Celestial ... 1.50
- ❑50, Jul 1994; Giant-size ... 2.00
- ❑50/Variant, Jul 1994; Giant-size; foil cover ... 2.95
- ❑51, Aug 1994 ... 1.50
- ❑52, Sep 1994 ... 1.50
- ❑53, Oct 1994; Drax vs. Wolfhound ... 1.50
- ❑54, Nov 1994; final fate of Spider-Man ... 1.50
- ❑55, Dec 1994; V: Ripjak ... 1.50
- ❑56, Jan 1995; V: Ripjak ... 1.50
- ❑57, Feb 1995 A: Bubonicus ... 1.50
- ❑58, Mar 1995 ... 1.50
- ❑59, Apr 1995 A: Silver Surfer ... 1.50
- ❑60, May 1995 A: Silver Surfer ... 1.50
- ❑61, Jun 1995 ... 1.50
- ❑62, Jul 1995; Giant-size; Final Issue ... 2.50
- ❑Ann 1, Jul 1991; Korvac Quest ... 4.00
- ❑Ann 2, ca. 1992; HT, BWi (a) ... 2.50
- ❑Ann 3, ca. 1993; 1: Cuchulain. trading card ... 2.95
- ❑Ann 4, ca. 1994; 1994 Ann ... 2.95

Guerrilla Groundhog
Eclipse

- ❑1, Jan 1987, b&w ... 1.50
- ❑2, Mar 1987 ... 1.50

Guerrilla War
Dell

- ❑12, Jul 1965, Series continued from Jungle War Stories #11 ... 10.00
- ❑13, Dec 1965 ... 10.00
- ❑14, Mar 1966, Final Issue ... 10.00

Guff!
Dark Horse

- ❑1, Apr 1998, b&w; bound-in Meanie Babies card ... 1.95

Gullivera
NBM

- ❑1, ca. 1996; Adult ... 13.95

Gumbo
Deadline Studios

- ❑1, Feb 1994, b&w ... 2.50
- ❑2, Sep 1994, b&w ... 2.50

Gumby 3-D
Blackthorne

- ❑1 ... 2.50
- ❑2 ... 2.50
- ❑3 ... 2.50
- ❑4; Blackthorne 3-D Series #21 ... 2.50
- ❑5 ... 2.50
- ❑6 ... 2.50
- ❑7 ... 2.50

Gumby's Summer Fun Special
Comico

- ❑1, Jul 1987; Wraparound cover ... 2.50

Gumby's Winter Fun Special
Comico

- ❑1 ... 2.50

Guncandy
Image

- ❑1, Aug 2005 ... 5.99
- ❑2, Mar 2006 ... 5.99

Gundam Seed Astray R
Tokyopop

- ❑1, Feb 2005, b&w ... 9.99
- ❑2, May 2005 ... 9.99
- ❑3, Jul 2005 ... 9.99
- ❑4, Nov 2005 ... 9.99

Gundam: The Origin
Viz

- ❑1, Apr 2002 ... 7.95
- ❑2, Jul 2002 ... 7.95

Gundam Wing: Blind Target
Viz

- ❑1, Feb 2001 ... 2.95
- ❑2, Mar 2001 ... 2.95
- ❑3, Apr 2001 ... 2.95
- ❑4, May 2001 ... 2.95

Gundam Wing: Episode Zero
Viz

- ❑1, Apr 2001 ... 2.95
- ❑2, May 2001 ... 2.95

Other grades: Multiply price above by 5/6 for VF/NM • 2/3 for VERY FINE • 1/3 for FINE • 1/5 for VERY GOOD • 1/8 for GOOD

Grifter

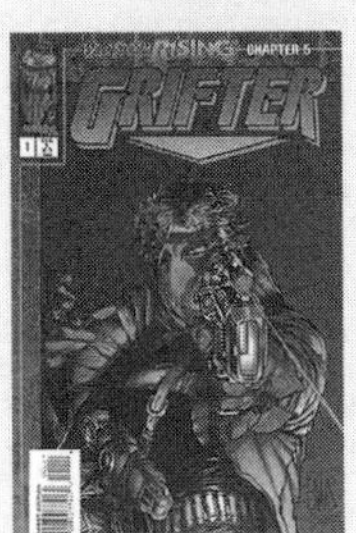

WildC.A.T.S member has solo outings

©Image

Grimjack

A bounty hunter in multiple dimensions

©First

Grimm's Ghost Stories

Gold Key horror series not too scary

©Gold Key

Groo

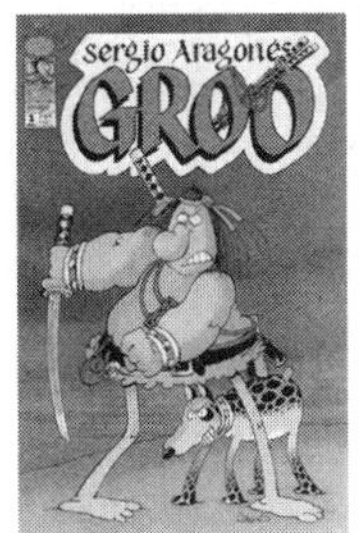

Wandering screw-up lands at Image for a time

©Image

Guardians of Metropolis

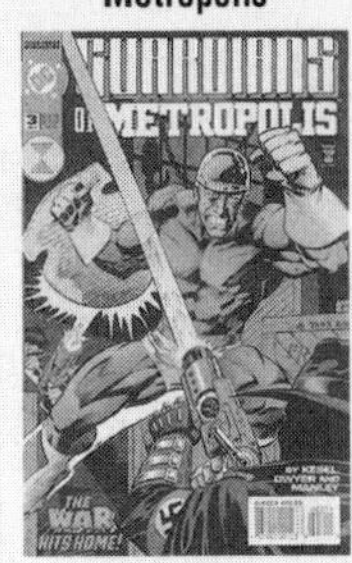

Aged Newsboy Legion reunites

©DC

N-MINT

❑3, Jun 2001 ... 2.95
❑4, Jul 2001 ... 2.95
❑5, Aug 2001 ... 2.95
❑6, Sep 2001 ... 2.95
❑7, Oct 2001 ... 2.95
❑8, Nov 2001 ... 2.95

Gun Fighters in Hell
Rebel

❑1; ca. 1993 ... 2.25
❑2 ... 2.25
❑3, b&w; ca. 1994 ... 2.25
❑4 ... 2.25
❑5; ca. 1997 ... 2.25

Gunfire
DC

❑0, Oct 1994; Continued in Gunfire #6 ... 2.00
❑1, May 1994 ... 2.00
❑2, Jun 1994 ... 2.00
❑3, Jul 1994 ... 2.00
❑4, Aug 1994 ... 2.00
❑5, Sep 1994; Continued in Gunfire #0 ... 2.00
❑6, Nov 1994 ... 2.00
❑7, Dec 1994 ... 2.00
❑8, Jan 1995 ... 2.00
❑9, Feb 1995 ... 2.00
❑10, Mar 1995 ... 2.00
❑11, Apr 1995 ... 2.00
❑12, May 1995 ... 2.00
❑13, Jun 1995; Final Issue ... 2.25

Gun Fury
Aircel

❑1, Jan 1989, b&w ... 1.95
❑2, Feb 1989, b&w ... 1.95
❑3, Mar 1989, b&w ... 1.95
❑4, Apr 1989, b&w ... 1.95
❑5, May 1989, b&w ... 1.95
❑6, Jun 1989, b&w ... 1.95
❑7, Jul 1989, b&w ... 1.95
❑8, Aug 1989, b&w ... 1.95
❑9, Sep 1989, b&w ... 1.95
❑10, Oct 1989, b&w ... 1.95

Gun Fury Returns
Aircel

❑1, Sep 1990, b&w ... 2.25
❑2, Oct 1990, b&w ... 2.25
❑3, Nov 1990, b&w ... 2.25
❑4, Dec 1990, b&w ... 2.25

Gun Fu: Showgirls Are Forever
Image

❑1, Apr 2006 ... 3.50

Gung Ho
Avalon

❑1, b&w; Reprints ... 2.95

Gunhawks
Marvel

❑1, Oct 1972, 1: Reno Jones and Kid Cassidy ... 50.00
❑2, Dec 1972 ... 18.00
❑3, Feb 1973 ... 8.00
❑4, Apr 1973 ... 8.00
❑5, Jun 1973, V: Reverend Mr. Graves ... 8.00
❑6, Aug 1973, D: Kid Cassidy ... 8.00
❑7, Oct 1973, Title changes to Gunhawk 8.00

N-MINT

Gunhed
Viz

❑1, Japanese ... 5.50
❑2, Japanese ... 5.50
❑3, Japanese ... 5.50

Gunner
Gun Dog

❑1, Mar 1999 ... 2.95

Gunparade March
ADV Manga

❑1, ca. 2004; Graphic novel; Read right to left; b&w ... 9.99
❑2, ca. 2004; Graphic novel; Read right to left; b&w ... 9.99
❑3, ca. 2005; Graphic novel; Read right to left; b&w ... 9.99

Gunpowder Girl & The Outlaw Squaw
Active Images

❑1, ca. 2005 ... 12.95

Gun Runner
Marvel

❑1, Oct 1993; four cards; Polybagged; wraparound cover ... 2.75
❑2, Nov 1993 ... 1.75
❑3, Dec 1993 ... 1.75
❑4, Jan 1994 ... 1.75
❑5, Feb 1994 ... 1.75
❑6, Mar 1994 ... 1.75

Gunslinger Girl
ADV Manga

❑1, ca. 2004; Read right to left; Graphic novel; b&w; Read right to left, back to front ... 9.99
❑2, ca. 2005; Read right to left; Graphic novel; b&w; Read right to left, back to front ... 9.99
❑3, ca. 2005; Read right to left; Graphic novel; b&w ... 9.99

Gunslingers
Marvel

❑1, Feb 2000; One-shot reprinting Western stories ... 2.99

Gunsmith Cats
Dark Horse / Manga

❑1, Sep 1995 ... 3.00
❑2, Sep 1995 ... 2.50
❑3, Sep 1995 ... 2.50
❑4, Sep 1995 ... 3.00
❑5, Sep 1995 ... 3.00
❑6, Oct 1995 ... 3.00
❑7, Nov 1995 ... 3.00
❑8, Dec 1995 ... 3.00
❑9, Jan 1996 ... 3.00
❑10, Feb 1996 ... 3.00

Gunsmith Cats: Bad Trip
Dark Horse / Manga

❑1, Jun 1998 ... 2.95
❑2, Jun 1998 ... 2.95
❑3, Aug 1998 ... 2.95
❑4, Sep 1998 ... 2.95
❑5, Oct 1998 ... 2.95
❑6, Nov 1998 ... 2.95

Gunsmith Cats: Bean Bandit
Dark Horse / Manga

❑1, Jan 1999 ... 2.95
❑2, Feb 1999 ... 2.95

N-MINT

❑3, Mar 1999 ... 2.95
❑4, Apr 1999 ... 2.95
❑5, May 1999 ... 2.95
❑6, Jun 1999 ... 2.95
❑7, Jul 1999 ... 2.95
❑8, Aug 1999 ... 2.95
❑9, Sep 1999 ... 2.95

Gunsmith Cats: Goldie vs. Misty
Dark Horse / Manga

❑1, Nov 1997 ... 2.95
❑2, Dec 1997 ... 2.95
❑3, Jan 1998 ... 2.95
❑4, Feb 1998 ... 2.95
❑5, Mar 1998 ... 2.95
❑6, Apr 1998 ... 2.95
❑7, May 1998 ... 2.95

Gunsmith Cats: Kidnapped
Dark Horse / Manga

❑1, Nov 1999 ... 2.95
❑2, Dec 1999 ... 2.95
❑3, Jan 2000 ... 2.95
❑4, Feb 2000 ... 2.95
❑5, Mar 2000 ... 2.95
❑6, Apr 2000 ... 2.95
❑7, May 2000 ... 2.95
❑8, Jun 2000 ... 2.95
❑9, Jul 2000 ... 2.95
❑10, Aug 2000 ... 2.95

Gunsmith Cats: Mister V
Dark Horse / Manga

❑1, Oct 2000 ... 3.50
❑2, Nov 2000 ... 3.50
❑3, Dec 2000 ... 3.50
❑4, Jan 2001 ... 3.50
❑5, Feb 2001 ... 3.50
❑6, Mar 2001 ... 3.50
❑7, Apr 2001 ... 3.50
❑8, May 2001 ... 3.50
❑9, Jun 2001 ... 3.50
❑10, Jul 2001 ... 3.50
❑11, Aug 2001 ... 3.50

Gunsmith Cats: Shades of Gray
Dark Horse / Manga

❑1, May 1997 ... 2.95
❑2, Jun 1997 ... 2.95
❑3, Jul 1997 ... 2.95
❑4, Aug 1997 ... 2.95
❑5, Sep 1997 ... 2.95

Gunsmith Cats Special
Dark Horse

❑1, Nov 2001, hardcover ... 2.99

Gunsmith Cats: The Return of Gray
Dark Horse / Manga

❑1, Aug 1996 ... 2.95
❑2, Sep 1996 ... 2.95
❑3, Oct 1996 ... 2.95
❑4, Nov 1996 ... 2.95
❑5, Dec 1996 ... 2.95
❑6, Jan 1997 ... 2.95
❑7, Feb 1997 ... 2.95

Gunsmoke
Gold Key

❑1, Feb 1969 ... 30.00
❑2, Apr 1969 ... 20.00

Other grades: Multiply price above by 5/6 for VF/NM • 2/3 for VERY FINE • 1/3 for FINE • 1/5 for VERY GOOD • 1/8 for GOOD

❑3, Jun 1969 ... 20.00
❑4, Aug 1969 ... 20.00
❑5, Nov 1969 ... 20.00
❑6, Feb 1970 ... 20.00

Guns of Shar-Pei
Caliber

❑1, b&w ... 2.95
❑2, b&w ... 2.95
❑3, b&w ... 2.95

Guns of the Dragon
DC

❑1, Oct 1998 ... 2.50
❑2, Nov 1998 ... 2.50
❑3, Dec 1998 ... 2.50
❑4, Jan 1999 ... 2.50

Gun That Won the West
Winchester

❑1; giveaway ... 24.00

Gun Theory
Marvel / Epic

❑1, Oct 2003 ... 2.50
❑2, Nov 2003 ... 2.50

Gunwitch: Outskirts of Doom
Oni

❑1 2001 ... 2.95

Gutwallow
Numbskull

❑1, Feb 1998, b&w ... 2.95
❑2, Apr 1998 ... 2.95
❑3, Jun 1998 ... 2.95
❑4, Aug 1998 ... 2.95
❑5, Dec 1998 ... 2.95
❑6, Feb 1999 ... 2.95
❑7, Apr 1999 ... 2.95
❑8, Jul 1999 ... 2.95
❑9, Sep 1999 ... 2.95
❑10, Dec 1999 ... 2.95
❑11, Mar 2000 ... 2.95
❑12, Jun 2000 ... 2.95

Gutwallow
Numbskull

❑1, Nov 2000 ... 2.95
❑2, Feb 2001 ... 2.95
❑3, Jun 2001 ... 2.95

Guy Gardner
DC

❑1, Oct 1992 JSa (a) ... 2.00
❑2, Nov 1992 JSa (a) ... 1.75
❑3, Dec 1992; JSa (a); (almost) wordless story ... 1.50
❑4, Jan 1993; JSa (a); Includes postage paid postcard survey from Dick Giordano (asking who bought book; Gender; Age; And which comic) ... 1.50
❑5, Feb 1993; JSa (a); V: Goldface ... 1.50
❑6, Mar 1993; JSa (a); V: Green Lantern (Hal Jordan) ... 1.25
❑7, Apr 1993; JSa (a); V: Goldface; V: Repo; Jocasta; And Piston ... 1.25
❑8, May 1993; JSa (a); V: Lobo, Lobo cover/appearance ... 1.25
❑9, Jun 1993; JSa (a); V: Green Lantern Boodikka ... 1.25
❑10, Jul 1993; JSa (a); V: Green Lantern Boodikka ... 1.25
❑11, Aug 1993; JSa (a); Team-up with General Glory ... 1.25
❑12, Sep 1993 JSa (a) ... 1.25
❑13, Oct 1993 JSa (a) ... 1.25
❑14, Nov 1993 JSa (a) ... 1.25
❑15, Dec 1993; Guest starring Justice League America; Story continued from JLA #83; Story continues into JLA#84 ... 1.50
❑16, Jan 1994; Series continued in Guy Gardner: Warrior #17 ... 1.50

Guy Gardner: Collateral Damage
DC

❑1, Feb 2007 ... 5.99
❑2, Mar 2007, Final Issue ... 5.99

Guy Gardner Reborn
DC

❑1, ca. 1992; V: Black Hand ... 4.95
❑2, ca. 1992; V: Weaponers of Qward ... 4.95
❑3, ca. 1992; Team-up with Lobo; Final book leads into new monthly Guy Gardner series ... 4.95

Guy Gardner: Warrior
DC

❑0, Oct 1994; O: Guy Gardner's Warrior persona ... 1.75
❑17, Feb 1994; Title changes to Guy Gardner: Warrior; Series continued from Guy Gardner #16 ... 1.50
❑18, Mar 1994; V: Militia ... 1.50
❑19, Apr 1994; V: Militia ... 1.50
❑20, May 1994; V: Parallax (Hal Jordan) ... 1.50
❑21, Jun 1994; V: Parallax ... 1.50
❑22, Jul 1994; V: Nazi Dinosaurs ... 1.50
❑23, Aug 1994; Zero Hour tie-in ... 1.50
❑24, Sep 1994; Zero Hour ... 1.50
❑25, Nov 1994; Giant-size; JSa (a); 25th anniversary issue; 6 artist pin-up pages ... 2.50
❑26, Dec 1994 ... 1.50
❑27, Jan 1995; V: Sledge ... 1.50
❑28, Feb 1995; V: Major Force; Green Lantern (Kyle Rayner) appearance/ team-up ... 1.50
❑29, Mar 1995; Giant-size ... 1.50
❑29/Variant, May 1995; Giant-size; enhanced foldout cover ... 2.95
❑30, Apr 1995; Continues from Action Comics #709 ... 1.50
❑31, Jun 1995; V: Dementor ... 1.75
❑32, Jul 1995 ... 1.75
❑33, Aug 1995 ... 1.75
❑34, Sep 1995 ... 1.75
❑35, Oct 1995 ... 1.75
❑36, Nov 1995; Underworld Unleashed; V: Earthworm; V: Cheetah; V: Blackguard ... 1.75
❑37, Dec 1995; Underworld Unleashed ... 1.75
❑38, Jan 1996 ... 1.75
❑39, Feb 1996; Christmas party at Warriors ... 1.75
❑40, Mar 1996; V: Gorilla Grodd; Guy's Mom shows up at Warriors ... 1.75
❑41, Apr 1996; V: Dungeon; Warrior (Guy Gardner) views a Warrior cartoon ... 1.75
❑42, May 1996; Guy becomes a woman ... 1.75
❑43, Jun 1996; V: Sledge; V: Major Force; V: Dementor ... 1.75
❑44, Jul 1996; JSa (a); V: Major Force; Arisia funeral; Final Issue ... 1.75
❑Ann 1, ca. 1995; Year One ... 3.50
❑Ann 2, ca. 1996; JSa (a); Legends of the Dead Earth ... 2.95

Guy Pumpkinhead
Saint Gray

❑1 ... 2.50

Guzzi Lemans
Antarctic

❑1, Aug 1996, b&w ... 2.95
❑2, Oct 1996, b&w; Final Issue ... 2.95

Gyre
Abaculus

❑1, Dec 1997, b&w ... 3.50
❑2, Feb 1998, b&w ... 2.95
❑3, Apr 1998 ... 2.95
❑Ashcan 1; Preview of Gyre #1 ... 0.50
❑Special 1 ... 4.50

Gyre: Traditions & Interruptions
Abaculus

❑1, b&w; Promotional book for series ... 1.00

Gyro Comics
Rip Off

❑1, ca. 1988, b&w ... 2.00
❑2, ca. 1988, b&w ... 2.00
❑3, ca. 1988, b&w ... 2.00

Gyro Gearloose
Dell

❑-207, Jul 1962; Cover code 01329-207 ... 50.00

Hacker Files
DC

❑1, Aug 1992, TS (a); 1: Jack Marshall ... 2.25
❑2, Sep 1992, TS (a) ... 1.95
❑3, Oct 1992, TS (a) ... 1.95
❑4, Nov 1992, TS (a) ... 1.95
❑5, Dec 1992, TS (a); Oracle arrested by Feds ... 1.95
❑6, Jan 1993, TS (a) ... 1.95
❑7, Feb 1993, TS (a) ... 1.95
❑8, Mar 1993, TS (a) ... 1.95
❑9, Apr 1993, TS (a) ... 1.95
❑10, May 1993, TS (a) ... 1.95
❑11, Jun 1993, TS (a); Cover credits incorrectly list Mark Buckingham ... 1.95
❑12, Jul 1993, TS (a); Cover credits incorrectly list Mark Buckingham ... 1.95

Hackmasters of EverKnight
Kenzer and Company

❑1, May 2000, b&w; Knights of the Dinner Table back-up story ... 3.50
❑2, Jul 2000, b&w; Knights of the Dinner Table back-up story ... 2.95
❑3, Sep 2000, b&w; Knights of the Dinner Table back-up story ... 2.95
❑4, Nov 2000, b&w; Knights of the Dinner Table back-up story ... 2.95
❑5, Jan 2001, b&w; Knights of the Dinner Table back-up story ... 2.95
❑6, Mar 2001, b&w ... 2.95
❑7, May 2001, b&w ... 2.95
❑8, Jul 2001, b&w ... 2.95
❑9, Aug 2001 ... 2.95
❑10, Sep 2001 ... 2.95

Hack Slash: Land of Lost Toys
Devil's Due / Chaos

❑1, Dec 2005 ... 3.25
❑2, Dec 2005 ... 3.25
❑3, Feb 2006 ... 3.25
❑3/Variant, Feb 2006 ... 3.25

Hack/Slash: Slice Hard
Devil's Due

❑1, Dec 2006 ... 4.95
❑1/Variant, Dec 2006 ... 4.95

Hack/Slash: Slice Hard 25-Cent Special
Devil's Due

❑1, Jun 2006 ... 0.25

Hack/Slash: Trailers
Devil's Due

❑1, Mar 2006 ... 3.25
❑1/Variant, Mar 2006 ... 3.25
❑1/2nd variant, Mar 2006 ... 3.25

Hairbat
Screaming Rice

❑1, b&w ... 2.50
❑2, b&w ... 2.50
❑3, b&w ... 2.50
❑4, b&w ... 2.50

Hairbat
Slave Labor

❑1, Jul 1995, b&w ... 2.95

Hair Bear Bunch
Gold Key

❑1, Feb 1972 ... 10.00
❑2, May 1972 ... 7.00
❑3, Aug 1972 ... 6.00
❑4, Nov 1972 ... 6.00
❑5, Feb 1973 ... 6.00
❑6, May 1973 ... 4.00
❑7, Aug 1973 ... 4.00
❑8, Nov 1973 ... 4.00
❑9, Feb 1974 ... 4.00

Hairbutt the Hippo
Rat Race

❑1, ca. 1992, b&w ... 2.95
❑2, ca. 1993, b&w ... 2.95
❑3, ca. 1993, b&w ... 2.95

Hairbutt the Hippo Crime Files
Rat Race

❑1, Dec 1995, b&w ... 3.50
❑2, ca. 1996, b&w ... 3.50
❑3, ca. 1996, b&w ... 3.50
❑4, ca. 1996, b&w ... 3.50
❑5, ca. 1996, b&w ... 3.50
❑6, ca. 1996, b&w ... 3.50

Hairbutt the Hippo: Private Eye
Ratrace

❑1, Spr 1997, b&w; no indicia ... 2.95
❑2, Sum 1997, b&w; no indicia ... 2.95
❑3, ca. 1997, b&w ... 2.95

Halifax Explosion
Halifax

❑1, Apr 1997, b&w ... 2.50

Hall of Fame
J.C.

❑1 ... 1.50

Guardians of the Galaxy

Jim Valentino revives '70s space team
©Marvel

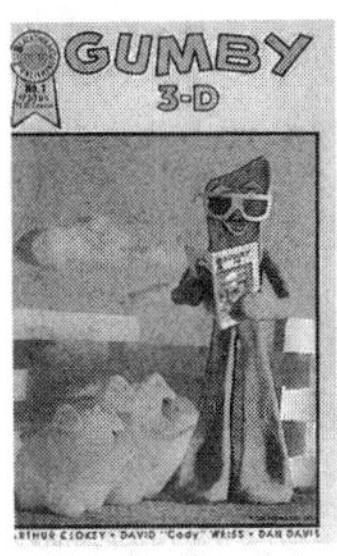

Gumby 3-D

Clay adventures that leap off the page
©Blackthorne

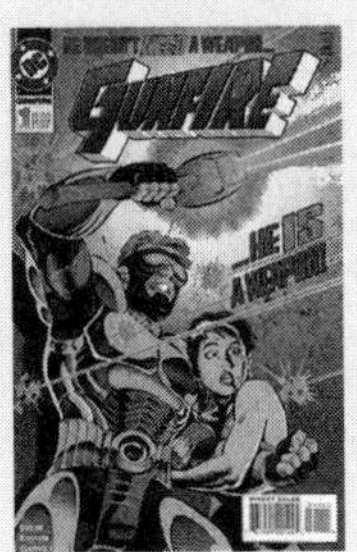

Gunfire

Short-lived "New Blood" spin-off
©DC

Gunhawks

D: partner reduces plural title
©Marvel

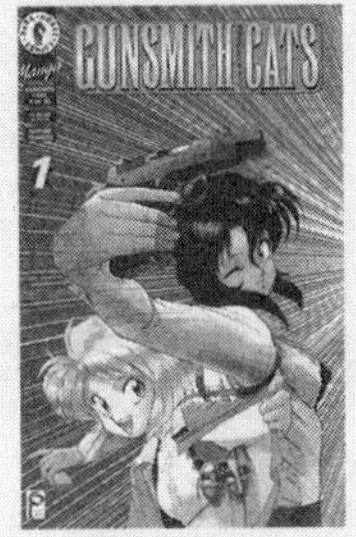

Gunsmith Cats

Female investigators team in manga series
©Dark Horse

N-MINT

❑2, Aug 1983; Reprints with new cover. 1.50
❑3, Dec 1983 1.50

Hall of Heroes
Hall of Heroes

❑1, May 1997, b&w 2.50
❑2 2.50
❑3 2.50

Hall of Heroes Halloween Special
Hall of Heroes

❑1, Oct 1997, b&w; NN; One-shot 2.50

Hall of Heroes Presents
Hall of Heroes

❑1, Aug 1993 2.50
❑2, Sep 1993 2.50
❑3, Nov 1993 2.50

Hall of Heroes Presents
Hall of Heroes

❑0/A, Mar 1997, b&w; Slingers cover 2.50
❑0/B, Mar 1997, b&w; Salamandroid cover 2.50
❑0/C, Mar 1997, b&w; The Fuzz cover 2.50
❑1, Jul 1996, b&w 2.50
❑2, Sep 1996, b&w 2.50
❑3/A, b&w; no indicia 2.50
❑3/B; alternate b cover with Nazi swastika in background 2.50
❑4, May 1997; Turaxx 2.50
❑5, Sep 1997; The Becoming; extra-wide 2.50

Hall of Horrors
Hall of Heroes

❑1, May 1997; Sinister and Grin pin-ups 2.50

Hallowed Knight
Shea

❑1, Apr 1997, b&w 2.95
❑2, Sep 1997, b&w 2.95

Halloween
Chaos

❑1, Nov 2000; based on movie 2.95

Halloween Horror
Eclipse

❑1, Oct 1987; JD (w); JD (a); a.k.a. Seduction of the Innocent #7 2.00

Halloween Megazine
Marvel

❑1, Dec 1996; reprints stories from Tomb of Dracula 2.99

Halloween Terror
Eternity

❑1, b&w 2.50

Halls of Horror
Eclipse

❑1, Jun 1985 1.75
❑2, Jun 1985 1.75
❑3 1.75

Halo, an Angel's Story
Sirius

❑1, Apr 1996 2.95
❑2, May 1996 2.95
❑3, Jun 1996 2.95
❑4, Jul 1996 2.95

Halo Graphic Novel
Marvel

❑1, Sep 2006 24.99

N-MINT

Halo: Uprising
Marvel

❑1, Sep 2007 3.99
❑2, Jan 2008 3.99

Hammer
Dark Horse

❑1, Oct 1997 2.95
❑2, Nov 1997 2.95
❑3, Dec 1997 2.95
❑4, Jan 1998 2.95

Hammerlocke
DC

❑1, Sep 1992; 1: Hammerlocke 1.75
❑2, Oct 1992 1.75
❑3, Nov 1992 1.75
❑4, Dec 1992 1.75
❑5, Jan 1993 1.75
❑6, Feb 1993 1.75
❑7, Mar 1993 1.75
❑8, Apr 1993 1.75
❑9, May 1993; Final Issue 1.75

Hammer of God
First

❑1, Feb 1990 1.95
❑2, Mar 1990 1.95
❑3, Apr 1990 1.95
❑4, May 1990 1.95

Hammer of God: Butch
Dark Horse

❑1, May 1994 2.50
❑2, Jul 1994 2.50
❑3, Aug 1994; Final Issue 2.50

Hammer of God: Pentathlon
Dark Horse

❑1; NN 2.50

Hammer of God: Sword of Justice
First

❑1, Feb 1991 4.95
❑2, Mar 1991 4.95

Hammer of the Gods
Insight

❑1, ca. 2001, b&w 2.95
❑2, ca. 2001, b&w 2.95
❑3, ca. 2001, b&w 2.95
❑4, ca. 2001, b&w 2.95
❑5, ca. 2001, b&w; Contains extra material about the four-issue mini-series 2.95

Hammer of the Gods Color Saga
Insight

❑nn, ca. 2001; Prints the internet daily strip that launched the series and a new color story 4.95

Hammer of the Gods: Hammer Hits China
Image

❑1, Feb 2003 2.95
❑2, May 2003 2.95
❑3, Oct 2003 2.95

Hammer: The Outsider
Dark Horse

❑1, Feb 1999 2.95
❑2, Mar 1999 2.95
❑3, Apr 1999 2.95

N-MINT

Hammer: Uncle Alex
Dark Horse

❑1, Aug 1998 2.95

Hamster Vice
Blackthorne

❑1, Jun 1986 1.50
❑2, Jul 1986 1.50
❑3, Sep 1986 1.50
❑4 1.50
❑5 1.50
❑6 1.50
❑7 1.50
❑8, Jul 1987 1.50
❑9 1.50
❑3D 1, Nov 1986 2.50
❑3D 2, Feb 1987; a.k.a. Blackthorne 3-D #15 2.50

Hamster Vice
Eternity

❑1, Apr 1989, b&w 1.95
❑2, b&w 1.95

Hana-Kimi
Viz

❑1, Sep 2004 9.95
❑2, Nov 2004 9.95
❑3, Jan 2005 9.95
❑4, Feb 2005 9.95
❑5, Apr 2005 9.99
❑6, Jun 2005 9.99
❑7, Aug 2005 9.99
❑8, Oct 2005 9.99

Hand Shadows
Doyan

❑1 1.50
❑2, Nov 1986 1.50

Hands Off!
Ward Sutton

❑1, b&w 2.95

Hands Off!
Tokyopop

❑1, Oct 2004 9.99
❑2, Feb 2005 9.99
❑3, May 2005 9.99
❑4, Aug 2005 9.99
❑5, Jan 2006 9.99

Hands of the Dragon
Atlas-Seaboard

❑1, Jun 1975 6.00

Hanna-Barbera All-Stars
Archie

❑1, Oct 1995, Anthology 2.00
❑2, Dec 1995, Anthology 2.00
❑3, Feb 1996, Anthology 2.00
❑4, Apr 1996, Anthology 2.00

Hanna-Barbera Bandwagon
Gold Key

❑1, Oct 1962 70.00
❑2, Jan 1963 50.00
❑3, Apr 1963 50.00

Hanna-Barbera Big Book
Harvey

❑1, Jun 1993 1.95
❑3 2.50

Other grades: Multiply price above by 5/6 for VF/NM • 2/3 for VERY FINE • 1/3 for FINE • 1/5 for VERY GOOD • 1/8 for GOOD

N-MINT

Hanna-Barbera Giant Size
Harvey

❑2, Nov 1992, Flip book ... 2.25

Hanna-Barbera Parade
Charlton

❑1, Sep 1971 ... 35.00
❑2, Nov 1971 ... 18.00
❑3, Dec 1971 ... 15.00
❑4, Jan 1972 ... 13.00
❑5, Feb 1972 ... 14.00
❑6, Apr 1972, A: Wilma Flintstone. A: Fred Flintstone. A: Pebbles Flintstone. Dixie cameo; Pixie cameo ... 12.00
❑7, May 1972 ... 12.00
❑8, Jul 1972 ... 12.00
❑9, Oct 1972 ... 12.00
❑10, Dec 1972 ... 12.00

Hanna-Barbera Presents
Archie

❑1, Nov 1995, Atom Ant and Secret Squirrel ... 1.50
❑2, Jan 1996, Wacky Races ... 1.50
❑3, Mar 1996, Yogi Bear ... 1.50
❑4, May 1996, Quick Draw McGraw and Magilla Gorilla ... 1.50
❑5, Jul 1996 ... 1.50
❑6, Aug 1996, Superstar Olympics ... 1.50
❑8, Oct 1996, Frankenstein Jr. and the Impossibles ... 1.50

Hanna-Barbera Presents All-New Comics
Harvey

❑1, giveaway promo ... 1.00

Hanna-Barbera Super TV Heroes
Gold Key

❑1, Apr 1968, Herculoids ... 58.00
❑2, Jul 1968, Birdman ... 36.00
❑3, Oct 1968, Shazzan, Space Ghost, Moby Dick, Birdman, Young Samson and Goliath ... 36.00
❑4, Jan 1969, Herculoids, Birdman, Shazzan, Moby Dick, Mighty Mightor ... 30.00
❑5, Apr 1969 ... 30.00
❑6, Jul 1969, Space Ghost ... 35.00
❑7, Oct 1969, Space Ghost ... 35.00

Hansi, the Girl Who Loved the Swastika
Spire

❑1, ca. 1973 ... 28.00

Hap Hazard
Fandom House

❑1, b&w ... 2.00

Happenstance Jack, III
-Ism

❑1, May 1998 ... 3.00

Happiest Millionaire
Gold Key

❑1, Apr 1968 ... 25.00

Happy
Wonder Comics

❑1, b&w ... 2.00

Happy Birthday Gnatrat!
Dimension

❑1 ... 1.95

Happy Birthday Martha Washington
Dark Horse / Legend

❑1, Mar 1995; FM (w); DaG (a); cardstock cover ... 3.00

Happydale: Devils in the Desert
DC / Vertigo

❑1; prestige format ... 6.95
❑2; prestige format ... 6.95

Happy Days
Gold Key

❑1, Mar 1979 ... 20.00
❑2, May 1979 ... 10.00
❑3, Jul 1979 ... 10.00
❑4, Sep 1979 ... 10.00
❑5 1979 ... 10.00
❑6, Feb 1980 ... 10.00

Harbinger
Valiant

❑0, Feb 1993; O: Sting. sendaway; Special issue given as a premium from coupons in Harbinger #1-6 ... 6.00
❑0/Pink, Feb 1993; Pink variant ... 65.00
❑0/2nd, Feb 1993; O: Sting. Included with Harbinger trade paperback ... 3.00
❑1, Jan 1992; O: Harbinger. 1: Flamingo. 1: Zeppelin. 1: Sting. 1: Kris. 1: Torque. 1: Harbinger kids. 1: Flamingo; Includes coupon for Harbinger #0; 1: Zephyr ... 30.00
❑2, Feb 1992; Includes coupon for Harbinger #0; 1: Rock; 1: Swallow; 1: Sparrow ... 8.00
❑3, Mar 1992; V: Ax; Includes coupon for Harbinger #0; 1: Ax ... 8.00
❑4, Apr 1992; Scarce ... 11.00
❑5, May 1992; A: Solar. Includes coupon for Harbinger #0 ... 10.00
❑6, Jun 1992; D: Torque; D: Torque (John Torkelson) ... 9.00
❑7, Jul 1992 ... 7.00
❑8, Aug 1992; FM (c); FM (a); Unity ... 4.00
❑9, Sep 1992; Unity; Birth of Magnus ... 4.00
❑10, Oct 1992; 1: H.A.R.D Corps. 1: H.A.R.D Corps; 1: H.A.R.D. Corps ... 4.00
❑11, Nov 1992 A: H.A.R.D Corps ... 2.00
❑12, Dec 1992 ... 1.00
❑13, Jan 1993; Dark Knight cover ... 1.00
❑14, Feb 1993 ... 1.00
❑15, Mar 1993 ... 1.00
❑16, Apr 1993 ... 1.00
❑17, May 1993 ... 1.00
❑18, Jun 1993; KN (c); 1: Screen ... 1.00
❑19, Jul 1993 ... 1.00
❑20, Aug 1993; Includes serial number coupon for contest ... 1.00
❑21, Sep 1993 ... 1.00
❑22, Oct 1993 A: Archer & Armstrong ... 1.00
❑23, Nov 1993 ... 1.00
❑24, Dec 1993 ... 1.00
❑25, Jan 1994; Giant-size; D: Rock. V: Harada. Sting vs. Harada; Harada put into coma; Sting loses powers ... 1.00
❑26, Feb 1994; 1: Sonix. 1: Anvil. 1: Amazon. 1: Microwave. 1: Jolt. new team; Zephyr rejoins Harbinger foundation ... 1.00
❑27, Mar 1994 ... 1.00
❑28, Apr 1994 ... 1.00
❑29, May 1994; trading card ... 2.00
❑30, Jun 1994 A: H.A.R.D.Corps ... 1.00
❑31, Aug 1994; A: H.A.R.D.Corps. Contiuned from H.A.R.D. Corps #19 ... 1.00
❑32, Sep 1994 A: Eternal Warrior ... 1.00
❑33, Oct 1994 A: Doctor Eclipse ... 1.00
❑34, Nov 1994; Chaos Effect Delta 1 ... 1.00
❑35, Dec 1994 ... 2.00
❑36, Jan 1995 A: Magnus ... 1.00
❑37, Feb 1995; Painted cover ... 1.00
❑38, Mar 1995 ... 1.00
❑39, Apr 1995 ... 3.00
❑40, May 1995 ... 4.00
❑41, Jun 1995; Final Issue ... 5.00

Harbinger: Acts of God
Acclaim

❑1, Jan 1998; Wraparound cover ... 3.95

Harbinger Files
Valiant

❑1, Aug 1994, O: Toyo Harada ... 2.00
❑2, Feb 1995, 1: The Harbinger ... 4.00

Hardball
Aircel

❑1, May 1991 ... 2.95
❑2, Jul 1991 ... 2.95
❑3, Aug 1991 ... 2.95
❑4, Aug 1991 ... 2.95

Hard Boiled
Dark Horse

❑1, Sep 1990 ... 4.95
❑2, Dec 1990 ... 5.95
❑3, Mar 1992 ... 5.95

Hardcase
Malibu / Ultraverse

❑1, Jun 1993, 1: NM-E. 1: Nicholas Lone (Solitaire). 1: Hardcase ... 2.50
❑1/Hologram, Jun 1993, Holographic cover ... 5.00
❑1/Ltd., Jun 1993, Ultrafoil limited edition ... 3.00
❑2, Jul 1993, 1: Choice. trading card ... 2.00
❑3, Aug 1993, 1: The Needler. 1: Gun Nut. 1: Trouble ... 2.00
❑4, Sep 1993, O: Hardcase. Fold-out cover ... 2.00
❑5, Oct 1993, Rune ... 2.00
❑6, Nov 1993 ... 1.95
❑7, Dec 1993, Break-Thru ... 1.95
❑8, Jan 1994, GP (a); A: Solution. O: Solitaire ... 1.95
❑9, Feb 1994, BA (c); BA (a) ... 1.95
❑10, Mar 1994 ... 1.95
❑11, Apr 1994 ... 1.95
❑12, May 1994, Wraparound cover; Anniversary Issue; Metalic Ink ... 1.95
❑13, Jun 1994, 1: Karr. 1: Wynn ... 1.95
❑14, Jul 1994 ... 1.95
❑15, Aug 1994 ... 1.95
❑16, Oct 1994, KB (w); Flip book with Ultraverse Premiere #7 ... 3.50
❑17, Nov 1994, 1: The Genius ... 1.95
❑18, Dec 1994 ... 1.95
❑19, Jan 1995, 1: Trauma. 1: Bismark ... 1.95
❑20, Feb 1995 ... 2.50
❑21, Mar 1995 ... 2.50
❑22, Apr 1995, D: Trouble ... 2.50
❑23, May 1995 ... 2.50
❑24, Jun 1995 ... 2.50
❑25, Jul 1995 ... 2.50
❑26, Aug 1995, Final Issue ... 2.95

Hardcore Station
DC

❑1, Jul 1998 ... 2.50
❑2, Aug 1998 ... 2.50
❑3, Sep 1998 ... 2.50
❑4, Oct 1998 ... 2.50
❑5, Nov 1998 ... 2.50
❑6, Dec 1998 ... 2.50

H.A.R.D. Corps
Valiant

❑1, Dec 1992, Fold-out cover ... 1.00
❑1/Gold, Dec 1992, Gold (promotional) edition; Fold-out cover ... 12.00
❑2, Jan 1993 ... 1.00
❑3, Feb 1993 ... 1.00
❑4, Apr 1993 ... 1.00
❑5, Apr 1993 ... 1.00
❑5/ComicDef, Apr 1993 ... 5.00
❑6, May 1993 ... 1.00
❑7, Jun 1993, V: Spider-Aliens ... 1.00
❑8, Jul 1993 ... 1.00
❑9, Aug 1993, Serial Number Contest! ... 1.00
❑10, Sep 1993, Serial Number Contest! ... 1.00
❑11, Oct 1993 ... 1.00
❑12, Nov 1993 ... 1.00
❑13, Dec 1993, D: Superstar ... 1.00
❑14, Jan 1994 ... 1.00
❑15, Feb 1994 ... 1.00
❑16, Mar 1994 ... 1.00
❑17, Apr 1994, V: Armorines ... 1.00
❑18, May 1994, trading card ... 2.00
❑19, Jun 1994, Harada awakes from coma ... 1.00
❑20, Jul 1994 ... 1.00
❑21, Sep 1994 ... 1.00
❑22, Oct 1994 ... 1.00
❑23, Nov 1994, Chaos Effect Delta 4 ... 1.00
❑24, Dec 1994 ... 1.00
❑25, Jan 1995 ... 1.00
❑26, Feb 1995 ... 2.00
❑27, Mar 1995 ... 2.00
❑28, Apr 1995 ... 2.00
❑29, May 1995 ... 3.00
❑30, Jun 1995, Final Issue ... 5.00

Hardkorr
Aircel

❑1, Jun 1991, b&w; Adult ... 2.50
❑2, Jul 1991, b&w; Adult ... 2.50
❑3, Aug 1991, b&w; Adult ... 2.50
❑4, Sep 1991, b&w; Adult ... 2.50

Hard Looks
Dark Horse

❑1, Mar 1992, b&w ... 2.50
❑2, May 1992, b&w ... 2.50
❑3, Jul 1992, b&w ... 2.50
❑4, Sep 1992, b&w ... 2.50
❑5, Nov 1992, b&w ... 2.50
❑6, Jan 1993, b&w ... 2.95
❑7, Mar 1993, b&w ... 2.95
❑8, May 1993, b&w ... 2.95
❑9, Jul 1993, b&w ... 2.95
❑10, Sep 1993, b&w ... 3.50

Other grades: Multiply price above by 5/6 for VF/NM • 2/3 for VERY FINE • 1/3 for FINE • 1/5 for VERY GOOD • 1/8 for GOOD

Gunsmoke (Gold Key)

Marshall Dillon cleans up Dodge
©Gold Key

Guy Gardner

Hot-headed GL with no finesse
©DC

Hair Bear Bunch

Trio of bruins scheme at zoo
©Gold Key

Halloween

Michael Myers makes comics debut
©Chaos

Hamster Vice

Another artifact of the Turtles craze
©Blackthorne

N-MINT

Hard Rock Comics
Revolutionary

❑1, Mar 1992, b&w; Metallica; early 5.00
❑2, Apr 1992, b&w; Motley Crue 4.00
❑3, May 1992, b&w; Jane's Addiction 3.00
❑4, Jun 1992, b&w; Nirvana 4.00
❑5, Jul 1992, b&w; Kiss: Tales From the Tours 8.00
❑5/2nd, Jul 1992; Kiss: Tales From the Tours 5.00
❑6, Sep 1992, b&w; Def Leppard II 2.50
❑7, Oct 1992, b&w; Red Hot Chili Peppers 2.50
❑8, Nov 1992, b&w; Soundgarden, Pearl Jam 2.50
❑9, Dec 1992, b&w; Queen II 2.50
❑10, Jan 1993, b&w; Birth of Punk 2.50
❑11, Feb 1993, b&w; Pantera 2.50
❑12, Mar 1993, b&w; Hendrix 2.50
❑13, Apr 1993, b&w; Dead Kennedys 3.00
❑14, May 1993, b&w; Van Halen II 2.50
❑15, Jun 1993, b&w; Megadeath, Motorhead; Dave Mustaine interview 2.50
❑16, Jul 1993, b&w; Joan Jett, Lita Ford 2.50
❑17; never published; British Metal 2.50
❑18, Sep 1993, b&w; Queensryche II 2.50
❑19, Oct 1993, b&w; Tesla, Spirit, UKJ 2.50
❑20, Nov 1993, b&w; Ratt, P-Funk, Sweet 2.50

Hard Time
DC / Focus

❑1, Apr 2004 2.50
❑2, May 2004 2.50
❑3, Jun 2004 2.50
❑4, Jul 2004 2.50
❑5, Aug 2004 2.50
❑6, Sep 2004 2.50
❑7, Oct 2004 2.50
❑8, Nov 2004 2.50
❑9, Dec 2004 2.50
❑10, Jan 2005 2.50
❑11, Feb 2005 2.50
❑12, Mar 2005 2.50

Hard Time: Season Two
DC

❑1, Jan 2006 2.50
❑2, Mar 2006 2.50
❑3, Mar 2006 2.50
❑4, May 2006 2.99
❑5, Jun 2006 2.50
❑6, Jul 2006, Price increase 2.99
❑7, Aug 2006, Final issue 2.99

Hardware
DC / Milestone

❑1, Apr 1993; O: Hardware. 1: Reprise. 1: Edwin Alva. 1: Hardware. newsstand 1.50
❑1/CS, Apr 1993; O: Hardware. 1: Reprise. 1: Edwin Alva. 1: Hardware. bagged 2.95
❑1/Platinum, Apr 1993; Platinum (promotional) edition; O: Hardware. 1: Reprise. 1: Edwin Alva. 1: Hardware. no cover price; platinum 3.00
❑2, May 1993; 1: Barraki Young 1.50
❑3, May 1993; 1: Systematic 1.50
❑4, Jun 1993 1.50
❑5, Jul 1993; 1: Deacon Stuart. 1: Deathwish 1.50
❑6, Aug 1993 1.50
❑7, Sep 1993; O: Deathwish 1.50
❑8, Oct 1993 1.50
❑9, Nov 1993; 1: Technique 1.50
❑10, Dec 1993; RB (a); 1: Harm. 1: Transit 1.50
❑11, Jan 1994; 1: Shadowspire. 1: Dharma. 1: The Star Chamber 1.50
❑12, Feb 1994 RB (a) 1.50
❑13, Mar 1994 1.50
❑14, Apr 1994 1.50
❑15, May 1994 1.50
❑16, Jun 1994; Giant-size; 1: Hardware Version 2.0. 1: Hardware Version 2.0. 2.50
❑16/Variant, Jun 1994; Giant-size; 1: Hardware Version 2.0. Fold-out cover 3.95
❑17, Jul 1994 A: Steel 1.50
❑18, Aug 1994 A: Steel 1.75
❑19, Sep 1994 1.75
❑20, Oct 1994 KP (a) 1.75
❑21, Nov 1994 1.75
❑22, Dec 1994 1.75
❑23, Jan 1995 1.75
❑24, Feb 1995 1.75
❑25, Mar 1995; Giant-size 2.95
❑26, Apr 1995 1.75
❑27, May 1995 1.75
❑28, Jun 1995 1.75
❑29, Jul 1995; cover has both .99 and 2.50 cover price 2.50
❑30, Aug 1995; Long Hot Summer 2.50
❑31, Sep 1995; D: Edwin Alva; The Long Hot Summer 2.50
❑32, Oct 1995 2.50
❑33, Nov 1995 HC (c) 2.50
❑34, Dec 1995 2.50
❑35, Jan 1996 2.50
❑36, Feb 1996 2.50
❑37, Mar 1996 2.50
❑38, Apr 1996 2.50
❑39, May 1996 2.50
❑40, Jun 1996 KP (a) 2.50
❑41, Jul 1996 2.50
❑42, Aug 1996 2.50
❑43, Sep 1996 2.50
❑44, Oct 1996 2.50
❑45, Nov 1996; return of Edwin Alva 2.50
❑46, Dec 1996 2.50
❑47, Jan 1997 2.50
❑48, Feb 1997 2.50
❑49, Mar 1997 2.50
❑50, Apr 1997; Giant-size; Final Issue 3.95

Hardwired
Bangtro

❑1, May 1994 2.25

Hardy Boys
Gold Key

❑1, Apr 1970, 1: Pete Jones; 1: Wanda Kay Breckinridge; Based on animated TV series 28.00
❑2, Jul 1970 18.00
❑3, Oct 1970 18.00
❑4, Jan 1971, DS (a); Final issue 18.00

Hari Kari
Black Out

❑0; indicia says "#0 #1" 2.95
❑1; ca. 1995 2.95

Hari Kari: Live & Untamed
Blackout

❑0; Includes photo feature 2.95
❑0/Variant; variant cover 4.00
❑1 2.95

Hari Kari Private Gallery
Blackout

❑0; Pin-Ups 2.95

Hari Kari: Rebirth
Black Out

❑1; 1996 2.95

Hari Kari Resurrection
Blackout

❑1 2.95

Hari Kari: The Beginning
Black Out

❑1; Green background; ca. 1996 2.95

Hari Kari: The Diary of Kari Sun
Blackout

❑½; prose accompanied with pin-ups 2.95

Hari Kari: The Silence of Evil
Black Out

❑0; 1996 2.95

Harlem Globetrotters
Gold Key

❑1, Apr 1972 13.00
❑2, Jul 1972 9.00
❑3, Oct 1972, A: Curly. A: Gip. A: Pabs. A: Geese. A: Granny. A: Dribbles. A: B.J.. A: Meadowlark 7.00
❑4, Jan 1973 7.00
❑5, Apr 1973 7.00
❑6, Jul 1973 5.00
❑7, Oct 1973 5.00
❑8, Jan 1974 5.00
❑9, Apr 1974 5.00
❑10, Jul 1974 5.00
❑11, Oct 1974 5.00
❑12, Jan 1975 5.00

Harlem Heroes
Fleetway-Quality

❑1, b&w 1.95
❑2, b&w 1.95
❑3, b&w 1.95
❑4, b&w 1.95
❑5, b&w 1.95
❑6, b&w 1.95

Harlequin
Caliber

❑1, May 1993, b&w; NN 2.95

Harley & Ivy: Love on the Lam
DC

❑1, Nov 2001, b&w 5.95

Harley Quinn
DC

❑1, Dec 2000; V: Joker; Harley Quinn breaks Joker out of Arkham Asylum 3.50
❑2, Jan 2001; V: Two-Face 3.00
❑3, Feb 2001 A: Catwoman 3.00
❑4, Mar 2001 3.00
❑5, Apr 2001; O: Harley Quinn 3.00
❑6, May 2001; V: Riddler; Harley Quinn robs Wayne Manor 2.50

Other grades: Multiply price above by 5/6 for VF/NM • 2/3 for VERY FINE • 1/3 for FINE • 1/5 for VERY GOOD • 1/8 for GOOD

❑7, Jun 2001; V: Big Barda; V: Riddler... 2.50
❑8, Jul 2001 2.50
❑9, Aug 2001 2.50
❑10, Sep 2001 2.50
❑11, Oct 2001 2.25
❑12, Nov 2001 2.95
❑13, Dec 2001; Joker: Last Laugh crossover 2.25
❑14, Jan 2002 2.25
❑15, Feb 2002 2.25
❑16, Mar 2002 A: Poison Ivy 2.25
❑17, Apr 2002 2.25
❑18, May 2002 2.25
❑19, Jun 2002 A: Superman 2.25
❑20, Jul 2002 2.25
❑21, Aug 2002 2.25
❑22, Sep 2002 2.25
❑23, Oct 2002 2.50
❑24, Nov 2002; Harley Quinn's spirit inhabits various bodies before Zatanna recreates Harley Quinn's physical body 2.50
❑25, Dec 2002; Batman V: Joker 2.50
❑26, Jan 2003 2.50
❑27, Feb 2003 2.50
❑28, Mar 2003 2.50
❑29, Apr 2003 2.50
❑30, May 2003 2.50
❑31, Jun 2003 2.50
❑32, Jul 2003 2.50
❑33, Aug 2003 2.50
❑34, Sep 2003 2.50
❑35, Oct 2003 2.50
❑36, Nov 2003 2.50
❑37, Dec 2003 2.50
❑38, Jan 2004, Final Issue 2.50

Harley Quinn: Our Worlds At War
DC

❑1, Oct 2001, b&w 2.95

Harley Rider
Hungness

❑1 2.00

Harold Hedd (Last Gasp)
Last Gasp Eco-Funnies

❑1, Adult 8.00
❑2; Adult 4.00

Harold Hedd in "Hitler's Cocaine"
Kitchen Sink

❑1, Jan 1984; Printed on coated paper .. 40.00
❑2, Jan 1984; Printed on coated paper .. 40.00

Harpy Pin-Up Special
Peregrine Entertainment

❑1, May 1998, b&w; Adult 3.00

Harpy Preview
Ground Zero

❑1, Oct 1996, b&w 3.00

Harpy: Prize of the Overlord
Ground Zero

❑1, Dec 1996, b&w 3.00
❑2, Feb 1997, b&w 3.00
❑3, Apr 1997, b&w; cover says Blood of the Demon 3.00
❑4 3.00
❑5 3.00
❑6 3.00

Harrier Preview
Harrier

❑1; 1: Cuirass; Night Bird 1.00

Harriers
Express / Entity

❑1; Foil stamped cover 2.95
❑2 2.95
❑3 2.95

Harrowers
Marvel / Epic

❑1, Dec 1993, glow in the dark cover 2.95
❑2, Jan 1994 2.50
❑3, Feb 1994 2.50
❑4, Mar 1994 2.50
❑5, Apr 1994 2.50
❑6, May 1994 2.50

Harry the Cop
Slave Labor

❑1, Apr 1992, b&w; Adult 2.95
❑1/2nd, Oct 1992, b&w; 2nd printing; Adult 2.95

Harsh Realm
Harris

❑1, Feb 1994 2.95
❑2, Mar 1994 2.95
❑3, Apr 1994 2.95
❑4, May 1994 2.95
❑5, Jun 1994 2.95
❑6, Jul 1994 2.95

Harte of Darkness
Eternity

❑1, b&w 2.50
❑2, b&w 2.50
❑3, b&w 2.50
❑4, b&w 2.50

Harvey
Marvel

❑1, Oct 1970, humor 50.00
❑2, Dec 1970, humor 18.00
❑3, Jun 1972, humor 8.00
❑4, Aug 1972, humor 6.00
❑5, Oct 1972, humor 6.00
❑6, Dec 1972, humor 6.00

Hate
Fantagraphics

❑1, Spr 1990, b&w; Spring 1990 8.00
❑1/2nd, Nov 1991; 2nd printing 3.50
❑1/3rd, Dec 1992; 3rd printing 2.00
❑2, Sum 1990 5.00
❑2/2nd; 2nd printing 3.00
❑2/3rd, May 1993; 3rd printing 2.50
❑3, Fal 1990 4.00
❑3/2nd; 2nd printing 2.50
❑3/3rd, Jul 1993; 3rd printing 2.50
❑4, Spr 1991 4.00
❑4/2nd, Mar 1992; 2nd printing 2.00
❑5, Sum 1991 4.00
❑5/2nd, May 1992; 2nd printing 2.00
❑6, Fal 1991 4.00
❑7, Win 1991 3.00
❑8, Spr 1992 3.00
❑9, Sum 1992 3.00
❑10, Fal 1992 3.00
❑11, Win 1993 2.50
❑12, Spr 1993 2.50
❑13, Sum 1993 2.50
❑14, Fal 1993 2.50
❑15, Spr 1994 2.50
❑16, Fal 1994; color story 2.95
❑17, Win 1994 2.95
❑18, Apr 1995 2.95
❑19, Jun 1995 2.95
❑20, Aug 1995; color and b&w 2.95
❑21, Oct 1995 2.95
❑22, Dec 1995 2.95
❑23, ca. 1996 2.95
❑24, ca. 1996 2.95
❑25, ca. 1996 2.95
❑26, ca. 1996 2.95
❑27, May 1997 2.95
❑28, Jul 1997 2.95
❑29, ca. 1997 2.95
❑30, ca. 1997; color and b&w 2.95

Hateball
Fantagraphics

❑1; giveaway; NN; Giveaway 1.00

Hate Jamboree!
Fantagraphics

❑1, Oct 1998, newsprint cover 3.95

Haunted
Charlton

❑1, Sep 1971, SD (w); SD (a) 12.00
❑2, Nov 1971, SD (c) 6.00
❑3, Jan 1972 6.00
❑4, Feb 1972, SD (c) 5.00
❑5, Apr 1972, SD (c) 5.00
❑6, Jun 1972, WH (a) 5.00
❑7, Aug 1972, SD (c) 4.00
❑8, Oct 1972, SD (c) 4.00
❑9, Dec 1972 4.00
❑10, Jan 1973, JAb (a) 4.00
❑11, Mar 1973 3.00
❑12, May 1973, PM (a) 3.00
❑13, Jul 1973, SD (a) 3.00
❑14, Sep 1973 3.00
❑15, Nov 1973, SD, JAb (a) 3.00
❑16, Jun 1974, SD, WH (a) 3.00
❑17, Jul 1974, PM (a) 3.00
❑18, Oct 1974, JSa (c); WH (w); WH (a) 3.00
❑19, Dec 1974, PM (a) 3.00
❑20, Feb 1975, TS (w); TS (a) 3.00
❑21, Apr 1975, TS (w); TS (a); Title becomes Baron Weirwulf's Haunted Library 3.00
❑22, Jun 1975, TS, JSa (a) 3.00
❑23, Sep 1975, TS (c); TS, SD, PM (a) .. 3.00
❑24, Nov 1975, SD (a) 3.00
❑25, Jan 1976, TS (c) 3.00
❑26, Mar 1976 3.00
❑27, May 1976 3.00
❑28, Jul 1976, MZ (c) 3.00
❑29, Sep 1976 3.00
❑30, Nov 1976 3.00
❑31, Jan 1977, Cover says Sep 77 3.00
❑32, Oct 1977, WH (a) 3.00
❑33, Dec 1977, JSa, PM (a) 3.00
❑34, Feb 1978 3.00
❑35, Apr 1978, DN, DH, JSa (a); Cover reprinted from #12 3.00
❑36, May 1978, TS (a) 3.00
❑37, Jul 1978, TS (a); "Fiendish Females" issue 3.00
❑38, Oct 1978 3.00
❑39, Dec 1978, SD (a); Cover reprinted from #10 3.00
❑40, Feb 1979, SD, JAb (a); Cover reprinted from #8 3.00
❑41, Apr 1979 3.00
❑42, Jun 1979, Cover reprinted from #15 3.00
❑43, Jul 1979, WH (a); Reprints Haunted #9 3.00
❑44, Sep 1979, Cover reprinted from #20 3.00
❑45, Oct 1979, DN, JSa, WH (a) 3.00
❑46, Dec 1979 3.00
❑47, Jan 1980, SD, MZ (a) 3.00
❑48, Mar 1980, SD (c); Cover reprinted from #3 3.00
❑49, May 1980 3.00
❑50, Jul 1980 3.00
❑51, Oct 1980, All Ditko Issue 2.50
❑52, Dec 1980 2.50
❑53, Jan 1981, Doctor Graves issue 2.50
❑54, Mar 1981 2.50
❑55, May 1981, TS (w); TS, PM (a); Reprints from Haunted #19 and 21 .... 2.50
❑56, Jul 1981, SD (c) 2.50
❑57, Sep 1981, SD (c) 2.50
❑58, Oct 1981 2.50
❑59, Jan 1982, DN, JSa (a) 2.50
❑60, Mar 1982 2.50
❑61, Apr 1982 2.50
❑62, Jul 1982, Infinity cover 2.50
❑63, Sep 1982, WH (c); WH (w); JSa, WH (a) 2.50
❑64, Nov 1982 2.50
❑65, Jan 1983 2.50
❑66, Mar 1983, TS (c) 2.50
❑67, May 1983, TS, SD (a) 2.50
❑68, Jul 1983 2.50
❑69, Sep 1983, Cover reprinted from #5 2.50
❑70, Nov 1983 2.50
❑71, Jan 1984 2.50
❑72, Mar 1984 2.50
❑73, May 1984, TS (c) 2.50
❑74, Jul 1984 2.50
❑75, Sep 1984, Final Issue 2.50

Haunted
Chaos

❑1, Jan 2002 2.95
❑1/Ltd., Jan 2002; premium edition; Limited to 3,000 copies 2.95
❑2, Feb 2002 2.95
❑3, Mar 2002 2.95
❑4, Apr 2002 2.95

Haunted Man
Dark Horse

❑1, Mar 2000 2.95
❑2 2.95
❑3 2.95

Haunted Mansion
Slave Labor

❑1, Nov 2005 2.95

Other grades: Multiply price above by 5/6 for VF/NM • 2/3 for VERY FINE • 1/3 for FINE • 1/5 for VERY GOOD • 1/8 for GOOD

Hansi, the Girl Who Loved the Swastika

Young German girl is saved by religion
©Spire

Harbinger

Valiant series got very hot, then very cold
©Valiant

Hard Rock Comics

More unauthorized rock biographies
©Revolutionary

Hardware

One of the first DC Milestone titles
©DC

Hardy Boys

Live action version predated Shaun Cassidy
©Gold Key

N-MINT

Haunt of Fear (Gladstone)
Gladstone

❑1, May 1991; Reprints stories from The Haunt of Fear #17, Weird Science-Fantasy #28 .... 2.50
❑2, Jul 1991 .... 2.50

Haunt of Fear (RCP)
Cochran

❑1, Sep 1991; Giant-size; Reprints Haunt of Fear #14, Weird Fantasy #13 .... 2.00
❑2, Nov 1991; Giant-size; Giant-size 2.00
❑3, Jan 1992; Giant-size; Giant-size 2.00
❑4, Mar 1992; Giant-size; Giant-size 2.00
❑5, May 1992; Giant-size; Giant-size 2.00

Haunt of Fear (RCP)
Gemstone

❑1, Nov 1992; Reprints The Haunt of Fear (EC) #1 .... 2.00
❑2, Feb 1993; Reprints The Haunt of Fear (EC) #2 .... 2.00
❑3, May 1993; Reprints The Haunt of Fear (EC) #3 .... 2.00
❑4, Aug 1993; Reprints The Haunt of Fear (EC) #4 .... 2.00
❑5, Nov 1993; Reprints The Haunt of Fear (EC) #5 .... 2.00
❑6, Feb 1994; Reprints The Haunt of Fear (EC) #6 .... 2.00
❑7, May 1994; Reprints The Haunt of Fear (EC) #7 .... 2.00
❑8, Aug 1994; Reprints The Haunt of Fear (EC) #8 .... 2.00
❑9, Nov 1994; Reprints The Haunt of Fear (EC) #9 .... 2.00
❑10, Feb 1995; Reprints The Haunt of Fear (EC) #10 .... 2.00
❑11, May 1995; Reprints The Haunt of Fear (EC) #11 .... 2.00
❑12, Aug 1995; Reprints The Haunt of Fear (EC) #12 .... 2.00
❑13, Nov 1995; Reprints The Haunt of Fear (EC) #13 .... 2.00
❑14, Feb 1996; Reprints The Haunt of Fear (EC) #14 .... 2.00
❑15, May 1996; Reprints The Haunt of Fear (EC) #15 .... 2.00
❑16, Aug 1996; Ray Bradbury story; Reprints The Haunt of Fear (EC) #16; Ray Bradbury adaptation 2.50
❑17, Nov 1996; Reprints The Haunt of Fear (EC) #17 .... 2.50
❑18, Feb 1997; Ray Bradbury story; Reprints The Haunt of Fear (EC) #18 .... 2.50
❑19, May 1997; Reprints The Haunt of Fear (EC) #19; Mentioned in Seduction of the Innocent "A comic book baseball game" 2.50
❑20, Aug 1997; Reprints The Haunt of Fear (EC) #20 .... 2.50
❑21, Nov 1997; Reprints The Haunt of Fear (EC) #21 .... 2.50
❑22, Feb 1998; Reprints The Haunt of Fear (EC) #22 .... 2.50
❑23, May 1998; Reprints The Haunt of Fear (EC) #23 .... 2.50
❑24, Aug 1998; Reprints The Haunt of Fear (EC) #24 .... 2.50
❑25, Nov 1998; Reprints The Haunt of Fear (EC) #25 .... 2.50
❑26, Feb 1999; Reprints The Haunt of Fear (EC) #26 .... 2.50

N-MINT

❑27, May 1999; Reprints The Haunt of Fear (EC) #27 .... 2.50
❑28, Aug 1999; Reprints The Haunt of Fear (EC) #28 .... 2.50
❑Ann 1; Reprints The Haunt of Fear #1-5 .... 8.95
❑Ann 2; Reprints The Haunt of Fear #6-10 .... 9.95
❑Ann 3; Reprints The Haunt of Fear #11-15 .... 10.95
❑Ann 4; Reprints The Haunt of Fear #16-20 .... 10.50
❑Ann 5; Reprints The Haunt of Fear #21-25 .... 11.95
❑Ann 6; Reprints The Haunt of Fear #26-28 .... 8.95

Haunt of Horror
Marvel

❑1, May 1974 .... 8.00
❑2, Jul 1974 .... 6.00
❑3, Sep 1974 .... 5.00
❑4, Nov 1974 .... 5.00
❑5, Jan 1975 .... 5.00

Haunt of Horror: Edgar Allan Poe
Marvel

❑1, Aug 2006, b&w 3.99
❑2, Sep 2006 .... 3.99
❑3, Sep 2006; b&w 3.99

Haven: The Broken City
DC

❑1, Feb 2002 .... 2.50
❑2, Mar 2002 .... 2.50
❑3, Apr 2002 .... 2.50
❑4, May 2002 .... 2.50
❑5, Jun 2002 .... 2.50
❑6, Jul 2002 .... 2.50
❑7, Aug 2002 .... 2.50
❑8, Sep 2002 .... 2.50
❑9, Oct 2002 .... 2.50

Havoc, Inc.
Radio

❑1, Mar 1998 .... 2.95
❑2, Jun 1998 .... 2.95
❑3, Sep 1998 .... 2.95
❑4, Dec 1998 .... 2.95
❑5 1999 .... 2.95
❑6 1999 .... 2.95
❑7 .... 2.95
❑8, Jul 2000 .... 2.95
❑9 .... 2.95

Havok & Wolverine: Meltdown
Marvel / Epic

❑1, Mar 1989 .... 4.00
❑2, ca. 1989 .... 4.00
❑3, ca. 1989 .... 4.00
❑4, Oct 1989 .... 4.00

Hawaiian Dick
Image

❑1, Dec 2002 .... 2.95
❑2, Jan 2003 .... 2.95
❑3, Feb 2003 .... 2.95

Hawaiian Dick: The Last Resort
Image

❑1, Aug 2004 .... 2.95
❑2, Dec 2004 .... 2.95

N-MINT

Hawk & the Dove
DC

❑1, Aug 1968, SD (c); SD (a) 60.00
❑2, Oct 1968, SD (c); DG (w); SD (a) 40.00
❑3, Dec 1968, GK (c); DG (w); GK (a) 40.00
❑4, Feb 1969, GK (c); DG (w); GK (a) 40.00
❑5, Mar 1969, GK (c); DG, GK (w); GK (a); A: Teen Titans 40.00
❑6, Jun 1969, GK (c); DG, GK (w); GK (a); Final Issue 30.00

Hawk and Dove
DC

❑1, Oct 1988; RL (c); RL (a); 1: Dove II. 1: Dove II 3.00
❑2, Nov 1988 RL (c); RL (a) 2.50
❑3, Dec 1988 RL (c); RL (a) 2.00
❑4, Win 1988; RL (c); RL (a); Winter 1988 .... 2.00
❑5, Hol 1989; RL (c); RL (a); O: Dove. Hol 1989 .... 2.00

Hawk and Dove
DC

❑1, Jun 1989 .... 1.50
❑2, Jul 1989 .... 1.00
❑3, Aug 1989 .... 1.00
❑4, Sep 1989 .... 1.00
❑5, Oct 1989 .... 1.00
❑6, Nov 1989 .... 1.00
❑7, Dec 1989 .... 1.00
❑8, Jan 1990 .... 1.00
❑9, Feb 1990 .... 1.00
❑10, Mar 1990 .... 1.00
❑11, Apr 1990 .... 1.00
❑12, May 1990 A: New Titans 1.00
❑13, Jun 1990 .... 1.00
❑14, Jul 1990 .... 1.00
❑15, Aug 1990 .... 1.00
❑16, Sep 1990 .... 1.00
❑17, Oct 1990 .... 1.00
❑18, Nov 1990 .... 1.00
❑19, Dec 1990 .... 1.00
❑20, Jan 1991 .... 1.00
❑21, Feb 1991 .... 1.00
❑22, Mar 1991 .... 1.00
❑23, Apr 1991 .... 1.00
❑24, May 1991 .... 1.00
❑25, Jun 1991; Giant-size 2.00
❑26, Aug 1992; O: Hawk and Dove 1.25
❑27, Sep 1991 .... 1.25
❑28, Oct 1991; Giant-size; War of the Gods 2.00
❑Ann 1, Oct 1990; Titans West 3.00
❑Ann 2, Sep 1991; Armageddon 2001 .... 2.00

Hawk and Dove
DC

❑1, Nov 1997; O: new team 2.50
❑2, Dec 1997 .... 2.50
❑3, Jan 1998 .... 2.50
❑4, Feb 1998; V: Count Vertigo 2.50
❑5, Mar 1998; Final Issue 2.50

Hawk & Windblade
Warp

❑1, Aug 1997 .... 2.95
❑2, Sep 1997 .... 2.95

Other grades: Multiply price above by 5/6 for VF/NM • 2/3 for VERY FINE • 1/3 for FINE • 1/5 for VERY GOOD • 1/8 for GOOD

Hawkeye
Marvel

❑1, Sep 1983, O: Hawkeye 2.50
❑2, Oct 1983 2.00
❑3, Nov 1983, 1: Oddball 2.00
❑4, Dec 1983 2.00

Hawkeye
Marvel

❑1, Jan 1994 1.75
❑2, Feb 1994 1.75
❑3, Mar 1994 1.75
❑4, Apr 1994 1.75

Hawkeye
Marvel

❑1, Dec 2003 2.99
❑2, Jan 2004 2.99
❑3, Feb 2004 2.99
❑4, Mar 2004 2.99
❑5, Apr 2004 2.99
❑6, May 2004 2.99
❑7, Jun 2004 2.99
❑8, Aug 2004 2.99

Hawkeye: Earth's Mightiest Marksman
Marvel

❑1, Oct 1998; V: Taskmaster; Oddball; One-shot 2.99

Hawkgirl
DC

❑50, Jun 2006, During, DC's "One Year Later," series title changed from Hawkman (4th series) after #49 2.50
❑51, Jul 2006 2.50
❑52, Aug 2006, One Year Later 2.99
❑53, Sep 2006, V: Khimaera 2.99
❑54, Oct 2006, V: Khimaera 2.99
❑55, Nov 2006, V: Khimaera 2.99
❑56, Dec 2006, V: Khimaera 2.99
❑57, Jan 2007 2.99
❑58, Feb 2007 2.99
❑59, Mar 2007, V: Blackfire 2.99
❑60 2.99
❑61 2.99
❑62 2.99
❑63 2.99
❑64 2.99
❑65 2.99
❑66 2.99

Hawkman
DC

❑1, May 1964, MA (c); MA (a) 475.00
❑2, Jul 1964, MA (c); MA (a); Julius Schwartz autograph; Murphy Anderson autograph 200.00
❑3, Sep 1964, MA (c); MA (a) 75.00
❑4, Nov 1964, MA (c); MA (a); O: Zatanna. 1: Zatanna; Guy H. Lillian L.O.C 200.00
❑5, Jan 1965, MA (c); MA (a); 2: Shadow-Thief 65.00
❑6, Mar 1965, MA (c); MA (a); Mike Friedrich L.O.C 65.00
❑7, May 1965, MA (c); MA (a); reprint from Mystery in Space #87 65.00
❑8, Jul 1965, MA (c); MA (a); Guy H. Lillian L.O.C 65.00
❑9, Sep 1965, MA (c); MA (a); A: Atom. Atom & Hawkman learn identities 65.00
❑10, Nov 1965, MA (c); MA (a); 2: CAW 50.00
❑11, Jan 1966, MA (c); MA (a); 1: Shrike 50.00
❑12, Mar 1966, MA (c); MA (a) 50.00
❑13, May 1966, MA (c); MA (a); Dave Cockrum L.O.C 40.00
❑14, Jul 1966, MA (c); MA (a); Guy H. Lillian L.O.C 40.00
❑15, Sep 1966, MA (c); MA (a); Guy H. Lillian L.O.C 40.00
❑16, Nov 1966, MA (c); MA (a); Irene Vartanoff L.O.C.; Guy H. Lillian L.O.C. 36.00
❑17, Jan 1967, MA (c); MA (a); Irene Vartanoff L.O.C.; Guy H. Lillian L.O.C. 36.00
❑18, Mar 1967, MA (c); MA (a); A: Adam Strange. V: Manhawks. Part 1 36.00
❑19, May 1967, MA (c); MA (a); Part 2 36.00
❑20, Jul 1967, MA (c); MA (a); 1: Lion Mane; Steve Leialoha L.O.C 32.00
❑21, Sep 1967, MA (c); MA (a); 2nd Appearance of Lion Mane 32.00
❑22, Nov 1967, DD (c); DD (a) 32.00
❑23, Jan 1968, DD (c); DD (a) 32.00
❑24, Mar 1968, DD (c); DD (a); Reprint story 32.00
❑25, May 1968, DD (c); DD (a); Golden Age Hawkman reprint 32.00
❑26, Jul 1968, DD (c); JK (w); JK, DD (a); reprints 2-page Kirby story 32.00
❑27, Sep 1968, JKu (c); DD (a); Series continues in Atom and Hawkman #39; Final Issue 32.00

Hawkman
DC

❑1, Aug 1986; RHo (c); RHo (a); Shadow-Thief Who's Who bio page 2.50
❑2, Sep 1986; RHo (c); RHo (a); V: Shadow Thief 2.00
❑3, Oct 1986; RHo (c); RHo (a); V: Shadow Thief 2.00
❑4, Nov 1986 RHo (c); RHo (a); A: Zatanna 1.50
❑5, Dec 1986; RHo (c); RHo (a); V: Lionmane 1.50
❑6, Jan 1987; RHo (c); RHo (a); V: Lionmane 1.50
❑7, Feb 1987; V: Darkwing 1.50
❑8, Mar 1987; V: Darkwing 1.50
❑9, Apr 1987 1.50
❑10, May 1987 A: Superman 1.50
❑11, Jun 1987 1.50
❑12, Jul 1987 1.50
❑13, Aug 1987 1.50
❑14, Sep 1987 1.50
❑15, Oct 1987 1.50
❑16, Nov 1987 1.50
❑17, Dec 1987; Final Issue 1.50
❑Special 1, Mar 1986 RHo (c); RHo (w); RHo (a) 3.00

Hawkman
DC

❑0, Oct 1994; O: Hawkman (new) 2.50
❑1, Sep 1993; JDu (c); JDu (a); foil cover 2.50
❑2, Oct 1993 JDu (c); JDu (a) 1.75
❑3, Nov 1993 JDu (a) 1.75
❑4, Dec 1993 JDu (a) 1.75
❑5, Jan 1994 1.75
❑6, Feb 1994 1.75
❑7, Mar 1994 LMc (a) 1.75
❑8, Apr 1994 LMc (a) 1.75
❑9, May 1994 1.75
❑10, Jun 1994 1.75
❑11, Jul 1994 A: Carter Hall 1.75
❑12, Aug 1994 LMc (a) 1.95
❑13, Sep 1994; Zero Hour 1.95
❑14, Nov 1994 1.95
❑15, Dec 1994; A: Aquaman. D: Scavanger I 1.95
❑16, Jan 1995 A: Wonder Woman 1.95
❑17, Feb 1995 1.95
❑18, May 1995 1.95
❑19, Apr 1995 1.95
❑20, May 1995 1.95
❑21, Jun 1995; V: Shadow Thief. V: Gentleman Ghost 2.25
❑22, Jul 1995 2.25
❑23, Aug 1995; Story continues in Guy Gardner: Warrior #34 2.25
❑24, Sep 1995 2.25
❑25, Oct 1995 2.25
❑26, Nov 1995; A: Scarecrow. Underworld Unleashed 2.25
❑27, Dec 1995; A: Neuron. A: Silent Knight. Underworld Unleashed 2.25
❑28, Jan 1996; V: Dr. Polaris 2.25
❑29, Feb 1996 A: Vandal Savage 2.25
❑30, Mar 1996 2.25
❑31, Apr 1996 2.25
❑32, Jun 1996; Final issue 2.25
❑33, Jul 1996; A: Arion. D: Hawkman; Final Issue 2.25
❑Ann 1, ca. 1993; JDu (a); 1: Mongrel; Bloodlines; 1993 Ann 3.50
❑Ann 2, ca. 1995; BG (a); Year One 3.95

Hawkman
DC

❑1, May 2002 JRo (w) 3.00
❑2, Jun 2002 JRo (w) 2.50
❑3, Jul 2002 JRo (w) 2.50
❑4, Aug 2002; JRo (w); 1:ficer Isabella 2.50
❑5, Sep 2002 JRo (w) 2.50
❑6, Oct 2002; JRo (w); V: Alias the Spider 2.50
❑7, Nov 2002; JRo (w); Lives Past story; IR Nighthawk & Cinnamon are past Lives of Hawkman & Hawkgirl 2.50
❑8, Dec 2002 2.50
❑9, Jan 2003; JRo (w); Includes preview of Aquaman (6th Series) #1 2.50
❑10, Feb 2003 JRo (w) 2.50
❑11, Mar 2003 2.50
❑12, Apr 2003 2.50
❑13, May 2003 2.50
❑14, Jun 2003 2.50
❑15, Jul 2003 2.50
❑16, Aug 2003 2.50
❑17, Sep 2003 2.50
❑18, Oct 2003 2.50
❑19, Nov 2003, 1: Headhunter 2.50
❑20, Dec 2003 2.50
❑21, Jan 2004, DC: The New Frontier preview 2.50
❑22, Jan 2004, Hard Time preview 2.50
❑23, Feb 2004, Continued from JSA #56 & into #57 2.50
❑24, Mar 2004, Continued from JSA #57 & into #58 2.50
❑25, Apr 2004, Continued from JSA #58 2.50
❑26, May 2004; 1: Bishop (past life of Hawkman); 1: Bishop 2.50
❑27, Jun 2004 2.50
❑28, Jul 2004 2.50
❑29, Aug 2004 2.50
❑30, Sep 2004 2.50
❑31, Oct 2004; Includes Sky Captain and the World of Tomorrow promo CD; Includes Sky Captain and the World of Tomorrow promo poster 2.50
❑32, Nov 2004, Kevin Nowlan cover 2.50
❑33, Dec 2004 2.50
❑34, Jan 2005 2.50
❑35, Feb 2005 2.50
❑36, Mar 2005 2.50
❑37, Apr 2005; Return of Golden Eagle . 2.50
❑38, May 2005 2.50
❑39, Jun 2005; 1: Thought Terror 2.50
❑40, Jul 2005 2.50
❑41, Aug 2005 8.00
❑42, Sep 2005; V: Pilgrim 4.00
❑43, Oct 2005; O: post-crisis Golden Eagle 2.50
❑44, Sep 2005; Golden Eagle becomes Hawkman 2.50
❑45, Dec 2005; V: Golden Eagle 2.50
❑46, Jan 2006; Infinite Crisis tie-in 2.50
❑47, Feb 2006, Rann-Thanagr War tie-in 2.50
❑48, Mar 2006, Rann/Thanagr War tie-in 2.50
❑49, Apr 2006, During DC's "One Year Later," series name changes to Hawkgirl with #50 2.50

Hawkman Secret Files and Origins
DC

❑1, Oct 2002, b&w 4.95

Hawkmoon: The Jewel in the Skull
First

❑1, May 1986 1.75
❑2, Jul 1986 1.75
❑3, Sep 1986 1.75
❑4, Nov 1986 1.75

Hawkmoon: The Mad God's Amulet
First

❑1, Jan 1987 1.75
❑2, Feb 1987 1.75
❑3, Mar 1987 1.75
❑4, Apr 1987 1.75

Hawkmoon: The Runestaff
First

❑1, ca. 1988 2.00
❑2, ca. 1988 2.00
❑3, ca. 1988 2.00
❑4, ca. 1988 2.00

Hawkmoon: The Sword of the Dawn
First

❑1, Sep 1987 1.75
❑2, Nov 1987 1.75
❑3, Jan 1988 1.75
❑4, Mar 1988 1.75

Hawkshaws
Image

❑1, Mar 2000, b&w 2.95

Hawk, Street Avenger
Taurus

❑1, Jun 1996, b&w 2.50

Hawkworld
DC

❑1, Aug 1989; O: Hawkman. New costume 4.00

Harlem Globetrotters

Based on the Hanna-Barbera animated series
©Gold Key

Harley Quinn

More with the Joker's wacky sidekick
©DC

Hate

You don't want Buddy Bradley's life...
©Fantagraphics

Hawk & the Dove

Brothers who become crimefighters
©DC

Hawkeye

Marvel's archer gets starring role, finally
©Marvel

	N-MINT
❑2, Sep 1989; Truman	4.00
❑3, Oct 1989; Truman	4.00

Hawkworld
DC

	N-MINT
❑1, Jun 1990; 1: post-Crisis Kanjar Ro	2.50
❑2, Jul 1990	2.00
❑3, Aug 1990	2.00
❑4, Sep 1990	2.00
❑5, Oct 1990	2.00
❑6, Dec 1990	2.00
❑7, Jan 1991	2.00
❑8, Feb 1991	2.00
❑9, Mar 1991	2.00
❑10, Apr 1991	2.00
❑11, May 1991; 1: Killer Shark	1.50
❑12, Jun 1991	1.50
❑13, Jul 1991	1.50
❑14, Aug 1991	1.50
❑15, Sep 1991; War of the Gods	1.50
❑16, Oct 1991; War of the Gods	1.50
❑17, Nov 1991	1.50
❑18, Dec 1991	1.50
❑19, Jan 1992	1.50
❑20, Feb 1992	1.50
❑21, Mar 1992	1.50
❑22, Apr 1992; 1: Fel Andar (JLI's fake Hawkman; Father of Golden Eagle)	1.50
❑23, May 1992	1.50
❑24, Jul 1992	1.50
❑25, Aug 1992	1.50
❑26, Sep 1992	1.50
❑27, Oct 1992; JDu (a); 1: The White Dragon	1.75
❑28, Nov 1992 JDu (a)	1.75
❑29, Dec 1992 JDu (a)	1.75
❑30, Jan 1993; 1: Count Viper. 1: The Netherworld	1.75
❑31, Feb 1993	1.75
❑32, Mar 1993; Final Issue	1.75
❑Ann 1, Dec 1990 A: Flash	3.00
❑Ann 2, Aug 1991	2.95
❑Ann 2/2nd, Aug 1991; silver	2.95
❑Ann 3, ca. 1992; LMc (c); LMc (a); Eclipso	2.95

Haywire
DC

	N-MINT
❑1, Oct 1988; 1: Haywire	1.25
❑2, Nov 1988	1.25
❑3, Dec 1988	1.25
❑4, Dec 1988	1.25
❑5, Jan 1989	1.25
❑6, Jan 1989	1.25
❑7, Mar 1989; V: White Lotus	1.25
❑8, Apr 1989	1.25
❑9, May 1989	1.25
❑10, Jun 1989	1.25
❑11, Jul 1989	1.25
❑12, Aug 1989	1.25
❑13, Sep 1989; Final Issue	1.25

Hazard
Image

	N-MINT
❑1, Jun 1996	1.75
❑2, Jul 1996, cover says Jun, indicia says Jul	1.75
❑3, Jul 1996	1.75
❑4, Aug 1996	1.75
❑5, Sep 1996	1.75
❑6, Oct 1996, cover says Sep, indicia says Oct	2.25
❑7, Nov 1996, Final Issue	2.25

Hazard!
Motion

	N-MINT
❑1, b&w; Breakneck Blvd	2.50

Hazard!
Reckless Vision

	N-MINT
❑1, b&w; first Breakneck Blvd. Story	2.50

H-Bomb
Antarctic

	N-MINT
❑1, Apr 1993, b&w; Adult	2.95

Head
Fantagraphics

	N-MINT
❑1 2002	7.00
❑2	3.95
❑3	3.95
❑4	3.95
❑5	3.95
❑6	3.95
❑7	3.95
❑8, Jun 2004	3.95
❑9, Oct 2004	3.95
❑10, Jan 2005	3.95
❑11, Aug 2005; Computer-illustrated cover	3.95
❑12, Aug 2005	3.95
❑13, Dec 2005	3.95

Headbanger
Parody

	N-MINT
❑1	2.50

Headbuster
Antarctic

	N-MINT
❑1, Sep 1998, b&w	2.95

Headhunters
Image

	N-MINT
❑1, Apr 1997, b&w; cover says Mar, indicia says Apr	2.95
❑2, May 1997, b&w	2.95
❑3, Jun 1997, b&w	2.95

Headless Horseman
Eternity

	N-MINT
❑1, b&w	2.25
❑2, b&w	2.25

Headman
Innovation

	N-MINT
❑1	2.50

Health
David Tompkins

	N-MINT
❑1	1.00
❑2	1.50
❑3	1.50
❑4	2.00
❑5	2.00
❑6	5.00

Heap
Skywald

	N-MINT
❑1, Sep 1971 TS, JAb (a)	16.00

Heartbreak Comics
Eclipse

	N-MINT
❑1, b&w; magazine	3.95

Heartbreakers
Dark Horse

	N-MINT
❑1, Apr 1996; Trina Robbins pinup; Ron Randall pinup	2.95
❑2, May 1996; Alex Ross pinup; Matt Haley pinup	2.95
❑3, Jun 1996	2.95
❑4, Jul 1996; Final Issue	2.95

Heartbreakers Superdigest: Year Ten
Image

	N-MINT
❑1, Dec 1999	13.95

Heartland
DC / Vertigo

	N-MINT
❑1, Mar 1997; One-shot	4.95

Heart of Darkness
Hardline

	N-MINT
❑1	2.95

Heart of Empire
Dark Horse

	N-MINT
❑1, Apr 1999	2.95
❑2, May 1999	2.95
❑3, Jun 1999	2.95
❑4, Jul 1999	2.95
❑5, Aug 1999	2.95
❑6, Sep 1999	2.95
❑7, Oct 1999	2.95
❑8, Nov 1999	2.95
❑9, Dec 1999	2.95

Hearts of Darkness
Marvel

	N-MINT
❑1, Dec 1991; Ghost Rider, Wolverine, and Punisher vs. Blackheart	4.95

Heart Throbs
DC

	N-MINT
❑74, Nov 1961	27.00
❑75, Jan 1962	27.00
❑76, Mar 1962	27.00
❑77, May 1962	27.00
❑78, Jul 1962	27.00
❑79, Sep 1962	27.00
❑80, Nov 1962	27.00
❑81, Jan 1963	20.00
❑82, Mar 1963	20.00
❑83, May 1963	20.00
❑84, Jul 1963	20.00
❑85, Sep 1963	20.00
❑86, Nov 1963	20.00
❑87, Jan 1964	20.00
❑88, Mar 1964	20.00
❑89, May 1964	20.00
❑90, Jul 1964	20.00
❑91, Sep 1964	16.00
❑92, Nov 1964	16.00
❑93, Jan 1965	16.00
❑94, Mar 1965	16.00
❑95, May 1965	16.00
❑96, Jul 1965	16.00
❑97, Sep 1965	16.00
❑98, Nov 1965	16.00
❑99, Jan 1966	16.00
❑100, Mar 1966	16.00
❑101, May 1966, A: The Beatles. Beauty column begins; Beatles mentioned on cover	60.00

Other grades: Multiply price above by 5/6 for VF/NM • 2/3 for VERY FINE • 1/3 for FINE • 1/5 for VERY GOOD • 1/8 for GOOD

	N-MINT
❑102, Jul 1966	13.00
❑103, Sep 1966, 3 Girls: Their Lives, Their Loves	13.00
❑104, Nov 1966	13.00
❑105, Jan 1967, Mod fashion column debuts; 3 Girls: Their Lives, Their Loves	13.00
❑106, Mar 1967	13.00
❑107, May 1967	13.00
❑108, Jul 1967, 3 Girls: Their Lives, Their Loves	13.00
❑109, Sep 1967	13.00
❑110, Nov 1967	13.00
❑111, Jan 1968	10.00
❑112, Mar 1968	10.00
❑113, May 1968	10.00
❑114, Jul 1968	10.00
❑115, Sep 1968	10.00
❑116, Nov 1968	10.00
❑117, Jan 1969	10.00
❑118, Mar 1969	10.00
❑119, May 1969	10.00
❑120, Jul 1969	10.00
❑121, Sep 1969	10.00
❑122, Nov 1969	10.00
❑123, Jan 1970	10.00
❑124, Mar 1970	10.00
❑125, May 1970	10.00
❑126, Jul 1970	10.00
❑127, Sep 1970	10.00
❑128, Nov 1970	10.00
❑129, Jan 1971	10.00
❑130, Mar 1971	10.00
❑131, May 1971	9.00
❑132, Jul 1971	9.00
❑133, Sep 1971	9.00
❑134, Oct 1971	9.00
❑135, Nov 1971	9.00
❑136, Dec 1971	9.00
❑137, Jan 1972	9.00
❑138, Feb 1972	9.00
❑139, Mar 1972	9.00
❑140, Apr 1972	9.00
❑141, May 1972	9.00
❑142, Jun 1972	9.00
❑143, Jul 1972	9.00
❑144, Aug 1972	9.00
❑145, Sep 1972	9.00
❑146, Oct 1972, Series continues as Love Stories	9.00

Heartthrobs
DC / Vertigo

	N-MINT
❑1, Jan 1999	2.95
❑2, Feb 1999	2.95
❑3, Mar 1999	2.95
❑4, Apr 1999	2.95

Heathcliff
Marvel / Star

	N-MINT
❑1, Apr 1985	1.50
❑2, Jun 1985	1.00
❑3, Aug 1985	1.00
❑4, Oct 1985	1.00
❑5, Dec 1985	1.00
❑6, Feb 1986, Christmas storylines	1.00
❑7, Apr 1986	1.00
❑8, Jun 1986	1.00
❑9, Aug 1986	1.00
❑10, Sep 1986	1.00
❑11, Oct 1986	1.00
❑12, Nov 1986	1.00
❑13, Dec 1986	1.00
❑14, Feb 1987	1.00
❑15, Apr 1987	1.00
❑16, Jun 1987	1.00
❑17, Aug 1987	1.00
❑18, Sep 1987	1.00
❑19, Oct 1987	1.00
❑20, Nov 1987	1.00
❑21, Dec 1987	1.00
❑22, Feb 1988	1.00
❑23, Apr 1988	1.00
❑24, Jun 1988	1.00
❑25, Aug 1988	1.00
❑26, Sep 1988	1.00
❑27, Oct 1988	1.00
❑28, Nov 1988	1.00
❑29, Dec 1988	1.00
❑30, Feb 1989	1.00
❑31, Mar 1989	1.00
❑32, Apr 1989	1.00
❑33, May 1989	1.00
❑34, Jun 1989	1.00
❑35, Jul 1989	1.00
❑36, Aug 1989	1.00
❑37, Sep 1989	1.00
❑38, Oct 1989	1.00
❑39, Nov 1989	1.00
❑40, Nov 1989	1.00
❑41, Dec 1989	1.00
❑42, Dec 1989	1.00
❑43, Jan 1990	1.00
❑44, Feb 1990	1.00
❑45, Mar 1990	1.00
❑46, Apr 1990	1.00
❑47, May 1990; Batman parody	1.00
❑48, Jun 1990	1.00
❑49, Jul 1990	1.00
❑50, Aug 1990; Giant-size	1.50
❑51, Sep 1990	1.00
❑52, Oct 1990	1.00
❑53, Nov 1990	1.00
❑54, Dec 1990	1.00
❑55, Jan 1991	1.00
❑56, Feb 1991; Final Issue	1.00
❑Ann 1, ca. 1987	1.25

Heathcliff's Funhouse
Marvel / Star

	N-MINT
❑1, May 1987	1.25
❑2, Jun 1987	1.00
❑3, Jul 1987	1.00
❑4, Aug 1987	1.00
❑5, Sep 1987	1.00
❑6, Oct 1987	1.00
❑7, Nov 1987	1.00
❑8, Dec 1987	1.00
❑9, Jan 1988	1.00
❑10, Feb 1988	1.00

Heatseeker
Fantaco

	N-MINT
❑1; NN	5.95

Heaven Above Heaven
Tokyopop

	N-MINT
❑1, May 2005, b&w; Graphic novel	9.99
❑2, Aug 2005; Graphic novel; b&w	9.99
❑3, Nov 2005	9.99

Heaven LLC
Image

	N-MINT
❑1, ca. 2004	12.95

Heaven's Devils
Image

	N-MINT
❑1, Oct 2003	2.95
❑2, Nov 2003	3.50
❑3, Apr 2004	3.50
❑4, Sep 2004	3.50

Heaven Sent
Antarctic

	N-MINT
❑1, Jan 2004	2.99
❑2, Mar 2004	2.99
❑3, May 2004	2.99
❑4, Jul 2004	2.99
❑5, Sep 2004	2.99
❑6, Nov 2004	2.99
❑7, ca. 2005	2.99
❑8, ca. 2005	2.99
❑9, ca. 2005	2.99
❑10, ca. 2005	2.99
❑11, ca. 2005	2.99

Heaven's War
Image

	N-MINT
❑0, ca. 2003	12.95

Heavy Armor
Fantasy General

	N-MINT
❑1	1.70
❑2	1.70
❑3, b&w	1.70

Heavy Hitters
Marvel / Epic

	N-MINT
❑Ann 1 1993; Bound-in Heavy Hitters trading card #3 (Spyke); Wraparound cover	3.75

Heavy Liquid
DC / Vertigo

	N-MINT
❑1, Oct 1999; Adult	5.95
❑2, Nov 1999; Adult	5.95
❑3, Dec 1999; Adult	5.95
❑4, Jan 2000; Adult	5.95
❑5, Feb 2000; Adult	5.95

Heavy Metal Monsters
Revolutionary

	N-MINT
❑1, Jan 1992, b&w	3.00
❑2, ca. 1993; 3-D	3.95

Heck!
Rip Off

	N-MINT
❑1, b&w; Trade Paperback	7.95

Heckle and Jeckle
Gold Key

	N-MINT
❑1, Nov 1962	36.00
❑2, Jan 1963	18.00
❑3, Dec 1962	16.00
❑4, Feb 1963	16.00

Heckle and Jeckle
Dell

	N-MINT
❑1, May 1966	25.00
❑2, Oct 1966	13.00
❑3, Aug 1967	13.00

Heckler
DC

	N-MINT
❑1, Sep 1992	1.25
❑2, Oct 1992; Generic issue	1.25
❑3, Nov 1992	1.25
❑4, Dec 1992	1.25
❑5, Jan 1993	1.25
❑6, Feb 1993	1.25

Hectic Planet
Slave Labor

	N-MINT
❑6, Nov 1993, previously titled Pirate Corp$!	2.50
❑6/2nd, Jan 1996, 2nd printing	2.75

Hector Plasm
Image

	N-MINT
❑1, Jul 2006	5.99

Hector Heathcote
Gold Key

	N-MINT
❑1, Mar 1964, Based on Terrytoons cartoon series	30.00

Hedge Knight
Image

	N-MINT
❑1, Aug 2003	2.95
❑2, Sep 2003	2.95
❑2/A, Sep 2003; Vallejo cover	5.95
❑3, Feb 2004	2.95

Hee Haw
Charlton

	N-MINT
❑1, Aug 1970	13.00
❑2, Oct 1970	8.00
❑3, Dec 1970	6.00
❑4, Feb 1971	6.00
❑5, Apr 1971	6.00
❑6, Jun 1971	6.00
❑7, Aug 1971	6.00

Heirs of Eternity
Image

	N-MINT
❑1, Apr 2003	2.95
❑2, Jun 2003	2.95
❑3, Jul 2003	2.95
❑4, Aug 2003	2.95
❑5, Sep 2003	2.95

He Is Just a Rat
Exclaim! Brand Comics

	N-MINT
❑1, Spr 1995	2.75
❑2, Fal 1995	2.75
❑3, Spr 1996	2.75
❑4, Fal 1996	2.75
❑5, Spr 1997	2.75

Hell
Dark Horse

	N-MINT
❑1, Jul 2003	2.99
❑2, Sep 2003	2.99
❑3, Oct 2003	2.99
❑4, Mar 2004	2.99

Hellbender
Eternity

	N-MINT
❑1, b&w; Shuriken	2.25

Hawkman

Flier from The Brave and The Bold breaks out
©DC

Hawkworld

Mini-series remakes legend of Hawkman
©DC

Haywire

Stranger steals special super-suit
©DC

Heart Throbs

DC romance title inherited from Quality Comics
©DC

Heathcliff

Comic-panel cat has longest-running Star title
©Marvel

Hellblazer
DC

	N-MINT
❑1, Jan 1988; 40 pages	10.00
❑2, Feb 1988	5.00
❑3, Mar 1988	4.00
❑4, Apr 1988	4.00
❑5, May 1988	4.00
❑6, Jun 1988	4.00
❑7, Jul 1988	4.00
❑8, Aug 1988 AA (a)	4.00
❑9, Sep 1988; AA (a); A: Swamp Thing. Continues in Swamp Thing #76	4.00
❑10, Oct 1988; A: Swamp Thing, Abby. Continues from Swamp Thing #76	4.00
❑11, Nov 1988	3.50
❑12, Dec 1988	3.50
❑13, Dec 1988; References to British comics	3.50
❑14, Jan 1989	3.00
❑15, Jan 1989	3.00
❑16, Feb 1989	3.00
❑17, Apr 1989	3.00
❑18, May 1989 AA (a)	3.00
❑19, Jun 1989 AA (a)	3.00
❑20, Jul 1989 AA (a)	3.00
❑21, Aug 1989 AA (a)	2.50
❑22, Sep 1989 AA (a)	2.50
❑23, Oct 1989 A: Sherlock Holmes	2.50
❑24, Nov 1989	2.50
❑25, Jan 1990	2.50
❑26, Feb 1990	2.50
❑27, Mar 1990 NG (w)	9.00
❑28, Apr 1990; D: Thomas Constantine	3.00
❑29, May 1990	3.00
❑30, Jun 1990	3.00
❑31, Jul 1990	3.00
❑32, Aug 1990; Cover credits list incorrect writer	3.00
❑33, Sep 1990	3.00
❑34, Oct 1990	3.00
❑35, Nov 1990	3.00
❑36, Dec 1990	3.00
❑37, Jan 1991	3.00
❑38, Feb 1991	3.00
❑39, Mar 1991	3.00
❑40, Apr 1991; 52 pages; 8 page preview of Kid Eternity#1	3.50
❑41, May 1991; 1st Garth Ennis story	6.00
❑42, Jun 1991	4.00
❑43, Jul 1991	4.00
❑44, Aug 1991	4.00
❑45, Sep 1991	4.00
❑46, Oct 1991	4.00
❑47, Nov 1991	3.00
❑48, Dec 1991	3.00
❑49, Jan 1992	3.00
❑50, Feb 1992; Giant-size; 38 page special; Chaos preview insert; My Name is Chaos preview	4.00
❑51, Mar 1992	3.00
❑52, Apr 1992	3.00
❑53, May 1992	3.00
❑54, Jun 1992	3.00
❑55, Jul 1992	3.00
❑56, Aug 1992	3.00
❑57, Sep 1992	3.00
❑58, Oct 1992	3.00
❑59, Nov 1992	3.00
❑60, Dec 1992	3.00
❑61, Jan 1993	3.00
❑62, Feb 1993; NG (w); Death Talks About Life AIDS-awareness insert	3.00
❑63, Mar 1993	3.00
❑64, Apr 1993	3.00
❑65, May 1993	3.00
❑66, Jun 1993	3.00
❑67, Jul 1993	3.00
❑68, Aug 1993	3.00
❑69, Sep 1993	3.00
❑70, Oct 1993	3.00
❑71, Nov 1993	3.00
❑72, Dec 1993	3.00
❑73, Jan 1994	3.00
❑74, Feb 1994	3.00
❑75, Mar 1994; Double-size	3.50
❑76, Apr 1994	3.00
❑77, May 1994	3.00
❑78, Jun 1994	3.00
❑79, Jul 1994	3.00
❑80, Aug 1994	3.00
❑81, Sep 1994	3.00
❑82, Oct 1994	3.00
❑83, Nov 1994	3.00
❑84, Dec 1994	3.00
❑85, Jan 1995	3.00
❑86, Feb 1995	3.00
❑87, Mar 1995	3.00
❑88, Apr 1995	3.00
❑89, May 1995	3.00
❑90, Jun 1995	3.00
❑91, Jul 1995	3.00
❑92, Aug 1995	3.00
❑93, Sep 1995	3.00
❑94, Oct 1995	3.00
❑95, Nov 1995	3.00
❑96, Dec 1995	3.00
❑97, Jan 1996	3.00
❑98, Feb 1996	3.00
❑99, Mar 1996	3.00
❑100, Apr 1996	3.00
❑101, May 1996	2.50
❑102, Jun 1996	2.50
❑103, Jul 1996	2.50
❑104, Aug 1996	2.50
❑105, Sep 1996	2.50
❑106, Oct 1996	2.50
❑107, Nov 1996	2.50
❑108, Dec 1996	2.50
❑109, Jan 1997	2.50
❑110, Feb 1997	2.50
❑111, Mar 1997	2.50
❑112, Apr 1997	2.50
❑113, May 1997	2.50
❑114, Jun 1997	2.50
❑115, Jul 1997	2.50
❑116, Aug 1997	2.50
❑117, Sep 1997	2.50
❑118, Oct 1997	2.50
❑119, Nov 1997	2.50
❑120, Dec 1997; Giant-size; A: Alan Moore. 10th anniversary;	2.50
❑121, Jan 1998	2.50
❑122, Feb 1998	2.50
❑123, Mar 1998	2.50
❑124, Apr 1998	2.50
❑125, May 1998	2.50
❑126, Jun 1998	2.50
❑127, Jul 1998	2.50
❑128, Aug 1998	2.50
❑129, Sep 1998	2.50
❑130, Oct 1998	2.50
❑131, Nov 1998	2.50
❑132, Dec 1998	2.50
❑133, Jan 1999	2.50
❑134, Feb 1999	2.50
❑135, Mar 1999	2.50
❑136, Apr 1999	2.50
❑137, May 1999	2.50
❑138, Jun 1999	2.50
❑139, Jul 1999	2.50
❑140, Aug 1999	2.50
❑141, Oct 1999	2.50
❑142, Nov 1999	2.50
❑143, Dec 1999	2.50
❑144, Jan 2000	2.50
❑145, Feb 2000	2.50
❑146, Mar 2000	2.50
❑147, Apr 2000	2.50
❑148, May 2000	2.50
❑149, Jun 2000	2.50
❑150, Jul 2000	2.50
❑151, Aug 2000	2.50
❑152, Sep 2000	2.50
❑153, Oct 2000	2.50
❑154, Nov 2000	2.50
❑155, Dec 2000	2.50
❑156, Jan 2001	2.50
❑157, Feb 2001	2.50
❑158, Mar 2001	2.50
❑159, Apr 2001	2.50
❑160, May 2001	2.50
❑161, Jun 2001	2.50
❑162, Jul 2001	2.50
❑163, Aug 2001	2.50
❑164, Sep 2001	2.50
❑165, Oct 2001	2.50
❑166, Nov 2001	2.50
❑167, Dec 2001	2.50
❑168, Jan 2002	2.50
❑169, Feb 2002	2.50
❑170, Mar 2002	2.50
❑171, Apr 2002	2.50
❑172, May 2002	2.50
❑173, Jun 2002	2.50
❑174, Aug 2002	2.50
❑175, Sep 2002	2.50
❑176, Oct 2002	2.75
❑177, Dec 2002	2.75
❑178, Jan 2003	2.75
❑179, Feb 2003	2.75
❑180, Mar 2003	2.75
❑181, Apr 2003	2.75
❑182, May 2003	2.75
❑183, Jun 2003	2.75
❑184, Jul 2003	2.75
❑185, Aug 2003	2.75
❑186, Sep 2003	2.75
❑187, Oct 2003	2.75
❑188, Nov 2003	2.75
❑189, Dec 2003	2.75

Other grades: Multiply price above by 5/6 for VF/NM • 2/3 for VERY FINE • 1/3 for FINE • 1/5 for VERY GOOD • 1/8 for GOOD

N-MINT

❑190, Jan 2004 ... 2.75
❑191, Feb 2004 ... 2.75
❑192, Mar 2004 ... 2.75
❑193, Apr 2004 ... 2.75
❑194, May 2004 ... 2.75
❑195, Jun 2004 ... 2.75
❑196, Jul 2004 ... 2.75
❑197, Aug 2004 ... 2.75
❑198, Sep 2004 ... 2.75
❑199, Oct 2004 ... 2.75
❑200, Nov 2004 ... 4.50
❑201, Dec 2004 ... 2.75
❑202, Jan 2005 ... 2.75
❑203, Feb 2005 ... 2.75
❑204, Mar 2005 ... 2.75
❑205, Apr 2005 ... 2.75
❑206, May 2005 ... 2.75
❑207, Jun 2005 ... 2.75
❑208, Jul 2005 ... 2.75
❑209, Aug 2005 ... 2.75
❑210, Sep 2005 ... 2.75
❑211, Oct 2005 ... 2.75
❑212, Nov 2005 ... 2.75
❑213, Dec 2005 ... 2.75
❑214, Jan 2006 ... 2.75
❑215, Feb 2006 ... 2.75
❑216, Mar 2006 ... 2.99
❑217, Apr 2006 ... 2.75
❑218, Jun 2006 ... 2.75
❑219, Jun 2006 ... 2.75
❑220, Aug 2006, Price increase ... 2.99
❑221, Sep 2006, Cover by Lee Bermejo ... 2.99
❑222, Sep 2006 ... 2.99
❑223, Oct 2006 ... 2.99
❑224, Nov 2006 ... 2.99
❑225, Dec 2006 ... 2.99
❑226, Jan 2007 ... 2.99
❑227, Mar 2007 ... 2.99
❑228 ... 2.99
❑229 ... 2.99
❑230 ... 2.99
❑231 ... 2.99
❑232 ... 2.99
❑233 ... 2.99
❑234 ... 2.99
❑235 ... 2.99
❑236 ... 2.99
❑237 ... 2.99
❑238 ... 2.99
❑239 ... 2.99
❑240 ... 2.99
❑241 ... 2.99
❑242 ... 2.99
❑243 ... 2.99
❑244 ... 2.99
❑245 ... 2.99
❑246 ... 2.99
❑247 ... 2.99
❑248 ... 2.99
❑249 ... 2.99
❑250 ... 2.99
❑251 ... 2.99
❑252 ... 2.99
❑253 ... 2.99
❑254 ... 2.99
❑Ann 1, Oct 1989 BT (a) ... 6.00
❑Special 1, Jan 1993 CV (a) ... 5.00

Hellblazer Special: Bad Blood
DC / Vertigo

❑1, Sep 2000 ... 2.95
❑2, Oct 2000 ... 2.95
❑3, Nov 2000 ... 2.95
❑4, Dec 2000 ... 2.95

Hellblazer Special: Lady Constantine
DC / Vertigo

❑1, Feb 2003 ... 2.95
❑2, Mar 2003 ... 2.95
❑3, Apr 2003 ... 2.95
❑4, May 2003 ... 2.95

Hellblazer/The Books of Magic
DC / Vertigo

❑1, Dec 1997 ... 3.50
❑2, Jan 1998 ... 3.50

Hellboy: Almost Colossus
Dark Horse / Legend

❑1, Jun 1997 ... 2.95
❑2, Jul 1997 ... 2.95

Hellboy: Box Full of Evil
Dark Horse / Maverick

❑1, Aug 1999 ... 2.95
❑2, Sep 1999 ... 2.95

Hellboy Christmas Special
Dark Horse

❑1, Dec 1997, NN; One-shot ... 4.00

Hellboy: Conqueror Worm
Dark Horse / Maverick

❑1, May 2001 ... 2.99
❑2, Jun 2001 ... 2.99
❑3, Jul 2001 ... 2.99
❑4, Aug 2001 ... 2.99

Hellboy, the Corpse and The Iron Shoes
Dark Horse / Legend

❑1; collects the story serialized in the distributor catalog Advance Comics #75-82 ... 3.50

Hellboy: Makoma
Dark Horse

❑1, Jan 2006 ... 2.99
❑2, May 2006 ... 2.99

Hellboy: Seed of Destruction
Dark Horse / Legend

❑1, Mar 1994; JBy (w); O: Hellboy. 1: Monkeyman & O'Brien (in back-up story) ... 6.00
❑2, Apr 1994 JBy (w) ... 4.00
❑3, May 1994 JBy (w) ... 4.00
❑4, Jun 1994 JBy (w) ... 4.00

Hellboy: The Island
Dark Horse

❑1, Aug 2005; Hellboy comic #23 ... 2.99
❑2, Sep 2005 ... 2.99

Hellboy: The Third Wish
Dark Horse

❑1, Jul 2002 ... 2.90
❑2, Aug 2002 ... 2.90

Hellboy: The Wolves of Saint August
Dark Horse / Legend

❑1; prestige format; collects the story from Dark Horse Presents #88-91 ... 4.95

Hellboy: Wake the Devil
Dark Horse / Legend

❑1, Jun 1996; Silent as the Grave back-up ... 4.00
❑2, Jul 1996; Silent as the Grave back-up ... 3.50
❑3, Aug 1996; Silent as the Grave back-up ... 3.50
❑4, Sep 1996; Silent as the Grave back-up ... 3.50
❑5, Oct 1996; Silent as the Grave back-up ... 3.50

Hellboy: Weird Tales
Dark Horse

❑1, Feb 2003; Lobster Johnson begins ... 2.99
❑2, Apr 2003 ... 2.99
❑3, Jun 2003 ... 2.99
❑4, Aug 2003; Liz Sherman story ... 2.99
❑5, Oct 2003 ... 2.99
❑6, Dec 2003 ... 2.99
❑7, Feb 2004 ... 2.99
❑8, Apr 2004 ... 2.99

Hellboy Jr.
Dark Horse

❑1, Oct 1999 ... 2.95
❑2, Nov 1999 ... 2.95

Hellboy Jr. Halloween Special
Dark Horse

❑1, Oct 1997, Hellboy Jr. pinup; wraparound cover ... 3.95

Hell Car Comix
Alternating Crimes

❑1, Fal 1998 ... 2.95

Hellcat
Marvel

❑1, Sep 2000 ... 2.99
❑2, Oct 2000 ... 2.99
❑3, Nov 2000 ... 2.99

Hell City, Hell
Diablo Musica

❑1; shrinkwrapped with CD-ROM ... 2.25

Hellcop
Image

❑1, Aug 1998; cover says Oct, indicia says Aug ... 2.50
❑1/A, Aug 1998; Alternate cover; Man kneeling with gun, woman, faces in background ... 2.50
❑2, Nov 1998 ... 2.50
❑2/A, Nov 1998; alternate cover ... 2.50
❑3, Jan 1999 ... 2.50
❑4, Mar 1999 ... 2.50

Hell Eternal
DC / Vertigo

❑1; prestige format; NN; One-shot; Prestige format ... 6.95

Hellgate: London
Dark Horse

❑1, Nov 2006 ... 2.99
❑2, Jan 2007 ... 2.99

Hellgirl: Demonseed
Knight

❑1, Mar 1995 ... 2.95

Hellhole
Image

❑1, Jul 1999 ... 2.50
❑2, Oct 1999 ... 2.50
❑3, Dec 1999 ... 2.50

Hellhounds
Image

❑1, Aug 2003 ... 2.95
❑2, Sep 2003 ... 2.95
❑3, Oct 2003 ... 2.95
❑4, Feb 2004; b&w ... 2.95

Hellhounds: Panzer Corps
Dark Horse

❑1, Jan 1994, b&w ... 2.50
❑2, Feb 1994, b&w ... 2.50
❑3, Apr 1994, b&w ... 2.50
❑4, May 1994, b&w ... 2.50
❑5, Jun 1994, b&w ... 2.50
❑6, Jul 1994, b&w ... 2.50

Hellhound: The Redemption Quest
Marvel / Epic

❑1, Dec 1993 ... 2.25
❑2, Jan 1994 ... 2.25
❑3, Feb 1994 ... 2.25
❑4, Mar 1994 ... 2.25

Hellina
Lightning

❑1, Sep 1994, b&w ... 2.75

Hellina 1997 Pin-Up Special
Lightning

❑1, Feb 1997; b&w pin-ups; cover A ... 3.50

Hellina/Catfight
Lightning

❑1, Oct 1995, b&w ... 3.00
❑1/A, Oct 1995; Olive metallic edition ... 3.00
❑1/2nd, Aug 1997, b&w; reprints Hellina, Catfight ... 2.95

Hellina: Christmas in Hell
Lightning

❑1, Dec 1996, b&w ... 2.95
❑1/A, Dec 1996; nude cover A ... 4.00
❑1/B, Dec 1996; nude cover B ... 4.00

Hellina/Cynder
Lightning

❑1, Sep 1997 ... 2.95

Hellina/Double Impact
Lightning

❑1, Feb 1996 ... 2.75
❑1/A, Feb 1996, crossover with High Impact ... 3.00
❑1/B, Feb 1996, alternate cover ... 3.00
❑1/Nude, Feb 1996, Nude edition with certificate of authenticity; polybagged nude cover ... 4.00
❑1/Platinum, Feb 1996, Platinum edition ... 3.00

Hellina: Genesis
Lightning

❑1, Apr 1996, b&w; bagged with Hellina poster ... 3.50

Other grades: Multiply price above by 5/6 for VF/NM • 2/3 for VERY FINE • 1/3 for FINE • 1/5 for VERY GOOD • 1/8 for GOOD

Heckler

Villain from Hostess ad gets series

©DC

Hee Haw

"Doom, Despair, Agony, Oh Me..."

©Charlton

He Is Just a Rat

Part of a wave of "rave-and-rant" comics

©Exclaim! Brand Comics

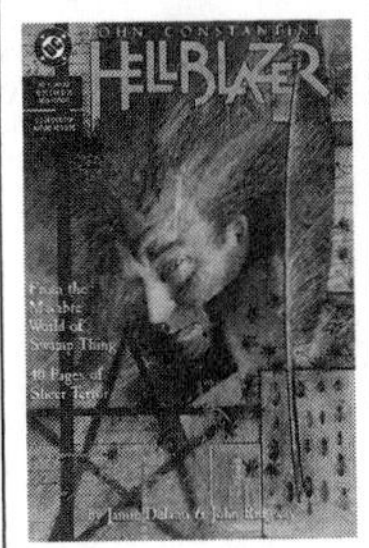

Hellblazer

The story of demon-foiler John Constantine

©DC

Hellboy: Seed of Destruction

Nazi-summoned demon turns investigator

©Dark Horse

N-MINT

Hellina: Heart of Thorns
Lightning

❑2, Sep 1996 ... 2.75
❑2/Nude, Sep 1996; nude cover edition ... 4.00

Hellina: Hellborn
Lightning

❑1, Dec 1997, b&w ... 2.95

Hellina: Hell's Angel
Lightning

❑1, Nov 1996, b&w ... 2.75
❑2, Dec 1996, b&w ... 2.75

Hellina: in the Flesh
Lightning

❑1, Aug 1997, b&w ... 2.95

Hellina: Kiss of Death
Lightning

❑1, Jul 1995, b&w ... 2.75
❑1/Gold; Gold edition ... 3.00
❑1/Nude, Jul 1995, b&w; Nude edition ... 4.00
❑1/2nd, Mar 1997; Encore edition; alternate cover ... 2.95

Hellina: Naked Desire
Lightning

❑1, May 1997; Abrams cover ... 2.95

Hellina/Nira X
Lightning

❑1, Aug 1996; crossover with Entity ... 3.00

Hellina: Skybolt Toyz Limited Edition
Lightning

❑1/A, Aug 1997, b&w; reprints Hellina #1 ... 1.50
❑1/B, Aug 1997; alternate cover ... 1.50

Hellina: Taking Back the Night
Lightning

❑1, Apr 1995 ... 4.50

Hellina: Wicked Ways
Lightning

❑1/A, Nov 1995, b&w; alternate cover; polybagged ... 2.75
❑1/B, Nov 1995; polybagged ... 3.00
❑1/Nude, Nov 1995; polybagged; Cover C ... 9.95
❑1/Silver; silver edition ... 2.75

Hell Magician
Fc9 Publishing

❑1, Aug 2005 ... 2.95

Hell Michigan
Fc9 Publishing

❑1, Aug 2005 ... 2.95
❑2, Sep 2005 ... 2.95
❑1/Ashcan, Aug 2005 ... 4.00

Hellraiser
Marvel / Epic

❑Holiday 1; Nude edition with certificate of authenticity; Dark Holiday Special ... 4.95
❑Summer 1; Giant-size; Summer Special; ca. 1992 ... 5.95
❑Spring 1; Spring Special ... 6.95

Hellraiser III: Hell on Earth
Marvel / Epic

❑1; Movie adaptation ... 5.00

Hellraiser Posterbook
Marvel / Epic

❑1 ... 4.95

N-MINT

Hellraiser: Spring Slaughter
Marvel / Epic

❑1 ... 6.95

Hellsaint
Black Diamond

❑1, Mar 1998 ... 2.50

Hell's Angel
Marvel

❑1, Jul 1993 ... 1.75
❑2, Aug 1993 ... 1.75
❑3, Sep 1993 ... 1.75
❑4, Oct 1993 ... 1.75
❑5, Nov 1993; Series continued as Dark Angel #6 ... 1.75

Hellshock
Image

❑1, Jul 1994 ... 2.00
❑2, Aug 1994 ... 2.00
❑3, Oct 1994; O: Hellshock ... 2.00
❑4; Pin-up by Adam Kubert and Jae Lee ... 2.00
❑4/A, Nov 1994; BSz (c); variant cover ... 2.00
❑4/B, Nov 1994 BSz (c) ... 1.95
❑Ashcan 1; ashcan ... 1.00

Hellshock
Image

❑1, Jan 1997 ... 2.95
❑1/A, Jan 1997 ... 2.95
❑2, Feb 1997 ... 2.95
❑3, Mar 1997 ... 2.95

Hellspawn
Image

❑1, Aug 2000 BMB (w) ... 3.00
❑2, Sep 2000 BMB (w) ... 2.50
❑3, Oct 2000 BMB (w) ... 2.50
❑4, Nov 2000 BMB (w) ... 2.50
❑5, Jan 2001 BMB (w) ... 2.50
❑6, Feb 2001 BMB (w) ... 2.50
❑7, Apr 2001 TMc (a) ... 2.50
❑8, May 2001 ... 2.50
❑9, Jun 2001 ... 2.50
❑10, Jul 2001 ... 2.50
❑11, Aug 2001 ... 2.50
❑12, Sep 2001 ... 2.50
❑13, May 2002 ... 2.50
❑14, Dec 2002 ... 2.50
❑15, Feb 2003 ... 2.50
❑16, Apr 2003 ... 2.50

Hellspock
Express / Parody

❑1, b&w; One-shot ... 2.95

Hellstalker
Rebel Creations

❑1 ... 2.25
❑2, Jul 1989 ... 2.25

Hellstorm: Prince of Lies
Marvel

❑1, Apr 1993; parchment cover ... 2.95
❑2, May 1993 ... 2.00
❑3, Jun 1993 ... 2.00
❑4, Jul 1993 ... 2.00
❑5, Aug 1993 ... 2.00
❑6, Sep 1993 ... 2.00
❑7, Oct 1993; Book 1 ... 2.00

N-MINT

❑8, Nov 1993; Book 1 ... 2.00
❑9, Dec 1993; Book 1 ... 2.00
❑10, Jan 1994; Book 1 ... 2.00
❑11, Feb 1994; Book 2 ... 2.00
❑12, Mar 1994 ... 2.00
❑13, Apr 1994 ... 2.00
❑14, May 1994; Includes trading cards ... 2.00
❑15, Jun 1994 ... 2.00
❑16, Jul 1994 ... 2.00
❑17, Aug 1994 ... 2.00
❑18, Sep 1994 ... 2.00
❑19, Oct 1994 ... 2.00
❑20, Nov 1994 ... 2.00
❑21, Dec 1994; Final Issue ... 2.00

Hellstorm: Son of Satan
Marvel

❑1, Dec 2006 ... 3.99
❑2, Feb 2007 ... 3.99
❑3, Mar 2007 ... 3.99

Helm Premiere
Helm

❑1, Mar 1995, b&w; Preview edition ... 2.95

Help
Jeff Levine

❑1 ...

Help
Warren

❑1, ca. 1964, HK (w) ... 45.00
❑2, ca. 1964, HK (w) ... 28.00
❑3, ca. 1964, HK (w) ... 20.00
❑4, ca. 1964, HK (w) ... 20.00
❑5, ca. 1964, HK (w) ... 20.00
❑6, ca. 1964, HK (w) ... 20.00
❑7, ca. 1964, HK (w) ... 20.00
❑8, ca. 1964, HK (w) ... 20.00
❑9, ca. 1964, HK (w) ... 20.00
❑10, ca. 1964, HK (w) ... 20.00
❑11, ca. 1964, HK (w) ... 20.00
❑12, HK (w) ... 20.00

Help
Warren

❑1 HK (w) ... 26.00
❑2 HK (w) ... 16.00
❑3 HK (w) ... 16.00

Helsing
Caliber

❑1, b&w ... 2.95
❑1/A; cover has woman in black standing ... 2.95
❑2, b&w; ca. 1998 ... 2.95

Helter Skelter
Antarctic

❑0, May 1997, b&w ... 2.95
❑1, Jun 1997, b&w ... 2.95
❑2, Sep 1997, b&w ... 2.95
❑3, Nov 1997, b&w ... 2.95
❑4, Dec 1997, b&w ... 2.95
❑6, Mar 1998, b&w ... 2.95
❑5, Jan 1998, b&w ... 2.95

Helyun: Bones of the Backwoods
Slave Labor

❑1, Nov 1991, b&w ... 2.95

Other grades: Multiply price above by 5/6 for VF/NM • 2/3 for VERY FINE • 1/3 for FINE • 1/5 for VERY GOOD • 1/8 for GOOD

Helyun Book 1
Slave Labor

	N-MINT
❑1, Aug 1990, b&w; NN; b&w	6.95

Hembeck
Fantaco

	N-MINT
❑1; Best of Dateline: @!!?#	2.50
❑2, Feb 1980 FH (a)	2.50
❑3, Jun 1980	1.50
❑4, Nov 1980	1.50
❑5, Feb 1981 FH (a)	2.50
❑6, Sep 1981; Jimmy Olsen's Pal	2.25
❑7, Jan 1983; Dial H for Hembeck	1.95

Hemp for Victory
Starhead

	N-MINT
❑1, Sep 1993, b&w; based on 1943 USDA film	2.50

Henry V
Caliber / Tome

	N-MINT
❑1, b&w	2.95

Hepcats
Double Diamond

	N-MINT
❑1, May 1989	5.00
❑2, Jul 1989	4.00
❑3, Aug 1989	3.00
❑4, Nov 1989	3.00
❑5, Feb 1989	3.00
❑6, Oct 1990	3.00
❑7, Mar 1991	3.00
❑8, Dec 1991	3.00
❑9, Jun 1992	3.00
❑10, Dec 1992	3.00
❑11, Jan 1994	3.00
❑12, Jul 1994	3.00
❑13	3.00
❑14	2.50
❑Special 1, May 1991; Reprints	4.00
❑Special 2, Sep 1994; Reprints	4.00

Hepcats
Antarctic

	N-MINT
❑0, Nov 1996	4.00
❑0/A; Comics Cavalcade Commemorative Edition	5.95
❑0/Deluxe, Nov 1996; Radio Hepcats edition; polybagged with compact disc	9.95
❑1, Dec 1996	3.50
❑2, Jan 1997	3.50
❑3, Feb 1997	3.00
❑4, Mar 1997	3.00
❑5, Apr 1997	3.00
❑6, Jan 1998	2.95
❑7, Mar 1998	2.95
❑8	2.95
❑9, Apr 1998	2.95
❑10, May 1998	2.95
❑11, May 1998	2.95
❑12, Jun 1998	2.95

Herbie
Dark Horse

	N-MINT
❑1, Oct 1992; Reprints	2.50
❑2, Nov 1992; Reprints	2.50

Herbie (A+)
A-Plus

	N-MINT
❑1; Reprints (including part of Herbie #8)	2.50
❑2; Reprints	2.50
❑3; Reprints	2.50
❑4; Reprints	2.50
❑5; Reprints	2.50
❑6; Reprints	2.50

Herbie
ACG

	N-MINT
❑1, Apr 1964, A: Castro. A: Lyndon Johnson. A: Sonny Liston. A: Khrushchev	95.00
❑2, Jun 1964, A: Marie Antoinette	60.00
❑3, Aug 1964, A: Churchill	48.00
❑4, Sep 1964, A: Doc Holliday. A: Clantons	48.00
❑5, Oct 1964, A: Frank Sinatra. A: Beatles. A: Dean Martin	48.00
❑6, Dec 1964, A: Gregory Peck. A: Ava Gardner	40.00
❑7, Feb 1965, A: Harry Truman. A: Mao. A: Khruschcev	40.00
❑8, Mar 1965, O: Fat Fury. A: George Washington. A: Barry Goldwater. A: Lyndon Johnson	50.00
❑9, Apr 1965	38.00
❑10, Jun 1965, Herbie's prehistoric girlfriend returns	38.00
❑11, Aug 1965, A: Adlai Stevenson. A: Queen Isabella. A: Columbus. A: Lyndon Johnson	30.00
❑12, Sep 1965, Fat Fury story	30.00
❑13, Oct 1965, Fat Fury imitator story	30.00
❑14, Dec 1965, A: Magicman. A: Fat Fury. A: Nemesis. Christmas story	30.00
❑15, Feb 1966, A: Josephine. A: Napoleon	30.00
❑16, Mar 1966, A: Mao Tse Tung. A: Fat Fury	30.00
❑17, Apr 1966	30.00
❑18, Jun 1966	30.00
❑19, Aug 1966, A: Cleopatra	30.00
❑20, Sep 1966, Fat Fury vs. Dracula	30.00
❑21, Oct 1966	30.00
❑22, Dec 1966, A: Charles de Gaulle. A: Queen Elizabeth. A: Ben Franklin. Fat Fury learns magic	30.00
❑23, Feb 1967, Final Issue	30.00

Hercules
Charlton

	N-MINT
❑1, Oct 1967, Thane of Bagarth by Steve Skeates and Jim Aparo; sell-through 46.6%, according to Charlton files	14.00
❑2, Dec 1967, Thane of Bagarth by Steve Skeates and Jim Aparo; sell-through 40.3%, according to Charlton files	9.00
❑3, Feb 1968, Sell-through 36.1%, according to Charlton files	6.00
❑4, Jun 1968, Sell-through 37.6%, according to Charlton files	6.00
❑5, Jul 1968, Sell-through 33.5%, according to Charlton files	6.00
❑6, Sep 1968, Sell-through 35.5%, according to Charlton files	5.00
❑7, Nov 1968	5.00
❑8, Dec 1968, JA (a); Thane of Bagarth by Steve Skeates and Jim Aparo; sell-through 47%, according to Charlton files	5.00
❑8/A, Dec 1968, Magazine-sized issue; Low distribution	10.00
❑9, Feb 1969, Sell-through 31.4%, according to Charlton files	5.00
❑10, Apr 1967, Sell-through 36.0%, according to Charlton files	5.00
❑11, May 1967, Sell-through 32.9%, according to Charlton files	5.00
❑12, Jul 1967, Sell-through 28%, according to Charlton files	5.00
❑13, Oct 1967, Final Issue	5.00

Hercules
Marvel

	N-MINT
❑1, Sep 1982, BL (c); BL (w); BL (a)	1.50
❑2, Oct 1982, BL (c); BL (w); BL, LMc (a)	1.50
❑3, Nov 1982, BL (c); BL (w); BL, LMc (a)	1.50
❑4, Dec 1982, BL (c); BL (w); BL (a)	1.50

Hercules
Marvel

	N-MINT
❑1, Mar 1984, BL (c); BL (w); BL (a)	1.50
❑2, Apr 1984, BL (c); BL (w); BL (a)	1.25
❑3, May 1984, BL (c); BL (w); BL (a)	1.25
❑4, Jun 1984, BL (c); BL (w); BL (a)	1.25

Hercules
Marvel

	N-MINT
❑1, Jun 2005	2.99
❑2, Jul 2005	2.99
❑3, Aug 2005	2.99
❑4, Sep 2005	2.99
❑5, Oct 2005	2.99

Hercules (Avalon)
Avalon

	N-MINT
❑1, Oct 2002, b&w; Reprints from Charlton series	5.95
❑2, Dec 2002; Reprints from Charlton series	5.95

Hercules: Heart of Chaos
Marvel

	N-MINT
❑1, Aug 1997; gatefold summary	2.50
❑2, Sep 1997; gatefold summary	2.50
❑3, Oct 1997; gatefold summary	2.50

Hercules: Official Comics Movie Adaptation
Acclaim

	N-MINT
❑1; digest; adapts movie	4.50

Hercules Project
Monster

	N-MINT
❑1, Aug 1991, b&w	1.95
❑2, b&w	1.95

Hercules: The Legendary Journeys
Topps

	N-MINT
❑1, Jun 1996, wraparound cover	3.00
❑2, Jul 1996	3.00
❑3/A, Aug 1996, A: Xena. art cover	3.00
❑3/B, Aug 1996, A: Xena. Photo cover	3.00
❑3/Gold, Aug 1996, 1: Xena. Gold logo variant	3.00
❑4, Sep 1996, 2: Xena. A: Xena	3.00
❑5, Oct 1996, A: Xena	3.00

Hercules Unbound
DC

	N-MINT
❑1, Nov 1975 WW, JL (a)	12.00
❑2, Jan 1976	7.00
❑3, Mar 1976	4.00
❑4, May 1976	3.00
❑5, Jul 1976	3.00
❑6, Sep 1976	2.50
❑7, Nov 1976	2.50
❑8, Jan 1977	2.50
❑9, Mar 1977	2.50
❑10, May 1977	2.50
❑11, Jul 1977	2.50
❑12, Sep 1977, Final Issue	2.50

Here Come the Big People
Event

	N-MINT
❑1, Sep 1997	2.95
❑1/A, Sep 1997; Alternate cover (large woman burping man)	2.95

Here Come the Lovejoys Again
Fantagraphics

	N-MINT
❑1, Sep 2005	3.95
❑2, Jan 2006	3.95

Here Is Greenwood
Viz

	N-MINT
❑1, Nov 2004	9.99
❑2, Jan 2005	9.99
❑3, Mar 2005	9.99
❑4, May 2005; Here is Devilwood backup feature	9.99
❑5, Jul 2005; Black Magic Woman backup feature	9.99
❑6, Sep 2005	9.99

Heretic
Dark Horse / Blanc Noir

	N-MINT
❑1, Nov 1996; Maximum Velocity back-up	2.95
❑2, Jan 1997; Maximum Velocity back-up	2.95
❑3, Feb 1997; Maximum Velocity back-up	2.95
❑4, Mar 1997; Maximum Velocity back-up	2.95

Heretics
Iguana

	N-MINT
❑1, Nov 1993; Foil-embossed logo	2.95

Hermes vs. the Eyeball Kid
Dark Horse

	N-MINT
❑1, Dec 1994, b&w	2.95
❑2, Jan 1995, b&w	2.95
❑3, Feb 1995, b&w	2.95

Hero
Marvel

	N-MINT
❑1, May 1990	1.50
❑2, Jun 1990	1.50
❑3, Jul 1990	1.50
❑4, Aug 1990	1.50
❑5, Sep 1990	1.50
❑6, Oct 1990	1.50

Hero Alliance
Wonder Color

	N-MINT
❑1, May 1987	1.95

Hero Alliance
Innovation

	N-MINT
❑1, Sep 1989	1.75
❑2, Oct 1989	1.75
❑3, Dec 1989	1.95
❑4, Feb 1990	1.95
❑5, Mar 1990	1.95
❑6, Apr 1990	1.95
❑7, May 1990	1.95
❑8, Jul 1990	1.95
❑9, Sep 1990	1.95
❑10, Oct 1990	1.95
❑11, Nov 1990	1.95
❑12, Dec 1990	1.95
❑13, Mar 1991	1.95
❑14, Apr 1991	1.95

Hellcat

Patsy Walker for the new millennium

©Marvel

Hellina/Cynder

From the late, unlamented "Bad Girl" era

©Lightning

Hellshock

Caught between Heaven and Hell

©Image

Hellstorm: Prince of Lies

Son of Satan gets own series again

©Marvel

Hepcats

Relationship story abandoned by creator

©Double Diamond

	N-MINT
❑15, May 1991	1.95
❑16, Jun 1991	1.95
❑17, Jul 1991	2.50
❑Ann 1, Sep 1990	2.75
❑Special 1	2.50

Hero Alliance & Justice Machine: Identity Crisis
Innovation

❑1, Oct 1990	2.75

Hero Alliance: End of the Golden Age
Innovation

❑1/2nd, Jul 1989; 2nd printing	1.75
❑1, Jul 1989	1.75
❑2, Jul 1989	1.75
❑3, Aug 1989	1.75

Hero Alliance Quarterly
Innovation

❑1, Sep 1991	2.75
❑2, Dec 1991	2.75
❑3, Mar 1992	2.75
❑4	2.75

Hero at Large
Speakeasy Comics

❑1, Sep 2005	2.99

Herobear And The Kid
Astonish

❑1, ca. 1999, B&w and red	2.95
❑1/2nd, ca. 2000, 2nd printing; B&w and red	2.95
❑2, ca. 2000	2.95
❑2/2nd, ca. 2000, b&w	2.95
❑3, ca. 2001, b&w	3.50
❑4, ca. 2002, b&w	3.50
❑5, ca. 2002, b&w	3.50

Hero Camp
Image

❑1, Jun 2005	2.95
❑2, Jul 2005	2.95
❑3, Aug 2005	2.95
❑4, Sep 2005	2.95

H-E-R-O
DC

❑1, Apr 2003	2.50
❑1/2nd, Sep 2003	4.95
❑2, May 2003	2.50
❑3, Jun 2003	2.50
❑4, Jul 2003	2.50
❑5, Aug 2003	2.50
❑6, Sep 2003	2.50
❑7, Oct 2003	2.50
❑8, Nov 2003	2.50
❑9, Dec 2003	2.50
❑10, Jan 2004	2.50
❑11, Feb 2004	2.50
❑12, Mar 2004	2.50
❑13, Apr 2004	2.50
❑14, May 2004	2.50
❑15, Jun 2004	2.50
❑16, Jul 2004	2.50
❑17, Aug 2004	2.50
❑18, Sep 2004	2.50
❑19, Oct 2004, Sky Captain and the World of Tomorrow promo CD	2.50
❑20, Nov 2004	2.50

	N-MINT
❑21, Jan 2005	2.50
❑22, Feb 2005, Final issue	2.50

Hero Double Feature
DC

❑1, Jun 2003; Collects Hero (DC) #1 & #2	4.95

Heroes (Blackbird)
Blackbird

❑1, Dec 1985	3.00
❑2, Mar 1986	1.75
❑3	1.75
❑4, Nov 1987	2.00
❑5, Apr 1988	2.00
❑6	2.00

Heroes (Milestone)
DC / Milestone

❑1, May 1996	2.50
❑2, Jun 1996, V: Shadow Cabinet	2.50
❑3, Jul 1996	2.50
❑4, Aug 1996	2.50
❑5, Sep 1996	2.50
❑6, Nov 1996	2.50

Heroes
Marvel

❑1, Dec 2001	7.00
❑1/2nd, Dec 2001; 2nd printing	3.50

Heroes Against Hunger
DC

❑1, Aug 1986; BSz, NA (c); JSn (w); DaG, CI, KG, JDu, GP, JK, JKu, RA, MR (a); Charity benefit comic for Ethiopian famine victims	3.00

Heroes Anonymous
Bongo

❑1, Jul 2003	2.99
❑2, Oct 2003	2.99
❑3, Dec 2003	2.99
❑4, Feb 2004	2.99
❑5, Jun 2004	2.99
❑6 2004	2.99

Heroes for Hire
Marvel

❑1, Jul 1997; Hulk, Hercules, Iron Fist, Luke Cage, Black Knight, White Tiger; wraparound cover	2.99
❑2/A, Aug 1997; gatefold summary; Jim Hammond (original Human Torch) joins team	1.99
❑2/B, Aug 1997; gatefold summary; alternate cover; Jim Hammond (original Human Torch) joins team	1.99
❑3, Sep 1997; gatefold summary	1.99
❑4, Oct 1997; gatefold summary; V: Controller	1.99
❑5, Nov 1997; gatefold summary	1.99
❑6, Dec 1997; gatefold summary	1.99
❑7, Jan 1998; gatefold summary	1.99
❑8, Feb 1998; gatefold summary	1.99
❑9, Mar 1998; gatefold summary	1.99
❑10, Apr 1998; gatefold summary	1.99
❑11, May 1998; gatefold summary; V: Wild Pack	1.99
❑12, Jun 1998; gatefold summary	2.99
❑13, Jul 1998; gatefold summary; Ant-Man inside Hammond's body	1.99
❑14, Aug 1998; gatefold summary; Black Knight vs. dragons	1.99

	N-MINT
❑15, Sep 1998; gatefold summary	1.99
❑16, Oct 1998; gatefold summary	1.99
❑17, Nov 1998; gatefold summary	1.99
❑18, Dec 1998; gatefold summary	1.99
❑19, Jan 1999; gatefold summary; Final Issue	1.99
❑Ann 1998; gatefold summary; Heroes for Hire/Quicksilver '98; wraparound cover	2.99

Heroes for Hire
Marvel

❑1, Nov 2006, Hulk, Hercules, Iron Fist, Luke Cage, Black Knight, White Tiger; Wraparound cover	2.99
❑2, Dec 2006	2.99
❑3, Jan 2007	2.99
❑4, Feb 2007	2.99
❑5, Mar 2007	2.99

Heroes for Hope
Marvel

❑1, Dec 1985, JSn (c); MGr, SL, AMo (w); BWr, GM, JB, JBy, BG, JR2, SR, BB, FM, BA, CV (a); famine relief	5.00

Heroes from Wordsmith
Special Studio

❑1, b&w	2.50

Heroes Incorporated
Double Edge

❑1, Mar 1995	2.95

Heroes, Inc. Presents Cannon
Armed Services

❑1 1969, WW (c); WW (w); SD, WW (a); NN; U.S.M.C. on inside back cover; 1: Cannon; 1: The Misfits; 1: Mystra; 1: Shag; 1: Glomb; 1: Dragonella; Includes Salute to a Medal of Honor Winner: Cpl. Robert E. O'Malley; Comic-size	12.50
❑2; Includes 1-page Dynamo pin-up by Wally Wood on on inside front cover, 2-page Ka-davahr pin-up and 1-page SF pin-up, both by John Byrne and 1-page Punisher/Huntress (Marvel)/Domino Fortune pin-up by Howard Chaykin on inside back cover; Magazine-size; Published and © by CPL/Gang; b&w; ca. 1976	10.00

Heroes of Faith
Coretoons

❑1, Jun 1992	2.50

Heroes of Rock 'n Fire
Wonder Comix

❑1, Apr 1987	1.95
❑2, Aug 1987, b&w	1.75

Heroes of the Equinox
Fantasy Flight

❑1	6.95

Heroes Reborn
Marvel

❑½ 1996; JPH (w); RL (a); With certificate of authenticity	3.00

Heroes Reborn: Ashema
Marvel

❑1, Jan 2000	1.99

Heroes Reborn: Doom
Marvel

❑1, Jan 2000	1.99

Other grades: Multiply price above by 5/6 for VF/NM • 2/3 for VERY FINE • 1/3 for FINE • 1/5 for VERY GOOD • 1/8 for GOOD

Heroes Reborn: Doomsday
Marvel

❑1, Jan 2000 .... 1.99

Heroes Reborn: Masters Of Evil
Marvel

❑1, Feb 1999 .... 1.99

Heroes Reborn Mini Comic
Marvel

❑1, Sep 1996 .... 1.00

Heroes Reborn: Rebel
Marvel

❑1, Jan 2000 .... 1.99

Heroes Reborn: Remnants
Marvel

❑1, Jan 2000 .... 1.99

Heroes Reborn: The Return
Marvel

❑1, Dec 1997 PD (w) 2.50
❑1/Variant, Dec 1997; PD (w); Franklin Richards on cover 3.00
❑2, Dec 1997 PD (w) 2.50
❑2/Variant, Dec 1997; PD (w); Spider-Man/Hulk variant cover 3.00
❑3, Dec 1997 PD (w) 2.50
❑3/Variant, Dec 1997; PD (w); Iron Man variant cover 3.00
❑4, Dec 1997 PD (w) 2.50
❑4/Variant, Dec 1997; PD (w); Reed Richards variant cover 3.00
❑Ashcan 1, Dec 1997 RL, JLee (a) 1.00

Heroes Reborn: Young Allies
Marvel

❑1, Jan 2000 .... 1.99

Hero for Hire
Marvel

❑1, Jun 1972, GT, JR (c); GT, JR (a); 1&O: Power Man II (Luke Cage). 1: Diamondback 125.00
❑2, Aug 1972, GT, JR (c); GT (a); V: Diamondback 30.00
❑3, Oct 1972, GT (a); 1: Mace. V: Mace . 14.00
❑4, Dec 1972 .... 12.00
❑5, Jan 1973, GT (a) 12.00
❑6, Feb 1973 .... 12.00
❑7, Mar 1973, GT (a) 9.00
❑8, Apr 1973, GT (a); A: Doctor Doom ... 9.00
❑9, May 1973, GT (a) 9.00
❑10, Jun 1973, GT (a); 1: Señor Muerte I (Ramon Garcia) 8.00
❑11, Jul 1973, GT (a); D: Señor Muerte I (Ramon Garcia) 9.00
❑12, Aug 1973, (c); GT (a); 1: Chemistro I (Curtis Carr) 9.00
❑13, Sep 1973, V: Lionfang 9.00
❑14, Oct 1973, O: Luke Cage. V: Big Ben 9.00
❑15, Nov 1973, BEv (w); BEv (a); Sub-Mariner back-up 9.00
❑16, Dec 1973, FMc (a); O: Stiletto. D: Rackham. V: Stiletto. series continues as Power Man 9.00

Hero Hotline
DC

❑1, Apr 1989 KS (a) 2.00
❑2, May 1989 .... 2.00
❑3, Jun 1989; 1: Snafu 2.00
❑4, Jul 1989 .... 2.00
❑5, Aug 1989 .... 2.00
❑6, Sep 1989 .... 2.00

Heroic
Lightning

❑1 .... 1.75

Heroic 17
Pennacle

❑1, Sep 1993 .... 2.95

Heroic Tales
Lone Star

❑1, Jun 1997, Amazon 2.50
❑2, Aug 1997, Amazon 2.50
❑3, Oct 1997 .... 2.50
❑4, Dec 1997 .... 2.50
❑5, Feb 1998 .... 2.50
❑6, May 1998, Amazon and Blackheart .. 2.50
❑7, Jul 1998, Amazon and Gunslinger ... 2.50
❑8, Aug 1998, Atlas 2.50
❑9, Apr 2000 .... 2.50
❑10, May 2000 .... 2.50

Heroines Inc.
Avatar

❑1, Apr 1989, b&w 1.75

Heroman
Dimension

❑1, Oct 1986 .... 1.75

Hero on a Stick
Big-Baby

❑1 .... 2.95

Hero Premiere Edition
Warrior

❑1, Jun 1993 .... 2.00
❑2; Batman/Grendel; Red Background; Has Hero Premier #2 on back 2.00
❑3, Jul 1993; Aliens/Predator: The Deadliest of the Species 2.00
❑4; AMo (w); 1963 #5 preview 2.00
❑5; Q-Unit 2.00
❑6; 1963 #5 preview 2.00

Heros
OK

❑1 .... 2.50

Hero Sandwich
Slave Labor

❑1, Feb 1987, b&w 2.00
❑2, May 1987, b&w 1.50
❑3, Aug 1987, b&w 1.50
❑4, Jan 1988, b&w 1.75
❑5, Oct 1988, b&w 1.75
❑6, Feb 1989, b&w 1.75
❑7, Mar 1990, b&w 2.25
❑8, Jun 1991, b&w 2.50
❑9, May 1992, b&w 2.50

Hero Squared
Boom Studios

❑1, Sep 2005 .... 3.99
❑1/Finger, Sep 2005 .... 3.99

Hero Zero
Dark Horse

❑0, Sep 1994 .... 2.50

Heru, Son of Ausar
Ania

❑1, Apr 1993; 1: Heru; Includes trading cards 1.95

He Said/She Said Comics
First Amendment

❑1; Amy Fisher/Joey Buttafuoco 3.00
❑2; Woody Allen/Mia Farrow 3.00
❑3; Bill Clinton/Gennifer Flowers 3.00
❑4; Tonya Harding/Jeff Gillooly 3.00
❑5; O.J. Simpson/Nicole Brown 3.00

Hex
DC

❑1, Sep 1985; 1&O: Hex (future Jonah Hex). 1: Stiletta. continued from Jonah Hex #92 .... 5.00
❑2, Oct 1985 .... 1.50
❑3, Nov 1985 .... 1.50
❑4, Dec 1985 .... 1.50
❑5, Jan 1986 .... 1.50
❑6, Feb 1986 .... 1.50
❑7, Mar 1986 .... 1.50
❑8, Apr 1986 .... 1.50
❑9, May 1986 .... 1.50
❑10, Jun 1986 A: Legion 1.50
❑11, Jul 1986 A: Batman of future 1.50
❑12, Aug 1986 A: Batman of future 1.50
❑13, Sep 1986; 1: Dogs of War 1.50
❑14, Oct 1986 .... 1.50
❑15, Nov 1986 KG (c); KG (a) 1.50
❑16, Dec 1986 KG (c); KG (a) 1.50
❑17, Jan 1987 KG (a) 1.50
❑18, Feb 1987; KG (a); Final Issue 1.50

Hexbreaker: A Badger Graphic Novel
First

❑1, Mar 1988 .... 8.95

Hex Of The Wicked Witch
Asylum

❑0/A, Aug 1999 .... 1.95
❑0/B, Aug 1999; Deluxe edition 3.95

Hey, Boss!
Visionary

❑1 .... 2.00

Hey, Mister
Insomnia

❑1, May 1997, b&w 2.50
❑2, Nov 1997, b&w 2.50
❑3, Aug 1998, b&w 2.95
❑4, Dec 1998, b&w 2.95

Hey Mister: After School Special
Top Shelf

❑1, b&w; digest; collects five-issue mini-comics series 4.95

Hi-Adventure Heroes
Gold Key

❑1, May 1969 .... 12.00
❑2, Aug 1969 .... 7.00

Hideo Li Files
Raging Rhino

❑1, b&w; Adult 2.95

Hiding Place
DC / Piranha

❑1 .... 12.95

Hiding Place (Spire)
Spire

❑1, ca. 1973, adapts book by Carrie Ten Boom 5.00

Hieroglyph
Dark Horse

❑1, Nov 1999 .... 2.95
❑2, Dec 1999 .... 2.95
❑3, Jan 2000 .... 2.95
❑4, Feb 2000 .... 2.95

High Adventure
Red Top

❑1, Oct 1957 .... 40.00

Highbrow Entertainment
Image

❑Ashcan 1; Ascan promotional edition .. 1.00

High Caliber
Caliber

❑1, b&w; Trade Paperback 9.95
❑2 .... 3.95
❑3 .... 3.95
❑4, Giant-size; flip book with Raven Chronicles #15 .... 3.95

High Chaparral
Gold Key

❑1, Aug 1968, Photo cover; One-shot; Based on TV series 40.00

High Octane Theatre
Infiniti

❑1; Includes sticker 2.50

High Roads
DC / Homage

❑1, Jun 2002 .... 2.95
❑2, Jul 2002 .... 2.95
❑3, Aug 2002 .... 2.95
❑4, Sep 2002 .... 2.95
❑5, Oct 2002 .... 2.95
❑6, Nov 2002 .... 2.95

High School Agent
Sun

❑1 .... 2.50

High Shining Brass
Apple

❑1, Nov 1990, b&w 2.75
❑2, Mar 1991, b&w 2.75
❑3, May 1991, b&w 2.75
❑4, Jun 1991 .... 2.75

High Stakes Adventures
Antarctic

❑1, Dec 1998 .... 2.95
❑1/Deluxe, Dec 1998; Deluxe edition 5.95

Hightop Ninja
Authority

❑1 .... 2.95
❑2 .... 2.95
❑3 .... 2.95

High Voltage
Black Out

❑0 .... 2.95

Hi Hi Puffy Amiyumi
DC

❑1, Apr 2006 .... 2.25

Other grades: Multiply price above by 5/6 for VF/NM • 2/3 for VERY FINE • 1/3 for FINE • 1/5 for VERY GOOD • 1/8 for GOOD

Herbie

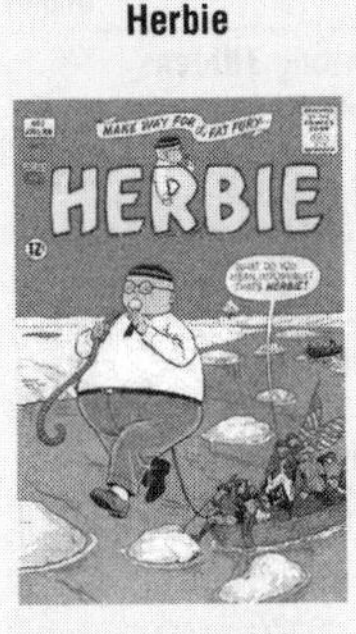

"You want I should bop you with this lollipop?"
©ACG

Hercules

Layton's funny take on Hercules in space
©Marvel

Hercules Unbound

DC awakens Hercules after World War III
©DC

Heroes Against Hunger

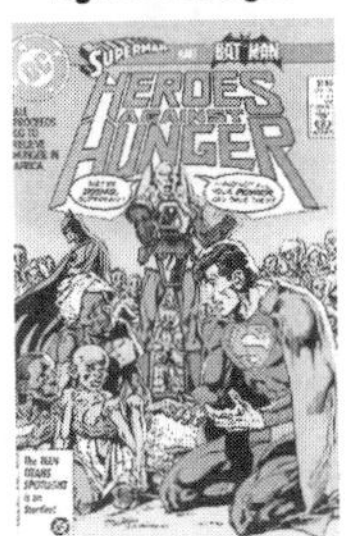

DC's famine relief project followed Marvel's
©DC

Heroes Reborn: The Return

Peter David undoes what Liefeld and Lee did
©Marvel

N-MINT

❑2, May 2006 .... 2.25
❑3, Jun 2006 .... 2.25

Hikaru No Go
Viz

❑1, Aug 2004, Reprints from Shonen Jump; Graphic novel; Reads right to left; b&w 7.95
❑2, Oct 2004; Reprints from Shonen Jump; Graphic novel; Reads right to left; b&w 7.95
❑3, Feb 2005; Reprints from Shonen Jump #21-25; Graphic novel; Reads right to left; b&w 7.95
❑4, May 2005; Reprints from Shonen Jump #25-29; Graphic novel; Reads right to left; b&w 7.95
❑5, Oct 2005; Reprints from Shonen Jump #30-32 .... 7.95

Hilly Rose
Astro

❑1, May 1995, b&w 3.00
❑1/A, May 1995, b&w 3.00
❑2, Jul 1995, b&w 4.00
❑3, Oct 1995, b&w 3.00
❑4, Dec 1995, b&w 3.00
❑5, Feb 1996, b&w 3.00
❑6, Apr 1996, b&w 3.00
❑7, Aug 1996, b&w 3.00
❑8, Dec 1996, b&w 3.00
❑9, Apr 1997, b&w 3.00

Hip Flask
Comicraft

❑½, Aug 1998, San Dego Comic-Con preview 2.95

Hip Flask: Elephantmen
Active Images

❑1/Desert, Jul 2003, Desert cover 6.00
❑1/Sushi, Jul 2003, Sushi bar cover 4.00
❑1/Street, Jul 2003, Alleyway cover 5.00
❑1/Townhouse, Jul 2003, Townhouse cover 6.00

Hip Flask: Ladronn Sketchbook
Active Images

❑1, ca. 2005 .... 10.00
❑2, ca. 2005 .... 10.00
❑3, ca. 2005 .... 10.00

His Name Is... Savage
Adventure House

❑1, magazine; GK (a); NN 24.00

History of Marvels Comics
Marvel

❑1, Jul 2000 .... 1.00

History of the DC Universe
DC

❑1, Sep 1986, GP (a) 3.25
❑2, Nov 1986, GP (a) 3.25

History of Violence
DC / Paradox

❑1, b&w; Introduction by John Wagner; 286 pages; ca. 1997 .... 9.95

Hitchhiker's Guide to the Galaxy
DC

❑1 .... 4.95
❑2, ca. 1993 .... 4.95
❑3, ca. 1993 .... 4.95

N-MINT

Hitman
DC

❑1, Apr 1996 A: Batman 3.00
❑2, Jun 1996; A: Joker. V: Joker 3.00
❑3, Jul 1996 .... 2.50
❑4, Aug 1996 .... 2.50
❑5, Sep 1996; V: Nightfist 2.50
❑6, Oct 1996; cover says Part 4 of 4 .... 2.50
❑7, Nov 1996; D: Nightfist. D: Johnny Navarone 2.50
❑8, Dec 1996; O: Hitman. Final Night 2.50
❑9, Dec 1996 .... 2.50
❑10, Jan 1997 .... 2.50
❑11, Feb 1997 .... 2.25
❑12, Mar 1997 A: Green Lantern 2.25
❑13, Apr 1997 .... 2.25
❑14, May 1997 .... 2.25
❑15, Jun 1997 .... 2.25
❑16, Jul 1997 A: Catwoman 2.25
❑17, Aug 1997 .... 2.25
❑18, Sep 1997 .... 2.25
❑19, Oct 1997 .... 2.25
❑20, Nov 1997; V: Mawzir; Demon (Etrigan) team-up 2.25
❑21, Dec 1997; Face cover 2.25
❑22, Jan 1998 .... 2.25
❑23, Feb 1998 .... 2.25
❑24, Mar 1998 .... 2.25
❑25, Apr 1998 .... 2.25
❑26, May 1998 .... 2.25
❑27, Jun 1998 .... 2.25
❑28, Jul 1998 .... 2.25
❑29, Aug 1998 .... 2.25
❑30, Sep 1998 .... 2.50
❑31, Oct 1998 .... 2.50
❑32, Dec 1998 .... 2.50
❑33, Jan 1999 .... 2.50
❑34, Feb 1999 A: Superman 2.50
❑35, Mar 1999; 1: Frances Monaghan 2.50
❑36, Apr 1999; 2: Frances Monaghan. D: Tommy's mother 2.50
❑37, May 1999 .... 2.50
❑38, Jun 1999 .... 2.50
❑39, Jul 1999 .... 2.50
❑40, Aug 1999 .... 2.50
❑41, Sep 1999 .... 2.50
❑42, Oct 1999 .... 2.50
❑43, Nov 1999 .... 2.50
❑44, Dec 1999 .... 2.50
❑45, Jan 2000 .... 2.50
❑46, Feb 2000 .... 2.50
❑47, Mar 2000 .... 2.50
❑48, Apr 2000 .... 2.50
❑49, May 2000 .... 2.50
❑50, Jun 2000 .... 2.50
❑51, Jul 2000 .... 2.50
❑52, Aug 2000 .... 2.50
❑53, Sep 2000 .... 2.50
❑54, Oct 2000 .... 2.50
❑55, Nov 2000 .... 2.50
❑56, Dec 2000 .... 2.50
❑57, Jan 2001 .... 2.50
❑58, Feb 2001 .... 2.50
❑59, Mar 2001 .... 2.50
❑60, Jun 2001; D: Hitman; Final Issue; Price increase 2.50

N-MINT

❑1000000, Nov 1998, b&w 3.00
❑Ann 1; Pulp Heroes; 1997 Ann 3.95

Hitman/Lobo: That Stupid Bastich
DC

❑1, Sep 2000 .... 3.95

Hitomi 2
Antarctic

❑1, Aug 1993, b&w 2.50
❑2, Oct 1993, b&w 2.75
❑3, Dec 1993, b&w 2.75
❑4, Feb 1994, b&w 2.75
❑5, Apr 1994, b&w 2.75
❑6, Jul 1994, b&w 2.75
❑7, Nov 1994, b&w 2.75
❑8, Mar 1995, b&w 2.75
❑9, May 1995, b&w 2.75
❑10, May 1997, b&w 3.95

Hitomi and Her Girl Commandos
Antarctic

❑1, Apr 1992, b&w 2.50
❑2, Jun 1992, b&w 2.50
❑3, Aug 1992, b&w 2.50
❑4, Oct 1992, b&w 2.50

Hit the Beach
Antarctic

❑1, Jul 1993, b&w 2.95
❑1/Gold, Jul 1993; Deluxe edition; gold foil 4.95
❑2, Jul 1994, b&w 2.95
❑3, Jul 1995, b&w 2.95
❑4, Jul 1997, b&w 2.95
❑5, Jul 1998, b&w; regular edition 2.95
❑5/CS, Jul 1998, b&w; Special edition; polybagged with postcard 4.95
❑6, Jul 1999 .... 3.95

Hobbit
Eclipse

❑1/2nd 4.95
❑1, Aug 1989 .... 4.95
❑2, ca. 1990 .... 4.95
❑3, ca. 1990 .... 4.95

Hockey Masters
Revolutionary

❑1, Dec 1993, b&w 2.95

Hoe
Thunderball

❑1 .... 2.50

Hogan's Heroes
Dell

❑1, Jun 1966 .... 50.00
❑2, Sep 1966, Photo still doctored for cover gag 40.00
❑3, Nov 1966, Photo still doctored for cover gag 32.00
❑4, Jan 1967 .... 32.00
❑5, Mar 1967 .... 32.00
❑6, May 1967 .... 26.00
❑7, Jul 1967 .... 26.00
❑8, Sep 1967 .... 26.00
❑9, Oct 1969, Cover reprinted from #1 .... 26.00

Hokum & Hex
Marvel

❑1, Sep 1993, O: Trip Munroe. Embossed cover 2.50

Other grades: Multiply price above by 5/6 for VF/NM • 2/3 for VERY FINE • 1/3 for FINE • 1/5 for VERY GOOD • 1/8 for GOOD

	N-MINT
❑2, Oct 1993, A: Felon Bale. A: Analyzer. A: Trip Monroe	1.75
❑3, Nov 1993	1.75
❑4, Dec 1993, O: Z-Man. D: Z-Man	1.75
❑5, Jan 1994, A: Hyperkind	1.75
❑6, Feb 1994	1.75
❑7, Mar 1994	1.75
❑8, Apr 1994	1.75
❑9, May 1994, Final Issue	1.95

Holed Up
Avatar

❑1, Apr 2004 ... 3.50

Holiday for Screams
Malibu

❑1, b&w; NN ... 4.95

Holiday Out
Renegade

❑1, Mar 1987, b&w ... 2.00
❑2, b&w ... 2.00
❑3, b&w ... 2.00

Hollow Earth
Vision

❑1, May 1996 ... 2.50
❑2, ca. 1996 ... 2.50
❑3, Jan 1997 ... 2.50

Hollow Grounds
DC

❑1, ca. 2004 ... 19.95

Hollywood Superstars
Marvel / Epic

❑1, Nov 1990 ... 2.95
❑2, Jan 1991 ... 2.25
❑3, Feb 1991 ... 2.25
❑4, Mar 1991 ... 2.25
❑5, Apr 1991 ... 2.25

Holo Brothers
Monster

❑1 1989, b&w ... 2.00
❑2, b&w ... 2.00
❑3 ... 2.25
❑4 ... 2.25
❑5 ... 2.25
❑6 ... 2.25
❑7 ... 2.25
❑8 ... 2.25
❑9 ... 2.25
❑10 ... 2.25
❑Special 1; O: Holo. Brothers ... 2.25

Holy Avenger
Slave Labor

❑1, Apr 1996 ... 4.95

Holy Cross
Fantagraphics

❑0, b&w ... 4.95
❑1 ... 2.95
❑2, Oct 1994, b&w ... 2.95

Holy Knight
Pocket Change

❑1, ca. 1994 ... 2.50
❑2, ca. 1994 ... 2.50
❑3, ca. 1994 ... 2.50
❑4, ca. 1994 ... 2.50
❑5, ca. 1995 ... 2.50
❑6, ca. 1995 ... 2.50
❑7, ca. 1995 ... 2.50
❑8, ca. 1995 ... 2.50

Holy Terror
Image

❑1, Aug 2002, b&w ... 2.95

Homage Studios Swimsuit Special
Image

❑1, Apr 1993; JLee (c); JLee (a); pin-ups ... 2.00

Home Grown Funnies
Kitchen Sink

❑1, Jan 1971; Adult ... 55.00
❑1/2nd; 2nd printing ... 22.00
❑1/3rd; 3rd printing ... 10.00
❑1/4th; 4th printing ... 6.00
❑1/5th; 5th printing ... 4.00
❑1/6th; 6th printing ... 4.00
❑1/7th; 7th printing ... 4.00
❑1/8th; 8th printing ... 4.00
❑1/9th; 9th printing ... 4.00
❑1/10th; 10th printing ... 4.00
❑1/11th; 11th printing ... 4.00
❑1/12th, Mar 1977; 12th printing; Adult ... 3.50
❑1/13th; 13th printing ... 3.50
❑1/14th; 14th printing ... 3.50
❑1/15th; 15th printing ... 3.50

Homelands on The World of Magic: The Gathering
Acclaim / Armada

❑1; prestige format; polybagged with Homelands card ... 5.95

Homer The Happy Ghost
Marvel

❑1, Nov 1969, DDC (c); SL (w); DDC (a) ... 40.00
❑2, Jan 1969, DDC (c); SL (w); DDC (a); Reprints cover from #21 of the Atlas series ... 30.00
❑3, Mar 1969, DDC (c); SL (w); DDC (a) ... 30.00
❑4, May 1970, DDC (c); SL (w); DDC (a) ... 30.00

Homicide
Dark Horse

❑1, Apr 1990, b&w ... 1.95

Homicide: Tears of the Dead
Chaos

❑1, Apr 1997 ... 2.95

Homo Patrol
Helpless Anger

❑1, b&w; NN; Adult ... 3.50

Honeymooners
Lodestone

❑1, Oct 1986; Photo cover ... 1.50

Honeymooners
Triad

❑1, Sep 1987; Photo cover ... 2.00
❑2, Sep 1987; reprints #1's indicia; photo back cover ... 2.00
❑3, Dec 1987; Deluxe edition; squarebound; wraparound cover ... 3.50
❑4, Jan 1988; photo back cover ... 2.00
❑5, Feb 1988; wraparound cover ... 2.00
❑6, Mar 1988; photo back cover ... 2.00
❑7, Apr 1988; wraparound cover ... 2.00
❑8, May 1988; wraparound cover ... 2.00
❑9, Jul 1988; squarebound; wraparound cover ... 2.00
❑10, Apr 1989; Photo cover ... 2.00
❑11, Jun 1989; Photo cover ... 2.00
❑12, Aug 1989; Photo cover ... 2.00
❑13 1989 ... 2.00

Honey Mustard
Tokyopop

❑1, Aug 2005, b&w; Read right to left; Graphic novel ... 9.99
❑2, Nov 2005 ... 9.99
❑3, Jan 2006 ... 9.99

Honey West
Gold Key

❑1, Sep 1966 ... 25.00

Hong Kong Phooey
Charlton

❑1, May 1975 ... 40.00
❑2, Aug 1975 ... 20.00
❑3, Oct 1975 ... 10.00
❑4, Dec 1975 ... 10.00
❑5, Feb 1976 ... 10.00
❑6, May 1976 ... 10.00
❑7, Jul 1976 ... 10.00
❑8, Sep 1976 ... 10.00
❑9, Nov 1976 ... 10.00

Hong on the Range
Image

❑1, Dec 1997 ... 2.50
❑2, Jan 1998 ... 2.50
❑3, Feb 1998 ... 2.50

Honk!
Fantagraphics

❑1, Nov 1986, b&w ... 2.25
❑2, Jan 1987, b&w ... 2.25
❑3, Mar 1987, b&w ... 2.25
❑4, May 1987, b&w ... 2.25
❑5, Jul 1987, b&w ... 2.25

Honko the Clown
C&T

❑1, b&w ... 2.00

Honor Among Thieves
Gateway

❑1, Mar 1987 ... 1.50

Honor of the Damned
-Ism

❑1, ca. 2005 ... 3.50

Hood
South Central

❑1, b&w ... 2.75

Hood
Marvel

❑1, Jul 2002 ... 2.99
❑2, Aug 2002 ... 2.99
❑3, Sep 2002 ... 2.99
❑4, Oct 2002 ... 2.99
❑5, Nov 2002 ... 2.99
❑6, Dec 2002 ... 2.99

Hood Magazine
Oakland

❑1 ... 3.00
❑2 ... 3.00

Hoodoo
3-D Zone

❑1, Nov 1988, b&w ... 2.50

Hook
Marvel

❑1, Feb 1992, CV (w); GM (a) ... 1.25
❑2, Feb 1992, CV (w) ... 1.25
❑3, Mar 1992, CV (w) ... 1.25
❑4, Mar 1992, CV (w) ... 1.25

Hook
Marvel

❑1; magazine; NN ... 2.95

Hoon
Eenieweenie

❑1, Jun 1995, b&w ... 2.50
❑2, Aug 1995, b&w ... 2.50
❑3, Oct 1995, b&w ... 2.50
❑4, Dec 1995, b&w ... 2.50
❑5, Feb 1996, b&w ... 2.50
❑6, Apr 1996, b&w ... 2.50

Hoon
Caliber / Tapestry

❑1, ca. 1996, b&w ... 2.95
❑2, ca. 1996, b&w ... 2.95

Hopeless Savages
Oni

❑1, Aug 2001, b&w ... 2.95
❑2 2001, b&w ... 2.95
❑3 2001, b&w ... 2.95
❑4 2001, b&w ... 2.95

Hopeless Savages: Ground Zero
Oni

❑1, Jul 2002, b&w ... 2.95
❑2, Aug 2002, b&w ... 2.95
❑3, Sep 2002, b&w ... 2.95
❑4, Oct 2002, b&w ... 2.95

Hopster's Tracks
Bongo

❑1, b&w ... 2.95
❑2, b&w ... 2.95

Horde
Swing Shift

❑1, b&w ... 2.00

Horde
DC

❑1, ca. 2004 ... 17.95

Horizontal Lieutenant
Dell

❑1, Oct 1962; adapts MGM film ... 30.00

Horny Biker Sluts
Last Gasp

❑1, b&w; Adult ... 2.95
❑2; Adult ... 2.95
❑3; Adult ... 2.95
❑4 1991; Adult; b&w ... 2.95
❑5, b&w pin-ups, cardstock cover ... 2.95
❑6; Adult ... 3.95
❑7; Adult ... 3.95
❑8; Adult ... 3.95
❑9; Adult ... 3.95

Other grades: Multiply price above by 5/6 for VF/NM • 2/3 for VERY FINE • 1/3 for FINE • 1/5 for VERY GOOD • 1/8 for GOOD

Hero for Hire

The series that turns into Power Man
©Marvel

Hex

Western star is pulled forward into 2050
©DC

Hilly Rose

Investigative reporter proves her worth
©Astro

Hitman

Contract killer has special skills
©DC

Hogan's Heroes

POW sitcom escapes into comics
©Dell

N-MINT

❑10; Adult ... 3.95
❑11; Adult ... 3.95
❑12; Adult ... 3.95
❑13; Adult ... 3.95

Horny Comix & Stories
Rip Off

❑1, Apr 1991, b&w; Adult ... 2.50
❑2, Jul 1991, b&w; Adult ... 2.50
❑3, Dec 1991, b&w; Adult ... 2.50
❑4, May 1992, b&w; Adult ... 2.50

Horny Tails
NBM

❑1; Adult ... 12.95

Horny Toads
Fantagraphics / Eros

❑1, b&w; Adult ... 2.95

Horobi Part 1
Viz

❑1, Mar 1990, b&w; Japanese ... 3.75
❑2, Apr 1990, b&w; Japanese ... 3.75
❑3, May 1990, b&w; Japanese ... 3.75
❑4, Jun 1990, b&w; Japanese ... 3.75
❑5, Jul 1990, b&w; Japanese ... 3.75
❑6, Aug 1990, b&w; Japanese ... 3.75
❑7, Sep 1990, b&w; Japanese ... 3.75
❑8, Oct 1990, b&w; Japanese ... 3.75

Horobi Part 2
Viz

❑1, Nov 1990, b&w; Japanese ... 4.25
❑2, Dec 1990, b&w; Japanese ... 4.25
❑3, Jan 1991, b&w; Japanese ... 4.25
❑4, Feb 1991, b&w; Japanese ... 4.25
❑5, Mar 1991, b&w; Japanese ... 4.25
❑6, Apr 1991, b&w; Japanese ... 4.25
❑7, May 1991, b&w; Japanese ... 4.25

Horrible Truth About Comics
Alternative

❑1, Jan 1999, b&w; NN ... 2.95

Horror House
AC

❑1, ca. 1994 ... 2.95

Horror Illustrated Book of Fears
Northstar

❑1; Adult ... 4.00
❑2, Feb 1990; Adult ... 4.00

Horror in the Dark
Fantagor

❑1, b&w; Adult ... 2.00
❑2, b&w; Adult ... 2.00
❑3, b&w; Adult ... 2.00
❑4, b&w; Adult ... 2.00

Horrorist
DC / Vertigo

❑1, Dec 1995 ... 5.95
❑2, Jan 1996 ... 5.95

Horror of Collier County
Dark Horse

❑1, Oct 1999 ... 2.95
❑2 ... 2.95
❑3 ... 2.95
❑4 ... 2.95
❑5 ... 2.95

N-MINT

Horror
Cross Plains

❑nn, Aug 2000 ... 5.95

Horror Show
Caliber

❑1, Oct 1991; Reprints stories from Dr. Wirtham's Comics & Stories #3-6 and Rocket's Blast Comic Collector #136.. 3.50

Horrors of the Haunter
AC

❑1, b&w; Reprints ... 2.95

Horse
Slave Labor

❑1, Sep 1989, b&w ... 2.95
❑2 ... 2.95
❑3 ... 2.95

Horseman
Kevlar

❑0, May 1996, b&w; Commemorative edition; no cover price; published after Crusade issue #1 ... 2.95
❑0/Gold, May 1996, gold foil-embossed cardstock cover; published after Crusade issue #1 ... 2.95
❑0/Silver, no cover price or indicia; published after Crusade issue #1 ... 2.95
❑0/A, May 1996, Woman holding sword facing forward on cover ... 2.95
❑1, Mar 1996, Published by Crusade ... 2.95
❑1/A, Nov 1996, Kevlar edition; Kevlar begins publishing ... 2.95
❑2, Jan 1997, b&w; no cover price or indicia ... 2.95

Hosie's Heroines
Slave Labor

❑1, Apr 1993; Adult ... 2.95

Hostile Takeover
Malibu

❑Ashcan 1, Sep 1994; ashcan; Ultraverse Preview ... 1.00

Hotel Harbour View
Viz

❑1, b&w; Japanese ... 9.95

Hothead Paisan: Homicidal Lesbian Terrorist
Giant Ass

❑13; Adult ... 3.50

Hot Line
Fantagraphics / Eros

❑1, Nov 1992; Adult ... 2.50

Hot Mexican Love Comics
Hot Mexican Love Comics

❑1 ... 3.95
❑2 ... 3.95

Hot N' Cold Heroes
A-Plus

❑1, b&w ... 2.50
❑2, Mar 1991, reprints O: Nemesis, Magicman ... 2.50

Hot Nights in Rangoon
Fantagraphics / Eros

❑1; Adult ... 2.95
❑2 1994; 24 pages; Adult ... 2.95
❑3, Nov 1994; Adult ... 2.95

N-MINT

Hot Rod Racers
Charlton

❑1, Dec 1965 ... 30.00
❑2, Feb 1965 ... 20.00
❑3, May 1965 ... 20.00
❑4, Jul 1965 ... 20.00
❑5, Sep 1965 ... 20.00
❑6, Nov 1965 ... 20.00
❑7, Jan 1966 ... 20.00
❑8, May 1966 ... 20.00
❑9, Jul 1966 ... 20.00
❑10 1966 ... 20.00
❑11, Nov 1966 ... 20.00
❑12, Jan 1967 ... 20.00
❑13, Mar 1967 ... 20.00
❑14 1967 ... 20.00
❑15, Jul 1967 ... 20.00

Hot Rods and Racing Cars
Charlton

❑54, Nov 1961 ... 18.00
❑55 1961 ... 18.00
❑56, Mar 1962, A: Road Knights. A: Clint Curtis ... 18.00
❑57, May 1962 ... 18.00
❑58, Jul 1962 ... 18.00
❑59, Sep 1962 ... 18.00
❑60, Nov 1962 ... 18.00
❑61, Jan 1963 ... 13.00
❑62, Mar 1963 ... 13.00
❑63, May 1963 ... 13.00
❑64, Jul 1963 ... 13.00
❑65, Sep 1963 ... 13.00
❑66, Nov 1963 ... 13.00
❑67, Jan 1964 ... 13.00
❑68, Mar 1964, A: Road Knights. A: Clint Curtis ... 13.00
❑69, Jun 1964 ... 13.00
❑70, Sep 1964, 1: Ken King ... 13.00
❑71 1964 ... 13.00
❑72 1965 ... 13.00
❑73 1965 ... 13.00
❑74 1965 ... 13.00
❑75, Aug 1965 ... 13.00
❑76, Oct 1965 ... 13.00
❑77, Dec 1965 ... 13.00
❑78, Mar 1966 ... 13.00
❑79, Jun 1966 ... 13.00
❑80, Aug 1966 ... 13.00
❑81, Oct 1966 ... 10.00
❑82, Dec 1966 ... 10.00
❑83, Feb 1967 ... 10.00
❑84, Apr 1967 ... 10.00
❑85, Jun 1967 ... 10.00
❑86, Aug 1967 ... 10.00
❑87, Oct 1967 ... 10.00
❑88 1967 ... 10.00
❑89, Feb 1968 ... 10.00
❑90, Jun 1968 ... 10.00
❑91, Aug 1968 ... 10.00
❑92, Oct 1968 ... 10.00
❑93, Dec 1968 ... 10.00
❑94, Feb 1969 ... 10.00
❑95, Apr 1969 ... 10.00
❑96, Jun 1969 ... 10.00
❑97, Aug 1969 ... 10.00
❑98, Oct 1969 ... 10.00

N-MINT

❑99, Dec 1969 .... 10.00
❑100, Feb 1970 .... 10.00
❑101, Apr 1970 .... 7.00
❑102, Jun 1970 .... 7.00
❑103, Aug 1970 .... 7.00
❑104, Oct 1970 .... 7.00
❑105, Dec 1970 .... 7.00
❑106, Feb 1971 .... 7.00
❑107, Apr 1971 .... 7.00
❑108, Jun 1971 .... 7.00
❑109, Aug 1971 .... 7.00
❑110, Oct 1971 .... 7.00
❑111, Dec 1971 .... 7.00
❑112, Feb 1972 .... 7.00
❑113, Apr 1972 .... 7.00
❑114, Jun 1972, A: Clint Curtis. A: Alex . 7.00
❑115, Aug 1972 .... 7.00
❑116, Oct 1972 .... 7.00
❑117, Dec 1972 .... 7.00
❑118, Feb 1973 .... 7.00
❑119, Apr 1973 .... 7.00
❑120, Jun 1973 .... 7.00

Hot Shots
Hot

❑1, Apr 1987 .... 2.00

Hot Shots: Avengers
Marvel

❑1, Oct 1995; pin-ups 2.95

Hot Shots: Spider-Man
Marvel

❑1, Jan 1996; pin-ups 2.95

Hot Shots: X-Men
Marvel

❑1, Jan 1996; pin-ups; Introduction by Scott Lobdell 2.95

Hotspur
Eclipse

❑1, Jun 1987 .... 1.75
❑2, Aug 1987 .... 1.75
❑3, Sep 1987 .... 1.75

Hot Stuf'
Sal Quartuccio

❑1 .... 4.00
❑2 .... 3.00
❑3, Dec 1976; RCo (w); RCo (a); Adult .. 3.00
❑4, Mar 1977; ATh, GM (w); ATh, GM, EC (a); Adult 3.00
❑5, Fal 1977 .... 3.00
❑6, Dec 1977 MN, EC (w); MN, EC (a) ... 3.00
❑7 .... 3.00
❑8, ca. 1978 .... 3.00

Hot Stuff
Harvey

❑1, Sep 1991 .... 1.50
❑2, Dec 1991 .... 1.25
❑3, Mar 1992 .... 1.25
❑4, Jun 1992 .... 1.25
❑5, Sep 1992 .... 1.25
❑6, Mar 1993 .... 1.25
❑7, May 1993 .... 1.25
❑8, Aug 1993 .... 1.25
❑9, Nov 1993 .... 1.50
❑10, Jan 1994 .... 1.50
❑11, Mar 1994 .... 1.50
❑12, Jun 1994 .... 1.50

Hot Stuff Big Book
Harvey

❑1, Nov 1992 .... 1.95
❑2, Jun 1993 .... 1.95

Hot Stuff Digest
Harvey

❑1, Jul 1992 .... 2.25
❑2, Nov 1992 .... 2.25
❑3, Apr 1993 .... 1.75
❑4 .... 1.75
❑5 .... 1.75

Hot Stuff Giant Size
Harvey

❑1, Oct 1992 .... 2.25
❑2, Jul 1993 .... 2.25
❑3, Oct 1993 .... 2.25

Hot Stuff Little Devil
Harvey

❑41, Nov 1961 .... 20.00
❑42, Dec 1961 .... 20.00
❑43, Jan 1962 .... 20.00
❑44, Feb 1962 .... 20.00
❑45, Mar 1962 .... 20.00
❑46, Apr 1962 .... 20.00
❑47, May 1962 .... 20.00
❑48, Jun 1962 .... 20.00
❑49 1962 .... 20.00
❑50, Oct 1962 .... 20.00
❑51, Dec 1962 .... 15.00
❑52, Feb 1963 .... 15.00
❑53, Apr 1963 .... 15.00
❑54, Jun 1963 .... 15.00
❑55, Aug 1963 .... 15.00
❑56, Oct 1963 .... 15.00
❑57, Dec 1963 .... 15.00
❑58, Feb 1964 .... 15.00
❑59, Apr 1964 .... 15.00
❑60, Jun 1964 .... 15.00
❑61, Aug 1964 .... 15.00
❑62, Oct 1964 .... 15.00
❑63, Dec 1964 .... 15.00
❑64, Feb 1965 .... 15.00
❑65, Apr 1965 .... 15.00
❑66, Jun 1965 .... 15.00
❑67, Aug 1965 .... 15.00
❑68, Oct 1965 .... 15.00
❑69, Dec 1965 .... 15.00
❑70, Feb 1966 .... 15.00
❑71, Apr 1966 .... 10.00
❑72, Jun 1966 .... 10.00
❑73, Aug 1966 .... 10.00
❑74, Oct 1966 .... 10.00
❑75, Dec 1966 .... 10.00
❑76, Feb 1967 .... 10.00
❑77, Apr 1967 .... 10.00
❑78, Jun 1967 .... 10.00
❑79, Aug 1967 .... 10.00
❑80, Oct 1967 .... 10.00
❑81, Dec 1967 .... 10.00
❑82, Feb 1968 .... 10.00
❑83, Apr 1968 .... 10.00
❑84, Jun 1968 .... 10.00
❑85, Aug 1968 .... 10.00
❑86, Oct 1968 .... 10.00
❑87, Dec 1968 .... 10.00
❑88, Feb 1969 .... 10.00
❑89, Apr 1969 .... 10.00
❑90, May 1969 .... 10.00
❑91, Jul 1969 .... 10.00
❑92, Sep 1969 .... 10.00
❑93, Oct 1969 .... 10.00
❑94, Dec 1969 .... 10.00
❑95, Jan 1970 .... 10.00
❑96, Mar 1970 .... 10.00
❑97, May 1970 .... 10.00
❑98, Jul 1970 .... 10.00
❑99, Sep 1970 .... 10.00
❑100, Oct 1970 .... 10.00
❑101, Nov 1970 .... 7.00
❑102, Jan 1971 .... 7.00
❑103, Mar 1971 .... 7.00
❑104, May 1971 .... 7.00
❑105, Jul 1971 .... 7.00
❑106, Sep 1971 .... 7.00
❑107, Nov 1971 .... 7.00
❑108, Jan 1972 .... 7.00
❑109, Mar 1972 .... 7.00
❑110, May 1972 .... 7.00
❑111, Jul 1972 .... 7.00
❑112, Sep 1972 .... 7.00
❑113, Nov 1972 .... 7.00
❑114, Jan 1973 .... 7.00
❑115, Mar 1973 .... 7.00
❑116, May 1973 .... 7.00
❑117, Jul 1973 .... 7.00
❑118, Sep 1973 .... 7.00
❑119, Nov 1973 .... 7.00
❑120, Jan 1974 .... 7.00
❑121, Mar 1974 .... 7.00
❑122, May 1974 .... 5.00
❑123, Jul 1974 .... 5.00
❑124, Sep 1974 .... 5.00
❑125, Nov 1974 .... 5.00
❑126, Jan 1975 .... 5.00
❑127, Mar 1975 .... 5.00
❑128, May 1975 .... 5.00
❑129, Jul 1975 .... 5.00
❑130, Sep 1975 .... 5.00
❑131, Nov 1975; Hostess Twinkies ad: Wendy vs. Gobble-Up Goblin 5.00
❑132, Jan 1976; Hostess Fruit Pies ad: Richie Rich 5.00
❑133, Mar 1976 .... 5.00
❑134, May 1976 .... 5.00
❑135, Jul 1976 .... 5.00
❑136, Sep 1976 .... 5.00
❑137, Nov 1976 .... 5.00
❑138, Jan 1977 .... 5.00
❑139, Mar 1977 .... 5.00
❑140, May 1977 .... 5.00
❑141, Jul 1977 .... 5.00
❑142, Feb 1978 .... 5.00
❑143, Apr 1978 .... 5.00
❑144, Jun 1978 .... 5.00
❑145, Sep 1978 .... 5.00
❑146, Dec 1978 .... 3.00
❑147, Feb 1979 .... 3.00
❑148, Apr 1979 .... 3.00
❑149, Jun 1979 .... 3.00
❑150, Aug 1979 .... 3.00
❑151, Oct 1979 .... 3.00
❑152, Jan 1980 .... 3.00
❑153, Mar 1980 .... 3.00
❑154, May 1980 .... 3.00
❑155, Jul 1980 .... 3.00
❑156, Sep 1980 .... 3.00
❑157, Nov 1980 .... 3.00
❑158, Jan 1981 .... 3.00
❑159, Mar 1981 .... 3.00
❑160, May 1981 .... 3.00
❑161, Jul 1981 .... 3.00
❑162, Sep 1981 .... 3.00
❑163, Nov 1981 .... 3.00
❑164 .... 3.00
❑165, Oct 1986 .... 3.00
❑166, Dec 1986 .... 3.00
❑167, Feb 1987 .... 3.00
❑168, Apr 1987 .... 3.00
❑169, Jun 1987 .... 3.00
❑170, Sep 1987 .... 3.00
❑171, Nov 1987 .... 3.00
❑172, Nov 1987 .... 3.00
❑173, Sep 1990 .... 3.00
❑174, Oct 1990 .... 3.00
❑175, Nov 1990 .... 3.00
❑176, Dec 1990 .... 3.00
❑177, Jan 1991 .... 3.00

Hot Tails
Fantagraphics / Eros

❑1; Adult 3.50

Hot Wheels
DC

❑1, Apr 1970 .... 45.00
❑2, Jun 1970 .... 30.00
❑3, Aug 1970, NA (c); ATh, NA, RE (a) .. 24.00
❑4, Oct 1970 .... 24.00
❑5, Dec 1970 .... 24.00
❑6, Feb 1971, NA (c); NA, RE (a) 30.00

Hourman
DC

❑1, Apr 1999; A: Amazo. A: Justice League of America. A: Snapper Carr. V: Amazo 2.50
❑1/Autographed; A: Amazo. A: Justice League of America. A: Snapper Carr. Autographed by David Meikis 15.95
❑2, May 1999 A: Tomorrow Woman 2.50
❑3, Jun 1999 .... 2.50
❑4, Jul 1999; V: Lord of Time 2.50
❑5, Aug 1999 A: Golden Age Hourman .. 2.50
❑6, Sep 1999; V: Amazo 2.50
❑7, Oct 1999; V: Amazo 2.50
❑8, Nov 1999; Day of Judgment 2.50
❑9, Dec 1999 .... 2.50
❑10, Jan 2000 .... 2.50
❑11, Feb 2000 .... 2.50
❑12, Mar 2000 .... 2.50
❑13, Apr 2000 .... 2.50
❑14, May 2000 .... 2.50
❑15, Jun 2000; V: Undersoul (21st century villian) 2.50
❑16, Jul 2000; Follow-up to Justice Leage of America #77 .... 2.50
❑17, Aug 2000 .... 2.50

Other grades: Multiply price above by 5/6 for VF/NM • 2/3 for VERY FINE • 1/3 for FINE • 1/5 for VERY GOOD • 1/8 for GOOD

Hollywood Superstars

Stuntman, comedian, and actress fight crime

©Marvel

Honeymooners

Ralph Kramden returns in 1980s relaunch

©Triad

Hot Rod Racers

More racing comics from Charlton

©Charlton

Hot Shots: X-Men

Pin-ups based on Fleer card series

©Marvel

Hot Stuff, The Little Devil

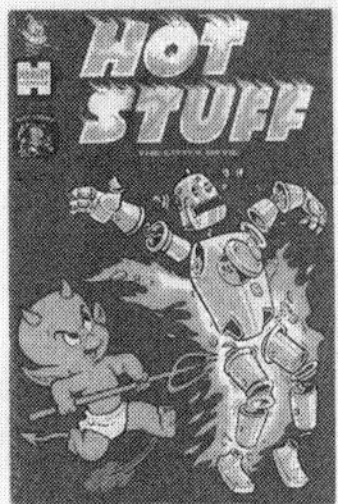

Annoying demon tortures Enchanted Forest

©Harvey

N-MINT

❑18, Sep 2000; V: Counter-Evolutionary ... 2.50
❑19, Oct 2000 ... 2.50
❑20, Nov 2000; Snapper Carr transported to his time with the Blasters ... 2.50
❑21, Dec 2000; V: Amazo; Hourman recovers timelost Snapper Carr ... 2.50
❑22, Jan 2001 ... 2.50
❑23, Feb 2001; Travels to 1950's and 2020's ... 2.50
❑24, Mar 2001; Hourman V: Hourman (Rex Tyler) in 853rd century ... 2.50
❑25, Apr 2001; Final isue ... 2.50

House II The Second Story
Marvel

❑1, Oct 1987; Movie adaptation ... 2.00

House of Frightenstein
AC

❑1, b&w; Reprints ... 2.95

House of M
Marvel

❑1, Jul 2005 ... 4.00
❑1/Quesada, Jul 2005 ... 30.00
❑1/DirCut, Jul 2005 ... 4.00
❑1/Gatefold, Jul 2005 ... 5.00
❑1/Madurera, Jul 2005 ... 12.00
❑2, Aug 2005 ... 2.99
❑2/Dodson 2005 ... 25.00
❑3, Aug 2005 ... 6.00
❑3/Cassaday, Aug 2005 ... 20.00
❑4, Sep 2005 ... 2.99
❑4/Peterson, Sep 2005 ... 15.00
❑5, Oct 2005 ... 5.00
❑5/McKone, Oct 2005 ... 15.00
❑6, Nov 2005 ... 2.99
❑6/Land, Nov 2005 ... 15.00
❑7, Dec 2005; Regular cover (Scarlet Witch holding fallen Quicksilver) ... 4.00
❑8, Jan 2006 ... 2.99

House of Mystery
DC

❑116, Nov 1961 ... 45.00
❑117, Dec 1961 ... 35.00
❑118, Jan 1962 ... 35.00
❑119, Feb 1962 ... 35.00
❑120, Mar 1962, ATh (a) ... 45.00
❑121, Apr 1962 ... 28.00
❑122, May 1962 ... 28.00
❑123, Jun 1962 ... 28.00
❑124, Jul 1962 ... 28.00
❑125, Aug 1962 ... 28.00
❑126, Sep 1962 ... 28.00
❑127, Oct 1962 ... 28.00
❑128, Nov 1962 ... 28.00
❑129, Dec 1962 ... 28.00
❑130, Jan 1963 ... 28.00
❑131, Feb 1963 ... 22.00
❑132, Mar 1963 ... 22.00
❑133, Apr 1963 ... 22.00
❑134, May 1963 ... 22.00
❑135, Jun 1963 ... 22.00
❑136, Jul 1963 ... 22.00
❑137, Sep 1963 ... 22.00
❑138, Oct 1963 ... 22.00
❑139, Dec 1963 ... 22.00
❑140, Jan 1964 ... 22.00
❑141, Mar 1964 ... 22.00

N-MINT

❑142, Apr 1964 ... 22.00
❑143, Jun 1964, DD (c); MM (a); J'onn J'onzz; Martian Manhunter begins ... 175.00
❑144, Jul 1964, J'onn J'onzz Martian Manhunter ... 75.00
❑145, Sep 1964, J'onn J'onzz Martian Manhunter ... 50.00
❑146, Oct 1964, J'onn J'onzz Martian Manhunter ... 50.00
❑147, Dec 1964, J'onn J'onzz Martian Manhunter ... 50.00
❑148, Jan 1965, J'onn J'onzz Martian Manhunter ... 50.00
❑149, Mar 1965, ATh (a); J'onn J'onzz Martian Manhunter ... 50.00
❑150, Apr 1965, J'onn J'onzz Martian Manhunter ... 50.00
❑151, Jun 1965, J'onn J'onzz Martian Manhunter ... 50.00
❑152, Jul 1965, J'onn J'onzz Martian Manhunter ... 50.00
❑153, Sep 1965, J'onn J'onzz ... 50.00
❑154, Oct 1965 ... 50.00
❑155, Dec 1965 ... 50.00
❑156, Jan 1966, O: Dial "H" For Hero. 1: Dial "H" For Hero. 1: Robby Reed ... 75.00
❑157, Mar 1966, Dial H For Hero; Martian Manhunter ... 50.00
❑158, Apr 1966, Dial H For Hero; Martian Manhunter ... 50.00
❑159, Jun 1966, Dial H For Hero; Martian Manhunter ... 50.00
❑160, Jul 1966, Dial "H" for Hero; Robby Reed becomes Plastic Man ... 90.00
❑161, Sep 1966, Dial "H" for Hero ... 35.00
❑162, Oct 1966, Dial H For Hero; Martian Manhunter ... 32.00
❑163, Dec 1966, Dial H For Hero; Martian Manhunter ... 32.00
❑164, Jan 1967, Dial H For Hero; Martian Manhunter ... 32.00
❑165, Mar 1967, V: Professor Hugo; Martian Manhunter; Dial H For Hero ... 32.00
❑166, Apr 1967, Dial H For Hero; Martian Manhunter ... 32.00
❑167, Jun 1967, Dial H For Hero; Martian Manhunter ... 32.00
❑168, Jul 1967, Dial H For Hero; Martian Manhunter ... 32.00
❑169, Sep 1967, 1: Gem Girl; Martian Manhunter; Dial H For Hero ... 32.00
❑170, Oct 1967, Dial H For Hero; Martian Manhunter ... 32.00
❑171, Dec 1967, Dial "H" for Hero ... 32.00
❑172, Feb 1968, Dial H For Hero; Martian Manhunter ... 32.00
❑173, Apr 1968, Last Dial H For Hero; Last Martian Manhunter in House of Mystery ... 32.00
❑174, Jun 1968, JO (w); CI, NA (a); Mystery format begins ... 50.00
❑175, Aug 1968, NA (c); SA, JO (w); JO, NA (a); 1: Cain ... 45.00
❑176, Oct 1968, NA (c); SA, JO (w); SA, JO, NA (a) ... 24.00
❑177, Dec 1968,NA (c); SA, JO (w); MM, SA, JO, NA (a) ... 24.00
❑178, Feb 1969, JO, NA (w); SA, JO, NA, JM (a) ... 45.00
❑179, Apr 1969, NA (c); SA, JO (w); SA, BWr, JO, NA (a); Bernie Wrightson's first professional work ... 60.00

N-MINT

❑180, Jun 1969, SA, GK (w); SA, BWr, JO, NA, GK, WW (a) ... 25.00
❑181, Aug 1969, NA (c); SA, JO (w); SA, BWr, NA, FS (a) ... 25.00
❑182, Oct 1969, SA, JO (w); SA, ATh, JO, NA, AT, WH (a) ... 18.00
❑183, Dec 1969, SA, JO (w); SA, BWr, JO, NA, WW (a) ... 25.00
❑184, Feb 1970, NA (c); SA, JO (w); SA, ATh, BWr, NA, GK, WW, AT (a) ... 18.00
❑185, Apr 1970,NA (c); SA, JO (w); AW, SA, BWr, JO, NA, WW, WH (a) ... 30.00
❑186, Jun 1970, NA (c); SA, JO (w); SA, BWr, NA (a) ... 75.00
❑187, Aug 1970, NA (c); SA, JO (w); SA, ATh, NA, AT, WH (a) ... 20.00
❑188, Oct 1970, NA (c); SA, JO (w); SA, BWr, NA, TD (a) ... 30.00
❑189, Dec 1970, NA (c); JO (w); SA, TS, NA, AT (a) ... 20.00
❑190, Feb 1971, JO (w); SA, ATh, NA, AT, RE (a) ... 20.00
❑191, Apr 1971, NA (c); SA (w); SA, BWr, NA, TD (a) ... 25.00
❑192, Jun 1971, NA (c); GM, DH, NA, JA (a) ... 20.00
❑193, Jul 1971, BWr (c); SA (w); SA, BWr, TD (a) ... 25.00
❑194, Sep 1971 BWr (c); SA (w); SA, ATh, BWr, NR, JK, RH (a) ... 30.00
❑195, Oct 1971; SA (w); MM, SA, BWr, NR (a); Swamp Thing prototype? ... 45.00
❑196, Nov 1971; JA (c); SA (w); SA, ATh, GM, NA, GK, NC, WH (a); The Alien Within Me reprinted from My Greatest Adventure #60; Dark Journey reprinted from issue #72 ... 20.00
❑197, Dec 1971; NA (c); NR, NA, DD, NC (a); Mr. Mortem reprinted from issue #20; The Guardian of the Past reprinted from House of Secrets #11 ... 20.00
❑198, Jan 1972; He Adopted a Martian Boy reprinted from Tales of the Unexpected #28; The Thing in the Telescope reprinted from issue #60 ... 20.00
❑199, Feb 1972; NA (c); SA (w); BO, SA, RB, JK, NA, WW (a); He Doomed The World! reprinted from My Greatest Adventure #17; The Haunting Wind! reprinted from Phantom Stranger (1st Series) #2 ... 20.00
❑200, Mar 1972; The Secret of Camp Galaxy reprinted from House of Secrets #26; The Forbidden Wish reprinted from Tales of the Unexpected #7 ... 20.00
❑201, Apr 1972; SA, JO (w); SA, BWr, JA, RMo (a); Million-Dollar Magic reprinted from issue #60; Hail the Conquering Aliens reprinted from issue #103 ... 20.00
❑202, May 1972; SA, NR, GC (a); Stay Away From Me óYou Might Die reprinted from My Greatest Adventure #72; The Phantom on Wheels reprinted from issue #58 ... 14.00
❑203, Jun 1972; The Golden Doom reprinted from issue #64 ... 14.00
❑204, Jul 1972, SA, BWr (w); SA, BWr, AN (a) ... 20.00
❑205, Aug 1972 ... 12.00
❑206, Sep 1972 ... 12.00
❑207, Oct 1972, JSn, BWr, NR, GT, JSt, DA (a) ... 40.00
❑208, Nov 1972 ... 12.00
❑209, Dec 1972, BWr, AA, JA (a) ... 10.00

Other grades: Multiply price above by 5/6 for VF/NM • 2/3 for VERY FINE • 1/3 for FINE • 1/5 for VERY GOOD • 1/8 for GOOD

	N-MINT
❑210, Jan 1973	10.00
❑211, Feb 1973, BWr, NR, DGr, AA (a)	10.00
❑212, Mar 1973, MA, AN (a)	10.00
❑213, Apr 1973, BWr (c); SA (w); SA, BWr, AN (a)	10.00
❑214, May 1973, BWr (c); ME (w); BWr, NR (a)	6.00
❑215, Jun 1973	6.00
❑216, Jul 1973	6.00
❑217, Sep 1973, BWr (c)	6.00
❑218, Oct 1973	6.00
❑219, Nov 1973, BWr, NR (a)	6.00
❑220, Dec 1973	6.00
❑221, Jan 1974, BWr (c); BWr, FT (a)	12.00
❑222, Feb 1974	6.00
❑223, Mar 1974	6.00
❑224, Apr 1974, 100-page giant; MM, BWr, FR, NA, DD, AN (a); A: Phantom Stranger. Phantom Stranger	35.00
❑225, Jun 1974, 100-page giant; AN (a)	18.00
❑226, Aug 1974, 100-page giant; BWr, NR, AA (a); A: Phantom Stranger	18.00
❑227, Oct 1974, 100-page giant; NR (a)	27.00
❑228, Dec 1974, 100-page giant; NR, NA, AT (a)	18.00
❑229, Feb 1975, 100-page giant	18.00
❑230, Apr 1975	5.00
❑231, May 1975	5.00
❑232, Jun 1975	5.00
❑233, Jul 1975	5.00
❑234, Aug 1975	5.00
❑235, Sep 1975	5.00
❑236, Oct 1975 SD, BWr, NA (a)	5.00
❑237, Nov 1975	5.00
❑238, Dec 1975	5.00
❑239, Feb 1976	5.00
❑240, Apr 1976	5.00
❑241, May 1976	5.00
❑242, Jun 1976	5.00
❑243, Jul 1976, Bicentennial #10	5.00
❑244, Aug 1976	5.00
❑245, Sep 1976	5.00
❑246, Oct 1976	5.00
❑247, Nov 1976	5.00
❑248, Dec 1976	5.00
❑249, Jan 1977	5.00
❑250, Feb 1977	5.00
❑251, Mar 1977; NA, WW (a); giant	4.00
❑252, May 1977; NA, AN (a); giant	4.00
❑253, Jul 1977; NA (c); NA, AN (a); giant	4.00
❑254, Sep 1977; SD, NA, WH (a); giant	4.00
❑255, Nov 1977; BWr (a); giant	4.00
❑256, Jan 1978; BWr (a); giant	4.00
❑257, Mar 1978; MG, RE, WH (a); giant	4.00
❑258, May 1978; SD (a); giant	4.00
❑259, Jul 1978; DN, MG (a); giant	4.00
❑260, Sep 1978	3.00
❑261, Oct 1978	3.00
❑262, Nov 1978, JO (c); RT (a)	3.00
❑263, Dec 1978	3.00
❑264, Jan 1979	3.00
❑265, Feb 1979	3.00
❑266, Mar 1979	3.00
❑267, Apr 1979	3.00
❑268, May 1979	3.00
❑269, Jun 1979	3.00
❑270, Jul 1979	3.00
❑271, Aug 1979	3.00
❑272, Sep 1979	3.00
❑273, Oct 1979	3.00
❑274, Nov 1979, JO (a)	3.00
❑275, Dec 1979	3.00
❑276, Jan 1980	3.00
❑277, Feb 1980	3.00
❑278, Mar 1980	3.00
❑279, Apr 1980	3.00
❑280, May 1980	3.00
❑281, Jun 1980	3.00
❑282, Jul 1980, JSn (a)	3.00
❑283, Aug 1980	3.00
❑284, Sep 1980	3.00
❑285, Oct 1980	3.00
❑286, Nov 1980	3.00
❑287, Dec 1980	3.00
❑288, Jan 1981	3.00
❑289, Feb 1981, 1: I, Vampire	3.00
❑290, Mar 1981, I, Vampire	3.00
❑291, Apr 1981, I, Vampire	3.00
❑292, May 1981	3.00
❑293, Jun 1981, I, Vampire	3.00
❑294, Jul 1981	3.00
❑295, Aug 1981	3.00
❑296, Sep 1981	3.00
❑297, Oct 1981, I, Vampire	3.00
❑298, Nov 1981	3.00
❑299, Dec 1981, I, Vampire	3.00
❑300, Jan 1982	3.00
❑301, Feb 1982	3.00
❑302, Mar 1982, I, Vampire	3.00
❑303, Apr 1982, I, Vampire	3.00
❑304, May 1982, I, Vampire	3.00
❑305, Jun 1982, I, Vampire	3.00
❑306, Jul 1982, I, Vampire	3.00
❑307, Aug 1982, I, Vampire	3.00
❑308, Sep 1982, I, Vampire	3.00
❑309, Oct 1982, I, Vampire	3.00
❑310, Nov 1982, I, Vampire	3.00
❑311, Dec 1982, I, Vampire	3.00
❑312, Jan 1983, I, Vampire	3.00
❑313, Feb 1983	3.00
❑314, Mar 1983, I, Vampire	3.00
❑315, Apr 1983, I, Vampire	3.00
❑316, May 1983	3.00
❑317, Jun 1983	3.00
❑318, Jul 1983, I, Vampire	3.00
❑319, Aug 1983, D: I, Vampire	3.00
❑320, Sep 1983	3.00
❑321, Oct 1983, Final Issue	3.00

House of Secrets
DC

	N-MINT
❑50, Nov 1961	65.00
❑51, Dec 1961	52.00
❑52, Jan 1962	52.00
❑53, Mar 1962	52.00
❑54, May 1962	52.00
❑55, Jul 1962	52.00
❑56, Sep 1962	52.00
❑57, Nov 1962	52.00
❑58, Jan 1963	52.00
❑59, Mar 1963	52.00
❑60, May 1963, Mark Merlin	52.00
❑61, Jul 1963, MM (a); 1: Eclipso	125.00
❑62, Sep 1963	60.00
❑63, Nov 1963, Mark Merlin; Eclipso	50.00
❑64, Jan 1964	50.00
❑65, Mar 1964, MM, ATh (a)	50.00
❑66, May 1964, MM, ATh (a); Eclipso cover	65.00
❑67, Jul 1964, MM, ATh (a); Eclipso cover	40.00
❑68, Sep 1964	36.00
❑69, Nov 1964	36.00
❑70, Jan 1965, Eclipso cover	36.00
❑71, Mar 1965	36.00
❑72, May 1965	36.00
❑73, Jul 1965, 1: Prince Ra-Man. Eclipso cover; Mark Merlin becomes Prince Ra-Man	36.00
❑74, Sep 1965, Prince Ra-Man	36.00
❑75, Nov 1965, Both Eclipso and Prince Ra-Man logos on cover	36.00
❑76, Jan 1966, Eclipso/Ra-Man crossover	36.00
❑77, Mar 1966	36.00
❑78, May 1966, Eclipso cover	36.00
❑79, Jul 1966, Eclipso/Ra-Man crossover	36.00
❑80, Sep 1966, Eclipso cover	45.00
❑81, Sep 1969, NA (c); 1: Abel. Mystery format begins	55.00
❑82, Nov 1969, NA (c); NA (a)	20.00
❑83, Jan 1970, ATh (a)	20.00
❑84, Mar 1970, NA (c)	20.00
❑85, May 1970, NA (c); DH, NA, GK (a)	32.00
❑86, Jul 1970, NA (c); GM (a)	20.00
❑87, Sep 1970, NA (c); BWr, DG, RA (a)	45.00
❑88, Nov 1970, NA (c); DG, DD (a)	40.00
❑89, Jan 1971, GM (c); GM (a); Harlequin-esque cover	40.00
❑90, Mar 1971, RB, GM, NA (a); 1st Buckler DC art	40.00
❑91, May 1971, MA, NA, WW (a)	40.00
❑92, Jul 1971, BWr (c); DD, ME (w); BWr, DD, TD (a); 1: Swamp Thing	450.00
❑93, Sep 1971 BWr (c); BWr, JA (a)	25.00
❑94, Nov 1971; BWr (c); SA, ATh, BWr, TD (a); Includes Abel's Fables by Aragones	25.00
❑95, Jan 1972	25.00
❑96, Mar 1972; BWr (c); SA, ATh, DD, WW (a); Includes Abel's Fables by Argones	25.00
❑97, May 1972; SA, JA (a); Includes Abel's Fables by Aragones	25.00
❑98, Jul 1972; 52 pages	25.00
❑99, Sep 1972 BWr, NR (a)	25.00
❑100, Oct 1972 BWr (c); SA, TP, TD (a)	27.00
❑101, Nov 1972 SA (w); SA, AN (a)	18.00
❑102, Dec 1972	18.00
❑103, Jan 1973 BWr (c); SA, AN (a)	18.00
❑104, Feb 1973	18.00
❑105, Mar 1973	18.00
❑106, Apr 1973, BWr (c)	18.00
❑107, May 1973, BWr (c); SA (a)	18.00
❑108, Jun 1973	18.00
❑109, Jul 1973	18.00
❑110, Aug 1973	18.00
❑111, Sep 1973	18.00
❑112, Oct 1973	18.00
❑113, Nov 1973	10.00
❑114, Dec 1973	10.00
❑115, Jan 1974	10.00
❑116, Feb 1974	10.00
❑117, Mar 1974, AA, AN (a)	10.00
❑118, Apr 1974, This issue's Statement of Ownership was also accidentally printed in Our Fighting Forces #148	10.00
❑119, May 1974	10.00
❑120, Jun 1974, TD (a)	10.00
❑121, Jul 1974	10.00
❑122, Aug 1974	10.00
❑123, Sep 1974, FR (c); ATh (a)	10.00
❑124, Oct 1974 FR (c); RMo (a)	10.00
❑125, Nov 1974	10.00
❑126, Dec 1974	10.00
❑127, Jan 1975	10.00
❑128, Feb 1975	10.00
❑129, Mar 1975	10.00
❑130, Apr 1975 SA, NR (a)	10.00
❑131, May 1975	10.00
❑132, Jun 1975	10.00
❑133, Jul 1975	10.00
❑134, Aug 1975	10.00
❑135, Sep 1975 BWr (c)	10.00
❑136, Nov 1975 BWr (c)	10.00
❑137, Jan 1976	10.00
❑138, Mar 1976	10.00
❑139, May 1976; BWr (c); SD (a); Halloween cover	10.00
❑140, Jul 1976; O: Patchwork Man	10.00
❑141, Sep 1976; O: Patchwork Man	10.00
❑142, Nov 1976	7.00
❑143, Jan 1977	7.00
❑144, Mar 1977	7.00
❑145, May 1977	7.00
❑146, Jul 1977 GM (c)	7.00
❑147, Sep 1977 GM (c)	7.00
❑148, Nov 1977	7.00
❑149, Jan 1978	7.00
❑150, Mar 1978, JSn (c)	7.00
❑151, May 1978 MG (a)	7.00
❑152, Jul 1978	7.00
❑153, Sep 1978 JA (c)	7.00
❑154, Nov 1978, TS, RT (a); Series merges with The Unexpected	7.00

House of Secrets
DC / Vertigo

	N-MINT
❑1, Oct 1996; 1: Rain	3.00
❑2, Nov 1996	3.00
❑3, Dec 1996	3.00
❑4, Jan 1997	3.00
❑5, Feb 1997	3.00
❑6, Mar 1997	3.00
❑7, Apr 1997	3.00
❑8, May 1997	3.00
❑9, Jun 1997	3.00
❑10, Jul 1997	3.00
❑11, Aug 1997	3.00
❑12, Sep 1997	3.00
❑13, Oct 1997	3.00
❑14, Nov 1997	3.00
❑15, Dec 1997	3.00
❑16, Feb 1998	3.00
❑17, Mar 1998; covers form triptych	3.00
❑18, Apr 1998; covers form triptych	3.00
❑19, May 1998; covers form triptych	3.00
❑20, Jun 1998	3.00
❑21, Jul 1998	2.50

Other grades: Multiply price above by 5/6 for VF/NM • 2/3 for VERY FINE • 1/3 for FINE • 1/5 for VERY GOOD • 1/8 for GOOD

Hot Wheels

DC gets license to drive in race series

©DC

Hourman

Series follows DC One Million story arc

©DC

House of M

Marvel universe upheaval from Bendis

©Marvel

House of Mystery

Horror series began back in 1951

©DC

House of Secrets

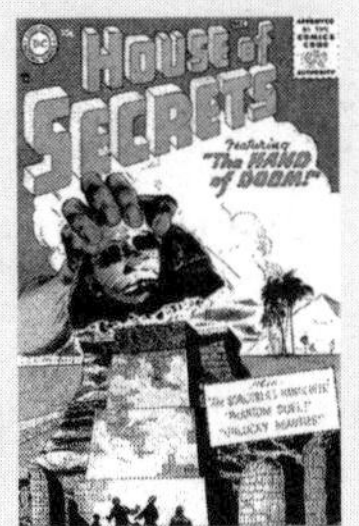

Witches, boogey men, and psychotics at large

©DC

N-MINT

❑22, Aug 1998 .... 2.50
❑23, Sep 1998 .... 2.50
❑24, Nov 1998 .... 2.50
❑25, Dec 1998 .... 2.50

House of Secrets: Façade
DC / Vertigo

❑1, May 2001 .... 5.95
❑2, Jun 2001 .... 5.95

House of Yang
Charlton

❑1, Jul 1975 .... 15.00
❑2, Oct 1975 .... 10.00
❑3, Dec 1975 .... 10.00
❑4, Feb 1976 .... 10.00
❑5, Apr 1976 .... 10.00
❑6, Jun 1976 .... 10.00

House of Yang
Modern

❑1, ca. 1978; reprints Charlton series 2.00
❑2, ca. 1978 .... 2.00

Housewives at Play
Fantagraphics / Eros

❑1 .... 2.95
❑2; b&w 2.95
❑3 .... 2.95

Howard the Duck
Marvel

❑1, Jan 1976, FB (c); FB (a); 1: Beverly. A: Spider-Man 5.00
❑2, Mar 1976, FB (c); FB (a) 2.00
❑3, May 1976, RB (c); JB (a) 2.00
❑3/A, May 1976; 30¢ cover 20.00
❑3/30¢, May 1976, (c); JB (a); 30¢ regional price variant 20.00
❑4, Jul 1976, (c); GC (a); Joey Cavalieri L.O.C 2.00
❑4/A, Jul 1976; 30¢ cover 20.00
❑4/30¢, Jul 1976, (c); GC (a); 30¢ regional price variant 20.00
❑5, Sep 1976, (c); GC (a) 2.00
❑6, Nov 1976, (c); GC (a) 2.00
❑7, Dec 1976, (c); GC (a) 2.00
❑8, Jan 1977, (c); GC (a) 2.00
❑9, Feb 1977, (c); GC (a) 2.00
❑10, Mar 1977, GC (c); GC (a); Spider-Man; Dr. Strange 2.00
❑11, Apr 1977, GC (c); GC (a) 2.00
❑12, May 1977, (c); GC (a); 1: Kiss (rock group) 6.00
❑13, Jun 1977, (c); GC (a); A: Kiss (rock group). Newsstand edition (distributed by Curtis); issue number in box 4.00
❑13/A, Jun 1977; 35¢ cover; 2: Kiss (rock group) 15.00
❑13/Whitman, Jun 1977, (c); GC (a); A: Kiss (rock group). Special markets edition (usually sold in Whitman bagged prepacks); price appears in a diamond; UPC barcode appears 5.00
❑13/35¢, Jun 1977, (c); GC (a); 35¢ regional price variant; newsstand edition (distributed by Curtis); issue number in box 15.00
❑14, Jul 1977, (c); GC, KJ (a) 2.00
❑14/A, Jul 1977; 35¢ cover 15.00
❑14/35¢, Jul 1977, (c); GC, KJ (a); 35¢ regional price variant 15.00

N-MINT

❑15, Aug 1977, (c); GC, KJ (a); 1: Doctor Bong 2.00
❑15/A, Aug 1977; 35¢ cover 15.00
❑15/35¢, Aug 1977, (c); GC, KJ (a); 1: Doctor Bong. 35¢ regional price variant 15.00
❑16, Sep 1977, (c); O: Doctor Bong. all-text issue 2.00
❑16/A, Sep 1977; 35¢ cover 15.00
❑16/35¢, Sep 1977, (c); O: Doctor Bong. 35¢ regional price variant; all-text issue 15.00
❑17, Oct 1977, (c); GC, KJ (a); O: Doctor Bong 2.00
❑17/A, Oct 1977; 35¢ cover 15.00
❑17/35¢, Oct 1977, (c); GC, KJ (a); O: Doctor Bong. 35¢ regional price variant 15.00
❑18, Nov 1977, (c); GC, KJ (a) 2.00
❑19, Dec 1977, (c); GC, KJ (a) 2.00
❑20, Jan 1978, (c); GC, KJ (a); V: Sudol 2.00
❑21, Feb 1978, (c); Cl, KJ (a); V: Soofi .. 2.00
❑22, Mar 1978, (c); VM (a) 2.00
❑23, Apr 1978, GC (c); VM (a) 2.00
❑24, May 1978, GC (c); GC, TP (a) 2.00
❑25, Jun 1978, GC, KJ (c); GC, KJ (a); A: Ringmaster 2.00
❑26, Jul 1978, GC, KJ (c); GC, KJ (a); A: Ringmaster 2.00
❑27, Sep 1978, (c); GC, KJ (a); A: Ringmaster 2.00
❑28, Nov 1978, (c); Cl (a) 2.00
❑29, Jan 1979, GC (c); ME (w) 2.00
❑30, Mar 1979, AM, GC (c); AM, GC (a); V: Doctor Bong 2.00
❑31, May 1979, AM, GC (c); AM, GC (a); V: Doctor Bong 2.00
❑32, Jan 1986, PS (a); O: Howard the Duck 2.00
❑33, Sep 1986, BB (c); VM (a); Final Issue 2.00
❑Ann 1, Oct 1977, GC, TP (c); VM (a) 4.00

Howard the Duck
Marvel / MAX

❑1, Mar 2002 .... 2.99
❑2, Apr 2002 .... 2.99
❑3, May 2002 .... 2.99
❑4, Jun 2002 .... 2.99
❑5, Jul 2002 .... 2.99
❑6, Aug 2002 .... 2.99

Howard the Duck
Marvel

❑1, Oct 1979, b&w; MG, GC, BMc, KJ (a); contains nudity 4.00
❑2, Dec 1979, b&w; VM (c); GC, KJ (a) . 3.00
❑3, Feb 1980, b&w; AM, GC (a) 3.00
❑4, Mar 1980, b&w; GC, JB, JBy, KJ (a); A: Kiss. A: Beatles 4.00
❑5, May 1980, b&w; MG, GC, BMc (a)... 3.00
❑6, Jul 1980, b&w; MG, BMc (a) 3.00
❑7, Sep 1980, b&w; GC, JBy, HC, AA, TP, MR (a); A: Man-Thing 3.00
❑8, Nov 1980, b&w; GC, MR (a); Batman parody 3.00
❑9, Mar 1981, b&w; GC (a) 3.00

Howard the Duck Holiday Special
Marvel

❑1, Feb 1997 .... 2.50

N-MINT

Howard the Duck: The Movie
Marvel

❑1, Dec 1986; O: Howard the Duck 1.00
❑2, Jan 1987 .... 1.00
❑3, Feb 1987 .... 1.00

Howl
Eternity

❑1, b&w; Reprints 2.25
❑2, Apr 1989, b&w; Reprints 2.25

Howl's Moving Castle Film Comics
Viz

❑1, Aug 2005 .... 9.99
❑2, Sep 2005 .... 9.99
❑3, Oct 2005 .... 9.99
❑4, Nov 2005 .... 9.99

How The West Was Won
Gold Key

❑1, Jul 1963, NN; Movie adaptation 18.00

How To Break Into Comics
Antarctic

❑1, ca. 2005 .... 2.99

How to Draw Comics Comic
Solson

❑1, ca. 1985 .... 1.95

How To Draw Felix The Cat And His Friends
Felix

❑1 1992, b&w 2.25

How to Draw Manga
Antarctic

❑1 .... 4.95
❑2 .... 4.95
❑3, Feb 2001 .... 4.95
❑4, Mar 2001 .... 4.95
❑5, Apr 2001 .... 4.95
❑6, Jun 2001 .... 4.95
❑7, Aug 2001 .... 4.95
❑8, Sep 2001 .... 4.95
❑9, Oct 2001 .... 4.95
❑10, Nov 2001 .... 4.95
❑11, Jan 2002 .... 4.95
❑12, Feb 2002 .... 4.95
❑13, Mar 2002 .... 4.95
❑14, Apr 2002 .... 4.95
❑15, May 2002 .... 4.95
❑16, Jun 2002 .... 4.95
❑17, Jul 2002 .... 4.95
❑18, Aug 2002 .... 4.95
❑19, Oct 2002 .... 4.95
❑20 2002 .... 4.95
❑21 2002 .... 4.95
❑22, Feb 2003 .... 4.95
❑23, Apr 2003 .... 4.95
❑24, May 2003 .... 4.95
❑25, Aug 2003 .... 4.95

How to Draw Manga: Next Generation
Antarctic

❑1/A, ca. 2005 .... 4.95
❑1/B, ca. 2005 .... 4.95
❑1/C, ca. 2005 .... 4.95
❑2, ca. 2005 .... 4.95
❑3, ca. 2005 .... 4.95
❑4, ca. 2005 .... 4.95

Other grades: Multiply price above by 5/6 for VF/NM • 2/3 for VERY FINE • 1/3 for FINE • 1/5 for VERY GOOD • 1/8 for GOOD

N-MINT

❑5, ca. 2005 ... 4.95
❑6, ca. 2005 ... 4.95
❑7, ca. 2005 ... 4.95
❑8, ca. 2005 ... 4.95
❑9, ca. 2005 ... 4.95
❑10, ca. 2005 ... 4.95

How to Draw Teenage Mutant Ninja Turtles
Solson

❑1 ... 2.25

How To Pick Up Girls If You're A Comic Book Geek
3 Finger Prints

❑1, Jul 1997; cardstock cover ... 3.95

How to Publish Comics
Solson

❑1 ... 2.00

How to Self-Publish Comics ... Not Just Create Them
Devil's Due

❑1, Mar 2006 ... 4.95
❑3, Apr 2006 ... 4.95
❑4, Jun 2006 ... 4.95

H.R. Pufnstuf
Gold Key

❑1, Oct 1970 ... 55.00
❑2, Jan 1971 ... 40.00
❑3, Apr 1971 ... 40.00
❑4, Jul 1971 ... 35.00
❑5, Oct 1971 ... 35.00
❑6, Jan 1972 ... 35.00
❑7, Apr 1972 ... 25.00
❑8, Jul 1972 ... 25.00

Hsu and Chan
Slave Labor

❑1, Jan 2003 ... 2.95
❑2 ... 2.95
❑3 ... 2.95
❑4 ... 2.95
❑5 ... 2.95
❑6 ... 2.95
❑7, Sep 2005 ... 2.95

Huckleberry Hound
Gold Key

❑14, Dec 1961, Yogi Bear cover ... 20.00
❑15 1962 ... 20.00
❑16 1962 ... 20.00
❑17, Jun 1962 ... 20.00
❑18, Oct 1962, Giant-size ... 26.00
❑19, Jan 1963, Giant-size ... 26.00
❑20, Apr 1963 ... 20.00
❑21, Jul 1963 ... 15.00
❑22, Oct 1963 ... 15.00
❑23, Jan 1964 ... 15.00
❑24, May 1964 ... 15.00
❑25, Aug 1964 ... 15.00
❑26, Nov 1964 ... 15.00
❑27, Jul 1965 ... 15.00
❑28 1966 ... 15.00
❑29, Apr 1967 ... 15.00
❑30, Jul 1967 ... 15.00
❑31, Oct 1967 ... 9.00
❑32, Jan 1968 ... 9.00
❑33, Apr 1968 ... 9.00
❑34, Jul 1968 ... 9.00
❑35, Oct 1968 ... 9.00
❑36, Jan 1969 ... 9.00
❑37, Apr 1969 ... 9.00
❑38, Jul 1969 ... 9.00
❑39, Oct 1969 ... 9.00
❑40, Jan 1970 ... 6.00
❑41, Apr 1970 ... 6.00
❑42, Jul 1970 ... 6.00
❑43, Oct 1970 ... 6.00

Huckleberry Hound & Quick Draw McGraw Giant-Size Flip Book
Harvey

❑1, Nov 1993 ... 2.25

Huey, Dewey, and Louie Junior Woodchucks
Gold Key

❑1, Aug 1966 ... 36.00
❑2, Aug 1967 ... 20.00
❑3, Dec 1968 ... 16.00
❑4, Jan 1970, Reprinted from Walt Disney's Comics #181 and 227 ... 12.00
❑5, Apr 1970, Reprinted from Walt Disney's Comics #125 and 132 ... 12.00
❑6, Jul 1970 ... 12.00
❑7, Oct 1970 ... 12.00
❑8, Jan 1971 ... 12.00
❑9, Apr 1971 ... 12.00
❑10, Jul 1971 ... 12.00
❑11, Oct 1971 ... 10.00
❑12, Jan 1972, CB (w) ... 10.00
❑13, Mar 1972 ... 10.00
❑14, May 1972 ... 10.00
❑15, Jul 1972 ... 10.00
❑16, Sep 1972 ... 10.00
❑17, Nov 1972 ... 10.00
❑18, Jan 1973 ... 10.00
❑19, Mar 1973 ... 10.00
❑20, May 1973 ... 10.00
❑21, Jul 1973 ... 8.00
❑22, Sep 1973 ... 8.00
❑23, Nov 1973 ... 8.00
❑24, Jan 1974 ... 8.00
❑25, Mar 1974, Includes reprinted story from Walt Disney's Comics & Stories #238 ... 8.00
❑26, May 1974, Reprinted from Walt Disney's Comics #232 ... 8.00
❑27, Jul 1974 ... 8.00
❑28, Sep 1974 ... 8.00
❑29, Nov 1974 ... 8.00
❑30, Jan 1975 ... 8.00
❑31, Mar 1975 ... 8.00
❑32, May 1975 ... 8.00
❑33, Jul 1975 ... 8.00
❑34, Sep 1975 ... 8.00
❑35, Nov 1975, Reprinted from Huey, Dewey and Louie Junior Woodchucks #7 ... 8.00
❑36, Jan 1976 ... 8.00
❑37, Mar 1976 ... 8.00
❑38, May 1976 ... 8.00
❑39, Jul 1976 ... 8.00
❑40, Sep 1976 ... 8.00
❑41, Nov 1976, Reprinted from Huey, Dewey and Louie Junior Woodchucks #6 ... 6.00
❑42, Mar 1977 ... 6.00
❑43, Apr 1977 ... 6.00
❑44, Jun 1977 ... 6.00
❑45, Aug 1977 ... 6.00
❑46, Sep 1977 ... 6.00
❑47, Dec 1977 ... 6.00
❑48, Feb 1978 ... 6.00
❑49, Apr 1978 ... 6.00
❑50, Jun 1978 ... 6.00
❑51, Aug 1978 ... 6.00
❑52, Sep 1978 ... 6.00
❑53, Dec 1978 ... 6.00
❑54, Feb 1979 ... 6.00
❑55, Apr 1979 ... 6.00
❑56, Jun 1979 ... 6.00
❑57, Jul 1979 ... 6.00
❑58, Aug 1979 ... 6.00
❑59, Sep 1979 ... 6.00
❑60, Dec 1979 ... 6.00
❑61, Feb 1980 ... 4.00
❑62, Mar 1980 ... 4.00
❑63, ca. 1980 ... 4.00
❑64, ca. 1980 ... 4.00
❑65, Sep 1980 ... 4.00
❑66, Nov 1980 ... 4.00
❑67, Jan 1981 ... 4.00
❑68, Jun 1981 ... 4.00
❑69, Aug 1981 ... 4.00
❑70, ca. 1981 ... 4.00
❑71, Dec 1981 ... 4.00
❑72, ca. 1982 ... 4.00
❑73, Mar 1982 ... 4.00
❑74, Mar 1982 ... 4.00
❑75, Apr 1983 ... 4.00
❑76, May 1983 ... 4.00
❑77, Jul 1983 ... 4.00
❑78, Aug 1983 ... 4.00
❑79, ca. 1984 ... 4.00
❑80, ca. 1984 ... 4.00
❑81, ca. 1984 ... 4.00

Hugga Bunch
Marvel / Star

❑1, Oct 1986 ... 1.00
❑2, Dec 1986 ... 1.00
❑3, Feb 1986 ... 1.00
❑4, Apr 1986 ... 1.00
❑5, Jun 1986 ... 1.00
❑6, Aug 1986 ... 1.00

Hugo
Fantagraphics

❑1 ... 1.95
❑2 ... 1.95
❑3, Jul 1985 ... 1.95

Hulk
Marvel

❑1, Apr 1999, JBy (w); JBy, DGr (a); wraparound cover ... 3.50
❑1/A, Apr 1999, JBy (w); JBy, DGr (a); Sunburst cover ... 5.00
❑1/Gold, Apr 1999, JBy (w); JBy, DGr (a); DFE gold foil cover ... 4.00
❑2, May 1999, DGr (c); JBy (w); DGr (a) ... 2.50
❑3, Jun 1999, DGr (c); JBy (w); DGr (a); Tyrannus revealed as mind-controlling rampaging Hulk ... 2.50
❑4, Jul 1999, DGr (c); JBy (w); DGr (a); V: Tyrannus; Rampaging Hulk downs an airliner ... 2.50
❑5, Aug 1999, JBy (w); SB (a); A: Avengers ... 2.50
❑6, Sep 1999, DGr (c); JBy (w); DGr (a); A: Man-Thing ... 2.50
❑7, Oct 1999, DGr (c); JBy (w); DGr (a); A: Man-Thing. A: Avengers ... 2.50
❑8, Nov 1999, DGr (c); EL (w); SB (a); V: Wolverine; Includes Spider-Man (Fast Lane) insert ... 2.50
❑9, Dec 1999, DGr (c); JOy (w); SB (a) . 2.50
❑10, Jan 2000, JOy (w); SB (a); V: Tyrannus ... 2.50
❑11, Feb 2000, SB (c); JOy (w); SB (a); becomes "Incredible Hulk (2nd series)" 2.50

Hulk
Marvel

❑1, Jan 2008 ... 6.00
❑1/2nd, Jan 2008 ... 3.00
❑2, Feb 2008 ... 4.00
❑3, Apr 2008 ... 3.00

Hulk
Marvel

❑10, Aug 1978; format changes to color magazine; VM (c);Title changes to The Hulk ... 7.00
❑11, Oct 1978; GC, TD (a); Wrapround cover; Moon Knight backup stories begin; 1: Marlene Alraune ... 7.00
❑12, Dec 1978; KP, JR2 (a); Wraparound cover; Cover date is December, indicia date is November; Lou Ferrigno interview 7.00
❑13, Feb 1979 BSz, BMc (a) ... 7.00
❑14, Apr 1979 BSz, MZ, BMc (a) ... 7.00
❑15, Jun 1979 BSz, GC, AA, BMc (a) ... 7.00
❑16, Aug 1979 MZ (a) ... 7.00
❑17, Oct 1979 BSz, GC, AA, KJ, BWi (a) 7.00
❑18, Dec 1979 BSz, AA, KJ (a) ... 7.00
❑19, Feb 1980 GC, HT, AA, JSe, BWi (a) 7.00
❑20, Apr 1980; BSz, AA (a); Kenneth Johnston interview ... 7.00
❑21, Jun 1980; HC, BA, BMc (a); Dominic Fortune begins ... 7.00
❑22, Aug 1980 HC, AA (a) ... 5.00
❑23, Oct 1980 JB, HC, BA, AA (a) ... 5.00
❑24, Dec 1980; GC, HC, AA (a); Begins Hulk stories in b&w, Dominic Fortune in color ... 5.00
❑25, Feb 1981; GC, HC, AA (a); Dominic Fortune ends ... 5.00
❑26, Apr 1981; JB (c); GC, AA (a); B&W 5.00
❑27, Jun 1981; GC (a); Final Issue; b&w 5.00

Hulk and Thing: Hard Knocks
Marvel

❑1, Nov 2004 ... 3.50
❑2, Dec 2004 ... 3.50
❑3, Jan 2005 ... 3.50
❑4, Feb 2005 ... 3.50

Hulk: Destruction
Marvel

❑1, Sep 2005 ... 2.99
❑2, Oct 2005 ... 2.99
❑3, Nov 2005 ... 2.99
❑4, Dec 2005 ... 2.99

Howard the Duck

Hip, hot comic from the 1970s
©Marvel

Howard the Duck: The Movie

Movie ruined all that was good in the world
©Marvel

How The West Was Won

Wide-screen epic comes to comics
©Gold Key

H.R. Pufnstuf

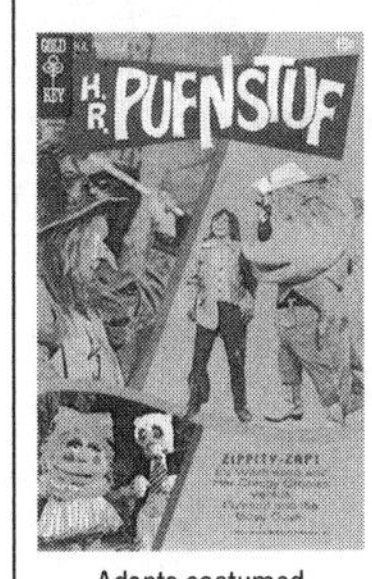

Adapts costumed TV acid trip
©Gold Key

Huckleberry Hound

Cornpone canine cracks wise
©Gold Key

N-MINT

Hulk: Gamma Games
Marvel

- ❑1, Feb 2004 ... 2.99
- ❑2, Mar 2004 ... 2.99
- ❑3, Apr 2004 ... 2.99

Hulk: Gray
Marvel

- ❑1, Nov 2003, JPH (w) ... 5.00
- ❑2, Dec 2003, JPH (w) ... 3.50
- ❑3, Jan 2004, JPH (w) ... 5.00
- ❑4, Feb 2004, JPH (w) ... 4.00
- ❑5, Mar 2004 ... 5.00
- ❑6, Apr 2004, JPH (w) ... 3.50
- ❑1/HC, ca. 2004 ... 21.99

Hulk Movie
Marvel

- ❑1, ca. 2003 ... 12.99

Hulk/Pitt
Marvel

- ❑1, Dec 1996; NN ... 5.99

Hulk: Project H.I.D.E.
Marvel

- ❑1, Aug 1998; No cover price; prototype for children's comic ... 2.00

Hulk Smash
Marvel

- ❑1, Mar 2001 ... 2.99
- ❑2, Apr 2001 ... 2.99

Hulk: The Movie Adaptation
Marvel

- ❑1, Aug 2003 ... 3.50

Hulk 2099
Marvel

- ❑1, Dec 1994 ... 2.50
- ❑2, Jan 1995 ... 1.50
- ❑3, Feb 1995 ... 1.50
- ❑4, Mar 1995 ... 1.50
- ❑5, Apr 1995 ... 1.50
- ❑6, May 1995 ... 1.50
- ❑7, Jun 1995; One Nation under Doom crossover ... 1.95
- ❑8, Jul 1995; V: Doom 2099; One Nation under Doom crossover ... 1.95
- ❑9, Aug 1995; One Nation under Doom crossover ... 1.95
- ❑10, Sep 1995; continued in 2099 A.D. Apocalypse #1 ... 1.95

Hulk: Unchained
Marvel

- ❑1, Feb 2004 ... 2.99
- ❑2, Apr 2004 ... 2.99
- ❑3, May 2004 ... 2.99

Hulk vs. Thing
Marvel

- ❑1, Dec 1999; Reprints Fantastic Four #24, 26, 112, Marvel Features #11 ... 3.99

Hulk/Wolverine: 6 Hours
Marvel

- ❑1, Feb 2003 ... 2.99
- ❑2, Mar 2003 ... 2.99
- ❑3, Apr 2003 ... 2.99
- ❑4, May 2003 ... 2.99

N-MINT

Human Defense Corps
DC

- ❑1, Jul 2003 ... 2.50
- ❑2, Aug 2003 ... 2.50
- ❑3, Sep 2003 ... 2.50
- ❑4, Oct 2003 ... 2.50
- ❑5, Nov 2003 ... 2.50
- ❑6, Dec 2003 ... 2.50

Human Fly
Marvel

- ❑1, Sep 1977, 1&O: Human Fly. A: Spider-Man ... 3.00
- ❑1/35¢, Sep 1977, 1&O: Human Fly. A: Spider-Man. 35¢ regional price variant ... 15.00
- ❑2, Oct 1977, CI (c); CI (a); A: Ghost Rider. Newsstand edition (distributed by Curtis); issue number in box ... 2.00
- ❑2/Whitman, Oct 1977, CI (a); A: Ghost Rider. Special markets edition (usually sold in Whitman bagged prepacks); price appears in a diamond; no UPC barcode. ... 2.00
- ❑2/35¢, Oct 1977, CI (c); CI (a); A: Ghost Rider. 35¢ regional price variant; newsstand edition (distributed by Curtis); issue number in box ... 15.00
- ❑3, Nov 1977 ... 1.50
- ❑4, Dec 1977 ... 1.50
- ❑5, Jan 1978 ... 1.50
- ❑6, Feb 1978 ... 1.50
- ❑7, Mar 1978 ... 1.50
- ❑8, Apr 1978 ... 1.50
- ❑9, May 1978, A: Daredevil ... 1.50
- ❑10, Jun 1978 ... 1.50
- ❑11, Jul 1978 ... 1.50
- ❑12, Aug 1978 ... 1.50
- ❑12/Whitman, Aug 1978, Special markets edition (usually sold in Whitman bagged prepacks); price appears in a diamond; no UPC barcode ... 1.50
- ❑13, Sep 1978, FR (a); Newsstand edition (distributed by Curtis); issue number in box ... 1.50
- ❑13/Whitman, Sep 1978, Special markets edition (usually sold in Whitman bagged prepacks); price appears in a diamond; UPC barcode appears ... 1.50
- ❑14, Oct 1978, FR (a); Newsstand edition (distributed by Curtis); issue number in box ... 1.50
- ❑14/Whitman, Oct 1978, Special markets edition (usually sold in Whitman bagged prepacks); price appears in a diamond; no UPC barcode ... 1.50
- ❑15, Nov 1978, Newsstand edition (distributed by Curtis); issue number in box ... 1.50
- ❑15/Whitman, Nov 1978, Special markets edition (usually sold in Whitman bagged prepacks); price appears in a diamond; no UPC barcode ... 1.50
- ❑16, Dec 1978 ... 1.50
- ❑17, Jan 1979 ... 1.50
- ❑18, Feb 1979, Newsstand edition (distributed by Curtis); issue number in box ... 1.50
- ❑18/Whitman, Feb 1979, Special markets edition (usually sold in Whitman bagged prepacks); price appears in a diamond; no UPC barcode ... 1.50
- ❑19, Mar 1979, Final Issue ... 1.50

N-MINT

Human Gargoyles
Eternity

- ❑1, Jun 1988, b&w ... 1.95
- ❑2, Aug 1988, b&w ... 1.95
- ❑3, b&w ... 1.95
- ❑4, b&w ... 1.95

Human Head Comix
Iconografix

- ❑1, b&w; Adult ... 2.50

Humankind
Image

- ❑1, Aug 2004 ... 4.00
- ❑1/A, Aug 2004, Sketch cover giveaway from Wizard World Chicago 2004 ... 2.00
- ❑2, Sep 2004 ... 3.00
- ❑3, Oct 2004 ... 3.00
- ❑4, Nov 2004 ... 2.99
- ❑5, Jan 2005 ... 2.99

Human Powerhouse
Pure Imagination

- ❑1, b&w ... 2.00

Human Race
DC

- ❑1, Apr 2005 ... 2.99
- ❑2, Jun 2005 ... 2.99
- ❑3, Jul 2005 ... 2.99
- ❑4, Aug 2005 ... 2.99
- ❑5, Sep 2005 ... 2.99
- ❑6, Oct 2005 ... 2.99
- ❑7 2005 ... 2.99

Human Remains
Black Eye

- ❑1 ... 3.50

Human Target
DC / Vertigo

- ❑1, Apr 1999 ... 2.95
- ❑2, May 1999 ... 2.95
- ❑3, Jun 1999 ... 2.95
- ❑4, Jul 1999 ... 2.95

Human Target
DC / Vertigo

- ❑1, Oct 2003 ... 2.95
- ❑2, Nov 2003 ... 2.95
- ❑3, Dec 2003 ... 2.95
- ❑4, Jan 2004 ... 2.95
- ❑5, Feb 2004 ... 2.95
- ❑6, Mar 2004 ... 2.95
- ❑7, Apr 2004 ... 2.95
- ❑8, May 2004 ... 2.95
- ❑9, Jun 2004 ... 2.95
- ❑10, Jul 2004 ... 2.95
- ❑11, Aug 2004 ... 2.95
- ❑12, Sep 2004 ... 2.95
- ❑13, Oct 2004 ... 2.95
- ❑14, Nov 2004 ... 2.95
- ❑15, Dec 2004 ... 2.95
- ❑16, Jan 2005 ... 2.95
- ❑17, Feb 2005 ... 2.95
- ❑18, Mar 2005 ... 2.95
- ❑19, Apr 2005 ... 2.95
- ❑20, May 2005 ... 2.95
- ❑21, Jun 2005; Final issue ... 2.99

Other grades: Multiply price above by 5/6 for VF/NM • 2/3 for VERY FINE • 1/3 for FINE • 1/5 for VERY GOOD • 1/8 for GOOD

Human Target Special
DC

❑1, Nov 1991; One-shot 2.00

Human Target: Strike Zone
DC

❑1, ca. 2004 9.95

Human Torch
Marvel

❑1, Sep 1974; JK (a); Torch vs. Torch reprinted from Strange Tales #101; Horror Hotel reprinted from The Human Torch (1st series) #33 9.00
❑2, Nov 1974; SL (w); JK (a); Reprints Torch story from Strange Tales #102 and The Human Torch (1st series) #30 4.00
❑3, Jan 1975; SL (w); JK (a); Reprints Torch story from Strange Tales #103, Sub-Mariner #23 3.00
❑4, Mar 1975; Reprints Torch story from Strange Tales #104, The Human Torch (1st series) #38 3.00
❑5, May 1975; Reprints Torch story from Strange Tales #105, The Human Torch (1st series) #38 3.00
❑6, Jul 1975; Reprints Torch story from Strange Tales #106, The Human Torch (1st series) #38 3.00
❑7, Sep 1975; Reprints Torch story from Strange Tales #107, Sub-Mariner #35 3.00
❑8, Nov 1975; JK (a); Reprints Torch story from Strange Tales #108, Marvel Super-Heroes #16 3.00

Human Torch
Marvel

❑1, Jun 2003 2.50
❑2, Jul 2003 2.50
❑3, Aug 2003 2.50
❑4, Sep 2003 2.50
❑5, Oct 2003 2.50
❑6, Nov 2003 2.99
❑7, Jan 2004 2.50
❑8, Feb 2004 2.99
❑9, Mar 2004 2.99
❑10, Apr 2004 2.99
❑11, May 2004 2.99
❑12, Jun 2004 2.99

Humants
Legacy

❑1 2.45
❑2 2.45

Hummingbird
Slave Labor

❑1, Jun 1996 4.95

Humongous Man
Alternative

❑1, Sep 1997, b&w 2.25
❑2, Nov 1997, b&w 2.25

Humor on the Cutting...Edge
Edge

❑1, b&w 2.95
❑2, b&w 2.95
❑3, b&w 2.95
❑4, b&w 2.95

Hunchback of Notre Dame
Marvel

❑1, Jul 1996; adapts movie; square binding; cardstock cover 4.95

Hunger
Speakeasy Comics

❑1 2005 2.99
❑2, Jul 2005 2.99
❑3, Sep 2005 2.99
❑4, Oct 2005 2.99

Hunter-Killer
Image

❑0, Dec 2004 1.00
❑0/Ltd., Dec 2004 4.99
❑0/Autographed, Dec 2004 19.99
❑0/Conv, Dec 2004; Sketch cover distributed at Wizard World Texas, 2004 6.00
❑1/Campbell, ca. 2005 3.00
❑1/Hairsine, ca. 2005, b&w 4.00
❑1/Silvestri, ca. 2005, b&w 5.00
❑2/Silvestri, ca. 2005 2.99
❑2/Linsner 2005 4.00
❑3 2005 2.99
❑4 2005 2.99
❑5, Jan 2006 2.99
❑6, Sep 2006 2.99
❑8, Nov 2006 2.99
❑8/Variant, Nov 2006 2.99
❑9, Nov 2006 2.99
❑9/Variant, Nov 2006 2.99
❑10, Jan 2007 2.99

Hunter-Killer Dossier
Image

❑0, Sep 2005 2.99

Hunter's Heart
DC / Paradox

❑1, b&w; digest 5.95
❑2, b&w; digest 5.95
❑3, b&w; digest 5.95

Hunter: The Age of Magic
DC / Vertigo

❑1, Sep 2001 3.50
❑2, Oct 2001 3.00
❑3, Nov 2001 3.00
❑4, Dec 2001 3.00
❑5, Jan 2002 3.00
❑6, Feb 2002 3.00
❑7, Mar 2002 3.00
❑8, Apr 2002 3.00
❑9, May 2002 3.00
❑10, Jun 2002 3.00
❑11, Jul 2002 2.50
❑12, Aug 2002 2.50
❑13, Sep 2002 2.50
❑14, Oct 2002 2.75
❑15, Nov 2002 2.75
❑16, Dec 2002 2.75
❑17, Jan 2003 2.75
❑18, Feb 2003 2.75
❑19, Mar 2003 2.75
❑20, Apr 2003 2.75
❑21, May 2003 2.75
❑22, Jun 2003 2.75
❑23, Jul 2003 2.75
❑24, Aug 2003 2.75
❑25, Sep 2003 2.75

Hunter x Hunter
Viz

❑1, Apr 2005 7.99
❑2, May 2005 7.99
❑3, Jul 2005 7.99
❑4, Sep 2005 7.99
❑5, Nov 2005 7.99

Hunt for Black Widow
Fleetway-Quality

❑1; Judge Dredd 2.95

Hunting
Northstar

❑1, Nov 1993 3.95

Huntress
DC

❑1, Apr 1989; JSa (c); JSa (a); 1&O: The Huntress III (Helena Bertinelli) 2.50
❑2, May 1989 JSa (a) 2.00
❑3, Jun 1989 2.00
❑4, Jul 1989 1.50
❑5, Aug 1989 1.50
❑6, Sep 1989 1.25
❑7, Oct 1989 1.25
❑8, Nov 1989 1.25
❑9, Dec 1989 1.25
❑10, Jan 1990 1.25
❑11, Feb 1990 1.25
❑12, Mar 1990 1.25
❑13, Apr 1990 1.25
❑14, May 1990 JSa (a) 1.25
❑15, Jun 1990 1.25
❑16, Jul 1990 1.25
❑17, Aug 1990 A: Batman 1.25
❑18, Sep 1990 A: Batman 1.25
❑19, Oct 1990; A: Batman. Final Issue 1.25

Huntress
DC

❑1, Jun 1994 2.00
❑2, Jul 1994 2.00
❑3, Aug 1994 2.00
❑4, Sep 1994 2.00

Hup
Last Gasp

❑1, ca. 1986, b&w; Adult 3.00
❑2; Adult 3.00
❑3; Adult 3.00
❑4, ca. 1992; Adult 3.00

Hurricane Girls
Antarctic

❑1, Jul 1995 3.50
❑2, Sep 1995 3.50
❑3, Nov 1995 3.50
❑4 3.50
❑5 3.50
❑6 3.50
❑7, Aug 1996; Final Issue 3.50

Hurricane LeRoux
Inferno

❑1; 1: Hurricane LeRoux 2.50

Hustler Comix
L.F.P.

❑1, Spr 1997; magazine; Adult 4.99
❑2, Sum 1997; magazine; Adult 4.99
❑3, Fal 1997; magazine; Adult 4.99
❑4, Win 1997; magazine; Adult 4.99

Hustler Comix
L.F.P.

❑1, Spr 1998; magazine; Adult 4.99
❑2, May 1998; magazine; Adult 4.99
❑3, Jul 1998; magazine; Adult 4.99
❑4, Sep 1998; magazine; Adult 4.99
❑5, Nov 1998; magazine; Final Issue; Adult 4.99

Hustler Comix XXX
L.F.P.

❑1, Jan 1999; magazine; Adult 5.99

Hutch Owen's Working Hard
New Hat

❑1, b&w 3.95

Hy-Breed
Division

❑1, ca. 1994, b&w; Continued from Motley Stories #3 2.25
❑2, ca. 1994, b&w 2.25
❑3, ca. 1994, b&w 2.25
❑4, b&w 2.50
❑5, b&w 2.50
❑6, b&w 2.50
❑7, b&w 2.50
❑8, ca. 1997 2.50
❑9, ca. 1997 2.50
❑10, ca. 1998, b&w 2.50

Hybrid: Etherworlds
Dimension 5

❑1 2.50
❑2 2.50
❑3 2.50

Hybrids
Continuity

❑0, Apr 1993, silver and red foil covers; title reads "Hybrids Deathwatch 2000" 1.00
❑1, Apr 1993, trading cards; diecut cardstock cover; title reads "Hybrids Deathwatch 2000" 2.50
❑2, Jun 1993, thermal cover; trading card; title reads "Hybrids Deathwatch 2000" 2.50
❑3, Aug 1993, trading card; Deathwatch 2000 dropped from indicia; Published out of sequence after #5 2.50
❑4, Published out of sequence after #5, #3 2.50
❑5, Includes trading card 2.50

Hybrids
Continuity

❑1, Jan 1994; Embossed cover 2.50

Hybrids: The Origin
Continuity

❑2, Jul 1993; "Revengers Special" on cover; #1 was actually Revengers: Hybrid Special 2.50
❑3, Sep 1993; "Revengers Special" on cover 2.50
❑4, Dec 1993 2.50
❑5, Jan 1994 2.50

Hyde-25
Harris

❑0, Apr 1995; Reprints Vampirella (Magazine) #1 in color; Reprints Vampirella (Magazine) #1 in color 2.95

Other grades: Multiply price above by 5/6 for VF/NM • 2/3 for VERY FINE • 1/3 for FINE • 1/5 for VERY GOOD • 1/8 for GOOD

Huey, Dewey, and Louie Junior Woodchucks

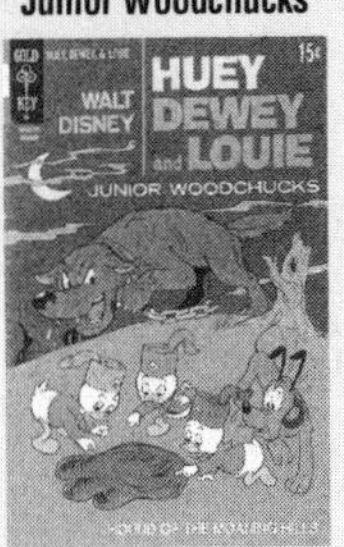

Carl Barks' diminutive trio solves problems
©Gold Key

Hulk

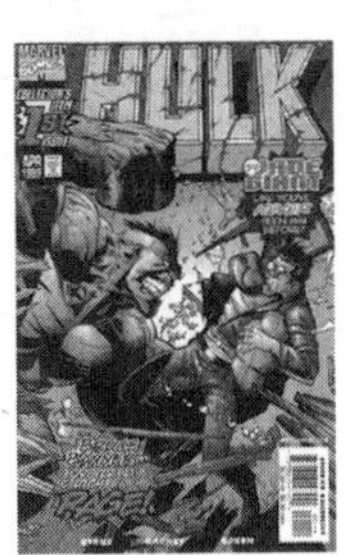

Became Incredible Hulk Vol. 2 after a year
©Marvel

Human Fly

Based on real-life Evel Knievel-type
©Marvel

Human Target

Mature-readers revival of 1970s character
©DC

Human Torch

Johnny Storm gets another solo shot
©Marvel

N-MINT

Hydrogen Bomb Funnies
Rip Off

- ❑1, Adult 5.00

Hydrophidian
NBM

- ❑1; Adult 10.95

Hyena
Tundra

- ❑1, b&w 3.95
- ❑2, b&w 3.95
- ❑3, b&w 3.95
- ❑4 .... 3.95

Hyperactives
Alias

- ❑0, Jan 2006 .... 0.75

Hyper Comix
Kitchen Sink

- ❑1, Mar 1979; Adult 5.00

Hyper Dolls
Ironcat

- ❑1 .... 2.95
- ❑2 .... 2.95

Hyper Dolls
Ironcat

- ❑1 .... 2.95
- ❑2, Sep 1998 .... 2.95
- ❑3 .... 2.95
- ❑4 .... 2.95
- ❑5 .... 2.95
- ❑6, Jul 1999 .... 2.95

Hyperkind
Marvel / Razorline

- ❑1, Sep 1993, Foil embossed cover 2.50
- ❑2, Oct 1993 .... 1.75
- ❑3, Nov 1993 .... 1.75
- ❑4, Dec 1993 .... 1.75
- ❑5, Jan 1994 .... 1.75
- ❑6, Feb 1994, Wrap-around cover 1.75
- ❑7, Mar 1994 .... 1.75
- ❑8, Apr 1994 .... 1.75
- ❑9, May 1994, Final Issue 1.75

Hyperkind Unleashed!
Marvel

- ❑1, Aug 1994 .... 2.95

Hyper Police
Tokyopop

- ❑1, Jan 2005, Graphic novel 9.99
- ❑2, Mar 2005; Graphic novel 9.99
- ❑3, Jun 2005; Graphic novel 9.99
- ❑4, Sep 2005 .... 9.99
- ❑5, Jan 2006 .... 9.99

Hyper Rune
Tokyopop

- ❑1, Nov 2004, Graphic novel 9.99
- ❑2, Jan 2005; Graphic novel 9.99
- ❑3, Apr 2005; Graphic novel 9.99
- ❑4, Oct 2005 .... 9.99

Hypersonic
Dark Horse

- ❑1, Nov 1997 .... 2.95
- ❑2, Dec 1997 .... 2.95
- ❑3, Jan 1998 .... 2.95
- ❑4, Feb 1998 .... 2.95

Hyper Violents
CFD

- ❑1, Jul 1996, b&w; Adult 2.95

Hypothetical Lizard
Avatar

- ❑1 2005 .... 3.50
- ❑1/Wraparound 2005 .... 5.00
- ❑1/Platinum 2005 .... 12.00
- ❑1/Tarot, Jun 2005; 1,250 copies printed. "Queen of Cups" tarot cover fits with Nightjar tarot cover to create a set based on the worlds of Alan Moore. Painted by Lorenzo Lorente and Sebastian Fiumara 3.99
- ❑2 2005 .... 3.50
- ❑2/Wraparound 2005 .... 5.00
- ❑3, Sep 2005 .... 3.50
- ❑3/Foil, Sep 2005 .... 6.00
- ❑3/Wraparound, Sep 2005 .... 5.00

Hysteria: One Man Gang
Image

- ❑1, Apr 2006 .... 2.99
- ❑2, May 2006 .... 2.99

i 4 N i
Mermaid

- ❑1 1994 .... 2.25
- ❑2, Feb 1995 .... 2.25

I Am Legend
Eclipse

- ❑1, b&w 5.95
- ❑2 .... 5.95
- ❑3 .... 5.95
- ❑4 .... 5.95

I am Legion: Dancing Faun
DC

- ❑1, Oct 2004 .... 6.95

I Before E
Fantagraphics

- ❑1, b&w 3.95
- ❑1/2nd, May 1994; 2nd printing 3.95
- ❑2, b&w 3.95

I-Bots
Tekno

- ❑1, Dec 1995, GP (c); HC (w); GP (a); 1: the I•Bots 2.00
- ❑2, Dec 1995, HC (c); HC (w); GP (a) 2.00
- ❑3, Jan 1996, GP (c); HC (w); GP (a) 2.25
- ❑4, Feb 1996, GP (c); HC (w); GP, GK (a) 2.25
- ❑5, Mar 1996, GP (c); HC (w); GP (a) 2.25
- ❑6, Apr 1996, GP (c); HC (w); GP (a) 2.25
- ❑7, May 1996, HC (w); GP, PB (a); A: Lady Justice 2.25

I-Bots
Big

- ❑1, Jun 1996 .... 2.25
- ❑2, Jul 1996 .... 2.25
- ❑3, Aug 1996 .... 2.25
- ❑4, Sep 1996 .... 2.25
- ❑5, Oct 1996 .... 2.25
- ❑6, Nov 1996, E.C. tribute cover 2.25
- ❑7, Dec 1996, forms triptych 2.25
- ❑8, Jan 1997, forms triptych 2.25
- ❑9, Feb 1997, forms triptych 2.25

iCandy
DC / Vertigo

- ❑1, Nov 2003 .... 2.50
- ❑2, Dec 2003 .... 2.50
- ❑3, Jan 2004 .... 2.50
- ❑4, Feb 2004 .... 2.50
- ❑5, Mar 2004 .... 2.50
- ❑6 .... 0.00

Icarus
Aircel

- ❑1, Apr 1987 .... 2.00
- ❑2, Apr 1987 .... 2.00
- ❑3, Jun 1987 .... 2.00
- ❑4, Jul 1987 .... 2.00
- ❑5, Aug 1987 .... 2.00

Icaru
Kardia

- ❑1, Jun 1992 .... 2.25

Ice Age on the World of Magic: The Gathering
Acclaim / Armada

- ❑1, Jul 1995; bound-in Magic card (Chub Toad) 2.50
- ❑2, Aug 1995; bound-in Chub Toad card from Ice Age 2.50
- ❑3, Sep 1995; polybagged with sheet of creature tokens 2.50
- ❑4, Oct 1995; polybagged with sheet of creature tokens 2.50

Iceman
Marvel

- ❑1, Dec 1984, MZ (c); O: Iceman 4.00
- ❑2, Feb 1985 .... 2.50
- ❑3, Apr 1985 .... 2.50
- ❑4, Jun 1985, MZ (c) 2.50

Iceman
Marvel

- ❑1, Dec 2001 .... 4.00
- ❑2, Jan 2002 .... 2.50
- ❑3, Feb 2002, Cover lists incorrect artist credit 2.50
- ❑4, Mar 2002 .... 2.50

Icicle
Hero

- ❑1, Jul 1992, b&w 4.95
- ❑2, Sep 1992, b&w 3.50
- ❑3, b&w 3.50
- ❑4, b&w 3.50
- ❑5, b&w 3.95

I Come In Peace
Greater Mercury

- ❑1 .... 1.50

Icon
DC / Milestone

- ❑1, May 1993, 1&O: Rocket. O: Icon. 1: S.H.R.E.D. 2.00
- ❑1/CS, May 1993, O: Rocket. O: Icon. poster; trading card 2.95
- ❑2, Jun 1993, 1: Payback 1.50
- ❑3, Jul 1993 .... 1.50
- ❑4, Aug 1993, A: Blood Syndicate. Rocket's pregnant 1.50
- ❑5, Sep 1993, V: Blood Syndicate 1.50
- ❑6, Oct 1993, V: Blood Syndicate 1.50

Other grades: Multiply price above by 5/6 for VF/NM • 2/3 for VERY FINE • 1/3 for FINE • 1/5 for VERY GOOD • 1/8 for GOOD

	N-MINT
❑7, Nov 1993	1.50
❑8, Dec 1993, O: Icon	1.50
❑9, Jan 1994	1.50
❑10, Feb 1994, V: Holocaust	1.50
❑11, Mar 1994, KB (w); 1: Todd Loomis	1.50
❑12, Apr 1994, 1: Gideon's Cord	1.50
❑13, May 1994, 1: Buck Wild	1.50
❑14, Jun 1994, JBy (c)	1.50
❑15, Jul 1994, A: Superboy	1.75
❑16, Aug 1994, A: Superman	1.75
❑17, Sep 1994	1.75
❑18, Oct 1994	1.75
❑19, Nov 1994	1.75
❑20, Dec 1994, A: Static. A: Wise Son. A: Dharma. A: Hardware	1.75
❑21, Jan 1995, Mothership Connection Conclusion	1.75
❑22, Feb 1995, 1: New Rocket. A: Static. A: Hardware. A: DMZ	1.75
❑23, Mar 1995	1.75
❑24, Apr 1995, Rocket's baby born	1.75
❑25, May 1995, Giant-size	2.95
❑26, Jun 1995, V: Oblivion	1.75
❑27, Jul 1995, Icon returns from space	2.50
❑28, Aug 1995	2.50
❑29, Sep 1995	2.50
❑30, Oct 1995, Funeral of Buck Wild	2.50
❑31, Nov 1995	1.00
❑32, Dec 1995	2.50
❑33, Jan 1996	2.50
❑34, Feb 1996	2.50
❑35, Mar 1996	2.50
❑36, Apr 1996	2.50
❑37, Sep 1996, Icon in the 1920s	2.50
❑38, Oct 1996, V: Holocaust	2.50
❑39, Nov 1996, V: Holocaust	2.50
❑40, Dec 1996, V: Blood Syndicate	2.50
❑41, Jan 1997	2.50
❑42, Feb 1997, Final Issue	2.50

Icon Devil
Spider

❑1	1.50
❑2	1.50

Iconografix Special
Iconografix

❑1, b&w	2.50

Iczer 3
CPM

❑1, Sep 1996, b&w	2.95
❑2, Oct 1996, b&w	2.95

Id
Fantagraphics / Eros

❑1, b&w; Adult	2.50
❑2, b&w; Adult	2.50
❑3, b&w; Adult	2.50
❑3/2nd, Jun 1995, b&w; 2nd printing; Adult	2.95

ID4: Independence Day
Marvel

❑0, Jun 1996; prequel to movie	2.50
❑1, Jul 1996; adapts movie	1.95
❑2, Aug 1996; adapts movie	1.95

Id_entity
Tokyopop

❑1, May 2005	9.99
❑2, Jul 2005	9.99
❑3, Sep 2005	9.99
❑4, Dec 2005	9.99

Identity Crisis
DC

❑1, Aug 2004; D: Sue Dibny	15.00
❑1/2nd, Aug 2004, Negative Sketch cover	6.00
❑1/3rd, Aug 2004, New Rags Morales cover	5.00
❑1/DF, Aug 2004	15.00
❑1/Sketch, Aug 2004; Sketch cover variant from Diamond 2004 Retailer Summit	225.00
❑2, Sep 2004	8.00
❑3, Oct 2004	7.00
❑4, Nov 2004	8.00
❑5, Dec 2004	7.00
❑6, Jan 2005	8.00
❑7, Feb 2005	7.00
❑7/DF Morales, Feb 2005	15.00
❑7/DF Turner, Feb 2005	25.00

Identity Disc
Marvel

	N-MINT
❑1, Aug 2004	2.99
❑2, Sep 2004	2.99
❑3, Oct 2004	2.99
❑4, Nov 2004	2.99
❑5, Dec 2004	2.99

I Die at Midnight
DC / Vertigo

❑1, ca. 2000	2.95

Idiotland
Fantagraphics

❑1, b&w; Adult	2.95
❑2, b&w; Adult	2.50
❑3, b&w; Adult	2.50
❑4, Dec 1993, b&w; Adult	2.50
❑5, b&w; Adult	2.50
❑6, Aug 1994, b&w; Adult	2.50

Idle Worship
Visceral

❑1	2.95

Idol
Marvel / Epic

❑1	2.95
❑2	2.95
❑3	2.95

I Dream of Jeannie
Dell

❑1, Apr 1966, Photo cover	60.00
❑2, Dec 1966	40.00

I Dream of Jeannie (Airwave)
Airwave

❑1, Aug 2002, b&w	2.95
❑Ann 1, ca. 2002, b&w; Tricks and Treat Ann; cardstock cover	3.50

I Feel Sick
Slave Labor

❑1, Aug 1999	3.95

If the Devil Would Talk
Impact

❑1, ca. 1958	450.00

Igrat
Verotik

❑1, Nov 1995; Adult	2.95

Igrat Illustrations
Verotik

❑1, Apr 1997; pin-ups; embossed cardstock cover	3.95

I Had a Dream
King Ink Empire

❑1, Jun 1995	2.95

I (Heart) Marvel: Marvel AI
Marvel

❑1, Apr 2006	2.99

I (Heart) Marvel: Masked Intentions
Marvel

❑1, May 2006	2.99

I (Heart) Marvel: My Mutant Heart
Marvel

❑1, Mar 2006	2.99

I (Heart) Marvel: Outlaw Love
Marvel

❑1, May 2006	2.99

I (Heart) Marvel: Web of Romance
Marvel

❑1, Apr 2006	2.99

I Hunt Monsters
Antarctic

❑1, Mar 2004	2.99
❑2, Apr 2004	2.99
❑3, May 2004	2.99
❑4, Jun 2004	2.99
❑5, Jul 2004	2.99
❑6, Aug 2004	2.99
❑7, Sep 2004	2.99
❑8, Oct 2004	2.99
❑9, Nov 2004	2.99

I Hunt Monsters
Antarctic

❑1, Jan 2005; Wraparound cover; B&w series	2.99

	N-MINT
❑2, Feb 2005	2.99
❑3, Mar 2005	2.99
❑4, Apr 2005	2.99
❑5, May 2005	2.99
❑6, Jun 2005	2.99
❑7, Jul 2005	2.99
❑8, ca. 2005	2.99
❑9, ca. 2005	2.99

Ike and Kitzi
A Capella

❑1	2.50

Iliad
Slave Labor / Amaze Ink

❑1, Dec 1997, b&w	2.95
❑2, Jan 1998, b&w	2.95

Iliad II
Micmac

❑1, Oct 1986, b&w	2.00
❑2, b&w	2.00
❑3, b&w	2.00

Illegal Aliens
Eclipse

❑1, Sep 1999, b&w; NN	2.50

Illuminations
Monolith

❑1	2.50
❑2	2.50
❑3	2.50
❑4	2.50
❑5, Feb 1995	2.50

Illuminator
Marvel / Nelson

❑1, ca. 1993, 1: Illuminator; O: Illuminator	4.99
❑2, ca. 1993	4.99
❑3, ca. 1993	2.95

Illuminatus
Eye-N-Apple

❑1; Adult	2.00
❑2; Adult	2.00

Illuminatus!
Rip Off

❑1, Oct 1990, b&w	2.50
❑2, Dec 1990, b&w	2.50
❑3, Apr 1991, b&w	2.50

Illustrated Classex
Comic Zone

❑1, Dec 1991, b&w; Adult	2.75

Illustrated Dore: Book of Genesis
Tome

❑1, b&w	2.50

Illustrated Dore: Book of the Apocrypha
Tome

❑1, b&w	2.50

Illustrated Editions
Thwack! Pow!

❑1, Feb 1995	1.95

Illustrated Kama Sutra
NBM

❑1; Adult	12.95

Illustrated Tales
FTR

❑1	1.95

I Love Lucy
Eternity

❑1, May 1990, b&w; strip reprint	2.95
❑2, Jun 1990, b&w; strip reprint	2.95
❑3, Jul 1990, b&w; strip reprint	2.95
❑4, Aug 1990, b&w; strip reprint	2.95
❑5, Sep 1990, b&w; strip reprint	2.95
❑6, Oct 1990, b&w; strip reprint	2.95

I Love Lucy Book Two
Eternity

❑1, Nov 1990, b&w; strip reprints	2.95
❑2, Dec 1990, b&w; strip reprints	2.95
❑3, Jan 1991, b&w; strip reprints	2.95
❑4, Feb 1991, b&w; strip reprints	2.95
❑5, Mar 1991, b&w; strip reprints	2.95
❑6, Apr 1991, b&w; strip reprints	2.95

Other grades: Multiply price above by 5/6 for VF/NM • 2/3 for VERY FINE • 1/3 for FINE • 1/5 for VERY GOOD • 1/8 for GOOD

Hunter: The Age of Magic

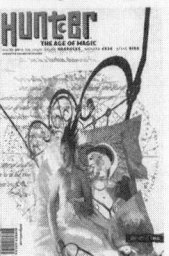

Continues the tales from Books of Magic
©DC

Hyperkind

Another artifact from the Clive Barker-verse
©Marvel

Iceman

Founding X-Man gets his own limited run
©Marvel

Icon

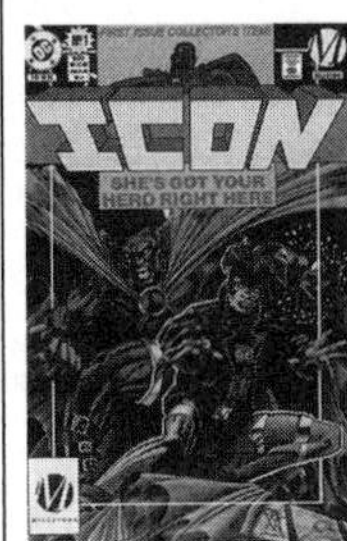

Alien visitor stars in Milestone series
©DC

I Love Lucy

Reprints comic strip by Lawrence Nadel
©Eternity

N-MINT

I Love Lucy in 3-D
Eternity

❑1 ... 3.95

I Love Lucy in Full Color
Eternity

❑1, comic book reprint; Collects I Love Lucy # 4,5,8,16 ... 5.95

I Love New York
Linsner.com

❑1, ca. 2002; A: Dawn. 9/11 benefit issue; title appears on cover, spray painted on World Trade Center ... 10.00

I Love You
Charlton

❑37 1961 ... 10.00
❑38, Jan 1962 ... 10.00
❑39 1962 ... 10.00
❑40 1962 ... 10.00
❑41 1962 ... 10.00
❑42, Oct 1962 ... 10.00
❑43, Dec 1963 ... 10.00
❑44, Feb 1963 ... 10.00
❑45, Apr 1963 ... 10.00
❑46, Jun 1963 ... 10.00
❑47, Aug 1963 ... 10.00
❑48, Oct 1963 ... 10.00
❑49, Feb 1964 ... 10.00
❑50, Apr 1964 ... 10.00
❑51, Jun 1964 ... 8.00
❑52, Aug 1964 ... 8.00
❑53, Oct 1964 ... 8.00
❑54, Jan 1965 ... 8.00
❑55, Mar 1965 ... 8.00
❑56, May 1965 ... 8.00
❑57, Jul 1965 ... 8.00
❑58, Sep 1965 ... 8.00
❑59, Nov 1965 ... 8.00
❑60, Jan 1966, Elvis Presley story ... 60.00
❑61, Mar 1966 ... 4.00
❑62, May 1966 ... 4.00
❑63, Jul 1966 ... 4.00
❑64, Sep 1966 ... 4.00
❑65, Nov 1966 ... 4.00
❑66, Feb 1967 ... 4.00
❑67, Apr 1967 ... 4.00
❑68, Jun 1967 ... 4.00
❑69, Aug 1967 ... 4.00
❑70, Oct 1967 ... 3.00
❑71, Dec 1967 ... 3.00
❑72, Feb 1968 ... 3.00
❑73, Jun 1968 ... 3.00
❑74, Aug 1968 ... 3.00
❑75, Oct 1968 ... 3.00
❑76, Dec 1968 ... 3.00
❑77, Jan 1969 ... 3.00
❑78, Mar 1969 ... 3.00
❑79, May 1969 ... 3.00
❑80, Jul 1969 ... 3.00
❑81, Sep 1969 ... 3.00
❑82, Nov 1969 ... 3.00
❑83, Jan 1970 ... 3.00
❑84, Mar 1970 ... 3.00
❑85, May 1970 ... 3.00
❑86, Jul 1970 ... 3.00
❑87, Sep 1970 ... 3.00

N-MINT

❑88, Nov 1970 ... 3.00
❑89, Jan 1971 ... 3.00
❑90, Mar 1971 ... 3.00
❑91, May 1971 ... 2.50
❑92, Jul 1971 ... 2.50
❑93, Sep 1971 ... 2.50
❑94, Nov 1971 ... 2.50
❑95, Jan 1972 ... 2.50
❑96, Mar 1972 ... 2.50
❑97, May 1972 ... 2.50
❑98, Jul 1972 ... 2.50
❑99, Sep 1972 ... 2.50
❑100, Dec 1972 ... 2.50
❑101, Jan 1973 ... 2.50
❑102, Mar 1973 ... 2.50
❑103, May 1973 ... 2.50
❑104, Jul 1973 ... 2.50
❑105, Sep 1973 ... 2.50
❑106, Nov 1973 ... 2.50
❑107, Jun 1974 ... 2.50
❑108, Sep 1974 ... 2.50
❑109, Nov 1974 ... 2.50
❑110, Jan 1975 ... 2.50
❑111, Mar 1975 ... 2.50
❑112, May 1975 ... 2.50
❑113, Jul 1975 ... 2.50
❑114, Oct 1975 ... 2.50
❑115, Dec 1975 ... 2.50
❑116, Feb 1976 ... 2.50
❑117, Apr 1976 ... 2.50
❑118, Jun 1976 ... 2.50
❑119, Aug 1976 ... 2.50
❑120, Oct 1976 ... 2.50
❑121, Dec 1976, End of original run (1976) ... 2.50
❑122, Mar 1979, Series begins again (1979) ... 1.50
❑123, Jun 1979 ... 1.50
❑124 1979 ... 1.50
❑125 1979 ... 1.50
❑126, Oct 1979 ... 1.50
❑127, Dec 1979 ... 1.50
❑128, Feb 1980 ... 1.50
❑129, Mar 1980 ... 1.50
❑130, May 1980, Final issue ... 1.50

I Love You
Avalon

❑1 ... 2.95

I Love You Special
Avalon

❑1, b&w ... 2.95

I, Lusiphur
Mulehide

❑1, b&w ... 20.00
❑2, b&w ... 12.00
❑3, b&w ... 15.00
❑4, b&w ... 12.00
❑5, b&w ... 10.00
❑6, b&w ... 8.00
❑7, b&w; series continues as Poison Elves ... 8.00

I Luv Halloween
Tokyopop

❑1, Oct 2005 ... 9.99

N-MINT

Image
Image

❑0, ca. 1993; TMc, RL, JLee, EL (w); TMc, RL, JLee, EL (a); Mail-away coupon-redemption promo from coupons in early Image comics ... 4.00

Image Comics Holiday Special 2005
Image

❑1, Jan 2006 ... 9.99

Image Introduces... Believer
Image

❑1, Dec 2001, b&w ... 2.95

Image Introduces... Cryptopia
Image

❑1, Apr 2002, b&w ... 2.95

Image Introduces... Dog Soldiers
Image

❑1, Jun 2002, b&w ... 2.95

Image Introduces... Legend of Isis
Image

❑1, Feb 2002, b&w ... 2.95

Image Introduces... Primate
Image

❑1/A, Sep 2001, b&w ... 2.95
❑1/B, Sep 2001 ... 2.95

Image of the Beast
Last Gasp

❑1, ca. 1979, 36 pages; Adult ... 3.00

Image Plus
Image

❑1, May 1993 ... 2.25

Images of a Distant Soil
Image

❑1, Feb 1997, b&w; pin-ups by various artists ... 2.95

Images of Omaha
Kitchen Sink

❑1, ca. 1992, b&w; benefit comic; intro by Harlan Ellison; afterword by Neil Gaiman; cardstock cover ... 3.95
❑2, ca. 1992, b&w; benefit comic; cardstock cover ... 3.95

Images of Shadowhawk
Image

❑1, Sep 1993 ... 1.95
❑2, Oct 1993 ... 1.95
❑3, Jan 1994 ... 1.95

Image Two-In-One
Image

❑1, Dec 2001, b&w ... 2.95

Imagi-Mation
Imagi-Mation

❑1; Gnatman ... 1.75
❑2; Star Wreck ... 1.75

Imaginaries
Image

❑1, Apr 2005; Mike Miller cover ... 2.95
❑1/A, Apr 2005; Greg Titus cover ... 2.95
❑2/A cover 2005 ... 2.95
❑2/B cover 2005 ... 2.95
❑3/A cover, Sep 2005 ... 2.95
❑3/B cover, Sep 2005 ... 2.95
❑4, Dec 2005 ... 2.95

Other grades: Multiply price above by 5/6 for VF/NM • 2/3 for VERY FINE • 1/3 for FINE • 1/5 for VERY GOOD • 1/8 for GOOD

N-MINT N-MINT N-MINT

Imagine
Star*Reach

❑1, May 1978, b&w NA, GD, MR (w); NA, GD, MR (a) 20.00
❑1/2nd, May 1978; NA, GD, MR (w); NA, GD, MR (a); Contains color centerspread 10.00
❑2, Jun 1978, b&w CR (c); CR, GD (w); CR, GD (a) 10.00
❑3, Aug 1978, b&w CR (c); CR (w); CR (a) 15.00
❑4, Nov 1978, SD (c); SD (a); Black & white with a color story 10.00
❑5, Apr 1979, b&w; CR (w); CR (a); Magazine size 6.00
❑6, Jul 1979, b&w CR (w); CR (a) 6.00

I'm Dickens... He's Fenster
Dell

❑1, May 1963 .... 25.00
❑2, Aug 1963 .... 20.00

Immortal Combat
Express / Entity

❑1, Feb 1995; Entity Illustrated Novella #5; cardstock cover 2.95

Immortal Doctor Fate
DC

❑1, Jan 1985; MN, KG, JSa (a); O: Doctor Fate 1.50
❑2, Feb 1985 KG (a) 1.50
❑3, Mar 1985 KG (a) 1.50

Immortal II
Image

❑1, Apr 1997, b&w; cover also says May, indicia says Apr 2.50
❑1/A, Apr 1997, b&w; cover says Immortal Two, indicia says Immortal II 2.50
❑2, Jun 1997, b&w; cover says Immortal Two, indicia says Immortal II 2.50
❑3, Aug 1997, b&w; cover says Immortal Two, indicia says Immortal II 2.50
❑4, Sep 1997, b&w; cover says Immortal Two, indicia says Immortal II 2.50
❑5, Feb 1998, b&w; cover says Immortal Two, indicia says Immortal II 2.50

Immortal Iron Fist
Marvel

❑1, Feb 2007 .... 8.00
❑2, Mar 2007 .... 6.00

Immortals
Comics By Day

❑1 .... 1.00

Imp
Slave Labor

❑1, Jun 1994 .... 2.95

Impact (RCP)
RCP

❑1, Apr 1999 .... 2.50
❑2, May 1999 .... 2.50
❑3, Jun 1999 .... 2.50
❑4, Jul 1999 .... 2.50
❑5, Aug 1999 .... 2.50
❑Ann 1; Collects Impact (RCP) #1-5 .... 13.50

Impact Christmas Special
DC / Impact

❑1 1991; Cover says "Impact Winter Special" 2.50

Impact Comics Who's Who
DC / Impact

❑1, Sep 1991 .... 4.95
❑2, Dec 1991 .... 4.95
❑3, May 1992; trading cards 4.95

Impaler
Image

❑1, Dec 2006 .... 2.99
❑2, Nov 2006 .... 2.99

Imperial Dragons
Alias

❑1, Sep 2005; Includes Dreamland Chronicles preview 0.75

Imperial Guard
Marvel

❑1, Jan 1997; Wraparound cover 1.99
❑2, Feb 1997; wraparound cover 1.99
❑3, Mar 1997; Final Issue 1.99

Impossible Man Summer Vacation Spectacular
Marvel

❑1, Aug 1990 .... 2.00
❑2, Aug 1991 .... 2.00

Impulse
DC

❑1, Apr 1995, MWa (w); O: Impulse 4.00
❑2, May 1995, MWa (w) 3.50
❑3, Jun 1995, MWa (w) 2.50
❑4, Jul 1995, MWa (w); 1: White Lightning 2.50
❑5, Aug 1995, MWa (w); V: White Lightning 2.50
❑6, Sep 1995, MWa (w); Child abuse 2.25
❑7, Oct 1995, MWa (w); V: Gridlock 2.25
❑8, Nov 1995, MWa (w); V: Blockbuster. Underworld Unleashed 2.25
❑9, Dec 1995, MWa (w); A: Xs. Continued into Flash (2nd Series) #109; V: Savitar 2.25
❑10, Jan 1996, MWa (w); continues in Flash #110 .... 2.00
❑11, Feb 1996, MWa (w); D: Johnny Quick; V: Savitar 2.00
❑12, Mar 1996, MWa (w); XS leaves 2.00
❑13, May 1996, MWa (w) 2.00
❑14, Jun 1996, MWa (w); V: White Lightning. V: Trickster 2.00
❑15, Jul 1996, MWa (w); V: White Lightning. V: Trickster 2.00
❑16, Aug 1996, MWa (w); more of Max Mercury's past revealed 2.00
❑17, Sep 1996, MWa (w); A: Zatanna 2.00
❑18, Oct 1996, V: thieves stealing NASA virtual reality technology 2.00
❑19, Nov 1996, MWa (w) 2.00
❑20, Dec 1996, MWa (w); Bart plays baseball 1.75
❑21, Jan 1997, MWa (w); A: Legion. LSH seek cosmic treadmill to return to 30th century 1.75
❑22, Feb 1997, MWa (w); A: Jesse Quick 1.75
❑23, Mar 1997, MWa (w); Impulse's mother returns 1.75
❑24, Apr 1997, MWa (w); Impulse goes to 30th century 1.75
❑25, May 1997, MWa (w); Impulse in 30th century 1.75
❑26, Jun 1997, MWa (w); SB (a); Impulse returns to 20th century 1.75
❑27, Jul 1997, MWa (w) 1.75
❑28, Aug 1997, 1: Arrowette 1.75
❑29, Sep 1997 .... 1.75
❑30, Oct 1997, Genesis; Impulse gains new powers 1.75
❑31, Nov 1997, V: Doctor Claiborne 1.75
❑32, Dec 1997, Face cover 1.95
❑33, Jan 1998, 1: Jasper Pierson. V: White Lightning; Thanksgiving 1.95
❑34, Feb 1998, Max and Impulse travel in time 1.95
❑35, Mar 1998, Max and Impulse turned into apes 1.95
❑36, Apr 1998 .... 1.95
❑37, May 1998, 1: Glory Shredder 1.95
❑38, Jun 1998, Manchester floods 1.95
❑39, Jul 1998, A: Trickster 1.95
❑40, Aug 1998 .... 1.95
❑41, Sep 1998, A: Arrowette 2.25
❑42, Oct 1998, Virtual pets 2.25
❑43, Dec 1998, Aids refugee inventor escape military forces 2.25
❑44, Jan 1999, Halloween 2.25
❑45, Feb 1999, A: Bart's mother. Christmas 2.25
❑46, Mar 1999, A: Flash II (Barry Allen). Chain Lightning tie-in 2.25
❑47, Apr 1999, A: Superman. Superboy cameo 2.25
❑48, May 1999, V: Riddler 2.25
❑49, Jun 1999 .... 2.25
❑50, Jul 1999, A: Batman. V: Joker; 1: Inertia 2.25
❑51, Aug 1999, V: Prince Fog 2.25
❑52, Sep 1999, V: Kalibak; V: Technoplasm 2.25
❑53, Oct 1999, V: Inertia. V: Kalibak 2.25
❑54, Nov 1999, Day of Judgment 2.25
❑55, Dec 1999, V: Sir Real 2.25
❑56, Jan 2000, A: Young Justice. Technoplasm duplicates Superboy and Robin abilities 2.25
❑57, Feb 2000, A: Plastic Man. V: Mr. Mxyzptlk; Christmas issue 2.25
❑58, Mar 2000 .... 2.25
❑59, Apr 2000, Valentine's Day issue 2.25
❑60, May 2000 .... 2.25
❑61, Jun 2000, V: Paintball; V: Gentleman Ghost; Day of Judgment follow-up 2.25
❑62, Jul 2000 .... 2.25
❑63, Aug 2000, Inertia (disguised as Impulse) V: Prince Fog 2.25
❑64, Sep 2000 .... 2.25
❑65, Oct 2000, Inertia (disguised as Impulse) accompanies Max Mercury into Speed Force 2.50
❑66, Nov 2000, V: Inertia; Max Mercury cured by Speed Force 2.50
❑67, Dec 2000 .... 2.50
❑68, Jan 2001, Green Lantern: Circle Of Fire tie-in; Adam Strange cover/appearance. 2.50
❑69, Feb 2001, Green Lantern: Circle Of Fire tie-in; Adam Strange cover/appearance. 2.50
❑70, Mar 2001 .... 2.50
❑71, Apr 2001 .... 2.50
❑72, May 2001 .... 2.50
❑73, Jun 2001 .... 2.50
❑74, Jul 2001 .... 2.50
❑75, Aug 2001 .... 2.50
❑76, Sep 2001 .... 2.50
❑77, Oct 2001, Story continued from Young Justice #36 .... 2.50
❑78, Nov 2001 .... 2.50
❑79, Dec 2001, Joker: Last Laugh tie-in 2.50
❑80, Jan 2002, V: White Lightning 2.50
❑81, Feb 2002 .... 2.50
❑82, Mar 2002 .... 2.50
❑83, Apr 2002 .... 2.50
❑84, May 2002 .... 2.50
❑85, Jun 2002 .... 2.50
❑86, Jul 2002 .... 2.50
❑87, Aug 2002 .... 2.50
❑88, Sep 2002 .... 2.50
❑89, Oct 2002, Final issue; V: Rival 2.50
❑1000000, Nov 1998, A: John Fox. V: Vandal Savage; Rescue of Jesse Quick 4.00
❑Ann 1, ca. 1996, MWa (w); Legends of the Dead Earth 5.00
❑Ann 2, ca. 1997, A: Vigilante. Pulp Heroes 3.95

Impulse/Atom Double-Shot
DC

❑1, Feb 1998, One-shot 1.95

Impulse: Bart Saves the Universe
DC

❑1, prestige format; Batman cameo; Flash I (Jay Garrick) cameo; Flash II (Barry Allen) cameo; Flash III (Wally West) cameo 5.95

Impulse Plus
DC

❑1, Sep 1997, continues in Superboy Plus #2 2.95

Imp-Unity
Spoof

❑1, b&w; parody 2.95

Incomplete Death's Head
Marvel

❑1, Jan 1993; Giant-size; Die-cut cover. 2.95
❑2, Feb 1993 .... 1.75
❑3, Mar 1993 .... 1.75
❑4, Apr 1993 .... 1.75
❑5, May 1993 .... 1.75
❑6, Jun 1993 .... 1.75
❑7, Jul 1993 .... 1.75
❑8, Aug 1993 .... 1.75
❑9, Sep 1993 .... 1.75
❑10, Oct 1993 .... 1.75
❑11, Nov 1993 .... 1.75
❑12, Dec 1993; double-sized 1.75

Incredible Hulk
Marvel

❑-1, Jul 1997, PD (w); O: Hulk. Flashback 2.25
❑1, May 1962, JK (c); SL (w); JK (a); 1&O: Hulk. 1: General "Thunderbolt" Ross. 1: Rick Jones. 1: Betty Ross. Hulk's skin is gray (printing mistake). 13000.00
❑2, Jul 1962, JK (c); SL (w); SD, JK (a); O: Hulk. Hulk's skin is printed in green 3500.00
❑3, Sep 1962, JK, (c); SL (w); JK (a); O: Hulk. 1: Ringmaster. 1: Cannonball (villain). 1: The Clown. 1: Teena the Fat Lady. 1: Bruto the Strongman 2000.00
❑4, Nov 1962, JK (c); SL (w); JK (a); O: Hulk. 1: Boris Monguski and Mongu (his robot) 1750.00
❑5, Jan 1963, JK (c); SL (w); JK (a); 1: Tyrannus; 1: General Fang 1750.00
❑6, Mar 1963, SD (c); SL (w); SD (a); 1: Metal Master. 1: Teen Brigade. Moves to "Tales To Astonish" following this issue 2250.00

Other grades: Multiply price above by 5/6 for VF/NM • 2/3 for VERY FINE • 1/3 for FINE • 1/5 for VERY GOOD • 1/8 for GOOD

I Love You (Charlton)

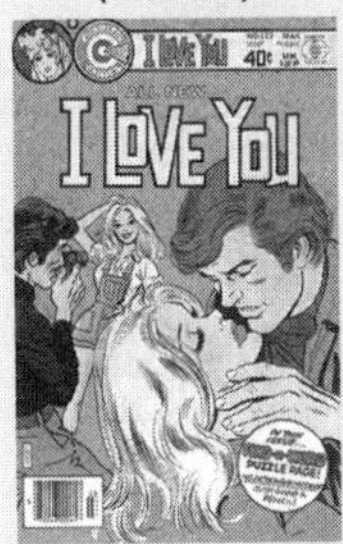

Long-running Charlton romance title

©Charlton

Images of Omaha

Benefit title for Omaha co-creator Reed Waller

©Kitchen Sink

Image Two-In-One

Cover styled like Marvel Two-in-One

©Image

Immortal Doctor Fate

Retells tales of the original Doctor Fate

©DC

Imperial Guard

Adventures of the Shi'ar enforcers

©Marvel

	N-MINT
❑102, Apr 1968, GT (a); O: Hulk. Numbering continued from "Tales To Astonish"	150.00
❑103, May 1968, 1: Space Parasite	100.00
❑104, Jun 1968, V: Rhino	75.00
❑105, Jul 1968, BEv (w); GT (a); 1: Missing Link. V: Gargoyle	70.00
❑106, Aug 1968, HT, GT (a); 1: Colonel Yuri Brevlov; 2: Missing Link	50.00
❑107, Sep 1968, HT (a); V: Mandarin. 2: Colonel Yuri Brevlov	50.00
❑108, Oct 1968, SL (w); HT, JSe (a); A: Nick Fury	50.00
❑109, Nov 1968, HT, (c); SL (w); HT, JSe (a); Tony Isabella L.O.C	50.00
❑110, Dec 1968, HT (c); SL (w); HT, JSe (a); Peter Sanderson L.O.C	50.00
❑111, Jan 1969, HT (c); SL (w); HT, DA (a); 1: Galaxy Master	50.00
❑112, Feb 1969, HT (c); SL (w); HT, DA (a); 2: Galaxy Master	50.00
❑113, Mar 1969, HT (c); SL (w); HT, DA (a); V: Sandman. V: Sandman	40.00
❑114, Apr 1969, HT (c); SL (w); HT, DA (a)	40.00
❑115, May 1969, HT (c); SL (w); HT, DA (a)	40.00
❑116, Jun 1969, HT (c); SL (w); HT, DA (a); 1: Super Humanoid	35.00
❑117, Jul 1969, HT (c); SL (w); HT, DA (a); 2: Super Humanoid	35.00
❑118, Aug 1969, HT (c); SL (w); HT (a); A: Sub-Mariner. 1: Mistress Fara; D: Mistress Fara	35.00
❑119, Sep 1969, HT (c); SL (w); HT (a)	35.00
❑120, Oct 1969, HT (c); SL (w); HT (a)	35.00
❑121, Nov 1969, HT (c); HT (a); 1: the Glob	35.00
❑122, Dec 1969, HT (c); HT (a); A: Thing. Hulk vs. Thing	55.00
❑123, Jan 1970, HT (c); HT (a)	30.00
❑124, Feb 1970, HT (c); SB, HT (a); V: Rhino	30.00
❑125, Mar 1970, HT (c); HT (a); V: Absorbing Man	30.00
❑126, Apr 1970, HT (c); HT (a); 1: The Night-Crawler; 1: Jack Van Nyborg; 1: Barbara Denton Norris (Valkyrie); 2: The Nameless One	25.00
❑127, May 1970, HT (c); HT (a); V: Mogol. 1: Mogol; D: Mogol	25.00
❑128, Jun 1970, HT (c); HT (a)	25.00
❑129, Jul 1970, HT (c); HT (a); 2: Glob	25.00
❑130, Aug 1970, HT (c); HT (a); 1: Raoul Stoddard; Neal Pozner L.O.C	25.00
❑131, Sep 1970, HT (c); HT, JSe (a); Iron Man	30.00
❑132, Oct 1970, HT (c); HT, JSe (a); V: Hydra. 2: Jim Wilson	25.00
❑133, Nov 1970, HT (c); HT, JSe (a); 1: Draxon	20.00
❑134, Dec 1970, HT (c); SB, HT (a)	16.00
❑135, Jan 1971, HT (c); SB, HT (a); V: Kang	16.00
❑136, Feb 1971, HT (c); SB, HT (a); 1: Xeron; 1: Klaatu	16.00
❑137, Mar 1971, HT (c); HT (a); 1: Captain Cybor; D: Captain Cybor; D: Klaatu; 2: Xeron; 2: Klaatu	20.00
❑138, Apr 1971, HT (c); HT (a)	20.00
❑139, May 1971, HT (c); HT (a)	20.00
❑140, Jun 1971, HT (c); HT (a); 1: Jarella. Written by Harlan Ellison	20.00
❑140/2nd, HT (c); HT (a); 1: Jarella. 2nd printing	2.50
❑141, Jul 1971, HT (c); HT, JSe (a); O: Doc Samson. 1: Doc Samson	20.00
❑142, Aug 1971, HT (c); HT, JSe (a); 2: Valkyrie	20.00
❑143, Sep 1971, HT (c); JSe (a); V: Doctor Doom. 2: Doc Samson	20.00
❑144, Oct 1971, HT (c); JSe (a); V: Doctor Doom. 2: Valeria	20.00
❑145, Nov 1971, Giant-size; HT (c); HT, JSe (a); O: Hulk	20.00
❑146, Dec 1971, HT (c); HT, JSe (a)	20.00
❑148, Feb 1972, HT (c); HT, JSe (a); 1: Peter Corbeau. Peter Corbeau	20.00
❑147, Jan 1972, HT (c); HT, JSe (a)	20.00
❑149, Mar 1972, HT (c); HT, JSe (a); 1: Inheritor	20.00
❑150, Apr 1972, HT (c); HT, JSe (a); 1: Viking. A: Lorna Dane. A: Havoc	20.00
❑151, May 1972, HT (c); HT, JSe (a)	20.00
❑152, Jun 1972, HT (c); HT (a); Steve Englehart work is uncredited	25.00
❑153, Jul 1972, HT (c); HT, JSe (a); A: Fantastic Four. A: Peter Parker. A: Matt Murdock. Mike W. Barr L.O.C.	20.00
❑154, Aug 1972, HT (c); HT, JSe (a); A: Ant-Man. V: Chameleon	20.00
❑155, Sep 1972, HT (c); HT, JSe (a); 1: Shaper of Worlds. V: Captain Axis	20.00
❑156, Oct 1972, HT (c); HT (a)	20.00
❑157, Nov 1972, HT (c); HT (a)	20.00
❑158, Dec 1972, HT (c); HT (a); A: Warlock. V: Rhino on Counter-Earth	20.00
❑159, Jan 1973, HT (c); HT (a); V: Abomination	20.00
❑160, Feb 1973, HT (c); HT (a)	20.00
❑161, Mar 1973, HT (c); HT (a); A: Mimic. D: Mimic. V: Beast. D: Mimic	30.00
❑162, Apr 1973, HT (c); HT (a); 1: Wendigo. V: Wendigo	55.00
❑163, May 1973, HT (c); HT (a); 1: Gremlin	15.00
❑164, Jun 1973, HT (c); HT (a); 1: Captain Omen	15.00
❑165, Jul 1973, HT (c); HT (a); V: Aquon	15.00
❑166, Aug 1973, HT (c); HT (a); 1: Zzzax	15.00
❑167, Sep 1973, HT (c); HT, JAb (a); V: Modok. V: M.O.D.O.K	15.00
❑168, Oct 1973, HT (c); HT, JAb (a); 1: Harpy	15.00
❑169, Nov 1973, HT (c); HT, JAb (a); 1: Bi-Beast I. V: Bi-Beast I	15.00
❑170, Dec 1973, HT (c); HT, JAb (a); D: Bi-Beast I	15.00
❑171, Jan 1974, HT (c); HT, JAb (a); V: Abomination. V: Rhino	15.00
❑172, Feb 1974, HT (c); HT, JAb (a); A: X-Men. Credit for Roy Thomas is mistake	25.00
❑173, Mar 1974, HT (c); HT (a); V: Cobalt Man	15.00
❑174, Apr 1974, HT (c); HT, JAb (a); V: Cobalt Man. Marvel Value Stamp #47: Green Goblin	15.00
❑175, May 1974, HT, JR (c); HT, JAb (a); A: Inhumans. V: Inhumans. Marvel Value Stamp #56: Rawhide Kid	15.00
❑176, Jun 1974, HT (c); HT, JAb (a); A: Warlock. Marvel Value Stamp #67: Cyclops	15.00
❑177, Jul 1974, HT (c); HT, JAb (a); D: Warlock. Marvel Value Stamp #39: Iron Fist	17.00
❑178, Aug 1974, HT (c); HT, JAb (a); D: Warlock. Warlock returns	17.00
❑179, Sep 1974, HT (c); HT, JAb (a); Marvel Value Stamp #16: Shang-Chi	16.00
❑180, Oct 1974, HT (c); HT, JAb (a); 1: Wolverine (cameo). A: Wendigo. Marvel Value Stamp #67: Cyclops	180.00
❑181, Nov 1974, HT (c); HT, JAb (a); 1: Wolverine (full appearance). A: Wendigo. Marvel Value Stamp #54: Shanna the She-Devil	750.00
❑181/Ace, Wizard Ace Edition; acetate cover	5.00
❑182, Dec 1974, HT (c); HT (a); 1&O: Hammer. 1&O: Anvil. 1: Crackajack. A: Wolverine. V: Hammer. V: Anvil. Marvel Value Stamp #59: Golem	100.00
❑183, Jan 1975, V: Zzzax. Marvel Value Stamp #4: Thing	12.00
❑184, Feb 1975, HT (c); HT (a); Marvel Value Stamp #58: Mandarin	10.00
❑185, Mar 1975, HT (c); HT (a)	10.00
❑186, Apr 1975, HT (c); HT (a); 1: Devastator I (Kirov Petrovna). D: Devastator I (Kirov Petrovna). Marvel Value Stamp #11: Deathlok	10.00
❑187, May 1975, HT (c); HT, JSa (a); V: Gremlin	10.00
❑188, Jun 1975, HT (c); HT, JSa (a); V: Gremlin	10.00
❑189, Jul 1975, HT (c); HT, JSa (a); V: Mole Man	10.00
❑190, Aug 1975, HT (c); HT (a); 1: Glorian. V: Toad Men	10.00
❑191, Sep 1975, HT (c); HT, JSa (a); V: Shaper of Worlds	8.00
❑192, Oct 1975, HT, JSa (a)	8.00
❑193, Nov 1975, GK, JR (c); HT, JSa (a); V: Doc Samson	8.00
❑194, Dec 1975, GK, JR (c); SB, JSa (a)	8.00
❑195, Jan 1976, SB, JSa (a); V: Abomination	8.00
❑196, Feb 1976, GK, JR (c); SB, JSa (a); V: Abomination	8.00
❑197, Mar 1976, BWr (c); SB, JSa (a); V: Man-Thing. V: Gardner	8.00
❑198, Apr 1976, GK, JR (c); SB, JSa (a); A: Man-Thing. V: Collector	8.00
❑198/30¢, Apr 1976, 30¢ regional variant	20.00
❑199, May 1976, RB (c); SB, JSa (a); V: Doc Samson	8.00
❑199/30¢, May 1976, 30¢ regional variant	20.00
❑200, Jun 1976, 200th anniversary issue; RB (c); SB, JSa (a); A: Surfer and others	11.00
❑200/30¢, Jun 1976, 200th anniversary issue; RB (c); SB, JSa (a); A: Surfer and others. 30¢ regional variant	30.00
❑201, Jul 1976, RB, JR (c); SB, JSa (a).	7.00
❑201/30¢, Jul 1976, 30¢ regional variant	20.00
❑202, Aug 1976, RB, JR (c); SB, JSa (a); A: Jarella	7.00
❑202/30¢, Aug 1976, RB (c); SB, JSa (a); 30¢ regional variant	20.00
❑203, Sep 1976, JR (c); SB, JSa (a); V: Psyklop	7.00
❑204, Oct 1976, HT (c); HT (w); HT, JSa (a); O: Hulk. 1: Kronus	7.00
❑205, Nov 1976, HT (c); SB, JSa (a)	7.00
❑206, Dec 1976, DC (c); SB, JSa (a)	7.00
❑207, Jan 1977, DC (c); SB, JSa (a); A: Defenders	7.00
❑208, Feb 1977, SB, JSa (a); Newsstand edition (distributed by Curtis); issue number in box	7.00

INCREDIBLE HULK

Other grades: Multiply price above by 5/6 for VF/NM • 2/3 for VERY FINE • 1/3 for FINE • 1/5 for VERY GOOD • 1/8 for GOOD

N-MINT

❑208/Whitman, Feb 1977, SB, JSa (a); Special markets edition (usually sold in Whitman bagged prepacks); price appears in a diamond; UPC barcode appears 7.00
❑209, Mar 1977, SB, JSa (a); V: Absorbing Man. Newsstand edition (distributed by Curtis); issue number in box 7.00
❑209/Whitman, Mar 1977, SB, JSa (a); V: Absorbing Man. Special markets edition (usually sold in Whitman bagged prepacks); price appears in a diamond; UPC barcode appears 7.00
❑210, Apr 1977, SB (a); A: Doctor Druid. Newsstand edition (distributed by Curtis); issue number in box 7.00
❑210/Whitman, Apr 1977, SB (a); A: Doctor Druid. Special markets edition (usually sold in Whitman bagged prepacks); price appears in a diamond; UPC barcode appears 7.00
❑211, May 1977, SB (a); A: Doctor Druid. Newsstand edition (distributed by Curtis); issue number in box 7.00
❑211/Whitman, May 1977, SB (a); A: Doctor Druid. Special markets edition (usually sold in Whitman bagged prepacks); price appears in a diamond; UPC barcode appears 7.00
❑212, Jun 1977, RB (c); SB (a); 1: Constrictor. V: Constrictor. Newsstand edition (distributed by Curtis); issue number in box 7.00
❑212/Whitman, Jun 1977, RB (c); SB (a); 1: Constrictor. V: Constrictor. Special markets edition (usually sold in Whitman bagged prepacks); price appears in a diamond; UPC barcode appears 7.00
❑212/35¢, Jun 1977, RB (c); SB (a); 1: Constrictor. V: Constrictor. 35¢ regional variant newsstand edition (distributed by Curtis); issue number in box 15.00
❑213, Jul 1977, RB (c); SB, TP (a); V: Quintronic Man. Newsstand edition (distributed by Curtis); issue number in box 7.00
❑213/Whitman, Jul 1977, SB, TP (a); V: Quintronic Man. Special markets edition (usually sold in Whitman bagged prepacks); price appears in a diamond; UPC barcode appears 7.00
❑213/35¢, Jul 1977, RB (c); SB, TP (a); V: Quintronic Man. 35¢ regional variant newsstand edition (distributed by Curtis); issue number in box 15.00
❑214, Aug 1977, RB (c); SB (a); Jack of Hearts; Newsstand edition (distributed by Curtis); issue number in box 7.00
❑214/Whitman, Aug 1977, SB (a); Special markets edition (usually sold in Whitman bagged prepacks); price appears in a diamond; UPC barcode appears 7.00
❑214/35¢, Aug 1977, RB (c); SB (a); Jack of Hearts; 35¢ regional variant newsstand edition (distributed by Curtis); issue number in box 15.00
❑215, Sep 1977, RB (c); SB (a); 1: Bi-Beast II. Newsstand edition (distributed by Curtis); issue number in box 7.00
❑215/Whitman, Sep 1977, SB (a); 1: Bi-Beast II. Special markets edition (usually sold in Whitman bagged prepacks); price appears in a diamond; UPC barcode appears 7.00
❑215/35¢, Sep 1977, RB (c); SB (a); 1: Bi-Beast II. 35¢ regional variant newsstand edition (distributed by Curtis); issue number in box 15.00
❑216, Oct 1977, RB (c); SB (a); V: Bi-Beast II. Newsstand edition (distributed by Curtis); issue number in box 7.00
❑216/Whitman, Oct 1977, SB (a); V: Bi-Beast II. Special markets edition (usually sold in Whitman bagged prepacks); price appears in a diamond; no UPC barcode 7.00
❑216/35¢, Oct 1977, RB (c); SB (a); V: Bi-Beast II. 35¢ regional variant newsstand edition (distributed by Curtis); issue number in box 15.00
❑217, Nov 1977, JSn (c); SB (a); V: Circus of Crime. Newsstand edition (distributed by Curtis); issue number in box 7.00
❑217/Whitman, Nov 1977, JSn (c); SB (a); V: Circus of Crime. Special markets edition (usually sold in Whitman bagged prepacks); price appears in a diamond; no UPC barcode 7.00
❑218, Dec 1977, KP, GT (a); Doc Samson vs. Rhino; Newsstand edition (distributed by Curtis); issue number in box 7.00

N-MINT

❑218/Whitman, Dec 1977, KP, GT (a); Special markets edition (usually sold in Whitman bagged prepacks); price appears in a diamond; no UPC barcode 7.00
❑219, Jan 1978, SB (a); V: Cap'n Barracuda 5.00
❑220, Feb 1978, SB (a); V: Cap'n Barracuda 5.00
❑221, Mar 1978, RB (c); SB, AA (a); A: Stingray 5.00
❑222, Apr 1978, JSn (w); JSn, AA (a); Newsstand edition (distributed by Curtis); issue number in box 5.00
❑222/Whitman, Apr 1978, JSn, AA (a); Special markets edition (usually sold in Whitman bagged prepacks); price appears in a diamond; UPC barcode appears 5.00
❑223, May 1978, RB (c); SB (a); Newsstand edition (distributed by Curtis); issue number in box 5.00
❑223/Whitman, May 1978, SB (a); Special markets edition (usually sold in Whitman bagged prepacks); price appears in a diamond; no UPC barcode 5.00
❑224, Jun 1978, SB (a); Newsstand edition (distributed by Curtis); issue number in box 5.00
❑224/Whitman, Jun 1978, SB (a); Special markets edition (usually sold in Whitman bagged prepacks); price appears in a diamond; no UPC barcode 5.00
❑225, Jul 1978, SB (a) 5.00
❑226, Aug 1978, SB, JSt (a); Newsstand edition (distributed by Curtis); issue number in box 5.00
❑226/Whitman, Aug 1978, SB, JSt (a); Special markets edition (usually sold in Whitman bagged prepacks); price appears in a diamond; UPC barcode appears 5.00
❑227, Sep 1978, HT (c); SB, KJ (a); Doc Samson; Newsstand edition (distributed by Curtis); issue number in box 5.00
❑227/Whitman, Sep 1978, HT (c); SB, KJ (a); Special markets edition (usually sold in Whitman bagged prepacks); price appears in a diamond; no UPC barcode 5.00
❑228, Oct 1978, HT, BMc (c); SB, BMc (a); O: Moonstone. 1: Moonstone. Newsstand edition (distributed by Curtis); issue number in box 5.00
❑228/Whitman, Oct 1978, HT, BMc (c); SB, BMc (a); O: Moonstone. 1: Moonstone. Special markets edition (usually sold in Whitman bagged prepacks); price appears in a diamond; no UPC barcode 5.00
❑229, Nov 1978, BL, HT (c); SB (a); A: Moonstone. A: Doc Samson. Newsstand edition (distributed by Curtis); issue number in box 5.00
❑229/Whitman, Nov 1978, BL, HT (c); SB (a); A: Moonstone. A: Doc Samson. Special markets edition (usually sold in Whitman bagged prepacks); price appears in a diamond; no UPC barcode 5.00
❑230, Dec 1978, BL (c); BL, JM (a); Newsstand edition (distributed by Curtis); issue number in box 5.00
❑230/Whitman, Dec 1978, BL (c); BL, JM (a); Special markets edition (usually sold in Whitman bagged prepacks); price appears in a diamond; no UPC barcode 5.00
❑231, Jan 1979, HT (c); SB (a); Newsstand edition (distributed by Curtis); issue number in box 5.00
❑231/Whitman, Jan 1979, HT (c); SB (a); Special markets edition (usually sold in Whitman bagged prepacks); price appears in a diamond; no UPC barcode 5.00
❑232, Feb 1979, (c); SB (a); A: Captain America. Newsstand edition (distributed by Curtis); issue number in box 5.00
❑232/Whitman, Feb 1979, (c); SB (a); A: Captain America. Special markets edition (usually sold in Whitman bagged prepacks); price appears in a diamond; no UPC barcode 5.00
❑233, Mar 1979, AM (c); SB (a); A: Marvel Man (Quasar). 5.00
❑234, Apr 1979, AM (c); SB, JAb (a); 1: Quasar. (Marvel Man changed name to Quasar) 5.00
❑235, May 1979, AM (c); SB (a); A: Machine Man. Newsstand edition (distributed by Curtis); issue number in box 5.00

N-MINT

❑235/Whitman, May 1979, AM (c); SB (a); A: Machine Man. Special markets edition (usually sold in Whitman bagged prepacks); price appears in a diamond; no UPC barcode 5.00
❑236, Jun 1979, AM (c); SB (a); A: Machine Man 5.00
❑237, Jul 1979, AM (c); SB, JAb (a) 5.00
❑238, Aug 1979, AM (c); SB, JAb (a) 5.00
❑239, Sep 1979, AM (c); SB (a) 5.00
❑240, Oct 1979, AM (c); SB, JSt (a) 5.00
❑241, Nov 1979, SB (a) 4.00
❑242, Dec 1979, BL (c); SB (a); V: Tyranus 4.00
❑243, Jan 1980, AM (c); SB (a); A: Power Man and Iron Fist 4.00
❑244, Feb 1980, AM (c); CI (a); D: It, the Living Colossus 4.00
❑245, Mar 1980, AM (c); SB (a) 4.00
❑246, Apr 1980, RB, JAb (c); SB (a); A: Captain Marvel 4.00
❑247, May 1980, AM (c); SB (a); A: Jarella 4.00
❑248, Jun 1980, MG (c); SB (a); V: Gardener 4.00
❑249, Jul 1980, SD (c); SD (a); A: Jack Frost 4.00
❑250, Aug 1980, Giant-sized; AM (c); SB (a); 1: Sabra (cameo). A: Silver Surfer 7.00
❑251, Sep 1980, MG (c); SB (a); A: 3-D Man 2.50
❑252, Oct 1980, RB, FS (c); SB (a); A: Changelings 2.50
❑253, Nov 1980, RB, FS (c); SB (a); A: Doc Samson. A: Changelings 2.50
❑254, Dec 1980, AM (c); SB (a); 1&O: X-Ray. 1&O: Vector. 1&O: U-Foes. 1&O: Ironclad 2.50
❑255, Jan 1981, AM, RB (c); SB (a); V: Thor 2.50
❑256, Feb 1981, AM, RB (c); SB (a); 1&O: Sabra 2.50
❑257, Mar 1981, AM, RB, TD (c); SB (a); 1&O: Arabian Knight 2.50
❑258, Apr 1981, AM, FM (c); SB (a); 1&O: Ursa Major 2.50
❑259, May 1981, AM, PB, FM (c); AM, SB (a); O: Presence. O: Vanguard. A: Soviet Super-Soldiers 2.50
❑260, Jun 1981, AM (c); SB (a) 2.50
❑261, Jul 1981, FM (c); SB (a); V: Absorbing Man 2.50
❑262, Aug 1981, AM (c); SB (a); 1: Glazier 2.50
❑263, Sep 1981, AM (c); SB (a); V: Landslide, Avalanche. V: Landslide, Avalanche 2.50
❑264, Oct 1981, FM (c); SB (a) 2.50
❑265, Nov 1981, AM (c); SB (a); 1: Shooting Star. 1: Firebird. V: Rangers 2.50
❑266, Dec 1981, AM (c); SB (a); V: High Evolutionary 2.50
❑267, Jan 1982, AM, FM (c); SB (a); O: Glorian. V: Glorian 2.50
❑268, Feb 1982, FM (c); SB (a); O: Rick Jones 2.50
❑269, Mar 1982, AM (c); SB (a) 2.50
❑270, Apr 1982, AM (c); SB (a) 2.50
❑271, May 1982, 20th Anniversary Issue; AM (c); SB (a); 1: Rocket Raccoon 2.50
❑272, Jun 1982, AM (c); SB (a); A: Alpha Flight 2.50
❑273, Jul 1982, SB (a); A: Alpha Flight .. 2.50
❑274, Aug 1982, AM (c); SB (a) 2.50
❑275, Sep 1982, SB, JSt (a); V: Megalith 2.50
❑276, Oct 1982, SB, JSt (a); V: U-Foes .. 2.50
❑277, Nov 1982, SB (c); SB (a); V: U-Foes 2.50
❑278, Dec 1982, AM, SB (c); SB, JSt (a); Hulk granted amnesty 2.50
❑279, Jan 1983 .... 2.50
❑280, Feb 1983, SB (a) 2.50
❑281, Mar 1983, SB, JSt (a) 2.50
❑282, Apr 1983, AM, JSt (c); SB, JSt (a); A: She-Hulk 2.50
❑283, May 1983, AM (c); SB, JSt (a); A: Avengers 2.50
❑284, Jun 1983, AM, JSt (c); SB, JSt (a); A: Avengers. V: Leader 2.50
❑285, Jul 1983, JSt (c); SB (a) 2.50
❑286, Aug 1983, BA (c); SB (a) 4.00
❑287, Sep 1983, AM (c); SB (a) 2.50
❑288, Oct 1983, AM, JSt (c); SB, JM (a); V: Modok. V: M.O.D.O.K 2.50
❑289, Nov 1983, AM (c); SB, JSt (a); V: A.I.M 2.50
❑290, Dec 1983, AM (c); SB (a); V: Modok. V: Modame. V: M.O.D.O.K 2.50

Impossible Man Summer Vacation Spectacular

Generally silly stories of the alien imp

©Marvel

Impulse

Tales of a speedy and impulsive teen-ager

©DC

Incomplete Death's Head

Early cyborg stories from Marvel UK

©Marvel

Incredible Hulk

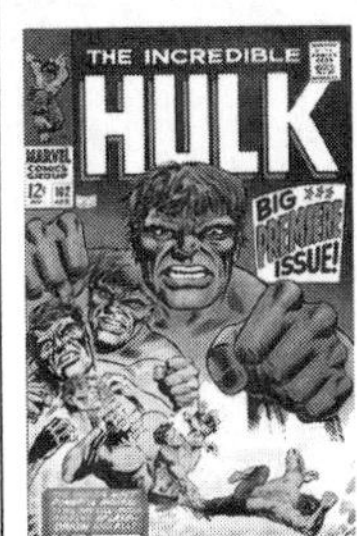

Title picks up Tales to Astonish numbering

©Marvel

Incredible Hulk

First 11 issues were simply titled "Hulk"

©Marvel

N-MINT

❑291, Jan 1984, SB (a); O: Thunderbolt Ross. Assistant Editor Month 2.50
❑292, Feb 1984, KN (c); SB, JSt (a)....... 2.50
❑293, Mar 1984, SB (a); V: Fantastic Four 2.50
❑294, Apr 1984, SB (a) 2.50
❑295, May 1984, BSz (c); SB (a); V: Boomerang. Secret Wars aftermath 2.50
❑296, Jun 1984, BSz (c); SB (a); V: ROM 5.00
❑297, Jul 1984, BSz (c); SB (a)............. 4.00
❑298, Aug 1984, KN (c); SB (a); A: Nightmare 2.50
❑299, Sep 1984, SB (a); A: Doctor Strange 2.50
❑300, Oct 1984, 300th anniversary edition; (c); SB (a); V: Everybody. Hulk banished to Crossroads...................... 4.00
❑301, Nov 1984, BSz (c); SB (a) 2.50
❑302, Dec 1984, SB (a).......................... 2.50
❑303, Jan 1985, SB (a) 2.50
❑304, Feb 1985, SB (a); NOTE4SUPPORT: cover ink listed as Mundelo alias for Nowlan 2.50
❑305, Mar 1985, SB (a); V: U-Foes 2.50
❑306, Apr 1985, SB (a) 2.50
❑307, May 1985, SB (a) 2.50
❑308, Jun 1985, SB (a) 2.50
❑309, Jul 1985, SB (a) 2.50
❑310, Aug 1985, AW (c); AW (a)........... 2.50
❑311, Sep 1985, AW (c)......................... 2.50
❑312, Oct 1985, BSz (c);Secret Wars II . 2.50
❑313, Nov 1985, A: Alpha Flight. Continued into Alpha Flight (1st Series) #29.......... 2.50
❑314, Dec 1985, JBy (c); JBy (w); JBy, BWi (a); A: Doc Samson.................... 2.50
❑315, Jan 1986, JBy (c); JBy (w); JBy (a); Hulk and Banner separated................ 3.00
❑316, Feb 1986, JBy (c); JBy (w); JBy (a); A: Avengers 3.00
❑317, Mar 1986, JBy (c); JBy (w); JBy (a) 3.00
❑318, Apr 1986, JBy (c); JBy (w); JBy (a) 3.00
❑319, May 1986, JBy (c); JBy (w); JBy (a); Wedding of Bruce Banner and Betty Ross 3.00
❑320, Jun 1986, AM, (c); AM (w); AM (a); V: Doc Samson.................................. 2.00
❑321, Jul 1986, AM, BWi (c); AM (w); AM (a); V: Avengers................................. 2.00
❑322, Aug 1986, AM (c); AM (w); AM (a) 2.00
❑323, Sep 1986, AM (c); AM (w); AM (a) 2.00
❑324, Oct 1986, AM (c); AM (w); AM (a); O: Hulk. 1: Grey Hulk (new); Hulk turns Grey.. 5.00
❑325, Nov 1986, AM (c); AM (w); AM, BMc (a); 1: Rick Jones as green Hulk. 3.00
❑326, Dec 1986, BMc (c); AM (w); Green Hulk vs. Grey Hulk............................. 3.50
❑327, Jan 1987, AM (c); AM (w); V: Zzzax 2.50
❑328, Feb 1987, BMc (c); PD (w); TD (a); 1st Peter David writing 2.50
❑329, Mar 1987, AM (c); AM (w); AM (a) 2.00
❑330, Apr 1987, TMc (c); AM, PD (w); AM, TMc (a); D: Thunderbolt Ross 5.00
❑331, May 1987, PD (w); TMc (a); 2nd Peter David issue; gray Hulk revealed. 5.00
❑332, Jun 1987, BMc (c); PD (w); TMc (a) 5.00
❑333, Jul 1987, (c); PD (w); TMc (a) 5.00
❑334, Aug 1987, TMc, (c); PD (w); TMc (a).. 5.00
❑335, Sep 1987, BMc (c); PD (w).......... 2.00
❑336, Oct 1987, BMc (c); PD (w); TMc (a); A: X-Factor 3.00

N-MINT

❑337, Nov 1987, BMc (c); PD (w); TMc (a); A: X-Factor 3.00
❑338, Dec 1987, (c); PD (w); TMc (a); 1: Mercy 3.00
❑339, Jan 1988, BMc (c); PD (w); TMc (a); A: Ashcan, Leader........................ 3.00
❑340, Feb 1988, TMc, BWi (c); PD (w); TMc (a); V: Wolverine........................ 14.00
❑341, Mar 1988, TMc (c); PD (w); TMc (a); V: Man-Bull 4.00
❑342, Apr 1988, TMc (c); PD (w); TMc (a); A: Leader 2.00
❑343, May 1988, TMc (c); PD (w); TMc (a) 2.00
❑344, Jun 1988, TMc, BWi (c); PD (w); TMc, BWi (a) 2.00
❑345, Jul 1988, Double-size; TMc (c); PD (w); TMc (a) 2.00
❑346, Aug 1988, TMc, EL (c); PD (w); TMc, EL (a) 2.00
❑347, Sep 1988, PD (w); MGu (a); in Vegas 2.00
❑348, Oct 1988, MGu (c); PD (w); MGu (a); V: Absorbing Man. V: Absorbing Man 2.00
❑349, Nov 1988, BMc (c); PD (w); A: Spider-Man 2.00
❑350, Dec 1988, PD (w); Hulk vs. Thing 5.00
❑351, Jan 1989, PD (w); BWi (a).......... 2.00
❑352, Feb 1989, PD (w)......................... 2.00
❑353, Mar 1989, PD (w) 2.00
❑354, Apr 1989, PD (w)......................... 2.00
❑355, May 1989, PD (w); HT (a); A: Glorian 2.00
❑356, Jun 1989, BMc (c); PD (w).......... 2.00
❑357, Jul 1989, BMc (c); PD (w) 2.00
❑358, Aug 1989, PD (w) 2.00
❑359, Sep 1989, JBy (c); PD (w) 2.00
❑360, Oct 1989, BMc (c); V: Nightmare. 2.00
❑361, Nov 1989, BMc (c); PD (w); Iron Man 2.00
❑362, Nov 1989, KN (c); PD (w); A: Werewolf by Night.......................... 2.00
❑363, Dec 1989, GC (c); PD (w); V: Grey Gargoyle. Acts of Vengeance............. 2.00
❑364, Dec 1989, PD (w); V: Abomination 2.00
❑365, Jan 1990, PD (w); V: Thing......... 2.00
❑366, Feb 1990, PD (w); V: Leader........ 2.00
❑367, Mar 1990, PD (w); V: Madman. 1st Dale Keown art............................. 2.00
❑368, Apr 1990, PD (w); 1: Pantheon. V: Mr. Hyde; 1: Agamemnon 2.00
❑369, May 1990, (c); PD (w); BMc (a); V: Freedom Force 2.00
❑370, Jun 1990, BMc (c); PD (w); BMc (a); A: Doctor Strange. A: Sub-Mariner 2.00
❑371, Jul 1990, BMc (c); PD (w); BMc (a); A: Doctor Strange. A: Sub-Mariner..... 2.00
❑372, Aug 1990, PD (w); BMc (a); Green Hulk returns 3.00
❑373, Sep 1990, BMc (c); PD (w).......... 2.00
❑374, Oct 1990, BMc (c); PD (w); BMc (a); V: Super Skrull............................ 2.00
❑375, Nov 1990, BMc (c); PD (w); BMc (a); V: Super Skrull............................ 2.00
❑376, Dec 1990, BMc (c); PD (w); BMc (a); 1: Agamemnon (as hologram). Green Hulk vs. Grey Hulk 2.00
❑377, Jan 1991, BMc (c); PD (w); BMc (a); 1: Hulk (new, smart). Fluorescent inks on cover...................................... 2.50

N-MINT

❑377/2nd, Jan 1991, BMc (c); PD (w); BMc (a); 1: Hulk (new, smart). Fluorescent inks on cover; 2nd printing (gold).................. 2.00
❑377/3rd, Jan 1991, BMc (c); PD (w); BMc (a); 3rd printing.......................... 2.00
❑378, Feb 1991, BMc (c); KB, PD (w); Rhino as Santa.................................. 3.00
❑379, Mar 1991, BMc (c); PD (w); A: Pantheon... 2.00
❑380, Apr 1991, PD (w); Doc Samson solo story 2.00
❑381, May 1991, PD (w); Hulk joins Pantheon.. 2.00
❑382, Jun 1991, BMc (c); PD (w) 2.00
❑383, Jul 1991, PD (w); V: Abomination 2.00
❑384, Aug 1991, PD (w); V: Abomination. Infinity Gauntlet; tiny Hulk.................. 2.00
❑385, Sep 1991, PD (w); Infinity Gauntlet 4.00
❑386, Oct 1991, PD (w); A: Sabra.......... 3.00
❑387, Nov 1991, PD (w); A: Sabra. V: Sabra 2.00
❑388, Dec 1991, PD (w); 1: Speedfreek. 2.00
❑389, Jan 1992, A: Man-Thing 2.00
❑390, Feb 1992, PD (w) 2.00
❑391, Mar 1992, PD (w); A: X-Factor..... 2.00
❑392, Apr 1992, PD (w); A: X-Factor 3.00
❑393, May 1992, 30th Anniversary of the Hulk, Green Foil Cover; PD (w); HT (a); A: X-Factor. Green Foil Cover............. 4.00
❑393/2nd, May 1992, 30th Anniversary of the Hulk; PD (w); HT (a); non-foil cover 2.50
❑394, Jun 1992, PD (w); 1: Trauma 3.00
❑395, Jul 1992, PD (w); A: Punisher 1.50
❑396, Aug 1992, PD (w); A: Punisher. V: Mr. Frost. V: Doctor Octopus.......... 1.50
❑397, Sep 1992, PD (w); V: U-Foes....... 1.50
❑398, Oct 1992, PD (w); V: Leader........ 1.50
❑399, Nov 1992, JDu (c); PD (w); JDu (a); D: Marlo 1.50
❑400, Dec 1992, SL, PD (w); SD, JDu (a); D: Leader. Marlo revived; Prism cover 3.00
❑400/2nd, Dec 1992, SL, PD (w); SD, JDu (a); 2nd printing; D: Leader; Marlo revived 2.50
❑401, Jan 1993, PD (w); JDu (a); 1: Agamemnon (physical). V: U-Foes. 1.50
❑402, Feb 1993, PD (w); JDu (a); A: Doc Samson. V: Juggernaut...................... 1.50
❑403, Mar 1993, PD (w); V: Juggernaut 1.50
❑404, Apr 1993, PD (w); A: Avengers. V: Juggernaut 1.50
❑405, May 1993, PD (w)......................... 1.50
❑406, Jun 1993, PD (w); A: Doc Samson. A: Captain America 1.50
❑407, Jul 1993, PD (w); 1: Piecemeal.... 1.50
❑408, Aug 1993, PD (w); D: Perseus. V: Madman... 1.50
❑409, Sep 1993, PD (w); A: Killpower. A: Motormouth................................. 1.50
❑410, Oct 1993, PD (w); A: Doctor Samson. A: S.H.I.E.L.D.. A: Nick Fury 1.50
❑411, Nov 1993, PD (w); A: Nick Fury... 1.50
❑412, Dec 1993, PD (w); A: She-Hulk. V: Bi-Beast... 1.50
❑413, Jan 1994, PD (w)......................... 1.50
❑414, Feb 1994, PD (w); A: Silver Surfer 1.50
❑415, Mar 1994, PD (w); A: Starjammers 1.50
❑416, Apr 1994, PD (w)......................... 1.50
❑417, May 1994, PD (w); Rick's bachelor party.. 1.50

❑418, Jun 1994, PD (w); D: Sandman. Wedding of Rick Jones and Marlo; Peter David (writer) puts himself in script....... 2.00

❑418/Variant, Jun 1994, PD (w); D: Sandman. Die-cut cover; Wedding of Rick Jones and Marlo; Peter David (writer) puts himself in script............ 3.00

❑419, Jul 1994, PD (w); V: Talos the Tamed 1.50

❑420, Aug 1994, PD (w); D: Jim Wilson 1.50

❑421, Sep 1994, PD (w); V: Thor; Pantheon and Hulk track Agamemnon to Asgard .. 1.50

❑422, Oct 1994, PD (w)........................ 1.50

❑423, Nov 1994, PD (w); A: Hel............ 1.50

❑424, Dec 1994, PD (w); Trial of Agamemnon.. 1.50

❑425, Jan 1995, Giant-size; PD (w); V: Endless Knights; Hulk reverts to Bruce Banner when enraged.............. 2.25

❑425/Variant, Jan 1995, Giant-size; PD (w); Hologram cover........................ 3.50

❑426, Feb 1995, PD (w); Hulk reverts to Banner.. 1.50

❑426/Deluxe, Feb 1995, Deluxe edition; PD (w); Mercy calms enraged Banner 1.95

❑427, Mar 1995, PD (w); A: Man-Thing. Bonus Hulk & Man-Thing Pin-Up....... 1.50

❑427/Deluxe, Mar 1995, PD (w); V: Man-Thing; Bonus Hulk & Man-Thing Pin-Up 1.95

❑428, Apr 1995, PD (w); A: Man-Thing.. 1.50

❑428/Deluxe, Apr 1995, PD (w); V: Man-Thing..................................... 1.95

❑429, May 1995, (c); PD (w)................ 1.50

❑429/Deluxe, May 1995, (c); PD (w)...... 1.95

❑430, Jun 1995, PD (w); V: Speedfreek. 1.95

❑431, Jul 1995, (c); PD (w); V: Abomination 1.95

❑432, Aug 1995, (c); PD (w); V: Abomination 1.95

❑433, Sep 1995, PD (w); A: Punisher. A: Nick Fury.. 1.95

❑434, Oct 1995, (c); PD (w); AM (a); A: Howling Commandoes. Funeral of Nick Fury; OverPower cards inserted.. 1.95

❑435, Nov 1995, AM (c); PD (w); AM (a); V: Rhino. Casey at the Bat tribute....... 1.95

❑436, Dec 1995, (c); PD (w); A: Maestro. continued in Cutting Edge #1............. 1.95

❑437, Jan 1996, AM (c); PD (w)............ 1.95

❑438, Feb 1996, (c); PD (w).................. 1.95

❑439, Mar 1996, (c); PD (w); Deranged Hulk destroys Mount Rushmore............ 1.95

❑440, Apr 1996, (c); PD (w); V: Thor..... 1.95

❑441, May 1996, (c); PD (w); A: She-Hulk. Pulp Fiction tribute cover.................. 1.95

❑442, Jun 1996, (c); PD (w); A: She-Hulk. A: Doc Samson. A: Molecule Man. no Hulk.. 1.95

❑443, Jul 1996, (c); PD (w); A: Janis..... 1.50

❑444, Aug 1996, PD (w); V: Cable. V: Cable 1.50

❑445, Sep 1996, PD (w); A: Avengers.... 1.50

❑446, Oct 1996, PD (w); post-Onslaught; Hulk turns savage and highly radioactive.. 1.50

❑447, Nov 1996, PD (w)........................ 1.50

❑448, Dec 1996, PD (w); A: Pantheon... 1.50

❑449, Jan 1997, PD (w); 1: The Thunderbolts 8.00

❑450, Feb 1997, Giant-size; PD (w); A: Doctor Strange. connection to Heroes Reborn universe revealed....... 5.00

❑451, Mar 1997, PD (w); Hulk takes over Duck Key.. 2.00

❑452, Apr 1997, PD (w); Hulk vs. Hurricane Betty.................................. 2.00

❑453, May 1997, PD (w); Hulk vs. Hulk. 2.00

❑454, Jun 1997, PD (w); V: Wolverine; In Savage Land...................................... 2.00

❑455, Aug 1997, gatefold summary; PD (w); DGr (a); A: Apocalypse. V: X-Men. Thunderbolt Ross returns.................. 2.00

❑456, Sep 1997, gatefold summary; PD (w); JKu (a); Apocalypse transforms Hulk into War.................................... 2.00

❑457, Oct 1997, gatefold summary; PD (w); V: Juggernaut; 1: Akhenaten (Amenhotep IV)................................. 2.00

❑458, Nov 1997, gatefold summary; PD (w); A: Mercy. V: Mr. Hyde................. 2.00

❑459, Dec 1997, gatefold summary; PD (w); A: Mercy. V: Abomination............ 2.00

❑460, Jan 1998, gatefold summary; (c); PD (w); The Hulk and Bruce Banner are reunited; return of Maestro................ 2.00

❑461, Feb 1998, gatefold summary; PD (w); V: Destroyer; V: Maestro-empowered Destroyer.......................... 2.00

❑462, Mar 1998, gatefold summary; PD (w) 2.00

❑463, Apr 1998, gatefold summary; PD (w); Troyjan kidnaps Hulk and Thunderbolt Ross............................. 2.00

❑464, May 1998, gatefold summary; JKu (c); PD (w); JKu (a); A: Silver Surfer.. 2.00

❑465, Jun 1998, gatefold summary; (c); PD (w); A: Reed Richards. A: Tony Stark 2.00

❑466, Jul 1998, gatefold summary; PD (w); D: Betty Banner.......................... 2.00

❑467, Aug 1998, gatefold summary; PD (w); final Peter David-written issue.... 2.00

❑468, Sep 1998, gatefold summary; 1st Joe Casey issue.......................... 2.00

❑469, Oct 1998, gatefold summary; (c); V: Super-Adaptoid............................. 2.00

❑470, Nov 1998, gatefold summary; (c); V: Circus of Crime............................ 2.00

❑471, Dec 1998, gatefold summary; V: Circus of Crime............................ 2.00

❑472, Jan 1999, gatefold summary; (c); A: Xantarean.. 2.00

❑473, Feb 1999, gatefold summary; A: Xanterean. A: Watchers.................. 1.99

❑474, Mar 1999, (c); A: Xanterean. A: Watchers. A: Abomination. A: Thunderbolt Ross. Final Issue........ 1.99

❑Ann 1, Oct 1968, JSo (c); SL (w); HT (a) 115.00

❑Ann 2, Oct 1969, SD, JK (a); Reprints from Incredible Hulk #3 and Tales to Astonish #62-66................................ 40.00

❑Ann 3, Jan 1971, Cover reads "King-Size Special"; SL (w); JK (a); Cover reads King-Size Special; Reprints from Tales to Astonish #70-74........................... 25.00

❑Ann 4, Jan 1972, HT (c); SL (w); JK, JR (a); Cover reads "Special"; Reprints from Tales to Astonish #75-77 and Not Brand Ecch #5.................................. 25.00

❑Ann 5, ca. 1976, SB, JK, (c); SB, JAb (a); V: Xemnu. V: Groot. V: Diablo. V: Diablo. V: Blip. V: Taboo. V: Goom................ 9.00

❑Ann 6, ca. 1977, HT, (c); HT (a); 1: Paragon. A: Warlock. A: Doctor Strange. Doctor Strange................... 7.00

❑Ann 7, ca. 1978, JBy, BL (c); JBy (w); JBy, BL (a); A: Iceman. A: Angel. V: Master Mold................................. 9.00

❑Ann 8, ca. 1979, AM, (c); JBy (w); SB, AA (a); Alpha Flight........................... 5.00

❑Ann 9, ca. 1980, SD, (c); AM, SD (a)... 3.00

❑Ann 10, ca. 1981, AM, (c); AM (a); Captain Universe.............................. 4.00

❑Ann 11, ca. 1982, AM (c); RB, FM (a); First Frank Miller Marvel pencils........ 3.00

❑Ann 12, ca. 1983, BA (c); HT, BA (a).... 2.50

❑Ann 13, ca. 1984.................................. 2.50

❑Ann 14, ca. 1985.................................. 2.50

❑Ann 15, ca. 1986, V: Abomination........ 2.50

❑Ann 16, ca. 1990, PD (w); HT (a); Lifeform 2.50

❑Ann 17, ca. 1991, Ann 1991................. 2.50

❑Ann 18, ca. 1992, JRo, PD (w); Return of Defenders...................................... 2.75

❑Ann 19, ca. 1993, 1: Lazarus. Polybagged with trading card............ 2.95

❑Ann 20, ca. 1994.................................. 4.00

❑Ann 1997, ca. 1997, Hulk vs. Gladiator; Incredible Hulk '97........................... 2.99

❑Ann 1998, ca. 1998, gatefold summary; wraparound cover; Hulk/Sub-Mariner '98 2.99

❑Ashcan 1, Spr 1994, ashcan edition; Date is actually Spring/Summer......... 1.00

Incredible Hulk
Marvel

❑12, Mar 2000; SB (c); SB (a); Was "Hulk" 2.50

❑13, Apr 2000 SB (c); SB (a)................ 2.50

❑14, May 2000 SB (c); SB (a).............. 2.50

❑15, Jun 2000 SB (c); SB (a)................ 2.50

❑16, Jul 2000; SB (c); SB (a); Hulk (Professor) confronts Nick Fury about General Ryker.................................... 2.50

❑17, Aug 2000; SB (c); SB (a); Hulk (Professor) V: Flux.......................... 2.50

❑18, Sep 2000; SB (c); SB (a); General Ryker captures Hulk (Professor)........ 2.50

❑19, Oct 2000; SB (a); General Ryker experiments on Hulk (Professor)....... 2.50

❑20, Nov 2000; SB (c); SB (a); Hulk (Professor) V: Flux; Thunderbolt Ross V: General Ryker................................ 2.50

❑21, Dec 2000.. 2.25

❑22, Jan 2001... 2.25

❑23, Feb 2001... 2.25

❑24, Mar 2001; JR2 (c); JR2, DG (a); A: Abomination. A: Thunderbolt Ross. lower cover price; part of Marvel's Slashback program.......................... 2.00

❑25, Apr 2001; double-sized; JR2 (c); JR2, TP (a); A: Abomination.............. 2.99

❑26, May 2001; Hulk (Savage Hulk) V: Killer Shrike................................... 2.25

❑27, Jun 2001 JR2 (c); JR2, TP (a)....... 2.25

❑28, Jul 2001 (c); JR2, TP (a).............. 2.25

❑29, Aug 2001... 2.25

❑30, Sep 2001 TP (a).............................. 2.25

❑31, Oct 2001 TP (a).............................. 2.25

❑32, Nov 2001 TP (a).............................. 2.25

❑33, Dec 2001... 2.25

❑34, Jan 2002 JR2, TP (a)..................... 12.50

❑35, Feb 2002; JR2, TP (a); 'Nuff Said silent story.. 6.00

❑36, Mar 2002 JR2, TP (a)..................... 5.00

❑37, Apr 2002 JR2, TP (a)..................... 5.00

❑38, May 2002; JR2, TP (a); Norman Rockwell spoof cover......................... 5.00

❑39, Jun 2002; JR2, TP (a); wraparound cover.. 4.00

❑40, Jul 2002; TP (a); wraparound cover 4.00

❑41, Aug 2002; TP (a); wraparound cover 4.00

❑42, Aug 2002; TP (a); wraparound cover 3.00

❑43, Sep 2002; JR2 (a); wraparound cover.. 3.00

❑44, Oct 2002; wraparound cover......... 3.00

❑45, Nov 2002; wraparound cover......... 3.00

❑46, Dec 2002; wraparound cover......... 2.50

❑47, Jan 2003; wraparound cover......... 2.25

❑48, Feb 2003; wraparound cover......... 2.25

❑49, Mar 2003; wraparound cover......... 2.25

❑50, Apr 2003; wraparound cover......... 5.00

❑51, May 2003.. 4.00

❑52, Jun 2003... 3.00

❑53, Jun 2003... 3.00

❑54, Jul 2003; V: Abomination............... 3.00

❑55, Aug 2003.. 2.00

❑56, Aug 2003, V: Absorbing Man......... 2.25

❑57, Sep 2003, V: Absorbing Man......... 2.25

❑58, Sep 2003, V: Absorbing Man......... 2.25

❑59, Oct 2003, V: Absorbing Man.......... 2.25

❑60, Nov 2003.. 2.25

❑61, Nov 2003.. 2.25

❑62, Dec 2003.. 2.25

❑63, Jan 2004... 2.25

❑64, Feb 2004... 2.99

❑65, Mar 2004.. 2.25

❑66, Apr 2004... 2.25

❑67, Apr 2004... 2.99

❑68, May 2004.. 2.99

❑69, May 2004.. 2.99

❑70, Jun 2004... 2.99

❑71, Jun 2004, A: . A: Tony Stark.......... 2.99

❑72, Jul 2004, A: Tony Stark................. 2.99

❑73, Aug 2004.. 2.25

❑74, Sep 2004... 2.25

❑75, Oct 2004; Giant-Size...................... 3.50

❑76, Nov 2004.. 3.50

❑77, Dec 2005.. 2.99

❑78, Feb 2005... 2.99

❑79, Mar 2005.. 2.99

❑80, Apr 2005... 2.99

❑81, May 2005; Homage cover to Frank Frazetta (Death Dealer)....................... 2.99

❑82, Jun 2005... 2.99

❑83, Jul 2005.. 5.00

❑83/Variant, Jul 2005............................. 4.00

❑84, Aug 2005; House of M tie-in; Picture of hulk is green.................................. 2.99

❑84/Variant, Aug 2005............................ 4.00

❑85, Sep 2005; House of M.................... 2.99

❑86, Oct 2005; House of M..................... 2.99

❑87, Dec 2005.. 2.99

❑88, Jan 2006... 2.99

❑89, Jan 2006... 2.99

❑90, Feb 2006... 2.99

❑91, Mar 2006.. 2.99

❑92, Apr 2006, Planet Hulk.................... 25.00

❑92/2nd, Apr 2006.................................. 6.00

❑93, Jun 2006, Planet Hulk.................... 2.99

❑94, Jul 2006, Planet Hulk..................... 2.99

❑95, Aug 2006, Planet Hulk.................... 2.99

❑96, Sep 2006, Planet Hulk.................... 2.99

❑97, Oct 2006, Planet Hulk.................... 2.99

❑98, Nov 2006, Planet Hulk.................... 2.99

Incredible Hulk and Wolverine

Reprints first Wolverine story
©Marvel

Incredible Hulk, The: Future Imperfect

Celebrated Peter David future tale
©Marvel

Incredible Hulk: Hercules Unleashed

Follow-up to the Onslaught storyline
©Marvel

Incredible Hulk Megazine

Giant-sized issue with plenty of reprints
©Marvel

Incredible Hulk vs. Quasimodo

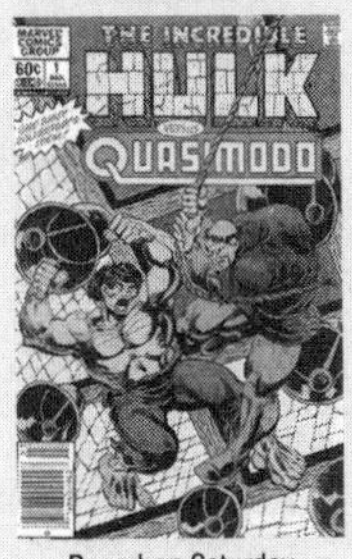

Based on Saturday morning cartoon episode
©Marvel

N-MINT

❑99, Dec 2006, V: Spikes; Planet Hulk ... 2.99
❑100, Jan 2007, Planet Hulk; Also includes Incredible Hulk (1st Series) #3, #152-153 ... 3.99
❑100/Variant, Jan 2007 ... 3.99
❑101, Feb 2007, Planet Hulk ... 2.99
❑102, Mar 2007, Planet Hulk ... 2.99
❑103 ... 2.99
❑104 ... 2.99
❑105 ... 2.99
❑106 ... 2.99
❑107 ... 2.99
❑108 ... 2.99
❑109 ... 2.99
❑110 ... 2.99
❑111 ... 2.99
❑112 ... 2.99
❑Ann 1999, Oct 1999 DGr (c); FH, JBy (w); FH, DGr, KJ (a) ... 5.00
❑Ann 2000; A: She-Hulk. A: Avengers. V: Avengers ... 3.50
❑Ann 2001, Nov 2001 (c); EL (w) ... 2.99

Incredible Hulk and Wolverine
Marvel

❑1, Oct 1986; Reprints The Incredible Hulk #181-182, other story ... 7.00
❑1/2nd; Reprints The Incredible Hulk #181-182, other story ... 4.00

Incredible Hulk: Future Imperfect
Marvel

❑1, Jan 1993; prestige format; GP (c); PD (w); GP (a); 1: The Maestro. Embossed cover; indicia lists date as Jan 93 ... 6.00
❑2, Feb 1993; prestige format; GP (c); PD (w); GP (a); Embossed cover; indicia lists date as Dec 92 ... 6.00

Incredible Hulk: Hercules Unleashed
Marvel

❑1, Oct 1996; follows events of Onslaught 2.50

Incredible Hulk Megazine
Marvel

❑1, Dec 1996; Reprints ... 3.95

Incredible Hulk: Nightmerica
Marvel

❑1, Aug 2003 ... 2.99
❑2, Sep 2003 ... 2.99
❑3, Oct 2003 ... 2.99
❑4, Nov 2003 ... 2.99
❑5, Mar 2004 ... 2.99
❑6, May 2004 ... 2.99

Incredible Hulk Poster Magazine
Marvel

❑1/A; comics ... 3.95
❑1/B; TV show ... 2.00

Incredible Hulk: The End
Marvel

❑1, Aug 2002 ... 5.95

Incredible Hulk vs. Quasimodo
Marvel

❑1, Mar 1983, SB (c); SB (a); Based on Saturday morning cartoon ... 1.50

Incredible Hulk vs. Superman
Marvel

❑1, Jul 1999; prestige format ... 6.00

N-MINT

Incredible Hulk vs. Venom
Marvel

❑1, Apr 1994; NN; Red foil embossed cover ... 3.00

Incredible Mr. Limpet
Dell

❑1, Jun 1964 ... 25.00

Incredibles
Dark Horse

❑1, Nov 2004 ... 2.99
❑2, Dec 2004 ... 2.99
❑3, Jan 2005 ... 2.99
❑4, Feb 2005 ... 2.99

Incubus
Palliard

❑1, b&w; Adult ... 2.95
❑2, b&w; Adult ... 2.95

Independent Publisher's Group Spotlight
Hero

❑0, Aug 1993, b&w; Bagged with card; no cover price ... 3.50

Independent Voices
Peregrine Entertainment

❑1, Sep 1998, b&w; SPX '98 anthology. 1.95
❑2/2nd, May 2000, b&w; CBLDF benefit comic book ... 2.95
❑2, Sep 1999, b&w; CBLDF benefit comic book ... 2.95
❑3, Aug 2001, b&w ... 2.95

Indiana Jones and the Arms of Gold
Dark Horse

❑1, Feb 1994 ... 2.50
❑2, Mar 1994 ... 2.50
❑3, Apr 1994 ... 2.50
❑4, May 1994 ... 2.50
❑5 ... 2.50
❑6, Apr 1994 ... 2.50

Indiana Jones and the Fate of Atlantis
Dark Horse

❑1, Mar 1991; trading cards ... 2.50
❑1/2nd; 2nd printing ... 2.50
❑2, May 1991; trading cards ... 2.50
❑3, Jul 1991 ... 2.50
❑4, Sep 1991 ... 2.50

Indiana Jones and the Golden Fleece
Dark Horse

❑1, Jun 1994 ... 2.50
❑2, Jul 1994 ... 2.50

Indiana Jones and the Iron Phoenix
Dark Horse

❑1, Dec 1994 ... 2.50
❑2, Jan 1995 ... 2.50
❑3, Feb 1995 ... 2.50
❑4, Mar 1995 ... 2.50

Indiana Jones and the Last Crusade
Marvel

❑1, Oct 1989; comic book ... 1.00
❑2, Oct 1989; comic book ... 1.00
❑3, Nov 1989; comic book ... 1.00
❑4, Nov 1989; comic book ... 1.00

N-MINT

Indiana Jones and the Last Crusade
Marvel

❑1, Aug 1989, b&w; magazine ... 2.95

Indiana Jones and the Sargasso Pirates
Dark Horse

❑1, Dec 1995 ... 2.50
❑2, Jan 1996 ... 2.50
❑3, Feb 1996 ... 2.50
❑4, Mar 1996; Final Issue ... 2.50

Indiana Jones and the Shrine of the Sea Devil
Dark Horse

❑1, Sep 1994; One-shot ... 2.50

Indiana Jones and the Spear of Destiny
Dark Horse

❑1, Apr 1995 ... 2.50
❑2, May 1995 ... 2.50
❑3, Jun 1995 ... 2.50
❑4, Jul 1995 ... 2.50

Indiana Jones and the Temple of Doom
Marvel

❑1, Sep 1984; BG (a); Movie adaptation 2.00
❑2, Oct 1984; BG (a); Movie adaptation. 2.00
❑3, Nov 1984; BG (a); Movie adaptation 2.00

Indiana Jones: Thunder in the Orient
Dark Horse

❑1, Sep 1993 ... 2.50
❑2, Oct 1993 ... 2.50
❑3, Nov 1993 ... 2.50
❑4, Dec 1993 ... 2.50
❑5, Mar 1994 ... 2.50
❑6, Apr 1994 ... 2.50

Indian Summer
NBM

❑1; Adult ... 21.95

Indigo Vertigo One Shot
Image

❑1 ... 4.95

In Dream World
Tokyopop

❑1, Apr 2005, Graphic novel; b&w ... 9.99
❑2, Jul 2005; Graphic novel; b&w ... 9.99
❑3, Oct 2005 ... 9.99

Industrial Gothic
DC / Vertigo

❑1, Dec 1995 ... 2.50
❑2, Jan 1996 ... 2.50
❑3, Feb 1996 ... 2.50
❑4, Mar 1996 ... 2.50
❑5, Apr 1996, Final Issue ... 2.50

Industrial Strength Preview
Silver Skull

❑1, b&w ... 1.50

Industry of War One-Shot
Image

❑1, Jan 2006 ... 7.99

Indy Buzz
Blindwolf

❑1, Mar 1999 ... 2.95

Other grades: Multiply price above by 5/6 for VF/NM • 2/3 for VERY FINE • 1/3 for FINE • 1/5 for VERY GOOD • 1/8 for GOOD

Inedible Adventures of Clint the Carrot
Hot Leg

❑1, Mar 1994, b&w 2.50

Infantry
Devil's Due

❑1, Dec 2004 3.00
❑1/Alternative, Dec 2004; "Team" cover, also known as B cover 4.00
❑1/Graham, Dec 2004; Graham Crackers exclusive; 1,000 printed. Skottie Young cover. Solicited December 2004 7.00
❑2, Jan 2005 2.95
❑3, Feb 2005 2.95

Infectious
Fantaco

❑1; One-shot 3.95

Inferior Five
DC

❑1, Apr 1967, Poliwko cover 24.00
❑2, Jun 1967 16.00
❑3, Aug 1967 14.00
❑4, Oct 1967 14.00
❑5, Dec 1967 14.00
❑6, Feb 1968, A: DC heroes 14.00
❑7, Apr 1968 14.00
❑8, Jun 1968 14.00
❑9, Aug 1968 14.00
❑10, Oct 1968, A: other heroes. Final issue of original run (1968) 14.00
❑11, Sep 1972, reprints Showcase #62; Series begins again (1972) 10.00
❑12, Nov 1972, reprints Showcase #63 . 10.00

Inferno
Aircel

❑1, Oct 1990, b&w; Adult 2.50
❑2, Nov 1990, b&w; Adult 2.50
❑3, Dec 1990, b&w; Adult 2.50
❑4, Jan 1991, b&w; Adult 2.50

Inferno
Caliber

❑1, Aug 1995, b&w 2.95

Inferno
DC

❑1, Oct 1997, spin-off from Legion of Super-Heroes 2.50
❑2, Nov 1997 2.50
❑3, Jan 1998 2.50
❑4, Feb 1998 2.50

Inferno: Hellbound
Image

❑0, Jul 2002 2.50
❑1, Feb 2002 2.50
❑2, Aug 2002 2.50
❑3, Nov 2002; Final issue 2.99

Infinite Crisis
DC

❑1/Perez, Dec 2005, b&w; Jim Lee cover; D: Black Condor 2; D: Phantom Lady 2; D: Human Bomb 1; D: Dr. Polaris; Wonder Woman holding sword 6.00
❑1/Lee, Dec 2005 6.00
❑1/2nd, Dec 2005 4.00
❑1/RRP, Dec 2005 450.00
❑2/Perez, Jan 2006; D: Royal Flush Gang; D: Mr. Atom; George Perez & Jerry Ordway not credited for p. 14-17 6.00
❑2/Lee, Jan 2006 6.00
❑3/Perez, Feb 2006, Jim Lee Batman/Superman cover; 1: Jaime Reyes; D: Atlantis; D: Neptune Perkins 6.00
❑3/Lee, Feb 2006 6.00
❑4/Perez, Mar 2006, Jim Lee cover; D: Pantha; D: Wildebeest; D: Bushido; 1: Crispus Allen as Spectre 6.00
❑4/Lee, Mar 2006 6.00
❑5/Perez, May 2006, George Perez cover 4.00
❑5/Lee, May 2006 4.00
❑6, Jun 2006, George Perez cover 3.99
❑7, Jul 2006, 1: Atom III; D: Alexander Luthor; D: Breach; D: Peacekeeper; D: Looker; D: Nightblade; D: Razorsharp; D: Ballistic; D: Baron Blitzkrieg; D: Charaxes; D: Geist; D: Mongrel; D: Earth 2 Superman; Jim Lee cover; 1: Atom (Ryan Choi) 3.99

Infinite Crisis Secret Files 2006
DC

❑1, May 2006 12.00

Infinite Kung Fu
Kagan McLeod

❑1, Aug 2000 4.50
❑1/2nd; 2nd printing, 2002 4.50

Infinity Abyss
Marvel

❑1, Aug 2002 2.99
❑2, Aug 2002 2.99
❑3, Sep 2002 2.99
❑4, Sep 2002 2.99
❑5, Oct 2002 2.99
❑6, Oct 2002 3.50

Infinity Charade
Parody

❑1/A 2.50
❑1/B 2.50
❑1/Gold; Gold limited edition (1500 printed) 4.00

Infinity Crusade
Marvel

❑1, Jun 1993, Gold foil cover 3.50
❑2, Jul 1993 2.50
❑3, Aug 1993 2.50
❑4, Sep 1993 2.50
❑5, Oct 1993 2.50
❑6, Nov 1993 2.50

Infinity Gauntlet
Marvel

❑1, Jul 1991, GP (c); JSn (w); GP (a); A: Thanos. A: Spider-Man. A: Avengers. A: Silver Surfer 3.00
❑2, Aug 1991, GP (c); JSn (w); GP (a); A: Thanos. A: Spider-Man. A: Avengers. A: Silver Surfer 2.50
❑3, Sep 1991, GP (c); JSn (w); GP (a); A: Thanos. A: Spider-Man. A: Avengers. A: Silver Surfer 2.50
❑4, Oct 1991, GP (c); JSn (w); GP (a); A: Thanos. A: Spider-Man. A: Avengers. A: Silver Surfer 2.50
❑5, Nov 1991, GP (c); JSn (w) 2.50
❑6, Dec 1991, GP (c); JSn (w) 2.50

Infinity Graphics Presents
Infinity

❑1, Jun 1987; Newsprint cover 1.75

Infinity, Inc.
DC

❑1, Mar 1984; JOy (c); JOy (a); O: Infinity Inc 2.50
❑2, May 1984; JOy (a); O: ends. V: Ultra-Humanite 2.00
❑3, Jun 1984; JOy (a); V: Solomon Grundy 2.00
❑4, Jul 1984 JOy, JKu (a) 2.00
❑5, Aug 1984 JOy (a) 2.00
❑6, Sep 1984 JOy (a) 1.50
❑7, Oct 1984 JOy (a); A: E-2 Superman. 1.50
❑8, Nov 1984 JOy (a) 1.50
❑9, Dec 1984 JOy (a) 1.50
❑10, Jan 1985 JOy (a) 1.50
❑11, Feb 1985; more on Infinity's origin 1.25
❑12, Mar 1985; 1: Yolanda Montez. Brainwave Junior's new powers 1.25
❑13, Apr 1985; V: Thorn 1.25
❑14, May 1985; TMc (c); TMc (a); 1: Chroma. 1: Marcie Cooper 3.50
❑15, Jun 1985 TMc (c); TMc (a); A: Chroma 2.50
❑16, Jul 1985; TMc (c); TMc (a); 1: Mr. Bones 2.50
❑17, Aug 1985; TMc (c); TMc (a); 1: Helix 2.50
❑18, Sep 1985; TMc (c); TMc (a); V: Helix. Crisis 2.50
❑19, Oct 1985; TMc (c); TMc (a); 1: Mekanique. A: Steel. A: JLA. Crisis. 2.50
❑20, Nov 1985; TMc (c); TMc (a); 1: Rick Tyler. Crisis 2.50
❑21, Dec 1985; TMc (c); TMc (a); 1: Doctor Midnight (new). 1: Hourman II (Rick Tyler). Crisis 2.50
❑22, Jan 1986; TMc (c); TMc (a); Crisis 2.50
❑23, Feb 1986; TMc (c); TMc (a); V: Solomon Grundy. Crisis 2.50
❑24, Mar 1986; TMc, DG (a); Star Spangled Kid, Jonni Thunder vs. Last Criminal; Crisis 2.50
❑25, Apr 1986; TMc (c); TMc (a); Crisis aftermath; Hourman II joins team; Doctor Midnight joins team; Wildcat II joins team 2.50
❑26, May 1986 TMc (c); TMc (a); A: Helix 2.50
❑27, Jun 1986; TMc (c); TMc (a); Lyta's memories erased 2.50
❑28, Jul 1986; TMc (a); V: Mr. Bones 2.50
❑29, Jul 1986; TMc (c); TMc (a); V: Helix 2.50
❑30, Sep 1986; TMc (c); TMc (a); JSA mourned 2.50
❑31, Oct 1986; TMc (a); 1: Skyman. A: Jonni Thunder 2.50
❑32, Nov 1986; TD (c); TMc (a); V: Psycho Pirate 2.50
❑33, Dec 1986; TMc (c); TMc (a); O: Obsidian 2.50
❑34, Jan 1987; TMc (a); V: Global Guardians 2.50
❑35, Feb 1987; TMc (a); V: Injustice Unlimited 2.50
❑36, Mar 1987; TMc (a); V: Solomon Grundy 2.50
❑37, Apr 1987; TMc (a); O: Northwing 2.50
❑38, May 1987; O: Helix; Trial of Helix; Mr. Bones remanded to custody of Infinity Inc 1.25
❑39, Jun 1987; O: Solomon Grundy 1.25
❑40, Jul 1987; V: Jonni Thunder's Thunderbolt 1.25
❑41, Aug 1987 1.25
❑42, Sep 1987; Fury leaves team 1.25
❑43, Oct 1987; V: Silver Scarab 1.25
❑44, Nov 1987 1.25
❑45, Dec 1987 A: Titans 1.25
❑46, Jan 1988; V: Floronic Man. Millennium 1.50
❑47, Feb 1988; V: Harlequin. Millennium 1.25
❑48, Mar 1988; O: Nuklon 1.25
❑49, Apr 1988 A: Sandman 1.25
❑50, May 1988; Giant-size 2.50
❑51, Jun 1988; D: Skyman; Injustice Unlimited reforms 1.25
❑52, Jul 1988; V: Helix 1.25
❑53, Aug 1988; V: Injustice Unlimited; Final Issue 1.75
❑Ann 1, Nov 1985; TMc (c); TMc (a); O: Jade and Obsidian. Crisis 2.50
❑Ann 2, Jul 1988; crossover with Young All-Stars Ann #1 2.50
❑Special 1, ca. 1987; cover forms diptych with Outsiders Special #1 1.50

Infinity of Warriors
Ominous

❑1, Oct 1994 1.95

Infinity War
Marvel

❑1, Jun 1992; gatefold cover 2.50
❑2, Jul 1992; gatefold cover 2.50
❑3, Aug 1992; gatefold cover 2.50
❑4, Sep 1992; gatefold cover 2.50
❑5, Oct 1992; gatefold cover 2.50
❑6, Nov 1992; gatefold cover 2.50

Infochameleon: Company Cult
Mediawarp

❑1, Feb 1997, b&w; One-shot 4.50

Inhumanoids
Marvel / Star

❑1, Jan 1987; 1: Earth Corps 1.00
❑2, Mar 1987 1.00
❑3, May 1987 1.00
❑4, Jul 1987 1.00

Inhumans
Marvel

❑1, Oct 1975, GK (c); GP (a); V: Blastaar 8.00
❑2, Dec 1976 4.00
❑3, Feb 1976, Ralph Macchio L.O.C.; Peter B. Gillis L.O.C.; Marvel Value Stamp Series B #36 4.00
❑4, Apr 1976 3.50
❑4/30¢, Apr 1976, 30¢ regional price variant 7.00
❑5, Jun 1976 3.50
❑6, Aug 1976, Wendy Pini L.O.C.; Marvel Value Stamp Series B #7 3.00
❑6/30¢, Aug 1976, 30¢ regional price variant 20.00
❑7, Oct 1976 3.00
❑8, Dec 1976 3.00
❑9, Feb 1977, Reprints Amazing Adventures (3rd Series) #1 & 2 3.00
❑10, Apr 1977 3.00
❑11, Jun 1977 3.00
❑11/35¢, Jun 1977, 35¢ regional price variant 15.00
❑12, Aug 1977, V: Hulk 3.00
❑12/35¢, Aug 1977, V: Hulk. 35¢ regional price variant 3.00
❑Special 1, Apr 1990, RHo (a); O: Medusa. A: Fantastic Four. O: Medusa 4.00

Other grades: Multiply price above by 5/6 for VF/NM • 2/3 for VERY FINE • 1/3 for FINE • 1/5 for VERY GOOD • 1/8 for GOOD

Indiana Jones and the Last Crusade

Marvel adaptation of third Indy film

©Marvel

Indiana Jones and the Spear of Destiny

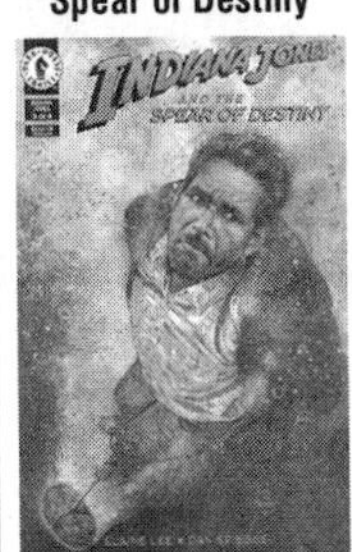

Original story picks up after Last Crusade

©Dark Horse

Indiana Jones and the Temple of Doom

1984 film adaptation by Marvel

©Marvel

Inferior Five

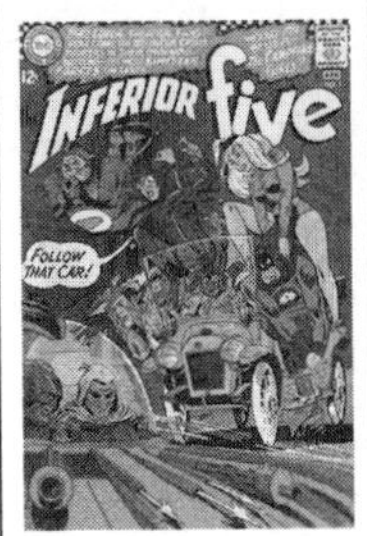

Merryman, Dumb Bunny, and company

©DC

Infinity, Inc.

Formed by the kids and wards of the JSA

©DC

N-MINT

Inhumans
Marvel

- ❑1, Nov 1998, gatefold summary; Includes trading card 4.00
- ❑1/Ltd., Nov 1998, DFE alternate cover signed 4.00
- ❑1/Variant, Nov 1998, DFE alternate cover 4.00
- ❑2/A, Dec 1998, gatefold summary; Woman in circle on cover 3.00
- ❑2/B, Dec 1998, gatefold summary 3.00
- ❑3, Jan 1999 .... 3.00
- ❑4, Feb 1999 .... 3.00
- ❑5, Mar 1999, Earth vs. Attilan war 3.00
- ❑6, Apr 1999 .... 3.00
- ❑7, May 1999 .... 3.00
- ❑8, Jun 1999 .... 3.00
- ❑9, Jul 1999 .... 3.00
- ❑10, Aug 1999 .... 3.00
- ❑11, Sep 1999 .... 3.00
- ❑12, Oct 1999 .... 3.00

Inhumans
Marvel

- ❑1, Jun 2000 .... 2.99
- ❑2, Jul 2000 .... 2.99
- ❑3, Aug 2000 .... 2.99
- ❑4, Oct 2000 .... 2.99

Inhumans
Marvel

- ❑1, Jun 2003, Marvel called this Vol. 6, counting the specials 2.50
- ❑2, Jul 2003 .... 2.50
- ❑3, Aug 2003 .... 2.50
- ❑4, Oct 2003 .... 2.99
- ❑5, Nov 2003 .... 2.99
- ❑6, Dec 2003 .... 2.99
- ❑7, Jan 2004 .... 2.99
- ❑8, Feb 2004 .... 2.99
- ❑9, Mar 2004 .... 2.99
- ❑10, Apr 2004 .... 2.99
- ❑11, May 2004 .... 2.99
- ❑12, Jun 2004 .... 2.99

Inhumans: The Great Refuge
Marvel

- ❑1, May 1995 .... 2.95

Inhumans: The Untold Saga
Marvel

- ❑1, Apr 1990 .... 1.50

Initial D
Tokyopop

- ❑1, May 2002, b&w 9.99
- ❑2, Jul 2002 .... 9.99
- ❑3, Oct 2002 .... 9.99
- ❑4, Jan 2003; Includes map 9.99
- ❑5, Apr 2003 .... 9.99
- ❑6, Jun 2003 .... 9.99
- ❑7, Aug 2003 .... 9.99
- ❑8, Oct 2003 .... 9.99
- ❑9, Dec 2003 .... 9.99
- ❑10, Feb 2004 .... 9.99
- ❑11, Apr 2004 .... 9.99
- ❑12, Jun 2004 .... 9.99
- ❑13, Aug 2004 .... 9.99
- ❑14, Oct 2004 .... 9.99
- ❑15, Dec 2004 .... 9.99
- ❑16, Feb 2005 .... 9.99

N-MINT

- ❑17, Apr 2005 .... 9.99
- ❑18, Jun 2005 .... 9.99
- ❑19, Aug 2005 .... 9.99
- ❑20, Oct 2005 .... 9.99

Inkpunks Quarterly
Funk-O-Tron

- ❑1 .... 2.95
- ❑2 .... 2.95
- ❑3 .... 2.95

Inmates Prisoners Of Society
Delta

- ❑1, Aug 1997 .... 2.95
- ❑2, Mar 1998 .... 2.95
- ❑3, Jul 1998 .... 2.95
- ❑4, Nov 1998 .... 2.95

Innercircle
Mushroom

- ❑0.1, Feb 1995 .... 2.50

Inner-City Products
Hype

- ❑1, b&w 2.00

Inner City Romance
Last Gasp

- ❑1 .... 5.00
- ❑2, Dec 1972; Wraparound cover; b&w. 3.00
- ❑3 .... 3.00
- ❑4; Wraparound Cover; b&w; ca. 1977. .... 3.00
- ❑5, Feb 1979 .... 3.00

Innocent Bystander
Ollie Ollie! Oxen Free

- ❑1; ca. 1995; 1: Lao Shan. 1: Balac-Soon 2.95
- ❑2; ca. 1996 .... 2.95
- ❑3; Winter 1996-1997; All Marx Brothers issue 2.95
- ❑4, Sum 1997; Tales of 2 Kitties 2.95
- ❑5, Win 1998 .... 2.95
- ❑6, Fal 1998 .... 2.95

Innocent Ones
Fantagraphics

- ❑1 2005 .... 7.95

Innocents
Image

- ❑1, Jul 2006 .... 2.99

Innovation Preview Special
Innovation

- ❑1, Jun 1989; sampler 1.00

Innovation Spectacular
Innovation

- ❑1, Dec 1990 .... 2.95
- ❑2, Jan 1991 .... 2.95

Innovation Summer Fun Special
Innovation

- ❑1; ca. 1991 .... 3.50

Inovators
Dark Moon

- ❑1, Apr 1995; cardstock cover 2.50

In Rage
CFD

- ❑1, ca. 1994, b&w; No cover price; Comic Book Legal Defense Fund fund-raiser comic 2.50

N-MINT

Insane
Dark Horse

- ❑1, Feb 1988 .... 1.75
- ❑2 .... 1.75

Insane Clown Posse
Chaos!

- ❑1, Jun 1999 .... 3.00
- ❑1/A, Jun 1999; Tower Reocrds variant. 4.00
- ❑2, Aug 1999; Listed as #1 Vol. 2 .... 3.00
- ❑2/CS, Aug 1999; Includes CD 4.00
- ❑3, Oct 1999; Listed as #1 Vol. 3 .... 3.00
- ❑3/A, Oct 1999; Tower Reocrds variant. 4.00
- ❑4, Jan 2000; Says #1 on cover with Pendulum below issue number; polybagged with first of 12 Pendulum CDs 3.00
- ❑4/CS, Jan 2000; Includes CD 4.00
- ❑5, ca. 2000 .... 3.00
- ❑5/CS, ca. 2000; Includes CD 4.00
- ❑6, ca. 2000 .... 3.00
- ❑6/CS, ca. 2000 .... 4.00
- ❑7, ca. 2000 .... 3.00
- ❑7/CS, ca. 2000; Includes CD 4.00
- ❑8, ca. 2001 .... 3.00
- ❑8/CS, ca. 2001; Includes CD 4.00
- ❑9, ca. 2001 .... 3.00
- ❑9/CS, ca. 2001; Includes CD 3.00
- ❑10, ca. 2001 .... 3.00
- ❑10/CS, ca. 2001; Includes CD 3.00
- ❑11, ca. 2001 .... 3.00
- ❑11/CS, ca. 2001; Includes CD 4.00
- ❑12, ca. 2001 .... 3.00
- ❑12/CS, ca. 2001; Includes CD 3.00

In Search of Shirley
NBM

- ❑1 .... 9.95

In Search of the Castaways
Gold Key

- ❑1, Mar 1963 .... 20.00

Insect Man's 25th Anniversary Special
Entertainment

- ❑1, Mar 1991 .... 2.00

Inside Out King
Free Fall

- ❑1 .... 2.95
- ❑1/2nd; 2nd printing 2.95

Insomnia
Fantagraphics

- ❑1, Aug 2005; 2nd book of Ignatz collection 7.95

Insomnia
Fantagraphics

- ❑1, Dec 2005 .... 7.95

Inspector
Gold Key

- ❑1, Jul 1974, (c); (w); (a); Cover code 90292-407 .... 20.00
- ❑2, Oct 1974, (c); (w); (a); Cover code 90292-410; unusual Pink Panther story without "Pink" in title; not Tufts art 10.00
- ❑3, Jan 1975, (c); (w); (a); Cover code 90292-501; includes 16-page toy catalog 5.00
- ❑4, Apr 1975, (c); (w); (a); Cover code 90292-504 .... 5.00

Other grades: Multiply price above by 5/6 for VF/NM • 2/3 for VERY FINE • 1/3 for FINE • 1/5 for VERY GOOD • 1/8 for GOOD

❑5, Jul 1975, (c); (w); (a); Cover code 90292-507 .... 5.00
❑6, Oct 1975, (c); (w); (a); Cover code 90292-510 .... 5.00
❑7, Jan 1976, (c); (w); Cover code 90292-601; includes Bugs Bunny in Hostess ad ("The Great Carrot Famine") 5.00
❑8, Mar 1976, (c); (w); (a); Cover code 90292-603 .... 5.00
❑9, May 1976, (c); (w); (a); Cover code 90292-605 .... 5.00
❑10, Jul 1976, (c); (w); Cover code 90292-607 .... 5.00
❑11, Sep 1976, (c); (w); Cover code 90292-609; includes Hulk in Hostess ad ("The Green Frog") 5.00
❑12, Nov 1976, (c); (w); (a); Cover code 90292-611 .... 5.00
❑13, Feb 1977, (c); (w); (a); Cover code 90292-702 .... 5.00
❑14, Apr 1977, (c); (w); Cover code 90292-704; includes Spider-Man in Hostess ad ("Will Power") 5.00
❑15, Jun 1977, (c); (w); Cover code 90292-706; includes Iron Man in Hostess ad ("A Dull Pain") 5.00
❑16, Aug 1977, (c); (w); (a); Cover code 90292-708 .... 5.00
❑17, Oct 1977, (c); (w); (a); Cover code 90292-710 .... 5.00
❑18, Dec 1977, (c); (w); (a); Cover code 90292-712; includes Daredevil in Hostess ad ("Because"); not Tufts art 5.00
❑19, Feb 1978, (c); (w); (a); Cover code 90292-802 .... 5.00

Inspector Gill of the Fish Police
Apple

❑0, Spr 1991 .... 2.50

Instant Piano
Dark Horse

❑1, Aug 1994, b&w 3.95
❑2, Dec 1994, b&w 3.95
❑3, Feb 1995, b&w 3.95
❑4, Jun 1995, b&w 3.95

Intense!
Pure Imagination

❑2, b&w; Reprints 3.00

Interactive Comics
Adventure

❑1; NN 4.95
❑2, b&w; NN 4.95

Interface
Marvel / Epic

❑1, Dec 1989 .... 5.00
❑2, Feb 1990 .... 4.00
❑3, Apr 1990 .... 4.00
❑4, Jun 1990 .... 4.00
❑5, Aug 1990 .... 4.00
❑6, Oct 1990 .... 9.00
❑7, Nov 1990 .... 9.00
❑8, Dec 1990, Final Issue 9.00

Internal Fury
Fierce Comics

❑4, Jan 2006; b&w 3.50
❑3, Nov 2005; b&w 3.50
❑2, Jan 2005 .... 2.00
❑1, Aug 2005 .... 2.00

International Cowgirl Magazine
Iconografix

❑1, b&w 2.95
❑2, b&w 2.95

Interplanetary Lizards of the Texas Plains
Leadbelly

❑0, O: Interplanetary Lizards 2.50
❑1, Apr 1991, b&w 2.00
❑2, Sep 1991, b&w 2.00
❑3 .... 2.00
❑8, Aug 1993, b&w 2.50

Interstellar Overdrive
Leonine

❑1 1990 .... 1.25
❑2, Apr 1990 .... 1.25

Interview With the Vampire
Innovation

❑1, ca. 1991 .... 2.50
❑2, ca. 1991 .... 2.50
❑3, ca. 1991 .... 2.50
❑4, ca. 1991 .... 2.50
❑5, ca. 1992 .... 2.50
❑6, ca. 1992 .... 2.50
❑7, ca. 1992 .... 2.50
❑8, ca. 1993 .... 2.50
❑9, ca. 1993 .... 2.50
❑10, ca. 1993 .... 2.50
❑11, ca. 1993 .... 2.50
❑12, ca. 1993 .... 2.50

In the Days of the Ace Rock 'n' Roll Club
Fantagraphics

❑1, b&w; NN 4.95

In The Days of the Mob
DC

❑1, Fal 1971 .... 50.00

In the Presence of Mine Enemies
Spire

❑1 .... 7.00

In Thin Air
Tome

❑1/A, b&w; With alternate ending #1 .... 2.95
❑1/B, b&w; With alternate ending #2 .... 2.95

Intimates
DC

❑1, Jan 2005 .... 2.95
❑2, Feb 2005 .... 2.95
❑3, Mar 2005 .... 2.95
❑4, Apr 2005 .... 2.95
❑5, May 2005 .... 2.95
❑6, Jun 2005 .... 2.95
❑7, Jun 2005 .... 2.99
❑8, Jul 2005 .... 2.99
❑9, Aug 2005 .... 2.99
❑10, Sep 2005 .... 2.99
❑11, Oct 2005 .... 2.99
❑12, Dec 2005 .... 2.99

Intimidators
Image

❑1, Jan 2006 .... 3.50
❑2, Feb 2006 .... 3.50
❑3, Mar 2006 .... 3.50
❑4, Apr 2006 .... 3.50

Intrazone
Brainstorm

❑1, Mar 1993, b&w 2.95
❑1/Ltd., Mar 1993; limited edition; Includes trading card 5.95
❑2, Apr 1993, b&w 2.95
❑2/Ltd., Apr 1993; limited edition; Includes trading card 5.95

Intrigue
Image

❑1/A, Aug 1999 .... 2.50
❑1/B, Aug 1999; alternate cover with woman firing directly at reader 2.50
❑2/A, Sep 1999; Woman posting next to target on cover 2.50
❑2/B, Sep 1999; alternate cover 2.50
❑3, Oct 1999 .... 2.95

Intruder Comics Module
TSR

❑1 .... 2.95
❑2 .... 2.95
❑3 .... 2.95
❑4 .... 2.95
❑5; "Intruder II" on cover 2.95
❑6; "Intruder II" on cover 2.95
❑7; Intruder II 2.95
❑8; Intruder II 2.95
❑9; Intruder II 2.95

Inu-Yasha
Viz

❑1, Apr 1997 .... 3.00
❑2, May 1997 .... 2.95
❑3, Jun 1997 .... 2.95
❑4, Jul 1997 .... 2.95
❑5, Aug 1997 .... 2.95
❑6, Sep 1997 .... 3.25
❑7, Oct 1997 .... 3.25
❑8, Nov 1997 .... 3.25
❑9, Dec 1997 .... 3.25
❑10, Jan 1998 .... 3.25
❑11, Feb 1998 .... 3.25
❑12, Mar 1998 .... 3.25
❑13, Apr 1998 .... 3.25
❑14, May 1998 .... 3.25
❑15, Jun 1998 .... 3.25

Inu-Yasha Part 2
Viz

❑1, Jul 1998; b&w 3.25
❑2, Aug 1998 .... 3.25
❑3, Sep 1998 .... 3.25
❑4, Oct 1998 .... 3.25
❑5, Nov 1998 .... 3.25
❑6, Dec 1998 .... 3.25
❑7, Jan 1999 .... 3.25
❑8, Feb 1999 .... 3.25
❑9, Mar 1999 .... 3.25

Inu-Yasha Part 3
Viz

❑1, Apr 1999; b&w 3.25
❑2, May 1999 .... 3.25
❑3, Jun 1999 .... 3.25
❑4, Jul 1999 .... 3.25
❑5, Aug 1999 .... 3.25
❑6, Sep 1999 .... 3.25
❑7, Oct 1999 .... 3.25

Inu-Yasha Part 4
Viz

❑1, Nov 1999; b&w 3.25
❑2, Dec 1999 .... 3.25
❑3, Jan 2000 .... 3.25
❑4, Feb 2000 .... 3.25
❑5, Mar 2000 .... 3.25
❑6, Apr 2000 .... 3.25
❑7, May 2000 .... 3.25

Inu-Yasha Part 5
Viz

❑1, Jun 2000; b&w 2.95
❑2, Jul 2000 .... 2.95
❑3, Aug 2000 .... 2.95
❑4, Sep 2000 .... 2.95
❑5, Oct 2000 .... 2.95
❑6, Nov 2000 .... 2.95
❑7, Dec 2000 .... 2.95
❑8, Jan 2001 .... 2.95
❑9, Feb 2001 .... 2.95
❑10, Mar 2001 .... 2.95
❑11, Apr 2001 .... 2.95

Inu-Yasha Part 6
Viz

❑1, May 2001; b&w 2.95
❑2, Jun 2001 .... 2.95
❑3, Jul 2001 .... 2.95
❑4, Aug 2001 .... 2.95
❑5, Sep 2001 .... 2.95
❑6, Oct 2001 .... 2.95
❑7, Nov 2001 .... 2.95
❑8, Dec 2001 .... 2.95
❑9, Jan 2002 .... 2.95
❑10, Feb 2002 .... 2.95
❑11, Mar 2002 .... 2.95
❑12, Apr 2002 .... 2.95
❑13, May 2002 .... 2.95
❑14, Jun 2002 .... 2.95
❑15, Jul 2002 .... 2.95

Inu-Yasha Part 7
Viz

❑1, Aug 2002 .... 2.95
❑2, Sep 2002 .... 2.95
❑3, Oct 2002 .... 2.95
❑4, Nov 2002 .... 2.95
❑5, Dec 2002 .... 2.95
❑6, Jan 2003 .... 2.95
❑7, Feb 2003 .... 2.95

Invaders
Gold Key

❑1, Oct 1967 .... 40.00
❑2, Jan 1968 .... 28.00
❑3, Jun 1968 .... 28.00
❑4, Oct 1968 .... 28.00

Invaders
Marvel

❑1, Aug 1975, continued from Giant-Size Invaders #1; FR (a); Marvel Value Stamp #37: Watcher 18.00

Inhumanoids

The Earth Corps battle plant monsters

©Marvel

Inhumans

Fantastic Four spinoff in its first series

©Marvel

Insane Clown Posse

Gross-out comic based on gross-out band

©Chaos!

Inspector

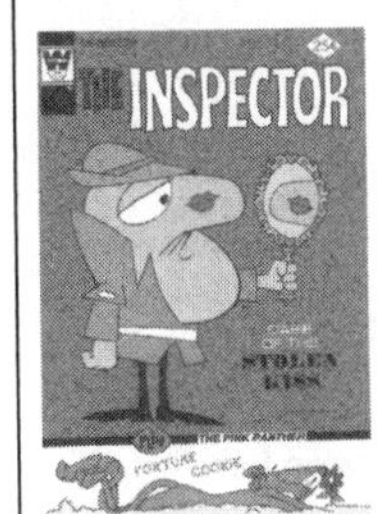

Includes some great Warren Tufts stories

©Gold Key

In the Presence of Mine Enemies

American POW in Vietnam tells spiritual story

©Spire

N-MINT

❑2, Oct 1975, 1: Mailbag. 1: Brain Drain. V: Donar 10.00
❑3, Nov 1975, 1: U-Man. Captain America vs. Namor vs. Torch; Marvel Value Stamp #97: Black Knight 6.00
❑4, Jan 1976, O: U-Man. V: U-Man 6.00
❑5, Mar 1976, 1: Fin. V: Red Skull 5.00
❑6, May 1976, A: Liberty Legion 5.00
❑6/30¢, May 1976, 30¢ regional price variant 20.00
❑7, Jul 1976, V: Baron Blood. 1: Baron Blood; 1: Freedom's Five; 1: Lady Crichton (Spitfire); 1&O: Union Jack I (James Montgomery); 1: Crimson Cavalier; 1: Sir Steel & Silver 5.00
❑7/30¢, Jul 1976, 30¢ regional price variant 20.00
❑8, Sep 1976, A: Union Jack 5.00
❑9, Oct 1976, O: Baron Blood. V: Baron Blood 5.00
❑10, Nov 1976, V: Reaper. reprints Captain America #22 .... 4.00
❑11, Dec 1976, O: Spitfire. 1: Blue Bullet. 1: Spitfire. V: Blue Bullet 4.00
❑12, Jan 1977, 1: Spitfire 4.00
❑13, Feb 1977, A: Golem. Newsstand edition (distributed by Curtis); issue number in box 4.00
❑13/Whitman, Feb 1977, A: Golem. Special markets edition (usually sold in Whitman bagged prepacks); price appears in a diamond; UPC barcode appears 4.00
❑14, Mar 1977, 1: Spirit of '76. 1: Dyna-Mite. 1: Crusaders. Newsstand edition (distributed by Curtis); issue number in box 4.00
❑14/Whitman, Mar 1977, 1: Spirit of '76. 1: Dyna-Mite. 1: Crusaders. Special markets edition (usually sold in Whitman bagged prepacks); price appears in a diamond; UPC barcode appears 4.00
❑15, Apr 1977, JK (c); FR, FS (a); V: Crusaders. Newsstand edition (distributed by Curtis); issue number in box 4.00
❑15/Whitman, Apr 1977, FR, FS (a); V: Crusaders. Special markets edition (usually sold in Whitman bagged prepacks); price appears in a diamond; UPC barcode appears 4.00
❑16, May 1977, V: Master Man 4.00
❑17, Jun 1977, 1: Warrior Woman. V: Warrior Woman. Newsstand edition (distributed by Curtis); issue number in box 4.00
❑17/Whitman, Jun 1977, 1: Warrior Woman. V: Warrior Woman. Special markets edition (usually sold in Whitman bagged prepacks); price appears in a diamond; UPC barcode appears 4.00
❑17/35¢, Jun 1977, 35¢ regional variant newsstand edition (distributed by Curtis); issue number in box 7.00
❑18, Jul 1977, 1: Mighty Destroyer. Newsstand edition (distributed by Curtis); issue number in box 4.00
❑18/Whitman, Jul 1977, 1: Mighty Destroyer. Special markets edition (usually sold in Whitman bagged prepacks); price appears in a diamond; UPC barcode appears 4.00

N-MINT

❑18/35¢, Jul 1977, 35¢ regional variant newsstand edition (distributed by Curtis); issue number in box 7.00
❑19, Aug 1977, O: Union Jack II (Brian Falsworth). 1: Sub-Mariner. 1: Union Jack II (Brian Falsworth). A: Hitler. Mighty Destroyer becomes Union Jack II; Reprints Motion Picture Funnies Weekly; Newsstand edition (distributed by Curtis); issue number in box 4.00
❑19/Whitman, Aug 1977, 1&O: Union Jack II (Brian Falsworth). 1: Sub-Mariner. A: Hitler. Special markets edition (usually sold in Whitman bagged prepacks); price appears in a diamond; UPC barcode appears 4.00
❑19/35¢, Aug 1977, 35¢ regional variant newsstand edition (distributed by Curtis); issue number in box 7.00
❑20, Sep 1977, O: Sub-Mariner. 1: Sub-Mariner. A: Spitfire. A: Union Jack. Reprints Sub-Mariner story from Motion Picture Funnies Weekly #1; Newsstand edition (distributed by Curtis); issue number in box 5.00
❑20/Whitman, Sep 1977, O: Sub-Mariner. 1: Sub-Mariner. A: Spitfire. A: Union Jack. Special markets edition (usually sold in Whitman bagged prepacks); price appears in a diamond; UPC barcode appears 5.00
❑20/35¢, Sep 1977, 35¢ regional variant newsstand edition (distributed by Curtis); issue number in box 10.00
❑21, Oct 1977, FR, FS (a); Reprints Sub-Mariner story from Marvel Mystery Comics #10; Newsstand edition (distributed by Curtis); issue number in box 3.00
❑21/Whitman, Oct 1977, FR, FS (a); Special markets edition (usually sold in Whitman bagged prepacks); price appears in a diamond; no UPC barcode 3.00
❑21/35¢, Oct 1977, 35¢ regional variant newsstand edition (distributed by Curtis); issue number in box 6.00
❑22, Nov 1977, O: Toro (new origin). V: Asbestos Lady 4.00
❑23, Dec 1977, 1: Scarlet Scarab. V: Scarlet Scarab 4.00
❑24, Jan 1978, reprints Marvel Mystery Comics #17 .... 4.00
❑25, Feb 1978, V: Scarlet Scarab 4.00
❑26, Mar 1978, 1: Destroyer II (Roger Aubrey). V: Agent Axis 4.00
❑27, Apr 1978 .... 4.00
❑28, May 1978, 1: Golden Girl. 1: Kid Commandos. 1: Human Top (David Mitchell) 4.00
❑29, Jun 1978, O: Invaders. 1: Teutonic Knight. V: Teutonic Knight 4.00
❑30, Jul 1978 .... 4.00
❑31, Aug 1978, V: Frankenstein. Newsstand edition (distributed by Curtis); issue number in box 3.00
❑31/Whitman, Aug 1978, V: Frankenstein. Special markets edition (usually sold in Whitman bagged prepacks); price appears in a diamond; no UPC barcode 3.00
❑32, Sep 1978, V: Thor 3.00
❑33, Oct 1978, V: Thor 4.00
❑34, Nov 1978, V: Destroyer 2.50
❑35, Dec 1978, A: Whizzer 2.50
❑36, Jan 1979, V: Iron Cross 2.50

N-MINT

❑37, Feb 1979, A: Liberty Legion. V: Iron Cross. Newsstand edition (distributed by Curtis); issue number in box 2.50
❑37/Whitman, Feb 1979, A: Liberty Legion. V: Iron Cross. Special markets edition (usually sold in Whitman bagged prepacks); price appears in a diamond; no UPC barcode 2.50
❑38, Mar 1979, 1: Lady Lotus. A: U-Man 2.50
❑39, Apr 1979 .... 2.50
❑40, May 1979, V: Baron Blood 2.50
❑41, Sep 1979, Double-size; V: Super Axis (Baron Blood, U-Man, Warrior Woman, Master Man). V: Super Axis (Baron Blood, U-Man, Warrior Woman, Master Man); Final Issue; Double-size 3.50
❑Ann 1, ca. 1977, Alex Schomburg cover; ca. 1977; 1: Agent Axis (Hiroyuki Kanegawa & Aldo Malvagio & Berthold Volker) 12.00

Invaders
Marvel

❑1, May 1993 .... 1.75
❑2, Jun 1993, V: Battle Axis 1.75
❑3, Jul 1993 .... 1.75
❑4, Aug 1993 .... 1.75

Invaders
Marvel

❑0, Sep 2004 .... 2.99
❑1, Oct 2004 .... 2.99
❑2, Nov 2004 .... 2.99
❑3, Dec 2004 .... 2.99
❑4, Jan 2005 .... 2.99
❑5, Feb 2005 .... 2.99
❑6, Mar 2005 .... 2.99
❑7, Apr 2005 .... 2.99
❑8, May 2005 .... 2.99
❑9, Jun 2005 .... 2.99

Invaders from Home
DC / Piranha

❑1 .... 2.50
❑2 .... 2.50
❑3 .... 2.50
❑4 .... 2.50
❑5 .... 2.50
❑6 .... 2.50

Invaders from Mars
Eternity

❑1, Feb 1990, b&w; Movie adaptation 2.50
❑2, Mar 1990, b&w; Movie adaptation 2.50
❑3, Apr 1990, b&w; Movie adaptation 2.50

Invaders from Mars (Book II)
Eternity

❑1, ca. 1990, b&w; sequel 2.50
❑2, ca. 1990, b&w; sequel 2.50
❑3, ca. 1990, b&w; sequel 2.50

Invasion!
DC

❑1, Jan 1989, 84 page giant; KG (w); TMc (a); 1&O: Blasters. 1: Garryn Bek. 1: Dominators. 1: Vril Dox II 3.00
❑2, Feb 1989, 84 page giant; KG (w); KG, TMc (a); 1: Strata. 1: L.E.G.I.O.N.. 1: Lyrissa Mallor 3.00
❑3, Mar 1989, 84 page giant; D: Scott Fisher; Return of Metamorpho 3.00

Invasion (Avalon)
Avalon

❑1 ... 2.95

Invasion '55
Apple

❑1, Oct 1990, b&w ... 2.25
❑2, b&w ... 2.25
❑3, b&w ... 2.25

Invasion of the Mind Sappers
Fantagraphics

❑1, Jan 1996, b&w; cardstock cover ... 8.95

Invasion of the Space Amazons from the Purple Planet
Grizmart

❑1, May 1997, b&w ... 2.25
❑2, Fal 1997, b&w ... 2.25
❑3, Win 1997, b&w ... 2.25

Invert
Caliber

❑1, b&w; NN ... 2.50

Invincible
Image

❑0, ca. 2005; O: Invincible ... 1.00
❑1, Jan 2003 ... 25.00
❑2, Feb 2003 ... 12.00
❑3, Mar 2003 ... 12.00
❑4, Apr 2003; Includes pin-ups ... 12.00
❑5, Jun 2003; Includes pin-ups ... 7.00
❑6, Oct 2003; Includes pin-ups ... 7.00
❑7, Nov 2003; Includes pin-ups ... 7.00
❑8, Jan 2004 ... 7.00
❑9, Feb 2004 ... 7.00
❑10, Mar 2004; Hector Plasm backup story ... 7.00
❑11, Apr 2004; Hector Plasm backup story ... 7.00
❑12, Apr 2004; Hector Plasm backup story ... 5.00
❑13, Aug 2004 ... 5.00
❑14, Sep 2004 ... 5.00
❑15, Oct 2004 ... 5.00
❑16, Nov 2004 ... 2.95
❑17, Dec 2004 ... 2.95
❑18, Jan 2005 ... 2.95
❑19, Mar 2005 ... 2.95
❑20, Apr 2005 ... 2.95
❑21, May 2005 ... 2.95
❑22, Jun 2005 ... 2.95
❑23, Jul 2005 ... 2.95
❑24, Aug 2005 ... 2.99
❑25, Oct 2005; Giant-size ... 4.95
❑26, Sep 2005 ... 2.99
❑27, Jan 2006; Backup story ... 2.99
❑28, Mar 2006 ... 2.99
❑29, Apr 2006 ... 2.99
❑30, May 2006 ... 2.99
❑31, Jun 2006 ... 2.99
❑32, Jul 2006 ... 2.99
❑33, Jul 2006 ... 2.99
❑34, Sep 2006 ... 2.99
❑35, Nov 2006 ... 2.99
❑36, Dec 2006, Includes preview of Capes ... 2.99
❑37, Jan 2007 ... 2.99

Invincible Ed (Summertime)
Summertime

❑1 2002 ... 3.50
❑2 2002 ... 3.95

Invincible Ed
Dark Horse

❑1 2003 ... 2.99
❑2 2003 ... 2.99
❑3, Jul 2003 ... 2.99
❑4, Feb 2004 ... 2.99

Invincible Four of Kung Fu & Ninja
Dr. Leung's

❑1 ... 2.00
❑2 ... 2.00
❑3 ... 2.00
❑4 ... 2.00
❑5 ... 2.00

Invincible Man
Junko / Dark Horse

❑1, Sum 1998, b&w; Glossy cover; 1500 printed ... 5.00
❑1/Ltd., b&w; has $100 cover price; 500 printed ... 8.00

Invincibles
CFD

❑1, May 1997 ... 2.95

Invincible Script Book
Image

❑1, Mar 2006 ... 3.99

Invisible 9
Flypaper

❑1, May 1998 ... 2.95

Invisible Dirty Old Man
Red Giant

❑1 ... 3.50

Invisible Frontier
NBM

❑1 ... 15.95
❑2 ...
❑3 ...

Invisible People
Kitchen Sink

❑1 ... 2.95
❑2 ... 2.95
❑3 ... 2.95

Invisibles
DC / Vertigo

❑1, Sep 1994; Giant-size; 1: King Mob ... 3.50
❑2, Oct 1994 ... 2.50
❑3, Nov 1994 ... 2.50
❑4, Dec 1994 ... 2.00
❑5, Jan 1995; There are at least four cover variants, denoted A through D ... 2.00
❑6, Feb 1995 ... 2.00
❑7, Mar 1995 ... 2.00
❑8, Apr 1995 ... 2.00
❑9, Jun 1995 ... 2.50
❑10, Jul 1995 ... 2.50
❑11, Aug 1995 ... 2.50
❑12, Sep 1995 ... 2.50
❑13, Oct 1995 ... 2.50
❑14, Nov 1995 ... 2.50
❑15, Dec 1995 ... 2.50
❑16, Jan 1996 ... 2.50
❑17, Feb 1996 ... 2.50
❑18, Mar 1996 ... 3.00
❑19, Apr 1996 ... 3.00
❑20, May 1996 ... 3.00
❑21, Jun 1996 ... 3.00
❑22, Jul 1996 BB (c) ... 3.00
❑23, Aug 1996 ... 3.00
❑24, Sep 1996 ... 3.00
❑25, Oct 1996; Final Issue ... 4.00

Invisibles
DC / Vertigo

❑1, Feb 1997 BB (c) ... 3.00
❑2, Mar 1997 BB (c) ... 2.50
❑3, Apr 1997 BB (c); BB (a) ... 2.50
❑4, May 1997 BB (c) ... 2.50
❑5, Jun 1997 BB (c); BB (a) ... 2.50
❑6, Jul 1997 BB (c) ... 2.50
❑7, Aug 1997 BB (c) ... 2.50
❑8, Sep 1997 BB (c) ... 2.50
❑9, Oct 1997 BB (c) ... 2.50
❑10, Nov 1997 BB (c); BB (a) ... 2.50
❑11, Dec 1997 BB (c) ... 2.50
❑12, Jan 1998 BB (c) ... 2.50
❑13, Feb 1998 BB (c) ... 2.50
❑14, Mar 1998 BB (c) ... 2.50
❑15, Apr 1998 BB (c) ... 2.50
❑16, May 1998 BB (c) ... 2.50
❑17, Aug 1998 BB (c) ... 2.50
❑18, Sep 1998 BB (c) ... 2.50
❑19, Oct 1998 BB (c) ... 2.50
❑20, Nov 1998 BB (c) ... 2.50
❑21, Jan 1999 BB (c) ... 2.50
❑22, Feb 1999 BB (c) ... 2.50

Invisibles
DC / Vertigo

❑12, Apr 1999; Issues count from 12 to 1 ... 2.95
❑11, May 1999; Issues count from 12 to 1 ... 2.95
❑10, Jun 1999; Issues count from 12 to 1 ... 2.95
❑9, Jul 1999; Issues count from 12 to 1 ... 2.95
❑8, Aug 1999; Issues count from 12 to 1 ... 2.95
❑7, Oct 1999; Issues count from 12 to 1 ... 2.95
❑6, Dec 1999; Issues count from 12 to 1 ... 2.95
❑5, Jan 2000; Issues count from 12 to 1 ... 2.95
❑4, Mar 2000; Issues count from 12 to 1 ... 2.95
❑3, Apr 2000; Issues count from 12 to 1 ... 2.95
❑2, May 2000; Issues count from 12 to 1 ... 2.95
❑1, Jun 2000; Issues count from 12 to 1 ... 2.95

Invisoworld
Eternity

❑1 ... 1.95

I.N.V.U.
Tokyopop

❑1, Feb 2003, b&w ... 9.99
❑2, Feb 2003, b&w ... 9.99

Io
Invictus

❑1, Oct 1994 ... 2.25
❑3, Win 1995, b&w; ashcan ... 2.25

Ion
DC

❑1, Jul 2006 ... 2.99
❑2, Aug 2006 ... 2.99
❑3, Sep 2006, A World of Trouble, Green Lantern (Mogo) cover/appearance ... 2.99
❑4, Sep 2006, V: Green Lantern (Hal Jordan) ... 2.99
❑5, Oct 2006, Team-up with Green Lantern (Hal Jordan); Hal Jordan vs. Alex Nero ... 2.99
❑6, Nov 2006 ... 2.99
❑7, Jan 2007 ... 2.99
❑8, Feb 2007, V: Hiddai champion ... 2.99
❑9, Mar 2007 ... 2.99

I, Paparazzi
DC / Vertigo

❑1 ... 29.95

Ironcat
Ironcat

❑1, Jul 1999 ... 2.95
❑2, Aug 1999 ... 2.95

Iron Corporal
Charlton

❑23, Oct 1985, Continues From Army War Heroes ... 1.50
❑24, Dec 1985, Reprints from Army War Heroes #25, Attack #54 ... 1.50
❑25, Feb 1985, Reprints from Fightin' Navy #82 ... 1.50

Iron Corporal
Avalon

❑1, b&w ... 2.95

Iron Devil
Fantagraphics / Eros

❑1, b&w; Adult ... 2.95
❑2, b&w; Adult ... 2.95
❑3, Mar 1994, b&w; Adult ... 2.95

Iron Fist
Marvel

❑1, Nov 1975, GK (c); JBy (a); A: Iron Man. Marvel Value Stamp #63: Sub-Mariner ... 35.00
❑2, Dec 1975, GK (c); JBy (a) ... 12.00
❑3, Feb 1976, KP (c); JBy (a) ... 10.00
❑4, Apr 1976, GK (c); JBy (a) ... 8.00
❑4/30¢, Apr 1976, GK (c); JBy (a); 30¢ regional price variant ... 20.00
❑5, Jun 1976, GK (c); JBy (a) ... 8.00
❑5/30¢, Jun 1976, GK (c); JBy (a); 30¢ regional price variant ... 20.00
❑6, Aug 1976, GK (c); JBy (a) ... 8.00
❑6/30¢, Aug 1976, GK (c); JBy (a); 30¢ regional price variant ... 20.00
❑7, Sep 1976, GK (c); JBy (a) ... 8.00
❑8, Oct 1976, JBy (c); JBy (a) ... 8.00
❑9, Nov 1976, DC (c); JBy (a) ... 8.00
❑10, Dec 1976, DC (c); JBy (a) ... 8.00
❑11, Feb 1977, GK (c); JBy (a) ... 8.00
❑12, Apr 1977, DC (c); JBy (a) ... 8.00
❑13, Jun 1977, DC (c); JBy (a); V: Boomerang ... 8.00
❑13/35¢, Jun 1977, 35¢ cover price; Limited distribution ... 10.00
❑14, Aug 1977, JBy (a); 1: Sabretooth ... 80.00

Inu-Yasha

Rumiko Takahashi's feudal fairy tale

©Viz

Invaders

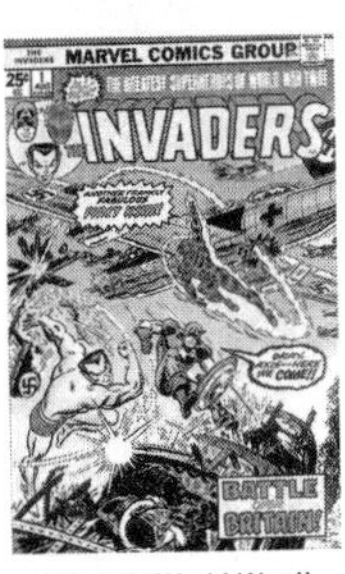

Marvel's World War II super-team

©Marvel

Invaders from Mars

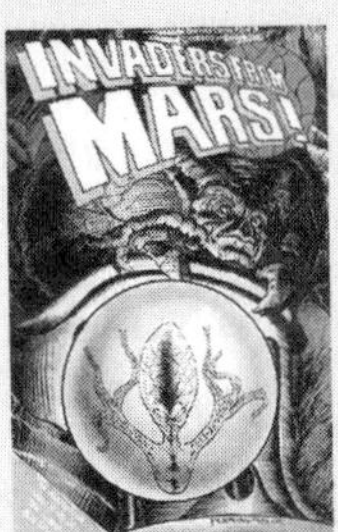

Based on the 1953 science-fiction film

©Eternity

Invincible

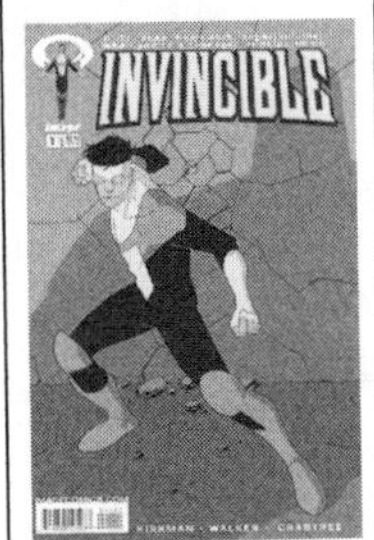

Son begins inheriting super-hero dad's power

©Image

Invisibles

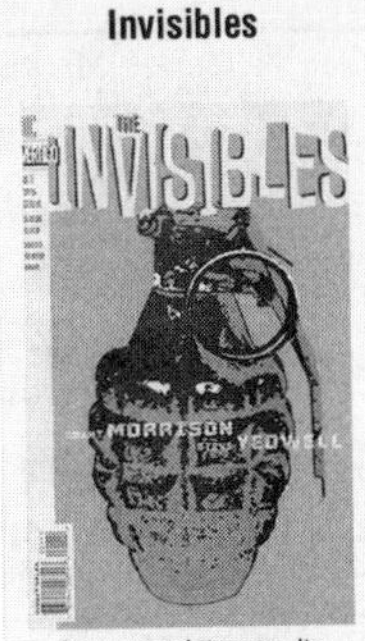

Secret society recruits problem kid

©DC

N-MINT

❑14/35¢, Aug 1977, JBy (a); 1: Sabretooth. 35¢ cover price; Limited distribution 150.00
❑15, Sep 1977, DC (c); JBy (a); A: X-Men. A: Wolverine. Final Issue 27.00
❑15/35¢, Sep 1977, DC (c); JBy (a); A: X-Men. 35¢ cover price; Limited distribution 75.00

Iron Fist
Marvel

❑1, Sep 1996 .... 2.00
❑2, Oct 1996 .... 1.50

Iron Fist
Marvel

❑1, Jul 1998; gatefold summary 2.50
❑2, Aug 1998; gatefold summary 2.50
❑3, Sep 1998; gatefold summary 2.50

Iron Fist
Marvel

❑1, May 2004 .... 2.99
❑2, Jun 2004 .... 2.99
❑3, Jul 2004 .... 2.99
❑4, Aug 2004 .... 2.99
❑5, Sep 2004 .... 2.99
❑6, Oct 2004 .... 2.99

Iron Fist: Wolverine
Marvel

❑1, Nov 2000; V: Hand 2.99
❑2, Dec 2000; V: Hand 2.99
❑3, Jan 2001; V: Hand 2.99
❑4, Feb 2001; V: Hand 2.99

Iron Ghost
Image

❑1, Apr 2005 .... 2.95
❑2, Jul 2005 .... 2.95
❑3, Oct 2005 .... 2.95
❑4 2005 .... 2.99
❑5, Feb 2006 .... 2.99
❑6, Apr 2006 .... 2.99

Ironhand of Almuric
Dark Horse

❑1, b&w 2.00
❑2, b&w 2.00
❑3, b&w 2.00
❑4, b&w 2.00

Ironjaw
Atlas-Seaboard

❑1, Jan 1975 NA (c); JAb (a) 9.00
❑2, Mar 1975 NA (c) 6.00
❑3, May 1975 .... 6.00
❑4, Jul 1975; O: Ironjaw 8.00

Iron Lantern
Marvel / Amalgam

❑1, Jun 1997 .... 1.95

Iron Man
Marvel

❑1, May 1968, GC (c); GC, JCr (a); O: Iron Man; 1: Mordius 365.00
❑2, Jun 1968, JCr (a); 1: Demolisher; 1: Janice Cord 75.00
❑3, Jul 1968, JCr (a); Walt Simonson L.O.C 60.00
❑4, Aug 1968, JCr, GT (a) 60.00

N-MINT

❑5, Sep 1968, JCr, GT (a); 1: Cerebus; 1: Krylla 55.00
❑6, Oct 1968, JCr, GT (a); 2: Crusher; Peter Sanderson L.O.C 50.00
❑7, Nov 1968, JCr, GT (a) 50.00
❑8, Dec 1968, JCr, GT (a) 40.00
❑9, Jan 1969, JCr, GT (a); V: Hulk (robot) 90.00
❑10, Feb 1969, JCr, GT (a); Walt Simonson L.O.C 42.00
❑11, Mar 1969, V: Mandarin; Peter Sanderson L.O.C 35.00
❑12, Apr 1969, O: The Controller. 1: Janice Cord. 1: The Controller 35.00
❑13, May 1969, V: Controller. 2: The Controller 27.00
❑14, Jun 1969, V: Night Phantom. 1: Night Phantom 27.00
❑15, Jul 1969, V: Unicorn. 1: Alex Niven 27.00
❑16, Aug 1969, V: Unicorn; Don McGregor L.O.C 27.00
❑17, Sep 1969, 1: Madame Masque I (Whitney Frost); 1: Midas; 2: Alex Niven 27.00
❑18, Oct 1969, O: Madame Masque I; 2: Midas 25.00
❑19, Nov 1969, O: Madame Masque I. Tony Stark's heart repaired 25.00
❑20, Dec 1969, V: Lucifer 25.00
❑21, Jan 1970, 1: Crimson Dynamo III (Alex Nevsky). Tony Stark quits as Iron Man 20.00
❑22, Feb 1970, D: Janice Cord. V: Crimson Dynamo 20.00
❑23, Mar 1970, 1: Mercenary; D: Vincent Sandhurst; D: Mercenary 20.00
❑24, Apr 1970, V: Minotaur. 1: Minotaur; D: Minotaur; Madame Masque appearnce 20.00
❑25, May 1970, A: Sub-Mariner. V: Sub-Mariner 20.00
❑26, Jun 1970, A: Val-Larr. 1: Val-Larr 20.00
❑27, Jul 1970, 1: Firebrand (Marvel). V: Firebrand 20.00
❑28, Aug 1970, V: Controller. 1: Meredith McCall 20.00
❑29, Sep 1970 .... 20.00
❑30, Oct 1970 .... 20.00
❑31, Nov 1970, 1: Kevin O'Brien (later Guardsman). V: Smashers 15.00
❑32, Dec 1970, V: Mechanoid. 1: Mechanoid 15.00
❑33, Jan 1971, 1: Spymaster. V: Spymaster; 2: Kevin O'Brian (later Guardsman) 15.00
❑34, Feb 1971, V: Spymaster. 2: Spymaster 15.00
❑35, Mar 1971, A: Daredevil. 1: Capricorn; 1: Aquarius; 1: Sagittarius; 2: Libra 15.00
❑36, Apr 1971, SB (c); DH (a); V: Ramrod. 1: Ramrod; 1: Marianne Rogers 15.00
❑37, May 1971, 2: Ramrod; 2: Marianne Rogers 15.00
❑38, Jun 1971, V: Jonah 15.00
❑39, Jul 1971, V: White Dragon. 1: White Dragon I; 1: Shara-Lee 15.00
❑40, Aug 1971, D: White Dragon I; D: Shara-Lee 15.00
❑41, Sep 1971, V: Slasher. 2: Mr. Kline 12.00
❑42, Oct 1971 .... 12.00

N-MINT

❑43, Nov 1971, Giant-size; GK (c); SL (w); GT, JM (a); 1: Guardsman. V: Mikas; V: Mikas; Giant-Man and Wasp: Tales to Astonish #52 .... 35.00
❑44, Jan 1972, GT, RA (a); V: Night Phantom; Ant-Man 12.00
❑45, Mar 1972, GT (a); Steve Englehart work is uncredited 15.00
❑46, May 1972, GT (a); 1: Marianne Rodgers. A: Guardsman. D: Guardsman 15.00
❑47, Jun 1972, JM (a); O: Iron Man 35.00
❑48, Jul 1972, V: Firebrand 12.00
❑49, Aug 1972, V: Adaptoid 12.00
❑50, Sep 1972, V: Princess Python 12.00
❑51, Oct 1972 .... 17.00
❑52, Nov 1972, V: Raga 10.00
❑53, Dec 1972, JSn, GT (a); 1: Black Lama. V: Black Lama 10.00
❑54, Jan 1973, 1: Moondragon (as Madame MacEvil). A: Sub-Mariner. V: Sub-Mariner 16.00
❑55, Feb 1973, JSn (w); JSn (a); 1: Mentor. 1: Drax the Destroyer. 1: Thanos. 1: Kronos. 1: Blood Brothers. 1: Starfox; 1: Mentor (A'Lars) 110.00
❑56, Mar 1973, JSn (w); JSn (a); 1: Fangor 15.00
❑57, Apr 1973 .... 15.00
❑58, May 1973, V: Mandarin 15.00
❑59, Jun 1973 .... 15.00
❑60, Jul 1973 .... 15.00
❑61, Aug 1973 .... 15.00
❑62, Sep 1973 .... 15.00
❑63, Oct 1973 .... 15.00
❑64, Nov 1973, survey 15.00
❑65, Dec 1973, O: Doctor Spectrum 15.00
❑66, Feb 1974, A: Thor. Marvel Value Stamp A80 .... 15.00
❑67, Apr 1974, A: Sunfire. Marvel Value Stamp #80: Ghost Rider 15.00
❑68, Jun 1974, GT (a); O: Iron Man. A: Sunfire. Marvel Value Stamp #29: Baron Mordo 10.00
❑69, Aug 1974, GT (a); V: Sunfire. V: Mandarin. V: Unicorn. V: Yellow Claw. Marvel Value Stamp #22: Man-Thing 10.00
❑70, Sep 1974, GT (a); Marvel Value Stamp #2: Hulk 10.00
❑71, Nov 1974, GT (a); Marvel Value Stamp #26: Mephisto 10.00
❑72, Jan 1975, GT, NA (a); comic con 10.00
❑73, Mar 1975, GK (c); KP (a) 10.00
❑74, May 1975, KP (a); V: Modok. V: M.O.D.O.K 10.00
❑75, Jun 1975 .... 10.00
❑76, Jul 1975, GT (a) 10.00
❑77, Aug 1975 .... 10.00
❑78, Sep 1975, in Vietnam 10.00
❑79, Oct 1975 .... 10.00
❑80, Nov 1975, JK (c) 10.00
❑81, Dec 1975, Marvel Value Stamp 10.00
❑82, Jan 1976, repeats letter column from #81; Marvel Value Stamp B2 .... 10.00
❑83, Feb 1976, HT (a); V: Red Ghost. Marvel Value Stamp B16 .... 10.00
❑84, Mar 1976, HT (a); Marvel Value Stamp B56 .... 10.00
❑85, Apr 1976, Deletion of nose from Iron Man's mask 10.00

Other grades: Multiply price above by 5/6 for VF/NM • 2/3 for VERY FINE • 1/3 for FINE • 1/5 for VERY GOOD • 1/8 for GOOD

	N-MINT
❑85/30¢, Apr 1976, 30¢ cover; Deletion of nose from Iron Man's mask	20.00
❑86, May 1976, 1: Blizzard. V: Blizzard. Marvel Value Stamp B84	10.00
❑86/30¢, May 1976, 30¢ cover; Marvel Value Stamp B84	20.00
❑87, Jun 1976, Marvel Value Stamp	10.00
❑87/30¢, Jun 1976, 30¢ cover; V: Blizzard; Marvel Value Stamp	20.00
❑88, Jul 1976, GT (a); Marvel Value Stamp 66	10.00
❑88/30¢, Jul 1976, 30¢ cover; Marvel Value Stamp 66	20.00
❑89, Aug 1976, GT (a); A: Daredevil	10.00
❑89/30¢, Aug 1976, 30¢ cover	20.00
❑90, Sep 1976	10.00
❑91, Oct 1976, GT (a)	10.00
❑92, Nov 1976, GT (a); V: Melter	10.00
❑93, Dec 1976	10.00
❑94, Jan 1977, HT (w); HT (a)	10.00
❑95, Feb 1977, Newsstand edition (distributed by Curtis); issue number in box	10.00
❑95/Whitman, Feb 1977, Special markets edition (usually sold in Whitman bagged prepacks); price appears in a diamond; UPC barcode appears	18.00
❑96, Mar 1977, GT (a); 1: New Guardsman. Michael O'Brien becomes New Guardsman; Newsstand edition (distributed by Curtis); issue number in box	10.00
❑96/Whitman, Mar 1977, GT (a); 1: New Guardsman. Special markets edition (usually sold in Whitman bagged prepacks); price appears in a diamond; UPC barcode appears	18.00
❑97, Apr 1977	10.00
❑98, May 1977, Newsstand edition (distributed by Curtis); issue number in box	8.00
❑98/Whitman, May 1977, Special markets edition (usually sold in Whitman bagged prepacks); price appears in a diamond; UPC barcode appears	18.00
❑99, Jun 1977, GT (a); V: Mandarin. Newsstand edition (distributed by Curtis); issue number in box	8.00
❑99/Whitman, Jun 1977, GT (a); V: Mandarin. Special markets edition (usually sold in Whitman bagged prepacks); price appears in a diamond; UPC barcode appears	18.00
❑99/35¢, Jun 1977, GT (a); V: Mandarin. 35¢ regional variant newsstand edition (distributed by Curtis); issue number in box	15.00
❑100, Jul 1977, 100th anniversary issue; JSn (c); GT (a); Mandarin; Newsstand edition (distributed by Curtis); issue number in box	12.00
❑100/Whitman, Jul 1977, JSn (c); GT (a); Special markets edition (usually sold in Whitman bagged prepacks); price appears in a diamond; UPC barcode appears	20.00
❑100/35¢, Jul 1977, 35¢ regional variant newsstand edition (distributed by Curtis); issue number in box	18.00
❑101, Aug 1977, VM (c); GT (a); 1: Dreadknight. Newsstand edition (distributed by Curtis); issue number in box	7.00
❑101/Whitman, Aug 1977, GT (a); 1: Dreadknight. Special markets edition (usually sold in Whitman bagged prepacks); price appears in a diamond; UPC barcode appears	14.00
❑101/35¢, Aug 1977, VM (c); GT (a); 1: Dreadknight. 35¢ regional variant newsstand edition (distributed by Curtis); issue number in box	12.00
❑102, Sep 1977, O: Dreadknight. 1: Dreadknight. Newsstand edition (distributed by Curtis); issue number in box	7.00
❑102/Whitman, Sep 1977, O: Dreadknight. 1: Dreadknight. Special markets edition (usually sold in Whitman bagged prepacks); price appears in a diamond; no UPC barcode	14.00
❑102/35¢, Sep 1977, O: Dreadknight. 1: Dreadknight. 35¢ regional variant newsstand edition (distributed by Curtis); issue number in box	12.00
❑103, Oct 1977, A: Jack of Hearts. Newsstand edition (distributed by Curtis); issue number in box	7.00

	N-MINT
❑103/Whitman, Oct 1977, A: Jack of Hearts. Special markets edition (usually sold in Whitman bagged prepacks); price appears in a diamond; no UPC barcode	14.00
❑103/35¢, Oct 1977, A: Jack of Hearts. 35¢ regional variant newsstand edition (distributed by Curtis); issue number in box	12.00
❑104, Nov 1977, Newsstand edition (distributed by Curtis); issue number in box	7.00
❑104/Whitman, Nov 1977, Special markets edition (usually sold in Whitman bagged prepacks); price appears in a diamond; no UPC barcode	14.00
❑105, Dec 1977, DC (c); GT (a); A: Jack of Hearts	7.00
❑106, Jan 1978	7.00
❑107, Feb 1978, KP (c); KP (a); V: Midas	7.00
❑108, Mar 1978, KP (c); CI (a)	7.00
❑109, Apr 1978, 1: Vanguard. V: Darkstar. V: Vanguard; 1: Crimson Dynamo (Dmitri Bukharin)	7.00
❑110, May 1978, DC (c); KP (a); A: Jack of Hearts	7.00
❑111, Jun 1978, Wundagore	7.00
❑112, Jul 1978, KP (c); KP, AA (a)	7.00
❑113, Aug 1978, JR2 (c); KP, HT (a); Newsstand edition (distributed by Curtis); issue number in box	7.00
❑113/Whitman, Aug 1978, HT (a); Special markets edition (usually sold in Whitman bagged prepacks); price appears in a diamond; no UPC barcode	14.00
❑114, Sep 1978, Newsstand edition (distributed by Curtis); issue number in box	7.00
❑114/Whitman, Sep 1978, Special markets edition (usually sold in Whitman bagged prepacks); price appears in a diamond; no UPC barcode	14.00
❑115, Oct 1978, JR2 (c); DGr, JR2 (a); Newsstand edition (distributed by Curtis); issue number in box	7.00
❑115/Whitman, Oct 1978, DGr (a); Special markets edition (usually sold in Whitman bagged prepacks); price appears in a diamond; no UPC barcode	14.00
❑116, Nov 1978, JR2 (c); BL (w); BL, JR2 (a); D: Ape-Man I (Gordon Monk Keefer). D: Frog-Man I (Francois LeBlanc). D: Count Nefaria. D: Cat-Man I (Townshend Patane). D: Bird-Man I (Henry Hawk). 1st David Michelinie written issue; Newsstand edition (distributed by Curtis); issue number in box	7.00
❑116/Whitman, Nov 1978, BL, JR2 (a); D: Ape-Man I (Gordon Monk Keefer). D: Frog-Man I (Francois LeBlanc). D: Count Nefaria. D: Cat-Man I (Townshend Patane). D: Bird-Man I (Henry Hawk). Special markets edition (usually sold in Whitman bagged prepacks); price appears in a diamond; no UPC barcode	14.00
❑117, Dec 1978, JR2 (c); BL (w); BL, JR2 (a); 1: Beth Cabe. Newsstand edition (distributed by Curtis); issue number in box	7.00
❑117/Whitman, Dec 1978, BL, JR2 (a); 1: Beth Cabe. Special markets edition (usually sold in Whitman bagged prepacks); price appears in a diamond; no UPC barcode	14.00
❑118, Jan 1979, BL (c); BL (w); JBy, BL (a); 1: James Rhodes (Rhodey). 1: Mrs. Arbogast. Newsstand edition (distributed by Curtis); issue number in box	7.00
❑118/Whitman, Jan 1979, JBy, BL (a); 1: James Rhodes (Rhodey). 1: Mrs. Arbogast. Special markets edition (usually sold in Whitman bagged prepacks); price appears in a diamond; no UPC barcode	14.00
❑119, Feb 1979, JR2 (c); BL, JR2 (a); Stark battles with alcohol; Newsstand edition (distributed by Curtis); issue number in box	7.00
❑119/Whitman, Feb 1979, BL, JR2 (a); Special markets edition (usually sold in Whitman bagged prepacks); price appears in a diamond; no UPC barcode	14.00
❑120, Mar 1979, 1: Justin Hammer. A: Sub-Mariner. Stark battles with alcohol	7.00
❑121, Apr 1979, A: Sub-Mariner. Stark battles with alcohol	7.00

	N-MINT
❑122, May 1979, O: Iron Man. A: Sub-Mariner. Stark battles with alcohol; Newsstand edition (distributed by Curtis); issue number in box	7.00
❑122/Whitman, May 1979, O: Iron Man. A: Sub-Mariner. Special markets edition (usually sold in Whitman bagged prepacks); price appears in a diamond; no UPC barcode	14.00
❑123, Jun 1979, Stark battles with alcohol	7.00
❑124, Jul 1979, BL (c); BL (w); JR2 (a); Stark battles with alcohol	7.00
❑125, Aug 1979, BL (c); BL (w); JR2 (a); A: Scott Lang (Ant-Man). Stark battles with alcohol	7.00
❑126, Sep 1979, V: Justin Hammer. Stark battles with alcohol	7.00
❑127, Oct 1979, Stark battles with alcohol	7.00
❑128, Nov 1979, BL (c); BL (w); BL, JR2 (a); Stark begins recovery from alcohol	7.00
❑129, Dec 1979, BL (c); SB (a); V: Dreadnought	7.00
❑130, Jan 1980	5.00
❑131, Feb 1980, A: Hulk. Jo Duffy L.O.C	5.00
❑132, Mar 1980, A: Hulk	5.00
❑133, Apr 1980, BL (c); BL (w); BL (a); A: Hulk. A: Ant-Man	5.00
❑134, May 1980, BL (c); BL (w); BL (a).	5.00
❑135, Jun 1980, BL (c); BL (w); BL (a); V: Titanium Man	5.00
❑136, Jul 1980, BL (c); BWi (a)	5.00
❑137, Aug 1980, BL (c); BL (w); BL (a) .	5.00
❑138, Sep 1980, BL (c); BL, TP (a); 1: Dreadnought (silver)	5.00
❑139, Oct 1980, BL (c); BL (a); Bethany Cabe knows Tony is Iron Man	5.00
❑140, Nov 1980, BL (c); BL (a)	5.00
❑141, Dec 1980, BL (c); BL (w); BL, JR2 (a)	5.00
❑142, Jan 1981, BL (c); BL (w); BL, JR2 (a); 1: Space Armor	5.00
❑143, Feb 1981, BL (c); BL (w); BL, JR2 (a); 1: Sunturion	5.00
❑144, Mar 1981, BL (c); BL (w); BL, JR2 (a); O: James Rhodes (Rhodey); O: James Rhodes	5.00
❑145, Apr 1981, BL (c); BL (w); BL, JR2 (a)	5.00
❑146, May 1981, BL (c); BL, JR2 (a); V: Blacklash	5.00
❑147, Jun 1981, BL (c); BL (w); BL, JR2 (a)	5.00
❑148, Jul 1981, BL (c); BL, JR2 (a)	5.00
❑149, Aug 1981, JR2 (c); BL (w); BL, JR2 (a); V: Doctor Doom	5.00
❑150, Sep 1981, double-sized; JR2 (c); BL (w); BL, JR2 (a); V: Doctor Doom. In Camelot	7.00
❑151, Oct 1981, BL (c); BL (w); BL, LMc (a); A: Ant-Man	5.00
❑152, Nov 1981, BL (c); BL (w); BL, JR2 (a); 1: Stealth Armor	5.00
❑153, Dec 1981, BL (c); BL (w); BL, JR2 (a)	5.00
❑154, Jan 1982, JR2 (c); BL, JR2 (a); D: Unicorn I (Milos Masaryk)	7.00
❑155, Feb 1982, BL, JR2 (a)	5.00
❑156, Mar 1982, JR2 (a)	5.00
❑157, Apr 1982	5.00
❑158, May 1982, BL (c); CI (a)	5.00
❑159, Jun 1982, PS (c); PS (a); Diablo..	5.00
❑160, Jul 1982, SD (a); Serpent Squad .	7.00
❑161, Aug 1982, LMc (a); Moon Knight	5.00
❑162, Sep 1982	5.00
❑163, Oct 1982, LMc (a); 1: Obadiah Stane (voice only). 1: Chessmen. 1: Indries Moomji. 1: Iron Monger (voice only)	5.00
❑164, Nov 1982, BA (c); LMc, BA (a)	5.00
❑165, Dec 1982, LMc (a)	5.00
❑166, Jan 1983, LMc (c); LMc (a); 1: Obadiah Stane (full appearance). 1: Iron Monger (full appearance); 1: Iron Monger (Obadiah Stane); 1: Obadiah Stane	5.00
❑167, Feb 1983, LMc (a); Alcohol problem returns	5.00
❑168, Mar 1983, LMc (a); Machine Man; Stark battles with alcohol	5.00
❑169, Apr 1983, LMc (a); Jim Rhodes takes over Stark's job as Iron Man; Stark battles with alcohol	5.00
❑170, May 1983, LMc (c); LMc (a); 1: Morley Erwin. 1: James Rhodes as Iron Man. Stark battles with alcohol...	5.00

Other grades: Multiply price above by 5/6 for VF/NM • 2/3 for VERY FINE • 1/3 for FINE • 1/5 for VERY GOOD • 1/8 for GOOD

Invisibles

Issues released in reverse order, counting down

©DC

Iron Fist

Short 1970s series introduced Sabretooth

©Marvel

Ironjaw

Metal-mandibled man from short-lived line

©Atlas-Seaboard

Iron Man

Billionaire inventor creates super suit

©Marvel

Iron Man

Jim Lee's "Heroes Reborn" take on Iron Man

©Marvel

	N-MINT
❑171, Jun 1983, LMc (c); LMc (a); 1: Clytemnestra Erwin. V: Thunderball. Stark battles with alcohol	2.50
❑172, Jul 1983, LMc (c); LMc (a); A: Captain America. Stark battles with alcohol	2.50
❑173, Aug 1983, LMc (a); Stark International becomes Stane International; Stark battles with alcohol	2.50
❑174, Sep 1983, LMc (c); LMc (a); V: Chessmen. S.H.I.E.L.D. acquires armor; Stark battles with alcohol	2.50
❑175, Oct 1983, LMc (c); LMc (a); Stark battles with alcohol	2.50
❑176, Nov 1983, LMc (c); LMc (a); Stark battles with alcohol	2.50
❑177, Dec 1983, LMc (c); LMc (a); V: Flying Tiger. Stark battles with alcohol (alcohol storyline continues through next several issues)	2.50
❑178, Jan 1984, LMc (c); LMc (a)	2.50
❑179, Feb 1984, LMc (c); LMc (a); V: Mandarin	2.50
❑180, Mar 1984, LMc (c); LMc (a); V: Mandarin	2.50
❑181, Apr 1984, LMc (c); LMc (a); V: Mandarin. Erroneously reprints 1982 Statement of Ownership	2.50
❑182, May 1984, LMc (c); LMc (a); alcoholism cured again	4.00
❑183, Jun 1984, LMc (c); LMc (a); V: Taurus	2.50
❑184, Jul 1984, LMc (c); LMc (a); Tony Stark founds new company in California	2.50
❑185, Aug 1984, LMc (c); LMc (a)	2.50
❑186, Sep 1984, LMc (c); LMc (a); O: Vibro. 1: Vibro. V: Vibro	4.00
❑187, Oct 1984, LMc (a); V: Vibro	2.50
❑188, Nov 1984, DP (a); 1: Circuits Maximus. V: Brothers Grimm	2.50
❑189, Dec 1984, LMc (a); V: Termite	2.50
❑190, Jan 1985, LMc (a); A: Scarlet Witch. V: Termite	2.50
❑191, Feb 1985, LMc (a); Tony Stark returns as Iron Man in original armor.	2.50
❑192, Mar 1985, Iron Man (Stark) vs. Iron Man (Rhodey)	4.00
❑193, Apr 1985, LMc (a); West Coast Avengers learn Tony is Iron Man	2.50
❑194, May 1985, LMc (a); 1: Scourge. A: West Coast Avengers. D: Enforcer (Marvel)	2.50
❑195, Jun 1985, A: Shaman	2.50
❑196, Jul 1985	2.50
❑197, Aug 1985, Secret Wars II	2.50
❑198, Sep 1985, SB (a); O: Obadiah Stane. O: Iron Monger	2.50
❑199, Oct 1985, HT (a); D: Morley Erwin. James Rhodes crippled	2.50
❑200, Nov 1985, double-sized; 1: Red and white battlesuit. D: Obadiah Stane. D: Iron Monger. Tony Stark returns as Iron Man; New armor (red & white)	3.00
❑201, Dec 1985	2.00
❑202, Jan 1986, A: Ka-Zar. V: Fixer	2.00
❑203, Feb 1986	2.00
❑204, Mar 1986	2.00
❑205, Apr 1986, V: Modok. V: M.O.D.O.K	2.00
❑206, May 1986	2.00
❑207, Jun 1986	2.00
❑208, Jul 1986	2.00

	N-MINT
❑209, Aug 1986	2.00
❑210, Sep 1986, A: Happy Hogan	2.00
❑211, Oct 1986	2.00
❑212, Nov 1986, 1: new Dominic Fortune; D: Dominic Fortune	2.00
❑213, Dec 1986, A: Dominic Fortune	2.00
❑214, Jan 1987, Construction of Stark Enterprises begins	2.00
❑215, Feb 1987	2.00
❑216, Mar 1987, D: Clytemnestra Erwin	2.00
❑217, Apr 1987, 1: undersea armor	2.00
❑218, May 1987, BL (c); BL (a); 1: Deep Sea armor	2.00
❑219, Jun 1987, BL (c); BL (a); 1: Ghost. V: Ghost	2.00
❑220, Jul 1987, D: Spymaster	2.00
❑221, Aug 1987	2.00
❑222, Sep 1987	2.00
❑223, Oct 1987, BL (c); 1: Rae LaCoste.	2.00
❑224, Nov 1987, BL (a)	2.00
❑225, Dec 1987, Giant-size	3.00
❑226, Jan 1988	2.50
❑227, Feb 1988, BL (w)	2.50
❑228, Mar 1988, BL (w)	2.50
❑229, Apr 1988, BL (w); D: Gremlin a.k.a Titanium Man II; D: Titanium Man (Topolov)	3.00
❑230, May 1988, BL (w); V: Firepower. apparent death of Iron Man	2.50
❑231, Jun 1988, V: Firepower. new armor	2.50
❑232, Jul 1988, offset	2.50
❑232/A, Jul 1988, Flexographic	2.50
❑233, Aug 1988, BL (w); BG (a); 1: Kathy Dare. A: Ant-Man	2.00
❑234, Sep 1988, BL (w); BG (a); A: Spider-Man	2.00
❑235, Oct 1988, BL (w); BG (a)	1.50
❑236, Nov 1988, BL (w); BG (a)	1.50
❑237, Dec 1988, BL (w); BG (a)	1.50
❑238, Jan 1989, BL (w); BG (a); 1: Madame Masque II	1.50
❑239, Feb 1989, BL (c); BG (a)	1.50
❑240, Mar 1989, BL (c); BL (w); BG (a).	1.50
❑241, Apr 1989, BL (c); BL (w)	1.50
❑242, May 1989, BL (c); BL (w); Stark shot by Kathy Dare	1.50
❑243, Jun 1989, BL (c); BL (w); BL (a); Stark crippled	2.00
❑244, Jul 1989, Giant-size; Carl Walker a.k.a. Force becomes Iron Man; New armor to allow Stark to walk again	3.00
❑245, Aug 1989, BL (c); PS (a)	1.50
❑246, Sep 1989, BL (c); BL (w); BL (a).	1.50
❑247, Oct 1989, BL (c); BL (w); BL (a)..	1.50
❑248, Nov 1989, BL (c); BL (w); BL (a); Stark cured by implanted bio-chip	1.50
❑249, Nov 1989, BL (c); BL (a); Doctor Doom	1.50
❑250, Dec 1989, double-sized; BL (c); BL (w); BL (a); V: Doctor Doom. Acts of Vengeance	1.75
❑251, Dec 1989, HT (a); V: Wrecker. Acts of Vengeance	1.25
❑252, Jan 1990, HT (a); V: Chemistro. Acts of Vengeance	1.25
❑253, Feb 1990, JBy (c); GC (a); Carnival of Death!	1.25
❑254, Mar 1990, BL (c); BL (w); BL (a).	1.25
❑255, Apr 1990, HT (a)	1.25

	N-MINT
❑256, May 1990, JR2 (c); BL (w); JR2 (a)	1.25
❑257, Jun 1990	1.25
❑258, Jul 1990, JR2 (c); JBy (w); JR2 (a)	1.50
❑259, Aug 1990, JR2 (c); JBy (w); JR2 (a)	1.50
❑260, Sep 1990, JR2 (c); JBy (w); JR2 (a)	1.50
❑261, Oct 1990, JR2 (c); JBy (w); JR2 (a)	1.50
❑262, Nov 1990, JR2 (c); JBy (w); JR2 (a)	1.50
❑263, Dec 1990, JR2 (c); JBy (w); JR2 (a)	1.50
❑264, Jan 1991, JR2 (c); JBy (w); JR2 (a)	1.50
❑265, Feb 1991, JR2 (c); JBy (w); JR2 (a)	1.50
❑266, Mar 1991, JR2 (c); JBy (w); JR2 (a)	1.50
❑267, Apr 1991, JBy (w)	1.50
❑268, May 1991, JBy (w); O: Iron Man..	1.50
❑269, Jun 1991, JBy (w)	1.50
❑270, Jul 1991, JBy (w)	1.50
❑271, Aug 1991, JBy (w)	1.50
❑272, Sep 1991, JBy (w)	1.50
❑273, Oct 1991, JBy (w)	1.50
❑274, Nov 1991, JBy (w); O: Fin Fang Foom. V: Fin Fang Foom	1.50
❑275, Dec 1991, Giant-size; JBy (w); V: Fin Fang Foom. V: Mandarin. V: Dragon Lords	1.50
❑276, Jan 1992, JBy (w)	1.50
❑277, Feb 1992, JBy (w)	1.50
❑278, Mar 1992, 1: new Space Armor. Galactic Storm	1.50
❑279, Apr 1992, V: Ronan the Accuser. Galactic Storm	1.50
❑280, May 1992, A: The Stark	1.50
❑281, Jun 1992, 1: War Machine armor	3.00
❑282, Jul 1992, 2: War Machine armor .	3.00
❑283, Aug 1992	1.50
❑284, Sep 1992, O: War Machine. 1: War Machine. D: Tony Stark	2.00
❑285, Oct 1992	1.25
❑286, Nov 1992	1.25
❑287, Dec 1992	1.25
❑288, Jan 1993, 30th anniversary special; Embossed cover; Tony Stark revived..	2.50
❑289, Feb 1993	1.25
❑290, Mar 1993, Metallic ink cover; New Armor	3.50
❑291, Apr 1993, James Rhodes leaves to become War Machine	1.25
❑292, May 1993	1.25
❑293, Jun 1993	1.25
❑294, Jul 1993	1.25
❑295, Aug 1993, Infinity Crusade	1.25
❑296, Sep 1993	1.25
❑297, Oct 1993, A: M.O.D.A.M. A: Omega Red	1.25
❑298, Nov 1993	1.25
❑299, Dec 1993, V: Ultimo	1.25
❑300, Jan 1994, Giant size; A: Iron Legion (all substitute Iron Men). V: Ultimo. Stark dons new (modular) armor	2.50
❑300/Variant, Jan 1994, Giant size; Special (embossed foil) cover edition; Stark dons new (modular) armor	3.95
❑301, Feb 1994	1.25
❑302, Mar 1994, A: Venom	1.25
❑303, Apr 1994	1.25
❑304, May 1994, 1: Hulkbuster Armor...	1.25
❑305, Jun 1994, A: Hulk	1.50
❑306, Jul 1994, Stark restructures company	1.50
❑307, Aug 1994	1.50

	N-MINT
❑308, Sep 1994	1.50
❑309, Oct 1994	1.50
❑310, Nov 1994, Includes animation cel, preview of Marvel Action Hour	1.50
❑310/CS, Nov 1994, polybagged with 16-page preview, acetate print, and other items	2.95
❑311, Dec 1994	1.50
❑312, Jan 1995	1.50
❑313, Feb 1995	1.50
❑314, Mar 1995	1.50
❑315, Apr 1995, V: Titanium Man	1.50
❑316, May 1995	1.50
❑317, Jun 1995, D: Titanium Man I. flip book with War Machine: Brothers in Arms part 3 back-up	2.50
❑318, Jul 1995	1.50
❑319, Aug 1995, O: Iron Man	1.50
❑320, Sep 1995	1.50
❑321, Oct 1995, OverPower cards inserted	1.50
❑322, Nov 1995	1.50
❑323, Dec 1995, A: Avengers. A: Hawkeye	1.50
❑324, Jan 1996	1.50
❑325, Feb 1996, Giant-size; wraparound cover; Tony Stark vs. young Tony Stark	3.00
❑326, Mar 1996	1.50
❑327, Apr 1996, V: Frostbite. reading of Tony Stark's will	1.50
❑328, May 1996	1.50
❑329, Jun 1996, Fujikawa International takes over Stark Enterprises	1.50
❑330, Jul 1996	1.50
❑331, Aug 1996	1.50
❑332, Sep 1996, Final Issue; Onslaught: Impact 2	1.50
❑Ann 1, Aug 1970, GC, DH, JK, WW, JAb (a); Reprints from Tales of Suspense #71, #79, and #80, and Tales to Astonish #82	27.00
❑Ann 2, Nov 1971, Reprints	20.00
❑Ann 3, ca. 1976, ca. 1976	10.00
❑Ann 4, ca. 1977, Cover reads "King-Size Special"; Cover reads King-Size Special	4.00
❑Ann 5, ca. 1982	3.00
❑Ann 6, ca. 1983, LMc (c); LMc (a); A: Eternals. D: Zuras (spirit leaves body). New Iron Man appears	3.00
❑Ann 7, ca. 1984, LMc (a); 1: Goliath III (Erik Josten). A: . A: West Coast Avengers. West Coast Avengers	3.00
❑Ann 8, ca. 1986, A: X-Factor	3.00
❑Ann 9, ca. 1987	3.00
❑Ann 10, ca. 1989, BL (c); GC, JBy, KP, BL, PS, DP (a); Atlantis Attacks	2.50
❑Ann 11, ca. 1990, A: Machine Man	2.00
❑Ann 12, ca. 1991, 1: Trapster II	2.00
❑Ann 13, ca. 1992, GC (a); A: Darkhawk, Avengers West Coast	2.00
❑Ann 14, ca. 1993, trading card	2.95
❑Ann 15, ca. 1994, GC (a); V: Controller; 1994 Ann	2.95
❑Ashcan 1, Nov 1994, Collectors' Preview; "Iron Man & Force Works" on cover	1.95

Iron Man
Marvel

	N-MINT
❑1, Nov 1996; Giant-size; JLee (w); O: Hulk (new). O: Iron Man (new); Giant-size; O: Hulk; O: Iron Man; 56 pages	3.00
❑1/A, Nov 1996; Giant-size; JLee (w); O: Iron Man (new). variant cover	3.00
❑2, Dec 1996; JLee (w); V: Hulk	2.00
❑3, Jan 1997; JLee (w); 1: Whirlwind. A: Fantastic Four	2.00
❑4, Feb 1997; JLee (w); V: Living Laser	2.00
❑4/A, Feb 1997; JLee (w); variant cover	2.00
❑5, Mar 1997; JLee (w); V: Whirlwind	1.95
❑6, Apr 1997; JLee (a); A: Onslaught. concludes in Captain America #6	1.95
❑7, May 1997 JPH, JLee (w)	1.95
❑8, Jun 1997 JPH (w)	1.95
❑9, Jul 1997 JPH (w)	1.95
❑10, Aug 1997; gatefold summary; JPH (w)	1.95
❑11, Sep 1997; gatefold summary; JPH, JLee (w); A: Doctor Doom	1.95
❑12, Oct 1997; gatefold summary; JPH, JLee (w); cover forms quadtych with Fantastic Four #12, Avengers #12, and Captain America #12	3.50
❑13, Nov 1997; gatefold summary; JRo (w); cover forms quadtych with Fantastic Four #13, Avengers #13, and Captain America #13	2.50

Iron Man
Marvel

	N-MINT
❑1, Feb 1998; Giant-size; KB (w); 1: Stark Solutions. wraparound cover	3.50
❑1/A, Feb 1998; gatefold summary; KB (w); 1: Stark Solutions. wraparound cover	4.00
❑2, Mar 1998; gatefold summary; KB (w)	2.00
❑2/Variant, Mar 1998; KB (w); variant cover	3.00
❑3, Apr 1998; gatefold summary; KB (w)	2.00
❑4, May 1998; gatefold summary; KB (w); V: Firebrand	2.00
❑5, Jun 1998; gatefold summary; KB (w); V: Firebrand	2.00
❑6, Jul 1998; gatefold summary; RHo, KB (w); A: Black Widow	2.00
❑7, Aug 1998; gatefold summary; RHo, KB (w); A: Warbird	2.00
❑8, Sep 1998; gatefold summary; KB (w); Tony beaten	2.00
❑9, Oct 1998; gatefold summary; KB (w); A: Winter Guard	2.00
❑10, Nov 1998; gatefold summary; KB (w)	2.00
❑11, Dec 1998; gatefold summary; KB (w); A: Warbird. V: War Machine armor. new home	2.00
❑12, Jan 1999; gatefold summary; KB (w); A: Warbird. V: War Machine armor	2.00
❑13, Feb 1999; double-sized; KB (w); A: Controller. V: Controller; Gatefold summary	3.00
❑14, Mar 1999; KB (w); A: Fantastic Four. A: S.H.I.E.L.D.. A: Watcher. V: Ronan. Fantastic Four crossover, part 2	1.99
❑15, Apr 1999; KB (w); V: Nitro	1.99
❑16, May 1999 KB (w)	1.99
❑17, Jun 1999 KB (w); A: Fin Fang Foom	1.99
❑18, Jul 1999 KB (w); A: Warbird	1.99
❑19, Aug 1999; KB (w); V: War Machine	1.99
❑20, Sep 1999; KB (w); V: War Machine	1.99
❑21, Oct 1999; KB (w); 1: Inferno. continues in Thor #17	1.99
❑22, Nov 1999; KB (w); 1: Carnivore. A: Thor. continues in Peter Parker, Spider-Man #11	1.99
❑23, Dec 1999 KB (w); A: Ultimo	1.99
❑24, Jan 2000	1.99
❑25, Feb 2000; double-sized; KB (w); BL (a); A: Warbird. A: Ultimo	2.25
❑26, Mar 2000	2.25
❑27, Apr 2000	2.25
❑28, May 2000	2.25
❑29, Jun 2000	2.25
❑30, Jul 2000	2.25
❑31, Aug 2000	2.25
❑32, Sep 2000; A: Wong-Chu. concludes in Iron Man Ann 2000	2.25
❑33, Oct 2000	2.25
❑34, Nov 2000	2.25
❑35, Dec 2000	2.25
❑36, Jan 2001	2.25
❑37, Feb 2001	2.25
❑38, Mar 2001	2.25
❑39, Apr 2001	2.25
❑40, May 2001 BL, JR, ES (a)	2.25
❑41, Jun 2001	2.25
❑42, Jul 2001	2.25
❑43, Aug 2001	2.25
❑44, Sep 2001	2.25
❑45, Oct 2001	2.25
❑46, Nov 2001; BL (w); BL, JR2, GT (a); Reprints Iron Man (1st Series) #78, 140 and 141; 100 page monster	3.50
❑47, Dec 2001	2.25
❑48, Jan 2002	2.25
❑49, Feb 2002; 'Nuff Said silent issue	2.25
❑50, Mar 2002; MGr (w); Giant-size	2.99
❑51, Apr 2002; MGr (w); wraparound cover	2.25
❑52, May 2002; MGr (w); wraparound cover	2.25
❑53, Jun 2002; MGr (w); wraparound cover	2.25
❑54, Jun 2002; MGr (w); wraparound cover	2.25
❑55, Jul 2002; MGr (w); wraparound cover	2.25
❑56, Aug 2002; MGr (w); wraparound cover	2.25
❑57, Sep 2002; MGr (w); wraparound cover	2.25
❑58, Oct 2002; MGr (w); wraparound cover	2.25
❑59, Nov 2002; MGr (c); MGr (w); MGr (a); wraparound cover	2.25
❑60, Dec 2002; MGr (c); MGr (w); MGr (a); wraparound cover	2.25
❑61, Jan 2003; MGr (c); MGr (w); MGr (a); wraparound cover	2.25
❑62, Feb 2003; MGr (w); wraparound cover	2.25
❑63, Feb 2003; MGr (w); wraparound cover	2.25
❑64, Mar 2003; MGr (w); wraparound cover	2.25
❑65, Apr 2003 MGr (w)	2.25
❑66, May 2003 MGr (w)	2.25
❑67, Jun 2003	2.99
❑68, Jul 2003	2.99
❑69, Aug 2003, (c)	2.99
❑70, Sep 2003	2.99
❑71, Oct 2003	2.99
❑72, Nov 2003	2.99
❑73, Dec 2003, JJM (w); Stark seeks cabinet post	2.99
❑74, Jan 2004, JJM (w); Stark nomination announced	2.99
❑75, Feb 2004, JJM (w)	2.99
❑76, Mar 2004, JJM (w); A: Crimson Dynamo III (Alex Nevsky). Stark rejected by Senate subcommittee	2.99
❑77, Apr 2004, JJM (w)	2.99
❑78, May 2004, JJM (w); Stark named Secretary of Defense	2.99
❑79, Jun 2004, JJM (w)	2.99
❑80, Jun 2004, JJM (w); Stark visits Iraq	2.99
❑81, Jul 2004, JJM (w)	2.99
❑82, Jul 2004, JJM (w); Force reconciled with Stark	2.99
❑83, Jul 2004 JJM (w)	2.99
❑84, Aug 2004; JJM (w); Avengers Dissasemble Prologue	8.00
❑85, Aug 2004; JJM (w); Avengers Dissasemble Prologue	5.00
❑86, Sep 2004	2.99
❑87, Oct 2004	2.99
❑88, Nov 2004	2.99
❑89, Dec 2004, Final issue	2.99
❑Ann 1998, ca. 1998; MWa (w); V: Modok. Iron Man/Captain America '98; wraparound cover	3.50
❑Ann 1999, Aug 1999; wraparound cover	3.50
❑Ann 2000, ca. 2000; D: Wong-Chu. wraparound cover	3.50
❑Ann 2001, ca. 2001	2.99

Iron Man
Marvel

	N-MINT
❑1, Jan 2004	3.50
❑2, Feb 2005	2.99
❑3, May 2005	2.99
❑4, Sep 2005	2.99
❑5, Mar 2006	2.99
❑6, Jun 2006	2.99
❑7, Jul 2006, Adi Granov cover	2.99
❑8, Aug 2006, Adi Granov cover; V: Graviton	2.99
❑9, Sep 2006, Adi Granov cover	2.99
❑10, Sep 2006, Adi Granov cover; V: Sentry	2.99
❑11, Oct 2006, Adi Granov cover	2.99
❑12, Nov 2006, Adi Granov cover	2.99
❑13, Jan 2007, Civil War tie-in	2.99
❑14, Feb 2007, Civil War tie-in	2.99
❑15, Mar 2007; The Initiative	2.99
❑16, Apr 2007; The Initiative	2.99
❑16/Variant, Apr 2007; Newsstand edition with repeated pages	14.00
❑17, May 2007; The Initiative	2.99
❑18	2.99
❑19	2.99
❑20	2.99
❑21	2.99
❑22	2.99
❑23	2.99

Iron Man

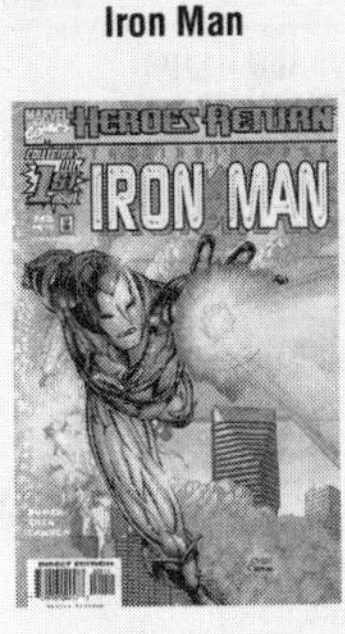

Series revealed Iron Man's identity
©Marvel

Iron Man & Sub-Mariner

Single-issue prequel to solo series launches
©Marvel

Iron Man: Bad Blood

Michelinie and Layton reteam on Iron Man
©Marvel

Iron Man: The Iron Age

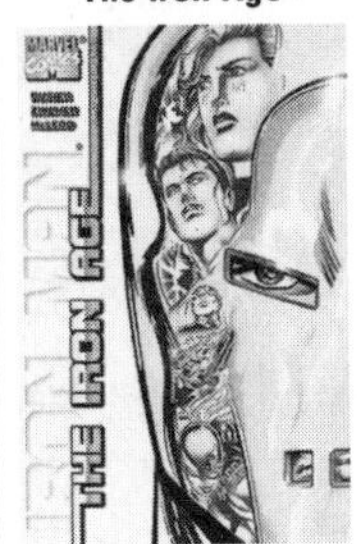

Retells early Iron Man adventures
©Marvel

Iron Manual

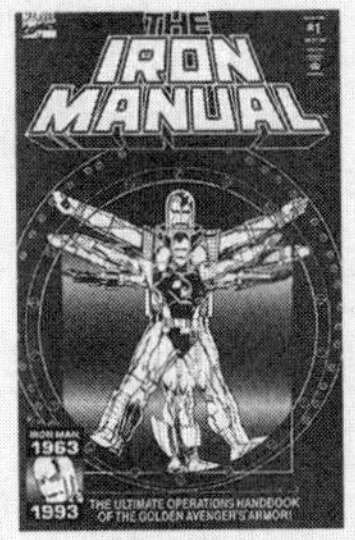

Shellhead's schematics with blueprint cover
©Marvel

	N-MINT
❑24	2.99
❑25	2.99
❑26	2.99
❑27	2.99
❑28	2.99
❑29	2.99
❑30	2.99
❑31	2.99
❑32	2.99
❑33	2.99
❑34	2.99
❑35	2.99

Iron Man & Sub-Mariner
Marvel

❑1, Apr 1968, BEv (c); GC, JCr (a); O: Destiny	100.00

Iron Man: Bad Blood
Marvel

❑1, Sep 2000	2.99
❑2, Oct 2000	2.99
❑3, Nov 2000	2.99
❑4, Dec 2000	2.99

Iron Man/Captain America: Casualties of War
Marvel

❑1, Mar 2007	3.99

Iron Man: House of M
Marvel

❑1, Aug 2005	5.00
❑1/Variant, Aug 2005	4.00
❑2, Sep 2005	2.99
❑3, Oct 2005	2.99

Iron Man: Hypervelocity
Marvel

❑1, Mar 2007	2.99

Iron Man: The Inevitable
Marvel

❑1, Feb 2006	2.99
❑2, Mar 2006	2.99
❑3, May 2006	2.99
❑4, Jun 2006	2.99
❑5, Jul 2006	2.99
❑6, Aug 2006	2.99

Iron Man: The Iron Age
Marvel

❑1, Aug 1998; prestige format; retells early Iron Man adventures	5.99
❑2, Sep 1998; prestige format; retells early Iron Man adventures	5.99

Iron Man: The Legend
Marvel

❑1, Sep 1996; wraparound cover; summation of history of character	3.95

Iron Man 2020
Marvel

❑1; One-shot	5.95

Iron Manual
Marvel

❑1, ca. 1993; no cover date; background info on Iron Man's armor	2.00

Iron Man/X-O Manowar: Heavy Metal
Marvel

	N-MINT
❑1, Sep 1996, crossover with Acclaim	2.50

Iron Marshal
Jademan

❑1, Jul 1990	1.75
❑2, Aug 1990	1.75
❑3, Sep 1990	1.75
❑4, Oct 1990	1.75
❑5, Nov 1990	1.75
❑6, Dec 1990	1.75
❑7, Jan 1991	1.75
❑8, Feb 1991	1.75
❑9, Mar 1991	1.75
❑10, Apr 1991	1.75
❑11, May 1991	1.75
❑12, Jun 1991	1.75
❑13, Jul 1991	1.75
❑14, Aug 1991	1.75
❑15, Sep 1991	1.75
❑16, Oct 1991	1.75
❑17, Nov 1991	1.75
❑18, Dec 1991	1.75
❑19, Jan 1992	1.75
❑20, Feb 1992	1.75
❑21, Mar 1992	1.75
❑22, Apr 1992	1.75
❑23, May 1992	1.75
❑24, Jun 1992	1.75
❑25, Jul 1992	1.75
❑26, Aug 1992	1.75
❑27, Sep 1992	1.75
❑28, Oct 1992	1.75
❑29, Nov 1992	1.75
❑30, Dec 1992	1.75
❑31, Jan 1993	1.75
❑32, Feb 1993	1.75

Iron Saga's Anthology
Iron Saga

❑1, Jan 1987	1.75

Iron West
Image

❑1, Jul 2006, b&w	14.99

Iron Wings
Action

❑1, May 1999	2.50

Iron Wings
Image

❑1, Apr 2000	2.50

Ironwolf
DC

❑1, ca. 1986; Reprints IronWolf adventures from Weird Worlds #8-10	2.00

Ironwood
Fantagraphics / Eros

❑1, Jan 1991, b&w; Adult	4.00
❑2, Mar 1991, b&w; Adult	2.25
❑3, May 1991, b&w; 24 pages; Adult	2.25
❑4, Jul 1991, b&w; Adult	2.25
❑5, Oct 1991, b&w; Adult	2.25
❑6, ca. 1992, b&w; Adult	2.25
❑7, Mar 1992, b&w; 24 pages; Adult	2.50
❑8, ca. 1992, b&w; Adult	2.50

	N-MINT
❑9, Aug 1993, b&w; Adult	2.50
❑10, Sep 1994, b&w; 24 pages; Adult	2.75

Irredeemable Ant-Man
Marvel

❑1, Dec 2006	2.99
❑2, Jan 2007	2.99
❑3, Feb 2007	2.99
❑4, Mar 2007	2.99

I Saw It
Educomics

❑1, b&w; Hiroshima	2.00

Isis
DC

❑1, Oct 1976, 1: Isis; 1: Andrea Thomas; 1: Scarab I (DC); Based on Saturday morning TV series	6.00
❑2, Dec 1976	4.00
❑3, Feb 1977	3.50
❑4, Apr 1977	3.50
❑5, Jun 1977, Begin $0.35 cover; Price increase; New direction	3.50
❑6, Aug 1977	3.50
❑7, Oct 1977, O: Isis	4.00
❑8, Dec 1977, Final Issue	3.50

Island of Dr. Moreau
Marvel

❑1, Oct 1977, Movie adaptation	3.00

Ismet
Canis

❑1, May 1981	1.25
❑2, Jul 1981	1.25
❑3, Sep 1981	1.25
❑4, Nov 1981	1.25
❑5	1.25

I Spy
Gold Key

❑1, Aug 1966, based on TV series	55.00
❑2, Apr 1967, based on TV series	40.00
❑3, Nov 1967, based on TV series	33.00
❑4, Feb 1968, based on TV series	33.00
❑5, Jun 1968, based on TV series	33.00
❑6, Sep 1968, based on TV series	33.00

Itchy & Scratchy Comics
Bongo

❑1, ca. 1993; Includes poster	2.50
❑2, ca. 1994; ca. 1993	2.00
❑3, ca. 1994; A: Bart Simpson. Includes decoder screen; ca. 1993	2.25
❑Holiday 1, ca. 1994; Itchy & Scratchy Holiday Hi-Jinx Special	2.00

Itchy Planet
Fantagraphics

❑1, Spr 1988	2.25
❑2, Sum 1988	2.25
❑3, Fal 1988	2.25

It's About Time
Gold Key

❑1, Jan 1967	25.00

Itsi Kitsi
Funny Book Institute

❑1, May 2000	3.00

Other grades: Multiply price above by 5/6 for VF/NM • 2/3 for VERY FINE • 1/3 for FINE • 1/5 for VERY GOOD • 1/8 for GOOD

It's Only a Matter of Life and Death
Fantagraphics

❑1, b&w 3.95

It's Science With Dr. Radium
Slave Labor

❑1, Sep 1986 .... 2.00
❑2, Jan 1987 .... 2.00
❑3, Mar 1987 .... 2.00
❑4, May 1987 .... 2.00
❑5, Jul 1987 .... 2.00
❑6, Oct 1987 .... 2.00
❑7, Feb 1988 .... 2.00
❑Special 1, Jan 1989, b&w 2.95

It! The Terror from Beyond Space
Millennium

❑1; Die-cut cover 2.50
❑2, Jan 1993 .... 2.50
❑3 .... 2.50
❑4 .... 2.50

I Want to Be Your Dog
Fantagraphics / Eros

❑1, Oct 1990, b&w; Adult 1.95
❑2, b&w; Adult 1.95
❑3, Dec 1990, b&w; Adult 1.95
❑4, b&w; Adult 1.95
❑5, Sep 1991, b&w; Adult 2.25

J2
Marvel

❑1, Oct 1998; gatefold summary; son of Juggernaut 2.00
❑1/A, Oct 1998; gatefold summary; Alternate cover with J2 alone in foreground 2.00
❑2, Nov 1998; gatefold summary; V: X-People 2.00
❑3, Dec 1998 A: Hulk. A: Dr. Strange. A: Doctor Strange. A: Sub-Mariner 2.00
❑4, Jan 1999; 1: Nemesus. A: Doc Magus 2.00
❑5, Feb 1999; 1: Wild Thing. A: Wolverine. A: Elektra 2.00
❑6, Mar 1999; A: Magneta. Wild Thing story 2.00
❑7, Apr 1999; A: Cyclops. A: Uncanny X-People. A: Parody. Wild Thing story 2.00
❑8, May 1999 .... 2.00
❑9, Jun 1999; 1: Big Julie 2.00
❑10, Jul 1999 A: Wolverine 2.00
❑11, Aug 1999 A: Sons of the Tiger. A: Iron Fist 2.00
❑12, Oct 1999 .... 2.00

Jab
Adhesive

❑1 .... 2.50
❑2 .... 2.50
❑3, Spr 1993; bullet hole 2.50
❑4 .... 2.50
❑5 .... 2.50

Jab
Cummings Design Group

❑3, Aut 1994, b&w; Fall 1994 .... 2.95

Jab
Funny Papers

❑1, b&w 2.50
❑2, b&w 2.50

Jack
Med Systems Company

❑1, Sep 1995 .... 2.95

Jackaroo
Eternity

❑1, Feb 1990, b&w; Australian 2.25
❑2, Mar 1990, b&w; Australian 2.25
❑3, Apr 1990, b&w; Australian 2.25

Jack Cross
DC

❑1, Oct 2005 .... 2.50
❑2, Nov 2005 .... 2.50
❑3, Dec 2005 .... 2.50
❑4, Jan 2006 .... 2.50

Jack Frost
Amazing

❑1, b&w 1.95
❑2, b&w 1.95

Jack Hunter
Blackthorne

❑1, Mar 1988 .... 1.25

Jackie Jokers
Harvey

❑1, Mar 1973 .... 12.00
❑2, May 1973, Richard Nixon appears on cover with Jackie 10.00
❑3, Jul 1973 .... 10.00
❑4, Sep 1973 .... 10.00

Jack Kirby's Galactic Bounty Hunters
Marvel

❑1, Sep 2006 .... 3.99
❑2, Nov 2006 .... 2.99
❑3, Dec 2006 .... 2.99

Jack of Fables
DC

❑1, Oct 2006 .... 2.99
❑2, Nov 2006 .... 2.99
❑3, Dec 2006 .... 2.99
❑4, Jan 2007 .... 2.99
❑5, Feb 2007 .... 2.99
❑6, Mar 2007, Jack Frost 2.99
❑7 .... 2.99
❑8 .... 2.99
❑9 .... 2.99
❑10 .... 2.99
❑11 .... 2.99
❑12 .... 2.99
❑13 .... 2.99
❑14 .... 2.99
❑15 .... 2.99
❑16 .... 2.99
❑17 .... 2.99
❑18 .... 2.99
❑19 .... 2.99
❑20 .... 2.99
❑21 .... 2.99
❑22 .... 2.99
❑23 .... 2.99
❑24 .... 2.99
❑25 .... 2.99
❑26 .... 2.99
❑27 .... 2.99
❑28 .... 2.99
❑29 .... 2.99
❑30 .... 2.99
❑31 .... 2.99
❑32 .... 2.99
❑33 .... 2.99
❑34 .... 2.99
❑35 .... 2.99

Jack of Hearts
Marvel

❑1, Jan 1984 .... 1.50
❑2, Feb 1984 .... 1.50
❑3, Mar 1984 .... 1.50
❑4, Apr 1984 .... 1.50

Jack's Luck Runs Out
Beekeeper Cartoon Amusements

❑1; NN 3.50

Jack Staff
Image

❑1, Feb 2003 .... 2.95
❑2, Apr 2003 .... 2.95
❑3, Aug 2003 .... 2.95
❑4, Nov 2003 .... 2.95
❑5, Aug 2004 .... 3.50
❑6, Dec 2004 .... 3.50
❑7, ca. 2005 .... 3.50
❑8, ca. 2005 .... 3.50
❑9 2005 .... 3.50
❑12, Dec 2006 .... 3.50

Jack the Ripper
Caliber / Tome

❑1 1998, b&w; One-shot 2.95

Jack the Ripper
Eternity

❑1, b&w 2.25
❑2, b&w 2.25
❑3, b&w 2.25

Jacquelyn the Ripper
Fantagraphics

❑1, Oct 1994, b&w; 24 pages; Adult 2.95
❑2, Oct 1994, b&w; 24 pages; Adult 2.95

Jacque's Voice of Doom
Doomed Comics

❑1, b&w; strip reprints 1.50

Jademan Collection
Jademan

❑1 .... 2.50
❑2 .... 2.50
❑3, Feb 1990 .... 2.50

Jademan Kung Fu Special
Jademan

❑1; Perviews of Jademan's Titles 1.50

Jade Warriors
Image

❑1, Ca, 1999 .... 2.50
❑1/A, Painted alternate cover 2.50
❑2, Jan 2000 .... 2.50

Jaguar
DC / Impact

❑1, Aug 1991; O: Jaguar. 1: The Jaguar (Maria de Guzman). 1: Timon de Guzman. 1: Tracy Dickerson. 1: Maxim Ruiz. 1: Maxx-13. 1: Luiza Timmerman 1.00
❑2, Sep 1991 .... 1.00
❑3, Oct 1991; V: Maxx-13 .... 1.00
❑4, Nov 1991; 1: Victor Drago. A: Black Hood 1.00
❑5, Dec 1991; 1: Void 1.00
❑6, Jan 1992 .... 1.00
❑7, Mar 1992 .... 1.00
❑8, Apr 1992 .... 1.00
❑9, May 1992; 1: Moonlighter. trading card 1.00
❑10, Jun 1992 .... 1.00
❑11, Jul 1992 .... 1.25
❑12, Aug 1992 .... 1.25
❑13, Sep 1992 .... 1.25
❑14, Oct 1992; Final Issue 1.25
❑Ann 1, ca. 1992; Includes trading card.; Shield story; Black Hood story 2.50

Jaguar God
Verotik

❑0, Feb 1996; FF (c); FF (a); Adult 4.00
❑1, Mar 1995; FF (c); FF (a); Adult 4.00
❑2, Aug 1995; Adult 4.00
❑3, Mar 1996; Adult 3.50
❑4 1996; Adult 3.50
❑5, Sep 1996; Adult 3.50
❑6, Apr 1997; Adult 2.95
❑7, Jun 1997; Adult 2.95
❑8 1997; Adult 2.95

Jaguar God Illustrations
Verotik

❑nn, Nov 2000 .... 3.95

Jaguar God: Return to Xibalba
Verotik

❑1, Feb 2003; Limited "Fan Club" edition 5.00

Jailbait
Fantagraphics / Eros

❑1, Dec 1998 .... 2.95

Jake Thrash
Aircel

❑1 .... 2.00
❑2 .... 2.00

Jam
Slave Labor

❑1, Nov 1989, b&w series 2.50
❑2, Jan 1990, b&w 2.00
❑3, Mar 1990, b&w 2.00
❑4, May 1990 .... 2.95
❑5, Mar 1991 .... 2.95
❑6 .... 2.50
❑7, Mar 1994, b&w 2.50
❑8, Feb 1995, b&w 2.95
❑9, Aug 1995, b&w 2.95
❑10, b&w 2.95
❑11, b&w 2.95
❑12 .... 2.95
❑13 .... 2.95

Other grades: Multiply price above by 5/6 for VF/NM • 2/3 for VERY FINE • 1/3 for FINE • 1/5 for VERY GOOD • 1/8 for GOOD

Ironwolf

Collects Chaykin's Weird Worlds space opera
©DC

I Spy

Tennis player and secret agent team up
©Gold Key

J2

Juggernaut's son wants to be a hero
©Marvel

Jack of Hearts

Excess energy poses potential problem
©Marvel

Jaguar

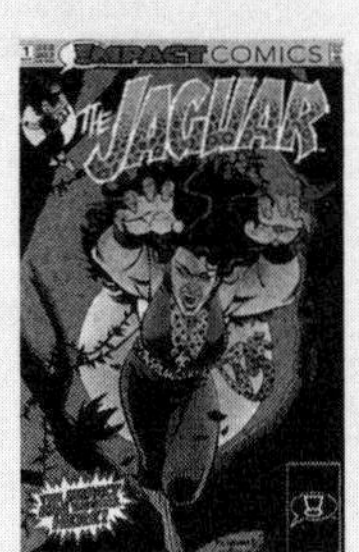

Brazilian student becomes were-creature
©DC

N-MINT

Jamar Chronicles
Sweat Shop
- ❑1, b&w ... 2.00

James Bond 007: A Silent Armageddon
Dark Horse
- ❑1, Mar 1993; cardstock cover ... 2.95
- ❑2, May 1993; cardstock cover ... 2.95

James Bond 007/Goldeneye
Topps
- ❑1, Jan 1996; Movie adaptation ... 2.95
- ❑2, Feb 1996 ... 2.95
- ❑3, Mar 1996 ... 2.95

James Bond 007: Serpent's Tooth
Dark Horse
- ❑1, Jul 1992, prestige format ... 4.95
- ❑2, Aug 1992, prestige format ... 4.95
- ❑3, Feb 1993, prestige format ... 4.95

James Bond 007: Shattered Helix
Dark Horse
- ❑1, Jun 1994 ... 2.50
- ❑2, Jul 1994 ... 2.50

James Bond 007: The Quasimodo Gambit
Dark Horse
- ❑1, Jan 1995; cardstock cover ... 3.95
- ❑2, Feb 1995; cardstock cover ... 3.95
- ❑3, May 1995; cardstock cover ... 3.95

James Bond for Your Eyes Only
Marvel
- ❑1, Oct 1981, HC (a); Movie adaptation . 1.50
- ❑2, Nov 1981, HC (a); Movie adaptation 1.50

James Bond Jr.
Marvel
- ❑1, Jan 1992, TV cartoon ... 1.00
- ❑2, Feb 1992, TV cartoon ... 1.00
- ❑3, Mar 1992, TV cartoon ... 1.00
- ❑4, Apr 1992, TV cartoon ... 1.00
- ❑5, May 1992, TV cartoon ... 1.00
- ❑6, Jun 1992, TV cartoon ... 1.00
- ❑7, Jul 1992, TV cartoon ... 1.00
- ❑8, Aug 1992, TV cartoon ... 1.00
- ❑9, Sep 1992, TV cartoon ... 1.00
- ❑10, Oct 1992, TV cartoon ... 1.00
- ❑11, Nov 1992, TV cartoon ... 1.00
- ❑12, Dec 1992, TV cartoon ... 1.00

James Bond: Permission to Die
Eclipse
- ❑1, ca. 1989 MGr (w); MGr (a) ... 4.00
- ❑2, ca. 1989 MGr (w); MGr (a) ... 4.00
- ❑3, ca. 1991 MGr (w); MGr (a) ... 5.00

Jam Quacky
JQ
- ❑1, b&w ... 2.00

Jam Special
Matrix
- ❑1 ... 2.50

Jam Super Cool Color-Injected Turbo Adventure from Hell
Comico
- ❑1, May 1988 ... 2.50

N-MINT

Jam Urban Adventure
Tundra
- ❑1, Jan 1992, Tundra publishes ... 2.95
- ❑2, Feb 1992 ... 2.95
- ❑3, Mar 1992 ... 2.95

Jane Bondage
Fantagraphics / Eros
- ❑1; Adult; b&w ... 2.50
- ❑2, Sep 1995 ... 2.95

Jane Bond: Thunderballs
Fantagraphics / Eros
- ❑1, Feb 1992, b&w; Adult ... 2.50

Jane Doe
Raging Rhino
- ❑1, b&w; Adult ... 2.95
- ❑2, b&w; Adult; ca. 1993 ... 2.95
- ❑3, b&w; Adult; ca. 1994 ... 2.95

Jane's World
Girl Twirl
- ❑1 2003 ... 2.95
- ❑2 2003 ... 2.95
- ❑3 2003 ... 2.95
- ❑4 2003 ... 2.95
- ❑5 2003 ... 2.95
- ❑6 2003 ... 2.95
- ❑7 2003 ... 2.95
- ❑8 2003 ... 2.95
- ❑9 2004 ... 5.95
- ❑10 2004 ... 5.95
- ❑11 2004 ... 5.95
- ❑12 2004 ... 5.95
- ❑13 2004 ... 5.95
- ❑14 2004 ... 5.95
- ❑15 2004 ... 5.95
- ❑16 2004 ... 5.95

Janx
Es Graphics
- ❑1 ... 1.00
- ❑2 ... 1.00

J.A.P.A.N.
Outerealm
- ❑1 ... 1.80

Jaq Hammer
Anubis
- ❑0, ca. 1994 ... 2.75
- ❑1 ... 3.00

Jar of Fools Part One
Penny Dreadful
- ❑1, Jun 1994, b&w ... 5.95

Jason and the Argonauts
Tome
- ❑1, b&w ... 2.50
- ❑2, b&w ... 2.50
- ❑3, b&w ... 2.50
- ❑4, b&w ... 2.50
- ❑5, b&w ... 2.50

Jason Goes to Hell: The Final Friday
Topps
- ❑1, Jul 1993; glowing cover ... 2.95
- ❑2, Aug 1993; Includes trading cards 2.95
- ❑3, Sep 1993; Includes trading cards 2.95

N-MINT

Jason Monarch
Oracle
- ❑1, Apr 1979, b&w ... 2.00

Jason vs. Leatherface
Topps
- ❑1, Oct 1995 ... 2.95
- ❑2, Nov 1995 ... 2.95
- ❑3, Dec 1995 ... 2.95

Java Town
Slave Labor
- ❑1, May 1992, b&w ... 2.95
- ❑2, Nov 1993, b&w ... 2.95
- ❑3, Jul 1994, b&w ... 2.95
- ❑4, Jul 1995, b&w ... 2.95
- ❑5, Nov 1995, b&w ... 2.95
- ❑6, Jun 1996, b&w ... 2.95

Javerts
Firstlight
- ❑1, ca. 1997, b&w; no cover price or indicia ... 2.95

Jax and the Hell Hound
Blackthorne
- ❑1, Nov 1986 ... 1.75
- ❑2, Feb 1987 ... 1.75
- ❑3 1987 ... 1.75
- ❑4 1987 ... 1.75

Jay Anacleto Sketchbook
Image
- ❑1, Apr 1999; no cover price ... 2.00
- ❑1/A, Apr 1999; Has cover price ... 2.00

Jay & Silent Bob
Oni
- ❑1, Jul 1998 KSm (w) ... 4.00
- ❑1/Variant, Jul 1998; KSm (w); Photo cover ... 5.00
- ❑1/2nd, Oct 1998; KSm (w); 2nd printing 2.95
- ❑2, Oct 1998 KSm (w) ... 3.00
- ❑3, Dec 1998; KSm (w); Photo cover 3.00
- ❑4, Oct 1999 KSm (w) ... 3.00

Jazz
High Impact
- ❑1, Mar 1996 ... 2.95
- ❑2, May 1996 ... 2.95

Jazz Age Chronicles (EF)
EF Graphics
- ❑1, Jan 1989 ... 1.50
- ❑2, Mar 1989 ... 1.50
- ❑3, May 1989 ... 1.50

Jazz Age Chronicles
Caliber
- ❑1, b&w ... 2.50
- ❑2, May 1990, b&w ... 2.50
- ❑3, b&w ... 2.50
- ❑4, b&w ... 2.50
- ❑5, b&w ... 2.50

Jazzbo Comics That Swing
Slave Labor
- ❑1, Nov 1994; Adult ... 2.95
- ❑2, Apr 1995; Replacement God preview 2.95

Other grades: Multiply price above by 5/6 for VF/NM • 2/3 for VERY FINE • 1/3 for FINE • 1/5 for VERY GOOD • 1/8 for GOOD

Jazz: Solitaire
High Impact

- ❑1, May 1998 .... 2.95
- ❑1/A, May 1998; wraparound cover 3.50
- ❑1/Gold, May 1998; gold foil logo; no cover price 3.50
- ❑2, May 1998 .... 3.00
- ❑2/A; no cover price 5.00
- ❑2/B; nude cover (blue background) 5.00
- ❑3 .... 3.00
- ❑3/A; Nude cover 5.00
- ❑3/B; wraparound nude cover 5.00

JCP Features
J.C.

- ❑1, Feb 1981; DG, NA (a); THUNDER Agents 3.00

Jeffrey Dahmer: An Unauthorized Biography of a Serial Killer
Boneyard

- ❑1, Mar 1992; Adult 4.00
- ❑1/2nd; Adult 3.00

Jeffrey Dahmer vs. Jesus Christ
Boneyard

- ❑1, Feb 1993; wraparound cover 4.00
- ❑1/Autographed; Adult 4.00

Jemm, Son of Saturn
DC

- ❑1, Sep 1984; GC (c); GC, KJ (a); 1: Jemm, Son of Saturn 1.50
- ❑2, Oct 1984 .... 1.00
- ❑3, Nov 1984; O: Jemm 1.00
- ❑4, Dec 1984 .... 1.00
- ❑5, Jan 1985 .... 1.00
- ❑6, Feb 1985 .... 1.00
- ❑7, Mar 1985 GC (c); GC, KJ (a) 1.00
- ❑8, Apr 1985 .... 1.00
- ❑9, May 1985 .... 1.00
- ❑10, Jun 1985 .... 1.00
- ❑11, Jul 1985 .... 1.00
- ❑12, Aug 1985; Final issue 1.00

Jennifer Daydreamer: Oliver
Top Shelf

- ❑1, ca. 2003, b&w; smaller than comic-book size 4.95

Jenny Finn
Oni

- ❑1, Jun 1999 .... 2.95
- ❑2, Sep 1999 .... 2.95
- ❑3, Nov 1999 .... 2.95
- ❑4, Feb 2000 .... 2.95

Jenny Finn: Messiah
Oni

- ❑1, Continued from Jenny Finn (Oni Press) Bk 1; ca. 2005 .... 6.99

Jenny Sparks: The Secret History of the Authority
DC / Wildstorm

- ❑1, Aug 2000 .... 2.50
- ❑2, Sep 2000 .... 2.50
- ❑3, Oct 2000 .... 2.50
- ❑4, Nov 2000 .... 2.50
- ❑5, Mar 2001 .... 2.50

Jeremiah: A Fistful of Sand
Adventure

- ❑1, Jun 1991, b&w 2.50
- ❑2, Jun 1991, b&w 2.50

Jeremiah: Birds of Prey
Adventure

- ❑1, Apr 1991, b&w 2.50
- ❑2, Apr 1991, b&w 2.50

Jeremiah: The Heirs
Adventure

- ❑1, b&w 2.50
- ❑2, b&w 2.50

Jerkbox & Punk'nhead
Jerkbox Studios

- ❑1, Sep 1999, b&w 2.95

Jersey Devil
South Jersey Rebellion

- ❑1 1992; no indicia 2.25
- ❑2; 48 pages 2.95
- ❑3 .... 2.25
- ❑4 1997 .... 2.25
- ❑5 1997 .... 2.25
- ❑6 1997 .... 2.25
- ❑7; no indicia 2.25

Jesse James
AC

- ❑1, b&w; Reprints 3.95

Jester's Moon
One Shot

- ❑1, Aug 1996, b&w; NN 1.00

Jesus Comics
Rip Off

- ❑1 .... 5.00
- ❑2 .... 4.00
- ❑3, Jul 1972 .... 4.00

Jet
Authority

- ❑1, Dec 1996 .... 2.95

Jet
DC / Wildstorm

- ❑1, Nov 2000 .... 2.50
- ❑2, Dec 2000 .... 2.50
- ❑3, Jan 2001 .... 2.50
- ❑4, Feb 2001 .... 2.50

Jet Black
Monolith

- ❑1, Sep 1997; O: Jet Black 2.50

Jet Comics
Slave Labor / Amaze Ink

- ❑1, Oct 1997, b&w; 1: Alex Chambers; 1: Spectrum; O: Spectrum 2.95
- ❑2, Feb 1998, b&w 2.95
- ❑3, Mar 1998; Final Issue 2.95

Jet Dream
Gold Key

- ❑1, Jun 1968, Painted cover 18.00

Jetsons
Gold Key

- ❑1, Jan 1963 .... 90.00
- ❑2, Apr 1963 .... 65.00
- ❑3, Jun 1963 .... 48.00
- ❑4, Jul 1963 .... 48.00
- ❑5, Sep 1963 .... 48.00
- ❑6, Nov 1963 .... 40.00
- ❑7, Jan 1964 .... 40.00
- ❑8, Mar 1964 .... 40.00
- ❑9, May 1964 .... 40.00
- ❑10, Jul 1964 .... 40.00
- ❑11, Sep 1964 .... 24.00
- ❑12, Nov 1964 .... 24.00
- ❑13, Jan 1965 .... 24.00
- ❑14, Mar 1965 .... 24.00
- ❑15, May 1965 .... 24.00
- ❑16, Jul 1965 .... 24.00
- ❑17, Sep 1965 .... 24.00
- ❑18, Nov 1965 .... 24.00
- ❑19, Jan 1966 .... 24.00
- ❑20, Mar 1966 .... 24.00
- ❑21, Jun 1966 .... 16.00
- ❑22, Sep 1966 .... 16.00
- ❑23, Jul 1967 .... 16.00
- ❑24, Oct 1967 .... 16.00
- ❑25, Jan 1968 .... 16.00
- ❑26, Apr 1968 .... 16.00
- ❑27, Jul 1968 .... 16.00
- ❑28, Oct 1968 .... 16.00
- ❑29, Jan 1969 .... 16.00
- ❑30, Apr 1969 .... 16.00
- ❑31, Jul 1969 .... 14.00
- ❑32, Oct 1969 .... 14.00
- ❑33, Jan 1970 .... 14.00
- ❑34, Apr 1970 .... 14.00
- ❑35, Jul 1970 .... 14.00
- ❑36, Oct 1970 .... 14.00

Jetsons
Charlton

- ❑1, Nov 1970 .... 35.00
- ❑2, Jan 1971 .... 22.00
- ❑3, Mar 1971 .... 14.00
- ❑4, May 1971 .... 14.00
- ❑5, Jul 1971 .... 14.00
- ❑6, Sep 1971 .... 10.00
- ❑7, Nov 1971 .... 10.00
- ❑8, Jan 1972 .... 10.00
- ❑9, Mar 1972 .... 10.00
- ❑10, May 1972 .... 10.00
- ❑11, Jul 1972 .... 7.00
- ❑12, Sep 1972 .... 7.00
- ❑13, Nov 1972 .... 7.00
- ❑14, Jan 1973 .... 7.00
- ❑15, Feb 1973 .... 7.00
- ❑16, Apr 1973 .... 7.00
- ❑17, Jun 1973 .... 7.00
- ❑18, Aug 1973 .... 7.00
- ❑19, Oct 1973 .... 7.00
- ❑20, Dec 1973 .... 7.00

Jetsons
Harvey

- ❑1, Sep 1992 .... 1.50
- ❑2, Jan 1993 .... 1.50
- ❑3, May 1993 .... 1.50
- ❑4, Sep 1993 .... 1.50
- ❑5, Nov 1993 .... 1.50

Jetsons
Archie

- ❑1, Sep 1995, A: The Flintstones 2.00
- ❑2, Oct 1995 .... 1.50
- ❑3, Nov 1995 .... 1.50
- ❑4, Dec 1995 .... 1.50
- ❑5, Jan 1996 .... 1.50
- ❑6, Feb 1996 .... 1.50
- ❑7, Mar 1996 .... 1.50
- ❑8, Apr 1996 .... 1.50
- ❑9, May 1996 .... 1.50
- ❑10, Jun 1996 .... 1.50
- ❑11, Jul 1996 .... 1.50
- ❑12, Aug 1996 .... 1.50

Jetsons Big Book
Harvey

- ❑1, Nov 1992 .... 1.95
- ❑2, Apr 1993 .... 1.95
- ❑3, ca. 1993 .... 1.95

Jetsons Giant Size
Harvey

- ❑1, Oct 1992 .... 3.00
- ❑2, Mar 1993 .... 2.50
- ❑3, ca. 1993 .... 2.50

Jew in Communist Prague, A
NBM

- ❑1; oversized graphic novel 11.95
- ❑2; oversized graphic novel 11.95

Jezebel Jade
Comico

- ❑1, Oct 1988; wraparound cover 2.00
- ❑2, Nov 1988; wraparound cover 2.00
- ❑3, Dec 1988; wraparound cover 2.00

Jezebelle
WildStorm

- ❑1/A, Mar 2001; Woman leaping backward on cover, two hands with energy glow 2.50
- ❑1/B, Mar 2001; Woman standing on cover, one hand in energy ball 2.50
- ❑2, Apr 2001 .... 2.50
- ❑3, May 2001 .... 2.50
- ❑4, Jun 2001 .... 2.50
- ❑5, Jul 2001 .... 2.50
- ❑6, Aug 2001 .... 2.50

JFK Assassination
Zone

- ❑1 .... 3.50

Jhereg
Marvel / Epic

- ❑1 .... 8.95

Jigaboo Devil
Millennium

- ❑0, b&w 2.95

Jigsaw
Harvey

- ❑1, Sep 1966, O: Jigsaw (Harvey). 1: Jigsaw (Harvey); 1: Jigsaw (Gary Jason); 1: Super Luck; O: Jigsaw (Gary Jason) 16.00
- ❑2, Dec 1966, 1: Man from SRAM 10.00

Jill: Part-Time Lover
NBM

- ❑1; Adult 11.95

Other grades: Multiply price above by 5/6 for VF/NM • 2/3 for VERY FINE • 1/3 for FINE • 1/5 for VERY GOOD • 1/8 for GOOD

James Bond 007/ Goldeneye	Jason vs. Leatherface	Jemm, Son of Saturn	Jetsons	Jingle Belle
		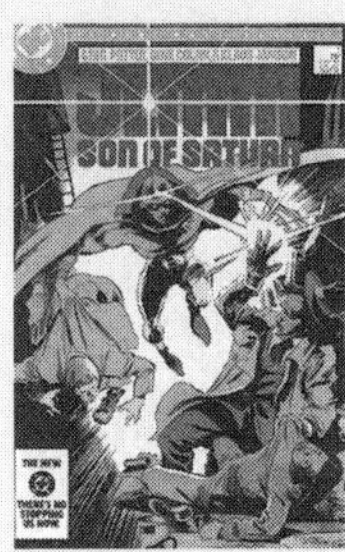		
Adapts Brosnan's first 007 outing	Horror icons don't play well together	Saturnian refugee seeks shelter on Earth	First family of future's comic capers	Santa's daughter's mischevious misadventures
©Topps	©Topps	©DC	©Gold Key	©Oni

N-MINT

Jim
Fantagraphics

❑1 .... 8.00
❑2 .... 6.00
❑3 .... 5.00
❑4 .... 5.00

Jim
Fantagraphics

❑1, Dec 1993, b&w 5.00
❑2, b&w 4.00
❑3, b&w 4.00
❑4, b&w 3.00
❑5, b&w 3.00
❑6, May 1996, b&w 3.00
❑Special 1; Frank's Real Pa Special Edition; Frank's Real Pa Special Edition 4.00

Jimbo
Bongo / Zongo

❑1, ca. 1995, b&w; Adult 2.95
❑2, ca. 1995, b&w; Adult 2.95
❑3, indicia says #2 .... 2.95
❑4, b&w; no indicia 2.95
❑5, Adult 2.95
❑6, Adult 2.95
❑7, Adult 2.95

Jim Hardy
United Feature

❑1, ca. 1947 .... 100.00
❑2, Jul 1947 .... 60.00

Jing: King of Bandits
Tokyopop

❑1, Jun 2003 .... 9.99
❑2, Aug 2003 .... 9.99
❑3, Dec 2003 .... 9.99
❑4, Jan 2004 .... 9.99
❑5, Mar 2004 .... 9.99
❑6, May 2004 .... 9.99
❑7, Jul 2004 .... 9.99

Jing: King of Bandits - Twilight Tales
Tokyopop

❑1, Sep 2004 .... 9.99
❑2, Dec 2004 .... 9.99
❑3, Mar 2005 .... 9.99
❑4, Jun 2005 .... 9.99
❑5, Sep 2005 .... 9.99
❑6, Dec 2005 .... 9.99

Jingle Belle
Oni

❑1, Nov 1999, b&w 2.95
❑2, Dec 1999, b&w 2.95

Jingle Belle
Dark Horse

❑1, Nov 2004 .... 2.99
❑2, Dec 2004 .... 2.99
❑3, Jan 2005 .... 2.99
❑4, Jun 2005 .... 3.00

Jingle Belle Jubilee
Oni

❑nn, Nov 2001, b&w 2.95

N-MINT

Jingle Belle's All-Star Holiday Hullabaloo
Oni

❑1, Nov 2000, b&w 4.95

Jingle Belle: The Fight Before Christmas
Dark Horse

❑1, Jan 2006 .... 2.99

Jingle Belle Winter Wingding
Oni

❑nn, Nov 2002, b&w 2.95

Jinn
Image

❑1, Feb 2000 .... 2.95
❑2, May 2000 .... 2.95
❑3, Oct 2000 .... 2.95

Jinx
Caliber

❑1, b&w; Caliber publishes 3.50
❑2, b&w 3.00
❑3, b&w 3.00
❑4, b&w 3.00
❑5, Nov 1996, b&w 3.00
❑6, b&w; series moves to Image 3.00
❑7 .... 3.00
❑8; Charity Special 4.95
❑9; Homeless Edition; Homeless Edition 4.95
❑10, b&w; Image publishes 2.95
❑11, b&w; Labeled issue Vol. 2, #2; b&w 2.95
❑12; Labeled issue Vol. 2, #3 .... 3.95
❑13, b&w; Labeled issue Vol. 2, #4; b&w 3.95
❑14, b&w; Labeled issue Vol. 2, #5; b&w 3.95
❑15 .... 3.95
❑16; Torso 3.95
❑17; Torso 3.95
❑18; Fire 2.95
❑19; Buried Treasures 2.95
❑20, b&w; True Crime Confessions 3.95
❑21; Torso 3.95
❑Special 1, ca. 1997, b&w 4.95

Jinx Pop Culture Hoo-Hah
Image

❑1, b&w; NN; One-shot 3.95

Jizz
Fantagraphics

❑1, b&w; Adult 2.00
❑2, b&w; Adult 2.00
❑3, b&w; Adult 2.00
❑4, b&w; Adult 2.00
❑5; Adult 2.25
❑6; Adult 2.25
❑7; Adult 2.25
❑8; Adult 2.50
❑9; Adult 2.95
❑10, b&w; Adult 2.50

JLA
DC

❑1, Jan 1997; Superman, Batman, Flash, Wonder Woman, Green Lantern, Martian Manhunter, Aquaman team ... 6.00
❑2, Feb 1997 .... 4.00
❑3, Mar 1997 .... 4.00
❑4, Apr 1997 .... 4.00

N-MINT

❑5, May 1997; V: Prof. Ivo. V: T.O. Morrow. Membership drive 4.00
❑6, Jun 1997; 1: Zauriel. A: Neron. A: Ghast. A: Abnegazar 4.00
❑7, Jul 1997; 1: Asmodel 3.00
❑8, Aug 1997; V: Key 3.00
❑9, Sep 1997; V: Key 3.00
❑10, Oct 1997; V: New Injustice Gang ... 3.00
❑11, Nov 1997 .... 2.50
❑12, Dec 1997 .... 2.50
❑13, Dec 1997; Face cover; Aquaman, Green Lantern, and Flash in future 2.50
❑14, Jan 1998 .... 2.50
❑15, Feb 1998; Giant-size; 48 pages 2.95
❑16, Mar 1998; V: Prometheus. Watchtower blueprints 2.00
❑17, Apr 1998; V: Prometheus; Orion joins; Big Barda joins 2.00
❑18, May 1998; MWa (w); 1: Julian September 2.00
❑19, Jun 1998 MWa (w); A: Atom 2.00
❑20, Jul 1998; MWa (w); V: Adam Strange; JLA: The Nail preview 2.00
❑21, Aug 1998; A: Aleaa. V: Adam Strange 2.00
❑22, Sep 1998; A: Daniel (Sandman). V: Star Conqueror 2.00
❑23, Oct 1998; A: Daniel. V: Star Conqueror. 1: Justice Legion A; 1: 853rd century versions of Aquaman; Wonder Woman rejoins; Hippolyta leaves; 1: Aquaman (853rd Century).. 2.00
❑24, Dec 1998; 1: Ultramarine Corps; 1: Warmaker One; 1: 4-D; 1: Flow; 1: Pulse 8 .... 2.00
❑25, Jan 1999; V: Ultramarine Corps; General Eiling becomes Shaggy Man . 2.00
❑26, Feb 1999; A: Ultra-Marines. A: Shaggy Man. V: Shaggy Man 2.00
❑27, Mar 1999; A: Justice Society of America. V: Amazo 2.00
❑28, Apr 1999 A: Justice Society of America. A: Triumph 2.00
❑29, May 1999 JSa (w); JSa (a); A: Justice Society of America. A: Captain Marvel 2.00
❑30, Jun 1999 A: Justice Society of America 2.00
❑31, Jul 1999 .... 2.00
❑32, Aug 1999; DGry, MWa (w); JLA in No Man's Land 2.00
❑33, Sep 1999 MWa (w) 2.00
❑34, Oct 1999 .... 2.00
❑35, Nov 1999; A: new Spectre. Day of Judgment 2.00
❑36, Dec 1999 .... 2.00
❑37, Jan 2000 .... 2.00
❑38, Feb 2000 .... 2.00
❑39, Mar 2000 .... 2.00
❑40, Apr 2000 .... 2.00
❑41, May 2000; Giant-size; D: Aztek; Big Barda quits; Orion quits; Giant-size; 52 pages 2.99
❑42, Jun 2000 .... 1.99
❑43, Jul 2000 MWa (w) 1.99
❑44, Aug 2000 MWa (w) 2.25
❑45, Sep 2000 MWa (w) 2.25
❑46, Oct 2000 MWa (w) 2.25
❑47, Nov 2000 MWa (w) 2.25
❑48, Dec 2000 MWa (w) 2.25
❑49, Jan 2001 MWa (w) 2.25

Other grades: Multiply price above by 5/6 for VF/NM • 2/3 for VERY FINE • 1/3 for FINE • 1/5 for VERY GOOD • 1/8 for GOOD

	N-MINT
❑50, Feb 2001; Giant-size; MWa (w); 48 pages	3.75
❑51, Apr 2001 MWa (w)	2.25
❑52, May 2001 MWa (w)	2.25
❑53, Jun 2001 MWa (w)	2.25
❑54, Jul 2001 MWa (w)	2.25
❑55, Aug 2001 MWa (w)	2.25
❑56, Sep 2001 MWa (w)	2.25
❑57, Oct 2001 MWa (w)	2.25
❑58, Nov 2001 MWa (w)	2.25
❑59, Dec 2001; BSz (c); Joker: Last Laugh tie-in; Death Queen & Jack of Royal Flush Gang	2.25
❑60, Jan 2002 MWa (w)	2.25
❑61, Feb 2002; Giant-size; KB (w); 1: The Power Company; 1: Josiah Power; 1: Striker Z; 1: Sapphire; 1: Witchfire; 1: Skyrocket; Includes preview of The Power Compan	2.25
❑62, Mar 2002	2.25
❑63, Apr 2002	2.25
❑64, May 2002	2.25
❑65, Jun 2002	2.25
❑66, Jul 2002; 1: Manitou Raven	2.25
❑67, Aug 2002	2.25
❑68, Sep 2002; The Obsidian Age Prelude	2.25
❑69, Oct 2002; 1: Faith; Join Hawkgirl II; Join Jason Blood; Join Major Disaster; Rejoin Green Arrow 1; Rejoin Firestorm; Join Nightwing; Faith joins team	2.25
❑70, Oct 2002; Return of Aquaman; Old JLA on ancient Earth	2.25
❑71, Nov 2002; New JLA on modern Earth	2.25
❑72, Nov 2002; Old JLA on ancient Earth	2.25
❑73, Dec 2002	2.25
❑74, Dec 2002	2.25
❑75, Jan 2003; 1: Dawn Raven; Giant-Size; V: Gamemnae; Aquaman sinks Atlantis	3.95
❑76, Feb 2003	2.25
❑77, Mar 2003	2.25
❑78, Apr 2003	2.25
❑79, May 2003	2.25
❑80, Jun 2003	2.25
❑81, Jul 2003	2.25
❑82, Aug 2003	2.25
❑83, Sep 2003	2.25
❑84, Oct 2003	2.25
❑85, Oct 2003	2.25
❑86, Nov 2003	2.25
❑87, Nov 2003	2.25
❑88, Dec 2003	2.25
❑89, Dec 2003	2.25
❑90, Jan 2004	2.25
❑91, Feb 2004	2.25
❑92, Mar 2004	2.25
❑93, Apr 2004	2.25
❑94, May 2004, JOy, JBy (c); JBy (w); JOy, JBy (a)	2.25
❑95, May 2004	2.25
❑96, Jun 2004	2.25
❑97, Jun 2004	2.25
❑98, Jul 2004	2.25
❑99, Jul 2004	2.25
❑100, Aug 2004; 52 pages	3.50
❑101, Sep 2004	2.25
❑102, Sep 2004	2.25
❑103, Oct 2004	2.25
❑104, Oct 2004	2.25
❑105, Nov 2004	2.25
❑106, Nov 2004	2.25
❑107, Dec 2004, 1: Power Ring III; V: Crime Syndicate of Amerika; Includes Heroscape #2: Trapped Behind Enemy Minds promo comic	5.00
❑108, Jan 2005, D: Power Ring II	5.00
❑109, Feb 2005	2.25
❑110, Mar 2005	2.25
❑111, Apr 2005	2.25
❑112, May 2005	2.25
❑113, Jun 2005	2.25
❑114, Jul 2005	2.25
❑115, Aug 2005; Identity Criss fall-out	12.00
❑116, Sep 2005; Identity Crisis fallout	5.00
❑117, Oct 2005; 1: Black Spider III; Identity Crisis fallout	2.50
❑118, Nov 2005; Identity Crisis fallout	2.50
❑119, Dec 2005; Identity Crisis fallout; Superboy Prime destroys Watchtower and captures Martian Manhunter	2.50
❑120, Dec 2005; Infinite Crisis Tie-In	2.50
❑121, Dec 2005; Infinite Crisis Tie-In	2.50
❑122, Jan 2006; Infinite Crisis tie-in; Omac Project tie-in	2.50
❑123, Feb 2006, Infinite Crisis Tie-In	2.50
❑124, Mar 2006, Infinite Crisis Tie-In	2.50
❑125, Apr 2006, Infinite Crisis Tie-In; Final issue	2.50
❑1000000, Nov 1998; One Million	2.00
❑Ann 1, ca. 1997; Pulp Heroes	6.00
❑Ann 2, Oct 1998; Ghosts	4.50
❑Ann 3, Sep 1999; JLApe	3.50
❑GS 1, Jul 1998; KG (w); 80 pages	4.95
❑GS 2, Nov 1999; 80 pages	4.95
❑GS 3, Oct 2000; 80 pages	5.95

JLA: Act of God
DC

	N-MINT
❑1, Jan 2001	4.95
❑2, Feb 2001	4.95
❑3, Mar 2001	4.95

JLA: Age of Wonder
DC

	N-MINT
❑1, Jun 2003	5.95
❑2, Jul 2003	5.95

JLA/Avengers
Marvel

	N-MINT
❑1, Nov 2003	7.00
❑3, Jan 2004	5.95
❑3/2nd, Apr 2004	7.00

JLA: Black Baptism
DC

	N-MINT
❑1, May 2001	2.50
❑2, Jun 2001	2.50
❑3, Jul 2001	2.50
❑4, Aug 2001	2.50

JLA: Classified
DC

	N-MINT
❑1, Jan 2005; Heroes Cover	6.00
❑2, Feb 2005	4.00
❑3, Mar 2005	2.95
❑4, Apr 2005	2.95
❑5, May 2005; Price increase	2.99
❑6, Jun 2005	2.99
❑7, Jul 2005	2.99
❑8, Aug 2005	2.99
❑9, Sep 2005	2.99
❑10, Oct 2005	2.99
❑11, Oct 2005	2.99
❑12, Nov 2005	2.99
❑13, Dec 2005; Reduced price issue	2.99
❑14, Jan 2006	2.99
❑15, Feb 2006	2.99
❑17, May 2006	2.99
❑18, May 2006	2.99
❑19, Jun 2006, 1: Soldat; 1: Marieke; 1: Velocista; 1: Dybbuk; 1: Jin Si; 1: Ghost Lion	2.99
❑20, Jun 2006	2.99
❑21, Aug 2006	2.99
❑22, Aug 2006, V: Royal Flush Gang; V: Amos Fortune; Cover by Mike Zeck and Jerry Ordway	2.99
❑23, Sep 2006, V: Royal Flush Gang; V: Amos Fortune	2.99
❑24, Sep 2006, V: Royal Flush Gang; V: Amos Fortune; Cover by Mike Zeck and Jerry Ordway	2.99
❑25, Oct 2006, V: Royal Flush Gang; V: Amos Fortune	2.99
❑26, Nov 2006	2.99
❑27, Nov 2006	2.99
❑28, Dec 2006	2.99
❑29, Jan 2007, Includes 3-D Heroscape glasses; Includes Teen Titans:Sparktop giveaway; Includes Teen Titans: Sparktop mini-comic	2.99
❑30, Feb 2007	2.99
❑31, Mar 2007, Early March release	2.99
❑32	2.99
❑33	2.99
❑34	2.99
❑35	2.99
❑36	2.99
❑37	2.99
❑38	2.99
❑39	2.99
❑40	2.99
❑41	2.99
❑42	2.99
❑43	2.99
❑44	2.99
❑45	2.99
❑46	2.99
❑47	2.99
❑48	2.99
❑49	2.99
❑50	2.99
❑51	2.99
❑52	2.99
❑53	2.99
❑54	2.99

JLA Classified: Cold Steel
DC

	N-MINT
❑1, Jan 2006	5.99
❑2, Mar 2006	5.99

JLA: Created Equal
DC

	N-MINT
❑1, ca. 2000; Elseworlds	5.95
❑2, ca. 2000; Elseworlds	5.95

JLA/Cyberforce
DC

	N-MINT
❑0, Oct 2005	5.99

JLA: Destiny
DC

	N-MINT
❑1, Aug 2002	5.95
❑2, Sep 2002	5.95
❑3, Oct 2002	5.95
❑4, Nov 2002	5.95

JLA: Foreign Bodies
DC

	N-MINT
❑1 1999; prestige format; One-shot	5.95

JLA Gallery
DC

	N-MINT
❑1, ca. 1997; pin-ups; wraparound cover	2.95

JLA: Gatekeeper
DC

	N-MINT
❑1, Dec 2001	4.95
❑2, Jan 2002	4.95
❑3, Feb 2002	4.95

JLA: Gods and Monsters
DC

	N-MINT
❑1, Aug 2001	6.95

JLA/Haven: Anathema
DC

	N-MINT
❑1, Nov 2002	5.95

JLA/Haven: Arrival
DC

	N-MINT
❑1, Jan 2002	5.95

JLA: Heaven's Ladder
DC

	N-MINT
❑1, ca. 2000; tabloid-sized one-shot	9.95

JLA: Incarnations
DC

	N-MINT
❑1, Jul 2001	3.50
❑2, Aug 2001	3.50
❑3, Sep 2001	3.50
❑4, Oct 2001	3.50
❑5, Nov 2001	3.50
❑6, Dec 2001	3.50
❑7, Feb 2002	3.50

JLA in Crisis Secret Files
DC

	N-MINT
❑1, Nov 1998; summaries of events from Crisis through One Million	4.95

JLA/JSA: Virtue & Vice
DC

	N-MINT
❑1, ca. 2003	17.95

JLA: Liberty & Justice
DC

	N-MINT
❑1, ca. 2004	9.95

JLA: Our Worlds At War
DC

	N-MINT
❑1, Sep 2001; Story continued From Superman (2nd Series) #172	2.95

JLA: Paradise Lost
DC

	N-MINT
❑1, Jan 1998	2.00

Other grades: Multiply price above by 5/6 for VF/NM • 2/3 for VERY FINE • 1/3 for FINE • 1/5 for VERY GOOD • 1/8 for GOOD

Jinx

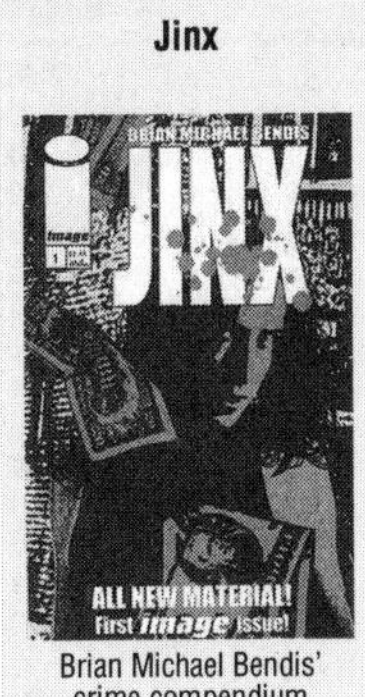

Brian Michael Bendis' crime compendium
©Caliber

JLA

Grant Morrison revives original team
©DC

JLA in Crisis Secret Files

Continuity fixes abound with single Earth
©DC

JLA: Our Worlds At War

Focuses on JLA's involvement in conflict
©DC

JLA: World without Grown-Ups

Adult heroes become kids and vice versa
©DC

N-MINT

❑2, Feb 1998 ... 2.00
❑3, Mar 1998 ... 2.00

JLA: Primeval
DC

❑1, ca. 1999 ... 5.95

JLA: Riddle of the Beast
DC

❑1, ca. 2003 ... 14.95

JLA: Scary Monsters
DC

❑1, May 2003 ... 2.50
❑2, Jun 2003 ... 2.50
❑3, Jul 2003 ... 2.50
❑4, Aug 2003 ... 2.50
❑5, Aug 2003 ... 2.50
❑6, Sep 2003 ... 2.50

JLA Secret Files
DC

❑1, Sep 1997, bios of team members and key villains; timeline ... 4.95
❑2, Aug 1998, bios of team members and key villains ... 3.95
❑3, Dec 2000 ... 4.95

JLA Secret Files 2004
DC

❑1, Jan 2004 ... 5.00

JLA: Secret Society of Super-Heroes
DC

❑1, ca. 2000 ... 5.95
❑2 ... 5.95

JLA: Seven Caskets
DC

❑1; One-shot ... 5.95

JLA: Shogun of Steel
DC

❑1, Apr 2002 ... 6.95

JLA Showcase
DC

❑GS 1, Feb 2000; 80-Page Giant ... 4.95

JLA/Spectre: Soul War
DC

❑1, Mar 2003 ... 5.95
❑2, Apr 2003 ... 5.95

JLA: Superpower
DC

❑1, Nov 1999; prestige format; One-shot; Mark Antaeus joins JLA ... 5.95

JLA: The Island of Dr. Moreau
DC

❑1, Oct 2002 ... 6.95

JLA: The Nail
DC

❑1, Aug 1998; Elseworlds ... 5.50
❑2, Sep 1998; Elseworlds ... 5.00
❑3, Oct 1998; Elseworlds ... 5.00

JLA/Titans
DC

❑1, Dec 1998 ... 3.00
❑1/Ltd., Dec 1998, Autographed ... 5.00

N-MINT

❑2, Jan 1999 ... 3.00
❑3, Feb 1999, Includes preview for new series ... 3.00

JLA: Tomorrow Woman
DC

❑1, Jun 1998; Girlfrenzy; set during events of JLA #5 ... 1.95

JLA V: Predator
DC

❑1, ca. 2000 ... 5.95

JLA: Welcome to Working Week
DC

❑1, ca. 2003 ... 6.95

JLA/WildC.A.T.s
DC

❑1, ca. 1997; prestige format; crossover with Image; Crime Machine ... 5.95

JLA/Witchblade
DC

❑1, ca. 2000 ... 5.95

JLA: World without Grown-Ups
DC

❑1, Aug 1998; prestige format; wraparound cover ... 5.50
❑2, Sep 1998 ... 5.00

JLA: Year One
DC

❑1, Jan 1998 MWa (w) ... 3.50
❑2, Feb 1998 MWa (w) ... 3.00
❑3, Mar 1998 MWa (w) ... 3.00
❑4, Apr 1998 MWa (w) ... 3.00
❑5, May 1998 MWa (w); A: Doom Patrol ... 3.00
❑6, Jun 1998 MWa (w) ... 1.95
❑7, Jul 1998 MWa (w); A: Superman ... 1.95
❑8, Aug 1998; MWa (w); Martian Manhunter monitoring of JLA revealed ... 1.95
❑9, Sep 1998 MWa (w) ... 1.95
❑10, Oct 1998 MWa (w) ... 1.99
❑11, Nov 1998 JSa, MWa (w); JSa (a); A: Metal Men. A: Blackhawks. A: Freedom Fighters. A: Challengers ... 1.99
❑12, Dec 1998; MWa (w); Final Issue ... 2.95

JLA-Z
DC

❑1, Nov 2003 ... 2.50
❑2, Dec 2003 ... 2.50
❑3, Jan 2004 ... 2.50

JLX
DC / Amalgam

❑1, Apr 1996 ... 1.95

JLX Unleashed
DC / Amalgam

❑1, Jun 1997 ... 1.95

Joe Dimaggio
Celebrity

❑1; trading cards ... 6.95

Joel Beck's Comics and Stories
Kitchen Sink

❑1 ... 2.00

N-MINT

Joe Psycho & Moo Frog
Goblin

❑1 ... 3.50
❑2, ca. 1996 ... 3.00
❑3, Sep 1997 ... 3.00
❑4 ... 3.00
❑5 ... 3.00
❑Ashcan 1, b&w; Kinko's Ashcan Edition; no cover price ... 1.50

Joe Psycho Full Color Extravagarbonzo
Goblin

❑1, ca. 1998; NN ... 2.95

Joe Sinn
Caliber

❑1, b&w ... 2.95
❑1/Ltd.; limited edition ... 3.00
❑2, b&w; Final issue (others never released) ... 2.95

John Carter of Mars
Gold Key

❑1, Apr 1964 ... 30.00
❑2, Jul 1964 ... 16.00
❑3, Oct 1964 ... 16.00

John Carter, Warlord of Mars
Marvel

❑1, Jun 1977, GK (c); GK, DC (a); O: John Carter, Warlord of Mars ... 8.00
❑1/35¢, Jun 1977, 35¢ regional price variant ... 15.00
❑2, Jul 1977, GK (a); V: White Apes. Newsstand edition (distributed by Curtis); issue number appears in box. ... 4.00
❑2/35¢, Jul 1977, 35¢ regional price variant; issue number appears in box. ... 8.00
❑2/Whitman, Jul 1977, GK (a); V: White Apes. Special markets edition (usually sold in Whitman bagged prepacks); price appears in a diamond; UPC barcode appears ... 4.00
❑3, Aug 1977, GK, TD (a); V: White Apes ... 3.00
❑3/35¢, Aug 1977, GK (c); GK, TD, AN (a); V: White Apes. 35¢ regional price variant ... 8.00
❑4, Sep 1977, GK (a) ... 3.00
❑4/35¢, Sep 1977, GK (a); 35¢ regional price variant ... 8.00
❑5, Oct 1977, GK (a); V: Stara Kan ... 3.00
❑5/35¢, Oct 1977, GK (a); V: Stara Kan. 35¢ regional price variant ... 8.00
❑6, Nov 1977 ... 2.50
❑7, Dec 1977 ... 2.50
❑8, Jan 1978 ... 2.50
❑9, Feb 1978 ... 2.50
❑10, Mar 1978 ... 2.50
❑11, Apr 1978, O: Dejah Thoris ... 2.50
❑12, May 1978 ... 2.50
❑13, Jun 1978 ... 2.50
❑14, Jul 1978 ... 2.50
❑15, Aug 1978 ... 2.50
❑16, Sep 1978 ... 2.50
❑17, Oct 1978 ... 2.50
❑18, Nov 1978, JBy (c); FM (a) ... 2.50
❑19, Dec 1978 ... 2.50
❑20, Jan 1979 ... 2.50
❑21, Feb 1979 ... 2.50
❑22, Mar 1979 ... 2.50
❑23, Apr 1979 ... 2.50

❑24, May 1979 ... 2.50
❑25, Jul 1979, FM (c); FM (a) ... 2.50
❑26, Aug 1979, FM (c); FM (a) ... 2.50
❑27, Sep 1979 ... 2.50
❑28, Oct 1979 ... 2.50
❑Ann 1, ca. 1977 ... 2.00
❑Ann 2, ca. 1978 ... 2.00
❑Ann 3, ca. 1979 ... 2.00

John Constantine — Hellblazer: Papa Midnite
DC / Vertigo

❑1, Apr 2005 ... 2.95
❑2, May 2005 ... 2.95
❑3, Jun 2005 ... 2.95
❑4, Jun 2005 ... 2.99
❑5, Aug 2005 ... 2.99

John F. Kennedy
Dell

❑1, Aug 1964, DG (a); 12-378-410; memorial comic book; Biography ... 45.00
❑1/2nd, ca. 1964, DG (a); Biography ... 30.00
❑1/3rd, ca. 1964, DG (a); Biography ... 22.00

John Law Detective
Eclipse

❑1, Apr 1983 WE (w); WE (a) ... 2.00

Johnny Atomic
Eternity

❑1, b&w ... 2.50
❑2, b&w ... 2.50
❑3, b&w ... 2.50

Johnny Comet
Avalon

❑1, Apr 1999 ... 2.95
❑2 1999 ... 2.95
❑3 1999 ... 2.95
❑4 1999 ... 2.95
❑5 1999 ... 2.95

Johnny Cosmic
Thorby

❑1; Flip-book with Spacegal Comics #2 . 2.95

Johnny Dynamite
Dark Horse

❑1, Sep 1994, Based on the Pete Morisi Comic Book Feature ... 2.95
❑2, Oct 1994, B&w and red ... 2.95
❑3, Nov 1994, B&w and red ... 2.95
❑4, Dec 1994, Based on the Pete Morisi Comic Book Feature; b&w and red ... 2.95

Johnny Gambit
Hot

❑1, Apr 1987 ... 1.75

Johnny Hazard (Pioneer)
Pioneer

❑1, Dec 1988, b&w ... 2.00

Johnny Hazard Quarterly
Dragon Lady

❑1 ... 5.95
❑2 ... 5.95
❑3 ... 5.95
❑4 ... 5.95

Johnny Jason, Teen Reporter
Dell

❑2, Aug 1962, First issue published as Dell's Four Color #1302 ... 20.00

Johnny Nemo Magazine
Eclipse

❑1, Sep 1995 ... 2.75
❑2, Nov 1985 ... 2.75
❑3, Feb 1986 ... 2.75
❑4; Exists? ... 2.75
❑5; Exists? ... 2.75
❑6; Exists? ... 2.75

Johnny the Homicidal Maniac
Slave Labor

❑1, Aug 1995, b&w A: Squee ... 13.00
❑1/2nd, Dec 1995, b&w; 2nd printing ... 4.00
❑1/3rd, Aug 1996, b&w; 3rd printing ... 3.00
❑1/4th, May 1997, b&w; 4th printing ... 3.00
❑2, Nov 1995, b&w ... 9.00
❑2/2nd, Jul 1996, b&w; 2nd printing ... 3.00
❑3, Feb 1996, b&w ... 7.00
❑3/2nd, Jul 1996, b&w; 2nd printing ... 3.00
❑4, May 1996, b&w ... 6.00
❑4/2nd, Apr 1997, b&w; 2nd printing ... 3.00
❑5, Aug 1996, b&w ... 5.00
❑5/2nd, Apr 1997, b&w; 2nd printing ... 3.00
❑6, Aug 1996, b&w ... 4.00
❑7, Aug 1996, b&w ... 4.00
❑Special 1; Limited to 2000; Reprints Johnny the Homicidal Maniac #1 with cardstock outer cover ... 20.00

Johnny Thunder
DC

❑1, Mar 1973 ... 12.00
❑2, May 1973 ... 8.00
❑3, Aug 1973 ... 8.00

John Steele, Secret Agent
Gold Key

❑1, Dec 1964 ... 18.00

Joker
DC

❑1, May 1975 DG, IN (a); A: Two-Face ... 16.00
❑2, Jul 1975 ... 12.00
❑3, Oct 1975 ... 8.00
❑4, Dec 1975; V: Green Arrow ... 8.00
❑5, Feb 1976; V: Royal Flush Gang ... 8.00
❑6, Apr 1976 ... 7.00
❑7, Jun 1976, V: Lex Luthor ... 7.00
❑8, Aug 1976, Bicentennial #7 ... 7.00
❑9, Sep 1976, A: Catwoman. Final Issue 7.00

Joker: Last Laugh
DC

❑1, Dec 2001 ... 2.95
❑2, Dec 2001 ... 2.95
❑3, Dec 2001 ... 2.95
❑4, Dec 2001 ... 2.95
❑5, Dec 2001 ... 2.95
❑6, Jan 2002 ... 2.95

Joker: Last Laugh Secret Files
DC

❑1, Dec 2001 ... 5.95

Joker/Mask
Dark Horse

❑1, May 2000 ... 2.95
❑2, Jun 2000 ... 2.95
❑3, Jul 2000 ... 2.95
❑4, Aug 2000 ... 2.95

Jolly Jack Starjumper Summer of '92 One-Shot
Conquest

❑1, b&w; NN ... 2.95

Jonah Hex
DC

❑1, Apr 1977 ... 28.00
❑2, Jun 1977, 1: El Papagayo. V: El Papagayo. 1: El Papagayo; V: El Papagayo ... 10.00
❑3, Aug 1977 ... 7.00
❑4, Sep 1977 ... 7.00
❑5, Oct 1977 ... 7.00
❑6, Nov 1977 ... 6.00
❑7, Dec 1977, O: Jonah Hex ... 7.00
❑8, Jan 1978, O: Jonah's facial scars ... 7.00
❑9, Feb 1978 ... 5.00
❑10, Mar 1978 ... 5.00
❑11, Apr 1978 ... 4.00
❑12, May 1978 ... 4.00
❑13, Jun 1978 ... 4.00
❑14, Jul 1978 ... 4.00
❑15, Aug 1978 ... 4.00
❑16, Sep 1978 ... 4.00
❑17, Oct 1978 ... 4.00
❑18, Nov 1978 ... 4.00
❑19, Dec 1978 ... 4.00
❑20, Jan 1979 ... 4.00
❑21, Feb 1979 ... 3.00
❑22, Mar 1979 ... 3.00
❑23, Apr 1979 ... 3.00
❑24, May 1979 ... 3.00
❑25, Jun 1979 ... 3.00
❑26, Jul 1979 ... 3.00
❑27, Aug 1979 ... 3.00
❑28, Sep 1979 ... 3.00
❑29, Oct 1979 ... 3.00
❑30, Nov 1979 ... 3.00
❑31, Dec 1979 ... 3.00
❑32, Jan 1980, O: Jonah Hex ... 3.00
❑33, Feb 1980 ... 3.00
❑34, Mar 1980 ... 3.00
❑35, Apr 1980 ... 3.00
❑36, May 1980 ... 3.00
❑37, Jun 1980, A: Stonewall Jackson ... 3.00
❑38, Jul 1980 ... 3.00
❑39, Aug 1980 ... 3.00
❑40, Sep 1980 ... 3.00
❑41, Oct 1980 ... 3.00
❑42, Nov 1980 ... 3.00
❑43, Dec 1980 ... 3.00
❑44, Jan 1981 ... 3.00
❑45, Feb 1981 ... 3.00
❑46, Mar 1981 ... 3.00
❑47, Apr 1981 ... 3.00
❑48, May 1981 ... 3.00
❑49, Jun 1981 ... 3.00
❑50, Jul 1981 ... 3.00
❑51, Aug 1981 ... 2.50
❑52, Sep 1981 ... 2.50
❑53, Oct 1981 ... 2.50
❑54, Nov 1981 ... 2.50
❑55, Dec 1981 ... 2.50
❑56, Jan 1982 ... 2.50
❑57, Feb 1982, El Diablo back-up ... 2.50
❑58, Mar 1982, El Diablo back-up ... 2.50
❑59, Apr 1982, El Diablo back-up ... 2.50
❑60, May 1982, El Diablo back-up ... 2.50
❑61, Jun 1982, in China ... 2.50
❑62, Jul 1982, in China ... 2.50
❑63, Aug 1982 ... 2.50
❑64, Sep 1982 ... 2.50
❑65, Oct 1982 ... 2.50
❑66, Nov 1982 ... 2.50
❑67, Dec 1982 ... 2.50
❑68, Jan 1983 ... 2.50
❑69, Feb 1983 ... 2.50
❑70, Mar 1983 ... 2.50
❑71, Apr 1983 ... 2.50
❑72, May 1983 ... 2.50
❑73, Jun 1983 ... 2.50
❑74, Jul 1983 ... 2.50
❑75, Aug 1983, RA (c); TD (a) ... 2.50
❑76, Sep 1983, TD (a) ... 2.50
❑77, Oct 1983, RA (c); TD (a) ... 2.50
❑78, Nov 1983, TD (a) ... 2.50
❑79, Dec 1983 ... 2.50
❑80, Jan 1984 ... 2.50
❑81, Feb 1984 ... 2.50
❑82, Mar 1984 ... 2.50
❑83, Apr 1984 ... 2.50
❑84, May 1984 ... 2.50
❑85, Jun 1984; V: Gray Ghost ... 2.50
❑86, Aug 1984 ... 2.50
❑87, Oct 1984 ... 2.50
❑88, Dec 1984 ... 2.50
❑89, Feb 1985; V: Gray Ghost ... 2.50
❑90, Apr 1985 ... 2.50
❑91, Jun 1985 ... 2.50
❑92, Aug 1985; events continue in Hex . 2.50

Jonah Hex
DC

❑1, Jan 2006 ... 2.50
❑2, Jan 2006 ... 2.50
❑3, Mar 2006 ... 2.99
❑4, Apr 2006 ... 2.99
❑5, May 2006 ... 2.99
❑6, Jun 2006 ... 2.99
❑7, Jul 2006 ... 2.99
❑8, Aug 2006 ... 2.99
❑9, Sep 2006 ... 2.99
❑10, Oct 2006 ... 2.99
❑11, Nov 2006 ... 2.99
❑12, Dec 2006 ... 2.99
❑13, Jan 2007 ... 2.99
❑14, Feb 2007 ... 2.99
❑15, Mar 2007 ... 2.99
❑16 ... 2.99
❑17 ... 2.99
❑18 ... 2.99
❑19 ... 2.99
❑20 ... 2.99
❑21 ... 2.99
❑22 ... 2.99
❑23 ... 2.99
❑24 ... 2.99
❑25 ... 2.99
❑26 ... 2.99

John Carter, Warlord of Mars

Adapts Burroughs' red planet adventures
©Marvel

John F. Kennedy

Tribute to slain leader
©Dell

Johnny the Homicidal Maniac

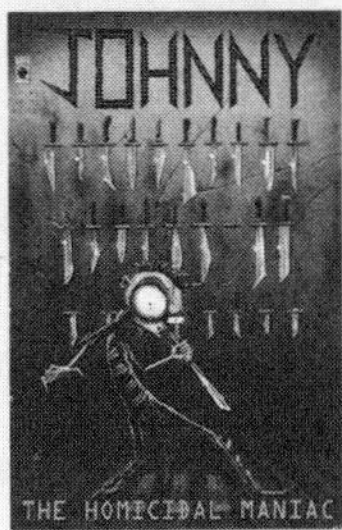

Jhonen Vasquez' pre-Invader Zim work
©Slave Labor

Jonah Hex

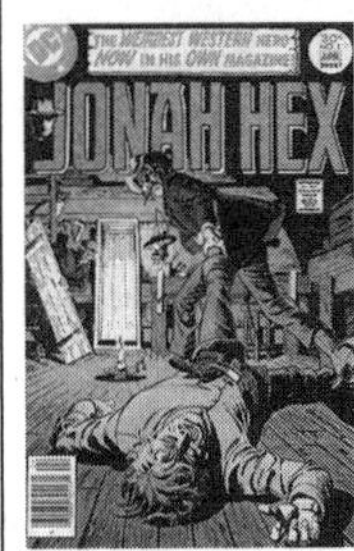

Scarred bounty hunter in Old West
©DC

Jonny Quest (Comico)

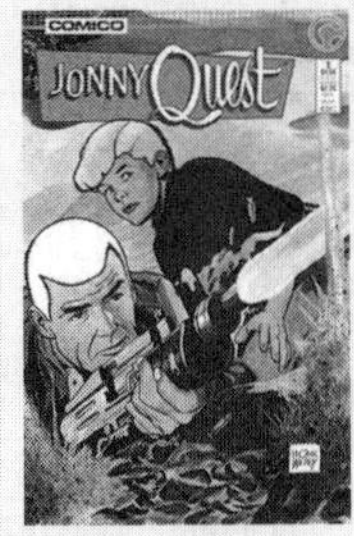

Son often extricates father from peril
©Comico

N-MINT

❑27 .... 2.99
❑28 .... 2.99
❑29 .... 2.99
❑30 .... 2.99
❑31 .... 2.99
❑32 .... 2.99
❑33 .... 2.99
❑34 .... 2.99
❑35 .... 2.99
❑36 .... 2.99
❑37 .... 2.99
❑38 .... 2.99
❑39 .... 2.99
❑40 .... 2.99
❑41 .... 2.99
❑42 .... 2.99
❑43 .... 2.99

Jonah Hex and Other Western Tales
DC

❑1, Oct 1979 .... 7.00
❑2, Dec 1979 .... 7.00
❑3, Feb 1980 .... 7.00

Jonah Hex: Riders of the Worm and Such
DC / Vertigo

❑1, Mar 1995 .... 3.00
❑2, Apr 1995 .... 3.00
❑3, May 1995 .... 3.00
❑4, Jun 1995 .... 3.00
❑5, Jul 1995 .... 3.00

Jonah Hex: Shadows West
DC / Vertigo

❑1, Feb 1999 .... 2.95
❑2, Mar 1999 .... 2.95
❑3, Apr 1999 .... 2.95

Jonah Hex: Two-Gun Mojo
DC / Vertigo

❑1, Aug 1993 .... 3.50
❑1/Silver, Aug 1993; Silver (limited promotional) edition 6.00
❑2, Sep 1993 .... 3.00
❑3, Oct 1993 .... 3.00
❑4, Nov 1993 .... 3.00
❑5, Dec 1993; Final Issue 3.00

Jonas! (Mike Deodato's...)
Caliber

❑1 .... 2.95

Jonathan Fox
Mariah Graphics

❑1 .... 2.00

Jones Touch
Fantagraphics / Eros

❑1, Apr 1993; Adult 2.75

Jonni Thunder
DC

❑1, Feb 1985; DG (a); O: Jonni Thunder. 1: Jonni Thunder 1.25
❑2, Apr 1985 DG (a) 1.25
❑3, Jun 1985 DG (a) 1.25
❑4, Aug 1985 DG (a) 1.25

N-MINT

Jonny Demon
Dark Horse

❑1, May 1994 .... 2.50
❑2, Jun 1994 .... 2.50
❑3, Jul 1994 .... 2.50

Jonny Double
DC / Vertigo

❑1, Sep 1998 .... 2.95
❑2, Oct 1998 .... 2.95
❑3, Nov 1998 .... 2.95
❑4, Dec 1998 .... 2.95

Jonny Quest
Gold Key

❑1, Dec 1964 .... 85.00

Jonny Quest
Comico

❑1, Jun 1986; Wraparound cover, pinup by Mark Wheatley and Marc Hempel 3.00
❑2, Jul 1986; Pinup by Adam Kubert 2.50
❑3, Aug 1986 DSt (c) 2.50
❑4, Sep 1986; MW (c); TY (a); Wraparound cover, pinup by Keith Wilson and Ken Feduniewicz 2.50
❑5, Oct 1986; DSt (c); Pinup by Robb Phipps, Mike Gustovich and Kurt Mausert 2.50
❑6, Nov 1986; Wraparound cover 2.00
❑7, Dec 1986; Wraparound cover, pinup by Marc Hempel and Mark Wheatley 2.00
❑8, Jan 1987; Wraparound cover, pinup by Tom Grindberg and Joe Matt 2.00
❑9, Feb 1987; MA (a); Wraparound cover, pinup by Sam Keith 2.00
❑10, Mar 1987 .... 2.00
❑11, Apr 1987; BSz (c); BA, JSa (a); Wraparound cover, pinup by Brent Anderson and Tom Vincent 1.50
❑12, May 1987; Wraparound cover, pinup by Ken Steacy 1.50
❑13, Jun 1987 CI (a) 1.50
❑14, Jul 1987; Wraparound cover 1.50
❑15, Aug 1987 .... 1.75
❑16, Sep 1987 .... 1.75
❑17, Oct 1987; ME (w); SR (a); Wraparound cover; Includes pinup by Harrison Fong, Bill Anderson and Marcus David 1.75
❑18, Nov 1987 .... 1.75
❑19, Dec 1987; Wraparound cover; Includes pinup by Sal Trapani and Joe Matt 1.75
❑20, Jan 1988; Pinup by Dick Ayers and Tom Reilly 1.75
❑21, Feb 1988 .... 1.75
❑22, Mar 1988 .... 1.75
❑23, Apr 1988 .... 1.75
❑24, May 1988 .... 1.75
❑25, Jun 1988 .... 1.75
❑26, Jul 1988 .... 1.75
❑27, Aug 1988 .... 1.75
❑28, Sep 1988 .... 1.75
❑29, Oct 1988 .... 1.75
❑30, Nov 1988; A Jonny Quest Classic 1.75
❑31, Dec 1988 .... 1.75

N-MINT

❑Special 1, Sep 1988; Special #1; Wraparound cover; Pinups by Ron Frenz and Will Blyberg, Jill Thompson and Terry Austin, Keith S. Wilson and Bill Anderson, Don Sherwood, Rod Whigham and Jack Torrance 1.75
❑Special 2, Oct 1988; Special #2; Wraparound cover; Pinups by Tim sale, Richard Howell, Rod Whigham and Rich Rankin, Don Sherwood 1.75

Jonny Quest Classics
Comico

❑1, May 1987 .... 2.00
❑2, Jun 1987 .... 2.00
❑3, Jul 1987 .... 2.00

Jon Sable, Freelance
First

❑1, Jun 1983; MGr (c); MGr (w); MGr (a); 1: Sable 3.00
❑2, Jul 1983 MGr (w); MGr (a) 2.00
❑3, Aug 1983; MGr (w); MGr (a); O: Sable 2.00
❑4, Sep 1983; MGr (w); MGr (a); O: Sable 2.00
❑5, Oct 1983; MGr (w); MGr (a); O: Sable 2.00
❑6, Nov 1983; MGr (w); MGr (a); O: Sable 2.00
❑7, Dec 1983 MGr (w); MGr (a) 2.00
❑8, Jan 1984 MGr (w); MGr (a) 2.00
❑9, Feb 1984 MGr (w); MGr (a) 2.00
❑10, Mar 1984 MGr (c); MGr (w); MGr (a) 2.00
❑11, Apr 1984 MGr (w); MGr (a) 2.00
❑12, May 1984 MGr (w); MGr (a) 2.00
❑13, Jun 1984 MGr (w); MGr (a) 2.00
❑14, Jul 1984 MGr (w); MGr (a) 2.00
❑15, Aug 1984 MGr (w); MGr (a) 2.00
❑16, Sep 1984 MGr (w); MGr (a) 2.00
❑17, Oct 1984 MGr (c); MGr (w); MGr (a) 2.00
❑18, Oct 1984 MGr (c); MGr (w); MGr (a) 2.00
❑19, Dec 1984 MGr (w); MGr (a) 2.00
❑20, Jan 1985 MGr (w); MGr (a) 2.00
❑21, Feb 1985 MGr (w); MGr (a) 1.75
❑22, Mar 1985 MGr (w); MGr (a) 1.75
❑23, Apr 1985 MGr (w); MGr (a) 1.75
❑24, May 1985 MGr (w); MGr (a) 1.75
❑25, Jun 1985; MGr (c); MGr (w); MGr (a); Shatter back-up story 1.75
❑26, Jul 1985; MGr (c); MGr (w); MGr (a); Shatter back-up story 1.75
❑27, Aug 1985; MGr (c); MGr (w); MGr (a); Shatter back-up story 1.75
❑28, Sep 1985; MGr (c); MGr (w); MGr (a); Shatter back-up story 1.75
❑29, Oct 1985; MGr (c); MGr (w); MGr (a); Shatter back-up story 1.75
❑30, Nov 1985; MGr (c); MGr (w); MGr (a); Shatter back-up story 1.75
❑31, Dec 1985 MGr (w); MGr (a) 1.75
❑32, Jan 1986 MGr (w); MGr (a) 1.75
❑33, Feb 1986 SA, MGr (c); MGr (w); SA, MGr (a) 1.75
❑34, Mar 1986 MGr (w); MGr (a) 1.75
❑35, Apr 1986 MGr (w); MGr (a) 1.75
❑36, May 1986 MGr (w); MGr (a) 1.75
❑37, Jun 1986 MGr (w); MGr (a) 1.75
❑38, Jul 1986 MGr (w); MGr (a) 1.75
❑39, Aug 1986 MGr (w); MGr (a) 1.75
❑40, Sep 1986 MGr (w); MGr (a) 1.75
❑41, Oct 1986 MGr (w); MGr (a) 1.75
❑42, Nov 1986 MGr (w); MGr (a) 1.75
❑43, Dec 1986 MGr (w); MGr (a) 1.75

N-MINT

❑44, Jan 1987 MGr (c); MGr (w); MGr (a) 1.75
❑45, Mar 1987 MGr (c); MGr (w); MGr (a) 1.75
❑46, Apr 1987 MGr (c); MGr (w); MGr (a) 1.75
❑47, May 1987 MGr (c); MGr (w); MGr (a) 1.75
❑48, Jun 1987 MGr (c); MGr (w); MGr (a) 1.75
❑49, Jul 1987 MGr (c); MGr (w); MGr (a) 1.75
❑50, Aug 1987 MGr (c); MGr (w); MGr (a) 1.75
❑51, Sep 1987 MGr (c); MGr (w); MGr (a) 1.75
❑52, Oct 1987 MGr (c); MGr (w); MGr (a) 1.75
❑53, Nov 1987 MGr (c); MGr (w); MGr (a) 1.75
❑54, Dec 1987 MGr (c); MGr (w); MGr (a) 1.75
❑55, Jan 1988 MGr (c); MGr (w); MGr (a) 1.75
❑56, Feb 1988; MGr (c); MGr (w); MGr (a); Final Issue 1.75

Jon Sable, Freelance: Bloodline
Idea & Design Works

❑1, ca. 2005 3.99
❑2 2005 3.99
❑3, Sep 2005 3.99
❑4, Oct 2005 3.99
❑5, Nov 2005 3.99
❑6, Dec 2005 3.99

Jontar Returns
Miller

❑1, b&w 2.00
❑2, b&w 2.00
❑3, b&w 2.00
❑4, b&w 2.00

Josie & the Pussycats
Archie

❑45, Dec 1969 12.00
❑46, Feb 1970 6.00
❑47, Apr 1970 6.00
❑48, Jun 1970 6.00
❑49, Aug 1970 6.00
❑50, Sep 1970 6.00
❑51, Oct 1970 6.00
❑52, Dec 1970 6.00
❑53, Feb 1971 6.00
❑54, Apr 1971 6.00
❑55, Jun 1971, Giant-size 6.00
❑56, Aug 1971, Giant-size 6.00
❑57, Sep 1971, Giant-size 6.00
❑58, Oct 1971, Giant-size 6.00
❑59, Dec 1971, Giant-size 6.00
❑60, Feb 1972, Giant-size 6.00
❑61, Apr 1972, Giant-size 5.00
❑62, Jun 1972, Giant-size 5.00
❑63, Aug 1972, Giant-size 5.00
❑64, Sep 1972, Giant-size 5.00
❑65, Oct 1972, Giant-size 5.00
❑66, Dec 1972, Giant-size 5.00
❑67, Feb 1973 5.00
❑68, Apr 1973 5.00
❑69, Jun 1973 5.00
❑70, Aug 1973 5.00
❑71, Sep 1973 4.00
❑72, Oct 1973 4.00
❑73, Dec 1973 4.00
❑74, Feb 1974 4.00
❑75, Apr 1974 4.00
❑76, Jun 1974 4.00
❑77, Aug 1974 4.00
❑78, Sep 1974 4.00
❑79, Oct 1974 4.00
❑80, Dec 1974 4.00
❑81, Feb 1975 4.00
❑82, Jun 1975 4.00
❑83, Aug 1975 4.00
❑84, Sep 1975 4.00
❑85, Oct 1975 4.00
❑86, Dec 1975 4.00
❑87, Feb 1976 4.00
❑88, Apr 1976 4.00
❑89, Jun 1976 4.00
❑90, Aug 1976 4.00
❑91, Sep 1976 3.00
❑92, Oct 1976 3.00
❑93, Dec 1976 3.00
❑94, Feb 1977 3.00
❑95, Aug 1977 3.00
❑96, Oct 1977 3.00
❑97 3.00
❑98 3.00
❑99, Aug 1979 3.00
❑100, Oct 1979 3.00
❑101, Aug 1980 3.00
❑102 3.00
❑103 3.00
❑104 3.00
❑105 3.00
❑106, Oct 1982 3.00

Josie & the Pussycats
Archie

❑1, ca. 1993 2.00
❑2, ca. 1993 2.00

Journey
Aardvark-Vanaheim

❑1, Mar 1983, b&w 4.00
❑2 1983, b&w 3.00
❑3 1983, b&w 2.50
❑4 1983, b&w 2.50
❑5 1983, b&w 2.50
❑6, b&w 2.50
❑7, b&w 2.50
❑8, Mar 1984, b&w 2.50
❑9, Apr 1984, b&w 2.50
❑10, May 1984, b&w 2.50
❑11, Jun 1984, b&w 2.00
❑12, Jul 1984, b&w 2.00
❑13, Aug 1984, b&w 2.00
❑14, Sep 1984, b&w 2.00
❑15, Apr 1985, b&w 2.00
❑16, May 1985, b&w 2.00
❑17, Jun 1985, b&w 2.00
❑18, Jul 1985, b&w 2.00
❑19, Aug 1985, b&w 2.00
❑20, Sep 1985, b&w 2.00
❑21, Oct 1985, b&w 2.00
❑22, Nov 1985, b&w 2.00
❑23, Dec 1985, b&w 2.00
❑24, Jan 1986, b&w 2.00
❑25, Feb 1986, b&w 2.00
❑26, Mar 1986, b&w 2.00
❑27, Jul 1986, b&w 2.00

Journey into Mystery
Marvel

❑83, Aug 1962, SL (w); SD, JK (a); 1&O: Thor; 1: Dr. Donald Blake; 1: Stone Men from Saturn 4500.00
❑83/Golden Recor, ca. 1966; SL (w); SD, JK (a); 1&O: Thor. Golden Records reprint (with record) 60.00
❑84, Sep 1962, SL (w); SD, DH, JK (a); 1: Executioner. 1: Loki. 1: Jane Foster 725.00
❑85, Oct 1962, SL (w); SD, DH, JK (a); 1: Balder. 1: Loki. 1: Odin. 1: Tyr. 1: Heimdall 450.00
❑86, Nov 1962, SL (w); SD, DH, JK (a); 1: Tomorrow Man. 1: Odin 400.00
❑87, Dec 1962, SL (w); SD, JK (a) 600.00
❑88, Jan 1963, SL (w); SD, DH, JK (a); A: Loki 250.00
❑89, Feb 1963, SL (w); SD, JK (a); O: Thor 300.00
❑90, Mar 1963, JK (c); SL (w); SD, JSt (a); 1: Carbon-Copy 150.00
❑91, Apr 1963, JK (c); SL (w); SD, JSt (a); 1: Sandu 130.00
❑92, May 1963, JK (c); SL (w); SD, JSt (a); 1: Frigga. A: Loki 130.00
❑93, Jun 1963, SL (w); SD, JK (a); 1: Radioactive Man (Dr. Chen Lu)-Marvel 160.00
❑94, Jul 1963, JK (c); SL (w); SD, JSt (a); Loki 130.00
❑95, Aug 1963, JK (c); SL (w); SD, JSt (a) 130.00
❑96, Sep 1963, JK (c); SL (w); SD, JSt (a); Merlin 130.00
❑97, Oct 1963, SL (w); DH, JK (a); 1: Surtur. 1: Lava Men. V: Ymir. V: Molto. Tales of Asgard backup stories begin 325.00
❑98, Nov 1963, JK (c); SL (w); DH, JK (a); 1: Cobra; 2: Ymir 120.00
❑99, Dec 1963, SL (w); DH, JK (a); 1: Mr. Hyde 105.00
❑100, Jan 1964, JK (c); SL (w); DH, JK (a); 1: Storm Giants; 1: Agnar 115.00
❑101, Feb 1964, SL (w); JK (a); A: Iron Man. A: Giant Man. 1: Geirrodur (King of the Trolls) 150.00
❑102, Mar 1964, SL (w); JK (a); 1: Hela. 1: Sif. 1: The Norns 75.00
❑103, Apr 1964, SL (w); JK (a); 1: Enchantress. V: Executioner; 1: Executioner 75.00
❑104, May 1964, SL (w); JK (a); giants 75.00
❑105, Jun 1964, SL (w); JK (a); V: Cobra. V: Hyde 75.00
❑106, Jul 1964, SL (w); JK (a); O: Balder 75.00
❑107, Aug 1964, SL (w); JK (a); 1&O: Grey Gargoyle; 1: Karnilla; O: Balder 75.00
❑108, Sep 1964, SL (w); JK (a); A: Doctor Strange 75.00
❑109, Oct 1964, SL (w); JK (a); A: Magneto 90.00
❑110, Nov 1964, JK (c); SL (w); JK (a); V: Loki. V: Cobra. V: Hyde 75.00
❑111, Dec 1964, SL (w); JK (a); V: Loki. V: Cobra. V: Hyde. 1: Hardol the Healer; 1: Sigurd 75.00
❑112, Jan 1965, SL (w); JK (a); V: Hulk; Thor fights Hulk 210.00
❑113, Feb 1965, SL (w); JK (a); V: Grey Gargoyle. 1: Honir the Hunter 75.00
❑114, Mar 1965, SL (w); JK (a); 1&O: Absorbing Man; 1: Fenris; 1: Haakun the Hunter; 1: Iduna 75.00
❑115, Apr 1965, SL (w); JK (a); O: Loki. 90.00
❑116, May 1965, SL (w); JK (a); A: Daredevil. A: Loki. 1: Yagg; 1: King Hymir; 1: Princess Rinda; Invincible slayer of Skornheim 75.00
❑117, Jun 1965, JK (c); SL (w); JK (a); A: Loki. 1: Owersword of Asgard (Odinsword) 70.00
❑118, Jul 1965, SL (w); JK (a); 1: The Destroyer 70.00
❑119, Aug 1965, JK (c); SL (w); JK (a); 1: Warriors Three. 1: Hogun. 1: Fandrall. 1: Volstagg; 1: Kroda; 1: Magrat; 1: Ularic; Tales of Asgard 70.00
❑120, Sep 1965, SL (w); JK (a) 70.00
❑121, Oct 1965, JK (c); SL (w); JK (a) 70.00
❑122, Nov 1965, SL (w); JK (a) 70.00
❑123, Dec 1965, JK (c); SL (w); JK (a); 1: Demon (witch doctor); Tales of Asgard storyline (back-up story) 70.00
❑124, Jan 1966, SL (w); JK (a); 1: Queen Ula; 1: Flying Trolls of Thryheim; 2: Demon; 2: Demon (witch doctor) 70.00
❑125, Feb 1966, SL (w); JK (a); Series continues in Thor #126 70.00
❑503, Nov 1996; A: Lost Gods. D: Red Norvell. Series continued from Thor #502 1.50
❑504, Dec 1996 A: Ulik 1.50
❑505, Jan 1997; A: Spider-Man. V: Wrecking Crew 1.50
❑506, Feb 1997 1.50
❑507, Mar 1997 1.50
❑508, Apr 1997; V: Red Norvell. V: Red Norvell; Includes 3 page b&w Cable Preview 1.50
❑509, May 1997; return of Loki 1.50
❑510, Jun 1997; V: Red Norvell 1.50
❑511, Aug 1997; gatefold summary; Loki vs. Seth 1.99
❑512, Sep 1997; gatefold summary 1.99
❑513, Oct 1997; gatefold summary; SB (a); Asgardian storyline concludes 1.99
❑514, Nov 1997; gatefold summary; Shang-Chi 1.99
❑515, Dec 1997; gatefold summary; Shang-Chi 1.99
❑516, Jan 1998; gatefold summary; Shang-Chi 1.99
❑517, Feb 1998; gatefold summary; Black Widow 1.99
❑518, Mar 1998; gatefold summary; Black Widow 1.99
❑519, Apr 1998; gatefold summary; Black Widow 1.99
❑520, May 1998; gatefold summary; Hannibal King 1.99
❑521, Jun 1998; gatefold summary; Hannibal King 1.99
❑Ann 1, ca. 1965; King-Size Ann; SL (w); JK (a); 1: Hercules. A: Zeus; New stories and reprints from JIM #85, 93 and 97; continues as Thor Ann 150.00

Journey into Mystery
Marvel

❑1, Oct 1972, JSn, GK, TP (a); Robert Howard adaptation: "Dig Me No Grave" 17.00
❑2, Dec 1972 7.00
❑3, Feb 1973 7.00
❑4, Apr 1973, H.P. Lovecraft adaptation: "Haunter of the Dark" 6.00
❑5, Jun 1973, Robert Bloch adaptation: "Shadow From the Steeple" 6.00
❑6, Aug 1973 5.00

Jon Sable, Freelance

Mike Grell mercenary series
©First

Josie & the Pussycats

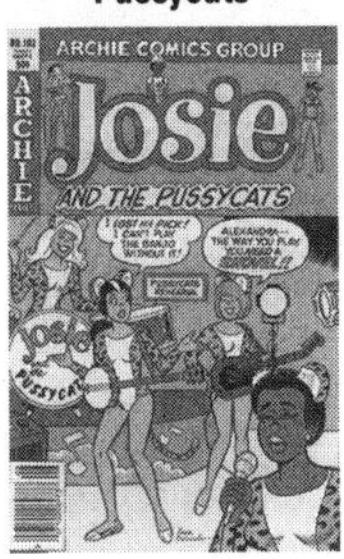

Leader named after co-creator DeCarlo's wife
©Archie

Journey

Frontier adventures from Wm. Messner-Loebs
©Aardvark-Vanaheim

Journey into Mystery

Moves from horror to Norse mythology at #83
©Marvel

JSA

Golden Age team trains new generation
©DC

N-MINT

❑7, Oct 1973 ... 5.00
❑8, Dec 1973 ... 5.00
❑9, Feb 1974 ... 5.00
❑10, Apr 1974 ... 5.00
❑11, Jun 1974 ... 5.00
❑12, Aug 1974 ... 5.00
❑13, Oct 1974 ... 5.00
❑14, Dec 1974 ... 5.00
❑15, Feb 1975 ... 5.00
❑16, Apr 1975 ... 5.00
❑17, Jun 1975 ... 5.00
❑18, Aug 1975 ... 5.00
❑19, Oct 1975; Final Issue ... 5.00

Journeyman
Image

❑1, Aug 1999 ... 2.95
❑2, Sep 1999 ... 2.95
❑3, Oct 1999 ... 2.95

Journeyman/Dark Ages
Lucid

❑1, Sum 1997, b&w; San Diego edition; NN ... 3.00

Journey: Wardrums
Fantagraphics

❑1, May 1987; sepia tones ... 2.00
❑1/2nd, Aug 1987, b&w; sepia dropped. 1.75
❑2, Oct 1990; Last issue ... 2.00

Jr. Carrot Patrol
Dark Horse

❑1, May 1989, b&w ... 2.00
❑2, b&w ... 2.00

JSA
DC

❑1, Aug 1999, JRo (w); D: Fate; D: Kid Eternity; Funeral Sandman 1 ... 5.00
❑2, Sep 1999, JRo (w); V: Mordru ... 2.50
❑3, Oct 1999, JRo (w); V: Mordru. 1: Dr. Fate IV; Join Hawkgirl II ... 2.50
❑4, Nov 1999, JRo (w); V: Mordru. identity of new Doctor Fate revealed ... 2.50
❑5, Dec 1999, JRo (w); 1: Geomancer ... 2.50
❑6, Jan 2000 ... 2.50
❑7, Feb 2000 ... 2.50
❑8, Mar 2000, D: Ian Karkull ... 2.50
❑9, Apr 2000, 1: new Injustice Gang ... 2.50
❑10, May 2000 ... 2.50
❑11, Jun 2000 ... 2.50
❑12, Jul 2000 ... 2.50
❑13, Aug 2000 ... 2.50
❑14, Sep 2000, Return Dove II ... 2.50
❑15, Oct 2000, Quit Starman VII ... 2.50
❑16, Nov 2000 ... 2.50
❑17, Dec 2000 ... 2.50
❑18, Jan 2001, 1: & Death Seven Shadows; Times Past issue; 1: Seven Shadows ... 2.50
❑19, Feb 2001 ... 2.50
❑20, Mar 2001 ... 2.50
❑21, Apr 2001 ... 2.50
❑22, May 2001 ... 2.50
❑23, Jun 2001, 1: Onimar Synn; Return Hawkman ... 2.50
❑24, Jul 2001 ... 2.50
❑25, Aug 2001 ... 2.50
❑26, Sep 2001 ... 2.50
❑27, Oct 2001 ... 2.50
❑28, Nov 2001 ... 2.50
❑29, Dec 2001, Joker: Last Laugh tie-in 2.50
❑30, Jan 2002 ... 2.50
❑31, Feb 2002, Power Girl returns ... 2.50
❑32, Mar 2002 ... 2.50
❑33, Apr 2002, AM, KG (a) ... 2.50
❑34, May 2002 ... 2.50
❑35, Jun 2002 ... 2.50
❑36, Jul 2002 ... 2.50
❑37, Aug 2002, Extra-sized issue; Crimson Avenger story ... 3.50
❑38, Sep 2002, Join Jakeem Thunder ... 2.50
❑39, Oct 2002, Power Girl V: Da Bomb .. 2.50
❑40, Nov 2002, 1: Shadower II; D: Shadower I ... 2.50
❑41, Dec 2002 ... 2.50
❑42, Jan 2003, Includes preview of Gotham Central #1 ... 2.50
❑43, Feb 2003 ... 2.50
❑44, Mar 2003, Return Dove II ... 2.50
❑45, Apr 2003 ... 2.50
❑46, May 2003 ... 2.50
❑47, Jun 2003 ... 2.50
❑48, Jul 2003 ... 2.50
❑49, Aug 2003 ... 2.50
❑50, Sep 2003, Princes of Darkness, Part 5 ... 3.95
❑51, Oct 2003, D: Kobra ... 2.50
❑52, Nov 2003 ... 2.50
❑53, Dec 2003 ... 2.50
❑54, Jan 2004, KB (w); Preview of Superman: Secret Identity ... 2.50
❑55, Jan 2004, Kinetic preview ... 2.50
❑56, Feb 2004, Continued in Hawkman #23 ... 2.50
❑57, Mar 2004, Continued in Hawkman #24 ... 2.50
❑58, Apr 2004, Concludes in Hawkman #25 ... 4.00
❑59, May 2004 ... 2.50
❑60, Jun 2004, D: Ice-Sickle ... 2.50
❑61, Jul 2004 ... 2.50
❑62, Aug 2004 ... 2.50
❑63, Sep 2004, JOy (a) ... 2.50
❑64, Oct 2004, JOy (a) ... 2.50
❑65, Nov 2004 ... 2.50
❑66, Dec 2004, D: Hourman III ... 2.50
❑67, Jan 2005, DaG (a) ... 7.00
❑68, Feb 2005, ARo (c); Diptych cover with #69 ... 5.00
❑69, Mar 2005 ... 4.00
❑70, Apr 2005, D: Chronos II ... 4.00
❑71, May 2005 ... 2.50
❑72, Jun 2005 ... 4.00
❑73, Jun 2005 ... 5.00
❑74, Jul 2005 ... 4.00
❑75, Aug 2005; Day of Vengeance tie-in; Extra Sized ... 2.50
❑76, Sep 2005; The OMAC Project tie-in 2.50
❑77, Oct 2005; Day of Vengeance tie-in. 2.50
❑78, Dec 2005; Infinite Crisis tie-in ... 2.50
❑79, Jan 2006; Infinite Crisis tie-in ... 2.50
❑80, Jan 2006, Infinite Crisis tie-in; D: Dr. Fate IV (Hector Hall); D: Fury II ... 2.50
❑81, Mar 2006, Hourman IV (Rick Tyler appearance) ... 2.50
❑82, Apr 2006, Infinite Crisis crossover 2.50
❑83, May 2006, One Year Later ... 2.50
❑84, Jun 2006, One Year Later ... 2.50
❑85, Jul 2006, Price increase; One Year Later ... 2.99
❑86, Aug 2006 ... 2.99
❑87, Sep 2006, Final issue; D: Gentleman Ghost ... 2.99
❑Ann 1, Oct 2000; 1: Nemesis. Planet DC 5.00

JSA: All Stars
DC

❑1, Jul 2003 ... 2.50
❑2, Aug 2003; Spotlight on Hawkgirl & Golden Age Hawkman ... 2.50
❑3, Sep 2003; Spotlight on Doctor Fate; Golden Age Doctor Fate ... 2.50
❑4, Oct 2003; Star-Spangled Kid II changes name to Stargirl ... 2.50
❑5, Nov 2003; Spotlight on Hourman & Golden Age Hourman ... 2.50
❑6, Dec 2003; V: jewel thieves; Spotlight on Doctor Midnight & Golden Age Doctor Midnight; Delivers baby at subway crash site ... 2.50
❑7, Jan 2004; Includes preview of The New Frontier #1; Spotlight on Golden Age Mister Terrific and Modern Mister Terrific ... 3.50
❑8, Feb 2004 ... 2.50

JSA: Classified
DC

❑1/Conner, Sep 2005 ... 16.00
❑1/Hughes, Sep 2005 ... 24.00
❑1/Sketch, Sep 2005; Sketch from Adam Hughes variant, 2nd print ... 7.00
❑2, Oct 2005; O: Powergirl ... 9.00
❑2/Sketch, Oct 2005 ... 4.00
❑3, Nov 2005; O: Powergirl; Huntress ... 5.00
❑4, Dec 2005; O: Powergirl ... 5.00
❑5, Jan 2006; Injustice Society reforms 2.50
❑6, Feb 2006 ... 2.50
❑8, Mar 2006 ... 2.50
❑9, Apr 2006 ... 2.50
❑10, Jun 2006, One Year Later ... 2.50
❑11, Jun 2006, One Year Later ... 2.50
❑12, Aug 2006, V: Vandal Savage; One Year Later ... 2.99
❑13, Sep 2006, V: Vandal Savage ... 2.99
❑14, Oct 2006, V: Gambler; V: Wizard; V: Amos Fortune; V: Sportsmaster ... 2.99
❑15, Oct 2006, V: Gambler; V: Wizard; V: Amos Fortune ... 2.99
❑16, Mar 2006, V: Gambler; V: Wizard; V: Amos Fortune; V: Sportsmaster ... 2.99
❑18, Jan 2007, V: Bane ... 2.99
❑19, Feb 2007 ... 2.99
❑20, Mar 2007 ... 2.99
❑21 ... 2.99
❑22 ... 2.99
❑23 ... 2.99
❑24 ... 2.99
❑25 ... 2.99
❑26 ... 2.99
❑27 ... 2.99
❑28 ... 2.99
❑29 ... 2.99
❑30 ... 2.99
❑31 ... 2.99
❑32 ... 2.99

Other grades: Multiply price above by 5/6 for VF/NM • 2/3 for VERY FINE • 1/3 for FINE • 1/5 for VERY GOOD • 1/8 for GOOD

N-MINT

❑33 ... 2.99
❑34 ... 2.99
❑35 ... 2.99
❑36 ... 2.99
❑37 ... 2.99
❑38 ... 2.99
❑39 ... 2.99

JSA: Our Worlds At War
DC

❑1, Sep 2001 ... 2.95

JSA Secret Files
DC

❑1, Aug 1999; background information on team's formation and members ... 4.95
❑2, Sep 1999; 1: Roulette ... 4.95

JSA: Strange Adventures
DC

❑1, Oct 2004 ... 3.50
❑2, Nov 2004 ... 3.50
❑3, Dec 2004 ... 3.50
❑4, Jan 2005 ... 3.50
❑5, Feb 2005 ... 3.50
❑6, Mar 2005 ... 3.50

JSA: The Liberty File
DC

❑1, Feb 2000 ... 6.95
❑2, Mar 2000 ... 6.95

JSA: Unholy Three
DC

❑1, Apr 2003 ... 6.95
❑2, May 2003 ... 6.95

Jubilee
Marvel

❑1, Nov 2004 ... 2.99
❑2, Dec 2004 ... 2.99
❑3, Jan 2005 ... 2.99
❑4, Feb 2005 ... 2.99
❑5, Feb 2005 ... 2.99
❑6, Mar 2005 ... 2.99

Judge Dredd vs. Aliens: Incubus
Dark Horse

❑1, Mar 2003 ... 2.99
❑2, Apr 2003 ... 2.99
❑3, May 2003 ... 2.99
❑4, Jun 2003 ... 2.99

Judge Child
Eagle

❑1 BB (a) ... 2.00
❑2 ... 2.00
❑3 ... 2.00
❑4 ... 2.00
❑5 ... 2.00

Judge Colt
Gold Key

❑1, Oct 1969 ... 15.00
❑2, Feb 1970 ... 10.00
❑3, May 1970, O: Judge Colt ... 10.00
❑4, Sep 1970 ... 10.00

Judge Dredd
Eagle

❑1, Nov 1983; BB (c); BB (a); 1: Judge Dredd (in U.S.). A: Judge Death) ... 4.00
❑2, Dec 1983 BB (c); BB (a) ... 3.00
❑3, Jan 1984; BB (a); A: Judge Anderson. V: Judge Death ... 2.50
❑4, Feb 1984 BB (c); BB (a) ... 2.50
❑5, Mar 1984 ... 2.50
❑6, Apr 1984 ... 2.50
❑7, May 1984 ... 2.50
❑8, Jun 1984 ... 2.50
❑9, Jul 1984 ... 2.50
❑10, Aug 1984 ... 2.50
❑11, Sep 1984 ... 2.00
❑12, Oct 1984 ... 2.00
❑13, Nov 1984 ... 2.00
❑14, Dec 1984 ... 2.00
❑15, Jan 1985; Umpty Candy ... 2.00
❑16, Feb 1985; V: Fink Angel ... 2.00
❑17, Mar 1985 ... 2.00
❑18, Apr 1985 ... 2.00
❑19, May 1985 ... 2.00
❑20, Jun 1985 ... 2.00
❑21, Jul 1985 ... 2.00
❑22, Aug 1985 ... 2.00
❑23, Sep 1985; BB (c); Combined issue with #24 ... 2.00
❑24, Oct 1985; DaG (c); Combined issue with #23 ... 2.00
❑25, Nov 1985 ... 2.00
❑26, Dec 1985 ... 2.00
❑27, Jan 1986 ... 2.00
❑28, Feb 1986; The Hotdog Run ... 2.00
❑29, Mar 1986 ... 2.00
❑30, Apr 1986 ... 2.00
❑31, May 1986; V: Judge Child. V: Mean Machine ... 2.00
❑32, Jun 1986; V: Mean Machine ... 2.00
❑33, Jul 1986; League of Fatties ... 2.00
❑34, Aug 1986 ... 2.00
❑35, Sep 1986; Final Issue ... 2.00

Judge Dredd
Fleetway-Quality

❑1, Oct 1986 ... 3.00
❑2, Nov 1986 ... 2.50
❑3, Dec 1986 ... 2.00
❑4, Jan 1987 ... 2.00
❑5, Feb 1987, poster ... 2.00
❑6, Mar 1987, Christmas issue ... 2.00
❑7 1987 ... 2.00
❑8, Jul 1987, wraparound cover ... 2.00
❑9, Aug 1987 ... 2.00
❑10, Sep 1987 ... 2.00
❑11, Oct 1987 ... 2.00
❑12, dropped publication date from cover and indicia for rest of series ... 2.00
❑13 ... 2.00
❑14, BB (a) ... 2.00
❑15 ... 2.00
❑16 ... 2.00
❑17 ... 2.00
❑18 ... 2.00
❑19 ... 2.00
❑20 ... 2.00
❑21, double issue #21, 22 ... 2.00
❑22 ... 2.00
❑23, double issue #23, 24 ... 2.00
❑24 ... 2.00
❑25 ... 2.00
❑26 ... 2.00
❑27 ... 2.00
❑28 ... 2.00
❑29 ... 2.00
❑30 ... 2.00
❑31 ... 2.00
❑32 ... 2.00
❑33 ... 2.00
❑34 ... 2.00
❑35 ... 2.00
❑36 ... 2.00
❑37 ... 2.00
❑38 ... 2.00
❑39 ... 2.00
❑40 ... 2.00
❑41, Reprints stories from 2000 A.D. #445, #447, and #449 ... 2.00
❑42, Reprints stories from 2000 A.D. #421, #422, and #434 ... 2.00
❑43, Reprints stories from 2000 A.D. #113-115 and #412 ... 2.00
❑44, Reprints stories from 2000 A.D. #60, #304, and #514 ... 2.00
❑45, BT (a); Reprints stories from 2000 A.D. #119, #457, #458, and #459 ... 2.00
❑46 ... 2.00
❑47 ... 2.00
❑48 ... 2.00
❑49, Reprints stories from 2000 A.D. #182, #490, #491, and #493 ... 2.00
❑50 ... 2.00
❑51 ... 2.00
❑52 ... 2.00
❑53, BB (a); Reprints stories from 2000 A.D. #25 and #519 ... 2.00
❑54, Reprints stories from 2000 A.D. #643-645 and 2000 A.D. 1990 Mega-Special ... 2.00
❑55 ... 2.00
❑56 ... 2.00
❑57 ... 2.00
❑58 ... 2.00
❑59 ... 1.95
❑60 ... 1.95
❑61, Series continued in Judge Dredd Classics #62 ... 1.95
❑Special 1 ... 2.50

Judge Dredd
DC

❑1, Aug 1994 ... 3.00
❑2, Sep 1994 ... 2.50
❑3, Oct 1994 ... 2.50
❑4, Nov 1994 ... 2.00
❑5, Dec 1994 ... 2.00
❑6, Jan 1995 ... 2.00
❑7, Feb 1995 ... 2.00
❑8, Mar 1995 ... 2.00
❑9, Apr 1995; homage to Judge Dredd #1 (first series) ... 2.00
❑10, May 1995; Judge Dredd sample trading card included ... 2.00
❑11, Jun 1995 ... 2.25
❑12, Jul 1995 ... 2.25
❑13, Aug 1995 ... 2.25
❑14, Sep 1995 ... 2.25
❑15, Oct 1995 ... 2.25
❑16, Nov 1995 ... 2.25
❑17, Dec 1995 ... 2.25
❑18, Jan 1996; Final Issue ... 2.25

Judge Dredd: America
Fleetway-Quality

❑1 ... 2.95
❑2 ... 2.95

Judge Dredd Classics
Fleetway-Quality

❑62 ... 1.95
❑63 ... 1.95
❑64 ... 1.95
❑65 ... 1.95
❑66 ... 1.95
❑67 ... 1.95
❑68 ... 1.95
❑69 ... 1.95
❑70 ... 1.95
❑71 ... 1.95
❑72 ... 1.95
❑73 ... 1.95
❑74 ... 1.95
❑75 ... 1.95
❑76 ... 1.95
❑77 ... 1.95

Judge Dredd: Emerald Isle
Fleetway-Quality

❑1, ca. 1991 ... 4.95

Judge Dredd: Legends of the Law
DC

❑1, Dec 1994 BA (a) ... 2.50
❑2, Jan 1995 BA (a) ... 2.00
❑3, Feb 1995 BA (a) ... 2.00
❑4, Mar 1995 BA (a) ... 2.00
❑5, Apr 1995 ... 2.00
❑6, May 1995 ... 2.00
❑7, Jun 1995 ... 2.25
❑8, Jul 1995 JBy (w); JBy (a) ... 2.25
❑9, Aug 1995 JBy (w); JBy (a) ... 2.25
❑10, Sep 1995 JBy (w); JBy (a) ... 2.25
❑11, Oct 1995 JBy (c) ... 2.25
❑12, Nov 1995 ... 2.25
❑13, Dec 1995; Final Issue ... 2.25

Judge Dredd: Raptaur
Fleetway-Quality

❑1; Judge Dredd ... 2.95
❑2; Judge Dredd ... 2.95

Judge Dredd's Crime File
Eagle

❑1, Aug 1985 ... 3.00
❑2 ... 3.00
❑3 ... 3.00
❑4, Nov 1985 ... 3.00
❑5 DaG (a) ... 3.00
❑6 ... 3.00

Judge Dredd's Crime File
Fleetway-Quality

❑1 ... 4.25
❑2 ... 4.25
❑3 ... 4.25
❑4 ... 4.25

Other grades: Multiply price above by 5/6 for VF/NM • 2/3 for VERY FINE • 1/3 for FINE • 1/5 for VERY GOOD • 1/8 for GOOD

JSA: All Stars

Golden Age ties to modern day
©DC

Judge Dredd

Mega City One's chief lawman's solo title
©Eagle

Judge Dredd

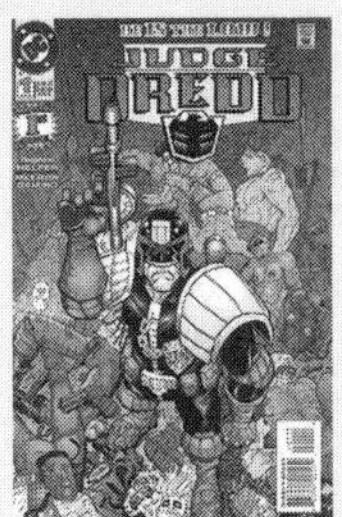

Dredd brings the law to DC
©DC

Judge Dredd's Crime File (Eagle)

Reprints early 2000 A.D. Dredd doings
©Eagle

Judgment Day

Liefeld heroes hold trial for one of their own
©Awesome

N-MINT

Judge Dredd's Hardcase Papers
Fleetway-Quality

❑1 .... 5.95
❑2 .... 5.95
❑3 .... 5.95
❑4 .... 5.95

Judge Dredd the Megazine
Fleetway-Quality

❑1 .... 4.95
❑2 .... 4.95
❑3 .... 4.95

Judge Dredd: The Official Movie Adaptation
DC

❑1; prestige format; NN; Movie adaptation; ca. 1995 .... 5.95

J.U.D.G.E.: Secret Rage
Image

❑1, Mar 2000 .... 2.95

Judgment Day
Lightning

❑1/A, Sep 1993, Red prism border; red foil cover 3.50
❑1/B, Sep 1993, purple foil cover 3.50
❑1/C, Sep 1993, misprint 3.50
❑1/D, Aug 1993, promotional copy; metallic ink 3.50
❑1/Gold, Sep 1993, Gold prism border; Gold foil cover 3.50
❑1/Platinum, Aug 1993, promotional copy; platinum 3.50
❑2, Oct 1993, trading card 2.95
❑3, Nov 1993, O: X-Treme 2.95
❑4, Dec 1993 .... 2.95
❑5, Jan 1994 .... 2.95
❑6, Feb 1994, O: Salubrio 2.95
❑7, Mar 1994, O: Safeguard 2.95
❑8, Apr 1994 .... 2.95

Judgment Day
Awesome

❑1, Jun 1997; Alpha 2.50
❑1/A, Jun 1997; Alpha; variant cover 2.50
❑1/2nd; Alpha 2.50
❑2, Jul 1997; Omega 2.50
❑2/A, Jul 1997; Omega; variant cover 2.50
❑3, Jul 1997; Final Judgment 2.50
❑3/A, Jul 1997; Final Judgment 2.50

Judgment Day: Aftermath
Awesome

❑1, Mar 1998 .... 2.50
❑1/A, Mar 1998; Purple cover by Evans 2.50

Judgment Day: Final Judgment
Awesome

❑3, Oct 1997; Continued from Judgment Day: Omega #2 .... 2.50

Judgment Day Sourcebook
Awesome

❑1; no cover price or indicia; American Entertainment exclusive preview of series 1.00

Judgment Pawns
Antarctic

❑1, Feb 1997, b&w 2.95
❑2, Apr 1997, b&w 2.95
❑3, Jul 1997, b&w 2.95

Judgments
NBM

❑1; Adult 14.95

Judo Girl
Alias

❑0/Conv 2005 .... 8.00
❑1/Balan 2005 .... 3.00
❑1/Taylor 2005 .... 4.00
❑2/Balan, Jul 2005 .... 3.00
❑2/Taylor, Jul 2005 .... 4.00
❑3/Balan, Aug 2005 .... 3.00
❑3/Taylor, Aug 2005 .... 4.00
❑4/Balan, Sep 2005 .... 3.00
❑4/Miller, Sep 2005 .... 4.00

Judomaster
Charlton

❑89, Jun 1966, Series continued from Gun Master #89 .... 12.00
❑90, Aug 1966, O: Thunderbolt (Peter Cannon) 9.00
❑91, Oct 1966, A: Sarge Steel. Letters page includes bio of Frank McLaughlin; 1: Tiger 9.00
❑92, Dec 1966, Bill Schelly L.O.C 9.00
❑93, Feb 1967, Bill Schelly L.O.C 9.00
❑94, Apr 1967 .... 9.00
❑95, Jun 1967, FMc (c); FMc (w); FMc, DG (a) 9.00
❑96, Aug 1967 .... 9.00
❑97, Oct 1967 .... 9.00
❑98, Dec 1967, Final Issue 9.00

Judomaster
Modern

❑93, ca. 1977; FMc (w); FMc (a); reprints Charlton series 2.00
❑94, ca. 1978 .... 2.00
❑96, ca. 1978 .... 2.00
❑98, ca. 1978 .... 2.00

Juggernaut
Marvel

❑1, Apr 1997; One-shot 2.99

Juggernaut
Marvel

❑1, Nov 1999 .... 2.99

Jughead
Archie

❑1, Aug 1987 .... 3.00
❑2, Oct 1987 .... 2.00
❑3, Dec 1987 .... 2.00
❑4, Feb 1988 .... 1.50
❑5, Apr 1988 .... 1.50
❑6, Jun 1988 .... 1.50
❑7, Aug 1988 .... 1.50
❑8, Oct 1988 .... 1.50
❑9, Dec 1988 .... 1.50
❑10, Feb 1989 .... 1.50
❑11, Apr 1989 .... 1.50
❑12, Jun 1989 .... 1.50
❑13, Aug 1989 .... 1.50
❑14, Oct 1989 .... 1.50
❑15, Dec 1989 .... 1.50
❑16, Feb 1990 .... 1.50
❑17, Apr 1990 .... 1.50
❑18, Jun 1990 .... 1.50
❑19, Aug 1990 .... 1.50
❑20, Oct 1990 .... 1.50
❑21, Dec 1990 .... 1.50
❑22, Feb 1991 .... 1.50
❑23, Apr 1991 .... 1.50
❑24, Jun 1991 .... 1.50
❑25, Aug 1991 .... 1.50
❑26, Oct 1991 .... 1.50
❑27, Nov 1991 .... 1.50
❑28, Dec 1991 .... 1.50
❑29, Jan 1992 .... 1.50
❑30, Feb 1992 .... 1.50
❑31, Mar 1992 .... 1.50
❑32, Apr 1992 .... 1.50
❑33, May 1992 .... 1.50
❑34, Jun 1992 .... 1.50
❑35, Jul 1992 .... 1.50
❑36, Aug 1992 .... 1.50
❑37, Sep 1992 .... 1.50
❑38, Oct 1992 .... 1.50
❑39, Nov 1992 .... 1.50
❑40, Dec 1992 .... 1.50
❑41, Jan 1993 .... 1.50
❑42, Feb 1993 .... 1.50
❑43, Mar 1993 .... 1.50
❑44, Apr 1993 .... 1.50
❑45, May 1993, Series continued in Archie's Pal Jughead #46 .... 1.50

Jughead and Friends Digest
Archie

❑1, May 2005 .... 2.39
❑2, Jun 2005 .... 2.39
❑3, Aug 2005 .... 2.39
❑4, Sep 2005 .... 2.39
❑5, Jan 2006 .... 2.39
❑6, Nov 2005 .... 2.39
❑7, Feb 2006 .... 2.39
❑8, Mar 2006 .... 2.39
❑9, May 2006 .... 2.39
❑10, Jun 2006 .... 2.49
❑11, Aug 2006 .... 2.49
❑12, Sep 2006 .... 2.49
❑13, Oct 2006 .... 2.49
❑14, Nov 2006 .... 2.49
❑15, Jan 2007 .... 2.49
❑16, Feb 2007 .... 2.49
❑17 .... 2.49
❑18 .... 2.49
❑19 .... 2.49
❑20 .... 2.49
❑21 .... 2.49
❑22 .... 2.49
❑23 .... 2.49
❑24 .... 2.49
❑25 .... 2.49
❑26 .... 2.49
❑27 .... 2.49
❑28 .... 2.49
❑29 .... 2.49
❑30 .... 2.49
❑31 .... 2.49
❑32 .... 2.49
❑33 .... 2.49

Jughead as Captain Hero
Archie

	N-MINT
❑1, Oct 1966	28.00
❑2, Dec 1966	15.00
❑3, Feb 1967	10.00
❑4, Apr 1967	7.00
❑5, Jun 1967	7.00
❑6, Aug 1967	7.00
❑7, Nov 1967	7.00

Jughead's Baby Tales
Archie

	N-MINT
❑1, Spr 1994, Spring 1994	2.00
❑2, Win 1994, Continued from Baby Tales #1	2.00

Jughead's Diner
Archie

	N-MINT
❑1, Apr 1990	2.00
❑2, Jun 1990	1.50
❑3, Aug 1990	1.50
❑4, Oct 1990	1.50
❑5, Dec 1990	1.50
❑6, Feb 1991	1.50
❑7, Apr 1991	1.50

Jughead's Double Digest
Archie

	N-MINT
❑1, Oct 1989	3.69
❑2, Jan 1990	4.00
❑3, ca. 1990	4.00
❑4, Aug 1990	4.00
❑5, Nov 1990	4.00
❑6, Feb 1991	3.00
❑7, May 1991	3.00
❑8, Aug 1991	3.00
❑9, Nov 1991	3.00
❑10, Feb 1992, DDC (c)	3.00
❑11, Apr 1992	3.00
❑12, Jul 1992	3.00
❑13, Oct 1992	3.00
❑14, Dec 1992	3.00
❑15, Feb 1993	3.00
❑16, ca. 1993	3.00
❑17, May 1993	3.00
❑18	3.00
❑19	3.00
❑20	3.00
❑21	3.00
❑22, ca. 1993	3.00
❑23	3.00
❑24	3.00
❑25	3.00
❑26, ca. 1994	3.00
❑27, Dec 1994	3.00
❑28, Jan 1995	3.00
❑29, Mar 1995	3.00
❑30, May 1995	3.00
❑31, Jul 1995	2.75
❑32, Sep 1995	2.75
❑33, Nov 1995	2.75
❑34, Jan 1996	2.75
❑35, Feb 1996	2.75
❑36, Apr 1996	2.75
❑37, Jun 1996	2.75
❑38, Aug 1996	2.75
❑39, Sep 1996	2.75
❑40, Nov 1996, duplicate pages at front	2.75
❑41, Jan 1997	2.75
❑42, Feb 1997	2.75
❑43, Apr 1997	2.75
❑44, Jun 1997	2.75
❑45, Jul 1997	2.75
❑46, Sep 1997	2.79
❑47, Nov 1997	2.79
❑48, Dec 1997	2.79
❑49, Feb 1998	2.79
❑50, Apr 1998	2.79
❑51, Jun 1998	2.79
❑52, Jul 1998	2.79
❑53, Aug 1998	2.79
❑54, Oct 1998	2.79
❑55, Nov 1998, DDC (a)	2.95
❑56, Jan 1999	2.95
❑57, Feb 1999	2.95
❑58, Apr 1999	2.95
❑59, Jun 1999	2.99
❑60, Jul 1999	2.99
❑61, Aug 1999	2.99
❑62, Oct 1999	2.99
❑63, Nov 1999	2.99
❑64, Jan 2000	2.99
❑65, Feb 2000	2.99
❑66, Apr 2000	2.99
❑67, May 2000	2.99
❑68, Jul 2000, O: Shield (1 page); O: Jaguar (1 page)	3.19
❑69, Aug 2000	3.19
❑70, Oct 2000	3.19
❑71, Nov 2000	3.19
❑72, Jan 2001	3.19
❑73, Feb 2001	3.19
❑74, Mar 2001	3.19
❑75, May 2001	3.29
❑76, Jun 2001	3.29
❑77, Aug 2001	3.29
❑78, Sep 2001	3.29
❑79, Oct 2001	3.29
❑80, Nov 2001	3.59
❑81, Jan 2002	3.59
❑82, Feb 2002	3.59
❑83, Mar 2002	3.59
❑84, May 2002	3.59
❑85, Jun 2002	3.59
❑86, Aug 2002	3.59
❑87, Sep 2002	3.59
❑88, Oct 2002	3.59
❑89, Nov 2002	3.59
❑90, Jan 2003	3.59
❑91, Feb 2003	3.59
❑92, Mar 2003	3.59
❑93, May 2003	3.59
❑94, Jun 2003	3.59
❑95, Aug 2003	3.59
❑96, Sep 2003	3.59
❑97, Oct 2003	3.59
❑98, Dec 2003	3.59
❑99, Jan 2004	3.59
❑100, Mar 2004, AM (a)	3.59
❑101, Apr 2004	3.59
❑102, May 2004	3.59
❑103, Jul 2004	3.59
❑104, Aug 2004	3.59
❑105, Sep 2004	3.59
❑106, Oct 2004	3.59
❑107, Nov 2004	3.59
❑108, Jan 2005	3.59
❑109, Feb 2005	3.59
❑110, Mar 2005	3.59
❑111, Apr 2005	3.59
❑112, May 2005	3.59
❑113, Aug 2005	3.59
❑114, Sep 2005	3.59
❑115, Oct 2005	3.59
❑116, Nov 2005	3.59
❑117, Dec 2005	3.59
❑118, Jan 2006	3.59
❑119, Feb 2006	3.59
❑120, May 2006	3.59
❑121, Jun 2006	3.69
❑122, Aug 2006	3.69
❑123, Aug 2006	3.69
❑124, Oct 2006	3.69
❑125, Nov 2006	3.69
❑126, Jan 2007	3.69
❑127, Feb 2007	3.69
❑128	3.69
❑129	3.69
❑130	3.69
❑131	3.69
❑132	3.69
❑133	3.69
❑134	3.69
❑135	3.69
❑136	3.69
❑137	3.69
❑138	3.69
❑139	3.69
❑140	3.69
❑141	3.69
❑142	3.69
❑143	3.69
❑144	3.69
❑145	3.69
❑146	3.69
❑147	3.69
❑148	3.69
❑149	3.69
❑150	3.69

Jughead's Jokes
Archie

	N-MINT
❑1, Aug 1967	60.00
❑2, Oct 1967	35.00
❑3, Jan 1968	25.00
❑4, Mar 1968	18.00
❑5, May 1968	18.00
❑6, Jul 1968	15.00
❑7, Sep 1968	15.00
❑8, Nov 1968	15.00
❑9, Jan 1969, Archie Giant	15.00
❑10, Mar 1969, Archie Giant	15.00
❑11, May 1969, Archie Giant	12.00
❑12, Jul 1969, Archie Giant	12.00
❑13, Sep 1969, Archie Giant	12.00
❑14, Nov 1969, Archie Giant	12.00
❑15, Jan 1970, Archie Giant	12.00
❑16, Mar 1970, Archie Giant	10.00
❑17, May 1970, Archie Giant	10.00
❑18, Jul 1970, Archie Giant	10.00
❑19, Sep 1970, Archie Giant	10.00
❑20, Nov 1970, Archie Giant	10.00
❑21, Jan 1971, Archie Giant	7.00
❑22, Mar 1971, Archie Giant	7.00
❑23, May 1971, Archie Giant	7.00
❑24, Jul 1971, Archie Giant	7.00
❑25, Sep 1971, Archie Giant	7.00
❑26, Oct 1971, Archie Giant	7.00
❑27, Jan 1972, Archie Giant	7.00
❑28, Apr 1972, Archie Giant	7.00
❑29, Jul 1972, Archie Giant	7.00
❑30, Sep 1972, Archie Giant	7.00
❑31, Oct 1972, Archie Giant	5.00
❑32, Jan 1973, Archie Giant	5.00
❑33, Apr 1973, Archie Giant	5.00
❑34, Jul 1973, Archie Giant	5.00
❑35, Sep 1973, Archie Giant	5.00
❑36, Oct 1973, Archie Giant	5.00
❑37, Jan 1974, Archie Giant	5.00
❑38, Apr 1974	5.00
❑39, Jul 1974	5.00
❑40, Sep 1974	5.00
❑41, Oct 1974	4.00
❑42, Jan 1975	4.00
❑43, Apr 1975	4.00
❑44, Jul 1975	4.00
❑45, Sep 1975	4.00
❑46, Oct 1975	4.00
❑47, Jan 1976	4.00
❑48, Apr 1976	4.00
❑49, Jul 1976	4.00
❑50, Sep 1976	4.00
❑51, Oct 1976	4.00
❑52, Jan 1977	4.00
❑53, Apr 1977	4.00
❑54, Jul 1977	4.00
❑55, Sep 1977	4.00
❑56, Oct 1977	4.00
❑57, Jan 1978	4.00
❑58, Apr 1978	4.00
❑59, Jul 1978	4.00
❑60, Sep 1978	4.00
❑61, Oct 1978	3.00
❑62, Jan 1979	3.00
❑63, Apr 1979	3.00
❑64, Jul 1979	3.00
❑65, Sep 1979	3.00
❑66, Oct 1979	3.00
❑67	3.00
❑68	3.00
❑69	3.00
❑70	3.00
❑71	3.00
❑72	3.00
❑73	3.00
❑74	3.00
❑75	3.00
❑76	3.00
❑77	3.00
❑78, Sep 1982	3.00

Judomaster

Charlton martial artist made Crisis appearance

©Charlton

Jughead (Vol. 2)

Archie's best pal's solo outings

©Archie

Jughead's Diner

Enabling setting for food fanatic

©Archie

Jughead's Time Police

Jughead lusts for female Archie descendant

©Archie

Jungle Action (Marvel)

Black Panther takes over with #5

©Marvel

Jughead's Pal Hot Dog
Archie

	N-MINT
❑1, Jan 1990	1.00
❑2, Jan 1990	1.00
❑3 1990	1.00
❑4 1990	1.00
❑5 1990	1.00

Jughead's Time Police
Archie

	N-MINT
❑1, Jul 1990	1.25
❑2, Sep 1990	1.00
❑3, Nov 1990	1.00
❑4, Jan 1991	1.00
❑5, Mar 1991, A: Abe Lincoln	1.00
❑6, May 1991, O: Time Beanie	1.00

Jughead with Archie Digest Magazine
Archie

	N-MINT
❑1, Mar 1974	12.00
❑2, May 1974	7.00
❑3, Jul 1974	7.00
❑4, Sep 1974	7.00
❑5, Nov 1974	7.00
❑6, Jan 1975	7.00
❑7, Mar 1975	7.00
❑8, May 1975	7.00
❑9, Jul 1975	7.00
❑10, Sep 1975	7.00
❑11, Nov 1975	4.00
❑12, Jan 1976	4.00
❑13, Mar 1976	4.00
❑14, May 1976	4.00
❑15, Jul 1976	4.00
❑16, Sep 1976	4.00
❑17, Nov 1976	4.00
❑18, Jan 1977	4.00
❑19, Mar 1977	4.00
❑20, May 1977	4.00
❑21, Jul 1977	2.50
❑22, Sep 1977	2.50
❑23, Nov 1977	2.50
❑24, Jan 1978	2.50
❑25, Mar 1978	2.50
❑26, May 1978	2.50
❑27, Jul 1978	2.50
❑28, Sep 1978	2.50
❑29, Nov 1978	2.50
❑30, Jan 1979	2.50
❑31, Mar 1979	2.50
❑32, May 1979	2.50
❑33, Jul 1979	2.50
❑34, Sep 1979	2.50
❑35, Nov 1979	2.50
❑36, Jan 1980	2.50
❑37, Mar 1980	2.50
❑38, May 1980	2.50
❑39, Jul 1980	2.50
❑40, Sep 1980	2.50
❑41, Nov 1980	2.50
❑42, Jan 1981, DDC (c)	2.50
❑43, Mar 1981	2.50
❑44, May 1981	2.50
❑45, Jul 1981	2.50
❑46, Sep 1981	2.50
❑47, Nov 1981	2.50
❑48, Jan 1982	2.50
❑49, Mar 1982	2.50
❑50, May 1982	2.50
❑51, Jul 1982	2.00
❑52, Sep 1982	2.00
❑53, Nov 1982	2.00
❑54, Jan 1983	2.00
❑55, Mar 1983	2.00
❑56, May 1983	2.00
❑57, Jul 1983	2.00
❑58, Sep 1983	2.00
❑59, Nov 1983	2.00
❑60, Jan 1984	2.00
❑61, Mar 1984	2.00
❑62, May 1984	2.00
❑63, Jul 1984	2.00
❑64, Sep 1984	2.00
❑65, Nov 1984, DDC (c)	2.00
❑66, Jan 1985	2.00
❑67, Mar 1985	2.00
❑68, May 1985	2.00
❑69, Jul 1985	2.00
❑70, Sep 1985	2.00
❑71, Nov 1985	2.00
❑72, Jan 1986	2.00
❑73, Mar 1986	2.00
❑74, May 1986	2.00
❑75, Jul 1986	2.00
❑76, Sep 1986	2.00
❑77, Nov 1986	2.00
❑78, Jan 1987	2.00
❑79, Mar 1987, DDC (c)	2.00
❑80, May 1987	2.00
❑81, Jul 1987	2.00
❑82, Sep 1987	2.00
❑83, Nov 1987	2.00
❑84, Jan 1988	2.00
❑85, Mar 1988	2.00
❑86, May 1988	2.00
❑87, Jul 1988	2.00
❑88, Sep 1988	2.00
❑89, Nov 1988	2.00
❑90, Jan 1989	2.00
❑91, Mar 1989	2.00
❑92, May 1989	2.00
❑93, Jul 1989	2.00
❑94, Sep 1989	2.00
❑95, Nov 1989	2.00
❑96, Jan 1990	2.00
❑97, Mar 1990	2.00
❑98, May 1990	2.00
❑99, Jul 1990	2.00
❑100, Sep 1990	2.00
❑101, Nov 1990	1.75
❑102, Jan 1991	1.75
❑103, Mar 1991	1.75
❑104, May 1991	1.75
❑105, Jul 1991	1.75
❑106, Sep 1991	1.75
❑107, Nov 1991	1.75
❑108, Jan 1992, DDC (c); GC (a)	1.75
❑109, Feb 1992, DDC (c)	1.75
❑110, Apr 1992	1.75
❑111, Jun 1992	1.75
❑112, Aug 1992	1.75
❑113, Nov 1992	1.75
❑114, Feb 1993	1.75
❑115, May 1993	1.75
❑116, Aug 1993	1.75
❑117, Nov 1993	1.75
❑118, Mar 1994	1.75
❑119, May 1994	1.75
❑120, Aug 1994	1.75
❑121, Nov 1994	1.75
❑122, Jan 1995	1.75
❑123, May 1995	1.75
❑124, Aug 1995	1.75
❑125, Oct 1995	1.75
❑126, Jan 1996	1.75
❑127, ca. 1996	1.75
❑128, Sep 1996	1.79
❑129, Oct 1996	1.79
❑130, Dec 1997	1.79
❑131, Feb 1997	1.79
❑132, Mar 1997	1.79
❑133, May 1997	1.79
❑134, Jul 1997	1.79
❑135, Aug 1997	1.79
❑136, Oct 1997	1.79
❑137, Dec 1997	1.79
❑138, Jan 1998	1.95
❑139, Mar 1998	1.95
❑140, May 1998	1.95
❑141, Jun 1998	1.95
❑142, Aug 1998	1.95
❑143, Oct 1998, DDC (a)	1.95
❑144, Nov 1998	1.95
❑145, Dec 1998	1.95
❑146, Feb 1999	1.95
❑147, Apr 1999	1.95
❑148, May 1999	1.95
❑149, Jun 1999	1.99
❑150, Aug 1999	1.99
❑151, Sep 1999	1.99
❑152, Nov 1999	1.99
❑153, Dec 1999	1.99
❑154, Feb 2000	1.99
❑155, Mar 2000	1.99
❑156, May 2000	1.99
❑157, Jul 2000	2.19
❑158, Aug 2000	2.19
❑159, Sep 2000	2.19
❑160, Nov 2000	2.19
❑161, Dec 2000	2.19
❑162, Jan 2001	2.19
❑163, Feb 2001	2.19
❑164, Mar 2001	2.39
❑165, Jun 2001, Little Archie stories	2.39
❑166, Jul 2001	2.39
❑167, Aug 2001	2.39
❑168, Oct 2001	2.39
❑169, Nov 2001	2.39
❑170, Jan 2002	2.39
❑171, Feb 2002	2.39
❑172, Mar 2002	2.39
❑173, May 2002	2.39
❑174, Jul 2002	2.39
❑175, Aug 2002	2.39
❑176, Sep 2002	2.39
❑177, Nov 2002	2.39
❑178, Dec 2002	2.39
❑179, Jan 2003	2.39
❑180, Mar 2003	2.39

Other grades: Multiply price above by 5/6 for VF/NM • 2/3 for VERY FINE • 1/3 for FINE • 1/5 for VERY GOOD • 1/8 for GOOD

N-MINT

- ❑181, Apr 2003 — 2.39
- ❑182, May 2003 — 2.39
- ❑183, Jul 2003 — 2.39
- ❑184, Aug 2003 — 2.39
- ❑185, Sep 2003, Pop Tate's first name revealed as Leo — 2.39
- ❑186, Oct 2003 — 2.39
- ❑187, Dec 2003 — 2.39
- ❑188, Jan 2004 — 2.39
- ❑189, Feb 2004 — 2.39
- ❑190, Apr 2004 — 2.39
- ❑191, May 2004 — 2.39
- ❑192, Jun 2004 — 2.39
- ❑193, Jul 2004 — 2.39
- ❑194, Aug 2004 — 2.39
- ❑195, Sep 2004 — 2.39
- ❑196, Oct 2004 — 2.39
- ❑197, Jan 2005 — 2.39
- ❑198, Feb 2005 — 2.39
- ❑199, Mar 2005 — 2.39

Jugular
Black Out

- ❑0 — 2.95

Jumper
Zav

- ❑1, b&w — 3.00
- ❑2, b&w — 3.00

Jun
Disney

- ❑1 — 1.50

Junction 17
Antarctic

- ❑1, Aug 2003; b&w — 3.50
- ❑2 2003 — 2.99
- ❑3 2003 — 2.99
- ❑4, Jan 2004 — 2.99

Jungle Action
Marvel

- ❑1, Oct 1972, Reprints — 15.00
- ❑2, Dec 1972, Reprints — 7.00
- ❑3, Feb 1973, Reprints — 7.00
- ❑4, Apr 1973, Reprints — 7.00
- ❑5, Jul 1973, Black Panther begins — 35.00
- ❑6, Sep 1973, Reprints Lorna; The Jungle Girl #6; Black Panther; Map of Wakanda — 12.00
- ❑7, Nov 1973, Reprints Lorna; The Jungle Girl #22; Black Panther — 8.00
- ❑8, Jan 1974, RB (c); RB, KJ (a); O: Black Panther. 1: Malice; 2: Venomm; Map of Wakanda; Guy H. Lillian III L.O.C. — 15.00
- ❑9, May 1974, A: Black Panther. Marvel Value Stamp #31 Modok — 7.00
- ❑10, Jul 1974, A: Black Panther. Marvel Value Stamp #38: Red Sonja — 6.00
- ❑11, Sep 1974, A: Black Panther. Marvel Value Stamp #43: Enchantress — 6.00
- ❑12, Nov 1974, A: Black Panther. Marvel Value Stamp #9: Captain Marvel — 6.00
- ❑13, Jan 1975, A: Black Panther. Marvel Value Stamp #33: Invisible Girl — 6.00
- ❑14, Mar 1975, A: Black Panther. Black Panther; Peter B. Gillis L.O.C. — 6.00
- ❑15, May 1975, A: Black Panther. 1: Salamander K'Ruel; Black Panther . — 6.00
- ❑16, Jul 1975, A: Black Panther. Black Panther — 6.00
- ❑17, Sep 1975, A: Black Panther. 2: Lord Karnaj; Baron Macabre appearace — 5.00
- ❑18, Nov 1975, A: Black Panther. 1: Madam Slay; Black Panther appearance — 5.00
- ❑19, Jan 1976, 1: Baron Macabre. A: Black Panther; 1: Kevin Trublood; Black Panther — 5.00
- ❑20, Mar 1976, A: Black Panther. 1: Kevin Trublood; Ralph Macchio L.O.C.; Marvel Value Stamp Series B #44 — 5.00
- ❑21, May 1976, A: Black Panther. Black Panther; Marvel Value Stamp Series B #81 — 5.00
- ❑21/30¢, May 1976, A: Black Panther. 30¢ regional variant — 20.00
- ❑22, Jul 1976, A: Black Panther. Black Panther — 5.00
- ❑22/30¢, Jul 1976, A: Black Panther. 30¢ regional variant — 20.00
- ❑23, Sep 1976, A: Black Panther. reprints Daredevil #69 — 5.00
- ❑24, Nov 1976, 1: Wind Eagle. A: Black Panther; Final Issue — 5.00

Jungle Book
Gold Key

- ❑1, Mar 1968 — 25.00

Jungle Book
Disney

- ❑1/A, Jun 1990; saddle-stitched — 2.95
- ❑1/B, Jun 1990; squarebound — 5.95

Jungle Book
NBM

- ❑1 — 16.95

Jungle Comics
A-List

- ❑1, Spr 1997, gatefold summary; Sheena; Reprints Sheena 3-D special #1 in color — 2.95
- ❑2, Fal 1997, Wambi — 2.95
- ❑3, Win 1997 — 2.95
- ❑4, Mar 1998 — 2.95
- ❑5, Oct 1998, Sheena — 2.95

Jungle Fantasy
Avatar

- ❑1, Feb 2003; Carrie Hall cover — 3.50
- ❑2, Mar 2003; Adrian Vixens cover — 3.50
- ❑3, Jul 2003; Ron Adrian cover; Fauna Cabrera — 3.50

Jungle Girls
AC

- ❑1, Aug 1988, b&w — 2.00
- ❑2 — 2.25
- ❑3 — 2.75
- ❑4 — 2.75
- ❑5 — 2.75
- ❑6; MB (a); Reprints — 2.95
- ❑7; MB (a); Reprints — 2.95
- ❑8, b&w — 2.95
- ❑9, b&w — 2.95
- ❑10, ca. 1992, b&w — 2.95
- ❑11, ca. 1992, b&w — 2.95
- ❑12, b&w — 2.95
- ❑13, ca. 1993, b&w — 2.95
- ❑14, ca. 1993, b&w — 2.95
- ❑15, ca. 1993, b&w — 2.95
- ❑16, b&w — 2.95

Jungle Girls!
Eternity

- ❑8 — 2.95

Jungle Jim
King

- ❑5, Dec 1967 — 9.00

Jungle Jim
Charlton

- ❑22, Feb 1969, Series continued from Jungle Jim (Dell) — 24.00
- ❑23, Apr 1969 — 18.00
- ❑24, Jun 1969 — 18.00
- ❑25, Aug 1969 — 16.00
- ❑26, Oct 1969 — 16.00
- ❑27, Dec 1969 — 16.00
- ❑28, Feb 1970, Final Issue — 16.00

Jungle Jim
Avalon

- ❑1; published in 1998, indicia says 1995 — 2.95

Jungle Love
Aircel

- ❑1, b&w; Adult — 2.95
- ❑2, b&w; Adult — 2.95
- ❑3, b&w; Adult — 2.95

Jungle Tales of Cavewoman
Basement

- ❑1; Adult — 2.95

Jungle Tales of Tarzan
Charlton

- ❑1, Jan 1965, Sam Glanzman credits — 45.00
- ❑2, Mar 1965, Sam Glanzman credits — 35.00
- ❑3, May 1965, Sam Glanzman credits — 35.00
- ❑4, Jul 1965, Bill Montes and Ernie Bache credits — 35.00

Jungle Twins
Gold Key

- ❑1, Apr 1972 — 10.00
- ❑2, Jul 1972 — 7.00
- ❑3, Oct 1972 — 4.00
- ❑4, Jan 1972 — 4.00
- ❑5, Apr 1972 — 4.00

- ❑6, Jul 1973 — 3.00
- ❑7, Oct 1973 — 3.00
- ❑8, Jan 1974 — 3.00
- ❑9, Apr 1974 — 3.00
- ❑10, Jul 1974 — 3.00
- ❑11, Oct 1974 — 3.00
- ❑12, Jan 1975 — 3.00
- ❑13, Mar 1975 — 3.00
- ❑14, May 1975 — 3.00
- ❑15, Jul 1975 — 3.00
- ❑16, Sep 1975 — 3.00
- ❑17, Nov 1975 — 3.00
- ❑18, ca. 1982, Final Issue — 2.00

Junior Carrot Patrol
Dark Horse

- ❑1, May 1989, b&w; Flaming Carrot stories — 2.00
- ❑2, ca. 1989 — 2.00

Junior Jackalope
Nevada City

- ❑1, b&w — 1.50
- ❑2, Dec 1983, b&w — 1.50

Junior Woodchucks
Disney

- ❑1, Jul 1991, Reprints — 1.50
- ❑2, Aug 1991 — 1.50
- ❑3, Sep 1991 — 1.50
- ❑4, Oct 1991 — 1.50

Junk Culture
DC / Vertigo

- ❑1, Jul 1997 — 2.50
- ❑2, Aug 1997 — 2.50

Junker
Fleetway-Quality

- ❑1 — 2.95
- ❑2 — 2.95
- ❑3 — 2.95
- ❑4 — 2.95

Junkfood Noir
Oktober Black

- ❑1, Jun 1996, b&w — 1.95

Junk Force
ComicsOne

- ❑1, Jan 2004; Reads right to left; b&w .. — 9.95

Junkyard Enforcer
Boxcar

- ❑1, Aug 1998, b&w — 2.95

Jupiter
Sandberg

- ❑1; Anthology — 2.95
- ❑2, Sep 1999 — 2.95
- ❑3, Oct 1999 — 2.95

Jurassic Lark Deluxe Edition
Parody

- ❑1, b&w — 2.95

Jurassic Park
Topps

- ❑0, Nov 1993; DG, GK (a); Polybagged with trade paperback; Flip book with two prequels to the movie — 2.95
- ❑0/Direct ed., Nov 1993; GP (c); GK (a); trading cards (came packed with trade paperback) — 3.00
- ❑1, Jun 1993; DC (c); GK (a); Movie Adaptation; Includes Trading Cards — 3.00
- ❑1/Direct ed., Jun 1993; DC (c); GK (a); trading cards — 3.00
- ❑2, Jul 1993; GK (a); Movie Adaptation; Includes Trading Cards — 3.00
- ❑2/Direct ed., Jul 1993; GK (c); GK (a); trading cards — 3.00
- ❑3, Jul 1993; GK (a); Movie Adaptation; Includes Trading Cards — 3.00
- ❑3/Direct ed., Jul 1993; GK (a); trading cards — 3.00
- ❑4, Aug 1993; GK (a); Movie Adaptation; Includes Trading Cards — 3.00
- ❑4/Direct ed., Aug 1993; GK (a); hologram card — 3.00

Jurassic Park Adventures
Topps

- ❑1, Jun 1994 — 2.00
- ❑2, ca. 1994 — 2.00
- ❑3, ca. 1994 — 2.00
- ❑4, ca. 1994 — 2.00

Other grades: Multiply price above by 5/6 for VF/NM • 2/3 for VERY FINE • 1/3 for FINE • 1/5 for VERY GOOD • 1/8 for GOOD

Jungle Book

Adapts Disney animated Kipling classic
©Gold Key

Jurassic Park

Simonson and Kane adapt Spielberg SF film
©Topps

Just a Pilgrim

Post-apocalyptic bounty hunter story
©Black Bull

Justice

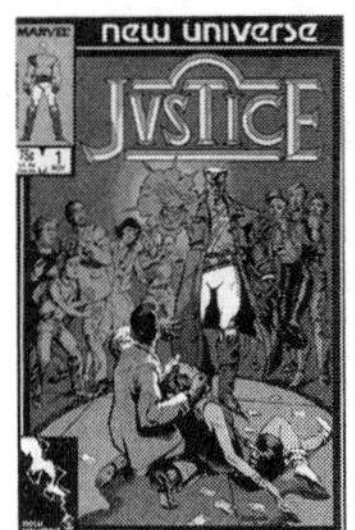

New Universe hero wields energy sword
©Marvel

Justice, Inc.

Pulp adventurer comes to comics
©DC

	N-MINT
❑5, ca. 1994	2.00
❑6, ca. 1994	2.00
❑7, ca. 1994	2.00
❑8, Dec 1994	2.00
❑9	2.00
❑10	2.00

Jurassic Park: Raptor
Topps

	N-MINT
❑1, Nov 1993; Zorro #0	2.95
❑2, Dec 1993; cards	2.95

Jurassic Park: Raptors Attack
Topps

	N-MINT
❑1, Mar 1994	2.50
❑2, Apr 1994	2.50
❑3, May 1994	2.50
❑4, Jun 1994	2.50

Jurassic Park: Raptors Hijack
Topps

	N-MINT
❑1, Jul 1994	2.50
❑2, Aug 1994	2.50
❑3	2.50
❑4	2.50

Just a Pilgrim
Black Bull

	N-MINT
❑1, May 2001	4.00
❑2, Jun 2001	2.99
❑3, Jul 2001 KN (c)	2.99
❑4, Aug 2001 BSz (c)	2.99
❑5, Sep 2001	2.99

Justice
Marvel

	N-MINT
❑1, Nov 1986; 1: Justice	1.25
❑2, Dec 1986	1.00
❑3, Jan 1987	1.00
❑4, Feb 1987, JSa (a)	1.00
❑5, Mar 1987	1.00
❑6, Apr 1987	1.00
❑7, May 1987	1.00
❑8, Jun 1987	1.00
❑9, Jul 1987	1.00
❑10, Aug 1987	1.00
❑11, Sep 1987	1.00
❑12, Oct 1987	1.00
❑13, Nov 1987	1.00
❑14, Dec 1987	1.00
❑15, Jan 1988	1.00
❑16, Feb 1988	1.00
❑17, Mar 1988	1.00
❑18, Apr 1988	1.25
❑19, May 1988	1.25
❑20, Jun 1988	1.25
❑21, Jul 1988	1.25
❑22, Aug 1988	1.25
❑23, Sep 1988	1.25
❑24, Oct 1988	1.25
❑25, Nov 1988	1.25
❑26, Dec 1988	1.50
❑27, Jan 1989	1.50
❑28, Feb 1989	1.50
❑29, Mar 1989	1.50
❑30, Apr 1989, PD (w); A: Psi-Force	1.50
❑31, May 1989	1.50
❑32, Jun 1989, Final Issue, Unauthorized Joker appearance (page 18)	1.50

Justice
Antarctic

	N-MINT
❑1, May 1994, b&w	3.50

Justice Brigade
TCB Comics

	N-MINT
❑1, b&w	1.50
❑2, b&w	1.50
❑3, b&w	1.50
❑4, b&w	1.50
❑5, b&w	1.50
❑6, b&w	1.50
❑7, b&w	1.50
❑8, b&w	1.50

Justice
DC

	N-MINT
❑1/Heroes, Sep 2005	5.00
❑1/Villains, Sep 2005	4.00
❑2, Dec 2005; Price increase	3.50
❑3, Feb 2006	3.50
❑4, Apr 2006	3.50
❑5, Jun 2006	3.50
❑6, Sep 2006	3.50
❑7, Nov 2006	3.50
❑8, Jan 2007	3.50
❑9, Mar 2007	3.50
❑10	3.50
❑11	3.50
❑12	3.50

Justice: Four Balance
Marvel

	N-MINT
❑1, Sep 1994	1.75
❑2, Oct 1994	1.75
❑3, Nov 1994	1.75
❑4, Dec 1994	1.75

Justice, Inc.
DC

	N-MINT
❑1, Jun 1975; JKu (c); O: The Avenger. adapts Justice Inc. novel	3.00
❑2, Aug 1975; JK (a); adapts The Skywalker	2.00
❑3, Oct 1975; JK (a); 1: Fergus MacMurdie	2.00
❑4, Dec 1975 JKu (c); JK (a)	2.00

Justice, Inc.
DC

	N-MINT
❑1 1989; prestige format; O: The Avenger	4.00
❑2 1989; prestige format	4.00

Justice League
DC

	N-MINT
❑1, May 1987; 1: Maxwell Lord	6.00
❑2, Jun 1987; 1: Silver Sorceress. 1: Bluejay. 1: Wandjina	2.50
❑3, Jul 1987; V: Rocket Reds. 1: Rocket Red 4	2.50
❑3/Ltd., Jul 1987; Superman logo on cover (limited edition); alternate cover	10.00
❑4, Aug 1987; V: Royal Flush Gang. Booster Gold joins team	2.50
❑5, Sep 1987; Batman vs. Guy Gardner.	2.00
❑6, Oct 1987; KG (w); KG (a); Series continues in Justice League International #7	2.00
❑Ann 1, ca. 1987, b&w; numbering continues with Justice League International Ann #2	3.00

Justice League Adventures
DC

	N-MINT
❑1, Jan 2002	2.50
❑2, Feb 2002	2.00
❑3, Mar 2002	2.00
❑4, Apr 2002	2.00
❑5, May 2002	2.00
❑6, Jun 2002	2.00
❑7, Jul 2002	2.00
❑8, Aug 2002	2.00
❑9, Sep 2002	2.00
❑10, Oct 2002	2.25
❑11, Nov 2002	2.25
❑12, Dec 2002	2.25
❑13, Jan 2003	2.25
❑14, Feb 2003	2.25
❑15, Mar 2003	2.25
❑16, Apr 2003	2.25
❑17, May 2003	2.25
❑18, Jun 2003	2.25
❑19, Jul 2003	2.25
❑20, Aug 2003	2.25
❑21, Sep 2003	2.25
❑22, Oct 2003	2.25
❑23, Nov 2003	2.25
❑24, Dec 2003	2.25
❑25, Jan 2004	2.25
❑26, Feb 2004	2.25
❑27, Mar 2004	2.25
❑28, Apr 2004	2.25
❑29, May 2004	2.25
❑30, Jun 2004	2.25
❑31, Jul 2004	2.25
❑32, Aug 2004	2.25
❑33, Sep 2004	2.25
❑34, Oct 2004	2.25

Justice League America
DC

	N-MINT
❑0, Oct 1994; New team begins: Wonder Woman, Flash III (Wally West), Fire, Metamorpho, Crimson Fox, Hawkman, Obsidian, Nuklon	2.00
❑26, May 1989; A: Huntress. Continued from Justice League International	1.75
❑27, Jun 1989; Exorcist homage cover	1.75
❑28, Jul 1989	1.75
❑29, Aug 1989	1.75
❑30, Sep 1989; Huntress II joins team	1.75
❑31, Oct 1989; A: Justice League Europe. Doctor Fate II joins team; Crossover with Justice League Europe #7-8	1.75
❑32, Nov 1989; A: Justice League Europe. Crossover with Justice League Europe #7-8	1.75
❑33, Dec 1989; A: Kilowog. 1: Kooey Kooey Kooey	1.75
❑34, Jan 1990	1.75
❑35, Feb 1990; 1: Power Girl's "the cat"	1.75
❑36, Mar 1990; 1: Mr. Nebula. 1: Scarlet Skier. A: G'Nort	1.75
❑37, Apr 1990; Booster Gold quits	1.75
❑38, May 1990; V: Despero. D: Steel II	1.75
❑39, Jun 1990; V: Despero	1.75
❑40, Jul 1990; V: Despero	1.75
❑41, Aug 1990	1.75

Other grades: Multiply price above by 5/6 for VF/NM • 2/3 for VERY FINE • 1/3 for FINE • 1/5 for VERY GOOD • 1/8 for GOOD

N-MINT

❑42, Sep 1990; membership drive; Return of Mr. Miracle; Orion joins team; Lightray joins team ... 1.75
❑43, Oct 1990 ... 1.75
❑44, Nov 1990 ... 1.75
❑45, Jan 1991 ... 1.75
❑46, Jan 1991; KG (w); 1: General Glory. Medley art begins ... 1.75
❑47, Feb 1991 ... 1.75
❑48, Mar 1991 ... 1.75
❑49, Apr 1991 ... 1.75
❑50, May 1991; Double-size; General Glory joins ... 1.75
❑51, Jun 1991 ... 1.25
❑52, Jul 1991; Guy Gardner vs. Blue Beetle ... 1.25
❑53, Aug 1991 ... 1.25
❑54, Sep 1991; Tasmanian Devil joins; Dr. Light IV joins; Blue Beetle quits; Ice quits ... 1.25
❑55, Oct 1991; V: Global Guardians. D: Jack O'Lantern II ... 1.25
❑56, Nov 1991; back to Happy Harbor ... 1.25
❑57, Dec 1991; KG (w); V: Extremists ... 1.25
❑58, Jan 1992; KG (w); A: Lobo. V: Lobo. V: Despero ... 1.25
❑59, Feb 1992 KG (w) ... 1.25
❑60, Mar 1992 KG (w) ... 1.25
❑61, Apr 1992; 1: Bloodwynd. V: Weapons Master. new JLA ... 1.25
❑62, May 1992; BG (a); V: Weapons Master. V: Weapons Master ... 1.25
❑63, Jun 1992; Bloodwynd joins team; Guy Gardner leaves team ... 1.25
❑64, Jul 1992; V: Starbreaker ... 1.25
❑65, Aug 1992; V: Starbreaker ... 1.25
❑66, Sep 1992; Guy returns ... 1.25
❑67, Oct 1992 ... 1.25
❑68, Nov 1992 ... 1.25
❑69, Dec 1992; Doomsday ... 3.00
❑69/2nd, Dec 1992; 2nd printing; Doomsday ... 1.75
❑70, Jan 1993; cover wrapper ... 2.00
❑70/2nd, Jan 1993; cover wrapper; Funeral for a Friend ... 1.75
❑71, Feb 1993; black cover wrapper; Wonder Woman joins team; Ray joins team; Agent Liberty joins team; Black Condor joins team ... 2.00
❑71/Variant, Feb 1993; New team begins; Split cover ... 2.00
❑72, Mar 1993; V: Doctor Destiny ... 1.50
❑73, Apr 1993; V: Doctor Destiny ... 1.50
❑74, May 1993; V: Doctor Destiny ... 1.50
❑75, Jun 1993; V: Doctor Destiny ... 1.50
❑76, Jul 1993; 1&O: Bloodwynd II ... 1.50
❑77, Jul 1993; O: Bloodwynd II ... 1.50
❑78, Aug 1993 RT (a); A: Jay Garrick ... 1.50
❑79, Aug 1993; V: new Extremists ... 1.50
❑80, Sep 1993; Booster gets new armor ... 1.50
❑81, Oct 1993; Ray vs. Captain Atom ... 1.50
❑82, Nov 1993 ... 1.50
❑83, Dec 1993 ... 1.50
❑84, Jan 1994 ... 1.50
❑85, Feb 1994 ... 1.50
❑86, Mar 1994; 1: Amazing Man II ... 1.50
❑87, Apr 1994 ... 1.50
❑88, May 1994 ... 1.50
❑89, Jun 1994 ... 1.50
❑90, Jul 1994 ... 1.50
❑91, Aug 1994; Funeral of Ice ... 1.50
❑92, Sep 1994; A: Triumph. Zero Hour ... 1.50
❑93, Nov 1994; 1: Scarabus ... 1.50
❑94, Dec 1994 ... 1.50
❑95, Jan 1995 ... 1.50
❑96, Feb 1995 ... 1.50
❑97, Mar 1995 ... 1.50
❑98, Apr 1995; Blue Devil joins team ... 1.50
❑99, May 1995 ... 1.50
❑100, Jun 1995; Giant-size anniversary edition ... 2.95
❑100/Variant, Jun 1995; Giant-size anniversary edition; Holo-grafix cover ... 3.95
❑101, Jul 1995 ... 1.75
❑102, Aug 1995 ... 1.75
❑103, Sep 1995 ... 1.75
❑104, Oct 1995 ... 1.75
❑105, Nov 1995; Underworld Unleashed ... 1.75
❑106, Dec 1995; Underworld Unleashed ... 1.75
❑107, Jan 1996 ... 1.75
❑108, Feb 1996; 1: Equinox; D: Scarabus ... 1.75

N-MINT

❑109, Mar 1996 A: Equinox ... 1.75
❑110, Apr 1996 A: El Diablo ... 1.75
❑111, Jun 1996 ... 1.75
❑112, Jul 1996 ... 1.75
❑113, Aug 1996; Final Issue ... 1.75
❑Ann 4, ca. 1990; Justice League Antarctica ... 3.00
❑Ann 5, ca. 1989; Armageddon 2001 ... 3.00
❑Ann 5/2nd, ca. 1990; Silver ink cover .. 2.50
❑Ann 6, ca. 1991; DC (a); Eclipso ... 2.50
❑Ann 7, ca. 1992; 1: Terrorsmith. Bloodlines ... 2.50
❑Ann 8, ca. 1993; Elseworlds ... 2.95
❑Ann 9, ca. 1994; Year One ... 3.50
❑Ann 10, ca. 1996; Legends of the Dead Earth; events continue in Ray #26; 1996 ... 2.95
❑Special 1, ca. 1990 ... 1.50
❑Special 2, ca. 1991 ... 2.95
❑SP 1/A, ca. 1992; Double-size; Justice League Spectacular; Green Lantern on cover ... 2.00
❑SP 1/B, ca. 1992; Double-size; Justice League Spectacular; Superman on cover ... 2.00

Justice League: A Midsummer's Nightmare
DC

❑1, Sep 1996; forms triptych with other two issues ... 2.95
❑2, Oct 1996; forms triptych with other two issues ... 2.95
❑3, Nov 1996; forms triptych with other two issues ... 2.95

Justice League Elite
DC

❑1, Sep 2004 ... 4.00
❑2, Oct 2004 ... 2.50
❑3, Nov 2004 ... 2.50
❑4, Dec 2004 ... 2.50
❑5, Jan 2005 ... 2.50
❑6, Feb 2005 ... 2.50
❑7, Mar 2005 ... 2.50
❑8, Apr 2005 ... 2.50
❑9, May 2005 ... 2.50
❑10, Jun 2005 ... 2.50
❑11, Jun 2005 ... 2.50

Justice League Europe
DC

❑1, Apr 1989; KG (w); KG (a); 1: Catherine Cobert ... 2.00
❑2, May 1989 ... 1.50
❑3, Jun 1989 ... 1.50
❑4, Jul 1989; V: Queen Bee ... 1.50
❑5, Aug 1989 A: Sapphire, Java ... 1.50
❑6, Sep 1989; 1: Crimson Fox ... 1.50
❑7, Oct 1989; A: Justice League America. Batman app.; JLA x-over ... 1.50
❑8, Nov 1989; A: Justice League America. Continued from Justice League America #32 ... 1.50
❑9, Dec 1989 A: Superman ... 1.50
❑10, Jan 1990; Crimson Fox joins team. ... 1.50
❑11, Feb 1990; Guy Gardner vs. Metamorpho ... 1.50
❑12, Mar 1990; Metal Men app ... 1.50
❑13, Apr 1990 ... 1.50
❑14, May 1990 ... 1.50
❑15, Jun 1990; 1: Extremists ... 1.50
❑16, Jun 1990; V: Extremists ... 1.50
❑17, Aug 1990; V: Extremists ... 1.50
❑18, Sep 1990; V: Extremists. 1: Bowman ... 1.50
❑19, Oct 1990; V: Extremists ... 1.50
❑20, Nov 1990; 1: The Beefeater ... 1.50
❑21, Dec 1990 ... 1.25
❑22, Jan 1991 ... 1.25
❑23, Feb 1991; Blue Jay joins: Silver Sorceress joins ... 1.25
❑24, Mar 1991 ... 1.25
❑25, Apr 1991 ... 1.25
❑26, May 1991 ... 1.25
❑27, Jun 1991 ... 1.25
❑28, Jul 1991 ... 1.25
❑29, Aug 1991 ... 1.25
❑30, Sep 1991; V: Jack O'Lantern. D: Little Mermaid ... 1.25
❑31, Oct 1991; evicted from JLI Embassy ... 1.25
❑32, Nov 1991 KG (w); KG (a) ... 1.25

N-MINT

❑33, Dec 1991; KG (w); A: Lobo. V: Lobo. V: Despero; Sonic the Hedgehog bonus book ... 1.25
❑34, Jan 1992; A: Lobo. V: Lobo. V: Despero ... 1.25
❑35, Feb 1992; KG (w); KG (a); V: Extremists; D: Silver Sorceress ... 1.25
❑36, Mar 1992 ... 1.25
❑37, Apr 1992; new team ... 1.25
❑38, May 1992 ... 1.25
❑39, Jun 1992 ... 1.25
❑40, Jul 1992 ... 1.25
❑41, Aug 1992 ... 1.25
❑42, Sep 1992; Wonder Woman joins team ... 1.25
❑43, Oct 1992 ... 1.25
❑44, Oct 1992 ... 1.25
❑45, Dec 1992 ... 1.25
❑46, Jan 1993 ... 1.25
❑47, Feb 1993 ... 1.25
❑48, Mar 1993 A: Justice Society of America ... 1.25
❑49, Apr 1993 ... 1.25
❑50, May 1993; Giant-size; A: Justice Society of America. V: Sonar. Series continues as Justice League International ... 2.50
❑Ann 1; ca. 1990; A: Global Guardians .. 2.00
❑Ann 2, Jan 1991; A: Demon. A: Elongated Man. A: Anthro. A: Bat Lash. A: Hex. A: General Glory. A: Legion. Armageddon 2001 ... 2.00
❑Ann 3; Eclipso; numbering continues as Justice League International Ann ... 2.50

Justice League International
DC

❑7, Nov 1987; Title changes to Justice League International; Captain Marvel leaves team; Captain Atom joins team; Rocket Red joins team ... 2.00
❑8, Dec 1987; 1: Catherine Cobert ... 1.50
❑9, Jan 1988; Millennium ... 1.50
❑10, Feb 1988; 1: G'Nort. Millennium ... 1.50
❑11, Mar 1988; Rocket Red 4 joins team 1.25
❑12, Apr 1988 ... 1.25
❑13, May 1988; A: Suicide Squad. Continues in Suicide Squad #10 ... 1.25
❑14, Jun 1988; 1: Lord Manga Khan; 1: L-Ron; Fire & Ice join team ... 1.25
❑15, Jul 1988; 1: Manga Khan. 1: L-Ron 1.25
❑16, Aug 1988 ... 1.25
❑17, Sep 1988; D: Thunderer ... 1.25
❑18, Oct 1988; A: Lobo. Bonus Book ... 1.25
❑19, Nov 1988; A: Lobo. Fake Hawkman & Hawkwoman join team (see Hawkworld #22) ... 1.25
❑20, Dec 1988 A: Lobo ... 1.25
❑21; A: Lobo. no month of publication .. 1.25
❑22; Invasion!; no month of publication; Oberon solo story ... 1.25
❑23, Jan 1989; 1: Injustice League. V: Injustice League. Invasion! ... 1.25
❑24, Feb 1989; Giant-size; 1: JL Europe. Bonus Book ... 2.00
❑25, Apr 1989; becomes Justice League America ... 1.25
❑51, Jun 1993; was Justice League Europe ... 1.25
❑52, Jul 1993 ... 1.25
❑53, Aug 1993; D: Crimson Fox I ... 1.25
❑54, Sep 1993 ... 1.25
❑55, Sep 1993 ... 1.25
❑56, Oct 1993 ... 1.25
❑57, Oct 1993 ... 1.25
❑58, Nov 1993 ... 1.25
❑59, Dec 1993 ... 1.50
❑60, Jan 1994 ... 1.50
❑61, Feb 1994 ... 1.50
❑62, Mar 1994; Metamorpho gets new look ... 1.50
❑63, Apr 1994 ... 1.50
❑64, May 1994 ... 1.50
❑65, Jun 1994 MWa (w) ... 1.50
❑66, Jul 1994 ... 1.50
❑67, Aug 1994 ... 1.50
❑68, Sep 1994; A: Triumph. Zero Hour .. 1.50
❑Ann 2, ca. 1988; A: Joker. V: Joker. numbering continued from Justice League Ann #1 ... 3.00
❑Ann 3, ca. 1989; ca. 1992 ... 3.00
❑Ann 4 ... 2.50
❑Ann ... 2.95

Other grades: Multiply price above by 5/6 for VF/NM • 2/3 for VERY FINE • 1/3 for FINE • 1/5 for VERY GOOD • 1/8 for GOOD

Justice League

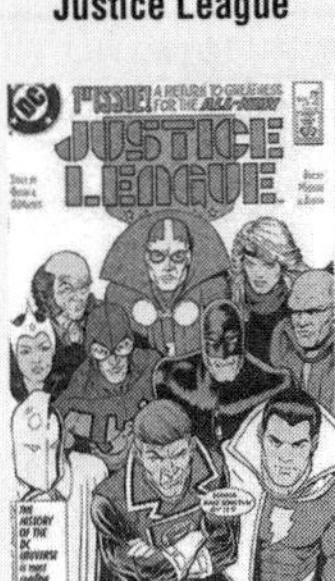

Bwah-ha-ha adventures begin
©DC

Justice League America

From Justice League to JL International to ...
©DC

Justice League Europe

Second Justice League team big in France
©DC

Justice League of America

Silver Age DC heroes formed super-team
©DC

Justice League Quarterly

Anthology allows longer adventures
©DC

N-MINT

❑Special 1; KG (w); KG (a); Mr. Miracle . 1.50
❑Special 2, Jan 1991; Huntress 2.95

Justice League of America
DC

❑1, Nov 1960; 1&O: Despero. Membership consists of Flash, Wonder Woman, J'onn J'onzz, Green Lantern, Superman, Batman and Aquaman...... 5000.00
❑2, Jan 1961; A: Merlin. Jerry Bails L.O.C 1250.00
❑3, Mar 1961; O: Kanjar Ro. 1: Kanjar Ro. 1: Hyathis; Jerry Bails L.O.C 1000.00
❑4, May 1961; Green Arrow joins team; Snapper Carr 700.00
❑5, Jul 1961; 1&O: Doctor Destiny 600.00
❑6, Sep 1961; 1: Professor Amos Fortune 400.00
❑7, Nov 1961 .... 400.00
❑8, Jan 1962, Roy Thomas L.O.C 400.00
❑9, Feb 1962, O: Justice League of America 1000.00
❑10, Mar 1962, 1: Lord of Time. 1: Felix Faust; 1: Abnegazar; 1: Rath; 1: Ghast; Roy Thomas L.O.C 400.00
❑11, May 1962 .... 250.00
❑12, Jun 1962, 1&O: Doctor Light I (Dr. Arthur Light); Paul Gambaccini L.O.C 250.00
❑13, Aug 1962 .... 250.00
❑14, Sep 1962, Atom joins Justice League of America 250.00
❑15, Nov 1962 .... 250.00
❑16, Dec 1962....................................... 225.00
❑17, Feb 1963, 1: Tornado Champion (Red Tornado) 225.00
❑18, Mar 1963 .... 225.00
❑19, May 1963, 2: Doctor Destiny; Jerry Bails L.O.C... 225.00
❑20, Jun 1963....................................... 225.00
❑21, Aug 1963, 1: Earth-2 (named). Return of Justice Society of America; Justice League of America teams up with Justice Society of America.......... 350.00
❑22, Sep 1963, Return of Justice Society of America; Justice League of America teams up with Justice Society of America 325.00
❑23, Nov 1963, 1: Queen Bee; Atom II cameo; Batman cameo; Superman cameo.. 150.00
❑24, Dec 1963, 2: Kanjar Ro; Dave Cockrum L.O.C.; Roy Thomas L.O.C... 150.00
❑25, Feb 1964 .... 150.00
❑26, Mar 1964 .... 150.00
❑27, May 1964, 2: Amazo; Guy H. Lillian L.O.C 150.00
❑28, Jun 1964.. 150.00
❑29, Aug 1964, 1&O: Crime Syndicate. 1: Earth-3. A: Justice Society of America 150.00
❑30, Sep 1964, Justice League of America teams up with Justice Society of America against the Crime Syndicate of America 150.00
❑31, Nov 1964, Hawkman joins team 100.00
❑32, Dec 1964, MA (c); O: Brainstorm. 1: Brainstorm. V: Brain Storm 90.00
❑33, Feb 1965, Roy Thomas L.O.C 90.00
❑34, Mar 1965, A: Joker. V: Doctor Destiny. 2: Chac................................. 75.00
❑35, May 1965....................................... 75.00
❑36, Jun 1965, 2: Brain Storm; Guy H. Lillian L.O.C.. 75.00

N-MINT

❑37, Aug 1965, 1: Earth-A. A: Justice Society of America 125.00
❑38, Sep 1965, A: Justice Society of America 125.00
❑39, Nov 1965; 80 page giant (#16); aka 80 Page Giant #G-16 (continuation of 80 Page Giant series' numbering as production codes); reprints Brave and the Bold #28, 30, and Justice League of America #5.. 125.00
❑40, Nov 1965, social issue................... 75.00
❑41, Dec 1965, MA (c); MA (a); 1: The Key. V: Key; 2: Invisible Destroyer...... 75.00
❑42, Feb 1966, MA (c); MA (a); A: Metamorpho 60.00
❑43, Mar 1966, MA (c); MA (a); 1: Royal Flush Gang 60.00
❑44, May 1966, MA (c); MA (a); Guy H. Lillian L.O.C.. 60.00
❑45, Jun 1966, MA (c); MA (a); 1: Shaggy Man. V: Shaggy Man 60.00
❑46, Aug 1966, 1: Sandman I (in Silver Age). A: Justice Society of America. V: Solomon Grundy, Blockbuster; Blockbuster; Justice League of America teams up with Justice Society of America 110.00
❑47, Sep 1966, A: Justice Society of America. V: Anti-Matter Man 95.00
❑48, Oct 1966; MA (c); MA (a); aka 80 Page Giant #G-29; reprints................. 140.00
❑49, Nov 1966, MA (c); MA (a)............. 60.00
❑50, Dec 1966, MA (c); MA (a); Robin apperance.. 60.00
❑51, Feb 1967, A: Elongated Man 60.00
❑52, Mar 1967 .... 60.00
❑53, May 1967.. 55.00
❑54, Jun 1967, 2: Royal Flush Gang; Mark Gruenwald L.O.C 55.00
❑55, Aug 1967, Justice League of America teams up with Justice Society of America 115.00
❑56, Sep 1967, Justice League of America teams up with Justice Society of America 100.00
❑57, Nov 1967 .... 55.00
❑58, Dec 1967; Giant-size; aka 80 Page Giant #G-41 .... 55.00
❑59, Dec 1968 .... 55.00
❑60, Feb 1968, 2: Queen Bee; Captain Comet reprint from Strange Adventures #38; Carl Gafford L.O.C.; Gerry Conway L.O.C 55.00
❑61, Mar 1968 .... 55.00
❑62, May 1968.. 55.00
❑63, Jun 1968.. 45.00
❑64, Aug 1968, DD (a); A: Justice Society of America. Return of Red Tornado.... 45.00
❑65, Sep 1968, DD (a); V: T.O.Morrow. Justice League of America teams up with Justice Society of America 45.00
❑66, Nov 1968, NA (c); DD (a)............ 45.00
❑67, Dec 1968; NA (c); DD (a); aka 80 Page Giant #G-53; reprints................. 60.00
❑68, Jan 1969, DD (a) 50.00
❑69, Feb 1969, CI (c); DD (a); Wonder Woman leaves Justice League of America 45.00
❑70, Mar 1969, NA (c); DD (a); A: Creeper 45.00
❑71, May 1969, DD (a); 1: Blue Jay. Martian Manhunter leaves Justice League of America 45.00

N-MINT

❑72, Jun 1969, JKu (c); DD (a); Martin Pasko L.O.C.; Mark Evanier L.O.C 45.00
❑73, Aug 1969, JKu (c); DD (a); A: Justice Society of America 35.00
❑74, Sep 1969, NA (c); DD (a); A: Justice Society. D: Larry Lance. Black Canary goes to Earth-1.................................. 35.00
❑75, Nov 1969, MA (c); DD (a); 1: Black Canary II (Dinah Lance)...................... 35.00
❑76, Dec 1969; MA, DD (a); aka Giant #G-65; reprints #7 and #12; pin-ups of Justice Society of America and Seven Soldiers.. 35.00
❑77, Dec 1969, MA, CI (c); DD (a); Jerry Bails L.O.C.; Alan Brennert L.O.C 35.00
❑78, Feb 1970, GK (c); DD (a); Guy Lillian L.O.C.; Mike Tiefenbacher L.O.C......... 35.00
❑79, Mar 1970, NA (c); DD (a); Martin Pasko L.O.C.; Alan Brennert L.O.C.; Flash II on cover only 35.00
❑80, May 1970, MA, CI (c); DD (a); Mark Gruenwald L.O.C 35.00
❑81, Jun 1970, NA (c); DD (a); Martin Pasko L.O.C.; Don McGregor L.O.C.... 35.00
❑82, Aug 1970, NA (c); DD (a); Justice Society of America team-up 45.00
❑83, Sep 1970, MA (c); DD (a); A: Spectre. Justice Society of America team-up ... 30.00
❑84, Nov 1970, MA, CS (c); MA, DD (a); V: The 100; Strange Adventures #30; Justice League of America 30.00
❑85, Dec 1970; Giant-size; aka Giant #G-77; reprints.. 40.00
❑86, Dec 1970, NA (c); DD (a) 25.00
❑87, Feb 1971, NA (c); DD (a); 1: Silver Sorceress; 1: Blue Jay; 1: Wandjina; 1: Jack B. Quick.................................. 25.00
❑88, Mar 1971, NA (c); DD (a) 25.00
❑89, May 1971, NA (c); DD (a); V: Harlequin Ellis (based on writer Harlan Ellison) 25.00
❑90, Jun 1971, MA, CI (c); DD (a); Guy H. Lillian L.O.C.. 25.00
❑91, Aug 1971; NA (c); CI, DD (a); Includes The Day the World Melted (reprinted from Mystery in Space #6); Hourman: The Hour Hourman Died! (reprinted from The Spectre (1st Series) #7) 35.00
❑92, Sep 1971; NA (c); CI, DD (a); 1: Starbreaker. 1: Earth-2 Robin costume designed by Neal Adams; V: Solomon Grundy; Includes Flash: The One-Man Justice League! (reprinted from Flash #158) 32.00
❑93, Nov 1971, Giant-size; aka Giant #G-89; reprints.. 25.00
❑94, Nov 1971; NA, DD (a); O: Sandman I (Wesley Dodds). 1: Merlyn. A: Deadman. Reprints Adventure Comics #40 .... 60.00
❑95, Dec 1971; MA, NA (c); DD (a); O: Doctor Midnight. O: Doctor Fate. Reprints More Fun Comics #67 and All-American Comics #25 .... 20.00
❑96, Feb 1972; NA (c); DD, BK (a); V: Cosmic Vampire. 1: Starbreaker; Adam Strange cameo; Includes reprints from Adventure Comics #48; Sensation Comics #84 .... 20.00
❑97, Mar 1972; NA (c); DD (a); O: Justice League of America; Includes pages reprinted from The Brave and the Bold #28; Sargon cameo 20.00

❑98, May 1972; NA (c); DD (a); A: Sargon. Justice League of America; Sargon; The sorcerer: Sensation Comics #70; Starman: Adventure Comics #92........ 20.00

❑99, Jun 1972; NC (c); DD (a); A: Sargon. Justice League Of America; The Sandman: Adventure Comics #51; The Atom I (Al Pratt): Flash Comics #98... 20.00

❑100, Aug 1972, NC (c); DD (a); Return of Seven Soldiers of Victory.............. 65.00

❑101, Sep 1972, NC (c); DD (a); Justice League of America teams up with Justice Society of America.......... 20.00

❑102, Oct 1972, DD (a); D: Red Tornado. Justice League of America teams up with Justice Society of America......... 20.00

❑103, Dec 1972, NC (c); DG, DD (a); A: Phantom Stranger......................... 20.00

❑104, Feb 1973, NC (c); DG, DD (a); V: Hector Hammond. V: Shaggy Man . 20.00

❑105, May 1973, DG, DD (a); Elongated Man joins the Justice League of America... 20.00

❑106, Aug 1973, NC (c); DG, DD (a); Red Tornado (new) joins the Justice League of America.. 20.00

❑107, Oct 1973, NC (c); DG, DD (a); 1: Freedom Fighters. 1: Earth-X. A: Justice Society of America............ 25.00

❑108, Dec 1973, NC (c); DG, DD (a); A: Justice Society of America. A: Freedom Fighters.......................... 25.00

❑109, Feb 1974, NC (c); DG, DD (a); Hawkman resigns from Justice League of America.. 20.00

❑110, Apr 1974, NC (c); ATh, CI, DG, DD (a); Justice Society of America pin-up 25.00

❑111, Jun 1974, NC (c); DG, DD (a); V: Libra; Seven Soldiers of Victory: Leading Comics #2; The Shining Knight: Leading Comics #2; The Star-Spangled Kid: Leading Comics #2; The Green Arrow (golden age): Leading Comics #2; JLA: Justice League of America #32; Justice League of America; 100 pages.......................... 25.00

❑112, Aug 1974, MM, DG, DD (a); V: Amazo; Seven Soldiers of Victory: Leading Comics #2; The Crimson Avenger: Leading Comics #2; Vigilante: Leading Comics #2; Starman: Adventure Comics #81; JLA: Justice League of America #19; Justice League of America; 100 pages...................... 25.00

❑113, Oct 1974, DG, DD (a); Justice Society of America: All-Star #41; Justice League of America: JLA #16; 100 pages.. 25.00

❑114, Dec 1974, DG, DD (a); V: Anakronus. Return of Snapper Carr 25.00

❑115, Feb 1975, DG, DD (a); Justice Society of America: All-Star Comics #44; Justice League of America: JLA #40; 100 pages................................. 25.00

❑116, Mar 1975, MA, DG, DD (a); V: Matter Master. Return of Hawkman 25.00

❑117, Apr 1975; FMc, DD (a); Hawkman rejoins JLA 15.00

❑118, May 1975 FMc, DD (a)................ 15.00

❑119, Jun 1975 FMc, DD (a)................. 15.00

❑120, Jul 1975; MGr (c); FMc, DD (a); A: Adam Strange. V: Kanjar Ro........... 15.00

❑121, Aug 1975; FMc, DD (a); V: Kanjar Ro; Wedding of Adam Strange and Alanna 15.00

❑122, Sep 1975; MGr (c); FMc, DD (a); V: Doctor Light. V: Dr. Light............... 15.00

❑123, Oct 1975; FMc, DD (a); 1: Earth-Prime (named). A: Justice Society of America.. 15.00

❑124, Nov 1975 FMc, DD (a); A: Justice Society of America 15.00

❑125, Dec 1975 FMc, DD (a)................ 15.00

❑126, Jan 1976; FMc, DD (a); Joker...... 10.00

❑127, Feb 1976 DG (c); FMc, DD (a)...... 10.00

❑128, Mar 1976; FMc, DD (a); Wonder Woman rejoins................................... 10.00

❑129, Apr 1976, FMc, DD (a); D: Red Tornado (new); Jo Duffy L.O.C........... 10.00

❑130, May 1976, FMc, DD (a)............... 10.00

❑131, Jun 1976, FMc, DD (a)................ 10.00

❑132, Jul 1976, FMc, DD (a); Bicentennial #6... 10.00

❑133, Aug 1976, FMc, DD (a) 10.00

❑134, Sep 1976, FMc, DD (a)................ 10.00

❑135, Oct 1976, FMc, DD (a); 1: Earth-S (named)... 10.00

❑136, Nov 1976, FMc, DD (a)............... 10.00

❑137, Dec 1976, FMc, DD (a); A: Marvel Family. Superman vs. Captain Marvel (Golden Age).................................... 20.00

❑138, Jan 1977, double-sized; NA (c); FMc, DD (a)... 7.00

❑139, Feb 1977, double-sized; NA (c); FMc, DD (a)... 7.00

❑140, Mar 1977, double-sized; RB (c); FMc, DD (a); A: Manhunters.............. 7.00

❑141, Apr 1977, double-sized; RB (c); FMc, DD (a); A: Manhunters.............. 7.00

❑142, May 1977, double-sized; RB (c); FMc, DD (a); 1: The Construct............ 7.00

❑143, Jun 1977, double-sized; FMc, DD (a); 1: Privateer 7.00

❑144, Jul 1977, double-sized; DD (c); FMc, DD (a); O: Justice League of America; 48 pages............................ 7.00

❑145, Aug 1977, DD (c); FMc, DD (a); 48 pages 7.00

❑146, Sep 1977, DD (c); FMc, DD (a); 48 pages; Red Tornado returns; Hawkgirl II joins Justice League of America...... 7.00

❑147, Oct 1977, RB (c); FMc, DD (a); A: Legion. V: Mordru; 48 pages.......... 7.00

❑148, Nov 1977, RB (c); FMc, DD (a); A: Legion. V: Mordru; 48 pages.......... 7.00

❑149, Dec 1977, RB (c); FMc, DD (a); 1: Star-Tsar; 48 pages 7.00

❑150, Jan 1978, RB (c); FMc, DD (a); V: Key; 48 pages.............................. 7.00

❑151, Feb 1978, FMc, DD (a); 48 pages 5.00

❑152, Mar 1978, RB (c); FMc, DD (a); 48 pages 5.00

❑153, Apr 1978, RB (c); FMc, GT, DD (a); 1: Ultraa; 48 pages.......................... 5.00

❑154, May 1978, FMc, DD (a); V: Doctor Destiny; 48 pages............................. 5.00

❑155, Jun 1978, JAb (c); FMc, DD (a); 48 pages; Double-sized 5.00

❑156, Jul 1978, RB (c); FMc, DD (a); A: Phantom Stranger. 48 pages; Double-sized 5.00

❑157, Aug 1978, JSa (c); FMc, DD (a); 48 pages; Wedding of Atom II (Ray Palmer) and Jean Loring........... 5.00

❑158, Sep 1978, RB (c); FMc, DD (a); Poison Ivy apperance........................... 5.00

❑158/Whitman, Sep 1978, FMc, DD (a); Whitman variant................................. 10.00

❑159, Oct 1978, RB (c); JSa (w); FMc, DD (a); A: Enemy Ace. A: Justice Society of America. A: Black Pirate. A: Viking Prince. A: Miss Liberty. A: Jonah Hex. 5.00

❑160, Nov 1978, DD (c); JSa (w); FMc, DD (a); A: Enemy Ace. A: Justice Society of America. A: Black Pirate. A: Viking Prince. A: Miss Liberty. A: Jonah Hex..................................... 5.00

❑160/Whitman, Nov 1978, JSa (w); FMc, DD (a); A: Enemy Ace. A: Justice Society of America. A: Black Pirate. A: Viking Prince. A: Miss Liberty. A: Jonah Hex. Whitman variant......... 10.00

❑161, Dec 1978, RB (c); FMc, DD (a); Zatanna joins the Justice League of America... 5.00

❑161/Whitman, Dec 1978, FMc, DD (a); Zatanna joins the Justice League of America; Whitman variant................. 10.00

❑162, Jan 1979, DD (c); FMc, DD (a) 5.00

❑162/Whitman, Jan 1979, FMc, DD (a); Whitman variant................................ 10.00

❑163, Feb 1979, RB (c); FMc, DD (a)..... 5.00

❑164, Mar 1979, RB (c); FMc, DD (a).... 5.00

❑165, Apr 1979, FMc, DD (a)................ 5.00

❑166, May 1979, DG (c); FMc, DD (a); V: Secret Society of Super-Villains.... 12.00

❑166/Whitman, May 1979, FMc, DD (a); V: Secret Society of Super-Villains. Whitman variant................................. 25.00

❑167, Jun 1979, DD (c); FMc, DD (a); V: Secret Society of Super-Villains..... 12.00

❑167/Whitman, Jun 1979, FMc, DD (a); Whitman variant................................. 25.00

❑168, Jul 1979, DD (c); FMc, DD (a); V: Secret Society of Super-Villains..... 25.00

❑168/Whitman, Jul 1979, FMc, DD (a); V: Secret Society of Super-Villains. Whitman variant................................. 35.00

❑169, Aug 1979, DD (c); FMc, DD (a).... 5.00

❑169/Whitman, Aug 1979, FMc, DD (a); Whitman variant.................................. 10.00

❑170, Sep 1979, DD (c); FMc, DD (a); A: Supergirl. Supergirl cameo 5.00

❑171, Oct 1979, DD (c); FMc, DD (a); A: Justice Society of America. D: Mr. Terrific; D: Mr. Terrific (Terry Sloane) . 5.00

❑171/Whitman, Oct 1979, FMc, DD (a); A: Justice Society of America. D: Mr. Terrific. Whitman variant.......... 10.00

❑172, Nov 1979, DD (c); FMc, DD (a); A: Justice Society of America............ 5.00

❑172/Whitman, Nov 1979, FMc, DD (a); A: Justice Society of America. Whitman variant... 10.00

❑173, Dec 1979, DD (c); FMc, DD (a); A: Black Lightning............................. 5.00

❑173/Whitman, Dec 1979, FMc, DD (a); A: Black Lightning. Whitman variant .. 10.00

❑174, Jan 1980, DD (c); FMc, DD (a); A: Black Lightning 5.00

❑175, Feb 1980, RA (c); FMc, DD (a); V: Doctor Destiny 5.00

❑176, Mar 1980, RA (c); FMc, DD (a); V: Doctor Destiny 5.00

❑176/Whitman, Mar 1980, FMc, DD (a); V: Doctor Destiny. Whitman variant.... 10.00

❑177, Apr 1980, RB (c); FMc, DD (a); A: J'onn J'onzz. V: Despero............... 5.00

❑177/Whitman, Apr 1980; Whitman variant... 10.00

❑178, May 1980, JSn (c); FMc, DD (a); V: Despero.. 5.00

❑178/Whitman, May 1980; Whitman variant... 10.00

❑179, Jun 1980, JSn (c); FMc, DD (a); Firestorm joins the Justice League of America... 5.00

❑179/Whitman, Jun 1980; Whitman variant... 10.00

❑180, Jul 1980, JSn (c); FMc, DD (a) 5.00

❑181, Aug 1980, RA (c); FMc, DD (a); A: Snapper Carr. Green Arrow leaves team 5.00

❑181/Whitman, Aug 1980, FMc, DD (a); A: Snapper Carr. Green Arrow leaves team; Whitman variant...................... 10.00

❑182, Sep 1980, DC (c); FMc, DD (a); A: Felix Faust. Elongated Man back-up 5.00

❑183, Oct 1980, JSn (c); JSa (w); FMc, DD (a); A: Orion. A: Justice Society of America. A: Metron. A: Mr. Miracle. V: Icicle. V: Shade. V: Fiddler. V: Darkseid; Dick Dillin's last published work... 5.00

❑184, Nov 1980, GP (c); FMc, GP (a); A: Justice Society of America. A: New Gods. V: Darkseid. V: Injustice Society 5.00

❑185, Dec 1980, JSn (c); FMc, GP (a); A: Justice Society of America. A: New Gods. V: Darkseid. V: Injustice Society. Has O.J. Simpson Dingo Boots ad on back cover... 5.00

❑186, Jan 1981, GP (c); FMc, GP (a); V: Shaggy Man 5.00

❑187, Feb 1981, DG, RA (c); FMc, DH, RA (a) 5.00

❑188, Mar 1981, DG, RA (c); FMc, RB, DH, RA (a) 5.00

❑189, Apr 1981, BB (c); FMc, RB (a); V: Starro... 5.00

❑190, May 1981, BB (c); RB (a); V: Starro 5.00

❑191, Jun 1981, RB, DG (c); RB (a); V: Amazo. V: The Key 5.00

❑192, Jul 1981, GP (c); GP (a); O: Red Tornado. A: T.O. Morrow 5.00

❑193, Aug 1981, RB, GP (a); 1: Danette Reilly. 1: All-Star Squadron; 16 page insert; Johnny Thunder appeaance..... 5.00

❑194, Sep 1981, GP (c); GP (a) 5.00

❑195, Oct 1981, GP (c); GP (a); A: Justice Society of America. V: Secret Society of Super-Villains 5.00

❑196, Nov 1981, GP (c); GP (a); A: Justice Society of America. V: Secret Society of Super-Villains 5.00

❑197, Dec 1981, GP (c); GP, KP (a); A: Justice Society of America. V: Secret Society of Super-Villains; Todd McFarlane L.O.C 5.00

❑198, Jan 1982, RA (c); DH (a); A: Scalphunter. A: Bat Lash. A: Cinnamon. A: Jonah Hex. V: Lord of Time... 5.00

❑199, Feb 1982, GP (c); DH (a); A: Scalphunter. A: Bat Lash. A: Cinnamon. A: Jonah Hex. V: Lord of Time 5.00

❑200, Mar 1982; Anniversary issue; CI, GP, PB, DG, JKu, BB, GK, TD, JA (a); O: JLA. A: Snapper Carr. Green Arrow rejoins 7.00

Other grades: Multiply price above by 5/6 for VF/NM • 2/3 for VERY FINE • 1/3 for FINE • 1/5 for VERY GOOD • 1/8 for GOOD

Justice Leagues: JL?

JLA founders form own teams
©DC

Justice League Task Force

Spin-off sanctions s pecial super-teams
©DC

Justice Machine (Comico)

Super-powered police force in space
©Comico

Justice Society of America

Early 1950s adventure spells finis for JSA
©DC

Justice Society of America

Short-lived series had animated look
©DC

	N-MINT
❏201, Apr 1982, GP (c); DH (a); V: Ultraa	3.00
❏202, May 1982, GP (c); DH (a)	3.00
❏203, Jun 1982, GP (c); DH (a); V: Hector Hammond. V: New Royal Flush Gang.	3.00
❏204, Jul 1982, GP (c); DH (a); V: Hector Hammond. V: New Royal Flush Gang.	3.00
❏205, Aug 1982, GP (c); DH (a); V: Hector Hammond. V: New Royal Flush Gang.	3.00
❏206, Sep 1982, DC (c); CI, DH, RT (a); V: Rath. V: Ghast. V: Abnegazar	3.00
❏207, Oct 1982, GP (c); JSa (w); DH, RT (a); A: Justice Society of America. A: All-Star Squadron. V: Per Degaton. V: Crime Syndicate. Justice Society of America, Justice League of America, and All-Star Squadron team up	3.00
❏208, Nov 1982, GP (c); JSa (w); DH, CS (a); A: Justice Society of America. A: All-Star Squadron. V: Per Degaton. V: Crime Syndicate. Justice Society of America, Justice League of America, and All-Star Squadron team up	3.00
❏209, Dec 1982, GP (c); JSa (w); DH (a); A: Justice Society of America. A: All-Star Squadron. V: Per Degaton. V: Crime Syndicate. Justice Society of America, Justice League of America, and All-Star Squadron team up	3.00
❏210, Jan 1983, RB (c); RB (a); first publication of story slated for 1977 DC tabloid	3.00
❏211, Feb 1983, RB (c); RB (a); first publication of story slated for 1977 DC tabloid	3.00
❏212, Mar 1983, GP (c); RB (a); concludes story slated for 1977 DC tabloid	3.00
❏213, Apr 1983, GP (c); DH, RT (a)	3.00
❏214, May 1983, GP (c); DH, RT (a)	3.00
❏215, Jun 1983, GP (c); DH, RT (a)	3.00
❏216, Jul 1983, DH (a)	3.00
❏217, Aug 1983, GP (c); D: Garn Daanuth	3.00
❏218, Sep 1983, A: Amazo. V: Prof. Ivo.	4.00
❏219, Oct 1983, GP (c); JSa (w); JSa (a); A: Justice Society of America. A: Thunderbolt	3.00
❏220, Nov 1983, GP (c); JSa (w); JSa (a); O: Black Canary. A: Justice Society of America. A: Sargon	4.00
❏221, Dec 1983	3.00
❏222, Jan 1984	3.00
❏223, Feb 1984	3.00
❏224, Mar 1984; KB (w); V: Paragon	3.00
❏225, Apr 1984	3.00
❏226, May 1984 RA (c)	3.00
❏227, Jun 1984	4.00
❏228, Jul 1984; J'onn J'onzz returns	3.00
❏229, Aug 1984	3.00
❏230, Sep 1984	3.00
❏231, Oct 1984 JSa, KB (w); JSa (a); A: Justice Society of America. A: Supergirl. A: Phantom Stranger	3.00
❏232, Nov 1984; JSa, KB (w); JSa (a); A: Justice Society of America. A: Supergirl. V: Crime Syndicate. V: Crime Syndicate	3.00
❏233, Dec 1984; A: Vibe. cover forms four-part poster with issues #234-236; New team begins	3.00
❏234, Jan 1985 A: Monitor. A: Vixen	3.00
❏235, Feb 1985; O: Steel. 1: The Cadre. V: Overmaster. V: The Cadre	3.00

	N-MINT
❏236, Mar 1985; A: Gypsy. V: Overmaster. V: The Cadre	3.00
❏237, Apr 1985; A: Wonder Woman. A: Superman. A: The Flash. V: Mad Maestro	3.00
❏238, May 1985; D: Anton Allegro	3.00
❏239, Jun 1985; D: General Mustapha Maksai. Wonder Woman leaves Justice League	3.00
❏240, Jul 1985; KB (w); 1: Doctor Anomaly	3.00
❏241, Aug 1985; GT (a); V: Amazo	3.00
❏242, Sep 1985; GT (a); V: Amazo. M.A.S.K. preview	3.00
❏243, Oct 1985; GT (a); V: Amazo. Aquaman leaves the Justice League of America	3.00
❏244, Nov 1985; JSa (w); JSa (a); A: Justice Society of America. A: Infinity, Inc.. Crisis; Steel vs. Steel	3.00
❏245, Dec 1985; LMc (c); LMc (a); A: Lord of Time. Crisis; Steel in future	3.00
❏246, Jan 1986; LMc (a); evicted from HQ	3.00
❏247, Feb 1986; LMc (a); back to Happy Harbor	3.00
❏248, Mar 1986; LMc (c); LMc (a); J'onn J'onzz solo story	3.00
❏249, Apr 1986 LMc (c); LMc (a)	3.00
❏250, May 1986; Giant-size; LMc (a); A: original JLA. Batman rejoins Justice League of America	3.00
❏251, Jun 1986; LMc (c); LMc (a); V: Despero	3.00
❏252, Jul 1986; LMc (c); LMc (a); V: Despero	3.00
❏253, Aug 1986; LMc (a); O: Despero	3.00
❏254, Sep 1986; LMc (c); JO (w); LMc (a); V: Despero; Includes Mask preview	3.00
❏255, Oct 1986; LMc (c); LMc (a); O: Gypsy	3.00
❏256, Nov 1986 LMc (a)	3.00
❏257, Dec 1986; LMc (a); Zatanna leaves Justice League	3.00
❏258, Jan 1987; LMc (a); D: Vibe; Legends, Chapter 5	3.00
❏259, Feb 1987; LMc (a); Gypsy leaves team	3.00
❏260, Mar 1987; LMc (c); LMc (a); D: Steel	3.00
❏261, Apr 1987; LMc (a); group disbands	4.00
❏Ann 1, Oct 1983; A: John Stewart. A: Sandman. V: Doctor Destiny	4.50
❏Ann 2, Oct 1984; 1&O: New JLA (Vixen, Vibe, Gypsy, Steel). 1: Gypsy.	3.50
❏Ann 3, Nov 1985; MGu (a); 1: Red Tornado (in current form). Crisis	3.50

Justice League of America: Another Nail
DC

❏1, Jul 2004	5.95
❏2, Aug 2004	5.95
❏3, Sep 2004	5.95

Justice League of America Index
Eclipse / Independent

❏1, Apr 1986	1.50
❏2, Apr 1986	1.50
❏3, May 1986	1.50
❏4, May 1986	1.50
❏5, Oct 1986	2.00
❏6, Nov 1986	2.00

	N-MINT
❏7, Jan 1987	2.00
❏8; Title changes to Justice League of America Index	2.00

Justice League of America
DC

❏0, Sep 2006, Michael Turner cover	6.00
❏1, Nov 2006	6.00
❏1/Variant, Nov 2006	6.00
❏2, Dec 2006	4.00
❏2/Variant, Dec 2006	4.00
❏3, Jan 2007, Cover by Michael Turner..	2.99
❏3/Variant, Jan 2007	2.99
❏4, Feb 2007, Michael Turner Cover	2.99
❏4/Variant, Feb 2007	2.99
❏5, Mar 2007	2.99
❏5/Variant, Mar 2007	2.99

Justice League of America Super Spectacular
DC

❏1, ca. 1999; Reprints	5.95

Justice League Quarterly
DC

❏1, Win 1990; 1: The Conglomerate; O: The Conglomerate	3.00
❏2, Spr 1991; V: Mr. Nebula	3.00
❏3, Jun 1991; cover says Sum, indicia says Jun	3.00
❏4, Fal 1991; Fall 1991; Cover says Aut; Indicia says Fall	3.00
❏5, Win 1991	3.00
❏6, Spr 1992	3.00
❏7, Sum 1992; Blue Beetle appearane	3.00
❏8, Sum 1992; cover says Aut, indicia says Sum; new Conglomerate	3.00
❏9, Win 1992	3.00
❏10, Spr 1993	3.00
❏11, Sum 1993	3.00
❏12, Sum 1993; covers says Aut, indicia says Sum; Conglomerate	3.00
❏13, Aut 1993; cover says Win, indicia says Aut	3.00
❏14, Spr 1994	3.00
❏15, Jun 1994; cover says Sum, indicia says Jun	3.00
❏16, Sep 1994; Titled Justice League International Quarterly	3.00
❏17, Win 1994; Final Issue; 1: Cascade.	3.00

Justice Leagues: JL?
DC

❏1, Mar 2001	2.50

Justice Leagues: JLA
DC

❏1, Mar 2001	2.50

Justice Leagues: Justice League of Aliens
DC

❏1, Mar 2001	2.50

Justice Leagues: Justice League of Amazons
DC

❏1, Mar 2001	2.50

N-MINT N-MINT N-MINT

Justice Leagues:Justice League of Arkham
DC

❑1, Mar 2001 .... 2.50

Justice Leagues: Justice League of Atlantis
DC

❑1, Mar 2001 .... 2.50

Justice League Task Force
DC

❑0, Oct 1994 MWa (w); A: Triumph 1.75
❑1, Jun 1993; membership card 2.00
❑2, Jul 1993 .... 1.50
❑3, Aug 1993 .... 1.50
❑4, Sep 1993 .... 1.50
❑5, Oct 1993 .... 1.50
❑6, Nov 1993 .... 1.25
❑7, Dec 1993; PD (w); transsexual J'onn J'onzz 1.50
❑8, Jan 1994; PD (w); transsexual J'onn J'onzz 1.50
❑9, Feb 1994 JPH (w); A: New Bloods 1.50
❑10, Mar 1994; V: Aryan Brigade; 1: Aryan Brigade 1.50
❑11, Apr 1994; V: Aryan Brigade 1.50
❑12, May 1994; Martian Manhunter appearance4 .... 1.50
❑13, Jun 1994 MWa (w) 1.50
❑14, Jul 1994 MWa (w) 1.50
❑15, Aug 1994 MWa (w) 1.50
❑16, Sep 1994; A: Triumph. Zero Hour 1.50
❑17, Nov 1994 MWa (w) 1.50
❑18, Dec 1994 MWa (w) 1.50
❑19, Jan 1995; MWa (w); V: Vandal Savage 1.50
❑20, Feb 1995 MWa (w) 1.50
❑21, Mar 1995 .... 1.50
❑22, Apr 1995 .... 1.50
❑23, May 1995 .... 1.50
❑24, Jun 1995 .... 1.75
❑25, Jul 1995 .... 1.75
❑26, Aug 1995 .... 1.75
❑27, Sep 1995 .... 1.75
❑28, Oct 1995 .... 1.75
❑29, Nov 1995 .... 1.75
❑30, Dec 1995; Underworld Unleashed 1.75
❑31, Jan 1996 .... 1.75
❑32, Feb 1996 .... 1.75
❑33, Mar 1996 .... 1.75
❑34, May 1996 .... 1.75
❑35, Jun 1996 A: Warlord. 1.75
❑36, Jul 1996 .... 1.75
❑37, Aug 1996; Final Issue 1.75

Justice League Unlimited
DC

❑1, Nov 2004 .... 2.25
❑2, Dec 2004; HeroScape bonus comic 1 of 2 .... 2.25
❑3, Jan 2005, 68 pages 2.25
❑4, Feb 2005 .... 2.25
❑5, Mar 2005 .... 2.25
❑6, Apr 2005 .... 2.25
❑7, May 2005 .... 2.25
❑8, Jun 2005 .... 2.25
❑9, Jun 2005 .... 2.25
❑10, Jul 2005 .... 2.25
❑11, Aug 2005 .... 2.25
❑12, Sep 2005; Includes Bionicle Special Edition 2.25
❑13, Oct 2005 .... 2.25
❑14, Dec 2005; Superman apperance 2.25
❑15, Jan 2006; Includes HeroScape #4 .... 2.25
❑16, Jan 2006 .... 2.25
❑17, Mar 2006 .... 2.25
❑18, Mar 2006 .... 2.25
❑19, May 2006 .... 2.25
❑20, Jun 2006 .... 2.25
❑21, Jul 2006 .... 2.25
❑22, Aug 2006 .... 2.25
❑23, Sep 2006, Includes HeroScape 2.25
❑24, Oct 2006 .... 2.25
❑25, Nov 2006 .... 2.25
❑27, Jan 2007, V: Parasite; Includes 3-D Heroscape glasses; Includes Teen Titans: Sparktop mini-comic 2.25
❑28, Feb 2007 .... 2.25
❑29, Mar 2007, Includes The Adventures of Finn & Friends backup story 2.25
❑30 .... 2.25
❑31 .... 2.25
❑32 .... 2.25
❑33 .... 2.25
❑34 .... 2.25
❑35 .... 2.25
❑36 .... 2.25
❑37 .... 2.25
❑38 .... 2.25
❑39 .... 2.25
❑40 .... 2.25
❑41 .... 2.25
❑42 .... 2.25
❑43 .... 2.25
❑44 .... 2.25
❑45 .... 2.25
❑46 .... 2.25

Justice Machine (Noble)
Noble

❑1, Jun 1981 JBy (c); MGu (w); MGu (a) 2.50
❑2, Dec 1981 TD (c); MGu (w); MGu (a) 2.50
❑3, Jun 1981 MGu (w); MGu (a) 2.50
❑4; MGu (w); MGu (a); Cobalt Blue back-up 2.50
❑5, Nov 1983; MGu (w); BL, MGu (a); Cobalt Blue back-up 2.50
❑Ann 1, Jan 1984; 1: Elementals. THUNDER Agents 5.00

Justice Machine
Comico

❑1, Jan 1987 MGu (a) 2.50
❑2, Feb 1987 MGu (a) 2.00
❑3, Mar 1987 MGu (a) 1.75
❑4, Apr 1987 MGu (a) 1.75
❑5, May 1987 MGu (a) 1.75
❑6, Jun 1987 MGu (a) 1.75
❑7, Jul 1987 MGu (a) 1.75
❑8, Aug 1987; MGu (a); D: Demon 1.75
❑9, Sep 1987 MGu (a) 1.75
❑10, Oct 1987 MGu (a) 1.75
❑11, Nov 1987 MGu (a) 1.75
❑12, Dec 1987 .... 1.75
❑13, Jan 1988 MGu (a) 1.75
❑14, Feb 1988 MGu (a) 1.75
❑15, Mar 1988; Wraparound cover 1.75
❑16, Apr 1988 .... 1.75
❑17, May 1988; Wraparound cover 1.75
❑18, Jun 1988; Wraparound cover 1.75
❑19, Jul 1988 .... 1.75
❑20, Aug 1988 .... 1.75
❑21, Sep 1988 .... 1.75
❑22, Oct 1988 .... 1.75
❑23, Nov 1988 .... 1.75
❑24, Dec 1988 .... 1.75
❑25, Jan 1989 .... 1.75
❑26, Feb 1989 .... 1.75
❑27, Mar 1989 .... 1.75
❑28, Apr 1989 .... 1.95
❑29, May 1989; Final Issue 1.95
❑Ann 1, Jun 1989 A: Elementals 2.75

Justice Machine
Innovation

❑1, Apr 1990 .... 1.95
❑2, May 1990 .... 1.95
❑3, Jul 1990 .... 1.95
❑4, Sep 1990 .... 1.95
❑5, Nov 1990 .... 1.95
❑6, Jan 1991 .... 2.25
❑7, Apr 1991 .... 2.25

Justice Machin
Millennium

❑1, ca. 1992; O: The Justice Machine 2.50
❑2, ca. 1992 .... 2.50

Justice Machine Featuring the Elementals
Comico

❑1, May 1986; Wraparound cover 2.00
❑2, Jun 1986 .... 1.75
❑3, Jul 1986; Wraparound cover 1.75
❑4, Aug 1986; Wraparound cover 1.75

Justice Machine Summer Spectacular
Innovation

❑1; ca. 1990 .... 2.75

Justice Riders
DC

❑1 1997, prestige format; Elseworlds; Justice League in old West 5.95

Justice Society of America
DC

❑1, Apr 1991; Flash 2.00
❑2, May 1991; Black Canary 1.75
❑3, Jun 1991; Green Lantern 1.75
❑4, Jul 1991; FMc (a); Hawkman 1.50
❑5, Aug 1991; Flash, Hawkman 1.50
❑6, Sep 1991; FMc (a); Green Lantern, Black Canary 1.50
❑7, Oct 1991; Green Lantern, Black Canary, Hawkman, Flash, Starman 1.50
❑8, Nov 1991; Green Lantern, Black Canary, Hawkman, Flash, Starman 1.50

Justice Society of America
DC

❑1, Aug 1992; 1: Jesse Quick 1.50
❑2, Sep 1992 .... 1.50
❑3, Oct 1992; V: Ultra-Humanite 1.50
❑4, Nov 1992; V: Ultra-Humanite 1.50
❑5, Dec 1992 .... 1.50
❑6, Jan 1993 .... 1.25
❑7, Feb 1993; in Bahdnesia 1.25
❑8, Mar 1993 .... 1.25
❑9, Apr 1993; Alan Scott vs. Guy Gardner 1.25
❑10, May 1993; Final Issue 1.25

Justice Society of America
DC

❑1, Jan 2007, 1: Liberty Belle II (Jesse Quick); 1: Starman VIII; 1: Mr. America II; 1: Cyclone (Maxine Hunkel) 6.00
❑1/Variant, Jan 2007 .... 6.00
❑2, Feb 2007, 1: Nathan Heywood (Commander Steel II); D: Mr. America II 4.00
❑3, Mar 2007, 1: Cyclone 3.00
❑4 .... 2.99
❑5 .... 2.99
❑6 .... 2.99
❑7 .... 2.99
❑8 .... 2.99
❑9 .... 2.99
❑10 .... 2.99
❑11 .... 2.99
❑12 .... 2.99
❑13 .... 2.99
❑14 .... 2.99
❑15 .... 2.99
❑16 .... 2.99
❑17 .... 2.99
❑18 .... 2.99
❑19 .... 2.99
❑20 .... 2.99
❑21 .... 2.99
❑22 .... 2.99
❑23 .... 2.99
❑24 .... 2.99
❑25 .... 2.99

Justice Society of America 100-Page Super Spectacular
DC

❑1; 2000 facsimile of 1975 100-Page Super Spectacular; reprints The Flash #137 and #201, All Star Comics #57, The Brave and the Bold #62, and Adventure Comics #418 .... 6.95

Just Imagine Comics and Stories
Just Imagine

❑1 1982 .... 2.00
❑2 1982 .... 2.00
❑3 1982 .... 2.00
❑4 1982 .... 2.00
❑5 1983 .... 2.00
❑6 1983 .... 2.00
❑7 1983 .... 2.00
❑8 1983 .... 2.00
❑9 .... 2.00
❑10, Jul 1984; b&w 2.00
❑11 1984 .... 2.00
❑Special 1 1983; gophers 2.00

Just Imagine's Special
Just Imagine

❑1, Jul 1986; 1: The Mildly Microwaved Pre-Pubescent Kung-Fu Gophers! 1.50

Other grades: Multiply price above by 5/6 for VF/NM • 2/3 for VERY FINE • 1/3 for FINE • 1/5 for VERY GOOD • 1/8 for GOOD

Kaboom

Teen acquires explosive powers

©Awesome

Kabuki

Highly stylized martial arts series

©Image

Kabuki Agents

Kabuki's sidekicks mount rescue of leader

©Image

Kabuki Gallery

Mixed media pin-ups from creator David Mack

©Caliber

Kamandi, the Last Boy on Earth

Apocalypse survivor's animal adventures

©DC

N-MINT

Just Imagine Stan Lee... Secret Files and Origins
DC

❑1, Mar 2002, DaG, JB, JOy, JBy, JKu, JLee (a) ... 4.95

Just Imagine Stan Lee With Chris Bachalo Creating Catwoman
DC

❑1, Jul 2002 ... 5.95

Just Imagine Stan Lee With Dave Gibbons Creating Green Lantern
DC

❑1, Dec 2001 ... 5.95

Just Imagine Stan Lee With Gary Frank Creating Shazam!
DC

❑1, May 2002 ... 5.95

Just Imagine Stan Lee With Jerry Ordway Creating JLA
DC

❑1, Feb 2002 ... 5.95

Just Imagine Stan Lee With Jim Lee Creating Wonder Woman
DC

❑1, Oct 2001 ... 5.95

Just Imagine Stan Lee With Joe Kubert Creating Batman
DC

❑1, Sep 2001 ... 5.95

Just Imagine Stan Lee With John Buscema Creating Superman
DC

❑1, Nov 2001 ... 5.95

Just Imagine Stan Lee With John Byrne Creating Robin
DC

❑1, Apr 2002 ... 5.95

Just Imagine Stan Lee With John Cassaday Creating Crisis
DC

❑1, Sep 2002 ... 5.95

Just Imagine Stan Lee With Kevin Maguire Creating The Flash
DC

❑1, Jan 2002 ... 5.95

Just Imagine Stan Lee With Scott McDaniel Creating Aquaman
DC

❑1, Jun 2002 ... 5.95

Just Imagine Stan Lee with Walter Simonson Creating Sandman
DC

❑1, Aug 2002 ... 5.95

Just Twisted
Necromics

❑1 ... 2.00

Justy
Viz

❑1, Dec 1988, b&w; Japanese ... 2.00
❑2, Dec 1988, b&w; Japanese ... 2.00
❑3, Jan 1989, b&w; Japanese ... 2.00
❑4, Jan 1989, b&w; Japanese ... 2.00
❑5, Feb 1989, b&w; Japanese ... 2.00
❑6, Feb 1989, b&w; Japanese ... 2.00
❑7, Mar 1989, b&w; Japanese ... 2.00
❑8, Mar 1989, b&w; Japanese ... 2.00
❑9, Apr 1989, b&w; Japanese ... 2.00

Kaboom
Awesome

❑1, Sep 1997; JPH (w); 1: Kaboom ... 2.50
❑1/A, Sep 1997; JPH (w); Dynamic Forces variant (marked as such); Purple Awesome logo ... 2.50
❑1/Gold, Sep 1997; Gold edition with silver logo; JPH (w); 1: Kaboom ... 2.50
❑2, Oct 1997 JPH (w) ... 2.50
❑2/Autographed, Oct 1997 JPH (w) ... 2.50
❑2/Gold, Oct 1997; Gold edition; JPH (w) ... 2.50
❑3, Nov 1997 JPH (w) ... 2.50
❑4, Feb 1998 JPH (w) ... 2.50
❑5, Mar 1998 JPH (w) ... 2.50
❑Ashcan 1, Feb 1998; Preview edition; JPH (w) ... 2.50
❑Ashcan 1/Gold, Feb 1998; Gold edition; JPH (w); Preview edition ... 2.50

Kabuki
Image

❑½, Sep 2001; Speckle-foil Wizard variant ... 3.00
❑½/A; Image's reprinting of the Wizard variant ... 4.00
❑1, Oct 1997; O: Kabuki ... 5.00
❑1/A, Oct 1997; JSo (c); JSo (a); O: Kabuki. alternate cover ... 5.00
❑2, Dec 1997 ... 4.00
❑3, Mar 1998 ... 4.00
❑4, Jun 1998 ... 3.50
❑5, Sep 1998 ... 2.95
❑6, Nov 1998 ... 2.95
❑7, Feb 1999 ... 2.95
❑7/Variant, Feb 1999; Alternate cover art ... 2.95
❑8, Jun 1999 ... 2.95
❑9, Mar 2000 ... 2.95

Kabuki Agents
Image

❑1, Aug 1999; Scarab ... 2.95
❑1/A, Aug 1999; Scarab alternate cover. ... 2.95
❑2, Oct 1999; Scarab ... 2.95
❑3, Nov 1999; Scarab ... 2.95
❑4, Apr 2000; Scarab ... 2.95
❑5, Nov 2000; Scarab ... 2.95
❑6, Jan 2001; Scarab ... 2.95
❑7, Mar 2001; Scarab ... 2.95
❑8, Aug 2001; Scarab ... 2.95

Kabuki: Circle of Blood
Caliber

❑1, Jan 1995, b&w; O: Kabuki ... 4.00
❑1/Ltd., Jan 1995; Limited edition with new, painted coverr; O: Kabuki ... 5.00
❑1/2nd, Jul 1995, b&w; enhanced cover ... 3.50
❑2, Mar 1995, b&w ... 3.50
❑3, May 1995, b&w; reprints #1's indicia ... 3.50
❑4, Jul 1995, b&w ... 3.00
❑5, Sep 1995, b&w ... 3.00
❑6, Nov 1995, b&w ... 3.00
❑6/Ltd., Nov 1995; New painted cover, signed ... 15.00

Kabuki Classics
Image

❑1, Feb 1999; Squarebound; Reprints Kabuki: Fear the Reaper ... 3.25
❑2, Mar 1999; Reprints Kabuki: Dance of Death ... 3.00
❑3, Mar 1999; Squarebound ... 4.95
❑4, Apr 1999 ... 3.25
❑5, Jul 1999 ... 3.25
❑6, Jul 1999 ... 3.25
❑7, Aug 1999 ... 3.25
❑8, Sep 1999 ... 3.25
❑9, Oct 1999 ... 3.25
❑10, Nov 1999 ... 3.25
❑11, Dec 1999 ... 3.25
❑12, Mar 2000; Reprints Kabuki: Masks of the Noh #4: In the Eye of the Storm ... 3.25

Kabuki Color Special
Caliber

❑1, Jan 1996 MGr (a) ... 3.50

Kabuki Compilation
Caliber

❑1, Jul 1995; Collects Kabuki: Dance of Death and Kabuki: Fear the Reaper ... 7.95

Kabuki: Dance of Death
London Night

❑1, Jan 1995, b&w; no cover price or indicia ... 3.50

Kabuki Dreams
Image

❑nn, Jan 1998, b&w; reprints Kabuki Color Special and Kabuki: Dreams of the Dead ... 5.00

Kabuki: Dreams of the Dead
Caliber

❑1, Jul 1996; NN; One-shot ... 2.95

Kabuki: Fear the Reaper
Caliber

❑1, Nov 1994 ... 3.50

Kabuki Gallery
Caliber

❑1, Aug 1995; pin-ups ... 2.95
❑1/A, Aug 1995; Comic Cavalcade edition ... 15.00

Kabuki: The Ghost Play
Image

❑1, Nov 2002; No issue number in indicia ... 2.95

Kabuki-Images
Image

❑1, Jul 1998; prestige format; pin-ups and story; Reprints Kabuki (Image) #1 with new pin-ups ... 4.95
❑2, Jan 1999; prestige format; Reprints Kabuki (Image) #2-3 ... 4.95

Kabuki
Marvel

❑1, Sep 2004 ... 4.00
❑1/Variant, Sep 2004 ... 5.00
❑2, Oct 2004 ... 2.99
❑3, Nov 2004 ... 2.99
❑4, Dec 2004 ... 2.99
❑4/Hughes, Dec 2004 ... 4.00
❑5, Dec 2005 ... 2.99
❑6, May 2006 ... 2.99

Other grades: Multiply price above by 5/6 for VF/NM • 2/3 for VERY FINE • 1/3 for FINE • 1/5 for VERY GOOD • 1/8 for GOOD

N-MINT

❑6/Variant, May 2006 ... 2.99
❑7, Nov 2006 ... 2.99

Kabuki: Masks of the Noh
Image

❑1, May 1996, b&w ... 3.00
❑2, Jun 1996, b&w ... 3.00
❑3, Sep 1996, b&w ... 3.00
❑4, Feb 1997, b&w ... 3.00

Kabuki Reflections
Image

❑1, Jul 1998; prestige format; no number on cover or in indicia ... 4.95
❑2, Dec 1998; prestige format ... 4.95
❑3, Jan 2000 ... 4.95
❑4, May 2002 ... 4.95

Kabuki: Reflections
Marvel

❑1, Mar 2007 ... 5.99

Kabuki: Skin Deep
Caliber

❑1, Oct 1996 ... 3.50
❑2, Feb 1997 ... 3.00
❑2/A, Feb 1997; alternate cover; white background ... 3.00
❑2/Ltd., Feb 1997; Wraparound cover by David Mack and Alex Ross ... 8.00
❑3, May 1997 ... 2.95

Kafka
Renegade

❑1, Apr 1987, b&w ... 3.00
❑2, May 1987, b&w ... 2.50
❑3, Jun 1987, b&w ... 2.50
❑4, Jul 1987, b&w ... 2.50
❑5, Aug 1987, b&w ... 2.50
❑6, Sep 1987, b&w ... 2.50

Kafka: The Execution
Fantagraphics

❑1, b&w; Duranona ... 2.95

Kaktus
Fantagraphics

❑1, b&w ... 2.50

Kalamazoo Comix
Discount Hobby

❑1 ... 1.95
❑2, Win 1996 ... 1.95
❑3, Win 1996 ... 1.95
❑4, Spr 1997 ... 2.95
❑5, Dec 1997 ... 2.95

Kalgan the Golden
Harrier

❑1, Mar 1988 ... 1.95

Kamandi: At Earth's End
DC

❑1, Jun 1993 ... 1.75
❑2, Jul 1993 ... 1.75
❑3, Aug 1993 ... 1.75
❑4, Sep 1993 ... 1.75
❑5, Oct 1993 ... 1.75
❑6, Nov 1993 ... 1.75

Kamandi, the Last Boy on Earth
DC

❑1, Nov 1972, JK (c); JK (w); JK (a); 1&O: Kamandi. 1: Dr. Canus. 1: Ben Boxer ... 20.00
❑2, Jan 1973, JK (c); JK (w); JK (a) ... 15.00
❑3, Feb 1973, JK (c); JK (w); JK (a); in Vegas ... 10.00
❑4, Mar 1973, JK (c); JK (w); JK (a); 1: Prince Tuftan ... 8.00
❑5, Apr 1973, JK (c); JK (w); JK (a) ... 8.00
❑6, Jun 1973, JK (c); JK (w); JK (a) ... 8.00
❑7, Jul 1973, JK (c); JK (w); JK (a) ... 8.00
❑8, Aug 1973, JK (c); JK (w); JK (a); In Washington, D.C ... 8.00
❑9, Sep 1973, JK (c); JK (w); JK (a) ... 8.00
❑10, Oct 1973, JK (c); JK (w); JK (a) ... 8.00
❑11, Nov 1973, JK (c); JK (w); JK (a) ... 7.00
❑12, Dec 1973, JK (c); JK (w); JK (a) ... 7.00
❑13, Jan 1974, JK (c); JK (w); JK (a) ... 7.00
❑14, Feb 1974, JK (c); JK (w); JK (a) ... 7.00
❑15, Mar 1974, JK (c); JK (w); JK (a) ... 7.00
❑16, Apr 1974, JK (c); JK (w); JK (a) ... 7.00
❑17, May 1974, JK (c); JK (w); JK (a) ... 7.00
❑18, Jun 1974, JK (c); JK (w); JK (a) ... 7.00
❑19, Jul 1974, JK (c); JK (w); JK (a); in Chicago ... 7.00
❑20, Aug 1974, JK (c); JK (w); JK (a); in Chicago ... 6.00
❑21, Sep 1974, JK (c); JK (w); JK (a) ... 6.00
❑22, Oct 1974, JK (c); JK (w); JK (a) ... 6.00
❑23, Nov 1974, JK (c); JK (w); JK (a) ... 6.00
❑24, Dec 1974, JK (c); JK (w); JK (a) ... 6.00
❑25, Jan 1975, JK (c); JK (w); JK (a) ... 6.00
❑26, Feb 1975, JK (c); JK (w); JK (a) ... 6.00
❑27, Mar 1975, JK (c); JK (w); JK (a) ... 6.00
❑28, Apr 1975, JK (c); JK (w); JK (a) ... 6.00
❑29, May 1975, JK (c); JK (w); JK (a); Superman's legend ... 6.00
❑30, Jun 1975, JK (c); JK (w); JK (a); 1: Pyra ... 6.00
❑31, Jul 1975, JK (c); JK (w); JK (a) ... 6.00
❑32, Aug 1975, JK (c); JK (w); JK (a); O: Kamandi. giant; Jack Kirby interview; New story and reprints Kamandi #1 ... 6.00
❑33, Sep 1975, JK (c); JK (w); JK (a) ... 6.00
❑34, Oct 1975, JKu (c); JK (w); JK (a) ... 6.00
❑35, Nov 1975, JKu (c); JK (w); JK (a) ... 6.00
❑36, Dec 1975, JKu (c); JK (w); JK (a) ... 6.00
❑37, Jan 1976, JKu (c); JK (w); JK (a) ... 6.00
❑38, Feb 1976, JKu (c); JK (w); JK (a) ... 6.00
❑39, Mar 1976, JKu (c); JK (w); JK (a) ... 5.00
❑40, Apr 1976, JKu (c); JK (w); JK (a) ... 5.00
❑41, May 1976, JKu (c) ... 4.00
❑42, Jun 1976, JL (c) ... 4.00
❑43, Jul 1976, Tales of the Great Disaster backup stories begin; Bicentennial #4 ... 4.00
❑44, Aug 1976, KG (a) ... 4.00
❑45, Sep 1976, MN, KG (a) ... 4.00
❑46, Oct 1976, MN, KG, JAb (a); Tales of the Great Disaster backup stories end ... 4.00
❑47, Nov 1976, RB (c); KG, AA (a) ... 4.00
❑48, Jan 1977 ... 4.00
❑49, Mar 1977, AA (a) ... 4.00
❑50, May 1977, RB, AA (c); AA (a); Kamandi reverts to OMAC ... 4.00
❑51, Jul 1977, RB, JAb (c); AA (a); 1: Kamarni; D: Arna.; Kamandi's and Arna's son ... 4.00
❑52, Sep 1977, RB, AA (c); AA (a) ... 4.00
❑53, Nov 1977, AM (c); AA (a) ... 4.00
❑54, Jan 1978, AM (c); AA (a) ... 4.00
❑55, Mar 1978, AM (c); V: Vortex Beast ... 2.50
❑56, May 1978, RB, JAb (c) ... 2.50
❑57, Jul 1978, JSn, (c);Jim Starlin cover; Continues in Karate Kid #15 ... 2.50
❑58, Sep 1978, (c); A: Karate Kid. Karate Kid ... 2.50
❑59, Oct 1978, JSn (c); JSn (w); JSn (a); OMAC back-up begins; continues in Warlord #37 ... 4.00

Kama Sutra
NBM

❑1 ... 12.95

Kama Sutra
Black Lace

❑1, Adult ... 2.95

Kamichama Karin
Tokyopop

❑1, Sep 2005 ... 9.99
❑2, Dec 2005 ... 9.99

Kamikaze
DC / Cliffhanger

❑1, Dec 2003 ... 2.95
❑2, Jan 2004 ... 2.95
❑3, Feb 2004 ... 2.95
❑4, Mar 2004 ... 2.95
❑5, Apr 2004 ... 2.95
❑6, May 2004 ... 2.95

Kamikaze Cat
Pied Piper

❑1, Jul 1987 ... 1.95

Kane
Dancing Elephant

❑1 ... 3.50
❑2 ... 3.50
❑3 ... 3.50
❑4 ... 3.50
❑5 ... 3.50
❑6 ... 3.50
❑7 ... 3.50
❑8 ... 3.50
❑9 ... 3.50
❑10 ... 3.50
❑11 ... 3.50
❑12 ... 3.50
❑13 ... 3.50
❑14 ... 3.50
❑15 ... 3.50
❑16 ... 3.50
❑17 ... 3.50
❑18 ... 3.50
❑19 ... 3.50
❑20 ... 3.50
❑21 ... 3.50
❑22 ... 3.50
❑23 ... 2.95
❑24 1998 ... 2.95
❑25, Jan 1999 ... 2.95
❑26, Apr 1999 ... 2.95
❑27, ca. 1999; Giant-size ... 5.00
❑28, ca. 2000 ... 2.95
❑29, ca. 2000 ... 2.95
❑30, Nov 2000 ... 2.95
❑31, Apr 2001 ... 2.95
❑32, Jul 2001 ... 2.95

Kanpai!
Tokyopop

❑1, Sep 2005 ... 9.99
❑2, Dec 2005 ... 9.99

Kansas Thunder
Red Menace

❑1, b&w ... 2.95

Kaos
Tommy Regalado

❑1, Aug 1994, b&w ... 2.00

Kaos Moon
Caliber

❑1, ca. 1996, b&w ... 2.95
❑2, Nov 1996, b&w ... 2.95
❑3, Jul 1997 ... 2.95
❑4, ca. 1997 ... 2.95

Kaptain Keen & Kompany
Vortex

❑1, Dec 1986 ... 1.75
❑2, ca. 1987 ... 1.75
❑3, ca. 1987 ... 1.75
❑4, ca. 1987 ... 1.75
❑5, ca. 1987 ... 1.75
❑6, Feb 1988 ... 1.75

Karas
Dark Horse

❑1, Jan 2005 ... 3.00

Karate Girl
Fantagraphics / Eros

❑1, ca. 1994, b&w; Adult ... 2.50
❑2, ca. 1994, b&w; Adult ... 2.50

Karate Girl Tengu Wars
Fantagraphics / Eros

❑1, ca. 1995 ... 2.95
❑2, ca. 1995 ... 2.95
❑3, Jun 1995 ... 2.95

Karate Kid
DC

❑1, Apr 1976 MGr (c); JSa, RE (a) ... 12.00
❑2, Jun 1976, Jim Shooter L.O.C ... 7.00
❑3, Aug 1976 ... 7.00
❑4, Oct 1976 ... 5.00
❑5, Dec 1976 ... 5.00
❑6, Feb 1977 ... 5.00
❑7, Apr 1977, MGr (a) ... 5.00
❑8, Jun 1977, MGr (c); MGr, JSa, RE (a); Mike W. Barr L.O.C ... 5.00
❑9, Aug 1977 ... 5.00
❑10, Oct 1977 ... 5.00
❑11, Dec 1977 ... 5.00
❑12, Feb 1978 ... 5.00
❑13, Apr 1978 ... 5.00
❑14, Jun 1978 ... 5.00
❑15, Aug 1978, Final Issue ... 5.00

Karate Kreatures
Ma

❑1, Sum 1989 ... 2.00
❑2, ca. 1989 ... 2.00

Other grades: Multiply price above by 5/6 for VF/NM • 2/3 for VERY FINE • 1/3 for FINE • 1/5 for VERY GOOD • 1/8 for GOOD

Kane

Anti-hero protects law and order in New Eden

©Dancing Elephant

Karate Kid

Not the movie with Arnold from Happy Days

©DC

Katmandu

Furry adventures with a realistic bent

©Antarctic

Ka-Zar

Tarzan-type battles dinos in Savage Land

©Marvel

Kendra: Legacy of the Blood

Short-lived comic from height of b&w glut

©Perrydog

N-MINT

Kare Kano
Tokyopop

❑1, Jan 2003, b&w; printed in Japanese format 9.99
❑2, Mar 2003, b&w; printed in Japanese format 9.99
❑3, May 2003, b&w; printed in Japanese format 9.99
❑4, Jul 2003; Graphic novel 9.99
❑5, Sep 2003; Graphic novel 9.99
❑6, Nov 2003; Graphic novel 9.99
❑7, Jan 2004; Graphic novel 9.99
❑8, Mar 2004; Graphic novel 9.99
❑9, May 2004; Graphic novel 9.99
❑10, Jul 2004; Graphic novel 9.99
❑11, Sep 2004; Graphic novel 9.99
❑12, Nov 2004; Graphic novel 9.99
❑13, Jan 2005; Graphic novel 9.99
❑14, Mar 2005; Graphic novel 9.99
❑15, May 2005; Graphic novel 9.99
❑16, Jul 2005; Graphic novel 9.99
❑17, Sep 2005; Graphic novel 9.99
❑18, Dec 2005; Graphic novel 9.99

Karma Incorporated
Viper

❑1, Sep 2005 2.95
❑2, Oct 2005 2.95

Karney
Idea & Design Works

❑1, ca. 2005 3.99
❑2, May 2005 3.99
❑3, Jun 2005 3.99
❑4, Sep 2005 3.99

Karza
Image

❑1, Feb 2003 2.95
❑2, Apr 2003 2.95
❑3, May 2003 2.95
❑4, May 2003 2.95

Katmandu
Antarctic

❑1, Nov 1993, b&w; Adul 2.75
❑2, Jan 1994, b&w; Adult 2.95
❑3, Apr 1994, b&w; Adult 2.95
❑4, Mar 1995, b&w; Adult 2.75
❑5, May 1995, b&w; Adult 2.75
❑6, Aug 1995; Adult 2.75
❑7, ca. 1996; Adult 2.75
❑8, Jul 1996, b&w; Adult 1.95
❑9, ca. 1996, b&w; Adult 1.95
❑10, ca. 1996, b&w; Adult 1.95
❑11, ca. 1997, b&w; Adult 1.95
❑12, ca. 1997, b&w; Adult 1.95
❑13, Sep 1997, b&w; Adult 2.95
❑14, ca. 1998; Adult 2.95
❑15, ca. 1998; Adult 2.95
❑16, Apr 1999, b&w; Adult 2.95
❑17, ca. 1999; Adult 2.95
❑18, ca. 1999; Adult 2.95
❑19, ca. 2000; Adult 2.95
❑20, Apr 2000; Adult 2.95
❑21, Jul 2000; Adult 2.95
❑22, ca. 2000; Adult 2.95
❑23 2001; Adult 2.95
❑24 2001; Adult 2.95

N-MINT

❑25 2001; Adult 2.95
❑26, Jun 2002; Adult 4.99
❑27, Aug 2002; Adult 4.99
❑28, ca. 2002; Adult 4.99
❑Ann 1, ca. 1999; Adult 4.99
❑Ann 2, ca. 2000; Adult 4.99
❑Ann 3, Dec 2001; Adult 4.99
❑Ann 4, Dec 2002; Adult 4.99

Kato of the Green Hornet
Now

❑1, Nov 1991 2.50
❑2, Dec 1991 2.50
❑3, Jan 1992 2.50
❑4, Feb 1992 2.50

Kato of the Green Hornet II
Now

❑1, Nov 1992 2.50
❑2, Dec 1992 2.50

Ka-Zar
Marvel

❑1, Aug 1970, SL (w); GC, JK, FS (a); 1: Ka-Zar. 1: Zabu. A: X-Men. giant; reprints X-Men #10 (first series) and Daredevil #24; Hercules back-up 35.00
❑2, Dec 1970, SL (w); GT, JK, JR (a); O: Ka-Zar. A: Daredevil. giant; Angel back-up; reprints Daredevil #12 and 13 15.00
❑3, Mar 1971, giant; reprints Amazing Spider-Man #57 and Daredevil #14; Angel back-up continues in Marvel Tales #30 15.00

Ka-Zar
Marvel

❑1, Jan 1974, O: Savage Land 17.00
❑2, Mar 1974, DH (a); Marvel Value Stamp #28: Hawkeye 7.00
❑3, May 1974, GK (c); DH (a); Marvel Value Stamp #46: Mysterio 5.00
❑4, Jul 1974, FB (c); DH (a); Marvel Value Stamp #9: Captain Marvel 5.00
❑5, Sep 1974, GK (c); DH (a); Marvel Value Stamp #18: Volstagg 5.00
❑6, Nov 1974, JB (a); Marvel Value Stamp #17: Black Bolt 5.00
❑7, Jan 1975, JB (a) 5.00
❑8, Mar 1975, GK (c); JB (a); Marvel Value Stamp #38: Red Sonja 3.00
❑9, Jun 1975, JB (a) 3.00
❑10, Aug 1975, GK (c); JB (a); Marvel Value Stamp #72: Lizard 3.00
❑11, Oct 1975 3.00
❑12, Nov 1975, Marvel Value Stamp #95: Moleman 3.00
❑13, Dec 1975 3.00
❑14, Feb 1976, A: Klaw 3.00
❑15, Apr 1976 3.00
❑15/30¢, Apr 1976, 30¢ regional price variant 20.00
❑16, Jun 1976; Marvel Value Stamp Series B #88 3.00
❑16/30¢, Jun 1976, 30¢ regional price variant 20.00
❑17, Aug 1976 3.00
❑17/30¢, Aug 1976, 30¢ regional price variant 20.00
❑18, Oct 1976 3.00
❑19, Dec 1976 3.00
❑20, Feb 1977, A: Klaw 3.00

N-MINT

Ka-Zar
Marvel

❑-1, Jul 1997, Flashback 2.00
❑1, May 1997, Black background on cover 2.50
❑2, Jun 1997 2.00
❑2/A, Jun 1997, alternate cover 2.00
❑3, Jul 1997 2.00
❑4, Aug 1997, gatefold summary 2.00
❑5, Sep 1997, gatefold summary; V: Rhino 2.00
❑6, Oct 1997, gatefold summary 2.00
❑7, Nov 1997, gatefold summary 2.00
❑8, Dec 1997, gatefold summary; Spider-Man CD-ROM inserted 2.00
❑9, Jan 1998, gatefold summary 2.00
❑10, Feb 1998, gatefold summary 2.00
❑11, Mar 1998, gatefold summary 1.99
❑12, Apr 1998, gatefold summary; V: High Evolutionary 1.99
❑13, May 1998, gatefold summary; V: High Evolutionary 1.99
❑14, Jun 1998, Flip-book; Gatefold summary; 48 pages 1.99
❑15, Jul 1998, gatefold summary; blinded 1.99
❑16, Aug 1998, gatefold summary 1.99
❑17, Sep 1998, gatefold summary 1.99
❑18, Oct 1998, gatefold summary 1.99
❑19, Nov 1998, gatefold summary 1.99
❑20, Dec 1998, gatefold summary; Final Issue 1.99
❑Ann 1997, ca. 1997, gatefold summary; wraparound cover 2.99

Kazar of the Savage Land
Marvel

❑1, Feb 1997; wraparound cover 2.50

Ka-Zar the Savage
Marvel

❑1, Apr 1981, BA (c); BA (a); O: Ka-Zar. 5.00
❑2, May 1981, BA (c); BA (a) 2.00
❑3, Jun 1981, BA (c); BA (a) 1.50
❑4, Jul 1981, BA (c); BA (a) 1.50
❑5, Aug 1981, BA (c); BA (a) 1.50
❑6, Sep 1981, BA (c); BA (w); BA (a) 1.50
❑7, Oct 1981, BA (c); BA (w); BA (a) 1.50
❑8, Nov 1981, BA (c); BA (a) 1.50
❑9, Dec 1981, BA (c); BA (w); BA (a) 1.50
❑10, Jan 1982; BA (c); BA (a); direct distribution 1.50
❑11, Feb 1982; BA (c); BA, GK (a); 1: Belasco. Zabu 1.50
❑12, Mar 1982; BA (c); BA, GK (a); panel missing 1.50
❑12/2nd, Mar 1982; Reprints 1.00
❑13, Apr 1982 BA (a) 1.50
❑14, May 1982; BA (c); BA, GK (a); Tales of Zabu back-up story 1.50
❑15, Jun 1982; BA (c); VM, BA (a); Tales of Zabu back-up story 1.50
❑16, Jul 1982; Tales of Zabu back-up story 1.50
❑17, Aug 1982; Tales of Zabu back-up story 1.50
❑18, Sep 1982; Tales of Zabu back-up story 1.50
❑19, Oct 1982; BA (c); VM, BA (a); Tales of Zabu back-up story; Wraparound cover 1.50
❑20, Nov 1982; Wraparound cover 1.50

Other grades: Multiply price above by 5/6 for VF/NM • 2/3 for VERY FINE • 1/3 for FINE • 1/5 for VERY GOOD • 1/8 for GOOD

N-MINT

❑21, Dec 1982; Tales of Zabu back-up story ... 1.50
❑22, Jan 1983; Tales of Zabu back-up story ... 1.50
❑23, Feb 1983; VM, BH (a); Tales of Zabu back-up story ... 1.50
❑24, Mar 1983; BH (a); Tales of Zabu back-up story ... 1.50
❑25, Apr 1983; Tales of Zabu back-up story ... 1.50
❑26, May 1983; Partial photo cover of New York City; Tales of Zabu back-up story ... 1.50
❑27, Aug 1983 ... 1.50
❑28, Oct 1983; Wraparound cover ... 1.50
❑29, Dec 1983; Double-size; Wedding of Ka-Zar, Shanna ... 1.50
❑30, Feb 1984 ... 1.50
❑31, Apr 1984 ... 1.50
❑32, Jun 1984 ... 1.50
❑33, Aug 1984 ... 1.50
❑34, Oct 1984; Final Issue ... 1.50

Keenspot Spotlight
Keenspot

❑2002, Apr 2002 ... 1.00
❑2003, May 2003, Free Comic Book Day edition ... 1.00

Keep
Idea & Design Works

❑1, Sep 2005 ... 3.99
❑2, Dec 2005 ... 3.99
❑3, Jan 2006 ... 3.99
❑4, Feb 2006 ... 3.99
❑5, Apr 2006 ... 3.99

Keif Llama
Oni

❑1, Mar 1999; NN ... 2.95

Keif Llama Xeno-Tech
Fantagraphics

❑1, ca. 1987 ... 2.00
❑2, ca. 1987 ... 2.00
❑3, ca. 1987 ... 2.00
❑4, ca. 1987 ... 2.00
❑5, ca. 1987 ... 2.00
❑6, ca. 1987 ... 2.00

Keif Llama: Xenotech
Aeon

❑1, ca. 2005 ... 2.95
❑2, ca. 2005 ... 2.95

Kekkaishi
Viz

❑1, May 2005 ... 9.99
❑2, Aug 2005 ... 9.99
❑3, Nov 2005 ... 9.99

Kelly Belle Police Detective
Newcomers

❑1 ... 2.95
❑2 ... 2.95
❑3 ... 2.95

Kelly Green
Dargaud

❑1; ca. 1982; 1&O: Kelly Green ... 15.00
❑2; ca. 1982 ... 15.00

Kelvin Mace
Vortex

❑1, ca. 1988 ... 3.00
❑2, ca. 1988 ... 1.75

Kendra: Legacy of the Blood
Perrydog

❑1, Feb 1987, b&w ... 2.00
❑2, Apr 1987, b&w ... 2.00

Kents
DC

❑1, Aug 1997; Clark Kent's ancestors in frontier Kansas ... 3.00
❑2, Sep 1997 ... 2.50
❑3, Oct 1997 ... 2.50
❑4, Nov 1997 (c) ... 2.50
❑5, Dec 1997 (c) ... 2.50
❑6, Jan 1998 (c) ... 2.50
❑7, Feb 1998 (c) ... 2.50
❑8, Mar 1998 ... 2.50
❑9, Apr 1998 ... 2.50
❑10, May 1998 ... 2.50
❑11, Jun 1998 ... 2.50
❑12, Jul 1998; D: Jeb Kent ... 2.50

Kerry Drake
Blackthorne

❑1, May 1986 ... 6.95
❑2, Jul 1986 ... 6.95
❑3, Dec 1986 ... 6.95
❑4, Feb 1987 ... 6.95
❑5, Jul 1987 ... 6.95

Keyhole
Millennium

❑1, Jun 1996 ... 2.95
❑2, Oct 1996 ... 2.95
❑3 1997 ... 2.95
❑4, May 1997 ... 2.95
❑5, Jun 1998 ... 2.95

Khan
Moonstone

❑1, Sep 2005 ... 2.95

Kick Ass
Marvel

❑1, Mar 2008 ... 8.00
❑2, Apr 2008 ... 4.00
❑3 ... 3.99
❑4 ... 3.99
❑5 ... 3.99
❑6 ... 3.99

Kickers, Inc.
Marvel

❑1, Nov 1986; 1&O: Kickers; Inc. ... 0.75
❑2, Dec 1986 ... 0.75
❑3, Jan 1987 ... 0.75
❑4, Feb 1987 ... 0.75
❑5, Mar 1987 ... 0.75
❑6, Apr 1987 ... 0.75
❑7, May 1987 ... 0.75
❑8, Jun 1987 ... 0.75
❑9, Jul 1987 ... 0.75
❑10, Aug 1987 ... 0.75
❑11, Sep 1987 ... 0.75
❑12, Oct 1987 ... 0.75

Kid's Joker
ADV Manga

❑1, ca. 2005 ... 9.99

Kid Anarchy
Fantagraphics

❑1, ca. 1990, b&w ... 2.50
❑2, ca. 1990, b&w ... 2.75
❑3, ca. 1990, b&w ... 2.75

Kid Blastoff
Slave Labor / Amaze Ink

❑1, Jun 1996 ... 2.75

Kid Cannibal
Eternity

❑1, Oct 1991 ... 2.50
❑2 1991 ... 2.50
❑3 1992 ... 2.50
❑4 1992 ... 2.50

Kid Colt Outlaw
Marvel

❑101, Nov 1961 ... 28.00
❑102, Jan 1962 ... 28.00
❑103, Mar 1962 ... 28.00
❑104, May 1962 ... 28.00
❑105, Jul 1962 ... 28.00
❑106, Sep 1962 ... 28.00
❑107, Nov 1962 ... 28.00
❑108, Jan 1963 ... 28.00
❑109, Mar 1963 ... 28.00
❑110, May 1963, SL (w) ... 28.00
❑111, Jul 1963 ... 18.00
❑112, Sep 1963, SL (w) ... 18.00
❑113, Nov 1963 ... 18.00
❑114, Jan 1964, V: Iron Mask ... 18.00
❑115, Mar 1964 ... 18.00
❑116, May 1964 ... 18.00
❑117, Jul 1964 ... 18.00
❑118, Sep 1964, V: Scorpion. V: Bull Barton. V: Doctor Danger ... 18.00
❑119, Nov 1964 ... 18.00
❑120, Jan 1965 ... 18.00
❑121, Mar 1965 ... 14.00
❑122, May 1965 ... 14.00
❑123, Jul 1965 ... 14.00
❑124, Sep 1965, V: Phantom Raider ... 14.00
❑125, Nov 1965, A: Two-Gun Kid ... 14.00
❑126, Jan 1966 ... 14.00
❑127, Mar 1966, V: Iron Mask. V: Fat Man. V: Doctor Danger ... 14.00
❑128, May 1966 ... 14.00
❑129, Jul 1966 ... 14.00
❑130, Sep 1966, SL (w); O: Kid Colt. giant ... 14.00
❑131, Nov 1966, SL (w); GC (a); giant ... 10.00
❑132, Jan 1967, giant ... 10.00
❑133, Mar 1967, V: Rammer Ramkin ... 10.00
❑134, May 1967 ... 10.00
❑135, Jul 1967 ... 10.00
❑136, Sep 1967 ... 10.00
❑137, Nov 1967 ... 10.00
❑138, Jan 1968 ... 10.00
❑139, Mar 1968, series goes on hiatus ... 10.00
❑140, Nov 1969, Reprints begin ... 5.00
❑141, Dec 1969 ... 5.00
❑142, Jan 1970 ... 5.00
❑143, Feb 1970 ... 5.00
❑144, Mar 1970 ... 5.00
❑145, Apr 1970 ... 5.00
❑146, May 1970 ... 5.00
❑147, Jun 1970 ... 5.00
❑148, Jul 1970 ... 5.00
❑149, Aug 1970 ... 5.00
❑150, Oct 1970 ... 5.00
❑151, Dec 1970 ... 5.00
❑152, Feb 1971 ... 5.00
❑153, Apr 1971 ... 5.00
❑154, Jul 1971 ... 5.00
❑155, Sep 1971 ... 5.00
❑156, Nov 1971 ... 5.00
❑157, Jan 1972 ... 5.00
❑158, Mar 1972 ... 5.00
❑159, May 1972 ... 5.00
❑160, Jul 1972 ... 5.00
❑161, Aug 1972 ... 5.00
❑162, Sep 1972 ... 5.00
❑163, Oct 1972 ... 5.00
❑164, Nov 1972 ... 5.00
❑165, Dec 1972 ... 5.00
❑166, Jan 1973 ... 5.00
❑167, Feb 1973 ... 5.00
❑168, Mar 1973 ... 5.00
❑169, Apr 1973 ... 5.00
❑170, May 1973, O: Kid Colt ... 5.00
❑171, Jun 1973, A: Two-Gun Kid ... 4.00
❑172, Jul 1973 ... 4.00
❑173, Aug 1973 ... 4.00
❑174, Sep 1973 ... 4.00
❑175, Oct 1973 ... 4.00
❑176, Nov 1973 ... 4.00
❑177, Dec 1973 ... 4.00
❑178, Jan 1974 ... 4.00
❑179, Feb 1974 ... 4.00
❑180, Mar 1974 ... 4.00
❑181, Apr 1974 ... 4.00
❑182, May 1974 ... 4.00
❑183, Jun 1974 ... 4.00
❑184, Jul 1974 ... 4.00
❑185, Aug 1974 ... 4.00
❑186, Sep 1974 ... 4.00
❑187, Oct 1974 ... 4.00
❑188, Nov 1974 ... 4.00
❑189, Dec 1974 ... 4.00
❑190, Jan 1975 ... 4.00
❑191, Feb 1975 ... 4.00
❑192, Mar 1975 ... 4.00
❑193, Apr 1975 ... 4.00
❑194, May 1975 ... 4.00
❑195, Jun 1975 ... 4.00
❑196, Jul 1975 ... 4.00
❑197, Aug 1975 ... 4.00
❑198, Sep 1975 ... 4.00
❑199, Oct 1975 ... 4.00
❑200, Nov 1975, GK (c); HT, JK (a); Jack Kirby pin-up ... 4.00
❑201, Dec 1975 ... 3.00
❑202, Jan 1976 ... 3.00
❑203, Feb 1976 ... 3.00
❑204, Mar 1976, Reprints Kid Colt Outlaw #72 ... 3.00
❑205, Apr 1976, Reprints from Kid Colt #134 ... 3.00

Other grades: Multiply price above by 5/6 for VF/NM • 2/3 for VERY FINE • 1/3 for FINE • 1/5 for VERY GOOD • 1/8 for GOOD

Kents, The

Adventures of Jonathan Kent's forebears
©DC

Kickers, Inc.

Enhanced football team from New Universe
©Marvel

Kid Colt Outlaw

Long-running western survived many others
©Marvel

Kid 'n Play

Based on stars of the House Party movie
©Marvel

King Conan

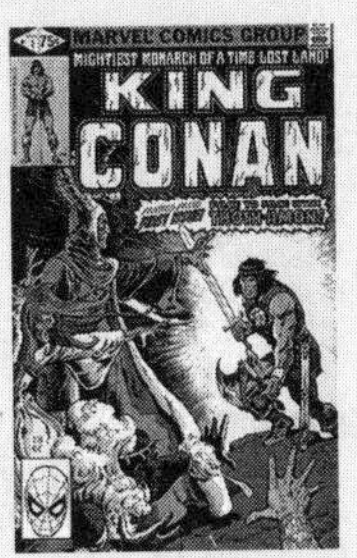

Series changes to "Conan the King" with #20
©Marvel

	N-MINT
❑205/30¢, Apr 1976, 30¢ regional price variant	20.00
❑206, May 1976	3.00
❑206/30¢, May 1976, 30¢ regional price variant	3.00
❑207, Jun 1976	3.00
❑207/30¢, Jun 1976, 30¢ regional price variant	3.00
❑208, Jul 1976	3.00
❑208/30¢, Jul 1976, 30¢ regional price variant	3.00
❑209, Aug 1976	3.00
❑209/30¢, Aug 1976, 30¢ regional price variant	3.00
❑210, Sep 1976, Reprints Kid Colt Outlaw #69 and #77	3.00
❑211, Oct 1976, Reprints KId Colt Outlaw # 89	3.00
❑212, Nov 1976	3.00
❑213, Dec 1976	3.00
❑214, Jan 1977	3.00
❑215, Feb 1977	3.00
❑216, Mar 1977	3.00
❑217, Apr 1977	3.00
❑218, Jun 1977	3.00
❑219, Aug 1977	3.00
❑219/35¢, Aug 1977, 35¢ regional price variant	15.00
❑220, Oct 1977	3.00
❑220/35¢, Oct 1977, 35¢ regional price variant	15.00
❑221, Dec 1977, Reprints Kid Colt #128; Gil Kane pin-up	3.00
❑222, Feb 1978	3.00
❑223, Apr 1978, Reprints Kid Colt #136; New Gil Kane pin-up	3.00
❑224, Jun 1978	3.00
❑225, Aug 1978	3.00
❑226, Oct 1978	3.00
❑227, Dec 1978	3.00
❑228, Feb 1979	3.00
❑229, Apr 1979, Final Issue	3.00

Kid Death & Fluffy: Halloween Special
Event

❑1, Oct 1997, Vampirella Cover - Quesada & Palmiotti; b&w	2.95

Kid Death & Fluffy Spring Break Special
Event

❑1, Jun 1996	2.50

Kid Eternity
DC / Vertigo

❑1, May 1991	4.95
❑2, Jul 1991	4.95
❑3, Oct 1991	4.95

Kid Eternity
DC / Vertigo

	N-MINT
❑1, May 1993	1.95
❑2, Jun 1993	1.95
❑3, Jul 1993	1.95
❑4, Aug 1993	1.95
❑5, Sep 1993	1.95
❑6, Oct 1993	1.95
❑7, Nov 1993	1.95
❑8, Dec 1993	1.95
❑9, Jan 1994	1.95
❑10, Feb 1994	1.95
❑11, Mar 1994	1.95
❑12, May 1994	1.95
❑13, Jun 1994	1.95
❑14, Jul 1994	1.95
❑15, Aug 1994	1.95
❑16, Sep 1994; Final Issue	1.95

Kid 'n Play
Marvel

❑1, Feb 1992	1.25
❑2, Mar 1992	1.25
❑3, Apr 1992	1.25
❑4, May 1992	1.25
❑5, Jun 1992	1.25
❑6, Jul 1992	1.25
❑7, Aug 1992	1.25
❑8, Sep 1992	1.25
❑9, Oct 1992	1.25

Kid Supreme
Image

❑1, Mar 1996; Kid Supreme with fist outstretched on cover	2.50
❑1/A, Mar 1996; Kid Supreme surounded by girls on cover	2.50
❑2, Apr 1996	2.50
❑3, Jul 1996	2.50
❑3/A, Jul 1996; alternate cover (green background)	2.50

Kid's WB Jam Packed Action
DC

❑1, ca. 2004	7.99

Kid Terrific
Image

❑1, Nov 1998, b&w	2.95

Kidz of the King
King

❑1, Mar 1994	2.95
❑2, May 1994	2.95
❑3, Apr 1995	2.95

Ki-Gorr the Killer
AC

❑1, Reprints	3.95

Kiku San
Aircel

❑1, Nov 1988	1.95
❑2, Dec 1988	1.95
❑3, Jan 1989	1.95
❑4, Feb 1989	1.95
❑5, Mar 1989	1.95
❑6, Apr 1989	1.95

Kilgore
Renegade

❑1, Nov 1987	2.00
❑2, Jan 1988	2.00
❑3, Mar 1988	2.00
❑4, May 1988	2.00

Kill Barny
Express / Parody

❑1, ca. 1992, b&w	2.50

Kill Barny 3
Express / Parody

❑1, ca. 1992, b&w	2.75

N-MINT

Killbox
Antarctic

❑1, Dec 2002	5.00
❑2, Jan 2003	5.00
❑3, Feb 2003	5.00

Killer Fly
Slave Labor

❑1, Mar 1995	2.95
❑2, Jun 1995	2.95
❑3, Sep 1995; Final Issue	2.95

Killer Instinct
Acclaim / Armada

❑1, Jun 1996, based on video game	2.50
❑2, Jul 1996, based on video game	2.50
❑3, Jul 1996, based on video game	2.50
❑4, Sep 1996, based on video game	2.50
❑5, Oct 1996, based on video game	2.50
❑6, Nov 1996, based on video game	2.50

Killer Instinct Tour Book
Image

❑1/A; Embossed cover	3.00
❑1/B; Embossed cover	3.00
❑1/Gold; Gold edition	3.00

Killer 7
Devil's Due

❑4/Special, Aug 2006	5.95
❑1, Feb 2006	2.95
❑2, Apr 2006	2.95
❑3, May 2006	2.95
❑3/Special, May 2006	5.95
❑4, Aug 2006	2.95

Killer Stunts, Inc.
Alias

❑1 2005	2.99
❑2, Jul 2005	2.99
❑3, Aug 2005	2.99
❑4, Nov 2005	2.99

Killer...Tales by Timothy Truman
Eclipse

❑1, Mar 1985	1.75

Kill Image
Boneyard

❑1, b&w; foil cover	3.50

Killing Stroke
Eternity

❑1, b&w	2.50
❑2, b&w	2.50
❑3, b&w	2.50
❑4, b&w	2.50

Kill Marvel
Boneyard

❑1/Ltd.; Special "Marvel Can'" edition	5.00

Killpower: The Early Years
Marvel

❑1, Sep 1993; foil cover	1.75
❑2, Oct 1993	1.75
❑3, Nov 1993	1.75
❑4, Dec 1993	1.75

Killraven
Marvel

❑1, Feb 2001	2.99

Other grades: Multiply price above by 5/6 for VF/NM • 2/3 for VERY FINE • 1/3 for FINE • 1/5 for VERY GOOD • 1/8 for GOOD

Killraven
Marvel

- ❑1, Dec 2002 ... 2.99
- ❑2, Jan 2003 ... 2.99
- ❑3, Feb 2003; Includes Incredible Hulk (2nd series) #50 preview ... 2.99
- ❑4, Mar 2003 ... 2.99
- ❑5, Apr 2003 ... 2.99
- ❑6, May 2003 ... 2.99

Kill Razor Special
Image

- ❑1, Aug 1995 ... 2.50

Kill Your Boyfriend
DC / Vertigo

- ❑1, Jun 1995; One-shot ... 4.95
- ❑1/2nd, May 1998; reprints 1995 one-shot with new afterword and other new material ... 5.95

Kilroy
Caliber

- ❑1, Apr 1998 ... 2.95
- ❑1/A, ca. 1998 ... 2.95

Kilroy Is Here
Caliber

- ❑0, ca. 1994, b&w ... 2.95
- ❑1, ca. 1995, b&w ... 2.95
- ❑2, ca. 1995, b&w ... 2.95
- ❑3, ca. 1995, b&w ... 2.95
- ❑4, ca. 1995, b&w ... 2.95
- ❑5, ca. 1995, #4 on cover ... 2.95
- ❑6, ca. 1996, includes pin-up gallery ... 2.95
- ❑7, ca. 1996, includes pin-up gallery ... 2.95
- ❑8, ca. 1996, includes pin-up gallery ... 2.95
- ❑9, ca. 1996, includes pin-up gallery ... 2.95
- ❑10, ca. 1996, includes pin-up gallery ... 2.95

Kilroy: Revelations
Caliber

- ❑1, ca. 1994, b&w; "Black light" cover ... 2.95

Kilroys
Avalon

- ❑1, ca. 2002 ... 2.95

Kilroy: The Short Stories
Caliber

- ❑1, ca. 1995, b&w; "Black light" cover ... 2.95

Kimber, Prince of the Feylons
Antarctic

- ❑1, Apr 1992, b&w ... 2.50
- ❑2, Jun 1992, b&w ... 2.50

Kimera
ADV Manga

- ❑1, ca. 2005 ... 9.99

Kimura
Nightwynd

- ❑1, ca. 1991, b&w ... 2.50
- ❑2, ca. 1991, b&w ... 2.50
- ❑3, ca. 1991, b&w ... 2.50
- ❑4, ca. 1991, b&w ... 2.50

Kin
Image

- ❑1, Sep 1999 ... 2.95
- ❑2, Oct 1999 ... 2.95
- ❑3, Nov 1999 ... 2.95
- ❑4, Jul 2000 ... 2.95
- ❑5, Aug 2000 ... 2.95
- ❑6, Sep 2000; Final Issue ... 3.95

Kindred
Image

- ❑1, Mar 1994 ... 2.50
- ❑2, Apr 1994 ... 1.95
- ❑3, May 1994 ... 1.95
- ❑3/A, May 1994; alternate cover ... 1.95
- ❑4, Jul 1994 ... 2.50

Kindred II
DC / Wildstorm

- ❑1, Mar 2002 ... 2.50
- ❑2, Apr 2002 ... 2.50
- ❑3, May 2002 ... 2.50
- ❑4, Jun 2002 ... 2.50

Kinetic
DC / Focus

- ❑1, May 2004 ... 2.50
- ❑2, Jun 2004 ... 2.50
- ❑3, Jul 2004 ... 2.50
- ❑4, Aug 2004 ... 2.50
- ❑5, Sep 2004 ... 2.50
- ❑6, Oct 2004 ... 2.50
- ❑7, Nov 2004 ... 2.50
- ❑8, Dec 2004 ... 2.50

King Arthur and the Knights of Justice
Marvel

- ❑1, Dec 1993 ... 1.25
- ❑2, Jan 1994 ... 1.25
- ❑3, Feb 1994 ... 1.25

King Comics Presents
King Comics

- ❑1 ... 1.95

King Conan
Marvel

- ❑1, Mar 1980; JB (c); JB (a); V: Thoth-Amon ... 5.00
- ❑2, Jun 1980 JB (c); JB (a) ... 1.50
- ❑3, Sep 1980; JB (c); JB (a); Adapting the story by L. Sprague De Camp & Lin Carter ... 1.50
- ❑4, Dec 1980; V: Thoth-Amon; Adapting the story by L. Sprague De Camp & Lin Carter ... 1.50
- ❑5, Mar 1981; Adapting Conan the Avenger by L. Sprague De Camp & Bjorn Nyberg ... 1.50
- ❑6, Jun 1981; Adapting Conan the Avenger by L. Sprague De Camp & Bjorn Nyberg ... 1.50
- ❑7, Sep 1981; JB (c); JB (a); Adapting Conan the Avenger by L. Sprague De Camp & Bjorn Nyberg ... 1.50
- ❑8, Dec 1981; JB (c); JB (a); Adapting Conan the Avenger by L. Sprague De Camp & Bjorn Nyberg ... 1.50
- ❑9, Mar 1982 ... 1.50
- ❑10, May 1982 ... 1.50
- ❑11, Jul 1982 ... 1.25
- ❑12, Sep 1982 ... 1.25
- ❑13, Nov 1982 ... 1.25
- ❑14, Jan 1983 ... 1.25
- ❑15, Mar 1983 ... 1.25
- ❑16, May 1983 ... 1.25
- ❑17, Jul 1983 ... 1.25
- ❑18, Sep 1983 ... 1.25
- ❑19, Nov 1983; Series continued in Conan the King #20 ... 1.25

King David
DC / Vertigo

- ❑1, May 2002 ... 19.95

Kingdom
DC

- ❑1, Feb 1999; MWa (w); MZ (a); Elseworlds ... 2.95
- ❑2, Feb 1999; MWa (w); MZ (a); Elseworlds ... 2.95

Kingdom Come
DC

- ❑1, ca. 1996; ARo (c); MWa (w); ARo (a); Elseworlds ... 5.00
- ❑1/2nd, ca. 1996; MWa (w); ARo (a); 2nd printing ... 4.95
- ❑2, ca. 1996; ARo (c); MWa (w); ARo (a); Elseworlds ... 5.00
- ❑3, ca. 1996; ARo (c); MWa (w); ARo (a); return of Captain Marvel; Elseworlds ... 5.00
- ❑4, ca. 1996; ARo (c); MWa (w); ARo (a); D: Captain Marvel. Elseworlds ... 5.00

Kingdom Hearts
Tokyopop

- ❑1, Oct 2005 ... 5.99

Kingdom: Kid Flash
DC

- ❑1, Feb 1999; Elseworlds ... 1.99

Kingdom: Nightstar
DC

- ❑1, Feb 1999; Elseworlds ... 1.99

Kingdom: Offspring
DC

- ❑1, Feb 1999; Elseworlds ... 1.99

Kingdom of the Dwarfs
Comico

- ❑1 ... 4.95

Kingdom of the Wicked
Caliber

- ❑1, ca. 1996, b&w ... 2.95
- ❑2, ca. 1996, b&w ... 2.95
- ❑3, ca. 1996, b&w ... 2.95
- ❑4, ca. 1996, b&w ... 2.95

Kingdom: Planet Krypton
DC

- ❑1, Feb 1999; Elseworlds ... 1.99

Kingdom: Son of the Bat
DC

- ❑1, Feb 1999; Elseworlds ... 1.99

King Kong
Gold Key

- ❑1, Sep 1968, adapts 1932 film ... 12.00

King Kong
Monster

- ❑1, Feb 1991, b&w; DSt (c); DSt (a) ... 2.50
- ❑2, ca. 1991, b&w ... 2.50
- ❑3, ca. 1991 ... 2.50
- ❑4, ca. 1991 ... 2.50
- ❑5, Nov 1991, AW (c) ... 2.50
- ❑6, Mar 1992 ... 2.50

King Leonardo and His Short Subjects
Gold Key

- ❑1, May 1962 ... 35.00
- ❑2, Oct 1962 ... 25.00
- ❑3, Mar 1963 ... 25.00
- ❑4, ca. 1963 ... 25.00

King Louie and Mowgli
Gold Key

- ❑1, May 1968 ... 20.00

King of Diamonds
Dell

- ❑1, Sep 1962, Based on TV show ... 30.00

King of Hell
Tokyopop

- ❑1, Jun 2003, b&w ... 9.99
- ❑2, Aug 2003 ... 9.99
- ❑3, Oct 2003 ... 9.99
- ❑4, Jan 2004 ... 9.99
- ❑5, Apr 2004 ... 9.99
- ❑6, Jul 2004 ... 9.99
- ❑7, Oct 2004 ... 9.99
- ❑8, Jan 2005 ... 9.99
- ❑9, Apr 2005 ... 9.99
- ❑10, Jul 2005 ... 9.99
- ❑11, Nov 2005 ... 9.99

King of the Dead
Fantaco

- ❑0, ca. 1988 ... 1.95
- ❑1, ca. 1988 ... 1.95
- ❑2, ca. 1988 ... 1.95
- ❑3, ca. 1988 ... 1.95
- ❑4, ca. 1988 ... 2.95

Kingpin
Marvel

- ❑1, Nov 1997; says "Spider-Man/Kingpin: To the Death" on cover ... 5.99

Kingpin
Marvel

- ❑1, Aug 2003 ... 2.50
- ❑2, Sep 2003 ... 2.50
- ❑3, Oct 2003 ... 2.99
- ❑4, Nov 2003 ... 2.99
- ❑5, Dec 2003 ... 2.99
- ❑6, Dec 2003 ... 2.99
- ❑7, Feb 2004 ... 2.99

Kings in Disguise
Kitchen Sink

- ❑1, Mar 1988, b&w ... 2.00
- ❑2, May 1988 ... 2.00
- ❑3, Jul 1988; b&w ... 2.00
- ❑4, Sep 1988; b&w ... 2.00
- ❑5, Mar 1989; b&w ... 2.00
- ❑6, Sep 1989; b&w ... 2.00

Kings of the Night
Dark Horse

- ❑1, ca. 1990 ... 2.25
- ❑2, ca. 1990 ... 2.25

Other grades: Multiply price above by 5/6 for VF/NM • 2/3 for VERY FINE • 1/3 for FINE • 1/5 for VERY GOOD • 1/8 for GOOD

Kingdom Come

Lauded Mark Waid/Alex Ross Elseworlds

©DC

King Kong (Gold Key)

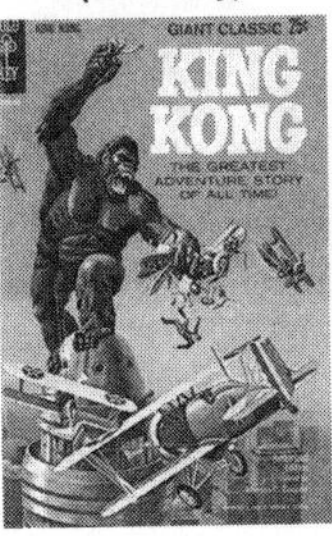

Gold Key version predates De Laurentiis

©Gold Key

Kiss: Psycho Circus

Circus freaks play music, make faces

©Image

Kitty Pryde & Wolverine

Series transforms Sprite into Shadowcat

©Marvel

Knights of the Dinner Table

Funny strip about role-playing gamers

©Kenzer

N-MINT

King Tiger & Motorhead
Dark Horse

❑1, Aug 1996 .... 2.95
❑2, Sep 1996 .... 2.95

Kinki Klitt Komics
Rip Off

❑1, Apr 1992, b&w; Adult 2.95
❑2, Jun 1992, b&w; Adult 2.50

Kinky Hook
Fantagraphics / Eros

❑1, b&w; Adult 2.50

Kip
Hammer & Anvil

❑1, b&w 2.50

Kirby King of the Serials
Blackthorne

❑1, Jan 1989, b&w 2.00

Kiss
Personality

❑1, b&w 3.50
❑2 .... 3.00
❑3 .... 3.00

Kiss
Dark Horse

❑1, Jun 2002 .... 2.99
❑1/Photo, Jun 2002 .... 2.99
❑2, Aug 2002, More Beast Now than Man cover 2.99
❑2/Photo, Aug 2002, Photo cover 2.99
❑3, Sep 2002 .... 2.99
❑3/Photo, Sep 2002, Photo cover 2.99
❑4, Nov 2002, Mel Rubi-c 2.99
❑4/Photo, Nov 2002, Photo cover 2.99
❑5, Nov 2002 .... 2.99
❑5/Photo, Nov 2002, Photo cover 2.99
❑6, Jan 2003 .... 2.99
❑6/Photo, Jan 2003, Photo cover 2.99
❑7, Feb 2003 .... 2.99
❑7/Photo, Feb 2003 .... 2.99
❑8, Mar 2003 .... 2.99
❑8/Photo, Mar 2003 .... 2.99
❑9, Apr 2003 .... 2.99
❑9/Photo, Apr 2003 .... 2.99
❑10, May 2003 .... 2.99
❑10/Photo, May 2003 .... 2.99
❑11, Jul 2003 .... 2.99
❑11/Photo, Jul 2003, Others appear in photo insets 2.99
❑12, Aug 2003 .... 2.99
❑12/Photo, Aug 2003, Others appear in photo insets 2.99
❑13, Sep 2003 .... 2.99
❑13/Photo, Sep 2003 .... 2.99

Kiss & Tell
Patricia Breen

❑1, Dec 1995, b&w; magazine 2.75

Kiss & Tell
Sirius

❑1, ca. 1996, b&w 2.50

Kiss Classics
Marvel

❑1; Reprints Marvel Super Special #1, #5 .... 10.00

N-MINT

Kisses
Spoof

❑1, Dec 1996, b&w 2.95

Kissing Canvas
MN Design

❑1, photos 5.50

Kiss Kiss Bang Bang
CrossGen

❑1, Feb 2004 .... 4.00
❑1/2nd, Mar 2004 .... 2.95
❑2, Mar 2004 .... 2.95
❑3, Apr 2004 .... 2.95
❑4, Jun 2004 .... 2.95
❑4/2nd, Jun 2004 .... 2.95
❑5, Aug 2004 .... 2.95

Kissnation
Marvel

❑1; A: X-Men. Reprints Marvel Super Specials with new editorial 11.00

Kiss of Death
Acme

❑1, Apr 1987 .... 2.00

Kiss of the Vampire
Brainstorm

❑1, ca. 1996 .... 2.95

Kiss Pre-History
Revolutionary

❑1, Apr 1993, b&w 3.00
❑2, May 1993, b&w 3.00
❑3, Jul 1993, b&w 3.00

Kiss: Psycho Circus
Image

❑1, Aug 1997 MG (c) 1.95
❑2, Sep 1997 MG (c) 1.95
❑3, Oct 1997 MG (c) 1.95
❑4, Nov 1997 MG (c) 1.95
❑5, Dec 1997 MG (c) 1.95
❑6, Jan 1998 .... 2.25
❑7, Mar 1998 .... 2.25
❑8, Apr 1998 .... 2.25
❑9, May 1998 .... 2.25
❑10, Jun 1998; covers of #10-12 form quadtych 2.25
❑11, Jul 1998; Covers of #10-13 form quadtych 2.25
❑12, Aug 1998; Covers of #10-13 form quadtych 2.25
❑13, Oct 1998; Covers of #10-13 form quadtych 2.25
❑14, Nov 1998 .... 2.25
❑15, Dec 1998 .... 2.25
❑16, Feb 1999 .... 2.25
❑17, Mar 1999 .... 2.25
❑18, Apr 1999 .... 2.25
❑19, May 1999 .... 2.25
❑20, Jun 1999 .... 2.25
❑21, Jul 1999 .... 2.25
❑22, Aug 1999 .... 2.25
❑23, Sep 1999 .... 2.25
❑24, Oct 1999 .... 2.25
❑25, Nov 1999 .... 2.25
❑26, Jan 2000 .... 2.25
❑27, Feb 2000 .... 2.25
❑28, Apr 2000 .... 2.25

N-MINT

❑29, Apr 2000 .... 2.50
❑30, May 2000 .... 2.50
❑31, Jun 2000 .... 2.50

Kiss: Satan's Music?
Celebrity

❑1; trading cards 4.00

Kissyfur
DC

❑1, ca. 1989 .... 2.00

Kiss: You Wanted the Best, You Got the Best
Wizard

❑1, Jun 1998 .... 1.00

Kitchen Sink Classics
Kitchen Sink

❑1, Jan 1994, b&w; reprints Omaha #0 . 4.50
❑2, b&w; reprints The People's Comics . 3.00
❑3, b&w; reprints D: Rattle #8 .... 3.00

Kitty Pryde & Wolverine
Marvel

❑1, Nov 1984 AM (a) 3.00
❑2, Dec 1984 AM (a) 2.50
❑3, Jan 1985 AM (a) 2.50
❑4, Feb 1985 AM (a) 2.50
❑5, Mar 1985 AM (a) 2.50
❑6, Apr 1985 AM (a) 2.50

Kitty Pryde, Agent of Shield
Marvel

❑1, Dec 1997, gatefold summary 2.50
❑2, Jan 1998, gatefold summary 2.50
❑3, Feb 1998, gatefold summary 2.50

Kitz 'n' Katz Komiks
Phantasy

❑1, ca. 1986 .... 1.50
❑2, ca. 1986, b&w 1.50
❑3, ca. 1987, b&w 1.50
❑4, ca. 1987, b&w 1.50
❑5, ca. 1987 .... 1.50
❑6, ca. 1987 .... 1.50

Kiwanni: Daughter of the Dawn
C&T

❑1, Feb 1988, b&w 2.25

Klor
Sirius

❑1, ca. 1998 .... 2.95
❑2, ca. 1998 .... 2.95
❑3, ca. 1998 .... 2.95

Klownshock
Northstar

❑1, Feb 1992, b&w; Indicia says January 1992 .... 2.75

Knewts of the Round Table
Pan

❑1, Jul 1998, b&w 2.50
❑2, Sep 1998, b&w 2.50
❑3, ca. 1998 .... 2.50
❑4, ca. 1999 .... 2.50
❑5, ca. 1999 .... 2.50

Knight
Bear Claw

❑0, Oct 1993 .... 2.50

Other grades: Multiply price above by 5/6 for VF/NM • 2/3 for VERY FINE • 1/3 for FINE • 1/5 for VERY GOOD • 1/8 for GOOD

N-MINT | N-MINT | N-MINT

Knightfool: The Fall of the Splatman
Parody

- ❑1 ... 2.95

Knighthawk
Acclaim / Windjammer

- ❑1, Sep 1995 ... 2.50
- ❑2, Sep 1995 ... 2.50
- ❑3, Oct 1995 ... 2.50
- ❑4, Oct 1995 ... 2.50
- ❑5, Nov 1995 ... 2.50
- ❑6, Nov 1995; Final Issue ... 2.50

Knightmare
Antarctic

- ❑1, Jul 1994, b&w ... 2.75
- ❑2, Sep 1994, b&w ... 2.75
- ❑3, Jan 1995, b&w ... 2.75
- ❑4, Mar 1995, b&w ... 2.75
- ❑5, Mar 1995, b&w ... 2.75
- ❑6, May 1995, b&w; Final Issue ... 2.75

Knightmare
Image

- ❑0, Aug 1995; chromium cover ... 3.50
- ❑1, Feb 1995 ... 2.50
- ❑2, Mar 1995 ... 2.50
- ❑3, Apr 1995 ... 2.50
- ❑4, May 1995 ... 2.50
- ❑4/A, May 1995; alternate cover ... 2.50
- ❑5, Jun 1995; Flip book with Warcry #1. ... 2.50
- ❑6, ca. 1995 ... 2.50
- ❑7, ca. 1995 ... 2.50
- ❑8, ca. 1995; Final Issue ... 2.50

Knightshift
London Night

- ❑1, ca. 1996; Adult; Chromium Wraparound Cover ... 3.00
- ❑2, Dec 1996; Adult ... 3.00

Knights' Kingdom
Lego

- ❑1; ca. 2000 ... 4.99

Knights of Pendragon
Marvel

- ❑1, Jul 1990 ... 2.50
- ❑2, Aug 1990 ... 2.00
- ❑3, Oct 1990 ... 2.00
- ❑4, Oct 1990 ... 2.00
- ❑5, Nov 1990 ... 2.00
- ❑6, Dec 1990 ... 2.00
- ❑7, Jan 1991 ... 2.00
- ❑8, Feb 1991 ... 2.00
- ❑9, Mar 1991 ... 2.00
- ❑10, Apr 1991 ... 2.00
- ❑11, May 1991, A: Iron Man ... 2.00
- ❑12, Jun 1991 ... 2.00
- ❑13, Jul 1991 ... 2.00
- ❑14, Aug 1991 ... 2.00
- ❑15, Sep 1991 ... 2.00
- ❑16, Oct 1991 ... 2.00
- ❑17, Nov 1991 ... 2.00
- ❑18, Dec 1991, A: Iron Man ... 2.00

Knights of Pendragon
Marvel

- ❑1, Jul 1992 A: Iron Man ... 2.00
- ❑2, Aug 1992 ... 1.75
- ❑3, Sep 1992 ... 1.75
- ❑4, Oct 1992 ... 1.75
- ❑5, Nov 1992; Title changes to The Knights of Pendragon; New armor ... 1.75
- ❑6, Dec 1992 ... 1.75
- ❑7, Jan 1993 A: Amazing Spider-Man ... 1.75
- ❑8, Feb 1993 ... 1.75
- ❑9, Mar 1993; Spider-Man ... 1.75
- ❑10, Apr 1993 ... 1.75
- ❑11, May 1993 ... 1.75
- ❑12, Jun 1993 ... 1.75
- ❑13, Jul 1993 ... 1.75
- ❑14, Aug 1993 A: Death's Head II ... 1.75
- ❑15, Sep 1993 A: Death's Head II ... 1.75

Knights of the Dinner Table
Kenzer

- ❑1, Jul 1994; b&w ... 150.00
- ❑2, Jan 1995; b&w ... 45.00
- ❑3, Apr 1995; b&w ... 25.00
- ❑4, Nov 1995; Gary Con issue ... 30.00
- ❑4/2nd, Feb 1997 ... 25.00
- ❑5, Mar 1997; b&w ... 25.00
- ❑6, Apr 1997; b&w ... 18.00
- ❑7, May 1997; b&w ... 18.00
- ❑8, Jun 1997; b&w ... 18.00
- ❑9, Jul 1997; b&w ... 18.00
- ❑10, Aug 1997 ... 18.00
- ❑11, Sep 1997; b&w ... 14.00
- ❑12, Oct 1997; b&w ... 14.00
- ❑13, Nov 1997; b&w ... 14.00
- ❑14, Dec 1997; b&w ... 14.00
- ❑15, Jan 1998; b&w ... 14.00
- ❑16, Feb 1998; b&w ... 10.00
- ❑17, Mar 1998; b&w ... 10.00
- ❑18, Apr 1998; b&w ... 10.00
- ❑19, May 1998; b&w ... 10.00
- ❑20, Jun 1998; b&w ... 10.00
- ❑21, Jul 1998; Gary Con issue ... 10.00
- ❑22, Aug 1998; b&w ... 6.00
- ❑23, Sep 1998; b&w ... 6.00
- ❑24, Oct 1998; b&w ... 6.00
- ❑25, Nov 1998; b&w ... 6.00
- ❑26, Dec 1998; b&w ... 6.00
- ❑27, Jan 1999; b&w ... 6.00
- ❑28, Feb 1999; b&w ... 6.00
- ❑29, Mar 1999; b&w ... 6.00
- ❑30, Apr 1999; b&w ... 6.00
- ❑31, May 1999; b&w ... 4.00
- ❑32, Jun 1999; b&w ... 4.00
- ❑33, Jul 1999; Wild Wild Hack ... 3.00
- ❑34, Aug 1999; b&w ... 2.95
- ❑35, Sep 1999; b&w ... 2.95
- ❑36, Oct 1999; b&w ... 2.95
- ❑37, Nov 1999; b&w ... 2.95
- ❑38, Dec 1999; b&w ... 2.95
- ❑39, Jan 2000; b&w ... 2.95
- ❑40, Feb 2000; b&w ... 2.95
- ❑41, Mar 2000; b&w ... 2.95
- ❑42, Apr 2000; b&w ... 2.95
- ❑43, May 2000; b&w ... 2.95
- ❑44, Jun 2000; b&w ... 2.95
- ❑45, Jul 2000; b&w ... 2.95
- ❑46, Aug 2000; b&w ... 2.95
- ❑47, Sep 2000; b&w ... 2.95
- ❑48, Oct 2000; b&w ... 2.95
- ❑49, Nov 2000; b&w ... 2.95
- ❑50, Dec 2000; double-sized ... 4.95
- ❑51, Jan 2001; b&w ... 2.95
- ❑52, Feb 2001; b&w ... 2.95
- ❑53, Mar 2001; b&w ... 2.95
- ❑54, Apr 2001; b&w ... 2.95
- ❑55, May 2001; b&w ... 2.95
- ❑56, Jun 2001; b&w ... 2.95
- ❑57, Jul 2001; b&w ... 2.95
- ❑58, Aug 2001; b&w ... 2.95
- ❑59, Sep 2001; b&w ... 2.95
- ❑60, Oct 2001; b&w; Players Handbook Errata Paste ups ... 2.99
- ❑61, Nov 2001; b&w ... 2.99
- ❑62, Dec 2001; b&w ... 2.99
- ❑63, Jan 2002; b&w ... 2.99
- ❑64, Feb 2002; b&w ... 2.99
- ❑65, Mar 2002; b&w ... 2.99
- ❑66, Apr 2002; b&w ... 2.99
- ❑67, May 2002; b&w ... 2.99
- ❑68, Jun 2002; b&w; The Hackmaster GM Shield Field Manual ... 2.99
- ❑69, Jul 2002; b&w ... 2.99
- ❑70, Aug 2002; b&w ... 3.99
- ❑71, Sep 2002; b&w ... 3.99
- ❑72, Oct 2002; b&w ... 3.99
- ❑73, Nov 2002; b&w ... 3.99
- ❑74, Dec 2002; b&w ... 3.99
- ❑75, Jan 2003; b&w ... 3.99
- ❑76, Feb 2003; b&w ... 3.99
- ❑77, Mar 2003; b&w ... 3.99
- ❑78, Apr 2003; b&w ... 3.99
- ❑79, May 2003; b&w ... 3.99
- ❑80, Jun 2003; b&w ... 3.99
- ❑81, Jul 2003; b&w ... 3.99
- ❑82, Aug 2003; b&w ... 3.99
- ❑83, Sep 2003; b&w ... 3.99
- ❑84, Oct 2003; b&w ... 3.99
- ❑85, Nov 2003; b&w ... 3.99
- ❑86, Dec 2003; b&w ... 3.99
- ❑87, Jan 2004; b&w ... 3.99
- ❑88, Feb 2004; b&w ... 3.99
- ❑89, Mar 2004; b&w ... 3.99
- ❑90, Apr 2004; b&w ... 3.99
- ❑91, May 2004; b&w ... 3.99
- ❑92, Jun 2004; b&w ... 3.99
- ❑93, Jul 2004; b&w ... 3.99
- ❑94, Aug 2004; b&w ... 3.99
- ❑95, Sep 2004; b&w ... 3.99
- ❑96, Oct 2004; b&w ... 3.99
- ❑97, Nov 2004; b&w ... 3.99
- ❑98, Dec 2004; b&w ... 3.99
- ❑99, Jan 2005; b&w ... 3.99
- ❑100, Feb 2005; b&w ... 7.99
- ❑101, Mar 2005, b&w ... 3.99
- ❑102, Apr 2005; b&w ... 3.99
- ❑103, May 2005; b&w ... 3.99
- ❑104, Jun 2005; b&w ... 3.99
- ❑105, Jul 2005; b&w ... 3.99
- ❑106, Aug 2005; b&w ... 3.99
- ❑107, Sep 2005; b&w ... 3.99
- ❑108, Oct 2005, b&w ... 3.99
- ❑109, Dec 2005; b&w ... 4.99
- ❑110 ... 4.99
- ❑111 ... 4.99
- ❑112 ... 4.99
- ❑113 ... 4.99
- ❑114 ... 4.99
- ❑115 ... 4.99
- ❑116 ... 4.99
- ❑117 ... 4.99
- ❑118 ... 4.99
- ❑119 ... 4.99
- ❑120 ... 4.99
- ❑121 ... 4.99
- ❑122 ... 4.99
- ❑123 ... 4.99
- ❑124 ... 4.99
- ❑125 ... 4.99
- ❑126 ... 4.99
- ❑127 ... 4.99
- ❑128 ... 4.99
- ❑129 ... 4.99
- ❑130 ... 4.99
- ❑131 ... 4.99
- ❑132 ... 4.99
- ❑133 ... 4.99
- ❑134 ... 4.99
- ❑135 ... 4.99
- ❑136 ... 4.99
- ❑137 ... 4.99
- ❑138 ... 4.99
- ❑139 ... 4.99
- ❑140 ... 4.99
- ❑141 ... 4.99
- ❑142 ... 4.99
- ❑143 ... 4.99
- ❑144 ... 4.99
- ❑145 ... 4.99
- ❑146 ... 4.99
- ❑147 ... 4.99
- ❑148 ... 4.99
- ❑149 ... 4.99

Knights of the Dinner Table: Black Hands Gaming Society Special
Kenzer and Company

- ❑1, ca. 2003 ... 2.99
- ❑2, ca. 2004 ... 2.99

Knights of the Dinner Table: Everknights
Kenzer and Company

- ❑-5, Feb 2002 ... 2.99
- ❑-4, Mar 2002 ... 2.99
- ❑-3, Apr 2002 ... 2.99
- ❑-2, May 2002 ... 2.99
- ❑-1, Jun 2002 ... 2.99
- ❑1, Jul 2002 ... 2.99
- ❑2, Sep 2002 ... 2.99
- ❑3, Nov 2002 ... 2.99
- ❑4, Jan 2003 ... 2.99
- ❑5, Mar 2003 ... 2.99
- ❑6, May 2003 ... 2.99
- ❑7, Jul 2003 ... 2.99
- ❑8, Sep 2003 ... 2.99
- ❑9, Nov 2003 ... 2.99
- ❑10, Jan 2004 ... 2.99
- ❑11, Mar 2004 ... 2.99
- ❑12, May 2004 ... 2.99
- ❑13, Jul 2004 ... 2.99

Other grades: Multiply price above by 5/6 for VF/NM • 2/3 for VERY FINE • 1/3 for FINE • 1/5 for VERY GOOD • 1/8 for GOOD

Knights of the Dinner Table Illustrated

Retells strip stories, with actual art

©Kenzer

Kobra

Twin brothers: one good, one evil

©DC

Kona

Caveman fights for survival on Monster Isle

©Dell

Konga

Steve Ditko adapts the 1961 monster film

©Charlton

Kong the Untamed

Kind of a 1970s version of Anthro

©DC

N-MINT

❑14, Nov 2004 .... 2.99
❑Special 1, Jun 2004 .... 2.99

Knights of the Dinner Table/Faans Crossover Special
Six Handed

❑1, Jul 1999, b&w 2.95

Knights of the Dinner Table Illustrated
Kenzer

❑1, Jun 2000, b&w 2.95
❑2, Aug 2000, b&w 2.95
❑3, Oct 2000, b&w 2.95
❑4, Dec 2000, b&w; creative team switches from Aaron Williams to Brendan and Brian Fraim 2.95
❑5, Feb 2001 .... 2.95
❑6, Apr 2001 .... 2.95
❑7, Jun 2001 .... 2.95
❑8, Aug 2001 .... 2.95
❑9, Oct 2001 .... 2.95
❑10, Dec 2001; reprints of original KoDT strips end 2.99
❑11, Feb 2002; cover forms triptych with other parts of crossover, Travelers and Knights of the Dinner Table Illustrated vs. Tony Digerolamo's The Travelers Crossover Special; references to where original strips can be found begin 2.99
❑12, Apr 2002 .... 2.99
❑13, Jun 2002 .... 2.99
❑14, Aug 2002 .... 2.99
❑15, Oct 2002 .... 2.99
❑16, Nov 2002 .... 2.99
❑17, Dec 2002; full-page panels throughout 2.99
❑18, Jan 2003 .... 2.99
❑19, Feb 2003 .... 2.99
❑20, Mar 2003 .... 2.99
❑21, Apr 2003 .... 2.99
❑22, May 2003; cover forms diptych with #23 .... 2.99
❑23, Jun 2003; cover forms diptych with #22 .... 2.99
❑24, Jul 2003 .... 2.99
❑25, Aug 2003 .... 2.99
❑26, Sep 2003 .... 2.99
❑27, Oct 2003 .... 2.99
❑28, Nov 2003 .... 2.99
❑29, Dec 2003 .... 2.99
❑30, Jan 2004 .... 2.99
❑31, Feb 2004 .... 2.99
❑32, Mar 2004 .... 2.99
❑33, Apr 2004 .... 2.99
❑34, May 2004 .... 2.99
❑35, Jun 2004 .... 2.99
❑36, Jul 2004 .... 2.99
❑37, Aug 2004 .... 2.99
❑38, Sep 2004 .... 2.99
❑39, Oct 2004 .... 2.99
❑40, Nov 2004 .... 2.99
❑41, Dec 2004 .... 2.99

Knights of the Jaguar Super Limited One Shot
Image

❑1, Jan 2004 .... 3.00

N-MINT

Knights of the Zodiac
Viz

❑1, Jan 2004 .... 7.95
❑2, Mar 2004 .... 7.95
❑3, May 2004 .... 7.95
❑4, Jul 8 .... 7.95
❑5, Sep 2004 .... 7.95
❑6, Nov 2004 .... 7.95
❑7, Jan 2005 .... 7.95
❑8, Mar 2005 .... 7.95
❑9, May 2005 .... 7.95
❑10, Jul 2005 .... 7.95
❑11, Sep 2005 .... 7.95
❑12, Nov 2005 .... 7.95

Knights on Broadway
Broadway

❑1, Jul 1996 .... 2.95
❑2, Aug 1996 .... 2.95
❑3, Oct 1996 .... 2.95

Knight's Round Table
Knight

❑1, Oct 1996, b&w; Anthology 2.95
❑1/A, ca. 1996; Photo cover 2.95

Knightstrike
Image

❑1, Dec 1995; polybagged with Sentinel card 2.50

Knight Watchman
Image

❑1, Jun 1998; cover says May, indicia says Jun 2.95
❑2, Jul 1998 .... 2.95
❑3, Aug 1998 .... 2.95
❑4, Oct 1998 .... 2.95

Knight Watchman: Graveyard Shift
Caliber

❑1, ca. 1994, b&w 2.95
❑2, ca. 1995 .... 2.95

Knight Wolf
Five Star

❑1 .... 2.50
❑2 .... 2.50
❑3 .... 2.50

Knuckles
Archie

❑1, Apr 1997 .... 4.00
❑2, May 1997 .... 3.00
❑3, Jun 1997 .... 3.00
❑4, Aug 1997 .... 2.25
❑5, Sep 1997 .... 2.25
❑6, Oct 1997 .... 2.25
❑7, Dec 1997 .... 2.25
❑8, Jan 1998 .... 2.25
❑9, Feb 1998 .... 2.25
❑10, Mar 1998 .... 2.25
❑11, Apr 1998 .... 2.25
❑12, May 1998 .... 2.25
❑13, Jun 1998 .... 2.25
❑14, Jul 1998 .... 2.25
❑15, Aug 1998 .... 2.25
❑16, Sep 1998 .... 2.25
❑17, Oct 1998 .... 2.25
❑18, Nov 1998 .... 2.25

N-MINT

❑19, Dec 1998 .... 2.25
❑20, Jan 1999 .... 2.25
❑21, Feb 1999 .... 2.25
❑22, Mar 1999, cover forms triptych with #23 and #24 .... 2.25
❑23, Apr 1999, cover forms triptych with #22 and #24 .... 2.25
❑24, May 1999, cover forms triptych with #22 and #23 .... 2.25
❑25, Jun 1999 .... 2.25
❑26, Jul 1999 .... 2.25
❑27, Aug 1999 .... 2.25
❑28, Sep 1999 .... 2.25
❑29, Oct 1999, The Echidna 2.25

Knuckles' Chaotix
Archie

❑1, Jan 1996 .... 3.00

Knuckles the Malevolent Nun
Fantagraphics

❑1, ca. 1991, b&w 2.25
❑2, ca. 1991 .... 2.25

Kobalt
DC / Milestone

❑1, Jun 1994 .... 1.75
❑2, Jul 1994 .... 1.75
❑3, Aug 1994 .... 1.75
❑4, Sep 1994, 1: Page 1.75
❑5, Oct 1994 .... 1.75
❑6, Nov 1994 .... 1.75
❑7, Dec 1994 .... 1.75
❑8, Jan 1995 .... 1.75
❑9, Feb 1995 .... 1.75
❑10, Mar 1995 .... 1.75
❑11, Apr 1995 .... 1.75
❑12, Jun 1995 .... 1.75
❑13, Jul 1995 .... 2.50
❑14, Jul 1995, Long Hot Summer 2.50
❑15, Aug 1995, Long Hot Summer 2.50
❑16, Sep 1995, Final Issue; Long Hot Summer 2.50

Kobra
DC

❑1, Mar 1976; JK (w); JK (a); 1&O: Kobra 9.00
❑2, May 1976 .... 3.00
❑3, Jul 1976, KG (a) 3.00
❑4, Sep 1976 .... 3.00
❑5, Dec 1976 .... 3.00
❑6, Feb 1977 .... 3.00
❑7, Apr 1977, Final Issue 3.00

Kodocha: Sana's Stage
Tokyopop

❑1, Jun 2002, b&w; printed in Japanese format 9.99
❑2, Jul 2002, b&w; printed in Japanese format 9.99
❑3, Sep 2002, b&w; printed in Japanese format 9.99

Kogaratsu: The Lotus of Blood
Acme

❑1 .... 5.95

N-MINT

Kolchak Tales: Black & White & Red All Over
Moonstone

❑1/A cover, Sep 2005 .... 4.95
❑1/B cover, Sep 2005 .... 4.95

Kolchak: Tales of the Night Stalker
Moonstone

❑1/A, ca. 2004 .... 3.50
❑1/B, ca. 2004 .... 3.50
❑2/A, ca. 2004 .... 3.50
❑2/B, ca. 2004 .... 3.50
❑3/A, ca. 2004 .... 3.50
❑3/B, ca. 2004 .... 3.50
❑4/A, ca. 2004 .... 3.50
❑4/B, ca. 2004 .... 3.50
❑5/A 2005 .... 3.50
❑5/B 2005 .... 3.50
❑6/A, Jun 2005 .... 3.50
❑6/B, Jun 2005 .... 3.50

Kolchak: The Night Stalker: Get of Belial
Moonstone

❑1, ca. 2002; Prestige format one-shot 6.95

Kolchak: The Night Stalker
Moonstone

❑1, ca. 2002; Prestige format one-shot 6.50

Komodo and the Defiants
Victory

❑1, ca. 1987 .... 1.50
❑2, ca. 1987 .... 1.50

Kona
Dell

❑2, Jul 1962, Numbering continued from appearance in Four Color Comics #1253 .... 18.00
❑3, Sep 1962 .... 15.00
❑4, Oct 1962, 1&O: Anak. Anak stories begin as back-up 15.00
❑5, Jan 1963 .... 15.00
❑6, Apr 1963 .... 12.00
❑7, Jul 1963 .... 12.00
❑8, Oct 1963 .... 12.00
❑9, Jan 1964 .... 12.00
❑10, Apr 1964 .... 12.00
❑11, Jul 1964 .... 12.00
❑12, Oct 1964 .... 12.00
❑13, Jan 1965 .... 12.00
❑14, Apr 1965 .... 12.00
❑15, Jul 1965 .... 10.00
❑16, Oct 1965 .... 10.00
❑17, Jan 1966 .... 10.00
❑18, Apr 1966 .... 10.00
❑19, Jul 1966 .... 10.00
❑20, Oct 1966 .... 10.00
❑21, Jan 1967, Final Issue 10.00

Konga
Charlton

❑1, ca. 1960, ca. 1960 .... 75.00
❑2, Aug 1961 .... 50.00
❑3, Oct 1961 .... 35.00
❑4, Dec 1961 .... 35.00
❑5, Mar 1962 .... 25.00
❑6, May 1962 .... 25.00
❑7, Jul 1962 .... 25.00
❑8, Sep 1962 .... 25.00
❑9, Nov 1962 .... 25.00
❑10, Jan 1963 .... 25.00
❑11, Mar 1963 .... 16.00
❑12, May 1963 .... 16.00
❑13, Jul 1963 .... 16.00
❑14, Sep 1963 .... 16.00
❑15, Nov 1963 .... 16.00
❑16, Jan 1964 .... 16.00
❑17, Mar 1964 .... 16.00
❑18, Jun 1964 .... 16.00
❑19, Sep 1964 .... 16.00
❑20, Dec 1965 .... 16.00
❑21, Feb 1965 .... 14.00
❑22, May 1965 .... 14.00
❑23, Nov 1965 .... 14.00

Konga's Revenge
Charlton

❑1, ca. 1963, Reprints Konga's Revenge #3; Published out of sequence 10.00

N-MINT

❑2, ca. 1963, ca. 1963 .... 7.00
❑3, ca. 1963, ca. 1963 .... 7.00

Kong, 8th Wonder of the World - Movie Adaptation
Dark Horse

❑1, Jan 2006 .... 3.99

Kong the Untamed
DC

❑1, Jul 1975; BWr (c); BWr, AA (a); O: Kong the Untamed 9.00
❑2, Sep 1975 .... 3.00
❑3, Nov 1975 AA (a) 3.00
❑4, Jan 1976 .... 3.00
❑5, Mar 1976; Final Issue 3.00

Konny and Czu
Antarctic

❑1, Sep 1994, b&w 2.75
❑2, Nov 1994, b&w 2.75
❑3, Jan 1995, b&w 2.75
❑4, Mar 1995, b&w 2.75

Koolau the Leper
Tome

❑1, b&w 2.50

Koosh Kins
Archie

❑1, Oct 1991 .... 1.00
❑2, Oct 1991 .... 1.00
❑3, Dec 1991 .... 1.00
❑4, Feb 1992 .... 1.00

Korak, Son of Tarzan
Gold Key

❑1, Jan 1964, RM (a); Gold Key begins publishing 65.00
❑2, Mar 1964, RM (a) 45.00
❑3, May 1964, RM (a) 45.00
❑4, Aug 1964, RM (a) 45.00
❑5, Oct 1964, RM (a) 45.00
❑6, Dec 1964, RM (a) 30.00
❑7, Mar 1965, RM (a) 30.00
❑8, May 1965, RM (a) 30.00
❑9, Jul 1965, RM (a) 30.00
❑10, Sep 1965, RM (a) 30.00
❑11, Nov 1965, RM (a) 30.00
❑12, Mar 1966 .... 25.00
❑13, Jun 1966 .... 25.00
❑14, Sep 1966 .... 25.00
❑15, Dec 1966 .... 25.00
❑16, Mar 1967 .... 25.00
❑17, Jun 1967 .... 25.00
❑18, Aug 1967 .... 25.00
❑19, Oct 1967 .... 20.00
❑20, Dec 1967, RM (a); 10101-712 .... 20.00
❑21, Feb 1968, RM (a) 20.00
❑22, Apr 1968 .... 20.00
❑23, Jun 1968 .... 20.00
❑24, Aug 1968 .... 20.00
❑25, Oct 1968 .... 20.00
❑26, Dec 1968 .... 20.00
❑27, Feb 1969 .... 20.00
❑28, Apr 1969 .... 20.00
❑29, Jun 1969 .... 20.00
❑30, Aug 1969 .... 20.00
❑31, Oct 1969 .... 20.00
❑32, Dec 1969 .... 20.00
❑33, Jan 1970 .... 20.00
❑34, Mar 1970 .... 20.00
❑35, May 1970 .... 20.00
❑36, Jul 1970 .... 20.00
❑37, Sep 1970 .... 20.00
❑38, Nov 1970 .... 17.00
❑39, Jan 1971 .... 17.00
❑40, Mar 1971 .... 17.00
❑41, May 1971 .... 17.00
❑42, Jul 1971 .... 17.00
❑43, Sep 1971 .... 17.00
❑44, Nov 1971 .... 17.00
❑45, Jan 1972 .... 17.00
❑46, May 1972, continues Gold Key numbering; DC begins publishing 17.00
❑47, Jul 1972 .... 15.00
❑48, Sep 1972 .... 15.00
❑49, Nov 1972 .... 15.00
❑50, Feb 1973 .... 15.00
❑51, Apr 1973, JKu (c); JKu (w); FT (a) 15.00
❑52, Jul 1973 .... 10.00

N-MINT

❑53, Sep 1973, JKu (c); Carson of Venus back-up 10.00
❑54, Nov 1973, JKu (c); MA (a); Carson of Venus back-up 10.00
❑55, Jan 1974, JKu (c);Carson of Venus back-up 10.00
❑56, Mar 1974, JKu (c);Carson of Venus back-up 10.00
❑57, Jun 1975 .... 10.00
❑58, Aug 1975 .... 10.00
❑59, Oct 1975, Series continued in Tarzan Family #60 .... 10.00

Kore
Image

❑1, Apr 2003 .... 2.95
❑2, Jun 2003 .... 2.95
❑3, Jul 2003 .... 2.95
❑4, Sep 2003 .... 2.95
❑5, Oct 2003 .... 2.95

Korg: 70,000 B.C.
Charlton

❑1, May 1975 .... 8.00
❑2, Aug 1975 .... 5.00
❑3, Oct 1975 .... 5.00
❑4, Dec 1975 .... 5.00
❑5, Feb 1976 .... 5.00
❑6, May 1976 .... 5.00
❑7, Jul 1976 .... 5.00
❑8, Sep 1976 .... 5.00
❑9, Nov 1976 .... 5.00

Korvus
Arrow

❑0, Jul 1999; Flip book with Spank the Monkey #1 .... 2.95
❑1, ca. 1998 .... 2.95
❑2, ca. 1998 .... 2.95
❑3, Spr 1998; Spring 1998 .... 2.95

Korvus
Arrow

❑1, Fal 1998 .... 2.95
❑2, ca. 1998 .... 2.95

Kosmic Kat
Image

❑1, Aug 1999 .... 2.95

Kosmic Kat Activity Book
Image

❑1, Aug 1999; O: Kosmic Kat 2.95

Krazy Kat
Gold Key

❑1, Jan 1964 .... 15.00

Kree-Skrull War Starring The Avengers
Marvel

❑1, Sep 1983; JB, NA (a); Reprints 3.00
❑2, Oct 1983; JB, NA (a); Reprints 3.00

Kremen
Grey Productions

❑1 .... 2.50
❑2 .... 2.50
❑3 .... 2.50

Krey
Gauntlet

❑1, ca. 1992, b&w 2.50
❑2, ca. 1992, b&w 2.50
❑3, ca. 1992, b&w 2.50
❑Special 1, ca. 1993; Flipbook 3.95

Krofft Supershow
Gold Key

❑1, Apr 1978 .... 6.00
❑2, May 1978 .... 4.00
❑3, Jun 1978 .... 4.00
❑4, Sep 1978 .... 4.00
❑5, Nov 1978 .... 4.00
❑6, Jan 1979 .... 4.00

Krull
Marvel

❑1, Nov 1983, Photo cover 1.25
❑2, Dec 1983 .... 1.25

Krusty Comics
Bongo

❑1, ca. 1995 .... 2.50
❑2, ca. 1995 .... 2.50
❑3, ca. 1995 .... 2.50

Other grades: Multiply price above by 5/6 for VF/NM • 2/3 for VERY FINE • 1/3 for FINE • 1/5 for VERY GOOD • 1/8 for GOOD

Korak, Son of Tarzan

A more youth-oriented version of Tarzan

©Gold Key

Kull the Conqueror

Barbarian series launched a year after Tarzan

©Marvel

Kyra

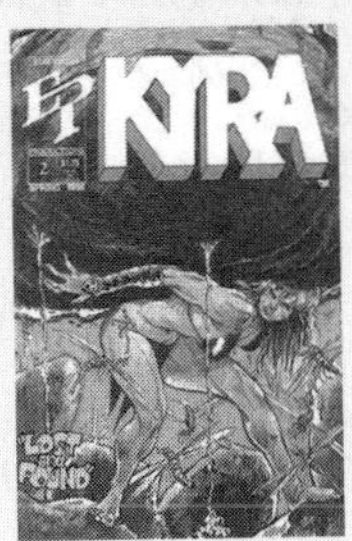

Woman wrestler in jungle comic

©Elsewhere

Lady Death

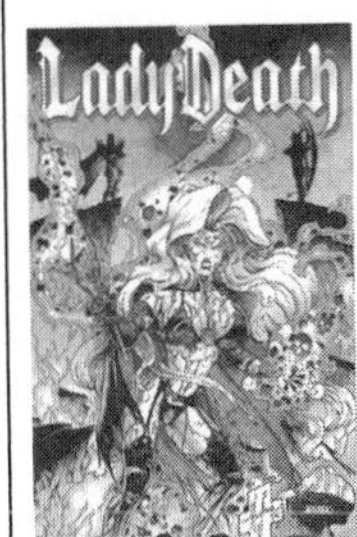

Origin story kicks off buxom "Bad Girl" wave

©Chaos!

Lady Justice

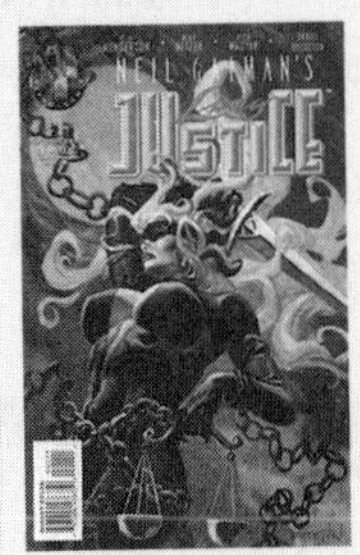

Spirit of Justice possesses, blinds females

©Tekno

N-MINT

Krypton Chronicles
DC

❑1, Sep 1981, RB (c); CS (a); A: Superman 1.50
❑2, Oct 1981, RA (c); CS (a); A: Black Flame 1.50
❑3, Nov 1981, RA (c); CS (a); O: name of Kal-El 1.50

Krypto the Super Dog
DC

❑1, Nov 2006 .... 2.25
❑2, Dec 2006 .... 2.99
❑3, Jan 2007, Includes 3-D Heroscape glasses; Includes Teen Titans: Sparktop mini-comic 2.25
❑4, Mar 2007 .... 2.25

Kull and the Barbarians
Marvel

❑1, May 1975, b&w; magazine; NA, GK, JSe, WW, RA (a); reprinted from Kull the Conqueror #1 and 2, Supernatural Thrillers #3 .... 16.00
❑2, Jul 1975, b&w; magazine; HC, NA, GK (a) 4.00
❑3, Sep 1975, b&w; magazine; O: Red Sonja 5.00

Kull in 3-D
Blackthorne

❑1; Blackthorne 3-D Series #51 .... 2.50
❑2 .... 2.50

Kull the Conqueror
Marvel

❑1, Jun 1971, WW, RA (a); O: Kull. 1: Brule the Spear-Slayer 20.00
❑2, Sep 1971, JSe (c); JSe (a) 12.00
❑3, Jul 1972, JSe (a); A: Thulsa Doom 8.00
❑4, Sep 1972, JSe (a) 8.00
❑5, Nov 1972, JSe (a) 7.00
❑6, Jan 1973, JSe (a) 5.00
❑7, Mar 1973 .... 5.00
❑8, May 1973 .... 5.00
❑9, Jul 1973 .... 5.00
❑10, Sep 1973, Continued as "Kull the Destroyer" 5.00

Kull the Conqueror
Marvel

❑1, Dec 1982; JB (a); Brule 5.00
❑2, Mar 1983; Misareena 3.00

Kull the Conqueror
Marvel

❑1, May 1983; JB, DGr, BWi (a); Iraina 2.00
❑2, Jul 1983 JB (a) 1.75
❑3, Dec 1983 JB (a) 1.75
❑4, Feb 1984; BSz, JB, CV (a); 48 pages 1.50
❑5, Aug 1984 .... 1.50
❑6, Oct 1984 .... 1.25
❑7, Dec 1984 .... 1.25
❑8, Feb 1985 .... 1.25
❑9, Apr 1985 .... 1.25
❑10, Jun 1985, Final Issue 1.25

Kull the Destroyer
Marvel

❑11, Nov 1973, Continued from Kull the Conqueror (1st Series) #10 .... 2.00
❑12, Jan 1974, SB, MP (a) 2.00
❑13, Mar 1974, MP (c); MP (a); Marvel Value Stamp #73: Kingpin 2.00
❑14, May 1974, JSn, MP (a); Marvel Value Stamp #40: Loki 2.00
❑15, Aug 1974, SL (w); SD, MP (a); series goes on hiatus; Marvel Value Stamp #42: Man Wolf 2.00
❑16, Aug 1976 .... 2.00
❑16/30¢, Aug 1976, 30¢ regional price variant 20.00
❑17, Oct 1976, AA (a) 2.00
❑18, Dec 1976, AA (a) 2.00
❑19, Feb 1977, JSe (c); AA (a) 2.00
❑20, Apr 1977, AA (a) 2.00
❑21, Jun 1977 .... 2.00
❑21/35¢, Jun 1977, 35¢ regional price variant 15.00
❑22, Aug 1977 .... 2.00
❑22/35¢, Aug 1977, 35¢ regional price variant 15.00
❑23, Oct 1977, Newsstand edition (disrtibuted by Curtis); issue number in box 2.00
❑23/Whitman, Oct 1977, Special markets edition (usually sold in Whitman bagged prepacks); price appears in a diamond; no UPC barcode 2.00
❑23/35¢, Oct 1977, 35¢ regional price variant 15.00
❑24, Dec 1977 .... 2.00
❑25, Feb 1978 .... 2.00
❑26, Apr 1978 .... 2.00
❑27, Jun 1978 .... 2.00
❑28, Aug 1978, Thulsa Doom returns 2.00
❑29, Oct 1978, A: Thulsa Doom. Final Issue 2.00

Kunoichi
Lightning

❑1, Sep 1996; also contains Sinja: Resurrection #1; indicia is for Sinja: Resurrection 3.00

Kwaiden
Dark Horse

❑1, ca. 2004 .... 14.95

Kyra
Elsewhere

❑1, ca. 1985, b&w 2.00
❑2, Spr 1986, b&w 2.00
❑3, Sum 1986, b&w 2.00
❑4, Dec 1986 .... 2.00
❑5, Jun 1987 .... 2.00
❑6, ca. 1987 .... 2.00

Kyrie
ADV Manga

❑1, ca. 2005 .... 9.99

K-Z Comics Presents
K-Z

❑1, Jun 1985 .... 1.50

Lab
Astonish

❑1, ca. 2001 .... 3.50
❑2, ca. 2003 .... 2.99

La Blue Girl
CPM / Bare Bear

❑1, Jul 1996, b&w; wraparound cover 2.95
❑2, Aug 1996, b&w; Adult 2.95
❑3, Sep 1996, b&w; Adult 2.95
❑4, Oct 1996, b&w; Adult 2.95
❑5, Nov 1996, b&w; Adult 2.95
❑6, Dec 1996, Adult 2.95
❑7, Jan 1997, Adult 2.95
❑8, Feb 1997, Adult 2.95
❑9, Mar 1997, Adult 2.95
❑10, Apr 1997, Adult 2.95
❑11, May 1997, Adult 2.95
❑12, Jun 1997, Adult 2.95

Labman
Image

❑1, Nov 1996; 1: Labman 3.50
❑1/A, Nov 1996; alternate cover 3.50
❑1/B, Nov 1996; alternate cover 3.50
❑1/C, Nov 1996; alternate cover 3.50
❑2, Dec 1996 .... 2.95
❑3, Jan 1997 .... 2.95

Labman Sourcebook
Image

❑1, Jun 1996; Limited edition giveaway from 1996 San Diego Comic-Con 1.00

Labor Force
Blackthorne

❑1, Sep 1986 .... 1.50
❑2 .... 1.50
❑3 .... 1.50
❑4 .... 1.75
❑5, Mar 1987 .... 1.75
❑6 .... 1.75
❑7 .... 1.75
❑8 .... 1.75

Labours of Hercules
Malan Classical Enterprises

❑1, b&w; NN 2.95

Lab Rats
DC

❑1, Jun 2002 .... 2.50
❑2, Jul 2002 .... 2.50
❑3, Aug 2002 .... 2.50
❑4, Sep 2002 .... 2.50
❑5, Oct 2002 .... 2.50
❑6, Nov 2002 .... 2.50
❑7, Dec 2002 .... 2.50

Labyrinth of Madness
TSR

❑1; ca. 1996 .... 1.00

Labyrinth: The Movie
Marvel

❑1, Nov 1986; JB, RT (a); Movie adaptation 1.50
❑2, Dec 1986; JB, RT (a); Movie adaptation 1.50
❑3, Jan 1987; JB, RT (a); Movie adaptation 1.50

Lackluster World
Gen: Eric Publishing

❑1, Mar 2005; b&w 3.95
❑2, Mar 2005; b&w 3.95
❑3, Aug 2005 .... 3.95

L.A. Comics
Los Angeles

❑1, Adult 3.00
❑2, Adult 3.00

Lad, A Dog
Dell

❑2, Sep 1962, First issue published as Dell's Four Color #1303; no photo cover on this issue 30.00

Lady and the Tramp
Dell

❑1, Jun 1955 .... 25.00

Lady and the Tramp
Gold Key

❑1, Jan 1963, adapts Disney animated film; reprints Four Color #629 .... 25.00
❑1, Mar 1972, adapts Disney animated film; reissued for re-release of film; reprints Four Color #629 .... 14.00

Lady and the Vampire
NBM

❑1; Adult 10.95

Lady Arcane
Hero Graphics

❑1, Jul 1992; O: Giant 4.95
❑2, Oct 1992, b&w 3.50
❑3, Jan 1993, b&w 3.50
❑4, b&w; Final Issue 2.95

Lady Crime
AC

❑1, ca. 1992, b&w; Bob Powell reprints 2.75

Lady Death
Chaos!

❑0, Nov 1997 .... 3.00
❑½, Dec 1994; Wizard mail-in promotional edition 4.00
❑½/A 1994; Wizard mail-in promotional edition; Black velvet edition 6.00
❑½/Gold 1994; Gold edition; Wizard mail-in promotional edition 5.00
❑1, Jan 1994; Chromium Cover 8.00
❑1/Ltd., Jan 1994; Signed limited edition 12.00
❑1/2nd, Feb 1994; Commemorative edition 2.75
❑2, Feb 1994 .... 8.00
❑3, Mar 1994 .... 5.00

Lady Death
Chaos!

❑1, Feb 1998 .... 7.00
❑1/Ltd., Feb 1998; premium limited edition; no cover price 9.00
❑2, Mar 1998 .... 2.95
❑3, Apr 1998; Signed edition; Signed edition 2.95
❑4, May 1998 .... 2.95
❑5, Jun 1998 .... 2.95
❑5/Variant, Jun 1998; variant cover 3.50
❑6, Jul 1998 .... 2.95
❑7, Aug 1998 .... 2.95
❑8, Sep 1998 .... 2.95
❑9, Oct 1998 .... 2.95
❑10, Nov 1998; cover says Oct, indicia says Nov 2.95
❑11, Dec 1998 .... 2.95
❑12, Jan 1999 .... 2.95
❑13, Feb 1999 .... 2.95
❑14, Mar 1999; Inferno 2.95
❑15, Apr 1999 .... 2.95
❑16, May 1999 .... 2.95

Lady Death: A Medieval Tale
CrossGen

❑1, Mar 2003 .... 2.95
❑2, Apr 2003 .... 2.95
❑3, May 2003 .... 2.95
❑4, Jun 2003 .... 2.95
❑5, Jul 2003 .... 2.95
❑6, Sep 2003 .... 2.95
❑7, Oct 2003 .... 2.95
❑8, Oct 2003 .... 2.95
❑9, Dec 2003 .... 2.95
❑10, Feb 2004 .... 2.95
❑11, Mar 2004 .... 2.95
❑12, Apr 2004 .... 2.95

Lady Death: Alive
Chaos

❑1, May 2001 .... 2.95
❑1/Ltd., May 2001; Premium Edition 2.95
❑2, Jun 2001 .... 2.95
❑3, Jul 2001 .... 2.95
❑4, Aug 2001 .... 2.95

Lady Death and the Women of Chaos! Gallery
Chaos

❑1, Nov 1996 .... 2.25

Lady Death/Bad Kitty
Chaos

❑1, Sep 2001 .... 2.99

Lady Death: Dark Millennium
Chaos

❑1, Feb 2000 .... 2.95
❑2, Mar 2000 .... 2.95

Lady Death: Dragon Wars
Chaos

❑1, Apr 1998 .... 2.95

Lady Death IV: The Crucible
Chaos!

❑½, Nov 1996; Wizard promotional edition 5.00
❑½/A, Jul 1996; Wizard promotional edition; Cloth alternate cover 8.00
❑1, Nov 1996 .... 3.00
❑1/A, Nov 1996; Leather edition 12.50
❑1/B, Nov 1996; All silver cover; Limited to 400; Comes with certificate of authenticity 16.00
❑1/Silver, Nov 1996; silver embossed cardstock wraparound cover 3.50
❑2, Jan 1997 .... 2.95
❑3, Mar 1997 .... 2.95
❑4, Apr 1997 .... 2.95
❑5, Aug 1997 .... 2.95
❑5/Variant, Aug 1997; Nightmare Premium Edition; no cover price 5.00
❑6, Oct 1997; What Is and What Should Never Be 2.95

Lady Death: Heartbreaker
Chaos

❑1, Mar 2002 .... 2.99
❑2 .... 2.99
❑3 .... 2.99
❑4 .... 2.99
❑Ashcan 1; ashcan edition 1.00

Lady Death in Lingerie
Chaos!

❑1, Aug 1995 .... 2.95
❑1/Ltd., Aug 1995, foil-stamped leather premium edition; no cover price; limited to 10, 000 copies 10.00

Lady Death: Judgement War
Chaos!

❑1, Nov 1999 .... 2.95
❑2, Dec 1999 .... 2.95
❑3, Jan 2000 .... 2.95

Lady Death: Judgement War Prelude
Chaos!

❑1, Oct 1999 .... 2.95

Lady Death: Retribution
Chaos!

❑1, Aug 1998 .... 2.95
❑1/A, Aug 1998; Painted alternate cover 3.50
❑1/Ltd., Aug 1998; premium edition 4.00

Lady Death Swimsuit Special
Chaos!

❑1, May 1994, b&w 2.50
❑1/Variant, May 1994; Red Velvet edition 8.00

Lady Death: The Gauntlet
Chaos

❑1, Apr 2002 .... 2.99
❑2, May 2002 .... 2.99

Lady Death: The Rapture
Chaos!

❑1, Jun 1999 .... 2.95
❑1/Dynamic, Jun 1999; Dynamic Forces cover 3.00
❑1/Ltd., Jun 1999; Premium Edition 3.00
❑2, Jul 1999 .... 2.95
❑3, Aug 1999 .... 2.95
❑4, Sep 1999 .... 2.95

Lady Death III: The Odyssey
Chaos!

❑-1, Apr 1996; Sneak Peek Preview; promotional piece for mini-series 1.50
❑1, Apr 1996; Gold foil cover 3.50
❑1/Variant, Apr 1996; foil embossed cardstock wraparound cover 5.00
❑2, May 1996 .... 3.00
❑3, Jun 1996 .... 3.00
❑4, Aug 1996 .... 3.00
❑4/A, Aug 1996; alternate cover 8.00

Lady Death: Tribulation
Chaos!

❑1, Dec 2000 .... 2.95
❑2, Jan 2001 .... 2.95

Lady Death II: Between Heaven & Hell
Chaos!

❑1, Mar 1995, O: Lady Death. chromium cover 3.50
❑1/A, Mar 1995, Gold edition 4.00
❑1/B, Mar 1995, Black velvet limited edition 5.00
❑1/Ltd., Mar 1995, Limited signed edition; Signed by Brian Pulido (w), Steven Hughes (a), & Jason Jensen (i) 5.00
❑1/2nd, Commemorative edition 2.75
❑2, Apr 1995 .... 3.00
❑3, May 1995 .... 3.00
❑4, Jun 1995 .... 3.00
❑4/Variant, Jun 1995, Lady Demon chase cover 5.00

Lady Death/Vampirella: Dark Hearts
Chaos!

❑1, Mar 1999; crossover with Harris 3.50
❑1/A, Mar 1999; Premium edition (5000 printed); Premium edition (5000 printed); Cover shows head and shoulders of Vampirella and Lady Death 8.00

Lady Death Vs. Purgatori
Chaos!

❑1/A, Dec 1999; Limited to 3,000 copies 5.00
❑1, Dec 1999; no cover price; red foil logo 3.00

Lady Death vs. Vampirella
Chaos

❑Ashcan 1, Feb 2000; Lady Death/Vampirella II Preview Book 1.00
❑1/Ltd., Feb 2000 .... 3.00
❑1, Feb 2000 .... 3.00

Lady Death: Wicked Ways
Chaos!

❑1, Feb 1998 .... 2.95
❑1/Variant, Feb 1998; premium edition; white background cover 5.00

Lady Death: Wild Hunt
CrossGen

❑1, Apr 2004 .... 2.95
❑2, May 2004 .... 2.95

Lady Dracula
Fantaco

❑1; Adult 4.95
❑2; Adult 4.95

Lady Justice
Tekno

❑1, Sep 1995, 1: Lady Justice 2.00
❑2, Oct 1995 .... 2.00
❑3, Nov 1995 .... 2.00
❑4, Dec 1995, begins new story-arc with new Lady Justice 2.00
❑5, Dec 1995 .... 2.00
❑6, Jan 1996 .... 2.25
❑7, Jan 1996, stand-alone story 2.25
❑8, Feb 1996 .... 2.25
❑9, Mar 1996 .... 2.25
❑10, Apr 1996 .... 2.25
❑11, May 1996, Final Issue 2.25

Lady Justice
Big

❑1, Jun 1996 .... 2.25
❑2, Jul 1996 .... 2.25
❑3, Aug 1996 .... 2.25
❑4, Sep 1996 .... 2.25
❑5, Oct 1996 .... 2.25
❑6, Nov 1996 .... 2.25
❑7, Dec 1996 .... 2.25
❑8, Jan 1997 .... 2.25
❑9, Feb 1997, Final Issue 2.25

Lady Pendragon Gallery Edition
Image

❑1, Oct 1999 .... 2.95
❑1/A, Oct 1999; alternate cover 2.95

Other grades: Multiply price above by 5/6 for VF/NM • 2/3 for VERY FINE • 1/3 for FINE • 1/5 for VERY GOOD • 1/8 for GOOD

Lady Pendragon

King Arthur's wife wields Excalibur
©Maximum

Lady Rawhide

Aptly named horse-riding Zorro gal pal
©Topps

Laff-a-Lympics

Battle of the Network Stars meets Olympics
©Marvel

Lancelot Link, Secret Chimp

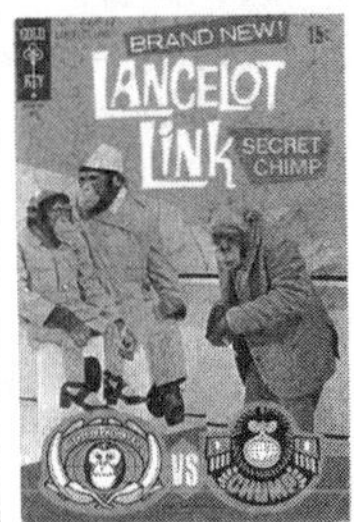

Simian secret agents oppose other apes
©Gold Key

Last Days of the Justice Society Special

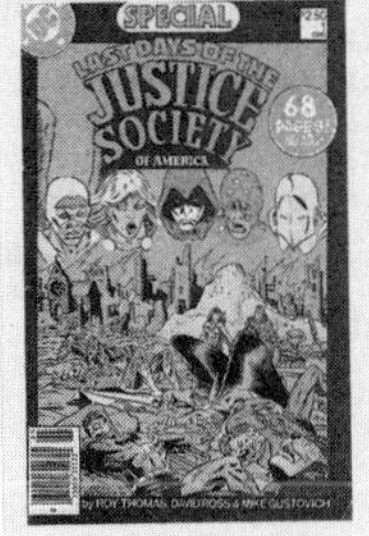

JSA fights Ragnarok over and over and ...
©DC

N-MINT

Lady Pendragon: Merlin
Image

❑1, Jan 2000 ... 2.95

Lady Pendragon/More Than Mortal
Image

❑1, May 1999 ... 2.50
❑1/A, May 1999, alternate cover; white background ... 4.00
❑1/B, May 1999, DF alternate cover (holding spear facing forward) ... 5.00
❑Ashcan 1, Feb 1999, b&w; no cover price; preview of upcoming crossover ... 2.00

Lady Pendragon
Maximum

❑1, Mar 1996; Rob Liefeld cover ... 2.50
❑1/A, Mar 1996; alternate cover ... 2.50
❑1/Autographed, Mar 1996; Alternate Cover, Autographed ... 6.00
❑1/2nd, Mar 1996; Remastered edition; Remastered edition; Rob Liefeld cover ... 2.50
❑Ashcan 1 ... 4.00

Lady Pendragon
Image

❑0, Mar 1999, flipbook with origin back-up ... 2.50
❑0/A, Mar 1999, Dynamic Forces sketch cover flipbook with origin back-up and certificate of Authenticity ... 4.00
❑1, Nov 1998 ... 3.00
❑1/A, Nov 1998, alternate cover; castle.. 3.00
❑1/B, Nov 1998, Dynamic Forces alternate cover; Swordswoman amid city ruins with sword pointing at sky ... 3.00
❑1/2nd, Feb 1999, Lady Pendragon Remastered; reprints #1 with corrections ... 2.50
❑2, Dec 1998, Drawn cover ... 4.00
❑2/A, Dec 1998, alternate cover ... 3.00
❑3, Jan 1999, crucified on cover ... 2.50
❑3/A, Jan 1999, manga-style cover ... 2.50
❑Ashcan 1, Jun 1998, Convention Preview Edition; no cover price ... 2.00

Lady Pendragon
Image

❑1, Mar 1999 ... 2.50
❑1/A, Apr 1999, "Stormkote"-covered flip book ... 2.50
❑1/B, Apr 1999, European Tour Edition.. 4.00
❑2, Apr 1999 ... 2.50
❑2/A, Apr 1999, alternate cover; Lady Pendragon vanquished ... 2.50
❑3, Jul 1999, 1: Alley Cat ... 2.50
❑4, Aug 1999, 1: Blue; Wraparound cover 2.50
❑5, Sep 1999 ... 2.50
❑6, Oct 1999 ... 2.50
❑7, Dec 1999, Giant-size; Flip-book ... 3.95
❑8, Feb 2000 ... 2.50
❑9, Apr 2000 ... 2.50
❑10, Aug 2000 ... 2.50

Lady Rawhide
Topps

❑1, Jul 1995 ... 2.95
❑2, Sep 1995 ... 2.95
❑3, Nov 1995 ... 2.95
❑4, Jan 1996 ... 2.95
❑5, Mar 1996; Final Issue ... 2.95

N-MINT

Lady Rawhide
Topps

❑½, ca. 1996; 1: Star Wolf ... 5.00
❑1, Oct 1996; 1: Scarlet Fever ... 2.95
❑2, Dec 1996; V: Scarlet Fever ... 2.95
❑3, Feb 1997 ... 2.95
❑4, Apr 1997, b&w ... 2.95
❑5, Jun 1997, b&w ... 2.95

Lady Rawhide Mini Comic
Topps

❑1, Jul 1995; Wizard supplement; no cover price ... 1.00

Lady Rawhide: Other People's Blood
Image

❑1, Mar 1999, b&w; Reprints Topps second series in b&w ... 2.95
❑2, Apr 1999, b&w; Reprints Topps second series in b&w ... 2.95
❑3, May 1999, b&w; Reprints Topps second series in b&w ... 2.95
❑4, Jun 1999, b&w; Reprints Topps second series in b&w ... 2.95
❑5, Jul 1999, b&w; Reprints Topps second series in b&w ... 2.95

Lady Rawhide Special Edition
Topps

❑1, Jun 1995; reprints Zorro #2 and 3... 3.95

Lady Spectra & Sparky Special
J. Kevin Carrier

❑1, Jan 1995 ... 2.50

Lady Supreme
Image

❑1, May 1996; aquamarine background cover ... 2.50
❑1/A, May 1996; brown background cover 2.50
❑2, Aug 1996; flip-book with New Men Special Preview Edition ... 2.50

Lady Vampré
Black Out

❑0 ... 2.95
❑1 ... 2.95

Lady Vampré: Pleasures of the Flesh
Black Out

❑1, b&w; 1: Black Lace ... 2.95

Lady Vampré vs. Black Lace
Black Out

❑1, Sep 1996, Flip-book ... 2.95

Laff-a-Lympics
Marvel

❑1, Mar 1978, based on Hanna-Barbera animated series ... 18.00
❑2, Apr 1978 ... 10.00
❑3, May 1978 ... 8.00
❑4, Jun 1978 ... 8.00
❑5, Jul 1978 ... 8.00
❑6, Aug 1978 ... 6.00
❑7, Sep 1978 ... 6.00
❑8, Oct 1978 ... 6.00
❑9, Nov 1978 ... 6.00
❑10, Dec 1978 ... 6.00
❑11, Jan 1979 ... 6.00
❑12, Feb 1979 ... 6.00
❑13, Mar 1979 ... 6.00

N-MINT

Laffin' Gas
Blackthorne

❑1, Jun 1986 ... 2.00
❑2 1986 ... 2.00
❑3 1986 ... 2.00
❑4 1986 ... 2.00
❑5 ... 2.00
❑6; 3-D; 3-D ... 2.00
❑7, Mar 1987 ... 2.00
❑8 1987 ... 2.00
❑9 1987 ... 2.00
❑10 1987 ... 2.00
❑11 ... 2.00
❑12 ... 2.00

Lagoon Engine Einsatz
ADV Manga

❑1, ca. 2005 ... 10.95

Lament of the Lamb
Tokyopop

❑1, May 2004; Graphic novel ... 9.99

Lance Barnes: Post Nuke Dick
Marvel / Epic

❑1, Apr 1993; Lance accidentally destroys the world ... 2.50
❑2, May 1993 ... 2.50
❑3, Jun 1993 ... 2.50
❑4, Jul 1993 ... 2.50

Lancelot Link, Secret Chimp
Gold Key

❑1, May 1971 ... 30.00
❑2, Aug 1971 ... 17.00
❑3, Nov 1971 ... 10.00
❑4, Feb 1972 ... 10.00
❑5, May 1972 ... 10.00
❑6, Aug 1972 ... 10.00
❑7, Nov 1972 ... 10.00
❑8, Feb 1973 ... 10.00

Lancelot Strong, the Shield
Archie / Red Circle

❑1, Jun 1983, RB (w); becomes Shield (Archie) ... 2.00

Lancer
Gold Key

❑1 1969 ... 25.00
❑2, Jun 1969 ... 20.00
❑3, Sep 1969 ... 20.00

Land of Nod
Dark Horse

❑1, Jul 1997, b&w; Jetcat story ... 2.95
❑2, Nov 1997, b&w ... 2.95
❑3, Feb 1998, b&w ... 2.95
❑4, Jun 1998, b&w ... 2.95

Land of Oz
Arrow

❑1, Nov 1998; Includes 3-D glasses ... 2.95
❑2, Jan 1999 ... 2.95
❑3, Mar 1999 ... 2.95
❑4, May 1999 ... 2.95
❑5, Jul 1999 ... 2.95
❑6, Sep 1999 ... 2.95
❑7, Nov 1999 ... 2.95
❑8, Mar 2000 ... 2.95
❑9, Apr 2000 ... 2.95

Other grades: Multiply price above by 5/6 for VF/NM • 2/3 for VERY FINE • 1/3 for FINE • 1/5 for VERY GOOD • 1/8 for GOOD

Land of the Giants
Gold Key
- ❑1, Nov 1968 .... 30.00
- ❑2, Jan 1969 .... 18.00
- ❑3, Mar 1969 .... 15.00
- ❑4, Jun 1969 .... 15.00
- ❑5, Sep 1969 .... 15.00

Landra Special
Alchemy
- ❑1, b&w; NN 2.00

Lann
Fantagraphics / Eros
- ❑1, Dec 1991, b&w; Adult 2.50

La Pacifica
DC / Paradox
- ❑1, b&w; digest 4.95
- ❑2, b&w; digest 4.95
- ❑3, b&w; digest 4.95

L.A. Phoenix
David G. Brown
- ❑1, Jul 1994, b&w 2.00
- ❑2, Jul 1995, b&w 2.00
- ❑3, Jul 1996, b&w 2.00

L.A. Raptor
Morbid
- ❑1, ca. 1995 .... 2.95

Lars of Mars 3-D
Eclipse
- ❑1, Apr 1987 .... 2.50

Laser Eraser & Pressbutton
Eclipse
- ❑1, Nov 1985 .... 1.50
- ❑2, Dec 1985 .... 1.50
- ❑3, Jan 1986 .... 1.50
- ❑4, Nov 1986 .... 1.50
- ❑5, May 1986 .... 1.50
- ❑6, Jul 1986 .... 1.50
- ❑3D 1, Aug 1986 .... 2.50

Lash Larue Western
AC
- ❑1; some color 3.50
- ❑Ann 1, b&w; Reprints 2.95

Lassie (Golden Press)
Golden Press
- ❑1, ca. 1978; Giant issue reprints stories from Lassie #19, 20, 21, 37, 38, 39, and 40; reprints painted cover from Lassie #30 .... 22.00

Last American
Marvel / Epic
- ❑1, Dec 1990 .... 2.25
- ❑2, Jan 1991 .... 2.25
- ❑3, Feb 1991 .... 2.25
- ❑4, Mar 1991 .... 2.25

Last Avengers
Marvel
- ❑1, Nov 1995; Alterniverse story 5.95
- ❑2, Dec 1995; Alterniverse story 5.95

Last Christmas
Image
- ❑1, Jun 2006 .... 2.99
- ❑2, Jul 2006 .... 2.99
- ❑3, Oct 2006 .... 2.99
- ❑4, Nov 2006 .... 2.99
- ❑5, Nov 2006 .... 2.99

Last Dangerous Christmas
Aeon
- ❑1, b&w; squarebound; benefit comic for neglected and abused children 5.95

Last Days of Hollywood, U.S.A.
Morgan
- ❑1 .... 2.95
- ❑2 .... 2.95
- ❑3 .... 2.95
- ❑4 .... 2.95
- ❑5 .... 2.95

Last Days of the Justice Society Special
DC
- ❑1, ca. 1986; JSA to Ragnarok after Crisis 3.00

Last Daze of the Bat-Guy
Mythic
- ❑1, b&w 2.95

Last Defender of Camelot
Zim
- ❑1, b&w; NN 1.95

Last Ditch
Edge
- ❑1, b&w 2.50

Last Gasp Comics and Stories
Last Gasp Eco-Funnies
- ❑1, ca. 1994 .... 3.95
- ❑2 .... 3.95
- ❑3, b&w; Anthology 3.95
- ❑4 .... 3.95

Last Generation
Black Tie
- ❑1 1987; Published by Black Tie Studios; ca. 1987 .... 1.95
- ❑2; ca. 1987 .... 1.95
- ❑3 .... 1.95
- ❑4; ca. 1988 .... 1.95
- ❑5 1989 .... 1.95

Last Hero Standing
Marvel
- ❑1, Aug 2005 .... 2.99
- ❑2, Aug 2005 .... 2.99
- ❑3, Aug 2005 .... 2.99
- ❑4, Aug 2005 .... 2.99
- ❑5, Aug 2005 .... 2.99

Last Kiss
Eclipse
- ❑1, ca. 1990, b&w 3.95

Last Kiss
Shanda
- ❑1, Feb 2001; Includes text piece, Was Joe Gill The Ann Landers of Comic Books? 4.95
- ❑2, Aug 2001 .... 4.95
- ❑3, Feb 2002 .... 4.95

Last Knight
NBM
- ❑1; ca. 2000 .... 15.95

Last Minute
-Ism
- ❑1, ca. 2004 .... 3.00
- ❑2, ca. 2004 .... 3.00
- ❑3, ca. 2004 .... 3.00
- ❑4, ca. 2004 .... 3.00
- ❑5, ca. 2005 .... 3.00
- ❑6, ca. 2005 .... 3.00

Last of the Dragons
Marvel / Epic
- ❑1; Ca 1988 .... 6.95

Last of the Viking Heroes
Genesis West
- ❑1, Mar 1987 .... 1.50
- ❑2, Jun 1987 .... 2.00
- ❑3, Aug 1987 .... 1.75
- ❑4, Nov 1987 .... 1.75
- ❑5/A, Jun 1988 .... 1.95
- ❑5/B, Jun 1988 .... 1.95
- ❑6, Jul 1988 .... 1.95
- ❑7, Jan 1989 .... 1.95
- ❑8, Jul 1989 .... 1.95
- ❑9, Jul 1991 .... 1.95
- ❑10, Oct 1991 .... 2.50
- ❑11, Feb 1992 .... 2.50
- ❑12, Jul 1992; Final Issue 2.50
- ❑Summer 1, Mar 1988; digest; Summer Special #1 .... 2.50
- ❑Summer 2, Apr 1990; Signed, numbered edition signed by authors; Summer Special #2 .... 2.50
- ❑Summer 3, Apr 1991; Wizard mail-in promotional edition; Summer Special #3 .... 2.50

Last One
DC / Vertigo
- ❑1, Jul 1993 .... 2.50
- ❑2, Aug 1993 .... 2.50
- ❑3, Sep 1993 .... 2.50
- ❑4, Oct 1993 .... 2.50
- ❑5, Nov 1993 .... 2.50
- ❑6, Dec 1993 .... 2.50

Last Planet
MBS
- ❑1 .... 2.50

Last Planet Standing
Marvel
- ❑1, Jul 2006 .... 2.99
- ❑2, Aug 2006 .... 2.99
- ❑3, Aug 206 .... 2.99
- ❑4, Sep 2006 .... 2.99
- ❑5, Sep 2006 .... 2.99

Last Shot
Image
- ❑1, Aug 2001 .... 2.95
- ❑2, Oct 2001 .... 2.95
- ❑3, Dec 2001 .... 2.95
- ❑4, Mar 2002 .... 2.95

Last Shot: First Draw
Image
- ❑1, May 2001 .... 2.95

Last Starfighter
Marvel
- ❑1, Oct 1984; Movie adaptation 2.00
- ❑2, Nov 1984; Movie adaptation 2.00
- ❑3, Dec 1984; Movie adaptation 2.00

Last Temptation
Marvel Music
- ❑1, May 1994 .... 4.95
- ❑1/A, May 1994; Variant cover with white background; came with the CD 4.95
- ❑2, Aug 1994 .... 4.95
- ❑3, Dec 1994 .... 4.95

Last Train to Deadsville: A Cal McDonald Mystery
Dark Horse
- ❑1, May 2004 .... 2.99
- ❑2, Jun 2004 .... 2.99
- ❑3, Jul 2004 .... 2.99
- ❑4, Nov 2004 .... 3.00

Latigo Kid Western
AC
- ❑1, b&w 1.95

Laugh
Archie
- ❑1, Jun 1987 .... 3.00
- ❑2, Aug 1987 .... 2.00
- ❑3, Oct 1987 .... 2.00
- ❑4, Dec 1987 .... 2.00
- ❑5, Feb 1988 .... 2.00
- ❑6, Apr 1988 .... 1.00
- ❑7, Jun 1988 .... 1.00
- ❑8, Jul 1988 .... 1.00
- ❑9, Aug 1988 .... 1.00
- ❑10, Oct 1988 .... 1.00
- ❑11, Dec 1988, DDC (a) 1.00
- ❑12, Feb 1989 .... 1.00
- ❑13, Apr 1989 .... 1.00
- ❑14, Jun 1989 .... 1.00
- ❑15, Jul 1989 .... 1.00
- ❑16, Aug 1989 .... 1.00
- ❑17, Oct 1989 .... 1.00
- ❑18, Dec 1989 .... 1.00
- ❑19, Feb 1990 .... 1.00
- ❑20, Apr 1990 .... 1.00
- ❑21, Jun 1990 .... 1.00
- ❑22, Jul 1990 .... 1.00
- ❑23, Aug 1990 .... 1.00
- ❑24, Oct 1990 .... 1.00
- ❑25, Dec 1990 .... 1.00
- ❑26, Feb 1991 .... 1.00
- ❑27, Apr 1991 .... 1.00
- ❑28, Jun 1991 .... 1.00
- ❑29, Aug 1991 .... 1.00

Laugh Comics
Archie
- ❑128, Nov 1961 .... 15.00
- ❑129, Dec 1961 .... 15.00
- ❑130, Jan 1962 .... 15.00
- ❑131, Feb 1962 .... 12.00
- ❑132, Mar 1962 .... 12.00
- ❑133, Apr 1962 .... 12.00
- ❑134, May 1962 .... 12.00
- ❑135, Jun 1962 .... 12.00
- ❑136, Jul 1962 .... 12.00
- ❑137, Aug 1962 .... 12.00

Other grades: Multiply price above by 5/6 for VF/NM • 2/3 for VERY FINE • 1/3 for FINE • 1/5 for VERY GOOD • 1/8 for GOOD

Last Kiss

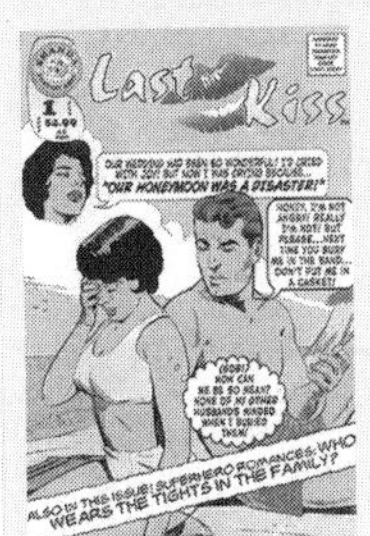

John Lustig's redialogued romance comics
©Shanda

Last of the Viking Heroes

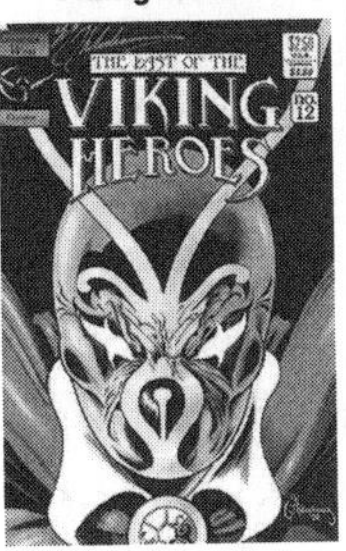

Conan Lite with more humor
©Genesis West

Last Starfighter

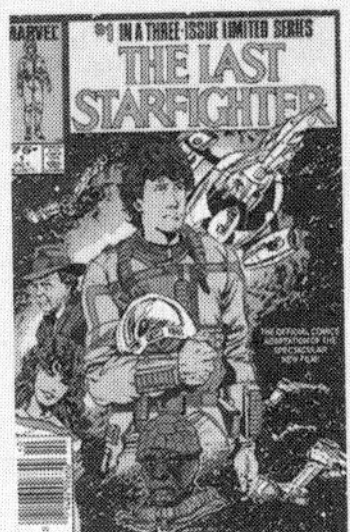

Videogame ranks potential defenders
©Marvel

Laugh Comics

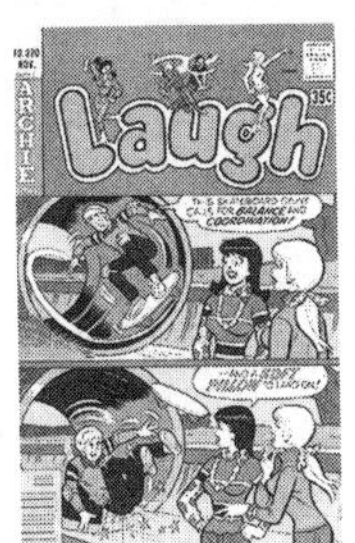

More misadventures of Archie and the gang
©Archie

Laurel & Hardy in 3-D

Stan and Ollie's multi-dimensional adventures
©Blackthorne

	N-MINT
❑138, Sep 1962	12.00
❑139, Oct 1962	12.00
❑140, Nov 1962	12.00
❑141, Dec 1962	12.00
❑142, Jan 1963	12.00
❑143, Feb 1963	12.00
❑144, Mar 1963	12.00
❑145, Apr 1963	12.00
❑146, May 1963	12.00
❑147, Jun 1963	12.00
❑148, Jul 1963	12.00
❑149, Aug 1963	12.00
❑150, Sep 1963	12.00
❑151, Oct 1963	12.00
❑152, Nov 1963	12.00
❑153, Dec 1963	12.00
❑154, Jan 1964	12.00
❑155, Feb 1964	12.00
❑156, Mar 1964	12.00
❑157, Apr 1964	12.00
❑158, May 1964	12.00
❑159, Jun 1964	12.00
❑160, Jul 1964	12.00
❑161, Aug 1964	12.00
❑162, Sep 1964	12.00
❑163, Oct 1964	12.00
❑164, Nov 1964	12.00
❑165, Dec 1964	12.00
❑166, Jan 1965	12.00
❑167, Feb 1965	12.00
❑168, Mar 1965	12.00
❑169, Apr 1965	12.00
❑170, May 1965, Two pages Decarlo pin-ups	12.00
❑171, Jun 1965	9.00
❑172, Jul 1965	9.00
❑173, Aug 1965	9.00
❑174, Sep 1965	9.00
❑175, Oct 1965	9.00
❑176, Nov 1965	9.00
❑177, Dec 1965	9.00
❑178, Jan 1966	9.00
❑179, Feb 1966	9.00
❑180, Mar 1966	9.00
❑181, Apr 1966, One page Decarlo pin-up	9.00
❑182, May 1966	9.00
❑183, Jun 1966	9.00
❑184, Jul 1966, Two pages Decarlo pin-ups; Fly and Captain Sprocket cameo in Lil Jinx story about appearing a comic book; Partially silent story	9.00
❑185, Aug 1966	9.00
❑186, Sep 1966	9.00
❑187, Oct 1966	9.00
❑188, Nov 1966	9.00
❑189, Dec 1966	9.00
❑190, Jan 1967	8.00
❑191, Feb 1967	8.00
❑192, Mar 1967	8.00
❑193, Apr 1967	8.00
❑194, May 1967	8.00
❑195, Jun 1967	8.00
❑196, Jul 1967, Decarlo pin-up only	8.00
❑197, Aug 1967, Decarlo pin-up only	8.00
❑198, Sep 1967	8.00
❑199, Oct 1967	8.00

	N-MINT
❑200, Nov 1967	8.00
❑201, Dec 1967	6.00
❑202, Jan 1968	6.00
❑203, Feb 1968	6.00
❑204, Mar 1968, Decarlo pin-up only	6.00
❑205, Apr 1968	6.00
❑206, May 1968	6.00
❑207, Jun 1968	6.00
❑208, Jul 1968	6.00
❑209, Aug 1968	6.00
❑210, Sep 1968	6.00
❑211, Oct 1968	6.00
❑212, Nov 1968	6.00
❑213, Dec 1968	6.00
❑214, Jan 1969	6.00
❑215, Feb 1969	6.00
❑216, Mar 1969	6.00
❑217, Apr 1969	6.00
❑218, May 1969	6.00
❑219, Jun 1969	6.00
❑220, Jul 1969	6.00
❑221, Aug 1969	6.00
❑222, Sep 1969	6.00
❑223, Oct 1969	6.00
❑224, Nov 1969	6.00
❑225, Dec 1969	6.00
❑226, Jan 1970, Title changes to Laugh	6.00
❑227, Feb 1970	6.00
❑228, Mar 1970	6.00
❑229, Apr 1970	6.00
❑230, May 1970	6.00
❑231, Jun 1970	6.00
❑232, Jul 1970	6.00
❑233, Aug 1970	6.00
❑234, Sep 1970	6.00
❑235, Oct 1970	6.00
❑236, Nov 1970	6.00
❑237, Dec 1970	6.00
❑238, Jan 1971	6.00
❑239, Feb 1971	6.00
❑240, Mar 1971	6.00
❑241, Apr 1971	6.00
❑242, May 1971	6.00
❑243, Jun 1971	6.00
❑244, Jul 1971	6.00
❑245, Aug 1971	6.00
❑246, Sep 1971	6.00
❑247, Oct 1971	6.00
❑248, Nov 1971	6.00
❑249, Dec 1971	6.00
❑250, Jan 1972	6.00
❑251, Feb 1972	4.00
❑252, Mar 1972	4.00
❑253, Apr 1972	4.00
❑254, May 1972	4.00
❑255, Jun 1972	4.00
❑256, Jul 1972	4.00
❑257, Aug 1972	4.00
❑258, Sep 1972	4.00
❑259, Oct 1972	4.00
❑260, Nov 1972	4.00
❑261, Dec 1972	4.00
❑262, Jan 1973	4.00
❑263, Feb 1973	4.00
❑264, Mar 1973	4.00
❑265, Apr 1973	4.00

	N-MINT
❑266, May 1973	4.00
❑267, Jun 1973	4.00
❑268, Jul 1973	4.00
❑269, Aug 1973	4.00
❑270, Sep 1973	4.00
❑271, Oct 1973	4.00
❑272, Nov 1973	4.00
❑273, Dec 1973	4.00
❑274, Jan 1974	4.00
❑275, Feb 1974	4.00
❑276, Mar 1974	4.00
❑277, Apr 1974	4.00
❑278, May 1974	4.00
❑279, Jun 1974	4.00
❑280, Jul 1974	4.00
❑281, Aug 1974	4.00
❑282, Sep 1974	4.00
❑283, Oct 1974	4.00
❑284, Nov 1974	4.00
❑285, Dec 1974	4.00
❑286, Jan 1975	4.00
❑287, Feb 1975	4.00
❑288, Mar 1975	4.00
❑289, Apr 1975	4.00
❑290, May 1975	4.00
❑291, Jun 1975	4.00
❑292, Jul 1975	4.00
❑293, Aug 1975	4.00
❑294, Sep 1975	4.00
❑295, Oct 1975	4.00
❑296, Nov 1975	4.00
❑297, Dec 1975	4.00
❑298, Jan 1976	4.00
❑299, Feb 1976	4.00
❑300, Mar 1976	4.00
❑301, Apr 1976	2.50
❑302, May 1976	2.50
❑303, Jun 1976	2.50
❑304, Jul 1976	2.50
❑305, Aug 1976	2.50
❑306, Sep 1976	2.50
❑307, Oct 1976	2.50
❑308, Nov 1976	2.50
❑309, Dec 1976	2.50
❑310, Jan 1977	2.50
❑311, Feb 1977	2.50
❑312, Mar 1977	2.50
❑313, Apr 1977	2.50
❑314, May 1977	2.50
❑315, Jun 1977	2.50
❑316, Jul 1977	2.50
❑317, Aug 1977	2.50
❑318, Sep 1977	2.50
❑319, Oct 1977	2.50
❑320, Nov 1977	2.50
❑321, Dec 1977	2.50
❑322, Jan 1978	2.50
❑323, Feb 1978	2.50
❑324, Mar 1978	2.50
❑325, Apr 1978	2.50
❑326, May 1978	2.50
❑327, Jun 1978	2.50
❑328, Jul 1978	2.50
❑329, Aug 1978	2.50
❑330, Sep 1978	2.50
❑331, Oct 1978	2.50

Other grades: Multiply price above by 5/6 for VF/NM • 2/3 for VERY FINE • 1/3 for FINE • 1/5 for VERY GOOD • 1/8 for GOOD

	N-MINT
❑332, Nov 1978	2.50
❑333, Dec 1978	2.50
❑334, Jan 1979	2.50
❑335, Feb 1979	2.50
❑336, Mar 1979	2.50
❑337, Apr 1979	2.50
❑338, May 1979	2.50
❑339, Jun 1979	2.50
❑340, Jul 1979	2.50
❑341, Aug 1979	2.50
❑342, Sep 1979	2.50
❑343, Oct 1979	2.50
❑344, Nov 1979	2.50
❑345, Dec 1979	2.50
❑346, Jan 1980	2.50
❑347, Feb 1980	2.50
❑348, Mar 1980	2.50
❑349, Apr 1980	2.50
❑350, May 1980	2.50
❑351, Jun 1980	2.00
❑352, Jul 1980	2.00
❑353, Aug 1980	2.00
❑354, Sep 1980	2.00
❑355, Oct 1980	2.00
❑356, Nov 1980	2.00
❑357, Dec 1980	2.00
❑358, Jan 1981	2.00
❑359, Feb 1981	2.00
❑360, Mar 1981, Reference to "Bolling Haunted House" in Lil Jinx story	2.00
❑361, Apr 1981	2.00
❑362, May 1981	2.00
❑363, Jun 1981	2.00
❑364, Jul 1981	2.00
❑365, Aug 1981	2.00
❑366, Sep 1981	2.00
❑367, Oct 1981	2.00
❑368, Nov 1981	2.00
❑369, Dec 1981	2.00
❑370, Jan 1982	2.00
❑371, Feb 1982	2.00
❑372, May 1982	2.00
❑373, Jul 1982	2.00
❑374, Sep 1982	2.00
❑375, Nov 1982	2.00
❑376, Jan 1983	2.00
❑377, Apr 1983	2.00
❑378, Jul 1983	2.00
❑379, Oct 1983	2.00
❑380, Dec 1983	2.00
❑381, Feb 1984	2.00
❑382, Apr 1984	2.00
❑383, Jun 1984	2.00
❑384, Aug 1984	2.00
❑385, Oct 1984	2.00
❑386, Dec 1984	2.00
❑387, Feb 1985	2.00
❑388, Apr 1985	2.00
❑389, Jun 1985	2.00
❑390, Aug 1985	2.00
❑391, Oct 1985	2.00
❑392, Dec 1985	2.00
❑393, Feb 1986	2.00
❑394, Apr 1986	2.00
❑395, Jun 1986	2.00
❑396, Aug 1986	2.00
❑397, Oct 1986	2.00
❑398, Dec 1986	2.00
❑399, Feb 1987, Circ figs are provided in Laugh, Vol. 2	2.00
❑400, Apr 1987, Circ figs are provided in Laugh, Vol. 2	2.00

Laugh Digest Magazine
Archie

	N-MINT
❑1, Aug 1974, NA (a)	10.00
❑2, Jan 1976	8.00
❑3, Mar 1976	8.00
❑4, May 1976	8.00
❑5, Jul 1976	8.00
❑6, Sep 1976	4.00
❑7, Nov 1976	4.00
❑8, Jan 1977	4.00
❑9, Mar 1977	4.00
❑10, May 1977	4.00
❑11, Jul 1977	3.00
❑12, Sep 1977	3.00
❑13, Nov 1977	3.00
❑14, Jan 1978	3.00
❑15, Mar 1978	3.00
❑16, May 1978	3.00
❑17, Jul 1978	3.00
❑18, Sep 1978	3.00
❑19, Nov 1978	3.00
❑20, Jan 1979	3.00
❑21, Mar 1979	2.00
❑22, May 1979	2.00
❑23, Jul 1979	2.00
❑24, Sep 1979	2.00
❑25, Nov 1979	2.00
❑26, Jan 1980	2.00
❑27, Mar 1980	2.00
❑28, May 1980	2.00
❑29, Jul 1980	2.00
❑30, Sep 1980	2.00
❑31, Nov 1980	2.00
❑32, Jan 1981	2.00
❑33, Mar 1981	2.00
❑34, May 1981	2.00
❑35, Jul 1981	2.00
❑36, Sep 1981	2.00
❑37, Nov 1981	2.00
❑38, Jan 1982	2.00
❑39, Mar 1982	2.00
❑40, May 1982	2.00
❑41, Jul 1982	1.50
❑42, Sep 1982	1.50
❑43, Nov 1982	1.50
❑44, Jan 1983	1.50
❑45, Mar 1983	1.50
❑46, May 1983	1.50
❑47, Jul 1983	1.50
❑48, Sep 1983	1.50
❑49, Nov 1983	1.50
❑50, Jan 1984	1.50
❑51, Mar 1984	1.50
❑52, May 1984	1.50
❑53, Jul 1984	1.50
❑54, Sep 1984	1.50
❑55, Nov 1984	1.50
❑56, Jan 1985	1.50
❑57, Mar 1985	1.50
❑58, May 1985	1.50
❑59, Jul 1985	1.50
❑60, Sep 1985	1.50
❑61, Nov 1985	1.50
❑62, Jan 1986	1.50
❑63, Mar 1986	1.50
❑64, May 1986	1.50
❑65, Jul 1986	1.50
❑66, Sep 1986	1.50
❑67, Nov 1986	1.50
❑68, Jan 1987	1.50
❑69, Mar 1987	1.50
❑70, May 1987	1.50
❑71, Jul 1987	1.50
❑72, Sep 1987	1.50
❑73, Nov 1987	1.50
❑74, Jan 1988	1.50
❑75, Mar 1988	1.50
❑76, May 1988	1.50
❑77, Jul 1988	1.50
❑78, Sep 1988	1.50
❑79, Nov 1988	1.50
❑80, Jan 1989	1.50
❑81, Mar 1989	1.50
❑82, May 1989	1.50
❑83, Jul 1989	1.50
❑84, Sep 1989	1.50
❑85, Nov 1989	1.50
❑86, Jan 1990	1.50
❑87, Mar 1990	1.50
❑88, May 1990	1.50
❑89, Jul 1990	1.50
❑90, Sep 1990	1.50
❑91, Nov 1990	1.50
❑92, Jan 1991	1.50
❑93, Mar 1991	1.50
❑94, ca. 1991	1.50
❑95, ca. 1991	1.50
❑96, ca. 1991	1.50
❑97, ca. 1991	1.50
❑98	1.50
❑99, ca. 1992	1.50
❑100, ca. 1992	1.50
❑101, ca. 1992	1.50
❑102, ca. 1992	1.50
❑103, ca. 1992	1.50
❑104, ca. 1992	1.50
❑105, ca. 1992	1.50
❑106, ca. 1993	1.50
❑107, May 1993	1.50
❑108, Jul 1993	1.50
❑109, Sep 1993	1.50
❑110, Nov 1993	1.50
❑111, Dec 1994	1.50
❑112, Feb 1994	1.50
❑113, ca. 1994	1.50
❑114, ca. 1994	1.50
❑115, ca. 1994	1.50
❑116, ca. 1994	1.50
❑117, Nov 1994	1.75
❑118, Jan 1995	1.75
❑119, Mar 1995	1.75
❑120, May 1995	1.75
❑121, Jul 1995	1.75
❑122, Sep 1995	1.75
❑123, Nov 1995	1.75
❑124, Dec 1995	1.75
❑125, Feb 1996	1.75
❑126, Apr 1996	1.75
❑127, May 1996	1.75
❑128, Jul 1996	1.75
❑129, Sep 1996	1.79
❑130, Oct 1996	1.79
❑131, Dec 1996	1.79
❑132, Feb 1997	1.79
❑133, Apr 1997	1.79
❑134, May 1997	1.79
❑135, Jul 1997	1.79
❑136, Sep 1997	1.79
❑137, Oct 1997	1.79
❑138, Dec 1997	1.79
❑139, Jan 1998	1.95
❑140, Mar 1998	1.95
❑141, May 1998	1.95
❑142, Jul 1998	1.95
❑143, Aug 1998	1.95
❑144, Oct 1998	1.95
❑145, Nov 1998, DDC (a)	1.95
❑146, Jan 1999	1.95
❑147, Mar 1999	1.95
❑148, Apr 1999	1.99
❑149, May 1999	1.99
❑150, Jul 1999	1.99
❑151, Aug 1999	1.99
❑152, Oct 1999	1.99
❑153, Nov 1999	1.99
❑154, Jan 2000	1.99
❑155, Mar 2000	1.99
❑156, May 2000	1.99
❑157, Jul 2000	2.19
❑158, Aug 2000	2.19
❑159, Oct 2000	2.19
❑160, Nov 2000	2.19
❑161, Dec 2000	2.19
❑162, Jan 2001	2.19
❑163, Feb 2001	2.19
❑164, Apr 2001	2.19
❑165, May 2001	2.19
❑166, Jul 2001	2.19
❑167, Aug 2001	2.19
❑168, Oct 2001	2.19
❑169, Nov 2001	2.19
❑170, Dec 2001	2.19
❑171, Jan 2002	2.19
❑172, Mar 2002	2.19
❑173, May 2002	2.19
❑174, Jul 2002	2.19
❑175, Aug 2002	2.19
❑176, Sep 2002	2.19
❑177, Nov 2002	2.19
❑178, Dec 2002	2.19
❑179, Jan 2003	2.19
❑180, Feb 2003	2.39
❑181, Mar 2003	2.39
❑182, May 2003	2.39
❑183, Jun 2003	2.39
❑184, Jul 2003	2.39
❑185, Sep 2003	2.39
❑186, Oct 2003	2.39
❑187, Nov 2003	2.39

Other grades: Multiply price above by 5/6 for VF/NM • 2/3 for VERY FINE • 1/3 for FINE • 1/5 for VERY GOOD • 1/8 for GOOD

L.A.W., The (Living Assault Weapons)

DC's Charlton heroes team again
©DC

League of Champions

Heroic heroes join forces
©Hero

League of Extraordinary Gentlemen

Victorian lit legends face threats
©DC

League of Super Groovy Crimefighters

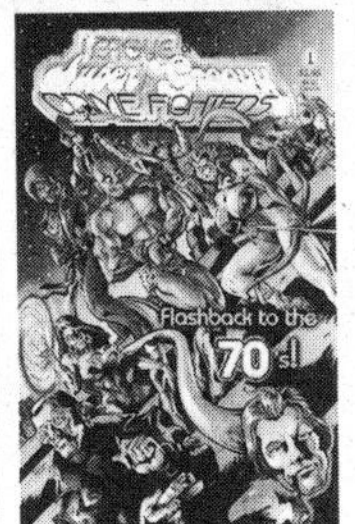

1970s comics ad items give losers powers
©Ancient

Leave It to Chance

Monster hunter's daughter faces own perils
©Image

N-MINT

❑188, Dec 2003 2.39
❑189, Feb 2004 2.39
❑190, Mar 2004 2.39
❑191, May 2004 2.39
❑192, Jun 2004 2.39
❑193, Jul 2004 2.39
❑194, Aug 2004 2.39
❑195, Sep 2004 2.39
❑196, Oct 2004 2.39
❑197, Nov 2004 2.39
❑198, Dec 2004 2.39
❑199, Jan 2005 2.39
❑200, Feb 2005 2.39

Launch!
Elsewhere

❑1; 1: Conscience 1.75

Laundryland
Fantagraphics

❑1, b&w 2.25
❑2, Jun 1991, b&w 2.50
❑3, b&w 2.50
❑4, b&w 2.50

Laurel and Hardy
Gold Key

❑1, Jan 1967 24.00
❑2, Oct 1967 18.00

Laurel and Hardy
DC

❑1, Aug 1972 40.00

Laurel & Hardy in 3-D
Blackthorne

❑1, Fal 1987; aka Blackthorne 3-D #23 2.50
❑2, Dec 1987; aka Blackthorne 3-D #34. 2.50

Lava
Crossbreed

❑1 2.95

Law
Asylum Graphics

❑1, b&w; no publication date 1.75

Law and Order
Maximum

❑1, Sep 1995; O: Law and Order 2.50
❑1/A, Sep 1995; Alternate cover with women standing atop body 2.50
❑2, Oct 1995 2.50
❑3, Nov 1995 2.50

Lawdog
Marvel / Epic

❑1, May 1993, Embossed cover 2.50
❑2, Jun 1993 1.95
❑3, Jul 1993 1.95
❑4, Aug 1993 1.95
❑5, Sep 1993 1.95
❑6, Oct 1993 1.95
❑7, Nov 1993 1.95
❑8, Dec 1993, trading card 1.95
❑9, Jan 1994, Trading card 1.95
❑10, Feb 1994, Final Issue 1.95

Lawdog and Grimrod: Terror at the Crossroads
Marvel / Epic

❑1, Sep 1993; Includes trading card 3.50

N-MINT

L.A.W. (Living Assault Weapons)
DC

❑1, Sep 1999 2.50
❑2, Oct 1999 2.50
❑3, Nov 1999 2.50
❑4, Dec 1999 2.50
❑5, Jan 2000 2.50
❑6, Feb 2000 2.50

Law of Dredd
Fleetway-Quality

❑1; BB (a); Reprints Judge Dredd stories from 2000 A.D. #149- 1.50
❑2 1.50
❑3 V: Judge Death 1.50
❑4 1.50
❑5 1.50
❑6 1.50
❑7 1.50
❑8 1.50
❑9 1.75
❑10 1.75
❑11 1.75
❑12 1.75
❑13 A: Judge Caligula 1.75
❑14 1.75
❑15 1.75
❑16 1.75
❑17 1.75
❑18 1.75
❑19 1.75
❑20 1.75
❑21 1.75
❑22 1.75
❑23 1.75
❑24 1.75
❑25 1.75
❑26 1.75
❑27 1.75
❑28 1.75
❑29 1.75
❑30 1.95
❑31 1.95
❑32 1.95
❑33 1.95

Lazarus Churchyard
Tundra

❑1 4.50
❑2 4.50
❑3 4.95

Lazarus Five
DC

❑1, Jul 2000 2.50
❑2, Aug 2000 2.50
❑3, Sep 2000 2.50
❑4, Oct 2000 2.50
❑5, Nov 2000 2.50

Lazarus Pits
Boneyard

❑1, Feb 1993, b&w pin-ups, cardstock cover 4.00

Leaf
Nab

❑1 1.95

N-MINT

❑1/Deluxe 4.95
❑2 1.95

League of Champions
Hero

❑1, Dec 1990; League of Champions: Continued from Champions #12; Sparkplug: Continued from Captain Thunder and Blue Bolt #10 3.00
❑2, Feb 1991; O: Malice (true origin); Giant: Continued from Champions Anl #1; O: Malice 3.00
❑3, Apr 1991; League of Champions; Madam Synn; Flare 3.00
❑4, Aug 1992, b&w; Sparkplug: continued fom League of Champions #1; League of Champions 3.50
❑5, Sep 1992, b&w; O: Flare; Marksman; Icicle; League of Champions 3.50
❑6, Oct 1992, b&w; League of Champions; Marksman 3.50
❑7, Nov 1992, b&w; A: Southern Knights. League of Champions; Marksman; Flare 3.50
❑8, Dec 1992, b&w 3.50
❑9, Jan 1993, b&w; League of Champions; Rose 3.50
❑10, Mar 1993, b&w; Rose; Icestar 3.50
❑11, May 1993, b&w; League of Champions; Mr. No; Bagged with trading card 3.95
❑12, Jul 1993; League of Champions; Soliloquy Jones; b&w 2.95

League of Extraordinary Gentlemen
DC / America's Best Comics

❑1, Mar 1999 AMo (w) 8.00
❑1/A, Apr 1999; AMo (w); DF Alternate; 5000 copies 5.00
❑2, Apr 1999 AMo (w) 5.00
❑3, Jun 1999; AMo (w); Cover says May, indicia says June 4.00
❑4, Nov 1999 AMo (w) 4.00
❑5, Jun 2000 AMo (w) 4.00
❑5/A, Jun 2000; AMo (w); Contained fake ad for The Marvel; All but est. 200 destroyed by DC 65.00
❑6, Sep 2000 AMo (w) 4.00

League of Extraordinary Gentlemen
America's Best

❑1, Sep 2002 4.00
❑2, Oct 2002 3.50
❑3, Nov 2002 3.50
❑4, Feb 2003, AMo (w) 3.50
❑5, Jul 2003 3.50
❑6, Nov 2003 3.50

League of Justice
DC

❑1, Jan 1996, prestige format; Elseworlds 5.95
❑2, Feb 1996, prestige format; Elseworlds 5.95

League of Rats
Caliber / Tome

❑1, b&w 2.95

Other grades: Multiply price above by 5/6 for VF/NM • 2/3 for VERY FINE • 1/3 for FINE • 1/5 for VERY GOOD • 1/8 for GOOD

League of Super Groovy Crimefighters
Ancient

❑1, Jun 2000; 1: Atlas (crimefighter); 1: Black Belt; 1: Cupid; 1: Mr. Phenomenal; 1: The Ring; 1: Thor (Crimefighter); 1: X 2.95
❑2, Dec 2000, b&w 2.95
❑3 2001, b&w 2.95
❑4, May 2001, b&w; published after #3, but dated before 2.95
❑5 2001 .... 2.95

Leather & Lace
Aircel

❑1/A, Aug 1989, b&w; Adult version 2.50
❑1/B, Aug 1989, b&w; Tame version 1.95
❑2/A, Sep 1989, b&w; Adult version 2.50
❑2/B, Sep 1989, b&w; Tame version 1.95
❑3/A, Oct 1989, b&w; Adult version 2.50
❑3/B, Oct 1989, b&w; Tame version 1.95
❑4/A, Nov 1989, b&w; Adult version 2.50
❑4/B, Nov 1989, b&w; Tame version 1.95
❑5/A, Dec 1989, b&w; Adult version 2.50
❑5/B, Dec 1989, b&w; Tame version 1.95
❑6/A, Jan 1990, b&w; Adult version 2.50
❑6/B, Jan 1990, b&w; Tame version 1.95
❑7/A, Feb 1990, b&w; Adult version 2.50
❑7/B, Feb 1990, b&w; Tame version 1.95
❑8/A, Mar 1990, b&w; Adult version 2.50
❑8/B, Mar 1990, b&w; Tame version 1.95
❑9, Apr 1990, b&w; Adult 2.50
❑10, May 1990, b&w; Adult 2.50
❑11, Jun 1990, b&w; Adult 2.50
❑12, Jul 1990, b&w; Adult 2.50
❑13, Aug 1990, b&w; Adult 2.50
❑14, Sep 1990, b&w; Adult 2.50
❑15, Oct 1990, b&w; Adult 2.50
❑16, Nov 1990, b&w; Adult 2.50
❑17, Dec 1990, b&w; Adult 2.50
❑18, Jan 1991, b&w; Adult 2.50
❑19, Feb 1991, b&w; Adult 2.50
❑20, Mar 1991, b&w; Adult 2.50
❑21, Apr 1991, b&w; Adult 2.50
❑22, May 1991, b&w; Adult 2.95
❑23, Jun 1991, b&w; Adult 2.95
❑24, Jul 1991, b&w; Adult 2.95
❑25, Aug 1991, b&w; Final Issue; Adult. 2.95

Leather & Lace: Blood, Sex, & Tears
Aircel

❑1, Oct 1991, b&w; Adult 2.95
❑2, Nov 1991, b&w; Adult 2.95
❑3, Dec 1991, b&w; Adult 2.95
❑4, Jan 1992; Adult 2.95

Leather & Lace Summer Special
Aircel

❑1, Jun 1990, b&w; Adult 2.50

Leatherboy
Fantagraphics / Eros

❑1, Jul 1994; Adult 2.95
❑2, Oct 1994; Adult 2.95
❑3, Nov 1994; Adult 2.95

Leatherface
Arpad

❑1, Apr 1991 .... 2.75

Leather Underwear
Fantagraphics

❑1, b&w 2.50

Leave it to Beaver
Dell

❑-207, Jul 1962, No number; cover says 01-428-207; previous issues appeared as Dell Four Color (2nd Series) #912, #999, #1103, #1191, and #1285 .... 100.00

Leave It to Chance
Image

❑1, Sep 1996 JRo (w); PS (a) 3.00
❑1/2nd, Sep 1996; JRo (w); PS (a); 2nd printing 2.50
❑2, Oct 1996 JRo (w); PS (a) 3.00
❑3, Nov 1996 PS (c); JRo (w); PS (a) 3.00
❑4, Feb 1997 PS (c); JRo (w); PS (a) 3.00
❑5, May 1997 JRo (w); PS (a) 3.00
❑6, Jul 1997 PS (c); JRo (w); PS (a) 2.50
❑7, Oct 1997 PS (c); JRo (w); PS (a) 2.50
❑8, Feb 1998 PS (c); JRo (w); PS (a) 2.50
❑9, Apr 1998 PS (c); JRo (w); PS (a) 2.50
❑10, Jun 1998 PS (c); JRo (w); PS (a) .. 2.50
❑11, Sep 1998 PS (c); JRo (w); PS (a) .. 2.95
❑13, Jul 2002; JRo (w); PS (a); Published by Image 4.95
❑12, Jun 1999; PS (c); JRo (w); PS (a); Final issue of original run (1999) 2.95

Led Zeppelin
Personality

❑1, b&w 2.95
❑2, b&w 2.95
❑3, b&w 2.95
❑4, b&w 2.95

Led Zeppelin Experience
Revolutionary

❑1, Aug 1992, b&w 2.50
❑2, Oct 1992, b&w 2.50
❑3, Dec 1992, b&w 2.50
❑4, Jan 1993, b&w 2.50
❑5, Feb 1993, b&w 2.50

Left-Field Funnies
Apex Novelties

❑1, Adult; ca. 1972 .... 4.00

Legacy
Majestic

❑0, Aug 1993 .... 2.25
❑0/Gold, Aug 1993, gold 2.25
❑1, Oct 1993, Glow-in-the-dark cover 2.25
❑2, Jan 1994 .... 2.25

Legacy
Antarctic

❑1, Aug 1999 .... 2.99

Legacy
Image

❑1, May 2003 .... 2.95
❑2, Jul 2003 .... 2.95
❑3, Nov 2003 .... 2.95
❑4, Apr 2004 .... 2.95

Legacy of Kain: Defiance One Shot
Image

❑1, Jan 2004 .... 2.99

Legacy of Kain: Soul Reaver
Top Cow

❑1, Oct 1999 .... 2.00

Legend
DC

❑1, May 2005 .... 5.95
❑2, Jun 2005 .... 5.99
❑3, Jun 2005 .... 5.99

Legend Lore
Arrow

❑1, b&w 2.00
❑2, b&w 2.00

Legendlore
Caliber

❑1 .... 2.95
❑2 .... 2.95
❑3 .... 2.95
❑4 .... 2.95

LegendLore: Wrath of the Dragon
Caliber

❑1; A.k.a. LegendLore #13 .... 2.95
❑2; A.k.a. LegendLore #14 .... 2.95

Legend of Isis
Alias

❑1, May 2005 .... 4.00
❑1/B cover, May 2005 .... 3.00
❑1/C cover, May 2005 .... 4.00
❑2, Jun 2005 .... 2.99
❑2/B cover, Jun 2005 .... 4.00
❑3, Sep 2005 .... 2.99
❑3/B cover, Sep 2005 .... 4.00
❑4, Nov 2005 .... 2.99
❑5, Dec 2005 .... 2.99
❑6, ca. 2005 .... 2.99
❑7, Jan 2006 .... 2.99

Legend of Jedit Ojanen on the World of Magic: The Gathering
Acclaim / Armada

❑1, Mar 1996; polybagged with card 2.50
❑2, Apr 1996; Final Issue 2.50

Legend of Jesse James
Gold Key

❑1, Feb 1966 .... 24.00

Legend of Kamui
Eclipse / Viz

❑1, May 1987, b&w; Japanese 3.00
❑1/2nd; 2nd printing 1.50
❑2, Jun 1987 .... 2.00
❑2/2nd; 2nd printing 1.50
❑3, Jun 1987 .... 2.00
❑3/2nd 1.50
❑4, Jul 1987 .... 1.50
❑5, Jul 1987 .... 1.50
❑6, Aug 1987 .... 1.50
❑7, Aug 1987 .... 1.50
❑8, Sep 1987 .... 1.50
❑9, Sep 1987 .... 1.50
❑10, Oct 1987 .... 1.50
❑11, Oct 1987 .... 1.50
❑12, Nov 1987 .... 1.50
❑13, Nov 1987 .... 1.50
❑14, Dec 1987 .... 1.50
❑15, Dec 1987 .... 1.50
❑16, Jan 1988 .... 1.50
❑17, Jan 1988 .... 1.50
❑18, Feb 1988; 48 pages 1.50
❑19, Feb 1988 .... 1.50
❑20, Mar 1988 .... 1.50
❑21, Mar 1988 .... 1.50
❑22, Apr 1988 .... 1.50
❑23, Apr 1988 .... 1.50
❑24, May 1988 .... 1.50
❑25, May 1988 .... 1.50
❑26, Jun 1988 .... 1.50
❑27, Jun 1988 .... 1.50
❑28, Jul 1988 .... 1.50
❑29, Jul 1988 .... 1.50
❑30, Aug 1988 .... 1.50
❑31, Aug 1988 .... 1.50
❑32, Sep 1988 .... 1.50
❑33, Sep 1988 .... 1.50
❑34, Oct 1988 .... 1.50
❑35, Oct 1988 .... 1.50
❑36, Nov 1988 .... 1.50
❑37, Nov 1988; Final Issue 1.50

Legend of Lemnear
CPM

❑1, Jan 1998; wraparound cover 3.00
❑2, Feb 1998 .... 3.00
❑3, Mar 1998 .... 3.00
❑4, Apr 1998 .... 3.00
❑5, May 1998 .... 3.00
❑6, Jun 1998; wraparound cover 3.00
❑7, Jul 1998; wraparound cover 3.00
❑8, Aug 1998 .... 2.95
❑9, Sep 1998 .... 2.95
❑10, Oct 1998 .... 2.95
❑11, Nov 1998 .... 2.95
❑12, Dec 1998 .... 2.95
❑13, Jan 1999; wraparound cover 2.95
❑14, Feb 1999 .... 2.95

Legend of Lilith
Image

❑0; no date 4.95

Legend of Mother Sarah
Dark Horse / Manga

❑1, Apr 1995, b&w 3.50
❑2, May 1995, b&w 3.00
❑3, Jun 1995, b&w 3.00
❑4, Jul 1995, b&w 2.50
❑5, Aug 1995, b&w 2.50
❑6, Sep 1995, b&w 2.50
❑7, Oct 1995, b&w 2.50
❑8, Nov 1995, b&w; Final Issue 2.50

Legend of Mother Sarah: City of the Angels
Dark Horse / Manga

❑1, Oct 1997 .... 3.95
❑2, Dec 1997 .... 3.95
❑3, Jan 1998 .... 3.95
❑4, Feb 1998 .... 3.95
❑5, Mar 1998 .... 3.95
❑6, Apr 1998 .... 3.95
❑7, May 1998 .... 3.95

Other grades: Multiply price above by 5/6 for VF/NM • 2/3 for VERY FINE • 1/3 for FINE • 1/5 for VERY GOOD • 1/8 for GOOD

Led Zeppelin Experience

Unauthorized bio series of British rockers
©Revolutionary

Legend of the Shield, The

Early Archie super-hero gets revamp
©DC

Legends

Becomes unlawful for heroes to take action
©DC

Legends of the DC Universe

Rotates creative teams and characters
©DC

L.E.G.I.O.N.

Acronym title changed annually as year turned
©DC

N-MINT

❑8, Jun 1998 .... 3.95
❑9, Jul 1998 .... 3.95

Legend of Mother Sarah, The: City of the Children
Dark Horse / Manga

❑1, Jan 1996 .... 3.95
❑2, Feb 1996 .... 3.95
❑3, Mar 1996 .... 3.95
❑4, Apr 1996 .... 3.95
❑5, May 1996 .... 3.95
❑6, Jun 1996 .... 3.95
❑7, Jul 1996 .... 3.95

Legend of Sleepy Hollow
Tundra

❑1; NN; Comics adaptation of The Legend of Sleepy Hollow by Washington Irving 6.95

Legend of Supreme
Image

❑1, Dec 1994; O: Supreme 2.50
❑2, Jan 1995; O: Supreme 2.50
❑3, Feb 1995; O: Supreme 2.50

Legend of the Elflord
Davdez

❑1, Jul 1998 .... 2.95
❑2, Sep 1998 .... 2.95
❑3 .... 2.95

Legend of the Hawkman
DC

❑1 2000; ca. 2000 .... 4.95
❑2 2000; ca. 2000 .... 4.95
❑3 2000; ca. 2000 .... 4.95

Legend of the Shield
DC / Impact

❑1, Jul 1991; O: Shield 1.50
❑2, Aug 1991 .... 1.00
❑3, Sep 1991; 1: Bert Watson; 1: Millie Mazda; 1: The Black Hood (Wayne Sidmonson); 1: The Weapon 1.00
❑4, Oct 1991; V: Weapon 1.00
❑5, Nov 1991; 1: Dusty Madigan 1.00
❑6, Dec 1991; 1: Theo Carver 1.00
❑7, Jan 1992 .... 1.00
❑8, Feb 1992; 1: The Shield I (Roger Higgins); V: Weapon 1.00
❑9, Mar 1992 .... 1.00
❑10, Apr 1992; Includes Trading Card 1.00
❑11, May 1992; trading card 1.00
❑12, Jun 1992 .... 1.00
❑13, Jul 1992 .... 1.00
❑14, Aug 1992 .... 1.00
❑15, Sep 1992 .... 1.00
❑16, Oct 1992; Final Issue 1.00
❑Ann 1; Includes trading card 2.50

Legend of Wonder Woman
DC

❑1, May 1986 KB (w) 1.50
❑2, Jun 1986 KB (w) 1.50
❑3, Jul 1986 KB (w) 1.50
❑4, Aug 1986 KB (w) 1.50

Legend of Young Dick Turpin
Gold Key

❑1, May 1966 .... 16.00

N-MINT

Legend of Zelda
Valiant

❑1, ca. 1990 .... 1.95
❑2, ca. 1990 .... 1.95
❑3, ca. 1990 .... 1.95
❑4, ca. 1990 .... 1.95
❑5, ca. 1990 .... 1.95

Legend of Zelda
Valiant

❑1, ca. 1990 .... 1.50
❑2, ca. 1990 .... 1.50
❑3, ca. 1990 .... 1.50
❑4, ca. 1990 .... 1.50
❑5, ca. 1990 .... 1.50

Legends
DC

❑1, Nov 1986; JBy (c); JBy (a); 1: Amanda Waller 2.00
❑2, Dec 1986 JBy (c); JBy (a) 1.50
❑3, Jan 1987; JBy (c); JBy (a); 1: Suicide Squad (modern) 2.00
❑4, Feb 1987 JBy (c); JBy (a) 1.50
❑5, Mar 1987 JBy (c); JBy (a) 1.50
❑6, Apr 1987; JBy (c); JBy (a); 1: Justice League 3.00

Legends and Folklore
Zone

❑1, Jul 1992, b&w 3.95
❑2, ca. 1992, b&w 2.95

Legends from Darkwood
Antarctic

❑1, Nov 2003; b&w 3.50
❑2, Jan 2004; b&w 3.50
❑3, Feb 2004; b&w 3.50

Legends from Darkwood: Summer Fun Special
Antarctic

❑0, Jun 2005 .... 2.99

Legends of Elfinwild
Wehner

❑1, b&w 1.75

Legends of Kid Death & Fluffy
Event

❑1, Feb 1997 .... 2.95

Legends of Luxura
Brainstorm

❑1, Feb 1996, b&w; collects Luxura stories 2.95
❑1/Ltd., Feb 1996; Special edition; no cover price; limited to 1000 copies 4.00

Legends of NASCAR
Vortex

❑1; Bill Elliott 3.50
❑1/2nd; Bill Elliott 2.00
❑1/3rd; Bill Elliott; Indicia marks it as 2nd Printing 3.00
❑2; Richard Petty; no indicia 2.00
❑2/Variant; hologram 3.00
❑3; Ken Shrader 2.00
❑4; Bobby Allison 2.00
❑5; Sterling Marlin 2.00
❑6 .... 2.00
❑7 .... 2.00

N-MINT

❑8; Benny Parsons 2.00
❑9; Rusty Wallace 2.00
❑10; Talladega Story 2.00
❑11; Morgan Shepherd 2.00
❑12 .... 2.00
❑13 .... 2.00
❑14 .... 2.00
❑15 .... 2.00
❑16; Final issue (?) 2.00

Legends of the Dark Claw
DC / Amalgam

❑1, Apr 1996; O: The Hyena. O: The Dark Claw 2.00

Legends of the DCU: Crisis on Infinite Earths
DC

❑1, Feb 1999; A: Flash II (Barry Allen). A: Supergirl. Takes place between Crisis on Infinite Earths #4 and #5 .... 4.95

Legends of the DC Universe
DC

❑1, Feb 1998; JRo (w); Superman 3.00
❑2, Mar 1998; JRo (w); Superman 2.50
❑3, Apr 1998; JRo (w); Superman 2.50
❑4, May 1998; SR (c);Wonder Woman 2.50
❑5, Jun 1998; Wonder Woman 2.50
❑6, Jul 1998; KN (a); Robin, Superman 2.25
❑7, Aug 1998; Green Lantern/Green Arrow 2.25
❑8, Sep 1998; Green Lantern/Green Arrow 2.25
❑9, Oct 1998; Green Lantern/Green Arrow 2.25
❑10, Nov 1998; O: Oracle. Batgirl 2.25
❑11, Dec 1998; O: Oracle. Batgirl 2.25
❑12, Jan 1999; JLA 2.25
❑13, Feb 1999; JLA 2.25
❑14, Mar 1999 SR (c); JK, ME (w); SR (a); A: Jimmy Olsen. A: Simyan. A: Superman. A: Darkseid. A: Guardian. A: Mokkari 2.25
❑15, Apr 1999 A: Flash II (Barry Allen). 2.25
❑16, May 1999 A: Flash II (Barry Allen). 2.25
❑17, Jun 1999 A: Flash II (Barry Allen). 2.25
❑18, Jul 1999; BG (a); Kid Flash, Raven 2.25
❑19, Aug 1999; Impulse; prelude to JLApe Anns 2.25
❑20, Sep 1999; MZ (a); Green Lantern: Abin Sur 2.25
❑21, Oct 1999; MZ (a); Green Lantern: Abin Sur 1.99
❑22, Nov 1999 SR (c) 1.99
❑23, Dec 1999 SR (c) 1.99
❑24, Jan 2000; Hunger Dog hunts a vandal on Apokolips 1.99
❑25, Feb 2000; Darkseid; Hunger Dog hunts a vandal on Apokolips 1.99
❑26, Mar 2000 TVE (a) 1.99
❑27, Apr 2000; TVE (a); Joker; Aquaman; Batman 1.99
❑28, May 2000; ARo (c); GK, KJ (a); Green Lantern & Atom 1.99
❑29, Jun 2000; ARo (c); GK, KJ (a); Green Lantern & Atom 1.99
❑30, Jul 2000 .... 1.99
❑31, Aug 2000 .... 2.50
❑32, Sep 2000 .... 2.50
❑33, Oct 2000; Hal Jordan: The Spectre 2.50
❑34, Nov 2000; Hal Jordan: The Spectre 2.50

N-MINT

❑35, Dec 2000; Hal Jordan: The Spectre ... 2.50
❑36, Jan 2001; Hal Jordan: The Spectre ... 2.50
❑37, Feb 2001; Green Lantern: Kyle Rayner ... 2.50
❑38, Mar 2001; Green Lantern: Kyle Rayner ... 2.50
❑39, Apr 2001 KN (c) ... 2.50
❑40, May 2001 ... 2.50
❑41, Jun 2001; Final issue ... 2.50
❑GS 1, Sep 1998; Spectre, Hawkman, Teen Titans, Adam Strange, Chronos, Doom Patrol, Rip Hunter, Linear Men. ... 4.95
❑GS 2, Jan 2000 KJ (a) ... 4.95

Legends of the DC Universe 3-D Gallery
DC

❑1, Dec 1998; pin-ups ... 2.95

Legends of the Legion
DC

❑1, Feb 1998; O: Ultra Boy ... 2.25
❑2, Mar 1998; O: Spark ... 2.25
❑3, Apr 1998; O: Umbra ... 2.25
❑4, May 1998; O: Star Boy ... 2.25

Legends of the Living Dead
Fantaco

❑1 ... 3.95

Legends of the Stargrazers
Innovation

❑1, Aug 1989 ... 1.95
❑2, Sep 1989 ... 1.95
❑3, Dec 1989 ... 1.95
❑4, Feb 1990 ... 1.95
❑5, Apr 1990 ... 1.95
❑6, Jun 1990 ... 1.95

Legends of the World's Finest
DC

❑1, ca. 1994, Prestige format ... 6.00
❑2, ca. 1994, Prestige format ... 4.95
❑3, ca. 1994, Superman, Batman; Prestige format ... 4.95

Legendz
Viz

❑1, Mar 2005 ... 7.99
❑2, Jun 2005 ... 7.99
❑3, Nov 2005 ... 7.99

L.E.G.I.O.N.
DC

❑1, Feb 1989; KG (w); O: L.E.G.I.O.N.. 1: Stealth. L.E.G.I.O.N. '89 starts ... 2.50
❑2, Mar 1989 ... 2.00
❑3, Apr 1989 ... 2.00
❑4, May 1989 A: Lobo ... 2.00
❑5, Jun 1989; Lobo joins team ... 2.00
❑6, Jul 1989 ... 1.75
❑7, Aug 1989 ... 1.75
❑8, Sep 1989 ... 1.75
❑9, Nov 1989 A: Phantom Girl ... 1.75
❑10, Dec 1989 ... 1.75
❑11, Jan 1990; L.E.G.I.O.N. '90 starts ... 1.50
❑12, Feb 1990 A: Emerald Eye ... 1.50
❑13, Mar 1990 ... 1.50
❑14, Apr 1990; L.E.G.I.O.N 90 ... 1.50
❑15, May 1990; 1: Lydea Darkstar; Lobo infiltrates criminal organization ... 1.50
❑16, Jun 1990; A: Lar Gand. Valor (Lar Gand) joins LEGION; Lobo exposed by criminal organization ... 1.50
❑17, Jul 1990 ... 1.50
❑18, Aug 1990; Lady Quark joins LEGION; LEGION V: criminal organization ... 1.50
❑19, Sep 1990; V: Lydea Darkstar ... 1.50
❑20, Oct 1990 ... 1.50
❑21, Nov 1990; D: Lyrissa Mallor ... 1.50
❑22, Dec 1990 A: Lady Quark ... 1.50
❑23, Jan 1991; L.E.G.I.O.N. '91 starts ... 2.50
❑24, Feb 1991 ... 1.50
❑25, Mar 1991 ... 1.50
❑26, Apr 1991 ... 1.50
❑27, May 1991 ... 1.50
❑28, Jun 1991; KG (c); KG (w); KG (a); Stealth Gives Birth ... 1.50
❑29, Jul 1991 ... 1.50
❑30, Aug 1991; 1: Ig'nea ... 1.50
❑31, Sep 1991; Painted cover; Lobo vs. Captain Marvel; Lobo vs. Capt. Marvel ... 1.50
❑32, Oct 1991; 1: Ice Man ... 1.50

N-MINT

❑33, Nov 1991 ... 1.50
❑34, Dec 1991 ... 1.50
❑35, Jan 1992; L.E.G.I.O.N. '92 starts ... 1.50
❑36, Feb 1992 ... 1.50
❑37, Mar 1992 ... 1.50
❑38, Apr 1992 ... 1.50
❑39, May 1992 ... 1.50
❑40, Jun 1992 ... 1.50
❑41, Jul 1992 ... 1.50
❑42, Jul 1992 ... 1.50
❑43, Aug 1992 ... 1.50
❑44, Aug 1992 ... 1.50
❑45, Sep 1992 ... 1.50
❑46, Nov 1992; V: alien-possessed Captain Comet ... 1.50
❑47, Dec 1992; Lobo vs. Green Lantern (Hal Jordan) ... 1.50
❑48, Jan 1993; L.E.G.I.O.N. '93 starts ... 1.50
❑49, Feb 1993 MWa (w) ... 1.75
❑50, Mar 1993; Double-size; L.E.G.I.O.N. '67 back-up ... 3.50
❑51, Apr 1993 ... 1.75
❑52, May 1993 ... 1.75
❑53, Jun 1993 ... 1.75
❑54, Jun 1993 MWa (w) ... 1.75
❑55, Jul 1993 MWa (w) ... 1.75
❑56, Jul 1993 ... 1.75
❑57, Aug 1993; MWa (w); Continued from Green Lantern #44 (3rd Series) ... 1.75
❑58, Sep 1993; Continued from Green Lantern #45 (3rd Series) ... 1.75
❑59, Oct 1993 MWa (w) ... 1.75
❑60, Nov 1993 MWa (w) ... 1.75
❑61, Dec 1993 ... 1.75
❑62, Jan 1994; L.E.G.I.O.N. '94 starts ... 1.75
❑63, Feb 1994; L.E.G.I.O.N. '94 ... 1.75
❑64, Mar 1994 ... 1.75
❑65, Apr 1994 ... 1.75
❑66, May 1994 ... 1.75
❑67, Jun 1994 ... 1.75
❑68, Jul 1994 ... 1.75
❑69, Aug 1994 A: Ultra Boy ... 1.75
❑70, Sep 1994; Giant-size; Zero Hour; story continues in R.E.B.E.L.S. '94 #0; L.E.G.I.O.N. goes renegade (becomes R.E.B.E.L.S.) ... 2.50
❑Ann 1, ca. 1990; A: Superman. Vril Dox vs. Brainiac ... 4.00
❑Ann 2, ca. 1991; Armageddon 2001 ... 2.95
❑Ann 3, ca. 1992; Eclipso: The Darkness Within ... 2.95
❑Ann 4, ca. 1993; MWa (w); 1: Pax; 1993 Ann; Bloodlines: Deathstorm ... 3.50
❑Ann 5, ca. 1994; CS (a); Elseworlds; L.E.G.I.O.N. 007 ... 3.50

Legion
DC

❑1, Dec 2001 ... 3.00
❑2, Jan 2002 ... 2.50
❑3, Feb 2002 ... 2.50
❑4, Mar 2002 ... 2.50
❑5, Apr 2002 ... 2.50
❑6, May 2002 ... 2.50
❑7, Jun 2002 ... 2.50
❑8, Jul 2002 ... 2.50
❑9, Aug 2002 ... 2.50
❑10, Sep 2002 ... 2.50
❑11, Oct 2002 ... 2.50
❑12, Nov 2002; Legion vs. JLA ... 2.50
❑13, Dec 2002 ... 2.50
❑14, Jan 2003; Includes preview of H-E-R-O #1 ... 2.50
❑15, Feb 2003 ... 2.50
❑16, Mar 2003 ... 2.50
❑17, Apr 2003 ... 2.50
❑18, May 2003; Ra's Al Ghul app ... 2.50
❑19, Jun 2003 ... 2.50
❑20, Jul 2003 ... 2.50
❑21, Aug 2003 ... 2.50
❑22, Sep 2003 ... 2.50
❑23, Oct 2003 ... 2.50
❑24, Nov 2003, Spotlight on Umbra ... 2.50
❑25, Dec 2003, 48 Page 45 Years of Legion issue; Garth (Lightening Lad) Returns ... 3.95
❑26, Jan 2004, Superboy (Kon-El Joins Legion); V: Darkseid minions; Superman (Clark Kent) joins Darkseid minions; Superboy (Conner Kent) joins Legion ... 2.50

N-MINT

❑27, Jan 2004, V: Darkseid minions ... 2.50
❑28, Feb 2004, V: Darkseid minions; Darkseid (8th century) arrives in 31st century; Darkseid (31st century) returns ... 2.50
❑29, Mar 2004 ... 2.50
❑30, Apr 2004, (c); Conclusion ... 2.50
❑31, May 2004 ... 2.50
❑32, Jun 2004 ... 2.50
❑33, Jul 2004 ... 2.50
❑34, Aug 2004 ... 2.50
❑35, Sep 2004 ... 2.50
❑36, Sep 2004 ... 2.50
❑37, Oct 2004 ... 2.50
❑38, Oct 2004; Final Issue ... 2.50

Legion Anthology
Limelight

❑1, b&w; manga ... 2.95
❑2 ... 2.95

Legion Lost
DC

❑1, May 2000; 1: Shikari (Lonestar) ... 2.50
❑2, Jun 2000 ... 2.50
❑3, Jul 2000 ... 2.50
❑4, Aug 2000; Erg-1 becomes Wildfire ... 2.50
❑5, Sep 2000 ... 2.50
❑6, Oct 2000 ... 2.50
❑7, Nov 2000 ... 2.50
❑8, Dec 2000 ... 2.50
❑9, Jan 2001 ... 2.50
❑10, Feb 2001 ... 2.50
❑11, Mar 2001; D: Monstress ... 2.50
❑12, Apr 2001; D: Element Lad ... 2.50

Legion Manga Anthology
Limelight

❑1 ... 2.95
❑2 ... 2.95
❑3 ... 2.95
❑4 ... 2.95

Legionnaires
DC

❑0, Oct 1994; MWa (w); revised Legion origin; continues in Legion of Super-Heroes #62 and Legionnaires #19 ... 2.25
❑1, Apr 1993; with trading card ... 3.00
❑2, May 1993; V: Fatal Five. covers of issues #2-6 form one image ... 2.00
❑3, Jun 1993; V: Fatal Five ... 2.00
❑4, Jul 1993; V: Fatal Five ... 2.00
❑5, Aug 1993; V: Fatal Five ... 2.00
❑6, Sep 1993; V: Fatal Five ... 1.50
❑7, Oct 1993 ... 1.50
❑8, Nov 1993; Brainiac 5 leaves team ... 1.50
❑9, Dec 1993; Lightning Lad V: Cosmic Boy ... 1.50
❑10, Jan 1994 ... 1.50
❑11, Feb 1994; Kid Quantum joins team ... 1.50
❑12, Mar 1994 ... 1.50
❑13, Apr 1994; Matter-Eater Lad becomes a girl ... 1.50
❑14, May 1994 ... 1.50
❑15, Jun 1994 ... 1.50
❑16, Jul 1994; MWa (w); Return of Dream Girl ... 1.50
❑17, Aug 1994; MWa (w); End of an Era Conclusion ... 1.50
❑18, Sep 1994; MWa (w); Zero Hour ... 1.50
❑19, Nov 1994 MWa (w) ... 1.50
❑20, Dec 1994; V: Mano ... 1.50
❑21, Jan 1995; 1: Work Force ... 1.50
❑22, Feb 1995 ... 1.50
❑23, Mar 1995 ... 1.50
❑24, Apr 1995 ... 1.50
❑25, May 1995 ... 1.50
❑26, Jun 1995 ... 1.75
❑27, Jul 1995 ... 2.25
❑28, Aug 1995; 1: Legion Espionage Squad ... 2.25
❑29, Sep 1995; 1: Dirk Morgna ... 2.25
❑30, Oct 1995; Lightning Lad turning point ... 2.25
❑31, Nov 1995; Future Tense, Part 3; Superboy made honorary member; Valor released into 30th century ... 2.25
❑32, Dec 1995; A: Chronos. Underworld Unleashed ... 2.25
❑33, Jan 1996; Kinetix finds Emerald Eye; [L1996-2] ... 2.25

Legion	Legionnaires	Legion of Super-Heroes	Legion of Super-Heroes	Legion of Super-Heroes
				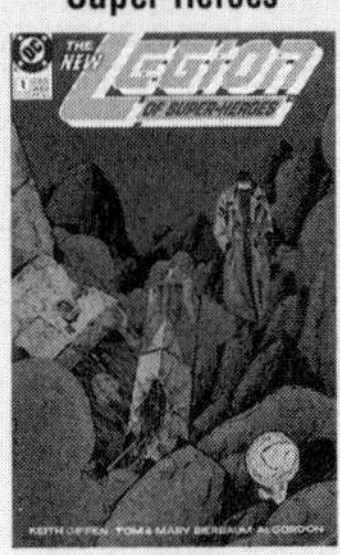
Shortened title resulted in three-year run ©DC	Futuristic teens defend domed cities ©DC	Quartet of reprint issues ©DC	Superboy leaves team and title ©DC	Keith Giffen shunts team five years ahead ©DC

	N-MINT
❑34, Feb 1996; [L1996-4]	2.25
❑35, Mar 1996; XS returns to 30th century; [L1996-6]	2.25
❑36, May 1996; [L1996-8]	2.25
❑37, Jun 1996; O: M'onel. [L1996-10]	2.25
❑38, Jul 1996; [L1996-12]	2.25
❑39, Aug 1996; Triad's three personalities become distinct; [L1996-14]	2.25
❑40, Sep 1996; [L1996-16]	2.25
❑41, Oct 1996; [L1996-18]	2.25
❑42, Nov 1996; [L1996-20]	2.25
❑43, Dec 1996; Legion try-outs; Magno joins team; Umbra joins team; Sensor joins team; [L1996-22]	2.25
❑44, Jan 1997; [L1997-1]	2.25
❑45, Feb 1997; V: Mantis Morlo. [L1997-3]	2.25
❑46, Mar 1997; [L1997-5]	2.25
❑47, Apr 1997; [L1997-7]	2.25
❑48, May 1997; V: Mordru. [L1997-9]	2.25
❑49, Jun 1997; A: Workforce. A: Heroes of Xanthu. D: Atom'x. V: Mordru. [L1997-11]	2.25
❑50, Jul 1997; Giant-size; V: Mordru. Poster; Mysa becomes young; [L1997-13]	3.95
❑51, Aug 1997; [L1997-15]	2.25
❑52, Sep 1997; Vi's new powers manifest; [L1997-17]	2.25
❑53, Oct 1997; Monstress joins team; Magno leaves team; [L1997-19]	2.25
❑54, Nov 1997; Golden Age story; [L1997-21]	2.25
❑55, Dec 1997; V: Composite Man. Face cover; [L1997-23]	2.25
❑56, Jan 1998; M'onel returns to Daxam; [L1998-1]	2.25
❑57, Feb 1998; [L1998-3]	2.25
❑58, Mar 1998; [L1998-5]	2.25
❑59, Apr 1998; [L1998-7]	2.25
❑60, May 1998; Chameleon leaves team; Sensor leaves team; Karate Kid joins team; Kid Quantum joins team; [L1998-9]	2.25
❑61, Jun 1998; A: Superman (from Time and Time Again). Multiple time shifts; [L1998-11]	2.25
❑62, Jul 1998; Dark Circle Rising, Part 1: Crossfire!; [L1998-13]	2.25
❑63, Aug 1998; Dark Circle Rising, Part 3: Resignation!; [L1998-15]	2.25
❑64, Sep 1998; Dark Circle Rising, Part 5: Enlightenment!; [L1998-17]	2.25
❑65, Oct 1998; Dark Circle falls; [L1998-19]	2.50
❑66, Dec 1998; 1: Charma. [L1998-21]	2.50
❑67, Jan 1999; A: Kono. [L1999-1]	2.50
❑68, Feb 1999; Monstress changes color; [L1999-3]	2.50
❑69, Mar 1999; A: Plasma. [L1999-5]	2.50
❑70, Apr 1999; Cosmic Boy vs. Domain; [L1999-7]	2.50
❑71, May 1999; V: Elements of Disaster. [L1999-9]	2.50
❑72, Jun 1999; [L1999-11]	2.50
❑73, Jul 1999; Star Boy solo; [L1999-13]	2.50
❑74, Aug 1999; [L1999-15]	2.50
❑75, Sep 1999; [L1999-17]	2.50
❑76, Oct 1999; O: Wildfire. [L1999-19]	2.50
❑77, Nov 1999; [L1999-21]	2.50
❑78, Dec 2000; [L1999-23]	2.50
❑79, Jan 2000; [L2000-1]	2.50
❑80, Feb 2000; [L2000-3]	2.50
❑1000000, Nov 1998; set 1, 000 years after events of One Million	4.00
❑Ann 1, ca. 1994; MWa (w); Elseworlds; Futuristic Camelot	5.00
❑Ann 2, ca. 1995; D: Apparition. Andromeda leaves team	3.95
❑Ann 3, ca. 1996; A: Barry Allen. Legends of the Dead Earth; XS' travels in time; 1996 Ann	2.95

Legionnaires Three
DC

	N-MINT
❑1, Feb 1986; KG (w); V: Time Trapper	1.25
❑2, Mar 1986; V: Time Trapper	1.00
❑3, Apr 1986; V: Time Trapper	1.00
❑4, May 1986; V: Time Trapper	1.00

Legion of Monsters
Marvel

	N-MINT
❑1, magazine, b&w	35.00

Legion of Night
Marvel

	N-MINT
❑1, Nov 1991; Adult	4.95
❑2, Dec 1991; Adult	4.95

Legion of Stupid Heroes
Alternate Concepts

	N-MINT
❑1, Jul 1997	2.50
❑2, Sep 1997	2.50
❑3	2.50
❑4, Mar 1998	2.50

Legion of Stupid Knights
Alternate Concepts

	N-MINT
❑Special 1, Feb 1998, b&w	2.50

Legion of Substitute Heroes Special
DC

	N-MINT
❑1; KG (c); KG (w); KG (a); ca. 1985	2.00

Legion of Super-Heroes
DC

	N-MINT
❑1, Feb 1973, Tales of the Legion of Super-Heroes; Tommy Tomorrow reprint	15.00
❑2, Mar 1973, Tales of the Legion of Super-Heroes; Tommy Tomorrow reprint	8.00
❑3, May 1973, V: Computo. Tales of the Legion of Super-Heroes; Tommy Tomorrow reprint	7.00
❑4, Aug 1973, V: Computo. Tales of the Legion of Super-Heroes; Tommy Tomorrow reprint	7.00

Legion of Super-Heroes
DC

	N-MINT
❑259, Jan 1980, Superboy leaves team; Continued from "Superboy and the Legion of Super-Heroes"	3.50
❑260, Feb 1980, V: Circus of Crime	2.75
❑261, Mar 1980, V: Circus of Crime	2.50
❑261/Whitman, Mar 1980, V: Circus of Crime. Whitman variant	5.00
❑262, Apr 1980	2.50
❑262/Whitman, Apr 1980, Whitman variant	5.00
❑263, May 1980	2.50
❑263/Whitman, May 1980, Whitman variant	5.00
❑264, Jun 1980	2.50
❑264/Whitman, Jun 1980, Whitman variant	5.00
❑265, Jul 1980, O: Tyroc. bonus Superman story starring the TRS-80 Computer Whiz Kids (Radio Shack sponsored story)	2.50
❑265/Whitman, Jul 1980, O: Tyroc. bonus Superman story starring the TRS-80 Computer Whiz Kids (Radio Shack sponsored story); Whitman variant	5.00
❑266, Aug 1980, Return of Bouncing Boy; Return of Duo Damsel	2.50
❑266/Whitman, Aug 1980, Return of Bouncing Boy; Return of Duo Damsel; Whitman variant	5.00
❑267, Sep 1980, O: Legion Flight Rings; Secret of the Legion Flight Rings	2.50
❑268, Oct 1980, GP (c); SD (a)	2.50
❑269, Nov 1980, V: Fatal Five	2.50
❑270, Dec 1980, Dark Man's identity revealed	2.50
❑271, Jan 1981, O: Dark Man	1.75
❑272, Feb 1981, O: Blok. 1: Dial 'H' for Hero (new). Blok joins Legion of Super-Heroes; Dial "H" For Hero preview story	1.75
❑273, Mar 1981	1.75
❑274, Apr 1981, RB (c); SD (a); Ultra Boy becomes pirate	1.75
❑275, May 1981	1.75
❑276, Jun 1981	1.75
❑277, Jul 1981, 1: Reflecto	1.75
❑278, Aug 1981, A: Reflecto. V: Grimbor. V: Grimbor	1.75
❑279, Sep 1981, Reflecto's identity revealed	1.75
❑280, Oct 1981, Superboy rejoins	1.75
❑281, Nov 1981, GP (c); SD (a); V: Molecule Master	1.75
❑282, Dec 1981, JA (c); O: Reflecto. Ultra Boy returns	1.75
❑283, Jan 1982, O: Wildfire. Wildfire story	1.75
❑284, Feb 1982	1.75
❑285, Mar 1982, KG, PB (a); Keith Giffen plots begin	2.50
❑286, Apr 1982, KG, PB (a); V: Doctor Regulus	2.00
❑287, May 1982, KG, PB (a); V: Kharlak	2.00
❑288, Jun 1982, KG (a)	2.00
❑289, Jul 1982, KG (c); Cl, KG (a)	2.00
❑290, Aug 1982, KG (a); Great Darkness Saga, Part 1	2.00
❑291, Sep 1982, KG (c); KG (a); Great Darkness Saga, Part 2	2.00
❑292, Oct 1982, KG (c); KG (a); Great Darkness Saga, Part 3	2.00
❑293, Nov 1982, KG (c); KG (w); KG (a); Great Darkness Saga, Part 4; Masters of the Universe preview story	2.00
❑294, Dec 1982; KG (c); KG (w); KG (a); Great Darkness Saga, Part 5; giant-size issue	2.00
❑295, Jan 1983, O: Universo (possible origin). A: Green Lantern Corps	1.50
❑296, Feb 1983, KG (c); KG (w); KG (a).	1.50
❑297, Mar 1983, O: Legion of Super-Heroes. Cosmic Boy solo story	3.00
❑298, Apr 1983, 1: Gemworld. 1: Dark Opal. 1: Amethyst. Amethyst, Princess of Gemworld preview story	1.50
❑299, May 1983, Invisible Kid II meets Invisible Kid I	1.50

Other grades: Multiply price above by 5/6 for VF/NM • 2/3 for VERY FINE • 1/3 for FINE • 1/5 for VERY GOOD • 1/8 for GOOD

	N-MINT
❑300, Jun 1983; Double-size; Tales of the Adult Legion; alternate futures	2.00
❑301, Jul 1983	1.50
❑302, Aug 1983, Lightning Lad vs. Lightning Lord	1.50
❑303, Sep 1983, V: Emerald Empress	1.50
❑304, Oct 1983, Legion Academy	1.50
❑305, Nov 1983, Shrinking Violet revealed as Durlan; real Shrinking Violet returns	1.50
❑306, Dec 1983; O: Star Boy	1.50
❑307, Jan 1984; V: Prophet	1.50
❑308, Feb 1984; V: Prophet	1.50
❑309, Mar 1984; V: Prophet	1.50
❑310, Apr 1984; V: Omen	3.00
❑311, May 1984	1.50
❑312, Jun 1984	1.50
❑313, Jul 1984; series continues as Tales of the Legion of Super-Heroes	1.50
❑Ann 1, ca. 1982; KG (c); KG (w); KG (a); 1: Invisible Kid II (Jacques Foccart)	2.50
❑Ann 2, ca. 1983; KG (c); KG (w); DaG, KG (a); Wedding of Karate Kid and Princess Projectra; Karate Kid and Princess Projectra leave Legion of Super-Heroes	2.00
❑Ann 3, ca. 1984; KG (c); KG (w); CS (a); O: Validus	2.00

Legion of Super-Heroes DC

	N-MINT
❑1, Aug 1984; KG (w); KG (a); V: Legion of Super-Villains. Silver ink cover	5.00
❑2, Sep 1984; KG (w); KG (a); 1: Kono. V: Legion of Super-Villains; 1: Cosmic King as teen; Reprinted in Tales of the Legion #327	4.00
❑3, Oct 1984; KG (w); V: Legion of Super-Villains; Reprinted in Tales of the Legion #328	4.00
❑4, Nov 1984; KG (w); D: Karate Kid. V: Legion of Super-Villains; Reprinted in Tales of the Legion #329	4.00
❑5, Dec 1984; KG (c); KG (w); D: Nemesis Kid; V: Legion of Super-Villians	4.00
❑6, Jan 1985; 1: Laurel Gand. Spotlight on Lightning Lass	2.25
❑7, Feb 1985	2.25
❑8, Mar 1985	2.25
❑9, Apr 1985; 1:Tellus	2.25
❑10, May 1985	2.25
❑11, Jun 1985; Bouncing Boy back-up	2.00
❑12, Jul 1985; Element Lad elected Leader	2.00
❑13, Aug 1985; 1: Myg (Karate Kid II)	2.00
❑14, Sep 1985; 1: Quislet. New members	2.00
❑15, Oct 1985	2.00
❑16, Nov 1985; Crisis	2.00
❑17, Dec 1985	2.00
❑18, Jan 1986; Crisis	2.00
❑19, Feb 1986	2.00
❑20, Mar 1986; V: Tyr	2.00
❑21, Apr 1986; V: Emerald Empress; Colossal Boy appeaance; Reprinted in Tales of the Legion #346	2.00
❑22, May 1986	2.00
❑23, Jun 1986	2.00
❑24, Jul 1986; Reprinted in Tales of the Legion #349	2.00
❑25, Aug 1986; Revealed Sensor Girl is Princess Projectra	2.00
❑26, Sep 1986	2.00
❑27, Oct 1986; V: Mordru	2.00
❑28, Nov 1986; Reprinted in Tales of the Legion #353	2.00
❑29, Dec 1986; V: Starfinger	2.00
❑30, Jan 1987	2.00
❑31, Feb 1987; Karate Kid, Princess Projectra, Ferro Lad story	1.75
❑32, Mar 1987; Universo Project, Chapter 1	1.75
❑33, Apr 1987; Universo Project, Chapter 2	1.75
❑34, May 1987; Universo Project, Chapter 3	1.75
❑35, Jun 1987; Universo Project, Chapter 4	1.75
❑36, Jul 1987; Legion elections	1.75
❑37, Aug 1987; Fate of Superboy revealed; Return of Star Boy and Sun Girl	5.00
❑38, Sep 1987; D: Superboy	5.00
❑39, Oct 1987; CS (a); O: Colossal Boy	1.75
❑40, Nov 1987; V: Starfinger	1.75
❑41, Dec 1987; V: Starfinger	1.75
❑42, Jan 1988; V: Laurel Kent. Millennium	1.75
❑43, Feb 1988; V: Laurel Kent. Millennium	1.75
❑44, Mar 1988; O: Quislet	1.75
❑45, Apr 1988; Double-size; 30th Anniversary Issue	3.00
❑46, May 1988	1.75
❑47, Jun 1988; V: Starfinger	1.75
❑48, Jul 1988; V: Starfinger	1.75
❑49, Aug 1988; V: Starfinger	1.75
❑50, Sep 1988; Giant-size; D: Duo Damsel (half). D: Time Trapper (possible death). D: Infinite Man. Mon-El wounded	2.00
❑51, Oct 1988	1.75
❑52, Nov 1988; Marriage of Mon-El and Shadow Lass	1.75
❑53, Dec 1988	1.75
❑54, Win 1988; no month of publication; cover says Winter	1.75
❑55, Hol 1989; no month of publication; cover says Holiday	1.75
❑56, Jan 1989; V: Inquisitor	1.75
❑57, Feb 1989	1.75
❑58, Mar 1989; D: Emerald Empress	1.75
❑59, Apr 1989; Sensor Girl elected leader	1.75
❑60, May 1989 KG (w); KG (a)	1.75
❑61, Jun 1989 KG (w); KG (a)	1.75
❑62, Jul 1989; KG (w); KG (a); D: Magnetic Kid	1.75
❑63, Aug 1989; KG (w); KG (a); Final Issue	1.75
❑Ann 1, Oct 1985; KG (c); KG (a); (10/85; 52 pgs)	3.00
❑Ann 2, ca. 1986; V: Validus	2.00
❑Ann 3, ca. 1987; O: new Legion of Substitute Heroes	2.00
❑Ann 4, ca. 1988; O: Starfinger. 1988 annual	2.50

Legion of Super-Heroes DC

	N-MINT
❑0, Oct 1994; KG, MWa (w); KG (a); O: Legion of Super-Heroes (revised). continues in Legion of Super-Heroes #62 and Legionnaires #19	2.00
❑1, Nov 1989; KG (c); KG (w); KG (a); Begins five years after previous series	2.50
❑2, Dec 1989; 1: Kono	2.00
❑3, Jan 1990; V: Roxxas. D: Blok	2.00
❑4, Feb 1990 KG (w); KG (a); A: Mon-El	2.00
❑5, Mar 1990	2.00
❑6, Apr 1990	2.00
❑7, May 1990	2.00
❑8, Jun 1990; origin	2.00
❑9, Jul 1990; Roxxas investigates history of Laurel Gand	2.00
❑10, Aug 1990; V: Roxxas. V: Roxxas	2.00
❑11, Sep 1990 A: Matter-Eater Lad	2.00
❑12, Oct 1990; Legion reformed	2.00
❑13, Nov 1990; poster	2.00
❑14, Jan 1991	2.00
❑15, Feb 1991	2.00
❑16, Mar 1991	2.00
❑17, Apr 1991; D: Tornado Twins (Don and Dawn Allen); V: Khunds	2.00
❑18, May 1991; V: Dark Circle	2.00
❑19, Jun 1991	2.00
❑20, Jul 1991	2.00
❑21, Aug 1991; Darkseid sends Lobo to recover Gemini Experiment	1.75
❑22, Sep 1991	1.75
❑23, Oct 1991; V: Lobo	1.75
❑24, Dec 1991; KG (a); 1: Batch Legion	1.75
❑25, Jan 1992	1.75
❑26, Feb 1992; KG (w); KG (a); contains map of Legion headquarters	1.75
❑27, Mar 1992; KG (w); KG (a); V: B.I.O.N	1.75
❑28, Apr 1992 KG (a); A: Sun Boy	1.75
❑29, May 1992 KG (w); KG (a)	1.75
❑30, Jun 1992; KG (w); KG (a); The Terra Mosaic	1.75
❑31, Jul 1992; KG (w); KG, CS (a); The Terra Mosaic; romance cover	1.75
❑32, Aug 1992; KG (w); KG (a); The Terra Mosaic	1.75
❑33, Sep 1992; The Terra Mosaic; Fate of Kid Quantum	1.75
❑34, Oct 1992; KG (w); KG (a); The Terra Mosaic; Timber Wolf mini-series preview	1.75
❑35, Nov 1992; KG (w); KG (a); The Terra Mosaic; Sun Boy meets Sun Boy	1.75
❑36, Nov 1992; KG (w); KG (a); The Terra Mosaic conclusion	1.75
❑37, Dec 1992; Star Boy and Dream Girl return	1.75
❑38, Dec 1992; KG (w); A: Death (Sandman). Earth destroyed	2.50
❑39, Jan 1993 KG (a)	1.75
❑40, Feb 1993; Wildfire returns	1.75
❑41, Mar 1993; 1: Legionnaires	1.75
❑42, Apr 1993	1.75
❑43, May 1993; White Witch returns	1.75
❑44, Jun 1993; 1: Firefist; 1: Veilmist; 1: Blood Claw; 1: Fleder-Web; Mordu reanimates dead; White Witch V: Mordu; LSH forced to include Khund members	1.75
❑45, Jul 1993; V: undead; V: Mordu	1.75
❑46, Aug 1993	1.75
❑47, Sep 1993; V: dead heroes	1.75
❑48, Oct 1993; V: Mordru	1.75
❑49, Nov 1993	1.75
❑50, Nov 1993; Wedding of Matter-Eater Lad and Saturn Queen	3.50
❑51, Dec 1993; Kent Shakespeare V: Chainmaster	1.75
❑52, Dec 1993; O: Timber Wolf	1.75
❑53, Jan 1994; V: Glorith	1.75
❑54, Feb 1994; Die-cut cover	2.95
❑55, Mar 1994	1.75
❑56, Apr 1994	1.75
❑57, May 1994	1.75
❑58, Jun 1994	1.75
❑59, Jul 1994; MWa (w); Insane Cosmic Boy attempts to recreate Earth	1.95
❑60, Aug 1994; MWa (w); Crossover with Legionnaires and Valor	1.95
❑61, Sep 1994; MWa (w); Zero Hour; end of original Legion of Super-Heroes	1.95
❑62, Nov 1994; MWa (w); D: Kid Quantum	1.95
❑63, Dec 1994; MWa (w); 1: Athramites, new Legion headquarters. Tenzil Kem hired as chef	1.95
❑64, Jan 1995; MWa (w); Return of Ultra Boy	1.95
❑65, Feb 1995 MWa (w)	1.95
❑66, Mar 1995; MWa (w); A: Laurel Gand. Andromeda, Shrinking Violet and Kinetix join team	1.95
❑67, Apr 1995 MWa (w)	1.95
❑68, May 1995	1.95
❑69, Jun 1995	2.25
❑70, Jul 1995 MWa (w)	2.25
❑71, Aug 1995; MWa (w); Trom destroyed	2.25
❑72, Sep 1995	2.25
❑73, Oct 1995 A: Mekt Ranz	2.25
❑74, Nov 1995; A: Superboy. A: Scavenger. Future Tense, Part 2; Concludes in Legionnaires #31	2.25
❑75, Dec 1995; A: Chronos. Underworld Unleashed	2.25
❑76, Jan 1996; Star Boy and Gates joins team; [L1996-1]	2.25
❑77, Feb 1996; O: Brainiac Five. [L1996-3]	2.25
❑78, Mar 1996; O: Fatal Five. 1: Fatal Five. [L1996-5]	2.25
❑79, Apr 1996; V: Fatal Five. [L1996-7]	2.25
❑80, May 1996; [L1996-9]	2.25
❑81, Jun 1996; Dirk Morgna becomes Sun Boy; Brainiac 5 quits; [L1996-11]	2.25
❑82, Jul 1996; Apparition returns; [L1996-13]	2.25
❑83, Aug 1996; D: Leviathan. Violet possessed by Emerald Eye; [L1996-15]	2.25
❑84, Sep 1996; [L1996-17]	2.25
❑85, Oct 1996; A: Superman. Seven Legionnaires, Inferno, and Shvaughn Erin in 20th century; [L1996-19]	2.25
❑86, Nov 1996; A: Ferro. Final Night; [L1996-21]	2.25
❑87, Dec 1996; A: Deadman. A: Phase. [L1996-23]	2.25
❑88, Jan 1997; A: Impulse. [L1997-2]	2.25
❑89, Feb 1997; A: Doctor Psycho. [L1997-4]	2.25
❑90, Mar 1997; V: Doctor Psycho. [L1997-6]	2.25
❑91, Apr 1997; Legion visits several DC eras; [L1997-8]	2.25
❑92, May 1997; 20th century group lands in 1958 Happy Harbor; [L1997-10]	2.25
❑93, Jun 1997; D: Douglas Nolan. [L1997-12]	2.25

Legion Worlds	Lensman	Lethal Foes of Spider-Man	Lethargic Comics	Life, the Universe and Everything
	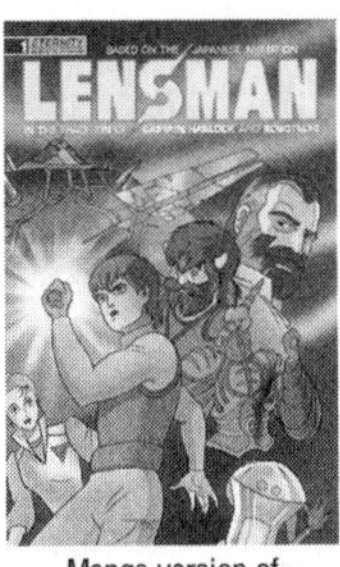	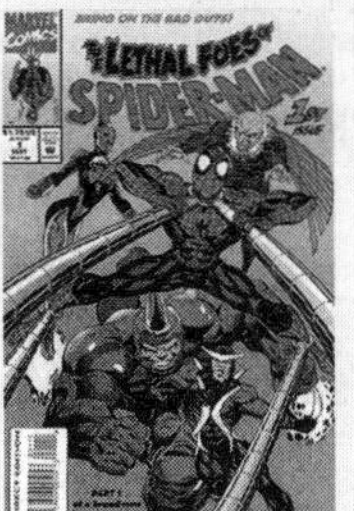		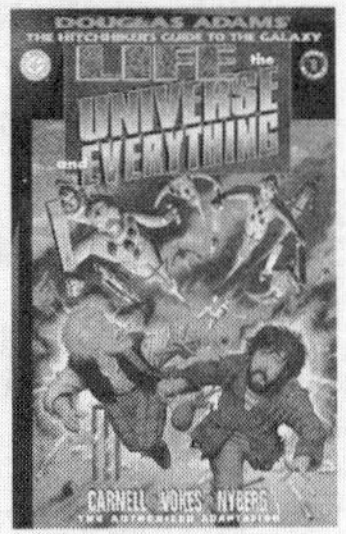
Travelogue of United Planets ©DC	Manga version of E.E. Smith SF classic ©Eternity	Doc Ock organizes new villainous group ©Marvel	Simple-looking parodies have surprising depth ©Alpha	Adaptation of the third Hitchhiker's novel ©DC

N-MINT

❑94, Jul 1997; [L1997-14] 2.25
❑95, Aug 1997; A: Metal Men. [L1997-16] 2.25
❑96, Sep 1997; Wedding of Ultra Boy and Apparition; Cosmic Boy revives; [L1997-18] 2.25
❑97, Oct 1997; V: Mantis. Genesis; Spark gains gravity powers; [L1997-20] 2.25
❑98, Nov 1997; Phase meets Apparition; [L1997-22] 2.25
❑99, Dec 1997; Face cover; [L1997-24]. 2.25
❑100, Jan 1998; Double-size; gatefold cover; Legionnaires return from 20th century; Pin-ups; [L1998-2] 5.95
❑101, Feb 1998; Spark gets her lightning powers back; [L1998-4] 2.25
❑102, Mar 1998; A: Heroes of Xanthu. [L1998-6] 2.25
❑103, Apr 1998; Karate Kid quits McCauley Industries; [L1998-8] 2.25
❑104, May 1998; A: Kono. time shifts to 2968; [L1998-10] 2.25
❑105, Jun 1998; V: Time Trapper. [L1998-12] 2.25
❑106, Jul 1998; Dark Circle Rising, Part 2: Assassination!; [L1998-14] 2.25
❑107, Aug 1998; Dark Circle Rising, Part 4: Duplicity!; [L1998-16] 2.25
❑108, Sep 1998; Dark Circle Rising, Part 6: Revelation!; [L1998-18] 2.25
❑109, Oct 1998; V: Emerald Eye. [L1998-20] 2.50
❑110, Dec 1998; Thunder joins team; [L1998-22] 2.50
❑111, Jan 1999; Karate Kid vs. M'onel; [L1999-2] 2.50
❑112, Feb 1999; [L1999-4] 2.50
❑113, Mar 1999; [L1999-6] 2.50
❑114, Apr 1999; 1: Bizarro Legion. [L1999-8] 2.50
❑115, May 1999; [L1999-10] 2.50
❑116, Jun 1999; Thunder vs. Pernisius; [L1999-12] 2.50
❑117, Jul 1999; [L1999-14] 2.50
❑118, Aug 1999; V: Pernisius. [L1999-16] 2.50
❑119, Sep 1999; M'Onel and Apparition tell a L.E.G.I.O.N. story; [L1999-18] 2.50
❑120, Oct 1999; V: Fatal Five. [L1999-20] 2.50
❑121, Nov 1999; [L1999-22] 2.50
❑122, Dec 1999; [L1999-24] 2.50
❑123, Jan 2000; [L2000-2] 2.50
❑1000000, Nov 1998; KG (a); set 1, 000 years after events of One Million+ E12681 4.00
❑Ann 1, ca. 1990; O: Glorith, Ultra Boy, Legion, Ultra Boy, Legion 5.00
❑Ann 2, ca. 1991; O: Valor; ca. 1997 3.50
❑Ann 3, ca. 1992; Timber Wolf goes to 20th century 3.50
❑Ann 4, ca. 1993; O: Jamm. 1: Jamm; 1993 annual; Bloodlines: Earthplague 3.50
❑Ann 5, ca. 1994; CS (a); Elseworlds; Legion in Oz 3.50
❑Ann 6, ca. 1995; MWa (w); O: Leviathan. O: Kinetix. Year One; 0: XS; Legion Headquarters Map; Legion Equipment 3.95
❑Ann 7, ca. 1996; A: Wildfire. Legends of the Dead Earth; 1996 annual 2.95

N-MINT

Legion of Super-Heroes
DC

❑1, Mar 2005 4.00
❑2, Apr 2005 2.95
❑3, May 2005 2.95
❑4, Jun 2005 2.95
❑5, Jun 2005 2.99
❑6, Jul 2005 2.99
❑7, Aug 2005 2.99
❑8, Sep 2005 2.99
❑9, Oct 2005 2.99
❑10, Nov 2005; D: Dream Girl III 2.99
❑11, Dec 2005 2.99
❑12, Jan 2006 2.99
❑13, Mar 2006, D: Dream Girl III 2.99
❑14, Mar 2006 2.99
❑15, May 2006, During DC's "One Year Later," series title changes to "Supergirl and the Legion of Super-Heroes with #16 2.99

Legion of Super-Heroes Index
Eclipse / Independent

❑1 2.00
❑2, Jan 1987 2.00
❑3, Feb 1987 2.00
❑4, Mar 1987 2.00
❑5, May 1987 2.00

Legion of Super-Heroes Secret Files
DC

❑1, Jan 1998; bios on members and villains 4.95
❑2, Jun 1999; bios on members and villains; Legion constitution 4.95

Legion of the Stupid-Heroes
Blackthorne

❑1, b&w; parody 1.75

Legion: Science Police
DC

❑1, Aug 1998 2.25
❑2, Sep 1998 2.25
❑3, Oct 1998 2.25
❑4, Nov 1998 2.25

Legion Secret Files 3003
DC

❑1, Jan 2004; Takes Place between The Legion #26 and #27 4.95

Legions of Ludicrous Heroes
C&T

❑1, b&w 2.00

Legion Worlds
DC

❑1, Jun 2001; V: Robotica; V: Tharok; LSH outpost reappears in Earth Orbit 3.95
❑2, Jul 2001 3.95
❑3, Aug 2001 3.95
❑4, Sep 2001; V: Robotica 3.95
❑5, Oct 2001 3.95
❑6, Nov 2001; Birth of Cub (Apparition's son) 3.95

Legion X-1
Silverwolf

❑1, Feb 1997, b&w 1.50
❑2, Mar 1987, b&w 1.50

N-MINT

Legion X-1
Greater Mercury

❑1, Aug 1989, b&w 2.00
❑2, Aug 1989, b&w; Cover says September 2.00
❑3, Jul 1990, b&w 2.00

Legion X-2
Greater Mercury

❑1, Aug 1989 2.00
❑2, May 1990 2.00
❑3, ca. 1990 2.00
❑4, ca. 1990 2.00
❑5, ca. 1990 2.00
❑6, ca. 1991 2.00
❑7, Mar 1991 2.00

Lejentia
Opus

❑1 1.95
❑2 2.25

Lemonade Kid
AC

❑1; Powell reprints 2.50

Lena's Bambinas
Fantagraphics

❑1 3.50

Lenore
Slave Labor

❑1, Feb 1998 3.25
❑2, Jun 1998 3.00
❑3, Sep 1998 2.95
❑4, Jan 1999 2.95
❑5, Mar 1999 2.95
❑6, Jul 1999 2.95
❑7, Dec 1999 2.95
❑12, Oct 2005 2.95

Lensman
Eternity

❑1, Feb 1990, b&w 2.25
❑1/Variant, Feb 1990, b&w; Special edition; cardstock cover; Includes Episode Guide; History; Story Timeline; Cycroader info; Galactic Patrol & Eddore Organizational charts; Vital Statistics on characters, vehicles and weapons 3.95
❑2, May 1990 2.25
❑3, Jun 1990 2.25
❑4, Jul 1990 2.25
❑5, Sep 1990 2.25
❑6, Oct 1990 2.25

Lensman: War of the Galaxies
Eternity

❑1, Nov 1990, b&w 2.25
❑2, Jan 1991, b&w 2.25
❑3, Mar 1991, b&w 2.25
❑4, Apr 1991, b&w 2.25
❑5, May 1991, b&w 2.25
❑6, Jun 1991, b&w 2.25
❑7, Jul 1991, b&w 2.25

Leonard Nimoy
Celebrity

❑1, b&w 5.95

Leonardo Teenage Mutant Ninja Turtle
Mirage

❑1, Dec 1986; continues in Teenage Mutant Ninja Turtles #10 .... 4.00

Leopold and Brink
Faultline

❑1, Jun 1997, b&w 2.50
❑2, Nov 1997, b&w 2.50
❑3, Jan 1998, b&w 2.95

Lester Girls: The Lizard's Trail
Eternity

❑1, b&w 2.50
❑2, b&w 2.50
❑3, b&w 2.50

Lethal
Image

❑1, Feb 1996 .... 2.50

Lethal Enforcer
Alias

❑1, ca. 2005 .... 0.75

Lethal Foes of Spider-Man
Marvel

❑1, Sep 1993 .... 2.00
❑2, Oct 1993 A: Answer. A: Hardshell. A: Doctor Octopus. A: Vulture 2.00
❑3, Nov 1993 KP (a) 2.00
❑4, Dec 1993 .... 2.00

Lethal Instinct
Alias

❑1, May 2005; Includes Tenth Muse preview 2.99
❑2, Jun 2005 .... 2.99
❑3, Sep 2005 .... 2.99
❑4, Nov 2005 .... 2.99
❑5, Jan 2006 .... 2.99

Lethal Orgasm
NBM

❑1; Adult 9.95

Lethal Strike
London Night

❑0; Commemorative edition 5.95
❑½; Includes promo card 3.00
❑1, Jun 1995 .... 3.00
❑2 .... 3.00
❑3 .... 3.00
❑Ann 1 .... 3.00

Lethal Strike/Double Impact: Lethal Impact
London Night

❑1, May 1996; crossover with High Impact 3.00

Lethargic Comics
Alpha

❑1, b&w; Spawn/Cerebus parody cover. 3.50
❑2, Feb 1994, b&w 3.00
❑3, Mar 1994, b&w 3.00
❑3.14, Apr 1994, b&w; Issue #pi 3.00
❑4, May 1994, b&w; Marvels #4 parody cover 3.00
❑5, Jul 1994, b&w; Dot-It-Yerself cover. 3.00
❑6, b&w; Sin City parody cover 2.50
❑7, b&w; Spawn/Batman parody cover .. 2.50
❑8, b&w 2.50
❑9, Apr 1995, b&w; Bone 2.50
❑10, b&w; Sin City parody cover 2.50
❑11, Aug 1995, b&w; Milk & Cheese 2.50
❑12, b&w; A: Shi. Shi cover 2.50
❑13 .... 2.50
❑14 .... 2.50

Lethargic Comics, Weakly
Lethargic

❑1, Jun 1991, b&w; 1: Guy with a Gun. 1: No Mutants. 1: Lethargic Lad. 1: Walrus Boy. 1: Him. 1: The Grad. 1: The Zit. Action Comics #601 parody cover 4.00
❑2, b&w; Detective Comics #27 parody cover 3.00
❑3, b&w; Spider-Man #1 parody cover .. 3.00
❑4, b&w; X-Men #1 parody cover 2.50
❑5, b&w; Dark Knight #1 parody cover .. 2.50
❑6, b&w; Dark Knight #4 parody cover .. 2.50
❑7; Crisis on Infinite Earths #12 parody cover 2.50
❑8; Avengers #4 parody cover 2.50
❑9; Spider-Man #16 parody cover; Issue reads sideways 2.50
❑10; Adventures of Captain America parody cover 2.50
❑11; Youngblood #1 parody cover 2.50
❑12, b&w; Alpha begins publishing; Superman #75 parody cover 2.50

Lethargic Lad
Crusade

❑1, Jun 1996, b&w 2.95
❑2, Jul 1996, b&w 2.95
❑3, Sep 1996, b&w; wraparound cover; Kingdom Come parody 2.95

Lethargic Lad
Crusade

❑1, Oct 1997; Team-up with Him 2.95
❑2, Dec 1997 .... 2.95
❑3, Mar 1998; Thieves & Kings 2.95
❑4, Apr 1998; Starro'David, The Captain Company (Starro and Avengers parodies); Batman origin parody 2.95
❑5, Jun 1998 .... 2.95
❑6, Sep 1998 .... 2.95
❑7, Nov 1998 .... 2.95
❑8, Jan 1999 .... 2.95
❑9, Mar 1999 .... 2.95

Level X
Caliber

❑1, b&w 3.95
❑2, b&w 3.95

Levi's World
Moordam

❑1, Jan 1998 .... 2.95
❑2, Mar 1998 .... 2.95
❑3, May 1998 .... 2.95
❑4, Aug 1998 .... 2.95

Lewd Moana
Fantagraphics / Eros

❑1; Adult 2.95

The Lexian Chronicles: Full Circle
APComics

❑1/Preview, May 2005 .... 5.00
❑1, Jun 2005 .... 3.50

Lex Luthor: Man of Steel
DC

❑1, May 2005 .... 2.99
❑2, Jun 2005 .... 2.99
❑3, Jun 2005 .... 2.99
❑4, Jul 2005 .... 2.99
❑5, Aug 2005 .... 2.99

Lex Luthor: The Unauthorized Biography
DC

❑1, Jul 1989; O: Luthor. Painted cover... 4.00

Lex Talionis: Jungle Tale One Shot
Image

❑1, Jan 2004 .... 5.95

Liaisons Delicieuses
Fantagraphics / Eros

❑1, b&w; Adult 1.95
❑2, Dec 1990, b&w; Adult 1.95
❑3; Adult 2.25
❑4, Mar 1991; Adult 2.25
❑5, May 1991; Adult 2.25
❑6, Jun 1991, Adult 2.25

Libby Ellis
Eternity

❑1, Jun 1988 .... 1.95
❑2, Jul 1988 .... 1.95
❑3, Aug 1988 .... 1.95
❑4, Sep 1988 .... 1.95

Libby Ellis
Malibu

❑1 .... 1.95
❑2 .... 1.95
❑3 .... 1.95
❑4 .... 1.95

Liberality For All
-Ism

❑1, ca. 2005 .... 2.99

Liberator
Malibu

❑1, Dec 1987, b&w; 1: Liberator 1.95
❑2, Feb 1988 .... 1.95
❑3, Mar 1988 .... 1.95
❑4, Jun 1988 .... 1.95
❑5, Oct 1988 .... 1.95
❑6, Dec 1988 .... 1.95

Liberator
Images & Realities

❑1 .... 2.00

Libertine
Fantagraphics / Eros

❑1, b&w; Adult 2.25
❑2; Adult 2.50

Liberty Meadows
Insight

❑1, Jun 1999, Reprints first eight weeks of Liberty Meadows 18.00
❑1/2nd, Reprints first eight weeks of Liberty Meadows 2.95
❑2, Aug 1999, Reprints weeks 9-16 of Liberty Meadows strip 10.00
❑3, Oct 1999, Reprints weeks 17-24 of Liberty Meadows strip 6.00
❑4, Nov 1999, Reprints weeks 25-32 of Liberty Meadows strip 6.00
❑5, Dec 1999, 42 strips plus 3 Sunday strip reprints 5.00
❑6, Jan 2000 .... 4.00
❑7, Feb 2000 .... 4.00
❑8, Mar 2000 .... 4.00
❑9, Apr 2000 .... 4.00
❑10, May 2000 .... 4.00
❑11, Jun 2000 .... 3.00
❑12, Jul 2000 .... 3.00
❑13, Aug 2000 .... 3.00
❑14, Sep 2000 .... 3.00
❑15, Nov 2000, reader requests 3.00
❑16, Dec 2000, Wiener Dog Race 3.00
❑17, Jan 2001 .... 3.00
❑18, Feb 2001 .... 3.00
❑19, Mar 2001 .... 2.95
❑20, May 2001, Adam Hughes cover 2.95
❑21, Jul 2001 .... 2.95
❑22 .... 2.95
❑23 .... 2.95
❑24 .... 2.95
❑25 .... 2.95
❑26, Oct 2001, .The wedding album 2.95
❑27, Aug 2002, Image begins as publisher 2.95
❑28, Oct 2002, b&w 2.95
❑29, Dec 2002, b&w 2.95
❑30, Feb 2003, b&w 2.95
❑31, Apr 2003, b&w 2.95
❑32, Jul 2003, b&w 2.95
❑33, Aug 2003, b&w 2.95
❑34, Oct 2003 .... 2.95
❑35, Jan 2004 .... 2.95
❑36, Apr 2004 .... 2.95
❑37, Jul 2006; Returns after two-year hiatus 2.99

Liberty Meadows Source Book
Image

❑1, Aug 2005 .... 4.95

Liberty Project
Eclipse

❑1, Jun 1987; KB (w); 1&O: The Liberty Project. 1: Cimmaron. 1: Burnout. 1: Crackshot. 1: Slick 2.00
❑2, Jul 1987 KB (w) 1.75
❑3, Aug 1987 KB (w) 1.75
❑4, Sep 1987 KB (w) 1.75
❑5, Oct 1987 KB (w) 1.75
❑6, Nov 1987 KB (w); A: Valkyrie 1.75
❑7, Dec 1987 KB (w) 1.75
❑8, May 1988 KB (w) 1.75

Libra
Eternity

❑1, Apr 1987 .... 1.95

Librarian
Fantagraphics

❑1, b&w 2.75

Photo Grading Guide

When comics are compared with the Photo Grading Guide, it's easy to see there are many comics which fall between categories in something of an infinite gradation. For example, a "Fair" condition comic book (which falls between "Good" and "Poor") may have a soiled, slightly damaged cover, a badly rolled spine, cover flaking, corners gone, tears, and the like. It is an issue with multiple problems but it is intact — and some collectors enjoy collecting in this grade for the fun of it. Tape may be present and is always considered a defect.

The condition of a comic book is a vital factor in determining its price.

MINT

(Abbreviated **M, Mt**)
This is a perfect comic book. Its cover has full luster, with edges sharp and pages like new. There are no signs of wear or aging. It is not imperfectly printed or off-center. "Mint" means just what it says.
Mint prices are 150% of the Near Mint prices listed in this guide.
[The term for this grade is the same one used for CGC's 10.0 grade.]

NEAR MINT

(Abbreviated **NM**)
This is a nearly perfect comic book.
Its cover shows barely perceptible signs of wear. Its spine is tight, and its cover has only minor loss of luster and only minor printing defects. Some discoloration is acceptable in older comics — as are signs of aging.
Near Mint prices are what are listed in this guide.
[The term for this grade is the same one used for CGC's 9.4 grade.]

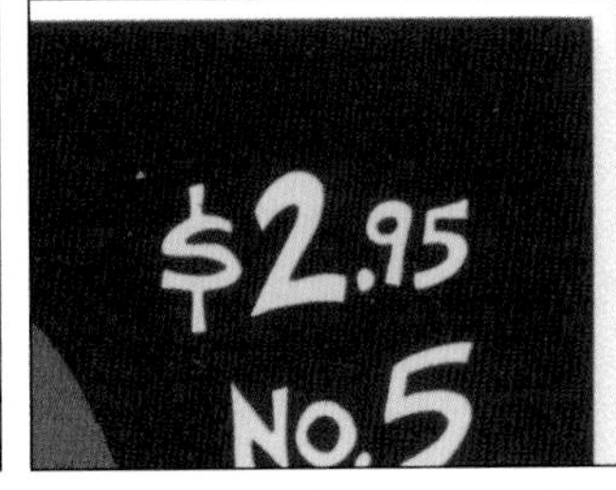

VERY FINE

(Abbreviated **VF**)

This is a nice comic book with beginning signs of wear. There can be slight creases and wrinkles at the staples, but it is a flat, clean issue with definite signs of being read a few times. There is some loss of the original gloss, but it is in general an attractive comic book.

Very Fine prices are 66.6% of the Near Mint prices listed in this guide.
[The term for this grade is the same one used for CGC's 8.0 grade.]

FINE

(Abbreviated **F, Fn**)

This comic book's cover is worn but flat and clean with no defacement. There is usually no cover writing or tape repair. Stress lines around the staples and more rounded corners are permitted. It is a good-looking issue at first glance.

Fine prices are 33.3% of the Near Mint prices listed in this guide.
[The term for this grade is the same one used for CGC's 6.0 grade.]

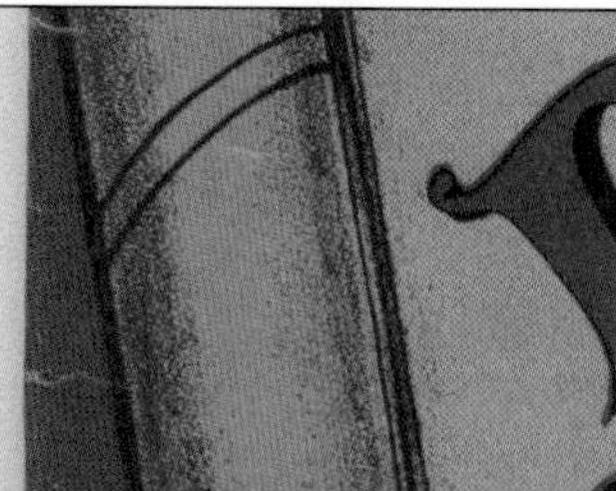

VERY GOOD

(Abbreviated **VG, VGd**)
Most of the original gloss is gone from this well-read issue.
There are minor markings, discoloration, and/or heavier stress lines around the staples and spine. The cover may have minor tears and/or corner creases, and spine-rolling is permissible.
Very Good prices are 20% of the Near Mint prices listed in this guide.
[The term for this grade is the same one used for CGC's 4.0 grade.]

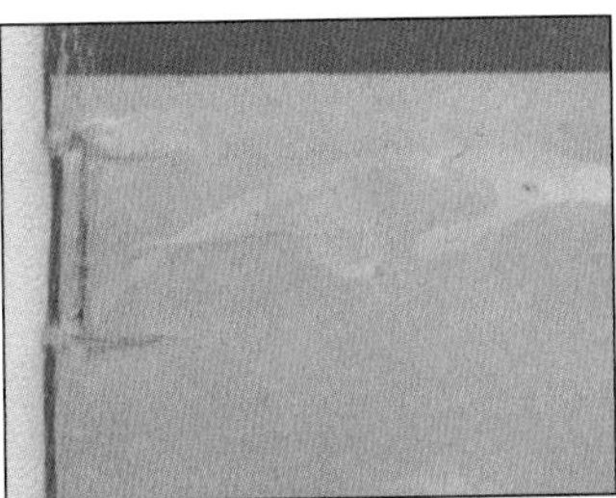

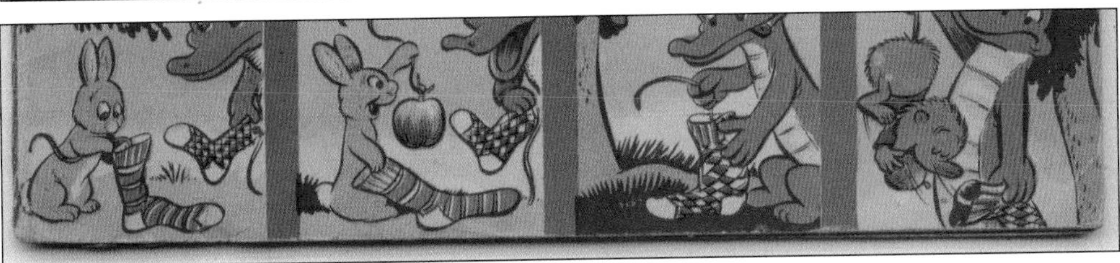

GOOD

(Abbreviated **G, Gd**)
This is a very worn comic book with nothing missing.
Creases, minor tears, rolled spine, and cover flaking are permissible. Older Golden Age comic books often come in this condition.
Good prices are 12.5% of the Near Mint prices listed in this guide.
[The term for this grade is the same one used for CGC's 2.0 grade.]

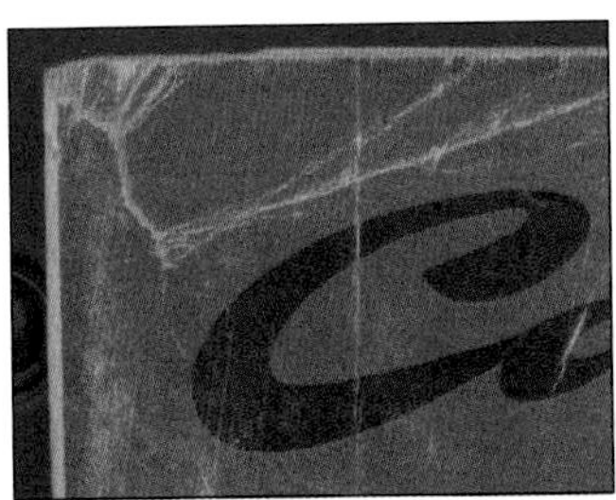
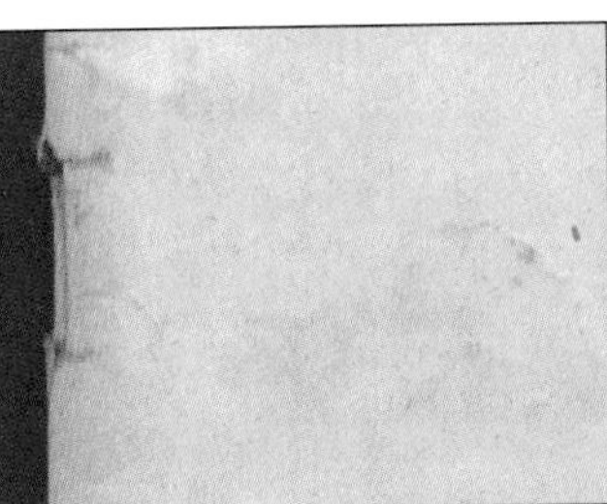
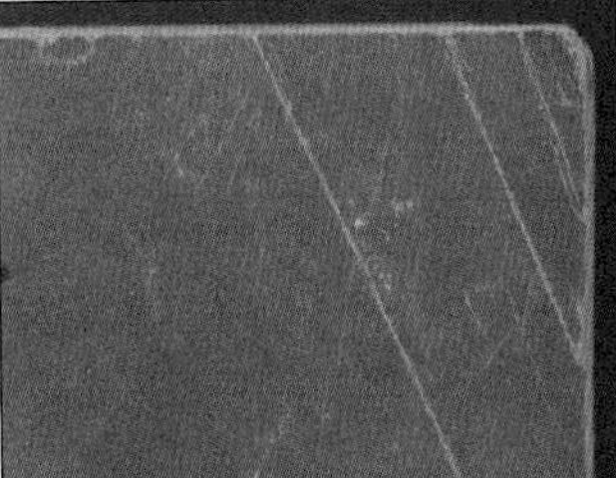

FAIR

(Abbreviated **FA, Fr**)

This comic book has multiple problems but is structurally intact. Copies may have a soiled, slightly damaged cover, a badly rolled spine, cover flaking, corners gone, and tears. Tape may be present and is always considered a defect.

Fair prices are 8% of the Near Mint prices listed in this guide.
[The term for this grade is the same one used for CGC's 1.0 grade.]

POOR

(Abbreviated **P, Pr**)

This issue is damaged and generally considered unsuitable for collecting. While the copy may still contain some readable stories, major defects get in the way. Copies may be in the process of disintegrating and may do so with even light handling.

Poor prices are 2% of the Near Mint prices listed in this guide.
[The term for this grade is the same one used for CGC's 0.5 grade.]

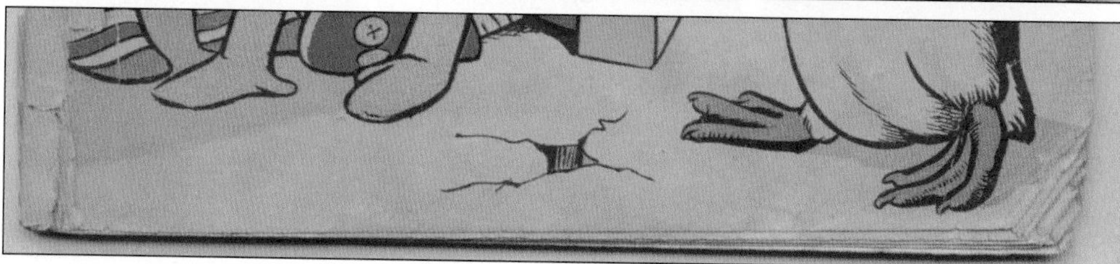

Guide to Defects

Theoretically, given a set of grading rules, determining the condition of a comic book should be simple. But flaws vary from item to item, and it can be difficult to pin one label on a particular issue — as with a sharp issue with a coupon removed. Another problem lies in grading historically significant vs. run-of-the-mill issues.

The examples shown here represent specific defects listed. These defects need to be taken into account when grading, but should *not* be the sole determinant of a comic's grade.

(For example, the comics with stamped arrival date, off-center staple are *not* in Mint condition aside from those defects.)

Stamped arrival date and off-center cover and off-center stapling.
Minor defects. Some will not call it "Mint"; some will.

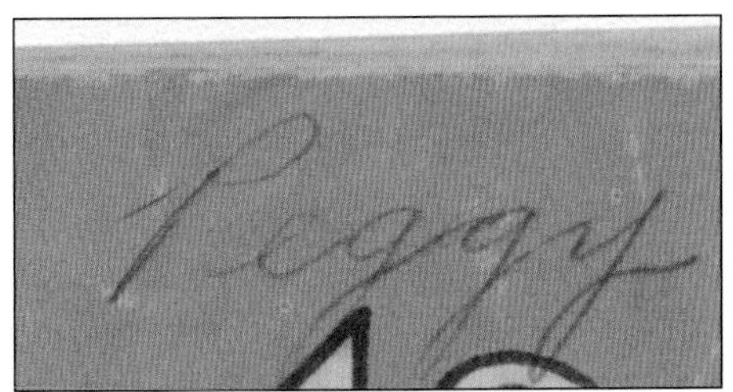

Writing defacing cover.
Marking can include filling in light areas or childish scribbling. Usually no better than "Good."

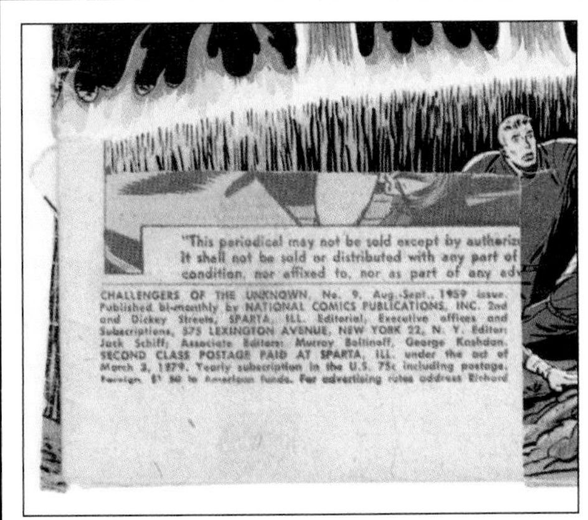

Clipped coupon.
A square or rectangular piece deliberately removed from the front or back cover or one of the interior pages.
No better than "Fair."

Subscription crease.
Comic books sent by mail were often folded down the middle, leaving a permanent crease. Definitely no better than "Very Good"; probably no better than "Good."

Water damage.
Varies from simple page-warping to staining shown here behind and on the logo. Less damage than this could be "Good"; this is no better than "Fair."

Missing pages and other material.
Ask before taking a comic book out of its bag, but most sellers should allow you to carefully flip through a comic book, looking for such items as clipped coupons from interior pages, scribbling on interior pages, a missing center section, or such lost extra material as trading cards or 3-D glasses.

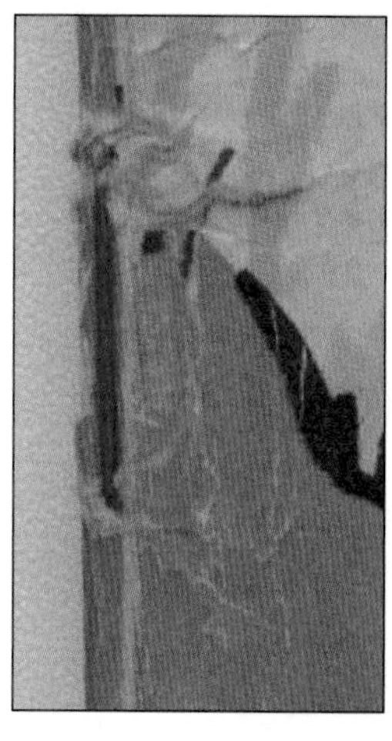

Rusty staple.
Caused by dampness during storage, rust stains around staples may be minor — or more apparent. No better than "Very Good."

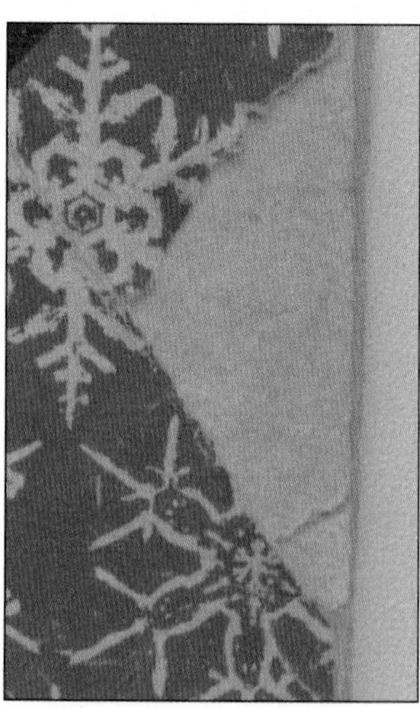

Chunk missing.
Sizable piece missing from the cover (front or back).
No better than "Fair."

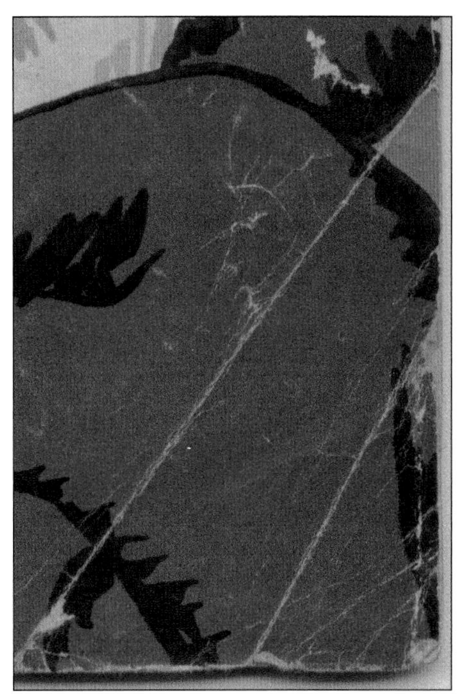

Multiple folds and wrinkles.
No better than "Fair" condition.

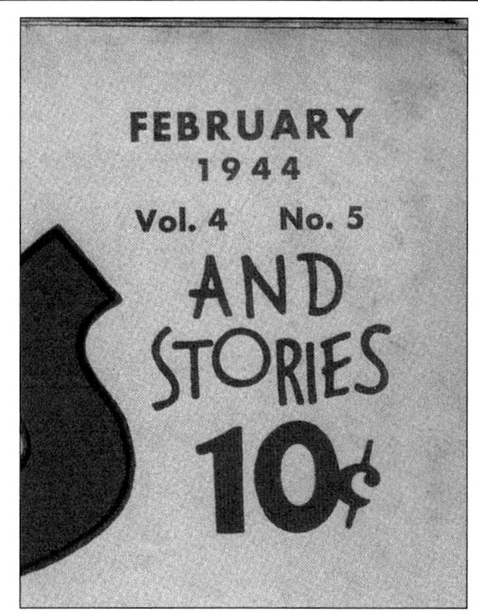

Stains.
Can vary widely, depending on cause. These look like dirt — but food, grease, and the like also stain. No better than "Good."

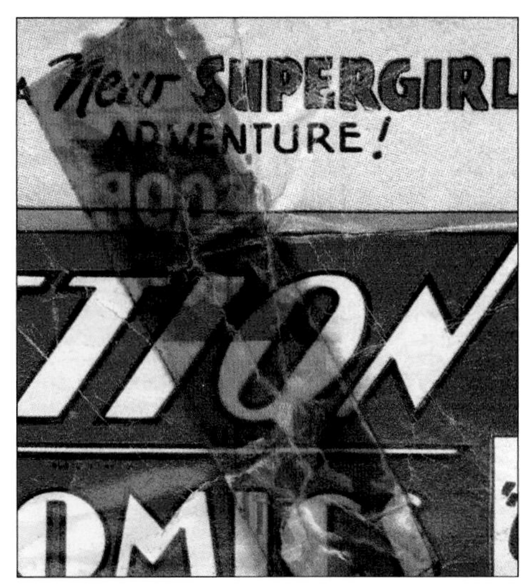

Tape.
This extreme example of tape damage is used to show ***why*** tape shouldn't be used on a comic book — or ***any*** book — for repairs. ***All*** tape (even so-called "magic" tape) ages badly — as does rubber cement. Use of tape usually means "Fair," at best.

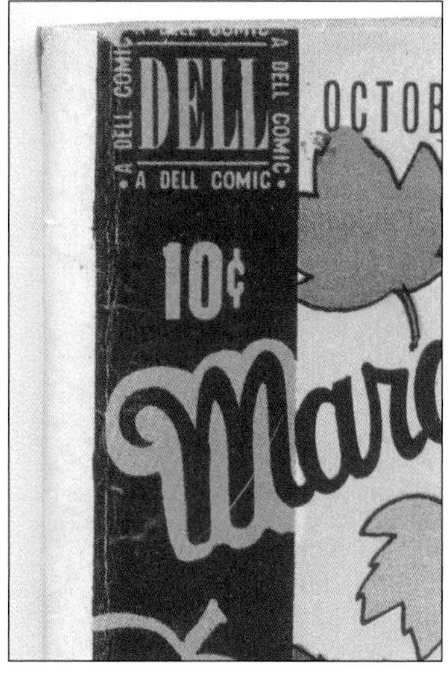

Rolled Spine.
Caused by folding back each page while reading — rather than opening the issue flat. Repeated folding permanently bent the spine. ***May*** be corrected, but the issue is no better than "Very Good."

Abbreviations

ISSUE DETAILS

(a) — Artist (interior)
(c) — Artist (cover)
(w) — Writer
A — Appearance of
D — Death of
DF — Dynamic Forces Edition
Giant — Giant Size
I — Introduction of
J — Joining of
JLA — Justice League of Amer.
JSA — Justice Society of Amer.
L — Leaving of
nn — no number
O — Origin of
rep. — reprint
V — versus
1 — first appearance of
2 — second appearance of

CREATOR INITIALS

AA — Alfredo Alcala
AAd — Art Adams
AF — Al Feldstein
AM — Al Milgrom
AMo — Alan Moore
AN — Alex Nino
AR — Alex Raymond
AT — Angelo Torres
ATh — Alex Toth
AW — Al Williamson

BA — Brent Anderson
BB — Brian Bolland
BE — Bill Elder
BEv — Bill Everett
BG — Butch Guice
BH — Bob Hall
BK — Bernie Krigstein
BL — Bob Layton
BMc — Bob McLeod
BO — Bob Oksner
BS — Barry Smith
BSz — Bill Sienkiewicz
BT — Bryan Talbot
BW — Basil Wolverton
BWa — Bill Ward
BWi — Bob Wiacek
BWr — Berni Wrightson

CB — Carl Barks
CCB — C.C. Beck
CI — Carmine Infantino
CR — P. Craig Russell
CS — Curt Swan
CV — Charles Vess

DA — Dan Adkins
DC — Dave Cockrum
DD — Dick Dillin
DaG — Dave Gibbons
DG — Dick Giordano
DGr — Dan Green
DGry — Devin Grayson
DH — Don Heck
DN — Don Newton
DP — Don Perlin
DR — Don Rosa
DS — Dan Spiegle
DSt — Dave Stevens

EC — Ernie Colon
EL — Erik Larsen

FB — Frank Brunner
FF — Frank Frazetta
FG — Floyd Gottfredson
FGu — Fred Guardineer
FH — Fred Hembeck
FM — Frank Miller
FMc — Frank McLaughlin
FR — Frank Robbins
FS — Frank Springer
FT — Frank Thorne

GC — Gene Colan
GD — Gene Day
GE — George Evans
GI — Graham Ingels
GK — Gil Kane
GM — Gray Morrow
GP — George Pérez
GT — George Tuska

HC — Howard Chaykin
HK — Harvey Kurtzman
HT — Herb Trimpe

IN — Irv Novick

JA — Jim Aparo
JAb — Jack Abel
JB — John Buscema
JBy — John Byrne
JCr — Johnny Craig
JD — Jayson Disbrow
JDu — Jan Duursema
JJ — Jeff Jones
JJM — John Jackson Miller
JK — Jack Kirby
JKa — Jack Kamen
JKu — Joe Kubert
JL — Jose Luis Garcia Lopez
JLee — Jim Lee
JM — Jim Mooney
JO — Joe Orlando
JOy — Jerry Ordway
JR — John Romita
JR2 — John Romita Jr.
JS — John Stanley
JSa — Joe Staton
JSe — John Severin
JSh — Jim Sherman
JSn — Jim Starlin
JSo — Jim Steranko
JSt — Joe Sinnott

KB — Kurt Busiek
KG — Keith Giffen
KGa — Kerry Gammill
KJ — Klaus Janson
KN — Kevin Nowlan
KP — Keith Pollard
KS — Kurt Schaffenberger

LMc — Luke McDonnell

MA — Murphy Anderson
MB — Matt Baker
MD — Mort Drucker
ME — Mark Evanier
MG — Michael Golden
MGr — Mike Grell
MGu — Mike Gustovich
MK — Mike Kaluta
MM — Mort Meskin
MN — Mike Nasser
MP — Mike Ploog
MR — Marshall Rogers
MW — Matt Wagner
MZ — Mike Zeck

NA — Neal Adams
NC — Nick Cardy
NG — Neil Gaiman
NR — Nestor Redondo

PB — Pat Broderick
PD — Peter David
PG — Paul Gulacy
PM — Pete Morisi
PS — Paul Smith

RA — Ross Andru
RB — Rich Buckler
RBy — Reggie Byers
RCo — Rich Corben
RE — Ric Estrada
RH — Russ Heath
RHo — Richard Howell
RK — Roy Krenkel
RL — Rob Liefeld
RM — Russ Manning
RMo — Ruben Moreira
RT — Romeo Tanghal

SA — Sergio Aragonés
SB — Sal Buscema
SD — Steve Ditko
SL — Stan Lee
SR — Steve Rude

TA — Tony DeZuniga
TMc — Todd McFarlane
TP — Tom Palmer
TS — Tom Sutton
TVE — Trevor Von Eeden
TY — Tom Yeates

VM — Val Mayerik

WE — Will Eisner
WH — Wayne Howard
WK — Walt Kelly
WP — Wendy Pini
WS — Walter Simonson
WW — Wally Wood

Life with Millie

More stories with Marvel's famous model
©Atlas

Lili

Brian Michael Bendis tale set in New Orleans
©Image

Limited Collectors' Edition

Oddly numbered treasury-sized comics
©DC

Linda Carter, Student Nurse

Clearly not the Wonder Woman actress
©Atlas

Little Audrey TV Funtime

More antics from Harvey's irrepressible youth
©Harvey

N-MINT

Licensable Bear
About

❑1, Nov 2003 .... 2.95
❑2, ca. 2005; b&w 2.95

License to Kill
Eclipse

❑1, ca. 1989 .... 7.95

Lidsville
Gold Key

❑1, Oct 1972 .... 20.00
❑2, Jan 1973, 16-page Kenner catalog insert 14.00
❑3, Apr 1973 .... 12.00
❑4, Jul 1973 .... 12.00
❑5, Oct 1973 .... 12.00

Lt. Robin Crusoe, U.S.N.
Gold Key

❑1, Oct 1966, Cover code -601; later reprinted in Walt Disney Showcase #26 .... 20.00

Life and Adventures of Santa Clause
Tundra

❑nn, ca. 1992 .... 24.95

L.I.F.E. Brigade
Blue Comet

❑1 .... 2.00
❑1/2nd; 2nd printing 2.00
❑2 .... 2.00
❑3; Title changes to New L.I.F.E. Brigade 2.00

Life Eaters
DC

❑1, ca. 2003 .... 29.95

Life of Captain Marvel
Marvel

❑1, Aug 1985; JSn (w); JSn, DC (a); Baxter reprint 3.00
❑2, Sep 1985; JSn (w); JSn, DGr, DC, JSt (a); Baxter reprint 2.50
❑3, Oct 1985; JSn (w); AM, JSn, DGr, JSt (a); Baxter reprint 2.50
❑4, Nov 1985; JSn (w); AM, JSn, DGr, DP, JSt (a); Baxter reprint 2.50
❑5, Dec 1985; JSn (w); JSn, DGr, KJ, JAb (a); Baxter reprint 2.50

Life of Christ
Marvel / Nelson

❑1, Feb 1993 .... 3.00

Life of Christ: The Easter Story
Marvel / Nelson

❑1 .... 3.00

Life of Pope John Paul II
Marvel

❑1, Jan 1983; JSt (a); 64 pages; No ads 2.50

Lifequest
Caliber

❑1, Dec 1997 .... 2.95
❑2, Feb 1998 .... 2.95
❑3, Jun 1998 .... 2.95
❑4, Nov 1998 .... 2.95
❑5, Jun 1999 .... 2.95

Life Under Sanctions
Fantagraphics

❑1, Feb 1994, b&w; NN 2.95

N-MINT

Life, the Universe and Everything
DC

❑1; prestige format; adapts Douglas Adams book 6.95
❑2; prestige format; adapts Douglas Adams book 6.95
❑3; prestige format; adapts Douglas Adams book 6.95

Life with Archie
Archie

❑1, Sep 1958 .... 225.00
❑2, Sep 1959 .... 110.00
❑3, Jul 1960 .... 85.00
❑4, Sep 1960 .... 85.00
❑5, Nov 1960 .... 85.00
❑6, Jan 1961 .... 55.00
❑7, Mar 1961 .... 55.00
❑8, May 1961 .... 55.00
❑9, Jul 1961 .... 55.00
❑10, Sep 1961 .... 55.00
❑11, Nov 1961 .... 32.00
❑12, Jan 1962 .... 32.00
❑13, Mar 1962 .... 32.00
❑14, May 1962 .... 32.00
❑15, Jul 1962 .... 32.00
❑16, Sep 1962 .... 32.00
❑17, Nov 1962 .... 32.00
❑18, Jan 1963 .... 32.00
❑19, Mar 1963 .... 32.00
❑20, May 1963 .... 32.00
❑21, Jul 1963 .... 25.00
❑22, Aug 1963 .... 25.00
❑23 1963 .... 25.00
❑24 1963 .... 25.00
❑25 1964 .... 25.00
❑26, Mar 1964 .... 25.00
❑27, May 1964 .... 25.00
❑28, Jul 1964 .... 25.00
❑29 1964 .... 25.00
❑30, Oct 1964 .... 25.00
❑31, Nov 1964 .... 25.00
❑32, Dec 1964 .... 16.00
❑33, Jan 1965 .... 16.00
❑34, Feb 1965 .... 16.00
❑35, Mar 1965 .... 16.00
❑36, Apr 1965 .... 16.00
❑37, May 1965 .... 16.00
❑38, Jun 1965 .... 16.00
❑39, Jul 1965 .... 16.00
❑40, Aug 1965 .... 16.00
❑41, Sep 1965 .... 12.00
❑42, Oct 1965 .... 12.00
❑43, Nov 1965 .... 12.00
❑44, Dec 1965 .... 12.00
❑45, Jan 1966 .... 12.00
❑46, Feb 1966 .... 12.00
❑47, Mar 1966 .... 12.00
❑48, Apr 1966 .... 12.00
❑49, May 1966 .... 12.00
❑50, Jun 1966 .... 12.00
❑51, Jul 1966 .... 8.00
❑52, Aug 1966 .... 8.00
❑53, Sep 1966 .... 8.00
❑54, Oct 1966 .... 8.00
❑55, Nov 1966 .... 8.00
❑56, Dec 1966 .... 8.00

N-MINT

❑57, Jan 1967 .... 8.00
❑58, Feb 1967 .... 8.00
❑59, Mar 1967 .... 8.00
❑60, Apr 1967 .... 8.00
❑61, May 1967 .... 5.00
❑62, Jun 1967 .... 5.00
❑63, Jul 1967 .... 5.00
❑64, Aug 1967 .... 5.00
❑65, Sep 1967 .... 5.00
❑66, Oct 1967 .... 5.00
❑67, Nov 1967 .... 5.00
❑68, Dec 1967 .... 5.00
❑69, Jan 1968 .... 5.00
❑70, Feb 1968 .... 5.00
❑71, Mar 1968 .... 4.00
❑72, Apr 1968 .... 4.00
❑73, May 1968 .... 4.00
❑74, Jun 1968 .... 4.00
❑75, Jul 1968 .... 4.00
❑76, Aug 1968 .... 4.00
❑77, Sep 1968 .... 4.00
❑78, Oct 1968 .... 4.00
❑79, Nov 1968 .... 4.00
❑80, Dec 1968 .... 4.00
❑81, Jan 1969 .... 3.00
❑82, Feb 1969 .... 3.00
❑83, Mar 1969 .... 3.00
❑84, Apr 1969 .... 3.00
❑85, May 1969 .... 3.00
❑86, Jun 1969 .... 3.00
❑87, Jul 1969 .... 3.00
❑88, Aug 1969 .... 3.00
❑89, Sep 1969 .... 3.00
❑90, Oct 1969 .... 3.00
❑91, Nov 1969 .... 2.50
❑92, Dec 1969 .... 3.00
❑93, Jan 1970 .... 3.00
❑94, Feb 1970 .... 3.00
❑95, Mar 1970 .... 3.00
❑96, Apr 1970 .... 3.00
❑97, May 1970 .... 3.00
❑98, Jun 1970 .... 3.00
❑99, Jul 1970 .... 3.00
❑100, Aug 1970 .... 3.00
❑101, Sep 1970 .... 2.50
❑102, Oct 1970 .... 2.50
❑103, Nov 1970 .... 2.50
❑104, Dec 1970 .... 2.50
❑105, Jan 1971 .... 2.50
❑106, Feb 1971 .... 2.50
❑107, Mar 1971 .... 2.50
❑108, Apr 1971 .... 2.50
❑109, May 1971 .... 2.50
❑110, Jun 1971 .... 2.50
❑111, Jul 1971 .... 2.50
❑112, Aug 1971 .... 2.50
❑113, Sep 1971 .... 2.50
❑114, Oct 1971 .... 2.50
❑115, Nov 1971 .... 2.50
❑116, Dec 1971 .... 2.50
❑117, Jan 1972 .... 2.50
❑118, Feb 1972 .... 2.50
❑119, Mar 1972 .... 2.50
❑120, Apr 1972 .... 2.50
❑121, May 1972 .... 2.00
❑122, Jun 1972 .... 2.00

Other grades: Multiply price above by 5/6 for VF/NM • 2/3 for VERY FINE • 1/3 for FINE • 1/5 for VERY GOOD • 1/8 for GOOD

N-MINT

❑123, Jul 1972 2.00
❑124, Aug 1972 2.00
❑125, Sep 1972 2.00
❑126, Oct 1972 2.00
❑127, Nov 1972 2.00
❑128, Dec 1972 2.00
❑129, Jan 1973 2.00
❑130, Feb 1973 2.00
❑131, Mar 1973 2.00
❑132, Apr 1973 2.00
❑133, May 1973 2.00
❑134, Jun 1973 2.00
❑135, Jul 1973 2.00
❑136, Aug 1973 2.00
❑137, Sep 1973 2.00
❑138, Oct 1973 2.00
❑139, Nov 1973 2.00
❑140, Dec 1973 2.00
❑141, Jan 1974 2.00
❑142, Feb 1974 2.00
❑143, Mar 1974 2.00
❑144, Apr 1974 2.00
❑145, May 1974 2.00
❑146, Jun 1974 2.00
❑147, Jul 1974 2.00
❑148, Aug 1974 2.00
❑149, Sep 1974 2.00
❑150, Oct 1974 2.00
❑151, Nov 1974 1.75
❑152, Dec 1974 1.75
❑153, Jan 1975 1.75
❑154, Feb 1975 1.75
❑155, Mar 1975 1.75
❑156, Apr 1975 1.75
❑157, May 1975 1.75
❑158, Jun 1975 1.75
❑159, Jul 1975 1.75
❑160, Aug 1975 1.75
❑161, Sep 1975 1.75
❑162, Oct 1975 1.75
❑163, Nov 1975 1.75
❑164, Dec 1975 1.75
❑165, Jan 1976 1.75
❑166, Feb 1976 1.75
❑167, Mar 1976 1.75
❑168, Apr 1976 1.75
❑169, May 1976 1.75
❑170, Jun 1976 1.75
❑171, Jul 1976 1.50
❑172, Aug 1976 1.50
❑173, Sep 1976 1.50
❑174, Oct 1976 1.50
❑175, Nov 1976 1.50
❑176, Dec 1976 1.50
❑177, Jan 1977 1.50
❑178, Feb 1977 1.50
❑179, Mar 1977 1.50
❑180, Apr 1977 1.50
❑181, May 1977 1.50
❑182, Jun 1977 1.50
❑183, Jul 1977 1.50
❑184, Aug 1977 1.50
❑185, Sep 1977 1.50
❑186, Oct 1977 1.50
❑187, Nov 1977 1.50
❑188, Dec 1977 1.50
❑189, Jan 1978 1.50
❑190, Feb 1978 1.50
❑191, Mar 1978 1.50
❑192, Apr 1978 1.50
❑193, May 1978 1.50
❑194, Jun 1978 1.50
❑195, Jul 1978 1.50
❑196, Aug 1978 1.50
❑197, Sep 1978 1.50
❑198, Oct 1978 1.50
❑199, Nov 1978 1.50
❑200, Dec 1978 1.50
❑201, Jan 1979 1.50
❑202, Feb 1979 1.50
❑203, Mar 1979 1.50
❑204, Apr 1979 1.50
❑205, Jun 1979 1.50
❑206, Jul 1979 1.50
❑207, Aug 1979 1.50
❑208, Sep 1979 1.50
❑209, Nov 1979 1.50
❑210, Dec 1979 1.50
❑211, Feb 1980 1.50
❑212, Mar 1980 1.50
❑213, Apr 1980 1.50
❑214, Jun 1980 1.50
❑215, Jul 1980 1.50
❑216, Aug 1980 1.50
❑217, Sep 1980 1.50
❑218, Nov 1980 1.50
❑219, Dec 1980 1.50
❑220, Feb 1981 1.50
❑221, Mar 1981 1.50
❑222, Apr 1981 1.50
❑223, Jun 1981 1.50
❑224, Jul 1981 1.50
❑225, Aug 1981 1.50
❑226, Sep 1981 1.50
❑227, Nov 1981 1.50
❑228, Dec 1981 1.50
❑229, Feb 1982 1.50
❑230, Mar 1982 1.50
❑231, May 1982 1.50
❑232, Jul 1982 1.50
❑233, Sep 1982 1.50
❑234, Nov 1982 1.50
❑235, Jan 1983 1.50
❑236, Apr 1983 1.50
❑237 1983 1.50
❑238 1983 1.50
❑239, Nov 1983 1.50
❑240, Jan 1984 1.50
❑241, Mar 1984 1.50
❑242, May 1984 1.50
❑243, Jul 1984 1.50
❑244, Sep 1984 1.50
❑245, Nov 1984 1.50
❑246, Jan 1985 1.50
❑247, Mar 1985 1.50
❑248, May 1985 1.50
❑249, Jul 1985 1.50
❑250, Sep 1985 1.50
❑251, Nov 1985 1.00
❑252, Jan 1986 1.00
❑253, Mar 1986 1.00
❑254, May 1986 1.00
❑255, Jul 1986 1.00
❑256, Sep 1986 1.00
❑257, Nov 1986 1.00
❑258, Jan 1987 1.00
❑259, Mar 1987 1.00
❑260, May 1987 1.00
❑261, Jul 1987 1.00
❑262, Sep 1987 1.00
❑263, Nov 1987 1.00
❑264, Jan 1988 1.00
❑265, Mar 1988 1.00
❑266, May 1988 1.00
❑267, Jul 1988 1.00
❑268, Sep 1988 1.00
❑269, Nov 1988 1.00
❑270, Jan 1989 1.00
❑271, Mar 1989 1.00
❑272, May 1989 1.00
❑273, Jul 1989 1.00
❑274, Sep 1989 1.00
❑275, Nov 1989 1.00
❑276, Jan 1990 1.00
❑277, Mar 1990 1.00
❑278, May 1990 1.00
❑279, Jul 1990 1.00
❑280, Sep 1990 1.00
❑281, Nov 1990 1.00
❑282, Jan 1991 1.00
❑283, Mar 1991 1.00
❑284, May 1991 1.00
❑285, Jul 1991, Final issue (?) 1.00

Life with Millie
Atlas

❑8, Dec 1960 35.00
❑9, Feb 1961 28.00
❑10, Apr 1961 28.00
❑11, Jun 1961 26.00
❑12, Aug 1961 26.00
❑13, Oct 1961 26.00
❑14, Dec 1961 26.00
❑15, Feb 1962 26.00
❑16, Apr 1962 26.00
❑17, Jun 1962 26.00
❑18, Aug 1962 26.00
❑19, Oct 1962 26.00
❑20, Dec 1962, SL (w) 26.00

Light and Darkness War
Marvel / Epic

❑1, Oct 1988 1.95
❑2, Nov 1988 1.95
❑3, Jan 1989 1.95
❑4, Feb 1989 1.95
❑5, Apr 1989 1.95
❑6, Sep 1989 1.95

Light Brigade
DC

❑1, Apr 2004 5.95
❑2, May 2004 5.95
❑3, Jun 2004 5.95
❑4, Jun 2004 5.95

Light Fantastic
Innovation

❑0, Movie adaptation; Novel adaptation 2.50
❑1, Jun 1992 2.50
❑2 2.50
❑3 2.50
❑4 2.50

Lightning Comics Presents
Lightning

❑1, May 1994 3.50

Lights Out
Tokyopop

❑1, Oct 2005, b&w 9.99

Lili
Image

❑0, ca. 1999 4.95

Liling-Po
Tokyopop

❑1, Feb 2005, Graphic novel; Read right to left 9.99
❑2, May 2005; Graphic novel; Read right to left 9.99
❑3, Oct 2005 9.99

Li'l Kids
Marvel

❑1, Jul 1970 35.00
❑2, Oct 1970 22.00
❑3, Nov 1971 22.00
❑4, Feb 1972 22.00
❑5, Apr 1972 22.00
❑6, Jun 1972 16.00
❑7, Aug 1972 16.00
❑8, Oct 1972 16.00
❑9 1973 16.00
❑10, Feb 1973 16.00
❑11, Apr 1973 16.00
❑12, Jun 1973 16.00

Lillith: Demon Princess
Antarctic

❑0, Mar 1998 1.95
❑0/Variant, Mar 1998; Special limited cover (Lilith flying w/green swish) 5.00
❑1, Aug 1996 5.00
❑2, Oct 1996 5.00
❑3, Feb 1997 5.00

Li'l Pals
Marvel

❑1, Sep 1972 25.00
❑2, Nov 1972 20.00
❑3, Jan 1973 20.00
❑4, Mar 1973 20.00
❑5, May 1973 20.00

Li'l Santa
NBM

❑1 14.95

Limited Collectors' Edition
DC

❑C-20; Rudolph the Red-Nosed Reindeer 32.00
❑C-21, Sum 1973; Shazam!; reprints Golden Age Marvel Family stories 16.00
❑C-22, Fal 1973; JKu (w); JK, JKu (a); Tarzan 14.00
❑C-23; House of Mystery 16.00
❑C-24; Rudolph the Red-Nosed Reindeer 26.00
❑C-25; NA (a); Batman 28.00

Other grades: Multiply price above by 5/6 for VF/NM • 2/3 for VERY FINE • 1/3 for FINE • 1/5 for VERY GOOD • 1/8 for GOOD

Little Dot

Obsessive-compulsive child acts out
©Harvey

Little Dot's Uncles and Aunts

Child has amazingly large family
©Harvey

Little Lotta

Nothing politically correct about this series
©Harvey

Little Lotta Foodland

May be overkill to say this title was giant-sized
©Harvey

Little Sad Sack

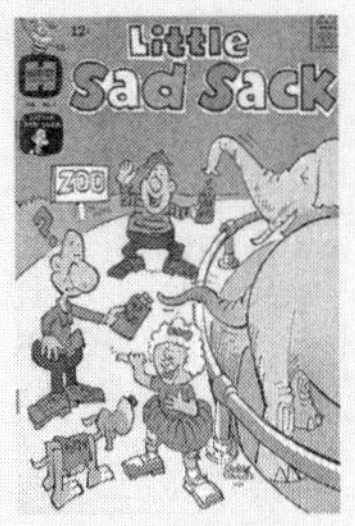

Adventures of a child before he's drafted
©Harvey

N-MINT

❑C-27; Shazam!; reprints Golden Age Marvel Family stories 16.00
❑C-29; JKu (w); JK, JKu (a); Tarzan 10.00
❑C-31, Nov 1974; Superman 15.00
❑C-32, Jan 1975; Ghosts 10.00
❑C-33, Feb 1975; Rudolph the Red-Nosed Reindeer 16.00
❑C-34, Mar 1975; Christmas With the Super-Heroes 12.00
❑C-35, May 1975; Shazam! 10.00
❑C-36, Jul 1975; NR, JK, JKu (a); The Bible 16.00
❑C-37, Sep 1975; Batman 20.00
❑C-38, Nov 1975; Superman 10.00
❑C-39, Nov 1975; CI, NA, DD, CCB (a); Secret Origins of Super Villains 10.00
❑C-40, Nov 1975; Dick Tracy 12.00
❑C-41, Jan 1976; ATh (w); ATh (a); Super Friends 10.00
❑C-42, Mar 1976; Rudolph the Red-Nosed Reindeer 10.00
❑C-43, Mar 1976; Christmas With the Super-Heroes 10.00
❑C-44, Jul 1976; Batman 12.00
❑C-45, Jul 1976; More Secret Origins of Super-Villains 10.00
❑C-46, Sep 1976; Justice League of America 10.00
❑C-47, Sep 1976; Superman Salutes the Bicentennial; reprints Tomahawk stories 10.00
❑C-48, Nov 1976; Superman vs. Flash... 12.00
❑C-49, Nov 1976; Legion 10.00
❑C-50; Rudolph the Red-Nosed Reindeer; poster 10.00
❑C-51, Aug 1977; Batman vs. Ra's Al Ghul 12.00
❑C-52; NA (a); Best of DC 10.00
❑C-57; Welcome Back, Kotter 14.00
❑C-59; Series continued in All-New Collectors' Edition; Batman's Strangest Cases 14.00

Lincoln-16
Skarwood

❑1, Aug 1997 .... 2.95
❑2, Oct 1997, b&w 2.95

Linda Carter, Student Nurse
Atlas

❑1, Sep 1961 .... 60.00
❑2, Nov 1961 .... 40.00
❑3, Jan 1962 .... 40.00
❑4, Mar 1962 .... 40.00
❑5, May 1962 .... 40.00
❑6, Jul 1962 .... 30.00
❑7, Sep 1962 .... 30.00
❑8, Nov 1962 .... 30.00
❑9, Jan 1963 .... 30.00

Linda Lark
Dell

❑1, Oct 1961 .... 15.00
❑2, Jan 1962 .... 10.00
❑3, Apr 1962 .... 10.00
❑4, Jul 1962 .... 10.00
❑5, Sep 1962 .... 10.00
❑6, Dec 1962 .... 10.00
❑7, Mar 1963 .... 10.00
❑8, Aug 1963 .... 10.00

N-MINT

Line the Dustbin Funnies
East Willis

❑1, Sum 1997 .... 2.95

Lionheart
Awesome

❑1/A, Aug 1999, JPH (w); Dynamic Forces variant 3.50
❑1/B, Aug 1999, JPH (w); Women, treasure chest on cover 3.00
❑Ashcan 1, Jul 1999, Wizard World '99 preview edition; JPH (w) 3.00

Lion King
Marvel

❑1, Jul 1994 .... 2.50

Lions, Tigers & Bears
Image

❑1, Mar 2005 .... 2.95
❑2, Apr 2005 .... 2.95
❑3, May 2005 .... 2.95

Lions, Tigers & Bears
Image

❑1, May 2006 .... 2.99
❑1/Variant, May 2006 .... 2.99
❑3, Nov 2006 .... 2.99

Lippy the Lion and Hardy Har Har
Gold Key

❑1, Mar 1963 .... 60.00

Lipstick
Rip Off

❑1, May 1992, b&w; Adult 2.50

Lisa Comics
Bongo

❑1; One-shot 2.25

Lita Ford: The Queen of Heavy Metal
Rock-It Comics

❑1; Includes guitar pick 5.00

Little Scrowlie
Slave Labor

❑1; b&w series 2.95
❑2 .... 2.95
❑3 .... 2.95
❑4 .... 2.95
❑5 .... 2.95
❑6, Jun 2004 .... 2.95
❑7 .... 2.95
❑8 .... 2.95
❑9 .... 2.95
❑10, Jul 2005 .... 2.95
❑11, Aug 2005 .... 2.95
❑12, Dec 2005 .... 2.95

Little Archie
Archie

❑21, Win 1961, Giant 32.00
❑22, Spr 1962, Giant 32.00
❑23, Sum 1962, Giant 32.00
❑24, Fal 1962, 1: Mad Doctor Doom. Giant 32.00
❑25, Win 1962, Giant 32.00
❑26, Spr 1963, Giant 32.00
❑27, Sum 1963, Giant 32.00
❑28, Fal 1963, Giant 32.00
❑29, Win 1963, Giant 32.00
❑30, Spr 1964, Giant 32.00

N-MINT

❑31, Sum 1964, Giant 32.00
❑32, Fal 1964, A: Mad Doctor Doom. Giant 32.00
❑33, Win 1964, Giant 32.00
❑34, Spr 1965, Giant 32.00
❑35, Sum 1965, Giant 32.00
❑36, Fal 1965, Giant 32.00
❑37, Win 1965, Giant 32.00
❑38, Spr 1966, Giant 32.00
❑39, Sum 1966, Giant 32.00
❑40, Fal 1966, Giant 32.00
❑41, Win 1966, Giant 22.00
❑42, Spr 1967, Giant 22.00
❑43, Sum 1967, Giant 22.00
❑44, Fal 1967, Giant 22.00
❑45, Win 1967, Giant 22.00
❑46, Spr 1968, Giant 22.00
❑47, Sum 1968, Giant 22.00
❑48, Jul 1968, Giant 22.00
❑49, Sep 1968, Giant; Jughead's and Miss Grundy's real first names used 22.00
❑50, Nov 1968, Giant 22.00
❑51, Jan 1969, Giant 22.00
❑52, Mar 1969, Giant 22.00
❑53, May 1969, Giant 22.00
❑54, Jul 1969, Giant 22.00
❑55, Sep 1969, Giant 22.00
❑56, Nov 1969, Giant 22.00
❑57, Jan 1970, Giant 22.00
❑58, Mar 1970, Giant 22.00
❑59, May 1970, Giant 22.00
❑60, Jul 1970, Giant 22.00
❑61, Sep 1970, Giant 16.00
❑62, Nov 1970, Giant 16.00
❑63, Jan 1971, Giant 16.00
❑64, Mar 1971, Giant 16.00
❑65, May 1971, Giant 16.00
❑66, Jul 1971, Giant 16.00
❑67, Sep 1971, Giant 16.00
❑68, Nov 1971, Giant 16.00
❑69, Jan 1972, Giant 16.00
❑70, Mar 1972, Giant 16.00
❑71, May 1972, Giant 16.00
❑72, Jul 1972, Giant 16.00
❑73, Sep 1972, Giant 16.00
❑74, Oct 1972, Giant 16.00
❑75, Dec 1972, Giant 16.00
❑76, Feb 1973, Giant 16.00
❑77, Apr 1973, Giant 16.00
❑78, May 1973, Giant 16.00
❑79, Jul 1973, Giant 16.00
❑80, Aug 1973, Giant 16.00
❑81, Sep 1973, Giant 11.00
❑82, Oct 1973, Giant 11.00
❑83, Dec 1973, Giant 11.00
❑84, Feb 1974, Giant 11.00
❑85, Apr 1974 .... 11.00
❑86, May 1974 .... 11.00
❑87, Jul 1974 .... 11.00
❑88, Aug 1974 .... 11.00
❑89, Sep 1974 .... 11.00
❑90, Oct 1974 .... 11.00
❑91, Dec 1974 .... 11.00
❑92, Feb 1975 .... 11.00
❑93, Mar 1975 .... 11.00
❑94, Apr 1975 .... 11.00
❑95, May 1975 .... 11.00

Other grades: Multiply price above by 5/6 for VF/NM • 2/3 for VERY FINE • 1/3 for FINE • 1/5 for VERY GOOD • 1/8 for GOOD

	N-MINT
❑96, Jul 1975	11.00
❑97, Aug 1975	11.00
❑98, Sep 1975	11.00
❑99, Oct 1975	11.00
❑100, Nov 1975	11.00
❑101, Dec 1975	6.00
❑102, Jan 1976	6.00
❑103, Feb 1976	6.00
❑104, Mar 1976	6.00
❑105, Apr 1976	6.00
❑106, May 1976	6.00
❑107, Jun 1976	6.00
❑108, Jul 1976	6.00
❑109, Aug 1976	6.00
❑110, Sep 1976	6.00
❑111, Oct 1976	6.00
❑112, Nov 1976	6.00
❑113, Dec 1976	6.00
❑114, Jan 1977	6.00
❑115, Feb 1977	6.00
❑116, Mar 1977	6.00
❑117, Apr 1977	6.00
❑118, May 1977	6.00
❑119, Jun 1977	6.00
❑120, Jul 1977	6.00
❑121, Aug 1977	4.00
❑122, Sep 1977	4.00
❑123, Oct 1977	4.00
❑124, Nov 1977	4.00
❑125, Dec 1977	4.00
❑126, Jan 1978	4.00
❑127, Feb 1978	4.00
❑128, Mar 1978	4.00
❑129, Apr 1978	4.00
❑130, May 1978	4.00
❑131, Jun 1978	4.00
❑132, Jul 1978	4.00
❑133, Aug 1978	4.00
❑134, Sep 1978	4.00
❑135, Oct 1978	4.00
❑136, Nov 1978	4.00
❑137, Dec 1978	4.00
❑138, Jan 1979	4.00
❑139, Feb 1979	4.00
❑140, Mar 1979	4.00
❑141, Apr 1979	3.00
❑142, May 1979	3.00
❑143, Jun 1979	3.00
❑144, Jul 1979	3.00
❑145, Aug 1979	3.00
❑146, Sep 1979	3.00
❑147, Oct 1979	3.00
❑148, Nov 1979	3.00
❑149, Dec 1979	3.00
❑150, Jan 1980	3.00
❑151, Feb 1980	3.00
❑152, Mar 1980	3.00
❑153, Apr 1980	3.00
❑154, May 1980	3.00
❑155, Jun 1980	3.00
❑156, Jul 1980	3.00
❑157, Aug 1980	3.00
❑158, Sep 1980	3.00
❑159, Oct 1980	3.00
❑160, Nov 1980	3.00
❑161, Dec 1980	3.00
❑162, Jan 1981	3.00
❑163, Feb 1981	3.00
❑164, Mar 1981	3.00
❑165, Apr 1981	3.00
❑166, May 1981	3.00
❑167, Jun 1981	3.00
❑168, Jul 1981	3.00
❑169, Aug 1981	3.00
❑170, Sep 1981	3.00
❑171, Oct 1981	3.00
❑172, Nov 1981	3.00
❑173 1982	3.00
❑174 1982	3.00
❑175 1982	3.00
❑176 1982	3.00
❑177 1982	3.00
❑178 1982	3.00
❑179 1982	3.00
❑180, ca. 1983	3.00

Little Archie Digest Magazine
Archie

	N-MINT
❑1 1991	3.00
❑2 1991	2.00
❑3 1991	2.00
❑4 1991	2.00
❑5 1992	2.00
❑6 1992	2.00
❑7 1992	2.00
❑8 1992	2.00
❑9 1992	2.00
❑10	2.00
❑11	1.75
❑12	1.75
❑13	1.75
❑14, Aug 1995	1.75
❑15, Oct 1995	1.75
❑16, Jun 1996	1.75
❑17, Sep 1996	1.79
❑18, Mar 1997	1.79
❑19, Jun 1997	1.79
❑20, Sep 1997	1.79
❑21, Mar 1998	1.95
❑22	1.95
❑23	1.95
❑24	1.95
❑25	1.95

Little Archie Mystery
Archie

	N-MINT
❑1, Aug 1963	60.00
❑2, Oct 1963	42.00

Little Audrey
Harvey

	N-MINT
❑1, Aug 1992	1.50
❑2 1992	1.25
❑3 1992	1.25
❑4 1992	1.25
❑5 1993	1.25
❑6 1993	1.25
❑7 1993	1.25
❑8 1993	1.25
❑9 1993	1.25

Little Audrey and Melvin
Harvey

	N-MINT
❑1, May 1962	45.00
❑2, Jul 1962	25.00
❑3, Sep 1962	18.00
❑4, Nov 1962	18.00
❑5, Jan 1963	18.00
❑6, Mar 1963	14.00
❑7, May 1963	14.00
❑8, Jul 1963	14.00
❑9, Sep 1963	14.00
❑10, Nov 1964	14.00
❑11 1964	12.00
❑12 1964	12.00
❑13 1964	12.00
❑14, Sep 1964	12.00
❑15, Nov 1964	12.00
❑16, Jan 1965	12.00
❑17, Mar 1965	12.00
❑18, May 1965	12.00
❑19, Jul 1965	12.00
❑20, Sep 1965	12.00
❑21, Nov 1965	9.00
❑22, Jan 1966	9.00
❑23, Mar 1966	9.00
❑24, May 1966	9.00
❑25, Jul 1966	9.00
❑26, Sep 1966	9.00
❑27, Oct 1966	9.00
❑28, Jan 1967	9.00
❑29, Mar 1967	9.00
❑30, May 1967	9.00
❑31, Jul 1967	6.00
❑32, Sep 1967	6.00
❑33, Nov 1967	6.00
❑34, Jan 1968	6.00
❑35, Sep 1968	6.00
❑36, Nov 1968	6.00
❑37, Jan 1969	6.00
❑38, Mar 1969	6.00
❑39, Apr 1969	6.00
❑40, Jun 1969	6.00
❑41, Aug 1969	4.00
❑42, Oct 1969	4.00
❑43, Dec 1969	4.00
❑44, Feb 1970	4.00
❑45, Apr 1970	4.00
❑46, Aug 1970	4.00
❑47, Oct 1970	4.00
❑48, Nov 1970	4.00
❑49 1971	4.00
❑50, Aug 1971	4.00
❑51, Sep 1971	4.00
❑52, Nov 1971	4.00
❑53 1972	4.00
❑54, Sep 1972	4.00
❑55, Nov 1972	4.00
❑56, Feb 1973	4.00
❑57, Apr 1973	4.00
❑58, Jun 1973	4.00
❑59, Aug 1973	4.00
❑60, Oct 1973	4.00
❑61, Dec 1973	4.00

Little Audrey TV Funtime
Harvey

	N-MINT
❑1, Sep 1962	45.00
❑2, Dec 1962	28.00
❑3, Mar 1963	24.00
❑4, Jun 1963	20.00
❑5, Sep 1963	20.00
❑6, Dec 1963	16.00
❑7, Mar 1964	16.00
❑8, Jun 1964	16.00
❑9, Sep 1964	16.00
❑10, Dec 1964	16.00
❑11, Mar 1965	12.00
❑12, Jun 1965	12.00
❑13, Sep 1965	12.00
❑14, Dec 1965	12.00
❑15, Mar 1966	12.00
❑16 1966	12.00
❑17, Nov 1966	12.00
❑18, Mar 1967	12.00
❑19 1967	12.00
❑20, Oct 1968	12.00
❑21, Dec 1968	9.00
❑22, May 1969	9.00
❑23, Jul 1969	9.00
❑24, Sep 1969	9.00
❑25, Nov 1969	9.00
❑26, Feb 1970	9.00
❑27, May 1970	9.00
❑28, Aug 1970	9.00
❑29, ca. 1970	9.00
❑30, Dec 1970	9.00
❑31 1971	9.00
❑32 1971	9.00
❑33 1971	9.00

Little Dot
Harvey

	N-MINT
❑74, Nov 1961	15.00
❑75, Dec 1961	15.00
❑76, Jan 1962	15.00
❑77, Feb 1962	15.00
❑78, Mar 1962	15.00
❑79, Apr 1962	15.00
❑80, May 1962	15.00
❑81, Jun 1962	10.00
❑82, Aug 1962	10.00
❑83, Oct 1962	10.00
❑84, Dec 1962	10.00
❑85, Feb 1963	10.00
❑86, Apr 1963	10.00
❑87, Jun 1963	10.00
❑88, Aug 1963	10.00
❑89, Oct 1963	10.00
❑90, Dec 1963	10.00
❑91, Feb 1964	10.00
❑92, Apr 1964	10.00
❑93, Jun 1964	10.00
❑94, Aug 1964	10.00
❑95, Oct 1964	10.00
❑96, Dec 1964	10.00
❑97, Feb 1965	10.00
❑98, Apr 1965	10.00
❑99, Jun 1965	10.00
❑100, Aug 1965	10.00
❑101, Oct 1965	7.00
❑102, Dec 1965	7.00
❑103, Feb 1966	7.00

Other grades: Multiply price above by 5/6 for VF/NM • 2/3 for VERY FINE • 1/3 for FINE • 1/5 for VERY GOOD • 1/8 for GOOD

Little Stooges

The son of a stooge is a stooge as well
©Gold Key

Lobo

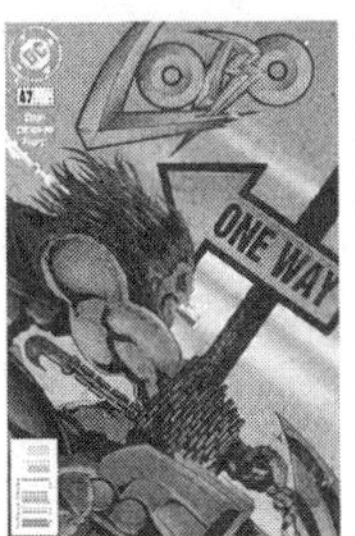

Hairy grouch gets title to himself
©DC

Logan's Run

Film adaptation had Thanos back-up story
©Marvel

Lois Lane

Main title was called "Superman's Girlfriend..."
©DC

Lone Ranger

Masked man restarted from the Dell series
©Gold Key

	N-MINT
❑104, Apr 1966	7.00
❑105, Jun 1966	7.00
❑106, Aug 1966	7.00
❑107, Oct 1966	7.00
❑108, Dec 1966	7.00
❑109, Feb 1967	7.00
❑110, Apr 1967	7.00
❑111, Jun 1967	7.00
❑112, Aug 1967	7.00
❑113, Oct 1967	7.00
❑114, Dec 1967	7.00
❑115, Feb 1968	7.00
❑116, Apr 1968	7.00
❑117, Jun 1968	7.00
❑118, Aug 1968	7.00
❑119, Oct 1968	7.00
❑120, Dec 1968	7.00
❑121, Feb 1969	7.00
❑122, Apr 1969	7.00
❑123, May 1969	7.00
❑124, Jul 1969	7.00
❑125 1969	7.00
❑126, Oct 1969	7.00
❑127, Dec 1969	7.00
❑128, Jan 1970	7.00
❑129, Mar 1970	7.00
❑130, May 1970	7.00
❑131, Jul 1970	7.00
❑132, Sep 1970	7.00
❑133, Oct 1970	7.00
❑134, Nov 1970	7.00
❑135, Jan 1971	7.00
❑136, Mar 1971	7.00
❑137, May 1971	7.00
❑138, Jul 1971	7.00
❑139, Sep 1971	7.00
❑140, Oct 1971	7.00
❑141, Nov 1971	7.00
❑142, Mar 1972, Giant-size	10.00
❑143, May 1972, Giant-size	10.00
❑144, Jul 1972, Giant-size	10.00
❑145, Sep 1972, Giant-size	10.00
❑146, Nov 1972	5.00
❑147, Jan 1973	5.00
❑148, Mar 1973	5.00
❑149, May 1973	5.00
❑150, Jul 1973	5.00
❑151, Sep 1973	5.00
❑152	5.00
❑153, Jun 1974	5.00
❑154, Aug 1974	5.00
❑155, Oct 1974	5.00
❑156, Dec 1974	5.00
❑157, Feb 1975	5.00
❑158, Apr 1975	5.00
❑159, Jun 1975	5.00
❑160, Aug 1975	5.00
❑161, Oct 1975	5.00
❑162, Dec 1975	5.00
❑163, Feb 1976	5.00
❑164, Apr 1976, Final Issue	5.00

Little Dot
Harvey

	N-MINT
❑1, Sep 1992	1.50
❑2	1.50
❑3, Jun 1993	1.50
❑4 1993	1.50
❑5, Jan 1994	1.50
❑6, Apr 1994	1.50
❑7, Jun 1994	1.50

Little Dot Dotland
Harvey

	N-MINT
❑1, Jul 1962	75.00
❑2, Sep 1962	40.00
❑3, Nov 1962	40.00
❑4, Jan 1963	35.00
❑5, Mar 1963	35.00
❑6, May 1963	24.00
❑7, Jul 1963	24.00
❑8, Sep 1963	24.00
❑9, Nov 1963	24.00
❑10, Jan 1964	24.00
❑11, Mar 1964	20.00
❑12, May 1964	20.00
❑13, Jul 1964	20.00
❑14, Sep 1964	20.00
❑15, Nov 1964	20.00
❑16, Jan 1965	20.00
❑17, Mar 1965	20.00
❑18, May 1965	20.00
❑19, Jul 1965	20.00
❑20, Sep 1965	20.00
❑21, Nov 1965	16.00
❑22, Jan 1966	16.00
❑23, Mar 1966	16.00
❑24, May 1966	16.00
❑25, Jul 1966	16.00
❑26, Sep 1966	16.00
❑27, Oct 1966	16.00
❑28, Jan 1967	16.00
❑29, Mar 1967	16.00
❑30, May 1967	12.00
❑31, Jul 1967	12.00
❑32, Sep 1967	12.00
❑33, Nov 1967	12.00
❑34, Jan 1968	12.00
❑35, Sep 1968	12.00
❑36, Nov 1968	12.00
❑37, Jan 1969	12.00
❑38, Mar 1969	12.00
❑39, Apr 1969	12.00
❑40, Jun 1969	10.00
❑41, Aug 1969	10.00
❑42, Oct 1969	10.00
❑43, Dec 1969	10.00
❑44, Feb 1970	10.00
❑45, Apr 1970	10.00
❑46, Aug 1970	10.00
❑47, Oct 1970	10.00
❑48, Jan 1971	10.00
❑49, Apr 1971	10.00
❑50, Aug 1971	10.00
❑51, ca. 1971	10.00
❑52, ca. 1972	10.00
❑53, Jun 1972	10.00
❑54, Sep 1972	10.00
❑55, Nov 1972	8.00
❑56, Feb 1973	8.00
❑57, Apr 1973	8.00
❑58, Jun 1973	8.00
❑59, Aug 1973	8.00
❑60, Nov 1973	8.00
❑61, Dec 1973, becomes Dot Dotland	8.00
❑62, Sep 1974, was Little Dot Dotland	10.00
❑63, Nov 1974	10.00

Little Dot in 3-D
Blackthorne

	N-MINT
❑1, Blackthorne 3-D Series #59; ca. 1988	2.50

Little Dot's Uncles and Aunts
Harvey

	N-MINT
❑1, Oct 1961	70.00
❑2, Aug 1962, A: Richie Rich	42.00
❑3, Nov 1962	42.00
❑4, Feb 1963	36.00
❑5, May 1963	36.00
❑6, Aug 1963	28.00
❑7, Nov 1963	28.00
❑8, Feb 1964	28.00
❑9, May 1964	28.00
❑10, Aug 1964	28.00
❑11, Nov 1964	22.00
❑12, Feb 1965	22.00
❑13, May 1965	22.00
❑14, Aug 1965	22.00
❑15, Nov 1965, Giant-Size	22.00
❑16, Feb 1966, Giant-Size	22.00
❑17 1966	22.00
❑18, Sep 1966	22.00
❑19, Nov 1966	22.00
❑20, Aug 1967	22.00
❑21, Nov 1967	22.00
❑22, Feb 1968	22.00
❑23, Jul 1968	22.00
❑24, Oct 1968	22.00
❑25, Dec 1968	22.00
❑26, Apr 1969, Giant-Size	22.00
❑27, Jun 1969	22.00
❑28, Aug 1969	22.00
❑29, Oct 1969	22.00
❑30, Nov 1969	22.00
❑31, Mar 1970	22.00
❑32, Jun 1970	22.00
❑33, Aug 1970	22.00
❑34, Oct 1970, Giant-Size	22.00
❑35, Nov 1970	22.00
❑36, Mar 1971	14.00
❑37 1971	14.00
❑38, Aug 1971	14.00
❑39, Oct 1971	14.00
❑40	14.00
❑41 1972	14.00
❑42, Jun 1972	14.00
❑43 1972, Giant-Size	14.00
❑44, Dec 1972	14.00
❑45, Feb 1973	14.00
❑46, Apr 1973	14.00
❑47, Jun 1973	14.00
❑48, Aug 1973	14.00
❑49, Oct 1973	14.00
❑50, Dec 1973	14.00
❑51, Feb 1974	14.00
❑52, Apr 1974	14.00

Other grades: Multiply price above by 5/6 for VF/NM • 2/3 for VERY FINE • 1/3 for FINE • 1/5 for VERY GOOD • 1/8 for GOOD

N-MINT

Little Ego
NBM

❑1; Adult 10.95

Little Endless Storybook
DC / Vertigo

❑1, Aug 2001 5.95

Little Gloomy
Slave Labor

❑1, Oct 1999 2.95

Little Gloomy's Super Scary Monster Show
Slave Labor

❑1 2005 2.95
❑2, Oct 2005 2.95

Little Greta Garbage
Rip Off

❑1, Jul 1990, b&w; Adult 2.50
❑2, Jun 1991, b&w; Adult 2.50

Little Grey Man
Image

❑1; graphic novel 6.95

Little Italy
Fantagraphics

❑1, b&w 3.95

Little Jim-Bob Big Foot
Jump Back

❑1, b&w 2.95
❑2, Jan 1998, b&w 2.95

Little Lotta
Harvey

❑38, Nov 1961 18.00
❑39, Jan 1962 18.00
❑40, Mar 1962 18.00
❑41, May 1962 15.00
❑42, Jul 1962 15.00
❑43, Sep 1962 15.00
❑44, Nov 1962 15.00
❑45, Jan 1963 15.00
❑46, Mar 1963 15.00
❑47, May 1963 15.00
❑48, Jul 1963 15.00
❑49, Sep 1963 15.00
❑50, Nov 1963 15.00
❑51, Jan 1964 12.00
❑52, Mar 1964 12.00
❑53, May 1964 12.00
❑54, Jul 1964 12.00
❑55, Sep 1964 12.00
❑56, Nov 1964 12.00
❑57, Jan 1965 12.00
❑58, Mar 1965 12.00
❑59, May 1965 12.00
❑60, Jul 1965 12.00
❑61, Sep 1965 12.00
❑62, Nov 1965 12.00
❑63, Jan 1966 12.00
❑64, Mar 1966 12.00
❑65, May 1966 12.00
❑66, Jul 1966 12.00
❑67, Sep 1966 12.00
❑68, Nov 1966 12.00
❑69, Jan 1967 12.00
❑70, Mar 1967 12.00
❑71, May 1967 8.00
❑72, Jul 1967 8.00
❑73, Sep 1967 8.00
❑74, Nov 1967 8.00
❑75, Jan 1968 8.00
❑76, Mar 1968 8.00
❑77, May 1968 8.00
❑78, Jul 1968 8.00
❑79, Sep 1968 8.00
❑80, Nov 1968 8.00
❑81, Jan 1969 8.00
❑82, Mar 1969 8.00
❑83, May 1969 8.00
❑84, Jul 1969 8.00
❑85, Sep 1969 8.00
❑86, Oct 1969 8.00
❑87, Dec 1969 8.00
❑88, Jan 1970 8.00
❑89, Apr 1970 8.00
❑90, Jul 1970 8.00
❑91, Sep 1970 5.00

N-MINT

❑92, Oct 1970 5.00
❑93, Nov 1970 5.00
❑94, Jan 1971 5.00
❑95, Mar 1971 5.00
❑96, May 1971 5.00
❑97, Jul 1971 5.00
❑98, Sep 1971 5.00
❑99, Nov 1971 6.00
❑100, Mar 1972 6.00
❑101, May 1972, Giant-size 6.00
❑102, Jul 1972 6.00
❑103, Sep 1972 3.00
❑104, Nov 1972 3.00
❑105, Jan 1973 3.00
❑106, Mar 1973 3.00
❑107, May 1973 3.00
❑108, Jul 1973 3.00
❑109, Sep 1973 3.00
❑110, Nov 1973 3.00
❑111, Sep 1974 3.00
❑112, Nov 1974 3.00
❑113, Jan 1975 3.00
❑114, Mar 1975 3.00
❑115, May 1975 3.00
❑116, Jul 1975 3.00
❑117, Sep 1975 3.00
❑118, Nov 1975 3.00
❑119, Jan 1976 3.00
❑120, Mar 1976, reprints #66 3.00

Little Lotta
Harvey

❑1, Oct 1992 1.50
❑2, Jan 1993 1.50
❑3, Apr 1993 1.50
❑4, Jul 1993 1.50

Little Lotta Foodland
Harvey

❑1, Sep 1963, Giant 45.00
❑2, Dec 1963, Giant 35.00
❑3, Mar 1964, Giant 35.00
❑4, Jun 1964, Giant 30.00
❑5, Sep 1964, Giant 30.00
❑6, Dec 1964, Giant 24.00
❑7, Mar 1965, Giant 24.00
❑8, Jul 1965, Giant 24.00
❑9, Oct 1965, Giant 24.00
❑10, Jan 1966, Giant 24.00
❑11, Apr 1966, Giant 16.00
❑12, Jul 1966, Giant 16.00
❑13, Oct 1966, Giant 16.00
❑14, Oct 1967, Giant 16.00
❑15, Sep 1968, Giant 16.00
❑16, Oct 1968, Giant 12.00
❑17, Nov 1968, Giant 12.00
❑18, Dec 1968, Giant 12.00
❑19, Sep 1969, Giant 12.00
❑20, Nov 1969, Giant 12.00
❑21, Feb 1970, Giant 8.00
❑22, May 1970, Giant 8.00
❑23, Aug 1970, Giant 8.00
❑24, Oct 1970, Giant 8.00
❑25, Dec 1970, Giant 8.00
❑26, Feb 1971, Giant 8.00
❑27, May 1971, Giant 8.00
❑28, Oct 1971, Giant 8.00
❑29, Oct 1972, Giant 8.00

Little Lulu
Dell / Gold Key/Whitman

❑159, ca. 1961 25.00
❑160, ca. 1961 25.00
❑161, ca. 1962 20.00
❑162, ca. 1962 20.00
❑163, May 1962 20.00
❑164, Jul 1962 20.00
❑165, Oct 1962, Giant-size; Little Lulu in Paris; back cover pin-up 70.00
❑166, Jan 1963, Giant-size 70.00
❑167, ca. 1963 20.00
❑168, ca. 1963 20.00
❑169, ca. 1963 20.00
❑170, Dec 1963 20.00
❑171, Mar 1964 20.00
❑172, Jun 1964 20.00
❑173, Sep 1964 20.00
❑174, Dec 1964 20.00
❑175, Mar 1965 20.00

N-MINT

❑176, Jun 1965 20.00
❑177, Sep 1965 20.00
❑178, Dec 1965 20.00
❑179, Mar 1966 20.00
❑180, Jun 1966 20.00
❑181, Sep 1966 15.00
❑182, Dec 1966 15.00
❑183, Mar 1967 15.00
❑184, Jun 1967 15.00
❑185, Sep 1967 15.00
❑186, Dec 1967 15.00
❑187, Mar 1968 15.00
❑188, Jun 1968 15.00
❑189, Sep 1968 15.00
❑190, Dec 1968 15.00
❑191, Mar 1969 15.00
❑192, Jun 1969 15.00
❑193, Sep 1969 15.00
❑194, Dec 1969 15.00
❑195, Mar 1970 15.00
❑196, Jun 1970 15.00
❑197, Sep 1970 15.00
❑198, Dec 1970 15.00
❑199, Mar 1971 15.00
❑200, Jun 1971 15.00
❑201, Sep 1971 9.00
❑202, Dec 197 9.00
❑203, Mar 1972 9.00
❑204, May 1972 9.00
❑205, Jul 1972 9.00
❑206, Aug 1972 9.00
❑207, Sep 1972 9.00
❑208, Nov 1972 9.00
❑209, Dec 1972 9.00
❑210, Jan 1973 9.00
❑211, Mar 1973 9.00
❑212, May 1973 9.00
❑213, Jul 1973 9.00
❑214, Sep 1973 9.00
❑215, Nov 1973 9.00
❑216, Jan 1974 9.00
❑217, Mar 1974 9.00
❑218, May 1974 9.00
❑219, Jul 1974 9.00
❑220, Aug 1974 9.00
❑221, Sep 1974 6.00
❑222, Nov 1974 6.00
❑223, Jan 1975 6.00
❑224, Mar 1975 6.00
❑225, May 1975 6.00
❑226, Jul 1975 6.00
❑227, Aug 1975 6.00
❑228, Sep 1975 6.00
❑229, Nov 1975 6.00
❑230, Jan 1976 6.00
❑231, Mar 1976 6.00
❑232, May 1976 6.00
❑233, ca. 1976 6.00
❑234, ca. 1976 6.00
❑235, ca. 1976 6.00
❑236, Nov 1976 6.00
❑237, Jan 1977 6.00
❑238, Mar 1977 6.00
❑239, May 1977 6.00
❑240, Jul 1977 6.00
❑241, Sep 1977 4.00
❑242, Nov 1977 4.00
❑243, ca. 1977 4.00
❑244, ca. 1978 4.00
❑245, ca. 1978 4.00
❑246, ca. 1978 4.00
❑247, ca. 1978 4.00
❑248, Sep 1978 4.00
❑249, Nov 1978 4.00
❑250, Jan 1979 4.00
❑251, Mar 1979 3.00
❑252, May 1979 3.00
❑253, Jul 1979 3.00
❑254, Aug 1979 3.00
❑255, ca. 1979 3.00
❑256, Nov 1979 3.00
❑257, Jan 1980 3.00
❑258, Mar 1980 12.00
❑259, May 1980 12.00
❑260, Sep 1980, Sold only in packs; extremely low distribution 325.00
❑261, Nov 1980, Sold only in packs 45.00

Other grades: Multiply price above by 5/6 for VF/NM • 2/3 for VERY FINE • 1/3 for FINE • 1/5 for VERY GOOD • 1/8 for GOOD

Lone Wolf and Cub

First (and first) U.S. printing of manga classic

©First

Longshot

Tousle-haired person inhabits Mojo-world

©Marvel

Looney Tunes

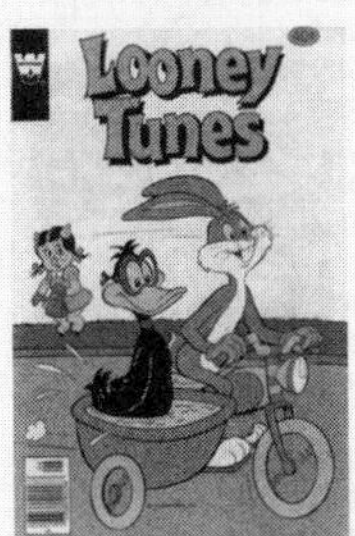

Gold Key version had some stories cross over

©Gold Key

Loose Cannon

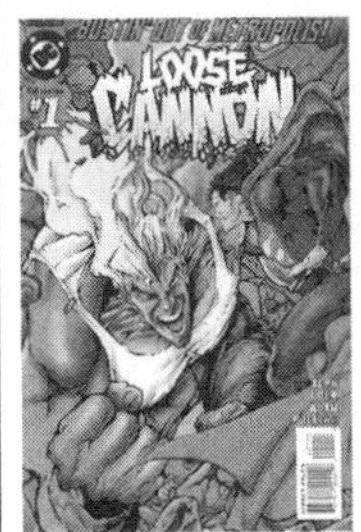

Cop turns into gigantic blue behemoth

©DC

Lost Universe

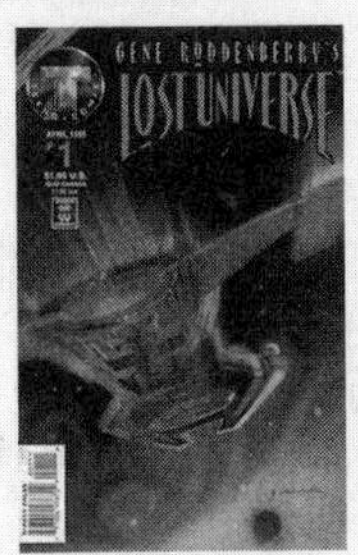

Producer creates comics series posthumously

©Tekno

	N-MINT
❑262, ca. 1981, Sold only in packs	12.00
❑263, ca. 1981, Sold only in packs	12.00
❑264, Feb 1982, Sold only in packs	12.00
❑265, ca. 1982, Sold only in packs	12.00
❑266, Jul 1983, Sold only in packs	15.00
❑267, ca. 1983, Sold only in packs	15.00
❑268 1984, Sold only in packs	15.00

Little Mermaid
Marvel

❑1, Sep 1994, Movie adaptation	2.50
❑2, Oct 1994	2.00
❑3, Nov 1994	2.00
❑4, Dec 1994	2.00
❑5, Jan 1995	2.00
❑6, Feb 1995	2.00
❑7, Mar 1995	2.00
❑8, Apr 1995	2.00
❑9, May 1995	2.00
❑10, Jun 1995	2.00
❑11, Jul 1995	2.00
❑12, Aug 1995, Final Issue	2.00

Little Mermaid Limited Series
Disney

❑1, Feb 1992	2.00
❑2, Mar 1992	2.00
❑3, May 1992	2.00
❑4, Jun 1992	2.00

Little Mermaid
W.D.

❑1; NN	3.50

Little Mermaid: Underwater Engagements
Acclaim

❑1; flip-book digest set before movie	4.50

Little Mermaid
Disney

❑1, stapled	2.50
❑1/Direct ed., squarebound	5.95

Little Miss Strange
Millennium

❑1	2.95

Little Mister Man
Slave Labor

❑1, Nov 1995, b&w	2.95
❑2, Dec 1995, b&w	2.95
❑3, Feb 1996, b&w; Final Issue	2.95

Little Monsters
Gold Key

❑1, Nov 1964	20.00
❑2, Feb 1965	12.00
❑3, Nov 1965	8.00
❑4 1966	8.00
❑5, Jul 1966	8.00
❑6, Oct 1966	6.00
❑7, Dec 1966	6.00
❑8, Feb 1967	6.00
❑9, Apr 1967	6.00
❑10, Jun 1967	5.00
❑11	5.00
❑12, Dec 1970	5.00
❑13, ca. 1971	5.00
❑14, Sep 1971	5.00
❑15, Dec 1971	5.00

	N-MINT
❑16, Mar 1972	5.00
❑17, Jun 1972	5.00
❑18, Sep 1972	5.00
❑19, Dec 1972	5.00
❑20, Mar 1973	5.00
❑21, Jun 1973	4.00
❑22, Sep 1973	4.00
❑23, Dec 1973	4.00
❑24, Mar 1974	4.00
❑25, Jun 1974	4.00
❑26, Sep 1974	4.00
❑27, Dec 1974	4.00
❑28, Mar 1975	4.00
❑29, Jun 1975	4.00
❑30, Sep 1975	4.00
❑31, Dec 1975	4.00
❑32, Feb 1976	4.00
❑33, Apr 1976	4.00
❑34, Jun 1976	4.00
❑35, Aug 1976	4.00
❑36, Oct 1976	4.00
❑37, Dec 1976	4.00
❑38, Feb 1977	4.00
❑39, Apr 1977	4.00
❑40, Jun 1977	4.00
❑41, Aug 1977	4.00
❑42, Oct 1977	4.00
❑43, Dec 1977	4.00
❑44, Feb 1978	4.00

Little Monsters
Now

❑1, Jan 1990; Movie adaptation	1.50
❑2, Feb 1990; Movie adaptation	1.50
❑3, Mar 1990; Movie adaptation	1.50
❑4, Apr 1990; Movie adaptation	1.50
❑5, May 1990; Movie adaptation	1.50
❑6, Jun 1990; Movie adaptation	1.50

Little Nemo in Slumberland 3-D
Blackthorne

❑1	2.50

Little Oz Squad
Patchwork

❑1, Jun 1995, b&w; Based on books by L. Frank Baum; No Indicia; no issue number	2.75

Little Red Hot: Bound
Image

❑1, Jul 2001	2.95
❑2, Sep 2001	2.95
❑3, Nov 2001	2.95

Little Red Hot: Chane of Fools
Image

❑1, Feb 1999	2.95
❑2, Mar 1999	2.95
❑3, Apr 1999	2.95

Little Ronzo in Slumberland
Slave Labor

❑1, Jul 1987	1.75

Little Sad Sack
Harvey

❑1, Oct 1964	7.00
❑2, Dec 1964	4.00
❑3, Feb 1964	4.00

	N-MINT
❑4, Apr 1965	4.00
❑5, Jun 1965	4.00
❑6, Aug 1965	3.00
❑7, Oct 1965	3.00
❑8, Dec 1965	3.00
❑9, Feb 1966	3.00
❑10, Apr 1966	3.00
❑11, Jun 1966	3.00
❑12, Sep 1966	3.00
❑13, Nov 1966	3.00
❑14, Jan 1966	3.00
❑15, Mar 1966	3.00
❑16, May 1966	3.00
❑17, Jul 1966	3.00
❑18, Sep 1966	3.00
❑19, Nov 1966	3.00

Little Shop of Horrors
DC

❑1, Mar 1987; Movie adaptation	2.00

Little Snow Fairy Sugar Manga
ADV Manga

❑1, ca. 2006	9.99
❑2, ca. 2006	9.99
❑3, ca. 2007	9.99

Little Star
Oni

❑1, Feb 2005, b&w	2.99
❑2, Jun 2005, b&w	2.99
❑3, Jun 2005, b&w	2.99
❑4, Oct 2005, b&w	2.99
❑5, Nov 2005; b&w	2.99

Little Stooges
Gold Key

❑1, Sep 1972	16.00
❑2, Dec 1972	12.00
❑3, Mar 1973	12.00
❑4, Jun 1973	9.00
❑5, Sep 1973	9.00
❑6, Dec 1973	9.00
❑7, Mar 1974	9.00

Little White Mouse
Caliber

❑1, Nov 1997, b&w	2.95
❑2, Jan 1998, b&w	2.95
❑3, Mar 1998	2.95
❑4, May 1998	2.95

Little White Mouse
Caliber

❑1, Aug 1998, b&w; Includes Sketchbook	2.95
❑2, Feb 1999, b&w	2.95
❑3, Apr 1999, b&w; "Letters to Home" reprinted from A Caliber Christmas 1998	2.95
❑4, ca. 1999, b&w	2.95

Livewires
Marvel

❑1, Apr 2005	2.99
❑2, May 2005	2.99
❑3, Jun 2005	2.99
❑4, Jul 2005	2.99
❑5, Aug 2005	2.99
❑6, Sep 2005	2.99

Other grades: Multiply price above by 5/6 for VF/NM • 2/3 for VERY FINE • 1/3 for FINE • 1/5 for VERY GOOD • 1/8 for GOOD

N-MINT

Livingstone Mountain
Adventure

❑1, Jul 1991, b&w ... 2.50
❑2, Aug 1991, b&w ... 2.50
❑3, Sep 1991, b&w ... 2.50
❑4, Oct 1991, b&w ... 2.50

Living with Zombies
Frightworld Studios

❑1, Dec 2005; b&w ... 2.50
❑2, Apr 2005; b&w ... 2.50
❑3, Aug 2005 ... 2.50

Liz and Beth
Fantagraphics / Eros

❑1, Feb 1991, b&w; Adult ... 3.00
❑2, May 1991, b&w; Adult ... 3.00
❑3, Aug 1991, b&w; Adult ... 3.00
❑4; Adult ... 3.00

Liz and Beth
Fantagraphics / Eros

❑1, b&w; Adult ... 2.50
❑2, Aug 1992, b&w; Adult ... 2.50
❑3, b&w; Adult ... 2.50
❑4; Adult ... 2.50

Liz and Beth
Fantagraphics / Eros

❑1, b&w; Adult ... 2.50
❑2, b&w; Adult ... 2.50
❑3, b&w; Adul ... 2.50
❑4, b&w; Adult ... 2.50
❑5, b&w; Adult ... 2.50
❑6, b&w; Adult ... 2.50
❑7, b&w; Adult ... 2.50

Lizard Lady
Aircel

❑1, b&w; Adult ... 2.95
❑2, Sep 1991, b&w; Adult ... 2.95
❑3, b&w; Adult ... 2.95
❑4, b&w; Adult ... 2.95

Lizards Summer Fun Special
Caliber

❑1, b&w; Adult ... 3.50

Lizzie McGuire Cine-Manga
Tokyopop

❑1, May 2003, fumetti with photos from the TV show ... 7.99

Llisica
NBM

❑1; Adult ... 9.95

Lloyd Llewellyn
Fantagraphics

❑1, Apr 1986 ... 2.25
❑2, Jun 1986 ... 2.25
❑3, Aug 1986 ... 2.25
❑4, Oct 1986 ... 2.25
❑5, Jan 1987 ... 2.25
❑6, Jun 1987 ... 2.25
❑Special 1 ... 2.50
❑Special 1/2nd, Oct 1992; 2nd printing.. 2.75

Loaded
Interplay

❑1 ... 1.00

Lobo
DC

❑1, Nov 1990, KG (a) ... 3.00
❑1/2nd, Nov 1990, KG (a); 2nd printing. 2.00
❑2, Dec 1990, KG (a) ... 2.00
❑3, Jan 1991, KG (a) ... 2.00
❑4, Feb 1991, KG (a) ... 2.00

Lobo
DC

❑0, Oct 1994; O: Lobo. 10/94 ... 2.50
❑1, Dec 1993; foil cover ... 3.50
❑2, Feb 1994 ... 2.50
❑3, Mar 1994; Mar on cover, Feb inside. 2.50
❑4, Apr 1994 ... 2.50
❑5, May 1994; 1: Gold Star ... 2.50
❑6, Jun 1994 ... 2.50
❑7, Jul 1994 ... 2.50
❑8, Aug 1994 ... 2.50
❑9, Sep 1994 ... 2.50
❑10, Nov 1994 ... 2.50
❑11, Dec 1994 ... 2.00
❑12, Jan 1995 ... 2.00

N-MINT

❑13, Feb 1995 ... 2.00
❑14, Mar 1995 ... 2.00
❑15, Apr 1995 ... 2.00
❑16, Jun 1995 ... 2.25
❑17, Jul 1995 ... 2.25
❑18, Aug 1995 ... 2.25
❑19, Sep 1995 ... 2.25
❑20, Oct 1995 ... 2.25
❑21, Nov 1995 A: Space Cabby ... 2.25
❑22, Dec 1995; Underworld Unleashed . 2.25
❑23, Jan 1996 ... 2.25
❑24, Feb 1996 ... 2.25
❑25, Mar 1996 ... 2.25
❑26, Apr 1996 ... 2.25
❑27, May 1996 ... 2.25
❑28, Jun 1996 ... 2.25
❑29, Jul 1996 ... 2.25
❑30, Aug 1996 ... 2.25
❑31, Sep 1996 ... 2.25
❑32, Oct 1996; Lobo's body is destroyed 2.25
❑33, Nov 1996; Sammy, The Flesh-Crazed Snale ... 2.25
❑34, Dec 1996 ... 2.25
❑35, Jan 1997 ... 2.25
❑36, Feb 1997 A: Hemingway. A: Poe. A: Mark Twain. A: Chaucer. A: Shakespeare ... 2.25
❑37, Mar 1997 ... 2.25
❑38, Apr 1997 ... 2.25
❑39, May 1997; Lobo as a pirate ... 2.25
❑40, Jun 1997; Lobo inside a whale ... 2.25
❑41, Jul 1997 ... 2.25
❑42, Aug 1997 ... 2.25
❑43, Sep 1997 ... 2.25
❑44, Oct 1997; Genesis ... 2.25
❑45, Nov 1997; V: Jackie Chin ... 2.25
❑46, Dec 1997; Face cover ... 2.25
❑47, Jan 1998 ... 2.25
❑48, Feb 1998 ... 2.25
❑49, Mar 1998 ... 2.25
❑50, Apr 1998; A: Keith Giffen. D: Everyone ... 2.25
❑51, May 1998 ... 2.25
❑52, Jun 1998 ... 2.25
❑53, Jul 1998 ... 2.25
❑54, Aug 1998 ... 2.25
❑55, Sep 1998 ... 2.25
❑56, Oct 1998 ... 2.50
❑57, Dec 1998; at police convention ... 2.50
❑58, Jan 1999; KG (a); A: Orion. A: Superman. Lobo hunts body-hopping alien on Earth ... 2.50
❑59, Feb 1999; A: Bad Wee Bastards. in miniature world ... 2.50
❑60, Mar 1999; 1: Superbo. Lobo reforms 2.50
❑61, Apr 1999; 2: Superbo. A: Savage Six 2.50
❑62, May 1999 ... 2.50
❑63, Jun 1999 A: Demon ... 2.50
❑64, Jul 1999; A: Demon. Final Issue ... 2.50
❑1000000, Nov 1998; 1: Layla ... 4.00
❑Ann 1, ca. 1993 ... 5.00
❑Ann 2, ca. 1994; SA (a); Elseworlds ... 3.50
❑Ann 3, ca. 1995; Year One ... 3.95

Lobo: A Contract on Gawd
DC

❑1, Apr 1994 ... 2.00
❑2, May 1994 ... 2.00
❑3, Jun 1994 ... 2.00
❑4, Jul 1994 ... 2.00

Lobo: Blazing Chain of Love
DC

❑1, Sep 1992 KG (a) ... 2.00

Lobo: Bounty Hunting for Fun and Profit
DC

❑1; prestige format; NN ... 4.95

Lobo: Chained
DC

❑1, May 1997; Lobo goes to jail ... 2.50

Lobo Convention Special
DC

❑1; KG (w); Set at 1993 San Diego Comic Convention ... 2.00

N-MINT

Lobo/Deadman: The Brave and the Bald
DC

❑1, Feb 1995; NN; One-shot ... 3.50

Lobo: Death and Taxes
DC

❑1, Oct 1996 ... 2.25
❑2, Nov 1996 ... 2.25
❑3, Dec 1996 ... 2.25
❑4, Jan 1997; Final Issue ... 2.25

Lobo/Demon: Helloween
DC

❑1, Dec 1996; One-shot ... 2.25

Lobo: Fragtastic Voyage
DC

❑1, ca. 1998; prestige format; NN; One-shot ... 5.95

Lobo Gallery: Portraits of a Bastich
DC

❑1, Sep 1995; pin-ups ... 3.50

Lobo Goes to Hollywood
DC

❑1, Aug 1996; One-shot ... 2.25

Lobo: Infanticide
DC

❑1, Oct 1992 KG (c); KG (w); KG (a) ... 2.00
❑2, Nov 1992 KG (c); KG (w); KG (a) ... 2.00
❑3, Dec 1992 KG (c); KG (w); KG (a) ... 2.00
❑4, Jan 1993 KG (c); KG (w); KG (a) ... 2.00

Lobo: in the Chair
DC

❑1, Aug 1994; One-shot ... 1.95

Lobo: I Quit
DC

❑1, Dec 1995; Lobo stops smoking ... 2.75

Lobo/Judge Dredd: Psycho-Bikers Vs. The Mutants from Hell
DC

❑1; prestige format; NN ... 4.95

Lobo/Mask
DC

❑1, Feb 1997, prestige format crossover with Dark Horse ... 5.95
❑2, Mar 1997, prestige format crossover with Dark Horse ... 5.95

Lobo Paramilitary Christmas Special
DC

❑1, Jan 1991; KG (w); KG (a); D: Santa Claus. D: Santa Claus ... 3.00

Lobo: Portrait of a Victim
DC

❑1, ca. 1993 ... 2.00

Lobo's Back
DC

❑1, May 1992, KG (a); 1: Ramona. Variant covers exist ... 2.00
❑2, Jun 1992, KG (a) ... 2.00
❑3, Oct 1992, KG (a) ... 2.00
❑4, Nov 1992, KG (a) ... 2.00

Lobo's Big Babe Spring Break Special
DC

❑1, Spr 1995; NN ... 1.95

Lobo the Duck
DC / Amalgam

❑1, Jun 1997 ... 1.95

Lobo: Un-American Gladiators
DC

❑1, Jun 1993 ... 2.00
❑2, Jul 1993 ... 2.00
❑3, Aug 1993 ... 2.00
❑4, Sep 1993 ... 2.00

Lobo Unbound
DC

❑1, Aug 2003 ... 2.95
❑2, Sep 2003 ... 2.95
❑3, Nov 2003; Hits the Spot ... 2.95
❑4, Jan 2004 ... 2.95
❑5, Mar 2004 ... 2.95
❑6, May 2004 ... 2.95

Other grades: Multiply price above by 5/6 for VF/NM • 2/3 for VERY FINE • 1/3 for FINE • 1/5 for VERY GOOD • 1/8 for GOOD

Louder than Words

Sergio series goes without saying... anything
©Dark Horse

Love & Rockets

Celebrated title from Los Bros Hernandez
©Fantagraphics

Love and Romance

Charlton title tried to have hip 1970s feel
©Charlton

Lucifer

Devilish Sandman character gets series
©DC

Lucy Show

Lucy's 1960s series spawns comic spinoff
©Gold Key

N-MINT

Lobocop
DC

❑1, Feb 1994 ... 2.00

Local
Oni

❑1, Nov 2005 ... 2.99
❑2, Jan 2006 ... 2.99

Loco vs. Pulverine
Eclipse

❑1, Jul 1992, b&w; wraparound cover; parody ... 2.50

Logan: Path of the Warlord
Marvel

❑1, Feb 1996 ... 6.00

Logan: Shadow Society
Marvel

❑1, Dec 1996; NN ... 6.00

Logan's Run
Marvel

❑1, Jan 1977, GP (a); Movie adaptation ... 5.00
❑2, Feb 1977, GP (c); GP (a) ... 2.00
❑3, Mar 1977, GP (a) ... 2.00
❑4, Apr 1977, GP (c); GP (a) ... 2.00
❑5, May 1977, GP (a) ... 2.00
❑6, Jun 1977, GP, PG (c); TS (a); A: Thanos. New stories begin; Back-up story is first solo story featuring Thanos ... 4.00
❑6/35¢, Jun 1977, PG (c); TS (a); A: Thanos. New stories begin; Back-up story is first solo story featuring Thanos; 35¢ regional price variant ... 15.00
❑7, Jul 1977, GP (a) ... 2.00
❑7/35¢, Jul 1977, GP (a); 35¢ regional price variant ... 5.00

Logan's Run
Adventure

❑1; PG (c); PG (a); Introduction by William F. Nolan ... 2.50
❑2, Jul 1990 ... 2.50
❑3 ... 2.50
❑4, Oct 1990 ... 2.50
❑5, Mar 1991 ... 2.50
❑6, Apr 1991 ... 2.50

Logan's World
Adventure

❑1, May 1991, b&w ... 2.50
❑2, Aug 1991, b&w ... 2.50
❑3, Sep 1991, b&w ... 2.50
❑4, Nov 1991, b&w ... 2.50
❑5, Jan 1992, b&w ... 2.50
❑6, Mar 1992, b&w ... 2.50

Lois Lane
DC

❑1, Aug 1986; GM (c); GM (a); 48 pages ... 2.00
❑2, Sep 1986; GM (c); GM (a); 48 pages ... 2.00

Loki
Marvel

❑1, Sep 2004 ... 12.00
❑2, Sep 2004 ... 6.00
❑3, Oct 2004 ... 3.50
❑4, Nov 2004 ... 3.50

N-MINT

Lolita
NBM

❑1; Adult ... 10.95
❑2; Adult ... 10.95
❑3; Adult ... 9.95
❑4; Adult ... 9.95

Lone
Dark Horse

❑1, Sep 2003 ... 2.99
❑2, Oct 2003 ... 2.99
❑3, Nov 2003 ... 2.99
❑4, Feb 2004 ... 2.99
❑5, Mar 2004 ... 2.99
❑6, Apr 2004 ... 2.99

Lone Gunmen
Dark Horse

❑Special 1, Jun 2001 ... 2.99

Lonely Nights Comics
Last Gasp

❑1; Adult; ca. 1986 ... 2.00

Lonely Tombstone One Shot
Image

❑1, Nov 2005 ... 5.99

Lonely War of Willy Schultz
Avalon

❑1, b&w; Reprints ... 2.95
❑2 ... 2.95
❑3 ... 2.95
❑4 ... 2.95

Lone Ranger
Gold Key

❑1, Sep 1964 ... 35.00
❑2, Sep 1965 ... 18.00
❑3, Mar 1966 ... 14.00
❑4, Aug 1966 ... 12.00
❑5, Jan 1967 ... 12.00
❑6, Apr 1967 ... 12.00
❑7, Jul 1967, Reprints ... 10.00
❑8, Oct 1967 ... 10.00
❑9, Jan 1968 ... 10.00
❑10, Apr 1968 ... 10.00
❑11, Jul 1968 ... 9.00
❑12, Oct 1968 ... 9.00
❑13, Mar 1969 ... 9.00
❑14, Jun 1969 ... 9.00
❑15, Sep 1969 ... 9.00
❑16, Dec 1969 ... 9.00
❑17, ca. 1972 ... 9.00
❑18, Sep 1974 ... 9.00
❑19, Dec 1974 ... 9.00
❑20, Mar 1975, Reprints ... 9.00
❑21, Jun 1975 ... 5.00
❑22, Sep 1975 ... 5.00
❑23, Dec 1975 ... 5.00
❑24, Mar 1976 ... 5.00
❑25, Jun 1976 ... 5.00
❑26, Sep 1976 ... 5.00
❑27, Dec 1976 ... 5.00
❑28, Mar 1977, Final Issue ... 5.00

Lone Ranger
Pure Imagination

❑1 1996, b&w; reprints newspaper strip ... 3.00

N-MINT

Lone Ranger and Tonto
Topps

❑1, Aug 1994 ... 2.50
❑1/Variant, Aug 1994; foil edition; Limited edition ... 4.00
❑2, Sep 1994 ... 2.50
❑2/Variant, Sep 1994; limited edition ... 3.50
❑3, Oct 1994 ... 2.50
❑3/Variant, Oct 1994; limited edition ... 3.00
❑4, Nov 1994 ... 2.50
❑4/Variant, Nov 1994; limited edition ... 3.00

Lone Ranger Golden West
Gold Key

❑1, ca. 1966 ... 45.00

Lone Wolf 2100: Red Files
Dark Horse

❑1, Feb 2003 ... 2.99

Lone Wolf and Cub
First

❑1, May 1987, FM (c); Introduction by Frank Miller ... 6.00
❑1/2nd, FM (c); FM (a); 2nd printing ... 2.50
❑1/3rd, FM (c); FM (a); 3rd printing ... 2.50
❑2, Jun 1987, FM (c); FM (a) ... 4.00
❑2/2nd, Jun 1987, FM (c); FM (a); 2nd printing ... 2.50
❑3, Jul 1987, FM (c); FM (a) ... 4.00
❑3/2nd, FM (c); FM (a); 2nd printing ... 2.50
❑4, Aug 1987, FM (c); FM (a) ... 3.00
❑5, Sep 1987, FM (c); FM (a) ... 3.00
❑6, Oct 1987, FM (c); FM (a); O: Lone Wolf ... 3.00
❑7, Nov 1987, FM (c); FM (a); O: Lone Wolf ... 3.00
❑8, Dec 1987, FM (c) ... 3.00
❑9, Jan 1988, FM (c) ... 3.00
❑10, Feb 1988, FM (c) ... 3.00
❑11, Mar 1988, FM (c) ... 2.50
❑12, Apr 1988, FM (c); FM (a) ... 2.50
❑13, May 1988, BSz (c); BSz (a) ... 2.50
❑14, Jun 1988, BSz (c); BSz (a) ... 2.50
❑15, Jul 1988, BSz (c); BSz (a) ... 2.50
❑16, Aug 1988, BSz (c); BSz (a) ... 2.50
❑17, Sep 1988, BSz (c); BSz (a) ... 2.50
❑18, Oct 1988, BSz (c); BSz (a) ... 2.50
❑19, Nov 1988, BSz (c); BSz (a) ... 2.50
❑20, Dec 1988, BSz (c); BSz (a) ... 2.50
❑21, Jan 1989, BSz (c) ... 2.50
❑22, Feb 1989, BSz (c) ... 2.50
❑23, Mar 1989, BSz (c) ... 2.50
❑24, Apr 1989, BSz (c) ... 2.50
❑25, May 1989, MW (c) ... 2.50
❑26, Jun 1989, MW (c) ... 2.95
❑27, Jul 1989, MW (c) ... 3.00
❑28, Aug 1989, MW (c) ... 3.00
❑29, Sep 1989, MW (c) ... 3.00
❑30, Oct 1989, MW (c) ... 3.00
❑31, Jan 1990, MW (c) ... 3.00
❑32, Apr 1990, MW (c) ... 3.00
❑33, May 1990, MW (c) ... 3.00
❑34, Jun 1990, MW (c) ... 3.25
❑35, Jun 1990, MW (c) ... 3.25
❑36, Jul 1990, MW (c) ... 3.25
❑37, Aug 1990, MP (c) ... 3.25
❑38, Sep 1990, MP (c) ... 3.25
❑39, Oct 1990, Giant-size; MP (c) ... 6.00
❑40, Nov 1990, MP (c) ... 3.25

Other grades: Multiply price above by 5/6 for VF/NM • 2/3 for VERY FINE • 1/3 for FINE • 1/5 for VERY GOOD • 1/8 for GOOD

N-MINT

❑41, Dec 1990, MP (c) ... 4.00
❑42, Jan 1991, MP (c) ... 4.00
❑43, Feb 1991, MP (c) ... 4.00
❑44, Mar 1991, MP (c) ... 4.00
❑45, Apr 1991, MP (c) ... 4.00
❑46, May 1991, MP (c); MP (a) ... 4.00
❑47, Jun 1991, MP (c); MP (a) ... 4.00
❑48, Jul 1991 ... 4.00
❑49, Aug 1991 ... 4.00

Lone Wolf and Cub
Dark Horse

❑1, Aug 2000; The Assassin's Road ... 9.95
❑2, Sep 2000; The Gateless Barrier ... 9.95
❑3, Nov 2000; The Flute of the Fallen Tiger ... 9.95
❑4, Dec 2000; The Bell Warden ... 9.95
❑5, Jan 2001; Black Wind; Samurai Executioner crossover ... 9.95
❑6, Feb 2001; Lanterns for the Dead ... 9.95
❑7, Mar 2001; Cloud Dragon, Wind Tiger ... 9.95
❑8, Apr 2001; Chains of Death ... 9.95
❑9, May 2001; Echo of the Assassin ... 9.95
❑10, Jun 2001; Hostage Child ... 9.95
❑11, Jul 2001; Talisman of Hades ... 9.95
❑12, Aug 2001; Shattered Stones ... 9.95
❑13, Sep 2001; The Moon in the East, The Sun in the West ... 9.95
❑14, Oct 2001; Day of the Demons ... 9.95
❑15, Nov 2001; Brothers of the Grass ... 9.95
❑16, Dec 2001; Gateway into Winter ... 9.95
❑17, Jan 2002; The Will of the Fang ... 9.95
❑18, Feb 2002; Twilight of the Kurokuwa ... 9.95
❑19, Mar 2002; The Moon in Our Hearts ... 9.95
❑20, Apr 2002; A Taste of Poison ... 9.95
❑21, May 2002; Fragrance of Death ... 9.95
❑22, Jun 2002; Heaven and Earth ... 9.95
❑23, Jul 2002; Tears of Ice ... 9.95
❑24, Aug 2002; In These Small Hands ... 9.95
❑25, Sep 2002; Perhaps in Death ... 9.95
❑26, Oct 2002; Struggle in the Dark ... 9.95
❑27, Nov 2002; Battle's Eve ... 9.95
❑28, Dec 2002; The Lotus Throne ... 9.95

Lone Wolf 2100
Dark Horse

❑1, May 2002 ... 2.99
❑2, Jun 2002 ... 2.99
❑3, Jul 2002 ... 2.99
❑4, Aug 2002 ... 2.99
❑5, Nov 2002 ... 2.99
❑6, Dec 2002 ... 2.99
❑7, Jan 2003 ... 2.99
❑8, May 2003 ... 2.99
❑9, Sep 2003 ... 2.99
❑10, Oct 2003 ... 2.99
❑11, Jan 2004 ... 2.99

Long, Hot Summer
DC / Milestone

❑1, Jul 1995; enhanced cover ... 2.95
❑2, Aug 1995 ... 2.50
❑3, Sep 1995; Final Issue ... 2.50

Longshot
Marvel

❑1, Sep 1985; 1: Longshot ... 3.50
❑2, Oct 1985; 1: Ricochet Rita ... 3.00
❑3, Nov 1985; 1: Mojo. 1: Spiral ... 2.50
❑4, Dec 1985 A: Spider-Man ... 2.50
❑5, Jan 1986 ... 2.00
❑6, Feb 1986; Double-size ... 2.50

Longshot
Marvel

❑1, Feb 1998; wraparound cover ... 3.99

Longshot Comics
Slave Labor

❑1, Jun 1995 ... 2.95
❑1/2nd, Feb 1996; 2nd printing ... 2.95
❑2, Jul 1997, b&w ... 2.95

Lookers
Avatar

❑1, Feb 1997 ... 3.00
❑2, Mar 1997 ... 3.00

Lookers: Slaves of Anubis
Avatar

❑1, Nov 1998; Adult ... 3.50

N-MINT

Looking Glass Wars: Hatter M
Image

❑1, Jan 2006 ... 3.99
❑2, Apr 2006 ... 3.50
❑3, Oct 2006 ... 3.50
❑4, Nov 2006 ... 3.99

Looney Tunes: Back in Action The Movie
DC

❑1, ca. 2003 ... 3.95

Looney Tunes
Gold Key

❑1, Apr 1975 ... 12.00
❑2, Jun 1975 ... 7.00
❑3, Aug 1975 ... 5.00
❑4, Oct 1975 ... 5.00
❑5, Dec 1975 ... 5.00
❑6, Feb 1976 ... 3.50
❑7, Apr 1976 ... 3.50
❑8, Jun 1976 ... 3.50
❑9, Aug 1976 ... 3.50
❑10, Oct 1976 ... 3.50
❑11, Dec 1976 ... 2.50
❑12, Feb 1977 ... 2.50
❑13, Apr 1977, Cover code 90296-704; Cracky in Hostess ad "Time on My Hands" ... 2.50
❑14, Jun 1977 ... 2.50
❑15, Aug 1977 ... 2.50
❑16, Oct 1977 ... 2.50
❑17, Dec 1977 ... 2.50
❑18, Feb 1978 ... 2.50
❑19, Apr 1978 ... 2.50
❑20, Jun 1978 ... 2.50
❑21, Aug 1978 ... 2.00
❑22, Oct 1978, Cover code 90296-810 ... 2.00
❑23, Dec 1978 ... 2.00
❑24, Feb 1979 ... 2.00
❑25, Apr 1979 ... 2.00
❑26, Jun 1979 ... 2.00
❑27, Aug 1979 ... 2.00
❑28, Oct 1979 ... 2.00
❑29, Dec 1979 ... 2.00
❑30, Feb 1980 ... 2.00
❑31, Apr 1980 ... 2.00
❑32, Jun 1980, Includes Incredible Hulk Hostess ad "Hulk Gets Even" by John Byrne never published in Marvel Comics ... 2.00
❑33, Aug 1980 ... 25.00
❑34, Oct 1980 ... 40.00
❑35, Dec 1980 ... 30.00
❑36, Feb 1981 ... 2.00
❑37, Apr 1981 ... 2.00
❑38, Jun 1981 ... 2.00
❑39, Aug 1981 ... 2.00
❑40, Oct 1981 ... 2.00
❑41, Jan 1982 ... 1.50
❑42, Feb 1982 ... 1.50
❑43, Apr 1982 ... 15.00
❑44, Jun 1982 ... 15.00
❑45, Aug 1982 ... 20.00
❑46, Mar 1984 ... 20.00
❑47, Jun 1984 ... 20.00

Looney Tunes
DC

❑1, Apr 1994, A: Marvin Martian ... 2.25
❑2, May 1994, Road Runner, Coyote ... 2.00
❑3, Jun 1994, Baseball issue ... 2.00
❑4, Jul 1994, A: Witch Hazel ... 2.00
❑5, Aug 1994, Coyote, Martians ... 1.75
❑6, Sep 1994, Tazmanian Devil ... 1.50
❑7, Oct 1994 ... 1.50
❑8, Nov 1994 ... 1.50
❑9, Dec 1994 ... 1.50
❑10, Jan 1995, Christmas issue ... 1.50
❑11, Feb 1995 ... 1.50
❑12, Mar 1995 ... 1.50
❑13, Apr 1995, Coyote ... 1.50
❑14, May 1995 ... 1.50
❑15, Jun 1995 ... 1.50
❑16, Jul 1995, Daffy, Speedy Gonzales ... 1.50
❑17, Aug 1995 ... 1.50
❑18, Sep 1995, Duck Dodgers ... 1.50
❑19, Oct 1995 ... 1.50
❑20, Nov 1995, Yosemite Sam ... 1.50
❑21, Feb 1996, Tazmanian Devil ... 1.50

N-MINT

❑22, Apr 1996 ... 1.50
❑23, Jun 1996 ... 1.75
❑24, Aug 1996 ... 1.75
❑25, Oct 1996, Indiana Itz Mine ... 1.75
❑26, Nov 1996, indicia says Nov, cover says Dec ... 1.75
❑27, Jan 1997, indicia says Jan, cover says Feb ... 1.75
❑28, Feb 1997, cover says Apr 96, indicia says Feb 97; Valentine's issue ... 1.75
❑29, May 1997, Coyote ... 1.75
❑30, Jul 1997, Twilight Zone cover ... 1.75
❑31, Aug 1997 ... 1.75
❑32, Sep 1997, Hercules parody ... 1.75
❑33, Oct 1997, Back to School issue ... 1.75
❑34, Nov 1997, Daffy V: Dinky Downunder ... 1.75
❑35, Dec 1997, Agent Daffy ... 1.95
❑36, Jan 1998, Sylvester, Tweety ... 1.95
❑37, Feb 1998, V: Crusher ... 1.95
❑38, Mar 1998, A: Marvin Martian ... 1.95
❑39, Apr 1998, Foghorn Leghorn ... 1.95
❑40, May 1998, Sylvester ... 1.95
❑41, Jun 1998, Sylvester, Porky ... 1.95
❑42, Jul 1998, Speedy Gonzales, Sylvester ... 1.95
❑43, Aug 1998, Bugs and Daffy do Magic ... 1.95
❑44, Sep 1998, Tweety and Sylvester ... 1.99
❑45, Oct 1998, Marvin Martian ... 1.99
❑46, Nov 1998, Bugs and Taz ... 1.99
❑47, Dec 1998, Christmas issue ... 1.99
❑48, Jan 1999, A: Rocky and Mugsy ... 1.99
❑49, Feb 1999, Pepe is stalked ... 1.99
❑50, Mar 1999 ... 1.99
❑51, Apr 1999 ... 1.99
❑52, May 1999 ... 1.99
❑53, Jun 1999 ... 1.99
❑54, Jul 1999 ... 1.99
❑55, Aug 1999 ... 1.99
❑56, Sep 1999 ... 1.99
❑57, Oct 1999 ... 1.99
❑58, Nov 1999 ... 1.99
❑59, Dec 1999 ... 1.99
❑60, Jan 2000 ... 1.99
❑61, Feb 2000 ... 1.99
❑62, Mar 2000 ... 1.99
❑63, Apr 2000 ... 1.99
❑64, May 2000 ... 1.99
❑65, Jun 2000 ... 1.99
❑66, Jul 2000 ... 1.99
❑67, Aug 2000 ... 1.99
❑68, Sep 2000 ... 1.99
❑69, Oct 2000 ... 1.99
❑70, Nov 2000 ... 1.99
❑71, Dec 2000 ... 1.99
❑72, Jan 2001 ... 1.99
❑73, Feb 2001 ... 1.99
❑74, Mar 2001 ... 1.99
❑75, Apr 2001 ... 1.99
❑76, May 2001 ... 1.99
❑77, Jun 2001 ... 1.99
❑78, Jul 2001, DDC (w) ... 1.99
❑79, Aug 2001 ... 1.99
❑80, Sep 2001 ... 1.99
❑81, Oct 2001 ... 1.99
❑82, Nov 2001 ... 1.99
❑83, Dec 2001, KG (w) ... 1.99
❑84, Jan 2002 ... 1.99
❑85, Feb 2002 ... 1.99
❑86, Mar 2002 ... 1.99
❑87, Apr 2002 ... 1.99
❑88, May 2002 ... 1.99
❑89, Jun 2002 ... 1.99
❑90, Jul 2002 ... 1.99
❑91, Aug 2002 ... 1.99
❑92, Sep 2002 ... 1.99
❑93, Oct 2002 ... 2.25
❑94, Nov 2002 ... 2.25
❑95, Dec 2002 ... 2.25
❑96, Jan 2003 ... 2.25
❑97, Feb 2003 ... 2.25
❑98, Mar 2003 ... 2.25
❑99, Apr 2003 ... 2.25
❑100, May 2003 ... 2.25
❑101, Jun 2003 ... 2.25
❑102, Jul 2003 ... 2.25
❑103, Aug 2003 ... 2.25
❑104, Sep 2003 ... 2.25
❑105, Oct 2003 ... 2.25

Other grades: Multiply price above by 5/6 for VF/NM • 2/3 for VERY FINE • 1/3 for FINE • 1/5 for VERY GOOD • 1/8 for GOOD

Luftwaffe: 1946 (Vol. 1)

Set in the Tigers of Terra alternate universe

©Antarctic

Machine

Cyborg entry to the Comics' Greatest World line

©Dark Horse

Machine Man

Kirby spinoff from 2001: A Space Odyssey

©Marvel

Machine Man

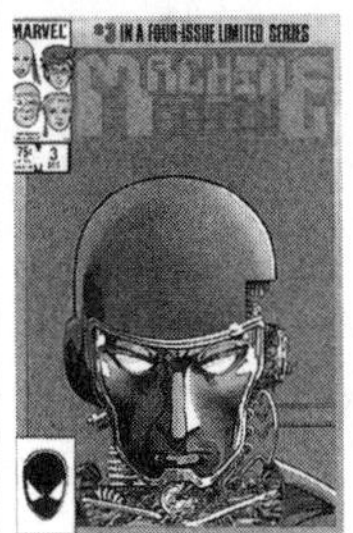

Series transports Machine Man to 2020

©Marvel

Madballs

As thin a reed on which a title has been based

©Marvel

N-MINT

❑106, Nov 2003 .... 2.25
❑107, Dec 2003 .... 2.25
❑108, Jan 2004 .... 2.25
❑109, Feb 2004 .... 2.25
❑110, Mar 2004 .... 2.25
❑111, Apr 2004 .... 2.25
❑112, May 2004 .... 2.25
❑113, Jun 2004 .... 2.25
❑114, Jul 2004 .... 2.25
❑115, Aug 2004 .... 2.25
❑116, Sep 2004 .... 2.25
❑117, Oct 2004 .... 2.25
❑118, Nov 2004 .... 2.25
❑119, Dec 2004 .... 2.25
❑120, Jan 2005 .... 2.25
❑121, Feb 2005 .... 2.25
❑122, Mar 2005 .... 2.25
❑123, Apr 2005 .... 2.25
❑124, May 2005 .... 2.25
❑125, Jun 2005 .... 2.25
❑126, Jul 2005 .... 2.25
❑127, Aug 2005 .... 2.25
❑128, Sep 2005 .... 2.25
❑129, Oct 2005; Includes Bionicle comic insert 2.25
❑130, Nov 2005 .... 2.25
❑131, Dec 2005 .... 2.25
❑132, Jan 2006 .... 2.25
❑133, Jan 2006 .... 2.25
❑134, Mar 2006 .... 2.25
❑135, Mar 2006 .... 2.25
❑136, May 2006 .... 2.25
❑137, Jun 2006 .... 2.25
❑138, Jul 2006 .... 2.25
❑139, Aug 2006 .... 2.25
❑140, Sep 2006 .... 2.25
❑141, Oct 2006 .... 2.25
❑142, Nov 2006 .... 2.25
❑144, Jan 2007, Includes 3-D Heroscape glasses; Includes Teen Titans: Sparktop mini-comic 2.25
❑145, Feb 2007 .... 2.25
❑146, Mar 2007 .... 2.25
❑147 .... 2.25
❑148 .... 2.25
❑149 .... 2.25
❑150 .... 2.25
❑151 .... 2.25
❑152 .... 2.25
❑153 .... 2.25
❑154 .... 2.25
❑155 .... 2.25
❑156 .... 2.25
❑157 .... 2.25
❑158 .... 2.25
❑159 .... 2.25
❑160 .... 2.25
❑161 .... 2.25
❑162 .... 2.25
❑163 .... 2.25
❑164 .... 2.25
❑165 .... 2.25
❑166 .... 2.25
❑167 .... 2.25
❑168 .... 2.25
❑169 .... 2.25

N-MINT

❑170 .... 2.25
❑171 .... 2.25
❑172 .... 2.25
❑173 .... 2.25

Looney Tunes Magazine
DC

❑1; Bugs Bunny 2.50
❑2; Batman parody 2.00
❑3 .... 2.00
❑4 .... 2.00
❑5 .... 2.00
❑6 .... 1.95
❑7 .... 1.95
❑8 .... 1.95
❑9 .... 1.95
❑10 .... 1.95
❑11; Title changes to Bugs Bunny & The Looney Tunes magazine; Title changes to Bugs Bunny & The Looney Tunes magazine 1.95
❑12 .... 1.95
❑13 .... 1.95
❑14 .... 1.95
❑15 .... 1.95
❑16; trading cards 1.95
❑17, Spr 1994 .... 1.95
❑19, Fal 1994 .... 1.50
❑20, Win 1995 .... 1.95

Loose Cannon
DC

❑1, Jun 1995 .... 1.75
❑2, Jul 1995; V: Bounty Inc 1.75
❑3, Aug 1995; V: Eradicator 1.75
❑4, Sep 1995; V: Eradicator; Final issue. 1.75

Loose Teeth
Fantagraphics

❑1, b&w 2.75
❑2, b&w 2.75
❑3, b&w 2.75

Lord Farris: Slavemaster
Fantagraphics / Eros

❑1, Feb 1996; Adult 2.95
❑2, May 1996; Adult 2.95

Lord Jim
Gold Key

❑1, Sep 1965; Photo cover; #10156-509 18.00

Lord of the Dead
Conquest

❑1, b&w 2.95

Lord Pumpkin
Malibu / Ultraverse

❑0, Oct 1994; Full body picture of Lord Pumpkin on cover 2.50
❑0/A, Oct 1994; Close-up of Lord Pumpkin's head on cover 2.50

Lord Pumpkin/NecroMantra
Malibu / Ultraverse

❑1, Apr 1995, b&w; Cover says Necromantra/Lord Pumpkin; flipbook 2.95
❑2, May 1995, b&w; Cover says Necromantra/Lord Pumpkin; flipbook 2.95

N-MINT

❑3, Jun 1995, b&w; Cover says Necromantra/Lord Pumpkin; flipbook 2.95
❑4, Jul 1995, b&w; Cover says Necromantra/Lord Pumpkin; flipbook 2.95

Lords
Legend (Not Dark Horse Imprint)

❑1 .... 2.25

Lords of Misrule
Dark Horse

❑1, Jan 1997, b&w 2.95
❑2, Feb 1997, b&w 2.95
❑3, Mar 1997, b&w 2.95
❑4, Apr 1997, b&w 2.95
❑5, May 1997, b&w 2.95
❑6, Jun 1997, b&w 2.95

Lords of Misrule
Atomeka

❑1 .... 6.95

Lords of the Ultra-Realm
DC

❑1, Jun 1987 .... 1.50
❑2, Jul 1986 .... 1.50
❑3, Aug 1986 .... 1.50
❑4, Sep 1986 .... 1.50
❑5, Oct 1986 .... 1.50
❑6, Nov 1986 .... 1.50
❑Special 1, ca. 1987 .... 2.25

Lore
Idea & Design Works

❑1, Dec 2003 .... 5.99
❑2, Mar 2004 .... 3.99
❑3, Jun 2004 .... 3.99
❑4, Jun 2004 .... 5.99

Lorelei
Starwarp

❑1, b&w 2.50

Lorelei of the Red Mist
Conquest

❑1, b&w 2.95
❑2, b&w 2.95

Lori Lovecraft: My Favorite Redhead
Caliber

❑1, Feb 1997 .... 3.95

Lori Lovecraft: Repression
A V

❑1, Jun 2002 .... 2.95

Lori Lovecraft: The Big Comeback
Caliber

❑1; Adult 2.95

Lori Lovecraft: The Dark Lady
Caliber

❑1 .... 2.95

Lortnoc
Radio

❑1, Aug 1998, b&w 2.95

Losers
DC / Vertigo

❑1, Aug 2003 .... 2.95
❑2, Sep 2003 .... 2.95
❑3, Oct 2003 .... 2.95
❑4, Nov 2003 .... 2.95

Other grades: Multiply price above by 5/6 for VF/NM • 2/3 for VERY FINE • 1/3 for FINE • 1/5 for VERY GOOD • 1/8 for GOOD

❑5, Dec 2003 2.95
❑6, Jan 2004 2.95
❑7, Feb 2004 2.95
❑8, Mar 2004 2.95
❑9, Apr 2004 2.95
❑10, May 2004 2.95
❑11, Jun 2004 2.95
❑12, Jul 2004 2.95
❑13, Aug 2004 2.95
❑14, Sep 2004 2.95
❑15, Oct 2004, Includes Sky Captain and the World of Tomorrow promotional disk 2.95
❑16, Nov 2004 2.95
❑17, Jan 2005 2.95
❑18, Feb 2005 2.95
❑19, Mar 2005 2.95
❑20, Apr 2005 2.95
❑21, May 2005 2.95
❑22, Jun 2005, Price increase 2.95
❑23, Jun 2005 2.99
❑24, Jul 2005 2.99
❑25, Aug 2005 2.99
❑26, Sep 2005 2.99
❑27, Oct 2005 2.99
❑28, Nov 2005 2.99
❑29, Dec 2005 2.99
❑30, Jan 2006 2.99
❑31, Mar 2006 2.99
❑32, Apr 2006, Final issue 2.99

Losers Special
DC

❑1, Sep 1985; O: Pooch (Gunner's Dog). O: Johnny Cloud. O: Captain Storm. D: The Losers. Crisis 2.50

Lost and Found Season of the Most PopeJoey
Abanne

❑1, Oct 2001 2.95

Lost Angel
Caliber

❑1, b&w 2.95

Lost
Caliber

❑1, Oct 1996, b&w 2.95
❑2 1996, b&w 2.95

Lost
Chaos

❑1, Dec 1997, b&w 2.95
❑2, Jan 1998, b&w 2.95
❑3, Feb 1998, b&w; cover says Feb 97; a misprint 2.95

Lost Continent
Eclipse

❑1, b&w; Japanese 3.50
❑2, b&w; Japanese 3.50
❑3, Nov 1990, b&w; Japanese 3.50
❑4, b&w; Japanese 3.50
❑5, b&w; Japanese 3.50
❑6, b&w; Japanese 3.50

Lost Girls
Kitchen Sink

❑1, Nov 1995; Oversized; cardstock cover 5.95
❑2, Feb 1996; Oversized; cardstock cover 5.95

Lost Heroes
Davdez

❑0, Mar 1998 2.95
❑1, Apr 1998 2.95
❑2, May 1998 2.95
❑3, Jun 1998 2.95
❑4, Aug 1998 2.95

Lost in Space
Innovation

❑1, Aug 1991 3.00
❑2, Nov 1991 2.75
❑3, Dec 1991 2.75
❑4, Feb 1992 2.50
❑5, Mar 1992 2.50
❑6, May 1992 2.50
❑7, Jun 1992 2.50
❑8, Aug 1992 2.50
❑9, Oct 1992 2.50
❑10, Nov 1992 2.50
❑11, Dec 1992; Judy's story 2.50
❑12, Apr 1993; Robinsons' Arrive at Alpha Centauri 2.50
❑13, Aug 1993 4.00
❑13/Gold, Aug 1993; Gold edition; enhanced cardstock cover 5.00
❑14, Sep 1993 2.50
❑15, Aug 1993; Includes preview of Zamindar #1 2.50
❑16, Sep 1993 2.50
❑17, Oct 1993 2.50
❑18, Nov 1993; Final Issue 2.50
❑Ann 1, ca. 1991 2.95
❑Ann 2, ca. 1992; PD (w) 2.95
❑Special 1; amended reprint of #1 4.00
❑Special 2; Amended reprint of #2 2.50

Lost in Space
Dark Horse

❑1, Apr 1998; Movie adaptation 2.95
❑2, May 1998; Movie adaptation 2.95
❑3, Jul 1998; Movie adaptation 2.95

Lost in Space: Project Robinson
Innovation

❑1, Nov 1993 2.50

Lost in the Alps
NBM

❑1 13.95

Lost Laughter
Bad Habit

❑1, b&w 2.50
❑2, b&w 2.50
❑3, b&w 2.50
❑4, Apr 1994, b&w 2.50

Lost Ones
Image

❑1, Mar 2000 2.95

Lost Ones: For Your Eyes Only
Image

❑1, Mar 2000; special preview; no price 1.00

Lost Planet
Eclipse

❑1, May 1987 2.00
❑2, Jul 1987 2.00
❑3, Sep 1987 2.00
❑4, Dec 1987 2.00
❑5, Feb 1988 2.00
❑6, Mar 1989; Final Issue 2.00

Lost Squad
Devil's Due

❑1, Sep 2005 2.95
❑2, Dec 2005 2.95
❑3, Mar 2006 2.95
❑4, May 2006 2.95
❑5, Jun 2006, b&w 2.95

Lost Universe
Tekno

❑0 2.25
❑1, Apr 1995, Bound-in trading card 1.95
❑2, May 1995, W/bound in game piece & trading card 1.95
❑3, Jun 1995, trading card 1.95
❑3/A, Jun 1995, variant cover 1.95
❑4, Jul 1995, bound-in trading card 1.95
❑5, Aug 1995, Flip cover; 1: Xander 1.95
❑6, Sep 1995, Flip cover 1.95
❑7, Oct 1995, Final Issue 1.95

Lost World
Millennium

❑1, Jan 1996; cover says Mar, indicia says Jan 2.95
❑2, Mar 1996 2.95

Lost World: Jurassic Park
Topps

❑1, May 1997 2.95
❑2, Jun 1997 2.95
❑3, Jul 1997 2.95

Loud Cannoli
Crazyfish / MJ-12

❑1; NN 2.95

Louder than Words
Dark Horse

❑1, Jul 1997 2.95
❑2, Aug 1997 2.95
❑3, Sep 1997 2.95
❑4, Oct 1997 2.95
❑5, Nov 1997 2.95
❑6, Dec 1997 2.95

Louie the Rune Soldier
ADV Manga

❑1, Mar 2004 9.99
❑2, ca. 2004 9.99
❑3, ca. 2004 9.99
❑4, ca. 2005 9.99

Louis Riel
Drawn & Quarterly

❑1 2.95
❑2 2.95
❑3 2.95
❑4 2.95
❑5, Sep 2000 2.95

Louis vs. Ali
Revolutionary

❑1, Dec 1993, b&w 2.95

Love & Rockets
Fantagraphics

❑1, Fal 1982 25.00
❑1/2nd; 2nd printing 4.00
❑1/3rd, Feb 1992; 3rd printing 3.95
❑1/4th, May 1995; 4th printing 4.95
❑1/5th, May 1995 4.95
❑2, Spr 1983 12.00
❑2/2nd; 2nd printing 3.95
❑2/3rd, May 1996 4.95
❑3, Fal 1983 9.00
❑3/2nd, Apr 1991; 2nd printing 3.95
❑4, Fal 1983 8.00
❑4/2nd, Apr 1991; 2nd printing 3.95
❑4/3rd; 3rd printing 3.95
❑5, Mar 1984 7.00
❑5/2nd, May 1991; 2nd printing 2.50
❑6, May 1984 5.00
❑6/2nd, May 1991; 2nd printing 2.50
❑7, Jul 1984 5.00
❑7/2nd, May 1991; 2nd printing 2.50
❑8, Sep 1984 5.00
❑8/2nd, Aug 1991; 2nd printing 2.50
❑9, Nov 1984 5.00
❑9/2nd, Oct 1991; 2nd printing 2.50
❑10, Jan 1985 5.00
❑10/2nd, Dec 1991; 2nd printing 2.95
❑11, Apr 1985; b&w 4.00
❑11/2nd, Feb 1992; 2nd printing 2.50
❑12, Jul 1985 4.00
❑12/2nd, Aug 1992; 2nd printing 2.50
❑13, Sep 1985; Lloyd Llewellyn 8 page preview 4.00
❑13/2nd, Oct 1992; 2nd printing 2.50
❑14, Nov 1985 4.00
❑14/2nd, Feb 1993; 2nd printing 2.50
❑15, Jan 1986 4.00
❑15/2nd, Aug 1993; 2nd printing 2.50
❑16, Mar 1986 3.00
❑16/2nd, Oct 1993; 2nd printing 2.95
❑17, Jun 1986 3.00
❑18, Sep 1986 3.00
❑19, Jan 1987 3.00
❑20, Apr 1987 3.00
❑21, Jul 1987 2.25
❑22, Aug 1987 2.25
❑23, Oct 1987 2.25
❑24, Dec 1987 2.25
❑25, Mar 1988 2.25
❑26, Jun 1988 2.25
❑27, Aug 1988 2.25
❑28, Dec 1988 2.95
❑28/2nd, Apr 1995; 2nd printing 2.95
❑29, Mar 1989 2.75
❑29/2nd, Mar 1992; 2nd printing 2.25
❑30, Jul 1989; 40 pages 2.95
❑30/2nd, Mar 1992; 2nd printing 2.95
❑31, Dec 1989 2.50
❑31/2nd, Apr 1992; 2nd printing 2.50
❑32, May 1990 2.50
❑33, Aug 1990 2.50
❑34, Nov 1990 2.50
❑35, Mar 1991 2.75
❑36, Nov 1991 2.75
❑37, Feb 1992 2.75
❑38, Apr 1992 2.75
❑39, Aug 1992 2.75

Mad-Dog

"Comic book" from a Bob Newhart series

©Marvel

Maelstrom

Executioner's life gets complicated

©Aircel

Mage

Mix of mythology and action-adventure

©Comico

Magical Mates

Manga story of three unusual girls

©Antarctic

Magic: The Gathering: Antiquities War

Early comic based on trading-card game

©Acclaim

N-MINT

❑40, Jan 1993; 48 pages 3.50
❑41, Apr 1993 2.95
❑42, Aug 1993 2.95
❑43, Nov 1993 2.95
❑44, Mar 1994 2.95
❑45, Jul 1994 2.95
❑46, Nov 1994 2.95
❑47, Apr 1995 2.95
❑48, Jul 1995 2.95
❑49, Nov 1995 2.95
❑50, Apr 1996, b&w; Final Issue; 56 pages; Wraparound cover featuring the the characters of the series; b&w 4.95

Love & Rockets
Fantagraphics

❑1, Spr 2001 6.00
❑2, Sum 2001 3.95
❑3, Fal 2001 3.95
❑4, Sum 2002 3.95
❑5, Sum 2002 3.95
❑6, ca. 2002 3.95
❑7, Spr 2003 3.95
❑8 3.95
❑9 3.95
❑10 5.95
❑11 4.50
❑12 4.50
❑13 4.50
❑14, Fal 2005 4.50
❑15, Jan 2006 4.50

Love & Rockets Bonanza
Fantagraphics

❑1, Mar 1989, b&w; Reprints 2.95
❑1/2nd, Feb 1992, b&w; 2nd printing 2.95

Love and Romance
Charlton

❑1, Sep 1971 24.00
❑2, Nov 1971 16.00
❑3, Jan 1972 12.00
❑4 1972 12.00
❑5, Apr 1972 12.00
❑6 1972 8.00
❑7, Aug 1972 8.00
❑8, Oct 1972 8.00
❑9, Dec 1972 8.00
❑10, Feb 1973 8.00
❑11, Apr 1973 6.00
❑12, May 1973 6.00
❑13 1973 6.00
❑14, Sep 1973 6.00
❑15, Nov 1973 6.00
❑16, Jan 1974 6.00
❑17, Jun 1974 6.00
❑18, Sep 1974 6.00
❑19, Nov 1974 6.00
❑20, Jan 1974 6.00
❑21, Mar 1974 4.00
❑22 1975 4.00
❑23, Jul 1975 4.00
❑24, Sep 1975 4.00

Love as a Foreign Language
Oni

❑1, Oct 2005 6.95
❑2, Feb 2005 6.95

N-MINT

❑3, Jun 2005 6.95
❑4, Nov 2005 6.95

Love Bites
Fantagraphics / Eros

❑1, Jun 1991, b&w; Adult 2.25
❑2, Jul 1991; Adult 2.25

Love Bites
Radio

❑1, Oct 2000 2.95

Love Bomb
Abaculus

❑1 2.95
❑2 2.95

Love Bug
Gold Key

❑1, Jun 1969 24.00

Lovebunny & Mr. Hell: Day in the Love Life
Image

❑1, Feb 2003 2.95

Lovebunny & Mr. Hell: Savage Love
Image

❑1, Apr 2003; 1: Industrielle; Preview of Misplaced 2.95

Lovecraft
Adventure

❑1 2.95
❑1/Ltd.; limited edition 3.00
❑2 2.95
❑3 2.95
❑4, May 1992 2.95

Love Diary
Charlton

❑19, Dec 1961 10.00
❑20, Mar 1962 10.00
❑21, May 1962 7.00
❑22, Jul 1962 7.00
❑23, Sep 1962 7.00
❑24, Nov 1962, DG (c) 7.00
❑25, Jan 1963 7.00
❑26, Mar 1963 7.00
❑27, May 1963 7.00
❑28, Jul 1963 7.00
❑29, Sep 1963 7.00
❑30, Nov 1963 7.00
❑31, ca. 1964 5.00
❑32, ca. 1964 5.00
❑33, ca. 1964 5.00
❑34, ca. 1964 5.00
❑35, Nov 1964 5.00
❑36, Jan 1965, Swimsuit cover 5.00
❑37, Apr 1965 5.00
❑38, Jul 1965 5.00
❑39, ca. 1965 5.00
❑40, Oct 1965 5.00
❑41, Dec 1965 4.00
❑42, Feb 1966 4.00
❑43, Apr 1966 4.00
❑44, Jun 1966 4.00
❑45, Sep 1966 4.00
❑46, Nov 1966 4.00
❑47, Jan 1967 4.00
❑48, Mar 1967 4.00

N-MINT

❑49, Jun 1967 4.00
❑50, Aug 1967 4.00
❑51, Oct 1967 4.00
❑52, Dec 1967 4.00
❑53, Feb 1968 4.00
❑54, Jun 1968 4.00
❑55, Aug 1968 4.00
❑56, Oct 1968, JL (c) 4.00
❑57, Dec 1968 4.00
❑58, Feb 1969 4.00
❑59, Apr 1969 4.00
❑60, Jun 1969 4.00
❑61, Aug 1969 2.50
❑62, Oct 1969 2.50
❑63, Dec 1969 2.50
❑64, Feb 1970 2.50
❑65, Apr 1970 2.50
❑66, Jun 1970 2.50
❑67, Aug 1970 2.50
❑68, Oct 1970 2.50
❑69, Dec 1970 2.50
❑70, Jan 1971 2.50
❑71, Mar 1971 2.50
❑72, May 1971 2.50
❑73, Jul 1971 2.50
❑74, Sep 1971 2.50
❑75, Nov 1971 2.50
❑76, Jan 1972 2.50
❑77, Mar 1972 2.50
❑78, May 1972 2.50
❑79, Jul 1972, David Cassidy "poster" inside 2.50
❑80, Sep 1972, Bobby Sherman "poster" inside 2.50
❑81, Dec 1972, Bobby Sherman "poster" inside 2.50
❑82, Jan 1973 2.50
❑83, Mar 1973, Susan Dey "poster" inside 2.50
❑84, May 1973 2.50
❑85, Jul 1973 2.50
❑86, Sep 1973 2.50
❑87, Nov 1973 2.50
❑88, Jun 1974 2.50
❑89, Sep 1974 2.50
❑90, Nov 1974 2.50
❑91, Jan 1975 2.50
❑92, Mar 1975 2.50
❑93, May 1975 2.50
❑94, Jul 1975 2.50
❑95, Sep 1975 2.50
❑96, Nov 1975 2.50
❑97, Feb 1976 2.50
❑98, Apr 1976 2.50
❑99, Jun 1976 2.50
❑100, Aug 1976 2.50
❑101, Oct 1976 2.50
❑102, Dec 1976, Final Issue 2.50

Love Eternal: A Tortured Soul
Vlad Ent.

❑1, b&w 2.00

Love Fantasy
Renegade

❑1, b&w 2.00

Other grades: Multiply price above by 5/6 for VF/NM • 2/3 for VERY FINE • 1/3 for FINE • 1/5 for VERY GOOD • 1/8 for GOOD

Love Hina
Tokyopop

- ❑1 2002 2.95
- ❑2 2002 2.95
- ❑3 2002 2.95
- ❑4 2002 2.95
- ❑5 2002 2.95

Love in Tights
Slave Labor

- ❑1, Nov 1998, b&w; First heart throbbin' issue 2.95

Loveless
DC / Vertigo

- ❑1, Nov 2005 2.99
- ❑2, Jan 2006 2.99
- ❑3, Feb 2006 2.99
- ❑4, Apr 2006 2.99
- ❑5, Jun 2006 2.99
- ❑6, Jun 2006 2.99
- ❑7, Aug 2006 2.99
- ❑8, Sep 2006 2.99
- ❑9, Oct 2006 2.99
- ❑10, Nov 2006 2.99
- ❑11, Dec 2006 2.99
- ❑12, Jan 2007 2.99
- ❑13, Feb 2007 2.99
- ❑14, Mar 2007 2.99
- ❑15 2.99
- ❑16 2.99
- ❑17 2.99
- ❑18 2.99
- ❑19 2.99
- ❑20 2.99
- ❑21 2.99
- ❑22 2.99
- ❑23 2.99
- ❑24 2.99

Love Letters in the Hand
Fantagraphics / Eros

- ❑1, May 1991, b&w; Adult 2.25
- ❑2, Jul 1991, b&w; Adult 2.25
- ❑3, b&w; Adult 2.50

Lovely as a Lie
Illustration

- ❑1, Nov 1994; Adult 3.25

Lovely Ladies
Caliber

- ❑1, b&w; pin-ups 3.50

Lovely Prudence
All the Rage

- ❑1, ca. 1995 2.95
- ❑2, ca. 1995 2.95
- ❑3, ca. 1995, b&w 2.95

Love Me Tenderloin
Dark Horse

- ❑1, Jan 2004, Cal McDonald Mystery One Shot 2.99

Love or Money
Tokyopop

- ❑1, Dec 2004, b&w 9.99
- ❑2, Mar 2005; b&w 9.99
- ❑3, Jun 2005; b&w 9.99
- ❑4, Dec 2005; b&w 9.99

Love Stories
DC

- ❑147, Nov 1972, Previous issues published as Heart Throbs 8.00
- ❑148, Jan 1973 8.00
- ❑149, Mar 1973 8.00
- ❑150, Jun 1973 8.00
- ❑151, Aug 1973 8.00
- ❑152, Oct 1973 8.00

Love Sucks
Ace

- ❑1 2.95

Lowlife
Caliber

- ❑1, b&w 2.50
- ❑2, b&w 2.50
- ❑3, b&w 2.50
- ❑4, Feb 1994, b&w 2.50

L.T. Caper
Spotlight

- ❑1 1.75

Luba
Fantagraphics

- ❑1, Feb 1998 2.95
- ❑2, Jul 1998 2.95
- ❑3, Dec 1998 2.95
- ❑4, Jan 2000 3.50
- ❑5, Oct 2000 3.50
- ❑6, Spr 2002 3.50
- ❑7, ca. 2002 3.50
- ❑8, ca. 2003 3.50
- ❑9, ca. 2004 3.50

Lucifer
DC / Vertigo

- ❑1, Jun 2000 3.50
- ❑2, Jul 2000 3.00
- ❑3, Aug 2000 3.00
- ❑4, Sep 2000 3.00
- ❑5, Oct 2000 3.00
- ❑6, Nov 2000 2.50
- ❑7, Dec 2000 2.50
- ❑8, Jan 2001 2.50
- ❑9, Feb 2001 2.50
- ❑10, Mar 2001 2.50
- ❑11, Apr 2001 2.50
- ❑12, May 2001 2.50
- ❑13, Jun 2001 2.50
- ❑14, Jul 2001 2.50
- ❑15, Aug 2001 2.50
- ❑16, Sep 2001 2.50
- ❑17, Oct 2001 2.50
- ❑18, Nov 2001 2.50
- ❑19, Dec 2001 2.50
- ❑20, Jan 2002 2.50
- ❑21, Feb 2002 2.50
- ❑22, Mar 2002 2.50
- ❑23, Apr 2002 2.50
- ❑24, May 2002 2.50
- ❑25, Jul 2002 2.50
- ❑26, Jul 2002 2.50
- ❑27, Aug 2002 2.50
- ❑28, Sep 2002 2.50
- ❑29, Oct 2002 2.50
- ❑30, Nov 2002 2.50
- ❑31, Dec 2002 2.50
- ❑32, Jan 2003 2.50
- ❑33, Feb 2003 2.50
- ❑34, Mar 2003 2.50
- ❑35, Apr 2003 2.50
- ❑36, May 2003 2.50
- ❑37, Jun 2003 2.50
- ❑38, Jul 2003 2.50
- ❑39, Aug 2003 2.50
- ❑40, Sep 2003 2.50
- ❑41, Oct 2003 2.50
- ❑42, Nov 2003 2.50
- ❑43, Dec 2003 2.50
- ❑44, Jan 2004 2.50
- ❑45, Feb 2004 2.50
- ❑46, Mar 2004 2.50
- ❑47, Apr 2004 2.50
- ❑48, May 2004 2.50
- ❑49, Jun 2004 2.50
- ❑50, Jul 2004 3.50
- ❑51, Aug 2004 2.50
- ❑52, Sep 2004 2.50
- ❑53, Oct 2004; Sky Captain and the World of Tomorrow promo CD 2.50
- ❑54, Nov 2004 2.50
- ❑55, Dec 2004 2.50
- ❑56, Jan 2005 2.50
- ❑57, Feb 2005 2.50
- ❑58, Mar 2005 2.50
- ❑59, Apr 2005 2.50
- ❑60, May 2005 2.50
- ❑61, Jun 2005 2.50
- ❑62, Jul 2005 2.50
- ❑63, Aug 2005 2.75
- ❑64, Sep 2005 2.75
- ❑65, Oct 2005 2.75
- ❑66, Nov 2005 2.75
- ❑67, Dec 2005 2.75
- ❑68, Jan 2006 2.99
- ❑69, Feb 2006 2.75
- ❑70, Mar 2006 2.99
- ❑71, May 2006 2.75
- ❑72, Jun 2006 2.75
- ❑73, Jul 2006 2.75
- ❑74, Aug 2006 2.99
- ❑75, Sep 2006, Final issue, Morpheus of the Endless appearance in flashback pages 19-23 3.99

Lucifer
Trident

- ❑1, Jul 1990, b&w 1.95
- ❑2, b&w 1.95
- ❑3, b&w 1.95

Lucifer: Nirvana
DC / Vertigo

- ❑1, Oct 2002, b&w 5.95

Lucifer's Hammer
Innovation

- ❑1, Nov 1993 2.50
- ❑2, Dec 1993 2.50
- ❑3 2.50
- ❑4 2.50
- ❑5 2.50
- ❑6 2.50

Luck of the Draw
Radio

- ❑1, Jun 2000, b&w; Adult 3.95

Lucky 7
Runaway Graphics

- ❑1, Apr 1993 1.95

Lucky Luke: Jesse James
Fantasy Flight

- ❑1 8.95

Lucky Luke: The Stage Coach
Fantasy Flight

- ❑1 8.95

Lucy Show
Gold Key

- ❑1, Jun 1963, Photo cover 65.00
- ❑2, Sep 1963 40.00
- ❑3, Dec 1963 32.00
- ❑4, Mar 1964 32.00
- ❑5, Jun 1964 32.00

Ludwig Von Drake
Dell

- ❑1, Nov 1961 16.00
- ❑2, Jan 1962 10.00
- ❑3, Mar 1962 8.00
- ❑4, Jun 1962 8.00

Luftwaffe: 1946 Technical Manual
Antarctic

- ❑1, Feb 1998; Projekt Saucer 4.00
- ❑2, Apr 1999; Hitler's Kamikazes 4.00

Luftwaffe: 1946
Antarctic

- ❑1, Jul 1996, b&w; Families of Altered Wars #39 5.00
- ❑2, Sep 1996, b&w; Families of Altered Wars #40 4.00
- ❑3, Nov 1996, b&w; Families of Altered Wars #41 4.00
- ❑4, Jan 1997, b&w; Families of Altered Wars #42; Storyline moves to Luftwaffe: 1946 (Vol. 2) #1; Final Issue 4.00
- ❑Ann 1, Apr 1998, b&w 4.00

Luftwaffe: 1946
Antarctic

- ❑1, Mar 1997; Families of Altered Wars #43 4.00
- ❑2, Apr 1997; contains indicia for issue #1 3.50
- ❑3, May 1997; Families of Altered Wars #45 3.50
- ❑4, Jul 1997; Families of Altered Wars #46 3.50
- ❑5, Aug 1997; Families of Altered Wars #47 3.00
- ❑6, Oct 1997; Families of Altered Wars #48 3.00
- ❑7, Nov 1997; Families of Altered Wars #49 3.00
- ❑8, Feb 1998; 50th "Families of Altered Wars" issue 3.00
- ❑9, Apr 1998; Families of Altered Wars #51 3.00
- ❑10, May 1998; Families of Altered Wars #52 3.00

Other grades: Multiply price above by 5/6 for VF/NM • 2/3 for VERY FINE • 1/3 for FINE • 1/5 for VERY GOOD • 1/8 for GOOD

Magilla Gorilla

Animated simian haunts pet store
©Gold Key

Magnus, Robot Fighter

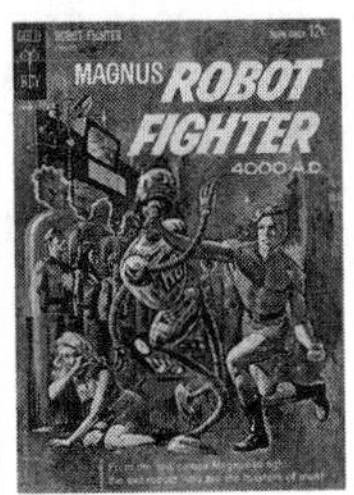

Robots gain free will and stage a revolution
©Gold Key

Magnus Robot Fighter

Valiant revives the old Gold Key series
©Valiant

Mai, the Psychic Girl

Wisdom Alliance pursues girl in manga import
©Eclipse

Maison Ikkoku Part 1

Rumiko Takahashi's long-running romance
©Viz

N-MINT

❑11, Jun 1998; Families of Altered Wars #53 ... 3.00
❑12, Jul 1998; Families of Altered Wars #54 ... 3.00
❑13, Aug 1998; Families of Altered Wars #55 ... 3.00
❑14, Oct 1998; Families of Altered Wars #56 ... 3.00
❑15, Feb 1999; Families of Altered Wars #57 ... 3.00
❑16, Mar 1999; Families of Altered Wars #58 ... 3.00
❑Ann 1, ca. 1998; 1998 Ann ... 3.00
❑Special 1, Apr 1998; Color Special ... 4.00
❑Special 2, Feb 1997, b&w; TriebflÉgel Special; German rocketry ... 4.00

Luftwaffe: 1946
Antarctic

❑1, Aug 2002; Families of Altered Wars #99; Storyline moves to Men's Altered Wars Chronicles ... 5.95
❑2, Oct 2002; Families of Altered Wars #101 ... 5.95
❑3, Oct 2002; Families of Altered Wars #102; Indicia says November 2002 ... 5.95
❑4, ca. 2002; Families of Altered Wars #103; Indicia says December 2002 ... 5.95
❑5, Jan 2003; Families of Altered Wars #104 ... 5.95
❑6, Feb 2003; Families of Altered Wars #105 ... 5.95
❑7, Mar 2003; Families of Altered Wars #106; Storyline moves to Families of Altered Wars Presents Luftwaffe: 1946 ... 5.95
❑8, Apr 2003 ... 5.95
❑9, May 2003 ... 5.95
❑10, Jun 2003 ... 5.95
❑11, Jul 2003 ... 5.95
❑12, Aug 2003 ... 5.95
❑13, Nov 2003 ... 5.95
❑14, Dec 2003 ... 5.95
❑15, Dec 2003 ... 5.95
❑16, Jan 2004 ... 5.95
❑17, Feb 2004 ... 5.95

Luftwaffe 1946
Antarctic

❑1, ca. 2005 ... 5.95
❑2, ca. 2005 ... 5.95
❑3, ca. 2005 ... 5.95

Luger
Eclipse

❑1, Oct 1986 TY (a) ... 2.00
❑2, Dec 1986 TY (a) ... 2.00
❑3, Feb 1987 TY (a) ... 2.00

Lugh, Lord of Light
Flagship

❑1, Feb 1987 ... 1.75
❑2, Jun 1987 ... 1.75
❑3 ... 1.75
❑4 ... 1.75

Lugo
Lost Boys

❑½; Promotional edition; Promotional edition ... 1.00

N-MINT

Lullaby
Alias

❑1, Dec 2005 ... 2.99

Lullaby: Wisdom Seeker
Image

❑1, ca. 2005 ... 2.95
❑1/B cover 2005 ... 4.00
❑2, ca. 2005; Includes Pakkins' Land preview ... 2.95
❑2/B cover 2005 ... 4.00
❑3, Apr 2005; Includes Valkyries preview ... 2.95
❑4, Sep 2005 ... 2.95

Lumenagerie
NBM

❑1; Adult ... 11.95

Lum Urusei*Yatsura
Viz

❑1, b&w; Japanese ... 5.00
❑2, b&w; Japanese ... 4.00
❑3, b&w; Japanese ... 4.00
❑4, b&w; Japanese ... 4.00
❑5 ... 3.50
❑6 ... 3.50
❑7 ... 3.50
❑8 ... 3.50

Lunar Donut
Lunar Donut

❑0, b&w; says (Honey-Glazed); cardstock cover ... 2.50
❑1, b&w; Flip-book; cover says (With Sprinkles) ... 2.50
❑2, b&w; Flip-book; cover says (Cherry-Filled) ... 2.50
❑3, b&w; Flip-book; cover says (Jelly-Filled) ... 2.50
❑4, ca. 1997 ... 2.50
❑5, ca. 1997 ... 2.50
❑6, Spr 1998 ... 2.50

Lunatic Binge
Eternity

❑1 ... 3.95
❑2 ... 3.95

Lunatic Fringe
Innovation

❑1, Jul 1989; O: Lunatic Fringe ... 1.75
❑2, Aug 1989 ... 1.75

Lunatik
Marvel

❑1, Dec 1995, 1&O: Lunatik II (alien); D: Lunatik I ... 1.95
❑2, Jan 1996, V: Avengers ... 1.95
❑3, Feb 1996, Final Issue ... 1.95

Lurid
Idea & Design Works

❑1, Jan 2003 ... 2.99
❑2, Mar 2003 ... 2.99
❑3, Jun 2003 ... 2.99

Lurid Tales
Fantagraphics / Eros

❑1, b&w; Adult ... 2.75

N-MINT

Lust
Fantagraphics / Eros

❑1, Apr 1997 ... 2.95
❑2, May 1997 ... 2.95
❑3, Jun 1997 ... 2.95
❑4, Jul 1997 ... 2.95
❑5, Aug 1997 ... 2.95
❑6, Sep 1997 ... 2.95

Lust for Life
Slave Labor

❑1, Feb 1997, b&w ... 2.95
❑2, May 1997, b&w ... 2.95
❑3, Aug 1997, b&w ... 2.95
❑4, Jan 1998 ... 2.95

Lust of the Nazi Weasel Women
Fantagraphics

❑1, b&w ... 2.25
❑2, b&w ... 2.25
❑3, Jan 1991, b&w ... 2.25
❑4, Apr 1991, b&w ... 2.25

Lux & Alby Sign on and Save the Universe
Dark Horse

❑1, Apr 1993, b&w ... 2.50
❑2, May 1993, b&w ... 2.50
❑3, Jun 1993, b&w ... 2.50
❑4, Jul 1993 ... 2.50
❑5, Aug 1993 ... 2.50
❑6, Sep 1993 ... 2.50
❑7, Oct 1993 ... 2.50
❑8, Oct 1993 ... 2.50
❑9, Dec 1993 ... 2.50

Luxura & Vampfire
Brainstorm

❑1 ... 2.95

Luxura Collection
Brainstorm

❑1, stories and pin-ups; cardstock cover ... 4.95

Luxura Leather Special
Brainstorm

❑1, Mar 1996; NN; Adult ... 2.95

Lycanthrope Leo
Viz

❑1, b&w ... 2.95
❑2, b&w ... 2.95
❑3, b&w ... 2.95
❑4, b&w ... 2.95
❑5, b&w ... 2.95
❑6, b&w ... 2.95
❑7, b&w ... 2.95

Lyceum
Hunter

❑1, Oct 1996, b&w; Adult ... 2.95
❑2, Aug 1997, b&w; Adult ... 2.95

Lycra-Woman and Spandex-Girl
Comic Zone

❑1, Dec 1992, b&w ... 2.95

Lycra Woman and Spandex Girl Christmas '77 Special
Comic Zone

❑1, b&w ... 2.95

N-MINT

Lycra Woman and Spandex Girl Halloween Special
Lost Cause

❑1, b&w ... 2.95

Lycra Woman and Spandex Girl Jurassic Dinosaur Special
Comic Zone

❑1, b&w ... 2.95

Lycra Woman and Spandex Girl Summer Vacation Special
Comic Zone

❑1, b&w ... 2.95

Lycra Woman and Spandex Girl Time Travel Special
Comic Zone

❑1, b&w ... 2.95

Lycra Woman and Spandex Girl Valentine Special
Comic Zone

❑1, b&w ... 2.95

Lynch
Image

❑1, May 1997; no indicia ... 2.50

Lynch Mob
Chaos

❑1, Jun 1994 ... 2.50
❑2, Jul 1994 ... 2.50
❑3, Aug 1994 ... 2.50
❑4, Sep 1994 ... 2.50

Lynx: An Elflord Tale
Peregrine Entertainment

❑1, Mar 1999, b&w ... 2.95

M
Eclipse

❑1, Jun 1990 ... 4.95
❑2 ... 4.95
❑3 ... 4.95
❑4 ... 5.95

Maburaho
ADV Manga

❑1, ca. 2005; Read right to left; Graphic novel; b&w ... 9.99

Macabre
Lighthouse

❑1 1989, b&w ... 2.50
❑2 1989, b&w ... 2.50
❑3 1989, b&w ... 2.50
❑4 1989 ... 2.50
❑5 1989 ... 2.50
❑6, Aug 1989 ... 2.50

Macabre
Lighthouse

❑1 1989 ... 2.50
❑2 1989 ... 2.50

Mace: Bounty Hunter
Image

❑1, Apr 2003 ... 2.99

M.A.C.H. 1
Fleetway-Quality

❑1, b&w 1: John Probe ... 2.00
❑2, b&w ... 2.00
❑3, b&w ... 2.00
❑4, b&w ... 2.00
❑5, b&w ... 2.00
❑6, b&w ... 2.00
❑7, b&w ... 2.00
❑8, b&w ... 2.00
❑9, b&w ... 2.00

Machine
Dark Horse

❑1, Nov 1994 ... 2.50
❑2, Dec 1994 ... 2.50
❑3, Jan 1995 ... 2.50
❑4, Feb 1995 ... 2.50

Machine Man
Marvel

❑1, Apr 1978, JK (c); JK (w); JK (a); 1: Machine Man ... 2.50
❑2, May 1978 ... 2.00
❑3, Jun 1978 ... 2.00
❑4, Jul 1978 ... 2.00
❑5, Aug 1978, Newsstand edition (distributed by Curtis); issue number in box ... 2.00
❑5/Whitman, Aug 1978, Special markets edition (usually sold in Whitman bagged prepacks); price appears in a diamond; UPC barcode appears ... 2.00
❑6, Sep 1978, Newsstand edition (distributed by Curtis); issue number in box ... 2.00
❑6/Whitman, Sep 1978, Special markets edition (usually sold in Whitman bagged prepacks); price appears in a diamond; UPC barcode appears ... 2.00
❑7, Oct 1978 ... 2.00
❑8, Nov 1978, Newsstand edition (distributed by Curtis); issue number in box ... 2.00
❑8/Whitman, Nov 1978, Special markets edition (usually sold in Whitman bagged prepacks); price appears in a diamond; no UPC barcode ... 2.00
❑9, Dec 1978, Storyline continues in Incredible Hulk, resuming eight months later ... 2.00
❑10, Aug 1979, Series resumes ... 2.00
❑11, Oct 1979 ... 2.00
❑12, Dec 1979 ... 2.00
❑13, Feb 1980 ... 2.00
❑14, Apr 1980 ... 2.00
❑15, Jun 1980, O: Ion. 1: Ion ... 2.00
❑16, Aug 1980, 1: Baron Brimstone ... 2.00
❑17, Oct 1980, 1: Madam Menace ... 2.00
❑18, Dec 1980, A: Alpha Flight ... 2.00
❑19, Feb 1981, FM (c); SD (a); 1: Jack O'Lantern I (Jason Macendale). Macendale becomes Hobgoblin II in Amazing Spider-Man #289 ... 12.50

Machine Man
Marvel

❑1, Oct 1984, HT (a) ... 1.50
❑2, Nov 1984, HT (a); 1: Iron Man 2020 ... 1.50
❑3, Dec 1984, HT (a) ... 1.50
❑4, Jan 1985, HT (a) ... 1.50

Machine Man/Bastion '98
Marvel

❑1, ca. 1998; gatefold summary; Marvel Ann; wraparound cover ... 2.99

Machine Man 2020
Marvel

❑1, Aug 1994; Reprints ... 2.00
❑2, Sep 1994; Reprints ... 2.00

Machine Teen
Marvel

❑1, Jul 2005 ... 2.99
❑2, Aug 2005 ... 2.99
❑3, Sep 2005 ... 2.99
❑4, Oct 2005 ... 2.99
❑5, Nov 2005 ... 2.99

Mack Bolan: The Executioner
Innovation

❑1, Jul 1993, enhanced cardstock cover; adapts War Against the Mafia ... 2.95
❑1/A, Jul 1993, Indestructible Tyvek cover ... 3.95
❑1/B, Jul 1993, Double-cover edition; black outer cover with red X ... 3.50
❑2, Aug 1993, Adapts War Against the Mafia ... 2.50
❑3, Nov 1993, Adapts War Against the Mafia ... 2.50
❑4 ... 2.50

Mackenzie Queen
Matrix

❑1 ... 1.50
❑2, b&w ... 1.50
❑3 ... 1.50
❑4 ... 1.50
❑5 ... 1.50

Mack the Knife: Monochrome Memories
Caliber

❑1, b&w ... 2.50

Macross II
Viz

❑1, ca. 1992 ... 3.00
❑2, ca. 1992 ... 2.75
❑3, ca. 1992 ... 2.75
❑4, ca. 1992 ... 2.75
❑5, ca. 1992 ... 2.75
❑6, ca. 1992 ... 2.75
❑7, ca. 1993 ... 2.75
❑8, ca. 1993 ... 2.75
❑9, ca. 1993 ... 2.75
❑10, ca. 1993 ... 2.75

Macross II: The Micron Conspiracy
Viz

❑1, b&w ... 3.00
❑2, b&w ... 2.75
❑3, b&w ... 2.75
❑4, b&w ... 2.75
❑5, b&w ... 2.75

Mad
E.C.

❑67, Dec 1961, b&w ... 48.00
❑68, Jan 1962, b&w ... 48.00
❑69, Mar 1962, b&w ... 48.00
❑70, Apr 1962, b&w ... 48.00
❑71, Jun 1962, b&w ... 36.00
❑72, Jul 1962, b&w ... 36.00
❑73, Sep 1962, b&w ... 36.00
❑74, Oct 1962, b&w ... 36.00
❑75, Dec 1962, b&w ... 36.00
❑76, Jan 1963, b&w ... 36.00
❑77, Mar 1963, b&w; JO, MD, WW (a); 48 pages ... 36.00
❑78, Apr 1963, b&w ... 36.00
❑79, Jun 1963, b&w ... 36.00
❑80, Jul 1963, b&w ... 36.00
❑81, Sep 1963, b&w ... 32.00
❑82, Oct 1963, b&w ... 32.00
❑83, Dec 1963, b&w ... 32.00
❑84, Jan 1964, b&w; SA, JO, MD, WW (a); 48 pages ... 32.00
❑85, Mar 1964, b&w ... 32.00
❑86, Apr 1964, b&w; 1: fold-in ... 32.00
❑87, Jun 1964, b&w ... 32.00
❑88, Jul 1964, b&w ... 32.00
❑89, Sep 1964, b&w ... 32.00
❑90, Oct 1964, b&w ... 32.00
❑91, Dec 1964, b&w ... 32.00
❑92, Jan 1965, b&w ... 32.00
❑93, Mar 1965, b&w ... 32.00
❑94, Apr 1965, b&w ... 32.00
❑95, Jun 1965, b&w ... 32.00
❑96, Jul 1965, b&w; JO, MD (a); 48 pages ... 32.00
❑97, Sep 1965, b&w ... 32.00
❑98, Oct 1965, b&w ... 32.00
❑99, Dec 1965, b&w ... 32.00
❑100, Jan 1966, b&w ... 32.00
❑101, Mar 1966, b&w ... 18.00
❑102, Apr 1966, b&w ... 18.00
❑103, Jun 1966, b&w ... 18.00
❑104, Jul 1966, b&w ... 18.00
❑105, Sep 1966, b&w; Batman TV-show parody ... 18.00
❑106, Oct 1966, b&w ... 18.00
❑107, Dec 1966, b&w ... 18.00
❑108, Jan 1967, b&w ... 18.00
❑109, Mar 1967, b&w ... 18.00
❑110, Apr 1967, b&w ... 18.00
❑111, Jun 1967, b&w ... 18.00
❑112, Jul 1967, b&w ... 18.00
❑113, Sep 1967, b&w ... 18.00
❑114, Oct 1967, b&w ... 18.00
❑115, Dec 1967, b&w ... 18.00
❑116, Jan 1968, b&w ... 18.00
❑117, Mar 1968, b&w ... 18.00
❑118, Apr 1968, b&w ... 18.00
❑119, Jun 1968, b&w ... 18.00
❑120, Jul 1968, b&w ... 18.00
❑121, Sep 1968, b&w; Beatles parody ... 22.00
❑122, Oct 1968, b&w ... 18.00
❑123, Dec 1968, b&w ... 15.00
❑124, Jan 1969, b&w ... 15.00
❑125, Mar 1969, b&w ... 15.00
❑126, Apr 1969, b&w ... 15.00
❑127, Jun 1969, b&w ... 15.00
❑128, Jul 1969, b&w ... 15.00
❑129, Sep 1969, b&w ... 15.00
❑130, Oct 1969, b&w ... 15.00
❑131, Dec 1969, b&w ... 15.00
❑132, Jan 1970, b&w ... 15.00
❑133, Mar 1970, b&w ... 15.00
❑134, Apr 1970, b&w ... 15.00
❑135, Jun 1970, b&w ... 15.00

Other grades: Multiply price above by 5/6 for VF/NM • 2/3 for VERY FINE • 1/3 for FINE • 1/5 for VERY GOOD • 1/8 for GOOD

Major Bummer

Called by DC "The First Inaction Hero"
©DC

Man-Frog

Life in the carny in another book from the 1980s glut
©Mad Dog

Man from Atlantis

Bobby Ewing stars in so-so SF TV effort
©Marvel

Man from U.N.C.L.E., The

TV spy drama had a nice comics run
©Gold Key

Man of Steel (Mini-Series)

Byrne series rebooted Superman's history
©DC

	N-MINT
❑136, Jul 1970, b&w	15.00
❑137, Sep 1970, b&w	15.00
❑138, Oct 1970, b&w	15.00
❑139, Dec 1970, b&w	15.00
❑140, Jan 1971, b&w	15.00
❑141, Mar 1971, b&w	12.00
❑142, Apr 1971, b&w	12.00
❑143, Jun 1971, b&w	12.00
❑144, Jul 1971, b&w	12.00
❑145, Sep 1971, b&w	12.00
❑146, Oct 1971, b&w	12.00
❑147, Dec 1971, b&w	12.00
❑148, Jan 1972, b&w	12.00
❑149, Mar 1972, b&w	12.00
❑150, Apr 1972, b&w	12.00
❑151, Jun 1972, b&w	9.00
❑152, Jul 1972, b&w	9.00
❑153, Sep 1972, b&w	9.00
❑154, Oct 1972, b&w	9.00
❑155, Dec 1972, b&w	9.00
❑156, Jan 1973, b&w	9.00
❑157, Mar 1973, b&w	9.00
❑158, Apr 1973, b&w	9.00
❑159, Jun 1973, b&w	9.00
❑160, Jul 1973, b&w	9.00
❑161, Sep 1973, b&w	8.00
❑162, Oct 1973, b&w	8.00
❑163, Dec 1973, b&w	8.00
❑164, Jan 1974, b&w	8.00
❑165, Mar 1974, b&w	8.00
❑166, Apr 1974, b&w	8.00
❑167, Jun 1974, b&w	8.00
❑168, Jul 1974, b&w	8.00
❑169, Sep 1974, b&w	8.00
❑170, Oct 1974, b&w	8.00
❑171, Dec 1974, b&w	6.50
❑172, Jan 1975, b&w	6.50
❑173, Mar 1975, b&w	6.50
❑174, Apr 1975, b&w	6.50
❑175, Jun 1975, b&w	6.50
❑176, Jul 1975, b&w	6.50
❑177, Sep 1975, b&w	6.50
❑178, Oct 1975, b&w	6.50
❑179, Dec 1975, b&w	6.50
❑180, Jan 1976, b&w; Jaws parody	6.50
❑181, Mar 1976, b&w	6.50
❑182, Apr 1976, b&w	6.50
❑183, Jun 1976, b&w	6.50
❑184, Jul 1976, b&w	6.50
❑185, Sep 1976, b&w	6.50
❑186, Oct 1976, b&w; Star Trek parody	6.50
❑187, Dec 1976, b&w	6.50
❑188, Jan 1977, b&w	6.50
❑189, Mar 1977, b&w	6.50
❑190, Apr 1977, b&w	5.00
❑191, Jun 1977, b&w	5.00
❑192, Jul 1977, b&w	5.00
❑193, Sep 1977, b&w	5.00
❑194, Oct 1977, b&w	5.00
❑195, Dec 1977, b&w	5.00
❑196, Jan 1978, b&w	5.00
❑197, Mar 1978, b&w	5.00
❑198, Apr 1978, b&w	5.00
❑199, Jun 1978, b&w	5.00
❑200, Jul 1978, b&w	5.00
❑201, Sep 1978, b&w	4.00

	N-MINT
❑202, Oct 1978, b&w	4.00
❑203, Dec 1978, b&w	4.00
❑204, Jan 1979, b&w; Jaws II Parody	4.00
❑205, Mar 1979, b&w	4.00
❑206, Apr 1979, b&w	4.00
❑207, Jun 1979, b&w	4.00
❑208, Jul 1979, b&w	4.00
❑209, Sep 1979, b&w	4.00
❑210, Oct 1979, b&w	4.00
❑211, Dec 1979, b&w	4.00
❑212, Jan 1980, b&w	4.00
❑213, Mar 1980, b&w	4.00
❑214, Apr 1980, b&w	4.00
❑215, Jun 1980, b&w	4.00
❑216, Jul 1980, b&w	4.00
❑217, Sep 1980, b&w	4.00
❑218, Oct 1980, b&w	4.00
❑219, Dec 1980, b&w	4.00
❑220, Jan 1981, b&w	4.00
❑221, Mar 1981, b&w	3.00
❑222, Apr 1981, b&w	3.00
❑223, Jun 1981, b&w	3.00
❑224, Jul 1981, b&w	3.00
❑225, Sep 1981, b&w	3.00
❑226, Oct 1981, b&w	3.00
❑227, Dec 1981, b&w	3.00
❑228, Jan 1982, b&w	3.00
❑229, Mar 1982, b&w	3.00
❑230, Apr 1982, b&w	3.00
❑231, Jun 1982, b&w	3.00
❑232, Jul 1982, b&w	3.00
❑233, Sep 1982, b&w	3.00
❑234, Oct 1982, b&w	3.00
❑235, Dec 1982, b&w	3.00
❑236, Jan 1983, b&w	3.00
❑237, Mar 1983, b&w	3.00
❑238, Apr 1983, b&w	3.00
❑239, Jun 1983, b&w	3.00
❑240, Jul 1983, b&w	3.00
❑241, Sep 1983, b&w	2.50
❑242, Oct 1983, b&w	2.50
❑243, Dec 1983, b&w	2.50
❑244, Jan 1984, b&w	2.50
❑245, Mar 1984, b&w	2.50
❑246, Apr 1984, b&w	2.50
❑247, Jun 1984, b&w	2.50
❑248, Jul 1984, b&w	2.50
❑249, Sep 1984, b&w	2.50
❑250, Oct 1984, b&w	2.50
❑251, Dec 1984, b&w	2.50
❑252, Jan 1985, b&w	2.50
❑253, Mar 1985, b&w	2.50
❑254, Apr 1985, b&w	2.50
❑255, Jun 1985, b&w	2.50
❑256, Jul 1985, b&w	2.50
❑257, Sep 1985, b&w	2.50
❑258, Oct 1985, b&w	2.50
❑259, Dec 1985, b&w	2.50
❑260, Jan 1986, b&w	2.50
❑261, Mar 1986, b&w	2.25
❑262, Apr 1986, b&w	2.25
❑263, Jun 1986, b&w	2.25
❑264, Jul 1986, b&w	2.25
❑265, Sep 1986, b&w	2.25
❑266, Oct 1986, b&w	2.25
❑267, Dec 1986, b&w	2.25

	N-MINT
❑268, Jan 1987, b&w	2.25
❑269, Mar 1987, b&w	2.25
❑270, Apr 1987, b&w	2.25
❑271, Jun 1987, b&w	2.25
❑272, Jul 1987, b&w	2.25
❑273, Sep 1987, b&w	2.25
❑274, Oct 1987, b&w	2.25
❑275, Dec 1987, b&w	2.25
❑276, Jan 1988, b&w	2.25
❑277, Mar 1988, b&w	2.25
❑278, Apr 1988, b&w	2.25
❑279, Jun 1988, b&w	2.25
❑280, Jul 1988, b&w	2.25
❑281, Sep 1988, b&w	2.25
❑282, Oct 1988, b&w	2.25
❑283, Dec 1988, b&w	2.25
❑284, Jan 1989, b&w	2.25
❑285, Mar 1989, b&w	2.25
❑286, Apr 1989, b&w	2.25
❑287, Jun 1989, b&w	2.25
❑288, Jul 1989, b&w	2.25
❑289, Sep 1989, b&w; Batman parody	2.25
❑290, Oct 1989, b&w	2.25
❑291, Dec 1989, b&w; Teenage Mutant Ninja Turtles parody	2.25
❑292, Jan 1990, b&w	2.25
❑293, Mar 1990, b&w	2.25
❑294, Apr 1990, b&w	2.25
❑295, Jun 1990, b&w	2.25
❑296, Jul 1990, b&w	2.25
❑297, Sep 1990, b&w	2.25
❑298, Oct 1990, b&w; Gremlins II; Teenage Mutant Ninja Turtles; Robocop II	2.25
❑299, Dec 1990, b&w	2.25
❑300, Jan 1991, b&w	2.25
❑301, Mar 1991, b&w	2.00
❑302, Apr 1991, b&w	2.00
❑303, Jun 1991, b&w	2.00
❑304, Jul 1991, b&w	2.00
❑305, Sep 1991, b&w	2.00
❑306, Oct 1991, b&w	2.00
❑307, Dec 1991, b&w	2.00
❑308, Jan 1992, b&w	2.00
❑309, Mar 1992, b&w	2.00
❑310, Apr 1992, b&w	2.00
❑311, Jun 1992, b&w	2.00
❑312, Jul 1992, b&w	2.00
❑313, Sep 1992, b&w	2.00
❑314, Oct 1992, b&w	2.00
❑315, Dec 1992, b&w	2.00
❑316, Jan 1993, b&w	2.00
❑317, Mar 1993, b&w	2.00
❑318, Apr 1993, b&w	2.00
❑319, Jun 1993, b&w	2.00
❑320, Jul 1993, b&w; A Fold in Cover	2.00
❑321, Sep 1993, b&w; Star Trek: Deep Space Nine parody	2.00
❑322, Oct 1993, b&w; Alfred E. Neman Lookalike Contest	2.00
❑323, Dec 1993, b&w	2.00
❑324, Jan 1994, b&w	2.00
❑325, Feb 1994, b&w	2.00
❑326, Mar 1994, b&w; Special Economic Recovery Issue	2.00
❑327, May 1994, b&w	2.00
❑328, Jun 1994, b&w; Love Connection	2.00

Other grades: Multiply price above by 5/6 for VF/NM • 2/3 for VERY FINE • 1/3 for FINE • 1/5 for VERY GOOD • 1/8 for GOOD

	N-MINT
❑329, Jul 1994, b&w	2.00
❑330, Sep 1994, b&w	2.00
❑331, Oct 1994, b&w	1.75
❑332, Dec 1994, b&w	1.75
❑333, Jan 1995, b&w	1.75
❑334, Mar 1995, b&w	1.75
❑335, May 1995, b&w	1.75
❑336, Jun 1995, b&w	1.75
❑337, Jul 1995, b&w	1.75
❑338, Aug 1995, b&w	1.75
❑339, Sep 1995, b&w	1.75
❑340, Oct 1995, b&w	1.75
❑341, Dec 1995, b&w	1.75
❑342, Jan 1996, b&w	2.00
❑343, Mar 1996, b&w	2.50
❑344, Apr 1996, b&w	2.50
❑345, May 1996, b&w	2.50
❑346, Jun 1996, b&w	2.50
❑347, Jul 1996, b&w	2.50
❑348, Aug 1996, b&w	2.50
❑349, Sep 1996, b&w	2.50
❑350, Oct 1996, b&w	2.50
❑351, Nov 1996, b&w	2.50
❑352, Dec 1996, b&w	2.50
❑353, Jan 1997, b&w	2.50
❑354, Feb 1997, b&w	2.50
❑355, Mar 1997, b&w	2.50
❑356, Apr 1997, b&w	2.50
❑357, May 1997, b&w	2.50
❑358, Jun 1997, b&w	2.50
❑359, Jul 1997, b&w	2.50
❑360, Aug 1997, b&w	2.50
❑361, Sep 1997, b&w	2.50
❑362, Oct 1997, b&w	2.50
❑363, Nov 1997, b&w	2.50
❑364, Dec 1997, b&w	2.50
❑365, Jan 1998, b&w	2.50
❑366, Feb 1998, b&w	2.50
❑367, Mar 1998, b&w; Buffy the Vampire Slayer parody; Starship Troopes parody	2.50
❑368, Apr 1998, b&w	2.50
❑369, May 1998, b&w	2.50
❑370, Jun 1998, b&w	2.50
❑371, Jul 1998, b&w	2.50
❑372, Aug 1998, b&w	2.50
❑373, Sep 1998, b&w	2.50
❑374, Oct 1998, b&w	2.50
❑375, Nov 1998, b&w	2.50
❑376, Dec 1998, b&w	2.50
❑377, Jan 1999, b&w	2.95
❑378, Feb 1999, b&w	2.50
❑379, Mar 1999, b&w	2.50
❑380, Apr 1999, b&w	2.75
❑381, May 1999, b&w	2.75
❑382, Jun 1999, b&w	2.75
❑383, Jul 1999, b&w; Alfred E. Neuman as Anakin Skywalker's shadow cover .	2.75
❑384, Aug 1999, b&w	2.75
❑385, Sep 1999, b&w	2.75
❑386, Oct 1999, b&w	2.75
❑387, Nov 1999, b&w	2.75
❑388, Dec 1999, b&w	2.75
❑389, Jan 2000, b&w	2.75
❑390, Feb 2000, b&w	2.75
❑391, Mar 2000, b&w	2.75
❑392, Apr 2000, b&w	2.75
❑393, May 2000, b&w	2.75
❑394, Jun 2000, b&w	2.99
❑395, Jul 2000, b&w; Al Gore cover	2.99
❑396, Aug 2000, b&w	2.99
❑397, Sep 2000, b&w	2.99
❑398, Oct 2000, b&w	2.99
❑399, Nov 2000, b&w	2.99
❑400, Dec 2000	2.99
❑401, Jan 2001	2.99
❑402, Feb 2001	2.99
❑403, Mar 2001	2.99
❑404, Apr 2001	2.99
❑405, May 2001	2.99
❑406, Jun 2001	2.99
❑407, Jul 2001	2.99
❑408, Aug 2001	2.99
❑409, Sep 2001	2.99
❑410, Oct 2001	2.99
❑411, Nov 2001	2.99
❑412, Dec 2001; MD (c); MD (a); Special Harry Potter issue	2.99
❑413, Jan 2002	2.99

	N-MINT
❑414, Feb 2002	2.99
❑415, Mar 2002; Drucker (cover)	2.99
❑416, Apr 2002; Lord of the Rings	2.99
❑417, May 2002; Britney Spears	2.99
❑418, Jun 2002; MD (c);Spider-Man	3.50
❑419, Jul 2002; Star Wars: Attack of the Clones	3.50
❑420, Aug 2002	3.50
❑421, Sep 2002	3.50
❑422, Oct 2002; Sopranos	3.50
❑423, Nov 2002; Golden (50th) Anniversary issue	3.50
❑424, Dec 2002	3.50
❑425, Jan 2003	3.50
❑426, Feb 2003; Graft Theft Auto	3.50
❑427, Mar 2003	3.50
❑428, Apr 2003	3.50
❑429, May 2003	3.50
❑430, Jun 2003	3.50
❑431, Jul 2003; Big Hulk on cover	3.50
❑432, Aug 2003	3.50
❑433, Sep 2003	3.50
❑434, Oct 2003	3.50
❑435, Nov 2003	3.50
❑436, Dec 2003; The Matrix	3.50
❑437, Jan 2004	3.50
❑438, Feb 2004; Guest artists special; "Superheroes" by Bruce Timm	3.50
❑439, Mar 2004	3.50
❑440, Apr 2004; American Idol	3.50
❑441, May 2004; Poster insert	3.50
❑442, Jun 2004	3.50
❑443, Jul 2004; "Snitch" cover	3.50
❑444, Aug 2004	3.50
❑445, Sep 2004	3.50
❑446, Oct 2004	3.50
❑447, Nov 2004	3.50
❑448, Dec 2004	3.50
❑449, Jan 2005	3.50
❑450, Feb 2005; Spy vs. Spy calendar	3.50
❑451, Mar 2005	3.50
❑452, Apr 2005	3.50
❑453, May 2005	3.50
❑454, Jun 2005; Cover price increase	3.99
❑455, Jul 2005; Batman with Alfred E. Neuman as bat cover	3.99
❑456, Aug 2005	3.99
❑457, Sep 2005	3.99
❑458, Oct 2005	3.99
❑459, Nov 2005	3.99
❑460, Dec 2005	3.99
❑461, Jan 2006	3.99
❑462, Mar 2006	3.99
❑463, Apr 2006	3.99
❑464, May 2006	3.99
❑465, Jun 2006	3.99
❑466, Jul 2006, Includes bonus poster	3.99
❑467, Aug 2006	3.99
❑468, Sep 2006	3.99
❑469, Oct 2006	3.99
❑470, Nov 2006	3.99
❑471, Dec 2006	3.99
❑472, Jan 2007	3.99
❑473, Feb 2007	3.99
❑474	3.99
❑475	3.99
❑476	3.99
❑477	3.99
❑478	3.99
❑479	3.99
❑480	3.99
❑481	3.99
❑482	3.99
❑483	3.99
❑484	3.99
❑485	3.99
❑486	3.99
❑487	3.99
❑488	3.99
❑489	3.99
❑490	3.99
❑491	3.99
❑492	3.99
❑493	3.99
❑494	3.99
❑495	3.99
❑496	3.99
❑497	3.99

	N-MINT
❑498	3.99
❑499	3.99

Madagascar
Tokyopop

❑1, Nov 2005	7.99

Madame Xanadu
DC

❑1, Jul 1981; BB, MR (a); O: Madame Xanadu. O" Madame Xanadu; Includes poster of Madame Xanadu	3.00

Madballs
Marvel / Star

❑1, Sep 1986; O: Madballs. 1: Madballs. 1: Colonel Corn	1.00
❑2, Oct 1986	1.00
❑3, Nov 1986	1.00
❑4, Jun 1987	1.00
❑5, Aug 1987	1.00
❑6, Oct 1987	1.00
❑7, Dec 1987	1.00
❑8, Feb 1988	1.00
❑9, Apr 1988	1.00
❑10, Jun 1988	1.00

Mad Classics
DC

❑1, Jan 2005	4.99
❑2, Jan 2005	4.99
❑3, Feb 2006	4.99
❑4, Feb 2006; King Kong special	4.99
❑5, Mar 2006	4.99
❑6, May 2006	4.99
❑7, Jul 2006	4.99
❑8, Sep 2006	4.99
❑9, Oct 2006	4.99
❑10, Nov 2006	4.99
❑11, Dec 2006	4.99
❑12, Feb 2007	4.99

Mad-Dog
Marvel

❑1, May 1993	1.25
❑2, Jun 1993; O: Mad-Dog	1.25
❑3, Jul 1993	1.25
❑4, Aug 1993	1.25
❑5, Sep 1993; 1: Karnivorrr	1.25
❑6, Oct 1993; Final Issue	1.25

Mad Dog Magazine
Blackthorne

❑1, Nov 1986	1.75
❑2	1.75
❑3, Mar 1987	1.75

Mad Dogs
Eclipse

❑1, Feb 1992; b&w	2.50
❑2, Mar 1992; b&w	2.50
❑3, Jul 1992; b&w	2.50

Mad Follies
E.C.

❑1, ca. 1963; NN; Paperback Book Covers	250.00
❑2, ca. 1964; Includes "Mad Mischief" Stickers	200.00
❑3, ca. 1965; Mischief Stickers	150.00
❑4, ca. 1966; Includes Mad mobile	100.00
❑5, ca. 1967; Includes Mad stencils	100.00
❑6, ca. 1968; Includes "Mad Mischief" Stickers	100.00
❑7, ca. 1969; Includes "Nasty Cards" postcards	100.00

Madhouse Glads
Archie

❑73, May 1970, Previous issues published as Madhouse Ma-ad Freakout	3.00
❑74, Jul 1970	3.00
❑75, Sep 1970	3.00
❑76, Nov 1970	3.00
❑77, Feb 1971	3.00
❑78, May 1971, 48 pages	5.00
❑79, Aug 1971, 48 pages	5.00
❑80, Sep 1971, 48 pages	5.00
❑81, Nov 1971, 48 pages	5.00
❑82, Feb 1972, 48 pages	5.00
❑83, May 1972, 48 pages	5.00
❑84, Aug 1972, 48 pages	5.00
❑85, Oct 1972, 48 pages	5.00
❑86, Dec 1972, 48 pages	5.00

Other grades: Multiply price above by 5/6 for VF/NM • 2/3 for VERY FINE • 1/3 for FINE • 1/5 for VERY GOOD • 1/8 for GOOD

Man-Thing (Vol. 1)

Swamp monster ruins lives, carpets
©Marvel

Mantra

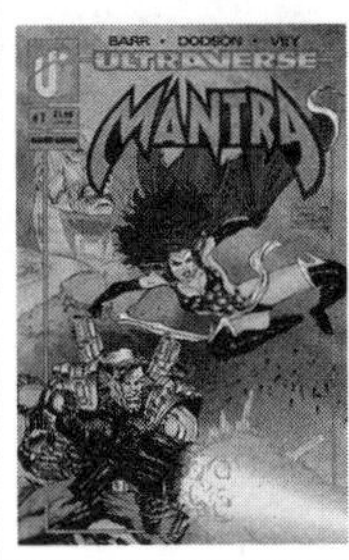

Warrior's mind is transplanted into woman's body
©Malibu

Marc Spector: Moon Knight

Third comics series for man with many identities
©Marvel

Marines Attack

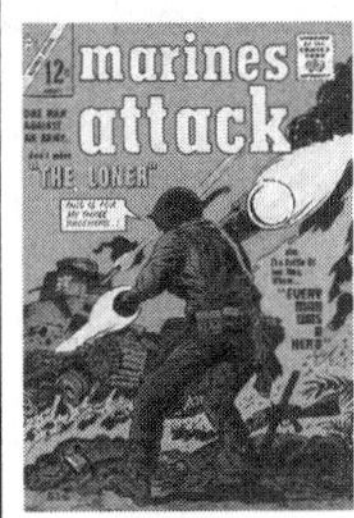

Interesting stories from veteran Sam Glanzman
©Charlton

Mark of Charon

Negation spin-off features soulless hunter
©CrossGen

	N-MINT
❑87, Feb 1973, 48 pages	5.00
❑88, May 1973, 48 pages	5.00
❑89, Aug 1973, 48 pages	5.00
❑90, Oct 1973, 48 pages	5.00
❑91, Dec 1973, 48 pages	5.00
❑92, Feb 1974, 48 pages	5.00
❑93, May 1974	3.00
❑94, Aug 1974, Later issues published as Madhouse	3.00

Madhouse Ma-ad Freakout
Archie

	N-MINT
❑71, ca. 1969, Earlier issues published as Madhouse Ma-ad Jokes	3.00
❑72, Jan 1970, Later issues published as Madhouse Glads	3.00

Madhouse Ma-ad Jokes
Archie

	N-MINT
❑66, Feb 1969, Previous issues published as Archie's Madhouse	3.50
❑67, Apr 1969	3.50
❑68, Jun 1969	3.50
❑69, Aug 1969	3.50
❑70, Oct 1969, Series continues as Madhouse Ma-ad Freakout	3.50

Mad Kids
DC

	N-MINT
❑1, Dec 2005	4.99
❑2, Apr 2006	4.99
❑4, Jun 2006; Includes fake Yu-Gi-Oh cards	4.99
❑5, Jan 2007; Includes "Make Your Own Holiday Ornament"	4.99

Madman
Tundra

	N-MINT
❑1/4th, Double-acetate cover	5.00
❑1, Mar 1992, b&w; prestige format; flip-action corners	8.00
❑1/2nd, 2nd printing	5.00
❑1/3rd, Kitchen Sink publishes	4.00
❑2, Apr 1992	6.00
❑3, May 1992	6.00

Madman Adventures
Tundra

	N-MINT
❑1, ca. 1992; ca. 1993	5.00
❑2, ca. 1993	4.00
❑3, ca. 1993	4.00

Madman Comics
Dark Horse

	N-MINT
❑1, Apr 1994; FM (c); O: Madman	4.00
❑2, Jun 1994	3.50
❑3, Aug 1994	3.50
❑4, Oct 1994	3.00
❑5, Jan 1995; Hellboy Appears	3.00
❑6, Mar 1995; FM (w); Big Guy appears	3.00
❑7, May 1995; FM (w); Big Guy appears	3.00
❑8, Jul 1995	3.00
❑9, Oct 1995	3.00
❑10, Jan 1996 ARo (c)	2.95
❑11, Oct 1996	2.95
❑12, Apr 1999; Doctor Robot back-up	2.95
❑13, May 1999; Doctor Robot back-up	2.95
❑14, Jun 1999; Doctor Robot back-up	2.95
❑15, Jul 1999; Doctor Robot back-up	2.95
❑16, Dec 1999; 1: Mr. Gum	2.95
❑17, Aug 2000; Madman is convinced to rescue the G-Men from Hell but is taken captive	2.95
❑18, Sep 2000; O: G-Men from Hell	2.95
❑19, Oct 2000; O: G-Men from Hell continued	2.99
❑20, Dec 2000; O: G-Men from Hell continued; V: Monstadt; G-Men from Hell rescue Madman	2.99
❑YB 1995, Jan 1996; YB '95; collects Madman Comics #1-5	17.95

Madman Picture Exhibition
AAA Pop

	N-MINT
❑1, Apr 2002	3.95
❑2, May 2002	3.95
❑3, Jun 2002	3.95
❑4, Jul 2002	3.95

Madman/The Jam
Dark Horse

	N-MINT
❑1, Jul 1998	2.95
❑2, Aug 1998	2.95

Mad Monster Party Adaptation
Black Bear

	N-MINT
❑1	2.95
❑2	2.95
❑3	2.95
❑4	2.95

Madonna
Personality

	N-MINT
❑1, b&w	2.95
❑1/Autographed, b&w	3.95
❑2, b&w	2.95
❑2/Autographed, b&w	3.95

Madonna Sex Goddess
Friendly

	N-MINT
❑1, ca. 1990	2.95
❑2, ca. 1991	2.95
❑3, ca. 1991	2.95

Madonna Special
Revolutionary

	N-MINT
❑1, Aug 1993, b&w	2.50

Madonna vs. Marilyn
Celebrity

	N-MINT
❑1	2.95

Mad Raccoons
Mu

	N-MINT
❑1, Jul 1991	2.50
❑2, Sep 1992	2.50
❑3, Aug 1993	2.50
❑4, Aug 1994	2.95
❑5, Aug 1995; cardstock cover	2.95
❑6, Jul 1996; cardstock cover	2.95

Madraven Halloween Special
Hamilton

	N-MINT
❑1, Oct 1995; NN; One-shot	2.95

Madrox
Marvel

	N-MINT
❑1, Nov 2004	2.99
❑2, Dec 2004	2.99
❑3, Jan 2005	2.99
❑4, Feb 2005	2.99
❑5, Mar 2005, Final issue	2.99

Mad Super Special
E.C.

	N-MINT
❑1, Fal 1970, b&w	90.00
❑2, Spr 1971, b&w	54.00
❑3 1971, b&w	44.00
❑4 1971, b&w	44.00
❑5 1971, b&w	44.00
❑6 1971, b&w	38.00
❑7 1972, b&w	38.00
❑8, b&w	38.00
❑9 1972, b&w	38.00
❑10 1973, b&w	38.00
❑11 1973, b&w	26.00
❑12 1974, b&w	26.00
❑13 1974, b&w	26.00
❑14 1974, b&w	26.00
❑15 1974, b&w	26.00
❑16 1975, b&w	20.00
❑17 1975, b&w	20.00
❑18 1975, b&w	20.00
❑19 1976, b&w	20.00
❑20 1976, b&w	20.00
❑21 1976, b&w	16.00
❑22 1977, b&w	16.00
❑23 1977, b&w	16.00
❑24 1977, b&w	16.00
❑25 1978, b&w	16.00
❑26 1978, b&w	12.00
❑27 1978, b&w	12.00
❑28, Fal 1979, b&w; Reprints items from past issues as well as new material; Reprints Mad #7	12.00
❑29, Win 1979, b&w;	12.00
❑30, Spr 1980, b&w	12.00
❑31, Sum 1980, b&w	10.00
❑32, Fal 1980, b&w	10.00
❑33, Win 1980, b&w	10.00
❑34, Spr 1981, b&w	10.00
❑35, Sum 1981, b&w	10.00
❑36, Fal 1981, b&w	10.00
❑37, Win 1981, b&w	10.00
❑38, Spr 1982, b&w	10.00
❑39, Sum 1982, b&w	10.00
❑40, Fal 1982, b&w	10.00
❑41, Win 1982, b&w	6.00
❑42, Win 1983, b&w	6.00
❑43, Spr 1983, b&w	6.00
❑44, Sum 1983, b&w	6.00
❑45, Fal 1983, b&w	6.00
❑46, Spr 1984, b&w	6.00
❑47, Sum 1984, b&w	6.00
❑48, Fal 1984, b&w	6.00
❑49, Win 1984, b&w	6.00
❑50, Spr 1985, b&w	6.00
❑51, Sum 1985, b&w	4.50
❑52, Fal 1985, b&w	4.50
❑53, Win 1985, b&w	4.50
❑54, Spr 1986, b&w	4.50
❑55, Sum 1986, b&w	4.50
❑56, Fal 1986, b&w	4.50
❑57, Win 1986, b&w	4.50
❑58, Spr 1987, b&w	4.50
❑59, Sum 1987, b&w	4.50
❑60, Fal 1987, b&w	4.50
❑61, Win 1987, b&w	4.00
❑62, Spr 1988, b&w	4.00

Other grades: Multiply price above by 5/6 for VF/NM • 2/3 for VERY FINE • 1/3 for FINE • 1/5 for VERY GOOD • 1/8 for GOOD

N-MINT

❑63, Sum 1988, b&w ... 4.00
❑64, Fal 1988, b&w ... 4.00
❑65, Win 1988, b&w ... 4.00
❑66, Spr 1989, b&w ... 4.00
❑67, Sum 1989, b&w ... 4.00
❑68, Fal 1989, b&w ... 4.00
❑69, Win 1989, b&w ... 4.00
❑70, Spr 1990, b&w ... 4.00
❑71, Sum 1990, b&w ... 3.50
❑72, Fal 1990, b&w ... 3.50
❑73, Win 1990, b&w ... 3.50
❑74, Spr 1991, b&w; Spring 1991 ... 3.50
❑75, Sum 1991, b&w ... 3.50
❑76, Fal 1991, b&w ... 3.50
❑77, Win 1991, b&w ... 3.50
❑78, Jan 1992, b&w ... 3.50
❑79, Feb 1992, b&w ... 3.50
❑80, Mar 1992, b&w ... 3.50
❑81, May 1992, b&w ... 3.50
❑82, Jul 1992, b&w ... 3.50
❑83, Sep 1992, b&w ... 3.50
❑84, Nov 1992, b&w ... 3.50
❑85, Jan 1993, b&w ... 3.50
❑86, Mar 1993, b&w ... 3.50
❑87, May 1993, b&w ... 3.50
❑88, Jul 1993, b&w ... 3.50
❑89, Sep 1993, b&w ... 3.50
❑90, Nov 1993, b&w ... 3.50
❑91, Jan 1994, b&w ... 3.50
❑92, Mar 1994, b&w ... 3.50
❑93, May 1994, b&w ... 3.50
❑94, Jul 1994, b&w; 49 Silly Sweepstakes Stickers and 36 Mad "No-Postage" Stamps ... 3.50
❑95, Sep 1994, b&w; Mania 3 ... 3.50
❑96, Spr 1994, b&w ... 3.50
❑97, b&w ... 3.50
❑98, b&w; Gross-Outs #2 ... 3.50
❑99, b&w; Movie Classics ... 3.50
❑100, b&w ... 3.99
❑101, b&w ... 3.99
❑102, Spr 1995, b&w ... 3.99
❑103, Apr 1995, b&w ... 3.99
❑104, Jun 1995, b&w ... 3.99
❑105, Jul 1995, b&w; O.J. Pod Stickers Included ... 3.99
❑106 1995, b&w ... 3.99
❑107, Oct 1995, b&w ... 3.99
❑108, Nov 1995, b&w ... 3.99
❑109, Dec 1996, b&w ... 3.99
❑110, Jan 1996, b&w ... 3.99
❑111, Mar 1996, b&w ... 3.99
❑112, Apr 1996, b&w ... 3.99
❑113, Jun 1996, b&w ... 3.99
❑114, Jul 1996, b&w ... 3.99
❑115, Sep 1996, b&w ... 3.99
❑116, Oct 1996, b&w ... 3.99
❑117, Dec 1996, b&w ... 3.99
❑118, Feb 1997, b&w ... 3.99
❑119, Apr 1997, b&w ... 3.99
❑120, Apr 1997, b&w ... 3.99
❑121, Jun 1997, b&w ... 3.99
❑122, Aug 1997, b&w ... 3.99
❑123, Sep 1997, b&w ... 3.99
❑124, Oct 1997, b&w ... 3.99
❑125, Dec 1997, b&w ... 3.99
❑126, Jan 1998, b&w ... 3.99
❑127, Mar 1998, b&w ... 3.99
❑128, Jun 1998, b&w ... 3.99
❑129, Jul 1998, b&w ... 3.99
❑130, Aug 1998 ... 3.99
❑131, Oct 1998 ... 3.99
❑132, Nov 1998 ... 3.99
❑133, Jan 1998 ... 3.99
❑134, Mar 1999 ... 3.99
❑135, Jun 1999 ... 3.99

Mael's Rage
Ominous

❑2, Aug 1994 ... 2.50
❑2/Variant, Aug 1994; cardstock outer cover ... 2.50

Maelstrom
Aircel

❑1, Jun 1987 ... 1.70
❑2, Jul 1987 ... 1.70
❑3, Aug 1987 ... 1.70
❑4, Sep 1987 ... 1.70

N-MINT

❑5, Oct 1987 ... 1.50
❑6, Nov 1987 ... 1.50
❑7, Dec 1987 ... 1.50
❑8, Jan 1988 ... 1.50
❑9, Feb 1988 ... 1.50
❑10, Mar 1988 ... 1.50

Magdalena
Image

❑1, Apr 2000, Regular cover with Magdalena standing, cross at bottom center of design ... 2.50
❑1/A, Apr 2000, 2000 Megacon Exclusive 2.50
❑1/B, Apr 2000, Alternate cover with Magdalena standing, cross at bottom center of design ... 2.50
❑2, Jun 2000 ... 2.50
❑3, Jan 2001 ... 2.50
❑3/A, Jan 2001, Alternate cover with Eruptor logo and foil additions ... 2.50

Magdalena
Image

❑1, Jul 2003 ... 2.99
❑1/A, Jul 2003 ... 5.00
❑2, Aug 2003 ... 2.99
❑3, Oct 2003 ... 2.99
❑4, Dec 2003 ... 2.99

Magdalena/Angelus
Image

❑0 ... 2.95
❑½, Nov 2001 ... 2.95

Magdalena/Vampirella
Image

❑1, Jun 2003; Magdalena w/blades drawn by Joe Benitez and Martin Montiel ... 2.99

Mage
Comico

❑1, May 1984; MW (c); MW (w); MW (a); 1: Kevin Matchstick ... 5.00
❑2, Jul 1984 MW (c); MW (w); MW (a). 4.00
❑3, Sep 1984 MW (c); MW (w); MW (a) 3.00
❑4, Nov 1984 MW (c); MW (w); MW (a) 3.00
❑5, Jan 1985 MW (c); MW (w); MW (a) 3.00
❑6, Mar 1985; MW (c); MW (w); MW (a); 1: Grendel I (Hunter Rose) (in color). Grendel ... 15.00
❑7, May 1985 MW (w); MW (a); A: Grendel I (Hunter Rose) ... 8.00
❑8, Jul 1985 MW (c); MW (w); MW (a); A: Grendel I (Hunter Rose) ... 4.00
❑9, Sep 1985 MW (c); MW (w); MW (a); A: Grendel I (Hunter Rose) ... 3.00
❑10, Dec 1985 MW (c); MW (w); MW (a); A: Grendel I (Hunter Rose) ... 3.00
❑11, Feb 1986 MW (c); MW (w); MW (a); A: Grendel I (Hunter Rose) ... 3.00
❑12, Apr 1986 MW (c); MW (w); MW (a); A: Grendel I (Hunter Rose) ... 3.00
❑13, Jun 1986; MW (c); MW (w); MW (a); D: Grendel I (Hunter Rose); D: Grendel I (Hunter Rose) ... 4.00
❑14, Aug 1986 MW (c); MW (w); MW (a); A: Grendel ... 3.00
❑15, Dec 1986; Giant-size; MW (c); MW (w); MW (a); Final Issue ... 6.00

Mage
Image

❑0, Jul 1997; MW (c); MW (w); MW (a); American Entertainment Exclusive ... 3.00
❑0/Autographed, Jul 1997; MW (c); MW (w); MW (a); Autographed by Matt Wagner ... 5.00
❑1, Jul 1997 MW (c); MW (w); MW (a). 4.00
❑1/3D, Feb 1998; 3-D edition; MW (c); MW (w); MW (a); with glasses ... 4.95
❑2, Aug 1997 MW (c); MW (w); MW (a) 3.50
❑3, Sep 1997 MW (c); MW (w); MW (a) 3.50
❑4, Nov 1997 MW (c); MW (w); MW (a) 3.00
❑5, Jan 1998 MW (c); MW (w); MW (a) 3.00
❑6, Mar 1998 MW (c); MW (w); MW (a) 2.50
❑7, Apr 1998 MW (c); MW (w); MW (a) 2.50
❑8, Jun 1998 MW (c); MW (w); MW (a) 2.50
❑9, Sep 1998 MW (c); MW (w); MW (a) 2.50
❑10, Dec 1998 MW (c); MW (w); MW (a) 2.50
❑11, Feb 1999 MW (c); MW (w); MW (a) 2.50
❑12, Apr 1999 MW (c); MW (w); MW (a) 2.50
❑13/A, Jun 1999; MW (c); MW (w); MW (a); covers form triptych ... 2.50
❑13/B, Jun 1999; MW (c); MW (w); MW (a); Mage cover ... 2.50

N-MINT

❑13/C, Jun 1999; MW (c); MW (w); MW (a); Mage cover ... 2.50
❑14, Aug 1999 MW (c); MW (w); MW (a) 2.50
❑15, Oct 1999 MW (c); MW (w); MW (a) 2.50
❑15/Variant, Oct 1999; MW (c); MW (w); MW (a); Special acetate double-cover 5.95

Mage Knight: Stolen Destiny
Idea & Design Works

❑1 2002 ... 3.50
❑2 2002 ... 3.50
❑3, Dec 2002 ... 3.50
❑4, Feb 2003 ... 3.50
❑5, Mar 2003 ... 3.50

Mage: The Hero Discovered
Image

❑1, Oct 1998; Reprints #1-2 of the Comico series ... 4.95
❑2, Dec 1998; Reprints #3-4 of the Comico series ... 4.95
❑3, Feb 1999; Reprints #5-6 of the Comico series ... 4.95
❑4, Apr 1999; Reprints #7-8 of the Comico series ... 4.95
❑5, Jun 1999; Reprints #9-10 of the Comico series ... 4.95
❑6, Jul 1999; Reprints #11-12 of the Comico series ... 4.95
❑7, Aug 1999; Reprints #13-14 of the Comico series ... 4.95
❑8, Sep 1999; Reprints #15 of the Comico series plus other material ... 4.95

Maggie and Hopey Color Special
Fantagraphics

❑1, May 1997 ... 3.50

Maggie the Cat
Image

❑1, Jan 1996 ... 2.50
❑2, Mar 1996 ... 2.50
❑3 1996, Exists? ... 2.50
❑4 1996, Exists? ... 2.50

Maggots
Hamilton

❑1, Nov 1991, b&w ... 3.95
❑2, Jan 1992, b&w ... 3.95
❑3, Mar 1992, b&w ... 3.95

Magical Mates
Antarctic

❑1, Feb 1996 ... 2.95
❑2, Apr 1996 ... 2.95
❑3, Jun 1996 ... 2.95
❑4, Aug 1996 ... 2.95
❑5, Oct 1996 ... 2.95
❑6, Dec 1996 ... 2.95
❑7 1997 ... 2.95
❑8 1997 ... 2.95
❑9 1997 ... 2.95

Magical Nymphini
Rip Off

❑1, Feb 1991, b&w; Adult ... 2.50
❑1/2nd; 2nd printing; Adult ... 2.50
❑2, Apr 1991, b&w; Adult ... 2.50
❑2/2nd; 2nd printing; Adult ... 2.50
❑3, Aug 1991, b&w; Adult ... 2.50
❑3/2nd; 2nd printing; Adult ... 2.50
❑4, Dec 1991, b&w; Adult ... 2.95
❑4/2nd; 2nd printing; Adult ... 2.95
❑5, Aug 1992, b&w; Adult ... 2.95
❑5/2nd; 2nd printing; Adult ... 2.95

Magical Twilight
Graphic Visions

❑1; Adult ... 2.95

Magic Boy and Girlfriend
Top Shelf

❑1, Jul 1998, b&w; NN ... 8.95

Magic Boy & the Robot Elf
Slave Labor

❑1, May 1996 ... 9.95

Magic Carpet
Shanda Fantasy Arts

❑1, Apr 1999, b&w ... 4.50

Magic Flute
Eclipse

❑1, ca. 1990; Part of Eclipse's Night Music series ... 4.95

Other grades: Multiply price above by 5/6 for VF/NM • 2/3 for VERY FINE • 1/3 for FINE • 1/5 for VERY GOOD • 1/8 for GOOD

Married...With Children (Vol. 1)

Fox's first dysfunctional family comes to comics

©Now

Mars Attacks (Vol. 1)

1950s card set inspires 1990s comic book

©Topps

Marshal Law

Judge Dredd-like hero hunter

©Marvel

Martian Manhunter

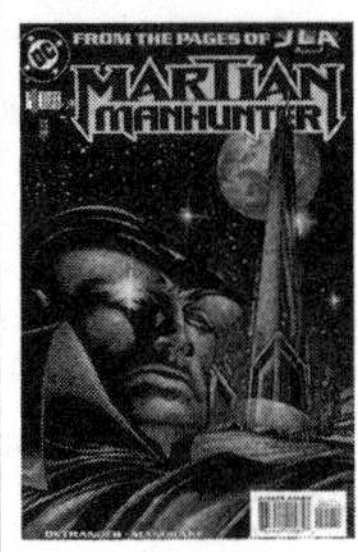

Early Silver Age hero finally gets series

©DC

Marvel Age

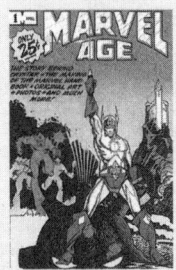

Fred Hembeck featured in house organ

©Marvel

	N-MINT
❑2, ca. 1990	4.95
❑3, ca. 1990; Night Music #11	4.95

Magicians' Village
Mad Monkey

❑1, ca. 1995	2.45

Magic Inkwell Comic Strip Theatre
Moordam

❑1, Mar 1998	2.95

Magicman
A-Plus

❑1, b&w; Reprints	2.95

Magic Pickle
Oni

❑1, Sep 2001	2.95
❑2 2001	2.95
❑3 2001	2.95
❑4	2.95

Magic Priest
Antarctic

❑1, Jun 1998, b&w	2.95

Magic: The Gathering: Antiquities War
Acclaim / Armada

❑1, Nov 1995	2.50
❑2, Dec 1995	2.50
❑3, Jan 1996	2.50
❑4, Feb 1996	2.50

Magic: The Gathering: Elder Dragons
Acclaim / Armada

❑1, Apr 1996	2.50
❑2, May 1996	2.50

Magic: The Gathering: Gerard's Quest
Dark Horse

❑1, Mar 1998	2.95
❑2, Apr 1998	2.95
❑3, May 1998	2.95
❑4, Sep 1998	2.95

Magic: The Gathering: Nightmare
Acclaim / Armada

❑1, ca. 1995	2.50

Magic: The Gathering: Shandalar
Acclaim / Armada

❑1, Mar 1996	2.50
❑2, Apr 1996	2.50

Magic: The Gathering: The Shadow Mage
Acclaim / Armada

❑1, Jul 1995; bound-in Fireball card	2.50
❑2, Aug 1995; bound-in Blue Elemental card	2.50
❑3, Sep 1995; bagged with Magic: The Gathering tokens and counters	2.50
❑4, Oct 1995; polybagged with sheet of creature tokens	2.50

Magic: The Gathering: Wayfarer
Acclaim / Armada

❑1, Nov 1995	2.50
❑2, Dec 1995	2.50
❑3, Jan 1996	2.50
❑4, Feb 1996	2.50
❑5, Mar 1996	2.50

Magic Whistle
Alternative

	N-MINT
❑1, Mar 1998, b&w	2.95
❑2, Aug 1998, b&w	2.95

Magic Words
Avatar

❑1, Nov 2002, b&w	6.95

Magik
Marvel

❑1, Dec 1983, JB (c); JB, TP (a)	2.25
❑2, Jan 1984, JB, TP (a)	2.00
❑3, Feb 1984, TP (a)	2.00
❑4, Mar 1984, SB, TP (a)	2.00

Magik
Marvel

❑1, Dec 2000	2.99
❑2, Jan 2001	2.99
❑3, Feb 2001	2.99
❑4, Mar 2001	2.99

Magilla Gorilla
Gold Key

❑1, ca. 1964	30.00
❑2, ca. 1964	15.00
❑3, Dec 1964	12.00
❑4, ca. 1965	12.00
❑5, ca. 1965	12.00
❑6, Aug 1965	10.00
❑7, Nov 1965	10.00
❑8, Jul 1966	10.00
❑9, Oct 1966	10.00
❑10, Dec 1968, Final Issue	10.00

Magna-Man: The Last Superhero
Comics Interview

❑1, b&w	1.95
❑2, Sum 1988, b&w	1.95
❑3, Sum 1988, b&w	1.95

Magnesium Arc
Iconografix

❑1	3.50

Magnetic Men Featuring Magneto
Marvel / Amalgam

❑1, Jun 1997	1.95

Magneto
Marvel

❑0, Sep 1993, retailer giveaway; BSz (c); JDu, JBy (a); O: Magneto. no cover price; Promotional give-away; Reprints "A Fire in the Sky" from X-Men Classic #19; Reprints "I Magneto" From X-Men Classic #12	3.00

Magneto
Marvel

❑1, Nov 1996	2.00
❑2, Dec 1996	2.00
❑3, Jan 1997	2.00
❑4, Feb 1997, Final Issue	2.00

Magneto and the Magnetic Men
Marvel / Amalgam

❑1, Apr 1996	1.95

Magneto Ascendant
Marvel

	N-MINT
❑1, Apr 1999; Reprints Magneto Stories from X-Men (1st Series)	3.99

Magneto: Dark Seduction
Marvel

❑1, Jun 2000; Magneto consolidates control over Genoshoa	2.99
❑2, Jul 2000; Scarlet Witch is sent by United Nations to investigate Genoshoa	2.99
❑3, Aug 2000; V: Avengers; V: She-Hulk; V: Triathalon; V: Warbird; V: Iron Man; V: Wasp; V: Giant-Man	2.99
❑4, Sep 2000; V: Avengers; V: She-Hulk; V: Triathalon; V: Warbird; V: Iron Man; V: Wasp; V: Giant-Man; Genoshoan technology restores Magneto's powers	2.99

Magneto Rex
Marvel

❑1, Apr 1999; 1: Zealot (Thomas Moreau); Magneto consolidates control of Genosha	2.50
❑2, Jun 1999; V: Zealot	2.50
❑3, Jul 1999; V: Zealot	2.50

Magnets: Robot Dismantler
Parody

❑1, b&w; Foil-embossed cover	2.50

Magnus, Robot Fighter
Gold Key

❑1, Feb 1963, 1&O: Magnus. 1: Leeja Clane	200.00
❑2, May 1963	125.00
❑3, Aug 1963	125.00
❑4, Nov 1963	60.00
❑5, Feb 1964	60.00
❑6, May 1964	60.00
❑7, Aug 1964	60.00
❑8, Nov 1964	60.00
❑9, Feb 1965	60.00
❑10, May 1965	60.00
❑11, Aug 1965	35.00
❑12, Nov 1965	35.00
❑13, Feb 1966, 1: Doctor Noel	35.00
❑14, May 1966	35.00
❑15, Aug 1966	35.00
❑16, Nov 1966	35.00
❑17, Feb 1967	35.00
❑18, May 1967	35.00
❑19, Aug 1967	35.00
❑20, Nov 1967	35.00
❑21, Feb 1968	20.00
❑22, May 1968, 1&O: Magnus. 1: Leeja Clane. Reprints Magnus, Robot Fighter (Gold Key) #1	20.00
❑23, Aug 1968, DS (a); Reprints	20.00
❑24, Nov 1968, Destruction of Malev-6	20.00
❑25, Feb 1969	20.00
❑26, May 1969	20.00
❑27, Aug 1969	20.00
❑28, Nov 1969, goes on hiatus	20.00
❑29, Nov 1971	10.00
❑30, Jan 1972	10.00
❑31, Apr 1972	10.00
❑32, Jul 1972	10.00
❑33, Oct 1972	10.00
❑34, Jan 1973	10.00

Other grades: Multiply price above by 5/6 for VF/NM • 2/3 for VERY FINE • 1/3 for FINE • 1/5 for VERY GOOD • 1/8 for GOOD

❑35, May 1974 ... 10.00
❑36, Aug 1974 ... 10.00
❑37, Nov 1974 ... 10.00
❑38, Feb 1975 ... 10.00
❑39, May 1975 ... 10.00
❑40, Aug 1975, Reprint of issue #17 ... 10.00
❑41, Nov 1975 ... 10.00
❑42, Jan 1976 ... 10.00
❑43, May 1976 ... 10.00
❑44, Aug 1976 ... 10.00
❑45, Oct 1976 ... 10.00
❑45/Whitman, Oct 1976 ... 18.00
❑46, Jan 1977 ... 10.00

Magnus Robot Fighter
Valiant

❑0/card, ca. 1992 ... 40.00
❑0/no card, ca. 1992 ... 30.00
❑1, May 1991; O: Magnus. trading cards ... 10.00
❑2, Jul 1991; Includes trading card; Includes coupon for #0 issue ... 8.00
❑3, Aug 1991; 1: Tekla; Includes trading card; Includes coupon for #0 issue ... 5.00
❑4, Sep 1991; Includes trading card; Includes coupon for #0 issue ... 5.00
❑5, Oct 1991; Flip-book; 1: Rai. Flip-book with Rai #1 ... 6.00
❑6, Nov 1991; Flip-book; A: Rai. A: Solar. Includes trading card; Includes coupon for #0 issue ... 6.00
❑7, Dec 1991; Flip-book; A: Rai. V: Rai; Includes trading card; Includes coupon for #0 issue ... 4.00
❑8, Jan 1992; Flip-book; A: Rai. Includes trading card; Includes coupon for #0 issue ... 4.00
❑9, Feb 1992 ... 3.00
❑10, Mar 1992 ... 3.00
❑11, Apr 1992 ... 6.00
❑12, May 1992; Giant-size; 1: Turok (Valiant) ... 20.00
❑13, Jun 1992 ... 3.00
❑14, Jul 1992 ... 3.00
❑15, Aug 1992; FM (c); FM (a); Unity ... 3.00
❑16, Sep 1992; Unity ... 3.00
❑17, Nov 1992 ... 2.00
❑18, Nov 1992 SD (c); SD (w); SD (a) ... 2.00
❑19, Dec 1992 SD (c); SD (w); SD (a) ... 2.00
❑20, Jan 1993 ... 2.00
❑21, Feb 1993; New logo ... 2.00
❑21/Gold, Feb 1993; Gold edition; New logo ... 20.00
❑22, Mar 1993 ... 2.00
❑23, Apr 1993 ... 2.00
❑24, May 1993; Story leads into Rai and the Future Force #9 ... 2.00
❑25, Jun 1993; BL (c); Silver embossed cover ... 2.00
❑25/VVSS, Jun 1993 ... 15.00
❑26, Jul 1993 ... 1.00
❑27, Aug 1993; Includes serial number coupon for contest ... 1.00
❑28, Sep 1993; Includes serial number coupon for contest ... 1.00
❑29, Oct 1993 A: Eternal Warrior ... 1.00
❑30, Nov 1993 A: X-O ... 1.00
❑31, Dec 1993 ... 1.00
❑32, Jan 1994 ... 1.00
❑33, Feb 1994 A: Timewalker ... 1.00
❑34, Mar 1994 ... 1.00
❑35, Apr 1994 ... 1.00
❑36, May 1994; trading card ... 2.00
❑37, Jun 1994 A: Starwatchers. A: Rai ... 1.00
❑38, Aug 1994 ... 1.00
❑39, Sep 1994 A: Torque ... 1.00
❑40, Oct 1994 ... 1.00
❑41, Nov 1994; Chaos Effect Epsilon 4 ... 1.00
❑42, Dec 1994 ... 1.00
❑43, Jan 1995 ... 1.00
❑44, Feb 1995; Includes a "Valiant Sneak Peek" card ... 3.00
❑45, Mar 1995 ... 2.00
❑46, Apr 1995 ... 2.00
❑47, May 1995 ... 2.00
❑48, Jun 1995 ... 2.00
❑49, Jul 1995; Birthquake ... 2.00
❑50, Jul 1995; Birthquake ... 2.00
❑51, Aug 1995; Birthquake ... 2.00
❑52, Aug 1995; Birthquake ... 2.00
❑53, Sep 1995 ... 2.00
❑54, Sep 1995 ... 2.00
❑55, Oct 1995 ... 3.00
❑56, Oct 1995 ... 3.00
❑57, Nov 1995 ... 3.00
❑57/error, Nov 1995 ... 10.00
❑58, Nov 1995 ... 3.00
❑59, Dec 1995 ... 3.00
❑60, Dec 1995 ... 3.00
❑61, Jan 1996 ... 4.00
❑62, Jan 1996; Torque becomes a Psi-Lord ... 4.00
❑63, Feb 1996 ... 5.00
❑64, Feb 1996; D: Magnus, Robot Fighter (Valiant); Final Issue ... 12.00
❑YB 1, ca. 1994; cardstock cover ... 5.00

Magnus Robot Fighter
Acclaim

❑1, May 1997 ... 2.50
❑1/Variant, May 1997, b&w; alternate painted cover ... 2.50
❑2, Jun 1997; V: Damon Angel ... 2.50
❑3, Jul 1997 ... 2.50
❑4, Aug 1997; V: androids in Hall of President's amusement park exhibit ... 2.50
❑5, Sep 1997 ... 2.50
❑6, Oct 1997 ... 2.50
❑7, Nov 1997; Gold Key homage cover ... 2.50
❑8, Dec 1997 ... 2.50
❑9, Jan 1998 ... 2.50
❑10, Feb 1998 ... 2.50
❑11, Mar 1998 ... 2.50
❑12, Apr 1998 ... 2.50
❑13, Jan 1998; No cover date; indicia says Jan ... 2.50
❑14, Feb 1998; No cover date; indicia says Feb ... 2.50
❑15, Mar 1998; V: Albania's artificial intelligence ... 2.50
❑16, Apr 1998; RT (a); Whitcraft has artificial heart implanted ... 2.50
❑17, May 1998 ... 2.50
❑18, Jun 1998 ... 2.50
❑Ashcan 1, Jan 1997, b&w; No cover price; preview of upcoming series ... 1.00

Magnus Robot Fighter/Nexus
Valiant / Dark Horse

❑0/Preview, ca. 1994 ... 10.00
❑1, Dec 1993; covers says Mar, indicia says Dec ... 3.00
❑2, Apr 1994; SR (c); SR (w); SR (a); Painted Cardstock cover ... 3.00

Magus
Caliber

❑1 ... 2.95
❑1/A; Variant cover of Girl praying in foreground, Magus behind ... 2.95
❑2 ... 2.95

Mahoromatic: Automatic Maiden
Tokyopop

❑1, May 2004 ... 9.99
❑2, Jul 2004 ... 9.99
❑3, Sep 2004 ... 9.99
❑4, Dec 2004 ... 9.99
❑5, Mar 2005 ... 9.99
❑6, Jan 2005 ... 9.99
❑7, Oct 2005 ... 9.99

Maine Zombie Lobstermen
Maine Stream Comics

❑1, b&w ... 2.50
❑2, b&w ... 2.50
❑3, b&w ... 3.50

Mai, the Psychic Girl
Eclipse / Viz

❑1, May 1987, b&w; Japanese ... 3.50
❑1/2nd 1987; 2nd printing ... 2.00
❑2, Jun 1987 ... 2.50
❑2/2nd 1987; 2nd printing ... 2.00
❑3, Jun 1987 ... 2.50
❑4, Jul 1987 ... 2.00
❑5, Jul 1987 ... 2.00
❑6, Aug 1987 ... 1.75
❑7, Aug 1987 ... 1.75
❑8, Sep 1987 ... 1.75
❑9, Sep 1987 ... 1.75
❑10, Oct 1987 ... 1.75
❑11, Oct 1987 ... 1.75
❑12, Nov 1987 ... 1.75
❑13, Nov 1987 ... 1.75
❑14, Dec 1987 ... 1.75
❑15, Dec 1987 ... 1.75
❑16, Jan 1988 ... 1.75
❑17, Jan 1988 ... 1.75
❑18, Feb 1988 ... 1.75
❑19, Feb 1988 ... 1.75
❑20, Mar 1988 ... 1.75
❑21, Mar 1988 ... 1.75
❑22, Apr 1988 ... 1.75
❑23, Apr 1988 ... 1.75
❑24, May 1988 ... 1.75
❑25, May 1988 ... 1.75
❑26, Jun 1988 ... 1.75
❑27, Jun 1988 ... 1.75
❑28, Jul 1988; Final Issue ... 1.75

Maison Ikkoku Part 1
Viz

❑1, Jun 1992 ... 4.00
❑2, Jul 1992 ... 3.50
❑3, Aug 1992 ... 3.50
❑4, Sep 1992 ... 3.50
❑5, Oct 1992 ... 3.50
❑6, Nov 1992 ... 3.50
❑7, Dec 1992 ... 3.50

Maison Ikkoku Part 2
Viz

❑1, Jan 1993 ... 3.50
❑2, Feb 1993 ... 3.00
❑3, Mar 1993 ... 3.00
❑4, Apr 1993 ... 3.00
❑5, May 1993 ... 3.00
❑6, Jun 1993 ... 3.00

Maison Ikkoku Part 3
Viz

❑1, Jul 1993 ... 3.00
❑2, Aug 1993 ... 3.00
❑3, Sep 1993 ... 3.00
❑4, Oct 1993 ... 3.00
❑5, Nov 1993 ... 3.00
❑6, Dec 1993 ... 3.00

Maison Ikkoku Part 4
Viz

❑1, Jan 1994 ... 2.95
❑2, Feb 1994 ... 2.95
❑3, Apr 1994 ... 2.95
❑4, May 1994 ... 2.95
❑5, Jun 1994 ... 2.95
❑6, Jul 1994 ... 2.95
❑7, Aug 1994 ... 2.95
❑8, Sep 1994 ... 2.95
❑9, Oct 1994 ... 2.95
❑10, Nov 1994 ... 2.95

Maison Ikkoku Part 5
Viz

❑1, Nov 1995; b&w ... 2.95
❑2, Dec 1995 ... 2.95
❑3, Jan 1996 ... 3.50
❑4, Feb 1996 ... 3.50
❑5, Mar 1996 ... 3.50
❑6, Apr 1996 ... 2.95
❑7, May 1996 ... 3.50
❑8, Jun 1996 ... 3.50
❑9, Jul 1996 ... 2.75

Maison Ikkoku Part 6
Viz

❑1, Aug 1996; b&w ... 3.50
❑2, Sep 1996 ... 2.95
❑3, Oct 1996 ... 3.50
❑4, Nov 1996 ... 3.50
❑5, Dec 1996 ... 2.95
❑6, Jan 1997 ... 3.50
❑7, Feb 1997 ... 2.95
❑8, Mar 1997 ... 2.95
❑9, Apr 1997 ... 2.95
❑10, May 1997 ... 2.95
❑11, Jun 1997 ... 3.50

Maison Ikkoku Part 7
Viz

❑1, Jul 1997 ... 3.50
❑2, Aug 1997 ... 3.50
❑3, Sep 1997 ... 3.25
❑4, Oct 1997 ... 3.25
❑5, Nov 1997 ... 3.25
❑6, Dec 1997 ... 3.25

Marvel Chillers

Modred the Mystic first featured
©Marvel

Marvel Classics Comics

Classics Illustrated for Marvel zombies
©Marvel

Marvel Collector's Edition

Mail-away from Charleston Chew
©Marvel

Marvel Collectors' Item Classics

Squarebound reprint title featured FF
©Marvel

Marvel Comics Presents

Biweekly serials featured Wolverine, others
©Marvel

N-MINT

❑7, Jan 1998 .... 3.25
❑8, Feb 1998 .... 3.25
❑9, Mar 1998 .... 3.25
❑10, Apr 1998 .... 3.25
❑11, May 1998 .... 3.25
❑12, Jun 1998 .... 3.25
❑13, Jul 1998 .... 3.25

Maison Ikkoku Part 8
Viz

❑1, Aug 1998 .... 3.25
❑2, Sep 1998 .... 3.50
❑3, Oct 1998 .... 2.95
❑4, Nov 1998 .... 3.50
❑5, Dec 1998 .... 3.50
❑6, Jan 1999 .... 3.50
❑7, Feb 1999 .... 3.50
❑8, Mar 1999 .... 3.25

Maison Ikkoku Part 9
Viz

❑1, Apr 1999 .... 3.25
❑2, May 1999 .... 3.25
❑3, Jun 1999 .... 3.25
❑4, Jul 1999 .... 3.25
❑5, Aug 1999 .... 3.25
❑6, Sep 1999 .... 3.25
❑7, Oct 1999 .... 3.25
❑8, Nov 1999 .... 3.25
❑9, Dec 1999 .... 3.25
❑10, Jan 2000; Final issue 2.95

Majcans
P.S.

❑1 .... 1.00

Majestic
DC

❑1, Oct 2004 .... 2.95
❑2, Nov 2004 .... 2.95
❑3, Dec 2004 .... 2.95
❑4, Jan 2005 .... 2.95
❑5, Jun 2005 .... 2.99

Majestic
DC / Wildstorm

❑1, Feb 2005 .... 2.95
❑2, Mar 2005 .... 2.95
❑3, Apr 2005; Price increase 2.95
❑4, May 2005 .... 2.95
❑5, Jun 2005 .... 2.95
❑6, Jul 2005 .... 2.99
❑7, Aug 2005 .... 2.99
❑8, Sep 2005 .... 2.99
❑9, Oct 2005 .... 2.99
❑10, Dec 2005 .... 2.99
❑11, Jan 2006 .... 2.99
❑12, Feb 2006 .... 2.99
❑13, Mar 2006 .... 2.99
❑14, Apr 2006 .... 2.99
❑15, May 2006 .... 2.99
❑16, Jun 2006 .... 2.99

Major Bummer
DC

❑1, Aug 1997; O: Major Bummer. 1: The Gecko. 1: Major Bummer 3.00
❑2, Sep 1997 .... 2.50
❑3, Oct 1997 .... 2.50
❑4, Nov 1997 .... 2.50

N-MINT

❑5, Dec 1997; Face cover 2.50
❑6, Jan 1998 .... 2.50
❑7, Feb 1998 .... 2.50
❑8, Mar 1998 .... 2.50
❑9, Apr 1998 .... 2.50
❑10, May 1998 .... 2.50
❑11, Jun 1998 .... 2.50
❑12, Jul 1998 .... 2.50
❑13, Aug 1998 .... 2.50
❑14, Sep 1998 .... 2.50
❑15, Oct 1998; Last Issue 2.50

Major Damage
Invictus

❑1, Oct 1994 .... 2.25
❑2 .... 2.25

Major Power And Spunky
Fantagraphics / Eros

❑1, Oct 1994; one shot 3.50

Makebelieve
Liar

❑1 .... 2.95

Malcolm-10
Onli

❑1, b&w 2.00

Malcolm X
Millennium

❑1, Jun 1993 .... 3.95

Malcolm X Angriest Man in America
London Publishing

❑1; British 6.50

Malibu Ashcan: UltraForce
Malibu / Ultraverse

❑1, Jun 1994; NN 0.75

Malibu Signature Series
Malibu

❑1993; autograph book giveaway 1.00
❑1994; autograph book giveaway 1.00

Malice in Wonderland
Fantagraphics / Eros

❑1, Aug 1993, b&w; Adult 2.75

Malinky Robot Bicycle
Slave Labor

❑1, Dec 2005 .... 2.95

Mallimalou
Chance

❑1 .... 1.50

Man Against Time
Image

❑1, May 1996 .... 2.25
❑1/A, May 1996 .... 2.25
❑2, Jun 1996 .... 2.25
❑3, Jul 1996 .... 2.25
❑4, Aug 1996 .... 2.25
❑5, Sep 1996 .... 2.25
❑6, Oct 1996 .... 2.25

Man-Bat
DC

❑1, Dec 1975 JA (c); SD (a) 10.00
❑2, Feb 1976 JA (c); SD (a) 4.00

N-MINT

Man-Bat
DC

❑1, Dec 1984; Reprints 2.50

Man-Bat
DC

❑1, Feb 1996 .... 2.50
❑2, Mar 1996, A: Killer Croc 2.50
❑3, Apr 1996 .... 2.50

Man-Bat
DC

❑1, Jun 2006 .... 2.50
❑3, Sep 2006 .... 2.99
❑4, Sep 2006 .... 2.99
❑5, Nov 2006 .... 2.99

Man Called A-X
Malibu / Bravura

❑0, Feb 1995; Published between #3 and #4 .... 2.95
❑1, Nov 1994 .... 2.95
❑1/A, Nov 1994 .... 2.95
❑2, Dec 1994 .... 2.95
❑3, Jan 1995 .... 2.95
❑4, Feb 1995 .... 2.95
❑5, Apr 1995 .... 2.95

Man Called A-X
DC

❑1, Oct 1997; follows events in Malibu/ Bravura series 2.50
❑2, Nov 1997 .... 2.50
❑3, Dec 1997 .... 2.50
❑4, Jan 1998 .... 2.50
❑5, Feb 1998 .... 2.50
❑6, Mar 1998 .... 2.50
❑7, Apr 1998 .... 2.50
❑8, May 1998; Final Issue 2.50

Man Called Loco, A
Avalon

❑1 .... 2.50

Mandrake the Magician
King

❑1, Sep 1966 .... 32.00
❑2, Nov 1966 .... 20.00
❑3, Jan 1967 .... 14.00
❑4, Mar 1967 .... 13.00
❑5, May 1967, Flying saucer story 13.00
❑6, Jul 1967 .... 10.00
❑7, Aug 1967 .... 10.00
❑8, Sep 1967, JJ (a) 16.00
❑9, Oct 1967, Brick Bradford back-up 9.00
❑10, Nov 1967, AR (a) 24.00

Mandrake the Magician
Marvel

❑1, Apr 1995; cardstock cover 2.95
❑2, May 1995; cardstock cover 2.95

Man-Eating Cow
NEC

❑1, Jul 1992 .... 4.50
❑2, Nov 1992 .... 3.50
❑3, Jan 1993 .... 3.50
❑4, Apr 1993; Scarcer 3.50
❑5, Jun 1993 .... 3.00
❑6, Aug 1993 .... 2.75
❑7, Nov 1993 .... 2.75

Other grades: Multiply price above by 5/6 for VF/NM • 2/3 for VERY FINE • 1/3 for FINE • 1/5 for VERY GOOD • 1/8 for GOOD

❑8, Jan 1994 .... 2.75
❑9 1994 A: The Tick 3.00
❑10, Jun 1994 A: The Tick 3.00

Man-Frog
Mad Dog

❑1, Jul 1987, b&w 2.00
❑2, b&w 2.00

Man from Atlantis
Marvel

❑1, Feb 1978; Giant-size; TS, FR, MZ, JSt (a); TV series 3.00
❑2, Mar 1978, FR (a) 2.00
❑3, Apr 1978 .... 2.00
❑4, May 1978, FR (a) 2.00
❑5, Jun 1978 .... 2.00
❑6, Jul 1978 .... 2.00
❑7, Aug 1978, FR (a); Final Issue 2.00

Man from U.N.C.L.E.
Gold Key

❑1, Feb 1965, based on TV series 150.00
❑2, Oct 1965 .... 75.00
❑3, Nov 1965 .... 50.00
❑4, Jan 1966 .... 50.00
❑5, Mar 1966 .... 50.00
❑6, May 1966 .... 35.00
❑7, Jul 1966 .... 35.00
❑8, Sep 1966, 10146-609 .... 35.00
❑9, Nov 1966 .... 35.00
❑10, Jan 1967 .... 35.00
❑11, Mar 1967 .... 35.00
❑12, May 1967 .... 35.00
❑13, Jul 1967 .... 35.00
❑14, Sep 1967 .... 35.00
❑15, Nov 1967 .... 35.00
❑16, Jan 1968 .... 35.00
❑17, Mar 1968 .... 35.00
❑18, May 1968 .... 35.00
❑19, Jul 1968 .... 35.00
❑20, Oct 1968 .... 35.00
❑21, Jan 1969, Reprints 25.00
❑22, Apr 1969, Reprints 25.00

Man from U.N.C.L.E.
Entertainment

❑1, Jan 1987, b&w 2.00
❑2, Feb 1987 .... 2.00
❑3, Apr 1987 .... 2.00
❑4, Aug 1987 .... 2.00
❑5, Dec 1987 .... 2.00
❑6, Feb 1988 .... 2.00
❑7, May 1988 .... 2.00
❑8, Jul 1988 .... 2.00
❑9, Aug 1988 .... 2.00
❑10, Sep 1988 .... 2.00
❑11, Sep 1988 .... 2.00

Man From U.N.C.L.E.: The Birds of Prey Affair
Millennium

❑1, Mar 1993 .... 2.95
❑2, Sep 1993 .... 2.95

Manga Caliente
Fantagraphics

❑1, Dec 2003 .... 3.95
❑2, Dec 2004 .... 3.95
❑3, Dec 2004 .... 3.95

Manga Darkchylde
Dark Horse

❑1, Feb 2005 .... 2.99
❑2, Jul 2005 .... 2.99

Manga Horror
Avalon

❑1, b&w; reprints Ghostly Tales 2.95

Mangaphile
Radio

❑1, Aug 1999, b&w 2.95
❑2, Oct 1999, b&w 2.95
❑3, Dec 1999, b&w 2.95
❑4, Feb 2000, b&w 2.95
❑5, Apr 2000, b&w 2.95
❑6, Jun 2000, b&w 2.95
❑7, Aug 2000, b&w; Rod Espinosa Interview 2.95

Manga Shi
Crusade

❑1, Aug 1996 .... 3.00

Manga Shi: Shiseji
Crusade

❑1 .... 2.95

Manga Shi 2000
Crusade

❑1, Feb 1997; flip book with Shi: Heaven and Earth preview back-up; In the Killer Skies 2.95
❑1/A, Feb 1997; "Virgin" cover without price or logo 3.00
❑1/B, Feb 1997; Rising Sun Edition; Rising Sun Edition; Black and White without cover price or flipbook material 3.00
❑2, Apr 1997 .... 2.95
❑3, Jun 1997 .... 2.95

Manga Surprise!
Morning & Afternoon, Kodansha Ltd.

❑1, Jul 1996, b&w; NN 2.00

Manga Vizion
Viz

❑1, Mar 1995 .... 5.00
❑2, Apr 1995 .... 5.00
❑3, May 1995 .... 5.00
❑4, Jun 1995 .... 5.00
❑5, Jul 1995 .... 5.00
❑6, Aug 1995 .... 5.00
❑7, Sep 1995 .... 5.00
❑8, Oct 1995 .... 5.00
❑9, Nov 1995 .... 5.00
❑10, Dec 1995 .... 5.00

Manga Vizion
Viz

❑1, Jan 1996 .... 5.00
❑2, Feb 1996 .... 5.00
❑3, Mar 1996 .... 5.00
❑4, Apr 1996 .... 5.00
❑5, May 1996 .... 5.00
❑6, Jun 1996 .... 5.00
❑7, Jul 1996 .... 5.00
❑8, Aug 1996 .... 5.00
❑9, Sep 1996 .... 5.00
❑10, Oct 1996 .... 5.00
❑11, Nov 1996 .... 5.00
❑12, Dec 1996 .... 5.00

Manga Vizion
Viz

❑1, Jan 1997 .... 4.95
❑2, Feb 1997 .... 4.95
❑3, Mar 1997 .... 4.95
❑4, Apr 1997 .... 4.95
❑5 1997 .... 4.95
❑6 1997 .... 4.95
❑7 1997 .... 4.95
❑8 1997 .... 4.95

Manga Vizion
Viz

❑1 .... 4.95
❑2 .... 4.95
❑3 .... 4.95
❑4 .... 4.95
❑5 .... 4.95
❑6 .... 4.95
❑7 .... 4.95
❑8 .... 4.95

Manga Zen
Zen Comics

❑1, b&w 2.50

Mangazine
Antarctic

❑1, ca. 1985, b&w; first Antarctic publication; newsprint cover; company name misspelled throughout 4.00
❑1/2nd; 2nd printing 2.00
❑2, ca. 1985 .... 3.50
❑3, ca. 1986 .... 1.75
❑4, ca. 1986 .... 3.50
❑5, ca. 1986 .... 3.50

Mangazine
Antarctic

❑1, Jan 1989, b&w 3.50
❑2, Jun 1989, b&w 3.00
❑3 1989, b&w 2.00
❑4, b&w 2.00
❑5, ca. 1990, b&w 2.00
❑6 .... 3.00
❑7 .... 3.00
❑8 .... 3.00
❑9 .... 3.00
❑10, Jul 1991 .... 3.00
❑11, Sep 1991 .... 3.00
❑12, Nov 1991 .... 3.00
❑13, Jan 1992 .... 3.00
❑14, Mar 1992 .... 3.00
❑15, May 1992 .... 3.00
❑16, ca. 1992 .... 3.00
❑17, Nov 1992 .... 3.00
❑18, Nov 1992; Urusei Yatsura special issue 3.00
❑19, Jan 1993 .... 3.00
❑20, Feb 1993 .... 3.00
❑21, Mar 1993 .... 3.00
❑22, Apr 1993 .... 3.00
❑23, May 1993 .... 3.00
❑24, Jun 1993 .... 3.00
❑25, Jul 1993 .... 3.00
❑26, Aug 1993 .... 3.00
❑27, Sep 1993 .... 3.00
❑28, Oct 1993 .... 3.00
❑29, Nov 1993 .... 3.00
❑30, Dec 1993 .... 3.00
❑31, Jan 1994 .... 2.95
❑32, Feb 1994; Super Cat Nuku-Nuku 2.95
❑33, May 1994 .... 2.95
❑34, Jul 1994 .... 2.95
❑35, Sep 1994 .... 2.95
❑36, Nov 1994 .... 2.95
❑37, Jan 1995 .... 2.95
❑38, Mar 1995 .... 2.95
❑39, May 1995 .... 2.95
❑40, Sep 1995 .... 2.95
❑41, Sep 1995; Samurai Troopers 2.95
❑42, Sep 1995 .... 2.95
❑43, Sep 1995; Samurai Troopers Episode Guide, Part 2 .... 2.95
❑44, May 1996 .... 2.95

Mangle Tangle Tales
Innovation

❑1; Intro by Harlan Ellison 2.95

Manhunter
DC

❑1, ca. 1984; Double-size; reprints serial from Detective Comics; Archie Goodwin 2.50

Manhunter
DC

❑1, Jul 1988; O: Manhunter II (Mark Shaw) 1.50
❑2, Aug 1988 .... 1.25
❑3, Sep 1988 .... 1.25
❑4, Oct 1988 .... 1.25
❑5, Nov 1988 .... 1.25
❑6, Dec 1988 .... 1.25
❑7, Dec 1988; V: Count Vertigo 1.25
❑8, Jan 1989; A: Flash. Invasion! 1.25
❑9, Jan 1989; A: Flash. Invasion! 1.25
❑10, Feb 1989 A: Checkmate 1.25
❑11, Mar 1989 .... 1.25
❑12, Apr 1989 .... 1.25
❑13, May 1989 .... 1.25
❑14, Jun 1989; The Janus Directive 1.25
❑15, Jul 1989 .... 1.25
❑16, Aug 1989 .... 1.25
❑17, Sep 1989 A: Batman 1.25
❑18, Oct 1989 .... 1.25
❑19, Nov 1989 .... 1.25
❑20, Dec 1989 .... 1.25
❑21, Jan 1990 .... 1.25
❑22, Feb 1990 .... 1.25
❑23, Mar 1990 .... 1.25
❑24, Apr 1990; Final Issue 1.25

Manhunter
DC

❑0, Oct 1994; 1: Manhunter III (Chase Lawler) 2.25
❑1, Nov 1994; O: Manhunter III (Chase Lawler) 2.25
❑2, Dec 1994; O: Manhunter III (Chase Lawler) 2.00
❑3, Jan 1995 .... 2.00
❑4, Feb 1995 .... 2.00
❑5, Mar 1995; Giarrano cover is credited after Kirby 2.00

Marvel Double Feature

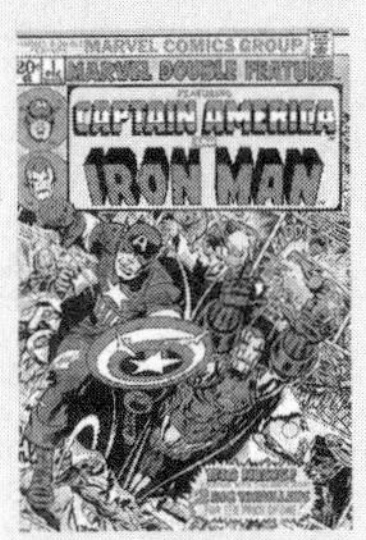

Reprints of Tales of Suspense hero stories
©Marvel

Marvel Fanfare

Bimonthly deluxe outings from various creators
©Marvel

Marvel Feature

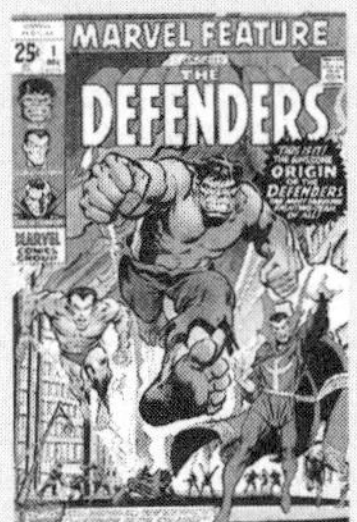

Test-bed for Defenders, Ant-Man
©Marvel

Marvel Feature

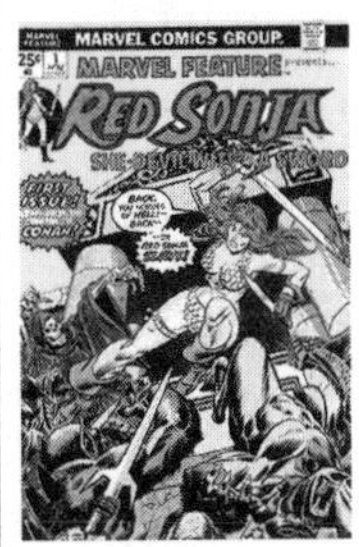

Conan takes over series' second run
©Marvel

Marvel: Heroes & Legends

Major Marvel events told from different POV
©Marvel

	N-MINT
❑6, Apr 1995	2.00
❑7, Jun 1995	2.00
❑8, Jul 1995	2.25
❑9, Aug 1995	2.25
❑10, Sep 1995	2.25
❑11, Oct 1995	2.25
❑12, Nov 1995; Underworld Unleashed	2.25

Manhunter
DC

	N-MINT
❑1, Oct 2004; 1: Manhunter VI (Kate Spencer); D: Copperhead; Kate Spencer takes up role as Manhunter	2.50
❑2, Nov 2004, Shadow Thief	2.50
❑3, Dec 2004, Shadow Thief	2.50
❑4, Jan 2005	2.50
❑5, Feb 2005; Identity Crisis Tie-In; Hawkman apeparance	4.00
❑6, Mar 2005, Trial of Shadow Thief for killing Firestorm	8.00
❑7, Apr 2005	2.50
❑8, May 2005	2.50
❑9, Jun 2005; D: Monocle; Phobia; Trial of Shadowthief	2.50
❑10, Jul 2005; D: Chase Lawler; Trial of Shadow-Thief; Dumas; Mark Shaw; Phobia; Merlyn	2.50
❑11, Aug 2005	2.50
❑12, Sep 2005	2.50
❑13, Oct 2005; Omac Project tie-in	2.50
❑14, Nov 2005; The OMAC Project Tie-In	2.50
❑15, Dec 2005; O: Manhunter VI suit (Darkstar armor)	2.50
❑16, Jan 2006	2.50
❑17, Feb 2006, Mr. Bones; Identity of Kate's Dad revealed	2.50
❑18, Mar 2006	2.50
❑19, Apr 2006	2.50
❑20, Jun 2006, One Year Later	2.50
❑21, Jun 2006, One Year Later	2.50
❑23, Sep 2006, Original Phantom Lady apperance	2.99
❑24, Sep 2006	2.99
❑25, Oct 2006	2.99
❑26, Feb 2007	2.99
❑26/Variant, Feb 2007	2.99
❑27, Mar 2007	2.99
❑28	2.99
❑29	2.99
❑30	2.99
❑31	2.99
❑32	2.99
❑33	2.99
❑34	2.99
❑35	2.99
❑36	2.99
❑37	2.99
❑38	2.99

Manhunter: The Special Edition
DC

	N-MINT
❑1, ca. 1999; collects serial from Detective Comics plus new story	9.95

Manic One-Shot
Image

	N-MINT
❑1, Feb 2004	3.50

Manifest Eternity
DC / Wildstorm

	N-MINT
❑1, Aug 2006	2.99
❑2, Sep 2006	2.99
❑3, Oct 2006	2.99
❑4, Nov 2006	2.99
❑5, Dec 2006	2.99
❑6, Jan 2007	2.99

Manik
Millennium

	N-MINT
❑1, Sep 1995; foil cover	2.95
❑2 1995	2.95
❑3 1996	2.95

Manimal
Renegade

	N-MINT
❑1, Jan 1986, b&w	1.70

Man in Black
Recollections

	N-MINT
❑1, b&w; ca. 1990	2.00
❑2, Jul 1991, b&w	2.00

Mankind
Chaos

	N-MINT
❑1, Sep 1999	2.95

Mann and Superman
DC

	N-MINT
❑1, ca. 2000	5.95

Man of Many Faces
Tokyopop

	N-MINT
❑1, May 2003, b&w; printed in Japanese format	9.99

Man of Rust
Blackthorne

	N-MINT
❑1/A, Nov 1986	1.50
❑1/B, Nov 1986	1.50

Man of Steel
DC

	N-MINT
❑1, Oct 1986; JBy (c); JBy (w); JBy (a); newsstand	2.50
❑1/Variant, Oct 1986; JBy (w); JBy, DG (a); direct	2.50
❑1/Silver, Oct 1986; silver edition; JBy (w); JBy (a)	2.50
❑2, Oct 1986; JBy (c); JBy (w); JBy (a); Introducing Lois lane	2.50
❑2/Silver, Nov 1986; silver edition; JBy (c); JBy (w); JBy (a)	2.50
❑3, Nov 1986; JBy (c); JBy (w); JBy (a); A: Batman. Face to Face with the Dark Knight	2.50
❑3/Silver, Nov 1986; silver edition; JBy (c); JBy (w); JBy (a); A: Batman	2.50
❑4, Nov 1986; JBy (c); JBy (w); JBy (a); Lex Luthor Strikes	2.50
❑4/Silver, Nov 1986; silver edition; JBy (c); JBy (w); JBy (a)	2.50
❑5, Dec 1986; JBy (c); JBy (w); JBy (a); The Beast Within	2.50
❑5/Silver, Dec 1986; silver edition; JBy (c); JBy (w); JBy (a)	2.50
❑6, Dec 1986; JBy (c); JBy (w); JBy (a); Return to Smallville—The Epic Conclusion	2.50
❑6/Silver, Jan 1986; silver edition; JBy (c); JBy (w); JBy (a)	2.50

Man of the Atom
Acclaim / Valiant

	N-MINT
❑1, Jan 1997; No cover price; preview of upcoming one-shot	3.95

Man of War
Eclipse

	N-MINT
❑1, Aug 1987, O: Man of War	1.75
❑2, Dec 1987	1.75
❑3, Feb 1988	1.75
❑4	1.75
❑5	1.75

Man of War
Malibu

	N-MINT
❑1/Direct ed., Apr 1993; Direct Market edition with different cover, no UPC code	2.50
❑1, ca. 1993; Includes poster	1.95
❑2, ca. 1993; Includes poster	2.50
❑3, ca. 1993; Includes poster	2.50
❑4, ca. 1993; Includes poster	2.50
❑5, ca. 1993; Includes poster of The Ferret	2.50
❑6, ca. 1993; Kevin Maguire cover; O: Man of War	2.25
❑7, ca. 1994	2.25
❑8, ca. 1994	2.25

Manosaurs
Express / Entity

	N-MINT
❑1	2.95
❑2	2.95

Mantech Robot Warriors
Archie

	N-MINT
❑1, Sep 1984, O: The Mantechs. 1: The Mantechs	1.00
❑2, Dec 1984	1.00
❑3, Feb 1985	1.00
❑4, May 1985, Final Issue	1.00

Man-Thing
Marvel

	N-MINT
❑1, Jan 1974, FB, VM, JM (a); 2: Howard the Duck	30.00
❑2, Feb 1974, VM (a)	14.00
❑3, Mar 1974, VM, JAb (a); 1: FoolKiller I (Greg Everbest). Marvel Value Stamp #60: Ka-Zar	10.00
❑4, Apr 1974, VM, JAb (a); O: FoolKiller I (Greg Everbest). D: FoolKiller I (Greg Everbest). Marvel Value Stamp #17: Black Bolt	8.00
❑5, May 1974; MP (a); Marvel Value Stamp #83: Dragon Man	10.00
❑6, Jun 1974; MP (a); Marvel Value Stamp #55: Medusa	5.00
❑7, Jul 1974; MP (a); Marvel Value Stamp #19: Balder, Hogun, Fandral	5.00
❑8, Aug 1974; MP (a); Marvel Value Stamp #37: Watcher	5.00
❑9, Sep 1974; MP (a); Marvel Value Stamp #53: Grim Reaper	5.00
❑10, Oct 1974 MP (w); MP (a)	5.00
❑11, Nov 1974; MP (a); Marvel Value Stamp #28: Hawkeye	2.50
❑12, Dec 1974 JB, KJ (a)	2.50
❑13, Jan 1975; TS, JB (a); Marvel Value Stamp #54: Shanna	2.50
❑14, Feb 1975; AA (a); Marvel Value Stamp #64: Sif	2.50
❑15, Mar 1975	2.50

Other grades: Multiply price above by 5/6 for VF/NM • 2/3 for VERY FINE • 1/3 for FINE • 1/5 for VERY GOOD • 1/8 for GOOD

N-MINT

❑16, Apr 1975 JB, TP (a) 2.50
❑17, May 1975 JM (a)........................... 2.50
❑18, Jun 1975 JM (a) 2.50
❑19, Jul 1975 JM, FS (a); 1: Scavenger . 2.50
❑20, Aug 1975 JM (a) 2.50
❑21, Sep 1975 JM (a); O: Scavenger 2.50
❑22, Oct 1975 JM (a); A: Howard the Duck 3.00

Man-Thing
Marvel

❑1, Nov 1979, JM, BWi (a).................... 2.50
❑2, Jan 1980, VM (a) 2.00
❑3, Mar 1980, JM, BWi (a)..................... 2.00
❑4, May 1980, DP, BWi (a); A: Dr. Strange 2.00
❑5, Jul 1980, DP, BWi (a)...................... 2.00
❑6, Sep 1980, DP, BWi (a)..................... 2.00
❑7, Nov 1980, DP, BWi (a) 2.00
❑8, Jan 1981 .... 2.00
❑9, Mar 1981 .... 2.00
❑10, May 1981 .... 2.00
❑11, Jul 1981 .... 2.00

Man-Thing
Marvel

❑1, Dec 1997, gatefold summary; wraparound cover 2.99
❑2, Jan 1998, gatefold summary 2.99
❑3, Feb 1998, gatefold summary 2.99
❑4, Mar 1998, gatefold summary........... 2.99
❑5, Apr 1998, gatefold summary 2.99
❑6, May 1998, gatefold summary 2.99
❑7, Jun 1998, gatefold summary........... 2.99
❑8, Jul 1998, gatefold summary 2.99

Man-Thing
Marvel

❑1, Sep 2004.. 2.99
❑2, Oct 2004 .... 2.99
❑3, Nov 2004 .... 2.99

Mantra
Malibu / Ultraverse

❑1, Jul 1993; 1&O: Mantra I (Eden Blake). 1: Boneyard. 1: Warstrike 2.50
❑1/Hologram, Jul 1993; 1&O: Mantra I (Eden Blake). 1: Boneyard. 1: Warstrike. Hologram cover................................ 6.00
❑1/Ltd., Jul 1993; Ultra Limited edition.. 3.00
❑2, Aug 1993 .... 2.25
❑3, Sep 1993; 1: Kismet Deadly 2.25
❑4, Oct 1993; ME (w); SA (a); Rune....... 2.50
❑5, Nov 1993 .... 2.00
❑6, Dec 1993; Break-Thru 2.00
❑7, Jan 1994; O: Prototype; O: Mantra... 2.00
❑8, Feb 1994; Direct Edition.................. 2.00
❑9, Mar 1994 .... 2.00
❑10, Apr 1994; Flip-book with Ultraverse Premiere #2.. 3.50
❑11, May 1994.. 1.95
❑12, Jun 1994; Wrap Around Cover....... 1.95
❑13, Aug 1994; D: Boneyard's Wives. issue has two different covers............ 1.95
❑13/A; D: Boneyard's Wives. variant cover 1.95
❑14, Sep 1994; 1: Mantra II (Lauren). D: Archimage.................................... 1.95
❑15, Oct 1994; A: Prime. D: Notch......... 1.95
❑16, Nov 1994 .... 1.95
❑17, Dec 1994; 1: NecroMantra. V: Necro Mantra 1.95
❑18, Feb 1995... 2.50
❑19, Mar 1995 .... 1.95
❑20, Apr 1995; 1: Overlord. D: Overlord 1.95
❑21, May 1995.. 2.50
❑22, Jun 1995... 2.50
❑23, Jul 1995.. 2.50
❑24, Aug 1995; Final Issue.................... 2.50
❑GS 1, ca. 1994; Giant-Size Mantra #1; GP (c); 1: Topaz. 1: Opal Queen. 1: Sapphire Queen 3.50

Mantra
Malibu / Ultraverse

❑0, Sep 1995; O: New Mantra. # Infinity 1.50
❑0/A, Sep 1995; O: New Mantra. alternate cover 1.50
❑1, Oct 1995; 1&O: Coven 2.00
❑2, Nov 1995; Flip Book w/ The Phoenix Resurrection - chapter 4.................... 1.50
❑3, Dec 1995; V: Necro Mantra............. 1.50
❑4, Jan 1996 .... 1.50
❑5, Feb 1996; V: N-ME........................... 1.50

N-MINT

❑6, Mar 1996; A: Rush. Mantra gets new costume 1.50
❑7, Apr 1996.. 1.50

Mantra: Spear of Destiny
Malibu / Ultraverse

❑1, Apr 1995; 1: The Herronvolk............ 2.50
❑2, May 1995... 2.50

Mantus Files
Eternity

❑1, b&w.. 2.50
❑2, b&w.. 2.50
❑3, b&w.. 2.50
❑4, b&w.. 2.50

Man with the Screaming Brain
Dark Horse

❑1/A cover, Jun 2005........................... 2.99
❑1/B cover, Jun 2005........................... 2.99
❑2/A cover, Jul 2005............................ 2.99
❑2/B cover, Jul 2005............................ 2.99
❑3/A cover, Aug 2005 .... 2.99
❑3/B cover, Aug 2005 .... 2.99
❑4/A cover, Sep 2005........................... 2.99
❑4/B cover, Sep 2005........................... 2.99

Many Reincarnations of Lazarus
Fisher

❑1, Dec 1998 .... 3.00
❑Ashcan 1, b&w; no cover price........... 1.00

Many Worlds of Tesla Strong
DC

❑1, May 2003.. 3.00

Mara
Aircel

❑1, May 1991; Adult 2.50
❑2; Adult.. 2.50
❑3, Oct 1991; Adult............................... 2.50
❑4, Jan 1992; Adult............................... 2.95

Mara Celtic Shamaness
Fantagraphics / Eros

❑1, Jul 1995; Adult 2.95
❑2; Adult.. 2.95
❑3; Adult.. 2.95
❑4; Adult.. 2.95
❑5, May 1997; Adult 2.95
❑6; Adult.. 2.95

Mara of the Celts Book 1
Rip Off

❑Special 1, Sep 1993, b&w; Adult 2.95

Mara of the Celts Book 2
Fantagraphics / Eros

❑1, Feb 1995; Adult............................... 2.95

Marauder
Silverline

❑1, Jan 1998.. 2.95
❑2 1998 .... 2.95
❑3 1998 .... 2.95
❑4 1998 .... 2.95

March Hare
Lodestone

❑1, b&w.. 1.50

Marc Silvestri Sketchbook
Image

❑1, Jan 2004.. 2.99

Marc Silvestri Sketchbook
Image

❑1, Dec 2006 .... 2.99

Marc Spector: Moon Knight
Marvel

❑1, Jun 1989.. 2.50
❑2, Jul 1989... 2.00
❑3, Mar 1989.. 2.00
❑4, Sep 1989.. 2.00
❑5, Oct 1989.. 2.00
❑6, Nov 1989; Brother Voodoo 2.00
❑7, Nov 1989; Brother Voodoo 2.00
❑8, Dec 1989 A: Punisher...................... 3.00
❑9, Dec 1989 A: Punisher...................... 3.00
❑10, Jan 1990; 1: Ringer II..................... 2.00
❑11, Feb 1990... 2.00
❑12, Mar 1990... 2.00
❑13, Apr 1990... 2.00
❑14, May 1990.. 2.00
❑15, Jun 1990... 2.00

N-MINT

❑16, Jul 1990.. 2.00
❑17, Aug 1990.. 2.00
❑18, Sep 1990 .... 2.00
❑19, Oct 1990 A: Punisher. A: Spider-Man 3.00
❑20, Nov 1990 A: Punisher. A: Spider-Man 3.00
❑21, Dec 1990 A: Punisher. A: Spider-Man 3.00
❑22, Jan 1991 .... 3.00
❑23, Feb 1991 .... 3.00
❑24, Mar 1991 .... 3.00
❑25, Apr 1991; Giant-size; TP (a); A: Ghost Rider 2.50
❑26, May 1991 TP (a) 2.00
❑27, Jun 1991... 2.00
❑28, Jul 1991.. 2.00
❑29, Aug 1991 .... 2.00
❑30, Sep 1991 .... 2.00
❑31, Oct 1991 .... 2.00
❑32, Nov 1991 A: Hobgoblin.................. 3.00
❑33, Dec 1991 A: Hobgoblin.................. 3.00
❑34, Jan 1992 .... 2.00
❑35, Feb 1992 A: Punisher..................... 2.00
❑36, Mar 1992 A: Punisher..................... 2.00
❑37, Apr 1992 A: Punisher..................... 2.00
❑38, May 1992 A: Punisher 2.00
❑39, Jun 1992; V: Doctor Doom 2.00
❑40, Jul 1992.. 2.00
❑41, Aug 1992; Infinity War Crossover.. 2.00
❑42, Sep 1992 .... 2.00
❑43, Oct 1992 .... 2.00
❑44, Nov 1992 .... 2.00
❑45, Dec 1992 .... 2.00
❑46, Jan 1993 .... 2.00
❑47, Feb 1993 .... 2.00
❑48, Mar 1993 .... 2.00
❑49, Apr 1993 .... 2.00
❑50, May 1993; Die-cut cover................ 2.95
❑51, Jun 1993... 1.75
❑52, Jul 1993.. 1.75
❑53, Aug 1993 .... 1.75
❑54, Sep 1993 .... 1.75
❑55, Oct 1993; 1: Sunstreak. 1st professional Stephen Platt art 2.50
❑56, Nov 1993 .... 2.50
❑57, Dec 1993 .... 2.50
❑58, Jan 1994... 2.00
❑59, Feb 1994... 2.00
❑60, Mar 1994; Final Issue 2.00
❑Special 1, ca. 1992; Team-up with Shang-Chi, Master of Kung Fu 2.50

Margie
Dell

❑2, Sep 1962, First issue published as Dell's Four Color #1307..................... 25.00

Marie-Gabrielle
NBM

❑1; Adult 15.95

Marilyn Monroe: Suicide or Murder?
Revolutionary

❑1, Sep 1993, b&w................................. 2.50

Marines Attack
Charlton

❑1, Aug 1964 .... 16.00
❑2 .... 12.00
❑3 .... 9.00
❑4 .... 9.00
❑5 .... 9.00
❑6 .... 6.00
❑7 .... 6.00
❑8 .... 6.00
❑9 .... 6.00

Marionette
Raven

❑1 1987, b&w 1.00
❑3, b&w.. 1.00

Marionette
Alpha Productions

❑1, b&w.. 2.50
❑2, b&w.. 2.50
❑3 .... 2.50

Mark
Dark Horse

❑1, Sep 1987 .... 2.00
❑2, Dec 1987 .... 2.00
❑3, Aug 1988; b&w................................ 2.00
❑4, Sep 1988; b&w................................ 2.00

MAN-THING

Other grades: Multiply price above by 5/6 for VF/NM • 2/3 for VERY FINE • 1/3 for FINE • 1/5 for VERY GOOD • 1/8 for GOOD

Marvel Knights

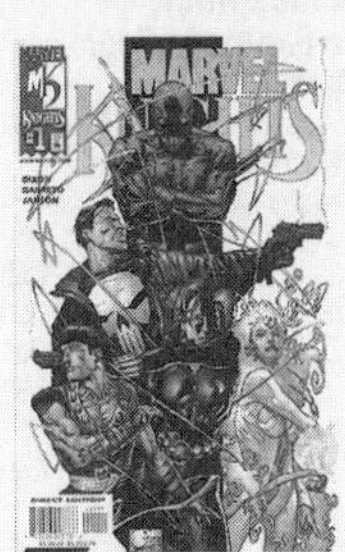

Marvel Knights characters cross over
©Marvel

Marvel Knights 4

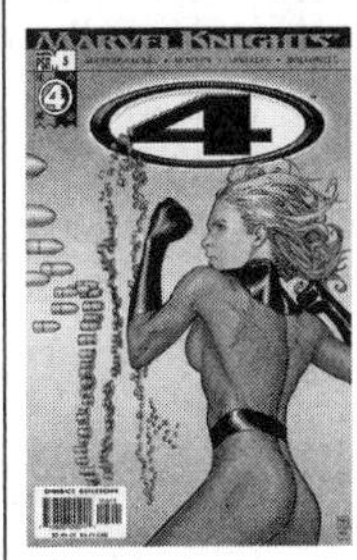

Fantastic adventures of Fantastic Four
©Marvel

Marvel Knights Spider-Man

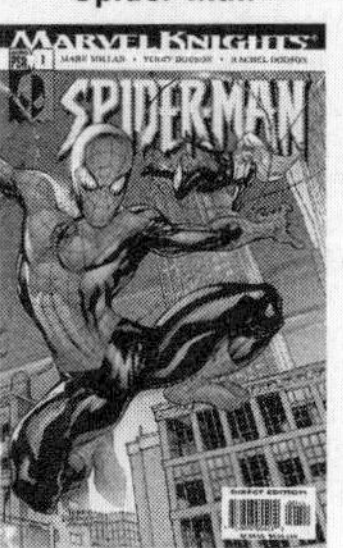

Mark Millar's take on the wallcrawler
©Marvel

Marvel Mangaverse

Manga-ized heroes failed to excite Marvelites
©Marvel

Marvel Premiere

Try-out title yielded Iron Fist, 3-D Man, others
©Marvel

N-MINT

❑5, Nov 1988 ... 2.00
❑6, Jan 1989; b&w ... 2.00

Mark
Dark Horse

❑1, Dec 1993 ... 2.50
❑2, Jan 1994 ... 2.50
❑3, Feb 1994 ... 2.50
❑4, Mar 1994 ... 2.50

Markam
Gauntlet

❑1 ... 2.50

Mark Hazzard: Merc
Marvel

❑1, Nov 1986, PD (w); GM (a); 1: Mark Hazzard ... 1.25
❑2, Dec 1986 ... 1.00
❑3, Jan 1987 ... 1.00
❑4, Feb 1987 ... 1.00
❑5, Mar 1987 ... 1.00
❑6, Apr 1987 ... 1.00
❑7, May 1987 ... 1.00
❑8, Jun 1987 ... 1.00
❑9, Jul 1987 ... 1.00
❑10, Aug 1987, GM (a) ... 1.00
❑11, Sep 1987 ... 1.00
❑12, Oct 1987 ... 1.00
❑Ann 1, Nov 1987, D: Hazzard ... 1.25

Mark of Charon
CrossGen

❑1, Apr 2003 ... 2.95
❑2, May 2003 ... 2.95
❑3, Jun 2003 ... 2.95
❑4, Jul 2003 ... 2.95
❑5, Sep 2003 ... 2.95

Mark of the Succubus
Tokyopop

❑1, Nov 2005 ... 9.99

Marksman
Hero

❑1, Jan 1988; O: The Marksman ... 1.95
❑2, Feb 1988 ... 1.95
❑3, Apr 1988 ... 1.95
❑4, Jun 1988 ... 1.95
❑5, Aug 1988 ... 1.95
❑Ann 1, Dec 1988 ... 2.75

Marmalade Boy
Tokyopop

❑1, Mar 2001; printed in Japanese format 2.95
❑2, Jun 2001; printed in Japanese format 2.95
❑3, Sep 2001; printed in Japanese format 2.95

Marooned!
Fantagraphics / Eros

❑1, b&w; Adult ... 1.95

Marquis: Danse Macabre
Oni

❑1, b&w ... 2.95
❑2, Jul 2000, b&w ... 2.95
❑3, Oct 2000, b&w ... 2.95

Marriage of Hercules and Xena
Topps

❑1, Jul 1998 ... 2.95

N-MINT

Married...With Children
Now

❑1, Jun 1990 ... 2.50
❑1/2nd; 2nd printing ... 2.00
❑2, Jul 1990; Photo cover ... 2.00
❑3, Aug 1990; Photo cover ... 2.00
❑4, Sep 1990 ... 2.00
❑5, Oct 1990; Photo cover ... 2.00
❑6, Nov 1990; Photo cover ... 2.00
❑7, Feb 1991; Photo cover; Final Issue .. 2.00

Married...With Children
Now

❑1, Sep 1991; Photo cover ... 2.50
❑2, Oct 1991; Peggy invents bon-bon filling detector ... 2.25
❑3, Nov 1991; Al turns into Psychodad . 2.25
❑4, Dec 1991; Photo cover ... 2.00
❑5, Jan 1992 ... 2.00
❑6, Mar 1992; Photo cover ... 2.00
❑7, Apr 1992; Final Issue ... 2.00
❑Ann 1994, ca. 1994; Ann ... 2.50
❑Special 1, Jul 1992; Special; with poster 2.00

Married...With Children: Buck's Tale
Now

❑1, ca. 1994; O: Buck (the Bundy Family dog) ... 2.00

Married...With Children: Bud Bundy, Fanboy in Paradise
Now

❑1; Includes poster ... 2.95

Married...With Children: Flashback Special
Now

❑1, Jan 1993; Al & Peg's First Date ... 2.00
❑2, Feb 1993; Al & Peg's Wedding ... 2.00
❑3, Mar 1993 ... 2.00

Married...With Children: Kelly Bundy
Now

❑1, Aug 1992; Photo cover ... 2.25
❑2, Sep 1992; Photo cover; Includes centerfold poster ... 2.25
❑3, Oct 1992; Photo cover ... 2.25

Married...With Children: Kelly Goes to Kollege
Now

❑1; Includes poster ... 2.95
❑2 ... 2.95
❑3 ... 2.95

Married...With Children: Off Broadway
Now

❑1, Sep 1993 ... 2.00

Married...With Children: Quantum Quartet
Now

❑1, Oct 1993; parody ... 2.00
❑2, Nov 1993; parody ... 2.00
❑3, Fal 1994; The Big Wrap-Up; combines issues #3 and 4 into flipbook; no indicia; parody ... 2.95

Married...With Children 3-D Special
Now

❑1, Jun 1993 ... 2.95

N-MINT

Married...With Children: 2099
Now

❑1, Jun 1993; Terminator spoof ... 2.00
❑2, Jul 1993 ... 2.00
❑3, Aug 1993 ... 2.00

Mars
First

❑1, Jan 1984 ... 1.50
❑2, Feb 1984 ... 1.25
❑3, Mar 1984 ... 1.25
❑4, Apr 1984 ... 1.25
❑5, May 1984 ... 1.25
❑6, Jun 1984 ... 1.25
❑7, Jul 1984 ... 1.25
❑8, Aug 1984 ... 1.25
❑9, Sep 1984 ... 1.25
❑10, Oct 1984 ... 1.25
❑11, Nov 1984 ... 1.25
❑12, Dec 1984 ... 1.25

Mars
Tokyopop

❑1, Mar 2002, b&w; printed in Japanese format ... 9.99
❑2, Jun 2002, b&w; printed in Japanese format ... 9.99
❑3, Aug 2002, b&w; printed in Japanese format ... 9.99

Mars Attacks
Topps

❑1, May 1994; KG (w); KG (a); Flip-book format ... 4.00
❑1/Ace, May 1994; Wizard Ace Edition #11; acetate overlay cover; sendaway from Wizard #65 ... 4.00
❑1/Ltd., May 1994; Limited edition promotional edition (5,000 printed); Flip-book format ... 4.00
❑2, Jun 1994; Flip cover ... 3.00
❑3, Aug 1994; Flip cover ... 3.00
❑4, Sep 1994; Flip cover ... 3.00
❑5, Oct 1994; Flip cover; Includes free Temporary Tattoo ... 3.00

Mars Attacks
Topps

❑1, Aug 1995 KG (w) ... 3.50
❑2, Sep 1995 ... 3.00
❑3, Oct 1995 ... 3.00
❑4, Jan 1996 ... 3.00
❑5, Jan 1996 ... 3.00
❑6, Mar 1996 ... 3.00
❑7, May 1996 ... 3.00
❑8, Jul 1996 ... 3.00

Mars Attacks Baseball Special
Topps

❑1, Jun 1996; Simon Bisley cover; One-shot ... 2.95

Mars Attacks High School
Topps

❑1, May 1997 ... 2.95
❑2, Sep 1997 ... 2.95

Mars Attacks Image
Image

❑1, Dec 1996; crossover with Topps ... 2.50
❑2, Jan 1997 ... 2.50

Other grades: Multiply price above by 5/6 for VF/NM • 2/3 for VERY FINE • 1/3 for FINE • 1/5 for VERY GOOD • 1/8 for GOOD

N-MINT

❑3, Mar 1997 ... 2.50
❑4, Apr 1997; D: U.S. Male ... 2.50

Mars Attacks the Savage Dragon
Topps

❑1, Dec 1996; crossover with Image; trading cards ... 2.95
❑2, Jan 1997; crossover with Image ... 2.95
❑3, Feb 1997; crossover with Image ... 2.95
❑4, Mar 1997; crossover with Image ... 2.95

Marshal Law
Marvel / Epic

❑1, Oct 1987 ... 3.50
❑2, Feb 1988 ... 2.50
❑3, Apr 1988 ... 2.50
❑4, Aug 1988 ... 2.50
❑5, Dec 1988 ... 2.50
❑6, Apr 1989 ... 2.50

Marshal Law: Kingdom of the Blind
Apocalypse

❑1; newsstand ... 3.95
❑1/Direct ed.; squarebound ... 5.95

Marshal Law: Secret Tribunal
Dark Horse

❑1, Sep 1993; cardstock cover ... 2.95
❑2, Apr 1994; cardstock cover ... 2.95

Marshal Law: Super Babylon
Dark Horse

❑1, May 1992; prestige format; NN ... 4.95

Marshal Law: The Hateful Dead
Apocalypse

❑1; prestige format; NN ... 5.95

M.A.R.S. Patrol Total War
Gold Key

❑3, Sep 1966, WW (a); Series continued from Total War #2 ... 50.00
❑4, Oct 1967, back cover pin-up ... 35.00
❑5, May 1968 ... 35.00
❑6, Aug 1968 ... 25.00
❑7, Nov 1968 ... 25.00
❑8, Feb 1969 ... 25.00
❑9, May 1969 ... 25.00
❑10, Aug 1969 ... 25.00

Martha Splatterhead's Weirdest Stories Ever Told
Monster

❑1, b&w; Adult, includes The Accused record ... 3.50

Martha Washington Goes to War
Dark Horse / Legend

❑1, May 1994; DaG (c); FM (w); DaG (a); cardstock cover ... 3.00
❑2, Jun 1994; DaG (c); FM (w); DaG (a); cardstock cover ... 3.00
❑3, Jul 1994; DaG (c); FM (w); DaG (a); cardstock cover ... 3.00
❑4, Aug 1994; DaG (c); FM (w); DaG (a); cardstock cover ... 3.00
❑5, Nov 1994; FM (w); DaG (a); cardstock cover ... 3.00

Martha Washington Saves the World
Dark Horse

❑1, Dec 1997; DaG (c); FM (w); DaG (a); cardstock cover ... 4.00
❑2, Jan 1998; DaG (c); FM (w); DaG (a); cardstock cover ... 4.00
❑3, Feb 1998; DaG (c); FM (w); DaG (a); cardstock cover ... 4.00

Martha Washington: Stranded in Space
Dark Horse / Legend

❑1, Nov 1995; DaG (c); FM (w); DaG (a); A: The Big Guy. reprints story from Dark Horse Presents; cardstock cover ... 3.00

Martian Manhunter
DC

❑1, May 1988; O: Martian Manhunter ... 1.50
❑2, Jun 1988 ... 1.50
❑3, Jul 1988 ... 1.50
❑4, Aug 1988 ... 1.50

Martian Manhunter
DC

❑0, Oct 1998 ... 3.00
❑1, Dec 1998 ... 2.50
❑2, Jan 1999 ... 2.00
❑3, Feb 1999 A: Bette Noir ... 2.00
❑4, Mar 1999; D: Karen Smith ... 2.00
❑5, Apr 1999 JDu (a) ... 2.00
❑6, May 1999; V: JLA ... 2.00
❑7, Jun 1999 ... 2.00
❑8, Jul 1999 ... 2.00
❑9, Aug 1999 A: JLA ... 2.00
❑10, Sep 1999 A: Fire ... 2.00
❑11, Oct 1999 ... 2.00
❑12, Nov 1999; A: Steel. A: Crimson Fox. A: Ice. A: Vibe. Day of Judgment ... 2.00
❑13, Dec 1999 ... 2.00
❑14, Jan 2000 ... 1.99
❑15, Feb 2000 ... 1.99
❑16, Mar 2000 ... 1.99
❑17, Apr 2000 ... 1.99
❑18, May 2000 A: JSA ... 1.99
❑19, Jun 2000 ... 1.99
❑20, Jul 2000; Superman Appearance (As Baby Kal-El, Young Clark Kent, and as a new Superman) ... 1.99
❑21, Aug 2000 ... 1.99
❑22, Sep 2000 ... 2.50
❑23, Oct 2000; Spectre (Jim Corrigan) Appearance, Phantom Stranger Apperance ... 2.50
❑24, Nov 2000 ... 2.50
❑25, Dec 2000 ... 2.50
❑26, Jan 2001 ... 2.50
❑27, Feb 2001 ... 2.50
❑28, Mar 2001 ... 2.50
❑29, Apr 2001 ... 2.50
❑30, May 2001 ... 2.50
❑31, Jun 2001 ... 2.50
❑32, Jul 2001 ... 2.50
❑33, Aug 2001 ... 2.50
❑34, Sep 2001; Metron; Lightray ... 2.50
❑35, Oct 2001 ... 2.50
❑36, Nov 2001; Final Issue ... 2.50
❑1000000, Nov 1998, b&w ... 4.00
❑Ann 1, ca. 1998; Ghosts ... 2.95
❑Ann 2, Oct 1999; JLApe ... 2.95

Martian Manhunter: American Secrets
DC

❑1, ca. 1992; prestige format ... 4.95
❑2, ca. 1992; prestige format ... 4.95
❑3, ca. 1992; prestige format ... 4.95

Martian Manhunter
DC

❑1, Oct 2006 ... 2.99
❑2, Nov 2006 ... 2.99
❑3, Dec 2006 ... 2.99
❑4, Jan 2007 ... 2.99
❑5, Feb 2007 ... 2.99

Martian Manhunter Special
DC

❑1, ca. 1996 ... 3.50

Martin Mystery
Dark Horse

❑1, Mar 1999 ... 4.95
❑2, Apr 1999 ... 4.95
❑3, May 1999 ... 4.95
❑4, Jun 1999 ... 4.95
❑5, Jul 1999 ... 4.95
❑6, Aug 1999 ... 4.95

Martin the Satanic Racoon
Gabe Martinez

❑1 ... 1.00
❑2 ... 2.00

Marvel Westerns: Western Legends
Marvel

❑1, Sep 2006 ... 3.99

Marvel Action Hour, Featuring Iron Man
Marvel

❑1, Nov 1994 ... 1.50
❑1/CS, Nov 1994; Collector's set: includes animation cel ... 2.95
❑2, Dec 1994 ... 1.50
❑3, Jan 1995 ... 1.50
❑4, Feb 1995 ... 1.50
❑5, Mar 1995; O: Iron Man ... 1.50
❑6, Apr 1995; O: The Mandarin ... 1.50
❑7, May 1995 ... 1.50
❑8, Jun 1995 ... 1.50

Marvel Action Hour, Featuring the Fantastic Four
Marvel

❑1, Nov 1994 ... 1.50
❑1/CS, Nov 1994; Collector's set: includes animation cel ... 2.95
❑2, Dec 1994 ... 1.50
❑3, Jan 1995 ... 1.50
❑4, Feb 1995 ... 1.50
❑5, Mar 1995 ... 1.50
❑6, Apr 1995 ... 1.50
❑7, May 1995 ... 1.50
❑8, Jun 1995 ... 1.50

Marvel Action Universe
Marvel

❑1, Jan 1989; Reprints Spider-Man and His Amazing Friends #1 ... 1.00

Marvel Adventure
Marvel

❑1, Dec 1975, GC (c); SL (w); GC (a); Reprints Daredevil #22 ... 8.00
❑2, Feb 1976, Reprints Daredevil #23 ... 5.00
❑3, Apr 1976, Reprints Daredevil #24 ... 5.00
❑3/30¢, Apr 1976, 30¢ regional price variant; reprints Daredevil #24 ... 20.00
❑4, Jun 1976, Reprints Daredevil #25 ... 5.00
❑4/30¢, Jun 1976, 30¢ regional price variant; reprints Daredevil #25 ... 20.00
❑5, Aug 1976, Reprints Daredevil #26 ... 4.00
❑5/30¢, Aug 1976, 30¢ regional price variant; reprints Daredevil #26 ... 20.00
❑6, Oct 1976, Reprints Daredevil #27 ... 4.00

Marvel Adventures
Marvel

❑1, Apr 1997, A: Hulk. V: Leader ... 2.00
❑2, May 1997, A: Spider-Man. V: Scorpion ... 1.50
❑3, Jun 1997, A: X-Men. V: Magneto ... 1.50
❑4, Jul 1997, A: Hulk. V: Brotherhood of Evil Mutants ... 1.50
❑5, Aug 1997, A: X-Men. A: Spider-Man. V: Abomination. V: Magneto ... 1.50
❑6, Sep 1997, A: Torch. A: Spider-Man. V: Lava Men ... 1.50
❑7, Oct 1997, A: Hulk. V: Tyrannus ... 1.50
❑8, Nov 1997, A: X-Men ... 1.50
❑9, Dec 1997, A: Fantastic Four ... 1.50
❑10, Jan 1998, A: Silver Surfer. V: Gladiator ... 1.50
❑11, Feb 1998, A: Spider-Man. V: Sandman ... 1.50
❑12, Mar 1998 ... 1.50
❑13, Apr 1998 ... 1.50
❑14, May 1998, A: Hulk. A: Doctor Strange. A: Juggernaut ... 1.50
❑15, Jun 1998, A: Wolverine ... 1.50
❑16, Jul 1998, A: Silver Surfer. V: Skrulls ... 1.50
❑17, Aug 1998, A: Iron Man. A: Spider-Man. V: Grey Gargoyle ... 1.50
❑18, Sep 1998, Final Issue ... 1.50

Marvel Adventures: Avengers
Marvel

❑1, Aug 2006 ... 2.99
❑2, Sep 2006 ... 2.99
❑3, Sep 2006 ... 2.99
❑4, Oct 2006 ... 2.99
❑5, Nov 2006 ... 2.99
❑6, Dec 2006 ... 2.99
❑7, Jan 2007 ... 2.99
❑8, Mar 2007 ... 2.99
❑9 ... 2.99
❑10 ... 2.99
❑11 ... 2.99
❑12 ... 2.99
❑13 ... 2.99
❑14 ... 2.99
❑15 ... 2.99
❑16 ... 2.99
❑17 ... 2.99
❑18 ... 2.99
❑19 ... 2.99
❑20 ... 2.99
❑21 ... 2.99
❑22 ... 2.99
❑23 ... 2.99
❑24 ... 2.99
❑25 ... 2.99
❑26 ... 2.99

Other grades: Multiply price above by 5/6 for VF/NM • 2/3 for VERY FINE • 1/3 for FINE • 1/5 for VERY GOOD • 1/8 for GOOD

Marvel Presents

Guardians of the Galaxy returned, expanded
©Marvel

Marvel Preview

Magazine-sized catch-all title
©Marvel

Marvel Riot

Aped Age of Apocalypse
©Marvel

Marvel Saga

Cohesive timeline applied to Marvel universe
©Marvel

Marvels Comics: Spider-Man

Comics as seen in the Marvel universe
©Marvel

N-MINT

- ❑27 2.99
- ❑28 2.99
- ❑29 2.99
- ❑30 2.99
- ❑31 2.99
- ❑32 2.99
- ❑33 2.99
- ❑34 2.99
- ❑35 2.99
- ❑36 2.99
- ❑37 2.99
- ❑38 2.99
- ❑39 2.99

Marvel Adventures: Fantastic Four
Marvel

- ❑0, Jun 2005 2.50
- ❑1, Jul 2005 2.50
- ❑2, Aug 2005 2.50
- ❑3, Sep 2005 2.50
- ❑4, Oct 2005 2.50
- ❑5, Nov 2005 2.50
- ❑6, Jan 2006 2.50
- ❑7, Feb 2006 2.50
- ❑8, Mar 2006 2.99
- ❑9, Apr 2006 2.50
- ❑10, May 2006 2.50
- ❑11, Jun 2006 2.99
- ❑12, Jul 2006 2.99
- ❑13, Aug 2006 2.99
- ❑14, Sep 2006 2.99
- ❑15, Oct 2006 2.99
- ❑16, Nov 2006 2.99
- ❑17, Dec 2006 2.99
- ❑18, Jan 2007 2.99
- ❑19, Feb 2007 2.99
- ❑20 2.99
- ❑21 2.99
- ❑22 2.99
- ❑23 2.99
- ❑24 2.99
- ❑25 2.99
- ❑26 2.99
- ❑27 2.99
- ❑28 2.99
- ❑29 2.99
- ❑30 2.99
- ❑31 2.99
- ❑32 2.99
- ❑33 2.99
- ❑34 2.99
- ❑35 2.99
- ❑36 2.99
- ❑37 2.99
- ❑38 2.99
- ❑39 2.99
- ❑40 2.99
- ❑41 2.99
- ❑42 2.99
- ❑43 2.99
- ❑44 2.99
- ❑45 2.99
- ❑46 2.99
- ❑47 2.99
- ❑48 2.99

N-MINT

Marvel Adventures Flip Magazine
Marvel

- ❑1, Jul 2005 3.99
- ❑2, Aug 2005 3.99
- ❑3, Sep 2005 3.99
- ❑4, Nov 2005; Collects Marvel Adventures Spider-Man #4 and Marvel Adventures Fantastic Four #4; Flipbook 3.99
- ❑5, Dec 2005; Collects Marvel Adventures Spider-Man #5 and Marvel Adventures Fantastic Four #5; Flipbook; Includes poster 3.99
- ❑6, Jan 2006; Collects Marvel Adventures Spider-Man #6 and Marvel Adventures Fantastic Four #6; Includes poster 3.99
- ❑7, Feb 2006, Includes poster; Collects Marvel Adventures: Fantastic Four #7 and Marvel Adventures: Spider-Man #7 3.99
- ❑8, Mar 2006, Includes poster; Collects Marvel Adventures: Fantastic Four #8 and Marvel Adventures: Spider-Man #8 3.99
- ❑9, Apr 2006, Includes poster; Collects Marvel Adventures: Fantastic Four #9 and Marvel Adventures: Spider-Man #9 3.99
- ❑10, May 2006; Includes poster; Collects Marvel Adventures: Fantastic Four #10 and Marvel Adventures: Spider-Man #10 3.99
- ❑11, Jul 2006, Includes poster; Collects Marvel Adventures: Fantastic Four #10 and Marvel Adventures: Spider-Man #10 3.99
- ❑13, Aug 2006, Includes poster; Collects from Marvel Adventures Spider-Man # 13, X-Men and Power Pack # 3 and Franklin Richards: Son of a Genius 4.99
- ❑15, Oct 2006, Includes poster; Collects Marvel Adventures: Fantastic Four #11 and Marvel Adventures: Spider-Man #15 4.99
- ❑16, Nov 2006, Includes Poster; Collects Marvel Adventures Spider-Man #16, Marvel Adventures Fantastic Four #12, and Franklin Richards: Son of a Genius 4.99
- ❑17, Dec 2006, Collects Marvel Adventures Spider-Man #17, Marvel Adventures Fantastic Four #13, and Franklin Richards: Son of a Genius; Poster Included 4.99
- ❑18, Jan 2007; Collects Marvel Adventures Spider-Man #18 and Marvel Adventures Fantastic Four #14; Includes Guiding Light Back up story and Poster 4.99
- ❑19, Feb 2007; Collects Marvel Adventures Spider-Man #19 and Marvel Adventures Fantastic Four #15; Spider-Man Poster included 4.99
- ❑20, Mar 2007 4.99
- ❑21 4.99
- ❑22 4.99
- ❑23 4.99
- ❑24 4.99
- ❑25 4.99
- ❑26 4.99

Marvel Adventures: Spider-Man
Marvel

- ❑1, Apr 2005 2.50
- ❑2, May 2005 2.50
- ❑3, Jun 2005 2.50
- ❑4, Jul 2005 2.50
- ❑5, Aug 2005 2.50

N-MINT

- ❑6, Sep 2005 2.50
- ❑7, Oct 2005 2.50
- ❑8 2005 2.50
- ❑9, Jan 2006 2.50
- ❑10, Feb 2006 2.50
- ❑11, Mar 2006 2.99
- ❑12, Mar 2006 2.50
- ❑13, May 2006 2.50
- ❑14, Jun 2006 2.99
- ❑15, Jul 2006 2.99
- ❑16, Aug 2006 2.99
- ❑17, Sep 2006 2.99
- ❑18, Oct 2006 2.99
- ❑19, Nov 2006 2.99
- ❑20, Dec 2006 2.99
- ❑21, Jan 2007 2.99
- ❑22, Feb 2007 2.99
- ❑23, Mar 2007 2.99
- ❑24 2.99
- ❑25 2.99
- ❑26 2.99
- ❑27 2.99
- ❑28 2.99
- ❑29 2.99
- ❑30 2.99
- ❑31 2.99
- ❑32 2.99
- ❑33 2.99
- ❑34 2.99
- ❑35 2.99
- ❑36 2.99
- ❑37 2.99
- ❑38 2.99
- ❑39 2.99
- ❑40 2.99
- ❑41 2.99
- ❑42 2.99
- ❑43 2.99
- ❑44 2.99
- ❑45 2.99
- ❑46 2.99
- ❑47 2.99
- ❑48 2.99
- ❑49 2.99
- ❑50 2.99
- ❑51 2.99
- ❑52 2.99
- ❑53 2.99

Marvel Adventures: The Thing
Marvel

- ❑1, Apr 2005 2.25
- ❑2, May 2005 2.50
- ❑3, Jun 2005 2.50

Marvel Age
Marvel

- ❑1, Apr 1983 2.00
- ❑2, May 1983 1.00
- ❑3, Jun 1983; Micronauts 1.00
- ❑4, Jul 1983; Return of the Jedi; Rock & Rule graphic novel 1.00
- ❑5, Aug 1983; Daredevil; The Hobgoblin 1.00
- ❑6, Sep 1983; Cloak & Dagger 1.00
- ❑7, Oct 1983; X-Men and Micronauts Ltd. Series 1.00

Other grades: Multiply price above by 5/6 for VF/NM • 2/3 for VERY FINE • 1/3 for FINE • 1/5 for VERY GOOD • 1/8 for GOOD

❑8, Nov 1983; Stan Lee, Jim Shooter interviews 1.00
❑9, Dec 1983; Super Boxers 1.00
❑10, Jan 1984; Star Wars cover 1.00
❑11, Feb 1984; Kitty Pryde & Wolverine 1.00
❑12, Mar 1984; Secret Wars 1.00
❑13, Apr 1984; Dreadstar; Feature on coloring comics 1.00
❑14, May 1984; FH (w); FH (a); John Byrne; Power Pack; Six From Sirius; Fred Hembeck strips begin 1.00
❑15, Jun 1984, FH (w); FH (a); Archie Goodwin on Epic Comics 1.00
❑16, Jul 1984, BSz (c); FH (w); FH (a) ... 1.00
❑17, Aug 1984, FH (w); FH (a); Muppets 1.00
❑18, Sep 1984, FH (w); FH (a); Questprobe 1.00
❑19, Oct 1984, FH (w); FH (a); Star Comics 1.00
❑20, Nov 1984, FH (w); FH (a); Letters to Marvel Super-Hero Secret Wars 1.00
❑21, Dec 1984, VM (c); FH (w); FH (a); Void Indigo 1.00
❑22, Jan 1985, JR (c); FH (w); FH (a); Sol Brodsky Remembered 1.00
❑23, Feb 1985, FH (w); FH (a); ROM 1.00
❑24, Mar 1985, FH (w); FH (a) 1.00
❑25, Apr 1985, FH (w); FH (a); Rocket Raccoon; Cloak & Dagger; Gargoyle... 1.00
❑26, May 1985, FH (w); FH (a); Starstruck 1.00
❑27, Jun 1985, FH (w); AM, FH (a); Secret Wars II 1.00
❑28, Jul 1985, FH (w); FH (a) 1.00
❑29, Aug 1985, FH, KB (w); FH (a); Vision & Scarlet Witch; West Coast Avengers (Ltd. Series) 1.00
❑30, Sep 1985, FH (w); FH (a) 1.00
❑31, Oct 1985, FH (w); FH (a) 1.00
❑32, Nov 1985, FH (w); FH (a) 1.00
❑33, Dec 1985, FH (w); FH (a); X-Factor 1.00
❑34, Jan 1986, FH (w); FH (a); G.I. Joes 1.00
❑35, Feb 1986, FH (w); FH (a); A Day in the Life of Marvel Comics 1.00
❑36, Mar 1986, FH (w); FH (a) 1.00
❑37, Apr 1986, FH (w); FH (a) 1.00
❑38, May 1986, FH (w); FH (a); He-Man 1.00
❑39, Jun 1986, FH (w); FH (a) 1.00
❑40, Jul 1986, FH (w); FH (a) 1.00
❑41, Aug 1986, FH (w); FH (a) 1.00
❑42, Sep 1986, FH (w); FH (a) 1.00
❑43, Oct 1986, FH (w); FH (a) 1.00
❑44, Nov 1986, FH (w); FH (a) 1.00
❑45, Dec 1986, FH (w); FH (a) 1.00
❑46, Jan 1987, FH (w); FH (a) 1.00
❑47, Feb 1987, FH (w); FH (a) 1.00
❑48, Mar 1987, FH (w); FH (a) 1.00
❑49, Apr 1987, FH (w); FH (a) 1.00
❑50, May 1987, FH (w); FH (a); Marvel Try-Out Book contest winners 1.00
❑51, Jun 1987, FH (w); FH (a) 1.00
❑52, Jul 1987, FH (w); FH (a) 1.00
❑53, Aug 1987, FH (w); FH (a) 1.00
❑54, Sep 1987, FH (w); FH (a); Spider-Man wedding 1.00
❑55, Oct 1987, FH (w); FH (a) 1.00
❑56, Nov 1987, FH (w); FH (a) 1.00
❑57, Dec 1987, FH (w); FH (a) 1.00
❑58, Jan 1988, FH (w); FH (a) 1.00
❑59, Feb 1988, FH (w); FH (a); New Universe 1.00
❑60, Mar 1988, FH (w); FH (a) 1.00
❑61, Apr 1988, FH (w); FH (a) 1.00
❑62, May 1988, FH (w); FH (a); The Shadow Line Saga 1.00
❑63, Jun 1988, FH (w); FH (a) 1.00
❑64, Jul 1988, FH (w); FH (a) 1.00
❑65, Aug 1988, FH (w); FH (a) 1.00
❑66, Sep 1988, FH (w); FH (a) 1.00
❑67, Oct 1988, FH (w); FH (a) 1.00
❑68, Nov 1988, FH (w); FH (a) 1.00
❑69, Dec 1988, FH (w); FH (a) 1.00
❑70, Jan 1989, FH, SL (w); FH (a) 1.00
❑71, Feb 1989, FH (w); FH (a) 1.00
❑72, Mar 1989, FH (w); FH (a) 1.00
❑73, Apr 1989, FH, JBy (w); FH, JBy (a) 1.00
❑74, May 1989, FH (w); FH (a) 1.00
❑75, Jun 1989, FH (w); FH (a) 1.00
❑76, Jul 1989, FH (w); FH (a); Atlantis Attacks 1.00
❑77, Aug 1989, FH (w); FH (a) 1.00
❑78, Sep 1989, FH (w); FH (a) 1.00
❑79, Oct 1989 FH, HC (w); FH, HC (a) ... 1.00
❑80, Nov 1989 FH (w); FH (a) 1.00
❑81, Nov 1989 FH (w); FH (a) 1.00
❑82, Dec 1989; FH (w); FH (a); Squadron Supreme 1.00
❑83, Dec 1989 FH (w); FH (a) 1.00
❑84, Jan 1990 FH (w); FH (a) 1.00
❑85, Feb 1990 FH (w); FH (a) 1.00
❑86, Mar 1990 FH (w); FH (a) 1.00
❑87, Apr 1990 FH (w); FH (a) 1.00
❑88, May 1990; FH (w); FH (a); Guardians of the Galaxy 1.00
❑89, Jun 1990 FH (w); FH (a) 1.00
❑90, Jul 1990 FH, TMc (w); FH, TMc (a) 1.00
❑91, Aug 1990 FH (w); FH (a) 1.00
❑92, Sep 1990 FH (w); FH (a) 1.00
❑93, Oct 1990 FH (w); FH (a) 1.00
❑94, Nov 1990 FH (w); FH (a) 1.00
❑95, Dec 1990; FH (w); FH (a); Captain America issue 1.00
❑96, Jan 1991 FH (w); FH (a) 1.00
❑97, Feb 1991 FH (w); FH (a) 1.00
❑98, Mar 1991; FH (w); FH (a); Toxic Avenger 1.00
❑99, Apr 1991; JSn, FH (w); FH, GP (a); Black Panther 1.00
❑100, May 1991; 100th anniversary issue; FH (w); FH (a); Alan Davis interview... 1.00
❑101, Jun 1991; JSn, FH (w); FH, BWr (a); Punisher: P.O.V. preview 1.00
❑102, Jul 1991; FH (w); FH, RL (a); X-Force 1.00
❑103, Aug 1991; FH (w); FH (a); Wonder Man 1.00
❑104, Sep 1991; FH (w); FH (a); Jim Lee 1.00
❑105, Oct 1991; FH (w); FH, GC (a); Wolverine, Tomb of Dracula 1.00
❑106, Nov 1991; Daredevil 300th anniversary; FH (w); FH (a) 1.00
❑107, Dec 1991; FH (w); FH (a); Clive Barker 1.00
❑108, Jan 1992; FH (w); FH (a); John Romita Jr. interview 1.00
❑109, Feb 1992; FH (w); FH (a); Groo, Christmas 1.00
❑110, Mar 1992; FH (w); FH (a); Cage; WCW feature 1.00
❑111, Apr 1992; FH (w); FH (a); John Romita Sr. interview 1.00
❑112, May 1992; Captain America 400th Anniversary; FH (w); FH (a) 1.00
❑113, Jun 1992; FH (w); FH (a); Captain America, Punisher 1.00
❑114, Jul 1992; Spider-Man's 30th anniversary; FH (w); FH (a) 1.00
❑115, Aug 1992; FH (w); FH (a); Rise of the midnight Sons, Tek World 1.00
❑116, Sep 1992; FH (w); FH (a); X-Men. 1.00
❑117, Oct 1992; FH (w); FH (a); 2099.... 1.00
❑118, Nov 1992; FH (w); FH (a); with card 1.00
❑119, Dec 1992; FH (w); FH (a); Hulk: Future Imperfect 1.00
❑120, Jan 1993; Tenth anniversary special; FH (w); FH (a) 1.00
❑121, Feb 1993; FH (w); FH (a); Ren & Stimpy 1.00
❑122, Mar 1993; X-Men 30th anniversary special; FH (w); FH (a) 1.00
❑123, Apr 1993; FH (w); FH (a); Thunderstrike 1.00
❑124, May 1993; FH (w); FH (a); Infinity Crusade 1.00
❑125, Jun 1993; FH (w); FH (a); 2099, Hunt for Magneto 1.00
❑126, Jul 1993; FH (w); FH (a); Video Games 1.00
❑127, Aug 1993; FH (w); FH (a); Holograms 1.00
❑128, Sep 1993; FH (w); FH (a); Includes Hunt for Magneto trading card; Peter David Interview on Epic; Fantastic Four Movie 1.00
❑129, Oct 1993; Flip-book; GP (c); FH (w); FH, GP (a); 1/2 X-Men/Avengers crossover poster; Biker Mice from Mars preview; Hellraiser/Marshal Law preview; Heavy Hitters Preview 1.25
❑130, Nov 1993; FH (w); ARo, FH (a); Marvels; poster 1.25
❑131, Dec 1993; FH (w); FH (a); Excalibur 1.25
❑132, Jan 1994; FH (w); FH (a); Force Works, ClanDestine 1.25
❑133, Feb 1994; FH (w); FH (a); X-Wedding, War Machine 1.25
❑134, Mar 1994; FH (w); FH (a); Beavis & Butt-Head 1.50
❑135, Apr 1994; FH (w); FH (a); Ghost Rider 2099; Conan the Adventurer 1.25
❑136, May 1994; FH (w); FH (a); New Warriors 1.25
❑137, Jun 1994; FH (w); FH (a); Spider-Man animated series 1.50
❑138, Jul 1994; Giant-size; FH (w); FH (a); remembering Jack Kirby; Spider-Man Animated Series, Blaze 1.50
❑139, Aug 1994; FH (w); FH (a); Batman and the Punisher 1.25
❑140, Sep 1994; FH (w); FH (a); Marvel Action Hour 1.25
❑Ann 1, Sep 1985, KB (w) 1.00
❑Ann 2, Sep 1986, AM, SL (w); AM, FH, JB, JK, KGa (a) 1.00
❑Ann 3, Sep 1987 FH, JB, TD, MR (a) ... 1.00
❑Ann 4, Sep 1988; Wolverine 1.00

Marvel Age: Fantastic Four
Marvel

❑1, Jun 2004 .... 2.99
❑2, Jul 2004 .... 2.25
❑3, Aug 2004 .... 2.25
❑4, Sep 2004 .... 2.25
❑5, Oct 2004 .... 2.25
❑6, Nov 2004 .... 2.25
❑7, Dec 2004 .... 2.25
❑8, Jan 2005 .... 2.25
❑9, Feb 2005 .... 2.25
❑10, Mar 2005 .... 2.25
❑11, Mar 2005 .... 2.25
❑12, Apr 2005 .... 2.25

Marvel Age: Fantastic Four Tales - The Thing
Marvel

❑1, Apr 2005 .... 2.25

Marvel Age Hulk
Marvel

❑1, Nov 2004 .... 1.75
❑2, Dec 2004 .... 1.75
❑3, Jan 2005 .... 1.75
❑4, Feb 2005 .... 1.75

Marvel Age Preview
Marvel

❑1, Apr 1990 .... 1.50
❑2; 1992 Preview 2.25

Marvel Age: Runaways
Marvel

❑1, ca. 2004 .... 7.99

Marvel Age: Sentinel
Marvel

❑1, ca. 2004 .... 7.99

Marvel Age: Spider-Girl
Marvel

❑1, ca. 2004 .... 7.99

Marvel Age: Spider-Man
Marvel

❑1, May 2004, SD, SL (w) 2.99
❑1/FCBD, Aug 2004 .... 2.00
❑2, Jun 2004, SD, SL (w) 2.99
❑3, Jul 2004, SD, SL (w) 2.99
❑4, Jul 2004, SD, SL (w) 2.99
❑5, Aug 2004 .... 2.25
❑6, Aug 2004 .... 2.25
❑7, Sep 2004 .... 2.25
❑8, Sep 2004 .... 2.25
❑9, Oct 2004 .... 2.25
❑10, Oct 2004 .... 2.25
❑11, Nov 2004 .... 2.25
❑12, Nov 2004 .... 2.25
❑13, Dec 2004 .... 2.25
❑14, Dec 2004 .... 2.25
❑15, Jan 2005 .... 2.25
❑16, Jan 2005 .... 2.25
❑17, Feb 2005 .... 2.25
❑18, Feb 2005 .... 2.25
❑19, Mar 2005 .... 2.25
❑20, Apr 2005 .... 2.25

Marvel Age Spider-Man Team Up
Marvel

❑1, Nov 2004 .... 1.75
❑2, Dec 2004 .... 1.75
❑3, Jan 2005 .... 1.75

Other grades: Multiply price above by 5/6 for VF/NM • 2/3 for VERY FINE • 1/3 for FINE • 1/5 for VERY GOOD • 1/8 for GOOD

Marvel's Greatest Comics

Continues Marvel Collector's Item Classics
©Marvel

Marvel: Shadows & Light

Black-and-white one-shot anthology
©Marvel

Marvel 1602

Neil Gaiman spins 17th century tale
©Marvel

Marvel Spectacular

Short-lived Thor reprint title
©Marvel

Marvel Super Action

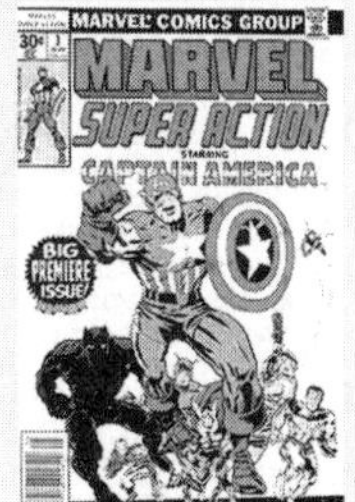

Mostly Captain America reprints
©Marvel

N-MINT

❑4, Mar 2005 ... 1.75
❑5, Apr 2005 ... 2.25

Marvel and DC Present
Marvel

❑1, Nov 1982; TD (a); X-Men & Titans; Early Marvel/DC crossover ... 12.00

Marvel Boy
Marvel

❑1/A, Aug 2000; Dynamic Forces cover ... 5.00
❑1, Aug 2000 ... 2.99
❑2, Sep 2000 ... 2.99
❑3, Oct 2000 ... 2.99
❑4, Nov 2000 ... 2.99
❑5, Dec 2000 ... 2.99
❑6, Mar 2001 ... 2.99

Marvel Chillers
Marvel

❑1, Nov 1975, GK (c); 1: The Other (Chthon). 1: Modred the Mystic; Reprint from Mystical Tales #7 ... 12.00
❑2, Jan 1976, A: Tigra. Modred ... 7.00
❑3, Mar 1976, O: Tigra. 1: The Darkhold. Tigra ... 10.00
❑4, May 1976, A: Tigra. A: Kraven ... 7.00
❑4/30¢, May 1976, 30¢ regional price variant ... 20.00
❑5, Jun 1976, A: Tigra ... 7.00
❑5/30¢, Jun 1976, 30¢ regional price variant ... 20.00
❑6, Aug 1976, RB (c); JBy (a); A: Tigra. Ralph Macchio L.O.C ... 5.00
❑6/30¢, Aug 1976, 30¢ regional price variant ... 20.00
❑7, Oct 1976, A: Tigra. Ralph Macchio L.O.C ... 5.00

Marvel Chillers: Shades of Green Monsters
Marvel

❑1, Mar 1997; mostly text story ... 2.99

Marvel Chillers: The Thing in the Glass Case
Marvel

❑1, Mar 1997; mostly text story ... 2.99

Marvel Classics Comics
Marvel

❑1, Jan 1976, GK (c); NR (a); Doctor Jekyll and Mr. Hyde ... 7.00
❑2, Feb 1976 ... 5.00
❑3, Mar 1976 ... 5.00
❑4, Apr 1976 ... 5.00
❑5, May 1976, Anna Sewell portrait by Larkin ... 5.00
❑6, Jun 1976, Jonathan Swift portrait by Bob Larkin ... 4.00
❑7, Jul 1976, Samuel Clemens portrait by Bob Larkin ... 4.00
❑8, Aug 1976, Herman Melville portrait by Bob Larkin ... 4.00
❑9, Sep 1976, Bram Stoker portrait by Dan Adkins ... 4.00
❑10, Oct 1976, Stephen Craine portrait by Dan Adkins ... 4.00
❑11, Nov 1976, AM, GK (c); DA (a); Adapts Jules Verne's Mysterious Island; Jules Verne portrait by Dan Adkins ... 4.00

N-MINT

❑12, Dec 1976, Three Musketeers; Last reprint issue; Alexandre Dumas portrait by Dan Adkins ... 4.00
❑13, Jan 1977, Last of the Mohicans; Brand new adaptations begin; James Fenimore Cooper portrait by Dan Adkins ... 4.00
❑14, Feb 1977, War of the Worlds; Pin-up by Dave Cockrum ... 4.00
❑15, Mar 1977, Treasure Island; Robert Louis Stevenson portrait by Howard Chaykin ... 4.00
❑16, Apr 1977, Ivanhoe; Sir Walter Scott portrait by Marie Severin ... 4.00
❑17, May 1977, Count of Monte Cristo ... 4.00
❑18, Jun 1977, Odyssey ... 4.00
❑19, Jul 1977 ... 4.00
❑20, Aug 1977 ... 4.00
❑21, Sep 1977, Master of the World ... 4.00
❑22, Oct 1977, Food of the Gods ... 4.00
❑23, Nov 1977 ... 4.00
❑24, Dec 1977 ... 4.00
❑25, Jan 1978, Invisible Man ... 4.00
❑26, Feb 1978, PG (a); Iliad ... 4.00
❑27, Mar 1978 ... 4.00
❑28, Apr 1978, MG (a); Mike Golden's first professional art ... 8.00
❑29, May 1978, Prisoner of Zenda ... 4.00
❑30, Jun 1978 ... 4.00
❑31, Jul 1978, First Man in the Moon ... 4.00
❑32, Aug 1978, White Fang ... 4.00
❑33, Sep 1978 ... 4.00
❑34, Oct 1978, AA (a) ... 4.00
❑35, Nov 1978 ... 4.00
❑36, Dec 1978, BH (c) ... 4.00

Marvel Collectible Classics: Amazing Spider-Man
Marvel

❑300, TMc (a); 1: Venom. Chromium wraparound cover; Reprints Amazing Spider-Man #300 ... 13.50
❑300/Autographed, TMc (a); 1: Venom. Chromium wraparound cover; Reprints Amazing Spider-Man #300 ... 29.99

Marvel Collectible Classics: Avengers
Marvel

❑1, Nov 1998, Chromium wraparound cover ... 13.50

Marvel Collectible Classics: X-Men
Marvel

❑1, Aug 1998, Chromium wraparound cover; Reprints X-Men #1 ... 13.50
❑GS 1, Nov 1998, Reprints GS X-Men #1; Chromium wraparound cover ... 13.50

Marvel Collectible Classics: X-Men
Marvel

❑1, Oct 1998, JLee (a); Chromium wraparound cover ... 13.50
❑1/Autographed, Oct 1998, JLee (a); Chromium wraparound cover ... 29.99

Marvel Collector's Edition
Marvel

❑1, Jan 1992; RHo (w); Spider-Man, Wolverine, Ghost Rider; Charleston Chew promotion, $.50 and a candy bar wrapper; Flip-book format ... 2.50

N-MINT

Marvel Collectors' Item Classics
Marvel

❑1, Feb 1966; Fantastic Four #2; Ant-Man: Tales to Astonish #36; Journey into Mystery (1st Series) #97; Amazing Spider-Man #3 ... 125.00
❑2, Apr 1966; Fantastic Four #3; Ant-Man: Tales to Astonish #37; Amazing Spider-Man #4 ... 70.00
❑3, Jun 1966; reprints Fantastic Four (Vol. 1) #4, Tales of Suspense #40, Incredible Hulk #3, Tales of Suspense #49, Strange Tales #110 ... 45.00
❑4, Aug 1966; Fantastic Four #7; Iron Man: Tales of Suspense #41; Dr. Strange: Strange Tales #111; Incredible Hulk #4 ... 45.00
❑5, Oct 1966; Fantastic Four #8; Iron Man: Tales of Suspense #42; Tales of the Watcher: Tales of Suspense #50; Dr. Strange: Strange Tales #114; Incredible Hulk #4 ... 30.00
❑6, Dec 1966; Fantastic Four #9; Iron Man: Tales of Suspense #43; Dr. Strange: Strange Tales #116; Incredible Hulk #5 ... 30.00
❑7, Feb 1967; Fantastic Four #13; Iron Man: Tales of Suspense #44; Dr. Strange: Strange Tales #117; Incredible Hulk #5 ... 15.00
❑8, Apr 1967; Fantastic Four #10; Iron Man: Tales of Suspense #45; Dr. Strange: Strange Tales #118; Incredible Hulk #2 (Chapter 1) ... 15.00
❑9, Jun 1967; Fantastic Four #14; Iron Man: Tales of Suspense #46; Dr. Strange: Strange Tales #119; Tales of the Watcher: Tales of Suspense #53; Incredible Hulk #2 (Chapters 2 and 3) ... 15.00
❑10, Aug 1967; Fantastic Four #15; Iron Man: Tales of Suspense #47; Tales of the Watcher: Tales of Suspense #54; Incredible Hulk #2 ... 15.00
❑11, Oct 1967; Fantastic Four #16; Iron Man: Tales of Suspense #51; Dr. Strange: Strange Tales #120; Incredible Hulk #6 (part 1) ... 12.00
❑12, Dec 1967; Reprints from Fantastic Four #17, Tales of Suspense #52, Strange Tales #121, Hulk #6 (part 2) ... 12.00
❑13, Feb 1968; Reprints from Fantastic Four #18, Tales of Suspense #52, 53, Strange Tales #122, Incredible Hulk #6 (part 3) ... 12.00
❑14, Apr 1968; Fantastic Four #20; Iron Man: Tales of Suspense #56; Dr. Strange: Strange Tales #123; Incredible Hulk #1 (part 1) ... 12.00
❑15, Jun 1968; Fantastic Four #21; Iron Man: Tales of Suspense #55; Dr. Strange: Strange Tales #124; The Hulk #1 (part 3); The Hulk #1 (part 4) ... 12.00
❑16, Aug 1968; Fantastic Four #22; Iron Man: Tales of Suspense #59; Dr. Strange: Strange Tales #125; Incredible Hulk #1 (part 5) ... 12.00
❑17, Oct 1968; Fantastic Four #23; Dr. Strange: Strange Tales #126; Iron Man: Tales of Suspense #57 ... 12.00
❑18, Dec 1968; Fantastic Four #24; Iron Man: Tales of Suspense #58; Dr. Strange: Strange Tales #127 ... 12.00

❑19, Feb 1969; SL (w); SD, DH, JK (a); Fantastic Four #27; Iron Man: Tales of Suspense #61; Tales of the Watcher: Tales of Suspense #51; Dr. Strange: Strange Tales #128 ... 12.00
❑20, Apr 1969; Fantastic Four #28; Iron Man: Tales of Suspense #60; Tales of the Watcher: Tales of Suspense #55; Dr. Strange: Strange Tales #129 ... 12.00
❑21, Jun 1969; Fantastic Four #29; Iron Man: Tales of Suspense #62; Tales of the Watcher: Tales of Suspense #56; Dr. Strange: Strange Tales #130 ... 15.00
❑22, Aug 1969; Series continued in Marvel's Greatest Comics #23 ... 17.00
❑23, Oct 1969 ... 20.00

Marvel Comics Presents
Marvel

❑1, Sep 1988; AM (w); AM, TS, JB, DC, KJ (a); Wolverine features begin ... 4.00
❑2, Sep 1988; KJ (c); AM (w); AM, TS, JB, DC, KJ (a); Wolverine ... 2.50
❑3, Sep 1988; JR2, BWi (c); AM (w); AM, TS, JB, DC, KJ (a); Wolverine ... 2.50
❑4, Oct 1988; AM, CR (c); AM (w); AM, TS, JB, DC, KJ (a); Wolverine ... 2.50
❑5, Oct 1988; TS, JB, DC, MGu, KJ (a); Wolverine ... 2.50
❑6, Nov 1988; TS, JB, DC, KJ (a); A: Sub-Mariner. Wolverine ... 2.00
❑7, Nov 1988; BL (c); SD (w); TS, SD, JB, DC, KJ (a); Wolverine ... 2.00
❑8, Dec 1988; CV (c); TS, JB, DC, KJ (a); Wolverine ... 2.00
❑9, Dec 1988; TS, JB, KJ (a); Wolverine ... 2.00
❑10, Jan 1989; SD (w); TS, SD, JB, CR, KJ (a); Wolverine; Colossus features begin ... 2.00
❑11, Jan 1989; TS, BL, CR (a); Colossus ... 1.50
❑12, Feb 1989; TS, DH, CR, FS (a); Colossus, Man-Thing ... 1.50
❑13, Feb 1989; GC (c); GC, TP, CR (a); Colossus ... 1.50
❑14, Mar 1989; SD (w); SD, GC, TP, CR (a); Colossus ... 1.50
❑15, Mar 1989; AM, GC, MGu, TP (a); Colossus ... 1.50
❑16, Mar 1989; KN (c); AM, GC, TP, CR, JM (a); Colossus ... 1.50
❑17, Apr 1989; RB (c); TS, GC (a); Cyclops features begin ... 1.50
❑18, Apr 1989; JBy (c); JBy (w); RHo, GC, JBy (a); She-Hulk, Cyclops ... 1.50
❑19, May 1989; RL (c); GC (a); 1: Damage Control. Cyclops ... 1.50
❑20, May 1989; GC (a); Cyclops ... 1.50
❑21, Jun 1989; GC (a); Cyclops ... 1.50
❑22, Jun 1989; MR (c); GC, DC (a); Cyclops ... 1.50
❑23, Jul 1989; GC, DC (a); Cyclops ... 1.50
❑24, Jul 1989; EL (c); RB, GC (a); Cyclops, Havok ... 1.50
❑25, Aug 1989; RB, GC (a); O: Nth Man. 1: Nth Man. Havok ... 1.50
❑26, Aug 1989; PG (c); RB, GC, PG (a); 1: Coldblood. Havok ... 1.50
❑27, Sep 1989; AM (c); RB, GC, PG (a); Havok ... 1.50
❑28, Sep 1989; RB, GC, PG (a); Havok ... 1.50
❑29, Sep 1989; RB, GC, PG (a); Havok ... 1.50
❑30, Oct 1989; RB, GC, PG (a); A: Wolverine. Havok ... 1.50
❑31, Oct 1989; RB, GC, PG, EL (a); O: Coldblood. Havok, Excalibur ... 1.50
❑32, Nov 1989; TMc (c); GC, DH, PG, DC, TP, EL (a); Excalibur ... 1.50
❑33, Nov 1989; GC, PG, TP, JLee, EL (a); Excalibur ... 1.50
❑34, Dec 1989; PS (c); GC, PG, TP, EL (a); Excalibur ... 1.50
❑35, Dec 1989; GC, PG, TP, EL (a); 1: Starduster. Excalibur ... 1.50
❑36, Jan 1989; BSz (c); GC, TP, EL (a); Excalibur ... 1.50
❑37, Jan 1989; DC (c); GC, TP, EL (a); Excalibur ... 1.50
❑38, Feb 1989; JB, EL, MR, DA (a); Excalibur ... 2.00
❑39, Feb 1989; BL (w); JB, BL, EL (a); Wolverine ... 1.50
❑40, Mar 1989; MR (c); BL (w); JB, BL, DH (a); Wolverine ... 1.50
❑41, Mar 1990; BL (w); JB, BL, DC (a); Wolverine ... 1.50
❑42, Mar 1990; BL (c); JB, DA (a); Wolverine ... 1.50
❑43, Apr 1990; EL (c); JB (a); Wolverine ... 1.50
❑44, Apr 1990; JB, BWi (a); Wolverine ... 1.50
❑45, May 1990; PD (w); JB, HT (a); Wolverine ... 1.50
❑46, May 1990; RL (c); JB (a); Wolverine ... 1.50
❑47, Apr 1990; JBy (c); JB, DP (a); Wolverine; cover dates, which only appeared in the indicia or in Marvel's catalog copy, actually do go backwards for a while at this point ... 1.50
❑48, Apr 1990; EL (c); EL (w); EL, ES (a); Spider-Man, Wolverine ... 2.00
❑49, May 1990; EL (c); EL (w); DH, EL (a); 1: Whiplash II. Spider-Man, Wolverine ... 2.00
❑50, May 1990; O: Captain Ultra. Spider-Man, Wolverine ... 2.00
❑51, Jun 1990; PG (c); RL (w); DH, RL (a); Wolverine ... 2.00
❑52, Jun 1990; RHo (c); RHo, RL (w); RHo, RL (a); Wolverine ... 2.00
❑53, Jul 1990; RL (w); RL (a); Wolverine ... 2.00
❑54, Jul 1990; SD (w); SD (a); Wolverine & Hulk ... 2.50
❑55, Jul 1990; Wolverine & Hulk ... 2.50
❑56, Aug 1990; SD (w); SD (a); Wolverine & Hulk ... 2.50
❑57, Aug 1990; Wolverine & Hulk ... 2.50
❑58, Sep 1990; DC (c); SD (w); SD (a); Wolverine & Hulk ... 2.50
❑59, Sep 1990; Wolverine & Hulk ... 2.50
❑60, Oct 1990; RHo (w); RHo (a); Wolverine & Hulk ... 2.50
❑61, Oct 1990; RHo (w); RHo (a); Wolverine & Hulk ... 2.50
❑62, Nov 1990; RHo (w); RHo, BG (a); Wolverine ... 2.50
❑63, Nov 1990; RHo (w); RHo, DH (a); Wolverine ... 2.00
❑64, Dec 1990; Wolverine, Ghost Rider ... 2.00
❑65, Dec 1990; Wolverine, Ghost Rider ... 2.00
❑66, Dec 1990; Wolverine, Ghost Rider ... 2.00
❑67, Jan 1991; Wolverine, Ghost Rider ... 2.00
❑68, Jan 1991; PG (a); Wolverine, Ghost Rider ... 2.00
❑69, Feb 1991; PG (a); Wolverine, Ghost Rider ... 2.00
❑70, Feb 1991; RL (c); PG (a); Wolverine, Ghost Rider ... 2.00
❑71, Mar 1991; PG (a); Wolverine, Ghost Rider ... 2.00
❑72, Mar 1991; PG (a); Weapon X ... 4.00
❑73, Mar 1991; PG, DC, JM (a); Weapon X ... 3.00
❑74, Apr 1991; PG, JSa (a); Weapon X ... 3.00
❑75, Apr 1991; MW (c); PG, DC (a); Weapon X ... 3.00
❑76, May 1991; PG, DC (a); Weapon X ... 3.00
❑77, May 1991; PG (a); Weapon X ... 3.00
❑78, Jun 1991; AM (c); Weapon X ... 3.00
❑79, Jun 1991; JBy (a); Weapon X ... 3.00
❑80, Jul 1991; SD (w); SD (a); Weapon X ... 3.00
❑81, Jul 1991; SD (w); SD, MR (a); Weapon X; Daredevil ... 3.00
❑82, Aug 1991; EL (c);Weapon X ... 3.00
❑83, Aug 1991; SD (w); EL (a); Weapon X ... 3.00
❑84, Sep 1991; Weapon X ... 3.00
❑85, Sep 1991; PD (w); RL (a); 1: Cyber. Wolverine; 1st Kieth art on Wolverine ... 3.00
❑86, Oct 1991; PD (w); RL (a); Wolverine ... 2.50
❑87, Oct 1991; PD (w); RL (a); Wolverine ... 2.00
❑88, Nov 1991; PD (w); Wolverine ... 2.00
❑89, Nov 1991; PD (w); Wolverine ... 2.00
❑90, Dec 1991; PD (w); A: Ghost Rider. A: Cable. Flip-book covers begin; Wolverine ... 2.00
❑91, Dec 1991; PD (w); A: Ghost Rider. A: Cable. Wolverine ... 1.50
❑92, Dec 1991; PD (w); A: Ghost Rider. A: Cable. Wolverine ... 1.50
❑93, Jan 1992; A: Ghost Rider. A: Cable. Wolverine ... 1.50
❑94, Jan 1992; A: Ghost Rider. A: Cable. Wolverine ... 1.50
❑95, Feb 1992; A: Ghost Rider. A: Cable. Wolverine ... 1.50
❑96, Feb 1992; A: Ghost Rider. A: Cable. Wolverine ... 1.50
❑97, Mar 1992; A: Ghost Rider. A: Cable. Wolverine ... 1.50
❑98, Mar 1992; Wolverine ... 1.50
❑99, Apr 1992; RL (w); Wolverine ... 1.50
❑100, Apr 1992; Anniversary issue; A: Ghost Rider. V: Doctor Doom. Wolverine ... 1.50
❑101, May 1992; TS, GC (a); Wolverine, Nightcrawler ... 1.50
❑102, May 1992; TS, GC (a); Wolverine, Nightcrawler ... 1.50
❑103, May 1992; TS, GC (a); Wolverine, Nightcrawler ... 1.50
❑104, Jun 1992; TS, GC (a); Wolverine, Nightcrawler ... 1.50
❑105, Jun 1992; TS, GC (a); Wolverine, Nightcrawler ... 1.50
❑106, Jul 1992; TS, GC (a); Wolverine, Nightcrawler ... 1.50
❑107, Jul 1992; TS, GC (a); Wolverine, Nightcrawler ... 1.50
❑108, Aug 1992; JSn (w); TS, GC (a); Wolverine, Ghost Rider ... 1.50
❑109, Aug 1992; JSn (w); A: Typhoid Mary. Wolverine, Ghost Rider ... 1.50
❑110, Sep 1992; JSn (w); A: Typhoid Mary. Wolverine, Ghost Rider ... 1.50
❑111, Sep 1992; JSn (w); A: Typhoid Mary. Infinity War; Wolverine, Ghost Rider ... 1.50
❑112, Oct 1992; JSn (w); GC (a); A: Typhoid Mary. Wolverine, Ghost Rider ... 1.50
❑113, Oct 1992; A: Typhoid Mary. Wolverine, Ghost Rider ... 1.50
❑114, Oct 1992; A: Typhoid Mary. Wolverine, Ghost Rider ... 1.50
❑115, Nov 1992; A: Typhoid Mary. Wolverine, Ghost Rider ... 1.50
❑116, Nov 1992; GK (a); A: Typhoid Mary. Wolverine, Ghost Rider ... 1.50
❑117, Dec 1992; SL (w); 1: Ravage 2099. A: Venom. Wolverine, Ghost Rider; Ravage 2099 preview ... 1.50
❑118, Dec 1992; PB (a); 1: Doom 2099. A: Venom. Wolverine; Doom 2099 preview ... 1.50
❑119, Jan 1993; A: Venom. Wolverine ... 1.50
❑120, Jan 1993; A: Venom. Wolverine ... 1.50
❑121, Feb 1993; Wolverine ... 1.50
❑122, Feb 1993; Wolverine ... 1.50
❑123, Mar 1993; Wolverine ... 1.50
❑124, Mar 1993; Wolverine ... 1.50
❑125, Apr 1993; Wolverine ... 1.50
❑126, Apr 1993; Wolverine ... 1.50
❑127, May 1993; DP (a); Wolverine ... 1.50
❑128, May 1993; Wolverine ... 1.50
❑129, May 1993; Wolverine ... 1.50
❑130, Jun 1993; Wolverine ... 1.50
❑131, Jun 1993; Wolverine ... 1.50
❑132, Jul 1993; Wolverine ... 1.50
❑133, Jul 1993; Wolverine ... 1.50
❑134, Aug 1993; Wolverine ... 1.50
❑135, Aug 1993; Wolverine ... 1.50
❑136, Sep 1993; Wolverine ... 1.50
❑137, Sep 1993; EL (w); Wolverine ... 1.50
❑138, Sep 1993 EL (w); A: Masters of Silence. A: Ghost Rider. A: Wolverine. A: Wusin. A: Spellbound. A: Nightcrawler ... 1.50
❑139, Oct 1993 EL (w); A: Masters of Silence. A: Ghost Rider. A: Wolverine. A: Wusin. A: Foreigner. A: Spellbound. A: Zxaxz ... 1.50
❑140, Oct 1993; EL (w); O: Captain Universe. A: Masters of Silence. A: Ghost Rider. A: Wolverine. A: Wusin. A: Captain Universe. A: Spellbound. A: Zxaxz ... 1.50
❑141, Nov 1993 EL (w) ... 1.50
❑142, Nov 1993 EL (w) ... 1.50
❑143, Dec 1993; Ghost Rider ... 1.75
❑144, Dec 1993; Ghost Rider ... 1.75
❑145, Jan 1994; Ghost Rider ... 1.75
❑146, Jan 1994 ... 1.75
❑147, Feb 1994 ... 1.75
❑148, Feb 1994 ... 1.75
❑149, Mar 1994; Vengeance, StarJammers, Daughters of the Dragon, Namor ... 1.75
❑150, Mar 1994 ... 1.75
❑151, Apr 1994; Wolverine, Daredevil, Vengeance, Typhoid Mary ... 1.75
❑152, Apr 1994 ... 1.75
❑153, May 1994 ... 1.75
❑154, May 1994 ... 1.75
❑155, May 1994 ... 1.75
❑156, Jun 1994 ... 1.75

Other grades: Multiply price above by 5/6 for VF/NM • 2/3 for VERY FINE • 1/3 for FINE • 1/5 for VERY GOOD • 1/8 for GOOD

Marvel Super Hero Contest of Champions

Wrong contender was handed victory
©Marvel

Marvel Super-Heroes

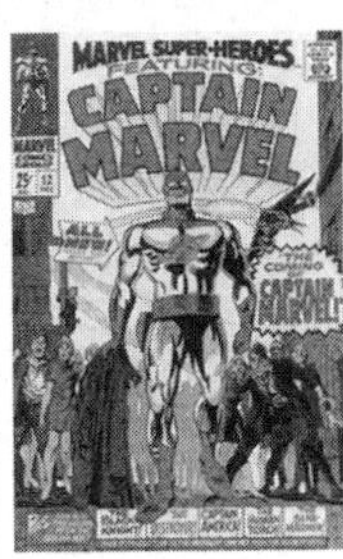

Introduces Kree Captain Mar-Vell
©Marvel

Marvel Super-Heroes

Seasonal super-hero anthology
©Marvel

Marvel Super-Heroes Megazine

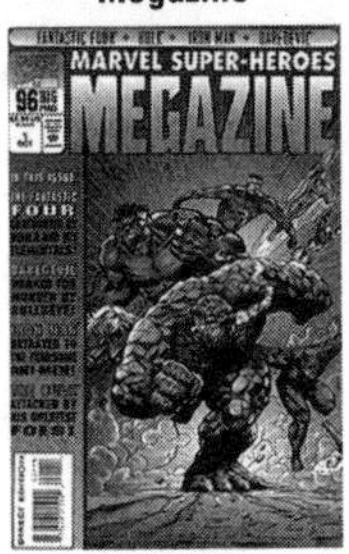

Back to square-bound anthologies
©Marvel

Marvel Super Heroes Secret Wars

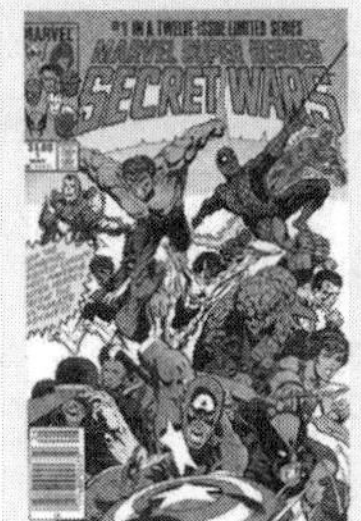

Event affected entire Marvel universe
©Marvel

	N-MINT
❑157, Jun 1994	1.75
❑158, Jul 1994	1.75
❑159, Jul 1994	1.75
❑160, Aug 1994	1.75
❑161, Aug 1994	1.75
❑162, Sep 1994; Tigra; Mace; Vengeance; New Warriors	1.75
❑163, Sep 1994; New Warriors; Tigra; Vengeance; Mace	1.75
❑164, Oct 1994; Vengeance; Tigra; Man-Thing; The Thing	1.75
❑165, Oct 1994; Man-Thing; Mr. Fantastic; Vengeance; Tigra	1.75
❑166, Oct 1994; Man-Thing; Spider-Woman; Vengeance; Turbo	1.75
❑167, Nov 1994	1.75
❑168, Nov 1994	1.75
❑169, Dec 1994	1.75
❑170, Dec 1994	1.75
❑171, Jan 1995	1.75
❑172, Jan 1995	1.75
❑173, Feb 1995	1.75
❑174, Feb 1995 KG (w); KG (a)	1.75
❑175, Mar 1995; KG (w); KG (a); Final Issue; New Genix; Vengeance; Steel Raven; Lunat!k	1.75

Marvel Comics: 2001
Marvel

	N-MINT
❑1, Jul 2001	1.00

Marvel Double Feature
Marvel

	N-MINT
❑1, Dec 1973	40.00
❑2, Feb 1974	20.00
❑3, Apr 1974	15.00
❑4, Jun 1974	10.00
❑5, Aug 1974, Reprints Tales of Suspense #81 (Captain America) & #88 (Iron Man)	10.00
❑6, Oct 1974, Reprints from Tales of Suspense #82 and #89	10.00
❑7, Dec 1974, Reprints Tales of Suspense #83 (Captain America) & #90 (Iron Man)	10.00
❑8, Feb 1975, Reprints Tales of Suspense #84 (Captain America) & #91 (Iron Man)	10.00
❑9, Apr 1975, Reprints Tales of Suspense #85 (Captain America) & #92 (Iron Man)	8.00
❑10, Jun 1975	8.00
❑11, Aug 1975	8.00
❑12, Oct 1975	8.00
❑13, Dec 1975	8.00
❑14, Feb 1976, V: Red Skull; V: Whiplash	8.00
❑15, Apr 1976	8.00
❑15/30¢, Apr 1976, 30¢ regional price variant	20.00
❑16, Jun 1976	8.00
❑16/30¢, Jun 1976, 30¢ regional price variant	20.00
❑17, Aug 1976, Reprints Iron Man vs. Sub-Mariner #1	8.00
❑17/30¢, Aug 1976, Reprints Iron Man vs. Sub-Mariner #1; 30¢ regional price variant	20.00
❑18, Oct 1976, Reprints story from Iron Man #1	8.00
❑19, Dec 1976	6.00
❑20, Feb 1977	6.00
❑21, Apr 1977, Reprints Tales of Suspense #98 & #99	6.00

Marvel Double Shot
Marvel

	N-MINT
❑1, Jan 2003; Thor/Hulk	2.99
❑2, Feb 2003; Avengers/Doom	2.99
❑3, Mar 2003; Ant-Man/Fantastic Four	2.99
❑4, Apr 2003; Dr. Strange/Iron Man	2.99

Marvel Encyclopedia
Marvel

	N-MINT
❑1, ca. 2004; magazine-sized; compiles information from other Marvel Encyclopedias; sold in department stores	5.99

Marvel Fanfare
Marvel

	N-MINT
❑1, Mar 1982; MG, FM (c); MG, PS, FM, TD (a); 1: Vertigo II. Spider-Man; Daredevil; Angel	4.50
❑2, May 1982; MG (c); MG, TVE (a); Spider-Man; Angel; Ka-Zar; Fantastic Four	3.25
❑3, Jul 1982; DC (c); DC, TVE (a); X-Men	3.25
❑4, Sep 1982; PS (c); MG, PS, TD (a); X-Men; Deathlok	2.50
❑5, Nov 1982; MR (c); LMc, CR, MR (a); Doctor Strange	2.50
❑6, Jan 1983; CV, CR (c); CV (a); Spider-Man; Doctor Strange; Scarlet Witch	2.00
❑7, Mar 1983; DD (a); Hulk; Daredevil	2.00
❑8, May 1983; CI, CR (c); GK (w); CI, GK (a); Doctor Strange; Mowgli	2.00
❑9, Jul 1983; AM (c); GK (w); GK (a); Man-Thing; Mowgli	2.00
❑10, Aug 1983; GP (c); GP (w); GP, BL, GK (a); Black Widow; Mowgli	2.00
❑11, Nov 1983; GP, CR (c); GP, GK (a); Black Widow	2.00
❑12, Jan 1984; AM, GP (c); AM, GP (a); Black Widow	2.00
❑13, Mar 1984; CV (c); GP, CV (a); Black Widow	2.00
❑14, May 1984; Vision; Quicksilver	2.00
❑15, Jul 1984; Thing	2.00
❑16, Sep 1984; DC (c); DC (a); Skywolf	2.00
❑17, Nov 1984; DC (c); DC (a); Skywolf	2.00
❑18, Jan 1985; FM (c); FM, KN (a); Captain America	2.00
❑19, Mar 1985; KGa (c); JSn (a); Cloak & Dagger	2.00
❑20, May 1985; AM, JSn (c); JSn (w); JSn (a); Thing; Hulk; Doctor Strange	2.00
❑21, Jul 1985; JSn (c); JSn (w); JSn (a); Thing; Hulk	2.00
❑22, Sep 1985; JSn (a); Thing; Hulk; Iron Man	2.00
❑23, Nov 1985; JSn (a); Thing; Hulk; Iron Man	2.00
❑24, Jan 1986; Weirdworld	2.00
❑25, Mar 1986; PB (a); Dave Sim pin-up section; Weirdworld	2.00
❑26, May 1986; PB (a); Weirdworld	2.00
❑27, Jul 1986; AM (w); AM, BMc (a); Weirdworld; Spider-Man; Daredevil	2.00
❑28, Sep 1986; Alpha Flight	2.00
❑29, Nov 1986; JBy (c); JBy (w); JBy (a); D: Hammer. D: Anvil. Hulk	2.00
❑30, Jan 1987; BA (c); BA (a); Moon Knight; Painted cover	2.00
❑31, Mar 1987; KGa (c); AM, KGa (w); AM, KGa (a); Captain America	2.00
❑32, May 1987; Captain America	2.00
❑33, Jul 1987; Wolverine; X-Men	2.00
❑34, Sep 1987; Warriors Three	2.00
❑35, Nov 1987; CV (c); CV (a); Warriors Three	2.00
❑36, Jan 1988; Warriors Three	2.00
❑37, Mar 1988; Warriors Three	2.00
❑38, Apr 1988; Moon Knight	2.00
❑39, Aug 1988; Hawkeye; Moon Knight	2.00
❑40, Oct 1988; Angel; Storm	2.00
❑41, Dec 1988; DaG (c); DaG, DG (a); Doctor Strange	2.00
❑42, Feb 1989; AM (w); AM, BH (a); Spider-Man	2.00
❑43, Apr 1989; Sub-Mariner; Human Torch	2.00
❑44, Jun 1989; Iron Man; Iron Man vs. Doctor Doom	2.00
❑45, Aug 1989; JBy (c); MG, JB, BL, HC, BA, JLee, KJ, KN (a); all pin-ups	2.00
❑46, Oct 1989; Fantastic Four	2.00
❑47, Nov 1989; Spider-Man; Hulk	2.00
❑48, Dec 1989; She-Hulk	2.00
❑49, Feb 1990; Doctor Strange	2.00
❑50, Apr 1990; JSa (c); AM (w); AM, JSa (a); X-Factor	2.25
❑51, Jun 1990; Silver Surfer	2.95
❑52, Aug 1990; Black Knight; Fantastic Four	2.25
❑53, Oct 1990; Black Knight; Doctor Strange	2.25
❑54, Dec 1990; Black Knight; Wolverine	2.25
❑55, Feb 1991; Power Pack; Wolverine	2.25
❑56, Apr 1991; CI, DH (a); Shanna the She-Devil	2.25
❑57, Jun 1991; Captain Marvel; Shanna the She-Devil	2.25
❑58, Aug 1991; Shanna the She-Devil; Vision II (android); Scarlet Witch	2.25
❑59, Oct 1991; RHo (w); RHo, TD (a); Shanna the She-Devil	2.25
❑60, Jan 1992; PS (c); PS (w); PS (a); Black Panther; Rogue; Daredevil	2.25

Marvel Fanfare
Marvel

	N-MINT
❑1, Sep 1996; A: Captain America. A: Deathlok. A: Falcon. Flipbook with Professor Xavier and the X-Men #11	1.50
❑2, Oct 1996 A: Wendigo. A: Hulk. A: Wolverine	1.00
❑3, Nov 1996 A: Ghost Rider. A: Spider-Man	1.00
❑4, Dec 1996 A: Longshot	1.00
❑5, Jan 1997; A: Dazzler. A: Longshot. V: Spiral	1.00
❑6, Feb 1997; A: Sabretooth. A: Power Man. A: Iron Fist. V: Sabretooth	1.00

Marvel Feature
Marvel

	N-MINT
❑1, Dec 1971, NA (c); DH, RA (a); O: Defenders. 1: Omegatron. D: Yandroth (physical body); Sub-Mariner reprint; Giant-Size	125.00
❑2, Mar 1972, BEv, RA (a); 2: Defenders. Sub-Mariner reprint	60.00

Other grades: Multiply price above by 5/6 for VF/NM • 2/3 for VERY FINE • 1/3 for FINE • 1/5 for VERY GOOD • 1/8 for GOOD

❑3, Jun 1972, GK (c); BEv, RA (a); A: Defenders. V: Xemnu the Titan...... 30.00
❑4, Jul 1972, A: Peter Parker. A: Ant-Man 25.00
❑5, Sep 1972, A: Ant-Man...................... 10.00
❑6, Nov 1972, A: Ant-Man. Mike W. Barr L.O.C 10.00
❑7, Jan 1973, GK (c); GK, CR (a); A: Ant-Man. David Michelinie L.O.C.............. 10.00
❑8, Mar 1973, O: Wasp. A: Ant-Man; Wasp appearance 10.00
❑9, May 1973, CR (a); A: Iron Man. A: Ant-Man 10.00
❑10, Jul 1973, CR (a); A: Ant-Man. Includes two backup reprint Stories from Marvel's Macabre Past; Mystic #14 and 35 .... 10.00
❑11, Sep 1973, Thing vs. Hulk.............. 55.00
❑12, Nov 1973, A: Thing. A: Iron Man. A: Thanos 35.00

Marvel Feature
Marvel

❑1, Nov 1975, GK (c); DG, NA (a); Red Sonja stories begin; Reprints Savage Sword of Conan #1.............................. 10.00
❑2, Jan 1976, FT (c); FT (a) 3.00
❑3, Mar 1976, FT (c); FT (a); Marvel Value Stamp Series B #53........................... 3.00
❑4, May 1976, FT (c); FT (a) 3.00
❑4/30¢, May 1976, 30¢ regional price variant 35.00
❑5, Jul 1976, FT (c); FT (a) 3.00
❑5/30¢, Jul 1976, 30¢ regional price variant 20.00
❑6, Sep 1976, A: Conan. Story continues in Conan the Barbarian #66; Ralph Macchio L.O.C 3.00
❑7, Nov 1976, Red Sonja vs. Conan....... 3.00

Marvel Frontier Comics Unlimited
Marvel

❑1, Jan 1994 .... 2.95

Marvel Fumetti Book
Marvel

❑1, Apr 1984, b&w; photos with balloon captions.. 2.00

Marvel Graphic Novel
Marvel

❑1, ca. 1982; JSn (w); JSn (a); D: Captain Marvel 13.00
❑1/2nd; JSn (w); JSn (a); D: Captain Marvel 6.00
❑1/3rd; JSn (w); JSn (a); D: Captain Marvel 6.00
❑2; CR (c); CR (a); Elric 7.00
❑3; JSn (c); JSn (w); JSn (a); Dreadstar 7.50
❑4; BMc (a); O: Sunspot. 1&O: New Mutants. 1: Mirage II (Danielle "Dani" Moonstar).. 12.00
❑4/2nd; BMc (a); 1&O: Mirage II (Danielle "Dani" Moonstar). 1&O: Sunspot. 1&O: New Mutants........................... 6.00
❑4/3rd; BMc (a)..................................... 5.00
❑5, Mar 1982; BA (a); X-Men: God Loves, Man Kills 20.00
❑5/2nd; BA (a); X-Men: God Loves, Man Kills 7.00
❑5/3rd; BA (c); BA (a); X-Men: God Loves, Man Kills 6.00
❑5/4th; BA (a); X-Men: God Loves, Man Kills 6.00
❑5/5th; BA (a); X-Men: God Loves, Man Kills 6.00
❑6; Star Slammers 6.00
❑7; CR (a); Killraven............................. 6.00
❑8; BSz (c); JBy (w); JBy (a); Super Boxers 6.00
❑9; DC (w); DC (a); The Futurians.......... 6.95
❑10; Heartburst...................................... 6.00
❑11; VM (a); Void Indigo........................ 6.00
❑12; FS (a); Dazzler: The Movie 6.95
❑13; Starstruck 6.95
❑14; BG (a); Swords of the Swashbucklers 6.00
❑15; CV (c); CV (a); Raven Banner......... 6.00
❑16; Aladdin Effect................................. 6.00
❑17; Living Monolith............................... 6.00
❑18; JBy (w); JBy (a); She-Hulk............. 7.00
❑19; Conan the Barbarian....................... 7.00
❑20, Oct 1985; Greenberg the Vampire.. 7.00
❑21; Marada the She-Wolf 7.00
❑22; BWr (a); Amazing Spider-Man 9.00
❑23; DGr (a); Dr. Strange 7.00
❑24; Daredevil.. 7.50
❑25; Dracula 7.00
❑26; Alien Legion.................................... 7.00
❑27; D: The Purple Man. Avengers 6.95
❑28; Conan the Reaver............................ 6.95
❑29; Thing vs. Hulk................................ 8.00
❑30, A Sailor's Story 5.95
❑31; 1&O: Wolfpack................................ 6.95
❑32 D: Groo 10.00
❑33; Thor.. 6.95
❑34; Cloak & Dagger................................ 6.95
❑35; Hardcover; Shadow 1941 .... 12.95
❑36; Willow... 6.95
❑37; Hercules.. 7.00
❑38; Silver Surfer.................................. 16.00

Marvel Graphic Novel: Arena
Marvel

❑1 .... 5.95

Marvel Graphic Novel: Cloak and Dagger and Power Pack: Shelter From the Storm
Marvel

❑1 .... 7.95

Marvel Graphic Novel: Emperor Doom: Starring the Mighty Avengers
Marvel

❑1 .... 5.95

Marvel Graphic Novel: Ka-Zar: Guns of the Savage Land
Marvel

❑1 .... 8.95

Marvel Graphic Novel: Rick Mason, the Agent
Marvel

❑1 1989.. 9.95

Marvel Graphic Novel: Roger Rabbit in the Resurrection of Doom
Marvel

❑1 .... 8.95

Marvel Graphic Novel: Who Framed Roger Rabbit?
Marvel

❑1 .... 6.95

Marvel Guide to Collecting Comics
Marvel

❑1, Sep 1982; no cover price................ 3.00

Marvel Halloween Ashcan 2006
Marvel

❑1, ca. 2006; reprints Marvel Adventures The Avengers #1 in smaller format..... 1.00

Marvel Halloween: Supernaturals Tour Book
Marvel

❑1, Nov 1998.. 2.99

Marvel: Heroes & Legends
Marvel

❑1, Oct 1996; backstory on Reed and Sue's wedding; wraparound cover 2.95
❑2, Nov 1997; untold Avengers story; Hawkeye, Quicksilver, Scarlet Witch joins team 2.99

Marvel Heroes Flip Magazine
Marvel

❑1, Jul 2005... 3.99
❑2, Aug 2005 .... 3.99
❑3, Sep 2005 .... 3.99
❑4, Nov 2005; Collects New Avengers #4, Captain America (5th Series) #4......... 3.99
❑5, Dec 2005; Collects New Avengers #5, Captain America (5th Series) #5.......... 3.99
❑6, Jan 2006; Collects New Avengers #6, Captain America (5th Series) #6; Includes poster 3.99
❑7, Feb 2006, D: Jack Monroe................ 3.99
❑8, Mar 2006, Includes poster................ 3.99
❑9, Apr 2006, Reprints New Avengers #9 and Captain America #9; Includes New Avengers poster 3.99
❑10, May 2006; Includes poster............ 3.99
❑11, Jul 2006, Includes poster 3.99
❑13, Aug 2006, Includes poster; Collects from New Avengers # 13, Captain America #14 and House of M # 2........ 4.99
❑14, Sep 2006; Includes poster; Collects from New Avengers #14, Young Avengers #1, and House of M #3 .... 4.99
❑15, Oct 2006; Includes poster; Collects from New Avengers #15, Young Avengers #2, and House of M #4 .... 4.99
❑16, Nov 2006, Includes poster; Collects New Avengers #16, Young Avengers #3, and House of M #5..................... 4.99
❑17, Dec 2006, Collects New Avengers #17, House of M #6, and Young Avengers #4; Includes Poster............... 4.99
❑18, Jan 2007; Collects New Avengers #18 and Young Avengers #5; Guiding Light Bonus Story; Includes Poster.... 4.99
❑19, Feb 2007; Collects New Avengers #19, Young Avengers #19 and House of M #7; Includes Young Avengers Poster... 4.99
❑20, Mar 2007 .... 4.99
❑21 .... 4.99
❑22 .... 4.99
❑23 .... 4.99
❑24 .... 4.99
❑25 .... 4.99
❑26 .... 4.99

Marvel Holiday Special
Marvel

❑1; SB, DC, KJ (a); no cover date or date in indicia... 3.00
❑1992, Jan 1993; for 1992 holiday season 3.00
❑1993, Jan 1994; JSn, SL, PD (w); AM, MG, DC, KGa (a); for 1993 holiday season.. 3.00
❑1994, Jan 1995; GP (c); KB (w); GM, SB (a); for 1994 holiday season 3.00
❑1996, Jan 1997 GP, SL, MWa (w)........ 2.95

Marvel Holiday Special 2005
Marvel

❑1, Jan 2006... 3.99

Marvel Holiday Special 2006
Marvel

❑1, Feb 2007... 3.99

Marvel Illustrated: Swimsuit Issue
Marvel

❑1, Mar 1991 .... 3.95

Marvel Knights
Marvel

❑1, Jul 2000; V: Ulik.............................. 3.50
❑1/A, Jul 2000; Daredevil close-up cover 5.00
❑2/Barreto, Aug 2000, b&w; A: Ulik. Barreto cover; Cloak and Dagger........ 4.00
❑2/Quesada, Aug 2000, b&w; Variant cover by Joe Quesada; Dagger in foreground 5.00
❑3, Sep 2000 A: Ulik 2.99
❑4, Oct 2000; Zaran steals biological weapon from AIM; Zaran hired to kill Shang-Chi 2.99
❑5, Nov 2000; Punisher V: alien............ 2.99
❑6, Dec 2000; Punisher V: alien; Zaran V: Shang-Chi 2.99
❑7, Jan 2001; V: Cloak.......................... 2.99
❑8, Feb 2001; V: Cloak.......................... 2.99
❑9, Mar 2001; V: Cloak; V: Nightmare; Cloak is depowered 2.99
❑10, Apr 2001; Black Widow and Dagger bond.. 2.99
❑11, May 2001; Heroes enlist Luke Cage 2.99
❑12, Jun 2001; V: Tombstone; V: Bengal; V: Bullet; V: Big Ben 2.99
❑13, Jul 2001; V: Zartan; V: Yellow Claw 2.99
❑14, Aug 2001; V: Yellow Claw; Heroes disband 2.99
❑15, Sep 2001 .... 2.99

Marvel Knights
Marvel

❑1, May 2002.. 2.99
❑2, Jun 2002.. 2.99
❑3, Jul 2002... 2.99
❑4, Aug 2002 .... 2.99
❑5, Sep 2002 .... 2.99
❑6, Oct 2002 .... 2.99

Marvel Knights 4
Marvel

❑1, Apr 2004.. 4.00
❑2, Apr 2004.. 2.99
❑3, May 2004... 2.99
❑4, May 2004... 2.99

Marvel Super Special

Movie adaptation magazine
©Marvel

Marvel Swimsuit Special

Characters in tighter, lesser outfits
©Marvel

Marvel Tails

Anthropomorphic version of arachnid hero
©Marvel

Marvel Tales (2nd Series)

Key Marvel moments reprints give way to Spidey
©Marvel

Marvel Team-Up

Mostly Spider-Man meetings
©Marvel

N-MINT

❑5, Jun 2004 ... 2.99
❑6, Jun 2004 ... 2.99
❑7, Sep 2004 ... 2.99
❑8, Sep 2004 ... 2.99
❑9, Oct 2004 ... 2.99
❑10, Nov 2004 ... 2.99
❑11, Dec 2004 ... 2.99
❑12, Jan 2004 ... 2.99
❑13, Feb 2005 ... 2.99
❑14, Mar 2005 ... 2.99
❑15, Apr 2005 ... 2.99
❑16, May 2005 ... 2.99
❑17, Jun 2005; V: Dr. Doom ... 2.99
❑18, Jul 2005 ... 2.99
❑19, Aug 2005 ... 2.99
❑20, Sep 2005 ... 2.99
❑21, Oct 2005 ... 2.99
❑22, Nov 2005 ... 2.99
❑23, Dec 2005 ... 2.99
❑24, Jan 2006 ... 2.99
❑25, Feb 2006 ... 2.99
❑26, Mar 2006 ... 3.00
❑27, Apr 2006, V: Nicholas Scratch; V: Salem Seven ... 3.00
❑28, May 2006, Title changes to "4" ... 2.99
❑29, Jul 2006, V: Godseye ... 2.99

Marvel Knights Double-Shot
Marvel

❑1, Jun 2002 ... 2.99
❑2, Jul 2002 ... 2.99
❑3, Aug 2002 ... 2.99
❑4, Sep 2002 ... 2.99

Marvel Knights Magazine
Marvel

❑1 ... 3.99
❑2 ... 3.99
❑3, Jul 2001 ... 3.99
❑4 ... 3.99
❑5 ... 3.99
❑6 ... 3.99

Marvel Knights/Marvel Boy Genesis Edition
Marvel

❑1, Jun 2000; Polybagged with Punisher (5th Series) #3 ... 1.00

Marvel Knights: Millennial Visions
Marvel

❑1, Feb 2002 ... 3.99

Marvel Knights Sketchbook
Marvel

❑1; KSm (w); BWr (a); Bundled with Wizard #84 ... 1.00

Marvel Knights Spider-Man
Marvel

❑1, Jun 2004; Wraparound cover ... 5.00
❑2, Jul 2004 ... 4.00
❑3, Aug 2004 ... 2.99
❑4, Sep 2004 ... 2.99
❑5, Oct 2004 ... 2.25
❑6, Nov 2004 ... 2.99
❑7, Dec 2004 ... 2.99
❑8, Jan 2005 ... 2.99
❑9, Feb 2005 ... 2.99
❑10, Mar 2005 ... 2.99

N-MINT

❑11, Apr 2005 ... 2.99
❑12, May 2005 ... 2.99
❑13, Jun 2005 ... 2.99
❑14, Jul 2005 ... 2.99
❑15, Aug 2005 ... 2.99
❑16, Sep 2005 ... 2.99
❑17, Oct 2005 ... 2.99
❑18, Nov 2005 ... 2.99
❑19, Dec 2005; Peter Parker holding Mary Jane, red cover ... 2.99
❑20, Jan 2006 ... 2.99
❑21, Feb 2006 ... 2.99
❑22, Mar 2006; Final Issue—continues in Sensational Spider-Man (3rd Series) . 2.99

Marvel Knights Tour Book
Marvel

❑1, Oct 1998; previews and interviews .. 2.99

Marvel Knights 2099: Black Panther
Marvel

❑1 2004 ... 4.00

Marvel Knights 2099: Daredevil
Marvel

❑1 2004 ... 4.00

Marvel Knights 2099: Inhumans
Marvel

❑1 2004 ... 4.00

Marvel Knights 2099: Mutant
Marvel

❑1 2004 ... 4.00

Marvel Knights 2099: Punisher
Marvel

❑1 2004 ... 4.00

Marvel Knights Wave 2 Sketchbook
Marvel

❑1; Special free edition from Marvel in Wizard #90; DGry (w); Sketchbook 1.00

Marvel Legacy: The 1960s Handbook
Marvel

❑1, Apr 2006 ... 4.99

Marvel Mangaverse
Marvel

❑1, Jun 2002 ... 2.25
❑2, Jul 2002 ... 2.25
❑3, Aug 2002 ... 2.25
❑4, Sep 2002 ... 2.25
❑5, Oct 2002 ... 2.25
❑6, Nov 2002 ... 2.25

Marvel Mangaverse: Avengers Assemble!
Marvel

❑1, Mar 2002 ... 2.25

Marvel Mangaverse: Eternity Twilight
Marvel

❑1, Mar 2002 ... 2.25
❑1/A, Mar 2002 ... 3.50

Marvel Mangaverse: Fantastic Four
Marvel

❑1, Mar 2002 ... 2.25

Marvel Mangaverse: Ghost Riders
Marvel

❑1, Mar 2002 ... 2.25

N-MINT

Marvel Mangaverse: New Dawn
Marvel

❑1, Mar 2002 ... 3.50

Marvel Mangaverse: Punisher
Marvel

❑1, Mar 2002 ... 2.25

Marvel Mangaverse: Spider-Man
Marvel

❑1, Mar 2002 ... 2.25

Marvel Mangaverse: X-Men
Marvel

❑1, Mar 2002 ... 2.25

Marvel Masterpieces 2 Collection
Marvel

❑1, Jul 1994; Pin-ups ... 2.95
❑2, Aug 1994; Pin-ups ... 2.95
❑3, Sep 1994; Pin-ups ... 2.95

Marvel Masterpieces Collection
Marvel

❑1, May 1993 ... 2.95
❑2, Jun 1993 ... 2.95
❑3, Jul 1993 ... 2.95
❑4, Aug 1993 ... 2.95

Marvel Milestone Edition: Amazing Fantasy
Marvel

❑15, Mar 1992, Reprints of Amazing Fantasy # 15: Spider-man's Origin 2.95

Marvel Milestone Edition: Amazing Spider-Man
Marvel

❑1, Jan 1993; Reprints Amazing Spider-Man #1 ... 2.95
❑3, Mar 1995; Reprints Amazing Spider-Man #3 ... 2.95
❑129; Reprints Amazing Spider-Man #129 ... 2.95
❑149, Nov 1994; indicia says Marvel Milestone Edition: Amazing Spider-Man #1; Reprints Amazing Spider-Man #149 ... 2.95

Marvel Milestone Edition: Avengers
Marvel

❑1, Sep 1993; Reprints The Avengers #1; Thor, Iron Man, Ant-man, Wasp, Hulk 2.95
❑4, Mar 1995; Reprints The Avengers #4; Captain America Joins ... 2.95
❑16; Reprints The Avengers #16; New team begins: Captain America, Hawkeye, Quicksilver, and Scarlet Witch ... 2.95

Marvel Milestone Edition: Captain America
Marvel

❑1, Mar 1995; Reprints Captain America #1 ... 3.95

Marvel Milestone Edition: Fantastic Four
Marvel

❑1, Nov 1991; Reprints 1961's Fantastic Four #1 (including Ads) ... 2.95
❑5, Nov 1992 ... 2.95

Other grades: Multiply price above by 5/6 for VF/NM • 2/3 for VERY FINE • 1/3 for FINE • 1/5 for VERY GOOD • 1/8 for GOOD

Marvel Milestone Edition: Giant-Size X-Men
Marvel

❑1 1991; Reprints Giant-Size X-Men in its entirety; Includes back-up reprints from X-Men (1st Series) # 43, 47, 57; ca. 1991 .... 3.95

Marvel Milestone Edition: Incredible Hulk
Marvel

❑1, Mar 1991; Reprints Incredible Hulk #1 2.95

Marvel Milestone Edition: Iron Fist
Marvel

❑14, 1: Sabretooth 2.95

Marvel Milestone Edition: Iron Man
Marvel

❑55, Nov 1992, Reprints Iron Man #55.. 2.95

Marvel Milestone Edition: Iron Man, Ant-Man & Captain America
Marvel

❑1, May 2005........ 3.99

Marvel Milestone Edition: Tales of Suspense
Marvel

❑39, Nov 1994; Reprints Tales of Suspense #39........ 2.95

Marvel Milestone Edition: X-Men
Marvel

❑1 1991; reprint (first series)........ 2.95
❑9, Oct 1993; Reprints X-Men (1st Series) #9........ 2.95
❑28, Nov 1994; indicia says Marvel Milestone Edition: X-Men #1; Reprints X-Men (1st Series) #28........ 2.95

Marvel Milestones: Beast & Kitty
Marvel

❑1, Jul 2006........ 3.99

Marvel Milestones: Black Panther, Storm, and Ka-Zar
Marvel

❑1, Aug 2006........ 3.99

Marvel Milestones: Blade, Man-Thing & Satana
Marvel

❑1........ 3.99

Marvel Milestones: Bloodstone, X-51, Captain Marvel II

❑1, Mar 2006........ 4.99

Marvel Milestones: Captain Britain, Psylocke, and Golden Age Sub-Mariner
Marvel

❑1, Oct 2005........ 3.99

Marvel Milestones: Dragon Lord, Speedball, and Man in the Sky
Marvel

❑1, May 2006........ 3.99

Marvel Milestones: Dr. Doom, Sub-Mariner, & Red Skull
Marvel

❑0, Jul 2005........ 3.99

Marvel Milestones: Dr. Strange, Silver Surfer, Sub-Mariner, Hulk
Marvel

❑1, Sep 2005........ 3.99

Marvel Milestones: Ghost Rider, Black Widow & Iceman
Marvel

❑1 2005; Reprints stories from Marvel Spotlight #5, Daredevil #81, and X-Men #47; O: Ghost Rider; ca. 2005........ 3.99

Marvel Milestones: Jim Lee and Chris Claremont X-Men and The Starjammers Part #17
Marvel

❑1, Nov 2006........ 3.99

Marvel Milestones: Legion of Monsters, Spider-Man, and Brother Voodoo
Marvel

❑1, Dec 2006........ 3.99

Marvel Milestones: Millie the Model & Patsy Walker
Marvel

❑1, Oct 2006, Collects Millie the Model #100, Defenders #65 and Patsy Walker #119; ca.2006........ 3.99

Marvel Milestones: Onslaught
Marvel

❑1, Feb 2007, Collects Onslaught: Marvel Universe........ 3.99

Marvel Milestones: Rawhide Kid and Two-Gun Kid
Marvel

❑1, Sep 2006........ 3.99

Marvel Milestones: Star Brand and Quasar
Marvel

❑1, May 2006........ 3.99

Marvel Milestones: Ultimate Spider-Man, Ultimate X-Men, Microman & Mantor
Marvel

❑1, Jan 2006, Reprints stories from Ultimate Spider-Man #1/2, Ultimate X-Men #1/2, Human Torch #2........ 3.99

Marvel Milestones: X-Men & The Starjammers Part 2
Marvel

❑1, Dec 2006........ 3.99

Marvel Monsters: Devil Dinosaur
Marvel

❑1, Dec 2005; Included reprint from Journey into Mystery (1st Series) #62 3.99

Marvel Monsters Fin Fang Four
Marvel

❑1, Dec 2005, b&w........ 3.99

Marvel Monsters: From the Files of Ulysses Bloodstone
Marvel

❑1, Jan 2006........ 3.99

Marvel Monsters: Monsters On the Prowl
Marvel

❑1, Dec 2005........ 3.99

Marvel Monsters: Where Monsters Dwell
Marvel

❑1, Dec 2005........ 3.99

Marvel Movie Premiere
Marvel

❑1, b&w; magazine........ 3.00

Marvel Movie Showcase
Marvel

❑1, Nov 1982, b&w; Reprints Star Wars (Marvel series) #1-3........ 1.25
❑2, Dec 1982, b&w; Reprints Star Wars (Marvel series) # 4-6........ 1.25

Marvel Movie Spotlight
Marvel

❑1, Nov 1982, JB, KJ (a); Reprints Raiders Of The Lost Ark # 1-3........ 4.00

Marvel Must Haves
Marvel

❑1, Dec 2001, Reprints Wolverine: The Origin #1, Startling Stories: Banner #1, Cable #97, Spider-Man's Tangled Web #4........ 3.99
❑2........ 3.99

Marvel Must Haves: Amazing Spider-Man #30-32
Marvel

❑1, ca. 2003; Reprints Amazing Spider-Man (Vol. 2) #30-32........ 3.99

Marvel Must Haves: Avengers #500-502
Marvel

❑1, ca. 2004........ 3.99

Marvel Must Haves: Incredible Hulk #50-52
Marvel

❑1, ca. 2003; Reprints Incredible Hulk (2nd series) #50-52........ 3.99

Marvel Must Haves: Incredible Hulk #34-36
Marvel

❑1, ca. 2003; Reprints Incredible Hulk (2nd series) #34-36........ 3.99

Marvel Must Haves: New Avengers #1-3
Marvel

❑1 2005........ 3.99

Marvel Must Haves: New X-Men #114-116
Marvel

❑1, ca. 2003; Reprints New X-Men #114-116........ 3.99

Marvel Must Haves: NYX #4-5
Marvel

❑0, Jul 2005........ 3.99

Marvel Must Haves: Sentinel #1 & #2 and Runaways #1 & #2
Marvel

❑1, ca. 2003; Reprints Sentinel #1-2, Runaways #1-2........ 3.99

Marvel Must Haves: Spider-Man & Black Cat #1-#3
Marvel

❑1, Jan 2006........ 4.99

Marvel Must Haves: The Ultimates #1-3
Marvel

❑1, ca. 2003; Reprints The Ultimates #1-3 3.99

Marvel Must Haves: Truth: Red, White and Black
Marvel

❑1, Apr 2003........ 3.99

Marvel Must Haves: Ultimate Spider-Man #1-3
Marvel

❑1, ca. 2003; Reprints Ultimate Spider-Man #1-3........ 3.99

Marvel Must Haves: Ultimate Venom
Marvel

❑1, May 2003........ 3.99

Marvel Must Haves: Ultimate War
Marvel

❑1, May 2003........ 3.99

Marvel Must Haves: Ultimate X-Men #1-3
Marvel

❑1, ca. 2003; Reprints Ultimate X-Men #1-3........ 3.99

Marvel Must Haves: Ultimate X-Men #34 & #35
Marvel

❑1, ca. 2003; Reprints Ultimate X-Men #34-35........ 2.99

Marvel Must Haves: Wolverine #20-22
Marvel

❑1 2005........ 0.00

Marvel Must Haves: Wolverine #1-3
Marvel

❑1, ca. 2003; no indicia; reprints Wolverine (3rd series) #1-3........ 3.99

Marvel Mystery Comics
Marvel

❑1, Dec 1999; Reprints........ 3.95

Marvel Nemesis: The Imperfects
Marvel

❑1, Jun 2005........ 4.00
❑2, Jul 2005........ 2.99
❑3, Aug 2005........ 2.99
❑4, Sep 2005........ 2.99
❑5, Oct 2005........ 2.99
❑6, Nov 2005........ 2.99

Marvel No-Prize Book
Marvel

❑1, Jan 1983; SL (w); JK (a); mistakes.. 3.00

Marvelous Adventures of Gus Beezer and Spider-Man
Marvel

❑1, Feb 2004........ 2.99

Marvel Team-Up

Spider-Man teams again
©Marvel

Marvel Team-Up

More Marvel-ous meetings
©Marvel

Marvel: The Lost Generation

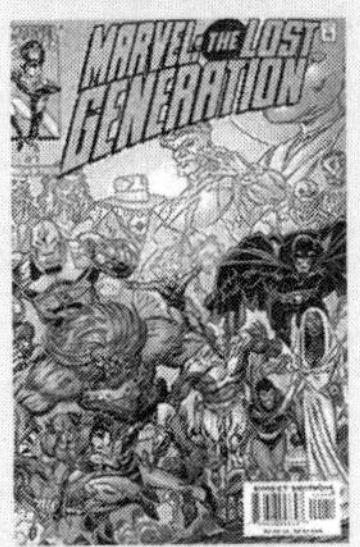

Time-traveling series numbered backwards
©Marvel

Marvel Treasury Edition

Life-sized reprints hard to hold in small hands
©Marvel

Marvel Treasury of Oz

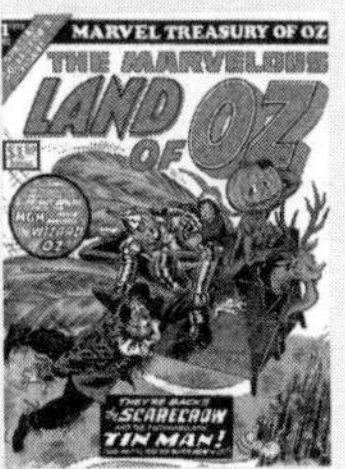

Adapts Baum's Land of Oz
©Marvel

N-MINT

Marvelous Adventures of Gus Beezer: Hulk
Marvel

❑1, May 2003 .... 2.99

Marvelous Adventures of Gus Beezer: Spider-Man
Marvel

❑1, May 2003 .... 2.99

Marvelous Adventures of Gus Beezer: X-Men
Marvel

❑1, May 2003 .... 2.99

Marvelous Dragon Clan
Lunar

❑1, Jul 1994, b&w........ 2.50
❑2, Sep 1994, b&w 2.50

Marvelous Wizard of Oz
Marvel

❑1, treasury-sized movie adaptation; ca. 1975 .... 16.00

Marvel: Portraits of a Universe
Marvel

❑1, Mar 1995 .... 2.95
❑2, Apr 1995........ 2.95
❑3, May 1995........ 2.95
❑4, Jun 1995........ 2.95

Marvel Poster Book
Marvel

❑1, Jan 1991; Marvel's First-Ever Poster Book........ 2.50

Marvel Poster Magazine
Marvel

❑2, Dec 2001, Winter 2001 .... 3.50

Marvel Premiere
Marvel

❑1, Apr 1972, GK (c); GK (a); O: Counter-Earth. O: Warlock........ 35.00
❑2, May 1972, GK (c); JK (w); JK, GK (a); A: Warlock. Yellow Claw 12.00
❑3, Jul 1972, SL (w); A: Doctor Strange 30.00
❑4, Sep 1972, FB (a); A: Doctor Strange 10.00
❑5, Nov 1972, MP, CR (a); A: Doctor Strange. Artist credited/corrected in issue #7 L.O.C 8.00
❑6, Jan 1973, MP (c); FB, MP (a); A: Doctor Strange........ 8.00
❑7, Mar 1973, MP (c); MP, CR (a); A: Doctor Strange........ 15.00
❑8, May 1973, JSn (a); A: Doctor Strange 10.00
❑9, Jul 1973, FB (c); FB (w); FB (a); A: Doctor Strange........ 6.00
❑10, Sep 1973, FB (c); FB (w); FB, NA (a); A: Doctor Strange. D: The Ancient One 9.00
❑11, Oct 1973, FB (c); FB, SL (w); SD, FB, NA (a); A: Doctor Strange........ 5.00
❑12, Nov 1973, FB (c); FB (w); FB, NA (a); A: Doctor Strange. Ralph Macchio L.O.C 5.00
❑13, Jan 1974, FB (c); FB (w); FB, NA (a); 1: Sise-Neg (as Cagliostro). A: Doctor Strange........ 8.00
❑14, Mar 1974, FB (c); FB (w); FB, NA (a); A: Sise-Neg. A: Doctor Strange 12.00
❑15, May 1974, GK (c); GK (a); O: Iron Fist. 1: Iron Fist. Marvel Value Stamp #94: Electro 80.00
❑16, Jul 1974, GK (c); 2: Iron Fist. 2: Iron Fist. Marvel Value Stamp #71: Vision. 20.00
❑17, Sep 1974, GK (c); A: Iron Fist. Marvel Value Stamp #32: Red Skull 12.00
❑18, Oct 1974, GK (c); A: Iron Fist. Marvel Value Stamp #74: Stranger 12.00
❑19, Nov 1974, GK (c); 1: Colleen Wing. A: Iron Fist. Marvel Value Stamp #6: Thor 10.00
❑20, Jan 1975, A: Iron Fist. Marvel Value Stamp #73: Kingpin........ 10.00
❑21, Mar 1975, A: Iron Fist........ 10.00
❑22, Jun 1975, A: Iron Fist. Ralph Macchio L.O.C........ 10.00
❑23, Aug 1975, GK (c); PB (a); A: Iron Fist. Marvel Value Stamp #27: Black Widow 10.00
❑24, Sep 1975, GK (c); PB (a); A: Iron Fist. Marvel Value Stamp #74: Stranger..... 10.00
❑25, Oct 1975, GK (c); JBy (a); A: Iron Fist. Marvel Value Stamp #6: Thor 15.00
❑26, Nov 1975, JK (c); GT, JK (a); A: Hercules........ 4.00
❑27, Dec 1975, A: Satana 10.00
❑28, Feb 1976, A: Werewolf. A: Man-Thing. A: Ghost Rider. A: Legion of Monsters. A: Morbius........ 13.00
❑29, Apr 1976, JK (c); DH, JK (a); O: Whizzer. O: Red Raven. O: Thin Man. O: Blue Diamond. O: Miss America; Marvel Value Stamp Series B #62 ...... 3.00
❑29/30¢, Apr 1976, JK (c); DH, JK (a); 30¢ regional price variant........ 20.00
❑30, Jun 1976, JK (c); DH, JK (a); A: Liberty Legion. Marvel Value Stamp Series B #87........ 2.50
❑30/30¢, Jun 1976, JK (c); DH, JK (a); A: Liberty Legion. 30¢ regional price variant........ 20.00
❑31, Aug 1976, JK (c); KG, JK (a); 1&O: Woodgod 3.00
❑31/30¢, Aug 1976, JK (c); KG, JK (a); 1&O: Woodgod. 30¢ regional price variant........ 20.00
❑32, Oct 1976, HC (w); HC (a); Monark Starstalker........ 3.00
❑33, Dec 1976, HC (a); A: Solomon Kane. Monark........ 3.00
❑34, Feb 1977, HC (a); A: Solomon Kane 3.00
❑35, Apr 1977, JK (c); 1&O: 3-D Man.... 3.00
❑36, Jun 1977, GK (c); A: 3-D Man........ 3.00
❑36/35¢, Jun 1977, GK (c); A: 3-D Man. 35¢ regional price variant........ 15.00
❑37, Aug 1977, GK (c); A: 3-D Man. Newsstand edition (distributed by Curtis); issue number in box 3.00
❑37/Whitman, Aug 1977, A: 3-D Man. Special markets edition (usually sold in Whitman bagged prepacks); price appears in a diamond; UPC barcode appears 3.00
❑37/35¢, Aug 1977, GK (c); A: 3-D Man. 35¢ regional price variant; newsstand edition (distributed by Curtis); issue number in box........ 15.00
❑38, Oct 1977, 1: Weirdworld. Newsstand edition (distributed by Curtis); issue number in box........ 3.00
❑38/Whitman, Oct 1977, 1: Weirdworld. Special markets edition (usually sold in Whitman bagged prepacks); price appears in a diamond; no UPC barcode 3.00
❑38/35¢, Oct 1977, 1: Weirdworld. 35¢ regional price variant; newsstand edition (distributed by Curtis); issue number in box........ 15.00
❑39, Dec 1977, A: Torpedo 3.00
❑40, Feb 1978, 1: Bucky II (Fred Davis). A: Torpedo........ 3.00
❑41, Apr 1978, DC (c); TS (a); 1: Seeker 3000........ 3.00
❑42, Jun 1978, DC (c); A: Tigra 3.00
❑43, Aug 1978, TS (a); 1: Paladin........ 3.00
❑44, Oct 1978, KG (a); A: Jack of Hearts 3.00
❑45, Dec 1978, A: Man-Wolf........ 3.00
❑46, Feb 1979, GP (c); GP (a); A: Man-Wolf. War God........ 3.00
❑47, Apr 1979, BL (c); JBy (a); 1: Ant-Man II (Scott Lang)........ 3.00
❑48, Jun 1979, DC (c); JBy, BL (a); A: Ant-Man........ 3.00
❑49, Aug 1979, FM (c); ME (w); SB, FM (a); A: The Falcon........ 3.00
❑50, Oct 1979, 1: Alice Cooper........ 12.50
❑51, Dec 1979, A: Black Panther. D: Windeagle........ 3.00
❑52, Feb 1980, A: Black Panther. 1: Soul Strangler; James Owsley L.O.C........ 3.00
❑53, Apr 1980, FM (c); FM (a); A: Black Panther........ 3.00
❑54, Jun 1980, GD (a); 1: Caleb Hammer 3.00
❑55, Aug 1980, A: Wonder Man........ 3.00
❑56, Oct 1980, HC (c); HC (w); HC, TD (a); A: Dominic Fortune 3.00
❑57, Dec 1980, DaG (a); 1: Doctor Who (in U.S.); Actual indicia: Marvel Premiere Featuring Dr. Who; Colorized reprints from Doctor Who Mag. UK; Pin-up art by Cockrum; Giacoia; Rubenstein........ 5.00
❑58, Feb 1981, FM (c); DaG (a); A: Doctor Who. Indicia reads: Marvel Premiere Featuring Doctor Who Colorized reprints from Doctor Who Mag. UK ... 3.00
❑59, Apr 1981, A: Doctor Who. Indicia reads: Marvel Premiere Featuring Doctor Who Colorized reprints from Doctor Who Mag. UK 3.00
❑60, Jun 1981, DaG (a); A: Doctor Who. Indicia reads: Marvel Premiere Featuring Doctor Who Colorized reprints from Doctor Who Mag. UK ... 3.00
❑61, Aug 1981, TS (a); A: Star-Lord. 3.00

Marvel Presents
Marvel

❑1, Oct 1975, GK (c); 1&O: Bloodstone. 11.00
❑2, Dec 1975, O: Bloodstone 5.00
❑3, Feb 1976, A: Guardians of the Galaxy. Marvel Value Stamp Series B #35 ...... 10.00
❑4, May 1976, 1&O: Nikki. A: Guardians of the Galaxy........ 4.00
❑4/30¢, May 1976, 30¢ regional price variant........ 20.00
❑5, Jun 1976, A: Guardians of the Galaxy. Marvel Value Stamp Series B #56 ...... 4.00
❑5/30¢, Jun 1976, 30¢ regional price variant........ 20.00
❑6, Aug 1976, A: Guardians of the Galaxy. V: Planetary Man........ 3.50
❑6/30¢, Aug 1976, 30¢ regional price variant........ 20.00
❑7, Nov 1976, A: Guardians of the Galaxy 3.50

Other grades: Multiply price above by 5/6 for VF/NM • 2/3 for VERY FINE • 1/3 for FINE • 1/5 for VERY GOOD • 1/8 for GOOD

❑8, Dec 1976, A: Guardians of the Galaxy. reprints Silver Surfer #2 .... 3.50
❑9, Feb 1977, O: Starhawk II (Aleta). A: Guardians of the Galaxy 3.50
❑10, Apr 1977, O: Starhawk II (Aleta). A: Guardians of the Galaxy 3.50
❑11, Jun 1977, A: Guardians of the Galaxy 3.50
❑11/35¢, Jun 1977, A: Guardians of the Galaxy. 35¢ regional price variant....... 3.50
❑12, Aug 1977, A: Guardians of the Galaxy 3.50
❑12/35¢, Aug 1977, A: Guardians of the Galaxy. 35¢ regional price variant....... 3.50

Marvel Preview
Marvel

❑1, Sum 1975; Man Gods From Beyond the Stars 15.00
❑2 1975; O: The Punisher. 1: Dominic Fortune; Don Pendleton interview; b&w; ca. 1975; First Punisher solo story 60.00
❑3, Sep 1975; Blade the Vampire Slayer 10.00
❑4, Jan 1976; 1&O: Star-Lord 7.00
❑5; Sherlock Holmes 5.00
❑6; Sherlock Holmes 5.00
❑7, Sep 1976; 1: Rocket Raccoon. Satana 5.00
❑8, Fal 1976; A: Legion of Monsters. Morbius, Blade 5.00
❑9, Apr 1977; O: Star Hawk. Man-God... 5.00
❑10, Jul 1977; JSn (a); Thor 5.00
❑11, Oct 1977; Star-Lord 5.00
❑12, Jan 1978; Haunt of Horror 5.00
❑13, Apr 1978; UFO 5.00
❑14, Aug 1978; Star-Lord 5.00
❑15, Oct 1978; CI, BWi (a); Star-Lord; Joe Jusko's first major comics work......... 5.00
❑16, Mar 1979; Detectives 5.00
❑17, May 1979; Blackmark 5.00
❑18, Aug 1979; Star-Lord 5.00
❑19, Nov 1979 A: Kull 5.00
❑20, Mar 1980; Bizarre Adventures........ 5.00
❑21, May 1980; A: Moon Knight. b&w ... 5.00
❑22, Aug 1980; Merlin; King Arthur 5.00
❑23, Nov 1980; GC, JB, FM (a); Bizarre Adventures 5.00
❑24, Feb 1981; Paradox; Title continues as "Bizarre Adventures" with #25 .... 5.00

Marvel Preview '93
Marvel

❑1, ca. 1993 .... 3.95

Marvel Riot
Marvel

❑1, Dec 1995; parodies Age of Apocalypse; wraparound cover 1.95

Marvel Romance Redux: But He Said He Loved Me
Marvel

❑1, Mar 20006 .... 2.99

Marvel Romance Redux: Guys & Dolls
Marvel

❑1, Jun 2006, Alters original stories to comic effect...................................... 2.99

Marvel Romance Redux: I Should Have Been a Blonde
Marvel

❑1, Jul 2006 .... 2.99

Marvel Romance Redux: Love Is a Four Letter Word
Marvel

❑1, Aug 2006 .... 2.99

Marvel Romance Redux: Restraining Orders Are for Other Girls
Marvel

❑1, Jun 2006 .... 2.99

Marvels
Marvel

❑0, Aug 1994, KB (w); ARo (a); Collects promo art and Human Torch story from Marvel Age; Fully painted 4.00
❑1, Jan 1994, ARo (c); KB (w); ARo (a); wraparound acetate outer cover; Torch, Sub-Mariner, Captain America; Fully painted 5.95
❑1/2nd, Apr 1996, KB (w); ARo (a); 2nd printing 2.95
❑2, Feb 1994, KB (w); ARo (a); Fully painted; wraparound acetate outer cover 5.95
❑2/2nd, May 1996, KB (w); ARo (a); 2nd printing 2.95
❑3, Mar 1994, KB (w); ARo (a); Coming of Galactus; Fully painted; wraparound acetate outer cover 5.95
❑3/2nd, May 1996, KB (w); ARo (a); wraparound cover 5.95
❑4, Apr 1994, KB (w); ARo (a); D: Gwen Stacy. Fully painted; wraparound acetate outer cover.............................. 5.95
❑4/2nd, Jun 1996, KB (w); ARo (a); wraparound cover 2.95

Marvel Saga
Marvel

❑1, Dec 1985; JBy, SL (w); SB, JBy, DH, JK, JSt (a); O: X-Men. O: Fantastic Four. O: Alpha Flight; Wraparound cover..... 2.50
❑2, Jan 1986; SL (w); SD, JK, BWi (a); O: Hulk. O: Spider-Man. Wrap around cover 2.00
❑3, Feb 1986; O: Sub-Mariner. O: Doom 2.00
❑4, Mar 1986; SL (w); ATh, JB, JBy, HT, JK, FM, BA, DC, BH, BWi (a); O: Thor 2.00
❑5, Apr 1986; O: Iceman. O: Angel 2.00
❑6, May 1986; SL (w); JB, DH, GT, JK, GK (a); O: Iron Man. O: Asgard. O: Odin .. 2.00
❑7, Jun 1986; SL (w); SD, BL, JR2, DH, JK, JM (a); O: Iron Man conclusion; Thor; The Hulk; Fantastic Four; Ant-Man; Egghead 2.00
❑8, Jul 1986; SL (w); SD, DH, JK (a); First Encounters: Cyclops & Iceman Vs. The Angel; Hulk and Spiderman's First Battles with the Fantastic Four 2.00
❑9, Aug 1986; O: Vulture; Fantastic Four; Sub-Mariner; Thor.............................. 2.00
❑10, Sep 1986; SL (w); SD, JB, BEv, JK (a); O: Marvel Girl. O: Beast. O: Avengers...................................... 2.00
❑11, Oct 1986; O: Molecule Man 1.50
❑12, Nov 1986; Captain America revived 1.50
❑13, Dec 1986; KJ (c); FM, SL (w); SD, GC, JB, BEv, KP, DH, SR, JK, FM, TP, KJ (a); O: Daredevil 1.50
❑14, Jan 1987; AW, KP (c); SL (w); AM, SD, JBy, DGr, JR2, JK, JSt (a); O: Scarlet Witch. O: Quicksilver 1.50
❑15, Feb 1987; O: Wonder Man. O: Hawkeye 1.50
❑16, Mar 1987; AW, KP (c); SL (w); SD, GC, PS, DH, JK, GK, DA (a); O: Frightful Four. O: Dormammu.......................... 1.50
❑17, Apr 1987; AW (c); SL (w); SD, VM, DH, JK, GK, JSt (a); O: Ka-Zar. O: Leader; O: Inhumans 1.50
❑18, May 1987; AM (c); SD, SL (w); SD, DH, JK, JSo, JSt (a); O: S.H.I.E.L.D.... 1.50
❑19, Jun 1987; new Avengers team....... 1.50
❑20, Jul 1987; Thor; Avengers; Fantastic Four; Hulk.. 1.50
❑21, Aug 1987; X-Men.......................... 1.50
❑22, Sep 1987; O: Mary Jane 1.50
❑23, Oct 1987; Inhumans 1.50
❑24, Nov 1987; BL (c); JK, SL (w); JB, JK, JSt (a); O: Galactus 1.50
❑25, Dec 1987; JK, SL (w); JB, JK, JSt (a); O: Silver Surfer; Final Issue 1.50

Marvels Comics: Captain America
Marvel

❑1, Jul 2000... 2.25

Marvels Comics: Daredevil
Marvel

❑1, Jun 2000... 2.25

Marvels Comics: Fantastic Four
Marvel

❑1, May 2000.. 2.25

Marvels Comics: Spider-Man
Marvel

❑1, Jul 2000... 2.25

Marvels Comics: Thor
Marvel

❑1, Jul 2000... 2.25

Marvels Comics: X-Men
Marvel

❑1, Jun 2000... 2.25

Marvel Select Flip Magazine
Marvel

❑1, Jul 2005... 3.99
❑2, Aug 2005 .... 3.99
❑3, Sep 2005 .... 3.99
❑4, Nov 2005; Reprints Astonishing X-Men #4 and New X-Men: Academy X #4 3.99
❑5, Dec 2005; Reprints Astonishing X-Men #5 and New X-Men: Academy X #5; Includes poster 3.99
❑6, Jan 2006; Reprints Astonishing X-Men #6 and New X-Men: Academy X #6; Includes poster 3.99
❑7, Feb 2006, Reprints Astonishing X-Men #7 and New X-Men: Academy X #7; Includes poster 3.99
❑8, Mar 2006, Reprints Astonishing X-Men #8 and New X-Men: Academy X #8; Includes poster 3.99
❑9, Apr 2006, Reprints Astonishing X-Men #9 and New X-Men: Academy X #9; Includes poster 3.99
❑10, May 2006; Reprints Astonishing X-Men #10 and New X-Men: Academy X #10; Includes poster 3.99
❑11, Jun 2006; Reprints Astonishing X-Men #11 and New X-Men: Academy X #11; Includes poster 3.99
❑12, Jul 2006; Reprints Astonishing X-Men #12 and X-Men: Phoenix—Endsong #1; Includes Poster 4.99
❑13, Aug 2006, Reprints X-Men: Deadly Genesis #1, X-Men: Phoenix—Endsong #2, and House of M #2 .... 4.99
❑14, Sep 2006, Reprints X-Men: Deadly Genesis #2, X-Men: Phoenix—Endsong #3, and House of M: #3 .... 4.99
❑15, Oct 2006, Reprints X-Men: Deadly Genesis #3, X-Men: PhoenixóEndsong #4, and House of M #4.......................... 4.99
❑16, Nov 2006; Reprints X-Men: Deadly Genesis #4, X-Men: Phoenix—Endsong #5, and House of M #5; Includes poster 4.99
❑17, Dec 2006; Reprints X-Men: Deadly Genesis #5, New X-Men: Academy X #12, and House of M #6; Includes poster 4.99
❑18, Jan 2007; Reprints X-Men: Deadly Genesis #6 and New X-Men: Academy X #13; Includes poster 4.99
❑19, Feb 2007; Reprints Astonishing X-Men #13, New X-Men: Academy X #14, and House of M #7.......................... 4.99
❑20, Mar 2007 .... 4.99

Marvel Selects: Fantastic Four
Marvel

❑1, Jan 2000; Reprints Fantastic Four (Vol. 1) #107 .... 2.75

Marvel Selects: Spider-Man
Marvel

❑1, Jan 2000; Reprints Amazing Spider-Man #100 .... 2.75
❑2, Feb 2000 .... 2.75
❑3, Mar 2000 .... 2.75

Marvel's Greatest Comics
Marvel

❑23, Oct 1969, Giant-size; Title continued from "Marvel Collector's Item Classics" 15.00
❑24, Dec 1969, Giant-size; Fantastic Four: Fantastic Four #32; Iron Man: Tales of Suspense #66; Tales of the Watcher: Tales of Suspense #58; Dr. Strange: Strange Tales #133........................... 15.00
❑25, Feb 1970, Giant-size 15.00
❑26, Apr 1970, Giant-size; Fantastic Four: Fantastic Four #34; Iron Man: Tales of Suspense #68; Captain America: Tales of Suspense #60; Dr. Strange: Strange Tales #137 .... 15.00
❑27, Jun 1970, Giant-size; Fantastic Four: Fantastic Four #35; Captain America: Tales of Suspense #62; Iron Man: Tales of Suspense #69; Dr. Strange: Strange Tales #138 .... 15.00
❑28, Aug 1970, Giant-size; Fantastic Four: Fantiastic Four #36; Captain America: Tales of Suspense #76; Iron Man: Tales of Suspense #70; Dr. Strange: Strarnge Tales #139.. 15.00
❑29, Dec 1970, Giant-size; Reprints Fantastic Four #12 and 31 .... 15.00
❑30, Mar 1971, Giant-size; Reprints Fantastic Four #37 and 38................. 15.00
❑31, Jun 1971, Giant-size; Reprints Fantastic Four #39 and 40................. 15.00
❑32, Sep 1971, Giant-size; Reprints Fantastic Four #41 and 42 .... 15.00
❑33, Dec 1971, Giant-size; Reprints Fantastic Four #44 and 45 .... 15.00

Marvel Triple Action

Fantastic Four and Avengers reprints
©Marvel

Marvel Two-In-One

The Thing's team-up tour de force
©Marvel

Marvel Universe

Invaders, Monster Hunters massacre series
©Marvel

Marvel Valentine Special

Romance blooms in Marvel universe
©Marvel

Marville

Series ended with Epic invitation
©Marvel

N-MINT

- ❑34, Mar 1972, Giant-size; Reprints Fantastic Four #46 and 47 .... 15.00
- ❑35, Jun 1972, A: Silver Surfer. Reprints Fantastic Four #48 .... 10.00
- ❑36, Jul 1972, Reprints Fantastic Four #49 .... 10.00
- ❑37, Sep 1972, Reprints Fantastic Four #50 .... 10.00
- ❑38, Oct 1972, Reprints Fantastic Four #51 .... 3.50
- ❑39, Nov 1972, Reprints Fantastic Four #52 .... 3.50
- ❑40, Jan 1973, Reprints Fantastic Four #53 .... 3.50
- ❑41, Mar 1973, Reprints Fantastic Four #54 .... 3.50
- ❑42, May 1973, Reprints Fantastic Four #55 .... 3.50
- ❑43, Jul 1973, Reprints Fantastic Four #56 .... 3.50
- ❑44, Sep 1973, Reprints Fantastic Four #61 .... 3.50
- ❑45, Oct 1973, Reprints Fantastic Four #62 .... 3.50
- ❑46, Nov 1973, Reprints Fantastic Four #63 .... 3.50
- ❑47, Jan 1974, Reprints Fantastic Four #64 .... 3.50
- ❑48, Mar 1974, Reprints Fantastic Four #65 .... 3.50
- ❑49, May 1974, Reprints Fantastic Four #66 .... 3.50
- ❑50, Jul 1974, SL (w); JK, JSt (a); A: Warlock (Him). Reprints Fantastic Four #67 .... 4.00
- ❑51, Sep 1974, Reprints Fantastic Four #68 .... 3.00
- ❑52, Oct 1974, Reprints Fantastic Four #69 .... 2.50
- ❑53, Nov 1974, Reprints Fantastic Four #70 .... 2.50
- ❑54, Jan 1975, Reprints Fantastic Four #71 .... 2.50
- ❑55, Mar 1975, Reprints Fantastic Four #73 .... 2.50
- ❑56, May 1975, Reprints Fantastic Four #74 .... 2.50
- ❑57, Jul 1975, Reprints Fantastic Four #75 .... 2.50
- ❑58, Sep 1975, Reprints Fantastic Four #76 .... 2.50
- ❑59, Oct 1975, Reprints Fantastic Four #77 .... 2.50
- ❑60, Nov 1975, Reprints Fantastic Four #78 .... 2.50
- ❑61, Jan 1976, Reprints Fantastic Four #79 .... 2.50
- ❑62, Mar 1976, Reprints Fantastic Four #80 .... 2.50
- ❑63, May 1976, Reprints Fantastic Four #81 .... 2.50
- ❑63/30¢, May 1976, 30¢ regional price variant; Reprints Fantastic Four #81 .... 20.00
- ❑64, Jul 1976, Reprints Fantastic Four #82 .... 2.50
- ❑64/30¢, Jul 1976, 30¢ regional price variant; Reprints Fantastic Four #82 .... 20.00
- ❑65, Sep 1976, Reprints Fantastic Four #83 .... 2.50
- ❑66, Oct 1976, Reprints Fantastic Four #84 .... 2.50

N-MINT

- ❑67, Nov 1976, Reprints Fantastic Four #85 .... 2.50
- ❑68, Jan 1977, Reprints Fantastic Four #86 .... 2.50
- ❑69, Mar 1977, Reprints Fantastic Four #87 .... 2.50
- ❑70, May 1977, Reprints Fantastic Four #88; newsstand edition (distributed by Curtis); issue number in box 2.50
- ❑70/Whitman, May 1977, Reprints Fantastic Four #88; special markets edition (usually sold in Whitman bagged prepacks); price appears in a diamond; UPC barcode appears 2.50
- ❑71, Jul 1977, Reprints Fantastic Four #89; newsstand edition (distributed by Curtis); issue number in box 2.00
- ❑71/Whitman, Jul 1977, Reprints Fantastic Four #89; special markets edition (usually sold in Whitman bagged prepacks); price appears in a diamond; UPC barcode appears 2.00
- ❑71/35¢, Jul 1977, Reprints Fantastic Four #89; 35¢ regional price variant; newsstand edition (distributed by Curtis); issue number in box 15.00
- ❑72, Sep 1977, Reprints Fantastic Four #90; newsstand edition (distributed by Curtis); issue number in box 2.00
- ❑72/Whitman, Sep 1977, Reprints Fantastic Four #90; special markets edition (usually sold in Whitman bagged prepacks); price appears in a diamond; UPC barcode appears 2.00
- ❑72/35¢, Sep 1977, Reprints Fantastic Four #90; 35¢ regional price variant; newsstand edition (distributed by Curtis); issue number in box 15.00
- ❑73, Oct 1977, Reprints Fantastic Four #91; newsstand edition (distributed by Curtis); issue number in box 2.00
- ❑73/Whitman, Oct 1977, Reprints Fantastic Four #91; special markets edition (usually sold in Whitman bagged prepacks); price appears in a diamond; no UPC barcode 2.00
- ❑73/35¢, Oct 1977, Reprints Fantastic Four #91; 35¢ regional price variant; newsstand edition (distributed by Curtis); issue number in box 15.00
- ❑74, Nov 1977, Reprints Fantastic Four #92; newsstand edition (distributed by Curtis); issue number in box 2.00
- ❑74/Whitman, Nov 1977, Reprints Fantastic Four #92; special markets edition (usually sold in Whitman bagged prepacks); price appears in a diamond; no UPC barcode 2.00
- ❑75, Jan 1978, Reprints Fantastic Four #93 .... 2.00
- ❑76, Mar 1978, Reprints Fantastic Four #95 .... 2.00
- ❑77, May 1978, Reprints Fantastic Four #96 .... 2.00
- ❑78, Jul 1978, Reprints Fantastic Four #97 .... 2.00
- ❑79, Sep 1978, Reprints Fantastic Four #98 .... 2.00
- ❑80, Nov 1978, Reprints Fantastic Four #99; newsstand edition (distributed by Curtis); issue number in box 2.00

N-MINT

- ❑80/Whitman, Nov 1978, Reprints Fantastic Four #99; special markets edition (usually sold in Whitman bagged prepacks); price appears in a diamond; no UPC barcode 2.00
- ❑81, Jan 1979, Reprints Fantastic Four #100 .... 2.00
- ❑82, Mar 1979, Reprints Fantastic Four #102 .... 2.00
- ❑83, Dec 1979, Reprints Fantastic Four #103 .... 2.00
- ❑84, Jan 1980, Reprints Fantastic Four #104 .... 2.00
- ❑85, Feb 1980, Reprints Fantastic Four #105 .... 2.00
- ❑86, Mar 1980, Reprints Fantastic Four #116 .... 2.00
- ❑87, Apr 1980, Reprints Fantastic Four #107 .... 2.00
- ❑88, May 1980, Reprints Fantastic Four #108 .... 2.00
- ❑89, Jun 1980, Reprints Fantastic Four #109 .... 2.00
- ❑90, Jul 1980, Reprints Fantastic Four #110 .... 2.00
- ❑91, Aug 1980, Reprints Fantastic Four #111 .... 2.00
- ❑92, Sep 1980, Reprints Fantastic Four #112 .... 2.00
- ❑93, Oct 1980, Reprinted from Fantastic Four #113 .... 2.00
- ❑94, Nov 1980, Reprinted from Fantastic Four #114; Reprinted from Tales to Astonish #40 .... 2.00
- ❑95, Dec 1980, Reprinted from Fantastic Four #115; Reprinted from Tales to Astonish #40; Reprints from Fantastic Four #115, Tales to Astonish #40 .... 2.00
- ❑96, Jan 1981, Reprinted from Fantastic Four #116 (edited to fit into normal-sized issue) 2.00

Marvel's Greatest Comics: Fantastic Four #52
Marvel

- ❑1, Sep 2006 .... 2.99

Marvel: Shadows & Light
Marvel

- ❑1, Feb 1997, b&w; Wolverine, Dracula, Doctor Strange, Captain Marvel; wraparound cover 2.95

Marvel 1602
Marvel

- ❑1, Nov 2003, NG (w) 6.00
- ❑2, Nov 2003, NG (w) 5.00
- ❑3, Dec 2003, NG (w) 6.00
- ❑4, Jan 2004, NG (w) 5.00
- ❑5, Feb 2004, NG (w) 6.00
- ❑6, Mar 2004, NG (w) 5.00
- ❑7, Apr 2004, NG (w) 4.00
- ❑8, Jun 2004, NG (w) 5.00

Marvel 1602: New World
Marvel

- ❑1, Sep 2005 .... 3.50
- ❑2, Oct 2005 .... 3.50
- ❑3, Nov 2005 .... 3.50
- ❑4, Dec 2005 .... 3.50
- ❑5, Jan 2006 .... 3.50

Other grades: Multiply price above by 5/6 for VF/NM • 2/3 for VERY FINE • 1/3 for FINE • 1/5 for VERY GOOD • 1/8 for GOOD

Marvel 1602: Fantastik Four
Marvel

- ❑1, Nov 2006 ... 3.50
- ❑2, Dec 2006 ... 3.50
- ❑3, Jan 2007 ... 3.50
- ❑4, Mar 2007 ... 3.50

Marvel 65th Anniversary Special
Marvel

- ❑1, Sep 2004, reprints stories from Marvel Mystery Comics #8-10 ... 4.99

Marvel Special Edition Featuring Close Encounters of the Third Kind
Marvel

- ❑3, ca. 1978; treasury-sized; adapts Close Encounters of the Third Kind ... 9.00

Marvel Special Edition Featuring Spectacular Spider-Man
Marvel

- ❑1, ca. 1975; treasury-sized; Treasury-sized; Includes pin-up by John Romita; The Sinister Six reprinted from Amazing Spider-Man Ann #1, several pages omitted; Face-to-Face withÒthe Lizard! reprinted from Amazing Spider-Man #6; The Molten Man RegretsÓ! reprinted from Amazing Spider-Man #35, one page omitted ... 12.00

Marvel Special Edition Featuring Star Wars
Marvel

- ❑1, ca. 1977; treasury-sized adaption of Star Wars ... 14.00
- ❑2, ca. 1977; treasury-sized adaption of Star Wars ... 12.00
- ❑3, ca. 1978; treasury-sized; collects previous two issues ... 14.00

Marvel Spectacular
Marvel

- ❑1, Aug 1973, SL (w); JK (a); reprints Thor #128 ... 5.00
- ❑2, Sep 1973, SL (w); JK (a); reprints Thor #129 ... 3.00
- ❑3, Oct 1973, JK (c); SL (w); JK (a); 1: Tana Nile (in real form). reprints Thor #130 ... 3.00
- ❑4, Nov 1973, SL (w); JK (a); reprints Thor #133 ... 3.00
- ❑5, Jan 1974, SL (w); JK (a); reprints Thor #134 ... 3.00
- ❑6, Mar 1974, SL (w); JK (a); reprints Tales of Asgard from Journey Into Mystery #121 and Thor #135 ... 3.00
- ❑7, May 1974; SL (w); JK (a); reprints Thor #136 ... 3.00
- ❑8, Jul 1974; SL (w); JK (a); reprints Thor #137 ... 3.00
- ❑9, Sep 1974; SL (w); JK (a); reprints Thor #138 ... 3.00
- ❑10, Oct 1974; SL (w); JK (a); reprints Thor #139 ... 3.00
- ❑11, Nov 1974; SL (w); JK (a); reprints Thor #140 ... 2.50
- ❑12, Dec 1974; SL (w); JK (a); reprints Thor #141 ... 2.50
- ❑13, Jan 1975; SL (w); JK (a); reprints Thor #142 ... 2.50
- ❑14, Mar 1975; SL (w); JK (a); reprints Thor #143 ... 2.50
- ❑15, Jun 1975; SL (w); JK (a); reprints Thor #144 ... 2.50
- ❑16, Jul 1975; SL (w); JK (a); reprints Thor #145 ... 2.50
- ❑17, Sep 1975; SL (w); JK (a); reprints Thor #146 ... 2.50
- ❑18, Oct 1975; SL (w); JK (a); reprints Thor #147 ... 2.50
- ❑19, Nov 1975; SL (w); JK (a); reprints Thor #148 ... 2.50

Marvel Spotlight
Marvel

- ❑1, Nov 1971, NA (c); NA, WW (a); O: Red Wolf. A: Red Wolf ... 25.00
- ❑2, Feb 1972, NA (c); BEv (w); BEv, FM, MP (a); O: Werewolf. 1: Werewolf; Includes reprint from Venus #16 ... 130.00
- ❑3, May 1972, A: Werewolf ... 30.00
- ❑4, Jun 1972, A: Werewolf ... 30.00
- ❑5, Aug 1972, FM, MP (c); SD, FM, MP (a); 1&O: Ghost Rider I (Johnny Blaze). 1: Zarathos (Ghost Rider's Spirit of Vengeance) ... 275.00
- ❑6, Oct 1972, A: Ghost Rider ... 45.00
- ❑7, Dec 1972, FM (c); FM, MP (a); A: Ghost Rider ... 35.00
- ❑8, Feb 1973, FM, MP, JM (a); A: Ghost Rider ... 25.00
- ❑9, Apr 1973, A: Ghost Rider ... 30.00
- ❑10, Jun 1973, A: Ghost Rider ... 35.00
- ❑11, Aug 1973, A: Ghost Rider ... 22.00
- ❑12, Oct 1973, HT (c); SD, HT (a); 1&O: Son of Satan ... 22.00
- ❑13, Jan 1974, O: Satana. A: Son of Satan ... 12.00
- ❑14, Mar 1974, A: Son of Satan. Marvel Value Stamp #5: Dracula ... 10.00
- ❑15, May 1974, A: Son of Satan. Marvel Value Stamp #21: Kull ... 10.00
- ❑16, Jul 1974, A: Son of Satan. Marvel Value Stamp #83: Dragon Man ... 7.00
- ❑17, Sep 1974, A: Son of Satan. Marvel Value Stamp #45: Mantis ... 7.00
- ❑18, Oct 1974, A: Son of Satan. Marvel Value Stamp #81: Rhino ... 7.00
- ❑19, Dec 1974, A: Son of Satan. Marvel Value Stamp #14: Living Mummy ... 7.00
- ❑20, Feb 1975, A: Son of Satan. Marvel Value Stamp #26: Mephisto ... 5.00
- ❑21, Apr 1975, A: Son of Satan ... 5.00
- ❑22, Jun 1975, A: Ghost Rider. A: Son of Satan ... 6.00
- ❑23, Aug 1975, A: Son of Satan ... 5.00
- ❑24, Oct 1975, A: Son of Satan. Last Son of Satan in Marvel Spotlight ... 5.00
- ❑25, Dec 1975, A: Sinbad. Adaptation of "The Seventh Voyage of Sinbad" movie ... 3.00
- ❑26, Feb 1976, A: Scarecrow (Marvel). Marvel Value Stamp Series B #23 ... 3.00
- ❑27, Apr 1976, A: Sub-Mariner. Marvel Value Stamp Series B #69 ... 3.00
- ❑27/30¢, Apr 1976, 30¢ regional price variant ... 20.00
- ❑28, Jun 1976, A: Moon Knight. 1st solo story for Moon Knight ... 10.00
- ❑28/30¢, Jun 1976, 30¢ regional price variant ... 18.00
- ❑29, Aug 1976, JK (c); JK, DP (a); A: Moon Knight ... 9.00
- ❑29/30¢, Aug 1976, 30¢ regional price variant ... 15.00
- ❑30, Oct 1976, JB (c); JB (a); A: Warriors Three ... 3.00
- ❑31, Dec 1976, HC (c); JSn (w); HC (a); A: Nick Fury ... 3.00
- ❑32, Feb 1977, GK (c); SB, JM (a); O: Spider-Woman I (Jessica Drew). 1: Spider-Woman I (Jessica Drew) ... 50.00
- ❑33, Apr 1977, 1: Devil-Slayer. A: Deathlok ... 3.00

Marvel Spotlight
Marvel

- ❑1, Jul 1979, PB (a); A: Captain Marvel ... 3.00
- ❑2, Sep 1979, FM (c); PB, TD (a); A: Captain Marvel ... 2.00
- ❑3, Nov 1979, AM (c); PB (a); A: Captain Marvel ... 2.00
- ❑4, Jan 1980, SD, FM (c); SD (a); A: Dragon Lord ... 2.00
- ❑5, Mar 1980, FM (c); SD, FM (a); A: Dragon Lord. A: Captain Marvel ... 2.00
- ❑6, May 1980, TS, BSz (a); O: Star-Lord ... 2.00
- ❑7, Jul 1980, BWi (c); TS, FM (a); A: Star-Lord ... 2.00
- ❑8, Sep 1980, FM (c); FM, TD (a); A: Captain Marvel ... 2.00
- ❑9, Nov 1980, SD (c); SD (a); A: Captain Universe ... 2.00
- ❑10, Jan 1981, SD (c); SD, FM (a); A: Captain Universe. 1 page Frank Miller ad for Dr. Strange series which never saw print ... 2.00
- ❑11, Mar 1981, SD (c); SD (a); A: Captain Universe ... 2.00

Marvel Spotlight: Brian Michael Bendis/Mark Bagley
Marvel

- ❑1, Feb 2007 ... 2.99

Marvel Spotlight: Daniel Way/Oliver Coipel
Marvel

- ❑1, Jun 2006 ... 2.99

Marvel Spotlight: David Finch/Roberto Aguirre-Sacasa
Marvel

- ❑1, Jun 2006 ... 2.99

Marvel Spotlight: Ed Brubaker/Billy Tan
Marvel

- ❑1, Nov 2006 ... 2.99

Marvel Spotlight: Heroes Reborn/Onslaught Reborn
Marvel

- ❑1, Jan 2007 ... 2.99

Marvel Spotlight: John Cassaday/Sean McKeever
Marvel

- ❑1, Feb 2006 ... 2.99

Marvel Spotlight: Joss Whedon/ Michael Lark
Marvel

- ❑1, May 2006 ... 2.99

Marvel Spotlight: Mark Millar/Steve McNiven
Marvel

- ❑1, Aug 2006 ... 2.99

Marvel Spotlight: Neil Gaiman/ Salvador Larroca
Marvel

- ❑1, Sep 2006 ... 2.99

Marvel Spotlight: Robert Kirkman/Greg Land
Marvel

- ❑1, Oct 2006 ... 2.99

Marvel Spotlight: Stan Lee/Jack Kirby
Marvel

- ❑1, Nov 2006, ca. 2006 ... 2.99

Marvel Spotlight: Warren Ellis/Jim Cheung
Marvel

- ❑1, Mar 2006 ... 2.99

Marvel Spring Special
Marvel

- ❑1, Nov 1988; Elvira ... 2.50

Marvel Super Action
Marvel

- ❑1, May 1977, JK (c); SL (w); JK (a); reprints Captain America #100; newsstand edition (distributed by Curtis); issue number in box ... 8.00
- ❑1/Whitman, May 1977, JK (a); Special markets edition (usually sold in Whitman bagged prepacks); price appears in a diamond; UPC barcode appears ... 8.00
- ❑2, Jul 1977, JK (c); SL (w); JK (a); Reprints Captain America #101 ... 2.50
- ❑2/35¢, Jul 1977, JK (c); SL (w); JK (a); Reprints Captain America #101; 35¢ regional price variant ... 15.00
- ❑3, Sep 1977, SL (w); JK (a); Reprints Captain America #102; newsstand edition (distributed by Curtis); issue number in box ... 2.50
- ❑3/Whitman, Sep 1977, JK (a); Special markets edition (usually sold in Whitman bagged prepacks); price appears in a diamond; UPC barcode appears ... 2.50
- ❑3/35¢, Sep 1977, 35¢ regional price variant; reprints Captain America #102 ... 15.00
- ❑4, Nov 1977, BEv, SL (w); BEv, JK, RH (a); O: Marvel Boy. Reprints Marvel Boy #1; newsstand edition (distributed by Curtis); issue number in box ... 2.50
- ❑4/Whitman, Nov 1977, JK (a); O: Marvel Boy. Special markets edition (usually sold in Whitman bagged prepacks); price appears in a diamond; no UPC barcode ... 2.50
- ❑5, Jan 1978, SL (w); JK (a); Reprints Captain America #103 ... 2.00
- ❑6, Mar 1978, SL (w); JK (a); Reprints Captain America #104 ... 2.00
- ❑7, Apr 1978, SL (w); JK (a); Reprints Captain America #105 ... 2.00
- ❑8, Jun 1978, SL (w); JK (a); Reprints Captain America #106 ... 2.00
- ❑9, Aug 1978, SL (w); JK (a); Reprints Captain America #107 ... 2.00
- ❑10, Oct 1978, SL (w); JK (a); Reprints Captain America #108; newsstand edition (distributed by Curtis); issue number in box ... 2.00

Mary Poppins

Practically perfect adaptation
©Gold Key

Mask

Toy and cartoon tie-in featured teen drivers
©DC

Mask

Mischevious mayhem made by facial appliance
©Dark Horse

Master of Kung Fu

Shang-Chi fights father's fakery
©Marvel

Masters of the Universe

First comics based on somewhat silly TV show
©DC

N-MINT

❑10/Whitman, Oct 1978, JK (a); Special markets edition (usually sold in Whitman bagged prepacks); price appears in a diamond; no UPC barcode ... 2.00
❑11, Dec 1978, SL (w); JK (a); Reprints Captain America #109; newsstand edition (distributed by Curtis); issue number in box ... 2.00
❑11/Whitman, Dec 1978, JK (a); Special markets edition (usually sold in Whitman bagged prepacks); price appears in a diamond; UPC barcode appears ... 2.00
❑12, Feb 1979, SL (w); JSo (a); A: Hulk. Reprints Captain America #110 ... 2.00
❑13, Apr 1979, JSo (c); SL (w); JSo (a); Reprints Captain America #111 ... 2.00
❑14, Dec 1979, reprints Avengers #55 ... 1.50
❑15, Jan 1980, reprints Avengers #56 ... 1.50
❑16, Feb 1980, reprints Avengers Ann #2 1.50
❑17, Mar 1980, reprints Avengers Ann #2 1.50
❑18, Apr 1980, reprints Avengers #57 ... 1.50
❑19, May 1980, reprints Avengers #58 .. 1.50
❑20, Jun 1980, reprints Avengers #59 ... 1.50
❑21, Jul 1980, reprints Avengers #60 .... 1.50
❑22, Aug 1980, reprints Avengers #61 ... 1.50
❑23, Sep 1980, reprints Avengers #62 ... 1.50
❑24, Oct 1980, reprints Avengers #63 ... 1.50
❑25, Nov 1980, reprints Avengers #64 ... 1.50
❑26, Dec 1980, reprints Avengers #65 ... 1.50
❑27, Jan 1981, reprints Avengers #66 ... 1.50
❑28, Feb 1981, reprints Avengers #67 ... 1.50
❑29, Mar 1981, reprints Avengers #68 ... 1.50
❑30, Apr 1981, reprints Avengers #69 ... 1.50
❑31, May 1981, reprints Avengers #70 .. 1.50
❑32, Jun 1981, reprints Avengers #71 ... 1.50
❑33, Jul 1981, reprints Avengers #72 .... 1.50
❑34, Aug 1981, reprints Avengers #73 ... 1.50
❑35, Sep 1981, reprints Avengers #74 ... 1.50
❑36, Oct 1981, reprints Avengers #75 ... 1.50
❑37, Nov 1981, reprints Avengers #76 ... 1.50

Marvel Super Action
Marvel

❑1, Jan 1976, b&w; O: Dominic Fortune. 1: Mockingbird (as Huntress). 2: Dominic Fortune. Weird World and Punisher stories ... 35.00

Marvel Super Hero Contest of Champions
Marvel

❑1, Jun 1982, BL, JR2 (c); JR2 (a); 1: Shamrock. 1: Le Peregrine. 1: Blitzkrieg. 1: Talisman I. 1: Collective Man. Alpha Flight ... 4.00
❑2, Jul 1982, BL, JR2 (c); JR2 (a); X-Men 3.50
❑3, Aug 1982, AM (c); JR2 (a); X-Men .. 3.50

Marvel Super-Heroes
Marvel

❑12, Dec 1967, 1&O: Captain Marvel. Title continued from "Fantasy Masterpieces"; Captain Marvel original story; reprints. 95.00
❑13, Mar 1968, 1: Carol Danvers. Captain Marvel original story; reprints ... 50.00
❑14, May 1968, BEv, SL (w); BEv, JK, RA (a); A: Spider-Man. Spider-Man original story; reprints 1st Kirby art at Marvel. 75.00
❑15, Jul 1968, BEv, SL (w); GC, BEv, JR (a); Medusa original story; reprints ... 42.00

N-MINT

❑16, Sep 1968, BEv, SL (w); BEv, HT, JR (a); 1&O: Phantom Eagle. Phantom Eagle original story; reprints ... 25.00
❑17, Nov 1968, BEv, SL (w); BEv (a); O: Black Knight III (Dane Whitman). D: Black Knight I (Sir Percy of Scandia). Black Knight original story; reprints All-Winners Squad #21 ... 30.00
❑18, Jan 1969, 1&O: Vance Astro. 1&O: Guardians of the Galaxy. 1: Yondu. 1: Charlie-27. 1: Zarek. Guardians of the Galaxy original story; reprints ... 40.00
❑19, Mar 1969, BEv, SL (w); BEv, GT (a); A: Ka-Zar. Ka-Zar original story; reprints ... 20.00
❑20, May 1969, A: Doctor Doom. Doctor Doom original story; reprints ... 35.00
❑21, Jul 1969, SL (w); JK (a); Reprints Avengers #3 and X-Men #2; new cover from new design ... 12.00
❑22, Sep 1969, SL (w); JO, JK (a); Reprints X-Men #3 and Daredevil #2; new cover based on design from X-Men #3 cover ... 12.00
❑23, Nov 1969, SL (w); JO, JK, TP (a); Reprints X-Men #4 and Daredevil #3; uses cover from X-Men #4, retouched with character moved ... 12.00
❑24, Jan 1970, SL (w); JO, JK, JSt (a); Reprints X-Men #5 and Daredevil #4; uses cover from Daredevil #4, recolored and retouched ... 12.00
❑25, Mar 1970, SD, JK, WW (a); Reprints X-Men #6, Daredevil #5, and Tales to Astonish #60; uses cover from X-Men #6, recolored and retouched ... 12.00
❑26, May 1970, SL (w); SD, JK, WW (a); Reprints X-Men #7, Daredevil #6, and Tales to Astonish #67; new cover adapts parts of Tales to Astonish #67 and Daredevil #6 covers ... 12.00
❑27, Jul 1970, SL (w); JK, WW (a); Reprints X-Men #8, Daredevil #7, and Tales to Astonish #68; new cover from new design ... 12.00
❑28, Oct 1970, SL (w); GC, JCr, WW (a); Reprints Daredevil #8, Tales of Suspense #73 and #74; new cover from new design ... 10.00
❑29, Jan 1971, SL (w); SD, GC, WW (a); Reprints Daredevil #9, Tales of Suspense #75 and #76; new cover from new design ... 10.00
❑30, Apr 1971, SL (w); SD, GC, JR (a); Reprints Daredevil #15, Tales of Suspense #77 and #78; new cover from new design ... 10.00
❑31, Nov 1971, SL (w); SD, GC, JR (a); Reprints Daredevil #19, Tales of Suspense #89 and #90; old cover, recolored with Iron Man added in inset 20.00
❑32, Sep 1972, SB (c); SL (w); GC, JK (a); Reprints from Tales to Astonish begin (#69 and #77); new cover from new design ... 6.00
❑33, Nov 1972, Reprints Tales to Astonish #78; new cover from new design ... 5.00
❑34, Jan 1973, Reprints Tales to Astonish #79; new cover from new design ... 5.00
❑35, Mar 1973, Reprints Tales to Astonish #80; new cover from new design ... 5.00
❑36, May 1973, Reprints Tales to Astonish #81; old cover, recolored ... 5.00

N-MINT

❑37, Jul 1973, Reprints Tales to Astonish #82; old cover, recolored ... 5.00
❑38, Sep 1973, Reprints Tales to Astonish #83; old cover, recolored ... 5.00
❑39, Oct 1973, Reprints Tales to Astonish #84; old cover, recolored ... 4.00
❑40, Nov 1973, Reprints Tales to Astonish #85; old cover, recolored ... 4.00
❑41, Jan 1974, Reprints Tales to Astonish #86; new cover from new design ... 4.00
❑42, Mar 1974, Reprints Tales to Astonish #87; old cover, recolored ... 4.00
❑43, May 1974, Reprints Tales to Astonish #88; new cover based on old design, with Hulk added ... 4.00
❑44, Jul 1974, Reprints Tales to Astonish #89; old cover, recolored ... 4.00
❑45, Sep 1974, Reprints Tales to Astonish #90; new cover from new design ... 4.00
❑46, Oct 1974, Reprints Tales to Astonish #91; old cover, recolored ... 3.00
❑47, Nov 1974, Reprints Tales to Astonish #92; new cover from new design ... 3.00
❑48, Jan 1975, Reprints Tales to Astonish #93; old cover, recolored ... 3.00
❑49, Mar 1975, Reprints Tales to Astonish #94; new cover from new design ... 3.00
❑50, May 1975, Reprints Tales to Astonish #95; new cover based on the original. 3.00
❑51, Jul 1975, Reprints Tales to Astonish #96; new cover from new design ... 3.00
❑52, Sep 1975, Reprints Tales to Astonish #97; old cover, recolored ... 2.50
❑53, Oct 1975, Reprints Tales to Astonish #98; new cover from new design ... 2.50
❑54, Nov 1975, Reprints Tales to Astonish #99; new cover from new design ... 2.50
❑55, Jan 1976, Reprints Tales to Astonish #101; old cover, retouched and recolored ... 2.50
❑56, Mar 1976, Reprints Incredible Hulk #102; new cover, based on original ... 2.50
❑57, May 1976, Reprints Incredible Hulk #103; old cover, recolored ... 2.50
❑57/30¢, May 1976, 30¢ regional price variant; reprints Incredible Hulk #103 20.00
❑58, Jul 1976, Reprints Incredible Hulk #104; old cover, recolored ... 2.50
❑58/30¢, Jul 1976, 30¢ regional price variant; reprints Incredible Hulk #104 20.00
❑59, Sep 1976, Reprints Incredible Hulk #105; old cover, recolored ... 2.50
❑60, Oct 1976, Reprints Incredible Hulk #106; old cover, recolored ... 2.50
❑61, Nov 1976, Reprints Incredible Hulk #107; old cover, partially redrawn ... 2.50
❑62, Jan 1977, Reprints Incredible Hulk #108; old cover, recolored ... 2.50
❑63, Mar 1977, Reprints Incredible Hulk #109; old cover, recolored ... 2.50
❑64, May 1977, Reprints Incredible Hulk #110; old cover, recolored; newsstand edition (distributed by Curtis); issue number in box ... 2.50
❑64/Whitman, May 1977, Special markets edition (usually sold in Whitman bagged prepacks); price appears in a diamond; UPC barcode appears ... 2.50
❑65, Jun 1977, Reprints Incredible Hulk #111; old cover, recolored; newsstand edition (distributed by Curtis); issue number in box ... 2.50

❑65/Whitman, Jun 1977, Special markets edition (usually sold in Whitman bagged prepacks); price appears in a diamond; UPC barcode appears 2.50
❑65/35¢, Jun 1977, 35¢ variant newsstand edition (distributed by Curtis); issue number in box 15.00
❑66, Sep 1977, Reprints Incredible Hulk #112; new cover, based on the original; newsstand edition (distributed by Curtis); issue number in box 2.50
❑66/Whitman, Sep 1977, Special markets edition (usually sold in Whitman bagged prepacks); price appears in a diamond; UPC barcode appears 2.50
❑66/35¢, Sep 1977, 35¢ variant newsstand edition (distributed by Curtis); issue number in box 15.00
❑67, Oct 1977, Reprints Incredible Hulk #113; new cover, based on the original; newsstand edition (distributed by Curtis); issue number in box 2.50
❑67/Whitman, Oct 1977, Special markets edition (usually sold in Whitman bagged prepacks); price appears in a diamond; no UPC barcode 2.50
❑68, Nov 1977, Reprints Incredible Hulk #114; new cover, based on the original 2.50
❑69, Jan 1978, Reprints Incredible Hulk #115; new cover from new design 2.50
❑70, Mar 1978, Reprints Incredible Hulk #116; new cover, based on the original 2.50
❑71, May 1978, Reprints Incredible Hulk #117; new cover, based on the original 2.50
❑72, Jul 1978, Reprints Incredible Hulk #119; new cover, based on the original, also by Trimpe 2.50
❑73, Aug 1978, Reprints Incredible Hulk #120; old cover, recolored 2.50
❑74, Sep 1978, Reprints Incredible Hulk #122; old cover, recolored; newsstand edition (distributed by Curtis); issue number in box 2.50
❑74/Whitman, Sep 1978, Special markets edition (usually sold in Whitman bagged prepacks); price appears in a diamond; UPC barcode appears 2.50
❑75, Oct 1978, Reprints Incredible Hulk #123; new cover from new design; newsstand edition (distributed by Curtis); issue number in box 2.50
❑75/Whitman, Oct 1978, Special markets edition (usually sold in Whitman bagged prepacks); price appears in a diamond; UPC barcode appears 2.50
❑76, Nov 1978, Reprints Incredible Hulk #124; old cover, recolored; newsstand edition (distributed by Curtis); issue number in box 2.50
❑76/Whitman, Nov 1978, Special markets edition (usually sold in Whitman bagged prepacks); price appears in a diamond; no UPC barcode 2.50
❑77, Dec 1978, Reprints Incredible Hulk #125; new cover, based on the original; newsstand edition (distributed by Curtis); issue number in box 2.50
❑77/Whitman, Dec 1978, Special markets edition (usually sold in Whitman bagged prepacks); price appears in a diamond; no UPC barcode 2.50
❑78, Jan 1979, Reprints Incredible Hulk #126; old cover, recolored; newsstand edition (distributed by Curtis); issue number in box 2.50
❑78/Whitman, Jan 1979, Special markets edition (usually sold in Whitman bagged prepacks); price appears in a diamond; no UPC barcode 2.50
❑79, Mar 1979, Reprints Incredible Hulk #127; old cover, recolored 2.50
❑80, May 1979, Reprints Incredible Hulk #128; old cover, recolored; newsstand edition (distributed by Curtis); issue number in box 2.50
❑80/Whitman, May 1979, Special markets edition (usually sold in Whitman bagged prepacks); price appears in a diamond; no UPC barcode 2.50
❑81, Jul 1979, Reprints Incredible Hulk #129; old cover, recolored 2.00
❑82, Aug 1979, Reprints Incredible Hulk #130; new cover from new design 2.00
❑83, Sep 1979, Reprints Incredible Hulk #131; old cover, recolored 2.00
❑84, Oct 1979, Reprints Incredible Hulk #132; old cover, recolored 2.00
❑85, Nov 1979, Reprints Incredible Hulk #133; old cover, recolored 2.00
❑86, Jan 1980, Reprints Incredible Hulk #134; old cover, recolored 2.00
❑87, Mar 1980, Reprints Incredible Hulk #135; old cover, recolored 2.00
❑88, May 1980, Reprints Incredible Hulk #138; old cover, recolored 2.00
❑89, Jul 1980, Reprints Incredible Hulk #139; old cover, recolored 2.00
❑90, Aug 1980, SB (a); Reprints Avengers #88; old cover, recolored 2.00
❑91, Sep 1980, HT (a); Reprints Incredible Hulk #140; old cover, recolored 2.00
❑92, Oct 1980, Reprints Incredible Hulk #141; old cover, recolored 2.00
❑93, Nov 1980, Reprints Incredible Hulk #142; old cover, recolored and relettered 2.00
❑94, Jan 1981, Reprints Incredible Hulk #145; old cover, recolored 2.00
❑95, Mar 1981, Reprints Incredible Hulk #146; new cover, from new design 2.00
❑96, Apr 1981, Reprints Incredible Hulk #147; old cover, recolored 2.00
❑97, May 1981, Reprints Incredible Hulk #148; old cover, recolored 2.00
❑98, Jun 1981, Reprints Incredible Hulk #149; old cover, recolored 2.00
❑99, Jul 1981, Reprints Incredible Hulk #150; old cover, recolored 2.00
❑100, Aug 1981, Reprints Incredible Hulk #151-152; cover from #152, recolored and retouched 2.00
❑101, Sep 1981, Reprints Incredible Hulk #153; old cover, recolored 2.00
❑102, Oct 1981, Reprints Incredible Hulk #154; old cover, horizontally flipped and recolored 2.00
❑103, Nov 1981, Reprints Incredible Hulk #155; old cover, recolored 2.00
❑104, Dec 1981, Reprints Incredible Hulk #156; old cover, recolored 2.00
❑105, Jan 1982, Reprints Incredible Hulk #157; old cover, recolored 2.00
❑Special 1, Oct 1966; SL (w); BEv, JK (a); 1&O: Daredevil. One-shot from 1966; Reprints stories from Avengers #2, Daredevil #1, Marvel Mystery Comics #8; Human Torch meets Sub-Mariner 40.00

Marvel Super-Heroes
Marvel

❑1, May 1990; JLee (c); SD, FH, KP, MGu (a); O: Raptor. Spring Special 3.50
❑2, Jul 1990; Summer Special; Iron Man, Rogue, Falcon, Speeball, Tigra, Daredevil 3.25
❑3, Oct 1990; Fall Special; Captain America, Hulk, Wasp, Blue Shield, Speedball, Captain Marvel 3.25
❑4, Dec 1990; Winter Special; Nick Fury, Daredevil, Spider-Man, Black Knight, Spitfire, Speedball 3.25
❑5, Apr 1991; SD (w); SD (a); Spring Special; Thing, Thor, Dr. Strange, Speedball, She-Hulk 3.25
❑6, Jul 1991; SD (w); RB, SD (a); Summer Special; X-Men, Sabra, Speedball, Power Pack 3.25
❑7, Oct 1991; PD (w); SD (a); Fall Special: X-Men, Shroud, Marvel Boy, Cloak and Dagger 3.25
❑8, Dec 1991; EL (c); SD (w); JSn, SD (a); Winter Special: X-Men, Namor, Iron Man 3.25
❑9, Apr 1992; KB (w); A: Cupid. Spring Special: Iron Man, West Coast Avengers, Thor 3.25
❑10, Jul 1992; Oversized format; A: Sabretooth. Summer Special: Ms. Marvel, Vision & Scarlet Witch, Namor 3.25
❑11, Oct 1992; MGu (a); Fall Special: Giant Man, Ghost Rider, Ms. Marvel... 3.00
❑12, Jan 1993; KB (w); Winter Special: Falcon, Dr. Strange, Iron Man 2.50
❑13, Apr 1993; KB (w); GC, DH (a); Spring Special: All-Iron Man issue 2.75
❑14, Jul 1993; BMc (a); Summer Special: Speedball, Dr. Strange, Iron Man 2.75
❑15, Oct 1993; KP, DH (a); A: Iron Man. A: Thor. Fall Special: Iron Man, Thor, Hulk 2.75

Marvel Super-Heroes Megazine
Marvel

❑1, Oct 1994 2.95
❑2, Nov 1994 2.95
❑3, Dec 1994 2.95
❑4, Jan 1995 2.95
❑5, Feb 1995 2.95
❑6, Mar 1995; O: Iron Man; Final Issue.. 2.95

Marvel Super Heroes Secret Wars
Marvel

❑1, May 1984; MZ (c); MZ (a); 1: Beyonder (voice only). X-Men, Avengers, Fantastic Four in all 4.00
❑2, Jun 1984 MZ (c); MZ (a) 2.00
❑3, Jul 1984; MZ (c); MZ (a); O: Volcana. 1: Volcana 3.00
❑4, Aug 1984 BL (c); BL (a) 4.00
❑5, Sep 1984 BL (c); BL (a) 3.00
❑6, Oct 1984; BL (c); MZ (a); D: Wasp... 4.00
❑7, Nov 1984; BL (c); MZ (a); 1: Spider-Woman II (Julia Carpenter). 3.00
❑8, Dec 1984; MZ (c); MZ (a); O: Spider-Man's black costume. 1: Alien costume (later Venom) 15.00
❑9, Jan 1985 MZ (c); MZ (a) 2.00
❑10, Feb 1985 MZ (c); MZ (a) 2.00
❑11, Mar 1985 MZ (c); MZ (a) 3.00
❑12, Apr 1985; Giant-size; MZ (c); MZ (a); Conclusion 2.00

Marvel Super Hero Island Adventures
Marvel

❑1, Apr 1999; SB (a); Giveaway at Universal Studios Island of Adventure 3.00

Marvel Super Special
Marvel

❑1, Sep 1977; RB, JB, SB (a); O: Kiss (rock group). Kiss; Group mixed drops of their blood into the printer's ink in publicity stunt; title begins as Marvel Comics Super Special 85.00
❑2, Mar 1978; Conan 8.00
❑3, Jun 1978; Close Encounters of the Third Kind 8.00
❑4, Aug 1978; The Beatles 30.00
❑5, Dec 1978; Title changes to Marvel Super Special; Kiss 55.00
❑6, Dec 1978; Jaws 2; #7, Marvel's adaptation of Sgt. Pepper's Lonely Hearts Club Band, was pulled from circulation 7.00
❑8, ca. 1979; Battlestar Galactica; tabloid 8.00
❑9, Feb 1979; Conan 7.00
❑10, Jun 1979; Star-Lord 6.00
❑11, Sep 1979; Warriors of Shadow Realm; Weirdworld 5.00
❑12, Nov 1979; Warriors of Shadow Realm; Weirdworld 5.00
❑13, Jan 1980; Warriors of Shadow Realm; Weirdworld 5.00
❑14, Feb 1980; GC, TP (a); Meteor 5.00
❑15, Mar 1980; Star Trek: The Motion Picture 5.00
❑16, Aug 1980; Empire Strikes Back 7.00
❑17, Nov 1980; Xanadu 3.50
❑18, Sep 1981; Raiders of the Lost Ark . 3.50
❑19, Oct 1981; For Your Eyes Only 3.50
❑20, Oct 1981; Dragonslayer 3.50
❑21, Aug 1982; Conan movie 3.50
❑22, Sep 1982; Comic size; Blade Runner 3.50
❑23, Sep 1982; Annie 3.50
❑24, Mar 1983; Dark Crystal 3.50
❑25, Aug 1983; Comic size; Rock & Rule 3.50
❑26, Sep 1983; Octopussy 3.50
❑27, Sep 1983; BSz (c); AW, TP (a); Return of the Jedi 3.50
❑28, Oct 1983; Krull 3.50
❑29, Jul 1984; Tarzan of the Apes 3.50
❑30, Aug 1984; Indiana Jones and the Temple of Doom 3.50
❑31, Sep 1984; The Last Starfighter 3.50
❑32, Oct 1984; The Muppets Take Manhattan 3.50
❑33, Nov 1984; Buckaroo Banzai 3.50
❑34, Nov 1984; Sheena 3.50
❑35, Dec 1984; Conan the Destroyer 3.50
❑36, Apr 1985; Dune 3.50
❑37, Apr 1985; 2010 3.50
❑38, Nov 1985; Red Sonja 3.50
❑39, Mar 1985; Santa Claus: the Movie . 3.50
❑40, Oct 1986; Labyrinth 3.50
❑41, Nov 1986; Howard the Duck movie adaptation 3.50

Marvel Swimsuit Special
Marvel

❑1, ca. 1992; in Wakanda 4.00
❑2, ca. 1993; on Monster Island 4.50

Masters of the Universe	Maverick	Max the Magnificent	Maxx	'Mazing Man
			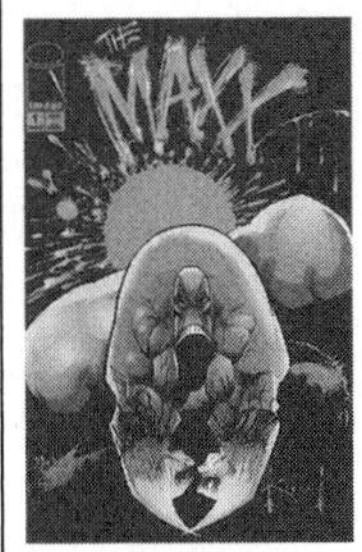	
Marvel's kiddie comics version of TV series ©Marvel	Luck is his companion, gambling is his game ©Dell	Jim Valentino's SF story was never completed ©Slave Labor	It's just not easy being purple ©Image	Cutesy super-hero antics from DC ©DC

N-MINT

❑3, ca. 1994; Oversize 4.50
❑4, ca. 1995; JDu, CR (a) 5.00

Marvel Tails
Marvel

❑1, Nov 1983, 1: Peter Porker 1.50

Marvel Tales
Marvel

❑1, ca. 1964, Giant-size; SL (w); SD, DH, JK (a); O: Iron Man. O: Ant-Man. 1&O: Spider-Man. O: The Hulk. O: Giant-Man. Reprints Amazing Fantasy #15; Listed as Marvel Tales Ann #1 in indicia 175.00
❑2, ca. 1965, Giant-size; O: X-Men. Reprints Uncanny X-Men #1, Incredible Hulk #3, Avengers #1 .... 85.00
❑3, Jul 1966, Giant-size; reprints Amazing Spider-Man #6 .... 45.00
❑4, Sep 1966, Giant-size; SD (a); Reprints Amazing Spider-Man #7 .... 30.00
❑5, Nov 1966, Giant-size; SL (w); SD, JK (a); Reprints Amazing Spider-Man #8 30.00
❑6, Jan 1967, Giant-size; SL (w); SD, JK (a); Reprints Amazing Spider-Man #9 25.00
❑7, Mar 1967, Giant-size; SL (w); SD, JK (a); Reprints Amazing Spider-Man #10 25.00
❑8, May 1967, Giant-size; SD (a); Reprints Amazing Spider-Man #13 .... 25.00
❑9, Jul 1967, Giant-size; SD (a); Reprints Amazing Spider-Man #14 .... 25.00
❑10, Sep 1967, Giant-size; SD (a); Reprints Amazing Spider-Man #15 .... 30.00
❑11, Nov 1967, Giant-size; SL (w); SD, JK, JSt (a); Reprints Amazing Spider-Man #16 .... 25.00
❑12, Jan 1968, Giant-size; SL (w); SD, DH (a); 1: The Trapster (Paste-Pot Pete). Reprints stories from Amazing Spider-Man #17, Strange Tales #110, Tales to Astonish #58, Tales to Astonish #98 .. 25.00
❑13, Mar 1968, Giant-size; SL (w); SD, DH, RH (a); O: Marvel Boy. Reprints Amazing Spider-Man #18 and Marvel Boy #1 .... 25.00
❑14, May 1968, Giant-size; SD (a); Marvel Boy; Reprints Amazing Spider-Man #19 25.00
❑15, Jul 1968, Giant-size; SL (w); SD (a); Marvel Boy; Reprints Amazing Spider-Man #20 .... 25.00
❑16, Sep 1968, Giant-size; SL (w); SD, JK (a); Marvel Boy; Reprints Amazing Spider-Man #21 .... 25.00
❑17, Nov 1968, Giant-size; SD (a); Reprints Amazing Spider-Man #22 .... 20.00
❑18, Jan 1969, Giant-size; SL (w); SD, JK (a); Reprints Amazing Spider-Man #23 20.00
❑19, Mar 1969, Giant-size; SL (w); SD, JK (a); Reprints Amazing Spider-Man #24 20.00
❑20, May 1969, Giant-size; SD, SL (w); SD, JK (a); Reprints Amazing Spider-Man #25 .... 20.00
❑21, Jul 1969, Giant-size; SD, SL (w); SD, JK (a); Reprints Amazing Spider-Man #26 .... 20.00
❑22, Sep 1969, Giant-size; SD, SL (w); SD, JK (a); Reprints Amazing Spider-Man #27 .... 15.00
❑23, Nov 1969, Giant-size 15.00
❑24, Jan 1970, Giant-size; SD (a); Reprints Amazing Spider-Man #31 .... 15.00
❑25, Mar 1970, Giant-size; SL (w); SD, JK (a); Amazing Spider-Man #32 .... 15.00
❑26, May 1970, Giant-size; SD (a); Reprints Amazing Spider-Man #33 .... 15.00
❑27, Jul 1970, Giant-size; SL (w); SD, JK (a); Reprints Amazing Spider-Man #34 15.00
❑28, Oct 1970, Giant-size; SL (w); SD (a); Reprints Amazing Spider-Man #35 and #36 .... 15.00
❑29, Jan 1971, Giant-size; JR (a); O: Green Goblin. Reprints Amazing Spider-Man #39 and #40 .... 15.00
❑30, Apr 1971, Giant-size; SL (w); DH, GT, JR (a); Reprints Amazing Spider-Man #58 and #41; conclusion of Angel back-up from Ka-Zar #3 .... 15.00
❑31, Jul 1971, Giant-size; SL (w); SD, JR (a); Reprints Amazing Spider-Man #37 and #42 .... 15.00
❑32, Nov 1971, Last giant-size issue; SL (w); JR (a); Amazing Spider-Man #43; Amazing Spider-Man #44; Tales of Suspense #83; Last giant-size issue .. 15.00
❑33, Feb 1972, SL (w); JR (a); Reprints Amazing Spider-Man #45 and #47 .... 12.00
❑34, Apr 1972, GK (c); SL (w); JR (a); Reprints Amazing Spider-Man #48 .... 12.00
❑35, Jun 1972, GK (c); SL (w); JR (a); Reprints Amazing Spider-Man #49 .... 12.00
❑36, Aug 1972, SL (w); JR (a); Reprints Amazing Spider-Man #51 .... 12.00
❑37, Sep 1972, SL (w); JR (a); Reprints Amazing Spider-Man #52 .... 12.00
❑38, Oct 1972, SL (w); JR (a); Reprints Amazing Spider-Man #53 .... 12.00
❑39, Nov 1972, SL (w); JR (a); Reprints Amazing Spider-Man #54 .... 12.00
❑40, Dec 1972, SL (w); JR (a); Reprints Amazing Spider-Man #55 .... 12.00
❑41, Feb 1973, JR (a); Reprints Amazing Spider-Man #56 .... 12.00
❑42, Apr 1973, JR (a); Reprints Amazing Spider-Man #59 .... 12.00
❑43, Jun 1973, JR (a); Reprints Amazing Spider-Man #60 .... 12.00
❑44, Aug 1973, Reprints Amazing Spider-Man #61 .... 12.00
❑45, Sep 1973, Reprints Amazing Spider-Man #62 .... 10.00
❑46, Oct 1973, Reprints Amazing Spider-Man #63 .... 10.00
❑47, Nov 1973, Reprints Amazing Spider-Man #64 .... 10.00
❑48, Dec 1973, Reprints Amazing Spider-Man #65 .... 10.00
❑49, Feb 1974, Reprints Amazing Spider-Man #66 .... 10.00
❑50, Apr 1974 .... 10.00
❑51, Jun 1974, Reprints Amazing Spider-Man #68 .... 10.00
❑52, Aug 1974 .... 10.00
❑53, Sep 1974 .... 10.00
❑54, Oct 1974, Reprints Amazing Spider-Man #73 .... 10.00
❑55, Nov 1974, Reprints Amazing Spider-Man #74 .... 10.00
❑56, Dec 1974, Reprints Amazing Spider-Man #75 .... 10.00
❑57, Feb 1975 .... 10.00
❑58, Apr 1975, Reprints Amazing Spider-Man #77 .... 10.00
❑59, Jun 1975, Amazing Spider-Man #78 10.00
❑60, Aug 1975, Amazing Spider-Man #79 10.00
❑61, Sep 1975, Reprints Amazing Spider-Man #80 .... 10.00
❑62, Oct 1975, Reprints Amazing Spider-Man #81 .... 10.00
❑63, Nov 1975 .... 10.00
❑64, Jan 1976, Amazing Spider-Man #83 10.00
❑65, Mar 1976, Amazing Spider-Man #84 10.00
❑66, Apr 1976 .... 10.00
❑66/30¢, Apr 1976, 30¢ regional price variant 20.00
❑67, May 1976, Amazing Spider-Man #86 10.00
❑67/30¢, May 1976, 30¢ regional price variant 20.00
❑68, Jun 1976, Reprints Amazing Spider-Man #87 .... 10.00
❑68/30¢, Jun 1976, 30¢ regional price variant; reprints Amazing Spider-Man #87 .... 20.00
❑69, Jul 1976, Amazing Spider-Man #88 10.00
❑69/30¢, Jul 1976, 30¢ regional price variant 20.00
❑70, Aug 1976, Amazing Spider-Man #89 10.00
❑70/30¢, Aug 1976, 30¢ regional price variant 20.00
❑71, Sep 1976, Amazing Spider-Man #90 10.00
❑72, Oct 1976, Reprints Amazing Spider-Man #91 .... 7.00
❑73, Nov 1976, Reprints Amazing Spider-Man #92 .... 7.00
❑74, Dec 1976, Reprints Amazing Spider-Man #93 .... 7.00
❑75, Jan 1977, Reprints Amazing Spider-Man #94 .... 7.00
❑76, Feb 1977, Amazing Spider-Man #95 7.00
❑77, Mar 1977, Amazing Spider-Man #96 7.00
❑78, Apr 1977, Amazing Spider-Man #97 7.00
❑79, May 1977, Newsstand edition (distributed by Curtis); issue number in box 7.00
❑79/Whitman, May 1977, Special markets edition (usually sold in Whitman bagged prepacks); price appears in a diamond; UPC barcode appears 10.00
❑80, Jun 1977, Newsstand edition (distributed by Curtis); issue number in box 7.00
❑80/Whitman, Jun 1977, Special markets edition (usually sold in Whitman bagged prepacks); price appears in a diamond; UPC barcode appears 10.00
❑80/35¢, Jun 1977, 35¢ regional price variant; newsstand edition (distributed by Curtis); issue number in box 18.00
❑81, Jul 1977, Newsstand edition (distributed by Curtis); issue number in box 7.00
❑81/Whitman, Jul 1977, Special markets edition (usually sold in Whitman bagged prepacks); price appears in a diamond; UPC barcode appears 14.00
❑81/35¢, Jul 1977, 35¢ regional price variant; newsstand edition (distributed by Curtis); issue number in box 15.00
❑82, Aug 1977, Newsstand edition (distributed by Curtis); issue number in box 7.00
❑82/Whitman, Aug 1977, Special markets edition (usually sold in Whitman bagged prepacks); price appears in a diamond; UPC barcode appears 14.00

Other grades: Multiply price above by 5/6 for VF/NM • 2/3 for VERY FINE • 1/3 for FINE • 1/5 for VERY GOOD • 1/8 for GOOD

	N-MINT
❑82/35¢, Aug 1977, 35¢ regional price variant; newsstand edition (distributed by Curtis); issue number in box	15.00
❑83, Sep 1977, Newsstand edition (distributed by Curtis); issue number in box	7.00
❑83/Whitman, Sep 1977, Special markets edition (usually sold in Whitman bagged prepacks); price appears in a diamond; UPC barcode appears	10.00
❑83/35¢, Sep 1977, 35¢ regional price variant; newsstand edition (distributed by Curtis); issue number in box	15.00
❑84, Oct 1977, Newsstand edition (distributed by Curtis); issue number in box	7.00
❑84/Whitman, Oct 1977, Special markets edition (usually sold in Whitman bagged prepacks); price appears in a diamond; no UPC barcode	7.00
❑84/35¢, Oct 1977, 35¢ regional price variant; newsstand edition (distributed by Curtis); issue number in box	15.00
❑85, Nov 1977, Newsstand edition (distributed by Curtis); issue number in box	7.00
❑85/Whitman, Nov 1977, Special markets edition (usually sold in Whitman bagged prepacks); price appears in a diamond; no UPC barcode	7.00
❑86, Dec 1977, Amazing Spider-Man #107	5.00
❑87, Jan 1978, Amazing Spider-Man #108	5.00
❑88, Feb 1978, Amazing Spider-Man #109	5.00
❑89, Mar 1978, Amazing Spider-Man #110	5.00
❑90, Apr 1978, Amazing Spider-Man #111	5.00
❑91, May 1978, Newsstand edition (distributed by Curtis); issue number in box	5.00
❑91/Whitman, May 1978, Special markets edition (usually sold in Whitman bagged prepacks); price appears in a diamond; no UPC barcode	5.00
❑92, Jun 1978, Reprints Amazing Spider-Man #113	5.00
❑93, Jul 1978, Amazing Spider-Man #114	5.00
❑94, Aug 1978, Newsstand edition (distributed by Curtis); issue number in box	5.00
❑94/Whitman, Aug 1978, Special markets edition (usually sold in Whitman bagged prepacks); price appears in a diamond; UPC barcode appears	5.00
❑95, Sep 1978, Newsstand edition (distributed by Curtis); issue number in box	5.00
❑95/Whitman, Sep 1978, Special markets edition (usually sold in Whitman bagged prepacks); price appears in a diamond; UPC barcode appears	5.00
❑96, Oct 1978, Newsstand edition (distributed by Curtis); issue number in box	5.00
❑96/Whitman, Oct 1978, Special markets edition (usually sold in Whitman bagged prepacks); price appears in a diamond; no UPC barcode	5.00
❑97, Nov 1978, Newsstand edition (distributed by Curtis); issue number in box	5.00
❑97/Whitman, Nov 1978, Special markets edition (usually sold in Whitman bagged prepacks); price appears in a diamond; no UPC barcode	5.00
❑98, Dec 1978, D: Gwen Stacy. Newsstand edition (distributed by Curtis); issue number in box	5.00
❑98/Whitman, Dec 1978, D: Gwen Stacy. Special markets edition (usually sold in Whitman bagged prepacks); price appears in a diamond; UPC barcode appears	5.00
❑99, Jan 1979, D: Green Goblin. Newsstand edition (distributed by Curtis); issue number in box	5.00
❑99/Whitman, Jan 1979, D: Green Goblin. Special markets edition (usually sold in Whitman bagged prepacks); price appears in a diamond; no UPC barcode	5.00
❑100, Feb 1979, MN, SD, GK, JR, TD (a); Amazing Spider-Man #123; Hawkeye and Two-Gun Kid	5.00
❑101, Mar 1979, Reprints Amazing Spider-Man #124; Man-Wolf	5.00
❑102, Apr 1979, Amazing Spider-Man #125	5.00
❑103, May 1979, Reprints Amazing Spider-Man #126	5.00
❑104, Jun 1979, Reprints Amazing Spider-Man #127	5.00
❑105, Jul 1979, Reprints Amazing Spider-Man #128	5.00
❑106, Aug 1979, 1: Punisher. 1: Jackal. Reprints Amazing Spider-Man #129	5.00
❑107, Sep 1979, Reprints Amazing Spider-Man #130	5.00
❑108, Oct 1979, Reprints Amazing Spider-Man #131	5.00
❑109, Nov 1979, Reprints Amazing Spider-Man #132	5.00
❑110, Dec 1979, Reprints Amazing Spider-Man #133	5.00
❑111, Jan 1980, Punisher	5.00
❑112, Feb 1980, Punisher	5.00
❑113, Mar 1980, Reprints Amazing Spider-Man #136	5.00
❑114, Apr 1980, Reprints Amazing Spider-Man #137	5.00
❑115, May 1980, Amazing Spider-Man #138; Reprints Amazing Spider-Man #138	5.00
❑116, Jun 1980, Reprints Amazing Spider-Man #139	5.00
❑117, Jul 1980, Reprints Amazing Spider-Man #140	5.00
❑118, Aug 1980, Reprints Amazing Spider-Man #141	5.00
❑119, Sep 1980, Reprints Amazing Spider-Man #142	5.00
❑120, Oct 1980, Reprints Amazing Spider-Man #143	5.00
❑121, Nov 1980, Reprints Amazing Spider-Man #144 and Sub-Mariner (Vol. 1) #35	5.00
❑122, Dec 1980, Reprints Amazing Spider-Man #145	5.00
❑123, Jan 1981, Reprints Amazing Spider-Man #146	4.00
❑124, Feb 1981, Reprints Amazing Spider-Man #147	4.00
❑125, Mar 1981, Reprints Amazing Spider-Man #148	4.00
❑126, Apr 1981, Reprints Amazing Spider-Man #149; Reprints Thor #150	4.00
❑127, May 1981, Reprints Amazing Spider-Man #150; Reprints Thor #157	4.00
❑128, Jun 1981, Reprints Amazing Spider-Man #151	4.00
❑129, Jul 1981, Reprints Amazing Spider-Man #152	4.00
❑130, Aug 1981, Reprints Amazing Spider-Man #153	4.00
❑131, Sep 1981, Reprints Amazing Spider-Man #154; Captain Britain	4.00
❑132, Oct 1981, Reprints Amazing Spider-Man #155; Captain Britain	4.00
❑133, Nov 1981, Reprints Amazing Spider-Man #156; Captain Britain	4.00
❑134, Dec 1981, Reprints Amazing Spider-Man #157; Dr. Strange: Strange Tales #110; Reprints from Amazing Spider-Man #157, Strange Tales #110	4.00
❑135, Jan 1982, Amazing Spider-Man #158; Dr. Strange: Strange Tales #111	4.00
❑136, Feb 1982, Amazing Spider-Man #159; Dr. Strange: Strange Tales #114	4.00
❑137, Mar 1982, O: Spider-Man. 1: Spider-Man. Reprints Amazing Fantasy #15	7.00
❑138, Apr 1982, Reprints Amazing Spider-Man #1	5.00
❑139, May 1982, Reprints Amazing Spider-Man #2	5.00
❑140, Jun 1982, Reprints Amazing Spider-Man #3	5.00
❑141, Jul 1982, Reprints Amazing Spider-Man #4	5.00
❑142, Aug 1982, Reprints Amazing Spider-Man #5	5.00
❑143, Sep 1982, Reprints Amazing Spider-Man #6	5.00
❑144, Oct 1982, Reprints Amazing Spider-Man #7	5.00
❑145, Nov 1982, Amazing Spider-Man #8	4.00
❑146, Dec 1982, Amazing Spider-Man #9	4.00
❑147, Jan 1983, Amazing Spider-Man #10	4.00
❑148, Feb 1983, Reprints Amazing Spider-Man #11	4.00
❑149, Mar 1983, Amazing Spider-Man #12	4.00
❑150, Apr 1983, Giant-size; Reprints Amazing Spider-Man Ann #1	4.00
❑151, May 1983, Amazing Spider-Man #13	4.00
❑152, Jun 1983, Amazing Spider-Man #14	4.00
❑153, Jul 1983, Amazing Spider-Man #15	4.00
❑154, Aug 1983, Amazing Spider-Man #16	4.00
❑155, Sep 1983, Amazing Spider-Man #17	4.00
❑156, Oct 1983, Amazing Spider-Man #18	4.00
❑157, Nov 1983, Amazing Spider-Man #19	4.00
❑158, Dec 1983, Amazing Spider-Man #20	4.00
❑159, Jan 1984, Amazing Spider-Man #21	4.00
❑160, Feb 1984, Amazing Spider-Man #22	4.00
❑161, Mar 1984, Amazing Spider-Man #23	4.00
❑162, Apr 1984, Reprints Amazing Spider-Man #24	4.00
❑163, May 1984, Reprints Amazing Spider-Man #25	4.00
❑164, Jun 1984, Reprints Amazing Spider-Man #26	4.00
❑165, Jul 1984, Reprints Amazing Spider-Man #27	4.00
❑166, Aug 1984, Amazing Spider-Man #28	4.00
❑167, Sep 1984, Amazing Spider-Man Ann #2	4.00
❑168, Oct 1984, Amazing Spider-Man #29	4.00
❑169, Nov 1984, Reprints Amazing Spider-Man #30	4.00
❑170, Dec 1984, Amazing Spider-Man #31	4.00
❑171, Jan 1985, Amazing Spider-Man #32	4.00
❑172, Feb 1985, Amazing Spider-Man #33	4.00
❑173, Mar 1985, Amazing Spider-Man #34	4.00
❑174, Apr 1985, Amazing Spider-Man #35	4.00
❑175, May 1985, Amazing Spider-Man #36	4.00
❑176, Jun 1985, Reprints Amazing Spider-Man #37	4.00
❑177, Jul 1985, Reprints Amazing Spider-Man #38	4.00
❑178, Aug 1985, Amazing Spider-Man #39	4.00
❑179, Sep 1985, Amazing Spider-Man #40	4.00
❑180, Oct 1985, Amazing Spider-Man #41	4.00
❑181, Nov 1985, Amazing Spider-Man Ann #3	4.00
❑182, Dec 1985, Amazing Spider-Man #42	4.00
❑183, Jan 1986, Amazing Spider-Man #43	4.00
❑184, Feb 1986, Amazing Spider-Man #44	2.00
❑185, Mar 1986, Amazing Spider-Man #45	2.00
❑186, Apr 1986, Reprints Amazing Spider-Man #46	2.00
❑187, May 1986, Reprints Amazing Spider-Man #47	2.00
❑188, Jun 1986, Reprints Amazing Spider-Man #48	2.00
❑189, Jul 1986, Reprints Amazing Spider-Man #49	2.00
❑190, Aug 1986, Reprints Amazing Spider-Man #50	2.00
❑191, Sep 1986, Reprints Amazing Spider-Man 96,97,98	2.00
❑192, Oct 1986, Giant-size; Reprints Amazing Spider-Man #121-122	3.00
❑193, Nov 1986, Reprints Marvel Team-Up #59	2.00
❑194, Dec 1986, Reprints Marvel Team-Up #60	2.00
❑195, Jan 1987, Reprints Marvel Team-Up #61	2.00
❑196, Feb 1987, Reprints Marvel Team-Up #62	2.00
❑197, Mar 1987, Reprints Marvel Team-Up #63	2.00

Other grades: Multiply price above by 5/6 for VF/NM • 2/3 for VERY FINE • 1/3 for FINE • 1/5 for VERY GOOD • 1/8 for GOOD

Mega Dragon & Tiger

Life after the asteroids devastate the earth

©Image

Megaton

Holiday Special had first mention Image series

©Megaton

Megaton Man

Don Simpson's super-hero parody

©Kitchen Sink

Mekanix

One of Marvel's less successful toy comics

©Marvel

Men in Black

Nearly forgotten comic later spawns movies

©Aircel

N-MINT

❑198, Apr 1987, Reprints Marvel Team-Up #64; ...and the Daughters of the Dragon ... 2.00
❑199, May 1987, Reprints Marvel Team-Up #56 ... 2.00
❑200, Jun 1987, Giant-size; TMc, FM (c); FM (a); Reprints Amazing Spider-Man Ann #14 ... 2.00
❑201, Jul 1987, TMc (c); JBy (a); Reprints Marvel Team-Up #65 ... 1.50
❑202, Aug 1987, TMc (c); JBy (a); Reprints Marvel Team-Up #66; Spider-Ham ... 1.50
❑203, Sep 1987, TMc (c); JBy (a); Reprints Marvel Team-Up #67; Spider-Ham ... 1.50
❑204, Oct 1987, TMc (c); JBy, BWi (a); Reprints Marvel Team-Up #68; Spider-Ham ... 1.50
❑205, Nov 1987, TMc, DC (c); JBy (a); Reprints Marvel Team-Up #69 ... 1.50
❑206, Dec 1987, TMc (c); JBy (a); Reprints Marvel Team-Up #70 ... 1.50
❑207, Jan 1988, TMc (c); JBy (a); Reprints Marvel Team-Up #75 ... 1.50
❑208, Feb 1988, TMc (c) ... 1.50
❑209, Mar 1988, TMc (c); 1: Punisher. 1: Jackal. Reprints Amazing Spider-Man #129 ... 2.00
❑210, Apr 1988, TMc (c); RA (a); A: Punisher. Reprints Amazing Spider-Man #134 ... 2.00
❑211, May 1988, TMc (c); A: Punisher ... 1.50
❑212, Jun 1988, TMc (c); A: Punisher ... 1.50
❑213, Jul 1988, TMc (c); A: Punisher ... 1.50
❑214, Aug 1988, TMc (c); A: Punisher ... 1.50
❑215, Sep 1988, TMc (c); A: Punisher ... 1.50
❑216, Oct 1988, TMc (c); FH (w); FH, RA (a); A: Punisher. Reprints Amazing Spider-Man #174; Spider-Ham ... 1.50
❑217, Nov 1988, TMc (c); FH (w); FH, RA (a); A: Punisher. Reprints Amazing Spider-Man #175; Spider-Ham ... 1.50
❑218, Dec 1988, TMc (c); KP (a); A: Punisher. Reprints Amazing Spider-Man #201; Spider-Ham ... 1.50
❑219, Jan 1989, TMc (c); KP (a); A: Punisher. Reprints Amazing Spider-Man #202; Spider-Ham ... 1.50
❑220, Feb 1989, TMc (c); AM (a); A: Punisher. Reprints Spectacular Spider-Man #81 ... 1.50
❑221, Mar 1989, TMc (c); AM (a); A: Punisher. Reprints Spectacular Spider-Man #82 ... 1.50
❑222, Apr 1989, TMc (c); A: Punisher. Reprints Spectacular Spider-Man #83 ... 1.50
❑223, May 1989, TMc (c); SL (w); TMc, JR (a); Reprints Amazing Spider-Man #88; Spider-Ham ... 1.50
❑224, Jun 1989, TMc (c); FH, SL (w); FH, TMc, GK (a); Reprints Amazing Spider-Man #89; Spider-Ham ... 1.50
❑225, Jul 1989, TMc (c); FH, SL (w); FH, TMc, GK (a); Reprints Amazing Spider-Man #90; D: Captain Stacy; Spider-Ham ... 1.50
❑226, Aug 1989, TMc (c); FH, SL (w); FH, TMc, GK (a); Reprints Amazing Spider-Man #91; Spider-Ham ... 1.50
❑227, Sep 1989, TMc (c); SL (w); TMc, GK (a); Reprints Amazing Spider-Man #92; Spider-Ham ... 1.50

N-MINT

❑228, Oct 1989, TMc (c); SB, TMc (a); Reprints Spectacular Spider-Man #17; Angel apperance; Spider-Ham ... 1.50
❑229, Nov 1989, TMc (c); SB, TMc (a); Reprints SpectacularSpider-Man #18; Spider-Ham ... 1.50
❑230, Nov 1989, TMc (c); TMc (a) ... 1.50
❑231, Dec 1989, TMc (c); TMc, HT (a) ... 1.50
❑232, Dec 1989, TMc (c); TMc (a) ... 1.50
❑233, Jan 1990, TMc (c); TMc (a); Spider-Ham ... 1.50
❑234, Feb 1990, TMc (c); TMc, GK (a) ... 1.50
❑235, Mar 1990, TMc (c); TMc (a) ... 1.50
❑236, Apr 1990, TMc (c); TMc (a) ... 1.50
❑237, May 1990, TMc (c); TMc (a); Reprints Marvel Team-Up #150 ... 1.50
❑238, Jun 1990, TMc (c); TMc (a) ... 1.50
❑239, Jul 1990, TMc (c); TMc (a) ... 1.50
❑240, Aug 1990 ... 1.50
❑241, Sep 1990, Reprints Marvel Team-Up #124 ... 1.50
❑242, Oct 1990 ... 1.50
❑243, Nov 1990, Reprints Marvel Team-Up #117; Spider-Man & Wolverine ... 1.50
❑244, Dec 1990 ... 1.50
❑245, Jan 1991, Reprints Marvel Team-Up #135; V: Morlocks; Spider-Man & Kitty Pryde ... 1.50
❑246, Feb 1991, Reprints Marvel Team-Up #149 ... 1.50
❑247, Mar 1991, Reprints Marvel Team-Up Ann #6 ... 1.50
❑248, Apr 1991, Reprints Marvel Team-Up Ann #6 ... 1.50
❑249, May 1991, GK (a); Reprints Marvel Team-Up #14 ... 1.50
❑250, Jun 1991, Giant-size; FM (c); FM (a); O: Storm. Reprints Marvel Team-Up #100 ... 1.50
❑251, Jul 1991, MR (c); SL (w); GK (a); Reprints Amazing Spider-Man #100 ... 1.50
❑252, Aug 1991, MR (c); GK, SL (w); GK (a); 1: Morbius. Reprints Amazing Spider-Man #101 ... 1.50
❑253, Sep 1991, Giant-size; GK, SL (w); GK (a); O: Morbius. Reprints Amazing Spider-Man #102 ... 1.50
❑254, Oct 1991, RA (a); A: Ghost Rider. Reprints Marvel Team-Up #15 ... 1.50
❑255, Nov 1991, SB (a); Reprints Marvel Team-Up #58 ... 1.50
❑256, Dec 1991, PB (a); A: Ghost Rider. Reprints Marvel Team-Up #91 ... 1.50
❑257, Jan 1992, JR2, JR (a); Reprints Amazing Spider-Man #238 ... 1.50
❑258, Feb 1992, JR2 (a); Reprints Amazing Spider-Man #239 ... 1.50
❑259, Mar 1992, JR2 (a); Reprints Amazing Spider-Man #249 ... 1.50
❑260, Apr 1992, JR2, KJ (a); Reprints Amazing Spider-Man #250 ... 1.50
❑261, May 1992, KJ (a); Reprints Amazing Spider-Man #251 ... 1.50
❑262, Jun 1992, JBy (a); A: X-Men ... 1.50
❑263, Jul 1992, JBy (a); O: Woodgod ... 1.50
❑264, Aug 1992, SL (w); reprints Amazing Spider-Man Ann #5 ... 1.50
❑265, Sep 1992, reprints Amazing Spider-Man Ann #6 ... 1.50
❑266, Oct 1992, Reprints Amazing Spider-Man #252 ... 1.50

N-MINT

❑267, Nov 1992, Reprints Amazing Spider-Man #253 ... 1.50
❑268, Dec 1992, Reprints Amazing Spider-Man #254 ... 1.50
❑269, Jan 1993, Reprints Amazing Spider-Man #255 ... 1.50
❑270, Feb 1993, Reprints Amazing Spider-Man #256; 1: Puma ... 1.50
❑271, Mar 1993, Reprints Amazing Spider-Man #257 ... 1.50
❑272, Apr 1993, Reprints Amazing Spider-Man #258 ... 1.50
❑273, May 1993, Reprints Amazing Spider-Man #259 ... 1.50
❑274, Jun 1993, Reprints Amazing Spider-Man #260 ... 1.50
❑275, Jul 1993, Reprints Amazing Spider-Man #261 ... 1.50
❑276, Aug 1993, A: Spider-Kid. Reprints Amazing Spider-Man #263 ... 1.50
❑277, Sep 1993, 1: Silver Sable. Reprints Amazing Spider-Man #265 ... 1.50
❑278, Oct 1993, A: Kingpin. A: Beyonder. Reprints Amazing Spider-Man #268 ... 1.50
❑279, Nov 1993, A: Firelord. Reprints Amazing Spider-Man #269 ... 1.50
❑280, Dec 1993, Reprints Amazing Spider-Man #270 ... 1.50
❑281, Jan 1994, Reprints Amazing Spider-Man #271 ... 1.50
❑282, Feb 1994, SB (a); Reprints Amazing Spider-Man #272 ... 1.50
❑283, Mar 1994, double-sized; O: Spider-Man. Reprints Amazing Spider-Man #275; Hobgoblin story ... 1.50
❑284, Apr 1994, A: Hobgoblin. D: Fly. Reprints Amazing Spider-Man #276 ... 1.50
❑285, May 1994, Reprints Amazing Spider-Man #277 ... 1.50
❑286, Jun 1994, PD (a); D: Wraith. Reprints Amazing Spider-Man #278 ... 1.50
❑286/CS, Jun 1994, PD (a); Collector's Set;Reprints Amazing Spider-Man #278 ... 2.95
❑286/2nd, Jun 1994, Collector's set; Includes animation cel, 16 page preview ... 2.95
❑287, Jul 1994, Jack O'Lantern cover/story; Reprints Amazing Spider-Man #279 ... 1.50
❑288, Aug 1994, Reprints Amazing Spider-Man #280 ... 1.50
❑289, Sep 1994, A: Jack O'Lantern. Reprints Amazing Spider-Man #281 ... 1.50
❑290, Oct 1994, A: X-Factor. Reprints Amazing Spider-Man #282 ... 1.50
❑291, Nov 1994, BL (a); Amazing Spider-Man #283 ... 1.50

Marvel Tales Flip Magazine
Marvel

❑1, Sep 2005 ... 3.99
❑2, Oct 2005 ... 3.99
❑3, Nov 2005 ... 3.99
❑4, Dec 2005 ... 3.99
❑6, Jan 2006 ... 3.99
❑7, Mar 2006, Reprints Spider-Man 9/11 issue and Runaways #1; Includes poster ... 3.99
❑8, Mar 2006, Includes poster ... 3.99
❑9, May 2006; Includes poster ... 3.99
❑10, Jun 2006; Includes poster ... 3.99

Other grades: Multiply price above by 5/6 for VF/NM • 2/3 for VERY FINE • 1/3 for FINE • 1/5 for VERY GOOD • 1/8 for GOOD

	N-MINT
❑11, Jul 2006; Includes poster	4.99
❑12, Aug 2006	4.99
❑13, Sep 2006, Reprints Amazing Spider-Man #42, Runaways #7, House of M #3	4.99
❑15, Oct 2006, Reprints Amazing Spider-Man #44, Runaways #9, and House of M #5	4.99
❑16, Nov 2006, Reprints Amazing Spider-Man #45, Runaways #10, and House of M #6; Poster Included	4.99
❑17, Jan 2007; Reprints Amazing Spider-Man #46 and Runaways #11; Includes poster	4.99
❑18, Feb 2007; Reprints Amazing Spider-Man #47, Runaways #12 and Hosue of M #7; Includes poster	4.99
❑19, Mar 2007	4.99

Marvel Team-Up
Marvel

	N-MINT
❑1, Mar 1972, GK (c); RA (a); 1: Misty Knight. V: Sandman. Spider-Man; Human Torch	185.00
❑2, May 1972, GK (c); RA, JM (a); A: Human Torch. Spider-Man; Human Torch	30.00
❑3, Jul 1972, GK (c); RA (a); A: Morbius. Spider-Man; Human Torch	25.00
❑4, Sep 1972, GK (c); GK (a); A: Morbius. Spider-Man; X-Men	45.00
❑5, Nov 1972, GK (c); GK (a); 1: Ballox (The Monstroid). Spider-Man; Vision	18.00
❑6, Jan 1973, GK (c); GK (a); O: Puppet Master. Spider-Man; Thing	16.00
❑7, Mar 1973, GK (c); RA, JM (a); 1: Kryllk the Cruel. Spider-Man; Thor	16.00
❑8, Apr 1973, JM (a); 1: The Man-Killer. Spider-Man; The Cat	16.00
❑9, May 1973, GK, JR (c); RA (a); A: Iron Man. Spider-Man; Iron Man	16.00
❑10, Jun 1973, JR (c); JM (a); A: Human Torch. Spider-Man; Human Torch	16.00
❑11, Jul 1973, JR (c); JM (a); A: The Inhumans. Spider-Man; Inhumans	13.00
❑12, Aug 1973, GK (c); DP, RA (a); 1: Moondark. Spider-Man; Werewolf	18.00
❑13, Sep 1973, GK (c); GK (a); A: Captain America. Spider-Man; Captain America	13.00
❑14, Oct 1973, GK (c); GK, WH (a); 1: The Aquanoids. Spider-Man; Sub-Mariner	13.00
❑15, Nov 1973, GK, JR (c); DP, RA (a); 1&O: Orb. Spider-Man; Ghost Rider	13.00
❑16, Dec 1973, JR (c); GK, JM (a); 1&O: The Basilisk I (Basil Elks). Spider-Man; Captain Marvel	13.00
❑17, Jan 1974, GK (c); GK (a); V: Basilisk. V: Mole Man. Spider-Man; Mr. Fantastic	13.00
❑18, Feb 1974, GK (a); A: The Hulk. Human Torch; Hulk	13.00
❑19, Mar 1974, GK (c); GK (a); 1: Stegron, the Dinosaur Man. Spider-Man; Ka-Zar; Marvel Value Stamp #90: Hercules	13.00
❑20, Apr 1974, GK, JR (c); SB (a); A: Black Panther. Spider-Man; Black Panther; Marvel Value Stamp #25: Torch	13.00
❑21, May 1974, GK (c); SB (a); A: Doctor Strange. Spider-Man; Doctor Strange; Marvel Value Stamp #33: Invisible Girl	8.00
❑22, Jun 1974, JR (c); SB (a); A: Hawkeye. Spider-Man; Hawkeye; Marvel Value Stamp #92: Byrrah	8.00
❑23, Jul 1974, GK (c); GK (a); A: X-Men. Human Torch; Iceman; X-Men; Marvel Value Stamp #28: Hawkeye	8.00
❑24, Aug 1974, GK, JR (c); JM (a); A: Brother Voodoo. Spider-Man; Brother Voodoo; Marvel Value Stamp #90: Hercules	8.00
❑25, Sep 1974, GK (c); JM (a); A: Daredevil. Spider-Man; Daredevil; Marvel Value Stamp #87: J. Jonah Jameson	8.00
❑26, Oct 1974, GK (c); JM (a); A: Thor. Human Torch; Thor; Marvel Value Stamp #56: Rawhide Kid	8.00
❑27, Nov 1974, JSn (c); JM (a); A: The Hulk. Spider-Man; Hulk; Marvel Value Stamp #68: Son of Satan	8.00
❑28, Dec 1974, GK (c); JM (a); A: Hercules. Spider-Man; Hercules; Marvel Value Stamp #43: Enchantress	8.00
❑29, Jan 1975, JR (c); JM (a); A: Iron Man. Human Torch; Iron Man; Marvel Value Stamp #11: Deathlok	8.00
❑30, Feb 1975, GK (c); JM (a); A: Falcon. Spider-Man; The Falcon; Marvel Value Stamp #89: Hammerhead	8.00
❑31, Mar 1975, GK (c); JM (a); A: Iron Fist. Spider-Man; Iron Fist	8.00
❑32, Apr 1975, GK (c); SB (a); A: Son of Satan. Human Torch; Son of Satan	5.00
❑33, May 1975, GK (c); SB (a); V: Meteor Man. Spider-Man; Nighthawk; Marvel Value Stamp #84: Dr. Doom	5.00
❑34, Jun 1975, GK (c); SB (a); V: Meteor Man. Spider-Man; Valkyrie	5.00
❑35, Jul 1975, GK (c); SB (a); A: Human Torch. A: Doctor Strange. Human Torch; Doctor Strange	5.00
❑36, Aug 1975, JR (c); SB (a); A: Frankenstein. Spider-Man; Frankenstein	5.00
❑37, Sep 1975, SB (a); A: Man-Wolf. Spider-Man; Man-Wolf	5.00
❑38, Oct 1975, SB (a); A: Beast. Spider-Man; Beast	5.00
❑39, Nov 1975, SB (a); A: Human Torch. Spider-Man; Human Torch; Marvel Value Stamp #87: J. Jonah Jameson	5.00
❑40, Dec 1975, SB (a); A: Sons of the Tiger. Spider-Man; Sons of Tiger; Human Torch	5.00
❑41, Jan 1976, GK (c); SB (a); A: Scarlet Witch. Spider-Man; Scarlet Witch	5.00
❑42, Feb 1976, SB (a); A: Vision. Spider-Man; Scarlet Witch; Vision	5.00
❑43, Mar 1976, GK (c); SB (a); A: Doctor Doom. Spider-Man; Doctor Doom	5.00
❑44, Apr 1976, GK (c); SB (a); A: Moondragon. Spider-Man; Moondragon	5.00
❑44/30¢, Apr 1976, A: Moondragon. Spider-Man; Moondragon	20.00
❑45, May 1976, GK (c); SB (a); A: Killraven. Spider-Man; Killraven	5.00
❑45/30¢, May 1976, A: Killraven. Spider-Man; Killraven	20.00
❑46, Jun 1976, RB (c); SB (a); A: Deathlok. Spider-Man; Deathlok	5.00
❑46/30¢, Jun 1976, A: Deathlok. Spider-Man; Deathlok	20.00
❑47, Jul 1976, GK (c); V: Basilisk. Spider-Man; Thing	3.50
❑47/30¢, Jul 1976, V: Basilisk. Spider-Man; Thing	20.00
❑48, Aug 1976, JR (c); SB (a); 1: Wraith. Spider-Man; Iron Man	3.50
❑48/30¢, Aug 1976, 1: Wraith. Spider-Man; Iron Man	20.00
❑49, Sep 1976, JR (c); SB (a); O: Wraith. Spider-Man; Iron Man; Doctor Strange	3.50
❑50, Oct 1976, GK (c); SB (w); SB (a); A: Iron Man. Spider-Man; Doctor Strange; Iron Man	3.50
❑51, Nov 1976, GK (c); SB (a); A: Iron Man. Spider-Man; Iron Man	3.50
❑52, Dec 1976, SB (a); A: Batroc. Spider-Man; Captain America	3.50
❑53, Jan 1977, DC (c); JBy (a); A: X-Men. A: Woodgod. Spider-Man; Hulk; Woodgod; X-Men; 1st John Byrne art on X-Men	15.00
❑54, Feb 1977, GK (c); JBy (a); A: Woodgod. Spider-Man; Hulk; newsstand edition (distributed by Curtis); issue number in box	4.00
❑54/Whitman, Feb 1977, GK (c); JBy (a); A: Woodgod. Special markets edition (usually sold in Whitman bagged prepacks); price appears in a diamond; UPC barcode appears	4.00
❑55, Mar 1977, DC (c); JBy (a); 1: Gardener. V: Gardener. Spider-Man; Warlock; newsstand edition (distributed by Curtis); issue number in box	4.00
❑55/Whitman, Mar 1977, DC (c); JBy (a); 1: Gardener. V: Gardener. Special markets edition (usually sold in Whitman bagged prepacks); price appears in a diamond; UPC barcode appears	4.00
❑56, Apr 1977, JR2, JR (c); SB (a); V: Blizzard. V: Electro. Spider-Man; Daredevil; newsstand edition (distributed by Curtis); issue number in box	4.00
❑56/Whitman, Apr 1977, JR2 (c); SB (a); V: Blizzard. V: Electro. Special markets edition (usually sold in Whitman bagged prepacks); price appears in a diamond; UPC barcode appears	4.00
❑57, May 1977, DC (c); SB (a); A: Black Widow. Spider-Man; Black Widow; newsstand edition (distributed by Curtis); issue number in box	4.00
❑57/Whitman, May 1977, DC (c); SB (a); A: Black Widow. Special markets edition (usually sold in Whitman bagged prepacks); price appears in a diamond; UPC barcode appears	4.00
❑58, Jun 1977, AM (c); SB (a); A: Ghost Rider. Spider-Man; Ghost Rider; newsstand edition (distributed by Curtis); issue number in box	4.00
❑58/Whitman, Jun 1977, AM (c); SB (a); A: Ghost Rider. Special markets edition (usually sold in Whitman bagged prepacks); price appears in a diamond; UPC barcode appears	4.00
❑58/35¢, Jun 1977, AM (c); SB (a); A: Ghost Rider. 35¢ regional price variant newsstand edition (distributed by Curtis); issue number in box; Spider-Man; Ghost Rider	15.00
❑59, Jul 1977, DC (c); JBy (a); A: Wasp. Spider-Man; Yellowjacket; The Wasp; newsstand edition (distributed by Curtis); issue number in box	4.00
❑59/Whitman, Jul 1977, DC (c); JBy (a); A: Wasp. Special markets edition (usually sold in Whitman bagged prepacks); price appears in a diamond; UPC barcode appears	4.00
❑59/35¢, Jul 1977, DC (c); JBy (a); A: Wasp. 35¢ regional price variant newsstand edition (distributed by Curtis); issue number in box; Spider-Man; Yellowjacket; The Wasp	15.00
❑60, Aug 1977, AM (c); JBy (a); A: Yellowjacket. Spider-Man; The Wasp; newsstand edition (distributed by Curtis); issue number in box	4.00
❑60/Whitman, Aug 1977, AM (c); JBy (a); A: Yellowjacket. Special markets edition (usually sold in Whitman bagged prepacks); price appears in a diamond; UPC barcode appears	4.00
❑60/35¢, Aug 1977, AM (c); JBy (a); A: Yellowjacket. 35¢ regional price variant newsstand edition (distributed by Curtis); issue number in box; Spider-Man; The Wasp	15.00
❑61, Sep 1977, RA (c); JBy (a); V: Super-Skrull. Spider-Man; Human Torch; newsstand edition (distributed by Curtis); issue number in box	4.00
❑61/Whitman, Sep 1977, RA (c); JBy (a); V: Super-Skrull. Special markets edition (usually sold in Whitman bagged prepacks); price appears in a diamond; no UPC barcode	4.00
❑61/35¢, Sep 1977, RA (c); JBy (a); V: Super-Skrull. 35¢ regional price variant newsstand edition (distributed by Curtis); issue number in box; Spider-Man; Human Torch	15.00
❑62, Oct 1977, GK (c); JBy (a); V: Super-Skrull. Spider-Man; Ms. Marvel; newsstand edition (distributed by Curtis); issue number in box	4.00
❑62/Whitman, Oct 1977, GK (c); JBy (a); V: Super-Skrull. Special markets edition (usually sold in Whitman bagged prepacks); price appears in a diamond; no UPC barcode	4.00
❑62/35¢, Oct 1977, GK (c); JBy (a); V: Super-Skrull. 35¢ regional price variant newsstand edition (distributed by Curtis); issue number in box; Spider-Man; Ms. Marvel	15.00
❑63, Nov 1977, DC (c); JBy (a); A: Iron Fist. Spider-Man; Iron Fist; newsstand edition (distributed by Curtis); issue number in box	4.00
❑63/Whitman, Nov 1977, DC (c); JBy (a); A: Iron Fist. Special markets edition (usually sold in Whitman bagged prepacks); price appears in a diamond; no UPC barcode	4.00
❑64, Dec 1977, DC (c); JBy (a); A: Daughters of Dragon. Spider-Man; Daughters of Dragon; newsstand edition (distributed by Curtis); issue number in box	4.00
❑64/Whitman, Dec 1977, DC (c); JBy (a); A: Daughters of Dragon. Special markets edition (usually sold in Whitman bagged prepacks); price appears in a diamond; UPC barcode appears	4.00

Other grades: Multiply price above by 5/6 for VF/NM • 2/3 for VERY FINE • 1/3 for FINE • 1/5 for VERY GOOD • 1/8 for GOOD

Men of War

War series focused on good writing
©DC

Meridian

One of four CrossGen flagship titles
©CrossGen

Merlin

Early years in the life of the fabled magician.
©Adventure

Metal Men

Robots from the Magnus that didn't fight robots
©DC

Metamorpho

Man becomes freak, but he's not bitter
©DC

	N-MINT
❑65, Jan 1978, GP (c); JBy (a); 1: Arcade. 1: Captain Britain (U.S.). Spider-Man; Captain Britain	4.00
❑66, Feb 1978, JBy (a); V: Arcade. Spider-Man; Captain Britain	7.00
❑67, Mar 1978, JBy (a); A: Tigra. V: Kraven. Spider-Man; Tigra	4.00
❑68, Apr 1978, JBy (c); JBy (a); 1: D'Spayre. A: Man-Thing. Spider-Man; Man-Thing	4.00
❑69, May 1978, DC (c); JBy (a); A: Havok. Spider-Man; Havok; newsstand edition (distributed by Curtis); issue number in box	4.00
❑69/Whitman, May 1978, DC (c); JBy (a); A: Havok. Special markets edition (usually sold in Whitman bagged prepacks); price appears in a diamond; no UPC barcode	4.00
❑70, Jun 1978, JBy (a); V: Living Monolith. Spider-Man; Thor	4.00
❑71, Jul 1978, A: The Falcon. Spider-Man; The Falcon	4.00
❑72, Aug 1978, JBy (c); JM (a); A: Iron Man. Spider-Man; Iron Man; newsstand edition (distributed by Curtis); issue number in box	4.00
❑72/Whitman, Aug 1978, JBy (c); JM (a); A: Iron Man. Special markets edition (usually sold in Whitman bagged prepacks); price appears in a diamond; UPC barcode appears	4.00
❑73, Sep 1978, KP (c); KGa (a); A: Daredevil. Spider-Man; Daredevil; newsstand edition (distributed by Curtis); issue number in box	4.00
❑73/Whitman, Sep 1978, KP (c); A: Daredevil. Special markets edition (usually sold in Whitman bagged prepacks); price appears in a diamond; no UPC barcode	4.00
❑74, Oct 1978, DC (c); BH (a); A: Not Ready For Prime Time Players (Saturday Night Live). Spider-Man; The Not-Ready-For-Prime-Time-Players (SNL)	4.00
❑75, Nov 1978, BH (c); JBy (a); A: Power Man. Spider-Man; Power Man; newsstand edition (distributed by Curtis); issue number in box	4.00
❑75/Whitman, Nov 1978, BH (c); JBy (a); A: Power Man. Special markets edition (usually sold in Whitman bagged prepacks); price appears in a diamond; no UPC barcode	4.00
❑76, Dec 1978, JBy (c); HC (a); A: Doctor Strange. Spider-Man; Doctor Strange; newsstand edition (distributed by Curtis); issue number in box	4.00
❑76/Whitman, Dec 1978, JBy (c); HC (a); A: Doctor Strange. Special markets edition (usually sold in Whitman bagged prepacks); price appears in a diamond; no UPC barcode	4.00
❑77, Jan 1979, JR2 (c); HC (a); A: Ms. Marvel. Spider-Man; Ms. Marvel; newsstand edition (distributed by Curtis); issue number in box	4.00
❑77/Whitman, Jan 1979, JR2 (c); HC (a); A: Ms. Marvel. Special markets edition (usually sold in Whitman bagged prepacks); price appears in a diamond; no UPC barcode	4.00
❑78, Feb 1979, AM (c); DP (a); A: Wonder Man. Spider-Man; Wonder Man; newsstand edition (distributed by Curtis); issue number in box	4.00
❑78/Whitman, Feb 1979, AM (c); DP (a); A: Wonder Man. Special markets edition (usually sold in Whitman bagged prepacks); price appears in a diamond; no UPC barcode	4.00
❑79, Mar 1979, JBy (c); JBy (a); A: Red Sonja. Spider-Man; Red Sonja	4.00
❑80, Apr 1979, RB (c); A: Clea. Spider-Man; Doctor Strange; Clea	4.00
❑81, May 1979, AM (c); D: Satana. Spider-Man; Satana; newsstand edition (distributed by Curtis); issue number in box	4.00
❑81/Whitman, May 1979, AM (c); D: Satana. Special markets edition (usually sold in Whitman bagged prepacks); price appears in a diamond; no UPC barcode	4.00
❑82, Jun 1979, RB (c); SB (a); A: Black Widow. Spider-Man; Black Widow	4.00
❑83, Jul 1979, RB (c); SB (a); A: Nick Fury. Spider-Man; Nick Fury	4.00
❑84, Aug 1979, SB (a); A: Shang-Chi. Spider-Man; Shang-Chi	4.00
❑85, Sep 1979, AM (c); SB (a); A: Nick Fury. Spider-Man; Shang-Chi; Nick Fury; Black Widow	4.00
❑86, Oct 1979, BMc (c); BMc (a); A: Guardians of the Galaxy. Spider-Man; Guardians of Galaxy	4.00
❑87, Nov 1979, AM (c); GC (a); 1: Hellrazor. Spider-Man; Black Panther	4.00
❑88, Dec 1979, RB (c); SB (a); A: Invisible Girl. Spider-Man; Invisible Girl	4.00
❑89, Jan 1980, RB (c); MN, RB (a); 1: Cutthroat. Spider-Man; Nightcrawler	4.00
❑90, Feb 1980, AM (c); A: Beast. Spider-Man; Beast	4.00
❑91, Mar 1980, RB (c); PB (a); A: Ghost Rider. Spider-Man; Ghost Rider	4.00
❑92, Apr 1980, AM (c); CI (a); 1: Mister Fear IV (Alan Fagan). Spider-Man; Hawkeye	4.00
❑93, May 1980, DP (c); TS, CI (a); A: Werewolf. Spider-Man; Werewolf by Night	4.00
❑94, Jun 1980, AM (c); MZ (a); A: The Shroud. Spider-Man; Shroud	4.00
❑95, Jul 1980, FM (c); FM (a); 1: Mockingbird. 1: Huntress as Mockingbird. Spider-Man	3.00
❑96, Aug 1980, A: Howard the Duck. Spider-Man; Howard the Duck	3.00
❑97, Sep 1980, CI (a); A: Spider-Woman. Hulk; Spider-Woman	3.00
❑98, Oct 1980, AM (c); A: Black Widow. Spider-Man; Black Widow	3.00
❑99, Nov 1980, FM (c); FM (a); A: Machine Man. Spider-Man; Machine Man	3.00
❑100, Dec 1980, double-sized; FM (c); JBy, FM (w); JBy, FM (a); O: Karma. O: Storm. 1: Karma. Spider-Man; Fantastic Four; Black Panther	6.00
❑101, Jan 1981, SD (a); A: Nighthawk. Spider-Man; Nighthawk	3.00
❑102, Feb 1981, FM (c); FS (a); A: Doctor Samson. Spider-Man; Doc Samson	3.00
❑103, Mar 1981, A: Ant-Man. Spider-Man; Ant-Man	3.00
❑104, Apr 1981, AM (c); A: The Hulk. Hulk; Ka-Zar	3.00
❑105, May 1981, AM (c); CI (a); A: Power Man and Iron Fist. Power Man; Iron Fist; Hulk	3.00
❑106, Jun 1981, FM (c); HT (a); V: Scorpion. Spider-Man; Captain America	3.00
❑107, Jul 1981, HT (a); A: She-Hulk. Spider-Man; She-Hulk	3.00
❑108, Aug 1981, HT (c); HT (a); A: Paladin. Spider-Man; Paladin	3.00
❑109, Sep 1981, JR2 (c); HT (a); A: Dazzler. Spider-Man; Dazzler	3.00
❑110, Oct 1981, BL (c); HT (w); HT (a); A: Iron Man. Spider-Man; Iron Man	3.00
❑111, Nov 1981, HT (a); A: Devil-Slayer. Spider-Man; Devil-Slayer	3.00
❑112, Dec 1981, JSe (c); HT (a); A: King Kull. Spider-Man; King Kull	3.00
❑113, Jan 1982, A: Quasar. Spider-Man; Quasar	3.00
❑114, Feb 1982, A: The Falcon. Spider-Man; The Falcon	3.00
❑115, Mar 1982, A: Thor. Spider-Man; Thor	3.00
❑116, Apr 1982, A: Valkyrie. Spider-Man; Valkyrie	3.00
❑117, May 1982, 1: Professor Power. Spider-Man; Wolverine	3.00
❑118, Jun 1982, JR2 (c); HT (a); O: Professor Power. Spider-Man; Professor X	3.00
❑119, Jul 1982, KGa (c); KGa (a); A: Gargoyle. Spider-Man; Gargoyle	3.00
❑120, Aug 1982, KGa (c); KGa (a); A: Dominic Fortune. Spider-Man; Dominic Fortune	3.00
❑121, Sep 1982, KGa (a); 1: Frog-Man II. Spider-Man; Human Torch	3.00
❑122, Oct 1982, KGa (a); A: Man-Thing. Man-Thing	3.00
❑123, Nov 1982, KGa (a); A: Daredevil. Man-Thing; Daredevil	3.00
❑124, Dec 1982, KGa (a); O: Professor Power. Spider-Man; The Beast	3.00
❑125, Jan 1983, JR2 (c); KGa (a); A: Tigra. Spider-Man; Tigra	3.00
❑126, Feb 1983, JR2 (c); BH (a); A: Son of Satan. Spider-Man; Hulk; Power Man; Son of Satan	3.00
❑127, Mar 1983, KGa (a); A: The Watcher. Spider-Man; The Watcher	3.00
❑128, Apr 1983, KGa (a); A: Captain America. Spider-Man; Captain America	3.00
❑129, May 1983, KGa (a); A: Vision. Spider-Man; Vision; The Vision	3.00
❑130, Jun 1983, JR2 (c); SB (a); A: Scarlet Witch. Spider-Man; Scarlet Witch; The Scarlet Witch	3.00
❑131, Jul 1983, PS (c); KGa (a); A: Frogman. Spider-Man; Frogman	3.00
❑132, Aug 1983, A: Mr. Fantastic. Spider-Man; Mr. Fantastic	3.00
❑133, Sep 1983, JBy (c); SB (a); A: Fantastic Four. Spider-Man; Fantastic Four	3.00
❑134, Oct 1983, A: Jack of Hearts. Spider-Man; Jack of Hearts	3.00
❑135, Nov 1983, A: Kitty Pryde. Spider-Man; Kitty Pryde	3.00
❑136, Dec 1983, PS (c); A: Wonder Man. Spider-Man; Wonder Man	3.00

Other grades: Multiply price above by 5/6 for VF/NM • 2/3 for VERY FINE • 1/3 for FINE • 1/5 for VERY GOOD • 1/8 for GOOD

❑137, Jan 1984, O: Doctor Faustus. Spider-Man; Aunt May; Franklin Richards; Assistant Editor's Month..... 4.00
❑138, Feb 1984, AM (c); A: Sandman. Spider-Man; Sandman (Marvel); Nick Fury 3.00
❑139, Mar 1984, A: Nick Fury. Spider-Man; Sandman (Marvel); Nick Fury 3.00
❑140, Apr 1984, A: Black Widow. Spider-Man; Black Widow..... 3.00
❑141, May 1984, A: Daredevil. Spider-Man new costume; Daredevil 3.00
❑142, Jun 1984, A: Captain Marvel. Spider-Man; Captain Marvel (female, new) 3.00
❑143, Jul 1984, A: Starfox. Spider-Man; Starfox..... 3.00
❑144, Aug 1984, A: Moon Knight. Spider-Man; Moon Knight..... 4.00
❑145, Sep 1984, A: Iron Man. Spider-Man; Iron Man..... 3.00
❑146, Oct 1984, A: Nomad. Spider-Man; Nomad..... 3.00
❑147, Nov 1984, A: Human Torch. Spider-Man; Human Torch..... 3.00
❑148, Dec 1984, A: Thor. Spider-Man; Thor..... 3.00
❑149, Jan 1985, A: Cannonball. Spider-Man; Cannonball..... 3.00
❑150, Feb 1985, Giant-size; A: the X-Men. Spider-Man; X-Men..... 3.00
❑Ann 1, ca. 1976, DC (c); SB (a); Spider-Man; X-Men..... 30.00
❑Ann 2, ca. 1979, AM (c); SB (a); Spider-Man; Hulk..... 6.00
❑Ann 3, ca. 1980, FM (c); HT, FM (a); Hulk; Power Man; Iron Fist; Machine Man... 4.00
❑Ann 4, ca. 1981, FM (c); FM (w); HT, FM (a); Spider-Man; Iron Fist; Power Man; Daredevil; Moon Knight..... 3.00
❑Ann 5, Nov 1981, Spider-Man; Thing; Scarlet Witch; Vision; Quasar 2.50
❑Ann 6, Oct 1983, New Mutants; Cloak & Dagger..... 2.50
❑Ann 7, Oct 1984, Alpha Flight 2.00

Marvel Team-Up
Marvel

❑1, Sep 1997; gatefold summary; Spider-Man; Generation X; Story takes place before Generation X #32..... 2.00
❑2, Oct 1997; gatefold summary; AM (a); Spider-Man; Hercules..... 2.00
❑3, Nov 1997; gatefold summary; A: Silver Sable. Spider-Man; Sandman 2.00
❑4, Dec 1997; gatefold summary; Spider-Man; Man-Thing..... 2.00
❑5, Jan 1998; A: Authority. V: Authority. Spider-Man..... 2.00
❑6, Feb 1998; A: Wrecking Crew. V: Wrecking Crew. Spider-Man; Sub-Mariner..... 2.00
❑7, Mar 1998; Spider-Man; Blade 2.00
❑8, Apr 1998; Sub-Mariner; Doctor Strange..... 2.00
❑9, May 1998; Sub-Mariner; Captain America..... 2.00
❑10, Jun 1998; Sub-Mariner; Thing..... 2.00
❑11, Jul 1998; A: Wrecking Crew. V: Wrecking Crew. Sub-Mariner; Iron Man..... 2.00

Marvel Team-Up
Marvel

❑1, Dec 2004..... 2.25
❑2, Jan 2005..... 2.25
❑3, Feb 2005..... 2.25
❑4, Mar 2005; Iron Man and The Hulk... 2.25
❑5, Apr 2005; Spider-Man; X-23..... 2.25
❑6, May 2005; Captain America; Black Widow..... 2.25
❑7, Jun 2005; Spider-Man; Moon Knight 2.25
❑8, Jul 2005..... 2.25
❑9, Aug 2005..... 2.99
❑10, Sep 2005..... 2.99
❑11, Oct 2005, Triptych cover; Giant image forms with Marvel Team-Up (3rd series) #12 & #13..... 2.99
❑12, Nov 2005, Triptych cover; Giant image forms with Marvel Team-Up (3rd series) #11 & #13..... 2.99
❑13, Dec 2005, Triptych cover; Giant image forms with Marvel Team-Up (3rd series) #11 & #12..... 2.99
❑14, Jan 2006, Invincible (Image Comics) appearance..... 2.99
❑15, Feb 2006..... 2.99
❑16, Mar 2006..... 2.99
❑17, Mar 2006..... 2.99
❑18, May 2006..... 2.99
❑19, Jun 2006, Wolverine & Cable..... 2.99
❑20, Jul 2006..... 2.99
❑21, Aug 2006..... 2.99
❑22, Sep 2006..... 2.99
❑23, Oct 2006..... 2.99
❑24, Nov 2006..... 2.99
❑25, Dec 2006, Final Issue..... 2.99

Marvel: The Lost Generation
Marvel

❑12, Mar 2000; JBy (w); JBy (a); #1 in sequence..... 2.99
❑11, Apr 2000; JBy (w); JBy (a); #2 in sequence..... 2.99
❑10, May 2000; JBy (w); AM, JBy (a); #3 in sequence..... 2.99
❑9, Jun 2000; JBy (w); JBy (a); #4 in sequence..... 2.99
❑8, Jul 2000; JBy (w); JBy (a); #5 in sequence..... 2.99
❑7, Aug 2000; JBy (c); JBy (w); JBy (a); A: Fantastic Four. A: Sub-Mariner. #6 in sequence..... 2.99
❑6, Sep 2000; JBy (w); JBy (a); #7 in sequence..... 2.99
❑5, Oct 2000; JBy (w); JBy (a); A: Venus. A: Thor. A: Odin. #8 in sequence..... 2.99
❑4, Nov 2000; JBy (w); JBy (a); #9 in sequence..... 2.99
❑3, Dec 2000; JBy (w); JBy (a); A: Yellow Claw. A: Sub-Mariner. #10 in sequence 2.99
❑2, Jan 2001; JBy (w); JBy (a); #11 in sequence..... 2.99
❑1, Feb 2001; JBy (w); JBy (a); #12 in sequence..... 2.95

Marvel Treasury Edition
Marvel

❑1, ca. 1974; SL (w); SD, BEv, JK, GK, JR, RA (a); The Spectacular Spider-Man .. 15.00
❑2, Dec 1974; JR (c); SL (w); JK, JSt (a); 1: Galactus. 1: The Silver Surfer. A: Sub-Mariner. The Fabulous Fantastic Four; Reprints early Fantastic Four issues... 10.00
❑3, ca. 1974; JR (c); SL (w); JB, JK (a); V: Hercules. The Mighty Thor; reprints Thor #125-130..... 10.00
❑4, ca. 1975; SB (a); Conan..... 10.00
❑5, ca. 1975; SL (w); JSn, HT, JSe, JSt, DA (a); reprints Hulk #3, 139, 141, Tales to Astonish #79, 100, and Marvel Feature #11..... 10.00
❑6, ca. 1975; SL (w); SD, GC, FB, BEv, DA (a); O: The Ancient One. Doctor Strange 10.00
❑7, ca. 1975; Avengers..... 10.00
❑8, Hol 1975; SL (w); SD, GC, HT, GT, FS (a); Giant Super-Hero Holiday Grab Bag; The Incredible Hulk #147, Luke Cage, Hero for Hire #7..... 10.00
❑9, ca. 1976; JB, SL (w); JB, JK (a); Giant Superhero Team-up; Reprints Prince Namor, the Sub-Mariner #8, Journey into Mystery #112, Silver Surfer (Vol. 1) #14, Daredevil #43; Namor vs. Human-Torch; Daredevil vs. Captain America; Thor vs. Hulk; Silver Surfer vs. Spider-Man..... 10.00
❑10, ca. 1976; SL (w); JK (a); The Mighty Thor; Reprints Thor #154-157 ..... 10.00
❑11, ca. 1976; SL (w); FF, JK, JSt (a); Fantastic Four..... 10.00
❑12, ca. 1976; Reprints Howard the Duck #1, Giant-Size Man-Thing #4, 5, with new Defenders story; FB, VM, SB, TP, KJ (a); Howard the Duck..... 10.00
❑13, ca. 1976; Giant Super-Hero Holiday Grab-Bag..... 10.00
❑14, ca. 1977; Amazing Spider-Man; reprints Amazing Spider-Man #100-102 and Not Brand Echh #6 ..... 10.00
❑15, ca. 1977; JB, FT, DG, NA, GK (a); Conan; Red Sonja..... 10.00
❑16, ca. 1977; Defenders..... 10.00
❑17, ca. 1978; SB, HT, JSe (a); The Incredible Hulk; Reprints The Incredible Hulk #121, 134, 150..... 10.00
❑18, ca. 1978; Spider-Man; X-Men..... 10.00
❑19, ca. 1978; Conan..... 10.00
❑20 1979; Hulk; reprints Incredible Hulk #136, 137, 143, 144; pin-up gallery... 10.00
❑21, ca. 1979; SL (w); JB, FF (a); Fantastic Four..... 10.00
❑22, ca. 1979; Spider-Man 10.00
❑23, ca. 1979; Conan; newsstand edition (distributed by Curtis); issue number in box..... 10.00
❑23/Whitman, ca. 1979; Conan; special markets edition; price appears in a diamond; UPC barcode appears 10.00
❑24 1979; Incredible Hulk; reprints Incredible Hulk #167-170; Wolverine and Hercules new back-up story; newsstand edition (distributed by Curtis); issue number in box..... 10.00
❑24/Whitman 1979; Incredible Hulk; special markets edition; price appears in a diamond; UPC barcode appears .. 10.00
❑25, ca. 1980; Spider-Man and Hulk at Winter Olympics..... 10.00
❑26, ca. 1980; Hulk; Wolverine; Hercules 12.00
❑27, ca. 1980; Marvel Team-Up; reprints MTU #9-11 and 27; new Angel story.. 10.00
❑28, Jul 1981; A: Wonder Woman. A: Hulk. V: Parasite. V: Doctor Doom. Spider-Man and Superman..... 25.00

Marvel Treasury of Oz
Marvel

❑1, ca. 1975; adapts Baum's Land of Oz 15.00

Marvel Treasury Special Featuring Captain America's Bicentennial Battles
Marvel

❑1, ca. 1976; JK (c); JK (w); JK (a); Captain America's Bicentennial Battles 16.00

Marvel Treasury Special, Giant Superhero Holiday Grab-Bag
Marvel

❑1, ca. 1974; JB (c); SL (w); GC, BEv, JK, WW, RA (a); Giant Super-Hero Holiday Grab Bag; reprints Marvel Team-Up #1, Fantastic Four #25-26, Daredevil #7, and Amazing Adventures..... 10.00

Marvel Triple Action
Marvel

❑1, Feb 1972, SL (w); JK, JSt (a); reprints Fantastic Four #55 and #57..... 20.00
❑2, Apr 1972, SL (w); JK, JSt (a); reprints Fantastic Four #58..... 12.00
❑3, Jun 1972, SL (w); JK, JSt (a); reprints Fantastic Four #59..... 12.00
❑4, Aug 1972, SL (w); JK, JSt (a); reprints Fantastic Four #60..... 12.00
❑5, Sep 1972, Avengers #10..... 12.00
❑6, Oct 1972, SL (w); DH (a) 8.00
❑7, Nov 1972, Avengers #13..... 8.00
❑8, Jan 1973, Avengers #14..... 8.00
❑9, Feb 1973, Avengers #15..... 8.00
❑10, Apr 1973, Avengers #16..... 8.00
❑11, Jun 1973, Avengers #17..... 8.00
❑12, Aug 1973, Avengers #18..... 8.00
❑13, Sep 1973, Avengers #19..... 8.00
❑14, Oct 1973, SL (w); DH (a); Reprints Avengers #20..... 8.00
❑15, Nov 1973, Avengers #21..... 8.00
❑16, Jan 1974, Avengers #22..... 8.00
❑17, Mar 1974, Avengers #23..... 8.00
❑18, May 1974, Avengers #24..... 8.00
❑19, Jul 1974, Avengers #25..... 8.00
❑20, Sep 1974, Avengers #26..... 8.00
❑21, Oct 1974, Avengers #27 ..... 8.00
❑22, Nov 1974, SL (w); DH (a); reprints Avengers #28..... 8.00
❑23, Jan 1975, Avengers #29..... 8.00
❑24, Mar 1975, Avengers #30..... 8.00
❑25, Sep 1975, Avengers #33..... 8.00
❑26, Nov 1975, Avengers #34; Reprints Avengers #34..... 8.00
❑27, Jan 1976, Reprint Avengers #35; Reprints Avengers #35..... 8.00
❑28, Mar 1976, Reprint Avengers #36; Reprints Avengers #36..... 8.00
❑29, May 1976, Avengers #37..... 8.00
❑29/30¢, May 1976, 30¢ regional price variant..... 20.00
❑30, Jul 1976, Avengers #38..... 5.00
❑30/30¢, Jul 1976, 30¢ regional price variant..... 20.00
❑31, Sep 1976, Avengers #39..... 5.00
❑32, Nov 1976, Avengers #40..... 5.00
❑33, Jan 1977, Avengers #41..... 5.00
❑34, Mar 1977, Avengers #42..... 5.00

Other grades: Multiply price above by 5/6 for VF/NM • 2/3 for VERY FINE • 1/3 for FINE • 1/5 for VERY GOOD • 1/8 for GOOD

Meteor Man

Tie-in to forgotten super-hero movie

©Marvel

Miami Mice

Miami Mice, meet Hamster Vice. Oy...

©Rip Off

Mickey Mouse

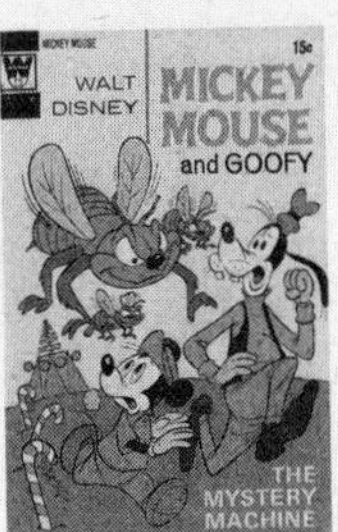

Look for the Floyd Gottfredson reprints

©Dell

Microbots

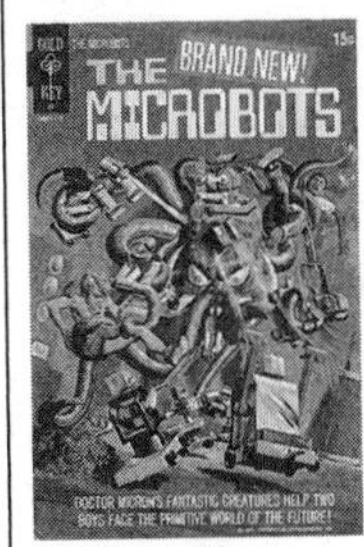

Doctor Micron's fantastic creatures

©Gold Key

Micronauts

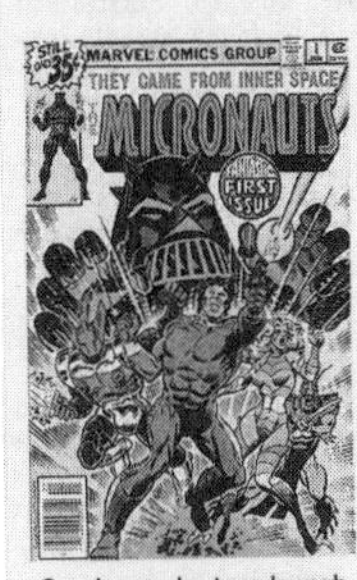

Semi-popular toys launch popular comics

©Marvel

	N-MINT
❑35, May 1977, Newsstand edition (distributed by Curtis); issue number in box	5.00
❑35/Whitman, May 1977, Special markets edition (usually sold in Whitman bagged prepacks); price appears in a diamond; UPC barcode appears	5.00
❑36, Jul 1977, Avengers #44	5.00
❑36/35¢, Jul 1977, 35¢ regional price variant	15.00
❑37, Sep 1977, Avengers #45	5.00
❑37/35¢, Sep 1977, 35¢ regional price variant	15.00
❑38, Nov 1977, Newsstand edition (distributed by Curtis); issue number in box	5.00
❑38/Whitman, Nov 1977, Special markets edition (usually sold in Whitman bagged prepacks); price appears in a diamond; no UPC barcode	5.00
❑39, Jan 1978, Avengers #47	5.00
❑40, Mar 1978, Avengers #48	5.00
❑41, Apr 1978, Avengers #49	5.00
❑42, Jun 1978, Avengers #50	5.00
❑43, Aug 1978, Avengers #51	5.00
❑44, Oct 1978, Avengers #52; Reprints Avengers #52	5.00
❑45, Dec 1978, A: X-Men. X-Men appearance, Reprint X-Men #45; Reprints X-Men #45	5.00
❑46, Feb 1979, Reprints Avengers (1st Series) #53	5.00
❑47, Apr 1979, Avengers #54 with new cover by Steve Ditko; Coverless	5.00
❑GS 1, ca. 1975	10.00
❑GS 2, ca. 1975	10.00

Marvel Two-In-One
Marvel

	N-MINT
❑1, Jan 1974, Man-Thing	55.00
❑2, Mar 1974, Namor; Marvel Value Stamp #63: Sub-Mariner	15.00
❑3, May 1974, A: Black Widow. Daredevil; Marvel Value Stamp #89: Hammerhead	10.00
❑4, Jul 1974, Captain America; Marvel Value Stamp #88: Leader	7.00
❑5, Sep 1974, Guardians of the Galaxy; Marvel Value Stamp #93: Silver Surfer	8.00
❑6, Nov 1974, Doctor Strange; Marvel Value Stamp #47: Green Goblin	8.00
❑7, Jan 1975, A: Doctor Strange. Valkyrie; Marvel Value Stamp #45: Mantis	5.00
❑8, Mar 1975, Ghost Rider	5.00
❑9, May 1975, Thor	5.00
❑10, Jul 1975, Black Widow	5.00
❑11, Sep 1975, GK (c); JAb (a); Golem	3.00
❑12, Nov 1975, JK (c); Iron Man; Marvel Value Stamp #45: Mantis	3.00
❑13, Jan 1976, Power Man	3.00
❑14, Mar 1976, HT (c); HT (a); Son of Satan	3.00
❑15, May 1976, DG (a); Morbius	3.00
❑15/30¢, May 1976, DG (a); 30¢ regional price variant	30.00
❑16, Jun 1976, DA (a); Ka-Zar	3.00
❑16/30¢, Jun 1976, DA (a); 30¢ regional price variant	30.00
❑17, Jul 1976, JSt (c); SB (a); A: Basilisk I (Basil Elks). Spider-Man	3.00
❑17/30¢, Jul 1976, JSt (c); SB (a); 30¢ regional price variant	30.00
❑18, Aug 1976, JSt (c); JM, DA (a); Scarecrow; Spider-Man	3.00
❑18/30¢, Aug 1976, JSt (c); JM, DA (a); 30¢ regional price variant; Scarecrow; Spider-Man	30.00
❑19, Sep 1976, Tigra	3.00
❑20, Oct 1976, Liberty Legion; continued from Marvel Two-In-One Ann #1	3.00
❑21, Nov 1976, A: Human Torch. Doc Savage	3.00
❑22, Dec 1976, Human Torch; Thor	3.00
❑23, Jan 1977, Human Torch; Thor	3.00
❑24, Feb 1977, SB (a); Black Goliath; newsstand editon (distributed by Curtis); issue number in box	3.00
❑24/Whitman, Feb 1977, SB (a); Special markets edition (usually sold in Whitman bagged prepacks); price appears in a diamond; UPC barcode appears	3.00
❑25, Mar 1977, JK (c); Iron Fist; newsstand editon (distributed by Curtis); issue number in box	3.00
❑25/Whitman, Mar 1977, Special markets edition (usually sold in Whitman bagged prepacks); price appears in a diamond; UPC barcode appears	3.00
❑26, Apr 1977, Nick Fury; newsstand editon (distributed by Curtis); issue number in box	2.00
❑26/Whitman, Apr 1977, Special markets edition (usually sold in Whitman bagged prepacks); price appears in a diamond; UPC barcode appears	2.00
❑27, May 1977, JK, JSt (c); Deathlok	2.00
❑28, Jun 1977, GK (c); Sub-Mariner; newsstand editon (distributed by Curtis); issue number in box	2.00
❑28/Whitman, Jun 1977, GK (c); Special markets edition (usually sold in Whitman bagged prepacks); price appears in a diamond; UPC barcode appears	2.00
❑28/35¢, Jun 1977, GK (c); 35¢ regional price variant newsstand editon (distributed by Curtis); issue number in box	20.00
❑29, Jul 1977, Shang-Chi; newsstand editon (distributed by Curtis); issue number in box	2.00
❑29/Whitman, Jul 1977, Special markets edition (usually sold in Whitman bagged prepacks); price appears in a diamond; UPC barcode appears	2.00
❑29/35¢, Jul 1977, 35¢ regional price variant newsstand editon (distributed by Curtis); issue number in box	20.00
❑30, Aug 1977, AM, RB (c); JB (a); 2: Spider-Woman I (Jessica Drew); newsstand editon (distributed by Curtis); issue number in box	2.00
❑30/Whitman, Aug 1977, AM, RB (c); JB (a); 2: Spider-Woman I (Jessica Drew). Special markets edition (usually sold in Whitman bagged prepacks); price appears in a diamond; UPC barcode appears	2.00
❑30/35¢, Aug 1977, AM, RB (c); JB (a); 2: Spider-Woman I (Jessica Drew). 35¢ regional price variant newsstand editon (distributed by Curtis); issue number in box	20.00
❑31, Sep 1977, Spider-Woman I (Jessica Drew); newsstand editon (distributed by Curtis); issue number in box	2.00
❑31/Whitman, Sep 1977, Special markets edition (usually sold in Whitman bagged prepacks); price appears in a diamond; UPC barcode appears	2.00
❑31/35¢, Sep 1977, 35¢ regional price variant newsstand editon (distributed by Curtis); issue number in box	20.00
❑32, Oct 1977, GP (c); Invisible Girl; newsstand editon (distributed by Curtis); issue number in box	2.00
❑32/Whitman, Oct 1977, GP (c); Special markets edition (usually sold in Whitman bagged prepacks); price appears in a diamond; no UPC barcode	2.00
❑33, Nov 1977, Mordred; newsstand editon (distributed by Curtis); issue number in box	2.00
❑33/Whitman, Nov 1977, Special markets edition (usually sold in Whitman bagged prepacks); price appears in a diamond; no UPC barcode	2.00
❑34, Dec 1977, Nighthawk	2.00
❑35, Jan 1978, Skull the Slayer	2.00
❑36, Feb 1978, Mr. Fantastic	2.00
❑37, Mar 1978, JSt (c); Matt Murdock	2.00
❑38, Apr 1978, JM (a); Daredevil	2.00
❑39, May 1978, Vision; Daredevil; newsstand editon (distributed by Curtis); issue number in box	2.00
❑39/Whitman, May 1978, Special markets edition (usually sold in Whitman bagged prepacks); price appears in a diamond; no UPC barcode	2.00
❑40, Jun 1978, Black Panther	2.00
❑41, Jul 1978, Brother Voodoo	2.00
❑42, Aug 1978, GP (c); SB, AA (a); Captain America; newsstand editon (distributed by Curtis); issue number in box	2.00
❑42/Whitman, Aug 1978, GP (c); SB, AA (a); Special markets edition (usually sold in Whitman bagged prepacks); price appears in a diamond; UPC barcode appears	2.00
❑43, Sep 1978, JBy (c); JBy (a); Man-Thing; newsstand editon (distributed by Curtis); issue number in box	2.00
❑43/Whitman, Sep 1978, JBy (c); JBy (a); Special markets edition (usually sold in Whitman bagged prepacks); price appears in a diamond; no UPC barcode	2.00
❑44, Oct 1978, BH (c); BH (a); Hercules; newsstand editon (distributed by Curtis); issue number in box	2.00
❑44/Whitman, Oct 1978, BH (c); BH (a); Special markets edition (usually sold in Whitman bagged prepacks); price appears in a diamond; no UPC barcode	2.00
❑45, Nov 1978, GD (a); Captain Marvel; newsstand editon (distributed by Curtis); issue number in box	2.00
❑45/Whitman, Nov 1978, Special markets edition (usually sold in Whitman bagged prepacks); price appears in a diamond; no UPC barcode	2.00
❑46, Dec 1978, Hulk; newsstand editon (distributed by Curtis); issue number in box	2.00
❑46/Whitman, Dec 1978, Special markets edition (usually sold in Whitman bagged prepacks); price appears in a diamond; no UPC barcode	2.00

Other grades: Multiply price above by 5/6 for VF/NM • 2/3 for VERY FINE • 1/3 for FINE • 1/5 for VERY GOOD • 1/8 for GOOD

N-MINT

❑47, Jan 1979, 1: Machinesmith. Yancy Street Gang; newsstand editon (distributed by Curtis); issue number in box 2.00

❑47/Whitman, Jan 1979, 1: Machinesmith. Special markets edition (usually sold in Whitman bagged prepacks); price appears in a diamond; no UPC barcode 2.00

❑48, Feb 1979, Jack of Hearts; newsstand editon (distributed by Curtis); issue number in box 2.00

❑48/Whitman, Feb 1979, Special markets edition (usually sold in Whitman bagged prepacks); price appears in a diamond; no UPC barcode 2.00

❑49, Mar 1979, AM (c); GD (a); Doctor Strange 2.00

❑50, Apr 1979, GP, JSt (c); JBy (w); JBy, JSe, JSt (a); Thing vs. Thing 2.00

❑51, May 1979, GP, JSt (c); FM, BMc (a); Beast; Wonder Man; Ms. Marvel; Nick Fury; newsstand editon (distributed by Curtis); issue number in box 3.00

❑51/Whitman, May 1979, GP, JSt (c); FM, BMc (a); Special markets edition (usually sold in Whitman bagged prepacks); price appears in a diamond; no UPC barcode 3.00

❑52, Jun 1979, GP, JSt (c); Moon Knight 2.00

❑53, Jul 1979, JBy, JSt (c); JBy, JSt (a); Quasar 2.00

❑54, Aug 1979, GP (c); JBy, JSt (a); 1: Screaming Mimi. 1: Poundcakes. D: Deathlok I (Luther Manning). Deathlok 3.50

❑55, Sep 1979, GP (c); JBy, JSt (a); Giant Man II (Bill Foster) 2.00

❑56, Oct 1979, JBy (c); GP, GD (a); 1: Letha. Thundra 1.50

❑57, Nov 1979, AM, GP (c); GP, GD (a); Wundarr 1.50

❑58, Dec 1979, GP (c); GP, GD (a); Aquarian; Quasar 1.50

❑59, Jan 1980, Human Torch 1.50

❑60, Feb 1980, GP, GD (a); 1: Impossible Woman. Impossible Man 1.50

❑61, Mar 1980, GP (c); GD (a); 1: Her. Starhawk 1.50

❑62, Apr 1980, GP, JSt (c); GD (a); Moondragon 1.50

❑63, May 1980, GP (c); GD (a); Warlock 1.50

❑64, Jun 1980, GP (c); GP, GD (a); 1: Black Mamba. 1: Anaconda. 1: Death-Adder. Stingray 1.50

❑65, Jul 1980, GP, GD (a); Triton 1.50

❑66, Aug 1980, GP (c); GD (a); A: Arcade. Scarlet Witch 1.50

❑67, Sep 1980, Hyperion; Thundra 1.50

❑68, Oct 1980, A: Arcade. Angel 1.50

❑69, Nov 1980, Guardians of the Galaxy 1.50

❑70, Dec 1980, Inhumans 1.50

❑71, Jan 1981, 1: Maelstrom. 1: Gronk. 1: Phobius. 1: Helio. Mr. Fantastic 1.50

❑72, Feb 1981, Stingray 1.50

❑73, Mar 1981, Quasar 1.50

❑74, Apr 1981, Puppet Master 1.50

❑75, May 1981, O: Blastaar. Avengers ... 1.50

❑76, Jun 1981, O: Ringmaster. Iceman.. 1.50

❑77, Jul 1981, Man-Thing 1.50

❑78, Aug 1981, Wonder Man 1.50

❑79, Sep 1981, 1: Star-Dancer. Blue Diamond 1.50

❑80, Oct 1981, Ghost Rider 1.50

❑81, Nov 1981, Sub-Mariner 1.50

❑82, Dec 1981, Captain America 1.50

❑83, Jan 1982, Sasquatch 1.50

❑84, Feb 1982, Alpha Flight 1.50

❑85, Mar 1982, Giant-Man; Spider-Woman 1.50

❑86, Apr 1982, Sandman (Marvel) 1.50

❑87, May 1982, Ant-Man 1.50

❑88, Jun 1982, She-Hulk 1.50

❑89, Jul 1982, Torch; Human Torch 1.50

❑90, Aug 1982, JM (a); Spider-Man 1.50

❑91, Sep 1982, Sphinx 1.50

❑92, Oct 1982, V: Ultron. Jocasta; Machine Man 1.50

❑93, Nov 1982, A: Machine Man. D: Jocasta. Machine Man 1.50

❑94, Dec 1982, Power Man; Iron Fist 1.50

❑95, Jan 1983, Living Mummy 1.50

❑96, Feb 1983, Marvel Heroes; Sandman (Marvel) 1.50

N-MINT

❑97, Mar 1983, Iron Man 1.50

❑98, Apr 1983, Franklin Richards 1.50

❑99, May 1983, BH (a); ROM 1.50

❑100, Jun 1983, Double-size; JSt (c); JBy (w); Ben Grimm 2.50

❑Ann 1, ca. 1976, JK (c); SB (a); Liberty Legion 4.00

❑Ann 2, Dec 1977, JSn (c); JSn (w); JSn (a); 1: Lord Chaos. 1: Champion of the Universe. 1: Master Order. D: Warlock. D: Thanos. Thanos transformed to stone; Spider-Man; Avengers; Captain Marvel 15.00

❑Ann 3, Aug 1978, SB (a); Nova 2.00

❑Ann 4, Oct 1979, Black Bolt 2.00

❑Ann 5, Sep 1980, Hulk 2.50

❑Ann 6, Oct 1981, 1: American Eagle 2.00

❑Ann 7, Oct 1982, 1: Champion of the Universe 2.00

Marvel Universe
Marvel

❑1, Jun 1998; gatefold summary; Invaders 2.99

❑2, Jul 1998; gatefold summary; JBy (c);Invaders 1.99

❑2/A, Jul 1998; gatefold summary; DaG, JBy (c);alternate cover; Invaders 1.99

❑3, Aug 1998; gatefold summary; PS (c); Invaders 1.99

❑4, Sep 1998; gatefold summary; Monster Hunters 1.99

❑5, Oct 1998; gatefold summary; Monster Hunters 1.99

❑6, Nov 1998; gatefold summary; Monster Hunters 1.99

❑7, Dec 1998; gatefold summary; O: Mole Man. Monster Hunters 1.99

Marvel Universe: Millennial Visions
Marvel

❑1, Feb 2002; Wraparound cover 3.99

Marvel Universe: The End
Marvel

❑1, May 2003; AM, JSn (c); JSn (w); AM, JSn (a); 48 pages 3.50

❑2, May 2003 AM, JSn (c); JSn (w); AM, JSn (a) 3.50

❑3, Jun 2003 AM, JSn (c); JSn (w); AM, JSn (a) 3.50

❑4, Jun 2003 AM, JSn (c); JSn (w); AM, JSn (a) 3.50

❑5, Jul 2003; AM, JSn (c); JSn (w); AM, JSn (a); Includes preview of Ultimate X-Men #34 .... 3.50

❑6, Aug 2003, AM, JSn (c); JSn (w); AM, JSn (a) 3.50

Marvel Valentine Special
Marvel

❑1, Apr 1997; DDC (a); A: Cyclops. A: Venus. A: Daredevil. A: Spider-Man. A: Phoenix. A: Absorbing Man. romance anthology 2.00

Marvel vs. DC/DC vs. Marvel
DC / Marvel

❑1, Mar 1996; 1: Access (out of costume). crossover with Marvel; continues in Marvel vs. DC #2; cardstock cover 4.00

❑2, Mar 1996; PD (w); crossover with DC; cardstock cover 4.00

❑3, Apr 1996; 1: Access. cardstock cover; crossover with DC; voting results; Marvel and DC universes joined; Stories continued in Amalgam titles ... 4.00

❑4, Apr 1996; PD (w); continued from Marvel vs. DC #3; cardstock cover 4.00

❑Ashcan 1; Consumer Preview; free preview of crossover series; with trading card and ballot 1.00

Marvel Westerns: Kid Colt and Arizona Girl
Marvel

❑1 .... 0.00

Marvel Westerns: Outlaw Files
Marvel

❑1, Sep 2006 .... 3.99

Marvel Westerns: Strange Westerns Starring Black Rider
Marvel

❑1, Oct 2006 .... 3.99

N-MINT

Marvel Westerns: Two-Gun Kid
Marvel

❑1, Aug 2006 .... 3.99

Marvel X-Men Collection
Marvel

❑1, Jan 1994; Pin-Ups 2.95

❑2, Feb 1994; Pin-Ups 2.95

❑3, Mar 1994; Pin-Ups 2.95

Marvel Year in Review
Marvel

❑1, ca. 1989 .... 3.95

❑2, ca. 1990 .... 3.95

❑3, ca. 1991 .... 3.95

❑4, ca. 1992 .... 3.95

❑5, ca. 1993 .... 3.95

❑6, ca. 1994 .... 2.95

Marvel Zombies
Marvel

❑1, Feb 2006, Amazing Fantasy #15 homage cover 55.00

❑1/2nd, Feb 2006, Spider-Man #1 homage cover 35.00

❑1/3rd, Feb 2006, Amazing Spider-Man #50 homage cover 12.00

❑2, Mar 2006, Avengers #4 homage cover 16.00

❑3, Apr 2006, Incredible Hulk #340 homage cover 6.00

❑3/2nd, Apr 2006, Daredevil #179 homage cover 4.00

❑4, May 2006, X-Men #1 homage cover 3.00

❑5, Jun 2006, Zombie tribute cover to Amazing Spider-Man Ann #21 .... 2.99

Marvel Zombies vs. Army of Darkness
Marvel

❑1, Feb 2007; Uncanny X-Men #141 homage 5.00

❑1/2nd, Feb 2007; Captain America Comics #1 homage 2.99

❑2, Mar 2007; Uncanny X-Men #268 homage 2.99

❑3, Apr 2007; Superman vs. Amazing Spider-Man homage 2.99

❑4, May 2007; Captain America #100 homage 2.99

❑5, Jun 2007 .... 2.99

Marville
Marvel

❑1, Nov 2002; Man with M on chest on cover 2.25

❑2, Dec 2002 .... 2.25

❑3, Jan 2003 .... 2.25

❑4, Feb 2003 .... 2.25

❑5, Mar 2003 .... 2.25

❑6, May 2003 .... 2.25

❑7, Jul 2003; Introduction and submission guidelines to Marvel's Epic imprint 2.25

Mary Jane
Marvel

❑1, Aug 2004 .... 2.25

❑2, Sep 2004 .... 2.25

❑3, Oct 2004 .... 2.25

❑4, Nov 2004 .... 2.25

Mary Jane: Homecoming
Marvel

❑1, Apr 2005 .... 2.99

❑2, May 2005 .... 2.99

❑3, Jun 2005 .... 2.99

Mary Poppins
Gold Key

❑1, Jan 1965 .... 28.00

Mask
DC

❑1, Dec 1985 CS, KS (a) 1.00

❑2, Jan 1986 CS, KS (a) 1.00

❑3, Feb 1986 HC (c); CS, KS (a) 1.00

❑4, Mar 1986 CS, KS (a) 1.00

Mask
DC

❑1, Feb 1987 .... 1.00

❑2, Mar 1987 .... 1.00

❑3, Apr 1987 .... 1.00

❑4, May 1987 .... 1.00

❑5, Jun 1987 .... 1.00

❑6, Jul 1987 .... 1.00

❑7, Aug 1987 .... 1.00

Mightyguy

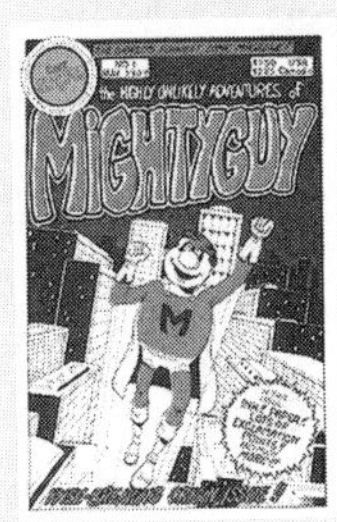

Tim Corrigan's minicomics character gets series
©C&T

Mighty Hercules

Stop saying "The Mighty Hercules"!
©Gold Key

Mighty Heroes

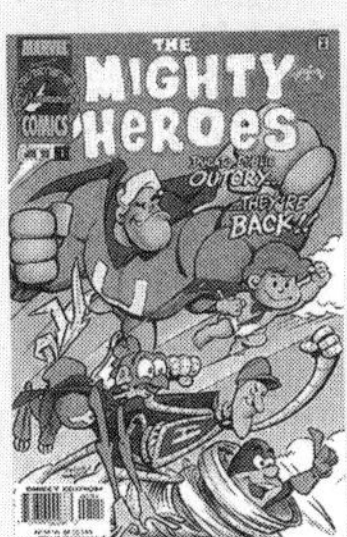

Based on long-ago Saturday morning cartoon
©Marvel

Mighty Marvel Western

Giant-sized reprint title for Marvel's westerns
©Marvel

Mighty Samson

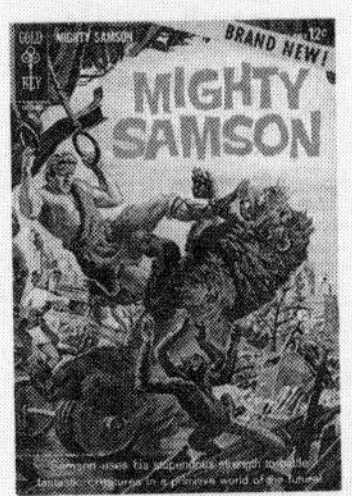

Gold Key hero didn't make it to Valiant
©Gold Key

N-MINT

❑8, Sep 1987 .... 1.00
❑9, Oct 1987 .... 1.00

Mask
Dark Horse

❑0, ca. 1991; Reprints Mask stories from Mayhem 4.95
❑1, Aug 1991 .... 4.00
❑2, Sep 1991 .... 3.50
❑3, Oct 1991 .... 3.00
❑4, Nov 1991 .... 3.00

Mask
Dark Horse

❑1, Feb 1995 .... 3.00
❑2, Mar 1995 .... 2.50
❑3, Apr 1995 .... 2.50
❑4, May 1995 .... 2.50
❑5, Jun 1995 .... 2.50
❑6, Jul 1995 .... 2.50
❑7, Aug 1995 .... 2.50
❑8, Sep 1995 .... 2.50
❑9, Oct 1995 .... 2.50
❑10, Dec 1995 A: Hero Zero, King Tiger. 2.50
❑11, Jan 1996 A: Barb Wire, The Machine 2.50
❑12, Feb 1996 A: X, Ghost, King Tiger ... 2.50
❑13, Mar 1996 A: Warmaker, King Tiger, Vortex 2.50
❑14, Apr 1996 .... 2.50
❑15, May 1996 A: Lt. Kellaway 2.50
❑16, Jun 1996 .... 2.50
❑17, Jul 1996 .... 2.50

Mask: Official Movie Adaptation
Dark Horse

❑1, Jul 1994 .... 2.50
❑2, Aug 1994 .... 2.50

Mask Returns
Dark Horse

❑1, Dec 1992; with Mask mask 4.00
❑2, Jan 1993 .... 3.00
❑3, Feb 1993 .... 3.00
❑4, Mar 1993; Walter dons Mask 3.00

Mask: Toys in the Attic
Dark Horse

❑1, Aug 1998 .... 2.95
❑2, Sep 1998; 40 pages; Pages out of order 2.95
❑3, Oct 1998 .... 2.95
❑4, Nov 1998 .... 2.95

Mask: Virtual Surreality
Dark Horse

❑1, Jul 1997; NN; One-shot 2.95

Mask Conspiracy
Ink & Feathers

❑1; Includes Big Lou back-up feature 6.95

Masked Man
Eclipse

❑1, Dec 1984, O: Masked Man. O: Masked Man 2.00
❑2, Feb 1985 .... 2.00
❑3, Apr 1985 .... 2.00
❑4, Jun 1985 .... 2.00
❑5, Aug 1985 .... 2.00
❑6, Oct 1985 .... 2.00
❑7, Dec 1985 .... 2.00

N-MINT

❑8, Feb 1986 .... 2.00
❑9, Apr 1986 .... 2.00
❑10, b&w 2.00
❑11, b&w 2.00
❑12, Apr 1988, b&w 2.00

Masked Rider
Marvel

❑1, Apr 1996, based on Saban television series, one-shot 2.95

Masked Warrior X
Antarctic

❑1, Apr 1996, b&w 3.50
❑2, Jun 1996, b&w 2.95
❑3, Aug 1996, b&w; 40-page special 3.50
❑4, Oct 1996, b&w 2.95

Mask/Marshal Law
Dark Horse

❑1, Feb 1998 .... 2.95
❑2, Mar 1998; Law dons the Mask 2.95

Mask of Zorro
Image

❑1, Aug 1998 .... 2.95
❑1/Variant, Sep 1998, alternate cover 2.95
❑2, Sep 1998 .... 2.95
❑2/Variant, Sep 1998, alternate cover 2.95
❑3, Oct 1998, indicia says Oct 2.95
❑3/Variant, Oct 1998, alternate cover 2.95
❑4, Dec 1998, cover says Jan, indicia says Dec 2.95
❑4/Variant, Dec 1998, Photo cover 2.95

Masks: Too Hot for TV
DC

❑1, ca. 2003 .... 4.95

Masque of the Red Death
Dell

❑1, Oct 1964, Photo cover 20.00

Masquerade
Mad Monkey

❑1 .... 3.95
❑2 .... 3.95
❑Ashcan 1 .... 2.00

Masques
Innovation

❑1, Jul 1992 .... 4.95
❑2 .... 4.95

Master Darque
Acclaim

❑1, Feb 1998, Suggested for Mature Readers 6.00
❑Ash 1, Oct 1997, Review edition (black and white) 4.00

Master of Kung Fu
Marvel

❑17, Apr 1974, Series continued from "Special Marvel Edition"; JSn (w); JSn (a); 1: Black Jack Tarr. Marvel Value Stamp #53: Grim Reaper 15.00
❑18, Jun 1974, PG (a); Marvel Value Stamp #62: Plunderer 7.00
❑19, Aug 1974, PG (a); A: Man-Thing; Marvel Value Stamp #11: Deathlok 6.00
❑20, Sep 1974, PG (a) 6.00
❑21, Oct 1974, Marvel Value Stamp #62: Plunderer 5.00

N-MINT

❑22, Nov 1974, PG (a); Marvel Value Stamp #79: Kang 5.00
❑23, Dec 1974, Marvel Value Stamp #97: Black Knight 5.00
❑24, Jan 1975, JSn (a); Marvel Value Stamp #15: Iron Man 5.00
❑25, Feb 1975, PG (a); Marvel Value Stamp #41: Gladiator 5.00
❑26, Mar 1975 .... 5.00
❑27, Apr 1975 .... 5.00
❑28, May 1975 .... 5.00
❑29, Jun 1975, PG (a); 1: Razor-Fist I. D: Razor-Fist I 5.00
❑30, Jul 1975, PG (a) 5.00
❑31, Aug 1975, GK (c); PG (a); Marvel Value Stamp #85: Lilith 5.00
❑32, Sep 1975 .... 4.00
❑33, Oct 1975, GK (c); PG (a); 1: Leiko Wu 4.00
❑34, Nov 1975, PG (a) 4.00
❑35, Dec 1975, PG (a) 4.00
❑36, Jan 1976 .... 4.00
❑37, Feb 1976 .... 4.00
❑38, Mar 1976, PG (a) 4.00
❑39, Apr 1976, GK (c); PG (w); PG (a); Marvel Value Stamp Series B #71 .... 4.00
❑39/30¢, Apr 1976, PG (a); 30¢ regional price variant 20.00
❑40, May 1976, PG (a) 3.00
❑40/30¢, May 1976, PG (a); 30¢ regional price variant 20.00
❑41, Jun 1976 .... 3.00
❑41/30¢, Jun 1976, 30¢ regional price variant 20.00
❑42, Jul 1976, PG (a); 1: Shockwave 3.00
❑42/30¢, Jul 1976, PG (a); 30¢ regional price variant 20.00
❑43, Aug 1976, RB (c); PG (a); (Regular.25-c) 3.00
❑43/30¢, Aug 1976, 30¢ regional price variant 20.00
❑44, Sep 1976, JB (c); PG (a) 3.00
❑45, Oct 1976, GK (c); PG (a) 3.00
❑46, Nov 1976, PG (a) 3.00
❑47, Dec 1976, DC (c); PG (a) 3.00
❑48, Jan 1977, PG (a) 3.00
❑49, Feb 1977, PG (a) 3.00
❑50, Mar 1977, PG (a) 3.00
❑51, Apr 1977, PG (c); PG (a) 3.00
❑52, May 1977 .... 3.00
❑53, Jun 1977, PG (a); reprints Master of Kung Fu #20 .... 3.00
❑53/35¢, Jun 1977, PG (a); 35¢ regional price variant 15.00
❑54, Jul 1977 .... 3.00
❑54/35¢, Jul 1977, 35¢ regional price variant 15.00
❑55, Aug 1977, PG (c); MZ (a) 3.00
❑55/35¢, Aug 1977, PG (c); MZ (a); 35¢ regional price variant 15.00
❑56, Sep 1977, 35¢ regional price variant 15.00
❑56/35¢, Sep 1977, 35¢ regional price variant 15.00
❑57, Oct 1977 .... 3.00
❑57/35¢, Oct 1977, 35¢ regional price variant 15.00
❑58, Nov 1977 .... 3.00
❑59, Dec 1977 .... 3.00
❑60, Jan 1978, V: Doctor Doom. Dr. Doom 3.00
❑61, Feb 1978 .... 3.00

Other grades: Multiply price above by 5/6 for VF/NM • 2/3 for VERY FINE • 1/3 for FINE • 1/5 for VERY GOOD • 1/8 for GOOD

N-MINT

❑62, Mar 1978 3.00
❑63, Apr 1978 3.00
❑64, May 1978, PG (c); MZ (a) 3.00
❑65, Jun 1978 3.00
❑66, Jul 1978 3.00
❑67, Aug 1978, PG (c); MZ (a) 3.00
❑68, Sep 1978, V: The Cat 3.00
❑69, Oct 1978 3.00
❑70, Nov 1978 3.00
❑71, Dec 1978 3.00
❑72, Jan 1979 3.00
❑73, Feb 1979 3.00
❑74, Mar 1979 3.00
❑75, Apr 1979 3.00
❑76, May 1979 3.00
❑77, Jun 1979, 1&O: Zaran 3.00
❑78, Jul 1979 3.00
❑79, Aug 1979 3.00
❑80, Sep 1979 3.00
❑81, Oct 1979 3.00
❑82, Nov 1979 3.00
❑83, Dec 1979, V: Fu Manchu 3.00
❑84, Jan 1980 3.00
❑85, Feb 1980 3.00
❑86, Mar 1980 3.00
❑87, Apr 1980, V: Fu Manchu 3.00
❑88, May 1980, V: Fu Manchu 3.00
❑89, Jun 1980, V: Fu Manchu 3.00
❑90, Jul 1980 3.00
❑91, Aug 1980, MZ, GD (a) 3.00
❑92, Sep 1980, MZ, GD (a) 3.00
❑93, Oct 1980, MZ (c); MZ, GD (a) 3.00
❑94, Nov 1980, MZ, GD (a) 3.00
❑95, Dec 1980, MZ, GD (a) 3.00
❑96, Jan 1981, MZ, GD (a) 3.00
❑97, Feb 1981, MZ, GD (a) 3.00
❑98, Mar 1981, MZ, GD (a) 3.00
❑99, Apr 1981, MZ, GD (a) 3.00
❑100, May 1981, Giant-size; MZ, GD (a); Double-sized 4.00
❑101, Jun 1981, MZ, GD (a) 2.00
❑102, Jul 1981, GD (a); 1: Day pencils 2.00
❑103, Aug 1981, GD (a) 2.00
❑104, Sep 1981 2.00
❑105, Oct 1981, 1: Razor-Fist II. 1: Razor-Fist III. D: Razor-Fist III 2.00
❑106, Nov 1981, GD (a); O: Razor-Fist II. O: Razor-Fist III. A: Velcro 2.00
❑107, Dec 1981, GD (a); A: Sata 2.00
❑108, Jan 1982, GD (a) 2.00
❑109, Feb 1982, GD (a) 2.00
❑110, Mar 1982, GD (a) 2.00
❑111, Apr 1982, GD (a) 2.00
❑112, May 1982, GD (a) 2.00
❑113, Jun 1982, GD (a) 2.00
❑114, Jul 1982 2.00
❑115, Aug 1982, GD (a) 2.00
❑116, Sep 1982, GD (a) 2.00
❑117, Oct 1982, GD (a) 2.00
❑118, Nov 1982, double-sized; GD (a); D: Fu Manchu 2.00
❑119, Dec 1982, GD (a) 2.00
❑120, Jan 1983, GD (a) 2.00
❑121, Feb 1983 2.00
❑122, Mar 1983 2.00
❑123, Apr 1983 2.00
❑124, May 1983 2.00
❑125, Jun 1983; Double-size; Final Issue 3.00
❑Ann 1, ca. 1976, KP (a); 1976 Ann 20.00

Master of Kung Fu: Bleeding Black
Marvel

❑1, Feb 1991; Wraparound cover 3.00

Master of Mystics: The Demoncraft
Chakra

❑1 1.50
❑2 1.50

Master of Rampling Gate
Innovation

❑1, Jun 1991 6.95

Masters of the Universe: Icons of Evil: Beast Man
Image

❑1, Jun 2003 4.95

Master of the Void
Iron Hammer

❑1, Dec 1993 2.95

N-MINT

Masters of Horror
Idea & Design Works

❑1, Dec 2005 3.99
❑3, Mar 2006 3.99
❑4, Apr 2006 3.99

Masters of the Universe
DC

❑1, Dec 1982 GT, AA (a) 3.00
❑2, Jan 1983 2.00
❑3, Feb 1983 2.00

Masters of the Universe
Marvel / Star

❑1, May 1986 4.00
❑2, Jul 1986 2.50
❑3, Sep 1986 2.50
❑4, Nov 1986 2.50
❑5, Jan 1987 2.50
❑6, Mar 1987 2.50
❑7, May 1987 2.50
❑8, Jul 1987 2.50
❑9, Sep 1987 2.50
❑10, Nov 1987 2.50
❑11, Jan 1988 2.50
❑12, Mar 1988 2.50
❑13, May 1988; Final Issue 3.00

Masters of the Universe
Image

❑1, Nov 2002, Cover A 2.95
❑1/B, Nov 2002, Cover B 2.95
❑1/Gold, Nov 2002, Gold foil logo on cover 5.95
❑2, Dec 2002, Cover A 2.95
❑2/B, Dec 2002, Cover B 2.95
❑3, Jan 2003, Cover A 2.95
❑3/B, Jan 2003, Cover B 2.95
❑4, Feb 2003, Cover A 2.95
❑4/B, Feb 2003, Cover B 2.95

Masters of the Universe
Image

❑1, Mar 2003 5.95
❑1/A, Jun 2003, Cover A; Wraparound 2.95
❑2, Apr 2003 2.95
❑3, May 2003 2.95
❑4, Jun 2003 2.95
❑4/A, Jun 2003, Edwards Holofoil cover 5.95
❑4/B, Jun 2003, Santalucia cover 5.95
❑4/C, Jun 2003, Vallejo Bell cover 5.95
❑5, Jul 2003, Skeletor solo cover 2.95
❑6, Aug 2003, Man-At-Arms reflected in shattered mirror cover 2.95
❑7 2.95
❑8 2.95
❑8/Graham, Graham Crackers exclusive; 500 copies created. Wraparound Faker cover by Randy Green. Offered December 2004 for $7.99 8.00

Master's Series
Avalon

❑1; Wally Wood War 2.50

Masterworks Series of Great Comic Book Artists
DC / Seagate

❑1, Spr 1983, FF (a); Reprints Shining Knight stories from Adventure Comics (1950-1951) 2.50
❑2, Jul 1983, FF (a); Reprints from Adventure #161 2.50
❑3, Oct 1983, BWr (a) 2.50

Matador
DC

❑1, Jun 2005 2.99
❑2, Jul 2005 2.99
❑3, Aug 2005 2.99
❑4, Sep 2005 2.99
❑5, Oct 2005 2.99

Matt Champion
Metro

❑1 2.00

Matterbaby
Antarctic

❑1, Feb 1997, b&w 2.95
❑Ann 1 2.95

N-MINT

Maverick
Dell

❑7, Oct 1959 50.00
❑8, Jan 1960 50.00
❑9, Mar 1960 50.00
❑10, May 1960 50.00
❑11, Jul 1960 40.00
❑12, Sep 1960 40.00
❑13, Nov 1960 40.00
❑14, Jan 1961 40.00
❑15, Jun 1961 40.00
❑16, Sep 1961 30.00
❑17, Dec 1961 30.00
❑18, Mar 1962 30.00
❑19, Jun 1962 30.00

Maverick
Marvel

❑1, Jan 1997, Giant-size; One-shot 2.95

Maverick
Marvel

❑1, Sep 1997; gatefold summary; wraparound cover 3.00
❑2, Oct 1997; gatefold summary; wraparound cover 1.95
❑2/Variant, Oct 1997; variant cover 1.95
❑3, Nov 1997; gatefold summary; A: Alpha Flight. wraparound cover 1.99
❑4, Dec 1997; gatefold summary; A: Alpha Flight. wraparound cover 1.99
❑5, Jan 1998; gatefold summary; A: Wolverine; The Blob 1.99
❑6, Feb 1998; gatefold summary 1.99
❑7, Mar 1998; gatefold summary 1.99
❑8, Apr 1998; gatefold summary 1.99
❑9, May 1998; gatefold summary 1.99
❑10, Jun 1998; gatefold summary 1.99
❑11, Jul 1998; gatefold summary 1.99
❑12, Aug 1998; Giant-size; Final Issue; Gatefold summary 2.99

Mavericks
Dagger

❑1, Jan 1994 2.50
❑2, Feb 1994 2.50
❑3, Mar 1994 2.50
❑4, Apr 1994 2.50
❑5, May 1994 2.50

Mavericks: The New Wave
Dagger

❑1 2.50
❑2 2.50
❑3 2.50

Max Brewster: The Universal Soldier
Fleetway-Quality

❑1 2.95
❑2 2.95
❑3 2.95

Max Burger PI
Graphic Image

❑1, b&w; 1: Max Burger 2.00
❑2, b&w 2.50

Max Damage: Panic!
Head

❑1, Jul 1995, b&w 2.75

Maximage
Image

❑1, Dec 1995; 1&O: Maximage; 1: The Ancient 2.50
❑2, Jan 1996; polybagged with card 2.50
❑3, Feb 1996 2.50
❑4, Mar 1996; continued from Glory #10 2.50
❑5, Apr 1996 2.50
❑6, May 1996 2.50
❑7, Jun 1996 2.50
❑8, Jul 1996 2.50
❑9, Aug 1996 2.50
❑10, Sep 1996 2.50

Maximo One-Shot
Dreamwave

❑1, Feb 2004 3.95

Maximortal
Tundra

❑1, Aug 1992 4.00
❑2, Oct 1992 4.00
❑3, Dec 1992, A: Holmes 4.00

Other grades: Multiply price above by 5/6 for VF/NM • 2/3 for VERY FINE • 1/3 for FINE • 1/5 for VERY GOOD • 1/8 for GOOD

Mike Danger (Vol. 1) (Mickey Spillane's...)

Mickey Spillane back in comics after 40 years
©Tekno

Milk & Cheese

Foul-mouthed dairy products go bad
©Slave Labor

Millennium

DC's mega-crossover event of 1988
©DC

Millennium Edition: Action Comics

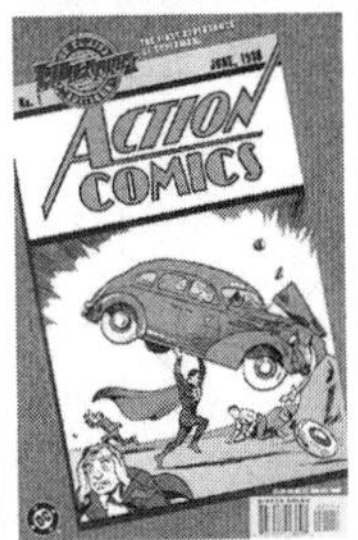

One of many reprints DC did in 2000
©DC

Minimum Wage

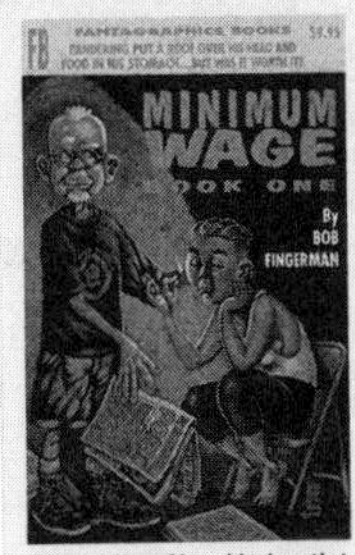

Struggling New York artist tries to make a living
©Fantagraphics

N-MINT

- ❑4, Mar 1993 — 4.00
- ❑5, May 1993 — 3.00
- ❑6, Jul 1993 — 3.00
- ❑7, Dec 1993 — 2.95

Maximum Security
Marvel

- ❑1, Dec 2000; V: Piledriver; V: Ronan the Accuser — 2.99
- ❑2, Dec 2000; V: Ego the Living Planet — 2.99
- ❑3, Jan 2001 — 2.99

Maximum Security Dangerous Planet
Marvel

- ❑1, Oct 2000, lead-in to Maximum Security — 2.99

Maximum Security: Thor vs. Ego
Marvel

- ❑1, Nov 2000; reprints Thor #133, #160, and #161 — 2.99

Maximum Volume
Kitchen Sink

- ❑1 — 14.95

Maxion
CPM Manga

- ❑1, Dec 1999, b&w — 2.95
- ❑2, Jan 2000, b&w — 2.95
- ❑3, Feb 2000, b&w — 2.95
- ❑4, Mar 2000, b&w — 2.95
- ❑5, Apr 2000, b&w — 2.95
- ❑6, May 2000, b&w — 2.95
- ❑7, Jun 2000 — 2.95
- ❑8, Jul 2000 — 2.95
- ❑9, Aug 2000 — 2.95
- ❑10, Sep 2000 — 2.95
- ❑11, Oct 2000 — 2.95
- ❑12, Nov 2000 — 2.95
- ❑13, Dec 2000 — 2.95
- ❑14, Jan 2001; b&w — 2.95
- ❑15, Feb 2001; b&w — 2.95
- ❑16, Mar 2001 — 2.95
- ❑17, Apr 2001 — 2.95
- ❑18, May 2001 — 2.95
- ❑19, Jun 2001 — 2.95
- ❑20, Jul 2001 — 2.95

Max of the Regulators
Atlantic

- ❑1 — 1.50
- ❑2 — 1.75
- ❑3 — 1.75
- ❑4 — 1.75

Max Rep in the Age of the Astrotitans
Dumbbell

- ❑1, Jun 1997, b&w — 2.75
- ❑2, Mar 1998, b&w — 2.75

Max the Magnificent
Slave Labor

- ❑1, Jul 1987 — 1.50
- ❑2 — 1.50
- ❑3 — 1.50

Maxwell Mouse Follies
Renegade

- ❑1, Feb 1986, b&w — 2.00
- ❑2, Apr 1986, b&w — 2.00
- ❑3, Jun 1986, b&w — 2.00
- ❑4, Sep 1986, b&w — 2.00
- ❑5, Dec 1986 — 2.00
- ❑6, Mar 1987 — 2.00

Maxwell the Magic Cat
Acme

- ❑1 — 4.95
- ❑2 — 4.95
- ❑3 — 4.95
- ❑4 — 5.95

Maxx
Image

- ❑½, Jun 1993; Wizard promotional edition — 5.00
- ❑½/Gold, Jun 1993; Gold edition; Promotional edition in slipcover with certificate of authenticity — 16.00
- ❑1, Mar 1993 — 3.00
- ❑1/3D, Jan 1998; 3-D edition; bound-in glasses — 5.00
- ❑1/Variant, Mar 1993; Glow-in-the-dark promotional edition — 6.00
- ❑2, Apr 1993 — 3.00
- ❑3, May 1993 — 2.50
- ❑4, Aug 1993 — 2.50
- ❑5, Sep 1993 — 2.50
- ❑6, Nov 1993; cover says Oct, indicia says Nov — 2.50
- ❑7, Mar 1994 A: Pitt — 2.50
- ❑8, May 1994 A: Pitt — 2.50
- ❑9, Jun 1994 — 2.50
- ❑10, Aug 1994 — 2.50
- ❑11, Oct 1994 — 2.00
- ❑12, Dec 1994 — 2.00
- ❑13, Jan 1995 — 2.00
- ❑14, Feb 1995 — 2.00
- ❑15, Apr 1995; cover says February, indicia says Apr — 2.00
- ❑16, Jun 1995; cover says Feb, indicia says Jun — 2.00
- ❑17, Jul 1995 — 2.00
- ❑18, Aug 1995 — 2.00
- ❑19, Sep 1995 — 2.00
- ❑20, Nov 1995 — 2.00
- ❑21, Jan 1996 — 2.00
- ❑22, Feb 1996 — 2.00
- ❑23, Mar 1996 — 2.00
- ❑24, May 1996 — 2.00
- ❑25, Jun 1996; cover says Jul, indicia says Jun — 2.00
- ❑26, Aug 1996; O: Mr. Gone — 2.00
- ❑27, Sep 1996 — 2.00
- ❑28, Jan 1997 — 2.00
- ❑29, Apr 1997 — 2.00
- ❑30, Jun 1997 — 2.00
- ❑31, Jul 1997 — 2.00
- ❑32, Sep 1997 — 2.00
- ❑33, Oct 1997 — 2.00
- ❑34, Dec 1997 — 2.00
- ❑35, Feb 1998; Final Issue — 2.00

Maxx
DC

- ❑1, ca. 2003 — 17.95
- ❑2, ca. 2004 — 17.95
- ❑3, ca. 2004 — 17.95

Mayhem
Dark Horse

- ❑1, May 1989, b&w — 4.00
- ❑2, Jun 1989, b&w — 3.50
- ❑3, Jul 1989, b&w — 3.50
- ❑4, Aug 1989, b&w — 3.50

Mayhem
Kelva

- ❑1, Dec 1977; Adult — 1.25

Maze
Metaphrog

- ❑1, Aug 1997, b&w; no indicia — 3.75

Maze Agency
Idea & Design Works

- ❑1, Jan 2006 — 3.99
- ❑2, Jan 2006 — 3.99
- ❑3, Mar 2006 — 3.99

Maze Agency
Comico

- ❑1, Dec 1988, 1: The Maze Agency; Comico publishes — 3.00
- ❑2, Jan 1989 — 2.50
- ❑3, Feb 1989 — 2.50
- ❑4, Mar 1989 — 2.00
- ❑5, Apr 1989 — 2.00
- ❑6, May 1989 — 2.00
- ❑7, Jun 1989 — 2.50
- ❑8, Dec 1989, Innovation begins as publisher — 2.00
- ❑9, Feb 1990, Ellery Queen — 2.00
- ❑10, Apr 1990 — 2.00
- ❑11, Apr 1990 — 2.00
- ❑12, May 1990 — 2.00
- ❑13, Jun 1990 — 2.00
- ❑14, Jul 1990 — 2.00
- ❑15, Aug 1990 — 2.00
- ❑16, Oct 1990, RH (c) — 2.50
- ❑17, Dec 1990 — 2.50
- ❑18, Feb 1991 — 2.50
- ❑19, Mar 1991 — 2.50
- ❑20, May 1991 — 2.50
- ❑21, Jun 1991 — 2.50
- ❑22, Jul 1991 — 2.50
- ❑23, Aug 1991 — 2.50
- ❑Ann 1, Aug 1990, MP (c); Spirit parody — 3.00
- ❑Special 1, May 1990, JSa (a) — 3.00
- ❑Xmas 1, Special edition; Christmas Special — 3.00

Maze Agency
Caliber

- ❑1, ca. 1997 — 2.95
- ❑2, ca. 1997 — 2.95
- ❑3, ca. 1997 — 2.95

'Mazing Man
DC

- ❑1, Jan 1986, 1: 'mazing Man — 1.00
- ❑2, Feb 1986 — 1.00
- ❑3, Mar 1986 — 1.00
- ❑4, Apr 1986 — 1.00
- ❑5, May 1986 — 1.00
- ❑6, Jun 1986 — 1.00
- ❑7, Jul 1986, 1: Zoot Sputnik — 1.00
- ❑8, Aug 1986 — 1.00
- ❑9, Sep 1986 — 1.00

Other grades: Multiply price above by 5/6 for VF/NM • 2/3 for VERY FINE • 1/3 for FINE • 1/5 for VERY GOOD • 1/8 for GOOD

	N-MINT
❑10, Oct 1986	1.00
❑11, Nov 1986	1.00
❑12, Dec 1986, FM (c); Frank Miller Dark Knight cover	1.00
❑Special 1, Jul 1987	2.00
❑Special 2, Apr 1988	2.00
❑Special 3, Sep 1990	2.00

McHale's Navy
Dell

❑1, May 1963 ... 40.00
❑2, Aug 1963 ... 32.00
❑3, Nov 1963 ... 26.00

M.D.
Gemstone

❑1, Sep 1999 ... 2.50
❑2, Oct 1999 ... 2.50
❑3, Nov 1999 ... 2.50
❑4, Dec 1999 ... 2.50
❑5, Jan 2000 ... 2.50

M.D. Geist
CPM

❑1, Jun 1995 ... 2.95
❑2, Jul 1995 ... 2.95
❑3, Aug 1995 ... 2.95

M.D. Geist: Ground Zero
CPM

❑1, Mar 1996; prequel to M.D. Geist, Armored Trooper Votoms preview back-up ... 2.95
❑2, Apr 1996; prequel to M.D. Geist, Armored Trooper Votoms preview back-up ... 2.95
❑3, May 1996; prequel to M.D. Geist, Armored Trooper Votoms preview back-up ... 2.95

Mea Culpa
Four Walls Eight Windows

❑1, Oct 1990 ... 12.95

Me-A Day With Elvis
Invincible

❑1 ... 1.00

Meadowlark
Parody

❑1, b&w; Shadowhawk silver foil cover parody ... 2.95

Me and Her
Fantagraphics / Eros

❑1, b&w; Adult ... 2.00
❑1/2nd; 2nd printing; Adult ... 2.00
❑2, b&w; Adult ... 2.00
❑3, Apr 1991; Adult ... 2.00
❑Special 1, b&w; Special edition; Adult ... 2.50

Mean, Green Bondo Machine
Mu

❑1, Jul 1992 ... 2.50

Mean Machine
Fleetway-Quality

❑1; Judge Dredd; no date of publication; Reprints Mean Machine stories from 2000 A.D. #730-736 ... 4.95

Meanwhile...
Crow

❑1, b&w ... 2.95
❑2, b&w ... 2.95

Measles
Fantagraphics

❑1 1998; Christmas 1998 ... 2.95
❑2 1999; Easter 1999 ... 2.95
❑3, Sum 1999 ... 2.95
❑4, Sum 1999 ... 2.95
❑5, Win 2000 ... 2.95
❑6, Spr 2000 ... 2.95
❑7 2000; New Year 2001 ... 2.95
❑8, Aug 2001 ... 2.95

Meat Cake
Fantagraphics

❑1, b&w; Adult ... 2.50
❑2, b&w; Adult ... 2.50
❑3, b&w; Adult ... 2.50
❑4, b&w; Adult ... 2.50
❑5, Nov 1995, b&w; Adult ... 2.95
❑6, Jan 1996, b&w; Adult ... 2.95
❑7 1997, b&w; Adult ... 2.95
❑8, Jun 1998, b&w; Adult ... 2.95

N-MINT

❑9, Apr 1999; Adult; b&w ... 2.95
❑10; Adult; b&w ... 2.95
❑11; Adult; b&w ... 3.95

Meat Cake
Iconografix

❑1, b&w ... 2.50

Meatface the Amazing Flesh Monster

❑1, b&w ... 2.50

Mecha
Dark Horse

❑1, Jun 1987 ... 1.75
❑2, Aug 1987 ... 1.75
❑3, Oct 1987, b&w ... 1.75
❑4, Dec 1987, b&w ... 1.75
❑5, Feb 1988, b&w ... 1.75
❑6, Apr 1988 ... 1.75

Mechanic
Image

❑1 1998; prestige format; NN; One-shot ... 5.95

Mechanical Man Blues
Radio

❑1, Dec 1998, b&w ... 2.95

Mechanics
Fantagraphics

❑1, Oct 1985; Introduction by Alan Moore ... 2.00
❑2, Nov 1985; Introduction by Wendy Pini ... 2.00
❑3, Dec 1985 ... 2.00

Mechanimals
Novelle

❑1, b&w ... 3.50
❑2, b&w ... 2.50

Mechanimoids Special X Anniversary
Mu

❑1, b&w; cardstock cover ... 3.50

Mechanoids
Caliber

❑1, b&w ... 2.50
❑2 ... 2.50
❑3 ... 2.50

Mech Destroyer
Image

❑1, Mar 2001 ... 2.95
❑2, Jun 2001; Indicia lists as March issue ... 2.95
❑3, Jul 2001 ... 2.95
❑4, Sep 2001 ... 2.95

Mechoverse
Airbrush

❑1; Airbrushed ... 1.50
❑2; Airbrushed ... 1.50
❑3; Airbrushed ... 1.50

Mechthings
Renegade

❑1, Jul 1987, b&w ... 2.00
❑2, Sep 1987, b&w ... 2.00
❑3, Nov 1987, b&w ... 2.00
❑4, Feb 1988, b&w ... 2.00

Medabots Part 1
Viz

❑1, Apr 2002, b&w ... 2.75
❑2, Apr 2002, b&w ... 2.75
❑3, May 2002, b&w ... 2.75
❑4, May 2002, b&w ... 2.75

Medabots Part 2
Viz

❑1, Jun 2002, b&w ... 2.75
❑2, Jun 2002, b&w ... 2.75
❑3, Jul 2002, b&w ... 2.75
❑4, Jul 2002, b&w ... 2.75

Medabots Part 3
Viz

❑1, Aug 2002, b&w ... 2.75
❑2, Aug 2002, b&w ... 2.75
❑3, Sep 2002, b&w ... 2.75
❑4, Sep 2002, b&w ... 2.75

Medabots Part 4
Viz

❑1, Oct 2002, b&w ... 2.75
❑2, Oct 2002, b&w ... 2.75
❑3, Nov 2002, b&w ... 2.75
❑4, Nov 2002, b&w ... 2.75

N-MINT

Medal of Honor
Dark Horse

❑1, Oct 1994 ... 2.50
❑2, Nov 1994 ... 2.50
❑3, Dec 1994 ... 2.50
❑4, Jan 1995 ... 2.50
❑5 ... 2.50
❑Special 1, Apr 1994, Special edition ... 2.50

Media*Starr
Innovation

❑1, Jul 1989 ... 1.95
❑2, Aug 1989 ... 1.95
❑3, Sep 1989 ... 1.95

Medieval Spawn
Image

❑1; three-part story; polybagged with Fan ... 2.00
❑2; three-part story; polybagged with Fan ... 2.00
❑3; three-part story; polybagged with Fan ... 2.00

Medieval Spawn/Witchblade
Image

❑1, May 1996 ... 3.00
❑1/AmEnt; American Entertainment exclusive; Gold cover ... 4.00
❑1/Gold, May 1996; Gold edition ... 6.00
❑1/Platinum; Platinum edition ... 15.00
❑2, Jun 1996 ... 3.50
❑3, Jun 1996; cover says Jul, indicia says Jun ... 3.00

Medieval Witchblade
Image

❑1 ... 5.90
❑2 ... 5.90
❑3 ... 5.90

Medora
Lobster

❑1, Dec 1999; Adult ... 2.95

Medusa Comics
Triangle

❑1 ... 1.50

MeetTheBank
Abaculus

❑1 ... 0.00

Meet the Bank
Custom

❑1, ca. 1995; Educational comic about banking ... 1.00

Megacity 909
Devil's Due

❑1 ... 6.00
❑1/Variant ... 5.00
❑2 ... 2.95
❑2/Variant ... 2.95
❑3 ... 2.95
❑3/Variant ... 2.95
❑4 ... 2.95
❑4/Variant ... 2.95
❑5 ... 2.95
❑5/Variant ... 2.95
❑6 ... 2.95
❑6/Variant ... 2.95
❑7 ... 2.95
❑7/Variant ... 2.95
❑8, Oct 2005 ... 2.95
❑8/Variant, Oct 2005 ... 2.95

Mega Dragon & Tiger
Image

❑1, Mar 1999 ... 2.95
❑2, Apr 1999 ... 2.95
❑3, May 1999 ... 2.95
❑4, Jun 1999 ... 2.95
❑5, Jul 1999 ... 2.95

Megahurtz
Image

❑1, Aug 1997, b&w ... 2.95
❑1/A, Aug 1997; no cover price ... 2.95
❑1/B, Aug 1997; no cover price ... 2.95
❑2, Sep 1997 ... 2.95
❑3, Oct 1997 ... 2.95

Megalith
Continuity

❑1 1989 ... 2.00
❑2 1989 ... 2.00
❑3 1990 ... 2.00

Other grades: Multiply price above by 5/6 for VF/NM • 2/3 for VERY FINE • 1/3 for FINE • 1/5 for VERY GOOD • 1/8 for GOOD

Minx

Imaginary childhood friend returns
©DC

Miracleman

Series had first Neil Gaiman work
©Eclipse

Mission: Impossible

Your mission, should you choose to accept it...
©Dell

Mr. and Mrs. J. Evil Scientist

Based on the Hanna-Barbera cartoon
©Gold Key

Mister Miracle

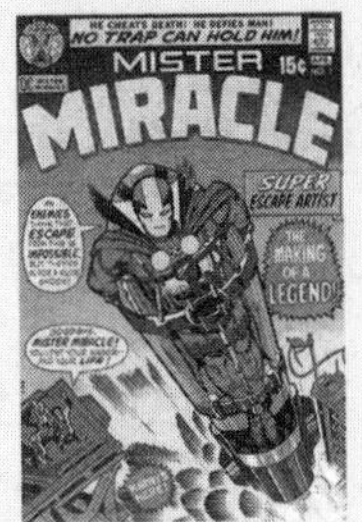

Son of the rulers of New Genesis
©DC

N-MINT

- ❑4, Nov 1990 ... 2.00
- ❑5, Jan 1991; NA (c); NA (w); MN, NA, TVE (a); Rise of Magic storyline ... 2.50
- ❑6, Jun 1991 ... 2.50
- ❑7, Jul 1991 ... 2.50
- ❑8, Dec 1991 ... 2.50
- ❑9, Mar 1992 ... 2.50

Megalith
Continuity

- ❑0, Apr 1993; silver foil issue number; prelude to Deathwatch 2000 ... 1.00
- ❑0/A, Apr 1993; red foil cover ... 1.00
- ❑1, Apr 1993; trading cards ... 2.50
- ❑2, Jun 1993; trading cards ... 2.50
- ❑3, Aug 1993; Wraparound cover ... 2.50
- ❑4, Oct 1993 ... 2.50
- ❑5, Dec 1993; Embossed cover ... 2.50
- ❑6, Dec 1993; Embossed cover ... 2.50
- ❑7, Jan 1994; Embossed cover ... 2.50

Megalomaniacal Spider-Man
Marvel

- ❑1, Jun 2002 ... 2.99

Megaman
Dreamwave

- ❑1, Sep 2003 ... 2.95
- ❑1/Dynamic, Sep 2003, Holofoil cover ... 5.95
- ❑2, Oct 2003 ... 2.95
- ❑3, Nov 2003 ... 2.95
- ❑4, Dec 2003 ... 2.95

Mega Morphs
Marvel

- ❑1, Sep 2005 ... 2.99
- ❑2, Oct 2005 ... 2.99
- ❑3, Nov 2005 ... 2.99
- ❑4, Dec 2005 ... 2.99

Megaton
Megaton

- ❑1, Nov 1983; BG, MGu, GD, EL (a); 1: Megaton. A: Vanguard ... 3.00
- ❑2, Oct 1985; EL (w); EL (a); One-page "Dragon" cameo by Erik Larsen ... 2.50
- ❑3, Feb 1986; EL (w); MGu, EL (a); 1: Savage Dragon ... 5.00
- ❑4, Apr 1986 ... 2.00
- ❑5, Jun 1986 ... 2.00
- ❑6, Dec 1986 ... 2.00
- ❑7, Apr 1987 ... 2.00
- ❑8, Aug 1987; 1: Youngblood in pin-up ... 2.50
- ❑Holiday 1; says 1994 on cover, 1993 in indicia ... 4.00

Megaton Man
Kitchen Sink

- ❑1, Nov 1984; O: Megaton Man ... 3.00
- ❑1/2nd; 2nd printing ... 2.00
- ❑2, Feb 1985 ... 2.50
- ❑3, Apr 1985 ... 2.50
- ❑4, Jun 1985 ... 2.50
- ❑5, Aug 1985 ... 2.50
- ❑6, Oct 1985; Border Worlds storyline begins ... 2.50
- ❑7, Dec 1985 ... 2.50
- ❑8, Feb 1986; Border Worlds back-up ... 2.50
- ❑9, Apr 1986 ... 2.50
- ❑10, Jun 1986; Final Issue ... 2.50

N-MINT

Megaton Man: Bombshell
Image

- ❑1, Jul 1999 ... 2.95

Megaton Man: Hardcopy
Image

- ❑1, Feb 1999, b&w; collects Internet strips ... 2.95
- ❑2, Apr 1999, b&w; collects Internet strips ... 2.95

Megaton Man Meets the Uncategorizable X+Thems
Kitchen Sink

- ❑1, Apr 1989, b&w; X-Men parody ... 2.00

Megaton Man vs. Forbidden Frankenstein
Fiasco

- ❑1, Apr 1996; aka Bizarre Heroes #16 ... 2.95

Megazzar Dude
Slave Labor

- ❑Special 1, Nov 1991, b&w ... 2.95

Mekanix
Marvel

- ❑1, Dec 2002; 1: Shola Inkose ... 2.99
- ❑2, Jan 2003 ... 2.99
- ❑3, Feb 2003 ... 2.99
- ❑4, Mar 2003 ... 2.99
- ❑5, Apr 2003 ... 2.99
- ❑6, May 2003 ... 2.99

Melissa Moore: Bodyguard
Draculina

- ❑1, b&w ... 2.95

Melody
Kitchen Sink

- ❑1, May 1988, b&w; Adult ... 2.50
- ❑2, Oct 1988, b&w; Adult ... 2.25
- ❑3, Mar 1989, b&w; Adult ... 2.00
- ❑4, Sep 1989, b&w; Adult ... 2.00
- ❑5, Apr 1990, b&w; Wraparound cover; Adult ... 2.00
- ❑6, Dec 1990, b&w; Adult ... 2.00
- ❑7, Feb 1992, b&w; Adult ... 2.25
- ❑8, Jan 1993, b&w; Adult ... 2.25

Melonpool Chronicles
Para-Troop

- ❑1 ... 2.95

Meltdown
Image

- ❑1, Jan 2007 ... 5.99

Melting Pot
Kitchen Sink

- ❑1, Dec 1993 ... 3.50
- ❑2, Feb 1994 ... 3.00
- ❑3 1994 ... 3.00
- ❑4, Sep 1994 ... 3.50

Melty Feeling
Antarctic / Venus

- ❑1, Oct 1996, b&w; Adult ... 3.50
- ❑2, Dec 1996, b&w; Adult ... 3.50
- ❑3, Jan 1997, b&w; Adult ... 3.50
- ❑4, Feb 1997, b&w; Adult ... 3.50

N-MINT

Melvin Monster
Dell

- ❑1, Apr 1965, JS (c); JS (w); JS (a) ... 60.00
- ❑2, Jul 1965, JS (c); JS (w); JS (a) ... 45.00
- ❑3, Dec 1965, JS (c); JS (w); JS (a) ... 40.00
- ❑4, Jul 1966, JS (c); JS (w); JS (a) ... 32.00
- ❑5, Oct 1966, JS (c); JS (w); JS (a) ... 32.00
- ❑6, Jan 1967, JS (c); JS (w); JS (a) ... 26.00
- ❑7, Apr 1967, JS (c); JS (w); JS (a) ... 26.00
- ❑8, May 1967, JS (c); JS (w); JS (a) ... 26.00
- ❑9, Aug 1967, JS (c); JS (w); JS (a) ... 26.00
- ❑10, Oct 1969, JS (c); JS (w); JS (a) ... 26.00

Melvis
Chameleon

- ❑1, Jul 1994; 2,500 copies ... 2.00
- ❑2 1994 ... 2.00
- ❑3 1994 ... 2.00
- ❑4 1994 ... 2.00

Memento Mori
Memento Mori

- ❑1 1995 ... 2.00
- ❑2, Mar 1995, b&w; no cover price ... 2.00

Memories
Marvel / Epic

- ❑1, ca. 1992, b&w; Japanese ... 2.50

Memory
NBM

- ❑1; Adult ... 25.00

Memoryman
David Markoff

- ❑1/Ashcan; Ashcan edition given as promo at 1995 San Diego Comicon; 1: Memoryman ... 1.00

Menagerie
Chrome Tiger

- ❑1, Nov 1987, b&w ... 1.95
- ❑2, Feb 1988, b&w ... 2.00

Mendy and the Golem
Mendy

- ❑1, Sep 1981 ... 2.50
- ❑2, Nov 1981 ... 2.00
- ❑3 1982 ... 2.00
- ❑4, Mar 1982 ... 2.00
- ❑5 1982 ... 2.00
- ❑6, Jul 1982 ... 2.00
- ❑7, Sep 1982; Numbered Vol. 2 #1 ... 2.00
- ❑8, Jan 1983; Numbered Vol. 2 #2 ... 2.00
- ❑9, Mar 1983; Says Vol. 2 #3 in indicia only ... 2.00
- ❑10, May 1983 ... 2.00
- ❑11, Jul 1983 ... 2.00
- ❑12, Sep 1983 ... 2.00
- ❑13, Nov 1983 ... 2.00
- ❑14, Jan 1984 ... 2.00
- ❑15, May 1984 ... 2.00
- ❑16, Sep 1984 ... 2.00
- ❑17, Feb 1985 ... 2.00
- ❑18, Mar 1985 ... 2.00
- ❑19, Apr 1985 ... 2.00

Men from Earth
Future-Fun

- ❑1 ... 2.00

Men in Black
Aircel

❑1, Jan 1990, b&w 15.00
❑2, Feb 1990, b&w 10.00
❑3, Mar 1990, b&w 8.00

Men in Black
Aircel

❑1, May 1991, b&w 14.00
❑2, Jun 1991, b&w 10.00
❑3, Jul 1991, b&w 8.00

Men in Black: Far Cry
Marvel

❑1, Aug 1997; Jay and Kay are reunited 3.99

Men in Black: Retribution
Marvel

❑1, Dec 1997 3.99

Men in Black: The Movie
Marvel

❑1, Oct 1997; adapts movie 3.99
❑1/AmEnt, ca. 1997, b&w; American Entertainment variant; reprints story from Aircel series 5.00

Men of Mystery
AC

❑1 6.95
❑2 6.95
❑3 6.95
❑4 6.95
❑5, ca. 1997; Golden-Age 6.95
❑6, ca. 1998; Golden-Age 6.95
❑7 6.95
❑8 6.95
❑9 6.95
❑10 6.95
❑11 6.95
❑12 6.95
❑13 6.95
❑14 6.95
❑15 6.95
❑16 6.95
❑17 6.95
❑18 6.95
❑19 6.95
❑20 6.95
❑21 6.95
❑22 6.95
❑23 6.95
❑24 6.95
❑25 6.95
❑26 6.95
❑27 6.95
❑28 6.95
❑29 6.95
❑30 6.95
❑31 6.95
❑32 6.95
❑33 6.95
❑34 6.95
❑35 6.95
❑36 6.95
❑37 6.95
❑38 6.95
❑39 6.95
❑40 6.95
❑41 6.95
❑42 6.95
❑43 6.95
❑44 6.95
❑45 6.95
❑46 6.95
❑47 6.95
❑48 6.95
❑49 6.95
❑50 6.95
❑51, ca. 2005 6.95
❑52, ca. 2005 6.95
❑53, ca. 2005 6.95
❑54, ca. 2005 6.95
❑55, ca. 2005 6.95
❑56, ca. 2005 6.95
❑Ann 15/Silver/3, ca. 2005 7.95

Men of War
DC

❑1, Aug 1977, 1&O: Gravedigger. Enemy Ace back-up 15.00
❑2, Sep 1977, JKu (c); Enemy Ace back-up 6.00
❑3, Nov 1977, JKu (c); Enemy Ace back-up 6.00
❑4, Jan 1978, JKu (c); Dateline: Frontline back-up 6.00
❑5, Mar 1978 6.00
❑6, May 1978 6.00
❑7, Jul 1978 6.00
❑8, Sep 1978, Enemy Ace story 6.00
❑9, Oct 1978, Enemy Ace backup story 6.00
❑10, Nov 1978, JKu (c); Enemy Ace and Dateline: Frontline back-ups 6.00
❑11, Dec 1978 6.00
❑12, Jan 1979, Enemy Ace story 6.00
❑13, Feb 1979, JKu (c); HC, RT (a); Enemy Ace story 4.00
❑14, Mar 1979, JKu (c); HC (a); Enemy Ace back-up 4.00
❑15, Apr 1979, JKu (c); JAb (a) 4.00
❑16, May 1979, JKu (c); Code Name: Gravedigger story 4.00
❑17, Jun 1979 4.00
❑18, Jul 1979 4.00
❑19, Aug 1979 4.00
❑20, Sep 1979, JKu (c); HC (a) 4.00
❑21, Oct 1979 4.00
❑22, Nov 1979 4.00
❑23, Dec 1979 4.00
❑24, Jan 1980 4.00
❑25, Feb 1980 4.00
❑26, Mar 1980, Final Issue 4.00

Men's Adventure Comix
Penthouse International

❑1, May 1995; Comic-sized; 1&O: Miss Adventure. 1&O: Hericane, Adult 6.00
❑2, Jul 1995; Adult 5.00
❑3, Sep 1995; Adult 5.00
❑4, Nov 1995; Adult 5.00
❑5, Dec 1995; Ringworld Throne preview; Adult 5.00
❑6, Feb 1996; Adult 5.00
❑7, Apr 1996; Adult 5.00

Menthu
Black Inc!

❑1, Jan 1998 2.95
❑2 1998 2.95
❑3 1998 2.95
❑4 1998 2.95

Menz Insana
DC / Vertigo

❑1; prestige format; NN; One-shot 7.95

Mephisto Vs.
Marvel

❑1, Apr 1987, AM (w); JB (a); Fantastic Four 2.50
❑2, May 1987, AM (w); JB (a); X-Factor 2.00
❑3, Jun 1987, AM (w); JB (a); X-Men 2.00
❑4, Jul 1987, AM (w); JB (a); Avengers 2.00

Mercedes
Angus

❑1 1995 2.95
❑2, Jan 1996 2.95
❑3, Feb 1996 2.95
❑4, Mar 1996 2.95
❑5, Apr 1996 2.95
❑6 2.95
❑7 2.95
❑8 2.95
❑9 2.95
❑10 2.95
❑11 2.95
❑12 2.95

Merchants of Death
Eclipse

❑1, Jul 1988, magazine 3.50
❑2, Aug 1988, magazine 3.50
❑3, Oct 1988, magazine 3.50
❑4, magazine 3.50

Merchants of Venus
DC

❑1 6.00

Mercy
DC / Vertigo

❑1; NN 6.00

Meridian
CrossGen

❑1, Jul 2000 3.50
❑2, Aug 2000 3.00
❑3, Sep 2000 3.00
❑4, Oct 2000 3.00
❑5, Nov 2000 3.00
❑6, Dec 2000 2.95
❑7, Jan 2001 2.95
❑8, Feb 2001 2.95
❑9, Mar 2001 2.95
❑10, Apr 2001 2.95
❑11, May 2001 2.95
❑12, Jun 2001 2.95
❑13, Jul 2001 2.95
❑14, Aug 2001 2.95
❑15, Sep 2001 2.95
❑16, Oct 2001 2.95
❑17, Nov 2001 2.95
❑18, Dec 2001 2.95
❑19, Jan 2002 2.95
❑20, Feb 2002 2.95
❑21, Mar 2002 2.95
❑22, Apr 2002 2.95
❑23, May 2002 2.95
❑24, Jun 2002 2.95
❑25, Jul 2002 2.95
❑26, Aug 2002 2.95
❑27, Sep 2002 2.95
❑28, Oct 2002 2.95
❑29, Nov 2002 2.95
❑30, Dec 2002 2.95
❑31, Jan 2003 2.95
❑32, Feb 2003 2.95
❑33, Mar 2003 2.95
❑34, Apr 2003 2.95
❑35, May 2003 2.95
❑36, Jun 2003 2.95
❑37, Jul 2003 2.95
❑38, Sep 2003 2.95
❑39, Nov 2003 2.95
❑40, Dec 2003 2.95
❑41, Jan 2004 2.95
❑42, Jan 2004 2.95
❑43, Mar 2004 2.95
❑44, Apr 2004; Final issue 2.95

Merlin
Adventure

❑1, Dec 1990, b&w 2.50
❑2, Jan 1991, b&w 2.50
❑3, Feb 1991, b&w 2.50
❑4, Mar 1991, b&w 2.50
❑5, Apr 1991, b&w 2.50
❑6, May 1991, b&w; Final Issue 2.50

Merlin: Idylls of the King
Adventure

❑1, Oct 1992, b&w 2.50
❑2, Nov 1992, b&w 2.50

Merlin Jones As The Monkey's Uncle
Gold Key

❑1, Oct 1965; Adapts Disney movie The Misadventures of Merlin Jones; photo stills on front cover, back cover, and inside covers 10.00

Merlinrealm 3-D
Blackthorne

❑1, Oct 1985 2.25

Mermaid
Alternative

❑1, May 1998, b&w; NN 2.95

Mermaid Forest
Viz

❑1, b&w 2.75
❑2, b&w 2.75
❑3, b&w 2.75
❑4, b&w 2.75

Mermaid's Dream
Viz

❑1, Oct 1985, b&w 2.75
❑2, b&w 2.75
❑3, b&w 2.75

Mr. T and the T-Force

He pities da fools that mess with him

©Now

Mister X

Angst-ridden independent comic

©Vortex

Misty

The niece of Millie the Model

©Marvel

Moby Duck

Crusty sea captain sails from Duckburg

©Gold Key

Mod Wheels

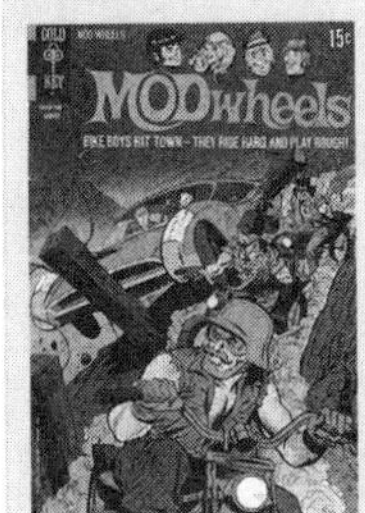

Mutton-chop sideburns and bell-bottom slacks

©Gold Key

N-MINT

Mermaid's Gaze
Viz

❑1, b&w 2.75
❑2, b&w 2.75
❑3, b&w 2.75
❑4, b&w 2.75

Mermaid's Mask
Viz

❑1, b&w 2.75
❑2, b&w 2.75
❑3, b&w 2.75
❑4 ..... 2.75

Mermaid's Promise
Viz

❑1, b&w 2.75
❑2, b&w 2.75
❑3, b&w 2.75
❑4, b&w 2.75

Mermaid's Scar
Viz

❑1, ca. 1994, b&w 2.75
❑2, b&w 2.75
❑3, b&w 2.75
❑4, b&w 2.75

Merton of the Movement
Last Gasp

❑1 ..... 3.50

Meru Puri
Viz

❑1, Jul 2005 ..... 8.99
❑2, Oct 2005 ..... 8.99

Merv Pumpkinhead, Agent of D.R.E.A.M.
DC / Vertigo

❑nn, ca. 2000; Prestige one-shot; cover says Sandman Presents..., but not indicia 5.95

Messenger
Image

❑1, Jul 2000 ..... 5.95

Messenger 29
September

❑1, Sep 1989, b&w 2.00

Messiah
Pinnacle

❑1, b&w 1.50

Messozoic
Kitchen Sink

❑1; NN 2.95

Meta-4
First

❑1, Feb 1991; 1&O: Meta-4 ..... 3.95
❑2, Mar 1991 ..... 2.25
❑3, Apr 1991 ..... 2.25

Metabarons
Humanoids

❑1, Jan 2000 ..... 4.00
❑2 2000 ..... 3.50
❑3 2000 ..... 3.50
❑4 2000 ..... 3.00
❑5, Jun 2000 ..... 3.00
❑6, Jul 2000 ..... 3.00
❑7, Aug 2000 ..... 3.00
❑8, Oct 2000 ..... 3.00
❑9, Dec 2000 ..... 3.00
❑10, Jan 2001 ..... 3.00
❑11, Feb 2001 ..... 2.95
❑12, Mar 2001 ..... 2.95
❑13, May 2001 ..... 2.95
❑14, May 2001 ..... 2.95

Metacops
Fantagraphics / Monster

❑1, Feb 1991, b&w 1.95
❑2, Mar 1991, b&w 1.95
❑3, Jul 1991, b&w 1.95

Metadocs: The Super E.R.
Antarctic

❑1, ca. 2005 ..... 4.95

Metal Bikini
Eternity

❑1, Oct 1990, b&w 2.25
❑2, Jun 1990, b&w 2.25
❑3 1991, b&w 2.25
❑4 1991, b&w 2.25
❑5 1991, b&w 2.25
❑6 1991, b&w 2.25

Metal Gear Solid
Idea & Design Works

❑1, Sep 2004 ..... 3.99
❑1/Silver, Sep 2004; Diamond 2004 Retailer Summit silver foil edition 7.00
❑1/2nd, Sep 2004; Woman with gun 3.99
❑1/Incentive, Sep 2004 ..... 35.00
❑2, Oct 2004 ..... 3.99
❑3, Nov 2004 ..... 3.99
❑4, Dec 2004 ..... 3.99
❑5, Jan 2005 ..... 3.99
❑6, Feb 2005 ..... 3.99
❑7, Mar 2005 ..... 3.99
❑8, Apr 2005 ..... 3.99
❑9, Jun 2005 ..... 3.99
❑10, Jul 2005 ..... 3.99
❑11, Aug 2005 ..... 3.99
❑12, Sep 2005 ..... 3.99
❑Ashcan 0, Jun 2004 ..... 1.00

Metal Gear Solid: Sons of Liberty
Idea & Design Works

❑0, Sep 2005 ..... 3.99
❑2, Dec 2005 ..... 3.99
❑3, Feb 2006 ..... 3.99
❑4, Feb 2006 ..... 3.99
❑5, Apr 2006 ..... 3.99
❑6, Jun 2006 ..... 3.99
❑7, Aug 2006 ..... 3.99
❑8, Nov 2006 ..... 3.99

Metal Guardian Faust
Viz

❑1, Mar 1997 ..... 2.95
❑2, Apr 1997 ..... 2.95
❑3, May 1997 ..... 2.95
❑4, Jun 1997 ..... 2.95
❑5, Jul 1997 ..... 2.95
❑6, Aug 1997 ..... 2.95
❑7, Sep 1997 ..... 2.95
❑8, Oct 1997 ..... 2.95

Metal Hurlant
DC

❑1; The Revolution has begun 8.00
❑2; Invasion! 8.00
❑3 ..... 8.00
❑4; By tomorrow I'll be dead 7.00
❑5 ..... 7.00
❑6, Jun 2003; War Holes 7.00
❑7, Jul 2003; Fragile 5.00
❑8, Sep 2003; The Zombies That Ate The World 5.00
❑9, Nov 2003 ..... 4.00
❑10, Jan 2004 ..... 4.00
❑11, Apr 2004 ..... 4.00
❑12, Sep 2004 ..... 4.00
❑13, Oct 2004 ..... 3.95
❑14, Jan 2005 ..... 3.95

Metallica
Celebrity

❑1/A 2.95
❑1/B; trading cards 6.95

Metallica
Forbidden Fruit

❑1, b&w; Adult 2.95
❑2, b&w; Adult 2.95

Metallica
Rock-It Comics

❑1; Includes guitar pick 5.00

Metallica's Greatest Hits
Revolutionary

❑1, Sep 1993, b&w 2.50

Metallix
Future

❑0, May 2003 ..... 3.50
❑1, Dec 2002 ..... 3.50
❑2 2003 ..... 3.50
❑3 2003 ..... 3.50
❑4, Apr 2003 ..... 3.50
❑5, Jun 2003 ..... 3.50
❑6, Jul 2003 ..... 2.99

Metal Men
DC

❑1, May 1963, 1: The Missile Men 500.00
❑2, Jul 1963, D: Tina (robot) 225.00
❑3, Sep 1963, 1: Tina (robot) II 150.00
❑4, Nov 1963, Tin (robot) leaves Earth .. 150.00
❑5, Jan 1964, 1: Mammoth Robots; 1: Mammoth Mechanical Queen 150.00
❑6, Mar 1964, 1: Doc Magnus (robot); 1: The Gas Gang 80.00
❑7, May 1964, Guy Lillian L.O.C.; 1: The Solar Brain 80.00
❑8, Jul 1964 ..... 80.00
❑9, Sep 1964 ..... 80.00
❑10, Nov 1964, 2: The Gas Gang; Metal Men appear next in Brave and the Bold #55 ..... 80.00
❑11, Jan 1965 ..... 55.00
❑12, Mar 1965, 2: The Missile Men 55.00
❑13, May 1965, 1: Tin's girlfriend. V: Skyscraper Robot 55.00
❑14, Jul 1965, 2: Chemo 55.00
❑15, Sep 1965, 1: B.O.L.T.S 55.00
❑16, Nov 1965 ..... 55.00
❑17, Jan 1966 ..... 55.00

Other grades: Multiply price above by 5/6 for VF/NM • 2/3 for VERY FINE • 1/3 for FINE • 1/5 for VERY GOOD • 1/8 for GOOD

N-MINT

❑18, Mar 1966 .... 55.00
❑19, May 1966, 1: The Man-Horse of Hades 55.00
❑20, Jul 1966, 1: Dr. Yes 55.00
❑21, Sep 1966, 1: Professor Bravo; 1: The Plastic Perils; 1: Ethylene; 1: Styrene; 1: Silicone; 1: Methacrylate; 1: Polyethylene 45.00
❑22, Nov 1966, 1: The Sizzler; Metal Men transformed into humans; Doc Magnus transformed into a robot 45.00
❑23, Jan 1967, 1: Profesor Snakelocks; 1: The Lizard (DC) 45.00
❑24, Mar 1967, 1: The Balloon Man 45.00
❑25, May 1967, D: The Sizzler 45.00
❑26, Jul 1967, 1: The Metal Mods 45.00
❑27, Sep 1967, O: Metal Men (partial reprint from Showcase #37) 80.00
❑28, Nov 1967, 1: The Leopard Mask gang 42.00
❑29, Jan 1968, 1: The Robot Eater of Metalas 5 .... 42.00
❑30, Mar 1968, 1: King Dymond 42.00
❑31, May 1968, 1: Back-Up Metal Men; 1: Metal Men (back-up team); 1: Silver; 1: Cobalt; 1: Zinc; 1: Osmium; 1: Gallium; 1: Iridia; 1: Darzz 24.00
❑32, Jul 1968, 1: The Robot Amazons; Last appearance of Nameless (robot) 24.00
❑33, Sep 1968 .... 24.00
❑34, Nov 1968 .... 24.00
❑35, Jan 1969 .... 24.00
❑36, Mar 1969 .... 24.00
❑37, May 1969, 1: Mr. Conan; 1: Dr. Pygmalion; Metal Men get human identites 24.00
❑38, Jul 1969, 1: The Black Coven 24.00
❑39, Sep 1969 .... 24.00
❑40, Nov 1969, Begin $0.15 cover; Price increase; Doc Will Magnus comes out of coma 24.00
❑41, Dec 1969, series put on hiatus 24.00
❑42, Mar 1973, Series begins again (1973); reprints 12.00
❑43, May 1973, Reprints 12.00
❑44, Jul 1973, V: Missile Men. back to hiatus; reprints 12.00
❑45, May 1976, DG (c); Series begins again (1976) 6.00
❑46, Jul 1976, DG (c); V: Chemo 6.00
❑47, Sep 1976, V: Plutonium Man; 1: Joanne Rome 6.00
❑48, Nov 1976, V: Eclipso 6.00
❑49, Jan 1977, V: Eclipso 6.00
❑50, Mar 1977, JSa, RA (a); Partial reprint, issue #6; Reprints Metal Men #6; Includes new framing sequence 6.00
❑51, May 1977, JSa (a); V: Vox; 1: Vox 6.00
❑52, Jul 1977, JSa (a); Begin $0.35 cover; 1: Dr. Strangelove (Norman Technmo); 1: The Brain Children; Price increase 6.00
❑53, Sep 1977, 2: Dr. Strangelove (Norman Technmo); 2: The Brain Children 6.00
❑54, Nov 1977, A: Green Lantern. 1: M-1; V: Missile Men 6.00
❑55, Jan 1978, V: Missile Men; 1: Z-1 .... 6.00
❑56, Mar 1978, V: Inheritor; Final Issue; 1: The Inheritor 6.00

Metal Men
DC

❑1, Oct 1993; foil cover 2.50
❑2, Nov 1993 .... 1.50
❑3, Dec 1993 .... 1.50
❑4, Jan 1994 .... 1.50

Metal Men of Mars & Other Improbable Tales
Slave Labor

❑1, Jan 1989, b&w; A: Tasma. A: Captain Daring 2.00

Metal Militia
Express / Entity

❑1/Ashcan, ca. 1995, b&w; enhanced cover 1.00
❑1, Aug 1995 .... 2.50
❑1/A, Aug 1995, b&w; enhanced cover; came w/PC game 6.95
❑2, Sep 1995 .... 2.50
❑3 1995 .... 2.50

Metamorpho
DC

❑1, Aug 1965 .... 75.00
❑2, Oct 1965 .... 45.00
❑3, Dec 1965 .... 40.00
❑4, Feb 1966, Metamorpho in Mexico 30.00
❑5, Apr 1966, Metamorpho vs. Metamorpho 30.00
❑6, Jun 1966 .... 30.00
❑7, Aug 1966 .... 30.00
❑8, Oct 1966, V: Doc Dread 30.00
❑9, Dec 1966 .... 30.00
❑10, Feb 1967, 1: Element Girl 25.00
❑11, Apr 1967 .... 25.00
❑12, Jun 1967 .... 25.00
❑13, Aug 1967 .... 25.00
❑14, Oct 1967 .... 25.00
❑15, Dec 1967 .... 25.00
❑16, Feb 1968 .... 25.00
❑17, Apr 1968, Final Issue 25.00

Metamorpho
DC

❑1, Aug 1993 .... 1.50
❑2, Sep 1993 .... 1.50
❑3, Oct 1993 .... 1.50
❑4, Nov 1993 .... 1.50

Metaphysique
Malibu

❑1, Apr 1995 .... 2.95
❑2, May 1995 .... 2.95
❑3, Jun 1995 .... 2.95
❑4, Aug 1995 .... 2.95
❑5, ca. 1995 .... 2.95
❑6, ca. 1995; A: Superius 2.95
❑Ashcan 1 .... 1.00

Metaphysique
Eclipse

❑1, Apr 1992 .... 2.50

Meteor Man
Marvel

❑1, Aug 1993; Movie tie-in 1.25
❑2, Sep 1993 .... 1.25
❑3, Oct 1993 .... 1.25
❑4, Nov 1993 .... 1.25
❑5, Dec 1993 .... 1.25
❑6, Jan 1994 .... 1.25

Meteor Man: The Movie
Marvel

❑1, Apr 1993; Movie adaptation 2.00

Metropolis S.C.U.
DC

❑1, Nov 1994 .... 1.50
❑2, Dec 1994 .... 1.50
❑3, Jan 1995 .... 1.50
❑4, Feb 1995 .... 1.50

Metropol
Marvel / Epic

❑1, ca. 1991 .... 2.95
❑2, ca. 1991 .... 2.95
❑3, ca. 1991 .... 2.95
❑4, ca. 1991 .... 2.95
❑5, ca. 1991 .... 2.95
❑6, ca. 1991 .... 2.95
❑7, ca. 1991 .... 2.95
❑8, ca. 1991 .... 2.95
❑9, ca. 1991 .... 2.95
❑10, ca. 1991 .... 2.95
❑11, ca. 1992 .... 2.95
❑12, ca. 1992, Final issue 2.95

Metropol A.D.
Marvel / Epic

❑1, Oct 1992 .... 3.50
❑2, Nov 1992 .... 3.50
❑3, Dec 1992 .... 3.50

Mez
C.A.P.

❑1, May 1997, b&w; Canadian cover price only 2.00
❑2, Mar 1998, b&w; Canadian cover price only 2.00

Mezz: Galactic Tour 2494
Dark Horse

❑1, May 1994, b&w; Nexus spin-off 2.50

M Falling
Vagabond

❑1; NN 3.50

MFI: The Ghosts of Christmas
Image

❑1, Dec 1999 .... 3.95

Miami Mice
Rip Off

❑1, Apr 1986 .... 2.00
❑1/2nd, May 1986; 2nd printing 2.00
❑1/3rd, May 1986; 3rd printing 2.00
❑2, Jul 1986, b&w 2.00
❑3, Oct 1986, b&w 2.00
❑3/A, Oct 1986, b&w; flexi-disc; w/soundsheet 5.00
❑4, Jan 1987, b&w 2.00

Michaelangelo Christmas Special
Mirage

❑1, Dec 1990, b&w 2.00

Michaelangelo Teenage Mutant Ninja Turtle
Mirage

❑1; Wraparound cover 2.50

Michael Jordan Tribute
Revolutionary

❑1 .... 2.95

Mickey and Donald
Gladstone

❑1, Mar 1988, CB, DR (w); CB, DR (a) 2.00
❑2, May 1988, WK (c); CB (w); CB (a) 2.00
❑3, Jul 1988, CB (w); CB (a) 2.00
❑4, Aug 1988, CB (w); CB, FG (a) 2.00
❑5, Sep 1988, WK (c); CB (w); CB (a) 2.00
❑6, Oct 1988, CB (w); CB (a) 2.00
❑7, Nov 1988, CB (a) 2.00
❑8, Dec 1988, CB (a) 2.00
❑9, Mar 1989, CB (a) 2.00
❑10, May 1989, CB (a) 2.00
❑11, Jul 1989, CB (a) 2.00
❑12, Aug 1989, CB (a) 2.00
❑13, Sep 1989, WK (c); CB (w); CB, FG (a); Reprints Donald Duck newspaper strips 2.00
❑14, Oct 1989, CB (a) 2.00
❑15, Nov 1989, CB (a) 2.00
❑16, Jan 1990, CB (a) 2.00
❑17, Mar 1990, CB, FG, DR (a) 1.95
❑18, May 1990, WK (c); CB, FG (a); series continues as Donald and Mickey 1.95

Mickey and Goofy Explore Energy
Dell

❑1, ca. 1976; giveaway; no indicia or cover price 2.00

Mickey & Minnie
W.D.

❑1; NN 3.50

Mickey Mantle
Magnum

❑1, Dec 1991; JSt (a); Photo cover 2.00
❑2 .... 2.00

Mickey Mouse
Dell / Gold Key/Whitman

❑80, Nov 1961 .... 14.00
❑81, Jan 1962 .... 12.00
❑82, Mar 1962 .... 12.00
❑83, Jun 1962 .... 12.00
❑84, Sep 1962 .... 12.00
❑85, Nov 1962, Gold Key Begins as Publisher 12.00
❑86, Feb 1963 .... 12.00
❑87, May 1963 .... 12.00
❑88, Jul 1963 .... 12.00
❑89, Sep 1963 .... 12.00
❑90, Nov 1963 .... 12.00
❑91, Dec 1963 .... 12.00
❑92, Feb 1964 .... 12.00
❑93, ca. 1964 .... 12.00
❑94, ca. 1964 .... 12.00
❑95, Jul 1964 .... 12.00
❑96, ca. 1964 .... 12.00
❑97, Oct 1964 .... 12.00
❑98, Nov 1964 .... 12.00
❑99, Feb 1965 .... 12.00
❑100, Apr 1965 .... 12.00

Monarchy, The

A new approach to changing the universe
©DC

Monkees

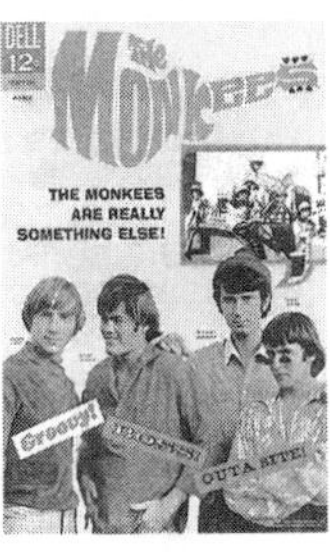

They may be coming to your town
©Gold Key

Monsters on the Prowl

Previously titled Chamber of Darkness
©Marvel

Moon Knight

Batman variant has multiple identities
©Marvel

Moonshadow

A fairy tale for grown-ups
©Marvel

	N-MINT
❑101, Jun 1965	11.00
❑102, Aug 1965	11.00
❑103, Oct 1965	11.00
❑104, Dec 1965	11.00
❑105, Feb 1966	11.00
❑106, Apr 1966	11.00
❑107, Jun 1966	11.00
❑108, Aug 1966	11.00
❑109, Oct 1966	11.00
❑110, Dec 1966	11.00
❑111, Feb 1967	11.00
❑112, Apr 1967	11.00
❑113, Jun 1967	11.00
❑114, Aug 1967	11.00
❑115, Nov 1967	11.00
❑116, Feb 1968, 10027-802	11.00
❑117, May 1968	11.00
❑118, Aug 1968	11.00
❑119, Nov 1968	11.00
❑120, Feb 1969	11.00
❑121, May 1969	10.00
❑122, Aug 1969	10.00
❑123, Nov 1969	10.00
❑124, Feb 1970	10.00
❑125, May 1970	10.00
❑126, Aug 1970	10.00
❑127, Nov 1970	10.00
❑128, Feb 1971	10.00
❑129, Apr 1971	10.00
❑130, Jun 1971	10.00
❑131, Aug 1971	10.00
❑132, Oct 1971	10.00
❑133, Dec 1971	10.00
❑134, Feb 1972	10.00
❑135, Apr 1972	10.00
❑136, Jun 1972	10.00
❑137, Aug 1972	10.00
❑138, Oct 1972	10.00
❑139, Dec 1972	10.00
❑140, Feb 1973	10.00
❑141, Apr 1973	8.00
❑142, Jun 1973	8.00
❑143, Aug 1973	8.00
❑144, Sep 1973	8.00
❑145, Oct 1973	8.00
❑146, Dec 1973	8.00
❑147, Feb 1974	8.00
❑148, Apr 1974	8.00
❑149, Jun 1974	8.00
❑150, Aug 1974	8.00
❑151, Sep 1974	8.00
❑152, Oct 1974	8.00
❑153, Dec 1974	8.00
❑154, Feb 1975	8.00
❑155, Apr 1975	8.00
❑156, Jun 1975	8.00
❑157, Aug 1975	8.00
❑158, Sep 1975	8.00
❑159, Oct 1975	8.00
❑160, Nov 1975	8.00
❑161, Jan 1976	7.00
❑162, Apr 1976	7.00
❑163, Jun 1976	7.00
❑164, Aug 1976	7.00
❑165, Sep 1976	7.00
❑166, Oct 1976	7.00

	N-MINT
❑167, Nov 1976	7.00
❑168, Dec 1976	7.00
❑169, Feb 1977	7.00
❑170, Apr 1977	7.00
❑171, May 1977	7.00
❑172, Jun 1977	7.00
❑173, Jul 1977	7.00
❑174, Aug 1977	7.00
❑175, Sep 1977	7.00
❑176, Oct 1977	7.00
❑177, Nov 1977	7.00
❑178, Dec 1977	7.00
❑179, Jan 1978	7.00
❑180, Feb 1978	7.00
❑181, Mar 1978	6.00
❑182, Apr 1978	6.00
❑183, May 1978	6.00
❑184, Jun 1978	6.00
❑185, Jul 1978	6.00
❑186, Aug 1978	6.00
❑187, Sep 1978	6.00
❑188, Oct 1978	6.00
❑189, Nov 1978	6.00
❑190, Dec 1978	6.00
❑191, Jan 1979	6.00
❑192, Feb 1979, Gold Key	6.00
❑193, Mar 1979	6.00
❑194, Apr 1979	6.00
❑195, May 1979	6.00
❑196, Jun 1979	6.00
❑197, Jul 1979	6.00
❑198, Aug 1979	6.00
❑199, Sep 1979	6.00
❑200, Oct 1979	6.00
❑201, Nov 1979	5.00
❑202, Dec 1979	5.00
❑203, Jan 1980	5.00
❑204, Feb 1980	8.00
❑205, Apr 1980	5.00
❑206, Jun 1980	5.00
❑207, Jul 1980	20.00
❑208, Aug 1980	50.00
❑209	20.00
❑210	7.00
❑211, Jun 1981	7.00
❑212, Aug 1981	7.00
❑213, Sep 1981	7.00
❑214, Dec 1981	7.00
❑215, Feb 1982	10.00
❑216	10.00
❑217	10.00
❑218	10.00
❑219, Oct 1986, FG (w); FG (a)	12.00
❑220, Nov 1986, FG (a)	4.00
❑221, Dec 1986, FG (a)	3.00
❑222, Jan 1987, FG (a)	3.00
❑223, Feb 1987, FG (a)	3.00
❑224, Mar 1987, FG (a)	3.00
❑225, Apr 1987, FG (a)	3.00
❑226, May 1987, FG (a)	3.00
❑227, Jun 1987, FG (a)	3.00
❑228, Jul 1987, FG (a)	3.00
❑229, Aug 1987, FG (a)	3.00
❑230, Sep 1987, FG (a)	3.00
❑231, Oct 1987, FG (a)	3.00
❑232, Nov 1987, FG (a)	3.00

	N-MINT
❑233, Dec 1987 FG (a)	3.00
❑234, Jan 1988, FG (a)	3.00
❑235, Mar 1988, FG (a)	3.00
❑236, Apr 1988, FG (a)	3.00
❑237, Jun 1988, FG (a)	3.00
❑238, Jul 1988, FG (a)	3.00
❑239, Aug 1988, FG (a)	3.00
❑240, Sep 1988, FG (a)	3.00
❑241, Oct 1988, FG (a)	2.00
❑242, Nov 1988, FG (a)	2.00
❑243, Dec 1988, FG (a)	2.00
❑244, Jan 1989, 60th anniversary, 100 pages; FG (a); Daily Strips compilation	2.00
❑245, Mar 1989, FG (a)	2.00
❑246, Apr 1989, FG (a)	2.00
❑247, Jun 1989, FG (a)	2.00
❑248, Jul 1989, FG (a)	2.00
❑249, Aug 1989, FG (a)	2.00
❑250, Sep 1989, FG (a)	2.00
❑251, Oct 1989, FG (w); FG (a)	2.00
❑252, Nov 1989, FG (a)	2.00
❑253, Dec 1989, FG (a)	2.00
❑254, Jan 1990, FG (a)	2.00
❑255, Feb 1990	2.00
❑256, Apr 1990	2.00

Mickey Mouse and Friends
Gemstone

	N-MINT
❑257, Sep 2003	2.95
❑258, Oct 2003	2.95
❑259, Nov 2003	2.95
❑260, Dec 2003	2.95
❑261, Jan 2004	2.95
❑262, Feb 2004	2.95
❑263, Mar 2004	2.95
❑264, Apr 2004	2.95
❑265, May 2004	2.95
❑266, Jun 2004	2.95
❑267, Jul 2004	2.95
❑268, Aug 2004	2.95
❑269, Sep 2004	2.95
❑270, Oct 2004	2.95
❑271, Nov 2004	2.95
❑272, Dec 2004; "The Happener" Strikes Again! reprinted from MM #30 (Also appears in MM #117)	2.95
❑273, Jan 2005	2.95
❑274, Feb 2005	2.95
❑275, Mar 2005	2.95
❑276, Apr 2005	2.95
❑277, May 2005	2.95
❑278, Jun 2005	2.95
❑279, Jul 2005	2.95
❑280, Aug 2005	2.95
❑281, Sep 2005	2.95
❑282, Oct 2005	2.95
❑283, Nov 2005	2.95
❑284, Dec 2005	2.95

Mickey Mouse
Disney

	N-MINT
❑1; in Russian	4.00

Mickey Mouse Adventures
Disney

	N-MINT
❑1, Jun 1990; Reprints from Mickey Mouse #45, 73	2.50
❑2, Jul 1990	2.00

Other grades: Multiply price above by 5/6 for VF/NM • 2/3 for VERY FINE • 1/3 for FINE • 1/5 for VERY GOOD • 1/8 for GOOD

❑3, Aug 1990; V: Phantom Blot 2.00
❑4, Sep 1990; Reprint from Mickey Mouse #83 .... 2.00
❑5, Oct 1990 .... 2.00
❑6, Nov 1990 .... 2.00
❑7, Dec 1990 .... 2.00
❑8, Jan 1991 JBy (c) 2.00
❑9, Feb 1991; Fantasia 2.00
❑10, Mar 1991; Reprint from Four Color Comics (2nd Series) #214 .... 2.00
❑11, Apr 1991 .... 2.00
❑12, May 1991 .... 2.00
❑13, Jun 1991; Reprints from Mickey Mouse #41 .... 2.00
❑14, Jul 1991 .... 2.00
❑15, Aug 1991 .... 2.00
❑16, Sep 1991 KB (w); KB (a) 2.00
❑17, Oct 1991; Dinosaur 2.00
❑18, Nov 1991; Dinosaur 2.00

Mickey Mouse Album
Gold Key

❑-210, Oct 1962, Cover code 01-518-210; no number 25.00
❑1, Sep 1963, Cover code 10082-309.... 20.00

Mickey Mouse and Goofy Explore Energy Conservation
Dell

❑1, ca. 1978, giveaway; no indicia or cover price 2.00

Mickey Mouse and Goofy Explore Energy Conservation
Disney

❑1, ca. 1978; Giveaway from Exxon; no indicia or cover price 2.00

Mickey and Goofy Explore the Universe of Energy
Disney

❑1, ca. 1985, Giveaway from Exxon available at Epcot; no indicia or cover price 3.00

Mickey Mouse Club
Gold Key

❑1, Jan 1964 .... 25.00

Mickey Mouse Digest
Gladstone

❑1, ca. 1986 .... 5.00
❑2, ca. 1986 .... 4.00
❑3, ca. 1986 .... 3.00
❑4, ca. 1986 .... 3.00
❑5, ca. 1987 .... 3.00

Mickey Mouse Surprise Party
Gold Key

❑1, Jan 1969, Reprints from Silly Symphonies #1, 2, Mickey Mouse #49, 58 .... 18.00

Mickey Rat
Los Angeles Comic Book Co.

❑1, May 1972, b&w; Adult 25.00
❑2, Oct 1972, b&w; Adult 20.00
❑3, Jul 1980, b&w; Adult 15.00
❑4, ca. 1982, b&w; Adult 15.00

Micra: Mind Controlled Remote Automaton
Comics Interview

❑1, Nov 1986; 1: MICRA; O: MICRA; b&w 1.75
❑2, Jan 1987; b&w 1.75
❑3, Feb 1987; b&w 1.75
❑4 1987; b&w 1.75
❑5 1987; b&w 1.75
❑6 1987; b&w 1.75
❑7 1987; b&w; ca. 1988 .... 1.75

Microbots
Gold Key

❑1, Dec 1971 .... 10.00

Micronauts
Marvel

❑1, Jan 1979, DC (c); MG (a); 1&O: Micronauts. 1: Baron Karza. 1: Space Glider. 1: Biotron. 1: Marionette. Newsstand edition (distributed by Curtis); issue number in box 4.00
❑1/Whitman, Jan 1979, MG (a); 1&O: Micronauts. 1: Baron Karza. 1: Space Glider. 1: Biotron. 1: Marionette. Special markets edition (usually sold in Whitman bagged prepacks); price appears in a diamond; no UPC barcode 4.00
❑1/2nd, Jan 1979, 2nd printing from Whitman; 1: Baron Karza; 1: Biotron; 1: Marionette; 1: Space Glider; 1: The Micronauts; O: Micronauts; 1: Arcoyear 2.00
❑2, Feb 1979, MG (c); MG (a); Newsstand edition (distributed by Curtis); issue number in box 3.00
❑2/Whitman, Feb 1979, MG (a); Special markets edition (usually sold in Whitman bagged prepacks); price appears in a diamond; no UPC barcode 3.00
❑3, Mar 1979, MG (c); MG (a); Newsstand edition (distributed by Curtis); issue number in box 2.50
❑3/Whitman, Mar 1979, MG (a); Special markets edition (usually sold in Whitman bagged prepacks); price appears in a diamond; no UPC barcode 2.50
❑4, Apr 1979, MG (c); MG (a) 2.50
❑5, May 1979, MG (c); MG (a); Newsstand edition (distributed by Curtis); issue number in box 2.50
❑5/Whitman, May 1979, MG (a); Special markets edition (usually sold in Whitman bagged prepacks); price appears in a diamond; no UPC barcode 2.50
❑6, Jun 1979, MG (c); MG (a) 2.00
❑7, Jul 1979, MG (c); MG (a); A: Man-Thing 2.00
❑8, Aug 1979, MG (c); MG (a); 1: Captain Universe 2.25
❑9, Sep 1979, MG (c); MG (a) 2.00
❑10, Oct 1979, MG (c); MG (a) 2.00
❑11, Nov 1979, MG (c); MG (a); V: Baron Karza 1.50
❑12, Dec 1979, MG (c); MG (w); MG (a) 1.50
❑13, Jan 1980 .... 1.50
❑14, Feb 1980 .... 1.50
❑15, Mar 1980, A: Fantastic Four. D: Microtron 1.50
❑16, Apr 1980, A: Fantastic Four 1.50
❑17, May 1980, A: Fantastic Four. D: Jasmine 1.50
❑18, Jun 1980 .... 1.50
❑19, Jul 1980 .... 1.50
❑20, Aug 1980, A: Ant-Man 1.50
❑21, Sep 1980, Tales of the Microverse. 1.50
❑22, Oct 1980, Tales of the Microverse.. 1.50
❑23, Nov 1980, V: Molecule Man; Tales of the Microverse 1.50
❑24, Dec 1980, Map of Homeworld; Tales of the Microverse 1.50
❑25, Jan 1981, O: Baron Karza. V: Mentallo; Tales of the Microverse... 1.50
❑26, Feb 1981, PB (c); PB (a) 1.50
❑27, Mar 1981, PB (c); PB (a); D: Biotron 1.50
❑28, Apr 1981, PB (c); PB (a); A: Nick Fury 1.50
❑29, May 1981, PB (c); PB (a); A: Nick Fury 1.50
❑30, Jun 1981, PB (c); PB (a) 1.50
❑31, Jul 1981, FM (c); PB, FM (a); A: Doctor Strange 1.50
❑32, Aug 1981, PB (c); PB (a); A: Doctor Strange 1.50
❑33, Sep 1981, BL (c); PB (a); A: Doctor Strange 1.50
❑34, Oct 1981, BL (c); PB (a); A: Doctor Strange 1.50
❑35, Nov 1981; double-sized; O: Microverse. A: Doctor Strange 1.50
❑36, Dec 1981 .... 1.50
❑37, Jan 1982, A: X-Men. A: Nightcrawler. 1: Huntarr 1.50
❑38, Feb 1982; Direct sales (only) begin 1.50
❑39, Mar 1982 .... 1.50
❑40, Apr 1982 A: Fantastic Four 1.50
❑41, May 1982; V: Dr. Doom 1.50
❑42, Jun 1982 .... 1.50
❑43, Jul 1982 .... 1.50
❑44, Aug 1982 .... 1.50
❑45, Sep 1982 .... 1.50
❑46, Oct 1982 .... 1.50
❑47, Nov 1982; Wraparound cover 1.50
❑48, Dec 1982; BG (a); 1st Guice 1.50
❑49, Jan 1983 .... 1.50
❑50, Feb 1983 .... 1.50
❑51, Mar 1983 .... 1.50
❑52, May 1983 .... 1.50
❑53, Jul 1983 .... 1.50
❑54, Sep 1983 .... 1.50
❑55, Nov 1983 .... 1.50
❑56, Jan 1984 .... 1.50
❑57, Mar 1984; double-sized 1.50
❑58, May 1984 .... 1.50
❑59, Aug 1984; Final Issue 3.00
❑Ann 1, Dec 1979 SD (c); SD (a) 4.00
❑Ann 2, Oct 1980; SD (c); RB, SD (a); V: Toymaster 3.00
❑Special 1, Dec 1983; Reprints material from Micronauts #1-3; New wraparound cover; Reprints from Micronauts #1-3 .... 2.00
❑Special 2, Jan 1984; Reprints material from Micronauts #3-5; New splash page and wraparound cover by Guice; Reprints from Micronauts #3-5; Map of Homeworld 2.00
❑Special 3, Feb 1984; Reprints material from Micronauts #6-8; Wraparound cover 2.00
❑Special 4, Mar 1984; Reprints material from Micronauts #8-10; New splash and wraparound cover by Guice; Reprints from Micronauts #8-10 .... 2.00
❑Special 5, Apr 1984; Reprints Micronauts #11 and #12, plus excerpts from #23 and #25; Wraparound cover; Reprints from Micronauts #11 and #12, plus excerpts from #23 and #25 .... 2.00

Micronauts
Marvel

❑1, Oct 1984, MG (c); Makers 3.00
❑2, Nov 1984 .... 1.50
❑3, Dec 1984 .... 1.50
❑4, Jan 1985 .... 1.50
❑5, Feb 1985 .... 1.50
❑6, Mar 1985 .... 1.50
❑7, Apr 1985 .... 1.50
❑8, May 1985 .... 1.50
❑9, Jun 1985 .... 1.50
❑10, Jul 1985 .... 1.50
❑11, Aug 1985 .... 1.50
❑12, Sep 1985 .... 1.50
❑13, Oct 1985 .... 1.50
❑14, Nov 1985 .... 1.50
❑15, Dec 1985 .... 1.50
❑16, Jan 1986, Secret Wars II 1.50
❑17, Feb 1986 .... 1.50
❑18, Mar 1986 KP (c) 1.50
❑19, Apr 1986 .... 1.50
❑20, May 1986 .... 1.50

Micronauts
Image

❑1, ca. 2002 .... 2.95
❑2, ca. 2002 .... 2.95
❑3, ca. 2002 .... 2.95
❑4, Dec 2002 .... 2.95
❑5, Feb 2003 .... 2.95
❑6, Mar 2003 .... 2.95
❑7, Apr 2003; Final issue 2.95
❑8, Jun 2003 .... 2.95
❑9, Jul 2003, Invasion, Part 2 .... 2.95
❑10, Aug 2003, Invasion, Part 3 .... 2.95
❑11, Oct 2003, Final issue 2.95

Middle Class Fantasies
Cartoonists Co-Op

❑1, b&w 3.00
❑2 .... 3.00

Middleman
Viper

❑1, Aug 2005 .... 2.95
❑2, Sep 2005 .... 2.95
❑3, Oct 2005 .... 2.95
❑4, Nov 2005 .... 2.95

Midnight
Ajax

❑1, Apr 1957 .... 54.00
❑2, Jul 1958 .... 38.00

Morbius: The Living Vampire

Vampire got his start in Spider-Man
©Marvel

More Than Mortal

Fantasy had heat briefly in 1997
©Liar

Mort the Dead Teenager

More uplifting fare for our nation's youth
©Marvel

Mother Teresa of Calcutta

Companion to Marvel's Pope John Paul comic
©Marvel

Ms. Marvel

Liberated heroine keeps changing her name
©Marvel

	N-MINT
❑3, Sep 1957	26.00
❑4	26.00
❑5, Feb 1958	26.00
❑6, Jun 1958	26.00

Midnighter
DC / Wildstorm

	N-MINT
❑1, Jan 2007	2.99
❑1/Variant, Jan 2007	2.99
❑1/2nd variant, Jan 2007	2.99
❑2, Feb 2007	2.99
❑2/Variant, Feb 2007	2.99
❑3, Mar 2007	2.99
❑3/Variant, Mar 2007	2.99

Midnight Eye Gokü
Viz

	N-MINT
❑1	4.95
❑2	4.95
❑3	4.95
❑4	4.95
❑5	4.95
❑6	4.95

Midnight Kiss
APComics

	N-MINT
❑1, ca. 2005	3.50

Midnight, Mass
DC / Vertigo

	N-MINT
❑1, Jun 2002	2.50
❑2, Jul 2002	2.50
❑3, Aug 2002	2.50
❑4, Sep 2002	2.50
❑5, Oct 2002	2.50
❑6, Nov 2002	2.50
❑7, Dec 2002	2.50
❑8, Jan 2003	2.50

Midnight Mass
DC / Vertigo

	N-MINT
❑1, Mar 2004	2.95
❑2, Apr 2004	2.95
❑3, May 2004	2.50
❑4, Jun 2004	2.50
❑5, Jul 2004	2.95
❑6, Aug 2004	2.95

Midnight Men
Marvel / Epic

	N-MINT
❑1, Jun 1993; Embossed cover	2.50
❑2, Jul 1993	1.95
❑3, Aug 1993	1.95
❑4, Sep 1993	1.95

Midnight Nation
Image

	N-MINT
❑½, Mar 2001, Wizard send-away promotional edition	5.00
❑½/Gold, Mar 2001, Gold edition; Wizard send-away promotional edition	9.00
❑1/A, Oct 2000, Cover A	4.00
❑1/B, Oct 2000, Dynamic Forces Exclusive; Cover B	5.00
❑1/C, Oct 2000, Dynamic Forces limited, numbered edition	8.00
❑1/D, Oct 2000, Convention exclusive edition; Convention exclusive edition	4.50
❑2, Nov 2000	3.00
❑3, Dec 2000	3.00
❑4, Jan 2001	3.00
❑5, Mar 2001	3.00
❑6, Apr 2001	2.50
❑7, May 2001	2.50
❑8, Jun 2001	2.50
❑9, Jul 2001, World Trade Center cover.	2.50
❑10, Aug 2001	2.50
❑11, Sep 2001	2.50
❑12, Oct 2001, Final issue	2.95

Midnight Panther
CPM

	N-MINT
❑1, Apr 1997; Adult; b&w	2.95
❑2, May 1997; Adult; b&w	2.95
❑3, Jun 1997; Adult; b&w	2.95
❑4, Jul 1997; Adult; b&w	2.95
❑5, Aug 1997; Adult; b&w	2.95
❑6, Sep 1997; Adult	2.95
❑7, Oct 1997; Adult	2.95
❑8, Nov 1997; Adult	2.95
❑9, Dec 1997; Adult	2.95
❑10, Jan 1998; Adult	2.95
❑11, Feb 1998; Adult	2.95
❑12, Mar 1998; Adult	2.95

Midnight Panther: Feudal Fantasy
CPM

	N-MINT
❑1, Sep 1998; wraparound cover	2.95
❑2, Oct 1998; Adult	2.95

Midnight Panther: School Daze
CPM

	N-MINT
❑1, Apr 1998; wraparound cover	2.95
❑2, May 1998; Adult; b&w	2.95
❑3, Jun 1998; wraparound cover	2.95
❑4, Jul 1998; Adult; b&w	2.95
❑5, Aug 1998; Adult; b&w	2.95

Midnight Screams
Mystery Graphix

	N-MINT
❑1	2.50
❑2, Jan 1992	2.50

Midnight Sons Unlimited
Marvel

	N-MINT
❑1, Apr 1993 KJ (a)	4.00
❑2, Jul 1993 BSz (c)	4.00
❑3, Oct 1993 JR2 (c); JR2 (a); A: Spider-Man	4.00
❑4, Jan 1994	3.95
❑5, Apr 1994	3.95
❑6, Jul 1994	3.95
❑7, Oct 1994	3.95
❑8, Jan 1995	3.95
❑9, May 1995 ARo (c); A: Destroyer. A: Union Jack. A: Blazing Skull	3.95
❑Ashcan 1; Previews the Midnight Sons titles	0.75

Midnite
Blackthorne

	N-MINT
❑1, Nov 1986	1.75
❑2, Jan 1987	1.75
❑3, Mar 1987	1.75

Midnite Skulker
Target

	N-MINT
❑1, Jun 1986; b&w series	1.75
❑2, Aug 1986, b&w	1.75
❑3, Oct 1986	1.75
❑4, Dec 1986, b&w	1.75
❑5, Feb 1987	1.75
❑6, Apr 1987	1.75
❑7, Aug 1987	1.75

Midnite's Quickies
One Shot

	N-MINT
❑1, b&w	3.50
❑2, b&w	2.95
❑Special 1, Oct 1997, b&w; No cover price; no indicia; published in Oct 97 .	3.00
❑Special 1/A, Jan 1998, b&w; No cover price; center color poster	3.00
❑Special 1/B, Oct 1997, b&w; foil variant cover	3.00

Midori Days
Viz

	N-MINT
❑1, Aug 2005	9.99
❑2, Oct 2005	9.99

Midvale
Mu

	N-MINT
❑1, b&w	2.50
❑2, Oct 1990, b&w	2.50

Mightily Murdered Power Ringers
Express / Parody Press

	N-MINT
❑1, b&w	2.50

Mighty Ace
Omega 7

	N-MINT
❑1	2.00
❑2; indicia indicates 1992 copyright, probably not year of publication	2.00

Mighty Bomb
Antarctic

	N-MINT
❑1, Jul 1997, b&w	2.95

Mighty Bombshells
Antarctic

	N-MINT
❑1, Sep 1993, b&w	2.75
❑2, Oct 1993, b&w	2.75

Mighty Cartoon Heroes
Karl Art

	N-MINT
❑0	2.95

Mighty Comics
Archie

	N-MINT
❑40, Nov 1966, Series continued from Fly Man #39	15.00
❑41, Dec 1966	15.00
❑42, Jan 1967	15.00
❑43, Feb 1967, 1: The Storm King. 1: The Stunner. A: The Web. A: The Shield. Black Hood appearace	15.00
❑44, Mar 1967	15.00
❑45, Apr 1967	15.00
❑46, May 1967	15.00
❑47, Jun 1967	15.00
❑48, Jul 1967	15.00
❑49, Aug 1967	15.00
❑50, Oct 1967, Final Issue	15.00

Mighty Crusaders
Archie

	N-MINT
❑1, Nov 1965, O: The Shield	24.00
❑2, Jan 1966, O: The Comet	15.00
❑3, Mar 1966, O: Fly Man	12.00
❑4, Apr 1966, "Too Many Superheroes"	10.00
❑5, Jun 1966, 1: The Terrific Three	10.00
❑6, Aug 1966	10.00
❑7, Oct 1966, O: Fly Girl	10.00

Other grades: Multiply price above by 5/6 for VF/NM • 2/3 for VERY FINE • 1/3 for FINE • 1/5 for VERY GOOD • 1/8 for GOOD

Mighty Crusaders
Archie / Red Circle

- ❑4, Nov 1983, RB (c); RB (w); RB (a); Previously titled All New Adventures of the Mighty Crusaders 1.25
- ❑5, Jan 1984, b&w 1.25
- ❑6, Mar 1984, b&w 1.25
- ❑7, May 1984, b&w 1.25
- ❑8, Jul 1984, b&w 1.25
- ❑9, Sep 1984, b&w 1.25
- ❑10, Dec 1984, b&w 1.25
- ❑11, Mar 1985, b&w 1.25
- ❑12, Jun 1985, b&w 1.25
- ❑13, Sep 1985, b&w 1.25

Mightyguy
C&T

- ❑1, May 1987; 1&O: Mightyguy 1.50
- ❑2 1987 .... 1.50
- ❑3 1987 .... 1.50
- ❑4 1987 .... 1.50
- ❑5 1987 .... 1.50

Mighty Hercules
Gold Key

- ❑1, Jul 1963 .... 40.00
- ❑2, Oct 1963, Back cover pin-up 40.00

Mighty Heroes
Dell

- ❑1, Mar 1967, O: The Mighty Heroes. based on Terrytoons feature 125.00
- ❑2, ca. 1967 .... 60.00
- ❑3, ca. 1967 .... 60.00
- ❑4, ca. 1967 .... 60.00

Mighty Heroes
Marvel / Paramount

- ❑1, Jan 1998; based on Terrytoons feature 2.99

Mighty I
Image

- ❑1, May 1995; Image Comics Fan Club.. 1.25
- ❑2, Jul 1995; Image Comics Fan Club.... 1.25

Mighty Love
DC

- ❑1, ca. 2005; Softcover 17.95
- ❑1/HC, ca. 2004; Hardcover 24.95

Mighty Magnor
Malibu

- ❑1, Apr 1993; ME (w); SA (a); 1: The Mighty Magnor 2.25
- ❑1/Variant, Apr 1993; ME (w); SA (a); 1: The Mighty Magnor. Pop-up cover . 3.95
- ❑2, May 1993 ME (w); SA (a) 1.95
- ❑3, Jun 1993 ME (w); SA (a) 1.95
- ❑4, Jul 1993 ME (w); SA (a) 1.95
- ❑5, Dec 1993 ME (w); SA (a) 1.95
- ❑6, Apr 1994; ME (w); SA (a); Final Issue 1.95

Mighty Man
Image

- ❑1, Mar 2005 .... 7.95

Mighty Marvel Must Haves: Astonishing X-Men #1-3
Marvel

- ❑1 2004 .... 0.00

Mighty Marvel Western
Marvel

- ❑1, Oct 1968, giant; Rawhide Kid, Kid Colt, Two-Gun Kid 45.00
- ❑2, Dec 1968, giant; Rawhide Kid, Kid Colt, Two-Gun Kid 30.00
- ❑3, Feb 1969, giant; Rawhide Kid, Kid Colt, Two-Gun Kid 25.00
- ❑4, Apr 1969, giant; Rawhide Kid, Kid Colt, Two-Gun Kid 25.00
- ❑5, Jun 1969, giant; Rawhide Kid, Kid Colt, Two-Gun Kid 25.00
- ❑6, Nov 1969, Reprints from Rawhide Kid #28, 31, Two-Gun Kid #66, Kid Colt Outlaw #111; Giant 20.00
- ❑7, Jan 1970, Reprints from Rawhide Kid #50, Two-Gun Kid #80, Kid Colt Outlaw #72, 112; Giant 20.00
- ❑8, May 1970, Reprints from Rawhide Kid #52, Two-Gun Kid #81, Kid Colt Outlaw #117; Giant 20.00
- ❑9, Jul 1970, Reprints from Rawhide Kid #54, Two-Gun Kid #62, Kid Colt Outlaw #78, 118; Giant 20.00
- ❑10, Sep 1970, Reprints from Rawhide Kid #54, 55, Two-Gun Kid #91, Kid Colt Outlaw #119; Giant 20.00
- ❑11, Nov 1970, Reprints from Rawhide Kid #58, Two-Gun Kid #72, Kid Colt Outlaw #80; Giant 20.00
- ❑12, Jan 1971, Reprints from Rawhide Kid #20, Two-Gun Kid #83, Kid Colt Outlaw #86; Giant 20.00
- ❑13, May 1971, Reprints from Rawhide Kid #21, Two-Gun Kid #84, Kid Colt Outlaw; Giant 20.00
- ❑14, Sep 1971, Reprints from Rawhide Kid #30, 31, Two-Gun Kid #54, Kid Colt Outlaw; Giant 20.00
- ❑15, Dec 1971, Reprints from Rawhide Kid #60, Two-Gun Kid #54, 55, Kid Colt Outlaw #64, Ringo Kid #14; Giant 20.00
- ❑16, Mar 1972, Reprints from Rawhide Kid #7, 10, Two-Gun Kid #59, Kid Colt Outlaw 15.00
- ❑17, Jun 1972, Reprints from Rawhide Kid #7, 10, Two-Gun Kid #52, Kid Colt Outlaw #44 .... 15.00
- ❑18, Jul 1972, Reprints from Rawhide Kid #11, Two-Gun Kid #50, Kid Colt Outlaw #44 .... 15.00
- ❑19, Sep 1972, Reprints from Rawhide Kid #11, Two-Gun Kid #50, Kid Colt Outlaw #45 .... 15.00
- ❑20, Oct 1972, Reprints from Rawhide Kid #7, 10, Two-Gun Kid #50, Kid Colt Outlaw #88 .... 15.00
- ❑21, Nov 1972, SL (w); JSe (a); Reprints from Rawhide Kid #34, Two-Gun Kid #52, Kid Colt Outlaw #88 .... 15.00
- ❑22, Jan 1973, SL (w); Reprints from Rawhide Kid #34, Kid Colt Outlaw #92, Outlaw Kid #8 .... 10.00
- ❑23, Mar 1973, Reprints from Rawhide Kid #15, Two-Gun Kid #56, Kid Colt Outlaw #75, Wyatt Earp #25 .... 10.00
- ❑24, May 1973, RB (c); SL (w); JSe (a); Reprints from Rawhide Kid #33, Kid Colt Outlaw #62, Matt Slade, Gunfighter #4 .... 10.00
- ❑25, Jul 1973, Reprints from Rawhide Kid #26, 40, Two-Gun Kid #10, Matt Slade, Gunfighter #4 .... 10.00
- ❑26, Sep 1973, Reprint from Rawhide Kid #31 .... 10.00
- ❑27, Oct 1973, Reprints from Rawhide Kid #25, Two-Gun Kid #51, Matt Slade, Gunfighter #4 .... 10.00
- ❑28, Dec 1973, Reprints from Rawhide Kid #26, Two-Gun Kid #65 .... 10.00
- ❑29, Jan 1974, Reprints from Rawhide Kid #23, Two-Gun Kid #51 .... 10.00
- ❑30, Mar 1974, Reprints from Rawhide Kid, Two-Gun Kid #49, Kid Slade, Gunfighter #5 .... 10.00
- ❑31, May 1974, Reprints from Rawhide Kide #15, Two-Gun Kid #55, Kid Slade, Gunfighter #5 .... 10.00
- ❑32, Jul 1974, Reprints from Rawhide Kid #23, Gunsmoke Western #58, Kid Slade, Gunfighter #7 .... 10.00
- ❑33, Aug 1974, Reprints from Rawhide Kid #25, Two-Gun Kid #11, Kid Slade, Gunfighter #7, Cowboy Action #5 ...... 10.00
- ❑34, Sep 1974, Reprints from Rawhide Kid #29, Two-Gun Kid #11, Kid Slade, Gunfighter #7 .... 10.00
- ❑35, Oct 1974, Reprints from Rawhide Kid #25, Two-Gun Kid #60, Kid Slade, Gunfighter #7, Western Kid #15 .... 10.00
- ❑36, Dec 1974, Reprints from Rawhide Kid #29, Two-Gun Kid #11, Kid Slade, Gunfighter #6 .... 10.00
- ❑37, Jan 1975, Reprints from Rawhide Kid #29, Two-Gun Kid #42, 51, Kid Slade, Gunfighter #6 .... 10.00
- ❑38, Mar 1975, New cover; Reprints stories from Rawhide Kid #19, Kid Slade #6, Two Gun Kid #65, #64; Reprints from Rawhide Kid #19, Two Gun Kid #64, 65, Kid Slade, Gunfighter #6 .... 10.00
- ❑39, May 1975, Reprints from Rawhide Kid #26, Two-Gun Kid #51, Kid Slade, Gunfighter #8 .... 10.00
- ❑40, Jul 1975, Reprints from Rawhide Kid #28, Two-Gun Kid #91, Kid Slade, Gunfighter #8 .... 10.00
- ❑41, Sep 1975, New cover; Reprints stories from Rawhide Kid #28, Kid Slade #8, Two-Gun Kid #51, and Western Outlaws #70; Reprints from Rawhide Kid #28, Two-Gun Kid #51, Kid Slade, Gunfigher #8, Western Outlaws and Sheriffs #70 .... 10.00
- ❑42, Oct 1975, Reprints from Rawhide Kid #27, Two-Gun Kid #41, Kid Slade, Gunfighter #5 .... 10.00
- ❑43, Dec 1975, Reprints from Rawhide Kid #30, Two-Gun Kid #41, Kid Colt Outlaw #91 .... 10.00
- ❑44, Mar 1976, Reprints from Rawhide Kid #28, Two-Gun Kid #41, Kid Slade, Gunfighter #8 .... 10.00
- ❑45, Jun 1976, Reprints Rawhide Kid #30, #67 and Two-Gun Kid #61 .... 10.00
- ❑45/30¢, Jun 1976, 30¢ regional price variant 20.00
- ❑46, Sep 1976, Final Issue; Reprints from Rawhide Kid #17, Two-Gun Kid #38, Kid Colt Outlaw #63 .... 10.00

Mighty Mites
Eternity

- ❑1, Oct 1986; X-Men parody 2.00
- ❑2/A, Jan 1987; Batman parody 2.00
- ❑2/B, Jan 1987; Batman parody 2.00
- ❑3, Mar 1987, B&w and color 2.00

Mighty Mites
Eternity

- ❑1, May 1987 .... 1.95
- ❑2, Jul 1987 .... 1.95

Mighty Morphin Power Rangers
Marvel

- ❑1, Nov 1995 .... 2.50
- ❑2, Dec 1995 .... 2.00
- ❑3, Dec 1995, cover says Jan, indicia says Dec 2.00
- ❑4, Feb 1996 .... 2.00
- ❑5, Mar 1996 .... 2.00
- ❑6, Apr 1996 .... 2.00
- ❑7, May 1996 .... 2.00
- ❑8, Jun 1996 .... 2.00
- ❑9, Jul 1996 .... 2.00

Mighty Morphin Power Rangers: Ninja Rangers/VR Troopers
Marvel

- ❑1, Dec 1995, flip book with VR Troopers back-up 2.50
- ❑2, Jan 1996, Power Rangers cover says Dec 95 .... 2.00
- ❑3, Feb 1996, flip book with VR Troopers back-up 2.00
- ❑4, Mar 1996, SD (a); flip book with VR Troopers back-up 2.00
- ❑5, Apr 1996, SD (a); flip book with VR Troopers back-up 2.00
- ❑6, May 1996 .... 2.00
- ❑7, Jun 1996 .... 2.00
- ❑8, Jul 1996, Final Issue 2.00

Mighty Morphin Power Rangers Saga
Hamilton

- ❑1, Dec 1994, O: Power Rangers 2.50
- ❑2, Jan 1995 .... 2.50
- ❑3, Feb 1995 .... 2.50

Mighty Morphin Power Rangers: The Movie
Marvel

- ❑1, Sep 1995; NN; Movie adaptation 2.95
- ❑1/Variant, Sep 1995; cardstock cover .. 3.95

Mighty Mouse
Gold Key

- ❑161, Oct 1964, Previous issues published as Adventures of Mighty Mouse (2nd Series) 30.00
- ❑162, Jan 1965 .... 30.00
- ❑163, Mar 1965 .... 30.00
- ❑164, Jul 1965 .... 30.00
- ❑165, Sep 1965, Series later revived with continued numbering as Adventures of Mighty Mouse (Gold Key) 30.00
- ❑167 .... 40.00
- ❑168, Sep 1966 .... 40.00
- ❑169, Dec 1966 .... 40.00

Mighty Mouse
Spotlight

- ❑1, ca. 1987 .... 2.00
- ❑2, ca. 1987 .... 2.00

Ms. Mystic

One of a long line of delayed titles
©Pacific

Ms. Tree

Mysteries by Max Allan Collins and Terry Beatty
©Eclipse

Munsters

TV family made seamless transition to comics
©Gold Key

Muppet Babies

Apparently the real Muppets were too "mature"
©Marvel

Mutant X

It's just too complicated to explain
©Marvel

N-MINT

Mighty Mouse
Marvel / Star

❑1, Oct 1990; Dark Knight parody cover 2.00
❑2, Nov 1990; Mighty Mouse Chronology 1.50
❑3, Dec 1990; JBy (c); 1: Bat-Bat. Sub-Mariner parody 1.50
❑4, Jan 1991; GP (c);Crisis parody 1.50
❑5, Feb 1991; Crisis parody 1.50
❑6, Mar 1991; McFarlane parody 1.50
❑7, Apr 1991; computer art 1.50
❑8, May 1991 1.50
❑9, Jun 1991 1.50
❑10, Jul 1991; Letterman parody 1.50

Mighty Mouse Adventure Magazine
Spotlight

❑1, b&w; ca. 1987 2.00

Mighty Mouse and Friends Holiday Special
Spotlight

❑1 2.00

Mighty Mutanimals
Archie

❑1, May 1991; TMNT spin-off 1.50
❑2 1991; TMNT spin-off 1.25
❑3 1991; TMNT spin-off 1.25

Mighty Mutanimals
Archie

❑1, Apr 1992 1.25
❑2, Jun 1992 1.25
❑3, Aug 1992 1.25
❑4, Sep 1992 1.25
❑5, Oct 1992 1.25
❑6, Dec 1992 1.25
❑7, Feb 1993; 1: Armaggon; 1: Merdude 1.25
❑8, Apr 1993 1.25

Mighty Samson
Gold Key

❑1, Jul 1964, O: Samson. 1: Samson. back cover pin-up 75.00
❑2, Jun 1965, 1: Terra of Jerz. back cover pin-up 45.00
❑3, Sep 1965, back cover pin-up 45.00
❑4, Dec 1965, back cover pin-up 45.00
❑5, Mar 1966, back cover pin-up 30.00
❑6, Jun 1966, back cover pin-up 30.00
❑7, Sep 1966, back cover pin-up 30.00
❑8, Dec 1966 30.00
❑9, Mar 1967, In Washington, D.C. 30.00
❑10, Jun 1967 30.00
❑11, Aug 1967 20.00
❑12, Nov 1967 20.00
❑13, Feb 1968 20.00
❑14, May 1968 20.00
❑15, Aug 1968 20.00
❑16, Nov 1968 20.00
❑17, Feb 1969 20.00
❑18, May 1969 20.00
❑19, Aug 1969, N'Yark floods 20.00
❑20, Nov 1969 20.00
❑21, Aug 1972, Reprints from Mighty Samson #7 15.00
❑22, Dec 1973, Reprints from Mighty Samson #2 15.00
❑23, Mar 1974 15.00

N-MINT

❑24, Jun 1974 15.00
❑25, Sep 1974 15.00
❑26, Dec 1974 15.00
❑27, Mar 1975 15.00
❑28, Jun 1975 15.00
❑29, Sep 1975 15.00
❑30, Dec 1975, In Macy's 15.00
❑31, Mar 1976, V: giant moths 15.00
❑32, Apr 1982, 1982 revival 10.00

Mighty Thor: Godstorm
Marvel

❑1, Nov 2001 3.50
❑2, Dec 2001; No indicia inside whatsoever 3.50
❑3, Jan 2002 3.50

Mighty Tiny
Antarctic

❑1, b&w 2.00
❑2, b&w 2.00
❑3, b&w 2.00
❑4, b&w 2.00
❑5; b&w 2.50

Mighty Tiny: The Mouse Marines
Antarctic

❑1, b&w 2.50

Mike Danger
Tekno

❑1, Sep 1995, FM (c) 1.95
❑2, Oct 1995 1.95
❑3, Nov 1995 1.95
❑4, Dec 1995 1.95
❑5, Dec 1995 2.25
❑6, Jan 1996 2.25
❑7, Jan 1996 2.25
❑8, Feb 1996 2.25
❑9, Mar 1996 2.25
❑10, Apr 1996 2.25
❑11, May 1996, RB (a) 2.25

Mike Danger
Big

❑1, Jun 1996 2.25
❑2, Jul 1996, Mike's head is separated from his body 2.25
❑3, Aug 1996 2.25
❑4, Sep 1996, V: Mann 2.25
❑5, Oct 1996 2.25
❑6, Nov 1996 2.25
❑7, Dec 1996 2.25
❑8, Jan 1997 2.25
❑9, Feb 1997 2.25
❑10, Apr 1997 2.25

Mike Mauser Files
Avalon

❑1 1999 2.95

Mike Mist Minute Mist-Eries
Eclipse

❑1, Apr 1981, b&w 1.50

Mike Regan
Hardboiled

❑1, b&w 2.95

N-MINT

Mike Shayne Private Eye
Dell

❑1, Nov 1962 16.00
❑2, Feb 1962 10.00
❑3, May 1962 10.00

Milikardo Knights
Mad Badger

❑1, Mar 1997, b&w 3.00
❑2, Jan 1998, b&w 3.00

Milk
Radio

❑1, Sep 1997, b&w 2.95
❑2, Nov 1997, b&w 2.95
❑3, Jan 1998, b&w 2.95
❑4, Mar 1998, b&w 2.95
❑5, May 1998, b&w 2.95
❑6, Jul 1998, b&w 2.95
❑7, Sep 1998, b&w 2.95
❑8, Nov 1998, b&w 2.95
❑9, Jan 1999, b&w 2.95
❑10, Mar 1999, b&w 2.95
❑11, May 1999, b&w 2.95
❑12, Jul 1999, b&w 2.95
❑13, Sep 1999, b&w 2.95
❑14, Nov 1999, b&w 2.95
❑15, Jan 2000, b&w 2.95
❑16, Mar 2000, b&w 2.95
❑17, May 2000, b&w 2.95
❑18, Jul 2000, b&w 2.95
❑19, Sep 2000, b&w 2.95
❑20, Nov 2001 2.95
❑21, Jan 2001 2.99
❑22, Mar 2001 2.99
❑23, May 2001 2.99
❑24, Jul 2001 2.99
❑25, Sep 2001 2.99
❑26, Nov 2001 2.99
❑27, Jan 2002 2.99
❑28, Mar 2002 2.99
❑29, May 2002 2.99
❑30, Jul 2002 2.99
❑31, Sep 2002 2.99
❑32, Nov 2002 2.99
❑33, Mar 2003 2.99
❑34, May 2003 2.99
❑35, Jul 2003 2.99
❑36, Sep 2003 2.99
❑37, Nov 2003 2.99
❑38, Jan 2004 2.99
❑39, Apr 2004 2.99
❑40, May 2004 2.99
❑41, Jul 2004 3.50
❑42, Sep 2004 3.50
❑43, Nov 2004 3.50

Milk & Cheese
Slave Labor

❑1, Mar 1991, b&w 65.00
❑1/2nd, Sep 1991, b&w; 2nd printing 6.00
❑1/3rd, Sep 1992, b&w; 3rd printing 5.00
❑1/4th, Aug 1993, b&w; 4th printing 3.00
❑1/5th, Oct 1994, b&w; 5th printing; b&w 3.00
❑1/6th, Sep 1995, b&w; 6th printing 3.00
❑1/7th, Feb 1997, b&w; 7th printing 2.75
❑2, Mar 1992, b&w; Other Number One; has Doctor Radium ad on back cover. 35.00

Other grades: Multiply price above by 5/6 for VF/NM • 2/3 for VERY FINE • 1/3 for FINE • 1/5 for VERY GOOD • 1/8 for GOOD

N-MINT

❑2/2nd, Jun 1993; has Fine Dairy Products ad on back cover 5.00
❑2/3rd, Oct 1994; has APE II ad on back cover 4.00
❑2/4th, Jan 1996; 4th printing 2.75
❑2/5th; 5th printing 2.75
❑3, Aug 1992, b&w; Third #1; has Rats ad on back cover 28.00
❑3/2nd, May 1993; has Fine Dairy Products ad on back cover 4.00
❑3/3rd, Oct 1994; has APE II ad on back cover 3.00
❑3/4th, Feb 1996; 4th printing 2.75
❑3/5th; 5th printing 2.75
❑4, Apr 1993, b&w; Fourth #1; has Fine Dairy Products ad on back cover 16.00
❑4/2nd, Mar 1995; has APE II ad on back cover 3.00
❑4/3rd, Aug 1996; 3rd printing 2.50
❑5, Apr 1994, b&w; First Second Issue; has APE ad on back cover 15.00
❑5/2nd, Nov 1994; has APE II ad on back cover 3.00
❑5/3rd, Feb 1996; 3rd printing 3.00
❑5/4th; 4th printing 2.75
❑6, Apr 1995, b&w; Six Six Six 8.00
❑6/2nd, Sep 1996; 2nd printing 2.75
❑7, Jun 1997, b&w; Latest Thing! 3.00

Milkman Murders
Dark Horse

❑1 2004 .... 3.00
❑2 2004 .... 3.00
❑3 2004 .... 3.00
❑4 2004 .... 3.00

Millennium
DC

❑1, Jan 1988 JSa (c); JSa (a) 2.00
❑2, Jan 1988 JSa (c); JSa (a) 1.50
❑3, Jan 1988 JSa (c); JSa (a) 1.50
❑4, Jan 1988 JSa (c); JSa (a) 1.50
❑5, Feb 1988 JSa (c); JSa (a) 1.50
❑6, Feb 1988 JSa (c); JSa (a) 1.50
❑7, Feb 1988 JSa (c); JSa (a) 1.50
❑8, Feb 1988 JSa (c); JSa (a) 1.50

Millennium 2.5 A.D.
Avalon

❑1 .... 2.95

Millennium Edition: Action Comics
DC

❑1, Feb 2000, 1: Superman; O: Superman; B&w and color 3.95

Millennium Edition: Adventure Comics
DC

❑61, Dec 2000; 1: Starman I (Ted Knight) 3.95
❑247, Nov 2000; The Legion of Super-Heroes; The 13 Superstition Arrows; Aquaman's Super Sea-Squad; Reprints Adventure Comics #247 .... 2.50

Millennium Edition: All Star Comics
DC

❑3, Jun 2000; 1: Justice Society of America. Reprints 3.95
❑3/Variant, Jun 2000; 1: Justice Society of America. chromium cover 10.00
❑8, Feb 2001; 1&O: Wonder Woman 3.95

Millennium Edition: All-Star Western
DC

❑10, Apr 2000, Reprints All-Star Western #10 .... 2.50

Millennium Edition: Batman
DC

❑1, Feb 2001, Reprints Batman: The Dark Knight Returns 3.95
❑1/Chrome, Feb 2001 .... 5.00

Millennium Edition: Batman: The Dark Knight Returns
DC

❑1, Oct 2000; Reprints Batman: The Dark Knight #1 .... 5.95

Millennium Edition: Crisis on Infinite Earths
DC

❑1, Feb 2000; Reprints Crisis on Infinite Earths #1 .... 2.50
❑1/Chrome, Feb 2000 .... 5.00

N-MINT

Millennium Edition: Detective Comics
DC

❑1, Jan 2001; Reprints Detective Comics #1 .... 3.95
❑27, Feb 2000; 1: Batman; 1: Commissioner Gordon 3.95
❑38, ca. 2000; 1: Robin I (Dick Grayson) 3.95
❑225, Dec 2000; 1: Martian Manhunter; O: Martian Manhunter 2.50
❑359, Oct 2000 .... 3.95
❑327, Mar 2000; New look Batman 3.95

Millennium Edition: Flash Comics
DC

❑1, Sep 2000; Reprints Flash Comics #1 3.95

Millennium Edition: Gen13
WildStorm

❑1, Apr 2000; Reprints Gen13 (Mini-Series) #1 .... 2.50

Millennium Edition: Green Lantern
DC

❑76, ca. 2000; Reprints Green Lantern (2nd Series) #76 .... 2.50

Millennium Edition: Hellblazer
DC

❑1, Jul 2000; Reprints Hellblazer #1 .... 2.95

Millennium Edition: House of Mystery
DC

❑1, Sep 2000; Reprints House of Mystery #1 .... 2.50

Millennium Edition: House of Secrets
DC

❑92, May 2000; 1: Swamp Thing 2.50

Millennium Edition: JLA
DC

❑1, ca. 2000; Reprints JLA #1 .... 2.50

Millennium Edition: Justice League
DC

❑1, Jul 2000; KG (w); KG (a); Reprints Justice League #1 .... 2.50
❑1/Chrome, Jul 2000 .... 5.00

Millennium Edition: Kingdom Come
DC

❑1, Aug 2000; Reprints Kingdom Come #1 .... 5.95

Millennium Edition: Mad
DC

❑1, Feb 2000 .... 2.00
❑1/Recalled, Feb 2000 .... 25.00

Millennium Edition: Military Comics
DC

❑1, Oct 2000; Reprints Military Comics #1 3.95

Millennium Edition: More Fun Comics
DC

❑73, Jan 2001; Reprints More Fun Comics #73 .... 3.95
❑101, Nov 2000; Reprints More Fun Comics #101 .... 2.95

Millennium Edition: Mysterious Suspense
DC

❑1, Sep 2000; 1: The Question;Reprints Mysterious Suspense #1 .... 2.50

Millennium Edition: New Gods
DC

❑1, Jun 2000; Reprints New Gods #1 .... 2.50

Millennium Edition: Our Army at War
DC

❑81, Jun 2000; 1: Sgt. Rock 2.50

Millennium Edition: Plop!
DC

❑1, Jul 2000; Reprints Plop! #1 .... 2.50

Millennium Edition: Police Comics
DC

❑1, Sep 2000; Reprints Police Comics #1 3.95

Millennium Edition: Preacher
DC

❑1, Oct 2000 .... 2.95

Millennium Edition: Sensation Comics
DC

❑1, Oct 2000; Reprints Sensation Comics #1 .... 3.95

N-MINT

Millennium Edition: Showcase
DC

❑4, ca. 2000; Reprints Showcase #4 .... 2.50
❑9, Jan 2001; Reprints Showcase #9 .... 2.50
❑22, Dec 2000; Reprints Showcase #22 2.50

Millennium Edition: Superboy
DC

❑1, Feb 2001 .... 2.95

Millennium Edition: Superman
DC

❑75, ca. 2000 .... 2.95

Millennium Edition: Superman
DC

❑1, Dec 2000; Reprints Superman (1st Series) #1 .... 2.95
❑1/Chrome, Dec 2000 .... 2.95
❑76, ca. 2000; ca. 2000 .... 2.95
❑233, Jan 2001 .... 2.50

Millennium Edition: Superman's Pal Jimmy Olsen
DC

❑1, Apr 2000; Reprints Superman's Pal Jimmy Olsen #1 .... 2.95

Millennium Edition: Tales Calculated to Drive You Mad
DC

❑1, ca. 2000 .... 2.95

Millennium Edition: The Brave and the Bold
DC

❑28, Feb 2000; 1: Snapper Carr; 1: The Justice League of America; 1: Justice League of America 2.50
❑85, Nov 2000 .... 2.50

Millennium Edition: The Flash
DC

❑123, May 2000; Reprints The Flash (1st Series) #1 .... 2.50

Millennium Edition: The Man of Steel
DC

❑1, ca. 2000 .... 2.50

Millennium Edition: The New Teen Titans
DC

❑1, Dec 2000 .... 2.50

Millennium Edition: The Saga of the Swamp Thing
DC

❑21, Feb 2000; Reprints Sandman #1 .... 2.50

Millennium Edition: The Sandman
DC

❑1, Feb 2000; Reprints Sandman #1 .... 2.95

Millennium Edition: The Shadow
DC

❑1, Feb 2001 .... 2.50

Millennium Edition: The Spirit
DC

❑1, Jul 2000; Reprints The Spirit #1 .... 2.95

Millennium Edition: Watchmen
DC

❑1, ca. 2000; Reprints Watchmen #1 .... 2.50

Millennium Edition: Whiz Comics
DC

❑2, Mar 2000; Reprints Whiz Comics #2 3.95

Millennium Edition: WildC.A.T.S
DC

❑1, ca. 2000 .... 2.50

Millennium Edition: Wonder Woman
DC

❑1, Aug 2000; Reprints Wonder Woman (1st Series) #1 .... 3.95

Millennium Edition: Wonder Woman
DC

❑1, May 2000; Reprints Wonder Woman (2nd Series) #1 .... 2.50

Millennium Edition: World's Finest
DC

❑71 .... 2.50

Other grades: Multiply price above by 5/6 for VF/NM • 2/3 for VERY FINE • 1/3 for FINE • 1/5 for VERY GOOD • 1/8 for GOOD

My Favorite Martian

1960s era's Mork, or ALF, or Third Rock
©Gold Key

My Greatest Adventure

Adventure title gives Doom Patrol its start
©DC

Mys-Tech Wars

Includes more characters than a keyboard
©Marvel

Mystery in Space

Infantino's Adam Strange was the draw
©DC

Mystic

Another of the first four CrossGen titles
©CrossGen

N-MINT

Millennium Edition: Young Romance Comics
DC

❑1, Apr 2000; Reprints Young Romance (DC) #1; 1st romance comic 2.95

Millennium Fever
DC / Vertigo

❑1, Oct 1995 .... 2.50
❑2, Nov 1995 .... 2.50
❑3, Dec 1995 .... 2.50
❑4, Jan 1996; Final Issue 2.50
❑Ashcan 1 .... 0.75

Millennium Index
Eclipse

❑1, Mar 1988 .... 2.00
❑2, Mar 1988 .... 2.00

Millie the Model Comics
Marvel

❑105, Nov 1961 .... 15.00
❑106, Jan 1962 .... 15.00
❑107, Mar 1962 .... 15.00
❑108, May 1962 .... 15.00
❑109, Jul 1962 .... 15.00
❑110, Sep 1962 .... 15.00
❑111, Nov 1962 .... 15.00
❑112, Jan 1963 .... 15.00
❑113, Mar 1963 .... 15.00
❑114, May 1963 .... 15.00
❑115, Jul 1963 .... 15.00
❑116, Sep 1963 .... 15.00
❑117, Nov 1963 .... 15.00
❑118, Jan 1964 .... 15.00
❑119, Mar 1964, Reprint from Patsy and Hedy #5 .... 15.00
❑120, May 1964 .... 15.00
❑121, Jul 1964 .... 15.00
❑122, Sep 1964 .... 15.00
❑123, Oct 1964 .... 15.00
❑124, Nov 1964 .... 15.00
❑125, Dec 1964 .... 15.00
❑126, Jan 1965 .... 15.00
❑127, Mar 1965 .... 15.00
❑128, May 1965 .... 15.00
❑129, Jul 1965 .... 15.00
❑130, Sep 1965 .... 15.00
❑131, Oct 1965 .... 12.00
❑132, Nov 1965 .... 12.00
❑133, Dec 1965 .... 12.00
❑134, Jan 1966 .... 12.00
❑135, Feb 1966 .... 12.00
❑136, Apr 1966 .... 12.00
❑137, May 1966 .... 12.00
❑138, Jun 1966 .... 12.00
❑139, Jul 1966 .... 12.00
❑140, Aug 1966 .... 12.00
❑141, Sep 1966 .... 12.00
❑142, Oct 1966 .... 12.00
❑143, Nov 1966 .... 12.00
❑144, Dec 1966 .... 12.00
❑145, Jan 1967 .... 12.00
❑146, Feb 1967 .... 12.00
❑147, Mar 1967 .... 12.00
❑148, Apr 1967 .... 12.00
❑149, May 1967 .... 12.00
❑150, Jun 1967 .... 12.00

N-MINT

❑151, Jul 1967 .... 12.00
❑152, Aug 1967 .... 12.00
❑153, Sep 1967 .... 12.00
❑154, Oct 1967, New Millie begins 12.00
❑155, Nov 1967 .... 10.00
❑156, Dec 1967 .... 10.00
❑157, Feb 1968 .... 10.00
❑158, Apr 1968 .... 10.00
❑159, Jun 1968 .... 10.00
❑160, Jul 1968 .... 10.00
❑161, Aug 1968 .... 10.00
❑162, Sep 1968 .... 10.00
❑163, Oct 1968 .... 10.00
❑164, Nov 1968 .... 10.00
❑165, Dec 1968 .... 10.00
❑166, Jan 1969 .... 10.00
❑167, Feb 1969 .... 10.00
❑168, Mar 1969 .... 10.00
❑169, Apr 1969 .... 10.00
❑170, May 1969 .... 10.00
❑171, Jun 1969 .... 10.00
❑172, Jul 1969 .... 10.00
❑173, Aug 1969 .... 10.00
❑174, Sep 1969 .... 10.00
❑175, Oct 1969 .... 10.00
❑176, Nov 1969 .... 10.00
❑177, Dec 1969 .... 10.00
❑178, Jan 1970 .... 10.00
❑179, Feb 1970 .... 10.00
❑180, Mar 1970 .... 10.00
❑181, Apr 1970 .... 8.50
❑182, May 1970 .... 8.50
❑183, Jun 1970 .... 8.50
❑184, Jul 1970 .... 8.50
❑185, Aug 1970 .... 8.50
❑186, Oct 1970 .... 8.50
❑187, Dec 1970 .... 8.50
❑188, Feb 1970 .... 8.50
❑189, Apr 1970 .... 8.50
❑190, Jun 1970 .... 8.50
❑191, Aug 1970 .... 8.50
❑192, Oct 1970 .... 8.50
❑193, Dec 1970 .... 8.50
❑194, Feb 1971 .... 8.50
❑195, Apr 1971 .... 8.50
❑196, Jun 1971 .... 8.50
❑197, Aug 1971 .... 8.50
❑198 .... 8.50
❑199 1972 .... 8.50
❑200 1972 .... 8.50
❑201, Apr 1972 .... 8.50
❑202, Jun 1973 .... 8.50
❑203, Aug 1973 .... 8.50
❑204, Sep 1973 .... 8.50
❑205, Oct 1973 .... 8.50
❑206, Nov 1973 .... 8.50
❑207, Dec 1973 .... 8.50
❑Ann 1, ca. 1962 .... 140.00
❑Ann 2, ca. 1963 .... 95.00
❑Ann 3, ca. 1964 .... 70.00
❑Ann 4, ca. 1965 .... 70.00
❑Ann 5, Sep 1966 .... 65.00
❑Ann 6, ca. 1967 .... 45.00
❑Ann 7, ca. 1968 .... 45.00
❑Ann 8, Sep 1969 .... 45.00
❑Ann 9, ca. 1970 .... 45.00

N-MINT

❑Ann 10, ca. 1971 .... 45.00
❑Ann 11; "Queen-Size" #11 .... 25.00
❑Ann 12; "Queen-Size" #12;1975 .... 25.00

Milton the Monster and Fearless Fly
Gold Key

❑1, ca. 1966 .... 60.00

Mindbenders
MBS

❑1 .... 2.50

Mindgame Gallery
Mindgame

❑1, b&w 1.95

Mind Probe
Rip Off

❑1, b&w 3.25

Minerva
NBM

❑1; Adult 9.95

Minimum Wage
Fantagraphics

❑1, Oct 1995 .... 2.95
❑2, Dec 1995 .... 2.95
❑3, Mar 1996 .... 2.95
❑4, Jun 1996; pin-ups 2.95
❑5, Nov 1996; b&w 2.95
❑6, Mar 1997 .... 2.95
❑7, Aug 1997 .... 2.95
❑8, Feb 1998 .... 2.95
❑9, Jun 1998; b&w 2.95
❑10, Jan 1999 .... 2.95

Ministry of Space
Image

❑1, Apr 2001 .... 2.95
❑2, Sep 2001 .... 2.95
❑3, May 2004 .... 2.95

Mink
Tokyopop

❑1, Apr 2004; 184 pages; Reads right to left; b&w 9.99

Minkenstein
Mu

❑0, Aug 2005 .... 2.95

Minotaur
Labyrinth

❑1, Feb 1996, b&w 2.50
❑2, Apr 1996, b&w 2.50
❑3, Jun 1996, b&w; cover says Jul, indicia says Jun 2.50
❑4, Sep 1996, b&w; Final Issue; b&w 2.50

Minx
DC / Vertigo

❑1, Oct 1998 .... 2.50
❑2, Nov 1998 .... 2.50
❑3, Dec 1998 .... 2.50
❑4, Jan 1999 .... 2.50
❑5, Feb 1999 .... 2.50
❑6, Mar 1999 .... 2.50
❑7, Apr 1999 .... 2.50
❑8, May 1999 .... 2.50

Other grades: Multiply price above by 5/6 for VF/NM • 2/3 for VERY FINE • 1/3 for FINE • 1/5 for VERY GOOD • 1/8 for GOOD

Miracle Girls
Tokyopop

❑1, ca. 2000 .... 2.95
❑2, ca. 2000 .... 2.95
❑3 .... 2.95
❑4 .... 2.95
❑5, ca. 2001 .... 2.95
❑6, ca. 2001 .... 2.95
❑7, ca. 2001 .... 2.95
❑8, ca. 2001 .... 2.95
❑9, ca. 2001 .... 2.95
❑10, ca. 2001 .... 2.95
❑11, ca. 2001 .... 2.95
❑12, ca. 2001 .... 2.95
❑13, ca. 2001 .... 2.95
❑14 .... 2.95
❑15 .... 2.95
❑16, ca. 2002 .... 2.95
❑17, ca. 2002 .... 2.95
❑18, ca. 2002 .... 2.95
❑19, ca. 2002 .... 2.95

Miracleman
Eclipse

❑1, Aug 1985; AMo (w); Reprints from Warrior #1-3 .... 10.00
❑2, Oct 1985; AMo (w); Reprints from Warrior #5-8 .... 8.00
❑3, Nov 1985; HC (c); AMo (w); Reprints from Warrior #9-11 .... 8.00
❑4, Dec 1985; JSn (c); AMo (w); Reprints from Warrior #13-15, 17 .... 8.00
❑4/Gold, Dec 1985 .... 15.00
❑5, Jan 1986; PG (c); AMo (w); Reprints from Warrior #16-18, 20 .... 8.00
❑5/Platinum, Jan 1986 .... 15.00
❑6, Feb 1986; AMo (w); Reprints from Warrior #12, 21; Pinups by Chuck Beckum 8.00
❑7, Apr 1986; PG (c); AMo (w); D: Gargunza; Tales of the First Empire story 8.00
❑8, Jun 1986; AMo (w); 1: The New Wave; Includes The New Wave preview 8.00
❑8/Gold, Jun 1986 .... 15.00
❑9, Jul 1986; AMo (w); birth 10.00
❑10, Dec 1986; AMo (w); Miracleman story; Laser Eraser and Pressbutton story 10.00
❑11, May 1987; AMo (w); Miracleman story; Laser Eraser and Pressbutton story 14.00
❑12, Sep 1987; AMo (w); Miracleman story; Laser Eraser and Pressbutton story 14.00
❑13, Nov 1987; AMo (w); Reprints from Young Miracleman #332 .... 18.00
❑14, Apr 1988 AMo (w) 24.00
❑15, Nov 1988; AMo (w); Scarce 35.00
❑16, Dec 1988; AMo (w); last Moore 16.00
❑17, Jun 1990; NG (w); 1st Neil Gaiman 25.00
❑17/Gold, Jun 1990 .... 40.00
❑18, Aug 1990 NG (w) 20.00
❑19, Nov 1990; NG (w); cardstock cover 15.00
❑20, Mar 1991; NG (w); cardstock cover 15.00
❑21, Jul 1991 NG (w) 15.00
❑22, Aug 1991 NG (w) 15.00
❑23, Jun 1992 NG (w) 16.00
❑24, Aug 1993; scarcer 25.00
❑3D 1, Dec 1985; Giant-size; AMo (w); 3-D Special #1 .... 10.00
❑3D 1/Gold, Dec 1985 .... 18.00

Miracleman: Apocrypha
Eclipse

❑1, Nov 1991 JRo, MW, NG (w); MW (a) 3.00
❑2, Jan 1992 KB, NG (w) 3.00
❑3, Apr 1991 NG (w); ARo, VM (a) 3.00

Miracleman Family
Eclipse

❑1, May 1988; O: Young Miracleman 3.00
❑2, Sep 1988; PG (c); Reprints from Marvelman Family #4, Young Marvelman #347 .... 3.00

Miracle Squad
Upshot

❑1 .... 2.00
❑2 .... 2.00
❑3, b&w 2.00
❑4, b&w 2.00

Miracle Squad: Blood and Dust
Apple

❑1, Jan 1989, b&w 2.00
❑2, Mar 1989, b&w 2.00
❑3, May 1989, b&w 2.00
❑4, Jul 1989, b&w 2.00

Mirrorwalker
Now

❑1, Oct 1990; semi-fumetti 2.95
❑2 .... 2.95

Mirrorworld: Rain
Netco

❑0, Apr 1997 .... 3.25
❑1, Feb 1997 .... 3.25

Misadventures Of Breadman And Doughboy
Hemlock Park

❑1, Oct 1999; no cover price 2.95
❑2 .... 2.95

Miseroth: Amok Hell
Northstar

❑1; Includes poster; Adult; b&w 4.95
❑2; Adult 4.95
❑3; Adult 4.95

Misery
Image

❑1, Dec 1995; One-shot 2.95

Misplaced
Image

❑1, May 2003; Cover A by Josh Blaylock, Clayton Brown & UDON 2.95
❑2, Aug 2003 .... 2.95

Miss Fury
Adventure

❑1, Nov 1991, 1&O: Miss Fury 2.50
❑1/Ltd., Nov 1991; limited edition 4.95
❑2, Dec 1991 .... 2.50
❑3 .... 2.50
❑4 .... 2.50

Miss Fury
Avalon

❑1 .... 2.95
❑2 .... 2.95

Missing Beings Special
Comics Interview

❑1, b&w 2.25

Mission: Impossible
Dell

❑1, May 1967 .... 24.00
❑2, Sep 1967 .... 18.00
❑3, Dec 1967 .... 18.00
❑4, Oct 1968 .... 18.00
❑5, Oct 1969, Same cover as #1; Reprints 12.00

Mission Impossible
Marvel

❑1, May 1996; prequel to movie 2.95

Missions in Tibet
Dimension

❑1, Jul 1995 .... 2.50

Miss Peach
Dell

❑1, Oct 1963 .... 60.00

Misspent Youths
Brave New Words

❑1 .... 2.50
❑2 .... 2.50
❑3, Jul 1991 .... 2.50

Miss Victory Golden Anniversary Special
AC

❑1, Nov 1991, reprint 1: Miss Victory 5.00

Mister America
Endeavor

❑1 .... 2.95
❑2, Apr 1994 .... 2.95

Mr. and Mrs. J. Evil Scientist
Gold Key

❑1, Nov 1963 .... 50.00
❑2, ca. 1964 .... 30.00
❑3, ca. 1965 .... 20.00
❑4, Sep 1966 .... 20.00

Mr. Average
B.S.

❑1 .... 2.25
❑2 .... 2.25
❑3 .... 2.25

Mr. Beat Adventures
Moordam

❑1, Jan 1997, b&w 2.95

Mr. Beat/Craybaby/Weirdsville Post Halloween Leftover Monster Thanksgiving Special
Blindwolf

❑1, Oct 1998 .... 2.95

Mr. Beat — Existential Cool
Moordam

❑0, Jun 1998; flip-book with Gyro-Man 2.95

Mr. Beat's Babes and Bongos Annual
Moordam

❑1/Blue, Oct 1998; Blue cover with Patty-Cake 2.95
❑1/Red, Oct 1998; Red cover with Betty Page 2.95

Mr. Beat's House of Burning Jazz Love
Moordam

❑1, Dec 1997, b&w 2.95

Mr. Beat's Two-Fisted Atomic Action Super Special
Moordam

❑1, Sep 1997, b&w; V: Roswell 2.95

Mr. Beat Superstar
Moordam

❑1, Jun 1998 O: Mr. Beat 3.00

Mister Blank
Slave Labor / Amaze Ink

❑0, Jan 1997; Published one month prior to issue #1; b&w 2.95
❑1, May 1997 .... 2.95
❑2, May 1997 .... 2.95
❑3, Aug 1997 .... 2.95
❑4, Nov 1997 .... 2.95
❑5, Feb 1998 .... 2.95

Mr. Cream Puff
Blackthorne

❑1, May 1987; b&w 1.75

Mr. Day & Mr. Night
Slave Labor

❑1, Apr 1993 .... 3.95

Mr. Doom
Pied Piper

❑1, Jul 1987 .... 1.95

Mister E
DC

❑1, Jun 1991 .... 2.00
❑2, Jul 1991 .... 2.00
❑3, Aug 1991 .... 2.00
❑4, Sep 1991; Tim Hunter; Zatanna; Dr. Fate 2.00

Mr. Fixitt
Apple

❑1, Jan 1989, b&w 1.95
❑2, Mar 1990 .... 1.95

Mr. Fixitt
Heroic

❑1, b&w; trading card 2.95

Mr. Hero-The Newmatic Man
Tekno

❑1, Mar 1995, game piece; trading card 1.95
❑2, Apr 1995, game piece; trading card 1.95
❑3, May 1995, game piece; trading card 1.95
❑4, Jun 1995, coupon 1.95
❑5, Jul 1995 .... 1.95
❑6, Aug 1995 .... 1.95
❑7, Sep 1995 .... 1.95
❑8, Oct 1995 .... 1.95
❑9, Nov 1995 .... 1.95
❑10, Dec 1995 .... 1.95
❑11, Dec 1995 .... 1.95
❑12, Jan 1996 .... 2.25
❑13, Jan 1996 .... 2.25
❑14, Feb 1996 .... 2.25
❑15, Mar 1996 .... 2.25

'Nam

Marvel's retelling of the Vietnam War

©Marvel

Names of Magic

Continuing stories featuring Neil Gaiman characters

©DC

Namor

Bill Jemas' solo Subby title didn't last long

©Marvel

Namor, The Sub-Mariner

Old Fishface returns as a businessman

©Marvel

Nash

Adventures featuring the wrestling icon

©Image

N-MINT

❑16, Apr 1996 .... 2.25
❑17, May 1996, Final Issue 2.25

Mr. Hero-The Newmatic Man
Big

❑1, Jun 1996, D: Mr. Hero 2.25
❑2, Jul 1996 .... 2.25
❑3, Aug 1996 .... 2.25
❑4, Sep 1996 .... 2.25

Mr. Jigsaw Special
Ocean

❑1, Spr 1988; O: Mr. Jigsaw. blue paper 2.00

Mr. Lizard 3-D
Now

❑1, May 1993; instant Mr. Lizard capsule 3.50

Mr. Lizard Annual
Now

❑1, Sep 1993; Ralph Snart capsule 2.95

Mr. Majestic
DC / Wildstorm

❑1, Sep 1999 .... 3.00
❑2, Oct 1999 .... 2.50
❑3, Nov 1999 .... 2.50
❑4, Dec 1999 .... 2.50
❑5, Jan 2000 .... 2.50
❑6, Feb 2000 .... 2.50
❑7, Mar 2000 .... 2.50
❑8, Apr 2000 .... 2.50
❑9, May 2000, Final Issue 2.50

Mister Miracle
DC

❑1, Apr 1971, JK (c); JK (w); JK (a); 1: Oberon; 1: Mister Miracle (Scott Free); 1: Steel Hand; 1: Mister Miracle (Thaddeus Brown) 50.00
❑2, Jun 1971, JK (c); JK (w); JK (a); 1: Doctor Bedlam. 1: Granny Goodness 25.00
❑3, Aug 1971, JK (c); JK (w); JK (a); V: Doctor Bedlam. Boy Commandos reprint 20.00
❑4, Oct 1971; Giant-size; JK (c); JK (w); JK (a); 1: Big Barda, Boy Commandos reprint. Boy Commandos reprint (Detective Comics #82) 25.00
❑5, Dec 1971; Giant-size; JK (c); JK (w); JK (a); Boy Commandos reprint (Detective Comics #76) 30.00
❑6, Feb 1972; Giant-size; JK (c); JK (w); JK (a); 1: Funky Flashman. 1: Lashina. 1: Female Furies. reprints Boy Commandos #1 .... 22.00
❑7, Apr 1972; Giant-size; JK (c); JK (w); JK (a); reprints Boy Commandos #3 .. 20.00
❑8, Jun 1972; Giant-size; JK (c); JK (w); JK (a); Boy Commandos reprint (Detective Comics #64) 20.00
❑9, Aug 1972, JK (c); JK (w); JK (a); 1: Himon 15.00
❑10, Oct 1972, JK (c); JK (w); JK (a) 15.00
❑11, Dec 1972, JK (c); JK (w); JK (a) 15.00
❑12, Feb 1973, JK (c); JK (w); JK (a) 15.00
❑13, Apr 1973, JK (c); JK (w); JK (a) 15.00
❑14, Jul 1973, JK (c); JK (w); JK (a); 1: Madame Evil Eye 15.00
❑15, Sep 1973, JK (c); JK (w); JK (a); 1: Mister Miracle II (Shilo Norman) 12.00
❑16, Nov 1973, JK (c); JK (w); JK (a) 12.00
❑17, Jan 1974, JK (c); JK (w); JK (a) 10.00

N-MINT

❑18, Mar 1974, JK (c); JK (w); JK (a); series goes on hiatus; Wedding of Mister Miracle and Barda 10.00
❑19, Sep 1977, MR (c); MR (a) 7.00
❑20, Oct 1977, MR (c); MR (a) 7.00
❑21, Dec 1977, MR (c); MR (a) 7.00
❑22, Feb 1978, MR (c); MR (a) 7.00
❑23, Apr 1978, MR (c); MG (a) 7.00
❑24, Jun 1978, MR (c); MG, RH (a) 7.00
❑25, Sep 1978, AM, RH, (c); MG, RH (a); Final Issue 7.00
❑Special 1, ca. 1987 .... 3.50

Mister Miracle
DC

❑1, Jan 1989; O: Mister Miracle. A: Doctor Bedlam 2.50
❑2, Feb 1989 .... 1.50
❑3, Mar 1989 .... 1.50
❑4, Apr 1989 .... 1.50
❑5, Jun 1989 .... 1.50
❑6, Jul 1989 .... 1.25
❑7, Aug 1989 .... 1.25
❑8, Sep 1989 .... 1.25
❑9, Oct 1989; 1&O: Maxi-Man 1.25
❑10, Nov 1989 .... 1.25
❑11, Dec 1989 .... 1.25
❑12, Jan 1990; Continued in Justice League Spaecial #1 .... 1.25
❑13, Mar 1990 A: Lobo 1.25
❑14, Apr 1990; A: Lobo. V: Lobo 1.25
❑15, May 1990; V: Lobo 1.25
❑16, Jun 1990 .... 1.25
❑17, Jul 1990 .... 1.25
❑18, Aug 1990 .... 1.25
❑19, Sep 1990 .... 1.25
❑20, Oct 1990 .... 1.25
❑21, Nov 1990; Return of Shilo Norman (Mister Miracle III) 1.25
❑22, Dec 1990 .... 1.25
❑23, Jan 1991 .... 1.25
❑24, Feb 1991 .... 1.25
❑25, Mar 1991 .... 1.25
❑26, Apr 1991 .... 1.25
❑27, May 1991 .... 1.25
❑28, Jun 1991; 1: Big Breeda; Final Issue 1.25

Mister Miracle
DC

❑1, Apr 1996 .... 1.95
❑2, May 1996; V: JLA; Dwayne Turner pin-up of Big Barda & Oberon follows story; Dwayne Turner pin-up of Big Barda & Oberon 1.95
❑3, Jun 1996 .... 1.95
❑4, Jul 1996; V: Black Racer 1.95
❑5, Aug 1996 .... 1.95
❑6, Sep 1996 .... 1.95
❑7, Oct 1996; Final Issue 1.95

Mr. Monster
Dark Horse

❑1, Feb 1988; O: Mr. Monster; Reprint from Triumph Comics #31; b&w 2.00
❑2, Apr 1988; Reprint from Super Duper Comics #3; b&w 2.00
❑3, Jun 1988; Reprint from Commando Comics #21; b&w 2.00
❑4, Nov 1988; b&w 2.00
❑5, Mar 1989; b&w 2.00

N-MINT

❑6, Oct 1989; has indicia for #5 .... 2.00
❑7, Apr 1990; b&w 2.00
❑8, Sep 1990; Giant-size; D: Mr. Monster; Final Issue 5.00

Mr. Monster Attacks!
Tundra

❑1, Aug 1992; Simon Bisley back cover. 3.95
❑2, Sep 1992 .... 3.95
❑3, Oct 1992 .... 3.95

Mr. Monster (Doc Stearn...)
Eclipse

❑1, Jan 1985; 1: Mr. Monster. Reprints Mr. Monster story from Vanguard Illustrated #7 .... 2.50
❑2, Aug 1985 DSt (c) 2.00
❑3, Oct 1985 BW, AMo (w); BW (a) 2.00
❑4, Dec 1985; Reprint from Ranger Comics #55 .... 2.00
❑5, Feb 1986 .... 2.00
❑6, Jun 1986 .... 2.00
❑7, Dec 1986 .... 2.00
❑8, Mar 1987 .... 2.00
❑9, Apr 1987 A: Wolff & Byrd. 2.00
❑10, Jun 1987; BW, AMo (w); BW (a); 6-D 2.00

Mr. Monster Presents (Crack-A-Boom!)
Caliber

❑1, Jun 1997 .... 2.95
❑2, Jul 1997 .... 2.95
❑3, Sep 1997 .... 2.95

Mr. Monster's Gal Friday... Kelly!
Image

❑1, Jan 2000 .... 3.50
❑2, Mar 2002 .... 3.50
❑3, May 2002 .... 3.50

Mr. Monster's High-Octane Horror
Eclipse

❑1, May 1986; A.K.A. Super Duper Special #2 .... 2.00
❑3D 1, May 1986; A.K.A. Super Duper Special #1 .... 2.50

Mr. Monster's Hi-Shock Schlock
Eclipse

❑1, Mar 1987; FH (w); FH (a); A.K.A. Super Duper Special #6 .... 2.00
❑2, May 1987; A.K.A. Super Duper Special #7 .... 2.00

Mr. Monster's Hi-Voltage Super Science
Eclipse

❑1, Jan 1987; A.K.A. Super Duper Special #5 .... 2.00

Mr. Monster's Triple Threat 3-D
3-D Zone

❑1, Jul 1993; NN 3.95

Mr. Monster's True Crime
Eclipse

❑1, Sep 1986; A.K.A. Super Duper Special #3 .... 2.00
❑2, Oct 1986; A.K.A. Super Duper Special #4 .... 2.00

Other grades: Multiply price above by 5/6 for VF/NM • 2/3 for VERY FINE • 1/3 for FINE • 1/5 for VERY GOOD • 1/8 for GOOD

N-MINT | N-MINT | N-MINT

Mr. Monster's Weird Tales of the Future
Eclipse

❑1, BW (c); BW (w); BW (a); A.K.A. Super Duper Special #8 ..... 2.00

Mr. Monster vs. Gorzilla
Image

❑1, Jul 1998; red, white, and blue 2.95

Mr. Mxyzptlk (Villains)
DC

❑1, Feb 1998; New Year's Evil 1.95

Mr. Natural
Kitchen Sink

❑1; 28 pages; Adult 90.00
❑1/2nd; 2nd printing; Adult 75.00
❑1/3rd; 3rd printing 50.00
❑1/4th, ca. 1970, 4th printing; 1970; Adult 35.00
❑2, Oct 1971 ..... 50.00
❑3, Jan 1977 ..... 45.00
❑3/2nd; 2nd printing 22.00
❑3/3rd; 3rd printing 10.00
❑3/4th; 4th printing 4.50
❑3/5th, ca. 1980; 5th printing 4.00
❑3/6th; 6th printing 4.00
❑3/7th; 7th printing 4.00
❑3/8th; 8th printing 4.00
❑3/9th; 9th printing 4.00
❑3/10th, Feb 1998; 10th printing 4.00

Mr. Night
Slave Labor

❑1, Nov 2005 ..... 2.95

Mr. Nightmare's Winter Special
Moonstone

❑1, Dec 1995, b&w; NN 3.50

Mr. Nightmare's Wonderful World
Moonstone

❑1, Jun 1995, b&w 2.95
❑2, Aug 1995, b&w 2.95
❑3, Oct 1995, b&w 2.95
❑4, Nov 1995, b&w 2.95
❑5, Feb 1996, b&w 2.95

Mister Planet
Mr. Planet

❑1, b&w 3.00
❑2, b&w 3.00

Mister Sixx
Imagine Nation

❑1 ..... 1.95

Mr. T and the T-Force
Now

❑1, Jun 1993; NA (c); NA (w); NA (a); trading card 3.00
❑1/Gold; Gold logo promotional edition; NA (w); NA (a); gold, advance 4.00
❑2, Sep 1993; trading card 2.00
❑3, Oct 1993; trading card 2.00
❑4, Nov 1993; trading card 2.00
❑5, Dec 1993; trading card 2.00
❑6, Jan 1994; trading card 2.00
❑7, Feb 1994; trading card 2.00
❑8, Mar 1994; trading card 2.00
❑9, Apr 1994; trading card; cover says Aug, indicia says Apr 2.00
❑10, May 1994 ..... 2.00

Mister X
Vortex

❑1, Jun 1984 1: Mister X 4.00
❑2, Aug 1984 ..... 2.75
❑3 ..... 2.75
❑4 ..... 2.50
❑5 ..... 2.50
❑6 ..... 2.50
❑7 ..... 2.50
❑8 ..... 2.50
❑9 ..... 2.50
❑10, Oct 1986 BSz (c) 2.50
❑11 ..... 2.50
❑12, Jan 1988 ..... 2.50
❑13, Mar 1988 ..... 2.50
❑14 ..... 2.50

Mister X
Vortex

❑1, b&w 3.00
❑2, b&w 2.50
❑3, b&w 2.50
❑4, b&w 2.50
❑5, b&w 2.50
❑6, b&w 2.25
❑7, b&w 2.25
❑8, b&w 2.25
❑9, b&w 2.25
❑10, b&w 2.25
❑11, b&w 2.25
❑12, b&w 2.50

Mister X
Caliber

❑1, ca. 1996, b&w 2.95
❑2, ca. 1996 ..... 2.95
❑3, Sep 1996 ..... 2.95
❑4, Dec 1996 ..... 2.95

Mistress of Bondage
Fantagraphics / Eros

❑1, b&w; Adult 2.95
❑2, b&w; Adult 2.95
❑3, b&w; Adult 2.95

Misty
Marvel / Star

❑1, Dec 1985 ..... 1.00
❑2, Feb 1986 ..... 1.00
❑3, Apr 1986 ..... 1.00
❑4, Jun 1986 ..... 1.00
❑5, Aug 1986 ..... 1.00
❑6, Oct 1986 ..... 1.00

Misty Girl Extreme
Fantagraphics / Eros

❑1, Jan 1997 ..... 2.95
❑2, Feb 1997 ..... 2.95

Mites
Continuüm

❑1, b&w 1.50
❑2 ..... 1.75

MixxZine
Mixx

❑1, Aug 1997; Issue #1-1 ..... 4.99
❑2, Oct 1997; Issue #1-2 ..... 4.99
❑3, Dec 1997; Issue #1-3 ..... 4.99
❑4, Feb 1998; Issue #1-4 ..... 4.99
❑5, Apr 1998; Issue #1-5 ..... 4.99
❑6, Jun 1998; Issue #1-6 ..... 4.99

Mnemovore
DC / Vertigo

❑1, May 2005 ..... 2.99
❑2, Jun 2005 ..... 2.99
❑3, Jul 2005 ..... 2.99
❑4, Aug 2005 ..... 2.99
❑5, Sep 2005 ..... 2.99
❑6, Oct 2005 ..... 2.99

Mobfire
DC / Vertigo

❑1, Dec 1994 ..... 2.50
❑2, Jan 1995 ..... 2.50
❑3, Feb 1995 ..... 2.50
❑4, Mar 1995 ..... 2.50
❑5, Apr 1995, A: John Constantine 2.50
❑6, May 1995 ..... 2.50
❑Ashcan 1, "Ashcan" preview given away by DC at shows 0.50

Mobile Police Patlabor Part 1
Viz

❑1, Jul 1997, b&w 2.95
❑2, Aug 1997, b&w 2.95
❑3, Sep 1997, b&w 2.95
❑4, Oct 1997, b&w 2.95
❑5, Nov 1997, b&w 2.95
❑6, Dec 1997, b&w 2.95

Mobile Police Patlabor Part 2
Viz

❑1, Jan 1998, b&w 2.95
❑2, Feb 1998, b&w 2.95
❑3, Mar 1998, b&w 2.95
❑4, Apr 1998, b&w 2.95
❑5, May 1998, b&w 2.95
❑6, Jun 1998, b&w 2.95

Mobile Suit Gundam 0079
Viz

❑1, Mar 1999; b&w 2.95
❑2, Apr 1999; b&w 2.95
❑3, May 1999; b&w 2.95
❑4, Jun 1999; b&w 2.95
❑5, Jul 1999; b&w 2.95
❑6, Aug 1999; b&w 2.95
❑7, Sep 1999; b&w 2.95
❑8, Oct 1999; b&w 2.95

Mobile Suit Gundam 0083
Viz

❑1, Nov 1999 ..... 4.95
❑2, Dec 1999 ..... 4.95
❑3, Jan 2000 ..... 4.95
❑4, Feb 2000 ..... 4.95
❑5, Mar 2000 ..... 4.95
❑6, Apr 2000 ..... 4.95
❑7, May 2000 ..... 4.95
❑8, Jun 2000 ..... 4.95
❑9, Jul 2000 ..... 4.95
❑10, Aug 2000 ..... 4.95
❑11, Sep 2000 ..... 4.95
❑12, Oct 2000 ..... 4.95
❑13, Nov 2000 ..... 4.95

Mobile Suit Gundam Seed Astray
Tokyopop

❑1, May 2004 ..... 9.99

Mobile Suit Gundam Wing: Ground Zero
Viz

❑1, Jun 2000 ..... 2.95
❑2, Jul 2000, b&w 2.95
❑3, Aug 2000, b&w 2.95
❑4, Sep 2000, b&w 2.95

Mobsters and Monsters Magazine
Original Syndicate

❑1, Jul 1995 ..... 3.00

Moby Dick
NBM

❑1 ..... 15.95

Moby Duck
Gold Key / Whitman

❑1, Oct 1967 ..... 12.00
❑2, Jun 1968 ..... 6.00
❑3, Sep 1968, Production code 10209-809 ..... 5.00
❑4, Dec 1968 ..... 5.00
❑5, Mar 1969, Production code 10209-903 ..... 5.00
❑6, Jun 1969 ..... 3.50
❑7, Oct 1969 ..... 3.50
❑8, Jan 1970 ..... 3.50
❑9, Apr 1970 ..... 3.50
❑10, Jul 1970, Production code 10209-007 ..... 3.50
❑11, Oct 1970 ..... 3.00
❑12, Jan 1974 ..... 3.00
❑13, Apr 1974, Production code 90209-404 ..... 3.00
❑14, Jul 1974 ..... 3.00
❑15, Oct 1974 ..... 3.00
❑16 1975 ..... 3.00
❑17 1975 ..... 3.00
❑18 1975 ..... 3.00
❑19, Aug 1975 ..... 3.00
❑20, Oct 1975 ..... 3.00
❑21, Jan 1976, Reprints from Moby Duck #7, 9 ..... 2.50
❑22, Apr 1976 ..... 2.50
❑23, Jul 1976 ..... 2.50
❑24, Oct 1976 ..... 2.50
❑25, Jan 1977 ..... 2.50
❑26, Apr 1977 ..... 2.50
❑27, Jul 1977 ..... 2.50
❑28, Oct 1977, Reprints from Moby Duck #8, 10 ..... 2.50
❑29, Jan 1978 ..... 2.50
❑30, Mar 1978, Reprint from Moby Duck #11 ..... 2.50

Mod
Kitchen Sink

❑1; 1: Adventures in Limbo; b&w 5.00

Other grades: Multiply price above by 5/6 for VF/NM • 2/3 for VERY FINE • 1/3 for FINE • 1/5 for VERY GOOD • 1/8 for GOOD

National Velvet

Based on the TV series, not the movie
©Dell

Navy War Heroes

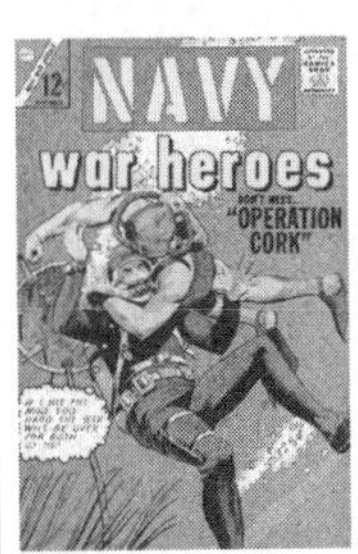

Yet another service-branch-centric war series
©Charlton

NBC Saturday Morning Comics

An NBC promo for its 1991 cartoon line-up
©Harvey

Negative Burn

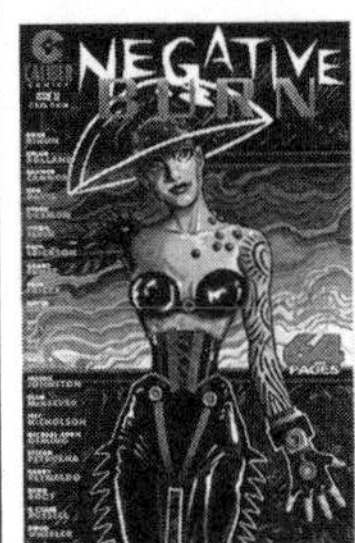

Many new creators came from this anthology
©Caliber

Neil the Horse Comics and Stories

Happy-go-lucky horse usually comes out OK
©Aardvark-Vanaheim

N-MINT

Model
Tokyopop

❑1, May 2004 .... 9.99

Model
NBM

❑1, Oct 2002 .... 24.95

Model By Day
Rip Off

❑1, Jul 1990, b&w; Adult 2.50
❑2, Oct 1990, b&w; Adult 2.50

Modeling with Millie
Marvel

❑21, Feb 1963, Reprint from Love Romances #84 .... 65.00
❑22, Apr 1963, Reprint from My Own Romance #49 .... 48.00
❑23, Jun 1963, Reprint from Nurse Helen Grant #1 .... 48.00
❑24, Aug 1963, Reprint from Hedy Wolfe #1 .... 48.00
❑25 1963 .... 48.00
❑26 1963, Reprint from Patsy Walker #85 .... 48.00
❑27, Nov 1963 .... 48.00
❑28, Reprint from Love Romances #83 . ... 48.00
❑29, ca. 1964 .... 48.00
❑30, ca. 1964, Reprint from Love Romances #62 .... 48.00
❑31, ca. 1964 .... 36.00
❑32, Jul 1964, Reprint from Love Romances #53 .... 36.00
❑33, ca. 1964, Reprint from Miss America #89 .... 36.00
❑34, ca. 1964, Reprint from Miss America #89 .... 36.00
❑35, ca. 1964 .... 36.00
❑36, Dec 1964 .... 36.00
❑37, Feb 1965 .... 36.00
❑38, Apr 1965 .... 36.00
❑39, Jun 1965 .... 36.00
❑40 1965 .... 36.00
❑41 1965 .... 30.00
❑42, Oct 1965 .... 30.00
❑43, Nov 1965 .... 30.00
❑44 .... 30.00
❑45, Feb 1966 .... 30.00
❑46, Apr 1966 .... 30.00
❑47, Jun 1966 .... 30.00
❑48, Aug 1966 .... 30.00
❑49, Sep 1966 .... 30.00
❑50, Oct 1966 .... 30.00
❑51, Nov 1966 .... 30.00
❑52, Dec 1966 .... 30.00
❑53, Apr 1967 .... 30.00
❑54 .... 30.00

Modern Grimm
Symptom

❑1, Dec 1996, b&w 2.75

Modern Pulp
Special Studio

❑1, b&w 2.75

Modern Romans
Fantagraphics / Eros

❑1, b&w; Adult 2.25
❑2, b&w; Adult 2.25
❑3, b&w; Adult 2.25

N-MINT

Modest Proposal, A
Tome

❑1, b&w 2.50
❑2, b&w 2.50

Modniks
Gold Key

❑1, ca. 1967 .... 8.00
❑2 .... 4.00

Mod Wheels
Gold Key

❑1, Feb 1971 .... 30.00
❑2, May 1971 .... 20.00
❑3, Aug 1971 .... 20.00
❑4, Nov 1971 .... 20.00
❑5, Feb 1972 .... 20.00
❑6, Jun 1972 .... 20.00
❑7, Jan 1973 .... 20.00
❑8, Apr 1973 .... 20.00
❑9, Jul 1973, DS (a) 20.00
❑10, Oct 1973 .... 15.00
❑11, Jan 1974 .... 15.00
❑12, Apr 1974 .... 15.00
❑13, Jul 1974 .... 15.00
❑14, Oct 1974 .... 15.00
❑15, Jan 1975 .... 15.00
❑16, Apr 1975 .... 15.00
❑17, Jul 1975 .... 10.00
❑18, Oct 1976 .... 10.00
❑19, Jan 1976 .... 10.00

Moebius Comics
Caliber

❑1, May 1996 .... 3.00
❑2, Jul 1996 .... 3.00
❑3, Sep 1996 .... 3.00
❑4, Nov 1996 .... 3.00
❑5, Jan 1997 .... 3.00
❑6, Mar 1997 .... 3.00

Moebius: Exotics
Dark Horse

❑1; prestige format; NN; One-shot 6.95

Moebius: H.P.'s Rock City
Dark Horse

❑1 1996; smaller than a normal comic book; squarebound 7.95

Moebius: Madwoman of the Sacred Heart
Dark Horse

❑1, Aug 1996 .... 12.95

Moebius: The Man from the Ciguri
Dark Horse

❑1 1996, smaller than a normal comic book; squarebound 7.95

Mogobi Desert Rats
Studio 91

❑1, Jan 1991 .... 2.25

Mojo Action Companion Unit
Exclaim

❑1, Spr 1997, b&w 2.75

Mojo Mechanics
Syndicate

❑1, ca. 1999; b&w 2.95
❑2 .... 2.95

N-MINT

Moment of Silence, A
Marvel

❑1, Feb 2002; BMB, KSm (w); ARo, JR2 (a); An introduction by Mayor Rudolph W. Giuliani 4.00

Moment of Freedom, A
Caliber / Tome

❑nn, ca. 1997, b&w 4.95

Mona
Kitchen Sink

❑1 .... 4.95

Monarchy
DC / Wildstorm

❑1, Apr 2001 .... 2.50
❑2, Jun 2001 .... 2.50
❑3, Jul 2001 .... 2.50
❑4, Aug 2001 .... 2.50
❑5, Sep 2001 .... 2.50
❑6, Sep 2001 .... 2.50
❑7, Oct 2001 .... 2.50
❑8, Nov 2001 .... 2.50
❑9, Dec 2001 .... 2.50
❑10, Jan 2002 .... 2.50
❑11, Feb 2002 .... 2.50
❑12, Mar 2002 .... 2.50

Mondo 3-D
3-D Zone

❑1; NN 3.95

Mondo Bondo
LCD

❑1; Adult 2.95

Money Talks
Slave Labor

❑1, Jun 1996 .... 3.50
❑2, Aug 1996 .... 2.95
❑3, Oct 1996 .... 2.95
❑4, Dec 1996 .... 2.95
❑5, Feb 1997 .... 2.95

Mongrel
Northstar

❑1/A, Dec 1994, b&w 3.95
❑2 .... 3.95
❑3 .... 3.95

Monica's Story
Alternative

❑1, Feb 1999, b&w; NN 3.50

Monkees
Gold Key

❑1, Mar 1967, based on TV series 45.00
❑2, May 1967 .... 30.00
❑3, Jul 1967 .... 24.00
❑4, Sep 1967 .... 20.00
❑5, Oct 1967 .... 20.00
❑6, Nov 1967 .... 18.00
❑7, Dec 1967 .... 18.00
❑8, Jan 1968 .... 18.00
❑9, Feb 1968 .... 18.00
❑10, Mar 1968 .... 18.00
❑11, May 1968 .... 12.00
❑12, Jun 1968 .... 12.00
❑13, Jul 1968 .... 12.00
❑14, Aug 1968 .... 12.00
❑15, Sep 1968 .... 12.00

Other grades: Multiply price above by 5/6 for VF/NM • 2/3 for VERY FINE • 1/3 for FINE • 1/5 for VERY GOOD • 1/8 for GOOD

N-MINT N-MINT N-MINT

❑16, Oct 1969 .... 12.00
❑17, Oct 1969, Reprints from The Monkees #1 .... 12.00

Monkey Business
Parody

❑1, b&w 2.50
❑2; Ren & Stimpy parody 2.50

Monkey In A Wagon Vs. Lemur On A Big Wheel
Alias

❑1, ca. 2005; Lullaby: Wisdom Seeker #1 preview 2.99

Monkeyman and O'Brien
Dark Horse / Legend

❑1, Jul 1996; V: Shrewmanoid; O: Shrewmanoid 3.50
❑2, Aug 1996; V: Froglodytes 3.00
❑3, Sep 1996; A: Shrewmanoid; Final Issue 2.95
❑Special 1, Feb 1996; O: Monkeyman and O'Brien; Reprints from Hellboy: Seed of Destruction #1-4; O: Monkeyman (Axewell Tiberius); O: Ann O'Brien 2.95

Monnga
Daikaiju

❑1, Aug 1995 .... 3.95

Monolith
Comico

❑1, Oct 1991 .... 2.50
❑2, Nov 1991 .... 2.50
❑3 .... 2.50
❑4, Aug 1992 .... 2.50

Monolith
DC

❑1, Apr 2004 .... 4.00
❑2, May 2004 (c) 2.95
❑3, Jun 2004 .... 2.95
❑4, Jul 2004 .... 2.95
❑5, Aug 2004 .... 2.95
❑6, Sep 2004 .... 2.95
❑7, Oct 2004 .... 2.95
❑8, Nov 2004 .... 2.95
❑9, Dec 2004 .... 2.95
❑10, Jan 2005 .... 2.95
❑11, Feb 2005 .... 2.95
❑12, Mar 2005, Final issue 2.95

Monolith
Last Gasp

❑1, Adult 3.00

Monroe
Conquest

❑1, b&w; poster; cards 4.95

Monster
Slave Labor

❑1, b&w; Adult 2.95

Monster
Ring

❑1 .... 2.00

Monster Boy
Monster

❑1, Sep 1991, b&w 2.50

Monster Boy Comics
Slave Labor

❑1, Sep 1997, b&w 2.95
❑2, Dec 1997, b&w 2.95
❑3; b&w 2.95

Monster Club
APComics

❑1, ca. 2002 .... 6.00
❑2 .... 5.00
❑3 .... 3.50
❑4 .... 3.50
❑5 .... 3.50
❑6 .... 3.50
❑7 .... 3.50
❑8 .... 3.50
❑9 .... 3.50

Monster Club
APComics

❑0, ca. 2004 .... 3.00
❑1, ca. 2004 .... 3.50
❑2 2004 .... 3.50
❑3, Aug 2004; Glossy cardstock cover 3.50

❑4, Sep 2004 .... 3.50
❑5, Oct 2004 .... 3.50

Monster Fighters Inc.
Image

❑1, Apr 1999; Wraparound cover 3.50

Monster Fighters Inc.: The Black Book
Image

❑1, Sep 2000; One-shot 3.50

Monster Fighters Inc.: The Ghosts of Christmas
Image

❑1, Dec 1999; One-shot 3.95

Monster Frat House
Eternity

❑1, Oct 1989, b&w 2.25

Monster House
Idea & Design Works

❑1, Jun 2006 .... 7.99

Monster in My Pocket
Harvey

❑1, Mar 1991 EC (a) 1.50
❑2, May 1991; The Exterminator 1.50
❑3, Jul 1991 GK (c); GK (a) 1.50
❑4, Sep 1991 GK (c); GK (a) 1.50

Monster Island
Compass

❑1, Nov 1998, b&w; wraparound cover 3.95

Monster Love
Kitchen Sink

❑1 .... 2.50

Monsterman
Image

❑1, Sep 1997, b&w 2.95

Monster Massacre
Atomeka

❑1; NN 7.95

Monster Massacre Special
Blackball

❑1; Simon Bisley cover 2.50

Monster Matinee
Chaos!

❑1, Oct 1997; monster pin-ups; commentary by Forrest J. Ackerman 2.50
❑1/Variant, Oct 1997; premium edition; alternate logoless cover; monster pin-ups; commentary by Forrest J. Ackerman 2.50
❑2, Oct 1997; monster pin-ups; commentary by Forrest J. Ackerman 2.50
❑3, Oct 1997; monster pin-ups; commentary by Forrest J. Ackerman 2.50

Monster Menace
Marvel

❑1, Dec 1993; SL (w); SD, JK (a); Reprints 1.50
❑2, Jan 1994; SD (c); SL (w); SD, JK (a); Reprints 1.50
❑3, Feb 1994; SD (c); SL (w); SD, JK (a); Reprints from Tales to Astonish #8, Uncanny Tales #6, Strange Tales #88 .... 1.50
❑4, Mar 1994; SL (w); SD, JK (a); Includes reprints from Strange Tales #75; Reprints from Strange Tales #75, 90, Journey into Mystery #64 .... 1.50

MonsterMen
Dark Horse

❑1, Aug 1999 .... 2.50

Monster Posse
Adventure

❑1, b&w 2.50
❑2, Nov 1992 .... 2.50
❑3 .... 2.50

Monsters from Outer Space
Adventure

❑1, Dec 1992, b&w 2.50
❑2, Jan 1993, b&w 2.50
❑3, Feb 1993, b&w 2.50

Monsters on the Prowl
Marvel

❑9, Feb 1971, Title changes to Monsters on the Prowl; Series continued from Chamber of Darkness #8 .... 25.00
❑10, Apr 1971, Reprints 15.00
❑11, Jun 1971, Reprints 15.00
❑12, Aug 1971, Reprints 15.00
❑13, Oct 1971; Reprints from Journey into Mystery #61, 70, Tales to Astonish #30, 31 .... 15.00
❑14, Dec 1971; Reprints from Journey into Mystery #66, 79, Tales to Astonish #23, 25, Strange Tales #73 .... 15.00
❑15, Feb 1972, JSe (c); DH, JK (a); Reprints from Strange Tales #82, Journey into Mystery #68 .... 15.00
❑16, Apr 1972, JSe (c); SL (w); SD, JK, JSe (a); King Kull 18.00
❑17, Jun 1972, HT (c); JK, JSt (a); Reprint from Tales of Suspense #14 .... 12.00
❑18, Aug 1972, Reprints from Tales of Suspense #22 .... 12.00
❑19, Oct 1972, Reprints from Tales of Suspense #23, 30 .... 12.00
❑20, Dec 1972, GK (c); SD, JK (a); Reprints from Tales of Suspense 18, 27, Journery into Mystery #63, Tales to Astonish #4 .... 12.00
❑21, Feb 1973, Reprints from Tales of Suspense #29, Marvel Tales #105 .... 12.00
❑22, Apr 1973, Reprints from Strange Tales #80, 93, Tales to Astonish #23 .... 12.00
❑23, Jun 1973, Reprints from Strange Tales #87, Adventures into Terror #15 .... 12.00
❑24, Aug 1973, Reprints from Strange Tales #84, Journey into Unknown Worlds #55 .... 12.00
❑25, Sep 1973, Reprints from Tales of Suspense #14, Strange Stories of Suspense #13, Journey into Mystery #4 .... 12.00
❑26, Oct 1973, Reprints from Strange Tales #95, Journey into Mystery #80, Adventures into Weird Worlds #5 .... 12.00
❑27, Nov 1974, Reprints from Amazing Adventures, Strange Tales #93 .... 12.00
❑28, Jun 1975; Reprints from Amazing Adventures #5, Adventures into Terror #14 .... 12.00
❑29, Aug 1975; Reprints from Tales to Astonish #34, Mystic #8, World of Suspense #3, Amazing Adventures #5 .... 12.00
❑30, Oct 1975; Final Issue; Reprints from Tales of Suspense #9, Tales to Astonish #34, Menace #11, Uncanny Tales #42 .... 12.00

Monsters to Laugh With
Marvel

❑1, ca. 1964 .... 40.00
❑2, ca. 1964 .... 30.00
❑3, ca. 1965 .... 30.00

Monsters Unleashed
Marvel

❑1, Jul 1973, b&w; magazine; Reprints from Journey into Mystery #1, 16 .... 40.00
❑2, Sep 1973; Frankenstein 18.00
❑3, Nov 1973; Frankenstein, Man-Thing, Son of Satan 15.00
❑4, Jan 1974; Frankenstein 15.00
❑5, Mar 1974; Frankenstein, Man-Thing 15.00
❑6, May 1974; Frankenstein, Werewolf 10.00
❑7, Jul 1974; Frankenstein, Werewolf 10.00
❑8, Sep 1974; Frankenstein, Man-Thing 10.00
❑9, Nov 1974; Frankenstein, Man-Thing, Wendigo 7.00
❑10, Jan 1975; Frankenstein, Tigra 7.00
❑11, Mar 1975; Gabriel 7.00
❑Ann 1, ca. 1975; Reprints 12.00

Monster War: Magdalena vs. Dracula
Image

❑1, ca. 2005 .... 2.99

Monster War: Tomb Raider vs. Wolf Men
Image

❑2, Jul 2005 .... 2.99

Monster War: Witchblade vs. Frankenstein
Image

❑3/A cover, Sep 2005; Joyce Chin cover 2.99
❑3/B cover, Sep 2005; Richard Ebas cover 2.99

Monster War: Darkness vs. Mr. Hyde
Image

❑4/A cover, Oct 2005; Richard Ebas cover 2.99
❑4/B cover, Oct 2005; Joyce Chin cover 2.99

Monster World
DC / Wildstorm

❑1, Jul 2001 .... 2.50
❑2, Aug 2001 .... 2.50

Other grades: Multiply price above by 5/6 for VF/NM • 2/3 for VERY FINE • 1/3 for FINE • 1/5 for VERY GOOD • 1/8 for GOOD

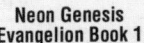

Neon Genesis Evangelion Book 1

Giant robots fight aliens in manga import
©Viz

Nevada

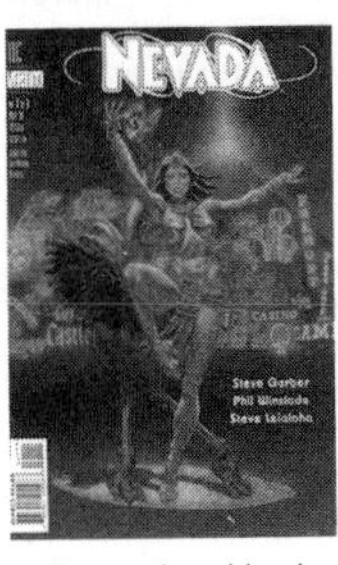

Reuses showgirl and ostrich from "Howard"
©DC

New Adventures of Huck Finn

Adapts television series episodes
©Gold Key

New Adventures of Superboy

Played fast and loose with continuity
©DC

New Adventures of the Phantom Blot

Short series gives birth to Super Goof
©Gold Key

N-MINT

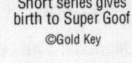

❑3, Sep 2001 .... 2.50
❑4, Oct 2001 .... 2.95

Monstrosity
Slap Happy

❑1, Oct 1998, b&w 4.95

Moon Beast
Avalon

❑1 .... 2.95

Moonchild
Forbidden Fruit

❑1, Jan 1992, b&w; Adult 2.95
❑2, Mar 1992, b&w; Adult 2.95

Moon Child
Forbidden Fruit

❑1, b&w 3.50
❑2, b&w 3.50
❑3, b&w 3.50

Moonfighting
Harrier

❑1, Mar 1988, b&w 1.95

Moon Knight
Marvel

❑1, Nov 1980, BSz (c); BSz (a); O: Moon Knight 10.00
❑2, Dec 1980, BSz (c); BSz (a) 7.00
❑3, Jan 1981, BSz (c); BSz (a); 1: Midnight Man (Anton Mogart) 5.00
❑4, Feb 1981, BSz (c); BSz (a); V: Committee 5.00
❑5, Mar 1981, BSz (c); BSz (a) 2.50
❑6, Apr 1981, BSz (a); Painted cover 2.50
❑7, May 1981, BSz (c); BSz (a) 2.50
❑8, Jun 1981, BSz (c); BSz (a); V: Moon Kings 2.50
❑9, Jul 1981, FM (c); BSz, FM (a); V: Midnight Man 2.50
❑10, Aug 1981, BSz (c); BSz (a); V: Midnight Man 2.50
❑11, Sep 1981, BSz (c); BSz (a); V: Creed 2.50
❑12, Oct 1981, FM (c); BSz, FM (a); 1: Morpheus (Robert Markham) 2.50
❑13, Nov 1981, BSz, FM (a); A: Daredevil 2.50
❑14, Dec 1981, BSz (c); BSz (a); 1: Stained Glass Scarlet Fasinera 2.50
❑15, Jan 1982; FM (c); BSz, FM (a); A: Thing. direct 2.50
❑16, Feb 1982; BSz (c); BSz (a); V: Blacksmith 2.50
❑17, Mar 1982; BSz (a); No ads 2.50
❑18, Apr 1982; BSz (c); BSz (a); V: Slayers Elite; "The Many Phases of Moon Knight" text pages by Allen Zelenetz; 1: Arsenal (Nimrod Strange) 2.50
❑19, May 1982; BSz (c); BSz (a); V: Arsenal 2.50
❑20, Jun 1982; BSz (c); BSz (a); V: Arsenal; D: Arsenal (Nimrod Strange) 2.50
❑21, Jul 1982; BSz (c); BSz (a); Tale of Konshu 2.00
❑22, Aug 1982; BSz (c); BSz (a); Tale of Konshu 2.00
❑23, Sep 1982; BSz (c); BSz (a); V: Morpheus 2.00
❑24, Oct 1982; BSz (c); BSz (a); 2: Scarlet 2.00
❑25, Nov 1982; double-sized; BSz (c); BSz (w); BSz (a); 1: Black Spectre (Carson Knowles); 48 pages 2.50

N-MINT

❑26, Dec 1982 BSz (c); BSz, KP (a) 2.00
❑27, Jan 1983 FM (c) 2.00
❑28, Feb 1983 BSz (c); BSz, KN (a) 2.00
❑29, Mar 1983 BSz (c); BSz, KN (a) 2.00
❑30, Apr 1983 BSz (c); BSz (a) 2.00
❑31, May 1983 BSz (c); BSz, KN (a) 2.00
❑32, Jul 1983 BSz (c); BSz, KN (a) 2.00
❑33, Sep 1983; BSz (c); BSz, KN (a); V: Druid Walsh 2.00
❑34, Nov 1983 BSz (c); RHo, BSz (a) 2.00
❑35, Jan 1984; double-sized; BMc, KN (a); A: X-Men. V: Bora; V: The Fly; 1: Bora; 48 pages 2.50
❑36, Mar 1984 .... 2.00
❑37, May 1984; BSz (a); "Crawley" portfolio by Bill Sienkiewicz 2.00
❑38, Jul 1984; Final Issue 2.00

Moon Knight
Marvel

❑1, Jun 1985; Double-size; O: Moon Knight; 48 pages 2.50
❑2, Aug 1985 .... 2.00
❑3, Sep 1985 .... 2.00
❑4, Oct 1985 .... 2.00
❑5, Nov 1985 .... 2.00
❑6, Dec 1985, BSz (c); Painted cover 2.00

Moon Knight
Marvel

❑1, Jan 1998; Indicia says "Moon Knight Vol.3, No.1" 2.50
❑2, Feb 1998; Indicia says "Moon Knight vol.2, No.2" 2.50
❑3, Mar 1998; V: Black Spectre; Indicia says "Moon Knight vol.2, No.3" 2.50
❑4, Apr 1998; V: Bushman; V: Morpheus; Indicia says "Moon Knight vol.2, No.4" 2.50

Moon Knight
Marvel

❑1, Jan 1999; says Feb on cover, Jan in indicia 2.99
❑2, Feb 1999; Cover incorrectly says "High Strangers" instead of "High Strangeness" 2.99
❑3, Feb 1999; Cover incorrectly says "High Strangers" instead of "High Strangeness" 2.99
❑4, Feb 1999; Cover incorrectly says "High Strangers" instead of "High Strangeness" 2.99

Moon Knight: Divided We Fall
Marvel

❑1, ca. 1992, b&w; NN 4.95

Moon Knight
Marvel

❑1, Jun 2006 .... 2.99
❑3, Sep 2006 .... 2.99
❑4, Oct 2006 .... 2.99
❑5, Nov 2006 .... 2.99
❑6, Jan 2007 .... 2.99

Moon Knight Special
Marvel

❑1; Shang-Chi 2.50

N-MINT

Moon Knight Special Edition
Marvel

❑1, Nov 1983; Reprints from Hulk (magazine); BSz (c); BSz (a); Reprints from Hulk (magazine); Includes new pin-ups and wraparound cover by Sienkiewicz; Reprints from Hulk (magazine) #13-14 .... 2.50
❑2, Dec 1983; BSz (c); BSz (a); Reprints 2.50
❑3, Jan 1984; BSz (c); BSz (a); Reprints 2.50

Moonshadow
Marvel / Epic

❑1, Mar 1985 O: Moonshadow 3.50
❑2, May 1985 .... 2.50
❑3, Jul 1985 .... 2.50
❑4, Sep 1985 .... 2.00
❑5, Nov 1985 .... 2.00
❑6, Jan 1986 .... 2.00
❑7, Mar 1986 .... 2.00
❑8, Jun 1986 .... 2.00
❑9, Aug 1986 .... 2.00
❑10, Oct 1986 .... 2.00
❑11, Jan 1987 O: Moonshadow 2.00
❑12, Feb 1987 .... 2.00

Moonshadow
DC / Vertigo

❑1, Sep 1994, O: Moonshadow 3.00
❑2, Oct 1994 .... 2.50
❑3, Nov 1994 .... 2.50
❑4, Dec 1994 .... 2.50
❑5, Jan 1995 .... 2.50
❑6, Feb 1995 .... 2.25
❑7, Mar 1995 .... 2.25
❑8, Apr 1995 .... 2.25
❑9, May 1995 .... 2.25
❑10, Jun 1995 .... 2.25
❑11, Jul 1995, O: Moonshadow 2.25
❑12, Aug 1995, Final Issue 2.95

Moon Shot, the Flight of Apollo 12
Pepper Pike Graphix

❑1, Jun 1994; One-shot 2.95

Moonstone Monsters: Zombies
Moonstone

❑1, Jun 2005 .... 2.95

Moonstruck
White Wolf

❑1, May 1987 .... 2.00

Moontrap
Caliber

❑1, b&w; Movie adaptation 2.00

Moonwalker 3-D
Blackthorne

❑1 .... 2.50

Moordam Christmas Comics
Moordam

❑1, Dec 1999 .... 2.95

Mora
Image

❑1, Mar 2005, b&w 2.95
❑2, Apr 2005; b&w 2.95
❑3, Jun 2005; b&w 2.95
❑4, Dec 2005 .... 2.95

Morbid Angel
London Night

❑½, Jul 1996 .... 3.00
❑1, Oct 1996 .... 3.00

Morbid Angel: Penance
London Night

❑1, Sep 1996 .... 3.95

Morbius Revisited
Marvel

❑1, Aug 1993; Reprints Fear #27 .... 2.00
❑2, Sep 1993; FR (a); Reprints Fear #28 .... 2.00
❑3, Oct 1993; DH (a); A: Helleyes. A: Simon Stroud. Reprints Fear #29 .... 2.00
❑4, Nov 1993; GE (a); Reprints Fear #30 .... 2.00
❑5, Dec 1993; FR (w); FR (a); Reprints Fear #31 .... 2.00

Morbius: The Living Vampire
Marvel

❑1, Sep 1992; Without poster 1.50
❑1/CS, Sep 1992; Polybagged w/poster 3.00
❑2, Oct 1992 .... 2.00
❑3, Nov 1992 .... 2.00
❑4, Dec 1992 .... 2.00
❑5, Jan 1993; 1: Basilisk II 2.00
❑6, Feb 1993 .... 1.75
❑7, Mar 1993 .... 1.75
❑8, Apr 1993 .... 1.75
❑9, May 1993; V: Nightmare 1.75
❑10, Jun 1993 .... 1.75
❑11, Jul 1993 .... 1.75
❑12, Aug 1993; Double cover 2.25
❑13, Sep 1993 .... 1.75
❑14, Oct 1993 .... 1.75
❑15, Nov 1993 .... 1.75
❑16, Dec 1993; Neon ink/matte finish cover 1.75
❑17, Jan 1994; Spot-varnished cover 1.75
❑18, Feb 1994 .... 1.75
❑19, Mar 1994 .... 1.75
❑20, Apr 1994 .... 1.75
❑21, May 1994 .... 1.75
❑22, Jun 1994 .... 1.95
❑23, Jul 1994 .... 1.95
❑24, Aug 1994 .... 1.95
❑25, Sep 1994; Giant-size 2.50
❑26, Oct 1994 .... 1.95
❑27, Nov 1994 .... 1.95
❑28, Dec 1994 .... 1.95
❑29, Jan 1995 .... 1.95
❑30, Feb 1995 .... 1.95
❑31, Mar 1995 .... 1.95
❑32, Apr 1995; Final Issue 1.95

More Fetish
Boneyard

❑1, Nov 1993; Adult 2.95

More Secret Origins Replica Edition
DC

❑1, Dec 1999; reprints 80-Page Giant #8; Reprints 80-Page Giant #8; O: Superman; O: The Atom II (Ray Palmer); O: The Justice League of America; O: Aquaman; O: The Atom (Ray Palmer); O: Justice League of America 4.95

More Starlight To Your Heart
ADV Manga

❑1, ca. 2004; Read right to left; Graphic novel; b&w 9.99
❑2, ca. 2004; Read right to left; Graphic novel; b&w 9.99

More Tales from Gimbley
Harrier

❑1, Feb 1988 .... 1.95

More Tales From Sleaze Castle
Gratuitous Bunny

❑1 .... 4.00
❑2 .... 3.00
❑3 1990 .... 3.00
❑4, Jan 1991 .... 3.00
❑5, Jan 1992 .... 3.00
❑6, Jan 1993 .... 3.00

More Than Mortal
Liar

❑1, Jun 1997 .... 3.00
❑1/2nd, Jun 1997; 2nd printing 2.95
❑2, Sep 1997 .... 3.00
❑2/Variant, Sep 1997; logoless cover 2.95
❑3, Dec 1997 .... 3.00
❑4, Apr 1998 .... 3.00
❑5, Dec 1999 .... 3.00
❑6, Mar 2000 .... 2.95
❑Deluxe 1; Collects More than Mortal #1-4 .... 14.95

More Than Mortal/Lady Pendragon
Image

❑1, Jun 1999 .... 2.50
❑1/A, Jun 1999; alternate cover 3.00

More Than Mortal: Otherworlds
Image

❑1, Jul 1999; Woman leaning on half-wall 3.00
❑1/A, Jul 1999; alternate cover 3.00
❑2, Aug 1999; Woman and man kneeling on cover, large figure standing behind 3.00
❑2/A, Aug 1999; alternate cover 3.00
❑3, Oct 1999; Woman holding sword on cover, red top left background 3.00
❑3/A, Oct 1999; alternate cover 3.00
❑4, Dec 1999; Woman neeling with fairy wings 3.00

More Than Mortal: Sagas
Liar

❑1, Aug 1998; O: Morlock. 1: Morlock 2.95
❑1/A, Aug 1998; variant cover for New Dimension Comics 3.00
❑2, Oct 1998 .... 2.95
❑3, Dec 1998 .... 2.95

More Than Mortal: Truths & Legends
Liar

❑1, Jun 1998; Cover has man with glowing eye at bow of ship 2.95
❑1/A, Jun 1998; Variant edition 3.00
❑1/Ltd., Jun 1998; Variant edition; Signed and numbered 4.00
❑2, Aug 1998 .... 2.95
❑3, Oct 1998 .... 2.95
❑4, Jan 1999 .... 2.95
❑5, Apr 1999 .... 2.95

More Trash from Mad
E.C.

❑1, ca. 1958, Magazine-sized; no number 275.00
❑2, ca. 1959, Magazine-sized; has Mad labels foldout 175.00
❑3, ca. 1960, Magazine-sized; has Mad textbook cover inserts 175.00
❑4, ca. 1961, Magazine-sized 175.00
❑5, ca. 1962, Magazine-sized; has window sticker inserts 175.00
❑6, ca. 1963, Magazine-sized; has color TV Guide parody insert 175.00
❑7, ca. 1964, Magazine-sized 150.00
❑8, ca. 1965, Magazine-sized 150.00
❑9, ca. 1966, Magazine-sized 150.00
❑10, ca. 1967, Magazine-sized 150.00
❑11, ca. 1968, Magazine-sized 150.00
❑12, ca. 1969, b&w; Magazine-sized; has "pocket medals" 150.00

Morlocks
Marvel

❑1, Jun 2002; 1: Angel Dust (Christine) 2.50
❑2, Jul 2002 .... 2.50
❑3, Aug 2002 .... 2.50
❑4, Sep 2002 .... 2.50

Morlock 2001
Atlas-Seaboard

❑1, Feb 1975; AM (c); AM (a); O: Morlock 9.00
❑2, Apr 1975 AM (a) 6.00
❑3, Jul 1975; RB (c); AM, SD, BWr (a); O: Midnight Men 8.00

Morning Glory
Radio

❑1, Nov 1998, b&w; Adult 2.95
❑2, Dec 1998, b&w; Adult 2.95
❑3, Jan 1999, b&w; Adult 2.95
❑4, Mar 1999; Adult; b&w 2.95
❑5, May 1999, b&w; Adult 2.95

Morningstar Special
Trident

❑1, Apr 1990, b&w 2.50

Morphing Period
Shanda

❑1 .... 4.95

Morphos the Shapechanger
Dark Horse

❑1, Jul 1996; prestige format; NN; One-shot 4.95

Morphs
Graphxpress

❑1, Apr 1987; b&w 2.00
❑2, Jul 1987; b&w 2.00
❑3; b&w 2.00
❑4; b&w 2.00

Morrigan
Dimension X

❑1, Aug 1993, b&w 2.75

Morrigan
Sirius

❑1, Jul 1997 .... 2.95

Mortal Coils: Bloodlines
Red Eye

❑1, Aug 2002 .... 2.50

Mortal Kombat
Malibu

❑1, Jul 1994, b&w; Blood and Thunder 3.00
❑1/A, Jul 1994, b&w; variant cover (Mortal Kombat logo) 3.00
❑2, Aug 1994, b&w; variant cover (Mortal Kombat logo); Blood and Thunder 3.00
❑3, Sep 1994, b&w; variant cover (Mortal Kombat logo); Blood and Thunder 3.00
❑4, Oct 1994, b&w; variant cover (Mortal Kombat logo); Blood and Thunder 3.00
❑5, Nov 1994, b&w; variant cover (Mortal Kombat logo); Blood and Thunder 3.00
❑6, Dec 1994, b&w; variant cover (Mortal Kombat logo) 3.00

Mortal Kombat: Baraka
Malibu

❑1, ca. 1995 .... 2.95

Mortal Kombat: Battlewave
Malibu

❑1, ca. 1995 .... 3.00
❑2, Mar 1995 .... 3.00
❑3, ca. 1995 .... 3.00
❑4, ca. 1995 .... 3.00
❑5, ca. 1995 .... 3.00
❑6, ca. 1995 .... 3.00

Mortal Kombat: Goro, Prince of Pain
Malibu

❑1, Sep 1994 .... 2.95
❑2, Oct 1994 .... 2.95
❑3, Nov 1994 .... 2.95

Mortal Kombat: Kitana & Mileena
Malibu

❑1, ca. 1995 .... 2.95

Mortal Kombat: Kung Lao
Malibu

❑1, ca. 1995 .... 2.95

Mortal Kombat: Rayden & Kano
Malibu

❑1, ca. 1995 .... 2.95
❑2, Apr 1995 .... 2.95
❑3 .... 2.95

Mortal Kombat Special Edition
Malibu

❑1, Nov 1994 .... 2.95
❑2 1994 .... 2.95

Mortal Kombat: Tournament Edition
Malibu

❑1, Dec 1994 .... 3.95
❑2 1995 .... 3.95

Mortal Kombat U.S. Special Forces
Malibu

❑1, Jan 1995 .... 3.50
❑2, Feb 1995 .... 3.50

Mortal Souls
Avatar

❑1/A, Apr 2002, b&w 3.50

Mortar Man
Marshall Comics

❑1, May 1993, b&w 1.95
❑2, ca. 1993, b&w 1.95
❑3, ca. 1993 .... 1.95

New Archies

Portrays the gang as younger teen-agers

©Archie

New Avengers

Bendis restarts classic series from beginning

©Marvel

New Gods

Jack Kirby's far-flung fantasy series

©DC

New Guardians

Series spinoff from Millennium event

©DC

New Mutants

X-Men farm team turned into X-Force

©Marvel

N-MINT

Mortigan Goth: Immortalis
Marvel

❑1, Sep 1993 .... 1.95
❑1/Variant, Sep 1993; foil cover 2.95
❑2, Oct 1993 .... 1.95
❑3, Jan 1994 .... 1.95
❑4, Mar 1994 .... 1.95

Mort the Dead Teenager
Marvel

❑1, Nov 1992 .... 1.75
❑2, Dec 1992 .... 1.75
❑3, Feb 1993 .... 1.75
❑4, Mar 1993 .... 1.75

Morty the Dog
Mu

❑1, b&w; digest 3.95
❑2, Spr 1991, b&w; digest 3.95

Morty the Dog
Starhead

❑1 .... 2.00

Mosaic
Sirius

❑1/A, Mar 1999 .... 2.95
❑1/B, Mar 1999; alternate cover; smaller logos 2.95
❑2, Apr 1999 .... 2.95
❑3, May 1999 .... 2.95
❑4, Jun 1999 .... 2.95
❑5, Jul 1999 .... 2.95

Mosaic: Hell City Ripper
Sirius

❑1 .... 2.95
❑1/Variant; alternate cover 2.95

Mostly Wanted
WildStorm

❑1, Jul 2000 .... 2.50
❑2, Aug 2000 .... 2.50
❑3, Sep 2000 .... 2.50
❑4, Nov 2000 .... 2.50

Moth (Steve Rude's)
Dark Horse

❑1, Apr 2004 .... 2.99
❑2, May 2004 .... 2.99
❑3, Aug 2004 .... 2.99
❑4, Oct 2004 .... 3.00

Moth (Steve Rude's) Double-Sized Special
Dark Horse

❑1, May 2004 .... 4.95

Motherless Child
Kitchen Sink

❑1 .... 2.95

Mother's Oats Comix
Rip Off

❑1, Adult; b&w 5.00
❑2, Adult; Cs. 1970; b&w 3.00

Mother Superion
Antarctic

❑1, Jul 1997 .... 2.95

N-MINT

Mother Teresa of Calcutta
Marvel

❑1, ca. 1984 .... 1.50

Motley Stories
Division

❑1, b&w 2.75

Motorbike Puppies
Dark Zulu Lies

❑1, Jun 1992; 1: The Humanals 2.50
❑2; Never published? 2.50

Motorhead
Dark Horse

❑1, Aug 1995, V: Predator 2.50
❑2, Sep 1995 .... 2.50
❑3, Oct 1995 .... 2.50
❑4, Nov 1995 .... 2.50
❑5, Dec 1995 .... 2.50
❑6, Jan 1996 .... 2.50
❑Special 1, Mar 1994 .... 3.95

Motormouth
Marvel

❑1, Jun 1992 1: Motormouth 2.00
❑2, Jul 1992 .... 1.75
❑3, Aug 1992; Punisher 1.75
❑4, Sep 1992 .... 1.75
❑5, Oct 1992 A: Punisher 1.75
❑6, Nov 1992; Title changes to Motormouth & Killpower 1.75
❑7, Dec 1992 A: Cable 1.75
❑8, Jan 1993 .... 1.75
❑9, Feb 1993 .... 1.75
❑10, Apr 1993 .... 1.75
❑11, Apr 1993 .... 1.75
❑12, May 1993 .... 1.75

Mountain
Underground

❑1, Flipbook High School Funnies 3.00

Mountain World
Icicle Ridge

❑1, b&w; ca. 1991 .... 2.00

Mouse Guard
Archaia Studios Press

❑1, Feb 2006 .... 90.00
❑1/2nd, Feb 2006 .... 18.00
❑2, Apr 2006 .... 25.00
❑3 .... 8.00
❑4 .... 8.00
❑5 .... 8.00
❑6 .... 8.00

Mouse on the Moon
Dell

❑1, Oct 1963 .... 15.00

Movie Star News
Pure Imagination

❑1; DSt (c); Bettie Page photos 6.00

Moxi
Lightning

❑1, Jul 1996 .... 3.00

Moxi's Friends: Bobby Joe & Nitro
Lightning

❑1, Sep 1996; b&w 2.75

N-MINT

Moxi: Strange Daze
Lightning

❑1, Nov 1996, b&w 3.00

M. Rex
Image

❑1, Nov 1999; Regular cover 2.95
❑1/A, Nov 1999; Alternate cover has large figure in background, boy, monkey on waterbike in foreground 5.00
❑2, Dec 1999 .... 2.95
❑Ashcan 1/A, Jul 1999; Flying car on cover 5.00
❑Ashcan 1/B, Jul 1999; Blue background on cover 5.00

Mr. T
APComics

❑1, Jun 2005; Sketch cover 3.50
❑2, ca. 2005 .... 3.50

Ms. Anti-Social
Helpless Anger

❑1, b&w; NN; 16 pages 1.75

Ms. Cyanide & Ice
Black Out

❑0 .... 2.95
❑1; Sly & Furious preview 2.95

Ms. Fantastic
Conquest

❑1, b&w; Adult 2.95
❑2, b&w; Adult 2.95
❑3, b&w; Adult 2.95
❑4, b&w; Adult 2.95

Ms. Fantastic Classics
Conquest

❑1, b&w; Adult 2.95

Ms. Fortune
Image

❑1, Jan 1998, b&w 2.95

Ms. Marvel
Marvel

❑1, Jan 1977, JR (c); JB (a); 1: Ms. Marvel 8.00
❑2, Feb 1977, 1: Destructor (Kerwin Korman) 3.00
❑3, Mar 1977 .... 3.00
❑4, Apr 1977, V: Doomsday Man 2.50
❑5, May 1977, A: Vision. O: Ms. Marvel (Carol Danvers) 2.50
❑6, Jun 1977 .... 2.50
❑6/35¢, Jun 1977, 35¢ regional variant 15.00
❑7, Jul 1977, V: Modok. V: M.O.D.O.K.; 1: Agent 17 .... 2.50
❑7/35¢, Jul 1977, 35¢ regional variant 15.00
❑8, Aug 1977 .... 2.50
❑8/35¢, Aug 1977, 35¢ regional variant 15.00
❑9, Sep 1977, 1: Deathbird 2.50
❑9/35¢, Sep 1977, 35¢ regional variant 15.00
❑10, Oct 1977 .... 2.50
❑10/35¢, Oct 1977, 35¢ regional variant 15.00
❑11, Nov 1977, 1: Hecate 2.00
❑12, Dec 1977, V: Hecate 2.00
❑13, Jan 1978 .... 2.00
❑14, Feb 1978, 1: Steeplejack II (Maxwell Plumm) 2.00
❑15, Mar 1978 .... 2.00
❑16, Apr 1978, 1: Mystique (cameo) 15.00

Other grades: Multiply price above by 5/6 for VF/NM • 2/3 for VERY FINE • 1/3 for FINE • 1/5 for VERY GOOD • 1/8 for GOOD

N-MINT

❑17, May 1978, 1: Centurion (Geoffrey Ballard) ... 8.00
❑18, Jun 1978, 1: Mystique (full appearance) ... 40.00
❑19, Aug 1978, A: Captain Marvel ... 2.50
❑20, Oct 1978, New costume ... 2.00
❑21, Dec 1978 ... 2.00
❑22, Feb 1979 ... 2.00
❑23, Apr 1979, Final Issue ... 2.00

Ms. Marvel
Marvel

❑1, May 2006 ... 2.99
❑2, Jun 2006, V: Brood; V: Cru ... 2.99
❑4, Aug 2006, Guest Starring Doctor.Strange ... 2.99
❑5, Sep 2006, V: Sir Warren Traveler ... 2.99
❑6, Oct 2006, Civil War Tie in; Arachne defects from pro-registration forces ... 2.99
❑7, Nov 2006, Civil War ... 2.99
❑8, Dec 2006, Civil War tie-in ... 2.99
❑10, Mar 2007 ... 2.99
❑11, Mar 2007 ... 2.99
❑12 ... 2.99
❑13 ... 2.99
❑14 ... 2.99
❑15 ... 2.99
❑16 ... 2.99
❑17 ... 2.99
❑18 ... 2.99
❑19 ... 2.99
❑20 ... 2.99
❑21 ... 2.99
❑22 ... 2.99
❑23 ... 2.99
❑24 ... 2.99
❑25 ... 2.99
❑26 ... 2.99
❑27 ... 2.99
❑28 ... 2.99
❑29 ... 2.99
❑30 ... 2.99
❑31 ... 2.99
❑32 ... 2.99
❑33 ... 2.99
❑34 ... 2.99
❑35 ... 2.99
❑36 ... 2.99
❑37 ... 2.99

Ms. Mystic
Pacific

❑1, Oct 1982; NA (c); NA (w); MN, NA (a); O: Ms. Mystic ... 4.00
❑2, Feb 1984; NA (c); NA (w); NA (a); 1&O: Ayre. 1&O: Fyre. 1&O: Watr. 1&O: Urth. 1&O: Urth 4; Tales of Zed . 3.00

Ms. Mystic
Continuity

❑1, Mar 1988; reprints Ms. Mystic (Pacific) #1 ... 2.00
❑2, Jun 1988; reprints Ms. Mystic (Pacific) #2 ... 2.00
❑3, Jan 1989 ... 2.00
❑4, May 1989 ... 2.00
❑5, Aug 1990; Comics Code ... 2.00
❑6, Nov 1990; Comics Code ... 2.00
❑7, Aug 1991 ... 2.00
❑8, Mar 1992 ... 2.00
❑9, May 1992; Double Cover ... 2.00

Ms. Mystic
Continuity

❑1, Oct 1993 ... 2.50
❑2, Nov 1993 ... 2.50
❑3, Dec 1993; Matte cover ... 2.50
❑4, Jan 1994, b&w; Orders were taken for #5 and #6 but they never appeared ... 2.50

Ms. Mystic Deathwatch 2000
Continuity

❑1, May 1993; Stereo diffusion cover ... 2.50
❑2, Jun 1993; trading card ... 2.50
❑3, Aug 1993; trading card; drops Deathwatch 2000 from indicia ... 2.50

Ms. PMS
Aaaahh!!

❑0, Mar 1992 ... 2.50
❑1, ca. 1992 ... 2.50

N-MINT

Ms. PMS
Aaaahh!!

❑1, ca. 2005 ... 3.50

Ms. Quoted Tales
Chance

❑1, Feb 1983 ... 1.50

Ms. Tree
Eclipse

❑1, Apr 1983; Eclipse publishes ... 4.00
❑2, Jun 1983; 1&O: The Scythe (Roger Loring); Frank Miller Famous Detective Pin-Up: Philip Marlowe ... 2.75
❑3, Aug 1983; Frank Miller Famous Detective Pin-Up: The Continental Op ... 2.75
❑4, Oct 1983; Frank Miller Famous Detective Pin-Up: Nancy Drew ... 2.50
❑5, Nov 1983 ... 2.50
❑6, Feb 1984; Mike Grell Famous Detective Pin-Up: Tiger Mann ... 2.00
❑7, Apr 1984; Mike Grell Famous Detective Pin-Up: Morgan the Raider . 2.00
❑8, May 1984 ... 2.00
❑9, Jul 1984 ... 2.00
❑10, Aug 1984; Aardvark-Vanaheim begins as publisher ... 2.00
❑11, Sep 1984 ... 2.00
❑12, Oct 1984 ... 2.00
❑13, Nov 1984 ... 2.00
❑14, Dec 1984 ... 2.00
❑15, Jan 1985 ... 2.00
❑16, Feb 1985 ... 2.00
❑17, Apr 1985 ... 2.00
❑18, May 1985 ... 2.00
❑19, Jun 1985; Renegade Press begins as publisher ... 2.00
❑20, Jul 1985 ... 2.00
❑21, Sep 1985 ... 2.00
❑22, Oct 1985; Abortion story ... 2.00
❑23, Nov 1985; Abortion story ... 2.00
❑24, Dec 1985 ... 2.00
❑25, Jan 1986 ... 2.00
❑26, Feb 1986 ... 2.00
❑27, Mar 1986 ... 2.00
❑28, Apr 1986 ... 2.00
❑29, May 1986 ... 2.00
❑30, Jun 1986 ... 2.00
❑31, Jul 1986 ... 2.00
❑32, Sep 1986 ... 2.00
❑33, Oct 1986 ... 2.00
❑34, Nov 1986 ... 2.00
❑35, Dec 1986 ... 2.00
❑36, Feb 1987 ... 2.00
❑37, Mar 1987 ... 2.00
❑38, Apr 1987 ... 2.00
❑39, May 1987 ... 2.00
❑40, Jun 1987 ... 2.00
❑41, Oct 1987; Johnny Dynamite backup 2.00
❑42, Nov 1987; Johnny Dynamite backup 2.00
❑43, Dec 1987; Johnny Dynamite backup 2.00
❑44, Feb 1988; Johnny Dynamite backup 2.00
❑45, Apr 1988; Johnny Dynamite back-up 2.00
❑46, May 1988; Luke Hennessy backup 2.00
❑47, Aug 1988 ... 2.00
❑48, Nov 1988; Johnny Dynamite backup 2.00
❑49, May 1989; Luke Hennessy backup 2.00
❑50, Jul 1989; WE, JK (a); Final Issue; Includes flexi-disc; Pin-Ups ... 2.75
❑3D 1, Aug 1985 ... 2.50
❑3D 2, Jul 1987; Ms. Tree's 1950's Three-Dimensional Crime ... 2.50
❑Summer 1, Aug 1986, b&w; Variant edition ... 2.00

Ms. Tree Quarterly
DC

❑1, Sum 1990, MGr (c); MGr (a); Batman, Midnight ... 4.00
❑2, Aut 1990, Butcher ... 4.00
❑3, Spr 1991, Butcher ... 4.00
❑4, Sum 1991 ... 4.00
❑5, Aut 1991, Fall 1991 ... 4.00
❑6, Win 1991 ... 4.00
❑7, Spr 1992 ... 4.00
❑8, Sum 1992, Cl (a) ... 4.00
❑9, Fal 1992, Listed as Ms. Tree Special in indicia ... 4.00
❑10, Win 1992, Listed as Ms. Tree Special; Final Issue; Winter 1992 ... 3.50

N-MINT

Ms. Victory Special
AC

❑1 ... 2.00

Mu
Devil's Due

❑1, Nov 2004 ... 2.95
❑1/Ropie, Nov 2004 ... 4.00
❑2, Dec 2004 ... 2.95
❑2/Suh, Dec 2004 ... 4.00
❑3, Jan 2005 ... 2.95
❑3/MLim, Jan 2005 ... 4.00
❑4, Aug 2005 ... 2.95
❑4/Hyung, Aug 2005 ... 4.00

Mucha Lucha
DC / Vertigo

❑1, Jun 2003 ... 2.25
❑2, Jul 2003 ... 2.25
❑3, Aug 2003 ... 2.25

Muktuk Wolfsbreath: Hard-Boiled Shaman
DC / Vertigo

❑1, Aug 1998 ... 2.50
❑2, Sep 1998 ... 2.50
❑3, Oct 1998 ... 2.50

Mullkon Empire
Tekno

❑1, Sep 1995 ... 1.95
❑2, Oct 1995 ... 1.95
❑3, Nov 1995 ... 1.95
❑4, Dec 1995 ... 1.95
❑5, Dec 1995 ... 1.95
❑6, Jan 1996 ... 1.95

Multiverse
DC / Helix

❑1, Nov 1997 ... 2.50
❑2, Dec 1997 ... 2.50
❑3, Jan 1998, Hitler appearance/story ... 2.50
❑4, Feb 1998 ... 2.50
❑5, Mar 1998 ... 2.50
❑6, Apr 1998 ... 2.50
❑7, May 1998 ... 2.50
❑8, Jun 1998 ... 2.50
❑9, Jul 1998 ... 2.50
❑10, Aug 1998 ... 2.50
❑11, Sep 1998 ... 2.50
❑12, Oct 1998, Final Issue ... 2.50

Mummy
Monster

❑1, b&w ... 2.00
❑2, b&w ... 2.00
❑3, b&w ... 2.00
❑4, b&w ... 2.00

Mummy
Dell

❑1, Reprints from Tales from the Tomb #1, Ghost Stories #1, Dracula #1 ... 25.00

Mummy Archives
Millennium

❑1, Jan 1992 ... 2.50

Mummy or Ramses the Damned
Millennium

❑1, Oct 1990 ... 3.00
❑2, Dec 1990 ... 2.50
❑3, ca. 1992 ... 2.50
❑4, ca. 1992 ... 2.50
❑5, ca. 1992 ... 2.50
❑6, ca. 1992 ... 2.50
❑7, ca. 1992 ... 2.50
❑8, ca. 1992 ... 2.50
❑9, ca. 1992 ... 2.50
❑10, ca. 1992 ... 2.50
❑11, ca. 1992 ... 2.50
❑12, ca. 1992 ... 2.50

Mummy's Curse
Aircel

❑1, Nov 1990, b&w ... 2.50
❑2, Dec 1990, b&w ... 2.50
❑3, Jan 1991, b&w ... 2.50
❑4, Feb 1991, b&w ... 2.50

Mummy: Valley of the Gods
Chaos

❑1, May 2001; Photo cover ... 2.99

New Mutants

Relaunch didn't last nearly as long
©Marvel

New Talent Showcase

DC break-in title lasted longer than others
©DC

New Teen Titans

Brought X-Men approach to DC universe
©DC

New Teen Titans

Restart was sold in comics shops only
©DC

New Terrytoons (2nd Series)

Your place to find Heckle and Jeckle
©Gold Key

N-MINT

❑2 2001 .... 2.99
❑3 2001 .... 2.99

Munden's Bar
First

❑Ann 1, Apr 1988; prestige format; Reprints from Grimjack #6, 10, 22 .... 2.95
❑Ann 2, Mar 1991; prestige format; Reprint from Grimjack #26 .... 5.95

Munsters
Gold Key

❑1, Jan 1965, Photo cover; Back cover pin-up 120.00
❑2, Apr 1965 .... 75.00
❑3, Jul 1965 .... 48.00
❑4, Oct 1965 .... 48.00
❑5, Jan 1966, back cover pin-up 48.00
❑6, Apr 1966 .... 34.00
❑7, Jun 1966 .... 34.00
❑8, Aug 1966 .... 34.00
❑9, Oct 1966 .... 34.00
❑10, Dec 1966 .... 34.00
❑11, Feb 1967 .... 30.00
❑12, Apr 1967 .... 30.00
❑13, Jun 1967 .... 30.00
❑14, Aug 1967, Cover reprints cover of #2, with green background rather than brown 30.00
❑15, Nov 1967, Cover the same image as #4, with yellow behind logo 30.00
❑16, Feb 1968 .... 30.00

Munsters
TV Comics

❑1, Aug 1997 .... 3.00
❑2/A, Oct 1997; blue background 3.00
❑2/B, Oct 1997; alternate cover (Marilyn); red background 3.00
❑3, Dec 1997 .... 3.00
❑4, Mar 1998 .... 3.00
❑4/Variant, Mar 1998; logoless 3.00
❑Special 1, Jul 1997; Comic Con 1997 Edition; Wraparound cover 3.00

Muppet Babies
Marvel / Star

❑1, May 1985 .... 1.50
❑2, Jul 1985 .... 1.00
❑3, Sep 1985 .... 1.00
❑4, Nov 1985 .... 1.00
❑5, Jan 1986 .... 1.00
❑6, Mar 1986 .... 1.00
❑7, May 1986 .... 1.00
❑8, Jul 1986 .... 1.00
❑9, Sep 1986 .... 1.00
❑10, Nov 1986 .... 1.00
❑11, Jan 1987 .... 1.00
❑12, Mar 1987 .... 1.00
❑13, May 1987 .... 1.00
❑14, Jul 1987 .... 1.00
❑15, Sep 1987 .... 1.00
❑16, Nov 1987 .... 1.00
❑17, Jan 1988 .... 1.00
❑18, Mar 1988; Marvel begins as publisher 1.00
❑19, May 1988 .... 1.00
❑20, Jul 1988 .... 1.00
❑21, Sep 1988 .... 1.00
❑22, Nov 1988 .... 1.00

N-MINT

❑23, Jan 1989 .... 1.00
❑24, Mar 1989 .... 1.00
❑25, May 1989 .... 1.00
❑26, Jul 1989 .... 1.00

Muppet Babies
Harvey

❑1, Jun 1993 .... 1.50
❑2, Sep 1993 .... 1.50
❑3, Dec 1993 .... 1.50
❑4, Mar 1994 .... 1.50
❑5, May 1994 .... 1.50
❑6, Aug 1994 .... 1.50

Muppet Babies Adventures
Harvey

❑1, Jul 1992; Cover date is 6/1/1992 in indicia 1.25

Muppet Babies Big Book
Harvey

❑1, Sep 1992 .... 1.95

Muppets Take Manhattan
Marvel / Star

❑1, Nov 1984, Reprints Marvel Super Special #32 .... 1.50
❑2, Dec 1984, Reprints Marvel Super Special #32 .... 1.50
❑3, Jan 1985, Reprints Marvel Super Special #32 .... 1.50

Murciélaga She-Bat
Heroic

❑1, Jan 1993, b&w; Reprints from Robo-Warriors #6, 7, 9 .... 1.50
❑2, Apr 1993, b&w 2.95
❑3, Jul 1993, b&w 2.95

Murder
Renegade

❑1, Aug 1986, b&w; variant cover (Mortal Kombat logo) 2.00
❑2, Oct 1986; b&w 2.00

Murder Can Be Fun
Slave Labor

❑1, Feb 1996, b&w 4.00
❑2, May 1996, b&w 3.50
❑3, Aug 1996, b&w 3.50
❑4, Nov 1996, b&w 3.50
❑5, May 1997, b&w 3.00
❑6, Jul 1997, b&w 3.00
❑7, Sep 1997, b&w 2.95
❑8, Jan 1998, b&w 2.95
❑9, Apr 1998, b&w 2.95
❑10, Aug 1998, b&w 2.95
❑11, Nov 1998, b&w 2.95
❑12, Feb 1999, b&w 2.95

Murder City
Eternity

❑1, b&w; Minute Movies 3.95

Murder Me Dead
El Capitán

❑1, Aug 2000; b&w 3.00
❑2, Oct 2000 .... 3.00
❑3, Dec 2000; b&w 3.00
❑4, Feb 2001; b&w 3.00
❑5, Apr 2001 .... 3.00

N-MINT

❑6, Jun 2001 .... 3.00
❑7, Jul 2001; b&w 3.00

Music Comics
Personality

❑2, ca. 1992; U2 .... 2.95
❑3, ca. 1992; The Red Hot Chili Peppers 2.95
❑4, ca. 1992; b&w; Elvis 2.50

Music Comics on Tour
Personality

❑1, b&w; Beatles 2.95

Mutant Aliens
NBM

❑1 .... 10.95

Mutant Book of the Dead
Starhead

❑1, b&w; Adult 2.50

Mutant Chronicles
Acclaim / Armada

❑1, May 1996; polybagged with Doom Trooper card; cardstock cover 2.95
❑2, Jun 1996; polybagged with Doom Trooper card; cardstock cover 2.95
❑3, Jul 1996; polybagged with Doom Trooper card; cardstock cover 2.95
❑4, Aug 1996; polybagged with Doom Trooper card; cardstock cover 2.95

Mutant Chronicles Sourcebook
Acclaim / Armada

❑1, Sep 1996; polybagged with card; cardstock cover 2.95

Mutant Earth
Image

❑1/A, Apr 2002; Flip book with Realm of the Claw #1 .... 2.95
❑1/B, Apr 2002; Flip book with Realm of the Claw #1 .... 2.95
❑2/A, Jun 2002, b&w; Flip book with Realm of the Claw #2 .... 2.95
❑2/B, Jun 2002, b&w; Flip book with Realm of the Claw #2 .... 2.95
❑3/A, Sep 2002, b&w; Flip book with Realm of the Claw #3 .... 2.95
❑3/B, Sep 2002, b&w; Flip book with Realm of the Claw #3 .... 2.95
❑4/A, ca. 2002, b&w; Flip book with Realm of the Claw #4 .... 2.95
❑4/B, ca. 2002, b&w; Flip book with Realm of the Claw #4 .... 2.95

Mutant Misadventures of Cloak & Dagger
Marvel

❑1, Oct 1988 A: X-Factor 2.00
❑2, Dec 1988 .... 1.50
❑3, Feb 1989 .... 1.50
❑4, Apr 1989; Inferno 1.50
❑5, Jun 1989; V: Ecstasy 1.50
❑6, Aug 1989; V: Ecstasy 1.50
❑7, Oct 1989; 1: Crimson Daffodil (Vernon Fernch) 1.50
❑8, Dec 1989 .... 1.50
❑9, Jan 1990; Avengers; Acts of Vengeance 2.50
❑10, Feb 1990; 1: X-Force (villains) 1.50
❑11, Apr 1990 .... 1.50
❑12, Jun 1990 .... 1.50

Other grades: Multiply price above by 5/6 for VF/NM • 2/3 for VERY FINE • 1/3 for FINE • 1/5 for VERY GOOD • 1/8 for GOOD

N-MINT

❑13, Aug 1990 1.50
❑14, Oct 1990; Title changes to Cloak & Dagger 1.50
❑15, Dec 1990 1.50
❑16, Feb 1991 1.50
❑17, Apr 1991; Spider-Man x-over 1.50
❑18, Jun 1991; Spider-Man, Ghost Rider 1.50
❑19, Aug 1991; Giant-size; O: Cloak and Dagger; Final Issue 2.50

Mutants and Misfits
Silverline

❑1, Jan 1987 2.00

Mutants vs. Ultras: First Encounters
Malibu / Ultraverse

❑1, Nov 1995; reprints Prime vs. Hulk, Night Man vs. Wolverine, and Exiles vs. X-Men 6.95

Mutant, Texas: Tales of Sheriff Ida Red
Oni

❑1, May 2002, b&w 2.95
❑2, ca. 2002, b&w 2.95
❑3, Oct 2002, b&w 2.95
❑4, Nov 2002, b&w; Final issue 2.95

Mutant X
Marvel

❑1, Oct 1998; gatefold summary; Mutant X, Iceman, Marvel Woman standing on cover 3.00
❑1/A, Oct 1998; alternate cover 4.00
❑2, Nov 1998; gatefold summary 2.50
❑2/A, Nov 1998; gatefold summary; alternate cover 2.50
❑3, Dec 1998; gatefold summary 2.50
❑4, Jan 1999; gatefold summary 2.50
❑5, Feb 1999; A: Havok. A: Madelyne Pryor. A: Marvel Woman. A: Brute. Gatefold summary 2.50
❑6, Mar 1999 A: Madelyne Pryor. A: Man-Spider. A: Brute 2.00
❑7, Apr 1999 A: Havok. A: Man-Spider. A: Brute. A: Green Goblin 2.00
❑8, May 1999 2.00
❑9, Jun 1999; A: Ben Grimm. A: Havok. A: Elektra. A: Mole Man. V: Goblin Queen 2.00
❑10, Jul 1999 A: X-Men. A: Magneto 1.99
❑11, Aug 1999 1.99
❑12, Sep 1999; giant-size 2.99
❑14, Nov 1999; V: Kree; V: Gladiator 1.99
❑13, Sep 1999; O: Bloodstorm; D: Kitty Pryde 1.99
❑15, Dec 1999 1.99
❑16, Jan 2000; V: anti-mutant SHIELD 1.99
❑17, Feb 2000; V: Mister Sinister 2.25
❑18, Mar 2000 2.25
❑19, Apr 2000 2.25
❑20, May 2000 2.25
❑21, Jun 2000 2.25
❑22, Aug 2000 2.25
❑23, Sep 2000 2.25
❑24, Oct 2000 2.25
❑25, Nov 2000 2.99
❑26, Dec 2000 MG (c) 2.25
❑27, Jan 2001; Bloodstorm V: Cloak and Dagger 2.25
❑29, Mar 2001; MG (c); D: Sabretooth; V: Sabretooth; Wolverine joins Six 2.25
❑28, Feb 2001; MG (c); Wolverine V: Sabretooth; Six rescue Wolverine 2.25
❑30, Apr 2001; MG (c); V: Avengers; V: Deathlok; V: Typhoid Mary; V: Hawkeye; V: Black Widow; V: Iron Man 2.25
❑31, May 2001; MG (c); Havok V: Captain America; Captain America empowered by Beyonder 2.25
❑32, Jun 2001; Final issue; D: Dracula; Bloodstorm V: Dracula; Havok V: Beyonder; Havok V: Goblin Queen 2.25
❑Ann 2001, ca. 2001; A: Beyonder 2.99

Mutant X
Marvel

❑1, Oct 2001 2.99

Mutant X: Dangerous Decisions
Marvel

❑1, Jun 2002 3.50

N-MINT

Mutant X: Origin
Marvel

❑1, May 2002 3.50

Mutant Zone
Aircel

❑1, Oct 1991, b&w 2.50
❑2, b&w 2.50
❑3, b&w 2.50

Mutation
Speakeasy Comics

❑1, Sep 2005 2.99
❑2, Oct 2005 2.99

Mutatis
Marvel / Epic

❑1, ca. 1992 2.50
❑2, ca. 1992 2.50
❑3, ca. 1992 2.50

Mutator
Checker

❑1, Sum 1998 1.95
❑2 1998 1.95

Muties
Marvel

❑1, Apr 2002 2.50
❑2, May 2002 2.50
❑3, Jun 2002 2.50
❑4, Jul 2002 2.50
❑5, Aug 2002 2.50
❑6, Sep 2002 2.50

Mutopia X
Marvel

❑1, Aug 2005 4.00
❑1/Variant, Aug 2005 2.99
❑2, Sep 2005 2.99
❑3, Oct 2005 2.99
❑4, Nov 2005 2.99
❑5, Jan 2006 2.99

My Faith in Frankie
DC / Vertigo

❑1, Mar 2004 2.95
❑2, Apr 2004 2.95
❑3, May 2004 2.95
❑4, Jun 2004; Conclusion 2.95

My Favorite Martian
Gold Key

❑1, Jan 1964, RM (a); Photo cover 55.00
❑2, Jul 1964, Photo in small box; cover has art 35.00
❑3, Feb 1965, Photo cover 30.00
❑4, May 1965 30.00
❑5, Aug 1965 24.00
❑6, Nov 1966 24.00
❑7, Apr 1966 24.00
❑8, Jul 1966 24.00
❑9, Oct 1966 24.00

My Flesh is Cool
Avatar

❑1, Feb 2004 3.50

My Greatest Adventure
DC

❑61, Nov 1961 DD (c); MM, ATh (a) 100.00
❑62, Dec 1961 75.00
❑63, Jan 1962 75.00
❑64, Feb 1962 75.00
❑65, Mar 1962 75.00
❑66, Apr 1962 75.00
❑67, May 1962 75.00
❑68, Jun 1962 75.00
❑69, Jul 1962 75.00
❑70, Aug 1962 75.00
❑71, Sep 1962 75.00
❑72, Oct 1962 75.00
❑73, Nov 1962 75.00
❑74, Dec 1962 75.00
❑75, Jan 1963 75.00
❑76, Feb 1963 75.00
❑77, Mar 1963, ATh, GC (a) 75.00
❑78, Apr 1963 75.00
❑79, May 1963 75.00
❑80, Jun 1963, 1&O: The Doom Patrol. O: Elastic-Girl. O: Negative Man. O: Robotman 425.00
❑81, Aug 1963, ATh (a); A: The Doom Patrol 150.00

N-MINT

❑82, Sep 1963, A: The Doom Patrol 150.00
❑83, Nov 1963, A: The Doom Patrol 150.00
❑84, Dec 1963, A: The Doom Patrol 150.00
❑85, Feb 1964, ATh (a); A: The Doom Patrol. Series continued in Doom Patrol (1st Series) #86 150.00

My Monkey's Name is Jennifer
Slave Labor

❑1, May 2002, b&w 2.95

My Name Is Chaos
DC

❑1, ca. 1992 5.00
❑2, ca. 1992 5.00
❑3, ca. 1992 5.00
❑4, ca. 1992 5.00

My Name Is Holocaust
DC / Milestone

❑1, May 1995 2.50
❑2, Jun 1995 2.50
❑3, Jul 1995 2.50
❑4, Aug 1995 2.50
❑5, Sep 1995 2.50

My Name is Mud
Incognito

❑1, Sum 1994 2.50

My Only Love
Charlton

❑1, Jul 1975 10.00
❑2, Sep 1975 4.00
❑3, Nov 1975 3.00
❑4, Jan 1976 3.00
❑5, Mar 1976 3.00
❑6, May 1976 3.00
❑7, Jul 1976 3.00
❑8, Sep 1976 3.00
❑9, Nov 1976 3.00

Myriad
Approbation

❑1, ca. 2005, b&w 2.99
❑2, ca. 2005, b&w 2.99
❑3, ca. 2005; b&w 2.99
❑4, ca. 2005; b&w 2.99
❑5, ca. 2005 2.99
❑6, ca. 2005 2.99

Myrmidon
Red Hills

❑1, Jul 1998, b&w 2.95

My Romantic Adventures?
Avalon

❑1 2.75

Myron Moose Funnies
Fantagraphics

❑1, Adult 1.75
❑2, Includes poster; Adult 1.75
❑3; Adult 1.75

Mysfits
Bon-a-Gram

❑1, Apr 1994 2.50

Mys-Tech Wars
Marvel

❑1, Mar 1993; Virtually all X-Men, Marvel UK characters appear 1.75
❑2, Apr 1993; Virtually all X-Men, Marvel UK characters appear 1.75
❑3, May 1993; Virtually all X-Men, Marvel UK characters appear 1.75
❑4, Jun 1993; Virtually all X-Men, Marvel UK characters appear 1.75

Mysterious Suspense
Charlton

❑1, Oct 1968, SD (c); SD (w); SD (a); Question 35.00

Mystery Date
Lightspeed

❑1, May 1999, b&w 2.95

Mystery in Space
DC

❑53, Aug 1959, GK (c); CI, GK (a); Adam Strange begins 1500.00
❑54, Sep 1959, GK (c); CI, GK (a) 425.00
❑55, Nov 1959, GK (c); CI (a) 250.00
❑56, Dec 1959, GK (c); CI, GK (a) 175.00
❑57, Feb 1960, GK (c); MA, CI (a) 175.00

Other grades: Multiply price above by 5/6 for VF/NM • 2/3 for VERY FINE • 1/3 for FINE • 1/5 for VERY GOOD • 1/8 for GOOD

New Titans

New Teen Titans without the "Teen"
©DC

New Vampire Miyu

Vampire princess and watcher of the dark
©Ironcat

New Warriors

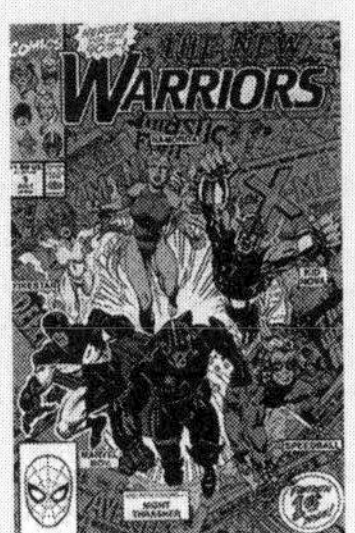

New team for younger super-heroes
©Marvel

New Wave

Scientists break the barrier between worlds
©Eclipse

Next Men

Only survivors of a bio-engineering project
©Dark Horse

N-MINT

❑58, Mar 1960, GK (c); CI, GK (a) 175.00
❑59, May 1960 GK (c); CI, GK (a) 175.00
❑60, Jun 1960, CI (c); CI, GK (a) 175.00
❑61, Aug 1960, CI (c); MA, CI, GK (a); 1: Tornado Tyrant. Later becomes Red Tornado 125.00
❑62, Sep 1960, CI (c); MA, CI (a) 125.00
❑63, Nov 1960, CI (c); MA, CI (a) 125.00
❑64, Dec 1960, CI (c); MA, CI (a) 125.00
❑65, Feb 1961, CI (c); CI (a) 125.00
❑66, Mar 1961, CI (c); CI (a); 1: Star Rovers (Homer Gint; Karel Sorensen; Rick Purvis) 125.00
❑67, May 1961, CI (c); CI, GK (a) 125.00
❑68, Jun 1961, CI (c); CI (a); 1: Dust Devil 125.00
❑69, Aug 1961, CI (c); CI (a) 125.00
❑70, Sep 1961, CI (c); MA, CI (a); 2: Dust Devil 125.00
❑71, Nov 1961, CI (c); CI (a) 125.00
❑72, Dec 1961, CI (c); CI (a); Gordon B. Love (L.O.C.) 100.00
❑73, Feb 1962, CI (c); CI (a) 100.00
❑74, Mar 1962, CI (c); CI (a); Paul Gambaccini L.O.C 100.00
❑75, May 1962, CI (c); CI (a); A: Justice League of America 225.00
❑76, Jun 1962, CI (c); CI (a); Paul Gambaccini L.O.C 100.00
❑77, Aug 1962, CI (c); CI (a) 100.00
❑78, Sep 1962, CI (c); CI (a) 100.00
❑79, Nov 1962, CI (c); CI (a) 100.00
❑80, Dec 1962, CI (c); CI (a); Buddy Saunders L.O.C 100.00
❑81, Feb 1963, CI (c); CI (a); Paul Gambaccini L.O.C.; Marv Wolfman L.O.C 75.00
❑82, Mar 1963, CI (c); CI (a); Buddy Saunders L.O.C.; Paul Gambaccini L.O.C 75.00
❑83, May 1963, CI (c); CI (a) 75.00
❑84, Jun 1963, CI (c); CI (a) 75.00
❑85, Aug 1963, CI (c); MA, CI (a); A: Adam Strange. Marv Wolfman L.O.C 75.00
❑86, Sep 1963, CI (c); CI (a) 75.00
❑87, Nov 1963, MA (c); MA, CI (a); A: Hawkman. 1: I.Q. Gang appearance; Joe Kubert L.O.C. 175.00
❑88, Dec 1963, CI (c); MA, CI (a); A: Hawkman 90.00
❑89, Feb 1964, MA (c); MA, CI (a); A: Hawkman 90.00
❑90, Mar 1964, CI (c); MA, CI (a); A: Hawkman 90.00
❑91, May 1964, CI (c); CI (a) 50.00
❑92, Jun 1964 50.00
❑93, Aug 1964 50.00
❑94, Sep 1964, 1: Adam Strange of 22nd Century; Adam Strange/Space Ranger crossover 40.00
❑95, Nov 1964 40.00
❑96, Dec 1964 40.00
❑97, Feb 1965 40.00
❑98, Mar 1965, 2: Adam Strange of the 22nd Century; Adam Strange/Space Ranger crossover 40.00
❑99, May 1965 40.00
❑100, Jun 1965, 1: Jan Vern 40.00
❑101, Aug 1965 40.00
❑102, Sep 1965 40.00

N-MINT

❑103, Nov 1965, 1&O: Ultra the Multi-Alien 40.00
❑104, Dec 1965 30.00
❑105, Feb 1966 30.00
❑106, Mar 1966 30.00
❑107, May 1966 30.00
❑108, Jun 1966 30.00
❑109, Aug 1966 30.00
❑110, Sep 1966, Original series ends 30.00
❑111, Sep 1980, Series begins again 5.00
❑112, Oct 1980 5.00
❑113, Nov 1980 5.00
❑114, Dec 1980 5.00
❑115, Jan 1981 5.00
❑116, Feb 1981 5.00
❑117, Mar 1981, Final Issue 5.00

Mystery in Space
DC

❑1, Nov 2006, O: The Weird; Rejuvenation of Captain Comet; Resurrection of The Weird; Captain Comet story; Rejuvenation of Captain Comet (Adam Blake) 3.99
❑1/Variant, Nov 2006 3.99
❑2, Dec 2006, 1: Lady Styx; D: Star Hawkins 3.99
❑3, Jan 2007 3.99
❑4, Feb 2007 3.99

Mystery Man
Slave Labor

❑1, Jul 1988, b&w 1.75
❑2, Nov 1988, b&w 1.75

Mystery Men Movie Adaptation
Dark Horse

❑1, Jul 1999 2.95
❑2, Aug 1999 2.95

Mysterymen Stories
Bob Burden

❑1, Sum 1996, b&w; prose story with illustrations 5.00

Mystery of Woolverine Woo-Bait
Fantagraphics

❑1, Dec 2004 4.95

Mystic
CrossGen

❑1, Jul 2000 3.25
❑2, Aug 2000 3.00
❑3, Sep 2000 3.00
❑4, Oct 2000 3.00
❑5, Nov 2000 3.00
❑6, Dec 2000 2.95
❑7, Jan 2001 2.95
❑8, Feb 2001 2.95
❑9, Mar 2001 2.95
❑10, Apr 2001 2.95
❑11, May 2001 2.95
❑12, Jun 2001 2.95
❑13, Jul 2001 2.95
❑14, Aug 2001 2.95
❑15, Sep 2001 2.95
❑16, Oct 2001 2.95
❑17, Nov 2001 2.95
❑18, Dec 2001 2.95
❑19, Jan 2002 2.95
❑20, Feb 2002 2.95

N-MINT

❑21, Mar 2002 2.95
❑22, Apr 2002 2.95
❑23, May 2002 2.95
❑24, Jun 2002 2.95
❑25, Jul 2002 2.95
❑26, Aug 2002 2.95
❑27, Sep 2002 2.95
❑28, Oct 2002 2.95
❑29, Nov 2002 2.95
❑30, Dec 2002 2.95
❑31, Jan 2003 2.95
❑32, Feb 2003 2.95
❑33, Mar 2003 2.95
❑34, Apr 2003 2.95
❑35, May 2003 2.95
❑36, Jun 2003 2.95
❑37, Jul 2003 2.95
❑38, Aug 2003 2.95
❑39, Sep 2003 2.95
❑40, Nov 2003 2.95
❑41, Nov 2003 2.95
❑42, Dec 2003 2.95
❑43, Jan 2004; Final Issue 2.95

Mystic Edge
Antarctic

❑1, Oct 1998; 1: Ena; 1: Evron; 1: Kyleen; 1: Risa; 1: Symattra 2.95

Mystic Trigger
Maelstrom

❑1; Tales of the Galactic Forces preview 3.25

Mystique
Marvel

❑1, Jun 2003 2.99
❑1/DF, Jun 2003 15.00
❑2, Jul 2003 2.99
❑3, Aug 2003, 1: Shortpack 2.99
❑4, Sep 2003 2.99
❑5, Oct 2003 2.99
❑6, Nov 2003 2.99
❑7, Dec 2003 2.99
❑8, Jan 2004 2.99
❑9, Feb 2004 2.99
❑10, Mar 2004 2.99
❑11, Apr 2004 2.99
❑12, May 2004 2.99
❑13, Jun 2004 2.99
❑14, Jul 2004 2.99
❑15, Jul 2004 2.99
❑16, Aug 2004 2.99
❑17, Sep 2004 2.99
❑18, Oct 2004 2.99
❑19, Nov 2004, V: Hydra 2.99
❑20, Dec 2004 2.99
❑21, Jan 2005 2.99
❑22, Feb 2005 2.99
❑23, Mar 2005 2.99
❑24, Apr 2005; Final Issue 2.99

Mystique & Sabretooth
Marvel

❑1, Dec 1996 1.95
❑2, Jan 1997 1.95
❑3, Feb 1997 1.95
❑4, Mar 1997 1.95

N-MINT

Myst: The Book of the Black Ships
Dark Horse

- ❑0, ca. 1997; American Entertainment Exclusive Edition; No cover price; based on video game ... 1.50
- ❑1, Aug 1997; based on video game ... 2.95
- ❑2, Sep 1997 ... 2.95
- ❑3, Oct 1997 ... 2.95
- ❑4, Nov 1997 ... 2.95

My Terrible Romance
NEC

- ❑1 ... 2.75
- ❑2, Jul 1994; Reprints from Hi-School Romance #9, My Desire #4, Voodoo #16, Romantic Love #8, All True Romance #17 ... 2.75

Myth
Fygmok

- ❑1, Dec 1996, b&w; wraparound cover ... 2.95
- ❑2, Feb 1997, b&w ... 2.95

Mythadventures
Warp

- ❑1, Mar 1984; Warp publishes ... 2.00
- ❑2, Jun 1984 ... 1.50
- ❑3, Sep 1984 ... 1.50
- ❑4, Dec 1984 ... 1.50
- ❑5, Mar 1985 ... 1.50
- ❑6, Jun 1985 ... 1.50
- ❑7, Sep 1985 ... 1.50
- ❑8, Dec 1985; PF (c); PF (w); PF (a); B&W ... 1.50
- ❑9, Mar 1986; b&w ... 1.50
- ❑10 1986; Apple begins as publisher ... 1.50
- ❑11 1986; Apple Publishes; b&w ... 1.50
- ❑12 1986; Final Issue; b&w ... 1.50

Myth Conceptions
Apple

- ❑1, Nov 1987; b&w ... 2.00
- ❑2, Jan 1988; b&w ... 1.75
- ❑3, Mar 1988; b&w ... 1.75
- ❑4, May 1988; b&w ... 1.75
- ❑5, Jul 1988; b&w ... 1.75
- ❑6, Sep 1988; b&w ... 1.75
- ❑7, Nov 1988; b&w ... 1.75
- ❑8, Jan 1989; b&w ... 1.75

Mythical Detective Loki
ADV Manga

- ❑1, ca. 2004 ... 9.99
- ❑2, ca. 2005 ... 9.99

Mythic Heroes
Chapterhouse

- ❑1, Sep 1996, b&w ... 2.50

Myth Maker
Cross Plains

- ❑1, Jun 1999, NN ... 6.95

Mythography
Bardic

- ❑1, Sep 1996; b&w ... 4.00
- ❑2, Feb 1997; b&w ... 4.00
- ❑3, Apr 1997; b&w ... 4.00
- ❑4, Jun 1997; b&w ... 4.00
- ❑5, Sep 1997; b&w ... 4.00
- ❑6, Nov 1997; Barr Girls story ... 4.00
- ❑7, Feb 1998; b&w ... 4.00
- ❑8, May 1998; b&w ... 4.00

Mythos
Wonder Comix

- ❑1, Jan 1987 ... 2.00
- ❑2, Apr 1987 ... 2.00
- ❑3, Aug 1987, b&w ... 2.00

Mythos: Hulk
Marvel

- ❑1, Nov 2006 ... 3.99

Mythos: The Final Tour
DC / Vertigo

- ❑1, Dec 1996; prestige format ... 5.95
- ❑2, Jan 1997; prestige format ... 5.95
- ❑3, Feb 1997; prestige format ... 5.95

Mythos: X-Men
Marvel

- ❑1, Mar 2006 ... 3.99

N-MINT

Mythstalkers
Image

- ❑1, Apr 2003 ... 2.95
- ❑2, May 2003 ... 2.95
- ❑3, Jun 2003 ... 2.95
- ❑4, Sep 2003 ... 2.95
- ❑5, Oct 2003; b&w ... 2.95
- ❑6, Dec 2003; b&w ... 2.95
- ❑7, Feb 2004 ... 2.95
- ❑8, May 2004 ... 2.95

My Uncle Jeff
Origin Comics

- ❑1, Feb 2003, b&w ... 3.95

My War With Brian
NBM

- ❑1 ... 16.95

Nadesico
CPM Manga

- ❑1, Jun 1999 ... 2.95
- ❑2, Jul 1999 ... 2.95
- ❑3, Aug 1999 ... 2.95
- ❑4, Sep 1999; Diptych cover ... 2.95
- ❑5, Oct 1999; Diptych cover ... 2.95
- ❑6, Nov 1999 ... 2.95
- ❑7, Dec 1999; Wraparound cover ... 2.95
- ❑8, Jan 2000; Wraparound cover ... 2.95
- ❑9, Feb 2000 ... 2.95
- ❑10, Mar 2000 ... 2.95
- ❑11, Apr 2000 ... 2.95
- ❑12, May 2000 ... 2.95
- ❑13, Jun 2000 ... 2.95
- ❑14, Jul 2000 ... 2.95
- ❑15, Aug 2000 ... 2.95
- ❑16, Sep 2000; Wraparound cover; Harlock ... 2.95
- ❑17, Oct 2000 ... 2.95
- ❑18, Nov 2000 ... 2.95
- ❑19, Dec 2000; Diptych cover ... 2.95
- ❑20, Jan 2001; Diptych cover ... 2.95
- ❑21, Feb 2001 ... 2.95
- ❑22, Mar 2001; Diptych cover ... 2.95
- ❑23, Apr 2001; Diptych cover ... 2.95
- ❑24, May 2001; Diptych cover ... 2.95
- ❑25, Jun 2001; Diptych cover ... 2.95
- ❑26, Jul 2001 ... 2.95

Nagasaki: The Forgotten Bomb
Antarctic

- ❑1, ca. 2004; Black Rain of Ruin #2 ... 3.95
- ❑2, ca. 2005 ... 3.99

Nail
Dark Horse

- ❑1, Aug 2004 ... 2.99
- ❑2, Sep 2004 ... 2.99
- ❑3, Oct 2004 ... 2.99
- ❑4, Nov 2004 ... 3.00

Naive Inter-Dimensional Commando Koalas
Eclipse

- ❑1, Oct 1986, b&w ... 1.50

Naked Angels
Fantagraphics / Eros

- ❑1 1996; Adult ... 2.95
- ❑2, May 1996; Adult ... 2.95

Naked Eye
Antarctic

- ❑1, Dec 1994, b&w; Adult ... 2.75
- ❑2, Feb 1995, b&w; Adult ... 2.75
- ❑3, Apr 1995, b&w; Adult ... 2.75

'Nam
Marvel

- ❑1, Dec 1986, MG (c); MG (a) ... 2.00
- ❑1/2nd, Dec 1986, MG (c); MG (a); 2nd printing ... 1.00
- ❑2, Jan 1987, MG (c); MG (a) ... 1.00
- ❑3, Feb 1987, MG (c); MG (a) ... 1.00
- ❑4, Mar 1987 ... 1.00
- ❑5, Apr 1987 ... 1.00
- ❑6, May 1987, MG (c); MG (a) ... 1.00
- ❑7, Jun 1987, MG (c); MG (a) ... 1.00
- ❑8, Jul 1987, MG (c); MG (a) ... 1.00
- ❑9, Aug 1987, D: Mike ... 1.00
- ❑10, Sep 1987 ... 1.00
- ❑11, Oct 1987 ... 1.00
- ❑12, Nov 1987 ... 1.00

N-MINT

- ❑13, Dec 1987 ... 1.00
- ❑14, Jan 1988 ... 1.00
- ❑15, Feb 1988 ... 1.00
- ❑16, Mar 1988 ... 1.00
- ❑17, Apr 1988 ... 1.00
- ❑18, May 1988 ... 1.25
- ❑19, Jun 1988 ... 1.25
- ❑20, Jul 1988 ... 1.25
- ❑21, Aug 1988 ... 1.25
- ❑22, Sep 1988 ... 1.25
- ❑23, Oct 1988 ... 1.25
- ❑24, Nov 1988 ... 1.25
- ❑25, Dec 1988 ... 1.25
- ❑26, Jan 1989 ... 1.50
- ❑27, Feb 1989 ... 1.50
- ❑28, Mar 1989 ... 1.50
- ❑29, Apr 1989 ... 1.50
- ❑30, May 1989 ... 1.50
- ❑31, Jun 1989 ... 1.50
- ❑32, Jul 1989 ... 1.50
- ❑33, Aug 1989 ... 1.50
- ❑34, Sep 1989 ... 1.50
- ❑35, Oct 1989, A: Bob Hope. Christmas issue ... 1.50
- ❑36, Nov 1989 ... 1.50
- ❑37, Nov 1989 ... 1.50
- ❑38, Dec 1989 ... 1.50
- ❑39, Dec 1989, A: Iron Man. A: Captain America. A: Thor ... 1.50
- ❑40, Jan 1990 ... 1.50
- ❑41, Feb 1990, A: Iron Man. A: Captain America. A: Thor ... 1.50
- ❑42, Mar 1990 ... 1.50
- ❑43, Apr 1990 ... 1.50
- ❑44, May 1990 ... 1.50
- ❑45, Jun 1990 ... 1.50
- ❑46, Jul 1990 ... 1.50
- ❑47, Aug 1990 ... 1.50
- ❑48, Sep 1990 ... 1.50
- ❑49, Oct 1990 ... 1.50
- ❑50, Nov 1990 ... 1.50
- ❑51, Dec 1990 ... 1.50
- ❑52, Jan 1991, A: Frank Castle (Punisher). 1.50
- ❑52/2nd, Jan 1991, A: Frank Castle (Punisher). 2nd printing ... 1.50
- ❑53, Feb 1991, A: Frank Castle (Punisher). 1.50
- ❑53/2nd, Feb 1991, A: Frank Castle (Punisher). 2nd printing ... 1.50
- ❑54, Mar 1991, TD (a) ... 1.50
- ❑55, Apr 1991, TD (a) ... 1.50
- ❑56, May 1991 ... 1.50
- ❑57, Jun 1991 ... 1.50
- ❑58, Jul 1991 ... 1.50
- ❑59, Aug 1991 ... 1.50
- ❑60, Sep 1991 ... 1.50
- ❑61, Oct 1991 ... 1.50
- ❑62, Nov 1991 ... 1.50
- ❑63, Dec 1991 ... 1.50
- ❑64, Jan 1992 ... 1.50
- ❑65, Feb 1992, RH (c); RH (a) ... 1.75
- ❑66, Mar 1992 ... 1.75
- ❑67, Apr 1992, A: Punisher ... 1.75
- ❑68, May 1992, A: Punisher ... 1.75
- ❑69, Jun 1992, A: Punisher ... 1.75
- ❑70, Jul 1992 ... 1.75
- ❑71, Aug 1992 ... 1.75
- ❑72, Sep 1992 ... 1.75
- ❑73, Oct 1992 ... 1.75
- ❑74, Nov 1992 ... 1.75
- ❑75, Dec 1992, HT (c); HT (a); Tells of Mai Lai Massacre from different points of view ... 2.25
- ❑76, Jan 1993 ... 1.75
- ❑77, Feb 1993 ... 1.75
- ❑78, Mar 1993 ... 1.75
- ❑79, Apr 1993 ... 1.75
- ❑80, May 1993, MG (c) ... 1.75
- ❑81, Jun 1993, MG (c) ... 1.75
- ❑82, Jul 1993 ... 1.75
- ❑83, Aug 1993 ... 1.75
- ❑84, Sep 1993, Told from Vietnamese point of view ... 1.75

Nameless
Image

- ❑1, May 1997; b&w ... 2.95
- ❑2, Jun 1997; b&w ... 2.95
- ❑3, Jul 1997, b&w ... 2.95

Nexus

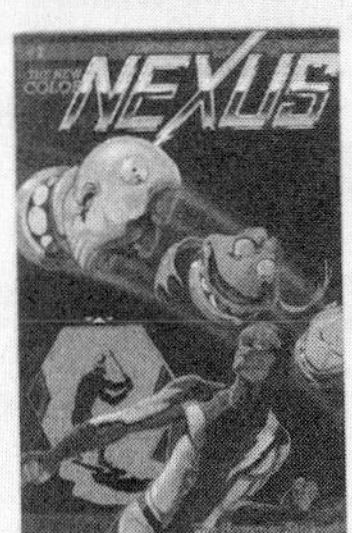

Distant worlds with Mike Baron, Steve Rude

©Capital

NFL Superpro

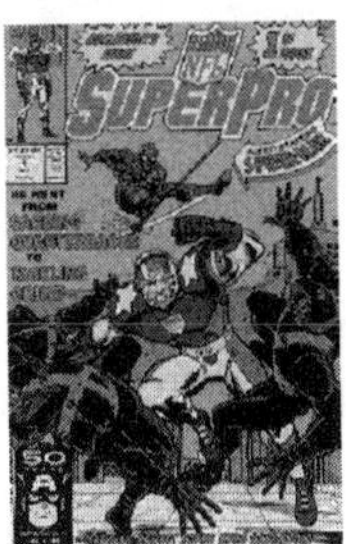

Failed attempt to get comics fans into sports

©Marvel

Nick Fury, Agent of SHIELD

Jim Steranko's celebrated and stylish series

©Marvel

Nick Fury vs. S.H.I.E.L.D.

Organization is invaded from within

©Marvel

Nightcrawler

Fanciful romp through alternate reality

©Marvel

N-MINT

❑4, Aug 1997, b&w 2.95
❑5, Sep 1997, b&w 2.95

Name of the Game
DC

❑1/HC 29.95

Names of Magic
DC / Vertigo

❑1, Feb 2001 .... 2.50
❑2, Mar 2001 .... 2.50
❑3, Apr 2001 .... 2.50
❑4, May 2001 .... 2.50
❑5, Jun 2001 .... 2.50

'Nam Magazine
Marvel

❑1, Aug 1988, b&w; MG (c); MG (a); Reprints 3.00
❑2, Sep 1988, b&w; Reprints 2.50
❑3, Oct 1988, b&w; Reprints 2.50
❑4, Nov 1988, b&w; Reprints 2.50
❑5, Dec 1988, b&w; Reprints 2.50
❑6, Dec 1988, b&w; Reprints 2.50
❑7, Jan 1989, b&w; Reprints 2.50
❑8, Feb 1989, b&w; Reprints 2.50
❑9, Mar 1989, b&w; Reprints 2.50
❑10, Apr 1989, b&w; Reprints 2.50

Namor
Marvel

❑1, Jun 2003 .... 3.00
❑2, Jun 2003 .... 2.25
❑3, Jul 2003 .... 2.25
❑4, Aug 2003 .... 2.25
❑5, Oct 2003 .... 2.99
❑6, Nov 2003 .... 2.99
❑7, Dec 2003 .... 2.99
❑8, Dec 2003 .... 2.99
❑9, Jan 2004 .... 2.99
❑10, Feb 2004 .... 2.99
❑11, Mar 2004 .... 2.99
❑12, Apr 2004 .... 2.99

Namor Sub-Mariner
Marvel

❑1, Apr 1990; JBy (c); JBy (w); JBy (a); O: Sub-Mariner 2.00
❑2, May 1990; JBy (c); JBy (w); JBy (a); 1: Headhunter; V: Griffin 1.50
❑3, Jun 1990 JBy (c); JBy (w); JBy (a) 1.50
❑4, Jul 1990 JBy (c); JBy (w); JBy (a) 1.50
❑5, Aug 1990 JBy (c); JBy (w); JBy (a) 1.50
❑6, Sep 1990 JBy (c); JBy (w); JBy (a) 1.25
❑7, Oct 1990 JBy (c); JBy (w); JBy (a) 1.25
❑8, Nov 1990; JBy (c); JBy (w); JBy (a); 1: Headhunter 1.25
❑9, Dec 1990 JBy (c); JBy (w); JBy (a) 1.25
❑10, Jan 1991 JBy (c); JBy (w); JBy (a) 1.25
❑11, Feb 1991 JBy (c); JBy (w); JBy (a) 1.25
❑12, Mar 1991; Giant-size; JBy (c); JBy (w); JBy (a); A: Human Torch. A: Captain America. A: Invaders. Return of The Invaders 1.25
❑13, Apr 1991 JBy (c); JBy (w); JBy (a) 1.00
❑14, May 1991 JBy (c); JBy (w); JBy (a) 1.00
❑15, Jun 1991 JBy (c); JBy (w); JBy (a) 1.00
❑16, Jul 1991; JBy (c); JBy (w); JBy (a); Punisher cameo 1.00
❑17, Aug 1991 JBy (c); JBy (w); JBy (a) 1.00
❑18, Sep 1991; JBy (c); JBy (w); JBy (a); V: Super-Skrull; Punisher cameo 1.00
❑19, Oct 1991 JBy (c); JBy (w); JBy (a) 1.00
❑20, Nov 1991; JBy (c); JBy (w); JBy (a); Iron Fist; O: Namorita (revealed as clone) 1.00
❑21, Dec 1991; JBy (c); JBy (w); JBy (a); The Thunderer; V: Thunderer; Namor searches for Iron Fist 1.00
❑22, Jan 1992; JBy (c); JBy (w); JBy (a); V: Thunderer; V: H'ythri; Namor searches for Iron Fist; Iron Fist located 1.00
❑23, Feb 1992; JBy (c); JBy (w); JBy (a); A: Wolverine. A: Iron Fist. Iron Fist returns; V: H'ythri; Namor searches for Iron Fist 1.25
❑24, Mar 1992; JBy (c); JBy (w); JBy (a); A: Wolverine. Namor fights Wolverine 1.25
❑25, Apr 1992 JBy (w); JBy (a); A: Wolverine 1.25
❑26, May 1992; JBy (w); 1st Jae Lee art 1.25
❑27, Jun 1992 JBy (w) 1.25
❑28, Jul 1992 JBy (w); A: Iron Fist 1.25
❑29, Aug 1992 JBy (w) 1.25
❑30, Sep 1992 JBy (w) 1.25
❑31, Oct 1992 JBy (w) 1.25
❑32, Nov 1992 JBy (w) 1.25
❑33, Dec 1992 .... 1.25
❑34, Jan 1993 .... 1.25
❑35, Feb 1993 .... 1.25
❑36, Mar 1993 .... 1.25
❑37, Apr 1993; foil cover 2.00
❑38, May 1993 .... 1.25
❑39, Jun 1993 .... 1.25
❑40, Jul 1993 .... 1.25
❑41, Aug 1993 .... 1.25
❑42, Sep 1993 A: Stingray 1.25
❑43, Oct 1993 A: Stingray 1.25
❑44, Nov 1993 .... 1.25
❑45, Dec 1993 .... 1.25
❑46, Jan 1994 .... 1.25
❑47, Feb 1994 .... 1.25
❑48, Mar 1994 .... 1.25
❑49, Apr 1994 .... 1.25
❑50, May 1994; Giant-size 1.75
❑50/Variant, May 1994; Giant-size; foil cover 2.95
❑51, Jun 1994 .... 1.75
❑52, Jul 1994 .... 1.50
❑53, Aug 1994 .... 1.50
❑54, Sep 1994; 1: Llyron 1.50
❑55, Oct 1994 .... 1.50
❑56, Nov 1994 .... 1.50
❑57, Dec 1994 .... 1.50
❑58, Jan 1995; V: Avengers 1.50
❑59, Feb 1995 .... 1.50
❑60, Mar 1995 .... 1.50
❑61, Apr 1995 .... 1.50
❑62, May 1995; Final Issue 1.50
❑Ann 1, ca. 1991; O: Namor 3.00
❑Ann 2, ca. 1992; A: The Defenders. Defenders; Namor's Top Ten Villains 2.25
❑Ann 3, ca. 1993; 1&O: The Assassin; 1993 Ann; Includes trading card 2.95
❑Ann 4, ca. 1994 .... 2.95

Nancy and Sluggo
Gold Key

❑188, Oct 1962, Back cover pin-up; Peanuts story 10.00
❑189, Jan 1963 .... 10.00
❑190, Apr 1963 .... 10.00
❑191, Jul 1963 .... 10.00
❑192, Oct 1963, Summer Camp 10.00

Nanny and the Professor
Dell

❑1, Aug 1970, based on TV show 16.00
❑2, Oct 1970 .... 10.00

Nanosoup
Millennium

❑1, ca. 1996, b&w; wraparound cover 2.95

Narcolepsy Dreams
Slave Labor

❑1, Feb 1995 .... 2.95
❑2, Aug 1995 .... 2.95
❑4; Mini-comic 1.00

Nard n' Pat
Cartoonists Co-Op

❑1, ca. 1974, b&w 3.00

Nascar Adventures
Vortex

❑1 1992; DH (a); Fred Lorenzen; regular cover 2.95
❑2 1992; Richard Petty 2.50
❑5 1992; Ernie Irvan 2.50
❑7 1992 .... 2.50

NASCUB Adventures
Vortex

❑1, Jun 1991 .... 2.00

Nash
Image

❑1, Jul 1999; regular cover 2.95
❑1/A, Jul 1999; Photo cover 2.95
❑1/B, Jul 1999; no cover price 2.95
❑2, Jul 1999; regular cover 2.95
❑2/A, Jul 1999; Photo cover 2.95
❑Ashcan 1, Jul 1999; Preview Book; regular cover 2.50
❑Ashcan 1/Varian, Jul 1999; Photo cover 2.50

Nasti: Monster Hunter
Schism

❑1, b&w; 1: Nasti 2.50
❑1/Autographed, limited edition (250 printed) with certificate of authenticity; 1: Nasti 3.00
❑2, b&w 2.50
❑3, b&w; ca. 1998 .... 2.50
❑Ashcan 1/Ltd., b&w; No cover price; preview of upcoming comic book on newsprint 1.00

Nathaniel Dusk
DC

❑1, Feb 1984, GC (c); GC (a); 1: Nathaniel Dusk 1.50
❑2, Mar 1984, GC (c); GC (a) 1.50
❑3, Apr 1984, GC (c); GC (a) 1.50
❑4, May 1984, GC (c); GC (a) 1.50

N-MINT

Nathaniel Dusk II
DC

❑1, Oct 1985 .... 2.00
❑2, Nov 1985 .... 2.00
❑3, Dec 1985 .... 2.00
❑4, Jan 1986 .... 2.00

Nathan Never
Dark Horse

❑1, Mar 1999; b&w 4.95
❑2, Apr 1999; b&w 4.95
❑3, May 1999; b&w 4.95
❑4, Jun 1999; b&w 4.95
❑5, Jul 1999; b&w 4.95
❑6, Aug 1999; b&w 4.95

National Comics
DC

❑1, May 1999; MWa (w); A: Flash. A: Justice Society. A: Mr. Terrific. Justice Society Returns 2.00

National Inquirer
Fantagraphics

❑1, Apr 1989 ....

National Velvet
Dell

❑1, Jul 1962, Code on cover ends in -207 .... 30.00
❑2, Oct 1962, Code on cover ends in -210 .... 30.00

National Velvet
Dell

❑1, Dec 1962; Based on the TV show 12.00
❑2, Mar 1963 .... 9.00

Nation of Snitches
DC / Piranha

❑1 .... 4.95

Nat Turner
Kyle Baker Publishing

❑1, Jul 2005 .... 3.00

Natural Inquirer
Fantagraphics

❑1, Apr 1989, b&w 2.00

Natural Selection
Atom

❑1, Jan 1998, b&w 2.95
❑2, Feb 1998, b&w 2.95

Nature of the Beast
Caliber

❑1, b&w 2.95
❑2, b&w 2.95

Naughty Bits
Fantagraphics

❑1, Mar 1991, b&w 7.00
❑1/2nd, Mar 1991, b&w; 2nd printing 2.50
❑2, Jun 1991, b&w 5.00
❑3, Sep 1991, b&w 4.00
❑4, Dec 1991, b&w 3.75
❑5, Apr 1992, b&w 3.75
❑6, Aug 1992, b&w 3.00
❑7, Nov 1992, b&w 3.00
❑8, Feb 1993, b&w 3.00
❑9, Jun 1993, b&w 3.00
❑10, Oct 1993, b&w 3.00
❑11, Jan 1994, b&w 2.50
❑12, Apr 1994, b&w 2.50
❑13, Jul 1994, b&w 2.95
❑14, Oct 1994, b&w 2.95
❑15, Feb 1995, b&w 2.95
❑16, May 1995, b&w 2.95
❑17, Aug 1995, b&w 2.95
❑18, Jan 1996, b&w 2.95
❑19, Apr 1996, b&w 2.95
❑20, Aug 1996, b&w 2.95
❑21, Nov 1996, b&w 2.95
❑22, Mar 1997, b&w 2.95
❑23, Jun 1997, b&w 2.95
❑24, Oct 1997, b&w 2.95
❑25, Mar 1998, b&w 2.95
❑26, Jun 1998 .... 2.95
❑27, Oct 1998 .... 2.95
❑28, ca. 1999 .... 2.95
❑29, Jul 1999 .... 2.95
❑30, Nov 1999 .... 2.95
❑31, Apr 2000 .... 2.95
❑32, Jul 2000 .... 2.95
❑33, Dec 2000 .... 2.95
❑34, May 2001 .... 2.95
❑35, Oct 2001 .... 2.95
❑36, Jul 2002 .... 2.95
❑37, Dec 2002 .... 2.95
❑38, Jul 2003 .... 2.95

Nausicaä of the Valley of Wind Part 1
Viz

❑1 .... 3.25
❑2 .... 3.25
❑3 .... 3.25
❑4 .... 3.25
❑5 .... 3.25
❑6 .... 3.25
❑7 .... 3.25

Nausicaä of the Valley of Wind Part 2
Viz

❑1 .... 2.95
❑2 .... 2.95
❑3 .... 2.95
❑4 .... 3.25

Nausicaä of the Valley of Wind Part 3
Viz

❑1 .... 3.95
❑2 .... 3.95
❑3 .... 3.95

Nausicaä of the Valley of Wind Part 4
Viz

❑1 .... 2.75
❑2 .... 2.75
❑3 .... 2.75
❑4 .... 2.75
❑5 .... 2.75
❑6 .... 2.75

Nausicaä of the Valley of Wind Part 5
Viz

❑1 .... 2.75
❑2 .... 2.75
❑3 .... 2.75
❑4 .... 2.75
❑5 .... 2.75
❑6 .... 2.75
❑7 .... 2.95
❑8 .... 2.95

Nautilus
Shanda Fantasy Arts

❑1, May 1999, b&w 2.95

Navy War Heroes
Charlton

❑1, Jan 1964 .... 12.00
❑2, Mar 1964 .... 8.00
❑3 1964 .... 6.00
❑4, Sep 1964 .... 6.00
❑5, Nov 1964 .... 6.00
❑6, Jan 1965 .... 6.00
❑7, Apr 1965 .... 6.00

Naza
Dell

❑1, Jan 1964 .... 15.00
❑2, Jun 1964 .... 8.00
❑3, Sep 1964 .... 8.00
❑4, Dec 1964 .... 8.00
❑5, Mar 1965 .... 8.00
❑6, Jun 1965 .... 6.00
❑7, Sep 1965 .... 6.00
❑8, Dec 1965 .... 6.00
❑9, Mar 1966 .... 6.00

Nazrat
Imperial

❑1; ca. 1986; b&w 2.00
❑2; b&w 2.00
❑3; b&w 2.00
❑4; b&w 2.00
❑5; b&w 2.00
❑6, Jun 1987, b&w 2.00

Nazz
DC

❑1, Oct 1990 .... 4.95
❑2, Nov 1990 .... 4.95
❑3, Dec 1990 .... 4.95
❑4, Jan 1991 .... 4.95

NBC Saturday Morning Comics
Harvey

❑1, Sep 1991; Toys "R" Us giveaway A: Geoffrey Giraffe 1.50

Near Myths
Rip Off

❑1, Jul 1990, b&w; Adult 2.50

Near to Now
Fandom House

❑1, b&w 2.00
❑2, b&w 2.00

Neat Stuff
Fantagraphics

❑1, Jul 1985; b&w 5.00
❑1/2nd; 2nd printing 2.50
❑2, Oct 1985 .... 4.00
❑2/2nd; 2nd printing 2.50
❑3, Mar 1986 .... 3.50
❑3/2nd; 2nd printing 2.50
❑4, Jul 1986 .... 3.00
❑4/2nd; 2nd printing 2.50
❑5, Dec 1986 .... 2.50
❑6, Apr 1987; all Bradley issue 2.50
❑7, Aug 1987 .... 2.50
❑8, Dec 1987 .... 2.50
❑9, Apr 1988 .... 2.50
❑10, Jul 1988 .... 2.50
❑11, Nov 1988 .... 2.50
❑12, Feb 1989; b&w 2.50
❑13, May 1989; b&w 2.50
❑14, Sep 1989; b&w 2.50
❑15, Dec 1989; b&w 2.50

Neck and Neck
Tokyopop

❑1, Dec 2004, b&w 9.99
❑2, Mar 2005; b&w 9.99
❑3, Jun 2005; b&w 9.99
❑4, Dec 2005; b&w 9.99

Necromancer
Anarchy

❑1, b&w; Adult 2.50
❑1/Deluxe; Deluxe edition; Adult 3.50
❑2, b&w; Adult 2.50
❑2/Deluxe; Deluxe edition; Adult 3.50
❑3, b&w; Adult 2.50
❑3/Deluxe; Deluxe edition; Adult 3.50
❑4, b&w; Adult 2.50
❑4/Deluxe; Deluxe edition; Adult 3.50

Necromancer
Anarchy

❑1, b&w 2.50
❑2, b&w 2.50
❑3, b&w 2.50
❑4, b&w 2.50

Necromancer
Image

❑1/Manapul, Sep 2005 .... 2.99
❑1/Horn, Sep 2005 .... 4.00
❑1/Bachalo, Sep 2005 .... 3.00
❑2 2005 .... 2.99
❑3, Jan 2006 .... 2.99
❑4, Feb 2006 .... 2.99
❑5, Jun 2006 .... 2.99
❑6, Jul 2006 .... 2.99

Necropolis
Fleetway-Quality

❑1 .... 2.95
❑2 .... 2.95
❑3 .... 2.95
❑4 .... 2.95
❑5 .... 2.95
❑6 .... 2.95
❑7 .... 2.95
❑8 .... 2.95
❑9 .... 2.95

Necroscope
Malibu

❑1, Oct 1992 .... 3.00
❑1/2nd, Dec 1992; Hologram cover 2.95
❑2, Dec 1992; bagged with tattoo 2.95
❑3, Feb 1993 .... 2.95
❑4 .... 2.95
❑5 .... 2.95

Night Force

Wolfman and Colan's horror crew
©DC

Night Man

Short-lived comic spawns long-lived TV show
©Malibu

Night Music

Fantasy from P. Craig Russell
©Eclipse

Nightstalkers

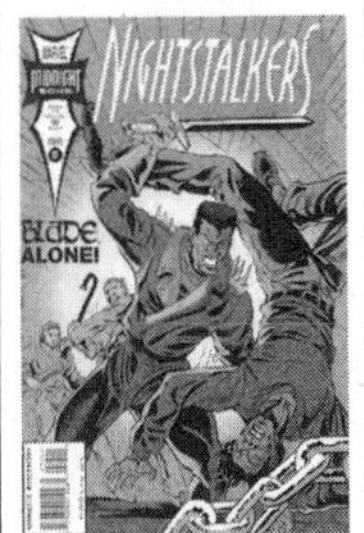

Frank Drake, Hannibal King, and Blade
©Marvel

Nightwatch

Scientist confronted by his future self
©Marvel

N-MINT

Necroscope Book II: Wamphyri
Malibu

❑1 ... 2.95
❑2, Nov 1994 ... 2.95
❑3, Jan 1994 ... 2.95
❑4 ... 2.95
❑5 ... 2.95

Necrowar
Dreamwave

❑1, Jul 2003 ... 2.95
❑2, Aug 2003 ... 2.95
❑3, Sep 2003 ... 2.95

Nefarismo
Fantagraphics / Eros

❑1 ... 2.95
❑2, b&w ... 2.95
❑3 ... 2.95
❑4 ... 2.95
❑5, May 1995 ... 2.95
❑6, Aug 1995, b&w ... 2.95
❑7, Sep 1995 ... 2.95
❑8, Oct 1995 ... 2.95

Negation
CrossGen

❑1, Jan 2002 ... 2.95
❑2, Feb 2002 ... 2.95
❑3, Mar 2002 ... 2.95
❑4, Apr 2002 ... 2.95
❑5, May 2002 ... 2.95
❑6, Jun 2002 ... 2.95
❑7, Jul 2002 ... 2.95
❑8, Aug 2002 ... 2.95
❑9, Sep 2002 ... 2.95
❑10, Oct 2002 ... 2.95
❑11, Nov 2002 ... 2.95
❑12, Dec 2002 ... 2.95
❑13, Jan 2003 ... 2.95
❑14, Feb 2003 ... 2.95
❑15, Mar 2003 ... 2.95
❑16, Apr 2003 ... 2.95
❑17, May 2003 ... 2.95
❑18, Jun 2003 ... 2.95
❑19, Jul 2003 ... 2.95
❑20, Aug 2003 ... 2.95
❑21, Oct 2003 ... 2.95
❑22, Nov 2003 ... 2.95
❑23, Nov 2003 ... 2.95
❑24, Dec 2003 ... 2.95
❑25, Jan 2004 ... 2.95
❑26, Feb 2004 ... 2.95
❑27, Mar 2004 ... 2.95

Negation War
CrossGen

❑1, Apr 2004 ... 2.95
❑1/2nd, May 2004 ... 2.95
❑2, May 2004 ... 2.95

Negation Prequel
CrossGen

❑1, Dec 2001 ... 2.95

N-MINT

Negative Burn
Caliber

❑1, ca. 1993, b&w; BB (w); BB (a); A: Flaming Carrot; Flip book ... 5.99
❑2, ca. 1993, b&w ... 5.99
❑3, Apr 1993, b&w A: Bone ... 4.00
❑4, ca. 1993, b&w ... 4.00
❑5, ca. 1993, b&w ... 4.00
❑6, ca. 1994, b&w ... 5.99
❑7, ca. 1994, b&w ... 4.00
❑8, ca. 1994, b&w ... 4.00
❑9, ca. 1994, b&w; BB, AMo (w); BB (a) ... 4.00
❑10, ca. 1994, b&w; BB, AMo (w); BB (a) ... 4.00
❑11, ca. 1994, b&w; BB, AMo, NG (w); BB (a) ... 4.00
❑12, ca. 1994, b&w; Jazz Age Chronicles ... 4.00
❑13, ca. 1994, b&w; BMB, BB, AMo, NG (w); BMB, BB, NG (a); A: Strangers in Paradise ... 6.50
❑14, ca. 1994, b&w ... 3.95
❑15, ca. 1994, b&w; BB (w); BB (a) ... 3.95
❑16, ca. 1994, b&w ... 3.95
❑17, ca. 1994, b&w; ca. 1995 ... 3.95
❑18, ca. 1994, b&w ... 3.95
❑19, Jan 1995, b&w ... 3.95
❑20, Feb 1995, b&w ... 3.95
❑21, Mar 1995, b&w ... 3.95
❑22, Apr 1995, b&w ... 3.95
❑23, May 1995, b&w ... 3.95
❑24, Jun 1995, b&w ... 3.95
❑25, Jul 1995, b&w ... 3.95
❑26, Aug 1995, b&w ... 3.95
❑27, Sep 1995, b&w ... 3.95
❑28, Oct 1995, b&w; Dusty Star ... 3.95
❑29, Nov 1995, b&w ... 3.95
❑30, Dec 1995, b&w ... 3.95
❑31, Jan 1996, b&w ... 3.95
❑32, Feb 1996, b&w ... 3.95
❑33, Mar 1996, b&w ... 3.95
❑34, Apr 1996, b&w ... 3.95
❑35, May 1996, b&w ... 3.95
❑36, Jun 1996, b&w ... 3.95
❑37, Jul 1996, b&w; BB, AMo (w); BMB, BB, CR (a); A: Dusty Star. Dusty Star; b&w ... 3.95
❑38, Aug 1996 ... 3.95
❑39, Sep 1996; b&w ... 4.00
❑40, Oct 1996 ... 3.95
❑41, Nov 1996 ... 3.95
❑42, Dec 1996 ... 3.95
❑43, Jan 1997 ... 3.95
❑44, Feb 1997 ... 3.95
❑45 1997 ... 3.95
❑46 1997 ... 3.95
❑47 1997 ... 3.95
❑48 1997 ... 4.95
❑49 1997 ... 4.95
❑50 1997; Final Issue ... 6.95

Negative Burn
Image

❑1, Jun 2006 ... 5.99
❑2, Jul 2006 ... 5.99
❑3, Sep 2006; b&w ... 5.99
❑4, Oct 2006; b&w ... 5.99
❑5, Dec 2006; b&w ... 5.99
❑6, Jan 2007 ... 5.99
❑7, Feb 2007; b&w ... 5.99

N-MINT

Negative Burn: Summer Special 2005
Image

❑1, Dec 2005 ... 9.95

Negative One
Eirich Olson

❑1, Sep 1999 ... 2.95

Neil & Buzz in Space and Time
Fantagraphics

❑1, Apr 1989, b&w ... 2.00

Neil the Horse Comics and Stories
Aardvark-Vanaheim

❑1, Feb 1983, b&w ... 2.50
❑2, Apr 1983, b&w ... 2.00
❑3, Jun 1983, b&w ... 2.00
❑4, Aug 1983, b&w ... 2.00
❑5, Nov 1983, b&w ... 2.00
❑6, Feb 1984, b&w ... 2.00
❑7, Apr 1984, b&w ... 2.00
❑8, Jun 1984, b&w ... 2.00
❑9, Sep 1984, b&w ... 2.00
❑10, Dec 1984, b&w ... 2.00
❑11, Apr 1985, b&w; Title changes to Neil the Horse ... 2.00
❑12, Jun 1985, b&w ... 2.00
❑13, Dec 1986, b&w ... 2.00
❑14, Jul 1988, b&w; giant ... 3.00
❑15, Aug 1988, b&w; giant ... 3.00

Nemesister
Cheeky

❑1, Apr 1997, b&w; cardstock cover ... 2.95
❑2, Jun 1997, b&w; cardstock cover ... 2.95
❑3, Sep 1997, b&w; cardstock cover ... 2.95
❑3/Ashcan; ashcan edition ... 0.50
❑4, Nov 1997, b&w; cardstock cover ... 2.95
❑5 ... 2.95
❑6 ... 2.95
❑7 ... 2.95
❑8 ... 2.95
❑9 ... 2.95

Nemesis the Warlock
Fleetway-Quality

❑1 1989, b&w ... 2.00
❑2, b&w ... 2.00
❑3, b&w ... 2.00
❑4, b&w ... 2.00
❑5, b&w ... 2.00
❑6, b&w ... 2.00
❑7, b&w ... 2.00
❑8, b&w ... 2.00
❑9, b&w BT (a) ... 2.00
❑10, b&w ... 2.00
❑11, b&w ... 2.00
❑12, b&w ... 2.00
❑13, b&w ... 2.00
❑14, b&w O: Torquemada ... 2.00
❑15, b&w ... 2.00
❑16, b&w ... 2.00
❑17, b&w ... 2.00
❑18, b&w ... 2.00
❑19, b&w ... 2.00

Neo
Excalibur
- ❑1, b&w; ca. 1989 ... 1.50

Neomen
Slave Labor
- ❑1, Oct 1987; no indicia ... 1.75
- ❑2, Jan 1988 ... 1.75

Neon City
Innovation
- ❑1, b&w ... 2.25

Neon City: After the Fall
Innovation
- ❑1, b&w ... 2.50

Neon Cyber
Image
- ❑1, Aug 1999 ... 2.50
- ❑1/Variant, Aug 1999; alternate cover ... 5.00
- ❑2, Sep 1999; Man facing giant on cover 2.50
- ❑2/Variant, Sep 1999; alternate cover ... 2.50
- ❑3, Oct 1999; alternate cover ... 2.50
- ❑4, Dec 1999 ... 2.50
- ❑5, Jan 2000 ... 2.50
- ❑6, Mar 2000 ... 2.50
- ❑7, May 2000 ... 2.50
- ❑8, Jun 2000 ... 2.50

Neon Genesis Evangelion Book 1
Viz
- ❑1/A, Sep 1997 ... 2.95
- ❑1/B, Sep 1997; Special collector's edition; printed in Japanese style (back to front) ... 2.95
- ❑2/A, Oct 1997 ... 2.95
- ❑2/B, Oct 1997; Special collector's edition; printed in Japanese style (back to front) ... 2.95
- ❑3/A, Nov 1997 ... 2.95
- ❑3/B, Nov 1997; Special collector's edition; printed in Japanese style (back to front) ... 2.95
- ❑4/A, Dec 1997 ... 2.95
- ❑4/B, Dec 1997; Special collector's edition; printed in Japanese style (back to front) ... 2.95
- ❑5/A, Jan 1998 ... 2.95
- ❑5/B, Jan 1998; Special collector's edition; printed in Japanese style (back to front) ... 2.95
- ❑6/A, Feb 1998 ... 2.95
- ❑6/B, Feb 1998; Special collector's edition; printed in Japanese style (back to front) ... 2.95

Neon Genesis Evangelion Book 2
Viz
- ❑1/A, Mar 1998 ... 3.50
- ❑1/B, Mar 1998; Special collector's edition; printed in Japanese style (back to front) ... 3.50
- ❑2/A, Apr 1998 ... 3.25
- ❑2/B, Apr 1998; Special collector's edition; printed in Japanese style (back to front) ... 3.25
- ❑3/A, May 1998 ... 2.95
- ❑3/B, May 1998; Special collector's edition; printed in Japanese style (back to front) ... 2.95
- ❑4/A, Jun 1998 ... 2.95
- ❑4/B, Jun 1998; Special collector's edition; printed in Japanese style (back to front) ... 2.95
- ❑5/A, Jul 1998 ... 2.95
- ❑5/B, Jul 1998; Special collector's edition; printed in Japanese style (back to front) 2.95

Neon Genesis Evangelion Book 3
Viz
- ❑1/A, Aug 1998 ... 2.95
- ❑1/B, Aug 1998; Special collector's edition; printed in Japanese style (back to front) ... 2.95
- ❑2/A, Sep 1998 ... 2.95
- ❑2/B, Sep 1998; Special collector's edition; printed in Japanese style (back to front) ... 2.95
- ❑3/A, Oct 1998 ... 2.95
- ❑3/B, Oct 1998; Special collector's edition; printed in Japanese style (back to front) ... 2.95
- ❑4/A, Nov 1998 ... 2.95
- ❑4/B, Nov 1998; Special collector's edition; printed in Japanese style (back to front) ... 2.95
- ❑5/A, Dec 1998 ... 2.95
- ❑5/B, Dec 1998; Special collector's edition; printed in Japanese style (back to front) ... 2.95
- ❑6/A, Jan 1999 ... 3.25
- ❑6/B, Jan 1999; Special collector's edition; printed in Japanese style (back to front) ... 3.25

Neon Genesis Evangelion Book 4
Viz
- ❑1/A, Feb 1999 ... 2.95
- ❑1/B, Feb 1999; Special collector's edition; printed in Japanese style (back to front) ... 2.95
- ❑2/A, Mar 1999 ... 2.95
- ❑2/B, Mar 1999; Special collector's edition; printed in Japanese style (back to front) ... 2.95
- ❑3/A, Apr 1999 ... 2.95
- ❑3/B, Apr 1999; Special collector's edition; printed in Japanese style (back to front) ... 2.95
- ❑4/A, May 1999 ... 2.95
- ❑4/B, May 1999, Special collector's edition; printed in Japanese style (back to front) ... 2.95
- ❑5/A, Jun 1999 ... 2.95
- ❑5/B, Jun 1999; Special collector's edition; printed in Japanese style (back to front) ... 2.95
- ❑6/A, Jul 1999 ... 2.95
- ❑6/B, Jul 1999; printed in Japanese style (back to front) ... 2.95
- ❑7, Aug 1999 ... 2.95
- ❑7/B, Aug 1999; printed in Japanese style (back to front) ... 2.95

Neon Genesis Evangelion Book 5
Viz
- ❑1, Oct 2000 ... 2.95
- ❑1/B, Oct 2000; printed in Japanese style (back to front) ... 2.95
- ❑2, Nov 2000 ... 2.95
- ❑2/B, Nov 2000; printed in Japanese style (back to front) ... 2.95
- ❑3, Dec 2000 ... 2.95
- ❑3/B, Dec 2000; printed in Japanese style (back to front) ... 2.95
- ❑4, Jan 2001 ... 2.95
- ❑4/B, Jan 2001; printed in Japanese style (back to front) ... 2.95
- ❑5, Feb 2001 ... 2.95
- ❑5/B, Feb 2001; printed in Japanese style (back to front) ... 2.95
- ❑6, Mar 2001 ... 2.95
- ❑6/B, Mar 2001; printed in Japanese style (back to front) ... 2.95
- ❑7, Apr 2001 ... 2.95
- ❑7/B, May 2001; printed in Japanese style (back to front) ... 2.95

Neon Genesis Evangelion Book 6
Viz
- ❑1, Jul 2001 ... 3.50
- ❑1/B, Jul 2001; printed in Japanese style (back to front) ... 3.50
- ❑2, Aug 2001 ... 3.50
- ❑2/B, Aug 2001; printed in Japanese style (back to front) ... 3.50
- ❑3, Sep 2001 ... 3.50
- ❑3/B, Sep 2001; printed in Japanese style (back to front) ... 3.50
- ❑4, Oct 2001 ... 3.50
- ❑4/B, Oct 2001; printed in Japanese style (back to front) ... 3.50

Neon Genesis Evangelion Book 7
Viz
- ❑1, May 2002 ... 2.95
- ❑1/B, May 2002; printed in Japanese style (back to front) ... 2.95
- ❑2, Jun 2002 ... 2.95
- ❑2/B, Jun 2002; printed in Japanese style (back to front) ... 2.95
- ❑3, Jul 2002 ... 2.95
- ❑3/B, Jul 2002; printed in Japanese style (back to front) ... 2.95
- ❑4, Aug 2002 ... 2.95
- ❑4/B, Aug 2002; printed in Japanese style (back to front) ... 2.95
- ❑5, Sep 2002 ... 2.95
- ❑5/B, Sep 2002; printed in Japanese style (back to front) ... 2.95
- ❑6, Oct 2002 ... 3.50
- ❑6/B, Oct 2002; printed in Japanese style (back to front) ... 3.50

Neotopia
Antarctic
- ❑1, Jan 2003 ... 3.95
- ❑2, Feb 2003 ... 3.95
- ❑3, Apr 2003 ... 3.95
- ❑4, May 2003 ... 3.95
- ❑5, Jun 2003 ... 3.95

Neotopia
Antarctic
- ❑1, Aug 2003 ... 2.99
- ❑2, Sep 2003 ... 2.99
- ❑3, Oct 2003 ... 2.99
- ❑4, Nov 2003 ... 2.99
- ❑5, Dec 2003 ... 2.99

Neotopia
Antarctic
- ❑1, Feb 2004 ... 2.99
- ❑2, Apr 2004 ... 2.99
- ❑3, May 2004 ... 2.99
- ❑4, Jun 2004 ... 2.99

Neotopia
Antarctic
- ❑1, Aug 2004 ... 2.99
- ❑2, Sep 2004 ... 2.99
- ❑3, Oct 2004 ... 2.99
- ❑4 2004 ... 2.99
- ❑5, ca. 2005 ... 2.99

Nerve
Nerve
- ❑1 ... 2.00
- ❑2 ... 1.50
- ❑3 ... 1.50
- ❑4 ... 1.50
- ❑5, Apr 1987 ... 1.50
- ❑6 1987 ... 1.50
- ❑7, Jul 1987 ... 1.50
- ❑8; oversize ... 4.00

Nervous Rex
Blackthorne
- ❑1, Aug 1985 ... 2.00
- ❑2, Oct 1985 ... 2.00
- ❑3, Dec 1985 ... 2.00
- ❑4, Feb 1986 ... 2.00
- ❑5, Apr 1986 ... 2.00
- ❑6, Jun 1986 ... 2.00
- ❑7, Aug 1986 ... 2.00
- ❑8, Oct 1986 ... 2.00
- ❑9, Dec 1986 ... 2.00
- ❑10, Feb 1987 ... 2.00

Nestrobber
Blue Sky Blue
- ❑1, Oct 1992, b&w ... 1.95
- ❑2, Jun 1994, b&w ... 1.95

Netherworld
Ambition
- ❑1, b&w ... 1.50

Netherworlds
Adventure
- ❑1, Aug 1988, b&w ... 1.95

Netman
Information Networks
- ❑0, Aug 1992 ... 0.50

Neuro Jack
Big
- ❑1, Aug 1996, all-digital art ... 2.25

Neuromancer: The Graphic Novel
Marvel / Epic
- ❑1 ... 8.95

Nevada
DC / Vertigo
- ❑1, May 1998 ... 2.50
- ❑2, Jun 1998 ... 2.50
- ❑3, Jul 1998 ... 2.50
- ❑4, Aug 1998 ... 2.50
- ❑5, Sep 1998 ... 2.50
- ❑6, Oct 1998 ... 2.50

Other grades: Multiply price above by 5/6 for VF/NM • 2/3 for VERY FINE • 1/3 for FINE • 1/5 for VERY GOOD • 1/8 for GOOD

Nightwing

Original Robin breaks out on his own

©DC

1963

Image Comics' homage to the Silver Age

©Image

Nine Volt

Motley group defends Earth from aliens

©Image

Ninja High School

Long-running spoof of Japanese comics

©Antarctic

Ninjak

Kurt Busiek's Valiant enforcer

©Valiant

N-MINT

Nevermen
Dark Horse

❑1, May 2000 ... 2.95
❑2, Jun 2000 ... 2.95
❑3, Jul 2000 ... 2.95

Nevermen: Streets of Blood
Dark Horse

❑1, Jan 2003 ... 2.99
❑2, Feb 2003 ... 2.99
❑3, May 2003 ... 2.99

Neverwhere
DC / Vertigo

❑1, Aug 2005 ... 2.99
❑2, Sep 2005 ... 2.99
❑3, Oct 2005 ... 2.99
❑4 2005 ... 2.99
❑5, Jan 2006 ... 2.99
❑6, Apr 2006 ... 2.99
❑7, Jul 2006 ... 2.99
❑8, Oct 2006 ... 2.99
❑9, Dec 2006 ... 2.99

New Adventures of Abraham Lincoln
Image

❑1 ... 19.95

New Adventures of Beauty and the Beast
Disney

❑1, Oct 1992 ... 1.50
❑1/Direct ed., Oct 1992 ... 2.00
❑2, Nov 1992 ... 1.50

New Adventures of Cholly and Flytrap: Till Death Do Us Part
Marvel / Epic

❑1, Dec 1990; prestige format ... 4.95
❑2, Jan 1991; prestige format ... 4.95
❑3, Feb 1991; prestige format ... 4.95

New Adventures of Felix the Cat
Felix

❑1, Oct 1992 ... 2.25
❑2 1992 ... 2.25
❑3 1992 ... 2.25
❑4 ... 2.25
❑5 1993 ... 2.25
❑6 ... 2.25
❑7 1993; becomes New Adventures of Felix the Cat and Friends ... 2.25

New Adventures of Huck Finn
Gold Key

❑1 ... 10.00

New Adventures of Jesus
Rip Off

❑1 ... 4.50

New Adventures of Judo Joe
Ace

❑1, Mar 1987, b&w; Reprints ... 1.75

New Adventures of Pinocchio
Dell

❑1, Oct 1962 ... 65.00
❑2, Jun 1963 ... 50.00
❑3 1963 ... 50.00

N-MINT

New Adventures of Rick O'Shay and Hipshot
Cottonwood

❑1 ... 4.95
❑2 ... 4.95

New Adventures of Shaloman
Mark 1

❑1, b&w; ca. 1991 ... 2.00
❑2; ca. 1992; b&w ... 2.50
❑3; ca. 1993; O: Shaloman; Reprint from Mark 1 Comics #2; ... 2.50
❑4, ca. 1994; b&w ... 2.50
❑5; indicia says #4 ... 2.95
❑8, b&w ... 2.50
❑Special 1, ca. 1995; b&w; Numbered X-Y; Issue Falls between #5 & 7 ... 2.50

New Adventures of Speed Racer
Now

❑0, Nov 1993; multi-dimensional cover. 3.95
❑1, Dec 1993 ... 1.95
❑2, Jan 1994 ... 1.95
❑3, Feb 1994 ... 1.95

New Adventures of Superboy
DC

❑1, Jan 1980, KS (c); KS (a) ... 4.00
❑1/Whitman, Jan 1980; Whitman variant 8.00
❑2, Feb 1980, KS (c); KS (a); Superboy's Secret Diary ... 1.50
❑2/Whitman, Feb 1980, KS (a); Whitman variant ... 3.00
❑3, Mar 1980, KS (c); KS (a); 1: Astralad (Joe Silver) ... 1.50
❑4, Apr 1980, RA, KS (c); KS (a) ... 1.50
❑4/Whitman, Apr 1980, KS (a); Whitman variant ... 3.00
❑5, May 1980, KS (c); KS (a) ... 1.50
❑5/Whitman, May 1980, KS (a); Whitman variant ... 3.00
❑6, Jun 1980, KS (c); KS (a) ... 1.50
❑6/Whitman, Jun 1980; Whitman variant 3.00
❑7, Jul 1980, RA, KS (c); JSn, KS (a); bonus Superman story ... 1.50
❑8, Aug 1980, RA, KS (c); KS (a) ... 1.50
❑8/Whitman, Aug 1980, KS (a); Whitman variant ... 3.00
❑9, Sep 1980, RA, KS (c); RB, KS (a); V: Phantom Zone villains; Superboy's Secret Diary ... 1.50
❑10, Oct 1980, KS (c); KS (a); Krypto back-up ... 1.50
❑11, Nov 1980, KS (c); KS (a); Superbaby back-up ... 1.50
❑12, Dec 1980, KS (c); KS, RT (a); Superboy's Secret Diary ... 1.50
❑13, Jan 1981, KS (c); KS (a) ... 1.50
❑14, Feb 1981, KS (c); DS, KS (a); Superboy; Superbaby ... 1.50
❑15, Mar 1981, KS (c); KS (a); Superboy; Strange Encounters for the First Time 1.50
❑16, Apr 1981, KS (c); KS (a); Superboy; Strange Encounters for the First Time 1.50
❑17, May 1981, KS (c); KS (a); Krypto back-up ... 1.50
❑18, Jun 1981, KS (c); KS (a); Superboy's Secret Diary ... 1.50
❑19, Jul 1981, KS (c); KS (a); Superboy; Superbaby; 1: Cory Renwald ... 1.50

N-MINT

❑20, Aug 1981, KS (c); KS (a); Superboy; Strange Encounters for the First Time 1.50
❑21, Sep 1981, KS (c); KS (a); Superboy; Strange Encounters for the First Time; 1: Huey McKay ... 1.00
❑22, Oct 1981, KS (c); KS, RT (a); Superboy; Krypto; Map of Smallville .. 1.00
❑23, Nov 1981, KS (c); KS (a); Superboy's Secret Diary ... 1.00
❑24, Dec 1981, KS (c); KS (a); Superboy; Superbaby ... 1.00
❑25, Jan 1982, KS (c); KS (a) ... 1.00
❑26, Feb 1982, KS (c); KS (a); Superboy; Strange Encounters for the First Time 1.00
❑27, Mar 1982, KS (c); KS (a); Superboy; Strange Encounters for the First Time; 1: Ralsa; 1: Sar-Ul ... 1.00
❑28, Apr 1982, KS (c); KS (a); Dial H for Hero back-up ... 1.00
❑29, May 1982, KS (c); KS (a); Dial H for Hero back-up ... 1.00
❑30, Jun 1982, RA (c); KS (a); Dial H for Hero back-up ... 1.00
❑31, Jul 1982, KS (c); KS (a); Dial H for Hero back-up ... 1.00
❑32, Aug 1982, GK (c); KS (a); Dial H for Hero back-up ... 1.00
❑33, Sep 1982, GK (c); KS (a); Dial H for Hero back-up ... 1.00
❑34, Oct 1982, RA (c); KS (a); 1: The Yellow Peril. Dial H for Hero back-up . 1.00
❑35, Nov 1982, GK (c); CS, KS (a); Dial H for Hero back-up ... 1.00
❑36, Dec 1982, RB (c); KS (a); Dial H for Hero back-up ... 1.00
❑37, Jan 1983, RA (c); KS (a); Dial H for Hero back-up ... 1.00
❑38, Feb 1983, RA (c); KS (a); Dial H for Hero back-up ... 1.00
❑39, Mar 1983, GK (c); KS (a); Dial H for Hero back-up ... 1.00
❑40, Apr 1983, KS (a); Dial H for Hero back-up ... 1.00
❑41, May 1983, GK (c); KS (a); Dial H for Hero back-up ... 1.00
❑42, Jun 1983, GK (c); KS (a); Dial H for Hero back-up ... 1.00
❑43, Jul 1983, GK (c); KS (a); Dial H for Hero back-up ... 1.00
❑44, Aug 1983, GK (c); KS (a); Dial H for Hero back-up ... 1.00
❑45, Sep 1983, GK (c); KS (a); 1: Sunburst. Dial H for Hero back-up . 1.00
❑46, Oct 1983, GK (c); KS (a); Dial H for Hero back-up ... 1.00
❑47, Nov 1983, GK (c); KS (a); Dial H for Hero back-up ... 1.00
❑48, Dec 1983; GK (c); KS (a); Dial H for Hero back-up ... 1.00
❑49, Jan 1984; GK (c); KS (a); Dial H for Hero back-up ... 1.00
❑50, Feb 1984; Giant-size; KG (c); KG, KS (a); A: Legion of Super-Heroes. Giant-size Anniversary Issue; 1: Nylor Truggs; 1: Cyclone; 1: Landslide; 1: Smasher; 1: High Roller; 1: Magaton; 1: Wisp; 1: Blizzard; 1: Man-Mountain ... 1.25
❑51, Mar 1984; FM (c); CS, KS (a); Reprints from Superman (1st Series) #362, 365, 366 ... 1.00
❑52, Apr 1984 KS (c); KS (a) ... 1.00

❑53, May 1984 KS (c); KS (a) 1.00
❑54, Jun 1984; KS (a); Final Issue 1.00

New Adventures of Terry & the Pirates
Avalon

❑1, ca. 1998 .... 2.95
❑2 .... 2.95
❑3 .... 2.95
❑4 .... 2.95
❑5 .... 2.95
❑6 .... 2.95

New Adventures of the Phantom Blot
Gold Key

❑1, Oct 1964 .... 18.00
❑2, Apr 1965, 1: Super Goof 16.00
❑3, Jul 1965 .... 12.00
❑4, Oct 1965 .... 8.00
❑5, Apr 1966 .... 8.00
❑6, Jul 1966 .... 8.00
❑7, Nov 1966 .... 8.00

New Age Comics
Fantagraphics

❑1, ca. 1985, Independent comics sampler 1.50

New America
Eclipse

❑1, Nov 1987 TY (c) 2.00
❑2, Dec 1987 .... 2.00
❑3, Jan 1988 TY (c) 2.00
❑4, Feb 1988 .... 2.00

New Archies
Archie

❑1, Oct 1987 .... 2.50
❑2, Jan 1988 .... 1.50
❑3, Feb 1988 .... 1.50
❑4, Apr 1988 .... 1.50
❑5, May 1988 .... 1.50
❑6, Jun 1988 .... 1.00
❑7, Aug 1988 .... 1.00
❑8, Sep 1988 .... 1.00
❑9, Oct 1988 .... 1.00
❑10, Dec 1988 .... 1.00
❑11, Jan 1989 .... 1.00
❑12, Feb 1989 .... 1.00
❑13, Apr 1989 .... 1.00
❑14, May 1989 .... 1.00
❑15, Jun 1989 .... 1.00
❑16, Aug 1989 .... 1.00
❑17, Sep 1989 .... 1.00
❑18, Oct 1989 .... 1.00
❑19, Dec 1989 .... 1.00
❑20, Jan 1990 .... 1.00
❑21, Feb 1990 .... 1.00
❑22, May 1990 .... 1.00

New Avengers
Marvel

❑0/Military 2005, Officially released on April 28th, 2005 at the Pentagon, this edition was made available only to the US Military 10.00
❑1, Feb 2005 .... 7.00
❑1/Retailer ed., Feb 2005, Spider-Man cover 70.00
❑1/DirCut, Feb 2005 .... 5.00
❑1/Quesada, Feb 2005 .... 12.00
❑1/Finch, Feb 2005, Third print cover 9.00
❑1/2nd, Feb 2005 .... 3.00
❑2, Mar 2005 .... 2.25
❑2/Hairsine, Mar 2005 .... 45.00
❑3, Apr 2005 .... 2.25
❑3/Wolverine, Apr 2005 .... 45.00
❑4, May 2005 .... 3.00
❑4/Cheung, May 2005, Jim Cheung variant cover 15.00
❑4/DF, May 2005, Signed by John Romita Jr 20.00
❑5, Jun 2005 .... 2.25
❑5/Granov, Jun 2005 .... 15.00
❑6, Jul 2005 .... 2.25
❑6/Hitch, Jul 2005 .... 15.00
❑7, Aug 2005 .... 8.00
❑7/Adams, Aug 2005 .... 25.00
❑8, Sep 2005 .... 2.50
❑8/Romita, Sep 2005 .... 20.00
❑9, Oct 2005 .... 2.50
❑9/Trimpe, Oct 2005 .... 15.00
❑10 2005 .... 2.50
❑11 2005 .... 2.50
❑12 2005 .... 2.50
❑13, Jan 2006 .... 2.50
❑14, Feb 2006 .... 2.50
❑15, Mar 2006 .... 2.50
❑16, Apr 2006 .... 2.50
❑17, Jun 2006 .... 2.50
❑18, Jun 2006 .... 2.99
❑19, Aug 2006 .... 2.99
❑20, Sep 2006 .... 2.99
❑21, Sep 2006 .... 2.99
❑22, Oct 2006 .... 2.99
❑23, Nov 2006 .... 2.99
❑24, Jan 2007 .... 2.99
❑25, Jan 2007 .... 2.99
❑26, Mar 2007 .... 2.99
❑27 .... 2.99
❑28 .... 2.99
❑29 .... 2.99
❑30 .... 2.99
❑31 .... 2.99
❑32 .... 2.99
❑33 .... 2.99
❑34 .... 2.99
❑35 .... 2.99
❑36 .... 2.99
❑37 .... 2.99
❑38 .... 2.99
❑39 .... 2.99
❑40 .... 2.99
❑41 .... 2.99
❑42 .... 2.99
❑43 .... 2.99
❑44 .... 2.99
❑45 .... 2.99
❑46 .... 2.99
❑47 .... 2.99
❑48 .... 2.99
❑49 .... 2.99
❑50 .... 2.99
❑51 .... 2.99
❑Ann 1, Jul 2006 .... 3.99

New Avengers: Illuminati
Marvel

❑1, Jan 2007; Road to Civil War 5.00

New Avengers/Illuminati Special
Marvel

❑1, Apr 2006 .... 14.00

New Avengers: Most Wanted Files
Marvel

❑1, Feb 2006 .... 3.99

New Beginning
Unicorn

❑1, b&w 2.00
❑2, b&w 2.00
❑3, b&w 2.00

New Bondage Fairies
Fantagraphics / Eros

❑1, Nov 1996; Adult 2.95
❑2, Dec 1996; Adult 2.95
❑3, Jan 1997; Adult 2.95
❑4, Feb 1997; Adult 2.95
❑5, Mar 1997; Adult 2.95
❑6, Apr 1997; Adult 2.95
❑7, May 1997; Adult 2.95
❑8, Jun 1997; Adult 2.95
❑9, Jul 1997; Adult 2.95
❑10, Aug 1997; Adult 2.95
❑11, Sep 1997; Adult 2.95
❑12, Oct 1997; Adult 2.95

New Crew
Personality

❑1, Jul 1991; Patrick Stewart 2.95
❑2; Jonathan Frakes 2.95
❑3; Brent Spiner 2.95
❑4; LeVar Burton 2.95
❑5; Denise Crosby 2.95
❑6; Michael Dorn 2.95
❑7; Marina Sertis 2.95
❑8; Gates McFadden 2.95
❑9; Whoopi Goldberg 2.95
❑10; Colm Meaney 2.95

New Crime Files of Michael Mauser, Private Eye
Apple

❑1, Jan 1992, b&w 2.50

New DNAgents
Eclipse

❑1, Oct 1985; ME (w); O: The DNAgents 1.50
❑2, Nov 1985 ME (w) 1.25
❑3, Nov 1985 ME (w) 1.25
❑4, Dec 1985 ME (w) 1.00
❑5, Jan 1986 ME (w) 1.00
❑6, Feb 1986 ME (w) 1.00
❑7, Apr 1986 ME (w) 1.00
❑8, Apr 1986 ME (w); DS (a) 1.00
❑9, Jun 1986 ME (w) 1.00
❑10, Jun 1986; JOy (c); ME (w); Includes Airboy Preview 1.00
❑11, Aug 1986 ME (w); RHo, DS (a) 1.00
❑12, Aug 1986 ME (w) 1.00
❑13, Oct 1986 EL (c); ME (w); EL (a) 1.00
❑14, Nov 1986 EL (c); ME (w); EL (a) 1.00
❑15, Dec 1986 EL (c); ME (w); EL (a) 1.00
❑16, Jan 1987 EL (c); ME (w); EL (a) 1.00
❑17, Mar 1987; EL (c); ME (w); DS, EL (a); Final Issue 1.00

New England Gothic
Visigoth

❑1, Dec 1986 .... 2.00
❑2, Jun 1987, b&w 2.00

New Excalibur
Marvel

❑1, Jan 2006 .... 2.99
❑2, Feb 2006 .... 2.99
❑3, Mar 2006 .... 2.99
❑4, Mar 2006 .... 2.99
❑5, May 2006 .... 2.99
❑6, Jun 2006 .... 2.99
❑7, Aug 2006 .... 2.99
❑8, Sep 2006 .... 2.99
❑9, Sep 2006 .... 2.99
❑10, Oct 2006 .... 2.99
❑11, Nov 2006 .... 2.99
❑12, Jan 2006 .... 2.99
❑13, Feb 2007 .... 2.99
❑14, Feb 2007 .... 2.99

Newforce
Image

❑1, Jan 1996; polybagged with Kodiak card 2.50
❑2, Feb 1996 .... 2.50
❑3, Mar 1996 .... 2.50
❑4, Apr 1996 .... 2.50

New Frontier
Dark Horse

❑1, Oct 1992, b&w 2.75
❑2, Nov 1992, b&w 2.75
❑3, Dec 1992, b&w 2.75

New Frontiers
Evolution

❑1, b&w; ca. 1989 .... 1.75
❑2, b&w; ca. 1991 .... 1.95

New Gods
DC

❑1, Mar 1971, JK (c); JK (w); JK (a); 1: Orion. 1: Apokolips. 1: Metron. 1: Kalibak. 1: Highfather. 1: Lightray .. 35.00
❑2, May 1971, JK (c); JK (w); JK (a); 1: Deep Six 18.00
❑3, Jul 1971, JK (c); JK (w); JK (a); 1: Black Racer 12.00
❑4, Sep 1971; Giant-size; JK (c); JK (w); JK (a); Reprints from Adventure Comics #73, Boy Commandos #12 .... 12.00
❑5, Nov 1971; Giant-size; JK (c); JK (w); JK (a); 1: Fastbak; Reprint from Adventure Comics #74 .... 12.00
❑6, Jan 1972; Giant-size; JK (c); JK (w); JK (a); 1: Fastbak; Reprints from Adventure Comics #75, Real Fact Comics #1 .... 12.00
❑7, Mar 1972; Giant-size; JK (c); JK (w); JK (a); 1: Steppenwolf; Reprints from Adventure Comics #76; O: Orion; O: Mr. Miracle; Real Fact Comics #2... 12.00
❑8, May 1972; Giant-size; JK (c); JK (w); JK (a); Reprint from Adventure Comics #77 .... 12.00

Nintendo Comics System

From Valiant's video-game beginnings
©Valiant

Noble Causes

A soap opera about super-heroes
©Image

Nobody

Nobody kills people like Nobody
©Oni

Nocturne

A hideous vigilante stalks the shadows
©Aircel

Nodwick

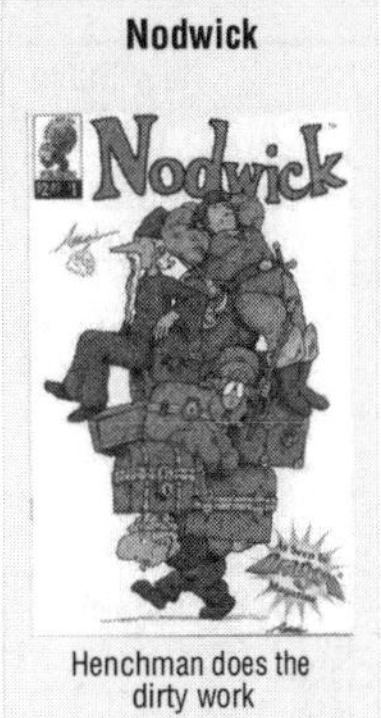

Henchman does the dirty work
©Henchman

	N-MINT
❑9, Jul 1972; Giant-size; JK (c); JK (w); JK (a); 1: Forager; Reprint from Adventure Comics #78	12.00
❑10, Sep 1972, JK (c); JK (w); JK (a)	12.00
❑11, Nov 1972, JK (c); JK (w); JK (a)	12.00
❑12, Jul 1977, AM (c); DN, DA (a); Series begins again	6.00
❑13, Aug 1977, AM (c); DN, DA (a)	6.00
❑14, Oct 1977, AM, RB (c); DN, DA (a)	6.00
❑15, Dec 1977, RB (c); RB, BMc (a)	6.00
❑16, Feb 1978, AM (c); DN (a)	6.00
❑17, Apr 1978, JSn (c); DN, DA (a)	6.00
❑18, Jun 1978, AM (c); DN, DA (a); Cover title changes to Return of the New Gods	6.00
❑19, Aug 1978, BL, JSa (c); DN, DA (a); Final Issue	6.00

New Gods
DC

	N-MINT
❑1, Jun 1984; New Gods (Vol. 1) reprints	2.00
❑2, Jul 1984; New Gods (Vol. 1) reprints	2.00
❑3, Aug 1984; New Gods (Vol. 1) reprints	2.00
❑4, Sep 1984; New Gods (Vol. 1) reprints	2.00
❑5, Nov 1984; New Gods (Vol. 1) reprints	2.00
❑6, Dec 1984; reprints New Gods (Vol. 1) #11, plus new stories	2.00

New Gods
DC

	N-MINT
❑1, Feb 1989 ME (w)	2.25
❑2, Mar 1989; JSn, ME (w); 1: Forager II	2.00
❑3, Apr 1989 JSn, ME (w)	2.00
❑4, May 1989 JSn, ME (w)	2.00
❑5, Jun 1989 ME (w)	2.00
❑6, Jul 1989 ME (w)	1.50
❑7, Aug 1989 ME (w)	1.50
❑8, Sep 1989 ME (w)	1.50
❑9, Oct 1989 ME (w)	1.50
❑10, Nov 1989 ME (w)	1.50
❑11, Dec 1989 ME (w)	1.50
❑12, Jan 1990 ME (w)	1.50
❑13, Feb 1990	1.50
❑14, Mar 1990	1.50
❑15, Apr 1990	1.50
❑16, May 1990	1.50
❑17, Jun 1990	1.50
❑18, Jul 1990	1.50
❑19, Aug 1990	1.50
❑20, Sep 1990	1.50
❑21, Dec 1990	1.50
❑22, Jan 1991	1.50
❑23, Feb 1991	1.50
❑24, Mar 1991; Guest Starring Forever People	1.50
❑25, Apr 1991; Guest Starring Forever People and Infinity Man	1.50
❑26, May 1991	1.50
❑27, Jul 1991	1.50
❑28, Aug 1991; Final Issue	1.50

New Gods
DC

	N-MINT
❑1, Oct 1995	2.00
❑2, Nov 1995	2.00
❑3, Dec 1995	2.00
❑4, Jan 1996	2.00
❑5, Feb 1996	2.00
❑6, Mar 1996	2.00
❑7, Apr 1996; Luke Ross pin-up follows story; Luke Ross pin-up	2.00
❑8, Jun 1996	2.00
❑9, Jul 1996 KG (c); KG (a)	2.00
❑10, Aug 1996 A: Superman	2.00
❑11, Sep 1996	2.00
❑12, Nov 1996 JBy (w); JBy (a)	1.00
❑13, Dec 1996 JBy (w); JBy (a)	2.00
❑14, Jan 1997 JBy (w); JBy (a); A: Forever People	2.00
❑15, Feb 1997; JBy (w); JBy (a); Final issue	2.00

New Gods Secret Files
DC

	N-MINT
❑1, Sep 1998	4.95

New Guardians
DC

	N-MINT
❑1, Sep 1988; Giant-size	2.00
❑2, Oct 1988	1.25
❑3, Nov 1988	1.25
❑4, Dec 1988	1.25
❑5, Dec 1988	1.25
❑6, Jan 1989; Invasion!	1.25
❑7, Feb 1989; Invasion!	1.25
❑8, Apr 1989	1.25
❑9, Jun 1989	1.25
❑10, Jul 1989	1.25
❑11, Aug 1989	1.25
❑12, Sep 1989; Final issue	1.25

New Hat
Black Eye

	N-MINT
❑1	1.00

New Hero Comics
Red Spade

	N-MINT
❑1, b&w	1.00

New Horizons
Shanda Fantasy Arts

	N-MINT
❑1, b&w; Anthology	4.95
❑2, b&w; Anthology	4.95
❑3, b&w; Anthology	4.50
❑4, b&w; Anthology	4.50
❑5, Apr 1999, b&w; Anthology	4.50

New Humans
Pied Piper

	N-MINT
❑1, Jul 1987, b&w; O: The New Humans	1.95
❑2 1987	1.95
❑3 1987	1.95

New Humans
Eternity

	N-MINT
❑1, Dec 1987; O: New Humans; Preview of Outlander #3; Preview of The Verdict #1; b&w	1.95
❑2, Jan 1988; Preview of The Rovers #6; b&w	1.95
❑3, Feb 1988	1.95
❑4, Mar 1988; Nude cover	1.95
❑5 1988	1.95
❑6 1988	1.95
❑7 1988	1.95
❑8, Sep 1988	1.95
❑9 1988	1.95
❑10 1989	1.95
❑11	1.95
❑12, Mar 1989	1.95
❑13	1.95
❑14; ca. 1989	1.95
❑15; ca. 1989	1.95
❑16	1.95
❑17; Final Issue	1.95
❑Ann 1, b&w; b&w The Shattered Earth Chronicles	2.95

New Justice Machine
Innovation

	N-MINT
❑1, Nov 1989	2.00
❑2, Jan 1990	2.00
❑3, Mar 1990	2.00

New Kids on the Block: Backstage Pass
Harvey

	N-MINT
❑1, ca. 1991	1.25

New Kids on the Block: Chillin'
Harvey

	N-MINT
❑1, ca. 1990	1.50
❑2, Jan 1991	1.25
❑3, ca. 1991	1.25
❑4, Apr 1991	1.25
❑5, Jun 1991	1.25
❑6, Oct 1991	1.25
❑7, Dec 1991	1.25

New Kids on the Block Comic Tour '90
Harvey

	N-MINT
❑1, ca. 1991	1.25

New Kids on the Block Magic Summer Tour
Harvey

	N-MINT
❑1, ca. 1991; NN	1.25
❑1/Ltd., ca. 1991; limited edition; NN	3.95

New Kids on the Block: NKOTB
Harvey

	N-MINT
❑1, Dec 1990	1.25
❑2, Jan 1991	1.25
❑3, Feb 1991	1.25
❑4, Mar 1991; Christmas cover	1.25
❑5, May 1991	1.25
❑6, Jul 1991	1.50

New Kids on the Block Step By Step
Harvey

	N-MINT
❑1, ca. 1991; NN; Fall 1990	1.25

New Kids on the Block: Valentine Girl
Harvey

	N-MINT
❑1, ca. 1991; NN; Fall 1990	1.25

New Love
Fantagraphics

	N-MINT
❑1, Aug 1996, b&w	2.95
❑2, Oct 1996, b&w	2.95
❑3, Mar 1997, b&w	2.95
❑4, Jun 1997, b&w	2.95
❑5, Sep 1997, b&w	2.95
❑6, Dec 1997, b&w	2.95

Newman
Image

	N-MINT
❑1, Jan 1996; polybagged with card; Extreme Destroyer Part 3	2.50
❑2, Feb 1996	2.50
❑3, Apr 1996	2.50
❑4, Apr 1996; V: Youngblood	2.50

Other grades: Multiply price above by 5/6 for VF/NM • 2/3 for VERY FINE • 1/3 for FINE • 1/5 for VERY GOOD • 1/8 for GOOD

New Mangaverse
Marvel

❑1, Mar 2006 .... 2.99
❑2, Apr 2006 .... 2.99
❑3, May 2006 .... 2.99
❑4, Jun 2006 .... 2.99

Newmen
Image

❑1, Apr 1994 RL (w) 2.50
❑2, May 1994 .... 2.25
❑3, Jun 1994 .... 2.25
❑4, Jul 1994 .... 2.25
❑5, Aug 1994 .... 2.50
❑6, Sep 1994 .... 2.50
❑7, Oct 1994 .... 2.50
❑8, Nov 1994 .... 2.50
❑9, Dec 1994; Extreme Sacrifice 2.50
❑10, Jan 1995; Includes trading card 2.50
❑11, Feb 1995; polybagged 2.50
❑11/A, Feb 1995; Alternate cover; polybagged 2.50
❑12, Mar 1995 .... 2.50
❑13, Apr 1995 .... 2.50
❑14, May 1995 .... 2.50
❑15, Jun 1995; no indicia 2.50
❑16, Jul 1995 .... 2.50
❑16/A, Jul 1995; alternate cover 3.00
❑17, Aug 1995 .... 2.50
❑18, Sep 1995 .... 2.50
❑19, Oct 1995 .... 2.50
❑20, Nov 1995; Babewatch 2.50
❑20/A, Nov 1995; Babewatch 2.50
❑21, Aug 1996 .... 2.50
❑22, Nov 1996; becomes Adventures of the New Men 2.50
❑23, Mar 1997 .... 2.50
❑24, Apr 1997 .... 2.50
❑25, May 1997 .... 2.50

New Mutants
Marvel

❑1, Mar 1983, BMc (c); BMc (a) 6.00
❑2, Apr 1983, BMc (c); BMc (a); V: Sentinels 2.00
❑3, May 1983, MGu (c); BMc (a); V: Brood 2.00
❑4, Jun 1983, BMc (c); SB (a) 1.50
❑5, Jul 1983, SB (a); A: Team America 1.50
❑6, Aug 1983, BMc (c); SB (a); A: Team America 1.50
❑7, Sep 1983, BMc (c); SB (a); 1: Axe 1.50
❑8, Oct 1983, BMc (c); SB, BMc (a); O: Magma. 1: Amara Aquila (Magma) 1.50
❑9, Nov 1983, BMc (c); SB (a); 1: Selene; 1: Selene Gallio 1.50
❑10, Dec 1983, BMc (c); SB (a); 1: Magma; 1: Magma (Amara Aquilla) 1.50
❑11, Jan 1984, SB (a); Assistant Editor Month 1.50
❑12, Feb 1984, SB (a) 1.50
❑13, Mar 1984, SB (a); 1: Cypher. A: Kitty Pryde; 1: Cypher (Doug Ramsey) 1.50
❑14, Apr 1984, SB (a); A: X-Men. V: Sy'm 1.50
❑15, May 1984, SB (a); A: X-Men. X-Men 1.50
❑16, Jun 1984, 1: Warpath. 1: Hellions; 1: Catseye; 1: Empath; 1: Jetstream 1.50
❑17, Jul 1984, SB (a); V: Hellions. The New Mutants vs. The Hellions 1.50
❑18, Aug 1984, BSz (c); BSz (a); 1: Warlock (machine); 1: Magus 1.50
❑19, Sep 1984, BSz (c); BSz (a); 1: Tom Corsi; 1: Sharon Friedlander 1.50
❑20, Oct 1984, BSz (c); BSz (a) 1.50
❑21, Nov 1984; Double-size; BSz (c); BSz (a); O: Warlock (machine) 1.50
❑22, Dec 1984, BSz (c); BSz (a) 1.50
❑23, Jan 1985, BSz (c); BSz (a); A: Cloak & Dagger 1.50
❑24, Feb 1985, BSz (c); BSz (a); A: Cloak & Dagger 1.50
❑25, Mar 1985, BSz (c); BSz (a); 1: Legion (cameo). A: Cloak & Dagger 2.50
❑26, Apr 1985, BSz (c); BSz (a); 1: Legion (psychic) 2.50
❑27, May 1985, BSz (c); BSz (a); A: Legion. V: Legion 2.00
❑28, Jun 1985, BSz (c); BSz (a); A: Legion 2.00
❑29, Jul 1985, BSz (c); BSz (a); 1: Guido Carosella (Strong Guy) 2.00
❑30, Aug 1985, BSz (c); BSz (a); Secret Wars II 1.50
❑31, Sep 1985, BSz (c); BSz (a) 1.50
❑32, Oct 1985, 1: Madripoor 1.50
❑33, Nov 1985 .... 1.50
❑34, Dec 1985 .... 1.50
❑35, Jan 1986; BSz (a); A: Magneto. Magneto begins as leader of New Mutants 1.50
❑36, Feb 1986; BSz (a); Secret Wars II tie-in; Price increase 1.50
❑37, Mar 1986; BSz (a); Secret Wars II tie-in 1.50
❑38, Apr 1986 .... 1.50
❑39, May 1986 KP (a) 1.50
❑40, Jun 1986 A: Captain America 1.50
❑41, Jul 1986 .... 1.50
❑42, Aug 1986; 1: Icarus (Joshua Guthrie); 1: Aero (Melody Guthrie) 1.50
❑43, Sep 1986 .... 1.50
❑44, Oct 1986 BG (a); A: Legion 1.50
❑45, Nov 1986; BG (a); Marvel 25th Anniversary frame cover 1.50
❑46, Dec 1986; BG (a); Mutant Massacre 1.50
❑47, Jan 1987 .... 1.50
❑48, Feb 1987 BG (a) 1.50
❑49, Mar 1987 .... 1.50
❑50, Apr 1987; Double-size; BG (a); Professor X returns as headmaster 1.50
❑51, May 1987 KN (c); KN (a); A: Star Jammers 1.50
❑52, Jun 1987 .... 1.50
❑53, Jul 1987 .... 1.50
❑54, Aug 1987; Karma leaves team 1.50
❑55, Sep 1987 .... 1.50
❑56, Oct 1987 KN (c) 1.50
❑57, Nov 1987 .... 1.50
❑58, Dec 1987; registration card 1.50
❑59, Jan 1988; 1: Ani-Mator (Frederick Animus); Fall of the Mutants 2.00
❑60, Feb 1988; double-sized; D: Cypher; Fall of the Mutants 2.00
❑61, Mar 1988; new costumes; (conclusion) 2.00
❑62, Apr 1988 .... 1.50
❑63, May 1988 A: X-Men 2.00
❑64, Jun 1988 .... 1.50
❑65, Jul 1988 .... 1.50
❑66, Aug 1988 .... 1.50
❑67, Sep 1988 .... 1.50
❑68, Oct 1988 .... 1.50
❑69, Nov 1988 .... 1.50
❑70, Dec 1988; Inferno 1.50
❑71, Jan 1989; O: N'astirh. Inferno 1.50
❑72, Feb 1989; Inferno 1.50
❑73, Mar 1989; Giant-size; Inferno 2.00
❑74, Apr 1989 .... 1.50
❑75, May 1989 .... 1.50
❑76, Jun 1989; RB (c); RB (a); A: X-Terminators. A: X-Factor. A: Sub-Mariner 1.50
❑77, Jul 1989 RB (c); RB (a) 1.50
❑78, Aug 1989 .... 1.50
❑79, Sep 1989 .... 1.50
❑80, Oct 1989 .... 1.50
❑81, Nov 1989; Hercules & Magma tale 1.50
❑82, Nov 1989 .... 1.50
❑83, Dec 1989 .... 1.50
❑84, Dec 1989; Acts of Vengeance 1.50
❑85, Jan 1990; TMc, RL (c); Acts of Vengeance 1.50
❑86, Feb 1990; TMc, RL (c); RL (a); 1: Zero. 1: Cable (cameo). Acts of Vengeance 3.00
❑87, Mar 1990; TMc, RL (c); RL, BWi (a); 1: Stryfe. 1: Cable 6.00
❑87/2nd, Mar 1990; TMc, RL (c); RL (a); 1: Cable. 2nd printing (gold) 2.00
❑88, Apr 1990; TMc, RL (c); RL (a); 2: Cable 2.50
❑89, May 1990 TMc, RL (c); RL (a) 2.00
❑90, Jun 1990 A: Sabretooth 2.00
❑91, Jul 1990 A: Sabretooth 2.00
❑92, Aug 1990 RL (c); BH (a) 2.00
❑93, Sep 1990; TMc, RL (c); RL (a); A: Wolverine. 1: Dragoness (Tamara Kurtz); 1: Kamikaze; 1: Sumo 2.00
❑94, Oct 1990 A: Wolverine 2.00
❑95, Nov 1990; D: Warlock (machine) 2.00
❑95/2nd, Nov 1990; D: Warlock (machine). 2nd printing (gold) 2.00
❑96, Dec 1990 .... 2.00
❑97, Jan 1991; D: Wipeout 2.00
❑98, Feb 1991; RL (c); RL (w); RL (a); 1: Deadpool. 1: Domino II. 1: Gideon; D: White Rook (Emmanuel da Costa) 5.00
❑99, Mar 1991; RL (c); RL (w); RL (a); 1: Feral. 1: Shatterstar (full appearance). A: Sunspot. Sunspot leaves 2.50
❑100, Apr 1991; Giant-size; RL (c); RL (w); RL (a); O: Shatterstar; D: Brute 2.00
❑100/2nd, Apr 1991; RL (c); RL (w); RL (a); 1: X-Force. 2nd printing (gold) 2.00
❑100/3rd, Apr 1991; RL (c); RL (w); RL (a); 1: X-Force. 3rd printing (silver) 2.00
❑Ann 1, ca. 1984; BSz (c); BMc (a); 1: Lila Cheney 3.00
❑Ann 2, Oct 1986; 1: Meggan. 1: Psylocke 4.00
❑Ann 3, ca. 1987; A: Impossible Man 2.00
❑Ann 4, ca. 1988 .... 2.00
❑Ann 5, ca. 1989; RL (c); RL (a) 2.00
❑Ann 6, ca. 1990; 1: Shatterstar (cameo) 2.50
❑Ann 7, ca. 1991; D: Super Sabre; Kings of Pain 2.00
❑Special 1, Dec 1985; 1: Brightwind; Dani becomes a Valkeryie 3.00
❑Summer 1, Jun 1990; Giant-size; Summer Special 2.00

New Mutants
Marvel

❑1, Jul 2003; 1: Wind Dancer 4.00
❑2, Aug 2003, 1: Hellion; 1: Mercury; 1: Wallflower; 1: Anole 2.50
❑3, Sep 2003, 1: Rockslide; 1: Wither 2.50
❑4, Oct 2003, 1: Prodigy 2.99
❑5, Nov 2003, 1: Elixer 2.99
❑6, Dec 2003 .... 2.99
❑7, Jan 2004, 1: Match; 1: Rockslide (Santo Vaccarro) 2.99
❑8, Apr 2004, 1: Surge 2.99
❑9, Apr 2004 .... 2.99
❑10, May 2004; 1: Tag 2.99
❑11, May 2004 .... 2.99
❑12, Jun 2004 .... 2.99
❑13, Jun 2004, Title becomes New X-Men: Academy X; Final Issue 2.99

New Mutants: Truth or Death
Marvel

❑1, Nov 1997; gatefold summary; original New Mutants travel through time and meet present-day counterparts 2.50
❑2, Dec 1997; gatefold summary 2.50
❑3, Jan 1998; gatefold summary 2.50

New Night of the Living Dead
Fantaco

❑0 .... 2.00
❑1 .... 3.95
❑2 .... 3.95
❑3 .... 3.95

New Order
Creative Force

❑1, Nov 1994 .... 2.95

New Paltz Comix
Moods

❑1; Adult; ca. 1973 .... 1.50
❑2 1974; Adult 1.50
❑3; Adult 1.50

New Partners in Peril
Blue Comet

❑1, b&w 2.25

New Partners in Peril
Tami

❑1 .... 2.25

New People
Dell

❑1, Jan 1970 .... 10.00
❑2, May 1970 .... 8.00

New Power Stars
Blue Comet

❑1, b&w; ca. 1989 .... 2.00

New Shadowhawk
Image

❑1, Jun 1995 .... 2.50
❑2, Aug 1995 .... 2.50
❑3, Sep 1995 .... 2.50
❑4, Nov 1995 .... 2.50

Nomad

Spinoff series from Captain America
©Marvel

No Need for Tenchi! Part 1

Hitoshi Okuda's hit comedy anime series
©Viz

Normalman

Jim Valentino's hilarious parody title
©Aardvark-Vanaheim

Nova

1970s hero just can't keep a series going
©Marvel

Nth Man, the Ultimate Ninja

N = The number of readers who remember...
©Marvel

N-MINT

❑5, Dec 1995 .... 2.50
❑6, Feb 1996 .... 2.50
❑7, Mar 1996 .... 2.50

New Statesmen
Fleetway-Quality

❑1 .... 4.00
❑2 .... 4.00
❑3 .... 4.00
❑4 .... 4.00
❑5 .... 4.00

Newstime
DC

❑1, May 1993; D: Superman Magazine .. 3.25

Newstralia
Innovation

❑1, Jul 1989 .... 2.00
❑2 .... 2.00
❑3 .... 2.25
❑4; b&w 2.25
❑5, b&w 2.25

New Talent Showcase
DC

❑1, Jan 1984 .... 1.50
❑2, Feb 1984 .... 1.50
❑3, Mar 1984 .... 1.50
❑4, Apr 1984 .... 1.50
❑5, May 1984 .... 1.50
❑6, Jun 1984 .... 1.50
❑7, Jul 1984 .... 1.50
❑8, Aug 1984 .... 1.50
❑9, Sep 1984 .... 1.50
❑10, Oct 1984 .... 1.50
❑11, Nov 1984 .... 1.25
❑12, Dec 1984 .... 1.25
❑13, Jan 1985 .... 1.25
❑14, Feb 1985; Extra Story called: The Roosevelt Project 1.25
❑15, Mar 1985 .... 1.25
❑16, Apr 1985; Title changes to Talent Showcase 1.25
❑17, May 1985 .... 1.25
❑18, Jun 1985 .... 1.25
❑19, Jul 1985; Final issue 1.25

New Teen Titans
DC

❑1, Nov 1980, GP (c); GP, RT (a); 1: Teen Titans; V: Gordanians 8.00
❑2, Dec 1980, GP (c); GP, RT (a); 1: Trigon. 1: Wintergreen. 1: Deathstroke the Terminator. D: The Ravager; 1: Ravager (Grant Wilson) 10.00
❑3, Jan 1981, GP (c); GP (w); GP (a); 1: Shimmer. 1: Gizmo. 1: Mammoth. 1: Fearsome Five. 1: Psimon. V: Doctor Light 3.00
❑4, Feb 1981, GP (c); GP (a); A: Justice League. 1: Arella (Raven's mother); O: Trigon 3.00
❑5, Mar 1981, GP (c); CS, RT (a); O: Raven. 1: Trigon; D: Goronn 3.00
❑6, Apr 1981, GP (c); GP (w); GP (a); O: Raven. V: Trigon; O: Arella 3.00
❑7, May 1981, GP (c); GP, RT (a); O: Cyborg. V: Fearsome Five. D: Cyborg's father; Kid Flash leaves team 3.00
❑8, Jun 1981, GP (c); GP (w); GP, RT (a); O: Kid Flash 3.00
❑9, Jul 1981, GP (c); GP, RT (a); V: Puppeteer; Deathstroke appearance 3.00
❑10, Aug 1981, GP (c); GP (w); GP, RT (a); O: Changeling. A: Deathstroke the Terminator 3.00
❑11, Sep 1981, GP (c); GP, RT (a) 2.00
❑12, Oct 1981, GP (c); GP, RT (a) 2.00
❑13, Nov 1981, GP (c); GP (w); GP, RT (a); A: Doom Patrol. A: Robotman 2.00
❑14, Dec 1981, GP (c); GP, RT (a); 1: Houngan. 1: Plasmus. 1: Phobia. A: Doom Patrol 2.00
❑15, Jan 1982, GP (c); GP (w); GP, RT (a); A: Doom Patrol. V: Brotherhood of Evil 2.00
❑16, Feb 1982, GP (c); GP (w); GP, RA, RT (a); 1: Yankee Poodle. 1: Pig-Iron. 1: Fastback. 1: Captain Carrot. 1: Rubberduck. 1: Alley-Kat-Abra. 1: Alley-Kat-Abra 2.00
❑17, Mar 1982, GP (c); GP, RT (a); 1: Francis Kane 2.00
❑18, Apr 1982, GP (c); GP, RT (a); 1: Maladi Maranova. A: Starfire (later Red Star) 2.00
❑19, May 1982, GP (c); GP, RT (a); A: Hawkman. V: Dr. Light; V: Statues of Vishnu incarnations brought to life 2.00
❑20, Jun 1982, GP (c); GP, RT (a); 1: The Disruptor 2.00
❑21, Jul 1982, GP (c); GC, GP, RT (a); 1: Monitor. 1: Harbinger. 1: Brother Blood. 1: Night Force. 1: Baron Winters. V: Brother Blood 2.00
❑22, Aug 1982, GP (c); GP, RT (a); V: Brother Blood; 1st App. of Komand'r (unnamed) 2.00
❑23, Sep 1982, GP (c); GP (w); GP, RT (a); 1: Komand'r (Blackfire) 2.00
❑24, Oct 1982, GP (c); GP (w); GP, RT (a); 1: X'Hal. A: Omega Men; 1: Blackfire (named as such) 2.00
❑25, Nov 1982, GP (c); GP (w); GP, CS, RT (a); 1: Masters of the Universe. A: Omega Men. Masters of the Universe preview 2.00
❑26, Dec 1982, GP (c); GP, RT (a); 1: Terra; 1: Terra (Tara Markov) 2.00
❑27, Jan 1983, GP (c); GP, RA, RT (a); 1: Howard Rondo. Atari Force preview 2.00
❑28, Feb 1983, GP (c); GP, RT (a); A: Terra. V: Brotherhood of Evil 2.00
❑29, Mar 1983, GP (c); GP, RT (a); A: Speedy. V: Brotherhood of Evil; Return of Speedy 2.00
❑30, Apr 1983, GP (c); GP, RT (a); A: Terra. Terra joins team 2.00
❑31, May 1983, GP (c); GP, RT (a); V: Brotherhood of Evil 2.00
❑32, Jun 1983, GP (c); GP, RT (a); O: Kid Flash; 1: Thunder (Gan Williams); 1: Lightning (Tavis Williams) 2.00
❑33, Jul 1983, GP (c); GP, RT (a); D: Trident 2.00
❑34, Aug 1983, GP (c); GP (a); A: Deathstroke the Terminator. V: Terminator 2.00
❑35, Oct 1983, GP (c); GP, KP, RT (a) 2.00
❑36, Nov 1983, GP (c); KP (a); A: Thunder and Lightning 2.00
❑37, Dec 1983; GP (c); GP (a); A: Outsiders. V: Doctor Light. V: Shimmer. V: Gizmo. V: Mammoth; V: Psimon 2.00
❑38, Jan 1984; GP (c); GP (w); GP (a); O: Wonder Girl 2.00
❑39, Feb 1984; GP (c); GP (w); GP (a); Dick Grayson quits as Robin; Wally West retires as Kid Flash 2.50
❑40, Mar 1984; GP (c); GP (w); GP (a); Series continued in Tales of the Teen Titans #41 .... 2.00
❑Ann 1, ca. 1982 GP (c); GP (w); GP (a); A: Omega Men 3.00
❑Ann 2, ca. 1983; GP (c); GP (w); GP (a); 1: Lyla (Harbinger). 1: Vigilante. A: Monitor; 1: Lyla Michaels 2.00
❑Ann 3, ca. 1984; D: Terra. Published as Tales of the Teen Titans Ann 2.00

New Teen Titans
DC

❑1, Aug 1984 GP (c); GP (w); GP (a) 3.00
❑2, Oct 1984 GP (c); GP (w); GP (a); A: Trigon 2.50
❑3, Nov 1984; GP (c); GP (w); GP (a); V: Trigon 2.50
❑4, Jan 1985; GP (c); GP (w); GP (a); V: Trigon 2.50
❑5, Feb 1985; GP (c); GP (w); GP (a); V: Trigon 2.50
❑6, Mar 1985 GP (c); GP (w) 2.00
❑7, Apr 1985; GP (c); JL (a); O: Lilith 2.00
❑8, May 1985 JL (a); A: Destiny 2.00
❑9, Jun 1985; JL (a); 1: Kole; 1: Kole Weathers 2.00
❑10, Jul 1985 RB (c); JL (a) 2.00
❑11, Aug 1985 JL (a) 2.00
❑12, Sep 1985 .... 2.00
❑13, Oct 1985; Crisis on Infinite Earths 2.00
❑14, Nov 1985; Crisis on Infinite Earths 2.00
❑15, Dec 1985; Tales of Tamaran 2.00
❑16, Jan 1986; DG (a); A: Omega Men. Tales of Tamaran 2.00
❑17, Feb 1986; Wedding of Starfire 2.00
❑18, Mar 1986 .... 2.00
❑19, Apr 1986 GP (c) 2.00
❑20, May 1986; GP (c); A: original Titans. A: Robin II (Jason Todd) 2.00
❑21, Jun 1986 GP (c); A: Cheshire 1.50
❑22, Jul 1986 GP (c) 1.50
❑23, Aug 1986; GP (c); V: Hybrids; Starfire vs. Blackfire 1.50
❑24, Oct 1986; V: Hybrids 1.50
❑25, Nov 1986; V: Hybrids 1.50
❑26, Dec 1986 KGa (a) 1.50
❑27, Jan 1987; KGa (a); V: Brotherhood of Evil 1.50
❑28, Feb 1987; V: Brother Blood 1.50
❑29, Mar 1987; V: Brother Blood 1.50
❑30, Apr 1987; V: Brother Blood 1.50
❑31, May 1987; A: Superman. A: Batman. V: Brother Blood 1.50
❑32, Jun 1987 .... 1.50
❑33, Jul 1987 JO (c); EL (a) 1.50
❑34, Aug 1987; V: Hybrid 1.50
❑35, Sep 1987 PB (c); PB (a) 1.50
❑36, Oct 1987; V: Wildebeest 1.50
❑37, Nov 1987; V: Wildebeest 1.75

Other grades: Multiply price above by 5/6 for VF/NM • 2/3 for VERY FINE • 1/3 for FINE • 1/5 for VERY GOOD • 1/8 for GOOD

❑38, Dec 1987; A: Infinity Inc.. V: Ultra-Humanite; Story continues in Infinity Inc. #45 ..... 1.75
❑39, Jan 1988 ..... 1.75
❑40, Feb 1988; V: I.Q.. V: Silver Fog. V: The Gentleman Ghost 1.75
❑41, Mar 1988; V: Wildebeest 1.75
❑42, Apr 1988; Brother Blood's child born 1.75
❑43, May 1988; GP (c); CS (a); V: Raven. Phobia vs. Raven 1.75
❑44, Jun 1988; V: Godiva 1.75
❑45, Jul 1988 A: Dial H for Hero 1.75
❑46, Aug 1988 A: Dial H for Hero 1.75
❑47, Sep 1988; O: Titans 1.75
❑48, Oct 1988; V: Red Star 1.75
❑49, Nov 1988; V: Red Star. Series continued in New Titans #50 ..... 1.75
❑Ann 1, ca. 1985; 1: Vanguard. A: Superman. V: Vanguard 2.50
❑Ann 2, Aug 1986; JBy (c); JBy (a); O: Brother Blood. 1: Cheshire. A: Doctor Light 2.75
❑Ann 3, ca. 1987; 1: Godiva. 1: Danny Chase. A: King Faraday. cover indicates '87 Ann, indicia says '86 ..... 2.50
❑Ann 4, ca. 1988; Private Lives 2.50

New Teen Titans (Giveaways and Promos)
DC

❑1; Beverage; DC drug issue 1.00
❑2; IBM/DC drug issue 1.00
❑3; GP, DC (a); Keebler; drug issue 1.00
❑4; DC (a); Keebler; drug issue 1.00
❑5 ..... 1.00

New Terrytoons
Gold Key

❑1, Oct 1962 ..... 35.00
❑2, Jan 1963, Summer Cruise 22.00
❑3 ..... 12.00
❑4, Sep 1969 ..... 8.00
❑5, Nov 1970 ..... 8.00
❑6, Jan 1970 ..... 6.00
❑7, Mar 1970 ..... 6.00
❑8, May 1970 ..... 6.00
❑9, Jul 1970 ..... 6.00
❑10, Oct 1970 ..... 6.00
❑11 1971 ..... 5.00
❑12 1971 ..... 5.00
❑13 1971 ..... 5.00
❑14, Nov 1971 ..... 5.00
❑15, Feb 1972 ..... 5.00
❑16, May 1972 ..... 5.00
❑17, Aug 1972 ..... 5.00
❑18, Nov 1972 ..... 5.00
❑19, Feb 1973 ..... 5.00
❑20, May 1973 ..... 5.00
❑21, Jul 1973 ..... 3.50
❑22 1973 ..... 3.50
❑23, Nov 1973 ..... 3.50
❑24, Jan 1974 ..... 3.50
❑25 ..... 3.50
❑26, Jun 1974 ..... 3.50
❑27, Aug 1974 ..... 3.50
❑28, Oct 1974 ..... 3.50
❑29, Dec 1974 ..... 3.50
❑30, Feb 1975 ..... 3.50
❑31, Apr 1976 ..... 2.50
❑32, Jun 1975 ..... 2.50
❑33, Aug 1975 ..... 2.50
❑34, Oct 1975 ..... 2.50
❑35, Dec 1975 ..... 2.50
❑36, Feb 1976 ..... 2.50
❑37, Apr 1976 ..... 2.50
❑38, Jun 1976 ..... 2.50
❑39, Aug 1976 ..... 2.50
❑40, Sep 1976 ..... 2.50
❑41, Nov 1976 ..... 2.00
❑42, Jan 1977 ..... 2.00
❑43, Mar 1977 ..... 2.00
❑44, May 1977 ..... 2.00
❑45, Jul 1977 ..... 2.00
❑46, Sep 1977 ..... 2.00
❑47, Nov 1977 ..... 2.00
❑48, Jan 1978 ..... 2.00
❑49, Mar 1978 ..... 2.00
❑50, May 1978 ..... 2.00
❑51, Jul 1979 ..... 2.00
❑52, Sep 1979 ..... 2.00
❑53, Nov 1979 ..... 2.00
❑54, Jan 1979 ..... 2.00

New Thunderbolts
Marvel

❑1, Dec 2004; Series continued from Thunderbolts; #82 ..... 2.99
❑2, Jan 2005; #83 ..... 2.99
❑3, Feb 2005; #84 ..... 2.99
❑4, Mar 2005; #85 ..... 2.99
❑5, Apr 2005; #86 ..... 2.99
❑6, May 2005; #87 ..... 2.99
❑7, May 2005; #88 ..... 2.99
❑8, Jun 2005; #89 ..... 2.99
❑9, Jul 2005 ..... 2.99
❑10, Aug 2005; #91 ..... 2.99
❑11, Sep 2005; #92; House of M tie-in 2.99
❑12, Oct 2005; A.k.a. Thunderbolts #93 2.99
❑13, Nov 2005; A.k.a. Thunderbolts #94 2.99
❑14, Dec 2005; A.k.a. Thunderbolts #95 2.99
❑15, Jan 2006; A.k.a. Thunderbolts #96 2.99
❑16, Feb 2006, A.k.a. Thunderbolts #97 2.99
❑17, Mar 2006, A.k.a. Thunderbolts #98 2.99
❑18, Apr 2006, A.k.a. Thunderbolts #99 2.99

New Titans
DC

❑0, Oct 1994; A: Terra. A: Nightwing. A: Impulse. A: Mirage. A: Damage. Series continued in New Titans #115;Titans get new headquarters 1.95
❑50, Dec 1988; GP (c); GP (w); GP (a); O: Wonder Girl (new origin). Series continued from New Teen Titans #49 . 2.00
❑51, Dec 1988; GP (c); GP (w); GP (a); 1: Cronus 2.00
❑52, Jan 1989; GP (c); GP (w); GP (a); V: Sparta 2.00
❑53, Feb 1989 GP (c); GP (w); GP (a).... 2.00
❑54, Mar 1989; GP (c); GP (w); GP (a); V: Sparta 2.00
❑55, Jun 1989; GP (c); GP (w); GP (a); 1: Troia 2.00
❑56, Jul 1989 GP (c); GP (w); A: Gnaark 2.00
❑57, Aug 1989; GP (c); GP (w); GP (a); V: Wildebeest 2.00
❑58, Sep 1989; GP (a); V: Wildebeest-controlled Cyborg 2.00
❑59, Oct 1989; GP (a); V: Wildebeest 2.00
❑60, Nov 1989 GP (c); GP (w); GP (a); A: Tim Drake 2.50
❑61, Dec 1989; GP (c); GP (w); GP (a); Part 5 in Batman #442 ..... 2.50
❑62, Jan 1990; A: Deathstroke the Terminator. V: were-creatures 2.00
❑63, Feb 1990; A: Deathstroke the Terminator. V: were-creatures 2.00
❑64, Mar 1990; A: Deathstroke the Terminator. V: were-creatures 2.00
❑65, Apr 1990; A: Robin III. A: Deathstroke the Terminator. Pre-Robin Tim Drake visits Nightwing 2.00
❑66, May 1990 GP (w) 2.00
❑67, Jul 1990; GP (w); V: Eric Forrester; Eric Forrester revealed as android 2.00
❑68, Jul 1990; V: Royal Flush Gang; V: Gambler 2.00
❑69, Sep 1990; V: Royal Flush Gang; V: Gambler 2.00
❑70, Oct 1990; A: Deathstroke the Terminator 2.00
❑71, Nov 1990; V: Wildebeest; Titans reunion 2.00
❑72, Jan 1991; A: Deathstroke the Terminator. D: Golden Eagle; Wildebeest attacks Aqualad and Golden Eagle 2.00
❑73, Feb 1991; 1: Phantasm. A: Deathstroke the Terminator; V: Wildebeest; Phantasm joins Titans 2.00
❑74, Mar 1991; 1: Pantha. A: Deathstroke the Terminator; V: Wildebeest 2.00
❑75, Apr 1991; A: Deathstroke the Terminator. V: Wildebeest 2.00
❑76, Jun 1991; A: Deathstroke the Terminator. destruction of Titans Tower 2.00
❑77, Jul 1991; A: Deathstroke the Terminator. Cyborg rebuilt 2.00
❑78, Aug 1991; A: Deathstroke the Terminator. V: Wildebeest 2.00
❑79, Sep 1991; CS (a); A: Team Titans. A: Deathstroke the Terminator. V: Wildebeest; Team Titans arrive in modern era 2.00
❑80, Nov 1991; KGa (c); KGa (a); A: Team Titans. Backstory of Team Titans and Lord Chaos 1.75
❑81, Dec 1991 KGa (c); CS (a); A: Pariah 1.75
❑82, Jan 1992 ..... 1.75
❑83, Feb 1992; D: Jericho 2.25
❑84, Mar 1992; O: Phantasm. D: Raven. 2.25
❑85, Apr 1992; 1: baby Wildebeest. A: Team Titans 2.25
❑86, May 1992; CS (a); Nightwing vs. Terminator for leadership of Titans..... 1.75
❑87, Jun 1992 ..... 1.75
❑88, Jul 1992 ..... 1.75
❑89, Aug 1992 ..... 1.75
❑90, Sep 1992 ..... 1.75
❑91, Oct 1992 A: Phantasm 1.75
❑92, Nov 1992 ..... 1.75
❑93, Dec 1992; follow-up to Titans Sell-Out Special 1.75
❑94, Feb 1993; covers of #94-96 form triptych 1.75
❑95, Mar 1993; Covers of #94-96 form triptych 1.75
❑96, Apr 1993; Covers of #94-96 form triptych; Injured Cyborg used in Boris Yeltsin assassination attempt 1.75
❑97, May 1993 ..... 1.75
❑98, Jun 1993; Against all odds 1.75
❑99, Jul 1993; 1: Arsenal 1.75
❑100, Aug 1993; Giant-size; V: Evil Raven. pin-ups; foil cover; wedding of Starfire II (Koriand'r) 3.00
❑101, Sep 1993 ..... 1.75
❑102, Oct 1993 ..... 1.75
❑103, Nov 1993 ..... 1.75
❑104, Dec 1993; final fate of Cyborg 1.75
❑105, Dec 1993 ..... 1.75
❑106, Jan 1994 ..... 1.75
❑107, Jan 1994 ..... 1.75
❑108, Feb 1994 ..... 1.75
❑109, Mar 1994 ..... 1.75
❑110, May 1994 ..... 1.75
❑111, Jun 1994 ..... 1.75
❑112, Jul 1994 ..... 1.95
❑113, Aug 1994 ..... 1.95
❑114, Sep 1994; new team; Series continued in The New Titans #0 ..... 1.95
❑115, Nov 1994 ..... 1.95
❑116, Dec 1994; A: Green Lantern. A: Psimon. Return of Psimon 1.95
❑117, Jan 1995; V: Psimon 1.95
❑118, Feb 1995 A: Thunder and Lightning 1.95
❑119, Mar 1995; V: Deathwing; Story continues in Showcase '98 #2 ..... 1.95
❑120, Apr 1995 A: Supergirl 1.95
❑121, May 1995 ..... 1.95
❑122, Jun 1995 ..... 2.25
❑123, Jul 1995 ..... 2.25
❑124, Aug 1995 ..... 2.25
❑125, Sep 1995; Giant-size 3.50
❑126, Oct 1995 ..... 2.25
❑127, Nov 1995 ..... 2.25
❑128, Dec 1995 ..... 2.25
❑129, Jan 1996 ..... 2.25
❑130, Feb 1996; GP (c); Final Issue 2.25
❑Ann 5, ca. 1989; See New Teen Titans Ann for previous issues; Who's Who entries 3.50
❑Ann 6, ca. 1990; CS (a); 1: Society of Sin. A: Starfire; 1: Trinity; O: Starfire; V: Society of Sin; V: Blackfire 3.50
❑Ann 7, ca. 1991; O: Team Titans. 1: Team Titans 3.50
❑Ann 8, ca. 1992; CS (a); (1992, 3.50); Eclipso: The Darkness Within 3.00
❑Ann 9, ca. 1993; O: Anima. 1: Anima ... 3.00
❑Ann 10, ca. 1994; Elseworlds 3.00
❑Ann 11, ca. 1995; Year One 3.95

New Triumph Featuring Northguard
Matrix

❑1 ..... 1.75
❑1/2nd; 2nd printing 1.75
❑2, ca. 1985 ..... 1.50
❑3 ..... 1.50
❑4 ..... 1.50
❑5 ..... 1.50

New Two-Fisted Tales
E.C. / Dark Horse

❑1; HK (c); HK (w); HK, WE (a); Reprints from Two-Fisted Tales #25 ..... 5.50

Other grades: Multiply price above by 5/6 for VF/NM • 2/3 for VERY FINE • 1/3 for FINE • 1/5 for VERY GOOD • 1/8 for GOOD

Occult Files of Dr. Spektor

Supernatural researcher becomes horror host
©Gold Key

October Yen

Juvenile artwork sullies SF story
©Antarctic

Odd Adventure-Zine

Delightfully surreal black-and-white title
©Zamboni

Official Handbook of the Marvel Universe

First encyclopedic work from the publisher
©Marvel

Official Marvel Index to the X-Men

Marvel makes Olshevsky's index official
©Marvel

N-MINT

New Two-Fisted Tales
Dark Horse

❑1, Oct 1993; NN ... 4.95

newuniversal
Marvel

❑1, Dec 2006 ... 8.00
❑2, Mar 2007 ... 6.00
❑3, Apr 2007 ... 4.00

New Vampire Miyu
Ironcat

❑1, Sep 1997 ... 3.00
❑2, Oct 1997 ... 3.00
❑3, Nov 1997 ... 3.00
❑4, Dec 1997 ... 3.00
❑5, Jan 1998 ... 3.00
❑6, Feb 1998 ... 3.00

New Vampire Miyu
Ironcat

❑1, Apr 1998 ... 2.95
❑2, May 1998 ... 2.95
❑3, Jun 1998 ... 2.95
❑4, Jul 1998 ... 2.95
❑5, Aug 1998 ... 2.95
❑6, Sep 1998 ... 2.95

New Vampire Miyu
Ironcat

❑1, Oct 1998 ... 2.95
❑2, Nov 1998 ... 2.95
❑3, Dec 1998 ... 2.95
❑4, Jan 1999 ... 2.95
❑5, Feb 1999 ... 2.95
❑6, Mar 1999 ... 2.95
❑7, Apr 1999 ... 2.95

New Vampire Miyu
Ironcat

❑1, May 1999 ... 2.95
❑2, Jun 1999 ... 2.95
❑3, Jul 1999 ... 2.95
❑4, Aug 1999 ... 2.95
❑5, Sep 1999 ... 2.95
❑6, Oct 1999 ... 2.95

New Warriors
Marvel

❑1, Jul 1990; O: New Warriors ... 1.50
❑1/2nd, Jul 1990; O: New Warriors. 2nd Printing (gold) ... 1.00
❑2, Aug 1990; O: Night Thrasher. 1&O: Silhouette ... 1.25
❑3, Sep 1990 ... 1.25
❑4, Oct 1990 ... 1.25
❑5, Nov 1990 ... 1.25
❑6, Dec 1990; Inhumans app ... 1.25
❑7, Jan 1991; A: Punisher. Punisher cameo ... 1.25
❑8, Feb 1991; O: Bengal. A: Punisher ... 1.25
❑9, Mar 1991 A: Punisher ... 1.25
❑10, Apr 1991 ... 1.25
❑11, May 1991; A: Wolverine. Wolverine ... 1.25
❑12, Jun 1991 ... 1.25
❑13, Jul 1991 ... 1.25
❑14, Aug 1991 A: Namor. A: Darkhawk ... 1.25
❑15, Sep 1991 ... 1.25
❑16, Oct 1991 ... 1.25
❑17, Nov 1991 A: Fantastic Four ... 1.25

N-MINT

❑18, Dec 1991 ... 1.25
❑19, Jan 1992 ... 1.25
❑20, Feb 1992 ... 1.25
❑21, Mar 1992 ... 1.25
❑22, Apr 1992 ... 1.25
❑23, May 1992; O: Night Thrasher. O: Silhouette. O: Chord ... 1.25
❑24, Jun 1992; O: Silhouette. O: Chord ... 1.25
❑25, Jul 1992; O: Chord. Die-cut cover ... 2.50
❑26, Aug 1992 ... 1.25
❑27, Sep 1992; Infinity War Crossover ... 1.25
❑28, Oct 1992; 1: Cardinal. 1: Turbo I (Michiko "Mickey" Musashi) ... 1.25
❑29, Nov 1992 ... 1.25
❑30, Dec 1992 ... 1.25
❑31, Jan 1993 ... 1.25
❑32, Feb 1993 ... 1.25
❑33, Mar 1993; 1: Turbo II (Mike Jeffries) ... 1.25
❑34, Apr 1993 ... 1.25
❑35, May 1993 ... 1.25
❑36, Jun 1993 ... 1.25
❑37, Jul 1993 ... 1.25
❑38, Aug 1993 ... 1.25
❑39, Sep 1993 ... 1.25
❑40, Oct 1993; A: Nova. A: Air-Walker. A: Super Nova. A: Firelord. Air-Walker appearnce ... 1.25
❑40/Variant, Oct 1993; A: Nova. A: Air-Walker. A: Super Nova. A: Firelord. Gold foil on cover ... 2.25
❑41, Nov 1993 ... 1.25
❑42, Dec 1993 ... 1.25
❑43, Jan 1994 ... 1.25
❑44, Feb 1994; Photo cover ... 1.25
❑45, Mar 1994; V: Gamemaster; V: Shinobi Shaw ... 1.25
❑46, Apr 1994 ... 1.25
❑47, May 1994; With Masterprint Cards ... 1.25
❑48, Jun 1994 ... 1.50
❑49, Jul 1994 ... 1.50
❑50, Aug 1994; Giant-size ... 2.00
❑50/Variant, Aug 1994; Giant-size; Glow-in-the-dark cover ... 2.95
❑51, Sep 1994 ... 1.50
❑52, Oct 1994 ... 1.50
❑53, Nov 1994 ... 1.50
❑54, Dec 1994 ... 1.50
❑55, Jan 1995 ... 1.50
❑56, Feb 1995 ... 1.50
❑57, Mar 1995 ... 1.50
❑58, Apr 1995 ... 1.50
❑59, May 1995 ... 1.50
❑60, Jun 1995; Giant-size ... 2.50
❑61, Jul 1995; Maximum Clonage Prologue ... 1.50
❑62, Aug 1995 A: Scarlet Spider ... 1.50
❑63, Sep 1995 ... 1.50
❑64, Oct 1995; A: Night Thrasher. A: Rage. Return of Night Thrasher and Rage ... 1.50
❑65, Nov 1995; A: Namorita. Return of Namorita ... 1.50
❑66, Dec 1995 A: Scarlet Spider. A: Speedball ... 1.50
❑67, Jan 1996; concludes in Web of Scarlet Spider #3 ... 1.50
❑68, Feb 1996 A: Guardians of the Galaxy ... 1.50
❑69, Mar 1996; D: Speedball ... 1.50
❑70, Apr 1996 ... 1.50

N-MINT

❑71, May 1996 ... 1.50
❑72, Jun 1996 A: Avengers ... 1.50
❑73, Jul 1996 ... 1.50
❑74, Aug 1996 ... 1.50
❑75, Sep 1996; Final Issue ... 1.50
❑Ann 1, ca. 1991; O: Night Thrasher ... 2.50
❑Ann 2, ca. 1992 ... 2.25
❑Ann 3, ca. 1993; Includes trading card; 1993 annual; ca. 1993 ... 2.95
❑Ann 4, ca. 1994 ... 2.95
❑Ashcan 1; "Ashcan" mini-comic ... 0.75

New Warriors
Marvel

❑1, Jul 2005 ... 4.00
❑2, Aug 2005 ... 2.99
❑3, Sep 2005 ... 2.99
❑4 2005 ... 2.99
❑5, Jan 2006 ... 2.99
❑6, Feb 2006 ... 2.99

New Warriors
Marvel

❑1, Oct 1999 ... 2.99
❑2, Nov 1999 ... 2.50
❑3, Dec 1999 ... 2.50
❑4, Jan 2000 ... 2.50
❑5, Feb 2000 ... 2.50
❑6, Mar 2000 ... 2.50
❑7, Apr 2000 ... 2.50
❑8, May 2000 ... 2.50
❑9, Jun 2000 ... 2.50
❑10, Jul 2000 ... 2.50

New Wave
Eclipse

❑1, Jun 1986 ... 2.00
❑1/A, misprint ... 2.00
❑2, Jul 1986 ... 1.50
❑3, Jul 1986 ... 1.50
❑4, Aug 1986 ... 1.00
❑5, Aug 1986, PG (c) ... 1.00
❑6, Sep 1986 ... 1.00
❑7, Sep 1986 ... 1.00
❑8, Sep 1986 ... 1.00
❑9, Oct 1986 ... 1.50
❑10, Nov 1986 ... 1.50
❑11, Dec 1986 ... 1.50
❑12, Feb 1987 ... 1.50
❑13, Mar 1987; Final Issue ... 1.50

New Wave V: The Volunteers
Eclipse

❑1, Apr 1987 ... 2.50
❑2, Jun 1987 ... 2.50

New World Order
Blazer

❑1, Nov 1992, b&w ... 3.00
❑2, b&w ... 2.75
❑3, b&w ... 2.75
❑4, Aug 1993, b&w ... 2.50
❑5, Jan 1994, b&w ... 2.50
❑6, May 1994, b&w; 1: Skinhead ... 2.50
❑7, Aug 1994, b&w; 1: Shining ... 2.50
❑8, Feb 1995, b&w ... 2.50

New World Order
Pig's Eye

❑1 ... 1.00

Other grades: Multiply price above by 5/6 for VF/NM • 2/3 for VERY FINE • 1/3 for FINE • 1/5 for VERY GOOD • 1/8 for GOOD

New Worlds Anthology
Caliber

- ❑1, ca. 1996, b&w 2.95
- ❑2, Jan 1996 3.95
- ❑3 3.95
- ❑4 3.95
- ❑5; ca, 1996; b&w 3.95
- ❑6 3.95

New X-Men (Academy X)
Marvel

- ❑1, Jul 2004; Cover says New X-Men: Academy X; indicia says New X-Men 4.00
- ❑2, Aug 2004 2.99
- ❑3, Sep 2004 2.99
- ❑4, Oct 2004 2.99
- ❑5, Nov 2004 2.99
- ❑6, Dec 2004 2.99
- ❑7, Jan 2005 2.99
- ❑8, Feb 2005 2.99
- ❑9, Mar 2005 2.99
- ❑10, Apr 2005 2.99
- ❑11, May 2005 2.99
- ❑12, May 2005 2.99
- ❑13, Jun 2005 2.99
- ❑14, Jul 2005 2.99
- ❑15, Aug 2005 2.99
- ❑16, Sep 2005 6.00
- ❑16/Variant, Sep 2005; 2nd print 4.00
- ❑17, Oct 2005 2.99
- ❑18, Nov 2005 2.99
- ❑19, Dec 2005 2.99
- ❑20, Jan 2006 2.99
- ❑21, Feb 2006 2.99
- ❑22, Mar 2006 2.99
- ❑23, May 2006 2.99
- ❑24, May 2006 2.99
- ❑25, Jun 2006 2.99
- ❑26, Jul 2006 2.99
- ❑27, Aug 2006 2.99
- ❑28, Sep 2006 2.99
- ❑29, Oct 2006 2.99
- ❑30, Nov 2006 2.99
- ❑31, Dec 2006 2.99
- ❑32, Jan 2007 2.99
- ❑33, Feb 2007 2.99
- ❑34, Mar 2007 2.99
- ❑35, Apr 2007 2.99
- ❑36, May 2007 2.99
- ❑37, Jun 2007 2.99
- ❑38, Jul 2007 2.99
- ❑39, Aug 2007 2.99
- ❑40, Sep 2007 2.99
- ❑41, Oct 2007 2.99
- ❑42, Nov 2007 2.99
- ❑43, Dec 2007 2.99
- ❑44, Jan 2008 2.99
- ❑45, Feb 2008 2.99
- ❑46, Mar 2008 2.99

New X-Men: Academy X Yearbook Special
Marvel

- ❑1, Dec 2005 3.99

New X-Men: Hellions
Marvel

- ❑1, Jul 2005 4.00
- ❑2, Aug 2005 2.99
- ❑3, Sep 2005 2.99
- ❑4, Oct 2005 2.99

New York City Outlaws
Outlaw

- ❑1, Feb 1984 2.00
- ❑2 2.00
- ❑3 2.00
- ❑4; ca. 1986; Astroman story; b&w 2.00

New York: Year Zero
Eclipse

- ❑1, Aug 1988 2.00
- ❑2, Aug 1988 2.00
- ❑3, Sep 1988 2.00
- ❑4, Oct 1988 2.00

Next
DC

- ❑1, Sep 2006 2.99
- ❑2, Oct 2006 2.99
- ❑3, Nov 2006 2.99
- ❑4, Dec 2006 2.99
- ❑5, Jan 2007 2.99
- ❑6, Feb 2007 2.99

Next Man
Comico

- ❑1, Mar 1985, 1&O: Next Man 2.00
- ❑2, Apr 1985 2.00
- ❑3, Jun 1985 2.00
- ❑4, Aug 1985 2.00
- ❑5, Oct 1985 2.00

Next Men
Dark Horse

- ❑0, Feb 1992; JBy (c); JBy (w); JBy (a); Reprints Next Men stories from Dark Horse Presents 3.00
- ❑1, Jan 1992; JBy (c); JBy (w); JBy (a); Embossed cover (silver logo) 3.00
- ❑1/2nd, Jan 1992; JBy (c); JBy (w); JBy (a); Embossed cover (gold logo) 2.50
- ❑2, Mar 1992; JBy (c); JBy (w); JBy (a); 1: Sathanus; Includes "Stock Certificate" 3.00
- ❑3, Apr 1992; JBy (c); JBy (w); JBy (a); Includes "Stock Certificate" 2.50
- ❑4, May 1992; JBy (c); JBy (w); JBy (a); Includes "Stock Certificate" 2.50
- ❑5, Jun 1992; JBy (c); JBy (w); JBy (a); Includes "Stock Certificate" 2.50
- ❑6, Jul 1992; JBy (c); JBy (w); JBy (a); Includes "Stock Certificate" 2.50
- ❑7, Sep 1992; JBy (c); JBy (w); JBy (a); 1: M4. flipbook with M4 #1 back-up story 2.50
- ❑8, Oct 1992; JBy (c); JBy (w); JBy (a); flipbook with M4 #2 back-up story 2.50
- ❑9, Nov 1992; JBy (c); JBy (w); JBy (a); flipbook with M4 #3 back-up story 2.50
- ❑10, Dec 1992; JBy (c); JBy (w); JBy (a); flipbook with M4 #4 back-up story 2.50
- ❑11, Jan 1993; JBy (c); JBy (w); JBy (a); M4 back-up story 2.50
- ❑12, Feb 1993; JBy (c); JBy (w); JBy (a); M4 back-up story 2.50
- ❑13, Mar 1993; JBy (c); JBy (w); JBy (a); M4 back-up story 2.50
- ❑14, Apr 1993; JBy (c); JBy (w); JBy (a); M4 back-up story 2.50
- ❑15, Jun 1993; JBy (c); JBy (w); JBy (a); M4 back-up story 3.00
- ❑16, Jul 1993; JBy (c); JBy (w); JBy (a); M4 back-up story 2.50
- ❑17, Aug 1993; FM (c); JBy (w); JBy (a); M4 back-up story 2.50
- ❑18, Sep 1993; JBy (c); JBy (w); JBy (a); M4 back-up story 2.50
- ❑19, Oct 1993; JBy (c); JBy (w); JBy (a); M4 back-up story 2.50
- ❑20, Nov 1993; JBy (w); JBy (a); M4 back-up story 2.50
- ❑21, Dec 1993; JBy (w); JBy (a); A: Hellboy. M4 back-up story 30.00
- ❑22, Jan 1994; JBy (c); JBy (w); JBy (a); M4 back-up story 2.50
- ❑23, Mar 1994; JBy (w); JBy (a); M4 back-up story 2.50
- ❑24, Apr 1994; JBy (w); JBy (a); M4 back-up story 2.50
- ❑25, May 1994 JBy (w); JBy (a); A: Cutter and Skywise (Elfquest characters). 2.50
- ❑26, Jun 1994 JBy (w); JBy (a) 2.50
- ❑27, Aug 1994 JBy (w); JBy (a) 2.50
- ❑28, Sep 1994 JBy (w); JBy (a) 2.50
- ❑29, Oct 1994 JBy (w); JBy (a) 2.50
- ❑30, Dec 1994; JBy (w); JBy (a); series goes on hiatus 2.50

Next Nexus
First

- ❑1, Jan 1989 SR (c); SR (a) 2.00
- ❑2, Feb 1989 SR (a) 2.00
- ❑3, Mar 1989 SR (a) 2.00
- ❑4, Apr 1989 SR (a) 2.00

Next Wave
Overstreet

- ❑1; Sampling of Five Self-Published comics 2.00

Nextwave
Marvel

- ❑1, Mar 2006 2.99
- ❑2, May 2006 2.99
- ❑3, Jun 2006 2.99
- ❑4, Jun 2006 2.99
- ❑5, Aug 2006 2.99
- ❑6, Sep 2006 2.99
- ❑7, Oct 2006, V: Mindless Ones 2.99
- ❑8, Nov 2006 2.99
- ❑9, Jan 2007 2.99
- ❑10, Feb 2007, V: Forbushman 2.99
- ❑11, Mar 2007 2.99

Nexus
Capital

- ❑1, Jan 1981, b&w; PG (c); SR (a); 1: Nexus; b&w 15.00
- ❑2, Jun 1982; PG (c); SR (a); O: Nexus 10.00
- ❑3, Oct 1982; SR (c); SR (a); O: Nexus; Includes record 15.00

Nexus
First

- ❑1 1983, SR (a); Nexus begins for first time in color 5.00
- ❑2, SR (a); O: Nexus; ca. 1983 4.00
- ❑3, SR (a); ca. 1983 2.50
- ❑4, Nov 1983, SR (a) 2.50
- ❑5, Jan 1983, SR (a) 2.50
- ❑6, Mar 1984, SR (a) 2.00
- ❑7, Apr 1985, SR (a); First Comics begins publishing 2.00
- ❑8, May 1985, SR (c); SR (a) 2.00
- ❑9, SR (a) 1.50
- ❑10, Jul 1985, SR (a) 1.75
- ❑11, Aug 1985, SR (a) 1.75
- ❑12, Sep 1985, SR (a) 1.75
- ❑13, Oct 1985, SR (c); SR (a) 1.75
- ❑14, Nov 1985, SR (c); SR (a) 1.75
- ❑15, Dec 1985, SR (c); SR (a) 1.75
- ❑16, Jan 1986, SR (c); SR (a) 1.75
- ❑17, Feb 1986, ES (a); Spotlight on Judah the Hammer 1.75
- ❑18, Mar 1986, SR (c); SR (a) 1.75
- ❑19, Apr 1986, SR (c); SR (a) 1.75
- ❑20, May 1986, SR (a) 1.75
- ❑21, Jun 1986 1.75
- ❑22, Jul 1986 1.75
- ❑23, Aug 1986 1.75
- ❑24, Sep 1986 1.75
- ❑25, Oct 1986 1.75
- ❑26, Nov 1986 1.75
- ❑27, Dec 1986, Clonezone story 1.75
- ❑28, Jan 1987, Judah the Hammer Backup Story 1.75
- ❑29, Feb 1987 1.75
- ❑30, Mar 1987, Judah story 1.75
- ❑31, Apr 1987, Judah The Hammer 1.75
- ❑32, May 1987, Judah The Hammer 1.75
- ❑33, Jun 1987, Judah The Hammer 1.75
- ❑34, Jul 1987, Judah The Hammer 1.75
- ❑35, Aug 1987, Judah The Hammer 1.75
- ❑36, Sep 1987, Judah The Hammer 1.75
- ❑37, Oct 1987 1.75
- ❑38, Nov 1987, Judah The Hammer 1.75
- ❑39, Dec 1987, Judah The Hammer 1.75
- ❑40, Jan 1988, SR (c); SR (a); Judah The Hammer 1.75
- ❑41, Feb 1988 1.75
- ❑42, Mar 1988 1.75
- ❑43, Apr 1988, PS (c); PS, SR (a) 1.75
- ❑44, May 1988 1.75
- ❑45, Jun 1988, A: Badger 1.75
- ❑46, Jul 1988, A: Badger 1.75
- ❑47, Aug 1988, A: Badger 1.75
- ❑48, Sep 1988, A: Badger 1.75
- ❑49, Oct 1988, A: Badger 1.75
- ❑50, Nov 1988, A: Badger. Crossroads 4.00
- ❑51, Dec 1988 1.95
- ❑52, Jan 1989 1.95
- ❑53, Feb 1989 1.95
- ❑54, Mar 1989 1.95
- ❑55, Apr 1989 1.95
- ❑56, May 1989, Judah The Hammer 1.95
- ❑57, Jun 1989, Judah The Hammer 1.95
- ❑58, Jul 1989, Judah The Hammer 1.95
- ❑59, Aug 1989 1.95
- ❑60, Sep 1989, Judah The Hammer 1.95
- ❑61, Oct 1989, Judah The Hammer 1.95
- ❑62, Nov 1989, Judah The Hammer 1.95
- ❑63, Dec 1989, Judah The Hammer 1.95
- ❑64, Jan 1990, Judah The Hammer 1.95
- ❑65, Feb 1990 1.95
- ❑66, Mar 1990, Judah The Hammer 1.95

Official Secret Agent	Offworld	Of Myths and Men	O.G. Whiz	Ohm's Law

Reprinting strips about G-Man Phil Corrigan	Science fiction anthology folded after one ish	The lighter side of magic and super-heroics	Boy owns his own toy company	"Mega-humans" brought back to life
©Pioneer	©Graphic Image	©Blackthorne	©Gold Key	©Imperial

	N-MINT
❑67, Apr 1990, Judah The Hammer	1.95
❑68, May 1990, Judah The Hammer	1.95
❑69, Jun 1990, Judah The Hammer	1.95
❑70, Jul 1990, Judah The Hammer	1.95
❑71, Aug 1990	1.95
❑72, Sep 1990, Judah The Hammer	1.95
❑73, Oct 1990, Judah The Hammer	2.25
❑74, Nov 1990, Judah The Hammer	2.25
❑75, Dec 1990	2.25
❑76, Jan 1991	2.25
❑77, Feb 1991	2.25
❑78, Mar 1991	2.25
❑79, Apr 1991	2.25
❑80, May 1991, Final issue of First series	2.25
❑81, Number not noted in indicia (was retroactive)	3.95
❑82, Number not noted in indicia (was retroactive)	3.95
❑83, Number not noted in indicia (was retroactive)	3.95
❑84, Number not noted in indicia (was retroactive)	3.95
❑85, Number not noted in indicia (was retroactive)	2.95
❑86, Number not noted in indicia (was retroactive)	2.95
❑87, Number not noted in indicia (was retroactive)	2.95
❑88, Number not noted in indicia (was retroactive)	2.95
❑89, Jun 1996, SR (a)	2.95
❑90, Jul 1996, SR (a)	2.95
❑91, Aug 1996, SR (a)	2.95
❑92, Sep 1996, SR (a)	2.95
❑93, Apr 1997, SR (a)	2.95
❑94, May 1997, SR (a)	2.95
❑95, Jul 1997, b&w; SR (c); SR (a)	2.95
❑96, Aug 1997, b&w; SR (a)	2.95
❑97, Sep 1997, b&w; SR (a)	2.95
❑98, Oct 1997, b&w; SR (a)	2.95

Nexus: Alien Justice
Dark Horse

❑1, Dec 1992; Retroactively numbered Nexus (Vol. 2) #82	3.95
❑2, Jan 1993; Retroactively numbered Nexus (Vol. 2) #83	3.95
❑3, Feb 1993; Retroactively numbered Nexus (Vol. 2) #84	3.95

Nexus Legends
First

❑1, May 1989, SR (a); Reprints Nexus (Vol. 2) #1 with new cover	2.50
❑2, Jun 1989, SR (a); Reprints Nexus (Vol. 2) #2 with new cover	2.00
❑3, Jul 1989, SR (a); Reprints Nexus (Vol. 2) #3 with new cover	2.00
❑4, Aug 1989, SR (a); Reprints	2.00
❑5, Sep 1989, SR (a); Reprints	2.00
❑6, Oct 1989, SR (a); Reprints	2.00
❑7, Nov 1989, SR (a); Reprints	2.00
❑8, Dec 1989, SR (a); Reprints	2.00
❑9, Jan 1990, SR (a); Reprints	2.00
❑10, Feb 1990, SR (a); Reprints	2.00
❑11, Mar 1990, SR (a); Reprints	2.00
❑12, Apr 1990, SR (a); Reprints	2.00
❑13, May 1990, SR (a); Reprints	2.00
❑14, Jun 1990, SR (a); Reprints	2.00
❑15, Jul 1990, SR (a); Reprints	2.00
❑16, Aug 1990, SR (a); Reprints	2.00
❑17, Sep 1990, SR (a); Reprints	2.00
❑18, Oct 1990, SR (a); Reprints	2.00
❑19, Nov 1990, SR (a); Reprints	2.00
❑20, Dec 1990, SR (a); Reprints	2.00
❑21, Jan 1991, SR (a); Reprints	2.00
❑22, Feb 1991, SR (a); Reprints	2.00
❑23, Mar 1991, SR (a); Final Issue	2.00

Nexus Meets Madman
Dark Horse

❑1, May 1996; NN; One-shot	2.95

Nexus the Liberator
Dark Horse

❑1, Aug 1992	2.50
❑2, Sep 1992	2.50
❑3, Oct 1992	2.50
❑4, Nov 1992	2.50

Nexus: The Origin
Dark Horse

❑1, ca. 1995; O: Nexus; This issue was retroactively numbered in the Nexus continuity as Nexus (Vol. 2) #81	3.95

Nexus: The Wages of Sin
Dark Horse

❑1, Mar 1995; cardstock cover	2.95
❑2, Apr 1995; cardstock cover	2.95
❑3, May 1995; cardstock cover	2.95
❑4, Jun 1995; Retroactively numbered Nexus (Vol. 2) #88	2.95

NFL Superpro
Marvel

❑1, Oct 1991; O: NFL SuperPro	1.00
❑2, Nov 1991	1.00
❑3, Dec 1991	1.00
❑4, Jan 1992	1.00
❑5, Feb 1992	1.00
❑6, Mar 1992	1.00
❑7, Apr 1992	1.00
❑8, May 1992; Captain America	1.00
❑9, Jun 1992	1.00
❑10, Jul 1992	1.00
❑11, Aug 1992	1.00
❑12, Sep 1992; Final Issue	1.00
❑Special 1, Sep 1991; Special collector's edition; Says "Special Edition" on cover	2.00
❑Special 1/Prest, Sep 1991; Says "Super Bowl Special" on cover; prestige format	3.95

Nick Fury, Agent of SHIELD
Marvel

❑1, Jun 1968, JSo (c); JSo (w); JSo (a); 1: Scorpio	75.00
❑2, Jul 1968, JSo (c); JSo (w); JSo (a); 1&O: Centuriu	40.00
❑3, Aug 1968, JSo (c); JSo (w); JSo (a)	40.00
❑4, Sep 1968, O: Nick Fury. S.H.I.E.L.D. origin issue	40.00
❑5, Oct 1968, JSo (c); JSo (w); JSo (a); Don McGregor L.O.C	40.00
❑6, Nov 1968, JSo (c); JSo, FS (a)	30.00
❑7, Dec 1968	30.00
❑8, Jan 1969, FS (c); HT, FS (a); D: Supremus. 1: Supremus	30.00
❑9, Feb 1969, FS (c); FS (a); 2: Hate-Monger	25.00
❑10, Mar 1969	25.00
❑11, Apr 1969, D: Hate-Monger; Don McGregor L.O.C	25.00
❑12, May 1969, 1: Robert Rickard; D: Robert Rickard; Don McGregor L.O.C	25.00
❑13, Jul 1969, HT (c); HT (a); 1: Super-Patriot; Don McGregor L.O.C	25.00
❑14, Aug 1969, HT (c); HT (a); Don McGregor L.O.C	20.00
❑15, Nov 1969, 1: Bullseye	50.00
❑16, Nov 1969; Giant-size; JK, SL (w); JK (a); Reprints from Strange Tales #136-138	20.00
❑17, Jan 1971; Giant-size; Reprints from Strange Tales #139-141	20.00
❑18, Mar 1971; Giant-size; Reprints from Strange Tales #142-144	20.00

Nick Fury, Agent of SHIELD
Marvel

❑1, Dec 1983; BH, JSo (c); JSo, SL (w); BH, JSo (a); Reprints from Nick Fury, Agent of SHIELD (1st series); wraparound cover	3.00
❑2, Jan 1984; Reprints from Nick Fury, Agent of SHIELD (1st series)	3.00

Nick Fury, Agent of S.H.I.E.L.D.
Marvel

❑1, Sep 1989 BH (c); BH (a)	2.25
❑2, Oct 1989; KP (c); KP (a); Death's Head	1.75
❑3, Nov 1989; KP (c); KP (a); Death's Head	1.75
❑4, Nov 1989; KP (c); KP (a); Sgt. Fury	1.50
❑5, Dec 1989 KP (c); KP (a)	1.50
❑6, Dec 1989 KP (c); KP (a)	1.50
❑7, Jan 1990 KP (c); KP (a)	1.50
❑8, Feb 1990	1.50
❑9, Mar 1990 KP (c); KP (a)	1.50
❑10, Apr 1990 KP (c); KP (a); A: Captain America	1.50
❑11, May 1990	1.50
❑12, Jun 1990	1.50
❑13, Jul 1990; KP (c); KP (a); Return of Yellow Claw	1.50
❑14, Aug 1990 KP (c); KP (a)	1.50
❑15, Sep 1990 KP (c); A: Fantastic Four	1.50
❑16, Oct 1990	1.50
❑17, Nov 1990 KP (c); HT (a)	1.50
❑18, Dec 1990	1.50
❑19, Jan 1991 HT (a)	1.50
❑20, Feb 1991	1.50
❑21, Mar 1991; BG (a); Baron Strucker revived	1.50
❑22, Apr 1991 BG (a)	1.50
❑23, May 1991 BG (a)	1.50
❑24, Jun 1991 A: Fantastic Four. A: Captain America	1.50
❑25, Jul 1991 BG (a)	1.50
❑26, Aug 1991 BG (a); A: Fantastic Four. A: Avengers	1.50
❑27, Sep 1991 A: Wolverine	2.00
❑28, Oct 1991 A: Wolverine	2.00
❑29, Nov 1991 A: Wolverine	2.00
❑30, Dec 1991 A: Deathlok	1.50
❑31, Jan 1992 A: Deathlok	1.50
❑32, Feb 1992 A: Weapon Omega	1.75
❑33, Mar 1992; 1: new agents (Psi-Borg, Violence, Knockabout, Ivory)	1.75

Other grades: Multiply price above by 5/6 for VF/NM • 2/3 for VERY FINE • 1/3 for FINE • 1/5 for VERY GOOD • 1/8 for GOOD

❑34, Apr 1992; V: Hydra. V: Baron Strucker 1.75
❑35, May 1992 1.75
❑36, Jun 1992; O: Constrictor. A: Cage. V: Constrictor 1.75
❑37, Jul 1992 1.75
❑38, Aug 1992 1.75
❑39, Sep 1992 1.75
❑40, Oct 1992 1.75
❑41, Nov 1992 1.75
❑42, Dec 1992 1.75
❑43, Jan 1993 1.75
❑44, Feb 1993 1.75
❑45, Mar 1993 1.75
❑46, Apr 1993 1.75
❑47, May 1993; D: Kate Neville (Nick Fury's Girlfriend); Final Issue 1.75

Nick Fury's Howling Commandos
Marvel

❑1, Dec 2005, b&w 2.99
❑1/DirCut, Jan 2006 3.99
❑2, Jan 2006 2.99
❑3, Feb 2006 2.99
❑4, Mar 2006 2.99
❑5, May 2006 2.99
❑6, Jun 2006 2.99

Nick Fury vs. S.H.I.E.L.D.
Marvel

❑1, Jun 1988 JSo (c) 4.00
❑2, Jul 1988 BSz (c) 3.50
❑3, Mar 1988 3.50
❑4, Sep 1988 3.50
❑5, Oct 1988 3.50
❑6, Nov 1988 3.50

Nick Hazard
Harrier

❑1, Jan 1988 1.95

Nicki Shadow
Relentless

❑0, Jul 1997 1.00
❑1, Nov 1997 2.50

Nick Noyz and the Nuisance Tour Book
Red Bullet

❑1, b&w 2.50

Nick Ryan the Skull
Antarctic

❑1, Dec 1994, b&w 2.75
❑2, Jan 1995, b&w; El Gato Negro back-up feature 2.75
❑3, Feb 1995, b&w; The Skull's Pal, Jake story 2.75

Night
Slave Labor / Amaze Ink

❑0, Nov 1995 1.50

Nightbird
Harrier

❑1, May 1988, b&w 1.95
❑2 1988, b&w 1.95

Night Breed
Marvel / Epic

❑1, Apr 1990 3.00
❑2, May 1990 2.50
❑3, Jun 1990 2.50
❑4, Jul 1990 2.50
❑5, Sep 1990 2.50
❑6, Nov 1990 2.50
❑7, Jan 1991 2.50
❑8, Mar 1991 2.50
❑9, May 1991 2.50
❑10, Jul 1991 2.50
❑11, Sep 1991 2.25
❑12, Nov 1991 2.25
❑13, Jan 1992, Rawhead Rex 2.25
❑14, Mar 1992, Rawhead Rex 2.25
❑15, May 1992, Rawhead Rex 2.25
❑16, Jun 1992, Rawhead Rex 2.25
❑17, Jul 1992 2.25
❑18, Aug 1992 2.25
❑19, Sep 1992 2.25
❑20, Oct 1992 2.50
❑21, Nov 1992 2.50
❑22, Dec 1992 2.50
❑23, Jan 1993 2.50
❑24, Feb 1993 2.50
❑25, Mar 1993, Final Issue 2.50

Night Brigade
Wonder Comix

❑1, Aug 1987, b&w 1.95

Nightcat
Marvel

❑1, Apr 1991; O: Nightcat 3.95

Night City
Thorby

❑1 2.95

Night Club
Image

❑1, ca. 2005 2.95
❑2, Jan 2006 2.99
❑3, May 2006 2.99
❑4, Jan 2007 2.99

Nightcrawler
Marvel

❑1, Nov 1985 DC (c); DC (w); DC (a) 2.00
❑2, Dec 1985 DC (c); DC (w); DC (a) 2.00
❑3, Jan 1986 DC (c); DC (w); DC (a) 2.00
❑4, Feb 1986 DC (c); DC (w); DC (a) 2.00

Nightcrawler
Marvel

❑1, Jan 2002 2.50
❑2, Feb 2002 2.50
❑3, Mar 2002 2.50
❑4, Apr 2002 2.50

Nightcrawler
Marvel

❑1, Nov 2004 2.99
❑2, Dec 2004 2.99
❑3, Jan 2005 2.99
❑4, Feb 2005 2.99
❑5, Apr 2005 2.99
❑6 2005 2.99
❑7, Aug 2005 2.99
❑8, Sep 2005 2.99
❑9, Oct 2005 2.99
❑10, Nov 2005; Preview of Nick Fury's Howling Commandos 2.99
❑11, Jan 2006 2.99
❑12, Jan 2006 2.99

Nightcry
CFD

❑1, b&w; cardstock cover 3.00
❑2, b&w; cardstock cover 3.00
❑3, b&w; cardstock cover 3.00
❑4, b&w; cardstock cover 3.00
❑5, May 1995, b&w; cardstock cover 3.00
❑6, May 1996, b&w; cardstock cover 3.00

Nightfall: The Black Chronicles
Homage

❑1, Dec 1999 2.95
❑2, Jan 2000 2.95
❑3, Feb 2000 2.95

Night Fisher
Fantagraphics

❑1, Nov 2005 12.95

Night Force
DC

❑1, Aug 1982, GC (c); GC (a); 1: Night Force 2.50
❑2, Sep 1982, GC (c); GC (a) 1.50
❑3, Oct 1982, GC (c); GC (a) 1.50
❑4, Nov 1982, GC (c); GC (a) 1.50
❑5, Dec 1982, GC (c); GC (a) 1.50
❑6, Jan 1983, GC (c); GC (a) 1.50
❑7, Feb 1983, GC (c); GC (a) 1.50
❑8, Mar 1983, GC (c); GC (a) 1.50
❑9, Apr 1983, GC (c); GC (a) 1.50
❑10, May 1983, GC (c); GC (a) 1.50
❑11, Jun 1983, GC (c); GC (a) 1.50
❑12, Jul 1983, GC (c); GC (a) 1.50
❑13, Aug 1983, GC (c); GC (a) 1.50
❑14, Sep 1983, GC (c); GC (a); Final Issue 1.50

Night Force
DC

❑1, Dec 1996, BA (c); BA (a) 2.50
❑2, Jan 1997, BA (c); BA (a) 2.25
❑3, Feb 1997, BA (a) 2.25
❑4, Mar 1997 2.25
❑5, Apr 1997 2.25
❑6, May 1997 2.25
❑7, Jun 1997 2.25
❑8, Jul 1997, continues in Challengers of the Unknown #6 2.25
❑9, Aug 1997 2.25
❑10, Sep 1997 2.25
❑11, Oct 1997 2.25
❑12, Nov 1997, Final Issue 2.50

Night Glider
Topps

❑1, Apr 1993; 1: Night Glider; Coupon for Secret City Saga #1; Includes trading card 2.95

Nighthawk
Marvel

❑1, Sep 1998; gatefold summary 2.99
❑2, Oct 1998; gatefold summary; V: Mephisto 2.50
❑3, Nov 1998; gatefold summary; V: Mephisto 2.50

Night in a Moorish Harem, A
NBM

❑1; ca. 1996; Adult 11.95
❑2; ca. 1997; Adult 10.95

Nightjar
Avatar

❑1, Mar 2004 3.00
❑1/Platinum 10.00
❑1/Wraparound 3.00
❑1/Tarot, Jun 2005; 1,250 copies printed. Tarot cover "Princess of Swords" fits with Hypothetical Lizard #1 Tarot cover 3.99
❑2 3.00
❑2/Platinum 10.00
❑2/Wraparound 4.00
❑3 3.00
❑3/Platinum 10.00
❑3/Wraparound 4.00
❑4 4.00
❑4/Tarot 5.00

Nightjar: Hollow Bones
Avatar

❑1, Jul 2004; Wrap around cover 4.00
❑1/Platinum 2004 10.00
❑1/Wraparound 2004 4.00

Night Life
Strawberry Jam

❑1, b&w; ca. 1986 1.50
❑2, b&w; ca. 1986 1.50
❑3, Feb 1987, b&w 1.50
❑4, Mar 1987, b&w 1.50
❑5, Apr 1987, b&w 1.50
❑6, May 1987, b&w 1.50
❑7, Mar 1988, b&w 1.50
❑8, Nov 1991, b&w; Published by Caliber Press 2.50

Nightlinger
Gauntlet

❑1, b&w 2.95
❑2, b&w 2.95

Nightly News
Image

❑1, Dec 2006 2.99
❑2, Jan 2007 2.99

Night Man
Malibu / Ultraverse

❑1, Oct 1993; ME (w); SA (a); 1&O: The Night Man. 1: Death Mask; Rune story; Flipbook 2.50
❑1/Ltd., Oct 1993; Ultra-limited edition; ME (w); SA (a); 1&O: The Night Man. 1: Death Mask; Ultra-limited edition of 5000; Rune Story; Mangor story; Flipbook 25.00
❑2, Nov 1993; 1: Mangle; Story continues in Freex #6 2.00
❑3, Dec 1993 A: Freex 2.00
❑4, Jan 1994; JRo (w); HC (a); O: Firearm 2.00
❑5, Feb 1994 2.00
❑6, Mar 1994 1.95
❑7, Apr 1994 1.95
❑8, May 1994 1.95
❑9, Jun 1994; D: Teknight I 1.95
❑10, Jul 1994; 1: Silver Daggers. 1: Chalk 1.95
❑11, Aug 1994; 1: Teknight II 1.95
❑12, Sep 1994 A: The Solution 1.95
❑13, Oct 1994; no indicia 1.95

Other grades: Multiply price above by 5/6 for VF/NM • 2/3 for VERY FINE • 1/3 for FINE • 1/5 for VERY GOOD • 1/8 for GOOD

Oh My Goddess!

Series numbering seems calculated to confuse

©Dark Horse

OMAC

One Man Army Corps serves world peace

©DC

Omaha The Cat Dancer

Cult favorite adults-only soap opera

©Kitchen Sink

Omega Men

Series guilty of the introduction of Lobo

©DC

Omega the Unknown

Storyline finally finished in The Defenders

©Marvel

N-MINT

- ❑14, Nov 1994; JRo (w); D: Torso 1.95
- ❑15, Dec 1994 1.95
- ❑16, Feb 1995; MZ (a); flipbook with Ultraverse Premiere #11 3.50
- ❑17, Feb 1995; 1: BloodyFly 2.50
- ❑18, Mar 1995 2.50
- ❑19, Apr 1995; D: Deathmask 2.50
- ❑20, May 1995; D: BloodyFly 2.50
- ❑21, Jun 1995 2.50
- ❑22, Jul 1995 A: Loki 2.50
- ❑23, Aug 1995; Final Issue 2.50
- ❑Ann 1, Jan 1995; 64 pages 3.95

Night Man
Malibu / Ultraverse

- ❑0, Sep 1995; Listed as issue #Infinity 1.50
- ❑0/A, Sep 1995; alternate cover 1.50
- ❑1, Oct 1995 1.50
- ❑2, Nov 1995; Flipbook 1.50
- ❑3, Dec 1995; V: Lord Pumpkin 1.50
- ❑4, Dec 1995; V: Lord Pumpkin; V: Mangle; Final Issue 1.50

Night Man/Gambit
Malibu / Ultraverse

- ❑1, Mar 1996; Foxfire story 1.95
- ❑2, Apr 1996 1.95
- ❑3, May 1996 1.95

Night Man vs. Wolverine
Malibu / Ultraverse

- ❑0, Aug 1995, no cover price 5.00

Nightmare
Innovation

- ❑1, Dec 1989 1.95

Nightmare
Marvel

- ❑1, Dec 1994 1.95
- ❑2, Jan 1995 1.95
- ❑3, Feb 1995 1.95
- ❑4, Mar 1995 1.95

Nightmare & Casper
Harvey

- ❑1, Aug 1963 60.00
- ❑2, Nov 1963 35.00
- ❑3, Feb 1964 35.00
- ❑4, May 1964 35.00
- ❑5, Aug 1964; becomes Casper and Nightmare 35.00

Nightmare on Elm Street
DC

- ❑1, Dec 2006 2.99
- ❑1/Variant, Dec 2006 2.99
- ❑2, Jan 2007 2.99
- ❑3, Feb 2007 2.99
- ❑4, Mar 2007 2.99

Nightmare on Elm Street, A
Marvel

- ❑1 3.00

Nightmare on Elm Street: The Beginning
Innovation

- ❑1 2.50
- ❑2 2.50

N-MINT

Nightmares
Eclipse

- ❑1, May 1985; PG (c); PG (a); Reprints from Eerie (Warren) #103, 109, 110 2.00
- ❑2, May 1985; PG (c); PG (a); Reprints from Eerie (Warren) #104, 105, 111 2.00

Nightmares & Fairy Tales
Slave Labor

- ❑1 2002 8.00
- ❑2 6.00
- ❑3 5.00
- ❑4 5.00
- ❑5 5.00
- ❑6 5.00
- ❑7 2.95
- ❑8 2.95
- ❑9 2.95
- ❑10 2.95
- ❑11 2.95
- ❑12 2.95
- ❑13, Aug 2005 2.95
- ❑14, Dec 2005 2.95

Nightmares on Elm Street
Innovation

- ❑1, Sep 1991 2.50
- ❑2, Nov 1991 2.50
- ❑3 2.50
- ❑4 2.50
- ❑5 2.50
- ❑6 2.50

Nightmare Theater
Chaos!

- ❑1, Nov 1997; horror anthology 2.50
- ❑2, Nov 1997; horror anthology 2.50
- ❑3, Nov 1997; horror anthology 2.50
- ❑4, Nov 1997; horror anthology 2.50

Nightmare Walker
Boneyard

- ❑1, Jul 1996, b&w 2.95

Nightmark
Alpha Productions

- ❑1, b&w 2.25

Nightmark: Blood & Honor
Alpha

- ❑1, Apr 1994 2.50
- ❑2 2.50
- ❑3 2.50

Nightmark Mystery Special
Alpha

- ❑1, b&w 2.50

Night Mary
Idea & Design Works

- ❑1, Sep 2005 3.99
- ❑2, Oct 2005 3.99
- ❑3, Dec 2005 3.99
- ❑4, Jan 2006 3.99
- ❑5, Jan 2006 3.99

Nightmask
Marvel

- ❑1, Nov 1986, AM (c); 1&O: Nightmask 1.00
- ❑2, Dec 1986 1.00
- ❑3, Jan 1987 1.00
- ❑4, Feb 1987 1.00

N-MINT

- ❑5, Mar 1987 1.00
- ❑6, Apr 1987 1.00
- ❑7, May 1987 1.00
- ❑8, Jun 1987 1.00
- ❑9, Jul 1987, Mark Bagley's first major comics work 1.00
- ❑10, Aug 1987 1.00
- ❑11, Sep 1987 1.00
- ❑12, Oct 1987, Final Issue 1.00

Night Masters
Custom Pic

- ❑1 1986; ca. 1985 1.50
- ❑2, Dec 1986 1.50
- ❑3, Jan 1986 1.50
- ❑4, Apr 1986 1.50
- ❑5, Aug 1986 1.50
- ❑6, Jan 1987 1.50

Night Music
Eclipse

- ❑1, Dec 1984 CR (w); CR (a) 2.00
- ❑2, Feb 1985 CR (w); CR (a) 2.00
- ❑3, Mar 1985; CR (w); CR (a); Rudyard Kipling adaptation 2.00
- ❑4, Dec 1985 CR (a) 2.00
- ❑5, Dec 1985 CR (a) 2.00
- ❑6 CR (a) 2.00
- ❑7, Feb 1988 CR (w); CR (a) 2.00
- ❑8, ca. 1989 3.95
- ❑9, ca. 1990 CR (a) 4.95
- ❑10, ca. 1990 CR (a) 4.95
- ❑11, ca. 1990 CR (a) 4.95

Night Nurse
Marvel

- ❑1, Nov 1972, 1: Linda Carter; 1: Georgia Jenkins; 1: Christine Palmer 110.00
- ❑2, Jan 1973, JR (c) 50.00
- ❑3, Mar 1973 50.00
- ❑4, May 1973 50.00

Night of the Living Dead
Fantaco

- ❑0, b&w 2.00
- ❑1, ca. 1991, b&w 4.95
- ❑2, b&w 4.95
- ❑3, b&w 5.95
- ❑4, b&w 5.95

Night of the Living Deadline USA
Dark Horse

- ❑1, Apr 1992, b&w; Anthology 2.95

Night of the Living Dead: Aftermath
Fantaco

- ❑1 1.95

Night of the Living Dead: London
Fantaco

- ❑1 5.95
- ❑2 5.95

Night of the Living Dead: Prelude
Fantaco

- ❑1, ca. 1991, b&w 1.50

Night Raven: House of Cards
Marvel

- ❑1, Aug 1991 5.95

Other grades: Multiply price above by 5/6 for VF/NM • 2/3 for VERY FINE • 1/3 for FINE • 1/5 for VERY GOOD • 1/8 for GOOD

Night Rider
Marvel

❑1, Oct 1974, Reprints Ghost Rider (Western) #1 ... 25.00
❑2, Dec 1974, GK (c); SL (w); Reprints Ghost Rider (Western) #2 ... 10.00
❑3, Feb 1975, Reprints Ghost Rider (Western) #3 ... 10.00
❑4, Apr 1975, Reprints Ghost Rider (Western) #4 ... 10.00
❑5, Jun 1975, Reprints Ghost Rider (Western) #5 ... 10.00
❑6, Aug 1975, Reprints Ghost Rider (Western) #6 ... 10.00

Night's Children
Fantaco

❑1, b&w ... 3.50
❑2, b&w ... 3.50
❑3, b&w ... 3.50
❑4, b&w ... 3.50

Night's Children: Double Indemnity
Fantaco

❑1, b&w ... 7.95

Night's Children Erotic Fantasies
Fantaco

❑1; Adult ... 4.50

Night's Children: Foreplay
Fantaco

❑1, b&w ... 4.95

Night's Children: The Vampire
Millennium

❑1 ... 2.95
❑2 ... 2.95

Night's Children: Vampyr!
Fantaco

❑1, b&w; Adult; ca. 1992 ... 3.50
❑2, b&w; Adult ... 3.50
❑3, b&w; Adult ... 3.50

Nightshade
No Mercy

❑1, Aug 1997; Adult ... 2.50

Nightshades
London Night

❑1; Adult ... 2.95

Nightside
Marvel

❑1, Dec 2001 ... 2.99
❑2, Jan 2002 ... 2.99
❑3, Feb 2002 ... 2.99
❑4, Mar 2002 ... 2.99

Nights into Dreams
Archie

❑1, Feb 1998 ... 1.75
❑2, Mar 1998 ... 1.75
❑3, Apr 1998 ... 1.75
❑4, Aug 1998 ... 1.75
❑5, Sep 1998 ... 1.75
❑6, Oct 1998 ... 1.75

Nightstalkers
Marvel

❑1, Nov 1992; Missing poster ... 1.00
❑1/CS, Nov 1992; Includes poster ... 2.75
❑2, Dec 1992 ... 2.00
❑3, Jan 1993 ... 2.00
❑4, Feb 1993 ... 1.75
❑5, Mar 1993 ... 1.75
❑6, Apr 1993 ... 1.75
❑7, May 1993 ... 1.75
❑8, Jun 1993 ... 1.75
❑9, Jul 1993 ... 1.75
❑10, Aug 1993; Double cover ... 2.25
❑11, Sep 1993 ... 1.75
❑12, Oct 1993; Gold cover ... 1.75
❑13, Nov 1993; 1: Short Circuit ... 1.75
❑14, Dec 1993; Neon ink on cover ... 1.75
❑15, Jan 1994; Spot-varnish cover ... 1.75
❑16, Feb 1994 ... 1.75
❑17, Mar 1994 ... 1.75
❑18, Apr 1994; Final Issue ... 1.75

Nightstreets
Arrow

❑1, Jul 1986; 1: Mr. Katt ... 2.50
❑2, Oct 1986 ... 2.00
❑3, Jan 1987 ... 2.00
❑4, Apr 1987 ... 2.00
❑5, Jul 1987 ... 2.00

Night Terrors
Chanting Monks

❑1 ... 2.75

Night Thrasher
Marvel

❑1, Aug 1993; foil cover ... 2.95
❑2, Sep 1993; 1: Tantrum ... 1.75
❑3, Oct 1993; 1: Aardwolf (Chon Li) ... 1.75
❑4, Nov 1993 ... 1.75
❑5, Dec 1993 ... 1.75
❑6, Jan 1994 ... 1.75
❑7, Feb 1994 ... 1.75
❑8, Mar 1994 ... 1.75
❑9, Apr 1994 ... 1.75
❑10, May 1994 ... 1.95
❑11, Jun 1994 ... 1.95
❑12, Jul 1994 ... 1.95
❑13, Aug 1994 ... 1.95
❑14, Sep 1994 ... 1.95
❑15, Oct 1994; V: Hulk ... 1.95
❑16, Nov 1994 ... 1.95
❑17, Dec 1994 ... 1.95
❑18, Jan 1995 ... 1.95
❑19, Feb 1995 ... 1.95
❑20, Mar 1995 ... 1.95
❑21, Apr 1995; Final Issue ... 1.95

Night Thrasher: Four Control
Marvel

❑1, Oct 1992 ... 2.00
❑2, Nov 1992 ... 2.00
❑3, Dec 1992 ... 2.00
❑4, Jan 1993 ... 2.00

Night Tribes
DC / Wildstorm

❑1, Jul 1999; NN; One-shot ... 4.95

Night Trippers
Image

❑1, Jul 2006 ... 16.99

Nightveil
AC

❑1, Feb 1984, PG (c) ... 2.00
❑2; ca. 1985; Nightveil story; Scarlet Scorpion story ... 2.00
❑3; ca. 1985; Nightviel story; Scarlet Scorpion story ... 2.00
❑4; ca. 1985; Nightviel story; Scarlet Scorpion story ... 2.00
❑5; ca. 1986; Nightviel story; Twice Told Tales of Nightviel, Reprint from More Fun #1; Tales of Nightviel ... 2.00
❑6; ca. 1986; Nightviel story; Scarlet Scorpion story; Twice Told Tales of Nightviel ... 2.00
❑7, Mar 1987; Nightviel story; Scarlet Scorpion story ... 2.00
❑Special 1, Aug 1988 ... 2.00

Nightveil's Cauldron of Horror
AC

❑1, b&w; Reprints ... 2.50
❑2; b&w ... 2.95
❑3, Sep 1991; b&w ... 2.95

Nightvenger
Axis

❑Ashcan 1, May 1994 ... 2.00

Nightvision
Rebel

❑1, Nov 1996; Adult ... 3.00
❑2 1997; Adult ... 2.50
❑3 1997; Adult ... 2.50
❑4 1997; Adult ... 2.50

Nightvision: All About Eve
London Night

❑1; Adult; ca. 1996; b&w ... 3.00

Nightvision
Atomeka

❑1, b&w; NN; Includes poster ... 2.95

Night Vixen
ABC

❑0/A, b&w ... 3.00
❑0/B; Eurotika Edition ... 4.00
❑0/C; Manga Flux Edition ... 4.00

Night Walker
Fleetway-Quality

❑1, Reprints Luke Kirby story from 2000 A.D ... 2.95
❑2, Reprints Luke Kirby story from 2000 A.D ... 2.95
❑3, Reprints Luke Kirby story from 2000 A.D ... 2.95

Night Warriors: Darkstalkers' Revenge the Comic Series
Viz

❑1, Nov 1998 ... 2.95
❑2, Dec 1998 ... 3.25
❑3, Jan 1999 ... 2.95
❑4, Feb 1999 ... 2.95
❑5, Mar 1999 ... 2.95
❑6, Apr 1999 ... 2.95

Nightwatch
Marvel

❑1, Apr 1994 ... 1.50
❑1/Variant, Apr 1994; foil cover ... 2.95
❑2, May 1994 ... 1.50
❑3, Jun 1994 ... 1.50
❑4, Jul 1994 ... 1.50
❑5, Aug 1994 ... 1.50
❑6, Sep 1994 ... 1.50
❑7, Oct 1994 ... 1.50
❑8, Nov 1994 ... 1.50
❑9, Dec 1994 ... 1.50
❑10, Jan 1995 ... 1.50
❑11, Feb 1995 ... 1.50
❑12, Mar 1995; Final Issue ... 1.50

Nightwing
DC

❑1, Sep 1995 ... 3.50
❑2, Oct 1995 ... 2.50
❑3, Nov 1995 ... 2.50
❑4, Dec 1995; Final issue ... 2.50

Nightwing
DC

❑½; 1997 ... 4.00
❑½/Platinum; Platinum edition; Includes certificate of authenticity; Autographed by Chuck Dixon ... 7.00
❑1, Oct 1996 ... 11.00
❑2, Nov 1996 ... 6.00
❑3, Dec 1996 ... 4.00
❑4, Jan 1997 ... 3.50
❑5, Feb 1997 ... 3.50
❑6, Mar 1997 ... 3.00
❑7, Apr 1997 ... 3.00
❑8, May 1997 ... 3.00
❑9, Jun 1997; V: Scarecrow ... 3.00
❑10, Jul 1997; V: Scarecrow ... 3.00
❑11, Aug 1997; V: Scarecrow ... 2.50
❑12, Sep 1997 ... 2.50
❑13, Oct 1997 ... 2.50
❑14, Nov 1997 A: Batman ... 2.50
❑15, Dec 1997; A: Batman. V: Two-Face. Face cover ... 2.50
❑16, Jan 1998 ... 1.95
❑17, Feb 1998 ... 1.95
❑18, Mar 1998 ... 1.95
❑19, Apr 1998; continues in Batman #553 ... 1.95
❑20, May 1998; continues in Batman #554 ... 1.95
❑21, Jun 1998; 1: Nitewing. A: Blockbuster ... 1.95
❑22, Jul 1998; V: Stallion. V: Brutale ... 1.95
❑23, Aug 1998; A: Lady Shiva. concludes in Green Arrow #135 ... 1.95
❑24, Sep 1998 ... 1.99
❑25, Oct 1998 ... 1.99
❑26, Dec 1998 A: Huntress ... 1.99
❑27, Jan 1999 A: Huntress ... 1.99
❑28, Feb 1999; 1: Torque. A: Huntress ... 1.99
❑29, Mar 1999 A: Huntress ... 1.99
❑30, Apr 1999 A: Superman ... 1.99
❑31, May 1999; Dick joins the Bludhaven police force ... 1.99
❑32, Jun 1999 ... 1.99
❑33, Jul 1999; V: Double Dare ... 1.99
❑34, Aug 1999; V: Double Dare; V: Electrocutioner; V: Stallion; V: Brutale ... 1.99
❑35, Sep 1999; No Man's Land ... 1.99
❑36, Oct 1999; No Man's Land ... 1.99

100 Bullets

It's the ammunition for revenge

©DC

Oni

Next, a title called "Dark Horse" from Oni Press

©Dark Horse

Oni Double Feature

Anthology flip-book from Oni Press

©Oni

Open Season

Jim Bricker's "slice of life" series

©Renegade

Open Space

Short-lived science-fiction anthology

©Marvel

N-MINT

❑37, Nov 1999; No Man's Land ... 1.99
❑38, Dec 2000; No Man's Land ... 1.99
❑39, Jan 2000; V: Huntress; V: rogue GCPD ... 1.99
❑40, Feb 2000 ... 1.99
❑41, Mar 2000 ... 1.99
❑42, Apr 2000 ... 1.99
❑43, May 2000 ... 1.99
❑44, Jun 2000 ... 1.99
❑45, Jul 2000; Continued in Birds of Prey #20 ... 1.99
❑46, Aug 2000; Continued in Birds of Prey #21 ... 2.25
❑47, Sep 2000; V: Nite-Wing; Nite-Wing kills FBI agent ... 2.25
❑48, Oct 2000 ... 2.25
❑49, Nov 2000 ... 2.25
❑50, Dec 2000; Extra-Sized issue ... 3.50
❑51, Jan 2001 ... 2.25
❑52, Feb 2001 A: Catwoman ... 2.25
❑53, Mar 2001 DGry (w) ... 2.25
❑54, Apr 2001 ... 2.25
❑55, May 2001 ... 2.25
❑56, Jun 2001 ... 2.25
❑57, Jul 2001; V: Shrike ... 2.25
❑58, Aug 2001; V: Shrike ... 2.25
❑59, Sep 2001 ... 2.25
❑60, Oct 2001 ... 2.25
❑61, Nov 2001 ... 2.25
❑62, Dec 2001; Joker: Last Laugh crossover ... 2.25
❑63, Jan 2002; V: Madmen ... 2.25
❑64, Feb 2002 ... 2.25
❑65, Mar 2002 ... 2.25
❑66, Apr 2002 MG (c) ... 2.00
❑67, May 2002 MG (c) ... 2.00
❑68, Jun 2002 MG (c) ... 2.25
❑69, Jul 2002 MG (c) ... 2.25
❑70, Aug 2002 MG (c) ... 2.25
❑71, Sep 2002 MG (c); DGry (w) ... 2.25
❑72, Oct 2002 MG (c); DGry (w) ... 2.25
❑73, Nov 2002 MG (c); DGry (w) ... 2.25
❑74, Dec 2002 MG (c); DGry (w) ... 2.25
❑75, Jan 2003; Giant-size; Extra-sized issue; Gotham Central #1 preview ... 2.00
❑76, Feb 2003 ... 2.25
❑77, Mar 2003 ... 2.25
❑78, Apr 2003 ... 2.25
❑79, May 2003 ... 2.25
❑80, Jun 2003 A: Deathstroke the Terminator ... 2.25
❑81, Jul 2003 A: Deathstroke the Terminator ... 2.25
❑82, Aug 2003 ... 2.25
❑83, Sep 2003 ... 2.25
❑84, Oct 2003 ... 2.25
❑85, Nov 2003 ... 2.25
❑86, Dec 2003 ... 2.25
❑87, Jan 2004, Supreman: Secret Identity preview; V: Tarantula II (Catalina Flores) ... 2.25
❑88, Feb 2004, Touch #1 preview; Painted cover; V: Firefly; Nightwing revisits Haly Circus ... 2.25
❑89, Mar 2004 ... 2.25
❑90, Apr 2004 ... 2.25
❑91, May 2004, DGry (w) ... 2.25
❑92, Jun 2004 ... 2.25
❑93, Jul 2004 ... 2.25

N-MINT

❑94, Aug 2004 ... 2.25
❑95, Sep 2004 ... 2.25
❑96, Oct 2004; Sky Captain and the World of Tomorrow demo CD; War Games: Act 1 Part 3 ... 2.25
❑97, Nov 2004, War Games: Act 2 Part 3 ... 2.25
❑98, Dec 2004, War Games; Act 3, Part 8 ... 2.25
❑99, Jan 2005 ... 3.00
❑100, Feb 2005, Extra Sized issue ... 4.00
❑101, Mar 2005 ... 6.00
❑102, Mar 2005 ... 5.00
❑103, Apr 2005 ... 6.00
❑104, May 2005 ... 6.00
❑105, Jun 2005 ... 5.00
❑106, May 2005; V: Killer Croc; Rescue Alfred disguised as Two-Face ... 6.00
❑107, Jun 2005 ... 2.25
❑108, Jun 2005 ... 2.25
❑109, Jul 2005 ... 2.50
❑110, Aug 2005; Villains United tie-in ... 2.50
❑111, Sep 2005 ... 2.50
❑112, Oct 2005 ... 2.50
❑113, Nov 2005; Nightwing trains Ravager ... 2.50
❑114, Jan 2006; Nightwing trains Ravager ... 2.50
❑115, Feb 2006 ... 2.50
❑116, Mar 2006, Infinite Crisis crossover ... 2.50
❑117, Apr 2006 ... 2.50
❑118, May 2006, One Year Later ... 2.50
❑119, Jun 2006, V: Jason Todd; One Year Later ... 2.50
❑120, Jul 2006, V: Jason Todd; One Year Later ... 2.99
❑121, Aug 2006 ... 2.99
❑122, Oct 2006, V: Pierce Brothers ... 2.99
❑123, Oct 2006 ... 2.99
❑124, Nov 2006 ... 2.99
❑125, Dec 2006, V: Raptor ... 2.99
❑126, Jan 2007, V: Raptor ... 2.99
❑127, Feb 2007 ... 2.99
❑128, Mar 2007, V: Raptor 2.0 ... 2.99
❑129 ... 2.99
❑130 ... 2.99
❑131 ... 2.99
❑132 ... 2.99
❑133 ... 2.99
❑134 ... 2.99
❑135 ... 2.99
❑136 ... 2.99
❑137 ... 2.99
❑138 ... 2.99
❑139 ... 2.99
❑140 ... 2.99
❑141 ... 2.99
❑142 ... 2.99
❑143 ... 2.99
❑144 ... 2.99
❑145 ... 2.99
❑146 ... 2.99
❑147 ... 2.99
❑148 ... 2.99
❑149 ... 2.99
❑150 ... 2.99
❑151 ... 2.99
❑152 ... 2.99
❑153 ... 2.99
❑1000000, Nov 1998 ... 2.00

N-MINT

❑Ann 1, ca. 1997; DGry (w); Pulp Heroes 5.00
❑GS 1, Dec 2000 ... 5.95

Nightwing: Alfred's Return
DC

❑1, Jul 1995; One-shot ... 3.50

Nightwing and Huntress
DC

❑1, May 1998, DGry (w) ... 2.00
❑2, Jun 1998, DGry (w); BSz (a) ... 2.00
❑3, Jul 1998 ... 2.00
❑4, Aug 1998, Final issue ... 2.00

Nightwing: Our Worlds at War
DC

❑1, Sep 2001; Our Worlds at War ... 2.95

Nightwing Secret Files
DC

❑1, Oct 1999; background information on series ... 4.95

Nightwing: The Target
DC

❑1, Sep 2001 ... 5.95

Nightwolf
Entropy

❑1 ... 1.50
❑2 ... 1.50

Nightwolf
Devil's Due

❑0, Jun 2006 ... 0.99
❑2, Sep 2006 ... 2.95
❑3, Dec 2006 ... 2.95

Night Zero
Fleetway-Quality

❑1, b&w ... 1.95
❑2, b&w ... 1.95
❑3, b&w ... 1.95
❑4, b&w ... 1.95

Nikki Blade Summer Fun
ABC

❑1/A, b&w; Adult ... 3.00
❑1/B; solo figure on cover ... 3.00

Nimrod
Fantagraphics

❑1, Jun 1998, b&w ... 2.95
❑2, Aug 1998, b&w ... 2.95

Nina's All-Time Greatest Collectors' Item Classic Comics
Dark Horse

❑1, Aug 1992, b&w ... 2.50

Nina's New & Improved All-Time Greatest Collectors' Item Classic Comics
Dark Horse

❑1, Feb 1994, b&w ... 2.50

9-11: Emergency Relief
Alternative

❑1, b&w; ca. 2002 ... 14.95

Nine Lives of Leather Cat
Forbidden Fruit

❑1, Aug 1993; 1: Leather Cat; O: Leather Cat; Adult ... 3.50
❑2; Adult ... 3.50

Other grades: Multiply price above by 5/6 for VF/NM • 2/3 for VERY FINE • 1/3 for FINE • 1/5 for VERY GOOD • 1/8 for GOOD

❑3; Adult 3.50
❑4; Adult 3.50
❑5; Adult 3.50
❑6; Adult 3.50

Nine Rings of Wu-Tang
Image

❑0, Nov 1999; Giveaway bundled with Wizard Magazine; Genesis Edition 2.00
❑1/A, Nov 1999; Woman with bow reclining on cover with jungle cats 4.00
❑1/B, Nov 1999; Tower Records variant 5.00
❑2, Dec 1999 2.95
❑3, Feb 2000 2.95
❑4, Apr 2000 2.95
❑5, Jul 2000 2.95

1984 Magazine
Warren

❑1, Jun 1978 6.00
❑2, Aug 1978 4.00
❑3, Sep 1978 4.00
❑4, Oct 1978 4.00
❑5, Feb 1979 4.00
❑6, Jun 1979 4.00
❑7, Aug 1979 4.00
❑8, Sep 1979 4.00
❑9, Oct 1979 4.00
❑10, Dec 1980; Series continued in 1994 #11 4.00

1994 Magazine
Warren

❑11, Feb 1980; Series continued from 1984 #10 3.00
❑12, Apr 1980; b&w 3.00
❑13, Jun 1980; b&w 3.00
❑14, Aug 1980; b&w 3.00
❑15, Oct 1980; b&w 3.00
❑16, Dec 1980; AN (a); B&W 3.00
❑17, Feb 1981; b&w 3.00
❑18, Apr 1981; FT (w); FT, AN (a); B&W 3.00
❑19, Jun 1981; b&w 3.00
❑20, Aug 1981; b&w 3.00
❑21, Oct 1981; FT (w); FT, AN (a); B&W 3.00
❑22, Dec 1981; b&w 3.00
❑23, Feb 1982; b&w 3.00
❑24, Apr 1982; b&w 3.00
❑25, Jun 1982; b&w 3.00
❑26, Aug 1982; b&w 3.00
❑27, Oct 1982; b&w 3.00
❑28, Dec 1982; b&w 3.00
❑29, Feb 1983; Final Issue; b&w 3.00

1963
Image

❑1, Apr 1993, AMo (w); DaG (a); Mystery Incorporated 2.00
❑1/BR, Apr 1993, Promotional limited edition; AMo (w); DaG (a); Bronze edition; Signed by Dave Gibbons 3.00
❑1/Gold, Apr 1993, Gold edition; AMo (w); DaG (a); Profits donated to cancer research 5.00
❑1/Silver, Apr 1993, silver edition; AMo (w); DaG (a); Profits donated to cancer research 3.00
❑2, May 1993, AMo (w); No One Escapes...the Fury 2.00
❑3, Jun 1993, AMo (w); Tales of the Uncanny 2.00
❑4, Jul 1993, AMo (w); Tales From Beyond; Johnny Beyond 2.00
❑5, Aug 1993, AMo (w); Horus, Lord of Light story 2.00
❑6, Oct 1993, AMo (w); DaG (a) 2.00

Ninety-Nine Girls
Fantagraphics / Eros

❑1, Apr 1991, b&w; Adult 2.25

Nine Volt
Image

❑1, Jul 1997; 1: Digit 2.50
❑1/A, Jul 1997; alternate cover 2.50
❑2, Aug 1997 2.50
❑3, Sep 1997 2.50
❑4, Oct 1997 2.50

Ninja
Eternity

❑1, Oct 1986 1.80
❑2, Nov 1986 1.80
❑3 1986 1.80
❑4 1986 1.80
❑5 1986 1.95
❑6 1986 1.95
❑7 1987 1.95
❑8 1987 1.95
❑9 1987 1.95
❑10 1987 1.95
❑11 1988 1.95
❑12, Sep 1988 1.95
❑13 1988 1.95
❑Special 1, Dec 1987, b&w 2.25

Ninja-Bots Super Special
Pied Piper

❑1 1.95

Ninja Boy
DC / Wildstorm

❑1, Oct 2001 3.50
❑2, Nov 2001 2.95
❑3, Dec 2001; Cover date says November, indicia says December 2.95
❑4, Jan 2002 2.95
❑5, Feb 2002 2.95
❑6, Mar 2002 2.95
❑Ashcan 1; Ashcan preview; Flip book with Out There Ash #1 1.00

Ninja Elite
Adventure

❑1; 7-1/2" x 8-1/2" version with black-and-white cover 1.50
❑1/2nd; 1st printing with color covers, full comic size 1.50
❑2, Jul 1987 1.50
❑3, ca. 1987 1.50
❑4, Dec 1987 1.50
❑5, ca. 1988 1.50
❑6, May 1988, b&w 1.50
❑7, Jul 1988, b&w 1.50
❑8, Aug 1988, b&w 1.50

Ninja Funnies
Eternity

❑1, Jan 1987 1.50
❑2 1.95
❑3 1.95
❑4 1.95
❑5 1.95

Ninja High School
Antarctic

❑0, May 1994, b&w; Antarctic publishes 3.00
❑0/Ltd., Jan 1994, b&w; foil cover edition (500 made) 4.00
❑1 7.00
❑1/2nd; 2nd printing 2.50
❑2 5.00
❑2/2nd; 2nd printing 2.00
❑3 4.00
❑3/2nd; 2nd printing 2.00
❑4 4.00
❑4/2nd; 2nd printing 2.00
❑5, Jun 1988, b&w; Eternity begins publishing 4.00
❑6 3.50
❑6/2nd; 2nd printing 2.00
❑7, Sep 1988 3.50
❑8, Dec 1988 3.50
❑9, Feb 1989 3.50
❑10, Mar 1989 3.50
❑11, May 1989 3.00
❑12, ca. 1989 3.00
❑13, ca. 1989 3.00
❑14, ca. 1989 3.00
❑15, ca. 1989 3.00
❑16, Dec 1989, b&w 2.50
❑17, Feb 1990, b&w 2.50
❑18, May 1990, b&w 2.50
❑19, Aug 1990, b&w 2.50
❑20, Sep 1990, b&w 2.50
❑21, Nov 1990, b&w 2.50
❑22, Jan 1991, b&w 2.50
❑23, Feb 1991; b&w 2.25
❑24, Apr 1991; b&w 2.25
❑25, ca. 1991; b&w 2.25
❑26, ca. 1991; b&w 2.25
❑27, ca. 1991; b&w 2.25
❑28, ca. 1991; b&w 2.25
❑29, Dec 1991; b&w 2.25
❑30, Jan 1992; b&w 2.25
❑31, ca. 1992; b&w 2.25
❑32, ca. 1992, b&w 2.50
❑33, May 1992, b&w 2.50
❑34, Oct 1992, b&w 2.50
❑35, Jan 1993, b&w 2.50
❑36, Jan 1993, b&w 2.50
❑37, Mar 1993, b&w 2.50
❑38, May 1993, b&w 2.50
❑39, ca. 1993, b&w 2.50
❑40, Jun 1994, b&w 2.75
❑40/Ltd., Jun 1994, b&w; gold foil logo edition (500 made) 3.00
❑41, Jul 1994, b&w 2.75
❑42, Sep 1994, b&w 2.75
❑43, Nov 1994, b&w 2.75
❑44, Jan 1995, b&w 2.75
❑45, Mar 1995, b&w 2.75
❑46, May 1995, b&w; 40 page special 2.75
❑47, Jul 1995, b&w 2.75
❑48, Sep 1995, b&w 2.75
❑49, Nov 1995, b&w 2.75
❑50, Jan 1996, b&w; Giant 64-Page Special 3.95
❑51, Apr 1996, b&w; April on cover, Febuary inside 2.95
❑52, Jun 1996, b&w 2.95
❑53, Sep 1996, b&w 2.95
❑54, Nov 1996, b&w 2.95
❑55, Jan 1997, b&w 2.95
❑56, Mar 1997, b&w 2.95
❑57, May 1997, b&w 2.95
❑58, Aug 1997, b&w 2.95
❑59, Oct 1997, b&w 2.95
❑60, Dec 1997, b&w 2.95
❑61, Feb 1998, b&w 2.95
❑62, Apr 1998, b&w 2.95
❑63, Jun 1998, b&w 2.95
❑64, Aug 1998, b&w 2.95
❑65, Oct 1998, b&w 2.95
❑66, Dec 1998, b&w 2.95
❑67, Mar 1999, b&w 2.95
❑68, Apr 1999, b&w 2.95
❑69, Jun 1999, b&w 2.95
❑70 1999; b&w 2.95
❑71 1999; b&w 2.95
❑72 1999; b&w 2.95
❑73 2000; b&w 2.95
❑74 2000; b&w 2.95
❑75 2000; b&w 2.95
❑76 2000; b&w 2.95
❑77 2000; b&w 2.95
❑78, Nov 2000; b&w 2.95
❑79 2000; b&w 2.95
❑80 2001; b&w 2.95
❑81 2001; b&w 2.95
❑82 2001; b&w 2.95
❑83 2001; b&w 2.95
❑84 2001; b&w 2.95
❑85 2001; b&w 2.95
❑86, Jul 2001; b&w 2.95
❑87 2001; b&w 2.95
❑88 2001; b&w 2.95
❑89 2001; b&w 2.95
❑90 2001; b&w 2.95
❑91 2002; b&w 2.95
❑92 2002; b&w 2.95
❑93 2002; b&w 2.95
❑94 2002; b&w 2.95
❑95 2002; b&w 2.95
❑96 2002; b&w 2.95
❑97 2002; b&w 2.95
❑98 2002; b&w 2.95
❑99 2002; b&w; Preview: Neotopia; Preview: Twilight X: Storm 2.95
❑100 2002 4.95
❑101 2002; b&w 3.50
❑102 2003; b&w 3.50
❑103 2003; b&w 3.50
❑104, Mar 2003; b&w 3.50
❑105 2003; b&w 3.50
❑106, Jun 2003; b&w 3.50
❑107, Jul 2003; b&w 3.50
❑108, Aug 2003; b&w 3.50
❑109, Sep 2003; b&w 3.50
❑110, Oct 2003; b&w 3.50
❑111, Dec 2003; b&w 3.50
❑112, Jan 2004; b&w 3.50
❑113, Feb 2004; b&w 3.50

Oriental Heroes

Convoluted storyline with careless art

©Jademan

Original Astro Boy

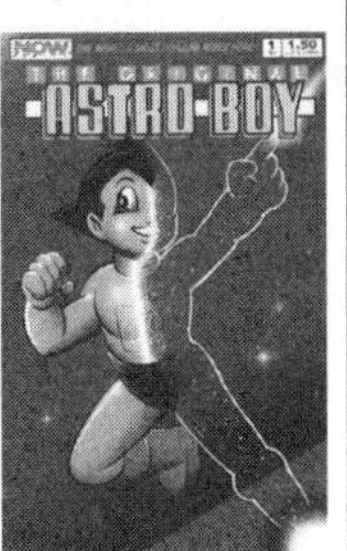

Child-sized robot with heart of gold

©Now

Orion

Walter Simonson's Jack Kirby tribute

©DC

Osborn Journals

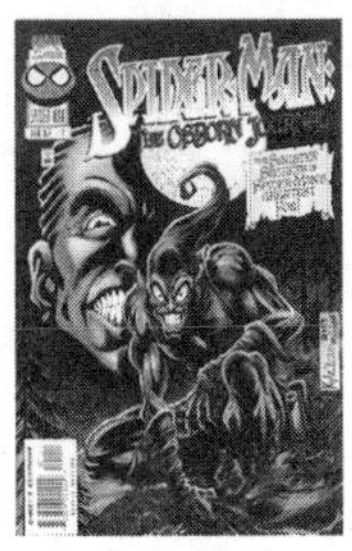

Explains the Spider-Clone saga

©Marvel

Our Army at War

Longest-running war title becomes Sgt. Rock

©DC

N-MINT

❑114, Mar 2004; b&w 3.50
❑115, Apr 2004; b&w 2.99
❑116, May 2004; b&w 2.99
❑117, Jun 2004; b&w 2.99
❑118, Jul 2004; b&w 2.99
❑119, Aug 2004; b&w 2.99
❑120, Sep 2004; b&w 2.99
❑121, Oct 2004 2.99
❑122, Nov 2004; b&w 2.99
❑123, Dec 2004; b&w 2.99
❑124, Jan 2005; b&w 2.99
❑125, Feb 2005; b&w 2.99
❑126, Mar 2005; b&w 2.99
❑127, Apr 2005; b&w 2.99
❑128, May 2005; b&w 2.99
❑129, Jun 2005 2.99
❑130, Jul 2005 2.99
❑131, ca. 2005 2.99
❑132, ca. 2005 2.99
❑133, ca. 2005 2.99
❑134, ca. 2005 2.99
❑YB 1, b&w 6.00
❑YB 2, 1990 YB; b&w 4.95
❑YB 3, 1991 YB; b&w 4.95
❑YB 4; 1992 YB; 8 pages color 4.95
❑YB 5, Oct 1993, b&w 3.95
❑YB 6, Oct 1994, b&w 3.95
❑YB 7, Oct 1995, b&w; cover says Oct 94, indicia says Oct 95 3.95
❑YB 8, Oct 1996, b&w; Front Cover by Jochen Weltjen; Inside Back Cover by Tyrone Ford; Back Cover by Kimiko Shimizu 3.95
❑YB 9/A, Oct 1997, b&w 3.95
❑YB 9/B, Oct 1997, b&w; alternate cover; Star Trek 3.95
❑YB 10/A, Oct 1998, b&w 2.95
❑YB 10/B, Oct 1998, b&w; "Titanic" themed cover 2.95
❑Summer 1, Jun 1999; Comic-sized; Summer Special (1999) 2.99
❑3D 1, Jul 1992; Trade Paperback; 3D Special 4.50

Ninja High School in Color
Eternity

❑1, Jul 1992 2.50
❑2 2.50
❑3, Sep 1992 2.50
❑4 2.00
❑5 2.00
❑6 2.00
❑7 2.00
❑8, ca. 1993 2.00
❑9, Jul 1993 2.00
❑10 2.00
❑11 2.00
❑12 2.00
❑13 2.00

Ninja High School Perfect Memory
Antarctic

❑1, b&w; sourcebook for series 5.00
❑1/2nd, Jun 1996; 2nd printing 5.95
❑2, Nov 1993; 1996 version 5.95
❑2/Platinum, Nov 1993; platinum 5.00

Ninja High School Spotlight
Antarctic

❑1; Indicia says #29 3.50
❑2, Oct 1996 2.95
❑3, Dec 1996; Ted Nomura 3.50
❑4, May 1999; Indicia says #1 2.99

Ninja High School Swimsuit Special
Antarctic

❑1, Dec 1992; Gold edition; JDu, JSt, KJ (a); two different covers 4.00
❑2, Dec 1993; 1998 YB; Ann 3.95
❑3, Dec 1994; Trade Paperback; Ann 3.95
❑4; Gold edition; 1995 Swimsuit Special 3.95
❑1996, Dec 1996, b&w; Platinum edition; No cover price; pinups 3.95

Ninja High School Talks About Comic Book Printing
Antarctic

❑1, giveaway 1.00

Ninja High School Talks About Sexually Transmitted Diseases
Antarctic

❑1, giveaway; ca. 1992 2.00

Ninja High School: The Prom Formula
Eternity

❑1, ca. 1989 2.95
❑2, May 1991, Flip-book 2.95

Ninja High School: The Prom Formula
Antarctic

❑1, Nov 2004, Flip-book 5.95

Ninja High School: The Special Edition
Eternity

❑1, b&w 2.50
❑2, b&w 2.50
❑3, b&w 2.50
❑4 2.50

Ninja High School Version 2
Antarctic

❑1, Jul 1999 2.50
❑2, Aug 1999 2.50

Ninjak
Valiant

❑0, Jun 1995; O: Doctor Silk. O: Ninjak. 3.00
❑0/A, Jun 1995; O: Doctor Silk. O: Ninjak. #00; cover forms diptych image with #0 4.00
❑1, Feb 1994; 1: Doctor Silk. chromium cover 2.00
❑1/Gold, Feb 1994; Gold edition; 1: Doctor Silk. wraparound chromium cover 20.00
❑2, Mar 1994 1.00
❑3, Apr 1994 1.00
❑4, May 1994; trading card 2.00
❑5, Jun 1994 A: X-O Manowar 1.00
❑6, Aug 1994 A: X-O Manowar 1.00
❑7, Sep 1994 1.00
❑8, Oct 1994; Chaos Effect Gamma 3 1.00
❑9, Nov 1994; new uniform 1.00
❑10, Dec 1994 1.00
❑11, Jan 1995; New Uniform 1.00
❑12, Feb 1995; trading card 2.00
❑13, Mar 1995; trading card 2.00
❑14, Apr 1995 1.00
❑15, May 1995 2.00
❑16, Jun 1995 2.00
❑17, Jul 1995; Birthquake 2.00
❑18, Jul 1995; Birthquake 2.00
❑19, Aug 1995; Birthquake 2.00
❑20, Aug 1995 2.00
❑21, Sep 1995 2.00
❑22, Sep 1995 2.00
❑23, Oct 1995 2.00
❑24, Oct 1995 2.00
❑25, Nov 1995 3.00
❑26, Nov 1995; Final Issue 5.00
❑YB 1, Dec 1994; cardstock cover 3.00

Ninjak
Acclaim / Valiant

❑1, Mar 1997, KB (w); 1&O: Ninjak II 2.50
❑1/Variant, Mar 1997, KB (w); 1&O: Ninjak. alternate painted cover 2.50
❑2, Apr 1997, KB (w) 2.50
❑3, May 1997, KB (w) 2.50
❑4, Jun 1997, KB (w); A: Colin King. real origin of Ninjak 2.50
❑5, Jul 1997, KB (w) 2.50
❑6, Aug 1997, KB (w); A: X-O Manowar 2.50
❑7, Sep 1997, KB (w); A: X-O Manowar. 2.50
❑8, Oct 1997, KB (w); A: Colin King 2.50
❑9, Nov 1997, KB (w) 2.50
❑10, Dec 1997, KB (w) 2.50
❑11, Jan 1998, KB (w) 2.50
❑12, Feb 1998, KB (w); Final Issue 2.50
❑Ashcan 1, Nov 1996, b&w; No cover price; preview of upcoming series 1.00

Ninja Scroll
DC

❑1, Dec 2006 2.99
❑1/Variant, Dec 2006 2.99
❑2, Jan 2007 2.99
❑2/Variant, Jan 2007 2.99
❑3, Feb 2007 2.99
❑3/Variant, Feb 2007 2.99
❑4, Mar 2007 2.99

Ninjutsu, Art of the Ninja
Solson

❑1, b&w 2.00

Nintendo Comics System
Valiant

❑1, Apr 1990; Trade paperback 4.95
❑2, Jul 1990; Trade paperback 4.95

Nintendo Comics System
Valiant

❑1, Feb 1991; Game Boy 2.00
❑2, Mar 1991; Game Boy 2.00
❑3, Apr 1991; Game Boy 2.00
❑4, May 1991; Game Boy 2.00
❑5, Jun 1991; Game Boy 2.00
❑6, Jul 1991; Game Boy 2.00
❑7, Aug 1991; Zelda 2.00
❑8, Sep 1991; Super Mario Bros 2.00
❑9, Oct 1991; Super Mario Bros 2.00

N.I.O.
Acclaim / Vertigo

❑1, Nov 1998 2.50

Nira X: Anime
Entity

❑0, Jan 1997 2.75

N-MINT N-MINT N-MINT

Nira X: Annual
Express / Entity

❑1/A, Sep 1996, b&w; Snowman 1944 preview ... 2.75
❑1/B, Sep 1996, b&w; Snowman 1944 preview ... 9.95

Nira X: Cyberangel
Express / Entity

❑1, Dec 1994; cardstock cover ... 3.00
❑2, Feb 1995 ... 2.50
❑3, Apr 1995 ... 2.50
❑4, Jun 1995 ... 2.50
❑Ashcan 1, Sum 1994, b&w; no cover price ... 1.00

Nira X: Cyberangel
Express / Entity

❑1, May 1996; 1: Delta-Void. 1: Millennia. 1: Paradoxx. 1: Quid. Gold foil logo ... 2.75
❑1/Ltd., May 1996; Limited commemorative edition; 1: Delta-Void. 1: Millennia. 1: Paradoxx. 1: Quid. 3000 printed ... 4.00
❑2, Jun 1996, b&w; 1: Talon. 1: Vex. 1: Cyberhood. 1: Solace ... 2.50
❑3, Jul 1996, b&w ... 2.50
❑4, Aug 1996, b&w; Final Issue ... 2.50

Nira X: Cyberangel
Express / Entity

❑1 ... 2.50

Nira X: Cyberangel - Cynder: Endangered Species
Express / Entity

❑1 ... 2.95
❑1/Ltd.; Commemorative edition; limited to 1500 copies; cardstock cover ... 12.95

Nira X: Exodus
Avatar / Entity

❑1, Oct 1997 ... 3.00

Nira X: Heatwave
Express / Entity

❑1, Jul 1995; enhanced wraparound cover ... 3.75
❑2, Aug 1995 ... 2.50
❑3, Sep 1995 ... 2.50

Nira X: Soul Skurge
Express / Entity

❑1, Nov 1996, b&w ... 2.75

Noble Armour Halberder
Academy

❑1, Jan 1997 ... 2.95

Noble Causes: Extended Family One Shot
Image

❑1, Jun 2003 ... 6.95

Noble Causes
Image

❑1/A, Jan 2002 ... 5.00
❑1/B, Jan 2002 ... 5.00
❑2/A, Mar 2002; Cover by Patrick Gleason ... 2.95
❑2/B, Mar 2002 ... 2.95
❑3/A, May 2002; Cover by Patrick Gleason ... 2.95
❑3/B, May 2002; Cover by Chriscross ... 2.95
❑4/A, May 2002; Bueno cover ... 2.95
❑4/B, May 2002; Ponce cover ... 2.95
❑5 ... 3.50

Noble Causes: Distant Relatives
Image

❑1, Aug 2003, b&w ... 2.95
❑2, Oct 2003, b&w ... 2.95
❑3, Oct 2003 ... 2.95
❑4, Dec 2003 ... 2.95

Noble Causes: Family Secrets
Image

❑1, Oct 2002 ... 2.95
❑2/A, Dec 2002, Cover by Mike Oeming ... 2.95
❑2/B, Dec 2002, Cover by Jim Valentino ... 2.95
❑3/A, Dec 2003, Cover by Mike Oeming ... 2.95
❑3/B, Dec 2003, Cover by Jim Valentino ... 2.95
❑4/A, Jan 2003, Cover by Mike Oeming ... 2.95
❑4/B, Jan 2003, Cover by Phil Hester, Ande Parks ... 2.95

Noble Causes: First Impressions
Image

❑1, Sep 2001 ... 2.95

Noble Causes
Image

❑1/A, Jul 2004 ... 3.50
❑1/B, Jul 2004 ... 3.50
❑2/A, Aug 2004 ... 3.50
❑2/B, Aug 2004 ... 3.50
❑3/A, Sep 2004 ... 3.50
❑3/B, Sep 2004 ... 3.50
❑4/A, Oct 2004 ... 3.50
❑4/B, Oct 2004 ... 3.50
❑5, Nov 2004 ... 3.50
❑6, Dec 2004 ... 3.50
❑7, Jan 2005 ... 3.50
❑8, Feb 2005 ... 3.50
❑9, Mar 2005 ... 3.50
❑10 2005 ... 3.50
❑11 2005 ... 3.50
❑12, Sep 2005 ... 3.50
❑13, Oct 2005 ... 3.50
❑14, Nov 2005 ... 3.50
❑15, Dec 2005 ... 3.50
❑16, Jan 2006 ... 3.50
❑17, Feb 2006 ... 3.50
❑18, Apr 2006 ... 3.50
❑19, May 2006 ... 3.50
❑20, Jul 2006 ... 3.50
❑21, Jul 2006 ... 3.50
❑22, Sep 2006 ... 3.50
❑23, Oct 2006 ... 3.50
❑24, Nov 2006 ... 3.50

Nobody
Oni

❑1, Nov 1998 ... 3.00
❑2, Dec 1998 ... 3.00
❑3, Jan 1999 ... 3.00
❑4, Feb 1999 ... 3.00

No Business Like Show Business
3-D Zone

❑1, b&w; not 3-D ... 2.50

Nocturnal Emissions
Vortex

❑1, b&w ... 2.50

Nocturnals
Malibu / Bravura

❑1, Jan 1995, 1: The Nocturnals ... 3.50
❑2, Feb 1995 ... 3.00
❑3, Apr 1995 ... 3.00
❑4, Apr 1995 ... 3.00
❑5, Jun 1995 ... 3.00
❑6, Aug 1995 ... 3.00

Nocturnals: Troll Bridge
Oni

❑1, Oct 2000; b&w and orange ... 4.95

Nocturnals: Witching Hour
Dark Horse

❑1, May 1998; NN; One-shot ... 4.95

Nocturne
Aircel

❑1, Jun 1991, b&w ... 2.50
❑2, Jul 1991, b&w ... 2.50
❑3, Aug 1991, b&w ... 2.50

Nocturne
Marvel

❑1, Jun 1995 ... 1.50
❑2, Jul 1995; indicia says Sep 95 ... 1.50
❑3, Aug 1995 ... 1.50
❑4, Sep 1995 ... 1.50

Nodwick
Henchman

❑1, Feb 2000, b&w ... 2.95
❑2, Mar 2000, b&w ... 2.95
❑3 2000, b&w ... 2.95
❑4, Aug 2000, b&w ... 2.95
❑5, Oct 2000, b&w ... 2.95
❑6, Dec 2000, b&w ... 2.95
❑7, Feb 2001, b&w ... 2.95
❑8, Apr 2001, b&w; Action Comics #1 cover spoof ... 2.95
❑9, Jun 2001, b&w ... 2.95
❑10, Aug 2001, b&w ... 2.95
❑11, Oct 2001, b&w ... 2.95
❑12, Dec 2001, b&w ... 2.99
❑13, Feb 2002, b&w ... 2.99
❑14, Apr 2002, b&w ... 2.99
❑15, Jun 2002, b&w ... 2.99
❑16, Jul 2002, b&w ... 2.99
❑17, Sep 2002, b&w ... 2.99
❑18, Nov 2002, b&w ... 2.99
❑19, Jan 2003, b&w ... 2.99
❑20 ... 2.99
❑21 ... 2.99
❑22 ... 2.99
❑23 ... 2.99
❑24 ... 2.99
❑25, Aug 2004 ... 2.99
❑26, Oct 2004 ... 2.99
❑27, Feb 2005 ... 2.99
❑28, Apr 2005 ... 2.99
❑29, Jul 2005 ... 2.99
❑30, Sep 2005 ... 2.99

No Escape
Marvel

❑1, Jun 1994, Movie adaptation ... 1.50
❑2, Jul 1994, Movie adaptation ... 1.50
❑3, Aug 1994, Movie adaptation ... 1.50

Nog the Protector of the Pyramides
Onli

❑1; NN ... 2.00

No Guts or Glory
Fantaco

❑1, ca. 1991, b&w ... 2.95

No Honor
Image

❑0 ... 3.00
❑1, Feb 2001; Marc Silvestri cover ... 2.50
❑2, Mar 2001 ... 2.50
❑3, Apr 2001 ... 2.50
❑4, May 2002; Final issue ... 2.50

No Hope
Slave Labor

❑1, Apr 1993 ... 2.95
❑1/2nd, Feb 1995; 2nd printing ... 2.95
❑2, Aug 1993 ... 2.95
❑2/2nd, Apr 1994; 2nd printing ... 2.95
❑3, Nov 1993 ... 2.95
❑3/2nd, Apr 1994; 2nd printing ... 2.95
❑4, Feb 1994 ... 2.95
❑4/2nd, Oct 1994; 2nd printing ... 2.95
❑5, Jun 1994 ... 2.95
❑6, Sep 1994 ... 2.95
❑7, Jan 1995 ... 2.95
❑8, Apr 1995 ... 2.95
❑9, Jul 1995 ... 2.95

Noid in 3-D
Blackthorne

❑1; Blackthorne 3-D series #74 ... 2.50
❑2; Blackthorne 3-D series #80 ... 2.50

No Illusions
Comics Defence Fund

❑1; Benefit for Comics Defence Fund (UK) ... 1.00

Noir
Alpha

❑1, Win 1994; text & comics ... 3.95

Noir
Creative Force

❑1, Apr 1995; Reprints story from Johnny Dynamite #12; Mickey Spillane interview; Queen preview ... 4.95

No Justice, No Piece!
Head

❑1, Oct 1997, b&w; benefit anthology for CBLDF ... 2.95
❑2, Jul 1998, b&w; benefit anthology for CBLDF ... 2.95

Nolan Ryan
Celebrity

❑1 ... 2.95

Nolan Ryan's 7 No-Hitters
Revolutionary

❑1, Aug 1993, b&w ... 2.95

Nomad
Marvel

❑1, Nov 1990 ... 2.00
❑2, Dec 1990, O: Nomad ... 2.00
❑3, Mar 1991 ... 2.00
❑4, Feb 1991 ... 2.00

Other grades: Multiply price above by 5/6 for VF/NM • 2/3 for VERY FINE • 1/3 for FINE • 1/5 for VERY GOOD • 1/8 for GOOD

Our Fighting Forces	Outbreed 999	Outcast, The	Outcasts	Outer Limits
				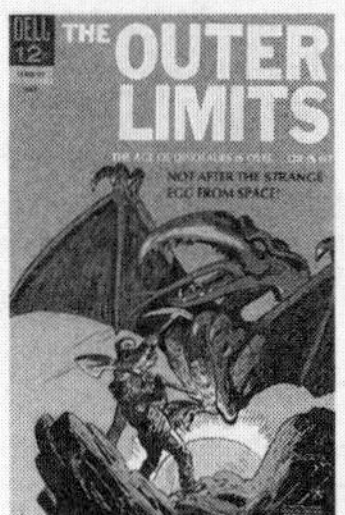
Launched Losers and Unknown Soldier ©DC	Prisoner subjected to experiments ©Blackout	Brain-damaged man has alien consciousness ©Acclaim	Mutants and undesireables rise up ©DC	Many stories based on the TV screenplays ©Dell

N-MINT

Nomad
Marvel

	N-MINT
❑1, May 1992; gatefold cover	2.50
❑2, Jun 1992	1.75
❑3, Jul 1992; Nomad vs. U.S.Agent	1.75
❑4, Aug 1992	1.75
❑5, Sep 1992	1.75
❑6, Oct 1992	1.75
❑7, Nov 1992; Infinity War	1.75
❑8, Dec 1992; L.A riots	1.75
❑9, Jan 1993	1.75
❑10, Feb 1993 A: Red Wolf	1.75
❑11, Mar 1993	1.75
❑12, Apr 1993 A: Hate-Monger	1.75
❑13, May 1993 A: Hate-Monger	1.75
❑14, Jun 1993 A: Hate-Monger	1.75
❑15, Jul 1993 A: Hate-Monger	1.75
❑16, Aug 1993 A: Gambit	1.75
❑17, Sep 1993	1.75
❑18, Oct 1993 A: Dr. Faustus	1.75
❑19, Nov 1993 MG (c)	1.75
❑20, Dec 1993	1.75
❑21, Jan 1994 A: Man-Thing	1.75
❑22, Feb 1994 MG (c)	1.75
❑23, Mar 1994 MG (c)	1.75
❑24, Apr 1994 MG (c)	1.75
❑25, May 1994; MG (c); Final Issue	1.75

Noman
Tower

❑1, Nov 1966; AW, WW (c); GK, WW (a); NoMan stories; Lightning story	40.00
❑2, Mar 1967; WW (c); WW (a); NoMan stories	28.00

No Man's Land
Tundra

❑1	14.95

Non
Red Ink

❑1	3.00
❑2	3.00
❑3	3.00

No Need for Tenchi! Part 1
Viz

❑1	3.00
❑2	3.00
❑3	3.00
❑4	3.00
❑5	3.00
❑6	3.00
❑7	3.00

No Need for Tenchi! Part 2
Viz

❑1	3.00
❑2	3.00
❑3	3.00
❑4	3.00
❑5	3.00
❑6	3.00
❑7	3.00

No Need for Tenchi! Part 3
Viz

❑1, Jun 1996	2.95
❑2, Jul 1996	2.95
❑3, Aug 1996	2.95
❑4, Sep 1996	2.95
❑5, Oct 1996	2.95
❑6, Nov 1996	2.95

N-MINT

No Need for Tenchi! Part 4
Viz

❑1, Dec 1997	2.95
❑2, Jan 1998	2.95
❑3, Feb 1998	2.95
❑4, Mar 1998	2.95
❑5, Apr 1998	2.95
❑6, May 1998	2.95

No Need for Tenchi! Part 5
Viz

❑1, Jun 1998	3.25
❑2, Jul 1998	2.95
❑3, Aug 1998	2.95
❑4, Sep 1998	2.95
❑5, Oct 1998	2.95

No Need for Tenchi! Part 6
Viz

❑1, Nov 1998	3.25
❑2, Dec 1998	2.95
❑3, Jan 1999	3.25
❑4, Feb 1999	3.25
❑5, Mar 1999	3.25

No Need for Tenchi! Part 7
Viz

❑1, Apr 1999	2.95
❑2, May 1999	2.95
❑3, Jun 1999	2.95
❑4, Jul 1999	2.95
❑5, Aug 1999	2.95
❑6, Sep 1999	2.95

No Need for Tenchi! Part 8
Viz

❑1, Oct 1999	3.25
❑2	3.25
❑3	3.25
❑4	3.25
❑5	3.25

No Need For Tenchi! Part 9
Viz

❑1, Mar 2000	2.95
❑2, Apr 2000	2.95
❑3, May 2000	2.95
❑4, Jun 2000	2.95
❑5, Jul 2000	2.95
❑6, Aug 2000	2.95

No Need for Tenchi! Part 10
Viz

❑1	2.95
❑2	2.95
❑3	2.95
❑4	2.95
❑5 2001	2.95
❑6 2001	2.95
❑7 2001	2.95

No Need For Tenchi! Part 11
Viz

❑1 2001	3.50
❑2 2001	3.50
❑3 2001	3.50
❑4 2001	3.50

N-MINT

No Need For Tenchi! Part 12
Viz

❑1 2001	2.95
❑2 2001	2.95
❑3 2001	2.95
❑4	2.95
❑5	2.95
❑6 2002	2.95

No Ninja Man
Custom Pic

❑1	1.50
❑1/2nd; 2nd printing	1.50

No No UFO
Antarctic / Venus

❑1, Aug 1996; Adult	2.95
❑2, May 1997, b&w; Adult	2.95
❑3, Sep 1997, b&w; Adult	2.95
❑4, May 1998, b&w; Adult	2.95

Noodle Fighter Miki
ADV Manga

❑1, ca. 2005; Read right to left; Graphic novel; b&w	9.99

No Pasaran!
NBM

❑1	13.95
❑2	11.95

No Profit for the Wise
CFD

❑1, Jul 1996, b&w; NN; Anthology	2.95

Norb
Mu

❑1, Jan 1992	8.95

Normalman
Aardvark-Vanaheim

❑1, Jan 1984; Aardvark-Vanaheim publishes	2.50
❑2, Apr 1984 O: Normalman	2.00
❑3, Jun 1984	2.00
❑4, Aug 1984	2.00
❑5, Oct 1984	2.00
❑6, Dec 1984	2.00
❑7, Feb 1985	2.00
❑8, Apr 1985	2.00
❑9, Jun 1985; Renegade begins as publisher	2.00
❑10, Aug 1985	2.00
❑11, Oct 1985	2.00
❑12, Dec 1985	2.00
❑3D 1; Double-size	2.50

Normalman 3-D
Renegade

❑1, Feb 1986	2.25

Normalman-Megaton Man Special
Image

❑1, Aug 1994	2.50

Northern's Hemisphere
Northern's Hemisphere

❑5, b&w	2.49
❑6, b&w	2.49
❑7, b&w	2.49

Other grades: Multiply price above by 5/6 for VF/NM • 2/3 for VERY FINE • 1/3 for FINE • 1/5 for VERY GOOD • 1/8 for GOOD

Northern's Hemisphere Undisguised
Northern's Hemisphere

❏1 ... 2.50

Northguard: The Mandes Conclusion
Caliber

❏1, Sep 1989, b&w ... 1.95
❏2, Oct 1989, b&w ... 1.95
❏3, Nov 1989, b&w ... 1.95

Northstar
Marvel

❏1, Apr 1994 ... 2.00
❏2, May 1994 ... 2.00
❏3, Jun 1994 ... 2.00
❏4, Jul 1994 ... 2.00

Northstar Presents
Northstar

❏1, Oct 1994 ... 2.50
❏2 ... 2.50

Northwest Cartoon Cookery
Starhead

❏1, ca. 1995, b&w; recipes from Pacific Northwest cartoonists ... 2.75

Northwest Passage
NBM

❏1, Sep 2005 ... 5.95

Nosferatu
Dark Horse

❏1, Mar 1991, b&w ... 3.95

Nosferatu
Tome

❏1, Jul 1991, b&w ... 2.75
❏2, Jul 1991, b&w ... 2.75

Nosferatu, Plague of Terror
Millennium

❏1, b&w; duotone ... 2.50
❏2, b&w; duotone ... 2.50
❏3, b&w; duotone ... 2.50
❏4, b&w; duotone ... 2.50

Nosferatu: The Death Mass
Antarctic / Venus

❏1, Dec 1997, b&w; Adult ... 2.95
❏2, Jan 1998, b&w; Adult ... 2.95
❏3, Feb 1998, b&w; Adult ... 2.95
❏4, Mar 1998, b&w; Adult ... 2.95

Nostradamus Chronicles: 1559-1821
Tome / Venus

❏1 ... 2.95

Not Approved Crime
Avalon

❏1 ... 2.95

Not Brand Echh
Marvel

❏1, Aug 1967, SL (w); BEv, JK, JSe, RA (a); 1: Forbush Man (on cover) ... 45.00
❏2, Sep 1967 ... 18.00
❏3, Oct 1967, O: Charlie America. O: Sore. O: Bulk ... 15.00
❏4, Nov 1967 ... 15.00
❏5, Dec 1967, TS (c); SL (w); GC, JK (a); 1&O: Forbush Man ... 15.00
❏6, Feb 1968 ... 10.00
❏7, Apr 1968, O: Stupor-Man. O: Fantastical Four ... 10.00
❏8, Jun 1968 ... 10.00
❏9, Aug 1968; Giant-size ... 25.00
❏10, Oct 1968; Giant-size; Reprints ... 25.00
❏11, Dec 1968; Giant-size ... 25.00
❏12, Feb 1969; Giant-size; TS, JB (a) ... 25.00
❏13, Apr 1969; Giant-size; Final Issue ... 25.00

Notenki Memoirs
ADV Manga

❏1, ca. 2005 ... 9.99

No Time for Sergeants
Dell

❏1, Feb 1965, cover code -502; based on TV show ... 40.00
❏2, May 1965, cover code -505; a drawn cover, yet actors' names appear with their drawings ... 40.00
❏3, Aug 1965, cover code -510 ... 30.00

(Not Only) The Best of Wonder Wart-Hog
Print Mint

❏1, ca. 1973, b&w ... 15.00
❏2, ca. 1973, b&w ... 12.00
❏3, ca. 1973, b&w ... 12.00

Not Quite Dead
Rip Off

❏1, Mar 1993, b&w; Adult ... 2.95
❏1/2nd; 2nd printing; Adult ... 2.95
❏2, b&w; Adult ... 2.95
❏3; Adult ... 2.95
❏4, ca. 1995; Adult ... 2.95

Nova
Marvel

❏1, Sep 1976, JB (c); JB, JSt (a); 1&O: Nova I (Richard Ryder) ... 8.00
❏2, Oct 1976, JB (c); JB, JSt (a); 1: Powerhouse; 1: Condor ... 4.00
❏3, Nov 1976, 1&O: Diamondhead ... 3.00
❏4, Dec 1976, V: Diamondhead ... 3.00
❏5, Jan 1977 ... 3.00
❏6, Feb 1977, 1: The Sphinx ... 3.00
❏7, Mar 1977, O: The Sphinx ... 3.00
❏8, Apr 1977, O: Megaman ... 3.00
❏9, May 1977 ... 3.00
❏10, Jun 1977 ... 3.00
❏10/35¢, Jun 1977, 35¢ regional variant ... 15.00
❏11, Jul 1977 ... 3.00
❏11/35¢, Jul 1977, 35¢ regional variant ... 15.00
❏12, Aug 1977, A: Spider-Man. Continued in Amazing Spider-Man #171 ... 3.00
❏12/35¢, Aug 1977, 35¢ regional variant ... 15.00
❏13, Sep 1977, 1: Crimebuster ... 3.00
❏13/35¢, Sep 1977, 35¢ regional variant ... 15.00
❏14, Oct 1977, 1: Inner Circle ... 3.00
❏14/35¢, Oct 1977, 35¢ regional variant ... 15.00
❏15, Nov 1977 ... 3.00
❏16, Dec 1977, V: Yellow Claw ... 3.00
❏17, Jan 1978 ... 3.00
❏18, Mar 1978 ... 3.00
❏19, May 1978, 1&O: Blackout I (Marcus Daniels) ... 3.00
❏20, Jul 1978 ... 3.00
❏21, Sep 1978 ... 3.00
❏22, Nov 1978, 1&O: Comet (Harris Moore) ... 3.00
❏23, Jan 1979 ... 3.00
❏24, Mar 1979, O: Crimebuster ... 3.00
❏25, May 1979, Final Issue ... 3.00

Nova
Marvel

❏1, Jan 1994 ... 2.25
❏1/Variant, Jan 1994; Special cover ... 2.95
❏2, Feb 1994 ... 2.00
❏3, Mar 1994 A: Spider-Man ... 1.75
❏4, Apr 1994 ... 1.75
❏5, May 1994 ... 1.75
❏6, Jun 1994 ... 1.95
❏7, Jul 1994 ... 1.95
❏8, Aug 1994 ... 1.95
❏9, Sep 1994 ... 1.95
❏10, Oct 1994 ... 1.95
❏11, Nov 1994; V: new Fantastic Four ... 1.95
❏12, Dec 1994 ... 1.95
❏13, Jan 1995 ... 1.95
❏14, Feb 1995 ... 1.95
❏15, Mar 1995 ... 1.95
❏16, Apr 1995 ... 1.95
❏17, May 1995 ... 1.95
❏18, Jun 1995; Final Issue ... 1.95

Nova
Marvel

❏1, May 1999; wraparound cover ... 2.99
❏2, Jun 1999; V: Diamondhead ... 1.99
❏2/Variant, Jun 1999 ... 1.99
❏3, Jul 1999; V: Quintronic Man ... 1.99
❏4, Aug 1999 ... 1.99
❏5, Sep 1999 ... 1.99
❏6, Oct 1999 ... 1.99
❏7, Nov 1999; 50th issue ... 1.99

Nova Hunter
Ryal

❏1; Includes coupon for trading cards ... 2.50
❏1/Autographed; Autographed limited edition; Includes coupon for trading cards ... 4.00

Novavolo
Jungle Boy

❏1, ca. 2000, b&w ... 3.95
❏Ann 2001, ca. 2001, b&w ... 3.95

Now Comics Preview
Now

❏1; 1: Thunderstar. 1: Valor. 1: Vector. 1: Syphons. 1: Ralph Snart ... 1.00

Nowheresville
Caliber

❏1, ca. 1995, b&w ... 3.50

Nowheresville: Death By Starlight
Caliber

❏1, ca. 1995; b&w ... 2.95
❏2, ca. 1996; b&w ... 2.95
❏3, b&w; flip book with Wordsmith #7 back-up ... 2.95
❏4; ca. 1996; b&w ... 2.95

Nowheresville: The History of Cool
Caliber

❏1; ca. 1997 ... 2.95

Now, on a More Serious Note...
Dawn

❏1, Sum 1994, b&w; no cover price ... 2.00

Now What?!
Now

❏1 ... 3.00
❏2 ... 2.00
❏3 ... 2.00
❏4 ... 2.00
❏5 ... 2.00
❏6 ... 2.00
❏7 ... 2.00
❏8 ... 2.00
❏9 ... 2.00
❏10 ... 2.00
❏11 ... 2.00

Nth Man, the Ultimate Ninja
Marvel

❏1, Aug 1989 ... 1.00
❏2, Sep 1989 ... 1.00
❏3, Oct 1989 ... 1.00
❏4, Nov 1989 ... 1.00
❏5, Nov 1989 ... 1.00
❏6, Dec 1989 ... 1.00
❏7, Dec 1989 ... 1.00
❏8, Jan 1990 ... 1.00
❏9, Feb 1990 ... 1.00
❏10, Mar 1990 ... 1.00
❏11, Apr 1990 ... 1.00
❏12, May 1990 ... 1.00
❏13, Jun 1990 ... 1.00
❏14, Jul 1990 ... 1.00
❏15, Aug 1990 ... 1.00
❏16, Sep 1990 ... 1.00

Nuance
Magnetic Ink

❏1, b&w ... 2.75
❏2, b&w ... 2.75
❏3, b&w ... 2.75

Nuclear War!
NEC

❏1 ... 3.50
❏2, Nov 2000 ... 3.50

Null Patrol
Escape Velocity

❏1; ca. 1986 ... 1.50
❏2 ... 1.50

Numidian Force
Kamite

❏4 ... 2.00

Nurses
Gold Key

❏1, Apr 1963 ... 50.00
❏2, Jul 1963 ... 40.00
❏3, Oct 1963 ... 30.00

Outlanders

Romantic space humor from Johji Manabe

©Dark Horse

Outlaw Kid

Attempted revival of the Atlas series

©Marvel

Outsiders

Team does without the Caped Crusader

©DC

Oz

Caliber's darker look at the fantasy world

©Caliber

Painkiller Jane

A supercop story with a voodoo touch

©Event

N-MINT

Nurture the Devil
Fantagraphics

❑2, Jul 1994, b&w 2.50
❑3, Dec 1994, b&w 2.50

Nut Runners
Rip Off

❑1, Sep 1991, b&w 2.50
❑2, Jan 1992, b&w 2.50

Nuts & Bots
Excel Graphics

❑1, Aug 1998, b&w; magazine 3.95

NYC Mech
Image

❑1, Apr 2004 .... 2.95
❑2, Aug 2004 .... 2.95
❑3, Jun 2004 .... 2.95
❑4, Jun 2004 .... 2.95
❑5, Aug 2004 .... 2.95
❑6, Dec 2004 .... 2.95

NYC Mech: Beta Love
Image

❑1, ca. 2005 .... 3.50
❑2, Jun 2005 .... 3.50
❑3, Oct 2005 .... 2.99
❑4, Jan 2006 .... 2.99
❑5, Mar 2006 .... 2.99

Nyght School
Brainstorm

❑2, b&w; Adult 2.95

NYX
Marvel

❑1, Dec 2003 .... 9.00
❑1/Variant, Dec 2003 .... 8.00
❑2, Jan 2004; 1: X-23 (Cameo) 7.00
❑2/Variant, Jan 2004 .... 5.00
❑3, Feb 2004; 1: X-23 .... 45.00
❑4, Jul 2004 .... 9.00
❑5, Aug 2004 .... 4.00
❑6, Sep 2005 .... 2.99
❑7, Oct 2005 .... 2.99

Obergeist: Ragnarok Highway
Image

❑1, May 2001 .... 2.95
❑2, Jun 2001 .... 2.95
❑3, Jul 2001 .... 2.95
❑4, Aug 2001 .... 2.95
❑5, Sep 2001 .... 2.95
❑6, Oct 2001 .... 2.95

Obergeist: The Empty Locket
Dark Horse

❑1, Mar 2002, b&w 2.95

Objective Five
Image

❑1, Jul 2000 .... 2.95
❑2, Aug 2000 .... 2.95
❑3, Sep 2000 .... 2.95
❑4, Nov 2000 .... 2.95
❑5, Dec 2000 .... 2.95
❑6, Jan 2001 .... 2.95

N-MINT

Oblivion
Comico

❑1, Jan 1996 .... 2.50
❑2, Mar 1996; Polybagged with one of two different cards 2.50
❑3, May 1996 .... 2.50

Oblivion City
Slave Labor

❑1, Mar 1991, b&w 2.50
❑2, May 1991, b&w 2.50
❑3, Jun 1991, b&w 2.50
❑4, Jun 1991, b&w 2.50
❑5, Sep 1991, b&w 2.50
❑6, Jan 1992, b&w 2.50
❑7, Apr 1992 .... 2.95
❑8, May 1992 .... 2.95
❑9, Jun 1992 .... 3.95

Obnoxio the Clown
Marvel

❑1, Apr 1983, X-Men 2.00

Occult Crimes Taskforce
Image

❑1, Aug 2006 .... 2.99
❑2, Oct 2006 .... 2.99

Occult Files of Dr. Spektor
Gold Key

❑1, Apr 1973, 1: Lakota Rainflower 32.00
❑2, Jun 1973 .... 14.00
❑3, Aug 1973 .... 14.00
❑4, Nov 1973 .... 14.00
❑5, Dec 1973 .... 14.00
❑6, Feb 1974 .... 8.00
❑7, Apr 1974, V: Ostellon Master of the Living Bones; Lakota Rainflower story 8.00
❑8, Jun 1974, 1: Valdemar Van Helsing; Elliot Kane story 8.00
❑9, Aug 1974, Simbar the were-lion story 8.00
❑10, Oct 1974 .... 8.00
❑11, Dec 1974 .... 5.00
❑12, Feb 1975, Fights werewolf 5.00
❑13, Apr 1975 .... 5.00
❑14, Jun 1975 .... 9.00
❑15, Aug 1975 .... 5.00
❑16, Oct 1975 .... 5.00
❑17, Dec 1975, 1: Anne Sara 5.00
❑18, Feb 1976, Rutland, Vermont story; Tom Fagan's name changed 7.00
❑19, Apr 1976 .... 5.00
❑20, Jun 1976 .... 5.00
❑21, Aug 1976 .... 3.00
❑22, Oct 1976 .... 3.00
❑23, Dec 1976 .... 7.00
❑24, Feb 1977 .... 3.00
❑25, May 1982, Whitman only 10.00

Ocean
DC

❑1, Dec 2004 .... 2.95
❑2, Jan 2005 .... 2.95
❑3, Feb 2005 .... 2.95
❑4, Mar 2005 .... 2.95
❑5, Apr 2005 .... 2.95
❑6, Jun 2005 .... 2.95

N-MINT

Ocean Comics
Ocean

❑1, b&w 1.75

Ocelot
Fantagraphics / Eros

❑1; Adult 2.75
❑2; Adult 2.75
❑3; Adult 2.75

Octavia
-Ism

❑1, ca. 2004 .... 2.95
❑2, ca. 2004 .... 2.95
❑3, ca. 2005 .... 2.95

Octavia Trilogy
-Ism

❑1, ca. 2005 .... 5.95

October Yen
Antarctic

❑1, Jul 1996, b&w 3.50
❑2, Sep 1996, b&w 2.95
❑3, Nov 1996, b&w 2.95

Octobriana
Revolution

❑1 .... 3.50
❑2 .... 2.95
❑3 .... 2.95
❑4 .... 2.95
❑5 .... 2.95

Octobriana: Filling in the Blanks
Artful Salamander

❑1, Win 1998, b&w 2.95

Odd Adventure-Zine
Zamboni

❑1, Jan 1997 .... 2.95
❑2, Apr 1997 .... 2.95
❑3, Jul 1997 .... 2.95
❑4, Dec 1997 .... 2.95

Oddballs
NBM

❑1, ca. 2002, b&w 2.95
❑2, ca. 2002, b&w 2.95
❑3, ca. 2002, b&w 2.95
❑4, ca. 2002, b&w 2.95
❑5, ca. 2002, b&w 2.95
❑6, ca. 2002, b&w 2.95
❑7, ca. 2003, b&w 2.95

Oddballz
NBM

❑1 2002 .... 2.95
❑2 2002 .... 2.95
❑3 .... 2.95
❑4 .... 2.95

Oddjob
Slave Labor

❑1, Spr 1999, b&w 2.95

Oddly Normal
Viper

❑1, Mar 2005 .... 2.95
❑2, Jun 2005 .... 2.95
❑3, Jul 2005 .... 2.95
❑4, Sep 2005 .... 2.95

Other grades: Multiply price above by 5/6 for VF/NM • 2/3 for VERY FINE • 1/3 for FINE • 1/5 for VERY GOOD • 1/8 for GOOD

Odd Tales
-Ism

❑1, ca. 2004 ... 3.95
❑2, ca. 2004 ... 3.95
❑3, ca. 2004 ... 3.95
❑4, ca. 2005; b&w ... 3.95

Oeming Sketchbook
Michael Avon Oeming

❑1; Adult ... 5.00

Of Bitter Souls
Speakeasy Comics

❑1, Sep 2005 ... 2.99
❑2, Oct 2005 ... 2.99

Offcastes
Marvel / Epic

❑1, Jul 1993; Embossed cover ... 2.50
❑2, Aug 1993 ... 1.95
❑3 ... 1.95

Offerings
Cry for Dawn

❑1, Feb 1993, b&w; Various Pin-ups; Adult ... 2.75
❑2, b&w; Adult, ca.1993, various Pin-ups 2.50

Official, Authorized Zen Intergalactic Ninja Sourcebook
Express / Entity

❑1, b&w ... 3.50
❑1/2nd; 94 revised edition ... 3.50

Official Buz Sawyer
Pioneer

❑1, Aug 1988, b&w ... 2.00
❑2, Sep 1988, b&w ... 2.00
❑3, Oct 1988, b&w ... 2.00
❑4, Nov 1988, b&w ... 2.00
❑5, Dec 1988, b&w ... 2.00

Official Handbook of the Conan Universe
Marvel

❑1, Jan 1986, Aesgaard to Zingara reference book ... 1.50
❑2, no price; sold with Conan Saga #75. 1.00

Official Handbook of the Invincible Universe
Image

❑1, Jan 2007 ... 4.99

Official Handbook of the Marvel Universe
Marvel

❑1, Jan 1983, Abomination to Avengers Quinjet ... 2.00
❑2, Feb 1983, Baron Mordo to The Collective Man ... 2.00
❑3, Mar 1983, The Collector to Dracula . 2.00
❑4, Apr 1983, Dragon Man to Gypsy Moth 2.00
❑5, May 1983, Hangman to Juggernaut. 2.00
❑6, Jun 1983, Kang to Man-Bull ... 2.00
❑7, Jul 1983, Mandarin to Mystique ... 2.00
❑8, Aug 1983, Namorita to Pyro ... 2.00
❑9, Sep 1983, Quasar to She-Hulk ... 2.00
❑10, Oct 1983, Shi'ar to Sub-Mariner ... 2.00
❑11, Nov 1983, Subterraneans to Ursa Major ... 2.00
❑12, Dec 1983, Valkyrie to Zzzax ... 2.00
❑13, Feb 1984, Book of the Dead: Air-Walker to Man-Wolf ... 2.00
❑14, Mar 1984, Book of the Dead: Marvel Boy to Zuras ... 2.00
❑15, May 1984, Weapons, Hardware, and Paraphernalia ... 2.00

Official Handbook of the Marvel Universe
Marvel

❑1, Dec 1985, Abomination to Batroc's Brigade ... 2.00
❑2, Jan 1986, Beast to Clea ... 2.00
❑3, Feb 1986, Cloak to Doctor Octopus . 2.00
❑4, Mar 1986, Doctor Strange to Galactus 2.00
❑5, Apr 1986, Gardener to Hulk ... 2.00
❑6, May 1986, Human Torch to Ka-Zar .. 2.00
❑7, Jun 1986, Khoryphos to Magneto ... 2.00
❑8, Jul 1986, Magus to Mole Man ... 2.00
❑9, Aug 1986, Molecule Man to Owl ... 2.00
❑10, Sep 1986, Paladin to The Rhino ... 2.00
❑11, Oct 1986, Richard Rider to Sidewinder ... 2.00
❑12, Nov 1986, Sif to Sunspot ... 2.00
❑13, Dec 1986, Super-Adaptoid to Umar 2.00
❑14, Jan 1987, Unicorn to Wolverine ... 2.00
❑15, Mar 1987, Wonder Man to Zzzax and Alien Races ... 2.00
❑16, Jun 1987, Book of the Dead: Air-Walker to Death-Stalker ... 2.00
❑17, Aug 1987, Book of the Dead: Destiny to Hobgoblin ... 2.00
❑18, Oct 1987, Book of the Dead: Hyperion to Nighthawk; Book of the Dead: Hyperion II to Nighthawk II ... 2.00
❑19, Dec 1987, Book of the Dead: Nuke to Obadiah Stane ... 2.00
❑20, Feb 1988, Book of the Dead: Stick to Zuras ... 2.00

Official Handbook of the Marvel Universe
Marvel

❑1, Jul 1989, Adversary to Chameleon .. 2.00
❑2, Aug 1989, Champion of the Universe to Ecstasy ... 2.00
❑3, Sep 1989, Eon to Hulk ... 2.00
❑4, Oct 1989, Human Torch I to Manikin 2.00
❑5, Nov 1989, Marauders to Power Princess ... 2.00
❑6, Nov 1989, Prowler to Serpent Society 2.00
❑7, Dec 1989, Set to Tyrak ... 2.00
❑8, Dec 1989, U-Man to Madelyne Pryor 2.00

Official Handbook of the Marvel Universe Master Edition
Marvel

❑1, Dec 1990, Three-hole punched looseleaf format ... 4.50
❑2, Jan 1991 ... 4.50
❑3, Feb 1991 ... 4.50
❑4, Mar 1991 ... 4.50
❑5, Apr 1991 ... 4.50
❑6, May 1991 ... 3.95
❑7, Jun 1991 ... 3.95
❑8, Jul 1991 ... 3.95
❑9, Aug 1991 ... 3.95
❑10, Sep 1991 ... 3.95
❑11, Oct 1991 ... 3.95
❑12, Nov 1991 ... 3.95
❑13, Dec 1991 ... 4.50
❑14, Jan 1992 ... 4.50
❑15, Feb 1992 ... 4.50
❑16, Mar 1992 ... 4.50
❑17, Apr 1992 ... 4.50
❑18, May 1992 ... 4.50
❑19, Jun 1992 ... 4.50
❑20, Jul 1992 ... 4.50
❑21, Aug 1992 ... 4.50
❑22, Sep 1992 ... 4.50
❑23, Oct 1992 ... 4.50
❑24, Nov 1992 ... 4.50
❑25, Dec 1992 ... 4.50
❑26, Jan 1993 ... 4.50
❑27, Feb 1993 ... 4.50
❑28, Mar 1993 ... 4.95
❑29, Apr 1993 ... 4.95
❑30, May 1993 ... 4.95
❑31, Jun 1993 ... 4.95
❑32, Jul 1993 ... 4.95
❑33, Aug 1993 ... 4.95
❑34, Sep 1993 ... 4.95
❑35, Oct 1993, KP (a) ... 4.95
❑36, Nov 1993 ... 4.95

Official Handbook of the Marvel Universe: Alternate Universes 2005
Marvel

❑1 2005 ... 3.99

Official Handbook of the Marvel Universe: Avengers 2005
Marvel

❑0, Sep 2005 ... 3.99

Official Handbook of the Marvel Universe: Book of the Dead 2004
Marvel

❑1, Oct 2004 ... 3.99

Official Handbook of the Marvel Universe Daredevil Elektra 2004
Marvel

❑1, Nov 2004 ... 3.50

Official Handbook of the Marvel Universe: Fantastic Four 2005
Marvel

❑0, Jul 2005 ... 3.99

Official Handbook of the Marvel Universe: Golden Age Marvel 2004
Marvel

❑1, ca. 2004 ... 3.99

Official Handbook of the Marvel Universe: Horror 2005
Marvel

❑1, Dec 2005, b&w ... 3.99

Official Handbook of the Marvel Universe: Hulk
Marvel

❑1, ca. 2004 ... 3.99

Official Handbook of the Marvel Universe: Spider-Man 2004
Marvel

❑1, ca. 2004 ... 3.99

Official Handbook of the Marvel Universe: The Avengers
Marvel

❑1, ca. 2004 ... 3.99

Official Handbook of the Marvel Universe: Wolverine 2004
Marvel

❑1 2004 ... 3.99

Official Handbook of the Marvel Universe: Women of Marvel 2005
Marvel

❑0 2005 ... 3.99

Official Handbook of the Marvel Universe: X-Men 2004
Marvel

❑1, ca. 2004 ... 3.99

Official Handbook of the Marvel Universe: X-Men - Age of Apocalypse 2005
Marvel

❑1, May 2005 ... 3.99

Official Handbook of the Marvel Universe: X-Men 2005
Marvel

❑1, Jan 2006 ... 3.99

Official Handbook: Ultimate Marvel Universe 2005
Marvel

❑0, Oct 2005 ... 3.99

Official Handbook: Ultimate Marvel Universe - Ultimates & X-Men 2005
Marvel

❑1, Feb 2006 ... 3.99

Official Hawkman Index
Eclipse / Independent

❑1, Nov 1986 ... 2.00
❑2, Dec 1986 ... 2.00

Official How to Draw G.I. Joe
Blackthorne

❑1, Nov 1987 ... 2.00
❑2, Jan 1988 ... 2.00
❑3, Mar 1988 ... 2.00

Official How to Draw Robotech
Blackthorne

❑1, Feb 1987, Cover by Dennis Francis and Paul Tallerday ... 2.00
❑2, Mar 1987 ... 2.00
❑3, Apr 1987 ... 2.00
❑4, May 1987 ... 2.00
❑5, Jun 1987 ... 2.00
❑6, Jul 1987 ... 2.00
❑7, Aug 1987 ... 2.00
❑8, Sep 1987 ... 2.00
❑9, Oct 1987 ... 2.00
❑10, Nov 1987 ... 2.00
❑11, Dec 1987 ... 2.00
❑12, Jan 1988 ... 2.00
❑13, Feb 1988 ... 2.00
❑14, Mar 1988 ... 2.00

Other grades: Multiply price above by 5/6 for VF/NM • 2/3 for VERY FINE • 1/3 for FINE • 1/5 for VERY GOOD • 1/8 for GOOD

Painkiller Jane/ Darkchylde

Scantily clad women held captive
©Event

Paradise X

Alex Ross' follow-up to Universe X
©Marvel

Paranoia

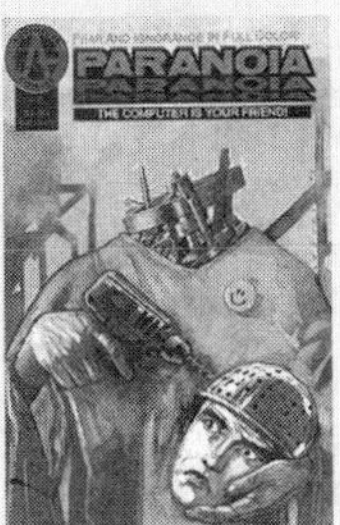

West End role-playing game comes to comics
©Adventure

Path

Set in a place very much like feudal Japan
©CrossGen

Patriots

WildStorm's elite force of super-agents
©WildStorm

N-MINT

Official How to Draw Transformers
Blackthorne

❑1, Sep 1987 .... 2.00
❑2, Nov 1987 .... 2.00
❑3, Jan 1988 .... 2.00
❑4, Mar 1988 .... 2.00

Official Johnny Hazard
Pioneer

❑1, Aug 1988, b&w; strips 2.00

Official Jungle Jim
Pioneer

❑1, Jun 1988, b&w 2.00
❑2, Jul 1988, b&w 2.00
❑3, Aug 1988, b&w 2.00
❑4, Sep 1988, b&w 2.00
❑5, Oct 1988, b&w 2.00
❑6, Nov 1988, b&w 2.00
❑7, Dec 1988, b&w 2.00
❑8, Jan 1989, b&w 2.00
❑9, Feb 1989, b&w 2.00
❑10, Apr 1989 .... 2.50
❑11, Apr 1989 .... 2.50
❑12 .... 2.50
❑13 .... 2.50
❑14 .... 2.50
❑15 .... 2.50
❑16 .... 2.50
❑Ann 1, Jan 1989, b&w 3.95

Official Justice League of America Index
ICG

❑1 .... 2.00
❑2 .... 2.00
❑3 .... 2.00
❑4 .... 2.00
❑5 .... 2.00
❑6 .... 2.00
❑7 .... 2.00
❑8; Title changes to Justice League of America Index; Covers Justice League of America #238-261, other related titles 2.00

Official Mandrake
Pioneer

❑1, Jun 1988, b&w 2.00
❑2, Jul 1988, b&w 2.00
❑3, Aug 1988, b&w 2.00
❑4, Sep 1988, b&w 2.00
❑5, Oct 1988, b&w 2.00
❑6, Nov 1988, b&w 2.00
❑7, Dec 1988, b&w 2.00
❑8, Jan 1989, b&w 2.00
❑9, Feb 1989, b&w 2.00
❑10, Apr 1989 .... 2.50
❑11, Apr 1989 .... 2.50
❑12 .... 2.50
❑13 .... 2.50
❑14 .... 2.50
❑15 .... 2.50

N-MINT

Official Marvel Index to Marvel Team-Up
Marvel

❑1, Jan 1986; Indexes Marvel Team-Up #1-20 .... 1.25
❑2, Feb 1986; Indexes Marvel Team-Up #21-42 .... 1.25
❑3, May 1986; Indexes Marvel Team-Up #43-59 and Ann #1 .... 1.25
❑4, Jul 1986; Indexes Marvel Team-Up #60-80 .... 1.25
❑5, Oct 1986; Indexes Marvel Team-Up #81-98, Ann #2 .... 1.25
❑6, Jul 1987; Indexes Marvel Team-Up #99 - 112, Ann 3 .... 1.25

Official Marvel Index to the Amazing Spider-Man
Marvel

❑1, Apr 1985; Indexes Amazing Fantasy #15, Amazing Spider-Man #1-29 .... 1.25
❑2, May 1985; Back cover is unpublished version of Amazing Spider-Man #10 cover; Indexes Amazing Spider-Man #30-59 and Ann #3-4 .... 1.25
❑3, Jun 1985; Indexes Amazing Spider-Man#59-84, King-Size Ann #5-6, Spectacular Spider-Man #1-2; Back cover is pin-up page from Amazing Spider-Man #3 .... 1.25
❑4, Jul 1985; Indexes Amazing Spider-Man#85-112, King-Size Ann #7-8 .... 1.25
❑5, Aug 1985; Indexes Amazing Spider-Man#114-137, King-Size Ann #9, Giant-Sized Super-Heroes #1 .... 1.25
❑6, Sep 1985; Indexes Amazing Spider-Man #138-155, Giant-Size Spider-Man #1-6 .... 1.25
❑7, Oct 1985; Indexes Amazing Spider-Man #156-174; Spider-Man Ann #10-11 .... 1.25
❑8, Nov 1985; Indexes issues #175-195, Ann #12 .... 1.25
❑9, Dec 1985; Indexes issues #196-215, Ann #13-14 .... 1.25

Official Marvel Index to the Avengers
Marvel

❑1, Jun 1987; Indexes Avengers #1-23 .... 2.95
❑2, Aug 1987; Indexes Avengers #24-45, Avengers Ann #1 .... 2.95
❑3, Oct 1987; Indexes Avengers #46-66, Ann #2, Marvel Super-Heroes #17 .... 2.95
❑4, Dec 1987; Indexes Avengers #67-87, Ann #3-5 and Ka-Zar #1 .... 2.95
❑5, Apr 1988; Indexes Avengers #88-108, Kree-Skrull War #1-2 .... 2.95
❑6, Jun 1988; Indexes Avengers #109-126, The Defenders #8-11, Giant-Size Avengers #1 .... 2.95
❑7, Aug 1988; Indexes Avengers #127-145, Giant-Size Avengers #2-5 .... 2.95

Official Marvel Index to The Avengers
Marvel

❑1, Oct 1994; Indexes Avengers #1 through #60 plus Anns #1 and #2 .... 1.95
❑2, Nov 1994; Indexes issues #61-122 .... 1.95
❑3, Dec 1994; Indexes issues #123-176, Ann #6-7, and Giant-Size #1-5 .... 1.95
❑4, Jan 1995; Indexes issues #177-230 .... 1.95

N-MINT

❑5, Feb 1995; Indexes issues #231-285, Anns #12-16 .... 1.95
❑6, Mar 1995; Indexes issues #286-333, Anns #17-20; Includes errata for earlier issues in the series 1.95

Official Marvel Index to the Fantastic Four
Marvel

❑1, Dec 1985; Indexes Fantastic Four #1-15 .... 1.25
❑2, Jan 1986 .... 1.25
❑3, Feb 1986; Indexes Fantastic Four #31-45 and Anns #2-3; Wraparound cover 1.25
❑4, Mar 1986; Indexes Fantastic Four #46-65, Ann #4 .... 1.25
❑5, Apr 1986; Indexes Fantastic Four #66-84, Ann #5-6 .... 1.25
❑6, May 1986; Indexes issues #85-106, Ann #7-8 .... 1.25
❑7, Jun 1986; Indexes issues #107-125, Ann #9 .... 1.25
❑8, Jul 1986; Indexes issues #126-141, Ann #10, Giant-Size Super-Stars #1 .... 1.25
❑9, Aug 1986 .... 1.25
❑10, Sep 1986; Indexes issues #161-176, Ann #11, Giant-Size Fantastic Four #4-6 .... 1.25
❑11, Oct 1986; Indexes issues #177-198 .... 1.25
❑12, Jan 1987; Indexes issues #199-214, Ann # 12-13 .... 1.25

Official Marvel Index to the X-Men
Marvel

❑1, May 1987; squarebound; cardstock cover 2.95
❑2, Jul 1987; Indexes X-Men #24 to #46 .... 2.95
❑3, Sep 1987; Indexes X-Men #47-66, Ka-Zar #2-3, Marvel Tales #30 .... 2.95
❑4, Nov 1987; Indexes X-Men #67-96, Ann #1-2, Giant-Size #1-2, Amazing Adventures (Comicbase 3rd series) #11-17, Hulk and Wolverine #1, X-Men Classics #1-3 .... 2.95
❑5, Mar 1988; Indexes X-Men #97-108, Classic X-Men #4-14 .... 2.95
❑6, May 1988; Indexes X-Men #109-124, Ann #3, Classic X-Men #15-19, Marvel Treasury Edition #26 .... 2.95
❑7, Jul 1988; Indexes X-Men #125-138, Ann #4, Classic X-Men #20-21, Amazing Adventures #1-14, Bizarre Adventures #27, and Phoenix The Untold Story #1 .... 2.95

Official Marvel Index to the X-Men
Marvel

❑1, Apr 1994 .... 1.95
❑2, May 1994 .... 1.95
❑3, Jun 1994 .... 1.95
❑4, Jul 1994 .... 1.95
❑5, Aug 1994 .... 1.95

Official Modesty Blaise
Pioneer

❑1, Jul 1988, b&w 2.00
❑2, Aug 1988, b&w 2.00
❑3, Sep 1988, b&w 2.00
❑4, Oct 1988, b&w 2.00
❑5, Nov 1988, b&w 2.00
❑6, Dec 1988, b&w 2.00
❑7, Dec 1988, b&w 2.00

❑8, Jan 1989, b&w.... 2.00
❑Ann 1, Dec 1988, b&w; O: Modesty.... 4.95

Official Prince Valiant
Pioneer

❑1, b&w; Hal Foster.... 2.00
❑2, Jul 1988, b&w; Hal Foster.... 2.00
❑3, Aug 1988, b&w; Hal Foster.... 2.00
❑4, Sep 1988, b&w; Hal Foster.... 2.00
❑5, Oct 1988, b&w; Hal Foster.... 2.00
❑6, Oct 1988, b&w; Hal Foster.... 2.00
❑7, Nov 1988; Foster.... 2.00
❑8, Dec 1988; Foster.... 2.00
❑9, Jan 1989; Foster.... 2.00
❑10, Feb 1989.... 2.50
❑11, Mar 1989.... 2.50
❑12, Apr 1989.... 2.50
❑13.... 2.50
❑14.... 2.50
❑15.... 2.50
❑16.... 2.50
❑17.... 2.50
❑18.... 2.50
❑Ann 1, Win 1988, b&w; Hal Foster.... 3.95
❑King Size 1, Apr 1989, b&w; Foster.... 3.95

Official Prince Valiant Monthly
Pioneer

❑1, Jun 1989, b&w.... 3.95
❑2, Jun 1989.... 3.95
❑3, ca. 1989.... 4.95
❑4, ca. 1989.... 4.95
❑5, ca. 1989.... 6.95
❑6.... 6.95
❑7.... 6.95
❑8.... 6.95

Official Rip Kirby
Pioneer

❑1, Aug 1988, b&w.... 2.00
❑2, Sep 1988, b&w.... 2.00
❑3, Oct 1988, b&w.... 2.00
❑4, Nov 1988, b&w.... 2.00
❑5, Dec 1988, b&w.... 2.00
❑6, Jan 1989, b&w.... 2.00

Official Secret Agent
Pioneer

❑1, Jun 1988, b&w.... 2.00
❑2, Jul 1988, b&w.... 2.00
❑3, Aug 1988, b&w.... 2.00
❑4, Sep 1988, b&w.... 2.00
❑5, Oct 1988, b&w.... 2.00
❑6, Nov 1988, b&w.... 2.00
❑7, Dec 1988, b&w.... 2.00

Official Teen Titans Index
Independent / Eclipse

❑1, Aug 1985.... 1.50
❑2, Sep 1985; Indexes Teen Titans #23-53, DC Super-Stars #1, Showcase #75, The Hawk and the Dove #1-6.... 1.50
❑3, Oct 1985; Indexes DC Comics Presents #26, New Teen Titans #1-25, Tales of the New Teen Titans #1-4, Marvel and DC Present #1.... 1.50
❑4, Nov 1985.... 1.50
❑5, Dec 1985.... 1.50

Offworld
Graphic Image

❑1.... 3.95

Of Mind and Soul
Rage

❑1, b&w.... 2.25

Of Myths and Men
Blackthorne

❑1, b&w.... 1.75
❑2, Mar 1987, b&w.... 1.75

Ogenki Clinic (Vol. 1)
Akita

❑1, Sep 1997.... 3.95
❑2, Oct 1997.... 3.95
❑3, Nov 1997.... 4.50
❑4, Dec 1997.... 4.50
❑5, Jan 1998.... 4.50
❑6, Feb 1998.... 4.50

Ogenki Clinic (Vol. 2)
Akita

❑1, Mar 1998.... 3.95
❑2, Apr 1998.... 3.95
❑3, May 1998.... 3.95
❑4, Jun 1998.... 3.95
❑5, Jul 1998.... 3.95
❑6, Aug 1998.... 3.95

Ogenki Clinic (Vol. 3)
Sexy Fruit

❑1, Sep 1998, Antonio Honduras translation.... 3.95
❑2, Oct 1998.... 3.95
❑3, Nov 1998.... 3.95
❑4, Dec 1998.... 3.95
❑5, Jan 1999.... 3.95
❑6, Feb 1999.... 3.95
❑7, Mar 1999.... 3.95

Ogenki Clinic (Vol. 4)
Sexy Fruit

❑1, Apr 1999.... 2.95
❑2, May 1999.... 2.95
❑3, Jun 1999.... 2.95
❑4, Jul 1999.... 2.95
❑5, Aug 1999.... 2.95
❑6, Sep 1999.... 2.95

Ogenki Clinic (Vol. 5)
Sexy Fruit

❑1, Oct 1999.... 2.95
❑2, Nov 1999.... 2.95
❑3, Dec 1999.... 2.95
❑4, Jan 2000.... 2.95
❑5, Feb 2000.... 2.95
❑6, Mar 2000.... 2.95
❑7, Apr 2000.... 2.95

Ogenki Clinic (Vol. 6)
Sexy Fruit

❑1, May 2000.... 2.95
❑2, Jun 2000.... 2.95
❑3, Jul 2000.... 2.95
❑4, Aug 2000.... 2.95
❑5, Sep 2000.... 2.95
❑6, Oct 2000.... 2.95
❑7, Nov 2000.... 2.95

Ogenki Clinic (Vol. 7)
Ironcat

❑1, Dec 2000.... 2.95
❑2, Jan 2001.... 2.95
❑3, Feb 2001.... 2.95
❑4, Mar 2001.... 2.95
❑5, Apr 2001.... 2.95
❑6, Jun 2001.... 2.95
❑7, Jul 2001.... 2.95

Ogenki Clinic (Vol. 8)
Ironcat

❑1, Aug 2001.... 2.95
❑2, Sep 2001.... 2.95
❑3, Oct 2001.... 2.95
❑4, Nov 2001.... 2.95
❑5, Dec 2001.... 2.95
❑6, Jan 2002.... 2.95
❑7, Feb 2002.... 2.95
❑8, Mar 2002.... 2.95

Ogenki Clinic (Vol. 9)
Ironcat

❑1, Apr 2002.... 2.95
❑2, May 2002.... 2.95
❑3, Jun 2002.... 2.95
❑4, Jul 2002.... 2.95
❑5, Aug 2002.... 2.95
❑6, Sep 2002.... 2.95
❑7, Oct 2002.... 2.95
❑8, Nov 2002.... 2.95

Ogre
Black Diamond

❑1, Jan 1994; 1: Barnacle Bill; 1: Felony; 1: Ogre.... 2.95
❑2, Mar 1994.... 2.95
❑3, May 1994.... 2.95
❑4, Jul 1994.... 2.95

O.G. Whiz
Gold Key

❑1, Feb 1971.... 25.00
❑2, May 1971.... 15.00
❑3, Aug 1971.... 10.00
❑4, Nov 1971.... 10.00
❑5, Feb 1972.... 10.00
❑6, May 1972, Final issue of original run (1972).... 10.00
❑7, May 1978, Series begins again (1978); giant-size issue; Time magazine parody cover ("Tike").... 3.00
❑8, Jul 1978.... 3.00
❑9, Sep 1978, A: Tubby.... 3.00
❑10, Nov 1978.... 3.00
❑11, Jan 1979, Final Issue.... 3.00

Oh.
B Publications

❑1; Magazine sized.... 2.95
❑2; Magazine sized.... 2.95
❑3; Magazine sized.... 2.95
❑4; Magazine sized.... 2.95
❑5; Magazine sized.... 2.95
❑6; Magazine sized.... 2.95
❑7; Magazine sized.... 2.95
❑8; Immola and the Luna Legion.... 2.95
❑9.... 2.95
❑10.... 2.95
❑11, Oct 1995.... 2.95
❑12.... 2.95
❑13.... 2.95
❑14.... 2.95
❑15.... 2.95
❑16.... 2.95
❑17.... 2.95
❑18.... 2.95
❑19.... 2.95
❑20.... 2.95
❑21.... 2.95
❑22.... 2.95

Ohm's Law
Imperial

❑1, 1: Black Hurrikan; 1: Drakkus; 1: Ohm.... 2.25
❑2, b&w; Black and White.... 1.95
❑3, b&w; Published out of sequence; Black and white.... 1.95

Oh My Goddess!
Dark Horse

❑1, Aug 1994, b&w.... 5.00
❑2, Sep 1994, b&w.... 3.00
❑3, Oct 1994, b&w.... 3.00
❑4, Nov 1994, b&w.... 3.00
❑5, Dec 1994, b&w.... 3.00
❑6, Jan 1995, b&w.... 3.00
❑88, Jul 2002, b&w; Numbering continued from combined Oh My Goddess! Part II-XI series.... 3.50
❑89, Aug 2002, b&w; Part XII #2.... 3.50
❑90, Sep 2002, b&w; Part XII #3.... 3.50
❑91, Oct 2002, b&w.... 3.50
❑92, Nov 2002, b&w.... 3.50
❑93, Dec 2002, b&w.... 3.50
❑94, Jan 2003, b&w.... 3.50
❑95, Feb 2003, b&w.... 3.50
❑96, Apr 2003, b&w.... 2.99
❑97, May 2003, b&w.... 2.99
❑98, Jun 2003, b&w.... 2.99
❑99, Jul 2003, b&w.... 2.99
❑100, Aug 2003, b&w.... 2.99
❑101, Sep 2003, b&w.... 2.99
❑102, Oct 2003, b&w.... 2.99
❑103, Nov 2003, b&w.... 2.99
❑104, Dec 2003, b&w.... 2.99
❑105, Feb 2004, b&w.... 2.99
❑106, Mar 2004, b&w.... 3.50
❑107, Apr 2004, b&w.... 2.99
❑108, May 2004, b&w.... 2.99
❑109, Aug 2004, b&w.... 2.99
❑110, Sep 2004, b&w.... 3.99
❑111, Oct 2004, b&w.... 3.99
❑112, Nov 2004, b&w.... 3.99

Oh My Goddess! Part II
Dark Horse

❑1, Feb 1995.... 3.00
❑2, Mar 1995.... 3.00
❑3, Apr 1995.... 2.75
❑4, May 1995.... 2.75
❑5, Jun 1995.... 2.75
❑6, Jul 1995.... 2.75
❑7, Aug 1995.... 3.00
❑8, Sep 1995.... 3.00

Paul the Samurai (Mini-Series)

Samurai takes job as security guard
©NEC

Peanuts (Dell)

Snoopy and company visit comic books
©Dell

Pebbles and Bamm-Bamm

Uses teen-age versions from CBS cartoon
©Charlton

Pep

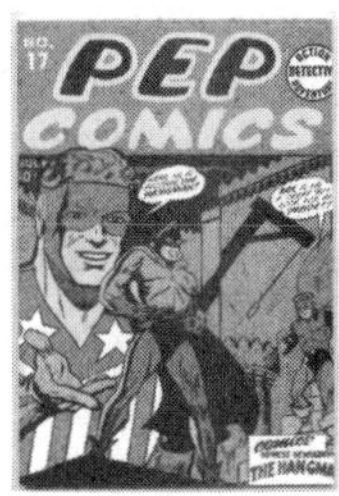

Long-running Archie series once had heroes
©Archie

Perry Mason

Courtroom drama didn't translate to comics page
©Dell

N-MINT

Oh My Goddess! Part III
Dark Horse / Manga

- ❑1, Nov 1995, Cover reads "Oh My Goddess Special" ... 3.00
- ❑2, Dec 1995, Cover reads "Oh My Goddess Special" ... 3.00
- ❑3, Jan 1996, Cover reads "Oh My Goddess Special" ... 3.00
- ❑4, Feb 1996, Cover reads "Oh My Goddess Special" ... 3.00
- ❑5, Mar 1996, Cover reads "Oh My Goddess Special" ... 3.00
- ❑6, Apr 1996, Cover reads "Oh My Goddess! 1 of 6" ... 3.00
- ❑7, May 1996, Cover reads "Oh My Goddess! 2 of 6" ... 3.00
- ❑8, Jun 1996, Cover reads "Oh My Goddess! 3 of 6" ... 3.00
- ❑9, Jul 1996, Cover reads "Oh My Goddess! 4 of 6" ... 3.00
- ❑10, Aug 1996, Cover reads "Oh My Goddess, part 5 of 6" ... 3.00
- ❑11, Sep 1996, Cover reads "Oh My Goddess! 6 of 6" ... 3.00

Oh My Goddess! Part IV
Dark Horse / Manga

- ❑1, Dec 1996, Cover reads "Oh My Goddess Special" ... 2.95
- ❑2, Jan 1997, Cover reads "Oh My Goddess! 1 of 3" ... 2.95
- ❑3, Feb 1997, Cover reads "Oh My Goddess! 2 of 3" ... 2.95
- ❑4, Mar 1997, Cover reads "Oh My Goddess! 3 of 3" ... 2.95
- ❑5, Apr 1997, Cover reads "Oh My Goddess Special" ... 2.95
- ❑6, May 1997, Cover reads "Oh My Goddess! 1 of 3" ... 2.95
- ❑7, Jun 1997, Cover reads Oh My Goddess! 2 of 3 ... 2.95
- ❑8, Jul 1997, Cover reads "Oh My Goddess! 3 of 3" ... 2.95

Oh My Goddess! Part V
Dark Horse / Manga

- ❑1, Sep 1997, Cover reads "Oh My Goddess Special" ... 2.95
- ❑2, Oct 1997, Cover reads "Oh My Goddess Special" ... 2.95
- ❑3, Nov 1997, Cover reads "Oh My Goddess Special" ... 3.95
- ❑4, Dec 1997, Cover reads "Oh My Goddess Special" ... 3.95
- ❑5, Jan 1998, 1: Kodama. Cover reads "Oh My Goddess! 1 of 2" ... 2.95
- ❑6, Feb 1998, 1: Hikari. Cover reads "Oh My Goddess! 2 of 2" ... 3.95
- ❑7, Mar 1998, Cover reads "Oh My Goddess! 1 of 2" ... 3.95
- ❑8, Apr 1998, Cover reads "Oh My Goddess! 2 of 2" ... 2.95
- ❑9, May 1998 ... 3.50
- ❑10, Jun 1998, Sakakibara. Cover reads "Oh My Goddess! One-Shot" ... 3.95
- ❑11, Jul 1998, Cover reads "Oh My Goddess! One-Shot" ... 3.95
- ❑12, Aug 1998, Cover reads "Oh My Goddess! One-Shot" ... 3.95

N-MINT

Oh My Goddess! Part VI
Dark Horse / Manga

- ❑1, Oct 1998 ... 3.50
- ❑2, Dec 1998 ... 2.95
- ❑3, Jan 1999 ... 2.95
- ❑4, Feb 1999 ... 2.95
- ❑5, Mar 1999 ... 2.95
- ❑6, Apr 1999 ... 2.95

Oh My Goddess! Part VII
Dark Horse / Manga

- ❑1, May 1999 ... 2.95
- ❑2, Jun 1999 ... 2.95
- ❑3, Jul 1999 ... 2.95
- ❑4, Aug 1999 ... 2.95
- ❑5, Sep 1999 ... 2.95
- ❑6, Oct 1999 ... 2.95
- ❑7, Nov 1999 ... 2.95
- ❑8, Dec 1999 ... 2.95

Oh My Goddess! Part VIII
Dark Horse / Manga

- ❑1, Jan 2000 ... 3.50
- ❑2, Feb 2000 ... 3.50
- ❑3, Mar 2000 ... 3.50
- ❑4, Apr 2000 ... 3.50
- ❑5, May 2000 ... 3.50
- ❑6, Jun 2000 ... 3.50

Oh My Goddess! Part IX
Dark Horse / Manga

- ❑1, Jul 2000 ... 3.50
- ❑2, Aug 2000 ... 3.50
- ❑3, Sep 2000 ... 3.50
- ❑4, Oct 2000 ... 3.50
- ❑5, Nov 2000 ... 3.50
- ❑6, Dec 2000 ... 3.50
- ❑7, Jan 2001 ... 3.50

Oh My Goddess! Part X
Dark Horse / Manga

- ❑1, Feb 2001 ... 3.50
- ❑2, Mar 2001 ... 3.50
- ❑3, Apr 2001 ... 3.50
- ❑4, May 2001 ... 3.50
- ❑5, Jun 2001 ... 3.50

Oh My Goddess! Part XI
Dark Horse

- ❑1, Aug 2001 ... 3.50
- ❑2, Sep 2001 ... 3.50
- ❑3, Oct 2001 ... 2.99
- ❑4, Nov 2001 ... 2.99
- ❑5, Dec 2001 ... 2.99
- ❑6, Feb 2002 ... 2.99

Oh My Goddess!: Adventures of the Mini-Goddesses
Dark Horse / Manga

- ❑1, May 2000 ... 9.95

Oh My Goth
Sirius / Dog Star

- ❑1 1998 ... 2.95
- ❑2, Oct 1998 ... 2.95
- ❑3, Jan 1999 ... 2.95
- ❑4, Apr 1999 ... 2.95

N-MINT

Oh My Goth: Humans Suck!
Sirius

- ❑1, Jun 2000, b&w ... 2.95
- ❑2, Aug 2000, b&w ... 2.95

Oink: Blood and Circus
Kitchen Sink

- ❑1, Apr 1998 ... 4.95
- ❑2, May 1998 ... 4.95
- ❑3, Jun 1998 ... 4.95
- ❑4, Jul 1998 ... 4.95

Oink: Heaven's Butcher
Kitchen Sink

- ❑1, Dec 1995 ... 4.95
- ❑2, Feb 1996 ... 4.95
- ❑3, Apr 1996 ... 4.95

OJ's Big Bust Out
Boneyard

- ❑1, Mar 1995, b&w; Adult ... 3.50

Oktane
Dark Horse

- ❑1, Aug 1995; Adult ... 2.50
- ❑2, Sep 1995; Adult ... 2.50
- ❑3, Oct 1995; Adult ... 2.50
- ❑4, Nov 1995; Final Issue; Adult ... 2.50

Oldblood
Parody

- ❑1 ... 2.50
- ❑1/2nd; 2nd printing ... 2.50

Olympians
Marvel / Epic

- ❑1, May 1991 ... 3.95
- ❑2, Jan 1992 ... 3.95

Olympus Heights
Idea & Design Works

- ❑1, Jul 2004 ... 3.99
- ❑2, Aug 2004 ... 3.99
- ❑3, Sep 2004 ... 3.99

OMAC
DC

- ❑1, Oct 1974, JK (c); JK (w); JK (a); O: Omac. 1: Omac ... 40.00
- ❑2, Dec 1974, JK (c); JK (w); JK (a); V: Mr. Big ... 15.00
- ❑3, Feb 1975, JK (c); JK (w); JK (a) ... 12.00
- ❑4, Apr 1975, JK (c); JK (w); JK (a) ... 10.00
- ❑5, Jun 1975 JK (c); JK (w); JK (a) ... 7.00
- ❑6, Aug 1975 JK (c); JK (w); JK (a) ... 7.00
- ❑7, Oct 1975 JK (c); JK (w); JK (a) ... 7.00
- ❑8, Dec 1975 JKu (c); JK (w); JK (a) ... 7.00

OMAC: One Man Army Corps
DC

- ❑1, Jan 1991, b&w; prestige format; JBy (c); JBy (w); JBy, JK (a) ... 4.00
- ❑2, Feb 1991, b&w; prestige format; JBy (c); JBy (w); JBy (a) ... 4.00
- ❑3, Mar 1991, b&w; prestige format; JBy (c); JBy (w); JBy (a) ... 4.00
- ❑4, Apr 1991, b&w; prestige format; JBy (c); JBy (w); JBy (a) ... 4.00

OMAC
DC

- ❑1, Sep 2006 ... 2.99
- ❑2, Oct 2006, V: Firestorm; V: Cyborg ... 2.99

Other grades: Multiply price above by 5/6 for VF/NM • 2/3 for VERY FINE • 1/3 for FINE • 1/5 for VERY GOOD • 1/8 for GOOD

❑3, Nov 2006 .... 2.99
❑4, Dec 2006 .... 2.99
❑5, Jan 2007 .... 2.99
❑6, Feb 2007 .... 2.99

OMAC Project
DC

❑1, Jun 2005 .... 22.00
❑1/2nd, Jun 2005 .... 7.00
❑1/3rd, Jun 2005 .... 3.00
❑2, Jul 2005 .... 6.00
❑2/2nd, Jul 2005 .... 3.00
❑3, Aug 2005 .... 4.00
❑4, Sep 2005 .... 2.50
❑5, Oct 2005 .... 2.50
❑6 2005 .... 2.50

OMAC Project: Infinite Crisis Special
DC

❑1, Jun 2006 .... 4.99

Omaha: Cat Dancer
Steeldragon

❑1, ca. 1984; Adult; b&w 12.00
❑1/Ashcan; preview 3.00
❑1/2nd; 2nd printing; Adult; b&w; ca. 1984 .... 4.00
❑2, ca. 1985; Series continued Omaha the Cat Dancer (Kitchen Sink) #3; Adult; b&w; ca. 1986 .... 8.00

Omaha The Cat Dancer
Kitchen Sink

❑0, Apr 1995, b&w; 1: Omaha the Cat Dancer. Reprints early Omaha stories from Vootie, Bizarre Sex #9 .... 4.00
❑1, Oct 1986, b&w; Reprint from Omaha: Cat Dancer #1 .... 10.00
❑1/2nd, b&w; 2nd printing 4.00
❑1/3rd, b&w; 3rd printing 3.00
❑2, Oct 1986, b&w; Reprint from Omaha: Cat Dancer #2 .... 5.00
❑3, Oct 1986, b&w 4.00
❑4, Jan 1987, b&w 4.00
❑5, Mar 1987, b&w 4.00
❑6, May 1987, b&w 3.00
❑6/2nd, Sep 1988 .... 2.50
❑7, Jul 1987, b&w 3.00
❑8, Oct 1987, b&w 3.00
❑9, Feb 1988, b&w 3.00
❑10, May 1988, b&w 3.00
❑11, Dec 1988, b&w 3.00
❑12, Jul 1989, b&w; Tales of Mipple City story 3.00
❑12/2nd, b&w; 2nd printing; Tales of Mipple City story 2.95
❑13, Sep 1989, b&w 3.00
❑13/2nd, b&w; 2nd printing 2.95
❑14, Mar 1990, b&w; Wendel back-up ... 3.00
❑15, Jan 1991, b&w; Wendel story 3.00
❑16, Nov 1991, b&w 2.50
❑17, Feb 1992, b&w; Tales of Mipple City story 2.50
❑18, Jan 1993, b&w 2.95
❑19, Jun 1993, b&w 2.50
❑20, Jun 1994, b&w; Final Kitchen Sink issue 2.95

Omaha The Cat Dancer
Fantagraphics

❑1, Jul 1994 .... 3.00
❑2, Aug 1994 .... 3.00
❑3, Nov 1994 .... 3.00
❑4, Feb 1995 .... 3.00

O'Malley and the Alley Cats
Gold Key

❑1, Apr 1971 .... 8.00
❑2, Jul 1971 .... 6.00
❑3, Jul 1972, Whitman publishes 6.00
❑4, Oct 1972 .... 4.00
❑5, Jan 1973 .... 4.00
❑6, Apr 1973 .... 4.00
❑7, Jul 1973 .... 4.00
❑8, Oct 1973 .... 4.00
❑9, Jan 1974, 16 pages; 16-page catalog insert 4.00

Omar Lennyx
Magnecom

❑1, ca. 1993; b&w; Omar Lennyx story; The Renegade story 2.95

Omega Elite
Blackthorne

❑1, b&w 3.50

Omega Flight
Marvel

❑1, Apr 2007 .... 7.00
❑2, May 2007 .... 5.00
❑3, Jun 2007 .... 4.00

Omega Force
South Star

❑1, Aug 1992 .... 2.00

Omega Force
Entity

❑1, ca. 1995, 1: Archetype; 1: Dual; 1: Flashback (Entity); 1: Karad the Godslayer; 1: Omega Force; 1: The Drakon; 1: The Earon Raider 2.50

Omega Knights
Underground

❑1 .... 2.00
❑2 .... 2.00
❑3 .... 2.00
❑4 .... 2.00
❑5 .... 2.00
❑6, Oct 1992 .... 2.00

Omega Man
Omega 7

❑0 .... 3.00
❑1, b&w; Simpson trial; no indicia 4.00
❑Ashcan 1, no cover price; no indicia; sideways format 1.00

Omega Men
DC

❑1, Apr 1983; KG (c); KG (w); KG (a); O: Omega Men 4.00
❑2, May 1983; KG (c); KG (w); KG (a); O: Broot 3.00
❑3, Jun 1983; 1: Lobo 2.00
❑4, Jul 1983; 1: Felicity; D: Demonia 1.50
❑5, Aug 1983; 2: Lobo 2.00
❑6, Sep 1983 .... 1.50
❑7, Oct 1983; O: Citadel 1.50
❑8, Nov 1983 .... 1.50
❑9, Dec 1983; A: Lobo. 3: Lobo 2.00
❑10, Jan 1984; 1st Lobo Full Story 2.00
❑11, Feb 1984 .... 1.25
❑12, Mar 1984 .... 1.25
❑13, Apr 1984; Primus gets eye back 1.25
❑14, May 1984 .... 1.25
❑15, Jun 1984 .... 1.25
❑16, Jul 1984 .... 1.25
❑17, Aug 1984 .... 1.25
❑18, Sep 1984 .... 1.25
❑19, Oct 1984 A: Lobo 1.25
❑20, Nov 1984 A: Lobo 2.00
❑21, Dec 1984 .... 1.25
❑22, Jan 1985 .... 1.25
❑23, Feb 1985 .... 1.25
❑24, Mar 1985 .... 1.25
❑25, Apr 1985 .... 1.25
❑26, May 1985; AMo (w); 1: Elu; Tales of Vega story 1.25
❑27, Jun 1985; AMo (w); Omega Men story; Tales of Vega story 1.25
❑28, Jul 1985; Omega Men story; Tales of Vega story 1.25
❑29, Aug 1985; Omega Men story; Tales of Vega story 1.25
❑30, Sep 1985; Omega Men story; Tales of Vega story 1.25
❑31, Oct 1985; Crisis 1.25
❑32, Nov 1985 DS (a) 1.25
❑33, Dec 1985; DaG (a); Omega Men story; Tales of Vega story 1.25
❑34, Jan 1986; RB (a); Tales of Vega story 1.25
❑35, Feb 1986; Omega Men story; Tales of Vega story 1.25
❑36, Mar 1986; JDu (a); Omega Men story; Tales of Vega story 1.25
❑37, Apr 1986; KG (w); KG (a); A: Lobo. Tales of Vega story 1.25
❑38, May 1986 .... 1.25
❑Ann 1, ca. 1984 .... 2.00
❑Ann 2, ca. 1985; O: Primus 1.75

Omega Men
DC

❑1, Dec 2006 .... 2.99
❑2, Jan 2007 .... 2.99
❑3, Mar 2007 .... 2.99

Omega the Unknown
Marvel

❑1, Mar 1976, JM (a); 1: James-Michael Starling (Omega the Unknown's counterpart). 1: Omega the Unknown 9.00
❑2, May 1976, A: Hulk. Marvel Value Stamp Series B #85 .... 6.00
❑2/30¢, May 1976, 30¢ regional price variant 20.00
❑3, Jul 1976, V: Electro 3.00
❑3/30¢, Jul 1976, 30¢ regional price variant 20.00
❑4, Sep 1976, 1: El Gato 2.00
❑5, Nov 1976, V: El Gato 2.00
❑6, Jan 1977, 1: The Wrench (Kurt Klemmer) 2.00
❑7, Mar 1977, V: Blockbuster (formerly Man-Brute); Man-Brute changes name to Blockbuster 2.00
❑8, May 1977, 1: Foolkiller II (Greg Salinger)-cameo; V: Nitro 2.00
❑9, Jul 1977, V: Blockbuster (formerly Man-Brute); D: Blockbuster 3.00
❑9/35¢, Jul 1977, 35¢ regional price variant 15.00
❑10, Oct 1977, D: Omega the Unknown; Final Issue; Storyline continues in Defenders #75 .... 2.00
❑10/35¢, Oct 1977, D: Omega the Unknown. 35¢ regional price variant.. 15.00

Omen
Chaos!

❑1, May 1998 .... 2.95
❑2, Jun 1998 .... 2.95
❑3, Jul 1998 .... 2.95
❑4, Aug 1998 .... 2.95
❑5, Sep 1998 .... 2.95

Omen
Northstar

❑1, b&w 2.00
❑2, b&w; ca. 1987 .... 2.00

Omen: Save the Chosen Preview
Chaos!

❑1, Sep 1997; preview of upcoming series 2.50

Omen: Vexed
Chaos!

❑1, Oct 1998 .... 2.95

Omicron: Astonishing Adventures on Other Worlds
Pyramid

❑1, b&w; flexi-disc 2.25
❑2, Sep 1987, b&w; flexi-disc 2.25

Omnibus: Modern Perversity
Blackbird

❑1, Jan 1992, b&w; squarebound 3.25

Omni Comix
Omni

❑1, Mar 1995, magazine; BWi (a); Mar '95 issue of Omni inserted 4.00
❑2, Apr 1995, magazine; insert in Apr. '95 issue of Omni with Omni Comix #2 cover 4.00
❑3, Oct 1995, magazine; T.H.U.N.D.E.R. Agents story 4.95

Omni Men
Blackthorne

❑1, Apr 1989, b&w 3.50

On a Pale Horse
Innovation

❑1, Jun 1991; Adapts Piers Anthony story from his Incarnations of Immortality series 4.95
❑2, Dec 1991 .... 4.95
❑3, Dec 1992 .... 4.95
❑4, Oct 1993 .... 4.95
❑5, Dec 1993 .... 4.95

Once Upon a Time in the Future
Platinum

❑1 .... 9.95

Peter Cannon-Thunderbolt

Tibetan-trained hero comes from Charlton
©DC

Peter Pan (Gold Key)

Perpetual pre-pubescents harass Hook
©Gold Key

Peter Parker: Spider-Man

Adjectiveless series restarts, adds proper name
©Marvel

Pete the P.O.'d Postal Worker

The Punisher takes philatelic tact
©Sharkbait

Phantom (1st Series)

Ghost Who Walks' longest-running series
©Gold Key

N-MINT

One
Tokyopop

❑1, Apr 2004 .... 9.99
❑2, Jun 2004 .... 9.99
❑3, Aug 2004 .... 9.99
❑4, Oct 2004 .... 9.99
❑5, Dec 2004 .... 9.99
❑6, Feb 2005 .... 9.99
❑7, Apr 2005 .... 9.99
❑8, Oct 2005 .... 9.99

One
Pacific

❑1, ca. 1977, b&w; 1st Pacific title 3.00

One
Marvel / Epic

❑1, Jul 1985; BA (a); 1&O: The One 2.00
❑2, Sep 1985 BA (a) 2.00
❑3, Nov 1985 BA (a) 2.00
❑4, Jan 1986 BA (a) 2.00
❑5, Mar 1986 BA (a) 2.00
❑6, May 1986 BA (a) 2.00

One-Arm Swordsman
Dr. Leung's

❑1 .... 1.80
❑2 .... 1.80
❑3 .... 1.80
❑4 .... 1.80
❑5 .... 1.80
❑6 .... 1.80
❑7 .... 1.80

One-Fisted Tales
Slave Labor

❑1, May 1990, b&w; brown paper wrapper 3.00
❑1/2nd, Nov 1990; 2nd printing; Adult... 2.50
❑2, Sep 1990, b&w; brown paper wrapper (some wrappers printed red in error). 3.00
❑2/2nd, Apr 1993; no brown paper wrapper 2.95
❑3, Feb 1991, b&w; brown paper wrapper; Cherry cover and story 2.50
❑3/2nd, Apr 1993; no brown paper wrapper 2.50
❑3/3rd, Aug 1993; no brown paper wrapper 2.95
❑4, Jun 1991, b&w; Adult 2.50
❑4/2nd, Jan 1992; 2nd printing; Adult ... 2.95
❑4/3rd, Aug 1993; no brown paper wrapper 2.95
❑5, Sep 1991, b&w; Adult 3.95
❑5/2nd, Feb 1992; 2nd printing; Adult ... 2.95
❑6, Apr 1992; Adult 2.95
❑7, Sep 1992, b&w; Adult 2.95
❑8, Mar 1993, b&w; Adult 2.95
❑9, Oct 1993, b&w; Adult 2.95
❑10, Feb 1994, b&w; Adult 2.95
❑11, Aug 1994, b&w; Adult 2.95

One Hundred and One Dalmatians
Disney

❑1, ca. 1991 .... 2.50

100 Bullets
DC / Vertigo

❑1, Aug 1999 .... 10.00
❑2, Sep 1999 .... 6.50
❑3, Oct 1999 .... 5.00
❑4, Nov 1999 .... 5.00
❑5, Dec 1999 .... 5.00
❑6, Jan 2000 .... 4.00
❑7, Feb 2000 .... 4.00
❑8, Mar 2000 .... 4.00
❑9, Apr 2000 .... 4.00
❑10, May 2000 .... 4.00
❑11, Jun 2000 .... 3.00
❑12, Jul 2000 .... 3.00
❑13, Aug 2000 .... 3.00
❑14, Sep 2000 .... 3.00
❑15, Oct 2000 .... 3.00
❑16, Nov 2000 .... 3.00
❑17, Dec 2000 .... 3.00
❑18, Jan 2001 .... 3.00
❑19, Feb 2001 .... 3.00
❑20, Mar 2001 .... 3.00
❑21, Apr 2001 .... 3.00
❑22, May 2001 .... 3.00
❑23, Jun 2001 .... 3.00
❑24, Jul 2001 .... 3.00
❑25, Aug 2001 .... 3.00
❑26, Sep 2001, DaG, FM, JLee (a) 3.00
❑27, Oct 2001 .... 3.00
❑28, Nov 2001 .... 3.00
❑29, Dec 2001 .... 3.00
❑30, Jan 2002 .... 3.00
❑31, Feb 2002 .... 2.50
❑32, Mar 2002 .... 2.50
❑33, Apr 2002 .... 2.50
❑34, May 2002 .... 2.50
❑35, Jun 2002 .... 2.50
❑36, Jul 2002, D: Milo Garrett 2.50
❑37, Sep 2002 .... 2.50
❑38, Oct 2002 .... 2.50
❑39, Nov 2002 .... 2.50
❑40, Jan 2003 .... 2.50
❑41, Feb 2003 .... 2.50
❑42, Mar 2003 .... 2.50
❑43, Apr 2003 .... 2.50
❑44, May 2003 .... 2.50
❑45, Jun 2003, The Losers preview 2.50
❑46, Jul 2003 .... 2.50
❑47, Oct 2003 .... 2.50
❑48, Dec 2003 .... 2.50
❑49, May 2004 .... 2.50
❑50, Aug 2004 .... 3.50
❑51, Sep 2004 .... 2.50
❑52, Oct 2004 .... 2.50
❑53, Nov 2004 .... 2.50
❑54, Dec 2004 .... 2.50
❑55, Jan 2005 .... 2.50
❑56, Feb 2005 .... 2.50
❑57, Mar 2005 .... 2.50
❑58, Apr 2005 .... 2.50
❑59, May 2005 .... 2.50
❑60, Jun 2005 .... 2.50
❑61, Jul 2005 .... 2.50
❑62, Aug 2005 .... 2.75
❑63, Sep 2005 .... 2.75
❑64, Oct 2005; Includes Loveless preview 2.75
❑65, Dec 2005 .... 2.75
❑66, Jan 2006 .... 2.75
❑67, Feb 2006 .... 2.75
❑68, Mar 2006 .... 2.75
❑69, Apr 2006 .... 2.75
❑70, May 2006 .... 2.75
❑71, Jun 2006 .... 2.75
❑72, Jul 2006 .... 2.99
❑73, Aug 2006, Cover by Dave Johnson 2.99
❑74, Sep 2006 .... 2.99
❑75, Oct 2006 .... 2.99
❑76, Nov 2006 .... 2.99
❑77, Dec 2006, Preview of Deathblow by Brian Azzarello and Carlos D'Anda 3.00
❑78, Jan 2007 .... 2.99
❑79 .... 2.99
❑80 .... 2.99
❑81 .... 2.99
❑82 .... 2.99
❑83 .... 2.99
❑84 .... 2.99
❑85 .... 2.99
❑86 .... 2.99
❑87 .... 2.99
❑88 .... 2.99
❑89 .... 2.99
❑90 .... 2.99
❑91 .... 2.99
❑92 .... 2.99
❑93 .... 2.99
❑94 .... 2.99
❑95 .... 2.99
❑96 .... 2.99
❑97 .... 2.99
❑98 .... 2.99
❑99 .... 2.99
❑100 .... 2.99

100 Degrees in the Shade
Fantagraphics / Eros

❑1, Feb 1992, b&w; Adult 2.50
❑2, May 1992, b&w; Adult 2.50
❑3, Jul 1992, b&w; Adult 2.50
❑4, Oct 1992, b&w; Adult 2.50

100 Girls
Arcana

❑1, Aug 2004 .... 5.00
❑1/Variant 5.00
❑2, Oct 2004 .... 2.95
❑3, Dec 2004 .... 2.95
❑4, Mar 2005; Red cover lettering 2.95
❑5, Aug 2005 .... 2.95
❑6, Oct 2005 .... 2.95

100 Greatest Marvels of All Time
Marvel

❑1, Dec 2001, reprints Uncanny X-Men #141, Fantastic Four (Vol. 1) #48, Amazing Spider-Man (Vol. 1) #1, Daredevil #181; cardstock cover 7.50
❑2, Dec 2001, reprints Avengers (Vol. 1) #1, Uncanny X-Men #350, Amazing Spider-Man (Vol. 1) #122, Captain America #109; cardstock cover 7.50
❑3, Dec 2001, reprints Incredible Hulk #181, X-Men #25, Amazing Spider-Man (Vol. 1) #33, Spider-Man #1; cardstock cover 7.50
❑4, Dec 2001, reprints Incredible Hulk (Vol. 1) #1, Ultimate X-Men #1, Daredevil #227, Wolverine #75; cardstock cover 7.50

Other grades: Multiply price above by 5/6 for VF/NM • 2/3 for VERY FINE • 1/3 for FINE • 1/5 for VERY GOOD • 1/8 for GOOD

❑5, Dec 2001, reprints Ultimate Spider-Man #1, X-Men (1st series) #1, Avengers (Vol. 1) #4, Amazing Spider-Man (Vol. 1) #121; cardstock cover ... 7.50
❑6, Dec 2001, reprints X-Men (2nd series) #1; cardstock cover ... 3.50
❑7, Dec 2001, reprints Giant-Size X-Men #1 ... 3.50
❑8, Dec 2001, reprints X-Men (1st series) #137; cardstock cover ... 3.50
❑9, Dec 2001, reprints Fantastic Four (Vol. 1) #1 ... 3.50
❑10, Dec 2001, reprints Amazing Fantasy #15 ... 3.50

101 Other Uses for a Condom
Apple

❑1, ca. 1991 ... 4.95

101 Ways to End the Clone Saga
Marvel

❑1, Jan 1997, One-shot ... 2.50

100%
DC / Vertigo

❑1, Aug 2002 ... 5.95
❑2, Sep 2002 ... 5.95
❑3, Oct 2002 ... 5.95
❑4, Nov 2002 ... 5.95
❑5, Dec 2002, Wraparound cover ... 5.95

100% True?
DC / Paradox Press

❑1, Sum 1996, b&w; magazine; excerpts from The Big Books of Death, Conspiracies, Weirdos, and Freaks ... 3.50
❑2, Win 1996, b&w; magazine; excerpts from The Big Books of Death, Conspiracies, Weirdos, and Freaks; Winter, 1996 issue ... 3.50

One Mile Up
Eclipse

❑1, Dec 1991, b&w Mad Dogs Preview 3 pages ... 2.50
❑2 ... 2.50

One Millennium
Hunter

❑1, b&w ... 2.50
❑2, b&w ... 2.50
❑3, ca. 1997, b&w ... 2.50
❑4, ca. 1997, b&w ... 2.50
❑5, ca. 1997, b&w ... 2.50

One Piece
Viz

❑1, Feb 2004, b&w ... 7.95
❑2, Apr 2004; b&w ... 7.95
❑3, Jun 2004 ... 7.95
❑5, Nov 2004; b&w ... 7.95
❑6, Mar 2005; b&w ... 7.95
❑7, Jul 2005; b&w ... 7.95
❑8, Oct 2005; I Won't Die ... 7.95

One-Pound Gospel
Viz

❑1 ... 3.50
❑2 ... 3.50
❑3 ... 2.95
❑4 ... 2.95

One-Pound Gospel Round 2
Viz

❑1, Jan 1997 ... 2.95
❑2, Feb 1997 ... 2.95
❑3, Mar 1997 ... 2.95
❑4 1997 ... 2.95
❑5 1997 ... 2.95
❑6 1997 ... 2.95

One-Shot Parody
Milky Way

❑1, ca. 1986, X-Men ... 1.50

One-Shot Western
Caliber

❑1, b&w ... 2.50

1001 Nights of Sheherazade
NBM

❑1; Adult; ca. 2002 ... 12.95

1111
Crusade

❑1, Oct 1996, b&w; prose story with facing page illustrations; illustrated story ... 2.95

1,001 Nights of Bacchus
Dark Horse

❑1, May 1993, b&w; NN; One-shot ... 4.50

...One to Go
Äardwolf

❑1 ... 2.50

Oni
Dark Horse

❑1, Feb 2001 ... 2.99
❑2, Feb 2001 ... 2.99
❑3, Feb 2001 ... 2.99

Oni Double Feature
Oni

❑1, Jan 1998; Flip-book; MW (c); KSm (w); MW (a); 1: Silent Bob. 1: Jay. Jay & Silent Bob, Milk & Cheese, Secret Broadcast ... 6.00
❑1/2nd, Mar 1998; 2nd printing ... 2.95
❑2, Feb 1998; Too Much Coffee Man, Car Crash, Secret Broadcast ... 4.00
❑3, Mar 1998; Frumpy the Clown, Bacon, Car Crash ... 3.50
❑4, Apr 1998; BSz (c); BSz (w); BSz (a); Bacon, A River in Egypt, Cheetahman; Judd Winick's first major comics work ... 3.50
❑5, May 1998 ... 3.50
❑6, Jun 1998; CR, NG (w); Only The End of the World Again, Zombie Kid ... 4.00
❑7, Jul 1998; Volcanic Revolver; Only the End of the World Again, Part 2; I Love Acne!! ... 2.95
❑8, Aug 1998; Only The End of the World Again, Satchel of Weltschmerz, Pip & Norton ... 2.95
❑9, Oct 1998 ... 2.95
❑10, Nov 1998; Sam & Max, Drive-By, Road Trip ... 2.95
❑11, Feb 1999; Usagi Yojimbo, Blue Monday, Drive-By ... 2.95
❑12, May 1999; The Harpooner, Bluntman & Chronic, The Honor Rollers ... 2.95

Onigami
Antarctic

❑1, Apr 1998 ... 2.95
❑2, Jun 1998 ... 2.95
❑3, Jul 1998; Includes preview of Far West by Richard Moore ... 2.95

Oni Press Color Special
Oni

❑2001, ca. 2001 ... 5.95
❑2002, ca. 2002 ... 5.95

Oni Press Summer Vacation Supercolor Fun Special
Oni

❑1, Jul 2000 ... 5.95

Only the End of the World Again
Oni

❑1, May 2000 ... 6.95

On Our Butts
Aeon

❑1, Apr 1995 ... 2.95

On Raven's Wings
Boneyard

❑1, Apr 1994; Adult ... 2.95
❑2, Sep 1994; Adult ... 2.95

Onslaught: Epilogue
Marvel

❑1, Feb 1997; 1: Nina; One-shot ... 2.95

Onslaught: Marvel
Marvel

❑1, Oct 1996; MWa (w); DGr (a); wraparound cover ... 6.00
❑1/Gold, Oct 1996 ... 12.00

Onslaught Reborn
Marvel

❑1, Dec 2006 ... 6.00
❑2, Mar 2007, Thor cover by Rob Liefield ... 4.00

Onslaught: X-Men
Marvel

❑1, Aug 1996; MWa (w); DGr (a); wraparound cover; set-up for Onslaught crossover in Marvel titles ... 5.00
❑1/Gold, Aug 1996 ... 10.00
❑1/Variant, Aug 1996; MWa (w); DGr (a); variant cover ... 8.00

On the Bus
Slave Labor

❑1, Aug 1994 ... 2.95

On the Road to Perdition
DC

❑1, May 2003 ... 7.95
❑2, Jan 2004 ... 7.95
❑3, Aug 2004; Detour ... 7.95

Onyx Overlord
Marvel / Epic

❑1, Oct 1992 ... 2.75
❑2, Nov 1992 ... 2.75
❑3, Dec 1992 ... 2.75
❑4, Jan 1993 ... 2.75

Oombah, Jungle Moon Man
Strawberry Jam

❑1, Aug 1992, b&w ... 2.50

Open Season
Renegade

❑1, Dec 1987, b&w ... 2.00
❑2 1987, b&w ... 2.00
❑3 1987, b&w ... 2.00
❑4, Oct 1987, b&w ... 2.00
❑5, Dec 1987, b&w ... 2.00
❑6, Apr 1988, b&w; black issue ... 2.00
❑7, b&w ... 2.00

Open Sore Funnies
Home-Made Euthanasia

❑1 ... 1.25

Open Space
Marvel

❑1, Dec 1989 KB (w) ... 5.00
❑2, Apr 1990 ... 5.00
❑3, Jun 1990 ... 5.00
❑4, Aug 1990 ... 5.00

Operation: Kansas City
Motion

❑1, Win 1993, b&w; Breakneck Blvd. Preview ... 2.50

Operation: Knightstrike
Image

❑1, May 1995 ... 2.50
❑1/A, May 1995; Purple background on cover ... 2.50
❑2, Jun 1995 ... 2.50
❑2/A, Jun 1995 ... 2.50
❑3, Jul 1995 ... 2.50

Operation: Stormbreaker
Acclaim / Valiant

❑1, Aug 1997; cover says Jul, indicia says Aug ... 3.95

Operative: Scorpio
Blackthorne

❑1, Jan 1989, b&w ... 3.50

Opposite Forces
Funnypages

❑1, ca. 2002; 1: Captain Dynamo ... 2.95
❑2, ca. 2003 ... 2.95
❑3, ca. 2004 ... 2.95
❑4, ca. 2004 ... 2.95

Opposite Forces
Alias

❑1, Sep 2005 ... 1.00
❑2, Nov 2005 ... 2.99
❑3, Dec 2005 ... 2.99

Optic Nerve
Drawn & Quarterly

❑1 ... 5.00
❑2 ... 3.00
❑3 ... 3.00
❑4, Mar 1997 ... 3.00
❑5, Feb 1998 ... 3.00
❑6, Jan 1999 ... 3.00
❑7, Jun 2000; Mini-Comic ... 3.00

Optimism of Youth
Fantagraphics

❑1, Oct 1991 ... 12.95

Ora
Son of a Treebob

❑1, Mar 1999, b&w ... 2.95

Phantom Jack

Pitched Epic series lands at Image
©Image

Phantom of Fear City

Fear City foundations established here
©Claypool

Phantom Stranger

Angelic agent tussles with Dr. 13
©DC

Phantom Zone

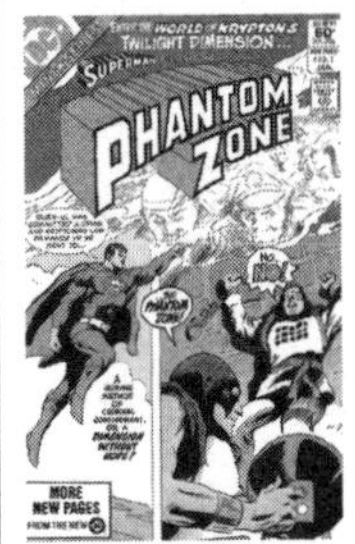

Superman tours spectral realm
©DC

Pink Panther

Comics discarded main character's silence
©Gold Key

N-MINT

Oracle
Oracle

❑1, Jun 1986, b&w; GP (a) 3.00

Oracle - A Trespassers Mystery
Amazing Montage

❑1, b&w 4.95

Oracle Presents
Oracle

❑1, b&w; GP (a); reprint of Oracle #1 3.00
❑2, Aug 1986, b&w; Critter Corps 3.00

Orbit
Eclipse

❑1; ca. 1990 4.95
❑2; ca. 1990 4.95
❑3; ca. 1990 4.95

Orbiter
DC

❑1, ca. 2003 24.95

Orb Magazine
Orb

❑1 1.25
❑2 1.25
❑3 1.25

Order
Marvel

❑1, Apr 2002 2.25
❑2, May 2002 2.25
❑3, Jun 2002 2.25
❑4, Jul 2002 2.25
❑5, Aug 2002 2.25
❑6, Sep 2002 2.25

Oriental Heroes
Jademan

❑1, Aug 1988 1.95
❑2, Sep 1988 1.95
❑3, Oct 1988 1.95
❑4, Nov 1988 1.95
❑5, Dec 1988 1.95
❑6, Jan 1989 1.95
❑7, Feb 1989 1.95
❑8, Mar 1989 1.95
❑9, Apr 1989 1.95
❑10, May 1989 1.95
❑11, Jun 1989 1.95
❑12, Jul 1989 1.95
❑13, Aug 1989 1.95
❑14, Sep 1989 1.95
❑15, Oct 1989 1.95
❑16, Nov 1989 1.95
❑17, Dec 1989 1.95
❑18, Jan 1990 1.95
❑19, Feb 1990 1.95
❑20, Mar 1990 1.95
❑21, Apr 1990 1.95
❑22, May 1990 1.95
❑23, Jun 1990 1.95
❑24, Jul 1990 1.95
❑25, Aug 1990 1.95
❑26, Sep 1990 1.95
❑27, Oct 1990 1.95
❑28, Nov 1990 1.95
❑29, Dec 1990 1.95
❑30, Jan 1991 1.95

N-MINT

❑31, Feb 1991 1.95
❑32, Mar 1991 1.95
❑33, Apr 1991 1.95
❑34, May 1991 1.95
❑35, Jun 1991 1.95
❑36, Jul 1991 1.95
❑37, Aug 1991 1.95
❑38, Sep 1991 1.95
❑39, Oct 1991 1.95
❑40, Nov 1991 1.95
❑41, Dec 1991 1.95
❑42, Jan 1992 1.95
❑43, Feb 1992 1.95
❑44, Mar 1992 1.95
❑45, Apr 1992 1.95
❑46, May 1992 1.95
❑47, Jun 1992 1.95
❑48, Jul 1992 1.95
❑49, Aug 1992 1.95
❑50, Sep 1992 1.95
❑51, Oct 1992 1.95
❑52, Nov 1992 1.95
❑53, Dec 1992 1.95
❑54, Jan 1993 1.95
❑55, Feb 1993; Final issue 1.95

Orient Gateway
NBM

❑1 13.95

Original Adventures of Cholly and Flytrap
Image

❑1, Mar 2006 5.99
❑2, Sep 2006 5.99

Original Astro Boy
Now

❑1, Sep 1987; O: Astro Boy; 42000 copies printed 2.00
❑2, Oct 1987 1.50
❑3, Nov 1987 1.50
❑4, Dec 1987 1.50
❑5, Jan 1988 1.50
❑6, Feb 1988 1.50
❑7, Mar 1988 1.50
❑8, Apr 1988 1.50
❑9, May 1988 1.50
❑10, Jun 1988 1.50
❑11, Aug 1988 1.50
❑12, Sep 1988 1.50
❑13, Oct 1988 1.50
❑14, Nov 1988 1.50
❑15, Jan 1989 1.50
❑16, Feb 1989 1.50
❑17, Mar 1989 1.50
❑18, Apr 1989 1.50
❑19, May 1989 1.50
❑20, Jun 1989; Final Issue 1.50

Original Black Cat
Recollections

❑1, Oct 1988; Reprints from Black Cat Comics #4, 14, 20 2.00
❑2, Mar 1989; MA (c); 1: Kit. Reprints... 2.00
❑3, Sep 1990; Reprints from Black Cat Comics #18, 29, Speed Comics #34; b&w 2.00

N-MINT

❑4, Jun 1991; Reprints from Black Cat Comics #9, 18, 21, Speed Comics #35 2.00
❑5, Jul 1991; Reprints from Black Cat Comics #10, 33, Green Hornet Fights Crime #38, Speed Comics #1 2.00
❑6, Aug 1991; reprints first Black Cat story from Pocket Comics #1 2.00
❑7, Nov 1991 2.00
❑8, Feb 1992; Title changes to Black Cat for one issue only 2.00
❑9; Title reverts to Original Black Cat 2.75
❑10; Title changes to Black Cat Comics for final issue 1.00

Original Boy: Day of Atonement
Omega 7

❑1; no cover price; no indicia; events deal with Million Man March on Washington 1.95

Original Crew
Personality

❑1, Jun 1991; William Shatner 3.00
❑2; Leonard Nimoy 3.00
❑3; DeForest Kelley 3.00
❑4; James Doohan 2.95
❑5; Walter Koenig 2.95
❑6; George Takei 2.95
❑7; Nichelle Nichols 2.95
❑8; Majel Barret 2.95
❑9; Bruce Hyde 2.95
❑10; Grace Lee Whitney 2.95

Original Dick Tracy
Gladstone

❑1, Sep 1990, Mrs. Pruneface 2.00
❑2, Nov 1990, Influence 2.00
❑3, Jan 1991, Gargles 2.00
❑4, Mar 1991, Itchy 2.00
❑5, May 1991, Shoulders 2.00

Original Doctor Solar, Man of the Atom
Valiant

❑1, Apr 1995, Cardstock cover; Reprints from Doctor Solar, Man of the Atom #1, 5 5.00

Original E-Man
First

❑1, Oct 1985; E-Man story, Reprints from E-Man (1st Series) #1, 2 2.00
❑2, Nov 1985; E-Man story, Reprint from E-Man (1st Series) #3; Michael Mauser, Private Eye story, Reprints from Vengeance Squad #1, 2 2.00
❑3, Dec 1985; E-Man story, Reprint from E-Man (1st Series) #4; Michael Mauser, Private Eye story, Reprints from Vengeance Squad #3, 4 2.00
❑4, Jan 1986; E-Man story, Reprints from E-Man (1st Series) #5, 6 2.00
❑5, Feb 1986; E-Man story, Reprint from E-Man (1st Series) #7; Michael Mauser, Private Eye story, Reprints from Vengeance Squad #5, 6 2.00
❑6, Mar 1986; E-Man story, Reprints from E-Man (1st Series) #8 2.00
❑7, Apr 1986; E-Man story, Reprint from E-Man (1st Series) #9, 10; Michael Mauser, Private Eye story, Reprints from Vengeance Squad #4 2.00

Original Ghost Rider
Marvel

- ❑1, Jul 1992; O: Ghost Rider; Reprint from Marvel Spotlight (Vol. 1) #5 .... 1.75
- ❑2, Aug 1992; Reprint from Marvel Spotlight (Vol. 1) #6 .... 1.75
- ❑3, Sep 1992; Reprints Marvel Spotlight #7; Phantom Rider back-up; Ghost Rider story, Reprint from Marvel Spotlight (Vol. 1) #7; Phantom Rider story 1.75
- ❑4, Oct 1992; Ghost Rider story, Reprint from Marvel Spotlight (Vol. 1) #8; Phantom Rider story 1.75
- ❑5, Nov 1992; Ghost Rider story, Reprint from Marvel Spotlight (Vol. 1) #9; Phantom Rider story 1.75
- ❑6, Dec 1992; Ghost Rider story, Reprint from Marvel Spotlight (Vol. 1) #10; Phantom Rider story 1.75
- ❑7, Jan 1993; Ghost Rider story, Reprint from Marvel Spotlight #11; Phantom Rider story 1.75
- ❑8, Feb 1993; Ghost Rider story, Reprint from Ghost Rider (Vol. 1) #1, Son of Satan (first appearance), Phantom Rider story 1.75
- ❑9, Mar 1993; Ghost Rider story; Reprint from Ghost Rider (Vol. 1) #2; Phantom Rider story 1.75
- ❑10, Apr 1993; Ghost Rider story; Reprint from Marvel Spotlight (Vol. 1) #12; Phantom Rider story 1.75
- ❑11, May 1993; O: the Phantom Rider (Carter Slade); Reprint from Ghost Rider (Vol. 1) #3 .... 1.75
- ❑12, Jun 1993; Ghost Rider story, Reprint from Ghost Rider (Vol. 1) #4; Phantom Rider story 1.75
- ❑13, Jul 1993; Ghost Rider story, Reprint from Ghost Rider (Vol. 1) #5; Phantom Rider story 1.75
- ❑14, Aug 1993; Reprint from Ghost Rider (Vol. 1) #6 .... 1.75
- ❑15, Sep 1993; Reprint from Ghost Rider (Vol. 1) #7; 1: Aguila (Paco Montoya) 1.75
- ❑16, Oct 1993; 1: Inferno; Reprint from Ghost Rider (Vol. 1) #8 .... 1.75
- ❑17, Nov 1993; Reprint from Ghost Rider (Vol. 1) #9 .... 1.75
- ❑18, Dec 1993; Reprint from Ghost Rider (Vol. 1) #11 .... 1.75
- ❑19, Jan 1994; Reprints Marvel Two-In-One #8 .... 1.75
- ❑20, Feb 1994; Reprint from Ghost Rider (Vol. 1) #12 .... 1.75

Original Ghost Rider Rides Again
Marvel

- ❑1, Jul 1991; Reprinted from Ghost Rider #68 .... 1.50
- ❑2, Aug 1991; Reprints from Ghost Rider (Vol. 1) #70, 71 .... 1.50
- ❑3, Sep 1991; Reprints from Ghost Rider (Vol. 1) #72, 73 .... 1.50
- ❑4, Oct 1991; Reprints from Ghost Rider (Vol. 1) #74, 75 .... 1.50
- ❑5, Nov 1991; Reprints from Ghost Rider (Vol. 1) #76, 77 .... 1.50
- ❑6, Dec 1991; Reprints from Ghost Rider (Vol. 1) #78, 79 .... 1.50
- ❑7, Jan 1992; Reprints from Ghost Rider (Vol. 1) #80, 81 .... 1.50

Original Magnus Robot Fighter
Valiant

- ❑1, Apr 1992, DG (c); RM (w); RM (a); Reprints Magnus, Robot Fighter 4000 A.D. #2; cardstock cover 4.00

Original Man
Omega 7

- ❑1 .... 3.50

Original Man: The Most Powerful Man In the Universe
Omega 7

- ❑1; Darkforce #0 as flip-side support story 1.95

Original Mysterymen Presents
Dark Horse

- ❑1, Jul 1999 .... 2.95
- ❑2, Aug 1999 .... 2.95
- ❑3, Sep 1999 .... 2.95
- ❑4, Oct 1999; All-Villian issue 2.95

Original Sad Sack Recollections

- ❑1, b&w 2.00

Original Shield
Archie

- ❑1, Apr 1984; Continued from Might Crusaders (2nd Series) #6 .... 1.00
- ❑2, Jun 1984 .... 1.00
- ❑3, Aug 1984 .... 1.00
- ❑4, Oct 1984 .... 1.00

Original Sin
Thwack! Pow!

- ❑1 .... 1.00
- ❑2 .... 1.00
- ❑3 .... 1.00

Original Street Fighter
Alpha

- ❑1, b&w 2.50

Original Tom Corbett
Eternity

- ❑1, Sep 1990, b&w; Reprinted from Field Enterprises strips Tom Corbett, Space Cadet; The Mercurian Invasion 2.95
- ❑2, Sep 1990, b&w; Reprinted from Field Enterprises strips Tom Corbett, Space Cadet; The Mercurian Invasion; Colonists on Titan 2.95
- ❑3, Oct 1990, b&w; Reprinted from Field Enterprises strips Tom Corbett, Space Cadet; Colonists on Titan 2.95
- ❑4, Nov 1990, b&w; Reprinted from Field Enterprises strips Tom Corbett, Space Cadet; The Revolt on Mars 2.95
- ❑5, Dec 1990, b&w; Reprinted from Field Enterprises strips Tom Corbett, Space Cadet; Slave Plantation of Venus; Issues #6-10 were planned but never published 2.95

Original Turok, Son of Stone
Valiant

- ❑1, Apr 1995, cardstock cover 4.00
- ❑2, May 1995, Reprints of Turok, Son of Stone #24, #33; cardstock cover 7.00

Original Tzu: Spirits of Death
Murim

- ❑1, Dec 1997, b&w; reprints manga series 2.95

O: Galactus
Marvel

- ❑1, Feb 1996, reprints Super-Villain Classics #1 .... 2.50

O: the Defiant Universe
Defiant

- ❑1, Feb 1994; O: Defiant Universe; Reprint from Defiant Genesis #1 .... 1.50

Orion
Dark Horse

- ❑1, Feb 1993, b&w; manga 3.95
- ❑2, Mar 1993, b&w; manga 2.95
- ❑3, Apr 1993, b&w; manga 2.95
- ❑4, May 1993, b&w; manga 2.95
- ❑5, Jun 1993, b&w; manga 2.95
- ❑6, Jul 1993, Manga 3.95

Orion
DC

- ❑1, Jun 2000 .... 2.50
- ❑2, Jul 2000 .... 2.50
- ❑3, Aug 2000; Tales of the New Gods story 2.50
- ❑4, Sep 2000; Tales of the New Gods story 2.50
- ❑5, Oct 2000 .... 2.50
- ❑6, Nov 2000; Tales of the New Gods story 2.50
- ❑7, Dec 2000; Tales of the New Gods story 2.50
- ❑8, Jan 2001; Tales of the New Gods story 2.50
- ❑9, Feb 2001 .... 2.50
- ❑10, Mar 2001; Tales of the New Gods story 2.50
- ❑11, Apr 2001 .... 2.50
- ❑12, May 2001; Tales of the New Gods back-up by Walter Simonson & Jim Lee; Tales of the New Gods story 2.50
- ❑13, Jun 2001; Tales of the New Gods story 2.50
- ❑14, Jul 2001; Tales of the New Gods story 2.50
- ❑15, Aug 2001; Mister Miracle appearance (disguised as Black Racer); Tales of the New Gods backup 2.50
- ❑16, Sep 2001 .... 2.50
- ❑17, Sep 2001; Orion surrenders anti-life equation 2.50
- ❑18, Oct 2001; Tales of the New Gods story 2.50
- ❑19, Nov 2001; V: Slig of Deep Six; Joker: Last Laugh crossover; Tales of the New Gods back-up by Eddie Campbell 2.50
- ❑20, Dec 2001 .... 2.50
- ❑21, Jan 2002; V: Arnicus Wolfram 2.50
- ❑22, Feb 2002 .... 2.50
- ❑23, Mar 2002 .... 2.50
- ❑24, Apr 2002 .... 2.50
- ❑25, May 2002; Final issue 2.50

Orlak Redux
Caliber

- ❑1, b&w 3.95

Ororo: Before the Storm
Marvel

- ❑1, Jul 2005 .... 2.99
- ❑2, Aug 2005 .... 2.99
- ❑3, Sep 2005 .... 2.99
- ❑4, Oct 2005 .... 2.99

Orphen
ADV Manga

- ❑1, ca. 2005; Read right to left; Graphic novel; b&w 9.99
- ❑2, ca. 2005; Read right to left; Graphic novel; b&w 9.99
- ❑3, ca. 2005 .... 9.99

Osborn Journals
Marvel

- ❑1, Feb 1997; summation of Clone Saga and return of Norman Osborn as Green Goblin 2.95

Othello
Tome

- ❑1, b&w; NN 3.50

Other Big Thing (Colin Upton's...)
Fantagraphics

- ❑1, Mar 1991, b&w 2.50
- ❑2, Jul 1991, b&w 2.25
- ❑3, Dec 1991, b&w 2.25
- ❑4, Jul 1992, b&w 2.50

Others
Image

- ❑0, Mar 1995; 16-page preview 1.00
- ❑1, Apr 1995 .... 2.50
- ❑2, May 1995 .... 2.50
- ❑3, Jul 1995 .... 2.50
- ❑4 .... 2.50

Others
Cormac

- ❑1 .... 1.50

Other Side
DC / Vertigo

- ❑1, Dec 2006 .... 2.99
- ❑2, Jan 2007 .... 2.99
- ❑3, Feb 2007 .... 2.99
- ❑4, Mar 2007 .... 2.99

Otherworld
DC / Vertigo

- ❑1, May 2005 .... 2.99
- ❑2, Jun 2005 .... 2.99
- ❑3, Jul 2005 .... 2.99
- ❑4, Aug 2005 .... 2.99
- ❑5, Sep 2005 .... 2.99
- ❑6, Oct 2005 .... 2.99
- ❑7, Nov 2005 .... 2.99

Otis Goes Hollywood
Dark Horse

- ❑1, Apr 1997, b&w 2.95
- ❑2, May 1997, b&w 2.95

Otto Space!
Manifest Destiny

- ❑1 .... 2.00
- ❑2 .... 2.00

Ouran High School Host Club
Viz

- ❑1, Jul 2005 .... 8.99
- ❑2, Sep 2005 .... 8.99
- ❑3, Nov 2005 .... 8.99

Other grades: Multiply price above by 5/6 for VF/NM • 2/3 for VERY FINE • 1/3 for FINE • 1/5 for VERY GOOD • 1/8 for GOOD

Pinky and the Brain

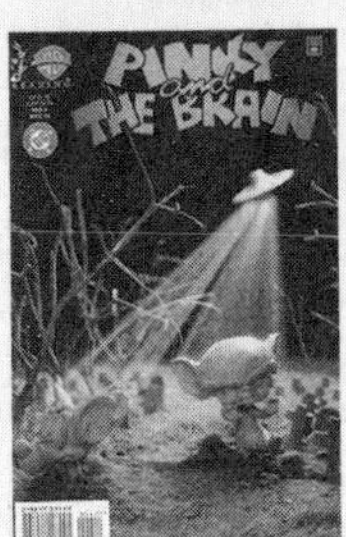

World domination plans derailed by dimwit
©DC

Pirates of Dark Water

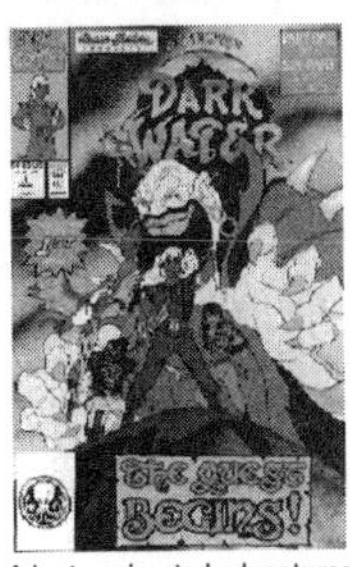

Adapts animated adventures on far-off world
©Marvel

Pitt

Dale Keown's creature seeks Earthly asylum
©Image

Planetary

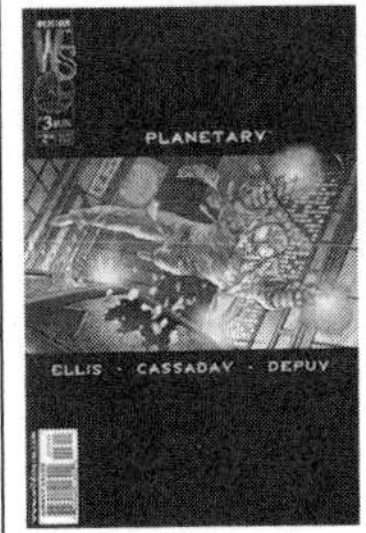

Pulp, pop culture references abound
©DC

Planet of the Apes

Magazine adapts movies, adds new stories
©Marvel

Our Army at War
DC

	N-MINT
❑81, Apr 1959; JKu, RA, RH, JAb (a); 1: Easy Co.. 1: Sgt. Rock	2500.00
❑82, May 1959; MD, RA, IN (a); 2: Sgt. Rock	650.00
❑83, Jun 1959; MD, JKu, RA (a); 1: Easy Company. 1st Kubert Sgt. Rock	1800.00
❑84, Jul 1959; Sgt Rock story	300.00
❑85, Aug 1959; O: The Ice Cream Soldier. 1: The Ice Cream Soldier; Sgt Rock story	350.00
❑86, Sep 1959; Sgt Rock story	300.00
❑87, Oct 1959; Sgt Rock story	300.00
❑88, Nov 1959; Sgt Rock story	325.00
❑89, Dec 1959; Sgt Rock story	300.00
❑90, Jan 1960; Sgt Rock story	300.00
❑91, Feb 1960; 1st full-length Sgt. Rock story; All-Rock issue	700.00
❑92, Mar 1960; Sgt Rock story	175.00
❑93, Apr 1960; Sgt Rock story	175.00
❑94, May 1960; Sgt Rock story	175.00
❑95, Jun 1960; Sgt Rock story	175.00
❑96, Jul 1960; Sgt Rock story	175.00
❑97, Aug 1960; Sgt Rock story	175.00
❑98, Sep 1960; Sgt Rock story	175.00
❑99, Oct 1960; Sgt Rock story	175.00
❑100, Nov 1960, Sgt Rock story	175.00
❑101, Dec 1960, Sgt Rock story	125.00
❑102, Jan 1961, Sgt Rock story	125.00
❑103, Feb 1961, Sgt Rock story	125.00
❑104, Mar 1961, Sgt Rock story	125.00
❑105, Apr 1961, Sgt Rock story	125.00
❑106, May 1961; Sgt Rock story	125.00
❑107, Jun 1961; Sgt Rock story	125.00
❑108, Jul 1961, Sgt Rock story	125.00
❑109, Aug 1961, Sgt Rock story	125.00
❑110, Sep 1961; Sgt Rock story	125.00
❑111, Oct 1961, Sgt Rock story	125.00
❑112, Nov 1961, Sgt Rock story	125.00
❑113, Dec 1961, Sgt Rock story	150.00
❑114, Jan 1962, Sgt Rock story	150.00
❑115, Feb 1962, Sgt Rock story	150.00
❑116, Mar 1962, Sgt Rock stroy	150.00
❑117, Apr 1962, 1: Sgt Mule (Millie); Sgt Rock story	150.00
❑118, May 1962, Sgt Rock story	150.00
❑119, Jun 1962, Sgt Rock story	125.00
❑120, Jul 1962, Sgt Rock story	80.00
❑121, Aug 1962, Sgt Rock story	80.00
❑122, Sep 1962, Sgt Rock story	75.00
❑123, Oct 1962, Sgt Rock story	75.00
❑124, Nov 1962, Sgt Rock story	75.00
❑125, Dec 1962, Sgt Rock story	75.00
❑126, Jan 1963, Sgt Rock story	100.00
❑127, Feb 1963, Sgt Rock story	75.00
❑128, Mar 1963, O: Sgt. Rock	275.00
❑129, Apr 1963, Sgt Rock story	75.00
❑130, May 1963, Sgt Rock story	75.00
❑131, Jun 1963, Sgt Rock story	75.00
❑132, Jul 1963, Sgt Rock story	75.00
❑133, Aug 1963, Sgt Rock story	75.00
❑134, Sep 1963, Sgt Rock story	60.00
❑135, Oct 1963, Sgt Rock story	60.00
❑136, Nov 1963, Sgt Rock story	60.00
❑137, Dec 1963, Sgt Rock story	60.00
❑138, Jan 1964, JKu (c); JKu, JAb (a); Sgt Rock story	50.00
❑139, Feb 1964, Sgt Rock story	50.00
❑140, Mar 1964, Sgt Rock story	50.00
❑141, Apr 1964, Sgt Rock story	50.00
❑142, May 1964, Sgt Rock story	50.00
❑143, Jun 1964, Sgt Rock story	50.00
❑144, Jul 1964, Sgt Rock story	50.00
❑145, Aug 1964, Sgt Rock story	50.00
❑146, Sep 1964, Sgt Rock story	50.00
❑147, Oct 1964, A: Sgt. Rock and Easy Co.. Sgt. Rock story	50.00
❑148, Nov 1964, A: Sgt. Rock and Easy Co.. Sgt. Rock story	50.00
❑149, Dec 1964, Sgt Rock story; Sgt Mule story	50.00
❑150, Jan 1965, Joe Kubert cover; Sgt Rock story	50.00
❑151, Feb 1965, JKu (c); JKu (a); 1: Enemy Ace. 1: Enemy Ace (Hans von Hammer); Sgt Rock story	350.00
❑152, Mar 1965, Sgt Rock story	50.00
❑153, Apr 1965, JKu (c); JKu (a); 2: Enemy Ace; Sgt Rock story	140.00
❑154, May 1965, Sgt Rock story	40.00
❑155, Jun 1965, JKu (c); JKu (a); A: Enemy Ace (next appearance is in Showcase #57). Sgt Rock story; 3: Enemy Ace	75.00
❑156, Jul 1965, Sgt Rock story	40.00
❑157, Aug 1965, A: Enemy Ace. Sgt Rock story	40.00
❑158, Sep 1965, JKu (c); JKu (a); 1: Iron Major; Sgt Rock story	60.00
❑159, Oct 1965, Sgt Rock story; Reprint from Our Army at War #91	40.00
❑160, Nov 1965, Sgt Rock story; Sgt Mule story	40.00
❑161, Dec 1965, Sgt Rock story	40.00
❑162, Jan 1966, A: Viking Prince. Sgt Rock story	40.00
❑163, Feb 1966, A: Viking Prince. Sgt Rock story	40.00
❑164, Feb 1966; Giant-size (80-Page Giant #G-19)	80.00
❑165, Mar 1966, V: Iron Major; Sgt Rock story	40.00
❑166, Apr 1966, Sgt Rock story	40.00
❑167, May 1966, Sgt Rock story	40.00
❑168, Jun 1966, Sgt Rock story	90.00
❑169, Jul 1966, JKu (c); GC, JKu (a); Sgt Rock story	30.00
❑170, Aug 1966, Sgt Rock story	30.00
❑171, Sep 1966, Sgt Rock story; Reprint from G.I. Combat #56	30.00
❑172, Oct 1966, Sgt Rock story; Reprint from G.I. Combat #59	30.00
❑173, Nov 1966, Sgt Rock story, Reprint from Our Army at War #99	30.00
❑174, Dec 1966, Sgt Rock story; Reprint from G.I. Combat #59	30.00
❑175, Jan 1967, Sgt Rock story; Reprint from G.I. Combat #57	30.00
❑176, Feb 1967, Sgt Rock story	30.00
❑177, Feb 1967; Giant-size (80-Page Giant #G-32)	50.00
❑178, Mar 1967, Sgt Rock story	30.00
❑179, Apr 1967, Sgt Rock story	30.00
❑180, May 1967, Sgt Rock story	30.00
❑181, Jun 1967, Sgt Rock story	30.00
❑182, Jul 1967, RH (c); NA, RH (a); Sgt Rock story	40.00
❑183, Aug 1967, JKu (c); NA, RH (a); Sgt Rock story	40.00
❑184, Sep 1967, Sgt Rock story; Reprint from Our Army at War #44	30.00
❑185, Oct 1967, Sgt Rock story	30.00
❑186, Nov 1967, JKu (c); JKu, NA (a); Joe Kubert cover; Sgt Rock story, Reprint from Our Army at War #90	40.00
❑187, Dec 1967, Sgt Rock story	30.00
❑188, Jan 1968, Sgt Rock story; Reprint from G.I. Combat #57	30.00
❑189, Feb 1968, Sgt Rock story; Reprint from Our Fighting Forces #1	30.00
❑190, Feb 1968; aka 80 Page Giant #G-44	40.00
❑191, Mar 1968, Sgt Rock story	25.00
❑192, Apr 1968, Sgt Rock story	25.00
❑193, May 1968, Sgt Rock story; Reprint from Our Fighting Forces #2	25.00
❑194, Jun 1968, 1: Unit 3 (kid guerrillas); 1: Kid Guerrillas of Unit 3 (Henri; Jon; Charlemagne; Danton; Jacques; Pierrot); Sgt Rock story	25.00
❑195, Jul 1968, Sgt Rock story; Reprint from G.I. Combat #97	25.00
❑196, Aug 1968, Sgt Rock story	25.00
❑197, Sep 1968, Sgt Rock story	25.00
❑198, Oct 1968, Sgt Rock story; Reprint from Star Spangled War Stories #88	25.00
❑199, Nov 1968, Sgt Rock story; Reprint from Our Army at War #42	20.00
❑200, Dec 1968, 200th issue	20.00
❑201, Jan 1969, Reprints from Our Army at War #14, 52; Sgt Rock story	20.00
❑202, Feb 1969, Sgt Rock story; Reprint from Our Army at War #39	20.00
❑203, Feb 1969; Giant-size; aka 80 Page Giant #G-56; last 80 Page Giant	35.00
❑204, Mar 1969, Reprints from Our Army at War #16, 17, 19, 58, Star Spangled War Stories #43	20.00
❑205, Apr 1969, Reprints from All-American Men of War #28, Star Spangled War Stories #34, Our Army at War #59	20.00
❑206, May 1969, Sgt Rock story; Reprint from All-American Men of War #7	20.00
❑207, Jun 1969, Sgt Rock story	20.00
❑208, Jul 1969, Sgt Rock story; Reprint from All-American Men of War #56	20.00
❑209, Aug 1969, Sgt Rock story	20.00
❑210, Sep 1969, Sgt Rock story	20.00
❑211, Oct 1969, Sgt Rock story	20.00
❑212, Nov 1969, Sgt Rock story; Reprint from Star Spangled War Stories #78	20.00
❑213, Dec 1969, Sgt Rock story	20.00
❑214, Jan 1970, Sgt Rock story	20.00
❑215, Feb 1970, Sgt Rock story	20.00
❑216, Feb 1970, Giant-size (80-Page Giant #G-80); JKu (c); RE (w); JKu, RA, RH, RE (a); aka Giant #G-68	55.00
❑217, Mar 1970, Sgt Rock story	15.00
❑218, Apr 1970, Sgt Rock story; Reprint from Our Fighting Forces #5; U.S.S. Stevens story	15.00
❑219, May 1970, JKu (c); MA, RH (a); Sgt Rock story	15.00
❑220, Jun 1970, Sgt Rock story; U.S.S. Stevens story	15.00

Other grades: Multiply price above by 5/6 for VF/NM • 2/3 for VERY FINE • 1/3 for FINE • 1/5 for VERY GOOD • 1/8 for GOOD

❑221, Jul 1970, JKu (c); JKu (w); JKu, RH (a); Sgt Rock story 15.00
❑222, Aug 1970, Sgt Rock story; U.S.S. Stevens story 15.00
❑223, Sep 1970, Sgt Rock story; U.S.S. Stevens story 15.00
❑224, Oct 1970, Sgt Rock story 15.00
❑225, Nov 1970, Sgt Rock story; U.S.S. Stevens story 15.00
❑226, Dec 1970, Sgt Rock story 15.00
❑227, Jan 1971, Sgt Rock story; U.S.S. Stevens story 15.00
❑228, Feb 1971, Sgt Rock story 15.00
❑229, Mar 1971; Giant-size; JKu (c); MD, JKu, RA, JAb (a); aka Giant #G-80 ...... 35.00
❑230, Mar 1971, JKu (c); JKu (w); RH (a); Sgt Rock story; U.S.S. Stevens story . 15.00
❑231, Apr 1971, Sgt Rock story; U.S.S. Stevens story 15.00
❑232, May 1971, Sgt Rock story; U.S.S. Stevens story 15.00
❑233, Jun 1971, Sgt Rock story 15.00
❑234, Jul 1971, Sgt Rock story 15.00
❑235, Aug 1971; Reprints from Our Army at War #52, Captain Storm #6; U.S.S. Stevens story; Sgt Rock story 25.00
❑236, Sep 1971; Reprints from Our Fighting Forces #45, Captain Storm #3; Sgt Rock story 25.00
❑237, Oct 1971; Reprints from Our Army at War #61, Our Fighting Forces #24; Sgt Rock story 25.00
❑238, Nov 1971; Sgt Rock story; U.S.S. Stevens story; Mlle. Marie story, Reprint from Star Spangled War Stories #90 .... 25.00
❑239, Dec 1971; Sgt Rock story; Reprint from Star Spangled War Stories #101, 102 .... 25.00
❑240, Jan 1972; 52 pages; Reprint from G.I. Combat #48; U.S.S. Stevens story; Sgt Rock story, Reprint from Our Army at War #86 .... 25.00
❑241, Feb 1972; 52 pages; Sgt Rock story; Reprint from G.I. Combat #55, 70; U.S.S. Stevens story 15.00
❑242, Feb 1972, JKu (c); MD, JKu, RA, RH, IN (a); a.k.a. DC 100-Page Super Spectacular #DC-9; wraparound cover 20.00
❑243, Mar 1972; Sgt Rock story; Reprint from G.I. Combat #62, Star Spangled War Stories #98 .... 15.00
❑244, Apr 1972; Reprints from Our Army at War #70, 77, Star Spangled War Stories #104; U.S.S. Stevens story; Sgt Rock story 15.00
❑245, May 1972; Reprints from All-American Men of War #61, G.I. Combat #77; U.S.S. Stevens story; Sgt Rock story 15.00
❑246, Jun 1972; Sgt Rock story; Reprint from All-American Men of War #63, Star Spangled War Stories #16 .... 15.00
❑247, Jul 1972, Sgt Rock story; U.S.S. Stevens story; Reprint from Our Army at War #91 .... 15.00
❑248, Aug 1972, Sgt Rock story; U.S.S. Stevens story 15.00
❑249, Sep 1972, Sgt Rock story 15.00
❑250, Oct 1972, Joe Kubert cover; Pearl Harbor Tabletop Diorama; Sgt Rock story 15.00
❑251, Nov 1972, Sgt Rock story 15.00
❑252, Dec 1972, Sgt Rock story 15.00
❑253, Jan 1973, Sgt Rock story 15.00
❑254, Feb 1973, Sgt Rock story 18.00
❑255, Mar 1973, Sgt Rock story 15.00
❑256, Apr 1973, Sgt Rock story; U.S.S. Stevens story 18.00
❑257, Jun 1973, Sgt Rock story; U.S.S. Stevens story 15.00
❑258, Jul 1973, Sgt Rock story; U.S.S. Stevens story 10.00
❑259, Aug 1973, Sgt Rock story; U.S.S. Stevens story 10.00
❑260, Sep 1973, Sgt Rock story 10.00
❑261, Oct 1973, Sgt Rock story; U.S.S. Stevens story 10.00
❑262, Nov 1973, Sgt Rock story; U.S.S. Stevens story 10.00
❑263, Dec 1973, Sgt Rock story 10.00
❑264, Jan 1974, Sgt Rock story 10.00
❑265, Feb 1974, Sgt Rock story; U.S.S. Stevens story 10.00
❑266, Mar 1974, Sgt Rock story; U.S.S. Stevens story 10.00
❑267, Apr 1974, Sgt Rock story; U.S.S. Stevens story 10.00
❑268, May 1974, Sgt Rock story 10.00
❑269, Jun 1974, Reprints from All-American Men of War #63, Star Spangled War Stories #65; 100 pages; Johnny Cloud story, Reprints from All-American Men of War #49, 97; Sgt Rock story, Reprint from Our Army at War #196; Lt. Hunter's Hellcats, Reprint from Our Fighting Forces #114 .... 10.00
❑270, Jul 1974, Sgt Rock story 10.00
❑271, Aug 1974, Sgt Rock story 10.00
❑272, Sep 1974, Sgt Rock story 15.00
❑273, Oct 1974, Sgt Rock story 10.00
❑274, Nov 1974, Sgt Rock story 10.00
❑275, Dec 1974, Reprints from All-American Men of War #22, Star Spangled War Stories #67, Our Army at War #39, 106; U.S.S. Stevens story; Sgt Rock story, Reprint from Showcase #45; 100 pages 10.00
❑276, Jan 1975; Sgt Rock story 10.00
❑277, Feb 1975; Sgt Rock story 10.00
❑278, Mar 1975; Sgt Rock story 10.00
❑279, Apr 1975; Sgt Rock story 10.00
❑280, May 1975; Reprints from All-American Men of War #52, Star Spangled War Stories #6; Sgt Rock story, Reprints from Our Army at War #81, 83; 64 pages 10.00
❑281, Jun 1975; Sgt Rock story; U.S.S. Stevens story 10.00
❑282, Jul 1975; Sgt Rock story; U.S.S. Stevens story 10.00
❑283, Aug 1975; Sgt Rock story 10.00
❑284, Sep 1975; Sgt Rock story 10.00
❑285, Oct 1975; Sgt Rock story 10.00
❑286, Nov 1975; Sgt Rock story 10.00
❑287, Dec 1975; Sgt Rock story 10.00
❑288, Jan 1976; Sgt Rock story 10.00
❑289, Feb 1976; Sgt Rock story 10.00
❑290, Mar 1976, Sgt Rock story; Medal of Honor story 10.00
❑291, Apr 1976, Sgt Rock story; Medal of Honor story 10.00
❑292, May 1976, Joe Kubert cover 10.00
❑293, Jun 1976, Sgt Rock story; U.S.S. Stevens story 10.00
❑294, Jul 1976, Sgt Rock story 10.00
❑295, Aug 1976, Sgt Rock story 10.00
❑296, Sep 1976, Sgt Rock story 10.00
❑297, Oct 1976, Sgt Rock story 10.00
❑298, Nov 1976, Sgt Rock story; U.S.S. Stevens story 10.00
❑299, Dec 1976, Sgt Rock story 10.00
❑300, Jan 1977, Sgt Rock story 10.00
❑301, Feb 1977, JKu (c); RE (a); Series is continued as "Sgt. Rock" 10.00

Our Fighting Forces
DC

❑64, Dec 1961; Gunner and Sarge story 28.00
❑65, Jan 1962, Gunner and Sarge story 18.00
❑66, Feb 1962, Gunner and Sarge story 18.00
❑67, Apr 1962, Gunner and Sarge story 18.00
❑68, Jun 1962, Gunner and Sarge story 18.00
❑69, Jul 1962, Gunner and Sarge story. 18.00
❑70, Aug 1962, Gunner and Sarge story 18.00
❑71, Oct 1962, Gunner and Sarge story 15.00
❑72, Nov 1962, Gunner and Sarge story 15.00
❑73, Jan 1963, Gunner and Sarge story 15.00
❑74, Feb 1963, Gunner and Sarge story 15.00
❑75, Apr 1963, Gunner and Sarge story 15.00
❑76, Jun 1963, Gunner and Sarge story 15.00
❑77, Jul 1963, Gunner and Sarge story. 15.00
❑78, Aug 1963, Gunner and Sarge story 15.00
❑79, Oct 1963, Gunner and Sarge story 15.00
❑80, Nov 1963, Gunner and Sarge story 15.00
❑81, Jan 1964, Gunner and Sarge story 10.00
❑82, Feb 1964, Gunner and Sarge story 10.00
❑83, Apr 1964, Gunner and Sarge story 10.00
❑84, May 1964, Gunner & Sarge 10.00
❑85, Jul 1964, Gunner and Sarge story. 10.00
❑86, Aug 1964, JKu (c); GC, JAb (a); Gunner and Sarge story 10.00
❑87, Oct 1964, Gunner and Sarge story 10.00
❑88, Nov 1964, Gunner and Sarge story 10.00
❑89, Jan 1965, Gunner and Sarge story 10.00
❑90, Feb 1965, Gunner and Sarge story 10.00
❑91, Apr 1965, JKu (c); JAb (a); Gunner and Sarge story 7.00
❑92, May 1965, Gunner and Sarge story 7.00
❑93, Jul 1965, Gunner and Sarge story. 7.00
❑94, Aug 1965, Gunner and Sarge story 7.00
❑95, Oct 1965, 1: Fighting Devil Dog (Lt. Larry Rock) 7.00
❑96, Nov 1965, Fighting Devil Dog story 7.00
❑97, Dec 1965, Fighting Devil Dog story 7.00
❑98, Jan 1966, Fighting Devil Dog story 7.00
❑99, Feb 1966, 1: Captain Phil Hunter ... 7.00
❑100, Apr 1966, JKu (c); GC, JAb (a); A: Captain Hunter. Captain Hunter story 6.00
❑101, Jun 1966, Captain Hunter story ... 6.00
❑102, Aug 1966, Captain Hunter story; Reprint from G.I. Combat #64 .... 6.00
❑103, Oct 1966, Captain Hunter story; Reprint from G.I. Combat #58 .... 6.00
❑104, Dec 1966, Captain Hunter story... 6.00
❑105, Feb 1967, Captain Hunter story ... 6.00
❑106, Apr 1967, IN (c); JAb (a); 1: Ben Hunter; 1: Hunter's Hellcats; Captain Hunter story 6.00
❑107, Jul 1967, Lt. Hunter's Hellcats story 6.00
❑108, Aug 1967, A: Lt. Hunter's Hellcats. Lt. Hunter's Hellcats story 6.00
❑109, Oct 1967, Lt. Hunter's Hellcats story 6.00
❑110, Dec 1967, Lt. Hunter's Hellcats story 6.00
❑111, Feb 1968, IN (c); JAb (a); Lt. Hunter's Hellcats story 6.00
❑112, Apr 1968, Lt. Hunter's Hellcats story 6.00
❑113, Jul 1968, IN (c); JAb (a); Lt. Hunter's Hellcats story 6.00
❑114, Aug 1968, Lt. Hunter's Hellcats story 6.00
❑115, Sep 1968, Reprints from Our Fighting Forces #77, Star Spangled War Stories #58; Lt. Hunter's Hellcats 6.00
❑116, Nov 1968, Lt. Hunter's Hellcats story; Reprint from Star Spangled War Stories #104 .... 6.00
❑117, Jan 1969, Lt. Hunter's Hellcats story; Reprint from Star Spangled War Stories #62 .... 6.00
❑118, Mar 1969, A: Lt. Hunter's Hellcats. Lt. Hunter's Hellcats story; Reprint from Our Army at War #41 .... 6.00
❑119, May 1969, JKu (c); GC (a); Lt. Hunter's Hellcats; Reprint from All-American Men of War #4 .... 6.00
❑120, Jul 1969, Lt. Hunter's Hellcats 6.00
❑121, Sep 1969, 1: Heller; Lt. Hunter's Hellcats story; Reprint from Star Spangled War Stories #103 .... 5.00
❑122, Nov 1969, Lt. Hunter's Hellcats ... 5.00
❑123, Jan 1970, Losers series begins ... 5.00
❑124, Mar 1970, JKu (c); JSe, RA (a); Losers story 5.00
❑125, May 1970, Losers story; Repriint from All-American Men of War #60.... 5.00
❑126, Jul 1970, Losers story; U.S.S. Stevens story 5.00
❑127, Sep 1970, JKu (c); RA (a); Losers 5.00
❑128, Nov 1970, Losers story; U.S.S. Stevens story; Repriint from G.I. Combat #63 .... 5.00
❑129, Jan 1971, Losers story 5.00
❑130, Mar 1971, Losers story 5.00
❑131, May 1971, Losers story; Reprint from Our Army at War #64 .... 5.00
❑132, Jul 1971, JKu (c); JSe, RE (a); Losers 5.00
❑133, Sep 1971; Reprints from Our Army at War #76, Our Fighting Forces #76; Balloon Buster story; Losers story 5.00
❑134, Nov 1971; Losers story; U.S.S. Stevens story; Reprint from Our Fighting Forces #90 .... 5.00
❑135, Jan 1972; Reprints from Our Army at War #22, 68; Losers story 5.00
❑136, Mar 1972; Reprints from G.I. Combat #52, Our Army at War #53; U.S.S. Stevens story; Losers story..... 5.00
❑137, May 1972; Giant-size; Losers 5.00
❑138, Jul 1972, Losers story; U.S.S. Stevens story; Reprint from Star Spangled War Stories #75 .... 5.00
❑139, Sep 1972, Losers story; U.S.S. Stevens story 5.00
❑140, Nov 1972, Losers story; U.S.S. Stevens story 5.00
❑141, Jan 1973, Losers story; U.S.S. Stevens story 5.00
❑142, Mar 1973, Losers story 5.00

Other grades: Multiply price above by 5/6 for VF/NM • 2/3 for VERY FINE • 1/3 for FINE • 1/5 for VERY GOOD • 1/8 for GOOD

Planet of the Apes

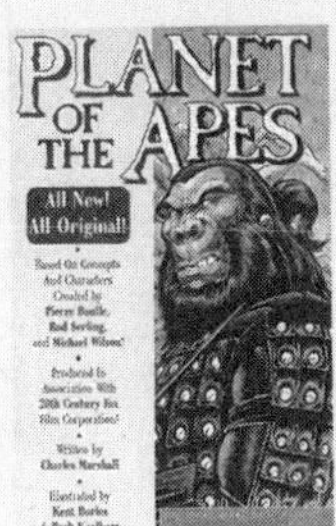

First issue had pink, yellow, or green overlays
©Adventure

Plasmer

Title caused Defiant change
©Marvel

Plastic Man

Silver Age revival featured original's son
©DC

Plop!

DC horror hosts offered humorous helpings
©DC

Poison Elves

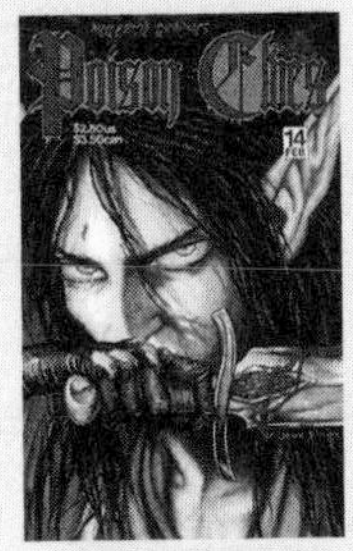

I, Lusiphur changes to ambiguous title
©Mulehide

	N-MINT
❑143, May 1973, Losers story; U.S.S. Stevens story	5.00
❑144, Jul 1973, Losers story	5.00
❑145, Sep 1973, Losers story	5.00
❑146, Nov 1973, Losers story	5.00
❑147, Jan 1974, Losers story	5.00
❑148, Mar 1974, Accidentally includes 1973 Statement of Ownership for House of Secrets	5.00
❑149, May 1974, Losers story	5.00
❑150, Jul 1974, Losers story	5.00
❑151, Sep 1974, Losers	4.00
❑152, Nov 1974, Losers	4.00
❑153, Feb 1975; Losers	4.00
❑154, Apr 1975; JK (c); JK (w); JK (a); Losers	4.00
❑155, May 1975; Losers	4.00
❑156, Jun 1975; Losers	4.00
❑157, Jul 1975; Losers	4.00
❑158, Aug 1975; JK (c); JK (w); JK (a); Losers	4.00
❑159, Sep 1975; JK (c); JK (w); JK (a); Losers	4.00
❑160, Oct 1975; JKu (c); JK (w); JK (a); Losers	4.00
❑161, Nov 1975; Losers	4.00
❑162, Dec 1975; JK (w); JK (a); Losers	4.00
❑163, Jan 1976; Losers story	4.00
❑164, Feb 1976; Losers story; Capt. Storm story	4.00
❑165, Mar 1976; Losers story; Gunner and Sarge story	4.00
❑166, Apr 1976; Losers story; Johnny Cloud story	4.00
❑167, Jun 1976, Losers story; Gunner and Sarge story	4.00
❑168, Aug 1976, Losers story; Johnny Cloud story	4.00
❑169, Oct 1976, Losers story; Johnny Cloud story	4.00
❑170, Dec 1976, Losers story; Sarge story	4.00
❑171, Feb 1977, Losers story; Gunner and Sarge story	4.00
❑172, Apr 1977, Losers story; Gunner and Sarge story	4.00
❑173, Jun 1977, Losers story; Capt. Storm story	4.00
❑174, Aug 1977, Losers story; Gunner and Sarge story	4.00
❑175, Oct 1977, Losers story; Gunner and Sarge story	4.00
❑176, Dec 1977, Losers story; Gunner and Sarge story	4.00
❑177, Feb 1978, Losers story; Gunner and Sarge story	4.00
❑178, Apr 1978, Losers story; Capt. Storm story	4.00
❑179, Jun 1978, Losers story; Johnny Cloud story	4.00
❑180, Aug 1978, Losers story; Johnny Cloud story	4.00
❑181, Oct 1978, Final Issue; Losers story; Capt. Storm story; H.Q. Confidential Super Spy	4.00

Our Love Story
Marvel

	N-MINT
❑1, Oct 1969, JR (c); JB, JR (a)	55.00
❑2, Dec 1969	25.00
❑3, Feb 1970	25.00
❑4, Apr 1970	25.00
❑5, Jun 1970, JR (c); SL (w); GC, JB, JSo (a)	75.00
❑6, Aug 1970	25.00
❑7, Oct 1970	25.00
❑8, Dec 1970	25.00
❑9, Feb 1971, Reprints from Teen-Age Romance #78, 84	35.00
❑10, Apr 1971, Reprint from Teen-Age romance #80	25.00
❑11, Jun 1971, Reprints from Love Romances #82, Teen-Age Romance #80	25.00
❑12, Aug 1971, Reprints from Love Romances #82, My Own Romance #74	35.00
❑13, Oct 1971, Reprints from Our Love Story #2, Teen-Age romance #83, My Love #1; Giant-size 52 pages	20.00
❑14, Dec 1971, Reprints from Our Love Story #2, My Own Romance #71	12.00
❑15, Feb 1972, SB, JAb (a)	12.00
❑16, Apr 1972, SL (w); JB, SB, JAb (a); Steve Englehart work is uncredited	12.00
❑17, Jun 1972	12.00
❑18, Aug 1972, JR (c); JR, JM (a); Reprint from My Love #2	12.00
❑19, Oct 1972, Reprints from My Love #3	12.00
❑20, Dec 1972, Reprints from My Love #5	12.00
❑21, Feb 1973, Reprints from Our Love Story #6, 7	8.00
❑22, Apr 1973	8.00
❑23, Jun 1973	8.00
❑24, Aug 1973	8.00
❑25, Oct 1973, Reprints from My Love #11, Teen-Age Romance #77, 80, Love Romances #82	8.00
❑26, Dec 1973	8.00
❑27, Feb 1974	8.00
❑28, Jun 1974	8.00
❑29, Aug 1974	8.00
❑30, Oct 1974	8.00
❑31, Dec 1974	8.00
❑32, Feb 1975	8.00
❑33, Apr 1975	8.00
❑34, Jun 1975	8.00
❑35, Aug 1975	8.00
❑36, Oct 1975	8.00
❑37, Dec 1975	8.00
❑38, Feb 1976, Final Issue	15.00

Outbreed 999
Blackout

	N-MINT
❑1, May 1994	2.95
❑2, Jul 1994	2.95
❑3, Aug 1994	2.95
❑4	2.95
❑5	2.95

Outcast
Acclaim / Valiant

	N-MINT
❑1, Dec 1995; One-shot	5.00

Outcasts
DC

	N-MINT
❑1, Oct 1987; 1: Kaine Salinger; 1: Outcasts	1.75
❑2, Nov 1987	1.75
❑3, Dec 1987	1.75
❑4, Jan 1988	1.75
❑5, Feb 1988	1.75
❑6, Mar 1988	1.75
❑7, Apr 1988; D: Kaine Salinger	1.75
❑8, May 1988	1.75
❑9, Jun 1988	1.75
❑10, Jul 1988	1.75
❑11, Aug 1988	1.75
❑12, Sep 1988; Final Issue	1.75

Outer Edge
Innovation

	N-MINT
❑1, b&w; Reprints from Son of Mutant World #4, 5, Twisted Tales #4, Den #6; b&w; ca. 1993	2.50

Outer Limits
Dell

	N-MINT
❑1, Jan 1964	125.00
❑2, Apr 1964	65.00
❑3, Jul 1964	65.00
❑4, Dec 1964	65.00
❑5, Jan 1965	65.00
❑6, Apr 1965	50.00
❑7, Jul 1965	50.00
❑8, Dec 1965	50.00
❑9, Jul 1966	50.00
❑10, Oct 1966	50.00
❑11, Jan 1967	35.00
❑12, Apr 1967	35.00
❑13, May 1967	35.00
❑14, Jul 1967	35.00
❑15, Sep 1967	35.00
❑16, Nov 1968	35.00
❑17, Oct 1968, Reprint of #1	35.00
❑18, Oct 1969, Final Issue; Reprint of #2	35.00

Outer Orbit
Dark Horse

	N-MINT
❑1, Jan 2007	2.99

Outer Space
Charlton

	N-MINT
❑1, Nov 1968	20.00

Outer Space Babes
Silhouette

	N-MINT
❑1	2.95

Out For Blood
Dark Horse

	N-MINT
❑1, Sep 1999	2.95
❑2, Oct 1999	2.95
❑3, Nov 1999	2.95
❑4, Dec 1999	2.95

Outlander
Malibu

	N-MINT
❑1, Oct 1987	1.95
❑2 1987	1.95
❑3, Dec 1987, b&w	1.95
❑4, Jan 1988	1.95
❑5, Mar 1988	1.95
❑6 1988	1.95
❑7 1988	1.95

Outlanders
Dark Horse

	N-MINT
❑0, Dec 1988; Includes poster	3.00
❑1, Jan 1989	2.50
❑2, Feb 1989	2.00
❑3, Mar 1989	2.00
❑4, Apr 1989	2.00

Other grades: Multiply price above by 5/6 for VF/NM • 2/3 for VERY FINE • 1/3 for FINE • 1/5 for VERY GOOD • 1/8 for GOOD

N-MINT

❏5, May 1989 2.00
❏6, Jun 1989 2.00
❏7, Jul 1989 2.00
❏8, Aug 1989 2.00
❏9, Sep 1989 2.25
❏10, Oct 1989 2.25
❏11, Nov 1989 2.25
❏12, Dec 1989 2.25
❏13, Jan 1990 2.25
❏14, Feb 1990 2.25
❏15, Mar 1990 2.25
❏16, Apr 1990 2.25
❏17, May 1990 2.25
❏18, Jun 1990 2.25
❏19, Jul 1990 2.25
❏20, Aug 1990 2.25
❏21, Sep 1990 2.25
❏22, Oct 1990 2.50
❏23, Nov 1990 2.50
❏24, Dec 1990 2.50
❏25, Jan 1991; Includes trading cards 2.50
❏26, Feb 1991; Includes trading cards 2.50
❏27, Mar 1991; Giant-size special; Includes trading cards 2.95
❏28, Apr 1991; Includes trading cards 2.50
❏29, May 1991; Includes trading cards 2.50
❏30, Jun 1991 2.50
❏31, Jul 1991 2.50
❏32, Aug 1991 2.50
❏33, Sep 1991; Final Issue 2.50
❏Special 1, b&w; manga; Epilogue 2.50

Outlanders Epilogue
Dark Horse

❏1, Mar 1994, b&w; NN 2.50

Outlaw 7
Dark Horse

❏1, Aug 2001, Wraparound cover 2.99
❏2, Sep 2001 2.99
❏3, Jan 2002 2.99

Outlaw Kid
Marvel

❏1, Aug 1970, JSe (c); JO (a); Reprints from the Outlaw Kid (1st Series) #3, Ringo Kid Western #12 25.00
❏2, Oct 1970, Reprints from the Outlaw Kid (1st Series) #5 10.00
❏3, Dec 1970, Reprints from the Outlaw Kid (1st Series) #2, 10 10.00
❏4, Feb 1971, Reprints from the Outlaw Kid (1st Series) #11 10.00
❏5, Apr 1971, Reprints from the Outlaw Kid (1st Series) #17, Apache Kid #6 10.00
❏6, Jun 1971, Reprints from the Outlaw Kid (1st Series) #3, 16 10.00
❏7, Aug 1971, Reprints from the Outlaw Kid (1st Series) #13, 16 10.00
❏8, Oct 1971, Giant-size; Reprints from the Outlaw Kid (1st Series) #18, 19, Kid Colt Outlaw #64 15.00
❏9, Dec 1971, Reprints from the Outlaw Kid (1st Series) #7, 8 8.00
❏10, Jun 1972, O: Outlaw Kid. series goes on hiatus 20.00
❏11, Aug 1972, Reprint from Quick-Trigger Western #17 8.00
❏12, Oct 1972 8.00
❏13, Dec 1972 8.00
❏14, Feb 1973 8.00
❏15, Apr 1973, Reprint from Western Outlaws #6 8.00
❏16, Jun 1973, Reprint from Kid Colt Outlaw #109 8.00
❏17, Aug 1973, Reprints from Outlaw Kid (1st Series) #3, Ringo Kid Western #12 8.00
❏18, Oct 1973, Reprints from the Outlaw Kid (1st Series) #5 8.00
❏19, Dec 1973, Reprints from the Outlaw Kid (1st Series) #10, Western Outlaws #4 8.00
❏20, Feb 1974, Reprints from the Outlaw Kid (1st Series) #11, Gunsmoke Western #46 8.00
❏21, Apr 1974, Reprints from the Outlaw Kid (1st Series) #17, Gunsmoke Western #46 5.00
❏22, Jun 1974, Reprints from the Outlaw Kid (1st Series) #3, 16 5.00
❏23, Aug 1974, Reprints from the Outlaw Kid (1st Series) #13, 16, 18 5.00
❏24, Oct 1974, Reprints from the Outlaw Kid (1st Series) #10, 11, 15, 19 5.00

N-MINT

❏25, Dec 1974, Reprints from the Outlaw Kid (1st Series) #8, 13 5.00
❏26, Feb 1975, Reprints from the Outlaw Kid (1st Series) #7, 18, 19, Texas Kid #8 5.00
❏27, Apr 1975; O: Outlaw Kid. Reprints from the Outlaw Kid (2nd Series) #10, Western Outlaws and Sheriffs #62; O: the Outlaw Kid (Lance Temple) 5.00
❏28, Jun 1975; Reprints from the Outlaw Kid (2nd Series) #11, Quick-Trigger Western #17 5.00
❏29, Aug 1975; Reprint from the Outlaw Kid (2nd Series) #12 5.00
❏30, Oct 1975; Reprint from the Outlaw Kid (2nd Series) #13 5.00

Outlaw Nation
DC / Vertigo

❏1, Nov 2000 2.50
❏2, Dec 2000 2.50
❏3, Jan 2001 2.50
❏4, Feb 2001 2.50
❏5, Mar 2001 2.50
❏6, Apr 2001 2.50
❏7, May 2001 2.50
❏8, Jun 2001 2.50
❏9, Jul 2001 2.50
❏10, Aug 2001 2.50
❏11, Sep 2001 2.50
❏12, Oct 2001 2.50
❏13, Nov 2001 2.50
❏14, Dec 2001 2.50
❏15, Jan 2002 2.50
❏16, Feb 2002 2.50
❏17, Mar 2002 2.50
❏18, Apr 2002 2.50
❏19, May 2002, Final issue 2.50

Outlaw Nation
Boneyard

❏1 1994; Adult; b&w 4.95
❏1/Platinum; Tim Bradstreet cover 5.00

Outlaw Overdrive
Blue Comet

❏1, Red Edition 2.95

Outlaws
DC

❏1, Sep 1991; LMc (c); LMc (a); 1: Hood 2.00
❏2, Oct 1991 LMc (c); LMc (a) 2.00
❏3, Nov 1991 LMc (c); LMc (a) 2.00
❏4, Dec 1991 LMc (c); LMc (a) 2.00
❏5, Jan 1992 LMc (c); LMc (a) 2.00
❏6, Feb 1992 LMc (c); LMc (a) 2.00
❏7, Mar 1992 LMc (c); LMc (a) 2.00
❏8, Apr 1992; LMc (c); LMc (a); D: Hood; Final Issue 2.00

Out of the Vortex
Dark Horse

❏5, Feb 1994, was Comics' Greatest World: Out of the Vortex 2.00
❏6, Mar 1994 2.00
❏7, Apr 1994 2.00
❏8, May 1994 2.00
❏9, Jun 1994 2.00
❏10, Jul 1994 2.00
❏11, Sep 1994 2.00
❏12, Oct 1994, Final Issue 2.00

Out of This World
Eternity

❏1, b&w; Reprints stories from Strange Worlds #9, Strange Planets #16, Tomb of Terror #6, and Weird Tales of the Future #1 3.50

Outposts
Blackthorne

❏1, Jun 1997 1.50

Outsiders
DC

❏1, Nov 1985; V: Nuclear Family 2.00
❏2, Dec 1985; 1: Untouchables; V: Nuclear Family; Looker story 1.50
❏3, Jan 1986; V: Force of July; Looker story 1.50
❏4, Feb 1986; Rescue Force of July; Metamorpho back-up 1.25
❏5, Mar 1986; Christmas Carol story 1.25
❏6, Apr 1986; V: Duke of Oil 1.25
❏7, May 1986; V: Duke of Oil 1.25
❏8, Jun 1986 1.25

N-MINT

❏9, Jul 1986; Halo and Tiger the Wondercat story 1.25
❏10, Aug 1986; Geo-Force story 1.25
❏11, Sep 1986; Halo story; Katana story 1.00
❏12, Oct 1986; V: Hammer & Sickle 1.00
❏13, Nov 1986; Geo-Force story; Black Lightning story; Metamorpho story 1.00
❏14, Dec 1986; Windfall story 1.00
❏15, Jan 1987 1.00
❏16, Feb 1987 1.00
❏17, Mar 1987; Batman returns 1.00
❏18, Apr 1987; V: Eclipso; Looker and Metamorpho story 1.00
❏19, May 1987; V: Masters of Disaster 1.00
❏20, Jun 1987; Geo-Force and Metamorpho story 1.00
❏21, Jul 1987; 1: Clayface IV 1.00
❏22, Aug 1987; EC parody back-up 1.00
❏23, Sep 1987 1.00
❏24, Oct 1987 1.00
❏25, Nov 1987 1.00
❏26, Dec 1987 1.00
❏27, Jan 1988; Millennium 1.00
❏28, Feb 1988; Millennium 1.00
❏Ann 1, Mar 1904; V: Kobra 2.50
❏Special 1, Jul 1987; Crossover continued in Infinity Inc. SE #1 1.50

Outsiders
DC

❏0, Oct 1994; New team begins 2.50
❏1/A, Nov 1993; Alpha version 4.00
❏1/B, Nov 1993; Omega version 3.00
❏2, Dec 1993 2.00
❏3, Jan 1994 A: Eradicator 2.00
❏4, Feb 1994 2.00
❏5, Mar 1994 2.00
❏6, Apr 1994 2.00
❏7, May 1994 2.00
❏8, Jun 1994 JA (a); A: Batman (Azrael) 2.00
❏9, Jul 1994 2.00
❏10, Aug 1994 2.00
❏11, Sep 1994; Zero Hour crossover 2.00
❏12, Nov 1994 2.00
❏13, Dec 1994; A: Superman. Continued from Action Comics #704 3.00
❏14, Jan 1995 2.00
❏15, Feb 1995 2.00
❏16, Mar 1995 2.00
❏17, Apr 1995 2.00
❏18, May 1995 2.00
❏19, Jun 1995 2.25
❏20, Jul 1995 2.25
❏21, Aug 1995 2.25
❏22, Sep 1995 2.25
❏23, Oct 1995 2.25
❏24, Nov 1995; Final Issue 2.25

Outsiders
DC

❏1, Aug 2003, 1: Thunder III; 1: Grace 2.50
❏2, Sep 2003 2.50
❏3, Oct 2003, Jade joins team 2.50
❏4, Nov 2003, V: Avalanche 2.50
❏5, Dec 2003, Brothers In Blood, Part 2 2.50
❏6, Jan 2004, 1: Brother Blood IX; D: Brother Blood VIII; D: Brother Blood VII 2.50
❏7, Feb 2004, O: Shift 2.50
❏8, Mar 2004, 1: Sabbac II; D: Sabbac I 2.50
❏9, Apr 2004, O: Sabbac II (Ishmael Gregor); V: Sabbac II 2.50
❏10, May 2004, A Family Matter, Part 3 2.50
❏11, Jun 2004 2.50
❏12, Jul 2004, Metamorpho II becomes Shift 2.50
❏13, Aug 2004, Return of Shimmer 2.50
❏14, Sep 2004, D: Gizmo 2.50
❏15, Oct 2004 2.50
❏16, Nov 2004, Join Starfire 2.50
❏17, Dec 2004, America's Most Wanted TV show 2.50
❏18, Jan 2005, America's Most Wanted TV show 2.50
❏19, Feb 2005; America's Most Wanted TV show 2.50
❏20, Mar 2005; Batman revealed to be funding Outsiders 2.50
❏21, Apr 2005; Batman revealed to be Deathstroke the Terminator 4.00
❏22, May 2005; Arsenal vs. Deathstroke 4.00

Other grades: Multiply price above by 5/6 for VF/NM • 2/3 for VERY FINE • 1/3 for FINE • 1/5 for VERY GOOD • 1/8 for GOOD

Poison Elves

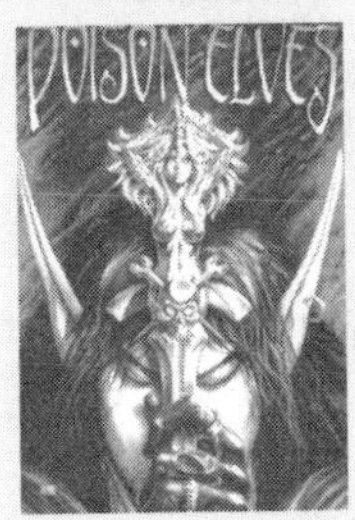

Sirius picks up odd fantasy series

©Sirius

Pokèmon: The Electric Tale of Pikachu

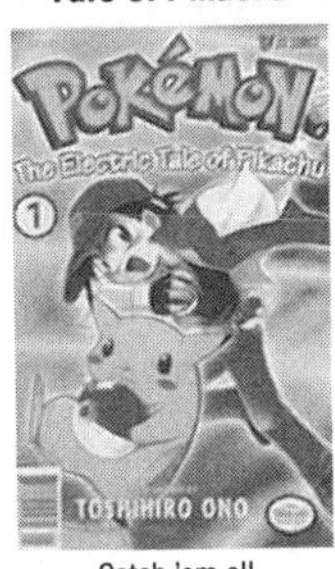

Catch 'em all creatures come to comics

©Viz

Popeye Special

Spinach addiction examined in origin story

©Ocean

Porky Pig

Stuttering star shows stout heart

©Gold Key

Power & Glory

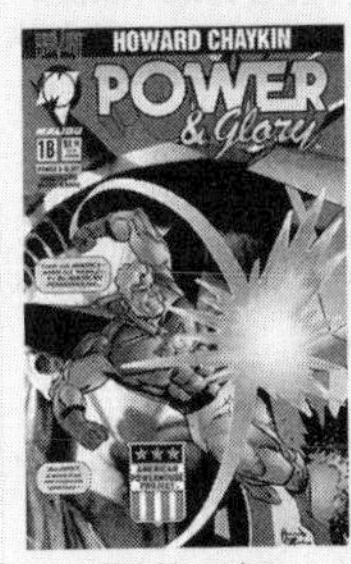

Chaykin makes corporate super-hero

©Malibu

N-MINT

	N-MINT
❑23, Jun 2005	4.00
❑24, Jul 2005; Crossover with Teen Titans #24-25; Indigo becomes Brainiac VIII	2.50
❑25, Aug 2005; Crossover with Teen Titans #24-25; D: Brainiac VIII	2.50
❑26, Sep 2005; Arsenal teams with original Outsiders	2.50
❑27, Oct 2005; Arsenal teams with original Outsiders	2.50
❑28, Nov 2005	2.50
❑29, Dec 2005; Infinite Crisis tie-in; Captain Marvel Jr. joins	2.50
❑30, Jan 2006; V: Sabbac II; V: Fearsome Five; Infinite Crisis tie-in	2.50
❑31, Jan 2006	2.50
❑32, Mar 2006, Infinate Crisis tie-in; Blackfire; Mirror Master; Captain Cold; Captain Boomerang; Katana; Captain Marvel, Jr	2.50
❑33, Mar 2006, Infinite Crisis cross-over; Blackfire; Mirror Master; Captain Cold; Captain Boomerang; Katana; Captain Marvel, Jr.; Mary Marvel	2.50
❑35, Jun 2006, One Year Later	2.50
❑36, Jul 2006, One Year Later; Price increase; Velocity	2.99
❑37, Aug 2006, Monsieur Mallah; The Brain	2.99
❑38, Sep 2006, Phobia; Monsieur Mallah; The Brain	2.99
❑39, Oct 2006, Monsieur Mallah; The Brain	2.99
❑40, Nov 2006, Monsieur Mallah; The Brain; Dr. Sivana	2.99
❑41, Dec 2006, Monsieur Mallah; The Brain; Dr. Sivana	2.99
❑42, Jan 2007, Dr. Sivana	2.99
❑43, Feb 2007, Dr. Sivana	2.99
❑44	2.99
❑45	2.99
❑46	2.99
❑47	2.99
❑48	2.99
❑49	2.99
❑50	2.99

Outsiders Double Feature
DC

	N-MINT
❑1, Oct 2003	4.95

Overkill: Witchblade/Aliens/ Darkness/Predator
Image

	N-MINT
❑1, Dec 2000	5.95
❑2, Mar 2001	5.95

Overload Magazine
Eclipse

	N-MINT
❑1, Apr 1987, b&w	1.50

Overmen
Excel

	N-MINT
❑1	2.95

Over the Edge
Marvel

	N-MINT
❑1, Nov 1995, Daredevil	1.25
❑2, Dec 1995, A: Doctor Strange	1.00
❑3, Jan 1996, Hulk	1.00
❑4, Feb 1996, Ghost Rider	1.00
❑5, Mar 1996, Punisher	1.00
❑6, Apr 1996, Daredevil and Black Panther	1.00
❑7, May 1996, Doctor Strange vs. Nightmare	1.00
❑8, Jun 1996, Elektra	1.00
❑9, Jul 1996, Ghost Rider, John Blaze	1.00
❑10, Aug 1996, Daredevil	1.00

Overture
Innovation / All-American

	N-MINT
❑1, Apr 1990, b&w; The Lunatic Fringe story; Sputnik the Spaceman story; The Blatherskite story	2.25
❑2, Jul 1990, b&w	2.25

Owl
Gold Key

	N-MINT
❑1, Apr 1967	50.00
❑2, Apr 1968	40.00

Owlhoots
Kitchen Sink

	N-MINT
❑1, ca. 1991; Two-color	2.50
❑2, ca. 1991; Two-color	2.50

Ox Cow O' War
Spoof

	N-MINT
❑1, b&w; parody	2.95

Oz
Caliber

	N-MINT
❑0; ca. 1995; b&w	4.00
❑1; ca. 1994	6.00
❑2; ca. 1994	4.00
❑3; ca. 1994	4.00
❑4	4.00
❑5; ca. 1995	3.50
❑6; ca. 1995	3.50
❑7; ca. 1995	3.50
❑8; ca. 1995	3.50
❑9; ca. 1995	3.50
❑10; ca. 1995	3.50
❑11; ca. 1995	3.00
❑12; ca. 1995	3.00
❑13; ca. 1996	3.00
❑14; ca. 1996	3.00
❑15 1996; Wraparound Cover	3.00
❑16, Jul 1996	3.00
❑17, Sep 1996	3.00
❑18, Nov 1996	2.95
❑19, Jan 1997	2.95
❑20, Mar 1997; Contains Map of the Marvelous Land of Oz	2.95

Oz Collection
Arrow

	N-MINT
❑1, b&w; ca. 1998	2.95

Oz: Daemonstorm
Caliber

	N-MINT
❑1, ca. 1997, b&w; intracompany crossover	3.95

Oz: Gale Force
Alias

	N-MINT
❑1, ca. 2005	4.99

Oz: Romance in Rags
Caliber

	N-MINT
❑1, ca. 1996, b&w	2.95
❑2, ca. 1996, b&w	2.95
❑3, ca. 1996, b&w	2.95

Oz Special: Freedom Fighters
Caliber

	N-MINT
❑1, b&w; ca. 1995	2.95

Oz Special: Lion
Caliber

	N-MINT
❑1, b&w; continues in Oz Special: Tin Man	2.95

Oz Special: Scarecrow
Caliber

	N-MINT
❑1, b&w; continues in Oz Special: Lion..	2.95

Oz Special: Tin Man
Caliber

	N-MINT
❑1, b&w; continues in Oz Special: Freedom Fighters	2.95

Oz Squad
Brave New Words

	N-MINT
❑1, Oct 1991	3.00
❑2, Jan 1992	2.50
❑3; ca. 1992	2.50
❑4	2.50

Oz Squad
Patchwork

	N-MINT
❑1	3.00
❑2	2.50
❑3	2.50
❑4, ca. 1994; b&w	2.75
❑5; ca. 1995	2.75
❑6; ca. 1995	2.95
❑7, Aug 1995	2.75
❑8, Oct 1995	2.75
❑9, Dec 1995; O: Tin Man	2.75
❑10, Feb 1996; O: Tin Man	2.75

Oz: Straw & Sorcery
Caliber

	N-MINT
❑1, Mar 1997, b&w	2.95
❑2 1997, b&w	2.95
❑3 1997, b&w	2.95

Oz: The Manga
Antarctic

	N-MINT
❑1, ca. 2005	2.99
❑2, ca. 2005	2.99
❑3, ca. 2005	2.99
❑4, ca. 2005	2.99
❑5, ca. 2005	2.99
❑6, ca. 2005	2.99

Oz-Wonderland Wars
DC

	N-MINT
❑1, Jan 1986	2.50
❑2, Feb 1986 A: Hoppy the Marvel Bunny	2.50
❑3, Mar 1986	2.50

Ozzy Osbourne
Rock-It Comics

	N-MINT
❑1, Dec 1993; Includes guitar pick	6.00

Pacific Presents
Pacific

	N-MINT
❑1, Oct 1982; SD, DSt (c); SD, DSt (w); SD, DSt (a); Rocketeer; Missing Man.	4.00
❑2, Apr 1983; DSt (c); SD, DSt (w); SD, DSt (a); Rocketeer; Missing Man	3.00
❑3, Mar 1984; SD (w); SD (a); Missing Man	1.50
❑4, Jun 1984; Doc.44 story; Mr Brinks story; Eerie Smith story; Last issue....	1.50

Pac (Preter-Human Assault Corps)
Artifacts
❑1, Oct 1993 ... 1.95

Pact
Image
❑1, Feb 1994 ... 1.95
❑2, Apr 1994; Wraparound/fold-out cover 1.95
❑3, Jun 1994; 1: Atrocity; Final Issue ... 1.95

Pact
Image
❑1, ca. 2005 ... 2.99
❑2, May 2005 ... 2.99
❑3, Jun 2005 ... 2.99
❑4, Jan 2006, Price change ... 2.99

Pagers Comics Anthology
No Talent
❑1, Spr 1997 ... 2.50
❑2, Sum 1997 ... 2.50
❑3, Fal 1997 ... 2.50
❑4, Win 1997 ... 2.50
❑5, Spr 1998 ... 2.50
❑6, Sum 1998 ... 2.50

Painkiller Jane
Event
❑0, Nov 1998; O: Painkiller Jane ... 3.95
❑0/Ltd.; O: Painkiller Jane; Autographed by Joe Quesada, Jimmy Palmiotti, Amanda Conner, and Brian Augustyn . 39.95
❑1, Jun 1997; MWa (w); wraparound cover ... 3.00
❑1/A, Jun 1997; MWa (w); variant cover 4.00
❑1/Red foil, Jun 1997; MWa (w); Red foil 25.00
❑2, Jul 1997; MWa (w); Standard cover: Jane in sunglasses close-up ... 3.00
❑2/A, Jul 1997; MWa (w); variant cover; Jane running ... 4.00
❑3, Aug 1997 MWa (w) ... 3.00
❑3/A, Aug 1997; MWa (w); variant cover 4.00
❑4, Sep 1997 MWa (w) ... 3.00
❑4/A, Sep 1997; MWa (w); variant cover 4.00
❑5, Oct 1997 MWa (w) ... 3.00
❑5/A, Oct 1997; MWa (w); variant cover 4.00

Painkiller Jane/Darkchylde
Event
❑0; European Preview book ... 4.00
❑0/Autographed; European Preview book 29.95
❑1, Oct 1998 ... 3.00
❑1/A, Oct 1998; DFE Omnichrome edition with COA ... 29.95
❑1/B, Oct 1998; DFE alternate cover ... 4.00
❑1/C, Oct 1998; Signed edition; Signed edition ... 39.95
❑Ashcan 1, Jul 1998; DF Exclusive; Sketches ... 5.00

Painkiller Jane/Hellboy
Event
❑1, Aug 1998; Cover by Mike Mignola ... 2.95
❑1/Ltd., Aug 1998; Signed edition; Signed edition ... 29.95
❑1/A, Aug 1998; Cover by Quesada/ Palmiotti ... 2.95

Painkiller Jane vs. The Darkness: Stripper
Event
❑1, Apr 1997; four alternate covers ... 2.95
❑1/A, Apr 1997; Jane facing forward, shooting on cover ... 3.00
❑1/B, Apr 1997; Diptych with 1/D; Quesada / Palmiotti Cover ... 3.00
❑1/C, Apr 1997; Hildebrandt cover ... 3.00
❑1/Ltd., Apr 1997; Signed edition ... 20.00

Paintball Universe 2000
Splattoons
❑1 ... 2.95

Pajama Chronicles
Blackthorne
❑1, Feb 1987 ... 1.75

Pakkins' Land
Caliber / Tapestry
❑0, Jun 1997 ... 1.95
❑1, Oct 1996 ... 2.95
❑1/2nd, ca. 1996, Labeled as "Special Edition" ... 2.95
❑2, Dec 1996 ... 2.95
❑2/2nd, ca. 1996, Labeled as "Special Edition" ... 2.95
❑3, Feb 1997 ... 2.95
❑4, May 1997 ... 2.95
❑5, Jun 1997 ... 2.95
❑6, Jul 1997 ... 2.95

Pakkins' Land: Forgotten Dreams
Caliber / Tapestry
❑1, Apr 1998 ... 2.95
❑2, ca. 1998 ... 2.95
❑3, ca. 1998 ... 2.95
❑4, Mar 2000, published by Image ... 2.95

Pakkins' Land: Quest for Kings
Caliber / Tapestry
❑1, Aug 1997 ... 2.95
❑1/A, Aug 1997 ... 2.95
❑2, Sep 1997 ... 2.95
❑2/A, Aug 1997, alternate cover ... 2.95
❑3, Nov 1997 ... 2.95
❑4, Dec 1997 ... 2.95
❑5, Jan 1998 ... 2.95
❑6, Mar 1998 ... 2.95

Pakkins' Land
Alias
❑1 2005 ... 2.99
❑2 2005 ... 2.99
❑3 2005 ... 2.99
❑4, Sep 2005 ... 2.99
❑5 2005 ... 2.99

Palatine
Gryphon Rampant
❑1 ... 2.50
❑2, Oct 1994 ... 2.50
❑3, Jan 1995 ... 2.50
❑4 ... 2.50
❑5 ... 2.50

Palestine
Fantagraphics
❑1, b&w ... 2.50
❑2, b&w ... 2.50
❑3, b&w ... 2.50
❑4, b&w ... 2.95
❑5 ... 2.50
❑6 ... 2.50
❑7, Sep 1994 ... 2.95
❑9, Oct 1995, b&w ... 2.95

Pal-Yat-Chee
Adhesive
❑1, Aug 1993, b&w ... 2.50

Pamela Anderson Uncovered
Pop
❑1 ... 2.95

Panda Khan Special
Abacus
❑1, Aug 1990, b&w ... 3.00

Pandemonium
Chaos!
❑1, Sep 1998 ... 2.95

Pandora Pill
Acid Rain
❑1 ... 2.50

Panic (RCP)
Gemstone
❑1, Mar 1997; Reprints Panic (EC) #1 ... 2.50
❑2, Jun 1997; Reprints Panic (EC) #2 ... 2.50
❑3, Sep 1997; Reprints Panic (EC) #3 ... 2.50
❑4, Dec 1997; Reprints Panic (EC) #4 ... 2.50
❑5, Mar 1998; Reprints Panic (EC) #5 ... 2.50
❑6, Jun 1998; Reprints Panic (EC) #6 ... 2.50
❑7, Sep 1998; Reprints Panic (EC) #7 ... 2.50
❑8, Dec 1998; Reprints Panic (EC) #8 ... 2.50
❑9, Mar 1999; Reprints Panic (EC) #9 ... 2.50
❑10, Jun 1999; Reprints Panic (EC) #10 2.50
❑11, Sep 1999; Reprints Panic (EC) #11 2.50
❑12, Dec 1999; Reprints Panic (EC) #12 2.50
❑Ann 1; Collects issues #1-4 ... 10.95
❑Ann 2; Collects issues #5-8 ... 10.95

Panorama
St.Eve Productions
❑1 ... 2.50
❑2, ca. 1991 ... 2.50

Pantera
Malibu / Rock-It
❑1, Aug 1994; magazine ... 4.00

Pantha: Haunted Passion
Harris / Rock-It
❑1, May 1997; Black & white reprints ... 2.95

Pantheon
Archer Books & Games
❑1, Oct 1995, b&w ... 2.95
❑2, Jun 1997; b&w ... 2.95

Pantheon
Lone Star
❑1, May 1998 ... 2.95
❑2, Jul 1998 ... 2.95
❑3, Sep 1998 ... 2.95
❑4, Jan 1999 ... 2.95
❑5, Jul 1999 ... 2.95
❑6, Aug 1999 ... 2.95

Pantheon: Ancient History
Lone Star
❑1, Aug 1999; Blackheart and Fandango story; Blackheart story Reprint from Heroic Tales #6 ... 3.95

Panzer 1946
Antarctic
❑1, Oct 2004 ... 5.95
❑2 ... 5.95
❑3, ca. 2005 ... 5.95
❑4, ca. 2005 ... 5.95
❑5, ca. 2005 ... 5.95

Paper Cinema: The Box
Grey Blossom Sequentials
❑3, Dec 1998 ... 3.55

Paper Cinema: Waves In Space
Grey Blossom Sequentials
❑2, Dec 1998 ... 3.55

Paper Dolls from the California Girls
Eclipse
❑1; paper dolls ... 5.95

Paper Museum
Jungle Boy
❑1, ca. 2002, b&w; magazine-sized ... 2.95

Paper Tales
CLG Comics
❑1, Sum 1993, b&w ... 2.50
❑2, Sum 1994, b&w ... 2.50

Para-Cops
Excel
❑1 ... 2.95

Paradax
Vortex
❑1 ... 1.75
❑2, Aug 1987 ... 1.75

Paradigm
Image
❑1, Sep 2002 ... 3.50
❑2, Oct 2002 ... 3.50
❑3, Nov 2002 ... 3.50
❑4, Dec 2002 ... 3.50
❑5, Jan 2003 ... 2.95
❑6, Feb 2003 ... 2.95
❑7, Mar 2003 ... 2.95
❑8, Apr 2003 ... 2.95
❑9, May 2003 ... 3.50
❑10, Jul 2003 ... 3.50
❑11, Oct 2003 ... 3.95
❑12, Dec 2003 ... 3.95

Paradigm
Gauntlet
❑1, ca. 1993 ... 2.95

Paradise Kiss
Tokyopop
❑1, May 2002, b&w; printed in Japanese format ... 9.99

Paradise Too
Abstract
❑nn, ca. 2000, b&w ... 2.75
❑2, ca. 2001, b&w ... 2.95
❑3, ca. 2001, b&w ... 2.95
❑4, ca. 2001, b&w ... 2.95
❑5, ca. 2002, b&w ... 2.95
❑6, ca. 2002, b&w ... 2.95
❑7, ca. 2002, b&w ... 2.95
❑8, ca. 2002, b&w ... 2.95
❑9, ca. 2002, b&w ... 2.95

Powerless

Psychiatrist sees through non-heroic world
©Marvel

Power Line

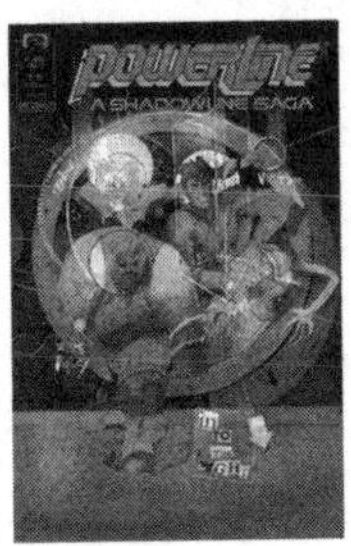

Shadow Dwellers tie Epic epics together
©Marvel

Power Man & Iron Fist

Hero for Hire gets a partner in Iron Fist
©Marvel

Power of Shazam, The

Jerry Ordway updates Captain Marvel
©DC

Power Pack

Alien gives Powers children powers
©Marvel

N-MINT

❑10, ca. 2002, b&w; 1: Wonderland....... 2.95
❑11, ca. 2003, b&w....... 2.95
❑12, Mar 2003, b&w; 1: Echo the Fairy; Wonderland story....... 2.95
❑13, Jul 2003, b&w; 1: Kaippe; Lady Supreme art; Poison Elves pin-up; Yankee Girl pin-up....... 2.95
❑14, Aug 2003, b&w; Final issue; Wonderland story....... 2.95

Paradise X
Marvel

❑0, Apr 2002....... 4.50
❑1, May 2002....... 2.99
❑2, Jun 2002....... 2.99
❑3, Aug 2002....... 2.99
❑4, Sep 2002....... 2.99
❑5, Oct 2002....... 2.99
❑6, Dec 2002....... 2.99
❑7, ca. 2003....... 2.99
❑8, ca. 2003....... 2.99
❑9, ca. 2003....... 2.99
❑10, Jun 2003....... 2.99
❑11, Jul 2003....... 2.99
❑12, Aug 2003....... 2.99

Paradise X: Devils
Marvel

❑1, Nov 2002....... 4.50

Paradise X: Heralds
Marvel

❑1, Dec 2001....... 3.50
❑2, Jan 2002....... 3.50
❑3, Feb 2002....... 3.50

Paradise X: A
Marvel

❑1, Oct 2003....... 2.99

Paradise X: X
Marvel

❑1, Nov 2003....... 2.99

Paradise X: Ragnarok
Marvel

❑1, Mar 2003....... 2.99
❑2, Apr 2003....... 2.99

Paradise X: Xen
Marvel

❑1, Jul 2002....... 4.50

Paradox Project: Genesis
Paradox Project

❑1, Dec 1998, b&w....... 2.95

Paragon: Dark Apocalypse
AC

❑1....... 2.95
❑2....... 2.95
❑3....... 2.95
❑4....... 2.95

Parallax: Emerald Night
DC

❑1, Nov 1996, D: Cyborg Superman. Final Night....... 15.00

Paranoia
Adventure

❑1, Oct 1991....... 2.95
❑2, Dec 1991....... 2.95

N-MINT

❑3, Feb 1992....... 2.95
❑4, Apr 1992....... 2.95
❑5, Jun 1992....... 2.95
❑6, Aug 1992....... 2.95

Paranoia
Co. & Sons

❑1, Adult; ca. 1972....... 4.00

Paraphernalia
Graphitti

❑1; Ordering Catalogue....... 2.00

Para Troop
Comics Conspiracy

❑0; ca. 1999....... 3.95
❑1....... 2.95
❑2....... 2.95
❑3, Oct 1998....... 2.95
❑4, Dec 1998....... 2.95
❑5, Feb 1999....... 2.95
❑Ashcan 1; Ashcan edition....... 2.95

Pardners
Cottonwood Graphics

❑1, Dec 1990, b&w....... 7.95
❑2, Dec 1991, b&w....... 7.95

Paris
Slave Labor

❑1, Nov 2005....... 2.95
❑2, Dec 2005....... 2.95

Paris the Man of Plaster
Harrier

❑1, May 1987; Paris the Man of Plaster story; Temptation story; Mr. Day and Mr. Night story....... 1.95
❑2, Aug 1987; Paris the Man of Plaster story; Temptation story; Mr. Day and Mr. Night story....... 1.95
❑3, Nov 1987; Paris the Man of Plaster story; Mr. Day and Mr. Night story....... 1.95
❑4, Dec 1987; Paris the Man of Plaster story; Temptation story; Pals of Paris story; Mr. Day and Mr. Night story....... 1.95
❑5, Mar 1987; Paris the Man of Plaster story; The Introspectre story....... 1.95
❑6, Sep 1987; Paris the Man of Plaster story; Mr Slugg story....... 1.95

Parliament of Justice
Image

❑1, Mar 2003, b&w....... 5.95

Paro-Dee
Parody

❑1, b&w; Adult....... 2.50

Parody Press Annual Swimsuit Special '93
Parody

❑1, Aug 1993....... 2.50

Particle Dreams
Fantagraphics

❑1, Oct 1986....... 2.25
❑2, Jan 1987....... 2.25
❑3, Apr 1987....... 2.25
❑4, Jun 1987....... 2.25
❑5 1987....... 2.25
❑6 1987....... 2.25

N-MINT

Partners in Pandemonium
Caliber

❑1, b&w....... 2.50
❑2, b&w....... 2.50
❑3, b&w....... 2.50

Partridge Family
Charlton

❑1, Mar 1971....... 30.00
❑2, May 1971....... 16.00
❑3, Jul 1971....... 14.00
❑4, Sep 1971....... 14.00
❑5, Sum 1971, Giant-size; Summer Special....... 20.00
❑6, Jan 1971....... 12.00
❑7, Feb 1972....... 12.00
❑8, Mar 1972....... 12.00
❑9, Apr 1972....... 12.00
❑10, May 1972....... 12.00
❑11, Aug 1972....... 12.00
❑12, Sep 1972....... 12.00
❑13, Nov 1972....... 12.00
❑14, Dec 1973....... 12.00
❑15, Jan 1973....... 10.00
❑16, ca. 1973....... 10.00
❑17, ca. 1973....... 10.00
❑18, ca. 1973....... 10.00
❑19, Jul 1973....... 10.00
❑20, Sep 1973....... 10.00
❑21, ca. 1973, Final Issue....... 10.00

Parts of a Hole
Caliber

❑1, b&w; Brian Michael Bendis' first major comics work....... 2.50

Parts Unknown
Eclipse

❑1, Aug 1995, b&w....... 2.50
❑2, Mar 1995, b&w; Blood is the Harvest #2 preview....... 2.50
❑3, Jun 1995, b&w....... 2.50
❑4, Oct 1995, b&w....... 2.50

Parts Unknown Convention Sketchbook
-Ism

❑1, ca. 2005....... 10.00

Parts Unknown: Dark Intentions
Knight

❑0, Aug 1995....... 2.95
❑1, Mar 1995....... 2.95
❑2, Jun 1995....... 2.95
❑3, Oct 1995....... 2.95
❑4 1995....... 2.95

Parts Unknown: Hostile Takeover
Image

❑1, Jun 2000....... 2.95
❑1/Ashcan, Jun 2000; Preview edition....... 4.95
❑2, Jul 2000....... 2.95
❑2/Ashcan, Jul 2000; Preview edition....... 4.95
❑3, Aug 2000....... 2.95
❑3/Ashcan, Aug 2000; Preview edition....... 4.95
❑4, Sep 2000....... 2.95
❑4/Ashcan, Sep 2000; Preview edition....... 4.95

N-MINT

Parts Unknown II: The Next Invasion
Eclipse

❑1, Dec 1993, b&w 2.95

Passover
Maximum

❑1, Dec 1996 ..... 2.99

Path
CrossGen

❑1, Apr 2002 ..... 2.95
❑2, May 2002 ..... 2.95
❑3, Jun 2002 ..... 2.95
❑4, Jul 2002 ..... 2.95
❑5, Aug 2002 ..... 2.95
❑6, Sep 2002 ..... 2.95
❑7, Oct 2002 ..... 2.95
❑8, Nov 2002 ..... 2.95
❑9, Dec 2002 ..... 2.95
❑10, Jan 2003 ..... 2.95
❑11, Feb 2003 ..... 2.95
❑12, Mar 2003 ..... 2.95
❑13, Apr 2003 ..... 2.95
❑14, May 2003 ..... 2.95
❑15, Jun 2003 ..... 2.95
❑16, Jul 2003 ..... 2.95
❑17, Sep 2003 ..... 2.95
❑18, Oct 2003 ..... 2.95
❑19, Nov 2003 ..... 2.95
❑20, Dec 2003 ..... 2.95
❑21, Jan 2004 ..... 2.95
❑22, Mar 2004 ..... 2.95
❑23, Apr 2004 ..... 2.95

Path Prequel
CrossGen

❑1, Mar 2002 ..... 2.95

Pathways to Fantasy
Pacific

❑1, Jul 1984, JJ (a) 2.00

Patient Zero
Image

❑1, Apr 2004 ..... 2.95
❑2, May 2004 ..... 2.95
❑3, Aug 2004 ..... 2.95
❑4, Sep 2004 ..... 3.00

Patrick Rabbit
Fragments West

❑1, Sum 1988 ..... 2.00
❑2 ..... 2.00
❑3 ..... 2.00
❑4 ..... 2.00
❑5 ..... 2.00
❑6 ..... 2.00
❑7 ..... 2.00

Patrick Stewart
Celebrity

❑1 ..... 2.95

Patrick Stewart vs. William Shatner
Celebrity

❑1, Jan 1992, b&w; With color paintings 5.95

Patriots
WildStorm

❑1, Jan 2000 ..... 2.50
❑2, Feb 2000 ..... 2.50
❑3, Mar 2000 ..... 2.50
❑4, Apr 2000 ..... 2.50
❑5, May 2000 ..... 2.50
❑6, Jun 2000 ..... 2.50
❑7, Jul 2000 ..... 2.50
❑8, Aug 2000 ..... 2.50
❑9, Sep 2000 ..... 2.50
❑10, Oct 2000 ..... 2.50

Pat Savage: The Woman of Bronze
Millennium

❑1, Oct 1992; NN 2.50

Patsy and Hedy
Marvel

❑79, Dec 1961, SL (w) 12.00
❑80, Feb 1962, SL (w) 12.00
❑81, Apr 1962 ..... 12.00
❑82, Jun 1962 ..... 12.00
❑83, Aug 1962 ..... 12.00
❑84, Oct 1962 ..... 12.00
❑85, Dec 1962 ..... 12.00
❑86, Feb 1963 ..... 12.00
❑87, Apr 1963 ..... 12.00
❑88, Jun 1963 ..... 12.00
❑89, Aug 1963 ..... 12.00
❑90, Oct 1963 ..... 12.00
❑91, Dec 1963 ..... 10.00
❑92, Feb 1964 ..... 10.00
❑93, Apr 1964 ..... 10.00
❑94, Jun 1964 ..... 10.00
❑95, Aug 1964, Graduation issue 10.00
❑96, Oct 1964, Patsy and Hedy "Career Girls" begins 10.00
❑97, Dec 1964 ..... 10.00
❑98, Feb 1965, SL (w) 10.00
❑99, Apr 1965, SL (w) 10.00
❑100, Jun 1965, SL (w) 10.00
❑101, Aug 1965 ..... 10.00
❑102, Oct 1965 ..... 10.00
❑103, Dec 1965 ..... 10.00
❑104, Feb 1966 ..... 10.00
❑105, Apr 1966 ..... 10.00
❑106, Jun 1966 ..... 10.00
❑107, Aug 1966 ..... 10.00
❑108, Oct 1966 ..... 10.00
❑109, Dec 1966 ..... 10.00
❑110, Feb 1967, "Girls on the Go-Go"; Peter and Gordon pin-up; celebrity interviews 10.00
❑Ann 1, ca. 1963 ..... 55.00

Patty Cake
Permanent Press

❑1, b&w; ca. 1994 ..... 3.00
❑2, b&w; ca. 1994 ..... 3.00
❑3, ca. 1995, b&w 3.00
❑4, ca. 1995, b&w 3.00
❑5, ca. 1996, b&w 3.00
❑6, ca. 1996, b&w 3.00
❑7, ca. 1996, b&w 3.00
❑8, ca. 1996, b&w 3.00
❑9, ca. 1996, b&w 3.00

Patty Cake
Caliber / Tapestry

❑1, ca. 1996, b&w 3.00
❑2, ca. 1997, b&w 3.00
❑3, ca. 1997, b&w 3.00
❑Holiday 1, Dec 1996, b&w 3.00

Patty Cake & Friends
Slave Labor

❑1, Nov 1997, b&w 3.00
❑2, Dec 1997, b&w 3.00
❑3, Jan 1998, b&w 3.00
❑4, Feb 1998, b&w 3.00
❑5, Mar 1998, b&w 3.00
❑6, Apr 1998, b&w 3.00
❑7, May 1998 ..... 2.95
❑8, Jun 1998 ..... 2.95
❑9, Aug 1998 ..... 2.95
❑10, Sep 1998 ..... 2.95
❑11, Nov 1998 ..... 2.95
❑12 ..... 2.95
❑Special 1, Oct 1997, NN 3.95

Patty Cake & Friends
Slave Labor

❑1, Nov 2000, b&w; cardstock cover 4.95
❑2 ..... 4.95
❑3 ..... 4.95
❑4 ..... 4.95
❑5 ..... 4.95
❑6 ..... 4.95
❑7 ..... 4.95
❑8 ..... 4.95
❑9 ..... 4.95
❑10 ..... 4.95
❑11 ..... 4.95
❑12 ..... 4.95
❑13, Jan 2005 ..... 4.95
❑15, Jan 2006; b&w 4.95

Paul the Samurai
New England

❑1, Jul 1992 ..... 4.00
❑2, Sep 1992 ..... 3.00
❑3, Nov 1992; Scarcer 6.00
❑4, Jan 1993 ..... 4.00
❑5, Mar 1993 ..... 2.75
❑6, May 1993 ..... 2.75
❑7, Jul 1993 ..... 2.75
❑8, Nov 1993 ..... 2.75
❑9, Mar 1994 A: The Tick 2.75
❑10, May 1994 A: The Tick 2.75

Paul the Samurai
NEC

❑1, Oct 1990 A: The Tick 3.50
❑2, Jul 1991 ..... 3.00
❑3, Dec 1991 ..... 3.00

Payne
Dream Catcher

❑1, Sep 1995, b&w 2.50

Peacemaker
Charlton

❑1, Mar 1967, Fightin' 5; Continued from Fightin' 5 #41 ..... 10.00
❑2, May 1967, Fightin' 5 back-up story 6.00
❑3, Jul 1967, Fightin' 5 ..... 6.00
❑4, Sep 1967, O: The Peacemaker; Fightin' 5 ..... 8.00
❑5, Nov 1967, Fightin' 5 ..... 6.00

Peacemaker Kurogane
ADV Manga

❑1, ca. 2004; Reads right to left; Graphic novel; b&w 9.99
❑2, ca. 2004; Reads right to left; Graphic novel; b&w 9.99
❑3, ca. 2005; Reads right to left; Graphic novel; b&w 9.99

Peacemaker
DC

❑1, Jan 1988 ..... 1.50
❑2, Feb 1988 ..... 1.50
❑3, Mar 1988 ..... 1.50
❑4, Apr 1988 ..... 1.50

Peace Party
Blue Corn

❑1; ca. 1999 ..... 2.95

Peace Posse
Mellon Bank

❑1 ..... 2.95

Peanut Butter and Jeremy
Alternative

❑1, Aug 2000, b&w; NN 2.95
❑2, Sep 2001, b&w 2.95
❑3, Oct 2002, b&w 2.95
❑4/FCBD, May 2003, b&w 2.00

Peanuts
Gold Key

❑1, May 1963, Reprints from Four Color Comics #878 ..... 125.00
❑2, Aug 1963, Reprints from Four Color Comics #969 ..... 75.00
❑3, Nov 1963, Interior artwork not by Schulz (most sources attribute this work to Schulz's assistant Anthony Pocmich), Reprints from Four Color Comics #1015 ..... 75.00
❑4, Feb 1964, Interior artwork not by Schulz (most sources attribute this work to Schulz's assistant Anthony Pocmich), Reprints from Peanuts (Dell) #4 ..... 75.00

Pebbles and Bamm-Bamm
Charlton

❑1, Jan 1972 ..... 18.00
❑2, Mar 1972 ..... 12.00
❑3, May 1972 ..... 9.00
❑4, Jul 1972 ..... 9.00
❑5, Aug 1972 ..... 9.00
❑6, Sep 1972 ..... 7.00
❑7, Oct 1972, No credits in issue 7.00
❑8, Nov 1972 ..... 7.00
❑9, Dec 1972 ..... 7.00
❑10, ca. 1973 ..... 7.00
❑11, ca. 1973 ..... 5.00
❑12, ca. 1973 ..... 5.00
❑13, ca. 1973 ..... 5.00
❑14, ca. 1973 ..... 5.00
❑15, Aug 1973 ..... 5.00
❑16, Oct 1973 ..... 5.00
❑17, Nov 1973 ..... 5.00
❑18, Jan 1974 ..... 5.00
❑19, Feb 1974 ..... 5.00
❑20, Jun 1974 ..... 5.00
❑21, Aug 1974 ..... 4.00
❑22, Nov 1974 ..... 4.00
❑23, Jan 1975 ..... 4.00

Other grades: Multiply price above by 5/6 for VF/NM • 2/3 for VERY FINE • 1/3 for FINE • 1/5 for VERY GOOD • 1/8 for GOOD

Powerpuff Girls

Sugar and spice combine with Chemical X

©DC

Powers

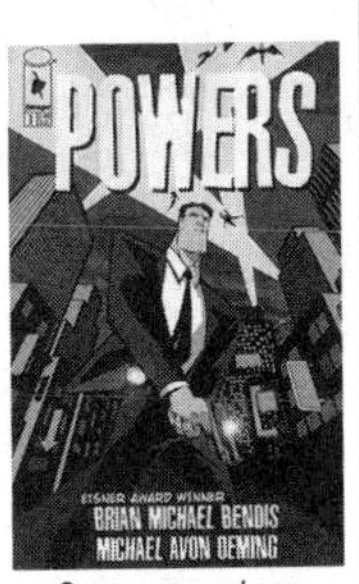

Super-powered cop solves super-crimes

©Image

Powers That Be

Broadway's debut featured Fatale, Star Seed

©Broadway

Predator

Alien hunters pay New York a visit

©Dark Horse

Pre-Teen Dirty-Gene Kung-Fu Kangaroos

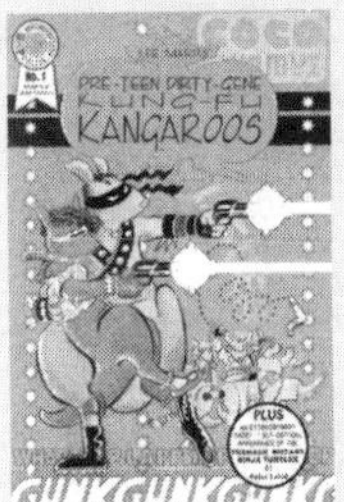

Turtles rip-off has Turtles appearance

©Blackthorne

	N-MINT
❑24, Feb 1975	4.00
❑25, Mar 1975	4.00
❑26, ca. 1975	4.00
❑27, ca. 1975	4.00
❑28, ca. 1975	4.00
❑29, ca. 1975	4.00
❑30, Dec 1975	4.00
❑31, Feb 1976	3.00
❑32, Apr 1976	3.00
❑33, Jun 1976	3.00
❑34, Aug 1976, No credits listed	3.00
❑35, Oct 1976	3.00
❑36, Dec 1976, No credits listed	3.00

Pebbles & Bamm-Bamm
Harvey

❑1, Nov 1993	1.50
❑2, Jan 1994	1.50
❑3, Mar 1994	1.50
❑Summer 1, Oct 1993	2.25

Pebbles Flintstone
Gold Key

❑1, Sep 1963	75.00

Pedestrian Vulgarity
Fantagraphics

❑1, b&w	2.50

Peek-A-Boo 3-D
3-D Zone

❑1; NN	3.95

Peepshow
Drawn & Quarterly

❑1	2.50
❑2, May 1992	2.50
❑3	2.50
❑4	2.50
❑5, Oct 1993	2.95
❑6, Apr 1994	2.95
❑7	2.95
❑8	2.95
❑9	2.95

Pellestar
Eternity

❑1, Sep 1987	1.95
❑2	1.95

Pendragon
Aircel

❑1, Nov 1991, b&w; Adult	2.95
❑2, Dec 1991, b&w; Adult	2.95

Pendulum
Adventure

❑1, Nov 1992, b&w	2.50
❑2, Dec 1992, b&w	2.50
❑3, b&w	2.50
❑4, b&w	2.50

Pendulum's Illustrated Stories
Pendulum

❑1; Moby Dick; No apparent cover price	4.95
❑2; Treasure Island	4.95
❑3; Doctor Jekyll	4.95
❑4; 20, 000 Leagues Under the Sea	4.95
❑5; Midsummer Night's Dream	4.95
❑6; Christmas Carol	4.95

Peng One Shot
Oni

	N-MINT
❑1, Sep 2005	5.95

Penguin & Pencilguin
Fragments West

❑1, Jan 1987	2.00
❑2, Feb 1987	2.00
❑3, Mar 1987	2.00
❑4, Apr 1987	2.00
❑5, May 1987	2.00
❑6, Jun 1987	2.00

Penguin Bros.
Labyrinth

❑1	2.50
❑2	2.50

Penny & Aggie
Alias

❑1, Jul 2005	2.99
❑2, Aug 2005	2.99
❑3, Sep 2005	2.99
❑4, ca. 2005	2.99

Penny Arcade: 1x 25 Cents
Dark Horse

❑1, Nov 2005	0.25

Penny Century
Fantagraphics

❑1, Dec 1997, b&w	2.95
❑2, Mar 1998, b&w	2.95
❑3, Sep 1998, b&w	2.95
❑4, Jan 1999, b&w	2.95
❑5, Jun 1999, b&w	2.95
❑6, Nov 1999, b&w	2.95
❑7, Jul 2000, b&w	2.95

Pentacle: The Sign of the Five
Eternity

❑1, Feb 1991	2.25
❑2 1991; b&w	2.25
❑3 1991; b&w	2.25
❑4 1991; b&w	2.25

Penthouse Comix
Penthouse International

❑1, Jun 1994; 1: Hericane	6.00
❑1/2nd, ca. 1995; subtitled Special Edition 1995; 2nd printing; 1: Hericane; 14 pages of new material	4.95
❑2, Jul 1994	4.95
❑3, Sep 1994; O: Hericane	4.95
❑4, Nov 1994	4.95
❑5, Jan 1995 KN (c); GM, CS, KN, RH (a)	4.95
❑6, Mar 1995; Comic size; GM (a)	4.95
❑6/A, Mar 1995; Magazine size; Omni Comix preview	4.95
❑7, May 1995; Comic size	4.95
❑7/A, May 1995; Magazine size	4.95
❑8, Jul 1995	4.95
❑9, Sep 1995	4.95
❑10, Nov 1995	4.95
❑11, Jan 1996; Jim Steranko pinups; Excerpt from Griffes d'Ange	4.95
❑12, Mar 1996; second anniversary issue	4.95
❑13, May 1996	4.95
❑14, Jul 1996	4.95
❑15, Sep 1996	4.95
❑16, Oct 1996; Dave Dorman cover	4.95

	N-MINT
❑17, Nov 1996; reprints Manara's Hidden Camera	4.95
❑18, Dec 1996; Wraparound cover	4.95
❑19, Jan 1997	4.95
❑20, Feb 1997; Joe Chiodo cover	4.95
❑21, Apr 1997	4.95
❑22, May 1997	4.95
❑23, Jun 1997	4.95
❑24, Jul 1997; Scott Hampton cover	4.95
❑25, Sep 1997; Sweet Chastity reprints begin; pin-ups of Chastity by various artists	4.95
❑26, Oct 1997	4.95
❑27, Nov 1997	4.95
❑28, Jan 1998	4.95
❑29, Feb 1998	4.95
❑30, Apr 1998	4.95
❑31, May 1998	4.95
❑32, Jun 1998	4.95
❑33, Jul 1998; Final Issue	4.95

Penthouse Max
Penthouse International

❑1, Jul 1996; Wraparound cover; Adult	4.95
❑2, Nov 1996; Adult	4.95
❑3, Spr 1997; Spring 1997; Wraparound cover; Adult	4.95

Penthouse Men's Adventure Comix
Penthouse

❑1, Apr 1995	4.95
❑2, Jun 1995	4.95
❑3, Aug 1995	4.95
❑4, Oct 1995	4.95
❑5, Dec 1995	4.95
❑6, Feb 1996	4.95
❑7, Apr 1996	4.95

People are Phony
Siegel and Simon

❑1, Sep 1976; Adult	4.00

People's Comics
Golden Gate

❑1, Sep 1972, D: Fritz the Cat; Adult	4.00

Pep
Archie

❑151, ca. 1961; A: The Fly. Archie; Betty and Veronica; Li'l Jinx; The Fly	15.00
❑152, Jan 1962, A: Jaguar. Archie; Moose; Jaguar; Li'l Jinx	15.00
❑153, Mar 1962, A: Fly Girl. Archie; Fly Girl; Li'l Jinx; Moose	15.00
❑154, May 1962, A: The Fly	15.00
❑155, Jun 1962, A: Fly Girl	15.00
❑156, Aug 1962, A: Fly Girl	15.00
❑157, Sep 1962, 1: Kree-Nal. A: Jaguar; Archie; Li'l Jinx	15.00
❑158, Oct 1962, A: Fly Girl. Archie; Reggie; Fly Girl; Li'l Jinx	15.00
❑159, ca. 1962, A: Jaguar	15.00
❑160, Jan 1963, A: The Fly	15.00
❑161, Mar 1963	7.00
❑162, May 1963	7.00
❑163, Jun 1963	7.00
❑164, Aug 1963	7.00
❑165, Sep 1963	7.00
❑166, Oct 1963	7.00
❑167, ca. 1963	7.00

Other grades: Multiply price above by 5/6 for VF/NM • 2/3 for VERY FINE • 1/3 for FINE • 1/5 for VERY GOOD • 1/8 for GOOD

	N-MINT
❑168, Jan 1964	7.00
❑169, Mar 1964	7.00
❑170, May 1964	7.00
❑171, Jun 1964	7.00
❑172, Aug 1964	7.00
❑173, Sep 1964	7.00
❑174, Oct 1964, Archie; Li'l Jinx; Betty and Veronica	7.00
❑175, Nov 1964	7.00
❑176, Dec 1964, Archie; Li'l Jinx; Josie	7.00
❑177, Jan 1965, Josie	7.00
❑178, Feb 1965	6.00
❑179, Mar 1965, Archie; Josie; Li'l Jinx	6.00
❑180, Apr 1965	6.00
❑181, May 1965, Archie; Betty and Veronica; Josie; Li'l Jinx	6.00
❑182, Jun 1965	6.00
❑183, Jul 1965, Betty and Veronica; Archie; Li'l Jinx	6.00
❑184, Aug 1965	6.00
❑185, Sep 1965	6.00
❑186, Oct 1965	6.00
❑187, Nov 1965	6.00
❑188, Dec 1965	6.00
❑189, Jan 1966	6.00
❑190, Feb 1966	6.00
❑191, Mar 1966	6.00
❑192, Apr 1966	6.00
❑193, May 1966, Archie; Professor Jughead; Li'l Jinx; Reggie; Betty and Veronica	6.00
❑194, Jun 1966	6.00
❑195, Jul 1966	6.00
❑196, Aug 1966	6.00
❑197, Sep 1966	6.00
❑198, Oct 1966, Archie; Li'l Jinx; Betty and Veronica	6.00
❑199, Nov 1966	6.00
❑200, Dec 1966	6.00
❑201, Jan 1967	5.00
❑202, Feb 1967	5.00
❑203, Mar 1967	5.00
❑204, Apr 1967	5.00
❑205, May 1967	5.00
❑206, Jun 1967	5.00
❑207, Jul 1967	5.00
❑208, Aug 1967, Archie; Li'l Jlnx; Betty and Veronica	5.00
❑209, Sep 1967	5.00
❑210, Oct 1967	5.00
❑211, Nov 1967	5.00
❑212, Dec 1967	5.00
❑213, Jan 1968	5.00
❑214, Feb 1968	5.00
❑215, Mar 1968	5.00
❑216, Apr 1968	5.00
❑217, May 1968	5.00
❑218, Jun 1968	5.00
❑219, Jul 1968	5.00
❑220, Aug 1968	5.00
❑221, Sep 1968, Archie; Li'l Jinx	4.00
❑222, Oct 1968	4.00
❑223, Nov 1968	4.00
❑224, Dec 1968	4.00
❑225, Jan 1969	4.00
❑226, Feb 1969	4.00
❑227, Mar 1969	4.00
❑228, Apr 1969	4.00
❑229, May 1969	4.00
❑230, Jun 1969	4.00
❑231, Jul 1969	4.00
❑232, Aug 1969	3.50
❑233, Sep 1969	3.50
❑234, Oct 1969	3.50
❑235, Nov 1969	3.50
❑236, Dec 1969	3.50
❑237, Jan 1970, Archie; Veronica; Li'l Jinx	3.50
❑238, Feb 1970, Archie; Li'l Jinx	3.50
❑239, Mar 1970	3.50
❑240, Apr 1970	3.50
❑241, May 1970	3.50
❑242, Jun 1970	3.50
❑243, Jul 1970, Archie; Moose; Li'l Jinx; Mr. Weatherbee	3.50
❑244, Aug 1970, Veronica; Archie; Li'l Jinx	3.50
❑245, Sep 1970	3.50
❑246, Oct 1970	3.50
❑247, Nov 1970, Archie; Hot Dog; Li'l Jinx	3.50

	N-MINT
❑248, Dec 1970	3.50
❑249, Jan 1971	3.50
❑250, Feb 1971	3.50
❑251, Mar 1971, Reggie; Archie; Li'l Jinx	1.75
❑252, Apr 1971	1.75
❑253, May 1971, Coach Cleats; Archie; Li'l Jinx; Dilton	1.75
❑254, Jun 1971	1.75
❑255, Jul 1971	1.75
❑256, Aug 1971	1.75
❑257, Sep 1971	1.75
❑258, Oct 1971	1.75
❑259, Nov 1971	1.75
❑260, Dec 1971	1.75
❑261, Jan 1972	1.75
❑262, Feb 1972	1.75
❑263, Mar 1972	1.75
❑264, Apr 1972	1.75
❑265, May 1972	1.75
❑266, Jun 1972	1.75
❑267, Jul 1972	1.75
❑268, Aug 1972, Archie; Li'l Jinx	1.75
❑269, Sep 1972	1.75
❑270, Oct 1972	1.75
❑271, Nov 1972	1.75
❑272, Dec 1972	1.75
❑273, Jan 1973	1.75
❑274, Feb 1973	1.75
❑275, Mar 1973	1.75
❑276, Apr 1973	1.75
❑277, May 1973	1.75
❑278, Jun 1973	1.75
❑279, Jul 1973	1.75
❑280, Aug 1973	1.75
❑281, Sep 1973	1.50
❑282, Oct 1973	1.50
❑283, Nov 1973	1.50
❑284, Dec 1973	1.50
❑285, Jan 1974	1.50
❑286, Feb 1974, Archie; Li'l Jinx; Betty and Veronica	1.50
❑287, Mar 1974	1.50
❑288, Apr 1974	1.50
❑289, May 1974	1.50
❑290, Jun 1974	1.50
❑291, Jul 1974	1.50
❑292, Aug 1974	1.50
❑293, Sep 1974	1.50
❑294, Oct 1974	1.50
❑295, Nov 1974	1.50
❑296, Dec 1974	1.50
❑297, Jan 1975	1.50
❑298, Feb 1975	1.50
❑299, Mar 1975	1.50
❑300, Apr 1975; Pop Tate; Li'l Jinx; Archie; Randy; Diston	1.50
❑301, May 1975	1.25
❑302, Jun 1975	1.25
❑303, Jul 1975	1.25
❑304, Aug 1975	1.25
❑305, Sep 1975	1.25
❑306, Oct 1975	1.25
❑307, Nov 1975	1.25
❑308, Dec 1975	1.25
❑309, Jan 1976	1.25
❑310, Feb 1976	1.25
❑311, Mar 1976	1.25
❑312, Apr 1976	1.25
❑313, May 1976	1.25
❑314, Jun 1976	1.25
❑315, Jul 1976	1.25
❑316, Aug 1976	1.25
❑317, Sep 1976	1.25
❑318, Oct 1976	1.25
❑319, Nov 1976	1.25
❑320, Dec 1976	1.25
❑321, Jan 1977	1.25
❑322, Feb 1977	1.25
❑323, Mar 1977	1.25
❑324, Apr 1977	1.25
❑325, May 1977	1.25
❑326, Jun 1977	1.25
❑327, Jul 1977	1.25
❑328, Aug 1977	1.25
❑329, Sep 1977	1.25
❑330, Oct 1977	1.25
❑331, Nov 1977	1.25
❑332, Dec 1977	1.25

	N-MINT
❑333, Jan 1978	1.25
❑334, Feb 1978	1.25
❑335, Mar 1978	1.25
❑336, Apr 1978	1.25
❑337, May 1978	1.25
❑338, Jun 1978	1.25
❑339, Jul 1978	1.25
❑340, Aug 1978	1.25
❑341, Sep 1978	1.25
❑342, Oct 1978	1.25
❑343, Nov 1978, Archie; Chuck; Li'l Jinx	1.25
❑344, Dec 1978	1.25
❑345, Jan 1979	1.25
❑346, Feb 1979, Archie; Reggie; Li'l Jinx and Mort the Worry Wart	1.25
❑347, Mar 1979	1.25
❑348, Apr 1979	1.25
❑349, May 1979	1.25
❑350, Jun 1979, Archie; Jughead; Li'l Jinx; Miss Beazly	1.25
❑351, Jul 1979	1.25
❑352, Aug 1979	1.25
❑353, Sep 1979	1.25
❑354, Oct 1979, Archie; Betty and Veronica; Li'l Jinx; Jughead	1.25
❑355, Nov 1979	1.25
❑356, Dec 1979	1.25
❑357, Jan 1980	1.25
❑358, Feb 1980	1.25
❑359, Mar 1980	1.25
❑360, Apr 1980	1.25
❑361, May 1980	1.25
❑362, Jun 1980	1.25
❑363, Jul 1980	1.25
❑364, Aug 1980	1.25
❑365, ca. 1980	1.25
❑366, ca. 1980	1.25
❑367, ca. 1980	1.25
❑368, Dec 1980	1.25
❑369, ca. 1981	1.25
❑370, ca. 1981	1.25
❑371, ca. 1981	1.00
❑372, ca. 1981	1.00
❑373, ca. 1981	1.00
❑374, ca. 1981	1.00
❑375, ca. 1981	1.00
❑376, ca. 1981	1.00
❑377, ca. 1981	1.00
❑378, ca. 1981	1.00
❑379, ca. 1981	1.00
❑380	1.00
❑381, ca. 1982	1.00
❑382, ca. 1982	1.00
❑383, Apr 1982	1.00
❑384	1.00
❑385, Aug 1982	1.00
❑386	1.00
❑387	1.00
❑388, Mar 1983	1.00
❑389, ca. 1983	1.00
❑390, ca. 1983	1.00
❑391, Nov 1983	1.00
❑392, Jan 1984	1.00
❑393, Mar 1984	1.00
❑394, May 1984	1.00
❑395, Jul 1984	1.00
❑396, Sep 1984, Archie; Marvelous Maureen; Moose	1.00
❑397, Nov 1984	1.00
❑398, Jan 1985	1.00
❑399, Mar 1985	1.00
❑400, May 1985	1.00
❑401, Jul 1985	1.00
❑402, Sep 1985	1.00
❑403, Nov 1985	1.00
❑404, Jan 1986	1.00
❑405, Mar 1986	1.00
❑406, May 1986	1.00
❑407, Jul 1986	1.00
❑408, Sep 1986	1.00
❑409, Nov 1986	1.00
❑410, Jan 1987	1.00
❑411, Mar 1987; Final Issue	1.00

Perazim
Antarctic

	N-MINT
❑1, Sep 1996, b&w	2.95

Other grades: Multiply price above by 5/6 for VF/NM • 2/3 for VERY FINE • 1/3 for FINE • 1/5 for VERY GOOD • 1/8 for GOOD

Prez

Keen teen becomes chief exec
©DC

Prime

Super shell turns to slime when done
©Malibu

Primer

Grendel premiered in Comico test title
©Comico

Primortals

Tekno title featured actual celebrity input
©Tekno

Prisoner

Unnumbered issues denoted by letter
©DC

N-MINT

❑2 ... 2.95
❑3 ... 2.95

Percevan: The Three Stars of Ingaar
Fantasy Flight

❑1 ... 8.95

Peregrine
Alliance

❑1, Apr 1994, b&w ... 2.50
❑2, Aug 1994, b&w ... 2.50

Perg
Lightning

❑1, Oct 1993, Glow-in the dark flip book ... 3.50
❑1/Gold, Oct 1993, Gold edition ... 3.50
❑1/Platinum, Oct 1993, Platinum edition ... 2.50
❑1/Variant, Oct 1993, glow cover ... 3.50
❑2, Nov 1993 ... 2.50
❑2/Platinum, Nov 1993, Platinum edition ... 2.50
❑3, Dec 1993 ... 2.50
❑3/Platinum, Dec 1993, Platinum edition ... 2.50
❑4, Jan 1994, O: Perg ... 2.50
❑4/Platinum, Jan 1994, Platinum edition ... 2.50
❑5, Feb 1994 ... 2.50
❑6, Mar 1994 ... 2.50
❑7, Apr 1994 ... 2.50
❑8, May 1994, Final Issue ... 2.50

Perhapanauts
Dark Horse

❑1, Nov 2005 ... 2.99
❑2, Dec 2005 ... 2.99
❑3, Jan 2006 ... 2.99
❑4, Apr 2006 ... 2.99

Perhapanauts: Second Chances
Dark Horse

❑1, Nov 2006 ... 2.99
❑2, Dec 2006 ... 2.99
❑3, Jan 2007 ... 2.99

Periphery
Arch-Type

❑1 ... 2.95

Perramus: Escape from the Past
Fantagraphics

❑1, Oct 1991, b&w ... 3.50
❑2, Jan 1992, b&w ... 3.50
❑3, Mar 1992, b&w ... 3.50
❑4, Apr 1992, b&w ... 3.50

Perry
Lightning

❑1, Oct 1997 ... 2.95

Perry Mason
Dell

❑1, Jun 1964 ... 40.00
❑2, Oct 1964 ... 40.00

Personality Classics
Personality

❑1; John Wayne ... 2.95
❑2; Marilyn Monroe ... 2.95
❑3; Elvis Presley ... 2.95
❑4 ... 2.95

Personality Comics Presents
Personality

❑1 1991; Paulina Porizkova ... 2.50
❑2, Apr 1991; Traci Lords ... 2.50

N-MINT

❑3 1991; Arnold Schwarzenegger ... 2.50
❑4 1991; Christina Applegate ... 2.50
❑5 1991; Patrick Swayze, Demi Moore ... 2.95
❑6 1991; Michael Jordan ... 2.95
❑7, Jul 1991; Samantha Fox ... 2.95
❑8, Aug 1991; Bettie Page, Jennifer Connelly ... 2.95
❑9, Sep 1991; Kim Basinger, Michael Keaton ... 2.95
❑10; Gloria Estefan ... 2.95
❑11 ... 2.95
❑12 ... 2.95
❑13 ... 2.95
❑14 ... 2.95
❑15 ... 2.95
❑16 ... 2.95
❑17 ... 2.95
❑18 ... 2.95

Pest
Pest Comics

❑1; Adult ... 1.95
❑2; Adult ... 1.95
❑3; Adult ... 1.95
❑4; Adult ... 1.95
❑5; Adult ... 1.95
❑6, b&w; Adult ... 1.95
❑7; Adult ... 1.95

Pet
Fantagraphics / Eros

❑1, May 1997; Adult ... 2.95

Peter Cannon-Thunderbolt
DC

❑1, Sep 1992; O: Thunderbolt ... 1.50
❑2, Oct 1992 ... 1.50
❑3, Nov 1992 ... 1.50
❑4, Dec 1992 ... 1.25
❑5, Jan 1993 ... 1.25
❑6, Feb 1993 ... 1.25
❑7, Mar 1993 ... 1.25
❑8, Apr 1993 ... 1.25
❑9, May 1993 ... 1.25
❑10, May 1993 ... 1.25
❑11, Jul 1993 ... 1.25
❑12, Aug 1993; Final Issue ... 1.25

Peter Kock
Fantagraphics / Eros

❑1, Jun 1994, b&w; Adult ... 3.50
❑2 1994, b&w; Adult ... 2.75
❑3 1994, b&w; Adult ... 2.75
❑4, May 1994, b&w; Adult ... 2.75
❑5, Jul 1994, b&w; Adult ... 2.75
❑6, Aug 1994, b&w; 24 pages; Adult ... 2.75

Peter Pan
Gold Key

❑1, Sep 1969, 10086-909 ... 20.00
❑2, Sep 1969, 10086-909 ... 12.00

Peter Pan (Tundra)
Tundra

❑1 ... 14.95
❑2 ... 14.95

Peter Pan
Disney

❑1, prestige format; Reprints ... 5.95

N-MINT

Peter Pan and the Warlords of Oz
Hand of Doom

❑1, Sep 1998 ... 2.95

Peter Pan & the Warlords of Oz: Dead Head Water
Hand of Doom

❑1, Feb 1999 ... 2.95

Peter Pan: Return to Never-Never Land
Adventure

❑1, Jul 1991 ... 2.50
❑2 ... 2.50

Peter Parker: Spider-Man
Marvel

❑1, Jan 1999; JR2 (a); V: Scorpion. wraparound cover ... 5.00
❑1/Sunburst, Jan 1999; JR2 (a); sunburst variant cover ... 6.00
❑1/Autographed, Jan 1999; JR2 (a); Autographed by Howard Mackie and John Romita Jr. ... 10.00
❑1/Dynamic, Jan 1999; JR2 (a); DFE alternate cover ... 14.00
❑2/A, Feb 1999; JR2 (a); A: Tocketts. A: Thor. Cover A ... 2.00
❑2/B, Feb 1999; JR2 (a); A: Tocketts. A: Thor. Cover B by Arthur Suydam ... 2.00
❑3, Mar 1999; JR2 (a); A: Shadrac. A: Iceman. A: Mary Jane. V: Shadrac. Continued from Amazing Spider-Man #3 ... 4.00
❑4, Apr 1999; JR2 (a); A: Marrow. #102 ... 4.00
❑5, May 1999; A: Black Cat. V: Spider-Woman. V: Spider-Woman ... 4.00
❑6, Jun 1999; V: Kingpin. V: Bullseye ... 4.00
❑7, Jul 1999 A: Blade ... 4.00
❑8, Aug 1999 A: Kingpin. A: Blade. A: Morbius ... 4.00
❑9, Sep 1999; V: Venom ... 4.00
❑10, Oct 1999; V: Venom ... 4.00
❑11, Nov 1999; continues in Juggernaut #1 ... 4.00
❑12, Dec 1999; #110; The Sandman ... 4.00
❑13, Jan 2000 ... 4.00
❑14, Feb 2000 ... 4.00
❑15, Mar 2000 ... 4.00
❑16, Apr 2000 ... 4.00
❑17, May 2000 ... 4.00
❑18, Jun 2000 ... 4.00
❑19, Jul 2000 ... 4.00
❑20, Aug 2000 ... 4.00
❑21, Sep 2000 ... 4.00
❑25/Variant, Sep 2000 ... 6.00
❑22, Oct 2000 ... 4.00
❑23, Nov 2000 ... 4.00
❑24, Dec 2000 ... 4.00
❑25, Jan 2001; V: Green Goblin; Giant-size ... 4.00
❑26, Feb 2001 ... 4.00
❑27, Mar 2001 A: Mendel Stromm ... 4.00
❑28, Apr 2001 A: Mendel Stromm ... 4.00
❑29, May 2001; continues in Amazing Spider-Man Ann 2001 ... 4.00
❑30, Jun 2001 ... 3.00
❑31, Jul 2001 ... 3.00
❑32, Aug 2001 ... 3.00
❑33, Sep 2001 ... 3.00
❑34, Oct 2001 ... 3.00

Other grades: Multiply price above by 5/6 for VF/NM • 2/3 for VERY FINE • 1/3 for FINE • 1/5 for VERY GOOD • 1/8 for GOOD

N-MINT

❑35, Nov 2001 ... 3.00
❑36, Dec 2001 ... 3.00
❑37, Jan 2002 ... 3.00
❑38, Feb 2002 ... 3.00
❑39, Mar 2002 ... 3.00
❑40, Apr 2002; Wraparound cover ... 3.00
❑41, May 2002; Wraparound cover ... 3.00
❑42, Jun 2002 ... 3.00
❑43, Jun 2002 ... 3.00
❑44, Jul 2002 ... 3.00
❑45, Aug 2002 ... 3.00
❑46, Sep 2002 ... 3.00
❑47, Oct 2002 ... 3.00
❑48, Nov 2002 ... 3.00
❑49, Dec 2002 ... 3.00
❑50, Jan 2003; Wraparound cover ... 3.50
❑51, Feb 2003; Hydro-Man and the Shocker ... 3.00
❑52, Mar 2003; Hydro-Man and the Shocker ... 3.00
❑53, Apr 2003 ... 3.00
❑54, May 2003 ... 3.00
❑55, Jun 2003 ... 3.00
❑56, Jul 2003 A: Sandman (Marvel). ... 3.00
❑57, Aug 2003, Final issue ... 3.00
❑Ann 1998, ca. 1998; gatefold summary; Peter Parker: Spider-Man/Elektra '98.. 4.00
❑Ann 1999, Aug 1999 A: Man-Thing ... 3.50

Peter Porker, the Spectacular Spider-Ham
Marvel / Star

❑1, May 1985, MG (c); 1: Spider-Ham. 1: J. Jonah Jackal. 1: Peter Porker. 1: Duck Doom ... 1.00
❑2, Jul 1985, 1: X-Bugs ... 1.00
❑3, Sep 1985, 1: Iron Mouse ... 1.00
❑4, Nov 1985, 1: Croctor Strange; Master of the Misfit Arts ... 1.00
❑5, Jan 1986, 1: Thrr; Dog of Thunder... 1.00
❑6, Mar 1986, 1: Awful Flight ... 1.00
❑7, May 1986, Deerdevil ... 1.00
❑8, Jul 1986, Silver Squirrel ... 1.00
❑9, Aug 1986 ... 1.00
❑10, Sep 1986 ... 1.00
❑11, Oct 1986 ... 1.00
❑12, Nov 1986, 1: Fantastic Fur ... 1.00
❑13, Jan 1987 ... 1.00
❑14, Mar 1987 ... 1.00
❑15, May 1987 ... 1.00
❑16, Jul 1987 ... 1.00
❑17, Sep 1987, Final Issue ... 1.00

Peter Rabbit 3-D
Eternity

❑1; Reprints from Peter Rabbit (Avon) stories ... 2.95

Peter the Little Pest
Marvel

❑1, Nov 1969, 1: Peter, The Little Pest. 1: Little Pixie ... 75.00
❑2, Jan 1970 ... 50.00
❑3, Mar 1970 ... 50.00
❑4, May 1970, titled Petey ... 50.00

Pete the P.O.'d Postal Worker
Sharkbait

❑1, Oct 1997 ... 3.50
❑2, Jan 1998 ... 3.00
❑3, Mar 1998 ... 3.00
❑4, Jun 1998 ... 3.00
❑5, Aug 1998; in England ... 3.00
❑6, Oct 1998 ... 2.95
❑7, Jan 1999; V: Teddy Cougar ... 2.95
❑8, Apr 1999; V: Teddy Cougar ... 2.95
❑9, Jun 1999; on Jerry Ringer Show ... 2.95
❑10, Aug 1999; V: Y2K. V: Y2K ... 2.95

Petticoat Junction
Dell

❑1, Oct 1964 ... 40.00
❑2, Jan 1965 ... 30.00
❑3, Apr 1965 ... 30.00
❑4, Jul 1965 ... 25.00
❑5, Oct 1965 ... 30.00

Petworks vs. WildK.A.T.S.
Parody

❑1 ... 2.50

N-MINT

Phaedra
Express / Entity

❑1, Sep 1994, b&w; cardstock cover; third in series of Entity illustrated novellas with Zen Intergalactic Ninja ... 2.95

Phage: ShadowDeath
Big

❑1, Jun 1996 ... 2.25
❑2, Aug 1996 ... 2.25
❑3, Sep 1996 ... 2.25
❑4, Sep 1996 ... 2.25
❑5, Oct 1996 ... 2.25
❑6, Nov 1996 ... 2.25

Phantacea: Phase One
Mcpherson

❑1, Nov 1987 ... 5.00

Phantasmagoria
Tome

❑1, b&w ... 2.50

Phantasy Against Hunger
Tiger

❑1, Sep 1987; KN (c); BSz, JO, GC, JOy, BA, JR, BMc, JA (a); Famine relief fundraiser ... 2.00

Phantom
Gold Key

❑1, Nov 1962, Gold Key publishes ... 90.00
❑2, Feb 1963, 1: Victor King; Francis Queen anf Jack Forest ... 55.00
❑3, May 1963, King, Queen and Jack ... 36.00
❑4, Aug 1963, King, Queen and Jack ... 36.00
❑5, Nov 1963, King, Queen and Jack ... 36.00
❑6, Feb 1964, King, Queen and Jack ... 36.00
❑7, May 1964, King, Queen and Jack ... 36.00
❑8, Aug 1964, King, Queen and Jack ... 36.00
❑9, Nov 1964, King, Queen and Jack ... 36.00
❑10, Feb 1965, King, Queen and Jack ... 36.00
❑11, Apr 1965, King, Queen and Jack ... 28.00
❑12, Jun 1965, 1: Track Hunter ... 28.00
❑13, Aug 1965, Track Hunter ... 28.00
❑14, Oct 1965, Track Hunter ... 28.00
❑15, Dec 1965, Track Hunter ... 28.00
❑16, Apr 1966, Track Hunter ... 28.00
❑17, Jul 1966, Track Hunter ... 28.00
❑18, Sep 1966, King Features Syndicate begins publishing ... 32.00
❑19, Nov 1966, Flash Gordon ... 24.00
❑20, Jan 1967 ... 24.00
❑21, Mar 1967, Mandrake the Magician ... 24.00
❑22, May 1967, Mandrake the Magician ... 24.00
❑23, Jul 1967, Mandrake the Magician.. 24.00
❑24, Aug 1967 ... 24.00
❑25, Sep 1967 ... 24.00
❑26, Oct 1967, Brick Bradford ... 24.00
❑27, Nov 1967 ... 24.00
❑28, Dec 1967, Freedom Fighters; Brick Bradford ... 24.00
❑30, Feb 1969, Charlton begins publishing (no issue #29) ... 15.00
❑31, Apr 1969 ... 15.00
❑32, Jun 1969 ... 15.00
❑33, Aug 1969, DP, JA (a) ... 15.00
❑34, Oct 1969 ... 15.00
❑35, Dec 1969 ... 15.00
❑36, Feb 1970 ... 15.00
❑37, Apr 1970 ... 15.00
❑38, Jun 1970 ... 15.00
❑39, Aug 1970 ... 15.00
❑40, Oct 1970 ... 15.00
❑41, Dec 1970 ... 12.00
❑42, Feb 1971 ... 12.00
❑43, Apr 1971 ... 12.00
❑44, Jun 1971 ... 12.00
❑45, Aug 1971 ... 12.00
❑46, Oct 1971, 1: Piranha ... 12.00
❑47, Dec 1971 ... 12.00
❑48, Feb 1972 ... 12.00
❑49, Apr 1972 ... 12.00
❑50, Jun 1972 ... 12.00
❑51, Aug 1972 ... 12.00
❑52, Oct 1972 ... 12.00
❑53, Nov 1972 ... 12.00
❑54, Feb 1973 ... 12.00
❑55, Apr 1973 ... 12.00
❑56, Jun 1973 ... 12.00
❑57, ca. 1973 ... 12.00

N-MINT

❑58, Oct 1973 ... 12.00
❑59, Dec 1973 ... 12.00
❑60, Jun 1974 ... 9.00
❑61, Aug 1974 ... 9.00
❑62, Nov 1974 ... 9.00
❑63, Jan 1975 ... 9.00
❑64, Mar 1975 ... 9.00
❑65, Jun 1975 ... 9.00
❑66, Aug 1975 ... 9.00
❑67, Oct 1975 ... 9.00
❑68, Dec 1975 ... 9.00
❑69, Feb 1976 ... 9.00
❑70, Apr 1976 ... 9.00
❑71, Jul 1976 ... 7.00
❑72, Aug 1976 ... 7.00
❑73, Oct 1976 ... 7.00
❑74, Jan 1977, Classic flag-cover; Final Issue ... 7.00

Phantom
Moonstone

❑1 2003 ... 3.50
❑2 ... 3.50
❑3 ... 3.50
❑4 ... 3.50
❑5 ... 3.50
❑6 ... 3.50
❑7 ... 3.50
❑8, Sep 2005 ... 3.50

Phantom 2040
Marvel

❑1, May 1995; 1&O: Phantom 2040; Includes poster ... 1.50
❑2, Jun 1995 ... 1.50
❑3, Jul 1995; Poster ... 1.50
❑4, Aug 1995; Poster ... 1.50

Phantom
DC

❑1, May 1988; JO (c); PD (w); JO, LMc (a); O: Phantom ... 2.00
❑2, Jun 1988 ... 2.00
❑3, Jul 1988 ... 2.00
❑4, Aug 1988 ... 2.00

Phantom
DC

❑1, May 1989 ... 2.00
❑2, Jun 1989 ... 1.50
❑3, Jul 1989 ... 1.50
❑4, Aug 1989 ... 1.50
❑5, Sep 1989 ... 1.50
❑6, Oct 1989 ... 1.50
❑7, Nov 1989 ... 1.50
❑8, Dec 1989 ... 1.50
❑9, Jan 1989 ... 1.50
❑10, Feb 1989 ... 1.50
❑11, Mar 1990 ... 1.50
❑12, Apr 1990 ... 1.50
❑13, May 1990; Final Issue ... 1.50

Phantom
Wolf

❑0/Ltd.; ca. 1993; limited edition subscribers' issue; Reprints of daily newspaper strip; b&w ... 3.50
❑1, Jul 1992 ... 2.50
❑2, Aug 1992 ... 2.25
❑3, Sep 1992 ... 2.25
❑4, Oct 1992 ... 2.25
❑5, Nov 1992; Poster across inside front and back cover ... 2.25
❑6, Dec 1992 ... 2.25
❑7, Jan 1992 ... 1.95
❑8, Feb 1992 ... 1.95

Phantom Force
Image

❑0, Mar 1994; Published by Genesis West; Includes trading card ... 2.50
❑1, Dec 1993; Published by Image; Includes trading card ... 2.50
❑2, Apr 1994; Published by Image ... 2.50
❑3, May 1994 ... 2.50
❑4, Jun 1994 ... 2.50
❑5, Jul 1994 ... 2.50
❑6, Aug 1994 ... 2.50
❑7, Sep 1994 ... 2.50
❑8, Oct 1994 ... 2.50
❑Ashcan 1; ashcan ... 2.50

Professor Xavier and the X-Men

Modern-day updates of X-Men adventures

©Marvel

Promethea

A female hero from the world of myths

©DC

Prophet

Nazi science experiment awakes today

©Image

Prototype

Corporate armored hero goes solo

©Malibu

Psi-Judge Anderson

Psychic Judge faces Death

©Fleetway-Quality

N-MINT

Phantom Force
Genesis West

❑0 .... 2.50

Phantom: The Ghost Killer
Moonstone

❑nn, ca. 2002 .... 5.95

Phantom Guard
Image

❑1, Oct 1997 .... 2.50
❑1/A, Oct 1997; alternate cover (white background) 2.50
❑2, Oct 1997 .... 2.50
❑3, Dec 1997 .... 2.50
❑4, Jan 1998 .... 2.50
❑4/Variant, Jan 1998; chromium cover 2.50
❑5, Feb 1998 .... 2.50
❑6, Mar 1998 .... 2.50

Phantom: The Hunt
Moonstone

❑nn, ca. 2003 .... 6.95

Phantom Jack
Image

❑1, Apr 2004 .... 2.95
❑2, May 2004 .... 2.95
❑3, Aug 2004 .... 2.95
❑4, Aug 2004 .... 2.95
❑4/Error, Aug 2004 .... 4.00
❑5, Jul 2004 .... 2.95

Phantom of Fear City
Claypool

❑1, May 1993 .... 2.50
❑2, Jul 1993; Soulsearchers and Company 2.50
❑3, Aug 1993 .... 2.50
❑4, Oct 1993; Tiberius Fox 2.50
❑5, Nov 1993; Tiberius Fox 2.50
❑6, Jan 1994; Tiberius Fox 2.50
❑7, Apr 1994; Tiberius Fox 2.50
❑8, Jul 1994 .... 2.50
❑9, Sep 1994; Tiberius Fox 2.50
❑10, Nov 1994; Tiberius Fox 2.50
❑11, Feb 1995; Tiberius Fox 2.50
❑12, May 1995; Final Issue 2.50

Phantom of the Opera
Eternity

❑1, b&w; Reprints from Scream #2 and 3 .... 2.00

Phantom of the Opera
Innovation

❑1, Dec 1991 .... 6.95

Phantom Quest Corp.
Pioneer

❑1, Mar 1997, b&w; wraparound cover 2.95

Phantom: The Singh Web
Moonstone

❑nn, ca. 2002 .... 6.95

N-MINT

Phantom Stranger
DC

❑1, May 1969, CI (a); A: Doctor 13. Phantom Stranger Reprint from Phantom Stranger (1st Series) #1; Doctor 13 Reprint from Star Spangled Comics #125 .... 125.00
❑2, Aug 1969, A: Doctor 13. Phantom Stranger Reprint from Phantom Stranger (1st Series) #1; Doctor 13 Reprint from Star Spangled Comics #128 .... 60.00
❑3, Oct 1969, A: Doctor 13. Phantom Stranger Reprint from Phantom Stranger (1st Series) #5; Doctor 13 Reprint from Star Spangled Comics #126 .... 60.00
❑4, Dec 1969, MA, NA (a); 1: Tala. A: Doctor 13 .... 70.00
❑5, Feb 1970, A: Doctor 13. .... 50.00
❑6, Apr 1970, A: Doctor 13. .... 50.00
❑7, Jun 1970, NA (c); JA (a); A: Doctor 13. .... 50.00
❑8, Aug 1970, A: Doctor 13. .... 40.00
❑9, Oct 1970, A: Doctor 13. Reprint from House of Mystery #24 .... 40.00
❑10, Dec 1970, A: Doctor 13. V: Tannarak; The Bewitched Clock! Reprint from House of Mystery #11 .... 40.00
❑11, Feb 1971 .... 40.00
❑12, Apr 1971, A: Doctor 13. .... 40.00
❑13, Jun 1971, A: Doctor 13 .... 40.00
❑14, Aug 1971, A: Doctor 13. .... 35.00
❑15, Oct 1971; Giant-size; A: Doctor 13. .... 35.00
❑16, Dec 1971; Giant-size; TD, JA (a); A: Doctor 13. A: Mark Merlin 35.00
❑17, Feb 1972; Giant-size; A: Doctor 13. Reprints "Suicide Tower!" from Star Spangled Comics #124; Reprints "I Was a Victim of Black Magic!" from House of Mystery #3; 52 pages 35.00
❑18, Apr 1972; Giant-size; 1: Cassandra Craft. A: Doctor 13. A: Mark Merlin; Reprint from Sensation Mystery #111; Mark Merlin Reprint from House of Secrets #59; Giant-size 52 pages 25.00
❑19, Jun 1972; Giant-size; A: Doctor 13. A: Mark Merlin. Mark Merlin Reprint from House of Secrets #60; Giant-size 52 pages 25.00
❑20, Aug 1972 .... 25.00
❑21, Oct 1972, A: Doctor 13. .... 25.00
❑22, Dec 1972, A: Doctor 13. .... 15.00
❑23, Feb 1973, 1: The Spawn of Frankenstein 15.00
❑24, Apr 1973, A: The Spawn of Frankenstein 15.00
❑25, Jul 1973, A: The Spawn of Frankenstein 15.00
❑26, Sep 1973, A: Doctor 13. A: The Spawn of Frankenstein 15.00
❑27, Nov 1973, A: The Spawn of Frankenstein 15.00
❑28, Jan 1974, A: The Spawn of Frankenstein 15.00
❑29, Mar 1974, A: The Spawn of Frankenstein 15.00
❑30, May 1974, A: The Spawn of Frankenstein 15.00
❑31, Jul 1974, A: Black Orchid 15.00
❑32, Sep 1974, A: Black Orchid. 15.00
❑33, Nov 1974, A: Deadman 15.00

N-MINT

❑34, Jan 1975, A: Black Orchid. A: Doctor 13 .... 15.00
❑35, Mar 1975 A: Black Orchid. 15.00
❑36, May 1975 A: Black Orchid 15.00
❑37, Jul 1975 .... 15.00
❑38, Sep 1975 A: Black Orchid. 15.00
❑39, Nov 1975 A: Deadman 15.00
❑40, Jan 1976 A: Deadman 15.00
❑41, Mar 1976; A: Deadman. Final Issue 15.00

Phantom Stranger
DC

❑1, Oct 1987 .... 3.00
❑2, Nov 1987 .... 2.50
❑3, Dec 1987 .... 2.50
❑4, Jan 1988 .... 2.50

Phantom: The Ghost Who Walks
Marvel

❑1, Feb 1995, cardstock cover 2.95
❑2, Mar 1995, cardstock cover 2.95
❑3, Apr 1995, cardstock cover 2.95

Phantom: The Treasure of Bangalla
Moonstone

❑nn, ca. 2002; Cover erroneously reads "Bagalla" 6.95

Phantom Zone
DC

❑1, Jan 1982, GC (a) 1.50
❑2, Feb 1982, GC (c); GC (a) 1.25
❑3, Mar 1982, GC (a) 1.25
❑4, Apr 1982, GC (a) 1.25

Phase One
Victory

❑1, Oct 1986 .... 1.50
❑2 .... 1.50
❑3 .... 1.50
❑4 .... 1.50
❑5 .... 1.50

Phathom
Blatant

❑1, Jun 1999; Parody of Michael Turner's Fathom 2.95

Phatwars
Bon

❑1 .... 2.00

Phaze
Eclipse

❑1, Apr 1988 .... 2.25
❑2, Oct 1988 .... 2.25

PhD: Phantasy Degree
Tokyopop

❑1, Jan 2005, Graphic novel; b&w 9.99
❑2, Apr 2005; Graphic novel; b&w 9.99
❑3, Jul 2005; Graphic novel; b&w 9.99
❑4, Oct 2005 .... 9.99

Phenomerama
Caliber

❑1 .... 2.95

Phigments
Amazing

❑1, b&w 1.95
❑2 .... 1.95

Other grades: Multiply price above by 5/6 for VF/NM • 2/3 for VERY FINE • 1/3 for FINE • 1/5 for VERY GOOD • 1/8 for GOOD

Philbert Desanex' Dreams
Rip Off
❑1, May 1993, b&w 2.95

Philistine
One Shot
❑1, Sep 1993, b&w 2.50
❑2, Apr 1994, b&w 2.50
❑3, Sep 1994, b&w 2.50
❑4 .... 2.50
❑5 .... 2.50
❑6 .... 2.50

Phineus: Magician for Hire
Piffle
❑1, Oct 1994, b&w; wraparound cover .. 2.95

Phobos
Flashpoint
❑1, Jan 1994 .... 2.50

Phoebe & the Pigeon People
Kitchen Sink
❑1 .... 3.00

Phoebe: Angel in Black
Angel
❑1 .... 2.95

Phoebe Chronicles
NBM
❑1; Adult 9.95
❑2; Adult 9.95

Phoenix
Atlas-Seaboard
❑1, Mar 1975, O: Phoenix (Atlas character) 7.00
❑2, Jun 1975 .... 5.00
❑3, Oct 1975, O: The Dark Avenger; Phoenix 3.00
❑4, Oct 1975 .... 3.00

Phoenix Restaurant
Fandom House
❑1, b&w 3.50

Phoenix Resurrection: Aftermath
Malibu / Ultraverse
❑1, Jan 1996, continues in Foxfire #1 .... 3.95

Phoenix Resurrection: Genesis
Malibu / Ultraverse
❑1, Dec 1995; Giant-size; wraparound cover; continues in The Phoenix Resurrection: Revelations; Phoenix force returns 3.95
❑2 .... 3.95

Phoenix Resurrection: Red Shift
Malibu / Ultraverse
❑0, Mar 1996; collects the seven flipbook chapters plus one new chapter 2.50
❑0/Ltd., Dec 1995; American Entertainment Edition; no cover price. 2.50

Phoenix Resurrection: Revelations
Malibu / Ultraverse
❑1, Dec 1995, wraparound cover; continues in The Phoenix Resurrection: Aftermath 3.95

Phoenix Square
Slave Labor
❑1, Aug 1997, b&w 2.95
❑2, Nov 1997 .... 2.95

Phoenix: The Untold Story
Marvel
❑1, Apr 1984; JBy (c); JBy (a); X-Men #137 with unpublished alternate ending 8.00

Phonogram
Image
❑1, Sep 2006, b&w 3.50
❑2, Oct 2006; b&w 3.50
❑3, Nov 2006; b&w 3.50

Phony Pages
Renegade
❑1, Apr 1986, Parody of Famous Comic Strips 2.00
❑2, May 1986, Parody of Famous Comic Books 2.00

Picture Taker
Slave Labor
❑1, Jan 1998, b&w 2.95

Pie
Wow Cool
❑1, b&w 2.95

Piece of Steak, A
Tome
❑1, b&w 2.50

Pieces
5th Panel
❑1, Apr 1997, b&w 2.50
❑2, Jul 1997, b&w 2.50
❑3 .... 2.50

Pied Piper Graphic Album
Pied Piper
❑1; Hero Alliance 6.95
❑2; < Never Published > 6.95
❑3; Beast Warriors 6.95

Pied Piper of Hamelin
Tome
❑1, b&w 2.95

Pigeonman
Above & Beyond
❑1, Oct 1997 .... 2.95

Pigeon-Man, the Bird-Brain
Ferry Tail
❑1, Apr 1993, b&w 2.50

Pighead
Williamson
❑1, b&w 2.95

Pigtale
Image
❑1, Mar 2005, b&w 2.95
❑2, Apr 2005; b&w 2.95
❑3, Sep 2005 .... 2.99
❑4, Jul 2006, b&w 2.99

Pilgrim's Progress
Marvel / Nelson
❑1, Dec 1992; adaptation 9.99

Pineapple Army
Viz
❑1, Dec 1988 .... 1.75
❑2, Dec 1988 .... 1.75
❑3, Jan 1989 .... 1.75
❑4, Jan 1989 .... 1.75
❑5, Feb 1989 .... 1.75
❑6, Feb 1989 .... 1.75
❑7, Mar 1989 .... 1.75
❑8, Mar 1989 .... 1.75
❑9, Apr 1989 .... 1.75
❑10, Apr 1989 .... 1.75

Pinhead
Marvel / Epic
❑1, Dec 1993; Embossed foil cover 2.95
❑2, Jan 1994; Adult 2.50
❑3, Feb 1994; Adult 2.50
❑4, Mar 1994; Adult 2.50
❑5, Apr 1994; Adult 2.50
❑6, May 1994; Final Issue; Adult 2.50

Pinhead vs. Marshal Law: Law in Hell
Marvel / Epic
❑1, Nov 1993; foil cover 2.95
❑2, Dec 1993; foil cover 2.95

Pink Dust
Kitchen Sink
❑1, Aug 1998; NN; Adult 3.50

Pink Floyd
Personality
❑1, b&w 2.95
❑2, b&w 2.95

Pink Floyd Experience
Revolutionary
❑1, Jun 1991, b&w 2.50
❑2, Aug 1991, b&w 2.50
❑3, Oct 1991, b&w 2.50
❑4, Dec 1991, b&w 2.50
❑5, Feb 1992, b&w 2.50

Pink Panther
Gold Key
❑1, Apr 1971, (c); (w); (a); Cover code 10266-104 .... 40.00
❑2, Jul 1971, (c); (w); (a); Cover code 10266-107 .... 17.00
❑3, Oct 1971, (c); (w); (a); Cover code 90266-110; Inspector referred to as "Clouzot" in newspaper 15.00
❑4, Jan 1972, (c); (w); (a); Cover code 90266-201 .... 15.00
❑5, Mar 1972, (c); (w); (a); Cover code 90266-203 .... 15.00
❑6, May 1972, (c); (w); (a); Cover code 90266-205 .... 8.00
❑7, Jul 1972, (c); (w); (a); Cover code 90266-207; has uncommon Pink Panther stories without "Pink" in title; no Inspector story 8.00
❑8, Sep 1972, (c); (w); (a); Cover code 90266-209 .... 8.00
❑9, Nov 1972, (c); (w); (a); Cover code 90266-211 .... 8.00
❑10, Jan 1973, (c); (w); (a); Cover code 90266-301 .... 8.00
❑11, Mar 1973, (c); (w); (a); Cover code 90266-303; has uncommon Pink Panther story without "Pink" in title ... 6.00
❑12, May 1973, (c); (w); (a); Cover code 90266-305 .... 6.00
❑13, Jul 1973, (c); (w); (a); Cover code 90266-307 .... 6.00
❑14, Sep 1973, (c); (w); (a); Cover code 90266-309; has uncommon Pink Panther stories without "Pink" in title 6.00
❑15, Oct 1973, (c); (w); (a); Cover code 90266-310 .... 6.00
❑16, Nov 1973, (c); (w); Cover code 90266-311; has uncommon Pink Panther story without "Pink" in title; Warren Tufts art begins 6.00
❑17, Jan 1974, (c); (w); Cover code 90266-401 .... 6.00
❑18, Mar 1974, (c); (w); Cover code 90266-403 .... 6.00
❑19, May 1974, (c); (w); Cover code 90266-405 .... 6.00
❑20, Jul 1974, (c); (w); Cover code 90266-407; rare Panther/Inspector crossover 6.00
❑21, Sep 1974, (c); (w); Cover code 90266-409 .... 4.00
❑22, Oct 1974, (c); (w); (a); Cover code 90266-410 .... 4.00
❑23, Nov 1974, (c); (w); (a); Cover code 90266-411 .... 4.00
❑24, Jan 1975, (c); (w); Cover code 90266-501 .... 4.00
❑25, Mar 1975, (c); (w); (a); Cover code 90266-503; has uncommon Pink Panther story without "Pink" in the title 4.00
❑26, May 1975, (c); (w); (a); Cover code 90266-505 .... 4.00
❑27, Jul 1975, (c); (w); (a); Cover code 90266-507 .... 4.00
❑28, Sep 1975, (c); (w); (a); Cover code 90266-509 .... 4.00
❑29, Oct 1975, (c); (w); (a); Cover code 90266-510 .... 4.00
❑30, Nov 1975, (c); (w); Cover code 90266-511 .... 4.00
❑31, Jan 1976, (c); (w); Cover code 90266-601 .... 4.00
❑32, Mar 1976, (c); (w); Cover code 90266-603 .... 4.00
❑33, Apr 1976, (c); (w); (a); Cover code 90266-604 .... 4.00
❑34, May 1976, (c); (w); (a); Cover code 90266-605 .... 4.00
❑35, Jun 1976, (c); (w); Cover code 90266-606; Tweety and Sylvester in Hostess ad ("A Tasty Trap!") 4.00
❑36, Jul 1976, (c); (w); (a); Cover code 90266-607 .... 4.00
❑37, Sep 1976, (c); (w); (a); Cover code 90266-609 .... 4.00
❑38, Oct 1976, (c); (w); (a); Cover code 90266-610 .... 4.00
❑39, Nov 1976, (c); (w); (a); Cover code 90266-611 .... 4.00
❑40, Jan 1977, (c); (w); Cover code 90266-701; Captain America in Hostess ad ("When It Rains It Pours") 4.00
❑41, Mar 1977, (c); (w); Cover code 90266-703; Casper in Hostess ad ("The Boogy-Woogy Man") 3.00
❑42, Apr 1977, (c); (w); Cover code 90266-704; Spider-Man Hostess ad ("Will Power") 3.00
❑43, May 1977, (w); (a); Cover code 90266-705; reprints part of #1 .... 3.00

PS238

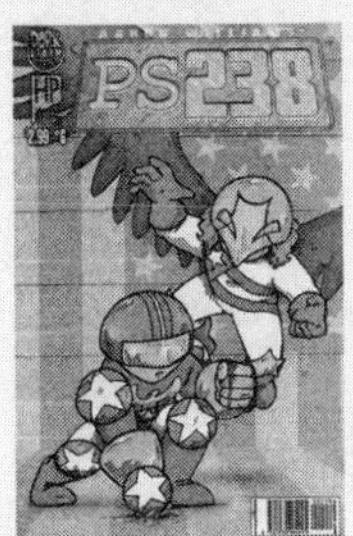
School days for super-hero offspring
©Dork Storm

Pulp

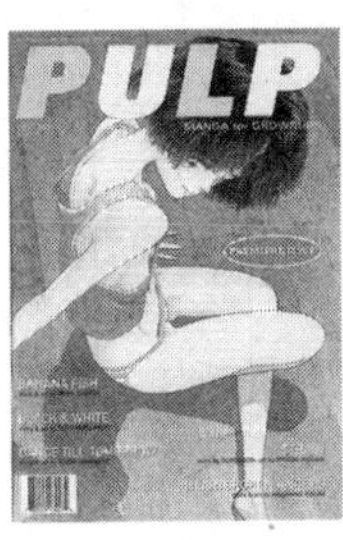
Large manga anthology with adult stories
©Viz

Pulse

Daily Bugle covers super-hero scene
©Marvel

Punisher

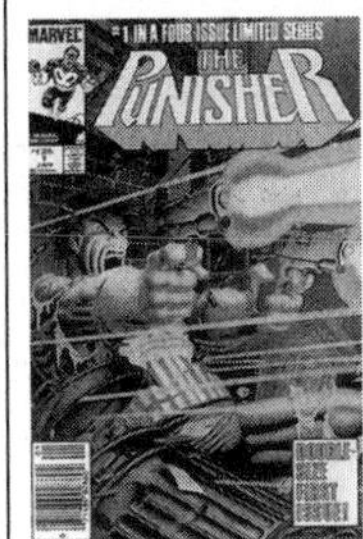
Mike Zeck draws Marvel merc's first mini
©Marvel

Punisher

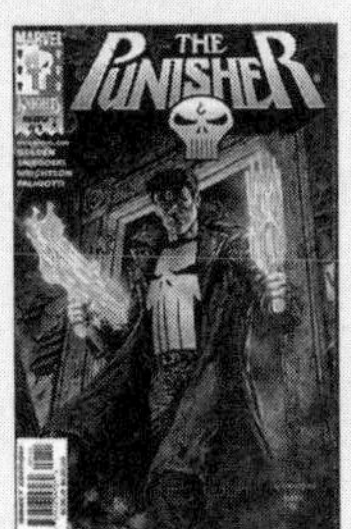
After-death adventure in afterlife
©Marvel

	N-MINT
❑44, Jun 1977, (c); (w); Cover code 90266-706; Iron Man in Hostess ad ("A Dull Pain"); No Inspector story	3.00
❑45, Jul 1977, (c); (w); Cover code 90266-707; Iron Man in Hostess ad ("A Dull Pain")	3.00
❑46, Sep 1977, (c); (w); Cover code 90266-709; Sad Sack in Hostess ad ("Sarge is a Bully"); "Snoring Pink" based on script from "Rock-a-Bye Pink" in #5	3.00
❑47, Oct 1977, (c); (w); Cover code 90266-710; Hulk in Hostess ad ("Up a Tree")	3.00
❑48, Nov 1977, (c); (w); Cover code 90266-711; Spider-Man in Hostess ad ("Break the Bank")	3.00
❑49, Jan 1978, (c); (w); Cover code 90266-801; Richie Rich in Hostess ad ("Brightens Up a Traffic Jam")	3.00
❑50, Mar 1978, (c); (w); Cover code 90266-803; Spider-Man in Hostess ad ("vs. the Chairman")	3.00
❑51, Apr 1978, (c); (w); Cover code 90266-804; Richie Rich Hostess ad ("A Real Treat")	3.00
❑52, May 1978, (c); (w); Cover code 90266-805; Captain America in Hostess ad "vs. the Aliens"	3.00
❑53, Jun 1978, (c); (w); Cover code 90266-806; Daredevil in Hostess ad ("The Peachy Keen Caper"); No Inspector story	3.00
❑54, Jul 1978, (c); (w); Cover code 90266-807; No Inspector story	3.00
❑55, Aug 1978, (c); (w); Cover code 90266-808; No Inspector story	3.00
❑56, Sep 1978, (c); (w); Cover code 90266-809; Captain America in Hostess ad "vs. the Aliens"	3.00
❑57, Oct 1978, (c); (w); Cover code 90266-810; Casper in Hostess ad ("A Real Oddball")	3.00
❑58, Nov 1978, (c); (w); Cover code 90266-811	3.00
❑59, Dec 1978, (c); (w); Cover code 90266-812	3.00
❑60, Jan 1979, (c); (w); (a); Cover code 90266-901; story directly adapts holiday cartoon special; Thor in Hostess ad ("The Storm Meets its Master")	3.00
❑61, Feb 1979, (c); (w); Cover code 90266-902	3.00
❑62, Mar 1979, (c); (w); Cover code 90266-903; Spider-Man in Hostess ad ("Meets June Jitsui!")	3.00
❑63, Apr 1979, (c); (w); Cover code 90266-904; Captain America in Hostess ad ("An Invading Army!"); no Inspector story	3.00
❑64, May 1979, (c); (w); Cover code 90266-905; No Inspector story	3.00
❑65, Jun 1979, (c); (w); (a); Cover code 90266-906; Thor in Hostess ad "Good Overcomes Evil"; no Inspector story	3.00
❑66, Jul 1979, (c); (w); (a); Cover code 90266-907; No Inspector story	3.00
❑67, Aug 1979, (c); (w); (a); Cover code 90266-908	3.00
❑68, Sep 1979, (c); (w); (a); Cover code 90266-909; Casper in Hostess ad "The Boo Keepers"; No Inspector story	3.00

	N-MINT
❑69, Oct 1979, (c); (w); (a); Cover code 90266-910; Captain Marvel in Hostess ad "Returns to Earth!"; no inspector story	3.00
❑70, Nov 1979, (c); (w); (a); Cover code 90266-911	3.00
❑71, Dec 1979, (c); (w); (a); Cover code 90266-912	3.00
❑72, Jan 1980, (c); (w); (a); Cover code 90266-001; Reprints #5 in entirety, recoloring art from cover	3.00
❑73, Feb 1980, (c); (w); (a); Cover code 90266-002; Captain America in Hostess ad ("The Deserted City"); No Inspector story	3.00
❑74, Jul 1980, (c); (w); (a); Cover code 90266-007; Casper in Hostess ad ("In Outer Space"); No Inspector story	3.00
❑75, Aug 1980, (c); (w); (a); Cover code 90266-008; Casper in Hostess ad ("Ghosts in the House")	15.00
❑76, Oct 1981, (c); (w); (a); Cover code 90266-010; Spider-Man in Hostess ad ("Meets the Bikers!"); No Inspector story	15.00
❑77, Dec 1981, (c); (w); (a); Cover code 90266-012	17.00
❑78, Jan 1981, (c); (w); (a); Cover code 90266-101; No Inspector Story	8.00
❑79, Jul 1981, (c); (w); (a); Cover code 90266-107	8.00
❑80, Sep 1981, (c); (w); (a); Cover code 90266-109	8.00
❑81, Feb 1982, (c); (w); (a); Cover code 90266-202; No Inspector story; "Pink in the Drink" reprinted from #1; "Pink on the Range" reprinted, probably from #4	8.00
❑82, Mar 1982, (c); (w); (a); Cover code 90266-203; No Inspector story; Pink Shoelacer reprinted from #6; Mr. Zap (rare story without Pink in title) reprinted from #7	8.00
❑83, Apr 1982, (c); (w); (a); Cover code 90266-204; "The Purloined Pink Lemonade" reprinted from #6	8.00
❑84, Jun 1983, (c); (w); (a)	15.00
❑85, ca. 1983, (c); (w); (a)	15.00
❑86, ca. 1983, (c); (w); (a)	15.00
❑87, ca. 1983, (c); (w); (a); Cover code 90266; issue number listed	15.00

Pink Panther
Harvey

❑1, Nov 1993	1.50
❑2, Dec 1993; Reprints Pink Panther (Gold Key) #50	1.50
❑3, Jan 1994; Reprints Pink Panther (Gold Key) #51	1.50
❑4, Feb 1994; Reprints Pink Panther (Gold Key) #52	1.50
❑5, Mar 1994	1.50
❑6, Apr 1994; Reprints Pink Panther (Gold Key) #53	1.50
❑7, May 1994; Reprints Pink Panther (Gold Key) #54	1.50
❑8, Jun 1994; Reprints Pink Panther (Gold Key) #55	1.50
❑9, Jul 1994; Reprints Pink Panther (Gold Key) #56	1.50
❑SS 1, ca. 1993; Super Special	2.25

Pinky and the Brain
DC

	N-MINT
❑1, Jul 1996; based on animated series.	2.50
❑2, Aug 1996; King Arthur Parody	2.00
❑3, Sep 1996	2.00
❑4, Oct 1996; Oz parody	1.75
❑5, Nov 1996; Western parody issue	1.75
❑6, Dec 1996; Ed Wood parody issue	1.75
❑7, Jan 1997; Faust parody	1.75
❑8, Feb 1997; Mission : Impossible parody	1.75
❑9, Mar 1997	1.75
❑10, Apr 1997	1.75
❑11, May 1997; Fantasia parody	1.75
❑12, Jun 1997; surfing parody	1.75
❑13, Jul 1997; Peter Pan parody; Aladdin parody cover; Ali-Baba parody	1.75
❑14, Aug 1997	1.75
❑15, Sep 1997; Bikers	1.75
❑16, Oct 1997; Terminator 2 parody	1.75
❑17, Nov 1997; Horror movies parody	1.75
❑18, Dec 1997; Manga parody	1.95
❑19, Jan 1998; Brain plays Santa	1.95
❑20, Feb 1998; Men in Black Parody; Mayberry R.F.D. parody	1.95
❑21, Mar 1998; Fantastic Voyage parody; Harper Valley PTA parody	1.95
❑22, May 1998; Man in the Iron Mask parody	1.95
❑23, Jun 1998; Jaws parody cover	1.95
❑24, Jul 1998; Zorro parody	1.95
❑25, Aug 1998; Batman: The Dark Night Returns parody	1.95
❑26, Oct 1998; Demi Moore parody issue	1.95
❑27, Nov 1998; Werewolf of London parody; Final issue	1.99
❑Holiday 1, Jan 1996; Giant-size; Christmas Special	3.00

Pinocchia
NBM

❑1; Adult	11.95

Pinocchio and the Emperor of the Night
Marvel

❑1, Mar 1988; Movie adaptation	1.25

Pinocchio Special
Gladstone

❑1, Mar 1990 WK (w); WK (a)	1.50

Pint-Sized X-Babies
Marvel

❑1, Aug 1998; gatefold summary	2.99

Pipsqueak Papers
Fantagraphics / Eros

❑1, b&w; Adult	2.75

Piracy
Gemstone

❑1, Mar 1998; Reprints	2.50
❑2, Apr 1998; Reprints	2.50
❑3, May 1998; Reprints	2.50
❑4, Jun 1998; Reprints	2.50
❑5, Jul 1998; Reprints	2.50
❑6, Aug 1998; Reprints	2.50
❑7, Sep 1998; Reprints Piracy (E.C.) #7	2.50

Other grades: Multiply price above by 5/6 for VF/NM • 2/3 for VERY FINE • 1/3 for FINE • 1/5 for VERY GOOD • 1/8 for GOOD

Piranha Is Loose!
Special Studio

- ❑1, b&w 2.75
- ❑2, b&w 2.75

Pirate Club
Slave Labor

- ❑1, Feb 2004; b&w 2.95
- ❑2, May 2004; b&w 2.95
- ❑3, Aug 2004; b&w 2.95
- ❑4, Nov 2004; b&w 2.95
- ❑5, Feb 2005; b&w 2.95
- ❑6, Jun 2005; b&w 2.95
- ❑8, Nov 2005 2.95

Pirate Corps
Eternity

- ❑1 2.50
- ❑2 2.50
- ❑3, Dec 1987 2.50
- ❑4, Feb 1988 2.50

Pirate Corp$!
Slave Labor

- ❑1, Jun 1989 2.50
- ❑1/2nd, Aug 1993; has Fine Dairy Products ad on back cover 2.50
- ❑2, Sep 1989 2.50
- ❑2/2nd, Feb 1993; has Fine Dairy Products ad on back cover 2.50
- ❑3, Feb 1991 2.50
- ❑3/2nd, Feb 1993; has Fine Dairy Products ad on back cover 2.50
- ❑4, Apr 1992 2.50
- ❑4/2nd, Sep 1993; has Fine Dairy Products ad on back cover 2.50
- ❑5, Dec 1992 2.50
- ❑5/2nd, Apr 1994; 2nd printing 2.50
- ❑Special 1, Mar 1989, b&w; has Futurama ad on back cover 1.95
- ❑Special 1/2nd, Aug 1993; has Fine Dairy Products ad on back cover 2.95

Pirate Queen
Comax

- ❑1, b&w; Adult 3.00

Pirates of Coney Island
Image

- ❑1, Nov 2006 2.99
- ❑1/Variant, Nov 2006 2.99
- ❑2, Nov 2006 2.99
- ❑3, Jan 2007 3.50
- ❑3/Variant, Jan 2007 3.50

Pirates of Dark Water
Marvel / Star

- ❑1, Nov 1991 1.00
- ❑2, Dec 1991 1.00
- ❑3, Jan 1992 1.00
- ❑4, Feb 1992 1.00
- ❑5, Mar 1992 1.00
- ❑6, Apr 1992 1.00
- ❑7, May 1992 1.25
- ❑8, Jun 1992 1.25
- ❑9, Jul 1992; Final Issue 1.25

P.I.'s: Michael Mauser and Ms. Tree
First

- ❑1, Jan 1985; MGr, JSa (a); Ms. Tree, E-Man 1.50
- ❑2, Mar 1985 JSa (a) 1.50
- ❑3, May 1985 JSa (a) 1.50

Pistolero
Eternity

- ❑1, ca. 1992; b&w; NN; 1: The Pistolero (John Hawke); One-shot 3.95

Pita Ten Official Fan Club Book
Tokyopop

- ❑1, Nov 2005, b&w 9.99

Pi: The Book of Ants
Artisan Entertainment

- ❑1, b&w; based on movie 2.95

Pitt
Image

- ❑½, Dec 1995 1.50
- ❑1, Jan 1993; 1: Pitt 3.00
- ❑1/Gold, Jan 1993; Gold edition 4.00
- ❑2, Jul 1993 1.95
- ❑3, Feb 1994 1.95
- ❑4, Apr 1994 1.95
- ❑5, Jun 1994 1.95
- ❑6, Sep 1994 1.95
- ❑7, Dec 1994 1.95
- ❑8, Apr 1994 1.95
- ❑9, Aug 1995 1.95
- ❑10, Jan 1996 1.95
- ❑11, May 1996 1.95
- ❑12, Dec 1996 1.95
- ❑13, Mar 1997 1.95
- ❑14, Jun 1997; Two green monsters on cover 2.50
- ❑15, Sep 1997 2.50
- ❑16, Dec 1997 2.50
- ❑17, Mar 1998 2.50
- ❑18, Jun 1998 2.50
- ❑19, Sep 1998 2.50
- ❑20, Oct 1998; Published by Full Bleed Studios 2.50

Pitt
Marvel

- ❑1; ca. 1987 3.25

Pitt Crew
Full Bleed

- ❑1, Aug 1998 3.00

Pitt: In the Blood
Full Bleed

- ❑1, Aug 1996 2.50

Pixy Junket
Viz

- ❑1, b&w 2.75
- ❑2, b&w 2.75
- ❑3, b&w 2.75
- ❑4, b&w 2.75
- ❑5, b&w 2.75
- ❑6, b&w 2.75

P.J. Warlock
Eclipse

- ❑1, Nov 1986, b&w 2.00
- ❑2, Jan 1987, b&w 2.00
- ❑3, Mar 1987, b&w 2.00

Places That Are Gone
Aeon

- ❑1, Jul 1994 2.75
- ❑2, Aug 1994 2.75

Plague
Tome

- ❑1, b&w 2.95

Plan 9 from Outer Space
Eternity

- ❑1, Oct 1990, b&w; Movie adaptation 4.95
- ❑1/2nd, Nov 1991; 2nd printing; Movie adaptation; Introduction by John Wooley; Inside back cover and bsack cover feature photos from film 4.95

Plan 9 from Outer Space: Thirty Years Later
Eternity

- ❑1, Jan 1991, b&w 2.50
- ❑2, Feb 1991, b&w 2.50
- ❑3, b&w 2.50

Planet 29
Caliber

- ❑1, b&w 2.50
- ❑2, b&w 2.50

Planetary
DC / Wildstorm

- ❑1, Apr 1999 8.00
- ❑2, May 1999 3.00
- ❑3, Jun 1999 3.00
- ❑4, Jul 1999 2.50
- ❑5, Sep 1999 2.50
- ❑6, Nov 1999 2.50
- ❑7, Jan 2000 2.50
- ❑8, Feb 2000 2.50
- ❑9, Apr 2000 2.50
- ❑10, Jun 2000 2.50
- ❑11, Sep 2000 2.50
- ❑12, Jan 2001 2.50
- ❑13, Feb 2001 2.50
- ❑14, Jun 2001 2.50
- ❑15, Jul 2001 2.50
- ❑16, Oct 2003 2.95
- ❑17, Dec 2003 2.95
- ❑18, Feb 2004 2.95
- ❑19, May 2004 2.95
- ❑20, Sep 2004 2.95
- ❑21, Dec 2004 2.95
- ❑22, Mar 2005 2.95
- ❑23, Jul 2005 2.99
- ❑24, Mar 2006 2.99
- ❑25, Jun 2006 2.99
- ❑26, Jan 2007 2.99

Planetary/Batman: Night on Earth
DC / Wildstorm

- ❑1, ca. 2003 5.95

Planetary/JLA: Terra Occulta
WildStorm

- ❑1, Nov 2002 5.95

Planetary/The Authority: Ruling the World
DC / Wildstorm

- ❑nn, Aug 2000 5.95

Planet Blood
Tokyopop

- ❑1, Feb 2005, b&w 9.99
- ❑2, Apr 2005; b&w 9.99
- ❑3, Oct 2005; b&w 9.99

Planet Comics
Blackthorne

- ❑1, Apr 1988 2.00
- ❑2, Jun 1988 2.00
- ❑3, Aug 1988 2.00

Planet Comic
A-List

- ❑1, Spr 1997 2.95
- ❑2, Fal 1997, b&w 2.95
- ❑3, Win 1997 2.95

Planet Comics
Avalon

- ❑1 5.95

Planet Hulk: Gladiator Guidebook
Marvel

- ❑1, Sep 2006 3.99

Planet Ladder
Tokyopop

- ❑1, Mar 2002, b&w; printed in Japanese format 9.99
- ❑2, Jul 2002, b&w; printed in Japanese format 9.99

Planet of Geeks
Starhead

- ❑1, b&w; Adult 2.75

Planet of Terror
Dark Horse

- ❑1, Jul 1987, AMo (c); BW (w); BW (a); Reprints from Journey into Unknown Worlds #7, Marvel Tales #102, Mystic #7, and Weird Tales of the Future #3 2.00

Planet of the Apes
Marvel

- ❑1, Aug 1974, b&w; magazine; GT, MP (a); adapts first movie plus new story 20.00
- ❑1/2nd; GT, MP (a); adapts first movie plus new story 5.00
- ❑2, Oct 1974, b&w; magazine; adapts first movie plus new story 10.00
- ❑3, Dec 1974, b&w; magazine; adapts first movie plus new stories 9.00
- ❑4, Jan 1975, b&w; magazine; adapts first movie plus new stories 8.00
- ❑5, Feb 1975, b&w; magazine; adapts first movie plus new stories 8.00
- ❑6, Mar 1975, b&w; magazine; concludes first movie adaptations plus new stories 6.00
- ❑7, Apr 1975, b&w; magazine 5.00
- ❑8, May 1975, b&w; magazine 5.00
- ❑9, Jun 1975 5.00
- ❑10, Jul 1975 5.00
- ❑11, Aug 1975 5.00
- ❑12, Sep 1975 5.00
- ❑13, Aug 1975 5.00
- ❑14, Nov 1975 5.00
- ❑15, Dec 1975 5.00
- ❑16, Jan 1976; D: Zira. D: Cornelius 5.00
- ❑17, Feb 1976 5.00
- ❑18, Mar 1976 5.00
- ❑19, Apr 1976, b&w; magazine 5.00
- ❑20, May 1976, b&w; magazine 5.00
- ❑21, Jun 1976, b&w; magazine 5.00

Punisher

Back from short supernatural outing
©Marvel

Punisher

Move to MAX increases body count
©Marvel

Punisher 2099

Frank Castle's legacy carries to future
©Marvel

Punisher War Journal

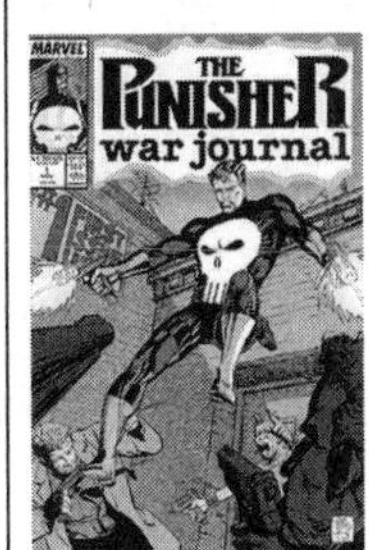

Narration creates own title
©Marvel

PvP

Pokes fun at popular culture
©Dork Storm

N-MINT

❑22, Jul 1976, b&w; magazine 5.00
❑23, Aug 1976, b&w; magazine 5.00
❑24, Sep 1976, b&w; magazine 5.00
❑25, Oct 1976, b&w; magazine 5.00
❑26, Nov 1976, b&w; magazine 5.00
❑27, Dec 1976, b&w; magazine 5.00
❑28, Jan 1977, b&w; magazine 5.00
❑29, Feb 1977, b&w; magazine 5.00
❑Ann 1 4.00

Planet of the Apes
Adventure

❑1, Apr 1990; extra cover in pink, yellow, or green 4.00
❑1/Ltd., Apr 1990; limited 4.00
❑1/2nd; 2nd printing 2.50
❑2, Jun 1990 3.00
❑3, Jul 1990 3.00
❑4, Aug 1990 3.00
❑5, Sep 1990 3.00
❑6, Oct 1990 3.00
❑7, Nov 1990 3.00
❑8, Dec 1990; Christmas 3.00
❑9, Jan 1991 3.00
❑10, Mar 1991 3.00
❑11, Apr 1991 2.50
❑12, May 1991; PG (c);Wedding of Alexander and Coure 2.50
❑13, Jun 1991 2.50
❑14, Jul 1991 2.50
❑15, Aug 1991 2.50
❑16, Sep 1991 2.50
❑17, Oct 1991 2.50
❑18, Nov 1991 2.50
❑19, Dec 1991 2.50
❑20, Jan 1992 2.50
❑21, Feb 1992 2.50
❑22, Apr 1992; sequel to Conquest of the Planet of the Apes 2.50
❑23, May 1992 2.50
❑24, Jul 1992 2.50
❑Ann 1, b&w 3.50

Planet of the Apes
Dark Horse

❑1, Jun 2001 2.99
❑1/Variant, Jun 2001, Photo cover 2.99
❑2, Jul 2001 2.99
❑2/Variant, Jul 2001, Photo cover 2.99
❑3, Aug 2001 2.99
❑3/Variant, Aug 2001, Photo cover 2.99

Planet of the Apes
Dark Horse

❑1, Sep 2001 2.99
❑1/Variant, Sep 2001; Photo cover 2.99
❑2, Oct 2001 2.99
❑2/Variant, Oct 2001; Photo cover 2.99
❑3, Nov 2001 2.99
❑3/Variant, Nov 2001; Photo cover 2.99
❑4, Dec 2001 2.99
❑4/Variant, Dec 2001; Photo cover 2.99
❑5, Jan 2002 2.99
❑5/Variant, Jan 2002; Photo cover 2.99
❑6, Feb 2002 2.99
❑6/Variant, Feb 2002; Photo cover 2.99

N-MINT

Planet of the Apes: Blood of the Apes
Adventure

❑1, Nov 1991, b&w 2.50
❑2, Dec 1991, b&w 2.50
❑3, Jan 1992, b&w 2.50
❑4, Feb 1992, b&w 2.50

Planet of the Apes: Forbidden Zone
Adventure

❑1, Dec 1992 2.50
❑2 2.50
❑3 2.50
❑4 2.50

Planet of the Apes: Sins of the Father
Adventure

❑1, Mar 1992, b&w 2.50

Planet of the Apes: Urchak's Folly
Adventure

❑1, Jan 1991, b&w 2.50
❑2, Feb 1991, b&w 2.50
❑3, Mar 1991, b&w 2.50
❑4, Apr 1991, b&w 2.50

Planet of Vampires
Atlas-Seaboard

❑1, Apr 1975 NA (c); PB (a) 12.00
❑2, Jul 1975 NA (c); PB (a) 8.00
❑3, Jul 1975 8.00

Planet Patrol
Edge / Seaboard

❑1 2.95

Planet Terry
Marvel / Star

❑1, Apr 1985, O: Planet Terry. 1: Planet Terry 1.00
❑2, May 1985 1.00
❑3, Jun 1985 1.00
❑4, Jul 1985 1.00
❑5, Aug 1985 1.00
❑6, Sep 1985 1.00
❑7, Oct 1985 1.00
❑8, Nov 1985 1.00
❑9, Dec 1985 1.00
❑10, Jan 1986 1.00
❑11, Feb 1986 1.00
❑12, Mar 1986, Final Issue 1.00

Planet-X
Eternity

❑1, b&w 2.50

Planet X Reprint Comic
Planet X

❑1, ca. 1987, reprints adaptation of The Man from Planet X; no cover price 2.00

Plaque X
Aholattafun

❑1, ca. 2004 2.95

Plasm
Defiant

❑0, Jun 1993; bound in Diamond Previews 1.00

Plasma Baby
Caliber

❑1, b&w 2.50

N-MINT

❑2, b&w 2.50
❑3, b&w 2.50

Plasmer
Marvel

❑1, Nov 1993; four trading cards 2.50
❑2, Dec 1993 1.95
❑3, Jan 1994 1.95
❑4, Feb 1994 1.95

Plastic Forks
Marvel / Epic

❑1, ca. 1990 4.95
❑2, ca. 1990 4.95
❑3, ca. 1990 4.95
❑4, ca. 1990 4.95
❑5, ca. 1990 4.95

Plastic Little
CPM

❑Ashcan 1, Jun 1997; Ashcan edition; Adult 3.00
❑1, Aug 1997 2.95
❑2, Sep 1997 2.95
❑3, Oct 1997 2.95
❑4, Nov 1997 2.95
❑5, Dec 1997 2.95

Plastic Man
DC

❑1, Dec 1966, GK (a); O: Plastic Man 150.00
❑2, Feb 1967, O: Plastic Man 50.00
❑3, Apr 1967 30.00
❑4, Jun 1967 20.00
❑5, Aug 1967 20.00
❑6, Oct 1967 15.00
❑7, Dec 1967, A: Plas' father (Plastic Man 1). A: Woozy Winks 15.00
❑8, Feb 1968 15.00
❑9, Apr 1968 15.00
❑10, Jun 1968, series goes on hiatus until 1976 15.00
❑11, Mar 1976; Series begins again: 1976 8.00
❑12, May 1976 8.00
❑13, Jul 1976 8.00
❑14, Sep 1976 8.00
❑15, Nov 1976 8.00
❑16, Mar 1977 8.00
❑17, May 1977 8.00
❑18, Jul 1977 8.00
❑19, Sep 1977 8.00
❑20, Nov 1977, Final Issue 8.00

Plastic Man
DC

❑1, Nov 1988; PF (w); O: Plastic Man 1.25
❑2, Dec 1988 PF (w) 1.25
❑3, Jan 1989 PF (w) 1.25
❑4, Feb 1989 PF (w) 1.25

Plastic Man
DC

❑1, Feb 2004 2.95
❑2, Mar 2004 2.95
❑3, Apr 2004 2.95
❑4, May 2004 2.95
❑5, Jun 2004 2.95
❑6, Jul 2004 2.95
❑7, Aug 2004 2.95
❑8, Sep 2004 2.95

❑9, Oct 2004 2.95
❑10, Nov 2004 2.95
❑11, Dec 2004, Includes free Heroscape #1: The Battle of All Time comic insert 2.95
❑12, Jan 2005 2.95
❑13, Feb 2005 2.95
❑14, Mar 2005 2.95
❑15, Apr 2005; Slight price increase 2.99
❑16, Jun 2005 2.99
❑17, Sep 2005 2.99
❑18, Nov 2005 2.99
❑19, Jan 2006 2.99
❑20, Mar 2006, Final issue 2.99

Plastic Man Lost Annual
DC

❑1, Feb 2004 6.95

Plastic Man Special
DC

❑1, Aug 1999; O: Woozy Winks 3.95

Plastron Café
Mirage

❑1, Dec 1992 2.25
❑2, Feb 1993 2.25
❑3, May 1993 2.25
❑4, Jul 1993 2.25

Platinum.44
Comax

❑1, b&w 2.95

Platinum Grit
Dead Numbat

❑1, Feb 1994 3.50
❑2 3.50
❑3, Dec 1994 3.50
❑4, Feb 1995, b&w 3.50
❑5; ca. 1996 3.50
❑6 3.50

Playbear
Fantagraphics / Eros

❑1; Adult 2.95
❑2, ca. 1995; Adult 2.95
❑3, Aug 1995; Adult 2.95

Playground
Caliber

❑1, b&w 2.50

Playgrounds
Fantagraphics

❑1, b&w 2.00

Pleasure & Passion
Brainstorm

❑1, Oct 1997, Adult 2.95

Pleasure Bound
Fantagraphics / Eros

❑1, Feb 1996; Adult 2.95

Plop!
DC

❑1, Oct 1973, BW (c); SA, FR (w); GE, SA, BWr (a) 18.00
❑2, Dec 1973, BW (c); SA (w); SA, NC (a) 8.00
❑3, Feb 1974, BW (c); SA (a) 8.00
❑4, Apr 1974, BW (c); SA (w); SA, BW, FR, NC (a) 7.00
❑5, Jun 1974, BW (c); SA, BWr (a) 7.00
❑6, Aug 1974, BW (c); SA (a) 6.00
❑7, Oct 1974, BW (c); SA, KS (a) 6.00
❑8, Dec 1974, BW (c); SA (a) 6.00
❑9, Feb 1975 BW (c); SA, BW, FR (a) 6.00
❑10, Mar 1975 BW (c); JO (w); SA, BW, RE (a) 6.00
❑11, Apr 1975 BW (c); SA (w); SA, ATh (a) 5.00
❑12, May 1975 BW (c); SA (a) 5.00
❑13, Jun 1975 WW (c); SA (w); SA (a) 5.00
❑14, Jul 1975 BW (c); SA (w); SA, WW (a) 5.00
❑15, Aug 1975 WW (c); SA (a) 5.00
❑16, Sep 1975 SA, SD, RE (a) 5.00
❑17, Oct 1975 BW (c); SA, FR (a) 5.00
❑18, Dec 1975 BW (c); SA, RE (a) 5.00
❑19, Feb 1976 WW (c); SA, FT (a) 5.00
❑20, Apr 1976 SA (a) 5.00
❑21, Jun 1976, Giant-size; JO (c); SA (a) 5.00
❑22, Aug 1976, Giant-size; JO (w); SA (a) 5.00
❑23, Oct 1976, Giant-size; Wally Wood's Lord of the Rings parody 5.00
❑24, Dec 1976, Giant-size; SA (w); SA, RE (a) 8.00

Pocahontas
Marvel

❑1, Jul 1995, prestige format one-shot 4.95

Poe
Cheese

❑1, Sep 1996; b&w 2.50
❑2, Oct 1996; b&w 2.50
❑3, Nov 1996; b&w 2.50
❑4, Dec 1996; b&w 2.50
❑5, Feb 1997, b&w 2.50
❑6, Apr 1997, b&w 2.50
❑7 2.50
❑8 2.50
❑9 2.50
❑10 2.50
❑11 2.50

Poe
Sirius

❑1, Oct 1997, b&w 2.50
❑2, Nov 1997, b&w 2.50
❑3, Dec 1997 2.50
❑4, Jan 1998 2.50
❑5, Feb 1998 2.50
❑6, Mar 1998 2.50
❑7, May 1998 2.50
❑8, Jun 1998 2.50
❑9, Jul 1998 2.50
❑10, Aug 1998 2.50
❑11, Sep 1998 2.50
❑12, Oct 1998 2.50
❑13, Nov 1998 2.50
❑14, Jan 1999 2.50
❑15, Feb 1999 2.50
❑16, Mar 1999 2.50
❑17, Apr 1999 2.50
❑18, Aug 1999 2.50
❑19, Sep 1999 2.50
❑20, Nov 1999 2.50
❑21, Jan 2000 2.95
❑22, Mar 2000 2.95
❑23, May 2000 2.95
❑24, Jul 2000 2.95
❑Special 1, Dec 1998; Color Special 2.95

Poets Prosper: Rhyme & Revelry
Tome

❑1 3.50

Point Blank
WildStorm

❑1, Oct 2002; Colin Wilson cover 2.95
❑2, Nov 2002 2.95
❑3, Dec 2002 2.95
❑4, Jan 2003 2.95
❑5, Feb 2003 2.95

Point-Blank
Eclipse

❑1, b&w 2.95
❑2, b&w 2.95

Point Pleasant
Ape Entertainment

❑1, ca. 2004 3.95

Poison Elves
Mulehide

❑8, Feb 1993; magazine-sized; Series continued from I, Lusiphur #7 15.00
❑9, Apr 1993; magazine-sized 12.00
❑10, Jun 1993; magazine-sized 12.00
❑11, Aug 1993 10.00
❑12, Oct 1993 10.00
❑13, Dec 1993 10.00
❑14, Feb 1994 10.00
❑15, Apr 1994; Scarcer 10.00
❑15/2nd 2.50
❑16, Jun 1994 8.00
❑17, Aug 1994 8.00
❑17/2nd 2.50
❑18, Oct 1994 5.00
❑19, Dec 1994 5.00
❑20, Feb 1995; Final Issue 5.00
❑Deluxe 1, ca. 2001; Poison Elves: The Mulehide Years 34.95

Poison Elves
Sirius

❑1, May 1995, b&w; 24,000 printed 6.00
❑1/2nd; 2nd printing; Drawn cover 2.50
❑2, Jun 1995, b&w 4.00
❑3, Jul 1995, b&w 4.00
❑4, Aug 1995, b&w 3.00
❑5, Oct 1995 3.00
❑6, Nov 1995 3.00
❑7, Dec 1995 2.50
❑8, Jan 1996 2.50
❑9, Jan 1996 2.50
❑10, Feb 1996 2.50
❑11, Mar 1996 2.50
❑12, Apr 1996 2.50
❑13, May 1996 2.50
❑14, Jun 1996 2.50
❑15, Jul 1996 2.50
❑16, Sep 1996 2.50
❑17, Oct 1996 2.50
❑18, Nov 1996 2.50
❑19, Dec 1996 2.50
❑20, Jan 1997 2.50
❑21, Feb 1997 2.50
❑22, Mar 1997 2.50
❑23, Apr 1997 2.50
❑24, May 1997 2.50
❑25, Jul 1997 2.50
❑26, Aug 1997 2.50
❑27, Sep 1997 2.50
❑28, Oct 1997 2.50
❑29, Nov 1997 2.50
❑30, Dec 1997 2.50
❑31, Jan 1998 2.50
❑32, Feb 1998 2.50
❑33, Mar 1998 2.50
❑34, Apr 1998 2.50
❑35, May 1998 2.50
❑36, Jun 1998 2.50
❑37, Jul 1998 2.50
❑38, Aug 1998 2.50
❑39, Sep 1998 2.50
❑40, Oct 1998 2.50
❑41, Nov 1998 2.50
❑42, Dec 1998 2.50
❑43, Jan 1999 2.50
❑44, Feb 1999 2.50
❑45, Mar 1999 2.50
❑46, Jun 1999 2.95
❑47, Jul 1999 2.50
❑48, Aug 1999 2.50
❑49, Sep 1999 2.50
❑50, Oct 1999 2.50
❑51, Nov 1999 2.50
❑52, Dec 1999 2.50
❑53, Jan 2000 2.95
❑54, Feb 2000 2.95
❑55, Mar 2000 2.95
❑56, Apr 2000 2.95
❑57, May 2000 2.95
❑58, Jun 2000 2.95
❑59, Jul 2000 2.95
❑60, Aug 2000 2.95
❑61, Sep 2000 2.95
❑62, Nov 2000 2.95
❑63, Jan 2001 2.95
❑64, Mar 2001 2.95
❑65, May 2001 2.95
❑66, Jul 2001 2.95
❑67, Sep 2001 2.95
❑68, Nov 2001 2.95
❑69, Jan 2002 2.95
❑70, Mar 2002 2.95
❑71, Feb 2003 2.95
❑72, Mar 2003 2.95
❑73, May 2003 2.95
❑74, Aug 2003 2.95
❑75, Dec 2003 2.95
❑76, Mar 2004 2.95
❑77, Mar 2004 2.95
❑79, Sep 2004 2.95
❑78, May 2004 2.95
❑Special 1, ca. 1998; Color Special 3.00

Poison Elves: Ventures
Sirius

❑1, Jul 2005 3.50

Poizon
London Night

❑0, Jul 1996 3.00
❑0/Nude, Jul 1996 3.50

Quack!

Indy series had early Dave Sim work

©Star*Reach

Quantum & Woody

Semi-serious super-hero fare

©Acclaim

Quantum Leap

Adventures based on NBC's SF series

©Innovation

Quasar

Third-rate hero gives Marvel a title under Q

©Marvel

Queen & Country

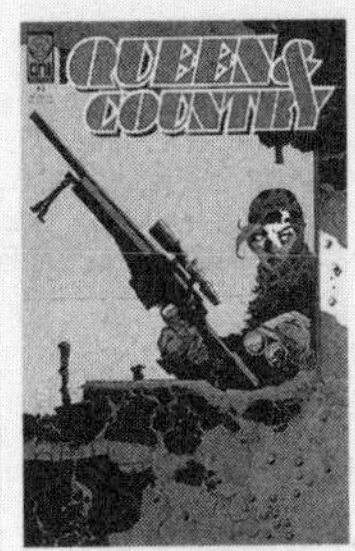

British espionage adventures with Tara

©Oni

N-MINT

❑½; ca. 1995 .... 3.00
❑1, Feb 1996 .... 3.00
❑1/A, Mar 1995; Green Death edition; Includes COA 15.00
❑1/Nude, Mar 1995; Adult 5.00
❑2, Apr 1996 .... 3.00
❑3, Jun 1996 .... 3.00

Pokémon: The Electric Tale of Pikachu
Viz

❑1, Nov 1998; 1: Pikachu 3.50
❑1/2nd; 2nd printing 3.25
❑1/3rd, Mar 1999; 3rd printing 3.25
❑2, Dec 1998 .... 3.25
❑2/2nd; 2nd printing 3.25
❑3, Jan 1999 .... 3.25
❑4, Feb 1999 .... 3.25

Pokémon Part 2
Viz

❑1, Mar 1999 .... 3.25
❑2, Apr 1999 .... 3.25
❑3, May 1999 .... 3.25
❑4, Jun 1999 .... 2.95

Pokémon Part 3
Viz

❑1, Jul 1999 .... 3.50
❑2, Aug 1999 .... 3.50
❑3, Sep 1999 .... 3.50
❑4, Oct 1999 .... 3.50

Pokémon Adventures
Viz

❑1, Sep 1999, Mysterious Mew 5.95
❑2, Oct 1999, Wanted: Pikachu 5.95
❑3, Nov 1999, Includes stickers 5.95
❑4, Dec 1999 .... 5.95
❑5, Jan 2000 .... 5.95

Pokémon Adventures Part 2
Viz

❑1 2000 .... 2.95
❑2 2000 .... 2.95
❑3 2000 .... 2.95
❑4 2000 .... 2.95
❑5 2000 .... 2.95
❑6 2000 .... 2.95

Pokémon Adventures Part 3
Viz

❑1 2000 .... 2.95
❑2 2000 .... 2.95
❑3 2000 .... 2.95
❑4 2000 .... 2.95
❑5 2000 .... 2.95
❑6, Jan 2001 .... 2.95
❑7, Feb 2001 .... 2.95

Pokémon Adventures Part 4
Viz

❑1, Mar 2001 .... 2.95
❑2, Apr 2001 .... 2.95
❑3, May 2001 .... 4.95
❑4, Jun 2001 .... 4.95

N-MINT

Pokémon Adventures Part 5
Viz

❑1, Jul 2001; Cover logo reads "Yellow Caballero" 4.95
❑2, Aug 2001; Cover logo reads "Yellow Caballero" 4.95
❑3, Sep 2001; Cover logo reads "Yellow Caballero" 4.95
❑4, Oct 2001; Cover logo reads "Yellow Caballero" 4.95
❑5, Nov 2001; Cover logo reads "Yellow Caballero" 4.95

Pokémon Adventures Part 6
Viz

❑1, Dec 2001; Cover logo reads "Yellow Caballero" 4.95
❑2, Jan 2002; Cover logo reads "Yellow Caballero" 4.95
❑3, Feb 2002; Cover logo reads "Yellow Caballero" 4.95
❑4, Mar 2002; Cover logo reads "Yellow Caballero" 4.95

Pokémon Adventures Part 7
Viz

❑1, Apr 2002; Cover logo reads "Yellow Caballero" 4.95
❑2, May 2002; Cover logo reads "Yellow Caballero" 4.95
❑3, Jun 2002; Cover logo reads "Yellow Caballero" 4.95
❑4, Jul 2002; Cover logo reads "Yellow Caballero" 4.95
❑5, Aug 2002; Cover logo reads "Yellow Caballero" 4.95

Police Academy
Marvel / Star

❑1, Oct 1989 .... 1.00
❑2, Nov 1989 .... 1.00
❑3, Dec 1989 .... 1.00
❑4, Jan 1990 .... 1.00
❑5, Feb 1990 .... 1.00
❑6, Mar 1990 .... 1.00

Police Action
Atlas-Seaboard

❑1, Feb 1975; MP (w); MP (a); Includes Mike Ploog story/art 11.00
❑2, Apr 1975; MP, FS (a); Includes Mike Ploog story/art 5.00
❑3, Jun 1975; FT (c); MP (a); Includes Mike Ploog story/art; Frank thorne cover 5.00

Polis
Brave New Words

❑1, b&w 2.50
❑2, b&w 2.50

Political Action Comics
Comicfix

❑1, ca. 2004, John Kerry/John Edwards parody comic for 2004 election campaign 4.99

Polly and Her Pals
Eternity

❑1, Oct 1990, b&w; strip reprints 2.95
❑2 1990, b&w; strip reprints 2.95
❑3 1991, b&w; strip reprints 2.95

N-MINT

❑4 1991, b&w; strip reprints 2.95
❑5 1991, b&w; strip reprints 2.95

Polly and the Pirates
Oni

❑1, Sep 2005 .... 2.99
❑2, Nov 2005 .... 2.99

Ponytail
Dell

❑-209, Sep 1962, Counted as #1 of the ongoing series 12.00
❑2, Jun 1963 .... 8.00
❑3, Sep 1963 .... 8.00
❑4, Dec 1963 .... 8.00
❑5, Mar 1964 .... 8.00
❑6, Jun 1964 .... 8.00
❑7, Sep 1964 .... 8.00
❑8, Dec 1964 .... 8.00
❑9, Mar 1965 .... 8.00
❑10, Jun 1965 .... 8.00
❑11, Sep 1965 .... 8.00
❑12, Dec 1965, Last Dell issue; moves to Charlton 8.00

Ponytail
Charlton

❑13, Nov 1969, First Charlton issue 6.00
❑14, Jan 1970 .... 4.00
❑15, Mar 1970 .... 4.00
❑16, May 1970 .... 4.00
❑17, Jul 1970 .... 4.00
❑18, Sep 1970 .... 4.00
❑19, Nov 1970 .... 4.00
❑20, Jan 1971 .... 4.00

Poot
Fantagraphics

❑1, Win 1997 .... 2.95
❑2, Spr 1998 .... 2.95
❑3, Sum 1998 .... 2.95
❑4, Win 1998 .... 3.95

Popbot
Idea & Design Works

❑1 2002 .... 7.99
❑2 2003 .... 7.99
❑3 2003 .... 7.99
❑4, Jun 2003 .... 7.99
❑5, Mar 2004 .... 9.99
❑7, May 2006 .... 9.99

Popcorn!
Discovery

❑1, b&w; cardstock cover 3.95

Popcorn Pimps
Fantagraphics

❑1, Jun 1996, b&w; squarebound 8.95

Popeye
Dell

❑62, Dec 1961 .... 40.00
❑63, Jan 1962 .... 40.00
❑64, Apr 1962 .... 40.00
❑65, Jul 1962, Last Dell issue 40.00
❑66, Oct 1962, First Gold Key issue 40.00
❑67, Jan 1963, 80-page 40.00
❑68, May 1963 .... 40.00
❑69, Jul 1963 .... 40.00
❑70, Nov 1963 .... 30.00

	N-MINT
❑71, Jan 1964	30.00
❑72, Apr 1964	30.00
❑73, Jul 1964	30.00
❑74, Nov 1964, Reprint from Popeye #10	30.00
❑75, Feb 1965	30.00
❑76, May 1965, Reprints	30.00
❑77, Aug 1965, Reprints	30.00
❑78, Nov 1965, Reprints from Popeye #43 and 45	30.00
❑79, Feb 1966, Reprints from Popeye #33 and 45	30.00
❑80, May 1966, Reprints from Popeye #29 and 41; Last Gold Key issue	30.00
❑81, Aug 1966, First King issue	25.00
❑82, Oct 1966	25.00
❑83, Dec 1966	25.00
❑84, Feb 1967	25.00
❑85, Apr 1967	25.00
❑86, Jun 1967	25.00
❑87, Jul 1967	25.00
❑88, Aug 1967	25.00
❑89, Sep 1967	25.00
❑90, Oct 1967	25.00
❑91, Nov 1967	25.00
❑92, Dec 1967, Last King issue	25.00
❑93 1968, First Charlton issue	20.00
❑94, Feb 1969	20.00
❑95, Apr 1969	20.00
❑96, Jun 1969	20.00
❑97, Aug 1969	20.00
❑98, Oct 1969	20.00
❑99, Dec 1969	20.00
❑100, Feb 1970	20.00
❑101, Apr 1970	15.00
❑102, Jun 1970	15.00
❑103, Aug 1970	15.00
❑104, Oct 1970	15.00
❑105, Dec 1970	15.00
❑106, Feb 1971, A: Sea Hag. A: Brutus. A: Junior Smith. A: Wimpy. A: Swee' Pea. A: Granny. A: Snuffy Smith. A: Pappy. A: Olive Oyl. A: Ma Smith	15.00
❑107, Apr 1971	15.00
❑108, Jun 1971	15.00
❑109, Aug 1971	15.00
❑110, Oct 1971	15.00
❑111, Dec 1971	15.00
❑112, Jan 1972	15.00
❑113, Mar 1972	15.00
❑114, May 1972	15.00
❑115, Jul 1972	15.00
❑116, Sep 1972	15.00
❑117, Nov 1972	15.00
❑118, Feb 1973	15.00
❑119, Apr 1973	15.00
❑120, Jun 1973	15.00
❑121, Aug 1973	10.00
❑122, Oct 1973	10.00
❑123, Nov 1973	10.00
❑124, ca. 1974	10.00
❑125, Sep 1974	10.00
❑126, Dec 1974	10.00
❑127, Feb 1975	10.00
❑128, Apr 1975	10.00
❑129, Jun 1975	10.00
❑130, Aug 1975	10.00
❑131, Oct 1975	10.00
❑132, Dec 1976	10.00
❑133, Feb 1976	10.00
❑134, ca. 1976	10.00
❑135, ca. 1976	10.00
❑136, ca. 1976	10.00
❑137, ca. 1976	10.00
❑138, Jan 1977, Last Chalton issue	10.00
❑139, May 1978, First issue of second Gold Key run	7.00
❑140, Jul 1978	7.00
❑141, Sep 1978	7.00
❑142, Nov 1978	7.00
❑143, Jan 1979	7.00
❑144, Mar 1979	7.00
❑145, Apr 1979	7.00
❑146, May 1979	7.00
❑147, Jun 1979	7.00
❑148, Jul 1979	7.00
❑149, Aug 1979	7.00
❑150, Sep 1979	5.00
❑151, Oct 1979	5.00
❑152, Nov 1980	5.00
❑153, Dec 1979	5.00
❑154, Jan 1980	5.00
❑155, Feb 1980, Last GoldKey label issue	5.00
❑156, Mar 1980, First Whitman-label issue	10.00
❑157 1980	10.00
❑158, Sep 1980	35.00
❑159, Nov 1980	30.00
❑162, Mar 1981, #160-161 never printed	10.00
❑163, ca. 1981	10.00
❑164, Aug 1981	10.00
❑165, ca. 1981	10.00
❑166, ca. 1982	10.00
❑167, ca. 1982	10.00
❑168, Jun 1983	18.00
❑169, ca. 1983	18.00
❑170, ca. 1983	18.00
❑171, ca. 1984	18.00
❑Special 1, Bold Detergent giveaway; Reprints issue #94	2.00

Popeye
Harvey

	N-MINT
❑1, Nov 1993	1.50
❑2, Jan 1994	1.50
❑3, Mar 1994	1.50
❑4, May 1994	1.50
❑5, Jun 1994	1.50
❑6, Jul 1994	1.50
❑Summer 1, Oct 1993	2.25

Popeye Special
Ocean

	N-MINT
❑1, Sum 1987; O: Popeye	2.00
❑2, Sep 1988	2.00

Pop Life
Fantagraphics

	N-MINT
❑1, Oct 1998; Adult	3.95
❑2, Mar 1999; Adult	3.95

Popples
Marvel / Star

	N-MINT
❑1, Dec 1986	1.00
❑2, Feb 1987	1.00
❑3, Apr 1987	1.00
❑4, Jun 1987	1.00

Pork Knight: This Little Piggy
Silver Snail

	N-MINT
❑1	2.00

Porky Pig
Gold Key

	N-MINT
❑1, Jan 1965	30.00
❑2, May 1965	14.00
❑3, Aug 1965	12.00
❑4, Nov 1965	12.00
❑5, Mar 1966	12.00
❑6, Jun 1966	8.00
❑7, Jul 1966	8.00
❑8, Sep 1966	8.00
❑9, Nov 1966; Cover code 10140-611	8.00
❑10, Jan 1967	8.00
❑11, Mar 1967	5.00
❑12, May 1967	5.00
❑13, Jul 1967	5.00
❑14, Sep 1967	5.00
❑15, Nov 1967	5.00
❑16, Jan 1968	5.00
❑17, ca. 1968	5.00
❑18, Jun 1968	5.00
❑19, Aug 1968	5.00
❑20, Oct 1968; Cover code 10140-810	5.00
❑21, Dec 1968	4.00
❑22, Feb 1969	4.00
❑23, Apr 1969	4.00
❑24, Jun 1969	4.00
❑25, Aug 1969	4.00
❑26, Oct 1969	4.00
❑27, Dec 1969; Cover code 10140-912	4.00
❑28, Feb 1970	4.00
❑29, Apr 1970	4.00
❑30, Jun 1970	4.00
❑31, Aug 1970, Cover code 10140-008	3.00
❑32, Oct 1970, Cover code 10140-010	3.00
❑33, Dec 1970, Cover code 10140-012	3.00
❑34, Feb 1971, Cover code 10140-102	3.00
❑35, Apr 1971, Cover code 10140-104	3.00
❑36, Jun 1971, Cover code 10140-106	3.00
❑37, Aug 1971, Cover code 10140-108	3.00
❑38, Oct 1971	3.00
❑39, Dec 1971	3.00
❑40, Feb 1972	3.00
❑41, Apr 1972, Cover code 90140-204	3.00
❑42, Jun 1972, Cover code 90140-206	3.00
❑43, Aug 1972, Cover code 90140-208	3.00
❑44, Oct 1972, Cover code 90140-210	3.00
❑45, Dec 1972, Cover code 90140-212	3.00
❑46, Feb 1973, Cover code 90140-302	3.00
❑47, Apr 1973, Cover code 90140-304	3.00
❑48, Jun 1973, Cover code 90140-306	3.00
❑49, Aug 1973, Cover code 90140-308	3.00
❑50, Oct 1973, Cover code 90140-310	3.00
❑51, Dec 1973, Cover code 90140-312	2.00
❑52, Feb 1974, Cover code 90140-402	2.00
❑53, Apr 1974, Cover code 90140-404	2.00
❑54, Jun 1974, Cover code 90140-406	2.00
❑55, Aug 1974, Cover code 90140-408	2.00
❑56, Oct 1974, Cover code 90140-410	2.00
❑57, Dec 1974, Cover code 90140-412	2.00
❑58, Feb 1975, Cover code 90140-502	2.00
❑59, Apr 1975, Cover code 90140-504	2.00
❑60, Jun 1975, Cover code 90140-506	2.00
❑61, Aug 1975	2.00
❑62, Sep 1975	2.00
❑63, Oct 1975	2.00
❑64, Nov 1975	2.00
❑65, Dec 1975	2.00
❑66, Apr 1976	2.00
❑67, Jun 1976	2.00
❑68, Jul 1976	2.00
❑69, Aug 1976	2.00
❑70, Sep 1976	2.00
❑71, Nov 1976	2.00
❑72, Jan 1977	2.00
❑73, Mar 1977	2.00
❑74, May 1977	2.00
❑75, Jul 1977	2.00
❑76, Aug 1977	2.00
❑77, Sep 1977	2.00
❑78, Nov 1977	2.00
❑79, Jan 1978	2.00
❑80, Mar 1978	2.00
❑81, May 1978	2.00
❑82, Jul 1978	2.00
❑83, Aug 1978	2.00
❑84, Sep 1978	2.00
❑85, Oct 1978	2.00
❑86, Nov 1978	2.00
❑87, Jan 1979	2.00
❑88, Mar 1979	2.00
❑89, May 1979	2.00
❑90, Jul 1979	2.00
❑91, Sep 1979	2.00
❑92, Nov 1979	2.00
❑93, Jan 1980	2.00
❑94, Mar 1980, Whitman begins as publisher	2.00
❑95, May 1980	2.00
❑96, Jul 1980	2.00
❑97, Sep 1980	2.00
❑98, Nov 1980	2.00
❑99, Jan 1981	2.00
❑100, Mar 1981	2.00
❑101, ca. 1981	2.00
❑102, Sep 1981	2.00
❑103, Nov 1981	2.00
❑104, Feb 1982	2.00
❑105, Apr 1982	2.00
❑106	2.00
❑107	2.00
❑108	2.00
❑109, ca. 1984	2.00

Pornotopia
Radio

	N-MINT
❑1, Aug 1999	2.95

Port
Silverwolf

	N-MINT
❑1, Feb 1987, b&w	1.50
❑2, Mar 1987, b&w	1.50

Portable Lowlife
Aeon

	N-MINT
❑1, Jul 1993; prestige format; NN	4.95

Other grades: Multiply price above by 5/6 for VF/NM • 2/3 for VERY FINE • 1/3 for FINE • 1/5 for VERY GOOD • 1/8 for GOOD

Question Quarterly

Only alliterative series beginning with Q

©DC

Quicksilver

Starring Scarlet Witch's speedster brother

©Marvel

Radioactive Man

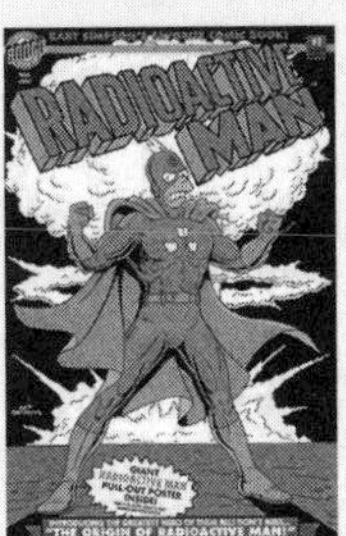

Bart Simpson's favorite super-hero

©Bongo

Ragman

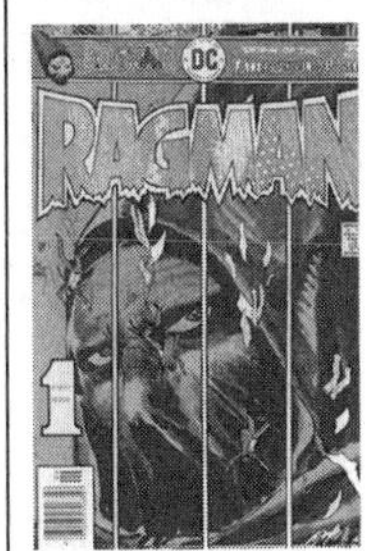

Pawnbroker by day, crimefighter by night

©DC

Rai

Series name adds then drops "Future Force"

©Valiant

N-MINT

Portals of Elondar
Storybook

❑1, Jul 1996, b&w 2.95

Portent
Image

❑1, Mar 2006 .... 2.99
❑2, May 2006 .... 2.99
❑3, Jul 2006 .... 2.99
❑4, Oct 2006 .... 2.99

Portia Prinz of the Glamazons
Eclipse

❑1, Dec 1986, b&w 2.00
❑2, Feb 1987, b&w 2.00
❑3, Apr 1987, b&w 2.00
❑4, Jun 1987, b&w 2.00
❑5, Aug 1987, b&w 2.00
❑6, Oct 1987, b&w 2.00

Portrait of a Young Man as a Cartoonist
Hammer & Anvil

❑1, Oct 1996 .... 2.95
❑2, Dec 1996 .... 2.95
❑3, Feb 1997 .... 2.95
❑4, Apr 1997 .... 2.95
❑5, Jun 1997 .... 2.95
❑6, Aug 1997 .... 2.95
❑7, Oct 1997 .... 2.95
❑8, Jan 1998 .... 2.95

Possessed
DC / Cliffhanger

❑1, Sep 2003 .... 2.95
❑2, Oct 2003 .... 2.95
❑3, Nov 2003 .... 2.95
❑4, Dec 2003 .... 2.95
❑5, Jan 2004 .... 2.95
❑6, Mar 2004 .... 2.95

Possibleman
Blackthorne

❑1, Jan 1987 .... 1.75
❑2, Apr 1987 .... 1.75

Post Apocalypse
Slave Labor

❑1, Dec 1994 .... 2.95

(Post-Atomic) Cyborg Gerbils
Trigon

❑1, Aug 1986 .... 2.50
❑2, Nov 1986 .... 2.50

Post Brothers
Rip Off

❑19, Apr 1991, b&w; Series continued from Those Annoying Post Brothers #18 .... 2.50
❑20, Jun 1991, b&w 2.50
❑21, Aug 1991, b&w 2.50
❑22, Oct 1991, b&w 2.50
❑23, Oct 1991, b&w 2.50
❑24, Dec 1991, b&w 2.50
❑25, Feb 1992, b&w 2.50
❑26, Apr 1992, b&w 2.50
❑27, Jun 1992, b&w 2.50
❑28, Aug 1992, b&w 2.50
❑29, Oct 1992, b&w 2.50
❑30, Dec 1992, b&w 2.50

N-MINT

❑31, Feb 1993, b&w 2.50
❑32, Apr 1993, b&w 2.50
❑33, Jun 1993, b&w; Listed as "Those Annoying Post Brothers" 2.50
❑34, Aug 1993, b&w 2.50
❑35, Oct 1993, b&w 2.50
❑36, Dec 1993, b&w 2.50
❑37, Feb 1994, b&w 2.50
❑38, Apr 1994, b&w; series continues as Those Annoying Post Bros 2.50

Potential
Slave Labor

❑1, Mar 1998, b&w; magazine-sized; Adult 3.50
❑2; Adult 3.50
❑3, Sep 1998; Adult 4.95
❑4, Feb 1999; Adult 3.50

Pound
Radio

❑1, Mar 2000, b&w 2.95

Pounded
Oni

❑1, Mar 2002 .... 2.95
❑2 2002 .... 2.95
❑3, Jun 2002 .... 2.95

Powder Burn
Antarctic

❑1, Mar 1999, b&w 2.99
❑1/A, Mar 1999, b&w; wraparound cover 2.99
❑1/CS, Mar 1999; Collector's Set 5.99

Power
Aircel

❑1, Mar 1991, b&w 2.25
❑2, Apr 1991, b&w 2.25
❑3, May 1991, b&w 2.25
❑4, Jun 1991, b&w 2.25

Power & Glory
Malibu / Bravura

❑1/A, Feb 1994, HC (w); HC (a); Alternate cover (marked) 2.50
❑1/B, Feb 1994, HC (w); HC (a); Alternate cover (marked) 2.50
❑1/Gold, Feb 1994, sendaway with gold ink on cover 3.00
❑1/Ltd., Feb 1994, serigraph cover 2.50
❑1/Variant, Feb 1994, blue foil 3.00
❑2, Mar 1994, HC (w); HC (a); Includes Bravura Gold Stamp coupon 2.50
❑3, Apr 1994, HC (w); HC (a); Includes Bravura Gold Stamp coupon 2.50
❑4, May 1994, HC (w); HC (a); Includes Bravura Gold Stamp coupon 2.50
❑WS 1, Dec 1994, Giant-size; HC (w); HC (a); Winter Special #1 .... 2.95

Power Brigade
Moving Target / Malibu

❑1 .... 1.75

Power Comics
Power

❑1, Aug 1977; 1st Dave Sim aardvark 2.00
❑1/2nd; 2nd printing; Nightwitch 2.00
❑2, Sep 1977; 1: Cobalt Blue; O: Cobalt Blue 2.00
❑3, Oct 1977 .... 2.00

N-MINT

❑4, Nov 1977 .... 2.00
❑5, Dec 1977; Bluebird 2.00

Power Comics
Eclipse

❑1, Mar 1988, b&w 2.00
❑2, May 1988, b&w 2.00
❑3, Jul 1988, b&w 2.00
❑4, Sep 1988, b&w 2.00

Power Company
DC

❑1, Apr 2002 KB (w) 3.00
❑2, May 2002 KB (w) 2.50
❑3, Jun 2002 KB (w) 2.50
❑4, Jul 2002 KB (w) 2.50
❑5, Aug 2002 KB (w) 2.50
❑6, Sep 2002 KB (w) 2.50
❑7, Oct 2002; KB (w); V: Aryn 2.75
❑8, Nov 2002 KB (w) 2.75
❑9, Dec 2002 KB (w) 2.75
❑10, Jan 2003; KB (w); Includes preview of Superman: Metropolis # 1 .... 2.75
❑11, Feb 2003; KB (w); Firestorms joins 2.75
❑12, Mar 2003 KB (w) 2.75
❑13, Apr 2003 .... 2.75
❑14, May 2003 .... 2.75
❑15, Jun 2003 .... 2.75
❑16, Jul 2003 .... 2.75
❑17, Aug 2003 .... 2.75
❑18, Sep 2003 .... 2.75

Power Company: Bork
DC

❑1, Mar 2002 .... 2.50

Power Company: Josiah Power
DC

❑1, Mar 2002 .... 2.50

Power Company: Manhunter
DC

❑1, Mar 2002 .... 2.50

Power Company: Sapphire
DC

❑1, Mar 2002 .... 2.50

Power Company: Skyrocket
DC

❑1, Mar 2002 .... 2.50

Power Company: Striker Z
DC

❑1, Mar 2002 .... 2.50

Power Company: Witchfire
DC

❑1, Mar 2002 .... 2.50

Power Defense
Miller

❑1, b&w 2.50

Power Factor
Wonder

❑1, May 1986; Wonder Color Publisher 1.95
❑2, Jun 1986; Pied Piper Publisher 1.95

Power Factor
Innovation

❑1, Oct 1990 .... 1.95
❑2, Dec 1990 .... 2.25

N-MINT

❑3, Feb 1991 .... 2.25
❑Special 1, Jan 1991 .... 2.75

Power Girl
DC

❑1, Jun 1988 .... 1.00
❑2, Jul 1988 .... 1.00
❑3, Aug 1988 .... 1.00
❑4, Sep 1988 .... 1.00

Powerless
Marvel

❑1, Aug 2004 .... 2.99
❑2, Sep 2004 .... 2.99
❑3, Oct 2004 .... 2.99
❑4, Nov 2004 .... 2.99
❑5, Dec 2004 .... 2.99
❑6, Jan 2005 .... 2.99

Power Line
Marvel / Epic

❑1, May 1988 BSz (c); BSz (a) 1.50
❑2, Jul 1988 .... 1.50
❑3, Sep 1988 .... 1.50
❑4, Nov 1988 .... 1.50
❑5, Jan 1989 .... 1.50
❑6, Mar 1989 .... 1.50
❑7, May 1989 GM (a) 1.50
❑8, Jul 1989 .... 1.50

Power Lords
DC

❑1, Dec 1983; O: Power Lords. 1: Power Lords. 1: Power Lords 1.00
❑2, Jan 1984 .... 1.00
❑3, Feb 1985 .... 1.00

Power Man & Iron Fist
Marvel

❑17, Feb 1974, GK (c); GT (a); A: Iron Man. Title continued from "Hero For Hire" .. 8.00
❑18, Apr 1974, GK (c); GT (a); Marvel Value Stamp #3: Conan 5.00
❑19, Jun 1974, GK (c); GT (a); Marvel Value Stamp #64: Sif 5.00
❑20, Aug 1974, GK (c); GT (a); Marvel Value Stamp #1: Spider-Man 5.00
❑21, Oct 1974, V: Power Man. Marvel Value Stamp #73: Kingpin 4.00
❑22, Dec 1974 .... 4.00
❑23, Feb 1975, RB (c); Marvel Value Stamp #3: Conan 4.00
❑24, Apr 1975, GK (c); GT (a); 1: Black Goliath. V: Circus of Crime. Marvel Value Stamp #27: Black Widow 4.00
❑25, Jun 1975, GK (c); V: Circus of Crime 4.00
❑26, Aug 1975, GK (c); GT (a) 4.00
❑27, Oct 1975, GP (w); GP (a) 4.00
❑28, Dec 1975 .... 4.00
❑29, Feb 1976 .... 4.00
❑30, Apr 1976 .... 4.00
❑30/30¢, Apr 1976, 30¢ regional price variant 20.00
❑31, May 1976, RB (c); SB, NA (a) 4.00
❑31/30¢, May 1976, RB (c); SB, NA (a); 30¢ regional price variant 20.00
❑32, Jun 1976 .... 3.00
❑32/30¢, Jun 1976, 30¢ regional price variant 20.00
❑33, Jul 1976 .... 3.00
❑33/30¢, Jul 1976, 30¢ regional price variant 20.00
❑34, Aug 1976 .... 3.00
❑34/30¢, Aug 1976, 30¢ regional price variant 20.00
❑35, Sep 1976 .... 3.00
❑36, Oct 1976, Reprint from Hero for Hire #12 .... 3.00
❑37, Nov 1976, 1: Chemistro II (Archibald "Arch" Morton) 3.00
❑38, Dec 1976, 2: Chemistro II (Archiblad Arch Morton) 3.00
❑39, Jan 1977 .... 3.00
❑40, Feb 1977 .... 3.00
❑41, Mar 1977, 1: Thunderbolt (William Carver); 1: Goldbug (Jack Smith) 3.00
❑42, Apr 1977 .... 3.00
❑43, May 1977 .... 3.00
❑44, Jun 1977 .... 3.00
❑44/35¢, Jun 1977, 35¢ regional price variant 15.00
❑45, Jul 1977, JSn (c); JSn (a); A: Mace 3.00
❑45/35¢, Jul 1977, JSn (c); JSn (a); A: Mace. 35¢ regional price variant 15.00
❑46, Aug 1977, GT (a); 1: Zzax 3.00
❑46/35¢, Aug 1977, GT (a); 1: Zzax. 35¢ regional price variant 15.00
❑47, Oct 1977, GK (c); GT (a); A: Iron Fist. Newsstand edition (distributed by Curtis); issue number in box 3.00
❑47/Whitman, Oct 1977, A: Iron Fist. Special markets edition (usually sold in Whitman bagged prepacks); price appears in a diamond; no UPC barcode 3.00
❑47/35¢, Oct 1977, GK (c); GT (a); A: Iron Fist. 35¢ regional price variant; newsstand edition (distributed by Curtis); issue number in box 15.00
❑48, Dec 1977, GK (c); JBy (a); 1: Power Man and Iron Fist 10.00
❑49, Feb 1978, JBy (a); A: Iron Fist. series continues as Power Man & Iron Fist .. 6.00
❑50, Apr 1978, DC (c); JBy (a) 6.00
❑51, Jun 1978 .... 3.00
❑52, Aug 1978 .... 3.00
❑53, Oct 1978, O: Nightshade 4.00
❑54, Dec 1978, O: Iron Fist 4.00
❑55, Feb 1979 .... 4.00
❑56, Apr 1979, O: Se-or Suerte II (Jaime Garcia). 1: Se-or Suerte II (Jaime Garcia) 3.00
❑57, Jun 1979, A: X-Men 12.00
❑58, Aug 1979, 1: El Aguila; 1: El Aguila (Alejandro Montoya) 3.00
❑59, Oct 1979, BL (c); BL, TVE (a) 3.00
❑60, Dec 1979, BL (c); BL (a) 3.00
❑61, Feb 1980, BL (c); BL, KGa (a) 3.00
❑62, Apr 1980, KGa (c); BL, KGa (a); D: Thunderbolt 3.00
❑63, Jun 1980, BL (c); BL, KGa (a) 3.00
❑64, Aug 1980, BL (c); BL, KGa (a) 3.00
❑65, Oct 1980, BL (c); BL, KGa (a); V: El Aguila 3.00
❑66, Dec 1980, FM (c); FM, KGa (a); 2: Sabretooth 20.00
❑67, Feb 1981, FM (c); BL (w); FM, KGa (a) 2.00
❑68, Apr 1981, FM (c); BL, FM (a) 2.00
❑69, May 1981 .... 2.00
❑70, Jun 1981, FM (c); FM, KGa (a); O: Colleen Wing 2.00
❑71, Jul 1981, FM (c); FM, KGa (a) 2.00
❑72, Aug 1981, FM (c); FM, KGa (a) 2.00
❑73, Sep 1981, FM (c); FM (a); A: ROM. Story continues in ROM #23 .... 2.00
❑74, Oct 1981, FM (c); KGa (a) 2.00
❑75, Nov 1981, origins 2.00
❑76, Dec 1981, FM (a) 2.00
❑77, Jan 1982, A: Daredevil 2.00
❑78, Feb 1982, A: Sabretooth. V: El Aguila 5.00
❑79, Mar 1982 .... 2.00
❑80, Apr 1982, FM (c); FM (a); V: Montenegro 2.00
❑81, May 1982 .... 2.00
❑82, Jun 1982 .... 2.00
❑83, Jul 1982 .... 2.00
❑84, Aug 1982, A: Sabretooth 6.00
❑85, Sep 1982 .... 2.00
❑86, Oct 1982, A: Moon Knight 2.00
❑87, Nov 1982, A: Moon Knight 2.00
❑88, Dec 1982 .... 2.00
❑89, Jan 1983 .... 2.00
❑90, Feb 1983, KB (w); A: Unus the Untouchable. V: Unus. Kurt Busiek's first Marvel work 2.00
❑91, Mar 1983 .... 2.00
❑92, Apr 1983, KB (w); 1: Eel II (Edward Lavell). V: Hammerhead 2.00
❑93, May 1983, KB (w); V: Chemistro ... 2.00
❑94, Jun 1983, KB (w); 1: Chemistro III (Calvin Carr) 2.00
❑95, Jul 1983, KB (w) 2.00
❑96, Aug 1983, KB (w); V: Chemistro 2.00
❑97, Sep 1983, KB (w); V: Fera 2.00
❑98, Oct 1983, KB (w) 2.00
❑99, Nov 1983, AM (c); KB (w); V: Fera. 2.00
❑100, Dec 1983, Giant-size; KB (w); V: Khan 2.00
❑101, Jan 1984 .... 2.00
❑102, Feb 1984, RHo (c); KB (w); RHo (a) 2.00
❑103, Mar 1984 .... 2.00
❑104, Apr 1984 .... 2.00
❑105, May 1984, KB (w); RHo (a) 2.00
❑106, Jun 1984 .... 2.00
❑107, Jul 1984 .... 2.00
❑108, Aug 1984 .... 2.00
❑109, Sep 1984, V: Reaper 2.00
❑110, Oct 1984 .... 2.00
❑111, Nov 1984 .... 2.00
❑112, Dec 1984 .... 2.00
❑113, Jan 1985, D: Solarr 2.00
❑114, Feb 1985, JBy (c) 2.00
❑115, Mar 1985 .... 2.00
❑116, Apr 1985 .... 2.00
❑117, May 1985 .... 2.00
❑118, Jul 1985 .... 2.00
❑119, Sep 1985 .... 2.00
❑120, Nov 1985 .... 2.00
❑121, Jan 1986, Secret Wars II 2.00
❑122, Mar 1986 .... 2.00
❑123, May 1986 .... 2.00
❑124, Jul 1986 .... 2.00
❑125, Sep 1986, D: Iron Fist (H'yithri double) 2.00
❑Ann 1, Jan 1976 .... 3.50

Power of Prime
Malibu / Ultraverse

❑1, Jul 1995; story continues in Prime #25 and #26 .... 2.50
❑2, Aug 1995; O: Prime 2.50
❑3, Sep 1995; O: Prime 2.50
❑4, Nov 1995; O: Prime 2.50

Power of Shazam
DC

❑1, Mar 1995 JOy (c); JOy (w) 3.00
❑2, Apr 1995; JOy (c); JOy (w); V: Arson Fiend 2.00
❑3, May 1995; JOy (c); JOy (w); V: Ibac 2.00
❑4, Jun 1995; JOy (c); JOy (w); Return of Mary Marvel, Tawky Tawny 2.00
❑5, Jul 1995 JOy (c); JOy (w) 2.00
❑6, Aug 1995; JOy (c); JOy (w); Return of Captain Nazi; Freddy Freeman and grandfather injured 2.00
❑7, Sep 1995; JOy (c); JOy (w); Return of Captain Marvel Jr 2.00
❑8, Oct 1995 JOy (c); JOy (w); CS (a); A: Minuteman. A: Bulletman. A: Spy Smasher 2.00
❑9, Nov 1995 JOy (c); JOy (w) 2.00
❑10, Dec 1995; JOy (c); JOy (w); JOy (a); O: Satanus. O: Blaze. O: Black Adam. O: Rock of Eternity. O: Shazam 2.00
❑11, Jan 1996; JOy (c); JOy (w); CS (a); A: Bulletman. Return of Ibis; Return of Uncle Marvel; Return of Marvel Family 1.75
❑12, Feb 1996; JOy (c); JOy (w); JOy (a); O: Seven Deadly Foes of Man 1.75
❑13, Mar 1996 JOy (c); JOy (w) 1.75
❑14, Apr 1996; JOy (c); JOy (w); GK (a); 1: Chain Lightning. Captain Marvel Jr. solo story 1.75
❑15, Jun 1996 JOy (c); JOy (w) 1.75
❑16, Jul 1996 JOy (c); JOy (w) 1.75
❑17, Aug 1996 JOy (c); JOy (w); CS (a) 1.75
❑18, Sep 1996 JOy (c); JOy (w) 1.75
❑19, Oct 1996; JOy (c); JOy (w); GK, JSa (a); A: Minuteman. Captain Marvel Jr. vs. Captain Nazi 1.75
❑20, Nov 1996; JOy (c); JOy (w); A: Superman. Final Night 1.75
❑21, Dec 1996 JOy (c); JOy (w); A: Plastic Man 1.75
❑22, Jan 1997 JOy (c); JOy (w); A: Batman 1.75
❑23, Feb 1997; JOy (c); JOy (w); V: Mr. Atom 1.75
❑24, Mar 1997 JOy (c); JOy (w); A: C.C. Batson. A: Baron Blitzkrieg. A: Spy Smasher 1.75
❑25, Apr 1997; JOy (c); JOy (w); V: Ibac. C.C. Batson as Captain Marvel 1.75
❑26, May 1997; Shazam attempts to set time right again 1.75
❑27, Jun 1997; JOy (c); JOy (w); A: Waverider. time is restored to proper course 1.75
❑28, Jul 1997 JOy (c); JOy (w); DG (a).. 1.75
❑29, Aug 1997 JOy (c); JOy (w); A: Hoppy the Marvel Bunny 1.75
❑30, Sep 1997; JOy (c); JOy (w); V: Mr. Finish. Mary receives new costume 1.75
❑31, Oct 1997; JOy (c); JOy (w); Genesis; Billy and Mary reveal their identities to the Bromfields 1.95
❑32, Nov 1997; 1: Windshear 1.95
❑33, Dec 1997; JOy (c); JOy (w); Face cover 1.95

Other grades: Multiply price above by 5/6 for VF/NM • 2/3 for VERY FINE • 1/3 for FINE • 1/5 for VERY GOOD • 1/8 for GOOD

Rain

Memories of Germany after World War II
©Tundra

Ralph Snart Adventures

Fed-up man decides to go insane
©Now

Rampaging Hulk

Magazine becomes simply "Hulk!"
©Marvel

Ranma 1/2

Boy turns into girl, dad turns into panda
©Viz

Ravage 2099

Stan Lee creates character for future line
©Marvel

N-MINT

❑34, Jan 1998 JOy (c); JOy (w); A: Gangbuster 1.95
❑35, Feb 1998; A: Starman. continues in Starman #40 1.95
❑36, Mar 1998 JOy (c); JOy (w); A: Starman 1.95
❑37, Apr 1998; JOy (c); JOy (w); CM3 vs. Doctor Morpheus 1.95
❑38, May 1998 JOy (c); JOy (w) 1.95
❑39, Jun 1998 1.95
❑40, Jul 1998 1.95
❑41, Aug 1998; JOy (c); JOy (w); D: Mr. Mind 1.95
❑42, Sep 1998 A: Chain Lightning 1.95
❑43, Oct 1998; kids on life support 2.50
❑44, Dec 1998 A: Black Adam. A: Thunder 2.50
❑45, Jan 1999 A: Justice League of America 2.50
❑46, Feb 1999; JOy (c); JOy (w); JOy (a); A: Superman. A: Black Adam. V: Superman 2.50
❑47, Mar 1999; JOy (w); JOy (a); A: Black Adam. Final Issue 2.50
❑1000000, Nov 1998 JOy (c); JOy (w); JOy (a) 4.00
❑Ann 1, ca. 1996; JOy (c); JOy (w); 1996; Legends of the Dead Earth 2.95

Power of Strong Man
AC

❑1, b&w; Reprints 2.50

Power of the Atom
DC

❑1, Aug 1988 1.00
❑2, Sep 1988 1.00
❑3, Oct 1988; V: Strobe 1.00
❑4, Nov 1988; Bonus Book #8 1.00
❑5, Dec 1988 1.00
❑6, Win 1988; V: Chronos 1.00
❑7, Hol 1988; Invasion! 1.00
❑8, Jan 1989; Invasion! 1.00
❑9, Feb 1989 1.00
❑10, Mar 1989; V: Humbug 1.00
❑11, Apr 1989 1.00
❑12, May 1989 1.00
❑13, Jun 1989 1.00
❑14, Jul 1989; V: Humbug 1.00
❑15, Aug 1989 1.00
❑16, Sep 1989 1.00
❑17, Oct 1989 1.00
❑18, Nov 1989; Last issue 1.00

Power Pachyderms
Marvel

❑1, Sep 1989; one-shot parody 1.00

Power Pack
Marvel

❑1, Aug 1984; Giant-size; 1&O: Mass Master. 1&O: Power Pack. 1&O: Lightspeed. V: Snarks 2.00
❑2, Sep 1984 1.50
❑3, Oct 1984 1.00
❑4, Nov 1984 1.00
❑5, Dec 1984 1.00
❑6, Jan 1985, A: Spider-Man 1.00
❑7, Feb 1985, A: Cloak & Dagger 1.00
❑8, Mar 1985, A: Cloak & Dagger 1.00
❑9, Apr 1985, BA (a) 1.00

N-MINT

❑10, May 1985, BA (a) 2.00
❑11, Jun 1985 1.00
❑12, Jul 1985, A: X-Men. 1: Annalee 1.00
❑13, Aug 1985, BA, BWi (c); BA, BWi (a) 1.00
❑14, Sep 1985, BWi (c); BWi (a) 1.00
❑15, Oct 1985, BWi (c); BWi (a) 1.00
❑16, Nov 1985, 1: Kofi 1.00
❑17, Dec 1985 1.00
❑18, Jan 1986, BA (a); Secret Wars II 1.00
❑19, Feb 1986; Giant-size; BA (a); A: Wolverine 1.50
❑20, Mar 1986 A: New Mutants 1.00
❑21, Apr 1986 BA (a) 1.00
❑22, May 1986 1.00
❑23, Jun 1986 1.00
❑24, Jul 1986 1.00
❑25, Aug 1986; Giant-size 1.25
❑26, Oct 1986 A: Cloak & Dagger 1.00
❑27, Dec 1986; A: Wolverine. A: Sabretooth. Mutant Massacre 4.00
❑28, Feb 1987 A: Fantastic Four. A: Avengers 1.00
❑29, Apr 1987; Giant-size DGr (c); DGr (a); A: Hobgoblin. A: Spider-Man 1.00
❑30, Jun 1987 VM (a) 1.00
❑31, Aug 1987; 1: Trash 1.00
❑32, Oct 1987 1.00
❑33, Nov 1987 1.00
❑34, Jan 1988 1.00
❑35, Feb 1988; Fall of Mutants 1.00
❑36, Apr 1988 1.00
❑37, May 1988 1.00
❑38, Jul 1988 1.00
❑39, Aug 1988 1.00
❑40, Sep 1988 1.00
❑41, Nov 1988 1.00
❑42, Dec 1988; Inferno 1.00
❑43, Jan 1989; Inferno 1.00
❑44, Mar 1989; Inferno 1.50
❑45, Apr 1989 1.50
❑46, May 1989 A: Punisher 1.50
❑47, Jul 1989 1.50
❑48, Sep 1989 1.50
❑49, Oct 1989 1.50
❑50, Nov 1989; Giant-size 2.00
❑51, Dec 1989; 1: Numinus 1.50
❑52, Dec 1989 1.50
❑53, Jan 1990; Acts of Vengeance 1.50
❑54, Feb 1990 1.50
❑55, Apr 1990 A: Mysterio 1.50
❑56, Jun 1990 1.50
❑57, Jul 1990; Nova apperance 1.50
❑58, Sep 1990; A: Galactus 1.50
❑59, Oct 1990 1.50
❑60, Nov 1990 1.50
❑61, Dec 1990 1.50
❑62, Jan 1991; Final Issue 2.00
❑Holiday 1, Feb 1992; magazine-sized 2.50

Power Pack
Marvel

❑1, Aug 2000 2.99

Power Pack
Marvel

❑1, May 2005 2.99
❑2, Jun 2005 2.99

N-MINT

❑3, Jul 2005 2.99
❑4, Aug 2005 2.99

Power Plays
Millennium

❑1, Feb 1995 2.95

Power Plays
AC

❑1, b&w; Summer 1985 1.75
❑2, Fal 1985, b&w 1.75

Power Plays
Extrava-Gandt

❑1, b&w 2.00
❑2 2.00
❑3, b&w 2.00

Powerpuff Girls
DC

❑1, May 2000 5.00
❑2, Jun 2000 3.00
❑3, Jul 2000 2.50
❑4, Aug 2000 2.00
❑5, Sep 2000 1.99
❑6, Oct 2000 1.99
❑7, Nov 2000 1.99
❑8, Dec 2000 1.99
❑9, Jan 2001 1.99
❑10, Feb 2001 1.99
❑11, Mar 2001 1.99
❑12, Apr 2001 1.99
❑13, May 2001 1.99
❑14, Jun 2001 1.99
❑15, Jul 2001 1.99
❑16, Aug 2001 1.99
❑17, Sep 2001 1.99
❑18, Oct 2001 1.99
❑19, Nov 2001 1.99
❑20, Dec 2001 1.99
❑21, Jan 2002 1.99
❑22, Feb 2002 1.99
❑23, Mar 2002 1.99
❑24, Apr 2002 1.99
❑25, May 2002, JBy (a) 1.99
❑26, Jun 2002 1.99
❑27, Jul 2002 1.99
❑28, Aug 2002 1.99
❑29, Oct 2002 2.25
❑30, Nov 2002 2.25
❑31, Dec 2002 2.25
❑32, Jan 2003 2.25
❑33, Feb 2003 2.25
❑34, Mar 2003 2.25
❑35, Apr 2003 2.25
❑36, May 2003 2.25
❑37, Jun 2003 2.25
❑38, Jul 2003 2.25
❑39, Aug 2003 2.25
❑40, Sep 2003 2.25
❑41, Oct 2003 2.25
❑42, Nov 2003 2.25
❑43, Dec 2003 2.25
❑44, Jan 2004 2.25
❑45, Feb 2004 2.25
❑46, Mar 2004 2.25
❑47, Apr 2004 2.25
❑48, May 2004 2.25

Other grades: Multiply price above by 5/6 for VF/NM • 2/3 for VERY FINE • 1/3 for FINE • 1/5 for VERY GOOD • 1/8 for GOOD

❑49, Jun 2004 ... 2.25
❑50, Jul 2004 ... 2.25
❑51, Aug 2004 ... 2.25
❑52, Sep 2004 ... 2.25
❑53, Oct 2004 ... 2.25
❑54, Nov 2004 ... 2.25
❑55, Dec 2004, Comes with free Heroscape #1: The Battle of All Time comic insert; Includes 2 Weird n' Wild Creatures trading cards ... 2.25
❑56, Jan 2005 ... 2.25
❑57, Feb 2005 ... 2.25
❑58, Mar 2005 ... 2.25
❑59, Apr 2005 ... 2.25
❑60, May 2005 ... 2.25
❑61, Jun 2005 ... 2.25
❑62, Jul 2005 ... 2.25
❑63, Aug 2005 ... 2.25
❑64, Sep 2005 ... 2.25
❑65, Oct 2005 ... 2.25
❑66, Nov 2005 ... 2.25
❑67, Dec 2005 ... 2.25
❑68, Jan 2006; Includes Heroscape #4 insert ... 2.25
❑69, Feb 2006 ... 2.25
❑70, Mar 2006, Reprints issue #1, new cover ... 2.25

Powerpuff Girls Double Whammy
DC

❑1, Dec 2000; Collects stories from Powerpuff Girls #1-2, Dexter's Laboratory #7 ... 5.00

Power Rangers Turbo: Into the Fire
Acclaim

❑1 ... 4.50

Power Rangers Zeo
Image

❑1, Sep 1996 ... 2.50
❑2, Oct 1996 ... 2.50

Powers
Image

❑1, Apr 2000 BMB (w) ... 7.00
❑2, May 2000 BMB (w) ... 6.00
❑3, Jun 2000; BMB (w); #1 in indicia ... 5.00
❑4, Aug 2000 BMB (w) ... 3.50
❑5, Sep 2000 BMB (w) ... 4.00
❑6, Oct 2000 BMB (w) ... 4.00
❑7, Nov 2000; BMB (w); Guest Starring Warren Ellis ... 4.00
❑8, Dec 2001 BMB (w) ... 4.00
❑9, Jan 2001 BMB (w) ... 4.00
❑10, Mar 2001 BMB (w) ... 4.00
❑11, Apr 2001 BMB (w) ... 2.95
❑12, Jun 2001 BMB (w) ... 2.95
❑13, Jun 2001 BMB (w) ... 2.95
❑14, Jul 2001 BMB (w) ... 2.95
❑15, Aug 2001 BMB (w) ... 2.95
❑16, Sep 2001 BMB (w) ... 2.95
❑17, Oct 2001 BMB (w) ... 2.95
❑18, Nov 2001 BMB (w) ... 2.95
❑19, Dec 2001 BMB (w) ... 2.95
❑20, Jan 2002 BMB (w) ... 2.95
❑21, ca. 2002 BMB (w) ... 2.95
❑22, ca. 2002 BMB (w) ... 2.95
❑23, ca. 2002 BMB (w) ... 2.95
❑24, ca. 2002 BMB (w) ... 2.95
❑25, ca. 2002 BMB (w) ... 2.95
❑26, Dec 2002 BMB (w) ... 2.95
❑27, Feb 2003 BMB (w) ... 2.95
❑28, Jan 2003 BMB (w) ... 2.95
❑29, Feb 2003 ... 2.95
❑30, Mar 2003 ... 2.95
❑31, Apr 2003 ... 2.95
❑32, Jun 2003 ... 2.95
❑33, Aug 2003 ... 2.95
❑34, Oct 2003 ... 2.95
❑35, Nov 2003 ... 2.95
❑36, Jan 2004 ... 2.95
❑37, Apr 2004 ... 2.95

Powers Coloring/Activity Book
Image

❑1, Feb 2001 ... 1.50

Powers
Marvel

❑1, Sep 2004 ... 2.95
❑2, Sep 2004 ... 2.95
❑3, Oct 2004 ... 2.95
❑4, Oct 2004 ... 2.95
❑5, Nov 2004 ... 2.95
❑6, Dec 2004 ... 2.95
❑7, Jan 2005 ... 2.95
❑8, Feb 2005 ... 2.95
❑9, Mar 2005 ... 2.95
❑10, Apr 2005 ... 2.95
❑11 2005 ... 2.95
❑12/Bendis, Oct 2005 ... 4.00
❑12/Oeming, Oct 2005 ... 2.95
❑13 2005 ... 2.95
❑14, Jan 2006 ... 2.95
❑15, Feb 2006 ... 2.95
❑16, Mar 2006 ... 2.95
❑17, May 2006 ... 2.95
❑18, Aug 2006 ... 2.95
❑19, Oct 2006 ... 2.95
❑20, Dec 2006 ... 2.95
❑21, Feb 2007 ... 2.95

Powers That Be
Broadway

❑1, Nov 1995; 1: Fatale. 1: Star Seed. Fatale and Star Seed; 1st comic from Broadway Comics ... 2.25
❑2, Dec 1995; Star Seed ... 2.50
❑2/Ashcan, Sep 1995, b&w; giveaway preview edition; Star Seed ... 1.00
❑3, Jan 1996; Star Seed ... 2.50
❑3/Ashcan, Oct 1995, b&w; giveaway preview edition; Star Seed ... 1.00
❑4, Feb 1996; Star Seed ... 2.50
❑5, Apr 1996; 1: Marnie. V: Gina and Charlotte. Star Seed ... 2.50
❑6, May 1996; 1: Ajax. Star Seed ... 2.95
❑7, Jul 1996; Title changes to Star Seed ... 2.95
❑8 1996 ... 2.95
❑9, Oct 1996 ... 2.95

Prairie Moon and Other Stories
Dark Horse

❑1, b&w; Rick Geary ... 2.25

Preacher
DC / Vertigo

❑1, Apr 1995; 1: Jesse Custer; 1: The Saint of Killers; 1: Cassidy; 1: Tulip ... 13.00
❑2, May 1995 1: The Saint of Killers ... 6.00
❑3, Jun 1995 ... 5.00
❑4, Jul 1995 ... 5.00
❑5, Aug 1995 ... 5.00
❑6, Sep 1995 ... 3.50
❑7, Oct 1995 ... 3.50
❑8, Nov 1995 ... 3.50
❑9, Dec 1995 ... 3.50
❑10, Jan 1996 ... 3.50
❑11, Feb 1996 ... 3.00
❑12, Mar 1996 ... 3.00
❑13, Apr 1996 ... 3.00
❑14, Jun 1996 ... 3.00
❑15, Jul 1996 ... 3.00
❑16, Aug 1996 ... 2.50
❑17, Sep 1996 ... 2.50
❑18, Oct 1996; Vietnam flashback story ... 2.50
❑19, Nov 1996 ... 2.50
❑20, Dec 1996 ... 2.50
❑21, Jan 1997 ... 2.50
❑22, Feb 1997 ... 2.50
❑23, Mar 1997 ... 2.50
❑24, Apr 1997 ... 2.50
❑25, May 1997; O: Cassidy ... 2.50
❑26, Jun 1997; O: Cassidy ... 2.50
❑27, Jul 1997 ... 2.50
❑28, Aug 1997 ... 2.50
❑29, Sep 1997 A: You-Know-Who ... 2.50
❑30, Oct 1997 A: You-Know-Who ... 2.50
❑31, Nov 1997 ... 2.50
❑32, Dec 1997 ... 2.50
❑33, Jan 1998 ... 2.50
❑34, Feb 1998 ... 2.50
❑35, Mar 1998 ... 2.50
❑36, Apr 1998 ... 2.50
❑37, May 1998 ... 2.50
❑38, Jun 1998 A: You-Know-Who ... 2.50
❑39, Jul 1998; Jesse loses an eye; Starr loses a leg ... 2.50
❑40, Aug 1998 ... 2.50
❑41, Sep 1998; six months later; Jesse becomes sheriff of Salvation, Texas ... 2.50
❑42, Oct 1998; 1: Odin Quincannon ... 2.50
❑43, Nov 1998; Jesse's mother's story ... 2.50
❑44, Dec 1998 ... 2.50
❑45, Jan 1999 ... 2.50
❑46, Feb 1999 ... 2.50
❑47, Mar 1999 ... 2.50
❑48, Apr 1999; D: Odin Quincannon ... 2.50
❑49, May 1999 ... 2.50
❑50, Jun 1999; Giant-size; JLee (a) ... 3.75
❑51, Jul 1999; 100 Bullets preview ... 4.00
❑52, Aug 1999 ... 4.00
❑53, Sep 1999 ... 4.00
❑54, Oct 1999 ... 4.00
❑55, Nov 1999 ... 4.00
❑56, Dec 1999 ... 4.00
❑57, Jan 2000 ... 4.00
❑58, Feb 2000 ... 4.00
❑59, Mar 2000 ... 4.00
❑60, Apr 2000 ... 4.00
❑61, May 2000 ... 4.00
❑62, Jun 2000 ... 4.00
❑63, Jul 2000 ... 4.00
❑64, Aug 2000 ... 4.00
❑65, Sep 2000; D: Cassidy; D: Jesse ... 4.00
❑66, Oct 2000; Giant-size; DaG, BB (a); Final Issue ... 3.75

Preacher Special: Cassidy: Blood & Whiskey
DC / Vertigo

❑1, Feb 1998, prestige format; One-shot ... 5.95

Preacher Special: One Man's War
DC / Vertigo

❑1, Mar 1998, O: Starr ... 5.00

Preacher Special: Saint of Killers
DC / Vertigo

❑1, Aug 1996 ... 3.00
❑2, Sep 1996 ... 3.00
❑3, Oct 1996 ... 3.00
❑4, Nov 1996 ... 3.00

Preacher Special: Tall in the Saddle
DC / Vertigo

❑1, Feb 2000 ... 4.95

Preacher Special: The Good Old Boys
DC / Vertigo

❑1, Aug 1997, One-shot ... 4.95

Preacher Special: The Story of You-Know-Who
DC / Vertigo

❑1, Dec 1996, O: You-Know-Who; One-shot ... 4.95

Precious Metal
Arts Industria

❑1, Dec 1990, b&w; Adult ... 2.50

Predator
Dark Horse

❑1, Jun 1989 ... 5.00
❑1/2nd; 2nd printing ... 2.50
❑2, Sep 1989 ... 3.50
❑3, Dec 1989 ... 3.00
❑4, Mar 1990 ... 3.00

Predator 2
Dark Horse

❑1, Feb 1991; Photo cover; Includes trading cards ... 3.00
❑2, Jun 1991; Photo cover; Includes trading cards ... 3.00

Predator: Bad Blood
Dark Horse

❑1, Dec 1993 ... 2.50
❑2, Feb 1994 ... 2.50
❑3, May 1994 ... 2.50
❑4, Jun 1994 ... 2.50

Predator: Big Game
Dark Horse

❑1, Mar 1991; trading cards ... 2.50
❑2, Apr 1991; no trading cards despite cover advisory ... 2.50
❑3, May 1991; trading cards ... 2.50
❑4, Jun 1991 ... 2.50

Predator: Captive
Dark Horse

❑1, Apr 1998; NN; One-shot ... 2.95

Raver

Guy occasionally visits parallel dimension
©Malibu

Rawhide Kid

Marvel's most successful Western character
©Marvel

Rawhide Kid

Pilloried revamp packed with gay jokes
©Marvel

Ray

His dad was exposed to a "light bomb"
©DC

Razor

Razor-wearing woman avenges father
©London Night

N-MINT

Predator: Cold War
Dark Horse

❑1, Sep 1991 .... 2.50
❑2, Oct 1991 .... 2.50
❑3, Nov 1991 .... 2.50
❑4, Dec 1991 .... 2.50

Predator: Dark River
Dark Horse

❑1, Jul 1996 .... 2.95
❑2, Aug 1996 .... 2.95
❑3, Sep 1996 .... 2.95
❑4, Oct 1996 .... 2.95

Predator: Hell & Hot Water
Dark Horse

❑1, Apr 1997; uninked pencils 2.95
❑2, May 1997; uninked pencils 2.95
❑3, Jun 1997; uninked pencils 2.95

Predator: Hell Come a Walkin'
Dark Horse

❑1, Feb 1998; Predator in Civil War 2.95
❑2, Mar 1998; Predator in Civil War 2.95

Predator: Homeworld
Dark Horse

❑1, Mar 1999 .... 2.95
❑2, Apr 1999 .... 2.95
❑3, May 1999 .... 2.95
❑4, Jun 1999 .... 2.95

Predator: Invaders from the Fourth Dimension
Dark Horse

❑1, Jul 1994; NN; One-shot 3.95

Predator: Jungle Tales
Dark Horse

❑1, Mar 1995; collects Predator: Rite of Passage from DHC #1 and 2; Predator: The Pride of Nghasa from DHC #10-12 .... 2.95

Predator: Kindred
Dark Horse

❑1, Dec 1996 .... 2.50
❑2, Jan 1997 .... 2.50
❑3, Feb 1997 .... 2.50
❑4, Mar 1997 .... 2.50

Predator: Nemesis
Dark Horse

❑1, Dec 1997 .... 2.95
❑2, Jan 1998 .... 2.95

Predator: Primal
Dark Horse

❑1, Jul 1997, Predator vs. bears 2.95
❑2, Aug 1997, Predator vs. bears 2.95

Predator: Race War
Dark Horse

❑0, Apr 1993 .... 2.50
❑1, Feb 1993 .... 2.50
❑2, Mar 1993 .... 2.50
❑3, Aug 1993 .... 2.50
❑4, Oct 1993 .... 2.50

Predator: Strange Roux
Dark Horse

❑1, Nov 1996; recipe for Strange Roux in back 2.95

N-MINT

Predator: The Bloody Sands of Time
Dark Horse

❑1, Feb 1992; Predator in WW I 2.75
❑2, Feb 1992; Predator in WW I 2.75

Predator vs. Judge Dredd
Dark Horse / Egmont

❑1, Oct 1997 .... 2.50
❑2, Nov 1997 .... 2.50
❑3, Dec 1997 .... 2.50

Predator vs. Magnus Robot Fighter
Dark Horse / Valiant

❑1, Nov 1992 .... 3.00
❑1/Platinum, Nov 1992; Platinum promotional edition 10.00
❑2, Dec 1993; trading cards 3.00

Predator: Xenogenesis
Dark Horse

❑1, Aug 1999 .... 2.95
❑2, Sep 1999 .... 2.95
❑3, Oct 1999 .... 2.95
❑4, Nov 1999 .... 2.95

Premiere
Diversity

❑1; 1500 printed 2.75
❑1/Gold; Gold limited edition (175 printed); Signed & numbered 4.00
❑1/Ltd.; Limited edition (175 printed); Signed & numbered 3.00
❑2; Includes poster 2.75

Preservation of Obscurity
Lump of Squid

❑1 .... 2.75
❑2 .... 2.75

President Dad
Tokyopop

❑1, Dec 2004 .... 9.99
❑2, Mar 2005 .... 9.99
❑3, Jun 2005 .... 9.99
❑4, Oct 2005 .... 9.99

Pressed Tongue
Fantagraphics

❑1, Feb 1994, b&w; Adult 2.95
❑3, Dec 1994, b&w; Adult 2.95

Presto Kid
AC

❑1, b&w; Reprints 2.50

Pretear
ADV Manga

❑1, ca. 2004 .... 9.99
❑2, ca. 2004 .... 9.99
❑3, ca. 2004 .... 9.99
❑4, ca. 2005 .... 9.99

Pre-Teen Dirty-Gene Kung-Fu Kangaroos
Blackthorne

❑1, Aug 1986 A: TMNT 2.00
❑2, Nov 1986 .... 2.00
❑3 1987 .... 2.00

Prey
Monster

❑1, b&w 2.25

N-MINT

❑2, b&w 2.25
❑3, b&w 2.25

Prey for Us Sinners
Fantaco

❑1, NN 4.95

Prez
DC

❑1, Sep 1973 .... 12.00
❑2, Nov 1973 .... 6.00
❑3, Jan 1974 .... 5.00
❑4, Mar 1974 .... 5.00

Pride & Joy
DC / Vertigo

❑1, Jul 1997 .... 2.50
❑2, Aug 1997 .... 2.50
❑3, Sep 1997 .... 2.50
❑4, Oct 1997 .... 2.50

Priest
Maximum

❑1, Aug 1996; 1: Priest 2.99
❑2, Sep 1996 .... 2.99
❑3, Oct 1996 .... 2.99

Primal
Dark Horse

❑1, Oct 1992 .... 2.50
❑2, Dec 1992 .... 2.50

Primal Force
DC

❑0, Oct 1994, 1&0: Primal Force 1.95
❑1, Nov 1994, 0: Leymen 1.95
❑2, Dec 1994 .... 1.95
❑3, Jan 1995 .... 1.95
❑4, Feb 1995 .... 1.95
❑5, Mar 1995 .... 1.95
❑6, Apr 1995 .... 1.95
❑7, May 1995 .... 1.95
❑8, Jun 1995, Black Condor II joins 2.25
❑9, Jul 1995 .... 2.25
❑10, Aug 1995 .... 2.25
❑11, Sep 1995 .... 2.25
❑12, Oct 1995 .... 2.25
❑13, Nov 1995, Underworld Unleashed 2.25
❑14, Dec 1995, Final Issue 2.25

Primal Rage
Sirius

❑1, Aug 1996, b&w 2.50
❑2, Oct 1996, b&w 2.50
❑3, Dec 1996, b&w 2.50
❑4, Feb 1997, b&w 2.50

Prime
Malibu / Ultraverse

❑½, May 1994; Wizard promotional edition 2.50
❑1, Jun 1993; 1: Prime. 1: Doctor Gross. Ultraverse 2.50
❑1/Hologram, Jun 1993; Holographic promotional edition; 1: Prime. 1: Doctor Gross 5.00
❑1/Ltd., Jun 1993; "Ultra-Limited" edition; 1: Prime. 1: Doctor Gross. foil stamped; $1.95 on cover 2.50
❑2, Jul 1993; Ultraverse; trading card 1.95
❑3, Aug 1993; 0: Prime 1.95

N-MINT

❑4, Sep 1993; 1: Maxi-Man. A: Prototype II (Jimmy Ruiz). V: Prototype. two different covers 1.95
❑5, Oct 1993; Rune 1.95
❑6, Nov 1993 .... 1.95
❑7, Dec 1993; Break-Thru 1.95
❑8, Jan 1994; O: Freex. A: Mantra 1.95
❑9, Feb 1994 .... 1.95
❑10, Mar 1994 A: Firearm 1.95
❑11, Apr 1994 .... 1.95
❑12, May 1994; flip-book with Ultraverse Premiere #3 .... 3.50
❑13, Jul 1994; Freex preview; two different covers 1.95
❑13/A, Jul 1994; variant cover 1.95
❑14, Sep 1994; 1: Papa Verite 1.95
❑15, Oct 1994 GP (c); GP (a) 1.95
❑16, Nov 1994; JOy, GP (c); 1: TurboCharge 1.95
❑17, Dec 1994 JOy (c) 1.95
❑18, Dec 1994 .... 1.95
❑19, Jan 1995 DC (a) 1.95
❑20, Mar 1995; 1: Phade 1.95
❑21, Apr 1995 JSa (a); A: Chelsea Clinton 1.95
❑22, May 1995 .... 1.95
❑23, Jun 1995 .... 1.95
❑24, Jun 1995 .... 1.95
❑25, Jul 1995; O: Prime. continued from Power of Prime #1 .... 1.95
❑26, Aug 1995; O: Prime. continues in Power of Prime #2 .... 1.95
❑Ann 1, Oct 1994; 1: new Prime. A: Hardcase. Prime: Gross and Disgusting 3.95
❑Ashcan 1, Aug 1994; ashcan edition 1.00

Prime
Malibu / Ultraverse

❑0, Sep 1995; Black September; #Infinity 1.50
❑0/A, Sep 1995; Black September; alternate cover 1.50
❑1, Oct 1995; Spider-Prime 1.50
❑2, Nov 1995 .... 1.50
❑3, Dec 1995 .... 1.50
❑4, Jan 1996; Kevin rejoins Prime body. 1.50
❑5, Feb 1996 .... 1.50
❑6, Mar 1996 .... 1.50
❑7, Apr 1996; Painted Cover 1.50
❑8, May 1996; Painted cover 1.50
❑9, Jun 1996 .... 1.50
❑10, Jul 1996 .... 1.50
❑11, Aug 1996 .... 1.50
❑12, Sep 1996 .... 1.50
❑13, Oct 1996 .... 1.50
❑14, Nov 1996 .... 1.50
❑15, Dec 1996; V: Lord Pumpkin; Final Issue 1.50

Prime 8 Creation
Two Morrows

❑1, Jul 2001, b&w 3.95

Prime/Captain America
Malibu / Ultraverse

❑1, Mar 1996 .... 3.95

Prime Cuts
Fantagraphics

❑1, Jan 1987; Adult 3.50
❑2, Mar 1987; Adult 3.50
❑3, May 1987; Adult 3.50
❑4 1987; Adult 3.50
❑5 1987; Adult 3.50
❑6 1987; Adult 3.50
❑7 1988; Adult 3.95
❑8, Apr 1988; Adult 3.95
❑9 1988; Adult 3.95
❑10, Dec 1988; Adult; b&w 3.95

Prime Cuts
Caliber

❑1 .... 2.95

Primer
Comico

❑1, Oct 1982, b&w; 1: Slaughterman. 1: Skrog. 1: Az 5.00
❑2 1982; MW (w); MW (a); 1: Argent. 1: Grendel I (Hunter Rose) 55.00
❑3 .... 4.00
❑4 1982, b&w; 1: Firebringer. 1: Laserman 4.00
❑5 1983; 1: The Maxx (original). 1st professional art by Sam Kieth 50.00
❑6, Feb 1984; RBy (a); 1: Evangeline 5.00

Primer
Comico

❑1, May 1996 .... 2.95

Prime Slime Tales
Mirage

❑1 1986, b&w; Published By Mirage Studio 1.50
❑2; Published By Mirage Studio 1.50
❑3, Nov 1986; Published By Now Comics 1.50
❑4, Jan 1987; Published By Now Comics 1.50

Prime vs. the Incredible Hulk
Malibu

❑0, Jul 1995; no cover price 5.00

Primitives
Sparetime

❑1, Jan 1995, b&w; 1: Primitives; O: Primitives 2.50
❑2, May 1995, b&w 2.50
❑3, Oct 1995, b&w 2.50

Primortals
Tekno

❑1, Mar 1995, Includes trading card 1.95
❑2, Apr 1995 .... 1.95
❑3, May 1995, Includes trading card 1.95
❑4, Jun 1995, Includes Steel Edition Teknophage #1 coupon 1.95
❑5, Jul 1995 .... 1.95
❑6, Aug 1995 .... 1.95
❑7, Sep 1995 .... 1.95
❑8, Oct 1995 .... 1.95
❑9, Nov 1995 .... 1.95
❑10, Dec 1995 .... 1.95
❑11, Dec 1995 .... 1.95
❑12, Jan 1996 .... 2.25
❑13, Mar 1996 .... 2.25
❑14, Apr 1996 .... 2.25
❑15, May 1996, Final Issue 2.25
❑16 .... 2.25

Primortals
Big

❑0, Jun 1996 .... 2.25
❑1, Jul 1996 .... 2.25
❑2, Aug 1996 .... 2.25
❑3, Sep 1996 .... 2.25
❑4, Oct 1996 .... 2.25
❑5, Nov 1996 .... 2.25
❑6, Dec 1996 .... 2.25
❑7, Jan 1997 .... 2.25
❑8, Feb 1997, b&w; Final Issue 2.25

Primortals Origins
Tekno

❑1, Jun 1995, O: Primortals 2.25
❑2, Jul 1995, O: Primortals 2.25

Primus
Charlton

❑1, Feb 1972 .... 7.00
❑2, Mar 1972 .... 4.00
❑3, May 1972 .... 4.00
❑4, Jun 1972 .... 4.00
❑5, Jul 1972 .... 3.00
❑6, Sep 1972 .... 3.00
❑7, Oct 1972 .... 3.00

Prince: Alter Ego
Piranha Music

❑1, Dec 1991 .... 2.00

Prince and the New Power Generation: Three Chains of Gold
DC / Piranha

❑1; NN 3.50

Prince and the Pauper
Dell

❑1, Jul 1962, 01-654-207 .... 15.00

Prince and the Pauper
Disney

❑1, squarebound 5.95

Prince Namor, the Sub-Mariner
Marvel

❑1, Sep 1984 .... 1.50
❑2, Oct 1984 .... 1.50
❑3, Nov 1984 .... 1.50
❑4, Dec 1984 .... 1.50

Prince Nightmare
Aaaargh!

❑1 .... 2.95

Princess and the Frog
NBM

❑1 .... 15.95

Princess Karanam and the Djinn of the Green Jug
Mu

❑1, b&w; NN 2.50

Princess Natasha
DC

❑1, Sep 2006 .... 2.25
❑2, Sep 2006 .... 2.25
❑3, Oct 2006 .... 2.25

Princess Prince
CPM Manga

❑1, Oct 2000 .... 2.95
❑1/A, Oct 2000; alternate wraparound cover 2.95
❑2, Nov 2000 .... 2.95
❑3, Dec 2000 .... 2.95
❑4, Jan 2001 .... 2.95
❑5, Feb 2001 .... 2.95
❑6, Mar 2001 .... 2.95
❑7, Apr 2001 .... 2.95
❑8, May 2001 .... 2.95
❑9, Jun 2001 .... 2.95
❑10, Jul 2001 .... 2.95

Princess Sally
Archie

❑1, Apr 1995 .... 1.50
❑2, May 1995 .... 1.50
❑3, Jun 1995 .... 1.50

Princess Tutu
ADV Manga

❑1, ca. 2005 .... 9.99
❑2, ca. 2005 .... 9.99

Prince Valiant
Marvel

❑1, Dec 1994; cardstock cover 3.95
❑2, Jan 1995; cardstock cover 3.95
❑3, Feb 1995; cardstock cover 3.95
❑4, Mar 1995; cardstock cover 3.95

Prince Valiant Monthly
Pioneer

❑1, b&w 4.95
❑2, b&w 4.95
❑3, b&w 4.95
❑4, b&w 4.95

Prince Vandal
Triumphant

❑1, Nov 1993; Unleashed! 2.50
❑2, Dec 1993; Unleashed! 2.50
❑3, Jan 1994 .... 2.50
❑4, Feb 1994 .... 2.50
❑5, Mar 1994 .... 2.50
❑6, Mar 1994 .... 2.50

Priority: White Heat
AC

❑1, Mar 1987 .... 1.75
❑2 .... 1.75

Prisoner
DC

❑1, Dec 1988; a 4.00
❑2, Jan 1989; b 4.00
❑3, Jan 1989; c 4.00
❑4, Feb 1989; d 4.00

Prisoner of Chillon
Tome

❑1, b&w 2.95

Prisonopolis
Mediawarp

❑1, Feb 1997, b&w 2.75
❑2, Apr 1997, b&w 2.75
❑3, Jun 1997 .... 2.75
❑4, Aug 1997 .... 2.75

Other grades: Multiply price above by 5/6 for VF/NM • 2/3 for VERY FINE • 1/3 for FINE • 1/5 for VERY GOOD • 1/8 for GOOD

Real Adventures of Jonny Quest

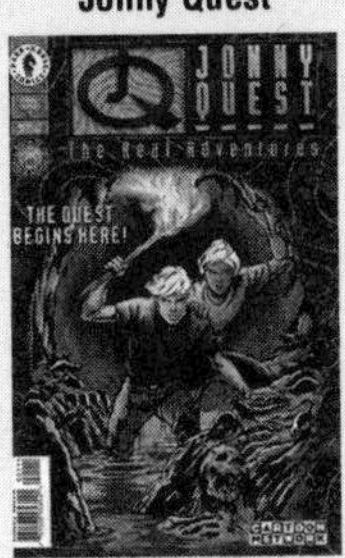

More with the TV cartoon hero
©Dark Horse

Real Ghostbusters

Based on cartoon version of film characters
©Now

Realm

Sword-and-sorcery themed series
©Arrow

Real Stuff

Critically acclaimed alternative comic
©Fantagraphics

R.E.B.E.L.S.

Once they were known as L.E.G.I.O.N.
©DC

	N-MINT

Private Beach: Fun and Perils in the Trudyverse
Antarctic

- ❑1, Jan 1995, b&w 2.75
- ❑2, Mar 1995, b&w 2.75
- ❑3, May 1995, b&w 2.75

Private Commissions
Forbidden Fruit

- ❑1, b&w; Adult 2.95
- ❑2, Mar 1992, b&w; Adult 2.95

Privateers
Vanguard

- ❑1, Aug 1987 ..... 1.50
- ❑2 ..... 1.50

Private Eyes
Eternity

- ❑1, Sep 1988, b&w; Saint reprints 1.95
- ❑2, Nov 1988, b&w; Saint reprints 1.95
- ❑3, Jan 1989, b&w; Saint reprints 1.95
- ❑4, May 1989 ..... 2.95
- ❑5, Aug 1989 ..... 3.50
- ❑6, Dec 1989 ..... 3.95

Pro
Image

- ❑1, Jul 2002, Adult 5.95

Pro Action Magazine
Marvel / NFL Properties

- ❑1, Jul 1994 ..... 2.95
- ❑2, Sep 1994 ..... 2.95
- ❑3, Nov 1994; magazine with bound-in Spider-Man comic book 2.95

Probe
Imperial

- ❑1 ..... 2.00
- ❑2 ..... 2.00
- ❑3 ..... 2.00

Prof. Coffin
Charlton

- ❑19, Oct 1985, WH (w); JSa, JAb, WH (a); Reprints from Midnight Tales #1 ..... 2.00
- ❑20, Dec 1985, Reprints from Midnight Tales #2 ..... 2.00
- ❑21, Feb 1986, TS, JSa, WH (a); Reprints from Midnight Tales #3 ..... 2.00

Professional: Golgo 13
Viz

- ❑1, Japanese 4.95
- ❑2, Japanese 4.95
- ❑3, Japanese 4.95

Professor Om
Innovation

- ❑1, May 1990 ..... 2.50

Professor Xavier and the X-Men
Marvel

- ❑1, Nov 1995; JDu (c); JDu (a); retells origin of team and first mission 1.50
- ❑2, Dec 1995; JDu (c); JDu (a); A: Vanisher. retells first Vanisher story 1.50
- ❑3, Jan 1996; retells first Blob story 1.50
- ❑4, Feb 1996; retells first meeting with Brotherhood of Evil Mutants 1.25
- ❑5, Mar 1996; retells first meeting with Brotherhood of Evil Mutants 1.25
- ❑6, Apr 1996 JDu (c); JDu (a) 1.25
- ❑7, May 1996; Sub-Mariner vs. Magneto 1.25
- ❑8, Jun 1996 ..... 1.25
- ❑9, Jul 1996 ..... 1.25
- ❑10, Aug 1996; V: Avengers 1.25
- ❑11, Sep 1996; A: Ka-Zar. Flipbook with Marvel Fanfare (2nd series) #1 ..... 1.00
- ❑12, Oct 1996; V: Juggernaut 1.00
- ❑13, Nov 1996; V: Juggernaut 1.00
- ❑14, Dec 1996 ..... 1.00
- ❑15, Jan 1997; V: Magneto. V: Stranger 1.00
- ❑16, Feb 1997; V: Sentinels 1.00
- ❑17, Mar 1997 ..... 1.00
- ❑18, Apr 1997; V: Sentinels; Final Issue 1.00

Profolio
Alchemy

- ❑1, Jul 1989, b&w 1.50
- ❑2; some color 2.50
- ❑3, b&w 2.50

Profolio
Alchemy

- ❑1 ..... 5.95

Progeny
Caliber

- ❑1, b&w; NN 4.95

Program Error: Battlebot
Phantasy

- ❑1 ..... 2.00

Project
DC / Paradox Press

- ❑1, ca. 1997, b&w; digest; short story collection 5.95
- ❑2, ca. 1997, b&w; digest; short story collection 5.95

Project A-Ko
Malibu

- ❑1, Mar 1994 ..... 2.95
- ❑2, Mar 1994 ..... 2.95
- ❑3, May 1994 ..... 2.95
- ❑4, Jun 1994 ..... 2.95

Project A-Ko 2
CPM

- ❑1, Apr 1995 ..... 2.95
- ❑2, Jun 1995 ..... 2.95
- ❑3, Aug 1995 ..... 2.95

Project A-Ko versus
CPM

- ❑1, Oct 1995 ..... 2.95
- ❑2, Dec 1995 ..... 2.95
- ❑3, Feb 1996 ..... 2.95
- ❑4, Apr 1996 ..... 2.95
- ❑5, Jun 1996; Final Issue 2.95

Project Arms
Viz

- ❑1, Sep 2002 ..... 3.25
- ❑2, Oct 2002 ..... 3.25
- ❑3, Nov 2002 ..... 3.25
- ❑4, Dec 2002 ..... 3.25
- ❑5, Jan 2003 ..... 3.25

Project: Dark Matter
Dimm Comics

- ❑1, Apr 1996, b&w 2.50
- ❑2, Jun 1996, b&w; cardstock cover 2.50
- ❑3, b&w; cardstock cover 2.50
- ❑4, Sep 1997, b&w 2.50

Project: Generation
Truth

- ❑1, Jun 2000, Distributed at San Diego Comic-Con 1.00
- ❑2, Sep 2000, Fall, 2000 ..... 1.00

Project: Hero
Vanguard

- ❑1, Aug 1987 ..... 1.50
- ❑2 ..... 1.50

Project Sex
Fantagraphics / Eros

- ❑1, Nov 1991, b&w; Adult 2.50

Project: Superior
Adhouse Books

- ❑1, ca. 2005 ..... 19.95

Project X
Kitchen Sink

- ❑1; Eastman/Bisley; bagged Thump'n Guts; poster; trading card 2.95

Promethea
DC / America's Best Comics

- ❑1, Aug 1999; ARo (c); AMo (w); O: Promethea 6.00
- ❑1/Variant, Aug 1999 ..... 7.00
- ❑2, Sep 1999 AMo (w) 4.00
- ❑3, Oct 1999 AMo (w) 2.95
- ❑4, Nov 1999 AMo (w); CV (a) 2.95
- ❑5, Dec 1999 AMo (w) 2.95
- ❑6, Mar 2000 AMo (w) 2.95
- ❑7, Apr 2000 AMo (w) 2.95
- ❑8, May 2000 AMo (w) 2.95
- ❑9, Sep 2000 AMo (w) 2.95
- ❑10, Oct 2000 AMo (w) 2.95
- ❑11, Dec 2000 AMo (w) 2.95
- ❑12, Feb 2001 AMo (w) 2.95
- ❑13, Apr 2001 AMo (w) 2.95
- ❑14, May 2001 AMo (w) 2.95
- ❑15, Jun 2001 AMo (w) 2.95
- ❑16, Jul 2001 AMo (w) 2.95
- ❑17, Aug 2001 AMo (w) 2.95
- ❑18, Sep 2001 AMo (w) 2.95
- ❑19, Oct 2001 AMo (w) 2.95
- ❑20, Nov 2001 AMo (w) 2.95
- ❑21, Aug 2002 AMo (w) 2.95
- ❑22, Nov 2002 AMo (w) 2.95
- ❑23, Dec 2002 AMo (w) 3.50
- ❑24, ca. 2003 ..... 2.95
- ❑25, May 2003 ..... 2.95
- ❑26, Aug 2003 ..... 2.95
- ❑27, Nov 2003 ..... 2.95
- ❑28, Feb 2004 ..... 2.95
- ❑29, May 2004, AMo (w) 2.95
- ❑30, Jul 2004 ..... 2.95
- ❑31, Oct 2004 ..... 2.95
- ❑32 2005; Final issue 4.00
- ❑32/Ltd 2005; Collects all 32 covers; signed by Alan Moore and J.H. Williams; 1,000 copies produced 125.00

Other grades: Multiply price above by 5/6 for VF/NM • 2/3 for VERY FINE • 1/3 for FINE • 1/5 for VERY GOOD • 1/8 for GOOD

N-MINT N-MINT N-MINT

Prometheus' Gift
Cat-Head
❑1, b&w; NN 2.25

Prometheus (Villains)
DC
❑1, Feb 1998; New Year's Evil 1.95

Promise
Viz
❑1, b&w; squarebound 5.95

Propellerman
Dark Horse
❑1, ca. 1993 2.95
❑2, ca. 1993; Includes trading cards 2.95
❑3, ca. 1993 2.95
❑4, ca. 1993 2.95
❑5, ca. 1994 2.95
❑6, ca. 1994 2.95
❑7, ca. 1994 2.95
❑8, ca. 1994; Includes trading cards 2.95

Prophecy of the Soul Sorcerer
Arcane
❑1, May 1999 2.95
❑2, Jul 1999 2.95
❑3, Jul 1999 2.95
❑Ashcan 1, Oct 1998 2.00

Prophecy of the Soul Sorcerer Preview Issue
Arcane
❑1 2.00

Prophecy of the Soul Sorcerer
Arcane
❑1, Mar 2000 2.95
❑2, Apr 2000 2.95
❑3, May 2000 2.95

Prophet
Image
❑0, Jul 1994 3.00
❑0/A, Jul 1994; San Diego Comic-Con edition 3.00
❑1, Oct 1993; RL (w); O: Prophet 3.00
❑1/Gold, Oct 1993; Gold edition 3.00
❑2, Nov 1993 FM (c); RL (w); FM (a) 2.50
❑3, Jan 1994 2.50
❑4, Feb 1994 2.50
❑4/Variant, Feb 1994; RL (w); Variant cover by Platt 3.00
❑5, Apr 1994 RL (w) 2.50
❑6, Jun 1994 RL (w) 2.50
❑7, Sep 1994 RL (w) 2.50
❑8, Nov 1994 2.50
❑9, Dec 1994 2.50
❑10, Jan 1995; Includes trading card 2.50

Prophet
Image
❑1, Aug 1995 3.50
❑1/Chromium, Aug 1995; Chromium cover 5.00
❑1/Holochrome, Aug 1995; Holochrome wraparound cover 6.00
❑2, Sep 1995 FM (c) 2.50
❑2/Platt, Sep 1995; alternate cover 4.00
❑3, Nov 1995 2.50
❑4, Feb 1996 A: NewMen 2.50
❑5, Feb 1996 2.50
❑6, Apr 1996 2.50
❑7, May 1996; A: Youngblood. Badrock in background on cover 2.50
❑8, Jul 1996 2.50
❑Ann 1/A, Sep 1995; polybagged with PowerCardz 4.00
❑Ann 1/B, Sep 1995; polybagged with PowerCardz 4.00

Prophet
Awesome
❑1, Mar 2000; Flip cover (McFarlane cover on back side) 2.99
❑1/A, Mar 2000; Red background, woman standing with sword, large man in background 2.99

Prophet Babewatch
Image
❑1, Dec 1995; cover says #1, indicia says #2 2.50

Prophet/Cable
Maximum
❑1, Jan 1997; crossover with Marvel 3.50
❑2, Mar 1997; cover says #1, indicia says #2; crossover with Marvel 3.50

Prophet/Chapel: Super Soldiers
Image
❑1/A, May 1996 2.50
❑1/B, May 1996; alternate cover (b&w) 2.50
❑2, Jun 1996 2.50

Proposition Player
DC / Vertigo
❑1, Dec 1999 2.50
❑2, Jan 2000 2.50
❑3, Feb 2000 2.50
❑4, Mar 2000 2.50
❑5, Apr 2000 2.50
❑6, May 2000 2.50

Protectors Handbook
Malibu
❑1, Nov 1992 2.50

Protectors
Malibu
❑1, Sep 1992; Split cover (in various colors) 1.95
❑1/CS, Sep 1992; with poster and wrapper 2.50
❑2, Oct 1992; with poster 2.50
❑3, Nov 1992; Includes poster 2.50
❑4, Dec 1992; Includes poster 2.50
❑5/A, Jan 1993; bullet hole; bagged 2.50
❑5/B, Jan 1993; Embossed cover; bullet hole 2.50
❑5/C, Jan 1993; Die-cut cover; bullet hole 2.95
❑6, Feb 1993; Includes poster 2.50
❑6/CS, Feb 1993; with poster 2.50
❑7, Mar 1993; 1: Night Mask II; Includes poster 2.50
❑8, Apr 1993 2.50
❑9, May 1993; Includes poster 2.50
❑10, Jun 1993; Includes poster 2.50
❑11, Jul 1993 2.50
❑12, Aug 1993; Includes poster 2.50
❑13, Sep 1993; Genesis 2.25
❑14, Oct 1993; Continued from Ex-Mutants #12 2.25
❑15, Nov 1993 2.25
❑16, Dec 1993 2.25
❑17, Jan 1994 2.50
❑18, Feb 1994 2.25
❑19, Mar 1994; Genesis 2.50
❑20, May 1994; Final Issue 2.50

Protectors
New York
❑1 1.70
❑2 1.70

Protheus
Caliber
❑1, ca. 1996, reprints Brazilian comic 2.95
❑2 2.95

Protista Chronicles
Xulu
❑1; no cover price 2.00

Prototykes Holiday Special/Hero Illustrated Holiday Special
Dark Horse
❑1 1.00
❑2, Dec 1994 JBy (w); JBy (a) 1.00

Prototype
Malibu / Ultraverse
❑0, Aug 1994; O: Prototype I (Bob Campbell). Reprints origin story from Malibu Sun plus new story 1.95
❑1, Aug 1993; 1: Prototype II (Jimmy Ruiz). 1: Prototype I (Bob Campbell). 1: Glare. 1: Veil. Ultraverse 2.50
❑1/Hologram, Aug 1993; Hologram cover limited edition; 1: Prototype II (Jimmy Ruiz). 1: Prototype I (Bob Campbell). 1: Glare. 1: Veil. hologram 5.00
❑2, Sep 1993; 1: Backstabber. A: Prime. 1.95
❑3, Oct 1993; Giant-size; Rune 2.50
❑4, Nov 1993; 1: Wrath 1.95
❑5, Dec 1993; A: Strangers. Break-Thru; Continued in Strangers #7 1.95
❑6, Jan 1994; 1: Arena 1.95
❑7, Feb 1994 1.95
❑8, Mar 1994 1.95
❑9, Apr 1994; 1: Prototype III (Donovan Jones) 1.95
❑10, May 1994 1.95
❑11, Jun 1994 1.95
❑12, Jul 1994 1.95
❑13, Aug 1994; KB (w); flipbook with Ultraverse Premiere #6 3.50
❑14, Oct 1994 1.95
❑15, Nov 1994 1.95
❑16, Dec 1994; 1: Wild Popes 1.95
❑17, Jan 1995 1.95
❑18, Feb 1995 2.50
❑GS 1, ca. 1994; Giant-Size edition 2.50

Prowler
Eclipse
❑1, Jul 1987; 1: Prowler 1.75
❑2, Aug 1987 1.75
❑3, Sep 1987 1.75
❑4, Oct 1987 1.75

Prowler
Marvel
❑1, Nov 1994 1.75
❑2, Dec 1994 1.75
❑3, Jan 1995 1.75
❑4, Feb 1995 1.75

Prowler in "White Zombie"
Eclipse
❑1, Oct 1988, b&w 2.00

Pro Wrestling's True Facts
Dan Pettiglio
❑1, Apr 1994, b&w; NN 2.95

Proximity Effect
Image
❑1, ca. 2004 9.99

Prudence & Caution
Defiant
❑1, May 1994, Double-size; English and Spanish versions 3.25
❑2, Jun 1994 2.50
❑3, Jul 1994 2.50
❑4, Aug 1994 2.50
❑5, Sep 1994 2.50
❑6, Oct 1994, Final Issue 2.50

Pryde & Wisdom
Marvel
❑1, Sep 1996 1.95
❑2, Oct 1996 1.95
❑3, Nov 1996; Final Issue 1.95

Pscythe
Image
❑1, Sep 2004, b&w 3.95
❑2, Oct 2004, b&w 3.95

Psi-Force
Marvel
❑1, Nov 1986 1.00
❑2, Dec 1986 1.00
❑3, Jan 1987 1.00
❑4, Feb 1987 1.00
❑5, Mar 1987 1.00
❑6, Apr 1987 1.00
❑7, May 1987 BH (a) 1.00
❑8, Jun 1987 1.00
❑9, Jul 1987 BH (a) 1.00
❑10, Aug 1987 1.00
❑11, Sep 1987 BH (a) 1.00
❑12, Oct 1987 BH (a) 1.00
❑13, Nov 1987 1.00
❑14, Dec 1987 BH (a) 1.00
❑15, Jan 1988 1.00
❑16, Feb 1988 1.00
❑17, Mar 1988 1.00
❑18, Apr 1988 1.00
❑19, May 1988 1.25
❑20, Jun 1988; Psi-Force; Spitfire 1.25
❑21, Jul 1988 1.25
❑22, Aug 1988; Psi-Force; DP-7 1.25
❑23, Sep 1988 1.25
❑24, Oct 1988 1.25
❑25, Nov 1988 1.25
❑26, Dec 1988 1.25
❑27, Jan 1989 1.25
❑28, Feb 1989 1.25

Other grades: Multiply price above by 5/6 for VF/NM • 2/3 for VERY FINE • 1/3 for FINE • 1/5 for VERY GOOD • 1/8 for GOOD

Redfox

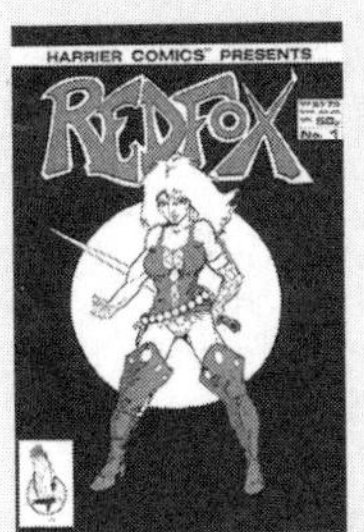

Fantasy title momentarily hot in 1980s boom
©Harrier

Red Sonja

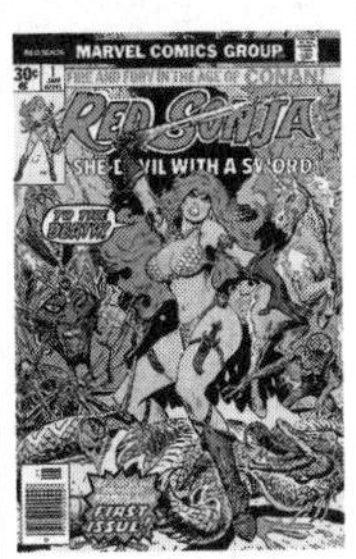

One of the early "hot" titles from the 1970s
©Marvel

Red Tornado

Hero's name sounds like bathroom cleanser
©DC

Red Wolf

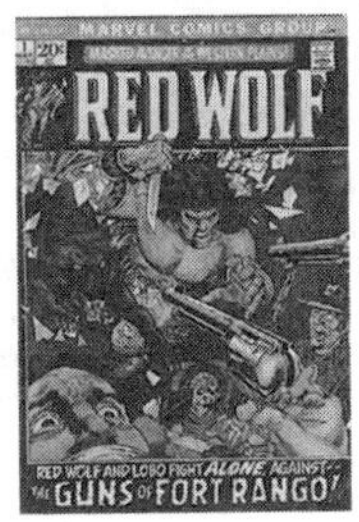

Billed as the first Native American super-hero
©Marvel

Ren & Stimpy Show

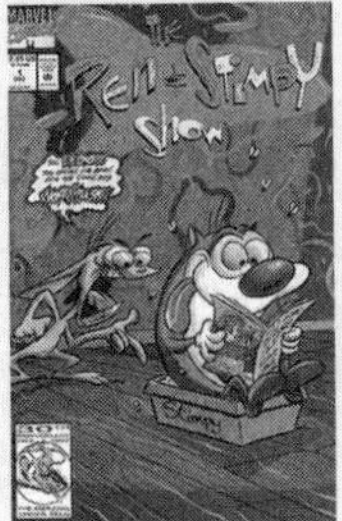

Tasteless show spawns many comics
©Marvel

N-MINT

❑29, Mar 1989 ... 1.25
❑30, Apr 1989 ... 1.25
❑31, May 1989 ... 1.25
❑32, Jun 1989; Final Issue ... 1.25
❑Ann 1, ca. 1987 ... 1.25

Psi-Judge Anderson
Fleetway-Quality

❑1 ... 2.00
❑2 ... 2.00
❑3 ... 2.00
❑4 ... 2.00
❑5 ... 2.00
❑6 ... 2.00
❑7 ... 2.00
❑8 ... 2.00
❑9 ... 2.00
❑10 ... 2.00
❑11 ... 2.00
❑12 ... 2.00
❑13 ... 2.00
❑14 ... 2.00
❑15 ... 2.00

Psi-Judge Anderson: Engrams
Fleetway-Quality

❑1, b&w ... 1.95
❑2, b&w ... 1.95

Psi-Judge Anderson: Psifiles
Fleetway-Quality

❑1 ... 2.95

Psi-Lords
Valiant

❑1, Sep 1994; Valiant Vision; chromium wrap-around cover ... 3.50
❑1/VVSS, Sep 1994 ... 70.00
❑1/Gold, Sep 1994; Gold edition; no cover price ... 20.00
❑2, Oct 1994; Valiant Vision ... 1.00
❑3, Nov 1994; Valiant Vision; Chaos Effect Epsilon 3 ... 1.00
❑4, Dec 1994; Valiant Vision ... 1.00
❑5, Jan 1995; Valiant Vision ... 2.00
❑6, Feb 1995 ... 2.00
❑7, Mar 1995 ... 2.00
❑8, Apr 1995; V: Destroyer ... 2.00
❑9, May 1995 ... 3.00
❑10, Jun 1995; Final Issue ... 5.00

PS238
Dork Storm

❑0, Nov 2002, b&w series ... 2.99
❑1, Mar 2003, b&w; 1: Captain Clarinet; Indicia says #2 ... 2.95
❑2, May 2003, b&w ... 2.95
❑3, Jul 2003, b&w ... 2.95
❑4, Sep 2003, b&w ... 2.95
❑5, Nov 2003, b&w ... 2.95
❑6, ca. 2004, b&w ... 2.95
❑7, ca. 2004, b&w ... 2.95
❑8, ca. 2004, b&w ... 2.95
❑9, Nov 2004, b&w ... 2.95
❑10 ... 2.95
❑11 ... 2.95
❑12 ... 2.95
❑13 ... 2.95
❑14 ... 2.95

N-MINT

❑15 ... 2.95
❑16 ... 2.95
❑17 ... 2.95
❑18 ... 2.95
❑19 ... 2.95
❑20 ... 2.95
❑21 ... 2.95
❑22 ... 2.95
❑23 ... 2.95
❑24 ... 2.95
❑25 ... 2.95
❑26 ... 2.95
❑27 ... 2.95
❑28 ... 2.95
❑29 ... 2.95
❑30 ... 2.95
❑31 ... 2.95
❑32 ... 2.95
❑33 ... 2.95
❑34 ... 2.95
❑35 ... 2.95
❑36 ... 2.95
❑37 ... 2.95
❑38 ... 2.95

Psyba-Rats
DC

❑1, Apr 1995; D: Channelman ... 2.50
❑2, May 1995 ... 2.50
❑3, Jun 1995 ... 2.50

Psychic Academy
Tokyopop

❑1, Mar 2004 ... 9.99
❑2, May 2004 ... 9.99
❑3, Jul 2004 ... 9.99
❑4, Sep 2004 ... 9.99
❑5, Nov 2004 ... 9.99
❑6, Jan 2005 ... 9.99
❑7, Mar 2005 ... 9.99
❑8, Jun 2005 ... 9.99
❑9, Sep 2005 ... 9.99
❑10, Dec 2005 ... 9.99

Psycho
DC

❑1, Sep 1991 ... 4.95
❑2, Oct 1991 ... 4.95
❑3, Dec 1991 ... 4.95

Psycho
Innovation

❑1 ... 2.50
❑2 ... 2.50
❑3 ... 2.50

Psychoanalysis
Gemstone

❑1, Aug 1999 ... 2.50
❑2, Sep 1999 ... 2.50
❑3, Oct 1999 ... 2.50
❑4, Nov 1999 ... 2.50
❑Ann 1, Collects series ... 10.95

Psychoblast
First

❑1, Nov 1987; 1: Psychoblast ... 1.75
❑2, Dec 1987 ... 1.75
❑3, Jan 1988 ... 1.75

N-MINT

❑4, Feb 1988 ... 1.75
❑5, Mar 1988 ... 1.75
❑6, Apr 1988 ... 1.75
❑7, May 1988 ... 1.75
❑8, Jun 1988 ... 1.75
❑9, Jul 1988; Final Issue ... 1.75

Psycho Killers
Comic Zone

❑1, b&w; Charles Manson ... 4.00
❑1/2nd; Charles Manson ... 3.00
❑2, b&w; David Berkowitz ("The Son of Sam") ... 3.50
❑2/2nd; David Berkowitz ("The Son of Sam") ... 3.00
❑3, b&w; Ed Gein ... 3.50
❑3/2nd; Ed Gein ... 2.95
❑4, Jul 1992; Henry Lee Lucas ... 2.95
❑5; Jeffrey Dahmer ... 3.25
❑6, Sep 1992; Richard Ramirez ("The Nightstalker") ... 2.95
❑7; Judias Buenoano ... 2.95
❑8, Nov 1992; John Wayne Gacy ... 2.95
❑9; Ted Bundy ... 2.95
❑10; Dean Corll ("The Candy Man") ... 2.95
❑11; The Hillside Strangler; A lawsuit was filed and resulted in this book being taken off the market ... 3.50
❑12; The Boston Strangler ... 2.95
❑13; Andrei Chikatilo ... 2.95
❑14, May 1993; Aileen Wuornos ... 2.95
❑15, Jul 1993; Charles Starkweather ... 2.95

Psycho Killers PMS Special
Zone

❑1, Jun 1993; Adult ... 3.25

Psychoman
Revolutionary

❑1; 1: Psychoman; O: Psychoman ... 2.50

Psychonaut
Fantagraphics

❑1, Mar 1996, b&w ... 3.95
❑3, b&w; flipbook with The Pursuers ... 3.50

Psychonauts
Marvel / Epic

❑1, Oct 1993 ... 4.95
❑2, Nov 1993 ... 4.95
❑3, Dec 1993 ... 4.95
❑4, Jan 1994 ... 4.95

Psycho-Path
Venusian

❑1, Jul 1990; b&w ... 2.00
❑2, Sep 1990, b&w ... 2.00

Psychotic Adventures Illustrated
Last Gasp

❑1, Published by Co. & Sons; b&w; ca. 1972 ... 3.00
❑2, Oct 1973, Published by Last Gasp ... 3.00
❑3, Jun 1974, Adult ... 3.00

Psy-Comm
Tokyopop

❑1, Nov 2005 ... 9.99

N-MINT

Psyence Fiction
Abaculus
- ❑½, Sum 1998, b&w; Ashcan preview edition ... 1.00
- ❑1 ... 2.95

Psylocke & Archangel: Crimson Dawn
Marvel
- ❑1, Aug 1997; gatefold summary; gatefold cover ... 2.50
- ❑2, Sep 1997; gatefold summary ... 2.50
- ❑3, Oct 1997; gatefold summary ... 2.50
- ❑4, Nov 1997; gatefold summary ... 2.50

Pteranoman
Kitchen Sink
- ❑1, Aug 1990 ... 2.00

Public Enemies
Eternity
- ❑1, b&w; Reprints ... 3.95
- ❑2, b&w; Reprints ... 3.95

Pubo
Dark Horse
- ❑1, Nov 2002, b&w ... 3.50
- ❑2, Jan 2003, b&w ... 3.50
- ❑3, Mar 2003, b&w ... 3.50

Puffed
Image
- ❑1, Jul 2003 ... 2.95
- ❑2, Aug 2003 ... 2.95
- ❑3, Sep 2003 ... 2.95

Puke & Explode
Northstar
- ❑1, Sep 1990; b&w ... 2.50
- ❑2 ... 2.50

Pulp (Vol. 1)
Viz
- ❑1, Dec 1997 ... 5.95

Pulp (Vol. 2)
Viz
- ❑1, Jan 1998 ... 5.95
- ❑2, Feb 1998 ... 5.95
- ❑3, Mar 1998 ... 5.95
- ❑4, Apr 1998 ... 5.95
- ❑5, May 1998 ... 5.95
- ❑6, Jun 1998 ... 5.95
- ❑7, Jul 1998 ... 5.95
- ❑8, Aug 1998 ... 5.95
- ❑9, Sep 1998 ... 5.95
- ❑10, Oct 1998 ... 5.95
- ❑11, Nov 1998 ... 5.95
- ❑12, Dec 1998 ... 5.95

Pulp (Vol. 3)
Viz
- ❑1, Jan 1999 ... 5.95
- ❑2, Feb 1999 ... 5.95
- ❑3, Mar 1999 ... 5.95
- ❑4, Apr 1999 ... 5.95
- ❑5, May 1999 ... 5.95
- ❑6, Jun 1999 ... 5.95
- ❑7, Jul 1999 ... 5.95
- ❑8, Aug 1999 ... 5.95
- ❑9, Sep 1999 ... 5.95
- ❑10, Oct 1999 ... 5.95
- ❑11, Nov 1999 ... 5.95
- ❑12, Dec 1999 ... 5.95

Pulp (Vol. 4)
Viz
- ❑1, Jan 2000 ... 5.95
- ❑2, Feb 2000 ... 5.95
- ❑3, Mar 2000 ... 5.95
- ❑4, Apr 2000 ... 5.95
- ❑5, May 2000 ... 5.95
- ❑6, Jun 2000 ... 5.95

Pulp (Vol. 5)
Viz
- ❑1, Jan 2001 ... 5.95
- ❑2, Feb 2001 ... 5.95
- ❑3, Mar 2001 ... 5.95
- ❑4, Apr 2001 ... 5.95
- ❑5, May 2001 ... 5.95
- ❑6, Jun 2001 ... 5.95
- ❑7, Jul 2001 ... 5.95
- ❑8, Aug 2001 ... 5.95
- ❑9, Sep 2001 ... 5.95
- ❑10, Oct 2001 ... 5.95
- ❑11, Nov 2001 ... 5.95
- ❑12, Dec 2001 ... 5.95

Pulp (Vol. 6)
Viz
- ❑1 ... 5.95
- ❑2 ... 5.95
- ❑3 ... 5.95
- ❑4 ... 5.95
- ❑5 ... 5.95
- ❑6 ... 5.95
- ❑7 ... 5.95
- ❑8 ... 5.95

Pulp Action
Avalon
- ❑1 ... 2.95
- ❑2 ... 2.95
- ❑3 ... 2.95
- ❑4 ... 2.95
- ❑5 ... 2.95
- ❑6 ... 2.95
- ❑7 ... 2.95
- ❑8 ... 2.95

Pulp Dreams
Fantagraphics / Eros
- ❑1, May 1991, b&w; Adult ... 2.50

Pulp Fantastic
DC / Vertigo
- ❑1, Feb 2000 ... 2.50
- ❑2, Mar 2000 ... 2.50
- ❑3, Apr 2000 ... 2.50

Pulp Fiction
A List
- ❑1, Spr 1997, b&w; reprints Golden Age material ... 2.50
- ❑2, Fal 1997, b&w; reprints Golden Age material ... 2.50
- ❑3, Win 1997, b&w; reprints Golden Age material ... 2.50
- ❑4 ... 2.50
- ❑5 ... 2.95
- ❑6 ... 2.95

Pulp Western
Avalon
- ❑1 ... 2.95

Pulse
Blackjack
- ❑1, Jun 1997, b&w; no cover price ... 2.00

Pulse
Marvel
- ❑1, Apr 2004, BMB (w) ... 5.00
- ❑2, May 2004, BMB (w) ... 3.00
- ❑3, Jul 2004, BMB (w) ... 2.99
- ❑4, Sep 2004 ... 2.99
- ❑5, Oct 2004 ... 2.25
- ❑6 ... 2.99
- ❑7 2005 ... 2.99
- ❑8, May 2005 ... 2.99
- ❑9 2005 ... 2.99
- ❑10, Sep 2005 ... 6.00
- ❑10/Variant, Sep 2005 ... 4.00
- ❑11, Oct 2005 ... 2.99
- ❑12, Jan 2006 ... 2.99
- ❑13, Mar 2006 ... 2.99
- ❑14, May 2006 ... 2.99

Pulse: House of M Special Edition
Marvel
- ❑1, Sep 2005 ... 1.00

Puma Blues
Aardvark One
- ❑1, Jun 1986, b&w; 10,000 copies printed; Aardvark One International Publisher ... 2.00
- ❑1/2nd, b&w; 2nd printing ... 2.00
- ❑2, Sep 1986, b&w; 10,000 copies printed ... 2.00
- ❑3, Dec 1986, b&w; 19,000 copies printed ... 2.00
- ❑4, Feb 1987, b&w; 13,000 copies printed ... 1.70
- ❑5, Mar 1987, b&w; 13,000 copies printed ... 1.70
- ❑6, Apr 1987, b&w; 13,000 copies printed ... 1.70
- ❑7, May 1987, b&w; 12,000 copies printed ... 1.70
- ❑8, May 1987, b&w ... 1.70
- ❑9, Jul 1987, b&w ... 1.70
- ❑10, Aug 1987, b&w ... 1.70
- ❑11, Sep 1987, b&w ... 1.70
- ❑12, Oct 1987, b&w ... 1.70
- ❑13, Nov 1987, b&w ... 1.70
- ❑14, Dec 1987, b&w ... 1.70
- ❑15, Jan 1988, b&w ... 1.70
- ❑16, Feb 1988, b&w ... 1.70
- ❑17, Mar 1988, b&w ... 1.70
- ❑18, Apr 1988, b&w; self-published ... 1.70
- ❑19 1988, b&w; self-published ... 1.70
- ❑20 1988, b&w; TS, AMo (w); self-published ... 1.70
- ❑21 1988, b&w; Mirage Studio Publisher 1.70
- ❑22 1988, b&w ... 1.70
- ❑23, b&w ... 1.70

Pummeler
Parody
- ❑1, Dec 1992, b&w; Foil embossed cover; Punisher parody ... 2.95

Pummeler $2099
Parody
- ❑1; Gold Trimmed Foil Cover ... 2.95

Pumpkinhead: The Rites of Exorcism
Dark Horse
- ❑1, ca. 1992 ... 2.50
- ❑2, ca. 1992 ... 2.50
- ❑3, ca. 1992 ... 2.50
- ❑4, ca. 1992 ... 2.50

Punisher
Marvel
- ❑1, Jan 1986; Double-size ... 13.00
- ❑2, Feb 1986 MZ (c); MZ (a) ... 7.00
- ❑3, Mar 1986 MZ (c); MZ (a) ... 7.00
- ❑4, Apr 1986 MZ (c); MZ (a) ... 6.00
- ❑5, May 1986 MZ (c); MZ (a) ... 6.00

Punisher
Marvel
- ❑1, Jul 1987 ... 7.00
- ❑2, Aug 1987 KJ (c); KJ (a) ... 4.00
- ❑3, Oct 1987 KJ (c); KJ (a) ... 4.00
- ❑4, Nov 1987 ... 3.00
- ❑5, Jan 1988 ... 3.00
- ❑6, Feb 1988 ... 3.00
- ❑7, Mar 1988 ... 3.00
- ❑8, May 1988 ... 3.00
- ❑9, Jun 1988 ... 3.00
- ❑10, Aug 1988 A: Daredevil ... 4.00
- ❑11, Sep 1988 ... 2.00
- ❑12, Oct 1988 ... 2.00
- ❑13, Nov 1988 ... 2.00
- ❑14, Dec 1988 A: Kingpin ... 2.00
- ❑15, Jan 1989 A: Kingpin ... 2.00
- ❑16, Feb 1989 A: Kingpin ... 2.00
- ❑17, Mar 1989 ... 2.00
- ❑18, Apr 1989; V: Kingpin ... 2.00
- ❑19, May 1989 ... 2.00
- ❑20, Jun 1989 ... 2.00
- ❑21, Jul 1989 EL (c); EL (a) ... 2.00
- ❑22, Aug 1989 EL (c); EL (a) ... 2.00
- ❑23, Sep 1989 EL (c); EL (a) ... 2.00
- ❑24, Oct 1989; EL (c); EL (a); 1: Shadowmasters ... 2.00
- ❑25, Nov 1989; Giant-sized; EL (c); EL (a); A: Shadowmasters ... 2.00
- ❑26, Nov 1989 RH (c); RH (a) ... 2.00
- ❑27, Dec 1989 ... 2.00
- ❑28, Dec 1989; Acts of Vengeance ... 2.00
- ❑29, Jan 1990; Acts of Vengeance ... 2.00
- ❑30, Feb 1990 ... 2.00
- ❑31, Mar 1990 ... 2.00
- ❑32, Apr 1990 ... 2.00
- ❑33, May 1990 ... 2.00
- ❑34, Jun 1990 ... 2.00
- ❑35, Jul 1990; Jigsaw Puzzle ... 2.00
- ❑36, Aug 1990; Jigsaw Puzzle ... 2.00
- ❑37, Aug 1990; Jigsaw Puzzle ... 2.00
- ❑38, Sep 1990; Jigsaw Puzzle ... 2.00
- ❑39, Sep 1990; Jigsaw Puzzle ... 2.00
- ❑40, Oct 1990; Jigsaw Puzzle ... 2.00
- ❑41, Oct 1990 ... 1.50
- ❑42, Nov 1990 ... 1.50
- ❑43, Dec 1990 ... 1.50
- ❑44, Jan 1991 ... 1.50
- ❑45, Feb 1991 ... 1.50
- ❑46, Mar 1991 ... 1.50
- ❑47, Apr 1991 ... 1.50
- ❑48, May 1991 ... 1.50

Other grades: Multiply price above by 5/6 for VF/NM • 2/3 for VERY FINE • 1/3 for FINE • 1/5 for VERY GOOD • 1/8 for GOOD

Replacement God

Kid runs from troubling prophecy

©Slave Labor

Resurrection Man

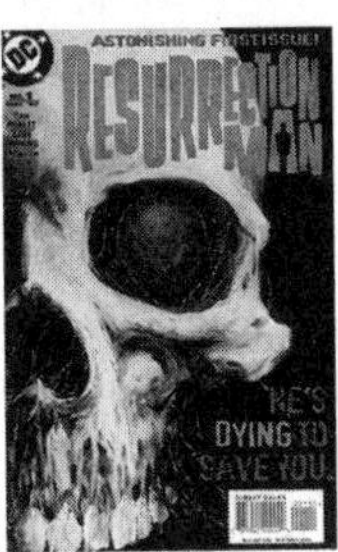

Amnesiac rediscovers bits of his past

©DC

Retaliator

Stranger intervenes on behalf of the abused

©Eclipse

Return of Lum Urusei*Yatsura

Alien princess with flying powers

©Viz

Revengers Featuring Armor and The Silverstreak

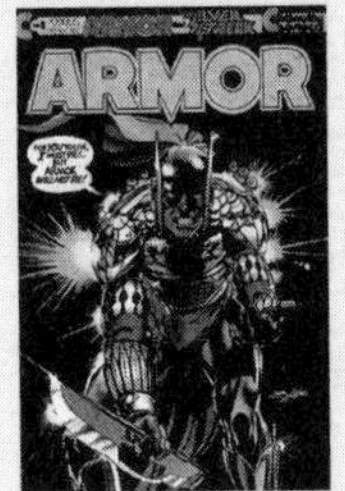

Cover title isn't actually the comic's name

©Continuity

	N-MINT
❑49, Jun 1991	1.50
❑50, Jul 1991; double-sized; MG (c)	2.00
❑51, Aug 1991; Credits are listed in issue 53	1.50
❑52, Sep 1991	1.50
❑53, Oct 1991 MG (c)	1.50
❑54, Nov 1991 AM (c)	1.50
❑55, Nov 1991	1.50
❑56, Dec 1991	1.50
❑57, Dec 1991; JLee (c); Two covers: outer wraparound cover, inner photo cover	2.00
❑58, Jan 1992 MG (c)	1.50
❑59, Jan 1992; Punisher becomes black	1.50
❑60, Feb 1992 VM (c); VM (a); A: Luke Cage	1.50
❑61, Mar 1992 VM (c); VM (a); A: Luke Cage	1.50
❑62, Apr 1992; VM (a); Punisher becomes white again	1.50
❑63, May 1992	1.25
❑64, Jun 1992	1.25
❑65, Jul 1992	1.25
❑66, Jul 1992	1.25
❑67, Aug 1992	1.25
❑68, Aug 1992	1.25
❑69, Sep 1992	1.25
❑70, Sep 1992	1.25
❑71, Oct 1992	1.25
❑72, Nov 1992	1.25
❑73, Dec 1992	1.25
❑74, Jan 1993	1.25
❑75, Feb 1993; VM (a); Embossed cover	2.75
❑76, Mar 1993	1.50
❑77, Apr 1993 VM (c); VM (w); VM (a)	1.50
❑78, May 1993 VM (c); VM (w); VM (a)	1.50
❑79, Jun 1993	1.50
❑80, Jul 1993	1.50
❑81, Aug 1993	1.25
❑82, Sep 1993	1.25
❑83, Oct 1993	1.25
❑84, Nov 1993	1.25
❑85, Dec 1993	1.25
❑86, Jan 1994; Giant-size; MG (c)	2.95
❑87, Feb 1994 MG (c)	1.25
❑88, Mar 1994	1.25
❑89, Apr 1994 RH (a)	1.25
❑90, May 1994 RH (a)	1.25
❑91, Jun 1994 RH (a)	1.50
❑92, Jul 1994 RH (a)	1.50
❑93, Aug 1994 BSz (c)	1.50
❑94, Sep 1994	1.50
❑95, Oct 1994	1.50
❑96, Nov 1994	1.50
❑97, Dec 1994	1.50
❑98, Jan 1995	1.50
❑99, Feb 1995	1.50
❑100, Mar 1995; Giant-size	2.95
❑100/Variant, Mar 1995; Giant-size; MG (c); foil cover	3.95
❑101, Apr 1995	4.00
❑102, May 1995	1.50
❑103, Jun 1995	1.50
❑104, Jul 1995; Final Issue	1.50
❑Ann 1, ca. 1988	3.50
❑Ann 2, ca. 1989; JLee (a); A: Moon Knight. V: Moon Knight. Atlantis Attacks	2.50
❑Ann 3, ca. 1990	2.50
❑Ann 4, ca. 1991; MG (c); JLee (a)	2.00
❑Ann 5, ca. 1992; PD (w); VM (a); System Bytes	2.25
❑Ann 6 1993; 1993 Ann; Polybagged	2.95
❑Ann 7, ca. 1994; 1994 Ann	2.95

Punisher
Marvel

	N-MINT
❑1, Nov 1995; foil cover	2.95
❑2, Dec 1995 A: Hatchetman	1.95
❑3, Dec 1995	1.95
❑4, Feb 1996; A: Daredevil. V: Jigsaw	1.95
❑5, Mar 1996 PB (a)	1.95
❑6, Apr 1996 PB (a)	1.95
❑7, May 1996	1.95
❑8, Jun 1996	1.95
❑9, Jul 1996	1.95
❑10, Aug 1996; V: Jigsaw	1.95
❑11, Sep 1996; S.H.I.E.L.D. helicarrier crashes	1.95
❑12, Oct 1996; V: X-Cutioner	1.95
❑13, Nov 1996; V: X-Cutioner	1.95
❑14, Dec 1996; V: X-Cutioner	1.50
❑15, Jan 1997; V: X-Cutioner	1.50
❑16, Feb 1997; V: X-Cutioner	1.50
❑17, Mar 1997	1.95
❑18, Apr 1997; Final Issue	1.95

Punisher
Marvel

	N-MINT
❑1, Nov 1998; gatefold summary	3.00
❑1/Variant, Nov 1998; DFE alternate cover	6.00
❑2, Dec 1998; gatefold summary	2.99
❑3, Jan 1999	2.99
❑4, Feb 1999	2.99

Punisher
Marvel

	N-MINT
❑1, Apr 2000	4.00
❑1/Variant, Apr 2000; White background on cover	8.50
❑2, May 2000	3.50
❑2/Variant, May 2000; White background on cover	6.00
❑3, Jun 2000; Polybagged with Marvel Knights/Marvel Boy Genesis Edition; Polybagged with Marvel Knights/ Marvel Boy Genesis Edition; V: Daredevil	3.50
❑4, Jul 2000; V: Ma Gnucci; Punisher cripples Ma Gnucci	3.00
❑5, Aug 2000	3.00
❑6, Sep 2000; V: Ma Gnucci army	2.99
❑7, Oct 2000	2.99
❑8, Nov 2000; 1: The Russian	2.99
❑9, Dec 2000	2.99
❑10, Jan 2001; V: Russian	2.99
❑11, Feb 2001; 1: The Vigilante Squad. D: The Russian	2.99
❑12, Mar 2001; D: Ma Gnucci	2.99

Punisher
Marvel

	N-MINT
❑1, Aug 2001	2.99
❑2, Sep 2001	2.99
❑3, Oct 2001	2.99
❑4, Nov 2001	2.99
❑5, Dec 2001	2.99
❑6, Jan 2002	2.99
❑7, Feb 2002; Silent issue	2.99
❑8, Mar 2002	2.99
❑9, Apr 2002	2.99
❑10, May 2002	2.99
❑11, Jun 2002	2.99
❑12, Jul 2002; D: Mr. Badwrench	2.99
❑13, Aug 2002	2.99
❑14, Sep 2002	2.99
❑15, Oct 2002	2.99
❑16, Nov 2002; V: Wolverine	2.99
❑17, Nov 2002; V: Wolverine	2.99
❑18, Dec 2002	2.99
❑19, Jan 2003	2.99
❑20, Feb 2003	2.99
❑21, Mar 2003	2.99
❑22, Apr 2003	2.99
❑23, May 2003	2.99
❑24, Jun 2003	2.99
❑25, Jun 2003	2.99
❑26, Jul 2003	2.99
❑27, Jul 2003	2.99
❑28, Aug 2003	2.99
❑29, Sep 2003	2.99
❑30, Oct 2003	2.99
❑31, Nov 2003	2.99
❑32, Nov 2003, O: Soap	2.99
❑33, Dec 2003	2.99
❑34, Dec 2003, V: Wolverine	2.99
❑35, Jan 2004	2.99
❑36, Jan 2004, V: Daredevil; V: Spiderman; V: Wolverine	2.99
❑37, Feb 2004, Indicia mistakenly says Feb 03; Final issue	2.99

Punisher
Marvel / MAX

	N-MINT
❑1, Mar 2004	5.00
❑1/DF, Mar 2004	15.00
❑2, Mar 2004	4.00
❑3, Apr 2004, TP (a)	2.99
❑4, May 2004, TP (a)	2.99
❑5, Jun 2004, TP (a)	2.99
❑6, Jul 2004	2.99
❑7, Aug 2004	2.99
❑8, Aug 2004	2.99
❑9, Sep 2004	2.99
❑10, Oct 2004	2.99
❑11, Oct 2004	2.99
❑12, Nov 2004	2.99
❑13, Dec 2004	2.99
❑14, Dec 2004	2.99
❑15, Jan 2005	2.99
❑16, Feb 2005	2.99
❑17, Mar 2005	2.99
❑18, Apr 2005	2.99
❑19, May 2005	2.99
❑20, Jun 2005	2.99
❑21, Jul 2005	2.99
❑22, Aug 2005	2.99
❑23, Sep 2005	2.99
❑24, Oct 2005	2.99
❑25, Nov 2005	2.99
❑26, Dec 2005	2.99
❑27, Jan 2006	2.99
❑28, Feb 2006	2.99
❑29, Mar 2006	2.99
❑30, Mar 2006	2.99

Other grades: Multiply price above by 5/6 for VF/NM • 2/3 for VERY FINE • 1/3 for FINE • 1/5 for VERY GOOD • 1/8 for GOOD

	N-MINT
❑31, May 2006	2.99
❑32, Jun 2006	2.99
❑33, Jul 2006	2.99
❑34, Aug 2006	2.99
❑35, Sep 2006	2.99
❑36, Oct 2006	2.99
❑37, Nov 2006	2.99
❑38, Dec 2006	2.99
❑39, Dec 2006	2.99
❑40, Jan 2007	2.99
❑42, Mar 2007	2.99
❑43	2.99
❑44	2.99
❑45	2.99
❑46	2.99
❑47	2.99
❑48	2.99
❑49	2.99
❑50	2.99
❑51	2.99
❑52	2.99
❑53	2.99
❑54	2.99
❑55	2.99
❑56	2.99
❑57	2.99
❑58	2.99
❑59	2.99
❑60	2.99
❑61	2.99
❑62	2.99

Punisher: A Man Named Frank
Marvel

❑1, Jun 1994; NN; One-shot ... 6.95

Punisher Anniversary Magazine
Marvel

❑1 ... 4.95

Punisher Armory
Marvel

❑1, Jul 1990; JLee (c); weapons ... 2.00
❑2, Jun 1991 JLee (c) ... 2.00
❑3, Apr 1991 ... 2.00
❑4, Oct 1992 ... 2.00
❑5, Feb 1992 ... 2.00
❑6 ... 2.00
❑7, Sep 1993 ... 2.00
❑8, Dec 1993 ... 2.00
❑9 ... 2.00
❑10, Nov 1994 ... 2.00

Punisher Back to School Special
Marvel

❑1, Nov 1992; BSz (c);1992 ... 3.50
❑2, Oct 1993; BSz (c); BSz (a) ... 3.00
❑3, Oct 1994 ... 3.00

Punisher/Batman: Deadly Knights
Marvel

❑1, Oct 1994; NN ... 4.95

Punisher/Black Widow: Spinning Doomsday's Web
Marvel

❑1; ca. 1992 ... 9.95

Punisher: Bloodlines
Marvel

❑1, ca. 1991; prestige format; NN ... 5.95

Punisher: Bloody Valentine
Marvel

❑1, Apr 2006 ... 3.99

Punisher: Die Hard in the Big Easy
Marvel

❑1, ca. 1992; prestige format one-shot .. 4.95

Punisher: Empty Quarter
Marvel

❑1, Nov 1994; prestige format one-shot 6.95

Punisher: G-Force
Marvel

❑1, ca. 1992; squarebound with cardstock cover ... 4.95

Punisher Holiday Special
Marvel

❑1, Jan 1993; foil cover ... 3.00
❑2, Jan 1994 BSz (c) ... 3.00
❑3, Jan 1995 ... 3.00

N-MINT

Punisher: Intruder
Marvel

❑1 ... 9.95
❑1/HC; ca. 1980 ... 14.95

Punisher Invades the 'Nam: Final Invasion
Marvel

❑1, Feb 1994; NN ... 6.95

Punisher Kills the Marvel Universe
Marvel

❑1, Nov 1995 ... 20.00
❑1/2nd, Mar 2000; 2nd printing ... 5.95

Punisher: Kingdom Gone
Marvel

❑1, Aug 1990 ... 16.95

Punisher Magazine
Marvel

❑1, Sep 1989, b&w; Reprints Punisher (Ltd. Series) #1 in black & white ... 3.00
❑2, Oct 1989, b&w; Reprints Punisher (Ltd. Series) #2-3 in black & white ... 2.50
❑3, Nov 1989, b&w; Reprints Punisher (Ltd. Series) #4-5 in black & white ... 2.50
❑4, Dec 1989, b&w; Reprints Punisher #1-2 in black & white ... 2.50
❑5, Dec 1989, b&w; Reprints Punisher #3-4 in black & white ... 2.50
❑6, Jan 1990, b&w; Reprints Punisher #5-6 in black & white ... 2.50
❑7, Feb 1990, b&w; Reprints Punisher #7-8 in black & white ... 2.50
❑8, Mar 1990, b&w; Reprints ... 2.50
❑9, Apr 1990, b&w; Reprints ... 2.50
❑10, May 1990, b&w; Reprints ... 2.50
❑11, Jun 1990, b&w; Reprints ... 2.50
❑12, Jul 1990, b&w; Reprints ... 2.50
❑13, Aug 1990, b&w; Reprints ... 2.50
❑14, Sep 1990, b&w; Reprints Punisher War Journal #1-2 ... 2.50
❑15, Oct 1990, b&w; Reprints ... 2.50
❑16, Nov 1990, b&w; Reprints ... 2.50

Punisher Meets Archie
Marvel

❑1, Aug 1994; JB (a); enhanced cover ... 4.00
❑1/Variant, Aug 1994; JB (c); JB (a); Die-cut cover ... 4.50

Punisher Movie Special
Marvel

❑1, Jun 1990; NN ... 5.95

Punisher: No Escape
Marvel

❑1, ca. 1990, prestige format; NN ... 4.95

Punisher: Official Movie Adaptation
Marvel

❑1, May 2004 ... 2.99
❑2, May 2004 ... 2.99
❑3, May 2004 ... 2.99

Punisher: Origin Micro Chip
Marvel

❑1, Jul 1993; O: Micro Chip ... 2.00
❑2, Aug 1993 ... 2.00

Punisher/Painkiller Jane
Marvel

❑1, Jan 2001; cardstock cover ... 3.50

Punisher: P.O.V.
Marvel

❑1, ca. 1991 BWr (c); JSn (w); BWr, BW (a) ... 5.00
❑2, ca. 1991 BWr (c); JSn (w); BWr, BW (a) ... 5.00
❑3, ca. 1991 BWr (c); JSn (w); BWr, BW (a) ... 5.00
❑4, ca. 1991 BWr (c); JSn (w); BWr, BW (a) ... 5.00

Punisher: Red X-Mas
Marvel

❑1, Jan 2004 ... 3.99

Punisher: Silent Night
Marvel

❑1, Feb 2006 ... 3.99

Punisher Summer Special
Marvel

❑1, Aug 1991 PD (w); VM (a) ... 3.00
❑2, Aug 1992 ... 3.00

N-MINT

❑3, Aug 1993 ... 2.50
❑4, Jul 1994 JR2 (c) ... 2.95

Punisher: The End
Marvel / MAX

❑1, Jun 2004 ... 4.50

Punisher: The Ghosts of Innocents
Marvel

❑1, ca. 1993 ... 5.95
❑2, ca. 1993 ... 5.95

Punisher: The Movie
Marvel

❑1, May 2004 ... 2.99
❑2, May 2004 ... 2.99
❑3, May 2004 ... 2.99

Punisher: The Prize
Marvel

❑1, ca. 1990; prestige format; NN ... 4.95

Punisher: The Tyger
Marvel

❑1, Aug 2006 ... 4.99

Punisher 2099
Marvel

❑1, Feb 1993; foil cover ... 1.75
❑2, Mar 1993; 1: Fearmaster ... 1.25
❑3, Apr 1993 ... 1.25
❑4, May 1993 ... 1.25
❑5, Jun 1993 ... 1.25
❑6, Jul 1993 ... 1.25
❑7, Aug 1993 ... 1.25
❑8, Sep 1993 ... 1.25
❑9, Oct 1993; D: Kerry Dowen ... 1.25
❑10, Nov 1993; 1: Jigsaw 2099 ... 1.25
❑11, Dec 1993 ... 1.25
❑12, Jan 1994 ... 1.25
❑13, Feb 1994 ... 1.25
❑14, Mar 1994 ... 1.25
❑15, Apr 1994 ... 1.25
❑16, May 1994 ... 1.50
❑17, Jun 1994 ... 1.50
❑18, Jul 1994 ... 1.50
❑19, Aug 1994; 1: Vendetta ... 1.50
❑20, Sep 1994 ... 1.50
❑21, Oct 1994 ... 1.50
❑22, Nov 1994 ... 1.50
❑23, Dec 1994 ... 1.50
❑24, Jan 1995 ... 1.50
❑25, Feb 1995; Giant-size ... 2.25
❑25/Variant, Feb 1995; Embossed cover 2.95
❑26, Mar 1995 ... 1.50
❑27, Apr 1995 ... 1.50
❑28, May 1995 ... 1.95
❑29, Jun 1995 ... 1.95
❑30, Jul 1995 ... 1.95
❑31, Aug 1995 ... 1.95
❑32, Sep 1995 ... 1.95
❑33, Oct 1995 ... 1.95
❑34, Nov 1995; continues in 2099 A.D. Apocalypse #1 ... 1.95

Punisher Vs Bullseye
Marvel

❑1, Jan 2006 ... 2.99
❑2, Feb 2006 ... 2.99
❑3, Mar 2006 ... 2.99
❑4, Apr 2006 ... 2.99
❑5, May 2006 ... 2.99

Punisher vs. Daredevil
Marvel

❑1, Jun 2000; Reprints ... 3.50

Punisher War Journal
Marvel

❑1, Nov 1988; JLee (a); O: Punisher ... 5.00
❑2, Dec 1988 JLee (a); A: Daredevil ... 3.00
❑3, Feb 1989 JLee (a); A: Daredevil ... 3.00
❑4, Mar 1989 JLee (c); JLee (a) ... 3.00
❑5, May 1989 JLee (c); JLee (a) ... 3.00
❑6, Jun 1989 JLee (c); JLee (a); A: Wolverine ... 3.00
❑7, Jul 1989 JLee (c); JLee (a); A: Wolverine ... 3.00
❑8, Sep 1989 JLee (c); JLee (a) ... 1.50
❑9, Oct 1989 JLee (c); JLee (a) ... 1.50
❑10, Nov 1989 JLee (c); JLee (a) ... 1.50
❑11, Dec 1989 JLee (c); JLee (a) ... 1.50

Other grades: Multiply price above by 5/6 for VF/NM • 2/3 for VERY FINE • 1/3 for FINE • 1/5 for VERY GOOD • 1/8 for GOOD

Revolver

British anthology repackaged for America
©Fleetway-Quality

Rhudiprrt, Prince of Fur

Get reincarnated with your cats
©Mu

Richard Dragon, Kung-Fu Fighter

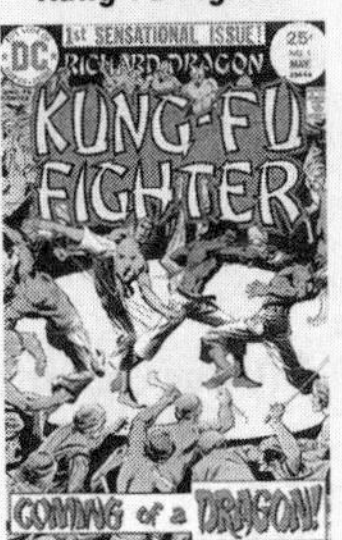

Sensei turns thief into good martial artist
©DC

Richie Rich

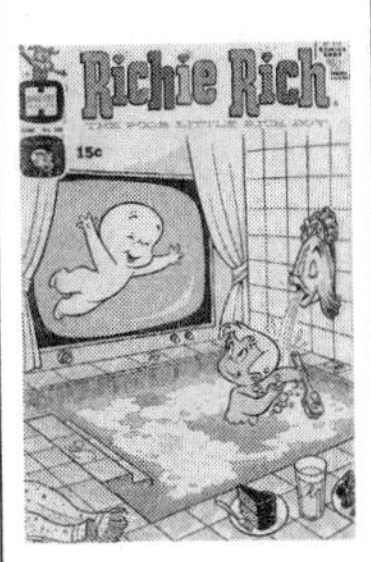

Poor little rich boy had many titles
©Harvey

Richie Rich

1990s Harvey restart didn't last as long
©Harvey

	N-MINT
❑12, Dec 1989; JLee (c); JLee (a); Acts of Vengeance	1.50
❑13, Dec 1989; JLee (c); JLee (a); Acts of Vengeance	1.50
❑14, Jan 1990 JLee (c); RH (a); A: Spider-Man	1.50
❑15, Feb 1990 JLee (c); RH (a); A: Spider-Man	1.50
❑16, Mar 1990	1.50
❑17, Apr 1990 JLee (c); JLee (a)	1.50
❑18, May 1990 JLee (c); JLee (a)	1.50
❑19, Jun 1990 JLee (c); JLee (a)	1.50
❑20, Jul 1990	1.50
❑21, Aug 1990	1.50
❑22, Sep 1990	1.50
❑23, Oct 1990	1.75
❑24, Nov 1990	1.75
❑25, Dec 1990 MG (c)	1.75
❑26, Jan 1991 MG (c)	1.75
❑27, Feb 1991 MG (c)	1.75
❑28, Mar 1991 MG (c)	1.75
❑29, Apr 1991 MG (c); A: Ghost Rider	1.75
❑30, May 1991 MG (c); A: Ghost Rider	1.75
❑31, Jun 1991; Painted cover	1.75
❑32, Jul 1991	1.75
❑33, Aug 1991 TP (c)	1.75
❑34, Sep 1991	1.75
❑35, Oct 1991	1.75
❑36, Nov 1991; Photo cover	1.75
❑37, Dec 1991	1.75
❑38, Jan 1992	1.75
❑39, Feb 1992	1.75
❑40, Mar 1992 MG (c)	1.75
❑41, Apr 1992 JR2 (c)	1.75
❑42, May 1992 JR2 (c)	1.75
❑43, Jun 1992 JR2 (c); VM (a)	1.75
❑44, Jul 1992 JR2 (c); VM (a)	1.75
❑45, Aug 1992 JR2 (c)	1.75
❑46, Sep 1992 JR2 (c)	1.75
❑47, Oct 1992	1.75
❑48, Nov 1992	1.75
❑49, Dec 1992	1.75
❑50, Jan 1993; 1: Punisher 2099. Embossed cover; Punisher 2099 Preview	2.95
❑51, Feb 1993	1.75
❑52, Mar 1993	1.75
❑53, Apr 1993	1.75
❑54, May 1993	1.75
❑55, Jun 1993	1.75
❑56, Jul 1993	1.75
❑57, Aug 1993 A: Ghost Rider. A: Daredevil	1.75
❑58, Sep 1993 A: Ghost Rider. A: Daredevil	1.75
❑59, Oct 1993 A: Max	1.75
❑60, Nov 1993 A: Cage	1.75
❑61, Dec 1993; Giant-size; MG (c); Embossed foil cover	2.95
❑62, Jan 1994 MG (c)	1.75
❑63, Feb 1994 MG (c)	1.75
❑64, Mar 1994; MG (c); regular cover	2.25
❑64/Variant, Mar 1994; MG (c); Die-cut cover	2.00
❑65, Apr 1994 BSz (c)	3.00
❑66, May 1994 BA (c); BA (a); A: Captain America	1.95
❑67, Jun 1994	1.95
❑68, Jul 1994	1.95
❑69, Aug 1994	1.95
❑70, Sep 1994	1.95
❑71, Oct 1994	1.95
❑72, Nov 1994	1.95
❑73, Dec 1994	1.95
❑74, Jan 1995	1.95
❑75, Feb 1995; Giant-size	4.00
❑76, Mar 1995; New Punisher (Lynn Michaels) begins	3.00
❑77, Apr 1995	1.95
❑78, May 1995	1.95
❑79, Jun 1995; D: Microchip	1.95
❑80, Jul 1995; D: Stone Cold; Final Issue	1.95

Punisher War Journal
Marvel

	N-MINT
❑1, Feb 2007	2.99
❑1/Variant, Feb 2007, b&w; Black-and-white version of the first issue	2.99
❑2, Mar 2007, Civil War tie-in	2.99
❑3, Apr 2007; Civil War tie-in	2.99
❑4, May 2007	2.99
❑5, Jun 2007	2.99
❑6, Jul 2007; The Initiative	6.00
❑7, Aug 2007; Punisher as Captain America on cover	2.99

Punisher War Zone
Marvel

	N-MINT
❑1, Mar 1992, JR2 (c); JR2 (a); Die-cut cover	2.50
❑2, Apr 1992, JR2 (c); JR2 (a)	1.75
❑3, May 1992, JR2 (c); JR2 (a)	1.75
❑4, Jun 1992, JR2 (c); JR2 (a)	1.75
❑5, Jul 1992, JR2 (c); JR2 (a)	1.75
❑6, Aug 1992, JR2 (c); JR2 (a)	1.75
❑7, Sep 1992, JR2 (c); JR2 (a)	1.75
❑8, Oct 1992, JR2 (c); JR2 (a)	1.75
❑9, Nov 1992	1.75
❑10, Dec 1992	1.75
❑11, Jan 1993	1.75
❑12, Feb 1993	1.75
❑13, Mar 1993	1.75
❑14, Apr 1992	1.75
❑15, May 1993	1.75
❑16, Jun 1993	1.75
❑17, Jul 1993, MG (c)	1.75
❑18, Aug 1993, MG (c)	1.75
❑19, Sep 1993, MG (c); A: Wolverine	1.75
❑20, Oct 1993	1.75
❑21, Nov 1993	1.75
❑22, Dec 1993	1.75
❑23, Jan 1994, Giant-size; MG (c); JB, VM (a); D: Rapido. Embossed foil cover	2.95
❑24, Feb 1994, MG (c); JB, VM (a)	1.75
❑25, Mar 1994, JB, VM (a)	2.25
❑26, Apr 1994, JB (a)	1.75
❑27, May 1994, JB (a)	1.75
❑28, Jun 1994, JB (a)	1.95
❑29, Jul 1994, JB (a)	1.95
❑30, Aug 1994, JB (a)	1.95
❑31, Sep 1994, JKu (a)	1.95
❑32, Oct 1994, JKu (a)	1.95
❑33, Nov 1994, JKu (c); JKu (a)	1.95
❑34, Dec 1994, JKu (a)	1.95
❑35, Jan 1995, JKu (a)	1.95
❑36, Feb 1995, JKu (a)	1.95
❑37, Mar 1995, O: Max (The Punisher's dog)	1.95
❑38, Apr 1995	1.95
❑39, May 1995	1.95
❑40, Jun 1995	1.95
❑41, Jul 1995, Final Issue	1.95
❑Ann 1, ca. 1993, MG (c); JB (a); trading card; pin-up gallery	2.95
❑Ann 2, ca. 1994, D: Roc	2.95

Punisher/Wolverine African Saga
Marvel

	N-MINT
❑1, ca. 1988; Reprints Punisher War Journal #6 & 7 in prestige format; NN	5.95

Punisher X-Mas Special
Marvel

	N-MINT
❑1, Feb 2007	3.99

Punisher: Year One
Marvel

	N-MINT
❑1, Dec 1994; O: Punisher	2.50
❑2, Jan 1995; O: Punisher	2.50
❑3, Feb 1995; O: Punisher	2.50
❑4, Mar 1995; O: Punisher	2.50

Punx
Acclaim / Valiant

	N-MINT
❑1, Nov 1995	2.50
❑2, Dec 1995	2.50
❑3, Jan 1996	2.50

Punx (Manga) Special
Acclaim / Valiant

	N-MINT
❑1, Mar 1996, to be read from back to front	2.50

Puppet Master
Eternity

	N-MINT
❑1	2.50
❑2	2.50
❑3	2.50
❑4	2.50

Puppet Master: Children of the Puppet Master
Eternity

	N-MINT
❑1	2.50
❑2	2.50

Pure Images
Pure Imagination

	N-MINT
❑1; some color	2.50
❑2; some color	2.50
❑3; monsters; some color	2.50
❑4; monsters; some color	2.50

Purgatori
Chaos!

	N-MINT
❑½, Dec 2000	2.95
❑1, Oct 1998	3.00
❑2, Nov 1998 V: Lady Death	2.95
❑3, Dec 1998	2.95
❑4, Jan 1999	2.95
❑5, Feb 1999	2.95
❑6, Mar 1999	2.95
❑7, Apr 1999; V: Dracula	2.95
❑Ashcan 1; ashcan preview; no cover price	3.00

Other grades: Multiply price above by 5/6 for VF/NM • 2/3 for VERY FINE • 1/3 for FINE • 1/5 for VERY GOOD • 1/8 for GOOD

Purgatori
Devil's Due / Chaos

❑1, Oct 2005 .... 3.00
❑2, Dec 2005, V: Lady Death 2.95
❑3, Jan 2006 .... 2.95
❑4, Feb 2006 .... 2.95
❑5, Mar 2006 .... 2.95
❑6, Sep 2006 .... 2.95

Purgatori: Empire
Chaos

❑1, May 2000 .... 2.95
❑2, Jun 2000 .... 2.95
❑3, Jul 2000 .... 2.95

Purgatori: Goddess Rising
Chaos!

❑1, Jul 1999 .... 2.95
❑1/Ltd., Jul 1999; limited edition 2.95
❑2, Aug 1999 .... 2.95
❑3, Sep 1999 .... 2.95
❑4, Dec 1999 .... 2.95

Purgatori: The Dracula Gambit
Chaos!

❑1, Aug 1997 .... 2.95
❑1/Variant, Aug 1997; Centennial Premium Edition; no cover price 3.00

Purgatori: The Dracula Gambit Sketchbook
Chaos!

❑1, Jul 1997; b&w preliminary sketches 2.95

Purgatori: The Vampires Myth
Chaos!

❑-1, Aug 1996 .... 1.50
❑1, Aug 1996; Red foil embossed 3.50
❑1/Ltd., Aug 1996; premium edition; limited to 10, 000 copies; wraparound acetate cover 5.00
❑1/Variant, Oct 1996; "Krome" edition (color) 8.00
❑2, Oct 1996 .... 3.00
❑3, Dec 1996 .... 2.95
❑4, Feb 1997 .... 2.95
❑5, Apr 1997 .... 2.95
❑6, Jun 1997 .... 2.95

Purgatori vs. Vampirella
Chaos

❑nn, Apr 2000 .... 2.95

Purgatory USA
Slave Labor

❑1, Mar 1989, b&w; Ed Brubaker's first published work 2.00

Purge
Ania

❑0 .... 1.95
❑1, Aug 1993 .... 1.95

Purge
Amara

❑0; Preview edition 1.50

Purple Claw Mysteries
AC

❑1, b&w; Reprints 2.95

Purr
Blue Eyed Dog

❑1; Adult; ca. 1993 .... 8.00

Pussycat
Marvel

❑1, ca. 1968, b&w; magazine; BWa, WW (a) 150.00

PvP
Dork Storm

❑1, Mar 2001 .... 2.95

PvP
Image

❑1, Mar 2003, b&w; Printed sideways 5.00
❑2, May 2003, b&w; Printed sideways 2.95
❑3, Jul 2003, b&w; Printed sideways 2.95
❑4, Oct 2003, b&w; Printed sideways 2.95
❑5, Dec 2003, b&w; Printed sideways 2.95
❑6, Jan 2004, b&w; Printed sideways 2.95
❑7, Apr 2004, b&w; Printed sideways 2.95
❑8, May 2004, b&w; Printed sideways 2.95
❑9, Jul 2004, b&w; Printed sideways 2.95
❑10, Aug 2004, b&w; Printed sideways 2.95
❑11, Sep 2004, b&w; EL (c);Printed sideways 2.95
❑12, Oct 2004, b&w; Printed sideways 2.95
❑13, Nov 2004, b&w; Printed sideways 2.95
❑14, ca. 2005 .... 2.95
❑15, ca. 2005 .... 2.95
❑16, ca. 2005 .... 2.95
❑17, ca. 2005 .... 2.95
❑18, Oct 2005 .... 2.95
❑19 2005 .... 2.95

PvP (Image 2nd Series)
Image

❑0, Sep 2005 .... 1.00
❑20, Dec 2005 .... 2.95
❑21, Jan 2006 .... 2.99
❑22, Feb 2006 .... 2.99
❑23, Mar 2006 .... 2.99
❑24, Apr 2006 .... 2.99
❑25, May 2006 .... 2.99
❑26, Jun 2006 .... 2.99
❑27, Jul 2006 .... 2.99
❑28, Nov 2006 .... 2.99
❑29, Dec 2006 .... 2.99
❑30 .... 2.99
❑31 .... 2.99
❑32 .... 2.99
❑33 .... 2.99
❑34 .... 2.99
❑35 .... 2.99
❑36 .... 2.99
❑37 .... 2.99
❑38 .... 2.99
❑39 .... 2.99
❑40 .... 2.99
❑41 .... 2.99
❑42 .... 2.99

Q-Loc
Chiasmus

❑1, Aug 1994 .... 2.50

Quack!
Star*Reach

❑1, Jul 1976, b&w; FB, HC, ME (w); FB, HC, DSt, ME (a) 2.50
❑2, Jan 1977, b&w SA (w); SA (a) 2.50
❑3, Apr 1977, b&w 2.50
❑4, Jun 1977, b&w 2.50
❑5, Sep 1977, b&w 2.50
❑6, Dec 1977, b&w FB (w); FB (a) 2.50

Quadrant
Quadrant

❑1, ca. 1983, b&w; Adult 1.95
❑2, ca. 1984, b&w; Adult 1.95
❑3, ca. 1984, b&w; Adult 1.95
❑4, ca. 1985, b&w; Adult 1.95
❑5, ca. 1985, b&w; Adult 1.95
❑6, ca. 1985, b&w; no cover date 1.95
❑7, ca. 1986, b&w; Adult 1.95
❑8, ca. 1986, b&w; Adult 1.95

Quadro Gang
Nonsense Unlimited

❑1, b&w 1.25

Quagmire
Kitchen Sink

❑1, Sum 1970, b&w; Adult 3.00

Quagmire U.S.A.
Antarctic

❑1, Mar 1994, b&w 2.75
❑2, May 1994, b&w 2.75
❑3, Jul 1994, b&w 2.75

Quagmire U.S.A.
Antarctic

❑1, Feb 2004 .... 2.99
❑2, Apr 2004 .... 2.99
❑3, Jun 2004 .... 2.99
❑4, Aug 2004 .... 2.99
❑5, Oct 2004 .... 2.99

Quality Special
Fleetway-Quality

❑1; Strontium Dog 2.00
❑2; Midnight Surfer 2.00

Quantum & Woody
Acclaim / Valiant

❑0/AmEnt, ca. 1997, American Entertainment exclusive 3.00
❑1, Jun 1997 .... 2.50
❑1/A, Jun 1997, Painted cover 2.50
❑2, Jul 1997 .... 2.50
❑3, Aug 1997, 1: The Goat; Indicia says July 1997 .... 2.50
❑4, Sep 1997 .... 2.50
❑5, Oct 1997 .... 2.50
❑6, Nov 1997 .... 2.50
❑7, Dec 1997 .... 2.50
❑8, Jan 1998 .... 2.50
❑9, Feb 1998, A: Troublemakers 2.50
❑10, Mar 1998 .... 2.50
❑11, Apr 1998 .... 2.50
❑12, Jan 1998, indicia says Jan; no cover date 2.50
❑13, Feb 1998, indicia says Feb; no cover date 2.50
❑14, Mar 1998, Indicia says March; No cover date 2.50
❑15, Apr 1998 .... 2.50
❑16, May 1998 .... 2.50
❑17, Jun 1998, Final Issue 2.50
❑Ashcan 1, Feb 1997, b&w preview of series; no cover price 1.00

Quantum Creep
Parody

❑1, ca. 1992, b&w 2.50

Quantum Leap
Innovation

❑1, Sep 1991; O: Doctor Sam Beckett (Quantum Leap). 1: Doctor Sam Beckett (Quantum Leap) 5.00
❑2, Dec 1991 .... 4.00
❑3, Mar 1992; Sam as Santa 4.00
❑4, Apr 1992; Sam on game show 4.00
❑5, May 1992; Superman theme cover 4.00
❑6, Sep 1992 .... 3.00
❑7, Oct 1992 .... 3.00
❑8, Dec 1992 .... 3.00
❑9, Feb 1993 .... 3.00
❑10, Apr 1993 .... 2.50
❑11, May 1993 .... 2.50
❑12, Jun 1993 .... 2.50
❑13, Aug 1993; Time and Space Special #1; foil-enhanced cardstock cover 2.95
❑Ann 1 1992; <Never published> 4.00
❑Special 1, Oct 1992; reprints #1 .... 5.00

Quantum: Rock of Ages
Dreamchilde Press

❑1, ca. 2003 .... 2.99
❑2, ca. 2003 .... 2.99
❑3, Apr 2004, Wraparound cover 2.99
❑4, Jun 2004 .... 2.99

Quasar
Marvel

❑1, Oct 1989, O: Quasar 1.50
❑2, Nov 1989 .... 1.00
❑3, Nov 1989, Human Torch Apperance 1.00
❑4, Dec 1989, O: Quantum 1.00
❑5, Dec 1989, V: Absorbing Man. Acts of Vengeance 1.00
❑6, Jan 1990, A: Venom. V: Red Ghost. V: Living Laser. Acts of Vengeance 1.00
❑7, Feb 1990, A: Spider-Man. Spider-Man has cosmic powers 1.00
❑8, Mar 1990, Secret War Tie-In 1.00
❑9, Apr 1990, 1: Captain Atlas 1.00
❑10, May 1990, O: Captain Atlas 1.00
❑11, Jun 1990, Phoenix 1.00
❑12, Jul 1990 .... 1.00
❑13, Aug 1990 .... 1.00
❑14, Sep 1990, TMc (c) 1.00
❑15, Oct 1990 .... 1.00
❑16, Nov 1990, 48 cosmic pages 1.00
❑17, Dec 1990 .... 1.00
❑18, Jan 1991 .... 1.00
❑19, Feb 1991, 1: Starlight 1.00
❑20, Mar 1991, Fantastic Four 1.00
❑21, Apr 1991 .... 1.00
❑22, May 1991, A: Ghost Rider 1.00
❑23, Jun 1991, A: Ghost Rider 1.00
❑24, Jul 1991, 1: Infinity (physical) 1.00
❑25, Aug 1991, new costume 1.00
❑26, Sep 1991, Infinity Gauntlet 1.00

Other grades: Multiply price above by 5/6 for VF/NM • 2/3 for VERY FINE • 1/3 for FINE • 1/5 for VERY GOOD • 1/8 for GOOD

Richie Rich & Casper

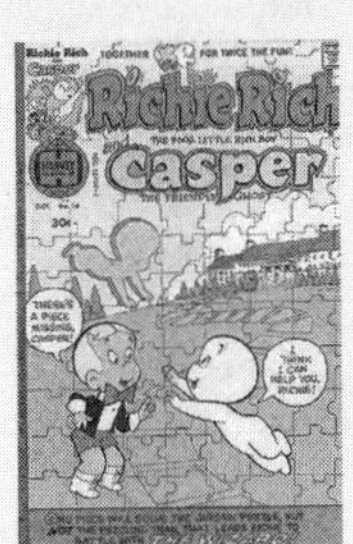

Richie went to the Enchanted Forest a lot
©Harvey

Richie Rich & Jackie Jokers

Stand-up comic appeared in many parodies
©Harvey

Richie Rich Big Book

1990s equivalent of the old 48-pagers
©Harvey

Richie Rich Cash

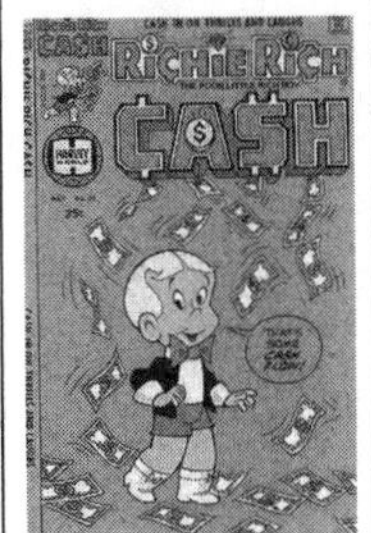

Cover gags usually involved currency
©Harvey

Richie Rich Diamonds

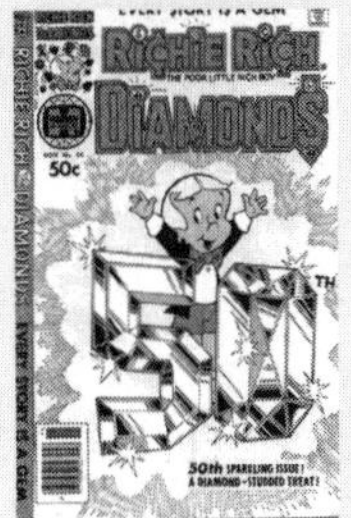

Cover gags usually involved diamonds
©Harvey

N-MINT

❑27, Oct 1991, 1: Epoch. Infinity Gauntlet 1.00
❑28, Nov 1991 1.00
❑29, Dec 1991 1.00
❑30, Jan 1992, PB (a) 1.00
❑31, Feb 1992, A: D.P.7. New Universe 1.25
❑32, Mar 1992, 1: Korath the Pursuer. A: Imperial Guard. A: Starfox. Galactic Storm 1.25
❑33, Apr 1992, V: Sh'iar Imperial Guard; Cover says #2; Galactic Storm 1.25
❑34, May 1992, A: Binary. Galactic Storm 1.25
❑35, Jun 1992, V: Shi'ar Starforce; V: Deathbird; Galactic Storm Aftermath 1.25
❑36, Jul 1992, A: Her. A: Makkari. V: Souleater 1.25
❑37, Aug 1992 1.25
❑38, Sep 1992, Infinity War 1.25
❑39, Oct 1992, Infinity War 1.25
❑40, Nov 1992, Infinity War 1.25
❑41, Dec 1992, 1: Kismet 1.25
❑42, Jan 1993 1.25
❑43, Feb 1993, V: Blue Marvel; Quasar escapes White Room 1.25
❑44, Mar 1993 1.25
❑45, Apr 1993 1.25
❑46, May 1993 1.25
❑47, Jun 1993, 1: Thunderstrike 1.75
❑48, Jul 1993 1.25
❑49, Aug 1993 1.25
❑50, Sep 1993, Giant-size; A: Silver Surfer. Holo-grafix cover 2.95
❑51, Oct 1993, A: Squadron Supreme. A: Anglemen 1.25
❑52, Nov 1993 1.25
❑53, Dec 1993 1.25
❑54, Jan 1994, Starblast Crossover 1.25
❑55, Feb 1994 1.25
❑56, Mar 1994 1.25
❑57, Apr 1994 1.25
❑58, May 1994 1.25
❑59, Jun 1994 1.25
❑60, Jul 1994, Final Issue 1.25
❑Special 1, Mar 1992, reprints Quasar #32 for newsstand distribution 1.50
❑Special 2, Apr 1992, reprints Quasar #33 for newsstand distribution 1.50
❑Special 3, May 1992, reprints Quasar #34 for newsstand distribution 1.50

Queen & Country
Oni

❑1, Mar 2001, b&w; Tim Sale cover 9.00
❑1/FCBD, Mar 2001 1.00
❑2, May 2001, b&w; Tim Sale cover 7.00
❑3, Jul 2001, b&w; Tim Sale cover 6.00
❑4, Sep 2001, b&w; Tim Sale cover 5.00
❑5, Nov 2001, b&w; John K. Snyder cover 5.00
❑6, Jan 2002, b&w; John K. Snyder cover 5.00
❑7, Mar 2002, b&w; John K. Snyder cover 5.00
❑8, May 2002, b&w 5.00
❑9, Jun 2002, b&w 5.00
❑10, Jul 2002, b&w 5.00
❑11, Aug 2002, b&w 5.00
❑12, Sep 2002, b&w 5.00
❑13, Jan 2003, b&w; Preview of Days Like This 5.00
❑14, Feb 2003, b&w; Preview of Midnight Mover 5.00

N-MINT

❑15, Apr 2003, b&w; Preview of Three Strikes 5.00
❑16, May 2003, b&w 4.00
❑17, Jun 2003, b&w 4.00
❑18, Oct 2003, b&w 4.00
❑19, Oct 2003, b&w 4.00
❑20, Nov 2004, b&w 4.00
❑21, Nov 2004, b&w 2.99
❑22, Dec 2004, b&w 2.99
❑23, Feb 2004, b&w 2.99
❑24, Apr 2004, b&w 2.99
❑25, Jun 2004, b&w; Note price 5.99
❑26, Jul 2004, b&w 2.99
❑27, Sep 2004, b&w 2.99
❑28, Nov 2004 2.99

Queen & Country: Declassified
Oni

❑1, Nov 2002, b&w 2.95
❑2, Dec 2002, b&w 2.95
❑3, Jan 2003, b&w 2.95

Queen & Country: Declassified
Oni

❑1, Jan 2005, b&w 2.99

Queen & Country: Declassified
Oni

❑1, Jun 2005; b&w 2.99
❑2, Sep 2005; b&w 2.99
❑3, Oct 2005; b&w 2.99

Queen of the Damned
Innovation

❑1, ca. 1991 2.50
❑2, ca. 1992 2.50
❑3, ca. 1992 2.50
❑4, ca. 1992 2.50
❑5, ca. 1992 2.50
❑6, ca. 1993 2.50
❑7, ca. 1993 2.50
❑8, Jul 1993 2.50
❑9, Sep 1993 2.50
❑10, Nov 1993 2.50
❑11, Dec 1993 2.50
❑12, Jan 1994 2.50

Queen's Greatest Hits
Revolutionary

❑1, Nov 1993, b&w 2.50

Quest for Camelot
DC

❑1, Jul 1998; Movie adaptation 4.95

Quest for Dreams Lost
Literacy Volunteers

❑1, ca. 1987, b&w; The Realm story 2.00

Question
DC

❑1, Feb 1987, Painted cover 2.00
❑2, Mar 1987 1.75
❑3, Apr 1987 1.75
❑4, May 1987 1.50
❑5, Jun 1987 1.50
❑6, Jul 1987 1.50
❑7, Aug 1987 1.50
❑8, Sep 1987 1.50
❑9, Oct 1987 1.50
❑10, Nov 1987 1.50

N-MINT

❑11, Dec 1987 1.50
❑12, Jan 1988 1.50
❑13, Feb 1988 1.50
❑14, Mar 1988 1.50
❑15, Apr 1988 1.50
❑16, May 1988 1.50
❑17, Jun 1988, Rorschach, Green Arrow 1.50
❑18, Jul 1988, Green Arrow 1.50
❑19, Aug 1988 1.50
❑20, Oct 1988 1.50
❑21, Nov 1988 1.50
❑22, Dec 1988 1.50
❑23, Win 1988 1.50
❑24, Jan 1989 1.50
❑25, Feb 1989 1.50
❑26, Mar 1989 1.50
❑27, Jun 1989 1.50
❑28, Jul 1989 1.50
❑29, Aug 1989 1.50
❑30, Sep 1989 1.50
❑31, Oct 1989 1.50
❑32, Nov 1989 1.50
❑33, Dec 1989 1.50
❑34, Jan 1990 1.50
❑35, Mar 1990 1.50
❑36, Apr 1990, Final Issue 1.50
❑Ann 1, ca. 1988, Batman, Green Arrow 2.50
❑Ann 2, ca. 1989, Green Arrow 3.50

Question
DC

❑1, Jan 2005 2.95
❑2, Feb 2005, 1: Subterraneans; 1: Minos; V: Subterraneans 2.95
❑3, Mar 2005 2.95
❑4, Apr 2005 2.95
❑5, May 2005 2.99
❑6, Jun 2005; D: Minos, V: Minos & Subterraneans 2.99

Question Quarterly
DC

❑1, Aut 1990 2.50
❑2, Sum 1991 2.50
❑3, Aut 1991 2.50
❑4, Win 1991 2.95
❑5, Spr 1992; Final Issue 2.95

Question Returns
DC

❑1, Feb 1997, One-shot 3.50

Quest of the Tiger Woman
Millennium

❑1 2.95

Quest Presents
Quest

❑1, Jul 1983; JD (w); JD (a); Wraparound cover 1.50
❑2, Sep 1983; JD (c); JD (w); JD (a); Wraparound cover 1.50
❑3, Nov 1983 JD (c); JD (w); JD (a) 1.50

Questprobe
Marvel

❑1, Aug 1984, JR (a); O: Chief Examiner. 1: Chief Examiner. Hulk 1.50

N-MINT

❑2, Jan 1985, AM (w); AM, JM (a); Spider-Man ... 1.50
❑3, Nov 1985, Human Torch; Thing ... 1.50

Quick Draw McGraw
Dell

❑2, Apr 1960 ... 15.00
❑3, Jul 1960 ... 10.00
❑4, Oct 1960 ... 10.00
❑5, Jan 1961 ... 10.00
❑6, Apr 1961 ... 10.00
❑7, Jul 1961 ... 10.00
❑8, Oct 1961 ... 8.00
❑9, Jan 1962 ... 8.00
❑10, Apr 1962 ... 8.00
❑11, Jul 1962 ... 8.00
❑12, Oct 1962 ... 8.00
❑13, Feb 1963 ... 6.00
❑14, ca. 1963 ... 6.00
❑15, Jun 1969 ... 10.00

Quick Draw McGraw
Charlton

❑1, Nov 1970 ... 10.00
❑2, Jan 1971 ... 7.00
❑3, Mar 1971 ... 5.00
❑4, May 1971 ... 5.00
❑5, Jul 1971 ... 5.00
❑6, Sep 1971 ... 4.00
❑7, Nov 1971 ... 4.00
❑8, Jan 1972 ... 4.00

Quicken Forbidden
Cryptic

❑1, ca. 1996, b&w ... 3.25
❑2, ca. 1996, b&w ... 3.00
❑3, ca. 1997, b&w ... 3.00
❑4, ca. 1997, b&w ... 3.00
❑5, ca. 1998, b&w ... 3.00
❑6, ca. 1998, b&w; ca. 1999 ... 3.00
❑7, ca. 1999, b&w ... 3.00
❑8, ca. 1999, b&w ... 3.00
❑9, ca. 2000, b&w ... 3.00
❑10, ca. 2000, b&w; ca. 2001 ... 2.95
❑11 ... 2.95
❑12 ... 2.95
❑13, Oct 2005 ... 2.95

Quicksilver
Marvel

❑1, Nov 1997, gatefold summary; wraparound cover ... 2.99
❑2, Dec 1997, gatefold summary ... 1.99
❑3, Jan 1998, gatefold summary ... 1.99
❑4, Feb 1998, gatefold summary ... 1.99
❑5, Mar 1998, gatefold summary ... 1.99
❑6, Apr 1998, gatefold summary ... 1.99
❑7, May 1998, gatefold summary ... 1.99
❑8, Jun 1998, gatefold summary; in Savage Land ... 1.99
❑9, Jul 1998, gatefold summary; V: Fenris; V: Random; V: Pyro; V: Feral; V: Avalanche; V: Omega Red; V: Alcoytes; In Savage Land ... 1.99
❑10, Aug 1998, gatefold summary; concludes in Avengers #7 ... 1.99
❑11, Sep 1998, gatefold summary ... 1.99
❑12, Oct 1998, double-sized; V: Exodus; Gatefold summary ... 1.99
❑13, Nov 1998, gatefold summary ... 1.99

Quincy Looks Into His Future
General Electric

❑1; giveaway; King Features strip ... 2.00

Quit City
Avatar

❑1, ca. 2004 ... 3.50
❑1/Foil, ca. 2004 ... 15.00

Quit Your Job
Alternative

❑1, b&w; NN; b&w ... 6.95

Quivers
Caliber

❑1, ca. 1991, b&w ... 2.95
❑2, ca. 1991, b&w ... 2.95

Q-Unit
Harris

❑1, Dec 1993; trading card; Polybagged with "layered reality cybercard" ... 2.95

N-MINT

Qwan
Tokyopop

❑1, Mar 2005 ... 9.99
❑2, Jul 2005 ... 9.99
❑3, Dec 2005 ... 9.99

Rabbit
Sharkbait

❑1 ... 2.50

Rabid
Fantaco

❑1; NN ... 5.95

Rabid Animal Komix
Krankin' Komix

❑1, Jun 1995 ... 2.95
❑2, May 1996 ... 2.95

Rabid Rachel
Miller

❑1, b&w ... 2.00

Race Against Time
Dark Angel

❑1, Jun 1997 ... 2.50
❑2, Aug 1997 ... 2.50

Race of Scorpions
Dark Horse

❑1, Mar 1990, b&w ... 4.50
❑2, Sep 1990, b&w ... 4.50

Race of Scorpions
Dark Horse

❑1, Jul 1991, b&w ... 2.25
❑2, Aug 1991 ... 2.50
❑3, Sep 1992 ... 2.50
❑4, Oct 1991 ... 2.50

Racer X
Now

❑1, Sep 1988 ... 2.00
❑2, Oct 1988 ... 1.75
❑3, Nov 1988 ... 1.75
❑4, Jan 1989 ... 1.75
❑5, Feb 1989 ... 1.75
❑6, Mar 1989 ... 1.75
❑7, Apr 1989 ... 1.75
❑8, May 1989; Comics Code ... 1.75
❑9, Jun 1989; Comics Code ... 1.75
❑10, Jul 1989; Comics Code ... 1.75
❑11, Aug 1989; Comics Code ... 1.75

Racer X
Now

❑1, Sep 1989 ... 2.00
❑2, Oct 1989 ... 1.75
❑3, Nov 1989 ... 1.75
❑4, Dec 1989 ... 1.75
❑5, Jan 1990 ... 1.75
❑6, Feb 1990 ... 1.75
❑7, Mar 1990 ... 1.75
❑8, Apr 1990 ... 1.75
❑9, May 1990 ... 1.75
❑10, Jun 1990 ... 1.75

Racer X
WildStorm

❑1, Oct 2000 ... 2.95
❑2, Nov 2000 ... 2.95
❑3, Dec 2000 ... 2.95

Racer X Premiere
Now

❑1, Aug 1988; NN ... 3.50

Rack & Pain
Dark Horse

❑1, Mar 1994; Dark Horse ... 2.50
❑2, Apr 1994 ... 2.50
❑3, May 1994 ... 2.50
❑4, Jun 1994 ... 2.50

Rack & Pain: Killers
Chaos

❑1, Sep 1996; Chaos ... 2.95
❑2, Oct 1996 ... 2.95
❑3, Dec 1996 ... 2.95
❑4, Jan 1996 ... 2.95

Radical Dreamer
Blackball

❑0, May 1994; poster comic ... 2.50
❑1, Jun 1994; poster comic ... 2.00
❑2, Jul 1994; poster comic ... 2.95

N-MINT

❑3, Sep 1994; poster comic ... 2.50
❑4, Nov 1994; foldout comic on cardstock ... 2.50

Radical Dreamer
Mark's Giant Economy Size

❑1, Jun 1995, b&w ... 2.95
❑2, Jul 1995, b&w ... 2.95
❑3, Aug 1995, b&w ... 2.95
❑4, Sep 1995, b&w ... 2.95
❑5, Dec 1995, b&w ... 2.95

Radioactive Man
Bongo

❑1, ca. 1993; O: Radioactive Man. glow cover ... 5.00
❑88; 2nd issue ... 5.00
❑216; 3rd issue ... 3.00
❑412, ca. 1994; 4th issue ... 3.00
❑679; 5th issue ... 3.00
❑1000, Jan 1995; 6th issue ... 3.00

Radioactive Man
Bongo

❑1, ca. 2000, #100 on cover ... 2.50
❑2, Nov 2000, #222 on cover ... 2.50
❑3, ca. 2001, DDC (a); #136 on cover ... 3.00
❑4, ca. 2001, March 1953 on cover ... 3.00
❑5, ca. 2002, #575 on cover ... 3.00
❑6, ca. 2002 ... 3.00
❑7, ca. 2003, 7th issue ... 3.00
❑8, ca. 2003, 8th issue; ca. 2004 ... 2.99
❑9, ca. 2004 ... 2.99

Radioactive Man 80 Page Colossal
Bongo

❑1, ca. 1995 ... 4.95

Radio Boy
Eclipse

❑1, Mar 1987, b&w ... 1.50

Radiskull & Devil Doll: Radiskull Love-Hate One Shot
Image

❑1, Apr 2003 ... 2.95

Radix
Image

❑1, Dec 2001; Wraparound cover ... 2.95
❑2, Feb 2002 ... 2.95

Radrex
Bullet

❑1, Jan 1990 ... 2.25

Ragamuffins
Eclipse

❑1, Jan 1985 GC (a) ... 2.00

Rage
Anarchy Bridgeworks

❑1 ... 2.95

Raggedy Ann and Andy
Dell

❑1, Oct 1964 ... 35.00
❑2 ... 20.00
❑3, Dec 1965 ... 20.00
❑4, Mar 1966 ... 20.00

Raggedy Ann and Andy
Gold Key

❑1, Dec 1971 ... 5.00
❑2, Mar 1972 ... 3.50
❑3, Dec 1972 ... 3.50
❑4, Mar 1973 ... 3.50
❑5, Jun 1973 ... 3.50
❑6, Sep 1973 ... 3.50

Raggedyman
Cult

❑1, b&w ... 2.50
❑1/Variant, b&w; Prism cover ... 2.75
❑2, b&w ... 1.95
❑3, b&w ... 1.95
❑4, b&w; BT (c); BT (a) ... 2.50
❑5, Jul 1993, b&w ... 2.50
❑6 ... 2.50

Raging Angels
Classic Hippie

❑1, b&w ... 2.50

Other grades: Multiply price above by 5/6 for VF/NM • 2/3 for VERY FINE • 1/3 for FINE • 1/5 for VERY GOOD • 1/8 for GOOD

Richie Rich Dollars & Cents

One of the earlier Richie Rich spinoffs
©Harvey

Richie Rich Fortunes

Series was bimonthly through the 1970s
©Harvey

Richie Rich Gold & Silver

Cover gags usually involved precious metals
©Harvey

Richie Rich Jackpots

Issue #25 had Richie marrying Mayda Munny
©Harvey

Richie Rich Millions

The earliest and longest-running Richie spinoff
©Harvey

N-MINT

Ragman
DC

❑1, Sep 1976, JKu (c); JKu (a); O: Ragman. 1: Ragman 5.00
❑2, Nov 1976, JKu (a) 3.00
❑3, Jan 1977, JKu (a) 3.00
❑4, Mar 1977, JKu (a) 3.00
❑5, Jul 1977, JKu (c); JKu (a); Final Issue 3.00

Ragman
DC

❑1, Oct 1991, PB (c); KG (w); KG, PB (a) 2.00
❑2, Nov 1991, PB (c); KG (w); KG, PB (a) 2.00
❑3, Dec 1991, PB (c); KG (w); KG, PB (a); O: Ragman 2.00
❑4, Jan 1992, PB (c); KG (w); KG, PB (a) 2.00
❑5, Feb 1992, PB (c); KG (w); KG, PB (a) 2.00
❑6, Mar 1992, PB (c); KG (w); KG, PB (a) 2.00
❑7, Apr 1992, PB (c); KG (w); KG, PB, RT (a) 2.00
❑8, May 1992, PB (c); KG (w); KG, PB, RT (a); A: Batman. Final Issue 2.00

Ragman: Cry of the Dead
DC

❑1, Aug 1993, JKu (c) 2.00
❑2, Sep 1993, JKu (c) 1.75
❑3, Oct 1993, JKu (c) 1.75
❑4, Nov 1993, JKu (c) 1.75
❑5, Dec 1993, JKu (c) 1.75
❑6, Jan 1994, JKu (c);Final Issue 1.75

Ragmop
Planet Lucy

❑1, Jun 1995 .... 2.75
❑1/2nd, Dec 1995; 2nd printing 3.10
❑2, Aug 1995 .... 2.75
❑2/2nd, Dec 1995; 2nd printing 2.95
❑3, Oct 1995 .... 2.95
❑4, Dec 1995 .... 2.95
❑5, Feb 1996 .... 2.95
❑6, Apr 1996 .... 2.95
❑7, Jun 1996 .... 2.95

Ragmop
Image

❑1, Sep 1997, b&w; synopsis of first series 2.95
❑2, Nov 1997, b&w 2.95
❑3, Feb 1998 .... 2.95

Ragnarok Guy
Sun

❑1 .... 2.50

Rahrwl
Northstar

❑1; Limited edition original print (1988). 32 pages. 500 copies produced 2.50
❑1/2nd; New edition with redrawn art, 2 additional pages; Splash page identifies it as a new printing 2.25

Rai
Valiant

❑0, Nov 1992; BL (w); 1&O: Rai. 1: Bloodshot; series continues as Rai and the Future Force; Foretells future of Valiant Universe 4.00
❑1, Mar 1992; Includes trading cards; Flip-book with Magnus Robot Fighter (Valiant) #5 .... 8.00
❑1/Companion, Mar 1992 .... 1.00
❑2, Apr 1992 .... 6.00
❑3, May 1992 .... 16.00
❑4, Jun 1992; Scarcer 15.00
❑5, Jul 1992 .... 6.00
❑6, Aug 1992; FM (c); Unity 3.00
❑7, Sep 1992; D: Rai (original). Unity 3.00
❑8, Oct 1992; Unity epilogue; Series continued in Rai and the Future Force #9 .... 3.00
❑25, Oct 1994; Series continued from Rai and the Future Force #24 .... 1.00
❑26, Nov 1994; Chaos Effect Epsilon 3 .... 1.00
❑27, Dec 1994 .... 1.00
❑28, Jan 1995 .... 1.00
❑29, Feb 1995 .... 2.00
❑30, Mar 1995 .... 2.00
❑31, Apr 1995 .... 2.00
❑32, May 1995 .... 3.00
❑33, Jun 1995; Final Issue 5.00

Rai and the Future Force
Valiant

❑9, May 1993; BL (w); A: X-O Commando. A: Eternal Warrior. A: Magnus. Series continued from Rai #8; gatefold cover; first Sean Chen work 1.00
❑9/Gold, May 1993; BL (w); Gold 18.00
❑9/VVSS, May 1993 .... 10.00
❑10, Jun 1993 .... 1.00
❑11, Jul 1993 .... 1.00
❑12, Aug 1993; Includes serial number coupon for contest 1.00
❑13, Sep 1993; Includes serial number coupon for contest 1.00
❑14, Oct 1993 A: X-O Manowar armor 1.00
❑15, Nov 1993; Contiuned in Magnus #30 .... 1.00
❑16, Dec 1993 .... 1.00
❑17, Jan 1994; X-O Manowar armor appearance 1.00
❑18, Feb 1994 .... 1.00
❑19, Mar 1994 .... 1.00
❑20, Apr 1994; Spylocke revealed as spider-alien 1.00
❑21, May 1994; trading card; series continues as Rai 2.00
❑21/VVSS, May 1994 .... 60.00
❑22, Jun 1994; D: Rai; Continued From Magnus #37 .... 1.00
❑23, Aug 1994 .... 1.00
❑24, Sep 1994; new Rai; Series continued in Rai #25 .... 1.00

Rai Companion
Valiant

❑1, Dec 1993; no cover price 1.00

Raiders of the Lost Ark
Marvel

❑1, Sep 1981, JB, KJ (a) 2.00
❑2, Oct 1981, JB, KJ (a) 2.00
❑3, Nov 1981, JB, KJ (a) 2.00

Raider 3000
Gauntlet

❑1, b&w 2.95
❑2, b&w 2.95

Raijin Comics
Gutsoon

❑1, Dec 2002 .... 4.95
❑2, Dec 2002 .... 4.95
❑3, Dec 2002 .... 4.95
❑4, Dec 2002 .... 4.95
❑5, Jan 2003 .... 4.95
❑6, Jan 2003 .... 4.95
❑7, Jan 2003 .... 4.95
❑8, Jan 2003 .... 4.95
❑9, Feb 2003 .... 4.95
❑10, Feb 2003 .... 4.95
❑11, Feb 2003 .... 4.95
❑12, Feb 2003 .... 4.95
❑13, Mar 2003 .... 4.95
❑14, Mar 2003 .... 4.95
❑15, Mar 2003 .... 4.95
❑16, Mar 2003 .... 4.95
❑17, Apr 2003 .... 4.95
❑18, Apr 2003 .... 4.95
❑19, Apr 2003 .... 4.95
❑20, Apr 2003 .... 4.95
❑21, May 2003 .... 4.95
❑22, May 2003 .... 4.95
❑23, May 2003 .... 4.95
❑24, May 2003 .... 4.95
❑25, Jun 2003 .... 4.95
❑26, Jun 2003 .... 4.95
❑27, Jun 2003 .... 4.95
❑28, Jun 2003 .... 4.95
❑29, Jul 2003 .... 4.95
❑30, Jul 2003 .... 4.95
❑31, Jul 2003 .... 4.95
❑32, Jul 2003 .... 4.95
❑33, Aug 2003 .... 4.95
❑34, Aug 2003 .... 4.95
❑35, Aug 2003 .... 4.95
❑36, Aug 2003 .... 4.95
❑37, Sep 2003 .... 5.95
❑38, Oct 2003 .... 5.95
❑39, Nov 2003 .... 5.95
❑40, Dec 2003 .... 5.95
❑41, Jan 2004 .... 5.95

Raika
Sun

❑1 .... 2.50
❑2 .... 2.50
❑3 .... 2.50
❑4 .... 2.50
❑5 .... 2.50
❑6 .... 2.50
❑7 .... 2.50
❑8 .... 2.50
❑9 .... 2.50
❑10 .... 2.50
❑11 .... 2.50
❑12 .... 2.50
❑13 .... 2.50
❑14 .... 2.50
❑15 .... 2.50
❑16 .... 2.50
❑17 .... 2.50
❑18 .... 2.50
❑19 .... 2.50
❑20 .... 2.50

Rain
Tundra

❑1; Introduction by Stephen R. Bissette 1.95
❑2 .... 1.95

Other grades: Multiply price above by 5/6 for VF/NM • 2/3 for VERY FINE • 1/3 for FINE • 1/5 for VERY GOOD • 1/8 for GOOD

❑3 .... 1.95
❑4 .... 1.95
❑5 .... 1.95
❑6 .... 1.95

Rainbow Brite and the Star Stealer
DC

❑1, ca. 1985, Official movie adaption 1.00

Raisin Pie
Fantagraphics

❑1, Sep 2002 .... 3.50
❑2 .... 3.50
❑3 .... 3.50
❑4 .... 3.50

Rak
Rak Graphics

❑1, b&w 5.00

Rakehell
Draculina

❑1; Adult 2.50

Ralfy Roach
Bugged Out

❑1, Jun 1993; NN 2.95

Ralph Snart Adventures
Now

❑1, Jun 1986; 1&O: Ralph Snart 3.00
❑2, Jul 1986 .... 2.00
❑3, Aug 1986 .... 2.00

Ralph Snart Adventures
Now

❑1, Nov 1986 .... 2.00
❑2, Dec 1986 .... 1.50
❑3, Jan 1987 .... 1.50
❑4, Feb 1987 .... 1.50
❑5, Mar 1987 .... 1.50
❑6, Apr 1987 .... 1.50
❑7, May 1987 .... 1.50
❑8, Jun 1987 .... 1.50
❑9, Jul 1987 .... 1.50

Ralph Snart Adventures
Now

❑1, Sep 1988 .... 2.00
❑1/3D, Nov 1992, bagged with no cards 2.95
❑1/CS, Nov 1992, 3-D; bagged with 12 cards 3.50
❑2, Oct 1988 .... 1.75
❑3, Nov 1988 .... 1.75
❑4, Jan 1989 .... 1.75
❑5, Feb 1989 .... 1.75
❑6, Mar 1989 .... 1.75
❑7, Apr 1989 .... 1.75
❑8, May 1989 .... 1.75
❑9, Jun 1989 .... 1.75
❑10, Jul 1989 .... 1.75
❑11, Aug 1989 .... 1.75
❑12, Sep 1989 .... 1.75
❑13, Oct 1989 .... 1.75
❑14, Nov 1989 .... 1.75
❑15, Dec 1989 .... 1.75
❑16, Jan 1990 .... 1.75
❑17, Feb 1990 .... 1.75
❑18, Mar 1990 .... 1.75
❑19, Apr 1990 .... 1.75
❑20, May 1990 .... 1.75
❑21, Jun 1990 .... 1.75
❑22, Jul 1990, Includes posters 1.75
❑23, Aug 1990, cover says May, indicia says Aug 1.75
❑24, Sep 1990, prestige format; with glasses 2.95
❑25, Oct 1990, The Early Years 1.75
❑26, Nov 1990 .... 1.75

Ralph Snart Adventures
Now

❑1, May 1992 .... 2.50
❑2, Jun 1992 .... 2.50
❑3, Jul 1992 .... 2.50

Ralph Snart Adventures
Now

❑1, Jul 1993 .... 2.50
❑2, Aug 1993; Includes trading card 2.50
❑3, Sep 1993; Includes trading card 2.50
❑4, Oct 1993; Includes trading card 2.50
❑5, Nov 1993; Includes trading card 2.50

Ralph Snart: The Lost Issues
Now

❑1, Apr 1993 .... 2.50
❑2, May 1993 .... 2.50
❑3, Jun 1993 .... 2.50

Ramblin' Dawg
Edge

❑1, Jul 1994 .... 2.95

Rambo
Blackthorne

❑1, Oct 1988, b&w 2.00

Rambo III
Blackthorne

❑1; Movie adaptation 2.00
❑3D 1; Movie adaptation; Blackthorne 3-D series #49 .... 2.50

Ramm
Megaton

❑1, May 1987 .... 1.50
❑2 .... 1.50

Rampage
Slap Happy

❑1, ca. 1997 .... 9.95

Rampaging Hulk
Marvel

❑1, Aug 1998, b&w; Giant-size 1.99
❑2, Sep 1998; gatefold summary; 1: Ravage; O: Ravage 1.99
❑2/A, Sep 1998; gatefold summary; variant cover 1.99
❑3, Oct 1998; gatefold summary; V: Ravage 1.99
❑4, Nov 1998; gatefold summary; Hulk rescues parent and child from avalanche 1.99
❑5, Dec 1998; gatefold summary; V: Fantastic Four 1.99
❑6, Jan 1999; gatefold summary; V: Puma; Final Issue 1.99

Rampaging Hulk
Marvel

❑1, Jan 1977, b&w; JB, AA (a); Bloodstone back-up 35.00
❑2, Apr 1977, b&w; AA (a); O: X-Men. Bloodstone back-up 14.00
❑3, Jun 1977, b&w; SB, AA (a); Bloodstone/Iron Man back-up story 5.00
❑4, Aug 1977, b&w; JSn (c); JSn (w); JSn, VM, AN (a); 1: Exo-Mind. Bloodstone/Iron Man back-up story 5.00
❑5, Oct 1977, b&w; JSn (c); VM, KP, AA, BWi (a); A: Sub-Mariner. Bloodstone back-up 5.00
❑6, Dec 1977, b&w; KP, TD (a); Bloodstone back-up 4.00
❑7, Feb 1978, b&w; JSn (c); JSn, KP, JM, BWi (a); A: Man-Thing. Man-Thing back-up 4.00
❑8, Apr 1978, b&w; HT, AA (a); A: Avengers. Bloodstone back-up 4.00
❑9, Jun 1978, b&w; SB, TD (a); Shanna back-up; later issues published as Hulk (magazine) 4.00

Ramthar
Caliber

❑1, Apr 1996, b&w; reprints Brazilian comic 2.95

Rana 7
NGNG

❑1 .... 2.95
❑2 .... 2.95
❑3 .... 2.95
❑4 .... 2.95

Rana 7: Warriors of Vengeance
NGNG

❑1, Dec 1995 .... 2.50
❑2, Mar 1996 .... 2.50

Random Encounter
Viper

❑1, Mar 2005; b&w 2.95
❑2, Jun 2005; b&w 2.95
❑3, Jul 2005; b&w 2.95
❑4, Sep 2005; b&w 2.95

Randy O'Donnell is the M@n
Image

❑1, May 2001; Flipbook with Mr. Right .. 2.95
❑2, Jul 2001 .... 2.95
❑3, Sep 2001 .... 2.95

Rango
Dell

❑1, Aug 1967, Tim Conway cover 25.00

Rank & Stinky
Parody

❑1, b&w 2.50
❑1/2nd; Rank & Stinky Eencore Eedition; Rank & Stinky Eencore Eedition 2.50
❑Special 1, b&w 2.75

Ranma 1/2 Part 1
Viz

❑1, ca. 1991; Comic in color 25.00
❑2, ca. 1991 .... 10.00
❑3, ca. 1991 .... 8.00
❑4, ca. 1991; Comics become b&w 6.00
❑5, ca. 1991 .... 6.00
❑6, ca. 1991 .... 5.00
❑7, ca. 1991 .... 5.00

Ranma 1/2 Part 2
Viz

❑1, Jan 1992 .... 7.00
❑2, Feb 1992 .... 5.00
❑3, Mar 1992 .... 4.00
❑4, Apr 1992 .... 4.00
❑5, May 1992 .... 4.00
❑6, Jun 1992 .... 3.50
❑7, Jul 1992 .... 3.50
❑8, Aug 1992 .... 3.50
❑9, Sep 1992 .... 3.50
❑10, Oct 1992 .... 3.50
❑11, Nov 1992 .... 3.50

Ranma 1/2 Part 3
Viz

❑1, Dec 1992 .... 3.00
❑2, Jan 1993 .... 3.00
❑3, Feb 1993 .... 3.00
❑4, Mar 1993 .... 3.00
❑5, Apr 1993 .... 3.00
❑6, May 1993 .... 3.00
❑7, Jun 1993 .... 3.00
❑8, Jul 1993 .... 3.00
❑9, Aug 1993 .... 3.00
❑10, Sep 1993 .... 3.00
❑11, Oct 1993 .... 3.00
❑12, Nov 1993 .... 3.00
❑13, Dec 1993 .... 3.00

Ranma 1/2 Part 4
Viz

❑1, Jan 1994 .... 3.00
❑2, Feb 1994 .... 3.00
❑3, Mar 1994 .... 3.00
❑4, Apr 1994 .... 3.00
❑5, May 1994 .... 3.00
❑6, Jun 1994 .... 3.00
❑7, Jul 1994 .... 3.00
❑8, Aug 1994 .... 3.00
❑9, Sep 1994 .... 3.00
❑10, Oct 1994 .... 3.00
❑11, Nov 1994 .... 3.00

Ranma 1/2 Part 5
Viz

❑1, Dec 1994 .... 3.00
❑2, Jan 1995 .... 3.00
❑3, Feb 1995 .... 3.00
❑4, Mar 1995 .... 3.00
❑5, Apr 1995 .... 3.00
❑6, May 1995 .... 3.00
❑7, Jun 1995 .... 3.00
❑8, Jul 1995 .... 3.00
❑9, Aug 1995 .... 3.00
❑10, Sep 1995 .... 3.00
❑11, Oct 1995 .... 3.00
❑12, Nov 1995 .... 3.00

Ranma 1/2 Part 6
Viz

❑1, Dec 1996 .... 2.95
❑2, Jan 1997 .... 2.95
❑3, Feb 1997 .... 2.95
❑4, Mar 1997 .... 2.95

Richie Rich Money World

Preteen plutocrat pitilessly shows off for poor
©Harvey

Richie Rich (Movie Adaptation)

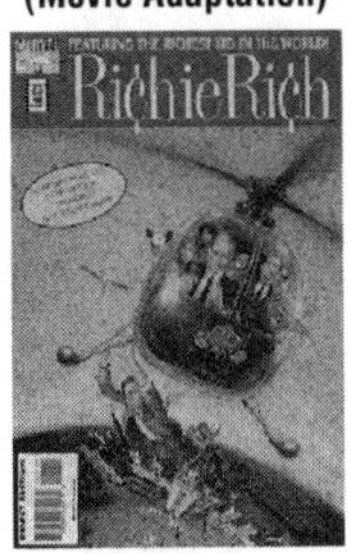

Culkin looked like he was in his 30s in this movie
©Marvel

Richie Rich Profits

More lavish displays of wealth
©Harvey

Richie Rich Riches

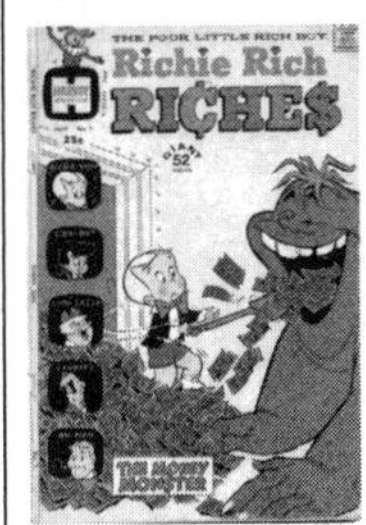

1970s spinoff added one more to the line
©Harvey

Richie Rich Success Stories

Logo dropped "Stories" for much of run
©Harvey

N-MINT

❑5, Apr 1997 2.95
❑6, May 1997 2.95
❑7, Jun 1997 2.95
❑8, Jul 1997 2.95
❑9, Aug 1997 2.95
❑10, Sep 1997 2.95
❑11, Oct 1997 2.95
❑12, Nov 1997 2.95
❑13, Dec 1997 2.95
❑14, Jan 1998 2.95

Ranma 1/2 Part 7
Viz

❑1, Feb 1998 2.95
❑2, Mar 1998 2.95
❑3, Apr 1998 2.95
❑4, May 1998 2.95
❑5, Jun 1998 2.95
❑6, Jul 1998 2.95
❑7, Aug 1998 2.95
❑8, Sep 1998 2.95
❑9, Oct 1998 2.95
❑10, Nov 1998 2.95
❑11, Dec 1998 2.95
❑12, Jan 1999 2.95
❑13, Feb 1999 2.95
❑14, Mar 1999 2.95

Ranma 1/2 Part 8
Viz

❑1, Apr 1999; b&w 2.95
❑2, May 1999 2.95
❑3, Jun 1999 2.95
❑4, Jul 1999 2.95
❑5, Aug 1999 2.95
❑6, Sep 1999; b&w 2.95
❑7, Sep 1999; b&w 2.95
❑8, Oct 1999; b&w 2.95
❑9, Nov 1999; b&w 2.95
❑10, Dec 1999; b&w 2.95
❑11, Jan 2000; b&w 2.95
❑12, Feb 2000; b&w 2.95
❑13, Mar 2000; b&w 2.95

Ranma 1/2 Part 9
Viz

❑1, May 2000 2.95
❑2, Jun 2000 2.95
❑3, Jul 2000 2.95
❑4, Aug 2000 2.95
❑5, Sep 2000 2.95
❑6, Oct 2000 2.95
❑7, Nov 2000 2.95
❑8, Dec 2000 2.95
❑9, Jan 2001 2.95
❑10, Feb 2001 2.95
❑11, Mar 2001 2.95

Ranma 1/2 Part 10
Viz

❑1, Apr 2001 2.95
❑2, May 2001 2.95
❑3, Jun 2001 2.95
❑4, Jul 2001 2.95
❑5, Aug 2001 2.95
❑6, Sep 2001 2.95
❑7, Oct 2001 2.95
❑8, Nov 2001 2.95
❑9, Dec 2001 2.95
❑10, Jan 2002 2.95
❑11, Feb 2002 2.95

Ranma 1/2 Part 11
Viz

❑1, Mar 2002 2.95
❑2, Apr 2002 2.95
❑3, May 2002 2.95
❑4, Jun 2002 2.95
❑5, Jul 2002 2.95
❑6, Aug 2002 2.95
❑7, Sep 2002 2.95
❑8, Oct 2002 2.95
❑9, Nov 2002 2.95
❑10, Dec 2002 2.95
❑11, Jan 2003 2.95

Ranma 1/2 Part 12
Viz

❑1, Mar 2003 2.95

Rann-Thanagar War
DC

❑1, Jun 2005 8.00
❑1/Variant, Jun 2005 5.00
❑2, Jul 2005 4.00
❑3, Aug 2005 2.50
❑4, Sep 2005 2.50
❑5, Oct 2005 2.50
❑6 2005 2.50

Rann/Thanagar War: Infinite Crisis Special
DC

❑1, Mar 2006, 1: Ion; D: Jade; Kyle Rayner becomes Ion 4.99

Rant
Boneyard

❑1, Nov 1994, b&w; JJ (a); Adult 2.95
❑2, Feb 1995, b&w; JJ (a); Adult 2.95
❑3; JJ (a); Adult 2.95
❑Ashcan 1; JJ (a); Ashcan version of issue #1. Black and white cover 2.50

Raphael Teenage Mutant Ninja Turtle
Mirage

❑1, Nov 1987; Oversized 2.50
❑1/2nd; 2nd printing 1.50

Rare Breed
Chrysalis

❑1, Nov 1995; 1: Ambush; 1: Ammo; 1: Buffalo Soldier; 1: Swede; 1: The Ravager 2.50
❑2, Mar 1996 2.50

Rascals in Paradise
Dark Horse

❑1, Aug 1994; magazine 4.00
❑2, Oct 1994; magazine 4.00
❑3, Dec 1994; magazine; Final Issue 4.00

Rat Bastard
Crucial

❑1, Jun 1997 2.50
❑1/Ashcan, Jun 1997; Black and white ashcan edition 2.50
❑2, Nov 1997 2.00
❑3, Apr 1998 2.00
❑4, Jul 1998 2.00
❑5, Oct 1998 1.95
❑6, Jul 1999 1.95

Rated X
Aircel

❑1, Apr 1991, b&w; Adult 2.95
❑2, Feb 1991, b&w; Adult 2.95
❑3, Apr 1991, b&w; Adult 2.95
❑Special 1, b&w; Adult 2.95

Rat Fink Comics
World of Fandom

❑1, b&w 2.50
❑2, b&w 2.50
❑3, b&w 2.50

Rat Fink Comix
Starhead

❑1 2.00

Ratfoo
Spit Wad

❑1, Sep 1997, b&w 2.95

Rat Patrol
Dell

❑1, Mar 1967 40.00
❑2, Apr 1967 40.00
❑3, May 1967 40.00
❑4, Aug 1967 40.00
❑5, Nov 1967 40.00
❑6, Oct 1969, Same cover as #1, slightly recolored 25.00

Rat Preview
Aeon / Backbone Press

❑1, May 1997, b&w; ashcan-sized; no cover price 1.00

Rats!
Slave Labor

❑1, Aug 1992, b&w 2.50

Ravage 2099
Marvel

❑1, Dec 1992; Metallic ink cover; foil cover 1.75
❑2, Jan 1993 1.25
❑3, Feb 1993 1.25
❑4, Mar 1993 1.25
❑5, Apr 1993 1.25
❑6, May 1993 1.25
❑7, Jun 1993 1.25
❑8, Jul 1993 1.25
❑9, Aug 1993 1.25
❑10, Sep 1993 1.25
❑11, Oct 1993 1.25
❑12, Nov 1993 1.25
❑13, Dec 1993 1.25
❑14, Jan 1994; Punisher 2099 appearance 1.25
❑15, Feb 1994 1.25
❑16, Mar 1994 1.25
❑17, Apr 1994 1.25
❑18, May 1994; Includes trading cards 1.25
❑19, Jun 1994 1.50
❑20, Jul 1994 1.50
❑21, Aug 1994 1.50
❑22, Sep 1994 1.50
❑23, Oct 1994 1.50
❑24, Nov 1994 1.50
❑25, Dec 1994 2.25

❑25/Variant, Dec 1994; enhanced cover. 2.95
❑26, Jan 1995 1.50
❑27, Feb 1995 1.50
❑28, Mar 1995 1.50
❑29, Apr 1995 1.50
❑30, May 1995 1.50
❑31, Jun 1995 1.95
❑32, Jul 1995; One Nation Under Doom crossover 1.95
❑33, Aug 1995; Final Issue; One Nation Under Doom crossover 1.95

Rave Master
Tokyopop

❑1, Feb 2003 9.99
❑2, Apr 2003 9.99
❑3, Jun 2003 9.99
❑4, Aug 2003 9.99
❑5, Oct 2003 9.99
❑6, Dec 2003 9.99
❑7, Feb 2004 9.99
❑8, Apr 2004 9.99
❑9, Jun 2004 9.99
❑10, Apr 2004 9.99
❑11, Oct 2004 9.99
❑12, Dec 2004 9.99
❑13, Feb 2005 9.99
❑14, Apr 2005 9.99
❑15, Jan 2005 9.99
❑16, Aug 2005 9.99
❑17, Oct 2005 9.99
❑18, Dec 2005 9.99

Raven
Renaissance

❑1, Sep 1993; 1: Ian Macauley; 1: Raven 2.50
❑2, Nov 1993 2.50
❑3, Apr 1994 2.50
❑4, Aug 1994 2.75

Raven Chronicles
Caliber

❑1, Jul 1995, b&w 2.95
❑2, b&w; ca. 1995 2.95
❑3, b&w; ca. 1995 2.95
❑4, b&w; ca. 1995 2.95
❑5; b&w; ca. 1995 2.95
❑6; b&w; ca. 1996 2.95
❑7; b&w; ca. 1996 2.95
❑8; b&w; ca. 1996 2.95
❑9; b&w; ca. 1996 2.95
❑10; b&w; ca. 1996 2.95
❑11; b&w; ca. 1996 2.95
❑12; b&w; ca. 1996 2.95
❑13; b&w; ca. 1997 2.95
❑14; b&w; ca. 1997 2.95
❑15; Giant-size; flip book with High Caliber 3.95

Ravens and Rainbows
Pacific

❑1, Dec 1983; Adult 1.50

Ravenwind
Pariah

❑1, Jun 1996, b&w 2.50

Raver
Malibu

❑1, Apr 1993; foil cover 2.95
❑2, May 1993 1.95
❑3, Jun 1993 1.95

Raw City
Dramenon

❑1; Adult 3.00

Rawhide
Dell

❑1, Aug 1962, No issue number: Cover code ends in -208, indicating this issue is from August 1962 200.00

Rawhide
Gold Key

❑1, Jul 1963 175.00
❑2, Jan 1964 150.00

Rawhide Kid
Marvel

❑25, Dec 1961 90.00
❑26, Feb 1962 90.00
❑27, Apr 1962 90.00
❑28, Jun 1962 90.00
❑29, Aug 1962 90.00
❑30, Oct 1962 90.00
❑31, Dec 1962 75.00
❑32, Feb 1963 75.00
❑33, Apr 1963 75.00
❑34, Jun 1963 75.00
❑35, Aug 1963 75.00
❑36, Oct 1963 75.00
❑37, Dec 1963 75.00
❑38, Feb 1964 75.00
❑39, Apr 1964 75.00
❑40, Jun 1964, A: Two-Gun Kid 75.00
❑41, Aug 1964 75.00
❑42, Oct 1964 75.00
❑43, Dec 1964 75.00
❑44, Feb 1965 75.00
❑45, Apr 1965, JK (c); SL (w); JK (a); O: Rawhide Kid 90.00
❑46, Jun 1965 60.00
❑47, Aug 1965 35.00
❑48, Oct 1965, V: Marko the Manhunter 35.00
❑49, Dec 1965, V: Masquerader; Reprint from Rawhide Kid (1st Series) #35 35.00
❑50, Feb 1966, A: Kid Colt. V: Masquerader, Reprint from Two-Gun Kid #65 35.00
❑51, Apr 1966, V: Aztecs; Reprint from Rawhide Kid (1st Series) #36 35.00
❑52, Jun 1966, SL (w); Reprint from Rawhide Kid (1st Series) #29 35.00
❑53, Aug 1966, Reprint from Kid Colt Outlaw #111 35.00
❑54, Oct 1966 35.00
❑55, Dec 1966, V: Plunderers; Reprint from Rawhide Kid (1st Series) #17 35.00
❑56, Feb 1967, V: Peacemaker 35.00
❑57, Apr 1967, V: Enforcerers (not Spider-Man villains); Reprint from Kid Cold Outlaw #105 35.00
❑58, Jun 1967, Reprint from Rawhide Kid (1st Series) #32 35.00
❑59, Aug 1967, V: Drako; Reprint from Rawhide Kid (1st Series) #41 35.00
❑60, Oct 1967, SL (w); HT (a); A: General George A. Custer. Two-Gun story reprinted from Two-Gun Kid #63 35.00
❑61, Dec 1967, A: Wild Bill Hickock. A: Calamity Jane 25.00
❑62, Feb 1968, V: Drako 25.00
❑63, Apr 1968, Reprint from Kid Colt Outlaw #105 25.00
❑64, Jun 1968, Kid Colt back-up 25.00
❑65, Aug 1968 25.00
❑66, Oct 1968, Two-Gun Kid back-up 25.00
❑67, Dec 1968, Rawhide Kid; Kid Colt 25.00
❑68, Feb 1969, V: Cougar; Reprint from Rawhide Kid (1st Series) #22 25.00
❑69, Apr 1969 25.00
❑70, Jun 1969 25.00
❑71, Aug 1969 18.00
❑72, Oct 1969 18.00
❑73, Dec 1969 18.00
❑74, Feb 1970 18.00
❑75, Apr 1970 18.00
❑76, May 1970 18.00
❑77, Jun 1970 18.00
❑78, Jul 1970 18.00
❑79, Aug 1970, Reprint from Kid Colt Outlaw #59 18.00
❑80, Oct 1970 18.00
❑81, Nov 1970 18.00
❑82, Dec 1970, Reprint from Rawhide Kid (1st Series) #59; Reprint from Kid Colt Outlaw #80 18.00
❑83, Jan 1971 18.00
❑84, Feb 1971, Reprints from Rawhide Kid (1st Series) #27 18.00
❑85, Mar 1971 18.00
❑86, Apr 1971, HT (c); SL (w); AW, JK (a); O: Rawhide Kid; Reprint from Rawhide Kid (1st Series) #17 18.00
❑87, May 1971 15.00
❑88, Jun 1971, Reprint from Two-Gun Kid #82 15.00
❑89, Jul 1971, Reprint form Kid Colt Outlaw #85 15.00
❑90, Aug 1971, Reprint from Two-Gun Kid #61 15.00
❑91, Sep 1971, O: Rawhide Kid; Reprint from Frontier Western #1 15.00
❑92, Oct 1971, Reprints from Rawhide Kid (1st Series) #18 15.00
❑93, Nov 1971, Reprints from Rawhide Kid (1st Series) #61 12.00
❑94, Dec 1971, Reprints from Rawhide Kid (1st Series) #10, 146 12.00
❑95, Jan 1972, Reprint from Two-Gun Kid #35; Reprint from Rawhide Kid (1st Series) #18 12.00
❑96, Feb 1972, 1: Missouri Kid (Herschel Wall); O: Missouri Kid (Herschel Wall); Reprint from Ringo Kid Western #15 12.00
❑97, Mar 1972, Reprint from Two-Gun Kid #59; Reprint from Ringo Kid Western #17 12.00
❑98, Apr 1972, SL (w); Reprint from Apache Kid #53; Reprint from Ringo Kid Western #16 12.00
❑99, May 1972, Reprint from Quick-Triggered Western #14 12.00
❑100, Jun 1972, O: Rawhide Kid; Reprint from Western Outlaws and Sheriffs #62 18.00
❑101, Jul 1972 12.00
❑102, Aug 1972, Reprint from Western Outlaws and Sheriffs #70 12.00
❑103, Sep 1972, Reprint from Western Outlaws #6 12.00
❑104, Oct 1972, Reprints from Rawhide Kid (1st Series) #63; Reprint from Frontier Western #1 12.00
❑105, Nov 1972, SL (w); JR (a); Reprint from Western Kid #10 12.00
❑106, Dec 1972, 1: Laura Prescott; Reprint from Western Outlaws #6 12.00
❑107, Jan 1973, Reprint from Rawhide Kid (1st Series) #39 12.00
❑108, Feb 1973, Reprint from Western Outlaws #15 12.00
❑109, Mar 1973, SL (w); JK (a); Reprint from Rawhide Kid (1st Series) #34 12.00
❑110, Apr 1973 12.00
❑111, May 1973, JK (c); SL (w); Reprint from Rawhide Kid (1st Series) #41; Reprint from Kid Cold Outlaw #60 12.00
❑112, Jun 1973, Reprint from Kid Cold Outlaw #95 12.00
❑113, Jul 1973, Reprint from Frontier Western #2 12.00
❑114, Aug 1973, Reprint from Western Outlaws #12 10.00
❑115, Sep 1973, Reprint from Frontier Western #10 10.00
❑116, Oct 1973 10.00
❑117, Nov 1973 10.00
❑118, Jan 1974 10.00
❑119, Mar 1974 10.00
❑120, May 1974 10.00
❑121, Jul 1974, reprints 7.00
❑122, Sep 1974, reprints 7.00
❑123, Nov 1974, reprints 7.00
❑124, Jan 1975, reprints 7.00
❑125, Mar 1975, reprints 7.00
❑126, May 1975, reprints 7.00
❑127, Jul 1975, reprints 7.00
❑128, Sep 1975, reprints 7.00
❑129, Oct 1975, reprints 7.00
❑130, Nov 1975, reprints 7.00
❑131, Jan 1976, reprints 7.00
❑132, Mar 1976, reprints 7.00
❑133, May 1976, reprints 7.00
❑133/30¢, May 1976, 30¢ regional price variant; reprints 20.00
❑134, Jul 1976, reprints 7.00
❑134/30¢, Jul 1976, 30¢ regional price variant; reprints 20.00
❑135, Sep 1976, reprints 7.00
❑136, Nov 1976, reprints 7.00
❑137, Jan 1977, reprints 7.00
❑138, Mar 1977, reprints 7.00
❑139, May 1977, reprints 7.00
❑140, Jul 1977, reprints 15.00
❑140/35¢, Jul 1977, reprints; 35¢ regional price variant 15.00
❑141, Sep 1977, reprints 6.00
❑142, Nov 1977, reprints 6.00
❑143, Jan 1978, reprints 6.00
❑144, Mar 1978, reprints 6.00
❑145, May 1978, reprints 6.00
❑146, Jul 1978, reprints 6.00
❑147, Sep 1978, PG (c); reprints 6.00
❑148, Nov 1978, reprints 6.00
❑149, Jan 1979, reprints 6.00
❑150, Mar 1979, reprints 6.00

Other grades: Multiply price above by 5/6 for VF/NM • 2/3 for VERY FINE • 1/3 for FINE • 1/5 for VERY GOOD • 1/8 for GOOD

Richie Rich Vaults of Mystery

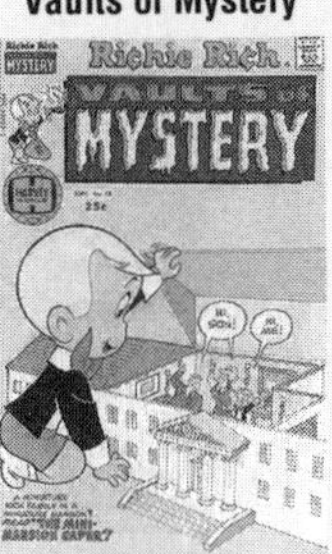

Showcase for spooky-themed adventures

©Harvey

Richie Rich Zillionz

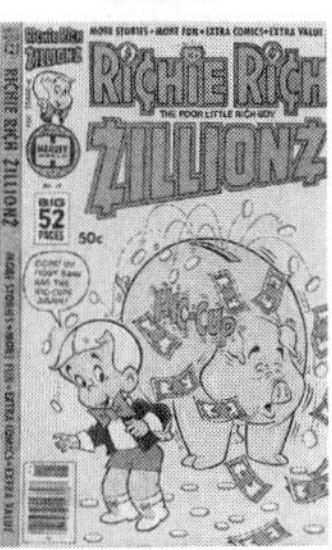

Once a 64-pager, page count soon dropped

©Harvey

Rima, the Jungle Girl

Intriguing jungle title by Nestor Redondo

©DC

Ripclaw (Vol. 1)

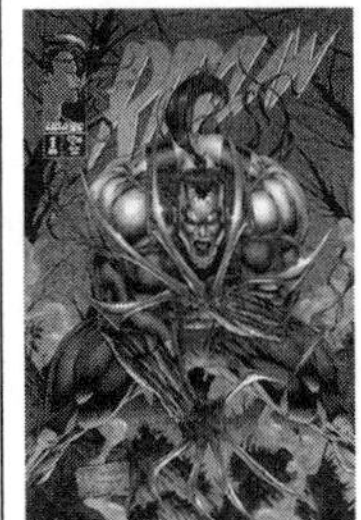

Native American hero from CyberForce

©Image

Rip Hunter... Time Master

Rip and crew solve mysteries in time

©DC

N-MINT

❑151, May 1979, Reprints Rawhide Kid #99 ..... 6.00
❑Special 1, Sep 1971; Reprints 12.00

Rawhide Kid
Marvel

❑1, Aug 1985; JBy (c); JBy, HT, JSe (a); O: Rawhide Kid 1.50
❑2, Sep 1985 KP (c); JBy, HT, JSe (a) 1.50
❑3, Oct 1985 KP (c); JBy, HT, JSe (a) 1.50
❑4, Nov 1985 KP (c); JBy, HT, JSe (a) 1.50

Rawhide Kid
Marvel / MAX

❑1, Apr 2003; JSe (a); Rawhide Kid recast as homosexual 5.00
❑2, May 2003 JSe (a) 4.00
❑3, May 2003 JSe (a) 3.00
❑4, Jun 2003 JSe (a) 3.00
❑5, Jun 2003 JSe (a) 2.99

Raw Media Illustrated
ABC

❑1, May 1998; wet T-shirt cover 3.25
❑1/Nude, May 1998; nude cover 3.25

Raw Media Mags
Rebel

❑1, b&w; Adult 5.00
❑2, ca. 1992; b&w; Adult 5.00
❑3, ca. 1992; b&w; Adult 5.00
❑4, May 1994, b&w; Adult 5.00

Raw Periphery
Slave Labor

❑1, b&w; Anthology; Adult 2.95

Ray
DC

❑1, Feb 1992; O: The Ray II (Ray Terrill) 3.00
❑2, Mar 1992 ..... 2.00
❑3, Apr 1992 ..... 1.50
❑4, May 1992 ..... 1.50
❑5, Jun 1992 ..... 1.50
❑6, Jul 1992 ..... 1.50

Ray
DC

❑0, Oct 1994; O: The Ray II (Ray Terrill) 1.95
❑1, May 1994 ..... 1.75
❑1/Variant, May 1994; foil cover 2.95
❑2, Jun 1994; O: The Ray II (Ray Terrill) 1.75
❑3, Jul 1994 ..... 1.75
❑4, Aug 1994 ..... 1.95
❑5, Sep 1994 ..... 1.95
❑6, Nov 1994 ..... 1.95
❑7, Dec 1994 ..... 1.95
❑8, Jan 1995; V: Lobo 1.95
❑9, Feb 1995 ..... 1.95
❑10, Mar 1995 ..... 1.95
❑11, Apr 1995 ..... 1.95
❑12, May 1995 ..... 1.95
❑13, Jun 1995 ..... 2.25
❑14, Jul 1995 ..... 2.25
❑15, Aug 1995; V: Deathmasque 2.25
❑16, Sep 1995 ..... 2.25
❑17, Oct 1995 ..... 2.25
❑18, Nov 1995; Underworld Unleashed 2.25
❑19, Dec 1995; Underworld Unleashed 2.25
❑20, Jan 1996 ..... 2.25
❑21, Feb 1996; V: Black Condor 2.25

N-MINT

❑22, Mar 1996 ..... 2.25
❑23, May 1996 ..... 2.25
❑24, Jun 1996 ..... 2.25
❑25, Jul 1996; Ray in the future 3.50
❑26, Aug 1996; continued from events in JLA Ann #10 ..... 2.25
❑27, Sep 1996 ..... 2.25
❑28, Oct 1996; secrets of both Ray's pasts revealed 2.25
❑Ann 1, ca. 1995; Year One 3.95

Ray
ADV Manga

❑1, ca. 2004 ..... 9.99
❑2, ca. 2005 ..... 9.99
❑3, ca. 2005 ..... 9.99

Ray Bradbury Comics
Topps

❑1, Feb 1993; AF, AW (w); AW, AT (a); Includes 3 trading cards; Reprint from Weird Science-Fantasy #25 ..... 3.50
❑2, Apr 1993; AF, MW, HK (w); MW, HK (a); Includes 3 trading cards; Reprint from Haunt of Fear #18 ..... 3.50
❑3, Jun 1993; Includes 3 trading cards 3.50
❑4, Aug 1993; Includes 3 trading cards 3.50
❑5, Oct 1993; Final issue (#6 canceled) 3.50
❑Special 1, ca. 1994; AF, CR, JKa (w); CR, JKa (a); Illustrated Man 3.50

Ray Bradbury Comics: Martian Chronicles
Topps

❑1, Jun 1994; Spaceman Special 3.25

Ray Bradbury Comics: Trilogy of Terror
Topps

❑1, May 1994 AF (w); WW (a) 3.25

Ray Bradbury Special: Tales of Horror
Topps

❑1, ca. 1994 ..... 2.50

Ray-Mond
Deep-Sea

❑1 ..... 2.95
❑2 ..... 2.95

Rayne
Sheet Happies

❑1, Jul 1995, b&w 2.50
❑2, Apr 1996, b&w; cover says Mar, indicia says Apr 2.50
❑3, Aug 1996, b&w 2.50
❑4, Jul 1997, b&w 2.95

Razor
London Night

❑0; London Night Edition; Green cover lettering; ca. 1996 ..... 3.99
❑0/A; Direct Market edition; Direct Market edition; Red title lettering 3.00
❑0/2nd; 2nd printing; Fathom Edition; Yellow title lettering 2.75
❑½; Promotional giveaway; 1: Poizon 3.00
❑1, Aug 1992 ..... 4.00
❑1/2nd; 2nd printing; Photo cover 3.00
❑2, Feb 1993 ..... 3.00
❑2/Platinum; Platinum edition 4.00

N-MINT

❑2/Variant; Signed, numbered edition (limited to 3,000 copies) with red or blue cover 5.00
❑3 ..... 3.00
❑3/CS; Includes posters 4.00
❑4 ..... 3.00
❑4/Platinum; Platinum edition 4.00
❑5 ..... 3.00
❑5/Platinum; Platinum edition 4.00
❑6 ..... 3.00
❑7 ..... 3.00
❑8 ..... 3.00
❑9, Aug 1994 ..... 3.00
❑10; O: Stryke 3.00
❑11, Sep 1994, b&w 3.00
❑12, b&w; Series continued in Razor Uncut #13 ..... 3.00
❑Ann 1, ca. 1993; 1: Shi 15.00
❑Ann 1/Gold; Gold limited edition; 1: Shi 20.00
❑Ann 2, b&w 3.50

Razor
London Night

❑1, Oct 1996, chromium cover 3.00
❑2, Nov 1996, Adult 3.00
❑3, Dec 1996, Adult 3.00
❑4, Mar 1997, Adult 3.00
❑5, Apr 1997, Adult 3.00
❑6, May 1997, Adult 3.00
❑7, Jun 1997, Final Issue; Adult; b&w 3.00

Razor & Shi Special
London Night

❑1; Crossover with Crusade 3.00
❑1/Platinum; Platinum edition; Adult 4.00

Razor Archives
London Night

❑1, May 1997; Adult 3.95
❑2, Jun 1997; Adult 5.00
❑3; Adult 5.00
❑4, Jul 1997; Adult 5.00

Razor: Burn
London Night

❑1; Adult 3.00
❑2; Adult 3.00
❑3; Adult 3.00
❑4; Adult 3.00

Razor/Cry No More
London Night

❑1 1995, b&w; NN; Adult 3.95

Razor/Dark Angel: The Final Nail
London Night

❑1, Jun 1994; Adult 2.95

Razorguts
Monster

❑1, b&w 2.25
❑2, Feb 1992, b&w 2.25
❑3, Mar 1992, b&w 2.25
❑4, b&w 2.25

Razorline: The First Cut
Marvel

❑1, Sep 1993, sampler; Previews Hokum & Hex, Hyperkind, Saint Sinner, and Ectokid 1.00

Other grades: Multiply price above by 5/6 for VF/NM • 2/3 for VERY FINE • 1/3 for FINE • 1/5 for VERY GOOD • 1/8 for GOOD

Razor/Morbid Angel
London Night

❑1, Aug 1996; Adult 3.00
❑2, Nov 1996; Adult 3.00
❑3, Dec 1996; Adult 3.00

Razor Nights
Caliber

❑1, Aug 1996, b&w 2.95

Razor's Edge
Innovation

❑1, b&w 2.50

Razor's Edge: Warblade
DC / Wildstorm

❑1, Jan 2005 .... 2.95
❑2, Feb 2005 .... 2.95
❑3, Mar 2005 .... 2.95
❑4, Apr 2005 .... 2.95
❑5, May 2005 .... 2.95

Razor: The Suffering
London Night

❑1; Adult 3.00
❑1/A; "Director's Cut" 3.00
❑2; Adult 3.00
❑2/A; "Director's Cut" 3.00
❑3; Adult 3.00

Razor: Torture
London Night

❑0, Dec 1995; enhanced wraparound cover; polybagged with card and catalog 3.95
❑1 1996; Adult 3.00
❑1/Variant 1996; alternate cover with no cover price 3.00
❑2 1996; Adult 3.00
❑2/Variant 1996; no cover price 3.00
❑3, Apr 1996; Adult 3.00
❑4, May 1996; Adult 3.00
❑5, Jun 1996; Adult 3.00
❑6, Jul 1996; Adult 3.00

Razor: Uncut
London Night

❑13 1995; Series continued from Razor #12 .... 3.00
❑14 1995; Adult 3.00
❑15, Jul 1995; Adult 3.00
❑16 1995; Adult 3.00
❑17, Oct 1995; Adult 3.00
❑18, Dec 1995; Adult 3.00
❑19 1995; Adult; ca. 1996 .... 3.00
❑20 1995, b&w; Adult 3.00
❑21, May 1996, b&w; Adult 3.00
❑22 1996, b&w; Adult 3.00
❑23 1996; Adult 3.00
❑24 1996; Adult 3.00
❑25, Aug 1996; Adult 3.00
❑26, Sep 1996; Adult 3.00
❑27, Oct 1996; Adult 3.00
❑28, Oct 1996; Adult 3.00
❑29, Nov 1996; Adult 3.00
❑30, Dec 1996; Adult 3.00
❑31, Jan 1997; Adult 3.00
❑32, Feb 1997; Adult 3.00
❑33, Feb 1997; Adult 3.00
❑34, Mar 1997; Adult 3.00
❑35, Apr 1997; Adult 3.00
❑36, May 1997; Adult 3.00
❑37, Jun 1997; Adult 3.00
❑38, Jul 1997; Adult 3.00
❑39, Aug 1997; Adult 3.00
❑40, Sep 1997; Adult 3.00
❑41, Oct 1997; Adult 3.00
❑42, Nov 1997; Adult 3.00
❑43, Dec 1997; Adult 3.00
❑44 1998; Adult 3.00
❑45 1998; Adult 3.00
❑46 1998; Adult 3.00
❑47, May 1998; Adult 3.00
❑48 1998; Adult 3.00
❑49 1998; Adult 3.00
❑50 1999; Adult 3.00
❑51, Mar 1999; Adult 3.00

Razor/Warrior Nun Areala: Faith
London Night

❑1, May 1996; one-shot crossover with Antarctic 3.95

Razorwire
5th Panel

❑1, Jun 1996, b&w 1.50
❑2, Jul 1997, b&w 1.50

Reaction: The Ultimate Man
Studio Archein

❑1; NN 2.95

Reacto-Man
B-Movie

❑1 .... 1.50
❑2 .... 1.50
❑3; 1: Warhead 1.50

Reactor Girl
Tragedy Strikes

❑1, Dec 1991, b&w; Adult 2.50
❑2, Apr 1992; Adult; b&w 2.95
❑3, Jun 1992; Adult; b&w 2.95
❑4, Aug 1992; Adult; b&w 2.95
❑5, Oct 1992; Adult 2.95

Reagan's Raiders
Solson

❑1, ca. 1986 .... 2.00
❑2, ca. 1986 .... 2.00
❑3, ca. 1987 .... 2.00

Real Adventures of Jonny Quest
Dark Horse

❑1, Sep 1996; based on 1996 animated series 3.00
❑2, Oct 1996 .... 2.95
❑3, Nov 1996 .... 2.95
❑4, Dec 1996 .... 2.95
❑5, Jan 1997 .... 2.95
❑6, Feb 1997 .... 2.95
❑7, Mar 1997 .... 2.95
❑8, May 1997 .... 2.95
❑9, Jun 1997 .... 2.95
❑10, Jul 1997 .... 2.95
❑11, Aug 1997 .... 2.95
❑12, Sep 1997; Final Issue 2.95

Real Americans Admit: "The Worst Thing I've Ever Done!"
NBM

❑1 .... 8.95

Real Bout High School
Tokyopop

❑1, Mar 2002, b&w; printed in Japanese format 9.99
❑2, Jun 2002, b&w; printed in Japanese format 9.99

Real Deal Magazine
Real Deal

❑5, b&w; magazine 2.00

Real Ghostbusters Summer Special
Now

❑1, Sum 1993; NN 2.95

Real Ghostbusters 3-D Summer Special
Now

❑1, Jul 1993; 3-D glasses included 2.95

Real Ghostbusters
Now

❑1, Aug 1988; Ghostbusters movie adaptation 2.00
❑2, Sep 1988 .... 1.75
❑3, Oct 1988 .... 1.75
❑4, Nov 1988 .... 1.75
❑5, Jan 1989 .... 1.75
❑6, Feb 1989 .... 1.75
❑7, Mar 1989 .... 1.75
❑8, Apr 1989 .... 1.75
❑9, May 1989 .... 1.75
❑10, Jun 1989 .... 1.75
❑11, Jul 1989 .... 1.75
❑12, Aug 1989 .... 1.75
❑13, Sep 1989 .... 1.75
❑14, Oct 1989 .... 1.75
❑15, Nov 1989 .... 1.75
❑16, Dec 1989 .... 1.75
❑17, Jan 1990 .... 1.75
❑18, Feb 1990 .... 1.75
❑19, Mar 1990 .... 1.75
❑20, Apr 1990; Includes pin-up poster 1.75
❑21, May 1990 .... 1.75
❑22, Jun 1990 .... 1.75
❑23, Jul 1990 .... 1.75
❑24, Aug 1990 .... 1.75
❑25, Sep 1990 .... 1.75
❑26, Oct 1990 .... 1.75
❑27, Nov 1990; Includes pin-up 1.75
❑28, Dec 1990; Final issue? 1.75
❑3D 1; gatefold summary; 3-D Special; Includes glasses 2.95

Real Ghostbusters
Now

❑1, Nov 1991 .... 1.75
❑1/3D, Oct 1991; polybagged; w/glasses 2.95
❑2, Dec 1991 .... 1.75
❑3, Jan 1992 .... 1.75
❑4, Feb 1992 .... 1.75
❑Ann 1992, Mar 1992 .... 1.00
❑Ann 1993, Dec 1992; 3-D 2.95

Real Girl
Fantagraphics

❑1, Oct 1990, b&w; Magazine sized 2.50
❑2, b&w; Adult 2.50
❑3, b&w; Adult 2.95
❑4, b&w; Adult 2.95
❑5, b&w; Adult 3.50
❑6, b&w; Adult 3.50
❑7, Aug 1994, b&w; Adult 3.50

Real Life
Fantagraphics

❑1, Mar 1990, b&w 2.50

Really Fantastic Alien Sex Frenzy
Fantagraphics / Eros

❑1, b&w; Adult 3.95

Realm Handbook
Caliber

❑1 .... 2.95

Realm of the Claw
Image

❑0, Oct 2003 .... 5.95
❑1/A, Nov 2003; Flip book with Mutant Earth #1/A 2.95
❑1/B, Nov 2003, Flip book with Mutant Earth #1/B 2.95
❑1/C, Nov 2003 .... 2.95
❑2/A, Jan 2004; Flip book with Mutant Earth #2/A 2.95
❑2/B, Jan 2004, Flip book with Mutant Earth #2 .... 2.95

Realm of the Dead
Caliber

❑1 .... 2.95
❑2 .... 2.95
❑3 .... 2.95

Realm
Arrow

❑1, ca. 1986 .... 5.00
❑2, ca. 1986; repeats indicia for #1 .... 2.00
❑3, ca. 1986 .... 2.00
❑4, Sep 1986; 1: Deadworld 4.00
❑5, Nov 1986 .... 1.75
❑6, Jan 1987 .... 1.75
❑7, Mar 1987 .... 1.75
❑8, May 1987 .... 1.75
❑9, Jul 1987 .... 1.75
❑10, Sep 1987 .... 1.75
❑11, Nov 1987 .... 1.75
❑12, Mar 1988 .... 1.75
❑13, Jun 1988; Published by WeeBee Comics 1.95
❑14, Feb 1989, b&w; Caliber begins publishing; b&w 1.95
❑15, Apr 1989, b&w 1.95
❑16, May 1989, b&w 2.50
❑17, Sep 1989 .... 2.50
❑18, Apr 1990 .... 2.50
❑19, Aug 1990; no publication date 2.50
❑20, Dec 1990 .... 2.50
❑21, Jan 1991; no publication date 2.50

Realm
Caliber

❑1, b&w 2.95
❑2, b&w 2.95
❑3, b&w 2.95
❑4, b&w 2.95
❑5, b&w 2.95

Other grades: Multiply price above by 5/6 for VF/NM • 2/3 for VERY FINE • 1/3 for FINE • 1/5 for VERY GOOD • 1/8 for GOOD

Rip Off Comix

A classic salute to everything 1970s
©Rip Off

Rising Stars

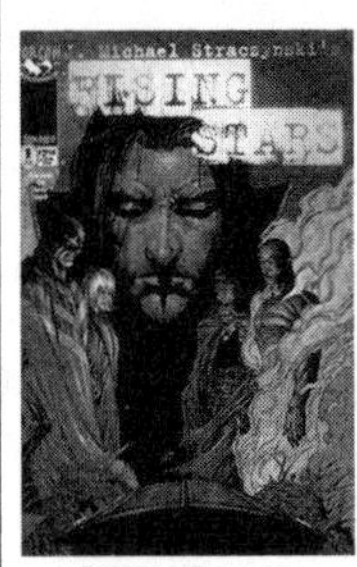

Babylon 5 creator does super-heroes
©Image

Robin (Mini-Series)

Third Robin gets first Robin mini-series
©DC

Robin

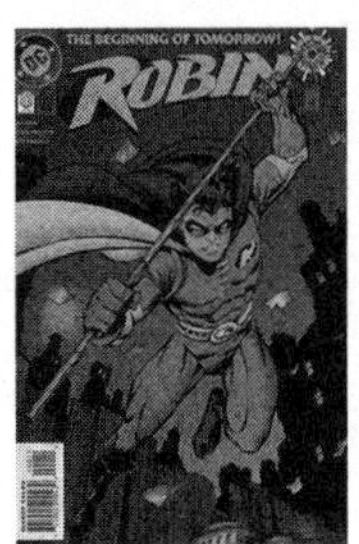

Sidekick finally gets ongoing series
©DC

Robin II

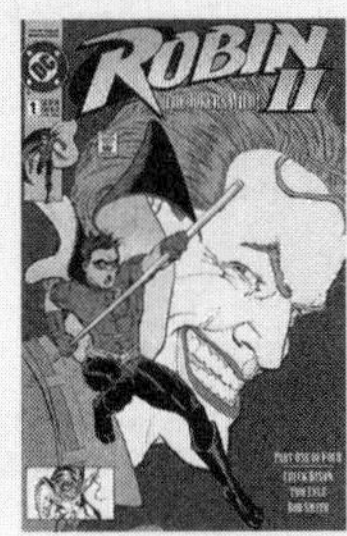

Second Robin mini has Joker on the loose
©DC

N-MINT

❑6, b&w ... 2.95
❑7, b&w ... 2.95
❑8, b&w ... 2.95
❑9, b&w ... 2.95
❑10, b&w ... 2.95
❑11, b&w ... 2.95
❑12, b&w ... 2.95
❑13, b&w ... 2.95

Real Schmuck
Starhead

❑1, b&w; Adult ... 2.95

Real Smut
Fantagraphics / Eros

❑1, b&w; Adult ... 2.50
❑2, b&w; Adult ... 2.50
❑3, b&w; Adult ... 2.50
❑4, Mar 1993, b&w; Adult ... 2.75
❑5, b&w; Adult ... 2.75
❑6, b&w; Adult ... 2.50

Real Stuff
Fantagraphics

❑1, Dec 1990, b&w ... 3.00
❑2, b&w ... 2.75
❑3, May 1991, b&w ... 2.50
❑4, Nov 1991, b&w ... 2.50
❑5, Feb 1992, b&w ... 2.50
❑6, Apr 1992, b&w ... 2.50
❑7, Jun 1992, b&w ... 2.50
❑8, Aug 1992, b&w ... 2.50
❑9, Oct 1992, b&w ... 2.50
❑10, Dec 1992, b&w ... 2.95
❑11, Feb 1993, b&w ... 2.50
❑12, Apr 1993, b&w ... 2.50
❑13, Jun 1993, b&w ... 2.50
❑14, Aug 1993, b&w ... 2.50
❑15, Oct 1993, b&w ... 2.50
❑16, Dec 1993, b&w ... 2.50
❑17, Mar 1994, b&w ... 2.50
❑18, May 1994 ... 2.50
❑19, Jul 1994, b&w ... 2.50
❑20, Oct 1994, b&w ... 2.95

Real War Stories
Eclipse

❑1, Jul 1987 ... 2.00
❑1/2nd, Feb 1988 ... 2.00
❑2, Jan 1991 ... 4.95

Real Weird War
Avalon

❑1; "Real Weird War" on cover ... 2.95

Real Weird West
Avalon

❑1 ... 2.95

Realworlds: Batman
DC

❑1; ca. 2000 ... 5.95

Realworlds: Justice League of America
DC

❑1, Jul 2000 ... 5.95

Realworlds: Superman
DC

❑1 ... 5.95

N-MINT

Realworlds: Wonder Woman
DC

❑1, Jun 2000 ... 5.95

Re-Animator
Aircel

❑1, Movie adaptation ... 2.95
❑2, Movie adaptation ... 2.95
❑3, Movie adaptation ... 2.95

Re-Animator: Dawn of the Re-Animator
Adventure

❑1, b&w ... 2.50
❑2, Apr 1992 ... 2.50
❑3, May 1992 ... 2.50
❑4 ... 2.50

Re-Animator in Full Color
Adventure

❑1, Nov 1991 ... 2.95
❑2 ... 2.95
❑3, Apr 1992 ... 2.95

Reaper One Shot
Image

❑1, May 2004 ... 6.95

Rear Entry
Fantagraphics / Eros

❑1 ... 3.50
❑2 ... 3.50
❑3 ... 3.50
❑4 ... 3.50
❑5 ... 3.95
❑6, Dec 2004 ... 3.95
❑7 ... 3.95
❑8, Dec 2004 ... 3.95
❑9, Apr 2005 ... 3.95
❑10, Dec 2005 ... 3.95

R.E.B.E.L.S.
DC

❑0, Oct 1994, story continued from L.E.G.I.O.N. '94 #70 ... 1.95
❑1, Nov 1994 ... 1.95
❑2, Dec 1994 ... 1.95
❑3, Jan 1995, Title changes to R.E.B.E.L.S. '95 ... 1.95
❑4, Feb 1995 ... 1.95
❑5, Mar 1995 ... 1.95
❑6, Apr 1995 ... 1.95
❑7, May 1995 ... 1.95
❑8, Jun 1995 ... 2.25
❑9, Jul 1995 ... 2.25
❑10, Aug 1995 ... 2.25
❑11, Sep 1995, return of Captain Comet ... 2.25
❑12, Oct 1995 ... 2.25
❑13, Nov 1995, Underworld Unleashed ... 2.25
❑14, Dec 1995, Title changes to R.E.B.E.L.S. '96 ... 2.25
❑15, Jan 1996 ... 2.25
❑16, Feb 1996 ... 2.25
❑17, Mar 1996, Final Issue ... 2.25

Rebel Sword
Dark Horse

❑1, Oct 1994, b&w ... 2.50
❑2, Nov 1994, b&w ... 2.50
❑3, Dec 1994, b&w ... 2.50

N-MINT

❑4, Jan 1995, b&w ... 2.50
❑5, Feb 1995, b&w ... 2.50

Rebirth
Tokyopop

❑1, Mar 2003, b&w; Graphic novel ... 9.99
❑2, Mar 2003; Graphic novel; b&w ... 9.99
❑3, Jul 2003; Graphic novel; b&w ... 9.99
❑4, Sep 2003; Graphic novel; b&w ... 9.99
❑5, Dec 2003; Graphic novel; b&w ... 9.99
❑6, Feb 2004; Graphic novel; b&w ... 9.99
❑7, Apr 2004; Graphic novel; b&w ... 9.99
❑8, Jun 2004; Graphic novel; b&w ... 9.99
❑9, Aug 2004; Graphic novel; b&w ... 9.99
❑10, Oct 2004; Graphic novel; b&w ... 9.99
❑11, Dec 2004; Graphic novel; b&w ... 9.99
❑12, Feb 2005; Graphic novel; b&w ... 9.99
❑13, Apr 2005; Graphic novel; b&w ... 9.99
❑14, Jun 2005; Graphic novel; b&w ... 9.99
❑15, Aug 2005; Graphic novel; Read right to left; b&w ... 9.99
❑16, Nov 2005 ... 9.99

Recollections Sampler
Recollections

❑1, b&w; Reprints ... 1.00

Record of Lodoss War: Chronicles of the Heroic Knight
CPM Manga

❑1, Sep 2000, b&w ... 2.95
❑2, Oct 2000, b&w ... 2.95
❑3, Nov 2000 ... 2.95
❑4, Dec 2000 ... 2.95
❑5, Jan 2001 ... 2.95
❑6, Feb 2001 ... 2.95
❑7, Mar 2001 ... 2.95
❑8, Apr 2001 ... 2.95
❑9, May 2001 ... 2.95
❑10, Jun 2001 ... 2.95
❑11, Jul 2001 ... 2.95

Record of Lodoss War: The Grey Witch
CPM

❑1, Nov 1998; wraparound cover ... 2.95
❑2, Dec 1998 ... 2.95
❑3, Jan 1999; wraparound cover ... 2.95
❑4, Feb 1999 ... 2.95
❑5, Mar 1999 ... 2.95
❑6, Apr 1999 ... 2.95
❑7, May 1999 ... 2.95
❑8, Jun 1999 ... 2.95
❑9, Jul 1999 ... 2.95
❑10, Aug 1999 ... 2.95
❑11, Sep 1999 ... 2.95
❑12, Oct 1999 ... 2.95
❑13, Nov 1999 ... 2.95
❑14, Dec 1999 ... 2.95
❑15, Jan 2000 ... 2.95
❑16, Feb 2000 ... 2.95
❑17, Mar 2000; wraparound cover ... 2.95
❑18, Apr 2000 ... 2.95
❑19, May 2000 ... 2.95
❑20, Jun 2000 ... 2.95
❑21, Jul 2000 ... 2.95
❑22, Aug 2000; wraparound cover ... 2.95

Record of Lodoss War: The Lady of Pharis
CPM

❑1 ... 2.95
❑2 ... 2.95
❑3 ... 2.95
❑4 ... 2.95
❑5 ... 2.95
❑6 ... 2.95
❑7 ... 2.95
❑8 ... 2.95

Rectum Errrectum
Boneyard

❑1; Adult ... 3.95

Red
DC / Homage

❑1, Sep 2003 ... 2.95
❑2, Oct 2003 ... 2.95
❑3, Feb 2004, Cover date indicates 2003 2.95

Redblade
Dark Horse

❑1, Apr 1993; gatefold cover ... 2.50
❑2, May 1993 ... 2.50
❑3, Jul 1993 ... 2.50

Red Circle Sorcery
Red Circle

❑6, Apr 1974; Series continued from Chilling Adventures in Sorcery #5 ... 10.00
❑7, Jun 1974 ... 5.00
❑8, Aug 1974 GM (c); ATh, GM, FT (a) ... 5.00
❑9, Oct 1974 ... 5.00
❑10, Dec 1974 GM, FT, HC, WW, JAb (a) 5.00
❑11, Feb 1975 ... 5.00

Reddevil
AC

❑1, no indicia ... 2.95

Red Diaries
Caliber

❑1, ca. 1997 ... 3.95
❑2, ca. 1997 ... 3.95
❑3, ca. 1997 ... 3.95
❑4, ca. 1997 ... 3.95

Red Dragon
Comico

❑1, Jun 1996 ... 2.95

Redeemer
Images & Realities

❑1 ... 2.95

Redeemers
Antarctic

❑1, Dec 1997, b&w ... 2.95

Red Flannel Squirrel
Sirius

❑1, Oct 1997, b&w ... 2.95

Redfox
Harrier

❑1, Jan 1986; 1: Redfox. Harrier publishes 4.00
❑1/2nd; 1: Redfox. Harrier publishes ... 1.75
❑2, Mar 1986 ... 3.00
❑3, May 1986 ... 2.50
❑4, Jul 1986 ... 1.75
❑5, Sep 1986 ... 1.75
❑6, Nov 1986 ... 1.75
❑7, Jan 1987 ... 1.75
❑8, Mar 1987 ... 1.75
❑9, May 1987 BT (c) ... 1.75
❑10, Jul 1987; Last Harrier issue ... 1.75
❑11, Sep 1987; Valkyrie begins publishing 2.00
❑12, Nov 1987 ... 2.00
❑13, Jan 1988 ... 2.00
❑14, Mar 1988 ... 2.00
❑15, May 1988; Luther Arkwright cameo 2.00
❑16, Jun 1988 ... 2.00
❑17, Aug 1988 ... 2.00
❑18, Oct 1988 ... 2.00
❑19, Feb 1989 ... 2.00
❑20, Jun 1989; NG (w); Final Issue ... 2.00

Red Heat
Blackthorne

❑1, Jul 1988, b&w; Movie adaptation ... 2.00
❑1/3D, Jul 1988; Movie adaptation ... 2.50

Redmask of the Rio Grande
AC

❑1, Reprints ... 2.95
❑2 ... 2.95
❑3; 3-D effects ... 2.95

Red Menace
DC

❑1, Feb 2007 ... 2.99
❑1/Variant, Feb 2007 ... 2.99
❑2, Mar 2007 ... 2.99
❑2/Variant, Mar 2007 ... 2.99

Red Moon
Millennium

❑1, Mar 1995, b&w ... 2.95
❑2 ... 2.95

Red Planet Pioneer
Inesco

❑1 ... 2.95

Red Prophet: The Tales of Alvin Maker
Marvel

❑1 ... 0.00

Red Razors: A Dreddworld Adventure
Fleetway-Quality

❑1 ... 2.95
❑2 ... 2.95
❑3 ... 2.95

Red Revolution
Caliber / Tome

❑1, b&w ... 2.95

Red Rocket 7
Dark Horse / Legend

❑1, Aug 1997 ... 2.95
❑2, Sep 1997 ... 2.95
❑3, Oct 1997 ... 2.95
❑4, Nov 1997 ... 2.95
❑5, Jan 1998 ... 2.95
❑6, Mar 1998 ... 3.95
❑7, Jun 1998 ... 3.95

Red Sonja
Marvel

❑1, Nov 1976, FT (c); FT, TD (a); O: Red Sonja ... 8.00
❑2, Jan 1977, FT (c); FT (a) ... 3.00
❑3, May 1977, FT (c); FT (a) ... 3.00
❑4, Jul 1977, FT (c); FT (a) ... 3.00
❑4/35¢, Jul 1977, 35¢ regional variant .. 20.00
❑5, Sep 1977, FT (c); FT (a); 35¢ regional price variant ... 20.00
❑5/35¢, Sep 1977, FT (a); 35¢ regional price variant ... 20.00
❑6, Nov 1977, FT (c); WP (w); FT (a) ... 3.00
❑7, Jan 1978, FT (c); FT (a) ... 1.50
❑8, Mar 1978, FT (c); FT (a) ... 1.50
❑9, May 1978, FT (c); FT (a) ... 1.50
❑10, Jul 1978, FT (c); FT (a) ... 1.50
❑11, Sep 1978, FT (c); FT (a) ... 1.50
❑12, Nov 1978 ... 1.50
❑13, Jan 1979 ... 1.50
❑14, Mar 1979 ... 1.50
❑15, May 1979 ... 1.50

Red Sonja
Marvel

❑1, Feb 1983, TD (a); Indicia reads Vol. 1 1.00
❑2, Mar 1983 ... 1.00

Red Sonja
Marvel

❑1, Aug 1983, giant ... 1.50
❑2, Oct 1983, giant ... 1.50
❑3, Dec 1983, giant ... 1.50
❑4, Feb 1984, giant ... 1.50
❑5, Jan 1985, PB (c); PB (a) ... 1.50
❑6, Feb 1985, PB (c); PB (a) ... 1.50
❑7, Mar 1985 ... 1.50
❑8, Apr 1985 ... 1.50
❑9, May 1985 ... 1.50
❑10, Aug 1985 ... 1.50
❑11, Nov 1985 ... 1.50
❑12, Feb 1986 ... 1.50
❑13, May 1986, Final Issue ... 1.50

Red Sonja
Dynamite Comics

❑0/Black 2005; Greg Land art. Promo comics priced at 25¢. Black background on cover ... 3.00
❑0/White 2005; Greg Land art. Promo comics priced at 25¢. White background on cover ... 3.00
❑0/Ross 2005; Alex Ross art. Retailer incentive provided 1 per 100 copies ordered ... 30.00
❑0/Sketch 2005; Greg Land sketch cover. Retailer incentive provided 1 per 1,000 copies ordered ... 150.00
❑0/Foil 2005 ... 10.00
❑0/Authentix 2005 ... 20.00
❑0/DF 2005 ... 25.00
❑1 2005 ... 20.00
❑1/Rivera 2005 ... 25.00
❑1/Adams 2005 ... 35.00
❑1/Linsner 2005 ... 125.00
❑1/Ross 2005 ... 40.00
❑1/Rubi 2005 ... 20.00
❑1/DF 2005 ... 35.00
❑2 2005 ... 0.00
❑3 2005 ... 0.00
❑4, Jan 2005 ... 0.00
❑5, Jan 2006 ... 2.99
❑6, Feb 2006 ... 0.00
❑7, Mar 2006 ... 0.00
❑8, Apr 2006 ... 0.00
❑9 ... 0.00

Red Sonja/Claw: Devil's Hands
DC

❑1, May 2006 ... 2.99
❑2, Jun 2006 ... 2.99
❑4, Aug 2006 ... 2.99

Red Sonja: Scavenger Hunt
Marvel

❑1, Dec 1995; One-shot ... 2.95

Red Sonja: The Movie
Marvel

❑1, Nov 1985; Movie adaptation ... 1.25
❑2, Dec 1985; Movie adaptation ... 1.25

Red Star
Image

❑1, Jun 2000 ... 3.50
❑2, Jul 2000 ... 3.00
❑3, Oct 2000 ... 2.95
❑4, Jan 2001 ... 2.95
❑5, Feb 2001 ... 2.95
❑6, Mar 2001 ... 2.95
❑7, Apr 2001 ... 2.95
❑8/A ... 2.95
❑8/B ... 3.00
❑9, Jun 2002 ... 3.00

Red Star
CrossGen

❑5, Jul 2004 ... 3.00
❑1, Feb 2003 ... 3.00
❑2, Jun 2003 ... 3.00
❑3, Oct 2003 ... 3.00
❑4, Mar 2004 ... 3.00

Red Tornado
DC

❑1, Jul 1985 CI (c); KB (w); CI (a) ... 1.00
❑2, Aug 1985 CI (c); KB (w); CI (a) ... 1.00
❑3, Sep 1985 CI (c); KB (w); CI (a) ... 1.00
❑4, Oct 1985 CI (c); KB (w); CI (a) ... 1.00

Red Wolf
Marvel

❑1, May 1972, 1: Red Wolf. 1: Lobo (Marvel) ... 35.00
❑2, Jul 1972 ... 18.00
❑3, Sep 1972 ... 15.00
❑4, Nov 1972, V: Man-Bear ... 15.00
❑5, Jan 1973 ... 15.00
❑6, Mar 1973 ... 10.00
❑7, May 1973 ... 10.00
❑8, Jul 1973 ... 10.00
❑9, Sep 1973, Final Issue ... 10.00

Reese's Pieces
Eclipse

❑1, ca. 1986 ... 1.75
❑2, ca. 1986 ... 1.75

Robin Hood (Dell)

More adventures with the merry men
©Dell

Robocop (Marvel)

Marvel continues the movie's adventures
©Marvel

Robotech

Beverly Hills 90210 with fighter jets in this series
©Antarctic

Robotech Masters

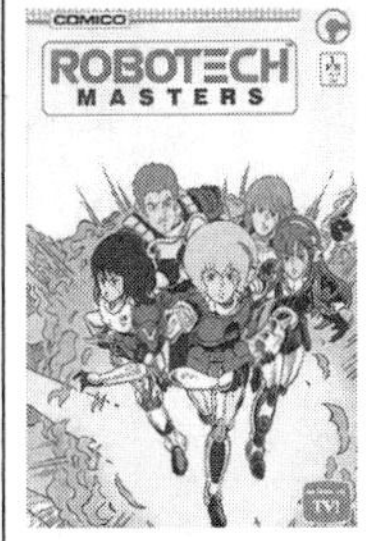

Early series based on big robot warriors
©Comico

Robotech: The Macross Saga

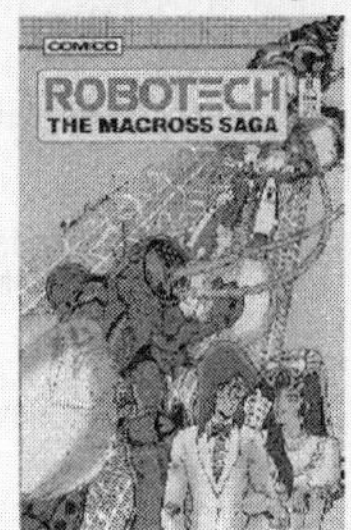

First issue is simply titled "Macross"
©Comico

N-MINT

Re:Gex
Awesome

❑0, Dec 1998; Woman with swords standing over figures 2.50
❑0/A, Jan 1999; Man with swords standing over figures 2.50
❑1, Sep 1998 .... 2.50
❑1/A, Sep 1998; White background; Two women with swords on cover 2.50

Reggie's Revenge
Archie

❑1, Spr 1994 .... 2.00
❑2, Fal 1994 .... 2.00
❑3, Spr 1995 .... 2.00

Regulators
Image

❑1, Jun 1995 .... 2.50
❑2, Jul 1995 .... 2.50
❑3, Aug 1995 .... 2.50
❑4 .... 2.50

Rehd
Antarctic

❑0, Jun 2003 .... 2.50

Reid Fleming
Boswell

❑1; 1: Reid Fleming 10.00
❑1/2nd; 2nd printing 4.00

Reid Fleming, World's Toughest Milkman
Eclipse

❑1, Oct 1986 .... 6.00
❑1/2nd; 2nd printing 3.00
❑1/3rd; 3rd printing 2.00
❑1/4th; 4th printing 2.00
❑1/5th; 5th printing 2.00
❑1/6th; 1996 .... 2.95
❑2, Mar 1987 .... 3.00
❑2/2nd; 2nd printing 2.00
❑2/3rd, Mar 1989; 3rd printing 2.00
❑3, Dec 1988; Indicia says #2:3 .... 2.00
❑4, Nov 1989 .... 2.00
❑5, Nov 1990 .... 2.00
❑6 .... 2.00
❑7, Jan 1997 .... 2.95
❑8, Aug 1997 .... 2.95
❑9, Apr 1998 .... 2.95

Reign of the Dragonlord
Eternity

❑1, Oct 1986 .... 1.80
❑2 .... 1.80

Reign of the Zodiac
DC / Homage

❑1, Oct 2003 .... 2.75
❑2, Nov 2003 .... 2.75
❑3, Dec 2003 .... 2.75
❑4, Jan 2004 .... 2.75
❑5, Feb 2004 .... 2.75
❑6, Mar 2004 .... 2.75
❑7, Apr 2004 .... 2.75
❑8, May 2004; Final issue 2.75

Reiki Warriors
Revolutionary

❑1, Aug 1993, b&w; Adult 2.95

N-MINT

Relative Heroes
DC

❑1, Mar 2000, 1: Relative Heroes 2.50
❑2, Apr 2000 .... 2.50
❑3, May 2000 .... 2.50
❑4, Jun 2000 .... 2.50
❑5, Jul 2000 .... 2.50
❑6, Aug 2000 .... 2.50

Relentless Pursuit
Slave Labor

❑1, Jan 1989, b&w 1.75
❑2, May 1989, b&w 1.75
❑3, Sep 1989, b&w 2.95
❑4, Jan 1990, b&w 3.95

Reload
DC / Homage

❑1, May 2003 .... 2.95
❑2, Jul 2003 .... 2.95
❑3, Sep 2003 .... 2.95

Remains
Idea & Design Works

❑1, May 2004 .... 3.99
❑2, Jun 2004 .... 3.99
❑3, Jul 2004 .... 3.99
❑4, Aug 2004 .... 3.99
❑5, Sep 2004 .... 3.99

Remarkable Worlds of Phineas B. Fuddle
Paradox

❑1, Jul 2000 .... 5.95
❑2, Aug 2000 .... 5.95
❑3, Sep 2000 .... 5.95
❑4, Oct 2000 .... 5.95

Remote
Tokyopop

❑1, Jan 2004, Graphic novel 9.99
❑2, Aug 2004; Graphic novel 9.99
❑3, Oct 2004; Graphic novel 9.99
❑4, Jan 2005; Graphic novel 9.99
❑5, Apr 2005; Graphic novel 9.99
❑6, Jul 2005; Graphic novel 9.99
❑7, Oct 2005 .... 9.99

Ren & Stimpy Show
Marvel

❑1/A, Dec 1992; Ren scratch&sniff card 2.50
❑1/B, Dec 1992; Stimpy scratch&sniff card 2.50
❑1/2nd; No air fouler 2.25
❑1/3rd; No air fouler 2.25
❑2, Jan 1993 .... 2.00
❑2/2nd; 2nd printing 1.75
❑3, Feb 1993 .... 2.00
❑3/2nd; 2nd printing 1.75
❑4, Mar 1993 A: Muddy Mudskipper 2.00
❑5, Apr 1993; in space 2.00
❑6, May 1993 A: Spider-Man 1.75
❑7, Jun 1993; Kid Stimpy 1.75
❑8, Jul 1993; Maltese Stimpy 1.75
❑9, Aug 1993 .... 1.75
❑10, Sep 1993 .... 1.75
❑11, Oct 1993 .... 1.75
❑12, Nov 1993; Stimpy cloned 1.75
❑13, Dec 1993; Halloween issue 1.75

N-MINT

❑14, Jan 1994 .... 1.75
❑15, Feb 1994; Christmas issue 1.75
❑16, Mar 1994; Elvis parody 1.75
❑17, Apr 1994 .... 1.75
❑18, May 1994; Powdered Toast Man 1.75
❑19, Jun 1994 .... 1.95
❑20, Jul 1994 A: Muddy Mudskipper 1.95
❑21, Aug 1994 .... 1.95
❑22, Sep 1994 .... 1.95
❑23, Oct 1994; wrestling 1.95
❑24, Nov 1994; box top collecting 1.95
❑25, Dec 1994; V: Dogzilla 1.95
❑25/Variant, Dec 1994; enhanced cover 2.95
❑26, Jan 1995 A: Sven Hoek 1.95
❑27, Feb 1995 .... 1.95
❑28, Mar 1995 A: Filthy the monkey 1.95
❑29, Apr 1995 .... 1.95
❑30, May 1995; Ren's birthday 1.95
❑31, Jun 1995 .... 1.95
❑32, Jul 1995 .... 1.95
❑33, Aug 1995 .... 1.95
❑34, Sep 1995 .... 1.95
❑35, Oct 1995 .... 1.95
❑36, Nov 1995 .... 1.95
❑37, Dec 1995; aliens 1.95
❑38, Jan 1996 .... 1.95
❑39, Feb 1996 .... 1.95
❑40, Mar 1996 .... 1.95
❑41, Apr 1996 .... 1.95
❑42, May 1996 .... 1.95
❑43, Jun 1996 .... 1.95
❑44, Jul 1996; Final Issue 1.95
❑Special 1, Jul 1994; Vol. 1, #1; Indicia reads: Ren & Stimpy Show Special: Powdered Toast Man 2.95
❑Special 2, Oct 1994; Summer Jobs 3.00
❑Special 3, Oct 1994; Masters of Time and Space! 3.00
❑Holiday 1, Feb 1995; NN 2.95

Ren & Stimpy Show: Radio Daze
Marvel

❑1, Nov 1995; based on audio release of same name 1.95

Ren & Stimpy Show Special: Around the World in a Daze
Marvel

❑1, Jan 1996; NN; One-shot 2.95

Ren & Stimpy Show Special: Eenteractive
Marvel

❑1, Jul 1995; NN 2.95

Ren & Stimpy Show Special: Four Swerks
Marvel

❑1, Jan 1995; NN 2.95

Ren & Stimpy Show Special: Powdered Toast Man
Marvel

❑1, Apr 1994; O: Crusto. Powdered Toast Man 3.00

Ren & Stimpy Show Special: Powdered Toastman's Cereal
Marvel

❑1, Apr 1995; NN 2.95

Ren & Stimpy Show Special: Sports
Marvel
- ❑1, Oct 1995; NN 2.95

Renegade
Rip Off
- ❑1, Aug 1991, b&w; Adult 2.50

Renegade!
Magnecom
- ❑1, Dec 1993 .... 2.95

Renegade Rabbit
Printed Matter
- ❑1 .... 1.75
- ❑2 .... 1.75
- ❑3 .... 1.75
- ❑4 .... 1.75
- ❑5; Cerebus parody 1.75

Renegade Romance
Renegade
- ❑1, Jun 1987, b&w 3.50
- ❑2, b&w; ca. 1988 .... 3.50

Renegades
Age of Heroes
- ❑1 .... 1.00
- ❑2 .... 1.00

Renegades of Justice
Blue Masque
- ❑1, ca. 1995, b&w 2.50
- ❑2, ca. 1995, b&w 2.50

Renfield
Caliber
- ❑1, ca. 1994 .... 2.95
- ❑1/Ltd.; Limited "special edition" with second cover 5.95
- ❑2, ca. 1994 .... 2.95
- ❑3, ca. 1995 .... 2.95
- ❑Ashcan 1, b&w; no cover price 1.00

Rennin Comics
Restless Muse
- ❑1, Sum 1997, b&w 2.95

Replacement God
Handicraft
- ❑6, Dec 1998 .... 6.95

Replacement God
Slave Labor / Amaze Ink
- ❑1, Jun 1995, b&w 6.00
- ❑1/2nd, Dec 1995, b&w; 2nd printing 3.00
- ❑2, Sep 1995, b&w 3.50
- ❑3, Dec 1995, b&w 3.00
- ❑4, Apr 1996, b&w 2.95
- ❑5, Jul 1996, b&w 2.95
- ❑6, Sep 1996, b&w 2.95
- ❑7, Dec 1996, b&w 2.95
- ❑8, Apr 1997, b&w 2.95

Replacement God and Other Stories
Image
- ❑1, May 1997, b&w; flip-book with Knute's Escapes back-up 2.95
- ❑2, Jul 1997, b&w; flip-book with Harris Thermidor back-up 2.95
- ❑3, Sep 1997, b&w; flip-book with Knute's Escapes back-up 2.95
- ❑4, Nov 1997, b&w; flip-book with Knute's Escapes back-up 2.95
- ❑5, Jan 1998, b&w; flip-book with Knute's Escapes back-up 2.95

Reporter
Reporter
- ❑1 .... 3.00

Requiem for Dracula
Marvel
- ❑1, Feb 1992; Reprints Tomb of Dracula #69, 70 .... 2.00

Rescueman
Best
- ❑1, b&w 2.95

Rescuers Down Under
Disney
- ❑1 .... 2.95

Resident Evil
Image
- ❑1, Mar 1998 .... 5.50
- ❑2, Jun 1998 .... 5.00
- ❑3, Sep 1998 .... 5.00
- ❑4, Dec 1998 .... 5.00
- ❑5, Feb 1999 .... 5.00

Resident Evil: Code Veronica
DC / Wildstorm
- ❑1, Aug 2002 .... 14.95
- ❑2, Oct 2002 .... 14.95
- ❑3, Dec 2002 .... 14.95

Resident Evil: Fire and Ice
WildStorm
- ❑1, Dec 2000 .... 2.50
- ❑2, Jan 2001 .... 2.50
- ❑3, Feb 2001 .... 2.50
- ❑4, May 2001 .... 2.50

Resistance
WildStorm
- ❑1, Nov 2002 .... 2.95
- ❑2, Dec 2002 .... 2.95
- ❑3, Jan 2003 .... 2.95
- ❑4, Feb 2003 .... 2.95
- ❑5, Mar 2003 .... 2.95
- ❑6, Apr 2003 .... 2.95
- ❑7, May 2003 .... 2.95
- ❑8, Jun 2003 .... 2.95

Restaurant at the End of the Universe
DC
- ❑1 1994; prestige format 6.95
- ❑2 1994; prestige format 6.95
- ❑3 1994; prestige format; Final Issue 6.95

Resurrection Man
DC
- ❑1, May 1997; Lenticular disc on cover 3.00
- ❑2, Jun 1997 A: Justice League of America 2.50
- ❑3, Jul 1997 .... 2.50
- ❑4, Aug 1997 BG (a) 2.50
- ❑5, Sep 1997 BG (a) 2.50
- ❑6, Oct 1997; Genesis; Resurrection Man powerless 2.50
- ❑7, Nov 1997 BG (a); A: Batman 2.50
- ❑8, Dec 1997; BG (a); Face cover 2.50
- ❑9, Jan 1998 BG (a); A: Hitman 2.50
- ❑10, Feb 1998 BG (a); A: Hitman 2.50
- ❑11, Mar 1998; BG (a); O: Resurrection Man 2.50
- ❑12, Apr 1998 BG (a) 2.50
- ❑13, May 1998 .... 2.50
- ❑14, Jun 1998 BG (a) 2.50
- ❑15, Jul 1998 .... 2.50
- ❑16, Aug 1998; A: Supergirl. Continued in Supergirl #24 .... 2.50
- ❑17, Sep 1998 A: Supergirl 2.50
- ❑18, Oct 1998 A: Deadman. A: Phantom Stranger 2.50
- ❑19, Dec 1998 .... 2.50
- ❑20, Jan 1999 .... 2.50
- ❑21, Feb 1999; BG (a); A: Justice League of America. V: Major Force 2.50
- ❑22, Mar 1999 BG (a) 2.50
- ❑23, Apr 1999; BG (c); BG (a); Mitch as a woman 2.50
- ❑24, May 1999 BG (a); A: Animal Man. A: Ray. A: Cave Carson. A: Ballistic. A: Vandal Savage. A: Vigilante 2.50
- ❑25, Jun 1999 BG (a); A: Forgotten Heroes 2.50
- ❑26, Jul 1999 A: Immortal Man 2.50
- ❑27, Aug 1999; BG (a); D: Immortal Man 2.50
- ❑1000000, Nov 1998 BG (c); BG (a) 4.00

Retaliator
Eclipse
- ❑1, Jul 1992, b&w; Includes game card 2.50
- ❑2, Aug 1992, b&w; Includes game card 2.50
- ❑3, Sep 1992, b&w 2.50
- ❑4, Oct 1992, b&w; Includes game card 2.50
- ❑5 .... 2.50

Retief
Mad Dog
- ❑1, Apr 1987 .... 2.00
- ❑2, Jun 1987 .... 2.00
- ❑3, Aug 1987 .... 2.00
- ❑4, Oct 1987 .... 2.00
- ❑5, Jan 1988 .... 2.00
- ❑6, Mar 1988 .... 2.00

Retief
Adventure
- ❑1, Dec 1989, b&w 2.25
- ❑2, Jan 1990, b&w 2.25
- ❑3, Feb 1990, b&w 2.25
- ❑4, May 1990, b&w 2.25
- ❑5, Jul 1990, b&w 2.25
- ❑6, Oct 1990, b&w 2.25

Retief and the Warlords
Adventure
- ❑1, b&w; Adult 2.50
- ❑2, b&w; Adult 2.50
- ❑3, b&w; Adult 2.50
- ❑4, b&w; Adult 2.50

Retief: Diplomatic Immunity
Adventure
- ❑1, b&w 2.50
- ❑2, b&w 2.50

Retief: Grime and Punishment
Adventure
- ❑1, Nov 1991, b&w 2.50

Retief of the C.D.T.
Mad Dog
- ❑1, b&w; ca. 1988 .... 2.00

Retief: The Garbage Invasion
Adventure
- ❑1, b&w 2.50

Retief: The Giant Killer
Adventure
- ❑1, Sep 1991, b&w 2.50

Retro 50's Comix
Edge
- ❑1, b&w 2.95
- ❑2, b&w 2.95
- ❑3, b&w; free fly 3.50

Retro Comics
AC
- ❑0, b&w; Cardstock cover; Cat-Man 5.95
- ❑1, b&w; Cardstock cover; Fighting Yank 5.95
- ❑2, b&w; Cardstock cover; Miss Victory 5.95
- ❑3, Original Cat-Man and Kitten 5.95

Retro-Dead
Blazer
- ❑1, Nov 1995, b&w 2.95

Retrograde
Eternity
- ❑1 .... 1.95
- ❑2 .... 1.95
- ❑3 .... 1.95

Retro Rocket
Image
- ❑1, Apr 2006 .... 2.99
- ❑3, Sep 2006 .... 2.99

Return of Disney's Aladdin
Disney
- ❑1 .... 1.50
- ❑2 .... 1.50

Return of Girl Squad X
Fantaco
- ❑1; NN 4.95

Return of Gorgo
Charlton
- ❑2, Sum 1963 .... 75.00
- ❑3, Fal 1964 .... 75.00

Return of Happy the Clown
Caliber
- ❑1, b&w; Adult; ca. 1995 .... 3.50
- ❑2, ca. 1995, b&w; Adult 2.95

Return of Herbie
Avalon
- ❑1, b&w; reprints and new story (originally scheduled for Dark Horse's Herbie #3) 2.50

Return of Lum Urusei*Yatsura, Part 1
Viz
- ❑1, Oct 1994, b&w 3.00
- ❑2, Nov 1994, b&w 3.00
- ❑3, Dec 1994, b&w 3.00
- ❑4, Jan 1995, b&w 3.00
- ❑5, Feb 1995, b&w 3.00
- ❑6, Mar 1995, b&w 3.00

Other grades: Multiply price above by 5/6 for VF/NM • 2/3 for VERY FINE • 1/3 for FINE • 1/5 for VERY GOOD • 1/8 for GOOD

Robotech Warriors

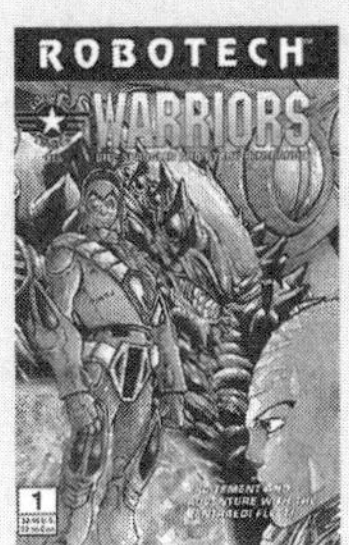

More with the Zentraedi race
©Academy

Rocketeer: The Official Movie Adaptation

Remarkably faithful movie adaptation
©Disney

Rocket Ranger

Lesser-known video game comic
©Adventure

Rock 'n' Roll Comics

Bios from the Beatles to Public Enemy
©Revolutionary

Roger Rabbit

Hit movie spawns comics title for Disney
©Disney

N-MINT

❑7, ca. 1995 .... 2.75
❑8, ca. 1995 .... 2.75

Return of Lum Urusei*Yatsura, Part 2
Viz

❑1, Apr 1995, b&w 3.00
❑2, May 1995, b&w 3.00
❑3, Jun 1995, b&w 3.00
❑4, Jul 1995, b&w 3.00
❑5, Aug 1995, b&w 3.00
❑6, Sep 1995, b&w 3.00
❑7, Oct 1995, b&w 3.00
❑8, Nov 1995, b&w 3.00
❑9, Dec 1995, b&w 3.00
❑10, Jan 1996, b&w 3.00
❑11, Feb 1996, b&w 3.00
❑12, Mar 1996, b&w 3.00
❑13, Apr 1996, b&w 3.00

Return of Lum Urusei*Yatsura, Part 3
Viz

❑1, May 1996, b&w 2.95
❑2, Jun 1996, b&w 2.95
❑3, Jul 1996, b&w 2.95
❑4, Aug 1996, b&w 2.95
❑5, Sep 1996, b&w 2.95
❑6, Oct 1996, b&w 2.95
❑7, Nov 1996, b&w 2.95
❑8, Dec 1996, b&w 2.95
❑9, Jan 1997, b&w 2.95
❑10, Feb 1997, b&w 2.95
❑11, Mar 1997, b&w 2.95

Return of Lum Urusei*Yatsura, Part 4
Viz

❑1, Apr 1997, b&w 2.95
❑2, May 1997, b&w 2.95
❑3, Jun 1997, b&w 2.95
❑4, Jul 1997, b&w 2.95
❑5, Aug 1997, b&w 2.95
❑6, Sep 1997, b&w 2.95
❑7, Oct 1997, b&w 2.95
❑8, Nov 1997, b&w 2.95
❑9, Dec 1997, b&w 2.95
❑10, Jan 1998, b&w 2.95
❑11, Feb 1998, b&w 2.95

Return of Megaton Man
Kitchen Sink

❑1, Jul 1988 .... 2.50
❑2, Aug 1988 .... 2.50
❑3, Sep 1988 .... 2.50

Return of Shadowhawk
Image

❑1, Nov 2004; One-shot 2.99

Return of Tarzan
Dark Horse

❑1, Apr 1997, adapts Burroughs novel .. 2.95
❑2, May 1997, adapts Burroughs novel . 2.95
❑3, Jun 1997, back cover has reproductions of New Story Magazine covers; adapts Burroughs novel; back cover has reproductions of New Story Magazine covers 2.95

Return of the Skyman
Ace

❑1, Sep 1987; Reprint from The Skyman #1 .... 1.75

N-MINT

Return of Valkyrie
Eclipse

❑1 .... 9.95

Return to Jurassic Park
Topps

❑1, Apr 1995 .... 2.50
❑2, May 1995 .... 2.50
❑3, Jun 1995 .... 2.95
❑4, Jul 1995 .... 2.95
❑5, Aug 1995 .... 2.95
❑6, Sep 1995 .... 2.95
❑7, Nov 1995 .... 2.95
❑8, Jan 1996 .... 2.95
❑9, Feb 1996; Final Issue 2.95

Return to the Eve
Monolith

❑1; Adult 2.50

Reveal
Dark Horse

❑1, Nov 2002; Squarebound anthology . 6.95

Revelations
Dark Horse

❑1/Ashcan, Mar 1995 KG (w) 1.00

Revelations
Golden Realm Unlimited

❑1 .... 2.75

Revelations
Eclipse

❑1 .... 7.95

Revelations
Dark Horse

❑1, Aug 2005 .... 2.99
❑2, Sep 2005 .... 2.99
❑3, Oct 2005 .... 2.99
❑4, Nov 2005 .... 2.99
❑5, Dec 2005 .... 2.99
❑6, Jan 2006 .... 2.99

Revelation: The Comic Book
Draw Near

❑1, b&w; No cover price; based on Book of Revelation 3.56
❑2, b&w; based on Book of Revelation .. 3.56
❑3, b&w; based on Book of Revelation .. 3.56
❑4, b&w; based on Book of Revelation .. 3.56
❑5 .... 3.56
❑6 .... 3.56

Revelry in Hell
Fantagraphics / Eros

❑1, Nov 1990, b&w; Adult; 2.50

Revenge of the Prowler
Eclipse

❑1, Feb 1988 .... 2.00
❑2, Mar 1988; Includes Flexi-disc 2.50
❑3, Apr 1988 .... 2.00
❑4, Jun 1988 .... 2.00

Revengers Featuring Armor and The Silverstreak
Continuity

❑1, Sep 1985; Revengers Featuring Armor and Silver Streak, The 2.00

N-MINT

❑2, Jun 1986; O: Armor 2.00
❑3, Feb 1987; Series continues as Armor (Continuity, 1st series) with #4; indicia for this issue accidentally reads "Revengers featuring Megalith"; who does not appear in the issue 2.00

Revengers Featuring Megalith
Continuity

❑1, Apr 1985; newsstand 2.00
❑1/Direct ed., Apr 1985 .... 2.00
❑2, Sep 1985; Revengers Featuring Megalith 2.00
❑3, Nov 1986 .... 2.00
❑4, Mar 1988 .... 2.00
❑5, Mar 1989 .... 2.00
❑6, ca. 1989 .... 2.00

Revengers: Hybrids Special
Continuity

❑1, Jul 1992; continues in Hybrids: The Origin #2 .... 4.95

Reverend Ablack: Adventures of the Antichrist
Creativeforce Designs

❑1 .... 2.50
❑2, Jul 1996, b&w 2.50

Revisionary
Moonstone

❑1, Sep 2005; b&w 2.95

Revolver
Fleetway-Quality

❑1 .... 2.50
❑2 .... 2.50
❑3 .... 2.50
❑4 .... 2.50
❑5 .... 2.50
❑6 .... 2.50
❑7 .... 2.50

Revolver
Renegade

❑1, Nov 1985, SD (a); Sci-Fi Adventure . 2.00
❑2, Dec 1985, Sci-Fi Adventure 2.00
❑3, Jan 1986, SD (w); SD (a); Sci-Fi Adventure 2.00
❑4, Feb 1986, Fantastic Fables 2.00
❑5, Mar 1986, Fantastic Fables 2.00
❑6, Apr 1986, Fantastic Fables 2.00
❑7, May 1986, Ditko's World: Static 2.00
❑8, Jun 1986, Ditko's World: Static 2.00
❑9, Jul 1986, Ditko's World: Static 2.00
❑10, Aug 1986, Murder 2.00
❑11, Sep 1986, Murder 2.00
❑12, Oct 1986, Murder 2.00
❑Ann 1, ca. 1986, b&w; ATh (c); SD (w); SD, EL, RT (a) 2.00

Revolving Doors
Blackthorne

❑1, Oct 1986 .... 1.75
❑2 .... 1.75
❑3 .... 1.75

Revved
Image

❑1, Aug 2006, Piers Anthony presents .. 9.99

Rex Libris
Slave Labor

❑1, Aug 2005, b&w ... 2.95
❑2, Dec 2005, b&w ... 2.95

Rex Mundi
Dark Horse

❑1, Sep 2006 ... 2.99
❑2, Nov 2006 ... 2.99
❑3, Jan 2007 ... 2.99

Rex Mundi
Image

❑1, Feb 2003 ... 2.99
❑2, Mar 2003 ... 2.99
❑3, Apr 2003 ... 2.99
❑4, Jun 2003 ... 2.95
❑5, Sep 2003 ... 2.95
❑6, Oct 2003 ... 2.95
❑7, Dec 2003 ... 2.95
❑8, Jan 2004 ... 2.95
❑9, May 2004 ... 2.95
❑10, Aug 2004 ... 2.95
❑11, Jun 2004 ... 2.95
❑12, Sep 2004 ... 2.95
❑13, Apr 2005 ... 2.95
❑14, Oct 2005 ... 2.99
❑15, Dec 2005; Story credits list it as issue #14 ... 2.99
❑16, Jan 2006; Indicia mistakenly shows date as January 2005 ... 2.99
❑17, Apr 2006; Indicia mistakenly shows date as March 2005 ... 2.99

RG Veda
Tokyopop

❑1, Apr 2005 ... 9.99
❑2, Jul 2005; Graphic novel; Read right to left ... 9.99
❑3, Oct 2005 ... 9.99

Rhaj
Mu

❑1, b&w ... 2.00
❑2, b&w ... 2.00
❑3, b&w ... 2.00
❑4 ... 2.25

Rhanes of Terror
Buffalo Nickel

❑1, Oct 1999 ... 2.99
❑2 ... 2.99
❑3 ... 2.99
❑4 ... 2.99

Rhudiprrt, Prince of Fur
Mu

❑1, Mar 1990, b&w ... 2.00
❑2, May 1990, b&w ... 2.00
❑3, Sep 1990; b&w ... 2.00
❑4, Nov 1990; b&w ... 2.25
❑5, Jun 1991; b&w ... 2.50
❑6, Nov 1991; b&w ... 2.50
❑7, Dec 1992, b&w ... 2.50
❑8, Jan 1994; b&w ... 2.50

Rib
Dilemma

❑1, Apr 1996, b&w ... 1.95

Ribit!
Comico

❑1 ... 1.95
❑2 ... 1.95
❑3 ... 1.95
❑4 ... 1.95

Richard Dragon
DC

❑1, Jul 2004 ... 2.50
❑2, Aug 2004 ... 2.50
❑3, Sep 2004 ... 2.50
❑4, Oct 2004 ... 2.50
❑5, Nov 2004 ... 2.50
❑6, Dec 2004 ... 2.50
❑7, Feb 2005 ... 2.50
❑8, Mar 2005 ... 2.50
❑9, Mar 2005 ... 2.50
❑10, Apr 2005 ... 2.50
❑11, May 2005 ... 2.50
❑12, Jun 2005; Final issue ... 2.50

Richard Dragon, Kung-Fu Fighter
DC

❑1, Apr 1975, DG (c); O: Richard Dragon, Kung Fu Fighter. 1: Richard Dragon, Kung Fu Fighter ... 10.00
❑2, Jul 1975, JSn (a) ... 4.00
❑3, Sep 1975 ... 4.00
❑4, Nov 1975 ... 3.00
❑5, Jan 1976, 1: Lady Shiva [Sandra Woosan] ... 3.00
❑6, Mar 1976 ... 2.00
❑7, Apr 1976 ... 2.00
❑8, May 1976 ... 2.00
❑9, Jun 1976 ... 2.00
❑10, Jul 1976 ... 2.00
❑11, Sep 1976 ... 1.50
❑12, Nov 1976 ... 1.50
❑13, Feb 1977 ... 1.50
❑14, Apr 1977 ... 1.50
❑15, Jun 1977 ... 1.50
❑16, Aug 1977 ... 1.50
❑17, Oct 1977 ... 1.50
❑18, Nov 1977, Final Issue, Ben Turner becomes the Bronze Tiger ... 1.50

Richard Speck
Boneyard

❑1, Mar 1993; Adult ... 2.75

Richie Rich
Harvey

❑1, Nov 1960 ... 3250.00
❑2, Jan 1961 ... 950.00
❑3, Mar 1961 ... 500.00
❑4, May 1961 ... 375.00
❑5, Jul 1961 ... 375.00
❑6, Sep 1961 ... 250.00
❑7, Nov 1961 ... 250.00
❑8, Jan 1962 ... 250.00
❑9, Mar 1962 ... 250.00
❑10, May 1962 ... 175.00
❑11, Jul 1962 ... 125.00
❑12, Sep 1962 ... 125.00
❑13, Oct 1962 ... 125.00
❑14, Nov 1962 ... 125.00
❑15, Jan 1963 ... 125.00
❑16, Mar 1963 ... 90.00
❑17, May 1963 ... 90.00
❑18, Jul 1963 ... 90.00
❑19, Sep 1963 ... 90.00
❑20, Nov 1963 ... 90.00
❑21, Jan 1964 ... 65.00
❑22, Mar 1964 ... 65.00
❑23, May 1964 ... 65.00
❑24, Jul 1964 ... 65.00
❑25, Sep 1964 ... 65.00
❑26, Oct 1964 ... 65.00
❑27, Nov 1964 ... 65.00
❑28, Dec 1964 ... 65.00
❑29, Jan 1965 ... 65.00
❑30, Feb 1965 ... 65.00
❑31, Mar 1965 ... 45.00
❑32, Apr 1965 ... 45.00
❑33, May 1965 ... 45.00
❑34, Jun 1965 ... 45.00
❑35, Jul 1965 ... 45.00
❑36, Aug 1965 ... 45.00
❑37, Sep 1965 ... 45.00
❑38, Oct 1965 ... 45.00
❑39, Nov 1965 ... 45.00
❑40, Dec 1965 ... 45.00
❑41, Jan 1966 ... 35.00
❑42, Feb 1966 ... 35.00
❑43, Mar 1966 ... 35.00
❑44, Apr 1966 ... 35.00
❑45, May 1966 ... 35.00
❑46, Jun 1966 ... 35.00
❑47, Jul 1966 ... 35.00
❑48, Aug 1966 ... 35.00
❑49, Sep 1966 ... 35.00
❑50, Oct 1966 ... 25.00
❑51, Nov 1966 ... 25.00
❑52, Dec 1966 ... 25.00
❑53, Jan 1967 ... 25.00
❑54, Feb 1967 ... 25.00
❑55, Mar 1967 ... 25.00
❑56, Apr 1967 ... 25.00
❑57, May 1967 ... 25.00
❑58, Jun 1967 ... 25.00
❑59, Jul 1967 ... 25.00
❑60, Aug 1967 ... 25.00
❑61, Sep 1967 ... 20.00
❑62, Oct 1967 ... 20.00
❑63, Nov 1967 ... 20.00
❑64, Dec 1967 ... 20.00
❑65, Jan 1968 ... 20.00
❑66, Feb 1968 ... 20.00
❑67, Mar 1968 ... 20.00
❑68, Apr 1968 ... 20.00
❑69, May 1968 ... 20.00
❑70, Jun 1968 ... 20.00
❑71, Jul 1968 ... 15.00
❑72, Aug 1968 ... 15.00
❑73, Sep 1968 ... 15.00
❑74, Oct 1968 ... 15.00
❑75, Nov 1968 ... 15.00
❑76, Dec 1968 ... 15.00
❑77, Jan 1969 ... 15.00
❑78, Feb 1969 ... 15.00
❑79, Mar 1969 ... 15.00
❑80, Apr 1969 ... 15.00
❑81, May 1969 ... 15.00
❑82, Jun 1969 ... 15.00
❑83, Jul 1969 ... 15.00
❑84, Aug 1969 ... 15.00
❑85, Sep 1969 ... 15.00
❑86, Oct 1969 ... 15.00
❑87, Nov 1969 ... 15.00
❑88, Dec 1969 ... 15.00
❑89, Jan 1970 ... 10.00
❑90, Feb 1970 ... 10.00
❑91, Mar 1970 ... 10.00
❑92, Apr 1970 ... 10.00
❑93, May 1970 ... 10.00
❑94, Jun 1970 ... 10.00
❑95, Jul 1970 ... 10.00
❑96, Aug 1970 ... 10.00
❑97, Sep 1970 ... 10.00
❑98, Oct 1970 ... 10.00
❑99, Nov 1970 ... 10.00
❑100, Dec 1970 ... 10.00
❑101, Jan 1971 ... 10.00
❑102, Feb 1971 ... 10.00
❑103, Mar 1971 ... 7.00
❑104, Apr 1971 ... 7.00
❑105, May 1971 ... 7.00
❑106, Jun 1971 ... 7.00
❑107, Jul 1971 ... 7.00
❑108, Aug 1971 ... 7.00
❑109, Sep 1971 ... 7.00
❑110, Oct 1971 ... 7.00
❑111, Nov 1971 ... 7.00
❑112, Jan 1972 ... 7.00
❑113, Mar 1972 ... 7.00
❑114, May 1972 ... 7.00
❑115, Jul 1972 ... 7.00
❑116, Sep 1972 ... 7.00
❑117, Nov 1972 ... 7.00
❑118, Jan 1973 ... 7.00
❑119, Mar 1973 ... 7.00
❑120, May 1973 ... 7.00
❑121, Jul 1973 ... 7.00
❑122, Sep 1973 ... 7.00
❑123, Nov 1973 ... 7.00
❑124, Jan 1974 ... 7.00
❑125, Mar 1974 ... 7.00
❑126, May 1974 ... 7.00
❑127, Jul 1974 ... 5.00
❑128, Sep 1974 ... 5.00
❑129, Nov 1974 ... 5.00
❑130, Jan 1975 ... 5.00
❑131, Mar 1975 ... 5.00
❑132, May 1975 ... 5.00
❑133, Jul 1975 ... 5.00
❑134, Sep 1975 ... 5.00
❑135, Oct 1975 ... 5.00
❑136, Nov 1975 ... 5.00
❑137, Dec 1975 ... 5.00
❑138, Jan 1976 ... 5.00
❑139, Feb 1976 ... 5.00
❑140, Mar 1976 ... 5.00
❑141, Apr 1976 ... 5.00
❑142, May 1976 ... 5.00
❑143, Jun 1976 ... 5.00
❑144, Jul 1976 ... 5.00
❑145, Aug 1976 ... 5.00

Other grades: Multiply price above by 5/6 for VF/NM • 2/3 for VERY FINE • 1/3 for FINE • 1/5 for VERY GOOD • 1/8 for GOOD

Rogue (1st Marvel series)

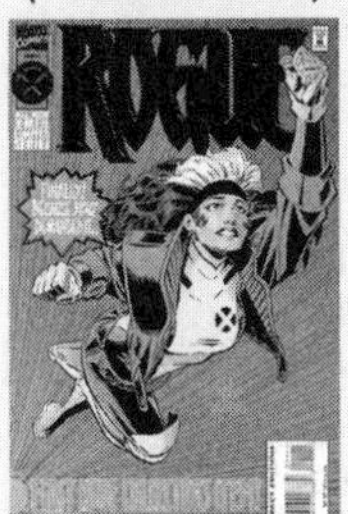

First limited series with Marvel's mutant misfit
©Marvel

Rom

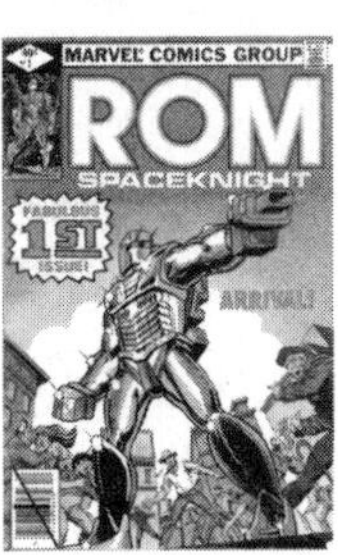

Forgotten toy results in long-running title
©Marvel

Ronald McDonald

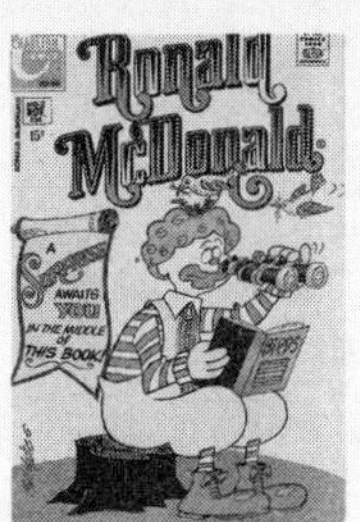

Hamburger stand mascot comes to comics
©Charlton

Ronin

If you intend to die, you can do anything...
©DC

Route 666

Girl sees ghosts, seeks same
©CrossGen

	N-MINT
❑146, Sep 1976	5.00
❑147, Oct 1976, Casper in Hostess ad: "...and the Fog")	5.00
❑148, Nov 1976	5.00
❑149, Dec 1976	5.00
❑150, Jan 1977	5.00
❑151, Feb 1977	5.00
❑152, Mar 1977	5.00
❑153, Apr 1977	5.00
❑154, May 1977	5.00
❑155, Jun 1977, Sad Sack in Hostess ad ("Oops")	5.00
❑156, Jul 1977	5.00
❑157, Aug 1977	5.00
❑158, Sep 1977	5.00
❑159, Oct 1977	5.00
❑160, Nov 1977	3.00
❑161, Dec 1977	3.00
❑162, Jan 1978, "Star Wars" reference on cover; Casper in Hostess ad ("Disguise")	3.00
❑163, Feb 1978	3.00
❑164, Mar 1978	3.00
❑165, Apr 1978	3.00
❑166, May 1978, Wendy in Hostess ad ("Give a Cheer")	3.00
❑167, Jun 1978	3.00
❑168, Jul 1978	3.00
❑169, Aug 1978	3.00
❑170, Sep 1978	3.00
❑171, Oct 1978	3.00
❑172, Nov 1978	3.00
❑173, Dec 1978	3.00
❑174, Jan 1979	3.00
❑175, Feb 1979	3.00
❑176, Mar 1979	3.00
❑177, Apr 1979, Hot Stuff in Hostess ad ("A Swell Party")	3.00
❑178, May 1979	3.00
❑179, Jun 1979	3.00
❑180, Jul 1979	3.00
❑181, Aug 1979	3.00
❑182, Sep 1979	3.00
❑183, Oct 1979	3.00
❑184, Nov 1979	3.00
❑185, Dec 1979	3.00
❑186, Jan 1980	3.00
❑187, Feb 1980, Holiday issue	3.00
❑188, Mar 1980	3.00
❑189, Apr 1980	3.00
❑190, May 1980	3.00
❑191, Jun 1980	3.00
❑192, Jul 1980	3.00
❑193, Aug 1980	3.00
❑194, Sep 1980	3.00
❑195, Oct 1980	3.00
❑196, Nov 1980	3.00
❑197, Dec 1980	3.00
❑198, Jan 1981	3.00
❑199, Feb 1981	3.00
❑200, Mar 1981	3.00
❑201, Apr 1981	1.75
❑202, May 1981	1.75
❑203, Jun 1981	1.75
❑204, Jul 1981	1.75
❑205, Aug 1981	1.75
❑206, Sep 1981	1.75
❑207, Oct 1981	1.75
❑208, Nov 1981	1.75
❑209, Dec 1981	1.75
❑210, Jan 1982	1.75
❑211, Feb 1982	1.75
❑212, Mar 1982	1.75
❑213, Apr 1982	1.75
❑214, May 1982	1.75
❑215, Jun 1982	1.75
❑216, Jul 1982	1.75
❑217, Aug 1982	1.75
❑218, Oct 1982	1.75
❑219, Oct 1986	1.75
❑220, Nov 1986	1.75
❑221, Dec 1986	1.75
❑222, Jan 1987	1.75
❑223, Feb 1987	1.75
❑224, Mar 1987	1.75
❑225, Apr 1987	1.75
❑226, May 1987	1.75
❑227, Jun 1987	1.75
❑228, Jul 1987	1.75
❑229, Aug 1987	1.75
❑230, Sep 1987	1.75
❑231, Nov 1987	1.75
❑232, Feb 1988	1.75
❑233, Apr 1988	1.75
❑234, Jun 1988	1.75
❑235, Aug 1988	1.75
❑236, Oct 1988	1.75
❑237, Dec 1989	1.75
❑238, Mar 1989	1.75
❑239, Jul 1989	1.75
❑240, Sep 1989	1.75
❑241, Oct 1989	1.75
❑242, Dec 1989	1.75
❑243, Feb 1990	1.75
❑244, Mar 1990	1.75
❑245, Apr 1990	1.75
❑246, May 1990	1.75
❑247, Jun 1990	1.75
❑248, Jul 1990	1.75
❑249, Aug 1990	1.75
❑250, Sep 1990	1.75
❑251, Oct 1990	1.75
❑252, Nov 1990	1.75
❑253, Dec 1990	1.75
❑254, Jan 1991, Final Issue	1.75

Richie Rich
Harvey

	N-MINT
❑1, Mar 1991	5.00
❑2, May 1991	3.00
❑3, Jul 1991	1.50
❑4, Sep 1991	1.50
❑5, Nov 1991	1.50
❑6, Jan 1992	1.50
❑7, Mar 1992	1.50
❑8, May 1992	1.50
❑9, Jul 1992	1.50
❑10, Sep 1992	1.50
❑11, Nov 1992	1.00
❑12, Jan 1993	1.00
❑13, Mar 1993	1.00
❑14, May 1993	1.00
❑15, Jul 1993	1.00
❑16, Sep 1993	1.00
❑17, Nov 1993	1.00
❑18, Jan 1994	1.00
❑19, Feb 1994	1.00
❑20, Mar 1994	1.00
❑21, Apr 1994	1.00
❑22, May 1994	1.00
❑23, Jun 1994	1.00
❑24, Jul 1994	1.00
❑25, Aug 1994	1.00
❑26, Sep 1994	1.00
❑27, Oct 1994	1.00
❑28, Nov 1994	1.00

Richie Rich Adventure Digest Magazine
Harvey

	N-MINT
❑1, May 1992	2.00
❑2, Feb 1993	1.75
❑3, Jun 1993	1.75
❑4, Oct 1993	1.75
❑5, Feb 1994	1.75
❑6, Jun 1994	1.75

Richie Rich and Billy Bellhops
Harvey

	N-MINT
❑1, Oct 1977, (c); (w); (a)	5.00

Richie Rich and Cadbury
Harvey

	N-MINT
❑1, Oct 1977	15.00
❑2, Sep 1978	10.00
❑3, Oct 1978	10.00
❑4, Nov 1978	10.00
❑5, Jan 1979	10.00
❑6, Mar 1979	10.00
❑7, May 1979	10.00
❑8, Jul 1979	10.00
❑9, Sep 1979	10.00
❑10, Nov 1979	10.00
❑11, Jan 1980	5.00
❑12, Apr 1980	5.00
❑13, Jul 1980	4.00
❑14, Sep 1980	4.00
❑15, Nov 1980	4.00
❑16 1981	4.00
❑17, May 1981	4.00
❑18, Aug 1981	4.00
❑19, Sep 1981	4.00
❑20, Nov 1981	3.00
❑21, Feb 1982	3.00
❑22, May 1982	3.00
❑23, Jul 1982	3.00
❑24, Jul 1990	3.00
❑25, Sep 1990	3.00
❑26, Oct 1990	3.00
❑27, Nov 1990	3.00
❑28, Dec 1990	3.00
❑29, Jan 1991	3.00

Richie Rich & Casper
Harvey

	N-MINT
❑1, Aug 1974	12.00
❑2, Oct 1974	6.00
❑3, Dec 1974	4.00
❑4, Feb 1975	4.00
❑5, Apr 1975	4.00
❑6, Jun 1975	3.00

Other grades: Multiply price above by 5/6 for VF/NM • 2/3 for VERY FINE • 1/3 for FINE • 1/5 for VERY GOOD • 1/8 for GOOD

	N-MINT
❑7, Aug 1975	3.00
❑8, Oct 1975	3.00
❑9, Dec 1975	3.00
❑10, Feb 1976	3.00
❑11, Apr 1976	2.00
❑12, Jun 1976	2.00
❑13, Aug 1976	2.00
❑14, Oct 1976	2.00
❑15, Dec 1977	2.00
❑16, Feb 1977	2.00
❑17, Apr 1977	2.00
❑18, Jun 1977	2.00
❑19, Aug 1977	2.00
❑20, Oct 1977	2.00
❑21, Dec 1977	2.00
❑22, Feb 1978	2.00
❑23, Apr 1978	2.00
❑24, Jul 1978	2.00
❑25, Sep 1978	2.00
❑26, Nov 1978	2.00
❑27, Mar 1979	2.00
❑28, May 1979	2.00
❑29, Jul 1979	2.00
❑30, Sep 1979	2.00
❑31, Nov 1979	2.00
❑32, Feb 1980; Has Wendy Hostess ad: "The Spell"	2.00
❑33, Apr 1980	2.00
❑34, Jun 1980	2.00
❑35, Sep 1980	2.00
❑36, Nov 1980	2.00
❑37, Dec 1980	2.00
❑38, Mar 1981	2.00
❑39, May 1981	2.00
❑40, Sep 1981	2.00
❑41, Nov 1981	2.00
❑42, Jan 1982	2.00
❑43, Mar 1982; Hot Stuff in Hostess ad ("Somethin' Else Cookin'")	2.00
❑44, Jun 1982	2.00
❑45, Sep 1982	2.00

Richie Rich and Casper in 3-D
Blackthorne

❑1/A, Dec 1987	2.50
❑1/B, Spanish; Burger King	2.50

Richie Rich & Dollar, the Dog
Harvey

❑1, Sep 1977	5.00
❑2, Feb 1978	3.00
❑3, Jun 1978	2.00
❑4, Oct 1978	2.00
❑5, Dec 1978	2.00
❑6, Feb 1979	1.50
❑7, Apr 1979	1.50
❑8, Jun 1979	1.50
❑9, Aug 1979	1.50
❑10, Oct 1979	1.50
❑11, Dec 1979	1.50
❑12, Mar 1980	1.50
❑13, May 1980	1.50
❑14, Aug 1980	1.50
❑15, Oct 1980	1.50
❑16, Nov 1980	1.50
❑17, Mar 1981	1.50
❑18, May 1981	1.50
❑19, Jul 1981	1.50
❑20, Oct 1981	1.50
❑21, Jan 1982	1.50
❑22, Mar 1982	1.50
❑23, Jun 1982	1.50
❑24, Aug 1982	1.50

Richie Rich and Dot
Harvey

❑1, Oct 1974, (c); (w); (a); Featuring Little Dot	20.00

Richie Rich and Gloria
Harvey

❑1, Sep 1977	10.00
❑2, Feb 1978	8.00
❑3, Aug 1978	8.00
❑4, Oct 1978	8.00
❑5, Nov 1978	8.00
❑6, Jan 1979	8.00
❑7, Mar 1979	8.00
❑8, May 1979	8.00
❑9, Jul 1979	8.00
❑10, Sep 1979	8.00
❑11, Nov 1979	5.00
❑12, Jan 1980	5.00
❑13, Apr 1980	5.00
❑14, Jun 1980	5.00
❑15, Aug 1980	5.00
❑16, Oct 1980	5.00
❑17, Dec 1980	5.00
❑18, Mar 1981	5.00
❑19, Jun 1981	5.00
❑20, Aug 1981	4.00
❑21, Oct 1981	4.00
❑22, Jan 1982	4.00
❑23, Mar 1982	4.00
❑24 1982	4.00
❑25, Sep 1982	4.00

Richie Rich and His Girlfriends
Harvey

❑1, Apr 1979	10.00
❑2, Nov 1979	8.00
❑3, Feb 1980	8.00
❑4, May 1980	8.00
❑5, Aug 1980	8.00
❑6, Oct 1980	8.00
❑7, Dec 1980	8.00
❑8, Feb 1981	8.00
❑9, Apr 1981	8.00
❑10, Jul 1981	8.00
❑11, Sep 1981	5.00
❑12, Dec 1981	5.00
❑13, Feb 1982	5.00
❑14, May 1982	5.00
❑15, Jul 1982	5.00
❑16, Dec 1982	5.00

Richie Rich and His Mean Cousin Reggie
Harvey

❑1, Apr 1979	10.00
❑2, Nov 1979	5.00
❑3, Jan 1980	5.00

Richie Rich & Jackie Jokers
Harvey

❑1, Nov 1973	18.00
❑2, Jan 1974	10.00
❑3, Mar 1974	6.00
❑4, May 1974	6.00
❑5, Jul 1974	6.00
❑6, Sep 1974	4.00
❑7, Nov 1974	4.00
❑8, Jan 1975	4.00
❑9, Mar 1975	4.00
❑10, May 1975	4.00
❑11, Sep 1975	3.00
❑12, Nov 1975	3.00
❑13, Jan 1976	3.00
❑14, Mar 1976	3.00
❑15, May 1976	3.00
❑16, Jul 1976	3.00
❑17, Sep 1976	3.00
❑18, Nov 1976	3.00
❑19, Jan 1977, Welcome Back Kotter parody	3.00
❑20, Apr 1977	3.00
❑21, Jun 1977, Laverne and Shirley parody; Casper in Hostess ad ("Over the Rainboo")	3.00
❑22, Aug 1977	3.00
❑23, Oct 1977	3.00
❑24, Dec 1977	3.00
❑25, Feb 1978	3.00
❑26, Apr 1978, Star Wars-based story	3.00
❑27, Jun 1978	3.00
❑28, Aug 1978	3.00
❑29, Oct 1978	3.00
❑30, Feb 1979	3.00
❑31, Apr 1979	2.00
❑32, Jun 1979	2.00
❑33, Aug 1979	2.00
❑34, Oct 1979	2.00
❑35, Dec 1979	2.00
❑36, Feb 1980	2.00
❑37, Apr 1980	2.00
❑38, Jul 1980	2.00
❑39, Sep 1980	2.00
❑40, Nov 1980	2.00
❑41, Jan 1981	2.00
❑42, Apr 1981	2.00
❑43, Jun 1981	2.00
❑44, Aug 1981	2.00
❑45, Nov 1981	2.00
❑46, Feb 1982	2.00
❑47, May 1982	2.00
❑48, Dec 1982	2.00

Richie Rich and Professor Keenbean
Harvey

❑1, Sep 1990	1.00
❑2, Nov 1990	1.00

Richie Rich and the New Kids on the Block
Harvey

❑1, Feb 1991	1.50

Richie Rich and Timmy Time
Harvey

❑1, ca. 1977, (c); (w); (a)	8.00

Richie Rich Bank Books
Harvey

❑1, Oct 1972	24.00
❑2, Dec 1972	10.00
❑3, Feb 1973	6.00
❑4, Apr 1973	6.00
❑5, Jun 1973	6.00
❑6, Aug 1973	4.00
❑7, Oct 1973	4.00
❑8, Dec 1973	4.00
❑9, Feb 1974	4.00
❑10, Apr 1974	4.00
❑11, Jun 1974	3.00
❑12, Aug 1974	3.00
❑13, Oct 1974	3.00
❑14, Dec 1974	3.00
❑15, Feb 1975	3.00
❑16, Apr 1975	3.00
❑17, Jun 1975	3.00
❑18, Aug 1975	3.00
❑19, Oct 1975	3.00
❑20, Dec 1975	3.00
❑21, Feb 1976	2.00
❑22, Apr 1976	2.00
❑23, Jun 1976	2.00
❑24, Aug 1976	2.00
❑25, Oct 1976	2.00
❑26, Dec 1976	2.00
❑27, Feb 1977	2.00
❑28, Apr 1977	2.00
❑29, Jun 1977	2.00
❑30, Aug 1977	2.00
❑31, Sep 1977	2.00
❑32, Nov 1977	2.00
❑33, Jan 1978	2.00
❑34, Mar 1978	2.00
❑35, May 1978, Has Wendy Hostess ad: "Give a Cheer"	2.00
❑36, Aug 1978	2.00
❑37, Oct 1978	2.00
❑38, Jan 1979	2.00
❑39, Mar 1979	2.00
❑40, May 1979	2.00
❑41, Jul 1979	2.00
❑42, Sep 1979	2.00
❑43, Oct 1979	2.00
❑44, Dec 1979	2.00
❑45, Mar 1980	2.00
❑46, May 1980	2.00
❑47, Aug 1980	2.00
❑48, Oct 1980	2.00
❑49, Nov 1980	2.00
❑50, Jan 1981	2.00
❑51, Apr 1981	2.00
❑52, Jun 1981	2.00
❑53, Aug 1981	2.00
❑54, Oct 1981	2.00
❑55, Dec 1981	2.00
❑56, Feb 1982	2.00
❑57, Apr 1982	2.00
❑58, Jul 1982	2.00
❑59, Sep 1982	2.00

Richie Rich Best of the Years
Harvey

❑1, ca. 1977	10.00
❑2, ca. 1978	6.00
❑3, ca. 1979	6.00

Other grades: Multiply price above by 5/6 for VF/NM • 2/3 for VERY FINE • 1/3 for FINE • 1/5 for VERY GOOD • 1/8 for GOOD

Runaways

Acclaimed Marvel series got a second chance
©Marvel

Rune

One of Malibu's last major launches
©Malibu

Ruse

Victorian detective world has fantasy elements
©CrossGen

Sable

Dropped the first name after the TV series
©First

Sabre

Post-apocalyptic adventure from Gulacy
©Eclipse

	N-MINT
❑4, ca. 1979	6.00
❑5, ca. 1980	6.00
❑6, ca. 1980	6.00

Richie Rich Big Book
Harvey

	N-MINT
❑1, Nov 1992	1.95
❑2, May 1993	1.95

Richie Rich Big Bucks
Harvey

	N-MINT
❑1, Apr 1991	2.00
❑2, Jun 1991	1.25
❑3, Aug 1991	1.25
❑4, Oct 1991	1.25
❑5, Dec 1991	1.25
❑6, Feb 1992	1.25
❑7, Apr 1992	1.25
❑8, Jul 1992	1.25

Richie Rich Billions
Harvey

	N-MINT
❑1, Oct 1974	12.00
❑2, Feb 1975	7.00
❑3, Apr 1975	6.00
❑4, Jun 1975	5.00
❑5, Sep 1975	5.00
❑6, Oct 1975	4.00
❑7, Dec 1975	4.00
❑8, Feb 1976	4.00
❑9, Apr 1976	4.00
❑10, May 1976	4.00
❑11, Jul 1976	3.00
❑12, Sep 1976	3.00
❑13, Nov 1976	3.00
❑14, Jan 1977	3.00
❑15, Mar 1977	3.00
❑16, Apr 1977	3.00
❑17, Jun 1977	3.00
❑18, Aug 1977	3.00
❑19, Oct 1977	3.00
❑20, Nov 1977	3.00
❑21, Jan 1978	3.00
❑22, Mar 1978	3.00
❑23, May 1978	3.00
❑24, Jul 1978; Hot Stuff in Hostess ad ("Devilishly Good")	3.00
❑25, Sep 1978	3.00
❑26, Nov 1978	3.00
❑27, Jan 1979	3.00
❑28, Feb 1979; Wendy in Hostess ad ("Wendy Puts Out the Fire")	3.00
❑29, Apr 1979	3.00
❑30, Jun 1979	3.00
❑31, Aug 1979	2.00
❑32, Oct 1979	2.00
❑33, Dec 1979	2.00
❑34, Apr 1980	2.00
❑35, Jun 1980	2.00
❑36, Aug 1980	2.00
❑37, Oct 1980	2.00
❑38, Dec 1980; Wendy in Hostess ad ("...and the Cherry-Dactyl")	2.00
❑39, Feb 1981	2.00
❑40, Apr 1981; Spooky in Hostess ad ("Pearl's Purse")	2.00
❑41, Jun 1981	2.00
❑42, Aug 1981	2.00
❑43, Oct 1981	2.00
❑44, Jan 1982	2.00
❑45, Mar 1982	2.00
❑46, May 1982	2.00
❑47, Jul 1982	2.00
❑48, Oct 1982	2.00

Richie Rich Cash
Harvey

	N-MINT
❑1, Sep 1974	10.00
❑2, Nov 1974	6.00
❑3, Jan 1975	4.00
❑4, Mar 1975	4.00
❑5, May 1975	4.00
❑6, Jul 1975	4.00
❑7, Sep 1975	4.00
❑8, Nov 1975	4.00
❑9, Jan 1976	4.00
❑10, Mar 1976	4.00
❑11, Apr 1976	3.00
❑12, Jun 1976	3.00
❑13, Aug 1976	3.00
❑14, Oct 1976	3.00
❑15, Dec 1976	3.00
❑16, Feb 1977	3.00
❑17, Apr 1977	3.00
❑18, Jun 1977	3.00
❑19, Aug 1977	3.00
❑20, Nov 1977	3.00
❑21, Jan 1977	3.00
❑22, Mar 1978	3.00
❑23, May 1978	3.00
❑24, Jul 1978	3.00
❑25, Sep 1978	3.00
❑26, Dec 1978	3.00
❑27, Feb 1979	3.00
❑28, Mar 1979	3.00
❑29, May 1979	3.00
❑30, Jul 1979	3.00
❑31, Sep 1979	2.00
❑32, Nov 1979	2.00
❑33, Jan 1980	2.00
❑34, Apr 1980	2.00
❑35, Jun 1980	2.00
❑36, Sep 1980	2.00
❑37, Nov 1980	2.00
❑38, Jan 1981	2.00
❑39, Mar 1981	2.00
❑40, May 1981	2.00
❑41, Jul 1981	2.00
❑42, Sep 1981	2.00
❑43, Nov 1981	2.00
❑44, Jan 1982	2.00
❑45, Apr 1982	2.00
❑46, Jun 1982	2.00
❑47, Aug 1982	2.00

Richie Rich Cash Money
Harvey

	N-MINT
❑1, ca. 1992	1.50
❑2, ca. 1992	1.50

Richie Rich Diamonds
Harvey

	N-MINT
❑1, Aug 1972	15.00
❑2, Oct 1972	9.00
❑3, Dec 1972	7.00
❑4, Feb 1973	7.00
❑5, Apr 1973	7.00
❑6, Jun 1973	5.00
❑7, Aug 1973	5.00
❑8, Oct 1973	5.00
❑9, Dec 1973	5.00
❑10, Feb 1974	5.00
❑11, Apr 1974	4.00
❑12, Jun 1974	4.00
❑13, Aug 1974	4.00
❑14, Oct 1974	4.00
❑15, Dec 1974	4.00
❑16, Feb 1975	4.00
❑17, Apr 1975	4.00
❑18, Jun 1975	4.00
❑19, Aug 1975	4.00
❑20, Oct 1975	4.00
❑21, Dec 1975	4.00
❑22, Feb 1976	4.00
❑23, Apr 1976	4.00
❑24, Jun 1976	4.00
❑25, Aug 1976	4.00
❑26, Oct 1976	4.00
❑27, Dec 1976	4.00
❑28, Feb 1977	4.00
❑29, Mar 1977	4.00
❑30, May 1977	4.00
❑31, Jul 1977	3.00
❑32, Sep 1977	3.00
❑33, Nov 1977	3.00
❑34, Jan 1978	3.00
❑35, Mar 1978	3.00
❑36, May 1978	3.00
❑37, Jul 1978	3.00
❑38, Sep 1978	3.00
❑39, Nov 1978	3.00
❑40, Jan 1979	3.00
❑41, Mar 1979	2.00
❑42, May 1979	2.00
❑43, Jul 1979	2.00
❑44, Sep 1979	2.00
❑45, Oct 1979	2.00
❑46, Feb 1980	2.00
❑47, May 1980	2.00
❑48, Jul 1980	2.00
❑49, Sep 1980	2.00
❑50, Nov 1980	2.00
❑51, Feb 1981	2.00
❑52, Apr 1981	2.00
❑53, Jun 1981	2.00
❑54, Sep 1981	2.00
❑55, Nov 1981	2.00
❑56, Jan 1982	2.00
❑57, Mar 1982	2.00
❑58, Jun 1982	2.00
❑59, Aug 1982	2.00

Richie Rich Digest Magazine
Harvey

	N-MINT
❑1, Oct 1986	4.00
❑2, Nov 1986	3.00
❑3, Dec 1986	3.00
❑4, Jan 1987	3.00
❑5, Feb 1987	3.00
❑6, Mar 1987	3.00
❑7, Apr 1987	3.00

Other grades: Multiply price above by 5/6 for VF/NM • 2/3 for VERY FINE • 1/3 for FINE • 1/5 for VERY GOOD • 1/8 for GOOD

❑8, May 1987 3.00
❑9, Jun 1987 3.00
❑10, Aug 1987 3.00
❑11, Oct 1987 2.00
❑12, Mar 1988 2.00
❑13, Jun 1988 2.00
❑14, Jul 1988 2.00
❑15, Sep 1988 2.00
❑16, Kops 'N' Krooks special 2.00
❑17, Jul 1989 2.00
❑18, Oct 1989 2.00
❑19, Mar 1990, Cover says "Holiday Digest" 2.00
❑20, Apr 1990 2.00
❑21, Jun 1990 2.00
❑22, Aug 1990 2.00
❑23, Sep 1990 2.00
❑24, Oct 1990 2.00
❑25, Nov 1990 2.00
❑26, Dec 1990 2.00
❑27, Jan 1991 2.00
❑28 1991 2.00
❑29, May 1991 2.00
❑30, Jul 1991 2.00
❑31, Sep 1991, Contains Star Trek parody 2.00
❑32 2.00
❑33, Feb 1992 2.00
❑34, Jun 1992 2.00
❑35, Sep 1992 2.00
❑36, Jan 1993 2.00
❑37, May 1993 2.00
❑38, Sep 1993 2.00
❑39 2.00
❑40 2.00
❑41, Jul 1994 2.00
❑42, Oct 1994 2.00

Richie Rich Digest Stories
Harvey

❑1, Oct 1977 10.00
❑2, Oct 1978 5.00
❑3, May 1979 5.00
❑4, Oct 1979, Infinity cover; Contains Lieutenant Columbo spoof 5.00
❑5, Feb 1980 5.00
❑6, Apr 1980 5.00
❑7, Jul 1980 5.00
❑8, Nov 1980 5.00
❑9, Mar 1981 5.00
❑10, Jul 1981 5.00
❑11, Oct 1981 3.00
❑12, Nov 1981 3.00
❑13, Feb 1982 3.00
❑14, Mar 1982 3.00
❑15 3.00
❑16, Jul 1982 3.00
❑17, Oct 1982 3.00

Richie Rich Digest Winners
Harvey

❑1, Dec 1977 10.00
❑2, Nov 1978 5.00
❑3, Aug 1979 5.00
❑4, Jan 1980 5.00
❑5, Mar 1980 5.00

Richie Rich Dollars & Cents
Harvey

❑1, Aug 1963 250.00
❑2 125.00
❑3, Jan 1964, Giant-Size 85.00
❑4 85.00
❑5, Jul 1964, Giant-Size 85.00
❑6 40.00
❑7, Giant-Size 40.00
❑8, Apr 1965 40.00
❑9, Jul 1965, Giant-Size 40.00
❑10, Oct 1965, Giant-Size 40.00
❑11, Jan 1966, Giant-Size 25.00
❑12, Apr 1966, Giant-Size 25.00
❑13, Jun 1966, Giant-Size 25.00
❑14, Aug 1966 25.00
❑15, Oct 1966 25.00
❑16, Dec 1966 25.00
❑17, Feb 1967 25.00
❑18, Apr 1967 25.00
❑19, Jun 1967 25.00
❑20, Oct 1967 25.00
❑21, Dec 1967 15.00
❑22, Feb 1968 15.00
❑23, Apr 1968 15.00
❑24, Jun 1968 15.00
❑25, Aug 1968 15.00
❑26, Oct 1968 15.00
❑27, Dec 1968 15.00
❑28, Feb 1969 15.00
❑29, Apr 1969 15.00
❑30, May 1969 15.00
❑31, Jul 1969 10.00
❑32, Sep 1969 10.00
❑33, Nov 1969 10.00
❑34, Jan 1970 10.00
❑35, Mar 1970 10.00
❑36, May 1970 10.00
❑37, Jul 1970 10.00
❑38, Sep 1970 10.00
❑39, Nov 1970 10.00
❑40, Jan 1971 10.00
❑41, Mar 1971 7.00
❑42, May 1971 7.00
❑43, Jul 1971 7.00
❑44, Sep 1971 7.00
❑45, Nov 1971 7.00
❑46, Jan 1972 7.00
❑47, Mar 1972 7.00
❑48, May 1972 7.00
❑49, Jun 1972 7.00
❑50, Aug 1972 7.00
❑51, Oct 1972 5.00
❑52, Dec 1972 5.00
❑53, Feb 1973 5.00
❑54, Apr 1973 5.00
❑55, Jun 1973 5.00
❑56, Aug 1973 5.00
❑57, Oct 1973 5.00
❑58, Dec 1973 5.00
❑59, Feb 1974 5.00
❑60, Apr 1974 5.00
❑61, Jun 1974 2.50
❑62, Aug 1974 2.50
❑63, Oct 1974 2.50
❑64, Dec 1974 2.50
❑65, Feb 1975 2.50
❑66, Apr 1975 2.50
❑67, Jun 1975 2.50
❑68, Aug 1975 2.50
❑69, Oct 1975 2.50
❑70, Dec 1975 2.50
❑71, Feb 1976 2.00
❑72, Apr 1976 2.00
❑73, Jun 1976 2.00
❑74, Aug 1976 2.00
❑75, Sep 1976 2.00
❑76, Nov 1976 2.00
❑77, Jan 1977 2.00
❑78, Mar 1977 2.00
❑79, May 1977 2.00
❑80, Jul 1977 2.00
❑81, Sep 1977 2.00
❑82, Oct 1977 2.00
❑83, Dec 1977 2.00
❑84, Feb 1978 2.00
❑85, Apr 1978 2.00
❑86, Jun 1978 2.00
❑87, Sep 1978 2.00
❑88, Oct 1978 2.00
❑89, Jan 1979 2.00
❑90, Mar 1979 2.00
❑91, May 1979 1.25
❑92, Jul 1979 1.25
❑93, Sep 1979 1.25
❑94, Nov 1979 1.25
❑95, Feb 1980 1.25
❑96, Apr 1980 1.25
❑97, Jun 1980 1.25
❑98, Sep 1980 1.25
❑99, Nov 1980 1.25
❑100, Jan 1981 1.25
❑101, Mar 1981 1.25
❑102, May 1981 1.25
❑103, Jul 1981 1.25
❑104, Oct 1981 1.25
❑105, Dec 1981 1.25
❑106, Feb 1982 1.25
❑107, Apr 1982 1.25
❑108, Jun 1982 1.25
❑109, Aug 1982, Final Issue 1.25

Richie Rich Fortunes
Harvey

❑1, Sep 1971 25.00
❑2, Nov 1971 10.00
❑3, Mar 1972 7.00
❑4, May 1972 7.00
❑5, Jul 1972 7.00
❑6, Sep 1972 5.00
❑7, Nov 1972 5.00
❑8, Jan 1973 5.00
❑9, Mar 1973 5.00
❑10, May 1973 5.00
❑11, Jul 1973 4.00
❑12, Sep 1973 4.00
❑13, Nov 1973 4.00
❑14, Jan 1974 4.00
❑15, Mar 1974 4.00
❑16, May 1974 4.00
❑17, Jul 1974 4.00
❑18, Sep 1974 4.00
❑19, Nov 1974 4.00
❑20, Jan 1975 4.00
❑21, Mar 1975 3.00
❑22, May 1975 3.00
❑23, Jul 1975 3.00
❑24, Sep 1975 3.00
❑25, Nov 1975 3.00
❑26, Jan 1976 3.00
❑27, Mar 1976 3.00
❑28, May 1976 3.00
❑29, Jul 1976 3.00
❑30, Sep 1976 3.00
❑31, Nov 1976 3.00
❑32, Jan 1977 3.00
❑33, Mar 1977 3.00
❑34, May 1977 3.00
❑35, Jul 1977 3.00
❑36, Sep 1977 3.00
❑37, Nov 1977 3.00
❑38, Jan 1978 3.00
❑39, Mar 1978 3.00
❑40, May 1978 3.00
❑41, Jul 1978 2.00
❑42, Sep 1978 2.00
❑43, Dec 1978 2.00
❑44, Feb 1979 2.00
❑45, Apr 1979 2.00
❑46, Jun 1979 2.00
❑47, Aug 1979 2.00
❑48, Oct 1979 2.00
❑49, Dec 1979 2.00
❑50, Mar 1980 2.00
❑51, May 1980 2.00
❑52, Aug 1980 2.00
❑53, Oct 1980 2.00
❑54, Nov 1980 2.00
❑55, Mar 1981 2.00
❑56, May 1981 2.00
❑57, Jul 1981 2.00
❑58, Sep 1981 2.00
❑59, Nov 1981 2.00
❑60, Jan 1982 2.00
❑61, Mar 1982 2.00
❑62, Jun 1982 2.00
❑63, Aug 1982 2.00

Richie Rich Gems
Harvey

❑1, Sep 1974 10.00
❑2, Nov 1974 6.00
❑3, Jan 1975 4.00
❑4, Mar 1975 4.00
❑5, May 1975 4.00
❑6, Jul 1975 3.00
❑7, Sep 1975 3.00
❑8, Nov 1975 3.00
❑9, Jan 1976 3.00
❑10, Mar 1976 3.00
❑11, May 1976 2.00
❑12, Jul 1976 2.00
❑13, Sep 1976 2.00
❑14, Nov 1976 2.00
❑15, Jan 1977 2.00
❑16, Mar 1977 2.00
❑17, May 1977 2.00

Sabretooth

Logan's chief nemesis captured
©Marvel

Sabrina the Teenage Witch

Magical teen moves from Madhouse
©Archie

Sachs & Violens

Photographer and model solve murder
©Marvel

Sad Sack

Reluctant draftee dodges responsibility
©Harvey

Sad Sack & The Sarge

C.O. gives Sack grief
©Harvey

	N-MINT
❑18, Jul 1977	2.00
❑19, Sep 1977	2.00
❑20, Nov 1977	2.00
❑21, Jan 1978	2.00
❑22, Mar 1978	2.00
❑23, Jun 1978	2.00
❑24, Nov 1978, Has Hot Stuff Hostess ad: "Devilishly Good"	2.00
❑25, Jan 1979	2.00
❑26, Jul 1979	2.00
❑27, Sep 1979	2.00
❑28, Nov 1979	2.00
❑29, Feb 1980	2.00
❑30, May 1980	2.00
❑31, Jul 1980	2.00
❑32, Sep 1980	2.00
❑33, Nov 1980	2.00
❑34, Jan 1981	2.00
❑35, Mar 1981	2.00
❑36, May 1981	2.00
❑37, Aug 1981	2.00
❑38, Oct 1981	2.00
❑39, Dec 1981	2.00
❑40, Feb 1982	2.00
❑41, Apr 1982	2.00
❑42, Jul 1982	2.00
❑43, Sep 1982	2.00

Richie Rich Giant Size
Harvey

	N-MINT
❑1, Oct 1992	2.25
❑2, Mar 1993	2.25
❑3, Jun 1993	2.25
❑4, Oct 1993	2.25

Richie Rich Gold & Silver
Harvey

	N-MINT
❑1, Sep 1975	10.00
❑2, Nov 1975	6.00
❑3, Jan 1976, Richie Rich in Hostess Ad (Untitled)	4.00
❑4, Mar 1976	4.00
❑5, May 1976, Sad Sack in Hostess Ad (Untitled)	4.00
❑6, Jul 1976	3.00
❑7, Aug 1976, Has Adam Awards promo panel	3.00
❑8, Oct 1976, Casper in Hostess ad ("Casper and the Fog")	3.00
❑9, Dec 1976, Casper in Hostess Ad ("Moo Boo")	3.00
❑10, Feb 1977, Wendy in Hostess ad ("Which Witch is Which?")	3.00
❑11, Apr 1977	2.00
❑12, May 1977, Casper in Hostess ad ("Over The Rainboo")	2.00
❑13, Jul 1977, Hot Suff in Hostess ad ("Lame Brain")	2.00
❑14, Sep 1977	2.00
❑15, Nov 1977	2.00
❑16, Jan 1978	2.00
❑17, Mar 1978	2.00
❑18, May 1978	2.00
❑19, Jul 1978	2.00
❑20, Sep 1978	2.00
❑21, Nov 1978	2.00
❑22, Jan 1979	2.00
❑23, Mar 1979	2.00
❑24, May 1979	2.00
❑25, Jul 1979	2.00
❑26, Sep 1979	2.00
❑27, Nov 1979	2.00
❑28, Feb 1980, Page count drops	2.00
❑29, Mar 1980	2.00
❑30, May 1980	2.00
❑31, Jul 1980	2.00
❑32, Sep 1980	2.00
❑33, Jan 1981	2.00
❑34, Mar 1981	2.00
❑35, May 1981, Burt Reynolds look-alike in story	2.00
❑36, Jul 1981	2.00
❑37, Sep 1981	2.00
❑38, Oct 1981	2.00
❑39, Dec 1981	2.00
❑40, May 1982	2.00
❑41, Jul 1982	2.00
❑42, Oct 1982	2.00

Richie Rich Gold Nuggets Digest Magazine
Harvey

	N-MINT
❑1, Dec 1990	2.50
❑2, Jan 1991	2.00
❑3, Apr 1991	2.00
❑4, Jun 1990	2.00

Richie Rich Holiday Digest
Harvey

	N-MINT
❑1, Jan 1980	3.00
❑2, Jan 1981	2.00
❑3, Jan 1982	2.00
❑4, Mar 1988	2.00
❑5, Feb 1989	2.00

Richie Rich Inventions
Harvey

	N-MINT
❑1, Oct 1977	10.00
❑2, May 1978	6.00
❑3, Aug 1978	6.00
❑4, Oct 1978	6.00
❑5, Dec 1978	6.00
❑6, Jan 1979	6.00
❑7, Mar 1979	6.00
❑8, May 1979	6.00
❑9, Jul 1979	6.00
❑10, Sep 1979	6.00
❑11, Nov 1979	4.00
❑12, Mar 1980	4.00
❑13, May 1980	4.00
❑14, Aug 1980	4.00
❑15, Oct 1980	4.00
❑16, Dec 1980	4.00
❑17, Feb 1981	4.00
❑18, Apr 1981, Spooky in Hostess ad ("Pearl's Purse")	4.00
❑19, Jun 1981	4.00
❑20, Aug 1981	3.00
❑21, Oct 1981	3.00
❑22, Feb 1981	3.00
❑23, Apr 1982	3.00
❑24, Jun 1982	3.00
❑25, Aug 1982	3.00
❑26, Oct 1982	3.00

Richie Rich Jackpots
Harvey

	N-MINT
❑1, Oct 1972	30.00
❑2, Dec 1972	12.00
❑3, Feb 1973	8.00
❑4, Apr 1973	8.00
❑5, Jun 1973	8.00
❑6, Aug 1973	6.00
❑7, Oct 1973	6.00
❑8, Dec 1973	6.00
❑9, Feb 1974	4.00
❑10, Apr 1974	4.00
❑11, Jun 1974	4.00
❑12, Aug 1974	4.00
❑13, Oct 1974	4.00
❑14, Dec 1974	4.00
❑15, Feb 1975	4.00
❑16, Apr 1975	4.00
❑17, Jun 1975	4.00
❑18, Aug 1975	4.00
❑19, Oct 1975	4.00
❑20, Dec 1975, Richie, Mayda legally married; Casper in Hostess ad (untitled, fights the No-Goodniks)	6.00
❑21, Feb 1976	3.00
❑22, Apr 1976	3.00
❑23, Jun 1976	3.00
❑24, Aug 1976	3.00
❑25, Oct 1976	3.00
❑26, Dec 1976	3.00
❑27, Feb 1977	3.00
❑28, Apr 1977	3.00
❑29, Jun 1977, Casper in Hostess ad ("Over the Rainboo")	3.00
❑30, Aug 1977	3.00
❑31, Oct 1977	3.00
❑32, Dec 1977	3.00
❑33, Feb 1978	3.00
❑34, Apr 1978	3.00
❑35, Jun 1978	3.00
❑36, Aug 1978	3.00
❑37, Oct 1978	3.00
❑38, Dec 1978	3.00
❑39, Feb 1979	3.00
❑40, Apr 1979	3.00
❑41, Jun 1979, Casper in Hostess ad ("Happy Boo-Day")	2.00
❑42, Aug 1979	2.00
❑43, Oct 1979	2.00
❑44, Dec 1980	2.00
❑45, Apr 1980	2.00
❑46, Jun 1980	2.00
❑47, Aug 1980	2.00
❑48, Oct 1980	2.00
❑49, Dec 1980, Casper in Hostess ad ("...Meets the Golden Ghost")	2.00
❑50, Feb 1981, Spooky in Hostess ad ("One Big Boo After Another")	2.00
❑51, Apr 1981, Spooky in Hostess ad ("Pearl's Purse")	2.00
❑52, Jun 1981, V: Leroy Blemish. Wendy in Hostess ad ("Catches the Good Taste Bandit")	2.00
❑53, Aug 1981	2.00
❑54, Oct 1981, Casper in Hostess ad ("Witches with a Heart of Gold")	2.00
❑55, Dec 1982	2.00

Other grades: Multiply price above by 5/6 for VF/NM • 2/3 for VERY FINE • 1/3 for FINE • 1/5 for VERY GOOD • 1/8 for GOOD

	N-MINT
❑56, Apr 1982	2.00
❑57, Jun 1982	2.00
❑58, Aug 1982	2.00

Richie Rich Million Dollar Digest
Harvey

	N-MINT
❑1, Oct 1980	10.00
❑2, Jan 1981	10.00
❑3, Apr 1981	10.00
❑4, Jul 1981	10.00
❑5, Nov 1981	10.00
❑6, Jan 1982	10.00
❑7, Mar 1982	10.00
❑8, Jun 1982	10.00
❑9, Aug 1982	10.00
❑10, Oct 1982	10.00

Richie Rich Million Dollar Digest
Harvey

	N-MINT
❑1, Nov 1986	5.00
❑2, Jan 1987	3.00
❑3, Mar 1987	3.00
❑4, May 1987	3.00
❑5, Jul 1987	3.00
❑6, Sep 1987	3.00
❑7, Nov 1987	3.00
❑8 1988	3.00
❑9 1988	3.00
❑10 1988	3.00
❑11, Oct 1988	2.00
❑12, Dec 1988	2.00
❑13, Aug 1989	2.00
❑14 1989	2.00
❑15 1990	2.00
❑16 1990	2.00
❑17 1990	2.00
❑18 1990	2.00
❑19 1990	2.00
❑20, Mar 1991	2.00
❑21 1991	2.00
❑22, Aug 1991	2.00
❑23, Oct 1991	2.00
❑24, Dec 1991	2.00
❑25, Mar 1992	2.00
❑26, Jul 1992	2.00
❑27, Nov 1992	2.00
❑28, Mar 1993	2.00
❑29, Jul 1993	2.00
❑30, Nov 1993	2.00
❑31, Mar 1994	2.00
❑32, May 1994	2.00
❑33, Aug 1994	2.00
❑34, Nov 1994	2.00

Richie Rich Millions
Harvey

	N-MINT
❑1, Sep 1961	200.00
❑2, Sep 1962	100.00
❑3, Dec 1962	100.00
❑4, Mar 1963	75.00
❑5, Jun 1963	75.00
❑6, Sep 1963	75.00
❑7, Dec 1963	75.00
❑8, Mar 1964	75.00
❑9, Jun 1964	75.00
❑10, Sep 1964	75.00
❑11, Dec 1964	50.00
❑12, Mar 1965, Giant-Size	50.00
❑13, Jun 1965	50.00
❑14, Sep 1965	50.00
❑15, Dec 1965	50.00
❑16, Mar 1966, V: Steve Rock. Story with Steve Rock, a James Bond send-up; Rocky and Bullwinkle in Cheerios ad	50.00
❑17, May 1966	50.00
❑18, Jul 1966	50.00
❑19, Sep 1966, V: Prof. Von Blitz. Rocky and Bullwinkle in Cheerios ad	50.00
❑20, Oct 1966	50.00
❑21, Jan 1967	40.00
❑22, Mar 1967, Giant-Size	40.00
❑23, Jun 1967	40.00
❑24, Aug 1967	40.00
❑25, Oct 1967	40.00
❑26, Dec 1967	40.00
❑27, Feb 1968	40.00
❑28, Apr 1968	40.00
❑29, Jun 1968	40.00
❑30, Aug 1968	40.00
❑31, Oct 1968	30.00
❑32, Dec 1968, UFO cover	30.00
❑33, Feb 1969	30.00
❑34, Apr 1969	30.00
❑35, May 1969	30.00
❑36, Jul 1969	30.00
❑37, Sep 1969	30.00
❑38, Nov 1969	25.00
❑39, Jan 1970	25.00
❑40, Mar 1970	25.00
❑41, May 1970	25.00
❑42, Jul 1970	25.00
❑43, Sep 1970	25.00
❑44, Nov 1970	25.00
❑45, Jan 1971	20.00
❑46, Mar 1971	20.00
❑47, May 1971	20.00
❑48, Jul 1971	20.00
❑49, Sep 1971	10.00
❑50, Nov 1971	10.00
❑51, Jan 1972	10.00
❑52, Mar 1972	10.00
❑53, May 1972	10.00
❑54, Jul 1972	10.00
❑55, Sep 1972	10.00
❑56, Nov 1972	10.00
❑57, Jan 1973	7.00
❑58, Mar 1973	7.00
❑59, May 1973	7.00
❑60, Jul 1973	7.00
❑61, Sep 1973	7.00
❑62, Nov 1973	5.00
❑63, Jan 1974	5.00
❑64, Mar 1974	5.00
❑65, May 1974	5.00
❑66, Jul 1974	5.00
❑67, Sep 1974	5.00
❑68, Nov 1974	5.00
❑69, Jan 1975	5.00
❑70, Mar 1975	5.00
❑71, May 1975, Robot attacks	5.00
❑72, Jul 1975	5.00
❑73, Sep 1975	5.00
❑74, Nov 1975	5.00
❑75, Jan 1976, Winter cover	5.00
❑76, Mar 1976	5.00
❑77, May 1976	5.00
❑78, Jul 1976	5.00
❑79, Sep 1976	5.00
❑80, Nov 1976	5.00
❑81, Jan 1977	2.50
❑82, Mar 1977, Casper in Hostess ad ("Haunted House for Sale")	2.50
❑83, May 1977	2.50
❑84, Jul 1977	2.50
❑85, Sep 1977	2.50
❑86, Nov 1977	2.50
❑87, Jan 1978	2.50
❑88, Mar 1978	2.50
❑89, May 1978	2.50
❑90, Aug 1978	2.50
❑91, Oct 1978	2.00
❑92, Dec 1978	2.00
❑93, Feb 1979	2.00
❑94, Apr 1979, V: Leroy Blemish. Hot Stuff in Hostess ad ("A Swell Party"); Richie in Grit ad ("Father Knows Best")	2.00
❑95, Jun 1979, Casper in Hostess ad ("Happy Boo-Day"); Richie in Grit ad ("Father Knows Best")	2.00
❑96, Aug 1979	2.00
❑97, Oct 1979	2.00
❑98, Dec 1979	2.00
❑99, Mar 1980	2.00
❑100, May 1980, 100th Issue Spectacular	2.00
❑101, Aug 1980	1.50
❑102, Oct 1980	1.50
❑103, Dec 1981	1.50
❑104, Feb 1981	1.50
❑105, Apr 1981	1.50
❑106, Jun 1981	1.50
❑107, Aug 1981	1.50
❑108, Oct 1981	1.50
❑109, Dec 1981	1.50
❑110, Apr 1982	1.50
❑111, Jun 1982	1.00
❑112, Aug 1982, Accordion cover	1.00
❑113, Oct 1982, Final Issue	1.00

Richie Rich Money World
Harvey

	N-MINT
❑1, Sep 1972	85.00
❑2, Nov 1972	35.00
❑3, Jan 1973	25.00
❑4, Mar 1973	20.00
❑5, May 1973	20.00
❑6, Jul 1973	15.00
❑7, Sep 1973	15.00
❑8, Nov 1973	15.00
❑9, Jan 1974	15.00
❑10, Mar 1974	15.00
❑11, May 1974	10.00
❑12, Jul 1974	10.00
❑13, Sep 1974	10.00
❑14, Nov 1974	10.00
❑15, Jan 1975	10.00
❑16, Mar 1975	10.00
❑17, May 1975	10.00
❑18, Jul 1975	10.00
❑19, Sep 1975	7.00
❑20, Nov 1975	7.00
❑21, Jan 1976	7.00
❑22, Mar 1976	7.00
❑23, May 1976	7.00
❑24, Jul 1976	7.00
❑25, Sep 1976	7.00
❑26, Nov 1976	7.00
❑27, Jan 1977	7.00
❑28, Mar 1977	7.00
❑29, May 1977	5.00
❑30, Jul 1977	5.00
❑31, Sep 1977	5.00
❑32, Nov 1977	5.00
❑33, Jan 1978	5.00
❑34, Mar 1978	5.00
❑35, May 1978	5.00
❑36, Aug 1978	5.00
❑37, Oct 1978	5.00
❑38, Jan 1979	5.00
❑39, Mar 1979	3.00
❑40, Jun 1979	3.00
❑41, Aug 1979	3.00
❑42, Sep 1979	3.00
❑43, Nov 1979	3.00
❑44, Jan 1980	3.00
❑45, Apr 1980	3.00
❑46, Jun 1980	3.00
❑47, Sep 1980	3.00
❑48, Oct 1980	3.00
❑49, Dec 1980	3.00
❑50, Feb 1981	3.00
❑51, Apr 1981	3.00
❑52, Jun 1981	3.00
❑53, Aug 1981	3.00
❑54, Oct 1981	3.00
❑55, Mar 1982	3.00
❑56, Mar 1982	3.00
❑57, May 1982	3.00
❑58 1982	3.00
❑59, Sep 1982	3.00

Richie Rich Money World Digest
Harvey

	N-MINT
❑1, Apr 1991	2.00
❑2, Dec 1991	1.75
❑3, Apr 1992	1.75
❑4, Aug 1992	1.75
❑5, Dec 1992	1.75
❑6, Apr 1993	1.75
❑7, Aug 1993	1.75
❑8, Dec 1993	1.75

Richie Rich (Movie Adaptation)
Marvel

	N-MINT
❑1, Feb 1995, Movie adaptation	2.95

Richie Rich Profits
Harvey

	N-MINT
❑1, Oct 1974; A: Richie Rich	25.00
❑2, Dec 1974	15.00
❑3, Feb 1975	15.00
❑4, Apr 1975	10.00
❑5, Jun 1975	10.00
❑6, Aug 1975	10.00
❑7, Oct 1975	10.00
❑8, Dec 1975	10.00
❑9, Feb 1976	10.00
❑10, Apr 1976	10.00

Other grades: Multiply price above by 5/6 for VF/NM • 2/3 for VERY FINE • 1/3 for FINE • 1/5 for VERY GOOD • 1/8 for GOOD

Sad Sack Army Life Parade

Anthology of Camp Swampy doings

©Harvey

Sad Sack Laugh Special

More messes with military mess-up

©Harvey

Sad Sack Navy, Gobs 'n' Gals

Sad Sack is all at sea in short-lived series

©Harvey

Sad Sack's Funny Friends

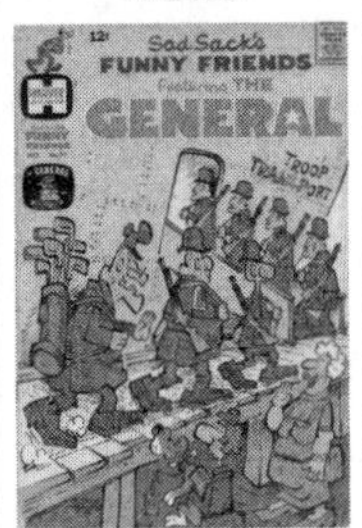

Solo spotlight shines on Sad Sack peers

©Harvey

Safety-Belt Man

Crash-test dummy gains life

©Sirius

	N-MINT
❑11, Jun 1976	8.00
❑12, Aug 1976	8.00
❑13, Oct 1976	8.00
❑14, Dec 1976	8.00
❑15, Feb 1977	8.00
❑16, Apr 1977	8.00
❑17, Jun 1977	8.00
❑18, Aug 1977	8.00
❑19, Oct 1977	8.00
❑20, Dec 1977	6.00
❑21, Feb 1978	6.00
❑22, Apr 1978	6.00
❑23, Jun 1978	6.00
❑24, Aug 1978	6.00
❑25, Oct 1978	6.00
❑26, Jan 1979	6.00
❑27, Feb 1979	6.00
❑28, Apr 1979	6.00
❑29, Jun 1979	6.00
❑30, Aug 1979	5.00
❑31, Oct 1979	5.00
❑32, Dec 1979	5.00
❑33, Feb 1980	5.00
❑34, Apr 1980	5.00
❑35, Jul 1980	5.00
❑36, Sep 1980	5.00
❑37, Nov 1980	5.00
❑38, Jan 1981	5.00
❑39, Mar 1981	5.00
❑40, May 1981, Sad Sack in Hostess ad ("Down and Out")	4.00
❑41, Jul 1981	4.00
❑42, Sep 1981	4.00
❑43, Nov 1981	4.00
❑44, Feb 1982	4.00
❑45, Apr 1982	4.00
❑46, Jun 1982	4.00
❑47, Sep 1982	4.00

Richie Rich Relics
Harvey

❑1, Jan 1988	2.50
❑2, May 1988	2.50
❑3, Sep 1988	2.50
❑4, Jan 1989	2.50

Richie Rich Riches
Harvey

	N-MINT
❑1, Jul 1972	28.00
❑2, Sep 1972	13.00
❑3, Nov 1972	8.00
❑4, Jan 1973	8.00
❑5, Mar 1973	8.00
❑6, May 1973	5.00
❑7, Jul 1973	5.00
❑8, Sep 1973	5.00
❑9, Nov 1973	5.00
❑10, Jan 1974	5.00
❑11, Mar 1974	4.00
❑12, May 1974	4.00
❑13, Jul 1974	4.00
❑14, Sep 1974	4.00
❑15, Nov 1974	4.00
❑16, Jan 1975	4.00
❑17, Mar 1975	4.00
❑18, May 1975	4.00
❑19, Jul 1975	4.00
❑20, Sep 1975	4.00
❑21, Nov 1975	3.00
❑22, Jan 1976	3.00
❑23, Mar 1976	3.00
❑24, May 1976	3.00
❑25, Jul 1976	3.00
❑26, Sep 1976	3.00
❑27, Nov 1976	3.00
❑28, Jan 1977; Casper in Hostess ad ("The Boohemians")	3.00
❑29, Mar 1977	3.00
❑30, May 1977	3.00
❑31, Jul 1977	2.00
❑32, Sep 1977	2.00
❑33, Nov 1977	2.00
❑34, Jan 1978	2.00
❑35, Mar 1978	2.00
❑36, May 1978	2.00
❑37, Jul 1978	2.00
❑38, Sep 1978	2.00
❑39, Dec 1978	2.00
❑40, Feb 1979	2.00
❑41, Apr 1979	2.00
❑42, Jun 1979	2.00
❑43, Aug 1979	2.00
❑44, Oct 1979	2.00
❑45, Dec 1979	2.00
❑46, Feb 1980	2.00
❑47, May 1980	2.00
❑48, Aug 1980	2.00
❑49, Oct 1980	2.00
❑50, Dec 1980	2.00
❑51, Feb 1981	2.00
❑52, Apr 1981	2.00
❑53, Jun 1981	2.00
❑54, Aug 1981	2.00
❑55, Oct 1981	2.00
❑56, Dec 1981	2.00
❑57, Mar 1982	2.00
❑58, Jun 1982	2.00
❑59, Aug 1982	2.00

Richie Rich Success Stories
Harvey

	N-MINT
❑1, Nov 1964	200.00
❑2, Feb 1965	100.00
❑3, May 1965	75.00
❑4, Aug 1965	75.00
❑5, Nov 1965	50.00
❑6, Feb 1966, Giant-Size	50.00
❑7, May 1966	50.00
❑8, Jul 1966	50.00
❑9, Aug 1966	50.00
❑10, Oct 1966	50.00
❑11, Dec 1966	25.00
❑12, Feb 1967	25.00
❑13, Apr 1967	25.00
❑14, Jun 1967	25.00
❑15, Sep 1967	25.00
❑16, Nov 1967	25.00
❑17, Jan 1968	25.00
❑18, Mar 1968	25.00
❑19, May 1968	25.00
❑20, Jul 1968, Giant-Size	25.00
❑21, Sep 1968	20.00
❑22, Nov 1968	20.00
❑23, Jan 1969	20.00
❑24, Mar 1969	20.00
❑25, Apr 1969	20.00
❑26, Jun 1969	15.00
❑27, Aug 1969	15.00
❑28, Oct 1969	15.00
❑29, Dec 1969	15.00
❑30, Feb 1970	15.00
❑31, Apr 1970	10.00
❑32, Jun 1970	10.00
❑33, Aug 1970	10.00
❑34, Oct 1970	10.00
❑35, Dec 1970	10.00
❑36, Feb 1971	10.00
❑37, Apr 1971	10.00
❑38, Jun 1971	10.00
❑39, Aug 1971	10.00
❑40, Oct 1971	10.00
❑41, Dec 1971	7.00
❑42, Feb 1972	7.00
❑43, Apr 1972	7.00
❑44, Jun 1972	7.00
❑45, Aug 1972	7.00
❑46, Oct 1972	7.00
❑47, Dec 1972	7.00
❑48, Feb 1973	7.00
❑49, Apr 1973	7.00
❑50, Jun 1973	7.00
❑51, Aug 1973	7.00
❑52, Oct 1973	7.00
❑53, Dec 1973	7.00
❑54, Feb 1974	7.00
❑55, Apr 1974	7.00
❑56, Jun 1974	7.00
❑57, Aug 1974	7.00
❑58, Oct 1974	7.00
❑59, Dec 1974	7.00
❑60, Feb 1975	7.00
❑61, Apr 1975	7.00
❑62, Jun 1975	7.00
❑63, Aug 1975	7.00
❑64, Oct 1975	7.00
❑65, Dec 1975	7.00
❑66, Feb 1976	7.00
❑67, Apr 1976	7.00
❑68, Jun 1976	7.00
❑69, Aug 1976	7.00
❑70, Oct 1976	7.00
❑71, Dec 1976	5.00
❑72, Feb 1977	5.00
❑73, Mar 1977	5.00
❑74, May 1977	5.00
❑75, Jul 1977	5.00
❑76, Sep 1977	5.00
❑77, Oct 1977	5.00
❑78, Dec 1977	5.00
❑79, Feb 1978	5.00
❑80, Apr 1978	5.00
❑81, Jun 1978	5.00
❑82, Aug 1978	5.00
❑83, Oct 1978	5.00
❑84, Dec 1978	5.00
❑85, Jan 1979	5.00
❑86, Mar 1979	5.00
❑87, May 1979	5.00
❑88, Jul 1979	5.00

Other grades: Multiply price above by 5/6 for VF/NM • 2/3 for VERY FINE • 1/3 for FINE • 1/5 for VERY GOOD • 1/8 for GOOD

	N-MINT
❑89, Sep 1979	5.00
❑90, Nov 1979, Wendy in Hostess ad ("Wendy Has a Visitor")	3.00
❑91, Jan 1980, Casper in Hostess ad ("Casper and the Ghnats")	3.00
❑92, Apr 1980, Casper in Hostess ad ("Casper Ends the Boo Hoos")	3.00
❑93, Jun 1980, Casper in Hostess ad ("Casper Plays Hide and Seek")	3.00
❑94, Sep 1980, Hot Stuff in Hostess ad ("Playing Cupid")	3.00
❑95, Nov 1980, Hot Stuff in Hostess ad ("Shut My Mouth!")	3.00
❑96, Jan 1981, Spooky in Hostess ad ("One Big Boo After Another")	3.00
❑97, Mar 1981, Hot Stuff in Hostess ad ("Too Much Mush!")	3.00
❑98, May 1981	3.00
❑99, Jul 1981	3.00
❑100, Sep 1981	3.00
❑101, Dec 1981	2.00
❑102, Feb 1982	2.00
❑103, May 1982	2.00
❑104, Jul 1982	2.00
❑105, Sep 1982	2.00

Richie Rich Vacation Digest
Harvey

❑1992, Oct 1992, #1 on cover	1.75
❑1993, Oct 1993, #1 on cover	1.75

Richie Rich Vacations Digest
Harvey

❑1, Oct 1980	10.00
❑2, Dec 1980	5.00
❑3, Feb 1981	5.00
❑4, Apr 1981	5.00
❑5, Jun 1981	5.00
❑6, Aug 1981	5.00
❑7, Oct 1981	5.00
❑8, Dec 1981, Infinity cover; Contains "Mork and Mindy" TV parody	5.00

Richie Rich Vaults of Mystery
Harvey

❑1, Nov 1974, Cover says "Vault"	25.00
❑2, Jan 1975, Cover says "Vault"	15.00
❑3, Mar 1975, Cover says "Vault"	8.00
❑4, May 1975, Cover says "Vault"	8.00
❑5, Jul 1975, Cover says "Vault"	8.00
❑6, Sep 1975, Cover title changes to "Vaults"	5.00
❑7, Nov 1975	5.00
❑8, Jan 1976	5.00
❑9, Mar 1976	5.00
❑10, May 1976	5.00
❑11, Jul 1976	4.00
❑12, Sep 1976	4.00
❑13, Nov 1976	4.00
❑14, Jan 1977	4.00
❑15, Mar 1977, Sad Sack in Hostess ad ("Sad vs. Merri")	4.00
❑16, May 1977	4.00
❑17, Jul 1977	4.00
❑18, Sep 1977	4.00
❑19, Nov 1977	4.00
❑20, Jan 1978	4.00
❑21, Mar 1978	3.00
❑22, May 1978	3.00
❑23, Jul 1978	3.00
❑24, Sep 1978	3.00
❑25, Nov 1978	3.00
❑26, Jan 1979	3.00
❑27, Mar 1979	3.00
❑28, May 1979	3.00
❑29, Jul 1979, Ghosts	3.00
❑30, Sep 1979	3.00
❑31, Nov 1979	3.00
❑32, Jan 1980, Casper in Hostess ad ("Casper and the Ghnats")	3.00
❑33, Apr 1980, Casper in Hostess ad ("Casper Ends the Boo Hoos")	3.00
❑34, Jun 1980	3.00
❑35, Aug 1980, Casper in Hostess ad ("Boo-tiful Endings")	3.00
❑36, Oct 1980, Hot Stuff in Hostess ad ("Mad, Mad, Mad World")	3.00
❑37, Dec 1980, Wendy in Hostess ad ("Cherry-Dactyl")	3.00
❑38, Feb 1981	3.00
❑39, Apr 1981	3.00
❑40, Jun 1981	3.00
❑41, Aug 1981	3.00
❑42, Oct 1981	3.00
❑43, Dec 1981	3.00
❑44, Feb 1982	3.00
❑45, Apr 1982, Irona	3.00
❑46, Jun 1982	3.00
❑47, Sep 1982	3.00

Richie Rich Zillionz
Harvey

❑1, Oct 1976	12.00
❑2, Jan 1977	6.00
❑3, Apr 1977	6.00
❑4, Jun 1977	6.00
❑5, Aug 1977	4.00
❑6, Oct 1977	3.00
❑7, Dec 1977	3.00
❑8, Feb 1978	3.00
❑9, Apr 1978	3.00
❑10, Jul 1978, Wendy in Hostess ad ("The Smart Wand")	3.00
❑11, Sep 1978	2.00
❑12, Nov 1978	2.00
❑13, Jan 1979	2.00
❑14, Mar 1979	2.00
❑15, May 1979	2.00
❑16, Jun 1979	2.00
❑17, Sep 1979	2.00
❑18, Nov 1979, Sad Sack in Hostess ad ("What a Trip")	2.00
❑19, Dec 1979, Casper in Hostess ad ("Ends the Boo Hoos")	2.00
❑20, Mar 1980	2.00
❑21, May 1980, Has Hostess ad (Wendy in "A Little Magic")	2.00
❑22, Jul 1980	2.00
❑23, Oct 1980, Has Hostess ad (Hot Stuff in "Mad Mad, Mad World")	2.00
❑24, Nov 1980, Hot Stuff in Hostess ad ("Shut My Mouth!")	2.00
❑25, Mar 1981	2.00
❑26, May 1981	2.00
❑27, Jul 1981	2.00
❑28, Sep 1981	2.00
❑29, Nov 1981	2.00
❑30, Jan 1982	2.00
❑31, Mar 1982	2.00
❑32, Jun 1982	2.00
❑33, Sep 1982	2.00

Ride
Image

❑1, Aug 2004	2.95
❑2 2004	2.95

Ride: 2 for the Road One Shot
Image

❑1, Oct 2005, b&w	2.95

Rifleman
Dell

❑2, Jan 1960, Series continued from Four Color Comics # 1009; Photo cover	85.00
❑3, Apr 1960	85.00
❑4, Jul 1960	70.00
❑5, Oct 1960	70.00
❑6, Jan 1961	70.00
❑7, Jun 1961	70.00
❑8, Sep 1961	70.00
❑9, Dec 1961	70.00
❑10, Jan 1962	70.00
❑11, Apr 1962	55.00
❑12, Jul 1962	55.00
❑13, Nov 1962	55.00
❑14, Feb 1963	55.00
❑15, May 1963	55.00
❑16, Aug 1963	55.00
❑17, Nov 1963	55.00
❑18, Apr 1964	55.00
❑19, Jul 1964	55.00
❑20, Oct 1964	55.00

Rima, the Jungle Girl
DC

❑1, May 1974, O: Rima, the Jungle Girl; Space Voyagers	13.00
❑2, Jul 1974, JKu (c); NR, JKu, AN (a); O: Rima, the Jungle Girl; Space Voyagers	7.00
❑3, Sep 1974, JKu (c); NR, JKu, AN (a); O: Rima, the Jungle Girl; Space Voyagers	7.00
❑4, Nov 1974, O: Rima, the Jungle Girl; Space Voyagers	7.00
❑5, Jan 1975, Rima; Space Voyagers	7.00
❑6, Mar 1975; Rima; Jungle Justice	7.00
❑7, May 1975; Final Issue; Rime; Space Marshal backup story	7.00

Rime of the Ancient Mariner
Tome

❑1, b&w; NN	3.95

Rimshot
Rip Off

❑1, Jun 1990, b&w; Adult	2.00
❑2, Feb 1991, b&w; Adult	2.00
❑3, Jul 1991, b&w; Adult	2.50

Ring of Roses
Dark Horse

❑1, b&w	2.50
❑2, b&w	2.50
❑3, b&w	2.50
❑4, b&w	2.50

Ring of the Nibelung
DC

❑1, ca. 1989	4.95
❑2; ca. 1990	4.95
❑3; ca. 1990	4.95
❑4; ca. 1990	4.95

Ring of the Nibelung (Vol. 1)
Dark Horse

❑1, Feb 2000	2.95
❑2, Mar 2000	2.95
❑3, Apr 2000	2.95
❑4, May 2000	2.95

Ring of the Nibelung (Vol. 2)
Dark Horse

❑1, Aug 2000	2.95
❑2, Sep 2000	2.95
❑3, Oct 2000	2.99

Ring of the Nibelung (Vol. 3)
Dark Horse

❑1, Dec 2000	2.99
❑2, Jan 2001	2.99
❑3, Feb 2001	2.99

Ring of the Nibelung, The (Vol. 4)
Dark Horse

❑1, Jun 2001	2.99
❑2, Jul 2001	2.99
❑3, Aug 2001	2.99
❑4, Sep 2001; Double-sized	2.99

Ringo Kid
Marvel

❑1, Jan 1970, SL (w); AW (a); Reprint from Ringo Kid Western	20.00
❑2, Mar 1970, JSe (a); Reprints from Ringo Kid Western #9	8.00
❑3, May 1970, Reprints from Ringo Kid Western #11 and 12	5.00
❑4, Jul 1970, Reprints from Ringo Kid Western #11 and 12	5.00
❑5, Sep 1970, Reprints from Ringo Kid Western #4	5.00
❑6, Nov 1970, Reprints from Ringo Kid Western #6	5.00
❑7, Jan 1971, HT (c); JSe, JAb (a); Reprints from Ringo Kid Western #7 .	5.00
❑8, Mar 1971	5.00
❑9, May 1971, Reprints from Ringo Kid Western #8 and Outlaw Kid #11	5.00
❑10, Jul 1971, Reprints from Ringo Kid Western #14	5.00
❑11, Sep 1971, Reprints from Ringo Kid Western #15	4.00
❑12, Nov 1971, Reprints from Ringo Kid Western #17, 18 and Rawhide Kid #28; Giant-size	10.00
❑13, Apr 1972, Reprints from Ringo Kid Western #17 and 18	4.00
❑14, May 1972, Reprints from Ringo Kid Western #16 and 19	4.00
❑15, Jul 1972, Reprints from Ringo Kid Western #16 and 19	4.00
❑16, Sep 1972, Reprints from Ringo Kid Western #19 and 20	4.00
❑17, Nov 1972, Reprints from Ringo Kid Western #20 and 21	4.00
❑18, Jan 1972, GK (c)	4.00
❑19, Mar 1973, SL (w)	4.00

Other grades: Multiply price above by 5/6 for VF/NM • 2/3 for VERY FINE • 1/3 for FINE • 1/5 for VERY GOOD • 1/8 for GOOD

Saga of Ra's Al Ghul

Extreme conservationist's early appearances
©DC

Sailor Moon Comic

Manga series of cosmically-named heroines
©Mixxzine

Sam and Twitch

More cases for Spawn investigators
©Image

Sam Slade, Robo-Hunter

A rogue hunter of rogue robots
©Fleetway-Quality

Samurai: Heaven and Earth

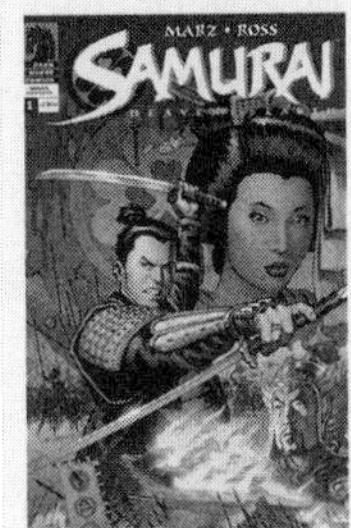

Swordsman seeks true love across world
©Dark Horse

N-MINT

❑20, May 1973, Reprints from Ringo Kid Western #10, 11 and Two-Gun Western #10 .... 4.00
❑21, Jul 1973, Reprints from Ringo Kid Western #9 .... 4.00
❑22, Sep 1973, Reprints from Ringo Kid Western #11 .... 4.00
❑23, Nov 1973, Reprints from Ringo Kid Western #11 and 12 .... 4.00
❑24, Nov 1975, Reprints from Ringo Kid Western #10 and 11 .... 4.00
❑25, Jan 1976, Reprints from Ringo Kid Western #11 and 12 .... 4.00
❑26, Mar 1976, Reprints from Ringo Kid Western #4 .... 4.00
❑27, May 1976, Reprints from Ringo Kid Western #6 .... 4.00
❑27/30¢, May 1976, 30¢ regional price variant 20.00
❑28, Jul 1976, Reprints from Ringo Kid Western #8 .... 4.00
❑28/30¢, Jul 1976, 30¢ regional price variant 20.00
❑29, Sep 1976, Reprints from Ringo Kid Western #19 .... 4.00
❑30, Nov 1976, Reprints from Ringo Kid Western #7; Final Issue 4.00

Rin Tin Tin & Rusty
Gold Key

❑1, Nov 1963 .... 50.00

Rio at Bay
Dark Horse

❑1, Aug 1992 .... 2.95
❑2, Aug 1992 .... 2.95

Rio Conchos
Gold Key

❑1, Mar 1965, Adapts film 22.00

Rio Graphic Novel
Comico

❑1, May 1987 .... 8.95

Rio Kid
Eternity

❑1, b&w 2.50
❑2, b&w 2.50
❑3, b&w 2.50

Rion 2990
Rion

❑1, b&w 1.50
❑2, b&w 1.50
❑3 .... 1.50
❑4 .... 1.50

Riot, Act 1
Viz

❑1, Oct 1995 .... 2.75
❑2, Nov 1995 .... 2.75
❑3, Dec 1995 .... 2.75
❑4, Jan 1996 .... 2.95
❑5, Feb 1996 .... 2.95
❑6, Mar 1996 .... 2.95

Riot, Act 2
Viz

❑1, Apr 1996 .... 2.95
❑2, May 1996 .... 2.95
❑3, Jun 1996 .... 2.95
❑4, Jul 1996 .... 2.95

N-MINT

❑5, Aug 1996 .... 2.95
❑6, Sep 1996 .... 2.95
❑7, Oct 1996 .... 2.95

Riot Gear
Triumphant

❑1, Sep 1993 .... 2.50
❑1/Ashcan, Sep 1993; Ashcan edition (color) 2.50
❑2, Oct 1993 .... 2.50
❑3, Nov 1993 .... 2.50
❑4, Dec 1993; Unleashed! 2.50
❑5, Jan 1994 .... 2.50
❑6, Feb 1994 .... 2.50
❑7, Mar 1994 .... 2.50
❑8, Apr 1994 .... 2.50
❑9, May 1994 .... 2.50
❑10, Jun 1994 .... 2.50
❑11, Jul 1994; Final issue? 2.50
❑Ashcan 1, ashcan 2.50

Riot Gear: Violent Past
Triumphant

❑1, Feb 1994 .... 2.50
❑2, Feb 1994; 14,000 printed 2.50

Ripclaw
Image

❑½; Wizard promotional edition; ca. 1995 .... 2.00
❑½/Gold; Gold edition; Wizard promotional edition; ca. 1995 .... 2.50
❑1, Apr 1995 .... 2.50
❑2, Jun 1995 .... 2.50
❑3, Jul 1995 .... 2.50
❑4, Aug 1995 .... 2.50

Ripclaw
Image

❑1, Dec 1995 .... 2.50
❑2, Jan 1996 .... 2.50
❑3, Feb 1996 .... 2.50
❑4, Mar 1996 .... 2.50
❑5, Apr 1996 .... 2.50
❑6, Jun 1996 .... 2.50
❑Special 1, Oct 1995; Special Edition #1 .... 2.50

R.I.P. Comics Module
TSR

❑1 .... 2.95
❑2 .... 2.95
❑3 .... 2.95
❑4 .... 2.95
❑5; Brasher 2.95
❑6; Brasher 2.95
❑7; Brasher 2.95
❑8; Brasher 2.95

R.I.P.D.
Dark Horse

❑1, Oct 1999 .... 2.95
❑2, Nov 1999 .... 2.95
❑3, Dec 1999 .... 2.95
❑4, Jan 2000 .... 2.95

Ripfire
Malibu

❑0, Jan 1995 .... 2.50

N-MINT

Rip Hunter...Time Master
DC

❑1, Mar 1961 .... 350.00
❑2, May 1961 .... 140.00
❑3, Jul 1961 .... 115.00
❑4, Sep 1961 .... 95.00
❑5, Nov 1961, Last $.10 issue 95.00
❑6, Jan 1962, NC (c); ATh (a) 85.00
❑7, Mar 1962, DD (c); ATh (a) 85.00
❑8, May 1962 .... 70.00
❑9, Jul 1962 .... 70.00
❑10, Sep 1962 .... 70.00
❑11, Nov 1962 .... 70.00
❑12, Jan 1963 .... 70.00
❑13, Mar 1963 .... 70.00
❑14, May 1963 .... 70.00
❑15, Jul 1963 .... 70.00
❑16, Sep 1963 .... 58.00
❑17, Nov 1963 .... 58.00
❑18, Jan 1964 .... 58.00
❑19, Mar 1964 .... 58.00
❑20, May 1964 .... 58.00
❑21, Jul 1964 .... 48.00
❑22, Sep 1964 .... 48.00
❑23, Nov 1964 .... 48.00
❑24, Jan 1965 .... 48.00
❑25, Mar 1965 .... 48.00
❑26, May 1965 .... 40.00
❑27, Jul 1965 .... 40.00
❑28, Sep 1965 .... 40.00
❑29, Nov 1965, Final Issue 40.00

Rip in Time
Fantagor

❑1, b&w; ca. 1986 .... 2.00
❑2, b&w; ca. 1986 .... 2.00
❑3, b&w; ca. 1987 .... 2.00
❑4, b&w; ca. 1987 .... 2.00
❑5, b&w; ca. 1987 .... 2.00

Ripley's Believe It or Not!
Gold Key

❑4, Apr 1967, Series continued from "Ripley's Believe it Or Not True War Stories" 26.00
❑5, Jun 1967 .... 16.00
❑6, Aug 1967 .... 16.00
❑7, Nov 1967 .... 16.00
❑8, Feb 1968, 10208-802 .... 16.00
❑9, May 1968 .... 16.00
❑10, Aug 1968, 10208-808 .... 16.00
❑11, Nov 1968, 10208-811 .... 12.00
❑12, Feb 1969 .... 12.00
❑13, Apr 1969 .... 12.00
❑14, Jun 1969 .... 12.00
❑15, Aug 1969, Production code 10208-908 .... 12.00
❑16, Oct 1969 .... 10.00
❑17, Dec 1969 .... 10.00
❑18, Feb 1970 .... 10.00
❑19, Apr 1970 .... 10.00
❑20, Jun 1970 .... 10.00
❑21, Aug 1970 .... 8.00
❑22, Oct 1970 .... 8.00
❑23, Dec 1970 .... 8.00
❑24, Feb 1971 .... 8.00
❑25, Apr 1971 .... 8.00

Other grades: Multiply price above by 5/6 for VF/NM • 2/3 for VERY FINE • 1/3 for FINE • 1/5 for VERY GOOD • 1/8 for GOOD

	N-MINT
❑26, Jun 1971	8.00
❑27, Aug 1971	8.00
❑28, Sep 1971	8.00
❑29, Oct 1971	8.00
❑30, Dec 1971	8.00
❑31, Feb 1972	5.00
❑32, Apr 1972	5.00
❑33, Jun 1972	5.00
❑34, Aug 1972, 90208-208	5.00
❑35, Sep 1972	5.00
❑36, Oct 1972	5.00
❑37, Dec 1972, 90208-212	5.00
❑38, Feb 1973	5.00
❑39, Apr 1973	5.50
❑40, Jun 1973	5.00
❑41, Aug 1973	5.00
❑42, Sep 1973	5.00
❑43, Oct 1973	5.00
❑44, Dec 1973	5.00
❑45, Feb 1974	5.00
❑46, Apr 1974	5.00
❑47, Jun 1974	5.00
❑48, Aug 1974	5.00
❑49, Sep 1974	5.00
❑50, Oct 1974	5.00
❑51, Dec 1974	4.00
❑52, Feb 1975	4.00
❑53, Apr 1975	4.00
❑54, Jun 1975	4.00
❑55, Jul 1975	4.00
❑56, Aug 1975	4.00
❑57, Sep 1975	4.00
❑58, Oct 1975	4.00
❑59, Dec 1975	4.00
❑60, Feb 1976	4.00
❑61, Apr 1976	4.00
❑62, Jun 1976	4.00
❑63, Jul 1976	4.00
❑64, Aug 1976	4.00
❑65, Oct 1976	4.00
❑66, Dec 1976	4.00
❑67, Jan 1977	4.00
❑68, Feb 1977	4.00
❑69, Apr 1977	4.00
❑70, Jun 1977	4.00
❑71, Jul 1977	3.00
❑72, Aug 1977	3.00
❑73, Oct 1977	3.00
❑74, Dec 1977, Reprints from Ripley's Believe It or Not! #16 and 18	3.00
❑75, Jan 1978	3.00
❑76, Feb 1978	3.00
❑77, Apr 1978, Reprints from Ripley's Believe It or Not! #14	3.00
❑78, Jun 1978, Reprints from Ripley's Believe It or Not! #15	3.00
❑79, Jul 1977, Reprints from Ripley's Believe It or Not! #17	3.00
❑80, Aug 1978, Reprints from Ripley's Believe It or Not! #1 and 12	3.00
❑81, Sep 1978, Reprints from Ripley's Believe It or Not! #1, 9 and 11	3.00
❑82, Oct 1978, Reprints from Ripley's Believe It or Not! #13; production code 90208-810; 48 pages	3.00
❑83, Nov 1978, Reprints from Ripley's Believe It or Not! #2 and 6	3.00
❑84, Dec 1978, Reprints from Ripley's Believe It or Not! #7 and 10	3.00
❑85, Jan 1979	3.00
❑86, Feb 1979	3.00
❑87, Apr 1979, Reprints from Ripley's Believe It or Not! #7 and 10	3.00
❑88, May 1979	3.00
❑89, Jul 1979	3.00
❑90, Aug 1979	3.00
❑91, Sep 1979, Reprints from Ripley's Believe It or Not! #8, 9 and 10	3.00
❑92, Oct 1979	3.00
❑93, Nov 1979, Reprints from Ripley's Believe It or Not! #28	3.00
❑94, Feb 1980, Final Issue	3.00

Ripley's Believe It or Not!
Dark Horse

❑1, May 2002	2.99
❑2, Oct 2002	2.99
❑3, Oct 2003	2.99
❑4 2003	2.99

Ripley's Believe It or Not!: Beauty & Grooming
Schanes

❑1	2.50

Ripley's Believe It or Not!: Child Prodigies
Schanes

❑1	2.50

Ripley's Believe It or Not!: Cruelty
Schanes Products

❑1, Jun 1993, b&w; says Crime & Murder on cover; reprints newspaper cartoons	2.50
❑2, Jun 1993, b&w; says Crime & Murder on cover; reprints newspaper cartoons	2.50

Ripley's Believe It or Not!: Fairy Tales & Literature
Schanes

❑1	2.50

Ripley's Believe It or Not!: Feats of Wonder
Schanes

❑1	2.50

Ripley's Believe It or Not!: Sports Feats
Schanes Products

❑1, Jun 1993, b&w; reprints newspaper cartoons	2.50

Ripley's Believe It or Not!: Strange Deaths
Schanes Products

❑1, Jun 1993, b&w; reprints newspaper cartoons	2.50

Ripley's Believe It or Not True War Stories
Gold Key

❑1, ca. 1966, #3 in overall series; Continued in Ripley's Believe It or Not #4	24.00

Rip Off Comix
Rip Off

❑1, Apr 1977	25.00
❑2, Jul 1977	16.00
❑3, Mar 1978	12.00
❑4, Nov 1978	8.00
❑5, Sep 1979	6.00
❑6, Mar 1980	6.00
❑6/2nd, Jan 1980; 2nd printing (1980)	2.50
❑7, Nov 1980	6.00
❑8, May 1981; 1981	5.00
❑9, Sep 1981; 1981	5.00
❑10, Mar 1982; b&w	5.00
❑11, Oct 1982	4.00
❑12, Apr 1983	4.00
❑13	4.00
❑14, Apr 1987	4.00
❑15, Jul 1987	4.00
❑16, Oct 1987	4.00
❑17, Jan 1988	4.00
❑18, Apr 1988	4.00
❑19, Jul 1988	4.00
❑20, Oct 1988	4.00
❑21, Jan 1989; 20th Anniversary	4.00
❑22, Apr 1989	4.00
❑23, Jul 1989	4.00
❑24, Oct 1989; San Diego Con	3.25
❑25, Jan 1990	3.25
❑26, Apr 1990	3.25
❑27, Jul 1990	3.95
❑28, Oct 1990	3.50
❑29, Jan 1991	3.50
❑30, Apr 1991	3.50
❑31, Mar 1992	3.50

Ripper
Aircel

❑1; 1&O: Ripper	2.50
❑2	2.50
❑3	2.50
❑4	2.50
❑5	2.50
❑6	2.50

Ripper Legacy
Caliber

❑1; Adult	2.95
❑2; Adult	2.95
❑3; Adult	2.95

Riptide
Image

❑1, Sep 1995	2.50
❑2, Oct 1995	2.50

Rise of Apocalypse
Marvel

❑1, Oct 1996; wraparound cover	1.95
❑2, Nov 1996; wraparound cover	1.95
❑3, Dec 1996; wraparound cover	1.95
❑4, Jan 1997; wraparound cover	1.95

Rising Stars
Image

❑0, Apr 2000; Wizard promotional edition	5.00
❑0/Gold 1999; Gold logo variant from Wizard promotion	12.00
❑½, Jul 2001; BA (c); Boy drawing on cover	2.95
❑1/Holofoil, Aug 1999; Holofoil edition	8.00
❑1/Chromium, Aug 1999; chromium cover	10.00
❑1/Kids, Aug 1999; Gold "Monster Edition"; Children running to house	7.00
❑1/Fighting, Aug 1999; Gold "Monster Edition"; Battle scene with blonde woman in foreground	6.00
❑1/Funeral, Aug 1999; Gold "Monster Edition"; Team standing over coffin	5.00
❑1/Wizard, Aug 1999; Another Universe/Wizard World variant (boy standing in foreground looking at large glowing sphere, Wizard World/AU markings)	3.50
❑2, Oct 1999	3.00
❑2/Dynamic, Dec 1999; Dynamic Forces variant cover	4.00
❑2/DF Gold, Dec 1999; Dynamic Forces gold variant cover (Dynamic Forces seal on cover)	7.00
❑3, Dec 1999	3.00
❑4 2000	3.00
❑5, Mar 2000	2.50
❑6, Apr 2000	2.50
❑7, May 2000	2.50
❑8 2000	2.50
❑9, Aug 2000	2.50
❑10, Oct 2000	2.50
❑11, Nov 2000	2.50
❑12, Jan 2001	2.50
❑13, Mar 2001	2.50
❑14, May 2001	2.50
❑15, Jun 2001; BA (c); BA (a); Flip-book with Universe preview	2.50
❑16, Jul 2001 BA (c); BA (a)	2.50
❑17, Jan 2002 BA (c); BA (a)	2.50
❑18, Jan 2002 BA (c); BA (a)	2.50
❑19, Sep 2002 BA (c); BA (a)	2.50
❑20, Oct 2002 BA (c); BA (a)	2.99
❑21, Jan 2003	2.99
❑22, Nov 2004	2.99
❑23, Dec 2004, Hunter Killer preview	2.99
❑24, Mar 2005; Series finale	2.99
❑Ashcan 1/Conven, Oct 2000; Convention Exclusive preview	6.00
❑Ashcan 1, Mar 1999; Prelude edition; Man sitting on cover	2.95

Rising Stars: Bright
Image

❑1, Feb 2003	2.99
❑2, Mar 2003	2.99
❑3, Apr 2003	2.99

Rising Stars: Untouchable
Image

❑1, Mar 2006	2.99
❑2, May 2006	2.99
❑3, May 2006	2.99
❑4, Jul 2006	2.99
❑5, Jul 2006	2.99
❑124, May 2006	2.99

Rising Stars: Visitations
Image

❑1, ca. 2002	8.99

Rising Stars: Voices of the Dead
Image

❑1, Jun 2005; City of Heroes preview	2.99
❑2, Jul 2005	2.99
❑3, Sep 2005	2.99

Samuree (1st Series)

Teen martial artist meets Revengers
©Continuity

Sandman

Short-lived Kirby creation
©DC

Sandman

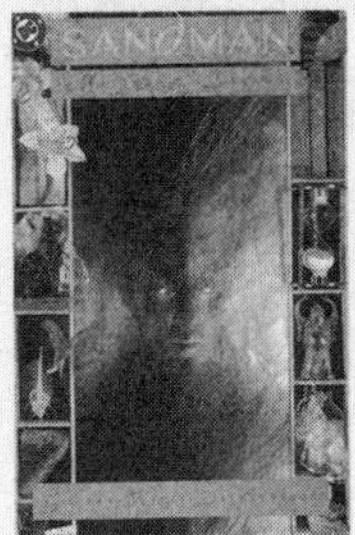

Lord of Dreams focus of fantasy series
©DC

Sandman Mystery Theatre

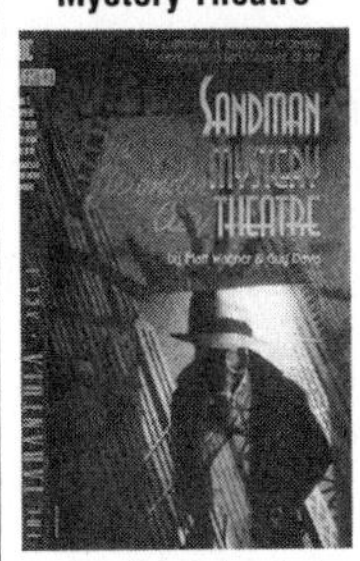

Darker stories of Golden Age hero
©DC

Sarge Snorkel

Beetle Bailey's C.O.'s solo stories
©Charlton

N-MINT

- ❑4, Oct 2005 ... 2.99
- ❑5, Nov 2005 ... 2.99
- ❑6, Dec 2005 ... 2.99

Riverdale High
Archie

- ❑1, Aug 1990 ... 1.50
- ❑2, Oct 1990 ... 1.00
- ❑3, Dec 1990 ... 1.00
- ❑4, Feb 1990 ... 1.00
- ❑5, Apr 1990 ... 1.00

Rivets & Ruby
Radio

- ❑1, Feb 1998 ... 2.95
- ❑2, Apr 1998 ... 2.95
- ❑3, Jul 1998 ... 2.95
- ❑4 ... 2.95

Rivit
Blackthorne

- ❑1 ... 1.75

Roach Killer
NBM

- ❑1 ... 11.95

Roachmill
Blackthorne

- ❑1, Dec 1986 ... 2.00
- ❑2, Feb 1987 ... 2.00
- ❑3, Apr 1987 ... 2.00
- ❑4, Jun 1987 ... 2.00
- ❑5, Sep 1987 ... 2.00
- ❑6, Oct 1987 ... 2.00

Roachmill
Dark Horse

- ❑1, May 1988 ... 2.00
- ❑2, Jun 1988 ... 1.75
- ❑3, Sep 1988 ... 1.75
- ❑4, Nov 1988 ... 1.75
- ❑5, Apr 1989 ... 1.75
- ❑6, Jun 1989 ... 1.75
- ❑7, Oct 1989 ... 1.75
- ❑8, Jan 1990; indicia says Jan 89; a misprint ... 1.75
- ❑9, Apr 1990 ... 1.95
- ❑10, Dec 1990; trading cards ... 1.95

Roadkill
Lighthouse

- ❑1, b&w ... 2.00
- ❑2, b&w ... 2.00

Roadkill: A Chronicle of the Deadworld
Caliber

- ❑1; text ... 2.95

Road to Hell
Idea & Design Works

- ❑1, Aug 2006 ... 3.99
- ❑2, Sep 2006 ... 3.99
- ❑3, Nov 2006; Includes War of the Undead backup story ... 3.99

Road Trip
Oni

- ❑1, Aug 2000, b&w; collects story from Oni Double Feature #9 and #10 ... 2.95

N-MINT

Roadways
Cult

- ❑1, May 1994, b&w ... 2.75
- ❑2, Jun 1994, b&w ... 2.75
- ❑3 ... 2.75
- ❑4 ... 2.75

Roarin' Rick's Rare Bit Fiends
King Hell

- ❑1, Jul 1994; Dave Sim ... 2.95
- ❑2, Aug 1994; Neil Gaiman ... 2.95
- ❑3, Sep 1994; Neil Gaiman ... 2.95
- ❑4, Oct 1994 ... 2.95
- ❑5, Nov 1994 ... 2.95
- ❑6, Dec 1994 ... 2.95
- ❑7, Jan 1995 ... 2.95
- ❑8, Feb 1995 ... 2.95
- ❑9, Mar 1995 ... 2.95
- ❑10, Apr 1995 ... 2.95
- ❑11, May 1995 ... 2.95
- ❑12, Jun 1995 ... 2.95
- ❑13, Aug 1995 ... 2.95
- ❑14, Sep 1995 ... 2.95
- ❑15, Nov 1995 ... 2.95
- ❑16, Dec 1995 ... 2.95
- ❑17, Jan 1996 ... 2.95
- ❑18, Mar 1996 ... 2.95
- ❑19, ca. 1996 ... 2.95
- ❑20, ca. 1996 ... 2.95
- ❑21, ca. 1996; Subtleman ... 2.95

Robbin' $3000
Parody

- ❑1, b&w ... 2.50

Rob Hanes
WCG

- ❑1, Jan 1991, b&w ... 2.50

Rob Hanes Adventures
WCG

- ❑1, Oct 2000 ... 2.50
- ❑2, Dec 2001 ... 2.50
- ❑3, Mar 2002 ... 2.50
- ❑4, Jul 2003 ... 2.75
- ❑5, Sep 2004 ... 2.95
- ❑6 2004; ca. 2004 ... 2.95
- ❑7 ... 2.95
- ❑8 ... 2.95
- ❑9 ... 2.95
- ❑10 ... 2.95
- ❑11 ... 2.95

Robin
DC

- ❑1, Jan 1991; BB (c); NA (a); 1: King Snake. poster ... 3.00
- ❑1/2nd, Jan 1991; BB (c); 1: King Snake. (no poster) ... 1.50
- ❑1/3rd, Jan 1991; BB (c); 1: King Snake. (no poster) ... 1.50
- ❑2, Feb 1991 BB (c) ... 2.50
- ❑2/2nd, Feb 1991; BB (c); 2nd printing.. 1.50
- ❑3, Mar 1991 BB (c) ... 2.00
- ❑4, Apr 1991; BB (c); V: Lady Shiva ... 2.00
- ❑5, May 1991; BB (c); V: King Shark ... 2.00
- ❑Ann 1, ca. 1992; Eclipso ... 2.50
- ❑Ann 2, ca. 1993 1: Razorsharp ... 2.50

N-MINT

Robin
DC

- ❑0, Oct 1994; O: Robin I (Dick Grayson). O: Robin III (Timothy Drake). O: Robin II (Jason Todd) ... 2.00
- ❑1, Nov 1993; 1: Shotgun Smith ... 4.00
- ❑1/Variant, Nov 1993; Embossed cover. 3.50
- ❑2, Jan 1994; Scott Hanna listed on credits listing (cover), but did not work on this issue ... 2.00
- ❑3, Feb 1994 ... 2.00
- ❑4, Mar 1994 A: Spoiler ... 2.00
- ❑5, Apr 1994 ... 2.00
- ❑6, May 1994; A: Huntress. Story continued from Showcase '94 #5, Story continues into Showcase '94 #6 ... 2.00
- ❑7, Jun 1994 ... 2.00
- ❑8, Jul 1994; Story continued from Legends Of The Dark Knight #62; Story continues into Catwoman #12; Nightwing cover/appearance ... 2.00
- ❑9, Aug 1994; KnightsEnd Aftermath ... 2.00
- ❑10, Sep 1994; Zero Hour; Tim Drake Robin teams with Dick Grayson Robin 2.00
- ❑11, Nov 1994; Contiunes in Batman #513 ... 1.75
- ❑12, Dec 1994 ... 1.75
- ❑13, Jan 1995; V: Steeljacket ... 1.75
- ❑14, Feb 1995 ... 1.75
- ❑14/Variant, Feb 1995; enhanced cardstock cover ... 2.50
- ❑15, Mar 1995 ... 1.75
- ❑16, Apr 1995 ... 1.75
- ❑17, Jun 1995 ... 2.00
- ❑18, Jul 1995; V: criminal sabotaging Gotham City structures ... 2.00
- ❑19, Aug 1995; V: Ulysses ... 2.00
- ❑20, Sep 1995; V: Ulysses ... 2.00
- ❑21, Oct 1995; Ninja camp ... 2.00
- ❑22, Nov 1995; Ninja camp ... 2.00
- ❑23, Dec 1995; V: Killer Moth a.k.a. Charaxes. Underworld Unleashed ... 2.00
- ❑24, Jan 1996; V: Killer Moth a.k.a. Charaxes. Underworld Unleashed ... 2.00
- ❑25, Feb 1996; anti-guns issue ... 2.00
- ❑26, Mar 1996 ... 2.00
- ❑27, Mar 1996; V: Catwoman ... 2.00
- ❑28, Apr 1996 ... 2.00
- ❑29, May 1996 ... 2.00
- ❑30, Jun 1996 ... 2.00
- ❑31, Jul 1996 A: Wildcat ... 2.00
- ❑32, Aug 1996; Nightwing and Robin track Ra's Al Ghul virus to Paris ... 2.00
- ❑33, Sep 1996; Nightwing, Robin and Huntress infiltrates Ra's Al Ghul yacht to decode virus ... 2.00
- ❑34, Oct 1996; self-contained story ... 2.00
- ❑35, Nov 1996; A: Spoiler. Final Night ... 2.00
- ❑36, Dec 1996; V: Toyman. V: Ulysses .. 2.00
- ❑37, Jan 1997; V: Toyman. V: Ulysses ... 2.00
- ❑38, Feb 1997; V: Slyfox ... 2.00
- ❑39, Mar 1997; V: Slyfox ... 2.00
- ❑40, Apr 1997 ... 1.95
- ❑41, May 1997 ... 1.95
- ❑42, Jun 1997; V: disgruntled television host ... 1.95
- ❑43, Jul 1997 ... 1.95
- ❑44, Aug 1997; A: Spoiler. V: The Baffler 1.95
- ❑45, Sep 1997; self-contained story ... 1.95

N-MINT

❑46, Oct 1997; self-contained story....... 1.95
❑47, Nov 1997; A: Nightwing. A: Batman. V: Ulysses.......... 1.95
❑48, Dec 1997; Face cover.......... 1.95
❑49, Jan 1998 A: King Snake.......... 1.95
❑50, Feb 1998; Giant-size; A: King Snake. A: Lady Shiva.......... 2.95
❑51, Mar 1998.......... 1.95
❑52, Apr 1998; continues in Batman: Blackgate-Isle of Men #1.......... 1.95
❑53, May 1998; V: Ventriloquist; V: Scarface.......... 1.95
❑54, Jun 1998; A: Spoiler. Aftershock.... 1.95
❑55, Jul 1998; continues in Nightwing #23.......... 1.95
❑56, Aug 1998; A: Spoiler. Tim breaks up with Ariana.......... 1.95
❑57, Sep 1998; Spoiler and Robin date.. 1.99
❑58, Oct 1998; V: Steeljacket.......... 1.99
❑59, Dec 1998; V: Steeljacket.......... 1.99
❑60, Jan 1999.......... 1.99
❑61, Feb 1999.......... 1.99
❑62, Mar 1999; A: Flash III (Wally West). Tim relocates to Keystone City.......... 1.99
❑63, Apr 1999 A: Riddler. A: Superman. A: Flash III (Wally West). A: Captain Boomerang.......... 1.99
❑64, May 1999; A: Flash III (Wally West). V: Riddler. V: Captain Boomerang....... 1.99
❑65, Jun 1999; Spoiler's child is born.... 1.99
❑66, Jul 1999; Tim returns to Gotham... 1.99
❑67, Aug 1999; A: Nightwing. No Man's Land.......... 1.99
❑68, Sep 1999; V: Ratcatcher. No Man's Land.......... 1.99
❑69, Oct 1999; V: Ratcatcher. No Man's Land.......... 1.99
❑70, Nov 1999; V: Mr. Freeze, No Man's Land.......... 1.99
❑71, Dec 1999; No Man's Land.......... 1.99
❑72, Jan 2000; V: Killer Croc, No Man's Land.......... 1.99
❑73, Feb 2000; No Man's Land.......... 1.99
❑74, Mar 2000.......... 1.99
❑75, Apr 2000; Giant-size.......... 2.95
❑76, May 2000.......... 1.99
❑77, Jun 2000; V: Manbat; V: Jaeger..... 1.99
❑78, Jul 2000.......... 1.99
❑79, Aug 2000; 1: Arrakhat.......... 2.25
❑80, Sep 2000.......... 2.25
❑81, Oct 2000.......... 2.25
❑82, Nov 2000.......... 2.25
❑83, Dec 2000.......... 2.25
❑84, Jan 2001; V: sea monster.......... 2.25
❑85, Feb 2001 A: Joker.......... 2.25
❑86, Mar 2001.......... 2.25
❑87, Apr 2001; Batman trains Spoiler; Batman reveals Robin (Tim Drake) identity to Spoiler.......... 2.25
❑88, May 2001; V: Kobra; Kobra kidnaps Robin friend.......... 2.25
❑89, Jun 2001; V: Kobra; Robin tracks kidnapped friend.......... 2.25
❑90, Jul 2001.......... 2.25
❑91, Aug 2001.......... 2.25
❑92, Sep 2001.......... 2.25
❑93, Oct 2001.......... 2.25
❑94, Nov 2001.......... 2.25
❑95, Dec 2001 BSz (c).......... 2.25
❑96, Jan 2002.......... 2.25
❑97, Feb 2002.......... 2.25
❑98, Mar 2002; Bruce Wayne, Murderer? Part 6.......... 2.25
❑99, Apr 2002; Bruce Wayne, Murderer? Part 11.......... 2.25
❑100, May 2002; Giant-size.......... 3.50
❑101, Jun 2002.......... 2.25
❑102, Jul 2002.......... 2.25
❑103, Aug 2002.......... 2.25
❑104, Sep 2002.......... 2.25
❑105, Oct 2002; No storyline given........ 2.25
❑106, Nov 2002; Batman and Robin recover stolen Batmobile.......... 2.25
❑107, Dec 2002; V: human Killer Moth.. 2.25
❑108, Jan 2003; Includes 8 page preview of Superman: Metropolis; Charaxes revealed as spawning human Killer Moths.......... 2.25
❑109, Feb 2003; V: Charaxes; V: human Killer Moth.......... 2.25
❑110, Mar 2003; V: Charaxes; V: Jaeger 2.25
❑111, Apr 2003; Spoiler deals with the death of her father (Cluemaster) during Suicide Squad mission.......... 2.25
❑112, May 2003.......... 2.25
❑113, Jun 2003; Spoiler talks to Riddler about her father (Cluemaster).......... 2.25
❑114, Jul 2003.......... 2.25
❑115, Aug 2003.......... 2.25
❑116, Sep 2003.......... 2.25
❑117, Oct 2003.......... 2.25
❑118, Nov 2003.......... 2.25
❑119, Dec 2003.......... 2.25
❑120, Jan 2004.......... 2.25
❑121, Feb 2004.......... 2.25
❑122, Mar 2004.......... 2.25
❑123, Apr 2004.......... 2.25
❑124, May 2004.......... 2.25
❑125, Jun 2004.......... 2.25
❑126, Jul 2004; Stephanie becomes Robin.......... 5.00
❑127, Aug 2004.......... 4.00
❑128, Sep 2004.......... 3.00
❑129, Oct 2004.......... 2.25
❑130, Nov 2004.......... 2.25
❑131, Dec 2004, Comes with free Heroscape #2: Trapped Behind Enemy Minds, comic insert.......... 2.25
❑132, Jan 2005.......... 2.25
❑133, Feb 2005.......... 2.25
❑134, Mar 2005.......... 2.25
❑135, Apr 2005.......... 2.25
❑136, May 2005.......... 2.25
❑137, Jun 2005.......... 2.25
❑138, Jul 2005.......... 2.25
❑139, Aug 2005.......... 2.50
❑140, Sep 2005.......... 2.50
❑141, Oct 2005.......... 2.50
❑142, Nov 2005.......... 2.50
❑143, Dec 2005; Omac Project Tie-In.... 2.50
❑144, Jan 2006; OMAC Project Tie-In.... 2.50
❑145, Feb 2006.......... 2.50
❑146, Mar 2006, Infinite Crisis crossover 2.50
❑147, Apr 2006, Infinite Crisis crossover 2.50
❑148, Jun 2006, One Year Later; New Costume.......... 2.50
❑149, Jun 2006, One Year Later.......... 2.50
❑151, Sep 2006.......... 2.99
❑152, Sep 2006.......... 2.99
❑153, Oct 2006, Captain Boomerang team-up.......... 2.99
❑154, Nov 2006.......... 2.99
❑155, Dec 2006.......... 2.99
❑156, Jan 2007, Includes 3-D Heroscape glasses; Includes Teen Titans: Sparktop mini-comic.......... 2.99
❑157, Feb 2007.......... 2.99
❑158, Mar 2007.......... 2.99
❑159, Apr 2007.......... 2.99
❑160, May 2007.......... 2.99
❑161, Jun 2007.......... 2.99
❑162, Jul 2007.......... 2.99
❑163, Aug 2007.......... 2.99
❑164, Sep 2007.......... 2.99
❑165, Sep 2007.......... 2.99
❑166, Oct 2007; Skill revealed to be Ravager.......... 2.99
❑167, Nov 2007.......... 2.99
❑168, Dec 2007; Story continues in Nightwing #138.......... 2.99
❑169, Jan 2008; Story continued from Batman #671; Story continues in Nightwing #139.......... 2.99
❑170.......... 2.99
❑171.......... 2.99
❑172.......... 2.99
❑173.......... 2.99
❑174.......... 2.99
❑175.......... 2.99
❑176.......... 2.99
❑177.......... 2.99
❑178.......... 2.99
❑179.......... 2.99
❑180.......... 2.99
❑181.......... 2.99
❑182.......... 2.99
❑183.......... 2.99
❑1000000, Nov 1998; A: Robin the Toy Wonder. Direct market edition.......... 4.00
❑Ann 3, ca. 1994; Elseworlds.......... 2.95
❑Ann 4, ca. 1995; Year One.......... 3.95
❑Ann 5, ca. 1996; Legends of the Dead Earth.......... 2.95
❑Ann 6, ca. 1997; Pulp Heroes.......... 3.95
❑Ann 7, ca. 2007.......... 5.00
❑GS 1, Sep 2000; Eighty Page Giant; Eighty Page Giant.......... 5.95

Robin II
DC

❑1, Oct 1991; CR (a); newsstand; no hologram.......... 1.00
❑1/A, Oct 1991; MW (c); CR (a); Robin Hologram; Joker in straight jacket...... 1.75
❑1/B, Oct 1991; DG (c); CR (a); Joker holding cover; Robin Hologram.......... 1.75
❑1/C, Oct 1991; CR (a); Robin Hologram; Batman cover.......... 1.75
❑1/CS, Oct 1991; set of all covers; extra hologram.......... 10.00
❑1/D, Oct 1991; CR (a); Joker standing cover; Robin Hologram.......... 1.75
❑2, Nov 1991; Normal cover; newsstand; no hologram.......... 1.00
❑2/A, Nov 1991; Joker with mallet cover; Batman Hologram.......... 1.75
❑2/B, Nov 1991; Joker with dart board cover; Batman Hologram.......... 1.75
❑2/C, Nov 1991; Joker with dagger cover; Batman Hologram.......... 1.75
❑2/CS, Nov 1991; Includes all variations of #2.......... 9.00
❑3, Nov 1991; Normal cover; newsstand; no hologram.......... 1.00
❑3/A, Nov 1991; Robin swinging cover; Joker Hologram.......... 1.50
❑3/B, Nov 1991; Joker Hologram; Robin perched.......... 1.50
❑3/CS, Nov 1991; Includes all variations of #3.......... 6.00
❑4, Dec 1991; Normal cover; newsstand, no hologram.......... 1.00
❑4/A, Dec 1991; Bat signal hologram.... 1.50
❑4/CS, Dec 1991; Includes all variations of #4.......... 4.25

Robin Plus
DC

❑1, Dec 1996.......... 2.95
❑2, Dec 1997; continues in Scare Tactics #10.......... 2.95

Robin 3000
DC

❑1, ca. 1992.......... 4.95
❑2, ca. 1992.......... 4.95

Robin: Year One
DC

❑1, Dec 2000.......... 4.95
❑2, Jan 2001.......... 4.95
❑3, Feb 2001.......... 4.95
❑4, Mar 2001.......... 4.95

Robin/Argent Double-Shot
DC

❑1, Feb 1998.......... 1.95

Robin III: Cry of the Huntress
DC

❑1, Dec 1992; newsstand.......... 1.25
❑1/Variant, Dec 1992; moving cover...... 2.50
❑2, Jan 1993; newsstand.......... 1.25
❑2/Variant, Jan 1993; moving cover...... 2.50
❑3, Jan 1993; newsstand.......... 1.25
❑3/Variant, Jan 1993; moving cover...... 2.50
❑4, Feb 1993; newsstand.......... 1.25
❑4/Variant, Feb 1993; moving cover...... 2.50
❑5, Feb 1993; newsstand.......... 1.25
❑5/Variant, Feb 1993; moving cover...... 2.50
❑6, Mar 1993; newsstand.......... 1.25
❑6/Variant, Mar 1993; moving cover...... 2.50

Robin Hood
Dell

❑1, ca. 1963.......... 20.00

Robin Hood
Eternity

❑1, Aug 1989, b&w.......... 2.25
❑2, Sep 1991, b&w.......... 2.25
❑3, b&w.......... 2.25
❑4, b&w.......... 2.25

Other grades: Multiply price above by 5/6 for VF/NM • 2/3 for VERY FINE • 1/3 for FINE • 1/5 for VERY GOOD • 1/8 for GOOD

Sarge Steel

New meaning for iron hand in velvet glove
©Charlton

Satan's Six

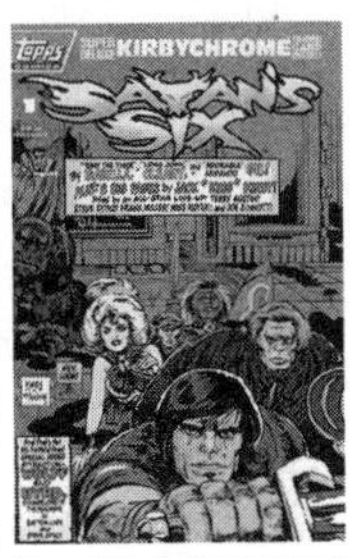

Topps' heroic line featured demonic team
©Topps

Savage Dragon

Multi-colored logos made collectors nuts
©Image

Savage Dragon

Fin-headed hero joins Chicago P.D.
©Image

Savage Dragon: God War

Hero forgets advice from Almighty
©Image

N-MINT

Robin Hood
Eclipse

- ❑1, Jul 1991 ... 2.50
- ❑2, Sep 1991 ... 2.50
- ❑3, Dec 1991 ... 2.50

Robin Red and the Lutins
Ace

- ❑1, Nov 1986 ... 1.75
- ❑2, Jan 1987 ... 1.75

Robinsonia
NBM

- ❑1; Adult ... 11.95

Robocop
Marvel

- ❑1, Oct 1987; Movie adaptation ... 2.50

Robocop
Marvel

- ❑1, Mar 1990 ... 3.00
- ❑2, Apr 1990 ... 2.00
- ❑3, May 1990 ... 1.50
- ❑4, Jun 1990 ... 1.50
- ❑5, Jul 1990 ... 1.50
- ❑6, Aug 1990 ... 1.50
- ❑7, Sep 1990 ... 1.50
- ❑8, Oct 1990 ... 1.50
- ❑9, Nov 1990 ... 1.50
- ❑10, Dec 1990 ... 1.50
- ❑11, Jan 1991 ... 1.50
- ❑12, Feb 1991 ... 1.50
- ❑13, Mar 1991 ... 1.50
- ❑14, Apr 1991 ... 1.50
- ❑15, May 1991 ... 1.50
- ❑16, Jun 1991 ... 1.50
- ❑17, Jul 1991 ... 1.50
- ❑18, Aug 1991 ... 1.50
- ❑19, Sep 1991 ... 1.50
- ❑20, Oct 1991 ... 1.50
- ❑21, Nov 1991 ... 1.50
- ❑22, Dec 1991 ... 1.50
- ❑23, Jan 1992; Final Issue ... 1.50

Robocop
Marvel

- ❑1, Jul 1990; prestige format; Movie adaptationt ... 4.95

Robocop 2
Marvel

- ❑1, Aug 1990; comic book ... 1.50
- ❑2, Sep 1990; comic book ... 1.50
- ❑3, Sep 1990; comic book ... 1.50

Robocop 2
Marvel

- ❑1, Aug 1990, b&w; magazine; Movie adaptation ... 2.50

Robocop 3
Dark Horse

- ❑1, Jul 1993; Movie adaptation ... 2.50
- ❑2, Sep 1993; Movie adaptation ... 2.50
- ❑3, Nov 1993; Movie adaptation ... 2.50

Robocop
Avatar

- ❑1, Aug 2003 ... 5.00
- ❑1/Platinum, Aug 2003 ... 7.00
- ❑1/Wraparound ... 5.00
- ❑2, Oct 2003 ... 3.50
- ❑2/Platinum ... 5.00
- ❑3, Nov 2003 ... 3.50
- ❑3/Platinum, Nov 2003 ... 6.00
- ❑3/Ryp ... 3.50
- ❑4, Dec 2003 ... 3.50
- ❑4/Miller ... 6.00
- ❑4/Platinum ... 5.00
- ❑5, Feb 2004 ... 3.50
- ❑5/Platinum ... 5.00
- ❑5/Wraparound ... 3.50
- ❑6 ... 3.50
- ❑6/Miller ... 6.00
- ❑6/Platinum ... 5.00
- ❑7 ... 3.50
- ❑7/Miller ... 6.00
- ❑7/Platinum ... 5.00
- ❑7/Wraparound ... 3.50
- ❑8 ... 3.50
- ❑8/Miller ... 6.00
- ❑8/Platinum ... 5.00
- ❑8/Wraparound ... 3.50

Robocop: Killing Machine
Avatar

- ❑1 ... 5.99
- ❑1/Platinum ... 15.00
- ❑1/Wraparound ... 6.00

Robocop: Mortal Coils
Dark Horse

- ❑1, Sep 1993 ... 2.50
- ❑2, Oct 1993 ... 2.50
- ❑3, Nov 1993 ... 2.50
- ❑4, Dec 1993 ... 2.50

Robocop: Prime Suspect
Dark Horse

- ❑1, Oct 1992 ... 2.50
- ❑2, Nov 1992 ... 2.50
- ❑3, Dec 1992 ... 2.50
- ❑4, Jan 1993 ... 2.50

Robocop: Roulette
Dark Horse

- ❑1, Dec 1993 ... 2.50
- ❑2, Jan 1994 ... 2.50
- ❑3, Feb 1994 ... 2.50
- ❑4, Mar 1994 ... 2.50

Robocop vs. the Terminator
Dark Horse

- ❑1, ca. 1992; FM (w); Includes RoboCop cut-out ... 3.00
- ❑1/Platinum, ca. 1992; Platinum promotional edition; FM (w); Includes RoboCop cut-out ... 4.00
- ❑2, ca. 1992; FM (w); Includes Terminator cut-out ... 2.50
- ❑3, ca. 1992; FM (w); Includes Flo cut-out ... 2.50
- ❑4, ca. 1992; FM (w); Includes ED-209 cut-out ... 2.50

Robocop: Wild Child
Avatar

- ❑1 2005 ... 2.99
- ❑1/Photo ... 4.00
- ❑1/Platinum ... 12.00
- ❑1/Rivalry ... 5.00
- ❑1/Wraparound ... 6.00

Robocop: Wild Child - Detroit's Finest
Avatar

- ❑1 2005 ... 5.99
- ❑1/Detroit 2005 ... 7.00
- ❑1/Photo 2005 ... 5.99
- ❑1/Platinum 2005 ... 15.00
- ❑1/Rivalry 2005 ... 7.00
- ❑1/Wraparound 2005 ... 5.99

Robo Dojo
DC / Wildstorm

- ❑1, Apr 2002 ... 2.95
- ❑2, May 2002 ... 2.95
- ❑3, Jun 2002 ... 2.95
- ❑4, Jul 2002 ... 2.95
- ❑5, Aug 2002 ... 2.95
- ❑6, Sep 2002 ... 2.95

Robo-Hunter
Eagle

- ❑1 ... 1.50
- ❑2 DaG (a) ... 1.25
- ❑3 DaG (a) ... 1.25
- ❑4 DaG (a) ... 1.25
- ❑5 ... 1.25

Robotech
Antarctic

- ❑1, Mar 1997 ... 2.95
- ❑2, May 1997 ... 2.95
- ❑3, Jul 1997 ... 2.95
- ❑4, Sep 1997 ... 2.95
- ❑5, Nov 1997 ... 2.95
- ❑6, Jan 1998 ... 2.95
- ❑7, Mar 1998 ... 2.95
- ❑8, May 1998 ... 2.95
- ❑9, Jul 1998 ... 2.95
- ❑10, Sep 1998 ... 2.95
- ❑11, Nov 1998 ... 2.95
- ❑Ann 1, Apr 1998, b&w ... 2.95

Robotech
DC / Wildstorm

- ❑0, Feb 2003; Pin-ups by various ... 2.50
- ❑1, Feb 2003 ... 2.95
- ❑2, Mar 2003 ... 2.95
- ❑3, Apr 2003 ... 2.95
- ❑4, May 2003 ... 2.95
- ❑5, Jun 2003 ... 2.95
- ❑6, Jul 2003 ... 2.95

Robotech: Amazon World-Escape from Praxis
Academy

- ❑1, Dec 1994 ... 2.95

Robotech: Class Reunion
Antarctic

- ❑1, Dec 1998, b&w ... 3.95

Robotech: Clone
Academy

- ❑0 ... 2.95
- ❑1 ... 2.95
- ❑2 ... 2.95
- ❑3 ... 2.95
- ❑4 ... 2.95
- ❑5 ... 2.95
- ❑Special 1 ... 3.50

Other grades: Multiply price above by 5/6 for VF/NM • 2/3 for VERY FINE • 1/3 for FINE • 1/5 for VERY GOOD • 1/8 for GOOD

Robotech: Covert-Ops
Antarctic
❑1, Aug 1998, b&w 2.95
❑2, Sep 1998, b&w 2.95

Robotech: Cyber World: Secrets of Haydon IV
Academy
❑1, Jul 1994 .... 2.95

Robotech Defenders
DC
❑1, Jan 1985 MA (a) 2.00
❑2, Apr 1985; MA (a); three-issue series was finished in two issues 2.00

Robotech: Escape
Antarctic
❑1, May 1998, b&w 2.95

Robotech: Final Fire
Antarctic
❑1, Dec 1998, b&w 2.95

Robotech: Firewalkers
Eternity
❑1, Jan 1993; Cover by Robert Chang; Follows Robotech: Invid War #6; Continues in Robotech: Moonwalkers 2.50

Robotech Genesis
Eternity
❑1, Mar 1992, trading cards 2.50
❑1/Ltd., Mar 1992; limited 5.95
❑2 .... 2.50
❑3 .... 2.50
❑4; trading cards 2.50
❑5, Sep 1992; trading cards 2.50
❑6 .... 2.50

Robotech in 3-D
Comico
❑1, Jul 1985 .... 2.50

RoboTech: Invasion
DC / Wildstorm
❑1, Mar 2004; Yashitaka Amano cover ... 2.95
❑2, Apr 2004 .... 2.95
❑3, May 2004 .... 2.95
❑4, Jun 2004 .... 2.95
❑5, Jul 2004 .... 2.95

Robotech: Invid War
Eternity
❑1, May 1992, b&w 2.50
❑2, Jun 1992, b&w 2.50
❑3, Jul 1992, b&w 2.50
❑4, Aug 1992, b&w 2.50
❑5, Sep 1992, b&w 2.50
❑6, Oct 1992, b&w 2.50
❑7, Nov 1992, b&w 2.50
❑8, Dec 1992, b&w 2.50
❑9, Jan 1993, b&w 2.50
❑10, Feb 1993, b&w 1.25
❑11, Mar 1993, b&w; Cover by John Waltrip 1.25
❑12, Apr 1993, b&w 1.25
❑13, May 1993, b&w 1.25
❑14, Jun 1993; b&w 2.50
❑15, Jul 1993; b&w 2.50
❑16, Aug 1993 .... 2.50
❑17, Sep 1993 .... 2.50
❑18, Oct 1993 .... 2.50

Robotech: Invid War Aftermath
Eternity
❑1, Dec 1993, b&w; Cover by Bruce Lewis, Tim Divar 2.50
❑2, Jan 1994, b&w 2.50

RoboTech: Love & War
DC / Wildstorm
❑1, Aug 2003 .... 2.95
❑2, Sep 2003 .... 2.99
❑3, Oct 2003 .... 2.95
❑4, Nov 2003 .... 2.95
❑5, Dec 2003 .... 2.95
❑6, Jan 2004 .... 2.95

RoboTech: Macross Saga
DC / Wildstorm
❑1, May 2003 .... 14.95
❑2, Jul 2003 .... 14.95
❑3, Sep 2003 .... 14.95
❑4, Nov 2003 .... 14.95

Robotech Masters
Comico
❑1, Jul 1985; Cover by Neil Vokes, Rich Rankin 2.00
❑2, Sep 1985 .... 1.50
❑3, Nov 1985; Cover by Neil D. Vokes, Rich Rankin 1.50
❑4, Nov 1985; Cover by Neil D. Vokes, Rich Rankin 1.50
❑5, Jan 1986; Cover by Neil D. Vokes, Rich Rankin 1.50
❑6, Feb 1986; Cover by Neil, Rich Rankin 1.50
❑7, Apr 1986; Cover by Neil, Rich Rankin 1.50
❑8, Apr 1986; Cover by I. D., Ken Steacy 1.50
❑9, Jul 1986; Cover by NDV, Rich Rankin 1.50
❑10, Aug 1986; Cover by NDV, Rich Rankin 1.50
❑11, Oct 1986; Cover by NDV, Rich Rankin 1.50
❑12, Nov 1986; Cover by NDV, Rich Rankin 1.50
❑13, Jan 1987; Cover by NDV, Rich Rankin 1.50
❑14, Feb 1987; Cover by NDV, Rich Rankin 1.50
❑15, Apr 1987; Cover by NDV, Rich Rankin 1.50
❑16, May 1987; Cover by NDV, Rich Rankin 1.50
❑17, Jul 1987; Cover by NDV, Rich Rankin 1.50
❑18, Aug 1987 .... 1.50
❑19, Dec 1987 .... 1.50
❑20 1987 .... 1.50
❑21, Jan 1988 .... 1.50
❑22, Feb 1988 .... 1.50
❑23 1988 .... 1.50

Robotech: Mechangel
Academy
❑1 .... 2.95
❑2 .... 2.95
❑3; O: Mechangel 2.95

Robotech: Megastorm
Antarctic
❑1, Aug 1998; wraparound cover 7.95

Robotech: Prelude to the Shadow Chronicles
DC
❑1, Dec 2005 .... 3.50
❑2, Dec 2005 .... 3.50
❑3, Jan 2006 .... 3.50
❑4, Feb 2006 .... 3.50
❑5, Mar 2006 .... 3.50

Robotech: Return to Macross
Eternity
❑1, Mar 1993, b&w 3.00
❑2, b&w 2.50
❑3, b&w 2.50
❑4, b&w 2.50
❑5, b&w 2.50
❑6, b&w 2.50
❑7, b&w 2.50
❑8, b&w 2.50
❑9, b&w 2.50
❑10, Jan 1994, b&w 2.50
❑11 .... 2.50
❑12 .... 2.50
❑13 .... 2.50
❑14 .... 2.50
❑15 .... 2.50
❑16 .... 2.50
❑17 .... 2.50
❑18 .... 2.50
❑19 .... 2.50
❑20 .... 2.50
❑21 .... 2.50
❑22 .... 2.50
❑23 .... 2.50
❑24 .... 2.50
❑25 .... 2.50
❑26 .... 2.50
❑27 .... 2.50
❑28 .... 2.50
❑29 .... 2.50
❑30 .... 2.50
❑31 .... 2.50
❑32, May 1996 .... 2.95

Robotech: Sentinels - Rubicon
Antarctic
❑1, Jun 1998, b&w 2.95
❑2 .... 2.95
❑3 .... 2.95
❑4 .... 2.95
❑5 .... 2.95
❑6 .... 2.95
❑7 .... 2.95

Robotech Special
Comico
❑1, May 1988; O: Dana Sterling 2.50

Robotech the Graphic Novel
Comico
❑1, Aug 1986; O: SDF-1Intro T.R. Edwards; The first Robotech graphic novel 5.95

Robotech: The Macross Saga
Comico
❑1, Dec 1984; "Macross" this issue 8.00
❑2, ca. 1985; Title changes to Robotech: The Macross Saga 4.00
❑3, ca. 1985 .... 3.00
❑4, ca. 1985 .... 3.00
❑5, ca. 1985 .... 3.00
❑6, Sep 1985 .... 2.00
❑7, Nov 1985 .... 2.00
❑8, Dec 1985 .... 2.00
❑9, ca. 1986 .... 2.00
❑10, ca. 1986 .... 2.00
❑11, ca. 1986; Cover by Mike Leeke and Chris Kalnick 2.00
❑12, ca. 1986 .... 2.00
❑13, ca. 1986; Cover by Mike Leeke and Chris Kalnick 2.00
❑14, ca. 1986; Cover by Mike Leeke and Chris Kalnick 2.00
❑15, ca. 1986; Cover by Mike Leeke and Chris Kalnick 2.00
❑16, ca. 1986; Cover by Mike Leeke and Mike Chen 2.00
❑17, ca. 1986 .... 2.00
❑18, Mar 1987 .... 2.00
❑19, May 1987 .... 2.00
❑20, Jun 1987 .... 2.00
❑21, Aug 1987 .... 2.00
❑22, ca. 1987 .... 2.00
❑23, ca. 1987 .... 2.00
❑24, ca. 1987 .... 2.00
❑25, ca. 1987 .... 2.00
❑26, ca. 1987 .... 2.00
❑27, ca. 1987 .... 2.00
❑28, Jun 1988 .... 2.00
❑29, Jul 1988 .... 2.00
❑30, Aug 1988 .... 2.00
❑31, Sep 1988 .... 2.00
❑32, Oct 1988 .... 2.00
❑33, ca. 1988 .... 2.00
❑34, ca. 1988 .... 2.00
❑35, Jan 1989 .... 2.00
❑36, ca. 1989; Final Issue 2.00

Robotech: The New Generation
Comico
❑1, Jul 1985 .... 2.00
❑2, Sep 1985 .... 1.50
❑3, Oct 1985 .... 1.50
❑4, Dec 1985 .... 1.50
❑5, Jan 1986 .... 1.50
❑6, Mar 1986 .... 1.50
❑7, Apr 1986 .... 1.50
❑8, Jun 1986 .... 1.50
❑9, Jul 1986 .... 1.50
❑10, Sep 1986 .... 1.50
❑11, Oct 1986; Dave Dorman Painted Cover 1.50
❑12, Dec 1986 .... 1.50
❑13, Jan 1987; Ken Steacy Painted Cover 1.50
❑14, Mar 1987 .... 1.50
❑15, Apr 1987 .... 1.50
❑16, Jun 1987 .... 1.50
❑17, Jul 1987 .... 1.50
❑18, Sep 1987 .... 1.50
❑19, Nov 1987 .... 1.50
❑20 .... 1.50
❑21, Jan 1988 .... 1.50
❑22, Mar 1988 .... 1.50
❑23, Apr 1988 .... 1.50
❑24, Jun 1988 .... 1.50
❑25 1988; last 1.50

Other grades: Multiply price above by 5/6 for VF/NM • 2/3 for VERY FINE • 1/3 for FINE • 1/5 for VERY GOOD • 1/8 for GOOD

Savage Hulk

CBG barrister Ingersoll makes appearance
©Marvel

Savage She-Hulk

Banner's blood changes cousin considerably
©Marvel

Savage Sword of Conan

Black-and-white sword-wielding adventures
©Marvel

Savage Tales

Early Marvel black-and-white fantasy title
©Marvel

Scamp

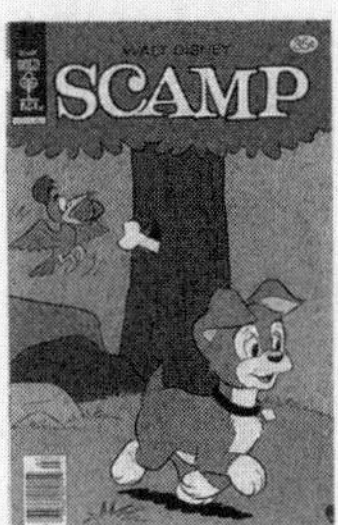

Lady and the Tramp's pup plays and plays
©Gold Key

N-MINT

Robotech II: Invid World, Assault on Optera
Academy

❑1, Oct 1994 .... 2.95

Robotech II: The Sentinels
Eternity

❑1, Nov 1988 .... 3.50
❑1/2nd; 2nd printing 2.00
❑2, Dec 1988 .... 2.50
❑3, Jan 1989 .... 2.50
❑3/2nd, Feb 1989; 2nd printing 2.00
❑4, Mar 1989 .... 2.25
❑5, Apr 1989 .... 2.25
❑6, May 1989 .... 2.00
❑7, Jun 1989 .... 2.00
❑8, Jul 1989 .... 2.00
❑9, Sep 1989 .... 2.00
❑10, Oct 1989 .... 2.00
❑11, Oct 1989 .... 2.00
❑12, Nov 1989 .... 2.00
❑13, Dec 1989 .... 2.00
❑14, Jan 1990 .... 2.00
❑15, Feb 1990 .... 2.00
❑16, Apr 1990; Final Issue 1.95

Robotech II: The Sentinels Book II
Eternity

❑1, May 1990 .... 2.25
❑2, Aug 1990 .... 2.25
❑3, Oct 1990 .... 2.25
❑4 .... 2.25
❑5 1991 .... 2.25
❑6 1991 .... 2.25
❑7 1991 .... 2.25
❑8 1991 .... 2.25
❑9 1991 .... 2.25
❑10 1991 .... 2.25
❑11, Dec 1991; Cover Jason Waltrip, Paul Mounts 2.25
❑12 .... 2.50
❑13, Mar 1992 .... 2.50
❑14 .... 2.50
❑15 .... 2.50
❑16, Oct 1992; Cover John Waltrip, Paul Mounts; b&w 2.50
❑17, Nov 1992; Cover Jason Waltrip, Paul Mounts; b&w 2.50
❑18, Jan 1993; Cover John Waltrip, Paul Mounts; b&w 2.50
❑19 .... 2.50
❑20, Apr 1993 .... 2.50

Robotech II: The Sentinels Book III
Eternity

❑1 .... 2.50
❑2 .... 2.50
❑3 .... 2.50
❑4 .... 2.50
❑5 .... 2.50
❑6 .... 2.50

Robotech II: The Sentinels Book IV
Academy

❑1 .... 2.95
❑2 .... 2.95
❑3 .... 2.95
❑4 .... 2.95
❑5 .... 2.95
❑6, May 1996 .... 2.95

Robotech II: The Sentinels Cyberpirates
Eternity

❑1, Mar 1991; b&w 2.25
❑2, Apr 1991 .... 2.25
❑3, May 1991 .... 2.25
❑4, Jul 1991 .... 2.25

Robotech II: The Sentinels Script Book
Eternity

❑1, b&w 9.95

Robotech II: The Sentinels Special
Eternity

❑1, Apr 1989 .... 1.95
❑2 .... 1.95

Robotech II: The Sentinels Swimsuit Spectacular
Eternity

❑1 .... 2.95

Robotech II: The Sentinels: The Illustrated Handbook
Eternity

❑1 .... 2.50
❑2 .... 2.50
❑3 .... 2.50

Robotech II: The Sentinels The Malcontent Uprisings
Malibu / Eternity

❑1, Aug 1989; b&w 2.00
❑2, Sep 1989; Cover by Michael Ling, Scott Bieser 2.00
❑3, Oct 1989; Cover by Michael Ling, Marcus David 2.00
❑4, Dec 1989; Cover by Michael C. Ling, Marcus Davis 2.00
❑5 .... 2.00
❑6 .... 2.00
❑7 .... 2.00
❑8, Aug 1990; b&w 2.00
❑9 .... 2.00
❑10 .... 2.00
❑11 .... 2.00
❑12 .... 2.00

Robotech II: The Sentinels: The Untold Story
Eternity

❑1, b&w 2.50

Robotech II: The Sentinels Wedding Special
Eternity

❑1, Apr 1989; Cover by Jason Waltrip, Scott Bieser 2.00
❑2, May 1989; Cover by Jason Waltrip, Scott Bieser 2.00

Robotech: Vermilion
Antarctic

❑1, Aug 1997 .... 2.95
❑2, Oct 1997 .... 2.95
❑3, Dec 1997 .... 2.95
❑4, Feb 1997 .... 2.95

Robotech Warriors
Academy

❑1, Feb 1995 .... 2.95

Robotech: Wings of Gibraltar
Antarctic

❑1, Aug 1998 .... 2.95
❑2, Sep 1998 .... 2.95

Robotix
Marvel

❑1, Feb 1986; HT (w); HT (a); 1: The Terrokors. 1: The Protectons 1.00

Robo Warriors
CFW

❑1; 1: Reiki 1.75
❑2; 0: Citation 1.95
❑3; 1: She-Bat 1.95
❑4 .... 1.95
❑5 .... 1.95
❑6 .... 1.95
❑7; 1: Mr. Slimey 1.95
❑8; Reiki becomes Mister No 1.95

Robyn of Sherwood
Caliber

❑1, Mar 1998, b&w 2.95

Rockers
Rip Off

❑1, Jul 1988, b&w; Adult 2.00
❑2, Oct 1988, b&w; Adult 2.00
❑3, Jan 1989, b&w; Adult 2.00
❑4, Feb 1989, b&w; Adult 2.00
❑5, May 1989, b&w; Adult 2.00
❑6, Jun 1989, b&w; Adult 2.00
❑7, Sep 1989, b&w; Adult 2.00
❑8, Feb 1990, b&w; Adult 2.00

Rocketeer 3-D Comic
Disney

❑1, Jun 1991; with audiotape; Based on The Rocketeer movie 5.00

Rocketeer Adventure Magazine
Comico

❑1, Jul 1988; CV, DSt (c); DSt (w); CV, DSt (a); Comico publishes 5.00
❑2, Jul 1989 DSt (c); DSt (w); DSt (a) ... 3.50
❑3, Jan 1995; DSt (c); DSt (w); PG, DSt (a); Dark Horse publishes 3.00

Rocketeer Special Edition
Eclipse

❑1, Nov 1984; Concludes Rocketeer story from Pacific Presents #2 .... 1.50

Rocketeer: The Official Movie Adaptation
Disney

❑1, Jun 1991; No cover date; stapled 2.95
❑1/Direct ed. 1991; No cover date; squarebound 5.95

Rocketman: King of the Rocket Men
Innovation

❑1 .... 2.50
❑2 .... 2.50
❑3 .... 2.50
❑4 .... 2.50

Other grades: Multiply price above by 5/6 for VF/NM • 2/3 for VERY FINE • 1/3 for FINE • 1/5 for VERY GOOD • 1/8 for GOOD

Rocketo
Speakeasy Comics

❑1, Sep 2005 2.99
❑2, Sep 2005 2.99
❑3, Oct 2005 2.99
❑4, Nov 2005 2.99
❑5 2005; Series moved to Image Comics with #6 2.99

Rocketo: Journey to the Hidden Sea
Image

❑6, Apr 2006 2.99
❑8, Jun 2006 2.99
❑9, Jul 2006 2.99
❑7, Jun 2006 2.99
❑10, Aug 2006 3.99
❑11, Oct 2006 3.99
❑12, Nov 2006 3.99

Rocket Raccoon
Marvel

❑1, May 1985 2.00
❑2, Jun 1985 1.00
❑3, Jul 1985 1.00
❑4, Aug 1985 1.00

Rocket Ranger
Adventure

❑1, Sep 1991 2.95
❑2, Dec 1991, b&w 2.95
❑3 1992, b&w 2.95
❑4 1992, b&w 2.95
❑5, Jul 1992, b&w 2.95
❑6 2.95

Rock Fantasy
Rock Fantasy

❑1; Pink Floyd 3.00
❑2; Rolling Stones 3.00
❑3; Led Zeppelin 3.00
❑4; New Kids on the Block; Stevie Nicks 3.00
❑5; Guns 'n Roses 3.00
❑6; Monstrosities of Rock 3.00
❑7; The Sex Pistols 3.00
❑8; Alice Cooper 3.00
❑9; Van Halen 3.00
❑10; Kiss 3.00
❑11; Jimi Hendrix 3.00
❑12, Sep 1990; Def Leppard 3.00
❑13; David Bowie 3.00
❑14; The Doors 3.00
❑15; Pink Floyd II 3.00
❑16; Double-size; The Great Gig in the Sky 5.00
❑17; Rock Vixens 3.00

Rockheads
Solson

❑1 1.95

Rockin' Bones
New England

❑1, Jan 1992, b&w 2.75
❑2, b&w 2.75
❑3, b&w 2.75
❑Holiday 1; Xmas Special 2.75

Rockinfreakapotamus Presents the Red Hot Chili Peppers Illustrated Lyrics
Telltale

❑1, Jul 1997, b&w; magazine-sized; NN 3.95

Rockin Rollin Miner Ants
Fate

❑1, Oct 1991 2.25

Rockmeez
Jzink Comics

❑1, Oct 1992 2.50
❑2, Nov 1992 2.50
❑3 2.50
❑4 2.50

Rock 'n' Roll Comics
Revolutionary

❑1, Jun 1989; Guns 'n' Roses 6.00
❑1/2nd, Jul 1989; Guns 'n' Roses 4.00
❑1/3rd, Aug 1989; Guns 'n' Roses 1.95
❑1/4th, Sep 1989; Guns 'n' Roses 1.95
❑1/5th, Oct 1989; Guns 'n' Roses 1.95
❑1/6th, Nov 1989; Guns 'n' Roses 1.95
❑1/7th, Dec 1989; Guns 'n' Roses; completely different than first six printings 1.95
❑2, Aug 1989; Metallica 3.00
❑2/2nd, Sep 1989; Metallica 1.95
❑2/3rd, Sep 1989; Metallica 1.95
❑2/4th, Sep 1989; Metallica 1.95
❑2/5th, Sep 1989; Metallica 1.95
❑1-2, Jul 1989; 2nd printing 4.00
❑1-3, Aug 1989; 3rd printing 1.95
❑2/6th, Metallica; 50% new material added 1.95
❑3, Sep 1989; Bon Jovi; Banned by Great Southern Co.; Rare 10.00
❑1-4, Sep 1989; 4th printing 1.95
❑1-5, Oct 1989; 5th printing 1.95
❑3/2nd, Oct 1989 1.95
❑1-6, Nov 1989; 6th printing 1.95
❑4, Oct 1989; Motley Crue; Banned by Great Southern Co.; 15,000 copies burned by Great Southern 50.00
❑4/2nd, Oct 1989; 2nd printing (no Ace Backwords); Banned by Great Southern Co. 3.00
❑1-7, Dec 1989; 7th printing; Color, completely different than first six printings 1.95
❑5, Nov 1989; Def Leppard 1.95
❑5/2nd, Nov 1989; Def Leppard 1.50
❑6, Dec 1989; Rolling Stones 1.95
❑6/2nd, Jan 1990; Rolling Stones 1.50
❑6/3rd, Jan 1990; Rolling Stones 1.50
❑2-2, Sep 1989; 2nd printing; Metallica. 1.95
❑2-3, Sep 1989; 3rd printing; Metallica . 1.95
❑6/4th, Feb 1990; Rolling Stones 1.50
❑2-4, Sep 1989; 4th printing; Metallica.. 1.95
❑7, Jan 1990; The Who 1.95
❑7/2nd, Feb 1990; The Who 1.50
❑2-5, Sep 1989; 5th printing; Metallica.. 1.95
❑7/3rd, Mar 1990; The Who 1.50
❑2-6, Oct 1990; 6th printing; 50% new material added; Metallica 1.95
❑8, Feb 1990; Skid Row; Never published: banned by injunction from Great Southern Company 1.50
❑9, Mar 1990; Kiss 5.00
❑9/2nd, Apr 1990; Kiss 1.95
❑9/3rd, May 1990; Kiss 1.95
❑10, Apr 1990; Two different versions printed, one with Whitesnake on cover, one with Warrant 1.95
❑10/2nd, May 1990; Whitesnake only on cover 1.50
❑3-2, Oct 1989 1.95
❑11, May 1990; Aerosmith 1.95
❑12, Jun 1990; New Kids on the Block.. 1.95
❑12/2nd, Aug 1990; New Kids On the Block 1.50
❑13, Jul 1990; Led Zeppelin 1.95
❑14, Aug 1990; Sex Pistols 1.95
❑15, Sep 1990, Poison 1.95
❑16, Oct 1990, Van Halen 1.95
❑17, Nov 1990, Madonna 3.00
❑18, Dec 1990; Alice Cooper; Full color. 1.95
❑19, Apr 1991, b&w; Public Enemy, 2 Live Crew 2.50
❑4-2, Oct 1989; 2nd printing (no Ace Backwords); Banned by Great Southern Co. 3.00
❑20, Apr 1991, b&w; Queensryche 2.50
❑21, Jan 1991, b&w; Prince 2.50
❑22, Feb 1991, AC/DC 2.50
❑23, Mar 1991, b&w; Living Colour 2.50
❑24, Mar 1991; Anthrax b&w 2.50
❑25, May 1991, b&w; ZZ Top 2.50
❑26, May 1991; Doors 2.50
❑27, Jun 1991; Doors 2.50
❑28, Jun 1991; Ozzy Osbourne; Black Sabbath 2.50
❑29, Jul 1991; Ozzy Osbourne; Black Sabbath 2.50
❑5-2, Nov 1989; 2nd printing; Def Leppard 1.50
❑30, Jul 1991; The Cure 2.50
❑31, Aug 1991; Vanilla Ice 2.50
❑32, Aug 1991; Frank Zappa 2.50
❑33, Sep 1991; Guns 'N' Roses II 2.50
❑34, Sep 1991; Black Crowes 2.50
❑35, Oct 1991; R.E.M 2.50
❑36, Oct 1991; Michael Jackson 2.50
❑37, Nov 1991; Ice-T 2.50
❑38, Nov 1991; Rod Stewart 2.50
❑39, Dec 1991; The Fall of the New Kids 2.50
❑6-2, Jan 1990; 2nd printing; Rolling Stones 1.50
❑6-3, Jan 1990; 3rd printing; Rolling Stones 1.50
❑40, Dec 1991; NWA; Ice Cube 2.50
❑41, Jan 1992; Paula Abdul 2.50
❑6-4, Feb 1990; 4th printing; Rolling Stones 1.50
❑42, Jan 1992; Metallica II 2.50
❑43, Feb 1992; Guns 'N' Roses: Tales from the Tour 2.50
❑44, Feb 1992; Scorpions 2.50
❑45, Mar 1992; Grateful Dead 2.50
❑46, Apr 1992; Grateful Dead II 2.50
❑47, May 1992; Grateful Dead III 2.50
❑48, Jun 1992; Queen 2.50
❑49, Jul 1992; Rush 2.50
❑7-2, Feb 1990; 2nd printing; The Who . 1.50
❑7-3, Mar 1990; 3rd printing; The Who . 1.50
❑50, Aug 1992; Bob Dylan 2.50
❑51, Sep 1992; Bob Dylan II 2.50
❑52, Oct 1992; Bob Dylan III 2.50
❑53, Nov 1992; Bruce Springsteen 2.50
❑54, Dec 1992; U2 2.50
❑55, Jan 1993; U2 II 2.50
❑56, Feb 1993; David Bowie 2.50
❑57, Mar 1993; Aerosmith 2.50
❑58, Apr 1993; Kate Bush 2.50
❑59, May 1993; Eric Clapton 2.50
❑60, Jun 1993; Genesis 2.50
❑61, Jul 1993; Yes 2.50
❑62, Aug 1993; Elton John 2.50
❑63, Sep 1993; Janis Joplin 2.50
❑64, Oct 1993; '60s San Francisco 2.50
❑65, Nov 1993; Sci-Fi Space Rockers 2.50

Rock N' Roll Comics Magazine
Revolutionary

❑1; Kiss 2.95
❑2; New Kids on the Block; b&w 2.95
❑3; Guns 'n' Roses 2.95
❑4; Metallica 2.95
❑5, Oct 1990; Aerosmith/Rolling Stones 2.95

Rock 'N' Roll
Image

❑1, Jan 2006 3.50

Rockola
Mirage

❑1 1.50

Rocko's Modern Life
Marvel

❑1, Jun 1994; TV cartoon 1.95
❑2, Jul 1994 1.95
❑3, Aug 1994 1.95
❑4, Sep 1994 1.95
❑5, Oct 1994 1.95
❑6, Nov 1994 1.95
❑7, Dec 1994; Final issue 1.95

Rocky and His Fiendish Friends
Gold Key

❑1, Oct 1962 100.00
❑2, Dec 1962 75.00
❑3, Mar 1963 75.00
❑4, Jun 1963 60.00
❑5, Sep 1963 60.00

Rocky Horror Picture Show: The Comic Book
Caliber

❑1, Jul 1990 7.00
❑1/2nd; new cover 3.00
❑2, Aug 1990 4.00
❑3, Jan 1991 4.00

Rocky Lane Western
AC

❑1, b&w; Reprints 2.50
❑2, b&w; Reprints 5.95
❑Ann 1, b&w; Reprints 2.95

Rocky: The One and Only
Fantagraphics

❑1, Jan 2006 12.95

Roel
Sirius

❑1, Feb 1997, b&w; cardstock cover 2.95

Scarlett

Post-Buffy movie, pre-Buffy TV
©DC

Scary Godmother

Jill Thompson's tricky treat of a series
©Sirius

Scavengers

Dinosaurs dumped in Dredd's domain
©Fleetway-Quality

Scene of the Crime

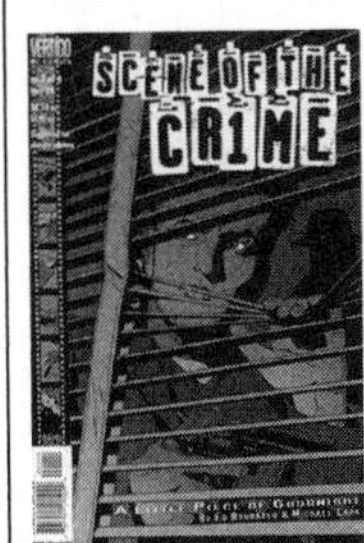

One-eyed P.I. seeks dame
©DC

Scion

Prince acquires power, incites war
©CrossGen

N-MINT

Rogan Gosh
DC / Vertigo

❑1; NN 6.95

Roger Fnord
Rip Off

❑1, Apr 1992, b&w; Adult 2.50

Roger Rabbit
Disney

❑1, Jun 1990; 1: Dick Flint 2.00
❑2, Jul 1990 .... 1.75
❑3, Aug 1990 .... 1.75
❑4, Sep 1990 .... 1.75
❑5, Oct 1990 .... 1.75
❑6, Nov 1990 .... 1.50
❑7, Dec 1990 .... 1.50
❑8, Jan 1991 .... 1.50
❑9, Feb 1991 .... 1.50
❑10, Mar 1991 .... 1.50
❑11, Apr 1991 .... 1.50
❑12, May 1991 .... 1.50
❑13, Jun 1991 .... 1.50
❑14, Jul 1991 .... 1.50
❑15, Aug 1991 .... 1.50
❑16, Sep 1991 .... 1.50
❑17, Oct 1991 .... 1.50
❑18, Nov 1991; Final Issue 1.50
❑Special 1; NN 3.50

Roger Rabbit in 3-D
Disney

❑1; with glasses; 3-D Zone reprints 2.50

Roger Rabbit's Toontown
Disney

❑1, Aug 1991 .... 1.50
❑2, Sep 1991; Winsor McCay tribute 1.50
❑3, Oct 1991 .... 1.50
❑4, Nov 1991; 1: Winnie Weasel 1.50
❑5, Dec 1991; Weasels solo story 1.50

Roger Wilco
Adventure

❑1 .... 2.95
❑2, Apr 1992, b&w 2.95

Rog-2000
Pacific

❑1 .... 2.00

Rogue Battlebook
Marvel

❑1 .... 3.99

Rogue
Marvel

❑1, Jan 1995; enhanced cover 4.00
❑2, Feb 1995; enhanced cover 2.95
❑3, Mar 1995; enhanced cover 2.95
❑4, Apr 1995; enhanced cover 2.95

Rogue
Marvel

❑1, Sep 2001 .... 2.50
❑2, Oct 2001 .... 2.50
❑3, Nov 2001 .... 2.50
❑4, Dec 2001 .... 2.50

N-MINT

Rogue
Marvel

❑1, Sep 2004 .... 2.99
❑2, Oct 2004 .... 2.99
❑3, Nov 2004 .... 2.99
❑4, Dec 2004 .... 2.99
❑5, Jan 2005 .... 2.99
❑6, Feb 2005 .... 2.99
❑7, Mar 2005 .... 2.99
❑8, Apr 2005 .... 2.99
❑9, May 2005 .... 2.99
❑10, Jun 2005 .... 2.99
❑11, Jul 2005 .... 2.99
❑12, Aug 2005 .... 2.99

Rogue
Monster

❑1, Aug 1991, b&w 1.95

Rogue Satellite Comics
Slave Labor

❑1, Aug 1996, b&w 2.95
❑2, b&w 2.95
❑3, Mar 1997, b&w 2.95
❑Special 1, b&w; Published by Modern; Flaming Carrot story 2.95

Rogues Gallery
DC

❑1; pin-ups 3.50

Rogues (Villains)
DC

❑1, Feb 1998; New Year's Evil 1.95

Rogue Trooper
Fleetway-Quality

❑1 DaG (a) 2.00
❑2 DaG (a) 2.00
❑3 DaG (a) 2.00
❑4 .... 2.00
❑5 DaG (a) 2.00
❑6 .... 1.75
❑7 AMo (w) 1.75
❑8 .... 1.75
❑9 .... 1.75
❑10 .... 1.75
❑11 .... 1.50
❑12 .... 1.50
❑13 .... 1.50
❑14 .... 1.50
❑15 .... 1.50
❑16 .... 1.50
❑17 .... 1.50
❑18 .... 1.50
❑19 .... 1.50
❑20 .... 1.50
❑21; double issue #21/22 .... 1.50
❑23; double issue #23/24 .... 1.50
❑25 .... 1.50
❑26 .... 1.50
❑27 .... 1.50
❑28 .... 1.50
❑29 .... 1.50
❑30 .... 1.75
❑31 .... 1.75
❑32 .... 1.75
❑33 .... 1.75
❑34 .... 1.75

N-MINT

❑35 .... 1.75
❑36 .... 1.75
❑37 .... 1.75
❑38 .... 1.75
❑39 .... 1.75
❑40 .... 1.75
❑41 .... 1.75
❑42 .... 1.75
❑43 .... 1.75
❑44 .... 1.75
❑45 .... 1.75
❑46 .... 1.75
❑47 .... 1.75
❑48 .... 1.75
❑49 .... 1.75

Rogue Trooper
Fleetway-Quality

❑1 .... 2.95
❑2 .... 2.95
❑3 .... 2.95
❑4 .... 2.95
❑5 .... 2.95
❑6 .... 2.95
❑7 .... 2.95
❑8 .... 2.95
❑9 .... 2.95

Roja Fusion
Antarctic

❑1, Apr 1995 .... 2.95

Rokkin
DC

❑1, Sep 2006 .... 2.99
❑2, Oct 2006 .... 2.99
❑3, Nov 2006 .... 2.99
❑4, Dec 2006 .... 2.99
❑5, Jan 2007 .... 2.99
❑6, Mar 2007 .... 2.99

Roland: Days Of Wrath
Terra Major

❑1, Jul 1999 .... 2.95

Rollercoaster
Fantagraphics

❑1, Sep 1996, b&w; magazine; cardstock cover 3.95

Rollercoasters Special Edition
Blue Comet

❑1 .... 2.00

Rolling Stones
Personality

❑1, b&w 2.95
❑2, b&w 2.95
❑3, b&w 2.95

Rolling Stones: Voodoo Lounge
Marvel / Marvel Music

❑1, ca. 1995; prestige format one-shot 6.95

Rom
Marvel

❑1, Dec 1979, SB (c); SB (a); O: ROM. 1: ROM 8.00
❑2, Jan 1980, AM, FM (c); SB, FM (a) 2.00
❑3, Feb 1980, FM (c); SB, FM (a); 1: Firefall 2.00
❑4, Mar 1980, SB (c); SB (a) 1.50
❑5, Apr 1980, AM (c); SB (a) 1.50

N-MINT

❑6, May 1980, AM (c); SB (a) 1.50
❑7, Jun 1980, MG (c); SB (a) 1.50
❑8, Jul 1980, MG (c); SB (a) 1.50
❑9, Aug 1980, MG (c); SB (a) 1.50
❑10, Sep 1980, MG (c); SB (a) 1.50
❑11, Oct 1980, MG (c); SB (a) 1.25
❑12, Nov 1980, MG (c); SB (a) 1.25
❑13, Dec 1980, MG (c); SB (a) 1.25
❑14, Jan 1981, DC (c); SB (a); V: Mad Thinker and His Awesome Android; The Saga of the Spaceknights backup feature 1.25
❑15, Feb 1981, BL (c); SB (a) 1.25
❑16, Mar 1981, SB (a); V: Watchwraith; Saga of the Spaceknights backup story 1.25
❑17, Apr 1981, FM (c); SB, FM (a); A: X-Men 1.50
❑18, May 1981, FM (c); SB, FM (a); A: X-Men 1.50
❑19, Jun 1981, MG (c); SB, JSt (a); A: X-Men 1.25
❑20, Jul 1981, AM (c); SB, JSt (a); V: Mentus; Saga of the Spaceknights backup story 1.25
❑21, Aug 1981, AM (c); SB, JSt (a); Saga of the Spaceknights backup story 1.25
❑22, Sep 1981, AM (c); SB (w); SB, JSt (a); V: Rocketeers; Saga of the Spaceknights backup story 1.25
❑23, Oct 1981, AM (c); SB (w); SB, JSt (a); A: Power Man. Story continued from Power Man & Iron Fist #73 .... 1.25
❑24, Nov 1981, AM (c); SB, JSt (a); D: Crimebuster. D: Powerhouse. D: Nova-Prime. D: Comet (Harris Moore). D: Protector; V: Skrulls 1.50
❑25, Dec 1981; Giant-size; SB (w); SB, JSt (a); Double-size; Back-up story 1.50
❑26, Jan 1982 .... 1.25
❑27, Feb 1982, V: Galactus 1.25
❑28, Mar 1982 .... 1.25
❑29, Apr 1982 .... 1.25
❑30, May 1982 .... 1.25
❑31, Jun 1982 .... 1.25
❑32, Jul 1982 .... 1.25
❑33, Aug 1982 .... 1.25
❑34, Sep 1982 .... 1.25
❑35, Oct 1982 .... 1.25
❑36, Nov 1982 .... 1.25
❑37, Dec 1982, Avalanche backup 1.25
❑38, Jan 1983 .... 1.25
❑39, Feb 1983 .... 1.25
❑40, Mar 1983 .... 1.25
❑41, Apr 1983 .... 1.25
❑42, May 1983 .... 1.25
❑43, Jun 1983 .... 1.25
❑44, Jul 1983, 1: Devastator II 1.25
❑45, Aug 1983 .... 1.25
❑46, Sep 1983 .... 1.25
❑47, Oct 1983 .... 1.25
❑48, Nov 1983 .... 1.25
❑49, Dec 1983 .... 1.25
❑50, Jan 1984; double-sized; SB (a); A: Skrulls. D: Torpedo 1.25
❑51, Feb 1984 .... 1.25
❑52, Mar 1984 .... 1.25
❑53, Apr 1984 .... 1.25
❑54, May 1984 .... 3.00
❑55, Jun 1984 .... 1.25
❑56, Jul 1984, A: Alpha Flight 3.00
❑57, Aug 1984, A: Alpha Flight 1.25
❑58, Sep 1984, Dire Wraiths 1.25
❑59, Oct 1984, PS (c); SD (a) 1.25
❑60, Nov 1984, SD (a) 1.25
❑61, Dec 1984, SD (a) 1.25
❑62, Jan 1985, MZ (c); SD (a) 1.25
❑63, Feb 1985, SD (a) 1.25
❑64, Mar 1985 .... 1.25
❑65, Apr 1985 .... 1.25
❑66, May 1985 .... 1.25
❑67, Jun 1985 .... 1.25
❑68, Jul 1985 .... 1.25
❑69, Aug 1985, V: Ego The Living Planet 1.25
❑70, Sep 1985, V: Unam the Unseen 1.25
❑71, Oct 1985, D: The Unseen 1.25
❑72, Nov 1985, Secret Wars II 1.25
❑73, Dec 1985 .... 1.25
❑74, Jan 1986; D: Seeker 1.25
❑75, Feb 1986; D: Trapper. D: Scanner... 2.00
❑Ann 1, ca. 1982; Stardust 1.00
❑Ann 2, ca. 1983 .... 1.00
❑Ann 3, ca. 1984; A: New Mutants 1.00
❑Ann 4, ca. 1985; A: Gladiator. D: Pulsar 1.00

Romancer
Moonstone

❑1, Dec 1996, b&w; NN 2.95

Roman Holidays
Gold Key

❑1, Feb 1973 .... 20.00
❑2, May 1973 .... 10.00
❑3, Aug 1973 .... 10.00

Romantic Tails
Head

❑1, Aug 1998, b&w 2.95

Romp One Shot
Image

❑1, Jan 2004 .... 6.95

Ronald McDonald
Charlton

❑1, Sep 1970 .... 52.00
❑2, Nov 1970 .... 35.00
❑3, Jan 1971 .... 35.00
❑4, Mar 1971 .... 35.00

Ronin
DC

❑1, Jul 1983 FM (c); FM (w); FM (a) 4.00
❑2, Sep 1983 FM (w); FM (a) 3.00
❑3, Nov 1983 FM (w); FM (a) 3.00
❑4, Jan 1984 FM (c); FM (w); FM (a) 3.00
❑5, Jan 1984 FM (w); FM (a) 3.00
❑6, Aug 1984; FM (w); FM (a); Scarcer.. 5.00

Rook
Harris

❑1, Jun 1995; NN 2.95
❑2, Sep 1995 .... 2.95

Rook Magazine
Warren

❑1, Oct 1979; Adult 4.00
❑2, Feb 1980; Adult 2.50
❑3, Jun 1980; Adult 2.50
❑4, Aug 1980; Adult 2.50
❑5, Oct 1980; Adult 2.50
❑6, Dec 1980; Adult 2.50
❑7, Feb 1981; Adult 2.50
❑8, Apr 1981; Adult 2.50
❑9, Jun 1981; Adult 2.50
❑10, Aug 1981; Adult 2.50
❑11, Oct 1981; Adult 2.00
❑12, Dec 1981; Adult 2.00
❑13, Feb 1982; Adult 2.00
❑14, Apr 1982; Adult 2.00

Room 222
Dell

❑1, Jan 1970 .... 30.00
❑2, Mar 1970 .... 20.00
❑3, Jul 1970 .... 20.00
❑4, Jan 1971, Same cover as #1, but white corner with price 20.00

Rooter
Custom

❑1, Aug 1996 .... 2.95
❑2, Dec 1996 .... 2.95
❑3, Feb 1997 .... 2.95
❑4, May 1997 .... 2.95
❑5, Jul 1997 .... 2.95
❑6, Oct 1997 .... 2.95

Rooter
Custom

❑1, b&w 2.95
❑2, ca. 1998, b&w 2.95

Roots of the Oppressor
Northstar

❑1, b&w 2.95

Roots of the Swamp Thing
DC

❑1, Jul 1986; Reprints 2.00
❑2, Aug 1986; Reprints 2.00
❑3, Sep 1986; reprints Swamp Thing #5 and #6 and House of Mystery #191 ... 2.00
❑4, Oct 1986; reprints Swamp Thing #7 and #8 and House of Mystery #221 ... 2.00
❑5, Nov 1986; Reprints stories from Swamp Thing #9, #10, House of Mystery #92 .... 2.00

Roscoe! The Dawg, Ace Detective
Renegade

❑1, Jul 1987, b&w 2.00
❑2, Oct 1987, b&w 2.00
❑3, Nov 1987, b&w 2.00
❑4, Jan 1988, b&w 2.00

Rose & Thorn
DC / Wildstorm

❑1, Feb 2004 .... 2.95
❑2, Mar 2004 .... 2.95
❑3, Apr 2004 .... 2.95
❑4, May 2004 .... 2.95
❑5, Jun 2004 .... 2.95
❑6, Jul 2004 .... 2.95

Rose
Hero

❑1, Dec 1992; Rose; Huntsman 3.50
❑2, Mar 1993; Rose; Huntsman 2.95
❑3, Jun 1993; Rose; Huntsman 3.95
❑4, Sep 1993; Rose; Huntsman 3.95
❑5, Dec 1993; Reprints from Marksman Ann #1, Marksman #3 and 4 .... 2.95

Rose
Cartoon Books

❑1, Nov 2000 .... 5.95
❑2, Apr 2001 .... 5.95
❑3, Feb 2002 .... 5.95

Rose & Gunn
Bishop

❑3, May 1995, b&w 2.95
❑4, Jun 1995, b&w 2.95
❑5, Aug 1995, b&w 2.95

Rose & Gunn Creator's Choice
Bishop

❑1, Sep 1995, b&w 2.95

Roswell: Little Green Man
Bongo

❑1, ca. 1996 .... 3.50
❑2, ca. 1996 .... 3.00
❑3, ca. 1996; V: Professor Von Sphinkter 3.00
❑4, ca. 1997; D: Shorty George 3.00
❑5, ca. 1998 .... 3.00
❑6, ca. 1999 .... 3.00

Rotogin Junkbotz
Image

❑0, Mar 2003 .... 2.50
❑1, May 2003 .... 2.95
❑2, Aug 2003 .... 2.95
❑3, Oct 2003 .... 2.95

Rough Raiders
Blue Comet

❑1 .... 2.00
❑2 .... 2.00
❑3 .... 2.00
❑Ann 1 .... 2.50

Roulette
Caliber

❑1, b&w 2.50

Route 666
CrossGen

❑1, Jun 2002 .... 2.95
❑2, Jul 2002 .... 2.95
❑3, Aug 2002 .... 2.95
❑4, Sep 2002 .... 2.95
❑5, Oct 2002 .... 2.95
❑6, Nov 2002 .... 2.95
❑7, Dec 2002 .... 2.95
❑8, Jan 2003 .... 2.95
❑9, Feb 2003 .... 2.95
❑10, Mar 2003 .... 2.95
❑11, Apr 2003 .... 2.95
❑12, May 2003 .... 2.95
❑13, Jul 2003 .... 2.95
❑14, Aug 2003 .... 2.95
❑15, Oct 2003 .... 2.95
❑16, Nov 2003 .... 2.95
❑17, Dec 2003 .... 2.95
❑18, Dec 2003 .... 2.95
❑19, Jan 2004 .... 2.95

Scooby-Doo

Crimes crushed by darned kids and dog
©DC

Scorpion

Atlas hero, not Marvel villain
©Annruel

Scorpio Rose

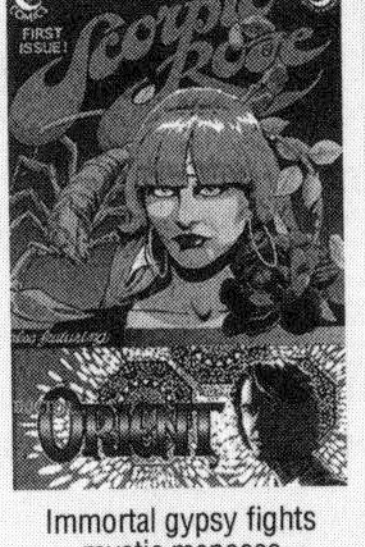

Immortal gypsy fights mystic menaces
©Eclipse

Scout

Post-apocalyptic Apache fights to survive
©Eclipse

Scud: The Disposable Assassin

Videogame suffered from limited marketing
©Fireman

N-MINT

❑20, Mar 2004 .... 2.95
❑21, Apr 2004 .... 2.95
❑22, May 2004; Final Issue 2.95

Rovers
Malibu

❑1, Sep 1987 .... 1.95
❑2 1987 .... 1.95
❑3 1987 .... 1.95
❑4 1988 .... 1.95
❑5, Jan 1988; b&w 1.95
❑6 1988, b&w 1.95
❑7 1988, b&w 1.95

Royal Roy
Marvel / Star

❑1, May 1985, 1: Royal Roy 1.00
❑2, Jul 1985 .... 1.00
❑3, Sep 1985 .... 1.00
❑4, Nov 1985 .... 1.00
❑5, Jan 1986 .... 1.00
❑6, Mar 1986, Final Issue 1.00

Roy Rogers Western
AC

❑1, b&w; Reprints 4.95

Roy Rogers Western Classics
AC

❑1; some color; reprints 2.95
❑2; some color; reprints 2.95
❑3; some color; reprints 3.95
❑4; some color; reprints 3.95
❑5; some color; reprints; photos 2.95

RTA: Personality Crisis
Image

❑0, Oct 2005 .... 3.50

Rubber Blanket
Rubber Blanket

❑1, b&w 5.75
❑2 .... 7.75
❑3 .... 7.95

Rubes Revue
Fragments West

❑1, b&w 2.00

Ruby Shaft's Tales of the Unexpurgated
Fantagraphics / Eros

❑1, b&w; Adult 2.50

Ruck Bud Webster and His Screeching Commandos
Pyramid

❑1, b&w; Adult 1.60

Rude Awakening
Dennis Mcmillan

❑1, Apr 1996, b&w 12.95

Rugrats Comic Adventures
Nickelodeon Magazines

❑1 1997; ca. 1997 .... 3.50
❑2 1997 .... 3.00
❑3 1998 .... 3.00
❑4 1998 .... 3.00
❑5 1998 .... 3.00
❑6, Apr 1998 .... 3.00
❑7 1998 .... 3.00

N-MINT

❑8, Jun 1998; magazine; no cover price 3.00
❑9 1998 .... 3.00
❑10, Aug 1998; magazine; no cover price 3.00

Rugrats Comic Adventures
Nickelodeon Magazines

❑1, Sep 1998; magazine; no cover price 3.00

Ruins
Marvel

❑1, Aug 1995; Acetate cover overlaying cardstock inner cover 4.95
❑2, Sep 1995; Acetate cover overlaying cardstock inner cover 4.95

Ruler of the Land
ADV Manga

❑1, ca. 2004; b&w 9.99
❑2, ca. 2004 .... 9.99
❑3, ca. 2004 .... 9.99
❑4, ca. 2005 .... 9.99
❑5, ca. 2005 .... 9.99

Rumble Girls: Silky Warrior Tansie
Image

❑1, Apr 2000 .... 3.50
❑2, Jun 2000 .... 3.50
❑3, Jul 2000 .... 3.50
❑4, Aug 2000 .... 3.50
❑5, Nov 2000 .... 3.50
❑6, Jan 2001 .... 3.50

Rumic World
Viz

❑1, b&w; Fire Tripper 3.25
❑2, b&w; Laughing Target 3.50

Rummage $2099
Parody

❑1; foil cover 2.95

Runaway
Dell

❑1, Oct 1964 .... 16.00

Runaway: A Known Associates Mystery
Known Associates

❑1, b&w 2.50

Runaways
Marvel

❑1, Jul 2003; 1: Alex Wilder; 1: Arsenic (Gertrude Yorkes); 1: Lucy In The Sky (Karolina Dean); 1: Talkback (Chase Stein); 1: Bruiser (Molly Hayes); 1: Sister Grimm (Nico Minoru) 4.00
❑2, Aug 2003, 1: Old Lace (Gertrude's dinosaur) 2.50
❑3, Sep 2003, 1: Old Lace (full); O: Karolina 2.50
❑4, Oct 2003 .... 2.50
❑5, Nov 2003 .... 2.99
❑6, Nov 2003 .... 2.99
❑7, Dec 2003, (c); 1: Topher 2.50
❑8, Jan 2004 .... 2.99
❑9, Feb 2004, Topher revealed to be a vampire 2.99
❑10, Mar 2004, D: Topher 2.99
❑11, Apr 2004 .... 2.99
❑12, Apr 2004 .... 2.99
❑13, May 2004, O: The Pride 2.99
❑14, Jun 2004, D: Lt. Flores 2.99

N-MINT

❑15, Jul 2004, V: The Pride 2.99
❑16, Aug 2004 .... 2.99
❑17, Oct 2004; D: Alex Wilder 2.99
❑18, Nov 2004 .... 2.99

Runaways
Marvel

❑1, Apr 2005 .... 6.00
❑1/Variant, Apr 2005 .... 5.00
❑2, May 2005 .... 2.99
❑3, Jun 2005 .... 2.99
❑4, Jul 2005 .... 2.99
❑5, Aug 2005 .... 2.99
❑6, Sep 2005 .... 2.99
❑7, Oct 2005 .... 2.99
❑8 2005 .... 2.99
❑9, Dec 2005 .... 2.99
❑10, Jan 2006 .... 2.99
❑11, Feb 2006 .... 2.99
❑12, Mar 2006 .... 2.99
❑13, Apr 2006 .... 2.99
❑14, May 2006 .... 2.99
❑15, Jul 2006 .... 2.99
❑16, Aug 2006 .... 2.99
❑17, Sep 2006 .... 2.99
❑18, Sep 2006 .... 2.99
❑19, Oct 2006 .... 2.99
❑20, Nov 2006 .... 2.99
❑21, Dec 2006 .... 2.99
❑22, Feb 2007 .... 2.99

Run, Buddy, Run
Gold Key

❑1, Jun 1967 .... 15.00

Rune
Malibu / Ultraverse

❑0, Jan 1994; Promotional edition (from redeeming coupons in early Ultraverse comics); no cover price 3.00
❑1, Jan 1994; Includes trading card 2.00
❑1/Variant, Jan 1994; Foil limited edition; silver foil logo 2.00
❑2, Feb 1994 .... 1.95
❑3, Mar 1994; 1: Ripfire. 1: Elven. Flip-book with Ultraverse Premiere #1 .... 3.50
❑4, Jun 1994 .... 1.95
❑5, Sep 1994 .... 1.95
❑6, Dec 1994 .... 1.95
❑7, Feb 1995 .... 1.95
❑8, Feb 1995 .... 1.95
❑9, Apr 1995; D: Sybil. D: Master Oshi. D: Tantalus 1.95
❑GS 1, Jan 1995; Giant-size Rune #1; O: Rune. 1: Sybil. 1: Master Oshi. 1: Tantalus. D: El Gato 2.50

Rune
Malibu / Ultraverse

❑0, Sep 1995; Black September; Rune #Infinity; black cover 1.50
❑0/Variant, Sep 1995; alternate cover; Rune #Infinity 2.00
❑1, Oct 1995 A: Gemini. A: Adam Warlock. A: Annihilus 1.50
❑2, Nov 1995 .... 1.50
❑3, Dec 1995 .... 1.50
❑4, Jan 1996 .... 1.50
❑5, Feb 1996 .... 1.50

N-MINT | N-MINT | N-MINT

❑6, Mar 1996 .... 1.50
❑7, Apr 1996; Final Issue 1.50

Rune: Hearts of Darkness
Malibu

❑1, Sep 1996; Flip-book 1.50
❑2, Oct 1996; Flip-book 1.50
❑3, Nov 1996; Flip-book; Feature the winner of the Wizard create a Villian contest 1.50

Rune/Silver Surfer
Marvel

❑1, Apr 1995; newsstand edition; crossover 3.00
❑1/Direct ed., Apr 1995; Direct Market edition; crossover; Squarebound with glossier paper 6.00

Runes of Ragnan
Image

❑1, Dec 2005 .... 3.50
❑2, Jan 2006 .... 3.50
❑3, Mar 2006 .... 3.50
❑4, Apr 2006 .... 2.99

Rune vs. Venom
Malibu / Ultraverse

❑1, Dec 1995; 48 pgs 3.95

Rune/Wrath
Malibu / Ultraverse

❑1; gold foil ashcan 1.00

Runners: Bad Goods
Serve Man Press

❑1, Jan 2003 .... 2.95
❑2, Sep 2003 .... 2.95
❑3, Jun 2004 .... 2.95
❑4, Aug 2004 .... 2.95
❑5, Feb 2005 .... 2.95

Rurouni Kenshin
Viz

❑1, Oct 2003 .... 7.95
❑2, Dec 2003 .... 7.95
❑3, Feb 2004 .... 7.95
❑4, Apr 2004 .... 7.95
❑5, Jun 2004 .... 7.95
❑6, Aug 2004 .... 7.95
❑7, Oct 2004 .... 7.95
❑8, Nov 2004 .... 7.95
❑9, Dec 2004 .... 7.95
❑10, Jan 2005 .... 7.95
❑11, Feb 2005 .... 7.95
❑12, Mar 2005 .... 7.95
❑13, Apr 2005 .... 7.95
❑14, May 2005 .... 7.95
❑15, Jun 2005 .... 7.95
❑16, Jul 2005 .... 7.95
❑17, Aug 2005 .... 7.95
❑18, Sep 2005 .... 7.95
❑19, Oct 2005 .... 7.95

Ruse
CrossGen

❑1, Nov 2001 .... 2.95
❑2, Dec 2001 .... 2.95
❑3, Jan 2002 .... 2.95
❑4, Feb 2002 .... 2.95
❑5, Mar 2002 .... 2.95
❑6, Apr 2002 .... 2.95
❑7, May 2002 .... 2.95
❑8, Jun 2002 .... 2.95
❑9, Jul 2002 .... 2.95
❑10, Aug 2002 .... 2.95
❑11, Sep 2002 .... 2.95
❑12, Oct 2002 .... 2.95
❑13, Nov 2002 .... 2.95
❑14, Dec 2002 .... 2.95
❑15, Jan 2003 .... 2.95
❑16, Feb 2003 .... 2.95
❑17, Mar 2003 .... 2.95
❑18, Apr 2003 .... 2.95
❑19, May 2003 .... 2.95
❑20, Jun 2003 .... 2.95
❑21, Jul 2003 .... 2.95
❑22, Aug 2003 .... 2.95
❑23, Sep 2003 .... 2.95
❑24, Nov 2003 .... 2.95
❑25, Nov 2003 .... 2.95
❑26, Jan 2004; Final issue 2.95

Ruse: Archard's Agents: Deadly Dare
CrossGen

❑1, Apr 2004 .... 2.95

Ruse: Archard's Agents: Pugilistic Pete
CrossGen

❑1, Nov 2003 .... 2.95

Rush City
DC

❑1, Sep 2006 .... 2.99
❑2, Nov 2006 .... 2.99
❑3, Feb 2007 .... 2.99

Rush Limbaugh Must Die
Boneyard

❑1, Nov 1993, b&w; NN; Adult 5.00

Rust
Now

❑1, Jul 1987 .... 2.00
❑2, Aug 1987 .... 2.00
❑3, Sep 1987 .... 2.00
❑4, Nov 1987 .... 2.00
❑5, Dec 1987 .... 2.00
❑6, Jan 1988 .... 2.00
❑7, Feb 1988 .... 2.00
❑8, Mar 1988 .... 2.00
❑9, Apr 1988 .... 2.00
❑10, May 1988 .... 2.00
❑11, Jul 1988 .... 2.00
❑12, Aug 1988; Terminator preview 2.00
❑13, Sep 1988 .... 2.00

Rust
Now

❑1, Feb 1989 .... 2.00
❑2, Mar 1989 .... 2.00
❑3, Apr 1989 .... 2.00
❑4, May 1989 .... 2.00
❑5, Jun 1989 .... 2.00
❑6, Aug 1989 .... 2.00
❑7, Sep 1989 .... 2.00

Rust
Adventure

❑1, Apr 1992, Adventure Comics 2.95
❑1/Ltd., Apr 1992; limited edition; Cardstock cover; rust-colored foil logo 4.95
❑2, Jun 1992 .... 2.95
❑3, Aug 1992 .... 2.95
❑4, Sep 1992 .... 2.95

Rust
Caliber

❑1 .... 2.95
❑2 .... 2.95

Ruule: Ganglords of Chinatown
Beckett

❑1, Nov 2003 .... 2.99
❑2, Dec 2003 .... 2.99
❑3, Jan 2004 .... 2.99
❑4, Feb 2004 .... 2.99
❑5, Mar 2004 .... 2.99

Saban Powerhouse
Acclaim

❑1, ca. 1997; digest; Power Rangers Turbo, Masked Rider, Samurai Pizza Cats; no indicia 4.50
❑2, ca. 1997; digest; Power Rangers Turbo, Masked Rider, Samurai Pizza Cats, BettleBorgs 4.50

Saban Presents Power Rangers Turbo vs. Beetleborgs Metallix
Acclaim

❑1, ca. 1997; digest; NN 4.50

Sabina
Fantagraphics / Eros

❑1 .... 2.95
❑2 .... 2.95
❑3, May 1994; b&w 2.95
❑4 .... 2.95
❑5 .... 2.95
❑6 .... 2.95
❑7, Jul 1996 .... 2.95

Sable
First

❑1, Mar 1988 .... 2.00
❑2, Apr 1988 .... 2.00
❑3, May 1988 .... 2.00
❑4, Jun 1988 .... 2.00
❑5, Jul 1988 .... 2.00
❑6, Aug 1988 .... 2.00
❑7, Sep 1988 .... 2.00
❑8, Oct 1988 .... 2.00
❑9, Nov 1988 .... 2.00
❑10, Dec 1988 .... 2.00
❑11, Jan 1989 .... 2.00
❑12, Feb 1989 .... 2.00
❑13, Mar 1989 .... 2.00
❑14, Apr 1989 .... 2.00
❑15, May 1989 .... 2.00
❑16, Jun 1989 .... 2.00
❑17, Jul 1989 .... 2.00
❑18, Aug 1989 .... 2.00
❑19, Sep 1989 .... 2.00
❑20, Oct 1989 .... 2.00
❑21, Nov 1989 .... 2.00
❑22, Dec 1989 .... 2.00
❑23, Jan 1990 .... 2.00
❑24, Feb 1990 .... 2.00
❑25, Mar 1990 .... 2.00
❑26, Apr 1990 .... 2.00
❑27, May 1990 .... 2.00

Sable
First

❑1, Mar 1990, MGr (w); MGr (a); Reprints Jon Sable, Freelance #1 .... 2.00
❑2, Apr 1990, MGr (w); MGr (a); Reprints 2.00
❑3, May 1990, MGr (w); MGr (a); Reprints 2.00
❑4, Jun 1990, MGr (w); MGr (a); Reprints 2.00
❑5, Jul 1990, MGr (w); MGr (a); Reprints 2.00
❑6, Aug 1990, MGr (w); MGr (a); Reprints 2.00
❑7, Sep 1990, MGr (w); MGr (a); Reprints 2.00
❑8, Oct 1990, MGr (w); MGr (a); Reprints 2.00
❑9, Nov 1990, MGr (w); MGr (a); Reprints 2.00
❑10, Dec 1990, MGr (w); MGr (a); Reprints 2.00

Sable & Fortune
Marvel

❑1, Mar 2006 .... 2.99
❑2, Mar 2006 .... 2.99
❑3, Jun 2006 .... 2.99
❑4, Jun 2006 .... 2.99

Sabra Blade
Draculina

❑1, Dec 1994, b&w 2.50
❑1/Variant, Dec 1994, b&w; alternate two-color cover 2.50

Sabre
Eclipse

❑1, Aug 1982; PG (c); PG, CV (a); 1: Sabre; Sabre: Reprint from Sabre Graphic Novel; Morrigan Tales 2.50
❑2, Oct 1982; PG (c); PG, CV (a); Sabre: Reprint from Sabre Graphic Novel; Morrigan Tales 2.00
❑3, Dec 1982; TS, PG (a); Sabre; Blackstar Blood 2.00
❑4, Mar 1983; Sabre; The Incredible Seven 2.00
❑5, Jul 1983; Sabre; The Incredible Seven 2.00
❑6, Oct 1983; Sabre; The Incredible Seven 2.00
❑7, Dec 1983; Sabre; Milissa Siren 2.00
❑8, Feb 1984; Sabre; Milissa Siren 2.00
❑9, Apr 1984; Sabre; Crimson Dawn 2.00
❑10, Jun 1984; MR (c); Sabre; Crimson Dawn 1.75
❑11, Aug 1984 GC (c) 1.75
❑12, Jan 1985; Sabre; Crimson Dawn 1.75
❑13, Apr 1985 .... 1.75
❑14, Aug 1985 .... 1.75

Sabre: 20th Anniversary Edition
Image

❑1, ca. 1998 .... 12.95

Sabretooth
Marvel

❑1, Aug 1993; Die-cut cover 3.00
❑2, Sep 1993 .... 3.00
❑3, Oct 1993; A: Mystique. cardstock cover 3.00
❑4, Nov 1993 .... 3.00
❑Special 1, Jan 1995; Special edition; MG (c); enhanced wraparound cover 4.95

Other grades: Multiply price above by 5/6 for VF/NM • 2/3 for VERY FINE • 1/3 for FINE • 1/5 for VERY GOOD • 1/8 for GOOD

Sea Devils

Quartet investigates underwater weirdness
©DC

Searchers

Descendants of lit characters form team
©Caliber

Second Life of Doctor Mirage

Slain psychic continues work after death
©Valiant

Secret Origins (2nd Series)

Precursor to Secret Files and Origins
©DC

Secret Six

Cover of #1 is story's splash page
©DC

N-MINT

Sabretooth
Marvel

❑1, Jan 1998, Prestige format one-shot. 5.99

Sabretooth
Marvel

❑1 2004 2.99
❑2 2.99
❑3 2.99
❑4 2005 2.99

Sabretooth Classic
Marvel

❑1, May 1994, reprints Power Man & Iron Fist #66 2.00
❑2, Jun 1994, KGa (a); reprints Power Man & Iron Fist #78 1.50
❑3, Jul 1994, reprints Power Man & Iron Fist #84 1.50
❑4, Aug 1994, reprints Peter Parker, The Spectacular Spider-Man #116 1.50
❑5, Sep 1994, PD (w); RB, BMc (a); reprints Peter Parker, The Spectacular Spider-Man #119 1.50
❑6, Oct 1994, reprints X-Factor #10 1.50
❑7, Nov 1994, SB (a); reprints The Mighty Thor #374 1.50
❑8, Dec 1994, reprints Power Pack #27. 1.50
❑9, Jan 1995, reprints Uncanny X-Men #212 1.50
❑10, Feb 1995, reprints Uncanny X-Men #213 1.50
❑11, Mar 1995, KJ (c); SB (a); reprints Daredevil #238 1.50
❑12, Apr 1995, reprints back-up stories from Classic X-Men #10 and Marvel Super-Heroes (no issue given) 1.50
❑13, May 1995, reprints Uncanny X-Men #219 1.50
❑14, Jun 1995, reprints Uncanny X-Men #221 1.50
❑15, Jul 1995, reprints Uncanny X-Men #222 1.50

Sabretooth: Mary Shelley Overdrive
Marvel

❑1, Aug 2002 2.99
❑2, Sep 2002 2.99
❑3, Oct 2002 2.99
❑4, Nov 2002 2.99

Sabrina
Archie

❑1, May 1997, DDC (c); DDC (a); Photo worked into cover art 2.50
❑2, Jun 1997, Photo worked into cover art 2.00
❑3, Jul 1997, Photo worked into cover art 2.00
❑4, Aug 1997, Photo worked into cover art 1.50
❑5, Sep 1997, Photo worked into cover art 1.50
❑6, Oct 1997, Photo worked into cover art 1.50
❑7, Nov 1997, Photo worked into cover art 1.50
❑8, Dec 1997, Photo worked into cover art 1.50
❑9, Jan 1998, Photo worked into cover art 1.75
❑10, Feb 1998, Photo worked into cover art 1.75
❑11, Mar 1998, Photo worked into cover art 1.75
❑12, Apr 1998, Photo worked into cover art 1.75
❑13, May 1998, Photo worked into cover art 1.75

N-MINT

❑14, Jun 1998, Photo worked into cover art 1.75
❑15, Jul 1998, Photo worked into cover art 1.75
❑16, Aug 1998, Photo worked into cover art 1.75
❑17, Sep 1998, A: Josie & the Pussycats. Photo worked into cover art 1.75
❑18, Oct 1998, Photo worked into cover art 1.75
❑19, Nov 1998, DDC (a); Photo worked into cover art; back to the '60s 1.75
❑20, Dec 1998, Photo worked into cover art 1.75
❑21, Jan 1999, Photo worked into cover art 1.75
❑22, Feb 1999, Photo worked into cover art 1.75
❑23, Mar 1999, Photo worked into cover art (hidden in crowd) 1.75
❑24, Apr 1999, Photo is inset on cover.. 1.79
❑25, May 1999, Photo worked into cover art 1.79
❑26, Jun 1999, Photo is inset on cover. 1.79
❑27, Jul 1999, Photo is inset on cover.. 1.79
❑28, Aug 1999, A: Sonic. Photo is inset on cover; continues in Sonic Super Special #10 1.79
❑29, Sep 1999, Photo is inset on cover. 1.79
❑30, Oct 1999, Photo is inset on cover.. 1.79
❑31, Nov 1999, Photo is inset on cover. 1.79
❑32, Dec 1999, DDC (c); DDC (a); Photo appears in inset 1.79

Sabrina
Archie

❑1, Jan 2000, based on the animated series 1.99
❑2, Feb 2000 1.99
❑3, Mar 2000 1.99
❑4, Apr 2000 1.99
❑5, May 2000 1.99
❑6, Jun 2000 1.99
❑7, Jul 2000 1.99
❑8, Aug 2000 1.99
❑9, Sep 2000 1.99
❑10, Oct 2000 1.99
❑11, Nov 2000 1.99
❑12, Dec 2000 1.99
❑13, Jan 2001 1.99
❑14, Feb 2001 1.99
❑15, Mar 2001 1.99
❑16, Apr 2001 1.99
❑17, May 2001 1.99
❑18, Jun 2001 1.99
❑19, Jul 2001 1.99
❑20, Aug 2001 1.99
❑21, Sep 2001 1.99
❑22, Oct 2001 1.99
❑23, Nov 2001 1.99
❑24, Dec 2001 1.99
❑25, Jan 2002 1.99
❑26, Jan 2002 1.99
❑27, Feb 2002 1.99
❑28, Mar 2002 1.99
❑29, Apr 2002 1.99
❑30, May 2002 1.99
❑31, Jun 2002 1.99
❑32, Jul 2002 1.99

N-MINT

❑33, Aug 2002 1.99
❑34, Sep 2002 1.99
❑35, Oct 2002 1.99
❑36, Nov 2002 1.99
❑37, Dec 2002 1.99
❑38, Jan 2003 1.99
❑39, Jan 2003 2.19
❑40, Feb 2003 2.19
❑41, Mar 2003 2.19
❑42, Apr 2003 2.19
❑43, May 2003 2.19
❑44, Jun 2003 2.19
❑45, Jul 2003 2.19
❑46, Aug 2003 2.19
❑47, Sep 2003 2.19
❑48, Oct 2003 2.19
❑49, Nov 2003 2.19
❑50, Dec 2003 2.19
❑51, Dec 2003 2.19
❑52, Jan 2004 2.19
❑53, Feb 2004 2.19
❑54, Mar 2004 2.19
❑55, Apr 2004 2.19
❑56, May 2004 2.19
❑57, Jul 2004, Listed as Sabrina the Teenage Witch on cover and indicia 2.19
❑58, Aug 2004, Begins Archie Manga series; Listed as Sabrina the Teenage Witch on cover and indicia 2.19
❑59, Sep 2004, Listed as Sabrina the Teenage Witch on cover and indicia 2.19
❑60, Oct 2004, Listed as Sabrina the Teenage Witch on cover and indicia 2.19
❑61, Nov 2004, Listed as Sabrina the Teenage Witch on cover and indicia 2.19
❑62, Jan 2005, Listed as Sabrina the Teenage Witch on cover and indicia 2.19
❑63, Feb 2005; Listed as Sabrina the Teenage Witch on cover and indicia 2.19
❑64, Mar 2005; Listed as Sabrina the Teenage Witch on cover and indicia 2.19
❑65, Apr 2005; Listed as Sabrina the Teenage Witch on cover and indicia 2.19
❑66, May 2005; Listed as Sabrina the Teenage Witch on cover and indicia 2.19
❑67, Aug 2005; Listed as Sabrina the Teenage Witch on cover and indicia, Josie & The Pussycats cover/ appearance 2.25
❑68, Sep 2005 2.25
❑69, Oct 2005 2.25
❑70, Nov 2005 2.25
❑71, Dec 2005 2.25
❑72, Jan 2006 2.25
❑73, Feb 2006 2.25
❑74, May 2006 2.25
❑75, Jun 2006 2.25
❑76, Aug 2006 2.25
❑77, Aug 2006 2.25
❑78, Oct 2006 2.25
❑79, Nov 2006 2.25
❑80, Jan 2007, Includes 3-D Heroscape glasses; Includes Teen Titans: Sparktop mini-comic 2.25
❑81, Feb 2007 2.25
❑82 2.50
❑83 2.50
❑84 2.50

Other grades: Multiply price above by 5/6 for VF/NM • 2/3 for VERY FINE • 1/3 for FINE • 1/5 for VERY GOOD • 1/8 for GOOD

	N-MINT
❑85	2.50
❑86	2.50
❑87	2.50
❑88	2.50
❑89	2.50
❑90	2.50
❑91	2.50
❑92	2.50
❑93	2.50
❑94	2.50
❑95	2.50
❑96	2.50
❑97	2.50
❑98	2.50
❑99	2.50
❑100	2.50
❑101	2.50
❑102	2.50

Sabrina Online
Vision

	N-MINT
❑2	3.50

Sabrina the Teenage Witch
Archie

	N-MINT
❑1, Apr 1971, Giant-size	45.00
❑2, Jul 1971, Giant-size	20.00
❑3, Sep 1971, Giant-size	12.00
❑4, Dec 1971, Giant-size	12.00
❑5, Feb 1972, Giant-size	12.00
❑6, Jun 1972, Giant-size	10.00
❑7, Aug 1972, Giant-size	10.00
❑8, Sep 1972, Giant-size	10.00
❑9, Oct 1972, Giant-size	10.00
❑10, Feb 1973, Giant-size	10.00
❑11, Apr 1973, Giant-size	8.00
❑12, Jun 1973, Giant-size	8.00
❑13, Aug 1973, Giant-size	8.00
❑14, Sep 1973, Giant-size	8.00
❑15, Oct 1973, Giant-size	8.00
❑16, Dec 1973, Giant-size	8.00
❑17, Feb 1974, Giant-size	8.00
❑18, Apr 1974	6.00
❑19, Jun 1974	6.00
❑20, Aug 1974	6.00
❑21, Sep 1974	5.00
❑22, Oct 1974	5.00
❑23, Feb 1975	5.00
❑24, Apr 1975	5.00
❑25, Jun 1975	5.00
❑26, Aug 1975	5.00
❑27, Sep 1975	5.00
❑28, Oct 1975	5.00
❑29, Dec 1975	5.00
❑30, Feb 1976	5.00
❑31, Apr 1976	4.00
❑32, Jun 1976	4.00
❑33, Aug 1976	4.00
❑34, Sep 1976	4.00
❑35, Oct 1976, A: Betty. A: Ethel. A: Jughead. A: Veronica	4.00
❑36, Dec 1977	4.00
❑37, Feb 1977	4.00
❑38, May 1977	4.00
❑39, Jun 1977	4.00
❑40, Aug 1977	4.00
❑41, Sep 1977	4.00
❑42, Oct 1977	4.00
❑43, Dec 1977	4.00
❑44, Feb 1978	4.00
❑45, May 1978	4.00
❑46, Jun 1978	4.00
❑47, Aug 1978	4.00
❑48, Sep 1978	4.00
❑49, Oct 1978	4.00
❑50, Dec 1978	4.00
❑51, Feb 1979	3.00
❑52, May 1979	3.00
❑53, Jun 1979	3.00
❑54, Aug 1979	3.00
❑55, Sep 1979	3.00
❑56, Oct 1979	3.00
❑57, Dec 1979	3.00
❑58, Feb 1980	3.00
❑59, Apr 1980	3.00
❑60, Jun 1980	3.00
❑61, Aug 1980	2.00
❑62, Sep 1980	2.00
❑63, Oct 1980	2.00
❑64, Dec 1980	2.00
❑65, Feb 1981	2.00
❑66, Apr 1981	2.00
❑67, Jun 1981	2.00
❑68, Aug 1981	2.00
❑69, Oct 1981	2.00
❑70, Dec 1981	2.00
❑71, Feb 1982	2.00
❑72, Apr 1982	2.00
❑73, Jun 1982	2.00
❑74, Aug 1982	2.00
❑75, Oct 1982	2.00
❑76, Dec 1982	2.00
❑77, Feb 1983	2.00
❑Holiday 1, ca. 1993, "Sabrina's Halloween Spoook-Tacular"	3.00
❑Holiday 2, ca. 1994	2.00
❑Holiday 3, ca. 1995	2.00

Sabrina the Teenage Witch
Archie

	N-MINT
❑1, ca. 1996, One-shot	2.00

Sachs & Violens
Marvel / Epic

	N-MINT
❑1, Nov 1993; GP (c); PD (w); GP (a); Embossed cover	3.00
❑1/Platinum, Nov 1993; Platinum promotional edition; GP (c); PD (w); GP (a); Embossed cover	3.00
❑2, May 1994; GP (c); PD (w); GP (a); Includes trading card	2.25
❑3, Jun 1994; GP (c); PD (w); GP (a); Sex, nudity	2.25
❑4, Jul 1994; GP (c); PD (w); GP (a); Includes trading card	2.25

Sacrificed Trees
Mansion

	N-MINT
❑1; ca. 2004	3.00

Sade/Razor
London Night

	N-MINT
❑1/2nd; Encore Edition; Adult	3.00

Sad Sack
Harvey

	N-MINT
❑123, Nov 1961	2.50
❑124, Dec 1961	2.50
❑125, Jan 1962	2.50
❑126, Feb 1962	2.50
❑127, Mar 1962	2.50
❑128, Apr 1962	2.50
❑129, May 1962	2.50
❑130, Jun 1962	2.50
❑131, Jul 1962	2.50
❑132, Aug 1962	2.50
❑133, Sep 1962	2.50
❑134, Oct 1962	2.50
❑135, Nov 1962	2.50
❑136, Dec 1962	2.50
❑137, Jan 1963	2.50
❑138, Feb 1963	2.50
❑139, Mar 1963	2.50
❑140, Apr 1963	2.50
❑141, May 1963	2.50
❑142, Jun 1963	2.50
❑143, Jul 1963	2.50
❑144, Aug 1963	2.50
❑145, Sep 1963	2.50
❑146, Oct 1963	2.50
❑147, Nov 1963	2.50
❑148, Dec 1963	2.50
❑149, Jan 1964	2.50
❑150, Feb 1964	2.50
❑151, Mar 1964	2.00
❑152, Apr 1964	2.00
❑153, May 1964	2.00
❑154, Jun 1964	2.00
❑155, Jul 1964	2.00
❑156, Aug 1964	2.00
❑157, Sep 1964	2.00
❑158, Oct 1964	2.00
❑159, Nov 1964	2.00
❑160, Dec 1964	2.00
❑161, Jan 1965	2.00
❑162, Feb 1965	2.00
❑163, Mar 1965	2.00
❑164, Apr 1965	2.00
❑165, May 1965	2.00
❑166, Jun 1965	2.00
❑167, Jul 1965	2.00
❑168, Aug 1965	2.00
❑169, Sep 1965	2.00
❑170, Oct 1965	2.00
❑171, Nov 1965	2.00
❑172, Dec 1965	2.00
❑173, Jan 1966	2.00
❑174, Feb 1966	2.00
❑175, Mar 1966	2.00
❑176, Apr 1966	2.00
❑177, May 1966	2.00
❑178, Jun 1966	2.00
❑179, Jul 1966	2.00
❑180, Aug 1966	2.00
❑181, Sep 1966	2.00
❑182, Oct 1966	2.00
❑183, Nov 1966	2.00
❑184, Dec 1966	2.00
❑185, Jan 1967	2.00
❑186, Feb 1967	2.00
❑187, Mar 1967	2.00
❑188, Apr 1967	2.00
❑189, May 1967	2.00
❑190, Jun 1967	2.00
❑191, Jul 1967	2.00
❑192, Aug 1967	2.00
❑193, Sep 1967	2.00
❑194, Oct 1967	2.00
❑195, Nov 1967	2.00
❑196, Dec 1967	2.00
❑197, Jan 1968	2.00
❑198, Mar 1968	2.00
❑199, May 1968	2.00
❑200, Jul 1968	2.00
❑201, Sep 1968	1.50
❑202, Oct 1968	1.50
❑203, Nov 1968	1.50
❑204, Jan 1969	1.50
❑205, Mar 1969	1.50
❑206, May 1969	1.50
❑207, Jul 1969	1.50
❑208, Sep 1969	1.50
❑209, Oct 1969	1.50
❑210, Nov 1969	1.50
❑211, Jan 1970	1.50
❑212, Mar 1970	1.50
❑213, May 1970	1.50
❑214, Jul 1970	1.50
❑215, Sep 1970	1.50
❑216, Oct 1970	1.50
❑217, Nov 1970	1.50
❑218, Jan 1971	1.50
❑219, Mar 1971	1.50
❑220, May 1971	1.50
❑221, Jul 1971	1.50
❑222, Sep 1971	1.50
❑223, Nov 1971	1.50
❑224, Jan 1972	1.50
❑225, Mar 1972	1.50
❑226, May 1972	1.50
❑227, Jul 1972	1.50
❑228, Sep 1972	1.50
❑229, Nov 1972	1.50
❑230, Jan 1973	1.50
❑231, Mar 1973	1.50
❑232, May 1973	1.50
❑233, Jul 1973	1.50
❑234, Sep 1973	1.50
❑235, Nov 1973	1.50
❑236, Jan 1974	1.50
❑237, Mar 1974	1.50
❑238, May 1974	1.50
❑239, Jul 1974	1.50
❑240, Sep 1974	1.50
❑241, Nov 1974	1.50
❑242, Jan 1975	1.50
❑243, Mar 1975	1.50
❑244, May 1975	1.50
❑245, Jul 1975	1.50
❑246, Sep 1975	1.50
❑247, Nov 1975	1.50
❑248, Jan 1976	1.50
❑249, Mar 1976	1.50
❑250, May 1976	1.50
❑251, Jul 1976	1.50
❑252, Sep 1976	1.50

Other grades: Multiply price above by 5/6 for VF/NM • 2/3 for VERY FINE • 1/3 for FINE • 1/5 for VERY GOOD • 1/8 for GOOD

Secret Society of Super-Villains

Super-villains form mutual aid group
©DC

Secret Wars II

Beyonder returns, seeking humanity
©Marvel

Seduction of the Innocent

Horror reprints mock title of expose
©Eclipse

Sensational Spider-Man

Web of Spidey subscribers' substitution
©Marvel

Sentry

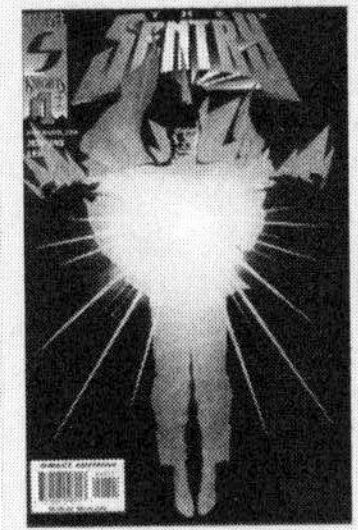

Imaginary precursor to Fantastic Four
©Marvel

	N-MINT
❑253, Nov 1976	1.50
❑254, Jan 1977	1.50
❑255, Mar 1977	1.50
❑256, May 1977	1.50
❑257, Jul 1977	1.50
❑258, Sep 1977	1.50
❑259, Nov 1977	1.50
❑260, Jan 1978	1.50
❑261, Mar 1978	1.50
❑262, May 1978	1.50
❑263, Jul 1978	1.50
❑264, Sep 1978	1.50
❑265, Nov 1978	1.50
❑266, Jan 1979	1.50
❑267, Mar 1979	1.50
❑268, May 1979	1.50
❑269, Jul 1979	1.50
❑270, Sep 1979	1.50
❑271, Nov 1979	1.50
❑272, Jan 1980	1.50
❑273, Mar 1980	1.50
❑274, May 1980	1.50
❑275, Jul 1980	1.50
❑276, Sep 1980	1.50
❑277, Nov 1980	1.50
❑278, Jan 1981	1.50
❑279, Mar 1981	1.50
❑280, May 1981	1.50
❑281, Jul 1981	1.50
❑282, Sep 1981	1.50
❑283, Nov 1981	1.50
❑284, Jan 1982	1.50
❑285, Mar 1982	1.50
❑286, May 1982	1.50
❑287, Jul 1982, Last Harvey Issue	1.50
❑288, ca. 1992	2.75
❑289, ca. 1992	2.75
❑290, ca. 1992, b&w	1.50
❑291, ca. 1993	1.50
❑292, ca. 1993; Fall 2005; Lorne-Harvey	9.95
❑293, ca. 1993	1.50
❑3D 1, ca. 1954; Harvey 3-D Hits	125.00

Sad Sack & The Sarge
Harvey

	N-MINT
❑28, Dec 1961	12.00
❑29, Feb 1962	12.00
❑30, Apr 1962	12.00
❑31, Jun 1962	9.00
❑32, Aug 1962	9.00
❑33, Oct 1962	9.00
❑34, Dec 1962	9.00
❑35, Feb 1963	9.00
❑36, Apr 1963	9.00
❑37, Jun 1963	9.00
❑38, Aug 1963	9.00
❑39, Oct 1963	9.00
❑40, Dec 1963	9.00
❑41, Feb 1964	7.00
❑42, Apr 1964	7.00
❑43, Jun 1964	7.00
❑44, Aug 1964	7.00
❑45, Oct 1964	7.00
❑46, Dec 1964	7.00
❑47, Feb 1965	7.00
❑48, Apr 1965	7.00
❑49, Jun 1965	7.00
❑50, Aug 1965	6.00
❑51, Oct 1965	6.00
❑52, Dec 1965	6.00
❑53, Feb 1966	6.00
❑54, Apr 1966	6.00
❑55, Jun 1966	6.00
❑56, Aug 1966	6.00
❑57, Sep 1966	6.00
❑58, Oct 1966	6.00
❑59, Dec 1966	6.00
❑60, Feb 1967	6.00
❑61, Apr 1967	5.00
❑62, Jun 1967	5.00
❑63, Aug 1967	5.00
❑64, Oct 1967	5.00
❑65, Dec 1967	5.00
❑66, Feb 1968	5.00
❑67, Apr 1968	5.00
❑68, Jun 1968	5.00
❑69, Aug 1968	5.00
❑70, Oct 1968	5.00
❑71, Dec 1968	5.00
❑72, Jan 1969	5.00
❑73 1969	5.00
❑74, May 1969	5.00
❑75, Jun 1969	5.00
❑76, Jul 1969	5.00
❑77, Sep 1969	5.00
❑78, Oct 1969	5.00
❑79, Dec 1969	5.00
❑80, Feb 1970	5.00
❑81, Apr 1970	3.00
❑82, Jun 1970	3.00
❑83, Aug 1970	3.00
❑84, Oct 1970	3.00
❑85, Nov 1970	3.00
❑86, Jan 1971	3.00
❑87, Feb 1971	3.00
❑88, Apr 1971	3.00
❑89, Jun 1971	3.00
❑90, Aug 1971	3.00
❑91, Oct 1971; Giant size; A: The General. A: Slob Slobinski	4.00
❑92, Dec 1971; Giant size	4.00
❑93, Feb 1972; Giant size	4.00
❑94, Apr 1972; Giant size	4.00
❑95, Jun 1972; Giant size	4.00
❑96, Aug 1972; Giant size	4.00
❑97, Oct 1972	3.00
❑98, Dec 1972	3.00
❑99, Feb 1973	3.00
❑100, Apr 1973	3.00
❑101, Jun 1973	2.00
❑102, Aug 1973	2.00
❑103, Oct 1973	2.00
❑104, Dec 1973	2.00
❑105, Feb 1974	2.00
❑106, Apr 1974	2.00
❑107, Jun 1974	2.00
❑108, Aug 1974	2.00
❑109, Oct 1974	2.00
❑110, Dec 1974	2.00
❑111, Feb 1975	2.00
❑112, Apr 1975	2.00
❑113, Jun 1975	2.00
❑114, Aug 1975	2.00
❑115, Oct 1975	2.00
❑116, Dec 1975	2.00
❑117, Feb 1976	2.00
❑118, Apr 1976	2.00
❑119, Jun 1976	2.00
❑120, Aug 1976	2.00
❑121, Oct 1976	2.00
❑122, Dec 1976	2.00
❑123, Feb 1977	2.00
❑124, Apr 1977	2.00
❑125, Jun 1977	2.00
❑126, Aug 1977	2.00
❑127, Oct 1977	2.00
❑128, Dec 1977	2.00
❑129, Feb 1978	2.00
❑130, Apr 1978	2.00
❑131, Jun 1978	2.00
❑132, Aug 1978	2.00
❑133, Oct 1978	2.00
❑134, Dec 1978	2.00
❑135, Feb 1979	2.00
❑136, Apr 1979	2.00
❑137, Jun 1979	2.00
❑138, Aug 1979	2.00
❑139, Oct 1979	2.00
❑140, Dec 1979	2.00
❑141, Feb 1980	2.00
❑142, Apr 1980	2.00
❑143, Jun 1980	2.00
❑144, Aug 1980	2.00
❑145, Oct 1980	2.00
❑146, Dec 1980	2.00
❑147, Feb 1981	2.00
❑148, Apr 1981	2.00
❑149, Jun 1981	2.00
❑150, Aug 1981	2.00
❑151, Oct 1981	2.00
❑152, Dec 1981	2.00
❑153, Feb 1982	2.00
❑154, Apr 1982	2.00
❑155, Jun 1982	2.00

Sad Sack Army Life Parade
Harvey

	N-MINT
❑1, Oct 1963; Giant-size	35.00
❑2, Feb 1964; Giant-size	20.00
❑3, May 1964; Giant-size	15.00
❑4, Aug 1964; Giant-size	12.00
❑5, Nov 1964; Giant-size	12.00
❑6, Feb 1965; Giant-size	10.00
❑7, May 1965; Giant-size	10.00
❑8, Aug 1965; Giant-size	10.00
❑9, Nov 1965; Giant-size	10.00
❑10, Feb 1966; Giant-size	10.00
❑11, May 1966; Giant-size	8.00
❑12, Jul 1966; Giant-size	8.00
❑13, Sep 1966; Giant-size	8.00
❑14, Oct 1966; Giant-size	8.00
❑15, Jan 1967; Giant-size	8.00
❑16, Mar 1967; Giant-size	8.00
❑17 1967; Giant-size	8.00
❑18, Nov 1967; Giant-size	8.00
❑19, Feb 1968; Giant-size	8.00
❑20, May 1968; Giant-size	8.00
❑21, Aug 1968; Giant-size	6.00

Other grades: Multiply price above by 5/6 for VF/NM • 2/3 for VERY FINE • 1/3 for FINE • 1/5 for VERY GOOD • 1/8 for GOOD

	N-MINT
❑22 1969; Giant-size	6.00
❑23, Feb 1969; Giant-size	6.00
❑24, Apr 1969; Giant-size	6.00
❑25, Aug 1969; Giant-size	6.00
❑26, Oct 1969; Giant-size	6.00
❑27, Dec 1969; Giant-size	6.00
❑28, Feb 1970; Giant-size	6.00
❑29, Apr 1970; Giant-size	6.00
❑30, Aug 1970; Giant-size	6.00
❑31, Oct 1970; Giant-size	5.00
❑32, Dec 1970; Giant-size	5.00
❑33, Feb 1971; Giant-size	5.00
❑34, Apr 1971; Giant-size	5.00
❑35, Aug 1971; Giant-size	5.00
❑36, Oct 1971; Giant-size	5.00
❑37, Dec 1971; Giant-size	5.00
❑38, Feb 1972; Giant-size	5.00
❑39, Apr 1972; Giant-size	5.00
❑40, Jun 1972; Giant-size	5.00
❑41, Aug 1972; Giant-size	4.00
❑42, Oct 1972; Giant-size	4.00
❑43, Dec 1972; Giant-size	4.00
❑44, Feb 1973; Giant-size	4.00
❑45, Apr 1973; Giant-size	4.00
❑46, Jun 1973; Giant-size	4.00
❑47, Aug 1973; Giant-size	4.00
❑48, Oct 1973; Giant-size	4.00
❑49, Dec 1973; Giant-size	4.00
❑50, Feb 1974; Giant-size	4.00
❑51, Apr 1974; Giant-size	2.50
❑52, Jun 1974; Giant-size	2.50
❑53, Aug 1974	2.50
❑54, Oct 1974	2.50
❑55, Dec 1974	2.50
❑56, Feb 1975	2.50
❑57, Apr 1975	2.50
❑58, Jul 1975	2.50
❑59, Sep 1975	2.50
❑60, Nov 1975	2.50
❑61, ca. 1976; Final Issue	2.50

Sad Sack at Home for the Holidays
Lorne-Harvey

	N-MINT
❑1, ca. 1992; Christmas cover	2.00

Sad Sack in 3-D
Blackthorne

	N-MINT
❑1, ca. 1988	2.00

Sad Sack Laugh Special
Harvey

	N-MINT
❑1, Win 1958; Giant-size	90.00
❑2, Spr 1959; Giant-size	45.00
❑3, Sum 1959; Giant-size	25.00
❑4, Apr 1960; Giant-size	25.00
❑5, Jul 1960; Giant-size	25.00
❑6, Oct 1960; Giant-size	25.00
❑7, Jan 1960; Giant-size	25.00
❑8, Apr 1960; Giant-size	25.00
❑9, Jul 1961; Giant-size	25.00
❑10, Oct 1961; Giant-size	25.00
❑11, Jan 1962; Giant-size	20.00
❑12, Apr 1962; Giant-size	20.00
❑13, Jul 1962; Giant-size	20.00
❑14, Oct 1962; Giant-size	20.00
❑15, Jan 1963; Giant-size	20.00
❑16, Apr 1963; Giant-size	20.00
❑17, Jul 1963; Giant-size	20.00
❑18, Oct 1963; Giant-size	20.00
❑19, Jan 1964; Giant-size	20.00
❑20, Apr 1964; Giant-size	20.00
❑21, Jul 1964; Giant-size	15.00
❑22, Sep 1964; Giant-size	15.00
❑23, Dec 1964; Giant-size	15.00
❑24, Mar 1965; Giant-size	15.00
❑25, Jun 1965; Giant-size	15.00
❑26, Sep 1965; Giant-size	15.00
❑27, Dec 1965; Giant-size	15.00
❑28, Mar 1966; Giant-size	15.00
❑29, Jun 1966; Giant-size	15.00
❑30, Aug 1966; Giant-size	15.00
❑31 1966; Giant-size	12.00
❑32, Oct 1966; Giant-size	12.00
❑33, Dec 1966; Giant-size	12.00
❑34, Feb 1967; Giant-size	12.00
❑35, Apr 1967; Giant-size	12.00
❑36, Jun 1967; Giant-size	12.00
❑37, Oct 1967; Giant-size	12.00
❑38, Nov 1967; Giant-size	12.00
❑39 1968; Giant-size	12.00
❑40, Apr 1968; Giant-size	12.00
❑41, Jun 1968; Giant-size	10.00
❑42, Aug 1968; Giant-size	10.00
❑43, Oct 1968; Giant-size	10.00
❑44, Dec 1968; Giant-size	10.00
❑45, Feb 1969; Giant-size	10.00
❑46, Apr 1969; Giant-size	10.00
❑47, May 1969; Giant-size	10.00
❑48, Jul 1969; Giant-size	10.00
❑49, Sep 1969; Giant-size	10.00
❑50, Nov 1969; Giant-size	10.00
❑51, Jan 1970; Giant-size	10.00
❑52, Mar 1970; Giant-size	10.00
❑53, May 1970; Giant-size	10.00
❑54, Jul 1970; Giant-size	10.00
❑55, Sep 1970; Giant-size	10.00
❑56, Nov 1970; Giant-size	10.00
❑57, Jan 1971; Giant-size	10.00
❑58, Mar 1971; Giant-size	10.00
❑59, May 1971; Giant-size	10.00
❑60, Jul 1971; Giant-size	10.00
❑61, Sep 1971; Giant-size	8.00
❑62, Nov 1971; Giant-size	8.00
❑63, Jan 1972; Giant-size	8.00
❑64, Mar 1972; Giant-size	8.00
❑65, May 1972; Giant-size	8.00
❑66, Jul 1972; Giant-size	8.00
❑67, Sep 1972; Giant-size	8.00
❑68, Nov 1972; Giant-size	8.00
❑69, Jan 1973; Giant-size	8.00
❑70, Mar 1973; Giant-size	8.00
❑71, May 1973; Giant-size	8.00
❑72, Jul 1973; Giant-size	8.00
❑73, Sep 1973; Giant-size	8.00
❑74, Nov 1973; Giant-size	8.00
❑75, Jan 1974; Giant-size	8.00
❑76, Mar 1974; Giant-size	8.00
❑77, May 1974; Giant-size	8.00
❑78, Jul 1974	8.00
❑79, Sep 1974	8.00
❑80, Nov 1974	8.00
❑81, Jan 1975	6.00
❑82, Mar 1975	6.00
❑83, Jun 1975	6.00
❑84, Aug 1975	6.00
❑85, Oct 1975	6.00
❑86, Dec 1975	6.00
❑87, Feb 1976	6.00
❑88, Apr 1976	6.00
❑89, Jun 1976	6.00
❑90, Aug 1976	6.00
❑91, Oct 1976	6.00
❑92, Dec 1976	6.00
❑93, Feb 1977	6.00

Sad Sack Navy, Gobs 'n' Gals
Harvey

	N-MINT
❑1, Aug 1972	12.00
❑2, Oct 1972	8.00
❑3, Dec 1972	6.00
❑4, Feb 1973	6.00
❑5, Apr 1973	6.00
❑6, Jun 1973	4.00
❑7, Aug 1973	4.00
❑8, Oct 1973	4.00

Sad Sack's Funny Friends
Harvey

	N-MINT
❑36, Nov 1961	8.00
❑37, Jan 1962	8.00
❑38, Mar 1962	8.00
❑39, May 1962	8.00
❑40, Jul 1962	8.00
❑41, Sep 1962	5.00
❑42, Nov 1962	5.00
❑43, Jan 1963	5.00
❑44, Mar 1963	5.00
❑45, May 1963	5.00
❑46, Jul 1963	5.00
❑47, Sep 1963	5.00
❑48, Nov 1963	5.00
❑49, Jan 1964	5.00
❑50, Mar 1964	5.00
❑51, May 1964	3.00
❑52, Jul 1964	3.00
❑53, Sep 1964	3.00
❑54, Nov 1964	3.00
❑55, Jan 1965	3.00
❑56, Mar 1965	3.00
❑57, May 1965	3.00
❑58, Jul 1965	3.00
❑59, Sep 1965	3.00
❑60, Nov 1965	3.00
❑61, Jan 1966	3.00
❑62, Mar 1966	3.00
❑63, May 1966	3.00
❑64 1966	3.00
❑65, Aug 1966	3.00
❑66, Oct 1966	3.00
❑67, Jan 1967	3.00
❑68, Mar 1967	3.00
❑69, May 1967	3.00
❑70 1967	3.00
❑71, Oct 1967, Featuring the General	3.00
❑72, Jan 1968	3.00
❑73, Apr 1968	3.00
❑74, Aug 1968	3.00
❑75, Oct 1968	3.00

Sad Sack U.S.A.
Harvey

	N-MINT
❑1, Nov 1972, New York	12.00
❑2, Jan 1973, Illinois	6.00
❑3, Mar 1973, Florida	6.00
❑4, May 1973, Texas	6.00
❑5, Jul 1973, Massachusetts; text feature printed out of order	6.00
❑6, Sep 1973, Washington	6.00
❑7, Nov 1973, Michigan	6.00
❑8, Oct 1974, Tennessee; Cover and indicia read Sad Sad U.S.A. Vacation .	6.00

Sad Sad Sack World
Harvey

	N-MINT
❑1, Oct 1964; Giant-size	45.00
❑2, Jan 1965; Giant-size	20.00
❑3, Apr 1965; Giant-size	20.00
❑4, Jul 1965; Giant-size	20.00
❑5, Oct 1965; Giant-size	20.00
❑6, Jan 1966; Giant-size	20.00
❑7, Apr 1966; Giant-size	20.00
❑8, Jun 1966; Giant-size	20.00
❑9, Aug 1966; Giant-size	20.00
❑10, Oct 1966; Giant-size	20.00
❑11, Dec 1966; Giant-size	15.00
❑12, Feb 1967; Giant-size	15.00
❑13, May 1967; Giant-size	15.00
❑14, Aug 1967; Giant-size	15.00
❑15, Nov 1967; Giant-size	15.00
❑16, Mar 1968; Giant-size	15.00
❑17, Jun 1968; Giant-size	15.00
❑18, Sep 1968; Giant-size	15.00
❑19, Nov 1968; Giant-size	15.00
❑20, Jan 1969; Giant-size	15.00
❑21, Apr 1969; Giant-size	15.00
❑22, Jun 1969; Giant-size	15.00
❑23, Oct 1969; Giant-size	15.00
❑24, Dec 1969; Giant-size	15.00
❑25, Mar 1970; Giant-size	15.00
❑26, Jun 1970; Giant-size	15.00
❑27, Sep 1970; Giant-size	15.00
❑28, Oct 1970; Giant-size	15.00
❑29, Dec 1970; Giant-size	15.00
❑30, Mar 1971; Giant-size	15.00
❑31, Jun 1971; Giant-size	12.00
❑32, Sep 1971; Giant-size	12.00
❑33, Oct 1971; Giant-size	12.00
❑34, Dec 1971; Giant-size	12.00
❑35, Feb 1972; Giant-size	12.00
❑36, Apr 1972; Giant-size	12.00
❑37, Jun 1972; Giant-size	12.00
❑38, Aug 1972; Giant-size	12.00
❑39, Oct 1972; Giant-size	12.00
❑39/A, Oct 1972, Giant-size; $0.35 cover price variant	12.00
❑40, Dec 1972	12.00
❑41, Feb 1973	10.00
❑42, Apr 1973	10.00
❑43, Jun 1973	10.00
❑44, Aug 1973	10.00
❑45, Oct 1973	10.00
❑46, Dec 1973	10.00

Serenity

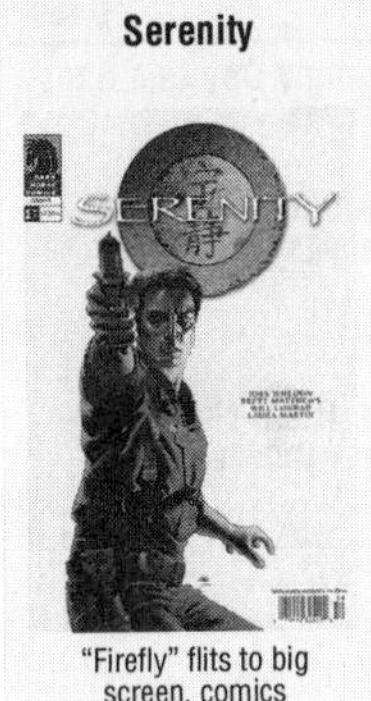

"Firefly" flits to big screen, comics

©Dark Horse

Sgt. Fury

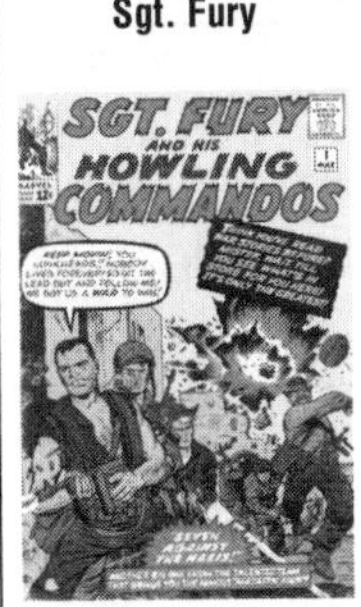

S.H.I.E.L.D. head in World War II

©Marvel

Sgt. Rock

Our Army at War acknowledges star

©DC

Sgt. Rock

Special reprints of Rock risks

©DC

Shade, The Changing Man

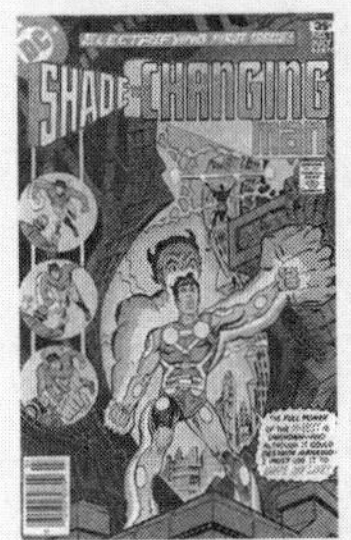

Other-dimensional traitor flees with M-vest

©DC

N-MINT

Safe Comics
Graphic Graphics

- ❑1, ca. 1998 .... 3.00
- ❑2, ca. 1999 .... 3.00

Safest Place in the World
Dark Horse

- ❑1, ca. 1993; NN 2.50

Safety-Belt Man
Sirius

- ❑1, Jun 1994, b&w 2.50
- ❑2, Oct 1994, b&w 2.50
- ❑3, Feb 1995, b&w 2.50
- ❑4, Jun 1995, b&w; color centerfold; Linsner back-up story 2.50
- ❑5, Aug 1995, b&w 2.50
- ❑6, Oct 1995, b&w 2.50

Safety-Belt Man: All Hell
Sirius

- ❑1, Jun 1996 .... 2.95
- ❑2, Jun 1996 .... 2.95
- ❑3 1996 .... 2.95
- ❑4, Sep 1996 .... 2.95
- ❑5, Jan 1997 .... 2.95
- ❑6, Aug 1997 .... 2.95

Saffire
Image

- ❑1, Apr 2000 .... 2.95
- ❑2, Dec 2000 .... 2.95
- ❑3, Feb 2001 .... 2.95

Saga
Odyssey

- ❑1, b&w 1.95

Saga of Crystar Crystal Warrior
Marvel

- ❑1, May 1983, 1&O: Crystar 2.00
- ❑2, Jul 1983, 1: Ika 1.00
- ❑3, Sep 1983, MG (c); A: Doctor Strange 1.00
- ❑4, Nov 1983, MG (c) 1.00
- ❑5, Jan 1984, MG (c); Assistant Editors' Month 1.00
- ❑6, Mar 1984, MG (c); A: Nightcrawler .. 1.00
- ❑7, May 1984, MG (c) 1.00
- ❑8, Jul 1984, MG (c) 1.00
- ❑9, Sep 1984, MG (c) 1.00
- ❑10, Nov 1984, MG (c) 1.00
- ❑11, Feb 1985, Double-size; MG (c); A: Alpha Flight. Final Issue 1.00

Saga of Ra's Al Ghul
DC

- ❑1, Jan 1988; Batman: Reprints from Detective Comics # 411 and Batman #232; El Diablo: Reprint from Weird Western #13 .... 2.50
- ❑2, Feb 1988; Reprints from Batman #345, 240 and Detective Comics #395 .... 2.50
- ❑3, Mar 1988; Batman: Reprints from Batman #242-243; Reprint from House of Mystery #179 .... 2.50
- ❑4, Apr 1988; Reprints from Batman #244, 245 and Detective Comics #410 .... 2.50

Saga of Seven Suns
DC / Wildstorm

- ❑1, ca. 2004 .... 24.95

N-MINT

Saga of Squadron Supreme
Marvel

- ❑1, Mar 2006, Based on Supreme Power #1-18, Supreme Power: Nighthawk #1-6, and Supreme Power: Hyperion #1-5 .... 3.99

Saga of the Man Elf
Trident

- ❑1, Aug 1989 .... 2.25
- ❑2 1989 .... 2.25
- ❑3, Mar 1989 .... 2.25
- ❑4 1990 .... 2.25
- ❑5 1990 .... 2.25

Saga of the Original Human Torch
Marvel

- ❑1, Apr 1990; O: The Human Torch I (android) 1.50
- ❑2, May 1990; O: Toro 1.50
- ❑3, Jun 1990; D: Hitler 1.50
- ❑4, Jul 1990 .... 1.50

Saga of the Sub-Mariner
Marvel

- ❑1, Nov 1988; RB (c); RB (a); O: Sub-Mariner 1.50
- ❑2, Dec 1988 .... 1.50
- ❑3, Jan 1989 .... 1.50
- ❑4, Feb 1989 A: Human Torch 1.50
- ❑5, Mar 1989 A: Human Torch. A: Captain America. A: Invaders 1.50
- ❑6, Apr 1989 A: Torch. A: Human Torch. A: Captain America. A: Invaders 1.50
- ❑7, May 1989 A: Fantastic Four 1.50
- ❑8, Jun 1989 A: Fantastic Four. A: Avengers 1.50
- ❑9, Jul 1989 A: Fantastic Four. A: Avengers 1.50
- ❑10, Aug 1989 .... 1.50
- ❑11, Sep 1989 .... 1.50
- ❑12, Oct 1989 .... 1.50

Saga of the Swamp Thing
DC

- ❑1, May 1982, TY (c); TY, DS (a); O: Swamp Thing; Continued from Swamp Thing (1st Series); Phantom Stranger 3.00
- ❑2, Jun 1982, TY, DS (a); Photo cover; Swamp Thing; Phantom Stranger 2.00
- ❑3, Jul 1982, TY, DS (a); Swamp Thing; Phantom Stranger 2.00
- ❑4, Aug 1982, TY, TD (a); Phantom Stranger back-up 2.00
- ❑5, Sep 1982, TY (c); TY (a); Phantom Strange back-up 2.00
- ❑6, Oct 1982, TY, DS (a); Swamp Thing; Phantom Stranger 2.00
- ❑7, Nov 1982, TY (a) 2.00
- ❑8, Dec 1982, TY (a); Phantom Stranger back-up 2.00
- ❑9, Jan 1983, TY (c); JDu (a) 2.00
- ❑10, Feb 1983, TY (a) 2.00
- ❑11, Mar 1983, TY (a) 2.00
- ❑12, Apr 1983, TY (a) 2.00
- ❑13, May 1983 .... 2.00
- ❑14, Jun 1983 .... 2.00
- ❑15, Jul 1983 .... 2.00
- ❑16, Aug 1983, TY (c) 2.00
- ❑17, Oct 1983, TY (c) 2.00
- ❑18, Nov 1983, TY (c); BWr (a) 2.00

N-MINT

- ❑19, Dec 1983, TY (c) 2.00
- ❑20, Jan 1984; TY (c); AMo (w); Alan Moore scripts begin 15.00
- ❑21, Feb 1984; TY (c); AMo (w); O: Swamp Thing (new origin) 12.00
- ❑22, Mar 1984 TY (c); AMo (w) 6.00
- ❑23, Apr 1984 TY (c); AMo (w) 6.00
- ❑24, May 1984 AMo (w); A: Justice League 6.00
- ❑25, Jun 1984 AMo (w) 6.00
- ❑26, Jul 1984 AMo (w) 4.00
- ❑27, Aug 1984 AMo (w) 4.00
- ❑28, Sep 1984 AMo (w) 4.00
- ❑29, Oct 1984 AMo (w) 4.00
- ❑30, Nov 1984 AMo (w); AA (a) 4.00
- ❑31, Dec 1984 AMo (w) 4.00
- ❑32, Jan 1985 AMo (w) 4.00
- ❑33, Feb 1985 AMo (w) 3.00
- ❑34, Mar 1985 AMo (w) 5.00
- ❑35, Apr 1985 AMo (w) 3.00
- ❑36, May 1985 AMo (w); BWr (a) 3.00
- ❑37, Jun 1985; AMo (w); 1: John Constantine 55.00
- ❑38, Jul 1985; AMo (w); 2: John Constantine 15.00
- ❑39, Aug 1985 AMo (w); A: John Constantine 9.00
- ❑40, Sep 1985 AMo (w); A: John Constantine 9.00
- ❑41, Oct 1985 AMo (w) 4.00
- ❑42, Nov 1985 AMo (w) 4.00
- ❑43, Dec 1985 AMo (w) 4.00
- ❑44, Jan 1986 AMo (w) 4.00
- ❑45, Feb 1986; AMo (w); AA (a); Series continued as "Swamp Thing (2nd Series) #46" 4.00
- ❑Ann 1, ca. 1982; TD (a); 1982 .... 3.00
- ❑Ann 2, ca. 1985; AMo (w); A: Demon. A: Spectre. A: Deadman. A: Phantom Stranger 4.00
- ❑Ann 3, ca. 1987; BB (c); A: Congorilla . 2.50

Saigon Chronicles
Avalon

- ❑1 .... 2.95

Saikano
Viz

- ❑1, Aug 2004, b&w 9.95
- ❑2, Oct 2004; b&w 9.95
- ❑3, Dec 2004; b&w 9.95
- ❑4, Apr 2005; b&w 9.95
- ❑5, Jul 2005; b&w 9.95
- ❑6, Oct 2005 .... 9.95

Sailor Moon Comic
Mixxzine

- ❑1, Oct 1998; Continued from MixxZine 15.00
- ❑1/A, Oct 1998; San Diego limited edition version; Pink with only logo on cover 12.00
- ❑2, Nov 1998 .... 8.00
- ❑3, Dec 1998 .... 8.00
- ❑4, Jan 1999 .... 8.00
- ❑5, Feb 1999 .... 6.00
- ❑6, Mar 1999 .... 6.00
- ❑7, Apr 1999 .... 6.00
- ❑8, May 1999 .... 5.00
- ❑9, Jun 1999 .... 4.00
- ❑10, Jul 1999 .... 3.00
- ❑11, Aug 1999 .... 3.00

❑12, Sep 1999 ... 3.00
❑13, Oct 1999 ... 3.00
❑14, Nov 1999 ... 3.00
❑15, Dec 1999 ... 3.00
❑16, Jan 2000 ... 3.00
❑17, Feb 2000 ... 3.00
❑18, Mar 2000 ... 3.00
❑19, Apr 2000 ... 3.00
❑20, May 2000 ... 3.00
❑21, Jun 2000 ... 3.00
❑22, Jul 2000 ... 3.00
❑23, Aug 2000 ... 3.00
❑24, Sep 2000 ... 3.00
❑25, Oct 2000; Giant-size ... 3.00
❑26, Nov 2000 ... 3.00
❑27, Dec 2000 ... 3.00
❑28, Jan 2001 ... 3.00
❑29, Feb 2001 ... 3.00
❑30, Mar 2001 ... 3.00
❑31, Apr 2001 ... 2.95
❑32, May 2001 ... 2.95
❑33, Jun 2001 ... 2.95

Sailor Moon SuperS
Mixx

❑1 ... 9.95

Sailor's Story, A
Marvel

❑1 ... 5.95

Sailor's Story, A: Winds, Dreams, and Dragons
Marvel

❑1; A Sailor's Story; ca. 1987 ... 6.95

Saint Angel
Image

❑0, Mar 2000 ... 2.95
❑1, Jun 2000 ... 3.95
❑2, Oct 2000 ... 3.95
❑3, Dec 2000 ... 3.95
❑4, Mar 2001, Flip book with Deity/ Catseye: Riftwave ... 3.95

St. George
Marvel / Epic

❑1, Jun 1988, BSz (c); BSz, KJ (a) ... 1.50
❑2, Aug 1988 ... 1.50
❑3, Oct 1988 ... 1.50
❑4, Dec 1988 ... 1.50
❑5, Feb 1989 ... 1.50
❑6, Apr 1989 ... 1.50
❑7, Jun 1989 ... 1.50
❑8, Aug 1989, Final Issue ... 1.50

Saint Germaine
Caliber

❑1, ca. 1997, b&w; Male figure cover ... 2.95
❑2 ... 2.95
❑3 ... 2.95
❑4 ... 2.95
❑5 ... 2.95

Saints
Saturn

❑0, Apr 1995, b&w ... 2.50
❑1, Fal 1996, b&w ... 2.50

Saint Sinner
Marvel

❑1, Oct 1993; foil cover ... 2.50
❑2, Nov 1993 ... 1.75
❑3, Dec 1993 ... 1.75
❑4, Jan 1994 ... 1.75
❑5, Feb 1994 ... 1.75
❑6, Mar 1994 ... 1.75
❑7, Apr 1994 ... 1.75
❑8, Apr 1994 ... 1.75

St. Swithin's Day
Trident

❑1, ca. 1990, b&w; One-shot ... 3.00
❑1/2nd, Mar 1998, b&w ... 2.95

St. Swithin's Day
Oni

❑1, Mar 1998 ... 2.95

Saiyuki
Tokyopop

❑1, Mar 2004 ... 9.99

Saiyuki Reload
Tokyopop

❑1, Aug 2005 ... 9.99
❑2, Dec 2005 ... 9.99

Sakura Taisen
Tokyopop

❑1, Jul 2005 ... 9.99
❑2, Dec 2005 ... 9.99

Salamander Dream
Adhouse Books

❑1, ca. 2005 ... 15.00

Salimba
Blackthorne

❑1, b&w ... 3.50
❑3D 1, Aug 1986, b&w ... 2.50
❑3D 2, Sep 1986 ... 2.50

Sally Forth
Fantagraphics / Eros

❑1, Sep 1993; Adult ... 2.95
❑1/2nd, Jun 1995; 2nd printing; Adult ... 2.95
❑2, Oct 1993; Adult ... 2.95
❑3, Feb 1994; Adult ... 2.95
❑4, Apr 1994; Adult ... 2.95
❑5, Jul 1994; Adult ... 2.95
❑6, Sep 1994, b&w; Adult ... 2.95
❑7, Nov 1994; Adult ... 2.95
❑8, Jan 1995; Adult ... 2.95

Sam & Max, Freelance Police
Marvel / Epic

❑1; NN ... 2.25

Sam and Max, Freelance Police Special
Fishwrap

❑1, ca. 1987, b&w ... 1.75

Sam & Max Freelance Police Special
Comico

❑1, ca. 1989 ... 2.75

Sam & Max Freelance Police Special Color Collection
Marvel / Epic

❑1; NN ... 4.95

Sam and Twitch
Image

❑1, Aug 1999 ... 2.50
❑2, Sep 1999 ... 2.50
❑3, Oct 1999 ... 2.50
❑4, Nov 1999 ... 2.50
❑5, Dec 1999 ... 2.50
❑6, Jan 2000 ... 2.50
❑7, Feb 2000 ... 2.50
❑8, Mar 2000 ... 2.50
❑9, Apr 2000 ... 2.50
❑10, May 2000 ... 2.50
❑11, Jun 2000 ... 2.50
❑12, Jul 2000 ... 2.50
❑13, Aug 2000 ... 2.50
❑14, Sep 2000 ... 2.50
❑15, Oct 2000 ... 2.50
❑16, Nov 2000 ... 2.50
❑17, Dec 2000 ... 2.50
❑18, Jan 2001 ... 2.50
❑19, Feb 2001 ... 2.50
❑20, Mar 2001 ... 2.50
❑21, Apr 2001 ... 2.50
❑22, May 2001 ... 2.50
❑23, Jan 2002 ... 2.50
❑24, Aug 2003 ... 2.50
❑25, Oct 2003 ... 2.50
❑26, Feb 2004 ... 2.50

Sam Bronx and the Robots
Eclipse

❑1, Dec 1989; hardcover ... 6.95

Sambu Gassho (A Chorus in Three Parts)
Bodo Genki

❑1, Aug 1994, b&w; no cover price ... 1.00

Sammy: Tourist Trap
Image

❑1, Feb 2003 ... 2.95
❑2, Mar 2003 ... 2.95
❑3, May 2003 ... 2.95
❑4, May 2003 ... 2.95

Sammy Very Sammy Day One Shot
Image

❑1, Aug 2004 ... 5.95

Sam Noir: Samurai Detective
Image

❑1, Oct 2006, b&w ... 2.99
❑2, Nov 2006; b&w ... 2.99
❑3, Nov 2006; b&w ... 2.99

Sam Slade, Robo-Hunter
Fleetway-Quality

❑1 ... 2.00
❑2 DaG (a) ... 1.50
❑3 DaG (a) ... 1.50
❑4 DaG (a) ... 1.50
❑5 DaG (a) ... 1.50
❑6 AMo (w) ... 1.50
❑7 ... 1.50
❑8 DaG (a) ... 1.50
❑9 ... 1.50
❑10 ... 1.50
❑11, no year of publication ... 1.50
❑12 DaG (a) ... 1.50
❑13 DaG (a) ... 1.50
❑14 DaG (a) ... 1.50
❑15 ... 1.50
❑16 ... 1.50
❑17 DaG (a) ... 1.50
❑18 DaG (a) ... 1.50
❑19 ... 1.50
❑20 ... 1.50
❑21; double issue #21/22 ... 1.50
❑22 ... 1.50
❑23; double issue #23/24 ... 1.50
❑24 ... 1.50
❑25 ... 1.50
❑26 ... 1.50
❑27 ... 1.50
❑28 ... 1.50
❑29 ... 1.50
❑30 ... 1.50
❑31 ... 1.50
❑32 ... 1.50
❑33 ... 1.50

Samson
Samson

❑½, Jan 1995; no indicia ... 2.50

Sam Stories: Legs
Image / Quality

❑1, Dec 1999 ... 2.50

Samurai
Aircel

❑1, Jan 1986 ... 3.00
❑1/2nd, 2nd printing ... 2.00
❑1/3rd, 3rd printing ... 2.00
❑2, Feb 1986 ... 2.00
❑3, Mar 1986 ... 2.00
❑4, Apr 1986 ... 2.00
❑5, May 1986 ... 2.00
❑6, Jun 1986 ... 2.00
❑7, Jul 1986 ... 2.00
❑8, Aug 1986 ... 2.00
❑9, Sep 1986 ... 2.00
❑10, Oct 1986 ... 2.00
❑11, Nov 1986 ... 2.00
❑12, Dec 1986 ... 2.00
❑13, Jan 1987, 1st Dale Keown art ... 3.00
❑14, Feb 1987 ... 3.00
❑15, Mar 1987 ... 3.00
❑16, Apr 1987 ... 3.00
❑17, May 1987 ... 2.00
❑18, Jun 1987 ... 2.00
❑19, Jul 1987 ... 2.00
❑20, Aug 1987, Splinters story; b&w ... 2.00
❑21, Sep 1987 ... 2.00
❑22, Oct 1987 ... 2.00
❑23, Nov 1987, Final Issue ... 2.00

Samurai (Vol. 2)
Aircel

❑1, Dec 1987 ... 2.00
❑2, Jan 1988 ... 2.00
❑3, Feb 1988 ... 2.00

Shadow

Archie series featured campy take

©Archie

Shadow

Kaluta returned Shadow to pulp roots

©DC

Shadow

Chaykin brought pulp avenger to today

©DC

Shadow

Sienkiewicz sent Shadow on strange trips

©DC

ShadowHawk

Valentino vigilante contracted HIV

©Image

N-MINT

Samurai (Vol. 3)
Aircel

- ❑1, Aug 1988; b&w 1.95
- ❑2, Sep 1988; b&w 1.95
- ❑3, Oct 1988; b&w 1.95
- ❑4, Nov 1988; b&w 1.95
- ❑5, Dec 1988; b&w 1.95
- ❑6, Dec 1988; b&w 1.95
- ❑7, Jan 1989; b&w 1.95

Samurai
Warp

- ❑1, May 1997, b&w 2.95

Samurai Cat
Marvel / Epic

- ❑1, Jun 1991 .... 2.25
- ❑2, Aug 1991 .... 2.25
- ❑3, Sep 1991 .... 2.25

Samurai Champloo
Tokyopop

- ❑1, Nov 2005 .... 9.99

Samurai Compilation Book
Aircel

- ❑1, b&w 4.95
- ❑2, b&w 4.95

Samurai Deeper Kyo
Tokyopop

- ❑1, Jun 2003, 202 pages 9.99
- ❑2, Aug 2003 .... 9.99
- ❑3, Oct 2003 .... 9.99
- ❑4, Dec 2003 .... 9.99
- ❑5, Feb 2004 .... 9.99
- ❑6, Apr 2004 .... 9.99
- ❑7, Jun 2004 .... 9.99
- ❑8, Aug 2004 .... 9.99
- ❑9, Oct 2004 .... 9.99
- ❑10, Dec 2004 .... 9.99
- ❑11, Feb 2005 .... 9.99
- ❑12, Apr 2005 .... 9.99
- ❑13, Jun 2005 .... 9.99
- ❑14, Jul 2005 .... 9.99
- ❑15, Aug 2005 .... 9.99
- ❑16, Nov 2005 .... 9.99

Samurai: Demon Sword
Night Wynd

- ❑1 .... 2.50
- ❑2 .... 2.50
- ❑3 .... 2.50
- ❑4 .... 2.50

Samurai Executioner
Dark Horse

- ❑1, Jul 2004; When the Demon Knife Weeps 9.95
- ❑2, Dec 2004; Two Bodies, Two Minds .. 9.95
- ❑3, Jan 2005; The Hell Stick 9.95
- ❑4, Apr 2005; Portrait of Death 9.95
- ❑5, Aug 2005; Ten Fingers, One Life 9.95
- ❑6, Sep 2005; Shinko the Kappa 9.95
- ❑7, Dec 2005; The Bamboo Splitter 9.95
- ❑8, Jan 2006; The Death Sign of Spring 9.95
- ❑9, Mar 2006; Facing Life and Death 9.95

N-MINT

Samurai Funnies
Solson

- ❑1; Texas chainsaw 2.00
- ❑2; Samurai 13th 2.00

Samurai Guard
Colburn

- ❑1, Nov 1999 .... 2.50
- ❑2, Jun 2000 .... 2.50
- ❑Ashcan 1 .... 1.00

Samurai: Heaven and Earth
Dark Horse

- ❑1, Dec 2004 .... 2.99
- ❑2, Jan 2005 .... 2.99
- ❑3, Feb 2005 .... 2.99
- ❑4, Sep 2005 .... 2.99

Samurai: Heaven and Earth
Dark Horse

- ❑1, Dec 2006 .... 2.99

Samurai Jack Special
DC

- ❑1, Sep 2002 .... 3.95
- ❑1/2nd, Jul 2004; reprint 3.95

Samurai Jam
Slave Labor

- ❑1, Jan 1994 .... 2.95
- ❑2, Apr 1994 .... 2.95
- ❑3, Jun 1994 .... 2.95
- ❑4, Sep 1994 .... 2.95

Samurai: Mystic Cult
Nightwynd

- ❑1, Nov 1992, b&w 2.50
- ❑2, Dec 1992, b&w 2.50
- ❑3, Jan 1993, b&w 2.50
- ❑4, Feb 1993, b&w 2.50

Samurai Penguin
Slave Labor

- ❑1, Jun 1986, b&w 1.50
- ❑2, Aug 1986, b&w 1.50
- ❑3, Feb 1987, b&w; pink logo version also exist 1.50
- ❑4, May 1987, b&w 1.50
- ❑5, Sep 1987, b&w 1.50
- ❑6, Mar 1988; D: Samurai Penguin 1.95
- ❑7, Jul 1988 .... 1.75
- ❑8, May 1989 .... 1.75

Samurai Penguin: Food Chain Follies
Slave Labor

- ❑1, Apr 1991; NN; One-shot 5.95

Samurai 7
Gauntlet

- ❑1, b&w 2.50
- ❑2, b&w 2.50
- ❑3, b&w 2.50

Samurai Squirrel
Spotlight

- ❑1, Sep 1986 .... 1.75
- ❑2, Jan 1987 .... 1.75

Samurai: Vampire's Hunt
Nightwynd

- ❑1, Jul 1992, b&w 2.50
- ❑2, Aug 1992, b&w 2.50

N-MINT

- ❑3, Sep 1992, b&w 2.50
- ❑4, Oct 1992, b&w 2.50

Samuree
Continuity

- ❑1, May 1987 .... 2.00
- ❑2, Aug 1987; Wrap around cover by Neal Adams 2.00
- ❑3, May 1988 .... 2.00
- ❑4, Jan 1989 .... 2.00
- ❑5, Apr 1989 .... 2.00
- ❑6, Aug 1989 .... 2.00
- ❑7, Feb 1990 .... 2.00
- ❑8, Nov 1990 .... 2.00
- ❑9, Jan 1991 .... 2.00

Samuree
Continuity

- ❑1, May 1993 .... 2.50
- ❑2, Sep 1993 .... 2.50
- ❑3, Dec 1993; Wrap-around cover 2.50
- ❑4, Jan 1994 .... 2.50

Samuree
Acclaim / Windjammer

- ❑1, Oct 1995 .... 2.50
- ❑2, Nov 1995 .... 2.50

Sanctuary Part 1
Viz

- ❑1, Jun 1993, b&w 6.00
- ❑2, Jul 1993, b&w 5.00
- ❑3, Aug 1993 .... 5.00
- ❑4, Sep 1993 .... 5.00
- ❑5, Oct 1993 .... 5.00
- ❑6, Nov 1993 .... 5.00
- ❑7, Dec 1993 .... 5.00
- ❑8, Jan 1994 .... 5.00
- ❑9, Feb 1994 .... 5.00

Sanctuary Part 2
Viz

- ❑1, Mar 1994 .... 5.00
- ❑2, Apr 1994 .... 5.00
- ❑3, May 1994 .... 5.00
- ❑4, Jun 1994 .... 5.00
- ❑5, Jul 1994 .... 5.00
- ❑6, Aug 1994 .... 5.00
- ❑7, Sep 1994 .... 5.00
- ❑8, Oct 1994 .... 5.00
- ❑9, Nov 1994 .... 5.00

Sanctuary Part 3
Viz

- ❑1, Dec 1994, b&w 3.25
- ❑2, Jan 1995, b&w 3.25
- ❑3, Feb 1995, b&w 3.25
- ❑4, Mar 1995, b&w 3.25
- ❑5, Apr 1995, b&w 3.25
- ❑6, May 1995, b&w 3.25
- ❑7, Jun 1995, b&w 3.25
- ❑8, Jul 1995, b&w 3.25

Sanctuary Part 4
Viz

- ❑1, Aug 1995 .... 3.25
- ❑2, Sep 1995 .... 3.25
- ❑3, Oct 1995 .... 3.25
- ❑4, Nov 1995 .... 3.25
- ❑5, Dec 1995 .... 3.25

Other grades: Multiply price above by 5/6 for VF/NM • 2/3 for VERY FINE • 1/3 for FINE • 1/5 for VERY GOOD • 1/8 for GOOD

	N-MINT
❑6, Jan 1996	3.50
❑7, Feb 1996	3.50

Sanctuary Part 5
Viz

❑1, Mar 1996	3.50
❑2, Apr 1996	3.50
❑3, May 1996	3.50
❑4, Jun 1996	3.50
❑5, Jul 1996	3.50
❑6, Aug 1996	3.50
❑7, Sep 1996	3.50
❑8, Oct 1996	3.50
❑9, Nov 1996	3.50
❑10, Dec 1996	3.50
❑11, Jan 1997	3.50
❑12, Feb 1997	3.50
❑13, Mar 1997	3.50

Sanctum
Blackshoe

❑1/Ltd.; Limited edition from 1999 San Diego Comic-Con	3.95

San Diego Comic-Con Comics
Dark Horse

❑1, ca. 1992; con giveaway; 1992 Comic-Con	3.25
❑2, Aug 1993; con giveaway; 1993 Comic-Con	2.95
❑3, Aug 1994; con giveaway; 1994 Comic-Con	2.50
❑4, Aug 1995; 1995 Comic-Con	2.50

Sandmadam
Spoof

❑1, b&w	2.95

Sandman
DC

❑1, Win 1974, JK (c); JK (a)	15.00
❑2, May 1975 JK (c); JK (a)	7.00
❑3, Jul 1975 JK (c); JK (a)	4.00
❑4, Sep 1975 JK (c); JK (a); A: Demon	4.00
❑5, Nov 1975 JK (c); JK (a)	4.00
❑6, Jan 1976; JK (a); Final Issue	4.00

Sandman
DC

❑1, Jan 1989; Giant-size; NG (w); 1: Sandman III (Morpheus)	25.00
❑2, Feb 1989 NG (w); A: Abel. A: Cain	12.00
❑3, Mar 1989 NG (w); A: John Constantine	12.00
❑4, Apr 1989 NG (w); A: Demon	3.50
❑5, May 1989 NG (w)	3.50
❑6, Jun 1989 NG (w)	3.50
❑7, Jul 1989 NG (w)	3.50
❑8, Aug 1989; Regular edition, no indicia in inside front cover; NG (w); 1: Death (Sandman), no indicia in inside front cover	15.00
❑8/Ltd., Aug 1989; limited edition; NG (w); 1: Death (Sandman). 1000 copies; Has indicia in inside front cover, editorial by Karen Berger	35.00
❑9, Sep 1989 NG (w)	3.50
❑10, Nov 1989 NG (w)	3.50
❑11, Dec 1989 NG (w)	3.50
❑12, Jan 1990 NG (w)	3.50
❑13, Feb 1990 NG (w)	3.50
❑14, Mar 1990 NG (w)	3.50
❑15, Apr 1990 NG (w)	2.50
❑16, Jun 1990 NG (w)	2.50
❑17, Jul 1990 NG (w)	2.50
❑18, Aug 1990 NG (w)	2.50
❑19, Sep 1990; NG (w); CV (a); properly printed; Midsummer Night's Dream	2.50
❑19/A, Sep 1990; NG (w); CV (a); pages out of order; Midsummer Night's Dream	2.50
❑20, Oct 1990; NG (w); D: Element Girl	2.50
❑21, Nov 1990 NG (w)	2.50
❑22, Jan 1991; NG (w); 1: Daniel (new Sandman)	3.50
❑23, Feb 1991 NG (w)	2.50
❑24, Mar 1991 NG (w)	2.50
❑25, Apr 1991 NG (w); MW (a)	2.50
❑26, May 1991 NG (w)	2.50
❑27, Jun 1991 NG (w)	2.50
❑28, Jul 1991 NG (w)	2.50
❑29, Aug 1991 NG (w)	2.50
❑30, Sep 1991 NG (w); BT (a)	2.50
❑31, Oct 1991 NG (w)	2.50
❑32, Nov 1991 NG (w)	2.50
❑33, Dec 1991 NG (w)	2.50
❑34, Jan 1992 NG (w)	2.50
❑35, Feb 1992 NG (w)	2.50
❑36, Apr 1992; Giant-size; NG (w); BT (a)	3.00
❑37, May 1992 NG (w)	2.50
❑38, Jun 1992 NG (w)	2.50
❑39, Jul 1992 NG (w)	2.50
❑40, Aug 1992 NG (w)	2.50
❑41, Sep 1992 NG (w)	2.50
❑42, Oct 1992 NG (w)	2.50
❑43, Nov 1992 NG (w)	2.50
❑44, Dec 1992 NG (w)	2.50
❑45, Jan 1993 NG (w)	2.50
❑46, Feb 1993; NG (w); Brief Lives	2.50
❑47, Mar 1993 NG (w)	2.50
❑48, Apr 1993 NG (w)	2.50
❑49, May 1993; NG (w); D: Orpheus	2.50
❑50, Jun 1993; Double-size; NG (w); CR (a); Bronze ink	4.50
❑50/Gold, Jun 1993; Gold edition; NG (w); CR (a)	20.00
❑51, Jul 1993 NG (w); BT, DG (a)	2.50
❑52, Aug 1993 NG (w); BT (a)	2.50
❑53, Sep 1993 NG (w); BT (a)	2.50
❑54, Oct 1993; NG (w); BT (a); O: Prez Rickard	2.50
❑55, Nov 1993 NG (w); BT (a)	2.50
❑56, Dec 1993 NG (w); BT (a)	2.50
❑57, Feb 1994; NG (w); Includes preview of American Freak: A Tale of the Un-Men	2.50
❑58, Mar 1994 NG (w)	2.50
❑59, Apr 1994 NG (w)	2.50
❑60, Jun 1994 NG (w)	2.50
❑61, Jul 1994 NG (w)	2.50
❑62, Aug 1994 NG (w); CV (a)	2.50
❑63, Sep 1994 NG (w)	2.50
❑64, Nov 1994 NG (w)	2.50
❑65, Dec 1994; NG (w); Vertigo Trading Preview Sample card Included	2.50
❑66, Jan 1995 NG (w)	2.50
❑67, Mar 1995 NG (w)	2.50
❑68, May 1995 NG (w)	2.50
❑69, Jul 1995; NG (w); D: Sandman III (Morpheus); 1: Sandman IV (Dream)	3.00
❑70, Aug 1995 NG (w)	2.50
❑71, Sep 1995 NG (w)	2.50
❑72, Nov 1995; NG (w); burial of Dream	2.50
❑73, Dec 1995 NG (w); A: Hob Gadling	2.50
❑74, Jan 1996 NG (w)	2.50
❑75, Mar 1996; NG (w); CV (a); A: William Shakespeare. contains timeline	4.00
❑Special 1, ca. 1991; Orpheus special edition; NG (w); SA, BT, CR (a); Glow-in-the-dark cover	5.00

Sandman: A Gallery of Dreams
DC / Vertigo

❑1, ca. 1994; NN	5.00

Sandman: Endless Nights
DC / Vertigo

❑1, Nov 2003	2.95

Sandman Midnight Theatre
DC / Vertigo

❑1, Sep 1995; prestige format; Morpheus meets Wesley Dodds	6.95

Sandman Mystery Theatre
DC / Vertigo

❑1, Apr 1993 MW (w)	4.00
❑2, May 1993 MW (w)	3.00
❑3, Jun 1993 MW (w)	3.00
❑4, Jul 1993 MW (w)	3.00
❑5, Aug 1993 MW (w)	3.00
❑6, Sep 1993 MW (w)	3.00
❑7, Oct 1993 MW (w)	3.00
❑8, Nov 1993 MW (w)	3.00
❑9, Dec 1993 MW (w)	3.00
❑10, Jan 1994 MW (w)	3.00
❑11, Feb 1994 MW (w)	2.75
❑12, Mar 1994 MW (w)	2.75
❑13, Apr 1994 MW (w)	2.75
❑14, May 1994 MW (w)	2.75
❑15, Jun 1994 MW (w)	2.75
❑16, Jul 1994 MW (w)	2.75
❑17, Aug 1994 MW (w)	2.75
❑18, Sep 1994 MW (w)	2.75
❑19, Oct 1994 MW (w)	2.75
❑20, Nov 1994 MW (w)	2.75
❑21, Dec 1994 MW (w)	2.50
❑22, Jan 1995 MW (w)	2.50
❑23, Feb 1995 MW (w)	2.50
❑24, Mar 1995 MW (w)	2.50
❑25, Apr 1995 MW (w)	2.50
❑26, May 1995 MW (w)	2.50
❑27, Jun 1995 MW (w)	2.50
❑28, Jul 1995 MW (w)	2.50
❑29, Aug 1995 MW (w)	2.50
❑30, Sep 1995 MW (w)	2.50
❑31, Oct 1995 MW (w)	2.50
❑32, Nov 1995 MW (w)	2.50
❑33, Dec 1995 MW (w)	2.50
❑34, Jan 1996 MW (w)	2.50
❑35, Feb 1996 MW (w)	2.50
❑36, Mar 1996 MW (w)	2.50
❑37, Apr 1996 MW (w)	2.50
❑38, May 1996 MW (w)	2.50
❑39, Jun 1996 MW (w)	2.50
❑40, Jul 1996; MW (w); Lead in to Starman (2nd series)	2.50
❑41, Aug 1996 MW (w)	2.50
❑42, Sep 1996 MW (w)	2.50
❑43, Oct 1996 MW (w); A: Crimson Avenger	2.50
❑44, Nov 1996 MW (w)	2.50
❑45, Dec 1996; MW (w); A: Blackhawk. Photo cover	2.50
❑46, Jan 1997 MW (w)	2.50
❑47, Feb 1997 MW (w)	2.50
❑48, Mar 1997; MW (w); Photo cover	2.50
❑49, Apr 1997 MW (w)	2.50
❑50, May 1997; Giant-size; MW (w); Includes Classic Sandman Tale (Golden Age style version of the Scarlet Ghost); Story credited to "Joe Kirby" as a tribute to Joe Simon and Jack Kirby who created The Sandman	3.50
❑51, Jun 1997 MW (w)	2.50
❑52, Jul 1997 MW (w)	2.50
❑53, Aug 1997 MW (w)	2.50
❑54, Sep 1997 MW (w)	2.50
❑55, Oct 1997 MW (w)	2.50
❑56, Nov 1997 MW (w)	2.50
❑57, Dec 1997 MW (w)	2.50
❑58, Jan 1998 MW (w)	2.50
❑59, Feb 1998 MW (w)	2.50
❑60, Mar 1998 MW (w)	2.50
❑61, Apr 1998	2.50
❑62, May 1998	2.50
❑63, Jul 1998	2.50
❑64, Aug 1998	2.50
❑65, Sep 1998	2.50
❑66, Oct 1998	2.50
❑67, Nov 1998	2.50
❑68, Dec 1998	2.50
❑69, Jan 1999	2.50
❑70, Feb 1999; Final Issue	2.50
❑Ann 1, Oct 1994 MW (w); ARo (a)	4.00

Sandman Mystery Theatre: Sleep of Reason
DC / Vertigo

❑1, Feb 2007	2.99

Sandman #1 Special Edition
DC / Vertigo

❑1, Dec 2006	0.50

Sandman Presents: Bast
DC / Vertigo

❑1, Mar 2003	2.95
❑2, Apr 2003	2.95
❑3, May 2003	2.95

Sandman Presents: Love Street
DC / Vertigo

❑1, Jul 1999; John Constantine in the '60s	2.95
❑2, Aug 1999	2.95
❑3, Sep 1999	2.95

Sandman Presents: Lucifer
DC / Vertigo

❑1, Mar 1999	2.95
❑2, Apr 1999	2.95
❑3, May 1999	2.95

Sandman Presents: Petrefax
DC / Vertigo

❑1, Mar 2000	2.95
❑2, Apr 2000	2.95

Other grades: Multiply price above by 5/6 for VF/NM • 2/3 for VERY FINE • 1/3 for FINE • 1/5 for VERY GOOD • 1/8 for GOOD

Shadowman

Big Easy jazz musician powered by voodoo

©Valiant

Shadow of the Batman

Reprints early 1970s Bat-stories

©DC

Shadow Strikes!

Shadow returns to 1930s adventures

©DC

Shadow War of Hawkman

Mistrust main focus of mini-series

©DC

Shanda the Panda

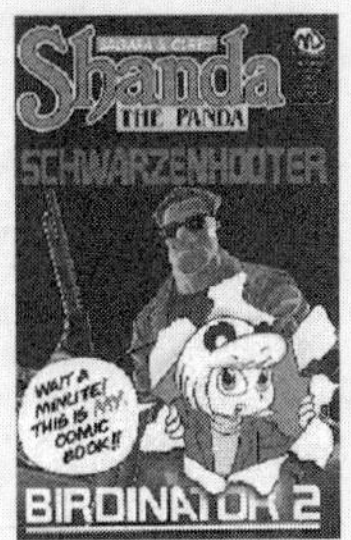

Anthropomorphic soap opera rivals real life

©Mu

N-MINT

❑3, May 2000 ... 2.95
❑4, Jun 2000 ... 2.95

Sandman Presents: Deadboy Detectives
DC / Vertigo

❑1, Aug 2001 ... 2.50
❑2, Sep 2001 ... 2.50
❑3, Oct 2001 ... 2.50
❑4, Nov 2001 ... 2.50

Sandman Presents: Everything You Always Wanted to Know About Dreams...But Were Afraid To Ask
DC / Vertigo

❑1, Jul 2001 ... 3.95

Sandman Presents: Thessaly - Witch for Hire
DC / Vertigo

❑1, Apr 2004 ... 2.95
❑2, May 2004 ... 2.95
❑3, Jun 2004 ... 2.95
❑4, Jul 2004 ... 2.95

Sandman Presents: The Corinthian
DC / Vertigo

❑1, Dec 2001 ... 2.50
❑2, Jan 2002 ... 2.50
❑3, Feb 2002 ... 2.50

Sandman Presents: The Thessaliad
DC / Vertigo

❑1, Mar 2002 ... 2.50
❑2, Apr 2002 ... 2.50
❑3, May 2002 ... 2.50
❑4, Jun 2002 ... 2.50

Sands
Black Eye

❑1, b&w; smaller than a normal comic book ... 2.50
❑2, b&w; smaller than a normal comic book ... 2.50
❑3, Feb 1997, b&w; smaller than a normal comic book ... 2.50

Sandscape
Dreamwave

❑1, Jan 2003 ... 2.95
❑2, Feb 2003 ... 2.95
❑3, Apr 2003 ... 2.95
❑4, Jun 2003 ... 2.95

San Francisco Comic Book
San Francisco Comic Book Co.

❑1, Jan 1970, Adult ... 6.00
❑2, Adult ... 4.00
❑3, Wraparound cover; Adult ... 4.00
❑4; Adult ... 4.00
❑5; Adult ... 4.00
❑6; Adult ... 4.00
❑7; Adult ... 4.00

Santa Claus Adventures
Innovation

❑1, Reprints ... 6.95

Santa Claws
Eternity

❑1, b&w ... 2.95

N-MINT

Santa Claws
Thorby

❑1; ca 1998 ... 2.95

Santana
Malibu / Rock-It

❑1, May 1994; magazine; TY (a) ... 5.00

Santa the Barbarian
Maximum

❑1, Dec 1996 ... 2.99

Sapphire
Aircel

❑1, Feb 1990; Adult ... 2.95
❑2, Mar 1990; Adult ... 2.95
❑3, Apr 1990; Adult ... 2.50
❑4, May 1990; Adult ... 2.50
❑5, Jun 1990; Adult ... 2.50
❑6, Jul 1990; Adult ... 2.50
❑7, Aug 1990; Adult ... 2.50
❑8; Adult ... 2.50
❑9, Sep 1990; Adult ... 2.50

Sapphire
NBM

❑1, Oct 2001; Adult ... 10.95
❑2; Adult ... 10.95

Sap Tunes
Fantagraphics

❑1, b&w ... 2.50
❑2, b&w ... 2.50

Sarah-Jane Hamilton Presents Superstars of Erotica
Re-Visionary

❑1; Adult ... 2.95

Sarge Snorkel
Charlton

❑1, Oct 1973 ... 8.00
❑2, Dec 1973 ... 5.00
❑3, Jun 1974 ... 4.00
❑4, Sep 1974 ... 4.00
❑5, Nov 1974 ... 4.00
❑6, Jan 1975 ... 3.00
❑7, Mar 1975 ... 3.00
❑8, May 1975 ... 3.00
❑9, Jul 1975 ... 3.00
❑10, Sep 1975 ... 3.00
❑11, Nov 1975 ... 3.00
❑12, Jan 1976 ... 3.00
❑13, Mar 1976 ... 3.00
❑14, May 1976 ... 3.00
❑15, Aug 1976 ... 3.00
❑16, Oct 1976 ... 3.00
❑17, Dec 1976 ... 3.00

Sarge Steel
Charlton

❑1, Dec 1964 ... 15.00
❑2, Feb 1965 ... 10.00
❑3, May 1965 ... 8.00
❑4, Jul 1965 ... 8.00
❑5, Sep 1965 ... 8.00
❑6, Nov 1965 ... 6.00
❑7, Apr 1966 ... 6.00
❑8, Oct 1966, Becomes Secret Agent ... 6.00
❑9 ... 6.00

N-MINT

Satanika
Verotik

❑0, ca. 1995; Adult ... 4.00
❑1, Jan 1995; Adult ... 5.00
❑2, Apr 1995; Adult ... 4.00
❑3, Jul 1995; Adult ... 4.00
❑4 1996 ... 3.00
❑5, Oct 1996 ... 3.00
❑6, Jan 1997 ... 2.95
❑7, Apr 1997 ... 2.95
❑8, Sep 1997 ... 2.95
❑9, Mar 1998 ... 2.95
❑10, Dec 1998 ... 2.95
❑11, May 1999 ... 3.95

Satanika Illustrations
Verotik

❑1, Sep 1996; Cardstock cover; pin-ups 3.95

Satanika Tales
Verotik

❑1 2005 ... 3.95
❑2, Sep 2005 ... 3.95

Satan Place
Thunderhill

❑1 ... 3.50

Satan's Six
Topps

❑1, Apr 1993; trading card; Wolff and Byrd, Counselors of the Macabre backup story ... 2.95
❑2, May 1993; trading cards ... 2.95
❑3, Jun 1993; trading cards ... 2.95
❑4, Jul 1993; trading cards ... 2.95

Satan's Six: Hellspawn
Topps

❑1, Jun 1994; Inside index lists it as issue #2 ... 2.50
❑2, Jun 1994 ... 2.50
❑3, Jul 1994 ... 2.50

Saturday Morning: The Comic
Marvel

❑1, Apr 1996 ... 1.95

Saturday Nite
Anson Jew

❑1, b&w ... 2.95

Saucy Little Tart
Fantagraphics / Eros

❑1, Dec 1995; Adult ... 2.95

Saurians: Unnatural Selection
CrossGen

❑1, Feb 2002 ... 2.95
❑2, Mar 2002 ... 2.95

Savage Combat Tales
Atlas-Seaboard

❑1, Feb 1975; O: Sgt. Stryker's Death Squad ... 16.00
❑2, Apr 1975 ... 10.00
❑3, Jul 1975 ... 10.00

N-MINT

Savage Dragon
Image

❑1, Jul 1992; four cover logo variants (bottom of logo is white, blue, green, or yellow) 3.00
❑2, Oct 1992; Centerfold Savage Dragon poster 2.50
❑3, Dec 1992; Centerfold Savage Dragon poster 2.50

Savage Dragon
Image

❑0, Aug 2006, O: The Savage Dragon 1.95
❑½, ca. 1997; EL (c); EL (w); EL (a); Includes Certificate of Authenticity 3.00
❑½/Platinum, ca. 1997; Platinum edition; EL (w); EL (a); Includes Certificate of Authenticity 4.00
❑1, Jun 1993 EL (c); EL (w); EL (a) 3.00
❑2, Jul 1993; EL (c); EL (w); EL (a); A: Teenage Mutant Ninja Turtles. Flip book with Vanguard #0 3.00
❑3, Aug 1993; EL (c); EL (w); EL (a); Mighty Man back-up feature 2.50
❑4, Sep 1993; EL (c); EL (w); EL (a); Flip book with Rapture and Ricochet 2.25
❑5, Oct 1993; EL (c); EL (w); EL (a); Flip book with Mighty Man #5 2.25
❑6, Nov 1993 EL (c); EL (w); EL (a) 2.25
❑7, Jan 1994 EL (c); EL (w); EL (a) 2.25
❑8, Mar 1994 EL (c); EL (w); EL (a) 2.00
❑9, Apr 1994 EL (c); EL (w); EL (a) 2.00
❑10, May 1994; EL (c); EL (w); EL (a); alternate cover; newsstand version 2.00
❑10/Direct ed., May 1994 EL (c); EL (w); EL (a) 2.00
❑11, Jul 1994 EL (c); EL (w); EL (a) 2.00
❑12, Aug 1994; EL (c); EL (w); EL (a); She Dragon 2.00
❑13, Jun 1995; JLee (c); EL (w); JLee, EL (a); 1: Condition Red 2.50
❑13/A, Jun 1995; EL (c); JLee, EL (w); JLee, EL (a); Image X month version 2.50
❑14, Oct 1994 EL (c); EL (w); EL (a) 1.95
❑15, Dec 1994 EL (c); EL (w); EL (a) 2.50
❑16, Jan 1995; EL (c); EL (w); EL (a); Savage Dragon on cover 2.50
❑17/A, Feb 1995; EL (c); EL (w); EL (a); One figure on cover; two different interior pages 2.50
❑17/B, Feb 1995; EL (c); EL (w); EL (a); Alternate cover; Two women on cover; Nudity; Two different interior pages 2.50
❑18, Mar 1995 EL (c); EL (w); EL (a) 2.50
❑19, Apr 1995 EL (c); EL (w); EL (a) 2.50
❑20, Jul 1995 EL (c); EL (w); EL (a) 2.50
❑21, Aug 1995 EL (c); EL (w); EL (a) 2.50
❑22, Sep 1995 EL (c); EL (w); EL (a); A: Teenage Mutant Ninja Turtles 2.50
❑23, Oct 1995 EL (c); EL (w); EL (a) 2.50
❑24, Dec 1995 EL (c); EL (w); EL (a) 2.50
❑25, Jan 1996; double-sized; EL (c); EL (w); EL (a) 3.95
❑25/A, Jan 1996; double-sized; EL (c); EL (w); EL (a); alternate cover 3.95
❑26, Mar 1996 EL (c); EL (w); EL (a) 2.50
❑27, Apr 1996 EL (c); EL (w); EL (a) 2.50
❑27/A, Apr 1996; EL (c); EL (w); EL (a); alternate cover only available at WonderCon 2.50
❑28, May 1996 EL (c); EL (w); EL (a); A: Maxx 2.50
❑29, Jul 1996 EL (c); EL (w); EL (a); A: Wildstar 2.50
❑30, Aug 1996 EL (c); EL (w); EL (a); A: Spawn 2.50
❑31, Sep 1996; EL (c); EL (w); EL (a); censored version says God is good inside Image logo on cover; God vs. The Devil 2.50
❑31/A, Sep 1996; EL (c); EL (w); EL (a); God vs. The Devil; uncensored version 2.50
❑32, Oct 1996 EL (c); EL (w); EL (a) 2.50
❑33, Nov 1996; EL (c); EL (w); EL (a); Birth of Dragon's son 2.50
❑34, Dec 1996 EL (c); EL (w); EL (a); A: Hellboy 2.50
❑35, Feb 1997 EL (c); EL (w); EL (a); A: Hellboy 2.50
❑36, Mar 1997; EL (c); EL (w); EL (a); 1: Zeek 2.50
❑37, Apr 1997 EL (c); EL (w); EL (a) 2.50
❑38, May 1997 EL (c); EL (w); EL (a) 2.50
❑39, Jun 1997 EL (c); EL (w); EL (a) 2.50

N-MINT

❑40, Jul 1997 EL (c); EL (w); EL (a) 2.50
❑40/A, Jul 1997; EL (c); EL (w); EL (a); She-Dragon cover 2.50
❑41, Sep 1997 EL (c); EL (w); EL (a); A: Wildstar. A: Monkeyman. A: Femforce. A: E-Man. A: Zot. A: Megaton. A: Madman. A: Vampirella. A: Hellboy. A: DNAgents 2.50
❑42, Oct 1997 EL (c); EL (w); EL (a) 2.50
❑43, Nov 1997 EL (c); EL (w); EL (a) 2.50
❑44, Dec 1997 EL (c); EL (w); EL (a) 2.50
❑45, Jan 1998 EL (c); EL (w); EL (a) 2.50
❑46, Feb 1998 EL (c); EL (w); EL (a) 2.50
❑47, Mar 1998 EL (c); EL (w); EL (a) 2.50
❑48, Apr 1998 EL (c); EL (w); EL (a) 2.50
❑49, May 1998 EL (c); EL (w); EL (a) 2.50
❑50, Jun 1998; EL (c); JPH, EL (w); TMc, RL, EL (a); 100 pages; Various Pin-Ups 5.95
❑51/A, Jul 1998; EL (c); EL (w); EL (a); red logo 2.50
❑51/B, Jul 1998; EL (c); EL (w); EL (a); yellow logo 2.50
❑52, Aug 1998 EL (c); EL (w); EL (a) 2.50
❑53, Sep 1998 EL (c); EL (w); EL (a) 2.50
❑54, Oct 1998 EL (c); EL (w); EL (a) 2.50
❑55, Nov 1998 EL (c); EL (w); EL (a) 2.50
❑56, Dec 1998 EL (c); EL (w); EL (a) 2.50
❑57, Jan 1999 EL (c); EL (w); EL (a) 2.50
❑58, Feb 1999 EL (c); EL (w); EL (a) 2.50
❑59, Mar 1999 EL (c); EL (w); EL (a) 2.50
❑60, Apr 1999 EL (c); EL (w); EL (a) 2.50
❑61, May 1999 EL (c); EL (w); EL (a) 2.50
❑62, Jun 1999 EL (c); EL (w); EL (a) 2.50
❑63, Jun 1999 EL (c); EL (w); EL (a) 2.50
❑64, Jul 1999 EL (c); EL (w); EL (a) 2.50
❑65, Aug 1999 EL (c); EL (w); EL (a) 2.50
❑66, Aug 1999 EL (c); EL (w); EL (a) 2.50
❑67, Sep 1999 EL (c); EL (w); EL (a) 2.50
❑68, Oct 1999 EL (c); EL (w); EL (a) 2.50
❑69, Nov 1999 EL (c); EL (w); EL (a) 2.50
❑70, Dec 1999 EL (c); EL (w); EL (a) 2.50
❑71, Jan 2000 EL (c); EL (w); EL (a) 2.50
❑72, Feb 2000 EL (c); EL (w); EL (a); A: Mighty Man 2.95
❑73, Mar 2000 EL (c); EL (w); EL (a) 2.95
❑74, Apr 2000 EL (c); EL (w); EL (a) 2.95
❑75, May 2000; Giant-size; EL (c); EL (w); EL (a) 5.95
❑76, Jun 2000 EL (c); EL (w); EL (a) 2.95
❑77, Jul 2000; EL (c); EL (w); EL (a); Larsen cover 2.95
❑78, Aug 2000 EL (c); EL (w); EL (a) 2.95
❑79, Sep 2000 EL (c); EL (w); EL (a) 2.95
❑80, Oct 2000 EL (c); EL (w); EL (a) 2.95
❑81, Nov 2000 EL (c); EL (w); EL (a) 2.95
❑82, Dec 2000 EL (c); EL (w); EL (a) 2.95
❑83, Jan 2001 EL (c); EL (w); EL (a); A: Madman 2.95
❑84, Feb 2001 EL (c); EL (w); EL (a) 2.95
❑85, Mar 2001 EL (c); EL (w); EL (a); A: Madman 2.95
❑86, Apr 2001 EL (c); EL (w); EL (a); A: Mighty Man 2.95
❑87, May 2001 EL (c); EL (w); EL (a) 2.95
❑88, Jun 2001 EL (c); EL (w); EL (a) 2.95
❑89, Jul 2001 EL (c); EL (w); EL (a) 2.95
❑90, Aug 2001 EL (c); EL (w); EL (a) 2.95
❑91, Sep 2001 EL (c); EL (w); EL (a) 2.95
❑92, Oct 2001 EL (c); EL (w); EL (a) 2.95
❑93, Nov 2001 EL (c); EL (w); EL (a); A: SuperPatriot 2.95
❑94, Dec 2001 EL (c); EL (w); EL (a) 2.95
❑95, Jan 2002 EL (c); EL (w); EL (a) 2.95
❑96, Feb 2002 EL (c); EL (w); EL (a) 2.95
❑97, Mar 2002 EL (c); EL (w); EL (a) 2.95
❑98, Apr 2002 EL (c); EL (w); EL (a) 2.95
❑99, May 2002 EL (c); EL (w); EL (a) 2.95
❑100, Jun 2002; EL (c); EL (w); JOy, FM, EL (a); Giant-size; 100 Pages 8.95
❑101, Jul 2002 EL (c); EL (w); EL (a) 2.95
❑102, Aug 2002; EL (c); EL (w); EL (a); V: Mother Mayhem 2.95
❑103, Sep 2002; EL (c); EL (w); EL (a); V: Universo; Destruction of Savage Dragon original world 2.95
❑104, Oct 2002; EL (c); EL (w); EL (a); Savage Dragon wedding 2.95
❑105, Nov 2002 EL (c); EL (w); EL (a) 2.95
❑106, Dec 2002; EL (c); EL (w); EL (a); Christmas issue 2.95

N-MINT

❑107, May 2003; EL (c); EL (w); EL (a); Flip book with Major Damage 3.95
❑108, Jul 2003 2.95
❑109, Jul 2003; V: Thor 2.95
❑110, Sep 2003 2.95
❑111, Oct 2003 2.95
❑112, Nov 2003 2.95
❑113, Feb 2004 2.95
❑114, May 2004 2.95
❑115, Jun 2004; 100 pages; Wraparound cover 2.95
❑116, Jul 2004 2.95
❑117, Aug 2004 2.95
❑118, Sep 2004 2.95
❑119, Oct 2004 2.95
❑120, ca. 2005 2.95
❑121, ca. 2005 2.95
❑122, Jan 2006 2.99
❑123, Mar 2006 2.99
❑125, Jun 2006 4.99
❑126, Jul 2006 2.99
❑127, Jul 2006 2.99
❑128, Oct 2006 2.99
❑129, Nov 2006 2.99
❑130, Jan 2007 2.99
❑131, Feb 2007 2.99
❑132 2.99
❑133 2.99
❑134 2.99
❑135 2.99
❑136 2.99
❑137 2.99
❑138 2.99
❑139 2.99
❑140 2.99
❑141 2.99
❑142 2.99
❑143 2.99
❑144 2.99
❑145 2.99
❑146 2.99
❑147 2.99
❑148 2.99
❑149 2.99
❑150 2.99

Savage Dragon Archives
Image

❑1, Jun 1998 2.95
❑2, Oct 1998; Reprints Graphic Fantasy #2 2.95
❑3, Dec 1998; b&w 2.95
❑4, Jan 1999 2.95

Savage Dragonbert: Full Frontal Nerdity
Image

❑1, Oct 2002 5.95

Savage Dragon Companion
Image

❑1, Jul 2002 2.95

Savage Dragon/Destroyer Duck
Image

❑1, Nov 1996 3.95

Savage Dragon: God War
Image

❑1, Mar 2004 2.95
❑2, Mar 2005 2.95
❑3, Jun 2005 2.95

Savage Dragon/Hellboy
Image

❑1, Oct 2002 5.95

Savage Dragon/Marshal Law
Image

❑1, Jul 1997, b&w; indicia says Savage Dragon/Marshall Law 2.95
❑2, Aug 1997, b&w 2.95

Savage Dragon: Red Horizon
Image

❑1, Feb 1997 2.50
❑2, Apr 1997 2.50
❑3, May 1997 2.50

Savage Dragon: Sex & Violence
Image

❑1, Aug 1997 2.50
❑2, Sep 1997 2.50

Other grades: Multiply price above by 5/6 for VF/NM • 2/3 for VERY FINE • 1/3 for FINE • 1/5 for VERY GOOD • 1/8 for GOOD

Shanna the She-Devil

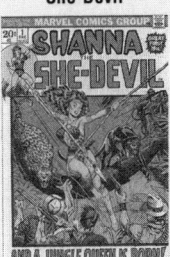

Ka-Zar's companion comes to jungle

©Marvel

Shatter

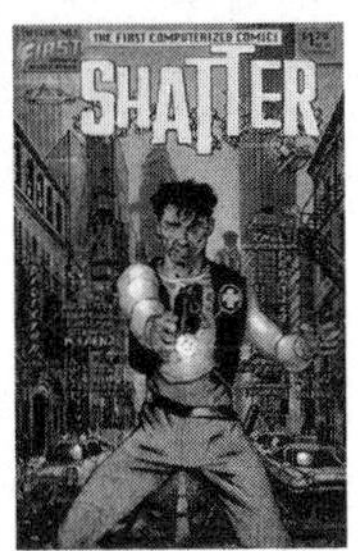

First computer-generated comic book

©First

Shazam!

Marvel Family returns after two decades

©DC

She-Hulk

Brains favored over brawn

©Marvel

Shi: The Way of the Warrior

Billy Tucci's female samurai seeks revenge

©Crusade

N-MINT

Savage Dragon/Teenage Mutant Ninja Turtles Crossover
Mirage

❑1, Sep 1993 ... 2.75

Savage Dragon Vs. The Savage Megaton Man
Image

❑1, Mar 1993 EL (c); EL (w); EL (a) ... 2.00
❑1/Gold, Mar 1993; EL (w); EL (a); Gold foil cover ... 3.00

Savage Fists of Kung Fu
Marvel

❑1; AM, JSn, JB, HT, DG, DA (a); O: The Sons of the Dragon ... 8.00

Savage Funnies
Vision

❑1, Jul 1996; Adult ... 1.95
❑2, Jul 1996; Adult ... 1.95

Savage Henry
Vortex

❑1, Jan 1987 ... 2.00
❑2, Feb 1987 ... 2.00
❑3, Apr 1987 ... 2.00
❑4 1987 ... 2.00
❑5 1987 ... 2.00
❑6, Jul 1988 ... 2.00
❑7, Sep 1988, b&w ... 2.00
❑8, Dec 1988 ... 2.00
❑9, Feb 1989 ... 2.00
❑10 ... 2.00
❑11 1990 ... 2.00
❑12 1990 ... 2.00
❑13 1990; Last Vortex issue ... 2.00
❑14, Mar 1991, b&w; Rip Off begins as publisher ... 2.50
❑15, May 1991, b&w ... 2.50
❑16, Jul 1991, b&w ... 2.50
❑17, Sep 1991, b&w ... 2.50
❑18, Nov 1991, b&w ... 2.50
❑19, Jan 1992, b&w ... 2.50
❑20, Mar 1992, b&w ... 2.50
❑21, May 1992, b&w ... 2.50
❑22, Jul 1992, b&w ... 2.50
❑23, Sep 1992, b&w ... 2.50
❑24, Nov 1992, b&w ... 2.50
❑25, Jan 1993, b&w ... 2.50
❑26, Mar 1993, b&w ... 2.50
❑27, May 1993 ... 2.50
❑28, Jul 1993, b&w ... 2.50
❑29, Sep 1993, b&w ... 2.50
❑30, Nov 1993, b&w ... 2.50

Savage Henry
Caliber / Iconografix

❑1, b&w ... 2.95
❑2, b&w ... 2.95
❑3, b&w ... 2.95

Savage Henry: Headstrong
Caliber

❑1, ca. 1995, b&w ... 2.95
❑2, ca. 1995, b&w ... 2.95
❑3, ca. 1995, b&w ... 2.95

N-MINT

Savage Hulk
Marvel

❑1, Jan 1996; prestige format; NN ... 6.95

Savage Ninja
Cadillac

❑1, Feb 1985; O: Savage Ninja ... 1.00

Savage Return of Dracula
Marvel

❑1, ca. 1992; Reprints Tomb of Dracula #1, 2 ... 2.00

Savages
Peregrine

❑1, ca. 2001 ... 2.95

Savages
Comax

❑1, b&w ... 2.50

Savage She-Hulk
Marvel

❑1, Feb 1980, JB (c); SL (w); JB (a); 1&O: She-Hulk ... 8.00
❑2, Mar 1980, JB (c); 1: Dan Zapper Ridge. 1: Morris Walters ... 5.00
❑3, Apr 1980 ... 2.50
❑4, May 1980 ... 2.50
❑5, Jun 1980 ... 2.50
❑6, Jul 1980, A: Iron Man ... 2.00
❑7, Aug 1980 ... 2.00
❑8, Sep 1980, A: Man-Thing ... 2.00
❑9, Oct 1980 ... 2.00
❑10, Nov 1980, 1: The Word; 1: Ultima ... 2.00
❑11, Dec 1980 ... 2.00
❑12, Jan 1981, V: Gemini ... 2.00
❑13, Feb 1981, FS (a); A: Man-Wolf ... 2.00
❑14, Mar 1981, FS (a); A: Man-Wolf. A: Hellcat ... 2.00
❑15, Apr 1981, FS (a) ... 2.00
❑16, May 1981, FS (a) ... 2.00
❑17, Jun 1981, V: Man-Elephant ... 2.00
❑18, Jul 1981, V: Grappler ... 2.00
❑19, Aug 1981 ... 2.00
❑20, Sep 1981 ... 2.00
❑21, Oct 1981 ... 2.00
❑22, Nov 1981, (c); FS (a); V: Radius ... 2.00
❑23, Dec 1981, FS (a) ... 2.00
❑24, Jan 1982, AM (a) ... 2.00
❑25, Feb 1982; Giant-size; Final Issue ... 2.00

Savage Sword of Conan
Marvel

❑1, Aug 1974, b&w; GK (w); JB, NA, GK, JSe, RA, BS (a); O: Red Sonja. O: Blackmark ... 60.00
❑2, Oct 1974 GK (w); JB, HC, GK, JSa (a); A: Kull ... 28.00
❑3, Dec 1974 ... 16.00
❑4, Feb 1975 GK (w); JB, NA, GK, AA (a) ... 12.00
❑5, Apr 1975 JB (a) ... 12.00
❑6, Jun 1975 ... 12.00
❑7, Aug 1975 GM, JB (a) ... 12.00
❑8, Oct 1975 ... 12.00
❑9, Dec 1975 ... 12.00
❑10, Feb 1976 JB (a) ... 12.00
❑11, Apr 1976; Magazine; Adapts Robert E. Howard story The Country of the Knife; b&w ... 8.00

N-MINT

❑12, Jun 1976; JB (a); Magazine; Adapts Robert E. Howard story The Slave Princess; b&w ... 8.00
❑13, Aug 1976; Reprints from Conan the Barbarian #17 and 18 ... 8.00
❑14, Sep 1976; Magazine; Adapts Robert E. Howard story; b&w ... 8.00
❑15, Oct 1976; JB (a); Magazine; Adapts Robert E. Howard story; b&w ... 8.00
❑16, Dec 1976; Conan; Bran Mak Morn ... 8.00
❑17, Feb 1977; Conan; Bran Mak Morn ... 8.00
❑18, Apr 1977; Conan; Solomon Kane ... 8.00
❑19, Jun 1977; Conan; Solomon Kane ... 8.00
❑20, Jul 1977; Magazine; b&w ... 8.00
❑21, Aug 1977; Magazine; Adapts unfinished Robert E. Howard story; b&w ... 6.00
❑22, Sep 1977; Solomon Kane ... 6.00
❑23, Oct 1977; Conan; King Kull; Red Sonja ... 6.00
❑24, Nov 1977; Magazine; Adapts Robert E. Howard story; b&w ... 6.00
❑25, Dec 1977; Conan; Solomon Kane ... 6.00
❑26, Jan 1978; Conan; Solomon Kane ... 6.00
❑27, Mar 1978; adapts Beyond the Black River ... 6.00
❑28, Apr 1978 ... 6.00
❑29, May 1978; Conan; Red Sonja ... 6.00
❑30, Jun 1978 ... 5.00
❑31, Jul 1978 ... 5.00
❑32, Aug 1978; adapts "The Flame Knife" ... 5.00
❑33, Sep 1978; Conan; Solomon Kane ... 5.00
❑34, Oct 1978; 1: Garth ... 5.00
❑35, Nov 1978 ... 5.00
❑36, Dec 1978 ... 5.00
❑37, Feb 1979; Conan; Solomon Kane ... 5.00
❑38, Mar 1979 JB, TD (a) ... 5.00
❑39, Apr 1979; Conan; Solomon Kane ... 5.00
❑40, May 1979 ... 5.00
❑41, Jun 1979; JB, TD (a); Conan; Solomon Kane ... 5.00
❑42, Jul 1979; JB, TD (a); Conan; Bran Mak Morn ... 5.00
❑43, Aug 1979; Conan; Bran Mak Morn ... 5.00
❑44, Sep 1979 SB, TD (a) ... 5.00
❑45, Oct 1979; Conan; Red Sonja ... 5.00
❑46, Nov 1979 TD (a) ... 5.00
❑47, Dec 1979 JB, GK (a) ... 5.00
❑48, Jan 1980 JB, TD (a) ... 5.00
❑49, Feb 1980 ... 5.00
❑50, Mar 1980 NR (c); JB, TD (a) ... 5.00
❑51, Apr 1980 ... 3.00
❑52, May 1980; NR (c); JB, TD (a); Conan crowned King of Aquilonia ... 3.00
❑53, Jun 1980 JB (a) ... 3.00
❑54, Jul 1980 JB (a) ... 3.00
❑55, Aug 1980 JB, AA (a) ... 3.00
❑56, Sep 1980 NR (c); JB, TD, GD (a) ... 3.00
❑57, Oct 1980 NR (c); JB, TD (a) ... 3.00
❑58, Nov 1980 NR (c); JB, TD, KGa (a) ... 3.00
❑59, Dec 1980 AA (a) ... 3.00
❑60, Jan 1981 JB (a) ... 3.00
❑61, Feb 1981 GD (w); JB (a) ... 3.00
❑62, Mar 1981 JB (a) ... 3.00
❑63, Apr 1981 GK (w); JB, GK, TP, BMc (a) ... 3.00
❑64, May 1981 ATh, GK (w); ATh, JB, GK (a) ... 3.00
❑65, Jun 1981 JB (w); JB, GK (a) ... 3.00

	N-MINT
❑66, Jul 1981 JB (w); JB (a)	3.00
❑67, Aug 1981 GK (w); JB, GK, AA (a)	3.00
❑68, Sep 1981 GD (a)	3.00
❑69, Oct 1981 GD (a)	3.00
❑70, Nov 1981; JB (a); Includes article on Conan movie	3.00
❑71, Dec 1981 JB (a)	3.00
❑72, Jan 1982 JB (a)	3.00
❑73, Feb 1982 JB (a)	3.00
❑74, Mar 1982 JB, VM, GD (a)	3.00
❑75, Apr 1982 AA (a)	3.00
❑76, May 1982 JB, AA (a)	3.00
❑77, Jun 1982 JB (a)	3.00
❑78, Jul 1982 JB, DG (a)	3.00
❑79, Aug 1982 JB (a)	3.00
❑80, Sep 1982 JB, AA (a)	3.00
❑81, Oct 1982 JB (a)	3.00
❑82, Nov 1982 AA (a)	3.00
❑83, Dec 1982 NA, AA (a); A: Red Sonja	3.00
❑84, Jan 1983 VM (a)	3.00
❑85, Feb 1983 GK (a)	3.00
❑86, Mar 1983 GK (a)	3.00
❑87, Apr 1983 JB (a)	3.00
❑88, May 1983 JB (a)	3.00
❑89, Jun 1983 GK (w); NR, AA (a)	3.00
❑90, Jul 1983 NR, JB (a)	3.00
❑91, Aug 1983 JB, VM (a)	3.00
❑92, Sep 1983 JB (a)	3.00
❑93, Oct 1983 JB (a)	3.00
❑94, Nov 1983 VM (c); VM (a)	3.00
❑95, Dec 1983 JB (a)	3.00
❑96, Jan 1984 JB (a)	3.00
❑97, Feb 1984	3.00
❑98, Mar 1984 JB (a)	3.00
❑99, Apr 1984 JB (a)	3.00
❑100, May 1984 JB (a)	3.00
❑101, Jun 1984 MG (c); JB (a)	2.50
❑102, Jul 1984 BSz (c)	2.50
❑103, Aug 1984 GD (a)	2.50
❑104, Sep 1984 VM, GD (a)	2.50
❑105, Oct 1984 MG (c)	2.50
❑106, Nov 1984 MG (c); GD (a)	2.50
❑107, Dec 1984	2.50
❑108, Jan 1985	2.50
❑109, Feb 1985	2.50
❑110, Mar 1985	2.50
❑111, Apr 1985	2.50
❑112, May 1985	2.50
❑113, Jun 1985	2.50
❑114, Jul 1985	2.50
❑115, Aug 1985 VM (a)	2.50
❑116, Sep 1985 SB (a)	2.50
❑117, Oct 1985 MG (c)	2.50
❑118, Nov 1985	2.50
❑119, Dec 1985	2.50
❑120, Jan 1986	2.50
❑121, Feb 1986	2.50
❑122, Mar 1986	2.50
❑123, Apr 1986	2.50
❑124, May 1986	2.50
❑125, Jun 1986	2.50
❑126, Jul 1986	2.50
❑127, Aug 1986	2.50
❑128, Sep 1986	2.50
❑129, Oct 1986	2.50
❑130, Nov 1986	2.50
❑131, Dec 1986	2.50
❑132, Jan 1987	2.50
❑133, Feb 1987	2.50
❑134, Mar 1987	2.50
❑135, Apr 1987	2.50
❑136, May 1987	2.50
❑137, Jun 1987	2.50
❑138, Jul 1987	2.50
❑139, Aug 1987	2.50
❑140, Sep 1987	2.50
❑141, Oct 1987	2.50
❑142, Nov 1987	2.50
❑143, Dec 1987	2.50
❑144, Jan 1988	2.50
❑145, Feb 1988 A: Red Sonja	2.50
❑146, Mar 1988	2.50
❑147, Apr 1988	2.50
❑148, May 1988	2.50
❑149, Jun 1988	2.50
❑150, Jul 1988 MG (c)	2.50
❑151, Aug 1988	2.50
❑152, Sep 1988	2.50
❑153, Oct 1988 LMc (a); A: Red Sonja	2.50
❑154, Nov 1988	2.50
❑155, Dec 1988	2.50
❑156, Jan 1989	2.50
❑157, Feb 1989	2.50
❑158, Mar 1989	2.50
❑159, Apr 1989	2.50
❑160, May 1989	2.50
❑161, Jun 1989	2.50
❑162, Jul 1989	2.50
❑163, Aug 1989	2.50
❑164, Sep 1989	2.50
❑165, Oct 1989	2.50
❑166, Nov 1989	2.50
❑167, Dec 1989	2.50
❑168, Dec 1989	2.50
❑169, Jan 1990	2.50
❑170, Feb 1990	2.50
❑171, Mar 1990	2.50
❑172, Apr 1990	2.50
❑173, May 1990	2.50
❑174, Jun 1990; Series continues as Savage Sword of Conan the Barbarian	2.25
❑175, Jul 1990	2.25
❑176, Aug 1990	2.25
❑177, Sep 1990	2.25
❑178, Oct 1990	2.25
❑179, Nov 1990 A: Red Sonja	2.25
❑180, Dec 1990	2.25
❑181, Jan 1991	2.25
❑182, Feb 1991	2.25
❑183, Mar 1991	2.25
❑184, Apr 1991 AA (a)	2.25
❑185, May 1991	2.25
❑186, Jun 1991	2.25
❑187, Jul 1991 A: Red Sonja	2.25
❑188, Aug 1991 DC (a)	2.25
❑189, Sep 1991 AA (a)	2.25
❑190, Oct 1991 JB (a)	2.25
❑191, Nov 1991 JB (a)	2.25
❑192, Dec 1991 JB (a)	2.25
❑193, Jan 1992 JB (a)	2.25
❑194, Feb 1992 JB (a)	2.25
❑195, Mar 1992 JB (a)	2.25
❑196, Apr 1992 JB (a)	2.25
❑197, May 1992 JB (a)	2.25
❑198, Jun 1992 JB (a)	2.25
❑199, Jul 1992 JB (a)	2.25
❑200, Aug 1992; JB (a); Conan meets Robert E. Howard	2.25
❑201, Sep 1992	2.25
❑202, Oct 1992 JB (a)	2.25
❑203, Nov 1992 JB (a)	2.25
❑204, Dec 1992 JB (a)	2.25
❑205, Jan 1993	2.25
❑206, Feb 1993	2.25
❑207, Mar 1993	2.25
❑208, Apr 199	2.25
❑209, May 1993	2.25
❑210, Jun 1993	2.25
❑211, Jul 1993	2.25
❑212, Aug 1993	2.25
❑213, Sep 1993	2.25
❑214, Oct 1993; Adapted from Robert E. Howard's "Red Nails"	2.25
❑215, Nov 1993	2.25
❑216, Dec 1993	2.25
❑217, Jan 1994	2.25
❑218, Feb 1994	2.25
❑219, Mar 1994	2.25
❑220, Apr 1994	2.25
❑221, May 1994, b&w	2.25
❑222, Jun 1994, b&w; JB (a)	2.25
❑223, Jul 1994, b&w; AA (a)	2.25
❑224, Aug 1994, b&w	2.25
❑225, Sep 1994, b&w; JB (a)	2.25
❑226, Oct 1994, b&w	2.25
❑227, Nov 1994, b&w; GE (w); GE (a)	2.25
❑228, Dec 1994, b&w; AN (a)	2.25
❑229, Jan 1995, b&w; AN (a)	2.25
❑230, Feb 1995, b&w	2.25
❑231, Mar 1995, b&w	2.25
❑232, Apr 1995, b&w	2.25
❑233, May 1995, b&w	2.25
❑234, Jun 1995, b&w; TS (c); TS, JB (a)	2.25
❑235, Jul 1995, b&w; JB (a); Final Issue	2.25
❑Ann 1, ca. 1975, b&w; reprinted from Conan the Barbarian (1st series) #10 and 13; Kull the Conqueror #3; Monsters on the Prowl #16	17.00
❑Special 1, ca. 1975	6.00

Savage Sword of Mike
Fandom House

	N-MINT
❑1, b&w	2.00

Savage Tales
Marvel

	N-MINT
❑1, May 1971, b&w magazine; SL (w); GM, GC, JB, JR, BS (a); 1&O: Man-Thing. A: Conan; Cover Painting by John Buscema	150.00
❑2, Oct 1973; JB (c); SL (w); AW, BWr, GM, FB (a); "Crusader" reprinted from The Black Knight #1	32.00
❑3, Feb 1974; SL (w); AW, FB, JR, JSt (a); Continues "Red Nails" story from issue #2	20.00
❑4, May 1974 SL (w); NA, GK (a)	20.00
❑5, Jul 1974; NA (c); DA, SL (w); JSn, JB, VM, NA, GK, DA (a); Conan; Brak: Reprint from Chamber of Chills #2; Ka-Zar: Reprint from Astonishing Tales #9	12.00
❑6, Sep 1974; Jann: Reprint from Jann of the Jungle #16; Ka-Zar: Reprint from Savage Tales (1st Series) #1	10.00
❑7, Nov 1974; Ka-Zar; Brak	10.00
❑8, Jan 1975; Ka-Zar; Brak	10.00
❑9, Mar 1975; Ka-Zar; Shanna the She-Devil	10.00
❑10, May 1975; Ka-Zar; Shanna the She-Devil	10.00
❑11, Jul 1975	10.00
❑12, Sum 1975	8.00
❑Ann 1, ca. 1975, b&w; GM, GK (a); O: Ka-Zar. Ka-Zar stories	25.00

Savage Tales
Marvel

	N-MINT
❑1, Oct 1985, b&w; magazine; MG (c); HT (w); MG, GM, HT, JSe (a); 1st 'Nam story	4.00
❑2, Dec 1985, HT (w); GM, HT, JSe (a); 2nd 'Nam story	3.00
❑3, Feb 1986, 2nd 'Nam story	2.50
❑4, Apr 1986, 'Nam	2.50
❑5, Jun 1986, JSe (a)	2.50
❑6, Aug 1986, JB, JSe (a)	2.00
❑7, Oct 1986, GM, JSe (a)	2.00
❑8, Dec 1986	2.00
❑9, Feb 1987, Final Issue	2.00

Savant Garde
Image

	N-MINT
❑1, Mar 1997	2.50
❑2, Apr 1997; 1: Innuendo	2.50
❑3, May 1997	2.50
❑4, Jun 1997	2.50
❑5, Jul 1997	2.50
❑6, Aug 1997	2.50
❑7, Sep 1997	2.50
❑Fan ed. 1/A, Feb 1997	1.00
❑Fan ed. 2/A, Mar 1997	1.00
❑Fan ed. 3/A, Apr 1997	1.00

Saved By the Bell
Harvey

	N-MINT
❑1, May 1992; Photo cover	1.25
❑2, Jun 1992	1.25
❑3, Jul 1992	1.25
❑4, Aug 1992	1.25
❑5, Sep 1992	1.25

Saviour
Trident

	N-MINT
❑1, Dec 1989, b&w; Adult	4.00
❑2, Feb 1990, b&w; Adult	1.95
❑3, Apr 1990, b&w; Adult	2.50
❑4, Aug 1990, b&w; Adult	2.50
❑5, Oct 1990, b&w; Adult	2.50

Saw: Rebirth
Idea & Design Works

	N-MINT
❑1	3.99

SB Ninja High School
Antarctic

	N-MINT
❑1/A, Aug 1992, b&w	2.50
❑1/B, Aug 1992, b&w; trading card	4.95
❑2/A, Feb 1993, b&w	2.95
❑2/B, Feb 1993, b&w; trading card	4.95
❑3/A, Sep 1994, b&w	2.75

Other grades: Multiply price above by 5/6 for VF/NM • 2/3 for VERY FINE • 1/3 for FINE • 1/5 for VERY GOOD • 1/8 for GOOD

Shockrockets

Elite space squadron action from Kurt Busiek

©Image

Shock Suspen Stories

Reprints E.C. crime classics

©Gemstone

Shogun Warriors

Toy tie-in has Marvel character appearances

©Marvel

Shonen Jump

Viz anthology features Yu-Gi-Oh!

©Viz

Shotgun Mary

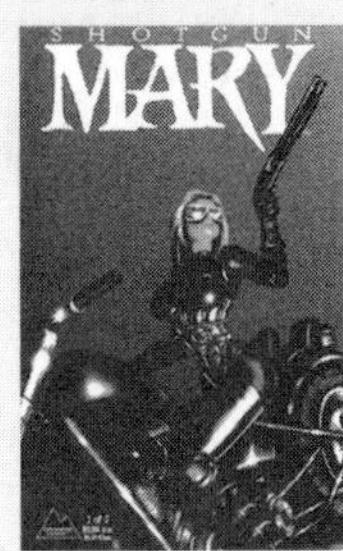

Double-barreled action with gun-wielding woman

©Antarctic

	N-MINT
❑3/B, Sep 1994, b&w; trading card	4.95
❑4, Feb 1995, b&w	2.75
❑5, May 1995, b&w	2.75
❑6, Aug 1995, b&w	2.75
❑7, Nov 1995, b&w	2.75

Scab
Fantaco

❑1, b&w	3.50
❑2, b&w	3.50

Scales of the Dragon
Sundragon

❑1, Mar 1997, b&w; Flip-book	1.95

Scalped
DC / Vertigo

❑1, Mar 2007	2.99

Scamp
Gold Key / Whitman

❑1, ca. 1968	8.00
❑2, Mar 1969	4.00
❑3, ca. 1970	4.00
❑4, Nov 1970	4.00
❑5, Feb 1971	4.00
❑6, Oct 1971	3.00
❑7, May 1972	3.00
❑8, Sep 1972	3.00
❑9, Nov 1972	3.00
❑10, Feb 1973	3.00
❑11, Jun 1973	2.50
❑12, Jul 1973	2.50
❑13, Sep 1973	2.50
❑14, Nov 1973	2.50
❑15, Jan 1974	2.50
❑16, Mar 1974	2.50
❑17, May 1974	2.50
❑18, Jul 1974	2.50
❑19, Sep 1974	2.50
❑20, Nov 1974	2.50
❑21, Jan 1975	2.00
❑22, Mar 1975	2.00
❑23, May 1975,	2.00
❑24, Jul 1975	2.00
❑25, Sep 1975	2.00
❑26, Nov 1975	2.00
❑27, Jan 1976	2.00
❑28, Mar 1976	2.00
❑29, May 1976	2.00
❑30, Jul 1976	2.00
❑31, Sep 1976	2.00
❑32, Nov 1976	2.00
❑33, Jan 1977	2.00
❑34, Mar 1977	2.00
❑35, May 1977	2.00
❑36, Jul 1977	2.00
❑37, Sep 1977	2.00
❑38, Nov 1977	2.00
❑39, Jan 1978	2.00
❑40, Mar 1978	2.00
❑41, May 1978	2.00
❑42, Jul 1978	2.00
❑43, Sep 1978	2.00
❑44, Nov 1978	2.00
❑45, Jan 1979	2.00

Scan
Iconografix

	N-MINT
❑1, b&w	2.95
❑2, b&w	2.95

Scandals
Thorby

❑1	2.95

Scandal Sheet
Arriba

❑1, b&w	2.50

Scarab
DC / Vertigo

❑0, Mar 1994	1.95
❑1, Nov 1993	1.95
❑2, Dec 1993	1.95
❑3, Jan 1994	1.95
❑4, Feb 1994	1.95
❑5, Mar 1994	1.95
❑6, Apr 1994	1.95
❑7, May 1994	1.95
❑8, Jun 1994	1.95

Scaramouch
Innovation

❑1, b&w	2.25
❑2, Feb 1991, b&w	2.25

Scarecrow of Romney Marsh
Gold Key

❑1, Apr 1964, No number; code on cover box ends in "404"	30.00
❑2, Jul 1965	20.00
❑3, Oct 1965	20.00

Scarecrow (Villains)
DC

❑1, Feb 1998; New Year's Evil	1.95

Scare Tactics
DC

❑1, Dec 1996; 1: Arnold Burnsteel; 1: Fang; 1: Grossout; 1: Screamqueen; 1: Slither; O: Scare Tactics	2.25
❑2, Jan 1997; Road Trip	2.25
❑3, Feb 1997	2.25
❑4, Mar 1997; O: Phil	2.25
❑5, Apr 1997; Valentine's Day Nightmare	2.25
❑6, May 1997	2.25
❑7, Jun 1997	2.25
❑8, Jul 1997	2.25
❑9, Aug 1997; series goes on hiatus; story continues in Impulse Plus #1	2.25
❑10, Jan 1998	2.25
❑11, Feb 1998; D: Slither	2.25
❑12, Mar 1998; Phil transforms	2.25

Scarface: Scarred for Life
Idea & Design Works

❑1, Jan 2007	3.99
❑1/Special, Jan 2007	19.99

Scarlet Crush
Awesome

❑1, Jan 1998; John Stinsman cover	2.50
❑2, Feb 1998; Cute cover	2.50

Scarlet in Gaslight
Eternity

	N-MINT
❑1, Mar 1988, b&w; Sherlock Holmes vs. Dracula	1.95
❑2, Apr 1988; b&w	1.95
❑3, May 1988; b&w	1.95
❑4, Jun 1988; b&w	1.95

Scarlet Kiss: The Vampyre
All American

❑1, b&w	2.95

Scarlet Scorpion/Darkshade
AC

❑1, Jul 1995	3.50
❑2 1995	3.50

Scarlet Spider
Marvel

❑1, Nov 1995, JR2 (c); GK (a)	2.00
❑2, Dec 1995, JR2 (c); JR2 (a); concludes in Spectacular Scarlet Spider #2	2.00

Scarlet Spider Unlimited
Marvel

❑1, Nov 1995	3.95

Scarlett
DC

❑1, Jan 1993; 1&O: Scarlett; 48 pages	3.00
❑2, Feb 1993	2.00
❑3, Mar 1993	2.00
❑4, Apr 1993	1.75
❑5, May 1993	1.75
❑6, Jun 1993	1.75
❑7, Jul 1993	1.75
❑8, Aug 1993	1.75
❑9, Sep 1993	1.75
❑10, Oct 1993	1.75
❑11, Nov 1993	1.75
❑12, Dec 1993	1.75
❑13, Jan 1994	1.75
❑14, Feb 1994; Final Issue	1.75

Scarlet Thunder
Slave Labor / Amaze Ink

❑1, Nov 1995	1.50
❑2, Feb 1996; 1: Blue Streak	1.50
❑3, May 1996; 1: Betty Joseph; 1: Oskar (cameo)	2.50
❑4, Dec 1996; 1: Lady Liberty; 1: Oskar (full)	2.50

Scarlett Pilgrim
Last Gasp

❑1; Adult	1.00

Scarlet Traces: The Great Game
Dark Horse

❑1, Jul 2006	2.99
❑2, Oct 2006	2.99
❑3, Nov 2006	2.99
❑4, Nov 2006	2.99

Scarlet Witch
Marvel

❑1, Jan 1994	1.75
❑2, Feb 1994	1.75
❑3, Mar 1994	1.75
❑4, Apr 1994	1.75

Scarlet Zombie
Comax
❑1, b&w; Adult 2.95

Scars
Avatar
❑1, Jan 2003 3.50
❑2, Feb 2003 3.50
❑2/A, Feb 2003; Wrap Cover 3.95
❑3, Mar 2003 3.50
❑4, Apr 2003 3.50
❑5, May 2003 3.50
❑5/A, May 2003; Wrap Cover 3.95
❑6, Jun 2003 3.50
❑6/A, Jun 2003; Wrap Cover 3.95

Scary!
Fantagraphics

Scary Book
Caliber
❑1, b&w 2.50
❑2, b&w 2.50

Scary Godmother
Sirius
❑1, May 2001; b&w 2.95
❑2, ca. 2001; b&w 2.95
❑3, ca. 2001; b&w 2.95
❑4, ca. 2001; b&w 2.95
❑5, ca. 2001; b&w 2.95
❑6, ca. 2001; b&w 2.95

Scary Godmother: Bloody Valentine
Sirius
❑1, Feb 1998 3.95

Scary Godmother Holiday Spooktacular
Sirius
❑1, Nov 1998, b&w; wraparound cover 2.95

Scary Godmother: Wild About Harry
Sirius
❑1, ca. 2000, b&w 2.95
❑2, ca. 2000, b&w 2.95
❑3, ca. 2000, b&w 2.95

Scary Tales
Charlton
❑1, Aug 1975, 1&O: Countess Von Bludd 5.00
❑2, Oct 1975 3.00
❑3, Dec 1975 3.00
❑4, Feb 1976 3.00
❑5, Apr 1976 3.00
❑6, Jun 1976 2.50
❑7, Sep 1976 2.50
❑8, Nov 1976 2.50
❑9, Jan 1977 2.50
❑10, Sep 1977 2.50
❑11, Jan 1978 2.00
❑12, Mar 1978 2.00
❑13, Apr 1978 2.00
❑14, May 1978 2.00
❑15, Jul 1978 2.00
❑16, Oct 1978 2.00
❑17, Dec 1978 2.00
❑18, Feb 1979 2.00
❑19, Apr 1979 2.00
❑20, Jun 1979 2.00
❑21, Aug 1980 2.00
❑22, Oct 1980 2.00
❑23, Dec 1980 2.00
❑24, Feb 1981, SD, JSa, MZ (a) 2.00
❑25, Apr 1981 2.00
❑26, Jun 1981 2.00
❑27, Aug 1981 2.00
❑28, Oct 1981 2.00
❑29, Dec 1981 2.00
❑30, Feb 1982 2.00
❑31, Apr 1982 2.00
❑32, Jun 1982 2.00
❑33, Aug 1982 2.00
❑34, Oct 1982 2.00
❑35, Dec 1982 2.00
❑36, Feb 1983 2.00
❑37, Apr 1983 2.00
❑38, Jun 1983 2.00
❑39, Aug 1983 2.00
❑40, Oct 1983 2.00
❑41, Dec 1983 2.00
❑42, Feb 1984 2.00
❑43, Apr 1984 2.00
❑44, Jun 1984 2.00
❑45, Aug 1984 2.00
❑46, Oct 1984, Final Issue 2.00

Scatterbrain
Dark Horse
❑1, Jun 1998 2.95
❑2, Jul 1998 2.95
❑3, Aug 1998 2.95
❑4, Sep 1998 2.95

Scavengers
Fleetway-Quality
❑1, Feb 1988; Judge Dredd 1.25
❑2, Mar 1988; Judge Dredd 1.25
❑3, Apr 1988; Judge Dredd 1.25
❑4, May 1988; Judge Dredd 1.25
❑5, Jun 1988 1.25
❑6, Jul 1988 1.50
❑7, Aug 1988 1.50
❑8, Sep 1988 1.50
❑9, Oct 1988 1.50
❑10, Nov 1988 1.50
❑11, Dec 1988 1.50
❑12, Jan 1989 1.50
❑13 1989 1.50
❑14 1989 1.50

Scavengers
Triumphant
❑0, Mar 1994; giveaway; 30, 000-copy edition 1.00
❑0/A, Mar 1994; 18, 000-copy edition 2.50
❑0/B, Mar 1994; 5000-copy edition 2.50
❑1, Jul 1993 2.50
❑1/Ashcan, Jul 1993; ashcan edition 2.50
❑2, Aug 1993 2.50
❑3, Sep 1993 2.50
❑4, Oct 1993 2.50
❑5, Nov 1993; D: Jack Hanal. Unleashed! 2.50
❑6, Dec 1993; Unleashed! 2.50
❑7, Jan 1994 2.50
❑8, Feb 1994 2.50
❑9, Mar 1994 2.50
❑10, Apr 1994 2.50
❑11, May 1994 2.50

SCC Convention Special
Super Crew
❑1; 1994 Convention Special 2.25

Scenario A
Antarctic
❑1, Jul 1998, b&w 2.95
❑2, Sep 1998, b&w 2.95

Scene of the Crime
DC / Vertigo
❑1, May 1999 2.50
❑2, Jun 1999 2.50
❑3, Jul 1999 2.50
❑4, Aug 1999 2.50

Schizo
Antarctic
❑1, Dec 1994, b&w 3.50
❑2, Jan 1996, b&w 3.95
❑3, Mar 1998, b&w 3.95

Science Affair, A
Antarctic
❑1, Mar 1994, b&w 2.75
❑1/Gold, Mar 1994; Gold edition 3.00
❑2, May 1994, b&w 2.75

Science Fair
Antarctic
❑1, ca. 2005 2.99
❑2, ca. 2005 2.99
❑3, ca. 2005 2.99

Science Fair Story of Electronics — The Discovery That Changed the World!
Radio Shack
❑1981, Fal 1981; Promotional giveaway from Radio Shack/Tandy; other editions exist as New Science Fair Story of Electronics; issue number indicates year of publication 1.00
❑1984, Spr 1984 1.00

Science Fiction Classics
Dragon Lady
❑1; Twin Earths 5.95

Sci-Fi
Rough Copy
❑1 2.95

Scimidar
Eternity
❑1, Jun 1988, b&w 2.50
❑2 1988, b&w 2.50
❑3 1988, b&w 2.50
❑4/A, Dec 1988; "mild" cover 2.00
❑4/B, Dec 1988; "hot" cover 2.00

Scimidar Book II
Eternity
❑1, May 1989, b&w; Adult 3.00
❑1/2nd; 2nd printing; Adult 3.00
❑2, b&w; PG (c); Adult 3.00
❑3, b&w; Adult 3.00
❑4, b&w; Adult 3.00

Scimidar Book III
Eternity
❑1, Jan 1990, b&w; Adult 3.00
❑1/2nd; 2nd printing; Adult 3.00
❑2, Feb 1990, b&w; Adult 3.00
❑3, b&w; Adult 3.00
❑4, b&w; Adult 3.00

Scimidar Book IV: "Wild Thing"
Eternity
❑1 3.00
❑1/Nude; Nude cover 3.00
❑2, b&w 3.00
❑3, b&w 3.00
❑4, b&w 3.00

Scimidar Book V: "Living Color"
Eternity
❑1, Apr 1991, b&w 2.50
❑1/Nude, Apr 1991, b&w; Nude cover 2.50
❑2, May 1991, b&w 2.50
❑3, Jun 1991, b&w 2.50
❑4, Sep 1991, b&w 2.50

Scimidar
CFD
❑1, b&w; ca. 1995 2.95
❑3 2.75

Scimidar Pin-Up Book
Eternity
❑1, Oct 1990, unstapled 3.75

Scion
CrossGen
❑1, Jul 2000 2.95
❑2, Aug 2000 2.95
❑3, Sep 2000 2.95
❑4, Oct 2000 2.95
❑5, Nov 2000 2.95
❑6, Dec 2000 2.95
❑7, Jan 2001 2.95
❑8, Feb 2001 2.95
❑9, Mar 2001 2.95
❑10, Apr 2001 2.95
❑11, May 2001 2.95
❑12, Jun 2001 2.95
❑13, Jul 2001 2.95
❑14, Aug 2001 2.95
❑15, Sep 2001 2.95
❑16, Oct 2001 2.95
❑17, Nov 2001 2.95
❑18, Dec 2001 2.95
❑19, Jan 2002 2.95
❑20, Feb 2002 2.95
❑21, Mar 2002 2.95
❑22, Apr 2002 2.95
❑23, May 2002 2.95
❑24, Jun 2002 2.95
❑25, Jul 2002 2.95
❑26, Aug 2002 2.95
❑27, Sep 2002 2.95
❑28, Oct 2002 2.95
❑29, Nov 2002 2.95
❑30, Dec 2002 2.95
❑31, Jan 2003 2.95
❑32, Feb 2003 2.95
❑33, Mar 2003 2.95
❑34, Apr 2003 2.95

Other grades: Multiply price above by 5/6 for VF/NM • 2/3 for VERY FINE • 1/3 for FINE • 1/5 for VERY GOOD • 1/8 for GOOD

Showcase

DC tryout title initiated Silver Age

©DC

Showcase '93

Trio of tales set in Gotham City

©DC

Showcase '95

Tales' focus moves to Metropolis

©DC

Shrek

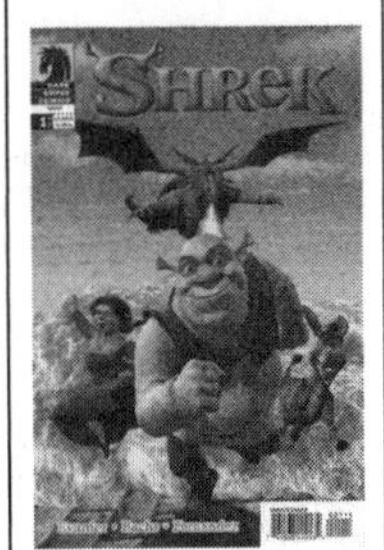

Animated adaptation definitely delayed

©Dark Horse

Sigil

One of the first four CrossGen titles

©CrossGen

	N-MINT
❑35, May 2003	2.95
❑36, Jun 2003	2.95
❑37, Jul 2003	2.95
❑38, Aug 2003; Asjleigh Pin-Up	2.95
❑39, Oct 2003	2.95
❑40, Nov 2003	2.95
❑42, Jan 2004	2.95
❑41, Dec 2003	2.95
❑43, Apr 2004; Final Issue	2.95

Sci-Spy
DC / Vertigo

❑1, Apr 2002	2.50
❑2, May 2002	2.50
❑3, Jun 2002	2.50
❑4, Jul 2002	2.50
❑5, Aug 2002	2.50
❑6, Sep 2002	2.50

Sci-Tech
DC / Wildstorm

❑1, Sep 1999	2.50
❑2, Oct 1999	2.50
❑3, Nov 1999	2.50
❑4, Dec 1999	2.50

Scooby-Doo
Marvel

❑1, Oct 1977	20.00
❑1/35¢, Oct 1977, 35¢ regional price variant	20.00
❑2, Dec 1977	7.00
❑3, Feb 1978	7.00
❑4, Apr 1978	7.00
❑5, Jun 1978	4.00
❑6, Aug 1978	4.00
❑7, Oct 1978	4.00
❑8, Dec 1978; Pages 1 and 30 printed out of order	4.00
❑9, Feb 1979; Final issue	4.00

Scooby-Doo
Harvey

❑1, ca. 1992	1.50
❑2, ca. 1992	1.50
❑3, ca. 1992	1.50
❑GS 1, ca. 1992	2.25
❑GS 2, ca. 1992	2.25
❑Special 1	1.95
❑Special 2	1.95

Scooby-Doo
Archie

❑1, Oct 1995	1.50
❑2, Nov 1995	1.50
❑3, Dec 1995	1.50
❑4, Jan 1996	1.50
❑5, Feb 1996	1.50
❑6, Mar 1996	1.50
❑7, Apr 1996	1.50
❑8, May 1996	1.50
❑10, Jul 1996	1.50
❑11, Aug 1996	1.50
❑12, Sep 1996	1.50
❑14, Nov 1996	1.50
❑15, Dec 1996	1.50
❑16, Jan 1997	1.50
❑17, Feb 1997	1.50
❑18, Mar 1997	1.50

	N-MINT
❑19, Apr 1997	1.50
❑20, May 1997	1.50
❑21, Jun 1997	1.50

Scooby-Doo
DC

❑1, Aug 1997 JSa (a)	2.50
❑2, Sep 1997	2.00
❑3, Oct 1997 JSa (a)	2.00
❑4, Nov 1997 JSa (c)	2.00
❑5, Dec 1997 JSa (a)	2.00
❑6, Jan 1998 A: Stetson Rogers (Shaggy's cousin).	2.00
❑7, Feb 1998	2.00
❑8, Mar 1998	2.00
❑9, Apr 1998	2.00
❑10, May 1998	2.00
❑11, Jun 1998	2.00
❑12, Jul 1998; JSa (a); mystery at a comic-book convention	2.00
❑13, Aug 1998	2.00
❑14, Sep 1998	2.00
❑15, Oct 1998	2.00
❑16, Nov 1998 A: Groovy Ghoulie	2.00
❑17, Dec 1998	2.00
❑18, Jan 1999	2.00
❑19, Feb 1999 JSa (a)	2.00
❑20, Mar 1999 JSa (a); A: Mystery, Inc.	2.00
❑21, Apr 1999 JSa (a); A: Mystery, Inc.	1.99
❑22, May 1999	1.99
❑23, Jun 1999 JSa (a)	1.99
❑24, Jul 1999 DP (a)	1.99
❑25, Aug 1999 DP (a)	1.99
❑26, Sep 1999 JSa (a)	1.99
❑27, Oct 1999 JSa (a)	1.99
❑28, Nov 1999 JSa (a)	1.99
❑29, Dec 1999 JSa, DP (a)	1.99
❑30, Jan 2000 JSa (a)	1.99
❑31, Feb 2000	1.99
❑32, Mar 2000	1.99
❑33, Apr 2000	1.99
❑34, May 2000 JSa (a)	1.99
❑35, Jun 2000 JSa (a)	1.99
❑36, Jul 2000	1.99
❑37, Aug 2000 JSa (a)	1.99
❑38, Sep 2000 JSa (a)	1.99
❑39, Oct 2000 JSa (a)	1.99
❑40, Nov 2000	1.99
❑41, Dec 2000 JSa (a)	1.99
❑42, Jan 2001 JSa (a)	1.99
❑43, Feb 2001 JSa (a)	1.99
❑44, Mar 2001 JSa (a)	1.99
❑45, Apr 2001 JSa (a)	1.99
❑46, May 2001 DDC (w); JSa (a)	1.99
❑47, Jun 2001 JSa (a)	1.99
❑48, Jul 2001 JSa (a)	1.99
❑49, Aug 2001	1.99
❑50, Sep 2001 JSa (c); JSa (a); A: Speed Buggy. A: Funky Phantom	1.99
❑51, Oct 2001 DDC (a)	1.99
❑52, Nov 2001 JSa (a)	1.99
❑53, Dec 2001 JSa (a)	1.99
❑54, Jan 2002 JSa (a)	1.99
❑55, Feb 2002 JSa (a)	1.99
❑56, Mar 2002 JSa (a)	1.99
❑57, Apr 2002 JSa (a)	1.99
❑58, May 2002	1.99

	N-MINT
❑59, Jun 2002 JSa (a)	1.99
❑60, Jul 2002 JSa (a)	1.99
❑61, Aug 2002 JSa (a)	1.99
❑62, Sep 2002 JSa (a)	1.99
❑63, Oct 2002 JSa (a)	1.99
❑64, Nov 2002	1.99
❑65, Dec 2002 JSa (c); JSa (a)	2.25
❑66, Jan 2003	2.25
❑67, Feb 2003	2.25
❑68, Mar 2003	2.25
❑69, Apr 2003	2.25
❑70, May 2003	2.25
❑71, Jun 2003	2.25
❑72, Jul 2003	2.25
❑73, Aug 2003	2.25
❑74, Sep 2003	2.25
❑75, Oct 2003	2.25
❑76, Nov 2003	2.25
❑77, Dec 2003	2.25
❑78, Jan 2004	2.25
❑79, Feb 2004	2.25
❑80, Mar 2004	2.25
❑81, Apr 2004	2.25
❑82, May 2004	2.25
❑83, Jun 2004	2.25
❑84, Jul 2004	2.25
❑85, Aug 2004	2.25
❑86, Sep 2004	2.25
❑87, Oct 2004	2.25
❑88, Nov 2004	2.25
❑89, Dec 2004	2.25
❑90, Jan 2005	2.25
❑91, Feb 2005	2.25
❑92, Mar 2005	2.25
❑93, Apr 2005	2.25
❑94, May 2005	2.25
❑95, Jun 2005	2.25
❑96, Jun 2005	2.25
❑97, Jul 2005	2.25
❑98, Aug 2005	2.25
❑99, Sep 2005	2.25
❑100, Oct 2005	2.25
❑101, Nov 2005; Includes Bioncle Preview	2.25
❑102, Jan 2006; Includes Heroscape #4 insert	2.25
❑103, Feb 2006	2.25
❑104, Mar 2006	2.25
❑105, Apr 2006	2.25
❑106, May 2006	2.25
❑107, Jun 2006	2.25
❑109, Sep 2006	2.25
❑110, Sep 2006	2.25
❑111, Oct 2006	2.25
❑112, Nov 2006	2.25
❑113, Dec 2006	2.25
❑114, Jan 2007, Includes 3-D Heroscape glasses; Includes Teen Titans: Sparktop mini-comic	2.25
❑115, Mar 2007	2.25
❑116	2.25
❑117	2.25
❑118	2.25
❑119	2.25
❑120	2.25
❑121	2.25

Other grades: Multiply price above by 5/6 for VF/NM • 2/3 for VERY FINE • 1/3 for FINE • 1/5 for VERY GOOD • 1/8 for GOOD

N-MINT

❑122 .... 2.25
❑123 .... 2.25
❑124 .... 2.25
❑125 .... 2.25
❑126 .... 2.25
❑127 .... 2.25
❑128 .... 2.25
❑129 .... 2.25
❑130 .... 2.25
❑131 .... 2.25
❑132 .... 2.25
❑133 .... 2.25
❑134 .... 2.25
❑135 .... 2.25
❑136 .... 2.25
❑137 .... 2.25
❑138 .... 2.25
❑138 .... 2.25
❑139 .... 2.25
❑140 .... 2.25
❑141 .... 2.25
❑142 .... 2.25
❑143 .... 2.25
❑144 .... 2.25
❑145 .... 2.25
❑Summer 1, Aug 2001; JSa (a); Super Scarefest! 3.95
❑Special 1, Oct 1999; JSa, EC (a); Spooky Spectacular 3.00
❑Special 2, Oct 2000 JSa (a) 3.95

Scooby-Doo Big Book
Harvey

❑1, Nov 1992 .... 1.95
❑2, Apr 2003 .... 1.95

Scooby-Doo Dollar Comic
DC

❑1, Oct 2003 .... 1.00

Scooby-Doo Super Scarefest
DC

❑1, Aug 2002 .... 3.95

Scooby Doo, Where Are You?
Gold Key

❑1, Mar 1970 .... 100.00
❑2, Jun 1970 .... 50.00
❑3, Sep 1970 .... 50.00
❑4, Dec 1970 .... 50.00
❑5, Mar 1971 .... 50.00
❑6, Jun 1971 .... 50.00
❑7, Aug 1971 .... 50.00
❑8, Oct 1971 .... 50.00
❑9, Dec 1971 .... 25.00
❑10, Feb 1972 .... 25.00
❑11, Apr 1972 .... 25.00
❑12, Jun 1972 .... 25.00
❑13, Aug 1972 .... 25.00
❑14, Oct 1972 .... 25.00
❑15, Dec 1972 .... 25.00
❑16, ca. 1973 .... 25.00
❑17, ca. 1973, Title changes to Scooby Doo Mystery Comics 25.00
❑18, ca. 1973 .... 25.00
❑19, Jul 1973 .... 25.00
❑20, Aug 1973 .... 15.00
❑21, Oct 1973 .... 15.00
❑22, Dec 1973 .... 15.00
❑23, Feb 1974 .... 15.00
❑24, Apr 1974 .... 15.00
❑25, Jun 1974, Indicia says Scooby-Doo ... Mystery Comics 15.00
❑26, ca. 1974, Reprints issue #6 .... 15.00
❑27, ca. 1974 .... 15.00
❑28, ca. 1974 .... 15.00
❑29, Dec 1974 .... 15.00
❑30, ca. 1975, Series moves to Charlton; Last issue 15.00

Scooby Doo, Where Are You?
Charlton

❑1, Apr 1975 .... 15.00
❑2, Jun 1975 .... 10.00
❑3, Aug 1975 .... 7.00
❑4, Oct 1975 .... 7.00
❑5, Dec 1975 .... 7.00
❑6, Feb 1976 .... 6.00
❑7, Apr 1976 .... 6.00
❑8, Jun 1976 .... 6.00
❑9, Aug 1976 .... 6.00
❑10, Oct 1976 .... 6.00
❑11, Dec 1976 .... 5.00

Scooterman
Wellzee

❑1, Apr 1996, b&w 2.75
❑2, Dec 1996, b&w; poster 2.75
❑3, Jul 1997, b&w 2.75

Scorched Earth
Tundra

❑1, Apr 1991 .... 2.95
❑2, Jun 1991 .... 2.95
❑3, Aug 1991; Last issue (issues #4-6 solicited but cancelled) 2.95

Scorchy
Forbidden Fruit

❑1, b&w; Adult 3.50

Score
DC / Piranha

❑1, ca. 1989; Adult 4.95
❑2, ca. 1989; Adult 4.95
❑3, ca. 1989; Adult 4.95
❑4, ca. 1989; Adult 4.95

Scorn: Deadly Rebellion
SCC Entertainment

❑0, Jul 1996, b&w 2.95

Scorn: Heatwave
SCC Entertainment

❑1, Jan 1997, b&w; follows events in Scorn: Deadly Rebellion 3.95

Scorpia
Miller

❑1 .... 2.50
❑2 .... 2.50

Scorpion
Annruel

❑1, b&w 2.50

Scorpion
Atlas-Seaboard

❑1, Feb 1975, HC (c); HC (w); HC (a); 1: The Scorpion I (Moro Frost). Scarce in high grade due to black cover 16.00
❑2, Apr 1975, HC (w); BWr, HC (a) 16.00
❑3, Jul 1975, 1: The Scorpion II (David Harper). Golem cover and story 10.00

Scorpion Corps
Dagger

❑1, Nov 1993; 1: Streik; Includes coupon for Dagger Universe #0 .... 2.50
❑2, Dec 1993; Includes coupon for Dagger Universe #0 .... 2.50
❑3, Jan 1994 .... 2.50
❑4, Feb 1994 .... 2.50
❑5, Mar 1994 .... 2.50
❑6, Apr 1994 .... 2.50
❑7, May 1994 .... 2.50
❑8, Jun 1994 .... 2.50
❑9, Jul 1994 .... 2.50
❑10, Aug 1994 .... 2.50

Scorpion King
Dark Horse

❑1, Mar 2002 .... 2.99
❑2, Apr 2002 .... 2.99

Scorpion Moon
Express / Entity

❑1, Oct 1994, b&w; Cardstock cover; 4th in a series of Entity illustrated novellas with Zen Intergalactic Ninja 2.95

Scorpio Rising
Marvel

❑1, Oct 1994; prestige format one-shot 5.95

Scorpio Rose
Eclipse

❑1, Jan 1983; MR (a); 1&O: Scorpio Rose. 1: Doctor Orient 2.00
❑2, Oct 1983 MR (a) 2.00

Scout
Eclipse

❑1, Nov 1985; Fashion in Action back-up 2.00
❑2, Dec 1985; Fashion in Action back-up 2.00
❑3, Jan 1985; Fashion in Action back-up 2.00
❑4, Feb 1986; Fashion in Action back-up 2.00
❑5, Mar 1986; Fashion in Action back-up 2.00
❑6, Apr 1986; Fashion in Action back-up 2.00
❑7, May 1986; TY (a); Fashion in Action back-up 2.00
❑8, Jun 1986; Fashion in Action back-up 2.00
❑9, Jul 1986; Airboy preview 2.00
❑10, Aug 1986; JDu, TY (a); Scout: XQB portfolio 2.00
❑11, Sep 1986; Monday: The Eliminator back-up begins 1.75
❑12, Oct 1986; Monday: The Eliminator back-up 1.75
❑13, Nov 1986; Monday: The Eliminator back-up 1.75
❑14, Dec 1986; Monday: The Eliminator back-up 1.75
❑15, Jan 1987; Swords of Texas back-up 1.75
❑16, Feb 1987; 3-D, glasses included 4.00
❑17, Mar 1987 A: Beanish 1.75
❑18, Apr 1987; Monday the Eliminator 1.75
❑19, May 1987; Flexidisc record by Tim Truman included 4.00
❑20, Jun 1987; Swords of Texas 1.75
❑21, Jul 1987; Beau LaDuke 1.75
❑22, Aug 1987 .... 1.75
❑23, Sep 1987 .... 1.75
❑24, Oct 1987 .... 1.75

Scout Handbook
Eclipse

❑1, ca. 1987; Details about characters and locations found in Scout and Scout: War Shaman 1.75

Scout: War Shaman
Eclipse

❑1, Mar 1988 .... 2.00
❑2, May 1988 .... 2.00
❑3, Jun 1988 .... 2.00
❑4, Jul 1988 .... 2.00
❑5, Aug 1988 .... 2.00
❑6, Sep 1988 .... 2.00
❑7, Oct 1988 .... 2.00
❑8, Nov 1988 .... 2.00
❑9, Dec 1988 .... 2.00
❑10, Jan 1989 .... 2.00
❑11, Feb 1989 .... 2.00
❑12, Mar 1989 .... 2.00
❑13, Apr 1989 .... 2.00
❑14, May 1989 .... 2.00
❑15, Jun 1989 .... 2.00
❑16, Jul 1989; D: Scout 2.00

Scrap City Pack Rats
Out of the Blue

❑1, b&w 1.50
❑2, b&w 1.50
❑3, b&w 1.50
❑4, b&w 1.75
❑5 1986, b&w 1.75

Scratch
Outside

❑1 1986 .... 1.75
❑2 1986 .... 1.75
❑3 1987 .... 1.75
❑4, Apr 1987 .... 1.75
❑5 1987 .... 1.75
❑6 1987 .... 1.75

Scratch
DC

❑1, Aug 2004 .... 2.50
❑2, Sep 2004 .... 2.50
❑3, Oct 2004 .... 2.50
❑4, Nov 2004 .... 2.50
❑5, Dec 2004 .... 2.50

Screamers
Fantagraphics / Eros

❑1 1995; Adult 2.95
❑2 1995; Adult 2.95
❑3, Oct 1995; Adult 2.95

Screen Monsters
Zone

❑1 .... 2.95

Screenplay
Slave Labor

❑1, Jun 1989, b&w 1.75

Screwball Squirrel
Dark Horse

❑1, Jul 1995, Wolf & Red back-up 2.50

Other grades: Multiply price above by 5/6 for VF/NM • 2/3 for VERY FINE • 1/3 for FINE • 1/5 for VERY GOOD • 1/8 for GOOD

Silencers (Image)

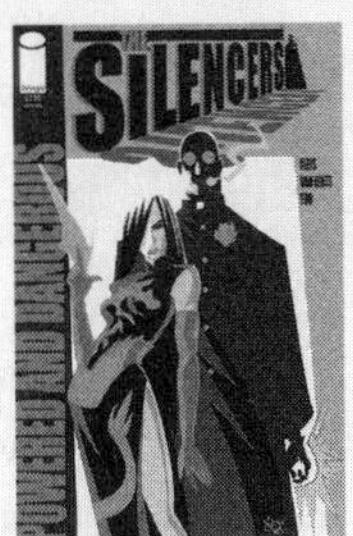

Adventure series from Steve Ellis
©Image

Silly Daddy

Slice of life stories with Joe Chiappetta
©Joe Chiappetta

Silver Age

Hearkening back to the 80-page giants
©DC

Silverblade

Maltese Falcon rolls back the years
©DC

Silver Sable

Female gun-for-hire spinoff from Spider-Man
©Marvel

N-MINT

❑2, Aug 1995, Droopy back-up 2.50
❑3, Sep 1995, Wolf & Red back-up 2.50

Screw Comics
Fantagraphics / Eros

❑1, b&w; Adult 3.50

Scrubs in Scrubland: The Reflex
Scrubland

❑1, b&w; Anthology 2.50

Scud: Tales from the Vending Machine
Fireman

❑1, Jan 1998 .... 3.00
❑2, Mar 1998 .... 2.50
❑3, May 1998; Photo Cover 2.50
❑4, Jul 1998 .... 2.50

Scud: The Disposable Assassin
Fireman

❑1, Feb 1994, b&w; 1: Scud; Includes trading card 10.00
❑1/2nd; 1: Scud. 2nd printing; Includes trading card 2.95
❑1/3rd 1997; 1: Scud. 3rd printing; Includes trading card 2.95
❑2, May 1994, b&w 4.00
❑3, b&w 4.00
❑4, b&w 4.00
❑5, b&w 4.00
❑6, b&w 2.95
❑7, b&w 2.95
❑8 1995, b&w 2.95
❑9, b&w 2.95
❑10, b&w 2.95
❑11 .... 2.95
❑12 .... 2.95
❑13 .... 2.95
❑14, Nov 1996 .... 2.95
❑15, Apr 1997 .... 2.95
❑16, Jun 1997 .... 2.95
❑17, Aug 1997 .... 2.95
❑18, Nov 1997 .... 2.95
❑19, Dec 1997 .... 2.95
❑20, Feb 1998 .... 2.95

Scum of the Earth
Aircel

❑1, Aug 1991, b&w; Movie adaptation; b&w 2.50
❑2, Oct 1991, b&w; Movie adaptation; b&w 2.50

Sea Devils
DC

❑1, Oct 1961, RH (a) 500.00
❑2, Dec 1961 .... 300.00
❑3, Feb 1962, RH (a) 200.00
❑4, Apr 1962 .... 125.00
❑5, Jun 1962 .... 125.00
❑6, Aug 1962 .... 75.00
❑7, Oct 1962 .... 75.00
❑8, Dec 1962 .... 75.00
❑9, Feb 1963 .... 75.00
❑10, Apr 1963 .... 75.00
❑11, Jun 1963 .... 75.00
❑12, Aug 1963 .... 75.00
❑13, Oct 1963, IN (c); GC, JKu, RA (a); Artists appear as themselves in the stories 75.00
❑14, Dec 1963 .... 50.00

N-MINT

❑15, Feb 1964 .... 50.00
❑16, Apr 1964 .... 50.00
❑17, Jun 1964 .... 50.00
❑18, Aug 1964 .... 50.00
❑19, Oct 1964 .... 50.00
❑20, Dec 1964 .... 50.00
❑21, Feb 1965 .... 35.00
❑22, Apr 1965 .... 35.00
❑23, Jun 1965 .... 35.00
❑24, Aug 1965 .... 35.00
❑25, Oct 1965 .... 35.00
❑26, Dec 1965 .... 35.00
❑27, Feb 1966 .... 35.00
❑28, Apr 1966 .... 35.00
❑29, Jun 1966 .... 35.00
❑30, Aug 1966 .... 35.00
❑31, Oct 1966 .... 35.00
❑32, Dec 1966 .... 35.00
❑33, Feb 1967 .... 35.00
❑34, Apr 1967 .... 35.00
❑35, Jun 1967, Final Issue 35.00

Seadragon
Elite

❑1, May 1986 .... 1.75
❑2, Jun 1986 .... 1.75
❑3, Aug 1986 .... 1.75
❑4 1986 .... 1.75
❑5 1986 .... 1.75
❑6, Jan 1986 .... 1.75

Seaguy
DC

❑1, Jul 2004 .... 2.95
❑2, Aug 2004 .... 2.95
❑3, Sep 2004 .... 2.95

Sea Hunt
Dell

❑4, Mar 1960, RM (a); numbering continues from Dell Four Color 30.00
❑5, Jun 1960, Photo cover 30.00
❑6, Sep 1960, Photo cover 30.00
❑7, Dec 1960, Photo cover 25.00
❑8, Mar 1961; no cover price 25.00
❑9, Jun 1961, Photo cover 25.00
❑10, Sep 1961, RM (a); Photo cover 20.00
❑11, Dec 1961, Photo cover 20.00
❑12, Mar 1962, Photo cover 20.00
❑13, Jun 1962, RM (a); Photo cover 20.00

Seals
Studio Aries

❑Ashcan 1, May 2000, b&w; preview 1.00

Sea of Red
Image

❑1, Apr 2005 .... 2.95
❑2, May 2005 .... 2.95
❑3, Jun 2005; Flip cover 2.95
❑4, Oct 2005 .... 2.95
❑5, Sep 2005 .... 2.95
❑6, Dec 2005 .... 2.95
❑8, Jan 2006 .... 2.99
❑9, Jun 2006 .... 2.99
❑10, Jul 2006 .... 2.99
❑11, Jul 2006 .... 2.99
❑12, Oct 2006 .... 2.99
❑13, Jan 2007 .... 3.50

N-MINT

seaQuest
Nemesis

❑1, Mar 1994; HC (c); KP (a); cardstock cover; based on TV show 2.50
❑2 1994 .... 2.25
❑3 1994 .... 2.25

Searchers
Caliber

❑1, May 1996, b&w 2.95
❑2 1996, b&w 2.95
❑3, ca. 1996, b&w 2.95
❑4, ca. 1996, b&w 2.95

Searchers: Apostle of Mercy
Caliber

❑1, ca. 1997, b&w; Giant-size 2.95
❑2, ca. 1997, b&w 3.95

Season of the Witch
Image

❑0 .... 2.50
❑1, Oct 2005 .... 3.50
❑2, Jan 2006 .... 3.50
❑3, Jan 2006 .... 3.50
❑4, Jun 2006 .... 3.50

Sebastian
Disney

❑1, Aug 1991 .... 2.00
❑2, Oct 1991 .... 2.00

Sebastian O
DC / Vertigo

❑1, May 1993; 1: Sebastian O 2.00
❑2, Jun 1993 .... 2.00
❑3, Jul 1993 .... 2.00

Second City
Harrier

❑1, Oct 1986 .... 1.95
❑2, Dec 1986 .... 1.95
❑3, Feb 1987 .... 1.95
❑4, Apr 1987 .... 1.95

Second Life of Doctor Mirage
Valiant

❑1, Nov 1993; D: Gwen Mirage; O: Doctor Mirage; Master Darque appearance 1.00
❑1/Gold, Nov 1993; Gold edition 15.00
❑2, Dec 1993 .... 1.00
❑3, Jan 1994 .... 1.00
❑4, Feb 1994 .... 1.00
❑5, Mar 1994 .... 1.00
❑6, Apr 1994 .... 1.00
❑7, May 1994; trading card 2.00
❑8, Jun 1994 .... 1.00
❑9, Aug 1994 .... 1.00
❑10, Sep 1994 .... 1.00
❑11, Oct 1994; Chaos Effect Beta 2 .... 1.00
❑12, Nov 1994 .... 1.00
❑13, Dec 1994 .... 1.00
❑14, Jan 1995 .... 2.00
❑15, Feb 1995 .... 2.00
❑16, Mar 1995 .... 2.00
❑17, Apr 1995 .... 2.00
❑18, May 1995; Final Issue 4.00

Second Rate Heroes
Foundation
❑1, b&w ... 2.50
❑2, b&w ... 2.50

Secret Agent
Charlton
❑9, Oct 1966, DG (c); FMc (w); FMc (a); 1: Mr. Ize!. Series continued from Sarge Steel #8 ... 8.00
❑10, Oct 1967, Tiffany Sinn ... 6.00

Secret Agent
Gold Key
❑1, Nov 1966, Photo cover ... 40.00
❑2, Jan 1968, Photo cover ... 25.00

Secret Agents
Personality
❑1, b&w ... 2.95
❑2, b&w ... 2.95
❑3, b&w ... 2.95

Secret City Saga
Topps
❑0, Apr 1993, Satan's Six backup story . 2.95
❑1, May 1993, trading cards ... 2.95
❑2, Jun 1993, trading cards ... 2.95
❑3, Jul 1993, trading cards ... 2.95
❑4, Aug 1993, trading cards ... 2.95

Secret Defenders
Marvel
❑1, Mar 1993; Story continued from Doctor Strange #50; foil cover ... 2.50
❑2, Apr 1993 ... 1.75
❑3, May 1993 ... 1.75
❑4, Jun 1993 ... 1.75
❑5, Jul 1993 A: Punisher ... 1.75
❑6, Aug 1993 ... 1.75
❑7, Sep 1993 ... 1.75
❑8, Oct 1993 A: Captain America. A: Spider-Man. A: Scarlet Witch. A: Doctor Strange. A: Xanadu ... 1.75
❑9, Nov 1993 ... 1.75
❑10, Dec 1993 ... 1.75
❑11, Jan 1994 ... 1.75
❑12, Feb 1994; foil cover ... 2.50
❑13, Mar 1994 ... 1.75
❑14, Apr 1994 ... 1.75
❑15, May 1994 ... 1.75
❑16, Jun 1994 ... 1.95
❑17, Jul 1994 TD (a) ... 1.95
❑18, Aug 1994 ... 1.95
❑19, Sep 1994 ... 1.95
❑20, Oct 1994 ... 1.95
❑21, Nov 1994 ... 1.95
❑22, Dec 1994 ... 1.95
❑23, Jan 1995 ... 1.95
❑24, Feb 1995; V: original Defenders ... 1.95
❑25, Mar 1995; Giant-size; Final Issue ... 2.50

Secret Doors
Dimension
❑1, b&w ... 1.50

Secret Fantasies
Bullseye
❑1, digest; B&w and red ... 2.25
❑2, b&w; normal-sized; cardstock cover ... 2.95

Secret Files
Angel
❑0, Jun 1996, b&w; Adult ... 2.95
❑0/Nude, Jun 1996, b&w; nude cover edition; cardstock cover ... 4.00
❑1, Fal 1996, b&w; Adult ... 2.95

Secret Files and Origins Guide to the DC Universe 2000
DC
❑1, Mar 2000 ... 6.95

Secret Files & Origins Guide to the DC Universe 2001-2002
DC
❑1, Feb 2002 ... 4.95

Secret Files: Invasion Day
Angel
❑1; Adult ... 5.00
❑1/Nude; Adult ... 5.00
❑2; Adult ... 5.00
❑2/Nude; Adult ... 5.00

Secret Files President Luthor
DC
❑1, Mar 2001 ... 4.95

Secret Files: The Strange Case
Angel
❑1; Adult ... 2.95

Secret Invasion
Marvel
❑1, Apr 2008 ... 5.00
❑1/2nd, Apr 2008 ... 4.00
❑2, May 2008 ... 4.00

Secret Killers
Bronze Man
❑1, Oct 1997, b&w ... 2.95
❑2 1997, b&w ... 2.95
❑3 1998, b&w ... 2.95
❑4 1998, b&w; becomes Exit from Shadow; indicia indicates name change 2.95

Secret Messages
NBM
❑1 2001 ... 2.95
❑2 ... 2.95
❑3 ... 2.95
❑4 ... 2.95
❑5, May 2002 ... 2.95

Secret Origins
DC
❑Ann 1, Aug 1961, second issue published as 80 Page Giant #8; CI, JK, GK, RA (c); CI, JK, GK, RA (a); reprints Silver Age origins of the Superman/ Batman team, Adam Strange, Green Lantern, Challengers of the Unknown, Green Arrow, Wonder Woman, Manhunter from Mars, and the Flash . 400.00

Secret Origins
DC
❑1, Mar 1973, NC (c); CI, JKu (a); O: Superman. O: Flash. O: Batman; The Flash: Showcase #4; Superman: Action Comics #1; Batman: Detective Comics #33; Hawkman I (Carter Hall): Flash Comics #88 ... 18.00
❑2, May 1973, O: Supergirl: Action Comics #252; O: Green Lantern: Showcase #22; O: The Atom: Showcase #34 ... 8.00
❑3, Aug 1973, O: Wonder Woman. O: Wildcat; Wonder Woman: Wonder Woman #1; Wildcat: Sensation Comics #1 ... 7.00
❑4, Oct 1973, O: Kid Eternity. O: Vigilante; Vigilante: Action Comics #42; Kid Eternity: Hit Comics #25 ... 7.00
❑5, Dec 1973, O: Spectre: ... 6.00
❑6, Feb 1974, O: The Legion of Super-Heroes; O: Blackhawk ... 6.00
❑7, Oct 1974, O: Robin I (Dick Grayson). O: Aquaman; Robin I (Dick Grayson): Detective Comics #38; Aquaman: More Fun Comics #73 ... 6.00

Secret Origins
DC
❑1, Apr 1986; O: Superman ... 5.00
❑2, May 1986; O: Blue Beetle. O: Blue Beetle I; O: Bluee Beetle II; O: Blue Beetle (Dan Garrett); O: Blue Beetle (Ted Kord) ... 2.00
❑3, Jun 1986; O: Captain Marvel ... 2.00
❑4, Jul 1986; O: Firestorm ... 2.00
❑5, Aug 1986; O: The Crimson Avenger. 2.00
❑6, Sep 1986; O: Halo. O: Batman (Golden Age); 52 pages ... 2.00
❑7, Oct 1986; BB (c); O: Sandman II (Dr. Garrett Sanford). O: Green Lantern (Guy Gardner). O: Sandman I (Wesley Dodds); 52 pages ... 2.00
❑8, Nov 1986; O: Doll Man. O: Shadow Lass ... 2.00
❑9, Dec 1986; O: Flash I (Jay Garrick). O: Skyman; O: Star Spangled Kid an Stripsey ... 2.00
❑10, Jan 1987; O: Phantom Stranger. Legends ... 2.00
❑11, Feb 1987; JOy (c); LMc (a); O: Power Girl. O: Hawkman (Golden Age) ... 2.00
❑12, Mar 1987; O: The Fury (Golden Age). O: Challengers of the Unknown; 52 pages ... 2.00
❑13, Apr 1987; O: Johnny Thunder. O: Nightwing. O: Whip ... 2.00
❑14, May 1987; O: Suicide Squad. Legends ... 2.00
❑15, Jun 1987; O: Spectre. O: Deadman; 52 pages ... 2.00
❑16, Jul 1987; O: Hourman I (Rex Tyler). O: Warlord; O: 'Mazing Man ... 2.00
❑17, Aug 1987; O: Adam Strange. O: Doctor Occult; 52 pages ... 2.00
❑18, Sep 1987; O: Creeper. O: Green Lantern I (Alan Scott). 52 pages ... 2.00
❑19, Oct 1987; JK (c); MA (a); O: Uncle Sam. O: Guardian ... 2.00
❑20, Nov 1987; O: Doctor Mid-Nite (Golden Age). O: Batgirl ... 2.00
❑21, Dec 1987; O: Black Condor. O: Jonah Hex ... 2.00
❑22, Jan 1988; O: Manhunters. Millennium ... 2.00
❑23, Feb 1988; O: Floronic Man. O: Guardians of the Universe. Millennium ... 2.00
❑24, Mar 1988; O: Blue Devil. O: Doctor Fate ... 2.00
❑25, Apr 1988; O: The Atom (Golden Age). O: the Legion of Super-Heroes; 52 pages ... 2.00
❑26, May 1988; O: Miss America. O: Black Lightning ... 2.00
❑27, Jun 1988; O: Zatara. O: Zatanna ... 2.00
❑28, Jul 1988; O: Nightshade. O: Midnight 2.00
❑29, Aug 1988; O: The Atom (Silver Age). O: Red Tornado (Golden Age). O: Mr. America ... 2.00
❑30, Sep 1988; O: Plastic Man. O: Elongated Man 52 pages ... 2.00
❑31, Oct 1988; O: Justice Society of America ... 2.00
❑32, Nov 1988; O: Justice League of America ... 2.00
❑33, Dec 1988; O: Icemaiden. O: Green Flame. O: Mr. Miracle; 52 pages ... 2.00
❑34, Dec 1988; O: Rocket Red. O: G'Nort. O: Captain Atom ... 2.00
❑35, Jan 1989; O: Booster Gold. O: Martian Manhunter. O: Max Lord ... 2.00
❑36, Jan 1989; O: Green Lantern (Silver Age). O: Poison Ivy ... 2.00
❑37, Feb 1989; O: Doctor Light. O: Legion of Substitute Heroes ... 2.00
❑38, Mar 1989; O: Speedy. O: Green Arrow 2.00
❑39, Apr 1989; O: Animal Man. O: Man-Bat; 52 pages ... 2.00
❑40, May 1989; O: Gorilla Grodd. O: Congorilla. O: Detective Chimp ... 2.00
❑41, Jun 1989; O: Flash's Rogue's Gallery; 52 pages ... 2.00
❑42, Jul 1989; O: Grim Ghost. O: Phantom Girl; 52 pages ... 2.00
❑43, Aug 1989; O: Chris KL-99. O: Hawk. O: Dove. O: Cave Carson ... 2.00
❑44, Sep 1989; O: Clayface III. O: Clayface I. O: Clayface IV. O: Clayface II; 52 pages; Continues in Detective Comics #604 ... 2.00
❑45, Oct 1989; O: Blackhawk. O: El Diablo 2.00
❑46, Dec 1989; Blueprints of Teen Titans Headquarters, Legion of Super-Heroes Headquarters ... 2.00
❑47, Feb 1990; O: Karate Kid. O: Chemical King. O: Ferro Lad ... 2.00
❑48, Apr 1990; O: Rex the Wonder Dog. O: Ambush Bug. O: Trigger Twins. O: Stanley and His Monster ... 2.00
❑49, Jun 1990; O: Newsboy Legion. O: Bouncing Boy. O: Silent Knight; 52 pages ... 2.00
❑50, Aug 1990; 100 Page giant; O: Robin I (Dick Grayson). O: Johnny Thunder (cowboy). O: Space Museum. O: Black Canary. O: Earth-2; O: Dolphin; Final Issue; 100 Page giant; 96 pages ... 2.00
❑Ann 1, ca. 1987; JBy (c); JBy (a); O: The Doom Patrol; O: Captain Comet ... 3.00
❑Ann 2, ca. 1988; O: Flash III (Wally West). O: Flash II (Barry Allen) 2.00
❑Ann 3, ca. 1989; O: Teen Titans. 1: Flamebird ... 2.00
❑GS 1, Dec 1998; O: Wonder Girl. O: Robin III (Tim Drake). O: Superboy. O: Impulse. O: Spoiler. O: Arrowette. O: Secret; 80-Page Giant ... 4.95
❑Special 1, Oct 1989; O: Riddler. O: Two-Face. O: Penguin ... 2.00

Secret Origins of Krankin' Komix
Krankin' Komix
❑1, Nov 1996 ... 1.00

Silver Surfer

Stan Lee and Jack Kirby's hip series
©Marvel

Silver Surfer

1987 relaunch lasted more than a decade
©Marvel

Silver Surfer

Surfer series had a short ride
©Marvel

Simpsons Comics

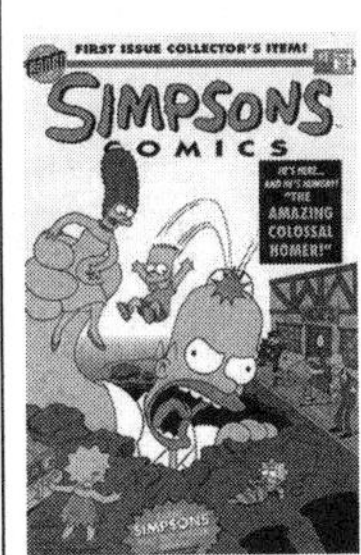

TV's favorite dysfunctional cartoon family
©Bongo

Simpsons Comics Presents Bart Simpson

Bimonhly antics from television terror
©Bongo

N-MINT

Secret Origins of Super-Villains
DC

❑GS 1, Dec 1999; O: Amazo; O: Echo; O: Encantadora; O: Granny Goodness; O: Johnny Sorrow; O: Sinestro; O: Tartarus 4.95

Secret Origins Of The World's Greatest Super Heroes
DC

❑1, ca. 1989; Reprints from Man of Steel #6, Secret Origins #36, Secret Origins #35, Secret Origins Ann #2, Secret Origins #32 .... 4.95

Secret Origins Replica Edition
DC

❑1, Feb 2000; Cardstock fold-out cover; reprints Secret Origins #1 (1st series) 4.95

Secret Plot
Fantagraphics / Eros

❑1, Oct 1997; Adult 2.95
❑2, Nov 1997; Adult 2.95

Secret Six
DC

❑1, May 1968, 1&O: The Secret Six. splash page is cover 45.00
❑2, Jul 1968 .... 15.00
❑3, Sep 1968 .... 12.00
❑4, Nov 1968 .... 12.00
❑5, Jan 1969 .... 12.00
❑6, Mar 1969 .... 15.00
❑7, May 1969, Final Issue 20.00

Secret Six
DC

❑1, Aug 2006, Splash page is cover; 1&O: The Secret Six 45.00
❑2, Sep 2006 .... 2.99
❑3, Oct 2006 .... 2.99
❑4, Dec 2006 .... 2.99
❑5, Jan 2007, V: Vandal Savage 2.99
❑6, Mar 2007 .... 2.99

Secret Society of Super-Villains
DC

❑1, Jun 1976, O: Secret Society 10.00
❑2, Aug 1976, DG (c); A: Captain Comet. Bicentennial #21 .... 5.00
❑3, Oct 1976 .... 5.00
❑4, Dec 1976 .... 5.00
❑5, Feb 1977, RB (a) 5.00
❑6, Apr 1977, RB (c); RB, BL (a) 5.00
❑7, Jun 1977, RB (c); RB, BL (a) 5.00
❑8, Aug 1977, RB, JAb (c); RB, BL (a) ... 5.00
❑9, Sep 1977, RB, JAb (c); RB, BMc (a) 2.50
❑10, Oct 1977, AM, JAb (c); JAb (a) 2.50
❑11, Dec 1977, RB (c); JO (a) 2.50
❑12, Jan 1978, RB, JAb (c); BMc (a) 2.50
❑13, Mar 1978, RB (c) 2.50
❑14, May 1978, RB, JAb (c) 2.50
❑15, Jul 1978, RB, DG (c);Final Issue 2.50

Secrets of Drawing Comics
Showcase

❑1, Jan 1994 .... 2.50
❑2 .... 2.50
❑3 .... 2.50
❑4 .... 2.50

N-MINT

Secrets of Haunted House
DC

❑1, Apr 1975; 1: Destiny; Eve apperance 35.00
❑2, Jun 1975 TD (a) 12.00
❑3, Aug 1975 NR (a) 12.00
❑4, Oct 1975 NR (a) 12.00
❑5, Dec 1975 .... 18.00
❑6, Jun 1977, Series resumes after 18-month hiatus 10.00
❑7, Aug 1977 .... 10.00
❑8, Oct 1977, SA (w); RT (a) 10.00
❑9, Dec 1977 .... 10.00
❑10, Feb 1978 .... 10.00
❑11, Apr 1978 .... 10.00
❑12, Jun 1978, JO (c); SD (a) 10.00
❑13, Aug 1978 .... 10.00
❑14, Oct 1978 .... 10.00
❑15, Aug 1979 .... 10.00
❑16, Sep 1979 .... 6.00
❑17, Oct 1979 .... 6.00
❑18, Nov 1979 .... 6.00
❑19, Dec 1979 .... 6.00
❑20, Jan 1980 .... 6.00
❑21, Feb 1980 .... 3.00
❑22, Mar 1980 .... 3.00
❑23, Apr 1980 .... 3.00
❑24, May 1980 .... 3.00
❑25, Jun 1980, TVE (a) 3.00
❑26, Jul 1980 .... 3.00
❑27, Aug 1980 .... 3.00
❑28, Sep 1980, DH (c) 3.00
❑29, Oct 1980 .... 3.00
❑30, Nov 1980 .... 3.00
❑31, Dec 1980, DS (a); 1: Mister E 5.00
❑32, Jan 1981 .... 3.00
❑33, Feb 1981 .... 3.00
❑34, Mar 1981 .... 3.00
❑35, Apr 1981 .... 3.00
❑36, May 1981 .... 3.00
❑37, Jun 1981 .... 3.00
❑38, Jul 1981 .... 3.00
❑39, Aug 1981 .... 3.00
❑40, Sep 1981 .... 3.00
❑41, Oct 1981, JKu (c); SD, DS (a) 3.00
❑42, Nov 1981 .... 3.00
❑43, Dec 1981 .... 3.00
❑44, Jan 1982, BWr (c) 3.00
❑45, Feb 1982 .... 3.00
❑46, Mar 1982, DG (c); RE (a); Final Issue 3.00

Secrets of Sinister House
DC

❑5, Jun 1972, Continues from Sinister House of Secret Love #4 .... 40.00
❑6, Aug 1972 .... 20.00
❑7, Nov 1972 .... 20.00
❑8, Dec 1972 .... 20.00
❑9, Feb 1973 .... 20.00
❑10, Mar 1973, NA (a) 25.00
❑11, Apr 1973 .... 15.00
❑12, Jun 1973 .... 15.00
❑13, Aug 1973 .... 15.00
❑14, Oct 1973 .... 15.00
❑15, Dec 1973 .... 15.00
❑16, Feb 1974 .... 12.00

N-MINT

❑17, Apr 1974, Death Has Five Guesses! reprinted from Sensation Mystery #112 12.00
❑18, Jun 1974, NC (c); MA, GK (a); Final Issue; Mad to Order reprinted from The Unexpected #116; The Baby That Had But 'One Year to Die' reprinted from The Unexpected #111; The Half-Lucky Charm! reprinted from Sensation Mystery #115 .... 15.00

Secrets of the House of M
Marvel

❑1, Sep 2005 .... 3.99

Secrets of the Legion of Super-Heroes
DC

❑1, Jan 1981, O: Legion of Super-Heroes 2.00
❑2, Feb 1981, O: Brainiac 5, Shrinking Violet, Sun-Boy, Bouncing Boy, Ultra-Boy, Matter Eater Lad, Mon-El & Dream Girl 2.00
❑3, Mar 1981, R.J. Brande revealed to be Chameleon Boy's father 2.00

Secrets of the Valiant Universe
Valiant

❑1, May 1994; Wizard Magazine promo; BL, BH (w); DP, BH (a); no price; bagged with Wizard Special 5.00
❑2, Oct 1994; BH (c); BH (w); Chaos Effect Beta 4 .... 3.00
❑3, Oct 1995; BL (w); future Rai; indicia says Oct; cover says Feb 3.00

Secretum Secretorum
Twilight Twins

❑0 .... 3.50

Secret Voice
Adhouse Books

❑1, ca. 2005 .... 4.95

Secret War
Marvel

❑1, Apr 2004, (c); BMB (w) 10.00
❑1/2nd, Apr 2004; Commorative Edition 5.00
❑1/3rd, Apr 2004 .... 3.99
❑2, Jul 2004 .... 6.00
❑2/2nd 2004 .... 3.50
❑3, Oct 2004 .... 5.00
❑4, Apr 2005 .... 3.99
❑5, Feb 2006, Foil lettering 3.99

Secret Wars II
Marvel

❑1, Jul 1985 A: X-Men. A: New Mutants 2.00
❑2, Aug 1985; A: Fantastic Four. A: Spider-Man. A: Power Man. A: Iron Fist. D: Hate-Monger III (H.M. Unger) 1.50
❑3, Sep 1985 .... 1.50
❑4, Oct 1985; 1&O: Kurse. A: Kursei; V: Avengers 1.50
❑5, Nov 1985; 1&O: Boomer (Boom Boom). V: X-Men. V: Fantastic Four. V: New Mutants. V: Avengers 2.50
❑6, Dec 1985 .... 1.50
❑7, Jan 1986; V: All villains 1.50
❑8, Feb 1986; O: Beyonder 1.50
❑9, Mar 1986; double-sized; D: Beyonder 1.50

Secret Weapons
Valiant

❑1, Sep 1993; 1&O: Doctor Eclipse. Serial number contest ... 1.00
❑2, Oct 1993; Wraparound cover ... 1.00
❑3, Nov 1993 ... 1.00
❑4, Dec 1993 ... 1.00
❑5, Jan 1994 A: Ninjak ... 1.00
❑6, Feb 1994 ... 1.00
❑7, Mar 1994 A: X-O Manowar. A: Turok ... 1.00
❑8, Apr 1994; V: Harbinger ... 1.00
❑9, May 1994; A: Bloodshot. trading card ... 1.00
❑10, Jun 1994 ... 1.00
❑11, Aug 1994; A: Bloodshot. Enclosed in manila envelope "For Your Eyes Only" cover; bagged cover ... 1.00
❑11/VVSS, Aug 1994 ... 30.00
❑12, Sep 1994 A: Bloodshot ... 1.00
❑13, Oct 1994; Chaos Effect Gamma 2 ... 1.00
❑14, Nov 1994 ... 1.00
❑15, Dec 1994 ... 1.00
❑16, Jan 1995 ... 2.00
❑17, Feb 1995 ... 2.00
❑18, Mar 1995 A: Ninjak ... 2.00
❑19, Apr 1995 ... 2.00
❑20, May 1995; (see Bloodshot #28) ... 4.00
❑21, May 1995; Final Issue ... 5.00

Sectaurs
Marvel / Star

❑1, Jun 1985 ... 1.00
❑2, Aug 1985 ... 1.00
❑3, Oct 1985 ... 1.00
❑4, Dec 1985 ... 1.00
❑5, Mar 1986 ... 1.00
❑6, May 1986 ... 1.00
❑7, Jul 1986 ... 1.00
❑8, Sep 1986 ... 1.00

Section 12
Mythic

❑1, b&w ... 2.95

Section Zero
Image

❑1, Jun 2000 ... 2.50
❑2, Jul 2000 ... 2.50
❑3, Sep 2000 ... 2.50

Seduction
Eternity

❑1, b&w ... 2.50

Seduction of the Innocent
Eclipse

❑1, Nov 1985; DSt (w); MM, ATh, TY (a); Reprints from Adventures into Darkness #6, Out of the Shadows #7, Fantastic Worlds #7, Out of the Shadows #9 ... 2.50
❑2, Dec 1985 MA, ATh, MB, NC, RMo (a) ... 2.00
❑3, Jan 1986; MM (c); MM, MA, ATh (w); MM, MA, ATh (a); Reprints from Who is Next? #5, The Unseen #10, Out of the Shadows #14, Lost Worlds #5 ... 2.00
❑4, Feb 1986 ATh (w); ATh, NC (a) ... 2.00
❑5, Mar 1986 ATh (w); ATh, TY (a) ... 2.00
❑6, Apr 1986; ATh, GT, FF, RA (w); Series continues, cross-listed as Christmas Classics (Walt Kelly's) #1, other titles from Eclipse ... 2.00
❑3D 1, ca. 1985; DSt (c); DSt (w); MM (a); ... 2.50
❑3D 2, ca. 1986; BWr (c); ATh, MB, NC (a) ... 2.50

Seeker
Caliber

❑1, Apr 1994, b&w ... 2.50
❑2 1994, b&w ... 2.95

Seekers into the Mystery
DC / Vertigo

❑1, Jan 1996 ... 2.50
❑2, Feb 1996 ... 2.50
❑3, Mar 1996 ... 2.50
❑4, Apr 1996 ... 2.50
❑5, Jun 1996 ... 2.50
❑6, Jul 1996 ... 2.50
❑7, Aug 1996 ... 2.50
❑8, Sep 1996 ... 2.50
❑9, Oct 1996 ... 2.50
❑10, Nov 1996 ... 2.50
❑11, Dec 1996 ... 2.50
❑12, Jan 1997 ... 2.50
❑13, Feb 1997 ... 2.50
❑14, Mar 1997 ... 2.50
❑15, Apr 1997, Final Issue ... 2.95

Seeker 3000
Marvel

❑1, Jun 1998, wraparound cover ... 2.99
❑2, Jul 1998, wraparound cover ... 2.99
❑3, Aug 1998, wraparound cover ... 2.99
❑4, Sep 1998, wraparound cover ... 2.99

Seeker 3000 Premiere
Marvel

❑1, Jun 1998; reprints Marvel Premiere #41 ... 1.50

Seeker: Vengeance
Sky

❑1, Nov 1993 ... 2.50
❑1/Gold, Nov 1993; Gold edition ... 3.00
❑2 1994 ... 2.50

Self-Loathing Comics
Fantagraphics

❑1 1996; Adult ... 2.95
❑2, May 1997; Adult ... 2.95

Semper Fi
Marvel

❑1, Dec 1988 JSe (c); JSe (a) ... 1.25
❑2, Jan 1989 JSe (c); JSe (a) ... 1.25
❑3, Feb 1989 JSe (c); JSe (a) ... 1.25
❑4, Mar 1989 JSe (c); JSe (a) ... 1.25
❑5, Apr 1989 JSe (c); JSe (a) ... 1.25
❑6, May 1989 JSe (c); JSe (a) ... 1.25
❑7, Jun 1989 JSe (c); JSe (a) ... 1.25
❑8, Jul 1989 JSe (a) ... 1.25
❑9, Aug 1989 JSe (a) ... 1.25

Sensational She-Hulk
Marvel

❑1, May 1989 JBy (c); JBy (w); JBy (a) ... 2.50
❑2, Jun 1989; JBy (c); JBy (w); JBy (a); V: Toad Men ... 2.00
❑3, Jul 1989 JBy (c); JBy (w); JBy (a); A: Spider-Man ... 2.00
❑4, Aug 1989; JBy (c); JBy (w); JBy (a); O: Blonde Phantom. A: Blonde Phantom ... 2.00
❑5, Sep 1989 JBy (c); JBy (w); JBy (a) ... 2.00
❑6, Oct 1989 JBy (c); JBy (w); JBy (a); A: Razorback ... 2.00
❑7, Nov 1989 JBy (c); JBy (w); JBy (a); A: Razorback ... 2.00
❑8, Nov 1989 JBy (c); JBy (w); JBy (a); A: Nick St. Christopher ... 2.00
❑9, Dec 1989; V: Madcap ... 1.75
❑10, Dec 1989 ... 1.75
❑11, Jan 1990 ... 1.75
❑12, Feb 1990 ... 1.75
❑13, Mar 1990 ... 1.75
❑14, Apr 1990 A: Howard the Duck ... 1.75
❑15, May 1990 A: Howard the Duck ... 1.75
❑16, Jun 1990 A: Howard the Duck ... 1.75
❑17, Jul 1990 A: Howard the Duck ... 1.75
❑18, Aug 1990 ... 1.75
❑19, Sep 1990 A: Nosferata the She-Bat ... 1.75
❑20, Oct 1990 ... 1.75
❑21, Nov 1990; Blonde Phantom ... 1.75
❑22, Dec 1990; Blonde Phantom ... 1.75
❑23, Jan 1991; Blonde Phantom ... 1.75
❑24, Feb 1991; Death's Head ... 1.75
❑25, Mar 1991; Hercules ... 1.75
❑26, Apr 1991 ... 1.75
❑27, May 1991; MZ (c); white inside covers ... 1.75
❑28, Jun 1991 ... 1.75
❑29, Jul 1991 MZ (c) ... 1.75
❑30, Aug 1991 ... 1.75
❑31, Sep 1991 JBy (c); JBy (w); JBy (a) ... 1.75
❑32, Oct 1991 JBy (c); JBy (w); JBy (a) ... 1.75
❑33, Nov 1991 JBy (c); JBy (w); JBy (a) ... 1.75
❑34, Dec 1991 JBy (c); JBy (w); JBy (a) ... 1.75
❑35, Jan 1992 JBy (c); JBy (w); JBy (a) ... 1.75
❑36, Feb 1992 JBy (c); JBy (w); JBy (a); A: Wyatt Wingfoot ... 1.75
❑37, Mar 1992 JBy (c); JBy (w); JBy (a) ... 1.75
❑38, Apr 1992; JBy (c); JBy (w); JBy (a); V: Mahkizmo ... 1.75
❑39, May 1992; JBy (c); JBy (w); JBy (a); A: Thing. V: Mahkizmo ... 1.75
❑40, Jun 1992 JBy (w); JBy (a) ... 1.75
❑41, Jul 1992 JBy (c); JBy (w); JBy (a) ... 1.75
❑42, Aug 1992 JBy (w); JBy (a) ... 1.75
❑43, Sep 1992 JBy (c); JBy (w); JBy (a) ... 1.75
❑44, Oct 1992 JBy (c); JBy (w); JBy (a) ... 1.75
❑45, Nov 1992 JBy (w); JBy (a) ... 1.75
❑46, Dec 1992 JBy (c); JBy (w); JBy (a) ... 1.75
❑47, Jan 1993 ... 1.75
❑48, Feb 1993 JBy (c); JBy (w); JBy (a) ... 1.75
❑49, Mar 1993 JBy (c); JBy (w); JBy (a) ... 1.75
❑50, Apr 1993; Double-size; JBy (c); JBy, FM (w); WP, DaG, JBy, HC, DG, FM (a); Green foil cover ... 2.95
❑51, May 1993; Savage She-Hulk vs. Sensational She-Hulk ... 1.75
❑52, Jun 1993 ... 1.75
❑53, Jul 1993 ... 1.75
❑54, Aug 1993 DC (a) ... 1.75
❑55, Sep 1993 ... 1.75
❑56, Oct 1993 A: Hulk ... 1.75
❑57, Nov 1993 A: Hulk ... 1.75
❑58, Dec 1993; A: Tommy the Gopher. V: Electro ... 1.75
❑59, Jan 1994 ... 1.75
❑60, Feb 1994; A: Millie the Model. Final Issue ... 1.75

Sensational She-Hulk in Ceremony
Marvel

❑1, ca. 1989; leg shaving ... 3.95
❑2, ca. 1989 ... 3.95

Sensational Spider-Man
Marvel

❑-1, Jul 1997; Flashback ... 2.00
❑0, Jan 1996; O: Spider-Man. 1: Armada. enhanced wraparound cardstock cover with lenticular animation card attached; new costume ... 5.00
❑1, Feb 1996; Series picks up subscribers from Web of Spider-Man ... 2.00
❑1/CS, Feb 1996 ... 4.00
❑2, Mar 1996 ... 2.00
❑3, Apr 1996 ... 2.00
❑4, May 1996; Ben Reilly revealed as Spider-Man ... 2.00
❑5, Jun 1996 V: Molten Man ... 2.00
❑6, Jul 1996 ... 2.00
❑7, Aug 1996 ... 2.00
❑8, Sep 1996 V: Looter ... 2.00
❑9, Oct 1996 A: Swarm ... 2.00
❑10, Nov 1996 ... 2.00
❑11, Dec 1996 ... 2.00
❑11/CS, Dec 1996 ... 6.99
❑12, Jan 1997 V: Trapster ... 2.00
❑13, Feb 1997 A: Ka-Zar. A: Shanna ... 2.00
❑14, Mar 1997 A: Ka-Zar. A: Shanna. A: Hulk ... 2.00
❑15, Apr 1997 A: Ka-Zar. A: Shanna. A: Hulk ... 2.00
❑16, May 1997 V: Prowler ... 2.00
❑17, Jun 1997 V: Vulture ... 2.00
❑18, Aug 1997; gatefold summary ... 2.00
❑19, Sep 1997; gatefold summary V: Living Pharaoh ... 2.00
❑20, Oct 1997; gatefold summary ... 2.00
❑21, Nov 1997; gatefold summary ... 1.99
❑22, Dec 1997; gatefold summary A: Doctor Strange ... 1.99
❑23, Jan 1998; gatefold summary ... 1.99
❑24, Feb 1998; gatefold summary V: Hydro-Man ... 1.99
❑25, Mar 1998; double-sized ... 2.99
❑25/A, Mar 1998; double-sized; Wanted poster cover ... 2.99
❑26, Apr 1998; gatefold summary; V: Hydro-Man. V: Sandman. Identity Crisis ... 1.99
❑27, May 1998; gatefold summary ... 1.99
❑27/A, May 1998; gatefold summary; variant cover ... 1.99
❑28, Jun 1998; gatefold summary A: Hornet ... 1.99
❑29, Jul 1998; gatefold summary A: Black Cat ... 1.99
❑30, Aug 1998; gatefold summary ... 1.99
❑31, Sep 1998; gatefold summary V: Rhino ... 1.99
❑32, Oct 1998; gatefold summary ... 1.99
❑33, Nov 1998; gatefold summary V: Override ... 1.99
❑Ann 1996, ca. 1996 O: Kraven the Hunter ... 3.00

Other grades: Multiply price above by 5/6 for VF/NM • 2/3 for VERY FINE • 1/3 for FINE • 1/5 for VERY GOOD • 1/8 for GOOD

Sinbad

Sailor from the Arabian Nights gets series
©Adventure

Sin City: A Dame to Kill For

Frank Miller continues his noir epic
©Dark Horse

Sinja: Deadly Sins

Series set in 13th century Japan
©Lightning

Sins of Youth: Wonder Girls

Wonder Woman and Wonder Girl switch ages
©DC

Sisterhood of Steel

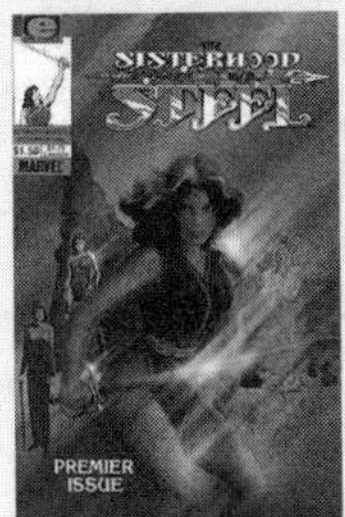

Life in the age of the longsword and crossbow
©Marvel

N-MINT

Sensation Comics
DC

❑1, May 1999; Justice Society Returns; Hawkgirl; Speed Saunders 1.99

Sensei
First

❑1, May 1989 .... 2.75
❑2, Jun 1989 .... 2.75
❑3, Jul 1989 .... 2.75
❑4, Dec 1989 .... 2.75

Sensual Phrase
Viz

❑1, Apr 2004, Graphic novel; Read right to left; Adult situations; b&w 9.95
❑2, Jun 2004 .... 9.95
❑3, Aug 2004 .... 9.95
❑4, Oct 2004 .... 9.95
❑5, Dec 2005 .... 9.95
❑6, Feb 2005 .... 9.99
❑7, Apr 2005 .... 9.99
❑8, Jun 2005 .... 9.99
❑9, Aug 2005 .... 9.99
❑10, Oct 2005 .... 9.99

Sentai
Antarctic

❑1, Feb 1994, b&w 2.95
❑2, Apr 1994, b&w 2.95
❑3, Jul 1994, b&w 2.95
❑4, Sep 1994, b&w 2.95
❑5, Nov 1994; Special 40-Page American Sentai Issue; First all color issue 2.95
❑6, Feb 1995, b&w 2.95
❑7, Apr 1995, b&w 2.95

Sentinel
Harrier

❑1, Dec 1986 .... 1.95
❑2, Feb 1987 .... 1.95
❑3, Apr 1987 .... 1.95
❑4, Jun 1987 .... 1.95

Sentinel
Marvel

❑1, Jun 2003 .... 2.99
❑2, Jul 2003 .... 2.99
❑3, Aug 2003 .... 2.50
❑4, Sep 2003 .... 2.50
❑5, Oct 2003 .... 2.50
❑6, Nov 2003 .... 2.99
❑7, Dec 2003 .... 2.50
❑8, Dec 2003 .... 2.99
❑9, Jan 2004 .... 2.99
❑10, Feb 2004 .... 2.99
❑11, Mar 2004 .... 2.99
❑12, Apr 2004 .... 2.99

Sentinel
Marvel

❑1, Jan 2006 .... 2.99
❑2, Feb 2006 .... 2.99
❑3, Mar 2006 .... 2.99
❑4, Mar 2006 .... 2.99
❑5, May 2006 .... 2.99

N-MINT

Sentinels of Justice
AC

❑1; Avenger 4.00
❑2; Jet Girl 5.95
❑3; Yankee Girl 4.00

Sentinels of Justice Compact
AC

❑1 .... 3.95
❑2 .... 3.95
❑3 .... 3.95

Sentinels Presents... Crystal World: Prisoners of Spheris
Academy

❑1 .... 2.95

Sentinel Squad O*N*E
Marvel

❑1, Mar 2006 .... 2.99
❑2, Apr 2006 .... 2.99
❑3, May 2006 .... 2.99
❑4, Jun 2006 .... 2.99
❑5, Jul 2006 .... 2.99

Sentry
Marvel

❑1, Sep 2000 .... 15.00
❑1/Variant, Sep 2000 .... 20.00
❑1/Conv, Sep 2000 .... 25.00
❑2, Oct 2000 .... 8.00
❑3, Nov 2000 A: Hulk. A: Spider-Man 4.00
❑4, Dec 2000 A: Doctor Strange 4.00
❑5, Jan 2001 A: Fantastic Four. A: Hulk. A: Spider-Man. A: Avengers 4.00

Sentry
Marvel

❑1 .... 2.99
❑2 2005 .... 2.99
❑3, Jan 2006 .... 2.99
❑4, Feb 2006 .... 2.99
❑5, Mar 2006 .... 2.99
❑6, May 2006 .... 2.99
❑7, Jun 2006 .... 2.99
❑8, Jul 2006 .... 2.99

Sentry/Fantastic Four
Marvel

❑1, Feb 2001 .... 2.99

Sentry/Hulk
Marvel

❑1, Feb 2001 .... 2.99

Sentry: Rough Cut
Marvel

❑1, Jan 2006 .... 3.99

Sentry Special
Innovation

❑1, Jun 1991 .... 2.75

Sentry/Spider-Man
Marvel

❑1, Feb 2001, V: Doctor Octopus; V: Void 2.99

Sentry/The Void
Marvel

❑1, Feb 2001 .... 5.00

N-MINT

Sentry/X-Men
Marvel

❑1, Feb 2001, V: General 2.99

Sepulcher
Illustration

❑1, Mar 2000 .... 2.99
❑2, May 2000 .... 2.99

Sequential
I Don't Get It

❑1 2000 .... 2.95
❑2 2000 .... 2.95
❑3, Jun 1999 .... 2.95

Seraphim
Innovation

❑1, May 1990 .... 2.50
❑2 1990 .... 2.50
❑3 1990 .... 2.50

Serenity
Dark Horse

❑1/Cassaday, Aug 2005; Cover: Mal by John Cassaday 12.00
❑1/Hitch, Aug 2005; Cover: Jayne by Brian Hitch 12.00
❑1/Jones, Aug 2005; Cover: Inara by J.G. Jones 12.00
❑2/Bradstreet, Sep 2005 .... 7.00
❑2/Chen, Sep 2005 .... 7.00
❑2/Quesada, Sep 2005 .... 7.00
❑2/DHP, Sep 2005 .... 7.00
❑3/Middleton, Oct 2005 .... 5.00
❑3/Phillips, Oct 2005 .... 5.00
❑3/Yu, Oct 2005 .... 5.00

Serenity: Better Days
Dark Horse

❑1, Mar 2008 .... 2.99
❑2, Apr 2008 .... 4.00

Sgt. Frog
Tokyopop

❑1, Mar 2004 .... 9.99
❑2, May 2004 .... 9.99
❑3, Jul 2004 .... 9.99
❑4, Sep 2004 .... 9.99
❑5, Nov 2004 .... 9.99
❑6, Jan 2005 .... 9.99
❑7, Mar 2005 .... 9.99
❑8, May 2005 .... 9.99
❑9, Jul 2005 .... 9.99
❑10, Dec 2005 .... 9.99

Sgt. Fury
Marvel

❑1, May 1963, 1: General Samuel Happy Sam Sawyer. 1: Dum Dum Dugan; 1: Sgt. Nick Fury; 1: Robert "Rebel" Ralston; 1: Junior Juniper; 1: Gabriel Jones; 1: Izzy Cohen; 1: Dino Manelli. 1500.00
❑2, Jul 1963 .... 400.00
❑3, Sep 1963, A: Reed Richards 225.00
❑4, Nov 1963, D: Junior Juniper 225.00
❑5, Jan 1964, JK (c); SL (w); JK (a); 1: Baron Strucker 225.00
❑6, Mar 1964 .... 150.00
❑7, May 1964, JK (c); SL (w); JK (a) 150.00
❑8, Jul 1964, JK (c); SL (w); 1: Percival Pinkerton. V: Doctor Zemo (later Baron Zemo); 1: Dr. Zemo 150.00

N-MINT

❑9, Aug 1964, JK (c); SL (w); 2: Baron Strucker; Dave Cockrum L.O.C 150.00
❑10, Sep 1964, 1: Captain Savage 150.00
❑11, Oct 1964, 1: Captain Flint.............. 100.00
❑12, Nov 1964 .... 100.00
❑13, Dec 1964, JK (c); SL (w); JK (a); A: Captain America 500.00
❑13/2nd, JK (c); SL (w); JK (a); A: Captain America. 2nd printing 2.00
❑14, Jan 1965, A: Baron Strucker. 1: Blitzkrieg Squad............................ 80.00
❑15, Feb 1965, JK (c); SL (w); 1: Hans Rooten. 1: Hans Rooten 80.00
❑16, Mar 1965, JK (c); SL (w); 2: Hans Rooten.. 75.00
❑17, Apr 1965, JK (c); SL (w) 75.00
❑18, May 1965, JK (c); SL (w); D: Pamela Hawley.. 75.00
❑19, Jun 1965, JK (c); SL (w)................ 75.00
❑20, Jul 1965, 2: Blitzkrieg Squad 50.00
❑21, Aug 1965, SL (w)........................... 50.00
❑22, Sep 1965... 50.00
❑23, Oct 1965, SL (w)............................. 50.00
❑24, Nov 1965, SL (w)............................ 30.00
❑25, Dec 1965, JK (c); SL (w)................ 50.00
❑26, Jan 1966, SL (w) 50.00
❑27, Feb 1966, SL (w); Explanation of Sgt. Fury's eye patch.............................. 50.00
❑28, Mar 1966, SL (w); V: Baron Strucker 40.00
❑29, Apr 1966, V: Baron Strucker 40.00
❑30, May 1966... 40.00
❑31, Jun 1966... 40.00
❑32, Jul 1966... 25.00
❑33, Aug 1966 .... 25.00
❑34, Sep 1966, O: General Samuel Happy Sam Sawyer. O: Howling Commandos 25.00
❑35, Oct 1966, Eric Koenig joins Howling Commandos 25.00
❑36, Nov 1966 .... 25.00
❑37, Dec 1966, GK (c) 25.00
❑38, Jan 1967, 1: Jim Morita 25.00
❑39, Feb 1967, 1: Colonel Klaue............ 20.00
❑40, Mar 1967 .... 20.00
❑41, Apr 1967, 2: Colonel Klaue............ 15.00
❑42, May 1967, 2: Ilsa Koenig 15.00
❑43, Jun 1967.. 15.00
❑44, Jul 1967, JSe (a)............................. 15.00
❑45, Aug 1967, 1: Paul Ryan 15.00
❑46, Sep 1967, Medics story 15.00
❑47, Oct 1967, Fury on furlough............. 15.00
❑48, Nov 1967, JSe (a); return of Blitz Squad 15.00
❑49, Dec 1967, JSe (a); Howlers in Pacific 15.00
❑50, Jan 1968, JSe (a); Howlers in Pacific 15.00
❑51, Feb 1968 .... 15.00
❑52, Mar 1968, in Treblinka 15.00
❑53, Apr 1968... 15.00
❑54, May 1968.. 15.00
❑55, Jun 1968... 15.00
❑56, Jul 1968... 15.00
❑57, Aug 1968, TS, JSe (a) 15.00
❑58, Sep 1968... 15.00
❑59, Oct 1968, Alan Kupperberg L.O.C .. 15.00
❑60, Nov 1968 .... 15.00
❑61, Dec 1968... 15.00
❑62, Jan 1969, O: Sgt. Fury. 1: Sgt. Bass 15.00
❑63, Feb 1969, 1: Jerry Larkin; D: Jerry Larkin 15.00
❑64, Mar 1969, Story continued from Captain Savage and his Leatherneck Raiders #11 .... 12.00
❑65, Apr 1969 .... 12.00
❑66, May 1969, 1: Coral Liebowitz......... 12.00
❑67, Jun 1969, JSe (c); 2: Coral Liebowitz 12.00
❑68, Jul 1969, Fury goes home on leave 12.00
❑69, Aug 1969, 1: Jacob Fury (later becomes Scorpio). 1: Von Steurer...... 12.00
❑70, Sep 1969, 1: Missouri Marauders.. 12.00
❑71, Oct 1969, 2: Missouri Marauders... 12.00
❑72, Nov 1969, Tony Isabella L.O.C 12.00
❑73, Dec 1969... 12.00
❑74, Jan 1970 .... 12.00
❑75, Feb 1970... 12.00
❑76, Mar 1970, BEv (w); Fury's father vs. The Red Baron.................................... 12.00
❑77, Apr 1970, BEv (w); 1: Hans Klaus.. 12.00
❑78, May 1970, BEv (w); 2: Hans Klaus. 12.00
❑79, Jun 1970, BEv (w); Alan Kupperberg L.O.C 12.00
❑80, Sep 1970, Reprints Sgt. Fury #21.. 12.00

N-MINT

❑81, Nov 1970, 1: Fred Jones................ 12.00
❑82, Dec 1970, SL (w); Reprints from Sgt. Fury #24... 12.00
❑83, Jan 1971, Dum-Dum Dugan vs. Man-Mountain McCoy......................... 12.00
❑84, Feb 1971, 2: Man-Mountain McCoy 12.00
❑85, Mar 1971, JK (c); SL (w); Reprint from Sgt. Fury #25............................ 12.00
❑86, Apr 1971... 12.00
❑87, May 1971, SL (w); Reprints from Sgt. Fury #26 .... 12.00
❑88, Jun 1971, A: Patton 12.00
❑89, Jul 1971, SL (w); Reprints from Sgt. Fury #27... 12.00
❑90, Aug 1971 .... 12.00
❑91, Sep 1971, SL (w); Reprints from Sgt. Fury #28... 12.00
❑92, Oct 1971, Giant-size; HT (c); 1: Tom Tanaka; D: Tom Tanaka; Reprint from Sgt. Fury #31 .... 12.00
❑93, Dec 1971, Reprints Sgt. Fury #32.. 12.00
❑94, Jan 1972, GK (c); Steve Englehart work was uncredited 12.00
❑95, Feb 1972, GK (c); SL (w); JK (a); reprints Sgt. Fury #2 .... 12.00
❑96, Mar 1972, GK (c) 12.00
❑97, Apr 1972, JSe (c);Steve Englehart work was uncredited 12.00
❑98, May 1972, JSe (c); 1: Dugan's Deadly Dozen.. 12.00
❑99, Jun 1972, JSe (c); Reprints from Sgt. Fury #33... 12.00
❑100, Jul 1972, GK (c); A: Gary Friedrich. A: Dick Ayers. A: Martin Goodman. A: Captain America. A: Stan Lee......... 25.00
❑101, Sep 1972, JSe (c); O: Howling Commandos. Reprints from Sgt. Fury #34 .... 12.00
❑102, Sep 1972, JR (c)........................... 10.00
❑103, Oct 1972, Reprints from Sgt. Fury #35.. 8.00
❑104, Nov 1972, HT (c); A: Combat Kelly and Deadly Dozen............................... 8.00
❑105, Dec 1972, Reprints from Sgt. Fury #36.. 8.00
❑106, Jan 1973, Continued (in part) from Combat Kelly #4 .... 8.00
❑107, Feb 1973, GK (c); Reprints from Sgt. Fury #37 .... 8.00
❑108, Mar 1973 .... 8.00
❑109, Apr 1973, Reprints from Sgt. Fury #38.. 8.00
❑110, May 1973, JSe (c) 8.00
❑111, Jun 1973, Reprints from Sgt. Fury #39.. 6.00
❑112, Jul 1973, V: Baron Strucker......... 6.00
❑113, Aug 1973, Reprints from Sgt. Fury #40.. 6.00
❑114, Sep 1973 .... 6.00
❑115, Oct 1973....................................... 6.00
❑116, Nov 1973....................................... 6.00
❑117, Jan 1974....................................... 6.00
❑118, Mar 1974, V: Rommel. Marvel Value Stamp #93: Silver Surfer 6.00
❑119, May 1974, RH (c); Marvel Value Stamp #79: Kang............................. 6.00
❑120, Jul 1974, Marvel Value Stamp #98: Puppet Master.................................. 6.00
❑121, Sep 1974, Reprints Sgt. Fury #19 6.00
❑122, Oct 1974, Reprints Sgt. Fury #20 5.00
❑123, Nov 1974, Reprints Sgt. Fury #21 5.00
❑124, Jan 1975, Reprints Sgt. Fury #22 5.00
❑125, Mar 1975, Reprints Sgt. Fury #23 5.00
❑126, May 1975, Reprints Sgt. Fury #24 5.00
❑127, Jul 1975, Reprints Sgt. Fury #25. 5.00
❑128, Sep 1975, Reprints Sgt. Fury #26 5.00
❑129, Oct 1975, Reprints Sgt. Fury #27 5.00
❑130, Nov 1975, Reprints Sgt. Fury #28 5.00
❑131, Jan 1976, Reprints Sgt. Fury #29 5.00
❑132, Mar 1976, Reprints Sgt. Fury #30 4.00
❑133, May 1976, Reprins Sgt. Fury #31 4.00
❑133/30¢, May 1976, 30¢ regional price variant... 20.00
❑134, Jul 1976, Reprints Sgt. Fury #32. 4.00
❑134/30¢, Jul 1976, 30¢ regional price variant.. 20.00
❑135, Sep 1976, Reprints Sgt. Fury #33 4.00
❑136, Oct 1976, Reprints Sgt. Fury #34 4.00
❑137, Nov 1976, Reprints Sgt.Fury #35 4.00
❑138, Jan 1977, Reprints Sgt. Fury #36 4.00
❑139, Mar 1977, Reprints Sgt. Fury #44 4.00
❑140, May 1977, Reprints Sgt. Fury #45 4.00

N-MINT

❑141, Jul 1977... 4.00
❑141/35¢, Jul 1977, 35¢ regional price variant.. 15.00
❑142, Sep 1977, Reprints Sgt. Fury #47 15.00
❑142/35¢, Sep 1977, 35¢ regional price variant.. 15.00
❑143, Nov 1977, Reprints Sgt. Fury #48 4.00
❑144, Jan 1978, Reprints Sgt. Fury #49 4.00
❑145, Mar 1978, Reprints Sgt. Fury #50 4.00
❑146, May 1978, Reprints Sgt. Fury #51 4.00
❑147, Jul 1978, Reprints Sgt. Fury #52. 4.00
❑148, Sep 1978, ReprintsSgt. Fury #53. 4.00
❑149, Nov 1978, Reprints Sgt. Fury #54 4.00
❑150, Jan 1979, Reprints Sgt. Fury #56 4.00
❑151, Mar 1979, Reprints Sgt. Fury #55 4.00
❑152, Jun 1979, Reprints Sgt. Fury #57 3.00
❑153, Aug 1979, Reprints Sgt. Fury #58 3.00
❑154, Oct 1979, Reprints Captain Savage #6.. 3.00
❑155, Dec 1979, Reprints Sgt. Fury #59 3.00
❑156, Feb 1980, Reprints Sgt. Fury #60 3.00
❑157, Apr 1980, Reprints Sgt. Fury #61 3.00
❑158, Jun 1980, Reprints Sgt. Fury #62 3.00
❑159, Aug 1980, Reprints Sgt. Fury #63 3.00
❑160, Oct 1980, Reprints Captain Savage #11.. 3.00
❑161, Dec 1980, Reprints Sgt. Fury #64 3.00
❑162, Feb 1981, Reprints Sgt. Fury #68 3.00
❑163, Apr 1981, Reprints Sgt. Fury #69; Reprint Not Brand Ecch #2................ 3.00
❑164, Jun 1981, Reprints Sgt. Fury #70 3.00
❑165, Aug 1981, Reprints Sgt. Fury #71 3.00
❑166, Oct 1981, Reprints Sgt. Fury #72 3.00
❑167, Dec 1981, Reprints Sgt. Fury #1.. 3.00
❑Ann 1, ca. 1965, Korea; reprints Sgt. Fury #4 and 5 .... 125.00
❑Ann 2, Aug 1966, O: S.H.I.E.L.D.. D-Day 55.00
❑Ann 3, Aug 1966, Cover reads "King-Size Special"; Vietnam 30.00
❑Ann 4, Apr 1968, Cover reads "King-Size Special"; Battle of the Bulge 22.00
❑Ann 5, Aug 1969, Cover reads "King-Size Special"; reprints from Sgt. Fury #6 and 7.. 10.00
❑Ann 6, Aug 1970, Cover reads "King-Size Special"... 9.00
❑Ann 7, ca. 1971, Cover reads "King-Size Special"... 9.00

Sgt. Fury: Peacemaker
Marvel

❑1, Mar 2006 .... 3.50
❑2, May 2006.. 3.50
❑3, Jul 2006.. 3.50
❑4, Jul 2006.. 3.50
❑5, Aug 2006 .... 3.50
❑6, Sep 2006 .... 3.50

Sgt. Rock
DC

❑302, Mar 1977, Series continued from "Our Army At War"............................ 25.00
❑303, Apr 1977....................................... 15.00
❑304, May 1977, Sgt Rock; USS Stevens 15.00
❑305, Jun 1977....................................... 15.00
❑306, Jul 1977.. 15.00
❑307, Aug 1977 .... 15.00
❑308, Sep 1977, Sgt Rock; USS Stevens 10.00
❑309, Oct 1977....................................... 10.00
❑310, Nov 1977 .... 10.00
❑311, Dec 1977 .... 10.00
❑312, Jan 1978, JKu (c) 10.00
❑313, Feb 1978....................................... 8.00
❑314, Mar 1978 .... 8.00
❑315, Apr 1978, JKu (c); RE (a) 8.00
❑316, May 1978, JKu (c) 8.00
❑317, Jun 1978.. 8.00
❑318, Jul 1978, Reprint from Our Army at War #220.. 8.00
❑319, Aug 1978, JKu (a)......................... 8.00
❑320, Sep 1978 .... 8.00
❑321, Oct 1978.. 6.00
❑322, Nov 1978 .... 6.00
❑323, Dec 1978 .... 6.00
❑324, Jan 1979, JKu (c) 6.00
❑325, Feb 1979, JKu (a) 6.00
❑326, Mar 1979, JKu (c).......................... 6.00
❑327, Apr 1979, JKu (c); RE (a) 6.00
❑328, May 1979, JKu (a) 6.00
❑329, Jun 1979, JKu (c) 6.00

Other grades: Multiply price above by 5/6 for VF/NM • 2/3 for VERY FINE • 1/3 for FINE • 1/5 for VERY GOOD • 1/8 for GOOD

Six From Sirius

Moench and Gulacy's space opera
©Marvel

Six Million Dollar Man

1970s TV hit was a good get for Charlton
©Charlton

Skull the Slayer

Dinosaurs and cavemen roam the earth
©Marvel

Slacker Comics

A tribute to high-school life and outcasts
©Slave Labor

Slash Maraud

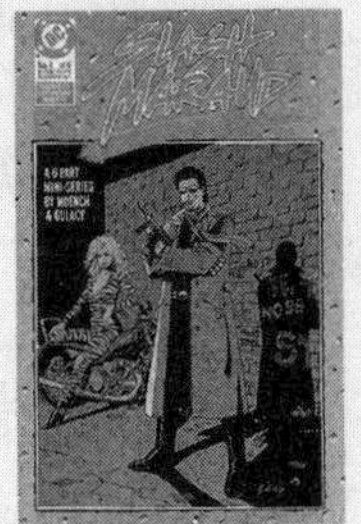

Earth is overrun by aliens in the future
©DC

N-MINT

❑329/Whitman, Jun 1979, Whitman variant ... 15.00
❑330, Jul 1979, JKu (c) ... 6.00
❑331, Aug 1979, JKu (c); TY, RE (a) ... 5.00
❑332, Sep 1979, JKu (c) ... 5.00
❑333, Oct 1979, JKu (c) ... 5.00
❑334, Nov 1979, JKu (c) ... 5.00
❑335, Dec 1979, JKu (a) ... 5.00
❑336, Jan 1980, JKu, RE (a) ... 5.00
❑337, Feb 1980, JKu (c); RE (a) ... 5.00
❑338, Mar 1980, JKu (a) ... 5.00
❑339, Apr 1980, JKu (c) ... 5.00
❑340, May 1980 ... 5.00
❑341, Jun 1980 ... 5.00
❑342, Jul 1980, JKu, RE (a) ... 4.00
❑343, Aug 1980, JKu (c) ... 4.00
❑344, Sep 1980, JKu (c) ... 4.00
❑345, Oct 1980, JKu (c) ... 4.00
❑346, Nov 1980, JKu (c); TY (w); TY (a) ... 4.00
❑347, Dec 1980, JKu (c); JDu, JSe (a) ... 4.00
❑348, Jan 1981 ... 4.00
❑349, Feb 1981, JKu (c); JDu (a) ... 4.00
❑350, Mar 1981 ... 4.00
❑351, Apr 1981 ... 3.00
❑352, May 1981 ... 3.00
❑353, Jun 1981 ... 3.00
❑354, Jul 1981, JKu (c) ... 3.00
❑355, Aug 1981, JKu (c) ... 3.00
❑356, Sep 1981, JKu (a) ... 3.00
❑357, Oct 1981, JKu (c); JDu (a) ... 3.00
❑358, Nov 1981, JKu (c); JDu (a) ... 3.00
❑359, Dec 1981, JKu (c); JDu (a) ... 3.00
❑360, Jan 1982, JKu (c); JDu (a) ... 3.00
❑361, Feb 1982, JKu (c) ... 3.00
❑362, Mar 1982, JKu (c); JDu (a) ... 3.00
❑363, Apr 1982, JKu (c) ... 3.00
❑364, May 1982 ... 3.00
❑365, Jun 1982 ... 3.00
❑366, Jul 1982, JKu (c) ... 3.00
❑367, Aug 1982, JKu (c) ... 3.00
❑368, Sep 1982, JKu (a) ... 3.00
❑369, Oct 1982, JKu (c) ... 3.00
❑370, Nov 1982 ... 3.00
❑371, Dec 1982 ... 2.50
❑372, Jan 1983 ... 2.50
❑373, Feb 1983, JKu (c) ... 2.50
❑374, Mar 1983, JKu (c) ... 2.50
❑375, Apr 1983 ... 2.50
❑376, May 1983 ... 2.50
❑377, Jun 1983, JKu (c); A: Worry Wart ... 2.50
❑378, Jul 1983, JKu (c); Christmas ... 2.50
❑379, Aug 1983, JKu (c) ... 2.50
❑380, Sep 1983, JKu (c) ... 2.50
❑381, Oct 1983, JKu (c) ... 2.50
❑382, Nov 1983 ... 2.50
❑383, Dec 1983 ... 2.50
❑384, Jan 1984; JKu (c); FT (a); Sgt Rock; USS Stevens ... 2.50
❑385, Feb 1984 JKu (c); ATh (a) ... 2.50
❑386, Mar 1984 JKu (c); FT (a) ... 2.50
❑387, Apr 1984; JKu (c); RE (a); Reprint from Our Army at War #263 ... 2.50
❑388, May 1984 ... 2.50
❑389, Jun 1984 ... 2.50
❑390, Jul 1984 JKu (c) ... 2.50
❑391, Aug 1984 ... 2.00
❑392, Sep 1984 JKu (c) ... 2.00
❑393, Oct 1984 JKu (c) ... 2.00
❑394, Nov 1984 JKu (c) ... 2.00
❑395, Dec 1984; JKu (a); Reprint from Our Army at War #269 ... 2.00
❑396, Jan 1985; JKu (c); RH (a); children in war ... 2.00
❑397, Feb 1985 ... 2.00
❑398, Mar 1985; JKu (a); Reprint from Wierd War Tales #6 ... 2.00
❑399, Apr 1985 ... 2.00
❑400, May 1985 ... 2.00
❑401, Jun 1985; Reprint from Weird War Tales #1 ... 2.00
❑402, Jul 1985; JKu (c); RE (a); Reprint from Our Army at War #269 ... 2.00
❑403, Aug 1985 ... 2.00
❑404, Sep 1985; V: Iron Major; Reprint from Our Army at War #158 ... 2.00
❑405, Oct 1985 ... 2.00
❑406, Nov 1985 ... 2.00
❑407, Dec 1985 ... 2.00
❑408, Feb 1986; Shelly Mayer tribute ... 2.00
❑409, Apr 1986 ... 2.00
❑410, Jun 1986 ... 2.00
❑411, Aug 1986 ... 2.00
❑412, Oct 1986 ... 2.00
❑413, Dec 1986 ... 2.00
❑414, Feb 1987; Christmas ... 2.00
❑415, Apr 1987 ... 2.00
❑416, Jun 1987 ... 2.00
❑417, Aug 1987; JKu (c); looking into future ... 2.00
❑418, Oct 1987; looking into future ... 2.00
❑419, Dec 1987 ... 2.00
❑420, Feb 1988 ... 2.00
❑421, Apr 1988 ... 2.00
❑422, Jul 1988; Final Issue ... 2.00
❑Ann 1 ... 4.00
❑Ann 2, Sep 1982 ... 4.00
❑Ann 3, Aug 1983 ... 3.00
❑Ann 4, Aug 1984 ... 3.00

Sgt. Rock
DC

❑14, Jul 1991; Series continued from Sgt. Rock Special #13 ... 2.00
❑15, Aug 1991; Sgt Rock: Reprint from Our Army at War #151; Reprint from Star Spangled War Stories #72; Enemy Ace: Reprint from Star Spangled War Stories #143 ... 2.00
❑16, Sep 1991; Sgt Rock: Reprint from Our Army at War #158; Ememy Ace: Reprint from Our Army at War #155; Reprint from Star Spangled War Stories #70 ... 2.00
❑17, Oct 1991; Sgt Rock: Reprint from Our Army at War #155; Enemy Ace: Reprint from Star Spangles War Stories #138 ... 2.00
❑18, Nov 1991; Sgt Rock: Reprint from Our Army at War #166; Enemy Ace: Reprint from Star Spangled War Stories #139 ... 2.00
❑19, Dec 1991; Sgt Rock: Reprint from Our Army at War #236; Enemy Ace: Reprint from Men of War #8; Batman and Sgt Rock: Reprint from Brave and the Bold #108 ... 2.00
❑20, Jan 1992; Sgt Rock: Reprint from Our Army at War #168 and 196; USS Stevens: Reprints from Our Army at War #235, 244 and 247 ... 2.00
❑21, Feb 1992; Sgt Rock: Reprints from Our Army at War #228 and 271; USS Stevens: Reprints from Our Army at War #257 and 262; Reprint from Our Army at War #236 ... 2.00
❑22, Mar 1992; Final issue ... 2.00
❑Special 1, Oct 1992; 1992 Special ... 2.95
❑Special 2, ca. 1994; Commemorates 50th anniversary of the Battle of the Bulge; 1994 Special ... 2.95

Sgt. Rock Special
DC

❑1, Sep 1988 A: Viking Prince ... 3.00
❑2, Dec 1988 ... 2.50
❑3, Mar 1989 ... 2.50
❑4, Jun 1989 ... 2.50
❑5, Sep 1989 ... 2.50
❑6, Dec 1989 ... 2.50
❑7, Mar 1990; reprints Our Fighting Forces #153 ... 2.50
❑8, Jun 1990 ... 2.50
❑9, Sep 1990; Enemy Ace guest stars ... 2.50
❑10, Dec 1990 ... 2.50
❑11, Mar 1991 ... 2.50
❑12, May 1991 ... 2.50
❑13, Jun 1991 ... 2.50

Sgt. Rock's Prize Battle Tales Replica Edition
DC

❑1, ca. 2000 ... 5.95

Sgt. Rock: The Prophecy
DC

❑1, Mar 2006, Andy Kubert cover; Sgt. Rock standing with guns in both hands ... 2.99
❑2, Apr 2006 ... 2.99
❑3, Jun 2006 ... 2.99
❑4, Jun 2006 ... 2.99
❑6, Sep 2006 ... 2.99

Sergio Aragonés Destroys DC
DC

❑1, Jun 1996; One-shot ... 3.50

Sergio Aragonés Massacres Marvel
Marvel

❑1, Jun 1996; wraparound cover ... 3.50

Sergio Aragonés Stomps Star Wars
Dark Horse

❑1, Feb 2000 ... 2.95

Serina
Antarctic

❑1, Mar 1996, b&w ... 2.95
❑2, May 1996, b&w ... 2.95
❑3, Jul 1996 ... 2.95

Serius Bounty Hunter
Blackthorne

❑1, Nov 1987, b&w ... 1.75
❑2, Jan 1988, b&w ... 1.75
❑3, Mar 1988, b&w ... 1.75

Serpentina
Lightning
- ❑1/A, Feb 1998, b&w 2.95
- ❑1/B, Feb 1998; Alternate cover 2.95

Serpentyne
Nightwynd
- ❑1, Apr 1992, b&w 2.50
- ❑2, May 1992, b&w 2.50
- ❑3, Jun 1992, b&w 2.50

Serra Angel on the World of Magic: The Gathering
Acclaim / Armada
- ❑1, Aug 1996; polybagged with oversized Serra Angel card; One-shot; Prestige format 5.95

Seth Throb Underground Artist
Slave Labor
- ❑1, Mar 1994 ..... 2.95
- ❑2, May 1994 ..... 2.95
- ❑3, Aug 1994 ..... 2.95
- ❑4, Dec 1994 ..... 2.95
- ❑5, Mar 1995 ..... 2.95
- ❑6, Jun 1995 ..... 2.95
- ❑7, Sep 1995 ..... 2.95

Settei
Antarctic
- ❑1, Feb 1993, b&w 7.95
- ❑2, Apr 1993, b&w 7.95

Settei Super Special Featuring: Project A-Ko
Antarctic
- ❑1, Feb 1994 ..... 2.95

Seven Block
Marvel / Epic
- ❑1, ca. 1990, b&w; prestige format; NN. 4.50

Seven Guys of Justice
False Idol
- ❑1, Apr 2000 ..... 2.00
- ❑2, ca. 2000 ..... 2.00
- ❑3, ca. 2000 ..... 2.00
- ❑4, ca. 2000 ..... 2.00
- ❑5, ca. 2000 ..... 2.00
- ❑6, ca. 2001; ca. 2000 ..... 2.00
- ❑7, ca. 2001 ..... 2.00
- ❑8, ca. 2001 ..... 2.00
- ❑9, ca. 2001 ..... 2.00
- ❑10, ca. 2001 ..... 2.00

777: Wrath/Faust Fearbook
Rebel
- ❑1 ..... 14.20

Seven Miles a Second
DC / Vertigo
- ❑1, ca. 1996; prestige format; NN; One-shot 7.95

Seven Soldiers
DC
- ❑0, Apr 2005 ..... 5.00
- ❑0/Faces, Apr 2005; 2nd print. Cover by J.H. Williams features the faces of the new Seven Soldiers team 2.95
- ❑1, Jan 2007 ..... 3.99

Seven Soldiers: Frankenstein
DC
- ❑1, Jan 2006 ..... 2.99
- ❑2, Feb 2006 ..... 2.99
- ❑3, May 2006 ..... 2.99
- ❑4, Jul 2006 ..... 2.99

Seven Soldiers: Guardian
DC
- ❑1, Jun 2005 ..... 2.99
- ❑2, Jul 2005 ..... 2.99
- ❑3, Aug 2005 ..... 2.99
- ❑4, Sep 2005 ..... 2.99

Seven Soldiers: Klarion the Witch Boy
DC
- ❑1, Jun 2005 ..... 4.00
- ❑2, Jul 2005 ..... 2.99
- ❑3, Aug 2005 ..... 2.99
- ❑4, Dec 2005 ..... 2.99

Seven Soldiers: Mister Miracle
DC
- ❑1, Nov 2005 ..... 2.99
- ❑2, Jan 2006 ..... 2.99
- ❑3, Mar 2006 ..... 2.99
- ❑4, May 2006 ..... 2.99

Seven Soldiers: Shining Knight
DC
- ❑1, May 2005 ..... 2.99
- ❑2, Jun 2005 ..... 2.99
- ❑3, Jul 2005 ..... 2.99
- ❑4, Oct 2005 ..... 2.99

Seven Soldiers: The Bulleteer
DC
- ❑1, Jan 2006 ..... 2.99
- ❑2, Feb 2006 ..... 2.99
- ❑3, Mar 2006 ..... 2.99
- ❑4, May 2006 ..... 2.99

Seven Soldiers: Zatanna
DC
- ❑1, Jun 2005; D: Doctor Thirteen 2.99
- ❑2, Aug 2005 ..... 2.99
- ❑3, Sep 2005 ..... 2.99
- ❑4, Jan 2006 ..... 2.99

7th Millennium
Allied
- ❑1 ..... 2.50
- ❑2 ..... 2.50
- ❑3 ..... 2.50
- ❑4 ..... 2.50

7th System
Sirius
- ❑1, Jan 1998, b&w 2.95
- ❑2, Feb 1998, b&w 2.95
- ❑3, Jul 1998, b&w 2.95
- ❑4, Dec 1998, b&w 2.95
- ❑6, Feb 1999, b&w 2.95
- ❑5, ca. 1999 ..... 2.95

77 Sunset Strip
Dell
- ❑1, Jul 1962 ..... 150.00

77 Sunset Strip
Gold Key
- ❑1, Nov 1962 ..... 100.00
- ❑2, Feb 1963 ..... 100.00

Sewage Dragoon
Parody
- ❑1 ..... 2.50
- ❑1/2nd; 2nd printing 2.50

Sex & Death
Acid Rain
- ❑1, b&w; Adult 3.95

Sex and Death
Acid Rain
- ❑1 ..... 2.50

Sexcapades
Fantagraphics / Eros
- ❑1, Dec 1996; Adult 2.95
- ❑2, Jan 1997; Adult 2.95
- ❑3, Feb 1997; Adult 2.95

Sex Drive
M.A.I.N.
- ❑1 ..... 3.00

Sexecutioner
Fantagraphics / Eros
- ❑1, Sep 1991, b&w; Adult 2.50
- ❑2, b&w; Adult 2.50
- ❑3, b&w; 24 pages; Adult 2.50

Sexhibition
Fantagraphics / Eros
- ❑1; Adult 2.95
- ❑2; Adult 2.95
- ❑3; Adult 2.95
- ❑4, Feb 1996; Adult 2.95

Sex in the Sinema
Comic Zone
- ❑1, Dec 1991, b&w; Adult 2.95
- ❑2, b&w; Indicia lists Feb 1992; Adult 2.95
- ❑3, b&w; Indicia says Sept 1992; Adult 2.95
- ❑4, b&w; Adult 2.95

Sex, Lies and Mutual Funds of the Yuppies From Hell
Marvel
- ❑1 ..... 2.95

Sex Machine
Fantagraphics / Eros
- ❑1, b&w; Adult 2.50
- ❑2, b&w; 24 pages; Adult 2.95
- ❑3, Dec 1997, b&w; Adult 2.95

Sexploitation Cinema: A Cartoon History
Revisionary
- ❑1, Nov 1998, b&w 3.50

Sex Trek: The Next Infiltration
Friendly
- ❑1, b&w; Adult 2.95

Sex Wad
Fantagraphics / Eros
- ❑1; Adult 2.95
- ❑2; Adult 2.95

Sex Warrior
Dark Horse
- ❑1 ..... 2.50
- ❑2 ..... 2.50

Sex Warrior Isane XXX
Fantagraphics
- ❑1, Dec 2004 ..... 3.95
- ❑2, Jan 2005 ..... 3.95
- ❑3, Feb 2005 ..... 3.95
- ❑4, Apr 2005 ..... 3.95
- ❑5, May 2005 ..... 3.95
- ❑6, Jul 2005 ..... 3.95
- ❑7, Sep 2005 ..... 3.95
- ❑8, Nov 2005 ..... 3.95

Sexx Wars
Immortal
- ❑1; Adult 2.95

Sexy Stories from the World Religions
Last Gasp
- ❑1; Adult 2.50

Sexy Superspy
Forbidden Fruit
- ❑1, Apr 1991, b&w; Adult 2.95
- ❑2, May 1991, b&w; Adult 2.95
- ❑3, b&w; Adult 2.95
- ❑4, b&w; Adult 2.95
- ❑5, b&w; Adult 2.95
- ❑6, b&w; Adult 2.95
- ❑7, b&w; Adult 2.95

Sexy Women
Celebrity
- ❑1 ..... 2.95
- ❑2 ..... 2.95

SFA International Presents
Shanda Fantasy Arts
- ❑1 ..... 0.00
- ❑2 ..... 0.00

SFA Spotlight
Shanda Fantasy Arts
- ❑1 ..... 2.95
- ❑2 ..... 2.95
- ❑3 ..... 2.95
- ❑4, May 1999, b&w 2.95
- ❑5, May 1999, b&w; Zebra Comics 4.50

Shade
DC
- ❑1, Apr 1997, JRo (w) 2.50
- ❑2, May 1997, JRo (w) 2.50
- ❑3, Jun 1997, JRo (w); A: Jay Garrick 2.50
- ❑4, Jul 1997, JRo (w) 2.50

Shade Changing Man
DC
- ❑1, Jul 1977, SD (c); SD (w); SD (a); O: Shade. 1: Shade 10.00
- ❑2, Sep 1977, SD (c); SD (w); SD (a) 4.00
- ❑3, Nov 1977, SD (c); SD (w); SD (a) 4.00
- ❑4, Jan 1978, SD (c); SD (w); SD (a) 4.00
- ❑5, Mar 1978, SD (c); SD (w); SD (a) 4.00
- ❑6, May 1978, SD (c); SD (w); SD (a); V: Khaos 4.00
- ❑7, Jul 1978, SD (c); SD (w); SD (a) 4.00
- ❑8, Sep 1978, SD (c); SD (w); SD (a) 4.00

Other grades: Multiply price above by 5/6 for VF/NM • 2/3 for VERY FINE • 1/3 for FINE • 1/5 for VERY GOOD • 1/8 for GOOD

Sliders

TV series was a modest SF hit
©Acclaim

Slimer!

Uses the "pet" ghost from Ghostbusters
©Now

Slingers

Characters based on aspects of Spider-Man
©Marvel

Smith Brown Jones

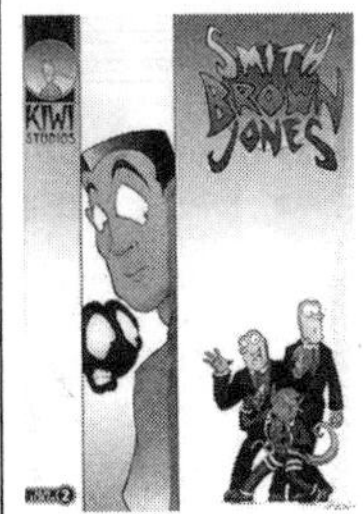

Goofy send-up of 1990s X-Files culture
©Kiwi

Smurfs

Relic from a long-dead period of madness
©Marvel

N-MINT

Shade Changing Man
DC

- ❑1, Jul 1990; 1: Kathy George. 1: American Scream 3.00
- ❑2, Aug 1990 .... 2.00
- ❑3, Sep 1990 .... 2.00
- ❑4, Oct 1990 .... 2.00
- ❑5, Nov 1990 .... 2.00
- ❑6, Dec 1990 .... 2.00
- ❑7, Jan 1991 .... 2.00
- ❑8, Feb 1991 .... 2.00
- ❑9, Mar 1991 .... 2.00
- ❑10, Apr 1991 .... 2.00
- ❑11, May 1991 .... 2.00
- ❑12, Jun 1991 .... 2.00
- ❑13, Jul 1991 .... 2.00
- ❑14, Aug 1991 .... 2.00
- ❑15, Sep 1991 .... 2.00
- ❑16, Oct 1991 .... 2.00
- ❑17, Nov 1991 .... 2.00
- ❑18, Dec 1991 .... 2.00
- ❑19, Jan 1992 .... 2.00
- ❑20, Jan 1992 JDu (a) 2.00
- ❑21, Mar 1992 .... 2.00
- ❑22, Apr 1992 .... 2.00
- ❑23, May 1992 .... 2.00
- ❑24, Jun 1992 .... 2.00
- ❑25, Jul 1992 .... 2.00
- ❑26, Aug 1992 .... 2.00
- ❑27, Sep 1992 .... 2.00
- ❑28, Oct 1992 .... 2.00
- ❑29, Nov 1992 .... 2.00
- ❑30, Dec 1992 .... 2.00
- ❑31, Jan 1993 .... 2.00
- ❑32, Feb 1993; Death Talks About Life AIDS insert 2.00
- ❑33, Mar 1993; Vertigo line starts 2.00
- ❑34, Apr 1993 .... 2.00
- ❑35, May 1993 .... 2.00
- ❑36, Jun 1993 .... 2.00
- ❑37, Jul 1993 .... 2.00
- ❑38, Aug 1993 .... 2.00
- ❑39, Sep 1993 .... 2.00
- ❑40, Oct 1993 .... 2.00
- ❑41, Nov 1993 .... 2.00
- ❑42, Dec 1993 .... 2.00
- ❑43, Jan 1994 .... 2.00
- ❑44, Feb 1994 .... 2.00
- ❑45, Mar 1994 .... 2.00
- ❑46, Apr 1994 .... 2.00
- ❑47, May 1994 .... 2.00
- ❑48, Jun 1994 .... 2.00
- ❑49, Jul 1994 .... 2.00
- ❑50, Aug 1994; Giant-size 3.00
- ❑51, Sep 1994 .... 2.00
- ❑52, Oct 1994 .... 2.00
- ❑53, Nov 1994 .... 2.00
- ❑54, Dec 1994 .... 2.00
- ❑55, Jan 1995 .... 2.00
- ❑56, Feb 1995 .... 2.00
- ❑57, Mar 1995 .... 2.00
- ❑58, Apr 1995 .... 2.00
- ❑59, May 1995 .... 2.25
- ❑60, Jun 1995 .... 2.25
- ❑61, Jul 1995 .... 2.25
- ❑62, Aug 1995 .... 2.25
- ❑63, Sep 1995 .... 2.25
- ❑64, Oct 1995 .... 2.25
- ❑65, Nov 1995 .... 2.25
- ❑66, Dec 1995 .... 2.25
- ❑67, Jan 1996 .... 2.25
- ❑68, Feb 1996 .... 2.25
- ❑69, Mar 1996 .... 2.25
- ❑70, Apr 1996; Final Issue 2.25

Shades and Angels
Candle Light

- ❑1, b&w 2.95

Shades of Blue
AMP

- ❑1, Jul 1999, b&w 2.50
- ❑2, Aug 2000; b&w 2.50

Shades of Gray
Lady Luck

- ❑1, ca. 1994 .... 2.50
- ❑2 .... 2.50
- ❑3 .... 2.50
- ❑4 .... 2.50
- ❑5 .... 2.50
- ❑6 .... 2.50
- ❑7 .... 2.50
- ❑8 .... 2.50
- ❑9 .... 2.50
- ❑10 .... 2.50
- ❑11 .... 2.50

Shades of Gray Comics and Stories
Tapestry

- ❑1, ca. 1996 .... 2.95
- ❑2 .... 2.95
- ❑3 .... 2.95
- ❑4 .... 2.95

Shade Special
AC

- ❑1, Oct 1984; Latigo Kid 1.50

Shado: Song of the Dragon
DC

- ❑1, ca. 1992, MGr (w) 5.00
- ❑2, ca. 1992, MGr (w) 5.00
- ❑3, ca. 1992, MGr (w) 5.00
- ❑4, ca. 1992, MGr (w) 5.00

Shadow
Archie

- ❑1, Aug 1964 .... 30.00
- ❑2, Sep 1964 .... 18.00
- ❑3, Nov 1964 .... 18.00
- ❑4, Jan 1965 .... 18.00
- ❑5, Mar 1965, O: Radiation Rogue. 1: Radiation Rogue 18.00
- ❑6, May 1965 .... 18.00
- ❑7, Jul 1965 .... 18.00
- ❑8, Sep 1965, Final Issue 18.00

Shadow
DC

- ❑1, Nov 1973 .... 12.00
- ❑2, Jan 1974, Alan Kupperberg L.O.C.; Mike Uslan L.O.C. 8.00
- ❑3, Mar 1974, BWr (a); Jack C. Harris L.O.C 8.00
- ❑4, May 1974 .... 6.00
- ❑5, Jul 1974 .... 4.00
- ❑6, Sep 1974 .... 5.00
- ❑7, Nov 1974 .... 4.00
- ❑8, Jan 1975 .... 4.00
- ❑9, Mar 1975 FR (c); FMc, FR (a) 4.00
- ❑10, May 1975 .... 4.00
- ❑11, Jul 1975; A: The Avenger. Robert Greenberger L.O.C. 4.00
- ❑12, Sep 1975 .... 4.00

Shadow
DC

- ❑1, May 1986; HC (c); HC (w); HC (a); The Shadow returns 3.00
- ❑2, Jun 1986 HC (c); HC (w); HC (a) 2.00
- ❑3, Jul 1986 HC (w); HC (a) 2.00
- ❑4, Aug 1986 HC (w); HC (a) 2.00

Shadow
DC

- ❑1, Aug 1987 BSz (c); BSz (a) 2.50
- ❑2, Sep 1987 BSz (c); BSz (a) 2.00
- ❑3, Oct 1987 BSz (c); BSz (a) 2.00
- ❑4, Nov 1987 BSz (c); BSz (a) 2.00
- ❑5, Dec 1987 BSz (c); BSz (a) 2.00
- ❑6, Jan 1988 BSz (c); BSz (a) 2.00
- ❑7, Feb 1988 .... 2.00
- ❑8, Mar 1988 .... 2.00
- ❑9, Apr 1988 .... 2.00
- ❑10, May 1988 .... 2.00
- ❑11, Jun 1988 .... 2.00
- ❑12, Jul 1988 .... 2.00
- ❑13, Aug 1988; D: Shadow 2.00
- ❑14, Sep 1988 .... 2.00
- ❑15, Oct 1988 .... 2.00
- ❑16, Nov 1988 .... 2.00
- ❑17, Dec 1988 A: Avenger 2.00
- ❑18, Dec 1988 A: Avenger 2.00
- ❑19, Jan 1989; Shadow alive again 2.00
- ❑Ann 1, ca. 1987; EC parody 2.50
- ❑Ann 2, ca. 1988 .... 2.50

Shadow
Dark Horse

- ❑1, Jun 1994 .... 2.50
- ❑2, Jul 1994 .... 2.50

Shadow Agents
Armageddon

- ❑1, May 1991 .... 2.50

Shadow and Doc Savage
Dark Horse

- ❑1, Jul 1995 .... 2.95
- ❑2, Aug 1995 .... 2.95

Shadow and the Mysterious 3
Dark Horse

- ❑1, Sep 1994; NN 2.95

Shadowblade
Hot

- ❑1 .... 1.75

Shadow: Blood and Judgment
DC

- ❑1 .... 12.95

	N-MINT

Shadow Cabinet
DC / Milestone

- ❑0, Jan 1994, Giant-size 2.50
- ❑1, Jun 1994, 1&O: Corpsicle; D: Corpsicle; O: Iron Butterfly; O: Sideshow 1.75
- ❑2, Jul 1994 .... 1.75
- ❑3, Aug 1994, 1: Telesthene 1.75
- ❑4, Sep 1994 .... 1.75
- ❑5, Oct 1994 .... 1.75
- ❑6, Nov 1994 .... 1.75
- ❑7, Dec 1994 .... 1.75
- ❑8, Jan 1995 .... 1.75
- ❑9, Feb 1995 .... 1.75
- ❑10, Mar 1995 .... 1.75
- ❑11, Apr 1995 .... 1.75
- ❑12, May 1995 .... 1.75
- ❑13, Jun 1995 .... 2.50
- ❑14, Jul 1995 .... 2.50
- ❑15, Aug 1995, Long Hot Summer 2.50
- ❑16, Sep 1995, The Long Hot Summer.. 2.50
- ❑17, Oct 1995, Final Issue 2.50

Shadow Comix Showcase
Shadow Comix

- ❑1, May 1996 .... 2.95

Shadow Cross
Darkside

- ❑1, Oct 1995 .... 2.75

Shadow Empires: Faith Conquers
Dark Horse

- ❑1, Aug 1994 .... 3.25
- ❑2, Sep 1994 .... 3.00
- ❑3, Oct 1994 .... 3.00
- ❑4, Nov 1994 .... 3.00

ShadowGear
Antarctic

- ❑1, Feb 1999 .... 2.99
- ❑2, Mar 1999 .... 2.99
- ❑3, Apr 1999 .... 2.99

ShadowHawk
Image

- ❑1, Aug 1992; 1: Shadowhawk. Embossed cover 3.00
- ❑1/A, Aug 1992; Newsstand edition (no gold stamp); 1: Shadowhawk. Embossed cover 2.00
- ❑2, Oct 1992 1: Arson. A: Spawn 2.50
- ❑3, Dec 1992; 1: The Others. 1: Liquefier. Glow-in-the-dark cover 2.50
- ❑4, Mar 1993 A: Savage Dragon 2.00

ShadowHawk
Image

- ❑1, May 1993, diecut foil cover 3.50
- ❑1/Gold, May 1993, Gold 3.00
- ❑2, Jul 1993, 1: Hawk's Shadow. ShadowHawk's identity revealed; Foil-embossed cover 2.00
- ❑2/Gold, Jul 1993, Gold edition 3.00
- ❑3, Aug 1993, 1: The Pact. 1: J.P. Slaughter. Cover perforated to allow folding out into poster 2.95

ShadowHawk
Image

- ❑0, Oct 1994, RL (w); RL (a); O: Shadowhawk. A: Mist. A: Bloodstrike. A: Mars Gunther. cover says September 2.50
- ❑1, Nov 1993, 1: Valentine. Foil-embossed cover 2.50
- ❑2, Dec 1993, 1: U.S. Male 2.00
- ❑3, Feb 1994, Fold-up cover 2.95
- ❑4, Mar 1994 .... 2.95
- ❑12, Aug 1994, (Numbering sequence follows from total of all ShadowHawk books published to this point) 1.95
- ❑13, Sep 1994, A: WildC.A.T.s 1.95
- ❑14, Oct 1994, A: 1963 heroes 2.50
- ❑15, Nov 1994, A: The Others 2.50
- ❑16, Jan 1995, A: Supreme 2.50
- ❑17, Mar 1995, A: Spawn 2.50
- ❑18, May 1995, D: Shadowhawk 2.50
- ❑Special 1, Dec 1994, Flip-book KB (w). 3.50

Shadowhawk
Image

- ❑1, May 2005 .... 2.99
- ❑2, Jun 2005 .... 2.99
- ❑3, Jul 2005 .... 2.99
- ❑4, Sep 2005 .... 2.99
- ❑5 2005 .... 2.99
- ❑6 2005 .... 2.99
- ❑7, Jan 2006 .... 2.99
- ❑8, Jan 2006 .... 3.50
- ❑9, Mar 2006 .... 3.50
- ❑10, Apr 2006 .... 3.50
- ❑11, Jun 2006 .... 3.50
- ❑12, Jul 2006 .... 3.50
- ❑13, Jul 2006 .... 3.50
- ❑14, Sep 2006 .... 3.50
- ❑15, Nov 2006 .... 3.50

Shadowhawk Gallery
Image

- ❑1, Apr 1994 .... 2.00

Shadowhawk One-Shot
Image

- ❑1, Oct 2006 .... 1.99

Shadowhawk Saga
Image

- ❑1; Includes numbered "Hero Original" seal; Hero Premiere Edition #8 .... 1.00

Shadowhawks of Legend
Image

- ❑1, Nov 1995 .... 4.95

Shadowhawk-Vampirella
Image / Harris

- ❑2, Feb 1995; crossover; continued from Vampirella - Shadowhawk #1 .... 4.95

Shadow: Hell's Heat Wave
Dark Horse

- ❑1, Apr 1995 .... 2.95
- ❑2, May 1995 .... 2.95
- ❑3, Jun 1995 .... 2.95

Shadow House
Shadow House

- ❑1, Aug 1997, b&w 2.95
- ❑2, Oct 1997, b&w 2.95
- ❑3, Dec 1997, b&w 2.95
- ❑4, Feb 1998, b&w 2.95

Shadowhunt Special
Image

- ❑1/A, Apr 1996; Part 1 of five-part crossover 2.50
- ❑1/B, Apr 1996; alternate cover; Part 1 of five-part crossover 2.50

Shadow: In the Coils of Leviathan
Dark Horse

- ❑1, Oct 1993; Poster by Michael W. Kaluta 2.95
- ❑2, Dec 1993; Poster by John Bolton.... 2.95
- ❑3, Feb 1994; Poster by Geof Darrow.... 2.95
- ❑4, Apr 1994; Poster by Gary Gianni 2.95

Shadow Lady
Dark Horse / Manga

- ❑1, Oct 1998, 1: Shadow Lady 3.00
- ❑2, Nov 1998 .... 2.50
- ❑3, Dec 1998 .... 2.50
- ❑4, Jan 1999 .... 2.50
- ❑5, Feb 1999 .... 2.50
- ❑6, Mar 1999 .... 2.50
- ❑7, Apr 1999 .... 2.50
- ❑8, May 1999 .... 2.50
- ❑9, Jun 1999 .... 2.50
- ❑10, Jul 1999 .... 2.50
- ❑11, Aug 1999 .... 2.50
- ❑12, Sep 1999 .... 2.50
- ❑13, Oct 1999 .... 2.50
- ❑14, Nov 1999 .... 2.50
- ❑15, Dec 1999 .... 2.50
- ❑16, Jan 2000 .... 2.50
- ❑17, Feb 2000 .... 2.50
- ❑18, Mar 2000 .... 2.50
- ❑19, Apr 2000 .... 2.50
- ❑20, May 2000 .... 2.50
- ❑21, Jun 2000 .... 2.50
- ❑22, Jul 2000 .... 2.50
- ❑23, Aug 2000 .... 2.50
- ❑24, Sep 2000 .... 2.50
- ❑Special 1, Oct 2000 .... 3.99

Shadowland
Fantagraphics

- ❑1, Oct 1989, b&w 2.25
- ❑2, b&w 2.25

Shadowline Special
Image

- ❑1 .... 1.00

Shadowlord/Triune
Jet City

- ❑1, Win 1986 .... 1.50

Shadowman
Valiant

- ❑0/Non-chromium 5.00
- ❑0/VVSS 45.00
- ❑0, Apr 1994; BH (c); BH (w); BH (a); O: Shadowman II (Jack Boniface). O: Shadowman I (Maxim St. James). Chromium cover 2.50
- ❑0/Gold, Apr 1994; Gold edition; BH (c); BH (w); BH (a); O: Shadowman II (Jack Boniface). O: Shadowman I (Maxim St. James); Yellow corner logo 20.00
- ❑1, May 1992; 1&O: Shadowman II (Jack Boniface) 8.00
- ❑2, Jun 1992 .... 5.00
- ❑3, Jul 1992 .... 5.00
- ❑4, Aug 1992; FM (c); FM (a); Unity 3.00
- ❑5, Sep 1992; BL (w); Unity 3.00
- ❑6, Oct 1992 SD (c); SD, DP, BH (w); SD (a) 3.00
- ❑7, Nov 1992 DP (c); BH (w); DP (a) 2.00
- ❑8, Dec 1992; BH (w); 1: Master Darque. V: Master Darque 4.00
- ❑9, Jan 1993 .... 2.00
- ❑10, Feb 1993 BH (c); BH (w); BH (a).... 1.00
- ❑11, Mar 1993 BH (c); BH (w); BH (a)... 1.00
- ❑12, Apr 1993; BH (c); BH (w); BH (a); V: Master Darque 1.00
- ❑13, May 1993 (c) 1.00
- ❑14, Jun 1993 BH (c); BH (w); BH (a) ... 1.00
- ❑15, Jul 1993 BH (c); BH (w); BH (a) ... 1.00
- ❑16, Aug 1993; BH (c); BH (w); BH (a); 1: Doctor Mirage 2.00
- ❑17, Sep 1993; BH (c); BH (w); BH (a); A: Archer & Armstrong. Serial number contest 1.00
- ❑18, Oct 1993 BH (c); BH (w); BH (a).... 1.00
- ❑19, Nov 1993; BH (c); BH (w); BH (a); A: Aerosmith 5.00
- ❑20, Dec 1993 BH (c); DP, BH (w); BH (a) 1.00
- ❑21, Jan 1994; BH (c); BH (w); BH (a); V: Master Darque; Indica says Jan 1993 1.00
- ❑22, Feb 1994 BH (c); BH (w); BH (a).... 1.00
- ❑23, Mar 1994; BH (c); BH (w); BH (a); A: Doctor Mirage. Continued from Dr. Mirage #5 .... 1.00
- ❑24, Apr 1994 BH (c); BH (w); BH (a).... 1.00
- ❑25, Apr 1994; BH (c); BH (w); BH (a); trading card 2.00
- ❑26, Jun 1994 BH (c); BH (w); BH (a) ... 1.00
- ❑27, Aug 1994 BH (c); BH (w); BH (a) ... 1.00
- ❑28, Sep 1994 BH (c); BH (w); BH (a) ... 1.00
- ❑29, Oct 1994; BH (c); BH (w); BH (a); Chaos Effect Beta 1 .... 1.00
- ❑30, Nov 1994 BH (c); BH (w); BH (a) ... 1.00
- ❑31, Dec 1994 BH (c); BH (w); BH (a) ... 1.00
- ❑32, Jan 1994 BH (c); BH (w); BH (a).... 2.00
- ❑33, Feb 1994 BH (c); BH (w); BH (a).... 2.00
- ❑34, Mar 1994 BH (c); BH (w); BH (a) ... 2.00
- ❑35, Apr 1995 BH (c) 2.00
- ❑36, May 1995 BH (c) 2.00
- ❑37, Jun 1995 BH (c); BH (w); BH (a) ... 2.00
- ❑38, Jul 1995; BH (c); BH (w); BH (a); Birthquake 2.00
- ❑39, Aug 1995; BH (c); BH (w); BH (a); Birthquake 2.00
- ❑40, Sep 1995 BH (c); BH (w); BH (a) ... 3.00
- ❑41, Oct 1995 BH (c); BH (w); BH (a) 3.00
- ❑42, Nov 1995 BH (c); BH (w); BH (a) ... 4.00
- ❑43, Dec 1995; BH (c); BH (w); BH (a); Final Issue 7.00
- ❑YB 1, Dec 1994; YB 1; YB 1 .... 3.95

Shadowman
Acclaim

- ❑1, Mar 1997 .... 2.50
- ❑1/Variant, Mar 1997, Painted cover...... 2.50
- ❑2, Apr 1997 .... 2.50
- ❑3, May 1997 .... 2.50
- ❑4, Jun 1997 .... 2.50
- ❑5, Jul 1997 .... 2.50
- ❑5/Ashcan, Mar 1997, b&w; No cover price; preview of upcoming issue....... 1.00
- ❑6, Aug 1997 .... 2.50
- ❑7, Sep 1997 .... 2.50

Other grades: Multiply price above by 5/6 for VF/NM • 2/3 for VERY FINE • 1/3 for FINE • 1/5 for VERY GOOD • 1/8 for GOOD

Snarf

Short black-and-white stories by top talent
©Kitchen Sink

Sock Monkey

Tony Millionaire's odd adventurer
©Dark Horse

Sojourn

Popular addition to the CrossGen universe
©CrossGen

Solar, Man of the Atom

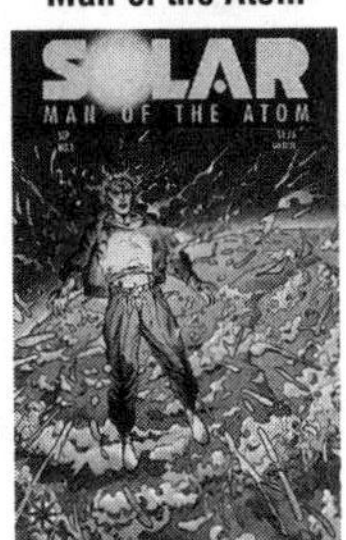

Popular relaunch of old Gold Key character
©Valiant

Solution

Quartet of ultra-powered heroes for hire
©Malibu

N-MINT

❑8, Oct 1997 ... 2.50
❑9, Nov 1997 ... 2.50
❑10, Dec 1997 ... 2.50
❑11, Jan 1998 ... 2.50
❑12, Feb 1998 ... 2.50
❑13, Mar 1998, Goat Month ... 2.50
❑14, Apr 1998 ... 2.50
❑15, Jan 1998, No cover date; indicia says Jan ... 2.50
❑16, Feb 1998, No cover date; indicia says Feb ... 2.50
❑Ashcan 1, Nov 1996, b&w; No cover price; preview of upcoming series ... 1.00

Shadowman
Acclaim

❑1, Jul 1999 ... 3.95
❑2, Aug 1999 ... 3.95
❑3, Sep 1999; Flipbook with Unity 2000 prelude story ... 3.95
❑4, Oct 1999; Flipbook with Unity 2000 prelude story, leads into Unity 2000 #1 ... 3.95

Shadow Master
Psygnosis / Manga

❑0; Preview ... 1.00

Shadowmasters
Marvel

❑1, Oct 1989; JLee (c); O: Shadow-masters ... 4.00
❑2, Nov 1989 ... 4.00
❑3, Dec 1989 ... 4.00
❑4, Jan 1990 ... 4.00

Shadowmen
Trident

❑1, b&w; Adult ... 2.25
❑2, b&w; Adult ... 2.25

Shadow of the Batman
DC

❑1, Dec 1985; MR (c); MR (a); Wrapaound cover; Reprints from Detective #469, 470, House of Mystery #274 ... 3.00
❑2, Jan 1986; MR (c); MR (a); Wrapaound cover; Reprint ... 2.00
❑3, Feb 1986; MR (c); MR (a); Wrapaound cover; Reprint ... 2.00
❑4, Mar 1986; MR (c); MR (a); Wrapaound cover; Reprint ... 2.00
❑5, Apr 1986; Wrapaound cover; Reprint; Final Issue ... 2.00

Shadow of the Torturer
Innovation

❑1, ca. 1991; Movie adaptation; Novel adaptation ... 2.50
❑2, ca. 1991; Movie adaptation; Novel adaptation ... 2.50
❑3, ca. 1991; Movie adaptation; Novel adaptation ... 2.50
❑4, ca. 1992 ... 2.50
❑5, ca. 1992 ... 2.50
❑6, ca. 1992 ... 2.50

Shadowpact
DC

❑1, Aug 2006 ... 2.99
❑2, Sep 2006 ... 2.99
❑3, Sep 2006, Phantom Stranger appearance (as narrator) ... 2.99
❑4, Oct 2006 ... 2.99
❑5, Nov 2006, Phantom Stranger appearance (as narrator) ... 2.99
❑6, Dec 2006 ... 2.99
❑7, Jan 2007, Phantom Stranger appearance (as narrator) ... 2.99
❑8, Mar 2007 ... 2.99

Shadowplay
Idea & Design Works

❑1 2005 ... 3.99
❑2 2005 ... 3.99
❑3, Dec 2005 ... 3.99
❑4, Jan 2006 ... 3.99

Shadow Raven
Poc-It

❑1, Jun 1995; 1: Shadow Raven ... 2.50

Shadow Reavers
Black Bull

❑1, Oct 2001 ... 2.99
❑2, Nov 2001 ... 2.99

Shadow Reigns
Aix C.C.

❑0, Dec 1997 ... 2.95

Shadow Riders
Marvel

❑1, Jun 1992; Embossed cover ... 2.50
❑2, Jul 1992 ... 1.75
❑3, Aug 1992 ... 1.75
❑4, Sep 1992 ... 1.75

Shadows
Image

❑1, Mar 2003 ... 2.95
❑2, Apr 2003 ... 2.95
❑3, Aug 2003 ... 2.95
❑4, Dec 2003 ... 2.95

Shadows & Light
Marvel

❑1, Feb 1998, b&w ... 2.99
❑2, Apr 1998, b&w ... 2.99
❑3, Jul 1998, b&w ... 2.99

Shadows and Light
NBM

❑1 ... 10.95
❑2 ... 10.95
❑3 ... 10.95
❑4 ... 10.95

Shadow's Edge
Lion

❑1 ... 3.95

Shadows Fall
DC / Vertigo

❑1, Nov 1994 ... 2.95
❑2, Dec 1994 ... 2.95
❑3, Jan 1995 ... 2.95
❑4, Feb 1995 ... 2.95
❑5, Mar 1995 ... 2.95
❑6, Apr 1995 ... 2.95

Shadows from the Grave
Renegade

❑1, b&w ... 2.00
❑2, Mar 1988, b&w ... 2.00

Shadow Slasher
Pocket Change

❑1; 1: Riplash ... 2.50

Shadow Slayer
Eternity

❑0 ... 1.95

Shadowstar
Shadowstar

❑1; Winter 1985 ... 2.00
❑2, Nov 1985; MGr (c); Published by ShadowStar Press ... 2.00
❑3, Dec 1985; first Slave Labor comic book ... 2.00

Shadow State
Broadway

❑1, Dec 1995, DC (a); 1: BloodS.C.R.E.A.M.. enhanced cardstock cover; BloodS.C.R.E.A.M., Fatale ... 2.50
❑2, Jan 1996, Till Death Do Us Part; Fatale ... 2.50
❑3, Mar 1996, Till Death Do Us Part ... 2.50
❑4, Apr 1996, Till Death Do Us Part ... 2.50
❑5, May 1996, Till Death Do Us Part ... 2.50
❑6, Jun 1996 ... 2.95
❑7, Jul 1996 ... 2.95
❑Ashcan 1, Sep 1995, b&w; giveaway preview edition; Till Death Do Us Part, Fatale ... 1.00

Shadow Strikes!
DC

❑1, Sep 1989 ... 2.50
❑2, Oct 1989 ... 2.25
❑3, Nov 1989 ... 2.00
❑4, Dec 1989 ... 2.00
❑5, Jan 1990 A: Doc Savage ... 2.00
❑6, Feb 1990 A: Doc Savage ... 2.00
❑7, Mar 1990 ... 2.00
❑8, Apr 1990; V: Shiwan Khan ... 2.00
❑9, May 1990; V: Shiwan Khan ... 2.00
❑10, Jun 1990; V: Shiwan Khan ... 2.00
❑11, Aug 1990 ... 2.00
❑12, Sep 1990 ... 2.00
❑13, Oct 1990 ... 2.00
❑14, Dec 1990 ... 2.00
❑15, Jan 1991 ... 2.00
❑16, Feb 1991 ... 2.00
❑17, Mar 1991 ... 2.00
❑18, Apr 1991 ... 2.00
❑19, May 1991 ... 2.00
❑20, Jun 1991 ... 2.00
❑21, Jul 1991 ... 2.00
❑22, Aug 1991 ... 2.00
❑23, Sep 1991 ... 2.00
❑24, Oct 1991 ... 2.00
❑25, Nov 1991 ... 2.00
❑26, Dec 1991 ... 2.00
❑27, Jan 1992 ... 2.00
❑28, Feb 1992 ... 2.00
❑29, Mar 1992 ... 2.00
❑30, Apr 1992 ... 2.00
❑31, May 1992 ... 2.00
❑Ann 1, Dec 1989 LMc, DS (a) ... 3.50

Shadowtown
Iconografix

❑1 ... 2.50

N-MINT | N-MINT | N-MINT

Shadowtown: Black Fist Rising
Madheart

❑1, b&w 2.50

Shadow War of Hawkman
DC

❑1, May 1985 RHo (c); RHo, AA (a) 1.50
❑2, Jun 1985 RHo (c); RHo (a) 1.25
❑3, Jul 1985 RHo (c); RHo (a); A: Elongated Man. A: Aquaman 1.25
❑4, Aug 1985 RHo (c); RHo (a) 1.25

Shadow Warrior
Gateway

❑1, b&w 1.95

Shaiana
Express / Entity

❑1, Jul 1995, b&w; enhanced cover 2.50
❑1/Chromium, Jul 1995 .... 10.00
❑1/Holochrome, Jul 1995 .... 15.00
❑2 .... 2.50
❑3 .... 2.50

Shaloman
Mark 1

❑1, b&w 1.75
❑2, b&w 1.75
❑3, b&w 1.75
❑4, b&w 1.75
❑5, b&w 1.75
❑6, b&w 1.75
❑7, b&w 1.75
❑8, b&w 1.75
❑9, b&w 1.75

Shaman
Continuity

❑0, Jan 1994; NA (w); NA, AN (a); Dealer incentive issue 2.00

Shaman's Tears
Image

❑0, Dec 1995, MGr (w); MGr (a); says 1996 indicia; meant 1995 .... 2.50
❑1, May 1993, MGr (w); MGr (a); foil cover 2.50
❑1/Platinum, May 1993, Platinum edition; MGr (w); MGr (a) 4.00
❑2, Jul 1993, MGr (w); MGr (a); cover says Aug; indicia says Jul 2.50
❑3, Nov 1994, MGr (w); MGr (a); Wrap-around cover 1.95
❑3/Ashcan, MGr (w); MGr (a); Limited "ashcan" run of Shaman's Tears #3 .... 3.00
❑4, Dec 1994, MGr (w); MGr (a); Title moves back to Image 1.95
❑5, Jan 1995, MGr (w); MGr (a) 1.95
❑6, Feb 1995, MGr (w); MGr (a) 1.95
❑7, May 1995, MGr (w); MGr (a) 1.95
❑8, May 1995, MGr (w); MGr (a) 1.95
❑9, Jun 1995, MGr (w); MGr (a) 1.95
❑10, Jul 1995, MGr (w); MGr (a) 1.95
❑11, Aug 1995, MGr (w); MGr (a) 1.95
❑12, Aug 1995, MGr (w); MGr (a); Final Issue 1.95

Shanda the Panda
Mu

❑1, May 1992, b&w 2.50

Shanda the Panda
Antarctic

❑1, Jun 1993 .... 2.50
❑2, Aug 1993 .... 2.50
❑3, Oct 1993 .... 2.75
❑4, Dec 1993 .... 2.75
❑5, Aug 1994 .... 2.75
❑6, Nov 1994 .... 2.75
❑7, Jan 1995 .... 2.75
❑8, Feb 1995 .... 2.75
❑9, May 1995 .... 2.75
❑10, Jul 1995 .... 2.75
❑11, Sep 1995 .... 2.75
❑12, Nov 1995; Vision Comics becomes publisher 2.75
❑13, Jan 1996; Backup story takes place between Shabda #2 and #3 .... 2.75
❑14, Mar 1996 .... 2.75
❑15, May 1996 .... 2.75
❑16, Jul 1996 .... 1.95
❑17, Jan 1997 .... 1.95
❑18, Mar 1997; Rocky Horror Picture Show spoof 1.95
❑19, May 1997 .... 1.95
❑20, Jul 1997 .... 1.95
❑21, Sep 1997; Demi Moore spoof cover 2.95
❑22 .... 2.95
❑23, Jan 1999 .... 2.95
❑24, Apr 1999; Totoro spoof cover 2.95
❑25, Jul 1999; Giant-size 4.95
❑26, Nov 1999 .... 2.95
❑27, Feb 2000 .... 2.95
❑28, May 2000 .... 2.95
❑29, Aug 2000 .... 2.95
❑30, Nov 2000 .... 2.95
❑31, Feb 2001 .... 2.99
❑32, May 2001 .... 2.99
❑33, Aug 2001 .... 2.99
❑34, Nov 2001; Giant-size 4.99
❑35, Aug 2002; Giant-size 4.99
❑36, ca. 2002; Giant-size 4.99
❑37, ca. 2003 .... 4.99
❑38, ca. 2003; Terri comes out 4.99
❑39, Dec 2003 .... 4.99
❑40, ca. 2004 .... 4.99
❑41, ca. 2004; b&w 4.99
❑42, ca. 2004; b&w 4.99
❑43, Mar 2005; Matrix-based cover 4.99
❑Ann 1 .... 4.00
❑Ann 2 .... 4.00
❑Ann 3 .... 4.50
❑Ann 4 .... 4.95

Shang Chi: Master of Kung Fu
Marvel

❑1, Nov 2002 .... 2.99
❑2, Dec 2002 .... 2.99
❑3, Jan 2003 .... 2.99
❑4, Feb 2003 .... 2.99
❑5, Mar 2003 .... 2.99
❑6, Apr 2003 .... 2.99

Shanghai: Big Machine
Brick House Digital

❑1, ca. 2000 .... 2.95

Shanghaied: The Saga of the Black Kite
Eternity

❑1, Jan 1987 .... 2.00
❑2 .... 2.00
❑3 .... 2.00

Shangri La
Image

❑1, ca. 2004 .... 7.95

Shanna the She-Devil
Marvel

❑1, Dec 1972, GT (a); 1: Shanna the She-Devil 27.00
❑2, Feb 1973, JSo (c); JSo (a) 6.00
❑3, Apr 1973 .... 3.50
❑4, Jun 1973 .... 3.50
❑5, Aug 1973 .... 3.50

Shanna the She-Devil
Marvel

❑1, Mar 2005 .... 6.00
❑2, Apr 2005 .... 3.50
❑3, May 2005 .... 3.50
❑4, Jun 2005 .... 3.50
❑5, Jul 2005 .... 3.50
❑6, Aug 2005 .... 3.50
❑7, Sep 2005 .... 3.50

Shaolin
Black Tiger

❑1; 1&O: The Tiger 2.95
❑2 .... 2.95
❑3 .... 2.95
❑4 .... 2.95
❑5 .... 2.95

Shaolin Cowboy
Burlyman

❑1 2005 .... 3.50
❑1/Variant 2005 .... 5.00
❑2 2005 .... 3.50
❑2/Mignola 2005 .... 8.00
❑3 2005 .... 3.50

Shaolin Sisters
Tokyopop

❑1, Feb 2003, b&w; printed in Japanese format 9.99
❑2, Apr 2003, b&w; printed in Japanese format 9.99

Shaolin Sisters: Reborn
Tokyopop

❑1, May 2005, b&w 9.99
❑2, Aug 2005 .... 9.99
❑3, Nov 2005 .... 9.99

Shaquille O'Neal vs. Michael Jordan
Personality

❑1 .... 2.95
❑2 .... 2.95

Shards
Ascension

❑1, Feb 1994 .... 2.50

Sharky
Image

❑1/A, Feb 1998 .... 2.50
❑1/B, Feb 1998; back cover pin-up 2.50
❑1/C, Feb 1998; signing tour edition 2.50
❑1/D, Feb 1998; no cover price; The $1,000,000 variant 2.50
❑2/A, Apr 1998 .... 2.50
❑2/B, Apr 1998; alternate wraparound cover (with Savage Dragon) 2.50
❑3, May 1998 .... 2.50
❑4, Jul 1998; gives date of publication as Late; Group charging on cover, "The Bad Guy!" inset 2.50
❑4/A, Jul 1998; Variant cover: monster breaking through road; Gives date of publication as Late 2.50

Shatter
First

❑1, Jun 1985; 1: Shatter. This is the first computer-generated comic book 2.50
❑1/2nd 2.00

Shatter
First

❑1, Dec 1985, Continued from Shatter one-shot 2.50
❑2, Feb 1986 .... 2.00
❑3, Jun 1986 .... 2.00
❑4, Aug 1986 .... 2.00
❑5, Oct 1986 .... 2.00
❑6, Dec 1986 .... 2.00
❑7, Feb 1987 .... 2.00
❑8, Apr 1987 .... 2.00
❑9, Jun 1987 .... 2.00
❑10, Aug 1987 .... 2.00
❑11, Oct 1987 .... 2.00
❑12, Dec 1987 .... 2.00
❑13, Feb 1988 .... 2.00
❑14, Apr 1988 .... 2.00

Shattered Earth
Eternity

❑1, Nov 1988 .... 1.95
❑2, Dec 1988 .... 1.95
❑3, Jan 1989 .... 1.95
❑4, Mar 1989 .... 1.95
❑5 1989 .... 1.95
❑6 1989 .... 1.95
❑7 1989 .... 1.95
❑8 1989 .... 1.95
❑9 1989 .... 1.95

Shattered Image
Image

❑1, Aug 1996 .... 2.50
❑2, Oct 1996; incorrect cover date 2.50
❑3, Nov 1996; cover says Oct, indicia says Nov 2.50
❑4, Dec 1996; Final Issue 2.50

Shatterpoint
Eternity

❑1, Dec 1990, b&w; Broid 2.25
❑2, Jan 1991, b&w; Broid 2.25
❑3, Feb 1991, b&w; Broid 2.25
❑4, Apr 1991, b&w; Broid 2.25

Shaun of the Dead
Idea & Design Works

❑1, Jul 2005 .... 3.99
❑2, Aug 2005 .... 3.99

Other grades: Multiply price above by 5/6 for VF/NM • 2/3 for VERY FINE • 1/3 for FINE • 1/5 for VERY GOOD • 1/8 for GOOD

Somerset Holmes

Amnesiac actress makes an escape
©Pacific

Sonic Disruptors

Uncompleted Baron title has pirate deejay
©DC

Sonic the Hedgehog

Long-running series based on Sega game
©Archie

Son of Ambush Bug

Ambush Bug in a variety of goofy vignettes
©DC

Soulsearchers and Company

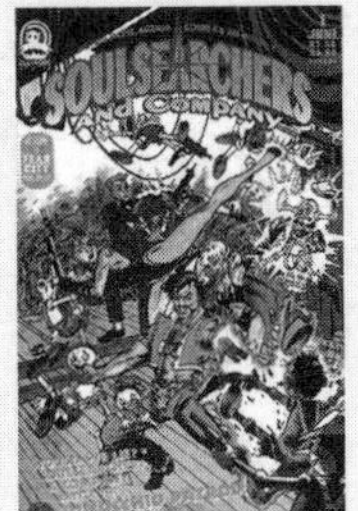

Peter David's group of paranormal researchers
©Claypool

	N-MINT
❑3, Aug 2005	3.99
❑4, Nov 2005	3.99

Shazam!
DC

	N-MINT
❑1, Feb 1973, CCB, NC (c); CCB (a); O: Captain Marvel (Golden Age)	20.00
❑2, Apr 1973, CCB (c); CCB (a); Partial photo cover; Infinity cover	10.00
❑3, Jun 1973, CCB (c); CCB (a)	10.00
❑4, Jul 1973, CCB (c); CCB (a); Reprint from Captain Marvel Adventures #97; Otto Binder L.O.C.; David Micheline L.O.C	10.00
❑5, Sep 1973, CCB (c); CCB (a); Captain Marvel Jr. Backup story	10.00
❑6, Oct 1973, CCB (c); CCB, KS (a); Photo cover	10.00
❑7, Nov 1973, CCB (c); CCB, KS (a)	10.00
❑8, Dec 1973, 100 Page giant; CCB (c); CCB (a); scheduled as DC 100-Page Super-Spectacular #DC-23	20.00
❑9, Jan 1974, CCB (c); DC, CCB (a)	10.00
❑10, Feb 1974, BO (c); BO (a); V: Aunt Minerva. Mary Marvel back-up	10.00
❑11, Mar 1974	10.00
❑12, Jun 1974, 100 Page giant	10.00
❑13, Aug 1974, 100 Page giant	10.00
❑14, Oct 1974, 100 Page giant; BO (c); CCB, KS (a); A: Monster Society	10.00
❑15, Dec 1974, 100 Page giant; A: Lex Luthor	10.00
❑16, Feb 1975, 100 Page giant; V: Seven Deadly Sins. Reprints from Marvel Family #29, 53, 59, Captain Marvel Adventures #103, 137, Captain Marvel Jr. #118	10.00
❑17, Apr 1975, 100 Page giant	10.00
❑18, Jun 1975	7.00
❑19, Aug 1975	7.00
❑20, Oct 1975	7.00
❑21, Dec 1975 CCB (w)	7.00
❑22, Feb 1976; V: King Kull	7.00
❑23, Win 1976; Reprint	7.00
❑24, Spr 1976, Spring 1976	7.00
❑25, Oct 1976, 1&O: Isis	7.00
❑26, Dec 1976	7.00
❑27, Feb 1977	7.00
❑28, Apr 1977, V: Black Adam	7.00
❑29, Jun 1977, V: Ibac	7.00
❑30, Aug 1977, Sivana makes a Superman robot	7.00
❑31, Oct 1977, A: Minute Man	7.00
❑32, Dec 1977	7.00
❑33, Feb 1978, V: Mr. Atom	7.00
❑34, Apr 1978, O: Captain Marvel Jr.. Captain Marvel Jr. vs. Captain Nazi	7.00
❑35, Jun 1978	7.00

Shazam! and the Shazam Family
DC

	N-MINT
❑Ann 1, Sep 2002, Reprints Golden Age stories including 1st Mary Marvel and 1st Black Adam	5.95

Shazam! Power of Hope
DC

	N-MINT
❑1, Nov 2000	9.95
❑1/2nd, 2nd printing (2002)	9.95

Shazam: The New Beginning
DC

	N-MINT
❑1, Apr 1987; O: Captain Marvel (Golden Age)-new origin	2.00
❑2, May 1987; V: Black Adam	2.00
❑3, Jun 1987; O: Black Adam	2.00
❑4, Jul 1987	2.00

Sheba
Sick Mind

	N-MINT
❑1, Jul 1996, b&w	2.50
❑2, Nov 1996, b&w	2.50
❑3, Feb 1997, b&w	2.50
❑4, Sep 1997, b&w	2.50

Sheba
Sirius

	N-MINT
❑1, Dec 1997, b&w; Dog Star publishes	2.50
❑2, Mar 1998, b&w	2.50
❑3, Jun 1998, b&w	2.50
❑4, Sep 1998, b&w	2.50
❑5 1999, b&w; Walter S. Crane publishes	2.50
❑6, May 1999, b&w	2.95
❑7	2.95
❑8	2.95

Sheba Pantheon
Sirius

	N-MINT
❑1, Aug 1998, b&w; collects strips and character bios	2.50

She Buccaneer
Monster

	N-MINT
❑1, Mar 1992, b&w	2.25
❑2, b&w	2.25

She-Cat
AC

	N-MINT
❑1, Jun 1989, b&w	2.50
❑2, Apr 1990, b&w	2.50
❑3, May 1990, b&w	2.50
❑4, Jun 1990, b&w	2.50

Sheedeva
Fantagraphics / Eros

	N-MINT
❑1, Aug 1994, b&w; 24 pages; Adult	2.95
❑2, Nov 1994, b&w; Adult	2.95

Sheena
Marvel

	N-MINT
❑1, Dec 1984; GM (c); GM (a); Movie adaptation	2.00
❑2, Feb 1985; GM (c); GM (a); Movie adaptation	2.00

Sheena 3-D Special
Blackthorne

	N-MINT
❑1, May 1985	2.00

Sheena-Queen of the Jungle
London Night

	N-MINT
❑1/A, ca. 1998; Alligator cover	5.00
❑1/B, ca. 1998; Leopard cover	5.00
❑1/C, ca. 1998; Zebra cover	5.00
❑1/D, ca. 1998; Ministry Edition; Adult	3.00
❑1/Ltd., ca. 1998; White leather edition	15.00

Sheena, Queen of the Jungle 3-D
Blackthorne

	N-MINT
❑1, May 1985, b&w; DSt (c); DSt (a)	2.50

She-Hulk
Marvel

	N-MINT
❑1, May 2004	12.00
❑2, Jun 2004	7.00
❑3, Jul 2004	4.00
❑4, Aug 2004	2.99
❑5, Sep 2004	2.99
❑6, Oct 2004	2.99
❑7, Nov 2004	2.99
❑8, Dec 2004	2.99
❑9, Jan 2005	2.99
❑10, Feb 2005	2.99
❑11, Mar 2005	2.99
❑12, Apr 2005; Final issue	2.99

She-Hulk
Marvel

	N-MINT
❑1, Dec 2005; Return of Hawkeye	2.99
❑2, Jan 2006; Franklin Richards back-up feature	2.99
❑3, Feb 2006; One hundredth solo She-Hulk comic	3.99
❑4, Mar 2006	2.99
❑5, Apr 2006	2.99
❑6, May 2006	2.99
❑7, Jun 2006	2.99
❑8, Jul 2006; Civil War tie-in; John Jameson proposes to Jennifer Walters	22.00
❑9, Aug 2006	2.99
❑10, Sep 2006	2.99

She Hulk 2
Marvel

	N-MINT
❑1, Dec 2005, b&w	2.99
❑2, Jan 2006	2.99
❑3, Feb 2006	3.99
❑4, Mar 2006	2.99
❑5, Apr 2006	2.99
❑6, Jun 2006	2.99
❑7, Jul 2006	2.99
❑8, Aug 2006	2.99
❑9, Sep 2006	2.99
❑10, Oct 2006	2.99
❑11, Nov 2006	2.99
❑12, Dec 2006	2.99
❑13, Jan 2007	2.99
❑14, Mar 2007	2.99

Sheila Trent: Vampire Hunter
Draculina

	N-MINT
❑1; 1&O: Sheila Trent	2.50
❑2	2.50

Shell Shock
Mirage

	N-MINT
❑1, Dec 1989	12.95

Sherlock Holmes
DC

	N-MINT
❑1, Oct 1975	8.00

Sherlock Holmes
Eternity

	N-MINT
❑1, b&w; strip reprints	2.00
❑2 1988, b&w; strip reprints	2.00
❑3 1988, b&w; strip reprints	2.00
❑4 1988, b&w; strip reprints	2.00
❑5, Oct 1988, b&w; strip reprints	2.00
❑6 1988, b&w; strip reprints	2.00
❑7 1988, b&w; strip reprints	2.00

Other grades: Multiply price above by 5/6 for VF/NM • 2/3 for VERY FINE • 1/3 for FINE • 1/5 for VERY GOOD • 1/8 for GOOD

❑8, Jan 1989, b&w; strip reprints 2.00
❑9 1989, b&w; strip reprints 2.00
❑10 1989, b&w; strip reprints 2.00
❑11 1989, b&w; strip reprints 2.00
❑12 1989, b&w; strip reprints 2.00
❑13 1989, b&w; strip reprints 2.00
❑14 1989, b&w; strip reprints 2.00
❑15 1989, b&w; strip reprints 2.00
❑16 1989 .... 2.25
❑17 1989 .... 2.25
❑18 1990 .... 2.25
❑19 1990 .... 2.25
❑20 1990 .... 2.25
❑21 1990 .... 2.50
❑22 1990 .... 2.50
❑23 1990, Final Issue 2.75

Sherlock Holmes
Avalon

❑1, ca. 1997, b&w 2.95

Sherlock Holmes: Adventures of the Opera Ghost
Caliber

❑1; ca. 1994 .... 2.95
❑2; ca. 1994 .... 2.95

Sherlock Holmes Casebook
Eternity

❑1; Originally published as New Adventures of Sherlock Holmes 2.25
❑2; Originally published as New Adventures of Sherlock Holmes 2.25

Sherlock Holmes: Dr. Jekyll & Mr. Holmes
Caliber / Tome

❑1 1998, b&w; NN; One-shot 2.95

Sherlock Holmes in the Case of the Missing Martian
Eternity

❑1, Jul 1990, b&w 2.25
❑2, Aug 1990, b&w 2.25
❑3, Sep 1990, b&w 2.25
❑4, Oct 1990, b&w 2.25

Sherlock Holmes in the Curious Case of the Vanishing Villain
Atomeka

❑1; NN 4.50

Sherlock Holmes Mysteries
Moonstone

❑1 .... 2.95

Sherlock Holmes of the '30s
Eternity

❑1, b&w; strip reprints 2.95
❑2, b&w; strip reprints 2.95
❑3, b&w; strip reprints 2.95
❑4, b&w; strip reprints 2.95
❑5, b&w; strip reprints 2.95
❑6, b&w; strip reprints 2.95
❑7, b&w; strip reprints 2.95

Sherlock Holmes Reader
Tome

❑1, ca. 1998, b&w 3.95
❑2, ca. 1999, b&w 3.95
❑3, ca. 2000, b&w 3.95
❑4, ca. 2000, b&w 3.95

Sherlock Holmes: Return of the Devil
Adventure

❑1, Sep 1992, b&w 2.50
❑2 1992, b&w 2.50

Sherlock Jr.
Eternity

❑1, b&w; strip reprints 2.50
❑2, Sep 1990, b&w; strip reprints 2.50
❑3, b&w; strip reprints 2.50

Sherman's Room
-Ism

❑1, ca. 2005 .... 2.95

Sherman's March Through Atlanta to the Sea
Heritage Collection

❑1; retells Civil War story; wraparound cover 3.50

Sheva's War
DC / Vertigo

❑1, Oct 1998 .... 2.95
❑2, Nov 1998 .... 2.95
❑3, Dec 1998 .... 2.95
❑4, Jan 1999 .... 2.95
❑5, Feb 1999 .... 2.95

Shi
Crusade

❑0, ca. 1996; Flipbook with Wolverine/Shi Night of Justice Preview 2.99
❑½, ca. 1996; Wizard promotional edition with COA 3.00

Shi: Art of War Tour Book
Crusade

❑1, ca. 1998 .... 4.95

Shi: Black, White, and Red
Crusade

❑1, Mar 1998, B&w and red 2.95
❑2, May 1998, B&w and red 2.95

Shi/Cyblade: The Battle for Independents
Crusade

❑1, Sep 1995, 1: The Atomik Angels. A: Cerebus. A: Bone. crossover; concludes Image's Cyblade/Shi: The Battle for Independents #1; Numerous other independent characters appear. 4.00
❑1/Variant, Sep 1995, alternate cover; crossover; concludes Image's Cyblade/Shi: The Battle for Independents #1 ... 5.00

Shi/Daredevil: Honor Thy Mother
Crusade

❑1, Jan 1997; flipbook with TCB Sneak Attack Edition #1; crossover with Marvel 2.95
❑1/Ltd., Jan 1997; "Banzai" edition; Banzai edition 6.00

Shidima
Image

❑0/A, Oct 2001 .... 2.95
❑0/B, Oct 2001 .... 2.95
❑1/A, Jan 2001; Many figures on cover, man center holding rope 2.95
❑1/B, Jan 2001; Four figures on cover, man front holding sword 2.95
❑2, Mar 2001 .... 2.95
❑3, May 2001 .... 2.95
❑4, Aug 2001 .... 2.95

Shi: East Wind Rain
Crusade

❑1, Nov 1997; Painted cover 3.50
❑2, Feb 1998 .... 3.50
❑Ashcan 1, Jul 1997; No cover price; Sneak Teaser Preview 1.00

SHIELD
Marvel

❑1, Feb 1973, JSo (c); SL (w); DH, JK (a); Nick Fury reprints from Strange Tales 15.00
❑2, Apr 1973, JSo (c); JK (w); DH, JK (a); Nick Fury reprints from Strange Tales 5.00
❑3, Jun 1973, JK (c); SL (w); JB, JK, JSo (a); Nick Fury reprints from Strange Tales 5.00
❑4, Aug 1973, JSo (c); SL (w); JK, JSo (a); Nick Fury reprints from Strange Tales 5.00
❑5, Oct 1973, JSo (c); JSo (w); JSo (a); Nick Fury reprints from Strange Tales 5.00

Shield
Archie / Red Circle

❑2, Aug 1983, was Lancelot Strong, the Shield; becomes Shield — Steel Sterling 1.00

Shield: Spotlight
Idea & Design Works

❑1, Jan 2004 .... 3.99
❑1/Photo, Jan 2004 .... 3.99
❑2, Feb 2004 .... 3.99
❑3, Mar 2004 .... 3.99
❑4, May 2004 .... 3.99
❑5, Jun 2004 .... 3.99

Shield — Steel Sterling
Archie / Red Circle

❑3, Dec 1983, was Shield; becomes Steel Sterling 1.00

Shi: Heaven & Earth
Crusade

❑1, Jul 1997 .... 2.95
❑1/A, Jul 1997; alternate cover 2.95
❑2, Nov 1997 .... 2.95
❑2/A, Nov 1997; logoless cover 2.95
❑3, Jan 1998 .... 2.95
❑4, Apr 1998 .... 2.95
❑4/A, Apr 1998; alternate cover (Shi facing right) 2.95
❑Ashcan 1, ca. 1997; Special Teaser Preview 2.95

Shi: Ju Nen
Dark Horse

❑1 2004 .... 2.99
❑2 2004 .... 2.99
❑3 2005 .... 2.99

Shi: Kaidan
Crusade

❑1, Oct 1996, b&w; VM (a); Japanese ghost stories 2.95
❑1/A, Oct 1996, b&w; alternate wraparound cover with no cover copy; Japanese ghost stories 3.00

Shiloh: The Devil's Own Day
Heritage Collection

❑1; retells Civil War battle; wraparound cover 3.50

Shi: Masquerade
Crusade

❑1, Mar 1998; wraparound painted cover 3.50

Shimmer
Avatar

❑1, Oct 1998 .... 3.50

Shi: Nightstalkers
Crusade

❑1, Sep 1997 .... 3.50

Shion: Blade of the Minstrel
Viz

❑1, Sep 1990, b&w 9.95

Shi: Pandora's Box
Avatar

❑1, Apr 2003 .... 3.50

Ship of Fools
Image

❑0, Aug 1997, b&w 2.95
❑1, Oct 1997, b&w 2.95
❑2, Dec 1997, b&w 2.95
❑3, Feb 1998, b&w 2.95

Ship of Fools
Caliber

❑1, b&w 3.00
❑2 .... 3.00
❑3, b&w 3.00
❑4 .... 3.00
❑5 .... 3.00
❑6 .... 3.00

Ship of Fools
NBM

❑1, Apr 1999; Adult 10.95

Shipwrecked!
Disney

❑1; NN; Movie adaptation 5.95

Shi: Rekishi
Crusade

❑1, Jan 1997; flipbook with Shi: East Wind Rain Sneak Attack Edition #1 .... 2.95
❑2, Apr 1997 .... 2.95

Shi: Sempo
Avatar

❑1, Aug 2003; Ryp cover 3.50
❑2, Oct 2003; Adrian cover 3.50

Shi: Senryaku
Crusade

❑1, Aug 1995 .... 3.25
❑1/Variant, Aug 1995; Variant "virgin" cover with no type 4.00
❑2, Oct 1995; Cover by William Tucci 3.00
❑3, Dec 1995 .... 3.00

Southern Knights

Long-running regional super-hero group

©Guild

Sovereign Seven

Claremont's less successful X-Men follow-up

©DC

Space Adventures

Science fiction tales and Steve Ditko

©Charlton

Space Family Robinson

The inspiration for "Lost in Space"

©Gold Key

Spacehawk

Basil Wolverton reprints plus new material

©Dark Horse

N-MINT

Shi: The Blood of Saints
Crusade

❑1, Nov 1996 .... 2.95
❑Fan ed. 1/A, Nov 1996; Promotional edition from FAN magazine 2.00

Shi: The Series
Crusade

❑1, Aug 1997 .... 3.50
❑1/A, Aug 1997; Sneak preview edition with photo cover with Tia Carrera; Sneak preview edition 3.50
❑2, Sep 1997 .... 3.00
❑3, Oct 1997 .... 3.00
❑4, Nov 1997 .... 3.00
❑5, Dec 1997 .... 3.00
❑6, Jan 1998 .... 2.95
❑7, Feb 1998; manga-style cover 2.95
❑8, Mar 1998 .... 2.95
❑9, Apr 1998 .... 2.95
❑9/A, Apr 1998; alternate cover (full moon in background) 2.95
❑9/B, Apr 1998; alternate cover (Shi on her back) 2.95
❑9/C, Apr 1998; alternate cover (manga-style) 2.95
❑10, May 1998; Regular cover (side profile, face and shoulder) 2.95
❑10/A, May 1998; alternate cover (in water) 2.95
❑10/B, May 1998; alternate cover (cherry blossoms) 2.95
❑10/C, May 1998; alternate cover (drawing sword) 2.95
❑11, Jun 1998, b&w 2.95
❑12, Jul 1998 .... 2.95
❑13, Aug 1998 .... 2.95
❑14, Aug 1998 .... 2.95
❑15, Sep 1998 .... 2.95
❑16, Sep 1998 .... 2.95

Shi: The Way of the Warrior
Crusade

❑½ 3.00
❑½/Platinum 4.00
❑1, Mar 1994 .... 6.00
❑1/A, Mar 1994; Fan Appreciation Edition 5.00
❑1/B, Mar 1994; "Fan Appreciation Edition" #1 with no logo on cover 8.00
❑1/C, Mar 1994; Commemorative edition from the 1994 San Diego Comic Con; Gold logo on cover 8.00
❑2, Jun 1994 .... 5.00
❑2/A, Jun 1994; Fan appreciation edition #2 .... 3.00
❑2/B, Jun 1994; San Diego Comicon edition 6.00
❑2/Ashcan, Jun 1994; Ashcan promotional edition of Shi: The Way of the Warrior #2 .... 5.00
❑3, Oct 1994 .... 4.00
❑4 1995 .... 4.00
❑4/2nd; acetate cover 3.00
❑5, Apr 1995; 1: Tomoe 3.00
❑5/Variant, Apr 1995; 1: Tomoe. Silvestri variant cover 5.00
❑6 1995 .... 3.00
❑6/A 1995; Fan Appreciation Edition 3.00
❑6/Ashcan 1995; Commemorative edition from 1995 San Diego Comic Con 4.00

N-MINT

❑7, Mar 1996; back-up crossover with Lethargic Lad 3.00
❑7/Variant, Mar 1996; chromium edition; No cover price; back-up crossover with Lethargic Lad; limited to 5, 000 copies 4.00
❑8, Jun 1996 .... 3.00
❑8/A, Jun 1996; Combo Gold Club version; 5000 publisher; With certificate of Authenticity 5.00
❑9, Sep 1996 .... 3.00
❑10, Oct 1996; wraparound cover 3.00
❑11, Dec 1996 .... 3.00
❑12, Apr 1997; contains Angel Fire preview 3.00
❑Fan ed. 1/A, Jan 1995; Included with Fan magazine; Overstreet Fan promotional edition #1; Included with Fan magazine 1.00
❑Fan ed. 2/A; Overstreet Fan promotional edition #2; Included with Fan magazine; Overstreet Fan promotional edition #2 .... 1.00
❑Fan ed. 3/A; Overstreet Fan promotional edition #3; Included with Fan magazine; Overstreet Fan promotional edition #3 .... 1.00

Shi/Vampirella
Crusade

❑1, Oct 1997; crossover with Harris 2.95

Shi vs. Tomoe
Crusade

❑1, Aug 1996; Foil wrap-around cover 3.95
❑1/Ltd., Aug 1996; Preview sold at San Diego Comic Con, black and white 5.00

Shi: Year of the Dragon
Crusade

❑1, Sep 2000 .... 2.99

Shock & Spank the Monkeyboys Special
Arrow

❑1, b&w 2.50

Shockrockets
Image

❑1, Apr 2000; A short Empire story 2.50
❑2, May 2000 .... 2.50
❑3, Jun 2000 .... 2.50
❑4, Jul 2000 .... 2.50
❑5, Aug 2000 .... 2.50
❑6, Oct 2000 .... 2.50

Shock SuspenStories
Gemstone

❑1, Sep 1992; AF (c); AF (w); JO, JKa, GI (a); Reprints Shock SuspenStories #1; Ray Bradbury adaptation; Electrocution cover 2.00
❑2, Dec 1992; Reprints Shock SuspenStories #2 .... 2.00
❑3, Mar 1993; Reprints Shock SuspenStories #3 .... 2.00
❑4, Jun 1993; AF (w); JO, WW, JKa (a); Reprints Shock SuspenStories #4 .... 2.00
❑5, Sep 1993; AF (w); JO, WW, JKa (a); Reprints Shock SuspenStories #5 .... 2.00
❑6, Dec 1993; AF, JO, WW, JKa, GI (w); JO, WW, JKa, GI (a); Reprints Shock SuspenStories #6 .... 2.00
❑7, Mar 1994; AF (c); AF, JO, WW, JKa, GI (w); GE, JO, JK, WW, JKa, GI (a); Reprints Shock SuspenStories #7 .... 2.00

N-MINT

❑8, Jun 1994; AF (c); AF, GE, AW, WW, JKa (w); GE, AW, WW, JKa (a); Reprints Shock SuspenStories #8 .... 2.00
❑9, Sep 1994; AF (c); AF, JO, WW, JKa (w); JO, WW, JKa (a); Reprints Shock SuspenStories #9 .... 2.00
❑10, Dec 1994; AF (c); AF, JO, WW, JKa (w); JO, WW, JKa (a); Reprints Shock SuspenStories #10 .... 2.00
❑11, Mar 1995; Reprints Shock SuspenStories #11 .... 2.00
❑12, Jun 1995; Reprints Shock SuspenStories #12 .... 2.00
❑13, Sep 1995; Reprints Shock SuspenStories #13 .... 2.00
❑14, Dec 1995; Reprints Shock SuspenStories #14 .... 2.00
❑15, Mar 1996; AF, GE, WW, JKa (w); GE, WW, JKa (a); Reprints Shock SuspenStories #15; Cannibalism story 2.00
❑16, Jun 1996; AF, GE, JO, JKa (w); GE, JO, JKa (a); Reprints Shock SuspenStories #16 .... 2.00
❑17, Sep 1996; AF, GE, JO, JKa (w); GE, JO, JKa (a); Reprints Shock SuspenStories #17 .... 2.50
❑18, Dec 1996; AF, GE, BK, JKa (w); GE, BK, JKa (a); Reprints Shock SuspenStories #18 .... 2.50
❑Ann 1; Reprints Shock SuspenStories #1-5 .... 8.95
❑Ann 2; AF, JO, WW, JKa, GI (w); GE, AW, JO, WW, JKa, GI (a); Reprints Shock SuspenStories #6-10 .... 9.95
❑Ann 3; Reprints Shock SuspenStories #11-14 .... 8.95
❑Ann 4; AF, GE, BK, JKa (w); GE, JO, WW, BK, JKa (a); Reprints Shock SuspenStories #15-18 .... 9.95

Shock the Monkey
Millennium

❑1 .... 2.95
❑2, b&w 3.95

Shock Therapy
Harrier

❑1, Nov 1986 .... 1.95
❑2, Dec 1986 .... 1.95
❑3, Jan 1987; b&w 1.95
❑4, Feb 1987 .... 1.95
❑5, Mar 1987 .... 1.95

Shogun Warriors
Marvel

❑1, Feb 1979, HT (c); HT (a); 1: Shogun Warriors. Newsstand edition (distributed by Curtis); issue number in box 5.00
❑1/Whitman, Feb 1979, HT (a); 1: Shogun Warriors. Special markets edition (usually sold in Whitman bagged prepacks); price appears in a diamond; no UPC barcode 5.00
❑2, Mar 1979, Newsstand edition (distributed by Curtis); issue number in box 2.00
❑2/Whitman, Mar 1979, Special markets edition (usually sold in Whitman bagged prepacks); price appears in a diamond; no UPC barcode 2.00
❑3, Apr 1979, Newsstand edition (distributed by Curtis); issue number in box 2.00

N-MINT | N-MINT | N-MINT

❑3/Whitman, Apr 1979, Special markets edition (usually sold in Whitman bagged prepacks); price appears in a diamond; no UPC barcode ... 2.00
❑4, May 1979, Newsstand edition (distributed by Curtis); issue number in box ... 2.00
❑4/Whitman, May 1979, Special markets edition (usually sold in Whitman bagged prepacks); price appears in a diamond; no UPC barcode ... 2.00
❑5, Jun 1979 ... 2.00
❑6, Jul 1979 ... 2.00
❑7, Aug 1979 ... 2.00
❑8, Sep 1979 ... 2.00
❑9, Oct 1979 ... 2.00
❑10, Nov 1979, V: Hand Of Five ... 2.00
❑11, Dec 1979 ... 1.50
❑12, Jan 1980 ... 1.50
❑13, Feb 1980 ... 1.50
❑14, Mar 1980, V: Dr. Demonicus ... 1.50
❑15, Apr 1980, V: Yakuza ... 1.50
❑16, May 1980, D: Followers ... 1.50
❑17, Jun 1980 ... 1.50
❑18, Jul 1980, V: Megatron ... 1.50
❑19, Aug 1980, A: Fantastic Four. V: Gigantauron ... 1.50
❑20, Sep 1980, A: Fantastic Four ... 1.50

Shojo Zen
Zen

❑1, Jan 1997 ... 2.50

Shonen Jump
Viz

❑0, Aug 2002 ... 5.00
❑1, Jan 2003 ... 4.95
❑2, Feb 2003 ... 4.95
❑3, Mar 2003 ... 4.95
❑4, Apr 2003 ... 4.95
❑5, May 2003 ... 4.95
❑6, Jun 2003 ... 4.95
❑7, Jul 2003 ... 4.95
❑8, Aug 2003 ... 4.95
❑9, Sep 2003 ... 4.95
❑10, Oct 2003 ... 4.95
❑11, Nov 2003 ... 4.95
❑12, Dec 2003 ... 4.95
❑13, Jan 2004 ... 4.95
❑14, Feb 2004 ... 4.95
❑15, Mar 2004 ... 4.95
❑16, Apr 2004 ... 4.95
❑17, May 2004 ... 4.95
❑18, Jun 2004 ... 4.95
❑19, Jul 2004 ... 4.95
❑20, Aug 2004 ... 4.95
❑21, Sep 2004 ... 4.95
❑22, Oct 2004 ... 4.95
❑23, Nov 2004 ... 4.95
❑24, Dec 2004 ... 4.95
❑25, Jan 2005 ... 4.95
❑26, Feb 2005 ... 4.99
❑27, Mar 2005 ... 4.99
❑28, Apr 2005 ... 4.99
❑29, May 2005 ... 4.99
❑30, Jun 2005 ... 4.99
❑31, Jul 2005 ... 4.99
❑32, Aug 2005 ... 4.99
❑33, Sep 2005 ... 4.99
❑34, Oct 2005 ... 4.99
❑35, Nov 2005 ... 4.99
❑36, Dec 2005 ... 4.99

Shooty Beagle
Fantagraphics / Eros

❑1, Apr 1991, b&w; Adult ... 2.25
❑2, May 1991, b&w; Adult ... 2.25
❑3, b&w; Adult ... 2.25

Short on Plot!
Mu

❑1, b&w; NN ... 2.50

Short Order
Head

❑1; Adult ... 20.00
❑2, Jan 1974; Adult ... 15.00

Shorts
Antarctic

❑1, Oct 1997 ... 2.95
❑2 ... 2.95

Shortstop Squad
Ultimate Sports Force

❑1, ca. 1999; Barry Larkin apperance ... 3.95

Shotgun Mary
Antarctic

❑1, Sep 1995 ... 4.00
❑1/CS, Sep 1995; CD edition; Includes CD of music ... 9.95
❑1/Variant, Sep 1995; alternate cover ... 2.95
❑2, Mar 1995 ... 3.00
❑3 1995; Exists? ... 3.00
❑Ashcan 1, Sep 1995; ashcan edition; Ashcan edition flipbook with Warriro Nun Areala ... 2.95

Shotgun Mary
Antarctic

❑1, Mar 1998 ... 2.95
❑1/Variant, Mar 1998; Limited edition cover (purple) ... 4.00
❑2, May 1998 ... 2.95
❑3, Jul 1998; Final Issue ... 2.95

Shotgun Mary: Blood Lore
Antarctic

❑1, Feb 1997 ... 2.95
❑2, Apr 1997 ... 2.95
❑3, Jun 1997 ... 2.95
❑4, Aug 1997 ... 2.95

Shotgun Mary: Deviltown
Antarctic

❑1, Jul 1996 ... 2.95
❑1/Ltd., ca. 1996; Commemorative edition ... 5.40

Shotgun Mary Shooting Gallery
Antarctic

❑1, Jun 1996; Anthology ... 2.95

Shotgun Mary: Son of the Beast
Antarctic

❑1, Oct 1997 ... 2.95

Shoujo
Antarctic

❑1, Jun 2003 ... 5.95
❑2, Aug 2003 ... 5.95
❑3, Oct 2003 ... 5.95

Showcase
DC

❑1, Apr 1956, Fire Fighters ... 3500.00
❑2, Jun 1956, IN (c); JKu, RA, RH (a); Kings of Wild ... 1000.00
❑3, Aug 1956; RH (a); Frogmen ... 1000.00
❑4, Oct 1956, CI (c); CI, JKu (a); 1&O: Flash II (Barry Allen). Begins DC Silver Age revival of heroes ... 27500.00
❑5, Dec 1956 RMo (c); MM, CS (a); A: Manhunters ... 1000.00
❑6, Feb 1957; JK (c); JK (a); 1&O: Challengers of the Unknown ... 4000.00
❑7, Apr 1957; JK (c); JK (a); 2: Challengers of the Unknown ... 2000.00
❑8, Jun 1957, CI (c); CI, GK (a); 1&O: Captain Cold ... 11500.00
❑9, Aug 1957 RMo (a); A: Lois Lane ... 7500.00
❑10, Oct 1957, A: Lois Lane ... 3000.00
❑11, Dec 1957; JK (c); JK (a); A: Challengers of the Unknown ... 1750.00
❑12, Feb 1958, JK (c); JK (a); A: Challengers of the Unknown ... 1750.00
❑13, Apr 1958, CI (c); CI (a); 1&O: Mr. Element. 1: Mr. Element. A: Flash II (Barry Allen) ... 4500.00
❑14, Jun 1958, CI (c); CI (a); 1&O: Doctor Alchemy. A: Flash II (Barry Allen) ... 4500.00
❑15, Aug 1958, 1: Space Ranger ... 2000.00
❑16, Oct 1958; 2: Space Ranger ... 1000.00
❑17, Dec 1958, GK (c); 1&O: Adam Strange; 1: Alanna; 1: Sardath ... 2750.00
❑18, Feb 1959; GK (c); 1: Rann ... 1200.00
❑19, Apr 1959 GK (c); A: Adam Strange ... 1500.00
❑20, Jun 1959, 1: Rip Hunter; Prehistoric Fun ... 1000.00
❑21, Aug 1959; 2: Rip Hunter; Doctor Rocket ... 500.00
❑22, Oct 1959; GK (a); 1&O: Green Lantern II (Hal Jordan. 1: Carol Ferris ... 5600.00
❑23, Dec 1959; GK (a); 1: Invisible Destroyer ... 1750.00
❑24, Feb 1960 GK (a); A: Green Lantern II ... 1750.00
❑25, Apr 1960 JKu (a); A: Rip Hunter ... 350.00
❑26, Jun 1960, JKu (a); A: Rip Hunter ... 350.00
❑27, Aug 1960; RH (a); 1: Sea Devils ... 900.00
❑28, Oct 1960, RH (a); 2: Sea Devils ... 400.00
❑29, Dec 1960; RH (a); A: Sea Devils. 3: Sea Devils ... 400.00
❑30, Feb 1961; O: Aquaman ... 800.00
❑31, Apr 1961, A: Aquaman ... 400.00
❑32, Jun 1961 A: Aquaman ... 400.00
❑33, Aug 1961 A: Aquaman ... 375.00
❑34, Oct 1961, GK (a); 1&O: Atom II (Ray Palmer) ... 1250.00
❑35, Dec 1961, GK (c); MA, GK (a); 2: Atom II (Ray Palmer) ... 700.00
❑36, Feb 1962, MA, GK (a); A: Atom II (Ray Palmer) ... 525.00
❑37, Apr 1962, 1: Metal Men ... 700.00
❑38, Jun 1962, A: Metal Men ... 400.00
❑39, Aug 1962, 1: Chemo. A: Metal Men ... 350.00
❑40, Oct 1962, A: Metal Men ... 300.00
❑41, Dec 1962, O: Tommy Tomorrow ... 150.00
❑42, Feb 1963, A: Tommy Tomorrow ... 150.00
❑43, Apr 1963, James Bond, Agent 007; movie adaptation ... 450.00
❑44, Jun 1963, A: Tommy Tomorrow ... 100.00
❑45, Aug 1963, RH (c); JKu (a); O: Sgt. Rock ... 325.00
❑46, Oct 1963, A: Tommy Tomorrow ... 100.00
❑47, Dec 1963, A: Tommy Tomorrow ... 100.00
❑48, Feb 1964, A: Cave Carson ... 80.00
❑49, Apr 1964, A: Cave Carson ... 80.00
❑50, Jun 1964, MA, CI (a); A: King Faraday. Reprints from World's Finest #64 and Danger Trail #2; I Spy ... 80.00
❑51, Aug 1964, MA, CI (a); A: King Faraday. Reprints from Danger Trail #1 and 3; I Spy ... 80.00
❑52, Oct 1964, A: Cave Carson ... 80.00
❑53, Dec 1964, JKu, RA, RH, IN (a); A: G.I. Joe. Reprints from GI Combat #52; 59 and 60 ... 100.00
❑54, Feb 1965, JKu, RA, RH, IN (a); A: G.I. Joe. Reprints from Our Army at War #75; Star Spangled War #50 and All-American Men of War #67 ... 100.00
❑55, Apr 1965, MA (a); O: Doctor Fate. Hourman ... 275.00
❑56, Jun 1965, MA (a); 1: Psycho-Pirate II (Roger Hayden). Doctor Fate, Hourman ... 125.00
❑57, Aug 1965, JKu (c); JKu (a); A: Enemy Ace ... 225.00
❑58, Oct 1965, JKu (c); JKu (a); A: Enemy Ace ... 150.00
❑59, Dec 1965, NC (c); NC (a); A: Teen Titans ... 125.00
❑60, Feb 1966, MA (a); O: The Spectre ... 225.00
❑61, Apr 1966, MA (a); A: Spectre ... 100.00
❑62, Jun 1966, JO (a); O: Inferior Five. 1: Earth-12. 1: Dumb Bunny. 1: Merryman. 1: Awkwardman. 1: Blimp. 1: White Feather. 1: Inferior Five ... 80.00
❑63, Aug 1966, JO (a); A: Inferior Five ... 50.00
❑64, Oct 1966, MA (a); A: Spectre. Mike Friedrich L.O.C.; Irene Vartanoff L.O.C ... 100.00
❑65, Dec 1966, A: Inferior Five. X-Men parody ... 50.00
❑66, Feb 1967, 1: B'wana Beast ... 30.00
❑67, Apr 1967, A: B'wana Beast ... 30.00
❑68, Jun 1967, A: Maniaks ... 30.00
❑69, Aug 1967, A: Maniaks ... 30.00
❑70, Oct 1967, A: Binky ... 30.00
❑71, Dec 1967, A: Maniaks ... 30.00
❑72, Feb 1968, RH (c); JKu (w); ATh, CI, JKu (a); A: Johnny Thunder. Trigger Twins, Texas Rangers ... 30.00
❑73, Apr 1968, SD (a); 1&O: Creeper ... 85.00
❑74, May 1968, 1: Anthro. Profile of Howie Post ... 45.00
❑75, Jun 1968, SD, DG (w); SD (a); 1&O: Dove I (Don Hall). 1&O: Hawk I (Hank Hall) ... 75.00
❑76, Aug 1968, 1: Bat Lash ... 50.00
❑77, Sep 1968, 1: Angel & Ape ... 50.00
❑78, Nov 1968, 1: Jonny Double ... 35.00
❑79, Dec 1968, 1: Dolphin; O: Aqualad; Reprinted from Adventure Comics #269 ... 45.00
❑80, Feb 1969, NA (c); CI (a); A: Phantom Stranger. Reprints from Phantom Stranger #2 and Star-Spangled Comics #122 ... 45.00
❑81, Mar 1969, Windy & Willy ... 45.00
❑82, May 1969, 1&O: Nightmaster ... 40.00

Other grades: Multiply price above by 5/6 for VF/NM • 2/3 for VERY FINE • 1/3 for FINE • 1/5 for VERY GOOD • 1/8 for GOOD

Space War

Ditko worked on science-fiction anthology
©Charlton

Space Wolf

Dan Flahive's anthropomorphic adventure
©Antarctic

Spanner's Galaxy

Wanted man doesn't know why he's wanted
©DC

Spawn

Todd McFarlane's flagship Image title
©Image

Spawn: The Dark Ages

Spawn series set in medieval times
©Image

N-MINT

❑83, Jun 1969, JKu (c); BWr (a); A: Nightmaster ... 40.00
❑84, Aug 1969, JKu (c); BWr (a); A: Nightmaster ... 40.00
❑85, Sep 1969, JKu (w); JKu (a); A: Firehair ... 20.00
❑86, Nov 1969, JKu (c); JKu, RE (w); JKu, RE (a); A: Firehair ... 20.00
❑87, Dec 1969, JKu (w); JKu (a); A: Firehair ... 20.00
❑88, Feb 1970, Jason's Quest ... 15.00
❑89, Mar 1970, Jason's Quest ... 15.00
❑90, May 1970, 1: Manhunter 2070 ... 15.00
❑91, Jun 1970 ... 15.00
❑92, Aug 1970, A: Manhunter 2070 ... 15.00
❑93, Sep 1970, A: Manhunter 2070 ... 15.00
❑94, Aug 1977, JA (c); JSa, JA (a); 1&O: Doom Patrol II. 1: Celsius ... 20.00
❑95, Oct 1977, \JA (c); JSa, JA (a); A: The Doom Patrol ... 8.00
❑96, Dec 1977, JA (c); JSa, JA (a); A: The Doom Patrol ... 8.00
❑97, Feb 1978, A: Power Girl ... 6.00
❑98, Mar 1978, JSa (c); JSa (a); O: Power Girl ... 6.00
❑99, Apr 1978, A: Power Girl ... 6.00
❑100, May 1978, Double-size; JSa (c); JSa (a); all-star issue ... 6.00
❑101, Jun 1978, JK, JKu (c); AM, MA (a); A: Hawkman ... 6.00
❑102, Jul 1978, JK, JKu (c); AM, MA (a); A: Hawkman. Adam Strange cover/appearance ... 6.00
❑103, Aug 1978, JK, JKu (c); AM, MA (a); A: Hawkman ... 6.00
❑104, Sep 1978, OSS Spies ... 5.00

Showcase '93
DC

❑1, Jan 1993; Catwoman, Cyborg, Blue Devil ... 2.25
❑2, Feb 1993; Catwoman, Cyborg, Blue Devil ... 2.25
❑3, Mar 1993; Catwoman, Flash, Blue Devil ... 2.25
❑4, Apr 1993; Catwoman, Geo-Force, Blue Devil ... 2.00
❑5, May 1993; Robin, Peacemaker, Blue Devil ... 2.00
❑6, Jun 1993; Robin, Peacemaker, Blue Devil ... 2.00
❑7, Jul 1993; Two-Face, Deathstroke, Jade, Obsidian, Peacemaker ... 2.50
❑8, Aug 1993; KJ (a); Two-Face, Batman, Deadshot, Fire and Ice ... 2.50
❑9, Sep 1993; HC (c); JRo (w); Huntress, Peacemaker, Shining Knight ... 2.00
❑10, Oct 1993; PG (c); JRo (w); Huntress, Deathstroke, Katana ... 2.00
❑11, Nov 1993; GP (c); BMc (a); Nightwing, Robin, Kobra Kronicles ... 2.00
❑12, Dec 1993; KG (w); KG, BMc (a); Nightwing, Robin, Green Lantern, Creeper ... 2.00

Showcase '94
DC

❑1, Jan 1994; Joker, New Gods, Gunfire ... 1.95
❑2, Feb 1994; Joker ... 1.95
❑3, Mar 1994; Arkham Asylum, Blue Beetle, Psyba-Rats ... 1.95

N-MINT

❑4, Apr 1994; Arkham Asylum, Blue Beetle, Psyba-Rats ... 1.95
❑5, May 1994; Huntress, Loose Cannon, Bloodwynd ... 1.95
❑6, Jun 1994; Robin ... 1.95
❑7, Jul 1994; Penguin, Arsenal, Terrorsmith ... 1.95
❑8, Aug 1994; Scarface, Zero Hour Prelude ... 1.95
❑9, Sep 1994; Scarface, Zero Hour Prelude ... 1.95
❑10, Oct 1994; Azrael, Zero Hour, Black Condor ... 1.95
❑11, Nov 1994; Man-Bat, Starfire, Black Condor ... 1.95
❑12, Dec 1994; 48 pages ... 1.95

Showcase '95
DC

❑1, Jan 1995; Supergirl, Alan Scott, Argus ... 2.50
❑2, Feb 1995; Supergirl, Metal Men, Argus ... 2.50
❑3, Mar 1995; Eradicator, Claw, The Question ... 2.50
❑4, Apr 1995 ... 2.50
❑5, Jun 1995; Rose and Thorn, Spoiler, Firehawk ... 2.50
❑6, Jul 1995; Bibbo, Lobo, Science Police, Legionnaires ... 2.95
❑7, Aug 1995; Mongul, Arion, New Gods ... 2.95
❑8, Sep 1995; Mongul, Spectre, Arsenal ... 2.95
❑9, Oct 1995; Lois Lane, Lobo, Martian Manhunter ... 2.95
❑10, Nov 1995; Gangbuster, Ferrin Colos, Hi-Tech ... 2.95
❑11, Nov 1995; Agent Liberty; Arkham Asylum; Hi-Tech ... 2.95
❑12, Dec 1995; Supergirl, Maitresse, The Shade ... 2.95

Showcase '96
DC

❑1, Jan 1996; Steel and Guy Gardner: Warrior, Aqualad, Metropolis S.C.U. ... 2.95
❑2, Feb 1996; Steel and Guy Gardner: Warrior, Circe, Metallo ... 2.95
❑3, Mar 1996; Lois Lane and Black Canary, Doctor Fate and The Shade, Lightray ... 2.95
❑4, Apr 1996; Guardian and Firebrand, Doctor Fate and The Shade, The Demon ... 2.95
❑5, Jun 1996; Green Arrow and Thorn, Doctor Fate and The Shade, New Gods ... 2.95
❑6, Jul 1996; Superboy and The Demon, Firestorm, The Atom ... 2.95
❑7, Aug 1996; Gangbuster and The Power of Shazam!, Fire, Firestorm ... 2.95
❑8, Sep 1996; Superboy and Superman, Legionnaires, Supergirl ... 2.95
❑9, Oct 1996; Shadowdragon and Lady Shiva, Doctor Light, Martian Manhunter ... 2.95
❑10, Nov 1996; Bibbo, Ultra Boy, Captain Comet ... 2.95
❑11, Dec 1996; Brainiac vs. Legion, Wildcat, Scare Tactics ... 2.95
❑12, Win 1996; Brainiac vs. Legion, Jesse Quick, King Faraday ... 2.95

Shred
CFW

❑1 ... 2.25
❑2 ... 2.25

N-MINT

❑3 ... 2.25
❑4 ... 2.25
❑5 ... 2.25
❑6, Sep 1989 ... 2.25
❑7 ... 2.25
❑8 ... 2.25

Shrek
Dark Horse

❑1, Sep 2003 ... 2.99
❑2, Dec 2003 ... 2.99
❑3, Dec 2003 ... 2.99

Shriek
Fantaco

❑1, b&w ... 4.95
❑2, b&w ... 4.95
❑Special 1, b&w ... 3.50
❑Special 2, b&w; Dangerbrain ... 3.50
❑Special 3, b&w ... 3.50

Shriek Show: Mark of Shadow
-Ism

❑1, ca. 2005 ... 2.99
❑2, ca. 2005 ... 2.99

Shrike
Victory

❑1, May 1987, b&w ... 1.50
❑2 ... 1.50

Shroud
Marvel

❑1, Mar 1994; O: The Shroud ... 1.75
❑2, Apr 1994 ... 1.75
❑3, May 1994 ... 1.75
❑4, Jun 1994 ... 1.75

Shugga
Fantagraphics / Eros

❑1, b&w; Adult ... 2.50
❑2, b&w; Adult ... 2.50

Shuriken
Blackthorne

❑1 ... 7.95

Shuriken
Victory

❑1, Win 1985 ... 1.50
❑2, Fal 1985 ... 1.50
❑3 ... 1.50
❑4, Nov 1986 ... 1.50
❑5 1987 ... 1.50
❑6, Feb 1987 ... 1.50
❑7, Mar 1987 ... 1.50
❑8, Apr 1987 ... 1.50

Shuriken
Eternity

❑1, Jun 1991, b&w ... 2.50
❑2, ca. 1991, b& ... 2.50
❑3, ca. 1991, b&w ... 2.50
❑4, ca. 1991, b&w ... 2.50
❑5, ca. 1991, b&w ... 2.50
❑6, ca. 1992, b&w ... 2.50

Shuriken: Cold Steel
Eternity

❑1, Jul 1989, b&w; 16 pgs ... 1.50
❑2, Aug 1989 ... 1.95
❑3, Sep 1989 ... 1.95

Other grades: Multiply price above by 5/6 for VF/NM • 2/3 for VERY FINE • 1/3 for FINE • 1/5 for VERY GOOD • 1/8 for GOOD

❑4, Oct 1989 ... 1.95
❑5, Nov 1989 ... 1.95
❑6, Dec 1989 ... 1.95

Shuriken Team-Up
Eternity

❑1, ca. 1989, b&w; Shuriken, Libra, Kokutai ... 1.95

Shut Up and Die!
Image

❑1, Jan 1998; b&w ... 2.95
❑2, Mar 1998; b&w ... 2.95
❑3, May 1998; b&w ... 2.95
❑4, Aug 1998 ... 2.95
❑5, ca. 1999 ... 2.95

Sick Smiles
Aiiie!

❑1, Jun 1994; Adult ... 2.50
❑2, Jul 1994; Adult ... 2.50
❑3, ca. 1994; Adult ... 2.50
❑4, ca. 1994; Adult ... 2.50
❑5, ca. 1994; Adult ... 2.50
❑6, ca. 1995; Adult ... 2.50
❑7, ca. 1995; Adult ... 2.50
❑8, Apr 1995; Adult ... 2.95

Sidekick
Image

❑1, Jul 2006 ... 3.50
❑2, Aug 2006 ... 3.50
❑3, Oct 2006 ... 3.50
❑4, Dec 2006 ... 3.99

Sidekicks
Fanboy

❑1, Jun 2000 ... 2.75

Sidekicks: The Substitute
Oni

❑1, Jul 2002 ... 2.95

Side Show
Mature Magic

❑1, Jun 1987 ... 1.75

Sideshow Comics
Pan Graphics

❑1, b&w; BT (w); BT (a) ... 1.75
❑2, b&w ... 1.75
❑3 ... 1.75
❑4 ... 1.75
❑5 ... 1.75

Siege
Image

❑1, Jan 1997 ... 2.50
❑2, Feb 1997 ... 2.50
❑3, Mar 1997 ... 2.50
❑4, Apr 1997 ... 2.50

Siegel and Shuster: Dateline 1930s
Eclipse

❑1, Nov 1984 ... 1.75
❑2, Sep 1985; b&w ... 1.75

Siege of the Alamo
Tome

❑1, Jul 1991, b&w ... 2.50

Sight Unseen
Fantagraphics

❑1, Apr 1997, b&w; collects story from The Stranger and The Philadelphia Weekly; wraparound cover ... 2.95

Sigil
CrossGen

❑1, Jul 2000 ... 4.00
❑2, Aug 2000 ... 3.00
❑3, Sep 2000 ... 3.00
❑4, Oct 2000 ... 3.00
❑5, Nov 2000 ... 3.00
❑6, Dec 2000 ... 2.95
❑7, Jan 2001 ... 2.95
❑8, Feb 2001 ... 2.95
❑9, Mar 2001 ... 2.95
❑10, Apr 2001 ... 2.95
❑11, May 2001 MWa (w) ... 2.95
❑12, Jun 2001 MWa (w) ... 2.95
❑13, Jul 2001 MWa (w) ... 2.95
❑14, Aug 2001 MWa (w) ... 2.95
❑15, Sep 2001 MWa (w) ... 2.95
❑16, Oct 2001 MWa (w) ... 2.95
❑17, Nov 2001 MWa (w) ... 2.95
❑18, Dec 2001 MWa (w) ... 2.95
❑19, Jan 2002 MWa (w) ... 2.95
❑20, Feb 2002 ... 2.95
❑21, Mar 2002 ... 2.95
❑22, Apr 2002 ... 2.95
❑23, May 2002 ... 2.95
❑24, Jun 2002 ... 2.95
❑25, Jul 2002 ... 2.95
❑26, Aug 2002 ... 2.95
❑27, Sep 2002 ... 2.95
❑28, Oct 2002 ... 2.95
❑29, Nov 2002 ... 2.95
❑30, Dec 2002 ... 2.95
❑31, Jan 2003 ... 2.95
❑32, Feb 2003 ... 2.95
❑33, Mar 2003 ... 2.95
❑34, Apr 2003 ... 2.95
❑35, May 2003 ... 2.95
❑36, Jun 2003 ... 2.95
❑37, Jul 2003 ... 2.95
❑38, Aug 2003 ... 2.95
❑39, Oct 2003 ... 2.95
❑40, Nov 2003 ... 2.95
❑41, Nov 2003 ... 2.95
❑42, Dec 2003; Final Issue ... 2.95

Sigma
Image

❑1, Apr 1996 ... 2.50
❑2, May 1996 ... 2.50
❑3, Jun 1996 ... 2.50

Silbuster
Antarctic

❑1, Jan 1994 ... 2.95
❑2, Feb 1994 ... 2.95
❑3, Mar 1994 ... 2.95
❑4, Apr 1994 ... 2.95
❑5, Oct 1994 ... 2.95
❑6, Nov 1994 ... 2.95
❑7, Dec 1994 ... 2.95
❑8, Jan 1995 ... 2.95
❑9, Feb 1995 ... 2.95
❑10, Aug 1995 ... 2.95
❑11, Oct 1995 ... 2.95
❑12, Oct 1995 ... 2.95
❑13, Oct 1995 ... 2.95
❑14, Oct 1995 ... 2.95
❑15, May 1996 ... 2.95
❑16, Jul 1996 ... 2.95
❑17, Sep 1996 ... 2.95
❑18, Sep 1996 ... 2.95
❑19, Jan 1997 ... 2.95

Silencers
Caliber

❑1, Jul 1991, b&w ... 2.50
❑2 1991, b&w ... 2.50
❑3 1991, b&w ... 2.50
❑4 1991, b&w ... 2.50

Silencers
Moonstone

❑1 2003 ... 3.50
❑2 2003 ... 3.50

Silencers
Image

❑1, Sep 2005 ... 2.95

Silent Hill: Paint It Black
Idea & Design Works

❑0 2005 ... 7.49

Silent City
Kitchen Sink

❑1, Oct 1995, b&w; oversized graphic novel ... 24.95

Silent Dragon
DC / Wildstorm

❑1, Sep 2005 ... 2.99
❑2, Oct 2005 ... 2.99
❑3, Nov 2005 ... 2.99
❑4, Dec 2005 ... 2.99
❑5, Jan 2006 ... 2.99
❑6, Feb 2006 ... 2.99

Silent Hill: Dead/Alive
Idea & Design Works

❑1, Dec 2005 ... 3.99
❑2, Feb 2006 ... 3.99
❑3, Mar 2006 ... 3.99
❑4, Apr 2006 ... 3.99

Silent Hill: Dying Inside
Idea & Design Works

❑1, Apr 2004 ... 3.99
❑2, Mar 2004 ... 3.99
❑3, Apr 2004 ... 3.99
❑3/Variant ... 5.00
❑4, May 2004 ... 3.99
❑5, Jun 2004 ... 3.99

Silent Invasion
Renegade

❑1, Apr 1986, b&w ... 2.00
❑2, Jun 1986, b&w ... 2.00
❑3, Aug 1986, b&w ... 2.75
❑4, Oct 1986, b&w ... 2.75
❑5, Dec 1986, b&w ... 2.75
❑6, Feb 1987, b&w ... 2.75
❑7, May 1987, b&w ... 2.75
❑8, Jul 1987, b&w ... 2.75
❑9, Sep 1987, b&w ... 2.75
❑10, Nov 1987, b&w ... 2.75
❑11, Jan 1988, b&w ... 2.75
❑12, Mar 1988, b&w ... 2.75

Silent Invasion: Abductions
Caliber

❑1, May 1998, b&w ... 2.95

Silent Mobius Part 1
Viz

❑1, ca. 1991 ... 4.95
❑2, ca. 1991 ... 4.95
❑3, ca. 1991 ... 4.95
❑4, ca. 1991 ... 4.95
❑5, ca. 1991 ... 4.95
❑6, ca. 1991 ... 4.95

Silent Mobius Part 2
Viz

❑1, ca. 1992 ... 4.95
❑2, ca. 1992 ... 4.95
❑3, ca. 1992 ... 4.95
❑4, ca. 1992 ... 4.95
❑5, ca. 1992 ... 4.95

Silent Mobius Part 3
Viz

❑1, ca. 1992 ... 2.75
❑2, ca. 1992 ... 2.75
❑3, ca. 1992 ... 2.75
❑4, ca. 1992 ... 2.75
❑5, ca. 1992 ... 2.75

Silent Mobius Part 4
Viz

❑1, ca. 1992 ... 2.75
❑2, ca. 1992 ... 2.75
❑3, ca. 1992 ... 2.75
❑4, ca. 1992 ... 2.75
❑5, ca. 1992 ... 2.75

Silent Mobius Part 5: Into the Labyrinth
Viz

❑1, May 1999 ... 2.95
❑2, Jun 1999 ... 2.95
❑3, Jul 1999 ... 2.95
❑4, Aug 1999 ... 2.95
❑5, Sep 1999 ... 2.95
❑6, Oct 1999 ... 2.95

Silent Mobius Part 6: Karma
Viz

❑1, Nov 1999; b&w ... 3.25
❑2, Dec 1999 ... 3.25
❑3, Jan 2000 ... 3.25
❑4, Feb 2000 ... 3.25
❑5, Mar 2000 ... 3.25
❑6, Apr 2000 ... 3.25
❑7, May 2000 ... 3.25

Silent Mobius Part 7: Catastrophe
Viz

❑1, Jun 2000 ... 2.95
❑2, Jul 2000 ... 2.95
❑3, Aug 2000 ... 2.95
❑4, Sep 2000 ... 2.95
❑5, Oct 2000 ... 2.95
❑6, Nov 2000 ... 2.95

Special Marvel Edition

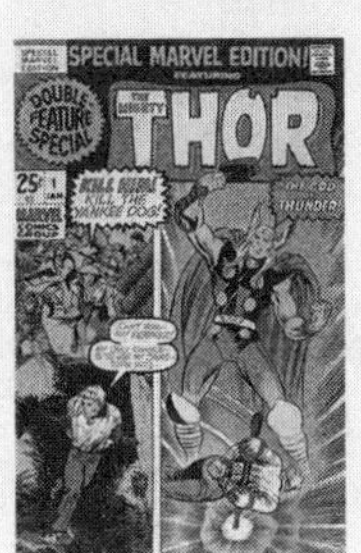

Gave birth to Master of Kung Fu
©Marvel

Spectacular Spider-Man

Two-issue 1968 attempt at magazine format
©Marvel

Spectacular Spider-Man

Title had "Peter Parker" in name for part of run
©Marvel

Spectacular Spider-Man

Relaunch opened with Venom storyline
©Marvel

Spectre

Some of Neal Adams' earliest work
©DC

N-MINT

Silent Mobius Part 8: Love & Chaos
Viz

❑1, Dec 2000 .... 2.95
❑2, Jan 2000 .... 2.95
❑3, Feb 2000 .... 2.95
❑4, Mar 2001 .... 2.95
❑5, Apr 2001 .... 2.95
❑6, May 2001 .... 2.95
❑7, Jun 2001 .... 2.95

Silent Mobius Part 9: Advent
Viz

❑1, Jul 2001 .... 2.95
❑2, Aug 2001 .... 2.95
❑3, Sep 2001 .... 2.95
❑4, Oct 2001 .... 2.95
❑5, Nov 2001 .... 2.95
❑6, Dec 2001 .... 2.95

Silent Mobius Part 10: Turnabout
Viz

❑1, Jan 2002 .... 2.95
❑2, Feb 2002 .... 2.95
❑3, Mar 2002 .... 2.95
❑4, Apr 2002 .... 2.95
❑5, May 2002 .... 2.95
❑6, Jun 2002 .... 2.95

Silent Mobius Part 11: Blood
Viz

❑1, Jul 2002 .... 2.95
❑2, Aug 2002 .... 2.95
❑3, Sep 2002 .... 2.95
❑4, Oct 2002 .... 2.95
❑5, Nov 2002 .... 2.95

Silent Mobius Part 12: Hell
Viz

❑1, Dec 2002 .... 2.95
❑2, Jan 2003 .... 2.95

Silent Rapture
Avatar

❑1, ca. 1997; Regular 3.00
❑2, ca. 1997; Regular 3.00

Silent Screamers: Nosferatu
Image

❑1, Oct 2000 .... 4.95

Silent Winter/Pineappleman
Limelight

❑1 .... 2.95

Silke
Dark Horse

❑1, Jan 2001 .... 2.95
❑2, Feb 2001 .... 2.99
❑3, Mar 2001 .... 2.99
❑4, Apr 2001 .... 2.99

Silken Ghost
CrossGen

❑1, Jun 2003 .... 2.95
❑2, Jul 2003 .... 2.95
❑3, Aug 2003 .... 2.95
❑4, Oct 2003 .... 2.95
❑5, Oct 2003 .... 2.95

Silly-Cat
Joe Chiappetta

❑1, Dec 1997 .... 1.00

N-MINT

Silly Daddy
Joe Chiappetta

❑1 .... 2.75
❑2, Sep 1995, b&w; flipbook with King Cat back-up 2.75
❑3 .... 2.75
❑4 .... 2.75
❑5 .... 2.75
❑6 .... 2.75
❑7 .... 2.75
❑8 .... 2.75
❑9 .... 2.75
❑10, Mar 1996, b&w 2.75
❑11 1996, b&w 2.75
❑12, b&w 2.75
❑13, b&w 2.75
❑14, b&w; no cover price 2.75
❑15 .... 2.75
❑16 .... 2.75
❑17 .... 2.75
❑18; ca. 1998 .... 2.75

Silver
Comicolor

❑1, Oct 1996 .... 2.00

Silver Age
DC

❑1, Jul 2000; 48 pages 2.50
❑GS 1, Jul 2000; O: Super-Turtle; Justice League of America; Batman; Jimmy Olsen; Wonder Woman; 80 pages 5.95

Silver Age: Challengers of the Unknown
DC

❑1, Jul 2000; Joe Kubert cover 2.50

Silver Age: Dial H for Hero
DC

❑1, Jul 2000 .... 2.50

Silver Age: Doom Patrol
DC

❑1, Jul 2000 .... 2.50

Silver Age: Flash
DC

❑1, Jul 2000 .... 2.50

Silver Age: Green Lantern
DC

❑1, Jul 2000; Gil Kane cover 2.50

Silver Age: Justice League of America
DC

❑1, Jul 2000 .... 2.50

Silver Age Secret Files
DC

❑1, Jul 2000 .... 4.95

Silver Age: Showcase
DC

❑1, Jul 2000 .... 2.50

Silver Age: Teen Titans
DC

❑1, Jul 2000; Nick Cardy cover 2.50

Silver Age: The Brave and the Bold
DC

❑1, Jul 2000 .... 2.50

N-MINT

Silverback
Comico

❑1, Oct 1989; O: Argent 2.50
❑2, Nov 1989; O: Argent 2.50
❑3, Dec 1989; O: Argent 2.50

Silverblade
DC

❑1, Sep 1987; 1: Silverblade; O: Silverblade; Includes poster 1.25
❑2, Oct 1987 .... 1.25
❑3, Nov 1987 .... 1.25
❑4, Dec 1987 .... 1.25
❑5, Jan 1988 .... 1.25
❑6, Feb 1988 .... 1.25
❑7, Mar 1988 .... 1.25
❑8, May 1988 .... 1.25
❑9, Jun 1988 .... 1.25
❑10, Jul 1988 .... 1.25
❑11, Aug 1988 .... 1.25
❑12, Sep 1988 .... 1.25

Silver Cross
Antarctic

❑1, Nov 1997 .... 2.95
❑2, Jan 1998 .... 2.95
❑3, Mar 1998 .... 2.95

Silverfawn
Caliber

❑1 .... 1.95

Silverhawks
Marvel / Star

❑1, Aug 1987 .... 1.00
❑2, Oct 1987 .... 1.00
❑3, Dec 1987 .... 1.00
❑4, Feb 1988 .... 1.00
❑5, Apr 1988 .... 1.00
❑6, Jun 1988; Final Issue 1.00
❑7, Jul 1988 .... 1.00

Silverheels
Pacific

❑1, Dec 1983 .... 1.50
❑2, Mar 1984; Includes portfolios by Scott Hampton and by Ken Steacy 1.50
❑3, May 1984 .... 1.50

Silver Sable
Marvel

❑1, Jun 1992; Embossed cover 2.00
❑2, Jul 1992 .... 1.50
❑3, Aug 1992 .... 1.50
❑4, Sep 1992; Infinity War crossover 1.50
❑5, Oct 1992; Infinity War crossover 1.25
❑6, Nov 1992 A: Deathlok 1.25
❑7, Dec 1992 A: Deathlok 1.25
❑8, Jan 1993 .... 1.25
❑9, Feb 1993; O: Wild Pack 1.25
❑10, Mar 1993 A: Punisher 1.25
❑11, Apr 1993 .... 1.25
❑12, May 1993 .... 1.25
❑13, Jun 1993 .... 1.25
❑14, Jul 1993 .... 1.25
❑15, Aug 1993 .... 1.25
❑16, Sep 1993 .... 1.25
❑17, Oct 1993; A: New Outlaws. A: Baron Von Strucker. A: Crippler. Infinity Crusade crossover 1.25

Other grades: Multiply price above by 5/6 for VF/NM • 2/3 for VERY FINE • 1/3 for FINE • 1/5 for VERY GOOD • 1/8 for GOOD

N-MINT

- ❑18, Nov 1993 ... 1.25
- ❑19, Dec 1993; Silver Sable; Man-Eater. ... 1.25
- ❑20, Jan 1994; Silver Sable; Sandman... 1.25
- ❑21, Feb 1994; Silver Sable; Wild Pack.. 1.25
- ❑22, Mar 1994 ... 1.25
- ❑23, Apr 1994; A: Daredevil. V: Deadpool 1.25
- ❑24, May 1994 ... 1.50
- ❑25, Jun 1994; Giant-size; Silver Sable; Li'l Silvie ... 2.00
- ❑26, Jul 1994 ... 1.50
- ❑27, Aug 1994 ... 1.50
- ❑28, Sep 1994 ... 1.50
- ❑29, Oct 1994 ... 1.50
- ❑30, Nov 1994 ... 1.50
- ❑31, Dec 1994 ... 1.50
- ❑32, Jan 1995 ... 1.50
- ❑33, Feb 1995 ... 1.50
- ❑34, Mar 1995 ... 1.50
- ❑35, Apr 1995; Final Issue ... 1.50

Silver Scream
Recollections

- ❑1, Jun 1991, b&w; Reprints ... 2.00
- ❑2, Aug 1991, b&w; Reprints ... 2.00
- ❑3, Nov 1991, b&w; Reprints ... 2.00

Silver Star
Pacific

- ❑1, Feb 1983; 1: Last of the Viking Heroes; Silver Star ... 1.00
- ❑2, Apr 1983; Silver Star; The Mocker ... 1.00
- ❑3, Jun 1983; Silver Star; Detective Flynn 1.00
- ❑4, Aug 1983; Silver Star; Detective Flynn 1.00
- ❑5, Nov 1983; Last of the Viking Heroes back-up ... 1.00
- ❑6, Jan 1984; Last of the Viking Heroes back-up ... 1.00

Silver Star
Topps

- ❑1, Oct 1993, trading cards; bagged; later planned issues do not exist ... 2.95

Silverstorm
Aircel

- ❑1, May 1990, b&w; 1: Silver Dollar; 1: Tempest ... 2.25
- ❑2, Jun 1990, b&w ... 2.25
- ❑3, Jul 1990, b&w ... 2.25
- ❑4, Aug 1990, b&w ... 2.25

Silverstorm
Silverline

- ❑1, Oct 1998 ... 2.95
- ❑2 1999 ... 2.95
- ❑3 1999 ... 2.95
- ❑4 1999 ... 2.95

Silver Surfer
Marvel

- ❑1, Aug 1968; Giant-size; JB (c); SL (w); GC, JB (a); O: Silver Surfer. adaptation from Tales of Suspense #53 ... 400.00
- ❑2, Oct 1968; Giant-size; JB (c); SL (w); GC, JB (a); adaptation from Amazing Adult Fantasy #8 ... 160.00
- ❑3, Dec 1968; Giant-size; JB (c); SL (w); GC, JB (a); 1: Mephisto. A: Thor. adaptation from Amazing Adult Fantasy #7 ... 135.00
- ❑4, Feb 1969; Giant-size; JB (c); SL (w); JB (a); Scarce; adaptation from Amazing Adult Fantasy #9 ... 265.00
- ❑5, Apr 1969; Giant-size; JB (c); SL (w); JB (a); adaptation from Tales to Astonish #26 ... 75.00
- ❑6, Jun 1969; Giant-size; JB (c); SL (w); FB, JB (a); adaptation from Amazing Adult Fantasy #13 ... 75.00
- ❑7, Aug 1969; Giant-size; JB (c); SL (w); JB (a); adaptation from Amazing Adult Fantasy #12 ... 90.00
- ❑8, Sep 1969, JB (c); SL (w); JB (a) ... 95.00
- ❑9, Oct 1969, JB (c); SL (w); JB (a) ... 60.00
- ❑10, Nov 1969, JB (c); SL (w); JB (a) ... 60.00
- ❑11, Dec 1969, JB (c); SL (w); JB (a) ... 65.00
- ❑12, Jan 1970, JB (c); SL (w); JB (a); V: Abomination ... 50.00
- ❑13, Feb 1970, JB (c); SL (w); JB (a); V: Doomsday Man ... 70.00
- ❑14, Mar 1970, JR (c); SL (w); JB (a); A: Spider-Man. Doug Moench L.O.C... 125.00
- ❑15, Apr 1970, SL (w); JB (a) ... 55.00
- ❑16, May 1970, JB (c); SL (w); JB (a) ... 55.00
- ❑17, Jun 1970, SL (w); JB (a) ... 55.00
- ❑18, Sep 1970, JK (c); SL (w); JK (a); A: Inhumans. Inhumans ... 55.00

Silver Surfer
Marvel / Epic

- ❑1, Dec 1988 SL (w) ... 3.00
- ❑2, Jan 1989 SL (w) ... 2.50

Silver Surfer
Marvel

- ❑-1, Jul 1997; A: Stan Lee. Flashback.... 3.00
- ❑½, ca. 1998; Wizard promotional edition (mail-in) ... 3.00
- ❑½/Platinum, ca. 1998; Wizard promotional edition (mail-in); Platinum edition ... 6.00
- ❑1, Jul 1987; Double-size; MR (c); MR (a) 7.00
- ❑2, Aug 1987 MR (c); MR (a) ... 6.00
- ❑3, Sep 1987 MR (c); MR (a) ... 4.00
- ❑4, Oct 1987 MR (c); MR (a); A: Mantis 4.00
- ❑5, Nov 1987; MR (c); MR (a); O: Skrulls. A: Mantis ... 4.00
- ❑6, Dec 1987 MR (c); MR (a) ... 3.50
- ❑7, Jan 1988 MR (c); MR (a) ... 3.50
- ❑8, Feb 1988 MR (c); MR (a) ... 3.50
- ❑9, Mar 1988 MR (c); MR (a) ... 3.50
- ❑10, Apr 1988 MR (a) ... 3.50
- ❑11, May 1988; MR (c); JSa (a); 1: Reptyl 3.00
- ❑12, Jun 1988 MR (c); MR (a) ... 3.00
- ❑13, Jul 1988 RB (c); JSa (a) ... 3.00
- ❑14, Aug 1988 JSa (a) ... 3.00
- ❑15, Sep 1988 ... 4.00
- ❑16, Oct 1988 A: Fantastic Four ... 3.00
- ❑17, Nov 1988 ... 3.00
- ❑18, Dec 1988 ... 3.00
- ❑19, Jan 1989 ... 3.00
- ❑20, Feb 1989 ... 3.00
- ❑21, Mar 1989 MR (c); MR (w); MR (a) 3.00
- ❑22, Apr 1989 ... 3.00
- ❑23, May 1989 ... 3.00
- ❑24, Jun 1989 ... 3.00
- ❑25, Jul 1989; Giant-size; V: new Super-Skrull ... 3.50
- ❑26, Aug 1989 ... 2.50
- ❑27, Sep 1989 ... 2.50
- ❑28, Oct 1989 ... 2.50
- ❑29, Nov 1989 ... 2.50
- ❑30, Nov 1989 ... 2.50
- ❑31, Dec 1989; Giant-size ... 3.00
- ❑32, Dec 1989 ... 2.00
- ❑33, Jan 1990 ... 2.00
- ❑34, Feb 1990 A: Thanos ... 5.00
- ❑35, Mar 1990; A: Thanos. Drax the Destroyer resurrected ... 3.50
- ❑36, Apr 1990 A: Thanos ... 3.00
- ❑37, May 1990 A: Thanos ... 3.00
- ❑38, Jun 1990 A: Thanos. A: Silver Surfer vs. Thanos ... 3.00
- ❑39, Jul 1990 A: Thanos ... 2.00
- ❑40, Aug 1990 ... 2.00
- ❑41, Sep 1990 ... 2.00
- ❑42, Oct 1990 ... 2.00
- ❑43, Nov 1990 ... 2.00
- ❑44, Dec 1990 ... 2.00
- ❑45, Jan 1991 ... 2.00
- ❑46, Feb 1991; A: Adam Warlock. Return of Adam Warlock ... 2.50
- ❑47, Mar 1991 JSn (w); A: Warlock ... 2.50
- ❑48, Apr 1991 ... 2.00
- ❑49, May 1991 ... 2.00
- ❑50, Jun 1991; JSn (w); O: Silver Surfer. Silver embossed cover ... 5.00
- ❑50/2nd, Jun 1991; JSn (w); O: Silver Surfer. Silver embossed cover ... 2.00
- ❑50/3rd, Jun 1991; JSn (w); O: Silver Surfer. Silver embossed cover ... 2.00
- ❑51, Jul 1991; Infinity Gauntlet crossover 2.00
- ❑52, Aug 1991; A: Firelord. A: Drax. Infinity Gauntlet crossover ... 2.00
- ❑53, Aug 1991; Infinity Gauntlet crossover ... 2.00
- ❑54, Sep 1991; Infinity Gauntlet crossover ... 2.00
- ❑55, Sep 1991; Infinity Gauntlet crossover ... 2.00
- ❑56, Oct 1991; Infinity Gauntlet crossover 2.00
- ❑57, Oct 1991; A: Thanos. Infinity Gauntlet crossover ... 2.00
- ❑58, Nov 1991; Infinity Gauntlet crossover ... 2.00
- ❑59, Nov 1991; Infinity Gauntlet crossover ... 2.00
- ❑60, Dec 1991 ... 2.00
- ❑61, Jan 1992 ... 2.00
- ❑62, Feb 1992 ... 2.00
- ❑63, Mar 1992 ... 2.00
- ❑64, Apr 1992 ... 2.00
- ❑65, May 1992 ... 2.00
- ❑66, Jun 1992; 1: Avatar ... 2.00
- ❑67, Jul 1992; Infinity war crossover 2.00
- ❑68, Aug 1992; Infinity war crossover... 2.00
- ❑69, Aug 1992; 1: Morg; Infinity war crossover ... 2.00
- ❑70, Sep 1992; O: Morg ... 2.00
- ❑71, Sep 1992 ... 2.00
- ❑72, Oct 1992 ... 2.00
- ❑73, Oct 1992 ... 2.00
- ❑74, Nov 1992 ... 2.00
- ❑75, Nov 1992; D: Nova (female). silver foil cover ... 3.50
- ❑76, Dec 1992 ... 1.50
- ❑77, Jan 1993 ... 1.50
- ❑78, Feb 1993 ... 1.50
- ❑79, Mar 1993 ... 1.50
- ❑80, Apr 1993 ... 1.50
- ❑81, May 1993 ... 1.50
- ❑82, Jun 1993 ... 1.75
- ❑83, Jul 1993; Infinity Crusade crossover 1.50
- ❑84, Aug 1993; Infinity Crusade crossover ... 1.50
- ❑85, Sep 1993; A: Wonder Man. A: Storm. A: Goddess. Infinity Crusade ... 1.50
- ❑85/CS, Sep 1993; A: Wonder Man. A: Storm. A: Goddess. "Dirtbag special"; Polybagged with Dirt #4; Infinity Crusade crossover ... 2.95
- ❑86, Oct 1993 ... 1.50
- ❑87, Nov 1993 ... 1.50
- ❑88, Jan 1994 ... 1.50
- ❑89, Feb 1994 ... 1.50
- ❑90, Mar 1994; Giant-size ... 1.95
- ❑91, Apr 1994 ... 1.25
- ❑92, May 1994 ... 1.50
- ❑93, Jun 1994 ... 1.50
- ❑94, Jul 1994 ... 1.50
- ❑95, Aug 1994 A: Fantastic Four ... 1.50
- ❑96, Sep 1994 A: Fantastic Four. A: Hulk 1.50
- ❑97, Oct 1994 ... 1.50
- ❑98, Nov 1994 ... 1.50
- ❑99, Dec 1994 ... 1.50
- ❑100, Jan 1995; Giant-size ... 2.50
- ❑100/Variant, Jan 1995; Giant-size; enhanced cover ... 3.95
- ❑101, Feb 1995 ... 1.50
- ❑102, Mar 1995 ... 1.50
- ❑103, Apr 1995 ... 1.50
- ❑104, May 1995 ... 1.50
- ❑105, Jun 1995; V: Super-Skrull ... 1.50
- ❑106, Jul 1995; Relinquishes Power Cosmic ... 1.50
- ❑107, Aug 1995 ... 1.50
- ❑108, Sep 1995; Regains Power Cosmic 1.50
- ❑109, Oct 1995 ... 1.50
- ❑110, Nov 1995 ... 1.50
- ❑111, Dec 1995 GP (w) ... 1.50
- ❑112, Jan 1996 ... 1.95
- ❑113, Feb 1996 ... 1.95
- ❑114, Mar 1996 GP (w) ... 1.95
- ❑115, Apr 1996 ... 1.95
- ❑116, May 1996 ... 1.95
- ❑117, Jun 1996 ... 1.95
- ❑118, Jul 1996 ... 1.95
- ❑119, Aug 1996 ... 1.95
- ❑120, Sep 1996 ... 1.95
- ❑121, Oct 1996 ... 1.95
- ❑122, Nov 1996; GP (w); V: Captain Marvel ... 1.95
- ❑123, Dec 1996; Surfer returns to Earth 1.95
- ❑124, Jan 1997 A: Kymaera ... 1.50
- ❑125, Feb 1997; Giant-size; V: Hulk. wraparound cover ... 2.99
- ❑126, Mar 1997 A: Doctor Strange ... 1.99
- ❑127, Apr 1997 ... 1.95
- ❑128, May 1997 A: Spider-Man, Daredevil 1.99
- ❑129, Jun 1997 ... 1.99
- ❑130, Aug 1997; gatefold summary ... 1.99
- ❑131, Sep 1997; gatefold summary ... 1.99
- ❑132, Oct 1997; gatefold summary ... 1.99

Other grades: Multiply price above by 5/6 for VF/NM • 2/3 for VERY FINE • 1/3 for FINE • 1/5 for VERY GOOD • 1/8 for GOOD

Spectre

Spectre given a second chance
©DC

Spectre

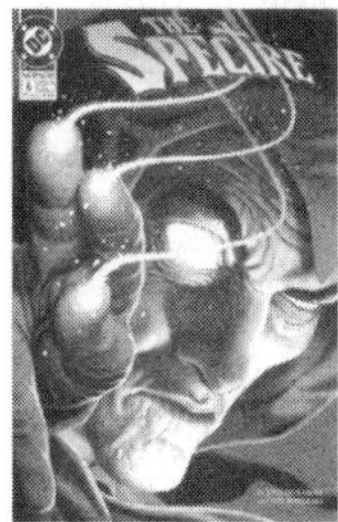

Character remains compelling in third series
©DC

Spectre

Hal Jordan dons the Spectre's cape
©DC

Speedball

Ditko's wacky teen-age speedster
©Marvel

Speed Racer

Anime liked by some, loathed by others
©Now

N-MINT

❑133, Nov 1997; gatefold summary; A: Puppet Master 1.99
❑134, Dec 1997; gatefold summary 1.99
❑135, Jan 1998; gatefold summary; A: Agatha Harkness 1.99
❑136, Feb 1998; gatefold summary 1.99
❑137, Mar 1998; gatefold summary; A: Agatha Harkness 1.99
❑138, Apr 1998; gatefold summary; A: Thing 1.99
❑139, May 1998; gatefold summary 1.99
❑140, Jun 1998; gatefold summary 1.99
❑141, Jul 1998; gatefold summary 1.99
❑142, Aug 1998; gatefold summary 1.99
❑143, Sep 1998; gatefold summary; V: Psycho-Man 1.99
❑144, Oct 1998; gatefold summary 1.99
❑145, Oct 1998; gatefold summary 1.99
❑146, Nov 1998; gatefold summary; Final Issue 1.99
❑Ann 1, ca. 1988; JSa (a) 4.00
❑Ann 2, ca. 1989 .... 3.00
❑Ann 3, ca. 1990 .... 2.50
❑Ann 4, ca. 1991; O: The Silver Surfer 2.50
❑Ann 5, ca. 1992; JSn, JB, JLee (a); O: Nebula 2.50
❑Ann 6, ca. 1993; 1: Legacy. A: Terrax. A: Jack of Hearts. A: Ronan the Accuser. A: Ganymede. trading card; Polybagged 2.95
❑Ann 7, ca. 1994 .... 2.95
❑Ann 1997, ca. 1997; wraparound cover 4.00
❑Ann 1998, ca. 1998; gatefold summary; V: Millennius. Silver Surfer/Thor '98; wraparound cover 2.99

Silver Surfer
Marvel

❑1, Sep 2003 .... 2.25
❑2, Dec 2003 .... 2.25
❑3, Jan 2004 .... 2.25
❑4, Feb 2004 .... 2.25
❑5, Mar 2004 .... 2.25
❑6, Apr 2004 .... 2.25
❑7, May 2004 .... 2.99
❑8, Jun 2004 .... 2.99
❑9, Jul 2004 .... 2.99
❑10, Aug 2004 .... 2.99
❑11, Sep 2004 .... 2.99
❑12, Oct 2004 .... 2.99
❑13, Nov 2004 .... 2.99
❑14, Dec 2004 .... 2.99

Silver Surfer (One-shot)
Marvel

❑1, Jun 1982 JBy, SL (w); JBy (a) 12.00

Silver Surfer: Dangerous Artifacts
Marvel

❑1, Jun 1996; One-shot 3.95

Silver Surfer: Inner Demons
Marvel

❑1, Apr 1998; collects Silver Surfer #123, 125, 126 .... 3.50

Silver Surfer: Loftier Than Mortals
Marvel

❑1, Oct 1999 .... 2.50
❑2, Nov 1999 .... 2.50

N-MINT

Silver Surfer/Superman
Marvel

❑1, Nov 1996; prestige format; crossover with DC 5.95

Silver Surfer: The Enslavers
Marvel

❑1, Mar 1990; hardcover 16.95

Silver Surfer vs. Dracula
Marvel

❑1, ca. 1994; Reprints Tomb of Dracula #50 .... 1.75

Silver Surfer/Warlock: Resurrection
Marvel

❑1, Mar 1993 .... 2.50
❑2, Apr 1993 .... 2.50
❑3, May 1993 .... 2.50
❑4, Jun 1993 .... 2.50

Silver Surfer/Weapon Zero
Marvel

❑1, Apr 1997; crossover with Image 2.95

Silver Sweetie
Spoof

❑1, b&w 2.95

Silverwing Special
Now

❑1, Jan 1987 .... 1.00

Simon and Kirby Classics
Pure Imagination

❑1, Nov 1986; new Vagabond Prince and reprints from Stuntman #1, All-New #13 and Green Hornet #39 .... 2.00

Simon Cat in Taxi
Slab-O-Concrete

❑1; Post card comics 1.50

Simon Spector
Avatar

❑1 2005 .... 3.50

Simpsons Comics
Bongo

❑1, ca. 1993; Fantastic Four #1 homage cover; Bart Simpsons' Creepy Crawly Tales back-up 5.00
❑2, ca. 1994; V: Sideshow Bob. Patty & Selma's Ill-Fated Romance Comics back-up 4.00
❑3, ca. 1994; Krusty, Agent of K.L.O.W.N. back-up 3.00
❑4, ca. 1994; infinity cover; trading card; Gnarly Adventures of Busman back-up 3.00
❑5, ca. 1994; wraparound cover 3.00
❑6, ca. 1994; Chief Wiggum's Pre-Code Crime Comics back-up 2.50
❑7, ca. 1994; McBain Comics back-up 2.50
❑8, ca. 1995; Edna; Queen of the Jungle back-up 2.50
❑9, ca. 1995; Lisa's diary; Barney Gumble back-up 2.50
❑10, ca. 1995; Apu's Kwik-E Comics back-up 2.50
❑11, ca. 1995; evil Flanders; Homer on the Range back-up 2.25
❑12, ca. 1995; White-Knuckled War Stories back-up 2.25
❑13, ca. 1995; Jimbo Jones' Wedgie Comics back-up 2.25

N-MINT

❑14, ca. 1995; Cantankerous Coot Classics back-up 2.25
❑15, ca. 1995; Heinous Funnies back-up 2.25
❑16, ca. 1996; SA (w); Bongo Grab Bag back-up 2.25
❑17, ca. 1996; Headlight Comics back-up 2.25
❑18, ca. 1996; Milhouse Comics back-up 2.25
❑19, ca. 1996; Roswell back-up 2.25
❑20, ca. 1996; Roswell back-up; Bad homage cover 2.25
❑21, ca. 1996; Roswell back-up 2.25
❑22, ca. 1996; Burns and Apu team up; Roswell back-up 2.25
❑23, ca. 1996; Reverend Lovejoy's Hellfire Comics back-up 2.25
❑24, ca. 1996; Li'l Homey back-up 2.25
❑25, ca. 1996; Marge gets her own talk show; Itchy & Scratchy back-up 2.25
❑26, ca. 1996; Speed parody 2.25
❑27, ca. 1996; Homer gets smart 2.25
❑28, ca. 1997; Krusty founds his own country 2.25
❑29, ca. 1997; Homer becomes a pro wrestler 2.25
❑30, ca. 1997; Burns clones Smithers 2.25
❑31, ca. 1997; Homer thinks he's Radioactive Man 2.25
❑32, ca. 1997; Krusty's coffee bar 2.95
❑33, ca. 1997; Alternate Springfield 2.25
❑34, ca. 1997; Burns sponsors Bart as a snowboarder 2.25
❑35, ca. 1998; Marge opens a daycare 2.25
❑36, ca. 1998; The return of the geeks 2.25
❑37, ca. 1998; El Grampo 2.25
❑38, ca. 1998; Burns makes addictive donuts 2.25
❑39, ca. 1998; Homer and Comic Book Guy on trial 2.25
❑40, ca. 1998; Krusty does live show from Simpsons house; Lard Lad back-up 2.50
❑41, ca. 1999 .... 2.50
❑42, ca. 1999; The Homer Show; Slobberwacky back-up 2.50
❑43, ca. 1999; story told backwards; Poochie back-up 2.50
❑44, ca. 1999; Lisa substitutes; Bartman back-up 2.50
❑45, ca. 1999; Hot Dog On A Schtick 2.50
❑46, ca. 1999 A: Sideshow Bob 2.50
❑47, ca. 2000 .... 2.50
❑48, ca. 2000 .... 2.50
❑49, ca. 2000 .... 2.50
❑50, ca. 2000; Giant-size 2.50
❑51, ca. 2000; Cletus back-up 2.50
❑52, ca. 2000 .... 2.50
❑53, ca. 2000; Ned Flanders back-up 2.50
❑54, ca. 2000 .... 2.50
❑55, ca. 2001 .... 2.50
❑55/2nd, ca. 2001 .... 2.50
❑56, ca. 2001 .... 2.50
❑56/2nd, ca. 1992 .... 2.50
❑57, ca. 2001 .... 2.50
❑58, ca. 2001 .... 2.50
❑59, ca. 2001 .... 2.50
❑60, ca. 2001 .... 2.50
❑61, ca. 2001 .... 2.50
❑62, ca. 2001 .... 2.50
❑63, ca. 2001; ca. 2002 .... 2.50

	N-MINT
❑64, ca. 2001; Malibu Stacy flip-book	2.50
❑65; ca. 2001	2.50
❑66, ca. 2002	2.50
❑67, ca. 2002	2.50
❑68, ca. 2002	2.50
❑69, ca. 2002	2.50
❑70, ca. 2002	2.50
❑71, ca. 2002	2.50
❑72, ca. 2002	2.50
❑73, ca. 2002	2.50
❑74, ca. 2002	2.50
❑75, ca. 2002	2.50
❑76, ca. 2002	2.50
❑77, Dec 2002	2.50
❑78, ca. 2003	2.50
❑79, ca. 2003	2.50
❑80, ca. 2003	2.50
❑81, ca. 2003	2.50
❑82, ca. 2003	2.50
❑83, Jun 2003	2.50
❑84, Jul 2003	2.50
❑85, Aug 2003	2.99
❑86, Sep 2003	2.99
❑87, Oct 2003	2.99
❑88, Nov 2003	2.99
❑89, Dec 2003	2.99
❑90, Jan 2004	2.99
❑91, Feb 2004	2.99
❑92, Mar 2004	2.99
❑93, Apr 2004	2.99
❑94, May 2004	2.99
❑95, Jun 2004	2.99
❑96, Jul 2004	2.99
❑97, Aug 2004	2.99
❑98, Sep 2004	2.99
❑99, Oct 2004	2.99
❑100, Nov 2004; Giant-sized	2.99
❑101, Dec 2004	2.99
❑102, Jan 2005	2.99
❑103, Feb 2005	2.99
❑104, Mar 2005	2.99
❑105, Apr 2005	2.99
❑106, May 2005	2.99
❑107, Jun 2005	2.99
❑108, Jul 2005	2.99
❑109, Sep 2005; Panel with Storm vs. Callisto in Morlock Sewers	2.99
❑110	2.99
❑111	2.99
❑112	2.99
❑113	2.99
❑114	2.99
❑115	2.99
❑116	2.99
❑117	2.99
❑118	2.99
❑119	2.99
❑120	2.99
❑121	2.99
❑122	2.99
❑123	2.99
❑124	2.99
❑125	2.99
❑126	2.99
❑127	2.99
❑128	2.99
❑129	2.99
❑130	2.99
❑131	2.99
❑132	2.99
❑133	2.99
❑134	2.99
❑135	2.99
❑136	2.99
❑137	2.99
❑138	2.99
❑139	2.99
❑140	2.99
❑141	2.99
❑142	2.99
❑143	2.99
❑144	2.99
❑145	2.99
❑146	2.99
❑147	2.99
❑148	2.99
❑149	2.99

	N-MINT
❑150	2.99
❑151	2.99
❑152	2.99
❑153	2.99
❑154	2.99
❑155	2.99

Simpsons Comics and Stories
Welsh

❑1, ca. 1993; O: Bartman. 1: The Simpsons. with poster	4.00

Simpsons Comics Presents Bart Simpson
Bongo

❑1, Aug 2000	2.50
❑2, Nov 2000	2.50
❑3, Feb 2001	2.50
❑4, May 2001	2.50
❑5, Aug 2001	2.50
❑6, Nov 2001	2.50
❑7, Feb 2002	2.50
❑8, May 2002	2.50
❑9, Aug 2002	2.50
❑10, Nov 2002	2.50
❑11, Mar 2003	2.50
❑12, Apr 2003	2.50
❑13, Sep 2003	2.99
❑14, Oct 2003	2.99
❑15, Dec 2003	2.99
❑16, Feb 2004	2.99
❑17, Apr 2004	2.99
❑18, Jun 2004	2.99
❑19, Aug 2004	2.99
❑20, ca. 2004	2.99
❑21 2005	2.99
❑22, Feb 2005	2.99
❑23, Apr 2005	2.99
❑24, Jun 2005	2.99
❑25, Oct 2005; Cover reads "Prince of Pranks"	2.99
❑26, Oct 2005; Cover reads "Big Spender"	2.99
❑27	2.99
❑28	2.99
❑29	2.99
❑30	2.99
❑31	2.99
❑32	2.99
❑33	2.99
❑34	2.99
❑35	2.99
❑36	2.99
❑37	2.99
❑38	2.99
❑39	2.99
❑40	2.99
❑41	2.99
❑42	2.99
❑43	2.99
❑44	2.99
❑45	2.99
❑46	2.99
❑47	2.99
❑48	2.99
❑49	2.99
❑50	2.99
❑51	2.99
❑52	2.99
❑53	2.99
❑54	2.99
❑55	2.99
❑56	2.99
❑57	2.99
❑58	2.99
❑59	2.99
❑60	2.99

Simpsons/Futurama Crossover Crisis Part 2
Bongo

❑1, Jan 2005	2.99

Simpsons Super Spectacular
Bongo

❑1, Oct 2005	4.99

Simulators
Neatly Chiseled Features

❑1	2.50

Sin
Tragedy Strikes

	N-MINT
❑1, Jun 1992, b&w	2.95
❑2, Aug 1992, b&w	2.95
❑3, Oct 1992, b&w	2.95

Sinbad
Adventure

❑1, Nov 1989, b&w; cardstock cover	2.25
❑2, Dec 1989, b&w; cardstock cover	2.25
❑3, Jan 1990, b&w; cardstock cover	2.25
❑4, Mar 1990, b&w	2.25

Sinbad Book II
Adventure

❑1, Mar 1991, b&w	2.50
❑2, Apr 1991, b&w	2.50
❑3, May 1991, b&w	2.50
❑4, Jun 1991, b&w	2.50

Sin City
Cozmic

❑1; Adult	1.50

Sin City: A Dame to Kill For
Dark Horse

❑1/2nd, Jul 1994; 2nd printing; b&w	2.95
❑1, Nov 1993, b&w; FM (c); FM (w); FM (a)	3.50
❑2, Jan 1994, b&w; FM (c); FM (w); FM (a)	3.25
❑3, Feb 1994, b&w; FM (c); FM (w); FM (a)	3.00
❑4, Mar 1994, b&w; FM (c); FM (w); FM (a)	3.00
❑5, Apr 1994, b&w; FM (c); FM (w); FM (a	3.00
❑6, May 1994, b&w; FM (c); FM (w); FM (a)	3.00

Sin City Angels
Fantagraphics

❑1, Dec 2004, Adult; b&w	3.95

Sin City: Family Values
Dark Horse

❑1, Oct 1997, b&w; FM (w); FM (a); NN; One-shot	15.00
❑1/A, Oct 1997, FM (w); FM (a); Cover has Roller-skating girl	18.00
❑1/Ltd., Oct 1997, Limited edition hardcover; FM (w); FM (a)	75.00

Sin City: Hell and Back
Dark Horse / Maverick

❑1, Jul 1999, b&w; cardstock cover	2.95
❑2, Aug 1999, b&w; cardstock cover	2.95
❑3, Sep 1999, b&w; cardstock cover	2.95
❑4, Oct 1999, b&w; cardstock cover	2.95
❑5, Nov 1999, b&w; cardstock cover	2.95
❑6, Dec 1999, b&w; cardstock cover	2.95
❑7, Jan 2000, b&w; cardstock cover	2.95
❑8, Feb 2000, b&w; cardstock cover	2.95
❑9, Apr 2000, b&w; cardstock cover	2.95

Sin City: Just Another Saturday Night
Dark Horse

❑½, Aug 1997, Wizard promotional edition; FM (c); FM (w); FM (a)	3.00
❑1, Oct 1998, b&w; FM (w); FM (a); NN; One-shot	2.50

Sin City: Lost, Lonely, & Lethal
Dark Horse / Legend

❑1, Dec 1996, Cardstock cover; b&w and blue	2.95

Sin City: Sex & Violence
Dark Horse

❑1, Mar 1997, b&w; cardstock cover	2.95

Sin City: Silent Night
Dark Horse / Legend

❑1, Nov 1995, b&w; cardstock cover	2.95

Sin City: That Yellow Bastard
Dark Horse / Legend

❑1, Feb 1996	2.95
❑2, Mar 1996	2.95
❑3, Apr 1996	2.95
❑4, May 1996	2.95
❑5, Jun 1996	2.95
❑6, Jul 1996	3.50

Sin City: The Babe Wore Red and Other Stories
Dark Horse

❑1, Nov 1994, NN; B&w and red	2.95

Other grades: Multiply price above by 5/6 for VF/NM • 2/3 for VERY FINE • 1/3 for FINE • 1/5 for VERY GOOD • 1/8 for GOOD

Spellbound

Rival spellbinders in a mystical universe
©Marvel

Spelljammer

Melds Dungeons & Dragons with science fiction
©DC

Spider-Girl

Spider-Man's daughter from alternate future
©Marvel

Spider-Man

"Adjectiveless" series created for McFarlane
©Marvel

Spider-Man & Wolverine

Popular characters in 2003 team-up
©Marvel

N-MINT

Sin City: The Big Fat Kill
Dark Horse

- ❑1, Nov 1994, b&w; Cardstock; Two page b&w gallery at back of book 2.95
- ❑2, Dec 1994, b&w; cardstock cover 2.95
- ❑3, Jan 1995, b&w; cardstock cover 2.95
- ❑4, Feb 1995, b&w; cardstock cover 2.95
- ❑5, Mar 1995, b&w; cardstock cover 2.95

Sindy
Forbidden Fruit

- ❑1, b&w; Adult 2.95
- ❑2, b&w; Adult 2.95
- ❑3, b&w; Adult 2.95
- ❑4, b&w; Adult 2.95
- ❑5, b&w; Adult 2.95

Sinergy
Caliber

- ❑1, ca. 1994, b&w 2.95
- ❑1/Ltd., ca. 1994; limited edition 5.95
- ❑2, ca. 1994, b&w 2.95
- ❑2/Ltd., ca. 1994; limited edition 5.95
- ❑3, ca. 1994, b&w 2.95
- ❑3/Ltd., ca. 1994; limited edition 5.95
- ❑4, ca. 1994, b&w 2.95
- ❑4/Ltd., ca. 1994; limited edition 5.95
- ❑5, ca. 1994, b&w 2.95
- ❑5/Ltd., ca. 1994; limited edition 5.95

Singularity 7
Idea & Design Works

- ❑1, Jul 2004 .... 3.99
- ❑2, Aug 2004 .... 3.99
- ❑3 2004 .... 3.99
- ❑4, Oct 2004 .... 3.99

Sinister House of Secret Love
DC

- ❑1, Oct 1971 .... 125.00
- ❑2, Dec 1971 JO (w); TD (a) 75.00
- ❑3, Feb 1972; White cover difficult to find in unaged condition 75.00
- ❑4, Apr 1972; TD (a); Series continued in Secrets of Sinister House #5 .... 75.00

Sinister Romance
Harrier

- ❑1, Jul 1988, b&w 2.00
- ❑2, Sep 1988, b&w 2.00
- ❑3, Jan 1988, b&w 1.95
- ❑4, Jun 1989, b&w 1.95

Sinja: Deadly Sins
Lightning

- ❑1, Jun 1996 .... 3.00
- ❑1/A; Commemorative edition 3.00
- ❑1/B; Nude edition 9.95

Sinja: Resurrection
Lightning

- ❑1, Aug 1996; flipbook with Kunoichi #1; indicia says Sinja: Resurrection; cover says Kunoichi 3.00

Sinnamon
Catfish

- ❑1, Dec 1995 .... 2.50

N-MINT

Sinnamon
Catfish

- ❑1 1996 .... 2.75
- ❑2 1996 .... 2.75
- ❑3 1996 .... 2.75
- ❑4 1996 .... 2.75
- ❑4/Variant 1996; Variant cover edition (500 printed) 5.00
- ❑5 1996 .... 2.75
- ❑5/Variant 1996; Variant cover edition (500 printed) 4.00
- ❑6 1996 .... 2.75
- ❑7 1996 .... 2.75
- ❑8 1996; Sinnamon vs. Aerobica 2.75

Sinner
Fantagraphics

- ❑1, Oct 1987 .... 2.95
- ❑2, Mar 1988 .... 2.95
- ❑3, May 1988 .... 2.95
- ❑4, Sep 1988 .... 2.95
- ❑5, Sep 1990 .... 2.95

Sinners
DC / Piranha

- ❑1 .... 9.95

Sinnin!
Fantagraphics / Eros

- ❑1, Apr 1991, b&w; Adult 2.25
- ❑2, b&w; Adult 2.25

Sin of the Mummy
Fantagraphics / Eros

- ❑1, b&w; Adult 2.50

Sins of Youth: Aquaboy/Lagoon Man
DC

- ❑1, May 2000 .... 2.50

Sins of Youth: Batboy and Robin
DC

- ❑1, May 2000 .... 2.50

Sins of Youth: JLA, Jr.
DC

- ❑1, May 2000 .... 2.50

Sins of Youth: Kid Flash/Impulse
DC

- ❑1, May 2000 .... 2.50

Sins of Youth Secret Files
DC

- ❑1, May 2000 .... 4.95

Sins of Youth: Starwoman and the JSA (Junior Society)
DC

- ❑1, May 2000 .... 2.50

Sins of Youth: Superman, Jr./ Superboy, Sr.
DC

- ❑1, May 2000 .... 2.50

Sins of Youth: The Secret/Deadboy
DC

- ❑1, May 2000 .... 2.50

Sins of Youth: Wonder Girls
DC

- ❑1, May 2000 .... 2.50

N-MINT

Sinthia
Lightning

- ❑1/A, Oct 1997 .... 2.95
- ❑1/B, Oct 1997; alternate cover 2.95
- ❑1/Platinum, Oct 1997; Platinum edition 4.00
- ❑2/A, Jan 1998 .... 3.00
- ❑2/B, Jan 1998 .... 3.00

Sir Charles Barkley and the Referee Murders
Hamilton

- ❑1, ca. 1993 .... 9.95

Siren
Malibu / Ultraverse

- ❑0, Sep 1995; Black September; #Infinity 1.50
- ❑0/A, Sep 1995; alternate cover 1.50
- ❑1, Oct 1995; V: War Machine; Line art style of illustration, lighter cover (but same design as 1/A); Standard Cover 1.50
- ❑2, Nov 1995; V: War Machine 1.50
- ❑3, Dec 1995; continues in Siren Special #1 .... 1.50
- ❑Special 1, Feb 1996; O: Siren 1.95

Siren: Shapes
Image

- ❑1, May 1998 .... 2.95
- ❑2, Sep 1998 .... 2.95
- ❑3, Nov 1998 .... 2.95

Sirens of the Lost World
Comax

- ❑1, b&w; Adult 2.95

Sirius Gallery
Sirius

- ❑1, ca. 1997; Limited edition 3.00
- ❑2, Apr 1999; cardstock cover; pin-ups 3.00
- ❑3, Jun 2000; no cover price; pin-ups 3.00

Sister Armageddon
Draculina

- ❑1; 1: Sister Armageddon 2.75
- ❑2, b&w 2.75
- ❑3, b&w 3.00
- ❑4 .... 3.00

Sisterhood of Steel
Marvel / Epic

- ❑1, Dec 1984 .... 2.00
- ❑2, Feb 1985 .... 2.00
- ❑3, Apr 1985 .... 2.00
- ❑4, Jun 1985 .... 2.00
- ❑5, Aug 1985 .... 2.00
- ❑6, Oct 1985 .... 2.00
- ❑7, Dec 1985 .... 2.00
- ❑8, Feb 1986 .... 2.00

Sister Red
ComicsOne

- ❑1, Feb 2004; Reads right to left 9.95
- ❑2, Apr 2004; Reads right to left 9.95

Sisters of Darkness
Illustration

- ❑1/A 1997; Adult cover 3.25
- ❑1/B 1997; tame cover 3.25
- ❑2/A 1997; Adult cover 3.25
- ❑2/B 1997; tame cover 3.25
- ❑3, Aug 1997 .... 3.25

Other grades: Multiply price above by 5/6 for VF/NM • 2/3 for VERY FINE • 1/3 for FINE • 1/5 for VERY GOOD • 1/8 for GOOD

Sisters of Mercy
Maximum
❑1, Dec 1995; 1: Doctor Vincent Casey; 1: Sisters of Mercy (super-heroes); Mature content; Adult 2.50
❑1/A, Dec 1995; alternate cover 2.50
❑2, Jan 1996; Mature content; Adult 2.50
❑3 1996; Adult 2.50
❑4 1996; Adult 2.50
❑5 1996; Adult 2.50

Sisters of Mercy
London Night
❑0, Mar 1997 .... 1.50

Sisters of Mercy: When Razors Cry Crimson Tears
No Mercy
❑1, Oct 1996 .... 2.50

Sister Vampire
Angel
❑1; Adult 2.95

Six
Image
❑0 2005 .... 5.99

6
Virtual
❑1, Oct 1996 .... 2.50
❑2, Nov 1996 .... 2.50
❑3, Dec 1996 .... 2.50

6: Lethal Origins
Virtual
❑1, May 1996, digest; NN 3.99

Six Degrees
Heretic
❑1, b&w 3.50
❑1/Autographed; Includes print, certificate of authenticity; Signed, numbered edition (100 copies) 6.00
❑2, b&w 2.95
❑3, b&w 2.95
❑4, b&w 2.95
❑5, b&w 2.95

Six From Sirius
Marvel / Epic
❑1, Jul 1984 PG (c); PG (a) 2.00
❑2, Aug 1984 PG (c); PG (a) 2.00
❑3, Sep 1984 PG (c); PG (a) 2.00
❑4, Oct 1984 PG (c); PG (a) 2.00

Six From Sirius 2
Marvel / Epic
❑1, Feb 1986 PG (c); PG (a) 2.00
❑2, Mar 1986 PG (c); PG (a) 2.00
❑3, Apr 1986 PG (c); PG (a) 2.00
❑4, May 1986 PG (c); PG (a) 2.00

Six-Gun Samurai
Alias
❑1, Sep 2005 .... 0.75
❑2, Nov 2005 .... 2.99

Six Million Dollar Man
Charlton
❑1, Jun 1976, JSa (c); JSa (a); 1&O: The Six Million Dollar Man 12.00
❑2, Aug 1976, NA (c); JSa (a); Nicola Cuti, Joe Staton credits; Action figure tie-in 6.00
❑3, Oct 1976, JSa (a); Nicola Cuti, Joe Staton credits 5.00
❑4, Dec 1977 .... 5.00
❑5, Oct 1977 .... 5.00
❑6, Feb 1978 .... 4.00
❑7, Mar 1978, Boyette and Himes credits 4.00
❑8, May 1978 .... 4.00
❑9, Jun 1978 .... 4.00

Six Million Dollar Man (Magazine)
Charlton
❑1, Jul 1976 .... 10.00
❑2, Sep 1976 .... 8.00
❑3, Nov 1976 .... 5.00
❑4, Jan 1977 .... 5.00
❑5, May 1977 .... 5.00
❑6, Jul 1977 .... 5.00
❑7 .... 5.00

666: The Mark of the Beast
Fleetway-Quality
❑1, ca. 1986 .... 2.50
❑2, ca. 1986 .... 2.00
❑3, ca. 1986 .... 2.00
❑4, ca. 1986 .... 2.00
❑5, ca. 1986 .... 2.00
❑6, ca. 1986 .... 2.00
❑7, ca. 1986 .... 2.00
❑8, ca. 1986 .... 2.00
❑9, ca. 1986 .... 2.00
❑10, ca. 1987 .... 2.00
❑11, ca. 1987 .... 2.00
❑12, ca. 1987; AMo (w); Alan Moore special 2.00
❑13, ca. 1987 .... 2.00
❑14, ca. 1987 .... 2.00
❑15, ca. 1987 .... 2.00
❑16, ca. 1987 .... 2.00
❑17, ca. 1987 .... 2.00
❑18, ca. 1987 .... 2.00

Six String Samurai
Awesome
❑1, Sep 1998 .... 2.95

68
Image
❑1, Feb 2007 .... 3.99

Sixty Nine
Fantagraphics / Eros
❑1, ca. 1993; Adult; b&w 2.75
❑2, Mar 1994; Adult; b&w 2.75
❑3, May 1994; Adult; b&w 2.75
❑4, Jul 1994, b&w; Adult 2.75

67 Seconds
Marvel / Epic
❑1; 68 pages 15.95

Sizzle Theatre
Slave Labor
❑1, Aug 1991, b&w; Adult 2.50

Sizzlin' Sisters
Fantagraphics / Eros
❑1 1997; Adult 2.95
❑2, Aug 1997; Adult 2.95

Skateman
Pacific
❑1, Nov 1983; Neal Adams cover; 1: Skateman; O: Skateman 1.50

Skeleton Girl
Slave Labor
❑1, Dec 1995; 1: J.J.; 1: Skeleton Girl; 1: Stacy the Maniacal; Skeleton Boy; Angst-Filled Hate Girl; Adult 2.95
❑2, Apr 1996; 2: J.J.; 2: Skeleton Girl; Skeleton Boy; Adult 2.95
❑3, Sep 1996; Adult 2.95

Skeleton Hand
Avalon
❑1 .... 2.99

Skeleton Key
Amaze Ink
❑1, Jul 1995 .... 2.00
❑2, Aug 1995 .... 2.00
❑3, Sep 1995 .... 2.00
❑4, Oct 1995 .... 2.00
❑5, Nov 1995 .... 2.00
❑6, Dec 1995 .... 2.00
❑7, Jan 1996 .... 2.00
❑8, Feb 1996 .... 2.00
❑9, Mar 1996 .... 2.00
❑10, Apr 1996 .... 2.00
❑11, May 1996 .... 1.75
❑12, Jun 1996 .... 1.75
❑13, Jul 1996 .... 1.75
❑14, Aug 1996 .... 1.75
❑15, Sep 1996, cover says Aug, indicia says Sep 1.75
❑16, Oct 1996 .... 1.75
❑17, Nov 1996 .... 1.75
❑18, Dec 1996 .... 1.75
❑19, Jan 1997 .... 1.75
❑20, Feb 1997 .... 1.75
❑21, Mar 1997 .... 1.75
❑22, Apr 1997 .... 1.75
❑23, May 1997 .... 1.75
❑24, Jun 1997 .... 1.75
❑25, Jul 1997 .... 1.75
❑26, Aug 1997 .... 1.75
❑27, Sep 1997 .... 1.75
❑28, Oct 1997 .... 1.75
❑29, Nov 1997 .... 1.75
❑30, Dec 1997 .... 1.75

Skeleton Warriors
Marvel
❑1, Apr 1995; 1: Baron Dark; 1: Doctor Cyborn; 1: Grimskull; 1: Prince Lightstar; 1: Talyn; O: The Skeleton Warriors 1.50
❑2, May 1995 .... 1.50
❑3, Jun 1995 .... 1.50
❑4, Jul 1995; Final Issue 1.50

Sketchbook Series
Tundra
❑1; Melting Pot 3.95
❑2; Totleben 3.95
❑3; Zulli 3.95
❑4 .... 3.95
❑5 .... 3.95
❑6; Screaming Masks 3.95
❑7 .... 3.95
❑8; Forg 3.95
❑9 .... 3.95
❑10 .... 4.95

Skidmarks
Tundra
❑0, b&w 2.95
❑1, b&w; ca. 1992 .... 2.95
❑2, b&w 2.95
❑3, b&w 2.95

Skid Roze
London Night
❑1, Jul 1998 .... 3.00

Skim Lizard
Puppy Toss
❑1; Adult 2.95

Skin
Tundra
❑1 .... 8.95

Skin Graft
Iconografix
❑1, b&w 3.50

Skin Graft: The Adventures of a Tattooed Man
DC / Vertigo
❑1, Jul 1993 .... 2.50
❑2, Aug 1993 .... 2.50
❑3, Sep 1993 .... 2.50
❑4, Oct 1993 .... 2.50

Skinheads in Love
Fantagraphics / Eros
❑1, Mar 1992, b&w; Adult 2.25

Skinners
Image
❑1/A 2.95
❑1/B 2.95
❑1/C 2.95

Skin13
Express / Parody
❑½/A, Oct 1995, b&w; Amazing SKIN Thir-Teen; reprints Skin13 #1 .... 2.50
❑½/B, Oct 1995, b&w; Barbari-SKIN; reprints Skin13 #1 .... 2.50
❑½/C, Oct 1995, b&w; SKIN-et Jackson; reprints Skin13 #1 .... 2.50
❑½/A/2nd; 2nd printing 2.50
❑½/B/2nd; 2nd printing 2.50
❑½/C/2nd; 2nd printing 2.50
❑1/A, b&w; ca. 1995 .... 2.50
❑1/B, b&w; Heavy Metal-style cover 2.50
❑1/C, b&w; Spider-Man #1-style cover 2.50

Skizz
Fleetway-Quality
❑1 .... 1.95
❑2 .... 1.95
❑3 .... 1.95

Other grades: Multiply price above by 5/6 for VF/NM • 2/3 for VERY FINE • 1/3 for FINE • 1/5 for VERY GOOD • 1/8 for GOOD

Spider-Man/Black Cat: The Evil That Men Do

Kevin Smith agrees to do series, forgets
©Marvel

Spider-Man: Blue

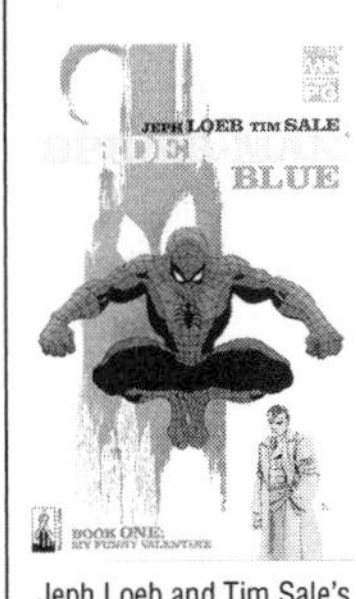

Jeph Loeb and Tim Sale's take on Spidey
©Marvel

Spider-Man: Chapter One

John Byrne tries to reboot Spider-Man
©Marvel

Spider-Man Megazine

Fun 96-page Spider-Man reprint series
©Marvel

Spider-Man: The Clone Journal

Special edition explains the Clone Saga
©Marvel

N-MINT

Skreemer
DC

❑1, May 1989 ... 2.00
❑2, Jun 1989 ... 2.00
❑3, Jul 1989 ... 2.00
❑4, Aug 1989 ... 2.00
❑5, Sep 1989 ... 2.00
❑6, Oct 1989 ... 2.00

Skrog
Comico

❑1, b&w ... 1.50

Skrog (Yip, Yip, Yay) Special
Crystal

❑1, b&w ... 2.50

Skrull Kill Krew
Marvel

❑1, Sep 1995; cardstock cover ... 2.95
❑2, Oct 1995; cardstock cover ... 2.95
❑3, Nov 1995; cardstock cover ... 2.95
❑4, Dec 1995; cardstock cover ... 2.95
❑5, Jan 1996; cardstock cover ... 2.95

Skulker
Thorby

❑1 ... 2.95

Skull & Bones
DC

❑1, ca. 1992 ... 4.95
❑2, ca. 1992 ... 4.95
❑3, ca. 1992 ... 4.95

Skull Comics
Last Gasp

❑1 ... 18.00
❑2, Jan 1970 ... 10.00
❑3 ... 6.00
❑4 ... 6.00
❑5, Jan 1972 ... 6.00
❑6, Jun 1972 ... 6.00

Skull the Slayer
Marvel

❑1, Aug 1975, GK (c); GK (a); O: Skull the Slayer ... 12.00
❑2, Nov 1975 ... 5.00
❑3, Jan 1976, Marvel Value Stamp Series B #22; Fred Hembeck L.O.C. ... 1.50
❑4, Mar 1976, RB (c); SB (a) ... 4.00
❑5, May 1976 ... 4.00
❑5/30¢, May 1976, 30¢ regional price variant ... 20.00
❑6, Jul 1976 ... 3.00
❑6/30¢, Jul 1976, 30¢ regional price variant ... 20.00
❑7, Sep 1976 ... 3.00
❑8, Nov 1976, Final issue ... 3.00

Skunk
Mu

❑1, Dec 1993, b&w; NN; Adult ... 2.50

Skunk
Express / Entity

❑1, ca. 1996 ... 2.75
❑2, ca. 1996 ... 2.75
❑3, Jul 1996, b&w; cover says #tree ... 2.75
❑4, Sep 1996, b&w ... 2.75

N-MINT

❑5, Sep 1996, b&w; cover says Cinco de Mayo ... 2.75
❑6, Oct 1996, b&w; cover says #sick ... 2.75
❑GN 1, ca. 1996, Collects issues #1-3 ... 4.75

Sky Ape (Les Adventures)
Slave Labor

❑1, Jun 1997, b&w ... 2.95
❑2, Sep 1997, b&w ... 2.95
❑3, Jan 1998, b&w ... 2.95

Sky Comics Presents Monthly
Sky Comics

❑1, b&w ... 2.50

Skye Blue
Mu

❑1, Apr 1992, b&w ... 2.50
❑2, Jul 1992, b&w ... 2.50
❑3, May 1993; b&w ... 2.50

Skye Runner
DC

❑1, Jul 2006 ... 2.99
❑2, Aug 2006 ... 2.99
❑3, Sep 2006 ... 2.99
❑4, Nov 2006 ... 2.99
❑5, Dec 2006 ... 2.99

Sky Gal
AC

❑1; some reprint; Reprints Sky Gal stories from Jumbo Comics #68, others plus new story ... 3.95
❑2; some color; some reprint; Reprints Sky Gal stories from Jumbo Comics plus new story ... 3.95
❑3; some color; some reprint; Reprints Sky Gal stories from Jumbo Comics plus new story ... 3.95

Sky Masters
Pure Imagination

❑1, ca. 1991, b&w; strip reprints ... 7.95

Skynn & Bones
Brainstorm

❑1; Adult ... 2.95

Skynn & Bones: Deadly Angels
Brainstorm

❑1, Apr 1996 ... 2.95

Skyscrapers of the Midwest
Adhouse Books

❑1, ca. 2004 ... 5.00
❑2, ca. 2005; b&w ... 5.00

Skywolf
Eclipse

❑1, Mar 1988 ... 2.00
❑2, May 1988 ... 2.00
❑3, Oct 1988; Contiunes in the pages of Airboy comics ... 2.00

Slacker Comics
Slave Labor

❑1, Aug 1994 ... 3.00
❑1/2nd, Apr 1995; 2nd printing ... 2.95
❑2, Nov 1994 ... 2.95
❑3, Feb 1995 ... 2.95
❑4, May 1995 ... 2.95
❑5, Sep 1995 ... 2.95
❑6, Dec 1995 ... 2.95

N-MINT

❑7, Feb 1996 ... 2.95
❑8, May 1996 ... 2.95
❑9, Aug 1996 ... 2.95
❑10 1996 ... 2.95
❑11, Jan 1997 ... 2.95
❑12 1997 ... 2.95
❑13, Apr 1997 ... 2.95
❑14, May 1997; Slacker Ann; Also titled "Ann #1" ... 2.95
❑15 1997; no indicia ... 2.95
❑16, Apr 1998 ... 2.95
❑17, Jul 1998 ... 2.95
❑18, Oct 1998 ... 2.95

Sláine the Berserker
Fleetway-Quality

❑1, Jul 1987 ... 1.50
❑2, Aug 1987 ... 1.50
❑3, Sep 1987 ... 1.50
❑4, Oct 1987 ... 1.50
❑5, Nov 1987 ... 1.50
❑6, Dec 1987 ... 1.50
❑7, Jan 1988 ... 1.50
❑8, Feb 1988 ... 1.50
❑9, Mar 1988 ... 1.50
❑10, Apr 1988 ... 1.50
❑11, May 1988 ... 1.50
❑12, Jun 1988 ... 1.50
❑13, Jul 1988 ... 1.50
❑14, Aug 1988; double issue #14/15 ... 1.50
❑16, Sep 1988; double issue #16/17 ... 1.50
❑18, Oct 1988 ... 1.50
❑19, Nov 1988 ... 1.50
❑20, Dec 1988 ... 1.50

Sláine the Horned God
Fleetway-Quality

❑1, ca. 1990 ... 3.50
❑2 ... 3.00
❑3 ... 3.00
❑4 ... 3.00
❑5 ... 3.00
❑6 ... 3.00

Sláine the King
Fleetway-Quality

❑21, Jan 1989 ... 1.50
❑22, Feb 1989 ... 1.50
❑23 1989 ... 1.50
❑24 1989 ... 1.50
❑25 1989 ... 1.50
❑26 1989 ... 1.50
❑27 1989 ... 1.50
❑28 1989 ... 1.50

Slam Dunk Kings
Personality

❑1, Mar 1992, b&w; Michael Jordan ... 2.95
❑2 1992, b&w ... 2.95
❑3 1992, b&w ... 2.95
❑4 1992, b&w ... 2.95

Slapstick
Marvel

❑1, Nov 1992, 1&O: Slapstick ... 1.25
❑2, Dec 1992 ... 1.25
❑3, Jan 1993 ... 1.25
❑4, Feb 1993 ... 1.25

Other grades: Multiply price above by 5/6 for VF/NM • 2/3 for VERY FINE • 1/3 for FINE • 1/5 for VERY GOOD • 1/8 for GOOD

Slash
Northstar
❑1, Aug 1993, b&w; Adult 2.75
❑1/Special, Aug 1993; Adult 4.95
❑2, Nov 1993, b&w; Adult 2.95
❑3, Feb 1993, b&w; Adult 2.95
❑4, Aug 1993, b&w; Adult 2.95
❑5, Oct 1993; Adult 2.95

Slash Maraud
DC
❑1, Nov 1987 PG (c); PG (a) 2.25
❑2, Dec 1987 PG (c); PG (a) 2.00
❑3, Jan 1988 PG (c); PG (a) 2.00
❑4, Feb 1988 PG (c); PG (a) 2.00
❑5, Mar 1988 PG (c); PG (a) 2.00
❑6, Apr 1988 PG (c); PG (a) 2.00

Slaughterman
Comico
❑1, b&w; Adult; ca. 1983 .... 3.50
❑2, b&w; Adult; ca. 1983 .... 3.50

Slave Girl
Eternity
❑1, Mar 1989, b&w; Reprints 2.25

Slave Labor Stories
Slave Labor
❑1, Feb 1992, b&w; Doctor Radium 2.95
❑2, Apr 1992, b&w; Milk & Cheese 2.95
❑3, Jul 1992, b&w; Bill the Clown 2.95
❑4, Nov 1992, b&w; Samurai Penguin ... 2.95

Slave Pit Funnies
Slave Pit
❑1; Adult 4.95

Slayers
CPM Manga
❑1, Oct 1998 .... 2.95
❑2, Nov 1998 .... 2.95
❑3, Dec 1998 .... 2.95
❑4, Jan 1999 .... 2.95
❑5, Feb 1999 .... 2.95

Slayers
Tokyopop
❑1, Sep 2004 .... 2.95
❑2, Dec 2004 .... 2.95
❑3, Mar 2005 .... 2.95
❑4, Jun 2005 .... 7.99
❑5, Sep 2005 .... 2.95
❑6, Dec 2005 .... 2.95

Sleazy Scandals of the Silver Screen
Kitchen Sink
❑1, Apr 1993, b&w pin-ups, cardstock cover 2.50

Sledge Hammer
Marvel
❑1, Feb 1988; TV tie-in 1.00
❑2, Mar 1988; TV tie-in 1.00

Sleeper
DC / Wildstorm
❑1, Mar 2003 .... 2.95
❑2, Apr 2003 .... 2.95
❑3, May 2003 .... 2.95
❑4, Jun 2003 .... 2.95
❑5, Jul 2003 .... 2.95
❑6, Aug 2003 .... 2.95
❑7, Oct 2003 .... 2.95
❑8, Oct 2003 .... 2.95
❑9, Nov 2003 .... 2.95
❑10, Jan 2004 .... 2.95
❑11, Feb 2004 .... 2.95
❑12, Mar 2004 .... 2.95

Sleeper: Season 2
DC / Wildstorm
❑1; Aug 2004 .... 2.95
❑2, Sep 2004 .... 2.95
❑3, Oct 2004 .... 2.95
❑4, Nov 2004 .... 2.95
❑5, Dec 2004 .... 2.95
❑6, Jan 2005 .... 2.95
❑7, Feb 2005 .... 2.95
❑8, Mar 2005 .... 2.95
❑9, Apr 2005 .... 2.95
❑10, May 2005 .... 2.95
❑11, Jun 2005 .... 2.99

Sleeping Dragons
Slave Labor / Amaze Ink
❑1 2000 .... 2.95
❑2 2000 .... 2.95
❑3, Mar 2001 .... 2.95
❑4, Jul 2001 .... 2.95

Sleepwalker
Marvel
❑1, Jun 1991, 1: Sleepwalker 1.50
❑2, Jul 1991, 1: 8-Ball 1.00
❑3, Aug 1991 .... 1.00
❑4, Sep 1991 .... 1.00
❑5, Oct 1991, A: Spider-Man 1.00
❑6, Nov 1991, A: Spider-Man 1.00
❑7, Dec 1991, Infinity Gauntlet 1.00
❑8, Jan 1992, A: Deathlok 1.25
❑9, Feb 1992 .... 1.25
❑10, Mar 1992 .... 1.25
❑11, Apr 1992, A: Ghost Rider 1.25
❑12, May 1992 .... 1.25
❑13, Jun 1992, 1: Spectra 1.25
❑14, Jul 1992 .... 1.25
❑15, Aug 1992 .... 1.25
❑16, Sep 1992 .... 1.25
❑17, Oct 1992 .... 1.25
❑18, Nov 1992, Infinity War crossover .. 1.25
❑19, Dec 1992, Die-cut cover 2.00
❑20, Jan 1993 .... 1.25
❑21, Feb 1993 .... 1.25
❑22, Mar 1993 .... 1.25
❑23, Apr 1993 .... 1.25
❑24, May 1993 .... 1.25
❑25, Jun 1993, Holo-grafix cover 2.95
❑26, Jul 1993 .... 1.25
❑27, Aug 1993 .... 1.25
❑28, Sep 1993 .... 1.25
❑29, Oct 1993, A: Spectra 1.25
❑30, Nov 1993 .... 1.25
❑31, Dec 1993 .... 1.25
❑32, Jan 1994 .... 1.25
❑33, Feb 1994, Final Issue 1.25
❑Holiday 1, Jan 1993 .... 2.00

Sleepwalking
Hall of Heroes
❑1, Jan 1996, b&w 2.50
❑1/Variant, Jan 1996, b&w; Black Magic edition; alternate logoless cover 9.95
❑2, Jun 1997, b&w 2.50
❑2/Variant, Jun 1997, b&w; alternate logoless cover 2.50
❑3, b&w 2.50

Sleepy Hollow
DC / Vertigo
❑1, Jan 2000 .... 7.95

Sleeze Brothers
Marvel / Epic
❑1, Aug 1989 .... 1.75
❑2, Sep 1989 .... 1.75
❑3, Oct 1989 .... 1.75
❑4, Nov 1989 .... 1.75
❑5, Dec 1989 .... 1.75
❑6, Jan 1990 .... 1.75

Sleeze Brothers
Marvel / Epic
❑1, ca. 1991; NN 3.95

Slice
Express / Entity
❑1, Oct 1996, b&w 2.75

Sliders
Acclaim / Armada
❑1, Jun 1996; DG (a); based on TV series 3.00
❑2, Jul 1996; DG (a); based on TV series 2.50
❑3, Sep 1996 .... 2.50
❑4, Sep 1996 .... 2.50
❑5, Oct 1996 VM, DG (a) 2.50
❑6, Nov 1996 VM (a) 2.50
❑7, Dec 1996 VM (a) 2.50
❑Special 1, Nov 1996; Narcotica 3.95
❑Special 2, Jan 1997 .... 3.95
❑Special 3, Mar 1997; Deadly Secrets ... 3.95

Slightly Bent Comics
Slightly Bent
❑1, Fal 1998, b&w 3.00
❑2, Win 1999, b&w 3.00

Slimer!
Now
❑1, May 1989 .... 2.00
❑2, Jun 1989 .... 2.00
❑3, Jul 1989 .... 2.00
❑4, Aug 1989 .... 1.75
❑5, Sep 1989 .... 1.75
❑6, Oct 1989 .... 1.75
❑7, Nov 1989 .... 1.75
❑8, Dec 1989 .... 1.75
❑9, Jan 1990 .... 1.75
❑10, Feb 1990 .... 1.75
❑11, Mar 1990 .... 1.75
❑12, Apr 1990 .... 1.75
❑13, May 1990 .... 1.75
❑14, Jun 1990 .... 1.75
❑15, Jul 1990 .... 1.75
❑16, Aug 1990 .... 1.75
❑17, Sep 1990 .... 1.75
❑18, Oct 1990 .... 1.75
❑19, Nov 1990 .... 1.75

Slingers
Marvel
❑0; Wizard promotional edition; ca. 1998 1.00
❑1/A, Dec 1998; gatefold summary; A: Ricochet. A: Dusk. A: Hornet. A: Prodigy. A: Black Marvel. variant cover with caption "Prodigy: Prepare for Justice!" 2.99
❑1/B, Dec 1998; gatefold summary; A: Ricochet. A: Dusk. A: Hornet. A: Prodigy. A: Black Marvel. Caption "Dusk Falls Over Manhattan" on cover 2.99
❑1/C, Dec 1998; gatefold summary; variant cover with caption "Hornet: Feel the Sting!" 2.99
❑1/D, Dec 1998; gatefold summary; variant cover with caption "Ricochet Springs into Action!" 2.99
❑2, Jan 1999; gatefold summary; Cover A 2.00
❑2/Variant, Jan 1999; Cover B 2.00
❑3, Feb 1999 A: Spider-Man. A: Prodigy 1.99
❑4, Mar 1999 A: Prodigy 1.99
❑5, Apr 1999 A: Black Marvel 1.99
❑6, May 1999 .... 1.99
❑7, Jun 1999; V: Griz 1.99
❑8, Jul 1999 .... 1.99
❑9, Aug 1999; Ricochet vs. Nanny and Orphanmaker 1.99
❑10, Sep 1999 .... 1.99
❑12, Nov 1999 .... 1.99

Sloth Park
Blatant
❑1, Jun 1998 .... 2.95

Slow Burn
Fantagraphics / Eros
❑1; Adult 2.95

Slow Death
Last Gasp
❑1, Apr 1970 .... 20.00
❑1/Silver, Apr 1970 .... 25.00
❑2, Jan 1970 .... 12.00
❑3, Nov 1971 .... 10.00
❑4, Jan 1972 .... 10.00
❑5, Jan 1973 .... 10.00
❑6, Jan 1974 .... 6.00
❑7, Dec 1976; Nude cover 6.00
❑8, Jul 1977; Greenpeace issue 6.00
❑9, Aug 1978 .... 6.00
❑10, Nov 1979 .... 6.00
❑11; Ca, 1992 .... 6.00

Slowpoke Comix
Alternative
❑1, Nov 1998, b&w; Adult 2.95

Sludge
Malibu / Ultraverse
❑1, Oct 1993, Rune 2.50
❑1/Ltd., Oct 1993, Ultra Ltd 3.00
❑2, Nov 1993, 1: Bloodstorm 2.00
❑3, Dec 1993, Break-Thru 2.00
❑4, Jan 1994, O: Mantra 2.00
❑5, Feb 1994 .... 2.00
❑6, Mar 1994, V: Lord Pumpkin 1.95
❑7, Jun 1994 .... 1.95
❑8, Jul 1994, V: Bloodstorm 1.95
❑9, Sep 1994, V: Lord Pumpkin 1.95

Other grades: Multiply price above by 5/6 for VF/NM • 2/3 for VERY FINE • 1/3 for FINE • 1/5 for VERY GOOD • 1/8 for GOOD

Spider-Man: The Manga

Import had some of Marvel's lowest sales ever
©Marvel

Spider-Man 2099

Flagship title of the futuristic 2099 line
©Marvel

Spider-Woman

Female version didn't fare so well
©Marvel

Spidey Super Stories

Educational series with The Electric Company
©Marvel

Spirit

Kitchen Sink takes over from Warren at #17
©Warren

N-MINT

❑10, Oct 1994, 1: Bash Brothers; 1: Organism 0.9B; 1: Vinaigrette ... 1.95
❑11, Nov 1994, V: Bash Brothers ... 1.95
❑12, Dec 1994, flipbook with Ultraverse Premiere #8 ... 3.50
❑13, Jan 1995, Final Issue ... 1.95

Sludge: Red X-Mas
Malibu / Ultraverse

❑1, Dec 1994 ... 2.50

Slug 'n' Ginger
Fantagraphics / Eros

❑1, b&w ... 2.25

Slutburger Stories
Rip Off

❑1/2nd, Oct 1992, b&w; 2nd printing; Adult ... 2.50
❑1, Jul 1990, b&w; Adult ... 2.50
❑2, Jul 1991, b&w; Adult ... 2.50

Small Favors
Fantagraphics / Eros

❑1, Nov 2000 ... 3.50
❑2, Feb 2001 ... 3.50
❑3, Jun 2001 ... 3.50
❑4, Oct 2001 ... 3.50

Small Gods
Image

❑1, Jun 2004, b&w ... 4.00
❑2, Jul 2004, b&w ... 2.95
❑3, Aug 2004, b&w ... 2.95
❑4, Sep 2004, b&w ... 2.95
❑5, Nov 2004, b&w ... 2.95
❑6, Feb 2005, b&w ... 2.95
❑7, Mar 2005; b&w ... 2.95
❑8, May 2005; b&w ... 2.95
❑9, Jun 2005; b&w ... 2.95
❑10, Sep 2005 ... 2.99
❑11, Oct 2005 ... 2.99
❑12, Feb 2006 ... 2.99

Small Gods Special
Image

❑0, Aug 2005 ... 2.99

Small Press Expo
Insight

❑1995, ca. 1995; Benefit Comic for American Cancer Society ... 2.95
❑1996, ca. 1996 ... 2.95
❑1997, ca. 1997; Benefit comic for Comic Legal Defense Fund ... 2.95

Small Press Swimsuit Spectacular
Allied

❑1, Jun 1995, b&w; pin-ups; benefit comic for American Cancer Society ... 2.95

Smallville
DC

❑1, May 2003; 48 pages ... 3.50
❑2, Jul 2003 ... 3.50
❑3, Sep 2003 ... 3.95
❑4, Nov 2003 ... 3.95
❑5, Jan 2004 ... 3.95
❑6, Mar 2004 ... 3.95
❑7, May 2004; Chloe Chronicles begins ... 3.95
❑8, Jul 2004 ... 3.95
❑9, Sep 2004 ... 3.95
❑10, Oct 2004 ... 3.95
❑11, Jan 2005 ... 3.95

Smash Comics
DC

❑1, May 1999; Justice Society Returns ... 1.99

Smax
DC / America's Best Comics

❑1, Oct 2003 ... 2.95
❑2, Nov 2003 ... 2.95
❑3, Dec 2003 ... 2.95
❑4, Feb 2004 ... 2.95
❑5, May 2004 ... 2.95

Smile
Mixx

❑1, Dec 1998; Sailor Moon ... 3.99
❑2 1999 ... 3.99
❑3 1999 ... 3.99
❑4 1999 ... 3.99
❑5 1999 ... 3.99
❑6 1999 ... 3.99
❑7, Dec 1999; Vol. 2 #1 ... 3.99
❑8; Vol. 2 #2 ... 3.99
❑9; Vol. 2 #3 ... 3.99
❑10; Vol. 2 #4 ... 3.99
❑11; Vol. 2 #5 ... 3.99
❑12; Vol. 2 #6 ... 3.99
❑13; Vol. 3 #1 ... 4.99
❑14; Vol. 3 #2 ... 4.99
❑15; Vol. 3 #3 ... 4.99
❑16; Vol. 3 #4 ... 4.99
❑17; Vol. 3 #5 ... 4.99
❑18; Vol. 3 #6 ... 4.99
❑19; Vol. 3 #7 ... 4.99
❑20; Vol. 3 #8 ... 4.99
❑21; Vol. 3 #9 ... 4.99
❑22; Vol. 3 #10 ... 4.99
❑23, Oct 2001; Vol. 3 #11 ... 4.99
❑24, Nov 2001; Vol. 3 #12 ... 4.99
❑25, Dec 2001; Vol. 4 #1 ... 4.99
❑26, Jan 2002; Vol. 4 #2 ... 4.99
❑27, Feb 2002; Vol. 4 #3 ... 4.99
❑28, Mar 2002; Vol. 4 #4 ... 4.99
❑29, Apr 2002; Vol. 4 #5 ... 4.99

Smile
Kitchen Sink

❑1, Adult ... 3.00

Smiley
Chaos

❑1, Jun 1998 ... 2.95

Smiley Anti-Holiday Special
Chaos!

❑1, Jan 1999 ... 2.95

Smiley's Spring Break
Chaos!

❑1, Apr 1999 ... 2.95

Smiley Wrestling Special
Chaos!

❑1, May 1999; NN; One-shot ... 2.95

Smilin' Ed
Fantaco

❑1 1982, b&w ... 1.25
❑2 1982, b&w ... 1.25
❑3 1982, b&w ... 1.25
❑4, Mar 1982, b&w ... 1.25

Smith Brown Jones
Kiwi

❑1, Jul 1997; b&w ... 4.00
❑2, Sep 1997; b&w ... 2.95
❑3, Nov 1997; b&w ... 2.95
❑4, Jan 1998; b&w ... 2.95
❑5, Apr 1998; b&w ... 2.95

Smith Brown Jones: Alien Accountant
Slave Labor

❑1, May 1998; b&w ... 2.95
❑2, Aug 1998; b&w ... 2.95
❑3, Nov 1998; b&w ... 2.95
❑4, Feb 1999; b&w ... 2.95

Smith Brown Jones: Halloween Special
Slave Labor

❑1, Oct 1998, b&w; Anthology ... 2.95

Smoke
Idea & Design Works

❑1, Jul 2005 ... 10.00
❑2, Aug 2005 ... 7.49
❑3, Sep 2005 ... 7.49

Smoke and Mirrors
Speakeasy Comics

❑1, Oct 2005 ... 2.99

Smokey Bear
Gold Key

❑1, Feb 1970 ... 8.00
❑2, May 1970 ... 5.00
❑3, Sep 1970 ... 4.00
❑4, Dec 1970 ... 3.00
❑5, Mar 1971 ... 3.00
❑6, Jun 1971 ... 3.00
❑7, Sep 1971, Production code 10249-109 ... 3.00
❑8, Dec 1971 ... 3.00
❑9, Mar 1972 ... 3.00
❑10, Jun 1972 ... 3.00
❑11, Sep 1972 ... 3.00
❑12, Dec 1972 ... 3.00
❑13, Mar 1973 ... 3.00

Smoot
Skip Williamson

❑1 ... 2.95

Smurfs
Marvel

❑1, Dec 1982 ... 4.00
❑2, Jan 1983 ... 4.00
❑3, Feb 1983 ... 4.00

Smut the Alternative Comic
Wiltshire

❑1; Adult ... 3.00

Snack Bar
Big Town

❑1 ... 2.95

Snagglepuss
Gold Key

❑1, Oct 1962 ... 45.00
❑2, Dec 1962 ... 30.00

Other grades: Multiply price above by 5/6 for VF/NM • 2/3 for VERY FINE • 1/3 for FINE • 1/5 for VERY GOOD • 1/8 for GOOD

❑3, Mar 1963 .... 30.00
❑4, Jun 1963 .... 30.00

Snake
Special Studio
❑1, Dec 1989, b&w 3.50

Snake Eyes
Fantagraphics
❑1, b&w 7.95
❑2, b&w 7.95
❑3, b&w 7.95

Snake Plissken Chronicles
CrossGen
❑1/A, Jun 2003 .... 2.99
❑1/B, Jun 2003 .... 2.99
❑2, Sep 2003 .... 2.99

Snakes on a Plane
DC
❑1, Nov 2006 .... 2.99
❑2, Dec 2006 .... 2.99

Snak Posse
HCOM
❑1, Jun 1994; 1st ap 1.95
❑2, Jul 1994 .... 1.95

Snap Dragons
Dork Storm
❑1, Aug 2002 .... 2.95
❑1/Variant, Aug 2002 .... 2.95
❑2, Oct 2002 .... 2.95
❑3, May 2003 .... 2.95

Snap the Punk Turtle
Super Crew
❑½ 2.25

Snarf
Kitchen Sink
❑1, Feb 1972, Adult 10.00
❑2, Aug 1972, Adult 8.00
❑3, Nov 1972, WE (c); WE (a); Adult 8.00
❑4, Mar 1973, Adult 8.00
❑5, Mar 1974, HK (c);Adult 6.00
❑6, Feb 1976; Adult 6.00
❑7, Feb 1977; Adult 6.00
❑8, Oct 1978; Adult 6.00
❑9, Feb 1981; Adult 6.00
❑10, Feb 1987; A: Omaha the Cat Dancer. Adult 6.00
❑11, Feb 1989; Adult 4.00
❑12, ca. 1989; Adult 4.00
❑13, Dec 1989; Adult 4.00
❑14, Mar 1990; Adult 4.00
❑15, Oct 1990; Adult 5.00

Snarl
Caliber
❑1, b&w 2.50
❑2, b&w 2.50
❑3, b&w 2.50

Snoid Comics
Kitchen Sink
❑1, Dec 1979 .... 2.00

Snooper and Blabber Detectives
Gold Key
❑1, Nov 1962 .... 100.00
❑2, Feb 1963 .... 75.00
❑3, May 1963 .... 75.00

S'Not for Kids
Vortex
❑1, b&w 6.95

Snowbuni
Mu
❑1, Jan 1991 .... 3.25

Snow Drop
Tokyopop
❑1, Jan 2004, b&w; Graphic novel; b&w 9.99
❑2, Mar 2004; Graphic novel; b&w 9.99
❑3, May 2004; Graphic novel; b&w 9.99
❑4, Jul 2004; Graphic novel; b&w 9.99
❑5, Sep 2004; Graphic novel; b&w 9.99
❑6, Nov 2004; Graphic novel; b&w 9.99
❑7, Jan 2005; Graphic novel; b&w 9.99
❑8, Mar 2005; Graphic novel; b&w 9.99
❑9, May 2005; Graphic novel; b&w 9.99
❑10, Aug 2005; Graphic novel; b&w 9.99
❑11, Nov 2005 .... 9.99

Snowman
Express / Entity
❑1, Nov 1996; 1: Snowman 5.00
❑1/A 1996; 1: Snowman. variant cover 6.00
❑1/2nd, Jul 1996, b&w; 1: Snowman. no cover price; given out at 1996 Comic Con International: San Diego 2.50
❑2 1996 .... 4.00
❑2/A, Mar 1996; variant cover 5.00
❑2/2nd 1996; 2nd printing 2.50
❑3, Jun 1996 .... 3.00
❑3/A 1996; variant cover 3.00

Snowman: 1944
Entity
❑1, Oct 1996 .... 2.75

Snow White
Marvel
❑1, Jan 1995; lead story is reprint of Dell Four Color #49 .... 2.00

Snow White and the Seven Dwarfs
Gladstone
❑1; Includes poster 3.50

Snuff
Boneyard
❑1, May 1997, b&w; Adult 2.95

Soap Opera Love
Charlton
❑1, Feb 1983 .... 25.00
❑2, Mar 1983 .... 15.00
❑3, Jun 1983 .... 15.00

Soap Opera Romances
Charlton
❑1, Jul 1982, Nurse Betsy Crane 12.00
❑2, Sep 1982, Nurse Betsy Crane 8.00
❑3, Dec 1983, Nurse Betsy Crane 8.00
❑4, Jan 1983, Nurse Betsy Crane 8.00
❑5, Mar 1983, Nurse Betsy Crane 8.00

SOB: Special Operations Branch
Promethean
❑1, May 1994, b&w; 1: Bandwidth; 1: Ferret (Prometheus); 1: Orion (Major James T. Greene); 1: Polymorph; 1: SOB; D: Bandwidth 2.25

Socketeer
Kardia
❑1, b&w; parody 2.25

Sock Monkey
Dark Horse
❑1, Sep 1998, b&w 2.95
❑2, Oct 1998, b&w 2.95

Sock Monkey
Dark Horse / Maverick
❑1, Jul 1999, b&w 2.95
❑2, Aug 1999, b&w 2.95

Sock Monkey
Dark Horse / Maverick
❑1, Nov 2000 .... 2.99
❑2, Dec 2000 .... 2.99

Sock Monkey
Dark Horse
❑1, May 2003 .... 2.99
❑2, Aug 2003 .... 2.99

Sock Monkey: The Inches Incident
Dark Horse
❑1, Nov 2006, b&w 2.99
❑2, Dec 2006, b&w 2.99

Socrates in Love
Viz
❑1, Oct 2005 .... 8.99

So Dark the Rose
CFD
❑1, Oct 1995; NN 2.95

Sofa Jet City Crisis
Visual Assault
❑1, b&w; NN 6.95

S.O.F.T. Corps
Spoof
❑1 .... 2.95

Sojourn
Dreamer
❑1, May 1998 .... 2.10
❑2 .... 2.10
❑3 .... 2.10
❑4 .... 2.10
❑5 .... 2.10
❑6 .... 3.15
❑7 .... 3.15
❑8 .... 3.15
❑9 .... 3.15
❑10 .... 3.15

Sojourn
CrossGen
❑1, Aug 2001 .... 5.00
❑2, Sep 2001 .... 2.95
❑3, Oct 2001 .... 2.95
❑4, Nov 2001 .... 2.95
❑5, Dec 2001 .... 2.95
❑6, Jan 2002 .... 2.95
❑7, Feb 2002 .... 2.95
❑8, Mar 2002 .... 2.95
❑9, Apr 2002 .... 2.95
❑10, May 2002 .... 2.95
❑11, Jun 2002 .... 2.95
❑12, Jul 2002 .... 2.95
❑13, Aug 2002 .... 2.95
❑14, Sep 2002 .... 2.95
❑15, Oct 2002 .... 2.95
❑16, Nov 2002 .... 2.95
❑17, Dec 2002 .... 2.95
❑18, Jan 2003 .... 2.95
❑19, Feb 2003 .... 2.95
❑20, Mar 2003 .... 2.95
❑21, Apr 2003 .... 2.95
❑22, May 2003 .... 2.95
❑23, Jun 2003 .... 2.95
❑24, Jul 2003 .... 2.95
❑25, Sep 2003 .... 1.00
❑26, Sep 2003 .... 2.95
❑27, Oct 2003 .... 2.95
❑28, Nov 2003 .... 2.95
❑29, Dec 2003 .... 2.95
❑30, Jan 2004 .... 2.95
❑31, Feb 2004; Kiss, Kiss, Bang, Bang preview 2.95
❑32, Mar 2004 .... 2.95
❑33, Apr 2004; Negaton War preview 2.95
❑34, May 2004 .... 2.95
❑34/2nd, Apr 2004 .... 2.95
❑Special 1, Sep 2001; Collects Prequel and #1 .... 3.95

Sojourn Prequel
CrossGen
❑1, Jul 2001; 32 page story 5.00

Solar Lord
Image
❑1, Mar 1999 .... 2.50
❑2, Apr 1999 .... 2.50
❑3, May 1999 .... 2.50
❑4, Jun 1999 .... 2.50
❑5, Jul 1999 .... 2.50
❑6, Aug 1999 .... 2.50
❑7, Sep 1999 .... 2.50

Solarman
Marvel
❑1, Jan 1989; O: Solarman 1.00
❑2, May 1990 .... 1.00

Solar, Man of the Atom
Valiant
❑1, Sep 1991; BL (w); O: Solar 7.00
❑2, Oct 1991; BL (w); DP (a); O: Solar 5.00
❑3, Nov 1991; BL (w); O: Solar. 1: Toyo Harada. 1: Harbinger Foundation 5.00
❑4, Dec 1991; DP (a); O: Solar 5.00
❑5, Jan 1992 EC (a) 5.00
❑6, Feb 1992; DP (a); V: Spider-Aliens 5.00
❑7, Mar 1992; DP (a); V: X-O armor 5.00
❑8, Apr 1992 .... 6.00
❑9, May 1992 .... 6.00
❑10, Jun 1992; 1: Eternal Warrior (cameo). All-black embossed cover 16.00
❑10/2nd, Jun 1992; 2nd printing 3.00
❑11, Jul 1992; SD (a); 1: Eternal Warrior (full appearance) 5.00
❑12, Aug 1992; FM (c); DP (a); Unity 4.00

Spirit of the Tao

D-Tron brings his style from Witchblade

©Image

Spirit: The New Adventures

Final ongoing title from Kitchen Sink

©Kitchen Sink

Splitting Image

Image decides to lampoon itself

©Image

Spooky

"Tuff Little Ghost" haunts, smokes

©Harvey

Spooky Spooktown

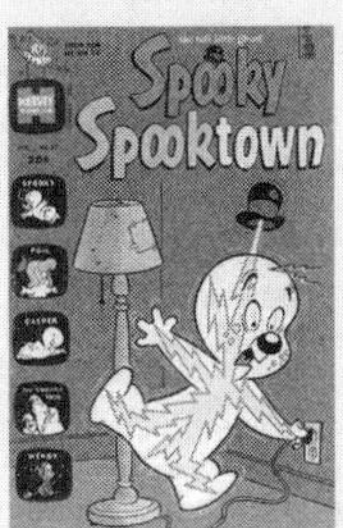

Series' name would not go over well today

©Harvey

N-MINT

❑13, Sep 1992; DP (w); DP (a); Unity 2.00
❑14, Oct 1992; 1: Fred Bender 4.00
❑15, Nov 1992 .... 2.00
❑16, Dec 1992; D: Lyja (Valiant)............ 2.00
❑17, Jan 1993 A: X-O Manowar 1.00
❑18, Feb 1993 .... 1.00
❑19, Mar 1993 .... 1.00
❑20, Apr 1993 .... 1.00
❑21, May 1993; V: Master Darque.......... 1.00
❑22, Jun 1993; V: Master Darque 1.00
❑23, Jul 1993; 1: Solar the Destroyer 1.00
❑24, Aug 1993; Serial Number Contest.. 1.00
❑25, Sep 1993; V: Doctor Eclipse. Secret Weapons x-over 1.00
❑26, Oct 1993 .... 1.00
❑27, Nov 1993 .... 1.00
❑28, Dec 1993; Solar the Destroyer vs. spiders 1.00
❑29, Jan 1994; Valiant Vision 1.00
❑30, Feb 1994 .... 1.00
❑31, Mar 1994 .... 1.00
❑32, Apr 1994 .... 1.00
❑33, May 1994; Valiant Vision; trading card 2.00
❑34, Jun 1994; Valiant Vision 1.00
❑35, Aug 1994; Valiant Vision 1.00
❑36, Sep 1994; V: Ravenus. V: Doctor Eclipse 1.00
❑37, Oct 1994; V: Ravenus. V: Doctor Eclipse 1.00
❑38, Nov 1994; Chaos Effect Epsilon 1 .. 1.00
❑39, Dec 1994 .... 1.00
❑40, Jan 1995 .... 1.00
❑41, Feb 1995 .... 1.00
❑42, Mar 1995 .... 2.00
❑43, Apr 1995 .... 2.00
❑44, May 1995 .... 2.00
❑45, Jun 1995 .... 2.00
❑46, Jul 1995 DG (a)............................ 2.00
❑47, Aug 1995 DG (a) 2.00
❑48, Sep 1995 DG (a) 2.00
❑49, Sep 1995 DG (a) 2.00
❑50, Oct 1995 DG (a) 2.00
❑51, Nov 1995 DG (a) 3.00
❑52, Nov 1995 DG (a) 3.00
❑53, Dec 1995 DG (a) 3.00
❑54, Dec 1995 DG (a) 3.00
❑55, Jan 1996 .... 3.00
❑56, Jan 1996 .... 3.00
❑57, Feb 1996 .... 4.00
❑58, Feb 1996 .... 4.00
❑59, Mar 1996; Texas destroyed 5.00
❑60, Apr 1996; Final Issue 10.00

Solar, Man of the Atom
Acclaim / Valiant

❑1, May 1997; lays groundwork for second Valiant universe 3.95

Solar, Man of the Atom: Hell on Earth
Acclaim

❑1, Jan 1998 .... 2.50
❑2, Feb 1998 .... 2.50
❑3, Mar 1998 .... 2.50
❑4, Apr 1998 .... 2.50

Solar, Man of the Atom: Revelations
Acclaim

❑1, Nov 1997 .... 3.95

N-MINT

Solar Stella
Sirius

❑1, Aug 2000, b&w; One-shot 2.95

Soldiers of Freedom
AC

❑1, Jul 1987............................ 1.75
❑2, Aug 1987 .... 1.95

Soldier X
Marvel

❑1, Sep 2002 .... 2.99
❑2, Oct 2002............................ 2.25
❑3, Nov 2002............................ 2.25
❑4, Dec 2002 .... 2.25
❑5, Jan 2003............................ 2.25
❑6, Feb 2003............................ 2.25
❑7, Mar 2003............................ 2.99
❑8, Apr 2003............................ 2.99
❑9, May 2003............................ 2.99
❑10, Jun 2003............................ 2.99
❑11, Jul 2003............................ 2.99
❑12, Aug 2003 .... 2.99

Sold Out
Fantaco

❑1, ca. 1986............................ 1.50
❑2, ca. 1987............................ 1.50

Solitaire
Malibu / Ultraverse

❑1, Nov 1993; 1: Solitaire. Comes polybagged with one of 4 "ace" trading cards 2.00
❑1/CS, Nov 1993; trading card.............. 2.50
❑2, Dec 1993; Break-Thru...................... 2.00
❑3, Feb 1994; O: Night Man.................. 2.00
❑4, Mar 1994; O: Solitaire...................... 2.00
❑5, Apr 1994............................ 2.00
❑6, May 1994............................ 1.95
❑7, Sep 1994; 1: Double Edge 1.95
❑8, Sep 1994; 1: The Degenerate.......... 1.95
❑9, Sep 1994; D: The Degenerate 1.95
❑10, Oct 1994............................ 1.95
❑11, Nov 1994............................ 1.95
❑12, Dec 1994; D: Jinn. D: Anton Lone; Final Issue 1.95

Solo
Marvel

❑1, Sep 1994; O: Solo........................ 1.75
❑2, Oct 1994............................ 1.75
❑3, Nov 1994............................ 1.75
❑4, Dec 1994; Final Issue...................... 1.75

Solo
Dark Horse

❑1, Jul 1996; Movie adaptation.............. 2.50
❑2, Aug 1996; Final Issue; Movie adaptation 2.50

Solo
DC

❑1, Jan 2005............................ 4.95
❑2, Feb 2005............................ 4.95
❑3, Mar 2005............................ 4.95
❑4, Jun 2005............................ 4.99
❑5, Jul 2005............................ 4.99
❑6, Oct 2005............................ 4.99
❑7, Dec 2005 .... 4.99
❑8, Feb 2006............................ 4.99

N-MINT

❑9, May 2006............................ 4.99
❑10, Jul 2006............................ 4.99
❑11, Sep 2006 .... 4.99
❑12, Nov 2006, Final issue.................... 4.99

Solo Avengers
Marvel

❑1, Dec 1987; JLee (a); I.D. card; 1st solo Mockingbird story............................ 1.00
❑2, Jan 1988; Captain Marvel 1.00
❑3, Feb 1988; BH (c); BH (a); V: Batroc. Moon Knight vs. Shroud 1.00
❑4, Mar 1988; Black Knight 1.00
❑5, Apr 1988; Scarlet Witch.................. 1.00
❑6, May 1988; Falcon 1.00
❑7, Jun 1988; Black Widow 1.00
❑8, Jul 1988; Hank Pym......................... 1.00
❑9, Aug 1988; Hellcat 1.00
❑10, Sep 1988; Doctor Druid 1.00
❑11, Oct 1988; Hercules 1.00
❑12, Nov 1988; Yellowjacket.................. 1.00
❑13, Dec 1988; Wonder Man 1.00
❑14, Jan 1989; Black Widow 1.00
❑15, Feb 1989; The Wasp 1.00
❑16, Mar 1989; Moondragon 1.00
❑17, Apr 1989; Sub-Mariner.................. 1.00
❑18, May 1989; Moondragon 1.00
❑19, Jun 1989; Black Panther................ 1.00
❑20, Jul 1989; Moondragon; series continues as Avengers Spotlight........ 1.00

Solo Ex-Mutants
Eternity

❑1 1987 .... 2.00
❑2, Feb 1988............................ 2.00
❑3, Apr 1988............................ 2.00
❑4 1988 .... 2.00
❑5 1988 .... 2.00
❑6, Jan 1989............................ 2.00

Solomon Kane
Marvel

❑1, Sep 1985; Double-size.................... 1.50
❑2, Nov 1985, KN (c) 1.25
❑3, Jan 1986, BSz (c) 1.25
❑4, Mar 1986 .... 1.25
❑5, May 1986............................ 1.25
❑6, Jul 1986 AW (a)............................ 1.25

Solomon Kane in 3-D
Blackthorne

❑1; Blackthorne 3-D Series #60 .... 2.50

Solson Christmas Special
Solson

❑1, ca. 1986; JLee (a); Samurai Santa; 1st Jim Lee art 3.00

Solson's Comic Talent Starsearch
Solson

❑1 .... 1.50
❑2 .... 1.50

Solus
CrossGen

❑1, Apr 2003............................ 2.95
❑2, May 2003............................ 2.95
❑3, Jun 2003............................ 2.95
❑4, Jul 2003............................ 2.95
❑5, Aug 2003 .... 2.95
❑6, Oct 2003............................ 2.95

Other grades: Multiply price above by 5/6 for VF/NM • 2/3 for VERY FINE • 1/3 for FINE • 1/5 for VERY GOOD • 1/8 for GOOD

N-MINT | N-MINT | N-MINT

❑7, Nov 2003 .... 2.95
❑8, Dec 2003 .... 2.95

Solution
Malibu / Ultraverse

❑0, Jan 1994; Promotional (coupon redemption) edition; no cover price.... 2.50
❑1, Sep 1993; 1: Quattro. 1: The Solution. 1: Outrage. 1: Dropkick. 1: Tech. 1: Shadowmage. 2.00
❑1/Ltd., Sep 1993; Ultra-Limited foil edition; 1: Quattro. 1: The Solution. 1: Outrage. 1: Dropkick. 1: Tech. 1: Shadowmage. 3.00
❑2, Oct 1993; Rune 2.50
❑3, Nov 1993 .... 2.00
❑4, Dec 1993; Break-Thru 2.00
❑5, Jan 1994; O: The Strangers. Dropkick solo story 1.95
❑6, Feb 1994; O: The Solution. O: Tech .. 1.95
❑7, Mar 1994; O: The Solution 1.95
❑8, Apr 1994; O: The Solution 1.95
❑9, Jun 1994 .... 1.95
❑10, Jul 1994 .... 1.95
❑11, Aug 1994 .... 1.95
❑12, Oct 1994 .... 1.95
❑13, Oct 1994 .... 1.95
❑14, Dec 1994 .... 1.95
❑15, Jan 1995 .... 1.95
❑16, Jan 1995; MZ (a); flipbook with Ultraverse Premiere #10 .... 3.50
❑17, Feb 1995 .... 2.50

Someplace Strange
Marvel / Epic

❑1; ca. 1988 .... 6.95

Somerset Holmes
Pacific

❑1, Sep 1983; BA (c); AW, BA (a); Published by Pacific Comics 2.50
❑2, Nov 1983 BA (c); AW, BA (a) 2.00
❑3, Feb 1984 BA (c); AW, BA (a) 2.00
❑4, Apr 1984 BA (c); AW, BA (a) 2.00
❑5, Nov 1984; BA (c); AW, BA (a); Eclipse begins publishing 2.00
❑6, Dec 1984 BA (c); AW, BA (a) 2.00

Some Tales from Gimbley
Harrier

❑1, Jun 1987 .... 1.95

Something
Strictly Underground

❑1 .... 2.95

Something at the Window is Scratching
Slave Labor

❑1 .... 9.95

Something Different
Wooga Central

❑1, b&w; Adult 2.00
❑2, Spr 1992; Spring 1992; Flexidisc; Adult 2.00
❑3, Win 1993, flexidisc 2.00

Something Wicked
Image

❑1, Nov 2003 .... 2.95
❑2, Dec 2003 .... 2.95
❑3, Apr 2004 .... 2.95

Some Trouble of a SeRRious Nature
Crusade

❑1, Nov 2001 .... 3.50

Somnambulo: Sleep of the Just
9th Circle

❑1, Aug 1996, b&w 2.95

Son of Vulcan
DC

❑1, Jul 2005 .... 2.99
❑2, Aug 2005 .... 2.99
❑3, Sep 2005 .... 2.99
❑4, Oct 2005 .... 2.99
❑5 2005 .... 2.99
❑6, Jan 2006 .... 2.99

Songbook (Alan Moore's...)
Caliber

❑1, Collected from issues of Negative Burn 5.95

Song of Mykal: Atlantis Fantasyworld 25th Anniversary Comic
Atlantis Fantasyworld

❑1, Nov 2001 .... 2.99

Song of the Cid
Tome

❑1, b&w 2.95
❑2, b&w 2.95

Song of the Sirens
Millennium

❑1, b&w 2.95
❑2, b&w 2.95

Songs of Bastards
Conquest

❑1, b&w 2.95

Sonic & Knuckles: Mecha Madness Special
Archie

❑1 1995 .... 2.00

Sonic & Knuckles Special
Archie

❑1, Aug 1995 .... 2.00

Sonic Blast Special
Archie

❑1, Oct 1996 .... 2.00

Sonic Disruptors
DC

❑1, Dec 1987 .... 1.00
❑2, Jan 1988 .... 1.00
❑3, Feb 1988 .... 1.00
❑4, Mar 1988 .... 1.00
❑5, May 1988 .... 1.00
❑6, Jun 1988 .... 1.00
❑7, Jul 1988; series goes on hiatus with unresolved storyline; Series cancelled 1.00

Sonic Live Special
Archie

❑1, Knuckles back-up continues in Sonic the Hedgehog #45 .... 2.00

Sonic Quest - The Death Egg Saga
Archie

❑2, Jan 1997 .... 1.50

Sonic's Friendly Nemesis Knuckles
Archie

❑1, Jul 1996 .... 3.00
❑2, Aug 1996 .... 2.00
❑3, Sep 1996 .... 2.00

Sonic the Hedgehog
Archie

❑1, ca. 1993 .... 20.00
❑2, ca. 1993 .... 10.00
❑3, ca. 1993 .... 10.00

Sonic the Hedgehog
Archie

❑0, Feb 1993 .... 9.00
❑1, Jul 1993 .... 12.00
❑2, Sep 1993 .... 9.00
❑3, Oct 1993 .... 9.00
❑4, Nov 1993 .... 7.00
❑5, Dec 1993 .... 7.00
❑6, Jan 1994 .... 6.00
❑7, Feb 1994 .... 6.00
❑8, Mar 1994 .... 6.00
❑9, Apr 1994 .... 6.00
❑10, May 1994 .... 6.00
❑11, Jun 1994 .... 4.00
❑12, Jul 1994 .... 4.00
❑13, Aug 1994 .... 4.00
❑14, Sep 1994 .... 4.00
❑15, Oct 1994 .... 4.00
❑16, Nov 1994 .... 4.00
❑17, Dec 1994 .... 4.00
❑18, Jan 1995 .... 4.00
❑19, Feb 1995 .... 4.00
❑20, Mar 1995 .... 4.00
❑21, Apr 1995 .... 3.00
❑22, May 1995 .... 3.00
❑23, Jun 1995 .... 3.00
❑24, Jul 1995 .... 3.00
❑25, Aug 1995 .... 3.00
❑26, Sep 1995 .... 3.00
❑27, Oct 1995 .... 3.00
❑28, Nov 1995 .... 3.00
❑29, Dec 1995 .... 3.00
❑30, Jan 1996 .... 3.00
❑31, Feb 1996 .... 3.00
❑32, Mar 1996 .... 3.00
❑33, Apr 1996 .... 3.00
❑34, May 1996 .... 3.00
❑35, Jun 1996 .... 3.00
❑36, Jul 1996 .... 3.00
❑37, Aug 1996, Bunnie Rabbot back-up story 3.00
❑38, Sep 1996, Tails solo story 3.00
❑39, Oct 1996 .... 3.00
❑40, Nov 1996 .... 3.00
❑41, Dec 1996 .... 3.00
❑42, Jan 1997 .... 3.00
❑43, Feb 1997 .... 3.00
❑44, Mar 1997 .... 3.00
❑45, Apr 1997 .... 3.00
❑46, May 1997 .... 3.00
❑47, Jun 1997 .... 3.00
❑48, Jul 1997 .... 3.00
❑49, Aug 1997 .... 3.00
❑50, Sep 1997 .... 3.00
❑51, Oct 1997 .... 1.50
❑52, Nov 1997, noir issue 1.50
❑53, Dec 1997 .... 1.50
❑54, Jan 1998 .... 1.50
❑55, Feb 1998 .... 1.50
❑56, Mar 1998 .... 1.50
❑57, Apr 1998 .... 1.50
❑58, May 1998 .... 1.50
❑59, Jun 1998 .... 1.50
❑60, Jul 1998 .... 1.50
❑61, Aug 1998 .... 1.50
❑62, Sep 1998 .... 1.50
❑63, Oct 1998 .... 1.50
❑64, Nov 1998 .... 1.75
❑65, Dec 1998 .... 1.75
❑66, Jan 1999 .... 1.75
❑67, Feb 1999 .... 1.75
❑68, Mar 1999 .... 1.75
❑69, Apr 1999 .... 1.79
❑70, May 1999 .... 1.79
❑71, Jun 1999 .... 1.79
❑72, Jul 1999 .... 1.79
❑73, Aug 1999 .... 1.79
❑74, Sep 1999 .... 1.79
❑75, Oct 1999 .... 1.79
❑76, Nov 1999 .... 1.79
❑77, Dec 1999 .... 1.79
❑78, Jan 2000 .... 1.79
❑79, Feb 2000 .... 1.79
❑80, Mar 2000 .... 1.79
❑81, Apr 2000 .... 1.79
❑82, May 2000 .... 1.79
❑83, Jun 2000 .... 1.99
❑84, Jul 2000 .... 1.99
❑85, Aug 2000 .... 1.99
❑86, Sep 2000 .... 1.99
❑87, Oct 2000 .... 1.99
❑88, Nov 2000 .... 1.99
❑89, Dec 2000 .... 1.99
❑90, Jan 2001 .... 1.99
❑91, Feb 2001 .... 1.99
❑92, Mar 2001 .... 1.99
❑93, Apr 2001 .... 1.99
❑94, May 2001 .... 1.99
❑95, Jun 2001 .... 1.99
❑96, Jul 2001 .... 1.99
❑97, Aug 2001 .... 1.99
❑98, Sep 2001 .... 1.99
❑99, Oct 2001 .... 1.99
❑100, Nov 2001 .... 1.99
❑101, Nov 2001 .... 2.19
❑102, Dec 2001 .... 2.19
❑103, Jan 2002 .... 2.19
❑104, Feb 2002 .... 2.19
❑105, Mar 2002 .... 2.19
❑106, Apr 2002 .... 2.19
❑107, May 2002 .... 2.19
❑108, May 2002 .... 2.19
❑109, Jun 2002 .... 2.19
❑110, Jul 2002 .... 1.99
❑111, Aug 2002 .... 2.19
❑112, Sep 2002 .... 2.19
❑113, Oct 2002 .... 2.19
❑114, Nov 2002 .... 2.19

Spring Break Comics

Beach humor from AC Comics
©AC

SpyBoy

Peter David series had three 13th issues
©Dark Horse

Squadron Supreme

Mark Gruenwald's look a t an alternate Earth
©Marvel

Squee!

Jhnoen Vazquez is the Tim Burton of comics
©Slave Labor

Stanley and His Monster

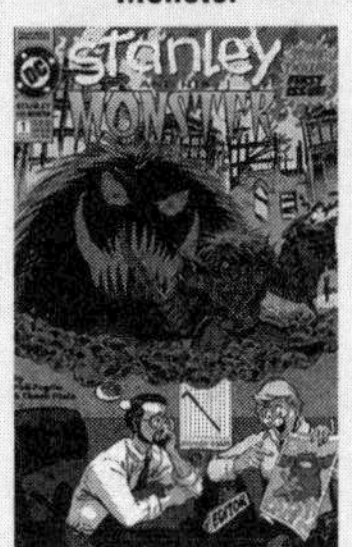
Phil Foglio's version of the 1960s silliness
©DC

N-MINT

❑115, Dec 2002 2.19
❑116, Jan 2003 2.19
❑117, Feb 2003 2.19
❑118, ca. 2003 2.19
❑119, Mar 2003 2.19
❑120, Apr 2003 2.19
❑121, May 2003 2.19
❑122, Jun 2003 2.19
❑123, Jul 2003 2.19
❑124, Aug 2003 2.19
❑125, Sep 2003 2.19
❑126, Oct 2003 2.19
❑127, Nov 2003 2.19
❑128, Dec 2003 2.19
❑129, Jan 2004 2.19
❑130, Feb 2004 2.19
❑131, Mar 2004 2.19
❑132, Mar 2004 2.19
❑133, Apr 2004 2.19
❑134, May 2004 2.19
❑135, Jun 2004 2.19
❑136, Jul 2004 2.19
❑137, Aug 2004 2.19
❑138, Sep 2004 2.19
❑139, Oct 2004 2.19
❑140, Nov 2004 2.19
❑141, Dec 2004 2.19
❑142, Jan 2005 2.19
❑143, Feb 2005 2.19
❑144, Feb 2005 2.19
❑145, Mar 2005 2.19
❑146, Apr 2005 2.19
❑147, May 2005 2.19
❑148, Jun 2005 2.19
❑149, Jul 2005 2.25
❑150, Aug 2005 2.25
❑151, Sep 2005 2.25
❑152, Oct 2005; Includes Bionicles insert comic 2.25
❑153, Nov 2005 2.25
❑154, Dec 2005 2.25
❑155, Jan 2006 2.25
❑156, Feb 2006 2.25
❑157, Feb 2006 2.25
❑158, Mar 2006 2.25
❑159, Apr 2006 2.25
❑160, May 2006 2.25
❑161, Jun 2006 2.25
❑163, Aug 2006 2.25
❑164, Aug 2006 2.25
❑165, Oct 2006 2.25
❑166, Nov 2006 2.25
❑167, Dec 2006 2.25
❑168, Jan 2007, Includes 3-D Heroscape glasses; Includes Teen Titans: Sparktop mini-comic 2.25
❑169, Jan 2007, Includes 3-D Heroscape glasses; Includes Teen Titans: Sparktop mini-comic 2.25
❑170, Feb 2007 2.25
❑171 2.25
❑172 2.25
❑173 2.25
❑174 2.25
❑175 2.25
❑176 2.25

N-MINT

❑177 2.25
❑178 2.25
❑179 2.25
❑180 2.25
❑181 2.25
❑182 2.25
❑183 2.25
❑184 2.25
❑185 2.25
❑186 2.25
❑187 2.25
❑188 2.25
❑189 2.25
❑190 2.25
❑191 2.25
❑192 2.25
❑193 2.25
❑194 2.25
❑195 2.25
❑196 2.25
❑197 2.25
❑Special 1, Nov 1997, ca.1997 3.00
❑Special 2, ca. 1997, Brave New World 2.00
❑Special 3, Jan 1998, Firsts 2.25
❑Special 4, Mar 1998 2.25
❑Special 5, Jun 1998, Sonic Kids 2.25
❑Special 6, Sep 1998, Director's Cut; expanded version of Sonic #50 2.25
❑Special 7, Dec 1998, crossover with Image 2.25
❑Special 8, Mar 1999 2.25
❑Special 9, Jun 1999 2.29
❑Special 10, Sep 1999, A: Sabrina 2.29
❑Special 11, Dec 1999 2.29
❑Special 12, Apr 2000 2.29
❑Special 13, Jun 2000 2.29
❑Special 14, Sep 2000 2.29
❑Special 15, Feb 2001 2.49

Sonic the Hedgehog in Your Face Special
Archie

❑1 2.00

Sonic the Hedgehog Triple Trouble Special
Archie

❑1, Oct 1995 2.00

Sonic vs. Knuckles Battle Royal Special
Archie

❑1, ca. 1997 2.00

Sonic X
Archie

❑1, Nov 2005 2.25
❑2, Nov 2005 2.25
❑3, Dec 2005 2.25
❑4, Jan 2006 2.25
❑5, Apr 2006 2.25
❑6, May 2006 2.25
❑7, May 2006 2.25
❑8, Jul 2006 2.25
❑9, Aug 2006 2.25
❑10, Aug 2006 2.25
❑11, Sep 2006 2.25
❑12, Nov 2006 2.25

N-MINT

❑13, Dec 2006 2.25
❑14, Jan 2007, Includes 3-D Heroscape glasses; Includes Teen Titans: Sparktop mini-comic 2.25
❑15, Feb 2007 2.25
❑16 2.25
❑17 2.25
❑18 2.25
❑19 2.25
❑20 2.25
❑21 2.25
❑22 2.25
❑23 2.25
❑24 2.25
❑25 2.25
❑26 2.25
❑27 2.25
❑28 2.25
❑29 2.25
❑30 2.25
❑31 2.25
❑32 2.25
❑33 2.25
❑34 2.25
❑35 2.25
❑36 2.25
❑37 2.25
❑38 2.25
❑39 2.25
❑40 2.25

Son of Ambush Bug
DC

❑1, Jul 1986 KG (c); KG (w); KG (a) 1.50
❑2, Aug 1986 KG (c); KG (w); KG (a) 1.50
❑3, Sep 1986 KG (c); KG (w); KG (a) 1.50
❑4, Oct 1986 KG (c); KG (w); KG (a) 1.50
❑5, Nov 1986 KG (c); KG (w); KG (a) 1.50
❑6, Dec 1986 KG (c); KG (w); KG (a) 1.50

Son of M
Marvel

❑1, Feb 2006 2.99
❑2, Mar 2006 2.99
❑3, Apr 2006 2.99
❑4, May 2006 2.99
❑5, Jun 2006 2.99
❑6, Aug 2006, Final Issue 2.99

Son of Mutant World
Fantagor

❑1, ca. 1990 3.00
❑2, ca. 1990 2.50
❑3, b&w; Black and white issues begin 2.00
❑4, b&w; ca. 1990 2.00
❑5, ca. 1990, b&w 2.00

Son of Rampage
Slap Happy

❑2, ca. 1998 13.95

Son of Satan
Marvel

❑1, Dec 1975, Marvel Value Stamp #13: Dr. Strange 20.00
❑2, Feb 1976 15.00
❑3, Apr 1976 10.00
❑3/30¢, Apr 1976, 30¢ regional variant 15.00
❑4, Jun 1976, CR (a) 10.00

Other grades: Multiply price above by 5/6 for VF/NM • 2/3 for VERY FINE • 1/3 for FINE • 1/5 for VERY GOOD • 1/8 for GOOD

❑4/30¢, Jun 1976, CR (a); 30¢ regional variant ... 15.00
❑5, Aug 1976 ... 10.00
❑5/30¢, Aug 1976, 30¢ regional variant. 15.00
❑6, Oct 1976 ... 10.00
❑7, Dec 1976 ... 10.00
❑8, Feb 1977 ... 10.00

Son of Yuppies From Hell
Marvel

❑1 ... 3.50

Sons of Katie Elder
Dell

❑1, Sep 1965, Photo cover with John Wayne, Dean Martin ... 125.00

Sophistikats Katch-Up Kollection
Silk Purrs

❑1, Jul 1995, b&w; NN ... 5.95

Sorcerer's Children
Sillwill

❑1, Dec 1998 ... 2.95
❑2, Feb 1999 ... 2.95
❑3, Apr 1999 ... 2.95
❑4, Jul 1999 ... 2.95

S.O.S.
Fantagraphics

❑1, b&w; NN; Adult ... 2.75

Soul
Flashpoint

❑1, Mar 1994 ... 2.50
❑1/Gold, Mar 1994; Gold edition ... 3.00

Soulfire
Aspen

❑0, May 2004 ... 5.00
❑0/Conv, May 2004 ... 7.00
❑0/Dynamic, May 2004 ... 15.00
❑1/Diamond, May 2004 ... 5.00
❑1, May 2004 ... 7.00
❑1/DF, May 2004 ... 15.00
❑1/Jay, May 2004 ... 6.00
❑1/Virgin, May 2004 ... 8.00
❑1/Wizard, May 2004 ... 5.00
❑2 ... 6.00
❑2/Rupps ... 10.00
❑3 ... 5.00
❑4 2005 ... 2.99
❑4/Variant ... 4.00
❑4/Campbell ... 3.00
❑4/Lee ... 4.00
❑4/Conv 2005; Wizard World Los Angeles (March 2004) convention. 3,500 created ... 10.00

Soulfire: Beginnings
Aspen

❑1, Jun 2003 ... 4.00
❑1/Conv, Jun 2003 ... 10.00

Soulfire: Dying of the Light
Aspen

❑0, Aug 2005 ... 2.50
❑0/Conv, Aug 2005 ... 15.00
❑1, Sep 2005 ... 2.99
❑2, Oct 2005 ... 2.99

Soulfire Preview
Aspen

❑1, Jun 2003 ... 4.00
❑1/Conv, Jun 2003; Pittsburgh Comic Con Edition ... 8.00

Soul of a Samurai
Image

❑1, Jun 2003 ... 5.95
❑2, Jul 2003 ... 5.95
❑3, Jan 2004 ... 5.95
❑4, Aug 2004; Final book ... 5.95

Soulquest
Innovation

❑1, Apr 1989 ... 3.95

Soul Saga
Top Cow

❑1, Feb 2000 ... 2.50
❑2, Apr 2000 ... 2.50
❑3, Aug 2000 ... 2.50
❑4, Oct 2000 ... 2.95
❑5, Apr 2001 ... 2.95

Soulsearchers and Company
Claypool

❑1, Jun 1993, b&w; RHo, PD (w) ... 4.00
❑2, Jul 1993, b&w RHo, PD (w); RHo (a) ... 3.00
❑3, Aug 1993, b&w; RHo, PD (w); Sandman parody ... 3.00
❑4, Sep 1993, b&w RHo, PD (w) ... 3.00
❑5, Oct 1993, b&w RHo, PD (w) ... 3.00
❑6, Feb 1994, b&w RHo, PD (w) ... 2.50
❑7, May 1994, b&w RHo, PD (w) ... 2.50
❑8, Jul 1994, b&w RHo, PD (w) ... 2.50
❑9, Oct 1995, b&w RHo, PD (w) ... 2.50
❑10, Jan 1995, b&w RHo, PD (w) ... 2.50
❑11, Feb 1995, b&w RHo, PD (w); RHo (a) ... 2.50
❑12, May 1995, b&w RHo, PD (w) ... 2.50
❑13, Jul 1995, b&w; RHo, PD (w); DC (a) ... 2.50
❑14, Oct 1995, b&w RHo, PD (w) ... 2.50
❑15, Dec 1995, b&w RHo, PD (w); DC (a) ... 2.50
❑16, Feb 1996, b&w RHo, PD (w) ... 2.50
❑17, Apr 1996, b&w RHo, PD (w); DC (a) ... 2.50
❑18, Jun 1996, b&w RHo, PD (w); DC (a) ... 2.50
❑19, Aug 1996, b&w RHo, PD (w); DC (a) ... 2.50
❑20, Oct 1996, b&w RHo, PD (w); DC (a) ... 2.50
❑21, Dec 1996, b&w RHo, PD (w); DC (a) ... 2.50
❑22, Feb 1997, b&w RHo, PD (w); DC (a) ... 2.50
❑23, Apr 1997, b&w RHo, PD (w); DC (a) ... 2.50
❑24, Jun 1997, b&w RHo, PD (w); DC (a) ... 2.50
❑25, Aug 1997, b&w RHo, PD (w); DC (a) ... 2.50
❑26, Oct 1997, b&w RHo, PD (w); DC (a) ... 2.50
❑27, Dec 1997, b&w RHo, PD (w); DC (a) ... 2.50
❑28, Feb 1998, b&w RHo, PD (w); DC (a) ... 2.50
❑29, Apr 1998, b&w; RHo, PD (w); DC, JM (a); O: Hot-2-Trot ... 2.50
❑30, Jun 1998, b&w RHo, PD (w); DC (a) ... 2.50
❑31, Aug 1998, b&w; RHo, PD (w); Li'l Soulsearchers ... 2.50
❑32, Sep 1998, b&w RHo, PD (w); DC (a) ... 2.50
❑33, Nov 1998, b&w RHo, PD (w); DC (a) ... 2.50
❑34, Jan 1999, b&w RHo, PD (w); DC (a) ... 2.50
❑35, Mar 1999, b&w RHo, PD (w); DC (a) ... 2.50
❑36, May 1999, b&w RHo, PD (w); DS (a) ... 2.50
❑37, Jul 1999, b&w RHo, PD (w); DC (a) ... 2.50
❑38, Sep 1999, b&w RHo, PD (w); DC (a) ... 2.50
❑39, Nov 1999, b&w RHo, PD (w) ... 2.50
❑40, Jan 2000, b&w PD (w); DC (a) ... 2.50
❑41, Mar 2000, b&w RHo, PD (w) ... 2.50
❑42, May 2000, b&w RHo, PD (w); DC (a) ... 2.50
❑43, Jul 2000, b&w DC, PD (w); DC (a). 2.50
❑44, Sep 2000, b&w RHo, PD (w); DC (a) ... 2.50
❑45, Nov 2000, b&w ... 2.50
❑46, Jan 2001, b&w ... 2.50
❑47, Mar 2001, b&w ... 2.50
❑48, May 2001, b&w ... 2.50
❑49, Jul 2001, b&w ... 2.50
❑50, Sep 2001, b&w ... 2.50
❑51, Nov 2001, b&w ... 2.50
❑52, Jan 2002, b&w ... 2.50
❑53, Mar 2002, b&w ... 2.50
❑54, May 2002, b&w ... 2.50
❑55, Jul 2002, b&w ... 2.50
❑56, Sep 2002, b&w ... 2.50
❑57, Nov 2002, b&w ... 2.50
❑58, Jan 2003, b&w ... 2.50
❑59, Mar 2003, b&w ... 2.50
❑60, May 2003, b&w ... 2.50
❑61, Jul 2003, b&w ... 2.50
❑62, Sep 2003, b&w ... 2.50
❑63, Nov 2003, b&w ... 2.50
❑64, Jan 2004, b&w ... 2.50
❑65, Mar 2004, b&w ... 2.50
❑66, May 2004, b&w ... 2.50
❑67, Jul 2004, b&w ... 2.50
❑68, ca. 2004 ... 2.50
❑69 2004 ... 2.50

Soul to Seoul
Tokyopop

❑1, Jan 2005, Graphic novel; b&w ... 9.99
❑2, Apr 2005; Graphic novel; b&w ... 9.99
❑3, Oct 2005 ... 9.99

Soul Trek
Spoof

❑1, Jul 1992, b&w; parody ... 2.95
❑2, b&w; parody ... 2.95

Soulwind
Image

❑1, Mar 1997, b&w ... 2.95
❑2, Apr 1997, b&w ... 2.95
❑3, May 1997, b&w ... 2.95
❑4, Jun 1997, b&w ... 2.95
❑5, Oct 1997, b&w ... 2.95
❑6, Dec 1997, b&w ... 2.95
❑7, Feb 1998, b&w ... 2.95
❑8, Apr 1998, b&w ... 2.95

Soupy Sales Comic Book
Archie

❑1, Jan 1965 ... 80.00

Southern Blood
Jm Comics

❑1, Aug 1992, b&w ... 2.50
❑2, b&w ... 2.50

Southern Cumfort
Fantagraphics / Eros

❑1 ... 2.95

Southern-Fried Homicide
Cremo / Shel-Tone

❑1, b&w; cardstock cover ... 7.95

Southern Knights
Guild

❑2, Apr 1983; Title changes to Southern Knights ... 2.00
❑3, Jul 1983; O: Electrode ... 2.00
❑4, Nov 1983 ... 2.00
❑5, Feb 1984 ... 2.00
❑6, Jun 1984; O: Connie Ronnin ... 2.00
❑7, Sep 1984 ... 2.00
❑8, Apr 1985; Publisher changed to Comics Interview ... 2.00
❑9, Jun 1985 ... 2.00
❑10, Aug 1985 ... 2.00
❑11, Oct 1985; Electrode ... 2.00
❑12, Dec 1985 ... 2.00
❑13, Feb 1986; Connie Ronnin ... 2.00
❑14, Apr 1986 ... 2.00
❑15, Jun 1986 ... 2.00
❑16, Aug 1986 ... 2.00
❑17, Oct 1986 ... 2.00
❑18, Dec 1986 ... 2.00
❑19, Feb 1987 ... 2.00
❑20, Apr 1987 ... 2.00
❑21, Jun 1987 ... 2.00
❑22, Aug 1987 ... 2.00
❑23, Dec 1987 ... 2.00
❑24, Dec 1987 ... 2.00
❑25, Feb 1988 ... 2.00
❑26, Apr 1988 ... 2.00
❑27, Jun 1988 ... 2.00
❑28, Aug 1988 ... 2.00
❑29, Aug 1988 ... 2.00
❑30, Sep 1988 ... 2.00
❑31, Oct 1988; Electrode and Dragon; Kristin and Connie Ronnin; Carl and Larry ... 2.00
❑32, Jan 1989 ... 2.00
❑33, Sep 1989 ... 2.00
❑34, Dec 1989 ... 2.25
❑35, Sep 1992, b&w; GP (c) ... 3.50
❑36, Nov 1992, b&w ... 3.50
❑Holiday 1, Oct 1988; Wizard promotional edition; Dread Halloween Special; b&w Reprint ... 2.25
❑Special 1, Apr 1989, b&w; Reprints ... 2.25

Southern Knights Primer
Comics Interview

❑1, b&w; Reprints ... 2.25

Southern Squadron
Aircel

❑1, Aug 1990; 1: Nightlifter; 1: Southern Squadron; 1: The Dingo ... 2.25
❑2, Sep 1990 ... 2.25
❑3, Sep 1990 ... 2.25
❑4, Nov 1990 ... 2.25

Southern Squadron
Eternity

❑1 1991; The Freedom of Information Act ... 2.50
❑2 1991 ... 2.50
❑3 1991 ... 2.50
❑4 1991 ... 2.50

Star Brand

Flagship title of ill-fated New Universe
©Marvel

Starjammers

Kevin Anderson's version failed to connect
©Marvel

Starman

Actually the fourth person to use the name
©DC

Starman

James Robinson delved into Golden Age lore
©DC

Star Rangers

Adventure title hit right at end of the b&w glut
©Adventure

N-MINT

Southern Squadron: The Freedom of Information Act
Eternity

❑1, Jan 1992; Fantastic Four #1 homage cover 2.50
❑2, Feb 1992 .... 2.50
❑3, Mar 1992 .... 2.50

Sovereign Seven
DC

❑1, Jul 1995; 1: Cascade; 1: Conal; 1: Cruiser; 1: Indigo; 1: Network; 1: Rampart; 1: Reflex; 1: Sovereign Seven 2.50
❑1/Variant, Jul 1995; foil edition; no cover price 4.00
❑2, Aug 1995 .... 2.00
❑3, Sep 1995 .... 2.00
❑4, Oct 1995 .... 2.00
❑5, Nov 1995 .... 2.00
❑6, Dec 1995 .... 2.00
❑7, Jan 1996 .... 2.00
❑8, Feb 1996 .... 2.00
❑9, Mar 1996 .... 2.00
❑10, Apr 1996 .... 2.00
❑11, Jun 1996 .... 1.95
❑12, Jul 1996 .... 1.95
❑13, Aug 1996 .... 1.95
❑14, Sep 1996 .... 1.95
❑15, Oct 1996 .... 1.95
❑16, Nov 1996; Final Night 1.95
❑17, Dec 1996 .... 1.95
❑18, Jan 1997; Cascade quits 1.95
❑19, Feb 1997; Cascade 1.95
❑20, Mar 1997; Cascade 1.95
❑21, Apr 1997; Cascade 1.95
❑22, May 1997; Cascade 1.95
❑23, Jun 1997; Cascade 1.95
❑24, Jul 1997 .... 1.95
❑25, Aug 1997 .... 1.95
❑26, Sep 1997 .... 2.25
❑27, Oct 1997; Genesis 2.25
❑28, Nov 1997 .... 2.25
❑29, Dec 1997; Face cover 2.25
❑30, Jan 1998 .... 2.25
❑31, Feb 1998 .... 2.25
❑32, Mar 1998 .... 2.25
❑33, Apr 1998 .... 2.25
❑34, May 1998 .... 2.25
❑35, Jun 1998 .... 2.25
❑36, Jul 1998; Final Issue 2.25
❑Ann 1, ca. 1995; Year One; Big Barda .. 3.95
❑Ann 2, ca. 1996; Legends of the Dead Earth; 1996 Ann 2.95

Sovereign Seven Plus
DC

❑1, Feb 1997 .... 2.95

Soviet Super Soldiers
Marvel

❑1, Nov 1992 .... 2.00

Space: 1999
Charlton

❑1, Nov 1975, JSa (c); JSa (a); O: Moonbase Alpha 10.00
❑2, Jan 1976, JSa (c); JSa (a) 7.00
❑3, Mar 1976, JBy (c); JBy, JSa (a) 7.00

N-MINT

❑4, May 1976, JBy (c); JBy (a) 7.00
❑5, Jul 1976, JBy (c); JBy (a) 5.00
❑6, Sep 1976, JBy (c); JBy (w); JBy (a). 5.00
❑7, Nov 1976, JSa (a) 5.00

Space: 34-24-34
MN Design

❑1, b&w; photos 4.50

Space: Above and Beyond
Topps

❑1, Jan 1996 .... 2.95
❑2, Feb 1996 .... 2.95
❑3, Mar 1996 .... 2.95

Space: Above and Beyond: The Gauntlet
Topps

❑1, May 1996 .... 2.95
❑2, Jun 1996 .... 2.95

Space Adventures
Charlton

❑33, Mar 1960, SD (c); SD (a); 1&O: Captain Atom 325.00
❑34, Jun 1960, SD (c); SD (a); 2: Captain Atom 150.00
❑35, Aug 1960, SD (c); SD (a); A: Captain Atom 125.00
❑36, Oct 1960, SD (c); SD (a); A: Captain Atom 125.00
❑37, Dec 1960, SD (c); SD (a); A: Captain Atom 125.00
❑38, Feb 1961, SD (c); SD (a); A: Captain Atom 125.00
❑39, Apr 1961, SD (c); SD (a); A: Captain Atom 125.00
❑40, Jun 1961, SD (a); A: Captain Atom 125.00
❑41, Aug 1961 .... 25.00
❑42, Oct 1961, SD (c); SD (a); A: Captain Atom 75.00
❑43, Dec 1961 .... 25.00
❑44, Feb 1962, Mercury Man 25.00
❑45, May 1962, Mercury Man 25.00
❑46, Jul 1962 .... 25.00
❑47, Sep 1962 .... 25.00
❑48, Nov 1962 .... 25.00
❑49, Jan 1963 .... 25.00
❑50, Mar 1963 .... 25.00
❑51, May 1963 .... 18.00
❑52, Jul 1963 .... 18.00
❑53, Sep 1963 .... 18.00
❑54, Nov 1963 .... 18.00
❑55, Mar 1964 .... 18.00
❑56, May 1964 .... 18.00
❑57, Jul 1964 .... 18.00
❑58, Sep 1964 .... 18.00
❑59, Nov 1964 .... 18.00
❑60, Oct 1967, JA (a); Vol. 3 #1 .... 18.00
❑61, Jul 1968, Vol. 3 #2 .... 12.00
❑62, Sep 1968, Vol. 3 #3 .... 12.00
❑63, Nov 1968, Vol. 3 #4 .... 12.00
❑64, Jan 1969, Vol. 3 #5 .... 12.00
❑65, Mar 1969, Vol. 3 #6 .... 12.00
❑66, May 1969, Vol. 3 #7 .... 12.00
❑67, Jul 1969, Vol. 3 #8 .... 12.00
❑68, May 1978, Vol. 3 #9; Captain Atom: Reprints from Space Adventures #33, 34 and 40 .... 12.00

N-MINT

❑69, Jul 1978, Vol. 3 #10; Reprints from Unusual Tales #8 and Haunted #32; Captain Atom: Repriints from Space Adventures #35 and 38 .... 12.00
❑70, Oct 1978, Vol. 3 #11; Captain Atom: Reprints from Space Adventures #36 and 37 .... 12.00
❑71, Jan 1979, Vol. 3 #12; Captain Atom: Reprints from Space Adventures #39, 40 and 42 .... 12.00
❑72, Mar 1979, SD (a); Indicia indicates Vol. 3 #13 .... 12.00

Space Ark
AC

❑1; ca. 1985 .... 1.75
❑2; ca. 1986 .... 1.75
❑3, b&w; Publisher changes to Apple; ca. 1987 .... 1.75
❑4, Jul 1987, b&w 1.75
❑5, Sep 1987, b&w 1.75

Space Bananas
Karl Art

❑0; Includes Captain Action #0 as insert 1.95

Space Beaver
Ten-Buck

❑1, Oct 1986 .... 1.50
❑2, Jan 1987 .... 1.50
❑3, Feb 1987 .... 1.50
❑4 1987; b&w 1.50
❑5 1987; b&w 1.50
❑6, Sep 1987; b&w 1.50
❑7, Oct 1987; b&w 1.50
❑8, Nov 1987; b&w 1.50
❑9, Dec 1987; b&w 1.50
❑10, Jan 1988; b&w 1.50
❑11, Feb 1988; b&w 1.50

Space Circus
Dark Horse

❑1, Jul 2000 .... 2.95
❑2, Aug 2000 .... 2.95
❑3, Sep 2000 .... 2.95
❑4, Oct 2000 .... 2.95

Space Cowboy Annual 2001
Vanguard

❑1/Frazetta, Dec 2001, Variant Frazetta cover 4.95
❑1/Williamson, Dec 2001, Variant Williamson cover 4.95

Spaced
Comics and Comix

❑1; ca. 1974; Adult; b&w 4.00

Spaced
Unbridled Ambition

❑1 .... 2.00
❑2 .... 2.00
❑3 .... 2.00
❑4 .... 2.00
❑5 .... 2.00
❑6 .... 2.00
❑7 .... 2.00
❑8 .... 2.00
❑9; Unbridled Ambition Publisher 2.00
❑10, b&w; Eclipse publisher 2.00
❑11, b&w 2.00

Other grades: Multiply price above by 5/6 for VF/NM • 2/3 for VERY FINE • 1/3 for FINE • 1/5 for VERY GOOD • 1/8 for GOOD

❑12, b&w 2.00
❑13, b&w 2.00

Spaced Out
Forbidden Fruit

❑1, Jul 1992; Adult 2.95

Spaced Out
Print Mint

❑1, Adult; ca. 1972 .... 3.00

Space Family Robinson
Gold Key

❑1, Dec 1962 .... 225.00
❑2, Mar 1963 .... 100.00
❑3, Jun 1963 .... 75.00
❑4, Sep 1963 .... 75.00
❑5, Dec 1963 .... 75.00
❑6, Feb 1964 .... 50.00
❑7, Apr 1964 .... 50.00
❑8, Jun 1964 .... 50.00
❑9, Aug 1964 .... 50.00
❑10, Oct 1964 .... 50.00
❑11, Dec 1964 .... 35.00
❑12, Apr 1965 .... 35.00
❑13, Jul 1965 .... 35.00
❑14, Oct 1965 .... 35.00
❑15, Jan 1966, Title changes to "Space Family Robinson Lost in Space" 35.00
❑16, Apr 1966 .... 25.00
❑17, Jul 1966 .... 25.00
❑18, Oct 1966 .... 25.00
❑19, Dec 1966 .... 25.00
❑20, Feb 1967 .... 25.00
❑21, Apr 1967 .... 20.00
❑22, Jun 1967 .... 20.00
❑23, Aug 1967 .... 20.00
❑24, Oct 1967 .... 20.00
❑25, Dec 1967 .... 20.00
❑26, Feb 1968 .... 20.00
❑27, Apr 1968 .... 20.00
❑28, Jun 1968 .... 20.00
❑29, Aug 1968 .... 20.00
❑30, Oct 1968 .... 20.00
❑31, Dec 1968 .... 20.00
❑32, Feb 1969 .... 20.00
❑33, Apr 1969 .... 20.00
❑34, Jun 1969 .... 20.00
❑35, Aug 1969 .... 20.00
❑36, Oct 1969, Final issue of original run 20.00
❑37, Oct 1973, Series begins again 20.00
❑38, Jan 1974, Title changes to "Space Family Robinson, Lost in Space on Space Station One" 20.00
❑39, Apr 1974 .... 20.00
❑40, Jul 1974 .... 20.00
❑41, Oct 1974 .... 20.00
❑42, Jan 1975 .... 20.00
❑43, Apr 1975 .... 20.00
❑44, Aug 1975 .... 20.00
❑45, Oct 1975 .... 10.00
❑46, Jan 1976 .... 10.00
❑47, Apr 1976 .... 10.00
❑48, Aug 1976 .... 10.00
❑49, Reprint from Space Family Robinson #38 .... 10.00
❑50 .... 10.00
❑51, Apr 1977 .... 10.00
❑52, ca. 1977 .... 10.00
❑53, ca. 1977 .... 10.00
❑54, Dec 1977 .... 10.00
❑55, ca. 1981, Series begins again 6.00
❑56, Jul 1981, Reprints Space Family Robinson #16 .... 6.00
❑57, Oct 1981, Reprints Space Family Robinson #17 .... 6.00
❑58, Feb 1982, Reprints from Space Family Robinson #18 .... 6.00
❑59, May 1982, Reprints from Space Family Robinson #50, 48; Final Issue. 6.00

Space Funnies
Archival

❑1, Jun 1990; Reprints from Target Comics #5-7; Spacehawk 5.95

Spacegal Comics
Thorby

❑1 .... 2.95
❑2; Flip-Book with Johnny Cosmic #1 .... 2.95

Space Ghost
Gold Key

❑1, Mar 1967 .... 150.00

Space Ghost
Comico

❑1, Dec 1987, Includes 5-page biography background on Space Ghost including early sketches by Alex Toth 3.50

Space Ghost
DC

❑1, Feb 2005 .... 22.00
❑2, Mar 2005 .... 10.00
❑3, Apr 2005 .... 2.95
❑4, May 2005 .... 2.95
❑5, Jun 2005 .... 2.95
❑6, Jun 2005 .... 2.99

Space Giants
Boneyard

❑1 .... 2.75

Spacegirl Comics
Bill Jones Graphics

❑1, Nov 1995, b&w 2.50
❑2, Nov 1995, b&w 2.50

Spacehawk
Dark Horse

❑1, ca. 1989; BW (w); BW (a); Reprints from Target Comics Vol. 1 #5-6 .... 2.00
❑2, ca. 1989; BW (c); BW (w); BW (a); Reprints from Target Comics Vol. 1 #7-8; b&w 2.00
❑3, ca. 1989; BW (w); BW (a); ca. 1990 2.25
❑4, ca. 1989; BW (w); BW (a) 2.25
❑5, Jan 1993 BW (w); BW (a) 2.50

Space Hustlers
Slave Labor

❑1, Mar 1997, b&w 2.95

Space Jam
DC

❑1, Oct 1996; prestige format; NN; Movie adaptation 5.95

Spaceknights
Marvel

❑1, Oct 2000 .... 2.99
❑2, Nov 2000 .... 2.99
❑3, Dec 2000 .... 2.99
❑4, Jan 2001 .... 2.99
❑5, Feb 2001 .... 2.99

Spaceman
Dell

❑2, Jun 1962 .... 40.00
❑3, Sep 1962 .... 32.00
❑4 1963 .... 24.00
❑5, Jun 1963 .... 24.00
❑6, Sep 1963 .... 24.00
❑7, Dec 1964 .... 22.00
❑8, Mar 1964 .... 22.00
❑9, ca. 1972, Reprints Space Man #1 .... 5.00
❑10, ca. 1972, Reprints Space Man #2 .... 5.00

Spaceman (Oni)
Oni

❑nn, Jul 2002 .... 2.95

Space: 1999
Charlton

❑1, Nov 1975, b&w GM (c); GM (a) 30.00
❑2, Jan 1976, b&w; GM (c); GM (a) 20.00
❑3, Mar 1976, b&w; GM (c); GM (a) 20.00
❑4, May 1976, b&w; GM (c) 20.00
❑5, Jul 1976, b&w 20.00
❑6, Aug 1976, b&w; GM (c); GM (a) 20.00
❑7, Sep 1976, b&w 20.00
❑8, Oct 1976, b&w 20.00

Space Patrol
Adventure

❑1 .... 2.50
❑2, b&w 2.50
❑3 .... 2.50

Space Slutz
Comic Zone

❑1, b&w; Adult 3.95

Space Time Shuffle a Trilogy
Alpha Productions

❑1, b&w 1.95
❑2, b&w 1.95

Space Trip to the Moon
Avalon

❑1, ca. 1999, b&w; adapts Destination: Moon 2.95

Space Usagi
Mirage

❑1, Jun 1992, b&w 3.00
❑2, Jul 1992, b&w 3.00
❑3, Aug 1992, b&w 3.00

Space Usagi
Mirage

❑1, Nov 1993 .... 3.00
❑2, Jan 1994 .... 3.00
❑3, Mar 1994 .... 3.00

Space Usagi
Dark Horse

❑1, Jan 1996, b&w 2.95
❑2, Feb 1996, b&w 2.95
❑3, Mar 1996, b&w 2.95

Space War
Charlton

❑14, Dec 1961 .... 30.00
❑15, Mar 1962 .... 30.00
❑16, May 1962 .... 16.00
❑17, Jul 1962 .... 16.00
❑18, Sep 1962 .... 16.00
❑19, Nov 1962 .... 16.00
❑20, Jan 1963 .... 16.00
❑21, Mar 1963 .... 16.00
❑22, May 1963 .... 16.00
❑23, Jul 1963 .... 16.00
❑24, Sep 1963 .... 16.00
❑25, Nov 1963 .... 16.00
❑26, Jan 1964 .... 16.00
❑27, Mar 1964, Series continued in Fightin' 5 #28 .... 16.00
❑28, Mar 1978, Series begins again (1978) 4.00
❑29, May 1978 .... 4.00
❑30, Jun 1978 .... 4.00
❑31, Oct 1978 .... 4.00
❑32, ca. 1979 .... 4.00

Space War Classics
Avalon

❑1, b&w 2.95

Space Wolf
Antarctic

❑1, Dec 1992, b&w 2.50
❑2, b&w 2.50

Spam
Alpha Productions

❑1, b&w; ca. 1989 .... 1.50
❑2, b&w 1.50

Spandex Tights
Lost Cause

❑1, Sep 1994, b&w 2.50
❑2, Nov 1994, b&w 2.25
❑3, b&w 2.25
❑4, Mar 1995, b&w 2.25
❑5, May 1995, b&w 2.25
❑6, Jul 1995, b&w; V: Mighty Awful Sour Rangers. false cover for Mighty Awful Sour Rangers #1 .... 2.50

Spandex Tights
Lost Cause

❑1, Jan 1997, b&w 2.95
❑2, Mar 1997, b&w 2.95
❑3, May 1997, b&w 2.95

Spanish Fly
Fantagraphics / Eros

❑1 .... 2.95
❑2 .... 2.95
❑3 .... 2.95
❑4 .... 2.95
❑5, May 1996 .... 2.95

Spank
Fantagraphics / Eros

❑2, b&w 2.25
❑3, b&w 2.25
❑4, b&w 2.25

Spank the Monkey
Arrow

❑1, Jul 1999, b&w; Flip book with Korvus #0 .... 2.95

Stars and S.T.R.I.P.E.

Stepfather and stepdaughter hero team
©DC

Star Slammers

Simonson tale began as Marvel Graphic Novel
©Malibu

Starslayer

Celtic barbarian whisked away to future
©Pacific

Star Spangled War Stories

Home to Enemy Ace and Unknown Soldier
©DC

Starstruck

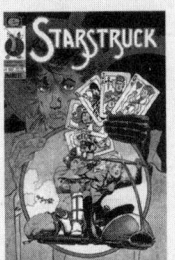

Tale of mystery, love, and cybernetics
©Marvel

N-MINT

Spanner's Galaxy
DC

❑1, Dec 1984; mini-series 1.00
❑2, Jan 1985 1.00
❑3, Feb 1985 1.00
❑4, Mar 1985 1.00
❑5, Apr 1985 1.00
❑6, May 1985 1.00

Sparkplug
Heroic

❑1, Mar 1993, b&w; Sparkplug; Murcielaga 2.95
❑2, May 1993, b&w; trading card 2.95
❑3 2.95

Sparky & Tim
Aaron Warner

❑1, Feb 1999 5.95

Sparrow
Millennium

❑1 1995, b&w 2.95
❑2, Apr 1995, b&w 2.95
❑3, May 1995, b&w 2.95
❑4, Jul 1995, b&w 2.95

Spartan: Warrior Spirit
Image

❑1, Jul 1995 2.50
❑2, Sep 1995 2.50
❑3, Oct 1995 2.50
❑4, Nov 1995 2.50

Spartan X: Hell-Bent-Hero-For-Hire
Image

❑1, Mar 1998 2.95
❑2, Apr 1998 2.95
❑3, May 1998, cover says Jun, indicia says May 2.95
❑4, Jul 1998, cover says Aug, indicia says Jul 2.95

Spartan X: The Armour of Heaven
Topps

❑1, May 1997 2.95

Spasm
Parody

❑1 9.95

Spasm
Rough Copy

❑1 2.95
❑2 2.95
❑3 2.95
❑4 2.95
❑5 2.95

Spawn
Image

❑1, May 1992; TMc (c); TMc (w); TMc (a); 1: Spawn 5.00
❑1/A, Sep 1997; TMc (c); TMc (w); TMc (a); promo with Spawn #65 2.95
❑2, Jul 1992; TMc (c); TMc (w); TMc (a); 1: Violator. cover says Jun, indicia says Jul 4.00
❑3, Aug 1992 TMc (c); TMc (w); TMc (a) 2.50
❑4, Sep 1992; TMc (c); TMc (w); TMc (a); with coupon 2.50

N-MINT

❑5, Oct 1992; TMc (c); TMc (w); TMc (a); Includes poster of Spawn mobile; Includes pin-ups 2.50
❑6, Nov 1992; TMc (c); TMc (w); TMc (a); 1: Overt-Kill 2.50
❑7, Jan 1993 TMc (c); TMc (w); TMc (a) 4.00
❑8, Mar 1993; TMc (c); AMo (w); TMc (a); cover says Feb, indicia says Mar 4.00
❑9, Mar 1993; TMc (c); NG (w); TMc (a); 1: Angela; Includes Jim Lee poster 4.00
❑10, May 1993 TMc (c); TMc (a); A: Cerebus 2.75
❑11, Jun 1993; TMc (c); FM (w); TMc (a); Includes poster 2.50
❑12, Jul 1993; TMc (c); TMc (w); TMc (a); Includes poster 2.50
❑13, Aug 1993; TMc (c); TMc (w); TMc (a); Spawn vs. Chapel 2.50
❑14, Sep 1993; TMc (c); TMc (w); TMc (a); A: Violator. Includes pin-up 2.50
❑15, Nov 1993; TMc (c); TMc (w); TMc (a); Includes pin-ups 2.50
❑16, Dec 1993; 1: Anti-Spawn; Includes pin-ups 2.50
❑17, Jan 1994; 1: Anti-Spawn. Spawn vs. Anti-Spawn 3.00
❑18, Feb 1994; Includes pin-ups 3.00
❑19, Oct 1994; Published out of sequence with fill-in art 3.00
❑20, Nov 1994; TMc (a); Published out of sequence with fill-in art 3.00
❑21, May 1994; TMc (c); TMc (w); TMc (a); Includes pin-ups 3.00
❑22, Jun 1994; TMc (c); TMc (w); TMc, EL (a); 8 page preview of WildC.A.T.S.- The Animated Series; Includes pin-up by Erik Larsen 3.00
❑23, Aug 1994; TMc (c); TMc (w); TMc (a); Includes pin-ups 3.00
❑24, Sep 1994 TMc (c); TMc (w); TMc (a) 3.00
❑25, Oct 1994; TMc (w); Includes pin-ups 3.00
❑26, Dec 1994 TMc (c); TMc (w); TMc (a) 3.00
❑27, Jan 1995 TMc (c); TMc (w); TMc (a) 3.00
❑28, Feb 1995 TMc (c); TMc (w); TMc (a) 3.00
❑29, Mar 1995 TMc (c); TMc (w); TMc (a) 3.00
❑30, Apr 1995 TMc (c); TMc (w); TMc (a) 3.00
❑31, May 1995 TMc (c); TMc (w); TMc (a) 3.00
❑32, Jun 1995 TMc (c); TMc (w); TMc (a) 3.00
❑33, Jul 1995 TMc (c); TMc (w); TMc (a) 3.00
❑34, Aug 1995 TMc (c); TMc (w); TMc (a) 3.00
❑35, Sep 1995 TMc (c); TMc (w); TMc (a) 3.00
❑36, Oct 1995 TMc (c); TMc (w); TMc (a) 3.00
❑37, Nov 1995 TMc (c); TMc, AMo (w); TMc (a) 3.00
❑38, Dec 1995; TMc (w); 1: Cy-Gor. cover says Aug, indicia says Dec 3.00
❑39, Dec 1995; TMc (c); TMc (w); TMc (a); Christmas story 3.00
❑40, Jan 1996 TMc (w) 3.00
❑41, Jan 1996 TMc (c); TMc (w); TMc (a) 3.00
❑42, Feb 1996 TMc (w) 3.00
❑43, Feb 1996 TMc (c); TMc (w); TMc (a) 3.00
❑44, Mar 1996 TMc (w) 3.00
❑45, Mar 1996 TMc (c); TMc (w); TMc (a) 3.00
❑46, Apr 1996 TMc (w) 3.00
❑47, Apr 1996 TMc (c); TMc (w); TMc (a) 3.00
❑48, May 1996 TMc (w) 3.00
❑49, May 1996 TMc (w); TMc (a) 3.00
❑50, Jun 1996 TMc (c); TMc (w); TMc (a) 2.95

N-MINT

❑51, Aug 1996; TMc (c); TMc (w); TMc (a); cover says Jul, indicia says Aug 1.95
❑52, Aug 1996 TMc (c); TMc (w); TMc (a) 1.95
❑53, Sep 1996 TMc (c); TMc (w); TMc (a) 1.95
❑54, Oct 1996 TMc (c); TMc (w); TMc (a) 1.95
❑55, Nov 1996 TMc (w); TMc (a) 1.95
❑56, Dec 1996 TMc (c); TMc (w); TMc (a) 1.95
❑57, Jan 1997 TMc (c); TMc (w); TMc (a) 1.95
❑58, Feb 1997 TMc (c); TMc (w); TMc (a) 1.95
❑59, Mar 1997 TMc (c); TMc (w); TMc (a) 1.95
❑60, Apr 1997 TMc (c); TMc (w); TMc (a) 1.95
❑61, May 1997 TMc (c); TMc (w); TMc (a) 1.95
❑62, Jun 1997; TMc (c); TMc (w); TMc (a); A: Angela. Angela appearance, dedicated to Clint Goldman 1.95
❑63, Jul 1997 TMc (c); TMc (w); TMc (a) 1.95
❑64, Aug 1997; TMc (c); TMc (w); TMc (a); polybagged with McFarlane Toys catalog 1.95
❑65, Sep 1997; TMc (w); TMc (a); Photo cover 1.95
❑66, Oct 1997 TMc (c); TMc (w); TMc (a) 1.95
❑67, Nov 1997; TMc (c); TMc (w); TMc (a); Dedicated to Gareb Shamus 1.95
❑68, Jan 1998 TMc (c); TMc (w); TMc (a) 1.95
❑69, Jan 1998 TMc (c); TMc (w); TMc (a) 1.95
❑70, Feb 1998 TMc (w); TMc (a) 1.95
❑71, Apr 1998 TMc (w); TMc (a) 1.95
❑72, May 1998 TMc (c); TMc (w); TMc (a) 1.95
❑73, Jun 1998 TMc (w); TMc (a) 1.95
❑74, Jul 1998 TMc (c); TMc (w) 1.95
❑75, Aug 1998 TMc (c); TMc (w) 1.95
❑76, Sep 1998 TMc (w) 1.95
❑77, Oct 1998 TMc (c); TMc (w) 1.95
❑78, Nov 1998 TMc (w) 1.95
❑79, Jan 1999 TMc (w) 1.95
❑80, Feb 1999 TMc (w) 1.95
❑81, Mar 1999 TMc (c); TMc (w) 1.95
❑82, Apr 1999 TMc (c); TMc (w) 1.95
❑83, May 1999 TMc (c); TMc (w) 1.95
❑84, Jun 1999 TMc (c); TMc (w) 1.95
❑85, Jul 1999 TMc (w) 1.95
❑86, Aug 1999 TMc (c); TMc (w) 1.95
❑87, Sep 1999 TMc (w) 1.95
❑88, Oct 1999 TMc (c); TMc (w) 1.95
❑89, Nov 1999 TMc (c); TMc (w) 1.95
❑90, Dec 1999 TMc (c); TMc (w) 1.95
❑91, Jan 2000 TMc (c); TMc (w) 1.95
❑92, Feb 2000 TMc (c); TMc (w) 1.95
❑93, Mar 2000 TMc (c); TMc (w) 1.95
❑94, Apr 2000; TMc (c); TMc (w); Child's art by Cyan and Kate McFarlane 1.95
❑95, May 2000 TMc (c); TMc (w) 1.95
❑96, Jun 2000 TMc (c); TMc (w) 1.95
❑97, Jul 2000; TMc (c); TMc (w); Angela apperance 1.95
❑98, Aug 2000; TMc (c); TMc (w); Angela apperance 2.50
❑99, Sep 2000; TMc (w); Angela apperance 2.50
❑100/A, Nov 2000; Giant-size; TMc (c); TMc (w); Todd McFarlane cover 6.00
❑100/B, Nov 2000; Giant-size; TMc (w); Ashley Wood cover 4.95
❑100/C, Nov 2000; Giant-size; FM (c); TMc (w); Frank Miller cover 4.95
❑100/D, Nov 2000; Giant-size; TMc (w); Mike Mignola Cover 4.95

	N-MINT
❑100/E, Nov 2000; Giant-size; ARo (c); TMc (w); Alex Ross cover	4.95
❑100/F, Nov 2000; Giant-size; TMc (w); Greg Capullo cover	4.95
❑101, Dec 2000 GP (c); TMc (w)	2.50
❑102, Jan 2001 TMc (c); TMc (w)	2.50
❑103, Feb 2001 TMc (w)	2.50
❑104, Feb 2001 TMc (c); TMc (w)	2.50
❑105, Feb 2001 TMc (c); TMc (w)	2.50
❑106, Mar 2001 TMc (c); TMc (w)	2.50
❑107, Apr 2001 TMc (c); TMc (w)	2.50
❑108, May 2001 TMc (c); TMc (w); TMc (a)	2.50
❑109, Jun 2001 TMc (c); TMc (w)	2.50
❑110, Jul 2001 TMc (c); TMc (w)	2.50
❑111, Aug 2001 TMc (c); TMc (w)	2.50
❑112, Sep 2001 TMc (c); TMc (w)	2.50
❑113, Oct 2001 TMc (c); TMc (w)	2.50
❑114, Nov 2001 TMc (c); TMc (w)	2.50
❑115, Dec 2001 TMc (c); TMc (w)	2.50
❑116, Jan 2002 TMc (c); TMc (w)	2.50
❑117, May 2002 TMc (c); TMc (w)	2.50
❑118, Jun 2002 TMc (c); TMc (w)	2.50
❑119, Aug 2002 TMc (c); TMc (w)	2.50
❑120, Sep 2002 TMc (c); TMc (w)	2.50
❑121, Dec 2002 TMc (w)	2.50
❑122, Feb 2003 TMc (w)	2.50
❑123, Mar 2003 TMc (w)	2.50
❑124, Apr 2003 TMc (w)	2.50
❑125, May 2003 TMc (w)	2.50
❑126, Jul 2003 TMc (w)	2.50
❑127, Aug 2003 TMc (w)	2.50
❑128, Sep 2003 TMc (w)	2.50
❑129, Oct 2003 TMc (w)	2.50
❑130, Nov 2003 TMc (w)	2.50
❑131, Dec 2003 TMc (c); TMc (w)	2.50
❑132, Feb 2004; TMc (w); Painted Cover	2.50
❑133, Apr 2004 TMc (w)	2.50
❑134, May 2004 TMc (w)	2.50
❑135, Aug 2004 TMc (w)	2.50
❑136, Sep 2004 TMc (w)	2.50
❑137, Oct 2004 TMc (w)	2.50
❑138, Nov 2004; TMc (w); Wraparound cover	2.50
❑139, Dec 2004 TMc (w)	2.50
❑140, Jan 2004, TMc (w)	2.50
❑141, Feb 2005 TMc (w)	2.50
❑142, Mar 2005	2.50
❑143, Apr 2005	2.50
❑144, May 2005	2.50
❑145, Jun 2005	2.50
❑146, Jul 2005	2.50
❑147, Aug 2005	2.50
❑148, Sep 2005	2.50
❑149, Oct 2005	2.50
❑150, Nov 2005	4.95
❑151, Dec 2005, Price increase; Spawn against empty white background; Wraparound	2.95
❑152, Jan 2006	2.95
❑153, Mar 2006	2.95
❑154, Apr 2006	2.95
❑155, May 2006	2.95
❑156, Jun 2006	2.95
❑157, Jul 2006	2.95
❑158, Sep 2006	2.95
❑159, Oct 2006	2.95
❑160, Nov 2006	2.99
❑161, Dec 2006	2.95
❑162, Jan 2007	2.95
❑163, Feb 2007	2.95
❑164	2.95
❑Ann 1, May 1999; squarebound	4.95
❑Fan ed. 1/A, Aug 1996, Promotional edition included in Overstreet Fan; Promotional edition included in Overstreet Fan #16	1.00
❑Fan ed. 1/B, Aug 1996	1.00
❑Fan ed. 2/A, Sep 1996, Promotional edition included in Overstreet Fan; Purple background	1.00
❑Fan ed. 2/B, Sep 1996	1.00
❑Fan ed. 3/A, Oct 1996, Promotional edition included in Overstreet Fan	1.00
❑Fan ed. 3/B, Oct 1996	1.00

Spawn-Batman
Image

	N-MINT
❑1, ca. 1994; TMc (c); FM (w); TMc (a); NN	4.00

Spawn Bible
Image

	N-MINT
❑1, Aug 1996; background on series	1.95

Spawn Blood and Salvation
Image

	N-MINT
❑1, Nov 1999	4.95

Spawn Blood Feud
Image

	N-MINT
❑1, Jun 1995	2.25
❑2, Jul 1995	2.25
❑3, Aug 1995	2.25
❑4, Sep 1995	2.25

Spawn: Godslayer
Image

	N-MINT
❑1, Dec 2006	6.99

Spawn Movie Adaptation
Image

	N-MINT
❑1, Dec 1997; prestige format; NN; Movie adaptation	4.95

Spawn #1 in 3-D
Image

	N-MINT
❑1, May 2006	5.95

Spawn: Simony One-Shot
Image

	N-MINT
❑1, Apr 2004	7.95

Spawn: The Dark Ages
Image

	N-MINT
❑1, Mar 1999; Painted Cover	3.00
❑1/Variant, Mar 1999; TMc (c); TMc (a); Variant cover by McFarlane	2.50
❑2, Apr 1999; TMc (c); TMc (a); Painted Cover	2.50
❑3, May 1999; Painted Cover	2.50
❑4, Jun 1999; Painted Cover	2.50
❑5, Jul 1999; Painted Cover	2.50
❑6, Aug 1999	2.50
❑7, Sep 1999	2.50
❑8, Oct 1999	2.50
❑9, Nov 1999	2.50
❑10, Dec 1999	2.50
❑11, Jan 2000	2.50
❑12, Feb 2000; Painted Cover	2.50
❑13, Mar 2000	2.50
❑14, Apr 2000	2.50
❑15, May 2000	2.50
❑16, Jun 2000; Painted Cover	2.50
❑17, Jul 2000; Painted Cover	2.50
❑18, Aug 2000; Painted Cover	2.50
❑19, Sep 2000; Painted Cover	2.50
❑20, Oct 2000	2.50
❑21, Nov 2000	2.50
❑22, Jan 2001	2.50
❑23, Feb 2001; Painted Cover	2.50
❑24, Mar 2001; Painted Cover	2.50
❑25, Apr 2001; TMc (c); Painted Cover	2.50
❑26, May 2001	2.50
❑27, Jun 2001	2.50
❑28, Jul 2001	2.50

Spawn the Impaler
Image

	N-MINT
❑1, Oct 1996	2.95
❑2, Nov 1996	2.95
❑3, Dec 1996	2.95

Spawn the Undead
Image

	N-MINT
❑1, Jun 1999	2.00
❑2, Jul 1999	1.95
❑3, Aug 1999	1.95
❑4, Sep 1999	1.95
❑5, Oct 1999	1.95
❑6, Nov 1999	1.95
❑7, Dec 1999; Painted Cover	1.95
❑8, Jan 2000	2.25
❑9, Feb 2000	2.25

Spawn/WildC.A.T.S
Image

	N-MINT
❑1, Jan 1996, AMo (w)	3.00
❑2, Feb 1996, AMo (w)	2.50
❑3, Mar 1996, AMo (w)	2.50
❑4, Apr 1996, AMo (w)	2.50

Spaztic Colon
-Ism

	N-MINT
❑1, ca. 2005; b&w	3.50
❑2, ca. 2005; b&w	3.50
❑3, ca. 2005; b&w	3.50

Special Hugging and Other Childhood Tales
Slave Labor

	N-MINT
❑1, Apr 1989, b&w	1.95

Special Marvel Edition
Marvel

	N-MINT
❑1, Jan 1971; SL (w); JK (a); reprints Thor stories from Journey into Mystery #117-119; Thor reprints begin	20.00
❑2, Apr 1971; reprints Thor stories from Journey into Mystery #120-122	15.00
❑3, Sep 1971; reprints Thor stories from Journey into Mystery #123-125	15.00
❑4, Feb 1972; reprints Thor #126 and #127; Thor reprints end	15.00
❑5, Jul 1972, Sgt. Fury reprints begin	7.00
❑6, Sep 1972, Reprint from Sgt. Fury #8	7.00
❑7, Nov 1972, Sgt. Fury	7.00
❑8, Jan 1973, JSe (c); SL (w); Reprint from Sgt. Fury #10	7.00
❑9, Mar 1973, Reprint from Sgt. Fury #11	7.00
❑10, May 1973, Reprint from Sgt. Fury #12	7.00
❑11, Jul 1973, A: Captain America. Reprint from Sgt. Fury #13	7.00
❑12, Sep 1973, Reprint from Sgt. Fury #14	7.00
❑13, Oct 1973, SL (w); SD (a); Reprint from Sgt. Fury #15	7.00
❑14, Nov 1973, Sgt. Fury reprints end	7.00
❑15, Dec 1973, JSn (c); JSn (w); JSn (a); 1: Shang-Chi, Master of Kung Fu. 1: Nayland Smith	45.00
❑16, Feb 1974, JSn (w); JSn (a); 1&O: Midnight. 2: Shang-Chi, Master of Kung Fu. series continues as Master of Kung Fu	18.00

Special War Series
Charlton

	N-MINT
❑1, Aug 1965, D-Day	10.00
❑2, Sep 1965, Attack!	8.00
❑3, Oct 1965, War and Attack	8.00
❑4, Nov 1965, 1&O: Judomaster; Sarge Steel	16.00

Species
Dark Horse

	N-MINT
❑1, Jun 1995; Movie adaptation	2.50
❑2, Jul 1995; Movie adaptation	2.50
❑3, Aug 1995; Movie adaptation	2.50
❑4, Sep 1995; Movie adaptation	2.50

Species: Human Race
Dark Horse

	N-MINT
❑1, Nov 1996	2.95
❑2, Dec 1996	2.95
❑3, Jan 1997	2.95
❑4, Feb 1997	2.95

Spectacles
Alternative

	N-MINT
❑1, Feb 1997, b&w	2.95
❑2, May 1997, b&w	2.95
❑3, Sep 1997, b&w	2.95
❑4, Jan 1998, b&w	2.95

Spectacular Scarlet Spider
Marvel

	N-MINT
❑1, Nov 1995	1.95
❑2, Dec 1995	1.95

Spectacular Spider-Man
Marvel

	N-MINT
❑1, Jul 1968, b&w; magazine; SL (w); JR (a); 1: Richard Raleigh, Man Monster	90.00
❑2, Nov 1968, color magazine; SL (w); JR (a); V: Green Goblin. V: Green Goblin.	75.00

Spectacular Spider-Man
Marvel

	N-MINT
❑-1, Jul 1997; Flashback	2.00
❑1, Dec 1976, SB (c); JR, SL (w); SB, JR (a); Tarantula	25.00
❑2, Jan 1977, SB (c); JR, SL (w); SB, JR, JM (a); Kraven	15.00
❑3, Feb 1977, AM (c); SB (a); 1&O: Lightmaster. Newsstand edition (distributed by Curtis); issue number in box	8.00

Other grades: Multiply price above by 5/6 for VF/NM • 2/3 for VERY FINE • 1/3 for FINE • 1/5 for VERY GOOD • 1/8 for GOOD

Startling Stories: The Thing

You could barely tell the real name of this title

©Marvel

Star Trek

Overseas artist hadn't seen the TV show

©Gold Key

Star Trek

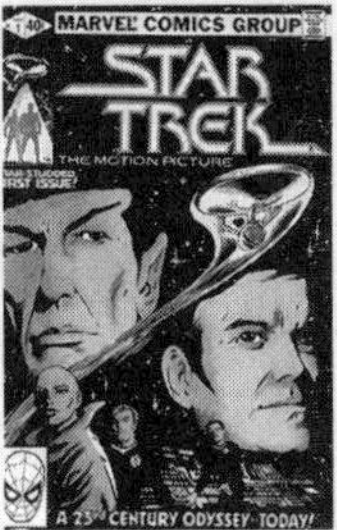

Marvel series followed the motionless picture

©Marvel

Star Trek

Peter David wrote many of the early issues

©DC

Star Trek: Deep Space Nine

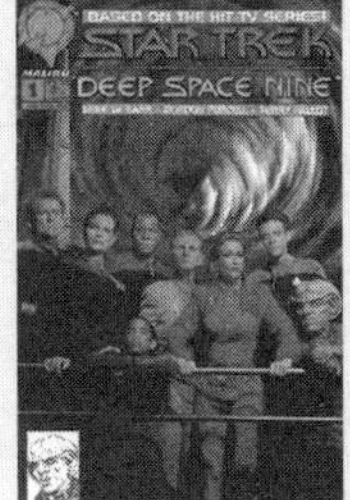

Title came before TV series got really good

©Malibu

	N-MINT
❑3/Whitman, Feb 1977, SB (a); 1&O: Lightmaster. Special markets edition (usually sold in Whitman bagged prepacks); price appears in a diamond; UPC barcode appears	8.00
❑4, Mar 1977, SB (a); V: Vulture. Newsstand edition (distributed by Curtis); issue number in box	5.00
❑4/Whitman, Mar 1977, SB (a); V: Vulture. Special markets edition (usually sold in Whitman bagged prepacks); price appears in a diamond; UPC barcode appears	5.00
❑5, Apr 1977, DC (c); SB (a); V: Vulture.	5.00
❑6, May 1977, A: Morbius. V: Morbius. Newsstand edition (distributed by Curtis); issue number in box	5.00
❑6/Whitman, May 1977, A: Morbius. V: Morbius. Special markets edition (usually sold in Whitman bagged prepacks); price appears in a diamond; UPC barcode appears	5.00
❑7, Jun 1977, A: Morbius. V: Morbius. Newsstand edition (distributed by Curtis); issue number in box	5.00
❑7/Whitman, Jun 1977, A: Morbius. V: Morbius. Special markets edition (usually sold in Whitman bagged prepacks); price appears in a diamond; UPC barcode appears	5.00
❑7/35¢, Jun 1977, A: Morbius. V: Morbius. 35¢ regional price variant newsstand edition (distributed by Curtis); issue number in box	15.00
❑8, Jul 1977, PG (c); SB (a); A: Morbius. V: Morbius. Newsstand edition (distributed by Curtis); issue number in box	5.00
❑8/Whitman, Jul 1977, PG (c); A: Morbius. V: Morbius. Special markets edition (usually sold in Whitman bagged prepacks); price appears in a diamond; UPC barcode appears	5.00
❑8/35¢, Jul 1977, PG (c); SB (a); A: Morbius. V: Morbius. 35¢ regional price variant newsstand edition (distributed by Curtis); issue number in box	15.00
❑9, Aug 1977, A: White Tiger. Newsstand edition (distributed by Curtis); issue number in box	5.00
❑9/Whitman, Aug 1977, A: White Tiger. Special markets edition (usually sold in Whitman bagged prepacks); price appears in a diamond; UPC barcode appears	5.00
❑9/35¢, Aug 1977, 35¢ regional price variant newsstand edition (distributed by Curtis); issue number in box	15.00
❑10, Sep 1977, A: White Tiger. Newsstand edition (distributed by Curtis); issue number in box	3.50
❑10/Whitman, Sep 1977, A: White Tiger. Special markets edition (usually sold in Whitman bagged prepacks); price appears in a diamond; no UPC barcode	3.50
❑10/35¢, Sep 1977, A: White Tiger. 35¢ regional price variant newsstand edition (distributed by Curtis); issue number in box	15.00
❑11, Oct 1977, AM (c); JM (a); Newsstand edition (distributed by Curtis); issue number in box	3.50
❑11/Whitman, Oct 1977, JM (a); Special markets edition (usually sold in Whitman bagged prepacks); price appears in a diamond; no UPC barcode	3.50
❑11/35¢, Oct 1977, AM (c); JM (a); 35¢ regional price variant newsstand edition (distributed by Curtis); issue number in box	15.00
❑12, Nov 1977, AM (c); SB (a); 1: Razorback (partial). A: Brother Power. Newsstand edition (distributed by Curtis); issue number in box	3.50
❑12/Whitman, Nov 1977, SB (a); 1: Razorback (partial). A: Brother Power. Special markets edition (usually sold in Whitman bagged prepacks); price appears in a diamond; no UPC barcode	3.50
❑13, Dec 1977, SB (c); SB (a); O: Razorback. 1: Razorback (full)	3.50
❑14, Jan 1978, SB (c); SB (a); V: Hatemongerr	3.50
❑15, Feb 1978, GK (c); SB (a); A: Razorback	3.50
❑16, Mar 1978, AM (c); SB (a); V: Beetle	3.50
❑17, Apr 1978, A: Iceman. A: Angel	3.50
❑18, May 1978, A: Iceman. A: Angel. Newsstand edition (distributed by Curtis); issue number in box	3.50
❑18/Whitman, May 1978, A: Iceman. A: Angel. Special markets edition (usually sold in Whitman bagged prepacks); price appears in a diamond; no UPC barcode	3.50
❑19, Jun 1978, V: Enforcers	3.50
❑20, Jul 1978, V: Light Master	3.50
❑21, Aug 1978, A: Moon Knight. Newsstand edition (distributed by Curtis); issue number in box	2.75
❑21/Whitman, Aug 1978, A: Moon Knight. Special markets edition (usually sold in Whitman bagged prepacks); price appears in a diamond; UPC barcode appears	2.75
❑22, Sep 1978, A: Moon Knight. Newsstand edition (distributed by Curtis); issue number in box	2.75
❑22/Whitman, Sep 1978, A: Moon Knight. Special markets edition (usually sold in Whitman bagged prepacks); price appears in a diamond; no UPC barcode	2.75
❑23, Oct 1978, A: Moon Knight	2.75
❑24, Nov 1978, Newsstand edition (distributed by Curtis); issue number in box	2.75
❑24/Whitman, Nov 1978, Special markets edition (usually sold in Whitman bagged prepacks); price appears in a diamond; no UPC barcode	2.75
❑25, Dec 1978, 1: Carrion I. Newsstand edition (distributed by Curtis); issue number in box	2.75
❑25/Whitman, Dec 1978, 1: Carrion I. Special markets edition (usually sold in Whitman bagged prepacks); price appears in a diamond; no UPC barcode	2.75
❑26, Jan 1979, A: Daredevil. Newsstand edition (distributed by Curtis); issue number in box	2.75
❑26/Whitman, Jan 1979, A: Daredevil. Special markets edition (usually sold in Whitman bagged prepacks); price appears in a diamond; no UPC barcode	2.75
❑27, Feb 1979, DC (c); FM, DC (a); A: Daredevil. Frank Miller's first Daredevil art; newsstand edition (distributed by Curtis); issue number in box	15.00
❑27/Whitman, Feb 1979, FM, DC (a); A: Daredevil. Frank Miller's first Daredevil art; special markets edition (usually sold in Whitman bagged prepacks); price appears in a diamond; no UPC barcode	15.00
❑28, Mar 1979, KP (c); FM (a); A: Daredevil	15.00
❑29, Apr 1979, V: Carrion	2.75
❑30, May 1979, V: Carrion. Newsstand edition (distributed by Curtis); issue number in box	2.75
❑30/Whitman, May 1979, V: Carrion. Special markets edition (usually sold in Whitman bagged prepacks); price appears in a diamond; no UPC barcode	2.75
❑31, Jun 1979, O: Carrion I. D: Carrion I	2.75
❑32, Jul 1979	2.75
❑33, Aug 1979, O: Iguana	2.75
❑34, Sep 1979, V: Lizard	2.75
❑35, Oct 1979	2.75
❑36, Nov 1979, V: Swarm	2.75
❑37, Dec 1979, V: Swarm	2.75
❑38, Jan 1980, A: Morbius. V: Morbius	2.75
❑39, Feb 1980, V: Schizoid Man	2.75
❑40, Mar 1980, V: Lizard	2.75
❑41, Apr 1980, V: Meteor Man	2.75
❑42, May 1980, A: Human Torch	2.75
❑43, Jun 1980, 1: Belladonna	2.75
❑44, Jul 1980	2.75
❑45, Aug 1980, Vulture	2.75
❑46, Sep 1980, FM (c); MZ (a); Cobra	2.75
❑47, Oct 1980	2.75
❑48, Nov 1980, FM (c)	2.75
❑49, Dec 1980, KP (c); JM (a); A: Prowler. Title changes to Peter Parker, The Spectacular Spider-Man	2.75
❑50, Jan 1981, FM (c); JR2, JM (a); Smuggler	2.75
❑51, Feb 1981, FM (c); JM (a); V: Mysterio	2.75
❑52, Mar 1981, FM (c); A: White Tiger	2.75
❑53, Apr 1981, JR2 (c); JM (a); V: Tinkerer	2.75
❑54, May 1981, FM (c)	2.75
❑55, Jun 1981, FM (c); LMc (a); V: Nitro	2.75
❑56, Jul 1981, FM (c); JM (a); 2: Jack O'Lantern II. V: Jack O'Lantern II	5.00
❑57, Aug 1981, FM (c); JM (a)	2.75
❑58, Sep 1981, JBy (a); V: Ringer	2.75
❑59, Oct 1981, BWi (c); JM (a)	2.75
❑60, Nov 1981; Giant-size; FM, JM (c); JM (a); O: Spider-Man. V: Beetle	2.75
❑61, Dec 1981, JM (a); A: Moonstone	2.75
❑62, Jan 1982, FM (c); FM, JM (a); V: Gold Bug	2.75
❑63, Feb 1982, V: Molten Man	2.75
❑64, Mar 1982, 1: Cloak & Dagger	5.00
❑65, Apr 1982, BL (c); BH, JM (a); V: Kraven	3.00
❑66, May 1982, V: Electro	3.00
❑67, Jun 1982, V: Kingpin	3.00
❑68, Jul 1982, V: Robot Master	3.00
❑69, Aug 1982, A: Cloak & Dagger	3.00
❑70, Sep 1982, A: Cloak & Dagger	3.00

Other grades: Multiply price above by 5/6 for VF/NM • 2/3 for VERY FINE • 1/3 for FINE • 1/5 for VERY GOOD • 1/8 for GOOD

N-MINT

❑71, Oct 1982, Gun control story 3.00
❑72, Nov 1982, V: Doctor Octopus 3.00
❑73, Dec 1982, V: Owl 3.00
❑74, Jan 1983, BH (c); BH (a); A: Black Cat 3.00
❑75, Feb 1983; Giant-size; A: Black Cat.. 2.75
❑76, Mar 1983, A: Black Cat 3.00
❑77, Apr 1983, A: Gladiator 3.00
❑78, May 1983, V: Doctor Octopus 3.00
❑79, Jun 1983, V: Doctor Octopus 3.00
❑80, Jul 1983, J. Jonah Jameson solo story 3.00
❑81, Aug 1983, AM (c); AM, JM (a); A: Punisher. A: Cloak & Dagger 3.00
❑82, Sep 1983, A: Punisher. A: Cloak & Dagger 2.75
❑83, Oct 1983, A: Punisher 7.00
❑84, Nov 1983 3.00
❑85, Dec 1983, A: Hobgoblin (Ned Leeds). V: Hobgoblin 5.00
❑86, Jan 1984, A: Fred Hembeck. Asst. Editor Month 3.00
❑87, Feb 1984, AM (c); AM (a); reveals identity 3.00
❑88, Mar 1984, A: Black Cat. V: Mr. Hyde. V: Cobra 3.00
❑89, Apr 1984, A: Fantastic Four. A: Kingpin. Fantastic Four appearance 3.00
❑90, May 1984, AM (w); AM, JM (a); new costume; Black Cat's new powers 3.00
❑91, Jun 1984, V: Blob 3.00
❑92, Jul 1984, 1: The Answer. V: Answer 3.00
❑93, Aug 1984, V: Answer 3.00
❑94, Sep 1984, A: Cloak & Dagger. V: Silvermane 3.00
❑95, Oct 1984, A: Cloak & Dagger. V: Silvermane 3.00
❑96, Nov 1984, A: Cloak & Dagger. V: Silvermane 3.00
❑97, Dec 1984, V: Hermit 3.00
❑98, Jan 1985, 1: Spot. V: Kingpin 3.00
❑99, Feb 1985, V: Spot 3.00
❑100, Mar 1985; Giant-size; V: Spot; 100th anniversary issue 5.00
❑101, Apr 1985, V: Blacklash 3.00
❑102, May 1985, V: Killer Shrike 2.25
❑103, Jun 1985 2.25
❑104, Jul 1985, O: Rocket Racer. V: Rocket Racer 2.25
❑105, Aug 1985, A: Wasp 2.25
❑106, Sep 1985, A: Wasp 2.25
❑107, Oct 1985, D: Jean DeWolff 2.25
❑108, Nov 1985 2.25
❑109, Dec 1985 2.25
❑110, Jan 1986, A: Daredevil 2.25
❑111, Feb 1986; Secret Wars II 2.25
❑112, Mar 1986; Christmas story 2.25
❑113, Apr 1986 2.25
❑114, May 1986 2.25
❑115, Jun 1986 A: Doctor Strange 2.25
❑116, Jul 1986 A: Sabretooth 3.00
❑117, Aug 1986 A: Doctor Strange 2.00
❑118, Sep 1986 2.00
❑119, Oct 1986 A: Sabretooth 2.00
❑120, Nov 1986 2.00
❑121, Dec 1986 2.00
❑122, Jan 1987 2.00
❑123, Feb 1987; PD (w); V: Blaze 2.00
❑124, Mar 1987; BH (c); V: Doctor Octopus 2.00
❑125, Apr 1987 A: Spider Woman 2.00
❑126, May 1987 A: Spider Woman 2.00
❑127, Jun 1987; AM (c); V: Lizard 2.00
❑128, Jul 1987 A: Silver Sable 2.00
❑129, Aug 1987; V: Foreigner 2.00
❑130, Sep 1987; A: Hobgoblin. V: Hobgoblin 3.00
❑131, Oct 1987; MZ (a); Kraven 5.00
❑132, Nov 1987; Kraven 4.00
❑133, Dec 1987 BSz (c); BSz (a) 3.00
❑134, Jan 1988; V: Sin Eater 2.00
❑135, Feb 1988; V: Sin Eater. V: Electro. Title returns to The Spectacular Spider-Man 2.00
❑136, Mar 1988; V: Sin Eater 2.00
❑137, Apr 1988; V: Tarantula 2.00
❑138, May 1988; A: Captain America. V: Tarantula 2.00
❑139, Jun 1988; O: Tombstone 2.00
❑140, Jul 1988 A: Punisher 2.00
❑141, Aug 1988 A: Punisher 2.00

N-MINT

❑142, Sep 1988 A: Punisher 2.00
❑143, Oct 1988 A: Punisher 4.00
❑144, Nov 1988; V: Boomerang. in San Diego 2.00
❑145, Dec 1988 2.00
❑146, Jan 1989; SB (a); Inferno 2.00
❑147, Feb 1989; 1: Hobgoblin III. Inferno 8.00
❑148, Mar 1989; Inferno 2.00
❑149, Apr 1989; O: Carrion II (Malcolm McBride). 1: Carrion II (Malcolm McBride) 3.00
❑150, May 1989; V: Tombstone 2.00
❑151, Jun 1989; V: Tombstone 2.00
❑152, Jul 1989; SB (a); V: Lobo Brothers 2.00
❑153, Aug 1989; V: Tombstone 2.00
❑154, Sep 1989; V: Puma 2.00
❑155, Oct 1989; V: Tombstone 2.00
❑156, Nov 1989; V: Banjo 2.00
❑157, Nov 1989; V: Electro 2.00
❑158, Dec 1989; V: Trapster. Acts of Vengeance; Spider-Man gets cosmic powers 5.00
❑159, Dec 1989; V: Brothers Grimm. Acts of Vengeance; Cosmic-powered Spider-Man 4.00
❑160, Jan 1990; V: Doctor Doom. Acts of Vengeance; Cosmic-powered Spider-Man 1.50
❑161, Feb 1990; A: Hobgoblin III. V: Hobgoblin III 1.50
❑162, Mar 1990; A: Hobgoblin III. V: Carrion 1.50
❑163, Apr 1990; A: Hobgoblin III. V: Hobgoblin III. V: Carrion 1.50
❑164, May 1990; V: Beetle 1.50
❑165, Jun 1990; D: Arranger; (Extra artists listed in Letter Column) 1.50
❑166, Jul 1990 SB (c); SB (a) 1.50
❑167, Aug 1990 SB (c); SB (a) 1.50
❑168, Sep 1990; Avengers 1.50
❑169, Oct 1990; Avengers 1.50
❑170, Nov 1990; Avengers 1.50
❑171, Dec 1990; SB (a); V: Puma 1.50
❑172, Jan 1991; V: Puma 1.50
❑173, Feb 1991; SB (a); Doctor Octopus 1.50
❑174, Mar 1991; SB (a); Doctor Octopus 1.50
❑175, Apr 1991; SB (a); Doctor Octopus 1.50
❑176, May 1991; KB (w); SB (a); O: Corona. 1: Corona 1.50
❑177, Jun 1991 KB (w); SB (a) 1.50
❑178, Jul 1991; SB (a); V: Vermin 1.50
❑179, Aug 1991; SB (a); V: Vermin 1.50
❑180, Sep 1991; SB (a); A: Green Goblin. V: Green Goblin 1.50
❑181, Oct 1991; SB (a); A: Green Goblin. V: Green Goblin 1.50
❑182, Nov 1991; SB (a); O: Vermin. A: Green Goblin. V: Green Goblin 1.50
❑183, Dec 1991; SB (a); A: Green Goblin. V: Green Goblin 1.50
❑184, Jan 1992 SB (a); A: Green Goblin 1.50
❑185, Feb 1992 SB (a); A: Frogman 1.50
❑186, Mar 1992; SB (a); V: Vulture 1.50
❑187, Apr 1992; SB (a); V: Vulture 1.50
❑188, May 1992; SB (a); V: Vulture 1.50
❑189, Jun 1992; 30th Anniversary Issue; SB, CV, BMc (a); O: Spider-Man. Silver hologram cover; Gatefold painted poster 4.00
❑189/2nd, Jun 1992; 30th Anniversary Issue; SB (a); O: Spider-Man. 2nd printing; Gold hologram cover; Double-size; Gatefold painted poster.. 3.00
❑190, Jul 1992; SB (c); SB (a); 1: Angela Cairn (later Nocturne) 1.50
❑191, Aug 1992 SB (a) 1.50
❑192, Sep 1992 SB (a) 1.50
❑193, Oct 1992; SB (a); V: Puma 1.50
❑194, Nov 1992; SB (a); V: Vermin 1.50
❑195, Dec 1992; SB (a); V: Vermin 1.50
❑195/CS, Dec 1992; Polybagged with Dirt Magazine #2, cassette sampler tape; SB (a); "Dirtbag Special" 2.50
❑196, Jan 1993 SB (a); D: Vermin 1.50
❑197, Feb 1993 SB (a); A: Spider-Man .. 1.50
❑198, Mar 1993 SB (a); A: X-Men 1.50
❑199, Apr 1993 SB (a); A: X-Men 1.50
❑200, May 1993; SB (c); SB (a); D: Green Goblin. foil cover 4.00
❑201, Jun 1993 SB (a); A: Carnage. A: Venom 1.50

N-MINT

❑202, Jul 1993 SB (c); SB (a); A: Carnage. A: Venom 1.50
❑203, Aug 1993 SB (c); SB (a); A: Carnage. A: Venom 1.50
❑204, Sep 1993; SB (a); A: Tombstone. V: Tombstone 1.50
❑205, Oct 1993; SB (a); A: Tombstone. V: Tombstone 1.50
❑206, Nov 1993; SB (a); V: Tombstone.. 1.50
❑207, Dec 1993; SB (a); V: Shroud 1.50
❑208, Jan 1994; SB (a); V: Shroud 1.50
❑209, Feb 1994; SB (a); A: Punisher. V: Foreigner 1.50
❑210, Mar 1994; SB (a); V: Foreigner 1.50
❑211, Apr 1994 SB (a) 1.50
❑212, May 1994 SB (a) 1.50
❑213, Jun 1994; V: Typhoid Mary. White cover with $1.50 cover price 1.50
❑213/CS, Jun 1994; V: Typhoid Mary. TV preview; print 2.95
❑214, Jul 1994; V: Bloody Mary 1.50
❑215, Aug 1994 SB (a) 1.50
❑216, Sep 1994; SB (a); V: Scorpion 1.50
❑217, Oct 1994 A: Ben Reilly 1.50
❑217/Variant, Oct 1994; Giant-size; O: Ben Reilly. A: Ben Reilly. flip-book with back-up story; enhanced cover... 2.95
❑218, Nov 1994; SB (c); SB (a); V: Puma 1.50
❑219, Dec 1994 SB (c); SB (a); A: Daredevil 1.50
❑220, Jan 1995; Giant-size; flip book with illustrated story from The Ultimate Spider-Man back-up 2.50
❑221, Feb 1995; BSz, SB (a); D: Doctor Octopus 3.00
❑222, Mar 1995 BSz, SB (c); BSz, SB (a) 1.50
❑223, Apr 1995; Giant-size 2.50
❑223/Variant, Apr 1995; Giant-size; enhanced cover 2.95
❑224, May 1995; The Mark Of Kaine, Part 4 1.50
❑225, Jun 1995; Giant-size; SB (a); 1: Green Goblin IV. Hologram cover... 5.00
❑225/Variant, Jun 1995; Hologram on cover 3.95
❑226, Jul 1995; identity of clone revealed 1.50
❑227, Aug 1995 1.50
❑228, Sep 1995; continues in Web of Spider-Man #129 1.50
❑229, Oct 1995; Giant-size; BSz, SB (a); the clone retires; wraparound cover... 2.50
❑229/Variant, Oct 1995; enhanced acetate outer cover; the clone retires 3.95
❑230, Jan 1996; Giant-size; V: D.K.. Special cover 3.95
❑231, Feb 1996 SB (c); SB (a) 1.50
❑232, Mar 1996; SB (a); New Doctor Octopus returns 1.50
❑233, Apr 1996 SB (a) 1.50
❑234, May 1996 1.50
❑235, Jun 1996; return of Will o' the Wisp 1.50
❑236, Jul 1996; V: Dragon-Man 1.50
❑237, Aug 1996; V: Lizard 1.50
❑238, Sep 1996; O: second Lizard 1.50
❑239, Oct 1996; V: Lizard 1.50
❑240, Nov 1996 1.50
❑240/A, Nov 1996; Variant cover showing pregnant Mary Jane 1.50
❑241, Dec 1996 1.50
❑242, Jan 1997; V: Chameleon 1.50
❑243, Feb 1997; V: Chameleon 1.50
❑244, Mar 1997; 1: Kangaroo II. V: Kraven 1.99
❑245, Apr 1997; V: Chameleon 1.99
❑246, May 1997; V: Legion of Losers (Gibbon, Spot, Kangaroo, Grizzly) 1.99
❑247, Jun 1997; V: Jack O' Lantern II 1.99
❑248, Aug 1997; gatefold summary; V: Jack O' Lantern 1.99
❑249, Sep 1997; gatefold summary; Norman Osborn buys Daily Bugle 1.99
❑250, Oct 1997; Giant-size; JR2 (c); wraparound cover 2.99
❑251, Nov 1997; gatefold summary; V: Kraven 1.99
❑252, Dec 1997; gatefold summary; V: Kraven 1.99
❑253, Jan 1998; gatefold summary; V: Kraven. V: Calypso 1.99
❑254, Feb 1998; gatefold summary 1.99
❑255, Mar 1998; gatefold summary 1.99
❑255/Variant, Mar 1998; Variant "Wanted Dead or Alive" cover 5.00

Other grades: Multiply price above by 5/6 for VF/NM • 2/3 for VERY FINE • 1/3 for FINE • 1/5 for VERY GOOD • 1/8 for GOOD

Star Trek: Early Voyages

Captain Pike thinks outside the box
©Marvel

Star Trek: Starfleet Academy

They almost did a TV show like this
©Marvel

Star Trek: The Next Generation

Jean-Luc Picard sips wine, gives orders
©DC

Star Trek Unlimited

Stories not restricted to one cast of characters
©Marvel

Star Wars

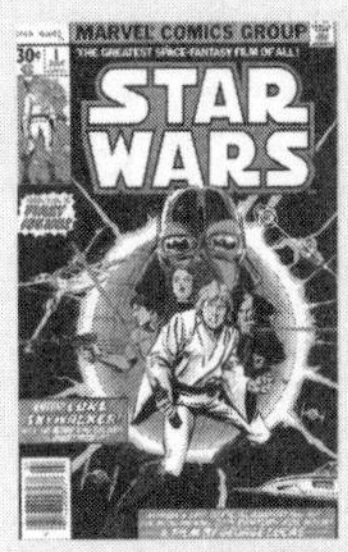

First issue was best-selling comic of the 1970s
©Marvel

N-MINT

❑256, Apr 1998; gatefold summary; V: White Rabbit ... 1.99
❑257, May 1998; gatefold summary; JR (c); Identity Crisis; has second cover with The Spectacular Prodigy #1 ... 1.99
❑258, Jun 1998; gatefold summary; V: Jack'OLantern & Conundrum ... 1.99
❑259, Jul 1998; gatefold summary ... 1.99
❑260, Aug 1998; gatefold summary ... 1.99
❑261, Sep 1998; gatefold summary ... 1.99
❑262, Oct 1998; gatefold summary ... 1.99
❑263, Nov 1998; gatefold summary; JBy (c); Final Issue ... 1.99
❑Ann 1, Dec 1979; RB, JM (a); Doctor Octopus ... 5.00
❑Ann 2, Sep 1980; JM (a); O: Rapier. 1: Rapier ... 4.00
❑Ann 3, Nov 1981 KP (a) ... 3.00
❑Ann 4, Nov 1984; O: Ben Parker ("Uncle Ben"). Title changes to Peter Parker, The Spectacular Spider-Man Ann ... 3.00
❑Ann 5, Oct 1985 ... 3.00
❑Ann 6, Oct 1986; series continues as Spectacular Spider-Man Ann ... 3.00
❑Ann 7, ca. 1987; V: Puma. Title returns to Spectacular Spider-Man Ann ... 3.00
❑Ann 8, ca. 1988 ... 4.00
❑Ann 9, ca. 1989; Atlantis Attacks ... 2.50
❑Ann 10, ca. 1990; SL (w); RB, TMc, RA (a); tiny Spider-Man ... 2.50
❑Ann 11, ca. 1991 EL (c); FH (w); FH (a) ... 2.50
❑Ann 12, ca. 1992; A: New Warriors. Venom back-up story ... 2.50
❑Ann 13, ca. 1993; AM, JR (a); trading card ... 2.95
❑Ann 14, ca. 1994; SB (a); V: Green Goblin; 1994 Ann ... 2.95
❑Ann 1997, ca. 1997; Peter Parker Spider-Man '97 ... 2.99
❑Special 1, ca. 1995; Flip-book; A: Scarlet Spider. A: The Lizard. A: Carnage. A: Venom. Super special ... 3.95

Spectacular Spider-Man
Marvel

❑1, Sep 2003, A: Venom ... 4.00
❑1/CanExpo, Sep 2003 ... 6.00
❑2, Sep 2003, A: Venom ... 3.00
❑3, Oct 2003, A: Venom ... 2.99
❑4, Nov 2003, A: Venom ... 4.00
❑5, Dec 2003, A: Venom ... 2.99
❑6, Jan 2004, A: Doctor Octopus ... 2.99
❑7, Jan 2004 ... 2.99
❑8, Feb 2004 ... 2.25
❑9, Mar 2004 ... 2.25
❑10, Apr 2004 ... 2.25
❑11, May 2004 ... 2.25
❑12, May 2005 ... 2.25
❑13, Jun 2004 ... 2.25
❑14, Jul 2004 ... 2.99
❑15, Aug 2004 ... 7.00
❑16, Aug 2004 ... 5.00
❑17, Sep 2004 ... 2.25
❑18, Oct 2004 ... 2.25
❑19, Nov 2004 ... 2.25
❑20, Dec 2004 ... 3.00
❑21, Jan 2005 ... 2.25
❑22, Feb 2005 ... 2.25
❑23, Mar 2005 ... 2.25

N-MINT

❑24, Apr 2005 ... 2.25
❑25, May 2005 ... 2.25
❑26, Jun 2005 ... 2.25
❑27, Jul 2005 ... 2.25

Spectacular Spider-Man Super Special
Marvel

❑1, Sep 1995; Flip-book; two of the stories conclude in Web of Spider-Man Super Special #1 ... 3.95

Spectre
DC

❑1, Dec 1967, MA, GC (a) ... 150.00
❑2, Feb 1968, NA (c); NA (a); 1pg "The Spectre interviews Neal Adams" ... 60.00
❑3, Apr 1968, NA (c); NA (a); Peter Sanderson L.O.C.; Carl Gafford L.O.C. ... 50.00
❑4, Jun 1968, NA (c); NA (w); NA (a); Klaus Janson L.O.C.; Irene Vartanoff L.O.C ... 50.00
❑5, Aug 1968, NA (c); NA (w); NA (a) ... 50.00
❑6, Oct 1968, MA (a) ... 40.00
❑7, Dec 1968, MA, DD (a); Klaus Janson L.O.C ... 40.00
❑8, Feb 1969, NC (c); MA (a) ... 40.00
❑9, Apr 1969, NC (c); BWr (a) ... 40.00
❑10, Jun 1969 ... 40.00

Spectre
DC

❑1, Apr 1987; GC (a); History of The Spectre two page treatise, Part 1 ... 3.00
❑2, May 1987; History of The Spectre two page treatise, Part 2 ... 2.50
❑3, Jun 1987 ... 2.50
❑4, Jul 1987 ... 2.50
❑5, Aug 1987 ... 2.50
❑6, Sep 1987 GC (a) ... 2.25
❑7, Oct 1987 A: Zatanna ... 2.25
❑8, Nov 1987 ... 2.25
❑9, Dec 1987 ... 2.25
❑10, Jan 1988; Millennium ... 2.25
❑11, Feb 1988; Millennium ... 2.00
❑12, Mar 1988 ... 2.00
❑13, Apr 1988 ... 2.00
❑14, May 1988 ... 2.00
❑15, Jun 1988 ... 2.00
❑16, Jul 1988 ... 2.00
❑17, Aug 1988 ... 1.75
❑18, Sep 1988 ... 1.75
❑19, Oct 1988 ... 1.75
❑20, Nov 1988 ... 1.75
❑21, Dec 1988 ... 1.50
❑22, Dec 1988 ... 1.50
❑23, Jan 1989; Invasion! ... 1.50
❑24, Feb 1989 ... 1.50
❑25, Apr 1989 ... 1.50
❑26, May 1989 ... 1.50
❑27, Jun 1989 ... 1.50
❑28, Aug 1989 ... 1.50
❑29, Sep 1989 ... 1.50
❑30, Oct 1989 ... 1.50
❑31, Nov 1989 ... 1.50
❑Ann 1, ca. 1988; A: Deadman. Madame Xanadu cameo; Kim Liang backup story ... 2.50

N-MINT

Spectre
DC

❑0, Oct 1994; O: The Spectre ... 2.50
❑1, Dec 1992; O: The Spectre. Glow-in-the-dark cover ... 6.00
❑2, Jan 1993 ... 5.00
❑3, Feb 1993 ... 4.00
❑4, Mar 1993 ... 3.00
❑5, Apr 1993 CV (c) ... 3.00
❑6, May 1993 ... 3.00
❑7, Jun 1993 ... 3.00
❑8, Jul 1993; Glow-in-the-dark cover ... 3.50
❑9, Aug 1993 MW (c) ... 3.00
❑10, Sep 1993 ... 3.00
❑11, Oct 1993 ... 3.00
❑12, Nov 1993 ... 3.00
❑13, Dec 1993; Glow-in-the-dark cover ... 3.00
❑14, Jan 1994 ... 2.50
❑15, Feb 1994 ... 2.50
❑16, Mar 1994 JA (a) ... 2.50
❑17, Apr 1994 ... 2.50
❑18, May 1994 ... 2.50
❑19, Jun 1994 ... 2.50
❑20, Jul 1994 BSz (c) ... 2.50
❑21, Aug 1994 ... 2.00
❑22, Sep 1994; ARo (c); A: Spear of Destiny. V: Superman ... 2.00
❑23, Nov 1994 ... 2.00
❑24, Dec 1994 ... 2.00
❑25, Jan 1995 ... 2.00
❑26, Feb 1995 ... 2.00
❑27, Mar 1995 ... 2.00
❑28, Apr 1995 ... 2.00
❑29, May 1995 ... 2.00
❑30, Jun 1995 ... 2.25
❑31, Jul 1995 ... 2.25
❑32, Aug 1995 ... 2.25
❑33, Sep 1995 ... 2.25
❑34, Oct 1995 ... 2.25
❑35, Nov 1995; Underworld Unleashed ... 2.25
❑36, Dec 1995; Underworld Unleashed ... 2.25
❑37, Jan 1996 ... 2.50
❑38, Feb 1996; O: Uncle Sam ... 2.50
❑39, Mar 1996; O: Shadrach; Continues in Man Of Steel #54 ... 2.50
❑40, Apr 1996; O: Captain Fear ... 2.50
❑41, May 1996 ... 2.50
❑42, Jun 1996 BB (c) ... 2.50
❑43, Jul 1996 ... 2.50
❑44, Aug 1996 ... 2.50
❑45, Sep 1996; homosexuality issues ... 2.50
❑46, Oct 1996; National Interest acquires Spear of Destiny ... 2.50
❑47, Nov 1996; Final Night ... 2.50
❑48, Dec 1996 ... 2.50
❑49, Jan 1997 ... 2.50
❑50, Feb 1997; 1: Patriot ... 2.50
❑51, Mar 1997 ... 2.50
❑52, Apr 1997; Gary Gianni cover ... 2.50
❑53, May 1997 ... 2.50
❑54, Jun 1997; 1: Mister Terrific II (Michael Holt) ... 2.50
❑55, Jul 1997 ... 2.50
❑56, Aug 1997 ... 2.50
❑57, Sep 1997 ... 2.50
❑58, Oct 1997; BWr (c); Genesis ... 2.50

Other grades: Multiply price above by 5/6 for VF/NM • 2/3 for VERY FINE • 1/3 for FINE • 1/5 for VERY GOOD • 1/8 for GOOD

❑59, Nov 1997 .... 2.50
❑60, Dec 1997; Face cover 2.50
❑61, Jan 1998 .... 2.50
❑62, Feb 1998; funeral of Jim Corrigan.. 2.50
❑Ann 1, ca. 1995; A: Doctor Fate. Year One 3.95

Spectre
DC

❑1, Mar 2001 .... 3.00
❑2, Apr 2001 .... 2.50
❑3, May 2001 .... 2.50
❑4, Jun 2001 .... 2.50
❑5, Jul 2001 A: Two-Face 2.50
❑6, Aug 2001 .... 2.50
❑7, Sep 2001 .... 2.50
❑8, Oct 2001 .... 2.50
❑9, Nov 2001 .... 2.50
❑10, Dec 2001; Joker: Last Laugh crossover 2.50
❑11, Jan 2002 .... 2.50
❑12, Feb 2002 .... 2.50
❑13, Mar 2002 .... 2.50
❑14, Apr 2002 .... 2.50
❑15, May 2002 .... 2.50
❑16, Jun 2002 .... 2.50
❑17, Jul 2002 .... 2.50
❑18, Aug 2002 .... 2.50
❑19, Sep 2002 CR (c) 2.50
❑20, Oct 2002 CR (c) 2.75
❑21, Nov 2002 CR (c) 2.75
❑22, Dec 2002 CR (c) 2.75
❑23, Jan 2003 .... 2.75
❑24, Feb 2003 .... 2.75
❑25, Mar 2003 .... 2.75
❑26, Apr 2003 .... 2.75
❑27, May 2003; Final issue 2.75

Spectrescope
Spectre

❑1, Mar 1994; giveaway; no cover price 1.00

Spectrum
New Horizons

❑1, Jul 1987, b&w 1.50

Spectrum Comics Previews
Spectrum

❑1, Feb 1983; 1: Survivors; Magazine size; Continued in Survivors #1 .... 3.00

Speedball
Marvel

❑1, Sep 1988; SD (c); SD (w); SD (a); O: Speedball 1.00
❑2, Oct 1988 SD (c); SD (w); SD (a) 1.00
❑3, Nov 1988 SD (c); SD (w); SD (a) 1.00
❑4, Dec 1988 SD (c); SD (w); SD (a) 1.00
❑5, Jan 1989 SD (c); SD (w); SD (a) 1.00
❑6, Feb 1989 SD (c); SD (w); SD (a) 1.00
❑7, Mar 1989 SD (c); SD (w); SD (a) 1.00
❑8, Apr 1989 SD (c); SD (w); SD (a) 1.00
❑9, May 1989 SD (c); SD (w); SD (a) 1.00
❑10, Jun 1989 SD (c); SD (w); SD (a) 1.00

Speed Buggy
Charlton

❑1, May 1975, 64 pages 12.00
❑2, Sep 1975 .... 8.00
❑3, Nov 1975 .... 8.00
❑4, Jan 1976 .... 8.00
❑5, Mar 1976 .... 8.00
❑6, May 1976 .... 8.00
❑7, Jul 1976 .... 8.00
❑8, Sep 1976 .... 8.00
❑9, Nov 1976 .... 8.00

Speed Demon
Marvel / Amalgam

❑1, Apr 1996, AM (a) 2.00

Speed Force
DC

❑1, Nov 1997; anthology series with stories of the various Flashes 3.95

Speed Racer
Now

❑1, Aug 1987; O: Speed Racer 2.50
❑1/2nd; O: Speed Racer. 2nd printing 1.50
❑2, Sep 1987 .... 2.00
❑3, Oct 1987 .... 2.00
❑4, Nov 1987 .... 1.75
❑5, Dec 1987 .... 1.75
❑6, Jan 1988 .... 1.75
❑7, Mar 1988 .... 1.75
❑8, Apr 1988 .... 1.75
❑9, May 1988 .... 1.75
❑10, Jun 1988 .... 1.75
❑11, Jul 1988 .... 1.75
❑12, Aug 1988 .... 1.75
❑13, Sep 1988 .... 1.75
❑14, Oct 1988 .... 1.75
❑15, Nov 1988 .... 1.75
❑16, Dec 1988 .... 1.75
❑17, Jan 1989 .... 1.75
❑18, Mar 1989 .... 1.75
❑19, Apr 1989 .... 1.75
❑20, May 1989 .... 1.75
❑21, Jun 1989 .... 1.75
❑22, Jul 1989 .... 1.75
❑23, Aug 1989; Includes poster 1.75
❑24, Sep 1989 .... 1.75
❑25, Oct 1989 .... 1.75
❑26, Nov 1989 .... 1.75
❑27, Dec 1989 .... 1.75
❑28, Jan 1990 .... 1.75
❑29, Feb 1990 .... 1.75
❑30, Mar 1990 .... 1.75
❑31, Apr 1990 .... 1.75
❑32, May 1990 .... 1.75
❑33, Jun 1990 .... 1.75
❑34, Jul 1990 .... 1.75
❑35, Aug 1990 .... 1.75
❑36, Sep 1990 .... 1.75
❑37, Oct 1990 .... 1.75
❑38, Nov 1990; Final Issue 1.75
❑Special 1, Mar 1988; O: The Mach 5 (Speed Racer's car) 2.50
❑Special 1/2nd, Sep 1988; 2nd printing. 1.75

Speed Racer
DC / Wildstorm

❑1, Oct 1999 .... 2.50
❑2, Nov 1999 .... 2.50
❑3, Dec 1999 .... 2.50

Speed Racer 3-D Special
Now

❑1, Jan 1993 .... 2.95

Speed Racer Classics
Now

❑1, Oct 1988, b&w 3.75
❑2, Feb 1989, b&w 3.95

Speed Racer Featuring Ninja High School
Now / Eternity

❑1, Aug 1993; trading card 2.50
❑2, Sep 1993; two trading cards 2.50

Speed Racer: Return of the GRX
Now

❑1, Mar 1994 .... 1.95
❑2, Apr 1994 .... 1.95

Speed Racer: The Original Manga
DC / Wildstorm

❑1 .... 9.95

Speed Tribes
Nemicron

❑1, Aug 1998 .... 2.95

Spellbinders
Fleetway-Quality

❑1, Dec 1986 .... 1.50
❑2, Jan 1986 .... 1.50
❑3, Feb 1986 .... 1.50
❑4, Mar 1986 .... 1.50
❑5, Apr 1986 .... 1.50
❑6, May 1986 .... 1.50
❑7, Jun 1986 .... 1.50
❑8, Jul 1986 .... 1.50
❑9, Aug 1986 .... 1.50
❑10, Sep 1986 .... 1.50
❑11, Oct 1986 .... 1.50
❑12, Nov 1986 .... 1.50

Spellbinders
Marvel

❑1, May 2005 .... 2.99
❑2, Jun 2005 .... 2.99
❑3, Jul 2005 .... 2.99
❑4, Aug 2005 .... 2.99
❑5, Sep 2005 .... 2.99
❑6, Oct 2005 .... 2.99

Spellbound
Marvel

❑1, Jan 1988 .... 1.50
❑2, Feb 1988 .... 1.50
❑3, Feb 1988 .... 1.50
❑4, Mar 1988 .... 1.50
❑5, Apr 1988 .... 1.50
❑6, Apr 1988; Double Size 2.25

Spellcaster
Medusa

❑1 .... 2.95
❑2 .... 2.95
❑3 .... 2.95

Spelljammer
DC

❑1, Sep 1990 .... 1.75
❑2, Oct 1990 .... 1.75
❑3, Nov 1990 .... 1.75
❑4, Dec 1990 .... 1.75
❑5, Jan 1991 .... 1.75
❑6, Feb 1991 .... 1.75
❑7, Mar 1991 .... 1.75
❑8, Apr 1991 .... 1.75
❑9, May 1991 .... 1.75
❑10, Jun 1991 .... 1.75
❑11, Jul 1991 .... 1.75
❑12, Aug 1991 .... 1.75
❑13, Sep 1991 .... 1.75
❑14, Oct 1991 .... 1.75
❑15, Nov 1991 .... 1.75
❑16, Dec 1991 .... 1.75
❑17, Jan 1992 .... 1.75
❑18, Feb 1992 .... 1.75

Spex-7
Shadow Shock

❑1, Sum 1994, b&w 1.50

Spicecapades
Fantagraphics

❑1, Spr 1999; magazine-sized; wraparound cover; Spice Girls parody 4.95

Spicy Adult Stories
Aircel

❑1, Mar 1991; pulp reprints 2.50
❑2, Apr 1991; pulp reprints 2.50
❑3, May 1991; pulp reprints 2.50
❑4, Jun 1991; pulp reprints 2.50

Spicy Tales
Eternity

❑1, Apr 1988, b&w; Reprints 1.95
❑2, Jun 1988, b&w; Reprints 1.95
❑3, Aug 1988, b&w; Reprints 1.95
❑4, Oct 1988, b&w; Reprints 1.95
❑5, Dec 1988, b&w; Reprints 1.95
❑6, Feb 1989, b&w; Reprints 1.95
❑7, May 1989, b&w; Reprints 1.95
❑8, Jun 1989, b&w; Reprints 1.95
❑9, Jul 1989, b&w; Reprints 1.95
❑10, Aug 1989 .... 1.95
❑11, Sep 1989 .... 1.95
❑12, Oct 1989 .... 1.95
❑13, Nov 1989 .... 1.95
❑14, Dec 1989 .... 2.25
❑15, Feb 1990 .... 2.25
❑16, Mar 1990 .... 2.25
❑17, Apr 1990 .... 2.25
❑18, May 1990 .... 2.95
❑19, Jun 1990 .... 2.95
❑20, Jul 1990 .... 2.95
❑Special 1, Feb 1989, b&w; Reprints 2.25
❑Special 2, Apr 1989, b&w; Reprints 2.25

Spider
Eclipse

❑1, Jun 1991; Wings 4.95
❑2, Aug 1991 .... 4.95
❑3, Oct 1991 .... 4.95

Spiderbaby Comix
Spiderbaby

❑1, Nov 1996 .... 3.95

Spider-Boy
Marvel / Amalgam

❑1, Apr 1996 .... 2.50

Other grades: Multiply price above by 5/6 for VF/NM • 2/3 for VERY FINE • 1/3 for FINE • 1/5 for VERY GOOD • 1/8 for GOOD

Star Wars

Dark Horse title turns into Star Wars: Republic
©Dark Horse

Star Wars: Dark Empire

Could be the basis of Episodes VII-IX
©Dark Horse

Star Wars: Dark Force Rising

Timothy Zahn novel comes to comics
©Dark Horse

Star Wars: Darth Maul

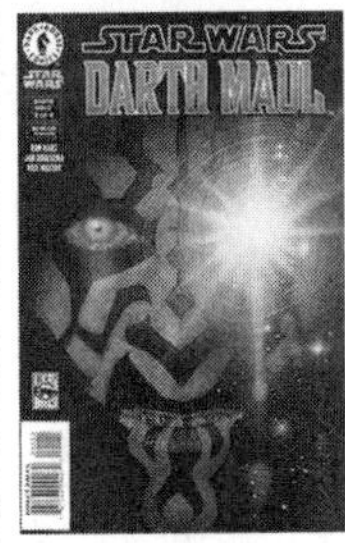

Short-lived Sith proved popular
©Dark Horse

Star Wars: Droids

Robotic Laurel and Hardy provided laughs
©Dark Horse

N-MINT

Spider-Boy Team-Up
Marvel / Amalgam

❑1, Jun 1997 ... 1.95

Spider-Femme
Spoof

❑1; parody ... 2.50

Spider Garden
NBM

❑1; Adult ... 12.95

Spider-Girl
Marvel

❑0, Oct 1998; O: Spider-Girl. reprints What If? #105 ... 2.00
❑½; Wizard promotional edition; V: Sabreclaw; V: Enthralla; Wizard promotional edition from Wizard #97; Includes certificate of authenticity; Story takes place between #12 & 13 of regular series; ca. 1999 ... 3.00
❑1, Oct 1998, White cover with Spider-Girl facing forward ... 4.00
❑1/A, Oct 1998, variant cover ... 4.00
❑2, Nov 1998, gatefold summary; 1: Crazy Eight; 1: Darkdevil; Standard cover: Darkdevil background ... 3.00
❑3, Dec 1998, gatefold summary; 1: Mr. Walters (Daily Bugle); 1: Fantastic Five; 1: Spyral; 1: Psi Lord; V: Spyral ... 3.00
❑4, Jan 1999, V: Dragon King; I: Dragon King ... 3.00
❑5, Feb 1999, 1: Spider-Venom. A: Venom ... 3.00
❑6, Mar 1999, A: Ladyhawk. A: Green Goblin ... 1.99
❑7, Apr 1999, A: Nova. A: Mary Jane Parker ... 1.99
❑8, May 1999, A: Kingpin. V: Mr. Nobody. V: Crazy Eight ... 1.99
❑9, Jun 1999, V: Killer Watt ... 1.99
❑10, Jul 1999, A: Spider-Man ... 1.99
❑11, Aug 1999, A: Human Torch. A: Spider-Man. V: Spider-Slayer; Includes Marvel Got Milk? card ... 1.99
❑12, Sep 1999, Includes Marvel Got Milk? card ... 1.99
❑13, Oct 1999 ... 1.99
❑14, Nov 1999, Gatefold cover; Includes Marvel Super Heroes Adventure featuring 8 page Spider-Man ... 1.99
❑15, Dec 1999, AW (a); 1: Mr. Abnormal ... 1.99
❑16, Jan 2000, Includes Marvel Super Heroes Adventure featuring 8-page Spider-Man bonus insert anti-drug promotion ... 2.25
❑17, Feb 2000, V: Kaine; Double sized issue; Peter Parker suits up ... 2.99
❑18, Mar 2000, 1: The Buzz; 1: Raptor (Brenda Drago); V: Mysterio; Bonus insert featuring Marvel Super-Heroes Spider-Man & Human Torch ... 2.25
❑19, Apr 2000 ... 2.25
❑20, May 2000 ... 2.25
❑21, Jun 2000, 1: Earthshaker ... 2.25
❑22, Jul 2000 ... 2.25
❑23, Aug 2000 ... 2.25
❑24, Sep 2000, 1: Dragonfist; V: Dragonfist ... 2.25
❑25, Oct 2000 ... 2.99
❑26, Nov 2000, Gatefold cover ... 2.25
❑27, Dec 2000 ... 2.25

N-MINT

❑28, Jan 2001 ... 2.25
❑29, Feb 2001 ... 2.25
❑30, Mar 2001 ... 2.25
❑31, Apr 2001, 1: G. W. Bridge (US President) ... 2.25
❑32, May 2001, 1: Spider-Man III (cameo); V: Soldiers of the Serpent ... 2.25
❑33, Jun 2001 ... 2.25
❑34, Jul 2001 ... 2.25
❑35, Aug 2001 ... 2.25
❑36, Sep 2001 ... 2.25
❑37, Oct 2001 ... 2.25
❑38, Nov 2001 ... 2.25
❑39, Dec 2001 ... 2.25
❑40, Jan 2002 ... 2.25
❑41, Feb 2002, 'Nuff Said Issue, No Dialogue; Script for wordless issue included in back book ... 2.25
❑42, Mar 2002 ... 2.25
❑43, Mar 2002 ... 2.25
❑44, Apr 2002 ... 2.25
❑45, May 2002, wraparound cover ... 2.25
❑46, Jun 2002 ... 2.25
❑47, Jul 2002 ... 2.25
❑48, Aug 2002 ... 2.25
❑49, Sep 2002 ... 2.25
❑50, Oct 2002 ... 2.25
❑51, Nov 2002 ... 2.25
❑52, Dec 2002 ... 2.25
❑53, Jan 2003 ... 2.25
❑54, Feb 2003 ... 2.25
❑55, Mar 2003 ... 2.25
❑56, Apr 2003 ... 2.25
❑57, May 2003 ... 2.25
❑58, Jun 2003 ... 2.25
❑59, Jun 2003 ... 2.99
❑60, Jul 2003, AW (c); AW (a) ... 2.99
❑61, Aug 2003, AW (c); AW (a) ... 2.99
❑62, Sep 2003, SB (a) ... 2.99
❑63, Oct 2003, SB (a) ... 2.99
❑64, Nov 2003, KJ (c); SB (a) ... 2.99
❑65, Dec 2003, KJ (c); SB (a) ... 2.99
❑66, Jan 2004, SB (c); SB (a) ... 2.99
❑67, Feb 2004, SB (c); SB (a) ... 2.99
❑68, Mar 2004, SB (c); SB (a) ... 2.99
❑69, Mar 2004 ... 2.99
❑70, Apr 2004, SB (a) ... 2.99
❑71, May 2004, SB (a) ... 2.99
❑72, Jun 2004, SB (a) ... 2.99
❑73, Jul 2004, SB (a) ... 2.99
❑74, Aug 2004, SB (a) ... 2.99
❑75, Sep 2004 ... 8.00
❑76, Sep 2004 ... 2.99
❑77, Oct 2004 ... 2.99
❑78, Oct 2004 ... 2.99
❑79, Nov 2004 ... 2.99
❑80, Dec 2004 ... 2.99
❑81, Jan 2005 ... 2.99
❑82, Feb 2005 ... 2.99
❑83, Mar 2005 ... 2.99
❑84, Apr 2005 ... 2.99
❑85, May 2005 ... 2.99
❑86, Jun 2005 ... 2.99
❑87, Jul 2005 ... 2.99
❑88, Aug 2005 ... 2.99
❑89, Sep 2005 ... 2.99

N-MINT

❑90, Oct 2005 ... 2.99
❑91, Nov 2005 ... 2.99
❑92, Jan 2006 ... 2.99
❑93, Feb 2006 ... 2.99
❑94, Mar 2006 ... 2.99
❑95, Mar 2006 ... 2.99
❑96, May 2006 ... 2.99
❑97, Jun 2006 ... 2.99
❑98, Jul 2006 ... 2.99
❑99, Aug 2006 ... 2.99
❑100, Sep 2006, Final Issue; Reprints Spider-Girl # 27 & 53 ... 3.99
❑Ann 1999, ca. 1999; Wraparound cover; Previews Wild Thing #1; Previews Fantastic Five #1 ... 3.99

Spider-Man
Marvel

❑-1, Jul 1997; Flashback ... 2.00
❑½, ca. 1999 ... 4.00
❑½/Platinum, ca. 1999; Platinum edition ... 6.00
❑1, Aug 1990; TMc (c); TMc (w); TMc (a); Green cover (newsstand) ... 5.00
❑1/CG, Aug 1990; TMc (c); TMc (w); TMc (a); bagged newsstand (green) ... 5.00
❑1/CS, Aug 1990; TMc (c); TMc (w); TMc (a); bagged silver cover ... 5.00
❑1/Platinum, Aug 1990; giveaway; TMc (c); TMc (w); TMc (a); Platinum edition ... 42.00
❑1/Silver, Aug 1990; TMc (c); TMc (w); TMc (a); silver cover ... 5.00
❑1/2nd; TMc (c); TMc (w); TMc (a); Gold cover; UPC box ... 50.00
❑1/Direct ed./2n, Aug 1990; TMc (c); TMc (w); TMc (a); Gold cover; direct sale ... 5.00
❑2, Sep 1990; TMc (c); TMc (w); TMc (a); Lizard ... 3.00
❑3, Oct 1990; TMc (c); TMc (w); TMc (a); Lizard ... 3.00
❑4, Nov 1990; TMc (c); TMc (w); TMc (a); Lizard ... 3.00
❑5, Dec 1990; TMc (c); TMc (w); TMc (a); Lizard ... 3.00
❑6, Jan 1991; TMc (c); TMc (w); TMc (a); A: Ghost Rider. V: Hobgoblin ... 3.00
❑7, Feb 1991; TMc (c); TMc (w); TMc (a); A: Ghost Rider. V: Hobgoblin ... 3.00
❑8, Mar 1991; TMc (c); TMc (w); TMc (a); A: Wolverine. V: Wendigo ... 2.50
❑9, Apr 1991; TMc (c); TMc (w); TMc (a); A: Wolverine. V: Wendigo ... 6.00
❑10, May 1991; TMc (c); TMc (w); TMc (a); A: Wolverine. V: Wendigo ... 4.00
❑11, Jun 1991; TMc (c); TMc (w); TMc (a); A: Wolverine. V: Wendigo ... 2.50
❑12, Jul 1991; TMc (c); TMc (w); TMc (a); A: Wolverine. V: Wendigo ... 2.50
❑13, Aug 1991; TMc (c); TMc (w); TMc (a); Spider-Man wears black costume ... 5.00
❑14, Sep 1991 TMc (c); TMc (w); TMc (a) ... 2.50
❑15, Oct 1991 EL (c); EL (w); EL (a); A: Beast ... 2.00
❑16, Nov 1991; TMc (c); TMc (w); TMc (a); X-Force; Sideways printing ... 2.00
❑17, Dec 1991; AW (a); A: Thanos. V: Thanos ... 2.00
❑18, Jan 1992; EL (c); EL (w); EL (a); Ghost Rider ... 2.00
❑19, Feb 1992 EL (c); EL (w); EL (a); A: Hulk ... 2.00

	N-MINT
❑20, Mar 1992 EL (c); EL (w); EL (a); A: Nova. A: Hulk. A: Solo. A: Deathlok	2.00
❑21, Apr 1992; EL (c); EL (w); EL (a); A: Solo. A: Deathlok. Deathlok appearance	2.00
❑22, May 1992 EL (c); EL (w); EL (a); A: Sleepwalker. A: Hulk. A: Ghost Rider. A: Deathlok	2.00
❑23, Jun 1992; EL (c); EL (w); EL (a); A: Fantastic Four. A: Hulk. A: Ghost Rider. A: Deathlok. Wraparound & gatefold cover	2.00
❑24, Jul 1992; Infinity War	2.00
❑25, Aug 1992 A: Phoenix	2.00
❑26, Sep 1992; 30th Anniversary Edition; O: Spider-Man. Gatefold poster; Hologram cover	4.00
❑27, Oct 1992 MR (c); MR (a)	2.00
❑28, Nov 1992	2.00
❑29, Dec 1992	2.00
❑30, Jan 1993	2.00
❑31, Feb 1993	2.00
❑32, Mar 1993 BMc (c); BMc (a)	2.00
❑33, Apr 1993 BMc (c); BMc (a); A: Punisher	2.00
❑34, May 1993 BMc (c); BMc (a); A: Punisher	2.00
❑35, Jun 1993 A: Carnage. A: Venom	2.00
❑36, Jul 1993 A: Carnage. A: Venom	2.00
❑37, Aug 1993 AM (a); A: Carnage. A: Venom	2.00
❑38, Sep 1993 KJ (c); KJ (a)	2.00
❑39, Oct 1993 KJ (c); KJ (a); A: Electro	2.00
❑40, Nov 1993; KJ (c); KJ (a); V: Electro	2.00
❑41, Dec 1993	2.00
❑42, Jan 1994; Iron Fist Apperance	2.00
❑43, Feb 1994; Iron Fist Apperance	2.00
❑44, Mar 1994	2.00
❑45, Apr 1994	2.00
❑46, May 1994	2.00
❑46/CS, May 1994; with print	3.00
❑47, Jun 1994; V: Hobgoblin	2.00
❑48, Jul 1994; V: Hobgoblin	2.00
❑49, Aug 1994	2.00
❑50, Sep 1994	2.50
❑50/Variant, Sep 1994; Holo-grafix cover	3.95
❑51, Oct 1994 A: Ben Reilly	2.50
❑51/Variant, Oct 1994; Giant-size; O: Ben Reilly. flip-book with back-up; enhanced cover	2.95
❑52, Nov 1994; The clone vs. Venom	2.00
❑53, Dec 1994; The clone defeats Venom	2.00
❑54, Jan 1995; flip book with illustrated story from The Ultimate Spider-Man back-up	2.00
❑55, Feb 1995; V: Grim Hunter	2.00
❑56, Mar 1995; Return of Gwen Stacy	2.00
❑57, Apr 1995; Giant-size; JR (c); JR2 (a)	2.50
❑57/Variant, Apr 1995; Giant-size; enhanced cardstock cover	2.95
❑58, May 1995	2.00
❑59, Jun 1995	2.00
❑60, Jul 1995; Kaine's identity revealed	2.00
❑61, Aug 1995	2.00
❑62, Sep 1995	2.00
❑63, Oct 1995; OverPower game cards bound-in	2.00
❑64, Jan 1996; V: Poison	2.00
❑65, Feb 1996	2.00
❑66, Mar 1996 JR2 (c); JR2 (a)	2.00
❑67, Apr 1996 JR2 (c); JR2 (w); AM, AW, JR2 (a)	2.00
❑68, May 1996	2.00
❑69, Jun 1996	2.00
❑70, Jul 1996 A: Hammerhead	2.00
❑71, Aug 1996; JR2 (c); JR2 (a); V: Hammerhead	2.00
❑72, Sep 1996; JR2 (c); JR2 (a); V: Sentinels	2.00
❑73, Oct 1996 JR2 (c); JR2 (a)	2.00
❑74, Nov 1996 JR2 (c); JR2 (a); A: Daredevil	2.00
❑75, Dec 1996; Giant-size; JR2 (c); JR2 (a); D: Ben Reilly. wraparound cover; return of original Green Goblin	3.50
❑76, Jan 1997; JR2 (c); JR2 (a); A: S.H.O.C.. V: S.H.O.C	2.00
❑77, Feb 1997; V: Morbius; Story continued in part from X-Man #24	2.00
❑78, Mar 1997; JR2 (c); JR2 (a); V: Morbius	2.00
❑79, Apr 1997; JR2 (c); JR2 (a); A: Morbius. V: S.H.O.C	2.00
❑80, May 1997; JR2 (c); JR2 (a); A: Morbius. V: Hammerhead	2.00
❑81, Jun 1997 JR2 (c); JR2 (a)	2.00
❑82, Aug 1997; gatefold summary; JR2 (c); JR2 (a)	2.00
❑83, Sep 1997; gatefold summary; JR2 (c); JR2 (a)	2.00
❑84, Oct 1997; gatefold summary; JR2 (c); JR2 (a); V: Juggernauty	2.00
❑85, Nov 1997; gatefold summary; V: Shocker	2.00
❑86, Dec 1997; gatefold summary; JR2 (c); JR2 (a); A: Trapster. V: Shocker	2.00
❑87, Jan 1998; gatefold summary; JR2 (c); JR2 (a); V: Shocker	2.00
❑88, Feb 1998; gatefold summary	2.00
❑89, Mar 1998; gatefold summary; JR2 (c); JR2 (a); V: Punisher. V: Shotgun	2.00
❑90, Apr 1998; gatefold summary; 1: Spidey as Dusk. V: Blastaar	2.00
❑91, May 1998; gatefold summary; Identity Crisis	2.00
❑92, Jun 1998; gatefold summary; JR2 (c); JR2 (a); Identity Crisis	2.00
❑93, Jul 1998; gatefold summary; A: Ghost Rider	2.00
❑94, Aug 1998; gatefold summary	2.00
❑95, Sep 1998; gatefold summary; V: Nitro	2.00
❑96, Oct 1998; gatefold summary; A: Madame Web	2.00
❑97, Nov 1998; gatefold summary; JBy (c); JR2 (a)	2.00
❑98/A, Nov 1998; gatefold summary; Series begins again as Peter Parker: Spider-Man; Spider-Man against stylized sun; Final Issue	2.00
❑98/B, Nov 1998; gatefold summary; JBy (c); JR2 (a); Alternate cover; series begins again as Peter Parker: Spider-Man	2.00
❑Ann 1997, ca. 1997	2.99
❑Ann 1998, ca. 1998; gatefold summary; A: Devil Dinosaur. A: Moon Boy. wraparound cover	2.99
❑GS 1, Dec 1998; Giant-Sized Spider-Man	3.99
❑Holiday 1995; A: Human Torch. A: Venom	2.95

Spider-Man Adventures
Marvel

	N-MINT
❑1, Dec 1994; adapts animated series	1.50
❑1/Variant, Dec 1994; Adapts animated series; enhanced cover	2.95
❑2, Jan 1995; adapts animated series	1.50
❑3, Feb 1995; adapts animated series	1.50
❑4, Mar 1995; adapts animated series	1.50
❑5, Apr 1995; adapts animated series	1.50
❑6, May 1995; adapts animated series	1.50
❑7, Jun 1995; adapts animated series	1.50
❑8, Jul 1995; Adapts animated series	1.50
❑9, Aug 1995; Adapts animated series	1.50
❑10, Sep 1995; Adapts animated series.	1.50
❑11, Oct 1995; Adapts animated series	1.50
❑12, Nov 1995; Adapts animated series	1.50
❑13, Dec 1995; Adapts animated series.	1.50
❑14, Jan 1996; Adapts animated series	1.50
❑15, Feb 1996; Adapts animated series; Continues in Adventures of Spider-Man #1	1.50

Spider-Man and Arana Special
Marvel

	N-MINT
❑1, Jun 2006	3.99

Spider-Man and Batman
Marvel

	N-MINT
❑1, Sep 1995; prestige format; NN	5.95

Spider-Man and Daredevil Special Edition
Marvel

	N-MINT
❑1, Mar 1984; Reprints from Spectacular Spider-Man #27 (with 4 extra pages) and 28	2.00

Spider-Man and Doctor Octopus: Negative Exposure
Marvel

	N-MINT
❑1, Dec 2003	2.99
❑2, Jan 2004	2.99
❑3, Feb 2004, Negative Exposure	2.99
❑4, Mar 2004	2.99
❑5, Apr 2004	2.99

Spider-Man and His Amazing Friends
Marvel

	N-MINT
❑1, Dec 1981, JR2 (c); DS (a); 1: Firestar. A: Iceman. A: Green Goblin. Adapted from television show	10.00

Spider-Man and Mysterio
Marvel

	N-MINT
❑1, Jan 2001; says Spider-Man: The Mysterio Manifesto on the cover	2.99
❑2, Feb 2001; says Spider-Man: The Mysterio Manifesto on the cover	2.99
❑3, Mar 2001; says Spider-Man: The Mysterio Manifesto on the cover	2.99

Spider-Man and Power Pack
Marvel

	N-MINT
❑1, Jan 2007	2.99
❑2, Feb 2007	2.99
❑3, Mar 2007	2.99

Spider-Man and the Dallas Cowboys
Marvel

	N-MINT
❑1, Sep 1983; Danger in Dallas giveaway; NN	10.00

Spider-Man and the Incredible Hulk
Marvel

	N-MINT
❑1, Sep 1981; Chaos in Kansas City giveaway; Denver Post giveaway	10.00

Spider-Man & the New Mutants
Marvel

	N-MINT
❑1; giveaway; child abuse	3.00

Spider-Man & Wolverine
Marvel

	N-MINT
❑1, Aug 2003	2.99
❑2, Sep 2003	2.99
❑3, Oct 2003	2.99
❑4, Nov 2003	2.99

Spider-Man and X-Factor: Shadowgames
Marvel

	N-MINT
❑1, May 1994; PB (c); KB (w); PB (a); O: Shadow Force. 1: Shadow Force	2.25
❑2, Jun 1994 KB (w); PB (a)	2.25
❑3, Jul 1994 PB (c); KB (w); PB (a)	2.25

Spider-Man/Badrock
Maximum

	N-MINT
❑1/A, Mar 1997; first part of story	2.99
❑1/B, Mar 1997; second part of story	2.99

Spider-Man/Black Cat: The Evil That Men Do
Marvel

	N-MINT
❑1, Aug 2002 KSm (w)	5.00
❑1/Dynamic, Aug 2002	7.00
❑2, Sep 2002; KSm (w); V: Scorpia	3.00
❑3, Oct 2002 KSm (w)	2.99
❑4, Feb 2006	2.99
❑5, Feb 2006	2.99
❑6, Mar 2006	2.99

Spider-Man: Blue
Marvel

	N-MINT
❑1, Jul 2002	6.00
❑2, Aug 2002	5.00
❑3, Sep 2002	3.50
❑4, Oct 2002; V: Vulture	3.50
❑5, Nov 2002	3.50
❑6, Apr 2003	3.50

Spider-Man: Breakout
Marvel

	N-MINT
❑1, Jun 2005	2.99
❑2, Jul 2005	2.99
❑3, Aug 2005	2.99
❑4, Sep 2005	2.99
❑5, Oct 2005	2.99

Spider-Man: Chapter One
Marvel

	N-MINT
❑0, May 1999; O: Lizard; O: Sandman; O: Vulture	2.50
❑1, Dec 1998; O: Doctor Octopus; O: Spider-Man	2.50
❑1/A, Dec 1998; DFE alternate cover	4.00
❑1/B, Dec 1998; Signed edition; O: Spider-Man; O: Doctor Octopus	14.00
❑1/C, Dec 1998; DFE alternate cover, signed	14.00

Star Wars: Episode I The Phantom Menace

In the comics, you can't hear Jar Jar
©Dark Horse

Star Wars Handbook

Guide to Stackpole's Rogue Squadron series
©Dark Horse

Star Wars: Infinities: A New Hope

How one tiny change can affect a universe
©Dark Horse

Star Wars: Jabba the Hutt

Should have had extra widescreen version
©Dark Horse

Star Wars: Jedi - Mace Windu

Polished, poised Jedi proves himself
©Dark Horse

	N-MINT
❑2/A, Dec 1998; Cover A	2.50
❑2/B, Dec 1998; Cover B	2.50
❑2/C, Dec 1998; Cover forms diptych with issue #1 DFE cover	4.00
❑3, Jan 1999; O: Vulture	2.50
❑4, Feb 1999; V: Doctor Doom; V: Doctor Octopus	2.50
❑5, Mar 1999; V: Lizard	2.50
❑6, Apr 1999; V: Electro	2.50
❑7, May 1999; V: Mysterio	2.50
❑8, Jun 1999; V: Green Goblin	2.50
❑9, Jul 1999; V: Kraven	2.50
❑10, Aug 1999; V: Green Goblin	2.50
❑11, Sep 1999	2.50
❑12, Oct 1999; V: Sandman; Final Issue	2.50
❑Deluxe 1; #1 & #2 Signed	29.95
❑Deluxe 1/Ltd.; #1 & #2 Pack, DFE alternate cover signed	29.95

Spider-Man: Christmas in Dallas
Marvel

❑1, Dec 1983; giveaway; NN	10.00

Spider-Man Classics
Marvel

❑1, Apr 1993; SD, SL (w); SD (a); 1&O: Spider-Man. O: Doctor Strange. Reprints Amazing Fantasy #15 & Strange Tales #115	2.00
❑2, May 1993; AM (c); SD, SL (w); SD (a); O: Spider-Man. 1: J. Jonah Jameson. 1: Chameleon. A: Fantastic Four. Reprints Amazing Spider-Man #1	1.50
❑3, Jun 1993; SD, SL (w); SD (a); 1: Mysterio (as alien). 1: Tinkerer. 1: Vulture. Reprints Amazing Spider-Man #2	1.50
❑4, Jul 1993; SD, SL (w); SD (a); O: Doctor Octopus. 1: Doctor Octopus. Reprints Amazing Spider-Man #3	1.50
❑5, Aug 1993; SD, SL (w); SD (a); O: Sandman (Marvel). 1: Betty Brant. 1: Sandman (Marvel). Reprints Amazing Spider-Man #4	1.50
❑6, Sep 1993; SD, SL (w); SD (a); A: Doctor Doom. Reprints Amazing Spider-Man #5	1.50
❑7, Oct 1993; SD, SL (w); SD (a); O: The Lizard. 1: The Lizard. Reprints Amazing Spider-Man #6	1.50
❑8, Nov 1993; SD, SL (w); SD (a); 2: The Vulture. Reprints Amazing Spider-Man #7	1.50
❑9, Dec 1993; SD, SL (w); SD (a); 1: The Living Brain. A: Human Torch. Reprints Amazing Spider-Man #8	1.50
❑10, Jan 1994; SD, SL (w); SD (a); O: Electro. 1: Electro. Reprints Amazing Spider-Man #9	1.50
❑11, Feb 1994; SD, SL (w); SD (a); 1: Big Man. 1: Enforcers. Reprints Amazing Spider-Man #10	1.50
❑12, Mar 1994; SD, SL (w); SD (a); 2: Doctor Octopus. Reprints Amazing Spider-Man #11	1.50
❑13, Apr 1994; Reprints Amazing Spider-Man #12 with new cover & 1-page cover gallery	1.25
❑14, May 1994; Reprints Amazing Spider-Man #13 with new cover & 1-page cover gallery; 1: Mysterio	1.25
❑15, Jun 1994; 1: Green Goblin I (Norman Osborn). Reprints Amazing Spider-Man #14 with new cover & 1-page cover gallery; Newsstand edition without extras	1.25
❑15/CS, Jun 1994; 1: Green Goblin I (Norman Osborn). polybagged with animation print	2.95
❑16, Jul 1994; Reprints Amazing Spider-Man #15 with new cover & 1-page cover gallery; 1: Kraven the Hunter; Final issue	1.25

Spider-Man Collectors' Preview
Marvel

❑1, Dec 1994	1.50

Spider-Man Comics Magazine
Marvel

❑1, Jan 1987; digest; Reprints from Amazing Spider-Man #51-53	1.50
❑2, Mar 1987; digest	1.50
❑3, May 1987; digest	1.50
❑4, Jul 1987; digest	1.50
❑5, Sep 1987; digest	1.50
❑6, Nov 1987; digest	1.50
❑7, Jan 1988; digest	1.50
❑8, Mar 1988; digest	1.50
❑9, May 1988; digest	1.50
❑10, Jul 1988; digest	1.50
❑11, Sep 1988; digest	1.50
❑12, Nov 1988; digest	1.50
❑13, Jan 1989; digest	1.50

Spider-Man/Daredevil
Marvel

❑1, Oct 2002	2.99

Spider-Man: Dead Man's Hand
Marvel

❑1, Apr 1997, wraparound cover	2.99

Spider-Man: Death and Destiny
Marvel

❑1, Aug 2000	2.99
❑2, Sep 2000	2.99
❑3, Oct 2000	2.99

Spider-Man/Doctor Octopus: Out of Reach
Marvel

❑1, Jan 2004	4.00
❑2, Feb 2004	2.99
❑3, Mar 2004	2.99
❑4, Apr 2004	2.99
❑5, May 2004	2.99

Spider-Man/Doctor Octopus: Year One
Marvel

❑1, Aug 2004	2.99
❑2, Aug 2004	2.99
❑3, Nov 2004	2.99
❑4, Dec 2004	2.99
❑5, Jan 2005	2.99

Spider-Man/Dr. Strange: The Way to Dusty Death
Marvel

❑1, ca. 1992, No cover price; graphic novel	6.95

Spider-Man Family
Marvel

❑1, Dec 2005, b&w; Spider-Girl; Spider-Woman: Reprint from Spider-Woman #20; Spider-Ham: Reprint from Marvel Tails #1; Spider-Man 2099: Reprint from Spider-Man 2099 #1; Peter Parker: Reprint from Untold Tales of Spider-Man '97 Ann; Spider-man: Reprint from Untold Tales of Spider-Man #1	4.99

Spider-Man Family: Amazing Friends
Marvel

❑1, Oct 2006	4.99

Spider-Man Family Featuring Spider-Clan
Marvel

❑1, Feb 2007, Collects Spider-Man 2099 #3, Amazing Spider-Man #252	4.99

Spider-Man: Fear Itself
Marvel

❑1, Feb 1992	12.95

Spider-Man: Friends & Enemies
Marvel

❑1, Jan 1995; 1: The Metahumes; O: The Metahumes	1.95
❑2, Feb 1995	1.95
❑3, Mar 1995	1.95
❑4, Apr 1995	1.95

Spider-Man: Funeral for an Octopus
Marvel

❑1, Mar 1995	1.50
❑2, Apr 1995	1.50
❑3, May 1995	1.50
❑4, Jun 1995	1.50

Spider-Man/Gen13
Marvel

❑1, Nov 1996; prestige format; NN	4.95

Spider-Man: Get Kraven
Marvel

❑1, Aug 2002	2.25
❑2, Sep 2002	2.25
❑3, Oct 2002	2.25
❑4, Nov 2002	2.25
❑5, Dec 2002	2.25
❑6, Jan 2003	2.25

Spider-Man: Hobgoblin Lives
Marvel

❑1, Jan 1997; wraparound cover	2.50
❑2, Feb 1997; wraparound cover	2.50
❑3, Apr 1997; wraparound cover; True identity of Hobgoblin I revealed	2.50

Spider-Man: House of M
Marvel

❑1, Jul 2005	6.00
❑1/Conv, Jul 2005	15.00
❑2, Aug 2005	5.00
❑2/Variant, Aug 2005	4.00
❑3, Sep 2005	2.99
❑4, Nov 2005	2.99
❑5, Jan 2006	2.99

Spider-Man/Human Torch
Marvel

❑1, Apr 2005 2.99
❑2, May 2005 2.99
❑3, Jun 2005 2.99
❑4, Jul 2005 2.99
❑5, Aug 2005 2.99

Spider-Man: India
Marvel

❑1, Dec 2004 2.99
❑2, Jan 2005 2.99
❑3, Feb 2005 2.99
❑4, Mar 2005 2.99

Spider-Man: Legacy of Evil
Marvel

❑1, Jun 1996; retells history of Green Goblin 3.95

Spider-Man Legends
Marvel

❑1, ca. 2003 0.00
❑2, ca. 2003 19.99
❑3, ca. 2004 24.99
❑4, ca. 2004 13.99

Spider-Man: Lifeline
Marvel

❑1, Apr 2001 2.99
❑2, May 2001 2.99
❑3, Jun 2001 2.99

Spider-Man Loves Mary Jane
Marvel

❑1, Feb 2006 2.99
❑2, Mar 2006 2.99
❑3, May 2006 2.99
❑4, Jun 2006 2.99
❑5, Jul 2006 2.99
❑6, Aug 2006 2.99
❑7, Sep 2006 2.99
❑8, Oct 2006 2.99
❑9, Nov 2006 2.99
❑10, Dec 2006 2.99
❑11, Jan 2007 2.99
❑12, Feb 2007 2.99
❑13, Mar 2007 2.99

Spider-Man: Made Men
Marvel

❑1, Aug 1999 5.99

Spider-Man Magazine
Marvel

❑1, Win 1994; X-Men 2.00
❑2, Jun 1994; NN; Winter 1994; X-Men, Profile Wolverine 2.00
❑3, Jul 1994; X-Men, Rogue and Gambit, Profile Doctor Octopus 2.00
❑4, Aug 1994; X-Men 2.00
❑5, Sep 1994; X-Men, Profile Hulk, Includes Cards 2.00
❑6, Oct 1994; X-Men 2.00
❑7, Nov 1994; X-Men, Profile Fantastic Four, Includes Cards 2.00
❑8, Dec 1994; Includes cards; Flip book with X-Men Magazine 2.00
❑9, Jan 1995; flip book with Iron Man back-up 2.00
❑10, Feb 1995; flip book with X-Men back-up 2.00

Spider-Man Magazine
Marvel

❑1, Spr 1995; NN 2.50

Spider-Man: Maximum Clonage Alpha
Marvel

❑1, Aug 1995; Acetate wraparound cover overlay 10.00

Spider-Man: Maximum Clonage Omega
Marvel

❑1, Aug 1995; D: The Jackal. enhanced wraparound cover 10.00

Spider-Man Megazine
Marvel

❑1, Oct 1994; Reprints from Amazing Spider-Man #224, 225, Marvel Team-Up #1 and Amazing Spider-Man #16 2.50
❑2, Nov 1994; Reprints from Amazing Spider-Man #226, 227, Marvel Team-Up #2 and Amazing Spider-Man #17 2.95
❑3, Dec 1994; Reprints from Amazing Spider-Man #229, 230, Marvel Team-Up #3 and Amazing Spider-Man #18 2.95
❑4, Jan 1995; Reprints from Amazing Spider-Man #231, 232, Marvel Team-Up #4 and Amazing Spider-Man #19 2.95
❑5, Feb 1995; Reprints from Amazing Spider-Man #233, 234, Marvel Team-Up #5 and Amazing Spider-Man #20 2.95
❑6, Mar 1995; Reprints from Amazing Spider-Man #235, 236, Marvel Team-Up #6 and Amazing Spider-Man #21; Final Issue 2.95

Spider-Man 2 Movie Adaptation
Marvel

❑1, Aug 2004 3.50

Spider-Man Mysteries
Marvel

❑1, Aug 1998; No cover price; prototype for children's comic 1.00

Spider-Man: Power of Terror
Marvel

❑1, Jan 1995 1.95
❑2, Feb 1995 1.95
❑3, Mar 1995 1.95
❑4, Apr 1995 1.95

Spider-Man, Power Pack
Marvel

❑1, Aug 1984; Giveaway from the National Committee for Prevention of Child Abuse; JBy (c); JM (a); No cover price; sexual abuse 1.00

Spider-Man/Punisher: Family Plot
Marvel

❑1, Feb 1996 2.95
❑2, Feb 1996 2.95

Spider-Man, Punisher, Sabretooth: Designer Genes
Marvel

❑1, ca. 1993; no cover price 8.95

Spider-Man: Quality of Life
Marvel

❑1, Jul 2002 2.99
❑2, Aug 2002 2.99
❑3, Sep 2002 2.99
❑4, Oct 2002 2.99

Spider-Man: Redemption
Marvel

❑1, Sep 1996, no ads 1.50
❑2, Oct 1996 1.50
❑3, Nov 1996 1.50
❑4, Dec 1996 1.50

Spider-Man: Reign
Marvel

❑1, Dec 2006; Spider-Man costume is grayish; Diamond warning of inapropriate material 20.00
❑2, Jan 2007 18.00

Spider-Man: Revenge of the Green Goblin
Marvel

❑1, Oct 2000 2.99
❑2, Nov 2000 2.99
❑3, Dec 2000; events lead in to Amazing Spider-Man #25 and Peter Parker, Spider-Man #25 2.99

Spider-Man Saga
Marvel

❑1, Nov 1991 2.95
❑2, Dec 1991 2.95
❑3, Jan 1992 2.95
❑4, Feb 1992; O: Venom 2.95

Spider-Man Special Edition
Marvel

❑1, Nov 1992; "The Trial of Venom" special edition to benefit Unicef; PD (w); A: Venom. Embossed cover 7.00

Spider-Man, Storm and Power Man
Marvel

❑1, Apr 1982; Smokescreen giveaway; NN; Marvel Comics Group green banner 2.00

Spider-Man Super Special
Marvel

❑1, Jul 1995; Flip-book; two of the stories continue in Venom Super Special #1 3.95

Spider-Man: Sweet Charity
Marvel

❑1, Aug 2002 4.99

Spider-Man Team-Up
Marvel

❑1, Dec 1995, MWa (w); A: X-Men. A: Cyclops. A: Archangel. A: Hellfire Club. A: Beast. A: Phoenix. A: Psylocke. 52 pages 3.00
❑2, Mar 1996, GP (w); A: Silver Surfer. 52 pages 3.00
❑3, Jun 1996, A: Fantastic Four. 52 pages 3.00
❑4, Sep 1996, A: Avengers. 68 pages 3.00
❑5, Dec 1996, A: Howard the Duck. A: Gambit. 68 pages 3.00
❑6, Mar 1997, TP, BMc (a); A: Dracula. A: Aquarian. A: Hulk. A: Doctor Strange. Minor price increase 3.00
❑7, Jun 1997, KB (w); SB, DG (a); A: Thunderbolts. 52 pages 3.00

Spider-Man Team-Up Special
Marvel

❑0 2005 2.99

Spider-Man: The Arachnis Project
Marvel

❑1, Aug 1994 2.00
❑2, Sep 1994 2.00
❑3, Oct 1994 2.00
❑4, Nov 1994 2.00
❑5, Dec 1994 2.00
❑6, Jan 1995 2.00

Spider-Man: The Clone Journal
Marvel

❑1, Mar 1995; SB (a); O: Ben Reilly; One-shot 3.00

Spider-Man: D: Captain Stacy
Marvel

❑1, Aug 2000, Reprints Amazing Spider-Man #88-90 3.50

Spider-Man: The Final Adventure
Marvel

❑1, Dec 1995, enhanced cardstock cover; clone returns to action one last time 3.00
❑2, Jan 1996, enhanced cardstock cover 3.00
❑3, Feb 1996, enhanced cardstock cover 3.00
❑4, Mar 1996, enhanced cardstock cover; Peter loses his powers 3.00

Spider-Man: The Jackal Files
Marvel

❑1, Aug 1995, files on main Spider-Man characters and equipment 1.95

Spider-Man: The Lost Years
Marvel

❑0, Jan 1996; JR2 (a); collects clone origin back-up stories; Collects prologue chapters to series 3.95
❑1, Aug 1995; JR2 (a); enhanced cardstock cover 3.00
❑2, Sep 1995; JR2 (a); enhanced cardstock cover 3.00
❑3, Oct 1995; JR2 (a); enhanced cardstock cover 3.00

Spider-Man: The Manga
Marvel

❑1, Dec 1997 3.99
❑2, Jan 1998; V: Electro 2.99
❑3, Feb 1998 2.99
❑4, Feb 1998 2.99
❑5, Mar 1998 2.99
❑6, Mar 1998 2.99
❑7, Mar 1998 2.99
❑8, Apr 1998 2.99
❑9, Apr 1998 2.99
❑10, May 1998 2.99
❑11, May 1998 2.99
❑12, Jun 1998 2.99
❑13, Jun 1998 2.99
❑14, Jul 1998; V: Mysterio 2.99
❑15, Jul 1998 2.99
❑16, Aug 1998; V: Mysterio 2.99
❑17, Aug 1998 2.99
❑18, Sep 1998 2.99
❑19, Sep 1998 2.99
❑20, Oct 1998 2.99
❑21, Oct 1998 2.99
❑22, ca. 1998 2.99
❑23, ca. 1998 2.99

Star Wars Tales

Anthology covered stories from different eras

©Dark Horse

Star Wars: X-Wing Rogue Squadron

Carries over characters from the prose novels

©Dark Horse

Star Western

Reprinted tales of western hero greats

©Avalon

Static

Most successful Milestone title

©DC

Static Shock!: Rebirth of the Cool

Milestone book resurrected in TV cartoon

©DC

	N-MINT
❑24, ca. 1998	2.99
❑25, ca. 1998	2.99
❑26, ca. 1999	2.99
❑27, ca. 1999	2.99
❑28, ca. 1999	2.99
❑29, ca. 1999	2.99
❑30, ca. 1999	2.99
❑31, ca. 1999	2.99

Spider-Man: The Mutant Agenda
Marvel

	N-MINT
❑0, Mar 1994; strip reprints; Spaces to paste in newspaper strip; cover says Feb, indicia says Mar	1.25
❑1, Mar 1994; Ties in with daily Spider-Man newspaper strip	1.75
❑2, Apr 1994; V: Hobgoblin	1.75
❑3, May 1994; V: Hobgoblin	1.75

Spider-Man: The Official Movie Adaptation
Marvel

	N-MINT
❑1, Jun 2002; Spider-Man crawling up building	5.95

Spider-Man: The Other Sketchbook
Marvel

	N-MINT
❑1 2005; ca. 2005	2.99

Spider-Man: The Parker Years
Marvel

	N-MINT
❑1, Nov 1995; retells events in the clone's life from Amazing Spider-Man #150 to the present	2.50

Spider-Man 2099
Marvel

	N-MINT
❑1, Nov 1992; PD (w); O: Spider-Man 2099. 1: Tyler Stone. foil cover	3.00
❑1/Autographed, Nov 1992; PD (w); AW (a); foil cover with certificate of authenticity	1.75
❑2, Dec 1992; PD (w); O: Spider-Man 2099	1.25
❑3, Jan 1993; PD (w); O: Spider-Man 2099	1.25
❑4, Feb 1993; PD (w); 1: The Specialist	1.25
❑5, Mar 1993 PD (w)	1.25
❑6, Apr 1993; PD (w); 1: Vulture 2099	1.25
❑7, May 1993 PD (w)	1.25
❑8, Jun 1993 PD (w)	1.25
❑9, Jul 1993 PD (w)	1.25
❑10, Aug 1993 PD (w)	1.25
❑11, Sep 1993 PD (w)	1.25
❑12, Oct 1993 PD (w)	1.25
❑13, Nov 1993 PD (w)	1.25
❑14, Dec 1993 PD (w)	1.25
❑15, Jan 1994 PD (w)	1.25
❑16, Feb 1994 PD (w)	1.25
❑17, Mar 1994 PD (w)	1.25
❑18, Apr 1994 PD (w)	1.25
❑19, May 1994 PD (w)	1.50
❑20, Jun 1994 PD (w)	1.50
❑21, Jul 1994 PD (w)	1.50
❑22, Aug 1994 PD (w)	1.50
❑23, Sep 1994; PD (w); Young Miguel O'Hara	1.50
❑24, Oct 1994 PD (w)	1.50
❑25, Nov 1994; Giant-size; PD (w); Hulk 2099	2.25
❑25/Variant, Nov 1994; Giant-size; PD (w); enhanced cover	2.95
❑26, Dec 1994; PD (w); Young Miguel O'Hara	1.50
❑27, Jan 1995; PD (w); Young Miguel O'Hara	1.50
❑28, Feb 1995; PD (w); Young Miguel O'Hara	1.50
❑29, Mar 1995; PD (w); Young Miguel O'Hara	1.50
❑30, Apr 1995; PD (w); Young Miguel O'Hara	1.50
❑31, May 1995 PD (w)	1.50
❑32, Jun 1995; PD (w); One Nation Under Doom crossover	1.95
❑33, Jul 1995; PD (w); A: Strange 2099. One Nation Under Doom crossover	1.95
❑34, Aug 1995; PD (w); One Nation Under Doom crossover	1.95
❑35, Sep 1995; PD (w); One Nation Under Doom crossover	1.95
❑35/Variant, Sep 1995; PD (w); alternate cover	1.95
❑36, Oct 1995; PD (w); KP (a); Spiderman 2099 on cover	1.95
❑36/Variant, Oct 1995; PD (w); KP (a); alternate cover; says Venom 2099; forms diptych	1.95
❑37, Nov 1995; PD (w); One Nation Under Doom crossover	1.95
❑37/Variant, Nov 1995; alternate cover; says Venom 2099	1.95
❑38, Dec 1995; PD (w); Spiderman 2099 on cover	1.95
❑38/Variant, Dec 1995; PD (w); alternate cover; says Venom 2099; forms diptych	1.95
❑39, Jan 1996 PD (w)	1.95
❑40, Feb 1996; PD (w); V: Goblin 2099	1.95
❑41, Mar 1996 PD (w)	1.95
❑42, Apr 1996 PD (w); BSz (a)	1.95
❑43, May 1996 PD (w)	1.95
❑44, Jun 1996	1.95
❑45, Jul 1996; V: Goblin 2099	1.95
❑46, Aug 1996; V: Vulture 2099. story continues in Fantastic Four 2099 #8	1.95
❑Ann 1, ca. 1994	2.95
❑Special 1, Nov 1995	3.95

Spider-Man 2099 Meets Spider-Man
Marvel

	N-MINT
❑1, Nov 1995; NN	5.95

Spider-Man Universe
Marvel

	N-MINT
❑1, Mar 2000; Reprints Peter Parker: Spider-Man #13, Webspinners #13, Spider-Woman (2nd Series) #8	4.99
❑2, Apr 2000	4.99
❑3, May 2000	4.99
❑4, Jun 2000	4.99
❑5, Jul 2000	4.99
❑6, Aug 2000	3.99
❑7, Sep 2000	3.99

Spider-Man Unlimited
Marvel

	N-MINT
❑1, May 1993	4.00
❑2, Aug 1993	4.00
❑3, Nov 1993; Doctor Octopus	4.00
❑4, Feb 1994; Mysterio	4.00
❑5, May 1994; Human Torch	4.00
❑6, Aug 1994	4.00
❑7, Nov 1994; Spider-Man and clone	4.00
❑8, Feb 1995; Spider-Man and clone	4.00
❑9, May 1995; Giant-sized	4.00
❑10, Sep 1995; V: Vulture	4.00
❑11, Jan 1996; 1: Skull Jacket	4.00
❑12, May 1996; V: Beetle; V: Boomerang; V: Jack O'Lantern; V: Scorpia; V: Shocker	4.00
❑13, Aug 1996; V: Scorpion	2.95
❑14, Dec 1996; D: Nightwatch; D: Polestar	2.99
❑15, Feb 1997; D: Nightwatc; V: Puma; D: Polestar	2.99
❑16, May 1997; V: Dreadknight	2.99
❑17, Aug 1997; gatefold summary; V: Robot Master	2.99
❑18, Nov 1997; gatefold summary; O: Doctor Octopus	2.99
❑19, Feb 1998; gatefold summary; V: Lizard	2.99
❑20, May 1998; gatefold summary	2.99
❑21, Aug 1998; gatefold summary	2.99
❑22, Nov 1998; gatefold summary; V: Scorpion; Final Issue	2.99

Spider-Man Unlimited
Marvel

	N-MINT
❑1, Dec 1999; based on animated television show	2.99

Spider-Man Unlimited
Marvel

	N-MINT
❑1, Mar 2004	2.99
❑2, May 2004	2.99
❑3, Jul 2004	2.99
❑4, Sep 2004	2.99
❑5, Oct 2004	2.99
❑6, Nov 2004	2.99
❑7, Dec 2004	2.99
❑8, Jan 2005	2.99
❑9, Jul 2005	2.99
❑10, Sep 2005	2.99
❑11, Oct 2005	2.99
❑12, Jan 2006	2.99
❑13, Mar 2006	2.99
❑14, May 2006	2.99
❑15, Jul 2006	2.99

Spider-Man Unmasked
Marvel

	N-MINT
❑1, Nov 1996; NN	5.95

Spider-Man: Venom Agenda
Marvel

	N-MINT
❑1, Jan 1998; gatefold summary; One-shot	2.99

Spider-Man vs. Dracula
Marvel

	N-MINT
❑1, Jan 1994; SL (w); RA (a); Reprints	2.00

Spider-Man vs. Punisher
Marvel

	N-MINT
❑1, Jul 2000	2.99

Spider-Man vs. the Hulk
Marvel

	N-MINT
❑1, ca. 1979; giveaway; NN	7.00

Spider-Man vs. Wolverine
Marvel

	N-MINT
❑1, Feb 1987; D: Ned Leeds	6.00
❑1/2nd, Aug 1990; D: Ned Leeds. cardstock cover	4.95

Other grades: Multiply price above by 5/6 for VF/NM • 2/3 for VERY FINE • 1/3 for FINE • 1/5 for VERY GOOD • 1/8 for GOOD

N-MINT

Spider-Man: Web of Doom
Marvel

- ❑1, Aug 1994 … 2.00
- ❑2, Sep 1994 … 2.00
- ❑3, Oct 1994 … 2.00

Spider: Reign of the Vampire King
Eclipse

- ❑1, ca. 1992 … 4.95
- ❑2, ca. 1992 … 4.95
- ❑3, ca. 1992 … 4.95

Spider Sneak Preview
Argosy

- ❑1, ca. 2001, b&w; prestige format one-shot … 5.00

Spider's Web
Blazing

- ❑1; Flip-book … 1.50

Spider-Woman
Marvel

- ❑1, Apr 1978, JSt (c); CI (a); O: Spider-Woman I (Jessica Drew) … 6.00
- ❑2, May 1978, 1: Morgan LeFay. Newsstand edition (distributed by Curtis); issue number appears in box … 3.00
- ❑2/Whitman, May 1978, 1: Morgan LeFay. Special markets edition (usually sold in Whitman bagged prepacks); price appears in a diamond; no UPC barcode … 3.00
- ❑3, Jun 1978, 1: Brothers Grimm … 2.50
- ❑4, Jul 1978 … 2.00
- ❑5, Aug 1978, Newsstand edition (distributed by Curtis); issue number appears in box … 2.00
- ❑5/Whitman, Aug 1978, Special markets edition (usually sold in Whitman bagged prepacks); price appears in a diamond; no UPC barcode … 2.00
- ❑6, Sep 1978, Newsstand edition (distributed by Curtis); issue number appears in box … 1.75
- ❑6/Whitman, Sep 1978, Special markets edition (usually sold in Whitman bagged prepacks); price appears in a diamond; no UPC barcode … 1.75
- ❑7, Oct 1978 … 1.75
- ❑8, Nov 1978 … 1.75
- ❑9, Dec 1978, 1&O: Needle … 1.75
- ❑10, Jan 1979, 1: Gypsy Moth … 1.75
- ❑11, Feb 1979, Newsstand edition (distributed by Curtis); issue number appears in box … 1.50
- ❑11/Whitman, Feb 1979, Special markets edition (usually sold in Whitman bagged prepacks); price appears in a diamond; no UPC barcode … 1.50
- ❑12, Mar 1979, D: Brothers Grimm … 1.50
- ❑13, Apr 1979 … 1.50
- ❑14, May 1979 … 1.50
- ❑15, Jun 1979 … 1.50
- ❑16, Jul 1979 … 1.50
- ❑17, Aug 1979 … 1.50
- ❑18, Sep 1979 … 1.50
- ❑19, Oct 1979, V: Werewolf … 1.50
- ❑20, Nov 1979, A: Spider-Man … 1.50
- ❑21, Dec 1979 … 1.50
- ❑22, Jan 1980 … 1.50
- ❑23, Feb 1980 … 1.50
- ❑24, Mar 1980, TVE (a) … 1.50
- ❑25, Apr 1980, JM (c) … 1.50
- ❑26, May 1980, JBy (c) … 1.50
- ❑27, Jun 1980 … 1.50
- ❑28, Jul 1980, A: Spider-Man … 1.50
- ❑29, Aug 1980, A: Spider-Man … 1.50
- ❑30, Sep 1980, 1: Doctor Karl Malus … 1.50
- ❑31, Oct 1980, FM (c); FM (a) … 1.50
- ❑32, Nov 1980, FM (c); FM (a) … 1.50
- ❑33, Dec 1980, 1&O: Turner D. Century … 1.50
- ❑34, Jan 1981 … 1.50
- ❑35, Feb 1981 … 1.50
- ❑36, Mar 1981 … 1.50
- ❑37, Apr 1981, 1: Siryn. A: X-Men … 4.00
- ❑38, Jun 1981, A: X-Men … 4.00
- ❑39, Aug 1981 … 1.25
- ❑40, Oct 1981, 1: Flying Tiger … 1.25
- ❑41, Dec 1981 … 1.25
- ❑42, Feb 1982 … 1.25
- ❑43, Apr 1982 … 1.25
- ❑44, Jun 1982 … 1.25
- ❑45, Aug 1982 … 1.25

N-MINT

- ❑46, Oct 1982 … 1.25
- ❑47, Dec 1982 … 1.25
- ❑48, Feb 1983 … 1.25
- ❑49, Apr 1983, 1: Poltergeist … 1.25
- ❑50, Jun 1983; Giant-size; D: Spider-Woman I (Jessica Drew). Photo cover; Final Issue … 4.00

Spider-Woman
Marvel

- ❑1, Nov 1993 … 1.75
- ❑2, Dec 1993; O: Spider-Woman … 1.75
- ❑3, Jan 1994 … 1.75
- ❑4, Feb 1994 … 1.75

Spider-Woman
Marvel

- ❑1, Jul 1999 JBy (w) … 2.99
- ❑2, Aug 1999; Spider-Man against blue city background on cover … 2.99
- ❑3, Sep 1999 … 1.99
- ❑4, Oct 1999 … 1.99
- ❑5, Nov 1999 … 1.99
- ❑6, Dec 1999 JBy (w) … 1.99
- ❑7, Jan 2000; Includes 8 page bonus Marvel Super Heroes insert … 1.99
- ❑8, Feb 2000 … 1.99
- ❑9, Mar 2000 … 1.99
- ❑10, Apr 2000 … 2.25
- ❑11, May 2000; 8 page bonus Marvel Super Heroes insert … 2.25
- ❑12, Jun 2000 … 2.25
- ❑13, Jul 2000 … 2.25
- ❑14, Aug 2000 … 2.25
- ❑15, Sep 2000 … 2.25
- ❑16, Oct 2000 … 2.25
- ❑17, Nov 2000 … 2.25
- ❑18, Dec 2000; JBy (w); Final Issue … 2.25

Spider-Woman: Origin
Marvel

- ❑1, Feb 2006, O: Spider-Woman … 2.99
- ❑2, Mar 2006, O: Spider-Woman … 2.99
- ❑3, Apr 2006, O: Spider-Woman … 2.99
- ❑4, May 2006, O: Spider-Woman … 2.99
- ❑5, Jun 2006, O: Spider-Woman … 2.99

Spidery-Mon: Maximum Carcass
Parody

- ❑1/A, b&w; Variant edition A; Covers of the three variants join together to form a mural … 3.25
- ❑1/B, b&w; Variant edition B; Covers of the three variants join together to form a mural … 3.25
- ❑1/C, b&w; Variant edition C; Covers of the three variants join together to form a mural … 3.25

Spidey and the Mini-Marvels
Marvel

- ❑1, May 2003 … 3.50

Spidey Super Stories
Marvel

- ❑1, Oct 1974, O: Spider-Man … 20.00
- ❑2, Nov 1974 … 6.00
- ❑3, Dec 1974, V: Circus of Crime … 5.00
- ❑4, Jan 1975 … 5.00
- ❑5, Feb 1975 … 5.00
- ❑6, Mar 1975 … 5.00
- ❑7, Apr 1975 … 5.00
- ❑8, May 1975 … 5.00
- ❑9, Jun 1975, V: Dr. Doom. Hulk … 5.00
- ❑10, Jul 1975 … 5.00
- ❑11, Aug 1975 … 5.00
- ❑12, Sep 1975 … 5.00
- ❑13, Oct 1975 … 5.00
- ❑14, Dec 1975, A: Shanna … 5.00
- ❑15, Feb 1976, A: Storm … 5.00
- ❑16, Apr 1976 … 5.00
- ❑17, Jun 1976 … 5.00
- ❑18, Aug 1976 … 5.00
- ❑19, Oct 1976 … 5.00
- ❑20, Dec 1976 … 5.00
- ❑21, Feb 1977 … 5.00
- ❑22, Apr 1977 … 5.00
- ❑23, Jun 1977 … 5.00
- ❑24, Jul 1977, A: Thundra … 5.00
- ❑25, Aug 1977 … 5.00
- ❑26, Sep 1977 … 5.00
- ❑27, Oct 1977 … 5.00
- ❑28, Nov 1977 … 5.00

N-MINT

- ❑29, Dec 1977, V: Kingpin … 5.00
- ❑30, Jan 1978, V: Kang the Conqueror … 5.00
- ❑31, Feb 1978 … 5.00
- ❑32, Mar 1978 … 5.00
- ❑33, Apr 1978, A: Hulk … 5.00
- ❑34, May 1978 … 5.00
- ❑35, Jul 1978, A: Shanna … 5.00
- ❑36, Sep 1978 … 5.00
- ❑37, Nov 1978, Newsstand edition (distributed by Curtis); issue number in box … 5.00
- ❑37/Whitman, Nov 1978, Special markets edition (usually sold in Whitman bagged prepacks); price appears in a diamond; no UPC barcode … 5.00
- ❑38, Jan 1979, Newsstand edition (distributed by Curtis); issue number in box … 5.00
- ❑38/Whitman, Jan 1979, Special markets edition (usually sold in Whitman bagged prepacks); price appears in a diamond; no UPC barcode … 5.00
- ❑39, Mar 1979, A: Thanos. A: Hellcat … 5.00
- ❑40, May 1979, Newsstand edition (distributed by Curtis); issue number in box … 5.00
- ❑40/Whitman, May 1979, Special markets edition (usually sold in Whitman bagged prepacks); price appears in a diamond; no UPC barcode … 5.00
- ❑41, Jul 1979 … 5.00
- ❑42, Sep 1979 … 5.00
- ❑43, Nov 1979 … 5.00
- ❑44, Jan 1980 … 5.00
- ❑45, Mar 1980, A: Doctor Doom. A: Silver Surfer … 5.00
- ❑46, May 1980 … 5.00
- ❑47, Jul 1980 … 5.00
- ❑48, Sep 1980 … 5.00
- ❑49, Nov 1980 … 5.00
- ❑50, Jan 1981 … 5.00
- ❑51, Mar 1981 … 5.00
- ❑52, May 1981 … 5.00
- ❑53, Jul 1981 … 5.00
- ❑54, Sep 1981 … 5.00
- ❑55, Nov 1981, V: Kingpin … 5.00
- ❑56, Jan 1982 … 5.00
- ❑57, Mar 1982, Final Issue … 5.00

Spike: Asylum
Idea & Design Works

- ❑1, Sep 2006 … 3.99
- ❑2, Oct 2006 … 3.99
- ❑3, Nov 2006 … 3.99
- ❑4, Dec 2006 … 3.99

Spike: Lost and Found
Idea & Design Works

- ❑1, May 2006 … 7.49

Spike: Old Times
Idea & Design Works

- ❑0, Sep 2005 … 7.49

Spike: Old Wounds
Idea & Design Works

- ❑1, Feb 2006 … 7.49

Spike vs. Dracula
Idea & Design Works

- ❑1, Mar 2006 … 3.99
- ❑2, Apr 2006 … 3.99
- ❑3, May 2006 … 3.99
- ❑4, Aug 2006 … 3.99
- ❑5, Aug 2006 … 3.99

Spineless-Man $2099
Parody

- ❑1 … 2.50

Spine-Tingling Tales
Gold Key

- ❑1, May 1975 … 20.00
- ❑2, Aug 1975 … 8.00
- ❑3, Nov 1975 … 8.00
- ❑4, Feb 1976 … 8.00

Spinworld
Slave Labor / Amaze Ink

- ❑1, Jul 1997, b&w … 2.95
- ❑2, Aug 1997, b&w … 2.95
- ❑3, Oct 1997, b&w … 2.95
- ❑4, Jan 1998, b&w … 2.95

Other grades: Multiply price above by 5/6 for VF/NM • 2/3 for VERY FINE • 1/3 for FINE • 1/5 for VERY GOOD • 1/8 for GOOD

Stealth Force

Operatives are killed...
and then revived
©Malibu

Steampunk

Nightmare techno-
Victorian world
©DC

Steel

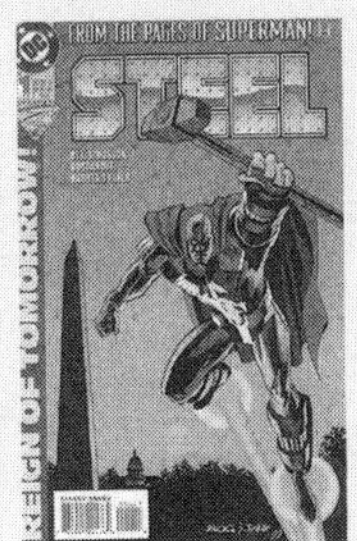

Steelworker filled
in for Superman
©DC

Stinz (1st Series)

Donna Barr's gutsy,
macho farmer centaurs
©Fantagraphics

Storm

X-Men star Ororo
gets limited series
©Marvel

N-MINT

Spiral Path
Eclipse

❑1, ca. 1986 .... 1.75
❑2, ca. 1986 .... 1.75

Spiral Zone
DC

❑1, Feb 1988 .... 1.00
❑2, Mar 1988 .... 1.00
❑3, Apr 1988 .... 1.00
❑4, May 1988 .... 1.00

Spirit
Harvey

❑1, Oct 1966; WE (c); WE (w); WE (a); O: The Spirit. Harvey 50.00
❑2, Mar 1967 WE (c); WE (w); WE (a) ... 42.00

Spirit
Kitchen Sink

❑1, Jan 1973, b&w; WE (c); WE (w); WE (a); Krupp/Kitchen Sink publishes 14.00
❑2, Sep 1973, WE (c); WE (w); WE (a); Adult 14.00

Spirit
Ken Pierce

❑1; WE (c); WE (w); WE (a); Reprints Daily Newspaper strips; ca. 1980 .... 18.00
❑2; WE (c); WE (w); WE (a); Reprints Daily Newspaper strips; ca. 1980 .... 18.00
❑3; WE (c); WE (w); WE (a); Reprints Daily Newspaper strips; ca. 1980 .... 18.00
❑4; WE (c); WE (w); WE (a); Reprints Daily Newspaper strips; ca. 1980 .... 18.00

Spirit (8th Series)
Kitchen Sink

❑1, Oct 1983, WE (c); WE (w); WE (a); O: The Spirit. Kitchen Sink publishes; reprints #291-294 .... 5.00
❑2, Dec 1983, WE (c); WE (w); WE (a); reprints #295-298 .... 4.00
❑3, Feb 1984, WE (c); WE (w); WE (a); reprints #299-302 .... 4.00
❑4, Mar 1984, WE (c); WE (w); WE (a); Reprints #303, 304, and Spirit story from Police Comics #98 .... 3.50
❑5, Jun 1984, WE (c); WE (w); WE (a); Reprints from #307, 308, 309, 310 .... 3.50
❑6, Aug 1984, WE (c); WE (w); WE (a); Reprints from #311, 312, 313, 314 .... 3.50
❑7, Oct 1984, WE (c); WE (w); WE (a); Reprints from #315, 316, 317, 318, 319 3.50
❑8, Feb 1985, WE (c); WE (w); WE (a); Reprints from #320, 321, 322, 323, 324 3.50
❑9, Apr 1985, WE (c); WE (w); WE (a); Reprints from #325, 326, 327, 328, 329 3.50
❑10, Jun 1985, WE (c); WE (w); WE (a); Reprints from #330, 331, 332, 333, 334 2.95
❑11, Aug 1985, WE (c); WE (w); WE (a); Reprints from #335, 336, 337, 338, 339 2.95
❑12, Oct 1985, b&w; WE (c); WE (w); WE (a); Reprints from #340, 341, 342, 343 2.00
❑13, Nov 1985, b&w; WE (c); WE (w); WE (a); Reprints from #344, 345, 346, 347 2.00
❑14, Dec 1985, b&w; WE (c); WE (w); WE (a); Reprints from #348, 349, 350, 351 2.00
❑15, Jan 1986, b&w; WE (c); WE (w); WE (a); reprints #356-359 .... 2.00
❑16, Feb 1986, b&w; WE (c); WE (w); WE (a); Reprints from #356, 357, 358, 359 2.00
❑17, Mar 1986, b&w; WE (c); WE (w); WE (a); Reprints from #360, 361, 362, 363 2.00
❑18, Apr 1986, b&w; WE (c); WE (w); WE (a); Reprints from #364, 365, 366, 367 2.00
❑19, May 1986, b&w; WE (c); WE (w); WE (a); Reprints from #368, 369, 370, 371 2.00
❑20, Jun 1986, b&w; WE (c); WE (w); WE (a); Reprints from #372, 373, 374, 375 2.00
❑21, Jul 1986, b&w; WE (c); WE (w); WE (a); Reprints from #376, 377, 378, 379 2.00
❑22, Aug 1986, b&w; WE (c); WE (w); WE (a); Reprints from #380, 381, 382, 383 2.00
❑23, Sep 1986, b&w; WE (c); WE (w); WE (a); Reprints from #384, 385, 386, 387 2.00
❑24, Oct 1986, b&w; WE (c); WE (w); WE (a); Reprints from #388, 389, 390, 391 2.00
❑25, Nov 1986, b&w; WE (c); WE (w); WE (a); Reprints from #392, 393, 394, 395 2.00
❑26, Dec 1986, b&w; WE (c); WE (w); WE (a); Reprints from #396, 397, 398, 399 2.00
❑27, Jan 1987, b&w; WE (c); WE (w); WE (a); Reprints from #400, 401, 402, 403 2.00
❑28, Feb 1987, b&w; WE (c); WE (w); WE (a); Reprints from #404, 405, 406, 407 2.00
❑29, Mar 1987, b&w; WE (c); WE (w); WE (a); Reprints from #408, 409, 410, 411 2.00
❑30, Apr 1987, b&w; WE (c); WE (w); WE (a); Reprints from #412, 413, 414, 415 2.00
❑31, May 1987, b&w; WE (c); WE (w); WE (a); Reprints from #416, 417, 418, 419 2.00
❑32, Jun 1987, b&w; WE (c); WE (w); WE (a); Reprints from #420, 421, 422, 423 2.00
❑33, Jul 1987, b&w; WE (c); WE (w); WE (a); Reprints from #424, 425, 426, 427 2.00
❑34, Aug 1987, b&w; WE (c); WE (w); WE (a); Reprints from #428, 429, 430, 431 2.00
❑35, Sep 1987, b&w; WE (c); WE (w); WE (a); Reprints from #432, 433, 434, 435 2.00
❑36, Oct 1987, b&w; WE (c); WE (w); WE (a); Reprints from #436, 437, 438, 439 2.00
❑37, Nov 1987, b&w; WE (w); WE (a) ... 2.00
❑38, Dec 1988, b&w; WE (w); WE (a).... 2.00
❑39, Jan 1988, b&w; WE (c); WE (w); WE (a) 2.00
❑40, Feb 1988, b&w; WE (c); WE (w); WE (a); Reprints from #452, 453, 454, 455 2.00
❑41, Mar 1988, b&w; WE (c); WE (w); WE (a); Wertham parody 2.00
❑42, Apr 1988, b&w; WE (c); WE (w); WE (a); Reprints from #460, 461, 462, 463 2.00
❑43, May 1988, b&w; WE (c); WE (w); WE (a); Reprints from #464, 465, 466, 467 2.00
❑44, Jun 1988, b&w; WE (c); WE (w); WE (a); Reprints from #468, 469, 470, 471 2.00
❑45, Jul 1988, b&w; WE (c); WE (w); WE (a); Reprints from #472, 473, 474, 475 2.00
❑46, Aug 1988, b&w; WE (c); WE (w); WE (a); Reprints from #476, 477, 478, 479 2.00
❑47, Sep 1988, b&w; WE (c); WE (w); WE (a); Reprints from #480, 481, 482, 483 2.00
❑48, Oct 1988, b&w; WE (c); WE (w); WE (a); Reprints from #484, 485, 486, 487 2.00
❑49, Nov 1988, b&w; WE (c); WE (w); WE (a) 2.00
❑50, Dec 1988, b&w; WE (c); WE (w); WE (a); Reprints from #492, 493, 494, 495 2.00
❑51, Jan 1989, b&w; WE (c); WE (w); WE (a); Reprints from #496, 497, 498, 499 2.00
❑52, Feb 1989, b&w; WE (c); WE (w); WE (a); Reprints from #500, 501, 502, 503 2.00
❑53, Mar 1989, b&w; WE (c); WE (w); WE (a); Reprints from #504, 505, 506, 507 2.00
❑54, Apr 1989, b&w; WE (c); WE (w); WE (a); Reprints from #508, 509, 510, 511 2.00
❑55, May 1989, b&w; WE (c); WE (w); WE (a) 2.00
❑56, Jun 1989, b&w; WE (c); WE (w); WE (a); Reprints from #516, 517, 518, 519 2.00
❑57, Jul 1989, b&w; WE (c); WE (w); WE (a); Reprints from #520, 521, 522, 523 2.00
❑58, Aug 1989, b&w; WE (c); WE (w); WE (a) 2.00
❑59, Sep 1989, b&w; WE (c); WE (w); WE (a) 2.00
❑60, Oct 1989, b&w; WE (c); WE (w); WE (a); Reprints #532-535 .... 2.00
❑61, Nov 1989, b&w; WE (c); WE (w); WE (a); Reprints #536-539 .... 2.00
❑62, Dec 1989, b&w; WE (c); WE (w); WE (a); Reprints from #540, 541, 542, 543 2.00
❑63, Jan 1990, b&w; WE (c); WE (w); WE (a); Reprints from #544, 545, 546, 547 2.00
❑64, Feb 1990, b&w; WE (c); WE (w); WE (a); Reprints from #548, 549, 550, 551 2.00
❑65, Mar 1990, b&w; WE (c); WE (w); WE (a); Reprints from #552, 553, 554, 555 2.00
❑66, Apr 1990, b&w; WE (c); WE (w); WE (a); Reprints from #556, 557, 558, 559 2.00
❑67, May 1990, b&w; WE (c); WE (w); WE (a); Reprints from #560, 561, 562, 563 2.00
❑68, Jun 1990, b&w; WE (c); WE (w); WE (a); Reprints from #564, 565, 566, 567 2.00
❑69, Jul 1990, b&w; WE (c); WE (w); WE (a); Reprints from #568, 569, 570, 571 2.00
❑70, Aug 1990, b&w; WE (c); WE (w); WE (a); Reprints from #572, 573, 574, 575 2.00
❑71, Sep 1990, b&w; WE (c); WE (w); WE (a); Reprints from #576, 577, 578, 579 2.00
❑72, Oct 1990, b&w; WE (c); WE (w); WE (a); Reprints from #580, 581, 582, 583 2.00
❑73, Nov 1990, b&w; Reprints from #584, 585, 586, 587 .... 2.00
❑74, Dec 1990, b&w; Reprints from #588, 589, 590, 591 .... 2.00
❑75, Jan 1991, b&w; Reprints from #592, 593, 594, 595 .... 2.00
❑76, Feb 1991, b&w; Reprints from #596, 597, 598, 599 .... 2.00
❑77, Mar 1991, b&w; Reprints from #600, 601, 602, 603 .... 2.00
❑78, Apr 1991, b&w; Reprints from #604, 605, 606, 607 .... 2.00
❑79, May 1991, b&w; reprints #608-611 2.00
❑80, Jun 1991, b&w; reprints #612-615 2.00
❑81, Jul 1991, b&w; reprints #616-619. 2.00
❑82, Aug 1991, b&w; reprints #620-623 2.00
❑83, Sep 1991, b&w; reprints #625-628 2.00
❑84, Oct 1991, b&w; reprints #629-631 2.00
❑85, Nov 1991, b&w; reprints #632-635 2.00
❑86, Dec 1991, b&w; Reprints from #636, 637, 638, 639, 640 .... 2.00
❑87, Jan 1992, b&w; Reprints from #641, 642, 643, 644, 645; Final Issue 2.00

Spirit
DC

❑1, Feb 2007 .... 2.99
❑2 .... 2.99

Spirit
Warren

❑1, Apr 1974, b&w WE (c); WE (w); WE (a) 22.00
❑2, Jun 1974, b&w WE (c); WE (w); WE (a) 10.00

❑3, Aug 1974, b&w WE (c); WE (w); WE (a) 7.00
❑4, Oct 1974, b&w WE (c); WE (w); WE (a) 6.00
❑5, Dec 1974, b&w WE (c); WE (w); WE (a) 6.00
❑6, Feb 1975, b&w WE (c); WE (w); WE (a) 6.00
❑7, Apr 1975, b&w WE (c); WE (w); WE (a) 6.00
❑8, Jun 1975, b&w WE (c); WE (w); WE (a) 6.00
❑9, Aug 1975, b&w WE (c); WE (w); WE (a) 6.00
❑10, Oct 1975, b&w WE (c); WE (w); WE (a) 6.00
❑11, Dec 1975, b&w WE (c); WE (w); WE (a) 6.00
❑12, Feb 1976, b&w WE (c); WE (w); WE (a) 6.00
❑13, Apr 1976, b&w WE (c); WE (w); WE (a) 5.00
❑14, Jun 1976, b&w WE (c); WE (w); WE (a) 5.00
❑15, Aug 1976, b&w WE (c); WE (w); WE (a) 5.00
❑16, Oct 1976, b&w WE (c); WE (w); WE (a) 7.00
❑17, Nov 1977, b&w; WE (c); WE (w); WE (a); Kitchen Sink begins as publisher; wraparound covers begin 4.00
❑18, May 1978, b&w; WE (c); WE (w); WE (a); Wraparound cover 4.00
❑19, Oct 1978, b&w; WE (c); WE (w); WE (a); Wraparound cover 4.00
❑20, Mar 1979, b&w; WE (c); WE (w); WE (a); Wraparound cover 4.00
❑21, Jul 1979, b&w; WE (c); WE (w); WE (a); Wraparound cover 4.00
❑22, Dec 1979, b&w; WE (c); WE (w); WE (a); Wraparound cover 4.00
❑23, Feb 1980, b&w; WE (c); WE (w); WE (a); Wraparound cover 4.00
❑24, May 1980, b&w; WE (c); WE (w); WE (a); Wraparound cover 4.00
❑25, Aug 1980, b&w; WE (c); WE (w); WE (a); Wraparound cover 4.00
❑26, Dec 1980, b&w; WE (c); WE, WW (w); WE, WW (a); Wraparound cover. 4.00
❑27, Feb 1981, b&w; WE (c); WE (w); WE (a); Wraparound cover 4.00
❑28, Apr 1981, b&w; WE (c); WE (w); WE (a); Wraparound cover 4.00
❑29, Jun 1981, b&w; WE (c); WE (w); WE (a); Wraparound cover 4.00
❑30, Jul 1981, b&w; WE (c); WE (w); WE (a); Featuring more than 50 artists; Wraparound cover 4.00
❑31, Oct 1981, b&w; WE (c); WE (w); WE (a); Wraparound cover 4.00
❑32, Dec 1981, b&w; WE (c); WE (w); WE (a); No wraparound cover 4.00
❑33, Feb 1982, b&w; WE (c); WE (w); WE (a); Wraparound cover 4.00
❑34, Apr 1982, b&w; WE (c); WE (w); WE (a); No wrapraround cover 4.00
❑35, Jun 1982, b&w; WE (c); WE (w); WE (a); No wraparound cover 4.00
❑36, Aug 1982, b&w; WE (c); WE (w); WE (a); Wraparound cover 4.00
❑37, Oct 1982, b&w; WE (c); WE (w); WE (a); Wraparound cover 4.00
❑38, Dec 1982, b&w; WE (c); WE (w); WE (a); Wraparound cover 4.00
❑39, Feb 1983, b&w; WE (c); WE (w); WE (a); Wraparound cover 4.00
❑40, Apr 1983, b&w; WE (c); WE (w); WE (a); Wraparound cover 4.00
❑41, Jun 1983, b&w; WE (c); WE (w); WE (a); Wraparound cover 4.00
❑Special 1 1975, b&w 35.00

Spirit Jam
Kitchen Sink

❑1, Aug 1998; Also was available as a hardcover and a Signed and numbered hardcover edition; Wraparound Jam Cover; Cerebus vs. The Spirit originally appeared in Cerebus Jam #1, published in April, 1985; The Spirit Jam originally appeared in The Spirit Magazine #30, published in July, 1981 5.95

Spirit of the Tao
Image

❑1, Jun 1998 2.50
❑2, Jul 1998 2.50
❑3, Aug 1998 2.50
❑4, Sep 1998 2.50
❑5, Nov 1998 2.50
❑6, Dec 1998 2.50
❑7, Feb 1999 2.50
❑8, Apr 1999 2.50
❑9, May 1999 2.50
❑10, Jun 1999 2.50
❑11, Aug 1999 2.50
❑12, Oct 1999 2.50
❑13, Nov 1999 2.50
❑Ashcan 1; 1: Jasmine. 1: Lance 5.00

Spirit of the Wind
Chocolate Mouse

❑1, b&w 2.00

Spirit of Wonder
Dark Horse / Manga

❑1, Apr 1996, b&w 2.95
❑2, May 1996, b&w 2.95
❑3, Jun 1996, b&w 2.95
❑4, Jul 1996, b&w 2.95
❑5, Aug 1996, b&w; Final Issue 2.95

Spirits
Mind Walker

❑3, Sep 1995, b&w 2.95

Spirits of Venom
Marvel

❑1 9.95

Spirit: The New Adventures
Kitchen Sink

❑1, Mar 1998 3.50
❑2, Apr 1998 3.50
❑3, May 1998; Brian Bolland cover 3.50
❑4, Jun 1998 3.50
❑5, Jul 1998 3.50
❑6, Sep 1998 3.50
❑7, Oct 1998 3.50
❑8, Nov 1998 3.50

Spirit: The Origin Years
Kitchen Sink

❑1, May 1992; O: The Spirit 2.95
❑2, Jul 1992 2.95
❑3, Sep 1992 2.95
❑4, Nov 1992 2.95
❑5, Jan 1993 2.95
❑6, Mar 1993 2.95
❑7, May 1993 2.95
❑8, Jul 1993 2.95
❑9, Sep 1993 2.95
❑10, Dec 1993 2.95

Spirit World
DC

❑1, Jul 1971; JK (w); JK (a); Includes poster 35.00

Spirou & Fantasio: Z Is for Zorglub
Fantasy Flight

❑1; graphic novel 8.95

Spitfire and the Troubleshooters
Marvel

❑1, Oct 1986, HT (a); Continued in Star Brand #2 1.00
❑2, Nov 1986 1.00
❑3, Dec 1986 1.00
❑4, Jan 1987, TMc (a) 1.00
❑5, Feb 1987 1.00
❑6, Mar 1987 1.00
❑7, Apr 1987 1.00
❑8, May 1987 1.00
❑9, Jun 1987, Series continued in "Code Name: Spitfire" 1.00

Spittin' Image
Eclipse

❑1; b&w parody 2.50

Spit Wad Comics
Spit Wad

❑1, Jun 1983, b&w 2.50

Splat!
Mad Dog

❑1, b&w 2.00
❑2, Mar 1987 2.00
❑3 2.00

Splatter
Arpad

❑1, b&w 2.50

Splatter
Northstar

❑1, May 1991, b&w; Adult 4.95
❑2, b&w; Adult 2.75
❑3, b&w; Adult 2.75
❑4, b&w; Adult 2.75
❑5, b&w; Adult 2.75
❑6, b&w; Adult 2.75
❑7, b&w; Adult 2.75
❑8; Adult 2.75
❑Ann 1; Adult 4.95

Splitting Image
Image

❑1, Mar 1993; parody 1.95
❑2, Apr 1993; parody 1.95

Spoof
Marvel

❑1, ca. 1970, Infinity cover 15.00
❑2, Nov 1972 7.00
❑3, Jan 1973 8.00
❑4, Mar 1973 7.00
❑5, May 1973, HT, JSe (c); Final Issue 7.00

Spoof Comics
Spoof

❑0, Jul 1992, b&w; Imp-Unity 2.50
❑1, Dec 1992, b&w; Spider-Femme 2.50
❑1/2nd 1992, Spider-Femme 2.95
❑2, Jan 1992, b&w; Batbabe 2.50
❑2/2nd 1992, Batbabe 2.50
❑3, Aug 1992, b&w; Wolverbroad 2.95
❑4, Sep 1992, b&w; Superbabe 2.95
❑5, Oct 1992, b&w; Daredame 2.95
❑6, Nov 1992, b&w; X-Babes 2.95
❑7 1993, b&w; Justice Broads 2.95
❑8 1993, b&w; Fantastic Femmes 2.95
❑9 1993, b&w; Hobo 2.95
❑10 1993, b&w; Wetshirts 2.95
❑11 1993, b&w; Mable 2.95
❑12, Mar 1993, b&w; Deathlocks 2.95

Spook City
Mythic

❑1, Nov 1997, b&w 2.95

Spookgirl
Slave Labor

❑1, ca. 2000 2.95

Spooky
Harvey

❑61, Nov 1961 12.00
❑62, Dec 1961 12.00
❑63, Jan 1962 12.00
❑64, Feb 1962 12.00
❑65, Mar 1962 12.00
❑66, Apr 1962 12.00
❑67, May 1962 12.00
❑68, Jun 1962 12.00
❑69, Aug 1962 12.00
❑70, Oct 1962 12.00
❑71, Dec 1962 8.00
❑72, Feb 1963 8.00
❑73, Apr 1963 8.00
❑74, Jun 1963 8.00
❑75, Aug 1963 8.00
❑76, Oct 1963 8.00
❑77, Dec 1963 8.00
❑78, Feb 1964 8.00
❑79, Apr 1964 8.00
❑80, Jun 1964 8.00
❑81, Aug 1964 8.00
❑82, Oct 1964 8.00
❑83, Dec 1964 8.00
❑84, Feb 1965 8.00
❑85, Apr 1965 8.00
❑86, Jun 1965 8.00
❑87, Aug 1965 8.00
❑88, Oct 1965 8.00
❑89, Dec 1965 8.00
❑90, Feb 1966 8.00
❑91, Apr 1966 6.00
❑92, Jun 1966 6.00
❑93, Aug 1966 6.00
❑94, Oct 1966 6.00
❑95, Dec 1966 6.00
❑96, Feb 1967 6.00
❑97, Apr 1967 6.00
❑98, Jun 1967 6.00

Stormwatch

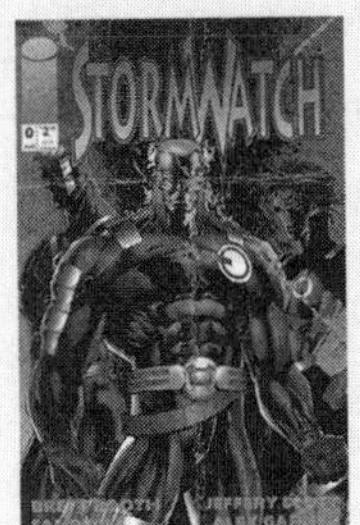

Sort of a super-powered U.N. task force
©Image

Stormwatch

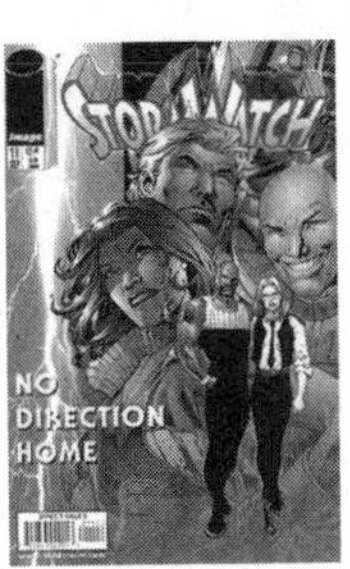

Laid groundwork for The Authority
©Image

Strange Adventures

Animal Man and Deadman got their start here
©DC

Strange Attractors

Curator finds mysterious amulet
©Retrografix

Strangehaven

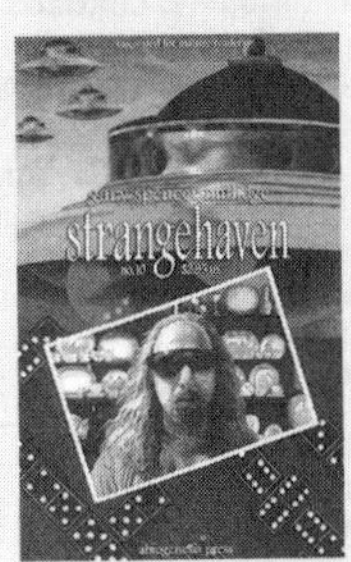

Acclaimed title from Gary Spencer Millidge
©Abiogenesis

N-MINT

❑99, Aug 1967 ... 6.00
❑100, Oct 1967 ... 6.00
❑101, Dec 1967 ... 6.00
❑102, Feb 1968 ... 6.00
❑103, Apr 1968 ... 6.00
❑104, Jun 1968 ... 6.00
❑105, Aug 1968 ... 6.00
❑106, Oct 1968 ... 6.00
❑107, Dec 1968 ... 6.00
❑108, Feb 1969 ... 6.00
❑109, Apr 1969 ... 6.00
❑110, May 1969 ... 6.00
❑111 1969 ... 5.00
❑112 1969 ... 5.00
❑113, Oct 1969 ... 5.00
❑114 1969 ... 5.00
❑115, Jan 1970 ... 5.00
❑116, Mar 1970 ... 5.00
❑117, May 1970 ... 5.00
❑118, Jul 1970 ... 5.00
❑119, Sep 1970 ... 5.00
❑120, Nov 1970 ... 5.00
❑121, Dec 1970 ... 5.00
❑122, Feb 1971 ... 5.00
❑123 1971 ... 5.00
❑124, Jun 1971 ... 5.00
❑125 1971 ... 5.00
❑126, Sep 1971 ... 5.00
❑127, Oct 1971 ... 5.00
❑128, Dec 1971 ... 5.00
❑129 ... 5.00
❑130, May 1972 ... 5.00
❑131, Jul 1972 ... 4.00
❑132, Sep 1972 ... 4.00
❑133, Nov 1972 ... 4.00
❑134, Jan 1973 ... 4.00
❑135, Mar 1973 ... 4.00
❑136, May 1973 ... 4.00
❑137, Jul 1973 ... 4.00
❑138, Sep 1973 ... 4.00
❑139, Nov 1973 ... 4.00
❑140, Jul 1974 ... 4.00
❑141, Sep 1974 ... 4.00
❑142, Nov 1974 ... 4.00
❑143, Jan 1975 ... 4.00
❑144, Mar 1975 ... 4.00
❑145, May 1975 ... 4.00
❑146, Jul 1975 ... 4.00
❑147, Sep 1975 ... 4.00
❑148, Nov 1975 ... 4.00
❑149, Jan 1976 ... 4.00
❑150, Mar 1976 ... 4.00
❑151, May 1976 ... 4.00
❑152, Jul 1976 ... 4.00
❑153, Sep 1976 ... 4.00
❑154, Nov 1976 ... 4.00
❑155, Jan 1977 ... 4.00
❑156, Dec 1977 ... 4.00
❑157, Feb 1978 ... 4.00
❑158, Apr 1978 ... 4.00
❑159, Sep 1978 ... 4.00
❑160, Oct 1979; Casper in Hostess ad ("Meets a Robot") ... 4.00
❑161, Sep 1980, (c); (w); (a) ... 4.00

N-MINT

Spooky
Harvey

❑1, ca. 1991 ... 1.25
❑2, ca. 1991 ... 1.25
❑3, ca. 1991 ... 1.25
❑4, ca. 1991 ... 1.25

Spooky Digest
Harvey

❑1, Oct 1992 ... 2.00
❑2 ... 2.00

Spooky Haunted House
Harvey

❑1, Oct 1972 ... 15.00
❑2, Dec 1972 ... 10.00
❑3, Feb 1973 ... 10.00
❑4, Apr 1973 ... 10.00
❑5, Jun 1973 ... 10.00
❑6, Aug 1973 ... 10.00
❑7, Oct 1973 ... 10.00
❑8, Dec 1973 ... 10.00
❑9, Feb 1974 ... 10.00
❑10, Apr 1974 ... 10.00
❑11, Jun 1974 ... 10.00

Spooky Spooktown
Harvey

❑1, Sep 1961 ... 85.00
❑2, Sep 1962 ... 45.00
❑3, Dec 1962 ... 30.00
❑4, ca. 1963 ... 30.00
❑5, ca. 1963 ... 30.00
❑6, ca. 1963 ... 22.00
❑7, ca. 1963 ... 22.00
❑8, ca. 1964 ... 22.00
❑9, ca. 1964 ... 22.00
❑10, ca. 1964 ... 22.00
❑11, ca. 1964 ... 15.00
❑12, Mar 1965, Giant-size ... 15.00
❑13, ca. 1965, Giant-Size ... 15.00
❑14, ca. 1965, Giant-Size ... 15.00
❑15, Sep 1965 ... 15.00
❑16, Mar 1966 ... 15.00
❑17, Sep 1966 ... 15.00
❑18, ca. 1967 ... 15.00
❑19, ca. 1967 ... 15.00
❑20, May 1967 ... 15.00
❑21, Sep 1967 ... 8.00
❑22, Nov 1967 ... 8.00
❑23, ca. 1968, Giant-Size ... 8.00
❑24, Apr 1968 ... 8.00
❑25, Jul 1968 ... 8.00
❑26, ca. 1968 ... 8.00
❑27, Dec 1968 ... 8.00
❑28, ca. 1969 ... 8.00
❑29, ca. 1969 ... 8.00
❑30, ca. 1969 ... 5.00
❑31, Oct 1969 ... 5.00
❑32, ca. 1970 ... 5.00
❑33, ca. 1970, Giant-Size ... 5.00
❑34, ca. 1970 ... 5.00
❑35, ca. 1970 ... 5.00
❑36, Oct 1970 ... 5.00
❑37, ca. 1971 ... 5.00
❑38, ca. 1971 ... 5.00
❑39, ca. 1971 ... 5.00

N-MINT

❑40, ca. 1971 ... 5.00
❑41, ca. 1971 ... 3.00
❑42, Dec 1971 ... 3.00
❑43, Mar 1972 ... 3.00
❑44, Jun 1972 ... 3.00
❑45, Sep 1972 ... 3.00
❑46, Dec 1972 ... 3.00
❑47, Feb 1973 ... 3.00
❑48, Apr 1973 ... 3.00
❑49, Jun 1973 ... 3.00
❑50, Aug 1973 ... 3.00
❑51, Oct 1973 ... 3.00
❑52, Dec 1973 ... 3.00
❑53, Oct 1974 ... 3.00
❑54, Dec 1974 ... 3.00
❑55, Feb 1975 ... 3.00
❑56, Apr 1975 ... 3.00
❑57, Jun 1975 ... 3.00
❑58, Aug 1975 ... 3.00
❑59, Oct 1975 ... 3.00
❑60, Dec 1975 ... 3.00
❑61, Feb 1976 ... 3.00
❑62, Apr 1976, A: Casper. A: Nightmare ... 3.00
❑63, Jun 1976 ... 3.00
❑64, Aug 1976 ... 3.00
❑65, Oct 1976 ... 3.00
❑66, Dec 1976 ... 3.00

Spooky the Dog Catcher
Paw Prints

❑1, Oct 1994, b&w ... 2.50
❑2, Jan 1995, b&w ... 2.50
❑3, May 1995, b&w ... 2.50

Sports Classics
Personality

❑1 ... 2.95
❑1/Ltd.; limited edition ... 5.95
❑2 ... 2.95
❑3 ... 2.95
❑4 ... 2.95
❑5 ... 2.95

Sports Comics
Personality

❑1; ca. 1992 ... 2.50
❑2 ... 2.50
❑3 ... 2.50
❑4 ... 2.50

Sports Hall of Shame in 3-D
Blackthorne

❑1; baseball ... 2.50

Sports Legends
Revolutionary

❑1, Sep 1992, b&w; Joe Namath ... 2.50
❑2, Oct 1992, b&w; Gordie Howe ... 2.50
❑3, Nov 1992, b&w; Arthur Ashe ... 2.50
❑4, Dec 1992, Muhammad Ali ... 2.50
❑5, Jan 1993, O.J. Simpson ... 2.50
❑6, Feb 1993, K.A. Jabbar ... 2.50
❑7, Mar 1993, b&w; Walter Payton ... 2.95
❑8, Apr 1993, b&w; Wilt Chamberlain ... 2.95
❑9, May 1993, b&w; Joe Louis ... 2.95

N-MINT

Sports Legends Special - Breaking the Color Barrier
Revolutionary

❑1, Oct 1993, b&w 2.95

Sports Personalities
Personality

❑1, Jul 1991; Bo Jackson 2.95
❑2, Aug 1991; Nolan Ryan 2.95
❑3; Rickey Henderson 2.95
❑4; Magic Johnson 2.95
❑5; Joe Montana 2.95
❑6; Lawrence Taylor 2.95
❑7 .... 2.95
❑8 .... 2.95
❑9 .... 2.95
❑10 .... 2.95
❑11 .... 2.95
❑12 .... 2.95
❑13 .... 2.95

Sports Superstars
Revolutionary

❑1, Apr 1992, b&w; Michael Jordan 2.50
❑2, May 1992, b&w; Wayne Gretzsky 2.50
❑3, Jun 1992, b&w; Magic Johnson 2.50
❑4, Jul 1992, b&w; Joe Montana 2.50
❑5, Aug 1992, b&w; Mike Tyson 2.50
❑6, Sep 1992, b&w; Larry Bird 2.50
❑7, Oct 1992, b&w; John Elway 2.50
❑8, Nov 1992, b&w; Julius Erving 2.50
❑9, Dec 1992, Barry Sanders 2.75
❑10, Jan 1993, Isiah Thomas 2.75
❑11, Feb 1992, Mario Lemieux 2.95
❑12, Mar 1993, b&w; Dan Marino 2.95
❑13, Apr 1993, b&w; Deion Sanders 2.95
❑14, May 1993, b&w; Patrick Ewing 2.95
❑15, Jun 1993, b&w; Charles Barkley 2.95
❑16, Aug 1993, b&w; Shaquille O'neal, Christian Laettner 2.95
❑Ann 1, Feb 1993, Michael Jordan II 2.75

Spotlight
Marvel

❑1, Sep 1978, Huckleberry Hound 8.00
❑2, Nov 1978 .... 6.00
❑3, Jan 1979 .... 6.00
❑4, Mar 1979, Magilla Gorilla; Snagglepuss 6.00

Spotlight on the Genius That Is Joe Sacco
Fantagraphics

❑1, b&w; NN 4.95

Spring Break Comics
AC

❑1, Mar 1987, b&w 1.50

Spring-Heel Jack
Rebel

❑1, b&w 2.25
❑2, b&w 2.25

Springtime Tales
Eclipse

❑1, Apr 1988; Peter Wheat 2.50

Spud
Spud

❑1, Sum 1996, b&w 3.50

Spunky Knight
Fantagraphics / Eros

❑1, May 1996 .... 2.95
❑2, Jun 1996 .... 2.95
❑3, Jul 1996 .... 2.95

Spunky Knight Extreme
Fantagraphics / Eros

❑1, Dec 2004 .... 3.95
❑2, Dec 2004 .... 3.95
❑3, Dec 2004 .... 3.95
❑4, Dec 2004 .... 3.95

Spunky Todd: The Psychic Boy
Caliber

❑1, b&w 2.95

SpyBoy
Dark Horse

❑1, Oct 1999 PD (w) 3.00
❑2, Nov 1999 PD (w) 2.75
❑3, Dec 1999 PD (w) 2.75
❑4, Jan 2000 PD (w) 2.75
❑5, Feb 2000 PD (w) 2.75
❑6, Mar 2000 PD (w) 2.50
❑7, Apr 2000 PD (w) 2.50
❑8, May 2000 PD (w) 2.50
❑9, Jun 2000 PD (w) 2.50
❑10, Jul 2000 PD (w) 2.50
❑11, Aug 2000 PD (w) 2.50
❑12, Sep 2000, b&w; PD (w); #13 skipped; story for that issue published as SpyBoy 13 miniseries 2.95
❑14, Nov 2000 PD (w) 2.99
❑15, Jan 2001; PD (w); Pop Mahn cover 2.99
❑16, Mar 2001 PD (w) 2.99
❑17, May 2001 PD (w) 2.99
❑Special 1, May 2002; PD (w); Special Edition #1 .... 4.99

Spyboy 13: Manga Affair
Dark Horse

❑1, Apr 2003; Series took the place of the 13th issue of SpyBoy 2.99
❑2, Jun 2003 .... 2.99
❑3, Aug 2003 .... 2.99

Spyboy: Final Exam
Dark Horse

❑1, May 2004 .... 2.99
❑2, Aug 2004 .... 2.99
❑3, Sep 2004 .... 2.99
❑4, Oct 2004 .... 2.99

Spyboy/Young Justice
Dark Horse

❑1, Feb 2002 .... 2.99
❑2, Mar 2002 .... 2.99
❑3, Apr 2002 .... 2.99

Spyke
Marvel / Epic

❑1, Jul 1993; Embossed cover 2.50
❑2, Aug 1993 .... 1.95
❑3, Sep 1993 .... 1.95
❑4, Oct 1993 .... 1.95

Spyman
Harvey

❑1, Sep 1966, 1&O: Spyman; Eye Spy 30.00
❑2, Dec 1966 .... 24.00
❑3, Feb 1967 .... 24.00

Squadron Supreme
Marvel

❑1, Sep 1985 BH (c); BH (a) 1.50
❑2, Oct 1985; BH (c); BH (a); V: Scarlet Centurion 1.00
❑3, Nov 1985; BH (c); BH (a); Death Nuke 1.00
❑4, Dec 1985 BH (c); BH (a) 1.00
❑5, Jan 1986; BH (c); BH (a); V: Institute of Evil. V: Institute of Evil; 1: Ape-X (Xina) 1.00
❑6, Feb 1986; BL (c); Quit Amphibian 1.00
❑7, Mar 1986 JB (a) 1.00
❑8, Apr 1986; BH (c); BH (a); Death Evil Hyperion 1.00
❑9, May 1986; D: Tom Thumb 1.00
❑10, Jun 1986; Death Doctor Decibel; Death Quagmire 1.00
❑11, Jul 1986 .... 1.00
❑12, Aug 1986; Death Nighthawk; Death Blue Eagle; Death Black Archer; Death Foxfire; Death Lamprey; Death Pinball 1.25

Squadron Supreme: New World Order
Marvel

❑1, Sep 1998 .... 5.99

Squadron Supreme
Marvel

❑1, Jun 2006, Team against blue background 2.99
❑2, Jun 2006 .... 2.99
❑3, Aug 2006 .... 2.99
❑4, Aug 2006 .... 2.99
❑5, Sep 2006 .... 2.99
❑6, Oct 2006 .... 2.99

Squalor
First

❑1, Dec 1989; 1st comics work by Stefan Petrucha 2.75
❑2, Jun 1990 .... 2.75
❑3, Jul 1990 .... 2.75
❑4, Aug 1990 .... 2.75

Squee!
Slave Labor

❑1, Apr 1997; b&w 7.00
❑1/2nd 1997; 2nd printing 2.95
❑2, Jul 1997 .... 5.00
❑3, Nov 1997 .... 3.50
❑4, Feb 1998 .... 3.50

Sri Krishna
Chakra

❑1 .... 3.50

Stacia Stories
Kitchen Sink

❑1, Jun 1995, b&w 2.95

Stagger Lee
Image

❑1, Jul 2006 .... 17.99

Stain
Fathom

❑1, Dec 1998 .... 2.95

Stainless Steel Armadillo
Antarctic

❑1, Feb 1995, b&w 2.95
❑2, Apr 1995, b&w 2.95
❑3, Jun 1995, b&w 2.95
❑4, Aug 1995, b&w 2.95
❑5, Oct 1995, b&w 2.95

Stainless Steel Rat
Eagle

❑1, Oct 1985; Reprinted from 2000 A.D. #140-145 .... 2.50
❑2, Nov 1985; Reprinted from 2000 A.D. #146-151 .... 2.50
❑3, Dec 1985 .... 2.50
❑4, Jan 1986 .... 2.50
❑5, Feb 1986 .... 2.50
❑6, Mar 1986 .... 2.50

Stalker
DC

❑1, Jul 1975; SD (c); SD, WW (a); O: Stalker. 1: Stalker 7.00
❑2, Sep 1975 .... 4.00
❑3, Nov 1975 .... 4.00
❑4, Jan 1976 .... 4.00

Stalkers
Marvel / Epic

❑1, Apr 1990; Paul Chadwick cover 1.50
❑2, May 1990 .... 1.50
❑3, Jun 1990 .... 1.50
❑4, Jul 1990 .... 1.50
❑5, Aug 1990 .... 1.50
❑6, Sep 1990 .... 1.50
❑7, Oct 1990 .... 1.50
❑8, Nov 1990 .... 1.50
❑9, Dec 1990 .... 1.50
❑10, Jan 1991 .... 1.50
❑11, Feb 1991 .... 1.50
❑12, Mar 1991 .... 1.50

Stalking Ralph
Aeon

❑1, Oct 1995; cardstock cover 4.95

Stand Up Comix
Grey

❑1, b&w 2.50

Stan Lee Meets Dr. Doom
Marvel

❑1, Feb 2007, Reprints from Fantastic Four #87 .... 3.99

Stan Lee Meets Dr. Strange
Marvel

❑1, Dec 2006 .... 3.99

Stan Lee Meets Silver Surfer
Marvel

❑1, Feb 2007, Also includes Silver Surfer #14 .... 3.99

Stan Lee Meets Spider-Man
Marvel

❑1, Dec 2006, Reprints Amazing Spider-Man #87 .... 3.99

Stan Lee Meets Thing
Marvel

❑1, Jan 2007 .... 3.99

Other grades: Multiply price above by 5/6 for VF/NM • 2/3 for VERY FINE • 1/3 for FINE • 1/5 for VERY GOOD • 1/8 for GOOD

Strangers

Cable car struck by energy, mutates riders
©Malibu

Strangers in Paradise

Long-running relationship title by Terry Moore
©Antarctic

Strange Sports Stories

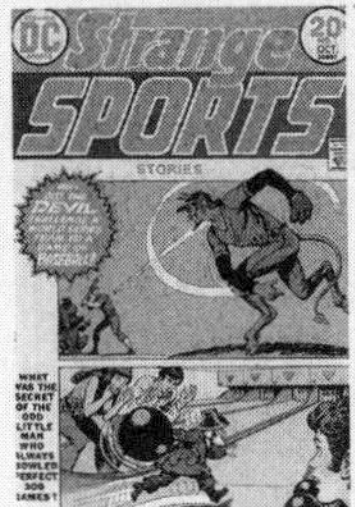

Mixed fantasy elements with sports themes
©DC

Strange Sports Stories (Adventure)

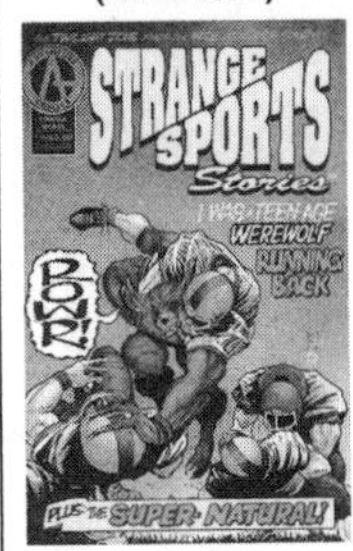

They might have seen the movie "Teen Wolf"
©Adventure

Strange Tales

Title gave birth to Dr. Strange and S.H.I.E.L.D.
©Marvel

N-MINT

Stanley & His Monster
DC

❑109, May 1968 20.00
❑110, Jul 1968 15.00
❑111, Sep 1968 15.00
❑112, Nov 1968 15.00

Stanley and His Monster
DC

❑1, Feb 1993 PF (w); PF (a) 2.50
❑2, Mar 1993 PF (w); PF (a) 2.00
❑3, Apr 1993 PF (w); PF (a) 2.00
❑4, May 1993 PF (w); PF (a) 2.00

Stanley the Snake with the Overactive Imagination
Emerald

❑1, b&w 1.50
❑2, b&w 1.50

Star
Image

❑1, Jun 1995 2.50
❑2, Jul 1995 2.50
❑3, Aug 1995 2.50
❑4, Oct 1995; cover says Aug, indicia says Oct 2.50

Starbikers
Renegade

❑1, b&w 2.00

Starblast
Marvel

❑1, Jan 1994; Story continues in Quasar #54 2.00
❑2, Feb 1994; Story continues in Quasar #55 1.75
❑3, Mar 1994; Story continues in Quasar #56 1.75
❑4, Apr 1994 1.75

Star Blazers
Comico

❑1, Apr 1987 2.00
❑2, ca. 1987 2.00
❑3, ca. 1987 2.00
❑4, ca. 1987 2.00

Star Blazers
Comico

❑1, ca. 1989 2.00
❑2, Jun 1989 PF (w) 2.00
❑3, Jul 1989 2.50
❑4, Aug 1989 2.50
❑5, Sep 1989 2.50

Star Blazers: The Magazine of Space Battleship Yamato
Argo

❑0 1995 2.95
❑1, Mar 1995 2.95

Star Blecch: Deep Space Diner
Parody

❑1/A; Star Blecch: Deep Space Diner cover 2.50
❑1/B; Star Blecch: The Degeneration cover 2.50

Star Blecch: Generation Gap
Parody

❑1, ca. 1995 3.95

N-MINT

Star Brand
Marvel

❑1, Oct 1986; JR2 (a); 1&O: Star Brand 1.00
❑2, Nov 1986 1.00
❑3, Dec 1986 1.00
❑4, Jan 1987 1.00
❑5, Feb 1987 1.00
❑6, Mar 1987 1.00
❑7, Apr 1987 1.00
❑8, May 1987 1.00
❑9, Jun 1987 1.00
❑10, Jul 1987 1.00
❑11, Jan 1988; JBy (w); JBy (a); Title changes to The Star Brand 1.00
❑12, Mar 1988; JBy (w); JBy (a); O: Star Brand. O: New Universe (explains "White Event"). Prelude to The Pitt 1.00
❑13, May 1988 JBy (w); JBy (a) 1.00
❑14, Jul 1988; JBy (w); JBy (a); Pitt tie in 1.00
❑15, Sep 1988 JBy (w); JBy (a) 1.00
❑16, Nov 1988; JBy (w); JBy (a); Nightmask 1.00
❑17, Jan 1989; JBy (w); JBy (a); Nightmask 1.00
❑18, Mar 1989; JBy (w); JBy (a); Justice 1.00
❑19, May 1989; JBy (w); JBy (a); Final Issue 1.00
❑Ann 1, ca. 1987 1.25

Starchild
Taliesen

❑0, Apr 1993, b&w 4.00
❑1, b&w; wraparound cover 4.00
❑1/2nd; 2nd printing 2.50
❑2 1993, b&w; wraparound cover 4.00
❑2/2nd, Feb 1994, b&w; wraparound cover 2.50
❑2/3rd, Feb 1994, b&w; wraparound cover 2.50
❑3 1993, b&w; wraparound cover 3.00
❑4 1993, b&w; wraparound cover 3.00
❑5, Jan 1994, b&w; wraparound cover 3.00
❑6, Feb 1994, b&w; wraparound cover 3.00
❑7, Mar 1994, b&w; wraparound cover 2.50
❑8, Apr 1994, b&w; wraparound cover 2.50
❑9, May 1994, b&w; wraparound cover 2.50
❑10, Aug 1994, b&w; wraparound cover 2.50
❑11, Dec 1994, b&w; wraparound cover 2.50
❑12, Jun 1995, b&w; wraparound cover 2.50
❑13 2.50
❑14; Final Issue 2.50

Starchild: Crossroads
Coppervale

❑1, Nov 1995, b&w 2.95
❑2, Jan 1996, b&w 2.95
❑3, Mar 1996, b&w 2.95

Starchild: Mythopolis
Image

❑0, Jul 1997, b&w 2.95
❑1, Sep 1997, b&w 2.95
❑2, Nov 1997, b&w 2.95
❑3, Jan 1998, b&w 2.95
❑4, Apr 1998, b&w 2.95
❑5 2.95
❑6 2.95

N-MINT

Starchy
Excel

❑1 1.95

Star Comics Magazine
Marvel / Star

❑1, Dec 1986; digest; Reprints 3.00
❑2, Feb 1987; digest; Reprints 2.00
❑3, Apr 1987; digest; Reprints 2.00
❑4, Jun 1987; digest; Reprints 2.00
❑5, Aug 1987; digest; Reprints 2.00
❑6, Oct 1987; digest; Reprints 2.00
❑7, Dec 1987; digest; Reprints 2.00
❑8, Feb 1988; digest; Reprints 2.00
❑9, Apr 1988; digest; Reprints 2.00
❑10, Jun 1988; digest; Reprints 2.00
❑11, Aug 1988; digest; Reprints 2.00
❑12, Oct 1988; digest; Reprints 2.00
❑13, Dec 1988; digest; Reprints 2.00

S.T.A.R. Corps
DC

❑1, Nov 1993 1.50
❑2, Dec 1993 1.50
❑3, Jan 1994 1.50
❑4, Feb 1994 1.50
❑5, Mar 1994 1.50
❑6, Apr 1994; Final Issue 1.50

Star Crossed
DC / Helix

❑1, Jun 1997 2.50
❑2, Jul 1997 2.50
❑3, Aug 1997 2.50

Stardust
DC / Vertigo

❑1, prestige format 6.50
❑2, prestige format; ca. 1988 6.00
❑3, prestige format 6.00
❑4, prestige format 6.00

Stardusters
Nightwynd

❑1, Sep 1991, b&w 2.50
❑2, Nov 1991, b&w 2.50
❑3, Jan 1992, b&w 2.50
❑4, Mar 1992, b&w 2.50

Stardust Kid
Image

❑1, May 2005 3.50
❑2, Oct 2005 3.50
❑3, Oct 2005 3.50

Starfire
DC

❑1, Sep 1976, 1&O: Starfire I 7.00
❑2, Nov 1976 3.00
❑3, Jan 1977 3.00
❑4, Mar 1977 3.00
❑5, May 1977 3.00
❑6, Jul 1977 3.00
❑7, Sep 1977 3.00
❑8, Nov 1977 3.00

Star Forces
The Other Faculty / Helix

❑1 3.00

Other grades: Multiply price above by 5/6 for VF/NM • 2/3 for VERY FINE • 1/3 for FINE • 1/5 for VERY GOOD • 1/8 for GOOD

Starforce Six Special
AC
- ❑1, Nov 1984 — 1.50

Stargate
Express / Entity
- ❑1, Jul 1996 — 2.95
- ❑1/Variant, Jul 1996; Photo cover — 3.50
- ❑2, Aug 1996; photo section back-up — 2.95
- ❑2/Variant, Aug 1996; photo section back-up — 3.50
- ❑3, Sep 1996; photo section back-up — 2.95
- ❑3/Variant, Sep 1996; photo section back-up — 3.50
- ❑4, Oct 1996; photo section back-up — 2.95
- ❑4/Variant, Oct 1996; photo section back-up — 3.50

Stargate Doomsday World
Entity
- ❑1, Nov 1996 — 2.95
- ❑2, Dec 1996 — 2.95
- ❑3, Jan 1997 — 2.95

Stargate SG1 Con Special 2003
Avatar
- ❑1, Sep 2003 — 3.95

Stargate SG1 Con Special 2004
Avatar
- ❑1, Apr 2004 — 2.99
- ❑1/A, Apr 2004; Wrap/Photo Cover — 3.99

Stargate SG-1: Daniel's Song
Avatar
- ❑1 2005 — 2.99
- ❑1/Photo — 4.00
- ❑1/Wraparound — 3.00
- ❑1/Glow, 1,000 copies printed — 20.00
- ❑1/Gold Foil; Retailer incentive. 500 copies printed — 6.00
- ❑1/PlatFoil; Retailer incentive. 700 copies printed — 10.00
- ❑1/Adversary — 5.99

Stargate SG1: Fall of Rome
Avatar
- ❑0/Preview — 6.00
- ❑1 — 3.99
- ❑1/Foil — 3.99
- ❑1/Platinum — 10.00
- ❑2 — 3.99
- ❑2/Painted — 5.99
- ❑2/Photo — 3.99
- ❑2/Platinum — 10.00
- ❑3 — 3.99
- ❑3/Painted — 5.99
- ❑3/Platinum — 10.00
- ❑3/Photo — 3.99

Stargate SG1: P.O.W.
Avatar
- ❑1, Feb 2004 — 3.50
- ❑2, Mar 2004 — 3.50
- ❑3, May 2004 — 3.50

Stargate: The New Adventures Collection
Entity
- ❑1, Dec 1997, b&w; Collects Stargate: One Nation Under Ra; Stargate: Underworld — 5.95

Stargate Underworld
Entity
- ❑1, ca. 1997; Bill Maus Cover — 2.95

Stargods
Antarctic
- ❑1, Jul 1998 — 2.95
- ❑1/CS, Jul 1998; poster; alternate cover — 5.95
- ❑2, Sep 1998 — 2.95
- ❑2/CS, Sep 1998; poster; alternate cover — 5.95

Stargods: Visions
Antarctic
- ❑1, Dec 1998; pin-ups — 2.95

Starhead Presents
Starhead
- ❑1 — 1.00
- ❑2, Apr 1987 — 1.00
- ❑3; Bad Teens — 1.00

Star Hunters
DC
- ❑1, Nov 1977 — 1.00
- ❑2, Jan 1978, RB (c); BL (a) — 1.00
- ❑3, Mar 1978, RB (c); MN, BL (a) — 1.00
- ❑4, May 1978 — 1.00
- ❑5, Jul 1978 — 1.00
- ❑6, Sep 1978 — 1.00
- ❑7, Nov 1978, Final Issue — 1.00

Star Jacks
Antarctic
- ❑1, Jun 1994, b&w — 2.75

Star Jam Comics
Revolutionary
- ❑1, Apr 1992, b&w; M.C. Hammer story — 2.50
- ❑2, Jun 1992, b&w; Janet Jackson story — 2.50
- ❑3, Aug 1992, b&w; Beverly Hills 90210 story — 2.50
- ❑4, Sep 1992, b&w; Beverly Hills 90210 story — 2.50
- ❑5, Oct 1992, b&w; Beverly Hills 90210 story — 2.50
- ❑6, Nov 1992, b&w; Kriss Kross story — 2.50
- ❑7, Dec 1992, b&w; Marky Mark story — 2.50
- ❑8, Jan 1993, b&w; Madonna story — 2.50
- ❑9, Feb 1993, b&w; Jennie Garth story — 2.50
- ❑10, Mar 1993, b&w; Melrose Place story — 2.50

Starjammers
Marvel
- ❑1, Oct 1995; OverPower cards bound-in; enhanced cardstock cover — 2.95
- ❑2, Nov 1995; enhanced cardstock cover — 2.95
- ❑3, Dec 1995; enhanced cardstock cover — 2.95
- ❑4, Jan 1996; enhanced cardstock cover — 2.95

Starjammers
Marvel
- ❑1, Sep 2004; Enhanced cardstock cover; OverPower cards bound-in — 2.99
- ❑2, Sep 2004; Enhanced cardstock cover — 2.99
- ❑3, Oct 2004 — 2.99
- ❑4, Oct 2004 — 2.99
- ❑5, Nov 2004 — 2.99
- ❑6, Nov 2004 — 2.99

Starjongleur
Trylvertel
- ❑1, Aug 1986, b&w — 2.00
- ❑2, Win 1987, b&w — 2.00

Starkid
Dark Horse
- ❑1, Jan 1998; prequel to movie — 2.95

Stark Raven
Endless Horizons
- ❑1, Sep 2000 — 2.95

Starkweather
Arcana
- ❑1, Aug 2004 — 3.95
- ❑1/Ltd. 2004 — 5.00
- ❑2, Oct 2004 — 3.95
- ❑3, Nov 2005 — 3.95
- ❑4, Feb 2005 — 3.95
- ❑5, Oct 2005; Price increase — 3.95

Starlight
Eternity
- ❑1, Oct 1987 — 1.95

Starlight Agency
Antarctic
- ❑1, Jun 1991, b&w — 2.50
- ❑2, Aug 1991, b&w — 2.50
- ❑3, Sep 1991, b&w — 2.50

Starlion: A Pawn's Game
Storm
- ❑1, Feb 1993 — 2.25

Starlord
Marvel
- ❑1, Dec 1996 — 2.50
- ❑2, Jan 1997 — 2.50
- ❑3, Feb 1997 — 2.50

Starlord Megazine
Marvel
- ❑1, Nov 1996, Reprints Star-Lord, The Special Edition #1; back cover pin-up — 2.95

Star-Lord Special Edition
Marvel
- ❑1, Feb 1982; DaG, MG, JBy (a); Star-Lord: Reprint from Marvel Preview #11; Doctor Who: Reprint from Doctor Who Monthly — 2.00

Starlove
Forbidden Fruit
- ❑1, b&w; Adult — 2.95
- ❑2, b&w; Adult — 3.50

Starman
DC
- ❑1, Oct 1988; 1&O: Starman IV (William Payton) — 2.00
- ❑2, Nov 1988 — 1.50
- ❑3, Dec 1988; V: Bolt — 1.50
- ❑4, Win 1988; V: Power Elite — 1.50
- ❑5, Hol 1989; Invasion! — 1.50
- ❑6, Jan 1989; Invasion! — 1.50
- ❑7, Feb 1989 — 1.50
- ❑8, Mar 1989 A: Lady Quark — 1.50
- ❑9, Apr 1989; O: Blockbuster. A: Batman — 1.50
- ❑10, May 1989; O: Blockbuster. A: Batman — 1.50
- ❑11, Jun 1989 — 1.25
- ❑12, Jul 1989 — 1.25
- ❑13, Aug 1989 — 1.25
- ❑14, Sep 1989; Superman — 1.25
- ❑15, Oct 1989; 1: Deadline — 1.25
- ❑16, Nov 1989 — 1.25
- ❑17, Dec 1989; Power Girl — 1.25
- ❑18, Jan 1990 — 1.25
- ❑19, Feb 1990 — 1.25
- ❑20, Mar 1990 — 1.25
- ❑21, Apr 1990 — 1.25
- ❑22, May 1990; V: Deadline — 1.25
- ❑23, Jun 1990 — 1.25
- ❑24, Jul 1990 — 1.25
- ❑25, Aug 1990 — 1.25
- ❑26, Sep 1990; 1: David Knight — 2.00
- ❑27, Oct 1990; O: Starman V (David Knight) — 1.25
- ❑28, Nov 1990; Superman — 1.25
- ❑29, Dec 1990 — 1.25
- ❑30, Jan 1991 — 1.25
- ❑31, Feb 1991 — 1.25
- ❑32, Mar 1991 — 1.25
- ❑33, Apr 1991 — 1.25
- ❑34, May 1991; Batman team-up — 1.25
- ❑35, Jun 1991 — 1.25
- ❑36, Jul 1991; Phantom Lady cover/appearance, Rampage cover/appearance — 1.25
- ❑37, Aug 1991 — 1.25
- ❑38, Sep 1991; War of the Gods — 1.25
- ❑39, Oct 1991 — 1.25
- ❑40, Nov 1991 — 1.25
- ❑41, Dec 1991 — 1.25
- ❑42, Jan 1992 — 1.25
- ❑43, Feb 1992 — 1.25
- ❑44, Mar 1992; Lobo — 1.25
- ❑45, Apr 1992; Lobo — 1.25

Starman
DC
- ❑0, Oct 1994; JRo (w); 1: Starman VI (Jack Knight); 1: Nash; D: Starman V (David Knight); 1: Mist II — 5.00
- ❑1, Nov 1994; JRo (w); 1: Hope; 1: Mason; 1: Barry; 1: Matthew O'Dare — 5.00
- ❑2, Dec 1994; JRo (w); 1: Charity — 4.00
- ❑3, Jan 1995; JRo (w); D: Kyle (Mist's son); Return Starman IV & II — 4.00
- ❑4, Feb 1995 JRo (w) — 3.00
- ❑5, Mar 1995; JRo (w); Jack appears b&w in story while David is in color — 3.00
- ❑6, Apr 1995; JRo (w); A Tale of Times Past — 3.00
- ❑7, May 1995 JRo (w) — 3.00
- ❑8, Jun 1995 JRo (w) — 3.00
- ❑9, Jul 1995 JRo (w) — 3.00
- ❑10, Aug 1995; JRo (w); V: Solomon Grundy. 1: Mist II; Nash becomes Mist II — 3.00
- ❑11, Sep 1995; JRo (w); JSA story; D: Ragdoll I; Cover Error Lists Harris and Von Grawbadger; A Tale of Times Past — 2.50
- ❑12, Oct 1995 JRo (w) — 2.50
- ❑13, Nov 1995; JRo (w); Underworld Unleashed — 2.50
- ❑14, Dec 1995 JRo (w) — 2.50

Other grades: Multiply price above by 5/6 for VF/NM • 2/3 for VERY FINE • 1/3 for FINE • 1/5 for VERY GOOD • 1/8 for GOOD

Strange Tales

Half Dr. Strange, half Cloak and Dagger
©Marvel

Strange Tales

Acetate-covered graphic novel
©Marvel

Strange Tales

Stars Werewolf by Night and Man-Thing
©Marvel

Stray Bullets

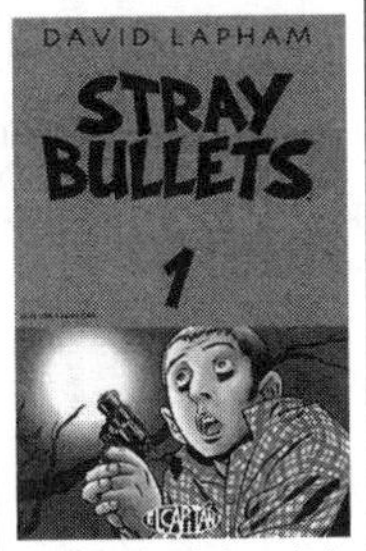

David Lapham's irregularly published crime hit
©El Capitan

Street Poet Ray

Marvel's worst-selling comic book ever
©Marvel

	N-MINT
❑15, Jan 1996 JRo (w)	2.50
❑16, Feb 1996 JRo (w)	2.50
❑17, Mar 1996 JRo (w)	2.50
❑18, Apr 1996; JRo (w); Original Starman V: The Mist	2.50
❑19, Jun 1996; JRo (w); Times Past	2.50
❑20, Jul 1996 JRo (w); A: Wesley Dodds appearance, Dian Belmont. A: Wesley Dodds. A: Dian Belmont	2.50
❑21, Aug 1996; JRo (w); Sandman Mystery Theatre crossover	2.50
❑22, Sep 1996; JRo (w); Sandman Mystery Theatre crossover	2.50
❑23, Oct 1996; JRo (w); Sandman Mystery Theatre crossover	2.50
❑24, Nov 1996; JRo (w); 1: Hamilton Drew	2.50
❑25, Dec 1996 JRo (w)	2.50
❑26, Jan 1997 JRo (w)	2.50
❑27, Feb 1997 JRo (w)	2.50
❑28, Mar 1997; JRo (w); A Tale of Times Past	2.50
❑29, Apr 1997; JRo (w); 1: Jake 'Bobbo' Benetti	2.50
❑30, May 1997 JRo (w)	2.50
❑31, Jun 1997 JRo (w)	2.50
❑32, Jul 1997; JRo (w); D: Solomon Grundy	2.50
❑33, Aug 1997 JRo (w); A: Solomon Grundy. A: Sentinel. A: Batman	2.50
❑34, Sep 1997 JRo (w); A: Ted Knight. A: Solomon Grundy. A: Sentinel. A: Batman. A: Jason Woodrue	2.50
❑35, Oct 1997; JRo (w); Genesis	2.50
❑36, Nov 1997; JRo (w); A: Will Payton. A Tale of Times Past	2.50
❑37, Dec 1997; JRo (w); Face cover	2.50
❑38, Jan 1998; JRo (w); 1: Baby Starman. Mist vs. Justice League Europe	2.50
❑39, Feb 1998; JRo (w); continues in Power of Shazam! #35; cover forms diptych with Starman #40	2.50
❑40, Mar 1998; JRo (w); cover forms diptych with Starman #39	2.50
❑41, Apr 1998; JRo (w); V: Doctor Phosphorus	2.25
❑42, May 1998; JRo (w); A: Demon. A Tale of Times Past	2.25
❑43, Jun 1998 JRo (w); A: Justice League of America	2.25
❑44, Jul 1998; JRo (w); A: Phantom Lady. A Tale of Times Past	2.25
❑45, Aug 1998 JRo (w)	2.25
❑46, Sep 1998; JRo (w); Cover states 1954 while title page states 1952; A Tale of Times Past	2.25
❑47, Oct 1998; JRo (w); 1: Spider II (in shadows)	2.50
❑48, Dec 1998 JRo (w); A: Solomon Grundy	2.50
❑49, Jan 1999 JRo (w)	2.50
❑50, Feb 1999 JRo (w); A: Legion	3.95
❑51, Mar 1999; JRo (w); A: Jor-El. on Krypton	2.50
❑52, Apr 1999; JRo (w); A: Turran Kha. A: Adam Strange. on Rann	2.50
❑53, May 1999; JRo (w); A: Adam Strange. on Rann	2.50
❑54, Jun 1999; JRo (w); Times Past	2.50
❑55, Jul 1999 JRo (w); A: Space Cabbie	2.50
❑56, Aug 1999 JRo (w)	2.50
❑57, Sep 1999; JRo (w); A: Fastbak. A: Tigorr. on Throneworld	2.50
❑58, Oct 1999 JRo (w); A: Will Payton	2.50
❑59, Nov 1999 JRo (w)	2.50
❑60, Dec 1999; Jack returns to Earth	2.50
❑61, Jan 2000 JRo (w)	2.50
❑62, Feb 2000 JRo (w)	2.50
❑63, Mar 2000 JRo (w)	2.50
❑64, Apr 2000 JRo (w)	2.50
❑65, May 2000; JRo (w); 1: Spider II (fully seen)	2.50
❑66, Jun 2000; JRo (w); O: Culp	2.50
❑67, Jul 2000 JRo (w)	2.50
❑68, Aug 2000 JRo (w)	2.50
❑69, Sep 2000; JRo (w)	2.50
❑70, Oct 2000 JRo (w)	2.50
❑71, Nov 2000; JRo (w); D: Culp; D: Solomon Grundy; Resurrection of Mist I; Black Pirate's (Jon Valor) spirit freed	2.50
❑72, Dec 2000; JRo (w); D: Starman I; D: Mist II; D: Barry O'Dare; D: Starman (Ted Knight); D: Mist I	2.50
❑73, Jan 2001; JRo (w); Funeral for Starman I; D: Matt O'Dare	2.50
❑74, Feb 2001; JRo (w); RH (a); Times Past	2.50
❑75, Mar 2001; JRo (w); Superman and Starman (Jack Knight) talk about Jor El and Starman (Ted Knight)	2.50
❑76, Apr 2001; JRo (w); Starman (Jack Knight) transported to 1951	2.50
❑77, May 2001; JRo (w); V: Mist I	2.50
❑78, Jun 2001; JRo (w); V: Mist I	2.50
❑79, Jul 2001 JRo (w)	2.50
❑80, Aug 2001; JRo (w); Final issue	2.50
❑1000000, Nov 1998 JRo (w)	3.50
❑Ann 1, ca. 1996; JRo (w); Legends of the Dead Earth; Shade tells stories of Ted Knight and Gavyn; 1996 Ann	5.00
❑Ann 2, ca. 1997; JRo (w); Pulp Heroes; 1997 annual	3.95
❑GS 1, Jan 1999; 80 page giant; JRo (w)	4.95

Starman: Secret Files
DC

	N-MINT
❑1, Apr 1998; background on series	4.95

Starman: The Mist
DC

	N-MINT
❑1, Jun 1998; Girlfrenzy	1.95

Star Masters
Marvel

	N-MINT
❑1, Dec 1995	1.95
❑2, Jan 1996	1.95
❑3, Feb 1996; continues in Cosmic Powers Unlimited #4	1.95

Starmasters
AC

	N-MINT
❑1, Mar 1989	1.50

Star Rangers
Adventure

	N-MINT
❑1, Oct 1987	1.95
❑2, Nov 1987; Painted cover by Dave Dorman; Backup story with early Adam Hughes work; b&w	1.95
❑3, Dec 1987; Death Hawk	1.95

Star*Reach
Star*Reach

	N-MINT
❑1, ca. 1974 JSn, HC (w); AM, JSn, HC (a)	2.00
❑2, ca. 1975 NA (c); JSn (w); JSn, DG (a)	2.00
❑3, ca. 1975	2.00
❑4, ca. 1976	2.00
❑5, ca. 1976 HC (c); FB (w); FB, HC, JSa (a)	1.50
❑6, Oct 1976 JJ (c); JSa, GD, AN (a)	1.50
❑7, ca. 1977 JSa (a)	1.50
❑8, ca. 1977; CR (c); GD (w); CR, GD (a); Adapts Wagner's Parsifal	1.50
❑9, ca. 1977	1.50
❑10, ca. 1977	1.50
❑11, ca. 1977	1.50
❑12, ca. 1978	1.50
❑13, ca. 1978	1.50
❑14, ca. 1978	1.50
❑15, ca. 1978	1.50
❑16, ca. 1979	1.50
❑17, ca. 1979	1.50
❑18, ca. 1979	1.50

Star*Reach Classics
Eclipse

	N-MINT
❑1, Mar 1984 JSn (w); DG (a)	2.00
❑2, Apr 1984	2.00
❑3, May 1984	2.00
❑4, Jun 1984	2.00
❑5, Jul 1984 HC (a)	2.00
❑6, Aug 1984 CR (a)	2.00

Starriors
Marvel / Star

	N-MINT
❑1, Nov 1984 BSz (c)	1.00
❑2, Dec 1984 BSz (c)	1.00
❑3, Jan 1985 BSz (c)	1.00
❑4, Feb 1985 BSz (c)	1.00

Star Rovers
Comax

	N-MINT
❑1, b&w; Pin-ups; Adult	2.95

Stars and S.T.R.I.P.E.
DC

	N-MINT
❑0, Jul 1999; JRo (w); A: Starman. 1st Geoff Johns work	2.95
❑1, Aug 1999; 1: Cindy Burman (Shiv); O: Star-Spangled Kid II	2.50
❑2, Sep 1999; 1: Paintball	2.50
❑3, Oct 1999; 1: Skeeter	2.50
❑4, Nov 1999; A: Captain Marvel. Day of Judgment	2.50
❑5, Dec 1999 A: Young Justice	2.95
❑6, Jan 2000	2.95
❑7, Feb 2000	2.95
❑8, Mar 2000	2.95
❑9, Apr 2000; 1: Crimson Avenger II; D: Spider I; D: Billy Gunn; D: Wing; Post-Crisis retelling of the Seven Soldiers of Victory's rescue by the JLA/JSA	2.95
❑10, May 2000	2.50
❑12, Jul 2000	2.50
❑11, Jun 2000	2.50
❑13, Aug 2000; D: Dragon King	2.50
❑14, Sep 2000; Final Issue	2.50

Other grades: Multiply price above by 5/6 for VF/NM • 2/3 for VERY FINE • 1/3 for FINE • 1/5 for VERY GOOD • 1/8 for GOOD

Star Seed
Broadway

❑7, Jul 1996; Series continued from Powers That Be #6 ... 2.95
❑8, Aug 1996 ... 2.95
❑9, Sep 1996; Final Issue ... 2.95

Starship Troopers
Dark Horse

❑1, Oct 1997 ... 2.95
❑2, Nov 1997 ... 2.95

Starship Troopers: Brute Creations
Dark Horse

❑1, Sep 1997; NN; One-shot; Movie prequel; Inspired by the classic Robert A. Heinlein novel ... 2.95

Starship Troopers: Dominant Species
Dark Horse

❑1, Aug 1998; Painted cover; Inspired by the classic Robert A. Heinlein novel ... 2.95
❑2, Sep 1998; Painted cover ... 2.95
❑3, Oct 1998; Painted cover ... 2.95
❑4, Nov 1998; Painted cover; Final issue 2.95

Starship Troopers: Insect Touch
Dark Horse

❑1, May 1997, cardstock cover ... 2.95
❑2, Jun 1997, cardstock cover ... 2.95
❑3, Jul 1997, cardstock cover ... 2.95

Star Slammers
Malibu / Bravura

❑1, May 1994; Includes coupon ... 2.50
❑1/Gold, May 1994 ... 3.00
❑2, Jun 1994; Cover by Walt Simonson; Includes coupon ... 2.50
❑3, Aug 1994; Includes coupon ... 2.50
❑4, Feb 1995; Includes coupon ... 2.50

Star Slammers Special
Dark Horse / Legend

❑1, Jun 1996; finishes Malibu/Bravura series ... 2.95

Starslayer
Pacific

❑1, Feb 1982; MGr (w); MGr (a); O: Starslayer. 1: Rocketeer (cameo) ... 2.00
❑2, Apr 1982; MGr (w); SA, MGr, DSt (a); 1&O: Rocketeer ... 4.00
❑3, Jun 1982; MGr (w); MGr, DSt (a); A: Rocketeer. Rocketeer backup story 2.00
❑4, Aug 1982 MGr (w); MGr (a) ... 1.00
❑5, Nov 1982 SA, MGr, ME (w); SA, MGr (a); A: Groo ... 2.00
❑6, Apr 1983 MGr (w); MGr (a) ... 1.00
❑7, Aug 1983; First Comics begins publishing ... 1.00
❑8, Sep 1983 ... 1.00
❑9, Oct 1983 ... 1.00
❑10, Nov 1983; 1: Grimjack ... 1.50
❑11, Dec 1983 A: Grimjack ... 1.00
❑12, Jan 1984 A: Grimjack ... 1.00
❑13, Feb 1984 A: Grimjack ... 1.00
❑14, Mar 1984 A: Grimjack ... 1.00
❑15, Apr 1984 A: Grimjack ... 1.00
❑16, May 1984 A: Grimjack ... 1.00
❑17, Jun 1984 A: Grimjack ... 1.00
❑18, Jul 1984 A: Grimjack ... 1.00
❑19, Aug 1984 ... 1.00
❑20, Sep 1984; Black Flame ... 1.00
❑21, Oct 1984; Black Flame ... 1.00
❑22, Nov 1984; Black Flame ... 1.25
❑23, Dec 1984; Black Flame ... 1.25
❑24, Jan 1985; Black Flame ... 1.25
❑25, Feb 1985; The Black Flame back-up story ... 1.25
❑26, Mar 1985; Black Flame ... 1.25
❑27, Apr 1985; TS (a); Black Flame (no Starslayer story) ... 1.25
❑28, May 1985; Black Flame ... 1.25
❑29, Jun 1985; Black Flame ... 1.25
❑30, Jul 1985; Black Flame ... 1.25
❑31, Aug 1985; Black Flame ... 1.25
❑32, Sep 1985; Black Flame ... 1.25
❑33, Oct 1985; Black Flame ... 1.25
❑34, Nov 1985; Final Issue ... 1.25

Starslayer: The Director's Cut
Acclaim / Windjammer

❑1, Jun 1995; New story and artwork ... 2.50
❑2, Jun 1995; Reprints Starslayer #1 ... 2.50
❑3, Jul 1995; Reprints Starslayer #2 ... 2.50
❑4, Jul 1995; Reprints Starslayer #3 ... 2.50
❑5, Aug 1995; Reprints Starslayer #4 ... 2.50
❑6, Sep 1995; cover says Aug, indicia says Sep; Reprints Starslayer #5 ... 2.50
❑7, Sep 1995; Reprints Starslayer #6 ... 2.50
❑8, Dec 1995; New story and artwork ... 2.50

Star Spangled Comics
DC

❑1, May 1999; A: Star Spangled Kid. A: Sandman. Justice Society Returns. 2.00

Star Spangled War Stories
DC

❑84, Aug 1959; 1&O: Mademoiselle Marie 125.00
❑85, Sep 1959 A: Mademoiselle Marie .. 80.00
❑86, Oct 1959 A: Mademoiselle Marie ... 80.00
❑87, Nov 1959 MD, JKu, RA (a); A: Mademoiselle Marie ... 80.00
❑88, Jan 1960; Mademoiselle Marie ... 65.00
❑89, Mar 1960; Mademoiselle Marie ... 65.00
❑90, May 1960; RA, IN (a); 1: Dinosaur Island, War That Time Forgot story ... 325.00
❑91, Jul 1960; Mademoiselle Marie ... 45.00
❑92, Sep 1960; Dinosaurs; War That Time Forgot ... 110.00
❑93, Nov 1960; Dinosaurs ... 45.00
❑94, Jan 1961; Dinosaurs; War That Time Forgot ... 110.00
❑95, Mar 1961; RA, RH, JAb (a); Dinosaurs; War That Time Forgot ... 110.00
❑96, May 1961; RA, JAb (a); Dinosaurs; War That Time Forgot ... 110.00
❑97, Jul 1961; RA, RH (a); Dinosaurs; War That Time Forgot ... 110.00
❑98, Sep 1961; JKu, RA, IN (a); Dinosaurs; War That Time Forgot ... 110.00
❑99, Nov 1961; RA, RH, JAb (a); Dinosaurs; War That Time Forgot ... 110.00
❑100, Jan 1962, RA, JAb (a); Dinosaurs; War That Time Forgot ... 145.00
❑101, Mar 1962, Dinosaurs; War That Time Forgot ... 60.00
❑102, May 1962, Dinosaurs; War That Time Forgot ... 60.00
❑103, Jul 1962, Dinosaurs; War That Time Forgot ... 60.00
❑104, Sep 1962, Dinosaurs; War That Time Forgot ... 60.00
❑105, Nov 1962, Dinosaurs; War That Time Forgot ... 60.00
❑106, Jan 1963, RA, JAb (a); Dinosaurs; War That Time Forgot ... 60.00
❑107, Mar 1963, RA, JAb (a); Dinosaurs; War That Time Forgot ... 60.00
❑108, May 1963, Dinosaurs; War That Time Forgot ... 60.00
❑109, Jul 1963, Dinosaurs; War That Time Forgot ... 60.00
❑110, Sep 1963, Dinosaurs; War That Time Forgot ... 60.00
❑111, Nov 1963, Dinosaurs; War That Time Forgot ... 60.00
❑112, Jan 1964, Dinosaurs; War That Time Forgot ... 60.00
❑113, Mar 1964, Dinosaurs; War That Time Forgot ... 60.00
❑114, May 1964, Dinosaurs; War That Time Forgot ... 60.00
❑115, Jul 1964, Dinosaurs; War That Time Forgot ... 60.00
❑116, Sep 1964, RA, IN (a); Dinosaurs; War That Time Forgot ... 60.00
❑117, Nov 1964, Dinosaurs; War That Time Forgot ... 60.00
❑118, Jan 1965, Dinosaurs; War That Time Forgot ... 60.00
❑119, Mar 1965, Dinosaurs; War That Time Forgot ... 60.00
❑120, Apr 1965, Dinosaurs; War That Time Forgot ... 60.00
❑121, Jun 1965, Dinosaurs; War That Time Forgot ... 60.00
❑122, Aug 1965, Dinosaurs; War That Time Forgot ... 60.00
❑123, Oct 1965, Dinosaurs; War That Time Forgot ... 60.00
❑124, Dec 1965, Dinosaurs; War That Time Forgot ... 60.00
❑125, Feb 1966, JKu, RA, JAb (a); Dinosaurs; War That Time Forgot ... 60.00
❑126, Apr 1966, JKu (c); JKu, JAb (a); 1: Sgt. Gorilla ... 60.00
❑127, Jun 1966, Dinosaurs; War That Time Forgot ... 60.00
❑128, Aug 1966, Dinosaurs; War That Time Forgot ... 60.00
❑129, Oct 1966, Dinosaurs; War That Time Forgot ... 60.00
❑130, Dec 1966, RH (c); JAb (a); Dinosaurs ... 60.00
❑131, Mar 1967, JAb (a); Dinosaurs; War That Time Forgot ... 60.00
❑132, May 1967, Dinosaurs; War That Time Forgot ... 60.00
❑133, Jul 1967, Dinosaurs; War That Time Forgot ... 60.00
❑134, Sep 1967, RH (c); NA, JAb (a); Dinosaurs ... 65.00
❑135, Nov 1967, RH (c); RH, JAb (a); Dinosaurs ... 60.00
❑136, Jan 1968, Dinosaurs ... 60.00
❑137, Mar 1968, RH (c); JKu (a); Dinosaurs ... 60.00
❑138, May 1968, JKu (a); Enemy Ace stories begin ... 60.00
❑139, Jul 1968, JKu (a); O: Enemy Ace. O: Enemy Ace ... 50.00
❑140, Sep 1968, JKu (c); JKu (a); Enemy Ace ... 24.00
❑141, Nov 1968, JKu (c); JKu (a); Enemy Ace ... 24.00
❑142, Jan 1969, JKu (c); JKu (a); Enemy Ace ... 24.00
❑143, Mar 1969, Enemy Ace ... 24.00
❑144, May 1969, JKu, NA (a); Enemy Ace 27.00
❑145, Jul 1969, Enemy Ace ... 35.00
❑146, Sep 1969, Enemy Ace ... 20.00
❑147, Nov 1969, JKu (c); JKu (a); Enemy Ace ... 20.00
❑148, Jan 1970, Enemy Ace ... 20.00
❑149, Mar 1970, JKu (c); JKu, RE (a); Enemy Ace; Viking Prince: Reprint from Brave and the Bold #11 ... 20.00
❑150, May 1970, JKu (c); JKu (w); JKu, RE (a); Enemy Ace, Viking Prince ... 20.00
❑151, Jul 1970, JKu (w); JKu (a); 1: Unknown Soldier ... 125.00
❑152, Sep 1970, 2: The Unknown Soldier; Battle Album; Enemy Ace ... 20.00
❑153, Nov 1970, JKu (c); JKu (w); JKu, IN (a); Reprints from Star Spangled War Stories #36, Our Army at War #155 20.00
❑154, Jan 1971, JKu (c); JKu (w); JKu (a); O: Unknown Soldier. Unknown Soldier; Enemy Ace ... 55.00
❑155, Mar 1971, JKu (c); JKu (a); reprints Enemy Ace story ... 16.00
❑156, May 1971, JKu (c); JKu, IN (a); Unknown Soldier; Enemy Ace back-up 14.00
❑157, Jul 1971, JKu (c); JKu (a); Unknown Soldier meets Easy Co.; Enemy Ace back-up ... 14.00
❑158, Sep 1971; JKu (c); JKu, RH, IN (a); Reprints from Our Fighting Forces 74 and All-American Men of War #57; Enemy Ace: Reprint from Our Army at War #151 ... 14.00
❑159, Nov 1971; JKu (a); Enemy Ace: Reprint from Showcase #58 ... 14.00
❑160, Jan 1972; Lt. Steve Savage: Reprint from All-American Men of War #112; Reprint from Our Army at War #70 ... 14.00
❑161, Mar 1972; Regular Enemy Ace stories end ... 14.00
❑162, May 1972; JKu (c); JKu (w); JKu, JSe (a); Reprint from Our Army at War #91; Lt. Steve Savage: Reprint from All-American Men of War #113 ... 6.00
❑163, Jul 1972; CI, JKu, DS (a); Lt. Steve Savage: Reprint from All-American Men of War #114; Reprint from All-American Men of War #8 ... 6.00
❑164, Sep 1972, ATh, DS (a) ... 6.00
❑165, Nov 1972 ... 6.00
❑166, Jan 1973, Unknown Soldier; Young Commandos ... 6.00
❑167, Feb 1973, HC (a); Unknown Soldier; U.S.S. Stevens ... 6.00
❑168, Mar 1973, JKu (c); TS (w); TS (a) 6.00
❑169, Apr 1973, JKu (c); GK (w); JKu, GK (a) ... 6.00
❑170, Jun 1973, JKu (c) ... 6.00
❑171, Jul 1973, JKu (c); JKu (a); O: The Unknown Soldier ... 6.00
❑172, Aug 1973, JKu (c); FR (w) ... 6.00
❑173, Sep 1973, JKu (c); FR (w); FT (a) 6.00
❑174, Oct 1973, JKu (c); FR (w); JKu (a) 6.00

Other grades: Multiply price above by 5/6 for VF/NM • 2/3 for VERY FINE • 1/3 for FINE • 1/5 for VERY GOOD • 1/8 for GOOD

Strontium Dog

Irradiated Johnny Alpha seeks bounties

©Fleetway-Quality

Stupid Comics

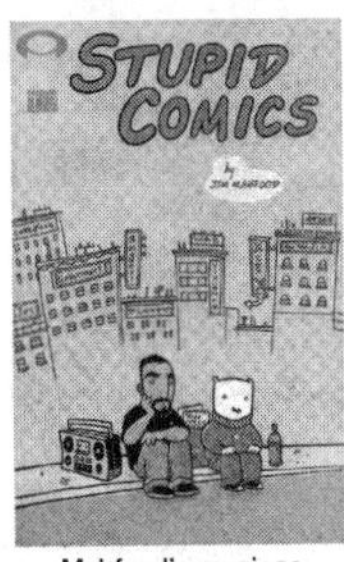

Mahfood's musings meander to Image

©Image

Stupid, Stupid Rat Tails

Bone prequel features Big Johnson Bone

©Cartoon Books

Sub-Mariner

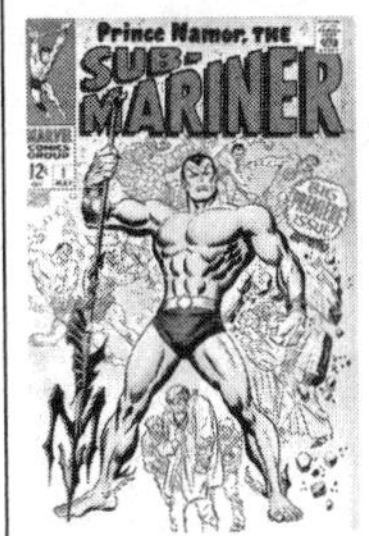

Angry Atlantean has control issues

©Marvel

Sugar & Spike

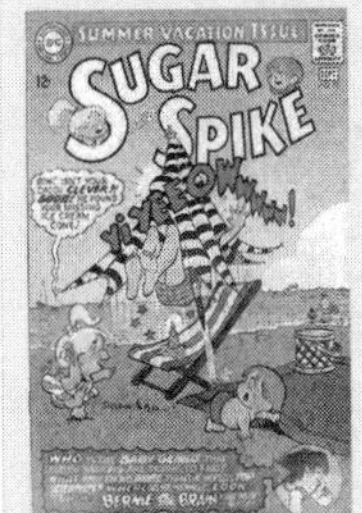

Child-like simplicity masks adult subtext

©DC

N-MINT

❑175, Nov 1973, JKu (c); FR (w); RE (a) 6.00
❑176, Dec 1973, FR (w); FT (a) 6.00
❑177, Jan 1974, FR (w); FT (a) 6.00
❑178, Feb 1974 6.00
❑179, Mar 1974, JKu (c); FR (w); RE (a); Joe Kubert cover; Unknown Soldier story 6.00
❑180, Jun 1974, JKu (c); FR (w) 6.00
❑181, Aug 1974, JKu (c); FR (w); FT (a) 5.00
❑182, Oct 1974, JKu (c); FR (w); FT (a) 5.00
❑183, Dec 1974 5.00
❑184, Feb 1975 SA (w); SA (a) 5.00
❑185, Mar 1975 5.00
❑186, Apr 1975 JKu (c) 5.00
❑187, May 1975 JKu (c) 5.00
❑188, Jun 1975 5.00
❑189, Jul 1975 JKu (c); JKu (a) 5.00
❑190, Aug 1975 JKu (c); JKu (a) 5.00
❑191, Sep 1975 JKu (c) 5.00
❑192, Oct 1975 JKu (c); JKu (a) 5.00
❑193, Nov 1975; JKu (c); Includes pre-CBG Alan Light newsletter ad 5.00
❑194, Dec 1975; JKu (c); Electric garotte story 5.00
❑195, Jan 1976 JKu (c) 5.00
❑196, Feb 1976 JKu (c) 5.00
❑197, Mar 1976 5.00
❑198, Apr 1976, JKu (c) 5.00
❑199, May 1976 5.00
❑200, Jul 1976, JKu (w); JKu (a); A: Mademoiselle Marie 5.00
❑201, Sep 1976, JKu (c); JKu (a) 5.00
❑202, Nov 1976 5.00
❑203, Jan 1977, JKu (c); JKu (a) 5.00
❑204, Mar 1977, JKu (c); BMc (a); Series continues as Unknown Soldier 5.00

Starstone
Aircel

❑1, b&w 1.70
❑2, b&w 1.70
❑3, b&w 1.70

Starstream
Gold Key / Whitman

❑1, ca. 1976 3.00
❑2 1976, Stories by Science-Fiction writers 3.00
❑3 1976 3.00
❑4 1976, JAb (a) 3.00

Starstruck (Epic)
Marvel / Epic

❑1, Feb 1985 2.50
❑2, Apr 1985 2.00
❑3, Jun 1985 2.00
❑4, Aug 1985 2.00
❑5, Oct 1985 2.00
❑6, Feb 1986 2.00

Starstruck
Dark Horse

❑1, Aug 1990, b&w 2.95
❑2, Oct 1990, b&w 2.95
❑3, Jan 1991, b&w 2.95
❑4, Mar 1991; trading cards 2.95

Startling Crime Illustrated
Caliber

❑1, Jan 1991, b&w 2.95

N-MINT

Startling Stories: Banner
Marvel

❑1, Sep 2001 2.99
❑2, Oct 2001 2.99
❑3, Nov 2001 2.99
❑4, Dec 2001 2.99

Startling Stories: The Thing
Marvel

❑1, ca. 2003 3.50

Startling Stories: The Thing -- Night Falls on Yancy Street
Marvel

❑1, Jun 2003 3.50
❑2, Jul 2003 3.50
❑3, Aug 2003 3.50
❑4, Sep 2003 3.50

Star Trek
Gold Key

❑1, Oct 1967, wraparound photo cover 350.00
❑2, Jun 1968, Front photo cover 125.00
❑3, Dec 1968, Front photo cover 100.00
❑4, Jun 1969, Photo cover 90.00
❑5, Sep 1969, Photo cover 75.00
❑6, Dec 1969, cover photo shows Spock from "Amok Time" 75.00
❑7, Mar 1970, Photo cover 60.00
❑8, Sep 1970, Photo cover 50.00
❑9, Feb 1971, last photo cover 50.00
❑10, May 1971 40.00
❑11, Aug 1971 30.00
❑12, Nov 1971 30.00
❑13, Feb 1972 30.00
❑14, May 1972 30.00
❑15, Aug 1972 30.00
❑16, Nov 1972 30.00
❑17, Feb 1973 30.00
❑18, May 1973 30.00
❑19, Jul 1973 30.00
❑20, Sep 1973 45.00
❑20/Whitman, Sep 1973 45.00
❑21, Nov 1973 30.00
❑22, Jan 1974 30.00
❑23, Mar 1974 30.00
❑23/Whitman, Mar 1974 45.00
❑24, May 1974 25.00
❑24/Whitman, May 1974 35.00
❑25, Jul 1974 35.00
❑25/Whitman, Jul 1974 35.00
❑26, Sep 1974 25.00
❑26/Whitman, Sep 1974 35.00
❑27, Nov 1974 20.00
❑27/Whitman, Nov 1974 30.00
❑28, Jan 1975 20.00
❑29, Mar 1975 30.00
❑29/Whitman, Mar 1975 30.00
❑30, May 1975 20.00
❑31, Jul 1975 20.00
❑31/Whitman, Jul 1975 30.00
❑32, Aug 1975 30.00
❑32/Whitman, Aug 1975 30.00
❑33, Sep 1975 30.00
❑33/Whitman, Sep 1975 30.00
❑34, Oct 1975 30.00
❑34/Whitman, Oct 1975 30.00

N-MINT

❑35, Nov 1975 30.00
❑35/Whitman, Nov 1975 30.00
❑36, Mar 1976 30.00
❑36/Whitman, Mar 1976 30.00
❑37, May 1976 20.00
❑38, Jul 1976 20.00
❑38/Whitman, Jul 1976 30.00
❑39, Aug 1976 30.00
❑39/Whitman, Aug 1976 30.00
❑40, Sep 1976 20.00
❑40/Whitman, Sep 1976 30.00
❑41, Nov 1976 25.00
❑41/Whitman, Nov 1976 25.00
❑42, Jan 1977 15.00
❑43, Feb 1977 15.00
❑44, May 1977 25.00
❑44/Whitman, May 1977, William Shatner and Leonard Nimoy photos in small boxes on cover 25.00
❑45, Jul 1977, reprints #7, including photo cover 25.00
❑45/Whitman, Jul 1977, reprints #7, including photo cover 25.00
❑46, Aug 1977 15.00
❑46/Whitman, Aug 1977 25.00
❑47, Sep 1977 25.00
❑47/Whitman, Sep 1977 25.00
❑48, Oct 1977 25.00
❑48/Whitman, Oct 1977 25.00
❑49, Nov 1977 15.00
❑50, Jan 1978 15.00
❑51, Mar 1978 15.00
❑51/Whitman, Mar 1978 25.00
❑52, May 1978 15.00
❑52/Whitman, May 1978 25.00
❑53, Jul 1978 25.00
❑53/Whitman, Jul 1978 25.00
❑54, Aug 1978 25.00
❑54/Whitman, Aug 1978 25.00
❑55, Sep 1978 25.00
❑55/Whitman, Sep 1978 25.00
❑56, Oct 1978 15.00
❑56/Whitman, Oct 1978 25.00
❑57, Nov 1978 25.00
❑57/Whitman, Nov 1978 25.00
❑58, Dec 1978 25.00
❑58/Whitman, Dec 1978 25.00
❑59, Jan 1979 25.00
❑59/Whitman, Jan 1979 25.00
❑60, Feb 1979 12.00
❑60/Whitman, Feb 1979 20.00
❑61, Mar 1979, A: Klingons. A: Harry Mudd. Final Issue 12.00

Star Trek
Marvel

❑1, Apr 1980, DC, KJ (a); adapts Star Trek: The Motion Picture 5.00
❑2, May 1980, DC, KJ (c); DC, KJ (a); adapts Star Trek: The Motion Picture 3.00
❑3, Jun 1980, BWi (c); DC, KJ (a); adapts Star Trek: The Motion Picture 2.00
❑4, Jul 1980, DC, KJ (c); DC, KJ (a) 2.00
❑5, Aug 1980, FM, KJ (c); DC, KJ (a) 2.00
❑6, Sep 1980, DC, KJ (c); DC, KJ (a) 2.00
❑7, Oct 1980, MN (c); MN, KJ (a) 2.00
❑8, Nov 1980, DC (c); DC (a) 2.00
❑9, Dec 1980, DC (c); DC, FS (a) 2.00

N-MINT

❑10, Jan 1981, FM (c); KJ (a); Starfleet files 2.00
❑11, Feb 1981, TP (c); TP (a) 2.00
❑12, Mar 1981, LMc, TP (a) 2.00
❑13, Apr 1981, TP (a); A: McCoy's daughter 2.00
❑14, Jun 1981, LMc, GD (a) 2.00
❑15, Aug 1981, DC (c); GK (a) 2.00
❑16, Oct 1981, AM, LMc (c); LMc, GD (a) 2.00
❑17, Dec 1981, TP (a) 2.00
❑18, Feb 1982, Final Issue 2.00

Star Trek
DC

❑1, Feb 1984; TS (a); 1: Nancy Bryce. 1: Konom. 1: Bearclaw. Kirk regains captaincy of Enterprise 4.00
❑2, Mar 1984; TS (a); Klingon Emperor Kahless IV declares war on Federation 3.00
❑3, Apr 1984 TS (a); A: Excalbians 3.00
❑4, May 1984 TS (c); TS (a); A: Organians 3.00
❑5, Jun 1984 TS (c); TS (a) 3.00
❑6, Jul 1984 TS (c); TS (a); A: Ambassador Robert Fox 2.50
❑7, Aug 1984; DG (c); O: Saavik. hints of Star Trek III dropped 2.50
❑8, Nov 1984; TS, JO (c); TS (a); V: Romulans. David Marcus and Saavik transfer to U.S.S. Grissom 2.50
❑9, Dec 1984; TS (c); TS (a); A: Mirror Universe Spock. A: Mirror Universe Kirk. A: Spock. Return of Mirror Universe; story set after events of Star Trek III: The Search for Spock 2.50
❑10, Jan 1985; TS (c); TS (a); A: U.S.S. Excelsior. A: Captain Styles. U.S.S. Excelsior vs. I.S.S. Enterprise 2.50
❑11, Feb 1985; TS (c); TS (a); A: Mirror Universe Spock. The two Spocks mind-meld 2.00
❑12, Mar 1985; TS (a); A: Mirror Universe Spock. Mirror Universe Enterprise's engineering hull destroyed 2.00
❑13, Apr 1985; TS (c); TS (a); 1: Mirror Universe David Marcus. New Frontiers, Part 5 2.00
❑14, May 1985; TS (c); TS (a); A: Mirror Universe Romulans. A: Mirror Universe Klingons. Spocks visit Mirror Universe Klingons 2.00
❑15, Jun 1985; TS (c); TS (a); 1: Mirror Universe U.S.S. Excelsior. New Frontiers, Part 7 2.00
❑16, Jul 1985; TS, KJ (c); TS (a); Kirk receives command of U.S.S. Excelsior 2.00
❑17, Aug 1985; TS, KJ (c); TS (a); Sulu, Uhura, and Bearclaw on shoreleave 2.00
❑18, Sep 1985; TS, KJ (c); TS (a); Scotty solo story 2.00
❑19, Oct 1985; TS (c); DS (a); Written by Walter Koenig 2.00
❑20, Nov 1985 TS (c); TS (a) 2.00
❑21, Dec 1985 TS (c); TS (a) 2.00
❑22, Jan 1986; TS (c); TS (a); return of Redjac 2.00
❑23, Feb 1986; KJ (c); TS (a); return of Redjac 2.00
❑24, Mar 1986 JSn (c); TS (a) 2.00
❑25, Apr 1986; JSn (c); TS (a); Ajir vs. Grond 2.00
❑26, May 1986 DG (c); TS (a) 2.00
❑27, Jun 1986 TS (a) 2.00
❑28, Jul 1986 GM (a) 2.00
❑29, Aug 1986 TS (a) 2.00
❑30, Sep 1986; KJ (c); CI (a); Uhura's early days on the Enterprise 2.00
❑31, Oct 1986 TS (a) 2.00
❑32, Nov 1986 TS (a) 2.00
❑33, Dec 1986; 20th Anniversary of Star Trek issue; TS (a); original Enterprise meets Excelsior 2.00
❑34, Jan 1987; TS (a); The Doomsday Bug, Part 1 2.00
❑35, Feb 1987; GM (a); The Doomsday Bug, Part 2 2.00
❑36, Mar 1987; GM (a); Kirk and company return to Vulcan; leads into Star Trek IV: The Voyage Home 2.00
❑37, Apr 1987; CS (a); Follows events of Star Trek IV: The Voyage Home 2.00
❑38, May 1987 2.00
❑39, Jun 1987; TS (a); return of Harry Mudd 2.00
❑40, Jul 1987 TS (a); A: Harry Mudd. 2.00
❑41, Aug 1987; TS (a); V: Orion pirates . 2.00

N-MINT

❑42, Sep 1987 TS (a) 2.00
❑43, Oct 1987; TS (a); The Return of the Serpent, Part 1 2.00
❑44, Nov 1987; TS (a); The Return of the Serpent, Part 2 2.00
❑45, Dec 1987; TS (a); The Return of the Serpent, Part 3 2.00
❑46, Jan 1988 TS (a) 2.00
❑47, Feb 1988 TS (a) 2.00
❑48, Mar 1988; PD (w); TS (a); 1: Moron. first Peter David script 2.00
❑49, Apr 1988 PD (w); TS (a) 2.00
❑50, May 1988; Giant-size; PD (w); TS (a); Konom and Nancy marry 2.00
❑51, Jun 1988 PD (w); TS (a) 2.00
❑52, Jul 1988; PD (w); TS (a); Dante's Inferno 2.00
❑53, Aug 1988 PD (w) 2.00
❑54, Sep 1988; PD (w); A: Sean Finnegan. Return of Finnegan 2.00
❑55, Oct 1988; PD (w); TS (a); Trial of Bearclaw 2.00
❑56, Nov 1988; GM (a); set during first five-year mission 2.00
❑Ann 1, ca. 1985; A: Captain Pike. Kirk's first mission on The Enterprise 3.00
❑Ann 2, ca. 1986; A: Captain Pike. The final mission of the first five-year mission 3.00
❑Ann 3, ca. 1988; GM (c); PD (w); CS (a); Scotty's romances 3.00

Star Trek
DC

❑1, Oct 1989; PD (w); 1: Salla. 1: M'yra. Set after the events of Star Trek V: The Final Frontier; Klingons place bounty on Kirk 5.00
❑2, Nov 1989 PD (w) 4.00
❑3, Dec 1989 PD (w) 3.00
❑4, Jan 1990; PD (w); 1: R.J. Blaise 3.00
❑5, Feb 1990 PD (w) 2.50
❑6, Mar 1990 PD (w) 2.50
❑7, Apr 1990 PD (w); 1: Sweeney 2.50
❑8, May 1990; PD (w); V: Sweeney 2.50
❑9, Jun 1990; PD (w); V: Sweeney 2.50
❑10, Jul 1990; PD (w); A: Areel Shaw. A: Samuel Cogsley. The Trial of James T. Kirk 2.50
❑11, Aug 1990; PD (w); A: Bella Oxmyx. A: Leonard James Akaar. The Trial of James T. Kirk 2.00
❑12, Sep 1990; PD (w); The Trial of James T. Kirk 2.00
❑13, Oct 1990; PD (w); Lost in Space homage 2.00
❑14, Dec 1990; PD (w); Lost in Space homage 2.00
❑15, Jan 1991; PD (w); Lost in Space homage 2.00
❑16, Feb 1991; Written by J. Michael Straczynski 2.00
❑17, Mar 1991 2.00
❑18, Apr 1991 2.00
❑19, May 1991; PD (w); final Peter David issue 2.00
❑20, Jun 1991 2.00
❑21, Jul 1991; Gods' Gauntlet, Part 2 2.00
❑22, Aug 1991; A: Harry Mudd. Return of Harry Mudd, Part 1 2.00
❑23, Sep 1991; A: Harry Mudd. Return of Harry Mudd; Part 2 2.00
❑24, Oct 1991; 25th anniversary of Star Trek; PD (w); BA, DC (a); A: Harry Mudd; Text pieces by Chris Claremont, Michael Jan Friedman, Peter David, and Howard Weinstein 3.00
❑25, Nov 1991 A: Saavik. A: Captain Styles 2.00
❑26, Dec 1991 2.00
❑27, Jan 1992 2.00
❑28, Feb 1992 2.00
❑29, Mar 1992 2.00
❑30, Apr 1992 2.00
❑31, May 1992; Veritas, Part 2 2.00
❑32, Jun 1992; Veritas, Part 3 2.00
❑33, Jul 1992; Veritas, Part 4 2.00
❑34, Aug 1992; JDu (a); Dream sequence 2.00
❑35, Sep 1992; Series goes biweekly; Sulu takes command of U.S.S. Excelsior 2.00
❑36, Sep 1992; The Tabukan Syndrome, Part 2 2.00
❑37, Oct 1992; The Tabukan Syndrome, Part 3 2.00

N-MINT

❑38, Oct 1992; The Tabukan Syndrome, Part 4 2.00
❑39, Nov 1992; The Tabukan Syndrome, Part 5 2.00
❑40, Nov 1992; Biweekly run ends 2.00
❑41, Dec 1992 2.00
❑42, Jan 1993 2.00
❑43, Feb 1993 2.00
❑44, Mar 1993 2.00
❑45, Apr 1993; A: Trelane. Return of Trelane 2.00
❑46, May 1993; Back to biweekly status 2.00
❑47, May 1993 2.00
❑48, Jun 1993 2.00
❑49, Jun 1993; RT (a); last biweekly issue 2.00
❑50, Jul 1993; Giant-size anniversary special; A: Gary Seven. Double-sized issue 3.50
❑51, Aug 1993; Saavik on secret mission 2.00
❑52, Sep 1993 2.00
❑53, Oct 1993; A: Lt. Worf. Time Crime, Part 1 2.00
❑54, Nov 1993; Time Crime, Part 2 2.00
❑55, Dec 1993; Time Crime, Part 3 2.00
❑56, Jan 1994; Time Crime, Part 4 2.00
❑57, Feb 1994; Time Crime, Part 5 2.00
❑58, Mar 1994; Chekov's first days on the Enterprise; cover forms triptych with issues #59 and 60 2.00
❑59, Apr 1994; Chekov's first days on the Enterprise; cover forms triptych with issues #57 and 58 2.00
❑60, Jun 1994; Chekov's first days on the Enterprise; cover forms triptych with issues #57 and 58 2.00
❑61, Jul 1994; return to Talos IV 2.00
❑62, Aug 1994; set near end of first five-year mission 2.00
❑63, Sep 1994 2.00
❑64, Oct 1994; follows events of Where No Man Has Gone Before 2.00
❑65, Nov 1994 2.00
❑66, Dec 1994 2.00
❑67, Jan 1995 2.00
❑68, Feb 1995 2.00
❑69, Mar 1995 2.00
❑70, Apr 1995 2.00
❑71, May 1995 2.50
❑72, Jun 1995 2.50
❑73, Jul 1995 2.50
❑74, Aug 1995 2.50
❑75, Sep 1995 3.95
❑76, Oct 1995 2.50
❑77, Nov 1995 2.50
❑78, Dec 1995 2.50
❑79, Jan 1996 2.50
❑80, Feb 1996; Final Issue 2.50
❑Ann 1, ca. 1990; PD (w); GM (a); Story by George Takei 3.50
❑Ann 2, ca. 1991; PD (w); CS (a); Kirk at Starfleet Academy 3.25
❑Ann 3, ca. 1992 3.50
❑Ann 4, ca. 1993; Spock on Enterprise with Captain Pike 3.50
❑Ann 5, ca. 1994; 1994 Ann 3.95
❑Ann 6, ca. 1995; D: Gary Seven. Convergence, Part 1; continues in Star Trek: The Next Generation Ann #6 3.95
❑Special 1, Spr 1994; BSz (c); PD (w); The Return of RJ Blaise 3.50
❑Special 2, Win 1994 3.50
❑Special 3, Win 1995 3.95

Star Trek: Debt of Honor
DC

❑1 14.95

Star Trek: Deep Space Nine
Malibu

❑0, Jan 1995; premium limited edition; QVC offer 3.00
❑1/A, Aug 1993; Newsstand cover 3.00
❑1/B, Aug 1993; line-drawing cover 3.00
❑1/C, Aug 1993; deluxe edition (black/foil) 4.00
❑2, Sep 1993; trading card 2.50
❑3, Oct 1993 2.50
❑4, Nov 1993; Part 1 2.50
❑5, Dec 1993; Part 2 2.50
❑6, Jan 1994 2.50
❑7, Feb 1994 2.50
❑8, May 1994; Part 1 2.50
❑9, Jun 1994; Part 2 2.50

Other grades: Multiply price above by 5/6 for VF/NM • 2/3 for VERY FINE • 1/3 for FINE • 1/5 for VERY GOOD • 1/8 for GOOD

Sugar Ray Finhead

A poor man's Savage Dragon
©Wolf

Suicide Squad

Team's name should have been dead giveaway
©DC

Sun-Runners

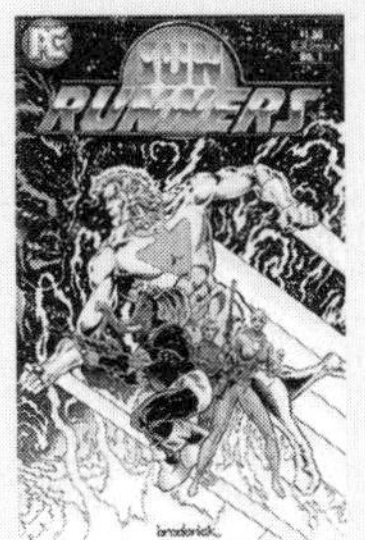

Solar power delivery on a galactic scale
©Pacific

Superboy

Boy of Steel's hometown was stuck in time
©DC

Superboy

TV series inspired second comics series
©DC

N-MINT

❑10, Jun 1994 ... 2.50
❑11, Jul 1994 ... 2.50
❑12, Jul 1994 ... 2.50
❑13, Aug 1994 ... 2.50
❑14, Sep 1994; Part 1 ... 2.50
❑15, Sep 1994; Part 2 ... 2.50
❑16, Nov 1994 ... 2.50
❑17, Dec 1994 ... 2.50
❑18, Jan 1995 ... 2.50
❑19, Feb 1995 ... 2.50
❑20, Mar 1995 ... 2.50
❑21, Apr 1995 ... 2.50
❑22, May 1995 ... 2.50
❑23, May 1995; The Secret of the Lost Orb, Part 1 ... 2.50
❑24, Jun 1995; The Secret of the Lost Orb, Part 2 ... 2.50
❑25, Jul 1995; The Secret of the Lost Orb, Part 3; Double-sized issue ... 3.50
❑26, Jul 1995; Part 1 ... 2.50
❑27, Aug 1995; Part 2 ... 2.50
❑28, Sep 1995 ... 2.50
❑29, Oct 1995; Part 1; Commander Riker; Mirror Tuvok ... 2.50
❑30, Nov 1995 ... 2.50
❑31, Dec 1995 ... 3.95
❑32, Jan 1996; Final Issue ... 3.50
❑Ann 1, ca. 1995 ... 3.95
❑Ashcan 1; limited edition ashcan; Hero Illustrated #2 as Hero Premiere Edition #1A ... 5.00
❑Special 1, ca. 1995 ... 3.50

Star Trek: Deep Space Nine
Marvel / Paramount

❑1, Nov 1996; Part 1; DS9 is drawn into the wormhole ... 2.00
❑2, Dec 1996; Part 2 ... 2.00
❑3, Jan 1997; Part 1 ... 2.00
❑4, Feb 1997; Part 1 ... 2.00
❑5, Mar 1997 ... 2.00
❑6, Apr 1997 ... 2.00
❑7, May 1997 ... 2.00
❑8, Aug 1997 ... 2.00
❑9, Sep 1997 ... 2.00
❑10, Oct 1997 ... 2.00
❑11, Nov 1997; gatefold summary; Telepathy War, Part 1; Crossover with ST: Starfleet Academy, ST: Telepathy War one-shot, ST Unlimited and ST: Voyager ... 2.00
❑12, Dec 1997; gatefold summary; Telepathy War, Part 2; Crossover with ST: Starfleet Academy, ST: Telepathy War one-shot, ST Unlimited and ST: Voyager ... 2.00
❑13, Jan 1998; gatefold summary ... 2.00
❑14, Feb 1998; gatefold summary; A: Tribbles ... 2.00
❑15, Mar 1998; gatefold summary; Final Issue ... 2.00

Star Trek: Deep Space Nine, the Celebrity Series: Blood and Honor
Malibu

❑1, May 1995; Written by Mark Lenard ... 2.95

Star Trek: Deep Space Nine Hearts and Minds
Malibu

❑1, Jun 1994; an original Deep Space Nine mini series ... 2.50
❑2, Jul 1994 ... 2.50
❑3, Aug 1994 ... 2.50
❑4, Sep 1994 ... 2.50

Star Trek: Deep Space Nine: Lightstorm
Malibu

❑1, Dec 1994 ... 3.50

Star Trek: Deep Space Nine: N-Vector
DC / Wildstorm

❑1, Aug 2000 ... 2.50
❑2, Sep 2000 ... 2.50
❑3, Oct 2000 ... 2.50
❑4, Nov 2000 ... 2.50

Star Trek: Deep Space Nine: Rules of Diplomacy
Malibu

❑1, Aug 1995; Co-Author Aron Eisenberg plays "Nog" in series ... 2.95

Star Trek: Deep Space Nine/ Star Trek: The Next Generation
Malibu

❑1, Oct 1994 ... 2.50
❑2, Nov 1994 ... 2.50
❑Ashcan 1; No cover price; Ashcan preview; flip-book with DC's Star Trek: The Next Generation/Star Trek: Deep Space Nine Ashcan ... 1.00

Star Trek: Deep Space Nine: Terok Nor
Malibu

❑0, Jan 1995; O: Deep Space Nine ... 2.95

Star Trek: Deep Space Nine Maquis
Malibu

❑1, Feb 1995; Soldier of Peace, Part 1 ... 2.50
❑2, Mar 1995; Soldier of Peace, Part 2 ... 2.50
❑3, Apr 1995; Soldier of Peace, Part 3 ... 2.50

Star Trek: Deep Space Nine, Ultimate Annual
Malibu

❑1, ca. 1995, Includes pinups ... 5.95

Star Trek: Deep Space Nine, Worf Special
Malibu

❑0, Dec 1995 ... 3.95

Star Trek: Divided We Fall
DC

❑1, Jul 2001 ... 2.95
❑2, Aug 2001 ... 2.95
❑3, Sep 2001 ... 2.95
❑4, Oct 2001 ... 2.95

Star Trek: Early Voyages
Marvel / Paramount

❑1, Feb 1997; Christopher Pike as Enterprise captain ... 2.99
❑2, Mar 1997; Battle with the Klingons ... 1.99
❑3, Apr 1997; prequel to The Cage ... 1.99
❑4, May 1997; Yeoman Colt's POV on The Cage ... 1.99
❑5, Jun 1997 ... 1.99
❑6, Jul 1997 ... 1.99
❑7, Aug 1997; gatefold summary; Pike vs. Kaaj ... 1.99
❑8, Sep 1997; gatefold summary ... 1.99
❑9, Oct 1997; gatefold summary ... 1.99
❑10, Nov 1997; gatefold summary; V: Chakuun ... 1.99
❑11, Dec 1997; gatefold summary ... 1.99
❑12, Jan 1998; gatefold summary ... 1.99
❑13, Feb 1998; gatefold summary ... 1.99
❑14, Mar 1998; gatefold summary; Pike vs. Kirk ... 1.99
❑15, Apr 1998; gatefold summary ... 1.99
❑16, May 1998; gatefold summary; Pike goes undercover ... 1.99
❑17, Jun 1998; gatefold summary; Final Issue ... 1.99

Star Trek: Enter the Wolves
WildStorm / Paramount

❑1, ca. 2001 ... 5.99

Star Trek: First Contact
Marvel / Paramount

❑1, Nov 1996; prestige format; Movie adaptation; cardstock cover ... 5.95

Star Trek Generations
DC

❑1; Movie adaptation; Newstand edition ... 3.95
❑1/Prestige; Movie adaptation; Prestige format one-shot ... 5.95

Star Trekker
Antarctic

❑1, Dec 1992, b&w; parody (never distributed) ... 2.95

Star Trek: Mirror Mirror
Marvel / Paramount

❑1, Feb 1997; one-shot sequel to original series episode ... 3.99

Star Trek Movie Special
DC

❑3, ca. 1984; Movie adaptation ... 2.00
❑4, ca. 1987; Movie adaptation ... 2.00
❑5, ca. 1989; Movie adaptation ... 2.00

Star Trek: New Frontier: Double Time
DC / Wildstorm

❑1, Nov 2000, Captain Calhoun on the USS Excalibur ... 5.95

Star Trek: Operation Assimilation
Marvel / Paramount

❑1, Apr 1997, Romulans as Borg ... 2.99

Star Trek VI: The Undiscovered Country
DC

❑1, ca. 1992; The Undiscovered Country Movie adaptation; Newsstand edition ... 2.95
❑1/Direct ed., ca. 1992; prestige format; The Undiscovered Country Movie adaptation ... 5.95

Star Trek Special
WildStorm

❑1 2001; Prestige format; stories for Star Trek, Next Generation, Deep Space Nine and Voyager ... 6.95

Other grades: Multiply price above by 5/6 for VF/NM • 2/3 for VERY FINE • 1/3 for FINE • 1/5 for VERY GOOD • 1/8 for GOOD

Star Trek: Starfleet Academy
Marvel / Paramount

- ❑1, Dec 1996 A: Nog 2.00
- ❑2, Jan 1997 .... 2.00
- ❑3, Feb 1997 .... 2.00
- ❑4, Mar 1997; Part 1 .... 2.00
- ❑5, Apr 1997; D: Kamilah. D: Kamilah Goldstein 2.00
- ❑6, May 1997 .... 2.00
- ❑7, Jun 1997 .... 2.00
- ❑8, Jul 1997; return of Charlie X 2.00
- ❑9, Aug 1997; gatefold summary; A: Pike. on Talos IV 2.00
- ❑10, Sep 1997; gatefold summary 2.00
- ❑11, Oct 1997; gatefold summary; cadets on trial for going to Talos IV 2.00
- ❑12, Nov 1997; gatefold summary; Part 1; Crossover with ST: Deep Space Nine, ST: Telepathy War one-shot; ST Unlimited and ST: Voyager 2.00
- ❑13, Dec 1997; gatefold summary 2.00
- ❑14, Jan 1998; gatefold summary; Part 1 .... 2.00
- ❑15, Feb 1998; gatefold summary; Part 2 .... 2.00
- ❑16, Mar 1998; gatefold summary; Part 3 .... 2.00
- ❑17, Apr 1998; gatefold summary 2.00
- ❑18/A, May 1998; English language edition 2.00
- ❑18/B, May 1998; Klingon language edition 2.00
- ❑19, Jun 1998; gatefold summary; Final Issue 2.00

Star Trek: Telepathy War
Marvel / Paramount

- ❑1, Nov 1997; concludes crossover between ST: Deep Space Nine, ST: Starfleet Academy; ST Unlimited and ST: Voyager 2.99

Star Trek: The Modala Imperative
DC

- ❑1, Jul 1991 .... 2.50
- ❑2, Aug 1991 .... 2.00
- ❑3, Aug 1991 .... 2.00
- ❑4, Sep 1991 .... 2.00

Star Trek: The Next Generation
DC

- ❑1, Feb 1988 .... 3.00
- ❑2, Mar 1988 .... 2.00
- ❑3, Apr 1988 .... 2.00
- ❑4, May 1988 .... 2.00
- ❑5, Jun 1988 D: Geordi 2.00
- ❑6, Jul 1988 .... 2.00

Star Trek: The Next Generation
DC

- ❑1, Oct 1989; Star Trek: The Next Generation Stardate Guide 5.00
- ❑2, Nov 1989 .... 4.00
- ❑3, Dec 1989 .... 3.00
- ❑4, Jan 1990 .... 3.00
- ❑5, Feb 1990 .... 3.00
- ❑6, Mar 1990 .... 2.50
- ❑7, Apr 1990 .... 2.50
- ❑8, May 1990 .... 2.50
- ❑9, Jun 1990 .... 2.50
- ❑10, Jul 1990 .... 2.50
- ❑11, Aug 1990 .... 2.50
- ❑12, Sep 1990 .... 2.50
- ❑13, Oct 1990 .... 2.50
- ❑14, Dec 1990 .... 2.50
- ❑15, Jan 1991; V: Ferengi 2.50
- ❑16, Feb 1991 .... 2.50
- ❑17, Mar 1991 .... 2.50
- ❑18, Apr 1991 .... 2.50
- ❑19, May 1991 .... 2.50
- ❑20, Jun 1991 .... 2.50
- ❑21, Jul 1991 .... 2.00
- ❑22, Aug 1991 .... 2.00
- ❑23, Sep 1991 .... 2.00
- ❑24, Oct 1991; Double-sized 25th Anniversary issue 2.00
- ❑25, Nov 1991; Giant-size 2.00
- ❑26, Dec 1991 .... 2.00
- ❑27, Jan 1992 .... 2.00
- ❑28, Feb 1992; Return of K'ehleyr 2.00
- ❑29, Mar 1992 .... 2.00
- ❑30, Apr 1992 .... 2.00
- ❑31, May 1992 .... 2.00
- ❑32, Jun 1992 .... 2.00
- ❑33, Jul 1992; Q turns the crew into Klingons 2.00
- ❑34, Jul 1992 .... 2.00
- ❑35, Aug 1992 .... 2.00
- ❑36, Aug 1992 .... 2.00
- ❑37, Sep 1992 .... 2.00
- ❑38, Sep 1992 .... 2.00
- ❑39, Oct 1992 .... 2.00
- ❑40, Nov 1992 .... 2.00
- ❑41, Dec 1992 .... 2.00
- ❑42, Jan 1993 .... 2.00
- ❑43, Feb 1993 .... 2.00
- ❑44, Mar 1993 .... 2.00
- ❑45, Apr 1993 .... 2.00
- ❑46, May 1993 .... 2.00
- ❑47, Jun 1993; Worst of Both Worlds, Part 1 .... 2.00
- ❑48, Jul 1993; Worst of Both Worlds, Part 2 .... 2.00
- ❑49, Aug 1993; Worst of Both Worlds, Part 3 .... 2.00
- ❑50, Sep 1993; Giant-size; Worst of Both Worlds, Part 4; Double-sized issue 3.50
- ❑51, Oct 1993 .... 2.00
- ❑52, Oct 1993; Dixon Hill story 2.00
- ❑53, Nov 1993 .... 2.00
- ❑54, Nov 1993 .... 2.00
- ❑55, Dec 1993 .... 2.00
- ❑56, Jan 1994 .... 2.00
- ❑57, Mar 1994 .... 2.00
- ❑58, Apr 1994 .... 2.00
- ❑59, May 1994 .... 2.00
- ❑60, Jun 1994 .... 2.00
- ❑61, Jul 1994 .... 2.00
- ❑62, Aug 1994 .... 2.00
- ❑63, Sep 1994 .... 2.00
- ❑64, Oct 1994 .... 2.00
- ❑65, Nov 1994 .... 2.00
- ❑66, Dec 1994 .... 2.00
- ❑67, Jan 1995 .... 2.00
- ❑68, Feb 1995 .... 2.00
- ❑69, Mar 1995 .... 2.00
- ❑70, Apr 1995 .... 2.00
- ❑71, May 1995 .... 2.00
- ❑72, Jun 1995; War and Madness, Part 1 .... 2.50
- ❑73, Jul 1995; War and Madness, Part 2 .... 2.50
- ❑74, Aug 1995; War and Madness, Part 3 .... 2.50
- ❑75, Sep 1995; Giant-size; V: Borg. War and Madness, Part 4; Double-sized issue 3.95
- ❑76, Oct 1995 .... 2.50
- ❑77, Nov 1995 .... 2.50
- ❑78, Dec 1995 .... 2.50
- ❑79, Jan 1996; Q transforms the crew into androids 2.50
- ❑80, Feb 1996; Final Issue 2.50
- ❑Ann 1, ca. 1990; Q story written by deLancie; Stardate back-up feature (puts comics & books in conjunction with TV series); 1990 Ann 3.50
- ❑Ann 2, ca. 1991 .... 3.50
- ❑Ann 3, ca. 1992 .... 3.50
- ❑Ann 4, ca. 1993 .... 3.50
- ❑Ann 5, ca. 1994 .... 3.50
- ❑Ann 6, ca. 1995; Part 2; continued from Star Trek Ann #6 .... 3.95
- ❑Special 1, ca. 1993 .... 4.50
- ❑Special 2, Sum 1994; Captain Bateson of the Bozeman 4.50
- ❑Special 3, Win 1995 .... 4.50

Star Trek: The Next Generation/ Deep Space Nine
DC

- ❑1, Dec 1994 .... 2.50
- ❑2, Jan 1995 .... 2.50
- ❑Ashcan 1; No cover price; flip-book with Malibu's Deep Space Nine/Star Trek: The Next Generation Ashcan 1.00

Star Trek: The Next Generation: Ill Wind
DC

- ❑1, Nov 1995 .... 2.50
- ❑2, Dec 1995 .... 2.50
- ❑3, Jan 1996 .... 2.50
- ❑4, Feb 1996 .... 2.50

Star Trek: The Next Generation: Perchance to Dream
DC / Wildstorm

- ❑1, Feb 2000 .... 2.50
- ❑2, Mar 2000 .... 2.50
- ❑3, Apr 2000 .... 2.50
- ❑4, May 2000 .... 2.50

Star Trek: The Next Generation: Riker
Marvel / Paramount

- ❑1, Jul 1998 .... 3.50

Star Trek:The Next Generation: Shadowheart
DC

- ❑1, Dec 1994 .... 1.95
- ❑2, Jan 1995 .... 1.95
- ❑3, Feb 1995 .... 1.95
- ❑4, Mar 1995 .... 1.95

Star Trek: The Next Generation: The Gorn Crisis
DC / Wildstorm

- ❑1, ca. 2002 .... 17.95
- ❑1/HC 29.95

Star Trek: The Next Generation: The Killing Shadows
DC / Wildstorm

- ❑1, Nov 2000 .... 2.50
- ❑2, Dec 2000 .... 2.50
- ❑3, Jan 2001 .... 2.50
- ❑4, Feb 2001 .... 2.50

Star Trek: The Next Generation: The Modala Imperative
DC

- ❑1, Sep 1991; Incorrect date in indicia 1.75
- ❑2, Aug 1991 .... 1.75
- ❑3, Aug 1991 .... 1.75
- ❑4, Oct 1991 .... 1.75

Star Trek: The Next Generation: The Series Finale
DC

- ❑1, ca. 1994; adapts final TV episode 3.95

Star Trek Unlimited
Marvel / Paramount

- ❑1, Nov 1996; Original crew story; Next Generation story 3.00
- ❑2, Jan 1997; Original crew story; Next Generation story 3.00
- ❑3, Apr 1997; Original crew story; Next Generation story 3.00
- ❑4, May 1997; Original crew story; Next Generation story; Original series and Next Generation stories crossover 3.00
- ❑5, Sep 1997; Original series and Next Generation stories crossover; Original crew story; Next Generation story 3.00
- ❑6, Nov 1997; Part 4; Crossover with ST: Deep Space Nine, ST: Starfleet Academy, ST: Telepathy War one-shot and ST: Voyager 3.00
- ❑7, Jan 1998 .... 3.00
- ❑8, Mar 1998; Kang vs. Sulu 3.00
- ❑9, May 1998; Chekov wins a Klingon cruiser 3.00
- ❑10, Jul 1998 .... 3.00

Star Trek: Untold Voyages
Marvel / Paramount

- ❑1, Mar 1998 .... 2.50
- ❑2, Apr 1998 .... 2.50
- ❑3, May 1998 .... 2.50
- ❑4, Jun 1998; Sulu takes command 2.50
- ❑5, Jul 1998; Final Issue 3.50

Star Trek: Voyager
Marvel / Paramount

- ❑1, Nov 1996 .... 2.00
- ❑2, Dec 1996 .... 2.00
- ❑3, Jan 1997 .... 2.00
- ❑4, Feb 1997; Part 1 .... 2.00
- ❑5, Mar 1997; Part 2 .... 2.00
- ❑6, Apr 1997; Part 1 .... 2.00
- ❑7, May 1997; Part 2 .... 2.00
- ❑8, Jun 1997 .... 2.00
- ❑9, Sep 1997; gatefold summary 2.00
- ❑10, Oct 1997; gatefold summary; replays events at Wolf 359 .... 2.00
- ❑11, Nov 1997; gatefold summary; V: Leviathan 2.00

Superboy and the Legion of Super-Heroes

Star shares series with futuristic team
©DC

Super DC Giant

Add an S before issue numbers for this one
©DC

Super Friends

Alex Toth also designed animated series
©DC

Supergirl

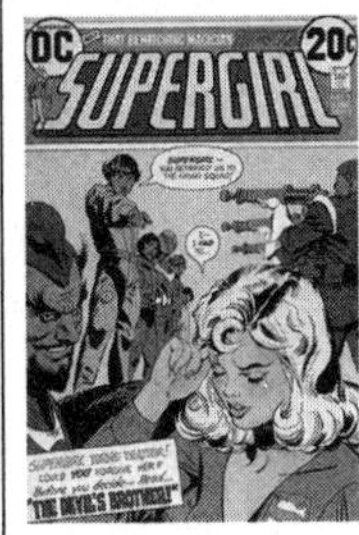

Short-lived series spun out of Adventure
©DC

Supergirl

Pocket universe heroine merges with delinquent
©DC

N-MINT

❑12, Dec 1997; gatefold summary 2.00
❑13, Jan 1998; gatefold summary; Part 5; Crossover with ST: Deep Space Nine, ST: Starfleet Academy, ST: Telepathy War one-shot and ST Unlimited 2.00
❑14, Feb 1998; gatefold summary; 1: Seven of Nine 2.00
❑15, Mar 1998; gatefold summary; Final Issue 2.00

Star Trek: Voyager: Avalon Rising
DC

❑1, Sep 2000 .... 5.95

Star Trek: Voyager: Encounters with the Unknown
DC

❑1; Collects Star Trek: Voyager—False Colors; Star Trek: Voyager—Avalon Rising; Star Trek: Voyager—Elite Force; Star Trek: Voyager—Planet Killer 19.95

Star Trek: Voyager: False Colors
DC / Wildstorm

❑1, Jan 2000 .... 5.95

Star Trek: Voyager: Splashdown
Marvel / Paramount

❑1, Apr 1998; gatefold summary 2.50
❑2, May 1998; gatefold summary 2.50
❑3, Jun 1998; gatefold summary 2.50
❑4, Jul 1998; gatefold summary; final Marvel Star Trek comic book 2.50

Star Trek: Voyager: The Planet Killer
DC / Wildstorm

❑1, Mar 2001 .... 2.95
❑2, Apr 2001 .... 2.95
❑3, May 2001 .... 2.95

Star Trek/X-Men
Marvel / Paramount

❑1, Dec 1996; X-Men meet original Enterprise crew 5.00

Star Trek/X-Men: Second Contact
Marvel / Paramount

❑1, May 1998, A: Kang. X-Men meet Next Generation crew; Sentinels; continues in Star Trek: The Next Generation/X-Men: Planet X novel 5.00
❑1/Variant, May 1998; Cover has Wolverine, Data, Riker, Sentinel in background 4.99

Star Wars
Marvel

❑1, Jul 1977, HC (c); HC (a); Newsstand edition (distributed by Curtis); issue number in box 20.00
❑1/35¢, Jul 1977, HC (c); HC (a); 35¢ regional price variant; Rare variation; Price is in a square area, and UPC code appears with no line drawn through it 800.00
❑1/2nd 1977, HC (c); HC (a); Newsstand reprint (distributed by Curtis); "reprint" in upper-left corner box and inside; price and issue number in square with Curtis Circulation (CC) logo 4.00
❑1/Whitman 2nd 1977; Special markets edition (usually sold in Whitman bagged prepacks); price appears in a diamond; no UPC barcode; 35¢ cover price; reprint on cover 4.00

N-MINT

❑1/Whitman 3rd 1977; Special markets edition (usually sold in Whitman bagged prepacks); price appears in a diamond; no UPC barcode; 35¢ cover price; reprint on cover 4.00
❑2, Aug 1977, HC (c); HC (a); Newsstand edition (distributed by Curtis); issue number in box 10.00
❑2/35¢, Aug 1977, HC (a); 35¢ regional price variant; newsstand edition (distributed by Curtis); issue number in box 150.00
❑2/2nd 1977, HC (c); HC (a); Newsstand reprint (distributed by Curtis); "reprint" in upper-left corner box and inside; price and issue number in square with Curtis Circulation (CC) logo 3.50
❑2/Whitman, Aug 1977, HC (a); Special markets edition (usually sold in Whitman bagged prepacks); price appears in a diamond; UPC barcode appears; 30¢ cover price 10.00
❑2/Whitman 2nd, Aug 1977, HC (a); Special markets edition (usually sold in Whitman bagged prepacks); price appears in a diamond; no UPC barcode; 35¢ cover price; reprint in indicia only 10.00
❑2/Whitman 3rd, Aug 1977, HC (a); Special markets edition (usually sold in Whitman bagged prepacks); price appears in a diamond; no UPC barcode; 35¢ cover price; reprint on cover 10.00
❑3, Sep 1977, DC (c); HC (a); Newsstand edition (distributed by Curtis); issue number in box 8.00
❑3/35¢, Sep 1977, HC (a); 35¢ regional price variant; newsstand edition (distributed by Curtis); issue number in box 150.00
❑3/2nd 1977, DC (c); HC (a); Newsstand reprint (distributed by Curtis); "reprint" in upper-left corner box and inside; price and issue number in square with Curtis Circulation (CC) logo 3.50
❑3/Whitman, Sep 1977, HC (a); Special markets edition (usually sold in Whitman bagged prepacks); price appears in a diamond; UPC barcode appears; 30¢ cover price 8.00
❑3/Whitman 2nd, Sep 1977, HC (a); Special markets edition (usually sold in Whitman bagged prepacks); price appears in a diamond; no UPC barcode; 35¢ cover price; reprint in indicia only 8.00
❑3/Whitman 3rd, Sep 1977, HC (a); Special markets edition (usually sold in Whitman bagged prepacks); price appears in a diamond; no UPC barcode; 35¢ cover price; reprint on cover 8.00
❑4, Oct 1977, GK (c); HC (a); Newsstand edition (distributed by Curtis); issue number in box; low distribution 7.00
❑4/35¢, Oct 1977, HC (a); 35¢ regional price variant; newsstand edition (distributed by Curtis); issue number in box 150.00
❑4/2nd 1977, GK (c); HC (a); Newsstand reprint (distributed by Curtis); "reprint" in upper-left corner box and inside; price and issue number in square with Curtis Circulation (CC) logo 3.50
❑4/Whitman, Oct 1977, HC (a); Special markets edition (usually sold in Whitman bagged prepacks); price appears in a diamond; no UPC barcode; 30¢ cover price 7.00

N-MINT

❑4/Whitman 2nd, Oct 1977, HC (a); Special markets edition (usually sold in Whitman bagged prepacks); price appears in a diamond; no UPC barcode; 35¢ cover price; reprint in indicia only 7.00
❑4/Whitman 3rd, Oct 1977, HC (a); Special markets edition (usually sold in Whitman bagged prepacks); price appears in a diamond; no UPC barcode; 35¢ cover price; reprint on cover 7.00
❑5, Nov 1977, HC (a); Newsstand edition (distributed by Curtis); issue number in box 7.00
❑5/2nd, Nov 1977, HC (a); Newsstand reprint (distributed by Curtis); "reprint" in upper-left corner box; price and issue number in square with Curtis Circulation (CC) logo 7.00
❑5/Whitman 1977, HC (a); Special markets edition (usually sold in Whitman bagged prepacks); price appears in a diamond; no UPC barcode 3.50
❑5/Whitman 2nd 1977, HC (a); Special markets reprint (usually sold in Whitman bagged prepacks); price appears in a diamond; no UPC barcode; reprint on cover 3.50
❑6, Dec 1977, HC (a); Newsstand edition (distributed by Curtis); issue number in box 7.00
❑6/2nd, Dec 1977, HC (a); Newsstand reprint (distributed by Curtis); "reprint" in upper-left corner box; price and issue number in square with Curtis Circulation (CC) logo 7.00
❑6/Whitman 1977, HC (a); Special markets edition (usually sold in Whitman bagged prepacks); price appears in a diamond; no UPC barcode 3.50
❑6/Whitman 2nd 1977, HC (a); Special markets reprint (usually sold in Whitman bagged prepacks); price appears in a diamond; no UPC barcode; reprint on cover 3.50
❑7, Jan 1978, GK (c); HC (a); Newsstand edition (distributed by Curtis); issue number in box 7.00
❑7/Whitman 1978, HC (a); Special markets edition (usually sold in Whitman bagged prepacks); price appears in a diamond; no UPC barcode
❑8, Feb 1978, GK (c); HC, TP (a); Newsstand edition (distributed by Curtis); issue number in box 7.00
❑8/Whitman 1978, HC, TP (a); Special markets edition (usually sold in Whitman bagged prepacks); price appears in a diamond; no UPC barcode 3.00
❑9, Mar 1978, GK (c); HC, TP (a); Newsstand edition (distributed by Curtis); issue number in box 7.00
❑9/Whitman 1978, HC, TP (a); Special markets edition (usually sold in Whitman bagged prepacks); price appears in a diamond; no UPC barcode 3.00
❑10, Apr 1978, HC (w); HC, TP (a); Newsstand edition (distributed by Curtis); issue number in box 7.00
❑10/Whitman, Apr 1978, HC, TP (a); Special markets edition (usually sold in Whitman bagged prepacks); price appears in a diamond; no UPC barcode 7.00
❑11, May 1978, GK (c); CI (a); Newsstand edition (distributed by Curtis); issue number in box 7.00

Other grades: Multiply price above by 5/6 for VF/NM • 2/3 for VERY FINE • 1/3 for FINE • 1/5 for VERY GOOD • 1/8 for GOOD

N-MINT

❑11/Whitman, May 1978, Cl (a); Special markets edition (usually sold in Whitman bagged prepacks); price appears in a diamond; UPC barcode appears ... 7.00
❑11/Whitman B, May 1978, Cl (a); Special markets edition (usually sold in Whitman bagged prepacks); price appears in a diamond; no UPC barcode ... 7.00
❑12, Jun 1978, Cl (a); Newsstand edition (distributed by Curtis); issue number in box ... 7.00
❑12/Whitman, Jun 1978, Cl (a); Special markets edition (usually sold in Whitman bagged prepacks); price appears in a diamond; no UPC barcode ... 7.00
❑13, Jul 1978, JBy (c); Cl, BWi (a); Newsstand edition (distributed by Curtis); issue number in box ... 7.00
❑13/Whitman, Jul 1978, Cl (a); Special markets edition (usually sold in Whitman bagged prepacks); price appears in a diamond; no UPC barcode ... 7.00
❑14, Aug 1978, Cl (c); Cl (a); Newsstand edition (distributed by Curtis); issue number in box ... 7.00
❑14/Whitman, Aug 1978, Cl (a); Special markets edition (usually sold in Whitman bagged prepacks); price appears in a diamond; UPC barcode appears ... 7.00
❑15, Sep 1978, Cl (a); D: Crimson Jack. Newsstand edition (distributed by Curtis); issue number in box ... 7.00
❑15/Whitman, Sep 1978, Cl (a); D: Crimson Jack. Special markets edition (usually sold in Whitman bagged prepacks); price appears in a diamond; no UPC barcode ... 7.00
❑16, Oct 1978, BWi (a); 1: Valance the bounty hunter. Newsstand edition (distributed by Curtis); issue number in box ... 7.00
❑16/Whitman, Oct 1978, BWi (a); 1: Valance the bounty hunter. Special markets edition (usually sold in Whitman bagged prepacks); price appears in a diamond; no UPC barcode ... 7.00
❑17, Nov 1978, DC (c); AM, HT (a); Newsstand edition (distributed by Curtis); issue number in box; low distribution; Tatooine adventure set before first movie ... 7.00
❑17/Whitman, Nov 1978, AM, HT (a); Special markets edition (usually sold in Whitman bagged prepacks); price appears in a diamond; no UPC barcode ... 7.00
❑18, Dec 1978, Newsstand edition (distributed by Curtis); issue number in box; low distribution ... 7.00
❑18/Whitman, Dec 1978, Special markets edition (usually sold in Whitman bagged prepacks); price appears in a diamond; no UPC barcode ... 7.00
❑19, Jan 1979, Cl (c); Cl, BWi (a); low distribution ... 7.00
❑20, Feb 1979, Cl (c); Cl, BWi (a) ... 6.00
❑21, Mar 1979, Cl (c); Cl, GD (a) ... 6.00
❑22, Apr 1979, Cl (c); Cl, BWi (a) ... 5.00
❑23, May 1979, Cl (c); Cl, BWi (a); Newsstand edition (distributed by Curtis); issue number in box ... 5.00
❑23/Whitman, May 1979, Cl, BWi (a); Special markets edition (usually sold in Whitman bagged prepacks); price appears in a diamond; no UPC barcode ... 5.00
❑24, Jun 1979, Cl (c); Cl, BWi (a); flashback to before first movie ... 4.00
❑25, Jul 1979, Cl (c); Cl, GD (a) ... 4.00
❑26, Aug 1979, Cl (c); Cl, GD (a) ... 4.00
❑27, Sep 1979, Cl, BWi (a) ... 4.00
❑28, Oct 1979, Cl (c); Cl, GD, BWi (a); A: Jabba the Hutt (not movie version). ... 4.00
❑29, Nov 1979, Cl, BWi (c); Cl, BWi (a); A: Darth Vader ... 4.00
❑30, Dec 1979, Cl (c); Cl, GD (a) ... 4.00
❑31, Jan 1980, Cl, BWi (c); Cl, BWi (a); return to Tatooine ... 4.00
❑32, Feb 1980, Cl (c); Cl, BWi (a) ... 4.00
❑33, Mar 1980, Cl (c); Cl, GD (a) ... 4.00
❑34, Apr 1980, Cl (c); Cl, BWi (a); D: Baron Tagge ... 4.00
❑35, May 1980, Cl (c); Cl, GD (a); A: Darth Vader. A: Luke Skywalker. 1st face-to-face mtg b/w Luke & Vader; Return of Orman & Silas Tagge ... 4.00
❑36, Jun 1980, Cl (c); Cl, GD (a) ... 4.00

N-MINT

❑37, Jul 1980, Cl, GD (a); 1st Vader/Luke duel ... 4.00
❑38, Aug 1980, MG (c); MG (w); MG (a); living spaceship ... 4.00
❑39, Sep 1980, AW (a); Empire Strikes Back adaptation ... 4.00
❑40, Oct 1980, AW (a); Empire Strikes Back adaptation ... 4.00
❑41, Nov 1980, AW (a); Empire Strikes Back adaptation ... 4.00
❑42, Dec 1980, AW (a); Empire Strikes Back adaptation ... 4.00
❑43, Jan 1981, AW (a); Empire Strikes Back adaptation ... 4.00
❑44, Feb 1981, AW (a); Empire Strikes Back adaptation ... 4.00
❑45, Mar 1981, Cl, GD (a); first post-Empire Strikes Back story ... 4.00
❑46, Apr 1981, Cl, TP (a) ... 4.00
❑47, May 1981, FM (c); Cl, GD (a) ... 4.00
❑48, Jun 1981, Cl, BWi (c); Cl (a) ... 4.00
❑49, Jul 1981, TP (a); low distribution .. 5.00
❑50, Aug 1981; double-sized; AW, TP (a); Giant-size ... 4.00
❑51, Sep 1981, TP (a); A: D: Star II. A: Tarkin. A: Star II appearance. D: D: Star II ... 4.00
❑52, Oct 1981, TP (a); A: D: Star II. A: Tarkin. A: Star II appearance. D: D: Star II ... 4.00
❑53, Nov 1981, Cl, TP (a) ... 4.00
❑54, Dec 1981, AM, Cl, TP (a) ... 4.00
❑55, Jan 1982, TP (a); 1st Plif ... 4.00
❑56, Feb 1982, TP (a) ... 4.00
❑57, Mar 1982, TP (a) ... 4.00
❑58, Apr 1982, TP (a); Return to Cloud City ... 4.00
❑59, May 1982, TP (a); 1: Orion Ferret .. 4.00
❑60, Jun 1982, TP (a) ... 4.00
❑61, Jul 1982, TP (a) ... 4.00
❑62, Aug 1982, TP (a); Luke kicked out of Alliance ... 4.00
❑63, Sep 1982, TP (c); TP (a) ... 4.00
❑64, Oct 1982, BA (c); D: Berl ... 4.00
❑65, Nov 1982, TP (c); TP (a); Luke skywalker stands trial for treason and leia fights alone ... 4.00
❑66, Dec 1982, TP (c); TP (a) ... 4.00
❑67, Jan 1983, TP (c); TP (a) ... 4.00
❑68, Feb 1983, TP, GD (a) ... 4.00
❑69, Mar 1983, TP (c); TP, GD (a); D: Suprema & Tobbi Dala ... 4.00
❑70, Apr 1983, TP (c); TP, KGa (a); Han Solo flashback story as told by Luke Skywalker ... 4.00
❑71, May 1983, TP (a) ... 4.00
❑72, Jun 1983, TP (a) ... 4.00
❑73, Jul 1983, TP (a) ... 4.00
❑74, Aug 1983, TP (c); TP (a); 1: Mone; Primor; Kendle; And Admiral Tower ... 4.00
❑75, Sep 1983, TP (c); TP (a) ... 4.00
❑76, Oct 1983, TP (c); TP (a); D: Admiral Tower; Copy 1 of 3 in ken's collection ... 4.00
❑77, Nov 1983, TP (a) ... 4.00
❑78, Dec 1983, BL (c); BL (w); BL, LMc (a) ... 4.00
❑79, Jan 1984, TP (a) ... 4.00
❑80, Feb 1984, TP (a) ... 4.00
❑81, Mar 1984, TP (c); TP (a); first post-Return of the Jedi story ... 4.00
❑82, Apr 1984 ... 4.00
❑83, May 1984, BMc (a) ... 4.00
❑84, Jun 1984, TP (a) ... 4.00
❑85, Jul 1984, BMc (c); TP, BMc (a) ... 4.00
❑86, Aug 1984, BMc (c); TP, BMc (a) ... 4.00
❑87, Sep 1984, TP (c); TP (a) ... 4.00
❑88, Oct 1984, BMc (c); TP, BMc (a); 1: Lumiya ... 4.00
❑89, Nov 1984 ... 4.00
❑90, Dec 1984, BMc (c); TP, BMc (a) ... 4.00
❑91, Jan 1985, TP (a) ... 4.00
❑92, Feb 1985; Giant-size; JDu (a) ... 4.00
❑93, Mar 1985, SB, TP (a) ... 4.00
❑94, Apr 1985, TP (a) ... 4.00
❑95, May 1985 ... 4.00
❑96, Jun 1985, BWi (a); Luke/Lumiya duel ... 4.00
❑97, Jul 1985 ... 4.00
❑98, Aug 1985, BSz (c); AW (a) ... 4.00
❑99, Sep 1985 ... 4.00
❑100, Oct 1985; Giant-size; TP (c) ... 4.00
❑101, Nov 1985, BSz (c) ... 4.00
❑102, Dec 1985, KGa (c); SB (a) ... 4.00

N-MINT

❑103, Jan 1986, D: Tai ... 4.00
❑104, Mar 1986 ... 4.00
❑105, May 1986 ... 4.00
❑106, Jul 1986 ... 4.00
❑107, Sep 1986; Final Issue; LOW distribution ... 25.00
❑Ann 1, Dec 1979 ... 8.00
❑Ann 2, ca. 1982; Cl (c); Cl (a) ... 5.00
❑Ann 3, ca. 1983; KJ (a ... 5.00

Star Wars
Dark Horse

❑1, Oct 1992, Includes trading cards ... 5.00
❑2, Nov 1992 ... 4.00
❑3, Dec 1992 ... 3.00
❑4, Jan 1993; Confrontation on Smugler's Moon ... 3.00
❑5, Feb 1993 ... 3.00
❑6, Mar 1993 ... 3.00
❑7, Apr 1993 ... 3.00
❑8, May 1993 ... 3.00
❑9, Jun 1993 ... 3.00
❑10, Jul 1993 ... 3.00

Star Wars
Dark Horse

❑0, Jun 1999; HC, TD (a); American Entertainment exclusive ... 10.00
❑1, Dec 1998 ... 4.00
❑2, Jan 1999 ... 3.00
❑3, Feb 1999 ... 3.00
❑4, Mar 1999 ... 3.00
❑5, Apr 1999 ... 3.00
❑6, May 1999 ... 3.00
❑7, Jun 1999 ... 2.50
❑8, Jul 1999 ... 2.50
❑9, Aug 1999 ... 2.50
❑10, Sep 1999 ... 2.50
❑11, Oct 1999 ... 2.50
❑12, Nov 1999 ... 2.50
❑13, Dec 1999 ... 2.50
❑14, Jan 2000 ... 2.50
❑15, Feb 2000 ... 2.50
❑16, Mar 2000 JDu (a) ... 2.50
❑17, Apr 2000 ... 2.50
❑18, May 2000 ... 2.50
❑19, Jun 2000 JDu (a) ... 2.50
❑20, Jul 2000 JDu (a) ... 2.50
❑21, Aug 2000 JDu (a) ... 2.50
❑22, Sep 2000 JDu (a) ... 2.50
❑23, Oct 2000 ... 2.50
❑24, Nov 2000 ... 2.50
❑25, Dec 2000 ... 2.50
❑26, Jan 2001 ... 2.50
❑27, Feb 2001 ... 2.99
❑28, Mar 2001 ... 2.99
❑29, Apr 2001 ... 2.99
❑30, May 2001 ... 2.99
❑31, Jun 2001 ... 2.99
❑32, Jul 2001 JDu (a) ... 2.99
❑33, Aug 2001 JDu (a) ... 2.99
❑34, Sep 2001 JDu (a) ... 2.99
❑35, Oct 2001 JDu (a) ... 2.99
❑36, Nov 2001 ... 2.99
❑37, Dec 2001 JDu (c) ... 2.99
❑38, Jan 2002 JDu (c) ... 2.99
❑39, Feb 2002 ... 2.99
❑40, Mar 2002 ... 2.99
❑41, Apr 2002 ... 2.99
❑42, May 2002 JDu (a) ... 2.99
❑43, Jun 2002 JDu (a) ... 2.99
❑44, Jul 2002 JDu (c); JDu (a) ... 2.99
❑45, Aug 2002; JDu (c); JDu (a); Tital Change to Star Wars: Republic ... 2.99
❑46, Sep 2002 ... 2.99
❑47, Oct 2002 ... 2.99
❑48, Nov 2002 ... 2.99
❑49, Dec 2002 ... 2.99
❑50, Jan 2003; Giant-size; The Epic Battle for Kamin ... 5.99
❑51, Mar 2003 ... 2.99
❑52, Apr 2003 ... 2.99
❑53, Apr 2003 ... 2.99
❑54, Jun 2003 ... 2.99
❑55, Jul 2003 ... 2.99
❑56, Jul 2003 ... 2.99
❑57, Sep 2003 ... 2.99
❑58, Dec 2003 ... 2.99
❑59, Dec 2003 ... 2.99

Supergirl

Betrayed by Luthor, Matrix seeks revenge
©DC

Super Goof

Ta-da! Powerful peanuts provide punch
©Gold Key

Super Heroes Stamp Album

DC does deal with Postal Service
©USPS

Super Information Hijinks: Reality Check

Reality didn't need checking, title did
©Tavicat

Superman

Silver Age silliness gave way to social concerns
©DC

	N-MINT
❑60, Jan 2004	2.99
❑61, Feb 2004	2.99
❑62, Mar 2004	2.99
❑63, Apr 2004	2.99
❑64, May 2004; One Jedi betrayed	2.99
❑65, Jun 2004	2.99
❑66, Jul 2004	2.99
❑67, Aug 2004	2.99
❑68, Sep 2004	2.99
❑69, Oct 2004	2.99
❑70, Nov 2004	2.99
❑71, Dec 2004; Republic	2.99
❑72, Jan 2005; Republic	2.99
❑73, Feb 2005	2.99
❑74, Mar 2005	2.99
❑75, May 2005	2.99
❑76, May 2005	2.99
❑77, Sep 2005	2.99
❑78, Oct 2005	2.99
❑79, Nov 2005	2.99
❑80, Dec 2005	2.99
❑81, Jan 2006	2.99
❑82, Feb 2006	2.99
❑83, Mar 2006, Final issue	2.99

Star Wars: A New Hope Manga
Dark Horse

	N-MINT
❑1, Jul 1998; b&w	9.95
❑2, Jul 1998; b&w	9.95
❑3, Sep 1998; b&w	9.95
❑4, Oct 1998; b&w	9.95

Star Wars: A New Hope: The Special Edition
Dark Horse

	N-MINT
❑1, Jan 1997	2.95
❑2, Feb 1997	2.50
❑3, Mar 1997	2.50
❑4, Apr 1997	2.50

Star Wars: Boba Fett
Dark Horse

	N-MINT
❑½, Dec 1997, Wizard mail-in edition	3.00
❑½/Gold, Dec 1997, Gold edition; Wizard promotional edition	5.00
❑1, Dec 1995, cardstock cover	3.95
❑2, Sep 1996, cardstock cover	3.95
❑3, Aug 1997, cardstock cover	3.95

Star Wars: Boba Fett: Agent of Doom
Dark Horse

	N-MINT
❑1, Nov 2000	2.99

Star Wars: Boba Fett: Enemy of the Empire
Dark Horse

	N-MINT
❑1, Jan 1999	2.95
❑2, Feb 1999	2.95
❑3, Mar 1999	2.95
❑4, Apr 1999	2.95

Star Wars: Boba Fett One-Shot
Dark Horse

	N-MINT
❑1, May 2006	2.99

Star Wars: Boba Fett: Twin Engines of Destruction
Dark Horse

	N-MINT
❑1, Jan 1997	2.95

Star Wars: Chewbacca
Dark Horse

	N-MINT
❑1, Jan 2000	2.95
❑2, Feb 2000	2.95
❑3, Mar 2000	2.95
❑4, Apr 2000	2.95

Star Wars: Crimson Empire
Dark Horse

	N-MINT
❑1, Dec 1997 PG (a)	6.00
❑2, Jan 1998 PG (a)	5.00
❑3, Feb 1998; PG (a); Carnor Jax appearance; Kir Kanos appearance	5.00
❑4, Mar 1998; PG (a); Carnor Jax appearance; Kir Kanos appearance	5.00
❑5, Apr 1998 PG (a)	5.00
❑6, May 1998 PG (a)	5.00

Star Wars: Crimson Empire II: Council of Blood
Dark Horse

	N-MINT
❑1, Nov 1998 PG (a)	4.00
❑2, Dec 1998 PG (a)	2.95
❑3, Jan 1999 PG (a)	2.95
❑4, Feb 1999 PG (a)	2.95
❑5, Mar 1999 PG (a)	2.95
❑6, Apr 1999 PG (a)	2.95

Star Wars: Dark Empire
Dark Horse

	N-MINT
❑1, Dec 1993; cardstock cover	6.00
❑1/2nd, Aug 1993; 2nd printing	3.00
❑1/Gold 1993	5.00
❑1/Platinum 1993	6.00
❑2, Feb 1993; cardstock cover	4.00
❑2/2nd, Aug 1993; 2nd printing	3.00
❑2/Gold 1993	4.00
❑2/Platinum 1993	5.00
❑3, Apr 1993; cardstock cover	4.00
❑3/2nd, Aug 1993; 2nd printing	3.00
❑3/Gold 1993	4.00
❑3/Platinum 1993	5.00
❑4, Apr 1993; cardstock cover	4.00
❑4/Gold 1993	4.00
❑4/Platinum 1993	5.00
❑5, Aug 1993; cardstock cover	3.00
❑5/Gold 1993	4.00
❑5/Platinum 1993	5.00
❑6, Oct 1993; cardstock cover	3.00
❑6/Gold 1993	4.00
❑6/Platinum 1993	5.00
❑Ashcan 1, Mar 1996; newsprint preview of trade paperback collection of mini-series; wraparound cover	1.00

Star Wars: Dark Empire II
Dark Horse

	N-MINT
❑1, Dec 1994; cardstock cover	2.95
❑1/Gold, Dec 1994	4.00
❑2, Jan 1995; cardstock cover	2.95
❑2/Gold, Jan 1995	4.00
❑3, Feb 1995; cardstock cover	2.95
❑3/Gold, Feb 1995	4.00
❑4, Mar 1995; cardstock cover	2.95
❑4/Gold, Mar 1995	4.00
❑5, Apr 1995; cardstock cover	2.95
❑5/Gold, Apr 1995	4.00
❑6, May 1995; cardstock cover	2.95
❑6/Gold, May 1995	4.00

Star Wars: Dark Force Rising
Dark Horse

	N-MINT
❑1, May 1997; adapts Timothy Zahn novel; cardstock cover	2.95
❑2, Jun 1997; adapts Timothy Zahn novel; cardstock cover	2.95
❑3, Jul 1997; adapts Timothy Zahn novel; cardstock cover	2.95
❑4, Aug 1997; adapts Timothy Zahn novel; cardstock cover	2.95
❑5, Sep 1997; adapts Timothy Zahn novel; cardstock cover	2.95
❑6, Oct 1997; adapts Timothy Zahn novel; cardstock cover	2.95

Star Wars: Dark Times
Dark Horse

	N-MINT
❑1, Dec 2006, General Dass Jennir; Bomo Greenbark	2.99

Star Wars: Darth Maul
Dark Horse

	N-MINT
❑1, Sep 2000	2.95
❑1/Variant, Sep 2000; Photo cover	2.95
❑2, Oct 2000	2.99
❑2/Variant, Oct 2000; Photo cover	2.99
❑3, Nov 2000	2.99
❑3/Variant, Nov 2000; Photo cover	2.99
❑4, Dec 2000	2.99
❑4/Variant, Dec 2000; Photo cover	2.99

Star Wars: Droids
Dark Horse

	N-MINT
❑1, Apr 1994; enhanced cover	3.00
❑2, May 1994	2.75
❑3, Jun 1994	2.75
❑4, Jul 1994	2.50
❑5, Aug 1994	2.50
❑6, Sep 1994	2.50
❑Special 1, Jan 1995; Special edition; Reprints serial from Dark Horse Comics	2.50

Star Wars: Droids
Dark Horse

	N-MINT
❑1, Apr 1995	2.50
❑2, May 1995	2.50
❑3, Jun 1995	2.50
❑4, Jul 1995	2.50
❑5, Sep 1995	2.50
❑6, Oct 1995	2.50
❑7, Nov 1995	2.50
❑8, Dec 1995	2.50

Star Wars: Empire
Dark Horse

	N-MINT
❑1, Sep 2002	2.99
❑2, Oct 2002	2.99
❑3, Nov 2002	2.99
❑4, Dec 2002	2.99
❑5, Jan 2003	2.99
❑6, Feb 2003	2.99
❑7, Mar 2003	2.99
❑8, Apr 2003	2.99
❑9, Jul 2003	2.99
❑10, Jul 2003	2.99
❑11, Aug 2003	2.99
❑12, Sep 2003	2.99
❑13, Oct 2003	2.99
❑14, Nov 2003	2.99
❑15, Dec 2003	2.99

Other grades: Multiply price above by 5/6 for VF/NM • 2/3 for VERY FINE • 1/3 for FINE • 1/5 for VERY GOOD • 1/8 for GOOD

❑16, Jan 2004 .... 2.99
❑17, Feb 2004 .... 2.99
❑18, Mar 2004 .... 2.99
❑19, Apr 2004 .... 2.99
❑20, May 2004 .... 2.99
❑21, Jun 2004 .... 2.99
❑22, Jul 2004 .... 2.99
❑23, Aug 2004 .... 2.99
❑24, Sep 2004 .... 2.99
❑25, Oct 2004 .... 2.99
❑26, Nov 2004 .... 2.99
❑27, Dec 2004 .... 2.99
❑28, Jan 2005 .... 2.99
❑29, Feb 2005 .... 2.99
❑30, Jun 2005 .... 2.99
❑31, Jul 2005 .... 2.99
❑32, Aug 2005 .... 2.99
❑33, Sep 2005 .... 2.99
❑34, Oct 2005 .... 2.99
❑35, Aug 2005 .... 2.99
❑36, Aug 2005 .... 2.99
❑37, Nov 2005 .... 2.99
❑38, Jan 2006 .... 2.99
❑39, Mar 2006 .... 2.99
❑40, Mar 2006, Series finale; Continued in Star Wars: Rebellion 2.99

Star Wars: Empire's End
Dark Horse

❑1, Oct 1995; cardstock cover 2.95
❑2, Nov 1995; cardstock cover 2.95

Star Wars: Episode I Anakin Skywalker
Dark Horse

❑1, May 1999; cardstock cover 2.95
❑1/Variant, May 1999; Photo cover 2.95

Star Wars: Episode III: Revenge of the Sith
Dark Horse

❑1 2005 .... 2.99
❑2 2005 .... 2.99
❑3, May 2005 .... 3.00
❑4, May 2005 .... 3.00

Star Wars: Episode I Obi-Wan Kenobi
Dark Horse

❑1, May 1999; cardstock cover 2.95
❑1/Variant, May 1999; Photo cover 2.95

Star Wars: Episode I Queen Amidala
Dark Horse

❑1, Jun 1999; cardstock cover 2.95
❑1/Variant, Jun 1999; Photo cover 2.95

Star Wars: Episode I Qui-Gon Jinn
Dark Horse

❑1, Jun 1999; cardstock cover 2.95
❑1/Variant, Jun 1999; Photo cover 2.95

Star Wars: Episode I The Phantom Menace
Dark Horse

❑1, May 1999; cardstock cover 2.95
❑1/Variant, May 1999; Photo cover 2.95
❑2, May 1999; cardstock cover 2.95
❑2/Variant, May 1999; Photo cover 2.95
❑3, May 1999; cardstock cover 2.95
❑3/Variant, May 1999; Photo cover 2.95
❑4, May 1999; cardstock cover 2.95
❑4/Variant, May 1999; Photo cover 2.95

Star Wars: Episode II: Attack of the Clones
Dark Horse

❑1 .... 3.99
❑1/Variant 3.99
❑2 .... 3.99
❑2/Variant 3.99
❑3 .... 3.99
❑3/Variant 3.99
❑4 .... 3.99
❑4/Variant 3.99

Star Wars: General Grievous
Dark Horse

❑1, Mar 2005 .... 2.99
❑2, May 2005 .... 2.99
❑3, May 2005 .... 2.99
❑4, Sep 2005 .... 2.99

Star Wars Handbook
Dark Horse

❑1, Jul 1998; X-Wing Rogue Squadron profiles 2.95
❑2, Jul 1999; Crimson Empire profiles 2.95

Star Wars: Heir to the Empire
Dark Horse

❑1, Oct 1995 .... 2.95
❑2, Nov 1995 .... 2.95
❑3, Dec 1995 .... 2.95
❑4, Jan 1996 .... 2.95
❑5, Mar 1996 .... 2.95
❑6, Apr 1996 .... 2.95

Star Wars in 3-D
Blackthorne

❑1, Dec 1987; a.k.a. Blackthorne in 3-D #30 .... 2.50

Star Wars: Infinities: A New Hope
Dark Horse

❑1, May 2001 .... 2.99
❑2, Jun 2001 .... 2.99
❑3, Jul 2001 .... 2.99
❑4, Aug 2001 .... 2.99

Star Wars: Infinities: Return of the Jedi
Dark Horse

❑1, Dec 2003 .... 2.99
❑2, Jan 2004 .... 2.99
❑3, Mar 2004 .... 2.99
❑4, Mar 2004 .... 2.99

Star Wars: Infinities: The Empire Strikes Back
Dark Horse

❑1, Jul 2002 .... 2.99
❑2, Aug 2002 .... 2.99
❑3, Sep 2002 .... 2.99
❑4, Oct 2002 .... 2.99

Star Wars: Jabba the Hutt
Dark Horse

❑1, Apr 1995 .... 2.50
❑2, Jun 1995 .... 2.50
❑3, Aug 1995 .... 2.50
❑4, Feb 1996; 3 page preview of Usagi Yojimbo #1 .... 2.50

Star Wars: Jango Fett: Open Seasons
Dark Horse

❑1, Apr 2002 .... 2.99
❑2, May 2002 .... 2.99
❑3, Jun 2002 .... 2.99
❑4, Jul 2002 .... 2.99

Star Wars: Jedi - Aayla Secura
Dark Horse

❑1, Aug 2003 .... 4.99

Star Wars: Jedi Academy: Leviathan
Dark Horse

❑1, Oct 1998 .... 2.95
❑2, Nov 1998 .... 2.95
❑3, Dec 1998 .... 2.95
❑4, Jan 1999 .... 2.95

Star Wars: Jedi Council: Acts of War
Dark Horse

❑1, Jun 2000 .... 2.95
❑2, Jul 2000 .... 2.95
❑3, Aug 2000 .... 2.95
❑4, Sep 2000 .... 2.95

Star Wars: Jedi - Dooku Clone Wars
Dark Horse

❑1, Dec 2003 .... 4.99

Star Wars: Jedi - Mace Windu
Dark Horse

❑1, Feb 2003 .... 4.99

Star Wars: Jedi Quest
Dark Horse

❑1, Sep 2001 .... 2.99
❑2, Oct 2001 .... 2.99
❑3, Nov 2001 .... 2.99
❑4, Dec 2001 .... 2.99

Star Wars: Jedi - Shaak Ti
Dark Horse

❑1, May 2003 .... 4.99

Star Wars: Jedi vs. Sith
Dark Horse

❑1, Apr 2001 .... 2.99
❑2, May 2001 .... 2.99
❑3, Jun 2001 .... 2.99
❑4, Jul 2001 .... 2.99
❑5, Aug 2001 .... 2.99
❑6, Sep 2001 .... 2.99

Star Wars: Jedi - Yoda
Dark Horse

❑1, Aug 2004 .... 5.00

Star Wars: Knights of the Old Republic
Dark Horse

❑1, Mar 2006, JJM (w) 12.00
❑2, Apr 2006, JJM (w) 6.00
❑3, May 2006, JJM (w) 6.00
❑4, Jun 2006, JJM (w) 6.00
❑5, Jul 2006, JJM (w) 5.00
❑6, Aug 2006, JJM (w) 5.00
❑7, Sep 2006, JJM (w) 4.00
❑8, Oct 2006, JJM (w) 4.00
❑9, Nov 2006, JJM (w); O: Lucien Draay 2.99
❑10, Dec 2006, JJM (w) 2.99
❑11, Jan 2007, JJM (w) 2.99
❑12, Feb 2006, JJM (w) 2.99
❑13 .... 2.99
❑14 .... 2.99
❑15 .... 2.99
❑16 .... 2.99
❑17 .... 2.99
❑18 .... 2.99
❑19 .... 2.99
❑20 .... 2.99
❑21 .... 2.99
❑22 .... 2.99
❑23 .... 2.99
❑24 .... 2.99
❑25 .... 2.99
❑26 .... 2.99
❑27 .... 2.99
❑28 .... 2.99
❑29 .... 2.99
❑30 .... 2.99
❑31 .... 2.99
❑32 .... 2.99
❑33 .... 2.99
❑34 .... 2.99
❑35 .... 2.99
❑36 .... 2.99
❑37 .... 2.99
❑38 .... 2.99
❑39 .... 2.99
❑40 .... 2.99
❑41 .... 2.99
❑42 .... 2.99

Star Wars: Knights of the Old Republic 25¢ Flip Book
Dark Horse

❑1, Mar 2006, JJM (w) 2.00

Star Wars: Legacy
Dark Horse

❑0, Jul 2006, Design Book 1.00
❑1, Jun 2006 .... 12.00
❑2, Jul 2006 .... 5.00
❑3, Nov 2006 .... 2.99
❑4, Nov 2006 .... 2.99
❑5, Dec 2006 .... 2.99
❑6, Dec 2006 .... 2.99
❑7, Feb 2007 .... 2.99
❑8 .... 2.99
❑9 .... 2.99
❑10 .... 2.99
❑11 .... 2.99
❑12 .... 2.99
❑13 .... 2.99
❑14 .... 2.99
❑15 .... 2.99
❑16 .... 2.99
❑17 .... 2.99
❑18 .... 2.99
❑19 .... 2.99
❑20 .... 2.99
❑21 .... 2.99
❑22 .... 2.99
❑23 .... 2.99

Superman

Revamped Man of Steel made for fresh start

©DC

Superman 3-D

Occasional 3-D only works from time to time

©DC

Superman Adventures

Animated tales provide fodder for spin-off

©DC

Superman: A Nation Divided

Civil War sees super-weapon from Kansas

©DC

Superman & Batman: Generations

Doing the decades with aging heroes

©DC

N-MINT

❑24 ... 2.99
❑25 ... 2.99
❑26 ... 2.99
❑27 ... 2.99
❑28 ... 2.99
❑29 ... 2.99
❑30 ... 2.99
❑31 ... 2.99
❑32 ... 2.99
❑33 ... 2.99
❑34 ... 2.99
❑35 ... 2.99
❑36 ... 2.99
❑37 ... 2.99

Star Wars: Mara Jade
Dark Horse

❑1, Aug 1998 ... 3.00
❑2, Sep 1998; 2: Mara Jade ... 2.95
❑3, Oct 1998 ... 2.95
❑4, Nov 1998; Darth Vader cameo; Luke Skywalker cameo; Emperor Palpatine cameo ... 2.95
❑5, Dec 1998 ... 2.95
❑6, Jan 1999 ... 2.95

Star Wars: Obsession
Dark Horse

❑1, Nov 2004 ... 8.00
❑2, Dec 2004 ... 4.00
❑3, Jan 2005 ... 2.99
❑4, Feb 2005 ... 2.99
❑5, Apr 2005 ... 2.99

Star Wars: Purge
Dark Horse

❑1, Dec 2005, One-shot ... 25.00

Star Wars: Qui-Gon & Obi-Wan: Last Stand on Ord Mantell
Dark Horse

❑1/A, Dec 2000; Obi-Wan leaping on cover, Qui-Gon standing ... 2.99
❑1/B, Dec 2000; Qui-gon and Obi-Wan standing on cover, Obi-Wan has light sabre out ... 2.99
❑1/C, Dec 2000 ... 2.99
❑2/A, Feb 2001; Drawn cover ... 2.99
❑2/B, Feb 2001 ... 2.99
❑3/A, Mar 2001; Drawn cover ... 2.99
❑3/B, Mar 2001 ... 2.99

Star Wars: Qui-Gon & Obi-Wan: The Aurorient Express
Dark Horse

❑1, Feb 2002 ... 2.99
❑2, May 2002 ... 2.99

Star Wars: Rebellion
Dark Horse

❑1, May 2006 ... 8.00
❑3, Jun 2006 ... 2.99
❑4, Aug 2006 ... 2.99
❑5, Jan 2007, Lt. Janek Sunber (Tank); Darth Vader ... 2.99

N-MINT

Star Wars: Return of the Jedi
Marvel

❑1, Oct 1983, BSz (c); AW (a); Reprints Marvel Super Special #27 ... 4.00
❑2, Nov 1983, BSz (c); AW (a); Reprints Marvel Super Special #27 ... 4.00
❑3, Dec 1983, BSz (c); AW (a); Reprints Marvel Super Special #27 ... 4.00
❑4, Jan 1984, BSz (c); AW (a); Reprints Marvel Super Special #27 ... 4.00

Star Wars: River of Chaos
Dark Horse

❑1, Jun 1995 ... 2.50
❑2, Jul 1995 ... 2.50
❑3, Sep 1995 ... 2.50
❑4, Nov 1995 ... 2.50

Star Wars: Shadows of Empire: Evolution
Dark Horse

❑1, Feb 1998 ... 2.95
❑2, Mar 1998 ... 2.95
❑3, Apr 1998 ... 2.95
❑4, May 1998 ... 2.95
❑5, Jun 1998 ... 2.95

Star Wars: Shadows of the Empire
Dark Horse

❑1, May 1996 ... 2.95
❑2, Jun 1996 ... 2.95
❑3, Jul 1996 ... 2.95
❑4, Aug 1996 ... 2.95
❑5, Sep 1996 ... 2.95
❑6, Oct 1996 ... 2.95

Star Wars: Shadow Stalker
Dark Horse

❑1, Sep 1997; NN; One-shot ... 2.95

Star Wars: Splinter of the Mind's Eye
Dark Horse

❑1, Dec 1995 ... 2.50
❑2, Feb 1996 ... 2.50
❑3, Apr 1996 ... 2.50
❑4, Jun 1996, Final Issue ... 2.50

Star Wars: Starfighter: Crossbones
Dark Horse

❑1, Jan 2002 ... 2.99
❑2, Feb 2002 ... 2.99
❑3, Mar 2002 ... 2.99

Star Wars: Tag & Bink are Dead
Dark Horse

❑1, Oct 2001 ... 2.99
❑2, Nov 2001 ... 2.99

Star Wars: Tag & Bink Episode I - Revenge of the Clone Menace
Dark Horse

❑1, May 2006 ... 2.99

Star Wars Tales
Dark Horse

❑1, Sep 1999 PD (w) ... 4.95
❑2, Dec 1999 ... 4.95
❑3, Mar 2000; Star Wars; Villie; Lando Calrissian ... 4.95
❑4, Jun 2000 ... 4.95
❑5, Sep 2000 ... 5.95
❑5/PH, Sep 2000 ... 5.95

N-MINT

❑6, Dec 2000 ... 5.95
❑7, Mar 2001 ... 5.99
❑8, Jun 2001 ... 5.99
❑9, Sep 2001 ... 5.99
❑10, Dec 2001 ... 5.99
❑11, Mar 2002 ... 5.99
❑12, Jun 2002 ... 5.99
❑13, Sep 2002 ... 5.99
❑14, Dec 2002 ... 5.99
❑15, Mar 2003 ... 5.99
❑16, Jun 2003 ... 5.99
❑17, Oct 2003 ... 5.99
❑18, Dec 2003 ... 5.99
❑19, Apr 2004 ... 5.99
❑20, Aug 2004 ... 5.99
❑21, Sep 2005; Cover reads: "Fly for the Glory of the Empire!" w/Vader in forefront ... 5.99
❑22/Art 2005 ... 7.00
❑22/Photo 2005 ... 5.99
❑23/Art 2005 ... 7.00
❑23/Photo 2005 ... 5.99
❑24/Art, Aug 2005 ... 7.00
❑24/Photo, Aug 2005 ... 5.99

Star Wars Tales-A Jedi's Weapon
Dark Horse

❑1 ... 1.00

Star Wars: Tales: A Jedi's Weapon
Dark Horse

❑1, May 2002 ... 2.00

Star Wars: Tales from Mos Eisley
Dark Horse

❑1, Mar 1996, NN ... 2.95

Star Wars: Tales of the Jedi
Dark Horse

❑1, Oct 1993 ... 4.00
❑1/Special, Oct 1993 ... 6.00
❑2, Nov 1993 ... 3.50
❑2/Special, Nov 1993 ... 5.00
❑3, Dec 1993 ... 3.25
❑3/Special, Dec 1993 ... 5.00
❑4, Jan 1994 ... 2.50
❑4/Special, Jan 1994 ... 5.00
❑5, Feb 1994 ... 2.50
❑5/Special, Feb 1994 ... 5.00

Star Wars: Tales of the Jedi: Dark Lords of the Sith
Dark Horse

❑1, Oct 1994 ... 3.00
❑2, Nov 1994 ... 3.00
❑3, Dec 1994 ... 3.00
❑4, Jan 1995 ... 3.00
❑5, Feb 1995 ... 3.00
❑6, Mar 1995 ... 3.00

Star Wars: Tales of the Jedi: Fall of the Sith Empire
Dark Horse

❑1, Jun 1997; Man with marionettes on cover ... 2.95
❑1/A, Jun 1997; Variant cover, flame in background ... 2.95
❑2, Jul 1997 ... 2.95
❑3, Aug 1997 ... 2.95

N-MINT | N-MINT | N-MINT

❑4, Sep 1997 ... 2.95
❑5, Oct 1997 ... 2.95

Star Wars: Tales of the Jedi: Redemption
Dark Horse

❑1, Jul 1998 ... 2.95
❑2, Aug 1998 ... 2.95
❑3, Sep 1998 ... 2.95
❑4, Oct 1998 ... 2.95
❑5, Nov 1998 ... 2.95

Star Wars: Tales of the Jedi: The Freedon Nadd Uprising
Dark Horse

❑1, Aug 1994 ... 2.50
❑2, Sep 1994 ... 2.50

Star Wars: Tales of the Jedi: The Golden Age of the Sith
Dark Horse

❑0, ca. 1996 ... 0.99
❑1, Oct 1996 ... 2.95
❑2, Nov 1996 ... 2.95
❑3, Dec 1996 ... 2.95
❑4, Jan 1997 ... 2.95
❑5, Feb 1997 ... 2.95

Star Wars: Tales of the Jedi: The Sith War
Dark Horse

❑1, Aug 1995 ... 2.50
❑2, Sep 1995 ... 2.50
❑3, Oct 1995 ... 2.50
❑4, Nov 1995 ... 2.50
❑5, Dec 1995 ... 2.50
❑6, Jan 1996 ... 2.50

Star Wars: The Bounty Hunters: Aurra Sing
Dark Horse

❑1, Jul 1999 ... 2.95

Star Wars: The Bounty Hunters: Kenix Kil
Dark Horse

❑1, Oct 1999; one shot ... 2.95

Star Wars: The Bounty Hunters: Scoundrel's Wages
Dark Horse

❑1, Aug 1999 ... 2.95

Star Wars: The Empire Strikes Back: Manga
Dark Horse

❑1, Jan 1999 ... 9.95
❑2, Feb 1999 ... 9.95
❑3, Mar 1999 ... 9.95
❑4, Apr 1999 ... 9.95

Star Wars: The Jabba Tape
Dark Horse

❑1, Dec 1998; NN ... 2.95

Star Wars: The Last Command
Dark Horse

❑1, Nov 1997 ... 3.50
❑2, Dec 1997 ... 3.00
❑3, Feb 1998 ... 3.00
❑4, Mar 1998 ... 3.00
❑5, Apr 1998 ... 3.00
❑6, Jul 1998 ... 2.95

Star Wars: The Protocol Offensive
Dark Horse

❑1, Sep 1997; prestige format; Co-written by Anthony Daniels, the actor who played C-3PO ... 4.95

Star Wars: The Return of Tag & Bink Special Edition
Dark Horse

❑1, May 2006 ... 2.99

Star Wars: Underworld: The Yavin Vassilika
Dark Horse

❑1/A, Dec 2000; Drawn cover with Han Solo, Lando Calrisian, and Boba Fett .. 2.99
❑1/B, Dec 2000; Painted cover with Jabba the Hutt ... 2.99
❑2/A, Jan 2001 ... 2.99
❑2/B, Jan 2001 ... 2.99
❑3/A, Feb 2001; Drawn cover with Han Solo, Lando Calrisian, and Boba Fett .. 2.99
❑3/B, Feb 2001 ... 2.99
❑4/A, Mar 2001 ... 2.99
❑4/B, Mar 2001 ... 2.99
❑5/A, Apr 2001 ... 2.99
❑5/B, Apr 2001 ... 2.99

Star Wars: Union
Dark Horse

❑1, Nov 1999; The wedding of Luke and Mara ... 14.00
❑2, Dec 1999 ... 10.00
❑3, Jan 2000 ... 7.00
❑4, Feb 2000; Wedding of Luke Skywalker & Mara Jade ... 5.00

Star Wars: Vader's Quest
Dark Horse

❑1, Feb 1999 ... 2.95
❑2, Mar 1999 ... 2.95
❑3, Apr 1999 ... 2.95
❑4, May 1999 ... 2.95

Star Wars: Valentines Story
Dark Horse

❑1, Feb 2003 ... 3.50

Star Wars: X-Wing Rogue Leader
Dark Horse

❑1 ... 2.99
❑2, Oct 2005 ... 2.99
❑3, Dec 2005 ... 2.99

Star Wars: X-Wing Rogue Squadron
Dark Horse

❑½, Feb 1997; Wizard mail-in edition; Wizard mail-in edition from Wizard #67; Includes certificate of authenticity ... 3.00
❑½/Platinum, Feb 1997; Platinum edition; Wizard mail-in edition from Wizard #67; Includes certificate of authenticity ... 5.00
❑1, Jul 1995 ... 4.00
❑2, Aug 1995 ... 3.50
❑3, Sep 1995 ... 3.50
❑4, Oct 1995 ... 3.50
❑5, Feb 1996 ... 3.00
❑6, Mar 1996 ... 3.00
❑7, Apr 1996 ... 3.00
❑8, Jun 1996 ... 3.00
❑9, Jul 1996 ... 3.00
❑10, Jul 1996 ... 3.00
❑11, Aug 1996 ... 3.00
❑12, Sep 1996 ... 3.00
❑13, Oct 1996 ... 3.00
❑14, Dec 1996 ... 3.00
❑15, Jan 1997 ... 3.00
❑16, Feb 1997 ... 3.00
❑17, Mar 1997 ... 3.00
❑18, Apr 1997 ... 3.00
❑19, May 1997 ... 3.00
❑20, Jun 1997 ... 3.00
❑21, Aug 1997 ... 3.00
❑22, Sep 1997 ... 3.00
❑23, Oct 1997 ... 3.00
❑24, Nov 1997 ... 3.00
❑25, Dec 1997; Giant-size; O: Baron Fel. 4.00
❑26, Jan 1998 ... 2.95
❑27, Feb 1998 ... 2.95
❑28, Mar 1998 ... 2.95
❑29, Apr 1998 ... 2.95
❑30, May 1998 ... 2.95
❑31, Jun 1998 ... 2.95
❑32, Jul 1998 ... 2.95
❑33, Aug 1998 ... 2.95
❑34, Sep 1998 ... 2.95
❑35, Nov 1998 ... 2.95
❑Special 1, Aug 1995; promotional giveaway with Kellogg's Apple Jacks; Promotional giveaway with Kellogg's Apple Jacks ... 1.00

Star Weevils
Rip Off

❑1 ... 1.00

Star Western
Avalon

❑1 ... 5.95
❑2; John Wayne feature ... 5.95
❑3; Clint Eastwood feature ... 5.95
❑4 ... 5.95
❑5 ... 5.95

S.T.A.T.
Majestic

❑1, Dec 1993 ... 2.25
❑1/Variant, Dec 1993; foil cover ... 2.25

Static
DC / Milestone

❑1, Jun 1993; 1: Hotstreak. 1: Frieda Goren. 1: Static. 1: Frieda Goren ... 2.00
❑1/CS, Jun 1993; 1: Hotstreak. 1: Frieda Goren. 1: Static. poster; trading card; Collector's Set ... 3.00
❑1/Silver, Jun 1993; Silver (limited promotional) edition; 1: Hotstreak. 1: Frieda Goren. 1: Static 3.00
❑2, Jul 1993; O: Static. 1: Tarmack ... 1.50
❑3, Aug 1993 ... 1.50
❑4, Sep 1993; 1: Don Giacomo Cornelius 1.50
❑5, Oct 1993; 1: Commando X ... 1.50
❑6, Nov 1993 ... 1.50
❑7, Dec 1993 ... 1.50
❑8, Jan 1994; Shadow War ... 1.50
❑9, Feb 1994; 1: Virus ... 1.50
❑10, Mar 1994; 1: Puff. 1: Coil ... 1.50
❑11, Apr 1994 ... 1.50
❑12, May 1994; KB (w); 1: Snakefinger . 1.50
❑13, Jun 1994 ... 1.50
❑14, Aug 1994; Giant-size; 48 pages ... 2.50
❑15, Sep 1994 ... 1.75
❑16, Oct 1994; 1: Joyride ... 1.75
❑17, Nov 1994 ... 1.75
❑18, Dec 1994 ... 1.75
❑19, Jan 1995 ... 1.75
❑20, Feb 1995 ... 1.75
❑21, Mar 1995 A: Blood Syndicate ... 1.75
❑22, Apr 1995 ... 1.75
❑23, Jun 1995 ... 1.75
❑24, Jul 1995 ... 1.75
❑25, Jul 1995; Double-size ... 3.95
❑26, Aug 1995 ... 2.50
❑27, Sep 1995 ... 2.50
❑28, Oct 1995 ... 2.50
❑29, Nov 1995 ... 2.50
❑30, Dec 1995; D: Larry ... 2.50
❑31, Jan 1996 GK (a) ... 0.99
❑32, Feb 1996 ... 2.50
❑33, Mar 1996 ... 2.50
❑34, Apr 1996 ... 2.50
❑35, May 1996 ... 2.50
❑36, Jun 1996 ... 2.50
❑37, Jul 1996 ... 2.50
❑38, Aug 1996 ... 2.50
❑39, Sep 1996 ... 2.50
❑40, Oct 1996 KP (a) ... 2.50
❑41, Nov 1996 ... 2.50
❑42, Dec 1996 ... 2.50
❑43, Jan 1997 ... 2.50
❑44, Feb 1997 ... 2.50
❑45, Mar 1997 ... 2.50
❑46, Apr 1997 ... 2.50
❑47, May 1997; Final Issue ... 2.50

Static Shock!: Rebirth of the Cool
DC / Milestone

❑1, Jan 2001 ... 2.50
❑2, Feb 2001 ... 2.50
❑3, May 2001 ... 2.50
❑4, Sep 2001 ... 2.50

Stay Puffed
Image

❑1, Jan 2004 ... 3.50

Steady Beat
Tokyopop

❑1, Oct 2005 ... 9.99

Stealth Force
Malibu

❑1, Jul 1987 ... 1.95
❑2, Aug 1987 ... 1.95
❑3, Sep 1987 ... 1.95
❑4, Oct 1987 ... 1.95
❑5, Nov 1987 ... 1.95
❑6, Dec 1987 ... 1.95
❑7, Jan 1988 ... 1.95
❑8, Feb 1988; Eternity begins as publisher 1.95

Other grades: Multiply price above by 5/6 for VF/NM • 2/3 for VERY FINE • 1/3 for FINE • 1/5 for VERY GOOD • 1/8 for GOOD

Superman & Batman: Generations II

Originals' descendants carry on legacy
©DC

Superman & Batman: Generations III

Century-long issues didn't seem like it
©DC

Superman & Bugs Bunny

Looney Tunes get powers, mayhem ensues
©DC

Superman/Batman

Select parts of stories play into continuity
©DC

Superman: Birthright

Mark Waid rethinks John Byrne's revamp
©DC

N-MINT

Stealth Squad
Petra

❑0, Jan 1995; O: Stealth Squad.............. 2.50
❑1; 1: Fire Flare; 1: Kid Mammoth; 1: Solar Blade; 1: Stealth One; 1: Stealth Squad; 1: Strikeforce Champion; 1: Swoop 2.50
❑2... 2.50
❑3... 2.50
❑4... 2.50

Steampunk
DC / Wildstorm

❑1, Apr 2000.. 2.50
❑2, May 2000.. 2.50
❑3, Jun 2000.. 2.50
❑4, Jul 2000.. 2.50
❑5, Oct 2000.. 3.50
❑6, Jan 2001.. 2.50
❑7, Apr 2001.. 2.50
❑8, Jun 2001.. 2.50
❑9, Sep 2001.. 2.50
❑10, Jan 2002.. 2.50
❑11, Apr 2002.. 2.50
❑12, Jul 2002... 3.50

Steampunk: Catechism
DC / Wildstorm

❑1, Jan 2000.. 2.50

Stech
Silverwolf

❑1, Dec 1986, b&w................................. 1.50

Steed and Mrs. Peel
Eclipse

❑1, Dec 1990.. 5.00
❑2, May 1991.. 5.00
❑3; ca. 1992... 5.00

Steel
DC

❑0, Oct 1994.. 1.50
❑1, Feb 1994.. 1.50
❑2, Mar 1994.. 1.50
❑3, Apr 1994.. 1.50
❑4, May 1994.. 1.50
❑5, Jun 1994.. 1.50
❑6, Jul 1994 A: Hardware...................... 1.50
❑7, Aug 1994; A: Icon. A: Hardware. Story continues into Blood Syndicate #17 ... 1.50
❑8, Sep 1994; V: Split........................... 1.50
❑9, Nov 1994.. 1.50
❑10, Dec 1994; V: Alter......................... 1.50
❑11, Jan 1995.. 1.50
❑12, Feb 1995.. 1.50
❑13, Mar 1995.. 1.50
❑14, Apr 1995.. 1.50
❑15, May 1995.. 1.50
❑16, Jun 1995; V: White Rabbit; V: Worm; V: Digit.. 1.95
❑17, Jul 1995; V: Chindi........................ 1.95
❑18, Aug 1995; V: Chindi...................... 1.95
❑19, Sep 1995; V: Team Hazard; Team-up with Chindi.. 1.95
❑20, Oct 1995.. 1.95
❑21, Nov 1995; Underworld Unleashed . 1.95
❑22, Dec 1995; A: Supergirl. A: Eradicator. Continues into Trial of Superman 1.95
❑23, Jan 1996.. 1.95
❑24, Feb 1996.. 1.95

N-MINT

❑25, Mar 1996.. 1.95
❑26, May 1996.. 1.95
❑27, Jun 1996; V: Team Hazard............. 1.95
❑28, Jul 1996; V: Plasmus..................... 1.95
❑29, Aug 1996.. 1.95
❑30, Sep 1996.. 1.95
❑31, Oct 1996.. 1.95
❑32, Nov 1996; V: Blockbuster.............. 1.95
❑33, Dec 1996 JA (a).............................. 1.95
❑34, Jan 1997; TP (a); A: Margot. new armor.. 1.95
❑35, Feb 1997 TP (a)............................. 1.95
❑36, Mar 1997 TP (a)............................. 1.95
❑37, Apr 1997.. 1.95
❑38, May 1997.. 1.95
❑39, Jun 1997 TP (a).............................. 1.95
❑40, Jul 1997; 1: new hammer............... 2.25
❑41, Aug 1997.. 1.95
❑42, Sep 1997 TP (a).............................. 1.95
❑43, Oct 1997; TP (a); A: Superman. Genesis... 1.95
❑44, Nov 1997.. 1.95
❑45, Dec 1997; TP (a); Face cover......... 1.95
❑46, Jan 1998 TP (a); A: Superboy........ 1.95
❑47, Feb 1998.. 2.50
❑48, Mar 1998; BSz (a); O: Crash.......... 2.50
❑49, Apr 1998 TP (a).............................. 2.50
❑50, May 1998; TP (a); A: Superman. Millennium Giants.............................. 2.50
❑51, Jun 1998... 2.50
❑52, Jul 1998; TP (a); Final Issue.......... 2.50
❑Ann 1, ca. 1994; Elseworlds................ 4.00
❑Ann 2, ca. 1995; Year One.................. 3.95

Steel Angel
Gauntlet

❑1; b&w.. 2.50

Steel Claw
Fleetway-Quality

❑1, Dec 1986... 1.50
❑2, Jan 1987... 1.50
❑3, Feb 1987... 1.50
❑4, Mar 1987... 1.50
❑5, Apr 1987... 1.50

Steeldragon Stories
Steeldragon

❑1; ca. 1983.. 1.50

Steele Destinies
Nightscapes

❑1, Apr 1995, b&w................................. 2.95
❑2, Jun 1995, b&w................................. 2.95
❑3, Sep 1995, b&w................................. 2.95

Steelgrip Starkey
Marvel / Epic

❑1, Jun 1986... 1.75
❑2, Aug 1986... 1.75
❑3, Nov 1986... 1.75
❑4, Dec 1986... 1.75
❑5, Jan 1987... 1.75
❑6, May 1987... 1.75

Steel Pulse
True Fiction

❑1, Mar 1986, b&w................................. 2.00
❑2, b&w.. 2.00

N-MINT

❑3, b&w.. 2.00
❑4... 3.50

Steel Sterling
Archie / Red Circle

❑4, Jan 1984; Red Circle publishes; was Shield — Steel Sterling........................ 1.00
❑5, Mar 1984; Archie publishes............ 1.00
❑6, May 1984... 1.00
❑7, Jul 1984... 1.00

Steel, the Indestructible Man
DC

❑1, Mar 1978, DH (c); DH (a); O: Steel. 1: Steel.. 5.00
❑2, Apr 1978.. 2.00
❑3, Jun 1978.. 2.00
❑4, Sep 1978.. 2.00
❑5, Nov 1978.. 2.00

Steel: The Official Comic Adaptation of the Warner Bros. Motion Picture
DC

❑1, Sep 1997; prestige format; NN; Movie adaptation.. 4.95

Steeltown Rockers
Marvel

❑1, Apr 1990.. 1.00
❑2, May 1990.. 1.00
❑3, Jun 1990.. 1.00
❑4, Jul 1990.. 1.00
❑5, Aug 1990.. 1.00
❑6, Sep 1990.. 1.00

Stellar Comics
Stellar

❑1... 2.50

Stellar Losers
Antarctic

❑1, Feb 1993, b&w................................. 2.50
❑2, Apr 1993, b&w................................. 2.50
❑3, Jun 1993, b&w................................. 2.50

Stephen Darklord
Rak

❑1, b&w.. 1.75
❑2, b&w.. 1.75
❑3, b&w.. 1.75

Steps to a Drug Free Life
David G. Brown

❑1, Feb 1998; promotional comic done for the Alcohol and Drug Council of Greater L.A. and Share Inc................................ 1.00

Stern Wheeler
Spotlight

❑1; Reprints from newspaper strips 25 Mar 1963-17 Apr 1963; ca. 1986....... 1.75

Steven
Kitchen Sink

❑1, b&w.. 3.00
❑2, b&w.. 3.00
❑3, May 1999, b&w................................ 3.00
❑4, b&w.. 3.00
❑5... 3.50
❑6, b&w.. 3.50
❑7... 3.50
❑8, Dec 1996, b&w; over-sized; cardstock cover.. 3.50

Other grades: Multiply price above by 5/6 for VF/NM • 2/3 for VERY FINE • 1/3 for FINE • 1/5 for VERY GOOD • 1/8 for GOOD

Steven Presents Dumpy
Fantagraphics
❑1, May 1999, b&w 2.95

Steven's Comics
DK Press / Yell Comics
❑3, b&w 3.00
❑1 ..... 1.00
❑2 ..... 2.00
❑4 ..... 3.50

Steve Zodiak and the Fireball XL-5
Gold Key
❑1, Jan 1964 ..... 65.00

Stewart the Rat
About
❑1, Feb 2003; Reprints Graphic Novel from 1980 originally published by Eclipse; b&w 3.95

Stickboy
Fantagraphics
❑1, b&w 2.50
❑1/2nd; 2nd printing 2.75
❑2, b&w 2.50
❑3, b&w 2.50
❑4, Nov 1990, b&w 2.95
❑5, Feb 1992, b&w 2.50

Stickboy
Revolutionary
❑1 ..... 2.95
❑2 ..... 2.95
❑3 ..... 2.95
❑4, Nov 1990 ..... 2.95

Stickboy
Starhead
❑1, b&w 2.50
❑2, b&w 2.50
❑3, b&w 2.50
❑4, b&w 2.50
❑5, b&w 2.50
❑6, b&w 2.50

Stig's Inferno
Vortex
❑1, ca. 1989 ..... 2.00
❑2 1989 ..... 2.00
❑3 1989 ..... 3.50
❑4 1989 ..... 3.50
❑5 1989 ..... 1.75
❑6 1989, b&w 1.50
❑7 1989, b&w 1.50

Stimulator
Fantagraphics / Eros
❑1, Nov 1991, b&w; Adult 2.50

Sting
Artline
❑1; flip book with Killer Synthetic Toads 2.50

Sting of the Green Hornet
Now
❑1, Jun 1992, bagged with poster 2.50
❑1/CS, Jun 1992, Includes poster and trading card 2.75
❑2, Jul 1992 ..... 2.50
❑2/CS, Jul 1992, bagged with poster 2.75
❑3, Aug 1992 ..... 2.50
❑3/CS, Aug 1992, bagged with poster 2.75
❑4, Sep 1992 ..... 2.50
❑4/CS, Sep 1992, stitched with poster 2.75

Stinktooth
Stinktooth
❑1, Nov 1991 ..... 1.00

Stinz
Fantagraphics
❑1, Aug 1989, b&w 4.00
❑2, Oct 1989, b&w 3.00
❑3, ca. 1989, b&w 3.00
❑4, Feb 1990, b&w; Moves to Brave New Words 2.50
❑5, ca. 1990; Published by Brave New Words 2.50

Stinz
Brave New Words
❑1, ca. 1990, b&w 2.50
❑3, ca. 1991; b&w 2.50
❑2, ca. 1991, b&w 2.50

Stinz
Mu
❑1, Oct 1994 ..... 2.50
❑2, Oct 1994 ..... 2.50
❑3, Feb 1995 ..... 2.50
❑4, Oct 1995 ..... 2.95
❑5, Jan 1997; Last Mu issue; moves to A Fine Line 4.95
❑6, Jun 1998; First A Fine Line Press issue 5.50
❑7, Aug 1998 ..... 4.95

Stoker's Dracula
Marvel
❑1 2004 ..... 3.99
❑2, ca. 2004 ..... 3.99
❑3 2005 ..... 3.99
❑4 2005 ..... 3.99

Stone
Image
❑1, Aug 1998 ..... 2.50
❑1/A, Aug 1998; Variant cover with white background 2.50
❑1/B, Aug 1998; Variant cover with side view of Stone, jewel showing in armband 2.50
❑2, Sep 1998 ..... 2.50
❑2/A, Sep 1998; DFE chrome cover; reprints indicia from #1 ..... 6.00
❑2/B, Sep 1998; alternate cover (white border) 4.00
❑3, Nov 1998 ..... 2.50
❑4, Apr 1999 ..... 2.50

Stone
Image
❑1, Aug 1999 ..... 2.50
❑1/Variant, Aug 1999; Chrome cover 6.95
❑2, Sep 1999 ..... 2.50
❑3, Dec 1999 ..... 2.50

Stone Cold Steve Austin
Chaos
❑1, Oct 1999; cover says Nov, indicia says Oct 2.95
❑2, Nov 1999 ..... 2.95
❑3, Dec 1999 ..... 2.95
❑4, Jan 2000 ..... 2.95

Stone Protectors
Harvey
❑1, May 1994; 1: the Stone Protectors; O: Stone Protectors 1.50
❑2, Jul 1994 ..... 1.50
❑3, Sep 1994 ..... 1.50

Stonewall in the Shenandoah
Heritage Collection
❑1; wraparound cover 3.50

Stoney Burke
Dell
❑1, Jun 1963 ..... 25.00
❑2, Sep 1963 ..... 20.00

Stories from Bosnia
Drawn and Quarterly
❑1, b&w; Oversized; cardstock cover 3.95

Storm
Marvel
❑1, Feb 1996; enhanced cardstock cover 2.95
❑2, Mar 1996; enhanced cardstock cover 2.95
❑3, Apr 1996; enhanced cardstock cover 2.95
❑4, May 1996; enhanced cardstock cover 2.95

Stormbreaker: The Saga of Beta Ray Bill
Marvel
❑1, Mar 2005 ..... 2.99
❑2, Apr 2005 ..... 2.99
❑3, May 2005 ..... 2.99
❑4, Jun 2005 ..... 2.99
❑5, Jul 2005 ..... 2.99
❑6, Aug 2005 ..... 2.99

Storm
Marvel
❑1, May 2006 ..... 2.99
❑2, Jun 2006 ..... 2.99
❑3, Jul 2006 ..... 2.99
❑4, Aug 2006 ..... 2.99
❑5, Sep 2006 ..... 2.99
❑6, Oct 2006 ..... 2.99

Stormquest
Caliber / Sky
❑1, Nov 1994; O: Stormquest 1.95
❑2, Dec 1994 ..... 1.95
❑3, ca. 1995 ..... 1.95
❑4, ca. 1995 ..... 1.95
❑5, ca. 1995 ..... 1.95
❑6, ca. 1955 ..... 1.95

Stormwatch
Image
❑0, Aug 1993; JLee (w); JLee (a); 1: Backlash. 1: Flashpoint. 1: Nautica. 1: Warguard. Polybagged 2.50
❑1, Mar 1993; 1: Hellstrike. 1: Battalion. 1: Diva. 1: Winter. 1: Strafe. 1: StormWatch. 1: Synergy. 1: Deathtrap. 1: Fuji 2.50
❑1/Gold, Mar 1993; Gold foil cover 3.00
❑2, May 1993; 1: Regent. 1: Cannon. 1: Fahrenheit. 1: Ion & Lance; 1: Regent; 1: Ion; 1: Lancer 1.95
❑3, Jul 1993; 1: LaSalle. A: Backlash 1.95
❑4, Aug 1993; V: Warguard. cover says Oct 1.95
❑5, Nov 1993 ..... 1.95
❑6, Dec 1993 ..... 1.95
❑7, Feb 1994; 1: Sunburst 1.95
❑8, Mar 1994; 1: Rainmaker 1.95
❑9, Apr 1994 ..... 2.50
❑10, Jun 1994 ..... 1.95
❑10/A, Jun 1994; Variant edition cover 3.00
❑10/B, Jun 1994; variant cover 3.00
❑11, Aug 1994 ..... 1.95
❑12, Aug 1994 ..... 1.95
❑13, Sep 1994 ..... 1.95
❑14, Sep 1994 ..... 1.95
❑15, Oct 1994 ..... 1.95
❑16, Nov 1994 ..... 1.95
❑17, Dec 1994 ..... 2.50
❑18, Jan 1995 ..... 2.50
❑19, Feb 1995 ..... 2.50
❑20, Mar 1995 ..... 2.50
❑21, Apr 1995; 1: Tao. cover says #1 ..... 2.50
❑22, May 1995; bound-in trading cards 2.50
❑23, Jun 1995 ..... 2.50
❑24, Jul 1995 ..... 2.50
❑25, May 1994; cover says Jun 95; Images of Tomorrow; Shipped out of sequence as preview to future events (after #9) 2.50
❑25/2nd, Aug 1995; 2nd printing 2.50
❑26, Aug 1995 ..... 2.50
❑27, Aug 1995 ..... 2.50
❑28, Sep 1995; 1: Swift. 1: Storm Force. 1: Flint. cover forms right half of diptych with issue #29 ..... 2.50
❑29, Oct 1995; indicia says Oct, cover says Nov 2.50
❑30, Nov 1995 ..... 2.50
❑31, Dec 1995 ..... 2.50
❑32, Jan 1996 ..... 2.50
❑33, Feb 1996 ..... 2.50
❑34, Mar 1996 ..... 2.50
❑35, Apr 1996 ..... 2.50
❑36, Jun 1996 ..... 2.50
❑37, Jul 1996; Giant-size; 1: Hawksmoor. 1: Jenny Sparks 3.50
❑38, Aug 1996 ..... 2.50
❑39, Aug 1996 ..... 2.50
❑40, Oct 1996 ..... 2.50
❑41, Oct 1996 ..... 2.50
❑42, Nov 1996 ..... 2.50
❑43, Dec 1996 ..... 2.50
❑44/A, Jan 1997; O: Jenny Sparks. Torrid Tales cover; homages to various comics eras 2.50
❑44/B, Jan 1997; GK (c); O: Jenny Sparks. Pop Art Masterpiece cover 2.50
❑44/C, Jan 1997; O: Jenny Sparks. Who Watches The Weathermen cover 2.50
❑45, Feb 1997 ..... 2.50
❑46, Mar 1997 ..... 2.50
❑47, Apr 1997 ..... 2.50
❑48, May 1997 ..... 2.50
❑49, Jun 1997 ..... 2.50
❑50, Jul 1997; Giant-size; Final Issue 4.50
❑Special 1, Jan 1994; 1: Argos 3.50
❑Special 2, May 1995 ..... 2.50

Other grades: Multiply price above by 5/6 for VF/NM • 2/3 for VERY FINE • 1/3 for FINE • 1/5 for VERY GOOD • 1/8 for GOOD

Superman Family

Jimmy and Lois' solo series moved to anthology
©DC

Super Manga Blast!

Manga serials include crazy cat capers
©Dark Horse

Superman: Metropolis

The life of a city that comes alive
©DC

Superman Red/ Superman Blue

Two Supermen are better than one
©DC

Superman's Girl Friend Lois Lane

Jimmy got his series first, but Lois wasn't far behind
©DC

N-MINT

Stormwatch
Image

	N-MINT
❑1, Oct 1997	2.50
❑1/A, Oct 1997; alternate cover (white background)	2.50
❑1/B, Oct 1997; Voyager pack	2.50
❑2, Nov 1997	2.50
❑3, Dec 1997	2.50
❑4, Feb 1998	2.50
❑5, Mar 1998	2.50
❑5/A, Mar 1998; alternate cover; group flying	2.50
❑6, Apr 1998	2.50
❑7, May 1998	2.50
❑8, Jun 1998	2.50
❑9, Jul 1998	2.50
❑10, Aug 1998	2.50
❑11, Sep 1998	2.50
❑12, Oct 1998	2.50

Stormwatcher
Eclipse

	N-MINT
❑1, Apr 1989, b&w	2.00
❑2, May 1989, b&w	2.00
❑3, b&w	2.00
❑4, b&w	2.00

Stormwatch: PHD
DC / Wildstorm

	N-MINT
❑1, Jan 2007	2.99
❑1/Variant, Jan 2007	2.99
❑1/2nd variant, Jan 2007	2.99
❑2, Feb 2007	2.99
❑2/Variant, Feb 2007	2.99

Stormwatch Sourcebook
Image

	N-MINT
❑1, Jan 1994	2.50

StormWatch: Team Achilles
WildStorm

	N-MINT
❑1, Aug 2002	2.95
❑2, Oct 2002	2.95
❑3, Nov 2002	2.95
❑4, Dec 2002	2.95
❑5, Jan 2003	2.95
❑6, Feb 2003	2.95
❑7, Mar 2003	2.95
❑8, Apr 2003	2.95
❑9, May 2003	2.95
❑10, Jun 2003	2.95
❑11, Jul 2003	2.95
❑12, Aug 2003	2.95
❑13, Sep 2003	2.95
❑14, Oct 2003	2.95
❑15, Nov 2003	2.95
❑16, Dec 2003	2.95
❑17, Jan 2004	2.95
❑18, Feb 2004	2.95
❑19, Mar 2004	2.95
❑20, May 2004	2.95
❑21, Jun 2004	2.95
❑22, Jul 2004	2.95
❑23, Aug 2004; Final Issue	2.95

Story of Electronics: The Discovery that Changed the World!
Radio Shack

	N-MINT
❑1, Sep 1980	2.50

N-MINT

Straitjacket Studios Presents
Straitjacket

	N-MINT
❑0	2.95

Strand
Trident

	N-MINT
❑1, Nov 1990, b&w	2.50
❑2, b&w	2.50

Stranded On Planet X
Radio

	N-MINT
❑1, Jun 1999	2.95

Strange
Marvel

	N-MINT
❑1, Nov 2004, Cardstock cover	3.50
❑2, Dec 2004, Cardstock cover	3.50
❑3, Dec 2004, Cardstock cover	3.50
❑4, Apr 2005, Cardstock cover	3.50
❑5, Jun 2005; Cardstock cover	3.50
❑6, Jul 2005; Cardstock cover	3.50

Strange Adventures
DC

	N-MINT
❑134, Nov 1961	65.00
❑135, Dec 1961	65.00
❑136, Jan 1962	50.00
❑137, Feb 1962	50.00
❑138, Mar 1962, A: The Atomic Knights	55.00
❑139, Apr 1962	50.00
❑140, May 1962	50.00
❑141, Jun 1962	55.00
❑142, Jul 1962	50.00
❑143, Aug 1962	50.00
❑144, Sep 1962, A: The Atomic Knights	50.00
❑145, Oct 1962	50.00
❑146, Nov 1962	40.00
❑147, Dec 1962, A: The Atomic Knights	50.00
❑148, Jan 1963	50.00
❑149, Feb 1963	40.00
❑150, Mar 1963, A: The Atomic Knights	50.00
❑151, Apr 1963	50.00
❑152, May 1963	50.00
❑153, Jun 1963, A: The Atomic Knights	50.00
❑154, Jul 1963	50.00
❑155, Aug 1963	50.00
❑156, Sep 1963, A: The Atomic Knights	50.00
❑157, Oct 1963	50.00
❑158, Nov 1963	50.00
❑159, Dec 1963	50.00
❑160, Jan 1964, A: The Atomic Knights.	50.00
❑161, Feb 1964	35.00
❑162, Mar 1964	35.00
❑163, Apr 1964	35.00
❑164, May 1964	35.00
❑165, Jun 1964	35.00
❑166, Jul 1964	35.00
❑167, Aug 1964	35.00
❑168, Sep 1964	30.00
❑169, Oct 1964	35.00
❑170, Nov 1964	50.00
❑171, Dec 1964	30.00
❑172, Jan 1965	30.00
❑173, Feb 1965	40.00
❑174, Mar 1965	30.00
❑175, Apr 1965	40.00
❑176, May 1965	30.00
❑177, Jun 1965, 1&O: Immortal Man	30.00
❑178, Jul 1965	25.00
❑179, Aug 1965	30.00
❑180, Sep 1965, 1&O: Animal Man (no costume)	150.00
❑181, Oct 1965	25.00
❑182, Nov 1965	30.00
❑183, Dec 1965	30.00
❑184, Jan 1966, A: Animal Man	60.00
❑185, Feb 1966, A: Immortal Man. A: Star Hawkins	25.00
❑186, Mar 1966	25.00
❑187, Apr 1966, 1&O: The Enchantress.	20.00
❑188, May 1966	25.00
❑189, Jun 1966	30.00
❑190, Jul 1966, 1: Animal Man (in costume)	100.00
❑191, Aug 1966	20.00
❑192, Sep 1966	25.00
❑193, Oct 1966	25.00
❑194, Nov 1966	20.00
❑195, Dec 1966, A: Animal Man	35.00
❑196, Jan 1967	25.00
❑197, Feb 1967	25.00
❑198, Mar 1967	20.00
❑199, Apr 1967	30.00
❑200, May 1967	25.00
❑201, Jun 1967, A: Animal Man	40.00
❑202, Jul 1967, CI (c); JO, JM (a)	20.00
❑203, Aug 1967	20.00
❑204, Sep 1967, Reprint from Strange Adventures #64	20.00
❑205, Oct 1967, 1&O: Deadman	125.00
❑206, Nov 1967, NA (a); 2: Deadman. Reprints from Strange Adventures #64	60.00
❑207, Dec 1967, NA (c); CI (w); CI, NA (a); Deadman	50.00
❑208, Jan 1968, NA (c); CI (w); CI, NA (a); Deadman	60.00
❑209, Feb 1968, NA (c); CI, NA (a); Deadman	60.00
❑210, Mar 1968, NA (c); NA, NC (a); Deadman	60.00
❑211, Apr 1968, NA (c); CI, NA (a); Deadman	60.00
❑212, Jun 1968, NA (c); NA (w); NA (a); Deadman	60.00
❑213, Aug 1968, NA (c); NA (w); NA (a); Deadman	40.00
❑214, Oct 1968, NA (c); NA (a); Deadman	60.00
❑215, Dec 1968, NA (c); NA (w); NA (a); 1: League of Assassins. 1: Sensei. Deadman	45.00
❑216, Feb 1969, NA (c); MD, NA (a); Deadman	40.00
❑217, Apr 1969, Adam Strange reprinted from Showcase #17; Atomic Knights reprinted from Strange Adventures #117; The Atomic Knights	20.00
❑218, Jun 1969, Reprints from Mystery in Space #16; Adam Strange reprinted from Showcase #17; Atomic Knights reprinted from Strange Adventures #117	20.00
❑219, Aug 1969, Adam Strange reprinted from Mystery in Space #53; Atomic Knights reprinted from Strange Adventures #123; Space Cabby reprinted from Mystery in Space #28.	20.00

Other grades: Multiply price above by 5/6 for VF/NM • 2/3 for VERY FINE • 1/3 for FINE • 1/5 for VERY GOOD • 1/8 for GOOD

N-MINT

❑220, Oct 1969, Reprints from Strange Adventure #34; Adam Strange reprinted from Mystery in Space #55; Atomic Knights reprinted from Strange Adventures #126 .... 25.00
❑221, Dec 1969, Reprints from Mystery in Space #22; All reprints; Adam Strange reprinted from Mystery in Space #59; Atomic Knights reprinted from Strange Adventure #129 .... 20.00
❑222, Feb 1970, MA, NA, GK (a); New Adam Strange story 20.00
❑223, Apr 1970, Reprints from Strange Adventures #21; Adam Strange reprinted from Mystery in Space #62; Atomic Knights reprinted from Strange Adventures #135; The Atomic Knights 20.00
❑224, Jun 1970, Reprints from Mystery in Space #41; Adam Strange reprinted from Mystery in Space #63; Atomic Knights reprinted from Strange Adventures #138 .... 15.00
❑225, Aug 1970, Reprints from Mystery in Space #33; Adam Strange reprinted from Mystery in Space #64; Atomic Knights reprinted from Strange Adventures #141 .... 15.00
❑226, Oct 1970; giant series begins 15.00
❑227, Dec 1970; JKu (c); MA, GC, CI, GK (a); Adam Strange; The Atomic Knights; Giant-Size 15.00
❑228, Feb 1971; Reprints from Mystery in Space #13, 28, 31, Strange Adventures #58 and 89; Atomic Knights reprinted from Strange Adventures #150; Adam Strange reprinted from Mystery in Space 68; Giant-Size 15.00
❑229, Apr 1971; Reprints from Strange Adventures #22, 54, 82, Mystery In Space #17 and 19; Atomic Knights reprinted from Strange Adventures #153; Adam Strange reprinted from Mystery In Space #69 .... 15.00
❑230, Jun 1971; Adam Strange reprinted from Mystery In Space #70; Atomic Knights reprinted from Strange Adventures #156; Strange Adventures #56, 67, 78, Mystery In Space #36 and 40 .... 15.00
❑231, Aug 1971; reprints from Strange Adventures #67, #83, #125, and #160, and Adam Strange from Mystery in Space #71 .... 10.00
❑232, Oct 1971; Reprints from Mystery In Space #14 and 17; Adam Strange reprinted from Mystery In Space #72; Star Rovers reprinted from Mystery In Space #66 .... 10.00
❑233, Dec 1971; Reprints from Strange Adventures #14, 51 and 161; Star Rovers reprinted from Mystery In Space #69; Adam Strange reprinted from Mystery In Space #73 .... 10.00
❑234, Feb 1972; Reprints from Strange Adventures #54 adn 59; Adam Strange reprinted from Mystery In Space #74; Star Rovers reprinted from Mystery In Space #74 .... 10.00
❑235, Apr 1972; Reprints from Strange Adventures #72 and 119; Adam Strange reprinted from Mystery in Space #75 .... 10.00
❑236, Jun 1972; Reprints from Mystery in Space #27 and Strange Adventures #98; Star Rovers reprinted from Mystery in Space #77; Adam Strange reprinted from Mystery in Space #76 . 10.00
❑237, Jun 1972, Reprints from Strange Adventures #72 and Mystery In Space #7; Adam Strange reprinted from Mystery In Space #77 .... 10.00
❑238, Oct 1972, MA, CI (a); Reprints from Strange Adventures #19 and 78; Adam Strange reprinted from Mystery In Space #78 .... 10.00
❑239, Dec 1972, Adam Strange reprinted from Mystery In Space #79; Reprint from Strange Adventures #100; Adam Strange: Mystery In Space #79 .... 10.00
❑240, Feb 1973, Reprints from Mystery In Space #40 and Strange Adventures #74; Adam Strange reprinted from Mystery In Space #80 .... 10.00
❑241, Apr 1973, Reprints Adam Strange from Mystery in Space #81 .... 10.00
❑242, Jul 1973, Reprints Adam Strange from Mystery in Space #82 .... 10.00
❑243, Sep 1973, reprints from Strange Adventures #131 and Adam Strange from Mystery in Space #83 .... 10.00
❑244, Nov 1973, Reprints Adam Strange from Mystery in Space #84; Reprints from Strange Adventures #52; Final Issue 10.00

Strange Adventures
DC / Vertigo

❑1, Nov 1999 .... 2.50
❑2, Dec 1999 .... 2.50
❑3, Jan 2000 .... 2.50
❑4, Feb 2000 .... 2.50

Strange Attractors
Retrografix

❑1, May 1993 .... 4.00
❑1/2nd, Jul 1994; 2nd printing 2.75
❑2, Aug 1993 .... 3.50
❑2/2nd, Jul 1993; 2nd printing 2.75
❑3, Nov 1993 .... 3.50
❑3/2nd, Jun 1993; 2nd printing 2.75
❑4, Feb 1994 .... 3.00
❑4/2nd, Jun 1994; 2nd printing 2.75
❑5, May 1994 .... 3.00
❑6, Aug 1994 .... 2.50
❑7, Nov 1994 .... 2.50
❑8, Jan 1995 .... 2.50
❑9, Apr 1995 .... 2.50
❑10, Jun 1995 .... 2.50
❑11, Sep 1995 .... 2.50
❑12, Nov 1995 .... 2.50
❑13, Feb 1996 .... 2.50
❑14, Jul 1996 .... 2.50
❑15, Feb 1997 .... 2.50

Strange Attractors: Moon Fever
Caliber

❑1, Feb 1997, b&w 2.95
❑2 1997 .... 2.95
❑3 1997 .... 2.95

Strange Avenging Tales
Fantagraphics

❑1, Feb 1997 .... 2.95

Strange Bedfellows
Hippy

❑1 2002; Adult 5.95
❑2, Jun 2002; Adult 5.95

Strange Brew
Aardvark-Vanaheim

❑1, b&w 3.00

Strange Combat Tales
Marvel / Epic

❑1, Oct 1993 .... 2.50
❑2, Nov 1993 .... 2.50
❑3, Dec 1993 .... 2.50
❑4, Jan 1984 .... 2.50

Strange Day
Alternative

❑1, ca. 2005 .... 3.95

Strange Days
Eclipse

❑1, Nov 1984 .... 1.50
❑2, Feb 1985 .... 1.50
❑3, Apr 1985 .... 1.50

Strange Detective Tales: Dead Love
Oddgod Press

❑1, Aug 2005 .... 3.95

Strange Embrace
Atomeka

❑1, Mar 1993, b&w 3.95
❑2, May 1993, b&w 3.95
❑3, Jul 1993, b&w 3.95

Strange Girl
Image

❑1, Jun 2005 .... 2.95
❑2, Jul 2005 .... 2.95
❑3, Oct 2005 .... 2.95
❑4, Aug 2005 .... 2.99
❑5, Jan 2006 .... 2.99
❑6, Feb 2006 .... 2.99
❑7, May 2006 .... 2.99
❑8, Jun 2006 .... 2.99
❑9, Jul 2006 .... 2.99
❑11, Nov 2006 .... 2.99
❑12, Jan 2007 .... 2.99

Strangehaven
Abiogenesis

❑1, Jun 1995 .... 5.00
❑1/2nd 2.95
❑2 .... 4.00
❑2/2nd 2.95
❑3, Dec 1995 .... 4.00
❑3/2nd 2.95
❑4, Jun 1996 .... 2.95
❑5, Nov 1996 .... 2.95
❑6, May 1997 .... 2.95
❑7 .... 2.95
❑8 1997 .... 2.95
❑9, Jun 1998 .... 2.95
❑10, Nov 1998 .... 2.95
❑11, Apr 1999 .... 2.95
❑12, Oct 1999 .... 2.95
❑13 .... 2.95
❑14 .... 2.95
❑15, May 2003 .... 2.95
❑16, ca. 2004 .... 2.95
❑17, Apr 2005 .... 2.95
❑18, ca. 2005; b&w 2.95

Strange Heroes
Lone Star

❑1, Jun 2000 .... 2.95
❑2 .... 2.95

Strange Killings: Body Orchard
Avatar

❑1 2002 .... 3.50
❑2 2002 .... 3.50
❑3 2002 .... 3.50
❑4 2002 .... 3.50
❑5 .... 3.50
❑6, Feb 2003 .... 3.50

Strange Killings: Necromancer
Avatar

❑1, Mar 2004 .... 3.50
❑2, Apr 2004 .... 3.50

Strange Killings: Strong Medicine
Avatar

❑1, Jul 2003 .... 3.50
❑2, Aug 2003 .... 3.50
❑2/A, Aug 2003; Wrap Cover 3.95
❑3, Oct 2003 .... 3.50

Strange Looking Exile
Robert Kirby

❑1 .... 2.00
❑2 .... 2.00
❑3 .... 2.00

Strangelove
Express / Entity

❑1, b&w 2.50
❑2, b&w 2.50

Stranger in a Strange Land
Rip Off

❑1, Jun 1989, b&w; Adult 2.00
❑2, May 1990, b&w; Adult 2.00
❑3, Sep 1991, b&w; Adult 2.50

Strangers
Malibu / Ultraverse

❑1, Jun 1993; O: The Strangers. 1: The Strangers. 1: The Night Man (out of costume) 2.00
❑1/Hologram, Jun 1993; hologram edition; Hologram edition 5.00
❑1/Ltd., Jun 1993; Ultra-limited edition . 4.00
❑2, Jul 1993; card 2.00
❑3, Aug 1993; 1: TNTNT 2.00
❑4, Sep 1993 A: Hardcase 2.00
❑5, Oct 1993; Rune 2.50
❑6, Nov 1993 .... 1.95
❑7, Dec 1993; Break-Thru 1.95
❑8, Jan 1994; O: The Solution 1.95
❑9, Feb 1994 .... 1.95
❑10, Mar 1994 .... 1.95
❑11, Apr 1994 .... 1.95
❑12, May 1994 .... 1.95
❑13, Jun 1994; KB (w); MGu (a); 1: Pilgrim. contains Ultraverse Premiere #4 .... 3.50
❑14, Jul 1994; 1: Byter 1.95

STRANGE ADVENTURES

Other grades: Multiply price above by 5/6 for VF/NM • 2/3 for VERY FINE • 1/3 for FINE • 1/5 for VERY GOOD • 1/8 for GOOD

Superman's Nemesis: Lex Luthor

A focal shift from good friends to bad enemies

©DC

Superman's Pal Jimmy Olsen

Cub reporter grows up, becomes Mr. Action

©DC

Superman: Speeding Bullets

First Superman Elseworlds casts Kal as Batman

©DC

Superman: The Dark Side

Man of Steel seduced by Apokolips' ruler

©DC

Superman: The Man of Steel

When three monthly titles just aren't enough

©DC

N-MINT

- ❑15, Aug 1994; 1: Lightshow. 1: Generator X. 1: Rodent ... 1.95
- ❑16, Sep 1994 ... 1.95
- ❑17, Oct 1994 A: Rafferty ... 1.95
- ❑18, Nov 1994 ... 1.95
- ❑19, Dec 1994 ... 1.95
- ❑20, Jan 1995; 1: Beater. 1: M.C. Zed ... 1.95
- ❑21, Feb 1995 ... 1.95
- ❑22, Mar 1995 ... 1.95
- ❑23, Apr 1995 ... 1.95
- ❑24, May 1995; Final Issue ... 1.95
- ❑Ann 1, Dec 1994; 64 pages ... 3.95

Strangers
Image

- ❑1, Mar 2003 ... 2.95
- ❑2, Apr 2003 ... 2.95
- ❑3, May 2003 ... 2.95
- ❑4, Jul 2003 ... 2.95
- ❑5, Aug 2003 ... 2.95
- ❑6, Sep 2003 ... 2.95

Strangers in Paradise
Antarctic

- ❑0, b&w ... 75.00
- ❑1, Nov 1993, b&w ... 65.00
- ❑1/2nd, Mar 1994, b&w; 2nd printing ... 5.00
- ❑1/3rd, Apr 1994, b&w; 3rd printing ... 3.00
- ❑2, Dec 1993, b&w ... 24.00
- ❑3, Feb 1994, b&w ... 18.00

Strangers in Paradise
Abstract

- ❑1, Sep 1994, b&w ... 30.00
- ❑1/Gold, Gold logo edition ... 4.00
- ❑1/2nd, Apr 1995, b&w; 2nd printing ... 2.75
- ❑2, Nov 1994, b&w ... 15.00
- ❑2/Gold, Gold logo edition ... 3.00
- ❑3, Jan 1995, b&w ... 12.00
- ❑3/Gold, Gold logo edition ... 3.00
- ❑4, Mar 1995, b&w ... 10.00
- ❑4/Gold, Gold logo edition ... 2.75
- ❑5, Jun 1995, b&w ... 10.00
- ❑5/Gold, Gold logo edition ... 2.75
- ❑6, Jul 1995, b&w ... 8.00
- ❑6/Gold, Gold logo edition ... 2.75
- ❑7, Sep 1995, b&w ... 8.00
- ❑7/Gold, Gold logo edition ... 2.75
- ❑8, Nov 1995, b&w ... 8.00
- ❑8/Gold, Gold logo edition ... 2.75
- ❑9, Jan 1996, b&w ... 8.00
- ❑9/Gold, Gold logo edition ... 2.75
- ❑10, Feb 1996, b&w ... 8.00
- ❑10/Gold, Gold logo edition ... 2.75
- ❑11 1996, b&w ... 5.00
- ❑11/Gold, Gold logo edition ... 2.75
- ❑12, May 1996, b&w ... 5.00
- ❑12/Gold, Gold logo edition ... 2.75
- ❑13, Jun 1996, b&w ... 4.00
- ❑13/Gold 1998; Gold logo edition ... 2.75
- ❑14, Jul 1996, b&w; continues in 3rd series (Image); Titled: Terry Moore's Strangers in Paradise; no gold logo edition ... 2.75

Strangers in Paradise
Homage

- ❑1, Oct 1996, JLee (a) ... 4.00
- ❑2, Dec 1996 ... 3.00
- ❑3, Jan 1997 ... 3.00
- ❑4, Feb 1997 ... 3.00
- ❑5, Apr 1997, cover says Mar, indicia says Apr ... 3.00
- ❑6, May 1997, b&w ... 3.00
- ❑7, Jul 1997, b&w ... 3.00
- ❑8, Aug 1997, b&w; Returns to Abstract ... 3.00
- ❑9, Sep 1997, b&w; returns to Abstract ... 3.00
- ❑10, Dec 1997, b&w ... 3.00
- ❑11, Dec 1997, b&w ... 3.00
- ❑12, Jan 1998, b&w ... 3.00
- ❑13, Mar 1998, b&w ... 3.00
- ❑14, Apr 1998, b&w ... 3.00
- ❑15, Jun 1998, b&w ... 3.00
- ❑16, Jul 1998, b&w ... 3.00
- ❑17, Sep 1998, b&w ... 3.00
- ❑18, Oct 1998, b&w ... 3.00
- ❑19, Nov 1998, b&w ... 3.00
- ❑20, Dec 1998, b&w ... 3.00
- ❑21, Feb 1999, b&w ... 3.00
- ❑22, Mar 1999, b&w ... 3.00
- ❑23, Mar 1999, b&w ... 3.00
- ❑24, Jun 1999, b&w ... 3.00
- ❑25, Jul 1999, b&w ... 3.00
- ❑26, Aug 1999, b&w ... 3.00
- ❑27, Sep 1999 ... 3.00
- ❑28, Nov 1999 ... 3.00
- ❑29, Dec 1999 ... 3.00
- ❑30, Feb 2000, b&w ... 3.00
- ❑31, Mar 2000 ... 2.95
- ❑32, May 2000 ... 2.95
- ❑33, May 2000 ... 2.95
- ❑34, Aug 2000 ... 2.95
- ❑35, Sep 2000 ... 2.95
- ❑36, Nov 2000 ... 2.95
- ❑37, Dec 2000 ... 2.95
- ❑38, Jan 2001 ... 2.95
- ❑39, Mar 2001 ... 2.95
- ❑40, Apr 2001 ... 2.95
- ❑41, Jun 2001 ... 2.95
- ❑42, Jul 2001 ... 2.95
- ❑43, Aug 2001 ... 2.95
- ❑44, Oct 2001 ... 2.95
- ❑45, Nov 2001 ... 2.95
- ❑46, Dec 2001 ... 2.95
- ❑47, Feb 2002 ... 2.95
- ❑48, Mar 2002 ... 2.95
- ❑49, Apr 2002 ... 2.95
- ❑50, May 2002 ... 2.95
- ❑51, Jun 2002 ... 2.95
- ❑52, Aug 2002 ... 2.95
- ❑53, Sep 2002 ... 2.95
- ❑54, Nov 2002 ... 2.95
- ❑55, Dec 2002 ... 2.95
- ❑56, Feb 2003 ... 2.95
- ❑57, Mar 2003 ... 2.95
- ❑58, May 2003 ... 3.00
- ❑59, Jul 2003 ... 3.00
- ❑60, Sep 2003 ... 3.00
- ❑61, Dec 2003 ... 3.00
- ❑62, Jan 2004 ... 3.00
- ❑63, Feb 2004 ... 3.00
- ❑64, May 2004 ... 3.00
- ❑65, Jun 2004 ... 2.95
- ❑66, Aug 2004 ... 2.95
- ❑67, Sep 2004 ... 2.95
- ❑68, Nov 2004 ... 2.95
- ❑69, Oct 2005 ... 2.95
- ❑70, Dec 2005 ... 3.00
- ❑71, Feb 2005 ... 3.00
- ❑72, Mar 2005 ... 3.00
- ❑73, Apr 2005 ... 3.00
- ❑74, Jun 2005 ... 3.00
- ❑75 2005 ... 3.00
- ❑76, Sep 2005 ... 3.00
- ❑77, Oct 2005 ... 3.00
- ❑78, Jan 2006 ... 2.95
- ❑Special 1, Feb 1999; Lyrics and Poems ... 4.00

Strangers in Paradise Sourcebook
Abstract

- ❑1, Oct 2003 ... 2.95

Stranger's Tale, A
Vineyard

- ❑1, b&w; cardstock cover ... 2.00

Stranger than Fiction
Impact

- ❑1 1998, b&w ... 1.99
- ❑2, Jul 1998, b&w ... 1.99
- ❑3 1998 ... 1.99
- ❑4 1998 ... 1.99

Strange Sports Stories
DC

- ❑1, Oct 1973, NC (c); FR (w); BO, DG, CS (a) ... 18.00
- ❑2, Dec 1973, FR (w); MA, DG, CS, IN (a) ... 9.00
- ❑3, Feb 1974, NC (c); FR (w); DG, CS (a) ... 7.00
- ❑4, Apr 1974, NC (c); DG, IN (a) ... 7.00
- ❑5, Jun 1974 ... 7.00
- ❑6, Aug 1974 ... 7.00

Strange Sports Stories
Adventure

- ❑1 ... 2.50
- ❑2, Jul 1992; Trading cards attached to cover ... 2.50
- ❑3 ... 2.50

Strange Stories
Avalon

- ❑1, b&w; reprints John Force and Magic Man stories ... 2.95

Strange Tales
Marvel

- ❑101, Oct 1962, JK (c); SL (w); SD, DH, JK (a); A: Human Torch. Human Torch features begin ... 900.00
- ❑102, Nov 1962, JK (c); SL (w); SD, DH, JK (a); A: Human Torch. A: Wizard. 1: Wizard ... 425.00
- ❑103, Dec 1962, JK (c); SL (w); SD, JK (a); A: Human Torch. 1: Zemu (ruler of the 5th Dimension) ... 300.00
- ❑104, Jan 1963, JK (c); SL (w); SD, JK (a); 1&O: Paste-Pot Pete. A: Human Torch ... 300.00
- ❑105, Feb 1963, JK (c); SL (w); SD, JK (a); A: Human Torch. V: Wizard. ... 300.00
- ❑106, Mar 1963, JK (c); SL (w); SD (a); A: Fantastic Four. A: Human Torch. V: Acrobat. Human Torch ... 225.00
- ❑107, Apr 1963, JK (c); SL (w); SD (a); A: Human Torch. A: Sub-Mariner. Human Torch vs. Sub-Mariner ... 250.00

N-MINT

❑108, May 1963, JK (c); SL (w); SD, JK (a); A: Fantastic Four. A: Human Torch ... 225.00
❑109, Jun 1963, JK (c); SL (w); SD, JK (a); 1: Circe (later becomes Sersi). A: Human Torch ... 225.00
❑110, Jul 1963, JK (c); SL (w); SD (a); 1: The Ancient One. 1: Doctor Strange. 1: Wong. A: Human Torch; 1: Nightmare ... 1250.00
❑111, Aug 1963, JK (c); SL (w); SD (a); 1: Asbestos. 1: Baron Mordo. 1: Eel I (Leopold Stryke). 2: Doctor Strange. A: Human Torch ... 350.00
❑112, Sep 1963, JK (c); SL (w); SD (a); A: Fantastic Four. A: Human Torch. 1: Eel ... 150.00
❑113, Oct 1963, SD (c); SL (w); SD (a); 1: Plantman. A: Human Torch; 1: Doris Evans ... 150.00
❑114, Nov 1963, JK (c); SL (w); SD, JK (a); A: Human Torch. A: Baron Mordo. A: Doctor Strange. V: Acrobat. Villain (The Acrobat) appears, dressed as Captain America ... 350.00
❑115, Dec 1963, SD (c); SL (w); SD (a); O: Doctor Strange. A: Human Torch. A: Sandman (Marvel) ... 450.00
❑116, Jan 1964, JK (c); SL (w); SD (a); A: Thing. A: Human Torch. A: Doctor Strange. V: Puppet Master ... 125.00
❑117, Feb 1964, SD (c); SL (w); SD (a); A: Fantastic Four. A: Human Torch. A: Doctor Strange. V: Baron Mordo. 2: Eel ... 100.00
❑118, Mar 1964, SD, JK (c); SL (w); SD (a); A: Fantastic Four. A: Human Torch. A: Doctor Strange. V: Wizard ... 100.00
❑119, Apr 1964, JK (c); SL (w); SD (a); A: Human Torch. A: Spider-Man. A: Doctor Strange. 1: Rabble Rouser; 1: Aggamo ... 125.00
❑120, May 1964, JK (c); SL (w); SD, JK (a); A: X-Men. A: Fantastic Four. A: Human Torch. A: Iceman. A: Doctor Strange ... 125.00
❑121, Jun 1964, SD, JK (c); SL (w); SD (a); A: Human Torch. A: Doctor Strange. V: Plantman ... 125.00
❑122, Jul 1964, SD, JK (c); SL (w); SD (a); A: Human Torch. A: Doctor Strange. A: Doctor Doom ... 125.00
❑123, Aug 1964, JK (c); SL (w); SD (a); 1&O: The Beetle. A: Thing. A: Human Torch. A: Thor ... 125.00
❑124, Sep 1964, SD (c); SL (w); SD (a); A: Thing. A: Human Torch ... 75.00
❑125, Oct 1964, JK (c); SL (w); SD (a); A: Human Torch ... 75.00
❑126, Nov 1964, JK (c); SL (w); SD (a); 1: Dormammu. 1: Clea. A: Human Torch ... 90.00
❑127, Dec 1964, SD, JK (c); SL (w); SD (a); A: Human Torch. 2: Clea; 2: Dormammu; 1: The Mindless Ones ... 75.00
❑128, Jan 1965, JK (c); SL (w); SD (a); A: Human Torch ... 75.00
❑129, Feb 1965, JK (c); SL (w); SD (a); A: Human Torch; 1: Tiboro ... 75.00
❑130, Mar 1965, JK (c); SL (w); SD (a); A: Human Torch. A: Beatles ... 90.00
❑131, Apr 1965, SD (c); SL (w); SD (a); A: Thing. A: Human Torch ... 75.00
❑132, May 1965, SD, JK (c); SL (w); SD (a); A: Thing. A: Human Torch ... 75.00
❑133, Jun 1965, JK (c); SL (w); SD (a); A: Thing. A: Human Torch. 1: Shazana ... 75.00
❑134, Jul 1965, JK (c); SL (w); SD (a); A: Torch. A: Human Torch. A: Watcher. Last Human Torch issue ... 75.00
❑135, Aug 1965, JK (c); SL (w); SD, JK (a); O: Nick Fury, Agent of SHIELD. 1: S.H.I.E.L.D.. 1: Nick Fury, Agent of SHIELD. 1: Hydra. A: Doctor Strange ... 125.00
❑136, Sep 1965, SD, JK (c); SD, SL (w); SD, JK (a); A: Doctor Strange. A: Nick Fury. 1: SHIELD barbershop; 1: Rama Kaliph; 1: Aged Genghis ... 75.00
❑137, Oct 1965, SD, JSe (c); SL (w); SD, JK (a); 1: Leslie Farrington; 1: Arnold Brown ... 50.00
❑138, Nov 1965, JSe (c); SL (w); SD, JK (a); 1: Eternity ... 50.00
❑139, Dec 1965, JK (c); SL (w); SD, JK (a) ... 50.00
❑140, Jan 1966, JK (c); SL (w); SD, DH, JK (a ... 50.00
❑141, Feb 1966, JK (c); SL (w); SD, JK (a); 1: The Fixer. 1: Mentallo; D: Arnold Brown ... 50.00
❑142, Mar 1966, JK (c); SL (w); SD, JK (a); 2: Mentallo; 2: The Fixer ... 50.00

N-MINT

❑143, Apr 1966, JK (c); SD, SL (w); SD, JK (a) ... 50.00
❑144, May 1966, JK (c); SD, SL (w); SD, JK (a); 1: The Druid. 1: Jasper Sitwell (SHIELD agent); 1: Asti the All-Seeing; 1: Tazza ... 50.00
❑145, Jun 1966, JK (c); SL (w); SD, DH, JK (a); 1: Mister Rasputin; 1: The Illusions of Ikonn ... 50.00
❑146, Jul 1966, SD (c); SD, JK, SL (w); SD, DH, JK (a); 1: Advanced Idea Mechanics (A.I.M.) ... 50.00
❑147, Aug 1966, JK (c); SL (w); BEv, DH, JK (a); 1&O: Kaluu ... 50.00
❑148, Sep 1966, BEv (c); JK (w); BEv, DH, JK (a); O: The Ancient One. 2: Kaluu; O: Kaluu ... 75.00
❑149, Oct 1966, JK (c); BEv, JK (a)s ... 50.00
❑150, Nov 1966, BEv (c); SL (w); JB, BEv, JK (a); 1: Umar. 1st John Buscema art at Marvel ... 50.00
❑151, Dec 1966, JK, JSo (c); SL (w); BEv, JK, JSo (a); 1st Jim Steranko art at Marvel ... 75.00
❑152, Jan 1967, BEv (c); SL (w); BEv, JK, JSo (a); 1: Emir Ali-Bey (Supreme Hydra); Doctor Strange; Nick Fury ... 50.00
❑153, Feb 1967, JSo (c); SL (w); JK, JSo (a); 1: Agent Bronson of SHIELD (Supreme Hydra); Doctor Strange; Nick Fury ... 50.00
❑154, Mar 1967, JSo, SL (w); JSo (a); 1: Dreadnought (original); 1: Veritas; 2: Agent Bronson of SHIELD (Supreme Hydra) ... 50.00
❑155, Apr 1967, JSo (c); JSo, SL (w); JSo (a); 1: Professor Anton Trojak; Doctor Strange; Nick Fury ... 50.00
❑156, May 1967, JSo, SL (w); JSo (a); A: Daredevil. 1: Zom ... 50.00
❑157, Jun 1967, JSo (c); JSo, SL (w); HT, JSo (a); 1: Living Tribunal; 2: Zom ... 50.00
❑158, Jul 1967, BEv (c); JSo (w); HT, JSo (a); D: Baron Strucker; 2: Living Tribunal ... 50.00
❑159, Aug 1967, JSo (c); JSo (w); HT, JSo (a); O: Nick Fury, Agent of SHIELD. 1: Val Fontaine. A: Captain America; 1: Gaff; O: Fury ... 60.00
❑160, Sep 1967, DA (c); JSo (w); HT, JSo (a); A: Captain America ... 50.00
❑161, Oct 1967, JSo (c); JSo (w); JSo, DA (a); A: Captain America. 1: Nebulos ... 50.00
❑162, Nov 1967, DA (c); JSo (w); JSo, DA (a); A: Captain America. 2: Val Fontaine; 2: Gaff; 2: Nebulos ... 50.00
❑163, Dec 1967, JSo (c); JSo (w); JSo, DA (a); 1: Clay Quartermain ... 50.00
❑164, Jan 1968, DA (c); JSo (w); BEv, JSo, DA (a); 1: Yandroth ... 50.00
❑165, Feb 1968, JSo (c); JSo (w); JSo, DA (a); 1: Voltorg; 2: Yandroth ... 50.00
❑166, Mar 1968, DA (c); JSo (w); GT, JSo, JSt, DA (a); 2: Voltorg ... 50.00
❑167, Apr 1968, JSo (c); JSo (w); JSo, DA (a); 1: Prime Mover; 2: Clay Quartermain ... 50.00
❑168, May 1968, DA (c); JSo (w); JSo, DA (a); original series continues as Doctor Strange; Nick Fury, Agent of SHIELD series ends ... 50.00
❑169, Jun 1973, 1&O: Brother Voodoo. second series begins ... 15.00
❑170, Aug 1973, 1: Bambu; D: Damballah; D: Papa Jambo; O: Brother Voodoo ... 10.00
❑171, Oct 1973, 1: Baron Samedi; D: Baron Samedi ... 7.00
❑172, Dec 1973, Brother Voodoo; Includes Voodoo, reprinted from Astonishing #56 ... 7.00
❑173, Feb 1974, RB (c); GC (a); 1: Black Talon I (Desmond Drew). Marvel Value Stamp #45: Mantis ... 7.00
❑174, Jun 1974, JB, JM (a); O: Golem. Marvel Value Stamp #44: Absorbing Man ... 7.00
❑175, Aug 1974, SL (w); SD, JK (a); reprints Amazing Adventures #1; Marvel Value Stamp #10: Power Man ... 7.00
❑176, Oct 1974, Marvel Value Stamp #94: Electro ... 7.00
❑177, Dec 1974, FB (c); TD (a); Golem series ends ... 7.00
❑178, Feb 1975, JSn (c); JSn (w); JSn (a); O: Warlock. 1: Magus; Reprinted in Warlock (2nd Series) #1 ... 15.00
❑179, Apr 1975, JSn (c); JSn (w); JSn (a); 1: Pip. A: Warlock ... 10.00

N-MINT

❑180, Jun 1975, JSn (c); JSn (w); JSn (a); 1: Gamora. A: Warlock; Reprinted in Warlock (2nd Series) #1 ... 10.00
❑181, Aug 1975, JSn (c); JSn (w); AM, JSn (a); A: Warlock ... 10.00
❑182, Oct 1975, reprinted from Strange Tales #123 and 124 ... 3.00
❑183, Dec 1975, reprinted from Strange Tales #130 and 131 ... 3.00
❑184, Feb 1976, reprinted from Strange Tales #132 and 133 ... 3.00
❑185, Apr 1976, reprinted from Strange Tales #134 and 135 ... 3.00
❑185/30¢, Apr 1976, 30¢ regional price variant; reprinted from Strange Tales #134 and 135 ... 20.00
❑186, Jun 1976, reprinted from Strange Tales #136 and 137 ... 3.00
❑186/30¢, Jun 1976, 30¢ regional price variant; reprinted from Strange Tales #136 and 137 ... 20.00
❑187, Aug 1976, reprinted from Strange Tales #138 and 139 ... 3.00
❑188, Oct 1976, reprinted from Strange Tales #140 and 141 ... 3.00
❑Ann 1, ca. 1962, reprinted from Journey Into Mystery #53, 55 and 59; Strange Tales #73, 76 and 78; Tales of Suspense #7 and 9; Tales to Astonish #1, 6 and 7 ... 325.00
❑Ann 2, ca. 1963, A: Human Torch. A: Spider-Man. Spider-Man new, all others reprinted from Strange Tales #67; Strange Worlds #1, 2 and 3; World of Fantasy #16 ... 350.00

Strange Tales
Marvel

❑1, Apr 1987; Doctor Strange, Cloak & Dagger ... 1.50
❑2, May 1987 ... 1.25
❑3, Jun 1987 ... 1.25
❑4, Jul 1987 ... 1.25
❑5, Aug 1987 ... 1.25
❑6, Sep 1987 ... 1.25
❑7, Oct 1987; Defenders ... 1.25
❑8, Nov 1987 ... 1.25
❑9, Dec 1987 ... 1.25
❑10, Jan 1988 ... 1.25
❑11, Feb 1988 ... 1.25
❑12, Mar 1988; Black Cat ... 1.25
❑13, Apr 1988 A: Punisher ... 1.75
❑14, May 1988 A: Punisher ... 1.75
❑15, Jun 1988 ... 1.25
❑16, Jul 1988 ... 1.25
❑17, Aug 1988 ... 1.50
❑18, Sep 1988; A: X-Factor ... 1.25
❑19, Oct 1988; Final Issue ... 1.25

Strange Tales
Marvel

❑1, Nov 1994; prestige format; acetate overlay cover ... 6.95

Strange Tales
Marvel

❑1, Sep 1998; gatefold summary; A: Werewolf. A: Man-Thing ... 4.99
❑2, Oct 1998; gatefold summary; A: Werewolf. A: Man-Thing ... 4.99
❑3, Jan 1999 ... 4.99
❑4, Dec 1998 ... 4.99

Strange Tales: Dark Corners
Marvel

❑1, May 1998; gatefold summary ... 3.99

Strange Weather Lately
Metaphrog

❑1 1997 ... 3.50
❑2, Dec 1997 ... 3.50
❑3, Feb 1998 ... 3.50
❑4 1998 ... 3.50
❑5, Jun 1998 ... 3.50
❑6, Aug 1998 ... 3.50
❑7, Oct 1998 ... 3.00
❑8 1999 ... 3.00
❑9 1999 ... 3.00
❑10, May 1999 ... 3.50

Other grades: Multiply price above by 5/6 for VF/NM • 2/3 for VERY FINE • 1/3 for FINE • 1/5 for VERY GOOD • 1/8 for GOOD

Superman: The Man of Tomorrow

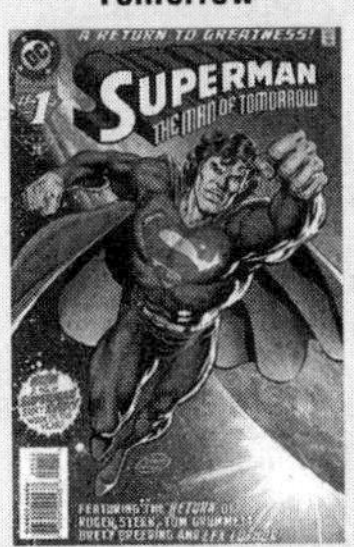

Fill-in for those pesky skip weeks
©DC

Superman: The Secret Years

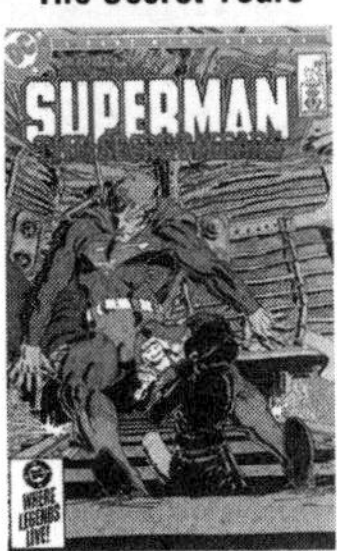

Bridges the gap between Boy and Man
©DC

Super Mario Bros.

Pre-hero Valiant plumbed videogame depths
©Valiant

Supernaturals

Monster masks highlight of each issue
©Marvel

Super-Villain Team-Up

Doom, Red Skull kept trying to make friends
©Marvel

N-MINT

Strange Wink
Dark Horse

❑1, Mar 1998, b&w; Reprints from A1 #4 and Pathways to Fantasy #1; Anthology 2.95
❑2, Apr 1998, b&w; Reprints from A1 #1, Epic Illustrated #24, A1 True Life Bikini Confidential #1 and Asylum #1; Anthology 2.95
❑3, May 1998, b&w; Anthology 2.95

Strange Worlds
Eternity

❑1, b&w; Reprints 3.95

Strange Worlds
North Coast

❑1, b&w; magazine; cardstock cover 4.00

Strangling Desdemona
Ningen Manga

❑1, b&w 2.95

Strapped
Gothic Images

❑1, Nov 1994 ..... 2.00
❑2, Jan 1995 ..... 2.00
❑3, May 1995 ..... 2.00
❑4, Jul 1995 ..... 2.00

Strata
Renegade

❑1, Jan 1986, b&w 2.00
❑2, Mar 1986, b&w 2.00
❑3 1986 ..... 2.00
❑4 1986 ..... 2.00
❑5 ..... 2.00

Stratonaut
Nightwynd

❑1, Oct 1991, b&w 2.50
❑2, Dec 1991, b&w 2.50
❑3, Feb 1992, b&w 2.50
❑4, Apr 1992, b&w 2.50

Stratosfear
Caliber

❑1 ..... 2.95

Strawberry Shortcake
Marvel / Star

❑1, Apr 1985 ..... 1.00
❑2, Jun 1985 ..... 1.00
❑3, Aug 1985 ..... 1.00
❑4, Oct 1985 ..... 1.00
❑5, Dec 1985 ..... 1.00
❑6, Feb 1986 ..... 1.00

Straw Men
All American

❑1, Oct 1989, b&w; Adult 1.95
❑2 1989, b&w; Adult 1.95
❑3 1989, b&w; Adult 1.95
❑4, Jan 1990, b&w; Adult 1.95
❑5 1990, b&w; Adult 1.95
❑6 1990, b&w; Adult 1.95
❑7 1990, b&w; Adult 1.95
❑8 1990, b&w; Adult 1.95

Stray Bullets
El Capitan

❑1, Mar 1995, b&w 4.00
❑1/2nd; 2nd printing 3.00
❑1/3rd; indicia says #3; third print 3.00

N-MINT

❑1/4th; 4th printing 3.00
❑2, Apr 1995, b&w 2.95
❑2/2nd; 2nd printing 2.95
❑2/3rd; 3rd printing 2.95
❑2/4th, Nov 1995; 4th printing 2.95
❑3, May 1995, b&w 2.95
❑3/2nd, Nov 1995; 2nd printing 2.95
❑4, Jun 1995, b&w; indicia contains information for issue #3 ..... 2.95
❑5 1995, b&w; indicia contains information for issue #4 ..... 2.95
❑6, Sep 1995, b&w 2.95
❑7, Nov 1995, b&w 2.95
❑8, Feb 1996, b&w 2.95
❑9, May 1996, b&w 2.95
❑10, Aug 1996, b&w 2.95
❑11, Oct 1996, b&w 2.95
❑12, Jan 1997, b&w 2.95
❑13, Apr 1997, b&w 2.95
❑14, Jun 1997, b&w 2.95
❑15, Jul 1998, b&w 2.95
❑16, Aug 1998, b&w 2.95
❑17, Nov 1998, b&w 2.95
❑18, Feb 1999, b&w 2.95
❑19, Apr 1999, b&w 2.95
❑20, Jul 1999, b&w 2.95
❑21 ..... 2.95
❑22 ..... 3.50
❑23 2002 ..... 3.50
❑24, Mar 2002 ..... 3.50
❑25 2002 ..... 3.50
❑26 2002 ..... 3.50
❑27 2002 ..... 3.50
❑28 2002 ..... 3.50
❑29 2003 ..... 3.50
❑30, Jan 2003 ..... 3.50
❑31, Jan 2003 ..... 3.50
❑32, Jan 2003 ..... 3.50
❑33, Jan 2004, b&w 3.50
❑34, Jan 2004 ..... 3.50
❑35, Jan 2004 ..... 3.50

Stray Cats
Twilight Twins

❑1, Jan 1999, b&w 2.50

Stray Toasters
Marvel / Epic

❑1, BSz (c); BSz (w); BSz (a) 4.50
❑2, BSz (c); BSz (w); BSz (a) 4.50
❑3, BSz (c); BSz (w); BSz (a) 4.50
❑4, BSz (w); BSz (a) 4.50

Street Fighter
Devil's Due

❑7 2004 ..... 2.95
❑7/Foil 2004 ..... 8.25
❑8 2004 ..... 2.95
❑8/Foil 2004 ..... 12.95
❑9 2004 ..... 2.95
❑9/Foil 2004 ..... 7.50
❑10 2004 ..... 2.95
❑10/Foil 2004 ..... 4.00
❑11 ..... 2.95
❑11/Variant 4.00
❑11/Foil 12.95
❑12 ..... 2.95
❑12/Variant 4.00

N-MINT

❑13 ..... 2.95
❑13/Variant 4.00
❑14 ..... 2.95
❑14/Variant 4.00

Streetfighter
Ocean

❑1, Aug 1986; 1: Streetfighter 2.00
❑2, Nov 1986; 2: Streetfighter 2.00
❑3, Feb 1987 ..... 2.00
❑4, May 1987 ..... 2.00

Street Fighter
Malibu

❑1, Sep 1993 ..... 2.95
❑1/Gold, Sep 1993; gold foil edition 5.00
❑2, Oct 1993 ..... 2.95
❑2/Gold, Oct 1993; gold foil edition 4.00
❑3, Nov 1993 ..... 2.95
❑3/Gold, Nov 1993; gold foil edition 4.00

Street Fighter
Image

❑1, Sep 2003 ..... 2.95
❑1/A/2nd, Sep 2003 ..... 5.00
❑1.1, Sep 2003; Madureira cover 2.25
❑1/A, Oct 2003 ..... 2.95
❑1/B, Nov 2003 ..... 2.95
❑1/2nd, Jan 2004 ..... 2.95
❑2, Oct 2003 ..... 2.95
❑2/A, Nov 2003 ..... 2.95
❑3, Nov 2003 ..... 2.95
❑3/C, Nov 2003; Chen cover 5.00
❑3/A, Dec 2003 ..... 2.95
❑3/B, Jan 2004 ..... 2.95
❑4, Dec 2003 ..... 2.95
❑4/C, Dec 2003; Chen cover 5.00
❑4/A, Jan 2004 ..... 2.95
❑5, Feb 2004 ..... 2.95
❑5/A, Feb 2004; Shinkiro cover 5.00
❑6, Apr 2004 ..... 2.95
❑6/Dynamic, Apr 2004; Foil Cover 5.00

Street Fighter: The Battle for Shadaloo
DC

❑1; polybagged with trading card and temporary tattoos 3.95

Street Fighter II
Tokuma Shoten

❑1, Apr 1994 ..... 2.95

Street Fighter II
Viz

❑1, Apr 1994 ..... 2.95
❑2, May 1994 ..... 2.95
❑3, Jun 1994 ..... 2.95
❑4, Jul 1994 ..... 2.95
❑5, Aug 1994 ..... 2.95
❑6, Sep 1994 ..... 2.95
❑7, Oct 1994 ..... 2.95
❑8, Nov 1994 ..... 2.95

Street Fighter II: The Animated Movie
Viz

❑1 ..... 2.95
❑2 ..... 2.95
❑3 ..... 2.95
❑4 ..... 2.95
❑5 ..... 2.95

Other grades: Multiply price above by 5/6 for VF/NM • 2/3 for VERY FINE • 1/3 for FINE • 1/5 for VERY GOOD • 1/8 for GOOD

Street Heroes 2005
Eternity

❑1, Jan 1989, b&w 1.95
❑2, Feb 1989, b&w 1.95
❑3, Mar 1989, b&w 1.95

Street Music
Fantagraphics

❑1, b&w 2.95
❑2, b&w 2.95
❑3, b&w 2.95
❑4, b&w 2.95
❑5, b&w 2.95
❑6, b&w 2.95

Street Poet Ray (Blackthorne)
Blackthorne

❑1, Apr 1989, b&w 2.00
❑2, b&w 2.00

Streets
DC

❑1, ca. 1993 4.95
❑2, ca. 1993 4.95
❑3, ca. 1993 4.95

Street Sharks
Archie

❑1, Jan 1996; based on toy line and animated series 1.50
❑2, Feb 1996 1.50
❑3, Mar 1996 1.50

Street Sharks
Archie

❑1, May 1996 1.50
❑3, Aug 1996 1.50

Street Wolf
Blackthorne

❑1, Jul 1986, b&w 2.00
❑2, Sep 1986, b&w 2.00
❑3, Dec 1986, b&w 2.00

Strike!
Eclipse

❑1, Aug 1987; 1: Strike; O: Sgt. Strike ... 1.75
❑2, Sep 1987; Reprints story from All-Thrill Comics #9 (9/1941); O: Sgt. Strike 1.75
❑3, Oct 1987; Reprints story from All-Thrill Comics #9 (9/1944) 1.75
❑4, Nov 1987; Reprints story from All-Thrill Comics, Vol. 2 #4 (5/1945) .. 1.75
❑5, Dec 1987; Reprints story from All-Thrill Comics #2, (1/1944) 1.75
❑6, Feb 1988; Reprints story from All-Thrill Comics Vol. 2 #8 (8/1946); O: Sgt. Strike; Final Issue 1.75

Strikeback!
Malibu / Bravura

❑1, Oct 1994 2.95
❑2, Nov 1994 2.95
❑3, Dec 1994; Final issue; series announced as six issues, but title cancelled after Marvel's purchase of Malibu 2.95

Strikeback!
Image

❑1, Jan 1996; Reprints Strikeback (Malibu) #1 with new cover 2.50
❑2, Feb 1996; Reprints Strikeback (Malibu) #2 with new cover 2.50
❑3, Mar 1996; Reprints Strikeback (Malibu) #3 with new cover 2.50
❑4, Apr 1996 2.50
❑5, Jun 1996; Final Issue 2.50
❑6 1996 2.50

Strike Force America
Comico

❑1, Aug 1992 2.50

Strike Force America
Comico

❑1; Polybagged with one of three different cards 2.95

Strike Force Legacy
Comico

❑1, Oct 1993 3.95

Strikeforce: Morituri
Marvel

❑1, Dec 1986; BA (c); BA (a); 1: Strikeforce: Morituri. Whilce Portacio's 1st pro work 2.00
❑2, Jan 1987 BA (c); BA (a) 1.50
❑3, Feb 1987 BA (c); BA (a) 1.50
❑4, Mar 1987 BA (c); BA (a) 1.75
❑5, Apr 1987 BA (c); BA (a) 1.25
❑6, May 1987 BA (c); BA (a) 1.25
❑7, Jun 1987 BA (c); BA (a) 1.25
❑8, Jul 1987 BA (c); BA (a) 1.25
❑9, Aug 1987 BA (c); BA (a) 1.25
❑10, Sep 1987; 1st full story by Whilce Portacio 1.25
❑11, Oct 1987 BA (c); BA (a) 1.25
❑12, Nov 1987 BA (c); BA (a) 1.25
❑13, Dec 1987; Giant-size; BA (c); BA (a) 1.50
❑14, Jan 1988 BA (c); BA (a) 1.25
❑15, Feb 1988 BA (c); BA (a) 1.25
❑16, Mar 1988 1.25
❑17, Apr 1988 1.25
❑18, May 1988 BA (c); BA (a) 1.25
❑19, Jun 1988 BA (c); BA (a) 1.25
❑20, Jul 1988 BA (c); BA (a) 1.25
❑21, Sep 1988 1.25
❑22, Oct 1988 1.25
❑23, Nov 1988 1.25
❑24, Dec 1988 1.50
❑25, Jan 1989 1.50
❑26, Feb 1989 1.50
❑27, Mar 1989 1.50
❑28, Apr 1989 1.50
❑29, May 1989 1.50
❑30, Jun 1989 1.50
❑31, Jul 1989; Final Issue 1.50

Strikeforce: Morituri: Electric Undertow
Marvel

❑1, Dec 1989; Strikeforce: Morituri 3.95
❑2, Dec 1989; Strikeforce: Morituri 3.95
❑3, Jan 1990; Strikeforce: Morituri 3.95
❑4, Feb 1990; Strikeforce: Morituri 3.95
❑5, Mar 1990; Strikeforce: Morituri 3.95

Striker
Viz

❑1, b&w 2.75
❑2, b&w 2.75
❑3, b&w 2.75
❑4, b&w 2.75

Striker: Secret of the Berserker
Viz

❑1, b&w 2.75
❑2, b&w 2.75
❑3, b&w 2.75
❑4, b&w 2.75

Strike! vs. Sgt. Strike Special
Eclipse

❑1, May 1988 1.95

Strippers and Sex Queens of the Exotic World
Fantagraphics

❑1; Adult 3.95
❑2; Adult 3.95
❑3, Jun 1994, b&w; cardstock cover 3.95
❑4, Oct 1994, b&w; Final Issue; 48 pages; Adult 3.95

Strips
Rip Off

❑1, Dec 1989, b&w; Adult 2.50
❑2, Feb 1990, b&w; Adult 2.50
❑3, Apr 1990, b&w; Adult 2.50
❑4, Jun 1990, b&w; Adult 2.50
❑5, Nov 1990, b&w; Adult 2.50
❑6, Dec 1990, b&w; Adult 2.50
❑7, Feb 1991, b&w; Adult 2.50
❑8, Mar 1991, b&w; Adult 2.50
❑9, Jun 1991, b&w; series goes on hiatus 2.50
❑10, b&w; series returns (1997); wraparound cover 2.95
❑11, b&w; wraparound cover 2.95
❑12, b&w; Adult 2.95
❑Special 1; reprints Rip Off issues with additional material 2.95
❑Special 2; reprints Rip Off issues with additional material 2.95

Strong Guy Reborn
Marvel

❑1, Sep 1997; gatefold summary; One-shot 2.99

Stronghold
Devil's Due

❑1, Oct 2005 4.95

Strontium Bitch
Fleetway-Quality

❑1 2.95
❑2 2.95

Strontium Dog
Eagle

❑1, Dec 1985; O: Johnny Alpha 1.50
❑2, Jan 1985 1.50
❑3, Feb 1985 1.50
❑4, Mar 1985 1.50

Strontium Dog
Fleetway-Quality

❑1 1987 1.50
❑2 1987 1.25
❑3 1987 1.25
❑4 1987 1.25
❑5 1987 1.25
❑6 1987 1.25
❑7 1988 1.25
❑8, Feb 1988 1.25
❑9, Mar 1988 1.25
❑10, Apr 1988 1.25
❑11 1988 1.25
❑12 1988 1.25
❑13 1988 1.50
❑14 1988; double issue #14/15 1.50
❑15 1988 1.50
❑16 1988; double issue #16/17 1.50
❑17 1988 1.50
❑18 1988 1.50
❑19 1.50
❑20, Dec 1988 1.50
❑21, Jan 1989 1.50
❑22, Feb 1989 1.50
❑23 1.50
❑24 1.50
❑25 1.50
❑26 1.50
❑27 1.50
❑28 1.50
❑29 1.50
❑Special 1; Special Edition #1; AMo (w); Reprints from 2000 A.D. #87-94 1.50

Strüdel War
Rough Copy

❑1; Flip-book 2.95

Stryfe's Strike File
Marvel

❑1, Jan 1993; Follows X-Cutioner's Song x-over series 1.75
❑1/2nd, Jan 1993; Gold cover 1.75

Stryke
London Night

❑0 3.00
❑0/A; alternate cover 4.00
❑1 3.00

Strykeforce
Image

❑1, May 2004 2.99
❑2, Apr 2004 2.99
❑3, Aug 2004 2.99
❑4 2004 2.99
❑5 2004 2.99

Students of the Unusual
3 Finger Prints

❑1, ca. 2005 2.95
❑2, ca. 2005 2.95
❑3, Dec. 2005 2.95
❑4, Mar 2006 2.95
❑5, Jun 2006 3.50
❑6, Sep 2006 3.50

Studio Comics Presents
Studio

❑1, May 1995; Battle Bunnies 2.50

Other grades: Multiply price above by 5/6 for VF/NM • 2/3 for VERY FINE • 1/3 for FINE • 1/5 for VERY GOOD • 1/8 for GOOD

Supreme

Image's answer to The Man of Steel
©Image

Supreme Power

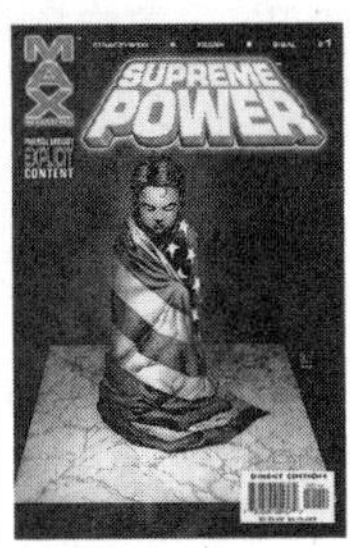

Straczynski provides Squadron Supreme origins
©Marvel

Swamp Thing

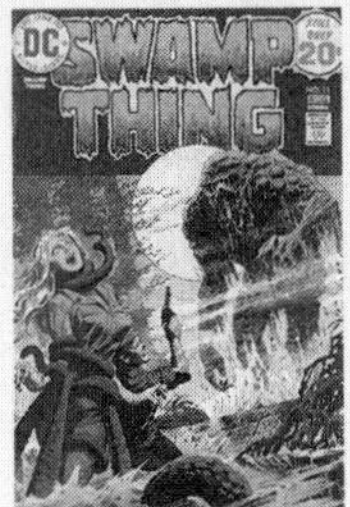

Wrightson and Wolfman's shambling hero
©DC

Swamp Thing

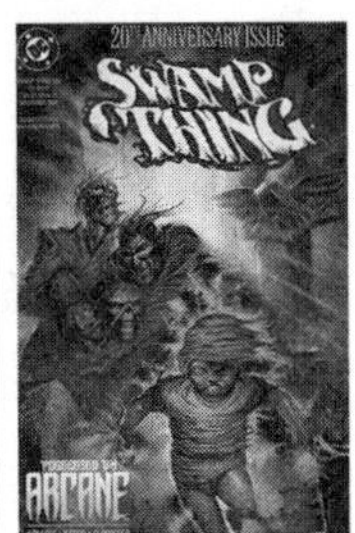

Elemental origins revealed in second series
©DC

Swamp Thing

Swamp Thing intervenes with rebellious teen
©DC

N-MINT

Stuff of Dreams
Fantagraphics

- ❑1 .... 3.95
- ❑2 .... 3.95
- ❑3 .... 3.95

Stunt Dawgs
Harvey

- ❑1, Mar 1993 .... 1.25

Stupid
Image

- ❑1, May 1993; parody 1.95

Stupid Comics
Oni

- ❑1, Jul 2000, b&w; collects Mahfood's strips from Java Magazine 2.95

Stupid Comics
Image

- ❑1, Sep 2003 .... 2.95
- ❑2, Oct 2003 .... 2.95
- ❑3, Sep 2005 .... 2.99

Stupid Heroes
Mirage / Next

- ❑1, Aug 1994; 1: Cinder; 1: Muscle Master; 1: Rock Boy; 1: Scott Poundstone; Includes trading cards ... 2.75
- ❑2, Oct 1994; 1: MISTer; Includes trading cards 2.75
- ❑3, Dec 1994; Includes trading cards 2.75

Stupidman
Parody

- ❑1 .... 2.50

Stupidman: Burial for a Buddy
Parody

- ❑1/A, b&w 2.50
- ❑1/B, b&w 2.50

Stupidman: Rain on the Stupidmen
Parody

- ❑1/A, b&w 2.50
- ❑1/B, b&w 2.95

Stupid, Stupid Rat Tails
Cartoon Books

- ❑1, Dec 1999 .... 2.95
- ❑2, Jan 2000 .... 2.95
- ❑3, Feb 2000; Happy Solstice reprinted from Bone Holiday Special 1993 .... 2.95

Stygmata
Express / Entity

- ❑0 1994; O: Stygmata 2.95
- ❑1, Jul 1994, b&w; enhanced cover 2.95
- ❑2 1994; Foil-stamped cover 2.95
- ❑3, Oct 1994, b&w 2.95

Subhuman
Dark Horse

- ❑1, Nov 1998 .... 2.95
- ❑2, Dec 1998 .... 2.95
- ❑3, Jan 1999 .... 2.95
- ❑4, Feb 1999 .... 2.95

Submarine Attack
Charlton

- ❑30 1961 .... 12.00
- ❑31, Dec 1962 .... 9.00
- ❑32, Mar 1962 .... 9.00
- ❑33 1962 .... 9.00
- ❑34, Jul 1962 .... 9.00
- ❑35 1962 .... 9.00
- ❑36, Nov 1962 .... 9.00
- ❑37, Jan 1963 .... 9.00
- ❑38, Mar 1963 .... 9.00
- ❑39, May 1963 .... 9.00
- ❑40, Jul 1963 .... 9.00
- ❑41, Sep 1963 .... 7.00
- ❑42, Nov 1963 .... 7.00
- ❑43, Jan 1964 .... 7.00
- ❑44, Mar 1964 .... 7.00
- ❑45, Jun 1964 .... 7.00
- ❑46 1964 .... 7.00
- ❑47, Nov 1964 .... 7.00
- ❑48, Jan 1965 .... 7.00
- ❑49, Mar 1965 .... 7.00
- ❑50 1965 .... 7.00
- ❑51, Aug 1965 .... 7.00
- ❑52, Oct 1965 .... 7.00
- ❑53, Dec 1965 .... 7.00
- ❑54, Feb 1966 .... 7.00

Sub-Mariner
Marvel

- ❑1, May 1968, JB (c); JB (a); O: Sub-Mariner, Carl Gafford L.O.C., Peter Sanderson, L.O.C.; Reprinted in Tales to Astonish (Vol. 2) #1 .... 125.00
- ❑2, Jun 1968, JB (c); JB (a); A: Triton. Richard Howell L.O.C 45.00
- ❑3, Jul 1968, JB (c); JB (a); A: Triton..... 35.00
- ❑4, Aug 1968, JB (c); JB (a) 35.00
- ❑5, Sep 1968, JB (c); JB (a); 1&O: Tiger Shark 1: Dr. Dorcas; 1: Diane Arliss; Reprinted in Tales to Astonish (Vol. 2) #5 .... 30.00
- ❑6, Oct 1968, JB (c); JB (a); Reprinted in Tales to Astonish (Vol. 2) #6 .... 25.00
- ❑7, Nov 1968, JB (c); JB (a); 1: Ikthon. Cover is black-and-white photo of New York parade; drawing of Namor superimposed 25.00
- ❑8, Dec 1968, JB (c); JB (a); V: Thing; Reprinted in Tales to Astonish (Vol. 2) #8 .... 75.00
- ❑8/2nd, JB (c); JB (a); V: The Thing. 2nd printing; Reprinted in Tales to Astonish (Vol. 2) #8 .... 1.50
- ❑9, Jan 1969, 1: Lemuria. 1: Naga 30.00
- ❑10, Feb 1969, O: Naga; Reprinted in Tales to Astonish (Vol. 2) #1 .... 25.00
- ❑11, Mar 1969 .... 20.00
- ❑12, Apr 1969 .... 20.00
- ❑13, May 1969, D: Naga 20.00
- ❑14, Jun 1969, A: Human Torch. D: Toro; Namor vs. Human Torch; Carl Gafford L.O.C.; Reprinted in Tales to Astonish (Vol. 2) #14 .... 50.00
- ❑15, Jul 1969 .... 20.00
- ❑16, Aug 1969, 1: Thakos; 2: Dr. Walter Newell 20.00
- ❑17, Sep 1969, 1: Kormok; 1: The Stalker 20.00
- ❑18, Oct 1969 .... 20.00
- ❑19, Nov 1969, 1&O: Stingray 20.00
- ❑20, Dec 1969 .... 20.00
- ❑21, Jan 1970, D: Seth (Namor's advisor) 20.00
- ❑22, Feb 1970, A: Doctor Strange. 1: The Nameless One 20.00
- ❑23, Mar 1970, 1&O: Orka 20.00
- ❑24, Apr 1970 .... 20.00
- ❑25, May 1970, O: Atlantis 20.00
- ❑26, Jun 1970, D: Red Raven 20.00
- ❑27, Jul 1970, SB (c); SB (a); 1: Commander Kraken 20.00
- ❑28, Aug 1970 .... 20.00
- ❑29, Sep 1970, SB (c); SB (a); V: Hercules 20.00
- ❑30, Oct 1970, SB (c); SB (a); A: Captain Marvel 20.00
- ❑31, Nov 1970, 2: Sting-Ray 15.00
- ❑32, Dec 1970, 1&O: Llyra 15.00
- ❑33, Jan 1971, SB (c); SB, JM (a); 1: Namora 15.00
- ❑34, Feb 1971, SB (c); SB, JM (a); A: Hulk. A: Silver Surfer. Leads into Defenders #1 .... 70.00
- ❑35, Mar 1971, SB (c); SB, JM (a); A: Hulk. A: Silver Surfer 35.00
- ❑36, Apr 1971, SB (c); BWr, SB (a); 1: The Octo-Meks. Wedding of Lady Dorma . 15.00
- ❑37, May 1971, SB (c); RA (a); D: Lady Dorma 15.00
- ❑38, Jun 1971, JSe, RA (a); O: Sub-Mariner 15.00
- ❑39, Jul 1971, RA, JM (a) 15.00
- ❑40, Aug 1971, A: Spider-Man. 1: Turalla 15.00
- ❑41, Sep 1971, GT (c); GT (a) 10.00
- ❑42, Oct 1971, GK (c); GT (a) 10.00
- ❑43, Nov 1971; Giant-size 10.00
- ❑44, Dec 1971, A: Human Torch 10.00
- ❑45, Jan 1972, Reprints Sub-Mariner Comics (Vol. 1) #42 .... 10.00
- ❑46, Feb 1972, GK (c); GC (a); D: Leonard McKenzie; 2: Sting-Ray 10.00
- ❑47, Mar 1972, GK (c); GC (a); 1: Cindy Jones 10.00
- ❑48, Apr 1972, GK (c); GC, BEv (a) 10.00
- ❑49, May 1972, GK (c); GC (a) 10.00
- ❑50, Jun 1972, GK (c); BEv (w); BEv (a); 1: Namorita 10.00
- ❑51, Jul 1972, GK (c); BEv (a) 10.00
- ❑52, Aug 1972, GK (c); BEv (w); BEv (a) 10.00
- ❑53, Sep 1972, SB (c); BEv (w); BEv (a); Reprinted from Sub-Mariner (Vol. 1) #41 .... 10.00
- ❑54, Oct 1972, JSt (c); BEv (w); BEv (a); 1: Lorvex. Reprinted from Sub-Mariner (Vol. 1) #39 .... 10.00
- ❑55, Nov 1972, BEv (c); BEv (w); BEv (a); 1: Torg 10.00
- ❑56, Dec 1972, 1: Tamara Rahn. 1: Coral; 1: Tamara Rahn 10.00
- ❑57, Jan 1973 .... 10.00
- ❑58, Feb 1973, GK (c); BEv (w); BEv (a) 10.00
- ❑59, Mar 1973, BEv (c); BEv (w); BEv (a); Namorita apperance 10.00
- ❑60, Apr 1973, RB (c); BEv (w); BEv (a) 10.00
- ❑61, May 1973, 1: Dr. Hydro 10.00
- ❑62, Jun 1973, Tales of Atlantis 10.00
- ❑63, Jul 1973, 1: Arkus. 1: Volpan. Tales of Atlantis 10.00
- ❑64, Aug 1973, 1: Madoxx. Tales of Atlantis 10.00
- ❑65, Sep 1973, Tales of Atlantis 10.00
- ❑66, Oct 1973, 1: Raman. Tales of Atlantis 10.00
- ❑67, Nov 1973, 2: Dr. Damon Walthers; 2: Clayton Wilson; New Black Costume for Namor 10.00

N-MINT

❑68, Jan 1974, 1: Force (Clayton Wilson); 1: Dr. Henry Croft; 1: Dr. Joseph Jennings.......... 10.00
❑69, Mar 1974, Marvel Value Stamp #20: Brother Voodoo.......... 10.00
❑70, May 1974; Marvel Value Stamp #98: Puppet Master.......... 10.00
❑71, Jul 1974; Marvel Value Stamp #52: Quicksilver.......... 10.00
❑72, Sep 1974; DA (a); Marvel Value Stamp #100: Galactus.......... 10.00
❑Special 1, ca. 1971; Sub-Mariner Special Edition #1; SB (c); SL (w); GC, BEv (a); Reprinted from Tales to Astonish #70-73.......... 10.00
❑Special 2, ca. 1972; Sub-Mariner Special Edition #2; BEv (c); SL (w); GC, BEv (a); Reprinted from Tales to Astonish #74-76.......... 15.00

Submissive Suzanne
Fantagraphics / Eros

❑1, b&w; 24 pages; Adult.......... 2.50
❑2, b&w; 24 pages; Adult.......... 2.50
❑3, b&w; Adult.......... 2.95
❑4, b&w; Adult.......... 2.95
❑5, b&w; Adult.......... 2.95
❑6, Aug 1998, b&w; Adult.......... 2.95

Subspecies
Eternity

❑1, May 1991.......... 2.50
❑2 1991.......... 2.50
❑3 1991.......... 2.50
❑4 1991.......... 2.50

Substance Affect
Crazyfish

❑1.......... 2.95

Substance Quarterly
Substance

❑1, Spr 1994, b&w; 1&o: Misfits.......... 3.00
❑2, Sum 1994, b&w; 1: Faerie King.......... 3.00
❑3, Fal 1994, b&w; 1: Nash; 1: Platt; O: Faerie King; Includes Nash sneak peek.......... 3.00

Subtle Violents
Cry for Dawn

❑1, ca. 1991; Adult.......... 15.00
❑1/A, ca. 1991; San Diego Comic-Con edition.......... 160.00

Suburban High Life
Slave Labor

❑1, Jun 1987; Adult.......... 1.75
❑1/2nd, Feb 1988; 2nd printing; Blue circle on front cover a darker blue; Adult.......... 1.75
❑2, Aug 1987; Adult.......... 1.75
❑3, Oct 1987; Adult.......... 1.75

Suburban High Life
Slave Labor

❑1, May 1988; Oversized.......... 5.95

Suburban Nightmares
Renegade

❑1, Jul 1988, b&w.......... 2.00
❑2, Jul 1988, b&w.......... 2.00
❑3, Aug 1988, b&w.......... 2.00
❑4, Aug 1988, b&w.......... 2.00

Suburban She-Devils
Marvel

❑1, Dec 1991; Cover reads Suburban Jersey Ninja She-Devils.......... 1.50

Suburban Voodoo
Fantagraphics

❑1, Nov 1992, b&w.......... 2.50

Succubus
Fantagraphics / Eros

❑1, b&w; Adult.......... 2.50

Sucker the Comic
Troma

❑1.......... 2.50

Suckle
Fantagraphics

❑1, Jan 1996, b&w; digest; NN; Adult.......... 14.95

Sugar & Spike
DC

❑1/2nd, Mar 2002; Facsimile Edition.......... 2.95
❑37, Nov 1961; Halloween issue.......... 125.00
❑38, Jan 1962, Christmas issue with Christmas cards.......... 125.00
❑39, Mar 1962, Valentine's issue with valentines.......... 125.00
❑40, May 1962, 1: Space Sprout.......... 125.00
❑41, Jul 1962.......... 75.00
❑42, Sep 1962, Vacation issue.......... 75.00
❑43, Nov 1962, Halloween issue.......... 75.00
❑44, Jan 1963, Christmas issue with Christmas cards.......... 75.00
❑45, Mar 1963, Valentine's issue with valentines.......... 75.00
❑46, May 1963, Wedding cover.......... 75.00
❑47, Jul 1963.......... 75.00
❑48, Sep 1963.......... 75.00
❑49, Nov 1963, Halloween issue.......... 75.00
❑50, Jan 1964, Christmas issue with Christmas cards.......... 75.00
❑51, Mar 1964, Valentine's issue with valentines.......... 55.00
❑52, May 1964.......... 55.00
❑53, Jul 1964.......... 55.00
❑54, Sep 1964.......... 55.00
❑55, Nov 1964, Halloween issue.......... 55.00
❑56, Jan 1965, Christmas issue with Christmas cards.......... 55.00
❑57, Mar 1965, Valentine's issue with valentines.......... 55.00
❑58, May 1965.......... 55.00
❑59, Jul 1965.......... 55.00
❑60, Sep 1965.......... 55.00
❑61, Nov 1965, A: Uncle Charley. Halloween issue.......... 50.00
❑62, Jan 1966, Christmas issue with Christmas cards.......... 50.00
❑63, Mar 1966, Valentine's issue with valentines.......... 50.00
❑64, May 1966.......... 50.00
❑65, Jul 1966, Summer issue.......... 50.00
❑66, Sep 1966.......... 50.00
❑67, Nov 1966, Halloween issue.......... 50.00
❑68, Jan 1967, Christmas issue.......... 50.00
❑69, Mar 1967, 1: Tornado Tot.......... 50.00
❑70, May 1967, Sugar & Spike become giants.......... 50.00
❑71, Jul 1967.......... 50.00
❑72, Sep 1967, 1: Bernie the Brain.......... 50.00
❑73, Nov 1967.......... 50.00
❑74, Jan 1968.......... 50.00
❑75, Mar 1968, 1: M.C.P. pellet.......... 50.00
❑76, May 1968.......... 50.00
❑77, Jul 1968, A: Bernie the Brain.......... 50.00
❑78, Sep 1968.......... 50.00
❑79, Nov 1968.......... 50.00
❑80, Jan 1969, A: Bernie the Brain.......... 50.00
❑81, Mar 1969.......... 35.00
❑82, May 1969, Sugar & Spike as grown-ups.......... 35.00
❑83, Jul 1969, super-powers.......... 35.00
❑84, Sep 1969.......... 35.00
❑85, Oct 1969; DC Giant F-2; reprints stories from #24, #41, #43, #48, and #72.......... 35.00
❑86, Nov 1969.......... 35.00
❑87, Jan 1970, 1: Marvin the Midget.......... 35.00
❑88, Mar 1970.......... 35.00
❑89, May 1970.......... 35.00
❑90, Jul 1970, 1: Flumsh.......... 35.00
❑91, Sep 1970.......... 35.00
❑92, Nov 1970.......... 35.00
❑93, Jan 1971.......... 35.00
❑94, Mar 1971, 1: Raymond.......... 35.00
❑95, May 1971.......... 35.00
❑96, Jul 1971; Reprints from Sugar & Spike #2 and 3.......... 35.00
❑97, Sep 1971.......... 35.00
❑98, Nov 1971; Final Issue.......... 35.00

Sugar Buzz
Slave Labor

❑1, Jan 1998, b&w.......... 2.95
❑2 1998.......... 2.95
❑3, Jun 1998.......... 2.95
❑4 1998.......... 2.95

Sugar Ray Finhead
Wolf

❑1.......... 2.50
❑2.......... 2.95
❑3.......... 2.95
❑4.......... 2.95
❑5; Publisher changes to Jump Back Productions.......... 2.95
❑6, Jul 1994.......... 2.95
❑7, Nov 1994, b&w.......... 2.95
❑8, Feb 1995, b&w.......... 2.95
❑9, Aug 1995, b&w.......... 2.95
❑10, Sep 1997.......... 2.95
❑11, Oct 1998.......... 2.95

Sugarvirus
Atomeka

❑1, b&w; NN.......... 3.95

Suicide Squad
DC

❑1, May 1987 HC (c); LMc (a).......... 1.25
❑2, Jun 1987.......... 1.00
❑3, Jul 1987; D: Mindboggler. V: Female Furies.......... 1.00
❑4, Aug 1987; Join Chronos; Join Nightshade.......... 1.00
❑5, Sep 1987; Join Penguin.......... 1.00
❑6, Oct 1987.......... 1.00
❑7, Nov 1987.......... 1.00
❑8, Dec 1987.......... 1.00
❑9, Jan 1988; 1: Duchess. Millennium Week 4.......... 1.00
❑10, Feb 1988; A: Batman. 1: Reverand Craemer.......... 1.00
❑11, Mar 1988 A: Speedy, Vixen.......... 1.00
❑12, Apr 1988; Join Vixen.......... 1.00
❑13, May 1988; A: Justice League International. continued from Justice League International #13; Suicide Squad view of Justice League.......... 1.00
❑14, Jun 1988.......... 1.00
❑15, Jul 1988.......... 1.00
❑16, Aug 1988 A: Shade, the Changing Man.......... 1.00
❑17, Sep 1988; V: Jihad.......... 1.00
❑18, Oct 1988; Ravan vs. Bronze Tiger.......... 1.00
❑19, Nov 1988.......... 1.00
❑20, Dec 1988.......... 1.00
❑21, Dec 1988.......... 1.00
❑22, Jan 1989.......... 1.00
❑23, Jan 1989; 1: Oracle; Invasion tie-in; Join Count Vertigo.......... 15.00
❑24, Feb 1989; Join Doctor Light; Join Punch & Jewlee; Join Shrike III; Join Ravan.......... 1.00
❑25, Mar 1989.......... 1.00
❑26, Apr 1989; D: Rick Flagg Jr.; D: Rustam.......... 1.00
❑27, May 1989; D: Mayflower; D: Sparkler; Crossover with Firestorm, Captain Atom, and Checkmate.......... 1.00
❑28, May 1989; V: Force of July; Crossover with Firestorm, Captain Atom, and Checkmate.......... 1.00
❑29, Jun 1989; Crossover with Firestorm, Captain Atom, and Checkmate.......... 1.00
❑30, Jun 1989; D: Lady Liberty; D: Silent Majority; Crossover with Firestorm, Captain Atom, and Checkmate.......... 1.00
❑31, Jul 1989.......... 1.00
❑32, Aug 1989; Join Major Victory.......... 1.00
❑33, Sep 1989; Join Poison Ivy.......... 1.00
❑34, Oct 1989; D: Briscoe.......... 1.00
❑35, Nov 1989; D: Doctor Light; D: Flo; D: Lashina; 1: Artemis III.......... 1.00
❑36, Dec 1989.......... 1.00
❑37, Jan 1990.......... 1.00
❑38, Feb 1990; Oracle revealed to be Barbara Gordon.......... 1.00
❑39, Mar 1990.......... 1.00
❑40, Apr 1990; Includes Batman poster.......... 1.00
❑41, May 1990.......... 1.00
❑42, Jun 1990.......... 1.00
❑43, Jul 1990.......... 1.00
❑44, Aug 1990; Flash.......... 1.00
❑45, Sep 1990.......... 1.00
❑46, Oct 1990.......... 1.00
❑47, Nov 1990; D: Ravan.......... 1.00
❑48, Dec 1990; Joker.......... 1.00
❑49, Jan 1991; Norm Breyfogle cover.......... 1.00
❑50, Feb 1991; 1: Thinker II (Cliff Carmichael); Giant-Size; 52 pages.......... 1.50
❑51, Mar 1991.......... 1.00
❑52, Apr 1991; Return Doctor Light.......... 1.00
❑53, May 1991; Join Stalnoivok.......... 1.00
❑54, Jun 1991; Join Thinker II.......... 1.00
❑55, Jul 1991.......... 1.00

Other grades: Multiply price above by 5/6 for VF/NM • 2/3 for VERY FINE • 1/3 for FINE • 1/5 for VERY GOOD • 1/8 for GOOD

Sword of Sorcery

Chaykin adapts Lieber's fantasy stories

©DC

Swords of Cerebus

Reprint series skipped an issue with #6

©Aardvark-Vanaheim

Swords of the Swashbucklers

Intergalactic pirates seek treasure

©Marvel

Tales Calculated to Drive You Mad

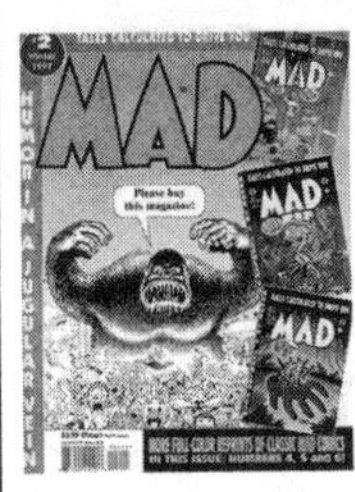

Takes the place of Mad Super Specials

©E.C.

Tales from the Crypt

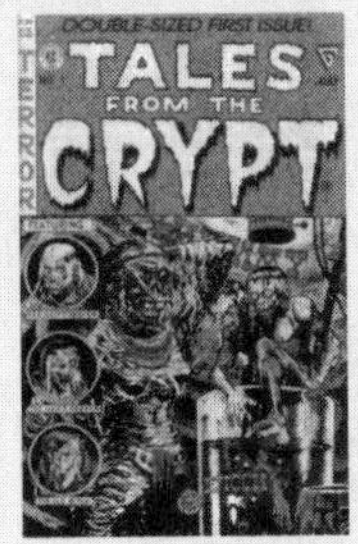

Crypt Keeper's origin appears in first issue

©Gladstone

	N-MINT
❑56, Aug 1991	1.00
❑57, Sep 1991	1.00
❑58, Oct 1991; A: Black Adam. D: The Writer (Grant Morrison); D: Enforcer; War of the Gods tie-in	1.00
❑59, Nov 1991; Batman; Story takes place before Adventures of Superman #484 an Aquaman (4th Series) #1	1.00
❑60, Dec 1991	1.00
❑61, Jan 1992	1.00
❑62, Feb 1992; D: Atom III (Adam Cray)	1.00
❑63, Mar 1992	1.00
❑64, Apr 1992	1.25
❑65, May 1992	1.25
❑66, Jun 1992; Final Issue	1.25
❑Ann 1, Dec 1988; A: Manhunter. secret of Argent revealed	1.50

Suicide Squad
DC

❑1, Nov 2001; D: Big Sir; D: Clock King; D: Multi-Man	2.50
❑2, Dec 2001	2.50
❑3, Jan 2002; Join Killer Frost; D: Bolt...	2.50
❑4, Feb 2002; D: Iron Major	2.50
❑5, Mar 2002	2.50
❑6, Apr 2002; Blackstar joins team	2.50
❑7, May 2002	2.50
❑8, Jun 2002	2.50
❑9, Jul 2002	2.50
❑10, Aug 2002	2.50
❑11, Oct 2002	2.50
❑12, Nov 2002; Final issue; D: Havana; D: Rustam (of Onslaught); V: Rustam (of Onslaught)	2.50

Suikoden III: The Successor of Fate
Tokyopop

❑1, May 2004	9.99
❑2, Jul 2004	9.99
❑3, Sep 2004	9.99
❑4, Nov 2004	9.99
❑5, Feb 2005	9.99
❑6, May 2005	9.99
❑7, Aug 2005	9.99
❑8, Nov 2005	9.99

Suit
Virtual

❑1/A, May 1996; Digest	3.99
❑1, May 1996	2.50
❑2/A, Jun 1997; Digest	3.99
❑2, Jun 1997	3.99

Sullengray
Ape Entertainment

❑1, ca. 2005	3.50

Sultry Teenage Super Foxes
Solson

❑1, b&w	2.00
❑2, b&w	2.00

Summer Love
Charlton

❑46, ca. 1965	95.00
❑47, Oct 1966, Beatles cover drawings in ad for Help! and Hard Days Night	70.00
❑48, ca. 1967	15.00

Sunburn
Alternative

	N-MINT
❑1, Aug 2000, b&w; smaller than normal comic book	2.95

Sun Devils
DC

❑1, Jul 1984	1.50
❑2, Aug 1984	1.50
❑3, Sep 1984	1.50
❑4, Oct 1984	1.50
❑5, Nov 1984	1.50
❑6, Dec 1984	1.50
❑7, Jan 1985	1.50
❑8, Feb 1985	1.50
❑9, Mar 1985	1.50
❑10, Apr 1985	1.50
❑11, May 1985	1.50
❑12, Jun 1985	1.50

Sundiata: A Legend of Africa
NBM

❑1	15.95

Sunfire & Big Hero Six
Marvel

❑1, Sep 1998	2.50
❑2, Oct 1998	2.50
❑3, Nov 1998	2.50

Sunglasses After Dark
Verotik

❑1, Nov 1995; Adult	2.95
❑2, Jan 1996; Adult	2.95
❑3, Mar 1996; Adult	2.95
❑4, Aug 1996; Adult	2.95
❑5, Oct 1996; Adult	2.95
❑6, Nov 1996; Adult	3.95

Sunrise
Harrier

❑1, Dec 1986	1.95
❑2, May 1987	1.95

Sun-Runners
Pacific

❑1, Feb 1984	1.50
❑2, Mar 1984; 1: Mike Mahogany	1.50
❑3, May 1984	1.50
❑4, Nov 1984; 1st issue at Eclipse	1.50
❑5, May 1984; Includes Sun Runners portfolio by Glenn Johnson (7 pages)	1.75
❑6, Oct 1984	1.75
❑7, Dec 1984; Series resumes with Tales of the Sun Runners #1 at Sirius Comics; Final Issue	1.75
❑Holiday 1; Double-size	1.95
❑Special 1; Special edition	1.95

Super Bad James Dynomite
Idea & Design Works

❑1, Jan 2006	3.99
❑2, Apr 2006	3.99
❑3, Aug 2006	3.99
❑4, Nov 2006	3.99

Superboy
DC

	N-MINT
❑93, Dec 1961, CS (c); A: Legion of Super-Heroes	90.00
❑94, Jan 1962	75.00
❑95, Mar 1962	75.00
❑96, Apr 1962	75.00
❑97, Jun 1962, Superbaby; Krypto	75.00
❑98, Jul 1962, CS (c); CS (a); 1&O: Ultra Boy. A: Legion of Super-Heroes; 1: Marla	100.00
❑99, Sep 1962	75.00
❑100, Oct 1962, 100th anniversary issue; CS (a); 1: Phantom Zone villains. A: Legion of Super-Heroes; Map Of Krypton	175.00
❑101, Dec 1962	60.00
❑102, Jan 1963, Superbaby back-up	60.00
❑103, Mar 1963, Red K story	60.00
❑104, Apr 1963, O: Phantom Zone	60.00
❑105, Jun 1963, Superboy; Krypto; Superbaby	60.00
❑106, Jul 1963, Superboy; Superbaby...	60.00
❑107, Sep 1963	60.00
❑108, Oct 1963	60.00
❑109, Dec 1963	60.00
❑110, Jan 1964	60.00
❑111, Mar 1964	60.00
❑112, Apr 1964	60.00
❑113, Jun 1964	60.00
❑114, Jul 1964	60.00
❑115, Sep 1964, Atomic Superboy	60.00
❑116, Oct 1964	60.00
❑117, Dec 1964, A: Legion	60.00
❑118, Jan 1965	60.00
❑119, Mar 1965	60.00
❑120, Apr 1965	60.00
❑121, Jun 1965, Clark loses his super-powers; Jor-El back-up	50.00
❑122, Jul 1965	50.00
❑123, Sep 1965	50.00
❑124, Oct 1965, CS (c); 1: Insect Queen	50.00
❑125, Dec 1965, CS (c); 1&O: Kid Psycho; Irene Vartanoff L.O.C.; Krypto reprinted in Superman Family #176	50.00
❑126, Jan 1966, O: Krypto	50.00
❑127, Mar 1966, 1: Bee-Boy	50.00
❑128, Apr 1966, A: Dev-Em. A: Kryptonite Kid. Imaginary Story	50.00
❑129, May 1966; Giant-size; aka 80 Page Giant #G-22	75.00
❑130, Jun 1966, Superbaby	40.00
❑131, Jul 1966	40.00
❑132, Sep 1966	40.00
❑133, Oct 1966, A: Robin. Hall of Fame Classic; Irene Vartanoff L.O.C.	40.00
❑134, Dec 1966, Krypto back-up	40.00
❑135, Jan 1967, Hall of Fame Classic	40.00
❑136, Mar 1967, CS (a); A: White Kryptonite. reprints story from Adventure Comics #279	40.00
❑137, Apr 1967	40.00
❑138, Jun 1967; Giant-size; aka 80 Page Giant #G-35	55.00
❑139, Jun 1967	40.00
❑140, Jul 1967	40.00
❑141, Sep 1967, 1: Ron-Avon	35.00
❑142, Oct 1967, A: Beppo. Superboy #80	35.00
❑143, Dec 1967, NA (c); Superboy #91	35.00
❑144, Jan 1968, CS (c)	35.00
❑145, Mar 1968, NA (c); FS (a); Ma and Pa Kent turn younger	35.00
❑146, Apr 1968, NA (c); CS (a)	35.00

Other grades: Multiply price above by 5/6 for VF/NM • 2/3 for VERY FINE • 1/3 for FINE • 1/5 for VERY GOOD • 1/8 for GOOD

❑147, Jun 1968; Giant-size; CS, JM (a); O: Saturn Girl. O: Cosmic Boy. aka 80 Page Giant #G-47; new story w/ reprints from Superboy #93 and #98, Action Comics #276, Adventure Comics #293, and Superman #147 50.00
❑148, Jun 1968, NA (c); CS, JAb (a); George Klein's last DC work 25.00
❑149, Jul 1968, NA (c); FR (w); Frank Robbins' first Superboy work 25.00
❑150, Sep 1968, NA (c); FR (w); JAb (a); V: Mr. Cipher 25.00
❑151, Oct 1968, NA (c); FR (w); JAb (a) 25.00
❑152, Dec 1968, NA (c); FR (w); WW (a) 25.00
❑153, Jan 1969, NA (c); FR (w); WW (a) 25.00
❑154, Mar 1969, NA, IN (c); FR (w); WW (a) 25.00
❑155, Apr 1969, NA (c); FR (w); WW (a); Letters column includes Frank Robbins autobiography 25.00
❑156, Jun 1969; Giant-size; aka Giant #G-59 65.00
❑157, Jun 1969, NA (c); FR (w); WW (a); 1: Bash Bashford; Includes material reprinted from Superman Ann #2 25.00
❑158, Jul 1969, NA (c); FR (w); WW (a); Letter column includes Bob Brown biography 25.00
❑159, Sep 1969, NA (c); FR (w); WW (a); V: Luthor; Letter page contains Wally Wood biography 25.00
❑160, Oct 1969, NA (c); FR (w); WW (a) 25.00
❑161, Dec 1969, NA (c); FR (w); WW (a); Mark Evanier L.O.C 25.00
❑162, Jan 1970 25.00
❑163, Mar 1970, NA (c); FR (w); CS (a); Includes material reprinted from Superboy #52 25.00
❑164, Apr 1970, NA (c); FR (w) 25.00
❑165, Jun 1970; Giant-size; CS (c); CS (a); aka Giant #G-71; reprints Adventure #210 & #283, and Superman #161 50.00
❑166, Jun 1970, NA (c); FR (w) 25.00
❑167, Jul 1970, NA (c); FR (w); Tony Isabella L.O.C 25.00
❑168, Sep 1970, NA (c); FR (w) 25.00
❑169, Oct 1970 20.00
❑170, Dec 1970 20.00
❑171, Jan 1971 20.00
❑172, Mar 1971, A: Legion of Super-Heroes. LSH back-ups begin 20.00
❑173, Apr 1971, NA (c); GT, DG (a); O: Cosmic Boy 20.00
❑174, Jun 1971; Giant-size; aka Giant #G-83; reprints Adventure #219, #225, and #262, Superboy #53 and #105 30.00
❑175, Jun 1971, NA (c); MA (a) 20.00
❑176, Jul 1971, NA (c); MA, GT, WW (a); A: Legion of Super-Heroes. O: Invisible Kid 20.00
❑177, Sep 1971; Giant-size; DG (c); MA (a); 48 pages 20.00
❑178, Oct 1971; Giant-size; NA (c); MA (a); 48 pages 20.00
❑179, Nov 1971; Giant-size; Reprint from Superboy (1st Series) #92 15.00
❑180, Dec 1971; Giant-size; 48 pages 15.00
❑181, Jan 1972; Giant-size; reprints Adventure #355 15.00
❑182, Feb 1972; Giant-size; 48 pages 20.00
❑183, Mar 1972; Giant-size; 52 pages; Superboy; Legion Of Super-Heroes 12.00
❑184, Apr 1972; Giant-size; O: Dial "H" For Hero; 48 pages; Dial H For Hero: House of Mystery #156; Superboy; Legion of Super-Heroes 12.00
❑185, May 1972, NC (c); CS (a); A: Legion of Super-Heroes. a.k.a. DC 100-Page Super Spectacular #185; Reprints from Adventure #208, #289 and 323, Brave and the Bold #60, Hit Comics #46, Sensation #1, and Star Spangled Comics #55; wraparound cover 12.00
❑186, May 1972; 48 pages; Dial 'H' For Hero: House of Mystery #157 12.00
❑187, Jun 1972; 48 pages; Superboy; Dial 'H' for Hero: House of Mystery #162; Bob Rozakis L.O.C 12.00
❑188, Jul 1972, O: Karkan 12.00
❑189, Aug 1972 12.00
❑190, Sep 1972, Superboy; Legion of Super-Heroes 12.00
❑191, Oct 1972, O: Sunboy; Legion of Super-Heroes; Superboy 12.00
❑192, Dec 1972, Superbaby 12.00
❑193, Feb 1973, New Costumes for Chameleon Boy, Shrinking Violet, Karate Kid, & Duo Damsel 12.00
❑194, Apr 1973 12.00
❑195, Jun 1973, 1: Wildfire. A: Legion of Super-Heroes. Wildfire joins team 12.00
❑196, Jul 1973, last Superboy solo story 12.00
❑197, Sep 1973, NC (c); MA, DC (a); Legion of Super-Heroes stories begin 20.00
❑198, Oct 1973, V: Fatal Five 12.00
❑199, Nov 1973 12.00
❑200, Feb 1974, Wedding of Bouncing Boy and Duo Damsel 15.00
❑201, Apr 1974 12.00
❑202, Jun 1974, 100-page giant; NC (c); MGr, DC, CS (a); New stories and reprints from Superboy #91 and Adventure #342, #344, and #345 30.00
❑203, Aug 1974, NC (c); MGr (a); D: Invisible Kid I (Lyle Norg). V: Validus; D: Invisible Kid (Lyle Norg) 12.00
❑204, Oct 1974, NC (c); MGr (a); 1: Anti Lad 12.00
❑205, Dec 1974, NC (c); MGr, DC, CS (a); reprints Superboy #88, Adventure #350 and #351 40.00
❑206, Jan 1975 NC (c); MGr (a) 12.00
❑207, Feb 1975 MGr (c); MGr (a) 12.00
❑208, Apr 1975, MGr (c); MGr, CS (a); Giant-Size; 68 pages 15.00
❑209, Jun 1975 MGr (c); MGr (a) 10.00
❑210, Aug 1975; MGr (c); MGr (a); O: Karate Kid 15.00
❑211, Sep 1975 MGr (c); MGr (a); A: Legion Subs 10.00
❑212, Oct 1975; MGr (c); MGr (w); MGr (a); Matter-Eater Lad leaves team 10.00
❑213, Dec 1975 A: Miracle Machine 7.00
❑214, Jan 1976 7.00
❑215, Mar 1976; V: Emerald Empress 7.00
❑216, Apr 1976, 1: Tyroc 7.00
❑217, Jun 1976, 1: Laurel Kent 7.00
❑218, Jul 1976, Tyroc joins team; Bicentennial #22 7.00
❑219, Sep 1976, V: Fatal Five 7.00
❑220, Oct 1976 7.00
❑221, Nov 1976, O: Charma. O: Grimbor. 1: Charma. 1: Grimbor 7.00
❑222, Dec 1976 5.00
❑223, Jan 1977, 1: Pulsar Stargrave. V: Time Trapper 5.00
❑224, Feb 1977, V: Stargrave 5.00
❑225, Mar 1977, 1: Dawnstar 5.00
❑226, Apr 1977, Dawnstar joins team; Stargrave's identity revealed 5.00
❑227, May 1977, Stargrave's identity revealed 5.00
❑228, Jun 1977, D: Chemical King. D: Chemical King 5.00
❑229, Jul 1977, Jeff Albrecht L.O.C 5.00
❑230, Aug 1977, Bouncing Boy's powers restored; series continues as Superboy and the Legion of Super-Heroes 5.00
❑Ann 1, Sum 1964 175.00
❑SP 1, ca. 1980; Superboy Spectacular; giant; 1st direct-sale only DC title; reprints; pin-up back cover 4.00

Superboy
DC

❑1, Jan 1990; JM (a); Photo cover from TV show 2.00
❑2, Feb 1990; Includes Bios of Actors 1.50
❑3, Mar 1990 1.50
❑4, Apr 1990 1.50
❑5, May 1990 1.50
❑6, Jun 1990 1.50
❑7, Jul 1990 MWa (w); JM (a) 1.50
❑8, Aug 1990; Bizarro 1.50
❑9, Sep 1990 CS (a) 1.50
❑10, Oct 1990 CS (a) 1.50
❑11, Nov 1990 CS (a) 1.50
❑12, Dec 1990 CS (a) 1.50
❑13, Jan 1991; Mxyzptlk 1.50
❑14, Feb 1991; V: Brimstone 1.50
❑15, Mar 1991 1.50
❑16, Apr 1991 A: Superman 1.50
❑17, May 1991 1.50
❑18, Jun 1991; Series continued in Adventures of Superboy #19 1.50
❑Special 1, ca. 1992; CS (a); One-shot associated with TV series 3.00

Superboy
DC

❑0, Oct 1994; O: Superboy (clone). Comes between issues #8 and 9 2.00
❑1, Feb 1994; V: Sidearm 2.50
❑2, Mar 1994; 1: Scavenger. 1: Knockout 2.00
❑3, Apr 1994; V: Scavenger 2.00
❑4, May 1994 2.00
❑5, Jun 1994; Story continues into Superman: The Man of Steel #35 2.00
❑6, Jul 1994; Worlds Collide, Part 3; crossover with Milestone Media 2.00
❑7, Aug 1994; Worlds Collide, Part 8; crossover with Milestone Media 2.00
❑8, Sep 1994; Zero Hour; meets original Superboy 2.00
❑9, Nov 1994; V: King Shark 2.00
❑10, Dec 1994; V: B.E.M 2.00
❑11, Jan 1995; V: Techno 2.00
❑12, Feb 1995; V: Copperhead 2.00
❑13, Mar 1995; Watery Grave, Part 1 2.00
❑14, Apr 1995; Watery Grave, Part 2 2.00
❑15, May 1995; Watery Grave, Part 3 2.00
❑16, Jun 1995; V: Loose Cannon 2.00
❑17, Jul 1995 2.00
❑18, Aug 1995; V: Valor; V: Champion 2.00
❑19, Sep 1995; Valor enters Phantom Zone 2.00
❑20, Oct 1995; A: Green Lantern. V: The Technician; V: Scavenger; V: Black Manta; Green Lantern (Kyle Rayner) cover/team-up 2.00
❑21, Nov 1995; Future Tense, Part 1; continues in Legion of Super-Heroes #74 2.00
❑22, Dec 1995; A: Killer Frost. Underworld Unleashed 2.00
❑23, Jan 1996 2.00
❑24, Feb 1996; V: Silver Sword. Knockout's past revealed 2.00
❑25, Mar 1996; Giant-size; Losin' It, Part 1; pin-up pages 3.00
❑26, Apr 1996; Losin' It, Part 2 2.00
❑27, May 1996; Losin' It, Part 3 2.00
❑28, Jun 1996; A: Supergirl. Losin' It, Part 4 2.00
❑29, Jul 1996; Losin' It, Part 5 2.00
❑30, Aug 1996; Losin' It, Part 6; Knockout captured 2.00
❑31, Sep 1996; V: Chuck Ho 2.00
❑32, Oct 1996; O: Superboy; V: King Shark 2.00
❑33, Nov 1996; Final Night 2.00
❑34, Dec 1996; Dubbilex regains powers 2.00
❑35, Jan 1997; 1: The Agenda; 1: Match 2.00
❑36, Feb 1997; V: Match 2.00
❑37, Mar 1997; SB (a); V: Sledge 2.00
❑38, Apr 1997; SB (a); V: Copperhead; Cover mistakenly lists S. Buscema and Kryssing as credits 2.00
❑39, May 1997 2.00
❑40, Jun 1997; continues in Superboy & the Ravers #10 2.00
❑41, Jul 1997 2.00
❑42, Aug 1997 2.00
❑43, Sep 1997 2.00
❑44, Oct 1997; Superboy goes to timeless island 2.00
❑45, Nov 1997; A: Legion of Super-Heroes. V: Silver Sword 2.00
❑46, Dec 1997; Face cover 2.00
❑47, Jan 1998; A: Green Lantern. Continued from Green Lantern #94 2.00
❑48, Feb 1998; V: King Kamehamayhem 2.00
❑49, Mar 1998; Martian Manhunter apperance 2.00
❑50, Apr 1998; Last Boy on Earth, Part 1 2.00
❑51, May 1998; Last Boy on Earth, Part 2 1.95
❑52, Jun 1998; Last Boy on Earth, Part 3; Superboy returns to Hawaii 1.95
❑53, Jul 1998; Last Boy on Earth, Part 4 1.95
❑54, Aug 1998 A: Guardian 1.95
❑55, Sep 1998; 1: new Hex. V: Grokk 1.95
❑56, Oct 1998; Mechanic takes over Cadmus 1.95
❑57, Dec 1998; Demolition Run, Part 1 1.99
❑58, Jan 1999; Demolition Run, Part 2 1.99
❑59, Feb 1999; A: Superman. A: Project: Cadmus. on Krypton 1.99
❑60, Mar 1999 1.99
❑61, Apr 1999; learns Superman's identity 1.99
❑62, May 1999; O: Black Zero 1.99
❑63, Jun 1999; V: Doomsdays 1.99

Other grades: Multiply price above by 5/6 for VF/NM • 2/3 for VERY FINE • 1/3 for FINE • 1/5 for VERY GOOD • 1/8 for GOOD

Tales from the Fridge

Cover homage to Tales from the Crypt #42

Tales of Asgard

Collects Journey into Mystery back-ups

Tales of G.I. Joe

Reprints joined recycled syndication

Tales of Suspense

Iron Man repulsed horror stories

Tales of Terror

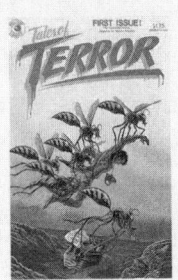

Horror tales eclipsed by other offerings

	N-MINT
❑64, Jul 1999	1.99
❑65, Aug 1999 A: Metal Men. A: Steel. A: Inferno. A: Green Lantern. A: Impulse. A: Creeper. A: Robin. A: Hero Hotline. A: Damage	1.99
❑66, Sep 1999; back to Wild Lands	1.99
❑67, Oct 1999; V: King Shark. V: King Shark	1.99
❑68, Nov 1999; Day of Judgment	1.99
❑69, Dec 1999	1.99
❑70, Jan 2000	1.99
❑71, Feb 2000	1.99
❑72, Mar 2000	1.99
❑73, Apr 2000	1.99
❑74, May 2000; Sins of Youth	1.99
❑75, Jun 2000	1.99
❑76, Jul 2000	1.99
❑77, Aug 2000	2.25
❑78, Sep 2000	2.25
❑79, Oct 2000	2.25
❑80, Nov 2000	2.25
❑81, Dec 2000	2.25
❑82, Jan 2001	2.25
❑83, Feb 2001	2.25
❑84, Mar 2001	2.25
❑85, Apr 2001	2.25
❑86, May 2001	2.25
❑87, Jun 2001	2.25
❑88, Jul 2001	2.25
❑89, Aug 2001	2.25
❑90, Sep 2001	2.25
❑91, Oct 2001	2.25
❑92, Nov 2001	2.25
❑93, Dec 2001; Joker: Last Laugh crossover	2.25
❑94, Jan 2002	2.25
❑95, Feb 2002	2.25
❑96, Mar 2002	2.25
❑97, Apr 2002	2.25
❑98, May 2002	2.25
❑99, Jun 2002	2.25
❑100, Jul 2002; Giant-size; BSz (c)	3.00
❑1000000, Nov 1998; Comes between issues #56 and 57	4.00
❑Ann 1, ca. 1994; Elseworlds; concludes story from Adventures of Superman Ann #6	3.00
❑Ann 2, ca. 1995; Year One; Identity of being who Superboy was cloned from is revealed	4.00
❑Ann 3, ca. 1996; Legends of the Dead Earth	2.95
❑Ann 4, ca. 1997; Pulp Heroes	3.95

Superboy and the Legion of Super-Heroes
DC

	N-MINT
❑231, Sep 1977, V: Fatal Five. Giant-Size	5.00
❑232, Oct 1977, 48 pages	5.00
❑233, Nov 1977, 1&O: Infinite Man; 48 pages	5.00
❑234, Dec 1977, 1: Composite Legionnaire; 48 pages	5.00
❑235, Jan 1978, 48 pages	5.00
❑236, Feb 1978, 48 pages	5.00
❑237, Mar 1978, MGr (c); Saturn Girl leaves team; Lightning Lad leaves team	5.00
❑238, Apr 1978, reprints Adventure Comics #359 and 360; wraparound cover	5.00
❑239, May 1978, 48 pages	5.00
❑240, Jun 1978, O: Dawnstar. V: Grimbor; 48 pages	5.00
❑241, Jul 1978, 48 pages	5.00
❑241/Whitman, Jul 1978, Whitman variant	8.00
❑242, Aug 1978, 48 pages	5.00
❑242/Whitman, Aug 1978, Whitman variant	8.00
❑243, Sep 1978, A: Legion Subs. 44 pages	5.00
❑243/Whitman, Sep 1978, A: Legion Subs. Whitman variant	8.00
❑244, Oct 1978, Mordru returns	5.00
❑244/Whitman, Oct 1978, Mordru returns; Whitman variant	8.00
❑245, Nov 1978, Lightning Lad and Saturn Girl rejoin	5.00
❑245/Whitman, Nov 1978, Lightning Lad and Saturn Girl rejoin; Whitman variant	8.00
❑246, Dec 1978	5.00
❑246/Whitman, Dec 1978, Whitman variant	8.00
❑247, Jan 1979	5.00
❑247/Whitman, Jan 1979, Whitman variant	8.00
❑248, Feb 1979	5.00
❑248/Whitman, Feb 1979, Whitman variant	8.00
❑249, Mar 1979	5.00
❑250, Apr 1979	5.00
❑251, May 1979	4.00
❑251/Whitman, May 1979, Whitman variant	7.00
❑252, Jun 1979	4.00
❑252/Whitman, Jun 1979, Whitman variant	7.00
❑253, Jul 1979, 1: Blok. V: League of Super-Assassins	4.00
❑253/Whitman, Jul 1979, 1: Blok. Whitman variant	7.00
❑254, Aug 1979, Whitman Cover	4.00
❑254/Whitman, Aug 1979, Whitman variant	7.00
❑255, Sep 1979, Legion visits Krypton before it's destroyed	4.00
❑255/Whitman, Sep 1979, Legion visits Krypton before it's destroyed; Whitman variant	7.00
❑256, Oct 1979, O: Brainiac 5	4.00
❑256/Whitman, Oct 1979, O: Brainiac 5. Whitman variant	7.00
❑257, Nov 1979, DG (c); SD, JSa (a); Return of Bouncing Boy; Return of Duo Damsel	4.00
❑257/Whitman, Nov 1979, SD (a); Return of Bouncing Boy; Return of Duo Damsel; Whitman variant	7.00
❑258, Dec 1979, V: Psycho Warrior. series continues as Legion of Super-Heroes	4.00
❑258/Whitman, Dec 1979, V: Psycho Warrior. series continues as Legion of Super-Heroes; Whitman variant	7.00

Superboy & the Ravers
DC

	N-MINT
❑1, Sep 1996	1.95
❑2, Oct 1996; Polybagged with issue of On the Edge	1.95
❑3, Nov 1996; 1: Half-Life	1.95
❑4, Dec 1996	1.95
❑5, Jan 1997; V: Scavenger	1.95
❑6, Feb 1997	1.95
❑7, Mar 1997	1.95
❑8, Apr 1997; V: Loophole; Batman cameo; Second story continues into Shadow of the Bat #62/Catwoman (2nd Series) #46	1.95
❑9, May 1997; Superman cover/appearance	1.95
❑10, Jun 1997; continued from Superboy #40, continues in Superboy #41	1.95
❑11, Jul 1997; V: The Red Shift	1.95
❑12, Aug 1997	1.95
❑13, Sep 1997; Dial H for Hero revels that he is gay	1.95
❑14, Oct 1997; Genesis	1.95
❑15, Nov 1997	1.95
❑16, Dec 1997	1.95
❑17, Jan 1998	1.95
❑18, Feb 1998	1.95
❑19, Mar 1998; Final Issue	1.95

Superboy Plus
DC

	N-MINT
❑1, Jan 1997	2.95
❑2, Fal 1997; continues in Catwoman Plus #1	2.95

Superboy/Risk Double-Shot
DC

	N-MINT
❑1, Feb 1998	1.95

Superboy/Robin: World's Finest Three
DC

	N-MINT
❑1, ca. 1996; prestige format; V: Metallo; V: Poison Ivy	4.95
❑2, ca. 1996; prestige format; V: Metallo; V: Poison Ivy	4.95

Superboy's Legion
DC

	N-MINT
❑1, Apr 2001; An Elseworlds Story	5.95
❑2, May 2001; An Elseworlds Story	5.95

Supercar
Gold Key

	N-MINT
❑1, Nov 1962	250.00
❑2, Feb 1963	200.00
❑3, May 1963	200.00
❑4, Aug 1963	200.00

Supercops
Now

	N-MINT
❑1, Sep 1990; double-sized	2.75
❑2, Oct 1990	1.75
❑3, Nov 1990	1.75
❑4, Feb 1991	1.75

Super Cops
Red Circle

	N-MINT
❑1, Jul 1974; GM (c); GM, FT (a); based on MGM movie	2.00

Super DC Giant
DC

	N-MINT
❑13, Sep 1970; really S-13; Binky	75.00
❑14, Sep 1970; JKu (c); CI, GK, RMo (a); really S-14; Top Guns of the West	30.00
❑15, Sep 1970; really S-15; Top Guns of the West	30.00

Other grades: Multiply price above by 5/6 for VF/NM • 2/3 for VERY FINE • 1/3 for FINE • 1/5 for VERY GOOD • 1/8 for GOOD

N-MINT N-MINT N-MINT

❑16, Sep 1970; really S-16; Brave & the Bold ... 30.00
❑17, Sep 1970; really S-17; Romance ... 125.00
❑18, Oct 1970; really S-18; Three Mouseketeers ... 50.00
❑19, Oct 1970; really S-19; Jerry Lewis ... 50.00
❑20, Oct 1970; really S-20; House of Mystery ... 40.00
❑21, Jan 1971; really S-21; Romance ... 175.00
❑22, Mar 1971; really S-22; Westerns ... 25.00
❑23, Mar 1971; really S-23; Unexpected ... 40.00
❑24, May 1971; CS (c); JM (a); really S-24; reprints Supergirl stories from Action Comics #295-298 ... 30.00
❑25, Aug 1971; really S-25; Challengers of the Unknown ... 25.00
❑26, Aug 1971; really S-26; Aquaman ... 25.00
❑27, Sum 1976; Flying Saucers ... 15.00

Super Deluxe Hero Happy Hour: The Lost Episode
Idea & Design Works

❑1, Sep 2006 ... 9.99

Superfan
Mark 1

❑1, b&w ... 1.95

Superfist Ayumi
Fantagraphics / Eros

❑1, Oct 1996; Adult ... 2.95
❑2, Nov 1996; Adult ... 2.95

Super Friends
DC

❑1, Nov 1976, ATh, RE (a) ... 20.00
❑2, Dec 1976 ... 9.00
❑3, Feb 1977 ... 7.00
❑4, Apr 1977 ... 7.00
❑5, Jun 1977, Colleen Doran L.O.C ... 7.00
❑6, Aug 1977, O: Atom ... 6.00
❑7, Oct 1977, 1: Wonder Twins. 1: Tasmanian Devil; 1: Wondertwins ... 6.00
❑8, Nov 1977, Jerry Siegel L.O.C ... 6.00
❑9, Dec 1977, 1: Iron Maiden ... 6.00
❑10, Mar 1978 ... 6.00
❑11, May 1978 ... 4.00
❑12, Jul 1978, 1: Doctor Mist; O: TNT; O: Dan the Dyna-Mite ... 4.00
❑13, Sep 1978 ... 4.00
❑13/Whitman, Sep 1978, Whitman variant ... 8.00
❑14, Nov 1978, O: Wondertwins ... 6.00
❑14/Whitman, Nov 1978, Whitman variant ... 12.00
❑15, Dec 1978 ... 4.00
❑15/Whitman, Dec 1978; Whitman variant ... 12.00
❑16, Jan 1979 ... 6.00
❑16/Whitman, Jan 1979, Whitman variant 12.00
❑17, Feb 1979 ... 4.00
❑18, Mar 1979 ... 4.00
❑19, Apr 1979 ... 4.00
❑20, May 1979 ... 4.00
❑20/Whitman, May 1979; Whitman variant ... 12.00
❑21, Jun 1979 ... 6.00
❑21/Whitman, Jun 1979; Whitman variant ... 12.00
❑22, Jul 1979 ... 6.00
❑22/Whitman, Jul 1979; Whitman variant 12.00
❑23, Aug 1979 ... 6.00
❑23/Whitman, Aug 1979; Whitman variant ... 12.00
❑24, Sep 1979 ... 4.00
❑25, Oct 1979, 1: Fire; 1: Fire (Beatriz DaCosta) ... 4.00
❑25/Whitman, Oct 1979, 1: Fire. Whitman variant ... 8.00
❑26, Nov 1979 ... 4.00
❑27, Dec 1979 ... 4.00
❑28, Jan 1980 ... 4.00
❑29, Feb 1980 ... 4.00
❑30, Mar 1980 ... 4.00
❑31, Apr 1980, A: Black Orchid ... 4.00
❑32, May 1980 ... 5.00
❑32/Whitman, May 1980, Whitman variant ... 10.00
❑33, Jun 1980 ... 4.00
❑34, Jul 1980 ... 4.00
❑35, Aug 1980 ... 4.00
❑36, Sep 1980, Wondertwins story ... 4.00
❑37, Oct 1980, Jack O'Lantern story ... 4.00
❑38, Nov 1980, Seraph story ... 4.00
❑39, Dec 1980, Wondertwins story ... 4.00
❑40, Jan 1981, Jack O'Lantern story ... 4.00
❑41, Feb 1981, Seraph story ... 4.00
❑42, Mar 1981, 1: Green Flame; Wondertwins story ... 4.00
❑43, Apr 1981, Jordan B. Gorfinkle L.O.C.; Plastic Man story ... 4.00
❑44, May 1981, Jack O'Lantern story ... 4.00
❑45, Jun 1981, Plastic Man story ... 4.00
❑46, Jul 1981, Jeff Albrecht L.O.C.; Seraph story ... 4.00
❑47, Aug 1981, O: Green Flame; Final Issue ... 4.00
❑Special 1, ca. 1981; giveaway; says A TV Comic on cover ... 5.00

Supergirl
DC

❑1, Nov 1972, Zatanna story ... 15.00
❑2, Jan 1973, Zatanna story ... 10.00
❑3, Feb 1973, BO (c); DH (a); Zatanna story ... 8.00
❑4, Apr 1973, Zatanna story ... 8.00
❑5, Jun 1973, BO (c); MA (a); origin of Zatana ... 8.00
❑6, Aug 1973, Melba Manton story ... 8.00
❑7, Oct 1973 ... 8.00
❑8, Nov 1973, Batman appearance, Hawkman appearance, Green Lantern appearance, Superman cameo ... 8.00
❑9, Jan 1974 ... 8.00
❑10, Sep 1974, A: Prez. Final Issue ... 8.00

Supergirl
DC

❑14, Dec 1983; Title changes to Supergirl; Series continued from "Daring New Adventures of Supergirl" ... 3.00
❑15, Jan 1984 ... 3.00
❑16, Feb 1984 KG (c); CI (a); A: Ambush Bug ... 3.00
❑17, Mar 1984 ... 3.00
❑18, Apr 1984 ... 3.00
❑19, May 1984 ... 3.00
❑20, Jun 1984 A: Teen Titans. A: Justice League of America ... 3.00
❑21, Jul 1984 CI (a) ... 3.00
❑22, Aug 1984 CI (a) ... 3.00
❑23, Sep 1984; CI (a); Final Issue ... 3.00
❑DOT 1, ca. 1984; Department of Transportation giveaway; AT (c); JO (w); AT (a) ... 4.00

Supergirl
DC

❑1, Sep 1996; PD (w); Matrix merges with Linda Danvers ... 10.00
❑1/2nd, Sep 1996; PD (w); 2nd printing 3.00
❑2, Oct 1996; PD (w); Matrix learns more of Linda Danvers' past ... 4.00
❑3, Nov 1996; PD (w); V: Gorilla Grodd. Final Night ... 3.50
❑4, Dec 1996; PD (w); V: Gorilla Grodd'; 1: Wally (God); Final Night ... 3.00
❑5, Jan 1997; PD (w); V: Chemo ... 3.00
❑6, Feb 1997; PD (w); A: Superman. V: Rampage ... 2.50
❑7, Mar 1997 PD (w) ... 2.50
❑8, Apr 1997 PD (w) ... 2.00
❑9, May 1997; PD (w); V: Tempus ... 2.00
❑10, Jun 1997 PD (w) ... 2.00
❑11, Jul 1997; PD (w); V: Silver Banshee 2.00
❑12, Aug 1997; PD (w); V: Silver Banshee 2.00
❑13, Sep 1997 PD (w) ... 2.00
❑14, Oct 1997; PD (w); Genesis ... 2.00
❑15, Nov 1997; PD (w); V: Extremists ... 2.00
❑16, Dec 1997; PD (w); V: Extremists. Face cover ... 2.00
❑17, Jan 1998; PD (w); V: Despero ... 2.00
❑18, Feb 1998; PD (w); V: Despero ... 2.00
❑19, Mar 1998; PD (w); V: Blastoff ... 2.00
❑20, Apr 1998; PD (w); Millennium Giants 2.00
❑21, May 1998 PD (w) ... 2.00
❑22, Jun 1998 PD (w) ... 2.00
❑23, Jul 1998 PD (w); A: Steel ... 2.00
❑24, Aug 1998; PD (w); A: Resurrection Man. Continued in Resurrection Man #17 ... 2.00
❑25, Sep 1998 PD (w) ... 2.00
❑26, Oct 1998; PD (w); O: Comet ... 2.00
❑27, Dec 1998; PD (w); V: Female Furies 2.00
❑28, Jan 1999; PD (w); V: Female Furies 2.00
❑29, Feb 1999 PD (w); A: Twilight. A: Female Furies. A: Granny Goodness 2.00
❑30, Mar 1999; PD (w); A: Matrix. V: Matrix ... 2.00
❑31, Apr 1999; PD (w); V: Matrix ... 1.99
❑32, May 1999 PD (w) ... 1.99
❑33, Jun 1999 PD (w) ... 1.99
❑34, Jul 1999; PD (w); V: Parasite ... 1.99
❑35, Aug 1999; PD (w); V: Parasite ... 1.99
❑36, Sep 1999; PD (w); A: Young Justice. Continued in Young Justice #13 ... 1.99
❑37, Oct 1999; PD (w); A: Young Justice. Continued from Young Justice #13 ... 1.99
❑38, Nov 1999; PD (w); A: Zauriel. Day of Judgment ... 1.99
❑39, Dec 1999 PD (w) ... 1.99
❑40, Jan 2000 PD (w) ... 1.99
❑41, Feb 2000 PD (w) ... 1.99
❑42, Mar 2000 PD (w) ... 1.99
❑43, Apr 2000 PD (w) ... 1.99
❑44, May 2000 PD (w) ... 1.99
❑45, Jun 2000 PD (w) ... 1.99
❑46, Jul 2000 PD (w) ... 1.99
❑47, Aug 2000 PD (w) ... 2.25
❑48, Sep 2000 PD (w) ... 2.25
❑49, Oct 2000 PD (w) ... 2.25
❑50, Nov 2000; Giant-size; PD (w) ... 3.95
❑51, Dec 2000 PD (w) ... 2.25
❑52, Jan 2001 PD (w) ... 2.25
❑53, Feb 2001 PD (w) ... 2.25
❑54, Mar 2001 PD (w) ... 2.25
❑55, Apr 2001 PD (w) ... 2.25
❑56, May 2001 PD (w) ... 2.25
❑57, Jun 2001 PD (w) ... 2.25
❑58, Jul 2001; PD (w); O: Buzz ... 2.25
❑59, Aug 2001; PD (w); Our Worlds At War: Prelude to War! ... 2.25
❑60, Sep 2001; PD (w); All-Out War!; Our Worlds At War: All-Out War! ... 2.25
❑61, Oct 2001; PD (w); Casualties of War!; Our Worlds At War: Casualties of War! 2.25
❑62, Nov 2001 PD (w); A: Two-Face ... 2.25
❑63, Dec 2001; PD (w); Joker: Last Laugh crossover ... 2.25
❑64, Jan 2002 PD (w) ... 2.25
❑65, Feb 2002 PD (w) ... 2.25
❑66, Mar 2002 PD (w); A: Demon ... 2.25
❑67, Apr 2002 PD (w); A: Demon ... 2.25
❑68, May 2002 PD (w) ... 2.25
❑69, Jun 2002 PD (w) ... 2.25
❑70, Jul 2002 PD (w) ... 2.25
❑71, Aug 2002 PD (w) ... 2.25
❑72, Sep 2002 PD (w) ... 2.25
❑73, Oct 2002 PD (w) ... 2.50
❑74, Nov 2002 PD (w) ... 2.50
❑75, Dec 2002 ... 2.50
❑75/Dynamic, Dec 2002; Dynamic Forces signed edition; Includes certificate of authenticity ... 19.95
❑76, Jan 2003; Crossover with Superman: The Man of Steel #132 ... 2.50
❑77, Feb 2003 ... 2.50
❑78, Mar 2003 ... 2.50
❑79, Apr 2003 ... 2.50
❑80, May 2003; D: Xenon; Final issue ... 2.50
❑1000000, Nov 1998 PD (w); A: R'E'L ... 4.00
❑Ann 1, ca. 1996; DG (a); Legends of the Dead Earth ... 2.95
❑Ann 2, ca. 1997; Pulp Heroes ... 3.95

Supergirl
DC

❑0, Aug 2005; Reprints Superman/Batman Issue #19 ... 5.00
❑1, Sep 2005; Supergirl standing over unconscious woman ... 7.00
❑1/Turner, Sep 2005 ... 10.00
❑1/Sketch, Sep 2005 ... 4.00
❑2, Nov 2005; Supergirl battling Teen Titans on cover ... 2.99
❑3, Jan 2006; Supergirl with red eyes cover ... 2.99
❑4, Apr 2006, Justice League heads cover 2.99
❑5, May 2006, Cover by Ian Churchill (Dark Supergirl) and Michael Turner (Normal Supergirl) where both of Dark Supergirl's hands in fists and orange background; 50/50 covers ... 3.99
❑6, Jul 2006, Masked Nightwing and Flamebird cover ... 2.99

Other grades: Multiply price above by 5/6 for VF/NM • 2/3 for VERY FINE • 1/3 for FINE • 1/5 for VERY GOOD • 1/8 for GOOD

Tales of the Beanworld

Simple, surreal, and high protein stories
©Eclipse

Tales of the Green Beret

No super-heroes here, just real heroes
©Dell

Tales of the Legion

First dozen issues fresh, rest reprints
©DC

Tales of the Teen Titans

Crisis caused continuity problem with reprints
©DC

Tales of the Unexpected

Science fiction turned to mystery, er, horror
©DC

N-MINT

❑7, Sep 2006, One Year Later; Cover by Ian Churchill and Aspen; Cover by Ian Churchill and Norm Rapmund 2.99
❑8, Oct 2006, One Year Later; Power Girl Apperance 2.99
❑9, Nov 2006, New title on cover: Supergirl Lost Daughter of Krypton.... 2.99
❑10, Dec 2006........... 2.99
❑11, Jan 2007........... 2.99
❑12, Feb 2007, 1: Terra II; V: Empathosaur 2.99
❑13, Mar 2007........... 2.99
❑14........... 2.99
❑15........... 2.99
❑16........... 2.99
❑17........... 2.99
❑18........... 2.99
❑19........... 2.99
❑20........... 2.99
❑21........... 2.99
❑22........... 2.99
❑23........... 2.99
❑24........... 2.99
❑25........... 2.99
❑26........... 2.99
❑27........... 2.99
❑28........... 2.99
❑29........... 2.99
❑30........... 2.99
❑31........... 2.99
❑32........... 2.99
❑33........... 2.99
❑34........... 2.99
❑35........... 2.99
❑36........... 2.99
❑37........... 2.99
❑38........... 2.99
❑39........... 2.99
❑40........... 2.99
❑41........... 2.99
❑42........... 2.99

Supergirl and the Legion of Super-Heroes
DC

❑17, Jul 2006........... 2.99
❑18, Aug 2006........... 2.99
❑19, Sep 2006, Cover by Kitson & Eyring 2.99
❑20, Sep 2006, Cover by Kitson........... 2.99
❑22, Dec 2006........... 2.99
❑23, Jan 2007, Regular edition Kitson cover........... 2.99
❑23/Variant, Jan 2007........... 2.99
❑24, Feb 2007........... 2.99
❑25, Mar 2007........... 2.99
❑26........... 2.99
❑27........... 2.99
❑28........... 2.99
❑29........... 2.99
❑30........... 2.99
❑31........... 2.99
❑32........... 2.99
❑33........... 2.99
❑34........... 2.99
❑35........... 2.99
❑36, Becomes Legion of Super-Heroes again........... 2.99

N-MINT

Supergirl/Lex Luthor Special
DC

❑1, ca. 1993; includes pin-up gallery; cover says Supergirl and Team Luthor 2.50

Supergirl
DC

❑1, Feb 1994; KGa (c); O: Supergirl (Matrix)........... 3.00
❑2, Mar 1994 KGa (c)........... 2.50
❑3, Apr 1994........... 2.50
❑4, May 1994........... 2.50

Supergirl Movie Special
DC

❑1, Movie adaptation........... 1.25

Supergirl Plus
DC

❑1, Feb 1997........... 2.95

Supergirl/Prysm Double Shot
DC

❑1, Feb 1998; One-shot........... 1.95

Supergirl: Wings
DC

❑1, Dec 2001........... 5.95

Super Goof (Walt Disney...)
Gold Key

❑1, ca. 1965, Gold Key publishes........... 24.00
❑2, ca. 1967, ca. 1967........... 12.00
❑3, May 1968........... 12.00
❑4, Sep 1968........... 10.00
❑5, Dec 1968........... 10.00
❑6, Mar 1969........... 10.00
❑7, Jun 1969........... 10.00
❑8, Sep 1969, V: The Beagle Boys........... 10.00
❑9, Dec 1969........... 10.00
❑10, Mar 1970........... 10.00
❑11, Jun 1970........... 7.00
❑12, Feb 1970........... 7.00
❑13, May 1970........... 7.00
❑14, Aug 1970........... 7.00
❑15, Nov 1970........... 7.00
❑16, Feb 1971........... 7.00
❑17, May 1971........... 7.00
❑18, Aug 1971........... 7.00
❑19, Nov 1971, A: Uncle Scrooge........... 7.00
❑20, Feb 1972........... 7.00
❑21, May 1972........... 5.00
❑22, Aug 1972........... 5.00
❑23, Nov 1972........... 5.00
❑24 1973........... 5.00
❑25 1973........... 5.00
❑26 1973........... 5.00
❑27, Oct 1973........... 5.00
❑28 1974........... 5.00
❑29 1974........... 5.00
❑30, Jun 1974........... 5.00
❑31, Aug 1974........... 3.00
❑32, Nov 1974........... 3.00
❑33 1975........... 3.00
❑34 1975........... 3.00
❑35, Sep 1975........... 3.00
❑36, Dec 1975........... 3.00
❑37, Feb 1976........... 3.00
❑38, Jun 1976........... 3.00
❑39, Sep 1976........... 3.00

N-MINT

❑40, Nov 1976........... 3.00
❑41, Feb 1977........... 3.00
❑42, Jun 1977........... 3.00
❑43, Sep 1977, Reprints stories from Super Goof #8 and #10........... 3.00
❑44, Nov 1977........... 3.00
❑45, Feb 1978........... 3.00
❑46, Apr 1978........... 3.00
❑47, Jun 1978........... 3.00
❑48, Aug 1978, Has Tarzan parody........... 3.00
❑49, Oct 1978, V: Emil Eagle. Casper in Hostess ad ("A Real Oddball")........... 3.00
❑50, Dec 1978........... 3.00
❑51, Feb 1979........... 2.50
❑52, Apr 1979........... 2.50
❑53, Jun 1979, A: Gus Goose. V: Emil Eagle. Thor in Hostess ad ("Good Overcomes Evil")........... 2.50
❑54, Aug 1979........... 2.50
❑55, Oct 1979........... 2.50
❑56, Dec 1979........... 2.50
❑57, Jan 1980........... 2.50
❑58, Mar 1980, A: Uncle Scrooge. Reprints stories from Super Goof #19; Chip 'n' Dale on cover; Spider-Man in Hostess ad ("Puts Himself in the Picture")........... 4.00
❑59, May 1980........... 4.00
❑60, Jul 1980........... 15.00
❑61, Oct 1980........... 70.00
❑62, Dec 1980........... 15.00
❑63, Jan 1981........... 2.50
❑64 1981........... 5.00
❑65 1981........... 5.00
❑66, Dec 1981........... 5.00
❑67, Feb 1982........... 8.00
❑68 1982........... 8.00
❑69 1982........... 8.00
❑70 1982........... 15.00
❑71 1982........... 15.00
❑72 1983........... 15.00
❑73, Jul 1983........... 15.00
❑74 1983, Final Issue........... 15.00

Super Green Beret
Milson

❑1, Apr 1967........... 30.00
❑2, Jun 1967........... 24.00

Super Heroes Battle Super Gorillas
DC

❑1, Win 1976, Reprints from Action Comics #238, Flash (1st Series) #172, Batman #75; Winter 1976........... 10.00

Super Heroes Puzzles and Games
Marvel

❑1, Apr 1980; giveaway; O: Captain America. O: Spider-Man. O: The Hulk. O: Spider-Woman. NN........... 2.00

Super Heroes Stamp Album
USPS / DC

❑1; JO, DG, JSa, AT, JA (a); 1900-1909. 3.00
❑2; 1910-1919........... 3.00
❑3; 1920-1929........... 3.00
❑4; 1930-1939; no Snow White coverage 3.00
❑5; 1940-1949........... 3.00
❑6; DG, JSa, TVE (a); 1950-1959; 3-D stamp........... 3.00

Other grades: Multiply price above by 5/6 for VF/NM • 2/3 for VERY FINE • 1/3 for FINE • 1/5 for VERY GOOD • 1/8 for GOOD

N-MINT

❑7; 1960-1969 ... 3.50
❑8; 1970-1979 ... 3.50
❑9; DG, JSa, TVE (a); 1980-1989 ... 3.50
❑10, Dec 2000; 1990-1999 ... 3.50

Super Heroes vs. Super Villains
Archie

❑1, ca. 1966, Reprints from Fly Man #31; 34 and 38 ... 50.00

Super Hero Happy Hour
GeekPunk

❑1, ca. 2002, b&w ... 3.00
❑2, ca. 2003, b&w ... 3.00
❑3, ca. 2003, b&w ... 3.00
❑4, ca. 2003, b&w; Series changes names to Hero Happy Hour due to trademark dispute with Marvel/DC over name Super-Hero ... 3.00

Super Information Hijinks: Reality Check
Tavicat

❑1, Oct 1995, b&w ... 2.95
❑2, Dec 1995, b&w ... 2.95
❑3 1996 ... 2.95
❑4 1996 ... 2.95
❑5 1996 ... 2.95

Super Information Hijinks: Reality Check!
Sirius

❑1, Sep 1996 ... 2.95
❑2, Oct 1996 ... 2.95
❑3, Nov 1996 ... 2.95
❑4, Dec 1996 ... 2.95
❑5, Jan 1997 ... 2.95
❑6, Feb 1997 ... 2.95
❑7, Mar 1997 ... 2.95
❑8, Jan 1998 ... 2.95
❑9, Mar 1998 ... 2.95
❑10, May 1998 ... 2.95
❑11, Jul 1998 ... 2.95
❑12, Oct 1998 ... 2.95

Superior Seven
Imagine This

❑1 ... 2.00
❑2 1992, b&w ... 2.00
❑3 1992, b&w ... 2.00
❑4 ... 2.00
❑5 ... 2.00

Superman
DC

❑149, Nov 1961 CS (a); A: Legion of Super-Heroes ... 125.00
❑150, Jan 1962 ... 68.00
❑151, Feb 1962 ... 68.00
❑152, Apr 1962, A: Legion of Super-Heroes ... 68.00
❑153, May 1962 ... 68.00
❑154, Jul 1962, CS (a) ... 68.00
❑155, Aug 1962 ... 68.00
❑156, Oct 1962 ... 68.00
❑157, Nov 1962, 1: Gold Kryptonite ... 68.00
❑158, Jan 1963, CS (a); 1: Nightwing. 1: Flamebird ... 68.00
❑159, Feb 1963, Imaginary story ... 68.00
❑160, Apr 1963, CS (a) ... 68.00
❑161, May 1963, D: Ma & Pa Kent ... 68.00
❑162, Jul 1963, KS (c); CS, KS (a) ... 58.00
❑163, Aug 1963 ... 58.00
❑164, Oct 1963, CS (a) ... 58.00
❑165, Nov 1963, 1: Sally Selwyn ... 58.00
❑166, Jan 1964 ... 58.00
❑167, Feb 1964, CS (a); O: Brainiac (new origin) ... 58.00
❑168, Apr 1964 ... 58.00
❑169, May 1964 ... 58.00
❑170, Jul 1964, A: John F. Kennedy. Imaginary story ... 58.00
❑171, Aug 1964, CS (a) ... 58.00
❑172, Oct 1964 ... 58.00
❑173, Nov 1964, Tales of Kryptonite No. 1 ... 58.00
❑174, Jan 1965 ... 58.00
❑175, Feb 1965, Imaginary Story ... 58.00
❑176, Apr 1965, CS (a); Tales of Kryptonite No. 2 ... 58.00
❑177, May 1965, Tales of Kryptonite No. 3 ... 58.00
❑178, Jul 1965 ... 58.00
❑179, Aug 1965, Tales of Kryptonite No. 4 ... 58.00

N-MINT

❑180, Oct 1965 ... 58.00
❑181, Nov 1965, CS (a); 1st Superman of 2965 ... 55.00
❑182, Jan 1966, V: Toyman. V: Toyman. ... 55.00
❑183, Jan 1966, Giant-size; aka 80 Page Giant #G-18; Golden Age reprints ... 55.00
❑184, Feb 1966 ... 55.00
❑185, Apr 1966 ... 55.00
❑186, May 1966, cCS (a) ... 55.00
❑187, Jun 1966, Giant-size; CS, KS (a); aka 80 Page Giant #G-23; Fortress stories; reprints from Superman #17, Action Comics #164, #233, #244, and #261, and Jimmy Olsen #53 (incl. Action covers) ... 60.00
❑188, Jul 1966, CS (c); CS (a) ... 55.00
❑189, Aug 1966, CS (c) ... 55.00
❑190, Oct 1966, CS (c); 1: Amalak ... 55.00
❑191, Nov 1966, V: D.E.M.O.N ... 55.00
❑192, Jan 1967, CS (a); Imaginary Story ... 55.00
❑193, Feb 1967, Giant-size; aka 80 Page Giant #G-31; reprints Action #223 and Superman #149 ... 60.00
❑194, Feb 1967, CS (a); Reprints Superman #133 ... 55.00
❑195, Apr 1967, CS (c); CS (a); Reprints Superman #133; 2: Amalak ... 55.00
❑196, May 1967 ... 55.00
❑197, Jul 1967, Giant-size; aka 80 Page Giant #G-36; All Clark Kent issue ... 55.00
❑198, Jul 1967, CS (a) ... 55.00
❑199, Aug 1967, 1: Superman/Flash race ... 180.00
❑200, Oct 1967, Imaginary story ... 60.00
❑201, Nov 1967, CS (a); The Jolly Jailhouse reprinted from issue #139 ... 24.00
❑202, Dec 1967, Giant-size; aka 80 Page Giant #G-42; Bizarro issue ... 30.00
❑203, Jan 1968, CS (c) ... 24.00
❑204, Feb 1968, NA (c); RA (a); 1: Q-energy. Includes reprint from Action Comics #222 ... 24.00
❑205, Apr 1968, 1: Black Zero ... 24.00
❑206, May 1968, Reprinted from issue #131 ... 24.00
❑207, Jun 1968, Giant-size; CS, KS (a); 30th Anniversary; aka 80 Page Giant #G-48; cover says July; reprints stories from Action Comics #265 and #266, Superman #135, and Superman's Girlfriend Lois Lane #15 ... 24.00
❑208, Jul 1968, NA (c); FR (w); CS, JAb (a); Reprint from Superman (1st Series) #130 ... 24.00
❑209, Aug 1968, RA (c); CS, JAb (a); Reprint from Superman (1st Series) #130 ... 24.00
❑210, Oct 1968, NA (c); CS (a) ... 24.00
❑211, Nov 1968, FR (w); CS, RA, JAb (a) ... 24.00
❑212, Jan 1969, Giant-size; CS (a); aka 80 Page Giant #G-54; Superbabies ... 50.00
❑213, Jan 1969, NA (c); CS, JAb (a); A: Lex Luthor. Includes reprint from issue #144 ... 24.00
❑214, Feb 1969, NA (c); CS, JAb (a); Includes How Perry White Hired Clark Kent! reprinted from issue #133 ... 24.00
❑215, Apr 1969, NA (c); CS, JAb (a); Imaginary Story; Superman as widower ... 24.00
❑216, May 1969, JKu (c); CS, RA, JAb (a); in Vietnam ... 24.00
❑217, Jul 1969; Giant-size; CS (c); CS (a); aka Giant #G-60 ... 30.00
❑218, Jul 1969, CS, JAb (a); Reprints The World of Mr. Mxyzptlk! from Action Comics #273 ... 20.00
❑219, Aug 1969, CS, JAb (a) ... 20.00
❑220, Oct 1969, CS (c); CS (a); Flash team-up ... 20.00
❑221, Nov 1969, CS (a) ... 20.00
❑222, Jan 1970; Giant-size; CS (c); CS (a); aka Giant #G-66 ... 30.00
❑223, Jan 1970, CS (a) ... 20.00
❑224, Feb 1970, CS (a); Imaginary Story ... 20.00
❑225, Apr 1970, CS (a) ... 20.00
❑226, May 1970, CS (a) ... 20.00
❑227, Jul 1970; Giant-size; CS (a); aka Giant #G-72 ... 30.00
❑228, Jul 1970, CS (c); CS, DA (a) ... 20.00
❑229, Aug 1970, CS, DA (a) ... 20.00
❑230, Oct 1970, CS, DA (a); Imaginary Story ... 20.00
❑231, Nov 1970, NA, CS (c); NA, CS, DA (a); Imaginary Story; Luthor reprint ... 20.00

N-MINT

❑232, Jan 1971; Giant-size; CS (c); CS (a); aka Giant #G-78 ... 30.00
❑233, Jan 1971, NA (c); RB, CS (a); 1: Sand Superman from Quarrm; World of Krypton back-up; First Sand Superman; All Kryptonite on Earth destroyed; Julius Schwartz begins as editor; How Jor-El met Lara ... 40.00
❑234, Feb 1971, NA, (c); MA, CS (a); A: Sand Superman. World of Krypton back-up ... 18.00
❑235, Mar 1971, NA (c); MA, CS (a); 1: Ferlin Nyxly ... 18.00
❑236, Apr 1971, NA (c); MA, DG, CS (a); World of Krypton back-up ... 18.00
❑237, May 1971, NA (c); MA, CS (a) ... 18.00
❑238, Jun 1971, MA, CI (c); MA, GM, CS (a); A: Sand Superman. World of Krypton back-up ... 18.00
❑239, Jul 1971, Giant-size; CS (c); MA, GM, CS (a); aka Giant #G-84; reprints Action #267 and #268, Superman #127 and #164 ... 30.00
❑240, Jul 1971, NA (c); DG, CS (a); A: I-Ching. World of Krypton back-up ... 18.00
❑241, Aug 1971, MA, CS (a); A: I-Ching. A: Sand Superman. Giant; Reprints Superman #112 and #176 ... 18.00
❑242, Sep 1971, NA (c); CI, CS (a); A: final. Reprints Superman #96, and Strange Adventures #54 ... 18.00
❑243, Oct 1971; NA (c); MA, CS (a); The Fabulous World of Krypton; Superman #38 ... 18.00
❑244, Nov 1971, CS (c); MA, CS (a); Reprints Superman #181 and Strange Adventures #34 ... 18.00
❑245, Jan 1972, CS (c); MA, CS, MR (a); a.k.a. DC 100-Page Super-Spectacular #DC-7; back cover pin-up; reprints from All-Star Western #117, The Atom #3, Detective #66, Kid Eternity #3, Mystery in Space #89, and Superman #87, and #167 ... 22.00
❑246, Dec 1971; CS (c); RB, MA, CS (a); There Is No Superman! reprinted from issue #40 ... 18.00
❑247, Jan 1972, CS (c); MA, CS (a); A: Guardians of the Universe. 1st Private Life of Clark Kent; Superman of Tomorrow back-up; Reprints Action #338 ... 18.00
❑248, Feb 1972; CS (c); DC, CS (a); Reprints Action #339 ... 18.00
❑249, Mar 1972; MA, NA, DD, CS (a); 1&O: Terra-Man; High Man on a Flagpole reprinted from issue #46 ... 18.00
❑250, Apr 1972; CS (a); Promotional Premium from 1955 ... 18.00
❑251, May 1972; MA, CS (a); Reprints from Superman #45; The Fabulous World of Krypton ... 18.00
❑252, Jun 1972, NA (c); MA, CS (a); a.k.a. DC 100-Page Super Spectacular #DC-13; wraparound cover ... 60.00
❑253, Jun 1972; MA, CS (a); Reprints ... 18.00
❑254, Jul 1972, NA, CS (a); Superman; The Private Life of Clark Kent ... 22.00
❑255, Aug 1972, CS (a); The Fabulous World of Superman ... 9.00
❑256, Sep 1972, CS (a); Superman; The Private Life of Clark Kent ... 9.00
❑257, Oct 1972, DD, CS (a); Superman; The Fabulous World of Krypton ... 9.00
❑258, Nov 1972, MA, DG, CS (a); Private Life of Clark Kent back-up ... 9.00
❑259, Dec 1972, CS (a) ... 9.00
❑260, Jan 1973, MA, DC, CS (a); World of Krypton back-up ... 9.00
❑261, Feb 1973, CS (a); A: Star Sapphire ... 9.00
❑262, Mar 1973, MA, CS (a); Private Life of Clark Kent back-up ... 9.00
❑263, Apr 1973, CS (a); Superman; The Fabulous World of Krypton ... 9.00
❑264, Jun 1973, DC, CS (a); 1: Steve Lombard; The Fabulous World of Krypton ... 9.00
❑265, Jul 1973, MA, CS (a) ... 8.00
❑266, Aug 1973, DD, CS (a); Superman; The Fabulous World of Krypton ... 8.00
❑267, Sep 1973, BO, MA, CS (a); Private Life of Clark Kent back-up ... 8.00
❑268, Oct 1973, DD, CS (a); The Fabulous World of Krypton ... 8.00
❑269, Nov 1973, CS (a) ... 8.00
❑270, Dec 1973, CS (a); Superman; The Private Life of Clark Kent ... 8.00

Other grades: Multiply price above by 5/6 for VF/NM • 2/3 for VERY FINE • 1/3 for FINE • 1/5 for VERY GOOD • 1/8 for GOOD

Tales of the Witchblade

Stories of weapon-wielding police officer

©Image

Tales to Astonish

Ant-Man, Giant-Man, Hulk anthology

©Marvel

Tales Too Terrible to Tell

Obscure pre-Code horror tales reprinted

©NEC

Tangled Web

Spider-Man stories from all over his career

©Marvel

Tank Girl

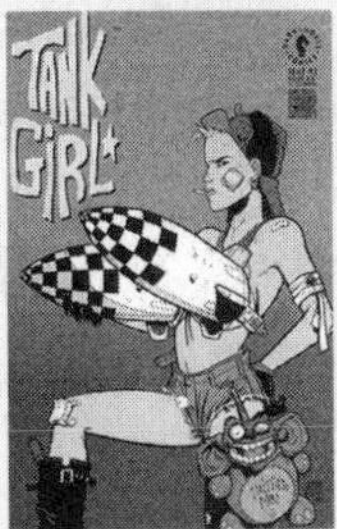

Jet Girl and Sub Girl forgot Jeep Girl

©Dark Horse

	N-MINT
❑271, Jan 1974, NC (c); DG, CS (a); V: Brainiac; The Fabulous World f Krypton	8.00
❑272, Feb 1974, NC (c); BO, GK, CS (a); Reprints Action #97, and Green Lantern (2nd series) #42	20.00
❑273, Mar 1974, BO, CS (a); Superman; The Private Life Of Clark Kent	7.00
❑274, Apr 1974, BO, CS (a)	7.00
❑275, May 1974, BO, DG, CS (a); Superman; The Fabulous World of Krypton	7.00
❑276, Jun 1974, NC (c); BO, CS (a); 1: Captain Thunder	7.00
❑277, Jul 1974, BO, CS (a); Private Life of Clark Kent back-up	7.00
❑278, Aug 1974, NC (c); BO, CS (a); Reprints Action #211 and #298, Superman #33 and #138, and World's Finest Comics #62	17.00
❑279, Sep 1974, CS (a); A: Batgirl. World of Krypton back-up	5.00
❑280, Oct 1974, BO, CS (a); Private Life of Clark Kent back-up	5.00
❑281, Nov 1974, CS (a); 1: Vartox	5.00
❑282, Dec 1974, CS, KS (a); World of Krypton back-up	5.00
❑283, Jan 1975, CS (a)	5.00
❑284, Feb 1975, NC (c); BO, CS (a); reprints Action #304, and Superman #25, #41, #42, and #148	7.00
❑285, Mar 1975; CS (a); A: Roy Raymond. The Private Life of Clark Kent	5.00
❑286, Apr 1975; CS (a); V: Luthor. V: Parasite; The Fabulous World of Krypton	5.00
❑287, May 1975, BO, CS (a); Return of Krypto; Private Life of Clark Kent back-up	4.00
❑288, Jun 1975 CS (a)	4.00
❑289, Jul 1975; CS (a); Superman; The Private Life Of Clark Kent	4.00
❑290, Aug 1975 CS (a)	4.00
❑291, Sep 1975, BO, CS (a)	4.00
❑292, Oct 1975, BO (c); BO, AM, CS (a); O: Lex Luthor. Private Life of Clark Kent back-up	4.00
❑293, Nov 1975, BO, CS (a)	2.50
❑294, Dec 1975; CS (a); Superman; The Private Life Of Clark Kent	2.50
❑295, Jan 1976 CS (a)	2.50
❑296, Feb 1976; CS (a); Superman loses powers when not in costume	2.50
❑297, Mar 1976 CS (a)	2.50
❑298, Apr 1976, BO, CS (a); Peter Sanderson LOC	2.50
❑299, May 1976, BO, CS (a)	2.50
❑300, Jun 1976, 300th anniversary issue; BO, CS (a); O: Superman of 2001; O:Superman	11.00
❑301, Jul 1976, CS (a); V: Solomon Grundy	2.50
❑302, Aug 1976, CS (a); V: Luthor	2.50
❑303, Sep 1976, CS (a); 1: Thunder and Lightning	2.50
❑304, Oct 1976, CS (a); V: The Parasite; Peter Sanderson LOC	2.50
❑305, Nov 1976, CS (a); D: Toyman II	2.50
❑306, Dec 1976, BO, CS (a); V: Bizarro; O: Bizarro	2.50
❑307, Jan 1977, NA (c); CS, FS, JL (a)	2.50
❑308, Feb 1977, NA (c); CS, FS, JL (a)	2.50

	N-MINT
❑309, Mar 1977, CS, FS, JL (a); Fred Hembeck LOC	2.50
❑310, Apr 1977, CS (a); 1: Metallo II; Fred Hembeck LOC	2.50
❑311, May 1977, CS (a); V: Amalak	2.50
❑312, Jun 1977, CS (a); V: Amalak	2.50
❑313, Jul 1977, NA, DD (c); CS, DA (a); V: Amalak; Peter Sanderson LOC	2.50
❑314, Aug 1977, CS (c); CS (a); V: Amalak	2.50
❑315, Sep 1977, AM (c); CS (a)	2.50
❑316, Oct 1977, CS (a)	2.50
❑317, Nov 1977, NA (c); CS, DA (a); Return of Lana Lang	2.50
❑318, Dec 1977 BO, RB (c); CS (a)	2.50
❑319, Jan 1978, RB (c); CS (a)	2.50
❑320, Feb 1978, CS (a)	2.50
❑321, Mar 1978, DG (c); CS (a)	2.50
❑321/Whitman, Mar 1978, DG (c); CS (a); Whitman variant	5.00
❑322, Apr 1978, CS (a); V: Parasite	2.50
❑322/Whitman, Apr 1978, CS (a); V: Parasite. Whitman variant	5.00
❑323, May 1978, CS, DA (a); 1: Atomic Skull	2.50
❑323/Whitman, May 1978, CS, DA (a); Whitman variant	5.00
❑324, Jun 1978, RB, DG (c); CS (a); O: Titano	2.50
❑324/Whitman, Jun 1978, RB, DG (c); CS (a); V: Titano. Whitman variant	5.00
❑325, Jul 1978, RB (c); CS (a)	2.50
❑325/Whitman, Jul 1978, RB (c); CS (a); Whitman variant	5.00
❑326, Aug 1978, RB (c); CS (a)	2.50
❑326/Whitman, Aug 1978, CS (a); Whitman variant	5.00
❑327, Sep 1978, RB (c); CS, KS (a); V: Kobra; Mr & Mrs Superman story	2.50
❑327/Whitman, Sep 1978, CS (a); Whitman variant	5.00
❑328, Oct 1978, DG (c); CS, KS (a); Private Life of Clark Kent back-up	2.50
❑328/Whitman, Oct 1978, DG (c); CS, KS (a); Whitman variant	5.00
❑329, Nov 1978, DG, RA (c); CS, KS (a); Mr. and Mrs. Superman back-up	2.50
❑329/Whitman, Nov 1978, DG, RA (c); CS, KS (a); ; Whitman variant	5.00
❑330, Dec 1978, RA (c); CS (a)	2.50
❑330/Whitman, Dec 1978, CS (a); Whitman variant	5.00
❑331, Jan 1979, RA (c); CS (a)	2.50
❑331/Whitman, Jan 1979, CS (a); Whitman variant	5.00
❑332, Feb 1979, RA (c); CS (a)	2.50
❑332/Whitman, Feb 1979, CS (a); Whitman variant	5.00
❑333, Mar 1979, RA (c); CS (a); O: Bizarro	2.50
❑333/Whitman, Mar 1979, CS (a); Whitman variant	5.00
❑334, Apr 1979, RA (c); CS (a)	2.50
❑334/Whitman, Apr 1979, CS (a); Whitman variant	5.00
❑335, May 1979, RA (c); CS (a); V: Mxyzptlk	2.50
❑335/Whitman, May 1979, CS (a); V: Mxyzptlk. Whitman variant	5.00
❑336, Jun 1979, RA (c); CS (a)	2.50
❑336/Whitman, Jun 1979, CS (a); Whitman variant	5.00

	N-MINT
❑337, Jul 1979, RA (c); CS (a)	2.50
❑337/Whitman, Jul 1979, CS (a); Whitman variant	5.00
❑338, Aug 1979, DG, RA (c); CS (a); Kandor enlarged	2.50
❑338/Whitman, Aug 1979, DG, RA (c); CS (a); Kandor enlarged; Whitman variant	5.00
❑339, Sep 1979 RA (c); CS (a)	2.50
❑339/Whitman, Sep 1979; CS (a); Whitman variant	5.00
❑340, Oct 1979 CS (a)	2.50
❑340/Whitman, Oct 1979; CS (a); Whitman variant	5.00
❑341, Nov 1979, DG, RA (c); CS (a); A: J. Wilbur Wolfingham	2.50
❑341/Whitman, Nov 1979, DG, RA (c); CS (a); A: J. Wilbur Wolfingham. Whitman variant	5.00
❑342, Dec 1979, RA (c); CS (a)	2.50
❑342/Whitman, Dec 1979, CS (a); Whitman variant	5.00
❑343, Jan 1980, RA (c); CS (a)	2.50
❑343/Whitman, Jan 1980, CS (a); Whitman variant	5.00
❑344, Feb 1980, CS (a)	2.50
❑344/Whitman, Feb 1980, CS (a); Whitman variant	5.00
❑345, Mar 1980, RA (c); CS (a)	2.50
❑345/Whitman, Mar 1980, CS (a); Whitman variant	5.00
❑346, Apr 1980, RA (c); CS (a)	2.50
❑346/Whitman, Apr 1980, CS (a); Whitman variant	5.00
❑347, May 1980, CS (a)	2.50
❑347/Whitman, May 1980, CS (a); Whitman variant	5.00
❑348, Jun 1980, RA (c); CS (a)	2.50
❑348/Whitman, Jun 1980, CS (a); Whitman variant	5.00
❑349, Jul 1980, RA (c); CS (a)	2.50
❑349/Whitman, Jul 1980, CS (a); Whitman variant	5.00
❑350, Aug 1980, RA (c); CS (a)	2.50
❑350/Whitman, Aug 1980, CS (a); Whitman variant	5.00
❑351, Sep 1980, RA (c); CS (a)	2.00
❑352, Oct 1980, RA (c); RB, CS (a); V: Destiny; The Fabulous World of Krypton	2.00
❑353, Nov 1980, RA (c); CS (a); V: The Demolisher; Just Imagine story	2.00
❑354, Dec 1980, RA (c); CS (a); Superman 2020 story	2.00
❑355, Jan 1981, JSn (c); JSn, CS (a); V: Momentus; Superman 2020 story .	2.00
❑356, Feb 1981, RB (c); CS (a); V: Vartox; The Fabulous World Of Krypton	2.00
❑357, Mar 1981, RA (c); CS (a); V: Vartox; Superman 2020 story	2.00
❑358, Apr 1981, DG, RA (c); CS (a); Imaginary story	2.00
❑359, May 1981, DC (c); CS (a); Superman: The In-Between Years	2.00
❑360, Jun 1981, RA (c); CS (a); Superman; The Fabulous World Of Krypton	2.00
❑361, Jul 1981, RA (c); CS (a); Superman 2020	2.00

Other grades: Multiply price above by 5/6 for VF/NM • 2/3 for VERY FINE • 1/3 for FINE • 1/5 for VERY GOOD • 1/8 for GOOD

❑362, Aug 1981, DG, RA (c); CS, KS, DA (a); Lana and Lois contract deadly virus that killed Kents; Superman The In-Between Years back-up 2.00
❑363, Sep 1981, RB, DG (c); RB, CS (a); A: Lex Luthor. Imaginary Story 2.00
❑364, Oct 1981, GP, DG (c); RB, CS (a); Superman 2020 back-up 2.00
❑365, Nov 1981, DG, RA (c); CS, KS (a); A: Supergirl. Superman the In-Between Years back-up 2.00
❑366, Dec 1981, RA (c); CS, KS (a); V: Superman Revenge Squad; Superman: The In-Between Years; Todd McFarlane L.O.C 2.00
❑367, Jan 1982, RA (c); GK, CS (a); V: Superman Revenge Squad; The Fabulous World of Krypton 2.00
❑368, Feb 1982, RB (c); CS (a); V: Superman Revenge Squad; Superman 2020 ..... 2.00
❑369, Mar 1982, RB (c); RB, CS (a); V: Parasite 2.00
❑370, Apr 1982, RA (c); CS (a); V: Chemo; Supernam: The In-Between Years 2.00
❑371, May 1982, RA (c); CS (a); Kandor repopulated by aliens; The Private Life of Clark Kent 2.00
❑372, Jun 1982, RA (c); GK, CS (a); Superman 2021 ..... 2.00
❑373, Jul 1982, RB (c); CS (a); The Private Life of Clark Kent 2.00
❑374, Aug 1982, GK (c); CS, KS (a); Superman: The In-Between Years 2.00
❑375, Sep 1982, GK (c); GK, CS (a); The Fabulous World of Krypton 2.00
❑376, Oct 1982, RB (c); BO, CI, CS, DA (a); Supergirl back-up 2.00
❑377, Nov 1982; GK (c); CS (a); V: Terra-Man; Masters of the Universe Preview; Includes Masters of the Universe Preview 2.00
❑378, Dec 1982; RB (c); CS (a); 1: Colonel Future (Ed Hamilton) 2.00
❑379, Jan 1983, DG, RA (c); CS (a); A: Bizarro. Graham Nolan L.O.C 2.00
❑380, Feb 1983, RA (c); CS (a); Crossover with New Adventures of Superboy #38 ..... 2.00
❑381, Mar 1983, GK (c); CS (a) 2.00
❑382, Apr 1983, GK (c); CS (a) 2.00
❑383, May 1983, CS (a) 2.00
❑384, Jun 1983, GK (c); CS (a) 2.00
❑385, Jul 1983, GK (c); CS (a); Continued from Action Comics #544 ..... 2.00
❑386, Aug 1983, GK (c); CS (a) 2.00
❑387, Sep 1983, GK (c); CS (a); Planeteer continued in Action Comics #547 ..... 2.00
❑388, Oct 1983, GK, (c); CS (a) 2.00
❑389, Nov 1983, GK (c); CS (a) 2.00
❑390, Dec 1983 GK (c); CS (a) 2.00
❑391, Jan 1984 CS (a) 2.00
❑392, Feb 1984 GK (c); CS (a) 2.00
❑393, Mar 1984 CS, IN (a) 2.00
❑394, Apr 1984 CS (a) 2.00
❑395, May 1984 CS (a) 2.00
❑396, Jun 1984 CS (a) 2.00
❑397, Jul 1984; CS (a); O: Kryptonite Man; Continued in Supergirl (2nd series) #21 ..... 2.00
❑398, Aug 1984, CS (a) 2.00
❑399, Sep 1984 CS (a) 2.00
❑400, Oct 1984, Giant-size; HC (c); JSo (w); JD, WP, AW, SD, BSz, BWr, JO, JOy, WE, JBy, MGr, JK, BB, FM, CS, JSo, KJ, MR (a); multiple short stories 5.00
❑401, Nov 1984; CS (a); V: Lex Luthor; Bonus Flash Force 2000; Bonus Insert: Flash Force 2000 ..... 2.00
❑402, Dec 1984, BO, CS (a) 2.00
❑403, Jan 1985; CS (a); T.M. Maple L.O.C 2.00
❑404, Feb 1985, BO, CI (a); imaginary story 2.00
❑405, Mar 1985 CS, KS (a) 2.00
❑406, Apr 1985 CS, IN (a) 2.00
❑407, May 1985, JOy (c); IN (a); powers passed along 2.00
❑408, Jun 1985, AW (c); AW, CS (a); nuclear nightmare 2.00
❑409, Jul 1985, AW (c); AW, CS, KS (a); T.M. Maple L.O.C.; Jerry Siegel L.O.C. 2.00
❑410, Aug 1985, KJ (c); AW, CS (a); V: Luthor 2.00
❑411, Sep 1985, DG (c); MA, CS (w); MA, CS (a); Julius Schwartz' birthday; MASK preview comic 2.00
❑412, Oct 1985; KJ (c); CS (a); V: Luthor 2.00
❑413, Nov 1985, KJ (c); AW, CS (a); V: Luthor; Lex Luthor continued in Crisis on Infinite Earths #6 ..... 2.00
❑414, Dec 1985, AW, CS (a); Crisis on Infinite Earths cross-over 2.00
❑415, Jan 1986, AW, CS (a); Crisis on Infinite Earths cross-over 2.00
❑416, Feb 1986, AW, CS (a); Superman learns Luthor's connection to Einstein 2.00
❑417, Mar 1986, CS (a); imaginary story 2.00
❑418, Apr 1986, CS (a) 2.00
❑419, May 1986, CS (a) 2.00
❑420, Jun 1986 CS (a) 2.00
❑421, Jul 1986, (c); JO (w); CS (a); MASK comic insert 2.00
❑422, Aug 1986, BB (c); TY, CS (a) 2.00
❑423, Sep 1986, CS (c); AMo (w); GP, CS (a); series continues as Adventures of Superman; imaginary story 5.00
❑Ann 1, Oct 1960; 1&O: Supergirl. 1: Supergirl reprinted. Reprints Action Comics #252 ..... 600.00
❑Ann 1/2nd, Oct 1998, Replica edition; CS (c); CS, KS (a); Cardstock cover; Replica Edition; reprints Giant Superman Ann #1 ..... 5.00
❑Ann 2, ca. 1960; O: Titano 325.00
❑Ann 3, Sum 1961; Strange Lives of Superman 210.00
❑Ann 4, Win 1961; O: Legion of Super-Heroes 180.00
❑Ann 5, Sum 1962, (c); (w); (a); Krypton related stories 105.00
❑Ann 6, Win 1962; 1: Legion of Super-Heroes. Reprints Adventure Comics #247 ..... 90.00
❑Ann 7, Jun 1963, 25th anniversary; (c); (w); (a); O: Superman-Batman team .. 62.00
❑Ann 8, Sum 1963, (c); (w); (a); Untold Stories and Secret Origins 46.00
❑Ann 9, ca. 1983 ..... 5.00
❑Ann 10, ca. 1984, MA, CS (a) 5.00
❑Ann 11, ca. 1985, DaG (c); AMo (w); DaG (a); A: Wonder Woman. A: Robin. A: Batman. V: Mongul 4.00
❑Ann 12, ca. 1986, BB (c); V: Luthor's Warsuit; Dave Gibbons L.O.C 3.00
❑Special 1, ca. 1983, GK, (c); GK (w); GK (a) 4.00
❑Special 2, Apr 1984; V: Brainiac 4.00
❑Special 3, Apr 1985, IN (a); V: Amazo.. 4.00

Superman
DC

❑0, Oct 1994, ▲1994-38 ..... 3.00
❑1, Jan 1987, JBy (c); JBy (w); JBy (a); 1: Metallo (new) 4.00
❑2, Feb 1987, JBy (c); JBy (w); JBy (a) . 3.50
❑3, Mar 1987, JBy (c); JBy (w); JBy (a); 1: Amazing Grace. Legends chapter 17 cross-over 3.00
❑4, Apr 1987, JBy (c); JBy (w); JBy (a); 1: Bloodsport 2.50
❑5, May 1987, JBy (c); JBy (w); JBy (a); Superman battles H'v'ler'ni 2.50
❑6, Jun 1987, JBy, (c); JBy (w); JBy (a); 1: A'x'lar; Beau Smith LOC 2.00
❑7, Jul 1987, JBy (c); JBy (w); JBy (a); 1&O: Rampage (DC) 2.00
❑8, Aug 1987, JBy (c); JBy (w); JBy (a); A: Superboy. A: Legion of Super-Heroes. Continued in Adventure Comics #591 ..... 2.00
❑9, Sep 1987, JBy (c); JBy (w); JBy (a); A: Joker. V: Joker. V: Luthor 3.50
❑10, Oct 1987, JBy (c); JBy (w); JBy (a); Superman's powers go crazy 2.00
❑11, Nov 1987, JBy (c); JBy (w); JBy (a); O: Mr. Mxyzptlk 2.00
❑12, Dec 1987, JBy, (c); JBy (w); JBy (a); O: Lori Lemaris; Manhunters capture the Kent parents 2.00
❑13, Jan 1988, JBy (c); JBy (w); JBy (a); Millennium Week 2 ..... 2.00
❑14, Feb 1988, JBy (c); JBy (w); JBy (a); A: Green Lantern. Millennium Week 6 2.00
❑15, Mar 1988, JBy (c); JBy (w); JBy (a); 1: Skyhook 2.00
❑16, Apr 1988, JBy (c); JBy (w); JBy (a); V: Prankster 2.00
❑17, May 1988, JBy (c); JBy (w); JBy (a); V: Silver Banshee 2.00
❑18, Jun 1988, JBy (w); Return to Krypton 2.00
❑19, Jul 1988, JOy (c); JBy (w); JBy (a); 1: Dreadnaught. 1: Psi-Phon; Continued in Adventures of Superman #442 ..... 2.00
❑20, Aug 1988, JBy (c); JBy (w); JBy (a); A: Doom Patrol 2.00
❑21, Sep 1988, JBy (c); JBy (w); JBy (a); Supergirl 2.00
❑22, Oct 1988, JBy, (c); JBy (w); JBy (a); Supergirl 2.00
❑23, Nov 1988, CR (a); A: Batman. V: Silver Banshee 2.00
❑24, Dec 1988, KGa (c); KGa (a); V: Rampage 2.00
❑25, Dec 1988, KGa (c); KGa (a); V: Milton Fine/Braniac 2.00
❑26, Jan 1989, KGa (c); KGa (a); Invasion! 2.00
❑27, Jan 1989, KGa (c); KGa (a); Invasion! 2.00
❑28, Feb 1989, KGa (c); KGa (a); in space 2.00
❑29, Mar 1989, KGa (c); JOy (w); in space 2.00
❑30, Apr 1989, KGa (c); KGa (a); in space 2.00
❑31, May 1989, KGa (c); Mxyzptlk vs. Luthor 2.00
❑32, Jun 1989, KGa (c); KGa (a); V: Mongul 2.00
❑33, Jul 1989, KGa (c); KGa (a) 2.00
❑34, Aug 1989, KGa (c); JOy (w); KGa (a); V: Skyhook 2.00
❑35, Sep 1989, KGa (c); JOy (w); CS, KGa (a); A: Black Racer. simultaneous stories 2.00
❑36, Oct 1989, JOy, KGa (c); JOy (w); JOy (a); V: Prankster 2.00
❑37, Nov 1989, JOy (c); JOy (w); JOy (a); A: Newsboys 2.00
❑38, Dec 1989, JOy (c); JOy (w); JOy (a) 2.00
❑39, Jan 1990, JOy (c); JOy (w); KGa, BMc (a); Lightning Racers insert 2.00
❑40, Feb 1990, JOy (c); JOy (w); JOy (a) 2.00
❑41, Mar 1990, JOy (c); JOy (w); JOy (a); A: Lobo. The Day of the Krypton Man part 1 ..... 2.00
❑42, Apr 1990, JOy (c); JOy (w); JOy (a); The Day of the Krypton Man part 4 .... 2.00
❑43, May 1990, JOy (c); JOy (w); JOy (a); V: Kryptonite Man 2.00
❑44, Jun 1990, JOy (c); JOy (w); JOy (a); A: Batman. Dark Knight over Metropolis 2.00
❑45, Jul 1990, JOy (c); JOy (w); JOy (a); Jimmy Olsen's Diary insert 2.00
❑46, Aug 1990, JOy (c); JOy (w); JOy (a); A: Jade. A: Obsidian. V: Terraman 2.00
❑47, Sep 1990, JOy, (c); JOy (w); JOy (a); V: Blaze. Soul Search - Chapter 2 ..... 2.00
❑48, Oct 1990, KGa, BMc (c); CS (a); A: Sinbad 2.00
❑49, Nov 1990, JOy (c); JOy (w); JOy (a) 2.00
❑50, Dec 1990, JOy (c); JOy (w); JOy, JBy, CS, KGa (a); Clark Kent proposes to Lois Lane 4.00
❑50/2nd, Dec 1990, JOy (c); JOy (w); JOy, JBy, CS, KGa (a); Clark Kent proposes to Lois Lane 1.75
❑51, Jan 1991, JOy (c); JOy (w); JOy (a); 1: Mister Z. ▲1991-1 ..... 2.00
❑52, Feb 1991, JOy (c); JOy (w); KGa (a); V: Terraman; ▲1991-4; V: Terra-Man. 2.00
❑52/2nd, Feb 1991, 2nd printing; ▲1991-4 ..... 1.00
❑53, Mar 1991, JOy (c); JOy (w); JOy (a); ▲1991-7; Lois reacts to Superman disclosing identity 2.50
❑53/2nd, Mar 1991, JOy (c); JOy (w); JOy (a); Lois reacts to Superman disclosing identity 1.50
❑54, Apr 1991, JOy (c); JOy (w); JOy (a); ▲1991-10; Time & Time Again, Part 3; Newsboy Legion back-up 1.75
❑55, May 1991, JOy (c); JOy (w); JOy (a); A: Demon. ▲1991-13; Time & Time Again, Part 6; Newboy Legion back-up 1.75
❑56, Jun 1991, ▲1991-16; Newsboy Legion backup 1.75
❑57, Jul 1991, Double-size; BMc (a); Krypton Man 2.00
❑58, Aug 1991, V: Bloodhounds. ▲1991-24 ..... 1.50
❑59, Sep 1991, ▲1991-28 ..... 1.50
❑60, Oct 1991, 1: Agent Liberty. V: Intergang. ▲1991-32 ..... 2.00
❑61, Nov 1991, A: Linear Men. A: Waverider. ▲1991-36 ..... 1.50
❑62, Dec 1991, ▲1991-40; Sonic the Hedgehog insert 1.50
❑63, Jan 1992, A: Aquaman. ▲1992-2.. 1.50

Tarzan

Manning masterpieces in majority of issues
©Gold Key

Tarzan

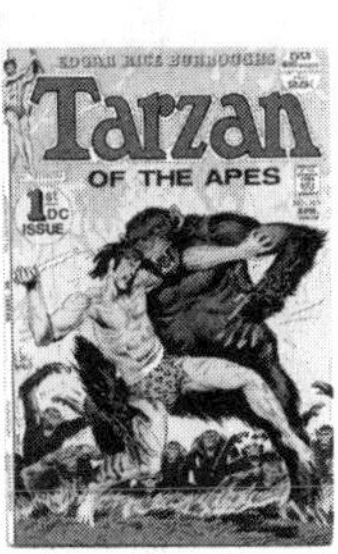

Joe Kubert adapted Burroughs' books
©DC

Tarzan

John Buscema covers post-World War I tales
©Marvel

Tarzan

Disney animation returned to ape man's roots
©Dark Horse

Tarzan/Carson of Venus

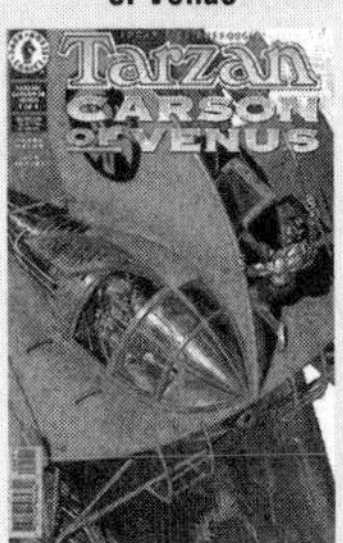

Jungle lord travels to planet of love
©Dark Horse

	N-MINT
❑64, Feb 1992, BG (a); Christmas issue.	1.50
❑65, Mar 1992, A: Guy Gardner. A: Deathstroke. A: Captain Marvel. A: Batman. A: Aquaman. ▲1992-10	1.50
❑66, Apr 1992, A: Guy Gardner. A: Deathstroke. A: Captain Marvel. A: Batman. A: Aquaman. ▲1992-14; Most DC characters appear	1.50
❑67, May 1992, ▲1992-18	1.50
❑68, Jun 1992, Deathstroke	1.50
❑69, Jul 1992, ▲1992-26	1.50
❑70, Aug 1992, Robin	1.50
❑71, Sep 1992, ▲1992-34	1.50
❑72, Oct 1992, ▲1992-38	1.50
❑73, Nov 1992, A: Doomsday. A: Waverider. ▲1992-42	3.00
❑73/2nd, Nov 1992, ▲1992-42	1.75
❑74, Dec 1992, Doomsday; ▲1992-74	4.00
❑74/2nd, Dec 1992, ▲1992-74	1.50
❑75, Jan 1993, D: Superman. newsstand; unbagged	5.00
❑75/CS, Jan 1993, D: Superman. ▲1993-2; Memorial Set; Includes poster, stamps, arm band, trading card, obituary	12.00
❑75/Platinum, Jan 1993, Platinum edition; D: Superman; ▲1993-2; RRP giveaway; Cover is identical to Memorial Edition but with silver platinum lettering; Includes poster, stamps, arm band, trading card, obituary	40.00
❑75/2nd, Jan 1993, D: Superman. 2nd printing; ▲1993-2; Gatefold back-cover	2.00
❑75/3rd, Jan 1993, D: Superman. 3rd printing; ▲1993-2; Gatefold back-cover	1.50
❑75/4th, Jan 1993, D: Superman. 4th printing; ▲1993-2; D: Superman; Gatefold back-cover	1.50
❑76, Feb 1993, ▲1993-6	2.50
❑77, Mar 1993, ▲1993-10	2.50
❑78, Jun 1993, 1: Cyborg Superman. ▲1993-14; Includes poster; 1: Man of Tomorrow; Reign of the Supermen!	2.00
❑78/CS, Jun 1993, 1: Cyborg Superman. Die-cut cover	2.50
❑79, Jul 1993, ▲1993-18; Reign of the Supermen!	2.00
❑80, Aug 1993, V: Mongul. Coast City destroyed; Cyborg Superman revealed as evil	2.00
❑81, Sep 1993, ▲1993-26; O: Cyborg Superman; Reign of the Supermen!	2.00
❑82, Oct 1993, return of Superman; Reign of the Superman ends; True Superman revealed	2.00
❑82/Variant, Oct 1993, Chromium cover; with poster; Reign of the Superman ends; True Superman revealed	3.50
❑83, Nov 1993, ▲1993-34; Funeral For a Friend Epilogue	2.00
❑84, Dec 1993, D: Adam Grant. V: Toyman. ▲1993-38; D: Adam Grant; V: Toyman; D: Adam Grant (Cat Grant's son)	2.00
❑85, Jan 1994, ▲1994-2	2.00
❑86, Feb 1994, ▲1994-6	2.00
❑87, Mar 1994, Bizarro	2.00
❑88, Apr 1994, Bizarro	2.00
❑89, May 1994, ▲1994-18	2.00

	N-MINT
❑90, Jun 1994, BA (a); ▲1994-22; The Battle For Metropolis!	2.00
❑91, Jul 1994, BA (a); ▲1993-26; The Fall of Metropolis!	2.00
❑92, Aug 1994, ▲1994-30	2.00
❑93, Sep 1994, Zero Hour	2.00
❑94, Nov 1994, ▲ 1994-42; Dead Again!	2.00
❑95, Dec 1994, A: Atom. ▲ 1994-46; Dead Again!	2.00
❑96, Jan 1995, ▲1995-2	2.00
❑97, Feb 1995, 1: Shadowdragon. ▲1995-6	2.00
❑98, Mar 1995, ▲1995-10	2.00
❑99, Apr 1995, A: Agent Liberty. ▲1995-14	2.00
❑100, May 1995, 100th anniversary edition; ▲1995-18	3.00
❑100/Variant, May 1995, 100th anniversary edition; enhanced cover; ▲1995-18	4.00
❑101, Jun 1995, ▲1995-22	2.00
❑102, Jul 1995, V: Captain Marvel. ▲1995-26	2.00
❑103, Aug 1995, V: Arclight. ▲1995-31	2.00
❑104, Sep 1995, Cyborg is released by Darkseid	2.00
❑105, Oct 1995, A: Green Lantern. ▲1995-39	2.00
❑106, Nov 1995, ▲1995-44; The Trial of Superman!	2.00
❑107, Dec 1995, ▲1995-48; The Trial of Superman!	2.00
❑108, Jan 1996, D: Mope; ▲1996-3	2.00
❑109, Feb 1996, Christmas story; return of Lori Lemaris; ▲1996-7	2.00
❑110, Mar 1996, JOy (w); A: Plastic Man. ▲1996-11	2.00
❑111, Apr 1996, ▲1996-16	2.00
❑112, Jun 1996, ▲1996-20	2.00
❑113, Jul 1996, ▲1996-24	2.00
❑114, Aug 1996, MWa (w); CS (a); ▲1996-29	2.00
❑115, Sep 1996, Lois becomes foreign correspondent	2.00
❑116, Oct 1996, Teen Titans preview	2.00
❑117, Nov 1996, Final Night; ▲1996-42	2.00
❑118, Dec 1996, A: Wonder Woman. Lois decides to return to Metropolis; ▲1996-46	2.00
❑119, Jan 1997, A: Legion. ▲1997-1	2.00
❑120, Feb 1997, ▲1997-6	2.00
❑121, Mar 1997, ▲1997-10	2.00
❑122, Apr 1997, energy powers begin to manifest	2.00
❑123, May 1997, New costume	3.00
❑123/Variant, May 1997, glow-in-the-dark cardstock cover; New costume	5.00
❑124, Jun 1997, A: Booster Gold. ▲1997-23	2.00
❑125, Jul 1997, A: Atom. in Kandor	2.00
❑126, Aug 1997, A: Batman. ▲1997-31	2.00
❑127, Sep 1997, Superman Revenge Squad leader's identity revealed	2.00
❑128, Oct 1997, V: Cyborg Superman. Genesis	2.00
❑129, Nov 1997, A: Scorn. ▲1997-44	2.00
❑130, Dec 1997, Face cover	2.00
❑131, Jan 1998, D: Mayor Berkowitz. birth of Lena Luthor	2.00
❑132, Feb 1998, ▲1998-7	2.00

	N-MINT
❑133, Mar 1998, ▲1998-12	2.00
❑134, Apr 1998, Millennium Giants	2.00
❑135, May 1998, leads into Superman Forever #1; End of Superman Red/Blue	2.00
❑136, Jul 1998, ▲1998-25	2.00
❑137, Aug 1998, V: Muto; ▲1998-29	2.00
❑138, Sep 1998, A: Kismet. V: Dominus. V: Dominus; ▲1998-33	2.00
❑139, Oct 1998, V: Dominus. ▲1998-37	1.99
❑140, Dec 1998, in Kandor; Inventor's identity revealed	1.99
❑141, Jan 1999, 1: Outburst. ▲1999-4.	1.99
❑142, Feb 1999, A: Outburst	1.99
❑143, Mar 1999, A: Supermen of America. A: Superman Robots. ▲1999-13	1.99
❑144, Apr 1999, Fortress destroyed	1.99
❑145, Jun 1999, ▲1999-23	1.99
❑146, Jul 1999, A: Toyman. ▲1999-27.	1.99
❑147, Aug 1999, Superman as Green Lantern	1.99
❑148, Sep 1999, ▲1999-36	1.99
❑149, Oct 1999, SB (a); ▲1999-40	1.99
❑150, Nov 1999, ▲1999-44	1.99
❑150/Variant, Nov 1999, Special cover	3.95
❑151, Dec 1999, Daily Planet reopens	1.99
❑152, Jan 2000, JPH (w); ▲2000-1	1.99
❑153, Feb 2000, JPH (w); ▲2000-5	1.99
❑154, Mar 2000, ▲2000-10; Y2K	1.99
❑155, Apr 2000, ▲2000-14	1.99
❑156, May 2000, JPH (w); ▲2000-18	1.99
❑157, Jun 2000, JPH (w); ▲2000-22	1.99
❑158, Jul 2000, ▲2000-26	1.99
❑159, Aug 2000, ▲2000-30; Green Lantern	1.99
❑160, Sep 2000, JPH (w); ▲2000-34; Superman: Arkham	2.25
❑161, Oct 2000, JPH (w); ▲2000-39	2.25
❑162, Nov 2000, JPH (w); ▲2000-43	2.25
❑163, Dec 2000, JPH (w); ▲2000-47	2.25
❑164, Jan 2001, JPH (w); ▲2001-1	2.25
❑165, Feb 2001, JPH (w); RL (a); ▲2001-6	2.25
❑166, Mar 2001, JPH (w); ▲2001-10	2.25
❑167, Apr 2001, JPH (w); ▲2001-14	2.25
❑168, May 2001, JPH (w); ▲2001-18	2.25
❑169, Jun 2001, ▲2001-22	2.25
❑170, Jul 2001, JPH (w); A: Krypto. ▲2001-26	2.25
❑171, Aug 2001, JPH (w); ▲2001-30	4.00
❑172, Sep 2001, JPH (w); ▲2001-34; Our Worlds at War; Our Worlds at War: All-Out War!; Continued in JLA: Our Worlds At War	2.25
❑173, Oct 2001, JPH (w); BSz (a); ▲2001-38; D: Strange Visitor; Our Worlds At War: Casualties of War	2.25
❑174, Nov 2001, JPH (w); ▲2001-42	2.25
❑175, Dec 2001, Giant-size; JPH (w); ▲2001-46; Joker: Last Laugh crossover	3.50
❑176, Jan 2002, JPH (w); ▲2002-1	2.25
❑177, Feb 2002, JPH (w)	2.25
❑178, Mar 2002, JPH (w)	2.25
❑179, Apr 2002, JPH (w)	2.25
❑180, May 2002, JPH (w)	2.25
❑181, Jun 2002, JPH (w)	2.25
❑182, Jul 2002, JPH (w)	2.25
❑183, Aug 2002, JPH (w)	2.25

Other grades: Multiply price above by 5/6 for VF/NM • 2/3 for VERY FINE • 1/3 for FINE • 1/5 for VERY GOOD • 1/8 for GOOD

❑184, Sep 2002 2.25
❑185, Oct 2002, BA (a); V: Major Force . 2.25
❑186, Nov 2002 2.25
❑187, Dec 2002 2.25
❑188, Jan 2003, Aquaman (6th series) #1 preview 2.25
❑189, Feb 2003 2.25
❑190, Apr 2003 2.25
❑190/A, Apr 2003, Reprints Superman: The 10-Cent Adventure #1; Double feature issue 3.95
❑191, May 2003 2.25
❑192, Jun 2003 3.00
❑193, Jul 2003 2.25
❑194, Aug 2003 2.25
❑195, Sep 2003 2.25
❑196, Oct 2003 2.25
❑197, Nov 2003 2.25
❑198, Dec 2003 2.25
❑199, Jan 2004 2.25
❑200, Feb 2004 3.50
❑201, Mar 2004 8.00
❑202, Apr 2004, Preview of Lex Luthor: Man of Steel #1 2.25
❑203, May 2004, Jim Lee sketchbook.... 6.00
❑204, Jun 2004, JLee (c); JLee (a) 4.00
❑204/Sketch, ca. 2004, JLee (c); JLee (a); Jim Lee Sketch Cover; Diamond Retailer Summit variant 250.00
❑204/DF Lee, Jun 2004; Dynamic Forces variant 30.00
❑204/DF Azzarell, Jun 2004; Dynamic Forces variant 25.00
❑205/Lee, Jul 2004, JLee (c); JLee (a)... 4.00
❑205/Turner, Jul 2004, JLee (a); Variant cover 3.00
❑205/DF Lee, Jul 2004, JLee (c); JLee (a); Dynamic Forces variant 2.50
❑205/DF Turner, Jul 2004, JLee (a); Dynamic Forces variant 25.00
❑206, Aug 2004, JLee (c); JLee (a) 2.50
❑207, Sep 2004, JLee (c); JLee (a) 2.50
❑208, Oct 2004, JLee (c); JLee (a) 5.00
❑209, Nov 2004, JLee (c); JLee (a) 4.00
❑210, Dec 2004, Intimates preview; Question preview 2.50
❑211, Jan 2005 2.50
❑212, Feb 2005 2.50
❑213, Mar 2005 2.50
❑214, Apr 2005 2.50
❑215, May 2005; Forms diptych cover with Superman (2nd Series) #215/A .. 2.99
❑216, Jun 2005; Continued from Adventures of Superman #639; Jean Loring becomes Eclipso II 5.00
❑217, Jul 2005 7.00
❑218, Aug 2005 5.00
❑219, Sep 2005; The OMAC Project tie-in; Continued in Action Comics #829 . 6.00
❑219/Variant, Sep 2005 2.50
❑220, Oct 2005 2.50
❑221, Nov 2005; Villains United tie-in 2.50
❑222, Dec 2005; OMAC Project tie-in 2.50
❑223, Jan 2006; Infinite Crisis tie-in 2.50
❑224, Jan 2006, Infinite Crisis tie-in 2.50
❑225, Mar 2006 2.50
❑226, Apr 2006, Infinite Crisis crossover; Continued in Action Comics #836 2.50
❑650, May 2006, Resumes numbering from Superman (1st series) 8.00
❑651, Jun 2006, One Year Later; Continued in Action Comics #838 2.50
❑652, Jul 2006, One Year Later; Continued in Action Comics #839 2.99
❑653, Aug 2006, Cover by Terry Dodson and Rachel Dodson; Continued in Action Comics #840 2.99
❑654, Sep 2006, Heroscape: Quest for Concan's Castle insert 2.99
❑655, Oct 2006 2.99
❑656, Nov 2006, V: Subjekt-17 2.99
❑657, Jan 2007 2.99
❑658 2.99
❑659 2.99
❑660 2.99
❑661 2.99
❑662 2.99
❑663 2.99
❑664 2.99
❑665 2.99
❑666 2.99
❑667 2.99
❑668 2.99
❑669 2.99
❑670 2.99
❑671 2.99
❑672 2.99
❑673 2.99
❑674 2.99
❑675 2.99
❑676 2.99
❑677 2.99
❑678 2.99
❑679 2.99
❑680 2.99
❑681 2.99
❑682 2.99
❑683 2.99
❑684 2.99
❑685 2.99
❑686 2.99
❑687 2.99
❑688 2.99
❑689 2.99
❑1000000, Nov 1998, Continued in JLA #1,000,000 4.00
❑1000000/Ltd., Nov 1998, Signed edition 14.99
❑Ann 1, ca. 1987, O: Titano 4.00
❑Ann 2, ca. 1988, Private Lives 3.00
❑Ann 3, ca. 1991; Armageddon 2001; Continued in Batman Ann #15 2.50
❑Ann 3/2nd, ca. 1991, 2nd printing; ca. 1991; Continued in Batman Ann #15.. 2.00
❑Ann 3/3rd, ca. 1991, silver 2.00
❑Ann 4, ca. 1992; Eclipso: The Darkness Within; Superman continued in Action Comics Ann #4 2.50
❑Ann 5, ca. 1993, 1: Myriad; Bloodlines; 1993 Ann; Bloodlines: Outbreak 2.50
❑Ann 6, ca. 1994, Elseworlds 2.95
❑Ann 7, ca. 1995, A: Dr. Occult. A: Doctor Occult. Year One 3.95
❑Ann 8, ca. 1996, Legends of the Dead Earth; The League of Supermen 2.95
❑Ann 9, Jul 1997, A: Doc Savage. Pulp Heroes 2.95
❑Ann 10, Oct 1998, A: Phantom Zone villains. Ghosts 2.95
❑Ann 11, Oct 1999, JLApe 2.95
❑Ann 12, Aug 2000, 2000 Ann; Planet DC 3.50
❑GS 1, Feb 1999, 80 page giant size; Superman 80-Page Giant 4.95
❑GS 2, Jun 1999, 80 page giant size; Superman 80-Page Giant 4.95
❑GS 3, Nov 2000, 80 page giant size; KN (c); Superman 80-Page Giant 5.95
❑Special 1, ca. 1992, MG, TMc, FM, CS (a); 1992 Special 4.00
❑3D 1 5.00

Superman 3-D
DC

❑1, Dec 1998; Includes glasses 4.00

Superman Adventures
DC

❑1, Nov 1996; based on animated series; follow-up to pilot episode 3.00
❑2, Dec 1996; V: Metallo 2.50
❑3, Jan 1997; V: Brainiac 2.50
❑4, Feb 1997 2.00
❑5, Mar 1997; V: Livewire 2.00
❑6, Apr 1997 2.00
❑7, May 1997; V: Mala. V: Jax-ur 2.00
❑8, Jun 1997; V: Mala. V: Jax-ur 2.00
❑9, Jul 1997 2.00
❑10, Aug 1997; V: Toyman 2.00
❑11, Sep 1997 2.00
❑12, Oct 1997 2.00
❑13, Nov 1997 2.00
❑14, Dec 1997; ME (w); Face cover 2.00
❑15, Jan 1998 ME (w); A: Bibbo 2.00
❑16, Feb 1998 2.00
❑17, Mar 1998 2.00
❑18, Apr 1998 DGry (w) 2.00
❑19, May 1998 2.00
❑20, Jun 1998; V: Mastertrax 2.00
❑21, Jul 1998; double-sized; adapts Supergirl episode 3.95
❑22, Aug 1998; V: Braniac 2.00
❑23, Sep 1998; A: Livewire. V: Brainiac. 2.00
❑24, Oct 1998; V: Parasite 2.00
❑25, Nov 1998 A: Batgirl 2.00
❑26, Dec 1998; V: Mxyzptlk. V: Mxyzptlk 2.00
❑27, Jan 1999; 1: Superior-Man 2.00
❑28, Feb 1999; A: Jimmy Olsen. Jimmy and Superman switch bodies 2.00
❑29, Mar 1999; A: Bizarro. A: Lobo. Lobo appearance 2.00
❑30, Apr 1999 2.00
❑31, May 1999 2.00
❑32, Jun 1999 2.00
❑33, Jul 1999 2.00
❑34, Aug 1999 A: Doctor Fate 2.00
❑35, Sep 1999; V: Toyman 2.00
❑36, Oct 1999 2.00
❑37, Nov 1999; V: Multi-Face 2.00
❑38, Dec 1999 2.00
❑39, Jan 2000 2.00
❑40, Feb 2000 2.00
❑41, Mar 2000 1.99
❑42, Apr 2000 1.99
❑43, May 2000 1.99
❑44, Jun 2000 1.99
❑45, Jul 2000 1.99
❑46, Aug 2000 1.99
❑47, Sep 2000 1.99
❑48, Oct 2000 1.99
❑49, Nov 2000 1.99
❑50, Dec 2000 1.99
❑51, Jan 2001 1.99
❑52, Feb 2001 1.99
❑53, Mar 2001 ME (w) 1.99
❑54, Apr 2001 1.99
❑55, May 2001 1.99
❑56, Jun 2001 1.99
❑57, Jul 2001 1.99
❑58, Aug 2001 1.99
❑59, Sep 2001 1.99
❑60, Oct 2001 1.99
❑61, Nov 2001 1.99
❑62, Dec 2001 1.99
❑63, Jan 2002 1.99
❑64, Feb 2002 1.99
❑65, Mar 2002 1.99
❑66, Apr 2002; Final issue 1.99
❑Ann 1, ca. 1997; JSa (c); JSa (a); ties in with Adventures in the DC Universe Ann #1 and Batman and Robin Adventures Ann #2 3.95
❑Special 1, Feb 1998; V: Lobo 2.95

Superman/Aliens 2: God War
DC

❑1, May 2002; Darkseid appearance 2.99
❑2, Jun 2002 2.99
❑3, Jul 2002; Cardstock cover 2.99
❑4, Aug 2002 2.99

Superman: A Nation Divided
DC

❑1; prestige format; Elseworlds; Superman in Civil War 4.95

Superman & Batman: Generations
DC

❑1, Jan 1999; Elseworlds story 4.95
❑2, Feb 1999; Elseworlds story 4.95
❑3, Mar 1999; Elseworlds story 4.95
❑4, Apr 1999; Elseworlds story 4.95

Superman & Batman: Generations II
DC

❑1, Oct 2001 5.95
❑2, Nov 2001 5.95
❑3, Dec 2001 5.95
❑4, Jan 2002 5.95

Superman & Batman: Generations III
DC

❑1, Mar 2003; Elseworlds 2.95
❑2, Apr 2003 2.95
❑3, May 2003 2.95
❑4, Jun 2003 2.95
❑5, Jul 2003 2.95
❑6, Aug 2003 2.95
❑7, Sep 2003 2.95
❑8, Oct 2003 2.95
❑9, Nov 2003 2.95
❑10, Dec 2003 2.95
❑11, Jan 2004 2.95
❑12, Feb 2004 2.95

Tarzan: The Lost Adventure

Previously unpublished tale captures pulp feel
©Dark Horse

Team Titans

Time-traveling team meets present-day Titans
©DC

Tech Jacket

Kirkman creation not Invincible
©Image

Teenage Hotrodders

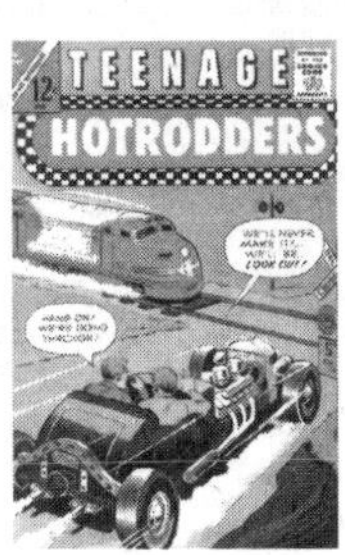

Thrill-seeking youngsters tightly tune heaps
©Charlton

Teenage Mutant Ninja Turtles

Irradiated amphibians trained by rodent master
©Mirage

N-MINT

Superman & Batman Magazine
Welsh

- ❑1, Sum 1993; bagged with poster 3.00
- ❑2, Fal 1993; Pullout features The Atom 2.00
- ❑3, Win 1993; trading cards 3.00
- ❑4, Spr 1994 .... 2.00
- ❑5, Sum 1994; magazine 2.00
- ❑7, Win 1995; magazine 2.00
- ❑8, Spr 1995; magazine 2.00

Superman and Batman: World's Funnest
DC

- ❑1, ca. 2000 .... 6.95

Superman & Bugs Bunny
DC

- ❑1, Jul 2000 .... 2.50
- ❑2, Aug 2000 .... 2.50
- ❑3, Sep 2000 .... 2.50
- ❑4, Oct 2000 .... 2.50

Superman & Savage Dragon: Chicago
DC

- ❑1, Dec 2002 .... 5.95

Superman & Savage Dragon: Metropolis
DC

- ❑nn, Nov 1999; Prestige-format one-shot crossover with Image 4.95

Superman: At Earth's End
DC

- ❑1, ca. 1995 .... 4.95

Superman/Batman Secret Files
DC

- ❑1, Dec 2003 .... 4.95

Superman/Batman
DC

- ❑1, Oct 2003; Batman cover 8.00
- ❑1/Retailer ed., Oct 2003; Retailer incentive edition (aka RRP edition); no cover price 125.00
- ❑1/2nd, Oct 2003 .... 4.00
- ❑1/3rd, Oct 2003 .... 4.00
- ❑2, Nov 2003 .... 6.00
- ❑3, Dec 2003 .... 5.00
- ❑3/2nd, Mar 2004 .... 2.95
- ❑4, Jan 2004 .... 4.00
- ❑5, Feb 2004 .... 2.95
- ❑6, Mar 2004 JPH (w) 4.00
- ❑7, Apr 2004 JPH (w) 2.95
- ❑8, May 2004; 1: Supergirl V (Kara Zor-El) 10.00
- ❑8/2nd, May 2004, Turner sketch cover. 7.00
- ❑8/3rd, May 2004, Wonder Woman cover by Michael Turner 6.00
- ❑8/4th, Aug 2004 .... 2.95
- ❑9, Jun 2004 .... 5.00
- ❑9/2nd, Jul 2004; reprint 4.00
- ❑9/3rd, Aug 2004 .... 2.95
- ❑10, Jul 2004; D: Harbinger 5.00
- ❑10/2nd, Aug 2004 .... 4.00
- ❑11, Sep 2004 .... 5.00
- ❑12, Oct 2004 .... 4.00
- ❑13, Dec 2004, Superman, Batman and Darkseid cover 5.00
- ❑13/Supergirl, Dec 2004 .... 7.00
- ❑14, Jan 2005 .... 5.00

N-MINT

- ❑15, Feb 2005 .... 4.00
- ❑16, Mar 2005 .... 5.00
- ❑17, Apr 2005 .... 4.00
- ❑18, May 2005; Final Page tribute to "Whatever Happened to the Man of Tomorrow?" 2.95
- ❑19, Jun 2005; Price increase 4.00
- ❑20, Jul 2005; Heroscape Insert #3: The New Recruit 2.99
- ❑21, Aug 2005 .... 4.00
- ❑22, Oct 2005 .... 2.99
- ❑23, Feb 2006 .... 2.99
- ❑24, Jun 2006 .... 2.99
- ❑26, Aug 2006, Superboy/Robin yellow cover; Sam Loeb tribute issue 3.99
- ❑27, Sep 2006 .... 2.99
- ❑28, Sep 2006, Heroescape Insert: Quest For Concan's Castle 2.99
- ❑29, Nov 2006, Green Lantern appearances/storyline (Kilowog; Hal Jordan; John Stewart) 2.99
- ❑30, Feb 2007, Kilowog V: Superman; Starfire V: Batman 2.99
- ❑31, Mar 2007 .... 2.99
- ❑32 .... 2.99
- ❑Ann 1, Jan 2007 .... 3.99

Superman: Birthright
DC

- ❑1, Sep 2003 .... 2.95
- ❑2, Oct 2003 .... 2.95
- ❑3, Nov 2003 .... 2.95
- ❑4, Jan 2004 .... 2.95
- ❑5, Feb 2004 .... 2.95
- ❑6, Mar 2004 .... 2.95
- ❑7, Apr 2004 .... 2.95
- ❑8, May 2004 .... 2.95
- ❑9, May 2004 .... 2.95
- ❑10, Jul 2004 .... 2.95
- ❑11, Aug 2004 .... 2.95
- ❑12, Sep 2004 .... 2.95

Superman: Blood of My Ancestors
DC

- ❑1, Nov 2003 .... 6.95

Superman Confidential
DC

- ❑1, Jan 2007, 1: Sara Hunter; Includes 3-D Heroscape glasses; Includes Teen Titans: Sparktop mini-comic 2.99
- ❑2, Feb 2007 .... 2.99
- ❑3, Mar 2007 .... 2.99
- ❑4 .... 2.99

Superman: Day of Doom
DC

- ❑1, ca. 2003; Includes preview of Gotham Central 9.95

Superman: Distant Fires
DC

- ❑1, Feb 1998; prestige format; Elseworlds 5.95

Superman/Doomsday: Hunter/Prey
DC

- ❑1, ca. 1994, prestige format 6.00
- ❑2, ca. 1994, prestige format; O: Doomsday 6.00
- ❑3, ca. 1994, prestige format; D: Doomsday 6.00

N-MINT

Superman: Emperor Joker
DC

- ❑1, Oct 2000; ▲2000-38 .... 3.50

Superman Family
DC

- ❑164, May 1974, NC (c); CS, JM, KS (a); Series continued from Superman's Pal Jimmy Olsen; reprints from Action #339, Adventure #272, Lois Lane #51, and Jimmy Olsen #76 .... 35.00
- ❑165, Jul 1974, reprints from Action #296, Jimmy Olsen #59, Lois Lane #47, Superboy #111, #133, and Superman #186 .... 13.00
- ❑166, Sep 1974, NC (c); CS, JM (a); Reprints w/ new Lois Lane story 13.00
- ❑167, Nov 1974, NC (c); KS (a); Reprints from Superboy (1st series) #100, and #124; Jimmy Olsen stories new 13.00
- ❑168, Jan 1975, Supergirl reprinted from Action #350; Bizarro Luthor reprinted from Adventure #293; Lois Lane story new 13.00
- ❑169, Mar 1975, NC (c); JM (a); Lois Lane; Jimmy Olsen: Superman's Pal Jimmy Olsen #63; Supergirl: Action Comics #350; Krypto: Adventure Comics #269; Superboy: Adventure Comics #236; Tales Of The Bizarro World: Adventure Comics #293; 100 Pages 13.00
- ❑170, May 1975, Jimmy Olsen; Supergirl: Action Comics #337; Lois Lane: Superman's Girl Friend Lois Lane #45; Mr Mxyzptlk: Superboy #120; 64 Pages 11.00
- ❑171, Jul 1975, Supergirl; Lois Lane: Superman's Girl Friend Lois Lane #29; Jimmy Olsen: Superman's Pal Jimmy Olsen #111; 64 pages; Reprints from Superman's Girl Friend Lois Lane #29, Superman's Pal Jimmy Olsen #111 .... 11.00
- ❑172, Sep 1975, KS (c); CS, KS (a); A: Green Lantern. Reprints from Action #364, and Jimmy Olsen #85 .... 11.00
- ❑173, Nov 1975, Jimmy Olsen; Supergirl: Action Comics #338; Krypto: Superboy #51; Lois Lane: Superman's Girl Friend Lois Lane #69; 64 pages; Reprints from Action Comics #338, Superboy #51, and Superman's Girl Friend Lois Lane #69; Jimmy Olsen story 11.00
- ❑174, Jan 1976, Supergirl; Lois Lane: Superman's Girl Friend Lois Lane #88; Jimmy Olsen: Superman's Pal Jimmy Olsen #9; Superman: Superman #102; 64 pages; Reprints from Superman's Girl Friend Lois Lane #88, Superman's Pal Jimmy Olsen #9, and Superman #102; Supergirl story 11.00
- ❑175, Mar 1976, Lois Lane; Supergirl: Action Comics #303; Jimmy Olsen: Superman's Pal Jimmy Olsen #21; Perry White: Superman #180; 64 pages; Reprints from Supergirl: Action Comics #303, Jimmy Olsen: Superman's Pal Jimmy Olsen #21, and Perry White: Superman #108; Lois Lane story 11.00
- ❑176, May 1976, Reprints from Superman's Girl Friend Lois Lane #98, Action Comics # 372, Superboy #125; 64 pages; Jimmy Olsen story; Lois Lane story; Supergirl story; Krypto story.... 11.00
- ❑177, Jul 1976, reprints from Jimmy Olsen #74 and Lois Lane #53 .... 11.00

Other grades: Multiply price above by 5/6 for VF/NM • 2/3 for VERY FINE • 1/3 for FINE • 1/5 for VERY GOOD • 1/8 for GOOD

❑178, Sep 1976, Reprints Action Comics #257 and Superman's Pal Jimmy Olsen #62; Lois Lane story; Supergirl story; Jimmy Olsen story 5.00
❑179, Oct 1976, Reprints Superman's Girl Friend Lois Lane #18 and Action Comics #255; Giant-size; Jimmy Olsen story; Lois Lane story; Supergirl story 5.00
❑180, Nov 1976, Supergirl; Jimmy Olsen: Superman's Pal Jimmy Olsen #71; Lois Lane: Superman's Girl Friend Lois Lane #17; Giant-size; Supergirl story; Jimmy Olsen: Superman's Pal Jimmy Olsen #71 reprint; Lois Lane: Superman's Girl Friend Lois Lane #17 reprint.............. 5.00
❑181, Jan 1977, Lois Lane; Jimmy Olsen: Superman's Pal Jimmy Olsen #57; Lois Lane story; Jimmy Olsen: Superman's Pal Jimmy Olsen #57 reprint 3.50
❑182, Apr 1977; Jimmy Olsen; Superbaby; Lois Lane; The Fabulous World of Krypton; Supergirl; Krypto; Jimmy Olsen stories; Superbaby story; Lois Lane story; The Fabulous World of Krypton story; Supergirl story; Krypto story.. 3.50
❑183, Jun 1977; Supergirl; Krypto; Jimmy Olsen; Perry White; Nightwing and Flamebird; Lois Lane; Supergirl story; Krypto story; Jimmy Olsen story; Perry White story; Nightwing and Flamebird story; Lois Lane story 3.50
❑184, Aug 1977; V: Prankster; Jimmy Olsen; Krypto; Lois Lane; Nightwing and Flamebird; Superman; Supergirl; O: Supergirl; Krypto story; Lois Lane story; Nightwing and Flamebird story; Superman story; Supergirl story; Jimmy Olsen story 3.50
❑185, Oct 1977; Jimmy Olsen; Superman; Lois Lane; Krypto; Nightwing and Flamebird; Supergirl; Jimmy Olsen story; Superman story; Lois Lane story; Krypto story; Nightwing and Flamebird story; Supergirl story 3.50
❑186, Dec 1977; A: Earth-2 Superman. Jimmy Olsen; Superman; Lois Lane; Krypto; Nightwing & Flamebird; Supergirl; 80 pages 3.50
❑187, Feb 1978; A: Earth-2 Superman. Jimmy Olsen; Superman; Lois Lane; Krypto; NIghtwing and Flamebird; Supergirl; 80 pages 3.50
❑188, Apr 1978; Red Kryptonite 3.50
❑189, Jun 1978; Jimmy Olsen; Superman; Lois Lane; Krypto; Nightwing and Flamebird; Supergirl; 80 pages.. 3.50
❑190, Aug 1978; Book Length Novel; Jimmy Olsen; Superman; Lois Lane; Krypto; Nightwing & Flamebird; Supergirl; Book Length Novel made up of individual stories; Jimmy Olsen story; Superman story; Lois Lane story; Krypto story; Nightwing & Flamebird story; Supergirl story 3.50
❑191, Oct 1978; Superboy; Jimmy Olsen; Krypto; Supergirl; Lois Lane; Superman; Nightwing and Flamebird; Superboy story; Jimmy Olsen story; Krypto story; Supergirl story; Lois Lane story; Superman story; Nightwing and Flamebird story 3.50
❑192, Dec 1978; Superboy; Supergirl; Krypto; Jimmy Olsen; Superman; Lois Lane; Nightwing & Flamebird; Wraparound cover; Superboy story; Supergirl story; Krypto story; Jimmy Olsen story; Superman story; Lois Lane story; Nightwing & Flamebird story.... 3.50
❑193, Feb 1979; Superboy; Jimmy Olsen; Lois Lane; Supergirl; Superman; Nightwing and Flamebird; Wraparound cover; Superboy story; Jimmy Olsen story; Lois Lane story; Supergirl story; Superman story; Nightwing and Flamebird story 3.50
❑194, Apr 1979; RA (c); DH, JSa, MR, KS (a); V: Jimmy clones. V: Jimmy clones; Nightwing and Flamebird; Jimmy Olsen and Lois Lane; Supergirl; Superboy; Wraparound cover; Nightwing and Flamebird story; Jimmy Olsen and Lois Lane story; Supergirl story; Superboy story.. 3.50
❑195, Jun 1979; Superboy; Lois Lane; The Private Life of Clark Kent; Mr. & Mrs. Superman; Supergirl; Wraparound cover; Superboy story; Lois Lane story; The Private Life of Clark Kent story; Mr. & Mrs. Superman story; Supergirl story 3.50
❑196, Aug 1979; Superboy; Lois Lane; The Private Life of Clark Kent; Jimmy Olsen; Mr & Mrs Superman; Supergirl; Wraparound cover; Superboy story; Lois Lane story; The Private Life of Clark Kent story; Jimmy Olsen story; Mr & Mrs Superman story; Supergirl story 3.50
❑197, Oct 1979; The Private Life of Clark Kent; The Private Life of Clark Kent story; Superboy story; Supergirl story; Lois Lane story; Jimmy Olsen story... 3.50
❑198, Dec 1979; Superboy; Mr. & Mrs Superman; Jimmy Olsen; Lois Lane; Supergirl; Superboy story; Mr. & Mrs Superman story; Jimmy Olsen story; Lois Lane story; Supergirl story; Tamsyn O'Flynn L.O.C 3.50
❑199, Feb 1980; Supergirl; Mr. & Mrs. Superman; The Private Life Of Clark Kent; Lois Lane; Jimmy Olsen; Supergirl story; Mr. & Mrs. Superman story; The Private Life Of Clark Kent story; Lois Lane story; Jimmy Olsen story; Tamsyn O'Flynn LOC 3.50
❑200, Apr 1980; Imaginary Story 3.50
❑201, Jun 1980; Supergirl; Mr. & Mrs. Superman; The Private Life of Clark Kent; Lois Lane; Jimmy Olsen; Supergirl story; Mr. & Mrs. Superman story; The Private Life of Clark Kent story; Lois Lane story; Jimmy Olsen story.. 3.00
❑202, Aug 1980; Supergirl; Mr. & Mrs. Superman; The Private Life of Clark Kent; Lois Lane; Jimmy Olsen; Supergirl story; Mr. & Mrs. Superman story; The Private Life of Clark Kent story; Lois Lane story; Jimmy Olsen story; Tamsyn O'Flynn LOC 3.00
❑203, Oct 1980; Supergirl; Mr. & Mrs Superman; The Private Life of Clark Kent; Lois Lane; Jimmy Olsen; 1: Lana Lang (Earth 2); Supergirl story; Mr. & Mrs Superman story; The Private Life of Clark Kent story; Lois Lane story; Jimmy Olsen story; Tamsyn O'Flynn LOC 3.00
❑204, Dec 1980; V: Enchantress. Supergirl; The Private Life of Clark Kent; Mr. & Mrs. Superman; Lois Lane; Jimmy Olsen; O: Enchantress; The Private Life of Clark Kent story; Mr. & Mrs. Superman story; Lois Lane story; Jimmy Olsen story; Supergirl story.... 3.00
❑205, Feb 1981; 1: H.I.V.E.. V: Enchantress; Mr. & Mrs. Superman; The Private Life of Clark Kent; Lois Lane and Jimmy Olsen; Supergirl; Mr. & Mrs. Superman story; The Private Life of Clark Kent story; Lois Lane and Jimmy Olsen story; Supergirl story 3.00
❑206, Apr 1981; A: Lesla-Lar. Supergirl; Mr & Mrs Superman; The Private Life of Clark Kent; Lois Lane; Jimmy Olsen; Supergirl story; Mr & Mrs Superman story; The Private Life of Clark Kent story; Lois Lane story; Jimmy Olsen story.. 3.00
❑207, Jun 1981; A: Legion. V: Universo. V: Universo; Mr. & Mrs. Superman; The Private Life of Clark Kent; Lois Lane; Jimmy Olsen; Supergirl; Mr. & Mrs. Superman story; The Private Life of Clark Kent story; Lois Lane story; Jimmy Olsen story; Supergirl story.... 3.00
❑208, Jul 1981; Supergirl relocates to New York.. 3.00
❑209, Aug 1981; Supergirl; Mr. & Mrs. Superman; The Private Life of Clark Kent; Lois Lane; Jimmy Olsen; Supergirl story; Mr. & Mrs. Superman story; The Private Life of Clark Kent story; Lois Lane story; Jimmy Olsen story.. 3.00
❑210, Sep 1981; Supergirl; Mr. & Mrs. Superman; The Private Life of Clark Kent; Lois Lane; Jimmy Olsen; Supergirl story; Mr. & Mrs. Superman story; The Private Life of Clark Kent story; Lois Lane story; Jimmy Olsen story.. 3.00
❑211, Oct 1981; Supergirl; Mr. & Mrs. Superman; The Private Life of Clark Kent; Lois Lane; Jimmy Olsen; Supergirl story; Mr. & Mrs. Superman story; The Private Life of Clark Kent story; Lois Lane story; Jimmy Olsen story.. 3.00
❑212, Nov 1981; Supergirl; Mr. & Mrs. Superman; The Private Life of Clark Kent; Lois Lane; Jimmy Olsen; Supergirl story; Mr. & Mrs. Superman story; The Private Life of Clark Kent story; Lois Lane story; Jimmy Olsen story.. 3.00
❑213, Dec 1981; 1: Insect Queen (Lana Lang). Supergirl; Mr. & Mrs Superman; The Private Life of Clark Kent; Lois Lane; Jimmy Olsen; Supergirl story; Mr. & Mrs Superman story; The Private Life of Clark Kent story; Lois Lane story; Jimmy Olsen story; Todd McFarlane LOC 3.00
❑214, Jan 1982; Supergirl; Mr. & Mrs. Superman; The Private Life of Clark Kent; Lois Lane; Jimmy Olsen; Supergirl story; Mr. & Mrs. Superman story; The Private Life of Clark Kent story; Lois Lane story; Jimmy Olsen story.. 3.00
❑215, Feb 1982; Supergirl; Mr. & Mrs. Superman; The Private Life Of Clark Kent; Lois Lane; Jimmy Olsen; Supergirl story; Mr. & Mrs. Superman story; The Private Life Of Clark Kent story; Lois Lane story; Jimmy Olsen story.. 3.00
❑216, Mar 1982; Supergirl; Mr. & Mrs. Superman; Superbaby; Lois Lane; Jimmy Olsen; Supergirl story; Mr. & Mrs. Superman story; Superbaby story; Lois Lane story; Jimmy Olsen story.. 3.00
❑217, Apr 1982; Mr. & Mrs. Superman; Supergirl; Jimmy Olsen; Lois Lane; Mr. & Mrs. Superman story; Supergirl story; Jimmy Olsen story; Lois Lane story.. 3.00
❑218, May 1982; Supergirl; Jimmy Olsen; Lois Lane; Mr. & Mrs. Superman; Supergirl story; Jimmy Olsen story; Lois Lane story; Mr. & Mrs. Superman story.. 3.00
❑219, Jun 1982; V: Master Jailer; Mr. & Mrs. Superman; Jimmy Olsen; Lois Lane; Supergirl; Mr. & Mrs. Superman story; Jimmy Olsen story; Lois Lane story; Supergirl story 3.00
❑220, Jul 1982; V: Master Jailer; Jimmy Olsen; Lois Lane; Mr. & Mrs. Superman; Supergirl; Jimmy Olsen story; Lois Lane story; Mr. & Mrs. Superman story; Supergirl story........ 3.00
❑221, Aug 1982; V: Master Jailer; Jimmy Olsen; Lois Lane; Mr. & Mrs. Superman; Supergirl; Jimmy Olsen story; Lois Lane story; Mr. & Mrs. Superman story; Supergirl story........ 3.00
❑222, Sep 1982; Supergirl; Jimmy Olsen; Lois Lane; Mr. & Mrs. Superman; Final Issue; Supergirl story; Jimmy Olsen story; Lois Lane story; Mr. & Mrs. Superman story................................ 3.00

Superman/Fantastic Four
DC

❑1, ca. 1999; Tabloid-sized crossover byDC and Marvel 9.95

Superman for All Seasons
DC

❑1, Sep 1998; prestige format 4.95
❑2, Oct 1998; prestige format.............. 4.95
❑3, Nov 1998; prestige format.............. 4.95
❑4, Dec 1998; prestige format 4.95

Superman for Earth
DC

❑1, Apr 1991; Wraparound cover, Prestige format 4.95

Superman Forever
DC

❑1, Jun 1998; newsstand edition; JBy, DG (a); Superman returns to normal powers 5.50
❑1/Variant, Jun 1998; prestige format; lenticular animation cover; Superman returns to normal powers.................. 7.00

Super Manga Blast!
Dark Horse

❑1, Mar 2000, b&w series 4.95
❑2, Apr 2000, b&w 4.95
❑3, May 2000, b&w 4.95
❑4, Jun 2000, b&w 4.95
❑5, Jul 2000, b&w 4.95
❑6, Aug 2000, b&w 4.95
❑7, Sep 2000, b&w 4.95

Teenage Mutant Ninja Turtles

Move to Image opens crossovers

©Image

Teenage Mutant Ninja Turtles Adventures

Lighter fare for Archie audience

©Archie

Teenage Mutant Ninja Turtles Movie II

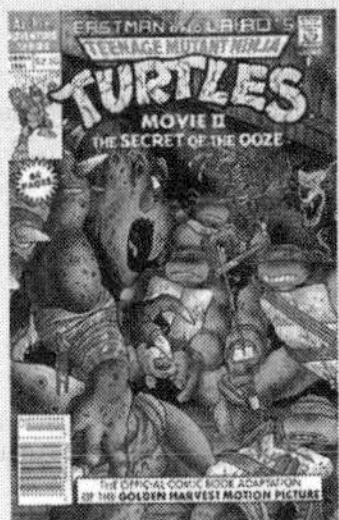

Turtles' true origins revealed

©Archie

Teen Comics

Unauthorized bios of youngsters' favorites

©Personality

Teen Confessions

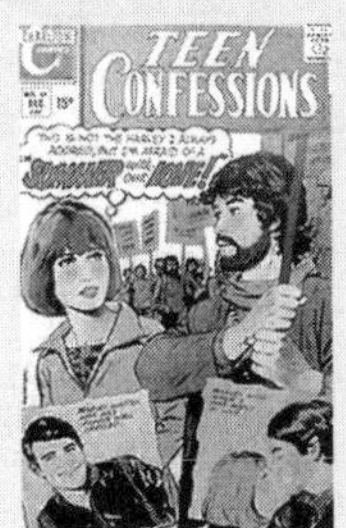

Romantic revelations of youths

©Charlton

N-MINT

❑8, Nov 2000, b&w 4.95
❑9, Jan 2001, b&w 4.95
❑10, Feb 2001, b&w 4.99
❑11, Mar 2001, b&w 4.99
❑12, May 2001, b&w 4.99
❑13, Jun 2001, b&w 4.99
❑14, Jul 2001, b&w 4.99
❑15, Aug 2001, b&w 4.99
❑16, Sep 2001, b&w 4.99
❑17, Oct 2001, b&w 4.99
❑18, Nov 2001, b&w 4.99
❑19, Feb 2002, b&w 5.99
❑20, Mar 2002, b&w 5.99
❑21, Apr 2002, b&w 5.99
❑22, May 2002, b&w; (128 pgs) 5.99
❑23, Jun 2002, b&w; (128 pgs) 5.99
❑24, Jul 2002, b&w; (128 pgs) 5.99
❑25, Sep 2002, b&w; (128 pgs) 5.99
❑26, Oct 2002, b&w; (128 pgs) 5.99
❑27, Nov 2002, b&w; (128 pgs) 5.99
❑28, Dec 2002, b&w; (128 pgs) 5.99
❑29, Jan 2003, b&w; (128 pgs) 5.99
❑30, Apr 2003, b&w 5.99
❑31, May 2003, b&w 5.99
❑32, Jun 2003, b&w 5.99
❑33, Jul 2003, b&w 5.99
❑34, Aug 2003, b&w 5.99
❑35, Oct 2003, b&w 5.99
❑36, Nov 2003, b&w 5.99
❑37, Jan 2004, b&w 5.99
❑38, Feb 2004, b&w 5.99
❑39, Feb 2004, b&w 5.99
❑40, Mar 2004, b&w 5.99
❑41, Mar 2004, b&w 5.99
❑42, May 2004, b&w 5.99
❑43, Jul 2004, b&w 5.99
❑44, Aug 2004, b&w 5.99
❑45, Sep 2004, b&w 5.99
❑46, Oct 2004, b&w 5.99
❑47, Nov 2004, b&w 5.99
❑48, Dec 2004, b&w 5.99
❑49, Jan 2005, b&w 5.99
❑50, Feb 2005 5.99
❑51, Jun 2005 5.99
❑52, Jul 2005 5.99
❑53, Aug 2005 5.99
❑54, Sep 2005 5.99
❑55, Oct 2005 5.99
❑56, Nov 2005 5.99
❑57, Nov 2005 5.99
❑58, Dec 2005 5.99
❑59, Mar 2006; Final issue 5.99

Superman Gallery
DC

❑1, ca. 1993, wraparound cover 2.95

Superman/Gen13
WildStorm

❑1, Jun 2000; $2.50, June 2000; Part 1 of 3 Mini-Series 2.50
❑1/A, Jun 2000; Fairchild opening shirt to show Supergirl costume on cover 2.50
❑2, Jul 2000; Supergirl/Fairchild cover 2.50

N-MINT

❑2/A, Jul 2000; Large figures looking down on cover 2.50
❑3, Aug 2000; Caitlin Fairchild gets her memory back thanks to a punch from Supergirl 2.50

Superman (Giveaways)
DC

❑1; game giveaway 1.00
❑2; Pizza Hut 1.00
❑3, Jul 1980; Radio Shack 1.00
❑4; Radio Shack 1.00
❑5; Radio Shack 1.00

Superman, Inc.
DC

❑1, Jan 2000 6.95

Superman IV Movie Special
DC

❑1, Oct 1987; Movie adaptation 2.00

Superman: Kal
DC

❑1; prestige format one-shot 5.95

Superman: Kansas Sighting
DC

❑1, Jan 2004 6.95
❑2, Feb 2004 6.95

Superman: King of the World
DC

❑1, Jun 1999, ▲1999-22 3.95
❑1/Gold, Jun 1999, enhanced cardstock cover; ▲1999-22 4.95

Superman: Last Son of Earth
DC

❑1, Sep 2000 5.95
❑2, Oct 2000 5.95

Superman: Last Stand on Krypton
DC

❑1, May 2003 6.95

Superman: Lex 2000
DC

❑1, Jan 2001; O: Lex Luthor 3.50

Superman: Lois Lane
DC

❑1, Jun 1998; Girlfrenzy 1.95

Superman/Madman Hullabaloo
Dark Horse / DC

❑1, Jun 1997; crossover with DC 2.95
❑2, Jul 1997; crossover with DC 2.95
❑3, Aug 1997; crossover with DC 2.95

Superman Meets the Motorsports Champions
DC

❑1, ca. 1999; TP (a); Promotional NASCAR comic 2.00

Superman Meets the Quik Bunny
DC

❑1; promotional giveaway from Nestle; CI (c); CI, DG (a); NN; Wraparound cover 1.00

Superman: Metropolis
DC

❑1, Apr 2003 2.95
❑2, May 2003 2.95

N-MINT

❑3, Jun 2003 2.95
❑4, Jul 2003 2.95
❑5, Aug 2003 2.95
❑6, Sep 2003 2.95
❑7, Oct 2003 2.95
❑8, Nov 2003 2.95
❑9, Dec 2003 2.95
❑10, Jan 2004 2.95
❑11, Feb 2004 2.95
❑12, Mar 2004 2.95

Superman Metropolis Secret Files
DC

❑1, Jul 2000 4.95

Superman Monster
DC

❑1; ca. 1999 5.95

Superman Movie Special
DC

❑1, Sep 1983; GM, CS (a); adapts Superman III 2.00

Superman: Our Worlds at War Secret Files
DC

❑1, Aug 2001 5.95

Superman: Peace on Earth
DC

❑1/2nd; 2nd printing; Oversized 9.95
❑1, Jan 1999; Oversized 9.95

Superman Plus
DC

❑1, Feb 1997 2.95

Superman: Red Son
DC

❑1, Jun 2003 7.00
❑2, Jul 2003 5.95
❑3, Aug 2003 5.95

Superman Red/Superman Blue
DC

❑1, Feb 1998; 1: Superman Red; Includes 3-D glasses 3.95
❑Deluxe 1, Feb 1998; one-shot with 3-D cover; Superman splits into two beings 4.95

Superman Returns: Krypton to Earth
DC

❑1, Aug 2006 3.99
❑2, Aug 2006 3.99
❑3, Sep 2006 3.99
❑4, Sep 2006 3.99

Superman Returns: The Movie Adaptation
DC

❑1, Sep 2006 6.99

Superman: Save the Planet
DC

❑1, Oct 1998; Daily Planet sold to Lex Luthor 2.95
❑1/Variant, Oct 1998; acetate overlay 3.95

Superman: Secret Files
DC

❑1, Jan 1998; background material 4.95
❑2, May 1999; background material 4.95

Other grades: Multiply price above by 5/6 for VF/NM • 2/3 for VERY FINE • 1/3 for FINE • 1/5 for VERY GOOD • 1/8 for GOOD

Superman: Secret Files 2004
DC

❑1, Aug 2004 .... 4.95

Superman Secret Files and Origins 2004
DC

❑0, Jul 2005 .... 6.00

Superman Secret Files 2005
DC

❑1, Jan 2006 .... 4.99

Superman: Secret Identity
DC

❑1, Mar 2004 .... 5.95
❑2, Apr 2004 .... 5.95
❑3, May 2004 .... 5.95
❑4, Jun 2004 .... 5.95

Superman's Girl Friend Lois Lane
DC

❑29, Nov 1961 .... 86.00
❑30, Jan 1962 CS (c); KS (a) 48.00
❑31, Feb 1962, Lana Lang cover 48.00
❑32, Apr 1962 .... 48.00
❑33, May 1962, A: Phantom Zone. A: Mon-El 48.00
❑34, Jul 1962 .... 48.00
❑35, Aug 1962, KS (c); CS, KS (a) 48.00
❑36, Oct 1962, KS (c); CS, KS (a) 48.00
❑37, Nov 1962, CS, KS (a) 48.00
❑38, Jan 1963 .... 48.00
❑39, Feb 1963, CS, KS (a) 48.00
❑40, Apr 1963, KS (a) 48.00
❑41, May 1963, CS, KS (a) 48.00
❑42, Jul 1963 .... 48.00
❑43, Aug 1963, KS (a) 48.00
❑44, Oct 1963 .... 48.00
❑45, Nov 1963 .... 48.00
❑46, Jan 1964, Imaginary Story; Sequel to "The Wife of Superman's Foe" in issue #34 .... 48.00
❑47, Feb 1964 .... 48.00
❑48, Apr 1964 .... 48.00
❑49, May 1964, KS (a) 48.00
❑50, Jul 1964 .... 48.00
❑51, Aug 1964, KS (a) 34.00
❑52, Oct 1964 .... 34.00
❑53, Nov 1964, KS (a); How Lois fell in love with Superman 34.00
❑54, Jan 1965, CS, KS (a); 1: Herko 34.00
❑55, Feb 1965 .... 34.00
❑56, Apr 1965 .... 34.00
❑57, May 1965, KS (a); 2: Herko 34.00
❑58, Jul 1965 .... 34.00
❑59, Aug 1965 .... 34.00
❑60, Oct 1965 .... 34.00
❑61, Nov 1965, KS (a) 34.00
❑62, Jan 1966 .... 34.00
❑63, Feb 1966, V: S.K.U.L.. Noel Neill interview 34.00
❑64, Apr 1966, Imaginary story 34.00
❑65, May 1966, Imaginary story 34.00
❑66, Jul 1966 .... 34.00
❑67, Aug 1966, The Bombshell of the Boulevards reprinted from issue #1 .... 34.00
❑68, Sep 1966, Giant-size; aka 80 Page Giant #G-26 .... 44.00
❑69, Oct 1966 .... 34.00
❑70, Nov 1966, A: Catwoman. 1st Catwoman in Silver Age 175.00
❑71, Jan 1967, A: Catwoman 105.00
❑72, Feb 1967, The Forbidden Box! reprinted from issue #37 .... 15.00
❑73, Apr 1967 .... 15.00
❑74, May 1967, 1: Bizarro Flash. 1: Bizarro Flash; Sweetheart of Robin Hood! reprinted from issue #22 .... 34.00
❑75, Jul 1967 .... 15.00
❑76, Aug 1967 .... 15.00
❑77, Sep 1967, Giant-size; aka 80 Page Giant #G-39 .... 24.00
❑78, Oct 1967, Superman's Forbidden Room reprinted from issue #2 .... 15.00
❑79, Nov 1967 .... 10.00
❑80, Jan 1968, Lois in mini-skirt cover.. .... 10.00
❑81, Feb 1968, How Lois Lane Got Her Job reprinted from issue #17 .... 10.00
❑82, Apr 1968, NA (c); IN (a) 10.00
❑83, May 1968, NA (c); FR (w); IN (a) ... 10.00
❑84, Jul 1968, NA (c); KS, IN (a); The Last Days of Lois Lane! reprinted from issue #27 .... 10.00
❑85, Aug 1968, NA (c); KS, IN (a); Reprint from Superman's Girl Friend Lois Lane #26 .... 10.00
❑86, Sep 1968; Giant-size; NA (c); NA, CS, KS (a); aka 80 Page Giant #G-51; Reprints stories from Lois Lane #37 and #41 .... 16.00
❑87, Oct 1968, NA (c); KS, IN (a); Reprint from Superman's Girl Friend Lois Lane #31 .... 10.00
❑88, Nov 1968, NA (c); KS, IN (a); Reprint from Superman's Girl Friend Lois Lane #24 .... 10.00
❑89, Jan 1969, Imaginary Story; Lois marries Batman 10.00
❑90, Feb 1969, NA (c); IN (a) 10.00
❑91, Apr 1969, NA (c); CS (a); Imaginary story 10.00
❑92, May 1969, CS, IN (a) 10.00
❑93, Jul 1969, CS (c); IN (a); A: Wonder Woman 10.00
❑94, Aug 1969, CS, KS, IN (a); Reprint from Superman's Girl Friend #20, minus top tier of page 9 .... 10.00
❑95, Sep 1969, b&w; Giant-size; CS (c); KS (a); aka Giant #G-63; Reprints stories from Lois Lane #8, #27, #36, and #40 .... 25.00
❑96, Oct 1969, CS, IN (a) 8.00
❑97, Nov 1969, KS, IN (a); Reprint from Superman's Girl Friend Lois Lane #16 .... 8.00
❑98, Jan 1970, CS, IN (a); Aka Giant #G-63 .... 8.00
❑99, Feb 1970, CS (c); KS, IN (a); Reprint from Superman's Girl Friend Lois Lane #3 .... 8.00
❑100, Apr 1970, CS (c); IN, RMo (a); Reprint from Showcase #9, originally titled "The New Lois Lane" 8.00
❑101, May 1970, CS (c); KS, IN (a); Reprint from Superman's Girl Friend Lois Lane #13, originally titled "Alias Lois Lane!" 8.00
❑102, Jul 1970, CS, KS, IN (a); Reprint from Superman's Girl Friend Lois Lane #10 .... 8.00
❑103, Aug 1970, CS, KS, IN (a); Reprint from Superman's Girl Friend Lois Lane #35 .... 8.00
❑104, Sep 1970, Giant-size; aka Giant #G-75 .... 16.00
❑105, Oct 1970, O: Rose & Thorn II (Rose Forrest). 1: Rose & Thorn II (Rose Forrest). 1: The 1,000; 1: The 100 .... 14.00
❑106, Nov 1970, Wonder Women of History: Martha G. Kimball reprinted from Wonder Woman (1st Series) #53 .... 14.00
❑107, Dec 1970 .... 6.00
❑108, Feb 1971, Includes 1971 Superman pin-up calendar 6.00
❑109, Apr 1971 .... 6.00
❑110, May 1971 .... 6.00
❑111, Jul 1971 .... 10.00
❑112, Aug 1971; DG, KS (a); Reprints from Lois Lane #30 .... 6.00
❑113, Sep 1971, Giant-size; aka Giant #G-87 .... 14.00
❑114, Sep 1971; KS (a); Reprints from Lois Lane #61 .... 6.00
❑115, Oct 1971; BO, DG (a); Reprints Lois Lane feature from Superman (1st series) #28, and Lady Danger feature from Sensation Comics #84 ... 6.00
❑116, Nov 1971; Reprint from Sensation Comics #94; Dr. Pat story; Rose and the Thorn story 6.00
❑117, Dec 1971; Reprint from Sensation Comics # 87 .... 6.00
❑118, Jan 1972; Reprint from Sensation Comics #95 .... 6.00
❑119, Feb 1972; Reprint from Sensation Comics #85 .... 6.00
❑120, Mar 1972; RB, KS (a); Reprints from Lois Lane #43, and Superman (1st series) #29 .... 6.00
❑121, Apr 1972; Reprint from Superman's Girl Friend Lois Lane #35 .... 5.00
❑122, May 1972; CS (a); Reprints from Lois Lane #35, and Superman (1st series) #30 .... 8.00
❑123, Jun 1972; Reprint from Batman #35 .... 8.00
❑124, Jul 1972, Lois Lane story; Rose and The Thorn story 5.00
❑125, Aug 1972, Lois Lane story; Rose and The Thorn story 5.00
❑126, Sep 1972, Lois Lane story; Rose and The Thorn story 5.00
❑127, Oct 1972, Lois Lane story; Rose and The Thorn story 5.00
❑128, Dec 1972 .... 5.00
❑129, Feb 1973, BO (c); DH (a) 5.00
❑130, Apr 1973 .... 5.00
❑131, Jun 1973, BO (c); KS (a); Reprints from Lois Lane #8 .... 5.00
❑132, Jul 1973 .... 5.00
❑133, Sep 1973 .... 5.00
❑134, Oct 1973 .... 5.00
❑135, Nov 1973 .... 5.00
❑136, Jan 1974, A: Wonder Woman 5.00
❑137, ca. 1974, Series combines with Superman's Pal Jimmy Olsen and Supergirl as Superman Family; Final Issue 5.00
❑Ann 1, Sum 1962 .... 75.00
❑Ann 2, Sum 1963 .... 50.00

Superman/Shazam: First Thunder
DC

❑1, Oct 2005 .... 3.50
❑2 2005 .... 3.50
❑3, Feb 2006 .... 3.50
❑4, May 2006 .... 3.50

Superman: Silver Banshee
DC

❑1, Dec 1998 .... 2.25
❑2, Jan 1999 .... 2.25

Superman's Metropolis
DC

❑1, Jan 1997; prestige format; Elseworlds 5.95

Superman's Nemesis: Lex Luthor
DC

❑1, Mar 1999 .... 2.50
❑2, Apr 1999; V: Demolitia 2.50
❑3, May 1999 .... 2.50
❑4, Jun 1999 .... 2.50

Superman's Pal Jimmy Olsen
DC

❑57, Dec 1961, CS (c); CS (a); A: Supergirl 30.00
❑58, Jan 1962 .... 30.00
❑59, Mar 1962, CS (a) 30.00
❑60, Apr 1962 .... 30.00
❑61, Jun 1962 .... 30.00
❑62, Jul 1962, Elastic Lad in Phantom Zone 30.00
❑63, Sep 1962 .... 30.00
❑64, Oct 1962 .... 30.00
❑65, Dec 1962 .... 30.00
❑66, Jan 1963 .... 30.00
❑67, Mar 1963 .... 30.00
❑68, Apr 1963 .... 30.00
❑69, Jun 1963, CS (a) 30.00
❑70, Jul 1963, Silver Kryptonite 30.00
❑71, Sep 1963 .... 25.00
❑72, Oct 1963, CS (a); A: Legion of Super-Heroes 30.00
❑73, Dec 1963 .... 30.00
❑74, Jan 1964, CS (a); A: Lex Luthor 25.00
❑75, Mar 1964, A: Supergirl 25.00
❑76, Apr 1964, CS (a); A: Lightning Lass. A: Saturn Girl, Lightning Lass, Triplicate Girl. A: Triplicate Girl. A: Saturn Girl ... 30.00
❑77, Jun 1964 .... 25.00
❑78, Jul 1964 .... 25.00
❑79, Sep 1964, Jimmy as Beatle 25.00
❑80, Oct 1964, 1: Bizarro-Jimmy Olsen. 25.00
❑81, Dec 1964 .... 25.00
❑82, Jan 1965 .... 25.00
❑83, Mar 1965 .... 25.00
❑84, Apr 1965, CS (c); CS (a); Gorilla cover 25.00
❑85, Jun 1965, CS (a) 25.00
❑86, Jul 1965 .... 25.00
❑87, Sep 1965, A: Legion of Super-Villains. A: Bizarro Jimmy 25.00
❑88, Oct 1965 .... 25.00
❑89, Dec 1965 .... 20.00
❑90, Jan 1966 .... 20.00
❑91, Mar 1966 .... 16.00
❑92, Apr 1966, A: Batman 16.00
❑93, Jun 1966 .... 16.00
❑94, Jul 1966 .... 16.00

Other grades: Multiply price above by 5/6 for VF/NM • 2/3 for VERY FINE • 1/3 for FINE • 1/5 for VERY GOOD • 1/8 for GOOD

Teen Titans

Sidekicks form group to help non-powered peers
©DC

Teen Titans

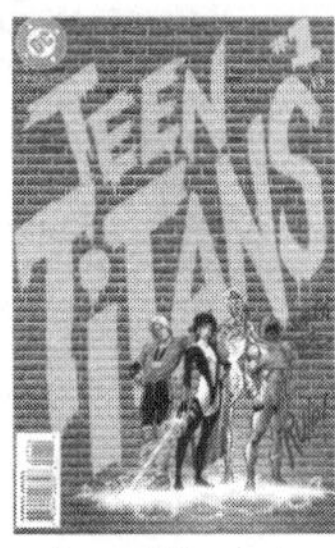

De-aged Atom leads adolescent adventurers
©DC

Teen Titans

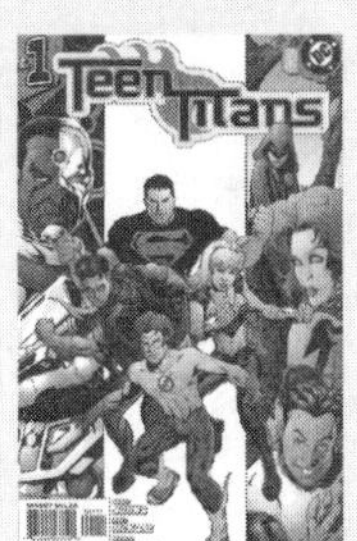

No longer Teens mentor new Teens
©DC

Tekworld

Shatner SF series features future cop
©Marvel

Tellos

Fantasy series plagued by delays
©Image

N-MINT

❑95, Aug 1966, Giant-size; aka 80 Page Giant #G-25 .... 25.00
❑96, Sep 1966 .... 16.00
❑97, Oct 1966 .... 16.00
❑98, Dec 1966 .... 16.00
❑99, Jan 1967, Jimmy as one-man Legion 16.00
❑100, Mar 1967, Wedding of Jimmy and Lucy Lane 25.00
❑101, Apr 1967 .... 12.00
❑102, Jun 1967 .... 12.00
❑103, Jul 1967 .... 12.00
❑104, Aug 1967; Giant-size; aka 80 Page Giant #G-38; Weird Adventures 35.00
❑105, Sep 1967 .... 12.00
❑106, Oct 1967, CS (a) 12.00
❑107, Dec 1967, CS (a) 12.00
❑108, Jan 1968, CS (a); Reprint from Superman's Pal Jimmy Olsen #41 .... 12.00
❑109, Mar 1968, A: Luthor. Imaginary story; Reprint from Superman's Pal Jimmy Olsen #41 .... 12.00
❑110, Apr 1968, NA (c); CS (a); Reprint from Superman's Pal Jimmy Olsen #35 12.00
❑111, Jun 1968 .... 12.00
❑112, Jul 1968, Reprint from Superman's Pal Jimmy Olsen #55 .... 12.00
❑113, Aug 1968; RA (c); CS (a); aka 80 Page Giant #G-50; Anti-Superman issue; Reprints from Jimmy Olsen #22, #27, and #28 .... 25.00
❑114, Sep 1968 .... 12.00
❑115, Oct 1968, A: Aquaman 12.00
❑116, Dec 1968, CS (a); Reprints from Jimmy Olsen #24 .... 12.00
❑117, Jan 1969, Includes reprint from #56 .... 12.00
❑118, Mar 1969 .... 12.00
❑119, Apr 1969, Reprint from Superman's Pal Jimmy Olsen #33 .... 12.00
❑120, Jun 1969 .... 10.00
❑121, Jul 1969 .... 10.00
❑122, Aug 1969; aka Giant #G-62 .... 10.00
❑123, Sep 1969 .... 10.00
❑124, Oct 1969 .... 10.00
❑125, Dec 1969, Reprint from Superman's Pal Jimmy Olsen #28 .... 10.00
❑126, Jan 1970, A: Kryptonite Plus. Kryptonite Plus appearance (hoax kryptonite) 10.00
❑127, Mar 1970 .... 16.00
❑128, Apr 1970, Reprint from Superman's Pal Jimmy Olsen #5 .... 10.00
❑129, Jun 1970, Reprint from Superman's Pal Jimmy Olsen #24 .... 10.00
❑130, Jul 1970, V: Brainiac 10.00
❑131, Aug 1970, aka Giant #G-74 .... 8.00
❑132, Sep 1970 .... 8.00
❑133, Oct 1970, JK (w); JK (a); 1: Newsboy Legion. 1: Habitat; 1: Newsboy Legion II 10.00
❑134, Dec 1970, 1: Darkseid 25.00
❑135, Jan 1971, 1: Project Cadmus 12.00
❑136, Mar 1971, O: Guardian (new) 12.00
❑137, Apr 1971 .... 12.00
❑138, Jun 1971 .... 12.00
❑139, Jul 1971, A: Don Rickles; 1: Goody Rickles 12.00
❑140, Aug 1971, aka Giant #G-86; reprints Jimmy Olsen #69, #72, and Superman #158 .... 12.00

N-MINT

❑141, Sep 1971; Reprint from Star Spangled Comics #7; 48 pages; Begins Newsboy Legion reprints by Jack Kirby, Joe Simon 10.00
❑142, Oct 1971; Includes reprint from Star-Spangled Comics #8 .... 10.00
❑143, Nov 1971; JK (w); JK (a); Includes reprint from Star-Spangled Comics #9 10.00
❑144, Dec 1971; JK (w); JK (a); Includes reprint from Star-Spangled Comics #10 10.00
❑145, Jan 1972; Includes reprint from Star-Spangled Comics #11 .... 10.00
❑146, Feb 1972; Includes reprint from Star-Spangled Comics #12 .... 10.00
❑147, Mar 1972; Includes reprint from Star-Spangled Comics #13 .... 10.00
❑148, Apr 1972; Last Kirby issue; Includes reprint from Star-Spangled Comics #14 .... 10.00
❑149, May 1972; BO (a); Includes reprint from Police Comics #75 .... 10.00
❑150, Jun 1972; Includes reprint from Police Comics #20 .... 10.00
❑151, Jul 1972 .... 8.00
❑152, Aug 1972 .... 7.00
❑153, Oct 1972, Includes two non-Jimmy Olsen backup inventory stories 7.00
❑154, Nov 1972 .... 7.00
❑155, Jan 1973, 1: Jimmy as Mr. Action 7.00
❑156, Feb 1973 .... 7.00
❑157, Mar 1973 .... 7.00
❑158, Jun 1973 .... 7.00
❑159, Aug 1973 .... 7.00
❑160, Oct 1973 .... 7.00
❑161, Nov 1973 .... 7.00
❑162, Dec 1973 .... 7.00
❑163, Feb 1974, Series continues as The Superman Family 7.00

Superman Spectacular
DC

❑1; V: Luthor. V: Brainiac. NN; A.k.a. DC Special Series (Vol. 1) #5 .... 3.00

Superman: Speeding Bullets
DC

❑1, ca. 1993; prestige format; Elseworlds 4.95

Superman: Strength
DC

❑1, Mar 2005 .... 5.95
❑2, Apr 2005 .... 5.95
❑3, May 2005 .... 5.95

Superman/Tarzan: Sons of the Jungle
Dark Horse

❑1, Oct 2001; Dark Horse Comics/DC Comics Elseworlds 2.99
❑2, Nov 2001; Dark Horse Comics/DC Comics Elseworlds 2.99
❑3, May 2002; Issue delayed until May 2002; Dark Horse Comics/DC Comics Elseworlds 2.99

Superman: The Dark Side
DC

❑1, Oct 1998 .... 4.95
❑2, Nov 1998 .... 4.95
❑3, Dec 1998 .... 4.95

N-MINT

Superman: The Doomsday Wars
DC

❑1, ca. 1999 .... 4.95
❑1/Ltd.; Signed edition 24.95
❑2, ca. 1999 .... 4.95
❑3, ca. 1999 .... 4.95

Superman: The Earth Stealers
DC

❑1, May 1988; NN; One-shot 2.95

Superman: The Greatest Stories Ever Told
DC

❑1, ca. 2004; Collects Superman (1st Series) #1, 65, 156, 164, 247, 400, Look Magazine 1940, Man of Steel #1, Superman (2nd Series) #18, and Action Comics #775 .... 19.95

Superman: The Last God of Krypton
DC

❑1, Aug 1999; prestige format; NN 4.95

Superman: The Legacy of Superman
DC

❑1, Mar 1993; Follows up after Superman's demise 2.50

Superman: The Man of Steel
DC

❑0, Oct 1994; ▲1994-37 .... 2.50
❑1, Jul 1991; BMc (a); 1: Cerberus. ▲1991-19 .... 6.00
❑2, Aug 1991; V: Sgt. Belcher. V: Rorc. ▲1991-23 .... 2.50
❑3, Sep 1991; War of the Gods 2.50
❑4, Oct 1991; V: Angstrom. ▲1991-31 . 2.00
❑5, Nov 1991; V: Atomic Skull. ▲1991-35 2.00
❑6, Dec 1991; ▲1991-39 .... 2.00
❑7, Jan 1992; V: Blockhouse. V: Jolt. ▲1992-1 .... 2.00
❑8, Feb 1992; V: Blockhouse. V: Jolt. ▲1992-5 .... 2.00
❑9, Mar 1992; ▲1992-9 .... 2.00
❑10, Apr 1992; ▲1992-13 .... 2.00
❑11, May 1992; ▲1992-17 .... 1.50
❑12, Jun 1992; ▲1992-21 .... 1.50
❑13, Jul 1992; ▲1992-25 .... 1.50
❑14, Aug 1992; A: Robin. ▲1992-29 ..... 1.50
❑15, Sep 1992; KG, KGa (a); A: Satanus. A: Blaze. ▲1992-33 .... 1.50
❑16, Oct 1992; ▲1992-37 .... 1.50
❑17, Nov 1992; 1: Doomsday (cameo). ▲1992-41 .... 3.00
❑18, Dec 1992; 1: Doomsday (full appearance). ▲1992-18 .... 4.00
❑18/2nd, Dec 1992; A: Doomsday. ▲1992-18 .... 2.00
❑18/3rd, Dec 1992; A: Doomsday. ▲1992-18 .... 1.50
❑19, Jan 1993; V: Doomsday. ▲1993-1 3.00
❑20, Feb 1993; ▲1993-5 .... 2.50
❑21, Mar 1993; Pa Kent has heart attack 2.50
❑22, Jun 1993; 1: Steel (John Henry Irons). ▲1993-13; 1; Reign of the Supermen! 2.00
❑22/Variant, Jun 1993; Die-cut cover 2.50
❑23, Jul 1993; Steel vs. Superboy 2.00
❑24, Aug 1993; Steel vs. Last Son of Krypton 2.00

Other grades: Multiply price above by 5/6 for VF/NM • 2/3 for VERY FINE • 1/3 for FINE • 1/5 for VERY GOOD • 1/8 for GOOD

N-MINT

❑25, Sep 1993; ▲1993-25; Reign of the Supermen! 2.00
❑26, Oct 1993; ▲1993-29; Reign of the Supermen!; Continued in Green Lantern v3 #46 2.00
❑27, Nov 1993; ▲1993-33 2.00
❑28, Dec 1993; ▲1993-37 2.00
❑29, Jan 1994; ▲1994-1; Spilled Blood 2.00
❑30, Feb 1994; Lobo 2.00
❑30/Variant, Feb 1994; vinyl clings cover 3.00
❑31, Mar 1994; ▲1994-9 2.00
❑32, Apr 1994; Bizarro 2.00
❑33, May 1994; ▲1994-17 2.00
❑34, Jun 1994; ▲1994-21; Battle for Metropolis; Kobalt preview 2.00
❑35, Jul 1994; crossover with Milestone Media 2.00
❑36, Aug 1994; A: Static. A: Icon. A: Hardware. ▲1994-29 2.00
❑37, Sep 1994; Zero Hour 2.00
❑38, Nov 1994; ▲1994-41; Dead Again! 2.00
❑39, Dec 1994; ▲1994-45; Dead Again! 2.00
❑40, Jan 1995; ▲1995-1 2.00
❑41, Feb 1995; ▲1995-5 2.00
❑42, Mar 1995; ▲1995-9 2.00
❑43, Apr 1995; A: Mr. Miracle. ▲1995-13 2.00
❑44, May 1995; ▲1995-17 2.00
❑45, Jun 1995; ▲1995-21 2.00
❑46, Jul 1995; ▲1995-25 2.00
❑47, Aug 1995; ▲1995-30 2.00
❑48, Sep 1995; A: Aquaman. ▲1995-34 2.00
❑49, Oct 1995; ▲1995-38 2.00
❑50, Nov 1995; Giant-size; Trial of Superman; ▲1995-43 3.00
❑51, Dec 1995; V: Freelance; Trial of Superman; ▲1995-47 2.00
❑52, Jan 1996; V: Cyborg; Trial of Superman; ▲1996-2; V: Cyborg Superman 2.00
❑53, Feb 1996; V: Brawl; ▲1996-6 2.00
❑54, Mar 1996; A: Spectre. ▲1996-10 2.00
❑55, Apr 1996; D: Jeb Friedman. ▲1996-15 2.00
❑56, May 1996; V: Mxyzptlk. Mr. Mxyzptlk cover; ▲1996-19; Memorial Tribute to Jerry Siegel 1914-1996 2.00
❑57, Jun 1996; A: Golden Age Flash. ▲1996-23 2.00
❑58, Jul 1996; ▲1996-28 2.00
❑59, Aug 1996; V: Parasite. ▲1996-32 2.00
❑60, Sep 1996; ▲ 1996-36 2.00
❑61, Oct 1996; polybagged with On the Edge; ▲1996-41 2.00
❑62, Oct 1996; O: Superman. Final Night; ▲1996-45 2.00
❑63, Dec 1996; Lois rescues Clark from terrorists; ▲1996-50 2.00
❑64, Jan 1997; ▲1997-4 2.00
❑65, Mar 1997; SB (a); V: Superman Revenge Squad. ▲1997-9 2.00
❑66, Apr 1997; ▲1997-14 2.00
❑67, May 1997; A: Scorn. destruction of old costume 2.00
❑68, Jun 1997; V: Metallo; ▲1997-22 2.00
❑69, Jul 1997; A: Atom. in Kandor 2.00
❑70, Aug 1997; A: Scorn. V: Saviourr; Back To Back With Scorn!; ▲1997-30 2.00
❑71, Sep 1997; 1: Baud. ▲1997-34 2.00
❑72, Oct 1997; V: Mainframe. Genesis 2.00
❑73, Nov 1997; V: Parademons. ▲1997-43 2.00
❑74, Dec 1997; A: Sam Lane. V: Rajiv. Face cover; ▲1997-47 2.00
❑75, Jan 1998; A: Mike Carlin. D: Mr. Mxyzptlk. ▲1998-1 2.00
❑76, Feb 1998; A: Simyan. A: Morgan Edge. A: Mokkari. ▲1998-5 2.00
❑77, Mar 1998; cover forms diptych with Action Comics #742 2.00
❑78, Apr 1998; Millennium Giants 2.00
❑79, May 1998; Millennium Giants aftermath 2.00
❑80, Jun 1998; set in late '30s 2.00
❑81, Jul 1998; set in late '30s 2.00
❑82, Aug 1998; A: Kismet. V: Dominus. ▲1998-32; Set in 1930s 2.00
❑83, Sep 1998; A: Waverider. ▲1998-36 2.00
❑84, Dec 1998; 1: Inventor. in Kandor 2.00
❑85, Jan 1999; V: Simyan. V: Mokkari; ▲1999-2 2.00
❑86, Feb 1999 2.00

N-MINT

❑87, Mar 1999 A: Steel. A: Superboy. A: Supergirl 2.00
❑88, May 1999; V: Robots. V: Robots 2.00
❑89, Jun 1999; V: Dominus. ▲1999-21 2.00
❑90, Jul 1999; ▲1999-26 2.00
❑91, Aug 1999; ▲1999-31 1.99
❑92, Sep 1999; Superman as Martian Manhunter; ▲1999-35 1.99
❑93, Oct 1999; ▲1999-39 1.99
❑94, Nov 1999; A: Strange Visitor. V: Parasite. ▲1999-43 1.99
❑95, Dec 1999; ▲1999-48 1.99
❑96, Jan 2000; ▲2000-3 1.99
❑97, Feb 2000; ▲2000-8 1.99
❑98, Mar 2000; ▲2000-12 1.99
❑99, Apr 2000; ▲2000-16 1.99
❑100, May 2000; Giant-size; ▲2000-20 2.99
❑100/Variant, May 2000; Giant-size; Special fold-out cover; ▲2000-20 3.99
❑101, Jun 2000 1.99
❑102, Jul 2000 1.99
❑103, Aug 2000; ▲2000-32 2.25
❑104, Sep 2000; ▲2000-36 2.25
❑105, Oct 2000; ▲2000-41 2.25
❑106, Nov 2000; ▲2000-45 2.25
❑107, Dec 2000; ▲2000-49 2.25
❑108, Jan 2001; ▲2001-4 2.25
❑109, Feb 2001; ▲2001-8 2.25
❑110, Mar 2001; A: Stars and S.T.R.I.P.E. ▲2001-12 2.25
❑111, Apr 2001; ▲2001-16 2.25
❑112, May 2001; ▲2001-20 2.25
❑113, Jun 2001; ▲2001-24 2.25
❑114, Jul 2001; ▲2001-28 2.25
❑115, Aug 2001; ▲2001-32; Our Worlds at War; Our Worlds at War: Prelude to War! 2.25
❑116, Sep 2001; ▲2001-36; Our Worlds at War: All-Out War 2.25
❑117, Oct 2001; ▲2001-40 2.25
❑118, Nov 2001; ▲2001-44 2.25
❑119, Dec 2001; JLee (c); ▲2001-48 2.25
❑120, Jan 2002; ▲2002-3 2.25
❑121, Feb 2002; Full Coverage 2.25
❑122, Mar 2002 2.25
❑123, Apr 2002 2.25
❑124, May 2002 2.25
❑125, Jun 2002 2.25
❑126, Jul 2002 2.25
❑127, Aug 2002 2.25
❑128, Sep 2002 2.25
❑129, Oct 2002 2.25
❑130, Nov 2002 2.25
❑131, Dec 2002 2.25
❑132, Jan 2003 2.25
❑133, Feb 2003 2.25
❑134, Mar 2003 2.25
❑1000000, Nov 1998; JOy (w); JOy (a); Published between issues #83 and #84 3.00
❑Ann 1, ca. 1992; A: Eclipso; Eclipso continued in Green Lantern Ann #1 3.00
❑Ann 2, ca. 1993; 1: Edge; Bloodlines; Bloodlines Outbreak 3.00
❑Ann 3, ca. 1994; Elseworlds 3.00
❑Ann 4, ca. 1995; A: Justice League. Year One 3.00
❑Ann 5, Nov 1996; JOy (c); KB (w); 1: Kaleb. Legends of the Dead Earth 3.00
❑Ann 6, Aug 1997; Pulp Heroes 3.95

Superman: The Man of Steel Gallery
DC

❑1, Dec 1995; pin-ups 3.50

Superman: The Man of Tomorrow
DC

❑1, Sum 1995; ▲1995-28 2.00
❑2, Fal 1995; A: Alpha Centurion ▲ 41 -1995; ▲1995-41 2.00
❑3, Win 1995; A: how Luthor regained strength and. Underworld Unleashed 2.00
❑4, Spr 1996; A: Captain Marvel. ▲1996-13 2.00
❑5, Sum 1996; Wedding of Lex Luthor and Contessa 2.00
❑6, Fal 1996; V: Jackal. ▲1996-38 2.00
❑7, Win 1997; V: Maxima. ▲1997-5 2.00
❑8, Sum 1997; V: Rock. ▲1997-13 2.00
❑9, Fal 1997; Ma and Pa Kent remember Superman's career 2.00
❑10, Win 1998; Obsession vs. Maxima 2.00

N-MINT

❑11, Fal 1998; Timewar 2.00
❑12, Win 1998; ▲1999-3 2.00
❑13, Spr 1999; ▲1999-16 2.00
❑14, Sum 1999; V: Riot. ▲1999-29 2.00
❑15, Fal 1999; V: Neron. Day of Judgment 3.00
❑1000000, Nov 1998 2.00

Superman: The Odyssey
DC

❑1, Jul 1999; prestige format; NN; One-shot 4.95

Superman: The Secret Years
DC

❑1, Feb 1985 FM (c); FM, CS (a) 1.50
❑2, Mar 1985; FM (c); FM, CS (a); A: Lori Lemaris. Clark reveals his secret to Billy Cramer 1.50
❑3, Apr 1985; FM (c); FM, CS (a); D: Billy Cramer 1.50
❑4, May 1985; FM (c); FM, CS (a); Superboy becomes Superman; Clark Kent meets Perry White 1.50

Superman: The Wedding Album
DC

❑1, Dec 1996; newsstand edition with gatefold back cover; JBy (c); JOy, GP, JBy, BG, DG, GK, CS, KGa, JM, BMc, NC (a): Wedding of Clark Kent and Lois Lane; ▲1996-47 6.00
❑1/Direct ed., Dec 1996; Wedding of Clark Kent and Lois Lane; white cardstock wraparound cover with gatefold back cover 4.95
❑1/Gold, Dec 1996; Gold Foil Edition; Retailer incentive; Limited to 250 copies 10.00

Superman/Thundercats
DC

❑1, ca. 2004 5.95

Superman/Toyman
DC

❑1, ca. 1996; promo for toy line 1.95

Superman: Under a Yellow Sun
DC

❑1, ca. 1994; prestige format one-shot 5.95

Superman vs. Aliens
DC / Dark Horse

❑1, Jul 1995; prestige format; crossover with Dark Horse 4.95
❑2, Aug 1995; prestige format; crossover with Dark Horse 4.95
❑3, Sep 1995; prestige format; crossover with Dark Horse 4.95

Superman Vs. Predator
DC / Dark Horse

❑1, Jul 2000 4.95
❑2, Aug 2000 4.95
❑3, Sep 2000 4.95

Superman vs. the Amazing Spider-Man
DC / Marvel

❑1; treasury-sized; DG, RA (a); V: Lex Luthor. V: Doctor Octopus. first DC/Marvel crossover 20.00

Superman vs. The Terminator: Death to the Future
Dark Horse

❑1, Dec 1999 2.95
❑2, Jan 2000 2.95
❑3, Feb 2000 2.95
❑4, Mar 2000 2.95

Superman Villains Secret Files
DC

❑1, Jun 1998; biographical info on Superman's Rogues Gallery 4.95

Superman vs. Darkseid: Apokolips Now
DC

❑1, Apr 2003 2.95

Superman: War of the Worlds
DC

❑1, Dec 1998; prestige format one-shot; Elseworlds 5.95

Terminator (1st Series)

Back to the future for T-1000s, resistance
©Now

Terminator: The Burning Earth

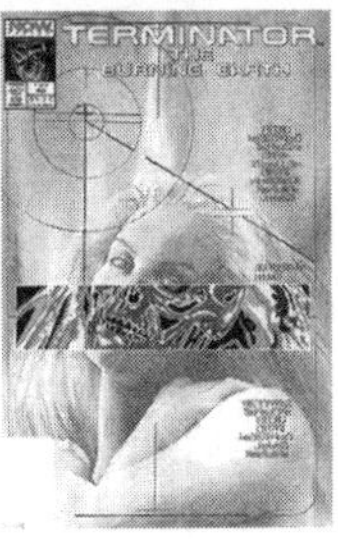

Alex Ross' early work already superb
©Now

Terra Obscura

The nadir of Nedor characters form team
©DC

Terror, Inc.

Mercenary acquires abilities with purloined parts
©Marvel

THB

Paul Pope's perplexing pieces in large format
©Horse

N-MINT

Superman: "Whatever Happened to the Man of Tomorrow?"
DC

❑39449, Nov 2006; Digest-sized reprint of the trade paperback that featured stories from Superman # 423 and Action Comics #583; Included in the 14 disc Superman Movies collector's tin set 5.95
❑1, Feb 1997; AMo (w); prestige format collection of Action Comics #583 and Superman #423 .... 5.95

Superman: Where is Thy Sting?
DC

❑1, Jul 2001 .... 6.95

Superman/Wonder Woman: Whom Gods Destroy
DC

❑1, Dec 1996; prestige format; Elseworlds 4.95
❑2, Jan 1997; prestige format; Elseworlds 4.95
❑3, Feb 1997; prestige format; Elseworlds 4.95
❑4, Mar 1997; prestige format; Elseworlds 4.95

Super Mario Bros.
Valiant

❑1, ca. 1991 .... 2.00
❑2, ca. 1991 .... 2.00
❑3, ca. 1991 .... 2.00
❑4, ca. 1991 .... 2.00
❑5, ca. 1991 .... 2.00
❑6, ca. 1991 .... 2.00
❑Special 1, ca. 1990 .... 2.50

Super Mario Bros.
Valiant

❑1, ca. 1991 .... 2.00
❑2, ca. 1991 .... 2.00
❑3, ca. 1991 .... 2.00
❑4, ca. 1991 .... 2.00
❑5, ca. 1991 .... 2.00

Supermarket
Idea & Design Works

❑1, Feb 2006 .... 3.99
❑2, Apr 2006 .... 3.99
❑3, Jun 2006, Monster House preview included 3.99
❑4, Aug 2006 .... 3.99

Supermen of America
DC

❑1, Mar 1999 .... 3.95
❑1/CS, Mar 1999; Collector's edition; Gatefold cardstock cover 4.95
❑2, Apr 1999 .... 2.50
❑3, May 1999 .... 2.50
❑4, Jun 1999 .... 2.50

Supermodels in the Rainforest
Sirius

❑1, Dec 1998, b&w 2.95
❑2, Feb 1999, b&w 2.95
❑3, Apr 1999 .... 2.95

Supernatural Freak Machine
Idea & Design Works

❑1, ca. 2005 .... 3.99
❑2, ca. 2005 .... 3.99

N-MINT

Supernatural Law
Exhibit A

❑24, Oct 1999, b&w; was Wolff & Byrd, Counselors of the Macabre 2.50
❑25, Feb 2000, b&w 2.50
❑26, May 2000, b&w 2.50
❑27, Jul 2000, b&w 2.50
❑28, Oct 2000, b&w 2.50
❑29, Feb 2001, b&w 2.50
❑30, Apr 2001, b&w 2.50
❑31, Oct 2001, b&w 2.50
❑32, Nov 2001 .... 2.50
❑33, Mar 2002 .... 2.50
❑34, May 2002 .... 2.50
❑35, Jul 2002 .... 2.50
❑36, Sep 2002 .... 2.50
❑37, Apr 2003 .... 2.50
❑38, Jul 2003 .... 2.50

Supernaturals
Marvel

❑1/A, Dec 1998; Includes Satana mask.. 3.99
❑1/B, Dec 1998; Includes Brother Voodoo mask 3.99
❑1/C, Dec 1998; Includes Gargoyle mask 3.99
❑1/D, Dec 1998; Includes Werewolf by Night Mask 3.99
❑1/E, Dec 1998; Includes Ghost Rider mask 4.50
❑1/Ltd., Dec 1998; DFE Signed 29.99
❑2/A, Dec 1998; Includes Satana mask.. 3.99
❑2/B, Dec 1998; Includes Brother Voodoo mask 3.99
❑2/C, Dec 1998 .... 3.99
❑2/D, Dec 1998; Includes Werewolf-by-Night mask 3.99
❑2/E, Dec 1998; Includes Ghost Rider mask 3.99
❑3/A, Dec 1998; Includes Satana mask.. 3.99
❑3/B, Dec 1998; Includes Brother Voodoo mask 3.99
❑3/C, Dec 1998 .... 3.99
❑3/D, Dec 1998; Includes Werewolf-by-Night mask 3.99
❑3/E, Dec 1998; Includes Ghost Rider mask 3.99
❑4/A, Dec 1998; Includes Satana mask.. 3.99
❑4/B, Dec 1998; Includes Brother Voodoo mask 3.99
❑4/C, Dec 1998 .... 3.99
❑4/D, Dec 1998 .... 3.99
❑4/E, Dec 1998; Includes Ghost Rider mask 3.99
❑Ashcan 1, Dec 1998; Character bios, sketches, creator bios 2.99

Supernaturals Tour Book
Marvel

❑1, Oct 1998; preview of series; cardstock cover 2.99

Supernatural Thrillers
Marvel

❑1, Dec 1972, JSo (c);It! (Theodore Sturgeon adaptation) 27.00
❑2, Feb 1973, Invisible Man 10.00
❑3, Apr 1973, GK (a); The Valley of the Worm 10.00
❑4, Jun 1973, Dr. Jekyll and Mr. Hyde... 10.00

N-MINT

❑5, Aug 1973, O: Living Mummy. 1: Living Mummy 27.00
❑6, Nov 1974, The Headless Horseman. 10.00
❑7, Jun 1974; A: Living Mummy. 2: Living Mummy; Reprint from Strange Tales #25 .... 10.00
❑8, Aug 1974; A: Living Mummy. Marvel Value Stamp #36: Ancient One 10.00
❑9, Oct 1974; A: Living Mummy. Marvel Value Stamp #29: Baron Mordo 10.00
❑10, Dec 1974; A: Living Mummy. Reprint from Adventures into Weird Worlds #10 .... 10.00
❑11, Feb 1975; A: Living Mummy. Marvel Value Stamp #86: Zemo 10.00
❑12, Apr 1975; A: Living Mummy. Marvel Value Stamp #49: Odin 10.00
❑13, Jun 1975 A: Living Mummy 10.00
❑14, Aug 1975 A: Living Mummy 10.00
❑15, Oct 1975; GK (c); TS (a); A: Living Mummy. Final issue 10.00

Superpatriot
Image

❑1, Jul 1993 KG, EL (w) 2.00
❑2, Sep 1993 .... 2.00
❑3, Oct 1993 .... 2.00
❑4, Nov 1993; cover says Dec, indicia says Nov 2.00

SuperPatriot: America's Fighting Force
Image

❑1, Jul 2002 .... 2.95
❑2, Aug 2002 .... 2.95
❑3, Sep 2002; August cover date 2.95
❑4, Oct 2002 .... 2.95

Superpatriot: Liberty & Justice
Image

❑1, Jun 1995 .... 2.50
❑2, Aug 1995 .... 2.50
❑3, Sep 1995 .... 2.50
❑4, Oct 1995 .... 2.50

Superpatriot: War on Terror
Image

❑1, Feb 2004 .... 4.00
❑2, Mar 2004 .... 2.95

Super Powers
DC

❑1, Jul 1984, JK (c); JK (w) 2.00
❑2, Aug 1984, JK (c); JK (w) 1.00
❑3, Sep 1984, JK (c); JK (w) 1.00
❑4, Oct 1984, JK (c); JK (w) 1.00
❑5, Nov 1984, JK (c); JK (w); JK (a) 1.00

Super Powers
DC

❑1, Sep 1985 JK (c); JK (a) 1.00
❑2, Oct 1985 JK (c); JK (a) 1.00
❑3, Nov 1985 JK (c); JK (a) 1.00
❑4, Dec 1985 JK (c); JK (a) 1.00
❑5, Jan 1986 JK (c); JK (a) 1.00
❑6, Feb 1986 JK (c); JK (a) 1.00

Super Powers
DC

❑1, Sep 1986 CI (c); CI (a) 1.00
❑2, Oct 1986; CI (c); CI (a); O: Captain Marvel; O: Plastic Man 1.00

Other grades: Multiply price above by 5/6 for VF/NM • 2/3 for VERY FINE • 1/3 for FINE • 1/5 for VERY GOOD • 1/8 for GOOD

N-MINT

❑3, Nov 1986; CI (c); JO (w); CI (a); MASK insert 1.00
❑4, Dec 1986 CI (c); CI (a) 1.00

Super Sexxx
Fantagraphics / Eros

❑1, b&w; Adult 3.25

Super Shark Humanoids
Fish Tales

❑1, Apr 1992 .... 2.75

Super Soldier
DC / Amalgam

❑1, Apr 1996; O: Super Soldier; Cover colors credited in Superman: The Man of Steel #58 .... 1.95

Super Soldier: Man of War
DC / Amalgam

❑1, Jun 1997 .... 1.95

Super Soldiers
Marvel

❑1, Apr 1993; foil cover 2.50
❑2, May 1993 .... 1.75
❑3, Jun 1993 .... 1.75
❑4, Jul 1993 .... 1.75
❑5, Aug 1993 .... 1.75
❑6, Sep 1993 .... 1.75
❑7, Oct 1993; X-Men cameo 1.75
❑8, Nov 1993 .... 1.75

Supersonic Soul Puddin Comics & Stories
Four Cats Funny Books

❑1, Jun 1995 .... 3.50

Super Sonic vs. Hyper Knuckles
Archie

❑1, One-shot; ca. 1996 .... 2.00

Superstar: As Seen on TV
Image

❑1, Jul 2001 .... 5.95

Superswine
Caliber

❑1, b&w 2.50
❑2, b&w 2.50

Super Taboo
Fantagraphics / Eros

❑1, Dec 1995; Adult 2.95
❑2, Jan 1996; Adult 2.95

Super-Team Family
DC

❑1, Nov 1975, Reprints from World's Finest Comics #175, Teen Titans (1st Series) #19, Flash #166 .... 12.00
❑2, Jan 1976, A: Speedy. A: Wildcat. A: Deadman. A: Superman. A: Green Arrow. A: Creeper. A: Batman. Includes reprints from Brave and the Bold #79; Adventure Comics #266 .... 6.00
❑3, Mar 1976, Robin apperarance; Includes reprints from Adventure Comics #267; World's Finest Comics #176 .... 6.00
❑4, May 1976, A: Justice Society of America. A: Superman. A: Solomon Grundy. A: Robin. A: Batman. Reprints from All Star Comics #33 and World's Finest Comics #98 .... 6.00
❑5, Jul 1976, Reprints; Reprints from The Brave and the Bold #64 and Superboy (1st Series) #47 .... 4.00
❑6, Sep 1976, V: Composite Superman; Reprints from World's Finest Comics #168 and Marvel Family #89; Superman/Batman story; Shazam! story 4.00
❑7, Nov 1976, Teen Titans 4.00
❑8, Jan 1977, A: Challengers of the Unknown. New stories begin 4.00
❑9, Mar 1977, A: Challengers of the Reprints from Adventure Comics #254 and Doom Patrol (1st Series) #88; Challengers of the Unknown story; Doom Patrol story; Green Arrow story 4.00
❑10, May 1977, A: Challengers of the Unknown. Reprint from Doom Patrol (1st Series) #88; Challengers of the Unknown story; Doom Patrol story 4.00
❑11, Jul 1977, Flash, Atom, Supergirl 3.00
❑12, Sep 1977, Green Lantern, Hawkman, Atom; Green Lantern, Hawkman, Atom story; Reprint from The Brave and the Bold #42; Jeff Albrecht LOC 3.00
❑13, Nov 1977, Atom, Aquaman, Captain Comet 3.00
❑14, Jan 1978, Wonder Woman, Atom; Continued from Secret Society of Super-Villains #10 .... 3.00
❑15, Apr 1978, Final Issue; Flash & The New Gods; Flash & The New Gods story 3.00

Super-Villain Classics
Marvel

❑1, May 1983, O: Galactus. Reprints 3.00

Super-Villain Team-Up
Marvel

❑1, Aug 1975, GE, BEv, GT (a); A: Doctor Doom. A: Sub-Mariner 7.00
❑2, Oct 1975, SB (a); A: Doctor Doom. A: Sub-Mariner 5.00
❑3, Dec 1975, A: Doctor Doom. A: Sub-Mariner 4.00
❑4, Feb 1976, A: Doctor Doom. A: Sub-Mariner 4.00
❑5, Apr 1976, HT (a); 1: Shroud. A: Doctor Doom. A: Sub-Mariner 4.00
❑5/30¢, Apr 1976, 30¢ cover; 1: Shroud 20.00
❑6, Jun 1976, HT (a); A: Doctor Doom. A: Sub-Mariner 3.00
❑6/30¢, Jun 1976, 30¢ cover 20.00
❑7, Aug 1976, HT (a); O: Shroud. A: Doctor Doom. A: Sub-Mariner 3.00
❑7/30¢, Aug 1976, 30¢ cover; O: Shroud 20.00
❑8, Oct 1976, KG (a); 1: Rajah. A: Doctor Doom. A: Sub-Mariner 3.00
❑9, Dec 1976, A: Doctor Doom. A: Sub-Mariner 3.00
❑10, Feb 1977, BH (a); A: Doctor Doom. A: Sub-Mariner 3.00
❑11, Apr 1977, BH (a) 3.00
❑12, Jun 1977, DC (c); BH (a); Newsstand edition (distributed by Curtis); issue number in box 3.00
❑12/Whitman, Jun 1977, BH (a); Special markets edition (usually sold in Whitman bagged prepacks); price appears in a diamond; UPC barcode appears 3.00
❑12/35¢, Jun 1977, DC (c); BH (a); 35¢ regional price variant; newsstand edition (distributed by Curtis); issue number in box 15.00
❑13, Aug 1977, 35¢ regional price variant 5.00
❑13/35¢, Aug 1977, 35¢ regional price variant 15.00
❑14, Oct 1977, JBy (c); BH (a); Newsstand edition (distributed by Curtis); issue number in box 3.00
❑14/Whitman, Oct 1977, BH (a); Special markets edition (usually sold in Whitman bagged prepacks); price appears in a diamond; no UPC barcode 3.00
❑14/35¢, Oct 1977, BH (a); 35¢ regional price variant; newsstand edition (distributed by Curtis); issue number in box 15.00
❑15, Nov 1977, A: Red Skull. A: Doctor Doom. Reprints from Astonishing Tales #4 and 5 .... 3.00
❑16, May 1979, A: Red Skull. A: Doctor Doom 3.00
❑17, Jun 1980, A: Red Skull. A: Doctor Doom 3.00

Suppressed!
Tome

❑1, b&w 2.95

Supreme
Image

❑0, Aug 1995 RL (c); RL (a) 2.50
❑1, Nov 1992; RL (w); Vol. 1 does not exist; Silver foil-embossed cover; Foil-embossed cover; Embossed cover; Says (Vol. 2) in indicia; Says (Vol. 2) in indicia but Vol. 1 does not exist; Infiniti story 2.50
❑1/Gold, Nov 1992; Gold promotional edition; Embossed cover 2.50
❑2, Feb 1993; 1: Grizlock. covers says May, indicia says Feb 2.00
❑3, Jun 1993; RL (w); 1: Khrome 2.00
❑4, Jul 1993; Pinups 2.00
❑5, Aug 1993; 1: Thor (Image); 1: Starguard; Pinups 2.00
❑6, Oct 1993; 1: Starguard; Pinups 2.00
❑7, Nov 1993 .... 2.00
❑8, Dec 1993; Pinup 2.00
❑9, Jan 1994; Pinup 2.00
❑10, Feb 1994; O: Supreme 2.00
❑11, Mar 1994; Quantum with arms in air on cover 2.00
❑12, Apr 1994; Pinup 2.00
❑13, Jun 1994; Pinup 2.50
❑14, Jun 1994; Pinup 2.50
❑15, Jul 1994; O: Supreme; O: Spawn 2.50
❑16, Jul 1994; Pinup; Todd Nauck art credit in #17 .... 2.50
❑17, Aug 1994; V: Pitt 2.50
❑18, Aug 1994; Kid Supreme Sneak Preview 2.50
❑19, Sep 1994; Pinup 2.50
❑20, Oct 1994; A: Kid Supreme. Pinup 2.50
❑21, Nov 1994; Pinup 2.50
❑22, Dec 1994 .... 2.50
❑23, Jan 1995; polybagged with trading card 2.50
❑24, Feb 1995 .... 2.50
❑25, May 1994; RL (w); Images of Tomorrow; Shipped out of sequence after #12 to give preview of future 2.50
❑26, Mar 1995; V: Kid Supreme 2.50
❑27, Apr 1995 .... 2.50
❑28, May 1995 .... 2.50
❑28/A, May 1995 A: Glory 2.50
❑28/B, May 1995 A: Glory 2.50
❑29, Jun 1995; polybagged with Power Cardz 2.50
❑30, Jul 1995; polybagged with Power Cardz 2.50
❑31, Aug 1995 .... 2.50
❑32, Oct 1995 .... 2.50
❑33, Nov 1995; Babewatch 2.50
❑34, Dec 1995 .... 2.50
❑35, Jan 1996; polybagged with Lady Supreme card 2.50
❑36, Feb 1996 .... 2.50
❑37, Mar 1996 .... 2.50
❑37/A, Mar 1996; alternate cover 2.50
❑37/B, Mar 1996; alternate cover 2.50
❑38, Apr 1996 .... 2.50
❑39, May 1996; V: Loki 2.50
❑40, Jul 1996 .... 2.50
❑41, Aug 1996; Newmen Special Preview Edition back-up; AMo (w); Newmen Special Preview Edition back-up 3.50
❑41/Ltd., Aug 1996; limited edition; alternate cover (Superman homage) 15.00
❑41/AmEnt, Aug 1996; alternate cover (American Entertainment exclusive) 9.00
❑41/2nd; 2nd printing 2.50
❑42, Sep 1996; AMo (w); Superman homage; moves to Maximum Press 3.00
❑43, Oct 1996; AMo (w); Superman homage 3.00
❑44, Jan 1997 AMo (w) 3.00
❑45, Jan 1997 AMo (w) 2.50
❑46, Feb 1997; AMo (w); 1: Suprema 2.50
❑47, Mar 1997; AMo (w); 1: Twilight 2.50
❑48, Apr 1997 AMo (w) 2.50
❑49, May 1997; AMo (w); cover says Jun, indicia says May 2.50
❑50, Jun 1997; Giant-size; AMo (w) 2.50
❑51, Jul 1997 AMo (w) 2.50
❑52/A, Sep 1997 AMo (w) 2.50
❑52/B, Sep 1997 AMo (w) 2.50
❑53, Sep 1997 AMo (w) 2.50
❑54, Nov 1997 AMo (w) 2.50
❑55, Nov 1997; AMo (w); GK (a); cover says Dec, indicia says Nov 2.50
❑56, Feb 1998; Mini-Supreme cover 2.50
❑Ann 1, May 1995 A: The Allies 4.00

Supreme: Glory Days
Image

❑1, Oct 1994, RL (w) 3.00
❑2, Dec 1994, RL (w); Final Issue 2.50

Supreme Power
Marvel

❑1, Oct 2003, 1: Blur; O: Hyperion 4.00
❑1/Special, Oct 2003 .... 4.99
❑2, Nov 2003, 1: Kingsley (Amphibian); 1: Zarda (Power Princess); 1: Nighthawk; 1: Dr. Spectrum 2.99
❑3, Dec 2003 .... 2.99
❑4, Jan 2003 .... 2.99
❑5, Feb 2004 .... 4.00

Thing: Freakshow

Solo stories reveal rocky road
©Marvel

Thing from Another World

John Carpenter remake of classic 50s horror film
©Dark Horse

Thing

From Two-in-One team-ups to solo adventures
©Marvel

30 Days of Night

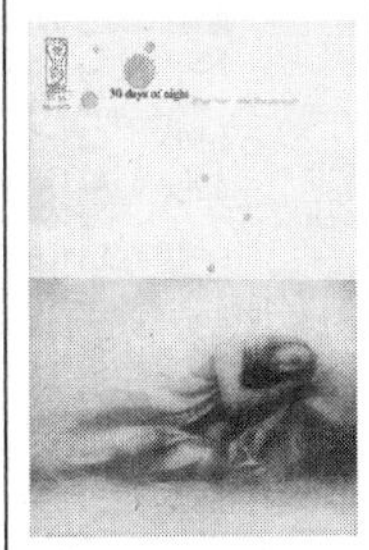

A vampire's paradise above the Arctic Circle
©Idea & Design Works

Thor

Thunder God journies to Marvel universe
©Marvel

	N-MINT
❑6, Mar 2004, (c)	2.99
❑7, Apr 2004	2.99
❑8, May 2004	2.99
❑9, Jun 2004	2.99
❑10, Jul 2004, 1: Princess Zarda	2.99
❑11, Sep 2004	2.99
❑12, Oct 2004, 1: Redstone	2.99
❑13, Nov 2004	2.99
❑14, Dec 2004	2.99
❑15, Jan 2005; 1: Tom Thumb	2.99
❑16, Apr 2005	2.99
❑17, May 2005	2.99
❑18, Oct 2005; 1: Arcanna; 1: Emil Burbank; 1: Nuke; 1: Shape; 1: Inertia; Final Issue	2.99

Supreme Power: Hyperion
Marvel / MAX

❑1, Nov 2005; Series takes place between Supreme Power #18 & Squadron Supreme #1; O: Emil Burbank	2.99
❑2, Dec 2005; 1: Blue Eagle; 1: Black Archer; 1: Lady Lark; 1: Haywire	2.99
❑3, Feb 2006	2.99
❑5, Jun 2006	2.99

Supreme Power: Nighthawk
Marvel

❑1, Oct 2005	2.99
❑2, Dec 2005	2.99
❑3, Jan 2006	2.99
❑4, Feb 2006	2.99
❑5, Mar 2006, Cover date follows date in indicia	2.99
❑6, Mar 2006	2.99

Supreme: The Return
Awesome

❑1, May 1999; continues story from Supreme #56	2.99
❑2, Jun 1999; infinite Darius Daxes	2.99
❑3; Brigade Preview Flip Book	2.99
❑4, Mar 2000; Back-up story featuring The League of Infinity	2.99
❑5, May 2000	2.99
❑6, Jun 2000; "The Return" dropped from cover	2.99

Supremie
Parody

❑1, b&w	2.50

Surfcrazed Comics
Pacifica

❑1	2.50
❑3; 3-D	3.95
❑4	2.50

Surf 'n' Wheels
Charlton

❑1, Nov 1969	12.00
❑2, Jan 1970	12.00
❑3, Mar 1970	12.00
❑4, May 1970	12.00
❑5, Jul 1970	12.00
❑6, Sep 1970	12.00

Surf Sumo
Star Tiger

	N-MINT
❑1	2.95
❑1/2nd, Jun 1997; 2nd printing with insert noting rights had reverted to Mighty Graphics; June 1997	2.95

Surge
Eclipse

❑1, Jul 1984 ME (w)	1.75
❑2, Aug 1984 ME (w); RHo (a)	1.75
❑3, Oct 1984 ME (w)	1.75
❑4, Jan 1985 ME (w); SR (a)	1.75

Surrogates
Top Shelf Productions

❑1, Jul 2005	2.95

Surrogate Saviour
Hot Brazen Comics

❑1, Sep 1995, b&w	2.50
❑2, Nov 1995, b&w	2.75
❑3, Jun 1996, b&w	2.95

Survive!
Apple

❑1, b&w	2.75

Survivors
Fantagraphics

❑1	2.50
❑2	2.50

Survivors
Prelude

❑1, Oct 1986; Story picks up from They Were Chosen To Be Survivors #4	1.95
❑2, Nov 1986; Last issue; Story continued in Survivors, The (Burnside) #1	1.95

Survivors
Burnside

❑1, Dec 1987; One-shot; Concludes story from Survivors, The (Prelude); b&w	1.95

Sushi
Shunga

❑1, Jan 1990, b&w; Adult	3.00
❑1/2nd; 2nd printing; Adult	2.50
❑2, b&w; Adult	3.00
❑3, b&w; Adult	3.00
❑4, Nov 1990, b&w; Adult	3.00
❑5, b&w; Adult	3.00
❑6, Aug 1991, b&w; Adult	3.00
❑7; Adult	2.50
❑8; Adult	2.50

Suspira: The Great Working
Chaos

❑1, Mar 1997	2.95
❑2, Apr 1997	2.95
❑3, May 1997	2.95
❑4, Jun 1997	2.95

Sussex Vampire
Caliber

❑1	2.95

Sustah-Girl: Queen of the Black Age
Onli

❑1, b&w	2.00

Swamp Fever
Big Muddy

	N-MINT
❑1, Adult; ca. 1972	3.00

Swamp Thing
DC

❑1, Nov 1972, BWr (c); BWr (a); O: Swamp Thing	60.00
❑2, Jan 1973, BWr (c); BWr (a)	30.00
❑3, Mar 1973, BWr (c); BWr (a); 1: Patchwork Man	20.00
❑4, May 1973, BWr (c); BWr (a)	20.00
❑5, Aug 1973, BWr (c); BWr (a)	15.00
❑6, Oct 1973, BWr (c); BWr (a)	15.00
❑7, Dec 1973, BWr (c); BWr (a); A: Batman. Batman	12.00
❑8, Feb 1974, BWr (c); BWr (a)	10.00
❑9, Apr 1974, BWr (c); BWr (a)	10.00
❑10, Jun 1974, BWr (c); BWr (a)	10.00
❑11, Aug 1974, NR (a)	5.00
❑12, Oct 1974, NR (a)	5.00
❑13, Dec 1974, NR (c); NR (a)	5.00
❑14, Feb 1975 NR (c); NR (a)	5.00
❑15, Apr 1975 NR (c); NR (a)	5.00
❑16, May 1975 NR (c); NR (a)	5.00
❑17, Jul 1975 NR (c); NR (a)	5.00
❑18, Sep 1975 NR (c); NR (a)	5.00
❑19, Oct 1975 NR (c); NR (a)	5.00
❑20, Jan 1976 NR (a)	5.00
❑21, Mar 1976 NR (c); NR (a)	5.00
❑22, May 1976, NR (a)	5.00
❑23, Jul 1976, NR (a)	5.00
❑24, Sep 1976, NR (a); Final Issue, continues as Saga of Swamp Thing	5.00

Swamp Thing
DC

❑46, Mar 1986; AMo (w); A: John Constantine. Crisis; Series continued from "Saga of the Swamp Thing"	4.00
❑47, Apr 1986; AMo (w); 1: Parliament of Trees	3.00
❑48, May 1986 AMo (w)	3.00
❑49, Jun 1986 AMo (w); AA (a)	3.00
❑50, Jul 1986; Giant-size; AMo (w); D: Sargon	4.00
❑51, Aug 1986 AMo (w)	3.00
❑52, Sep 1986; AMo (w); A: Arkham Asylum. A: Joker	4.00
❑53, Oct 1986; AMo (w); A: Batman. Arkham Asylum story	4.50
❑54, Nov 1986 AMo (w)	3.00
❑55, Dec 1986 AMo (w)	3.00
❑56, Jan 1987 AMo (w); AA (a)	3.00
❑57, Feb 1987 AMo (w)	3.00
❑58, Mar 1987; AMo (w); Spectre preview	3.00
❑59, Apr 1987 AMo (w)	3.00
❑60, May 1987; AMo (w); new format	3.00
❑61, Jun 1987 AMo (w)	3.00
❑62, Jul 1987	3.00
❑63, Aug 1987 AMo (w)	3.00
❑64, Sep 1987; AMo (w); TY (a); last with Moore	3.00
❑65, Oct 1987; 1: Sprout. Arkham Asylum	3.00
❑66, Nov 1987; Arkham Asylum	2.50
❑67, Dec 1987; 1: Hellblazer. Preview of Hellblazer; 6 Pg	2.50
❑68, Jan 1988	2.50
❑69, Feb 1988	2.50

N-MINT

- ❑70, Mar 1988 .... 2.50
- ❑71, Apr 1988 .... 2.50
- ❑72, May 1988 .... 2.50
- ❑73, Jun 1988 .... 2.50
- ❑74, Jul 1988 .... 2.50
- ❑75, Aug 1988 .... 2.50
- ❑76, Sep 1988; Continues from Hellblazer #9; continues in Hellblazer #10 .... 2.50
- ❑77, Oct 1988 AA (a) 2.50
- ❑78, Nov 1988 AA (a) 2.50
- ❑79, Dec 1988 A: Superman 2.50
- ❑80, Win 1988 .... 2.50
- ❑81, Hol 1989; Invasion! 2.50
- ❑82, Jan 1989; Sgt. Rock 2.25
- ❑83, Feb 1989; Enemy Ace 2.25
- ❑84, Mar 1989 A: Sandman 5.00
- ❑85, Apr 1989; Jonah Hex, Bat Lash 2.25
- ❑86, May 1989; Tomahawk, Rip Hunter, Demon 2.25
- ❑87, Jun 1989; Shining Knight, Demon . 2.25
- ❑88, Sep 1989 .... 2.25
- ❑89, Oct 1989 .... 2.25
- ❑90, Dec 1989; 1: Tefe Holland. Formerly known as Sprout 2.50
- ❑91, Jan 1990 A: Woodgod 2.25
- ❑92, Feb 1990 .... 2.25
- ❑93, Mar 1990 .... 2.25
- ❑94, Apr 1990 .... 2.25
- ❑95, May 1990 .... 2.25
- ❑96, Jun 1990 .... 2.25
- ❑97, Jul 1990 .... 2.25
- ❑98, Aug 1990 .... 2.25
- ❑99, Sep 1990 .... 2.25
- ❑100, Oct 1990; Giant-size 3.00
- ❑101, Nov 1990 .... 2.25
- ❑102, Dec 1990 .... 2.25
- ❑103, Jan 1991 .... 2.25
- ❑104, Feb 1991 .... 2.25
- ❑105, Mar 1991 .... 2.25
- ❑106, Apr 1991 .... 2.25
- ❑107, May 1991 .... 2.25
- ❑108, Jun 1991 .... 2.25
- ❑109, Jul 1991 .... 2.25
- ❑110, Aug 1991 .... 2.25
- ❑111, Sep 1991 .... 2.25
- ❑112, Oct 1991 .... 2.25
- ❑113, Nov 1991 .... 2.25
- ❑114, Dec 1991 .... 2.25
- ❑115, Jan 1992 .... 2.25
- ❑116, Feb 1992 .... 2.25
- ❑117, Mar 1992 JDu (a) 2.25
- ❑118, Apr 1992 .... 2.25
- ❑119, May 1992; 1: Lady Jane 2.25
- ❑120, Jun 1992 .... 2.25
- ❑121, Jul 1992 CV (c) 2.00
- ❑122, Aug 1992; CV (a); Includes pin-ups 2.00
- ❑123, Sep 1992 .... 2.00
- ❑124, Oct 1992 .... 2.00
- ❑125, Nov 1992; 20th Anniversary Issue; Arcane 3.25
- ❑126, Dec 1992 .... 2.00
- ❑127, Jan 1993 .... 2.00
- ❑128, Feb 1993; Vertigo line begins 2.00
- ❑129, Mar 1993 CV (c) 2.00
- ❑130, Apr 1993 .... 2.00
- ❑131, May 1993 .... 2.00
- ❑132, Jun 1993 .... 2.00
- ❑133, Jul 1993 CV (c) 2.00
- ❑134, Aug 1993 .... 2.00
- ❑135, Sep 1993 CV (c) 2.00
- ❑136, Oct 1993 CV (c) 2.00
- ❑137, Nov 1993; Pinup of Swamp Thing by Mike Mignola 2.00
- ❑138, Dec 1993 CV (c) 2.00
- ❑139, Jan 1994; CV (c);Continued from Black Orchid #5 .... 2.00
- ❑140, Mar 1994 .... 2.00
- ❑140/Platinum, Mar 1994 .... 6.00
- ❑141, Apr 1994 .... 2.00
- ❑142, May 1994 .... 2.00
- ❑143, Jun 1994 .... 2.00
- ❑144, Jul 1994 .... 2.00
- ❑145, Aug 1994 .... 2.00
- ❑146, Sep 1994 .... 2.00
- ❑147, Oct 1994 .... 2.00
- ❑148, Nov 1994 .... 2.00
- ❑149, Dec 1994; Includes trading card .. 2.00
- ❑150, Jan 1995; Giant-size 3.00
- ❑151, Feb 1995 BB (c) 2.00
- ❑152, Mar 1995 BB (c) 2.00
- ❑153, Apr 1995; BB (c) 2.00
- ❑154, May 1995 .... 2.25
- ❑155, Jun 1995 .... 2.25
- ❑156, Jul 1995 .... 2.25
- ❑157, Aug 1995 .... 2.25
- ❑158, Sep 1995 .... 2.25
- ❑159, Oct 1995; Photo cover 2.50
- ❑160, Nov 1995 .... 2.50
- ❑161, Dec 1995 .... 2.50
- ❑162, Jan 1996 .... 2.50
- ❑163, Feb 1996 .... 2.50
- ❑164, Mar 1996 .... 2.50
- ❑165, Apr 1996; CS (a); Imaginary story 2.50
- ❑166, May 1996 .... 2.50
- ❑167, Jun 1996 .... 2.50
- ❑168, Jul 1996 .... 2.50
- ❑169, Aug 1996 A: John Constantine 2.50
- ❑170, Sep 1996 .... 2.50
- ❑171, Oct 1996; Final Issue 2.50
- ❑Ann 4 A: Batman 3.50
- ❑Ann 5 A: Brother Power 3.50
- ❑Ann 6 .... 2.95
- ❑Ann 7; CV (c); Children's Crusade 3.95

Swamp Thing
DC / Vertigo

- ❑1, May 2000 .... 4.00
- ❑2, Jun 2000 .... 2.50
- ❑3, Jul 2000 .... 2.50
- ❑4, Aug 2000 .... 2.50
- ❑5, Sep 2000 .... 2.50
- ❑6, Oct 2000 .... 2.50
- ❑7, Nov 2000 .... 2.50
- ❑8, Dec 2000 .... 2.50
- ❑9, Jan 2001 .... 2.50
- ❑10, Feb 2001 .... 2.50
- ❑11, Mar 2001 .... 2.50
- ❑12, Apr 2001 .... 2.50
- ❑13, May 2001 .... 2.50
- ❑14, Jun 2001 .... 2.50
- ❑15, Jul 2001 .... 2.50
- ❑16, Aug 2001 .... 2.50
- ❑17, Sep 2001 .... 2.50
- ❑18, Oct 2001 .... 2.50
- ❑19, Nov 2001 .... 2.50
- ❑20, Dec 2001 .... 2.50

Swamp Thing
DC / Vertigo

- ❑1, May 2004 .... 4.00
- ❑2, Jun 2004 .... 2.95
- ❑3, Jul 2004 .... 2.95
- ❑4, Aug 2004 .... 2.95
- ❑5, Sep 2004; Includes preview of Books of Magick: Life During Wartime 2.95
- ❑6, Oct 2004 .... 2.95
- ❑7, Nov 2004 .... 2.95
- ❑8, Dec 2004 .... 2.95
- ❑9, Jan 2005 .... 2.95
- ❑10, Feb 2005 .... 2.95
- ❑11, Mar 2005 .... 2.95
- ❑12, Apr 2005 .... 2.95
- ❑13, May 2005 .... 2.95
- ❑14, Jun 2005 .... 2.95
- ❑15, Jul 2005 .... 2.99
- ❑16, Aug 2005 .... 2.99
- ❑17, Sep 2005 .... 2.99
- ❑18, Oct 2005 .... 2.99
- ❑19, Nov 2005 .... 2.99
- ❑20, Dec 2005 .... 2.99
- ❑21, Jan 2006 .... 2.99
- ❑22, Jan 2006 .... 2.99
- ❑23, Mar 2006 .... 2.99
- ❑24, Mar 2006 .... 2.99
- ❑25, May 2006 .... 2.99
- ❑26, Jun 2006 .... 2.99
- ❑27, Jul 2006 .... 2.99
- ❑28, Sep 2006, Cover by Eric Powell 2.99
- ❑29, Nov 2006, Eric Powell painted cover; Final Issue 2.99

Swamp Thing: Roots
DC / Vertigo

- ❑1; prestige format one-shot 7.95

Swan
Little Idylls

- ❑1, Jun 1995, b&w 2.95
- ❑2, Jun 1995, b&w 2.95
- ❑3 .... 2.95
- ❑4 .... 2.95

Sweatshop
DC

- ❑1, Jun 2003 .... 2.95
- ❑2, Jul 2003 .... 2.95
- ❑3, Aug 2003 .... 2.95
- ❑4, Sep 2003 .... 2.95
- ❑5, Oct 2003 .... 2.95
- ❑6, Nov 2003; Final issue 2.95

Sweet
Adept

- ❑1 .... 3.95

Sweetchilde
New Moon

- ❑1, b&w; Adult 2.95

Sweet Childe: Lost Confessions
Anarchy Bridgeworks

- ❑1; Adult 2.95

Sweet Lucy
Brainstorm

- ❑1, Jun 1993, b&w 2.95
- ❑2, b&w 2.95

Sweet Lucy: Blonde Steele
Brainstorm

- ❑1; Adult 2.95

Sweet Lucy Commemorative Edition
Brainstorm

- ❑1; Adult 3.95

Sweetmeats
Atomeka

- ❑1; b&w one-shot 3.95

Sweet XVI
Marvel

- ❑1, May 1991 .... 1.00
- ❑2, Jun 1991 .... 1.00
- ❑3, Jul 1991 .... 1.00
- ❑4, Aug 1991 .... 1.00
- ❑5, Sep 1991 .... 1.00
- ❑6, Oct 1991 .... 1.00
- ❑Special 1, Back to School Special 2.25

Swerve
Slave Labor / Amaze Ink

- ❑1, Dec 1995 .... 1.50
- ❑2, Mar 1996 .... 1.50

Swiftsure
Harrier

- ❑1, May 1985 .... 2.00
- ❑2 .... 2.00
- ❑3, Aug 1985 .... 2.00
- ❑4 .... 2.00
- ❑5, Nov 1985 .... 2.00
- ❑6, Jan 1986 .... 2.00
- ❑7, Mar 1986 .... 2.00
- ❑8, May 1986 .... 2.00
- ❑9, Jul 1986; Redfox 2.00
- ❑10, Sep 1986 .... 2.00
- ❑11, Nov 1986 .... 2.00
- ❑12, Jan 1987 .... 2.00
- ❑13, Mar 1987 .... 2.00
- ❑14, May 1987 .... 2.00
- ❑15, Jul 1987 .... 2.00
- ❑16, Sep 1987 .... 2.00
- ❑17, Nov 1987 .... 2.00
- ❑18, Jan 1988 .... 2.00

Swiftsure & Conqueror
Harrier

- ❑1 .... 2.00
- ❑2 .... 1.75
- ❑3, Aug 1985 .... 1.75
- ❑4, Sep 1985 .... 1.75
- ❑5, Nov 1985 .... 1.75
- ❑6 .... 1.75
- ❑7 .... 1.75
- ❑8, May 1986 .... 1.75
- ❑9, Jul 1986 A: Redfox 2.50
- ❑10, Sep 1986 .... 1.50
- ❑11, Nov 1986 .... 1.50

Other grades: Multiply price above by 5/6 for VF/NM • 2/3 for VERY FINE • 1/3 for FINE • 1/5 for VERY GOOD • 1/8 for GOOD

Thor

He used to be Mighty, but now he's just Thor
©Marvel

Thor Corps

Three different Thors team up
©Marvel

Thor: Son of Asgard

Teen-age version of the thunder god
©Marvel

Thor: Vikings

Garth Ennis' adult version of Thor
©Marvel

Those Magnificent Men In Their Flying Machines

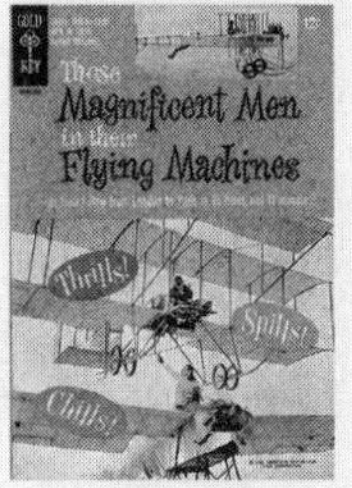

Adaptation of the movie by Gold Key
©Gold Key

N-MINT

❑12 1.50
❑13 1.95
❑14, May 1987 1.95
❑15, Jul 1987 1.95
❑16 1.95
❑17 1.95
❑18, Jan 1988 1.95

Swing with Scooter
DC

❑1, Jul 1966 30.00
❑2, Sep 1966 18.00
❑3, Nov 1966, JO (a) 15.00
❑4, Jan 1967 12.00
❑5, Mar 1967 12.00
❑6, May 1967 10.00
❑7, Jul 1967 10.00
❑8, Sep 1967 10.00
❑9, Nov 1967 10.00
❑10, Jan 1968 10.00
❑11, Mar 1968 8.00
❑12, May 1968 8.00
❑13, Jul 1968 8.00
❑14, Sep 1968 8.00
❑15, Nov 1968 8.00
❑16, Jan 1969 8.00
❑17, Mar 1969 8.00
❑18, May 1969 8.00
❑19, Jul 1969 8.00
❑20, Aug 1969 8.00
❑21, Sep 1969 6.00
❑22, Oct 1969 6.00
❑23, Nov 1969 6.00
❑24, Jan 1970 6.00
❑25, Feb 1970 6.00
❑26, Apr 1970 6.00
❑27, May 1970 6.00
❑28, Jul 1970 6.00
❑29, Aug 1970 6.00
❑30, Oct 1970 6.00
❑31, Nov 1970 5.00
❑32, Mar 1971 5.00
❑33, May 1971 5.00
❑34, Jul 1971 5.00
❑35, Sep 1971 5.00
❑36, Aug 1971, Final Issue 5.00

Switchblade
Silverline

❑1, Dec 1997 2.95

Sword in the Stone
Gold Key

❑1, Feb 1964, Adapts Disney animated feature 30.00

Sword of Damocles
Image

❑1, Mar 1996; 1: Fire From Heaven; 1: Sword of Damocles 2.50
❑2, Jul 1996 2.50

Sword of Dracula
Image

❑1, Oct 2003 2.95
❑2, Dec 2003 2.95
❑3, Apr 2004 2.99
❑4, Apr 2004 2.95

N-MINT

❑5 2004 2.95
❑6 2004 2.95

Sword of Sorcery
DC

❑1, Mar 1973, HC, NA (a); Fafhrd and The Gray Mouser 10.00
❑2, May 1973, HC (c); HC (a); Fafhrd and The Gray Mouser 8.00
❑3, Aug 1973, HC (a); Fafhrd and The Gray Mouser 8.00
❑4, Oct 1973, HC (c); HC (a); Fafhrd and The Gray Mouser 6.00
❑5, Dec 1973, AM, JSn, JSe (a); Fafhrd and The Gray Mouser 6.00

Sword of the Atom
DC

❑1, Sep 1983, GK (c); GK (a) 1.50
❑2, Oct 1983, GK (c); GK (a) 1.50
❑3, Nov 1983, GK (c); GK (a) 1.50
❑4, Dec 1983, GK (c); GK (a); Michael Eury L.O.C 1.50
❑Special 1, ca. 1984, GK (c); GK (a) 1.50
❑Special 2, ca. 1985, GK (c); GK (a) 1.50
❑Special 3, ca. 1988, PB (c); PB (a) 1.50

Sword of the Samurai
Avalon

❑1 1996, b&w; Reprints 2.50

Sword of Valor
A+

❑1 2.50
❑2 2.50
❑3 2.50
❑4 2.50

Swordsmen and Saurians
Eclipse

❑1, b&w 19.95

Swords of Cerebus
Aardvark-Vanaheim

❑1, b&w; Reprints Cerebus #1-4 5.00
❑1/2nd, b&w; Reprints Cerebus #1-4 5.00
❑1/3rd, b&w; Reprints Cerebus #1-4 5.00
❑2, b&w; Reprints Cerebus #5-8 5.00
❑2/2nd, b&w; Reprints Cerebus #5-8 5.00
❑3, b&w; Reprints Cerebus #9-12 6.00
❑3/2nd, b&w; Reprints Cerebus #9-12 6.00
❑3/3rd, b&w; Reprints Cerebus #9-12 6.00
❑4, b&w; Reprints Cerebus #13-16 6.00
❑4/2nd, b&w; Reprints Cerebus #13-16 6.00
❑5, b&w; Reprints Cerebus #17-20 5.00
❑6, b&w; Reprints Cerebus #21-24; first printing omitted issue #25 5.00

Swords of Cerebus Supplement
Aardvark-Vanaheim

❑1, b&w; giveaway to buyers of Swords of Cerebus #6 first printing; Giveawawy to buyers of Swords of Cerebus #6 first printing; reprints Cerebus #25 1.00

Swords of Shar-Pei
Caliber

❑1, b&w 2.50
❑2, b&w 2.50

N-MINT

Swords of Texas
Eclipse

❑1, Oct 1987 1.75
❑2, Nov 1987 1.75
❑3, Jan 1988 1.75
❑4, Mar 1988 1.75

Swords of the Swashbucklers
Marvel / Epic

❑1, May 1985 BG (a) 2.00
❑2, Jul 1985 BG (a) 1.75
❑3, Sep 1985 BG (a) 1.75
❑4, Nov 1985 BG (a) 1.50
❑5, Jan 1986 BG (a) 1.50
❑6, Mar 1986 BG (a) 1.50
❑7, May 1986 BG (a) 1.50
❑8, Jul 1986 BG (a) 1.50
❑9, Sep 1986 BG (a) 1.50
❑10, Nov 1986 BG (a) 1.50
❑11, Jan 1987 BG (a) 1.50
❑12, Mar 1987 BG (a) 1.50

Swords of Valor
A-Plus

❑1, b&w 2.50
❑2, b&w 2.50
❑3, b&w 2.50
❑4, b&w 2.50

Sylvia Faust
Image

❑1, Aug 2004 2.95
❑2, Oct 2004 2.95

Symbols of Justice
High Impact

❑1, Jun 1995; Wraparound cover 2.95

Syn
Dark Horse

❑1, Aug 2003 2.99
❑2, Oct 2003 2.99
❑3, Nov 2003 2.99
❑4, Jan 2004 2.99
❑5, Mar 2004 2.99

Synn, the Girl from LSD
AC

❑1, Aug 1990, b&w 3.95

Synthetic Assassin
Night Realm

❑1 1.50

Syphons
Now

❑1, Jul 1986, O: Syphons. 1: Syphons 2.00
❑2, Sep 1986 1.50
❑3, Nov 1986 1.50
❑4, Jan 1987 1.50
❑5, Mar 1987 1.50
❑6, Jul 1987 1.50
❑7, Aug 1987 1.50

Syphons
Now

❑0, Dec 1993; Preview edition 1.00
❑1, May 1994 2.50
❑2, Jun 1994 2.50
❑3, Jul 1994 2.50

Other grades: Multiply price above by 5/6 for VF/NM • 2/3 for VERY FINE • 1/3 for FINE • 1/5 for VERY GOOD • 1/8 for GOOD

Syphons: The Sygate Stratagem
Now

❑1, ca. 1994 ... 2.95
❑2, ca. 1994 ... 2.95
❑3, ca. 1994 ... 2.95

System
DC / Vertigo

❑1, May 1996 ... 2.95
❑2, Jun 1996 ... 2.95
❑3, Jul 1996 ... 2.95

System Seven
Arrow

❑1, Dec 1987 ... 1.50
❑2 ... 1.50
❑3 ... 1.50

Taboo
Spiderbaby / Tundra

❑1, b&w ... 9.95
❑2, b&w; ca. 1989 ... 9.95
❑3, b&w ... 9.95
❑4, b&w ... 14.95
❑5 ... 14.95
❑6; with booklet ... 14.95
❑7; with booklet ... 14.95
❑8, Jun 1995, b&w ... 14.95
❑9 ... 14.95

Taboux
Antarctic

❑1, Aug 1996; Adult ... 3.95
❑2, Aug 1996; Adult ... 3.95

Tabula Rasa
Image

❑1, Nov 2006, b&w ... 4.99

Tactics
ADV Manga

❑1, ca. 2004; Graphic novel; Reads right to left; b&w ... 9.99
❑2, ca. 2005; Graphic novel; Reads right to left; b&w ... 9.99

Tailgunner Jo
DC

❑1, Sep 1988 ... 1.25
❑2, Oct 1988 ... 1.25
❑3, Nov 1988 ... 1.25
❑4, Dec 1988 ... 1.25
❑5, Win 1988 ... 1.25
❑6, Jan 1989 ... 1.25

Tails
Archie

❑1, Dec 1995 ... 1.50
❑2, Jan 1996 ... 1.50
❑3, Feb 1996 ... 1.50

Tainted
DC / Vertigo

❑1, Feb 1995; Indicia says January 1995; Third Vertigo Voices title ... 4.95

Tainted Blood
Weirdling

❑1, Apr 1996 ... 2.95

Taken Under Compendium
Caliber

❑1, b&w; NN ... 2.95

Takion
DC

❑1, Jun 1996; 1: Takion ... 1.75
❑2, Jul 1996; V: Captain Atom; V: Flash; V: Green Lantern ... 1.75
❑3, Aug 1996 ... 1.75
❑4, Sep 1996 ... 1.75
❑5, Oct 1996 ... 1.75
❑6, Nov 1996; Final Night ... 1.75
❑7, Dec 1996; Lightray returns ... 1.75

Tale of Halima
Fantagraphics / Eros

❑1, b&w; Adult ... 2.75
❑2, b&w; Adult ... 2.75

Tale of Mya Rom
Aircel

❑1, b&w ... 1.70

Tale of One Bad Rat
Dark Horse

❑1, Oct 1994, BT, NG (w); BT (a); Introduction by Neil Gaiman ... 4.00
❑2, Nov 1994, BT (w); BT (a) ... 3.00
❑3, Dec 1994, BT (w); BT (a) ... 3.00
❑4, Jan 1995, BT (w); BT (a) ... 3.00

Tale of the Body Thief
Sicilian Dragon

❑1, Sep 1999 ... 2.95
❑2, Oct 1999 ... 2.95
❑3 1999 ... 2.95
❑4 2000 ... 2.95
❑5 2000 ... 2.95
❑6 2000 ... 2.95
❑7 2000 ... 2.95
❑8 2000 ... 2.95
❑9 2000 ... 2.95
❑10 2000 ... 2.95
❑11 2000 ... 2.95
❑12 2000 ... 2.95

Tales Calculated to Drive You Mad
E.C.

❑1, ca. 1997 ... 3.99
❑2, ca. 1997 ... 3.99
❑3, ca. 1997 ... 3.99
❑4, ca. 1998 ... 3.99
❑5, ca. 1998 ... 3.99
❑6, Mar 1999; Reprints Mad #16-18 ... 3.99
❑7, Nov 1999 ... 3.99
❑8, Jan 2000; Reprints Mad #22, 23 ... 3.99

Tales from Ground Zero
Excel

❑1, b&w ... 4.95

Tales From Necropolis
Brainstorm

❑1, b&w ... 2.95

Tales From ... Riverdale Digest Magazine
Archie

❑7, Dec 2005 ... 2.39
❑1, Jun 2005 ... 2.39
❑2, Jul 2005 ... 2.39
❑3, Aug 2005 ... 2.39
❑4, Sep 2005 ... 2.39
❑5, Oct 2005 ... 2.39
❑6, Nov 2005 ... 2.39
❑8, Jan 2006 ... 2.39
❑9, Apr 2006 ... 2.39
❑10, May 2006 ... 2.39
❑12, Aug 2006 ... 2.49
❑13, Oct 2006 ... 2.49
❑14, Nov 2006 ... 2.49
❑15, Dec 2006 ... 2.49
❑16, Jan 2007 ... 2.49
❑17, Mar 2007 ... 2.49

Tales from Shock City
Fantagraphics

❑nn, Oct 2001, b&w; Printed in black, white, and red ... 3.95

Tales From Sleaze Castle
Gratuitous Bunny

❑1 ... 2.50
❑2 ... 2.50
❑3 ... 2.50

Tales From the Age of Apocalypse
Marvel

❑1, Dec 1996 ... 5.95

Tales from the Age of Apocalypse: Sinister Bloodlines
Marvel

❑1, Dec 1997 ... 5.99

Tales from the Aniverse
Massive

❑1, Jan 1992, b&w ... 2.25
❑2 1992 ... 2.25
❑3 1992 ... 2.25

Tales from the Aniverse
Arrow

❑1 ... 2.00
❑2 ... 1.50
❑3 ... 1.50
❑4 ... 1.50
❑5 ... 1.50
❑6 ... 1.50

Tales from the Bog
Aberration

❑1, Nov 1995, b&w ... 3.00
❑2, Feb 1996, b&w ... 3.00
❑3, Jun 1996, b&w ... 3.00
❑4, Sep 1996, b&w ... 3.00
❑5, Apr 1997, b&w ... 3.00
❑6, Jun 1997, b&w ... 3.00
❑7, Nov 1997, b&w ... 3.00
❑Ashcan 1, Sep 1995, b&w ... 2.95

Tales from the Bog
Aberration

❑1 1998, b&w ... 2.95

Tales from the Bully Pulpit One Shot
Image

❑1 2004 ... 6.95

Tales from the Clonezone
Dark Horse

❑1 ... 1.75

Tales from the Crypt
Gladstone

❑1, Jul 1990; GE, AW, FF, BE, GI (w); GE, AW, JCr, FF, BE, JKa, GI (a); O: Crypt-Keeper. Reprints Tales From the Crypt #33, Crime SuspenStories #17 ... 3.00
❑2, Sep 1990; JO, JCr, JKa, GI (w); JO, JCr, JKa, GI (a); Reprints Tales From the Crypt #35, Crime SuspenStories #18 ... 2.50
❑3, Nov 1990; HK, JO, WW, JKa, GI (w); HK, JO, JCr, WW, JKa, GI (a); Reprints Tales From the Crypt #39, Crime SuspenStories #1 ... 2.50
❑4, Jan 1991; AF, AW, HK, JO, JCr, JKa (a); Reprints Tales From the Crypt #18, Crime SuspenStories #16 ... 2.50
❑5, Mar 1991; JCr, BK, JKa, GI (a); Reprints Tales From the Crypt #45, Crime SuspenStories #5 ... 2.50
❑6, May 1991; JCr, BK, JKa, GI (a); Reprints Tales From the Crypt #42, Crime SuspenStories #27 ... 2.50

Tales from the Crypt
Cochran

❑1, Jul 1991; over-sized reprint of Tales #31 and Crime SuspenStories #12; Over-sized reprint of Tales #31 and Crime SuspenStories #12 ... 3.95

Tales from the Crypt
Cochran

❑1, Sep 1991 ... 2.00
❑2, Oct 1991; Reprints Tales from the Crypt #34, Crime Suspenstories #15 ... 2.00
❑3, Dec 1991 ... 2.00
❑4, Feb 1992 ... 2.00
❑5, Mar 1992 ... 2.00
❑6, May 1992 ... 2.00
❑7, Jul 1992 ... 2.00

Tales from the Crypt
Gemstone

❑1, Sep 1992; AF, JCr (a); Reprints Crypt of Terror (EC) #17 ... 2.00
❑2, Dec 1992; Reprints Crypt of Terror (EC) #18 ... 2.00
❑3, Mar 1993; Reprints Crypt of Terror (EC) #19 ... 2.00
❑4, Jun 1993; AF, JCr, JKa, GI (a); Reprints Tales From the Crypt (EC) #20 ... 2.00
❑5, Sep 1993; AF, HK, WW, GI (a); Reprints Tales From the Crypt (EC) #21 ... 2.00
❑6, Dec 1993; AF, JCr, GI (a); Reprints Tales From the Crypt (EC) #22 ... 2.00
❑7, Mar 1994; AF, JCr, GI (a); Reprints Tales From the Crypt (EC) #23 ... 2.00
❑8, Jun 1994; AF (c); JCr, WW, GI (a); Reprints Tales From the Crypt (EC) #24 ... 2.00
❑9, Sep 1994; Reprints Tales From the Crypt (EC) #25 ... 2.00
❑10, Dec 1994; Reprints Tales From the Crypt (EC) #26 ... 2.00
❑11, Mar 1995; JO, JKa, GI (w); JO, JKa, GI (a); Reprints Tales From the Crypt (EC) #27 ... 2.00
❑12, Jun 1995; JO, JKa, GI (w); JO, JKa, GI (a); Reprints Tales From the Crypt (EC) #28 ... 2.00
❑13, Sep 1995; JO, JKa, GI (w); JO, JKa, GI (a); Reprints Tales From the Crypt (EC) #29 ... 2.00

3-D Substance

3-D comics from Jack Harris and Steve Ditko

©3-D Zone

3-D Zone

Get out your glasses for 3-D showcase

©3-D Zone

3 Geeks

Humor series about... well, three geeks

©3 Finger Prints

300

Ancient Greeks in action from Frank Miller

©Dark Horse

Three Stooges

Decent adaptation of Stooges' hilarity

©Gold Key

	N-MINT
❑14, Dec 1995; JO, JKa, GI (w); JO, JKa, GI (a); Reprints Tales From the Crypt (EC) #30	2.00
❑15, Mar 1996; AW, JKa, GI (w); AW, JKa, GI (a); Reprints Tales From the Crypt (EC) #31	2.00
❑16, Jun 1996; GE, GI (w); GE, GI (a); Reprints Tales From the Crypt (EC) #32	2.50
❑17, Sep 1996; GE, JKa, GI (w); GE, JKa, GI (a); O: the The Crypt Keeper. Reprints Tales From the Crypt (EC) #33	2.50
❑18, Dec 1996; GE, JKa, GI (w); GE, JKa, GI (a); Reprints Tales From the Crypt (EC) #34	2.50
❑19, Mar 1997; JO, JKa, GI (w); JO, JKa, GI (a); Reprints Tales From the Crypt (EC) #35	2.50
❑20, Jun 1997; GE, JKa, GI (w); GE, JKa, GI (a); Reprints Tales From the Crypt (EC) #36	2.50
❑21, Sep 1997; JO, BE, GI (w); JO, BE, GI (a); Reprints Tales From the Crypt (EC) #37	2.50
❑22, Dec 1997; BE, GI (w); BE, GI (a); Reprints Tales From the Crypt (EC) #38	2.50
❑23, Mar 1998; JO, JKa, GI (w); JO, JKa, GI (a); Reprints Tales From the Crypt (EC) #39	2.50
❑24, Jun 1998; GE, BK, GI (w); GE, BK, GI (a); Reprints Tales From the Crypt (EC) #40	2.50
❑25, Sep 1998; GE, JKa, GI (w); GE, JKa, GI (a); Reprints Tales From the Crypt (EC) #41	2.50
❑26, Dec 1998; Reprints Tales From the Crypt (EC) #42	2.50
❑27, Mar 1999; Reprints Tales From the Crypt (EC) #43	2.50
❑28, Jun 1999; Reprints Tales From the Crypt (EC) #44	2.50
❑29, Sep 1999; Reprints Tales From the Crypt (EC) #45	2.50
❑30, Dec 1999; Reprints Tales From the Crypt (EC) #46; material originally prepared for Crypt of Terror #1	2.50
❑Ann 1; Collects Tales From the Crypt #1-5	8.95
❑Ann 2	9.95
❑Ann 3	10.95
❑Ann 4	12.95
❑Ann 5; Collects Tales From the Crypt #37-41	13.50

Tales from the Edge!
Vanguard

❑1, Jun 1993, b&w; Flip-book; WW (w); WW (a)	3.50
❑2, Sep 1993, b&w	5.00
❑3, Dec 1993, b&w	3.00
❑4, Jul 1994, b&w	3.00
❑5, ca. 1994; Mature; b&w	3.00
❑6, ca. 1995	3.00
❑7, Jul 1995, b&w	3.00
❑8, b&w	4.00
❑9, b&w	5.00
❑10, b&w	4.00
❑11, Mar 1998; Steranko: Graphic Prince of Darkness special	5.00
❑12	4.00
❑13	3.00
❑14	5.00

	N-MINT
❑15; BSz (a); Bill Sienkiewicz Special	5.55
❑Summer 1, Aug 1994, b&w; cardstock cover	3.50

Tales from the Fridge
Kitchen Sink

❑1, Jun 1973, b&w	3.00

Tales from the Heart
Entropy

❑1 1988; no cover date	4.00
❑2 1988; ca. 1987	3.25
❑3, Dec 1988, b&w	3.00
❑4, Jan 1989, b&w	3.00
❑5, May 1989, b&w	2.95
❑6, Oct 1989, b&w	2.95
❑7, Nov 1990	2.95
❑8, Apr 1991	2.95
❑9, Aug 1992	2.95
❑10, Mar 1993, b&w	2.95
❑11, May 1994, b&w	2.95

Tales from the Heart of Africa: The Temporary Natives
Marvel / Epic

❑1, Aug 1990; NN; One-shot	3.95

Tales from the Kids
David G. Brown

❑1, Apr 1996, b&w; No cover price; anthology by children; produced for L.A. Cultural Affairs Dept	2.00

Tales From the Leather Nun
Last Gasp

❑1, 44 pages; Adult	14.00

Tales from the Outer Boroughs
Fantagraphics

❑1, b&w	2.25
❑2, b&w	2.25
❑3, b&w	2.25
❑4, b&w	2.50
❑5, b&w	2.50

Tales from the Plague
Eclipse

❑1; ca. 1986	3.95

Tales from the Ravaged Lands
Magi

❑0; no indicia; b&w introduction to series	2.00
❑1, b&w; no indicia or cover date	2.50
❑2, b&w; no indicia or cover date	2.50
❑3, Jan 1996, b&w	2.50
❑4, ca. 1996, b&w; no indicia or cover date	2.50
❑5, May 1996, b&w	2.50
❑6, Aug 1996, b&w	2.50

Tales from the Stone Troll Café
Planet X

❑1, ca. 1986	1.75

Tales from the Tomb
Dell

❑1, Oct 1962, JS (w); FS (a)	125.00

Tales of a Checkered Man
D.W. Brubaker

❑1, b&w; no cover price	2.00

N-MINT

Tales of Asgard
Marvel

❑1, Oct 1968; SL (w); JK (a); reprints "Tales of Asgard" stories from Journey Into Mystery #98-106	30.00

Tales of Asgard
Marvel

❑1, Feb 1984; SL (w); JK (a); reprints "Tales of Asgard" stories from Journey Into Mystery #129-136	1.50

Tales of Beatrix Farmer
Mu

❑1, Feb 1996, b&w; NN	2.95

Tales of Blue & Grey
Avalon

❑1, b&w	2.95

Tales of Evil
Atlas-Seaboard

❑1, Feb 1975	9.00
❑2, Apr 1975 TS (a)	7.00
❑3, Jul 1975 RB (w); RB (a)	7.00

Tales of Ghost Castle
DC

❑1, May 1975 SA (w); SA, NR (a)	10.00
❑2, Jul 1975 AN (a)	9.00
❑3, Sep 1975	9.00

Tales of G.I. Joe
Marvel

❑1, Jan 1988; Reprints G.I. Joe, A Real American Hero #1	1.00
❑2, Feb 1988; Reprints G.I. Joe, A Real American Hero #2	1.00
❑3, Mar 1988; Reprints G.I. Joe, A Real American Hero #3	1.00
❑4, Apr 1988; Reprints G.I. Joe, A Real American Hero #4	1.00
❑5, May 1988; Reprints G.I. Joe, A Real American Hero #5	1.00
❑6, Jun 1988; Reprints G.I. Joe, A Real American Hero #6	1.00
❑7, Jul 1988; Reprints G.I. Joe, A Real American Hero #7	1.00
❑8, Aug 1988; Reprints G.I. Joe, A Real American Hero #8	1.00
❑9, Sep 1988; Reprints G.I. Joe, A Real American Hero #9	1.00
❑10, Oct 1988; Reprints G.I. Joe, A Real American Hero #10	1.00
❑11, Nov 1988; Reprints G.I. Joe, A Real American Hero #11	1.00
❑12, Dec 1988; Reprints G.I. Joe, A Real American Hero #12	1.00
❑13, Jan 1989; Reprints G.I. Joe, A Real American Hero #13	1.00
❑14, Feb 1989; Reprints G.I. Joe, A Real American Hero #14	1.00
❑15, Mar 1989; Reprints G.I. Joe, A Real American Hero #15	1.00

Tales of Jerry
Hacienda

❑1, b&w; ca. 1978	2.50
❑2; ca. 1984	2.50
❑3	2.50
❑4	2.50
❑5	2.50
❑6	2.50

Other grades: Multiply price above by 5/6 for VF/NM • 2/3 for VERY FINE • 1/3 for FINE • 1/5 for VERY GOOD • 1/8 for GOOD

N-MINT | N-MINT | N-MINT

❑7 .... 2.50
❑8 .... 2.50
❑9 .... 2.50
❑10 .... 2.50

Tales of Lethargy
Alpha

❑1, b&w 2.50
❑2, b&w 2.50
❑3, b&w 2.50

Tales of Ordinary Madness
Dark Horse

❑1, b&w 2.50
❑2, b&w 2.50
❑3, b&w 2.50
❑4, b&w 2.50

Tales of Screaming Horror
Fantaco

❑1, ca. 1992, b&w 3.50

Tales of Sex and Death
Print Mint

❑1, Apr 1971, Adult 3.00
❑2; Adult 3.00

Tales of Shaundra
Rip Off

❑1; Adult 12.95

Tales of Suspense
Marvel

❑39, Mar 1963, JK (c); SL (w); GC, DH, JK (a); 1&O: Iron Man 3500.00
❑40, Apr 1963, JK (c); SL (w); SD, JK (a); 1: Iron Man gold armor; 1: Gargantus 1100.00
❑41, May 1963, SL (w); SD, JK (a); Iron Man 650.00
❑42, Jun 1963, SL (w); SD, DH (a); 1: Mad Pharoah; Iron Man 325.00
❑43, Jul 1963, 1&O: Kala; Iron Man 325.00
❑44, Aug 1963, Iron Man 325.00
❑45, Sep 1963, 1: Pepper Potts. 1: Happy Hogan. 1: Jack Frost II (Gregor Shapanka) 325.00
❑46, Oct 1963, 1: Crimson Dynamo; Iron Man 210.00
❑47, Nov 1963, JK (c); SL (w); SD, DH (a); 1&O: Melter 210.00
❑48, Dec 1963, SL (w); SD (a); New armor for Iron Man (red and gold) 265.00
❑49, Jan 1964, JK (c); SL (w); SD (a); A: Angel II. Watcher back-up 210.00
❑50, Feb 1964, JK (c); SL (w); DH (a); 1: The Mandarin. Watcher back-up 155.00
❑51, Mar 1964, JK (c); SL (w); DH (a); 1&O: Scarecrow (Marvel). Watcher back-up 105.00
❑52, Apr 1964, JK (c); SL (w); DH (a); 1: Black Widow. Watcher back-up 140.00
❑53, May 1964, JK (c); SL (w); DH (a); O: The Watcher. A: Black Widow. Watcher back-up 120.00
❑54, Jun 1964, JK (c); SL (w); DH (a); 1: Black Knight II (Nathan Garrett). Watcher back-up 62.00
❑55, Jul 1964, JK (c); SL (w); DH (a); A: The Mandarin. Watcher back-up 62.00
❑56, Aug 1964, JK (c); SL (w); DH (a); 1: Unicorn I (Milos Masaryk). Watcher back-up 62.00
❑57, Sep 1964, SL (w); DH (a); 1: Hawkeye. A: Black Widow. Watcher back-up 170.00
❑58, Oct 1964, JK (c); SL (w); DH, GT (a); A: Captain America. Watcher back-up 210.00
❑59, Nov 1964, JK (c); JK, SL (w); DH, JK (a); 1: Jarvis. V: Black Knight. Captain America second feature begins 210.00
❑60, Dec 1964, SL (w); DH, JK (a) 120.00
❑61, Jan 1965, SL (w); DH, JK (a) 82.00
❑62, Feb 1965, SL (w); DH, JK (a); O: Mandarin. redesign of Iron Man's helmet 82.00
❑63, Mar 1965, O: Bucky. O: Captain America. A: Dr. Erskine. A: General Phillips. A: Sgt. Duffy. 1: The Phantom 180.00
❑64, Apr 1965, 1: Agent 13 (Peggy Carter) 72.00
❑65, May 1965, A: Red Skull 125.00
❑66, Jun 1965, O: Red Skull. Red Skull returns 125.00
❑67, Jul 1965 .... 52.00
❑68, Aug 1965, 1: Morgan Stark 52.00
❑69, Sep 1965, 1: Titanium Man I (Boris Bullski); 1: Countess Stephanie de la Spiroza 52.00
❑70, Oct 1965, 2: Titanium Man I; 2: Countess Stephanie de la Spiroza .. 52.00
❑71, Nov 1965, SL (w); DH, GT, JK, WW (a) 42.00
❑72, Dec 1965, SL (w); DH, GT, JK (a) .. 42.00
❑73, Jan 1966, GC (c); SL (w); GC, GT, JK (a); D: Black Knight II (Nathan Garrett); D: Black Knight (Nathan Garrett) 42.00
❑74, Feb 1966, SL (w); GC, GT, JK (a); 1: The Freak (Happy Hogan) 42.00
❑75, Mar 1966, SL (w); GC, JK (a); 1: Second Agent 13 (Sharon Carter). 1: Batroc; 1: Peggy Carter; 1: THEM... 42.00
❑76, Apr 1966, JK (c); SL (w); GC, JR (a); 1: Ultimo (cameo). A: The Mandarin. A: Batroc; 1: THEM; 1: Batroc 42.00
❑77, May 1966, GC (c); SL (w); GC, JK, JR (a); 1&O: Ultimo 42.00
❑78, Jun 1966, JK (c); SL (w); GC, JK (a); A: Nick Fury. A: Ultimo. A: The Mandarin. 1: THEM 42.00
❑79, Jul 1966, GC (c); SL (w); GC, JK, JAb (a); 1: Cosmic Cube (Kubik). A: Namor. A: Red Skull 42.00
❑80, Aug 1966, SL (w); GC, DH, JK (a); A: Namor. A: Red Skull. Cosmic Cube; Sub-Mariner vs. Iron Man 42.00
❑81, Sep 1966, GC (c); JK, SL (w); GC, JK (a); A: Titanium Man. A: Red Skull 32.00
❑82, Oct 1966, JK (c); SL (w); GC, JK (a); 1: Adaptoid. A: Titanium Man. A: Scarlet Witch. A: Quicksilver 32.00
❑83, Nov 1966, GC (c); SL (w); GC, JK (a); A: Titanium Man. 1: The Tumbler 32.00
❑84, Dec 1966, JK (c); SL (w); GC, JK (a); 1: Super-Adaptoid. A: Goliath. A: Hawkeye. A: The Mandarin. A: The Wasp 32.00
❑85, Jan 1967, GC (c); SL (w); GC, JK (a); A: Batroc. V: Mandarin. Happy substitutes as Iron Man 32.00
❑86, Feb 1967, SL (w); GC, JK (a); 1: Colonel Kuro Chin (SHIELD SPecial Service Agent 60) 32.00
❑87, Mar 1967, 1: The Planner 32.00
❑88, Apr 1967, GK (c); SL (w); GC, GK (a); A: Mole Man. A: Swordsman. A: Power Man I (Erik Josten) 32.00
❑89, May 1967, GC (c); SL (w); GC, GK (a); A: Red Skull. A: Melter 32.00
❑90, Jun 1967, SL (w); GC, GK (a); O: Byrrah 32.00
❑91, Jul 1967, GC (c); SL (w); GC, GK (a); 1: Crusher 32.00
❑92, Aug 1967, SL (w); GC, JK, GK (a); 1: Half-Face; V: Mecho-Assassin 32.00
❑93, Sep 1967, SL (w); GC, JK, GK (a); 2: Half-Face 32.00
❑94, Oct 1967, 1: Modok. 1: M.O.D.O.K 32.00
❑95, Nov 1967, SL (w); GC, JK, GK (a); 1: Walter Newell (later becomes Stingray). Captain America's identity revealed 32.00
❑96, Dec 1967, JK (c); SL (w); GC, JK, GK (a) 32.00
❑97, Jan 1968, SL (w); GC, JK, GK (a); 1: Whiplash. A: Black Panther; 1: Big M; 1: Morgan Stark 32.00
❑98, Feb 1968, SL (w); GC, JK, GK (a); O: Whitney Frost. 1: Whitney Frost 32.00
❑99, Mar 1968, SL (w); GC, JK, GK (a); V: Red Skull. Series continued in Captain America #100, Iron Man #1 ... 32.00

Tales of Suspense: Captain America/Iron Man
Marvel

❑1, Feb 2005 .... 5.99

Tales of Suspense
Marvel

❑1, Jan 1995; prestige format one-shot; acetate outer cover 6.95

Tales of Tellos
Image

❑1, Nov 2004 .... 3.50
❑2, Dec 2004 .... 3.50
❑3, Feb 2005 .... 3.50

Tales of Terror
Eclipse

❑1, Jul 1985 .... 2.00
❑2, Sep 1985 .... 2.00
❑3, Nov 1985 .... 2.00
❑4, Jan 1986 .... 2.00
❑5, Mar 1986 .... 2.00
❑6, May 1986 .... 2.00
❑7, Jul 1986 .... 2.00
❑8, Sep 1986 .... 2.00
❑9, Nov 1986 .... 2.00
❑10, Jan 1987 .... 2.00
❑11, Mar 1987 .... 2.00
❑12, May 1987 .... 2.00
❑13, Jul 1987 .... 2.00

Tales of the Armorkins
Co. & Sons

❑1, Adult 3.00

Tales of the Beanworld
Eclipse

❑1, ca. 1985 .... 4.00
❑2, ca. 1985 .... 3.00
❑3, ca. 1986 .... 3.00
❑4, ca. 1986 .... 3.00
❑5, ca. 1986 .... 3.00
❑6, Apr 1987 .... 3.00
❑7, ca. 1987 .... 3.00
❑8, ca. 1987 .... 3.00
❑9, ca. 1988 .... 3.00
❑10, ca. 1988 .... 3.00
❑11, ca. 1988 .... 2.00
❑12, Feb 1989 .... 2.00
❑13, ca. 1989 .... 2.00
❑14, ca. 1989 .... 2.00
❑15, ca. 1990 .... 2.00
❑16, ca. 1990 .... 2.00
❑17, ca. 1990; b&w 2.00
❑18, ca. 1991; b&w 2.00
❑19, ca. 1991 .... 2.00
❑20, ca. 1993 .... 2.50
❑21, ca. 1993 .... 2.95

Tales of the Closet
Hetric-Martin

❑1, Sum 1987, b&w 2.50
❑2, b&w 2.50
❑3, b&w 2.50
❑4, b&w 2.50
❑5, b&w 2.50
❑6, b&w 2.50
❑7, Spr 1992 .... 2.50
❑8, Win 1992 .... 2.50

Tales of the Crimson Lion
Gary Lankford

❑1, Jul 1987 .... 1.95

Tales of the Cyborg Gerbils
Harrier

❑1, Nov 1987 .... 1.95

Tales of the Darkness
Image

❑½, Apr 1998, BSz (a); Female demon on cover 2.95
❑½/A, Apr 1998, BSz (a); Man atop demons on cover 4.00
❑1, Apr 1998 .... 2.95
❑2, Jun 1998 .... 2.95
❑3, Aug 1998 .... 2.95
❑4, Dec 1998 .... 2.95

Tales of the Fehnnik
Antarctic

❑1, Aug 1995, b&w 2.95

Tales of the Fehnnik
Radio

❑1, Jun 1998, b&w 2.95

Tales of the Great Unspoken
Top Shelf

❑1, b&w; no cover price 3.50

Tales of the Green Beret
Dell

❑1, Jan 1967 .... 25.00
❑2, Mar 1967 .... 18.00
❑3, Jun 1967 .... 18.00
❑4, Sep 1967 .... 18.00
❑5, ca. 1968, Reprints from Tales of the Green Beret #1 .... 18.00

Tales of the Green Berets
Avalon

❑1, "The Green Berets" in the indicia 2.95
❑2, "The Green Berets" in the indicia 2.95

Other grades: Multiply price above by 5/6 for VF/NM • 2/3 for VERY FINE • 1/3 for FINE • 1/5 for VERY GOOD • 1/8 for GOOD

THUNDER Agents

Classic art by Wood, Ditko, and Kane
©Tower

Thunderbolts

Supervillians hide out as super-heroes
©Marvel

Thunderbunny

Don't investigate strange lights on mountains
©Warp

Thundercats

Mildy popular cartoon series had later revival
©Marvel

Thunderstrike

When one Thor is never enough
©Marvel

N-MINT

❑3, "The Green Berets" in the indicia 2.95
❑4 ..... 2.95
❑5 ..... 2.95
❑6 ..... 2.95
❑7, "Green Berets" in the indicia 2.95

Tales of the Green Hornet
Now

❑1, Sep 1990 ..... 2.00
❑2, Oct 1990 ..... 2.00

Tales of the Green Hornet
Now

❑1, Jan 1992; Neal Adams cover 2.00
❑2, Feb 1992; O: The Green Hornet 2.00
❑3, Mar 1992; James Martin cover 2.00
❑4, Apr 1992; Eddie Newell cover 2.00

Tales of the Green Hornet
Now

❑1, Sep 1992; bagged with hologram card 2.75
❑2, Oct 1992 ..... 2.50
❑3, Nov 1992 ..... 2.50

Tales of the Green Lantern Corps
DC

❑1, May 1981, BB (c); FMc, JSa, JSe (a); O: Green Lantern; O: Krona 1.50
❑2, Jun 1981, BB (c); FMc, JSa, JSe (a) 1.25
❑3, Jul 1981, BB (c); FMc, JSa, JSe (a) . 1.25
❑Ann 1 ..... 1.50

Tales of the Jackalope
Blackthorne

❑1, Feb 1986 ..... 2.00
❑2, Apr 1986 ..... 2.00
❑3, May 1986 ..... 2.00
❑4, Sep 1986 ..... 2.00
❑5, Oct 1986 ..... 2.00
❑6, Dec 1986 ..... 2.00
❑7, Feb 1987 ..... 2.00

Tales of the Kung Fu Warriors
CFW

❑1; 1: Ethereal Black. 1: Squamous 2.00
❑2 ..... 2.00
❑3 ..... 2.00
❑4 ..... 2.00
❑5 ..... 2.00
❑6 ..... 2.00
❑7 ..... 2.00
❑8 ..... 2.00
❑9 ..... 2.00
❑10 ..... 2.25
❑11 ..... 2.25
❑12 ..... 2.25
❑13 ..... 2.25
❑14, Aug 1989; 1: Sumo 2.25

Tales of the Legion
DC

❑314, Aug 1984; O: White Witch 1.25
❑315, Sep 1984; KG (w); KG, GT (a); V: Dark Circle; O: White Witch 1.25
❑316, Oct 1984; O: White Witch 1.25
❑317, Nov 1984; Legion of Super-Heroes; Flash Force 2000 Bonus Comic; Heroes of Lallor story 1.25
❑318, Dec 1984; V: Persuader 1.25
❑319, Jan 1985 ..... 1.25

N-MINT

❑320, Feb 1985; Diagram of Legion headquarters 1.25
❑321, Mar 1985 ..... 1.25
❑322, Apr 1985 ..... 1.25
❑323, May 1985 ..... 1.25
❑324, Jun 1985; V: Dark Circle; Invisible Kid story 1.25
❑325, Jul 1985 ..... 2.00
❑326, Aug 1985; V: Legion of Super-Villains. begins reprints of Legion of Super-Heroes (3rd series) 1.00
❑327, Sep 1985; V: Legion of Super-Villains Mask Preview; Reprints Legion of Super-Heroes (3rd Series) #2 ..... 1.00
❑328, Oct 1985; V: Legion of Super-Villains; Reprints Legion of Super-Heroes (3rd Series) #3 ..... 1.00
❑329, Nov 1985; D: Karate Kid. V: Legion of Super-Villains; Reprints Legion of Super-Heroes (3rd Series) #4 ..... 1.00
❑330, Dec 1985; V: Legion of Super-Villains; Reprints Legion of Super-Heroes (3rd Series) #5 ..... 1.00
❑331, Jan 1986; O: Lightning Lord. O: Lightning Lass. O: Lightning Lad Reprints Legion of Super-Heroes (3rd Series) #6 ..... 1.00
❑332, Feb 1986; Reprints Legion of Super-Heroes (3rd Series) #7 ..... 1.00
❑333, Mar 1986; Reprints Legion of Super-Heroes (3rd Series) #8 ..... 1.00
❑334, Apr 1986; Reprints Legion of Super-Heroes (3rd Series) #9 ..... 1.00
❑335, May 1986; Reprints Legion of Super-Heroes (3rd Series) #10 ..... 1.00
❑336, Jun 1986; Reprints Legion of Super-Heroes (3rd Series) #11 ..... 1.00
❑337, Jul 1986; Reprints Legion of Super-Heroes (3rd Series) #12 ..... 1.00
❑338, Aug 1986; Reprints Legion of Super-Heroes (3rd Series) #13 ..... 1.00
❑339, Sep 1986; Magnetic Kid, Tellus, Polar Boy, Quislet, and Sensor Girl join team 1.00
❑340, Oct 1986; V: Doctor Regulus; Reprints Legion of Super-Heroes (3rd Series) #15 ..... 1.00
❑341, Nov 1986; Reprints Legion of Super-Heroes (3rd Series) #16 ..... 1.00
❑342, Dec 1986; Legionnaires' Fact File; Reprints Legion of Super-Heroes (3rd Series) #17; O: Legion of Super-Heroes 1.00
❑343, Jan 1987; O: Wildfire; The New Legionnaires' Fact File; "One-Shot Hero" reprinted from Superboy #195; "Betrayer" reprinted from Superboy #201 ..... 1.00
❑344, Feb 1987; Reprints Legion of Super-Heroes (3rd Series) #19; Invisible Kid story 1.00
❑345, Mar 1987; Reprints Legion of Super-Heroes (3rd Series) #20; Dream Girl story 1.00
❑346, Apr 1987; Reprints Legion of Super-Heroes (3rd Series) #21; Quislet story 1.00
❑347, May 1987; V: Universo; Reprints Legion of Super-Heroes (3rd Series) #22 ..... 1.00
❑348, Jun 1987; in Phantom Zone 1.00
❑349, Jul 1987; Reprints Legion of Super-Heroes (3rd Series) #24 ..... 1.00

N-MINT

❑350, Aug 1987; Sensor Girl's identity revealed 1.00
❑351, Sep 1987; V: Fatal Five; Reprints Legion of Super-Heroes (3rd Series) #26 ..... 1.00
❑352, Oct 1987; Reprints Legion of Super-Heroes (3rd Series) #27 ..... 1.00
❑353, Nov 1987; Reprints Legion of Super-Heroes (3rd Series) #28 ..... 1.00
❑354, Dec 1987; Final Issue; Reprints Legion of Super-Heroes (3rd Series) #29 ..... 1.00
❑Ann 4; Legion Checklist; ca. 1986; Reprints Legion of Super-Heroes (3rd Series) Anl 1 ..... 1.50
❑Ann 5; O: Validus. Double-cover; Reprints Legion of Super-Heroes (3rd Series) Anl 2; ca. 1987 ..... 1.50

Tales of the Marvels: Blockbuster
Marvel

❑1, Apr 1995; prestige format; acetate overlay outer cover 5.95

Tales of the Marvels: Inner Demons
Marvel

❑1, ca. 1995, acetate overlay outer cover 5.95

Tales of the Marvels: Wonder Years
Marvel

❑1, Aug 1995; wraparound acetate outer cover 4.95
❑2, Sep 1995; wraparound acetate outer cover 4.95

Tales of the Marvel Universe
Marvel

❑1, Feb 1997; wraparound cover 2.99

Tales of the New Teen Titans
DC

❑1, Jun 1982, GP (c); GP (a); O: Cyborg 1.50
❑2, Jul 1982, GP (c); GP (a); O: Raven .. 1.00
❑3, Aug 1982, GP (c); GP, GD (a); O: Changeling 1.00
❑4, Sep 1982, GP (c); GP (w); GP (a); O: Starfire II (Koriand'r). 1: Ryand'r ... 1.00

Tales of the Ninja Warriors
CFW

❑1, b&w 2.25
❑2, b&w 2.25
❑3, b&w 2.25
❑4, b&w 2.25
❑5, b&w 2.25
❑6, b&w; Magazine Format 2.25
❑7, b&w 2.25
❑8, b&w 2.25
❑9, b&w; Magazine Format 2.25
❑10, b&w; Magazine Format 2.25
❑11, b&w; Magazine Format 2.25
❑12, b&w 2.25
❑13, b&w 2.25
❑14, b&w 2.25
❑15, b&w 2.25
❑16, b&w 2.25

Tales of the Sun Runners
Sirius

❑1, Jul 1986 ..... 1.50

Other grades: Multiply price above by 5/6 for VF/NM • 2/3 for VERY FINE • 1/3 for FINE • 1/5 for VERY GOOD • 1/8 for GOOD

❑2, Sep 1986 ... 1.95
❑3 1986; Published by Amazing Comcis; Final issue; Sun Runners appear next in Sun-Runners HS #1; b&w ... 1.95

Tales of the Teenage Mutant Ninja Turtles
Mirage

❑1, May 1987 ... 3.00
❑2, Jul 1987 ... 2.00
❑3, Oct 1987 ... 2.00
❑4, Feb 1988; cover says Jan, indicia says Feb ... 2.00
❑5, May 1988 ... 2.00
❑6, Aug 1988 ... 2.00
❑7, Aug 1989; cover says Apr, indicia says Aug ... 2.00

Tales of the Teenage Mutant Ninja Turtles
Mirage

❑1 2004 ... 2.95
❑2 2004 ... 2.95
❑3 2004 ... 2.95
❑4 2004 ... 2.95
❑5 2004 ... 2.95

Tales of the Teen Titans
DC

❑41, Apr 1984; GP (c); GP (a); A: Brother Blood. Series continued from New Teen Titans (1st Series) #40 ... 2.00
❑42, May 1984; GP (c); GP (a); V: Deathstroke ... 2.00
❑43, Jun 1984; GP (c); GP (a); V: Deathstroke. V: H.I.V.E.; 1: Jericho (as Joseph Wilson); Beau Smith LOC. 3.00
❑44, Jul 1984; GP (c); GP (a); 1&O: Jericho. 1: Nightwing; O: Deathstroke; Continued in Tales of the Teen Titans Ann #3 ... 6.00
❑45, Aug 1984 GP (c); GP (a); A: Aquagirl. A: Aqualad. ... 1.50
❑46, Sep 1984; GP (c); GP (a); V: H.I.V.E.. V: H.I.V.E ... 1.50
❑47, Oct 1984; GP (c); GP (a); V: H.I.V.E.. V: H.I.V.E ... 1.50
❑48, Nov 1984; GP (c); GP, SR (a); V: Recombatants; Flash Force 2000 bonus comic ... 1.50
❑49, Dec 1984; GP (c); GP (w); CI, GP (a); V: Doctor Light ... 1.50
❑50, Feb 1985; Giant-size; GP (c); GP (w); GP (a); Wedding of Wonder Girl ... 2.00
❑51, Mar 1985; 1: Azrael (cameo, not Batman character). V: Cheshire ... 1.50
❑52, Apr 1985; GP (c); RB (a); 1: Azrael (full appearace, not Batman character). V: Cheshire ... 1.50
❑53, May 1985 GP (c); RB (a); A: Deathstroke ... 1.50
❑54, Jun 1985; RB, DG (a); A: Deathstroke. Trial of Deathstroke ... 1.50
❑55, Jul 1985; Changeling vs. Deathstroke ... 1.50
❑56, Aug 1985; V: Fearsome Five ... 1.50
❑57, Sep 1985; V: Fearsome Five. Cyborg transformed ... 1.50
❑58, Oct 1985; A: Monitor. A: Harbinger. V: Fearsome Five ... 1.50
❑59, Nov 1985; reprints DC Comics Presents #26 ... 1.50
❑60, Dec 1985; V: Trigon. series begins reprinting New Teen Titans (second series) ... 1.00
❑61, Jan 1986; V: Trigon; Reprints New Teen Titans (2nd Series) #2 ... 1.00
❑62, Feb 1986; V: Trigon; Reprints New Teen Titans (2nd Series) #3 ... 1.00
❑63, Mar 1986; V: Trigon; Reprints New Teen Titans (2nd Series) #4 ... 1.00
❑64, Apr 1986; V: Trigon; Reprints New Teen Titans (2nd Series) #5 ... 1.00
❑65, May 1986; Reprints New Teen Titans (2nd Series) #6 ... 1.00
❑66, Jun 1986; O: Lilith; Reprints New Teen Titans (2nd Series) #7; MASK insert ... 1.00
❑67, Jul 1986; Reprints New Teen Titans (2nd Series) #8 ... 1.00
❑68, Aug 1986; A: Kole. Reprints New Teen Titans (2nd Series) #9 ... 1.00
❑69, Sep 1986; Reprints New Teen Titans (2nd Series) #10 ... 1.00
❑70, Oct 1986; O: Kole ... 1.00
❑71, Nov 1986; Reprint from New Teen Titans (2nd Series) #12; Continued in New Teen Titans Ann #1 ... 1.00
❑72, Dec 1986; A: Outsiders. Reprint from New Teen Titans (2nd Series) #13; Crisis crossover ... 1.00
❑73, Jan 1987 ... 1.00
❑74, Feb 1987 ... 1.00
❑75, Mar 1987; A: Omega Men. Teen Titans; Tales of Tamaran ... 1.00
❑76, Apr 1987; Wedding of Starfire ... 1.00
❑77, May 1987 ... 1.00
❑78, Jun 1987; new team ... 1.00
❑79, Jul 1987 ... 1.00
❑80, Aug 1987 A: Cheshire, Lian ... 1.00
❑81, Sep 1987 ... 1.00
❑82, Oct 1987 ... 1.00
❑83, Nov 1987 ... 1.00
❑84, Dec 1987 ... 1.00
❑85, Jan 1988 ... 1.00
❑86, Feb 1988; V: Twister ... 1.00
❑87, Mar 1988; V: Brotherhood of Evil .. 1.00
❑88, Apr 1988; V: Brother Blood ... 1.00
❑89, May 1988; V: Brother Blood ... 1.00
❑90, Jun 1988 ... 1.00
❑91, Jul 1988; Final Issue ... 1.00
❑Ann 4; A: Superman. V: Vanguard. reprints New Teen Titans Ann #1 ... 1.50

Tales of the Unexpected
DC

❑67, Nov 1961 A: Space Ranger ... 85.00
❑68, Dec 1961, A: Space Ranger ... 85.00
❑69, Feb 1962, A: Space Ranger ... 85.00
❑70, Apr 1962, A: Space Ranger ... 85.00
❑71, Jun 1962, A: Space Ranger ... 60.00
❑72, Aug 1962, A: Space Ranger ... 60.00
❑73, Oct 1962, A: Space Ranger ... 60.00
❑74, Jan 1963, A: Space Ranger ... 60.00
❑75, Feb 1963, A: Space Ranger. Space Ranger story ... 50.00
❑76, Apr 1963, A: Space Ranger ... 50.00
❑77, Jun 1963, A: Space Ranger ... 50.00
❑78, Aug 1963, A: Space Ranger ... 50.00
❑79, Oct 1963, A: Space Ranger ... 50.00
❑80, Dec 1963, A: Space Ranger ... 50.00
❑81, Feb 1964, A: Space Ranger ... 50.00
❑82, Apr 1964, A: Space Ranger ... 50.00
❑83, Jun 1964, 1: Green Glob ... 30.00
❑84, Aug 1964 ... 30.00
❑85, Oct 1964 ... 30.00
❑86, Dec 1964 ... 30.00
❑87, Feb 1965 ... 30.00
❑88, Apr 1965 ... 30.00
❑89, Jun 1965 ... 30.00
❑90, Aug 1965 ... 30.00
❑91, Oct 1965, 1&O: Automan ... 22.00
❑92, Dec 1965 ... 22.00
❑93, Feb 1966 ... 22.00
❑94, Apr 1966 ... 22.00
❑95, Jun 1966 ... 22.00
❑96, Aug 1966 ... 22.00
❑97, Oct 1966, A: Automan ... 22.00
❑98, Dec 1966 ... 22.00
❑99, Feb 1967, Reprint from My Greatest Adventure #10 ... 22.00
❑100, Apr 1967 ... 22.00
❑101, Jun 1967, We Fought the Giant of Island X reprinted from My Greatest Adventure #9 ... 20.00
❑102, Aug 1967, The Doomsday Drum reprinted from House of Secrets #9 ... 20.00
❑103, Oct 1967, The Guardian of the Past reprinted from House of Secrets #11 . 20.00
❑104, Dec 1967, Series continues as The Unexpected ... 20.00

Tales of the Unexpected
DC

❑1, Dec 2006, Mignola cover; Includes Dr. Thirteen back-up story; 48 pages . 3.99
❑1/Variant, Dec 2006 ... 3.99
❑2, Jan 2007, Includes Dr. Thirteen back-up story; 48 pages ... 3.99
❑3, Feb 2007, Includes Dr. Thirteen back-up story; 48 pages ... 3.99

Tales of the Vampires
Dark Horse

❑1, Dec 2003 ... 2.99
❑2, Jan 2004 ... 2.99
❑3, Feb 2004 ... 2.99
❑4, Mar 2004 ... 2.99
❑5, Apr 2004 ... 2.99

Tales of the Witchblade
Image

❑½, Jun 1997; Wizard promotional item 4.00
❑½/A, Jun 1997; Wizard "Certified Authentic" exclusive ... 8.00
❑½/Gold, Jun 1997; Wizard promotional item; gold logo ... 5.00
❑1, Nov 1996 ... 2.95
❑1/A, Nov 1996; alternate cover; Green background with Witchblade front, arms behind back ... 2.95
❑1/B, Nov 1996; alternate cover (blue background with black panther) 2.95
❑1/Gold, Nov 1996; Gold edition ... 2.95
❑1/Platinum, Nov 1996; Platinum edition 5.00
❑2, Jun 1997 ... 2.95
❑3, Oct 1997 ... 2.95
❑4, Jan 1998 ... 2.95
❑5, May 1998 ... 2.95
❑6, Sep 1998 ... 2.95
❑7/A, Jun 1999; Woman turning around, eyes in background on cover ... 2.95
❑7/B, Jun 1999; Alternate cover (woman standing before pyramid) 2.95
❑7/C, Jun 1999; Alternate cover (Pharaoh Head cover) ... 2.95
❑8, Oct 1999 ... 2.95
❑9, Jan 2001 ... 2.95
❑Deluxe 1, Apr 2001; Collects Tales of the Witchblade #1-7; Witchblade: Distinctions ... 14.95

Tales of the Zombie
Marvel

❑1, Aug 1973, b&w; magazine; O: Zombie. Reprints from Menace #5, Journey into Mystery #1 and Chamber of Darkness #7 ... 25.00
❑2, Oct 1973; b&w ... 18.00
❑3, Jan 1974; b&w ... 15.00
❑4, Mar 1974; b&w ... 15.00
❑5, May 1974; b&w ... 15.00
❑6, Jul 1974; b&w ... 10.00
❑7, Sep 1974; b&w ... 10.00
❑8, Nov 1974; b&w ... 10.00
❑9, Jan 1975; b&w ... 10.00
❑10, Mar 1975; b&w ... 10.00
❑Ann 1; Reprints ... 15.00

Tales of Toad
Print Mint

❑1, Apr 1970, b&w ... 20.00
❑2, Jan 1971, b&w ... 15.00
❑3, Dec 1973, b&w A: Toadettes. A: Hoppy. A: Zippy the Pinhead. ... 15.00

Tales of Torment
Mirage

❑1, Apr 2004 ... 2.95

Tale Spin
Disney

❑1, Jun 1991 ... 1.50
❑2, Jul 1991 ... 1.50
❑3, Aug 1991 ... 1.50
❑4, Sep 1991 ... 1.50
❑5, Oct 1991 ... 1.50
❑6, Nov 1991 ... 1.50
❑7, Jan 1992 ... 1.50

Tale Spin Limited Series
Disney

❑1, Jan 1991 ... 1.50
❑2, Feb 1991 ... 1.50
❑3, Mar 1991 ... 1.50
❑4, Apr 1991 ... 1.50

Talespin
Disney

❑1; Sky-Raker ... 3.50

Tales Sleepy Hollow: The Lost Chronicles of "I Hunt Monsters"
Antarctic

❑1, ca. 2005 ... 2.99

Tales to Astonish
Marvel

❑27, Jan 1962; SL (w); SD, DH, JK (a); 1: Ant-Man (out of costume). 1: Hijacker ... 3600.00
❑28, Feb 1962, SD, GC, JK (a) ... 175.00

Tick

Big hero with IQ of tomato paste
©NEC

Tilazeus Meets the Messiah

Jesus Christ deals with a demon
©Aiiie

Timber Wolf

Solo outing for the Legionnaire
©DC

Time Breakers

Housewife uses thought to alter reality
©DC

Time Masters

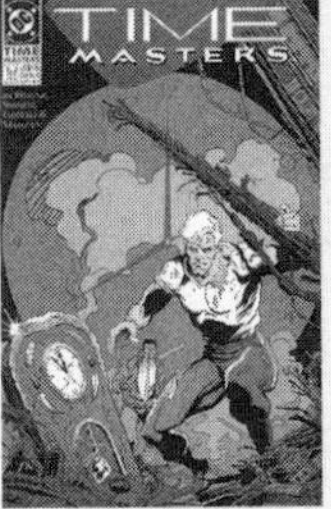

Post-Crisis updating of Rip Hunter
©DC

	N-MINT
❑29, Mar 1962, SD, JK (a)	175.00
❑30, Apr 1962, SD, DH, JK (a)	175.00
❑31, May 1962, SD, JK (a)	175.00
❑32, Jun 1962, SL (w); SD, DH, JK (a)	175.00
❑33, Jul 1962, SD, DH, JK (a)	175.00
❑34, Aug 1962, SD, DH, JK (a)	175.00
❑35, Sep 1962, SL (w); SD, DH, JK (a); 1: Ant-Man (in costume)	1900.00
❑36, Oct 1962, SL (w); SD, JK (a); 1: Comrade X (Madame X)	625.00
❑37, Nov 1962, SL (w); SD, DH, JK (a); 1: Protector (Gerald Marsh)	350.00
❑38, Dec 1962, SL (w); SD, DH, JK (a); 1: Egghead	350.00
❑39, Jan 1963, 1: Scarlet Beetle	350.00
❑40, Feb 1963	350.00
❑41, Mar 1963, JK (c); SL (w); SD, DH, JSt (a)	230.00
❑42, Apr 1963, JK (c); SL (w); SD, DH, JSt (a); O: The Voice. 1: The Voice	230.00
❑43, May 1963,JK (c); SL (w); SD, DH (a)	230.00
❑44, Jun 1963, SL (w); SD, JK (a); O: Wasp. 1: Wasp	500.00
❑45, Jul 1963, JK (c); SL (w); SD, DH (a); 2: Egghead	150.00
❑46, Aug 1963, JK (c); SL (w); SD, DH (a)	150.00
❑47, Sep 1963, JK (c); SL (w); SD, DH (a)	150.00
❑48, Oct 1963, JK (c); SL (w); SD, DH (a); 1&O: Porcupine	150.00
❑49, Nov 1963, DH (c); SL (w); DH, JK (a); 1: Giant Man. Ant-Man becomes Giant Man	250.00
❑50, Dec 1963, SL (w); SD, JK (a); 1&O: Human Top (later becomes Whirlwind	95.00
❑51, Jan 1964, SL (w); JK (a); Tale of the Wasp begins	95.00
❑52, Feb 1964, 1&O: Black Knight II (Nathan Garrett)	95.00
❑53, Mar 1964, 1: Giant Man and Wasp fan club	95.00
❑54, Apr 1964, 1: El Toro	95.00
❑55, May 1964	95.00
❑56, Jun 1964, V: Magician. 1: The Magician	95.00
❑57, Jul 1964, A: Spider-Man	125.00
❑58, Aug 1964	95.00
❑59, Sep 1964, JK (c); SL (w); Giant-Man vs. Hulk	150.00
❑60, Oct 1964, JK (c); SL (w); SD (a); Giant Man/Hulk double feature begins	175.00
❑61, Nov 1964, JK (c); SL (w); SD (a); 1: Major Glenn Talbot	75.00
❑62, Dec 1964, JK (c); SL (w); SD (a); 1: The Leader	90.00
❑63, Jan 1965, JK (c); SL (w); SD (a); O: The Leader. 1: The Wrecker II	75.00
❑64, Feb 1965, JK (c); SL (w); SD (a)	75.00
❑65, Mar 1965, JK (c); SL (w); SD, DH (a); Giant-Man's new costume	75.00
❑66, Apr 1965, JK (c); SL (w); SD (a); 1: Madame Macabre	70.00
❑67, May 1965, JK (c); SL (w); SD (a)	70.00
❑68, Jun 1965, JK (c); SL (w); JK (a); V: Leader	70.00
❑69, Jul 1965, JK (c); SL (w); JK (a); Giant Man feature ends	70.00
❑70, Aug 1965, JK (c); SL (w); GC, JK (a); Sub-Mariner begins	100.00
❑71, Sep 1965, GC (c); SL (w); GC, JK (a); 1: Vashti; 1: Seaweed Man	55.00

	N-MINT
❑72, Oct 1965, JK (c); SL (w); JK (a); 1: The Faceless Ones; 1: Zantor	55.00
❑73, Nov 1965, GC (c); SL (w); JK (a)	55.00
❑74, Dec 1965, GC (c); SL (w); JK (a)	55.00
❑75, Jan 1966, GC, JK (c); SL (w); GC, JK (a); 1: Behemoth; 1: King Arrkam	55.00
❑76, Feb 1966, GC (c); SL (w); GC, JK, GK (a)	55.00
❑77, Mar 1966, JK, JR (c); SL (w); JK, JR (a); Banner revealed as Hulk	55.00
❑78, Apr 1966, GC (c); SL (w); GC, BEv, JK (a); 1: Dr. Konrad Zaxon	55.00
❑79, May 1966, JK (c); SL (w); BEv, JK (a); D: Dr. Konrad Zaxon; 2: Dr. Konrad Zaxon	55.00
❑80, Jun 1966, GC (c); SL (w); GC, BEv, JK (a)	55.00
❑81, Jul 1966, BEv, JK (c); SL (w); GC, BEv, JK (a); 1: Boomerang; 1: Secret Empire	55.00
❑82, Aug 1966, GC (c); SL (w); GC, BEv, JK (a); Iron Man vs. Sub-Mariner; Hulk	78.00
❑83, Sep 1966, BEv, JK (c); SL (w); BEv, JK (a); Sub-Mariner, Hulk	55.00
❑84, Oct 1966, GC (c); SL (w); GC, BEv, JK (a); 1: Gorki	55.00
❑85, Nov 1966, BEv, JK (c); SL (w); GC, JB (a); 2: Gorki	55.00
❑86, Dec 1966, GC (c); SL (w); JB (a); 1: Hulk-Killer	55.00
❑87, Jan 1967, GK (c); SL (w); JB, BEv (a); 2: Hulk-Killer	55.00
❑88, Feb 1967, GC (c); SL (w); BEv, GK (a); 1: Servo-Robot; D: Boomerang	55.00
❑89, Mar 1967, GK (c); SL (w); BEv, GK (a); 2: Servo-Robot	55.00
❑90, Apr 1967, JK (c); SL (w); BEv, GK (a); 1: The Abomination. 1: Byrrah; O: Byrrah	55.00
❑91, May 1967, GK (c); SL (w); BEv, GK (a); Sub-Mariner story continues in Avengers #40	52.00
❑92, Jun 1967, DA (c); SL (w); DA (a); A: Silver Surfer. Sub-Mariner story continued from Avengers #40	75.00
❑93, Jul 1967, SL (w); DA (a); A: Silver Surfer. 2: It; The Silent One	75.00
❑94, Aug 1967, DA (c); SL (w); BEv, HT (a); Hulk story continues from Thor #135	50.00
❑95, Sep 1967, JK (c); SL (w); BEv, HT (a); Sub-Mariner story continues from Daredevil #24	50.00
❑96, Oct 1967, DA (c); SL (w); BEv, HT (a)	50.00
❑97, Nov 1967, JK (c); SL (w); HT (a); 1: Swamp Men of Skull Island; 1: Lord of the Living Lightning; 1: Living Lightning Legion	50.00
❑98, Dec 1967, DA (c); SL (w); HT (a); 1: Seth (Namor's advisor); 1: Seth	50.00
❑99, Jan 1968, SL (w); DA (a)	50.00
❑100, Feb 1968, SL (w); DA (a); Hulk vs. Sub-Mariner	75.00
❑101, Mar 1968, JK (c); SL (w); GC (a); Hulk feature continued in Incredible Hulk #102; Sub-Mariner feature continued in Iron Man & Sub-Mariner #1	85.00

Tales to Astonish
Marvel

	N-MINT
❑1, Dec 1979, JB (a); Reprints Sub-Mariner (Vol. 2) #1; O: Sub-Mariner	2.00
❑2, Jan 1980, JB (a); Reprints Sub-Mariner (Vol. 2) #2	1.50
❑3, Feb 1980, JB (a); Reprints Sub-Mariner (Vol. 2) #3	1.50
❑4, Mar 1980, JB (c); JB (a); Reprints Sub-Mariner (Vol. 2) #4	1.50
❑5, Apr 1980, JB (c); JB (a); Reprints Sub-Mariner (Vol. 2) #5	1.50
❑6, May 1980, JB (a); Reprints Sub-Mariner (Vol. 2) #6	1.50
❑7, Jun 1980, JB (a); Reprints Sub-Mariner (Vol. 2) #7	1.50
❑8, Jul 1980, JB (a); Reprints Sub-Mariner (Vol. 2) #8	1.50
❑9, Aug 1980, JB (a); Reprints Sub-Mariner (Vol. 2) #9	1.50
❑10, Sep 1980, GC (c); GC, JB (a); Reprints Sub-Mariner (Vol. 2) #10	1.50
❑11, Oct 1980, GC, JB (a); Reprints Sub-Mariner (Vol. 2) #11	1.50
❑12, Nov 1980, JB (a); Reprints Sub-Mariner (Vol. 2) #12; Vision story	1.50
❑13, Dec 1980, JB (a); Reprints Sub-Mariner (Vol. 2) #13; Nighthawk story	1.50
❑14, Jan 1981, JB, BEv, JK (a); Reprints Sub-Mariner (Vol. 2) #14; Pinups	1.50

Tales to Astonish
Marvel

	N-MINT
❑1, Dec 1994; prestige format one-shot; acetate outer cover	6.95

Tales to Offend
Dark Horse

	N-MINT
❑1, Jul 1997; Lance Blastoff	2.95

Tales Too Terrible to Tell
NEC

	N-MINT
❑1, Jan 1990, b&w; Reprints from Mister Mystery #13, Weird Chills #1, Weird Chills #3, Mister Mystery #16, Purple Claw #1, Strange Mysteries #7, Mister Mystery #17	2.95
❑1/2nd, May 1993; 2nd printing with new cover; Reprints from Mister Mystery #13, Weird Chills #1, Weird Chills #3, Mister Mystery #16, Purple Claw #1, Strange Mysteries #7, Mister Mystery #17	3.50
❑2, Mar 1991, b&w; Reprints from Strange Mysteries #6, Weird Mysteries #11, Unseen #14, Black Cat Mystery #45, Journey into Fear #5, Ghoul Tales #3, Dark Mysteries #13	3.50
❑3, Jun 1991, b&w; Reprints from Weird Chills #3, Weird Mysteries #10, Weird Chills #1, Adventures into Darkness #13, Horrific #5	3.50
❑4, Dec 1991, b&w; Reprints from Mister Mystery #13, Fantastic Fears #8, Unseen #14, Journey into Fear #12, Fantastic Fears #6, Purple Claw #1, Fantastic Fears #4, Dark Mysteries #19	3.50
❑5 1992, b&w; Reprints	3.50
❑6 1992, b&w; Reprints	3.50
❑7 1992, b&w; Reprints	3.50

Other grades: Multiply price above by 5/6 for VF/NM • 2/3 for VERY FINE • 1/3 for FINE • 1/5 for VERY GOOD • 1/8 for GOOD

Taleweaver
WildStorm

❑1, Nov 2001 .... 3.50
❑2, Dec 2001 .... 2.95
❑3, Jan 2002 .... 2.95
❑4, Feb 2002 .... 2.95
❑5, Mar 2002 .... 2.95
❑6, Apr 2002 .... 2.95

Talismen: SCSI Voodoo
Blink

❑1 .... 2.75
❑2 .... 2.75
❑3 .... 2.75

Talk Dirty
Fantagraphics / Eros

❑1, Jun 1992, b&w; Adult 2.50
❑2, Jul 1992, b&w; Adult 2.50
❑3, Aug 1992, b&w; Adult 2.95

Talking Orangutans in Borneo
GT-Labs

❑1, ca. 1999, b&w; efforts to educate orangutans to communicate via sign language 3.50

Tall Tails
Golden Realm

❑1, b&w 2.00
❑2, ca. 1993 .... 2.00
❑3 .... 2.95
❑4 .... 2.95
❑5 .... 2.95
❑6 .... 2.95
❑7 .... 2.95

Talonz
Stop Dragon

❑1, Jan 1987, b&w 1.50

Talos of the Wilderness Sea
DC

❑1, ca. 1985 .... 2.00

Tammas
Pandemonium

❑1, Dec 1986 .... 1.50

Tangent Comics/Doom Patrol
DC

❑1, Dec 1997, alternate universe 2.95

Tangent Comics/Green Lantern
DC

❑1, Dec 1997, alternate universe 2.95

Tangent Comics/JLA
DC

❑1, Sep 1998; alternate universe 1.95

Tangent Comics/Metal Men
DC

❑1, Dec 1997, alternate universe 2.95

Tangent Comics/Nightwing
DC

❑1, Dec 1997, alternate universe 2.95

Tangent Comics/Nightwing: Night Force
DC

❑1, Sep 1998; alternate universe 1.95

Tangent Comics/Powergirl
DC

❑1, Sep 1998; alternate universe 1.95

Tangent Comics/Sea Devils
DC

❑1, Dec 1997; alternate universe 2.95

Tangent Comics/Secret Six
DC

❑1, Dec 1997; alternate universe 2.95

Tangent Comics/Tales of the Green Lantern
DC

❑1, Sep 1998; alternate universe 1.95

Tangent Comics/The Atom
DC

❑1, Dec 1997, alternate universe 2.95

Tangent Comics/The Batman
DC

❑1, Sep 1998; alternate universe 1.95

Tangent Comics/The Flash
DC

❑1, Dec 1997; alternate universe 2.95

Tangent Comics/The Joker
DC

❑1, Dec 1997, alternate universe 2.95

Tangent Comics/The Joker's Wild
DC

❑1, Sep 1998; alternate universe 1.95

Tangent Comics/The Superman
DC

❑1, Sep 1998; alternate universe 1.95

Tangent Comics/The Trials of the Flash
DC

❑1, Sep 1998; alternate universe 1.95

Tangent Comics/Wonder Woman
DC

❑1, Sep 1998; alternate universe 1.95

Tangled Web
Marvel

❑1, Jun 2001; The Thousand 2.99
❑2, Jul 2001; The Thousand 2.99
❑3, Aug 2001; The Thousand 2.99
❑4, Sep 2001 .... 2.99
❑5, Oct 2001 .... 2.99
❑6, Nov 2001 .... 2.99
❑7, Dec 2001 .... 2.99
❑8, Jan 2002 .... 2.99
❑9, Feb 2002 .... 2.99
❑10, Mar 2002 .... 2.99
❑11, Apr 2002 .... 2.99
❑12, May 2002 .... 2.99
❑13, Jun 2002 .... 2.99
❑14, Jul 2002 .... 2.99
❑15, Aug 2002 .... 2.99
❑16, Sep 2002 .... 2.99
❑17, Oct 2002 .... 2.99
❑18, Nov 2002 .... 2.99
❑19, Dec 2002 .... 2.99
❑20, Jan 2003 .... 2.99
❑21, Feb 2003; Extra Sized Issue 2.99
❑22, Mar 2003 .... 2.99

Tank Girl
Dark Horse

❑1, May 1991, b&w; 1: Tank Girl (in American comics). trading cards; British 3.50
❑2, Jun 1991, b&w; British 3.00
❑3, Jul 1991, b&w; British 3.00
❑4, Aug 1991, b&w; British 3.00

Tank Girl 2
Dark Horse

❑1, Jun 1993, British 3.00
❑2, Jul 1993, British 3.00
❑3, Aug 1993, British 3.00
❑4, Sep 1993, British 3.00

Tank Girl: Apocalypse
DC / Vertigo

❑1, Nov 1995; Tank Girl becomes pregnant 2.25
❑2, Dec 1995 .... 2.25
❑3, Jan 1996 .... 2.25
❑4, Feb 1996; Tank Girl gives birth 2.25

Tank Girl Movie Adaptation
DC / Vertigo

❑1; prestige format one-shot 5.95

Tank Girl: The Odyssey
DC / Vertigo

❑1, Jun 1995 .... 2.95
❑2, Jul 1995 .... 2.95
❑3, Aug 1995 .... 2.95
❑4, Oct 1995 .... 2.95

Tank Vixens
Antarctic

❑1, Jan 1994 .... 2.95
❑2, Mar 1994 .... 2.95
❑3, ca. 1995 .... 2.95
❑4, Mar 1996 .... 2.95

Tantalizing Stories
Tundra

❑1, Oct 1992 .... 2.25
❑2, Dec 1992 .... 2.25
❑3, Feb 1993 .... 2.25
❑4, Apr 1993 .... 2.25
❑6, Jun 1993 .... 2.50

TaoLand
Sumitek

❑1, Nov 1994, b&w; cardstock cover 2.00
❑2, Aug 1995, b&w; cardstock cover 5.95
❑3, Sep 1995, b&w; cardstock cover 5.95
❑4, Feb 1996, b&w 5.95
❑5, Dec 1996; prestige format 5.95

TaoLand Adventures
Antarctic

❑1, Mar 1999 .... 3.50
❑2, May 1999 .... 3.50

Tap
Promethean

❑1, Sep 1994 .... 2.95
❑2, Jan 1995 .... 2.95
❑3, Jan 1995; indicia is for issue #2 .... 2.95

Tapestry
Superior Junk

❑1, b&w 1.50
❑1/2nd, Apr 1995; 2nd printing 1.50
❑2, Apr 1994, b&w 1.95
❑3, Jun 1994, b&w 1.95
❑4, Oct 1994, b&w 2.25
❑5, b&w 2.25

Tapestry Anthology
Caliber / Tapestry

❑1, Win 1997, b&w 2.95

Tapping the Vein
Eclipse

❑1; prestige format; CR (w); CR (a); foil-embossed logo 7.50
❑2; prestige format; KJ (a); foil-embossed logo 7.00
❑3; prestige format; foil-embossed logo 7.00
❑4; prestige format; foil-embossed logo 7.95
❑5; ca. 1992 .... 7.95

Target: Airboy
Eclipse

❑1, Mar 1988; A: Clint from A.R.B.B.H.. cardstock cover 2.00

Target: The Corruptors
Dell

❑2, Jun 1962, First issue published as Dell's Four Color #1306 .... 25.00
❑3, Dec 1962 .... 25.00

Targitt
Atlas-Seaboard

❑1, Mar 1975; O: Targitt 9.00
❑2, Apr 1975 .... 8.00
❑3, Jul 1975 .... 7.00

Tarot Cafe
Tokyopop

❑1, Mar 2005 .... 9.99
❑2, Jun 2005 .... 9.99
❑3, Sep 2005 .... 9.99
❑4, Dec 2005 .... 9.99

Tarot: Witch of the Black Rose
Broadsword

❑1, Mar 2000 .... 5.00
❑2, May 2000 .... 2.95
❑3, Jul 2000 .... 2.95
❑4, Sep 2000 .... 2.95
❑5, Nov 2000 .... 2.95
❑6, Jan 2001 .... 2.95
❑7, Mar 2001 .... 2.95
❑8, May 2001 .... 2.95
❑9, Jul 2001 .... 2.95
❑10, Sep 2001 .... 2.95
❑11, Nov 2001 .... 2.95
❑12, Jan 2002 .... 2.95
❑13, Mar 2002 .... 2.95
❑14, May 2002 .... 2.95
❑15, Jul 2002 .... 2.95
❑16, Sep 2002 .... 2.95
❑17, Nov 2002 .... 2.95
❑18, Jan 2003 .... 2.95
❑19, Mar 2003 .... 2.95
❑20, May 2003 .... 2.95
❑21 .... 2.95
❑22 .... 2.95
❑23 .... 2.95

Time Tunnel

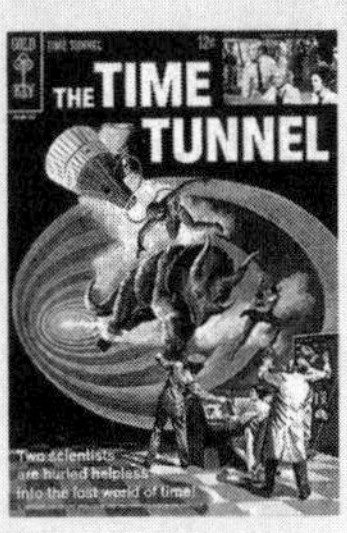

Stargate's 1960s television ancestor

©Gold Key

Time Twisters

Reprinted short stories from 2000 A.D.

©Fleetway-Quality

Titans

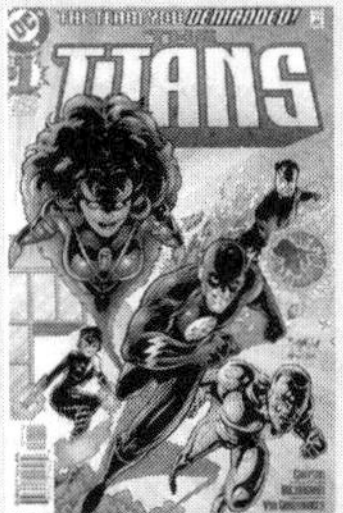

Back to basics with 1999 post-Teen relaunch

©DC

To Be Announced

"It's a Municipal Holiday, Charlie Brown!"

©Strawberry Jam

Tomahawk

Revolutionary-era hero raised by Indians

©DC

N-MINT

❑24 2.95
❑25 2.95
❑26 2.95
❑27 2.95
❑28 2.95
❑29 2.95
❑29/Variant 4.00
❑30 2005 2.95
❑30/Variant 2005 20.00
❑31 2005 2.95
❑31/Deluxe 2005 19.99
❑31/Photo 2005 15.00
❑32 2005 2.95
❑32/Variant 2005 5.00
❑33, Sep 2005 2.95
❑33/Deluxe, Sep 2005 19.99

Tarzan
Gold Key

❑132, Nov 1962, RM (a); Continued from Tarzan (Dell) #131 14.00
❑133, Jan 1963, RM (a); Brothers of the Spear story 14.00
❑134, Mar 1963, RM (a); Brothers of the Spear story 14.00
❑135, May 1963, RM (a); Brothers of the Spear story 14.00
❑136, Jul 1963, RM (a); Brothers of the Spear story 14.00
❑137, Aug 1963, RM (a); Brothers of the Spear story 14.00
❑138, Oct 1963, RM (a); Brothers of the Spear story; Ape-English Dictionary 14.00
❑139, Dec 1963, RM (a); Brothers of the Spear story; Ape-English Dictionary; Boy changes name to Korak 14.00
❑140, Feb 1964, RM (a); Brothers of the Spear story; Ape-English dictionary 14.00
❑141, Apr 1964, RM (a); Brothers of the Spear story; Ape-English dictionary 14.00
❑142, Jun 1964, RM (a); Brothers of the Spear story; Ape-English dictionary 14.00
❑143, Jul 1964, RM (a); Brothers of the Spear story 14.00
❑144, Aug 1964, RM (a); Brothers of the Spear story 14.00
❑145, Sep 1964, RM (a); Brothers of the Spear story 14.00
❑146, Oct 1964, (w); RM (a); Brothers of the Spear story 14.00
❑147, Dec 1964, RM (a); Brothers of the Spear story 14.00
❑148, Feb 1965, RM (a); Brothers of the Spear story 14.00
❑149, Apr 1965, RM (a); Brothers of the Spear story 14.00
❑150, Jun 1965, RM (a); Brothers of the Spear story 14.00
❑151, Aug 1965, RM (a); Brothers of the Spear story 14.00
❑152, Sep 1965, RM (a); Brothers of the Spear story 14.00
❑153, Oct 1965, RM (a); Brothers of the Spear story 14.00
❑154, Nov 1965, RM (a); Brothers of the Spear story; Ape-English dictionary 14.00
❑155, Dec 1965, RM (c); RM (a); O: Tarzan. adapts Tarzan of the Apes 18.00
❑156, Feb 1966, RM (c); RM (a); adapts Return of Tarzan 10.00

N-MINT

❑157, Apr 1966, RM (c); RM (a); adapts Beasts of Tarzan 10.00
❑158, Jun 1966, RM (a); adapts Son of Tarzan 10.00
❑159, Aug 1966, RM (c); RM, DS (a); adapts Jewels of Opar 10.00
❑160, Sep 1966, RM (c); RM (a); adapts Jewels of Opar 10.00
❑161, Oct 1966, RM (c); RM (a); adapts Jewels of Opar 10.00
❑162, Dec 1966, (w); TV Adventures on cover 10.00
❑163, Jan 1967, RM (c); RM (a); adapts Tarzan the Untamed 8.00
❑164, Feb 1967, RM (c); RM (a); adapts Tarzan the Untamed 8.00
❑165, Mar 1967, (w); DS (a); Photo cover; TV Adventures on cover 10.00
❑166, Apr 1967, RM (c); RM (a); adapts Tarzan the Terrible 8.00
❑167, May 1967, RM (c); RM (a); adapts Tarzan the Terrible 8.00
❑168, Jun 1967, (w); 10012-706 10.00
❑169, Jul 1967, adapts Jungle Tales of Tarzan 8.00
❑170, Aug 1967, adapts Jungle Tales of Tarzan 8.00
❑171, Sep 1967, TV Adventures 10.00
❑172, Oct 1967, RM (a); adapts Tarzan and the Golden Lion 7.00
❑173, Dec 1967, RM (a); adapts Tarzan and the Golden Lion 7.00
❑174, Feb 1968, RM (a); adapts Tarzan and the Ant Men 7.00
❑175, Apr 1968, RM (a); adapts Tarzan and the Ant Men 7.00
❑176, Jun 1968, RM (a); adapts Tarzan; Lord of the Jungle 7.00
❑177, Jul 1968, RM (a); adapts Tarzan; Lord of the Jungle 7.00
❑178, Aug 1968, RM (a); reprints issue #155 7.00
❑179, Sep 1968, adapts Tarzan at the Earth's Core 7.00
❑180, Oct 1968, adapts Tarzan at the Earth's Core 7.00
❑181, Dec 1968, adapts Tarzan at the Earth's Core 7.00
❑182, Feb 1969, adapts Tarzan the Invincible 7.00
❑183, Apr 1969, (c); adapts Tarzan the Invincible 7.00
❑184, Jun 1969, adapts Tarzan Triumphant 7.00
❑185, Jul 1969, adapts Tarzan Triumphant 7.00
❑186, Aug 1969, adapts Tarzan and the City of Gold 7.00
❑187, Sep 1969, adapts Tarzan and the City of Gold 7.00
❑188, Oct 1969, adapts Tarzan's Quest 7.00
❑189, Dec 1969, adapts Tarzan''s Quest 7.00
❑190, Feb 1970, adapts Tarzan and the Forbidden City 7.00
❑191, Apr 1970, RM, DS (a); adapts Tarzan and the Forbidden City 7.00
❑192, Jun 1970, RM, DS (a); adapts Tarzan and the Foreign Legion 7.00
❑193, Jul 1970, DS (a); adapts Tarzan and the Foreign Legion 7.00
❑194, Aug 1970, DS (a); adapts Tarzan and the Lost Empire 7.00

N-MINT

❑195, Sep 1970, adapts Tarzan and the Lost Empire 7.00
❑196, Oct 1970, RM (a); adapts Tarzan and the Tarzan Twins 7.00
❑197, Dec 1970, RM (a); Reprint from Tarzan (Dell) #120 7.00
❑198, Feb 1971, RM (a); Reprint from Tarzan (Dell) #121 7.00
❑199, Apr 1971, RM (a); Reprint from Tarzan (Dell) #122 7.00
❑200, Jun 1971, RM (a); Reprint from Tarzan (Dell) #123 7.00
❑201, Jul 1971, RM (a); Reprint from Tarzan (Dell) #124 6.00
❑202, Aug 1971, RM (a); astronauts land in jungle 6.00
❑203, Sep 1971, RM (a); Brothers of the Spear story 6.00
❑204, Oct 1971, RM (a); Ape-English dictionary; Reprint from Tarzan (Dell) #125 6.00
❑205, Dec 1971, RM (a); Reprint from Tarzan (Dell) #126 6.00
❑206, Feb 1972, moves to DC; Series continued in Tarzan (DC) #207 6.00

Tarzan
DC

❑207, Apr 1972; Giant-size; JKu (c); JKu (w); MA, GM, JKu (a); O: Tarzan. John Carter of Mars back-up; Series continued from Tarzan (Dell) 17.00
❑208, May 1972; JKu (c); JKu (w); GM, JKu (a); O: Tarzan. John Carter of Mars back-up 10.00
❑209, Jun 1972; JKu (c); JKu (w); MA, JKu (a); O: Tarzan. John Carter of Mars back-up continues in Weird Worlds #1 6.00
❑210, Jul 1972, JKu (c); JKu (w); JKu (a); O: Tarzan 6.00
❑211, Aug 1972, JKu (c); JKu (w); JKu (a); Reprints Newspaper strips 31 Jan 1932, 19 Apr 1942 - 5 Jul 1942; Tom Yeates L.O.C 4.00
❑212, Sep 1972, JKu (c); JKu (w); JKu (a) 4.00
❑213, Oct 1972, JKu (c); JKu (w); DGr, JKu (a); 1: Tangor (Lt. James Farnsworth); Beyond the Farthest Star story 4.00
❑214, Nov 1972, JKu (c); JKu (w); DGr, JKu (a); Beyond the Farthest Star back-up 4.00
❑215, Dec 1972, JKu (c); JKu (w); DGr, JKu (a); Beyond the Farthest Star back-up 4.00
❑216, Jan 1973, JKu (c); JKu (w); FT, HC, JKu (a); Beyond the Farthest Star back-up 4.00
❑217, Feb 1973, JKu (c); JKu (w); MA, JKu (a); Beyond the Farthest Star back-up 4.00
❑218, Mar 1973, JKu (c); JKu (w); MA, JKu (a); Beyond the Farthest Star back-up 4.00
❑219, May 1973, JKu (c); JKu (w); JKu (a) 4.00
❑220, Jun 1973, JKu (c); JKu (w); JKu (a) 4.00
❑221, Jul 1973, JKu (c); JKu (w); JKu (a); Reprint from Newspaper strip 3 Jan 1934 4.00
❑222, Aug 1973, JKu (c); JKu (w); JKu (a); Bob Rozakis L.O.C 4.00
❑223, Sep 1973, JKu (c); JKu (w); JKu (a) 4.00
❑224, Oct 1973, JKu (c); JKu (w); JKu (a) 4.00

Other grades: Multiply price above by 5/6 for VF/NM • 2/3 for VERY FINE • 1/3 for FINE • 1/5 for VERY GOOD • 1/8 for GOOD

❑225, Nov 1973, JKu (c); JKu (w); JKu (a) 4.00
❑226, Dec 1973, JKu (c); RM (w); JKu, RM (a); Reprints Newpaper strip 15 Nov 1970 - 7 Feb 1971 4.00
❑227, Jan 1974, JKu (c); JKu (w); JKu (a) 4.00
❑228, Feb 1974, JKu (c); JKu (w); JKu (a) 4.00
❑229, Mar 1974, JKu (c); JKu (w); JKu (a) 4.00
❑230, May 1974, 100 Page giant; JKu (c); JKu (w); CI, JKu, RM, RH (a); Reprints from Newspaper strip 6 Jul 1970 - 11 Aug 1970, Bomba #4, Action Comics #145, The Adventures of Rex the Wonder Dog #4 8.00
❑231, Jul 1974, 100 Page giant; JKu (c); JKu, RM (w); CI, JKu, RM, AN (a); Reprints from Newspaper strip 14 Mar 1971 - 1 Aug 1971, Action Comics #174, Bomba #3, The Adventures of Rex the Wonder Dog #6 8.00
❑232, Sep 1974, 100 Page giant; JKu (c); JKu, RM (w); NR, CI, JKu, GK, AA, RM, AN (a); Reprints from Newspaper strip 15 Aug 1971 - 5 Dec 1971, Action Comics #190, The Adventures of Rex the Wonder Dog #13 8.00
❑233, Nov 1974, 100 Page giant; JKu (c); JKu, RM (w); CI, JKu, GK, RM, AN (a); Reprints Newspaper strip 12 Dec 1971 - 2 Apr 1972, My Greatest Adventure #2, The Adventures of Rex the Wonder Dog #20, 34, Action Comics #199 8.00
❑234, Jan 1975, 100 Page giant; JKu (c); JKu, RM (w); CI, JKu, RM, AN, RMo (a); Reprints Newspaper strip 28 Jan 1969 - 11 Apr 1969, The Adventures of Rex the Wonder Dog #27, Action Comics #176, My Greatest Adventure #5, 14 8.00
❑235, Mar 1975, 100 Page giant; JKu (c); JKu, RM (w); CI, JKu, RM (a); Reprints Newspaper strip, Action Comics #189, Rex the Wonder Dog #35, My Greatest Adventure #4 8.00
❑236, Apr 1975 JKu (c); JKu, (w); JKu (a) 3.00
❑237, May 1975; JKu (c); RM, (w); JKu, RM (a); Reprints Newspaper strip 3.00
❑238, Jun 1975, JKu (c); RM, (w); RM (a); Reprints Newspaper strip; 68 pages; Giant-Size 3.00
❑239, Jul 1975, JKu (c); JKu, (w); JKu (a) 3.00
❑240, Aug 1975; JKu (c); JKu, (w); JKu (a); adapts The Castaways 3.00
❑241, Sep 1975 JKu (c); JKu, (w); JKu (a) 3.00
❑242, Oct 1975 JKu (c); JKu, (w); JKu (a) 3.00
❑243, Nov 1975 JKu (c); JKu, (w); JKu (a) 3.00
❑244, Dec 1975 JKu (c); JKu, (w); JKu (a) 3.00
❑245, Jan 1976 JKu (c); JKu, (w); JKu (a) 3.00
❑246, Feb 1976 JKu (c); JKu, (w); JKu (a) 3.00
❑247, Mar 1976, JKu (c); JKu, (w); JKu (a) 3.00
❑248, Apr 1976, JKu (c); JKu, (w); JKu (a); Tim Burgard L.O.C 3.00
❑249, May 1976, JKu (c); JKu, (w) 3.00
❑250, Jun 1976, JL (c); JL (a) 3.00
❑251, Jul 1976, JL (c); JL (a) 3.00
❑252, Aug 1976, JL (c); JKu (w); JKu, JL (a); Reprint from Tarzan #213 3.00
❑253, Sep 1976, JKu (c); JKu (w); JKu, JL (a); Tim Burgard L.O.C.; Reprint from Tarzan #213 3.00
❑254, Oct 1976, JL (c); FS, JL (a) 3.00
❑255, Nov 1976, FS, JL (a) 3.00
❑256, Dec 1976, adapts Tarzan the Untamed 3.00
❑257, Jan 1977, JKu (w); JKu (a); Reprint from Tarzan #214 3.00
❑258, Feb 1977, JKu (w); JKu (a); Final Issue; Reprint from Tarzan #216 3.00

Tarzan
Marvel

❑1, Jun 1977, JB (a) 3.00
❑1/35¢, Jun 1977, JB (a); 35¢ regional price variant 15.00
❑2, Jul 1977, Newsstand edition (distributed by Curtis); issue number in box 2.00
❑2/Whitman, Jul 1977, Special markets edition (usually sold in Whitman bagged prepacks); price appears in a diamond; UPC barcode appears 2.00
❑2/35¢, Jul 1977, 35¢ regional price variant; newsstand edition (distributed by Curtis); issue number in box 15.00
❑3, Aug 1977 2.00
❑3/35¢, Aug 1977, 35¢ regional price variant 15.00
❑4, Sep 1977 2.00
❑4/35¢, Sep 1977, 35¢ regional price variant 15.00
❑5, Oct 1977 2.00
❑5/35¢, Oct 1977, 35¢ regional price variant 15.00
❑6, Nov 1977 1.50
❑7, Dec 1977 1.50
❑8, Jan 1978 1.50
❑9, Feb 1978 1.50
❑10, Mar 1978 1.50
❑11, Apr 1978, Newsstand edition (distributed by Curtis); issue number in box 1.50
❑11/Whitman, Apr 1978, Special markets edition (usually sold in Whitman bagged prepacks); price appears in a diamond; no UPC barcode 1.50
❑12, May 1978, Newsstand edition (distributed by Curtis); issue number in box 1.50
❑12/Whitman, May 1978, Special markets edition (usually sold in Whitman bagged prepacks); price appears in a diamond; no UPC barcode 1.50
❑13, Jun 1978, Newsstand edition (distributed by Curtis); issue number in box 1.50
❑13/Whitman, Jun 1978, Special markets edition (usually sold in Whitman bagged prepacks); price appears in a diamond; no UPC barcode 1.50
❑14, Jul 1978 1.50
❑15, Aug 1978 1.50
❑15/Whitman, Aug 1978, Special markets edition (usually sold in Whitman bagged prepacks); price appears in a diamond; no UPC barcode 1.50
❑16, Sep 1978, Newsstand edition (distributed by Curtis); issue number in box 1.50
❑16/Whitman, Sep 1978, Special markets edition (usually sold in Whitman bagged prepacks); price appears in a diamond; UPC barcode appears 1.50
❑17, Oct 1978, Newsstand edition (distributed by Curtis); issue number in box 1.50
❑17/Whitman, Oct 1978, Special markets edition (usually sold in Whitman bagged prepacks); price appears in a diamond; no UPC barcode 1.50
❑18, Nov 1978, Newsstand edition (distributed by Curtis); issue number in box 1.50
❑18/Whitman, Nov 1978, Special markets edition (usually sold in Whitman bagged prepacks); price appears in a diamond; no UPC barcode 1.50
❑19, Dec 1978, Newsstand edition (distributed by Curtis); issue number in box 1.50
❑19/Whitman, Dec 1978, Special markets edition (usually sold in Whitman bagged prepacks); price appears in a diamond; no UPC barcode 1.50
❑20, Jan 1979, DC (c); SB, BH (a); Newsstand edition (distributed by Curtis); issue number in box 1.50
❑20/Whitman, Jan 1979, BH (a); Special markets edition (usually sold in Whitman bagged prepacks); price appears in a diamond; no UPC barcode 1.50
❑21, Feb 1979, Newsstand edition (distributed by Curtis); issue number in box 1.50
❑21/Whitman, Feb 1979, Special markets edition (usually sold in Whitman bagged prepacks); price appears in a diamond; no UPC barcode 1.50
❑22, Mar 1979 1.50
❑23, Apr 1979 1.50
❑24, May 1979, SB, BH (a); Newsstand edition (distributed by Curtis); issue number in box 1.50
❑24/Whitman, May 1979, BH (a); Special markets edition (usually sold in Whitman bagged prepacks); price appears in a diamond; no UPC barcode 1.50
❑25, Jun 1979, SB, BH (a) 1.50
❑26, Jul 1979, SB, BH (a) 1.50
❑27, Aug 1979 1.50
❑28, Sep 1979 1.50
❑29, Oct 1979 1.50
❑Ann 1, ca. 1977 3.00
❑Ann 2, ca. 1978, BH (c); BH (w); SB (a) 1.50
❑Ann 3, ca. 1979 1.50

Tarzan
Dark Horse

❑1, Jul 1996 3.00
❑2, Aug 1996 3.00
❑3, Aug 1996 3.00
❑4, Sep 1996 3.00
❑5, Nov 1996 3.00
❑6, Nov 1996 3.00
❑7, Jan 1997 3.00
❑8, Feb 1997 3.00
❑9, Mar 1997 3.00
❑10, Apr 1997 3.00
❑11, May 1997 3.00
❑12, Jun 1997 2.95
❑13, Aug 1997 2.95
❑14, Sep 1997 2.95
❑15, Sep 1997 2.95
❑16, Oct 1997 2.95
❑17, Dec 1997 TY (a) 2.95
❑18, Jan 1998 2.95
❑19, Feb 1998 2.95
❑20, Mar 1998 2.95

Tarzan
Dark Horse

❑1, Jul 1999 2.95
❑2, Jul 1999 2.95

Tarzan and the Jewels of Opar
Dark Horse

❑1, Jun 1999; digest; collects stories from Dell's Tarzan #159-161 plus pin-ups 10.95

Tarzan: A Tale of Mugambi
Dark Horse

❑1, Jun 1995; NN; One-shot 2.95

Tarzan/Carson of Venus
Dark Horse

❑1, May 1998 2.95
❑2, Jun 1998 2.95
❑3, Jul 1998 2.95
❑4, Aug 1998 2.95

Tarzan Digest
DC

❑1, Aut 1972, Sunday Strip reprints from Jan 14, 1968 - Jan 5, 1969 3.00

Tarzan Family
DC

❑60, Dec 1975, Series continued from Korak, Son of Tarzan #59; Korak; Carson of Venus; Tarzan Strip reprints Sep 4 - Oct 16 1932 5.00
❑61, Feb 1976, Korak; Tarzan; Carson of Venus 5.00
❑62, Apr 1976, Korak; John Carter of Mars; Tarzan; Carson of Venus 4.00
❑63, Jun 1976, Korak; John Carter of Mars; Carson of Venus; Tarzan strip reprints from Oct 11 - Dec 13 1931 4.00
❑64, Aug 1976, Korak; John Carter of Mars; Tarzan; Carson of Venus 4.00
❑65, Sep 1976, Korak; John Carter of Mars; Carson of Venus 4.00
❑66, Nov 1976, Korak; John Carter of Mars 4.00

Tarzan/John Carter: Warlords of Mars
Dark Horse

❑1, Jan 1996 2.50
❑2, Apr 1996, indicia says #3, cover says #2 2.50
❑3, May 1996, V: John Carter 2.50
❑4, Jul 1996, D: Taka; Final Issue 2.50

Tarzan, Lord of the Jungle
Gold Key

❑1, Sep 1965, Reprints from Tarzan (Dell) #13, 15, 17,18 and 41 40.00

Tarzan: Love, Lies and the Lost City
Malibu

❑1, Aug 1992; Flip-book; MW (w) 3.95
❑2, Sep 1992 3.95
❑3, Oct 1992 3.95

Tarzan of the Apes
Marvel

❑1, Jul 1984, ME (w); DS (a); O: Tarzan 3.00
❑2, Aug 1984, ME (w); DS (a); O: Tarzan 3.00

Other grades: Multiply price above by 5/6 for VF/NM • 2/3 for VERY FINE • 1/3 for FINE • 1/5 for VERY GOOD • 1/8 for GOOD

Tom & Jerry Comics

Long-running title went from Dell to Gold Key

©Dell

Tomb of Darkness

Horro SF title had been called "Beware"

©Marvel

Tomb of Dracula

Cult 1970s series gave birth to Blade

©Marvel

Tomb of Dracula

Black-and-white magazine version

©Marvel

Tomb Raider: The Series

Extremely healthy woman from video game

©Image

N-MINT

Tarzan of the Apes
Dark Horse

❑1, May 1999; digest; collects stories from Dell's Tarzan #155-158 and spot illustrations from Tarzan #154-156 .... 12.95

Tarzan: The Beckoning
Malibu

❑1, Nov 1992 .... 2.50
❑2, Dec 1992 .... 2.50
❑3, Jan 1993 .... 2.50
❑4, Feb 1993 .... 2.50
❑5, Mar 1993 .... 2.50
❑6, Apr 1993 .... 2.50
❑7, Jun 1993 .... 2.50

Tarzan: The Lost Adventure
Dark Horse

❑1, Jan 1995, b&w; squarebound 2.95
❑2, Feb 1995, b&w; squarebound 2.95
❑3, Mar 1995, b&w; squarebound 2.95
❑4, Apr 1995, b&w; squarebound 2.95

Tarzan: The Rivers of Blood
Dark Horse

❑1, Nov 1999 .... 2.95
❑2, Dec 1999 .... 2.95
❑3, Jan 2000 .... 2.95
❑4, Feb 2000; final issue of planned eight-issue mini-series 2.95

Tarzan: The Savage Heart
Dark Horse

❑1, Apr 1999 .... 2.95
❑2, May 1999 .... 2.95
❑3, Jun 1999 .... 2.95
❑4, Jul 1999 .... 2.95

Tarzan The Warrior
Malibu

❑1, Mar 1992 .... 2.50
❑2, May 1992 .... 2.50
❑3, Jun 1992 .... 2.50
❑4, Aug 1992 .... 2.50
❑5, Sep 1992 .... 2.50

Tarzan vs. Predator at the Earth's Core
Dark Horse

❑1, Jan 1996; Includes 3 page Aliens: Mondo Heat Preview 2.50
❑2, Feb 1996 .... 2.50
❑3, Mar 1996 .... 2.50
❑4, Jun 1996; D: Mahar Queen; Final Issue 2.50

Tarzan Weekly
Byblos

❑1 .... 5.00

T.A.S.E.R.
Comicreations

❑1, Sep 1992, b&w 2.00
❑2, Jun 1993, b&w 2.00

Task Force One
Image

❑1, Jul 2006 .... 3.50
❑2, Sep 2006 .... 3.50
❑3, Oct 2006 .... 3.50
❑4, Nov 2006 .... 3.50

N-MINT

Taskmaster
Marvel

❑1, Apr 2002 .... 2.99
❑2, May 2002 .... 2.99
❑3, Jun 2002 .... 2.99
❑4, Jul 2002 .... 2.99

Tasmanian Devil and His Tasty Friends
Gold Key

❑1, Nov 1962 .... 75.00

Tasty Bits
Avalon

❑1, Jul 1999 .... 2.95

Tattered Banners
DC / Vertigo

❑1, Nov 1998 .... 2.95
❑2, Dec 1998 .... 2.95
❑3, Jan 1999 .... 2.95
❑4, Feb 1999 .... 2.95

Tattoo
Caliber

❑1 .... 2.95
❑2 .... 2.95

Tattoo Man
Fantagraphics

❑1, b&w 2.75

Taxx
Express / Parody

❑½ 1.50
❑1, b&w 2.75

T-Bird Chronicles
Me Comix

❑1, b&w 1.50
❑2, b&w 1.50

Team 7
Image

❑1, Oct 1994 .... 3.00
❑1/A, Oct 1994; Variant cover by Whilce Portacio 3.00
❑2, Nov 1994 .... 2.50
❑3, Dec 1994 .... 2.50
❑4, Feb 1995 .... 2.50
❑Ashcan 1, Oct 1994, b&w; ashcan promo edition; Ashcan promo edition 1.00

Team 7: Dead Reckoning
Image

❑1, Jan 1996 .... 2.50
❑2, Feb 1996 .... 2.50
❑3, Mar 1996 .... 2.50
❑4, Apr 1996 .... 2.50

Team 7: Objective: Hell
Image

❑1, May 1995; with card 2.50
❑2, Jun 1995 .... 2.50
❑3, Jul 1995 .... 2.50

Team America
Marvel

❑1, Jun 1982, BL (c); O: Team America. 1.00
❑2, Jul 1982, LMc (a) 1.00
❑3, Aug 1982, LMc (c); LMc (a) 1.00
❑4, Sep 1982, LMc (c); LMc (a) 1.00
❑5, Oct 1982 .... 1.00

N-MINT

❑6, Nov 1982 .... 1.00
❑7, Dec 1982 .... 1.00
❑8, Jan 1983 .... 1.00
❑9, Feb 1983, A: Iron Man 1.00
❑10, Mar 1983 .... 1.00
❑11, Apr 1983, A: Ghost Rider 1.00
❑12, May 1983; Double-size; DP (a); Marauder unmasked 1.00

Team Anarchy
Dagger

❑1, Oct 1993; Adult 2.75
❑2, Nov 1993; Adult 2.50
❑3, Jan 1994; Adult 2.50
❑4, Feb 1994; Adult 2.50
❑5, Mar 1994; Adult 2.50
❑6, Apr 1994; Adult; Wraparound cover 2.50
❑7, May 1994; Adult 2.50

Team Nippon
Aircel

❑1, Jun 1989, b&w; 1: Team Nippon; O: Team Nippon 1.95
❑2, Jul 1989, b&w 1.95
❑3, Aug 1989, b&w 1.95
❑4, Sep 1989, b&w 1.95
❑5, Oct 1989, b&w 1.95
❑6, Nov 1989, b&w 1.95
❑7, Dec 1989, b&w; Final Issue 1.95

Team One: Stormwatch
Image

❑1, Jun 1995; cover says Jul, indicia says Jun 2.50
❑2, Aug 1995 .... 2.50

Team One: WildC.A.T.S
Image

❑1, Jul 1995 .... 2.50
❑2, Sep 1995 .... 2.50

Team Superman
DC

❑1, Jul 1999 .... 2.95

Team Superman Secret Files
DC

❑1, May 1998; biographical info on Superboy, Supergirl, Steel, and respective villains 4.95

Team Titans
DC

❑1/A, Sep 1992; KGa (a); O: Killowat. Comes in five different covers 4.00
❑1/B, Sep 1992; KGa (a); O: Mirage. Comes in five different covers 3.00
❑1/C, Sep 1992; O: Nightrider. Comes in five different covers 3.00
❑1/D, Sep 1992; O: Redwing. Comes in five different covers 3.00
❑1/E, Sep 1992; O: Terra. Comes in five different covers 3.00
❑2, Oct 1992; 1: Battalion; Continued from New Titans #91; Continued in Deathstroke the Terminator #16 .... 1.75
❑3, Nov 1992; Continued from New Titans #92 .... 1.75
❑4, Dec 1992; 1: Judge & Jury 1.75
❑5, Feb 1993; V: Death Penalty 1.75
❑6, Mar 1993 .... 1.75
❑7, Apr 1993; 1: Deathwing 1.75

N-MINT

❑8, May 1993; 1: Deathwing 1.75
❑9, Jun 1993 ..... 1.75
❑10, Jul 1993 ..... 1.75
❑11, Aug 1993 ..... 1.75
❑12, Sep 1993 ..... 1.75
❑13, Oct 1993 ..... 1.75
❑14, Nov 1993 ..... 1.75
❑15, Dec 1993 ..... 1.75
❑16, Jan 1994 ..... 1.75
❑17, Feb 1994 ..... 1.75
❑18, Mar 1994 ..... 1.75
❑19, Apr 1994 ..... 1.75
❑20, May 1994 ..... 1.75
❑21, Jun 1994 ..... 1.75
❑22, Jul 1994 ..... 1.75
❑23, Aug 1994 ..... 1.95
❑24, Sep 1994; Zero Hour 1.95
❑Ann 1; 1: Chimera; Bloodlines; Bloodlines: Deathstorm 3.50
❑Ann 2; Elseworlds 2.95

Team X
Marvel

❑2000, Feb 1999 ..... 3.50

Team X/Team 7
Marvel

❑1, Jan 1997, crossover with Image; squarebound 4.95

Team Yankee
First

❑1, Jan 1989 ..... 1.95
❑2, Jan 1989 ..... 1.95
❑3, Jan 1989 ..... 1.95
❑4, Feb 1989 ..... 1.95
❑5, Feb 1989 ..... 1.95
❑6, Feb 1989 ..... 1.95

Team Youngblood
Image

❑1, Sep 1993; 1: Dutch; 1: Masada; V: Giger 1.95
❑2, Oct 1993; V: Giger 1.95
❑3, Nov 1993; V: Giger 1.95
❑4, Dec 1993 ..... 1.95
❑5, Jan 1994; 1: Lynx 1.95
❑6, Feb 1994 ..... 1.95
❑7, Mar 1994; 1: Quantum 1.95
❑8, Apr 1994 ..... 1.95
❑9, May 1994 ..... 1.95
❑10, Jun 1994 ..... 2.50
❑11, Jul 1994 ..... 1.95
❑12, Aug 1994 ..... 2.50
❑13, Sep 1994 ..... 2.50
❑14, Oct 1994; Riptide poses nude 2.50
❑15, Nov 1994 ..... 2.50
❑16, Dec 1994; polybagged with trading card 2.50
❑17, Jan 1995; polybagged with trading card 2.50
❑18, May 1995 ..... 2.50
❑19, Jun 1995 ..... 2.50
❑20, Jul 1995 ..... 2.50
❑21, Mar 1996 ..... 2.50
❑22, Apr 1996; Final Issue; Continued from Youngblood #7; Continued in Newman #4 ..... 2.50

Team Zero
DC / Wildstorm

❑1, Jan 2006 ..... 2.99
❑2, Feb 2006 ..... 2.99
❑3, Mar 2006 ..... 2.99
❑4, May 2006 ..... 2.99
❑5, Jun 2006 ..... 2.99
❑6, Jul 2006 ..... 2.99

Tears
Boneyard

❑1, Oct 1992, b&w; Adult 2.95
❑2, Dec 1992, b&w; Adult 2.50

Teaser and the Blacksmith
Fantagraphics

❑1, b&w; Adult 3.50

Tech High
Virtually Real Enterprises

❑1, Fal 1996, b&w 2.50
❑2, Win 1996, b&w 2.50
❑3, Spr 1997, b&w 2.50

Tech Jacket
Image

❑1, Nov 2003 ..... 2.95
❑2, Dec 2003 ..... 2.95
❑3, Jan 2003 ..... 2.95
❑4, Feb 2003; Feb on cover, Jan inside 2.95
❑5, Apr 2003 ..... 2.95
❑6, May 2003 ..... 2.95

Techno Maniacs
Independent

❑1 ..... 1.95

Technopolis
Caliber

❑1 ..... 2.95
❑2 ..... 2.95
❑3 ..... 2.95
❑4 ..... 2.95

Technopriests
DC

❑1, ca. 2004; Trade paperback 14.95

Teenage Hotrodders
Charlton

❑1, Apr 1963 ..... 35.00
❑2, Jun 1963 ..... 20.00
❑3, Aug 1963 ..... 20.00
❑4, Oct 1963 ..... 20.00
❑5, Dec 1963 ..... 20.00
❑6, Feb 1964 ..... 20.00
❑7, May 1964 ..... 20.00
❑8, Jul 1964 ..... 20.00
❑9, Oct 1964 ..... 20.00
❑10, Dec 1964 ..... 20.00
❑11, Feb 1965 ..... 15.00
❑12, May 1965 ..... 15.00
❑13, Jul 1965 ..... 15.00
❑14, Sep 1965 ..... 15.00
❑15, Nov 1965 ..... 15.00
❑16, Jan 1966 ..... 15.00
❑17, Apr 1966 ..... 15.00
❑18, Jun 1966 ..... 15.00
❑19, Aug 1966 ..... 15.00
❑20, Oct 1966 ..... 15.00
❑21, Dec 1966 ..... 15.00
❑22, Feb 1967 ..... 15.00
❑23, May 1967 ..... 15.00
❑24, Jul 1967, Becomes Top Eliminator #25 ..... 15.00

Teen-Age Love
Charlton

❑23, Nov 1961 ..... 7.00
❑24, Jan 1962 ..... 7.00
❑25 1962 ..... 7.00
❑26 1962 ..... 7.00
❑27, Aug 1962 ..... 7.00
❑28, Oct 1962 ..... 7.00
❑29 1962 ..... 7.00
❑30 1963 ..... 7.00
❑31 1963 ..... 5.00
❑32, Jun 1963 ..... 5.00
❑33, Aug 1963 ..... 5.00
❑34, Oct 1963 ..... 5.00
❑35 1963, DG (c) 5.00
❑36, Feb 1964 ..... 5.00
❑37, May 1964 ..... 5.00
❑38, Jul 1964 ..... 5.00
❑39, Oct 1964 ..... 5.00
❑40 1964 ..... 5.00
❑41, ca. 1965 ..... 5.00
❑42, Jun 1965 ..... 5.00
❑43, Aug 1965 ..... 5.00
❑44, Oct 1965 ..... 5.00
❑45 1966 ..... 5.00
❑46, Mar 1966 ..... 5.00
❑47, May 1966 ..... 5.00
❑48, Jul 1966 ..... 5.00
❑49, Sep 1966 ..... 5.00
❑50, Nov 1966 ..... 5.00
❑51, Jan 1967 ..... 3.50
❑52, Mar 1967 ..... 3.50
❑53, May 1967 ..... 3.50
❑54, Jul 1967 ..... 3.50
❑55, Sep 1967 ..... 3.50
❑56, Nov 1967 ..... 3.50
❑57, Jan 1968 ..... 3.50
❑58, May 1968 ..... 3.50
❑59, Jul 1968 ..... 3.50
❑60, Sep 1968 ..... 3.50
❑61, Nov 1968 ..... 3.50
❑62, Jan 1969 ..... 3.50
❑63, Mar 1969 ..... 3.50
❑64, May 1969 ..... 3.50
❑65 1969 ..... 3.50
❑66, Sep 1969 ..... 3.50
❑67, Nov 1969 ..... 3.50
❑68, Jan 1970 ..... 3.50
❑69, Mar 1970 ..... 3.50
❑70, May 1970 ..... 3.50
❑71, Jul 1970 ..... 2.00
❑72, Sep 1970 ..... 2.00
❑73, Nov 1970 ..... 2.00
❑74, Jan 1971 ..... 2.00
❑75, Mar 1971 ..... 2.00
❑76, May 1971 ..... 2.00
❑77, Jul 1971 ..... 2.00
❑78, Sep 1971 ..... 2.00
❑79, Nov 1971 ..... 2.00
❑80, Dec 1971, David Cassidy pin-up 2.00
❑81, Jan 1972, Susan Dey pin-up 2.00
❑82, Feb 1972, Shirley Jones pin-up 2.00
❑83, Mar 1972 ..... 2.00
❑84, Jun 1972 ..... 2.00
❑85, Jul 1972 ..... 2.00
❑86, Aug 1972 ..... 2.00
❑87, Oct 1972 ..... 2.00
❑88, Nov 1972 ..... 2.00
❑89, Dec 1972 ..... 2.00
❑90, Jan 1973 ..... 2.00
❑91, Feb 1973 ..... 2.00
❑92, Apr 1973 ..... 2.00
❑93 1973 ..... 2.00
❑94, Aug 1973 ..... 2.00
❑95, Oct 1973 ..... 2.00
❑96, Dec 1973 ..... 2.00

Teenage Mutant Ninja Turtles
Mirage

❑1, ca. 1984; 1: Teenage Mutant Ninja Turtles. 1st printing-Beware of counterfeits 300.00
❑1/Counterfeit; Counterfeit of first printing; Most counterfeit copies have streak or scratch marks across center of back cover, black part of cover is slightly bluish instead of black 1.50
❑1/2nd, ca. 1984; 1: Teenage Mutant Ninja Turtles. 2nd printing 15.00
❑1/3rd, Feb 1985; 1: Teenage Mutant Ninja Turtles. 3rd printing 8.00
❑1/4th 1985; 1: Teenage Mutant Ninja Turtles. says Reprinting the first issue on cover 4.00
❑1/5th, Aug 1988; 1: Teenage Mutant Ninja Turtles. fifth printing 3.00
❑2, ca. 1984; 1st printing-Beware of counterfeits 28.00
❑2/Counterfeit; Counterfeit: Uses glossy cover stock 1.50
❑2/2nd 1984; 2nd printing 6.00
❑2/3rd 1986; 3rd printing 3.00
❑2/4th; 3rd printing 4.00
❑3 1985; first printing; correct 15.00
❑3/Misprint, ca. 1985; Giveaway, rare; first printing; misprints; Laird's photo appears in white instead of blue 15.00
❑3/2nd, Nov 1988; 2nd printing 3.00
❑4, ca. 1985 ..... 12.00
❑4/2nd, May 1987; 2nd printing 2.00
❑5, ca. 1985 ..... 4.00
❑5/2nd, Nov 1987; 2nd printing 2.00
❑6, ca. 1986 ..... 3.00
❑6/2nd, May 1987; 2nd printing 2.00
❑7, ca. 1986; First color Teenage Mutant Ninja Turtles (color insert) 5.00
❑7/2nd, Jan 1989; No color story 2.00
❑8, ca. 1986; A: Cerebus 4.00
❑9, Sep 1986 ..... 3.00
❑10, Apr 1987, b&w 3.00
❑11, Jun 1987, b&w 4.00
❑12, Sep 1987 ..... 3.00
❑13, Feb 1988 ..... 3.00
❑14, May 1988; cover says Feb, indicia says May 3.00
❑15, Sum 1988 ..... 3.00
❑16, Sep 1988; cover says Jul, indicia says Sep 2.00

Other grades: Multiply price above by 5/6 for VF/NM • 2/3 for VERY FINE • 1/3 for FINE • 1/5 for VERY GOOD • 1/8 for GOOD

Tom Mix Western	Tomoe	Tomorrow Stories	Tom Strong	Too Much Coffee Man
				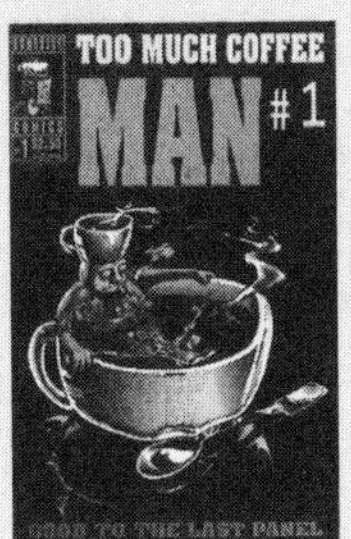
Reprinting tales of the old western hero ©AC	Series interacted with Crusade's Shi title ©Crusade	Showcases the stories of Alan Moore ©DC	Doc Savage quality to Alan Moore title ©DC	Cult favorite appeals to caffeine addicts ©Adhesive

	N-MINT
❑17, Jan 1989; cover says Nov, indicia says Jan	2.00
❑18, Feb 1989, b&w	2.00
❑18/2nd, Dec 1990, 2nd printing; Color reprint	2.00
❑19, Mar 1989; Return to NY	2.00
❑20, Apr 1989; Return to NY	2.00
❑21, May 1989; Return to NY	2.00
❑22, Jun 1989	2.00
❑23, Aug 1989; cover says Jul, indicia says Aug	2.00
❑24, Aug 1989	2.00
❑25, Sep 1989	2.00
❑26, Dec 1989; cover says Oct, indicia says Dec	2.00
❑27, Dec 1989; cover says Nov, indicia says Dec	2.00
❑28, Feb 1990	2.00
❑29, May 1990; cover says Mar, indicia says May	2.00
❑30, Jun 1990; cover says Apr, indicia says Jun	2.00
❑31, Jul 1990; Wraparound cover; b&w	2.00
❑32, Aug 1990	2.00
❑33, Jun 1990, In color	2.00
❑34, Sep 1990	2.00
❑35, Mar 1991; Wraparound cover	2.00
❑36, Aug 1991	2.00
❑37, Jun 1991	2.00
❑38, Jul 1991	2.00
❑39, Sep 1991	2.00
❑40, Oct 1991	2.00
❑41, Nov 1991	2.00
❑42, Dec 1991	2.00
❑43, Jan 1992	2.00
❑44, Feb 1992	2.00
❑45, Mar 1992	2.00
❑46, Apr 1992	2.00
❑47, May 1992	2.00
❑48, Jun 1992	2.00
❑49, Jul 1992	2.00
❑50, Aug 1992, b&w; City At War	2.00
❑51, Sep 1992, b&w	2.00
❑52, Oct 1992, b&w	2.25
❑53, Nov 1992, b&w	2.25
❑54, Dec 1992, b&w	2.25
❑55, Jan 1993, b&w	2.25
❑56, Feb 1993, b&w	2.25
❑57, Mar 1993, b&w	2.25
❑58, Apr 1993, b&w	2.25
❑59, May 1993, b&w	2.25
❑60, Jun 1993, b&w	2.25
❑61, Jul 1993, b&w	2.25
❑62, Aug 1993, b&w; Final Issue	2.25

Teenage Mutant Ninja Turtles
Mirage

❑1, Oct 1993	3.00
❑2, Dec 1993	3.00
❑3, Feb 1994	3.00
❑4, Apr 1994	3.00
❑5, Jun 1994	3.00
❑6, Aug 1994	2.75
❑7, Oct 1994	2.75
❑8, Nov 1994	2.75
❑9, Aug 1995	2.75
❑10, Aug 1995	2.75

	N-MINT
❑11, Sep 1995	2.75
❑12, Sep 1995	2.75
❑13, Oct 1995; Final Issue	2.75
❑Special 1, Jan 1993; Special	4.00

Teenage Mutant Ninja Turtles
Image

❑1, Jun 1996	3.50
❑2, Jul 1996	3.25
❑3, Sep 1996	3.25
❑4, Oct 1996	3.00
❑5, Dec 1996	3.00
❑6, Jan 1997	3.00
❑7, Feb 1997	3.00
❑8, Apr 1997; b&w	3.00
❑9, May 1997 A: Knight Watchman	3.00
❑10, Jul 1997	3.00
❑11, Oct 1997	2.95
❑12, Dec 1997	2.95
❑13, Feb 1998	2.95
❑14, Apr 1998	2.95
❑15, May 1998	2.95
❑16, Jul 1998	2.95
❑17, Sep 1998	2.95
❑18, Oct 1998	2.95
❑19, Jan 1999	2.95
❑20, Mar 1999	2.95
❑21, May 1999	2.95
❑22, Jul 1999	2.95
❑23, Oct 1999	2.95

Teenage Mutant Ninja Turtles Adventures
Archie

❑1, Aug 1988	3.00
❑2, Oct 1988	2.50
❑3, Dec 1988	2.50

Teenage Mutant Ninja Turtles Adventures
Archie

❑1, Mar 1989	3.00
❑2, May 1989	2.50
❑3, Jul 1989	2.50
❑4, Sep 1989	2.00
❑5, Oct 1989	2.00
❑6, Nov 1989	2.00
❑7, Dec 1989	2.00
❑8, Feb 1990	2.00
❑9, Mar 1990	2.00
❑10, May 1990	2.00
❑11, Jun 1990	1.50
❑12, Jul 1990	1.50
❑13, Oct 1990	1.50
❑14, Nov 1990	1.50
❑15, Dec 1990	1.50
❑16, Jan 1991	1.50
❑17, Feb 1991	1.50
❑18, Mar 1991	1.50
❑19, Apr 1991, 1: Mighty Mutanimals	1.50
❑20, May 1991	1.50
❑21, Jun 1991	1.50
❑22, Jul 1991	1.50
❑23, Aug 1991	1.50
❑24, Sep 1991	1.50
❑25, Oct 1991	1.50
❑26, Nov 1991	1.50

	N-MINT
❑27, Dec 1991	1.50
❑28, Jan 1992	1.50
❑29, Feb 1992	1.50
❑30, Mar 1992	1.50
❑31, Apr 1992	1.50
❑32, May 1992	1.50
❑33, Jun 1992	1.50
❑34, Aug 1992	1.50
❑35, Jul 1992	1.50
❑36, Sep 1992	1.50
❑37, Oct 1992	1.50
❑38, Nov 1992	1.50
❑39, Dec 1992	1.50
❑40, Jan 1993	1.50
❑41, Feb 1993	1.50
❑42, Mar 1993	1.50
❑43, Apr 1993	1.50
❑44, May 1993	1.50
❑45, Jun 1993	1.50
❑46, Jul 1993	1.50
❑47, Aug 1993	1.50
❑48, Sep 1993	1.50
❑49, Oct 1993	1.50
❑50, Nov 1993	1.50
❑51, Dec 1993	1.50
❑52, Jan 1994	1.50
❑53, Feb 1994	1.50
❑54, Mar 1994	1.50
❑55, Apr 1994	1.50
❑56, May 1994	1.50
❑57, Jun 1994	1.50
❑58, Jul 1994	1.50
❑59, Aug 1994	1.50
❑60, Sep 1994	1.50
❑61, Oct 1994	1.50
❑62, Nov 1994, Includes poster	1.50
❑63, Dec 1994	1.50
❑64, Jan 1995	1.50
❑65, Feb 1995	1.50
❑66, Mar 1995	1.50
❑67, Apr 1995	1.50
❑68, May 1995	1.50
❑69, Jun 1995	1.50
❑70, Jul 1995	1.50
❑71, Sep 1995	1.50
❑72, Oct 1995, Final Issue	1.50
❑Special 1, Sum 1992, Teenage Mutant Ninja Turtles Meet Archie	2.50
❑Special 2, Fal 1992	2.50
❑Special 3, Win 1992	2.50
❑Special 4, Spr 1993	2.50
❑Special 5, Sum 1993	2.50
❑Special 6, Fal 1993, Giant-Size Special #6	2.00
❑Special 7, Win 1993	2.00
❑Special 8, Spr 1994	2.00
❑Special 9, Sum 1994	2.00
❑Special 10, Fal 1994	2.00
❑Special 11, Teenage Mutant Ninja Turtles Special #11	2.00

Teenage Mutant Ninja Turtles Adventures
Archie

❑1, Jan 1996	1.50
❑2, Feb 1996	1.50
❑3, Mar 1996	1.50

Other grades: Multiply price above by 5/6 for VF/NM • 2/3 for VERY FINE • 1/3 for FINE • 1/5 for VERY GOOD • 1/8 for GOOD

Teenage Mutant Ninja Turtles Animated
Dreamwave

❑1, Jun 2003 2.95
❑2, Jul 2003 2.95
❑3, Aug 2003 2.95
❑4, Sep 2003 2.95
❑5, Oct 2003 2.95
❑6, Nov 2003 2.95
❑7, Dec 2003 2.95

Teenage Mutant Ninja Turtles Authorized Martial Arts Training Manual
Solson

❑1, Jan 1986 RB (w); RB (a) 2.50
❑2, Jan 1986 2.50
❑3, Jan 1986; Donatello 2.50
❑4, Jan 1986; Rafael 2.50

Teenage Mutant Ninja Turtles Classics Digest
Archie

❑1, ca. 1993 2.00
❑2, ca. 1993 1.75
❑3, ca. 1994 1.75
❑4, ca. 1994 1.75
❑5, ca. 1994 1.75
❑6, ca. 1994 1.75
❑7, Dec 1994; digest 1.75
❑8 1.75

Teenage Mutant Ninja Turtles/ Flaming Carrot Crossover
Mirage

❑1, Nov 1993 3.00
❑2, Dec 1993 3.00
❑3, Jan 1994 3.00
❑4, Feb 1994 3.00

Teenage Mutant Ninja Turtles III The Movie: The Turtles are Back...In Time
Archie

❑1; newsstand 2.50
❑1/Prestige; Prestige edition 4.95

Teenage Mutant Ninja Turtles II: The Secret of the Ooze
Mirage

❑1 5.95

Teenage Mutant Ninja Turtles Meet the Conservation Corps
Archie

❑1 2.50

Teenage Mutant Ninja Turtles Michaelangelo Christmas Special
Mirage

❑1, Dec 1990 1.75

Teenage Mutant Ninja Turtles Movie II
Archie

❑1, Jun 1991; NN 2.50

Teenage Mutant Ninja Turtles Mutant Universe Sourcebook
Archie

❑1 2.00
❑2 2.00
❑3 2.00

Teenage Mutant Ninja Turtles Present: April O'Neil
Archie

❑1, Apr 1993 1.25
❑2, May 1993 1.25
❑3, Jun 1993 1.25

Teenage Mutant Ninja Turtles Presents: Donatello and Leatherhead
Archie

❑1, Jul 1993 1.25
❑2, Aug 1993 1.25
❑3, Sep 1993 1.25

Teenage Mutant Ninja Turtles Presents Merdude and Michaelangelo
Archie

❑1, Oct 1993 1.25
❑2, Nov 1993 1.25
❑3, Dec 1993 1.25

Teenage Mutant Ninja Turtles-Savage Dragon Crossover
Mirage

❑1, Aug 1995 3.00

Teenage Mutant Ninja Turtles: The Movie
Archie

❑1, Sum 1990; newsstand 2.50
❑1/Direct ed., Sum 1990; prestige format 4.95
❑1/Prestige; Prestige edition 5.95

Teenage Mutant Ninja Turtles: The Movie
Mirage

❑1, b&w; NN 5.95

Teenagents
Topps

❑1, Aug 1993, three trading cards 2.95
❑2, Sep 1993, trading cards 2.95
❑3, Oct 1993, trading cards 2.95
❑4, Nov 1993, cards; Zorro preview 2.95

Teen Comics
Personality

❑1, ca. 1992; Beverly Hills 90210; Unauthorized biographies, text & pin-ups 2.50
❑2, ca. 1992 2.50
❑3, ca. 1992; Luke Perry; Unauthorized biography, text & pin-ups 2.50
❑4; Melrose Place; Unauthorized biographies, text & pin-ups 2.50
❑5; Marky Mark; Unauthorized biography, text & pin-ups 2.50
❑6; Madonna; Prince; Unauthorized biographies, text & pin-ups 2.50

Teen Confessions
Charlton

❑14, Nov 1961 25.00
❑15, Jan 1962 25.00
❑16, Mar 1962 25.00
❑17, May 1962 25.00
❑18, Jul 1962 25.00
❑19, Sep 1962 25.00
❑20, Nov 1962 25.00
❑21, Feb 1963 25.00
❑22, Apr 1963 25.00
❑23, Jun 1963 25.00
❑24, Aug 1963 25.00
❑25, Oct 1963 25.00
❑26, Dec 1963 25.00
❑27, ca. 1964 25.00
❑28, May 1964 25.00
❑29, Jul 1964 25.00
❑30, ca. 1964 25.00
❑31, ca. 1965 125.00
❑32, ca. 1965 20.00
❑33, May 1965 20.00
❑34, Jul 1965 20.00
❑35, Sep 1965 20.00
❑36, Nov 1965 20.00
❑37, Jan 1966 20.00
❑38, May 1966 20.00
❑39, Jul 1966 20.00
❑40, ca. 1966 20.00
❑41, Nov 1966 20.00
❑42, Jan 1967 20.00
❑43, Mar 1967 20.00
❑44, May 1967 20.00
❑45, Jul 1967 20.00
❑46, Sep 1967 20.00
❑47, Nov 1967 20.00
❑48, Jan 1968 20.00
❑49, Mar 1968 20.00
❑50, Jul 1968 20.00
❑51, Sep 1968 15.00
❑52, Nov 1968 15.00
❑53, Jan 1968 15.00
❑54, Mar 1969 15.00
❑55, ca. 1969 15.00
❑56, ca. 1969 15.00
❑57, Aug 1969 15.00
❑58, Nov 1969 15.00
❑59, ca. 1970 20.00
❑60, Feb 1970 12.00
❑61, Apr 1970 12.00
❑62, Jun 1970 12.00
❑63, Aug 1970 12.00
❑64, Oct 1970 12.00
❑65, Dec 1970 12.00
❑66, Feb 1971 12.00
❑67, Apr 1971 12.00
❑68, Jun 1971 12.00
❑69, Aug 1971 12.00
❑70, Oct 1971 12.00
❑71, Dec 1971, David Cassidy pin-up 12.00
❑72, Feb 1972 12.00
❑73, Apr 1972, Shirley Jones pin-up 12.00
❑74, Jun 1972, Bobby Sherman pin-up 12.00
❑75, Aug 1972 12.00
❑76, Oct 1972 12.00
❑77, Dec 1972 12.00
❑78, Feb 1973, Susan Dey pin-up 12.00
❑79, Apr 1973 12.00
❑80, Jun 1973 12.00
❑81, Jul 1973 12.00
❑82, Sep 1973 12.00
❑83, Nov 1973 12.00
❑84, Jan 1974 12.00
❑85, Sep 1974 12.00
❑86, ca. 1974 12.00
❑87, Feb 1975 12.00
❑88, Apr 1975 12.00
❑89, Jun 1975 12.00
❑90, Aug 1975 12.00
❑91, Oct 1975 12.00
❑92, Dec 1975 12.00
❑93, Feb 1976 12.00
❑94, Apr 1976 12.00
❑95, Jun 1976 12.00
❑96, Aug 1976 12.00
❑97, Oct 1976 12.00

Teens at Play
Fantagraphics

❑1 2005 4.95

Teen Tales: The Library Comic
David G. Brown

❑1, Oct 1997; promotional comic book done for the L.A. Public Library 1.00

Teen Titans
DC

❑1, Feb 1966, NC (c); NC (a); Peace Corps 260.00
❑2, Apr 1966, NC (c); NC (a); 1: Garn; V: Akkuru; The Caveman 100.00
❑3, Jun 1966, NC (c); NC (a) 40.00
❑4, Aug 1966, NC (c); NC (a); Reprinted in Teen Titans Ann 1999 40.00
❑5, Oct 1966, NC (c); NC (a) 40.00
❑6, Dec 1966, NC (c) 32.00
❑7, Feb 1967, NC (c); NC (a); 1: Mad Mod 32.00
❑8, Apr 1967, NC (c); IN, JAb (a) 32.00
❑9, Jun 1967, NC (c); NC, IN (a); V: Captain Tiger 32.00
❑10, Aug 1967, NC (c); NC, IN (a) 32.00
❑11, Oct 1967, NC (c); NC, IN (a) 28.00
❑12, Dec 1967, NC (c); NC, IN (a) 28.00
❑13, Feb 1968, NC (c); NC (a) 28.00
❑14, Apr 1968, NC (c); NC, FS (a); V: The Gargoyle 28.00
❑15, Jun 1968, NC (c); NC (a); V: Captain Rumble; V: Big Ernie; V: Tram the Trucker 28.00
❑16, Aug 1968, NC (c); NC (a) 28.00
❑17, Oct 1968, NC (c); NC (a); V: The Mad Mod 28.00
❑18, Dec 1968, NC (c); 1: Starfire I (Leonid Kovar); V: Andre Le Blanc 33.00
❑19, Feb 1969, NC (c); GK, WW (a); Reprinted in Super-Team Family #1 33.00
❑20, Apr 1969, NC (c); NA (w); NA, NC (a) 33.00
❑21, Jun 1969, NC (c); NA (w); NA, NC (a) 33.00
❑22, Aug 1969, NC (c); NA (w); NA, GK, NC (a); O: Wonder Girl; Klaus Janson L.O.C 33.00
❑23, Oct 1969, NC (c); GK, NC (a) 18.00
❑24, Dec 1969, NC (c); GK, NC (a); Klaus Janson L.O.C 18.00
❑25, Jan 1970, NC (c); DG (w); NC (a); 1: Lilith 18.00
❑26, Mar 1970, NC (c); DG (w); NC (a); 1: Mal Duncan; Alan Brennert LOC 12.00
❑27, May 1970, NC (c); DG (w); CI, GT, NC (a); in space 12.00
❑28, Jul 1970, NC (c); DG (w); NC (a) 12.00
❑29, Sep 1970, NC (c); DG (w); NC (a); A: Hawk & Dove. Credits from #32 12.00

Top Cat

Hanna-Barbera hipster felines wreak havoc
©Charlton

Top Cow Classics in Black and White: The Darkness

Top Cow gives readers a look at the inks
©Image

Top Dog

Talking canine becomes boy's best pal
©Marvel

Tor

The savage world of a million years ago
©DC

Torso

Eliot Ness' most horrifying case
©Image

N-MINT

❑30, Nov 1970, NC (c); DG (w); CI, NC (a); A: Aquagirl. Aqualad story 12.00
❑31, Jan 1971, NC (c); DG (w); GT, NC (a); Hawk and Dove story 20.00
❑32, Mar 1971, NC (c); DG (w); NC (a); 1: Gnaark; Mike W. Barr L.O.C 18.00
❑33, May 1971, NC (c); DG (w); GT, NC (a); Robin returns 18.00
❑34, Jul 1971, NC (c); GT, NC (a) 18.00
❑35, Sep 1971, Giant-size; NC (c); GT, NC (a); 1: Think Freak. Reprints material from World's Finest Comics #139; Reprints from Adventure Comics #263; 1: Think Freak 18.00
❑36, Nov 1971, Giant-size; NC (c); GT, NC, JA (a); Reprints from Adventure Comics #253 .... 18.00
❑37, Jan 1972, Giant-size; NC (c); GT, NC (a); Reprints Superboy Meets the Young Green Arrow from Adventure Comics #258; Includes reprints; Bob Rozakis L.O.C.; Green Arrow's costume mis-colored as Speedy's in reprint 18.00
❑38, Mar 1972, Giant-size; NC (c); GT, NC (a); Reprints Green Arrow's New Partner from Adventure Comics #260; Reprints Aqualad Goes to School from Adventure Comics #278; Lilith story .. 18.00
❑39, May 1972, Giant-size; NC (c); GT, GK, NC (a); Final 52-page issue 12.00
❑40, Jul 1972, NC (c); NC (a); 1: Black Moray. A: Aqualad; Bob Rozakis L.O.C 12.00
❑41, Sep 1972, NC (c); DC, NC (a); Lilith story 12.00
❑42, Nov 1972, NC (c); NC (a) 12.00
❑43, Jan 1973, NC (c); NC (a); series goes on hiatus 12.00
❑44, Nov 1976, 1: Guardian. V: Doctor Light. Series begins again (1976); New team: Kid Flash, Wonder Girl, Robin, Speedy, Mal 7.00
❑45, Dec 1976, IN (a); Includes Teen Titans appearance checklist 7.00
❑46, Feb 1977, RB (c); IN (a); V: Fiddler; Joker's Daughter joins the Titans; Teen Titans appearance checklist 7.00
❑47, Apr 1977, RB (c); 1: Darklight I. 1: Flamesplasher I. 1: Darklight II. 1: Flamesplasher II. 1: Sizematic II. 1: Darklight I; 1: Sizematic I 7.00
❑48, Jun 1977, RB, JAb (c); 1: Harlequin. 1: The Bumblebee 12.00
❑49, Aug 1977, RB, JAb (c); 1: Bryan the Brain 7.00
❑50, Oct 1977, RB, JAb (c); DH (a); Bat-Girl returns 20.00
❑51, Nov 1977, RB (c); DH (a); A: Titans West. V: Mr. Esper (as Captain Calamity) 6.00
❑52, Dec 1977, RB, JAb (c); DH (a); A: Titans West. V: Mr. Esper (as Captain Calamity) 6.00
❑53, Feb 1978, RB, JAb (c); O: Teen Titans. 1: The Antithesis; Final Issue 6.00

Teen Titans
DC

❑1, Oct 1996; GP (a); O: New team of four teen-agers led by Atom; 1: Argent II ... 4.00
❑2, Nov 1996; GP (a); V: Psions 3.00
❑3, Dec 1996; GP (a); A: Mr. Jupiter. A: Mad Mod. V: Jugular. team gets new costumes 3.00

N-MINT

❑4, Jan 1997 A: Captain Marvel Jr.. A: Nightwing. A: Robin 2.50
❑5, Feb 1997; GP (a); A: Captain Marvel Jr.. A: Supergirl. A: Nightwing. A: Robin. 1: Pylon; V: Veil 2.50
❑6, Mar 1997 GP (a) 2.50
❑7, Apr 1997; GP (a); 1: Dark Nemesis; 1: Carom; 1: Scorcher; 1: Vault; 1: Axis; 1: Blizzard; V: Dark Nemesis 2.50
❑8, May 1997; V: Dark Nemesis 2.50
❑9, Jun 1997; GP (a); A: Warlord. Prysm arrives in Skartaris; Titans followed ... 2.50
❑10, Jul 1997; A: Warlord. in Skartaris .. 2.50
❑11, Aug 1997; GP (a); A: Warlord. V: Motolla in Skartaris 2.00
❑12, Sep 1997; GP, DG, GK (a); flashback with original Titans 2.95
❑13, Oct 1997; flashback with original Titans 2.00
❑14, Nov 1997; GP (a); identity of Omen revealed 2.00
❑15, Jan 1998; GP (a); D: Joto. real identity of Omen revealed 2.00
❑16, Feb 1998 .... 2.00
❑17, Mar 1998; new members join 2.00
❑18, Apr 1998 .... 2.00
❑19, Apr 1998; A: Superman. Millennium Giants 2.00
❑20, May 1998 .... 2.00
❑21, Jun 1998 .... 2.00
❑22, Jul 1998; A: Changeling. V: Deathstroke; V: Veil 2.00
❑23, Aug 1998 A: Superman 1.95
❑24, Sep 1998; Final Issue; Titans Hunt Pt 4; Atom aged to adulthood; Joto resurrected 1.95
❑Ann 1, ca. 1997; Pulp Heroes 3.95
❑Ann 1999, ca. 1999; published in 1999 in style of '60s Ann; cardstock cover .. 4.95
❑42, Mar 2007 .... 2.99

Teen Titans
DC

❑½, Aug 2004, Wizard 1/2 redemption premium 16.00
❑1, Oct 2003; White cover; Mike McKone cover 12.00
❑1/2nd, Oct 2003; 2nd printing; Mike McKone cover 5.00
❑1/3rd, Oct 2003; 3rd printing; Cover homage to New Teen Titans #1 .... 4.00
❑1/4th, Oct 2003; sketch cover 8.00
❑2, Nov 2003 .... 2.50
❑3, Dec 2003 .... 2.50
❑4, Jan 2004; Impuse becomes Kid Flash II 2.50
❑5, Feb 2004 .... 2.50
❑6, Mar 2004 .... 2.50
❑7, Apr 2004 .... 2.50
❑8, May 2004; O: Raven 2.50
❑9, May 2004 .... 2.50
❑10, Jun 2004 .... 2.50
❑11, Jul 2004 .... 2.50
❑12, Aug 2004; Ravager loses her eye ... 2.50
❑13, Sep 2004; O: Beast Boy 2.50
❑14, Oct 2004 .... 2.50
❑15, Nov 2004 .... 2.50
❑16, Dec 2004, Continued in Teen Titans/Legion Special 5.00

N-MINT

❑17, Jan 2005, 1: Joker's Daughter, Includes Heroscape #2: Trapped behind Enemy Minds comic insert; Includes Heroscape #2: Trapped behind Enemy Minds comic insert 4.00
❑18, Feb 2005 .... 2.50
❑19, Mar 2005 .... 2.50
❑20, Apr 2005 .... 4.00
❑21, May 2005; Identity Crisis fall-out ... 2.50
❑22, Jun 2005; 1: Hawk III (Holly Granger); Identity Crisis fall-out; Includes Advent Rising #1 mini-comic insert 2.50
❑23, Jun 2005; Identity Crisis fall-out; Includes Heroscape #3: The New Recruit comic insert 2.50
❑24, Jul 2005; Crossover with Outsiders #24-25; Continued in Outsiders #24 .. 2.50
❑25, Aug 2005; Continued in Outsiders #25 .... 2.50
❑26, Sep 2005; Return of Omen 2.50
❑27, Oct 2005; Bionicle Metro Nui Battle For Metro Nui, Part 1 Reign of Darkness insert 2.50
❑28, Nov 2005 .... 2.50
❑29, Jan 2006 .... 2.50
❑30, Feb 2006, V: Dead Titans 2.50
❑31, Mar 2006, O: Kid Eternity 2.50
❑32, Apr 2006, Infinite Crisis crossover 2.50
❑33, May 2006, Infinite Crisis crossover; Continued in Infinite Crisis #6 .... 2.50
❑34, Jun 2006, One Year Later; Robin in new costume; Wonder Girl in new costume; Ravager and Kid Devil join team 2.50
❑35, Jul 2006, One Year Later 2.50
❑36, Aug 2006, One Year Later 2.99
❑37, Sep 2006, Cover by Daniels 2.99
❑38, Nov 2006 .... 2.99
❑39, Dec 2006 .... 2.99
❑40, Jan 2007 .... 2.99
❑41, Feb 2007, 1: Sara Hunter; Includes 3-D Heroscape glasses; Includes Teen Titans: Sparktop mini-comic 2.99
❑42 .... 2.99
❑43 .... 2.99
❑44 .... 2.99
❑45 .... 2.99
❑46 .... 2.99
❑47 .... 2.99
❑48 .... 2.99
❑49 .... 2.99
❑50 .... 2.99
❑51 .... 2.99
❑52 .... 2.99
❑53 .... 2.99
❑54 .... 2.99
❑55 .... 2.99
❑56 .... 2.99
❑57 .... 2.99
❑58 .... 2.99
❑59 .... 2.99
❑60 .... 2.99
❑61 .... 2.99
❑62 .... 2.99
❑63 .... 2.99
❑64 .... 2.99
❑65 .... 2.99
❑66 .... 2.99

Other grades: Multiply price above by 5/6 for VF/NM • 2/3 for VERY FINE • 1/3 for FINE • 1/5 for VERY GOOD • 1/8 for GOOD

- ❑67 2.99
- ❑68 2.99
- ❑69 2.99
- ❑70 2.99
- ❑71 2.99
- ❑72 2.99
- ❑Ann 1, May 2006 12.00

Teen Titans Go!
DC

- ❑1, Jan 2004 2.25
- ❑2, Feb 2004 2.25
- ❑3, Mar 2004 2.25
- ❑4, Apr 2004 2.25
- ❑5, May 2004 2.25
- ❑6, Jun 2004 2.25
- ❑7, Jul 2004 2.25
- ❑8, Aug 2004 2.25
- ❑9, Sep 2004 2.25
- ❑10, Oct 2004 2.25
- ❑11, Nov 2004 2.25
- ❑12, Dec 2004, Includes 2 Weird n' Wild Creatures collectible cards; Includes HeroScape insert 2.25
- ❑13, Jan 2005, Giant-Size; Captain Marvel back-up; 48 pages 2.95
- ❑14, Feb 2005 2.95
- ❑15, Mar 2005 2.25
- ❑16, Apr 2005 2.25
- ❑17, May 2005 2.25
- ❑18, Jun 2005; Includes HeroScape #3 insert 2.25
- ❑19, Jul 2005 2.25
- ❑20, Aug 2005 2.25
- ❑21, Sep 2005 2.25
- ❑22, Oct 2005; Includes Bionicle preview insert 2.25
- ❑23, Nov 2005 2.25
- ❑24, Dec 2005; Includes Bionicle insert 2.25
- ❑25, Jan 2006, Includes HeroScape insert #4 2.25
- ❑26, Feb 2006 2.25
- ❑27, Mar 2006 2.25
- ❑28, May 2006 2.25
- ❑30, Jul 2006 2.25
- ❑31, Aug 2006 2.25
- ❑32, Sep 2006 2.25
- ❑33, Oct 2006, Includes HeroScape insert 2.25
- ❑34, Nov 2006 2.25
- ❑35, Dec 2006 2.25
- ❑36, Jan 2007, Introducing Wonder Girl 2.25
- ❑37, Feb 2007, Includes 3-D Heroscape glasses; Includes Teen Titans: Sparktop mini-comic 2.25
- ❑38, Mar 2007 2.25

Teen Titans/Legion Special
DC

- ❑1, Nov 2004, 1: The Legion of Super-Heroes (5th Series) 4.00

Teen Titans/Outsiders Secret Files
DC

- ❑1, Dec 2003 5.95

Teen Titans/Outsiders Secret Files 2005
DC

- ❑1 2005 4.99

Teen Titans Spotlight
DC

- ❑1, Aug 1986; GP (c); Starfire 1.25
- ❑2, Sep 1986; Starfire 1.25
- ❑3, Oct 1986; RA (a); Jericho 1.25
- ❑4, Nov 1986; RA (a); Jericho 1.25
- ❑5, Dec 1986; RA (a); Jericho 1.25
- ❑6, Jan 1987; KN (c); RA (a); Jericho 1.00
- ❑7, Feb 1987; BG (a); Hawk 1.00
- ❑8, Mar 1987; BG (a); Hawk 1.00
- ❑9, Apr 1987; A: Robotman. Changeling 1.00
- ❑10, May 1987; BSz (c); EL (a); Aqualad 1.00
- ❑11, Jun 1987; JO (c); JO (a); Brotherhood of Evil 1.00
- ❑12, Jul 1987; Wonder Girl 1.00
- ❑13, Aug 1987; A: Two-Face. Cyborg; O: Two-Face 1.00
- ❑14, Sep 1987; Nightwing, Batman 1.00
- ❑15, Oct 1987; EL (c); EL (a); A: Komand'r. A: Ryand'r. Omega Men 1.00
- ❑16, Nov 1987; Thunder & Lightning 1.00
- ❑17, Dec 1987; DH (a); 1: Magenta 1.00
- ❑18, Jan 1988; Millennium; Aqualad 1.00
- ❑19, Feb 1988; GP (c); Millennium; Starfire 1.00
- ❑20, Mar 1988; Cyborg; Changeling 1.00
- ❑21, Apr 1988; DS (c); ME (w); DS (a); original Titans 1.00

Tekken Forever
Image

- ❑1/A, Dec 2001 2.95
- ❑1/B, Dec 2001 2.95

Tek Knights
Artline

- ❑1, b&w 2.95

Tekno*Comix Handbook
Tekno

- ❑1, May 1996, information on various Tekno characters 3.95

Teknophage
Tekno

- ❑1, Aug 1995 1.95
- ❑1/Variant, Jul 1995, Steel Edition; enhanced cover 3.00
- ❑2, Sep 1995 1.95
- ❑3, Oct 1995, BT (c); BT (a) 1.95
- ❑4, Nov 1995 1.95
- ❑5, Dec 1995 1.95
- ❑6, Dec 1995 1.95
- ❑7, Jan 1996 2.25
- ❑8, Feb 1996 2.25
- ❑9, Feb 1996 2.25
- ❑10, Mar 1996, Final Issue 2.25

Teknophage vs. Zeerus
Big

- ❑1, Jul 1996, One-shot 3.25

TEKQ
Gauntlet

- ❑1, b&w 2.95
- ❑2, b&w 2.95
- ❑3, b&w 2.95
- ❑4, b&w 2.95

Tekworld
Marvel / Epic

- ❑1, Sep 1992 2.50
- ❑2, Oct 1992 2.00
- ❑3, Nov 1992 2.00
- ❑4, Dec 1992 2.00
- ❑5, Jan 1993 2.00
- ❑6, Feb 1993 2.00
- ❑7, Mar 1993 2.00
- ❑8, Apr 1993 2.00
- ❑9, May 1993 2.00
- ❑10, Jun 1993 2.00
- ❑11, Jul 1993 1.75
- ❑12, Aug 1993 1.75
- ❑13, Sep 1993 1.75
- ❑14, Oct 1993; A: Jake Cardigan. Begins adaptation of TekLords 1.75
- ❑15, Nov 1993 1.75
- ❑16, Dec 1993 1.75
- ❑17, Jan 1994 1.75
- ❑18, Feb 1994 1.75
- ❑19, Mar 1994 1.75
- ❑20, Apr 1994 1.75
- ❑21, May 1994 1.75
- ❑22, Jun 1994 1.75
- ❑23, Jul 1994 1.75
- ❑24, Aug 1994; Partial photo cover 1.75

Telepathic Wanderers
Tokyopop

- ❑1, Nov 2005 9.99

Tellos
Image

- ❑1, May 1999 2.50
- ❑2, Jun 1999 2.50
- ❑3, Jul 1999 2.50
- ❑4, Oct 1999 2.50
- ❑4/A, Oct 1999; alternate cover w/moon in background 2.50
- ❑4/B, Oct 1999; alternate cover w/skeletons in bottom left 4.00
- ❑5, Dec 1999 2.50
- ❑6, Feb 2000 2.50
- ❑7, Apr 2000 2.50
- ❑8, Aug 2000 2.50
- ❑9, Sep 2000 2.50
- ❑10, Nov 2000 2.50
- ❑Ashcan 1; Dynamic Forces preview 2.00

Tellos: Maiden Voyage
Image

- ❑1, Mar 2001, Man atop demons on cover 5.95

Tellos: Sons & Moons
Image

- ❑1, Dec 2002, Man atop demons on cover 5.95

Tellos: The Last Heist
Image

- ❑1, Jun 2001, Man atop demons on cover 5.95

Tell Tale Heart and Other Stories
Fantagraphics

- ❑1, b&w 2.50

Telluria
Zub

- ❑1 2.50
- ❑2 2.50
- ❑3 2.50

Tempest
DC

- ❑1, Nov 1996, Tula returns 1.75
- ❑2, Dec 1996 1.75
- ❑3, Jan 1997, Aqualad's true origin revealed 1.75
- ❑4, Feb 1997 1.75

Template
Head

- ❑0; flip-book with Max Damage #0 2.95
- ❑1, Dec 1995, b&w 2.50
- ❑2, Feb 1996, b&w 2.50
- ❑3, Apr 1996, b&w 2.50
- ❑4, Jun 1996, b&w 2.50
- ❑5, Aug 1996, b&w 2.50
- ❑6, Nov 1996, b&w 2.50
- ❑7, Jul 1997, b&w 2.50
- ❑Special 1, Feb 1997, b&w 2.95
- ❑Spec 1/Ashcan, Feb 1997; Ashcan preview of special #1 2.00
- ❑Special 1/Varia, Feb 1997; alternate cover 5.90

Temple Snare
Mu

- ❑1, b&w; NN 2.25

Temptress: The Blood of Eve
Caliber

- ❑1 2.95

Tempus Fugitive
DC

- ❑1, ca. 1990; Wraparound cover 4.95
- ❑2, ca. 1990 4.95
- ❑3, ca. 1990 4.95
- ❑4, ca. 1990 4.95

Tenchi Muyo!
Pioneer

- ❑1, Mar 1997 2.95
- ❑2, Mar 1997 2.95
- ❑3, May 1997 2.95
- ❑4, Jul 1997 2.95
- ❑5, Aug 1997 2.95
- ❑6 2.95

Tender Love Stories
Skywald

- ❑1, Feb 1971 15.00
- ❑2, Apr 1971 10.00
- ❑3, Jun 1971 10.00
- ❑4, Jul 1971 10.00

Tenth
Image

- ❑0, Aug 1997; American Entertainment exclusive 3.00
- ❑½, Aug 1997; Wizard promotional edition with certificate of authenticity; Wizard promotional edition from Wizard #86 with certificate of authenticity 5.00
- ❑1, Jan 1997; cover says Mar, indicia says Jan 3.00
- ❑1/A, Jan 1997; American Entertainment exclusive cover 4.00
- ❑2, Feb 1997; cover says Apr, indicia says Feb 2.50
- ❑3, May 1997 2.50
- ❑4, Jun 1997 2.50

Toxic Crusaders

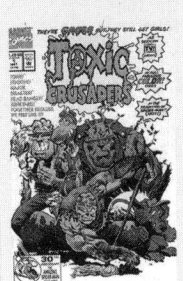

Comics with the Troma touch
©Marvel

Transformers

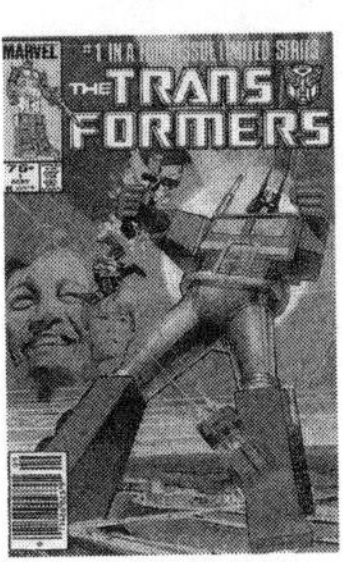

Series got hot years after it was canceled
©Marvel

Transformers: Armada

Spinoff series with the evolving robots
©Dreamwave

Transformers: Generation 1

Dreamwave captures wave of nostalgia
©Dreamwave

Transmetropolitan

Cyber-nightmare world of drugs and aliens
©DC

N-MINT

Tenth
Image

❑0, Aug 1997; O: The Tenth 3.00
❑0/A, Aug 1997; O: The Tenth; Autographed by Tony Daniel 8.00
❑0/AmEnt, Aug 1997; O: The Tenth. American Entertainment exclusive 4.00
❑1, Sep 1997 .... 3.00
❑1/AmEnt, Sep 1997; American Entertainment exclusive cover (logo at bottom right) 4.00
❑2, Oct 1997 .... 3.00
❑3, Nov 1997 .... 2.50
❑3/A, Nov 1997; Alternate "Adrenalyn" cover 3.00
❑3/B, Nov 1997; Wizard "Certified Authentic" limited edition; Autographed by Tony Daniel 8.00
❑4, Dec 1997 .... 2.50
❑5, Jan 1998 .... 2.50
❑6, Feb 1998 .... 2.50
❑7, Mar 1998 .... 2.50
❑8, Apr 1998 .... 2.50
❑9, Jun 1998 .... 2.50
❑10, Jul 1998 .... 2.50
❑10/A, Jul 1998; alternate cover (logo on right) 2.50
❑11, Aug 1998 .... 2.50
❑11/A, Aug 1998; alternate cover (white background) 2.50
❑12, Oct 1998 .... 2.50
❑13, Nov 1998 .... 2.50
❑14, Jan 1999 .... 2.50
❑14/A, Jan 1999; alternate cover (solo face) 2.50

Tenth
Image

❑1, Feb 1999 .... 2.95
❑1/A, Feb 1999; alternate cover 2.95
❑1/B, Feb 1999; DFE chromium edition; alternate cover 10.00
❑2, Apr 1999 .... 2.50
❑3, May 1999 .... 2.50
❑4, Jun 1999 .... 2.50

Tenth
Image

❑1, Sep 1999 .... 2.50
❑1/A, Sep 1999, Girl wearing shirt and panties on cover 6.00
❑1/B, Sep 1999, Another Universe exclusive cover 3.00
❑2, Oct 1999 .... 2.50
❑3, Nov 1999 .... 2.50
❑4, Dec 1999 .... 2.50

Tenth Configuration
Image

❑1, Aug 1998 .... 2.50

10th Muse
Image

❑1, Nov 2000, Rena Mero photo cover; Black background with orange border 2.95
❑2/A, Jan 2001, Character leaping from right on cover 2.95
❑2/B, Jan 2001, Character leaping from left on cover 2.95
❑2/C, Jan 2001, Photo cover 2.95
❑3/A, Mar 2001, Drawn cover with woman summoning lightning 2.95
❑3/B, Mar 2001, Cover with green border 2.95
❑3/C, Mar 2001, Drawn cover with woman leaping forward 2.95
❑3/D, Mar 2001, Wraparound Tower Records cover with red border 2.95
❑4, Mar 2001 .... 2.95
❑4/A, Mar 2001, Drawn cover 2.95
❑4/B, Mar 2001, Photo cover 2.95
❑5, Jul 2001, Cover by Ken Lashley; 10th Muse leaping in foreground, Savage Dragon in background 2.95
❑6, Sep 2001 .... 2.95
❑7, Oct 2001, Bonus Atlas story 2.95
❑8/A, Nov 2001, Drawn cover 2.95
❑8/B, Nov 2001, Photo cover 2.95
❑9/A, Dec 2001, Drawn cover 2.95
❑9/B, Dec 2001, Photo cover; Indicia lists as #8; Cover date says Jan, indicia says Dec 2.95

10th Muse
Alias

❑1, Feb 2005 .... 4.00
❑1/B cover, Feb 2005 .... 5.00
❑1/C cover, Feb 2005 .... 4.00
❑1/D cover, Feb 2005 .... 5.00
❑1/Photo foil, Feb 2005 .... 6.00
❑2 2005 .... 2.99
❑2/B cover 2005 .... 4.00
❑2/Photo foil 2005 .... 4.99
❑3, Jul 2005 .... 2.99
❑3/B cover, Jul 2005 .... 4.00
❑3/C cover, Jul 2005 .... 2.99
❑4, Sep 2005 .... 4.00
❑5, Nov 2005 .... 2.99
❑5/Special, Nov 2005 .... 19.99
❑6, Dec 2005 .... 2.99
❑8, Jan 2006 .... 2.99

Tenth: Resurrected
Dark Horse

❑1/A, Jul 2001; Lady standing in front of glowing skulls in background on cover 2.99
❑1/B, Jul 2001; Hulking figure on cover. 2.99
❑2, Aug 2001 .... 2.99
❑3, Nov 2001 .... 2.99
❑4, Feb 2002 .... 2.99

Ten Years of Love & Rockets
Fantagraphics

❑1, Sep 1992, b&w; NN 1.50

Terminal City
DC / Vertigo

❑1, Jul 1996 .... 2.50
❑1/Autographed, Jul 1996, Limited to 75 copies 5.00
❑2, Aug 1996 .... 2.50
❑3, Sep 1996 .... 2.50
❑4, Oct 1996 .... 2.50
❑5, Nov 1996 .... 2.50
❑6, Dec 1996 .... 2.50
❑7, Jan 1997 .... 2.50
❑8, Feb 1997 .... 2.50
❑9, Mar 1997, Final Issue 2.50

Terminal City: Aerial Graffiti
DC / Vertigo

❑1, Nov 1997 .... 2.50
❑2, Dec 1997 .... 2.50
❑3, Jan 1998 .... 2.50
❑4, Feb 1998 .... 2.50
❑5, Mar 1998 .... 2.50

Terminal Point
Dark Horse

❑1, Feb 1993, b&w 2.50
❑2, Mar 1993, b&w 2.50
❑3, Apr 1993, b&w 2.50

Terminator
Now

❑1, Sep 1988; movie tie-in 2.00
❑2, Oct 1988 .... 1.75
❑3, Nov 1988 .... 1.75
❑4, Jan 1989 .... 1.75
❑5, Feb 1989 .... 1.75
❑6, Mar 1989 .... 1.75
❑7, Apr 1989 .... 1.75
❑8, May 1989; Comics Code 1.75
❑9, Jun 1989; Comics Code 1.75
❑10, Jul 1989; PG (c); Comics Code 1.75
❑11, Aug 1989; Comics Code 1.75
❑12, Sep 1989; Comics Code 1.75
❑13, Oct 1989; Comics Code 1.75
❑14, Nov 1989; Comics Code 1.75
❑15, Dec 1989; Comics Code 1.75
❑16, Jan 1990; Comics Code 1.75
❑17, Feb 1990; Comics Code 1.75

Terminator
Dark Horse

❑1, Aug 1990 .... 3.00
❑2, Sep 1990 .... 3.00
❑3, Oct 1990 .... 3.00
❑4, Nov 1990 .... 3.00

Terminator
Dark Horse

❑1, ca. 1991; leads into 1998 series 2.95

Terminator
Dark Horse

❑1, Sep 1998; no month of publication 2.95
❑2, Oct 1998 .... 2.95
❑3, Nov 1998 .... 2.95
❑4, Dec 1998 .... 2.95

Terminator
Trident

❑1 .... 3.00
❑2 .... 3.00
❑3 .... 3.00
❑4 .... 3.00

Terminator 2: Judgment Day
Marvel

❑1, Sep 1991, KJ (a); Movie adaptation 2.00
❑2, Sep 1991, KJ (a); Movie adaptation 2.00
❑3, Oct 1991, KJ (a); Movie adaptation 2.00

Terminator 2: Judgment Day
Marvel

❑1, Sep 1991, b&w; magazine; NN; Movie adaptation 3.00

Terminator 3
Beckett

- ❑1, Jun 2003 ... 5.95
- ❑2, Jul 2003 ... 5.95
- ❑3, Aug 2003 ... 5.95
- ❑4, Sep 2003 ... 5.95
- ❑5, Nov 2003 ... 5.95
- ❑6, Dec 2003 ... 5.95

Terminator: All My Futures Past
Now

- ❑1, Aug 1990 ... 2.50
- ❑2, Sep 1990 ... 2.50

Terminator: Endgame
Dark Horse

- ❑1, Sep 1992 ... 2.50
- ❑2, Oct 1992 ... 2.50
- ❑3, Oct 1992 ... 2.50

Terminator: Hunters and Killers
Dark Horse

- ❑1, Mar 1992 ... 2.50
- ❑2, Apr 1992 ... 2.50
- ❑3, May 1992 ... 2.50

Terminator: One Shot
Dark Horse

- ❑1, Jul 1991; prestige format; pop-up ... 5.95

Terminator: Secondary Objectives
Dark Horse

- ❑1, Jul 1991 ... 2.50
- ❑2, Aug 1991 ... 2.50
- ❑3, Sep 1991 ... 2.50
- ❑4, Oct 1991 ... 2.50

Terminator: The Burning Earth
Now

- ❑1, Mar 1990; ARo (a); 1st comics work by Alex Ross ... 7.50
- ❑2, Apr 1990; ARo (a); Alex Ross ... 5.00
- ❑3, May 1990; ARo (a); Alex Ross ... 5.00
- ❑4, Jun 1990; ARo (a); Alex Ross ... 6.00
- ❑5, Jul 1990; ARo (a); Alex Ross ... 6.00

Terminator: The Dark Years
Dark Horse

- ❑1, Sep 1999 ... 2.95
- ❑2, Oct 1999 ... 2.95
- ❑3, Nov 1999 ... 2.95
- ❑4, Dec 1999 ... 2.95

Terminator: The Enemy Within
Dark Horse

- ❑1, Nov 1991 ... 2.50
- ❑2, Dec 1991 ... 2.50
- ❑3, Jan 1992 ... 2.50
- ❑4, Feb 1992 ... 2.50

Terraformers
Wonder Color

- ❑1, Apr 1987 ... 1.95
- ❑2 1987 ... 1.95

Terranauts
Fantasy General

- ❑1, ca. 1986 ... 1.75

Terra Obscura
DC / America's Best Comics

- ❑1, Aug 2003 ... 2.95
- ❑2, Sep 2003 ... 2.95
- ❑3, Oct 2003 ... 2.95
- ❑4, Dec 2003 ... 2.95
- ❑5, Jan 2004 ... 2.95
- ❑6, Feb 2004 ... 3.95

Terra Obscura, Book 2
DC / America's Best Comics

- ❑1, Oct 2004 ... 2.95
- ❑2, Nov 2004 ... 2.95
- ❑3, Dec 2004 ... 2.95
- ❑4, Jan 2005 ... 2.95
- ❑5, Feb 2005 ... 2.95
- ❑6, Mar 2005 ... 2.95

Terrarists
Marvel / Epic

- ❑1, Nov 1993 ... 2.50
- ❑2, Dec 1993; Includes trading card ... 2.50
- ❑3, Jan 1994 ... 2.50
- ❑4, Feb 1994 ... 2.50

Territory
Dark Horse

- ❑1, Jan 1999 ... 2.95
- ❑2, Feb 1999 ... 2.95
- ❑3, Mar 1999 ... 2.95
- ❑4, Apr 1999 ... 2.95

Terror
Leadslinger

- ❑1, b&w ... 2.50

Terroress
Helpless Anger

- ❑1, Dec 1990, b&w; Adult ... 2.50

Terror, Inc.
Marvel

- ❑1, Jul 1992; 1: Terror ... 2.00
- ❑2, Aug 1992; 1: Hellfire ... 1.75
- ❑3, Sep 1992 ... 1.75
- ❑4, Oct 1992 ... 1.75
- ❑5, Nov 1992 ... 1.75
- ❑6, Dec 1992 A: Punisher ... 1.75
- ❑7, Jan 1993 A: Punisher ... 1.75
- ❑8, Feb 1993 ... 1.75
- ❑9, Mar 1993 A: Wolverine ... 1.75
- ❑10, Apr 1993; JKu (c); A: Wolverine. Cover by Joe Kubert ... 1.75
- ❑11, May 1993; A: Punisher. A: Silver Sable. Continued in Cage #15 ... 1.75
- ❑12, Jun 1993; Continued in Cage #16 .. 1.75
- ❑13, Jul 1993; A: Ghost Rider. Final Issue 1.75

Terror on the Planet of the Apes
Adventure

- ❑1 1991, b&w ... 2.50
- ❑2, Jul 1991, b&w ... 2.50
- ❑3, Aug 1991, b&w; reprints Planet of the Apes (Marvel) #3 ... 2.50
- ❑4, Dec 1991, b&w; reprints Planet of the Apes (Marvel) #4 ... 2.50

Terror Tales
Eternity

- ❑1, Apr 1991, b&w ... 2.50

Terry and the Pirates
Avalon

- ❑1, b&w; strip reprints ... 2.95
- ❑2 ... 2.95

Testament
DC / Vertigo

- ❑1, Feb 2006 ... 2.99
- ❑2, Mar 2006 ... 2.99
- ❑3, Apr 2006 ... 2.99
- ❑4, Jun 2006 ... 2.99
- ❑5, Jun 2006 ... 2.99
- ❑6, Aug 2006 ... 2.99
- ❑7, Sep 2006 ... 2.99
- ❑8, Sep 2006 ... 2.99
- ❑9, Oct 2006 ... 2.99
- ❑10, Nov 2006 ... 2.99
- ❑11, Dec 2006 ... 2.99
- ❑12, Jan 2007 ... 2.99
- ❑13, Mar 2007 ... 2.99
- ❑14 ... 2.99
- ❑15 ... 2.99
- ❑16 ... 2.99
- ❑17 ... 2.99
- ❑18 ... 2.99
- ❑19 ... 2.99
- ❑20 ... 2.99
- ❑21 ... 2.99
- ❑22 ... 2.99

Test Dirt
Fantagraphics

- ❑1, b&w ... 2.50

Test Drive
M.A.I.N.

- ❑1; Flip Book Previews (Side A & B) ... 3.00

Texas Chainsaw Massacre
DC

- ❑1, Jan 2007 ... 2.99
- ❑1/Variant, Jan 2007 ... 2.99
- ❑2, Mar 2007 ... 2.99

Tex Benson
3-D Zone

- ❑1; b&w (not 3-D) ... 2.50
- ❑2; b&w (not 3-D) ... 2.50

Tex Benson
Metro

- ❑1, b&w ... 2.00
- ❑2 ... 2.00
- ❑3 ... 2.00
- ❑4 ... 2.00

Teykwa
Gemstone

- ❑1, Oct 1988, b&w ... 1.75

Thacker's Revenge
Explorer

- ❑1, b&w; Archie parody ... 2.95

Thane of Bagarth
Avalon

- ❑1 ... 2.95

Thanos
Marvel

- ❑1, Dec 2003, JSn (c); JSn (w); AM, JSn (a) ... 4.00
- ❑2, Jan 2004, JSn (c); JSn (w); AM, JSn (a) ... 2.99
- ❑3, Feb 2004, JSn, (c); JSn (w); AM, JSn (a) ... 2.99
- ❑4, Mar 2004, JSn (c); JSn (w); AM, JSn (a) ... 2.99
- ❑5, Mar 2004 ... 2.99
- ❑6, Apr 2004, Last Jim Starlin issue ... 2.99
- ❑7, May 2004, AM, JSn (c); KG (w); AM (a) 2.99
- ❑8, May 2004, KG (c); KG (w); AM (a)... 2.99
- ❑9, Jun 2004, KG, KJ (c); KG (w); AM (a) 2.99
- ❑10, Jul 2004, KG, KJ (c); KG (w); AM (a) 2.99
- ❑11, Aug 2004 ... 2.99
- ❑12, Sep 2004; Final issue ... 2.99

Thanos Quest
Marvel

- ❑1, Sep 1990, acetate overlay outer cover 4.95
- ❑1/2nd, ca. 1991, acetate overlay outer cover ... 4.95
- ❑2, Oct 1990, acetate overlay outer cover 4.95
- ❑2/2nd, ca. 1991, 2nd printing ... 4.95
- ❑Special 1, ca. 1999; Collects issues #1 and #2 ... 3.99

That Chemical Reflex
CFD

- ❑1; Adult ... 2.50
- ❑2; Adult ... 2.50
- ❑3; Adult ... 2.50

THB
Horse

- ❑1, Oct 1994, b&w ... 12.00
- ❑1/2nd, b&w; reprints THB #1 with revised and additional material ... 5.50
- ❑2, ca. 1994, b&w ... 10.00
- ❑3, Jan 1995, b&w ... 8.00
- ❑4, Feb 1995, b&w ... 8.00
- ❑5, Mar 1995, b&w ... 6.00
- ❑6 1996 ... 6.00
- ❑69, Oct 1994, b&w; promo edition; no cover price ... 5.00

T.H.E. Cat
Gold Key

- ❑1, Mar 1967, Photo cover ... 12.00
- ❑2, Apr 1967, Photo cover ... 10.00
- ❑3, Jun 1967, Photo cover ... 10.00
- ❑4, Oct 1967, Photo cover ... 10.00

TheComicStore.com Presents
TheComicStore.com

- ❑1 ... 1.00

There's a Madman in My Mirror
Bench

- ❑1, Mar 1999; cardstock cover ... 3.50

Thespian
Dark Moon

- ❑1, Apr 1995 ... 2.50

They Call Me...The Skul
Virtual

- ❑1, May 1996; digest; Only issue published ... 2.50
- ❑1/A, Oct 1996; digest ... 3.99
- ❑2, Nov 1996; Indicia says The Skul Vol. 1 No. 2 ... 2.50

They Came from the 50S
Eternity

- ❑1, b&w; Reprints ... 9.95

Treehouse of Horror

Annual comics tradition mirrors TV tradition

©Bongo

Tribe

Second and third issue came from Axis Comics

©Image

Trinity Angels

Nicely written characters and stylish art

©Acclaim

Triumph

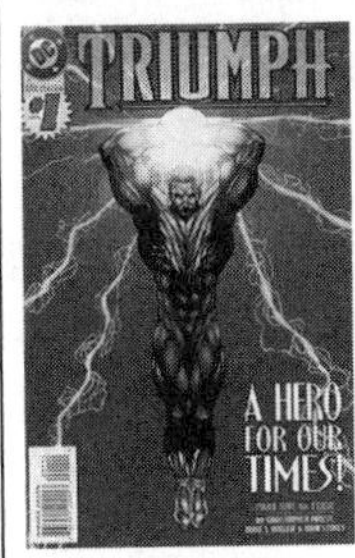

Character's father drove a getaway car

©DC

Troublemakers

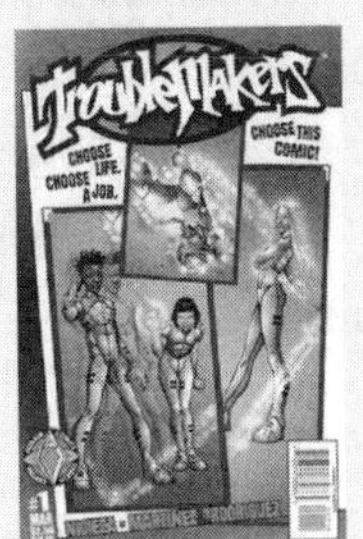

Characters more mellow than angst-ridden

©Acclaim

N-MINT

They Were 11
Viz

❑1, b&w ... 2.75
❑2, b&w ... 2.75
❑3, b&w ... 2.75
❑4, b&w ... 2.75

They Were Chosen to be the Survivors
Spectrum

❑1, Jun 1983, b&w ... 2.00
❑2, Sep 1983 ... 2.00
❑3, Dec 1983 ... 2.00
❑4, Mar 1984; Last issue; Story continued in Survivors, The (Prelude) #1 ... 2.00

Thief
Penguin Palace

❑1, Jul 1995, b&w ... 2.50

Thief of Sherwood
A-Plus

❑1, b&w; Reprints ... 2.25

Thieves
Silverwolf

❑1, Feb 1986, b&w ... 1.50

Thieves & Kings
I Box

❑1, Sep 1994 ... 4.00
❑1/2nd; 2nd printing ... 2.50
❑2, Nov 1994 ... 3.00
❑2/2nd; 2nd printing ... 2.50
❑3, Jan 1995 ... 3.00
❑3/2nd; 2nd printing ... 2.35
❑4, Mar 1995 ... 3.00
❑5, May 1995 ... 3.00
❑6, Jul 1995 ... 2.75
❑7, Sep 1995 ... 2.75
❑8, Nov 1995 ... 2.75
❑9, Jan 1996 ... 2.75
❑10, Mar 1996 ... 2.75
❑11, May 1996 ... 2.50
❑12, Jul 1996 ... 2.50
❑13, Sep 1996 ... 2.50
❑14, Nov 1996 ... 2.50
❑15, Jan 1997 ... 2.50
❑16, Mar 1997 ... 2.50
❑17, May 1997 ... 2.50
❑18, ca. 1997 ... 2.50
❑19, ca. 1997 ... 2.50
❑20, Nov 1997 ... 2.50
❑21, ca. 1998 ... 2.35
❑22, May 1998 ... 2.35
❑23, Jul 1998 ... 2.35
❑24, Sep 1998 ... 2.35
❑25, Nov 1998 ... 2.50
❑26, Jan 1999 ... 2.50
❑27, Mar 1999 ... 2.50
❑28, Jul 1999 ... 2.50
❑29, Oct 1999 ... 2.50
❑30, Jan 2000 ... 2.50
❑31, Mar 2000 ... 2.50
❑32, May 2000 ... 2.50
❑33, Aug 2000 ... 2.50
❑34, Nov 2000 ... 2.50
❑35, Feb 2001 ... 2.50
❑36, Jul 2001 ... 2.50

N-MINT

Thing: Freakshow
Marvel

❑1, Aug 2002 ... 2.99
❑2, Sep 2002 ... 2.99
❑3, Oct 2002; V: Paibok the Power-Skrull ... 2.99
❑4, Nov 2002 ... 2.99

Thing from Another World
Dark Horse

❑1, ca. 1993; cardstock cover ... 2.95
❑2, ca. 1993; cardstock cover ... 2.95
❑3 ... 2.99
❑4 ... 2.99

Thing From Another World: Climate of Fear
Dark Horse

❑1, ca. 1994 ... 2.50
❑2, ca. 1994 ... 2.50
❑3, ca. 1994 ... 2.50
❑4, ca. 1994 ... 2.50

Thing From Another World: Eternal Vows
Dark Horse

❑1, Dec 1993 ... 2.50
❑2, Jan 1994 ... 2.50
❑3, Feb 1994 ... 2.50
❑4, Mar 1994 ... 2.50

Thing
Marvel

❑1, Jan 2006 ... 2.99
❑2, Feb 2006 ... 2.99
❑3, Mar 2006 ... 2.99
❑4, May 2006 ... 2.99
❑5, Jun 2006 ... 2.99
❑6, Jul 2006 ... 2.99
❑7, Aug 2006 ... 2.99
❑8, Sep 2006 ... 2.99

Thing/She-Hulk: The Long Night
Marvel

❑1, May 2002, Man atop demons on cover ... 2.99

Thing
Marvel

❑1, Jul 1983, JBy (c); JBy (w); JBy (a); O: The Thing; O: Fantastic Four ... 6.00
❑2, Aug 1983, JBy (w); JBy (a); O: The Thing ... 1.50
❑3, Sep 1983, JBy (w); A: Inhumans ... 1.50
❑4, Oct 1983, BA (c); JBy (w); BA (a); A: Inhumans ... 1.50
❑5, Nov 1983, JBy (w); JBy (a); A: She-Hulk. A: Spider-Man ... 1.50
❑6, Dec 1983, BA (c); JBy (w); BA (a); V: Puppet Master. all-black issue ... 1.50
❑7, Jan 1984, JBy, BA (c); JBy (w); JBy, BA (a); Asst. Editor Month ... 1.50
❑8, Feb 1984, JBy (w) ... 1.50
❑9, Mar 1984, JBy (w) ... 1.50
❑10, Apr 1984, JBy (w); Secret Wars ... 1.50
❑11, May 1984, JBy (w); Secret Wars aftermath ... 1.25
❑12, Jun 1984, JBy (w) ... 1.25
❑13, Jul 1984, JBy (w) ... 1.25
❑14, Aug 1984 ... 2.00
❑15, Sep 1984, Beau Smith LOC ... 1.25
❑16, Oct 1984 ... 1.25

N-MINT

❑17, Nov 1984 ... 1.25
❑18, Dec 1984 ... 1.25
❑19, Jan 1985, JBy (w); Continued in Fantastic Four #274 ... 1.25
❑20, Feb 1985, JBy (w); Beau Smith LOC ... 1.25
❑21, Mar 1985, JBy (w) ... 1.25
❑22, Apr 1985, returns to Earth ... 1.25
❑23, May 1985, quits Fantastic Four ... 1.25
❑24, Jun 1985, D: Miracle Man (Marvel). V: Rhino ... 1.25
❑25, Jul 1985 ... 1.25
❑26, Aug 1985, V: Taskmaster ... 1.25
❑27, Sep 1985 ... 1.25
❑28, Oct 1985, 1: Demolition Dunphy (later becomes D-Man) ... 1.25
❑29, Nov 1985, Beau Smith LOC ... 1.25
❑30, Dec 1985, Secret Wars II ... 1.25
❑31, Jan 1986 ... 1.25
❑32, Feb 1986 ... 1.25
❑33, Mar 1986; D: Titania ... 1.25
❑34, Apr 1986; D: The Sphinx ... 1.25
❑35, May 1986; 1&O: Ms. Marvel II; Sharon Ventura becomes Ms. Marvel II ... 1.25
❑36, Jun 1986; Final Issue; Continued in West Coast Avengers #10 ... 1.25

3rd Degree
NBM

❑1 ... 2.95

Third Eye
Sirius

❑1 1998; prestige format; pin-ups ... 4.95
❑2, Dec 1998; pin-ups and stories; cardstock cover ... 4.95

Third World War
Fleetway-Quality

❑1 ... 2.50
❑2 ... 2.50
❑3 ... 2.50
❑4 ... 2.50
❑5 ... 2.50
❑6 ... 2.50

13: Assassin Comics Module
TSR

❑1 ... 2.00
❑2 ... 2.00
❑3 ... 2.00
❑4 ... 2.00
❑5 ... 2.00
❑6 ... 2.00
❑7 ... 2.00
❑8 ... 2.00

13 Days of Christmas: A Tale of the Lost Lunar Bestiary
Sirius

❑1, b&w; wraparound cover ... 2.95

Thirteen O'Clock
Dark Horse

❑1, b&w; NN ... 2.95

Thirteen Something!
Global

❑1 ... 1.95

N-MINT

13th Son: Worse Thing Waiting
Dark Horse

❑1, Oct 2005 2.99
❑2, Nov 2005 2.99
❑3, Dec 2005 2.99
❑4, Apr 2006 2.99

30 Days of Night
Idea & Design Works

❑1, Jun 2002 55.00
❑1/2nd, Aug 2002; 2nd printing 7.00
❑2, Aug 2002 25.00
❑3, Oct 2002 10.00
❑Ann 2004, Feb 2004 4.99

30 Days of Night: Bloodsucker Tales
Idea & Design Works

❑1, ca. 2004 3.99
❑2, ca. 2004 3.99
❑3, ca. 2004 3.99
❑4, ca. 2004 3.99
❑5, ca. 2005 3.99
❑6, ca. 2005 3.99
❑7, ca. 2005 3.99

30 Days of Night: Dead Space
Idea & Design Works

❑1, Feb 2006 3.99
❑2, Mar 2006 3.99
❑3, Apr 2006 3.99

30 Days of Night: Return to Barrow
Idea & Design Works

❑1, ca. 2004; Foil cover 12.00
❑1/2nd, Jun 2004 3.99
❑2, ca. 2004 8.00
❑3, ca. 2004 5.00
❑4, Jun 2004 3.99
❑5, Jul 2004 3.99
❑6, Aug 2004 3.99

Dark Days: A 30 Days of Night Sequel
Idea & Design Works

❑1, ca. 2003 8.00
❑2, ca. 2003 5.00
❑3, ca. 2003 4.00
❑4, ca. 2003 4.00
❑5, ca. 2003 4.00
❑6, ca. 2004 4.00

30 Days of Night: Spreading the Disease
Idea & Design Works

❑1, Jan 2007 3.99

39 Screams
Thunder Baas

❑1, ca. 1986 2.00
❑2, ca. 1986 2.00
❑3, ca. 1986 2.00
❑4, ca. 1986 2.00
❑5, ca. 1987 2.00
❑6, ca. 1987 2.00

32 Pages
Sirius

❑1, Jan 2001 2.95

This Is Heat
Aeon

❑1, b&w; NN 2.50

This Is Not an Exit
Draculina

❑1; Adult 2.95
❑2; Adult 2.95

This Is Sick!
Silver Skull

❑1, b&w; Zen; foil cover 2.95
❑2 2.95

Thor
Marvel

❑126, Mar 1966, JK (c); SL (w); JK (a); V: Hercules. Series continued from Journey into Mystery (Vol. 1) #125 125.00
❑127, Apr 1966, JK (c); SL (w); JK (a); 1: Volla. 1: Midgard Serpent. 1: Pluto 45.00
❑128, May 1966, JK (c); SL (w); JK (a) 45.00
❑129, Jun 1966, JK (c); SL (w); JK (a); 1: Ares. 1: Hela. 1: Tana Nile (disguised); 1: Harokin 45.00
❑130, Jul 1966, JK (c); SL (w); JK (a); 1: Tana Nile (in real form) 45.00

N-MINT

❑131, Aug 1966, JK (c); SL (w); JK (a); 1: Rigellian Colonizers; Tales of Asgard backup story 45.00
❑132, Sep 1966, JK (c); SL (w); JK (a); 1: Recorder. 1: Ego. V: Ego, the Living Planet 45.00
❑133, Oct 1966, JK (c); SL (w); JK (a) 45.00
❑134, Nov 1966, JK (c); SL (w); JK (a); 1: High Evolutionary 45.00
❑135, Dec 1966, JK (c); SL (w); JK (a); O: High Evolutionary 45.00
❑136, Jan 1967, JK (c); SL (w); JK (a); 1: Sif. Jane Foster denied immortality 45.00
❑137, Feb 1967, JK (c); SL (w); JK (a); 1: Ulik; 1: Mogul; 1: Saguta; D: Saguta 45.00
❑138, Mar 1967, JK (c); SL (w); JK (a) 45.00
❑139, Apr 1967, JK (c); SL (w); JK (a) 45.00
❑140, May 1967, JK (c); SL (w); JK (a); 1: Growing Man 45.00
❑141, Jun 1967, JK (c); SL (w); JK (a); 1: Replicus 32.00
❑142, Jul 1967, JK (c); SL (w); JK (a); Tales of Asgard backup story 32.00
❑143, Aug 1967, JK (c); SL (w); BEv, JK (a); 1: Forsung; 1: Magnir; 1: Brona; 1: The Spirit of the Living Talisman; 1: Mutaurus 32.00
❑144, Sep 1967, JK (c); SL (w); JK (a) 32.00
❑145, Oct 1967, JK (c); SL (w); JK (a); Tales of Asgard back-up story 32.00
❑146, Oct 1967, JK (c); SL (w); JK (a); O: Inhumans. A: Ringmaster. A: Circus of Crime. O: Inhumans backup story 32.00
❑147, Dec 1967, JK (c); SL (w); JK (a); O: Inhumans. O: Inhumans backup story 32.00
❑148, Jan 1968, JK (c); SL (w); JK (a); 1&O: The Wrecker III. O: Black Bolt 32.00
❑149, Feb 1968, JK (c); SL (w); JK (a); O: Maximus. O: Medusa. O: Black Bolt 32.00
❑150, Mar 1968, JK (c); SL (w); JK (a); O: Inhumans backup story 32.00
❑151, Apr 1968, JK (c); SL (w); JK (a); O: Inhumans backup story 32.00
❑152, May 1968, JK (c); SL (w); JK (a); O: Inhumans backup story 32.00
❑153, Jun 1968, JK (c); SL (w); JK (a) 32.00
❑154, Jul 1968, JK (c); SL (w); JK (a); V: Mangog. 1: Mangog 32.00
❑155, Aug 1968, JK (c); SL (w); JK (a) 32.00
❑156, Sep 1968, JK (c); SL (w); JK (a) 32.00
❑157, Oct 1968, JK (c); SL (w); JK (a); V: Mangog 32.00
❑158, Nov 1968, JK (c); SL (w); JK (a); O: Don Blake. O: Thor. Reprints 1: Thor in Journey into Mystery #83 (Aug 1962) 32.00
❑159, Dec 1968, JK (c); SL (w); JK (a); 1: Gondolff 32.00
❑160, Jan 1969, JK (c); SL (w); JK (a); V: Galactus 32.00
❑161, Feb 1969, JK (c); SL (w); JK (a); V: Galactus 25.00
❑162, Mar 1969, JK (c); SL (w); JK (a); O: Galactus 25.00
❑163, Apr 1969, JK (c); SL (w); JK (a) 25.00
❑164, May 1969, JK (c); SL (w); JK (a) 25.00
❑165, Jun 1969, JK (c); SL (w); JK (a); A: Him (Warlock). Warlock 40.00
❑166, Jul 1969, JK (c); SL (w); JK (a); A: Him (Warlock) 36.00
❑167, Aug 1969, JR (c); SL (w); JK, JR (a); A: Sif 24.00
❑168, Sep 1969, JK (c); SL (w); JK (a); O: Galactus. 1: Thermal Man; 36.00
❑169, Oct 1969, JK, JR (c); SL (w); JK (a); O: Galactus 36.00
❑170, Nov 1969, JR (c); SL (w); BEv, JK (a); 2: Thermal Man 20.00
❑171, Dec 1969, JK (c); SL (w); BEv, JK (a) 20.00
❑172, Jan 1970, JK (c); SL (w); BEv, JK (a) 20.00
❑173, Feb 1970, JK (c); SL (w); BEv, JK (a) 20.00
❑174, Mar 1970, JK (c); SL (w); BEv, JK (a); 1: Crypto-Man 20.00
❑175, Apr 1970, JK (c); SL (w); BEv, JK (a) 20.00
❑176, May 1970, BEv (c); SL (w); BEv, JK (a); V: Surtur the Fire Demon 20.00
❑177, Jun 1970, Alan Kupperberg L.O.C 20.00
❑178, Jul 1970 18.00
❑179, Aug 1970, Neal Pozner L.O.C. 18.00
❑180, Sep 1970, NA (c); SL (w); NA (a); V: Mephisto 24.00
❑181, Oct 1970, NA (c); SL (w); NA (a); V: Mephisto. V: Loki 23.00
❑182, Nov 1970 12.00

N-MINT

❑183, Dec 1970 12.00
❑184, Jan 1971, 1: Infinity (as force); 1: The Silent One 12.00
❑185, Feb 1971 12.00
❑186, Mar 1971, D: The Silent One 12.00
❑187, Apr 1971 12.00
❑188, May 1971 12.00
❑189, Jun 1971 12.00
❑190, Jul 1971 12.00
❑191, Aug 1971, 1: Durok the Demolisher 12.00
❑192, Sep 1971 12.00
❑193, Oct 1971, JR (c); JB, SB (a); A: Silver Surfer. Giant-size 55.00
❑194, Nov 1971 12.00
❑195, Dec 1971 12.00
❑196, Jan 1972 12.00
❑197, Feb 1972 12.00
❑198, Mar 1972, Mangog Kills Odin 12.00
❑199, Apr 1972, V: Pluto 12.00
❑200, Jun 1972, JB (a); Ragnarok 16.00
❑201, Jul 1972, JB, JM (a) 9.00
❑202, Aug 1972, JB (a); V: Ego-Prime 9.00
❑203, Sep 1972, JB (a) 9.00
❑204, Oct 1972, JB (a) 9.00
❑205, Nov 1972, JB (a) 9.00
❑206, Dec 1972, JB (a) 7.00
❑207, Jan 1973, JB (a) 7.00
❑208, Feb 1973, JB (a) 7.00
❑209, Mar 1973, JB (a); 1: Ultimus 7.00
❑210, Apr 1973, JB, DP (a) 7.00
❑211, May 1973, JB, DP (a) 7.00
❑212, Jun 1973, JB, DP (a) 7.00
❑213, Jul 1973, JB, DP (a) 7.00
❑214, Aug 1973 7.00
❑215, Sep 1973, 1: Xorr 7.00
❑216, Oct 1973, Battles the 4-D Man 7.00
❑217, Nov 1973 7.00
❑218, Dec 1973 7.00
❑219, Jan 1974 7.00
❑220, Feb 1974 7.00
❑221, Mar 1974, Marvel Value Stamp #1: Spider-Man 7.00
❑222, Apr 1974, Marvel Value Stamp #41: Gladiator 7.00
❑223, May 1974, Marvel Value Stamp #12: Daredevil 7.00
❑224, Jun 1974, Marvel Value Stamp #87: J. Jonah Jameson 7.00
❑225, Jul 1974, 1: Firelord. Marvel Value Stamp #17: Black Bolt 14.00
❑226, Aug 1974, Marvel Value Stamp #58: Mandarin 7.00
❑227, Sep 1974, Marvel Value Stamp #76: Dormammu 5.00
❑228, Oct 1974, Marvel Value Stamp #40: Loki 5.00
❑229, Nov 1974, Marvel Value Stamp #80: Ghost Rider 5.00
❑230, Dec 1974 5.00
❑231, Jan 1975, Marvel Value Stamp #83: Dragon Man 5.00
❑232, Feb 1975, Marvel Value Stamp #85: Lilith 5.00
❑233, Mar 1975 5.00
❑234, Apr 1975, V: Loki 5.00
❑235, May 1975, 1: The Possessor. Marvel Value Stamp #23: Sgt. Fury 5.00
❑236, Jun 1975, V: Absorbing Man 5.00
❑237, Jul 1975, Marvel Value Stamp #18: Volstagg 5.00
❑238, Aug 1975, JB, JSt (a); Marvel Value Stamp #94: Electro 5.00
❑239, Sep 1975, 1: Osiris. 1: Horus 5.00
❑240, Oct 1975, 1: Isis (Marvel). 1: Seth 5.00
❑241, Nov 1975, JK (c); JB (a) 5.00
❑242, Dec 1975, JB, JSt (a); V: The Servitor 5.00
❑243, Jan 1976, JB (a); V: ZarrkoThe Tomorrow Man, The Time-Twisters 5.00
❑244, Feb 1976, RB (c); JB (a); V: Time-Twisters 5.00
❑245, Mar 1976, RB (c); JB (a); V: Servitor 5.00
❑246, Apr 1976, RB (c); JB (a); A: Firelord. 5.00
❑246/30¢, Apr 1976, 30¢ regional price variant 20.00
❑247, May 1976, JB (a); A: Firelord. Peter Sanderson LOC 5.00
❑247/30¢, May 1976, 30¢ regional price variant 20.00
❑248, Jun 1976, JB (a); V: The Storm Giant 5.00

Other grades: Multiply price above by 5/6 for VF/NM • 2/3 for VERY FINE • 1/3 for FINE • 1/5 for VERY GOOD • 1/8 for GOOD

Trouble With Girls

Lots of tongue-in-cheek humor
©Malibu

Truth: Red, White & Black

Controversial storyline changed Cap's origin
©Marvel

TSR Worlds

DC special focused on role-playing universes
©DC

Turok, Dinosaur Hunter

Valiant revives Gold Key fighter
©Acclaim

Turok, Son of Stone

Long-running adventure character
©Dell

	N-MINT
❑248/30¢, Jun 1976, 30¢ regional price variant	20.00
❑249, Jul 1976, JK (c); JB (a); Sif trades places with Jane	5.00
❑249/30¢, Jul 1976, 30¢ regional price variant	5.00
❑250, Aug 1976, JK (c); JB (a)	5.00
❑250/30¢, Aug 1976, 30¢ regional price variant	5.00
❑251, Sep 1976, Thor journeys to Valhalla	5.00
❑252, Oct 1976, V: The Storm Giant, Ulik; Tales of Asgard story	5.00
❑253, Nov 1976, Thor and Ulik Vs. Trogg; Tales of Asgard story	5.00
❑254, Dec 1976, Reprinted from Thor #159	5.00
❑255, Jan 1977, V: The Stone Men from Saturn	5.00
❑256, Feb 1977, Newsstand edition (distributed by Curtis); issue number in box	5.00
❑256/Whitman, Feb 1977, Special markets edition (usually sold in Whitman bagged prepacks); price appears in a diamond; UPC barcode appears	5.00
❑257, Mar 1977, Newsstand edition (distributed by Curtis); issue number in box	5.00
❑257/Whitman, Mar 1977, Special markets edition (usually sold in Whitman bagged prepacks); price appears in a diamond; UPC barcode appears	5.00
❑258, Apr 1977, Newsstand edition (distributed by Curtis); issue number in box	5.00
❑258/Whitman, Apr 1977, Special markets edition (usually sold in Whitman bagged prepacks); price appears in a diamond; UPC barcode appears	5.00
❑259, May 1977, Newsstand edition (distributed by Curtis); issue number in box	5.00
❑259/Whitman, May 1977, Special markets edition (usually sold in Whitman bagged prepacks); price appears in a diamond; UPC barcode appears	5.00
❑260, Jun 1977, Newsstand edition (distributed by Curtis); issue number in box	5.00
❑260/Whitman, Jun 1977, Special markets edition (usually sold in Whitman bagged prepacks); price appears in a diamond; UPC barcode appears	5.00
❑260/35¢, Jun 1977, 35¢ regional price variant newsstand edition (distributed by Curtis); issue number in box	15.00
❑261, Jul 1977, Newsstand edition (distributed by Curtis); issue number in box	5.00
❑261/Whitman, Jul 1977, Special markets edition (usually sold in Whitman bagged prepacks); price appears in a diamond; UPC barcode appears	5.00
❑261/35¢, Jul 1977, 35¢ regional price variant newsstand edition (distributed by Curtis); issue number in box	15.00

	N-MINT
❑262, Aug 1977, JB (c); TD (a); Newsstand edition (distributed by Curtis); issue number in box	5.00
❑262/Whitman, Aug 1977, TD (a); Special markets edition (usually sold in Whitman bagged prepacks); price appears in a diamond; UPC barcode appears	5.00
❑262/35¢, Aug 1977, JB (c); TD (a); 35¢ regional price variant newsstand edition (distributed by Curtis); issue number in box	15.00
❑263, Sep 1977, JB (c); Newsstand edition (distributed by Curtis); issue number in box	5.00
❑263/Whitman, Sep 1977, Special markets edition (usually sold in Whitman bagged prepacks); price appears in a diamond; UPC barcode appears	5.00
❑263/35¢, Sep 1977, JB (c); 35¢ regional price variant newsstand edition (distributed by Curtis); issue number in box	15.00
❑264, Oct 1977, Newsstand edition (distributed by Curtis); issue number in box	5.00
❑264/Whitman, Oct 1977, Special markets edition (usually sold in Whitman bagged prepacks); price appears in a diamond; no UPC barcode	5.00
❑264/35¢, Oct 1977, 35¢ regional price variant newsstand edition (distributed by Curtis); issue number in box	15.00
❑265, Nov 1977, Newsstand edition (distributed by Curtis); issue number in box	2.50
❑265/Whitman, Nov 1977, Special markets edition (usually sold in Whitman bagged prepacks); price appears in a diamond; no UPC barcode	2.50
❑266, Dec 1977, TD (a); Loki; Return of Odin; The Destroyer	2.50
❑267, Jan 1978, TD (a); 1: Damocles.	2.50
❑268, Feb 1978, TD (a); V: Damocles	2.50
❑269, Mar 1978, TD (a); V: Stilt-Man	2.50
❑270, Apr 1978, TD (a); Newsstand edition (distributed by Curtis); issue number in box	2.50
❑270/Whitman, Apr 1978, Special markets edition (usually sold in Whitman bagged prepacks); price appears in a diamond; no UPC barcode	2.50
❑271, May 1978, TD (a); A: Iron Man. Newsstand edition (distributed by Curtis); issue number in box	2.50
❑271/Whitman, May 1978, A: Iron Man. Special markets edition (usually sold in Whitman bagged prepacks); price appears in a diamond; no UPC barcode	2.50
❑272, Jun 1978, JB, TP (a); Newsstand edition (distributed by Curtis); issue number in box	2.50
❑272/Whitman, Jun 1978, JB (a); Special markets edition (usually sold in Whitman bagged prepacks); price appears in a diamond; no UPC barcode	2.50
❑273, Jul 1978, 1: Red Norvell	2.50
❑274, Aug 1978, 1: Sigyn. 1: Frigga. D: Balder. Newsstand edition (distributed by Curtis); issue number in box	2.50

	N-MINT
❑274/Whitman, Aug 1978, 1: Sigyn. 1: Frigga. D: Balder. Special markets edition (usually sold in Whitman bagged prepacks); price appears in a diamond; no UPC barcode	2.50
❑275, Sep 1978, 1: Hermod. Newsstand edition (distributed by Curtis); issue number in box	2.50
❑275/Whitman, Sep 1978, 1: Hermod. Special markets edition (usually sold in Whitman bagged prepacks); price appears in a diamond; no UPC barcode	2.50
❑276, Oct 1978, Red Norvell named Thor; Newsstand edition (distributed by Curtis); issue number in box	2.50
❑276/Whitman, Oct 1978, Special markets edition (usually sold in Whitman bagged prepacks); price appears in a diamond; no UPC barcode	2.50
❑277, Nov 1978, Newsstand edition (distributed by Curtis); issue number in box	2.50
❑277/Whitman, Nov 1978, Special markets edition (usually sold in Whitman bagged prepacks); price appears in a diamond; no UPC barcode	2.50
❑278, Dec 1978, Newsstand edition (distributed by Curtis); issue number in box	2.50
❑278/Whitman, Dec 1978, Special markets edition (usually sold in Whitman bagged prepacks); price appears in a diamond; no UPC barcode	2.50
❑279, Jan 1979, Newsstand edition (distributed by Curtis); issue number in box	2.50
❑279/Whitman, Jan 1979, Special markets edition (usually sold in Whitman bagged prepacks); price appears in a diamond; no UPC barcode	2.50
❑280, Feb 1979, Newsstand edition (distributed by Curtis); issue number in box	2.50
❑280/Whitman, Feb 1979, Special markets edition (usually sold in Whitman bagged prepacks); price appears in a diamond; no UPC barcode	2.50
❑282, Apr 1979, 200th Journey into Mystery Tale featuring Thor	3.00
❑281, Mar 1979, A: Immortus	3.00
❑283, May 1979, A: Celestials. Newsstand edition (distributed by Curtis); issue number in box	3.00
❑283/Whitman, May 1979, A: Celestials. Special markets edition (usually sold in Whitman bagged prepacks); price appears in a diamond; no UPC barcode	3.00
❑284, Jun 1979, A: Externals	3.00
❑285, Jul 1979, V: Karkas	3.00
❑286, Aug 1979, V: Warlord Kro	3.00
❑287, Sep 1979	3.00
❑288, Oct 1979	3.00
❑289, Nov 1979	3.00
❑290, Dec 1979, V: El Toro Rojo	3.00
❑291, Jan 1980	3.00
❑292, Feb 1980	3.00
❑293, Mar 1980	3.00
❑294, Apr 1980, KP (a); O: Asgard. O: Odin. 1: Frey	3.00
❑295, May 1980, KP (c); KP (a)	3.00
❑296, Jun 1980, KP (a)	3.00
❑297, Jul 1980, KP (a); Thor as Siegfried	3.00
❑298, Aug 1980, KP (c); KP (a)	3.00

Other grades: Multiply price above by 5/6 for VF/NM • 2/3 for VERY FINE • 1/3 for FINE • 1/5 for VERY GOOD • 1/8 for GOOD

	N-MINT
❑299, Sep 1980, KP (a)	3.00
❑300, Oct 1980, KP (a); O: The Destroyer. O: Odin. D: Zuras (physical death). giant; Balder revived	8.00
❑301, Nov 1980, Thor meets other pantheons	2.00
❑302, Dec 1980	2.00
❑303, Jan 1981	2.00
❑304, Feb 1981, V: Wrecking Crew	2.00
❑305, Mar 1981, KP (c); KP (a)	2.00
❑306, Apr 1981, KP (c); KP (a); O: Firelord. 1: Air-Walker (real form). D: Air-Walker (real form); D: Nanna	2.00
❑307, May 1981, KP (a)	2.00
❑308, Jun 1981, KP (c); KP (a)	2.00
❑309, Jul 1981	2.00
❑310, Aug 1981, V: Mephisto	2.00
❑311, Sep 1981	2.00
❑312, Oct 1981, KP (c); KP, GD (a); V: Tyr	2.00
❑313, Nov 1981	2.00
❑314, Dec 1981, KP (c); KP, GD (a); 1: Shawna Lynde	2.00
❑315, Jan 1982, KP (c); KP (a)	2.00
❑316, Feb 1982	2.00
❑317, Mar 1982, KP (c); KP (a)	2.00
❑318, Apr 1982, GK (c); GK (a)	2.00
❑319, May 1982, KP (c); KP (a)	2.00
❑320, Jun 1982, AM (c); KP (a)	2.00
❑321, Jul 1982	2.00
❑322, Aug 1982, D: Darkoth	2.00
❑323, Sep 1982	2.00
❑324, Oct 1982	2.00
❑325, Nov 1982	2.00
❑326, Dec 1982, BA (c); BA (a)	2.00
❑327, Jan 1983	2.00
❑328, Feb 1983, 1: Megatak	2.00
❑329, Mar 1983	2.00
❑330, Apr 1983, BH (c); BH (w); BH (a); O: Crusader II (Arthur Blackwood). 1: Crusader II (Arthur Blackwood)	2.00
❑331, May 1983, BH (c); BH (w); BH (a)	2.00
❑332, Jun 1983	2.00
❑333, Jul 1983, BSz (c); V: Dracula	2.00
❑334, Aug 1983	2.00
❑335, Sep 1983, BSz (c); 1: The Possessor	2.00
❑336, Oct 1983, BL (c); HT (a)	2.00
❑337, Nov 1983, 1&O: Beta Ray Bill. 1st Simonson Thor	7.00
❑338, Dec 1983, A: Beta Ray Bill	3.00
❑339, Jan 1984, 1: Lorelei. A: Beta Ray Bill; Assistant Editors' Month	5.00
❑340, Feb 1984, A: Beta Ray Bill	4.00
❑341, Mar 1984, 1: Sigurd Jarlson	3.00
❑342, Apr 1984	4.00
❑343, May 1984	2.00
❑344, Jun 1984, 1: Malekith the Dark Elf	2.00
❑345, Jul 1984	2.00
❑346, Aug 1984	2.00
❑347, Sep 1984, 1: Algrim	2.00
❑348, Oct 1984	2.00
❑349, Nov 1984, O: Odin	3.00
❑350, Dec 1984, A: Beta Ray Bill	2.00
❑351, Jan 1985, A: Fantastic Four	2.00
❑352, Feb 1985, A: Fantastic Four. A: Beta Ray Bill. A: Avengers	2.00
❑353, Mar 1985	2.00
❑354, Apr 1985	2.00
❑355, May 1985, SB (a)	2.00
❑356, Jun 1985, BG (a); Hercules solo story	2.00
❑357, Jul 1985, Beau Smith LOC	2.00
❑358, Aug 1985, Beta Ray Bill vs. Titanium Man	2.00
❑359, Sep 1985, A: Loki. D: Megatak	2.00
❑360, Oct 1985	2.00
❑361, Nov 1985	2.00
❑362, Dec 1985, D: Executioner	2.00
❑363, Jan 1986, Secret Wars II; Thor's face scarred	2.00
❑364, Feb 1986	2.00
❑365, Mar 1986, Thor turned into frog	2.00
❑366, Apr 1986, Additional ink credits from #368	2.00
❑367, May 1986	2.00
❑368, Jun 1986, SB (a)	2.00
❑369, Jul 1986, SB (a)	2.00
❑370, Aug 1986, JB (c); JB (a)	2.00
❑371, Sep 1986, SB (a); A: Justice Peace. 1: Justice Peace	2.00
❑372, Oct 1986, SB (c); SB (a); Thor pinup	2.00
❑373, Nov 1986, SB (a); Mutant Massacre	2.00
❑374, Dec 1986, SB (a); A: X-Factor. Mutant Massacre	3.00
❑375, Jan 1987, SB (a)	2.00
❑376, Feb 1987, SB (a)	2.00
❑377, Mar 1987, SB (a)	2.00
❑378, Apr 1987, SB (a)	2.00
❑379, May 1987, SB (a)	2.00
❑380, Jun 1987	2.00
❑381, Jul 1987	1.50
❑382, Aug 1987, 300th Thor issue	2.00
❑383, Sep 1987, Secret Wars II	1.50
❑384, Oct 1987, 1: Dargo (future Thor)	1.50
❑385, Nov 1987, A: Hulk	1.50
❑386, Dec 1987, 1: Leir	1.50
❑387, Jan 1988	1.50
❑388, Feb 1988	1.50
❑389, Mar 1988	1.50
❑390, Apr 1988	1.50
❑391, May 1988, 1: Eric Masterson. A: Spider-Man	2.00
❑392, Jun 1988, 1: Quicksand; Daredevil appearance	1.50
❑393, Jul 1988	1.50
❑394, Aug 1988, BH (a)	1.50
❑395, Sep 1988, 1&O: Earth-Lord. 1&O: Wind Warrior	1.50
❑396, Oct 1988	1.50
❑397, Nov 1988	1.50
❑398, Dec 1988, 1: Caber	1.50
❑399, Jan 1989	1.50
❑400, Feb 1989, A: Avengers. V: Seth and Surtur. giant	2.00
❑401, Mar 1989	1.00
❑402, Apr 1989, Tales of Asgard story	1.00
❑403, May 1989, Tales of Asgard story	1.00
❑404, Jun 1989, Tales of Asgard story	1.00
❑405, Jul 1989, Tales of Asgard story	1.00
❑406, Aug 1989, Tales of Asgard story	1.00
❑407, Sep 1989, Title in indicia changes to The Mighty Thor	1.00
❑408, Oct 1989, Eric Masterson absorbs Thor's essence; series continues as The Mighty Thor through #490	1.00
❑409, Nov 1989, Title changes to The Mighty Thor	1.00
❑410, Nov 1989, Dr. Doom apperance; Tales of Asgard story	1.00
❑411, Dec 1989, 1: Night Thrasher. 1: New Warriors (cameo). 1: Chord. V: Juggernaut. Acts of Vengeance	3.00
❑412, Dec 1989, 1: New Warriors (full appearance). V: Juggernaut. Acts of Vengeance	2.00
❑413, Jan 1990, Acts of Vengeance; Beta Ray Thor story	1.00
❑414, Feb 1990	1.00
❑415, Mar 1990, O: Thor; Tales of Asgard story	1.00
❑416, Apr 1990, Tales of Asgard story	1.00
❑417, May 1990, Tales of Asgard story	1.00
❑418, Jun 1990, Tales of Asgard story	1.00
❑419, Jul 1990, O: Stellaris. 1: Stellaris. 1: Black Galaxy; Tales of Asgard story; Black Galaxy Saga	1.00
❑420, Aug 1990, 1&O: Nobilus; Tales of Asgard; Black Galaxy Saga	1.00
❑421, Aug 1990, Tales of Asgard story; Black Galaxy Saga	1.00
❑422, Sep 1990, O: Nobilus. 1: Analyzer; Black Galaxy Saga; Tales of Asgard story	1.00
❑423, Sep 1990, 1: Nobilus (full appearance); Black Galaxy Saga; Tales of Asgard	1.00
❑424, Oct 1990, Black Galaxy Saga; Tales of Asgard story	1.00
❑425, Oct 1990	1.00
❑426, Nov 1990	1.00
❑427, Dec 1990, A: Excalibur	1.00
❑428, Jan 1991, A: Excalibur	1.00
❑429, Feb 1991, A: Ghost Rider	1.00
❑430, Mar 1991, AM (a); A: Ghost Rider	1.00
❑431, Apr 1991	1.00
❑432, May 1991, Giant size; AM, JK (a); 1&O: Thor. 1: Thor II (Eric Masterson). A:300th. D: Loki. Reprints Journey Into Mystery (Vol. 1) #83; 350th appearance of Thor	2.00
❑433, Jun 1991, AM (a)	2.00
❑434, Jul 1991, AM (a)	1.00
❑435, Aug 1991	1.00
❑436, Sep 1991	1.00
❑437, Oct 1991, AM (a); Tales of Asgard story	1.00
❑438, Nov 1991, AM (a); V: Zarrko	1.00
❑439, Nov 1991, AM (a); Tales of Asgard story	1.00
❑440, Dec 1991, AM (a); 1: Thor Corps (Dargo, Beta Ray Bill, Eric Masterson); 1: Shatterfist; Tales of Asgard story	1.00
❑441, Dec 1991, AM (a); Tales of Asgard story	1.00
❑442, Jan 1992, AM (a); Return of Don Blake	1.00
❑443, Jan 1992, AM (a); A: Doctor Strange. A: Silver Surfer. V: Mephisto. V: Mephisto	1.00
❑444, Feb 1992, AM (a); Grinch parody	1.25
❑445, Mar 1992, V: Gladiator. Galactic Storm	1.25
❑446, Apr 1992, A: Avengers. Galactic Storm	1.25
❑447, May 1992, AM (a); A: Spider-Man. A: Absorbing Man. Tales of Asgard story	1.25
❑448, Jun 1992, AM (a); A: Spider-Man. Tales of Asgard story	1.25
❑449, Jul 1992, AM (a); 1&O: Bloodaxe	1.25
❑450, Aug 1992, Giant-size anniversary special; SL (w); AM, JK (a); O: Loki; Reprint of Journey Into Mystery #85; Tales of Asgard story	2.50
❑451, Sep 1992, AM (a); V: Bloodaxe	1.25
❑452, Oct 1992, V: BloodAxe; Tales of Asgard	1.25
❑453, Nov 1992, AM (a); Tales of Asgard	1.25
❑454, Nov 1992, AM (a)	1.25
❑455, Dec 1992, AM (a)	1.25
❑456, Dec 1992, AM (a)	1.25
❑457, Jan 1993, Original Thor returns	1.25
❑458, Jan 1993, Thor vs Thor	1.25
❑459, Feb 1993, AM (a)	1.25
❑460, Mar 1993, JSn (w); Painted cover	1.25
❑461, Apr 1993, JSn (w)	1.25
❑462, May 1993, JSn (w)	1.25
❑463, Jun 1993, Infinity Crusade Crossover	1.25
❑464, Jul 1993, Infinity Crusade crossover	1.25
❑465, Aug 1993, Infinity Crusade crossover	1.25
❑466, Sep 1993, Infinity Crusade crossover	1.25
❑467, Oct 1993, A: Lady Sif. A: Valkyrie. A: Pluto. Infinity Crusade crossover	1.25
❑468, Nov 1993	1.25
❑469, Dec 1993	1.25
❑470, Jan 1994	1.25
❑471, Feb 1994	1.25
❑472, Mar 1994	1.25
❑473, Apr 1994	1.25
❑474, May 1994	1.50
❑475, Jun 1994, Giant-size; O: Thor	2.00
❑475/Variant, Jun 1994, Giant-size; O: Thor. foil cover	2.50
❑476, Jul 1994	1.50
❑477, Aug 1994	1.50
❑478, Sep 1994, A: Red Norvell	1.50
❑479, Oct 1994	1.50
❑480, Nov 1994	1.50
❑481, Dec 1994, V: Grotesk	1.50
❑482, Jan 1995, Giant-size; Tales of Asgard story	2.95
❑483, Feb 1995	1.50
❑484, Mar 1995, A: War Machine	1.50
❑485, Apr 1995	1.50
❑486, May 1995	1.50
❑487, Jun 1995	1.50
❑488, Jul 1995	1.50
❑489, Aug 1995, V: Hulk	1.50
❑490, Sep 1995, V: Absorbing Man	1.50
❑491, Oct 1995, Title returns to Thor	1.50
❑492, Nov 1995, A: Enchantress	1.50
❑493, Dec 1995, A: Enchantress	1.50
❑494, Jan 1996	1.50
❑495, Feb 1996	1.50
❑496, Mar 1996, A: Captain America	1.50
❑497, Apr 1996	1.50
❑498, May 1996	1.50
❑499, Jun 1996	1.50

Other grades: Multiply price above by 5/6 for VF/NM • 2/3 for VERY FINE • 1/3 for FINE • 1/5 for VERY GOOD • 1/8 for GOOD

TV Western

AC spotlighted old western reprints
©AC

Tweety and Sylvester

Later issues had some clever pop culture gags
©Gold Key

22 Brides

Painkiller Jane plus twenty-one
©Event

Twilight Avenger

College football star avenges girlfriend
©Eternity

Twilight Zone

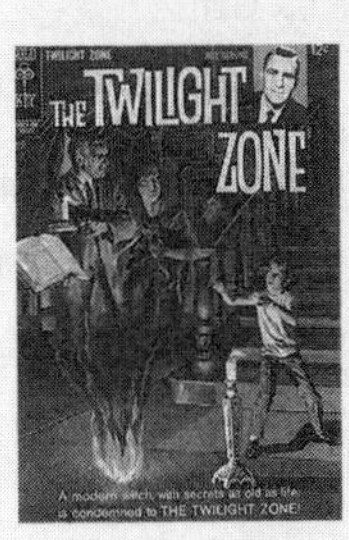

Rod Serling introduced these stories, too
©Gold Key

	N-MINT
❑500, Jul 1996, Giant-size; wraparound cover	2.50
❑501, Aug 1996, A: Red Norvell	1.50
❑502, Sep 1996, O: Thor. Series continued in Journey Into Mystery (Vol. 1) #503	1.50
❑Ann 2, Sep 1966, Cover reads "King Size Special"; SL (w); JK, JSt (a); reprints from Journey into Mystery #96 and #103	65.00
❑Ann 2/2nd, SL (w); JK, JSt (a); 2nd printing; Reprints from Journey into Mystery #96 and #103; Cover reads "King Size Special"	2.50
❑Ann 3, Jan 1971, JK (a); A: Grey Gargoyle. A: Absorbing Man. reprints Thor stories from Journey into Mystery #113 and #114; reprints Tales of Asgard from Journey into Mystery #107-110.	12.00
❑Ann 4, Cover reads "King Size Special"; SL (w); JK (a); reprints stories from Thor #131 and 132, and Journey Into Mystery #113	10.00
❑Ann 5, ca. 1976, JK (c); JB, JK (a); 1: Apollo; Story originally meant to be published in black and white magazine Thor the Mighty #1 (never published)	8.00
❑Ann 6, ca. 1977, JB (c); JB, JK (a)	8.00
❑Ann 7, ca. 1978	7.00
❑Ann 8, ca. 1979	6.00
❑Ann 9, ca. 1981, KP (c); LMc (a)	3.50
❑Ann 10, ca. 1982, BH (c); BH (a); O: Chthon. 1: Ahpuch. 1: Erishkegal. 1: Yama	3.50
❑Ann 11, ca. 1983, BL (c); BH (a); ca. 1983	3.50
❑Ann 12, ca. 1984, 1: Vidar	3.50
❑Ann 13, V: Mephisto	3.00
❑Ann 14, ca. 1989, Title changes to The Mighty Thor Ann	2.50
❑Ann 15, ca. 1990, O: Terminus	2.50
❑Ann 16, ca. 1991, AM (c); AM, HT (a); O: Thor. 1991 Ann	2.50
❑Ann 17, ca. 1992, Citizen Kang	2.50
❑Ann 18, ca. 1993, trading card	2.95
❑Ann 19, ca. 1994	2.95

Thor
Marvel

	N-MINT
❑1, Jul 1998; Giant-size; JR2 (c); JR2 (a)	5.00
❑1/A, Jul 1998; gatefold summary; JR2 (a); sketch cover	20.00
❑1/B, Jul 1998; gatefold summary; JR2 (a); Sunburst cover	5.00
❑1/C, Jul 1998; JR2 (a); DFE alternate cover	5.95
❑1/D, Jul 1998; JR2 (a); DFE alternate cover	8.00
❑1/E, Jul 1998; Rough Cut cover	5.00
❑2, Aug 1998; gatefold summary; JR2 (a); Thor receives new mortal identity	2.50
❑2/A, Aug 1998; JR2 (a); variant cover	2.50
❑3, Sep 1998; gatefold summary; JR2 (a); V: Sedna	2.00
❑4, Oct 1998; gatefold summary; JR2 (a); A: Namor	2.00
❑5, Nov 1998; gatefold summary; JR2 (a)	2.00
❑6, Dec 1998; gatefold summary; JR2 (a); A: Hercules	2.00
❑7, Jan 1999; gatefold summary; JR2 (a); A: Hercules	2.00
❑8, Feb 1999; gatefold summary; JR2 (a); A: Spider-Man. concludes in Peter Parker; Spider-Man #2	2.00
❑9, Mar 1999 JB (a)	2.00
❑10, Apr 1999; JR2 (a); V: Perrikus	2.00
❑11, May 1999; JR2 (a); A: Volstagg. V: Perrikus	1.99
❑12, Jun 1999; JR2, KJ (a); A: Hercules. A: Destroyer. A: Warriors Three. A: Replicus. V: Perrikus. wraparound cover	2.99
❑12/DF, Jun 1999	15.00
❑13, Jul 1999; JR2, KJ (a); V: Marnot	1.99
❑14, Aug 1999; A: Iron Man. V: Absorbing Man	1.99
❑15, Sep 1999 KJ (a); A: Warriors Three	1.99
❑16, Oct 1999 JR2, KJ (a)	1.99
❑17, Nov 1999 JR2, KJ (a)	1.99
❑18, Dec 1999 JR2 (a)	1.99
❑19, Jan 2000	1.99
❑20, Feb 2000	2.25
❑21, Mar 2000	2.25
❑22, Apr 2000	2.25
❑23, May 2000	2.25
❑24, Jun 2000	2.25
❑25, Jul 2000; Gold foil cover	2.25
❑25/Gold, Jul 2000	5.00
❑26, Aug 2000	2.25
❑27, Sep 2000	2.25
❑28, Oct 2000	2.25
❑29, Nov 2000 A: Wrecking Crew	2.25
❑30, Dec 2000 A: Malekith. A: Beta Ray Bill	2.25
❑31, Jan 2001	2.25
❑32, Feb 2001; SL (w); JB, JK (a); Reprints Thor Vol. 1 #136; Reprints Thor Vol. 1 #272; Reprints Thor Vol. 1 #363; 100 pages; Reprints from Thor Vol. 1 #127-128	3.50
❑33, Mar 2001; 1: Thor Girl	2.25
❑34, Apr 2001 A: Gladiator	2.25
❑35, May 2001 A: Gladiator	2.99
❑36, Jun 2001; V: Destroyer	2.25
❑37, Jul 2001	2.25
❑38, Aug 2001	2.25
❑39, Sep 2001	2.25
❑40, Oct 2001	2.25
❑41, Nov 2001	2.25
❑42, Dec 2001	2.25
❑43, Jan 2002	2.25
❑44, Feb 2002; Silent Issue	2.25
❑45, Mar 2002	2.25
❑46, Apr 2002; wraparound cover	2.25
❑47, May 2002; wraparound cover	2.25
❑48, Jun 2002; wraparound cover	2.25
❑49, Jul 2002	2.25
❑50, Aug 2002	2.25
❑51, Sep 2002	2.25
❑52, Oct 2002	2.25
❑53, Oct 2002	2.25
❑54, Nov 2002	2.25
❑55, Dec 2002	2.25
❑56, Jan 2003	2.25
❑57, Feb 2003; Multiple artists	2.25
❑58, Mar 2003	2.25
❑59, Apr 2003	2.25
❑60, May 2003	2.25
❑61, May 2003	2.25
❑62, Jun 2003	2.99
❑63, Jun 2003	2.99
❑64, Jul 2003	2.99
❑65, Aug 2003	2.99
❑66, Sep 2003	2.99
❑67, Oct 2003	2.99
❑68, Nov 2003	2.99
❑69, Nov 2003	2.99
❑70, Dec 2003	2.99
❑71, Jan 2004	2.99
❑72, Feb 2004	2.99
❑73, Mar 2004	2.99
❑74, Apr 2004	2.99
❑75, May 2004	2.99
❑76, May 2004	2.99
❑77, Jun 2004	2.99
❑78, Jul 2004	2.99
❑79, Jul 2004	2.99
❑80, Aug 2004	28.00
❑81, Aug 2004	5.00
❑82, Sep 2004	4.00
❑83, Oct 2004	4.00
❑84, Nov 2004	4.00
❑85, Dec 2004	2.99
❑Ann 1999, Mar 1999; V: Doom. set between Heroes Reborn and Heroes Return; wraparound cover	4.00
❑Ann 2001, Mar 2001; A: Hercules. A: Beta Ray Bill. wraparound cover	3.50

Thor
Marvel

	N-MINT
❑1, Sep 2007; Return of Don Blake and Thor.; Return of Don Blake and Thor	2.99
❑1/Suydam, Sep 2007; Arthur Suydam non-zombie variant cover	7.00
❑1/Turner, Sep 2007; Michael Turner variant cover	7.00
❑1/Zombie, Sep 2007; Arthur Suydam zombie cover	7.00
❑1/2nd, Sep 2007	4.00
❑1/3rd, Sep 2007	3.00
❑2, Oct 2007	2.99
❑2/Dell Otto, Oct 2007	5.00
❑2/2nd, Oct 2007	3.00
❑3, Nov 2007; Olivier Coipel Cover	2.99
❑4, Dec 2007	2.99
❑5, Jan 2008; Thor and woman (back turned) on cover; Loki returns as woman; Hela returns; Enchantress returns	2.99
❑6, Feb 2008	2.99
❑7	2.99
❑8	2.99
❑9	2.99
❑10	2.99
❑11	2.99
❑12	2.99

Thor: Blood Oath
Marvel

	N-MINT
❑1, Nov 2005	2.99
❑2, Dec 2005	2.99
❑3, Dec 2005	2.99
❑4, Jan 2006	2.99
❑5, Feb 2006	2.99
❑6, Feb 2006	2.99

Thor Corps
Marvel

	N-MINT
❑1, Sep 1993; Thor pinup	1.75
❑2, Oct 1993	1.75

Other grades: Multiply price above by 5/6 for VF/NM • 2/3 for VERY FINE • 1/3 for FINE • 1/5 for VERY GOOD • 1/8 for GOOD

N-MINT | N-MINT | N-MINT

❑3, Nov 1993 .... 1.75
❑4, Dec 1993 .... 1.75

Thorion of the New Asgods
Marvel / Amalgam

❑1, Jun 1997, Amalgam of Thor and New Gods 1.95

Thorr-Sverd
Vincent

❑1, b&w 1.00
❑2, b&w 1.00
❑3, b&w; ca. 1987 .... 1.00

Thor: Son of Asgard
Marvel

❑1, May 2004 .... 2.99
❑2, May 2004 .... 2.99
❑3, Jun 2004 .... 2.99
❑4, Jul 2004 .... 2.99
❑5, Aug 2004 .... 2.99
❑6, Sep 2004 .... 2.99
❑7, Oct 2004 .... 2.99
❑8, Nov 2004 .... 2.99
❑9, Dec 2004 .... 2.99
❑10, Jan 2005 .... 2.99
❑11, Feb 2005 .... 2.99
❑12, Mar 2005 .... 2.99

Thor: The Legend
Marvel

❑1, Sep 1996; information on Thor's career and supporting cast; wraparound cover 3.95

Thor: Vikings
Marvel

❑1, Sep 2003; cardstock cover 3.50
❑2, Oct 2003; cardstock cover 3.50
❑3, Nov 2003; cardstock cover 3.50
❑4, Dec 2003; cardstock cover 3.50
❑5, Jan 2004 .... 3.50

Those Annoying Post Bros.
Vortex

❑1 .... 3.00
❑2 .... 2.00
❑3 .... 2.00
❑4 .... 2.00
❑5 .... 2.00
❑6 .... 2.00
❑7 .... 2.00
❑8 .... 2.00
❑9 .... 2.00
❑10 .... 2.00
❑11 .... 2.00
❑12 .... 2.00
❑13 .... 2.00
❑14 .... 2.00
❑15 .... 2.00
❑16 .... 2.00
❑17 .... 2.00
❑18; Series continues as Post Brothers . 2.00
❑39, Aug 1994, b&w; Series continued from "Post Brothers" #38 .... 2.50
❑40, Oct 1994, b&w 2.50
❑41, Dec 1994, b&w 2.50
❑42, Feb 1995, b&w 2.50
❑43, Jun 1995, b&w 2.50
❑44, Jul 1995, b&w 2.50
❑45, Aug 1995, b&w 2.50
❑46, Oct 1995, b&w 2.50
❑47, Nov 1995, b&w 2.50
❑48, Feb 1996, b&w 2.50
❑Ann 1, Aug 1995, b&w; cardstock cover 4.95

Those Crazy Peckers
U.S.Comics

❑1, Feb 1987 .... 2.00

Those Magnificent Men In Their Flying Machines
Gold Key

❑1, Oct 1965, movie adaptation 25.00

Those Unstoppable Rogues
Original Syndicate

❑1, Mar 1995 .... 3.95

Those Who Hunt Elves
ADV Manga

❑1, ca. 2003; Reads right to left; b&w.... 9.99

Thrax
Event

❑1, Nov 1996 .... 2.95
❑2, Jan 1997 .... 2.95

Threat!
Fantagraphics

❑1, Jun 1986, b&w; Adult 2.25
❑2, Jul 1986, b&w; Adult 2.25
❑3, Aug 1986, b&w; Adult 2.25
❑4, Sep 1986, b&w; Adult 2.25
❑5, Oct 1986, b&w; Adult 2.25
❑6, Nov 1986, b&w; Adult 2.25
❑7, Dec 1986, b&w; Adult 2.25
❑8, Jan 1987, b&w; Adult 2.25
❑9, May 1987, b&w; Adult 2.25
❑10, Sep 1987, b&w; Adult 2.25

Three
Invincible

❑1 .... 2.00
❑2 .... 2.00
❑3 .... 2.00
❑4 .... 2.00

3-D Adventure Comics
Stats Etc.

❑1, Aug 1986; 1: Statman 2.00

3-D Alien Terror
Eclipse

❑1, Jun 1986; One-shot; Includes free 3-D glasses 2.50

3-D Exotic Beauties
3-D Zone

❑1, ca. 1990, NN 3.50

3-D Heroes
Blackthorne

❑1; In 3-D, glasses not included 2.50

3-D Hollywood
3-D Zone

❑1; paper dolls 2.95

3-D Space Zombies
3-D Zone

❑1; NN 3.95

3-D Substance
3-D Zone

❑1; NN 2.95
❑2 .... 3.95

3-D Three Stooges
Eclipse

❑1; Stuntgirl backup feature 2.50
❑2 .... 2.50
❑3 .... 2.50

3-D True Crime
3-D Zone

❑1, ca. 1992 .... 3.95

3-D Zone
3-D Zone

❑1, ca. 1986 .... 2.50
❑2, ca. 1986 .... 2.50
❑3, ca. 1987 .... 2.50
❑4, ca. 1987; Electric Fear 2.50
❑5, ca. 1987; Krazy Kat 2.50
❑6, ca. 1987; Rat Fink 2.50
❑7, ca. 1987; Hollywood 2.50
❑8, Sep 1987; High Seas 2.50
❑9, ca. 1987; Red Mask 2.50
❑10, ca. 1987; Jet 2.50
❑11, ca. 1987; Matt Fox 2.50
❑12, ca. 1987; Presidents 2.50
❑13, ca. 1988; Flash Gordon 2.50
❑14, ca. 1988; Tyranostar 2.50
❑15, ca. 1988; humor 2.50
❑16, ca. 1988; space vixens 2.50
❑17, ca. 1988; Thrilling Love 2.50
❑18, ca. 1988; Spacehawk 3-D 2.50
❑19, ca. 1989; Cracked 2.50
❑20, ca. 1989; Atomic Sub 2.50

.357!
Mu

❑1, Jul 1990, b&w 2.50

3 Geeks
3 Finger Prints

❑1, Sep 1997, b&w 3.00
❑1/2nd, b&w; 2nd printing 2.50
❑2, Oct 1997, b&w 2.50
❑3, Nov 1997, b&w; Brain Boy back-up . 2.50
❑4, Jan 1998, b&w; Brain Boy back-up.. 2.50
❑5, ca. 1998, b&w 2.50
❑6, ca. 1998, b&w 2.50
❑7, ca. 1998, b&w 2.50
❑8, Sep 1998, b&w; 48 pages 3.50
❑9, Feb 1999, b&w; movie night 2.50
❑10, Apr 1999, b&w; Allen's birthday 2.50
❑11, Jun 1999, b&w; Allen's redemption 2.50

300
Dark Horse

❑1, May 1998 FM (c); FM (w); FM (a).... 3.50
❑2, Jun 1998 FM (c); FM (w); FM (a)..... 3.50
❑3, Jul 1998 FM (c); FM (w); FM (a)...... 3.25
❑4, Aug 1998 FM (c); FM (w); FM (a) 3.25
❑5, Sep 1998 FM (c); FM (w); FM (a) 3.95

3 Little Kittens: Purr-Fect Weapons
Broadsword

❑1, Aug 2002; 3 Kittens cover 2.95
❑1/A, Aug 2002; Catress cover 2.95
❑2, Oct 2002; 3 Kittens cover 2.95
❑2/A, Oct 2002; Jaguara cover 2.95
❑3, Dec 2002; 3 Kittens cover 2.95
❑3/A, Dec 2002; Baby Cat cover 2.95

Three Mouseketeers
DC

❑1, May 1970 .... 35.00
❑2, Jul 1970 .... 18.00
❑3, Sep 1970 .... 18.00
❑4, Nov 1970 .... 18.00
❑5, Jan 1971 .... 22.00
❑6, Mar 1971 .... 22.00
❑7, May 1971 .... 22.00

Three Musketeers
Eternity

❑1, Dec 1988, b&w 1.95
❑2, Feb 1989, b&w 1.95
❑3, Apr 1989, b&w 1.95

Three Musketeers
Marvel

❑1, Dec 1993; Movie adaptation 1.50
❑2, Jan 1994; Movie adaptation 1.50

3 Ninjas Kick Back
Now

❑1, Jun 1994 .... 1.95
❑2 .... 1.95
❑3 .... 1.95

303
Avatar

❑0, Jul 2004 .... 1.00
❑1 2004 .... 5.00
❑1/Wraparound 2004 .... 10.00
❑2 2004 .... 4.00
❑2/Platinum 2004 .... 10.00
❑2/Wraparound 2004 .... 4.00
❑3 2005 .... 3.99
❑3/Wraparound 2005 .... 5.00
❑4 2005 .... 3.99
❑4/Wraparound 2005 .... 5.00
❑5, Oct 2005 .... 3.99
❑5/Incentive, Oct 2005 .... 7.00
❑5/Wraparound, Oct 2005 .... 3.99

Three Stooges
Gold Key

❑6, Nov 1961, Previous issues appeared as part of Dell Four Color 65.00
❑7, Jan 1962 .... 48.00
❑8, Mar 1962 .... 40.00
❑9, Aug 1962 .... 40.00
❑10, Oct 1962 .... 40.00
❑11, Jan 1963 .... 28.00
❑12, Apr 1963 .... 28.00
❑13, Jul 1963 .... 28.00
❑14, Oct 1963 .... 28.00
❑15, Jan 1964 .... 28.00
❑16, Mar 1964 .... 28.00
❑17, May 1964 .... 28.00
❑18, Jul 1964 .... 28.00
❑19, Sep 1964, Three Musketeers parody 28.00
❑20, Nov 1964 .... 28.00
❑21, Jan 1965 .... 22.00
❑22, Mar 1965 .... 22.00
❑23, May 1965 .... 22.00

Other grades: Multiply price above by 5/6 for VF/NM • 2/3 for VERY FINE • 1/3 for FINE • 1/5 for VERY GOOD • 1/8 for GOOD

Twilight Zone

Second series based on famous TV show
©Now

Twilight Zone Premiere

Many versions of this relaunch special
©Now

Two-Gun Kid

Marvel cowboy started back in the 1950s
©Marvel

2000 A.D. Presents

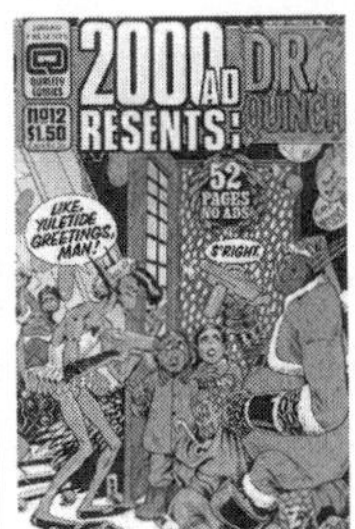

Second name for reprints of U.K. title
©Fleetway-Quality

2000 A.D. Showcase

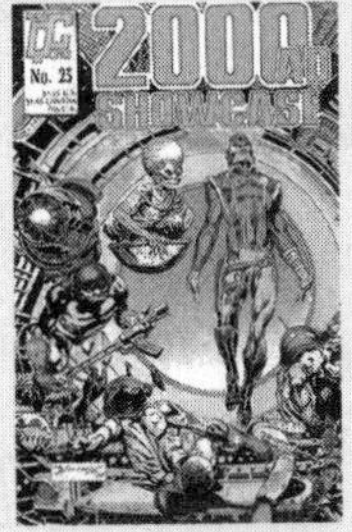

Title had changing name and double issues
©Fleetway-Quality

N-MINT

❑24, Jul 1965 .... 22.00
❑25, Sep 1965 .... 22.00
❑26, Nov 1965 .... 22.00
❑27, Mar 1966 .... 22.00
❑28, May 1966 .... 22.00
❑29, Jul 1966 .... 22.00
❑30, Sep 1966 .... 22.00
❑31, Nov 1966 .... 18.00
❑32, Jan 1967 .... 18.00
❑33, Mar 1967 .... 18.00
❑34, May 1967 .... 18.00
❑35, Jul 1967 .... 18.00
❑36, Sep 1967 .... 18.00
❑37, Dec 1967, Golden Goose 18.00
❑38, Mar 1968 .... 18.00
❑39, Jun 1968 .... 18.00
❑40, Sep 1968 .... 18.00
❑41, Dec 1968 .... 15.00
❑42, Mar 1969 .... 15.00
❑43, Jun 1969 .... 15.00
❑44, Sep 1969 .... 15.00
❑45, Dec 1969 .... 15.00
❑46, Mar 1970, reprints #16 .... 15.00
❑47, Jun 1970 .... 15.00
❑48, Sep 1970, reprints #13; Baseball ... 15.00
❑49, Dec 1970 .... 15.00
❑50, Mar 1971, as ape-men; Little Monsters back-up 15.00
❑51, Jun 1971 .... 15.00
❑52, Sep 1971 .... 15.00
❑53, Dec 1971 .... 15.00
❑54, Mar 1972 .... 15.00
❑55, Jun 1972, reprints #19; Three Musketeers parody 15.00

Three Stooges in 3-D
Eternity

❑1 .... 3.95

Three Stooges in Full Color
Eternity

❑1; Reprints 5.95

Three Stooges Meet Hercules
Dell

❑1, Aug 1962 .... 75.00

3x3 Eyes
Innovation

❑1, Sep 1991, b&w; Japanese 2.50
❑2, Oct 1991, b&w; Japanese 2.25
❑3, Nov 1991, b&w; Japanese 2.25
❑4, Dec 1991, b&w; Japanese 2.25
❑5, Jan 1992, b&w; Japanese 2.25

3x3 Eyes: Curse of the Gesu
Dark Horse / Manga

❑1, Oct 1995, b&w 2.95
❑2, Nov 1995, b&w 2.95
❑3, Dec 1995, b&w 2.95
❑4, Jan 1996, b&w 2.95
❑5, Feb 1996, b&w; Final Issue 2.95

3x3 Eyes: Descent of the Mystic City
Dark Horse

❑1, ca. 2004 .... 18.95

N-MINT

Threshold
Sleeping Giant

❑1, Oct 1996, b&w 2.50
❑2, Nov 1996, b&w; Final Issue 2.50

Threshold
Sleeping Giant

❑1, Dec 1997, b&w 2.50
❑2, Mar 1998, b&w 2.50
❑3 1998 .... 2.50
❑3/Autographed 1998; Autographed by David Yurkovich 2.50

Threshold
Avatar

❑1, Feb 1998; Snowman cover 4.95
❑2, Mar 1998; Snowman cover; b&w 4.95
❑3, Apr 1998; Ravening cover 4.95
❑4, May 1998; Donna Mia cover 4.95
❑5, Jun 1998; Widow cover 4.95
❑6, Jul 1998; Luna cover 4.95
❑7, Aug 1998; The Ravening cover 4.95
❑8, Sep 1998; Cyberangels cover 4.95
❑9, Oct 1998; Donna Mia cover 4.95
❑10, Nov 1998; Pandora cover 4.95
❑11, Dec 1998; Scythe cover 4.95
❑12, Jan 1999; Pandora cover 4.95
❑13, Feb 1999; Snowman cover 4.95
❑14, Mar 1999; Includes Kaos Moon story 4.95
❑15, Apr 1999; Avatars cover 4.95
❑16, May 1999; Avatars cover 4.95
❑17, Jun 1999; Nightvision cover 4.95
❑18, Jul 1999; Harpy cover 4.95
❑19, Aug 1999; Furies cover 4.95
❑20, Sep 1999; Includes Kaos Moon story 4.95
❑21, Oct 1999; Ana cover 4.95
❑22, Nov 1999; Ana cover 4.95
❑23, Dec 1999; Fauna cover 4.95
❑24, Jan 2000; Fauna cover 4.95
❑25, Feb 2000; Dark Blue cover 4.95
❑26, Mar 2000; Dark Blue cover 4.95
❑27, Apr 2000; Dark Blue cover 4.95
❑28, May 2000; Dark Blue cover 4.95
❑29, Jun 2000; Dark Blue cover 4.95
❑30, Jul 2000; Dark Blue cover 4.95
❑31, Aug 2000; Luna cover 4.95
❑32, Sep 2000; Ravening cover 4.95
❑33, Oct 2000; Pandora cover 4.95
❑34, Nov 2000; Pandora cover 4.95
❑35, Dec 2000; Fuzzy Dice cover 4.95
❑36, Jan 2001; Pandora cover 4.95
❑37, Feb 2001; Pandora cover 4.95
❑38, Mar 2001; Lookers cover 4.95
❑39, Apr 2001; Lookers cover 4.95
❑40, May 2001; Lookers cover 4.95
❑41, Jun 2001; Pandora cover 4.95
❑42, Jul 2001; Pandora cover 4.95
❑43, Aug 2001; Pandora cover 4.95
❑44, Sep 2001; Razor cover 4.95
❑45, Nov 2001; Pandora cover 4.95
❑46, Jan 2002; Pandora cover 4.95
❑47, Apr 2002; Demonslayer cover 4.95
❑48, Aug 2002; Demonslayer cover 4.95
❑49, Nov 2002; Demonslayer cover 4.95
❑50, May 2003; Hellina cover 4.95

N-MINT

Threshold of Reality
Maintech

❑1, Sep 1986 .... 1.00
❑2 .... 1.00
❑3 .... 1.00

Threshold: The Stamp Collector
Sleeping Giant

❑1, Mar 1997, b&w 2.50
❑2, May 1997, b&w 2.50

Thriller
DC

❑1, Nov 1983 TVE (c); TVE (a) 2.00
❑2, Dec 1983; O: Thriller 1.75
❑3, Jan 1984 .... 1.75
❑4, Feb 1984 .... 1.50
❑5, Mar 1984; Elvis satire 1.50
❑6, Apr 1984; Elvis satire 1.50
❑7, May 1984 .... 1.50
❑8, Jun 1984 .... 1.50
❑9, Jul 1984; David Goyer LOC 1.50
❑10, Aug 1984 .... 1.50
❑11, Sep 1984 .... 1.50
❑12, Oct 1984 .... 1.50

Thrilling Adventure Stories
Atlas-Seaboard

❑1, Feb 1975, b&w; magazine; RH (w); FT, EC, RH (a) 18.00
❑2, Aug 1975 .... 25.00

Thrilling Adventure Strips
Dragon Lady

❑5 1986; (formerly Best of Tribune Company) 2.95
❑6 1986 .... 2.95
❑7 1986 .... 2.95
❑8 1987 .... 2.95
❑9, Mar 1987 .... 2.95
❑10 1987 .... 2.95

Thrilling Comics
DC

❑1, May 1999; RH (a); A: Wildcat. A: Tigress. A: Hawkman. Manhunter apperance 2.00

Thrill Kill
Caliber

❑1, b&w 2.50

Thrillkiller
DC

❑1, Jan 1997; Elseworlds story 2.50
❑2, Feb 1997; Elseworlds story 2.50
❑3, Mar 1997; Elseworlds story 2.50

Thrillkiller '62
DC

❑1 1998; prestige format; Elseworlds; sequel to Thrillkiller 4.95

Thrillogy
Pacific

❑1, Jan 1984 .... 1.50

Through Gates of Splendor
Spire

❑1, ca. 1974, adapts book by Elisabeth Elliot 8.00

N-MINT

Thumb Screw
Caliber

❏1, b&w 3.50
❏2, b&w 3.50
❏3, b&w 3.50

Thump'n Guts
Kitchen Sink

❏1, ca. 1993; Poly-bag reads Project X, includes poster and trading card 2.95

Thun'Da, King of the Congo
AC

❏1, b&w; Reprints 2.50

Thun'da Tales
Fantagraphics

❏1, ca. 1986; Reprints from Thun'ds #1; O: Thun'da 2.00

T.H.U.N.D.E.R.
Solson

❏1 1.95

THUNDER Agents
Tower

❏1, Nov 1965; WW (c); GT, GK, WW (a); 1&O: Dynamo. 1&O: The THUNDER Squad. 1&O: Menthor. 1&O: NoMan 1: Iron Maiden 140.00
❏2, Jan 1966; WW (c); WW (a); 1: Lightning. D: Egghead. D: Agent Egghead 75.00
❏3, Mar 1966; WW (c); WW (a); 1: Vibraman 55.00
❏4, Apr 1966; WW, DA (a); O: Lightning 55.00
❏5, Jun 1966; WW (c); GK, WW (a); O: Demo 55.00
❏6, Jul 1966; WW (c); SD, WW (a); 1: Red Star; 1&O: Warp Wizard 42.00
❏7, Aug 1966; WW (c); SD, GT, WW (a); D: Menthor 42.00
❏8, Sep 1966; WW (c); DA (w); GT, WW, DA (a); 1&O: Raven 42.00
❏9, Oct 1966; 1: Mayven; 1: Spider 35.00
❏10, Nov 1966; 1: Tarlac 35.00
❏11, Mar 1967; WW (c); WW, DA (a); 1: Dr Forkliff 38.00
❏12, Apr 1967 WW (c); SD, WW (a) 38.00
❏13, Jun 1967; WW (c); GT, WW, DA (a); A: Undersea Agent. 1: Mockman 38.00
❏14, Jul 1967 GK (c); GK (w); SD, GT, GK, WW (a) 38.00
❏15, Sep 1967 GK (c); GT, WW (a) 38.00
❏16, Oct 1967 WW (c); WW (w); SD, GT, GK, WW, DA (a) 22.00
❏17, Dec 1967; DA (c); GT, WW (a); Reprint from THUNDER Agents #1 22.00
❏18, Sep 1968 SD, WW (a) 22.00
❏19, Nov 1968; GK, WW (c); GT, WW, DA (a); 1: The Ghost; Reprint from THUNDER Agents #12 22.00
❏20, Jan 1969; WW (a); O: Dynamo. Reprints 15.00

T.H.U.N.D.E.R. Agents
J.C.

❏1, May 1983 2.00
❏2, Jan 1984 2.00

Thunder Agents
Deluxe

❏1, Nov 1984; Includes pin-ups 2.00
❏2, Jan 1985 2.00
❏3, Nov 1985 2.00
❏4, Feb 1986 2.00
❏5, Oct 1986; Superman lookalike 2.00

Thunderbolt
Charlton

❏1, Jan 1966, PM (c); PM (w); PM (a); 1&O: Thunderbolt 16.00
❏51, Mar 1966, PM (c); PM (w); PM (a); Series continues after hiatus (Son of Vulcan #50?) 10.00
❏52, Jun 1966, PM (c); PM (w); FMc, PM (a) 9.00
❏53, Aug 1966, PM (c); PM (w); FMc, PM (a) 9.00
❏54, Oct 1966, PM (c); PM (w); PM (a) 9.00
❏55, Dec 1966, PM (c); PM (w); PM (a) 9.00
❏56, Feb 1967, PM (c); PM (w); PM (a) 9.00
❏57, May 1967, SD (w) 9.00
❏58, Jul 1967, PM (c); PM (w); PM (a) 9.00
❏59, Sep 1967, PM (c) 9.00
❏60, Nov 1967, JA (a); Final Issue 9.00

Thunderbolt Jaxon
DC / America's Best Comics

❏1, Mar 2006 2.99
❏2, May 2006 2.99
❏3, Jun 2006 2.99
❏4, Aug 2006 2.99
❏5, Sep 2006 2.99

Thunderbolts
Marvel

❏-1, Jul 1997; KB (w); A: Baron Zemo. A: Namor. Flashback 2.00
❏0, Jan 1997; KB (w); Free 1.00
❏1, Apr 1997; Giant-size; KB (w); Identities of Thunderbolts revealed 4.00
❏2, May 1997; KB (w); V: Mad Thinker 3.00
❏2/A, May 1997; Alternate cover 3.00
❏3, Jun 1997 KB (w) 3.00
❏4, Jul 1997; KB (w); 1: Jolt. Jolt joins team 2.50
❏5, Aug 1997; gatefold summary; KB (w); Atlas vs. Growing Man 2.50
❏6, Sep 1997; gatefold summary; KB (w) 2.00
❏7, Oct 1997; gatefold summary; KB (w); V: Elements of Doom. V: Elements of Doom 2.00
❏8, Nov 1997; gatefold summary; KB (w); A: Spider-Man 2.00
❏9, Dec 1997; gatefold summary; KB (w); A: Black Widow 2.00
❏10, Jan 1998; gatefold summary; KB (w); Thunderbolts revealed as Masters of Evil 2.00
❏11, Feb 1998; gatefold summary; KB (w) 2.00
❏12, Mar 1998; gatefold summary; KB (w); A: Fantastic Four. A: Avengers. Wraparound cover 6.00
❏13, Apr 1998; gatefold summary; KB (w) 2.00
❏14, May 1998; gatefold summary; KB (w) 2.00
❏15, Jun 1998; gatefold summary; KB (w) 2.00
❏16, Jul 1998; gatefold summary; KB (w); V: Lightning Rods (formerly Great Lakes Avengers) 2.00
❏17, Aug 1998; gatefold summary; KB (w); V: Graviton 2.00
❏18, Sep 1998; gatefold summary; KB (w) 2.00
❏19, Oct 1998; gatefold summary; KB (w); 1: Charcoal 2.00
❏20, Nov 1998; gatefold summary; KB (w); V: new Masters of Evil 2.00
❏21, Dec 1998; gatefold summary; KB (w); A: Hawkeye; O: Songbird 2.00
❏22, Jan 1999; gatefold summary; KB (w); Hercules vs. Atlas 2.00
❏23, Feb 1999 KB (w); A: U.S. Agent 2.00
❏24, Mar 1999; KB (w); A: Citizen V. O: Charcoal 2.00
❏25, Apr 1999; double-sized; KB (w); A: Masters of Evil. V: Masters of Evil; Wraparound cover 2.99
❏25/Autographed, Apr 1999; KB (w); A: Masters of Evil. Autographed by Mark Bagley 12.00
❏26, May 1999; Mach-1 in prison 1.99
❏27, Jun 1999 A: Archangel 1.99
❏28, Jul 1999; A: Archangel. V: Graviton 1.99
❏29, Aug 1999; A: Machine Man. V: Graviton 1.99
❏30, Sep 1999; Hawkeye and Moonstone caught in clinch 1.99
❏31, Oct 1999 1.99
❏32, Nov 1999; Spider-Man Fast Lane insert 1.99
❏33, Dec 1999; O: Jolt 1.99
❏34, Jan 2000; Spider-Man Fast Lane insert 1.99
❏35, Feb 2000 2.25
❏36, Mar 2000; 8 page bonus insert Marvel Super Heroes; 8 page bonus insert Marvel Super Heroes Spider-Man Fast Lane 2.25
❏37, Apr 2000 2.25
❏38, May 2000; V: V Battalion; Citizen V revealed as Dallas; Spider-Man Fast Lane insert 2.25
❏39, Jun 2000; Reprints from Tales of Suspense #57, 60, 64, Power Man #21; 100-Page Monster issue 2.25
❏40, Jul 2000; V: V-Battalion 2.25
❏41, Aug 2000 A: Sandman 2.25
❏42, Sep 2000; A: Wonder Man. Continued in Avengers #32 2.25
❏43, Oct 2000; KB (w); A: Black Widow. Continued in Avengers #33 2.25
❏44, Nov 2000; A: Nefaria. A: Avengers. Continued in Avengers #34 2.25
❏45, Dec 2000; Maximum Security 2.25
❏46, Jan 2001; return of Jolt 2.25
❏47, Feb 2001; A: Captain Marvel. V: Scourge; S.H.I.E.L.D. seizes Thunderbolts HQ 2.25
❏48, Mar 2001 2.25
❏49, Apr 2001; V: Henry Gyrich; Scourge revealed as mind-controlled Nomad; Fixer revealed alive 2.25
❏50, May 2001; double-sized; A: Citizen V. Double-sized; V: Henry Gyrich; V: Redeemers 2.99
❏51, Jun 2001; V: Doctor Doom 2.25
❏52, Jul 2001 2.25
❏53, Aug 2001; Charcoal spotlight 2.25
❏54, Sep 2001 2.25
❏55, Oct 2001 2.25
❏56, Nov 2001; D: Meteorite; D: Beetle (Leila Davis) 2.25
❏57, Dec 2001 2.25
❏58, Jan 2002 2.25
❏59, Feb 2002; 'Nuff Said issue 2.25
❏60, Mar 2002 2.25
❏61, Apr 2002 2.25
❏62, May 2002 2.25
❏63, Jun 2002 2.25
❏64, Jul 2002; Call of Duty preview 2.25
❏65, Aug 2002 2.25
❏66, Aug 2002 2.25
❏67, Sep 2002 2.25
❏68, Sep 2002; Interior contains same title artwork as previous issue 2.25
❏69, Oct 2002 2.25
❏70, Oct 2002 2.25
❏71, Nov 2002 2.25
❏72, Nov 2002 2.25
❏73, Dec 2002 2.25
❏74, Jan 2003; Uncanny X-Men #416 preview 2.25
❏75, Feb 2003; Incredible Hulk #50 preview 2.25
❏76, Mar 2003 2.25
❏77, Apr 2003 2.99
❏78, Jun 2003 2.99
❏79, Jul 2003 2.25
❏80, Aug 2003 2.25
❏81, Sep 2003; Title continued in New Thunderbolts #82 2.25
❏100, May 2006, Reprints Thunderbolts story from Tales Of The Marvel Universe #1; D: Photon II; "Origin" from Thundebolts'97; Credits for Tales story taken from original issue 3.99
❏101, Jun 2006 2.99
❏102, Jul 2006 2.99
❏103, Aug 2006, Civil War tie-in; Iron Man on cover 8.00
❏104, Sep 2006, Civil War tie-in; Zemo and Songbird with villains in darkness cover 2.99
❏105, Oct 2006, Civil War tie-in 2.99
❏106, Nov 2006 2.99
❏107, Dec 2006 2.99
❏108, Jan 2007; Incredible Hulk #100 preview 2.99
❏109, Mar 2007 2.99
❏110, Apr 2007; 1: new Thunderbolts team 5.00
❏111 2.99
❏112 2.99
❏113 2.99
❏114 2.99
❏115 2.99
❏116 2.99
❏117 2.99
❏118 2.99
❏119 2.99
❏120 2.99
❏121 2.99
❏122 2.99
❏123 2.99
❏124 2.99
❏125 2.99
❏126 2.99
❏127 2.99

Other grades: Multiply price above by 5/6 for VF/NM • 2/3 for VERY FINE • 1/3 for FINE • 1/5 for VERY GOOD • 1/8 for GOOD

2001 Nights

Possibly the best "hard" science-fiction comic

©Viz

2001, A Space Odyssey

Kirby series had little to do with the movie

©Marvel

Ultimate Adventures

Quesada's entry in "U-Decide" promotion

©Marvel

Ultimate Elektra

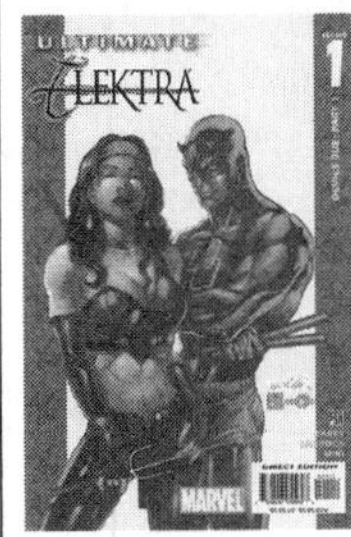

Series timed to help promote the movie

©Marvel

Ultimate Fantastic Four

Bendis starts the title Fantastic

©Marvel

N-MINT

❑128 ... 2.99
❑129 ... 2.99
❑130 ... 2.99
❑131 ... 2.99
❑132 ... 2.99
❑Ann 1997, Aug 1997; KB (w); GC, GP, BMc (a); O: Thunderbolts. 1997 Ann; wraparound cover ... 3.00
❑Ashcan 1; Ashcan preview; American Entertainment ... 2.50

Thunderbunny
Archie / Red Circle

❑1, Jan 1984 ... 2.00

Thunderbunny
Warp

❑1, Jun 1985; O: retold. Warp publishes ... 2.00
❑2, Aug 1985 ... 2.00
❑3, Oct 1985 ... 2.00
❑4, Dec 1985 ... 2.00
❑5, Feb 1986 ... 2.00
❑6, Apr 1986, b&w; Apple begins publishing ... 2.00
❑7, Jun 1986, b&w; Apple begins publishing ... 2.00
❑8, Aug 1987 ... 1.75
❑9, Oct 1987 ... 1.75
❑10, Jul 1987 ... 1.75
❑11, Sep 1987 A: THUNDER Agents ... 1.75
❑12, Nov 1987; last ... 1.75

Thundercats
Marvel / Star

❑1, Dec 1985, Collector's First Issue ... 4.00
❑2, Feb 1986 ... 2.00
❑3, Apr 1986 ... 2.00
❑4, Jun 1986 ... 2.00
❑5, Aug 1986 ... 2.00
❑6, Oct 1986 ... 2.00
❑7, Dec 1986 ... 1.50
❑8, Feb 1987 ... 1.50
❑9, Mar 1987 ... 1.50
❑10, Apr 1987 ... 1.50
❑11, May 1987 ... 1.50
❑12, Jun 1987 ... 1.50
❑13, Jul 1987 ... 1.50
❑14, Aug 1987 ... 1.50
❑15, Sep 1987 ... 1.50
❑16, Oct 1987 ... 1.50
❑17, Nov 1987 ... 1.50
❑18, Dec 1987 ... 1.50
❑19, Jan 1988 ... 1.50
❑20, Feb 1988 ... 1.50
❑21, Mar 1988 ... 1.50
❑22, Apr 1988 ... 1.50
❑23, May 1988 ... 1.50
❑24, Jun 1988; Final Issue ... 1.50

Thundercats/Battle of the Planets
DC / Wildstorm

❑1, ca. 2003 ... 4.95

Thundercats: Dogs of War
DC

❑1, Aug 2003 ... 2.95
❑2, Sep 2003 ... 2.95
❑3, Oct 2003 ... 2.95
❑4, Nov 2003 ... 2.95
❑5, Dec 2003 ... 2.95

N-MINT

Thundercats: Enemy's Pride
DC

❑1, Aug 2004 ... 2.95
❑2, Sep 2004 ... 2.95
❑3, Oct 2004 ... 2.95
❑4, Nov 2004 ... 2.95
❑5, Dec 2004 ... 2.95

Thundercats: Hammerhand's Revenge
DC

❑1, Dec 2003 ... 2.95
❑2, Jan 2004 ... 2.95
❑3, Feb 2004 ... 2.95
❑4, Mar 2004 ... 2.95
❑5, Apr 2004 ... 2.95

Thundercats Origins: Heroes & Villains
DC

❑1, Feb 2004 ... 3.50

Thundercats Origins: Villains & Heroes
DC

❑1, Feb 2004 ... 3.50

Thundercats: Reclaiming Thundera
DC

❑1, ca. 2003 ... 12.95

Thundercats: The Return
DC / Wildstorm

❑1, Apr 2003 ... 2.95
❑2, May 2003 ... 2.95
❑3, Jun 2003 ... 2.95
❑4, Jul 2003 ... 2.95
❑5, Aug 2003 ... 2.95

ThunderCats
DC / Wildstorm

❑0, Oct 2002; Campbell cover ... 2.50
❑1, Oct 2002; Lion-O raising his sword while group charges in all directions ... 2.50
❑2, Nov 2002; Jim Lee cover ... 2.95
❑3, Dec 2002 ... 2.95
❑4, Jan 2003 ... 2.95
❑5, Feb 2003; Cover shows Lion-O, Cheetara, Panthro, and Tygra in foreground over Grune the Destroyer in background ... 2.95

Thunder Girls
Pin & Ink

❑1, Sum 1997 ... 2.95
❑2, Sum 1999 ... 2.95
❑3, Fal 1999 ... 2.95

Thundergod
Crusade

❑1/A, Aug 1996; Alternate cover (drawn cover, man and woman clasping) ... 2.95
❑1, Aug 1996, b&w; Painted cover ... 2.95
❑2, Oct 1996, b&w ... 2.95
❑3, Dec 1996, b&w ... 2.95

Thundermace
Rak

❑1, Mar 1986, b&w ... 2.00
❑2, Dec 1986 ... 1.75
❑3, Apr 1987 ... 1.75
❑4 1987 ... 1.75
❑5 1987 ... 2.00

N-MINT

❑6 1987 ... 2.00
❑7 1987 ... 2.00

Thundersaurs: The Bodacious Adventures of Biff Thundersaur
Innovation

❑1, b&w ... 2.25

Thunderskull!
Slave Labor

❑1, Aug 1989, b&w ... 1.95

Thunderstrike
Marvel

❑1, Jun 1993; Prism cover ... 2.95
❑2, Nov 1993 ... 1.25
❑3, Dec 1993 ... 1.25
❑4, Jan 1994 ... 1.25
❑5, Feb 1994 ... 1.25
❑6, Mar 1994 ... 1.25
❑7, Apr 1994; V: Pandara ... 1.25
❑8, May 1994 ... 1.25
❑9, Jun 1994 ... 1.50
❑10, Jul 1994 ... 1.50
❑11, Aug 1994 ... 1.50
❑12, Sep 1994 ... 1.50
❑13, Oct 1994; 1: Bison ... 1.50
❑13/A, Oct 1994; flip-book with Code Blue back-up; second indicia gives title as Marvel Double Feature ... Thunderstrike/Code Blue ... 2.50
❑14, Nov 1994 ... 1.50
❑14/A, Nov 1994; flip-book with Code Blue back-up; second indicia gives title as Marvel Double Feature ... Thunderstrike/Code Blue ... 2.50
❑15, Dec 1994 ... 1.50
❑15/A, Dec 1994; flip-book with Code Blue back-up; second indicia gives title as Marvel Double Feature ... Thunderstrike/Code Blue ... 2.50
❑16, Jan 1995 ... 1.50
❑16/A, Jan 1995; flip-book with Code Blue back-up; second indicia gives title as Marvel Double Feature ... Thunderstrike/Code Blue ... 2.50
❑17, Feb 1995 ... 1.50
❑18, Mar 1995 ... 1.50
❑19, Apr 1995 ... 1.50
❑20, May 1995 ... 1.50
❑21, Jun 1995; Avengers #1 homage cover ... 1.50
❑22, Jul 1995; Identity of Bloodaxe revealed ... 1.50
❑23, Aug 1995; V: Avengers; V: Seth, Avengers, Thor; V: Thor; Thunderstrike kills Seth ... 1.50
❑24, Sep 1995; D: Eric Masterson; Final Issue ... 1.50

Tick
NEC

❑1, Jun 1988; Black background on cover ... 15.00
❑1/2nd; 2nd printing ... 3.00
❑1/3rd; 3rd printing ... 2.50
❑1/4th; 4th printing ... 2.25
❑1/5th; 5th printing ... 2.75
❑2, Sep 1988; Die-cut cover ... 8.00
❑2/Variant; Without die-cut cover ... 15.00
❑2/2nd; 2nd printing ... 3.00
❑2/3rd; 3rd printing ... 2.25

N-MINT N-MINT N-MINT

- ❑2/4th; 4th printing 2.25
- ❑2/5th; 5th printing 2.75
- ❑3, Dec 1988 .... 6.00
- ❑3/2nd, Nov 1989; Yellow stripe on cover saying "Encore Presentation" 3.00
- ❑3/3rd; 3rd printing 2.75
- ❑3/4th; 4th printing 2.75
- ❑4, Apr 1989; 1: Paul the Samurai 8.00
- ❑4/2nd; 1: Paul the Samurai. 2nd printing 2.25
- ❑4/3rd; 1: Paul the Samurai. 3rd printing 2.75
- ❑4/4th; 1: Paul the Samurai. 4th printing 2.75
- ❑4/5th; 1: Paul the Samurai. 5th printing 2.75
- ❑5, Aug 1989; Scarcer 8.00
- ❑5/2nd; 2nd printing 2.75
- ❑6, Nov 1989 .... 5.00
- ❑6/2nd 2.75
- ❑6/3rd 2.75
- ❑7, Feb 1990 .... 5.00
- ❑7/2nd; 2nd printing 2.75
- ❑7/3rd, Sep 1995; 3rd printing 2.75
- ❑8, Jul 1990; Has logo 8.00
- ❑8/Variant; No logo on cover 8.00
- ❑8/2nd; 2nd printing 2.75
- ❑9, Mar 1991; 1: The Chainsaw Vigilante 3.00
- ❑10, Oct 1991 .... 3.00
- ❑11, Aug 1992 .... 3.00
- ❑12, May 1993 .... 3.00
- ❑12/Ltd.; Gold spider foil on front 20.00
- ❑13, Nov 2000; Pseudo-Tick edition 3.50
- ❑Special 1, Mar 1988; Special edition; 1: The Tick 50.00
- ❑Special 2, Jun 1988; Special edition; 2: The Tick; Limited to 3000 copies 25.00

Tick & Arthur
NEC

- ❑1, Apr 1999 .... 3.50

Tick & Artie
NEC

- ❑1/A 2002; Tick, Arthur on cover 3.50
- ❑1/B 2002; Bugs on cover 3.50

Tick Big Blue Destiny
NEC

- ❑1, Oct 1997; Keen Edition; Arthur and Tick with #1 posing on cover 2.95
- ❑1/A, Oct 1997; Wicked Keen Edition; Die-cut cover 4.95
- ❑1/Ashcan, ca. 1997; ashcan edition; ashcan preview of mini-series 2.95
- ❑1/B, Oct 1997; Wicked Keen Edition without Die-Cut Cover; 500 printed 19.00
- ❑2, Dec 1997 .... 2.95
- ❑2/Variant, Dec 1997; Tick-buster cover 2.95
- ❑3, Mar 1998 .... 3.50
- ❑4, Apr 1998; Justice Cover 3.50
- ❑4/A, Apr 1998; Ocean cover 3.50
- ❑5, Jul 1998 .... 3.50

Tick Big Red-n-Green Christmas Spectacle
NEC

- ❑1, Dec 2001, Black background on cover 3.95

Tick Big Summer Annual
NEC

- ❑1, Jul 1999 .... 3.50

Tick: Circus Maximus
NEC

- ❑1, Mar 2000 .... 3.50
- ❑2, Apr 2000 .... 3.50
- ❑3, May 2000 .... 3.50
- ❑4, Jun 2000 .... 3.50

Tick: Days of Drama
New England

- ❑1, Sep 2005 .... 4.95

Tick: Heroes of the City
NEC

- ❑1, Feb 1999 .... 3.50

Tick Incredible Internet Comic
NEC

- ❑1, Jul 2001, Black background on cover 3.95

Tick: Karma Tornado
NEC

- ❑1, Oct 1993; Includes trading cards 4.00
- ❑1/2nd, Jan 1997; 2nd printing 2.95
- ❑2, Jan 1994 .... 3.50
- ❑2/2nd, Feb 1997; 2nd printing 2.95
- ❑3, May 1994; Scarce 5.00
- ❑3/2nd, Mar 1997; flip book with The Tick's Back back-up 2.95
- ❑4, Jul 1994; Scarce 5.00
- ❑4/2nd, Apr 1997; flip book with The Tick's Back back-up 2.95
- ❑5, Aug 1994; Scarce 5.00
- ❑5/2nd; 2nd printing 2.95
- ❑6, Oct 1994 .... 4.00
- ❑6/2nd, May 1997; 2nd printing 2.95
- ❑7, Nov 1994 .... 4.00
- ❑7/2nd; 2nd printing 2.95
- ❑8, Dec 1995 .... 4.00
- ❑8/2nd; 2nd printing 2.95
- ❑9, Mar 1995 .... 3.00
- ❑9/2nd; 2nd printing 2.95

Tick: Luny Bin Trilogy
NEC

- ❑0, Jul 1998; A.k.a. The Tick: Big Blue Destiny #6;Preview 1.50
- ❑1, Oct 1998 .... 3.50
- ❑2, Sep 1998 .... 3.50
- ❑3, Oct 1998 .... 3.50

Tick's Back
NEC

- ❑0, Aug 1997; Red cover 2.95
- ❑0/A, Aug 1997; Green Cover 5.00
- ❑0/B, Aug 1997; Gold Tick Cover 7.50
- ❑0/C, Aug 1997, b&w; no logo; gold cover 10.00

Tick's Big Back to School Special
NEC

- ❑1, ca. 1998; V: Stoolface Chippendale.. 3.50

Tick's Big Cruise Ship Vacation Special
NEC

- ❑1, Sep 2000 .... 3.50

Tick's Big Father's Day Special
NEC

- ❑1, Jun 2000; 1: Kid Tick 3.50

Tick's Big Halloween Special
NEC

- ❑1, Oct 1999 .... 3.50

Tick's Big Mother's Day Special
NEC

- ❑1, Apr 2000 .... 3.50

Tick's Big Romantic Adventure
NEC

- ❑1, Feb 1998 .... 2.95

Tick's Big Summer Fun Special
NEC

- ❑1, Aug 1998 .... 3.50

Tick's Big Tax Time Terror
NEC

- ❑1, Apr 2000 .... 3.50

Tick's Big Year 2000 Special
NEC

- ❑1, Mar 2000 .... 3.50

Tick's Big Yule Log Special
NEC

- ❑1/A, Dec 1997, b&w; Tick holding Arthur on cover 3.50
- ❑1, Dec 1997, b&w; Chritmas ornaments on Tick's Head on cover 3.50
- ❑1998, Feb 1998 .... 3.50
- ❑1999, Jan 1999 .... 3.50
- ❑2000, Nov 1999 .... 3.50
- ❑2000/Ltd., Nov 1999; Limited, autographed edition 4.95
- ❑2001 .... 3.50

Tick's Giant Circus of the Mighty
NEC

- ❑1, Sum 1992 .... 2.75
- ❑2, Sum 1992 .... 2.75

Tick's Golden Age Comic
NEC

- ❑1/A, May 2002; Red Timely-style cover 4.95
- ❑1/B, May 2002; Standing on top of world with Eagle cover 4.95
- ❑2/A, Aug 2002; Jungle cover 4.95
- ❑2/B, Aug 2002; EC spoof cover 4.95

Tick's Massive Summer Double Spectacle
NEC

- ❑1/B, Jul 2000; Limited Edition; Photo cover 3.50
- ❑1/A, Jul 2000; Special Edition; Photo cover 3.50
- ❑1, Jul 2000 .... 3.50
- ❑2/B 2001; Limited Edition; Photo cover 3.50
- ❑2/A 2001; Special Edition; Photo cover 3.50
- ❑2 2001 .... 3.50

Tick-Tock Follies
Slave Labor

- ❑1, Dec 1996 .... 2.95

Tic Toc Tom
Detonator Canada

- ❑1, Aut 1995, b&w; Fall 1995 .... 2.95
- ❑2, Win 1995, b&w 2.95
- ❑3, Spr 1996, b&w 2.95

Tiger 2021
Anubis

- ❑Ashcan 1, May 1994 .... 3.95

Tiger Girl
Gold Key

- ❑1, Sep 1968 .... 35.00

Tigerman
Atlas-Seaboard

- ❑1, Sep 1975; 1&O: Tigerman 9.00
- ❑2, Jun 1975 SD (a) 8.00
- ❑3, Sep 1975 SD (a) 8.00

Tigers of Terra
Mind-Visions

- ❑1, ca. 1992; Families of Altererd Wars #1 3.00
- ❑2, ca. 1992; Families of Altererd Wars #2 3.00
- ❑3, ca. 1992; Families of Altererd Wars #3 3.00
- ❑4, ca. 1992; Families of Altererd Wars #4 3.00
- ❑5, ca. 1992; Families of Altererd Wars #5 3.00
- ❑6, ca. 1992; Families of Altererd Wars #6 3.00
- ❑7, ca. 1992; Families of Altererd Wars #7 3.00
- ❑8, ca. 1993; Families of Altererd Wars #8 3.00
- ❑9, ca. 1993; two covers: a and b 3.75
- ❑10, ca. 1993, b&w; Families of Altererd Wars #10 .... 3.75
- ❑11, ca. 1993, b&w; Families of Altererd Wars #11 .... 3.95
- ❑12, Jul 1993, b&w; Families of Altererd Wars #12; Storyline moves to Tigers of Terra (Vol. 2) #1 .... 3.95

Tigers of Terra
Antarctic

- ❑0, Aug 1993; Families of Altered Wars #13; b&w 2.95
- ❑1, Oct 1993; Families of Altered Wars #14 3.00
- ❑2, Dec 1993; Families of Altered Wars #15 3.00
- ❑3, Feb 1994; Families of Altered Wars #16 3.00
- ❑4, Apr 1994; Families of Altered Wars #17 3.00
- ❑5, Jul 1994; Families of Altered Wars #18 3.00
- ❑6, Sep 1994; Families of Altered Wars #19 3.00
- ❑7, Dec 1994; Families of Altered Wars #20 3.00
- ❑8, Jan 1995; Families of Altered Wars #21 3.00
- ❑9, Mar 1995; Families of Altered Wars #22 3.00
- ❑10, Apr 1995; Families of Altered Wars #23 3.00
- ❑11, May 1995; Published as Tigers of Terra (Vol. 2) #11; Families of Altered Wars #24; b&w 2.75
- ❑12, Jun 1995; Families of Altered Wars #25 2.75
- ❑13, Jul 1995; Families of Altered Wars #26 2.75
- ❑14, Aug 1995; Families of Altered Wars #27 2.75
- ❑15, Sep 1995; Families of Altered Wars #28 2.75
- ❑16, Oct 1995; Families of Altered Wars #29 2.75
- ❑17, Nov 1995; Families of Altered Wars #30 2.75
- ❑18, Dec 1996; Families of Altered Wars #31 2.95
- ❑19, Jan 1996; Families of Altered Wars #32 2.95
- ❑20, Mar 1996; Families of Altered Wars #33 2.95
- ❑21, May 1996; Families of Altered Wars #34 2.95
- ❑22, Jul 1996; Families of Altered Wars #35 2.95
- ❑23, Sep 1996; Families of Altered Wars #36 2.95
- ❑24, Nov 1996; Families of Altered Wars #37 3.95
- ❑25, Jan 1997; Families of Altered Wars #38; Storyline moves to Luftwaffe: 1946 (Vol. 1) #1 .... 2.95

Tigers of Terra
Antarctic

- ❑1, Jul 2000; Families of Altered Wars #74 2.95

Ultimate Nightmare

X-Men vs. Ultimates in Tunguska
©Marvel

Ultimates

21st Century in-your-face Avengers
©Marvel

Ultimate Six

Ultimate Spidey joins the Sinister Six
©Marvel

Ultimate Spider-Man

Bendis reboot ushered in a new age
©Marvel

Ultimate X-Men

Turn-of-the-millennium spin on the mutants
©Marvel

N-MINT

Tigers of Terra: Technical Manual
Antarctic
- ❑1, Dec 1995, b&w ... 2.95
- ❑2, Jun 1996, b&w ... 2.95

Tiger Woman
Millennium
- ❑1, Sep 1994, no indicia ... 2.95
- ❑2, Apr 1995, no indicia; but title page says Tiger Woman #2, cover says Quest of the Tiger Woman #1 ... 2.95

Tiger-X
Eternity
- ❑1, Jul 1988, b&w; Story continued from Tiger-X Special #1 ... 2.00
- ❑2, Aug 1988, b&w ... 2.00
- ❑3, Sep 1988, b&w ... 2.00
- ❑Special 1, Jun 1988, b&w ... 2.25
- ❑Special 1/2nd, Dec 1988; 2nd printing. 2.25

Tiger-X Book II
Eternity
- ❑1, Jun 1989, b&w ... 2.00
- ❑2, Sep 1989, b&w ... 2.00
- ❑3, Dec 1989, b&w ... 2.00
- ❑4, Feb 1989, b&w ... 2.00

Tigra
Marvel
- ❑1, May 2002 ... 2.99
- ❑2, Jun 2002 ... 2.99
- ❑3, Jul 2002; Spider-Man/Kraven story included in several books this month. 2.99
- ❑4, Aug 2002 ... 2.99

Tigress
Hero
- ❑1, Aug 1992, b&w ... 2.95
- ❑2, Oct 1992, b&w ... 2.95
- ❑3, Dec 1992, b&w; 1: Mudpie ... 2.95
- ❑4, Feb 1993, b&w; Mudpie backup story 2.95
- ❑5, Apr 1993, b&w ... 2.95
- ❑6, Jun 1993; b&w ... 3.95

Tigress
Basement
- ❑1, Jul 1998 ... 2.95

Tijuana Bible
Starhead
- ❑1, b&w; Adult ... 2.50
- ❑2, b&w; Adult ... 2.50
- ❑3, b&w; Adult ... 2.50
- ❑4, b&w; Bluesie Toons ... 2.50
- ❑5; World's Fair ... 2.50
- ❑6; Fuller Brush Man ... 2.50
- ❑7; Royalty issue ... 2.50
- ❑8; Hollywood women ... 2.50
- ❑9; An Artist's Affaire ... 2.50

Tilazeus Meets the Messiah
Aiiie
- ❑1 ... 2.50

Timber Wolf
DC
- ❑1, Nov 1992 ... 1.50
- ❑2, Dec 1992 ... 1.50
- ❑3, Jan 1993; V: Creeper ... 1.50
- ❑4, Feb 1993 ... 1.50
- ❑5, Mar 1993 ... 1.50

N-MINT

Time Bandits
Marvel
- ❑1, Feb 1982; Movie adaptation ... 1.50

Time Breakers
DC / Helix
- ❑1, Jan 1997 ... 2.25
- ❑2, Feb 1997 ... 2.25
- ❑3, Mar 1997 ... 2.25
- ❑4, Apr 1997 ... 2.25
- ❑5, May 1997 ... 2.25

Time City
Rocket
- ❑1, Mar 1992; b&w ... 2.50

Timecop
Dark Horse
- ❑1, Sep 1994; Movie adaptation ... 2.50
- ❑2, Sep 1994; Movie adaptation ... 2.50

Timedrifter
Innovation
- ❑1, Dec 1990, b&w ... 2.25
- ❑2, b&w ... 2.25
- ❑3, b&w ... 2.25

Time Gates
Double Edge
- ❑1 ... 1.95
- ❑2 ... 1.95
- ❑3 ... 1.95

Timejump War
Apple
- ❑1, Oct 1989, b&w ... 2.25
- ❑2, b&w ... 2.25
- ❑3, b&w ... 2.25

Time Killers
Fleetway-Quality
- ❑1; Tales From Beyond Space: The Men In Red ... 2.95
- ❑2 ... 2.95
- ❑3 ... 2.95
- ❑4 ... 2.95
- ❑5 ... 2.95
- ❑6 ... 2.95
- ❑7 ... 2.95

Timeless Tales
Eclipse
- ❑1, Mar 1989, b&w ... 2.00

Timely Presents: All-Winners
Marvel
- ❑1, Dec 1999; Reprints All-Winners Comics #19 ... 3.99

Timely Presents: Human Torch
Marvel
- ❑1, Feb 1999; Painted cover; Contents reprinted from Human Torch Comics #5 3.99

Time Machine
Eternity
- ❑1, Apr 1990, b&w; Based on the story by H.G. Wells ... 2.50
- ❑2 1990, b&w ... 2.50
- ❑3 1990, b&w ... 2.50

N-MINT

Time Masters
DC
- ❑1, Feb 1990 ... 2.00
- ❑2, Mar 1990 ... 1.75
- ❑3, Apr 1990 ... 1.75
- ❑4, May 1990 ... 1.75
- ❑5, Jun 1990 A: Viking Prince ... 1.75
- ❑6, Jul 1990 A: Doctor Fate ... 1.75
- ❑7, Aug 1990 A: Arion ... 1.75
- ❑8, Sep 1990 ... 1.75

Time Out of Mind
Graphic Serials
- ❑1 ... 2.00
- ❑2 ... 1.75
- ❑3 ... 1.75

Timeslip Collection
Marvel
- ❑1, Nov 1998; collects short features from Marvel Vision; wraparound cover ... 2.99

Timeslip Special
Marvel
- ❑1, Oct 1998; cardstock cover ... 5.99

Timespell
Club 408 Graphics
- ❑0, ca. 1997, b&w; cardstock cover ... 2.95
- ❑1, ca. 1998, b&w; cardstock cover ... 2.95
- ❑2, ca. 1998, b&w; cardstock cover ... 2.95
- ❑3, ca. 1998, b&w; cardstock cover ... 2.95
- ❑4, ca. 1998, b&w; cardstock cover ... 2.95
- ❑Ashcan 1, ca. 1997; no cover price; ashcan preview of upcoming series ... 1.00

Timespell: The Director's Cut
Club 408 Graphics
- ❑1, ca. 1998, b&w; no price on cover; reprints #1 with revisions and additions 2.95

Timespirits
Marvel / Epic
- ❑1, Oct 1984 TY (c); TY (a) ... 2.00
- ❑2, Dec 1984 ... 1.75
- ❑3, Feb 1985 ... 1.75
- ❑4, Apr 1985 TY (c); AW, TY (a) ... 1.75
- ❑5, Jul 1985 ... 1.75
- ❑6, Sep 1985 ... 1.75
- ❑7, Dec 1985 ... 1.75
- ❑8, Mar 1986 ... 1.75

Time Traveler Ai
CPM Manga
- ❑1, Oct 1999, b&w ... 2.95
- ❑2, Nov 1999, b&w ... 2.95
- ❑3, Dec 1999, b&w ... 2.95
- ❑4, Jan 2000, b&w ... 2.95
- ❑5, Feb 2000, b&w ... 2.95
- ❑6, Mar 2000, b&w ... 2.95

Time Traveler Herbie
Avalon
- ❑1 ... 2.95

Time Tunnel
Gold Key
- ❑1, Feb 1967 ... 40.00
- ❑2, Jul 1967 ... 35.00

Other grades: Multiply price above by 5/6 for VF/NM • 2/3 for VERY FINE • 1/3 for FINE • 1/5 for VERY GOOD • 1/8 for GOOD

Time Twisted Tales
Rip Off

❑1, Reprints from Rip Off Comix #2 and 5; Adult 2.00

Time Twisters
Fleetway-Quality

❑1 AMo (w); DaG (a) 1.50
❑2 AMo (w); DaG (a) 1.50
❑3 AMo (w); BT (a) 1.50
❑4 AMo (w); DaG (a) 1.50
❑5 1.50
❑6 AMo (w) 1.50
❑7 AMo (w) 1.50
❑8 AMo (w); DaG (a) 1.50
❑9 AMo (w) 1.50
❑10 1.50
❑11 1.50
❑12 1.50
❑13 1.50
❑14 AMo (w); BB (a) 1.50
❑15 DaG (a) 1.50
❑16 1.50
❑17 NG (w) 1.50
❑18 NG (w) 1.50
❑19 1.50
❑20 1.50
❑21 AMo (w); DaG (a) 1.50

Timewalker
Acclaim / Valiant

❑0, Mar 1996; DP (c); BH (w); DP (a); O: Ivar; Wraparound Cover 5.00
❑1, Jan 1995; DP (c); BH (w); DP (a); cover has Dec 94 coverdate 2.00
❑1/VVSS 75.00
❑2, Feb 1995; DP (c); BH (w); DP (a); cover has Jan coverdate 1.00
❑3, Mar 1995; DP (c); BH (w); DP (a); cover has Feb coverdate 1.00
❑4, Apr 1995; BH (w); DP (a); cover has Mar coverdate 2.00
❑5, Apr 1995 BH (w); VM (a) 2.00
❑6, May 1995 2.00
❑7, Jun 1995 2.00
❑8, Jul 1995; Birthquake 2.00
❑9, Jul 1995; BH (w); DP (a); Birthquake 2.00
❑10, Aug 1995 2.00
❑11, Aug 1995 2.00
❑12, Sep 1995 DP (a) 2.00
❑13, Sep 1995 2.00
❑14, Oct 1995 2.00
❑15, Oct 1995; Final Issue 2.00
❑YB 1, May 1995; YB; A: H.A.R.D. Corps. Wraparound cover; YB 3.00

Time Wankers
Fantagraphics / Eros

❑1, Sep 1996, b&w; Adult 2.25
❑2, Jan 1991, b&w; Adult 2.25
❑3, Mar 1991, b&w; Adult 2.25
❑4, Apr 1991, b&w; Adult 2.25
❑5, Aug 1991, b&w; Adult 2.25

Time Warp
DC

❑1, Nov 1979 DN, TS, RB, SD, DG, JA, DA (a) 4.00
❑2, Jan 1980 2.00
❑3, Mar 1980 2.00
❑4, May 1980 2.00
❑5, Jul 1980; Final Issue 2.00

Time Warrior
Blazing

❑1 1993; Flipbookósee also Web-Man ... 2.50

Time Warriors: The Beginning
Fantasy General

❑1 1.50

Tim Holt Western Annual
AC

❑1, b&w; Reprints 2.95

Timmy the Timid Ghost
Charlton

❑1, Oct 1967 10.00
❑2, Feb 1968 6.00
❑3, Apr 1968 6.00
❑4, Jun 1968 6.00
❑5, Aug 1968 6.00
❑6, Oct 1968 6.00
❑7, Dec 1968 6.00
❑8, Feb 1969 6.00
❑9, Apr 1969 6.00
❑10, Jun 1969 6.00
❑11, Aug 1969 4.00
❑12, Oct 1969 4.00
❑13, Dec 1969 4.00
❑14, Jan 1970 4.00
❑15, Mar 1970 4.00
❑16, May 1970 4.00
❑17, Jul 1970 4.00
❑18, Sep 1970 4.00
❑19, Nov 1970 4.00
❑20, Jan 1971 4.00
❑21, Mar 1971 4.00
❑22, May 1971 4.00
❑23, Jul 1971 4.00
❑24, Sep 1985, reprints Timmy the Timid Ghost (1st series) #7 4.00
❑25, Nov 1985, reprints Timmy the Timid Ghost (1st series) #6 (cover reversed & recolored) 4.00
❑26, Jan 1986, reprints Timmy the Timid Ghost (1st series) #9 4.00

Tincan Man
Image / Valiant

❑1, Jan 2000 2.95
❑2, Feb 2000 2.95
❑Ashcan 1, Dec 1999; Preview issue 2.95

Tiny Deaths
YUGP

❑1 1.75
❑2, Jan 1997 1.75

Tipper Gore's Comics and Stories
Revolutionary

❑1, Oct 1989, b&w 1.95
❑2, Jan 1990, b&w 1.95
❑3, Mar 1990, b&w 1.95
❑4, May 1990, b&w 1.95
❑5, Jul 1990, b&w 1.95

Titan A.E.
Dark Horse

❑1, May 2000 2.95
❑2, Jun 2000 2.95
❑3, Jul 2000 2.95

Titans
DC

❑1, Mar 1999; DGry (w); A: H.I.V.E.. new team 3.00
❑1/Autographed, Mar 1999; DGry (w); A: H.I.V.E.. Autographed by Devin Grayson 15.95
❑2, Apr 1999 DGry (w); A: Superman. A: H.I.V.E. 2.50
❑3, May 1999; DGry (w); V: Goth 2.50
❑4, Jun 1999; DGry (w); V: Goth 2.50
❑5, Jul 1999; DGry (w); V: Siren 2.50
❑6, Aug 1999; DGry (w); A: Green Lantern. V: Red Panzer 2.50
❑7, Sep 1999 DGry (w) 2.50
❑8, Oct 1999 DGry (w) 2.50
❑9, Nov 1999; DGry (w); Day of Judgment 2.50
❑10, Dec 1999 DGry (w) 2.50
❑11, Jan 2000 DGry (w) 2.50
❑12, Feb 2000; 48 pages 2.50
❑13, Mar 2000 2.50
❑14, Apr 2000; DGry (w); Omen rescued from Tartarus 2.50
❑15, May 2000; DGry (w); V: Gargoyle 2.50
❑16, Jun 2000; V: Gargoyle 2.50
❑17, Jul 2000; V: Gordanians 2.50
❑18, Aug 2000 DGry (w) 2.50
❑19, Sep 2000 DGry (w) 2.50
❑20, Oct 2000 DGry (w) 2.50
❑21, Nov 2000; V: Hang-Men 2.50
❑22, Dec 2000; V: Deathstroke 2.50
❑23, Jan 2001; V: Dark Angel; Covers of #23-#25 form triptych 2.50
❑24, Feb 2001; V: Dark Angel; Covers of #23-#25 form triptych 2.50
❑25, Mar 2001; Giant-size; GP, NC (a); Giant-size; 48 pages; Covers of #23-#25 form triptych 3.95
❑26, Apr 2001; V: Shockwave 2.50
❑27, May 2001 2.50
❑28, Jun 2001 2.50
❑29, Jul 2001 2.50
❑30, Aug 2001 2.50
❑31, Sep 2001 2.50
❑32, Oct 2001 2.50
❑33, Nov 2001 2.50
❑34, Dec 2001; BSz (c); Joker: Last Laugh 2.50
❑35, Jan 2002 2.50
❑36, Feb 2002 2.50
❑37, Mar 2002 2.50
❑38, Apr 2002 2.50
❑39, May 2002 2.50
❑40, Jun 2002 2.50
❑41, Jul 2002 2.50
❑42, Aug 2002 2.50
❑43, Sep 2002 2.50
❑44, Oct 2002 2.75
❑45, Nov 2002 2.75
❑46, Dec 2002 2.75
❑47, Jan 2003 2.75
❑48, Feb 2003 2.75
❑49, Mar 2003 2.75
❑50, Apr 2003 2.75
❑Ann 1, Sep 2000; Planet DC 3.50

Titans/Legion of Super-Heroes: Universe Ablaze
DC

❑1, ca. 2000; Prestige format 4.95
❑2, ca. 2000; Prestige format 4.95
❑3, ca. 2000; Prestige format; 4.95
❑4 2000; Prestige format 4.95

Titan Special
Dark Horse

❑1, Jun 1994; D: Golden Boy; One-shot. 3.95

Titans: Scissors, Paper, Stone
DC

❑1 1997; prestige format; manga-style; Elseworlds 4.95

Titans Secret Files
DC

❑1, Mar 1999; 4.95
❑2, Oct 2000 4.95

Titans Sell-Out! Special
DC

❑1, Nov 1992 3.50

Titans/Young Justice: Graduation Day
DC

❑1, Jun 2003; V: Cybernetic android from the future; 1: Indigo 2.50
❑2, Jul 2003; D: Omen 2.50
❑3, Aug 2003; 1: Metamorpho II (becomes Shift); D: Donna Troy 2.50

Tiyu
Express / Entity

❑1, Oct 1996; Special picture-only cover 9.95

T-Minus-1
Renegade

❑1, Sep 1988, b&w 2.00

TMNT Mutant Universe Sourcebook
Archie

❑1, A-M 2.00
❑2, N-Z 2.00

TMNT: Teenage Mutant Ninja Turtles
Mirage

❑1, Dec 2001, Man atop demons on cover 2.95
❑2, Feb 2002 2.95
❑3, Apr 2002 2.95
❑4, Jun 2002 2.95
❑5, Aug 2002 2.95
❑6, Oct 2002 2.95
❑7, Dec 2002 2.95
❑8, Feb 2003, b&w 2.95
❑9, Apr 2003, b&w 2.95
❑10, Jun 2003, B&w, Extra length book. 3.95
❑11, Aug 2003 2.95
❑12, Oct 2003 2.95
❑13, Dec 2003 2.95
❑14, Feb 2004 2.95
❑15, Apr 2004 2.95
❑16, Nov 2004 2.95
❑17, Nov 2004 2.95
❑18, Nov 2004, b&w 2.95

To Be Announced
Strawberry Jam

❑1, ca. 1986, b&w 1.50
❑2, ca. 1986, b&w 1.50

UltraForce

Malibu's version of the Justice League
©Malibu

Ultraverse Origins

99¢ one-shot covering Malibu characters
©Malibu

Uncanny Origins

Straightforward approach for new readers
©Marvel

Uncanny X-Men

First 141 issues were "X-Men 1st Series"
©Marvel

Uncensored Mouse

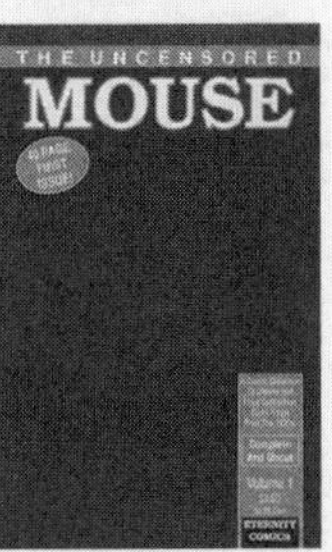

Uncopyrighted Mickey reprints led to fight
©Eternity

	N-MINT
❑3, ca. 1986, b&w	1.50
❑4, ca. 1986, b&w	1.50
❑5, ca. 1986, b&w	1.50
❑6, Feb 1987, b&w	1.50
❑7, ca. 1987, b&w	1.50

Todd McFarlane Presents: Kiss Psycho Circus
Image

❑1, Oct 1998; magazine; reprints #1-3 of comic book	6.95
❑2, Apr 1999; Includes Kiss: Psycho Circus #4, 5	4.95
❑3, Aug 1999; Includes Kiss: Psycho Circus #6, 7	4.95
❑4, Nov 1999; Includes Kiss: Psycho Circus #8, 9	4.95
❑5, Apr 2000	4.95

Todd McFarlane Presents: Ozzy Osbourne
Image

❑1, Jun 1999; magazine	4.95

Todd McFarlane Presents: The Crow Magazine
Image

❑1, Mar 2000, Includes James O'Barr interview	4.95

To Die For
Blackthorne

❑1, b&w; Movie adaptation	2.00
❑1/3D; Movie adaptation	2.50

Toe Tags Featuring George Romero
DC / Wildstorm

❑1, Dec 2004	2.95
❑2, Jan 2005	2.95
❑3, Feb 2005	2.95
❑4, Mar 2005	2.95
❑5, Apr 2005	2.95
❑6, May 2005	2.95

Tokyo Babylon
Tokyopop

❑1, May 2004; Graphic novel	9.99

Tokyo Boys & Girls
Viz

❑1, Jul 2005, b&w	8.99
❑2, Oct 2005	8.99

Tokyo Mew Mew
Tokyopop

❑1, Apr 2003, b&w; printed in Japanese format	9.99

TokyoPop
Mixx

❑1, Aug 1999	4.99
❑2, Oct 1999	4.99
❑3, Nov 1999	4.99
❑4, Dec 1999	4.99
❑5, Jan 2000	4.99
❑6	4.99
❑7	4.99

TokyoPop
Mixx

❑1	4.99
❑2, Oct 2000	4.99
❑3, Nov 2000	4.99

Tokyo Storm Warning
DC / Cliffhanger

	N-MINT
❑1, Aug 2003	2.95
❑2, Sep 2003	2.95
❑3, Dec 2003	2.95

Tokyo Tribes
Tokyopop

❑1, Sep 2004, Read right to left; Graphic novel	9.99
❑2, Feb 2005; Read right to left; Graphic novel; Foil cover lettering	9.99
❑3, Aug 2005; Foil cover; Graphic novel; Read right to left	9.99
❑4, Dec 2005	9.99

Tomahawk
DC

❑77, Nov 1961	32.00
❑78, Jan 1962	32.00
❑79, Mar 1962	32.00
❑80, May 1962	32.00
❑81, Jul 1962, 1: Miss Liberty	25.00
❑82, Sep 1962	25.00
❑83, Nov 1962	25.00
❑84, Jan 1963	25.00
❑85, Mar 1963	25.00
❑86, May 1963	25.00
❑87, Jul 1963	25.00
❑88, Sep 1963	25.00
❑89, Nov 1963	25.00
❑90, Jan 1964	25.00
❑91, Mar 1964	15.00
❑92, May 1964	15.00
❑93, Jul 1964	15.00
❑94, Sep 1964	15.00
❑95, Nov 1964	15.00
❑96, Jan 1965	15.00
❑97, Mar 1965	15.00
❑98, May 1965	15.00
❑99, Jul 1965	15.00
❑100, Sep 1965	15.00
❑101, Nov 1965	10.00
❑102, Jan 1966	10.00
❑103, Mar 1966	10.00
❑104, May 1966	10.00
❑105, Jul 1966	10.00
❑106, Sep 1966	10.00
❑107, Nov 1966	10.00
❑108, Jan 1967	10.00
❑109, Mar 1967	10.00
❑110, May 1967	10.00
❑111, Jul 1967	8.00
❑112, Sep 1967	8.00
❑113, Nov 1967, Reprint from Tomahawk #54	8.00
❑114, Jan 1968	8.00
❑115, Mar 1968, Reprint from Tomahawk #49	8.00
❑116, May 1968	8.00
❑117, Jul 1968	8.00
❑118, Sep 1968	8.00
❑119, Nov 1968, Tony Isabella L.O.C.	8.00
❑120, Jan 1969	8.00
❑121, Mar 1969	6.00
❑122, May 1969	6.00
❑123, Jul 1969, Reprint from Tomahawk #49	6.00
❑124, Sep 1969, Reprint from Tomahawk #31	6.00
❑125, Nov 1969	6.00
❑126, Jan 1970	6.00
❑127, Mar 1970	6.00
❑128, May 1970	6.00
❑129, Jul 1970, Includes General Tomahawk, reprinted from issue #51.	6.00
❑130, Sep 1970	6.00
❑131, Nov 1970, JKu (c); JKu (w); FT, FF, JKu (a); Series becomes "Son of Tomahawk"	6.00
❑132, Jan 1971, Says Son of Tomahawk on cover	6.00
❑133, Mar 1971, JKu (c); FT, JKu (a); Says Son of Tomahawk on cover; Includes pages from Ten Wagons for Tomahawk, reprinted from Tomahawk #26 with new framing sequence	4.50
❑134, May 1971, Says Son of Tomahawk on cover; Includes Pathway to Doom, reprinted from issue #27	4.50
❑135, Jul 1971, JKu (c); FT, JSe (a); Says Son of Tomahawk on cover	4.50
❑136, Sep 1971; Reprints from Tomahawk #87; Firehair; Wild Frontier; Hawk, Son of Tomahawk; 48 pages	4.50
❑137, Nov 1971; Reprints from Jimmy Wakely #1, Tomahawk #24, 85 and World's Finest Comics #67; Hawk, Son of Tomahawk; 48 pages	4.50
❑138, Jan 1972; Reprints from World's Finest Comics #70, All-American Western #124, and Legends of Daniel Boone #7; Hawk, Son of Tomahawk; 48 pages	4.50
❑139, Mar 1972; JKu (c); FT, FF, GK (a); says Son of Tomahawk on cover	4.50
❑140, May 1972; says Son of Tomahawk on cover	4.50

Tom & Jerry 50th Anniversary Special
Harvey

	N-MINT
❑1, Oct 1991; Reprints	2.50

Tom & Jerry Adventures
Harvey

❑1, May 1992; Reprints	1.25

Tom & Jerry and Friends
Harvey

❑1, Dec 1991; Reprints	1.25
❑2, Feb 1992; Reprints	1.25
❑3, Apr 1992; Reprints	1.25
❑4, Jul 1992; Reprints	1.25

Tom & Jerry Big Book
Harvey

❑1, Sep 1992	1.95
❑2, Jul 1993	1.95

Tom & Jerry Comics
Dell

❑208, Nov 1961	3.00
❑209, Jan 1962	3.00
❑210, Mar 1962	3.00
❑211, May 1962	3.00
❑212, Aug 1962	3.00
❑213, Nov 1962; Titled Tom and Jerry Funhouse	3.00
❑214, Feb 1963; Titled Tom and Jerry Funhouse	3.00

Other grades: Multiply price above by 5/6 for VF/NM • 2/3 for VERY FINE • 1/3 for FINE • 1/5 for VERY GOOD • 1/8 for GOOD

	N-MINT
❑215, May 1963, Titled Tom and Jerry Funhouse	3.00
❑216, Aug 1963	3.00
❑217, Nov 1963	3.00
❑218, Feb 1964	3.00
❑219, May 1964	3.00
❑220, Aug 1964	3.00
❑221, Nov 1964	3.00
❑222, Feb 1965, A: Professor Putter	3.00
❑223, Apr 1965	3.00
❑224, Jun 1965	3.00
❑225, Aug 1965, A: Professor Putter	3.00
❑226, Oct 1965	3.00
❑227, Dec 1965, A: Professor Putter	3.00
❑228, Feb 1966, A: Professor Putter	3.00
❑229, Apr 1966, A: Professor Putter	3.00
❑230, Jun 1966, A: Professor Putter	3.00
❑231, Aug 1966	2.00
❑232, Oct 1966	2.00
❑233, Dec 1966	2.00
❑234, Feb 1967, 10058-702; published by Gold Key	2.00
❑235, Apr 1967	2.00
❑236, Jun 1967, 10058-706; Published by Gold Key	2.00
❑237, Aug 1967	2.00
❑238, Nov 1967	2.00
❑239, Feb 1968	2.00
❑240, May 1968	2.00
❑241, Aug 1968	2.00
❑242, Nov 1968	2.00
❑243, Feb 1969, 10058-902	2.00
❑244, Apr 1969	2.00
❑245, Jun 1969	2.00
❑246, Aug 1969, 10058-908; published by Gold Key	2.00
❑247, Oct 1969, 10058-910; published by Gold Key	2.00
❑248, Dec 1969	2.00
❑249, Feb 1970	2.00
❑250, Apr 1970	2.00
❑251, Jun 1970	2.00
❑252, Aug 1970	2.00
❑253, Oct 1970	2.00
❑254, Dec 1970	2.00
❑255, Feb 1971	2.00
❑256, Apr 1971	2.00
❑257, Jun 1971	2.00
❑258, Aug 1971	2.00
❑259, Sep 1971	2.00
❑260, Dec 1971, 10058-110; published by Gold Key	2.00
❑261, Dec 1971	2.00
❑262, Feb 1972	2.00
❑263, Apr 1972, 90058-204	2.00
❑264, Jun 1972	2.00
❑265, Aug 1972	2.00
❑266, Sep 1972	2.00
❑267, Oct 1972	2.00
❑268, Dec 1972	2.00
❑269, Feb 1973	2.00
❑270, Apr 1973, 90058-304	2.00
❑271, Jun 1973	1.50
❑272, Jul 1973	1.50
❑273, Aug 1973	1.50
❑274, Sep 1973	1.50
❑275, Oct 1973	1.50
❑276, Nov 1973	1.50
❑277, Dec 1973	1.50
❑278, Jan 1974	1.50
❑279, Feb 1974	1.50
❑280, Mar 1974	1.50
❑281, Apr 1974	1.50
❑282, May 1974	1.50
❑283, Jun 1974	1.50
❑284, Jul 1974	1.50
❑285, Aug 1974	1.50
❑286, Sep 1974	1.50
❑287, Oct 1974	1.50
❑288, Nov 1974	1.50
❑289, Dec 1974	1.50
❑290, Jan 1975	1.50
❑291, Feb 1975	1.50
❑292, Mar 1977	1.50
❑293, Apr 1977	1.50
❑294, May 1977	1.50
❑295, Jun 1977	1.50
❑296, Jul 1977	1.50
❑297, Aug 1977	1.50
❑298, Sep 1977	1.50
❑299, Oct 1977	1.50
❑300, Nov 1977	1.50
❑301, Dec 1977	1.00
❑302, Jan 1978, 48 page issue	1.00
❑303, Feb 1978	1.00
❑304, Mar 1978	1.00
❑305, Apr 1978	1.00
❑306, May 1978	1.00
❑307, Jun 1978	1.00
❑308, Jul 1978	1.00
❑309, Aug 1978	1.00
❑310, Sep 1978	1.00
❑311, Oct 1978	1.00
❑312, Nov 1978	1.00
❑313, Dec 1978	1.00
❑314, Jan 1979	1.00
❑315, Feb 1979	1.00
❑316, Mar 1979	1.00
❑317, Apr 1979	1.00
❑318, May 1979	1.00
❑319, Jun 1979	1.00
❑320, Jul 1979	1.00
❑321, Aug 1979	1.00
❑322, Sep 1979	1.00
❑323, Oct 1979	1.00
❑324, Nov 1979	1.00
❑325, Dec 1979	1.00
❑326, Jan 1980	1.00
❑327, Feb 1980	1.00
❑328, Apr 1980	5.00
❑329, Jun 1980	5.00
❑330, Aug 1980	20.00
❑331, Oct 1980	7.00
❑332, Dec 1980	7.00
❑333, Feb 1981	7.00
❑334, Apr 1981	7.00
❑335, Jun 1981	7.00
❑336, Aug 1981	7.00
❑337, Oct 1981, 90058-110	7.00
❑338, ca. 1982	7.00
❑339, ca. 1982	7.00
❑340, ca. 1982	7.00
❑341, ca. 1982	7.00
❑342, ca. 1982	15.00
❑343, ca. 1983	15.00
❑344, ca. 1983, Final Issue	15.00

Tom & Jerry Digest
Harvey

	N-MINT
❑1, ca. 1992; Reprints	1.75

Tom & Jerry Giant Size
Harvey

	N-MINT
❑1, Oct 1992; Reprints	1.95
❑2, Oct 1993	2.25

Tom & Jerry Summer Fun
Gold Key

	N-MINT
❑1, Oct 1967, Droopy reprinted from Tom and Jerry Summer Fun (Dell) #1	35.00

Tom & Jerry
Harvey

	N-MINT
❑1, Sep 1991; Reprints	1.50
❑2, Nov 1991; Reprints	1.25
❑3, Jan 1992; Reprints	1.25
❑4, Mar 1992; Reprints	1.25
❑5, Jun 1992; Reprints	1.25
❑6, Jan 1993; Reprints	1.25
❑7, ca. 1993; Reprints	1.25
❑8, ca. 1993; Reprints	1.25
❑9, ca. 1993	1.50
❑10, Dec 1993	1.50
❑11, Jan 1994	1.50
❑12, Feb 1994	1.50
❑13, Mar 1994	1.50
❑14, Apr 1994	1.50
❑15, May 1994	1.50
❑16, Jun 1994	1.50
❑17, Jul 1994	1.50
❑18, Aug 1994	1.50
❑Ann 1, Sep 1994	2.25

Tomato
Starhead

	N-MINT
❑1, Apr 1994, b&w; Adult	2.75
❑2, Feb 1995, b&w; Adult	2.75

Tomb of Darkness
Marvel

	N-MINT
❑9, Jul 1974, Series continued from Beware #8	20.00
❑10, Sep 1974	10.00
❑11, Nov 1974	10.00
❑12, Jan 1975	10.00
❑13, Mar 1975	10.00
❑14, May 1975	10.00
❑15, Jul 1975	10.00
❑16, Sep 1975, Reprints from Tales of Suspense and Astonishing Tales	10.00
❑17, Nov 1975	10.00
❑18, Jan 1976	10.00
❑19, Mar 1976	10.00
❑20, May 1976	10.00
❑20/30¢, May 1976, 30¢ regional price variant	20.00
❑21, Jul 1976	10.00
❑21/30¢, Jul 1976, 30¢ regional price variant	20.00
❑22, Sep 1976, Reprints from Marvel Tales (1st Series) #113, Venus #19 and Strange Tales (1st Series) #16	10.00
❑23, Nov 1976, Final Issue	10.00

Tomb of Dracula
Marvel

	N-MINT
❑1, Apr 1972, NA (c); AW, GC (a); 1&O: Frank Drake. 1: Dracula (Marvel)	100.00
❑2, May 1972, JSe (c); GC (a)	35.00
❑3, Jul 1972, GC (c); GC (a); 1: Rachel Van Helsing	35.00
❑4, Sep 1972, GC (c); GC (a)	30.00
❑5, Nov 1972, GK (c); GC (a)	18.00
❑6, Jan 1973, NA (c); GC (a)	18.00
❑7, Mar 1973, GC (a); 1: Edith Harker	15.00
❑8, May 1973, GC (a)	12.00
❑9, Jun 1973, GC (a); 1: Lucas Brand	12.00
❑10, Jul 1973, GC (a); 1: Blade the Vampire Slayer	100.00
❑11, Aug 1973, GC (c); GC (a)	10.00
❑12, Sep 1973, FB (c); GC (a); A: Blade the Vampire Slayer	12.00
❑13, Oct 1973, GC (a); O: Blade the Vampire Slayer. 1: Deacon Frost	35.00
❑14, Nov 1973, GC (a); A: Blade the Vampire Slayer	12.00
❑15, Dec 1973, GC (a)	10.00
❑16, Jan 1974, GC (a)	10.00
❑17, Feb 1974, GC (a); A: Blade the Vampire Slayer	12.00
❑18, Mar 1974, GC (a); V: Werewolf by Night. Marvel Value Stamp #7: Werewolf	10.00
❑19, Apr 1974, GC (a); A: Blade the Vampire Slayer. Marvel Value Stamp #26: Mephisto	12.00
❑20, May 1974, GC (a); 1: Doctor Sun. Marvel Value Stamp #88: Leader	10.00
❑21, Jun 1974, GC (a); O: Doctor Sun. A: Blade the Vampire Slayer. Marvel Value Stamp #96: Dr. Octopus	10.00
❑22, Jul 1974, GC (a); Marvel Value Stamp #27: Black Widow	8.00
❑23, Aug 1974, GC, TP (a); Marvel Value Stamp #50 : Black Panther	8.00
❑24, Sep 1974, GC (a); Marvel Value Stamp #57: Vulture	8.00
❑25, Oct 1974, GC (a); 1&O: Hannibal King. Marvel Value Stamp #49: Odin	8.00
❑25/2nd, Oct 1974, GC (a); 1&O: Hannibal King. (part of Marvel Value Pack)	1.50
❑26, Nov 1974, GC (a); Marvel Value Stamp #80: Ghost Rider	8.00
❑27, Dec 1974, GC, TP (a); Marvel Value Stamp #69: Marvel Girl	8.00
❑28, Jan 1975, GC, TP (a); 1: Adri Nitall. Marvel Value Stamp #57: Vulture	8.00
❑29, Feb 1975, GC (c); GC, TP (a); Marvel Value Stamp #80: Ghost Rider	8.00
❑30, Mar 1975, GC (a); A: Blade the Vampire Slayer. Marvel Value Stamp #23: Sgt. Fury	10.00
❑31, Apr 1975, GC, TP (a); Marvel Value Stamp #45: Mantis	8.00
❑32, May 1975, GC (a)	8.00
❑33, Jun 1975, GC, TP (a)	7.00
❑34, Jul 1975, GC, TP (a); A: Brother Voodoo. Marvel Value Stamp #87: J. Jonah Jameson	7.00
❑35, Aug 1975, GC, TP (a); A: Brother Voodoo. Marvel Value Stamp #74: Stranger	7.00

Other grades: Multiply price above by 5/6 for VF/NM • 2/3 for VERY FINE • 1/3 for FINE • 1/5 for VERY GOOD • 1/8 for GOOD

Uncle Scrooge

Carl Bark's most popular creation

©Dell

Uncle Scrooge and Donald Duck

Gladstone spinoff ran two issues

©Gold Key

Uncle Slam & Fire Dog

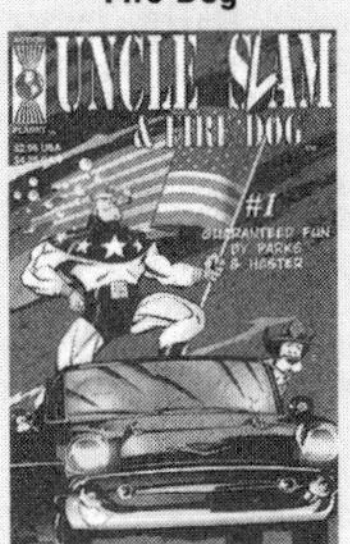

Hero has a hole in his head

©Action Planet

Underdog (Charlton)

Have no fear, animated canine is here

©Charlton

Underdog (Harvey)

Harvey reprints of older adventures

©Harvey

N-MINT

❑36, Sep 1975, GC (a); A: Brother Voodoo ... 7.00
❑37, Oct 1975, GC, TP (a); 1: Harold H. Harold. Marvel Value Stamp #12: Daredevil ... 7.00
❑38, Nov 1975, GC (c); GC, TP (a); A: Doctor Sun ... 7.00
❑39, Dec 1975, GC (c); GC, TP (a); D: Dracula. Marvel Value Stamp #77: Swordsman ... 7.00
❑40, Jan 1976, GC (c); GC, TP (a) ... 7.00
❑41, Feb 1976, GC (c); GC (a); A: Blade the Vampire Slayer ... 7.00
❑42, Mar 1976, GC (c); GC (a); A: Blade the Vampire Slayer. V: Doctor Sun ... 6.00
❑43, Apr 1976, BWr (c); GC (a) ... 6.00
❑43/30¢, Apr 1976, 30¢ regional price variant ... 18.00
❑44, May 1976, GC (c); GC (a); A: Hannibal King. A: Blade the Vampire Slayer. V: Doctor Strange ... 6.00
❑44/30¢, May 1976, GC (c); GC (a); 30¢ regional price variant ... 18.00
❑45, Jun 1976, GC (a); A: Hannibal King. Blade vs. Hannibal King ... 6.00
❑45/30¢, Jun 1976, GC (a); 30¢ regional price variant ... 18.00
❑46, Jul 1976, GC (c); GC (a); A: Blade. A: Blade the Vampire Slayer. Wedding of Dracula ... 6.00
❑46/30¢, Jul 1976, GC (c); GC (a); 30¢ regional price variant ... 18.00
❑47, Aug 1976, GC (c); GC (a); A: Blade the Vampire Slayer ... 6.00
❑47/30¢, Aug 1976, GC (c); GC (a); 30¢ regional price variant ... 18.00
❑48, Sep 1976, GC (c); GC (a); A: Hannibal King. A: Blade the Vampire Slayer ... 6.00
❑49, Oct 1976, GC (c); GC (a); A: Zorro. A: Tom Sawyer. A: D'Artagnan. A: Frankenstein. A: Blade the Vampire Slayer ... 6.00
❑50, Nov 1976, GC (c); GC (a); A: Blade the Vampire Slayer. A: Silver Surfer ... 10.00
❑51, Dec 1976, GC (c); GC, TP (a); 1: Janus. Blade vs. Hannibal King ... 6.00
❑52, Jan 1977, GC (c); GC (a) ... 6.00
❑53, Feb 1977, GC (c); GC (a); A: Son of Satan. Blade vs. Hannibal King and Deacon Frost ... 6.00
❑54, Mar 1977, GC (c); GC, TP (a); O: Janus. A: Blade. birth of Dracula's son ... 6.00
❑55, Apr 1977, GC, TP (c); GC (a) ... 6.00
❑56, May 1977, GC (c); GC (a) ... 6.00
❑57, Jun 1977, GC (c); GC, TP (a); 35¢ regional price variant ... 6.00
❑57/35¢, Jun 1977, GC, TP (a); 35¢ regional price variant ... 12.00
❑58, Jul 1977, GC (c); GC (a) ... 6.00
❑58/35¢, Jul 1977, 35¢ regional price variant ... 12.00
❑59, Aug 1977, GC (c); GC (a) ... 6.00
❑59/35¢, Aug 1977, GC (c); GC (a); 35¢ regional price variant ... 12.00
❑60, Sep 1977, GC (c); GC, TP (a) ... 6.00
❑60/35¢, Sep 1977, GC (c); GC, TP (a); 35¢ regional price variant ... 12.00
❑61, Nov 1977, GC (c); GC (a); O: Janus ... 5.00
❑62, Jan 1978, GC (c); GC (a) ... 5.00
❑63, Mar 1978, GC (c); GC (a) ... 5.00
❑64, May 1978, GC (c); GC, TP (a) ... 5.00
❑65, Jul 1978, GC (c); GC, TP (a) ... 5.00
❑66, Sep 1978, GC (c); GC, TP (a) ... 5.00
❑67, Nov 1978, GC (c); GC, TP (a); A: Lilith ... 5.00
❑68, Feb 1979, GC (c); GC (a) ... 5.00
❑69, Apr 1979, GC (c); GC, TP (a) ... 5.00
❑70, Aug 1979, Double-size; D: Dracula ... 8.00

Tomb of Dracula
Marvel

❑1 2004 ... 2.99
❑2 ... 2.99
❑3 ... 2.99
❑4 2005 ... 2.99

Tomb of Dracula
Marvel

❑1, Oct 1979, b&w; magazine; GC (a) ... 15.00
❑2, Dec 1979 SD, FR (a) ... 6.00
❑3, Feb 1980 GC, FM, TP (a) ... 6.00
❑4, Apr 1980 GC, JB, TP (a) ... 6.00
❑5, Jun 1980 GC, JB, TP (a) ... 6.00
❑6, Aug 1980 GC (a) ... 6.00

Tomb of Dracula
Marvel / Epic

❑1, Nov 1991 GC (c); AW, GC (a) ... 5.00
❑2, Dec 1991 GC (c); AW, GC (a) ... 5.00
❑3, Jan 1992 GC (c); AW, GC (a) ... 5.00
❑4, Feb 1992 GC (c); AW, GC (a) ... 5.00

Tomb of Ligeia
Dell

❑1, Jun 1965, Adapts movie Tomb of the Cat ... 12.00

Tomb Raider: Arabian Nights
Image

❑1, Aug 2004 ... 5.99

Tomb Raider Cover Gallery
Image

❑1, Apr 2006 ... 2.99

Tomb Raider/Darkness Special
Image

❑1, ca. 2001; Topcowstore.com exclusive ... 4.00
❑1/A, ca. 2001; Topcowstore.com exclusive; Gold foil logo on cover ... 6.00

Tomb Raider: Epiphany
Image

❑1, Jul 2003; Witchblade Animated; Special Preview, 6 pages ... 4.99

Tomb Raider Gallery
Image

❑1, Dec 2000 ... 2.95

Tomb Raider: Greatest Treasure of All One Shot
Image

❑1 ... 6.99

Tomb Raider: Journeys
Image

❑1, Feb 2002; Indicia says Jan, 2001; Cover A ... 2.95
❑2, Mar 2002 ... 2.95
❑3, May 2002; Adam Hughes cover ... 2.95
❑4, Jun 2002 ... 2.95
❑5, Aug 2002; Cover by Keu Cha ... 2.95
❑6, Sep 2002 ... 2.95
❑7, Oct 2002 ... 2.99
❑8, Dec 2002 ... 2.99
❑9, Feb 2003 ... 2.99
❑10, Feb 2003 ... 2.99
❑11, Apr 2003; Computer generated cover art by CORE/EIDOS ... 2.99
❑12, May 2003; Computer generated cover art by CORE/EIDOS; Final issue ... 2.99

Tomb Raider Magazine
Image

❑1, Jun 2001 ... 4.95

Tomb Raider: Takeover One Shot
Image

❑1, Dec 2003 ... 2.99

Tomb Raider: The Series
Image

❑0, Jun 2001 ... 2.50
❑0/Dynamic, Jun 2001; Painted cover; Dynamic Forces variant ... 5.00
❑½, Sep 2001; O: Lara Croft; Cover by Andy Park ... 2.50
❑1, Dec 1999; Lara Croft crouching on rock with setting sun ... 2.50
❑1/C, Dec 1999; Lara climbing mountain ... 2.50
❑1/D, Dec 1999; Lara standing in front of ruins ... 2.50
❑1/Holofoil, Dec 1999; Holofoil cover: Lara on rock, no sun in background ... 7.00
❑1/Another Unive, Dec 1999; Another Universe Exclusive ... 5.00
❑1/Tower Gold, Dec 1999; Tower Records exclusive; Gold foil Tomb Raider logo; Lara on rock, no sun in background ... 6.00
❑1/Tower, Dec 1999; Tower records exclusive w/o gold logo ... 5.00
❑2, Jan 2000; Cover by Andy Park ... 2.50
❑2/Tower, Jan 2000; Tower Records: Santa cover with blue background ... 5.00
❑2/Tower foil, Jan 2000; Tower Records: Santa cover with yellowish holo-foil background ... 6.50
❑3, Feb 2000 ... 2.50
❑3/Monster Mart, Feb 2000; Monster Mart Edition; Lara kneeling on ruins, Monster Mart logo in lower right ... 7.00
❑3/Gold Mart, Feb 2000; Gold Monster Mart edition; Lara kneeling on ruins, Monster Mart logo in lower right ... 125.00
❑4, Apr 2000; Lara sitting on root of tree, man standing, flames behind ... 2.50
❑4/Dynamic, Apr 2000; Lara in tree, DF logo at bottom left ... 4.00
❑4/Dynamic with, Apr 2000; Similar cover to 4, with Certificate of Authenticity ... 8.00
❑5, May 2000; Lara standing, dinosaur skeleton in background ... 2.50
❑5/Dynamic, May 2000; Dynamic Forces variant, Tomb Raider logo in upper right, DF logo below, Lara standing on Triceratops skull ... 6.00
❑6, Jul 2000; Painted cover by Joe Jusko ... 2.50
❑7, Jul 2000 ... 2.50
❑7/Museum, Jul 2000; Museum edition, limited to 25 copies.; Museum edition ... 125.00
❑8, Oct 2000 ... 2.50
❑9, Dec 2000; Lara sitting, faces in background ... 2.50
❑9/White, Dec 2000; White background, holding two guns ... 4.00

Other grades: Multiply price above by 5/6 for VF/NM • 2/3 for VERY FINE • 1/3 for FINE • 1/5 for VERY GOOD • 1/8 for GOOD

❑9/Dynamic, Dec 2000; Lara fighting crocodile, DF logo at top left............. 6.00
❑9/Dynamic blue, Dec 2000; Lara fighting crocodile, blue foil around DF logo at top left............. 7.00
❑9/Sketch, Dec 2000; Sketch cover, black and white............. 10.00
❑10, Jan 2001............. 2.50
❑10/Gold foil, Jan 2001; Gold foil around Tomb Raider logo, includes Certificate of Authenticity............. 12.00
❑10/Red foil, Jan 2001; Red foil around Tomb Raider logo, includes Certificate of Authenticity............. 10.00
❑11, Mar 2001............. 2.50
❑11/Graham, Mar 2001; Graham Crackers Blue Foil Edition; Limited to 1,000 copies; forms consecutive image with cover of exclusive Tomb Raider #12 Graham Crackers edition............. 7.00
❑12, Apr 2001............. 2.50
❑12/Graham, Apr 2001; 2,500 produced; forms single image with #11 Graham Crackers exclusive............. 8.00
❑13, May 2001............. 2.50
❑14, Jul 2001............. 2.50
❑15, Sep 2001............. 2.50
❑15/Dynamic, Sep 2001; DFE red foil cover............. 10.00
❑16, Oct 2001............. 2.50
❑17, Nov 2001............. 2.50
❑18, Dec 2001............. 2.50
❑19, Jan 2002............. 2.50
❑20, Feb 2002............. 2.50
❑21, May 2002............. 2.50
❑22, Jul 2002............. 2.50
❑23, Aug 2002; Cover by Randy Green.. 2.50
❑24, Oct 2002; Endgame Prelude............. 2.99
❑25, Nov 2002; Cover by Michael Turner (Black suit)............. 2.99
❑26, Feb 2003; Cover by Andy Park, Jonathan Sibal (Inks), Jonathan D. Smith (Color)............. 2.99
❑27, Feb 2003............. 2.99
❑28, Apr 2003............. 2.99
❑29, May 2003; Computer generated cover art by Eidos/Core............. 2.99
❑30, Jun 2003; Double sized issue; Cover by Tony Daniel; 1st Tony Daniel Tomb Raider art............. 2.99
❑31, Jun 2003............. 2.99
❑32, Aug 2003; Cover by Adam Hughes 2.99
❑33, Sep 2003............. 2.99
❑34, Oct 2003............. 2.99
❑35, Nov 2003............. 2.99
❑36, Jan 2004............. 2.99
❑37, Feb 2004............. 2.99
❑38, Apr 2004............. 2.99
❑39, Apr 2004............. 2.99
❑40, May 2004............. 2.99
❑41, May 2004............. 2.99
❑42, Aug 2004............. 2.99
❑43, Aug 2004............. 2.99
❑44, Aug 2004............. 2.99
❑45, Oct 2004............. 2.99
❑46, Nov 2004............. 2.99
❑47, Hughes cover............. 4.00
❑47/Variant, Basaldua cover............. 2.99
❑48, Hughes cover............. 4.00
❑48/Variant, Basaldua cover............. 2.99
❑49, Feb 2005............. 2.99
❑50, Mar 2005............. 2.99
❑Ashcan 1; Convention edition; Preview cover, with second outer cover (black & white) with Lara Croft on front, logo with white space on back............. 5.00

Tomb Raider/Witchblade
Image

❑1, Dec 1997; Green Cover............. 6.00
❑1/A, Dec 1997; Brown cover............. 6.00
❑1/B, Dec 1997; Includes certificate of authenticity; Autographed by Michael Turner............. 20.00
❑1/2nd, Dec 1998, titled "Tomb Raider/ Witchblade Revisited"............. 2.95

Tomb Tales
Cryptic

❑1, b&w; cardstock cover............. 3.00
❑2, Jun 1997, b&w; cardstock cover..... 3.00

Tom Corbett
Eternity

❑1, Jan 1990, b&w; Original material..... 2.25
❑2, Feb 1990, b&w; Original material..... 2.25
❑3, Mar 1990, b&w; Space Academy photo inside front cover............. 2.25
❑4, May 1990, b&w............. 2.25

Tom Corbett Book Two
Eternity

❑1, Sep 1990, b&w............. 2.25
❑2, Oct 1990, b&w............. 2.25
❑3, Oct 1990, b&w............. 2.25
❑4, Nov 1990, b&w............. 2.25

Tom Judge: End of Days
Image

❑1, Sep 2003............. 3.99

Tom Landry
Spire

❑1, ca. 1973; NN............. 3.00

Tommi Gunn
London Night

❑1, May 1996; Adult............. 3.00

Tommi Gunn: Killer's Lust
London Night

❑1, Feb 1997; Adult............. 3.00
❑1/Nude, Feb 1997; chromium cover..... 3.00

Tom Mix Western
AC

❑1; Reprints............. 2.95
❑2, b&w; Reprints............. 2.50

Tommy and the Monsters
New Comics

❑1, b&w; ca. 1989............. 1.95

Tomoe
Crusade

❑0, Mar 1996............. 3.00
❑0/Ltd., Mar 1996; Limited edition (5,000 printed); Limited edition............. 4.00
❑0/Variant, Mar 1996; variant cover....... 3.00
❑1, Apr 1996............. 3.00
❑1/Ltd., Apr 1996; Limited edition (5,000 printed)............. 4.00
❑1/2nd; Fan Appreciation Edition; contains preview of Manga Shi 2000. 3.00
❑2, May 1996............. 3.00
❑3, Jun 1996............. 3.00

Tomoe: Unforgettable Fire
Crusade

❑1, Jun 1997; prequel to Shi: The Series 2.95
❑1/Ltd., Jun 1997; American Entertainment Exclusive Edition; No cover price; prequel to Shi: The Series 3.50

Tomoe/Witchblade: Fire Sermon
Crusade

❑1, Sep 1996; one-shot crossover with Image............. 3.95
❑1/A, Sep 1996; Avalon edition; no cover price............. 5.00

Tomorrow Knights
Marvel / Epic

❑1, Jun 1990............. 1.95
❑2, Jul 1990............. 1.50
❑3, Sep 1990............. 1.50
❑4, Nov 1990............. 1.50
❑5, Jan 1991............. 1.50
❑6, Mar 1991............. 1.50

Tomorrow Man
Antarctic

❑1, Aug 1993, b&w; foil cover............. 2.95

Tomorrow Man & Knight Hunter: Last Rites
Antarctic

❑1, Jul 1994, b&w............. 2.75
❑2, Oct 1994, b&w............. 2.75
❑3, Dec 1994, b&w............. 2.75
❑4, Feb 1995, b&w............. 2.75
❑5, Apr 1995, b&w............. 2.75
❑6, Jun 1995, b&w............. 2.75

Tomorrow Stories
DC / America's Best Comics

❑1, Oct 1999; ARo (c); AMo (w); KN (a); 1: Greyshirt; 1: Jack B. Quick; 1: The Cobweb; 1: The First American; 1: U.S. Angel............. 4.00
❑1/Variant, Oct 1999............. 6.00
❑2, Nov 1999 AMo (w)............. 3.00
❑3, Dec 1999; KN (c); AMo (w); KN (a); O: Greyshirt............. 2.95
❑4, Jan 2000 AMo (w); KN (a)............. 2.95
❑5, Feb 2000 AMo (w)............. 2.95
❑6, Mar 2000; AMo (w); 1: Splash Brannigan............. 2.95
❑7, Apr 2000 AMo (w)............. 2.95
❑8, Jan 2001 AMo (w)............. 2.95
❑9, Feb 2001; AMo (w); O: The First American............. 2.95
❑10, Jun 2001 KN (c); AMo (w); KN (a). 2.95
❑11, Oct 2001 AMo (w)............. 2.95
❑12, Apr 2002 AMo (w)............. 2.95

Tomorrow Stories Special
DC

❑1, Jan 2006............. 6.99
❑2, May 2006............. 6.99

Tom Strong
DC / America's Best Comics

❑1, Jun 1999; 1&O: Tom Strong............. 4.00
❑1/Variant, Jun 1999............. 5.00
❑2, Jul 1999; V: Modular Man............. 3.00
❑3, Aug 1999; V: Aztech............. 2.95
❑4, Oct 1999; V: Ingrid Weiss, Nazi soldier; Tom Strong in WWII............. 2.95
❑5, Dec 1999; V: Pangaean, organism from prehistoric Earth............. 2.95
❑6, Feb 2000; V: Saveen............. 2.95
❑7, Mar 2000............. 2.95
❑8, Jul 2000............. 2.95
❑9, Sep 2000............. 2.95
❑10, Nov 2000............. 2.95
❑11, Jan 2001; 1: Tom Strange of Terra Obscura............. 2.95
❑12, Jun 2001; JLA homage cover........ 2.95
❑13, Jul 2001; Marvel Family homage cover............. 2.95
❑14, Oct 2001............. 2.95
❑15, Mar 2002; Fantastic Four homage cover............. 2.95
❑16, Apr 2002............. 2.95
❑17, Aug 2002............. 2.95
❑18, Dec 2002............. 2.95
❑19, Apr 2003............. 2.95
❑20, Jun 2003............. 2.95
❑21, Oct 2003............. 2.95
❑22, Dec 2003............. 2.95
❑23, Jan 2004............. 2.95
❑24, Feb 2004............. 2.95
❑25, May 2004............. 2.95
❑26, Jul 2004............. 2.95
❑27, Sep 2004............. 2.95
❑28, Oct 2004............. 2.95
❑29, Nov 2004............. 2.95
❑30, Feb 2005............. 2.95
❑31, Mar 2005............. 2.95
❑32, Apr 2005............. 2.99
❑33, Aug 2005............. 2.99
❑34, Oct 2005............. 2.99
❑35, Jan 2006............. 2.99
❑36, May 2006, Final Issue............. 2.99

Tom Strong's Terrific Tales
DC / America's Best Comics

❑1, Jan 2002; Jonni Future backup story; Arthur Adams (cover)............. 3.50
❑2, Mar 2002............. 2.95
❑3, Jun 2002............. 2.95
❑4, Nov 2002............. 2.95
❑5, Jan 2003; Story layout as if a set of bubblegum trading cards............. 2.95
❑6, Apr 2003............. 2.95
❑7, Jul 2003............. 2.95
❑8, Dec 2003............. 2.95
❑9, Apr 2004; Kaluta (cover)............. 2.95
❑10, Jun 2004............. 2.95
❑11, Sep 2004; Tesla Strong story......... 2.95
❑12, Jan 2005............. 2.95

Other grades: Multiply price above by 5/6 for VF/NM • 2/3 for VERY FINE • 1/3 for FINE • 1/5 for VERY GOOD • 1/8 for GOOD

Undersea Agent

Sister title for T.H.U.N.D.E.R. Agents
©Tower

Undertaker

World Wrestling Federation gets graphic
©Chaos

Underworld

Series of little dramas tied together
©DC

Underworld Unleashed: Apokolips: Dark Uprising

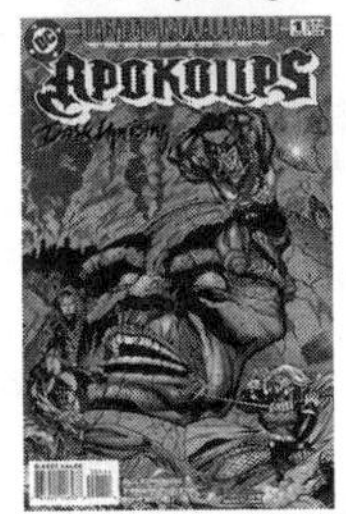

Villains sell souls for great power
©DC

Union

Strange soldier from another world's war
©Image

N-MINT

Tongue*Lash
Dark Horse

❑1, Aug 1996 .... 2.95
❑2, Sep 1996 .... 2.95

Tongue*Lash II
Dark Horse

❑1, Feb 1999; Adult 2.95
❑2, Mar 1999; Adult 2.95

Tony Bravado, Trouble-Shooter
Renegade

❑1, b&w 2.00
❑2, b&w 2.00
❑3, Dec 1989, b&w 2.50
❑4, b&w 2.50

Tool & Die
Flashpoint

❑1, Mar 1994 .... 2.50

Too Much Coffee Man
Adhesive

❑1, ca. 1993, b&w 12.00
❑2, b&w 8.00
❑3, b&w 6.00
❑4, b&w 5.00
❑5, b&w 5.00
❑6 .... 3.00
❑7 .... 3.00
❑8, Feb 1998 .... 3.00
❑MC 1; Mini-comic 10.00
❑MC 1/2nd; Mini-comic 3.00
❑MC 2; Mini-comic 8.00
❑MC 2/2nd; Mini-comic 3.00
❑MC 3; Mini-comic 8.00
❑MC 3/2nd; Mini-comic 3.00
❑MC 4; Mini-comic 6.00
❑MC 4/2nd; Mini-comic 3.00
❑Special 1, Jul 1997, b&w; NN 3.00
❑Special 2; Full-Color Special Edition 3.00

Too Much Hopeless Savages
Oni

❑1 2003, b&w 2.99
❑2 2003, b&w 2.99
❑3 2003, b&w 2.99
❑4 2003, b&w 2.99

Toon Warz: The Fandom Menace
Sirius

❑1/A, Jul 1999; Believe This Man cover 2.95
❑1/B, Jul 1999; Vain Affair cover 2.95
❑1/C, Jul 1999; Newspeak cover 2.95
❑1/D, Jul 1999; Primear cover 2.95

Tooth and Claw
Image

❑1, Aug 1999 .... 2.95
❑2, Sep 1999, Woman-cat holding skull on cover 2.95
❑2/A, Sep 1999, alternate cover 2.95
❑3, Oct 1999 .... 2.95
❑Ashcan 1 1999, DF Exclusive preview book 2.00

Top 10
DC / America's Best Comics

❑1, Sep 1999 .... 5.00
❑1/Variant, Sep 1999 .... 6.00
❑2, Oct 1999 .... 2.95
❑3, Nov 1999 .... 2.95
❑4, Dec 1999 .... 2.95
❑5, Jan 2000 .... 2.95
❑6, Feb 2000 .... 2.95
❑7, Apr 2000 .... 2.95
❑8, Jun 2000 .... 2.95
❑9, Oct 2000 .... 2.95
❑10, Jan 2001; D: Sung Li (Girl 1) 2.95
❑11, May 2001 .... 2.95
❑12, Oct 2001 .... 2.95

Top Cat
Dell

❑1, Dec 1961 .... 60.00
❑2, Mar 1962 .... 35.00
❑3, Jun 1962 .... 25.00
❑4, Oct 1962 .... 25.00
❑5, Jan 1963 .... 25.00
❑6, Apr 1963 .... 20.00
❑7, Jul 1963 .... 20.00
❑8, Oct 1963 .... 20.00
❑9, Jan 1964 .... 20.00
❑10, Apr 1964 .... 20.00
❑11, Jul 1964 .... 15.00
❑12, Oct 1964 .... 15.00
❑13, Jan 1965 .... 15.00
❑14, Apr 1965 .... 15.00
❑15, Jul 1965 .... 15.00
❑16, Oct 1965 .... 15.00
❑17, Jan 1966 .... 15.00
❑18, Apr 1966 .... 15.00
❑19 1966 .... 15.00
❑20 1967 .... 15.00
❑21, Dec 1967 .... 12.00
❑22, ca. 1968 .... 12.00
❑23, ca. 1968 .... 12.00
❑24, Dec 1968 .... 12.00
❑25, Mar 1969 .... 12.00
❑26, Jun 1969 .... 12.00
❑27, Sep 1969 .... 12.00
❑28, Dec 1969 .... 12.00
❑29, Mar 1970 .... 12.00
❑30, Jun 1970, 10004-006; Published by Gold Key 12.00
❑31, Sep 1970 .... 12.00

Top Cat
Charlton

❑1, Nov 1970 .... 20.00
❑2, Jan 1971 .... 12.00
❑3, Mar 1971 .... 8.00
❑4, May 1971 .... 8.00
❑5, Jul 1971 .... 8.00
❑6, Sep 1971 .... 5.00
❑7, Nov 1971 .... 5.00
❑8, Dec 1971 .... 5.00
❑9, Feb 1972 .... 5.00
❑10, Apr 1972 .... 5.00
❑11, Jun 1972 .... 4.00
❑12, Aug 1972 .... 4.00
❑13, Oct 1972 .... 4.00
❑14, Nov 1972 .... 4.00
❑15, Feb 1973 .... 4.00
❑16, Mar 1973 .... 4.00
❑17, May 1973 .... 4.00
❑18, Jul 1973 .... 4.00
❑19, Sep 1973 .... 4.00
❑20, Nov 1973 .... 4.00

Top Comics: Flintstones
Gold Key

❑1, ca. 1967 .... 10.00
❑2, ca. 1967 .... 10.00
❑3, ca. 1967 .... 15.00
❑4, ca. 1967 .... 15.00

Top Comics: Flipper
Gold Key

❑1, ca. 1967 .... 10.00

Top Comics: Lassie
Gold Key

❑1, ca. 1967, Reprints Lassie #68; no cover price 10.00

Top Comics: Mickey Mouse
Gold Key

❑1, ca. 1967 .... 10.00
❑2, ca. 1967 .... 10.00
❑3, ca. 1967 .... 15.00
❑4, ca. 1967 .... 15.00

Top Comics: Tweety & Sylvester
Gold Key

❑1, ca. 1967 .... 10.00
❑2, ca. 1967 .... 10.00

Top Comics: Yogi Bear
Gold Key

❑1, July 1967, reprints Yogi Bear (Gold Key) #30 .... 16.00

Top Cow 2003 Compilation Special
Image

❑1, Mar 2003 .... 3.00

Top Cow: Book of Revelation 2003
Image

❑1, Jun 2003 .... 3.99

Top Cow Classics in Black and White: Aphrodite IX
Image

❑1, Sep 2000 .... 2.95
❑1/A, Sep 2000; Sketch cover (marked as such) ....

Top Cow Classics in Black and White: Ascenscion
Image

❑1/A, Apr 2000; Sketch cover (marked as such) 2.95
❑1, Apr 2000 .... 2.95

Top Cow Classics in Black and White: Fathom
Image

❑1, May 2000 .... 2.95

Top Cow Classics in Black and White: Magdalena
Image

❑1, Oct 2002, Black background on cover 2.95

Top Cow Classics in Black and White: Midnight Nation
Image

❑1, Mar 2001 .... 2.95

Other grades: Multiply price above by 5/6 for VF/NM • 2/3 for VERY FINE • 1/3 for FINE • 1/5 for VERY GOOD • 1/8 for GOOD

Top Cow Classics in Black and White: Rising Stars
Image
❑1, Aug 2000 .... 2.95

Top Cow Classics in Black and White: The Darkness
Image
❑1, Mar 2000 .... 2.95

Top Cow Classics in Black and White: Tomb Raider
Image
❑1, Dec 2000........ 2.95

Top Cow Classics in Black and White: Witchblade
Image
❑1, Feb 2000........ 2.95
❑1/A; Sketch cover (marked as such) 5.00
❑25, Apr 2001........ 2.95

Top Cow Con Sketchbook 2004
Image
❑1, Aug 2004 .... 3.00

Top Cow Productions Inc./Ballistic Studios Swimsuit Special
Image
❑1, May 1995........ 2.95

Top Cow Secrets
Image
❑WS 1, Jan 1996; Special Winter Lingerie Edition; pin-ups 2.95

Top Cow Special
Image
❑1; Spring/Summer 2001 .... 2.95

Top Dog
Marvel / Star
❑1, Apr 1985, 1: Top Dog........ 1.00
❑2, Jun 1985........ 1.00
❑3, Aug 1985 .... 1.00
❑4, Oct 1985 .... 1.00
❑5, Dec 1985........ 1.00
❑6, Feb 1986........ 1.00
❑7, Apr 1986........ 1.00
❑8, Jun 1986........ 1.00
❑9, Aug 1986........ 1.00
❑10, Oct 1986 .... 1.00
❑11, Dec 1986........ 1.00
❑12, Feb 1987 .... 1.00
❑13, Apr 1987 .... 1.00
❑14, Jun 1987; Final Issue 1.00

Top Eliminator
Charlton
❑25 1967, From Teenage Hotrodders #24 10.00
❑26, Nov 1967, A: Scot Jackson and the Rod Masters........ 10.00
❑27, Jan 1968........ 10.00
❑28, Mar 1968 .... 10.00
❑29, Jul 1968, Becomes Drag 'n' Wheels with #30 .... 10.00

Topps Comics Presents
Topps
❑0, Jul 1993; Giveaway; Previewed Dracula vs. Zorro, Teenagents, Silver Star, Jack Kirby's Secret City Saga, Bill the Galactic Hero, etc 1.50
❑1, Sep 1993; giveaway 1.00

Top Shelf
Primal Groove
❑1, Win 1995, b&w 5.00

Top Shelf
Top Shelf
❑1, ca. 1996 .... 6.95
❑2, ca. 1997 .... 6.95
❑3, ca. 1997 .... 6.95
❑4, ca. 1997 .... 6.95
❑5, ca. 1998 .... 6.95
❑6, ca. 1998 .... 6.95
❑7, ca. 1998; ca. 1999 .... 6.95

Top 10: Beyond the Farthest Precinct
DC / America's Best Comics
❑1, Oct 2005 .... 2.99
❑2, Nov 2005 .... 2.99
❑3, Dec 2005........ 2.99
❑4, Jan 2006........ 2.99
❑5, Feb 2006........ 2.99

Tor
DC
❑1, Jun 1975; JKu (c); JKu (w); JKu (a); O: Tor 8.00
❑2, Aug 1975 JKu (w); JKu (a) 4.00
❑3, Oct 1975 JKu (w); JKu (a) 4.00
❑4, Dec 1975 JKu (c); JKu (w); JKu (a). 4.00
❑5, Feb 1976 JKu (c); JKu (w); JKu (a).. 4.00
❑6, Apr 1976; JKu (w); JKu (a); Final Issue 4.00

Tor
Marvel / Epic
❑1, Jun 1993, large size; O: Tor 5.95
❑2, Jul 1993, large size........ 5.95
❑3, Aug 1993, large size 5.95
❑4, Sep 1993, large size; Final issue...... 5.95

Tor 3-D
Eclipse
❑1, Jul 1986; Includes 3-D glasses........ 2.50
❑2, Aug 1987; Includes 3-D glasses 2.50

Torch of Liberty Special
Dark Horse
❑1, Jan 1995, NN; One-shot 2.50

Torchy
Bell Features
❑16, ca. 1964, Reprints #4 from Quality series 5.00

Torchy
Innovation
❑1, b&w; Reprints........ 2.50
❑2, b&w; Reprints........ 2.50
❑3, b&w; Reprints........ 2.50
❑4, b&w; Reprints........ 2.50
❑5, b&w; Reprints........ 2.50
❑9, b&w; Reprints; 1st Olivia cover 2.50
❑Summer 1, b&w; Summer Fun Special 2.50

Torg
Adventure
❑1, b&w........ 2.50
❑2, Mar 1992, b&w........ 2.50
❑3, Apr 1992, b&w 2.50
❑4, May 1992, b&w 2.50

Tori Do
Penguin Palace
❑1, Aug 1994, b&w........ 2.25
❑1/2nd, Mar 1995; 2nd printing........ 2.25

To Riverdale and Back Again
Archie
❑1, ca. 1990, NN........ 2.50

Tor Johnson: Hollywood Star
Monster
❑1, b&w........ 2.50

Tor Love Betty
Fantagraphics / Eros
❑1, Feb 1991, b&w; Adult 2.75

Torment
Aircel
❑1, b&w; Adult........ 2.95
❑2, b&w; Adult........ 2.95
❑3, b&w; Adult........ 2.95

Torpedo
Hard Boiled
❑1, Jul 1993, b&w; Reprints........ 2.95
❑2, Sep 1993, b&w; Reprints........ 2.95
❑3, b&w; Reprints........ 2.95
❑4, Mar 1994, b&w; Reprints 2.95

Torrid Affairs
Eternity
❑1 1988, b&w; Reprints........ 2.25
❑2/A, Feb 1989; tame cover 2.25
❑2/B, Feb 1989; sexy cover........ 2.25
❑3 1989........ 2.95
❑4 1989........ 2.95
❑5 1989........ 2.95

Torso
Image
❑1 1999; BMB (w); b&w........ 3.95
❑2 1999; BMB (w); b&w........ 3.95
❑3 1999; BMB (w); b&w........ 4.95
❑4 1999; BMB (w); b&w........ 4.95
❑5, Jun 1999; BMB (w); BMB (a); B&W 4.95
❑6 1999; BMB (w); BMB (a); 48 pages; b&w 4.95

Tortoise and The Hare
Last Gasp
❑1, Adult........ 3.00

To See the Stars
NBM
❑1; Adult........ 13.95

Total Eclipse
Eclipse
❑1, May 1988, V: Misery; V: Z........ 3.95
❑2, Aug 1988 .... 3.95
❑3, Dec 1988 .... 3.95
❑4, Jan 1989, 1: Doctor Eclipse; D: Strike!; Miracle Man appearance (scripted by Neil Gaiman) 3.95
❑5, Apr 1989, V: Misery........ 3.95

Total Eclipse: The Seraphim Objective
Eclipse
❑1, Nov 1988 .... 1.95

Total Justice
DC
❑1, Oct 1996; based on Kenner action figures........ 2.25
❑2, Nov 1996; based on Kenner action figures........ 2.25
❑3, Nov 1996; based on Kenner action figures........ 2.25

Totally Alien
Trigon
❑1, b&w........ 2.50
❑2, b&w........ 2.50
❑3, b&w........ 2.50
❑4, b&w........ 2.50
❑5, b&w........ 2.50

Totally Horses!
Painted Pony
❑1; magazine; horse stories........ 1.95
❑2, Spr 1997; magazine; horse stories .. 1.95
❑3; magazine; horse stories........ 1.95
❑4; magazine; horse stories........ 1.95
❑5, Sum 1998; magazine; horse stories. 1.95

Total Recall
DC
❑1, ca. 1990, Movie adaptation........ 2.95

Total War
Gold Key
❑1, Jul 1965........ 40.00
❑2, Oct 1965, Series continued in M.A.R.S. Patrol #3 .... 35.00

Totems
DC / Vertigo
❑1, Feb 2000........ 5.95

Totems
Cartoon Frolics
❑1 .... 2.95
❑2 .... 2.95
❑3 .... 2.95

Totem: Sign of the Wardog
Alpha Productions
❑1, b&w........ 2.25
❑2, b&w........ 2.25

Totem: Sign of the Wardog
Alpha Productions
❑1, Apr 1992, b&w 2.50
❑2, b&w........ 2.50
❑Ann 1........ 3.50

To the Heart of the Storm
DC
❑1, Sep 2000 .... 14.95

Touch
DC
❑1, Jun 2004........ 2.50
❑2, Jul 2004........ 2.50
❑3, Aug 2004........ 2.50
❑4, Sep 2004 .... 2.50
❑5, Oct 2004........ 2.50
❑6, Nov 2004........ 2.50

Touch of Silk, a Taste of Leather, A
Boneyard
❑1, Mar 1994, b&w; NN; Adult........ 2.95

Union Jack

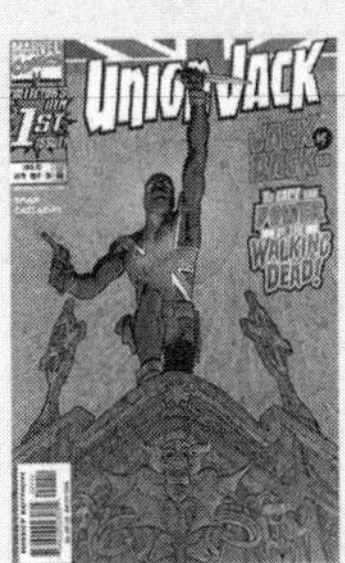

Fighting embodiment of the British spirit
©Marvel

Unity

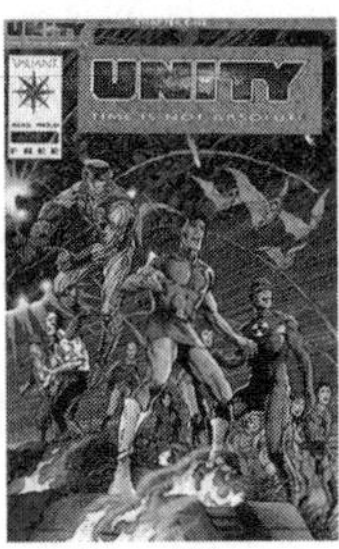

Very ambitious cross-over from Valiant
©Valiant

Universe X

Sequel limited series to Earth X
©Marvel

Unknown Soldier

Later name of Star Spangled War Stories
©DC

Untold Tales of Spider-Man

Excellent title filled in the early blanks
©Marvel

N-MINT

Touch of Silver, A
Image

❑1, Jan 1997, b&w 2.95
❑2, Mar 1997, b&w 2.95
❑3, May 1997, b&w 2.95
❑4, Jul 1997, b&w 2.95
❑5, Sep 1997; b&w with color section ... 2.95
❑6, Nov 1997, b&w 2.95

Tough
Viz

❑1, Jan 2005, b&w 9.99
❑2, Apr 2005; b&w 9.99
❑3, Jul 2005; Explicit content; b&w 9.99
❑4, Oct 2005 .... 9.99

Tough Guys and Wild Women
Eternity

❑1, Mar 1989, b&w; Saint reprints 2.25
❑2, b&w; Saint reprints 2.25

Tower of Shadows
Marvel

❑1, Sep 1969, JR (c); JCr, JSo, SL (w); JB, JCr, JSo (a) 55.00
❑2, Nov 1969, NA (w); JB, DH, NA (a) ... 25.00
❑3, Jan 1970, GC, GT (a) 25.00
❑4, Jan 1970 .... 25.00
❑5, May 1970, WW (w); WW (a) 25.00
❑6, Jul 1970, TS, WW, SL (w); TS, SD, GC, WW, DA (a); Reprint from Strange Tales #78 .... 15.00
❑7, Sep 1970, WW, SL (w); JK, WW (a); Reprint from Tales to Astonish #10 .... 15.00
❑8, Nov 1970, WW, SL (w); SD, DH, WW (a); Reprints from Tales to Astonish #13, 14 and 16 .... 15.00
❑9, Nov 1970, Series continued in Creatures On the Loose #10 .... 8.00
❑Special 1, Dec 1971; Reprints from Tower of Shadows #1, 2 and Journey into Mystery (1st Series) #61 .... 22.00

Townscapes
DC

❑1, ca. 2004 .... 17.95

Toxic!
Apocalypse

❑1; Marshal Law 2.50
❑2; Marshal Law 2.50
❑3; Marshal Law 2.50
❑4; Marshal Law 2.50
❑5; Marshal Law; Mutomatic; The Driver 2.50
❑6; Marshal Law 2.50
❑7; Marshal Law 2.50
❑8; Marshal Law 2.50
❑9; Marshal Law 2.50
❑10; Marshal Law 2.50
❑11; Marshal Law 2.50
❑12; Marshal Law 2.50
❑13; Marshal Law 2.50
❑14; Marshal Law 2.50
❑15; Marshal Law 2.50
❑16; Marshal Law 2.50
❑17; Marshal Law 2.50
❑18; Marshal Law 2.50
❑19; Marshal Law 2.50

N-MINT

Toxic Avenger
Marvel

❑1, Apr 1991, 1&O: Toxic Avenger 2.00
❑2, May 1991 .... 1.50
❑3, Jun 1991, Photo Cover 1.50
❑4, Jul 1991 .... 1.50
❑5, Aug 1991 .... 1.50
❑6, Sep 1991, VM (a) 1.50
❑7, Oct 1991, VM (c); VM (a) 1.50
❑8, Nov 1991, VM (c); VM (a) 1.50
❑9, Dec 1991 .... 1.50
❑10, Jan 1992, Photo cover 1.50
❑11, Feb 1992, VM (a); Photo cover 1.50

Toxic Crusaders
Marvel

❑1, May 1992; O: Toxic Avenger 1.25
❑2, Jun 1992 .... 1.25
❑3, Jul 1992 .... 1.25
❑4, Aug 1992 .... 1.25
❑5, Sep 1992 .... 1.25
❑6, Oct 1992 .... 1.25
❑7, Nov 1992 .... 1.25
❑8, Dec 1992 .... 1.25

Toxic Gumbo
DC / Vertigo

❑1, May 1998; prestige format; NN; One-shot 5.95

Toxic Paradise
Slave Labor

❑1, b&w; Love & Romance; cardstock cover 4.95

Toxin
Marvel

❑1, May 2005 .... 2.99
❑2, Jun 2005 .... 2.99
❑3, Jul 2005 .... 2.99
❑4, Aug 2005; New Avengers tie-in 2.99
❑5, Sep 2005 .... 2.99
❑6, Oct 2005; New Avengers Tie-In 2.99

Toxine
Nose

❑1, Jun 1991; Adult 3.00

Toyboy
Continuity

❑1, Oct 1986 .... 2.00
❑2, Aug 1987 .... 2.00
❑3, Nov 1987 .... 2.00
❑4, Feb 1988 .... 2.00
❑5, Jun 1988 .... 2.00
❑6, Nov 1988 .... 2.00
❑7, Mar 1989 .... 2.00

Toy Story
Marvel

❑1, Dec 1995 .... 4.95

Traci Lords: The Outlaw Years
Boneyard

❑1; Adult 3.00

Tracker
Blackthorne

❑1, May 1988, b&w 2.00
❑2, Jul 1988, b&w 2.00

N-MINT

Tragg and the Sky Gods
Whitman

❑1, Jun 1975; DS (a); 1&O 5.00
❑2, Sep 1975 .... 3.00
❑3, Dec 1975 .... 2.50
❑4, Feb 1976 .... 2.50
❑5, Apr 1976; Gold Key 2.50
❑6, Sep 1976 .... 2.50
❑7, Nov 1976 .... 2.50
❑8, Feb 1977 .... 2.50
❑9, May 1982, Reprint from Tragg and the Sky Gods #1 .... 2.50

Trailer Trash
Tundra

❑1, b&w; Adult 2.00
❑4, b&w; Adult 2.95
❑7, Jun 1996, b&w; Adult 2.95
❑8, Nov 1996, b&w; Adult 2.95

Trakk: Monster Hunter
Image

❑1, Nov 2003 .... 2.95
❑2, Apr 2004 .... 2.95

Tramps Like Us
Tokyopop

❑1, Aug 2004 .... 9.99
❑2, Oct 2004 .... 9.99
❑3, Dec 2004 .... 9.99
❑4, Feb 2005 .... 9.99
❑5, May 2005 .... 9.99
❑6, Aug 2005 .... 9.99
❑7, Nov 2005 .... 9.99

Tranceptor
NBM

❑1; Adult 11.95

Trancers
Eternity

❑1, Aug 1991, Movie adaptation 2.50
❑2, Movie adaptation 2.50

Tranquility
Dreamsmith

❑1, Sep 1998, b&w 2.50
❑2, Oct 1998, b&w 2.50
❑3, Nov 1998, b&w 2.50

Tranquilizer
Luxurious

❑1 .... 2.95
❑2 .... 2.95

Transformers
Marvel

❑1, Sep 1984; 1: Transformers. "Limited Series #1" 10.00
❑2, Nov 1984; "Limited Series #2" 5.00
❑3, Jan 1985; Spider-Man; "Limited Series #3" 5.00
❑4, Mar 1985; "Limited Series #4" 3.00
❑5, Jun 1985 .... 3.00
❑6, Jul 1985 .... 3.00
❑7, Aug 1985 .... 3.00
❑8, Sep 1985 A: Dinobots 3.00
❑9, Oct 1985 .... 3.00
❑10, Nov 1985; V: Devastator 3.00
❑11, Dec 1985; V: Jetfire 3.00
❑12, Jan 1986 .... 3.00

- ❑13, Feb 1986 — 3.00
- ❑14, Mar 1986 — 3.00
- ❑15, Apr 1986 — 3.00
- ❑16, May 1986 — 3.00
- ❑17, Jun 1986 — 3.00
- ❑18, Jul 1986 — 3.00
- ❑19, Aug 1986 — 3.00
- ❑20, Sep 1986 — 3.00
- ❑21, Oct 1986; 1: Aerialbots — 2.00
- ❑22, Nov 1986 — 2.00
- ❑23, Dec 1986 — 2.00
- ❑24, Jan 1987 — 2.00
- ❑25, Feb 1987 — 2.00
- ❑26, Mar 1987 — 2.00
- ❑27, Apr 1987 — 2.00
- ❑28, May 1987 — 2.00
- ❑29, Jun 1987 — 2.00
- ❑30, Jul 1987 — 2.00
- ❑31, Aug 1987 — 2.00
- ❑32, Sep 1987 — 2.00
- ❑33, Oct 1987 — 2.00
- ❑34, Nov 1987 — 2.00
- ❑35, Dec 1987 — 2.00
- ❑36, Jan 1988 — 2.00
- ❑37, Feb 1988 — 2.00
- ❑38, Mar 1988 — 2.00
- ❑39, Apr 1988 — 2.00
- ❑40, May 1988 — 2.00
- ❑41, Jun 1988 — 2.00
- ❑42, Jul 1988 — 2.00
- ❑43, Aug 1988 — 2.00
- ❑44, Sep 1988 — 2.00
- ❑45, Oct 1988 — 2.00
- ❑46, Nov 1988 — 2.00
- ❑47, Dec 1988 — 2.00
- ❑48, Jan 1989 — 2.00
- ❑49, Feb 1989 — 2.00
- ❑50, Mar 1989 — 2.00
- ❑51, Apr 1989 — 2.00
- ❑52, May 1989 — 2.00
- ❑53, Jun 1989 — 2.00
- ❑54, Jul 1989 — 2.00
- ❑55, Aug 1989 — 2.00
- ❑56, Sep 1989 — 2.00
- ❑57, Oct 1989 — 2.00
- ❑58, Nov 1989 — 2.00
- ❑59, Nov 1989 — 2.00
- ❑60, Dec 1989 — 2.00
- ❑61, Dec 1989 — 2.00
- ❑62, Jan 1990 — 2.00
- ❑63, Feb 1990 — 2.00
- ❑64, Mar 1990 — 2.00
- ❑65, Apr 1990 — 2.00
- ❑66, May 1990 — 2.00
- ❑67, Jun 1990 — 2.00
- ❑68, Jul 1990 — 2.00
- ❑69, Aug 1990 — 2.00
- ❑70, Sep 1990 — 5.00
- ❑71, Oct 1990 — 5.00
- ❑72, Nov 1990 — 5.00
- ❑73, Dec 1990 — 5.00
- ❑74, Jan 1991 — 5.00
- ❑75, Feb 1991; Double-size — 5.00
- ❑76, Mar 1991 — 5.00
- ❑77, Apr 1991 — 10.00
- ❑78, May 1991 — 10.00
- ❑79, Jun 1991 — 10.00
- ❑80, Jul 1991; Final Issue — 18.00

Transformers Animated Movie Adaptation
Idea & Design Works

- ❑1, Oct 2006 — 3.99
- ❑2, Nov 2006 — 3.99
- ❑3, Dec 2006 — 3.99

Transformers: Armada
Dreamwave

- ❑1, Jul 2002 (w) — 2.95
- ❑1/A, Jul 2002; (w); chromium cover — 2.95
- ❑2, Aug 2002 — 2.95
- ❑3, Oct 2002 — 2.95
- ❑4, Nov 2002 — 2.95
- ❑5, Dec 2002 — 2.95
- ❑6, Dec 2002 — 2.95
- ❑7, Jan 2003 — 2.95
- ❑7/A, Jan 2003; White background on cover — 3.50
- ❑8, Feb 2003 — 2.95
- ❑9, Mar 2003 — 2.95
- ❑10, Apr 2003 — 2.95
- ❑11, May 2003 — 2.95
- ❑12, Jun 2003 — 2.95
- ❑13, Jul 2003 — 2.95
- ❑14, Aug 2003 — 2.95
- ❑15, Sep 2003 — 2.95
- ❑16, Oct 2003 — 2.95
- ❑17, Nov 2003 — 2.95
- ❑18, Dec 2003 — 2.95

Transformers Armada: More Than Meets the Eye
Dark Horse

- ❑1, Mar 2004 — 4.95
- ❑2, Apr 2004 — 4.95
- ❑3, May 2004 — 4.95

Transformers: Beast Wars
Idea & Design Works

- ❑1, Feb 2006 — 2.99
- ❑2, Mar 2006 — 2.99
- ❑3, Apr 2006 — 2.99
- ❑4, May 2006 — 2.99

Transformers Comics Magazine
Marvel

- ❑1, Jan 1987; digest — 1.50
- ❑2, Mar 1987 — 1.50
- ❑3, May 1987 — 1.50
- ❑4, Jul 1987 — 1.50
- ❑5, Sep 1987 — 1.50
- ❑6, Nov 1987 — 1.50
- ❑7, Jan 1988 — 1.50
- ❑8, Mar 1988 — 1.50
- ❑9, May 1988 — 1.50
- ❑10, Jul 1988 — 1.50

Transformers: Energon
Dark Horse

- ❑19, Jan 2004 — 2.95
- ❑20, Feb 2004 — 2.95
- ❑21, Mar 2004 — 2.95
- ❑22, Apr 2004 — 2.95
- ❑23, May 2004 — 2.95
- ❑24, Jun 2004 — 2.95
- ❑25, Jul 2004 — 2.95
- ❑26, Aug 2004 — 2.95
- ❑27, Sep 2004 — 2.95
- ❑28, Oct 2004 — 2.95
- ❑29, Nov 2004 — 2.95
- ❑30, Dec 2004 — 2.95

Transformers: Escalation
Idea & Design Works

- ❑1, Nov 2006 — 3.99
- ❑1/Variant, Nov 2006 — 3.99
- ❑2, Dec 2006 — 3.99

Transformers: Evolutions
Idea & Design Works

- ❑1, May 2006 — 2.99
- ❑2, Jun 2006 — 2.99
- ❑3, Jul 2006 — 2.99
- ❑4, Sep 2006 — 2.99

Transformers/Gen13
Marvel

- ❑Ashcan 1 — 1.00

Transformers: Generation 1
Dreamwave

- ❑1/Autobot, Apr 2002; (w); Autobot cover — 4.00
- ❑1/Decepticon, Apr 2002; (w); Decepticon cover — 4.00
- ❑1/Chromium, Apr 2002; (w); chromium cover — 5.95
- ❑1/2nd, Apr 2002; (w); Optimus Prime and Bumblebee — 2.95
- ❑1/3rd, Apr 2002 (w) — 2.95
- ❑2/Autobot, May 2002; (w); Autobots cover — 3.50
- ❑2/Decepticon, May 2002; (w); Decepticon cover — 3.50
- ❑2/2nd, May 2002 (w) — 2.95
- ❑3/Autobot, Jun 2002; (w); Autobots cover — 2.95
- ❑3/Decepticon, Jun 2002; (w); Decepticon cover — 2.95
- ❑4/Autobot, Jul 2002; (w); Autobots cover — 2.95
- ❑4/Decepticon, Jul 2002; (w); Decepticon cover — 2.95
- ❑5/Autobot, Aug 2002; Autobots cover — 2.95
- ❑5/Decepticon, Aug 2002; Decepticon cover — 2.95
- ❑5/2nd, Nov 2002; 2nd printing — 2.95
- ❑6/Autobot, Oct 2002; (w); Autobots cover — 2.95
- ❑6/Decepticon, Oct 2002; (w); Decepticon cover — 2.95

Transformers: Generation 1
Dreamwave

- ❑1, Apr 2003 — 2.95
- ❑1/Counterfeit, Apr 2003, Chrome Cover — 5.95
- ❑2, May 2003 — 2.95
- ❑3, Jun 2003 — 2.95
- ❑4, Jul 2003 — 2.95
- ❑5, Aug 2003 — 2.95
- ❑6, Oct 2003 — 2.95

Transformers: Generation 1
Dreamwave

- ❑0, Dec 2003 — 2.95
- ❑1, Feb 2004 — 4.00
- ❑1/SilvSnail — 5.00
- ❑2, Feb 2004 — 2.95
- ❑3, Mar 2004 — 2.95
- ❑4, Apr 2004 — 2.95
- ❑5, Jun 2004 — 2.95
- ❑6, Jul 2004 — 2.95
- ❑7, Aug 2004 — 2.95
- ❑8, Sep 2004 — 2.95
- ❑9, Nov 2004 — 2.95
- ❑10, Dec 2005 — 2.95

Transformers: Generation 1 Preview
Dreamwave

- ❑1/A, Apr 2002; Autobot cover — 3.95
- ❑1/B, Apr 2002; Retailer Incentive Edition — 3.95

Transformers: Generation 2
Marvel

- ❑1, Nov 1993; O: Transformers — 1.75
- ❑1/Variant, Nov 1993; foil fold-out cover — 2.95
- ❑2, Dec 1993 — 1.75
- ❑3, Jan 1994 — 1.75
- ❑4, Feb 1994 — 1.75
- ❑5, Mar 1994 — 1.75
- ❑6, Apr 1994 — 1.75
- ❑7, May 1994 — 1.75
- ❑8, Jun 1994 — 1.75
- ❑9, Jul 1994 — 1.75
- ❑10, Aug 1994 — 1.75
- ❑11, Sep 1994 — 1.75
- ❑12, Oct 1994; double-sized; Final Issue — 2.25

Transformers: Generations
Idea & Design Works

- ❑1, Apr 2006 — 1.99
- ❑2, May 2006 — 1.99
- ❑3, Jun 2006 — 2.49
- ❑4, Jul 2006 — 2.49
- ❑5, Aug 2006 — 2.49
- ❑6, Aug 2006 — 2.49
- ❑7, Sep 2006 — 2.49
- ❑8, Oct 2006 — 2.49
- ❑9, Nov 2006 — 2.49
- ❑10, Dec 2006 — 2.99

Transformers/G.I.Joe
Dreamwave

- ❑1, Sep 2003 — 2.95
- ❑1/Dynamic, Sep 2003 — 1.48
- ❑1/H, Sep 2003; Holofoil cover — 5.95
- ❑2, Oct 2003 — 2.95
- ❑3, Nov 2003 — 2.95
- ❑4, Dec 2003 — 2.95
- ❑5, Jan 2004 — 2.95
- ❑6, Mar 2004 — 2.95

Transformers: Headmasters
Marvel

- ❑1, Jul 1987 — 1.00
- ❑2, Sep 1987 FS (a) — 1.00
- ❑3, Nov 1987 — 1.00
- ❑4, Jan 1988 — 1.00

Transformers
Idea & Design Works

- ❑0, Oct 2005 — 0.99

Other grades: Multiply price above by 5/6 for VF/NM • 2/3 for VERY FINE • 1/3 for FINE • 1/5 for VERY GOOD • 1/8 for GOOD

Usagi Yojimbo

Stan Sakai's wonderful samurai rabbit tale
©Fantagraphics

U.S. War Machine 2.0

Chuck Austen mature-readers title
©

V

Based on the 1980s NBC TV series
©DC

Valiant Vision Starter Kit

Full-color variant on 3-D comics
©Valiant

Valor (DC)

Interstellar teen-ager becomes super-hero
©DC

N-MINT

Transformers in 3-D
Blackthorne

❑1 ... 2.50
❑2, Dec 1987 ... 2.50
❑3, Apr 1988 ... 2.50

Transformers: Infiltration
Idea & Design Works

❑1, Jan 2006 ... 2.99
❑2, Feb 2006 ... 2.99
❑3, Mar 2006 ... 2.99
❑4, Apr 2006 ... 2.99
❑5, Jun 2006 ... 2.99
❑6, Jul 2006 ... 2.99

Transformers: Infiltration Cover Gallery
Idea & Design Works

❑1, Aug 2006 ... 5.99

Transformers: Micromasters
Dreamwave

❑1, Jun 2004 ... 2.95
❑2 2004 ... 2.95
❑3 2004 ... 2.95

Transformers: More than Meets the Eye Official Guide
Dreamwave

❑1, Apr 2003 ... 5.25
❑2, May 2003 ... 5.25
❑3, Jun 2003 ... 5.25
❑4, Jul 2003 ... 5.25
❑5, Sep 2003 ... 5.25
❑6, Sep 2003 ... 5.25
❑7, Oct 2003 ... 5.25
❑8, Nov 2003 ... 5.25

Transformers Movie
Marvel

❑1, Dec 1986 ... 1.00
❑2, Jan 1987 ... 1.00
❑3, Feb 1987 ... 1.00

Transformers Spotlight: Hot Rod
Idea & Design Works

❑1, Nov 2006 ... 3.99

Transformers Spotlight: Nightbeat
Idea & Design Works

❑1, Oct 2006 ... 3.99

Transformers Spotlight: Shockwave
Idea & Design Works

❑1, Sep 2006 ... 3.99

Transformers Spotlight: Six Shot
Idea & Design Works

❑1, Dec 2006 ... 3.99

Transformers: Stormbringer
Idea & Design Works

❑1, Jul 2006 ... 2.99
❑2, Aug 2006 ... 2.99
❑3, Sep 2006 ... 2.99
❑4, Oct 2006 ... 2.99

Transformers: The War Within
Dreamwave

❑Ashcan 1, Aug 2002; Preview issue ... 3.00
❑1, Oct 2002 ... 3.00
❑1/Variant, Oct 2002; lenticular animation cover ... 7.00
❑2, Nov 2002 ... 2.95
❑3, Dec 2002 ... 2.95
❑4, Jan 2003 ... 2.95
❑5, Feb 2003 ... 2.95
❑5/A, Feb 2003; Retailer Incentive edition; lenticular animation cover ... 5.00
❑6, Mar 2003 ... 2.95

Transformers: The War Within
Dreamwave

❑1, Oct 2003 ... 2.95
❑2, Nov 2003 ... 2.95
❑3, Dec 2003 ... 2.95
❑4, Jan 2004 ... 2.95
❑5, Mar 2004 ... 2.95
❑6, Apr 2004 ... 2.95

Transformers: The War Within
Dreamwave

❑1, Nov 2004 ... 2.95
❑2, Dec 2004 ... 2.95
❑3, Jan 2005 ... 2.95

Transformers Universe
Marvel

❑1, Dec 1986 ... 20.00
❑1/DirCut ... 10.00
❑2, Jan 1987 ... 10.00
❑2/OTFCC ... 20.00
❑2/FanClub ... 25.00
❑2/Conv ... 20.00
❑3, Feb 1987 ... 5.00
❑3/OTFCC ... 20.00
❑3/FanClub ... 20.00
❑3/Conv ... 20.00
❑4, Mar 1987 ... 2.00

Transit
Vortex

❑1, Mar 1987 ... 1.75
❑2, May 1987 ... 1.75
❑3, Jul 1987 ... 1.75
❑4, Sep 1987 ... 1.75
❑5, Nov 1987 ... 1.75

Transmetropolitan
DC / Helix

❑1, Sep 1997 ... 8.00
❑2, Oct 1997 ... 6.00
❑3, Nov 1997 ... 4.00
❑4, Dec 1997 ... 4.00
❑5, Jan 1998 ... 4.00
❑6, Feb 1998 ... 3.00
❑7, Mar 1998 ... 3.00
❑8, Apr 1998 ... 3.00
❑9, May 1998 ... 3.00
❑10, Jun 1998 ... 3.00
❑11, Jul 1998 ... 3.00
❑12, Aug 1998 ... 3.00
❑13, Sep 1998 ... 2.50
❑14, Oct 1998 ... 2.50
❑15, Nov 1998 ... 2.50
❑16, Dec 1998 ... 2.50
❑17, Jan 1999 ... 2.50
❑18, Feb 1999 ... 2.50
❑19, Mar 1999; The New Scum one: New Home ... 2.50
❑20, Apr 1999; The New Scum two: New city ... 2.50
❑21, May 1999 ... 2.50
❑22, Jun 1999 ... 2.50
❑23, Jul 1999; 100 Bullets preview ... 2.50
❑24, Aug 1999 ... 2.50
❑25, Sep 1999 ... 2.50
❑26, Oct 1999 ... 2.50
❑27, Nov 1999 ... 2.50
❑28, Dec 1999 ... 2.50
❑29, Jan 2000 ... 2.50
❑30, Feb 2000 ... 2.50
❑31, Mar 2000 ... 2.50
❑32, Apr 2000 ... 2.50
❑33, May 2000 ... 2.50
❑34, Jul 2000 ... 2.50
❑35, Aug 2000 ... 2.50
❑36, Sep 2000 ... 2.50
❑37, Oct 2000 ... 2.50
❑38, Nov 2000 ... 2.50
❑39, Dec 2000 ... 2.50
❑40, Jan 2001 ... 2.50
❑41, Feb 2001 ... 2.50
❑42, Mar 2001 ... 2.50
❑43, Apr 2001 ... 2.50
❑44, May 2001 ... 2.50
❑45, Jun 2001 ... 2.50
❑46, Aug 2001 ... 2.50
❑47, Sep 2001 ... 2.50
❑48, Oct 2001 ... 2.50
❑49, Nov 2001 ... 2.50
❑50, Dec 2001 ... 2.50
❑51, Jan 2002 ... 2.50
❑52, Feb 2002 ... 2.50
❑53, Mar 2002 ... 2.50
❑54, Apr 2002 ... 2.50
❑55, Jun 2002 ... 2.50
❑56, Jul 2002 ... 2.50
❑57, Aug 2002 ... 2.50
❑58, Sep 2002 ... 2.50
❑59, Oct 2002 ... 2.50
❑60, Nov 2002 ... 2.50

Transmetropolitan: Filth of the City
DC / Vertigo

❑1, Jul 2001, chromium cover ... 5.95

Transmetropolitan: I Hate it Here
DC / Vertigo

❑1, Jun 2000 ... 5.95

Transmutation of Ike Garuda
Marvel / Epic

❑1 ... 3.95
❑2, Jan 1992 ... 3.95

Trans Nubians
Adeola

❑1 ... 2.95

Trash
Fleetway-Quality

❑1 ... 2.95
❑2 ... 2.95

Trauma Corps
Anubis

❑1, Feb 1994 ... 2.75

Travelers
South Jersey Rebellion Productions
❑1, b&w; no indicia 2.25
❑2 .... 2.25
❑3 .... 2.25

Traveller's Tale, A
Antarctic
❑1, b&w 2.50
❑2, Aug 1992, b&w 2.50
❑3, Oct 1992, b&w 2.50

Travels of Jaimie McPheeters
Gold Key
❑1, Dec 1963, Kurt Russell photo on cover 12.00

Treasure Chests
Fantagraphics / Eros
❑1, Jun 1999; Adult 2.95
❑2 1999; Adult 2.95
❑3, Mar 2000; Adult 2.95
❑4, Feb 2000; Adult 2.95
❑5, Jul 2000; Adult 2.95

Treehouse of Horror
Bongo
❑1 1995; JRo (w); Halloween stories 3.50
❑2, Oct 1996; infinity cover; Halloween stories 2.50
❑3 1997; Halloween story 2.50
❑4 1998; Halloween stories 2.50
❑5 1999; SA (w); SA (a); Halloween stories; Eisner award winner 3.50
❑6 2000; DDC (a); Halloween stories 4.50
❑7, Oct 2001 .... 4.50
❑8, Oct 2002; Says #7 in indicia 3.50
❑9, Oct 2003 .... 4.99
❑10, Oct 2004 .... 4.99
❑11 .... 4.99
❑12 .... 4.99
❑13 .... 4.99
❑14 .... 4.99

Trekker
Dark Horse
❑1, May 1987, b&w 1.50
❑2, Jul 1987, b&w 1.50
❑3, Sep 1987 .... 1.75
❑4, Nov 1987 .... 1.50
❑5, Jan 1988 .... 1.50
❑6, Mar 1988 .... 1.50
❑7, May 1988 .... 1.50
❑8, Jul 1988 .... 1.50
❑9, Sep 1988 .... 1.50
❑Special 1, Color Special 2.95

Trekker
Image
❑Special 1, Jun 1999 .... 2.95

Trek Teens
Parody
❑1, Feb 1993, b&w 2.50
❑1/A, Feb 1993, b&w; alternate cover 2.50

Trenchcoat Brigade
DC / Vertigo
❑1, Mar 1999 .... 2.50
❑2, Apr 1999 .... 2.50
❑3, May 1999 .... 2.50
❑4, Jun 1999 .... 2.50

Trencher
Image
❑1, May 1993 KG (w); KG (a) 2.00
❑2, Jun 1993 KG (w); KG (a) 2.00
❑3, Jul 1993 KG (w); KG (a) 2.00
❑4, Oct 1993 KG (w); KG (a) 2.00

Trencher X-Mas Bites Holiday Blow-Out
Blackball
❑1, Dec 1993 .... 2.50

Trespassers
Amazing Montage
❑1 .... 2.50
❑2 .... 2.50
❑3 .... 2.50
❑4 .... 2.50
❑5 .... 2.50

Triad Universe
Triad
❑1, Jul 1994 .... 2.25
❑2, Aug 1994, b&w 2.25

Trial Run
Miller
❑1, b&w 2.00
❑2, b&w 2.00
❑3, b&w 2.00
❑4, b&w 2.00
❑5, b&w 2.00
❑6, b&w 2.00
❑7, b&w 2.00
❑14 .... 2.50
❑15 .... 2.50

Trials of Shazam!
DC
❑1, Nov 2006 .... 2.99
❑2, Dec 2006 .... 2.99
❑3, Jan 2007 .... 2.99
❑4, Feb 2007 .... 2.99
❑5 .... 2.99
❑6 .... 2.99
❑7 .... 2.99
❑8 .... 2.99
❑9 .... 2.99
❑10 .... 2.99
❑11 .... 2.99
❑12 .... 2.99

Triarch
Caliber
❑1, b&w; ca. 1990 .... 2.50
❑2, b&w; ca. 1991 .... 2.50

Tribe
Image
❑1, Mar 1993; Embossed cover; Only issue published by Image; cover says April, indicia says March 2.50
❑1/Variant, Mar 1993; gold logo; White cover; cover says April, indicia says March 2.95
❑2, Sep 1993; Axis begins publishing 1.95
❑3, Apr 1994; Final Issue 1.95

Tribe
Good
❑0, Oct 1996 .... 2.95

Trickster King Monkey
Eastern
❑1 .... 1.75

Trident
Trident
❑1, Aug 1989, b&w; Adult 3.50
❑2, Oct 1989, b&w; Adult 3.50
❑3, Dec 1989, b&w; Adult 3.50
❑4, Feb 1990, b&w; Adult 3.50
❑5, Apr 1990, b&w; Adult 3.50
❑6, Jun 1990, b&w; Adult 3.50
❑7, Aug 1990, b&w; Adult 3.50
❑8, Oct 1990, b&w; Adult 3.50

Trident Sampler
Trident
❑1 .... 1.00
❑2 NG (w) 1.00

Trigger
DC
❑1, Jan 2005 .... 2.95
❑2, Mar 2005 .... 2.95
❑3, Apr 2005 .... 2.95
❑4, May 2005 .... 2.95
❑5, Jun 2005 .... 2.99
❑6, Jul 2005 .... 2.99
❑7, Aug 2005 .... 2.99
❑8, Sep 2005; Final issue 2.99

Triggerman
Caliber
❑1, ca. 1996, b&w 2.95
❑2, ca. 1997, b&w 2.95

Trigger Twins
DC
❑1, Mar 1973, CI, RA (a); Reprints from All-Star Western #94, 81, 103 .... 18.00

Trilogy Tour
Cartoon
❑1, Sum 1997, b&w; promotional comic for Summer 1997 tour 1.50

Trilogy Tour II
Cartoon
❑1, Jun 1998, promotional comic for Summer 1998 tour 4.95

Trinity Angels
Acclaim / Valiant
❑1, Jul 1997; 1: Rubberneck. 1: Teresa Angelina Barbella. 1: Trenchmouth. 1: Gianna Barbella. 1: Maria Barbella 2.50
❑1/Variant, Jul 1997; alternate painted cover 2.50
❑2, Aug 1997; V: Prick 2.50
❑3, Sep 1997; Justice League America #1 homage cover 2.50
❑4, Oct 1997 .... 2.50
❑5, Nov 1997; new costumes 2.50
❑6, Dec 1997; 1: The Lounge Lizard 2.50
❑7, Jan 1998; Showgirls tribute cover 2.50
❑8, Feb 1998 .... 2.50
❑9, Mar 1998 .... 2.50
❑10, Apr 1998 .... 2.50
❑11, Jan 1998; No cover date; indicia says Jan 2.50
❑12, Feb 1998; No cover date; indicia says Feb 2.50
❑Ashcan 1, Mar 1997, b&w; No cover price; preview of upcoming series 1.00

Triple Dare
Alternative
❑1, May 1998, b&w; Anthology 2.95

Triple•X
Dark Horse
❑1, Dec 1994 .... 3.95
❑2, Jan 1995 .... 3.95
❑3, Feb 1995 .... 3.95
❑4, Mar 1995 .... 3.95
❑5, Apr 1995 .... 3.95
❑6, May 1995 .... 3.95
❑7, Jul 1995 .... 4.95

Triple-X Cinema: A Cartoon History
Re-Visionary
❑1, Mar 1997, b&w; Adult 3.50
❑2, Apr 1997, b&w; Adult 3.50
❑3, May 1997, b&w; Adult 3.50

Triumph
DC
❑1, Jun 1995 .... 1.75
❑2, Jul 1995 .... 1.75
❑3, Aug 1995 .... 1.75
❑4, Sep 1995 .... 1.75

Triumphant Unleashed
Triumphant
❑0, ca. 1993; Unleashed Prologue 2.50
❑0/A, ca. 1993; free; Unleashed Prologue 1.00
❑0/Variant, ca. 1993; Mail-in special-cover edition. Given as promo from coupons in first 9 Triumphant books; No cover price; Unleashed Prologue; red logo; mail-away version 4.00
❑1, Nov 1993 .... 2.50

Triumvirate
Catacomb
❑1, b&w; flipbook with Pinnacle #1 .... 2.50

Troll
Image
❑1, Dec 1993; Wraparound cover 2.50

Troll II
Image
❑1, Jul 1994 .... 3.95

Troll: Halloween Special
Image
❑1, Oct 1994 .... 2.95

Troll: Once a Hero
Image
❑1, Aug 1994 .... 2.50

Trollords: Death and Kisses
Apple
❑1 1989, b&w 2.25
❑2, Aug 1989, b&w 2.25
❑3 1989, b&w 2.25

Vampirella

Magazine became cult phenomenon

©Warren

Vampirella Classic

Revisiting the stories of yesteryear

©Harris

Vampirella Monthly

One cover was never enough

©Harris

Vampirella's Summer Nights

Followed the events of Morning in America

©Harris

Vampire Tales

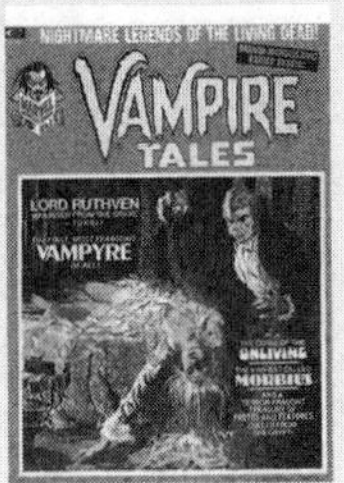

Comics, essays, and film commentary

©Marvel

N-MINT

❑4 1989, b&w 2.25
❑5 1989, b&w 2.25
❑6 .... 2.50

Trollords
Tru

❑1, Feb 1986, b&w; 1: Trollords 2.00
❑1/2nd, 1: Trollords. 2nd printing; $1.75 cover price 1.50
❑2, ca. 1986 .... 1.50
❑3, ca. 1986 .... 1.50
❑4, ca. 1986 .... 1.50
❑5, ca. 1986 .... 1.50
❑6, ca. 1986 .... 1.50
❑7, ca. 1986 .... 1.50
❑8, ca. 1987 .... 1.50
❑9, ca. 1987 .... 1.50
❑10, ca. 1987 .... 1.50
❑11, ca. 1987 .... 1.50
❑12, ca. 1987 .... 1.50
❑13, ca. 1987 .... 1.50
❑14, ca. 1987 .... 1.50
❑15, Feb 1988 .... 1.50
❑Special 1, Feb 1987, Jerry's Big Fun Book 2.00

Trollords
Comico

❑1, ca. 1988 .... 2.00
❑2, ca. 1988 .... 2.00
❑3, ca. 1989 .... 2.00
❑4, ca. 1989 .... 2.50

Troll Patrol
Harvey

❑1, Jan 1993 .... 1.95

Trombone
Knockabout

❑1; Adult 2.50

Tropo
Blackbird

❑1, b&w 2.75
❑2, b&w 2.75
❑3, b&w 2.75
❑4, b&w 2.75
❑5, b&w 2.75

Trouble
Marvel / Epic

❑1, Sep 2003; Photo cover 2.99
❑2, Oct 2003; Photo cover 2.99
❑3, Nov 2003; Photo cover 2.99
❑4, Dec 2003; Photo cover 2.99
❑5, Jan 2004, Photo cover 2.99

Trouble Express
Radio

❑1, Nov 1998; Will Allison cover (signed) 2.95
❑1/A, Nov 1998; Adam Warren cover 2.95
❑2, Jan 1999 .... 2.95

Trouble Magnet
DC

❑1, Feb 2000 .... 2.50
❑2, Mar 2000 .... 2.50
❑3, Apr 2000 .... 2.50
❑4, May 2000 .... 2.50

N-MINT

Troublemakers
Acclaim / Valiant

❑1, Apr 1997; 1: Troublemakers. 1: Calamity. 1: XL. 1: Rebound. 1: Blur. cover says Mar, indicia says Apr 2.50
❑1/Variant, Apr 1997; indicia and cover dates match 2.50
❑2, May 1997; cover says Apr, indicia says May 2.50
❑3, Jun 1997 .... 2.50
❑4, Jun 1997 .... 2.50
❑5, Aug 1997 .... 2.50
❑6, Sep 1997 .... 2.50
❑7, Oct 1997 .... 2.50
❑8, Nov 1997; Cover swipe from X-Men (1st Series) #100 .... 2.50
❑9, Dec 1997; teen sex issue 2.50
❑10, Jan 1998 .... 2.50
❑11, Feb 1998 .... 2.50
❑12, Mar 1998 .... 2.50
❑13, Apr 1998 .... 2.50
❑14, Jan 1998; no cover date; indicia says Jan 2.50
❑15, Feb 1998; no cover date; indicia says Feb 2.50
❑16, Mar 1998; month of publication repeated 2.50
❑17, Mar 1998; month of publication repeated 2.50
❑18, Mar 1998; month of publication repeated 2.50
❑19, Jun 1998; No cover date; Indicia says June 1998; Final Issue 2.50
❑Ashcan 1, Nov 1996, b&w; no cover price; preview of upcoming series 1.00

Troubleman
Image / Motown

❑1, Jun 1996 .... 2.25
❑2, Jul 1996 .... 2.25
❑3, Aug 1996 .... 2.25

Troubleshooters Inc.
Nightwolf

❑1, Win 1995, b&w 2.50
❑2, Spr 1995, b&w 2.50

Trouble With Girls
Malibu

❑1, Aug 1987, b&w 2.50
❑2, Sep 1987 .... 2.25
❑3, Oct 1987 .... 2.25
❑4, Nov 1987 .... 2.25
❑5, Dec 1987 .... 2.25
❑6, Jan 1988 .... 2.00
❑7, Feb 1988, b&w 2.00
❑8, Mar 1988, b&w 2.00
❑9, Apr 1988, b&w 2.00
❑10, May 1988, b&w 2.00
❑11, Jun 1988, b&w 2.00
❑12, Jul 1988, b&w 2.00
❑13, Aug 1988, b&w 2.00
❑14, Sep 1988, b&w 2.00
❑Ann 1, b&w 3.25
❑Holiday 1, b&w 2.95

Trouble With Girls
Comico

❑1, ca. 1989, Comico begins publishing 2.50
❑2, ca. 1989 .... 2.00

N-MINT

❑3, ca. 1989 .... 2.00
❑4, ca. 1989 .... 2.00
❑5, ca. 1989, b&w; Eternity begins publishing; Black & white format begins 1.95
❑6, ca. 1989, b&w 1.95
❑7, ca. 1989, b&w 1.95
❑8, ca. 1989, b&w 1.95
❑9, ca. 1990, b&w 1.95
❑10, ca. 1990, b&w 1.95
❑11, ca. 1990, b&w 1.95
❑12, ca. 1990, b&w 1.95
❑13, ca. 1990, b&w 1.95
❑14, ca. 1990, b&w 1.95
❑15, ca. 1990, b&w 2.25
❑16, ca. 1990 .... 2.25
❑17, ca. 1991 .... 2.25
❑18, ca. 1991 .... 2.25
❑19, ca. 1991 .... 2.25
❑20, ca. 1991 .... 2.25
❑21, ca. 1991 .... 2.25
❑22, ca. 1991 .... 2.25
❑23, ca. 1991 .... 2.25

Trouble With Girls: The Night of the Lizard
Marvel / Epic

❑1, Jun 1993; Embossed cover 2.50
❑2, Jul 1993 .... 2.25
❑3, Aug 1993 .... 2.25
❑4, Sep 1993 .... 2.25

Trouble with Tigers
Antarctic

❑1, Jan 1992, b&w 2.50
❑2, Feb 1992, b&w 2.50

Trout Fission
Tall Tale

❑1, Jul 1998, b&w 1.95
❑2, Oct 1998, b&w 1.95

Troy
Tome

❑1; Issue #1 preview for graphic novel .. 2.95

TRS-80 Computer Whiz Kids
Archie

❑1, giveaway 2.00

True Adventures of Adam and Bryon
American Mule

❑1, May 1998, b&w 2.50
❑2 1998 .... 2.50
❑3 1998 .... 2.50

True Confusions
Fantagraphics

❑1, b&w 2.50

True Faith
DC

❑1; squarebound; reprints Garth Ennis' first story from 1990 .... 12.95

True Gein
Boneyard

❑1, May 1993; Adult 3.00

True Glitz
Rip Off

❑1; Adult; ca. 1990 .... 2.50

Other grades: Multiply price above by 5/6 for VF/NM • 2/3 for VERY FINE • 1/3 for FINE • 1/5 for VERY GOOD • 1/8 for GOOD

True Love
Eclipse

❑1, Jan 1986; DSt (c); ATh, NC (a); Reprints stories from New Romances #17, Thrilling Romances #22, #24, and Intimate Love #20 .... 2.00
❑2, Jan 1986; BA (c); ATh, NC (a); Reprints stories from Popular Romance #22, New Romances #13, #15, and Thrilling Romances #24 .... 2.00

True North
Comic Legends Defense Fund

❑1, ca. 1988, b&w; Cardstock cover; benefit comic 3.50

True North II
Comic Legends Defense Fund

❑1, ca. 1990; cardstock foldout cover 4.50

True Sin
Boneyard

❑1; Adult 2.95

True Spy Stories
Caliber / Tome

❑1, b&w; bios 2.95

True Story, Swear to God
Image

❑1, Nov 2006 .... 2.99
❑2, Jan 2007 .... 2.99
❑3 .... 2.99
❑4 .... 2.99
❑5 .... 2.99
❑6 .... 2.99
❑7 .... 2.99
❑8 .... 2.99
❑9 .... 2.99
❑10 .... 2.99
❑11 .... 2.99

True Swamp
Peristaltic

❑1, Feb 1994, b&w; Adult 2.50
❑2, May 1994, b&w; Adult 2.50
❑3, ca. 1994; Adult 2.50
❑4, Oct 1994, b&w; Adult 2.50
❑5, Feb 1995, b&w; Adult 2.95

True Travel Tales
-Ism

❑1, ca. 2004 .... 2.95
❑2, ca. 2004 .... 2.95
❑3, ca. 2004 .... 2.95
❑4, ca. 2005 .... 2.95

Trufan Adventures Theatre
Paragraphics

❑1, ca. 1986, b&w 1.95
❑2, ca. 1986; 3-D 1.95

Truly Tasteless and Tacky
Caliber

❑1, b&w 2.50

Truth
Dark Horse

❑0, Jul 1999, b&w; ashcan-sized preview of upcoming graphic novel given out at Comic-Con International: San Diego in 1999 .... 1.00
❑1, Aug 1999; prestige format; includes CD soundtrack 17.95

Truth, Justin, and the American Way
Image

❑1, Apr 2006 .... 2.99
❑3, Jul 2006 .... 2.99
❑4, Oct 2006 .... 2.99

Truth: Red, White & Black
Marvel

❑1, Jan 2003; cardstock cover 5.00
❑2, Feb 2003; cardstock cover 3.50
❑3, Mar 2003; cardstock cover 3.50
❑4, Apr 2003; cardstock cover 3.50
❑5, May 2003; cardstock cover 3.50
❑6, Jun 2003; cardstock cover 3.50
❑7, Jul 2003; cardstock cover 3.50

Truth Serum
Slave Labor

❑1, Jan 2002, b&w; Smaller than comic-book size 2.95
❑2, Mar 2002, b&w; Smaller than comic-book size 2.95
❑3, May 2002, b&w; Smaller than comic-book size 2.95

Trypto the Acid Dog
Renegade

❑1, b&w 2.00

TSC Jams
TSC

❑0 .... 3.95
❑1; NN 3.95

TSR Worlds
DC

❑Ann 1, ca. 1990; 1: Meredith; 1: The Spelljammers 2.00

Tsukuyomi - Moon Phase
Tokyopop

❑1, Dec 2005 .... 9.99

Tsunami Girl
Image

❑1, Feb 1999, no month of publication 2.95
❑2, Apr 1999, no month of publication 2.95
❑3, Jun 1999 .... 2.95

Tsunami, the Irresistible Force
Epoch

❑1 .... 2.00

T2: Cybernetic Dawn
Malibu

❑0, Apr 1996; Flip-Book with T2 Nuclear Twilight #0 .... 3.00
❑1, Nov 1995; immediately follows events of T2 Judgment Day 2.50
❑2, Dec 1995 .... 2.50
❑3, Jan 1996 .... 2.50
❑4, Feb 1996 .... 2.50

T2: Nuclear Twilight
Malibu

❑0, Apr 1996; Flip-book with T2 Cybernetic Dawn #0 .... 3.00
❑1, Nov 1995; prequel to first Terminator movie 2.50
❑2, Dec 1995 .... 2.50
❑3, Jan 1996 .... 2.50
❑4, Feb 1996 .... 2.50

Tubby and the Little Men From Mars
Gold Key

❑1, Oct 1964 .... 75.00

Tuesday
Kim-Rehr

❑1, ca. 2003, b&w 2.95
❑2, ca. 2003, b&w 2.95
❑3, ca. 2004, b&w 2.95

Tuff Ghosts, Starring Spooky
Harvey

❑1, Jul 1962 .... 35.00
❑2, Sep 1962 .... 18.00
❑3, Nov 1962 .... 18.00
❑4, Jan 1963 .... 18.00
❑5, Mar 1963 .... 18.00
❑6, May 1963 .... 12.00
❑7, Jul 1963 .... 12.00
❑8, Sep 1963 .... 12.00
❑9, Nov 1963 .... 12.00
❑10, Jan 1964 .... 12.00
❑11, May 1964 .... 10.00
❑12, Jul 1964 .... 10.00
❑13, Nov 1964 .... 10.00
❑14, Jan 1965 .... 10.00
❑15, Mar 1965 .... 10.00
❑16, May 1965 .... 10.00
❑17, Jul 1965 .... 10.00
❑18, Sep 1965 .... 10.00
❑19, Nov 1965 .... 10.00
❑20, Jan 1966 .... 10.00
❑21, Mar 1966 .... 10.00
❑22, May 1966 .... 10.00
❑23, Jul 1966 .... 10.00
❑24, Sep 1966 .... 10.00
❑25, Nov 1966 .... 10.00
❑26, Jan 1967 .... 10.00
❑27, Mar 1967 .... 10.00
❑28, May 1967 .... 10.00
❑29, Jul 1967 .... 10.00
❑30, Sep 1967 .... 10.00
❑31, Nov 1967 .... 8.00
❑32, Jan 1968 .... 8.00
❑33, Jun 1968 .... 8.00
❑34, Aug 1968 .... 8.00
❑35, Oct 1968 .... 8.00
❑36, Nov 1968 .... 8.00
❑37, Apr 1969 .... 8.00
❑38, Sep 1969 .... 8.00
❑39, Nov 1969 .... 8.00
❑40, Sep 1971 .... 8.00
❑41, ca. 1972 .... 6.00
❑42, Jun 1972 .... 6.00
❑43, Oct 1972 .... 6.00

Tug & Buster
Art & Soul

❑1, Nov 1995 .... 3.00
❑2, Jan 1996 .... 3.00
❑3, Mar 1996 .... 3.00
❑4, May 1996 .... 3.00
❑5, Aug 1996 .... 3.00
❑6, May 1997 .... 3.00
❑7, Feb 1998 .... 3.00

Tug & Buster
Image

❑1, Aug 1998, b&w 2.95

Tumbling Boxes
Fantagraphics / Eros

❑1, Dec 1994, b&w; Adult 2.95

Tundra Sketchbook Series
Tundra

❑1; Melting Pot; Adult 3.95
❑2; Totleben; Adult 3.95
❑3; Noodles 3.95
❑4; Rick Bryant 3.95
❑5; Adult 3.95
❑6; Screaming Masks; Adult 3.95
❑7; Jon J. Muth; Adult 3.95
❑8; Forg 3.95
❑9; Michael Dooney; Adult 3.95
❑10; Skull Farmer 4.95
❑11; Adult 3.95
❑12; Adult 3.95

Turistas: Other Side of Paradise — Book One
Idea & Design Works

❑1, Nov 2006 .... 3.99

Turok
Acclaim

❑1, Mar 1998 .... 2.50
❑2, Apr 1998 .... 2.50
❑3, May 1998 .... 2.50
❑4, Jun 1998 .... 2.50

Turok Adon's Curse
Acclaim

❑1 .... 4.95

Turok: Child of Blood
Acclaim

❑1, Jan 1998; One-shot 3.95

Turok, Dinosaur Hunter
Acclaim / Valiant

❑0, Nov 1995; O: Andar; O: Lost Land; O: Turok 5.00
❑1, Jul 1993; chromium cover 2.00
❑1/Gold, Jul 1993; Gold edition; chromium cover 14.00
❑1/VVSS, Jul 1993 .... 20.00
❑2, Aug 1993 .... 1.00
❑3, Sep 1993 .... 1.00
❑4, Oct 1993 .... 1.00
❑5, Nov 1993 .... 1.00
❑6, Dec 1993 .... 1.00
❑7, Jan 1994 .... 1.00
❑8, Feb 1994 .... 1.00
❑9, Mar 1994 .... 1.00
❑10, Apr 1994 .... 1.00
❑11, May 1994; trading card 2.00
❑12, Jun 1994 .... 1.00
❑13, Aug 1994; V: Captain Red 1.00
❑14, Sep 1994; V: Captain Red 1.00
❑15, Oct 1994; V: Captain Red 1.00
❑16, Oct 1994; Chaos Effect 1.00
❑17, Nov 1994 .... 1.00
❑18, Dec 1994 .... 1.00
❑19, Jan 1995 .... 1.00

Other grades: Multiply price above by 5/6 for VF/NM • 2/3 for VERY FINE • 1/3 for FINE • 1/5 for VERY GOOD • 1/8 for GOOD

Vamps

Five beautiful women with the same problem

©DC

Vanguard

Created in the 1980s for the series Megaton

©Image

Vanguard Illustrated

Daring science-fiction anthology series

©Pacific

Vanity Angel

Kaori Asamo's adult pleasureland

©Antarctic

Vault of Horror

Reprints of classic E.C. comics

©Gladstone

	N-MINT
❑20, Feb 1995	2.00
❑21, Mar 1995	1.00
❑22, Apr 1995	2.00
❑23, May 1995	2.00
❑24, Jun 1995; back to the Lost Land	2.00
❑25, Jul 1995	2.00
❑26, Jul 1995; Birthquake	2.00
❑27, Aug 1995	2.00
❑28, Aug 1995	2.00
❑29, Sep 1995	2.00
❑30, Sep 1995	2.00
❑31, Oct 1995	2.00
❑32, Oct 1995	2.00
❑33, Nov 1995	2.00
❑34, Nov 1995	2.00
❑35, Dec 1995; Painted cover	2.00
❑36, Dec 1995	2.00
❑37, Jan 1996	2.00
❑38, Jan 1996	2.00
❑39, Feb 1996	3.00
❑40, Mar 1996	4.00
❑41, Apr 1996	4.00
❑42, Apr 1996	4.00
❑43, May 1996	3.00
❑44, May 1996	3.00
❑45, Jun 1996	6.00
❑46, Aug 1996	9.00
❑47, Aug 1996; Final Issue	18.00
❑Book 1	9.95
❑YB 1; YB 1; YB 1; Ca. 1994	3.95

Turok: Evolution
Acclaim

❑1, Aug 2002; Wraparound cover	2.50

Turok: Redpath
Acclaim

❑1, Oct 1997	3.95

Turok: Seeds of Evil
Acclaim

❑1; newsstand edition	4.99
❑1/Direct ed.; Direct cover	4.99

Turok/Shadowman
Acclaim / Valiant

❑1, Feb 1999	3.95

Turok: Shadow of Oblivion
Acclaim

❑1, Sep 2000; Based on the video game	4.95

Turok, Son of Stone
Dell / Gold Key

	N-MINT
❑26, Dec 1961	48.00
❑27, Mar 1962	48.00
❑28, Jun 1962	48.00
❑29, Sep 1962, Last Dell issue	48.00
❑30, Dec 1962, First Gold Key issue	48.00
❑31, Jan 1963	38.00
❑32, Mar 1963	38.00
❑33, May 1963	38.00
❑34, Jul 1963, 10030-307	38.00
❑35, Sep 1963	38.00
❑36, Nov 1963, reprints two Dell Turok stories	38.00
❑37, Jan 1964	38.00
❑38, Mar 1964	38.00
❑39, May 1964	38.00
❑40, Jul 1964	38.00
❑41, Sep 1964	28.00
❑42, Nov 1964	28.00
❑43, Jan 1965	28.00
❑44, Mar 1965	28.00
❑45, May 1965	28.00
❑46, Jul 1965, back cover pin-up	28.00
❑47, Sep 1965, 10030-509	28.00
❑48, Nov 1965	28.00
❑49, Jan 1966	28.00
❑50, Mar 1966	28.00
❑51, May 1966	22.00
❑52, Jul 1966	22.00
❑53, Sep 1966	22.00
❑54, Nov 1966, Reprints from Turok, Son of Stone #25	22.00
❑55, Jan 1967	22.00
❑56, Mar 1967	22.00
❑57, May 1967, Reprints from Turok, Son of Stone #17	22.00
❑58, Jul 1967	22.00
❑59, Oct 1967	22.00
❑60, Jan 1968	22.00
❑61, Apr 1968	15.00
❑62, Jul 1968	15.00
❑63, Oct 1968	15.00
❑64, Jan 1969	15.00
❑65, Apr 1969	15.00
❑66, Jul 1969	15.00
❑67, Oct 1969	15.00
❑68, Jan 1970	15.00
❑69, Apr 1970	15.00
❑70, Jul 1970	15.00
❑71, Oct 1970	10.00
❑72, Jan 1971	10.00
❑73, Apr 1971	10.00
❑74, Jul 1971	10.00
❑75, Oct 1971	10.00
❑76, Jan 1972	10.00
❑77, Mar 1972	10.00
❑78, May 1972	10.00
❑79, Jul 1972	10.00
❑80, Sep 1972	10.00
❑81, Nov 1972	10.00
❑82, Jan 1973, 90030-301	10.00
❑83, Mar 1973	10.00
❑84, May 1973	10.00
❑85, Jul 1973	10.00
❑86, Sep 1973	10.00
❑87, Nov 1973	10.00
❑88, Jan 1974	10.00
❑89, Mar 1974	10.00
❑90, May 1974	10.00
❑91, Jul 1974	8.00
❑92, Sep 1974	8.00
❑93, Nov 1974	8.00
❑94, Jan 1975	8.00
❑95, Mar 1975	8.00
❑96, May 1975	8.00
❑97, Jul 1975	8.00
❑98, Aug 1975	8.00
❑99, Sep 1975	8.00
❑100, Nov 1975	8.00
❑101, Jan 1976	8.00
❑102, Mar 1976	8.00
❑103, May 1976	8.00
❑104, Jul 1976	8.00
❑105, Sep 1976	8.00
❑106, Nov 1976	8.00
❑107, Jan 1977	8.00
❑108, Mar 1977	8.00
❑109, May 1977	8.00
❑110, Jul 1977	8.00
❑111, Sep 1977	6.00
❑112, Nov 1977, Reprints from Turok, Son of Stone #87	6.00
❑113, Jan 1978	6.00
❑114, Mar 1978, Reprint from Turok, Son of Stone #61	6.00
❑115, May 1978, Reprint from Turok, Son of Stone #63	6.00
❑116, Jul 1978	6.00
❑117, Sep 1978	6.00
❑118, Nov 1978	6.00
❑119, Jan 1979	6.00
❑120, Mar 1979	6.00
❑121, May 1979	6.00
❑122, Jul 1979	6.00
❑123, Sep 1979	6.00
❑124, Nov 1979	6.00
❑125, Jan 1980	6.00
❑126, Mar 1981	6.00
❑127, Oct 1981, Reprint from Turok, Son of Stone #101	6.00
❑128, Dec 1981, Reprints from Turok Sone of Stone #39	6.00
❑129, Feb 1982, Reprint from Turok, Son of Stone #26	6.00
❑130, Apr 1982, Final Issue; Reprint from Turok, Son of Stone #41	6.00
❑GS 1, Nov 1966; Reprints from Turok, Son of Stone #10, 11, 12 and 16	100.00

Turok: Spring Break in the Lost Land
Acclaim / Valiant

❑1, Jul 1997; One-shot	3.95

Turok: Tales of the Lost Land
Acclaim

❑1, Apr 1998; Tales of the Lost Land	3.95

Turok: The Empty Souls
Acclaim

❑1, Apr 1997	3.95
❑1/Variant, Apr 1997; alternate painted cover	3.95
❑Ashcan 1, Nov 1996, b&w; No cover price; preview of upcoming series	1.00

Turok the Hunted
Acclaim / Valiant

❑1, Mar 1996 MGr (w)	5.00
❑2, Mar 1996 MGr (w)	5.00

Turok, Timewalker: Seventh Sabbath
Acclaim / Valiant

❑1, Aug 1997; covers form diptych	2.50
❑2, Sep 1997; covers form diptych	2.50

Turtle Soup
Mirage

❑1, Sep 1987, b&w pin-ups, cardstock cover	5.00

Turtle Soup
Mirage

❑1, Nov 1991	2.50
❑2, Dec 1991	2.50

Other grades: Multiply price above by 5/6 for VF/NM • 2/3 for VERY FINE • 1/3 for FINE • 1/5 for VERY GOOD • 1/8 for GOOD

	N-MINT
❑3, Jan 1992	2.50
❑4, Feb 1992	2.50

Turtle Soup (Astonish)
Astonish

❑1, ca. 2003; Printed sideways with a cardstock cover	3.75

Tusk World Tour Book 2001
Tusk

❑nn, Apr 2001, b&w; Kaos Moon story..	4.95

Tutenstein
Marvel

❑1, Oct 2004; A: . A: . A: Cyclops. A: Wolverine. A: Storm. A: Spider-Man. Promotional giveaway promoting NBC/ Discovery Kids Saturday morning cartoon	1.00

Tuxedo Gin
Viz

❑1, Aug 2003	9.95
❑2, Oct 2003	9.95
❑3, Dec 2005	9.95
❑4, Feb 2004	9.95
❑5, Apr 2004	9.95
❑6, Jun 2004	9.95
❑7, Aug 2004	9.95
❑8, Oct 2004; Indicia says printed in 2003	9.95
❑9, Dec 2004; Indicia says printed in 2003	9.95
❑10, Feb 2005	9.95
❑11, Apr 2005	9.99
❑12, Jun 2005	9.99
❑13, Aug 2005	9.99
❑14, Oct 2005	9.99

TV Casper and Company
Harvey

❑1, Aug 1963, Harvey Giant	75.00
❑2, Oct 1963, Harvey Giant	30.00
❑3, Feb 1964, Harvey Giant	30.00
❑4 1964, Harvey Giant	30.00
❑5 1964, Harvey Giant	30.00
❑6 1964, Harvey Giant	20.00
❑7, Mar 1965, Harvey Giant	20.00
❑8 1965, Harvey Giant	20.00
❑9, Sep 1965, Harvey Giant	20.00
❑10, Dec 1965, Harvey Giant	20.00
❑11, Mar 1966, Harvey Giant	15.00
❑12, Jun 1966, Harvey Giant	15.00
❑13, Sep 1966, Harvey Giant	15.00
❑14 1967, Harvey Giant	15.00
❑15, Mar 1967, Harvey Giant	15.00
❑16, Nov 1967, Harvey Giant	15.00
❑17, Feb 1968, Harvey Giant	15.00
❑18, Apr 1968, Harvey Giant	15.00
❑19, Aug 1968, Harvey Giant	15.00
❑20, Nov 1968, Harvey Giant	15.00
❑21, Mar 1969, Harvey Giant	10.00
❑22, Apr 1969, Harvey Giant	10.00
❑23 1969, Harvey Giant	10.00
❑24, Oct 1969, Harvey Giant	10.00
❑25, Feb 1970, Harvey Giant	10.00
❑26, Apr 1970, Harvey Giant	10.00
❑27 1970, Harvey Giant	10.00
❑28, Oct 1970, Harvey Giant	10.00
❑29, Dec 1970, Harvey Giant	10.00
❑30, Feb 1971, Harvey Giant	10.00
❑31, Apr 1971, Harvey Giant	10.00
❑32, Aug 1971, Harvey Giant	8.00
❑33, Oct 1971, Harvey Giant	8.00
❑34, Dec 1971, Harvey Giant	8.00
❑35, Mar 1972, Harvey Giant	8.00
❑36, Aug 1972, Harvey Giant	8.00
❑37, Oct 1972, Harvey Giant	8.00
❑38, Dec 1972, Harvey Giant	8.00
❑39, Feb 1973, Harvey Giant	8.00
❑40, Apr 1973, Harvey Giant	8.00
❑41, Jun 1973, Harvey Giant	8.00
❑42, Aug 1973, Harvey Giant	8.00
❑43, Oct 1973, Harvey Giant	8.00
❑44, Dec 1973, Harvey Giant	8.00
❑45, Feb 1974, Harvey Giant	8.00
❑46, Apr 1974, Harvey Giant	8.00

TV Stars
Marvel

❑1, Aug 1978, 1: Captain Caveman (in comics). 1: Grape Ape (in comics)	15.00
❑2, Oct 1978	7.00
❑3, Dec 1978	7.00
❑4, Feb 1979, Final Issue	7.00

TV Western
AC

❑1, ca. 2001, b&w; reprints stories from Range Rider #17, Roy Rogers, and Wild Bill Hickok	5.95

Tweety and Sylvester
Gold Key / Whitman

❑1, ca. 1964	35.00
❑2, Feb 1966	20.00
❑3, Aug 1966	20.00
❑4, Nov 1966	20.00
❑5, Feb 1967	20.00
❑6, May 1967	8.00
❑7, Aug 1967	8.00
❑8, Nov 1967	8.00
❑9, Oct 1968	8.00
❑10, Mar 1969	8.00
❑11, Aug 1969	5.00
❑12, Nov 1969	5.00
❑13, Feb 1970	5.00
❑14, May 1970	5.00
❑15, Sep 1970	5.00
❑16, Dec 1970	5.00
❑17, Mar 1971	5.00
❑18, Jun 1971	5.00
❑19, Aug 1971	5.00
❑20, Oct 1971	5.00
❑21, Dec 1971	4.00
❑22, Jan 1972	4.00
❑23, Mar 1972	4.00
❑24, May 1972	4.00
❑25, Jul 1972	4.00
❑26, Sep 1972	4.00
❑27, Nov 1972	4.00
❑28, Jan 1973	4.00
❑29, Mar 1973	4.00
❑30, May 1973	4.00
❑31, Jul 1973	4.00
❑32, Aug 1973	4.00
❑33, Sep 1973	4.00
❑34, Nov 1973	4.00
❑35, Jan 1974	4.00
❑36, Mar 1974	4.00
❑37, May 1974	4.00
❑38, Jul 1974	4.00
❑39, Aug 1974	4.00
❑40, Sep 1974	4.00
❑41, Nov 1974	3.00
❑42, Jan 1975	3.00
❑43, Mar 1975	3.00
❑44, Apr 1975	3.00
❑45, May 1975	3.00
❑46, Jun 1975	3.00
❑47, Jul 1975	3.00
❑48, Aug 1975	3.00
❑49, Sep 1975	3.00
❑50, Oct 1975	3.00
❑51, Nov 1975	3.00
❑52, Dec 1975	3.00
❑53, Jan 1976	3.00
❑54, Feb 1976	3.00
❑55, Mar 1976	3.00
❑56, Apr 1976	3.00
❑57, May 1976	3.00
❑58, Jun 1976	3.00
❑59, Jul 1976	3.00
❑60, Aug 1976	3.00
❑61, Sep 1976	3.00
❑62, Oct 1976	3.00
❑63, Nov 1976	3.00
❑64, Dec 1976	3.00
❑65, Jan 1977	3.00
❑66, Feb 1977	3.00
❑67, Mar 1977	3.00
❑68, Apr 1977	3.00
❑69, May 1977	3.00
❑70, Jun 1977	3.00
❑71, Jul 1977	3.00
❑72, Aug 1977	3.00
❑73, Sep 1977	3.00
❑74, Oct 1977	3.00
❑75, Nov 1977	3.00
❑76, Dec 1977, Includes Daredevil Hostess ad "Because" by Gil Kane not published in Marvel Comics	3.00
❑77, Jan 1978	3.00
❑78, Feb 1978	3.00
❑79, Mar 1978	3.00
❑80, Apr 1978	3.00
❑81, May 1978	2.50
❑82, Jun 1978	2.50
❑83, Jul 1978	2.50
❑84, Aug 1978	2.50
❑85, Sep 1978	2.50
❑86, Oct 1978	2.50
❑87, Nov 1978	2.50
❑88, Dec 1978	2.50
❑89, Jan 1979	2.50
❑90, Feb 1979	2.50
❑91, Mar 1979	2.50
❑92, Apr 1979	2.50
❑93, May 1979	2.50
❑94, Jun 1979	2.50
❑95, Jul 1979	2.50
❑96, Aug 1979	2.50
❑97, Sep 1979	2.50
❑98, Oct 1979	2.50
❑99, Nov 1979	2.50
❑100, Dec 1979	2.50
❑101, Jan 1980	2.00
❑102, Feb 1980	2.00
❑103, ca. 1980	5.00
❑104, ca. 1980	5.00
❑105, ca. 1980	12.00
❑106, ca. 1980	12.00
❑107, ca. 1981	17.00
❑108, ca. 1981	8.00
❑109, ca. 1981	8.00
❑110, Aug 1981	8.00
❑111, Sep 1981	8.00
❑112, ca. 1981	8.00
❑113, Feb 1982	8.00
❑114, Hol 1982	8.00
❑115, Mar 1982	8.00
❑116, Apr 1982	8.00
❑117, ca. 1982	10.00
❑118, ca. 1982	10.00
❑119, ca. 1982	10.00
❑120, Oct 1982	10.00
❑121	10.00

24: Midnight Sun
Idea & Design Works

❑0, Sep 2005	7.49

24: Nightfall
Idea & Design Works

❑1, Nov 2006	3.99
❑2, Dec 2006	3.99

24 One-shot
Idea & Design Works

❑1, Jul 2004	6.99

20 Nude Dancers 20 Year Two
Tundra

❑1, b&w; NN	3.50

21
Image

❑1, Feb 1996	2.50
❑1/A, Feb 1996	2.50
❑2, Mar 1996	2.50
❑3, Apr 1996	2.50

21 Down
DC / Wildstorm

❑1, Nov 2002	2.95
❑2, Dec 2002	2.95
❑3, Jan 2003	2.95
❑4, Feb 2003	2.95
❑5, Mar 2003	2.95
❑6, Apr 2003	2.95
❑7, May 2003	2.95
❑8, Jun 2003	2.95
❑9, Jul 2003	2.95
❑10, Jun 2003	2.95
❑11, Jul 2003	2.95
❑12, Sep 2003	2.95

22 Brides
Event

❑1, Mar 1996	2.95
❑1/Ltd., Mar 1996; Limited, signed edition	3.50
❑2, Jun 1996	2.95
❑3, Sep 1996	2.95

Other grades: Multiply price above by 5/6 for VF/NM • 2/3 for VERY FINE • 1/3 for FINE • 1/5 for VERY GOOD • 1/8 for GOOD

Veils

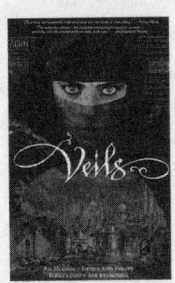

About the power of self-discovery
©DC

Vengeance of Vampirella

Led off the "bad girls" era of Vampirella
©Harris

Venom

Most successful title of Marvel's Tsunami line
©Marvel

Venom: Lethal Protector

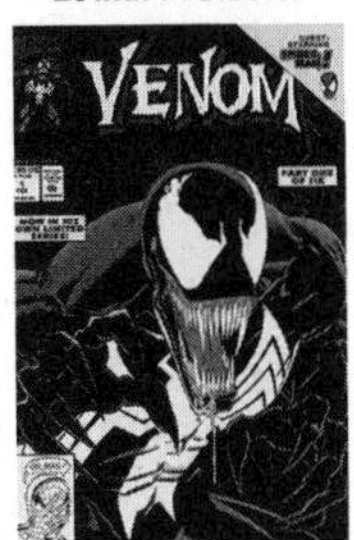

Some of #1's covers had a printing problem
©Marvel

Veronica

Rich girl waits until 1989 to get her solo series
©Archie

N-MINT

❑4, Jan 1997; Variant Painkiller Jane solo cover ... 2.95
❑4/A, Jan 1997; O: Painkiller Jane. Painkiller Jane on Dinosaur cover ... 3.50
❑CS 1, ca. 1997; Collector's Set. Includes #1-4, poster ... 34.95

Twice-Told Tales of Unsupervised Existence
Rip Off

❑1, Apr 1989, b&w ... 2.00

Twilight
DC

❑1, ca. 1991 ... 4.95
❑2, ca. 1991 ... 4.95
❑3, ca. 1991 ... 4.95

Twilight
Avatar

❑1, Mar 1997 ... 3.00
❑2, Mar 1997 ... 3.00

Twilight Avenger
Elite

❑1, Jul 1986 ... 1.75
❑2, Oct 1986 ... 1.75

Twilight Avenger
Eternity

❑1, Jul 1988, b&w ... 1.95
❑2, Aug 1988, b&w ... 1.95
❑3, Sep 1988, b&w ... 1.95
❑4, Nov 1988, b&w ... 1.95
❑5, Feb 1989, b&w ... 1.95
❑6, May 1989, b&w ... 1.95
❑7, Aug 1989, b&w ... 1.95
❑8, Feb 1990, b&w ... 1.95

Twilight Experiment
DC

❑1, Apr 2005 ... 2.95
❑2, May 2005 ... 2.95
❑3, Jun 2005 ... 2.95
❑4, Jun 2005 ... 2.99
❑5, Jul 2005 ... 2.99
❑6, Aug 2005 ... 2.99

Twilight Girl
Cross Plains

❑1, Nov 2000 ... 2.95
❑2, Dec 2000 ... 2.95
❑3, Jan 2001 ... 2.95

Twilight Man
First

❑1, Jun 1989 ... 2.75
❑2, Jul 1989 ... 2.75
❑3, Aug 1989 ... 2.75
❑4, Sep 1989 ... 2.75

Twilight People
Caliber

❑1, b&w ... 2.95
❑2, b&w ... 2.95

Twilight X
Pork Chop

❑1, b&w ... 2.00
❑2, b&w ... 2.00
❑3, b&w ... 2.00

N-MINT

Twilight X
Antarctic

❑1, b&w ... 2.50
❑2, b&w ... 2.50
❑3, b&w ... 2.50
❑4, Sep 1993, b&w ... 2.50
❑5, Feb 1994, b&w ... 2.75

Twilight-X: Interlude
Antarctic

❑1, Jul 1992, b&w ... 2.50
❑2, Sep 1992, b&w ... 2.50
❑3, Nov 1992, b&w ... 2.50
❑4, Jan 1993, b&w ... 2.50
❑5, Mar 1993, b&w ... 2.50
❑6, May 1993, b&w ... 2.50

Twilight-X: Interlude
Antarctic

❑1, Jun 1993, b&w ... 2.50
❑2, Jul 1993, b&w ... 2.50
❑3, Aug 1993, b&w ... 2.50
❑4, Sep 1993, b&w ... 2.50
❑5, Oct 1993, b&w ... 2.75

Twilight X Quarterly
Antarctic

❑1, Sep 1994, b&w ... 2.95
❑2, Nov 1994, b&w ... 2.95
❑3, Feb 1995, b&w ... 2.95

Twilight X: Storm
Antarctic

❑1 2003; b&w, ca. 2004 ... 3.50
❑2 2003; b&w, ca. 2004 ... 3.50
❑3, May 2003; b&w, ca. 2004 ... 3.50
❑4, Aug 2003; b&w, ca. 2004 ... 3.50
❑5, Sep 2003; b&w, ca. 2004 ... 3.50
❑6, Jan 2004; b&w, ca. 2004 ... 3.50

Twilight: X War
Antarctic

❑1, ca. 2005 ... 2.99

Twilight Zone
Dell

❑-207, Jul 1962, Cover code 01-860-297; earlier issues published as Dell Four Color #1173 and #1288 ... 250.00
❑-210, Oct 1962, Cover code 12-860-210 ... 200.00

Twilight Zone
Gold Key

❑1, Nov 1962, Published as Dell Four-Color #1173 ... 90.00
❑2, Feb 1963, Published as Dell Four-Color #1174 ... 55.00
❑3, May 1963 ... 42.00
❑4, Aug 1963 ... 35.00
❑5, Nov 1963 ... 35.00
❑6, Feb 1964 ... 35.00
❑7, May 1964 ... 35.00
❑8, Aug 1964 ... 35.00
❑9, Nov 1964 ... 35.00
❑10, Feb 1965 ... 35.00
❑11, May 1965 ... 30.00
❑12, Aug 1965 ... 30.00
❑13, Nov 1965 ... 30.00
❑14, Feb 1966, 10016-602 ... 30.00
❑15, May 1966 ... 30.00
❑16, Jul 1966 ... 30.00

N-MINT

❑17, Sep 1966 ... 30.00
❑18, Nov 1966 ... 30.00
❑19, Jan 1966, JO (a) ... 30.00
❑20, Mar 1966 ... 30.00
❑21, May 1967 ... 16.00
❑22, Jul 1967, 10016-707 ... 16.00
❑23, Oct 1967 ... 16.00
❑24, Jan 1968 ... 16.00
❑25, Apr 1968 ... 16.00
❑26, Jul 1968, 10016-807 ... 16.00
❑27, Dec 1968 ... 16.00
❑28, Mar 1969 ... 10.00
❑29, Jun 1969, 10016-906 ... 10.00
❑30, Sep 1969 ... 10.00
❑31, Dec 1969 ... 8.00
❑32, Mar 1970 ... 8.00
❑33, Jun 1970 ... 8.00
❑34, Sep 1970 ... 8.00
❑35, Dec 1970 ... 8.00
❑36, Mar 1971 ... 8.00
❑37, May 1971 ... 8.00
❑38, Jul 1971 ... 8.00
❑39, Sep 1971 ... 8.00
❑40, Nov 1971 ... 8.00
❑41, Jan 1972 ... 6.00
❑42, Mar 1972, 90016-203 ... 6.00
❑43, May 1972 ... 6.00
❑44, Jul 1972 ... 6.00
❑45, Sep 1972 ... 6.00
❑46, Nov 1972 ... 6.00
❑47, Jan 1973 ... 6.00
❑48, Mar 1973 ... 6.00
❑49, May 1973 ... 6.00
❑50, Jul 1973 ... 6.00
❑51, Aug 1973 ... 6.00
❑52, Sep 1973 ... 5.00
❑53, Nov 1973 ... 5.00
❑54, Jan 1974 ... 5.00
❑55, Mar 1974 ... 5.00
❑56, May 1974 ... 5.00
❑57, Jul 1974 ... 5.00
❑58, Aug 1974 ... 5.00
❑59, Sep 1974 ... 5.00
❑60, Nov 1974 ... 5.00
❑61, Jan 1975 ... 5.00
❑62, Mar 1975 ... 5.00
❑63, May 1975 ... 5.00
❑64, Jul 1975 ... 5.00
❑65, Aug 1975, AN (a) ... 5.00
❑66, Sep 1975 ... 5.00
❑67, Nov 1975, Cover code 90016-511 ... 5.00
❑68, Jan 1976 ... 5.00
❑69, Mar 1976 ... 5.00
❑70, May 1976 ... 5.00
❑71, Jul 1976, Reprints from Twilight Zone (Vol. 1) #45 ... 4.00
❑72, Aug 1976 ... 4.00
❑73, Sep 1976, Reprints from Twilight Zone (Vol. 1) #40 ... 4.00
❑74, Nov 1976 ... 4.00
❑75, Jan 1977 ... 4.00
❑76, Mar 1977 ... 4.00
❑77, May 1977 ... 4.00
❑78, Jul 1977 ... 4.00
❑79, Aug 1977, Reprints from Twilight Zone (Vol. 1) #39 ... 4.00

Other grades: Multiply price above by 5/6 for VF/NM • 2/3 for VERY FINE • 1/3 for FINE • 1/5 for VERY GOOD • 1/8 for GOOD

N-MINT N-MINT N-MINT

❑80, Sep 1977 .... 4.00
❑81, Nov 1977 .... 4.00
❑82, Jan 1978 .... 4.00
❑83, Apr 1978, Reprints from Twilight Zone (Vol. 1) #50 .... 4.00
❑84, Jun 1978, Reprints from Twilight Zone (Vol. 1) #52 .... 4.00
❑85, ca. 1978 .... 4.00
❑86, ca. 1978, Reprints from Twilight Zone (Vol. 1) #48 .... 4.00
❑87, ca. 1978 .... 4.00
❑88, ca. 1978 .... 4.00
❑89, Feb 1979 .... 4.00
❑90, Apr 1979 .... 4.00
❑91, Jun 1979 .... 4.00
❑92, ca. 1982, Reprints from Twilight Zone (Vol. 1) #1; Final Issue 4.00

Twilight Zone
Now

❑1, Nov 1991; two covers 2.50
❑1/Direct ed.; Direct Market edition 2.50
❑2, Dec 1991 .... 2.25
❑3, Jan 1992 .... 2.25
❑4, Feb 1992; Highways of the Night 2.00
❑5, Mar 1992; Queen of the Void 2.00
❑6, Apr 1992; Insecticide 2.00
❑7, May 1992; 2 Stories: The Outcast and Ghost Horse 2.00
❑8, Jun 1992; Survivor Types 2.00
❑9, Jul 1992; 3-D; Holographic cover; bagged; hologram; Partial 3-D art 2.95
❑9/Prestige, Jul 1992; 3-D; Holographic cover with glasses; hologram; Partial 3-D art; Extra stories 4.95
❑10, Aug 1992; Stairway to Heaven 1.95
❑11, Sep 1992 .... 1.95
❑12, Oct 1992 .... 1.95
❑13, Nov 1992 .... 1.95
❑14, Dec 1992 .... 1.95
❑15, Jan 1993 .... 1.95
❑16, Feb 1993 .... 1.95
❑SF 1, Mar 1993; hologram button; Science-Fiction Special 3.50

Twilight Zone
Now

❑1, May 1993 .... 2.50
❑2, Jun 1993; two different covers; computer special 2.50
❑3, Jul 1993 .... 2.50
❑4, Aug 1993 .... 2.50
❑Ann 1993, Apr 1993 .... 2.50

Twilight Zone 3-D Special
Now

❑1, Apr 1993; glasses 2.95

Twilight Zone Premiere
Now

❑1, Oct 1991; Introduction by Harlan Ellison 2.50
❑1/CS; Collector's Set (polybagged, gold logo); Not code approved; Introduction by Harlan Ellison 2.95
❑1/Direct ed., Oct 1991; Introduction by Harlan Ellison 2.50
❑1/Prestige; Prestige edition; Introduction by Harlan Ellison 4.95
❑1/2nd; Introduction by Harlan Ellison 2.50
❑1/Direct ed./2n; Not code-approved; Introduction by Harlan Ellison 2.50

Twin Earths
R. Susor

❑1, b&w; strip reprints 5.95
❑2, b&w; strip reprints 5.95

Twist
Kitchen Sink

❑1, b&w 2.00
❑2, May 1988 .... 2.00
❑3 .... 2.00

Twisted
Alchemy

❑1, b&w 3.95

Twisted 3-D Tales
Blackthorne

❑1; ca. 1986 .... 2.50

Twisted Sisters
Kitchen Sink

❑1, Apr 1994, b&w 3.50
❑2, May 1994; b&w 3.50

❑3 .... 3.50
❑4 .... 3.50

Twisted Tales
Pacific

❑1, Nov 1982; AA (a); Pacific publishes 3.50
❑2, Apr 1983 BWr (c); VM, MP (a) 2.50
❑3, Jun 1983 .... 2.50
❑4, Aug 1983 .... 2.50
❑5, Oct 1983 VM (a) 2.50
❑6, Jan 1983 .... 2.50
❑7, Mar 1954 .... 2.50
❑8, May 1954; BG (a); Eclipse publishes 2.50
❑9, Nov 1954; VM (a); Eclipse publishes 2.50
❑10, Dec 1984; BWr, GM (a); Eclipse publishes 2.50
❑3D 1, Aug 1986 .... 2.50

Twisted Tales of Bruce Jones
Eclipse

❑1, Feb 1985 .... 2.00
❑2, Jul 1986 .... 2.00
❑3, Mar 1986 .... 2.00
❑4, Feb 1986 .... 2.00

Twisted Tantrums of the Purple Snit
Blackthorne

❑1 .... 1.75
❑2 .... 1.75

Twister
Harris

❑1; trading card 3.00

Twitch
Aeon

❑1 .... 2.75

Two-Bits
Image

❑1, Feb 2005 .... 1.00

Two Faces of Tomorrow
Dark Horse

❑1, Aug 1997, b&w 2.95
❑2, Sep 1997, b&w; wraparound cover 2.95
❑3, Oct 1997, b&w 2.95
❑4, Nov 1997, b&w 2.95
❑5, Dec 1997, b&w 2.95
❑6, Jan 1998, b&w 2.95
❑7, Feb 1998, b&w 2.95
❑8, Mar 1998, b&w 2.95
❑9, Apr 1998, b&w 2.95
❑10, May 1998, b&w 2.95
❑11, Jun 1998, b&w 2.95
❑12, Jul 1998, b&w 2.95
❑13, Aug 1998, b&w 2.95

Two-Fisted Science
General Tektronics Labs

❑1, b&w; Excerpt of Bk 1; ca. 1997 .... 2.50

Two-Fisted Tales
Gemstone

❑1, Oct 1992; AF, HK, JCr, WW (a); Reprints Two-Fisted Tales (EC) #18 .... 2.00
❑2, Jan 1993; HK, JCr, JSe, WW (a); Reprints Two-Fisted Tales (EC) #19 .... 2.00
❑3, Apr 1993; HK, JSe, WW (a); Reprints Two-Fisted Tales (EC) #20 .... 2.00
❑4, Jul 1993; HK, JSe, WW (a); Reprints Two-Fisted Tales (EC) #21 .... 2.00
❑5, Oct 1993; HK, JSe, WW, AT (a); Reprints Two-Fisted Tales (EC) #22 .... 2.00
❑6, Jan 1994; HK, JSe, WW (a); Reprints Two-Fisted Tales (EC) #23 .... 2.00
❑7, Apr 1994; HK, JSe, WW (a); Reprints Two-Fisted Tales (EC) #24 .... 2.00
❑8, Jul 1994; Reprints Two-Fisted Tales (EC) #25 .... 2.00
❑9, Oct 1994; Reprints Two-Fisted Tales (EC) #26 .... 2.00
❑10, Jan 1995; Reprints Two-Fisted Tales (EC) #27 .... 2.00
❑11, Apr 1995; Reprints Two-Fisted Tales (EC) #28 .... 2.00
❑12, Jul 1995; Reprints Two-Fisted Tales (EC) #29 .... 2.00
❑13, Oct 1995; Reprints Two-Fisted Tales (EC) #30 .... 2.00
❑14, Jan 1996; Reprints Two-Fisted Tales (EC) #31 .... 2.00
❑15, Apr 1996; Reprints Two-Fisted Tales (EC) #32 .... 2.00
❑16, Jul 1996; Reprints Two-Fisted Tales (EC) #33 .... 2.50
❑17, Oct 1996; Reprints Two-Fisted Tales (EC) #34 .... 2.50
❑18, Jan 1997; Reprints Two-Fisted Tales (EC) #35 .... 2.50
❑19, Apr 1997; Reprints Two-Fisted Tales (EC) #36 .... 2.50
❑20, Jul 1997; Reprints Two-Fisted Tales (EC) #37 .... 2.50
❑21, Oct 1997; JSe (w); JSe (a); Reprints Two-Fisted Tales (EC) #38 .... 2.50
❑22, Jan 1998; Reprints Two-Fisted Tales (EC) #39 .... 2.50
❑23, Apr 1998; Reprints Two-Fisted Tales (EC) #40 .... 2.50
❑24, Jul 1998; Reprints Two-Fisted Tales (EC) #41 .... 2.50
❑Ann 1; Collects Two-Fisted Tales #1-5 .... 8.95
❑Ann 2; Collects Two-Fisted Tales #6-10 .... 9.95
❑Ann 3 .... 10.95
❑Ann 4 .... 12.95
❑Ann 5 .... 13.50

Two Fools
Last Gasp

❑1 .... 1.00

Two-Gun Kid
Marvel

❑60, Nov 1962, O: Two-Gun Kid 30.00
❑61, Jan 1963 .... 12.00
❑62, Mar 1963 .... 12.00
❑63, May 1963 .... 12.00
❑64, Jul 1963 .... 12.00
❑65, Sep 1963 .... 12.00
❑66, Nov 1963 .... 12.00
❑67, Jan 1964 .... 12.00
❑68, Mar 1964 .... 12.00
❑69, May 1964 .... 12.00
❑70, Jul 1964 .... 12.00
❑71, Sep 1964 .... 12.00
❑72, Nov 1964, V: Geronimo 12.00
❑73, Jan 1965 .... 12.00
❑74, Mar 1965 .... 12.00
❑75, May 1965, Reprint from Rawhide Kid #34 .... 12.00
❑76, Jul 1965, Reprint from Kid Colt Outlaw #95 .... 12.00
❑77, Sep 1965, Reprint from Kid Colt Outlaw #96 .... 12.00
❑78, Nov 1965, Reprint from Kid Colt Outlaw #101 .... 12.00
❑79, Jan 1966, V: Joe Goliath; Reprint from Two-Gun Kid #63 .... 12.00
❑80, Mar 1966, V: Billy the Kid; Reprint from Two-Gun Kid #64 .... 12.00
❑81, May 1966, Reprint from Kid Colt Outlaw #103 .... 8.00
❑82, Jul 1966, BEv (w); BEv (a) 8.00
❑83, Sep 1966, V: Durango; Reprint from Rawhide Kid #39 .... 8.00
❑84, Nov 1966, Reprint from Kid Cold Outlaw #109 .... 8.00
❑85, Jan 1967, Reprint from Rawhide Kid #40 .... 8.00
❑86, Mar 1967, V: Cole Younger; Reprint from Two-Gun Kid #67 .... 8.00
❑87, May 1967, Reprint from Two-Gun Kid #66 .... 8.00
❑88, Jul 1967, V: Rattler; Reprint from Kid Colt Outlaw #99 .... 8.00
❑89, Sep 1967, A: Rawhide Kid. A: Kid Colt 8.00
❑90, Nov 1967, Reprint from Two-Gun Kid #62 .... 8.00
❑91, Jan 1968, BEv (w); BEv (a); V: Silver Sidewinder 8.00
❑92, Mar 1968, series goes on hiatus 8.00
❑93, Jul 1970, Reprints begin 4.00
❑94, Sep 1970, Reprints from Two-Gun Kid #71 .... 4.00
❑95, Nov 1970, Reprint from Two-Gun Kid #75; Reprint from Rawhide Kid #34 .... 4.00
❑96, Jan 1971, Reprint from Two-Gun Kid #82 .... 4.00
❑97, Mar 1971, Reprints from Two-Gun Kid #86 and Kid Colt Outlaw #90 .... 4.00
❑98, May 1971, Reprints from Two-Gun Kid #92 .... 4.00
❑99, Jul 1971, Reprints from Two-Gun Kid #53 .... 4.00
❑100, Sep 1971, Reprints from Two-Gun Kid #35 and 61 .... 4.00
❑101, Nov 1971, JSe (c); SL (w); JK (a); O: Two Gun Kid. reprints origin story 4.00

Other grades: Multiply price above by 5/6 for VF/NM • 2/3 for VERY FINE • 1/3 for FINE • 1/5 for VERY GOOD • 1/8 for GOOD

Vertigo Jam

Better than most compliation efforts
©DC

Vertigo Preview

An early look at the then-new Vertigo line
©DC

Vertigo Secret Files & Origins: Swamp Thing

One-shot examines all things Swampy
©DC

V for Vendetta

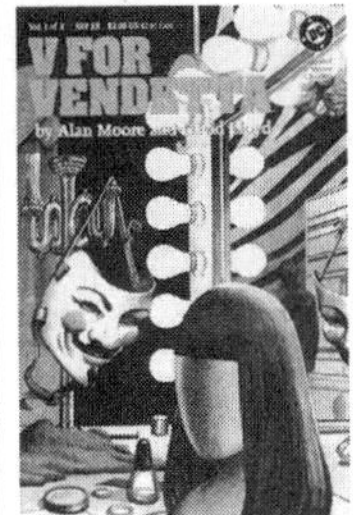

Life and death in totalitarian England
©DC

Victorian

Strangeness on the streets of New Orleans
©Penny-Farthing

N-MINT

- ❑102, Jan 1972, Reprint from Two-Gun Kid #38 ... 4.00
- ❑103, Mar 1972, SL (w); DH, JK (a); Reprints from Two-Gun Kid #58 and 59; Steve Englehart work is uncredited ... 4.00
- ❑104, May 1972, Reprint from Two-Gun Kid #43; Reprint from Quick-Trigger Western #14 ... 4.00
- ❑105, Jul 1972, Reprints from Two-Gun Kid #52 and #69 ... 4.00
- ❑106, Sep 1972, Reprints from Two-Gun Kid #70; Reprint from Ringo Kid #20 ... 4.00
- ❑107, Nov 1972, Reprints from Two-Gun Kid #50 and 74 ... 4.00
- ❑108, Jan 1973, Reprint from Two-Gun Kid #85; Reprint from Wyatt Earp #15 ... 4.00
- ❑109, Mar 1973, SL (w); GT (a); Reprints from Two-Gun Kid #84 and Wyatt Earp #3 ... 4.00
- ❑110, May 1973, Reprint from Two-Gun Kid #76 and Mat Slade, Gunfighter #1 ... 4.00
- ❑111, Jul 1973, Reprint from Two-Gun Kid #78; Reprint from Gunhawk #13 ... 4.00
- ❑112, Sep 1973, SL (w); Reprint from Two-Gun Kid #65 and Western Outlaws (Atlas) #4 ... 4.00
- ❑113, Oct 1973, Reprints from Two-Gun Kid #49 and #88 ... 4.00
- ❑114, Nov 1973, Reprints from Two-Gun Kid #43 and 79 ... 4.00
- ❑115, Dec 1973, Reprint from Two-Gun Kid #80 ... 4.00
- ❑116, Feb 1974, Reprint from Two-Gun Kid #67 ... 4.00
- ❑117, Apr 1974, Reprints from Two-Gun Kid #89 and Gunsmoke Western #47 ... 4.00
- ❑118, Jun 1974, Reprints from Two-Gun Kid #87 and Gunsmoke Western #46 ... 4.00
- ❑119, Aug 1974, Reprints from Two-Gun Kid #77 and Kid Colt Outlaw #96 ... 4.00
- ❑120, Oct 1974, Reprints from Two-Gun Kid #55 and #60 ... 4.00
- ❑121, Dec 1974, Reprints from Two-Gun Kid #73 and Wyatt Earp #29 ... 4.00
- ❑122, Feb 1975, Reprints from Two-Gun Kid #73 and Kid Colt Outlaw #62 ... 4.00
- ❑123, Apr 1975, Reprints from Two-Gun Kid #64 and #65 ... 4.00
- ❑124, Jun 1975, Reprints from Two-Gun Kid #42 and #88 ... 4.00
- ❑125, Aug 1975, Reprints from Two-Gun Kid #71 ... 4.00
- ❑126, Oct 1975, Reprints from Two-Gun Kid #85 ... 4.00
- ❑127, Dec 1975, Reprints from Two-Gun Kid #72 ... 4.00
- ❑128, Feb 1976, Reprints from Two-Gun Kid #92 ... 4.00
- ❑129, Apr 1976, Reprints from Two-Gun Kid #61 and Kid Colt Outlaw #141 ... 4.00
- ❑129/30¢, Apr 1976, 30¢ regional price variant ... 20.00
- ❑130, Jun 1976, Reprints from Two-Gun Kid #62 ... 4.00
- ❑130/30¢, Jun 1976, 30¢ regional price variant ... 20.00
- ❑131, Aug 1976, Reprints from Two-Gun Kid #83 ... 4.00
- ❑131/30¢, Aug 1976, 30¢ regional price variant ... 20.00
- ❑132, Sep 1976, Reprints from Two-Gun Kid #69 ... 4.00

N-MINT

- ❑133, Oct 1976, Reprints from Two-Gun Kid #70 ... 4.00
- ❑134, Dec 1976, Reprints from Two-Gun Kid #75 ... 4.00
- ❑135, Feb 1977, Reprints from Two-Gun Kid #66 ... 4.00
- ❑136, Apr 1977, Reprints from Two-Gun Kid #68; Final Issue ... 4.00

Two-Gun Kid: Sunset Riders
Marvel

- ❑1, Nov 1995; Painted cover ... 6.95
- ❑2, Dec 1995; Painted cover ... 6.95

2-Headed Giant
A Is A

- ❑1, Oct 1995, b&w; Anthology ... 2.95

2 Hot Girls on a Hot Summer Night
Fantagraphics / Eros

- ❑1, Apr 1991, b&w; Adult ... 3.00
- ❑2, May 1991, b&w; 24 pages; Adult ... 3.00
- ❑3, Jul 1991, b&w; 24 pages; Adult ... 3.00
- ❑4, Sep 1991, b&w; 24 pages; Adult ... 3.00

2 Live Crew Comics
Fantagraphics / Eros

- ❑1, b&w; Adult ... 2.95

Two Over Ten
Second 2 Some Studios

- ❑1, Nov 2001 ... 2.95
- ❑2, Dec 2001 ... 2.95
- ❑3, Jan 2002 ... 2.95
- ❑4, Feb 2002 ... 2.95
- ❑5, Mar 2002 ... 2.95

Two Step
DC

- ❑1, Dec 2003 ... 2.95
- ❑2, Mar 2004 ... 2.95
- ❑3, Jul 2004 ... 2.95

2000 A.D. Monthly
Eagle

- ❑1, Apr 1985 AMo (w) ... 2.00
- ❑2, May 1985 AMo (w) ... 2.00
- ❑3, Jun 1985 AMo (w) ... 2.00
- ❑4, Jul 1985 AMo (w) ... 2.00
- ❑5, Aug 1985 AMo (w) ... 2.00
- ❑6, Sep 1985 AMo (w); BB (a) ... 2.00

2000 A.D. Monthly
Eagle

- ❑1, Apr 1986; Judge Anderson, D.R. & Quinch, Skizz ... 2.00
- ❑2, May 1986 ... 2.00
- ❑3, Jun 1986 ... 2.00

2000 A.D. Presents
Fleetway-Quality

- ❑4, Jul 1986; Series continued from 2000 A.D. Monthly #3; Title changes to 2000 A.D. Presents; Quality begins publishing ... 1.50
- ❑5, Aug 1986 ... 1.50
- ❑6, Sep 1986 ... 1.50
- ❑7, Oct 1986 AMo (w); DaG (a) ... 1.50
- ❑8, Nov 1986 ... 1.50
- ❑9, Dec 1986 ... 1.50
- ❑10, Jan 1987 ... 1.50
- ❑11, Feb 1987 DaG (a) ... 1.50
- ❑12, Dec 1987 AMo (w); DaG (a) ... 1.50

N-MINT

- ❑13 ... 1.50
- ❑14, May 1988 ... 1.50
- ❑15 ... 1.50
- ❑16 ... 1.50
- ❑17 ... 1.50
- ❑18 ... 1.50
- ❑19 ... 1.50
- ❑20 DaG (a) ... 1.50
- ❑21 ... 1.50
- ❑22 ... 1.50
- ❑23 ... 1.50
- ❑24; Series continues as 2000 A.D. Showcase ... 1.50
- ❑25; Series continues as 2000 A.D. Showcase (1st Series) #25 ... 1.50

2000 A.D. Showcase
Fleetway-Quality

- ❑25; Series continued from 2000 A.D. Presents #24 ... 1.50
- ❑26 ... 1.50
- ❑27; DaG (a); double issue #27/28 ... 1.50
- ❑28; DaG (a); double issue #27/28 ... 1.50
- ❑29; double issue #29/30 ... 1.50
- ❑30; double issue #29/30 ... 1.50
- ❑31; Zenith ... 1.50
- ❑32; Zenith ... 1.50
- ❑33; Zenith ... 1.50
- ❑34; Zenith ... 1.50
- ❑35; Zenith ... 1.50
- ❑36; Zenith ... 1.50
- ❑37; Zenith ... 1.50
- ❑38; Zenith ... 1.50
- ❑39; Zenith ... 1.50
- ❑40; Zenith ... 1.50
- ❑41; Zenith ... 1.50
- ❑42; Zenith ... 1.50
- ❑43; Zenith ... 1.50
- ❑44; Zenith ... 1.50
- ❑45; Zenith ... 1.50
- ❑46 ... 1.50
- ❑47 ... 1.50
- ❑48 ... 1.75
- ❑49 ... 1.75
- ❑50 ... 1.75
- ❑51 ... 1.75
- ❑52 ... 1.75
- ❑53 ... 1.75
- ❑54 ... 1.75

2000 A.D. Showcase
Fleetway-Quality

- ❑1 ... 2.95
- ❑2 ... 2.95
- ❑3 ... 2.95
- ❑4; Axa ... 2.95
- ❑5; Axa ... 2.95
- ❑6; Strontium Dogs ... 2.95
- ❑7; Strontium Dogs ... 2.95
- ❑8 ... 2.95
- ❑9 ... 2.95
- ❑10 ... 2.95
- ❑11 ... 2.95

2002 Tokyopop Manga Sampler
Mixx

- ❑1, ca. 2002 ... 1.00

Other grades: Multiply price above by 5/6 for VF/NM • 2/3 for VERY FINE • 1/3 for FINE • 1/5 for VERY GOOD • 1/8 for GOOD

Two Thousand Maniacs
Aircel

- ❑1, b&w ... 2.50
- ❑2, b&w ... 2.50
- ❑3, b&w ... 2.50

2099 A.D.
Marvel

- ❑1, May 1995, enhanced cover ... 3.95

2099 A.D. Apocalypse
Marvel

- ❑1, Dec 1995, enhanced wraparound cover; continues in 2099 A.D. Genesis #1 ... 4.95

2099 A.D. Genesis
Marvel

- ❑1, Jan 1996, chromium cover ... 4.95

2099: Manifest Destiny
Marvel

- ❑1, Mar 1998, NN; One-shot ... 5.99

2099 Special: The World of Doom
Marvel

- ❑1, May 1995 ... 2.25

2099 Unlimited
Marvel

- ❑1, Jul 1993, 1: Hulk 2099. A: Spider-Man 2099 ... 3.95
- ❑2, Oct 1993, 1: R Gang 2099. Return of Hulk 2099 ... 3.95
- ❑3, Jan 1994 ... 3.95
- ❑4, Apr 1994 ... 3.95
- ❑5, Jul 1994, 1: Hazzard 2099; O: Duke Stratosphere ... 3.95
- ❑6, Aug 1994, 1: Galahad 2099 ... 3.95
- ❑7, Nov 1994 ... 3.95
- ❑8, Apr 1995 ... 3.95
- ❑9, Jul 1995 ... 3.95
- ❑10, Oct 1995 ... 3.95
- ❑Ashcan 1 1993, "2099 Limited" ashcan edition from Hero magazine; foil cover 1.00

2099: World of Tomorrow
Marvel

- ❑1, Sep 1996, wraparound cover; 2099 anthology ... 2.50
- ❑2, Oct 1996 ... 2.50
- ❑3, Nov 1996 ... 2.50
- ❑4, Dec 1996 ... 2.50
- ❑5, Jan 1997 ... 2.50
- ❑6, Feb 1997 ... 2.50
- ❑7, Mar 1997 ... 2.50
- ❑8, Apr 1997, Final Issue ... 2.50

2001 Nights
Viz

- ❑1, ca. 1990, b&w ... 4.00
- ❑2, ca. 1990, b&w ... 4.00
- ❑3, ca. 1990, b&w ... 4.00
- ❑4, ca. 1991, b&w ... 4.00
- ❑5, ca. 1991, b&w ... 4.00
- ❑6, ca. 1991, b&w ... 4.25
- ❑7, ca. 1991, b&w ... 4.25
- ❑8, ca. 1991, b&w ... 4.25
- ❑9, ca. 1991, b&w ... 4.25
- ❑10, ca. 1991, b&w; Final Issue ... 4.25

2001, A Space Odyssey
Marvel

- ❑1, Dec 1976, JK (c); JK (w); JK (a) ... 5.00
- ❑2, Jan 1977, JK (c); JK (w); JK (a) ... 5.00
- ❑3, Feb 1977, JK (c); JK (w); JK (a) ... 5.00
- ❑4, Mar 1977, JK (c); JK (w); JK (a) ... 5.00
- ❑5, Apr 1977, JK (c); JK (w); JK (a) ... 5.00
- ❑6, May 1977, JK (c); JK (w); JK (a) ... 5.00
- ❑7, Jun 1977, JK (w); JK (a) ... 5.00
- ❑7/35¢, Jun 1977, JK (w); JK (a); 35¢ price regional variant ... 20.00
- ❑8, Jul 1977, JK (w); JK (a); O: Machine Man (as Mister Machine). 1: Machine Man (as Mister Machine) ... 12.00
- ❑8/35¢, Jul 1977, JK (c); JK (w); JK (a); O: Machine Man (as Mister Machine). 1: Machine Man (as Mister Machine). 35¢ price regional variant ... 5.00
- ❑9, Aug 1977, JK (w); JK (a) ... 5.00
- ❑9/35¢, Aug 1977, JK (w); JK (a); 35¢ price regional variant ... 5.00
- ❑10, Sep 1977, JK (w); JK (a); O: Machine Man ... 5.00
- ❑10/35¢, Sep 1977, JK (c); JK (w); JK (a); O: Machine Man. 35¢ price regional variant ... 5.00
- ❑GS 1, ca. 1976, treasury-sized adaptation of movie; JK (c); JK (w); JK (a) ... 12.00

2010
Marvel

- ❑1, Apr 1984, TP (a); Movie adaptation. 1.50
- ❑2, May 1984, TP (a); Movie adaptation 1.50

2112
Dark Horse

- ❑1, Nov 1991; prestige format; 1: Sathanus; Prestige format ... 9.95
- ❑1/2nd; 2nd printing; 1: Sathanus ... 9.95
- ❑1/3rd; 3rd printing; 1: Sathanus ... 9.95

2024
NBM

- ❑1 ... 16.95

2020 Visions
DC / Vertigo

- ❑1, May 1997 ... 2.50
- ❑2, Jun 1997 ... 2.50
- ❑3, Jul 1997 ... 2.50
- ❑4, Aug 1997 ... 2.50
- ❑5, Sep 1997 ... 2.50
- ❑6, Oct 1997 ... 2.50
- ❑7, Nov 1997 ... 2.50
- ❑8, Dec 1997 ... 2.50
- ❑9, Jan 1998 ... 2.50
- ❑10, Feb 1998 ... 2.50
- ❑11, Mar 1998 ... 2.50
- ❑12, Apr 1998 ... 2.50

2 to Chest
Dark Horse

- ❑1, May 2004 ... 3.00

Two x Justice
Graphic Serials

- ❑1 ... 2.00

Tykes
Alternative

- ❑1, Nov 1997; Adult ... 2.95
- ❑Ashcan 1, Jul 1997; b&w and pink; smaller than normal comic book ... 2.95

Tyler Kirkham Sketchbook
Image

- ❑1, Oct 2006 ... 2.99

Typhoid
Marvel

- ❑1, Nov 1995; wraparound cardstock cover ... 3.95
- ❑2, Dec 1995; wraparound cardstock cover ... 3.95
- ❑3, Jan 1996; wraparound cardstock cover ... 3.95
- ❑4, Feb 1996; wraparound cardstock cover ... 3.95

Tyrannosaurus Tex
Monster

- ❑1, Jul 1991, b&w ... 2.50
- ❑2, Sep 1991, b&w ... 2.50
- ❑3, Nov 1991 ... 2.50

Tyrant
Spider Baby

- ❑1, Sep 1994, b&w ... 3.00
- ❑2, Nov 1994, b&w ... 3.00
- ❑3, Feb 1995, b&w ... 3.00
- ❑3/Gold, Feb 1995, b&w; Gold promotional edition, signed ... 3.50
- ❑4, Win 1996, b&w ... 3.00
- ❑5, ca. 1996, b&w ... 3.00
- ❑6, Dec 1996, b&w ... 3.00

Tzu the Reaper
Murim

- ❑1, Sep 1997; b&w ... 2.95
- ❑2, Oct 1997 ... 2.95
- ❑3, Dec 1997 ... 2.95

Uberdub
Caliber

- ❑1, Sep 1991 ... 2.50
- ❑2, Sep 1991 ... 2.50
- ❑3, Jan 1992 ... 2.50

UFO & Outer Space
Whitman

- ❑14, Jun 1978, Reprints UFO Flying Saucers #3 ... 8.00
- ❑15, Jul 1978, Reprints UFO Flying Saucers #4 ... 6.00
- ❑16, Aug 1978, Reprints ... 6.00
- ❑17, Sep 1978 ... 6.00
- ❑18, Nov 1978 ... 6.00
- ❑19, Jan 1979 ... 6.00
- ❑20, Apr 1979 ... 6.00
- ❑21, Jun 1979 ... 5.00
- ❑22, Aug 1979 ... 5.00
- ❑23, Oct 1979 ... 5.00
- ❑24, Dec 1979 ... 5.00
- ❑25, Feb 1980, Reprints UFO Flying Saucers #2 ... 5.00

UFO Encounters
Golden Press

- ❑1 ... 1.95

UFO Flying Saucers
Gold Key

- ❑1, Oct 1968, giant ... 25.00
- ❑2, Nov 1970 ... 15.00
- ❑3, Nov 1972 ... 15.00
- ❑4, Nov 1974 ... 15.00
- ❑5, Feb 1975 ... 10.00
- ❑6, May 1975 ... 10.00
- ❑7, Aug 1975 ... 10.00
- ❑8, Nov 1975 ... 10.00
- ❑9, Jan 1976 ... 10.00
- ❑10, May 1976 ... 10.00
- ❑11, Aug 1976 ... 10.00
- ❑12, Nov 1976 ... 10.00
- ❑13, Jan 1977, series continues as UFO & Outer Space ... 10.00

Ultiman Giant Annual
Image / Big Bang

- ❑1, Nov 2001 ... 4.95

Ultimate Adventures
Marvel

- ❑1, Nov 2002 ... 2.25
- ❑2, Dec 2002 ... 2.25
- ❑3, Mar 2003 ... 2.25
- ❑4, May 2003 ... 2.25
- ❑5, Jul 2003 ... 2.99
- ❑6, Sep 2003 ... 2.99

Ultimate Daredevil & Elektra
Marvel

- ❑1, Jan 2003 ... 3.00
- ❑2, Feb 2003 ... 2.25
- ❑3, Feb 2003 ... 2.25
- ❑4, Mar 2003 ... 2.25

Ultimate Elektra
Marvel

- ❑1, Oct 2004 ... 2.25
- ❑2, Nov 2004 ... 2.25
- ❑3, Dec 2004 ... 2.25
- ❑4, Jan 2005 ... 2.25
- ❑5, Feb 2005 ... 2.25

Ultimate Extinction
Marvel

- ❑1, Mar 2006 ... 2.99
- ❑2, Apr 2006 ... 2.99
- ❑3, May 2006 ... 2.99
- ❑4, Jun 2006 ... 2.99
- ❑5, Aug 2006 ... 2.99

Ultimate Fantastic Four
Marvel

- ❑1, Feb 2004, (c); BMB (w); 1: Ultimate Fantastic Four; 1: Ultimate Mister Fantastic; 1: Ultimate Invisible Woman; 1: Ultimate Human Torch; 1: Ultimate The Thing; O: Ultimate Fantastic Four 5.00
- ❑2, Mar 2004, 1: Ultimate Victor Van Damme; 1: Ultimate Mole Man ... 4.00
- ❑3, Apr 2004, (c); BMB (w) ... 3.00
- ❑4, May 2004, (c); BMB (w) ... 2.25
- ❑5, Jun 2004, (c); BMB (w) ... 3.00
- ❑6, Jul 2004 ... 2.25
- ❑7, Aug 2004, 1: Ultimate Doctor Doom 3.00
- ❑8, Sep 2004 ... 4.00
- ❑9, Sep 2004 ... 2.25
- ❑10, Oct 2004 ... 2.25
- ❑11, Nov 2004 ... 2.25
- ❑12, Dec 2004 ... 2.25

Vigilante

Adrian Chase chased bad guys
©DC

Vintage Magnus Robot Fighter

Reprints of the Gold Key Magnus comics
©Valiant

Violent Messiahs

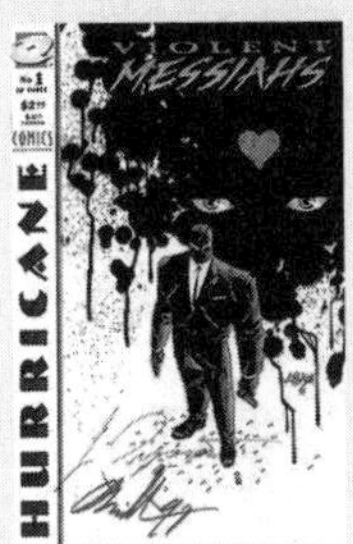

A gloomy black-and-white world
©Hurricane

Vision & Scarlet Witch

Part of Marvel's first wave of limited series
©Marvel

Visitor

Visitor from another world isn't accepted
©Valiant

N-MINT

- ❑13, Jan 2005 .... 2.25
- ❑13/Sketch, Jan 2005 .... 6.00
- ❑14, Feb 2005 .... 2.25
- ❑15, Mar 2005; 1: Nihil (Ultimate Annihilus) 2.25
- ❑16, Apr 2005 .... 2.25
- ❑17, May 2005 .... 2.25
- ❑18, Jun 2005 .... 2.25
- ❑19, Jul 2005; 1: Ultimate Mad Thinker. 5.00
- ❑20, Aug 2005; V: Rhona Burchill 4.00
- ❑21, Sep 2005; 1: Marvel Zombies 6.00
- ❑21/Variant, Sep 2005 .... 8.00
- ❑22, Oct 2005 .... 16.00
- ❑23, Nov 2005 .... 7.00
- ❑24, Dec 2005; 1: Ultimate Namor 2.50
- ❑25, Jan 2006, Flip book with Ultimate Vision #3 .... 2.50
- ❑26, Feb 2006, Flipbook with Ultimate Vision 2.50
- ❑27, Apr 2006, 1: Ultimate Super Skrull 2.50
- ❑28, Jun 2006 .... 2.90
- ❑29, Jul 2006, 1: Alicia Masters (Ultimate) 2.99
- ❑30, Aug 2006, Greg Land zombie cover 2.99
- ❑31, Sep 2006, Marvel Zombies tie-in ... 2.99
- ❑32, Oct 2006 .... 2.99
- ❑33, Nov 2006 .... 2.99
- ❑34, Nov 2006 .... 2.99
- ❑35, Dec 2006, 1: Ultimate Thanos 2.99
- ❑36, Jan 2007 .... 2.99
- ❑37, Mar 2007 .... 2.99
- ❑38 .... 2.99
- ❑39 .... 2.99
- ❑40 .... 2.99
- ❑41 .... 2.99
- ❑42 .... 2.99
- ❑43 .... 2.99
- ❑44 .... 2.99
- ❑45 .... 2.99
- ❑46 .... 2.99
- ❑47 .... 2.99
- ❑48 .... 2.99
- ❑49 .... 2.99
- ❑50 .... 2.99
- ❑51 .... 2.99
- ❑52 .... 2.99
- ❑53 .... 2.99
- ❑54 .... 2.99
- ❑55 .... 2.99
- ❑56 .... 2.99
- ❑57 .... 2.99
- ❑58 .... 2.99
- ❑59 .... 2.99
- ❑60 .... 2.99
- ❑Ann 1 2005 .... 3.99
- ❑Ann 2, Oct 2006 .... 4.00

Ultimate Fantastic Four/ X-Men Special
Marvel

- ❑1, Mar 2006 .... 2.99

Ultimate Iron Man
Marvel

- ❑1/Kubert, Apr 2005 .... 5.00
- ❑1/Hitch, Apr 2005 .... 4.00
- ❑1/Sketch, Apr 2005 .... 6.00
- ❑2, Aug 2005 .... 2.99
- ❑3, Sep 2005 .... 2.99
- ❑4, Nov 2005 .... 2.99
- ❑5, Feb 2006 .... 2.99

Ultimate Marvel Flip Magazine
Marvel

- ❑1, Jul 2005 .... 3.99
- ❑2, Aug 2005 .... 3.99
- ❑3, Sep 2005 .... 3.99
- ❑4, Oct 2005 .... 3.99
- ❑5, Nov 2005; Includes poster 3.99
- ❑6, Jan 2006; Includes poster 3.99
- ❑7, Feb 2006, Includes poster 3.99
- ❑8, Mar 2006, Includes poster 3.99
- ❑9, Mar 2006, Includes poster 3.99
- ❑10, May 2006, Includes poster 3.99
- ❑11, Jun 20006, Includes poster 3.99
- ❑12, Jul 2006, Includes poster 4.99
- ❑13, Aug 2006, Includes poster 4.99
- ❑14, Sep 2006, Includes Bonus Story: Ultimate Marvel Team-Up #1 .... 4.99
- ❑15, Oct 2006, Includes poster 4.99
- ❑16, Nov 2006, Reprints Ultimate Fantastic Four #16, Ultimate X-Men #16, and Ultimate Marvel Team-Up #3; Includes poster 4.99
- ❑17, Nov 2006; Reprints Ultimate Fantastic Four #17, Ultimate X-Men #17, and Ultimate Marvel Team-Up #3 4.99
- ❑18, Dec 2006; Collects Ultimate X-Men #18 and Ulltimate Fantastic Four #18 and Ultimate Marvel Team-Up #4; Poster Included 4.99
- ❑19, Jan 2007; Collects Ultimate X-Men #19 and Ultimate Fantastic Four #19; Includes Guiding Light backup story and poster 4.99
- ❑20, Feb 2007; Collects Ultimate X-Men #20, Ultimate Fantastic Four #20, and Marvel Team-Ups (3rd Series) #5 .... 4.99

Ultimate Marvel Magazine
Marvel

- ❑1, Feb 2001, BMB (w); reprints Ultimate Spider-Man #1 and #2 .... 6.00
- ❑2, Mar 2001, reprints Ultimate Spider-Man #3 and Ultimate X-Men #1 .... 4.00
- ❑3, Apr 2001, reprints Ultimate Spider-Man #4 and Ultimate X-Men #2 .... 4.00
- ❑4, May 2001 .... 3.99
- ❑5, Jun 2001, Reprints Ultimate Team-Up #1 & Ultimate X-Men #5 .... 3.99
- ❑6, Jul 2001 .... 3.99
- ❑7, Aug 2001 .... 3.99
- ❑8, Sep 2001 .... 3.99
- ❑9, Oct 2001 .... 3.99
- ❑10, Nov 2001 .... 3.99
- ❑11, Dec 2001 .... 3.99

Ultimate Marvel Team-Up
Marvel

- ❑1, Apr 2001, BMB (w); MW (a); A: Wolverine. A: Sabretooth. A: Spider-Man. Cardstock cover; Listed in indicia as Ultimate Spider-Man and Wolverine 2.99
- ❑2, May 2001, BMB (w); A: Hulk. A: Spider-Man 2.99
- ❑3, Jun 2001, Hulk 2.99
- ❑4, Jul 2001, Iron Man 2.99
- ❑5, Aug 2001, Iron Man 2.99
- ❑6, Sep 2001, Punisher, Daredevil 2.99
- ❑7, Oct 2001, Punisher, Daredevil 3.00
- ❑8, Nov 2001, Punisher, Daredevil 3.00
- ❑9, Dec 2001, Spider-Man & Fantastic Four 3.00
- ❑10, Jan 2002, Man-Thing 3.00
- ❑11, Feb 2002, Occurs before Ultimate X-Men #7; X-Men 3.00
- ❑12, Mar 2002, Doctor Strange 3.00
- ❑13, Apr 2002, Doctor Strange 3.00
- ❑14, May 2002, Black Widow 3.00
- ❑15, Jun 2002, Shang-Chi 3.00
- ❑16, Jul 2002, Final issue; Shang-Chi, Master of Kung Fu 3.00

Ultimate Nightmare
Marvel

- ❑1, Oct 2004 .... 3.00
- ❑2, Nov 2004 .... 2.25
- ❑3, Dec 2004, 1st Appearance Crimson Dynamo (Ultimate) 2.25
- ❑4, Jan 2005 .... 2.25
- ❑5, Feb 2005 .... 2.25

Ultimate Power
Marvel

- ❑1, Dec 2006, Ultimate Fantastic Four; Squadron Supreme 2.99
- ❑2, Feb 2007, Squadron Supreme; Ultimate Fantastic Four; Ultimate Spider-Man; Ultimates; Ultimate X-Men 2.99
- ❑3, Mar 2007, Squadron Supreme; Ultimate Fantastic Four; Ultimate Spider-Man; Ultimates; Ultimate X-Men 2.99

Ultimates
Marvel

- ❑1, Mar 2002, 1: Captain America (Ultimate); 1: Bucky (Ultimate); 1: Jarvis (Ultimate) 7.00
- ❑1/DF Millar, Mar 2002 .... 20.00
- ❑1/DF Quesada, Mar 2002; Dynamic Forces variant signed by Joe Quesada 25.00
- ❑2, Apr 2002, (c) 9.00
- ❑3, May 2002, (c) 6.00
- ❑4, Jun 2002, (c) 10.00
- ❑5, Jul 2002, (c) 8.00
- ❑6, Aug 2002, (c) 7.00
- ❑7, Sep 2002, (c); 1: Hawkeye (Ultimate) 6.00
- ❑8, Nov 2002, (c) 5.00
- ❑9, Apr 2003, (c) 6.00
- ❑10, Jul 2003, (c) 4.00
- ❑11, Sep 2003 (c) 3.00
- ❑12, Nov 2003, (c) 2.25
- ❑13, Jun 2004, (c); Final issueóreturns as Ultimates Vol. 2 .... 3.50
- ❑13/DF Millar, Jun 2004; Dynamic Forces variant signed by Mark Millar 20.00

Ultimates 2
Marvel

- ❑1, Feb 2005 .... 5.00
- ❑1/2nd, Feb 2005 .... 2.99
- ❑1/Sketch, Feb 2005 .... 35.00
- ❑2, Mar 2005 .... 2.99
- ❑3, Apr 2005 .... 2.99
- ❑4, May 2005 .... 2.99
- ❑5, Jun 2005 .... 2.99
- ❑6, Jul 2005 .... 2.99
- ❑7, Aug 2005 .... 2.99
- ❑8, Nov 2005 .... 2.99
- ❑9, Feb 2006 .... 2.99

❑10, May 2006 2.99
❑11, Sep 2006 2.99
❑12, Dec 2006 3.99
❑Ann 2, Nov 2006 3.99
❑Ann 1, Sep 2005 3.99

Ultimate Secret
Marvel

❑1, May 2005; 1: Captain Mahr-Vehl 2.99
❑2, Jun 2005 2.99
❑3, Aug 2005 2.99
❑4, Dec 2005 2.99

Ultimate Six
Marvel

❑1, Nov 2003 BMB (w) 4.00
❑2, Nov 2003 BMB (w) 3.00
❑3, Dec 2003 BMB (w) 2.25
❑4, Jan 2004 BMB (w) 3.00
❑5, Feb 2004, BMB (w) 2.25
❑6, Mar 2004 3.00
❑7, Jun 2004, BMB (w) 2.25

Ultimate Spider-Man
Marvel

❑½, ca. 2002, Wizard mail away incentive 8.00
❑½/A, ca. 2002, Wizard World East Con Edition 18.00
❑1, Oct 2000, BMB (w); O: Spider-Man. A: Mary Jane Watson. A: Norman Osborn 65.00
❑1/White, Oct 2000, BMB (w); White background on cover-otherwise same as #1 375.00
❑1/Dynamic, Oct 2000, BMB (w); Dynamic Forces cover 175.00
❑1/Kay-Bee, Jun 2001, BMB (w); K-B Toys Reprint 4.00
❑1/FCBD, May 2002, BMB (w); Free Comic Book Day Edition 3.00
❑1/Checkers 2000 7.00
❑1/Payless 6.00
❑1/Target 175.00
❑2, Dec 2000, BMB (w); Cardstock cover; Spider-Man lifting car on cover 30.00
❑2/Swinging, Dec 2000, BMB (w); Cardstock cover; Spider-Man swinging on cover 25.00
❑3, Jan 2001, BMB (w); O: Green Goblin. Cardstock cover; Spider-Man gets his costume 16.00
❑4, Feb 2001, BMB (w); D: Uncle Ben (off-panel). cardstock cover 8.00
❑5, Mar 2001, BMB (w); D: Uncle Ben (revealed). cardstock cover 55.00
❑6, Apr 2001, BMB (w); 1: Green Goblin (full). cardstock cover 9.00
❑6/Niagara, Apr 2001; Available only at Marvel SuperHeroes Adventure City in Niagara Falls, Canada. Reads Niagara Falls, Canada at bottom of cover 35.00
❑7, May 2001, BMB (w); A: Green Goblin. cardstock cover 9.00
❑8, Jun 2001, BMB (w) 8.00
❑8/Payless, Jun 2001; Spider-Man crawling up a wall; free with pair of shoes at Payless 6.00
❑8/Dynamic, Jun 2001, BMB (w); alternate cover with no cover price; Dynamic Forces signed and numbered edition 35.00
❑9, Jul 2001, BMB (w) 6.00
❑10, Aug 2001, BMB (w) 6.00
❑11, Sep 2001, BMB (w) 5.00
❑12, Oct 2001, BMB (w) 4.00
❑13, Nov 2001, BMB (w) 5.00
❑14, Jan 2002, BMB (w); "3-D" cover 4.00
❑15, Feb 2002, BMB (w) 5.00
❑16, Mar 2002, BMB (w) 3.00
❑17, Apr 2002, BMB (w) 3.00
❑18, May 2002, BMB (w) 3.00
❑19, May 2002, BMB (w) 3.00
❑20, Jun 2002, BMB (w) 3.00
❑21, Jun 2002, BMB (w) 3.00
❑22, Jul 2002, BMB (w) 3.50
❑23, Aug 2002, BMB (w) 3.00
❑24, Sep 2002, BMB (w) 3.00
❑25, Oct 2002, BMB (w); V: Green Goblin (Ultimate) 3.00
❑26, Nov 2002, BMB (w) 3.00
❑27, Nov 2002, BMB (w) 4.00
❑28, Dec 2002, BMB (w) 3.00
❑29, Dec 2002, BMB (w) 4.00
❑30, Jan 2003, BMB (w) 3.00
❑31, Jan 2003, BMB (w); D: Captain Stacy 4.00
❑32, Feb 2003, BMB (w) 3.00
❑33, Feb 2003, BMB (w); 1: Venom (Ultimate) 4.00
❑34, Mar 2003, BMB (w) 3.00
❑35, Mar 2003, BMB (w); A: Venom 3.00
❑36, Apr 2003, BMB (w); A: Venom 3.00
❑37, May 2003, BMB (w); A: Venom 3.00
❑38, May 2003, BMB (w); A: Venom 3.00
❑39, Jun 2003, BMB (w) 3.00
❑40, Jul 2003, BMB (w) 3.00
❑41, Jul 2003, BMB (w) 3.00
❑42, Aug 2003, BMB (w) 3.00
❑43, Sep 2003, BMB (w) 3.00
❑44, Oct 2003, BMB (w) 3.00
❑45, Nov 2003, BMB (w) 3.00
❑46, Nov 2003, BMB (w) 3.00
❑47, Dec 2003, BMB (w) 4.00
❑48, Dec 2003, (c); BMB (w) 3.00
❑49, Jan 2004, (c); BMB (w) 3.00
❑50, Feb 2004, (c); BMB (w) 4.00
❑51, Feb 2004, (c); BMB (w) 2.25
❑52, Mar 2004, (c); BMB (w) 2.25
❑53, Apr 2004 3.00
❑54, May 2004, BMB (w) 2.25
❑54/2nd, Sep 2004 2.25
❑55, May 2004, BMB (w) 2.25
❑56, Jun 2004, BMB (w) 4.00
❑57, Jun 2004, BMB (w) 2.25
❑58, Jul 2004, BMB (w) 2.25
❑59, Jul 2004, BMB (w) 2.25
❑60, Aug 2004 8.00
❑61, Sep 2004 5.00
❑62, Sep 2004, D: Gwen Stacy 8.00
❑63, Oct 2004 5.00
❑64, Oct 2004 4.00
❑65, Nov 2004 5.00
❑66, Dec 2004 2.25
❑67, Dec 2004 3.00
❑68, Jan 2005 2.25
❑69, Jan 2005 2.25
❑70, Feb 2005 2.25
❑71, Mar 2005 2.25
❑72, Apr 2005 4.00
❑73, May 2005 2.25
❑74, May 2005 2.25
❑75, Jun 2005 2.25
❑76, Jun 2005 2.25
❑77, Jul 2005 2.25
❑78, Aug 2005 2.50
❑79, Sep 2005 2.50
❑80, Oct 2005 2.50
❑81, Oct 2005 2.50
❑82, Nov 2005 2.50
❑83, Nov 2005 2.50
❑84, Dec 2005 2.50
❑85, Jan 2006 2.50
❑86, Jan 2006; Flip book with Ultimate Vision #1 2.50
❑87, Feb 2006 2.50
❑88, Feb 2006 2.50
❑89, Mar 2006 2.50
❑90, May 2006 2.50
❑91, May 2006 2.50
❑92, Jun 2006 2.50
❑93, Jun 2006 2.99
❑94, Jul 2006 2.99
❑95, Aug 2006, 1: Morbius 2.99
❑96, Sep 2006 2.99
❑97, Sep 2006, 1: Ultimate Scorpion 2.99
❑98, Oct 2006 2.99
❑99, Nov 2006 2.99
❑100, Dec 2006 3.99
❑101, Jan 2007, Fantastic Four vs. Nick Fury & Spider-Slayers 2.99
❑102, Feb 2007, O: Spider-Woman; Return of Doctor Octopus 2.99
❑103, Mar 2007, X-Men appearance 2.99
❑Ann 1, Oct 2005 3.99
❑Ann 2, Oct 2006 2.99
❑SP 1, Jul 2002 3.50

Ultimate Tales Flip Magazine
Marvel

❑1, Jul 2005 3.99
❑2, Aug 2005 3.99
❑3, Sep 2005 3.99
❑4, Oct 2005 3.99
❑5, Nov 2005 3.99
❑6, Jan 2006; Includes poster 3.99
❑7, Feb 2006, Includes poster 3.99
❑9, Mar 2006, Includes poster 3.99
❑10, May 2006, Includes poster 3.99
❑11, Jun 2006, Includes poster 3.99
❑12, Jul 2006, Includes poster 4.99
❑13, Aug 2006 4.99
❑14, Sep 2006, Reprints Ultimate Spider-man # 26 & #27; Includes poster 4.99
❑15, Oct 2006, Includes poster 4.99
❑16, Nov 2006; Reprints Ultimate Spider-man #30-31 and Ultimate Marvel Team-Up #3; Includes poster 4.99
❑17, Nov 2006; Collects Ultimate Spider-man #32, 33 and Ultimate Marvel Team-Up #4; Includes Poster 4.99
❑18, Dec 2006, Collects Ultimate Spider-Man #34 & #35 & Marvel Team-Up #4; Poster Included 4.99
❑19, Jan 2007, Collects Ultimate Spider-Man #36 & 37; Includes Guiding Light backup story and poster 4.99
❑20, Feb 2007; Collects Ultimate Spider-Man #38-39; Poster Included 4.99

Ultimate Vision
Marvel

❑0, Feb 2007 2.99
❑1, Feb 2007 2.99
❑2, Mar 2007 2.99

Ultimate War
Marvel

❑1, Feb 2003, chromium cover 2.50
❑2, Feb 2003 3.00
❑3, Mar 2003; 1: Unus (Ultimate) 3.00
❑4, Apr 2003 3.00

Ultimate Wolverine vs. Hulk
Marvel

❑1, Feb 2006 2.99
❑2, May 2006 2.99
❑3 2.99
❑4 2.99
❑5 2.99
❑6 2.99

Ultimate X-Men
Marvel

❑½, ca. 2002 5.00
❑1, Feb 2001, cardstock cover 14.00
❑1/Sketch, Feb 2001, sketch cover 20.00
❑1/Dynamic, Feb 2001, 7000 printed; DF alternate (color) cover 40.00
❑1/Checkers, Feb 2001, Checkers Reprint 30.00
❑1/NYPost, Feb 2001 8.00
❑1/Universal, Dec 2000; Features Wolverine on the cover; this preview was distributed in December 2000 at Universal Studios, Orlando. Features an Islands of Adventure ad on the back promoting Marvel attractions 60.00
❑2, Mar 2001, cardstock cover 7.00
❑3, Apr 2001, cardstock cover 6.00
❑4, May 2001 5.00
❑5, Jun 2001 5.00
❑6, Jul 2001 4.00
❑7, Aug 2001, 1: Nightcrawler (Ultimate); 1: Rogue (Ultimate); 1: S.H.I.E.L.D. (Ultimate) 4.00
❑8, Sep 2001, 1: Nick Fury (Ultimate); 1: Juggernaut (Ultimate) 4.00
❑9, Oct 2001 4.00
❑10, Nov 2001 4.00
❑11, Dec 2001, JKu (a) 3.00
❑12, Jan 2002 3.00
❑13, Feb 2002, 1: Gambit (Ultimate); 1: Hammerhead (Ultimate) 4.00
❑14, Mar 2002 3.00
❑15, Apr 2002 4.00
❑16, May 2002, 1: Betsy Braddock (Ultimate); 1: Moira MacTaggert (Ultimate); 1: Proteus (Ultimate) 3.00
❑17, Jun 2002 3.00
❑18, Jul 2002 5.00
❑19, Aug 2002, 1: Brian Braddock (Ultimate) 4.00
❑20, Sep 2002 3.00
❑21, Oct 2002 2.50
❑22, Nov 2002 2.50
❑23, Dec 2002, 1: Hellfire Club (Ultimate); 1: Sebastian Shaw (Ultimate) 2.50
❑24, Jan 2003 2.50

Void Indigo

Violent title was quickly canceled after protests
©Marvel

Voodoo (Image)

WildC.A.T.S member in web of dark magic
©Image

Wacky Adventures of Cracky

Starring Gold Key's own animal characters
©Gold Key

Wahoo Morris (Vol. 1)

Tales of an up-and-coming rock band
©Too Hip Gott Go Graphics

Walt Disney's Comics and Stories

Timeless stories in landmark series
©Dell

	N-MINT
❑25, Jan 2003	2.50
❑26, Feb 2003, (c)	2.50
❑27, Mar 2003, 1: Forge (Ultimate); 1: Multiple Man (Ultimate)	2.25
❑28, Apr 2003	2.25
❑29, Apr 2003	2.25
❑30, May 2003, Cover by Adam Kubert is "after Frazetta"	2.25
❑31, May 2003	2.25
❑32, Jun 2003, 1: Psylocke (Ultimate)	2.25
❑33, Jul 2003	5.00
❑34, Jul 2003, BMB (w)	4.00
❑35, Sep 2003, BMB (w)	3.00
❑36, Oct 2003, BMB (w)	4.00
❑37, Nov 2003, BMB (w)	3.00
❑38, Dec 2003, BMB (w)	2.25
❑39, Jan 2004, BMB (w); 1: Dum Dum Dugan (Ultimate)	3.00
❑40, Feb 2004, 1: Angel (Ultimate)	2.25
❑41, Mar 2004	5.00
❑42, Apr 2004, BMB (w); 1: Dazzler (Ultimate); 1: Emma Frost (Ultimate); 1: Karma (Ultimate)	4.00
❑43, May 2004, BMB (w); 1: Havok (Ultimate); 1: Polaris (Ultimate)	2.25
❑44, Jun 2004, BMB (w); 1: New Mutants (Ultimate); D: Beast (Ultimate)	2.25
❑45, Jul 2004, (c); BMB (w); Cover says New Mutants: Part 5	2.25
❑46, Jul 2004, 1: Sinister (Ultimate); 1: Northstar (Ultimate)	2.25
❑47, Aug 2004	2.25
❑48, Aug 2004, 1: Sunspot (Ultimate)	2.25
❑49, Sep 2004, 1: Apocalypse (Ultimate)	2.25
❑50, Oct 2004	5.00
❑50/Conv, Oct 2004	15.00
❑51, Nov 2004, 1: Fenris (Ultimate)	2.25
❑52, Dec 2004	2.25
❑53, Jan 2005	2.25
❑54, Feb 2005; 1: Longshot (Ultimate); 1: Mojo (Ultimate)	2.25
❑55, Mar 2005	2.25
❑56, Apr 2005	2.25
❑57, May 2005	2.25
❑58, Jun 2005	2.25
❑59, Jul 2005; 1: Lady Deathstrike (Ultimate)	2.25
❑60, Aug 2005	2.50
❑61, Sep 2005	2.50
❑61/Coipel, Sep 2005	5.00
❑62, Oct 2005; 1: Cannonball (Ultimate); 1: Doug Ramsey (Ultimate); 1: Mystique (Ultimate)	2.50
❑63, Nov 2005	2.50
❑64, Dec 2005	2.50
❑65, Jan 2006; Flip book with Ultiamte Vision #2	2.50
❑66, Mar 2006, 1: Liliandra (Ultimate); 1: Magician	2.50
❑67, Apr 2006	2.50
❑68, May 2006	2.50
❑69, Jun 2006, Price increase	2.99
❑71, Aug 2006	2.99
❑72, Sep 2006	2.99
❑73, Oct 2006	2.99
❑74, Nov 2006	2.99
❑75, Dec 2006, Note price	3.99
❑76, Jan 2007	2.99
❑77, Feb 2007	2.99
❑79	2.99
❑80	2.99
❑81	2.99
❑82	2.99
❑83	2.99
❑84	2.99
❑85	2.99
❑86	2.99
❑87	2.99
❑88	2.99
❑89	2.99
❑90	2.99
❑91	2.99
❑92	2.99
❑93	2.99
❑94	2.99
❑95	2.99
❑96	2.99
❑97	2.99
❑98	2.99
❑99	2.99
❑100	2.99
❑Ann 1, Oct 2005	3.99
❑Ann 2, Nov 2006	3.99

Ultimate X-Men/Fantastic Four Special
Marvel

	N-MINT
❑1, Feb 2006	2.99

Ultra
Image

	N-MINT
❑1, Aug 2004	4.00
❑2, Sep 2004	2.95
❑3, Oct 2004	2.95
❑4, Nov 2004	2.95
❑5, Dec 2004	2.95
❑6, Mar 2005	2.95
❑7, Apr 2005	2.95
❑8, May 2005	2.95

UltraForce
Malibu / Ultraverse

	N-MINT
❑0, Sep 1994 GP (c); GP (a)	2.50
❑0/Variant, Jul 1994; ashcan-sized; GP (a); no cover price	1.00
❑1, Aug 1994; GP (c); GP (a); 1: Atalon; Includes trading card	2.50
❑1/Hologram, Aug 1994; GP (a); Hologram cover	5.00
❑2, Oct 1994 GP (c); GP (a)	1.95
❑3, Nov 1994 GP (c); GP (a)	1.95
❑4, Jan 1995 GP (a)	1.95
❑5, Feb 1995 GP (a)	1.95
❑6, Mar 1995 GP (a)	2.50
❑7, Apr 1995 GP (c); GP (a)	2.50
❑8, May 1995 GP (a)	2.50
❑9, Jun 1995	2.50
❑10, Jul 1995	2.50
❑Ashcan 1; Ashcan	0.75

UltraForce
Malibu / Ultraverse

	N-MINT
❑0, Sep 1995; #Infinity	1.50
❑0/Variant, Sep 1995; #infinity on cover	1.50
❑1, Oct 1995; Drawn cover; Standard (non-painted) cover	1.50
❑2, Nov 1995; contains reprint of UltraForce #1	1.50
❑3, Dec 1995	1.50
❑4, Jan 1996	1.50
❑5, Feb 1996	1.50
❑6, Mar 1996	1.50
❑7, Apr 1996	1.50
❑8, May 1996	1.50
❑9, Jun 1996	1.50
❑10, Aug 1996	1.50
❑11, Aug 1996	1.50
❑12, Sep 1996	1.50
❑13, Oct 1996	1.50
❑14, Nov 1996	1.50
❑15, Dec 1996; D: Ripfire; Final Issue	1.50

UltraForce/Avengers
Malibu / Ultraverse

	N-MINT
❑1, Fal 1995; Fall 1995; Silver Foil Logo; Wraparound cover	3.95

UltraForce/Avengers Prelude
Malibu / Ultraverse

	N-MINT
❑1, Jul 1995; a.k.a. UltraForce #11	2.50

UltraForce/Spider-Man
Malibu / Ultraverse

	N-MINT
❑1, Jan 1996; alternate cover 1A	3.95
❑1/Variant, Jan 1996; alternate cover 1B	3.95

Ultragirl
Marvel

	N-MINT
❑1, Nov 1996	1.50
❑2, Dec 1996	1.50
❑3, Jan 1997; March 1997 on cover	1.50

Ultrahawk
D.M.S.

	N-MINT
❑1	1.50

Ultra Klutz
Onward

	N-MINT
❑1, Jun 1986	2.00
❑2, Sep 1986	2.00
❑3, Oct 1986	2.00
❑4, Nov 1986	2.00
❑5, Dec 1986	2.00
❑6, Jan 1987	2.00
❑7, Feb 1987	2.00
❑8, Mar 1987	2.00
❑9, Apr 1987	2.00
❑10, May 1987	2.00
❑11, Jun 1987	2.00
❑12, Jul 1987	2.00
❑13, Aug 1987	2.00
❑14, Sep 1987	2.00
❑15, Oct 1987	2.00
❑16, Nov 1987	1.50
❑17, Dec 1987	1.50
❑18, Jan 1988	1.75
❑19, Feb 1988	1.75
❑20 1988	1.75
❑21 1988	1.75
❑22 1988	1.75
❑23, Jul 1988	2.00
❑24, Aug 1988	2.00
❑25, Sep 1988	2.00
❑26, Nov 1988	2.00
❑27, Jan 1989	2.00
❑28 1989	2.00

Other grades: Multiply price above by 5/6 for VF/NM • 2/3 for VERY FINE • 1/3 for FINE • 1/5 for VERY GOOD • 1/8 for GOOD

N-MINT

❑29, Jun 1990 ... 2.00
❑30 1990 ... 2.00
❑31, May 1991 ... 2.00

Ultra Klutz '81
Onward

❑1, Jun 1981 ... 2.00

Ultraman
Harvey / Ultracomics

❑1, Jul 1993; O: Ultraman. newsstand ... 2.00
❑1/CS, Jul 1993 ... 2.50
❑1/Direct ed., Jul 1993; trading card; no type on cover ... 3.50
❑2 1993; newsstand ... 1.75
❑2/CS 1993 ... 2.50
❑2/Direct ed. 1993; direct sale; trading card ... 2.50
❑3, Sep 1993; newsstand ... 1.75
❑3/CS 1993 ... 2.50
❑3/Direct ed., Sep 1993; trading cards ... 2.50

Ultraman
Nemesis

❑-1, Mar 1994; negative image on cover ... 2.50
❑1, Apr 1994; Split cover ... 2.50
❑1/A, Apr 1994; alternate cover ... 2.25
❑2, May 1994; Regular cover (not split) ... 1.95
❑3, Aug 1994 ... 1.95
❑4, Sep 1994 ... 1.95
❑5 1994 ... 1.95

Ultraman Classic: Battle of the Ultra-Brothers
Viz

❑1, b&w ... 4.95
❑2, b&w ... 4.95
❑3, b&w ... 4.95
❑4, b&w ... 4.95
❑5, b&w ... 4.95

Ultraman Tiga
Dark Horse

❑1, Sep 2003 ... 3.99
❑2, Oct 2003 ... 3.99
❑3, Nov 2003 ... 3.99
❑4, Dec 2003 ... 3.99
❑5, Jan 2004 ... 3.99
❑6, Mar 2004 ... 2.99
❑7, Apr 2004 ... 2.99
❑8, May 2004 ... 3.99
❑9, May 2004 ... 3.99
❑10, Aug 2004 ... 3.99

Ultra Monthly
Malibu

❑1, Jun 1993, actually giveaway; Giveaway ... 0.50
❑2, Jul 1993, actually giveaway; Giveaway ... 0.50
❑3, Aug 1993, actually giveaway; cover says Sep, indicia says Aug ... 0.50
❑4, Sep 1993 ... 0.50
❑5, Oct 1993 ... 0.50
❑6, Nov 1993 ... 0.50

Ultraverse/Avengers Prelude
Malibu / Ultraverse

❑1, Jul 1995 ... 2.50

Ultraverse Double Feature: Prime and Solitaire
Malibu / Ultraverse

❑1, Jan 1995; 64 Pages! ... 3.95

Ultraverse: Future Shock
Malibu / Ultraverse

❑1, Feb 1997; final Ultraverse adventure ... 2.50

Ultraverse Origins
Malibu / Ultraverse

❑1, Jan 1994; O: Prime ... 1.25

Ultraverse Premiere
Malibu / Ultraverse

❑0, Nov 1993 ... 1.00

Ultraverse Unlimited
Malibu / Ultraverse

❑1, Jun 1996; 48 pgs ... 2.50
❑2, Sep 1996, b&w; Wraparound cvr ... 2.50

Ultraverse Year One
Malibu / Ultraverse

❑1, Sep 1994; Wraparound cover; Catalog of the stories and issues of the first year of the Ultraverse ... 4.95

Ultraverse Year Two
Malibu / Ultraverse

❑1, Aug 1995; Wraparound cover ... 4.95

Ultraverse Year Zero: The D: The Squad
Malibu / Ultraverse

❑1, Apr 1995; O: Hardcase; O: The Squad ... 2.95
❑2, May 1995 ... 2.95
❑3, Jun 1995 ... 2.95
❑4, Jul 1995 ... 2.95

Umbra
Image

❑1, Jul 2006, b&w ... 5.99
❑2, Jul 2006, b&w ... 5.99
❑3, Nov 2006, b&w ... 5.99

Umbrella Academy: Apocalypse Suite
Dark Horse

❑1, Sep 2007 ... 8.00
❑1/2nd, Sep 2007 ... 4.00
❑2, Oct 2007 ... 3.00
❑3, Nov 2007 ... 3.00
❑4, Dec 2007 ... 3.00
❑5, Jan 2008 ... 3.00
❑6, Feb 2008 ... 3.00

Unbound
Image

❑1, Jan 1998, b&w ... 2.95

Uncanny Origins
Marvel

❑1, Sep 1996; O: Cyclops ... 1.25
❑1/A, Sep 1996; O: Cyclops. No price on cover; variant cover ... 1.25
❑2, Oct 1996; O: Quicksilver ... 1.00
❑3, Nov 1996; O: Archangel ... 1.00
❑4, Dec 1996; O: Firelord ... 1.00
❑5, Jan 1997; O: Hulk ... 1.00
❑6, Feb 1997; O: Beast ... 1.00
❑7, Mar 1997; O: Venom. Flip book with Untold Tales of Spider-Man #19 ... 1.00
❑8, Apr 1997; O: Nightcrawler. Flip book with Untold Tales of Spider-Man #20 ... 1.00
❑9, May 1997; O: Storm ... 1.00
❑10, Jun 1997; O: Black Cat ... 1.00
❑11, Jul 1997; O: Black Knight ... 1.00
❑12, Aug 1997; O: Doctor Strange ... 1.00
❑13, Sep 1997; O: Daredevil ... 1.00
❑14, Oct 1997; O: Iron Fist ... 1.00

Uncanny Tales
Marvel

❑1, Dec 1973, All stories reprinted from Uncanny Tales (1st Series) #9 ... 20.00
❑2, Feb 1974 ... 12.00
❑3, Apr 1974, Reprints from Strange Tales #8, Adventures into Weird Worlds #17, Marvel Tales #114 and Uncanny Tales (1st Series) #38 ... 12.00
❑4, Jun 1974, Reprints from Weird Worlds #13, Mystic #16, 27 and Menace #3 ... 12.00
❑5, Aug 1974, Reprints from Mystic #26, Marvel Tales #117, Menace #2 and Adventure into Terror #12 ... 12.00
❑6, Oct 1974, Reprints from Astonishing #18, Adventures into Weird Worlds #5, 16 and Tales to Astonish #1 ... 12.00
❑7, Dec 1974, Reprints from Strange Tales #70, Marvel Tales #130 and Amazing Adult Fantasy #7 ... 12.00
❑8, Feb 1975, Reprints from Uncanny Tales #3, Astonishing #18 and Tales to Astonish #18 ... 12.00
❑9, Apr 1975 ... 12.00
❑10, Jun 1975, Reprints from Strange Tales #76, 77, 99 and World of Fantasy #10 ... 12.00
❑11, Aug 1975 ... 12.00
❑12, Oct 1975 ... 12.00

Uncanny X-Men
Marvel

❑-1, Jul 1997; Flashback ... 2.00
❑142, Feb 1981, JBy (w); JBy (a); A: Rachel Summers (Phoenix III). D: Colossus (future). D: Storm (future). D: Wolverine (future). Series continued from X-Men (1st Series) #141 ... 25.00
❑143, Mar 1981, JBy (w); JBy (a); Last Byrne art on X-Men ... 8.00
❑144, Apr 1981, BA (c); BA (a); A: Man-Thing. 1: Lee Forrester ... 6.00
❑145, May 1981, DC (c); DC (a) ... 7.00
❑146, Jun 1981, DC (c); DC (a) ... 6.00
❑147, Jul 1981, DC (c); DC (a) ... 6.00
❑148, Aug 1981, DC (c); DC (a); 1: Caliban. A: Dazzler. A: Spider-Woman ... 6.00
❑149, Sep 1981, DC (c); DC (a) ... 5.00
❑150, Oct 1981; double-sized; DC (c); DC, BWi (a); V: Magneto. Cyclops rejoins the X-Men ... 5.00
❑151, Nov 1981, DC, BMc (c); BMc (a) ... 5.00
❑152, Dec 1981, BMc (c); BMc (a) ... 5.00
❑153, Jan 1982, DC (c); DC (a) ... 5.00
❑154, Feb 1982, DC, BWi (c); DC, BWi (a) ... 5.00
❑155, Mar 1982, DC, BWi (c); DC, BWi (a); 1: Brood ... 5.00
❑156, Apr 1982, DC, BWi (c); DC, BWi (a) ... 5.00
❑157, May 1982, DC, BWi (c); DC, BWi (a); A: Phoenix ... 5.00
❑158, Jun 1982, DC, BWi (c); DC, BWi (a); A: Rogue ... 6.00
❑159, Jul 1982, BSz (c); BSz, BWi (a); A: Dracula ... 5.00
❑160, Aug 1982, BA, BWi (c); BA, BWi (a); 1: Magik (Illyana Rasputin as teenager). 1: Magik (Illyana Rasputin as teenager); 1: S'ym; 1: Illyana Rasputin (Magik) ... 5.00
❑161, Sep 1982, DC, BWi (c); DC, BWi (a); O: Professor X. O: Magneto ... 5.00
❑162, Oct 1982, DC, BWi (c); DC, BWi (a); Wolverine solo story ... 6.00
❑163, Nov 1982, DC, BWi (c); DC, BWi (a) ... 5.00
❑164, Dec 1982, DC, BWi (c); DC, BWi (a); 1: Binary ... 5.00
❑165, Jan 1983, PS (c); PS, BWi (a) ... 5.00
❑166, Feb 1983; Double-size; PS, BWi (c); PS, BWi (a); 1: Lockheed; D: Brood Queen ... 5.00
❑167, Mar 1983, PS, BWi (c); PS, BWi (a); A: New Mutants ... 4.00
❑168, Apr 1983, PS, BWi (c); PS, BWi (a); 1: Madelyne Pryor ... 5.00
❑169, May 1983, PS, BWi (c); PS, BWi (a); 1: Morlocks. 1: Sunder; 1: Callisto; 1: Masque; 1: Plague ... 5.00
❑170, Jun 1983, PS, BWi (c); PS, BWi (a) ... 5.00
❑171, Jul 1983, BWi (c); BWi (a); Rogue joins team ... 5.00
❑172, Aug 1983, PS (c); PS, BWi (a) ... 5.00
❑173, Sep 1983, PS, BWi (c); PS (a); O: Silver Samurai ... 5.00
❑174, Oct 1983, PS (c); PS, BWi (a) ... 5.00
❑175, Nov 1983; double-sized; PS (c); PS, JR2, BWi (a) ... 5.00
❑176, Dec 1983, JR2 (c); JR2, BWi (a); 1: Valerie Cooper; cover inker credit in letters page ... 4.00
❑177, Jan 1984, JR2 (c); JR2 (a); Assistant Editors' Month ... 4.00
❑178, Feb 1984, DGr, JR2 (c); JR2, BWi (a); Colleen Doran LOC ... 5.00
❑179, Mar 1984, DGr, JR2 (c); DGr, JR2 (a); 1: Leech; 1: Morlock Healer; 1: Plague ... 4.00
❑180, Apr 1984, JR2 (c); DGr, JR2, BWi (a); Secret Wars gateway ... 3.00
❑181, May 1984, JR2 (c); DGr, JR2 (a); 1: Amiko (Wolverine's adopted daughter) ... 4.00
❑182, Jun 1984, JR2 (c); DGr, JR2 (a); Rogue spotlight ... 5.00
❑183, Jul 1984, JR2 (c); DGr, JR2 (a) ... 5.00
❑184, Aug 1984, DGr, JR2 (c); DGr, JR2 (a); 1: Forge. A: Rachel. A: Selene. 1: Forge ... 4.00
❑185, Sep 1984, DGr, JR2 (c); DGr, JR2 (a); Storm loses powers ... 4.00
❑186, Oct 1984; double-sized; Storm ... 4.00
❑187, Nov 1984, DGr, JR2 (c); DGr, JR2 (a) ... 3.00
❑188, Dec 1984, JR2 (c); DGr, JR2 (a); 1: Adversary; Rachel Summers joins ... 3.00
❑189, Jan 1985, JR2 (c); JR2 (a) ... 4.00
❑190, Feb 1985, DGr, JR2 (c); DGr, JR2 (a); A: Spider-Man. A: Avengers ... 4.00
❑191, Mar 1985, DGr, JR2 (c); DGr, JR2 (a); A: Captain America. A: Spider-Man. A: Avengers. 1: Nimrod ... 5.00
❑192, Apr 1985, DGr, JR2 (c); DGr, JR2 (a); Magus ... 4.00
❑193, May 1985; double-sized; DGr, JR2 (c); DGr, JR2 (a); 20th anniv.; 100th New X-Men ... 5.00
❑194, Jun 1985, JR2 (c); DGr, JR2 (a); A: Juggernaut. V: Juggernaut. 1: Fenris ... 3.00

Other grades: Multiply price above by 5/6 for VF/NM • 2/3 for VERY FINE • 1/3 for FINE • 1/5 for VERY GOOD • 1/8 for GOOD

Walt Disney's Comics and Stories Penny Pincher

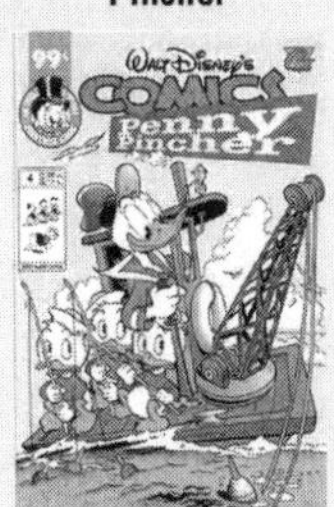

Barks' reprints in bargain package

©Gladstone

Walt Disney's Holiday Parade

Classic Christmas fare meets new treats

©Disney

Walt Disney Showcase

Mostly movie a daptations

©Gold Key

Walt Disney's World of Adventure

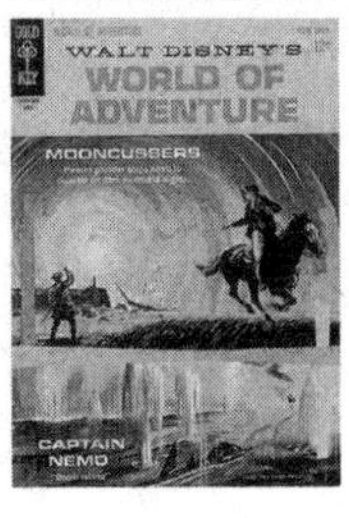

Action abounds in short-lived series

©Gold Key

Walter

Mask meanie gets solo shot

©Dark Horse

	N-MINT
❑195, Jul 1985, BSz, DGr (c); DGr, JR2 (a); A: Power Pack	3.00
❑196, Aug 1985, JR2 (c); DGr, JR2 (a); Secret Wars II	3.00
❑197, Sep 1985, DGr, JR2 (c); DGr, JR2 (a)	3.00
❑198, Oct 1985, Storm spotlight	3.00
❑199, Nov 1985, JR2 (c); DGr, JR2 (a); 1: Phoenix III (Rachel Summers) 1: Freedom Force	3.00
❑200, Dec 1985; Double-size; DGr, JR2 (c); DGr, JR2 (a)	6.00
❑201, Jan 1986, 1: Cable (as baby). 1st Whilce Portacio art in X-Men	5.00
❑202, Feb 1986; AW, JR2 (c); AW, JR2 (a); Secret Wars II	4.00
❑203, Mar 1986; AW, JR2 (c); AW, JR2 (a); Secret Wars II	4.00
❑204, Apr 1986; Nightcrawler solo story	4.00
❑205, May 1986; A: Power Pack. Wolverine solo story	4.00
❑206, Jun 1986; AW, JR2 (c); DGr, JR2 (a); V: Freedom Force	4.00
❑207, Jul 1986; DGr, JR2 (c); DGr, JR2 (a); Wolverine vs. Phoenix	4.00
❑208, Aug 1986 DGr, JR2 (c); DGr, JR2 (a)	4.00
❑209, Sep 1986; DGr, JR2 (c); JR2, CR (a); D: Harry Leland; D: Friedrich von Roehm	4.00
❑210, Oct 1986; JR2, BWi (c); DGr, JR2 (a); 1: Marauders; 1: Arclight; 1: Scalphunter; 1: Riptide; 1: Harpoon; 1: Scrambler	5.00
❑211, Nov 1986; AW, JR2 (c); AW, JR2 (a); 1: Cybelle	5.00
❑212, Dec 1986; DGr (c); DGr (a); Wolverine vs. Sabretooth	8.00
❑213, Jan 1987; Wolverine vs. Sabretooth	8.00
❑214, Feb 1987; BWi (a); Dazzler joins team	3.00
❑215, Mar 1987; DGr (c); DGr (a); 1: Crimson Commando; 1: Stonewall; 1: Super Sabre	3.00
❑216, Apr 1987 DGr, BG (a)	4.00
❑217, May 1987 BWi (c); BG (a); A: Juggernaut	3.00
❑218, Jun 1987; BWi (c); DGr (a); V: Juggernautt	3.00
❑219, Jul 1987; DGr (a); Havok joins X-Men	4.00
❑220, Aug 1987 DGr (c); DGr (a)	4.00
❑221, Sep 1987; DGr (c); DGr (a); 1: Mister Sinister. V: Mr. Sinister	7.00
❑222, Oct 1987; DGr (c); DGr (a); A: Sabretooth. V: Sabretooth	5.00
❑223, Nov 1987 DGr, KGa (c); DGr, KGa (a)	4.00
❑224, Dec 1987; BWi (c); BWi (a); registration card	3.00
❑225, Jan 1988; DGr (c); DGr (a); Fall of Mutants	3.00
❑226, Feb 1988; Double-size; DGr (c); DGr (a); Fall of Mutants; Storm regains powers	3.00
❑227, Mar 1988; DGr (c); DGr (a); Fall of Mutants	3.00
❑228, Apr 1988	3.00
❑229, May 1988; DGr (c); DGr (a); 1: The Reavers. 1: Gateway; 1: Jessan Hoan (Tiger Tyger); 1: Bonebreaker; 1: Skullbuster; 1: Pretty Boy	3.00
❑230, Jun 1988	3.00
❑231, Jul 1988 DGr (c); DGr (a)	3.00
❑232, Aug 1988 DGr (c); DGr (a)	4.00
❑233, Sep 1988 DGr (c); DGr (a)	3.00
❑234, Sep 1988 DGr (c)	3.00
❑235, Oct 1988; CR (c); CR (a); 1: Genosha; 1: Hawkshaw; 1: Pipeline; 1: Punchout; 1: Jenny Ransome	3.00
❑236, Oct 1988; DGr (c); DGr (a); 1: David Moreau	3.00
❑237, Nov 1988	3.00
❑238, Nov 1988 DGr (c); DGr (a)	3.00
❑239, Dec 1988; DGr (c); DGr (a); Inferno	3.00
❑240, Jan 1989; DGr (c); DGr (a); A: Sabretooth. Inferno	3.00
❑241, Feb 1989; DGr (c); DGr (a); Inferno	3.00
❑242, Mar 1989; Double-size; DGr (c); DGr (a); Inferno	3.00
❑243, Apr 1989; DGr (c);Inferno	3.00
❑244, May 1989; DGr (c); DGr (a); 1: Jubilee	5.00
❑245, Jun 1989; DGr, RL (c); DGr, RL (a); Invasion! parody	3.00
❑246, Jul 1989; DGr (c); DGr (a); 1: Sharon Kelly	3.00
❑247, Aug 1989; DGr (c); DGr (a); D: Sharon Kelly	3.00
❑248, Sep 1989; DGr, JLee (c); DGr, JLee (a); 1st Jim Lee art on X-Men	5.00
❑248/2nd, Sep 1989; JLee (c); JLee (a); 1st Jim Lee art on X-Men	1.50
❑249, Oct 1989 DGr (c); DGr (a)	3.00
❑250, Oct 1989 DGr (c)	3.00
❑251, Nov 1989 DGr (c); DGr (a)	3.00
❑252, Nov 1989 BSz, JLee (c)	2.50
❑253, Nov 1989 DGr (c)	2.50
❑254, Dec 1989; DGr (c); DGr (a); D: Sunder	2.50
❑255, Dec 1989; DGr (c); DGr (a); D: Destiny; D: Stonewall; 1: Matsuo Tsurayaba	2.50
❑256, Dec 1989; JLee (c); JLee (a); Acts of Vengeance	3.00
❑257, Jan 1990; JLee (c); JLee (a); Acts of Vengeance	3.00
❑258, Feb 1990; JLee (c); JLee (a); Acts of Vengeance	3.00
❑259, Mar 1990; DGr (c); DGr (a); Return of Colossus; Return of Dazzler	4.00
❑260, Apr 1990; JLee (c); DGr (a); 1: Cylla Markham (Skullbuster II)	3.00
❑261, May 1990 JLee (c); DGr (a)	2.50
❑262, Jun 1990; Forge battles mutant capable of creating grotesques	2.50
❑263, Jul 1990	2.50
❑264, Jul 1990; JLee (c);V: Genoshoa magistrates	2.50
❑265, Aug 1990; De-aged Storm lured into Shadow King trap	2.50
❑266, Aug 1990; 1: Gambit (full appearance); 1: Gambit (Remy LeBeau)	14.00
❑267, Sep 1990; JLee, BWi (c); JLee (a); Captain America, Wolverine, Black Widow team-up	6.00
❑268, Sep 1990; JLee (c); JLee (a); Wolverine; Captain America, Wolverine, Black Widow team-up	6.00
❑269, Oct 1990; JLee (c); JLee (a); Return of Rogue; Rogue V: Ms. Marvel; In Savage Land	3.00
❑270, Nov 1990; JLee (c); JLee (a); V: Cameron Hodge; V: Genoshoa magistrates	4.00
❑270/2nd, Nov 1990; JLee (a); Gold cover	2.00
❑271, Dec 1990; JLee (c); JLee (a); V: Cameron Hodge; V: Genoshoa magistrates; Storm turned into Genoshoa mutate	3.00
❑272, Jan 1991; JLee (c); JLee (a); V: Cameron Hodge; V: Genoshoa magistrates	3.00
❑273, Feb 1991 JLee (c); MG, JBy, JLee, KJ (a)	3.00
❑274, Mar 1991 JLee (c); JLee (a); A: Ka-Zar. A: Magneto. A: Nick Fury	3.00
❑275, Apr 1991; Double-size; JLee (c); JLee (a); X-Men and Starjammers V: Deathbird; SHIELD, Ka-Zar, Rogue and Magneto V: Zaladane and Savage Land mutates	3.00
❑275/2nd, Apr 1991; Double-size; JLee (c); JLee (a); gold logo	2.00
❑276, May 1991 JLee (c); JLee (w); JLee (a)	2.50
❑277, Jun 1991 JLee (c); JLee (w); JLee (a)	2.50
❑278, Jul 1991 PS (c); PS (a)	2.50
❑279, Aug 1991	2.50
❑280, Sep 1991; JLee (c);X-Factor crossover	2.50
❑281, Oct 1991; JBy, JLee (w); 1: Fitzroy. wraparound cover; new team	2.00
❑281/2nd, Oct 1991; JBy, JLee (w); 1: Fitzroy. 2nd printing (red); New team begins; wraparound cover	1.50
❑282, Nov 1991; JBy (w); 1: Bishop (cameo); D: Tarot	3.00
❑282/2nd, Nov 1991; JBy (w); 1: Bishop (cameo). Gold cover	1.25
❑283, Dec 1991; JBy (w); 1: Bishop (full); 1: Gamesmaster	5.00
❑284, Jan 1992 JBy (w)	4.00
❑285, Feb 1992; JBy, JLee (w); AM (a); 1: Mikhail Rasputin	2.50
❑286, Mar 1992 JLee (c); JLee (w); JLee (a)	2.00
❑287, Apr 1992; JLee (w); BSz, JR2, BWi (a); O: Bishop	2.50
❑288, May 1992 JBy, JLee (w); BSz (a).	2.00
❑289, Jun 1992; Bishop joins X-Men	2.00
❑290, Jul 1992	2.00
❑291, Aug 1992	2.00
❑292, Sep 1992 AM (a)	3.00
❑293, Oct 1992	2.00
❑294/CS, Nov 1992; Includes trading card	3.00
❑295/CS, Dec 1992; Includes trading card	2.00
❑296/CS, Jan 1993; Includes trading card	3.00
❑297, Feb 1993	1.50
❑298, Mar 1993; AM (c); AM (a); 1: Kleinstock Brothers; 1: Uniscone; D: Erik Kleinstock	2.00
❑299, Apr 1993; 1: Graydon Creed; 1: Fatale	1.50
❑300, May 1993; Double-size; DGr, JR2 (c); DGr, JR2 (a); holo-foil cover	3.00
❑301, Jun 1993 DGr, JR2 (c); DGr, JR2 (a)	1.50
❑302, Jul 1993 JR2 (c); DGr, JR2 (a)	1.50
❑303, Aug 1993; DGr (a); D: Illyana Rasputin	3.00
❑304, Sep 1993; 30th Anniversary Issue; JR2 (c); DGr, PS, JR2, TP (a); hologram	1.50
❑305, Oct 1993; JDu, (c); JDu (a); 1: Phalanx	1.50
❑306, Nov 1993 JR2 (c); DGr, JR2 (a)	2.00

Other grades: Multiply price above by 5/6 for VF/NM • 2/3 for VERY FINE • 1/3 for FINE • 1/5 for VERY GOOD • 1/8 for GOOD

	N-MINT
❑307, Dec 1993 DGr, JR2 (c); DGr, JR2 (a)	5.00
❑308, Jan 1994; DGr, JR2 (c); DGr, JR2 (a); Cyclops proposes to Jean Grey	1.50
❑309, Feb 1994 DGr, JR2 (c); DGr, JR2 (a)	1.50
❑310, Mar 1994; DGr, JR2 (c); DGr, JR2 (a); Includes trading cards	1.50
❑311, Apr 1994 JR2 (c); DGr, JR2 (a); A: Sabretooth	1.50
❑312, May 1994; DGr (c); DGr (a); Includes Marvel-Mart supplement	1.50
❑313, Jun 1994; DGr (c); DGr (a)	1.50
❑314, Jul 1994; BSz (a); V: White Queen	1.50
❑315, Aug 1994 DGr (a)	1.50
❑316, Sep 1994; DGr (c); DGr (a); Standard cover; Phalanx Covenant	1.50
❑316/Variant, Sep 1994; enhanced cover	1.50
❑317, Oct 1994; DGr (c); DGr (a); 1: Blink; 1: Skin; Standard cover: Phalanx Covenant; Standard cover	1.50
❑317/Variant, Oct 1994; enhanced cover	1.50
❑318, Nov 1994	2.00
❑318/Deluxe, Nov 1994; Deluxe edition	1.50
❑319, Dec 1994 DGr (a)	2.00
❑319/Deluxe, Dec 1994; Deluxe edition	1.50
❑320, Jan 1995 MWa (w)	2.00
❑320/Deluxe, Jan 1995; Deluxe edition; MWa (w)	1.50
❑320/Gold, Jan 1995; Wizard edition; No cover price; gold logo	2.00
❑321, Feb 1995 (c); MWa (w); DGr (a)	1.50
❑321/Deluxe, Feb 1995; Deluxe edition; MWa (w)	2.00
❑322, Jul 1995; AM, DGr (a); V: Onslaught. V: Juggernaut	2.00
❑323, Aug 1995; 1: Sack and Vessel	1.50
❑324, Sep 1995	2.00
❑325, Oct 1995; enhanced gatefold cardstock cover	2.00
❑326, Nov 1995; V: Sabretooth	2.00
❑327, Dec 1995; AM (a); A: Magneto. Magneto's fate revealed	2.00
❑328, Jan 1996; Psylocke vs. Sabretooth	2.00
❑329, Feb 1996 JPH (w)	4.00
❑330, Mar 1996 JPH (w)	2.00
❑331, Apr 1996; Iceman vs. White Queen	2.00
❑332, May 1996; V: Ozymandias	2.00
❑333, Jun 1996	2.00
❑334, Jul 1996 A: Juggernaut	2.00
❑335, Aug 1996 A: Uatu. A: Apocalypse.	2.00
❑336, Sep 1996	2.00
❑337, Oct 1996	2.00
❑338, Nov 1996; Angel regains his wings	2.00
❑339, Dec 1996; A: Spider-Man. Cyclops vs. Havok	2.00
❑340, Jan 1997	2.00
❑341, Feb 1997; Cannonball vs. Gladiator	2.00
❑342, Mar 1997	2.00
❑342/A, Mar 1997; Variant cover (Rogue)	2.00
❑343, Apr 1997	2.00
❑344, May 1997	2.00
❑345, Jun 1997	2.00
❑346, Aug 1997; gatefold summary; A: Spider-Man	2.00
❑347, Sep 1997; gatefold summary; AM (a)	2.00
❑348, Oct 1997; gatefold summary; AM (a)	2.00
❑349, Nov 1997; gatefold summary; V: Maggot	2.00
❑350, Dec 1997; gatefold summary	2.00
❑350/Variant, Dec 1997; gatefold summary; enhanced cover	2.00
❑351, Jan 1998; gatefold summary; V: Pyro. Cecilia joins team	2.00
❑352, Feb 1998; gatefold summary	2.00
❑353, Mar 1998; gatefold summary; Rogue vs. Wolverine	3.00
❑354, Apr 1998; gatefold summary; V: Sauron. Green-suited Pheonix on cover	1.99
❑355, May 1998; gatefold summary; A: Alpha Flight	1.99
❑356, Jun 1998; gatefold summary	1.99
❑357, Jul 1998; gatefold summary	1.99
❑358, Aug 1998; gatefold summary	1.99
❑359, Sep 1998; gatefold summary	1.99
❑360, Oct 1998; double-sized; Kitty Pryde, Colossus, Nightcrawler rejoin team	1.99
❑360/Variant, Oct 1998; Special cover	1.99
❑361, Nov 1998; gatefold summary; Return of Gambit	1.99

	N-MINT
❑362, Dec 1998; gatefold summary	1.99
❑363, Jan 1999; gatefold summary	4.00
❑364, Jan 1999; gatefold summary; Leinil Francis Yu's first major comics work	2.99
❑365, Mar 1999; gatefold summary; cover says Feb, indicia says Mar	1.99
❑366, Apr 1999; 1: Astra (identity unknown	1.99
❑367, Apr 1999 (c)	1.99
❑368, Jun 1999; Wolverine vs. Magneto; cover says May, indicia says Jun	1.99
❑369, Jun 1999; V: Juggernaut	1.99
❑370, Jul 1999	1.99
❑371, Aug 1999 A: Warlock	1.99
❑372, Sep 1999	1.99
❑373, Oct 1999	1.99
❑374, Nov 1999	1.99
❑375, Dec 1999; Giant-size	2.99
❑376, Jan 2000	1.99
❑377, Feb 2000; Jean Grey, Cyclops, and Apocalypse cover	1.99
❑378, Mar 2000	1.99
❑379, Apr 2000	2.99
❑380, May 2000 (c)	1.99
❑381, Jun 2000	2.25
❑381/Dynamic, Jun 2000, Dynamic Forces chromium variant; no UPC box on cover	7.00
❑382, Jul 2000	2.25
❑383, Aug 2000; Giant-size	2.99
❑384, Sep 2000	2.25
❑385, Oct 2000	2.25
❑386, Nov 2000	2.25
❑387, Dec 2000	2.99
❑388, Jan 2001	2.25
❑389, Feb 2001	2.25
❑390, Feb 2001; D: Colossus	2.25
❑391, Mar 2001 (c)	2.25
❑392, Apr 2001; Eve of Destruction	2.25
❑393, May 2001; Eve of Destruction	2.25
❑394, Jun 2001	2.25
❑395, Jul 2001	2.25
❑396, Aug 2001	2.25
❑397, Sep 2001	2.25
❑398, Oct 2001	2.25
❑399, Nov 2001; 1: Stacy-X (Miranda Leevald)	2.25
❑400, Dec 2001; Giant-size; (c);; Wraparound cover	3.50
❑401, Jan 2002; 1: X-Corps, 'Nuff Said month;; 'Nuff Said month	2.25
❑402, Feb 2002; 1: Nils Styger as Abyss (in 616 Universe)	2.25
❑403, Mar 2002 (c)	2.25
❑404, Apr 2002; D: Sunpyre	3.50
❑405, May 2002	2.25
❑406, Jun 2002; Call of Duty preview	2.25
❑407, Jul 2002	2.25
❑408, Aug 2002	2.25
❑409, Sep 2002	2.25
❑410, Oct 2002	2.25
❑411, Oct 2002	2.25
❑412, Nov 2002 (c)	2.25
❑413, Nov 2002	2.25
❑414, Dec 2002	2.25
❑415, Jan 2003; Uncanny X-Men #416 preview	2.25
❑416, Feb 2003; Studio Tron guest artwork	3.00
❑417, Mar 2003; Studio Tron guest artwork; No credits in issue	2.25
❑418, Mar 2003; Studio Tron guest artwork	2.25
❑419, Apr 2003; Studio Tron guest artwork	2.25
❑420, May 2003; D: Maximus Lobo	2.25
❑421, Jun 2003	2.25
❑422, Jun 2003; V: Alpha Flight	3.50
❑423, Jul 2003; D: Skin; D: Bedlam	2.25
❑424, Jul 2003; V: Church of Humanity	2.25
❑425, Aug 2003	2.25
❑426, Aug 2003	2.25
❑427, Sep 2003	2.25
❑428, Oct 2003; 1: Azazel; The Draco Prologue; Birth of Nightcrawler	2.25
❑429, Oct 2003	2.25
❑430, Oct 2003; O: Nightcrawler	2.99
❑431, Nov 2003; O: Nightcrawler; Polaris revealed to be Magneto's daughter	2.99
❑432, Dec 2003	2.99

	N-MINT
❑433, Jan 2004	2.99
❑434, Feb 2004	2.99
❑435, Feb 2004	2.99
❑436, Feb 2004, DGr (a)	2.99
❑437, Mar 2004	2.99
❑438, Mar 2004	2.99
❑439, Apr 2004	2.25
❑440, Apr 2004	2.99
❑441, May 2004	2.99
❑442, May 2004	2.25
❑443, Jun 2004, Professor X continued in Excalibur (2nd Series) #1	2.99
❑444, Jul 2004, (c)	4.00
❑445, Aug 2004	2.25
❑446, Sep 2004	2.25
❑447, Oct 2004	2.25
❑448, Oct 2004, Greg Land cover	2.25
❑449, Nov 2004	2.25
❑450, Dec 2004, X-23 appearance	7.00
❑451, Jan 2005, X-23 appearance	6.00
❑452, Feb 2005	3.00
❑453, Feb 2005	2.25
❑454, Mar 2005	2.25
❑455, Apr 2005	4.00
❑456, May 2005	2.25
❑457, Jun 2005	2.25
❑458, Jul 2005	2.25
❑459, Aug 2005	2.25
❑460, Sep 2005; Price increase	2.50
❑461, Sep 2005; Mojo on cover	2.50
❑461/Kubert, Sep 2005; Adam Kubert X-Babies incentive cover; available 1:15 copies	15.00
❑462, Oct 2005; House of M tie-in	2.50
❑463, Oct 2005; Nocturne Pete Wisdom.; Nocturne Pete Wisdom; House of M tie-in	2.50
❑464, Nov 2005; House of M tie-in; Nick Fury's Howling Commandos preview	2.50
❑465, Dec 2005; House of M tie-in	2.50
❑466, Jan 2006	2.50
❑467, Feb 2006	2.50
❑468, Mar 2006	2.50
❑469, Mar 2006	2.50
❑470, May 2006	2.50
❑471, Jun 2006	2.50
❑472, Jun 2006	2.99
❑473, Jul 2006, 1: The Foursaken	2.99
❑474, Sep 2006, Storm continued in Uncanny X-Men Ann 2006	2.99
❑475, Sep 2006, Wraparound cover	2.99
❑476, Sep 2006	2.99
❑477, Oct 2006	2.99
❑478, Nov 2006	2.99
❑479, Dec 2006, V: Korvus	2.99
❑480, Jan 2007	2.99
❑481, Feb 2007	2.99
❑482, Mar 2007	2.99
❑483, Apr 2007	2.99
❑484, May 2007	2.99
❑485, Jun 2007	2.99
❑486, Jul 2007; D: Corsair	2.99
❑487, Aug 2007	2.99
❑488, Sep 2007; Endangered Species continued in X-Factor #21	2.99
❑489, Oct 2007; Endangered Species continued in X-Factor (3rd Series) #22	2.99
❑490, Nov 2007; Endangered Species continued in X-Factor (3rd series) #23	2.99
❑491, Dec 2007; V: Morlocks; Endangered Species back-up story featuring the Beast; Endangered Species continued in (3rd series) X-Factor #24	2.99
❑492, Jan 2008; Continued From X-Men: Messiah Complex #1; Continues in X-Factor (3rd series) #25	6.00
❑493, Feb 2008	3.00
❑Ann 1, Dec 1970; Cover reads "King Size Special"; SL (w); JK (a); listed as X-Men in indicia, X-Men Special on cover; reprints X-Men #9 and 11	50.00
❑Ann 2, Nov 1971; Cover reads "King Size Special"; GK (c); reprints X-Men #22 and 23	45.00
❑Ann 3, Jan 1980; FM (c); GP, FM (a); 1: Arkon	14.00
❑Ann 4, Nov 1980; JR2 (c); JR2 (a); A: Doctor Strange. series continues as Uncanny X-Men Ann	6.00

Other grades: Multiply price above by 5/6 for VF/NM • 2/3 for VERY FINE • 1/3 for FINE • 1/5 for VERY GOOD • 1/8 for GOOD

Wanderers

Legion spin-off features revived adventurers

©DC

Wandering Star

Academy attendees flashback on events

©Pen and Ink

Wanted

Super-villain son embraces destiny

©Image

Wanted, the World's Most Dangerous Villains

Secret origins for super-villains

©DC

War

Appropriately enough, followed The Draft

©Marvel

N-MINT

❑Ann 5, Nov 1981 BA (c); BA, BMc (a); A: Fantastic Four 5.00
❑Ann 6, Nov 1982; BSz (c); BSz (a); A: Dracula. D: Rachel Van Helsing 7.00
❑Ann 7, ca. 1983 JR2 (c); MG (a) 5.00
❑Ann 8, ca. 1984 ..... 4.00
❑Ann 9, ca. 1985 ..... 10.00
❑Ann 10, Jan 1986; 1: Longshot 8.00
❑Ann 11, ca. 1987 ..... 4.00
❑Ann 12, ca. 1988; Evolutionary War 4.00
❑Ann 13, ca. 1989; Atlantis Attacks 3.00
❑Ann 14, ca. 1990; MG, KN (a); 1: Gambit (cameo) 6.00
❑Ann 15, ca. 1991 ..... 4.00
❑Ann 16, ca. 1992; Shattershot 2.25
❑Ann 17, ca. 1993; trading card 2.95
❑Ann 18, ca. 1994; JPH (w); JR2 (a); Includes pinup gallery; Bishop story 2.95
❑Ann 1995, Nov 1995; wraparound cover 3.95
❑Ann 1996, ca. 1996; wraparound cover 2.95
❑Ann 1997, Oct 1997; wraparound cover 2.99
❑Ann 1998, ca. 1998; Uncanny X-Men/ Fantastic Four '98; wraparound cover 2.99
❑Ann 2000, Feb 2001; Professor X 3.50
❑Ann 2001 2001 ..... 3.50

Uncensored Mouse
Eternity

❑1, Apr 1989, b&w; Mickey Mouse 2.50
❑2, Apr 1989; Mickey Mouse 2.50

Uncle Joe's Commie Book Featuring Cutey Bunny
Rip Off

❑1 1995, b&w; Adult 2.95

Uncle Sam
DC / Vertigo

❑1, ca. 1997; prestige format; ARo (a) 5.00
❑2, ca. 1997; prestige format; ARo (a) 5.00

Uncle Sam and the Freedom Fighters
DC

❑1, Sep 2006, Cover by Daniel AcuÒa 2.99
❑2, Nov 2006 ..... 2.99
❑3, Dec 2006, 1: Black Condor III (John Trujillo) 2.99
❑4, Jan 2007, 1: Americommando; 1: Barracuda; 1: Railgun; D: Spin Doctor 2.99
❑5, Feb 2007 ..... 2.99
❑6, Mar 2007 ..... 2.99
❑7 ..... 2.99
❑8 ..... 2.99

Uncle Scrooge
Dell / Gold Key/Whitman

❑36, Dec 1961, Old Number One Dime named as such 55.00
❑37, Mar 1962, "Cave of Ali Baba" reprinted in DuckTales #11 ..... 55.00
❑38, Jun 1962 ..... 55.00
❑39, Sep 1962 ..... 55.00
❑40, Dec 1962, Gold Key begins as publisher 55.00
❑41, Mar 1963 ..... 45.00
❑42, May 1963, CB (w); CB (a) 45.00
❑43, Jul 1963 ..... 45.00
❑44, Aug 1963,CB (w); CB (a) 45.00
❑45, Oct 1963, "Isle of Golden Geese" reprinted in Uncle Scrooge #352 ..... 45.00
❑46, Dec 1963 ..... 45.00

N-MINT

❑47, Feb 1964 ..... 45.00
❑48, Mar 1964, CB (w); CB (a) 45.00
❑49, May 1964 ..... 45.00
❑50, Jul 1964, Reprinted in US #187 ..... 45.00
❑51, Aug 1964 ..... 40.00
❑52, Sep 1964, CB (w); CB (a) 40.00
❑53, Oct 1964 ..... 40.00
❑54, Dec 1964 ..... 40.00
❑55, Feb 1965 ..... 40.00
❑56, Mar 1965 ..... 40.00
❑57, May 1965 ..... 40.00
❑58, Jul 1965 ..... 40.00
❑59, Sep 1965 ..... 40.00
❑60, Nov 1965 ..... 40.00
❑61, Jan 1966 ..... 40.00
❑62, Mar 1966 ..... 40.00
❑63, May 1966, "House of Haunts" reprinted in Uncle Scrooge #358 ..... 40.00
❑64, Jul 1966 ..... 40.00
❑65, Sep 1966 ..... 40.00
❑66, Nov 1966, CB (c); CB (w); CB (a); Gyro reprinted from Uncle Scrooge #22 ..... 40.00
❑67, Jan 1967 ..... 40.00
❑68, Mar 1967, "Hall of the Mermaid Queen" reprinted in Uncle Scrooge #356 ..... 40.00
❑69, May 1967 ..... 40.00
❑70, Jul 1967, CB (c); CB (w); CB (a) 40.00
❑71, Oct 1967 ..... 38.00
❑72, Dec 1967, Gyro reprinted from Uncle Scrooge #19 ..... 32.00
❑73, Feb 1968, Reprints stories from Uncle Scrooge #33 and 36 ..... 32.00
❑74, Apr 1968, (c); (w); (a) 32.00
❑75, Jun 1968 ..... 32.00
❑76, Aug 1968 ..... 32.00
❑77, Oct 1968 ..... 32.00
❑78, Dec 1968 ..... 32.00
❑79, Feb 1969 ..... 32.00
❑80, Apr 1969 ..... 32.00
❑81, Jun 1969, (c); (w); (a) 32.00
❑82, Aug 1969, Reprints story from Uncle Scrooge #34 ..... 32.00
❑83, Oct 1969 ..... 32.00
❑84, Dec 1969, Reprints story from Uncle Scrooge #14 ..... 32.00
❑85, Feb 1970, Reprints story from Uncle Scrooge #52 ..... 32.00
❑86, Apr 1970, CB (w); CB (a); Reprints story from Uncle Scrooge #35 ..... 32.00
❑87, Jun 1970, Reprints story from Uncle Scrooge #25 ..... 32.00
❑88, Aug 1970, Reprints story from Uncle Scrooge #38 ..... 32.00
❑89, Oct 1970, Reprints story from Uncle Scrooge #15 ..... 32.00
❑90, Dec 1970, Reprints stories from Uncle Scrooge #37 and 35 ..... 32.00
❑91, Feb 1971, Reprints stories from Uncle Scrooge #11 and 26 ..... 32.00
❑92, Apr 1971, Reprints stories from Uncle Scrooge #24, 31 and 32 ..... 32.00
❑93, Jun 1971, Reprints stories from Uncle Scrooge #34 and 36 ..... 32.00
❑94, Aug 1971, Reprints stories from Uncle Scrooge #35 and 53 ..... 32.00
❑95, Oct 1971, Reprints stories from Uncle Scrooge #30 and 51 ..... 32.00

N-MINT

❑96, Dec 1971, Reprints story from Uncle Scrooge #47 ..... 32.00
❑97, Feb 1972, Reprints stories from Uncle Scrooge #32 ..... 32.00
❑98, Apr 1972, Reprints story from Uncle Scrooge #41 ..... 32.00
❑99, Jun 1972, Reprints story from Uncle Scrooge #42 ..... 32.00
❑100, Aug 1972, Reprints story from Uncle Scrooge #30 ..... 32.00
❑101, Sep 1972, Reprints stories from Walt Disney's Comics & Stories #157 and 159 ..... 20.00
❑102, Nov 1972, Reprints stories from Uncle Scrooge #39 ..... 20.00
❑103, Feb 1973, CB (w); CB (a); Reprints story from Uncle Scrooge #16 ..... 20.00
❑104, Apr 1973, Reprints stories from Uncle Scrooge #9 and 42 ..... 20.00
❑105, Jun 1973, Reprints stories from Four Color Comics #495 and Uncle Scrooge #32 ..... 20.00
❑106, Aug 1973, Reprints stories from Uncle Scrooge #6 ..... 20.00
❑107, Sep 1973, Reprints story from Uncle Scrooge #21 ..... 20.00
❑108, Oct 1973, Reprints story from Uncle Scrooge #19 ..... 20.00
❑109, Dec 1973, Reprints story from Uncle Scrooge #13 ..... 20.00
❑110, Feb 1974, Reprints story from Uncle Scrooge #22 ..... 20.00
❑111, Jun 1974, Reprints story from Uncle Scrooge #8 ..... 20.00
❑112, Jun 1974, Reprints story from Uncle Scrooge #18 ..... 20.00
❑113, Aug 1974, CB (c); CB (w); CB (a); Reprints stories from Uncle Scrooge #24 and 44; cover reprinted from #20 ..... 20.00
❑114, Sep 1974, Reprints story from Uncle Scrooge #60 ..... 20.00
❑115, Oct 1974, Reprints story from Uncle Scrooge #58 ..... 20.00
❑116, Dec 1974, Reprints story from Uncle Scrooge #50 ..... 20.00
❑117, Feb 1975, Reprints stories from Uncle Scrooge #32 and 49 ..... 20.00
❑118, Apr 1975, Reprints stories from Uncle Scrooge #54 ..... 20.00
❑119, Jun 1975, Reprints stories from Uncle Scrooge #23 and 37 ..... 20.00
❑120, Jul 1975, Reprints stories from Uncle Scrooge #33 and 34 ..... 20.00
❑121, Aug 1975, Reprints story from Uncle Scrooge #55 ..... 18.00
❑122, Sep 1975, Reprints story from Uncle Scrooge #56 ..... 18.00
❑123, Oct 1975, Reprints story from Uncle Scrooge #57 ..... 18.00
❑124, Dec 1975, Reprints story from Uncle Scrooge #59 ..... 18.00
❑125, Jan 1976, Reprints story from Uncle Scrooge #68 ..... 18.00
❑126, Mar 1976, Reprints story from Uncle Scrooge #69 ..... 18.00
❑127, Apr 1976, Reprints story from Uncle Scrooge #61 ..... 18.00
❑128, May 1976, Reprints story from Uncle Scrooge #62 ..... 18.00
❑129, Jun 1976, Reprints story from Uncle Scrooge #63 ..... 18.00

Other grades: Multiply price above by 5/6 for VF/NM • 2/3 for VERY FINE • 1/3 for FINE • 1/5 for VERY GOOD • 1/8 for GOOD

N-MINT

❑130, Jul 1976, Reprints story from Uncle Scrooge #65 ... 18.00
❑131, Aug 1976, CB (c); CB (w); CB (a); Reprints story from Uncle Scrooge #66 ... 18.00
❑132, Sep 1976, CB (c); CB (w); CB (a); Reprints story from Uncle Scrooge #10; Hulk in Hostess ad ("vs. The Green Frog") ... 18.00
❑133, Oct 1976, CB (c); CB (w); CB (a); Reprints story from Uncle Scrooge #70; Casper in Hostess ad ("Spook-a-thon") ... 18.00
❑134, Nov 1976, Reprints story from Uncle Scrooge #64 ... 18.00
❑135, Dec 1976, Reprints stories from Uncle Scrooge #23 and 24 ... 18.00
❑136, Jan 1977, Reprints stories from Uncle Scrooge #37-39 ... 18.00
❑137, Feb 1977, Reprints story from Uncle Scrooge #31 ... 18.00
❑138, Mar 1977, CB (c); CB (w); CB (a); Reprints stories from Uncle Scrooge #28 and 48; Casper in Hostess ad ("The Boogy-Woogy Man") ... 18.00
❑139, Apr 1977, Reprints stories from Uncle Scrooge #45 ... 18.00
❑140, May 1977, Reprints story from Uncle Scrooge #43 ... 18.00
❑141, Jun 1977, CB (w); CB (a); Reprints story from Uncle Scrooge #42; Iron Man in Hostess ad ("A Dull Pain") ... 12.00
❑142, Jul 1977, Reprints story from Four Color Comics #456 ... 12.00
❑143, Aug 1977, Reprints stories from Uncle Scrooge #26 and 29 ... 12.00
❑144, Sep 1977, Reprints stories from Uncle Scrooge #28 ... 12.00
❑145, Oct 1977, Reprints story from Uncle Scrooge #71 ... 12.00
❑146, Nov 1977, Reprints story from Uncle Scrooge #30 ... 12.00
❑147, Dec 1977, Reprints stories from Uncle Scrooge #34-36 ... 12.00
❑148, Jan 1978, Reprints story from Uncle Scrooge #11 ... 12.00
❑149, Feb 1978, Reprints story from Uncle Scrooge #46 ... 12.00
❑150, Mar 1978, CB (c); CB (w); CB (a); Reprints stories from Uncle Scrooge #27; cover reprinted from #25; Spider-Man in Hostess ad ("vs. The Chairman") ... 12.00
❑151, Apr 1978, Reprints stories from Uncle Scrooge #25 ... 12.00
❑152, May 1978, CB (w); CB (a); Reprints stories from Uncle Scrooge #48 and 52; Captain America in Hostess ad ("vs. the Aliens") ... 12.00
❑153, Jun 1978, Reprints story from Uncle Scrooge #44 ... 12.00
❑154, Jul 1978, Reprints stories from Uncle Scrooge #35 and 53 ... 12.00
❑155, Aug 1978, CB (w); CB (a); Reprints stories from Uncle Scrooge #11 and 30 ... 12.00
❑156, Sep 1978, Reprints stories from Four Color Comics #456 (Uncle Scrooge #2) and Uncle Scrooge #38; Captain America in Hostess ad ("vs. the Aliens") ... 12.00
❑157, Oct 1978, CB (w); CB (a); Reprints stories from Uncle Scrooge #31, #52 and #53; Casper in Hostess ad ("A Real Oddball") ... 12.00
❑158, Nov 1978 ... 12.00
❑159, Dec 1978, CB (w); CB (a); Reprints stories from Uncle Scrooge #35 and #42 ... 12.00
❑160, Jan 1979 ... 12.00
❑161, Feb 1979 ... 10.00
❑162, Mar 1979, (c); (w); (a); Reprints from #81; Spider-Man in Hostess ad (June Jitsui) ... 10.00
❑163, Apr 1979 ... 10.00
❑164, May 1979 ... 10.00
❑165, Jun 1979 ... 10.00
❑166, Jul 1979, (c); (w); (a); Reprints story from Uncle Scrooge #74 ... 10.00
❑167, Aug 1979 ... 10.00
❑168, Sep 1979, Reprints story from Uncle Scrooge #79; Casper in Hostess ad ("The Boo Keepers") ... 10.00
❑169, Oct 1979 ... 10.00
❑170, Nov 1979 ... 10.00
❑171, Dec 1979 ... 10.00
❑172, Jan 1980 ... 15.00
❑173, Feb 1980 ... 15.00
❑174, Mar 1980 ... 15.00
❑175, Apr 1980 ... 15.00
❑176, May 1980 ... 15.00
❑177, Jun 1980, CB (c); CB (w); CB (a); Reprints story from Uncle Scrooge #16 and #103; Hulk in Hostess ad ("Hulk Gets Even") ... 25.00
❑178, Jul 1980 ... 25.00
❑179, Sep 1980 ... 225.00
❑180, Nov 1980 ... 35.00
❑181, Dec 1980 ... 15.00
❑182, Jan 1981, (c); (w); (a); V: The Beagle Boys ... 15.00
❑183, Feb 1981, CB (c); CB (w); CB (a); Cover reprinted from Uncle Scrooge #5; stories reprinted from #6 ... 15.00
❑184, Mar 1981, CB (c); CB (w); CB (a); Reprints stories from Uncle Scrooge #60 ... 15.00
❑185, Jun 1981 ... 15.00
❑186, Jul 1981 ... 10.00
❑187, Aug 1981 ... 10.00
❑188, Sep 1981 ... 10.00
❑189, Oct 1981 ... 10.00
❑190, Nov 1981 ... 10.00
❑191, Dec 1981 ... 10.00
❑192, Jan 1982 ... 10.00
❑193, Feb 1982 ... 10.00
❑194, Spr 1982 ... 10.00
❑195, Mar 1982 ... 10.00
❑196, Apr 1982 ... 10.00
❑197, May 1982 ... 10.00
❑198, ca. 1982 ... 15.00
❑199, May 1983 ... 10.00
❑200, ca. 1982 ... 10.00
❑201, ca. 1983 ... 6.00
❑202, ca. 1983 ... 6.00
❑203, Jul 1983 ... 6.00
❑204, Aug 1983 ... 6.00
❑205, Aug 1983 ... 6.00
❑206, ca. 1984 ... 6.00
❑207, May 1984 ... 6.00
❑208, Jun 1984 ... 6.00
❑209, Jul 1984 ... 6.00
❑210, Oct 1986, CB (w); CB (a); 1: Beagle Boys (reprint); 1st Gladstone issue ... 6.00
❑211, Nov 1986, CB (w); CB (a) ... 6.00
❑212, Dec 1986, CB (w); CB (a) ... 6.00
❑213, Jan 1987 ... 6.00
❑214, Feb 1987, CB (w); CB (a) ... 6.00
❑215, Mar 1987, CB (w); CB (a); Reprints story from Uncle Scrooge #17 ... 6.00
❑216, Apr 1987, CB (w); CB (a) ... 6.00
❑217, May 1987 ... 6.00
❑218, Jun 1987, CB (w); CB (a) ... 6.00
❑219, Jul 1987, DR (a); 1st Rosa Disney story ... 6.00
❑220, Aug 1987, CB (w); CB, DR (a) ... 5.00
❑221, Sep 1987, CB (w); CB (a) ... 5.00
❑222, Oct 1987, CB (w); CB (a) ... 5.00
❑223, Nov 1987, CB (w); CB (a) ... 5.00
❑224, Dec 1987, CB (w); CB, DR (a) ... 5.00
❑225, Feb 1988, CB (w); CB (a) ... 5.00
❑226, May 1988, CB (w); CB, DR (a) ... 5.00
❑227, Jul 1988, CB (w); CB (a) ... 5.00
❑228, Aug 1988, CB (w); CB (a) ... 5.00
❑229, Sep 1988, CB (w); CB (a) ... 5.00
❑230, Oct 1988, CB (w); CB (a) ... 5.00
❑231, Nov 1988, DR (c); CB (w); CB (a) ... 5.00
❑232, Dec 1988, CB (w); CB (a) ... 5.00
❑233, Feb 1989, CB (w); CB (a) ... 5.00
❑234, May 1989, CB (w); CB (a) ... 5.00
❑235, Jul 1989, CB (w); DR (a) ... 5.00
❑236, Aug 1989, CB (w); CB (a) ... 5.00
❑237, Sep 1989, CB (w); CB (a); Reprints story from Uncle Scrooge #11 ... 5.00
❑238, Oct 1989, CB (w); CB (a); "Trouble Indemnity" reprints from WDC&S #180; "Trouble Indemnity" reprints from WDC&S #180 ... 5.00
❑239, Nov 1989, CB (w); CB (a) ... 5.00
❑240, Dec 1989, CB (w); CB (a) ... 5.00
❑241, Feb 1990, CB (w); CB, DR (a) ... 4.00
❑242, Apr 1990, double-sized; CB (w); CB (a) ... 4.00
❑243, Jun 1990 ... 4.00
❑244, Jul 1990 ... 4.00
❑245, Aug 1990, CB (w); CB (a) ... 4.00
❑246, Sep 1990 ... 4.00
❑247, Oct 1990 ... 4.00
❑248, Nov 1990 ... 4.00
❑249, Dec 1990 ... 4.00
❑250, Jan 1991, CB (w); CB (a) ... 4.00
❑251, Feb 1991, CB (w); CB (a) ... 4.00
❑252, Mar 1991 ... 4.00
❑253, Apr 1991, CB (w); CB (a) ... 4.00
❑254, May 1991, CB (w); CB (a) ... 4.00
❑255, Jun 1991, CB (w); CB (a) ... 4.00
❑256, Jul 1991, CB (w); CB (a) ... 4.00
❑257, Aug 1991 ... 4.00
❑258, Sep 1991, CB (w); CB (a) ... 4.00
❑259, Oct 1991 ... 4.00
❑260, Nov 1991 ... 4.00
❑261, Dec 1991, CB, DR (w); CB, DR (a) ... 2.50
❑262, Jan 1992, DR (w); DR (a) ... 2.50
❑263, Feb 1992, DR (w); DR (a) ... 2.50
❑264, Mar 1992 ... 2.50
❑265, Apr 1992, CB (w); CB (a) ... 2.50
❑266, May 1992, CB (w); CB (a) ... 2.50
❑267, Jun 1992, CB (w); CB (a); contains Duckburg map piece 3 of 9 ... 2.50
❑268, Jul 1992, CB (w); CB (a); contains Duckburg map piece 6 of 9 ... 2.50
❑269, Aug 1992, CB (w); CB (a); contains Duckburg map piece 9 of 9 ... 2.50
❑270, Sep 1992, CB (w); CB (a); Olympics ... 2.50
❑271, Oct 1992, CB (w); CB (a) ... 2.50
❑272, Nov 1992, CB (w); CB (a) ... 2.50
❑273, Dec 1992, CB (w); CB (a) ... 2.50
❑274, Jan 1993, CB (w); CB (a) ... 2.50
❑275, Feb 1993, CB (w); CB (a) ... 2.50
❑276, Mar 1993, CB, DR (w); CB, DR (a) ... 2.50
❑277, Apr 1993, CB (w); CB (a) ... 2.50
❑278, May 1993, CB (w); CB, DR (a) ... 2.50
❑279, Jun 1993, CB (w); CB, DR (a) ... 2.50
❑280, Jul 1993 ... 2.50
❑281, Aug 1993, DR (c); CB (w); CB (a) ... 2.50
❑282, Oct 1993, CB (w); CB (a) ... 2.50
❑283, Dec 1993, CB (w); CB (a) ... 2.50
❑284, Feb 1994, CB (w); CB (a) ... 2.50
❑285, Apr 1994, DR (w); DR (a) ... 2.50
❑286, Jun 1994, DR (w); DR (a) ... 2.50
❑287, Aug 1994, DR (c); CB, DR (w); CB, DR (a) ... 2.50
❑288, Oct 1994, DR (c); DR (w); DR (a) ... 2.50
❑289, Dec 1994, DR (c); DR (w); DR (a) ... 2.50
❑290, Feb 1995, DR (c); DR (w); DR (a) ... 2.50
❑291, Apr 1995, DR (c); DR (w); DR (a) ... 2.50
❑292, Jun 1995, DR (c); DR (w); DR (a); Incide back cover reprints from Uncle Scrooge #41 ... 2.50
❑293, Aug 1995, CB, DR (w); DR (a) ... 2.50
❑294, Oct 1995, DR (w); DR (a); newsprint covers begin ... 2.50
❑295, Dec 1995, DR (w); DR (a) ... 2.50
❑296, Feb 1996, DR (w); DR (a) ... 2.50
❑297, Apr 1996, DR (w); DR (a) ... 2.50
❑298, Jun 1996 ... 2.50
❑299, Aug 1996 ... 2.50
❑300, Oct 1996, 48-Page Super Spectacular ... 2.25
❑301, Dec 1996, Reprints from Walt Disney Comics and Stories #138 ... 1.50
❑302, Feb 1997, CB (w); CB (a); reprints from WDC&S #297 ... 1.50
❑303, Apr 1997, newsprint covers end ... 1.50
❑304, Jun 1997, CB (w); CB (a); Reprints ... 1.50
❑305, Aug 1997, CB (w); CB (a); Reprints ... 1.50
❑306, Oct 1997, DR (c); DR (w); DR (a) ... 1.50
❑307, Dec 1997, Reprints from Uncle Scrooge #26 ... 1.50
❑308, Feb 1998 ... 1.50
❑309, May 1998, prestige format begins ... 6.95
❑310, Jun 1998 ... 6.95
❑311, Jul 1998 ... 6.95
❑312, Aug 1998 ... 6.95
❑313, Sep 1998 ... 6.95
❑314, Oct 1998 ... 6.95
❑315, Nov 1998 ... 6.95
❑316, Dec 1998 ... 6.95
❑317, Jan 1999 ... 6.95
❑318, Feb 1999, series goes on hiatus; Gemstone resumes publishing in 2003 ... 6.95

Uncle Scrooge
Gemstone

❑319, Jun 2003; prestige format ... 6.95
❑320, Jul 2003 ... 6.95
❑321, Aug 2003 ... 6.95
❑322, Sep 2003 ... 6.95
❑323, Oct 2003 ... 6.95
❑324, Nov 2003 ... 6.95

Other grades: Multiply price above by 5/6 for VF/NM • 2/3 for VERY FINE • 1/3 for FINE • 1/5 for VERY GOOD • 1/8 for GOOD

War Dancer

Mayan-like "god" comes to Earth
©Defiant

Warhammer Monthly

Ties in to Games Workshop's fantasy mini game
©Games Workshop

Warheads

Not the red-hot candy, but a Marvel UK comic
©Marvel

Warlock

Him got a series
©Marvel

Warlock and the Infinity Watch

Infinity Gems divvied up to diverse group
©Marvel

	N-MINT
❑325, Dec 2003	6.95
❑326, Jan 2004	6.95
❑327, Feb 2004	6.95
❑328, Mar 2004	6.95
❑329, Apr 2004	6.95
❑330, May 2004	6.95
❑331, Jun 2004	6.95
❑332, Jul 2004	6.95
❑333, Aug 2004	6.95
❑334, Sep 2004	6.95
❑335, Oct 2004	6.95
❑336, Nov 2004	6.95
❑337, Dec 2004	6.95
❑338, Jan 2005	6.95
❑339, Feb 2005	6.95
❑340, Mar 2005	6.95
❑341, Apr 2005	6.95
❑342, May 2005	6.95
❑343, Jun 2005	6.95
❑344, Jul 2005	6.95
❑345, Aug 2005	6.95
❑346, Sep 2005	6.95
❑347, Oct 2005	6.95
❑348, Nov 2005	6.95
❑349, Dec 2005	6.95

Uncle Scrooge Adventures
Gladstone

	N-MINT
❑1, Nov 1987 CB (w); CB (a)	5.00
❑2, Dec 1987 CB (w); CB (a)	3.00
❑3, Jan 1988 CB (w); CB (a)	2.00
❑4, Apr 1988 CB (w); CB (a)	2.00
❑5, Jun 1988 DR (w); DR (a)	6.00
❑6, Aug 1988 CB (w); CB (a)	2.00
❑7, Sep 1988 CB (w); CB (a)	2.00
❑8, Oct 1988 CB (w); CB (a)	2.00
❑9, Nov 1988 DR (w); DR (a)	5.00
❑10, Dec 1988 CB (w); CB (a)	2.00
❑11, Jan 1989 CB (w); CB (a)	2.00
❑12, Mar 1989 CB (w); CB (a)	2.00
❑13, Jun 1989 DR (c); CB (w); CB (a)	2.00
❑14, Aug 1989 DR (w); DR (a)	5.00
❑15, Sep 1989 CB (w); CB (a)	2.00
❑16, Oct 1989 CB (w); CB (a)	2.00
❑17, Nov 1989 CB (w); CB (a)	2.00
❑18, Dec 1989 CB (w); CB (a)	2.00
❑19, Jan 1990 DR (c); CB (w); CB (a)	2.00
❑20, Mar 1990; double-sized; CB, DR (w); CB, DR (a)	5.00
❑21, May 1990; double-sized; CB, DR (w); CB, DR (a)	5.00
❑22, Sep 1993; CB (w); CB (a); Reprints	1.50
❑23, Nov 1993; CB (w); CB (a); Reprints	2.95
❑24, Jan 1994; CB (w); CB (a); Reprints	1.50
❑25, Mar 1994; DR (c); CB (w); CB (a); Reprints	1.50
❑26, May 1994; CB (a); Reprints	2.95
❑27, Jul 1994; DR (a); O: Junior Woodchucks Handbook. O: Junior Woodchucks Handbook	1.50
❑28, Sep 1994; CB (a); A: Terries and Fermies. Reprints	2.95
❑29, Nov 1994	1.50
❑30, Jan 1995; 64 pages	2.95
❑31, Mar 1995	1.50
❑32, May 1995	1.50
❑33, Jul 1995; CB (w); CB (a); new story	2.95
❑34, Sep 1995	1.95
❑35, Nov 1995	1.95
❑36, Jan 1996	1.95
❑37, Mar 1996; newprint covers begin	1.50
❑38, May 1996	1.50
❑39, Aug 1996	1.50
❑40, Sep 1996	1.50
❑41, Nov 1996	1.95
❑42, Jan 1997	1.95
❑43, Feb 1997; CB (a); reprints The Queen of the Wild Dog Pack from US #62	1.50
❑44, Mar 1997	1.50
❑45, Apr 1997	1.50
❑46, May 1997; newprint covers end	1.95
❑47, Jun 1997; CB (a); Reprints	1.95
❑48, Jul 1997	1.95
❑49, Aug 1997	1.95
❑50, Sep 1997; CB (a); Reprints	1.95
❑51, Oct 1997 DR (w); DR (a)	1.95
❑52, Nov 1997	1.95
❑53, Dec 1997	1.95
❑54, Feb 1998	1.95

Uncle Scrooge and Donald Duck
Gold Key

	N-MINT
❑1, Jun 1965, Reprints stories from Four Color Comics #29 and 386	50.00

Uncle Scrooge & Donald Duck
Gladstone

	N-MINT
❑1, Jan 1998	2.00
❑2, Mar 1998	2.00

Uncle Scrooge and Money
Gold Key

	N-MINT
❑1, Mar 1967, CB (w); CB (a); Reprints story from Walt Disney's Comics #130; 10167-703	6.00

Uncle Scrooge Comics Digest
Gladstone

	N-MINT
❑1, Dec 1986; CB (a); reprints	3.00
❑2, Feb 1987; CB (a); reprints	2.00
❑3, Apr 1987; CB (a); reprints	2.00
❑4, Jun 1987; CB (a); reprints	2.00
❑5, Aug 1987; CB (a); reprints	2.00

Uncle Scrooge Goes to Disneyland
Gladstone

	N-MINT
❑1, Aug 1985, CB (w); CB (a); Dell Giant	275.00
❑1/A, Aug 1985, digest; Reprints from Uncle Scrooge Goes to Disney Land #1	5.00
❑1/A/2nd, digest CB (a)	5.00
❑1/2nd, Aug 1985, CB (w); CB (a); Reprints from Uncle Scrooge Goes to Disney Land #1	6.00

Uncle Scrooge the Golden Fleecing
Whitman

	N-MINT
❑1, Reprints	8.00

Uncle Slam & Fire Dog
Action Planet

	N-MINT
❑1, ca. 1997, b&w	2.95
❑2, b&w	2.95

Uncut Comics
Uncut Comics

	N-MINT
❑1, Apr 1997, b&w; free handout; Origins	1.00
❑1/A, Feb 1997, b&w; non-slick cover	1.50
❑1/B, Feb 1997, b&w; non-slick alternate cover	1.50
❑2, May 1997, b&w; flip-book with alternate cover back-up	1.95

Undercover Genie
DC

	N-MINT
❑1, ca. 2003	14.95

Underdog
Charlton

	N-MINT
❑1, Jul 1970, poster	60.00
❑2, Sep 1970	38.00
❑3, Nov 1970	30.00
❑4, Jan 1971	30.00
❑5, Mar 1971	30.00
❑6, May 1971	25.00
❑7, Jul 1971	25.00
❑8, Sep 1971	25.00
❑9, Nov 1971	25.00
❑10, Jan 1972	25.00

Underdog
Gold Key

	N-MINT
❑1, Mar 1975	35.00
❑2, Jun 1975	20.00
❑3 1975	12.00
❑4 1975	8.00
❑5 1976	8.00
❑6 1976	6.00
❑7, Jun 1976	6.00
❑8, Aug 1976	6.00
❑9, Oct 1976	6.00
❑10, Dec 1976	6.00
❑11, Feb 1976	5.00
❑12, Apr 1977	5.00
❑13, Jun 1977	5.00
❑14, Aug 1977	5.00
❑15, Oct 1977	5.00
❑16, Dec 1977	5.00
❑17, Feb 1978	5.00
❑18, Apr 1978	5.00
❑19, Jun 1978, Hostess Ad: Daredevil in The Peachy Keen Caper	5.00
❑20, Aug 1978	5.00
❑21, Oct 1978	4.00
❑22, Dec 1978	4.00
❑23, Feb 1979	4.00

Underdog
Spotlight

	N-MINT
❑1, ca. 1987	2.50
❑2, ca. 1987	2.50

Underdog
Harvey

	N-MINT
❑1, Nov 1993; No creator credits listed	1.50
❑2, Jan 1993; No creator credits listed	1.50
❑3, Mar 1994; No creator credits listed	1.50
❑4, May 1994; No creator credits listed	1.50
❑5, Jul 1994; No creator credits listed	1.50
❑Summer 1, Oct 1993	2.25

Underdog 3-D
Blackthorne

	N-MINT
❑1	2.50

Underground
Aircel

	N-MINT
❑1, b&w; NN; b&w	1.70

Underground
Dark Horse

❑1, Nov 1993 .... 3.95
❑2, Jan 1994 .... 3.95
❑3, Mar 1994 .... 3.95
❑4, May 1994 .... 3.95

Underground Classics
Rip Off

❑1, Dec 1985; Fabulous Furry Freak Brothers 6.00
❑2, Feb 1986; Dealer McDope 10.00
❑2/2nd 1986; 2nd printing; Adult 2.00
❑2/3rd 1986; 3rd printing; Adult 2.50
❑3, Mar 1986; Dealer McDope 8.00
❑3/2nd; 2nd printing; Adult 2.00
❑4, Sep 1987; Adult 2.50
❑5, Nov 1987; Wonder Warthog 7.50
❑6, Feb 1988; Adult 5.00
❑7, Apr 1988; Adult 6.00
❑8, Jun 1988; Adult 5.00
❑9, Feb 1989; Art of Greg Irons 4.00
❑10; Jesus 4.00
❑11; Jesus 4.00
❑12, Jul 1990; Shelton 3-D 5.00
❑12/2nd; 2nd printing; Adult 2.95
❑13; Jesus 4.00
❑14; Jesus 4.00
❑15; Adult 4.00

Underlords
Eidolon Entertainment

❑1 2005 .... 2.95
❑2 2005 .... 2.95
❑3 2005 .... 2.95
❑4, Aug 2005 .... 2.95

Undersea Agent
Tower

❑1, Jan 1966 .... 32.00
❑2, Apr 1966; Lt. Jones gains electrical powers 22.00
❑3, Jun 1966 .... 18.00
❑4, Aug 1966 .... 18.00
❑5, Oct 1966 .... 18.00
❑6, Mar 1967; Final Issue 18.00

Underside
Caliber

❑1 .... 2.95

Undertaker
Chaos

❑0, Feb 1999; Collector's issue; Wizard . 3.00
❑½, Mar 1999; Wizard collector's issue . 4.00
❑1, Apr 1999; Drawn cover 4.00
❑1/A, Apr 1999; DFE red foil cover 6.00
❑1/B, Apr 1999; DFE red foil cover; Autographed 8.00
❑1/Variant, Apr 1999; Photo cover 4.00
❑2, May 1999 .... 2.95
❑3, Jun 1999; Photo cover 2.95
❑4, Jul 1999 .... 2.95
❑5, Aug 1999 .... 2.95
❑6, Sep 1999; Photo cover 2.95
❑7, Oct 1999; Photo cover 2.95
❑8, Nov 1999 .... 2.95
❑9, Dec 1999 .... 2.95
❑10, Jan 2000 .... 2.95
❑Holiday 1, Oct 1999; digest 2.95

Under Terra
Predawn

❑2, b&w 2.45
❑3, b&w 2.45
❑4, b&w 2.45
❑5, b&w 2.45
❑6, b&w 1.75

Underwater
Drawn and Quarterly

❑1, Aug 1994 .... 2.95

Underworld
Marvel

❑1, Mar 2006 .... 2.99
❑2, May 2006 .... 2.99
❑3, Jun 2006 .... 2.99
❑4, Jul 2006 .... 2.99
❑5, Aug 2006 .... 2.99

Underworld
DC

❑1, Dec 1987 .... 2.99
❑2, Jan 1988 .... 2.99
❑3, Feb 1988 .... 2.99
❑4, Mar 1988 .... 2.99

Underworld
Death

❑1, b&w 2.00

Underworld: Evolution
Idea & Design Works

❑1, Feb 2006 .... 7.49

Underworld Unleashed
DC

❑1, Nov 1995; MWa (w); 1: Neron. D: Mongul. D: Boomerang. D: Weather Wizard. D: Mirror Master. D: Heat Wave. D: Captain Cold 3.50
❑2, Dec 1995; MWa (w); D: Marla Bloom 3.25
❑3, Dec 1995 MWa (w) 3.25

Underworld Unleashed: Abyss: Hell's Sentinel
DC

❑1, Dec 1995 .... 2.95

Underworld Unleashed: Apokolips: Dark Uprising
DC

❑1, Nov 1995 .... 1.95

Underworld Unleashed: Batman: Devil's Asylum
DC

❑1 1995 .... 2.95

Underworld Unleashed: Patterns of Fear
DC

❑1, Dec 1995; One-shot 2.95

Undie Dog
Halley's

❑1, b&w 1.50

Unexpected
DC

❑105, Feb 1968, GK, RMo (a); Series continued from Tales of the Unexpected #104 .... 50.00
❑106, Apr 1968, Reprint from Strange Adventure #32 .... 35.00
❑107, Jun 1968, Reprint from Strange Adventure #28 .... 35.00
❑108, Aug 1968 .... 35.00
❑109, Oct 1968 .... 35.00
❑110, Dec 1968 .... 35.00
❑111, Feb 1969 .... 35.00
❑112, Apr 1969 .... 35.00
❑113, Jun 1969, NA (c); CS (a) 35.00
❑114, Aug 1969 .... 30.00
❑115, Oct 1969 .... 30.00
❑116, Dec 1969 .... 30.00
❑117, Feb 1970 .... 25.00
❑118, Apr 1970, NA (c); MA, GT (a) 25.00
❑119, Jun 1970, NC (c); MA, BWr (a) 25.00
❑120, Aug 1970 .... 25.00
❑121, Oct 1970, NA (c); BWr, GT, DD (a) 25.00
❑122, Dec 1970 .... 25.00
❑123, Feb 1971 .... 25.00
❑124, Apr 1971 .... 25.00
❑125, Jul 1971 .... 25.00
❑126, Aug 1971; Reprints from house of Secrets #9 and House of Mystery #149 .... 25.00
❑127, Sep 1971; Reprints form House of Secrets #8, Sensation Comics #107 and 108 .... 25.00
❑128, Oct 1971; NC (c); BWr, NC (a); Reprints from House of Mystery #89 and 94 .... 45.00
❑129, Nov 1971; Reprints from House of Secrets #2 and House of Mystery #70 .... 20.00
❑130, Dec 1971; Reprints from Tales of the Unexpected #3 and 5 .... 20.00
❑131, Jan 1972; NC (c); DD, JM, NC (a); Reprints from House of Mystery #20 and My Greatest Adventure #30 .... 20.00
❑132, Feb 1972; Reprints from House of Secrets #1 and 6 .... 20.00
❑133, Mar 1972; Reprints from House of Mystery #8 and 21 .... 20.00
❑134, Apr 1972; Reprints from House of Mystery #18 and House of Secrets #58 .... 20.00
❑135, May 1972; Reprints from House of Mystery #96 and Tales of the Unexpected #9 .... 20.00
❑136, Jun 1972; Reprints from House of Secrets #52 and Tales of the Unexpected #16 .... 20.00
❑137, Jul 1972 .... 20.00
❑138, Aug 1972 .... 20.00
❑139, Sep 1972, NC (c); GT (a) 20.00
❑140, Oct 1972, NC (c) 15.00
❑141, Nov 1972 .... 15.00
❑142, Dec 1972, NC (c) 15.00
❑143, Jan 1973, NC (c) 15.00
❑144, Feb 1973 .... 15.00
❑145, Mar 1973 .... 15.00
❑146, Apr 1973, NC (c) 15.00
❑147, Jun 1973 .... 15.00
❑148, Jul 1973 .... 15.00
❑149, Aug 1973, NC (c) 15.00
❑150, Sep 1973 .... 15.00
❑151, Oct 1973, NC (c) 15.00
❑152, Nov 1973 .... 15.00
❑153, Dec 1973, NC (c) 15.00
❑154, Jan 1974, NC (c); DP (a) 15.00
❑155, Feb 1974 .... 15.00
❑156, Mar 1974 .... 15.00
❑157, Jun 1974, 100 Page giant; Reprints from House of Mystery #83, 92, 101, 118, House of Secrets #1, Tales of the Unexpected #7 and My Greatest Adventure #10; 100 Page giant 30.00
❑158, Aug 1974, 100 Page giant; Reprints from House of Secrets #18, house of Mystery #36, 144, Tales of the Unexpected 319 and Sensation Mystery #113; 100 Page giant 30.00
❑159, Oct 1974, 100 Page giant; Reprints from Tales of the Unexpected #15, 89, House of Mystery #2, 6, 30, My Greatest Adventure #67, House of Secrets #14 and The Unexpected #105; 100 Page giant 30.00
❑160, Dec 1974, 100 Page giant; NC (c); MM, MA, GC, PB (a); Reprints from Tales of the Unexpected #5, 18, 88, 93, My Greatest Adventure #74, House of Mystery #5, 56, House of Secrets #6 and The Unexpected #119; 100 Page giant 30.00
❑161, Feb 1975, 100 Page giant; Reprints from House of Secrets #11, The Unexpected #115, 116, 117 My Greatest Adventure #8 and 72; 100 Page giant 30.00
❑162, Mar 1975, 100 Page giant; Reprints from the Unexpected #109, 112, House of Mystery #1, 4, 72, My Greatest Adventure #71 and Tales of the Unexpected #104; 100 Page giant 30.00
❑163, Apr 1975 .... 10.00
❑164, May 1975 .... 10.00
❑165, Jun 1975 .... 10.00
❑166, Jul 1975 .... 10.00
❑167, Aug 1975 .... 10.00
❑168, Sep 1975 .... 10.00
❑169, Oct 1975 .... 10.00
❑170, Dec 1975 .... 10.00
❑171, Feb 1976 .... 10.00
❑172, Apr 1976 .... 10.00
❑173, Jun 1976 .... 10.00
❑174, Aug 1976 .... 10.00
❑175, Oct 1976 .... 10.00
❑176, Dec 1976 .... 10.00
❑177, Feb 1977 .... 10.00
❑178, Apr 1977 .... 10.00
❑179, Jun 1977 .... 10.00
❑180, Aug 1977 .... 10.00
❑181, Oct 1977 .... 10.00
❑182, Dec 1977 .... 10.00
❑183, Feb 1978 .... 10.00
❑184, Apr 1978 .... 10.00
❑185, Jun 1978 .... 10.00
❑186, Aug 1978 .... 10.00
❑187, Oct 1978 .... 10.00
❑188, Dec 1978 .... 10.00
❑189, Feb 1979 SD (a) 7.00
❑190, Apr 1979 .... 7.00
❑191, Jun 1979 JO (c); MR (a) 10.00
❑192, Aug 1979 RE, RT (a) 7.00
❑193, Oct 1979 RT (a) 7.00
❑194, Dec 1979 .... 7.00
❑195, Feb 1980 .... 7.00
❑196, Mar 1980 .... 7.00

Warlord	War Machine	War of the Gods	War of the Worlds	Warrior Nun Areala

Air Force pilot has adventures in lost world ©DC	Stark sidekick Rhodes gets own armor ©Marvel	Circe manipulates pantheons into conflict ©DC	Wells' classic updated to mid-1990s ©Caliber	A gun-wielding convent tenant ©Antarctic

N-MINT

❑197, Apr 1980 7.00
❑198, May 1980 7.00
❑199, Jun 1980 7.00
❑200, Jul 1980 7.00
❑201, Aug 1980 7.00
❑202, Sep 1980 7.00
❑203, Oct 1980 7.00
❑204, Nov 1980 7.00
❑205, Dec 1980 7.00
❑206, Jan 1981 7.00
❑207, Feb 1981 5.00
❑208, Mar 1981 5.00
❑209, Apr 1981 5.00
❑210, May 1981 5.00
❑211, Jun 1981 5.00
❑212, Jul 1981 5.00
❑213, Aug 1981 5.00
❑214, Sep 1981 5.00
❑215, Oct 1981 5.00
❑216, Nov 1981 5.00
❑217, Dec 1981, Abe Lincoln Astronaut cover 5.00
❑218, Jan 1982 5.00
❑219, Feb 1982 5.00
❑220, Mar 1982 5.00
❑221, Apr 1982 5.00
❑222, May 1982; Final Issue 5.00

Unforgiven
Mythic

❑1 2.75

Unfunnies
Avatar

❑1, Jan 2004 5.00
❑2, Mar 2004 3.50

Unfunny X-Cons
Parody

❑1, Sep 1992; three variant covers (X, Y, Z) 2.50
❑1/2nd; 2nd Printing with trading card 2.50

Unholy
Avatar

❑1 2005 3.99
❑1/Foil 2005 5.00
❑1/Platinum 2005 10.00
❑1/Haunted 2005 5.99
❑1/Premium 2005 8.00
❑1/Wraparound 2005 5.00
❑2 2005 3.50

Unicorn Isle
Apple

❑1, Oct 1986, b&w 2.00
❑2, Nov 1986, b&w 2.00
❑3, Dec 1986, b&w 2.00
❑4, Jan 1987 2.00
❑5, Feb 1987, b&w; While planned as a 12-issue series, #6-12 do not exist 2.00

Unicorn King
Kz Comics

❑1, Dec 1986, b&w 2.00

Union
Image

❑0, Jul 1994 2.50
❑0/A, Jul 1994; Variant edition cover; alternate cover 2.50
❑1, Jun 1993; Foil-embossed cover 2.50

N-MINT

❑2, Oct 1993 1.95
❑3, Dec 1993; V: Mnemo 1.95
❑4, Mar 1994 1.95

Union
Image

❑1, Feb 1995 2.50
❑2, Mar 1995 2.50
❑3, Apr 1995 2.50
❑4, May 1995; with cards 2.50
❑5, Jun 1995; 1: Rhiannon 2.50
❑6, Jul 1995 2.50
❑7, Aug 1995 2.50
❑8, Oct 1995 2.50
❑9, Feb 1996; Story continued in Union: Final Vengeance; covers says Dec, indicia says Feb 2.50

Union: Final Vengeance
Image

❑1, Oct 1997; concludes story from Union #9 2.50

Union Jack
Marvel

❑1, Dec 1998; gatefold summary 2.99
❑2, Jan 1999; gatefold summary 2.99
❑3, Feb 1999 2.99

Union Jacks
Anacom

❑1, b&w 2.00

Union Jack
Marvel

❑1, Nov 2006 2.99
❑2, Dec 2006 2.99
❑3, Jan 2007 2.99
❑4, Mar 2007 2.99

Unity
Valiant

❑0, Aug 1992; Blue cover (regular edition); BL (a) 5.00
❑0/Red, Aug 1992 75.00
❑1, Oct 1992 BL (w); BL (a) 4.00
❑1/Gold, Oct 1992; Gold edition; BL (w); BL (a) 10.00
❑1/Platinum, Oct 1992; Platinum edition; BL (w); BL (a) 12.00
❑YB 1, Feb 1994; YB 1; A: X-O Manowar. A: Solar. a.k.a. Unity: The Lost Chapter; cardstock cover 3.95

Unity: The Lost Chapter
Valiant

❑1, Feb 1995 5.00

Unity 2000
Acclaim

❑1, Nov 1999 JSn (c); JSn (a) 2.50
❑1/A, Nov 1999, Dynamic Forces variant; Includes certificate of authenticity 5.00
❑2, Dec 1999 JSn (a) 2.50
❑3, Jan 2000; JSn (c); JSn (a); series canceled 2.50

Universal Monsters: Dracula
Dark Horse

❑1 1993; Based on the classic Universal pictures film 4.95

N-MINT

Universal Monsters: Frankenstein
Dark Horse

❑1 1993; Based on the classic Universal pictures film 3.95

Universal Monsters: The Creature from the Black Lagoon
Dark Horse

❑1, Aug 1993; NN; Movie adaptation 4.95

Universal Monsters: The Mummy
Dark Horse

❑1 1993; Based on the classic Universal pictures film 4.95

Universal Pictures Presents Dracula
Dell

❑1, Sep 1963 160.00

Universal Soldier
Now

❑1, Sep 1992, newsstand 1.95
❑1/Direct ed., Sep 1992, Hologram cover; direct sale 2.50
❑1/Variant, Sep 1992, Waldenbooks; has UPC box and hologram 2.50
❑2, Oct 1992, newsstand 1.95
❑2/Direct ed., Oct 1992, direct-sale 2.50
❑3, Nov 1992, newsstand 1.95
❑3/Direct ed., Nov 1992, uncensored 2.50

Universe
Image

❑1, Aug 2001; Crain cover (monster clutching suspended man) 2.50
❑2, Oct 2001 2.50
❑3, Nov 2001 2.50
❑4, Jan 2002 2.50
❑5, Mar 2002 2.50
❑6, Apr 2002 2.50
❑7, Apr 2002 2.50
❑8, Jul 2002 4.95

Universe X
Marvel

❑0, Sep 2000; Cardstock cover; follows events of Earth X 3.99
❑1, Oct 2000; cardstock cover 3.50
❑2, Nov 2000; cardstock cover 3.50
❑3, Dec 2000; cardstock cover 3.50
❑4, Jan 2001; cardstock cover 3.50
❑5, Feb 2001; cardstock cover 3.50
❑6, Mar 2001; cardstock cover 3.50
❑7, Apr 2001; cardstock cover 3.50
❑8, May 2001; cardstock cover 3.50
❑9, Jun 2001; Cardstock cover 3.50
❑10, Jul 2001; Cardstock cover 3.50
❑11, Aug 2001; Cardstock cover 3.50
❑12, Sep 2001; Cardstock cover 3.50
❑X, Nov 2001 3.99

Universe X: Beasts
Marvel

❑1, Jun 2001 3.99

Universe X: Cap
Marvel

❑1, Feb 2001; ARo (c); TY (a); D: Captain America 5.00

Other grades: Multiply price above by 5/6 for VF/NM • 2/3 for VERY FINE • 1/3 for FINE • 1/5 for VERY GOOD • 1/8 for GOOD

Universe X: Iron Men
Marvel

❑1, Sep 2001 ... 3.99

Universe X: Omnibus
Marvel

❑1, Jun 2001 ... 3.99

Universe X: Spidey
Marvel

❑1, Jan 2001 ARo (c); ARo (w); BG, JR (a) ... 10.00
❑1/A, Jan 2001; ARo (c); ARo (w); BG, JR (a); Dynamic Forces variant ... 6.00
❑1/B, Jan 2001; ARo (c); ARo (w); BG, JR (a); Dynamic Forces variant sketch cover ... 10.00
❑1/C, Jan 2001; recalled edition with potentially libelous statement in background of one panel; ARo (c); ARo (w); BG, JR (a) ... 90.00

Unknown Soldier
DC

❑205, May 1977 ... 5.00
❑206, Jul 1977 ... 5.00
❑207, Sep 1977, AM (c); AM, RE (a) ... 5.00
❑208, Oct 1977 ... 5.00
❑209, Nov 1977, JKu (c); FT, JKu (a) ... 5.00
❑210, Dec 1977, JKu (c) ... 5.00
❑211, Jan 1978, JKu (c); JKu, RH (a) ... 4.00
❑212, Feb 1978, JKu (c) ... 4.00
❑213, Mar 1978 ... 4.00
❑214, Apr 1978, JKu (c); RT (a); A: Mademoiselle Marie ... 4.00
❑215, May 1978, JKu (c); JKu (a) ... 4.00
❑216, Jun 1978, RT (a) ... 4.00
❑217, Jul 1978, JKu (c); JKu (a) ... 4.00
❑218, Aug 1978 ... 4.00
❑219, Sep 1978, JKu (c); JKu, FM, RT (a) ... 4.00
❑220, Oct 1978, JKu (c); JKu, RE (a) ... 4.00
❑221, Nov 1978, RT (a) ... 4.00
❑222, Dec 1978, JKu (c); JKu (a) ... 4.00
❑223, Jan 1979, RT (a) ... 4.00
❑224, Feb 1979, JKu (c); DA, RT (a) ... 4.00
❑225, Mar 1979 ... 4.00
❑226, Apr 1979, JKu (c); JKu (a) ... 4.00
❑227, May 1979, JKu (c); JKu (a) ... 4.00
❑228, Jun 1979, JKu (c); JKu (a) ... 4.00
❑229, Jul 1979, JKu (c); JKu (a) ... 4.00
❑230, Aug 1979 ... 3.00
❑231, Sep 1979, JKu (c); JKu (a) ... 3.00
❑232, Oct 1979, JKu (c); JKu (a) ... 3.00
❑233, Nov 1979, JKu (c); JKu (a) ... 3.00
❑234, Dec 1979 ... 3.00
❑235, Jan 1980, RT (a) ... 3.00
❑236, Feb 1980 ... 3.00
❑237, Mar 1980 ... 3.00
❑238, Apr 1980 ... 3.00
❑239, May 1980 ... 3.00
❑240, Jun 1980 ... 3.00
❑241, Jul 1980, JKu (c); JKu (a) ... 3.00
❑242, Aug 1980, JKu (c) ... 3.00
❑243, Sep 1980, RE (a) ... 3.00
❑244, Oct 1980, JKu (c); TY, JKu, RE (a); A: Captain Storm ... 3.00
❑245, Nov 1980, RE (a) ... 3.00
❑246, Dec 1980 ... 3.00
❑247, Jan 1981, JKu (c); JKu (a) ... 3.00
❑248, Feb 1981, O: Unknown Soldier ... 5.00
❑249, Mar 1981, JKu (c); JKu (a); O: Unknown Soldier ... 5.00
❑250, Apr 1981 ... 3.00
❑251, May 1981, JSe (a) ... 3.00
❑252, Jun 1981, JSe (a) ... 3.00
❑253, Jul 1981, JKu (c); JSe (a) ... 3.00
❑254, Aug 1981 ... 3.00
❑255, Sep 1981 ... 3.00
❑256, Oct 1981 ... 3.00
❑257, Nov 1981, JKu (c); JKu (a); O: Capt. Storm. A: John F. Kennedy ... 3.00
❑258, Dec 1981, DS (a); A: John F. Kennedy ... 3.00
❑259, Jan 1982, DS (a); A: John F. Kennedy ... 3.00
❑260, Feb 1982, JKu (c); RE (a) ... 3.00
❑261, Mar 1982, RE (a) ... 3.00
❑262, Apr 1982 ... 3.00
❑263, May 1982 ... 3.00
❑264, Jun 1982, JKu (c); JKu, DS (a) ... 3.00
❑265, Jul 1982 ... 3.00
❑266, Aug 1982 ... 3.00
❑267, Sep 1982 ... 3.00
❑268, Oct 1982, JKu (c); JKu (a); D: Chat Noir. D: Hitler. D: The Unknown Soldier. Fall of Berlin ... 5.00

Unknown Soldier
DC

❑1, Win 1988; O: Unknown Soldier ... 2.50
❑2, Hol 1988 ... 2.50
❑3, Jan 1989 ... 2.50
❑4, Mar 1989 ... 2.50
❑5, Apr 1989 ... 2.50
❑6, May 1989 ... 2.50
❑7, Jul 1989 ... 2.50
❑8, Aug 1989 ... 2.50
❑9, Sep 1989 ... 2.50
❑10, Oct 1989 ... 2.50
❑11, Nov 1989 ... 2.50
❑12, Dec 1989 ... 2.50

Unknown Soldier
DC / Vertigo

❑1, Apr 1997 ... 2.50
❑2, May 1997 ... 2.50
❑3, Jun 1997 ... 2.50
❑4, Jul 1997 ... 2.50

Unknown Worlds
ACG

❑1, Aug 1960 ... 90.00
❑2, Sep 1960 ... 60.00
❑3, Oct 1960 ... 45.00
❑4, Dec 1960 ... 40.00
❑5, Feb 1961 ... 40.00
❑6, Mar 1961 ... 35.00
❑7, Apr 1961 ... 35.00
❑8, Jun 1961 ... 35.00
❑9, Aug 1961; Dinosaurs ... 50.00
❑10, Sep 1961 ... 35.00
❑11, Oct 1961 ... 28.00
❑12, Dec 1961, CCB (a) ... 28.00
❑13, Feb 1962 ... 28.00
❑14, Mar 1962 ... 28.00
❑15, Apr 1962 ... 28.00
❑16, Jun 1962 ... 28.00
❑17, Aug 1962 ... 28.00
❑18, Sep 1962, CCB (a) ... 28.00
❑19, Oct 1962 ... 28.00
❑20, Dec 1962 ... 28.00
❑21, Feb 1963 ... 20.00
❑22, Mar 1963 ... 20.00
❑23, Apr 1963 ... 20.00
❑24, Jun 1963 ... 20.00
❑25, Aug 1963 ... 20.00
❑26, Sep 1963 ... 20.00
❑27, Oct 1963 ... 20.00
❑28, Dec 1963 ... 20.00
❑29, Feb 1964 ... 20.00
❑30, Mar 1964 ... 20.00
❑31, Apr 1964, avg sales of 143,258;cites 300,000 avg press run;Statement of Ownership for 1963 appears ... 16.00
❑32, Jun 1964 ... 16.00
❑33, Aug 1964 ... 16.00
❑34, Sep 1964 ... 16.00
❑35, Oct 1964 ... 16.00
❑36, Dec 1964, JCr (a) ... 16.00
❑37, Feb 1965 ... 16.00
❑38, Mar 1965 ... 16.00
❑39, Apr 1965 ... 16.00
❑40, Jun 1965 ... 16.00
❑41, Aug 1965 ... 12.00
❑42, Sep 1965 ... 12.00
❑43, Oct 1965 ... 12.00
❑44, Dec 1965 ... 12.00
❑45, Feb 1966 ... 12.00
❑46, Mar 1966 ... 12.00
❑47, Apr 1966, KS (c); AW, JCr (a) ... 12.00
❑48, Jun 1966 ... 12.00
❑49, Aug 1966, SD (a) ... 12.00
❑50, Nov 1966, SD (a) ... 12.00
❑51, Oct 1966 ... 12.00
❑52, Dec 1966 ... 12.00
❑53, Feb 1967 ... 12.00
❑54, Mar 1967 ... 12.00
❑55, Apr 1967 ... 12.00
❑56, Jun 1967 ... 12.00
❑57, Aug 1967, Final Issue ... 12.00

Unknown Worlds of Frank Brunner
Eclipse

❑1, Aug 1985 ... 1.75
❑2, Aug 1985 ... 1.75

Unknown Worlds of Science Fiction
Marvel

❑1, Jan 1975, b&w; magazine ... 12.00
❑2, Mar 1975, b&w; magazine ... 7.00
❑3, May 1975, b&w; magazine ... 7.00
❑4, Jul 1975, b&w; magazine ... 7.00
❑5, Sep 1975, b&w; magazine ... 7.00
❑6, Nov 1975, b&w; magazine ... 7.00
❑Special 1 1976, Reprints ... 10.00

Unleashed!
Triumphant

❑1 ... 2.50

Unlimited Access
Marvel

❑1, Dec 1997, A: Wonder Woman. A: Spider-Man. A: Juggernaut. crossover with DC ... 2.50
❑2, Jan 1998, A: X-Men. A: Legion of Super-Heroes. crossover with DC ... 2.00
❑3, Feb 1998, A: Justice League of America. A: Avengers. crossover with DC ... 2.00
❑4, Mar 1998, crossover with DC; new Amalgams ... 3.00

Unsupervised Existence
Fantagraphics

❑1, b&w ... 2.00
❑2, b&w ... 2.00
❑3 ... 2.00
❑4 ... 2.00
❑5 ... 2.00
❑6 ... 2.00
❑7 ... 2.00
❑7/2nd; 2nd printing ... 2.00

Untamed
Marvel / Epic

❑1, Jun 1993; Embossed cover ... 2.50
❑2, Jul 1993 ... 1.95
❑3, Aug 1993 ... 1.95

Untamed Love
Fantagraphics

❑1, Nov 1987 ... 2.00

Untold Legend of Captain Marvel
Marvel

❑1, Apr 1997 ... 2.50
❑2, May 1997; V: Imperial Guard ... 2.50
❑3, Jun 1997; V: Brood ... 2.50

Untold Legend of the Batman
DC

❑1, Jul 1980, JBy, JA (a); O: Batman ... 3.00
❑1/2nd, JL (c); JBy, JA (a) ... 1.00
❑1/3rd, ca. 1980; JL (c); JBy, JA (a); Smaller-sized reprint with cardboard cover. Says "Special MPI audio edition" on cover ... 2.00
❑2, Aug 1980, JA (a); O: Robin (Dick Grayson); O: Alfred; O: Joker; O: Two-Face ... 2.00
❑3, Sep 1980, DG (c); JSa, JA (a); O: Commissioner Gordon; O: Batgirl (Barbara Gordon) ... 2.00

Untold Origin of Femforce
AC

❑1 1989; O: Femforce; Collects origins of members and reprints parts of Femforce #1-2, plus an additional framing sequence, all in color ... 12.95

Untold Origin of Ms. Victory
AC

❑1, Dec 1989, b&w; O: Ms. Victory ... 2.50

Untold Tales of Chastity
Chaos

❑1, Nov 2000 ... 2.95

Untold Tales of Lady Death
Chaos

❑1, Nov 2000, O: Lady Death ... 2.95

Untold Tales of Purgatori
Chaos

❑1, Nov 2000 ... 2.95

Warriors of Plasm	Watchmen	Way of the Rat	Weapon X	Web
	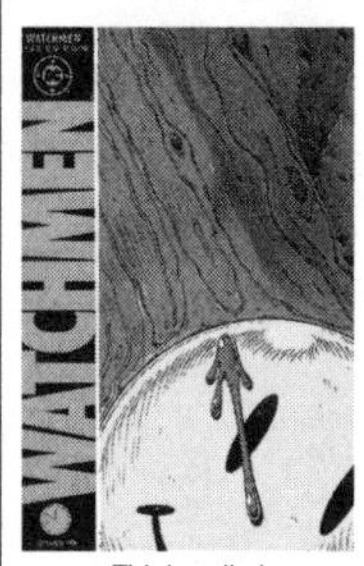			
Trading cards contain true first appearances ©Defiant	Thinly veiled Charlton copies regroup ©DC	Apprentice thief and monkey steal magic ring ©CrossGen	Wolverine's enemies unite against him ©Marvel	Government agents used tech for powers ©DC

N-MINT

Untold Tales of Spider-Man
Marvel

- ❑-1, Jul 1997; JR (c); FH (w); FH, JR (a); Flashback ... 1.00
- ❑1, Sep 1995; KB (w); O: Spider-Man ... 1.50
- ❑2, Oct 1995 KB (w) ... 1.25
- ❑3, Nov 1995; KB (w); V: Sandman ... 1.25
- ❑4, Dec 1995; KB (w); V: J. Jonah Jameson. Flip book with Avengers Unplugged #2 ... 1.00
- ❑5, Jan 1996; KB (w); V: Vulture ... 1.00
- ❑6, Feb 1996 KB (w); A: Human Torch ... 1.00
- ❑7, Mar 1996; KB (w); O: Electro. Flip book with Fantastic Four Unplugged #4 ... 1.00
- ❑8, Apr 1996; KB (w); V: Enforcers. Flip book with Avengers Unplugged #4 ... 1.00
- ❑9, May 1996; KB (w); V: Lizard ... 1.00
- ❑10, Jun 1996 KB (w) ... 1.00
- ❑11, Jul 1996 KB (w) ... 1.00
- ❑12, Aug 1996; KB (w); O: Betty Brant; V: Vulture; Takes place after Amazing Spider-Man #12; Betty Brant family background revealed ... 1.00
- ❑13, Sep 1996; KB (w); D: Bluebird. V: Black Knight. D: Bluebird (Sally Avril); V: Black Knight; Takes place after Amazing Spider-Man #12; Human Torch II (Johnny Storm) cameo ... 1.00
- ❑14, Oct 1996; KB (w); V: The Scorcher; Takes place after Amazing Spider-Man #13 ... 1.00
- ❑15, Nov 1996 KB (w) ... 1.00
- ❑16, Dec 1996 KB (w); A: Mary Jane ... 1.00
- ❑17, Jan 1997; KB (w); AW (a); O: Hawkeye. A: Hawkeye. V: Hawkeye; V: Hawkeye I (Clint Barton) ... 1.00
- ❑18, Feb 1997; KB (w); AW (a); A: Headsman. V: Headsman ... 1.00
- ❑19, Mar 1997; KB (w); AW (a); V: Doctor Octopus. Flip book with Uncanny Origins #7 ... 1.00
- ❑20, Apr 1997; KB (w); AW (a); O: The Vulture. V: Vulture. Flip book with Uncanny Origins #8 ... 1.00
- ❑21, May 1997; A: X-Men. V: Menace; Takes place after Amazing Spider-Man #18 pages 1-2 ... 1.00
- ❑22, Jun 1997; KB (w); V: Scarecrow; V: Green Goblin I (Norman Osborn); Takes place concurrently with Amazing Spider-Man #18 pages 3-22 ... 1.00
- ❑23, Aug 1997; KB (w); V: Crime Master; Takes place after Amazing Spider-Man #20 ... 1.00
- ❑24, Sep 1997; KB (w); BMc (a); V: Batwing; Takes place after Amazing Spider-Man #22 ... 1.00
- ❑25, Oct 1997; KB (w); BMc (a); V: Green Goblin. cover says Sep, indicia says Oct ... 1.00
- ❑Ann 1996, ca. 1996; KB (w); GK, KJ (a); A: Namor. A: Fantastic Four. Untold Tales of Spider-Man '96 ... 1.95
- ❑Ann 1997, ca. 1997; FH, KB (w); FH (a); Untold Tales of Spider-Man '97 ... 1.95

Untold Tales of the New Universe: Justice
Marvel

- ❑1, May 2006 ... 2.99

N-MINT

Untold Tales of the New Universe: D.P. 7
Marvel

- ❑1, Jun 2006 ... 2.99

Untold Tales of the New Universe: Nightmask
Marvel

- ❑1, May 2006 ... 2.99

Untold Tales of the New Universe: Psi-Force
Marvel

- ❑1, Jun 2006 ... 2.99

Untold Tales of the New Universe: Star Brand
Marvel

- ❑1, May 2006 ... 2.99

Untouchables
Dell

- ❑3, Jul 1962 ... 50.00
- ❑4, Aug 1962 ... 50.00

Untouchables
Caliber

- ❑1, Aug 1997 ... 2.95
- ❑2, Sep 1997 ... 2.95
- ❑3, Oct 1997 ... 2.95
- ❑4, Nov 1997 ... 2.95

Untouchables
Eastern

- ❑1 ... 1.00
- ❑2 ... 1.00

Up from Bondage
Fantagraphics / Eros

- ❑1, Jul 1991, b&w; Adult ... 2.95

Up From the Deep
Rip Off

- ❑1, ca. 1971 ... 3.00

Urban Hipster
Alternative

- ❑1, Oct 1998, b&w ... 2.95

Urban Legends
Dark Horse

- ❑1 1993, b&w ... 3.00

Urotsukidoji: Legend of the Overfiend
CPM

- ❑1, Jul 1998; b&w ... 2.95
- ❑2, Aug 1998 ... 2.95
- ❑3, Sep 1998 ... 2.95

Urth 4
Continuity

- ❑1, May 1989 ... 2.00
- ❑2, Apr 1990 ... 2.00
- ❑3, Oct 1990 ... 2.00
- ❑4, Dec 1990 ... 2.00

Urza-Mishra War on the World of Magic: The Gathering
Acclaim / Armada

- ❑1, Sep 1996; squarebound; polybagged with Soldevi Steam Beast card ... 5.95
- ❑2, Sep 1996; squarebound; polybagged with Soldevi Steam Beast and Phyrexian War Beast cards ... 5.95

N-MINT

U.S. 1
Marvel

- ❑1, May 1983, AM (c); AM (w); HT (a); O: U.S. 1 ... 1.00
- ❑2, Jun 1983, BSz (c); AM (w); HT (a) ... 1.00
- ❑3, Jul 1983, MG (c); AM (w); FS (a) ... 1.00
- ❑4, Aug 1983, MG (c); AM (w); FS (a) ... 1.00
- ❑5, Sep 1983, MG (c); AM (w); FS (a) ... 1.00
- ❑6, Oct 1983, MG (c); AM (w); FS (a) ... 1.00
- ❑7, Dec 1983, MG (c); AM (w); FS (a) ... 1.00
- ❑8, Feb 1984, MG (c); AM (w); FS (a) ... 1.00
- ❑9, Apr 1984 ... 1.00
- ❑10, Jun 1984, MG (c); AM (w); FS (a) . 1.00
- ❑11, Aug 1984, MG (c); AM (w); FS (a) . 1.00
- ❑12, Oct 1984, AM (w); SD (a) ... 1.00

U.S.Agent
Marvel

- ❑1, Jun 1993 ... 2.00
- ❑2, Jul 1993 ... 2.00
- ❑3, Aug 1993 ... 2.00
- ❑4, Sep 1993 ... 2.00

USAgent
Marvel

- ❑1, Aug 2001; D: Machete ... 2.99
- ❑2, Sep 2001 ... 2.99
- ❑3, Oct 2001 ... 2.99

Usagi Yojimbo
Fantagraphics

- ❑1, Jul 1987, b&w ... 8.00
- ❑1/2nd, Jul 1987; 2nd printing ... 2.50
- ❑2, Sep 1987, b&w ... 5.00
- ❑3, Oct 1987, b&w ... 5.00
- ❑4, Nov 1987, b&w ... 3.50
- ❑5, Jan 1988, b&w ... 3.50
- ❑6, Feb 1988, b&w ... 3.00
- ❑7, Mar 1988, b&w; Patrick Rabbit story 3.00
- ❑8, May 1988, b&w; Rockhoppers story 3.00
- ❑9, Jul 1988, b&w ... 3.00
- ❑10, Aug 1988, b&w; A: Teenage Mutant Ninja Turtles ... 3.00
- ❑10/2nd, Aug 1988; 2nd printing ... 2.00
- ❑11, Sep 1988, b&w; SA (w); SA (a) ... 2.50
- ❑12, Oct 1988, b&w; Lionheart story ... 2.50
- ❑13, Jan 1989, b&w; ME (w); indicia says Jan 88; a misprint ... 2.50
- ❑14, Jan 1989, b&w; indicia says Jan 89 2.50
- ❑15, Mar 1989, b&w ... 2.50
- ❑16, May 1989, b&w ... 2.50
- ❑17, Jul 1989, b&w ... 2.50
- ❑18, Oct 1989, b&w ... 2.50
- ❑19, Dec 1989, b&w ... 2.50
- ❑20, Feb 1990, b&w ... 2.50
- ❑21, Apr 1990, b&w; Panda Khan story. 2.50
- ❑22, May 1990, b&w; Space Ark story .. 2.50
- ❑23, Jul 1990, b&w; Lionheart story ... 2.50
- ❑24, Sep 1990, b&w; Lone Goat & Kid .. 2.50
- ❑25, Nov 1990, b&w; Lionheart story ... 2.50
- ❑26, Jan 1991, b&w; indicia says Jan 90; another misprint ... 2.50
- ❑27, Mar 1991, b&w; Coyote story ... 2.50
- ❑28, May 1991, b&w; Plato Potts story . 2.50
- ❑29, Jul 1991, b&w ... 2.50
- ❑30, Sep 1991, b&w; back cover reproduces front cover without logos ... 2.50

Other grades: Multiply price above by 5/6 for VF/NM • 2/3 for VERY FINE • 1/3 for FINE • 1/5 for VERY GOOD • 1/8 for GOOD

	N-MINT
❑31, Nov 1991, b&w; Penrod & Balboa story	2.50
❑32, Feb 1992, b&w	2.50
❑33, Apr 1992, b&w	2.50
❑34, Jun 1992, b&w, Panda Khan story.	2.50
❑35, Aug 1992, b&w, Lionheart story	2.50
❑36, Nov 1992, b&w; Lionheart story	2.50
❑37, Feb 1993, b&w; Hepcats story	2.50
❑38, Mar 1993, b&w; Final Issue; b&w	2.50
❑Special 1, Nov 1989; Color special #1	3.50
❑Special 2, Oct 1991; Color special #2	3.50
❑Special 3, Oct 1992; Color special #3	3.50
❑Summer 1, Oct 1986, b&w; SA (a); introduction by Mark Evanier	5.00

Usagi Yojimbo
Mirage

❑1, Mar 1993, A: Teenage Mutant Ninja Turtles	4.50
❑2, May 1993 A: Teenage Mutant Ninja Turtles	3.50
❑3, Jul 1993 A: Teenage Mutant Ninja Turtles	3.50
❑4, Sep 1993	3.50
❑5, Nov 1993; Indica states September 1993	3.50
❑6, Jan 1994	3.00
❑7, Apr 1994	3.00
❑8, Jun 1994	3.00
❑9, Aug 1994	3.00
❑10, Oct 1994	3.00
❑11, Dec 1994	2.75
❑12, Feb 1995	2.75
❑13, Apr 1995	2.75
❑14, Jun 1995	2.75
❑15, Aug 1995; 1: Lionheart (in color)	2.75
❑16, Oct 1995; Final Issue	2.75

Usagi Yojimbo
Dark Horse

❑1, Apr 1996, Cover marked 1 of 3; b&w series	4.00
❑2, May 1996, Cover marked 2 of 3	3.00
❑3, Jun 1996, Cover marked 3 of 3	3.00
❑4, Jul 1996	3.00
❑5, Aug 1996	3.00
❑6, Oct 1996	3.00
❑7, Nov 1996	3.00
❑8, Dec 1996	3.00
❑9, Jan 1997	3.00
❑10, Feb 1997, b&w	3.00
❑11, Mar 1997, b&w	3.00
❑12, Apr 1997, b&w	3.00
❑13, Aug 1997, b&w	3.00
❑14, Sep 1997, b&w	2.95
❑15, Oct 1997, b&w	2.95
❑16, Nov 1997, b&w	2.95
❑17, Jan 1998, b&w	2.95
❑18, Feb 1998, b&w	2.95
❑19, Mar 1998, b&w	2.95
❑20, Apr 1998, b&w	2.95
❑21, Jun 1998, b&w	2.95
❑22, Jul 1998, b&w	2.95
❑23, Sep 1998, b&w	2.95
❑24, Oct 1998, b&w	2.95
❑25, Nov 1998, Momo-Usagi-Taro	2.95
❑26, Jan 1999, b&w	2.95
❑27, Feb 1999, b&w	2.95
❑28, Apr 1999, b&w	2.95
❑29, May 1999, b&w	2.95
❑30, Jul 1999	2.95
❑31, Sep 1999, b&w	2.95
❑32, Oct 1999, b&w	2.95
❑33, Nov 1999, b&w	2.95
❑34, Dec 1999, b&w	2.95
❑35, Jan 2000, b&w	2.95
❑36, Feb 2000, b&w	2.95
❑37, Apr 2000	2.95
❑38, May 2000	2.95
❑39, Jul 2000, b&w	2.95
❑40, Aug 2000, b&w	2.95
❑41, Sep 2000, b&w	2.95
❑42, Oct 2000, b&w	2.95
❑43, Nov 2000, b&w	2.95
❑44, Dec 2000, b&w	2.95
❑45, Jan 2001, b&w	2.99
❑46, Mar 2001, Wraparound, dyptych cover	2.99
❑47, Apr 2001, Wraparound, dyptych cover	2.99

	N-MINT
❑48, May 2001, b&w	2.99
❑49, Jun 2001, b&w	2.99
❑50, Jul 2001, b&w	2.99
❑51, Aug 2001, b&w	2.99
❑52, Oct 2001, b&w	2.99
❑53, Dec 2001, b&w	2.99
❑54, Jan 2002, b&w	2.99
❑55, Feb 2002, b&w	2.99
❑56, Mar 2002, b&w	2.99
❑57, Apr 2002, b&w	2.99
❑58, May 2002, b&w	2.99
❑59, Jul 2002, b&w	2.99
❑60, Aug 2002, b&w	2.99
❑61, Oct 2002, b&w	2.99
❑62, Nov 2002, b&w	2.99
❑63, Jan 2003, b&w	2.99
❑64, Feb 2003, b&w	2.99
❑65, Mar 2003, b&w	2.99
❑66, Jun 2003, b&w	2.99
❑67, Jul 2003, b&w	2.99
❑68, Jul 2003, Space Usagi pinup by Guy Davis; b&w	2.99
❑69, Oct 2003, b&w	2.99
❑70, Nov 2003, b&w	2.99
❑71, Nov 2003, b&w	2.99
❑72, Dec 2004, b&w	2.99
❑73, Feb 2004, b&w	2.99
❑74, Mar 2004, b&w	2.99
❑75, Apr 2004, b&w	2.99
❑76, May 2004, b&w	2.99
❑77, Aug 2004, b&w	2.99
❑78, Sep 2004, b&w	2.99
❑79, Oct 2004, b&w	2.99
❑80, Nov 2004, b&w	2.99
❑81, Dec 2004, b&w	2.99
❑82, Mar 2005, b&w	2.99
❑83, Jun 2005, b&w	2.99
❑84, Jul 2005, b&w	2.99
❑85, Aug 2005, b&w	2.99
❑86, Sep 2005, b&w	2.99
❑87, Sep 2005; b&w	2.99
❑88, Oct 2005; b&w	2.99
❑90, Feb 2006, b&w	2.99
❑91, Mar 2006, b&w	2.99
❑92, Apr 2006, b&w	2.99
❑93, May 2006; b&w	2.99
❑94, Jun 2006, b&w	2.99
❑95, Sep 2006, b&w	2.99
❑96, Oct 2006; b&w	2.99
❑97, Nov 2006; b&w	2.99
❑98, Dec 2006, b&w	2.99
❑99	2.99
❑100	2.99
❑101	2.99
❑102	2.99
❑103	2.99
❑104	2.99
❑105	2.99
❑106	2.99
❑107	2.99
❑108	2.99
❑109	2.99
❑110	2.99
❑111	2.99
❑112	2.99
❑113	2.99
❑114	2.99
❑115	2.99
❑116	2.99
❑117	2.99
❑118	2.99
❑119	2.99
❑120	2.99
❑121	2.99
❑122	2.99
❑123	2.99
❑124	2.99
❑125	2.99
❑126	2.99
❑127	2.99
❑128	2.99
❑129	2.99
❑130	2.99
❑Special 4, ca. 1997, Color Special	3.50

U.S. Fighting Men
Super

	N-MINT
❑10, ca. 1963, JSe (c)	15.00
❑11	15.00
❑12	12.00
❑13	12.00
❑14	12.00
❑15, ca. 1964, JAb (c); RH (a)	12.00
❑16, ca. 1964	12.00
❑17, ca. 1964	12.00
❑18	12.00

U.S. War Machine 2.0

❑1, Sep 2003	2.99
❑2, Sep 2003	2.99
❑3, Sep 2003	2.99

V
DC

❑1, Feb 1985, Cl (a); Based on TV series	1.50
❑2, Mar 1985, Cl (a)	1.00
❑3, Apr 1985, Cl (a)	1.00
❑4, May 1985, TD (c); Cl (a)	1.00
❑5, Jun 1985	1.00
❑6, Jul 1985, Cl (a)	1.00
❑7, Aug 1985, Cl (a)	1.00
❑8, Sep 1985, Cl (a)	1.00
❑9, Oct 1985, Cl (a)	1.00
❑10, Nov 1985, Cl (a)	1.00
❑11, Dec 1985, Cl (a)	1.00
❑12, Jan 1986, Cl (a)	1.00
❑13, Feb 1986, Cl (a)	1.00
❑14, Mar 1986, Cl (a)	1.00
❑15, Apr 1986, Cl (a)	1.00
❑16, May 1986, Cl (a)	1.00
❑17, Jun 1986, DG (a)	1.00
❑18, Jul 1986, DG (a); Final Issue	1.00

Vagabond
Image

❑1/A, Aug 2000; Pat Lee cover	2.95
❑1/B, Aug 2000; Ryan Benjamin cover	2.95

Vagabond
Viz

❑1, Dec 2001; b&w	4.95
❑2, Dec 2001; b&w	4.95
❑3, Jan 2002; b&w	4.95
❑4, Feb 2002; b&w	4.95
❑5, Mar 2002; b&w	4.95
❑6, Apr 2002; b&w	4.95
❑7, May 2002; b&w	4.95
❑8, Jun 2002; b&w	4.95
❑9, Jul 2002; b&w	4.95
❑10, Aug 2002; b&w	4.95
❑11, Sep 2002; b&w	4.95
❑12, Oct 2002; b&w	4.95
❑13, Nov 2002; b&w	4.95
❑14, Dec 2002; b&w	4.95
❑15, Jan 2003; b&w	4.95

Vaistron
Slave Labor

❑1 2005	2.95
❑2, Jan 2006	2.95

Valentine
Redeye

❑1, Sep 1997, b&w	2.95

Valentino
Renegade

❑1, Apr 1985, b&w; NN	2.00
❑2, Apr 1987, b&w; Valentino Too	2.00
❑3, Apr 1988, b&w; Valentino the 3rd	2.00

Valerian
Fantasy Flight

❑1, Jul 1996, b&w; Heroes of the Equinox	2.95

Valeria, the She-Bat
Continuity

❑1, May 1993; Promotional edition, never available for ordering; NA (c); NA (w); NA (a); no cover price	3.00
❑2 1993; Promotional edition, never available for ordering; Promotional edition, never available for ordering	3.00
❑3 1993; Published out of sequence (after #5)	2.50
❑4 1993; Published out of sequence	2.50
❑5, Nov 1993; A: Knighthawk. Tyvek wraparound cover	2.00

Other grades: Multiply price above by 5/6 for VF/NM • 2/3 for VERY FINE • 1/3 for FINE • 1/5 for VERY GOOD • 1/8 for GOOD

Web of Spider-Man

A slender thread to hang a Spider-title from
©Marvel

Webspinners: Tales of Spider-Man

Updated early adventures for Spider-Man
©Marvel

Weird Melvin

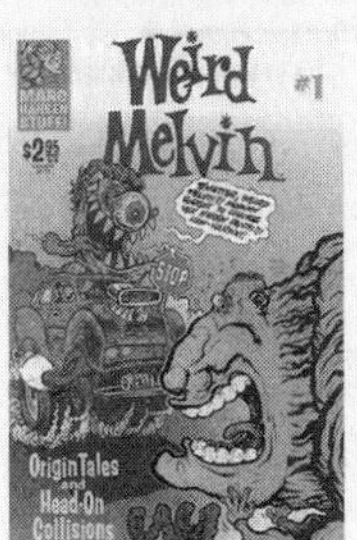

CBG strip inspires ongoing comic book
©Marc Hansen Stuff!

Weird Science

Final reprint series does E.C. stories in order
©Gemstone

Weird Secret Origins 80-Page Giant

More esoteric origins collected
©DC

N-MINT

Valeria the She-Bat
Acclaim / Windjammer

❑1, Sep 1995 ..... 2.50
❑2, Sep 1995 ..... 2.50

Valhalla
Antarctic

❑1, Feb 1999 ..... 2.99

Valiant Efforts
Valiant Comics

❑1, May 1991 ..... 1.95

Valiant Reader
Valiant

❑1 1993; background 0.50

Valiant Varmints
Shanda Fantasy Arts

❑1, b&w 4.50

Valiant Vision Starter Kit
Valiant

❑1, Jan 1994; comic book, glasses, poster 2.95

Valkyr
Ironcat

❑1, ca. 1999; Adult 2.95
❑2, ca. 1999; Adult 2.95
❑3, ca. 1999; Adult 2.95
❑4, ca. 1999 ..... 2.95
❑5, Aug 1999 ..... 2.95

Valkyrie
Eclipse

❑1, May 1987 PG (c); PG (a) 2.00
❑2, Jun 1987 PG (c); PG, BA (a) 2.00
❑3, Aug 1987 PG (c); PG, BA (a) 2.00

Valkyrie
Eclipse

❑1, Jul 1988 BA (a) 2.00
❑2, Aug 1988 BA (a) 2.00
❑3, Sep 1988 BA (a) 2.00

Valkyrie
Marvel

❑1, Jan 1997; Pinups 2.95

Valley of the Dinosaurs
Harvey

❑1, Apr 1975 ..... 10.00
❑2, Jun 1975 ..... 6.00
❑3, Jul 1975 ..... 6.00
❑4, Oct 1975 ..... 6.00
❑5, Dec 1975 ..... 6.00
❑6, Feb 1976 ..... 4.00
❑7, Apr 1976 ..... 4.00
❑8, Jun 1976 ..... 4.00
❑9, Aug 1976 ..... 4.00
❑10, Oct 1976 ..... 4.00
❑11, Dec 1976; Final Issue 4.00

Valor
DC

❑1, Nov 1992; Eclipso The Darness Within: Aftermath tie-in 1.25
❑2, Dec 1992 ..... 1.25
❑3, Jan 1993 ..... 1.25
❑4, Feb 1993; Lobo 1.25
❑5, Mar 1993 ..... 1.25
❑6, Apr 1993 ..... 1.25
❑7, May 1993 ..... 1.25
❑8, Jun 1993 ..... 1.25
❑9, Jul 1993 ..... 1.25
❑10, Aug 1993 ..... 1.25
❑11, Sep 1993 ..... 1.25
❑12, Oct 1993 ..... 1.25
❑13, Nov 1993 ..... 1.50
❑14, Dec 1993 ..... 1.50
❑15, Jan 1994 ..... 1.50
❑16, Feb 1994 ..... 1.50
❑17, Mar 1994 ..... 1.50
❑18, Apr 1994 ..... 1.50
❑19, May 1994 ..... 1.50
❑20, Jun 1994 ..... 1.50
❑21, Jul 1994; Continued in Legionnaires #16 ..... 1.50
❑22, Aug 1994; Continued in Legion of Super-Heroes #60 ..... 1.50
❑23, Sep 1994; Final Issue; Zero Hour Tie-in; End of an Era continued in Legion of Super-Heroes #61 ..... 1.50

Valor
Gemstone

❑1, Oct 1998 ..... 2.50
❑2, Nov 1998 ..... 2.50
❑3, Dec 1998 ..... 2.50
❑4, Jan 1999 ..... 2.50
❑5, Feb 1999 ..... 2.50

Valor Thunderstar and His Fireflies
Now

❑1, Dec 1986 ..... 1.50
❑2 1987 ..... 1.50
❑3 1987 ..... 1.50

Vamperotica
Brainstorm

❑1, ca. 1994, b&w 8.00
❑1/Gold 1994; Gold edition 10.00
❑1/Platinum 1994; Platinum edition 10.00
❑1/2nd, Sep 1994; 2nd printing 4.00
❑1/3rd, Dec 1994; 3rd printing 3.00
❑2 1995, b&w 5.00
❑3 1995, b&w 3.00
❑4 1995, b&w 3.00
❑5 1995, b&w 3.00
❑6 1995, b&w 3.00
❑7 1995, b&w 3.00
❑8, Oct 1995, b&w 3.00
❑9, Nov 1995, b&w 3.00
❑10, Dec 1995, b&w 3.00
❑11, Jan 1996, b&w 3.00
❑12, Feb 1996, b&w 3.00
❑13, Mar 1996, b&w 3.00
❑14, Apr 1996, b&w 3.00
❑15, May 1996, b&w 3.00
❑16, Jun 1996 ..... 3.00
❑16/Nude, Jun 1996; Nude cover 5.00
❑17, Jul 1996 ..... 2.95
❑17/A, Jul 1996; chromium cover 4.95
❑18, Aug 1996 ..... 2.95
❑18/Nude, Aug 1996; Nude cover 5.00
❑19, Sep 1996 ..... 2.95
❑19/A, Sep 1996; variant cover 2.95
❑19/Nude, Sep 1996; Nude cover 5.00
❑20, Oct 1996 ..... 2.95
❑20/Nude, Oct 1996; Nude cover 5.00
❑21, Nov 1996 ..... 2.95
❑22, Dec 1996 ..... 2.95
❑22/Nude, Dec 1996; Nude cover 5.00
❑23, Jan 1997 ..... 3.00
❑24, Feb 1997 ..... 3.00
❑24/Nude, Feb 1997; Nude cover 5.00
❑25, Mar 1997 ..... 3.00
❑26, Apr 1997 ..... 3.00
❑27, May 1997 ..... 3.00
❑28, Jun 1997 ..... 3.00
❑29, Jul 1997 ..... 3.00
❑30, Aug 1997 ..... 3.00
❑31, Sep 1997 ..... 3.00
❑32, Oct 1997 ..... 3.00
❑33, Nov 1997 ..... 3.00
❑34, Dec 1997 ..... 3.00
❑35, Jan 1998 ..... 3.00
❑36, Feb 1998 ..... 3.00
❑37, Mar 1998 ..... 3.00
❑38, Apr 1998 ..... 3.00
❑39, May 1998 ..... 3.00
❑40, Jun 1998 ..... 3.00
❑41, Jul 1998 ..... 3.00
❑42, Aug 1998 ..... 3.00
❑43, Sep 1998 ..... 3.00
❑44, Oct 1998 ..... 3.00
❑45, Nov 1998 ..... 3.00
❑45/Variant, Nov 1998; Photo cover 4.00
❑46, Dec 1998 ..... 3.00
❑47, Jan 1999 ..... 3.00
❑48, Feb 1999 ..... 3.00
❑49, Mar 1999 ..... 3.00
❑Ann 1; Ann #1 ..... 3.95
❑Ann 1/Gold; Ann #1-Gold Edition 8.00
❑SS 1, Oct 1994; Blue cover (regular edition) 4.00

Vamperotica Magazine
Brainstorm

❑1; Adult 4.95
❑1/Nude; Nude cover 6.00
❑1/Variant; Julie Strain Commemorative cover 10.00
❑2; Adult 4.95
❑2/Nude; Nude cover 6.00
❑2/Variant; Photo cover; Adult 5.95
❑3; Adult 4.95
❑3/Nude; Nude cover 6.00
❑3/Variant; Photo cover; Adult 6.00
❑4; Adult 5.95
❑4/Nude; Nude cover 6.00
❑4/Variant; Photo cover; Adult 5.95
❑5; Adult 5.95
❑5/Nude; Nude cover 6.00
❑6; Adult 5.95
❑6/Variant; Photo cover; Adult 5.95
❑7; Adult 5.95
❑7/Variant; Photo cover; Adult 5.95
❑8; Adult 5.95
❑8/Variant; Photo cover; Adult 5.95
❑9; Adult 5.95
❑9/Variant; Photo cover; Adult 5.95
❑10; Adult 5.95
❑10/Variant; Photo cover; Adult 5.95
❑11; Adult 2.50
❑11/Nude; Nude cover 3.00
❑12; Adult 2.50
❑12/Nude; Nude cover 3.00

Other grades: Multiply price above by 5/6 for VF/NM • 2/3 for VERY FINE • 1/3 for FINE • 1/5 for VERY GOOD • 1/8 for GOOD

Vamperotica Presents Countess Vladimira
Brainstorm

- ❑1, Dec 2001, b&w; Adult 3.00

Vampfire
Brainstorm

- ❑1, Sep 1996, b&w; Adult 2.95

Vampfire: Erotic Echo
Brainstorm

- ❑1; Adult 2.95
- ❑2, Feb 1997; Adult 2.95
- ❑2/Nude, Feb 1997; Adult 2.95

Vampfire: Necromantique
Brainstorm

- ❑1, Aug 1997; Adult 2.95
- ❑2; Adult 2.95

Vampire Companion
Innovation

- ❑1; cardstock cover 2.50
- ❑2; cardstock cover 2.50
- ❑3 2.50

Vampire Game
Tokyopop

- ❑1, Jun 2003 9.99
- ❑2, Aug 2003 9.99
- ❑3, Oct 2003 9.99
- ❑4, Jan 2004 9.99
- ❑5, Mar 2004 9.99
- ❑6, May 2004 9.99
- ❑7, Jul 2004 9.99
- ❑8, Sep 2004 9.99
- ❑9, Nov 2004 9.99
- ❑10, Feb 2005 9.99
- ❑11, May 2005 9.99
- ❑12, Aug 2005 9.99
- ❑13, Nov 2005 9.99

Vampire Girls: Bubble Gum & Blood
Angel

- ❑1; Adult 2.95
- ❑2; Adult 2.95

Vampire Girls: California 1969
Angel Entertainment

- ❑0, May 1996, b&w; Adult 2.95
- ❑0/A, May 1996, b&w; nude embossed foil cardstock cover; no indicia 5.00
- ❑0/Nude, May 1996, b&w; Nude cover 5.00
- ❑1, Aug 1996, b&w; Adult 2.95

Vampire Girls, Poets of Blood: San Francisco
Angel

- ❑1; Adult 5.00
- ❑1/Nude; Adult 5.00
- ❑2; Flipbook Previews of Angel 5.00
- ❑2/Nude; Flipbook Previews of Angel 5.00

Vampire Lestat
Innovation

- ❑1, Jan 1990 5.00
- ❑1/2nd; 2nd printing 2.50
- ❑2, Feb 1990 3.00
- ❑2/2nd; 2nd printing 2.50
- ❑2/3rd; 3rd printing 2.50
- ❑3, May 1990 3.00
- ❑3/2nd; 2nd printing 2.50
- ❑4, Jun 1990 2.50
- ❑5, Sep 1990 2.50
- ❑6, Nov 1990 2.50
- ❑7, Jan 1991 2.50
- ❑8, Mar 1991 2.50
- ❑9, May 1991 2.50
- ❑10 1991 2.50
- ❑11 1991 2.50
- ❑12 1991 2.50

Vampirella
Warren

- ❑1, Sep 1969, b&w; FF (c); TS, NA (a); 1: Vampirella 325.00
- ❑1/2nd, Oct 2001, b&w; FF (c); TS, NA (a); 2nd printing; 1969 Commemorative Edition; Pink lettering 15.00
- ❑2, Nov 1969, b&w 125.00
- ❑3, Jan 1970, b&w; Scarce 200.00
- ❑4, Mar 1970, b&w 75.00
- ❑5, May 1970, b&w 75.00
- ❑6, Jul 1970, b&w 70.00
- ❑7, Sep 1970, b&w FF (c); TS, FF (a) 70.00
- ❑8, Nov 1970, b&w; Horror format begins 70.00
- ❑9, Jan 1971, b&w WW (c); WW (w); TS, WW (a) 70.00
- ❑10, Mar 1971, b&w; WW (w); NA (a); 1st published comics work by Steve Englehart 30.00
- ❑11, May 1971, b&w; O: Pendragon. 1: Pendragon 43.00
- ❑12, Jul 1971, b&w; 1st Jose Gonzales art 43.00
- ❑13, Sep 1971, b&w 43.00
- ❑14, Nov 1971, b&w 43.00
- ❑15, Jan 1972, b&w 43.00
- ❑16, Apr 1972, b&w 30.00
- ❑17, Jun 1972, b&w 30.00
- ❑18, Aug 1972, b&w 30.00
- ❑19, Sep 1972, b&w; 1973 annual 30.00
- ❑20, Oct 1972, b&w 30.00
- ❑21, Dec 1972, b&w 30.00
- ❑22, Mar 1973, b&w 30.00
- ❑23, Apr 1973, b&w 30.00
- ❑24, May 1973, b&w 30.00
- ❑25, Jun 1973, b&w 30.00
- ❑26, Aug 1973, b&w 20.00
- ❑27, Sep 1973, b&w; 1974 annual 30.00
- ❑28, Nov 1973, b&w 25.00
- ❑29, Dec 1973, b&w 25.00
- ❑30, Jan 1974, b&w 25.00
- ❑31, Mar 1974, b&w FF (c); FF (a) 25.00
- ❑32, Apr 1974, b&w 25.00
- ❑33, May 1974, b&w 25.00
- ❑34, Jun 1974, b&w 25.00
- ❑35, Aug 1974, b&w 25.00
- ❑36, Sep 1974, b&w 25.00
- ❑37, Oct 1974, b&w; 1975 annual 20.00
- ❑38, Dec 1974, b&w 20.00
- ❑39, Feb 1974, b&w 20.00
- ❑40, Mar 1975, b&w 20.00
- ❑41, Apr 1975, b&w 20.00
- ❑42, May 1975, b&w 20.00
- ❑43, Jun 1975, b&w 20.00
- ❑44, Aug 1975, b&w 20.00
- ❑45, Sep 1975, b&w 20.00
- ❑46, Oct 1975, b&w; O: Vampirella; One story in color 25.00
- ❑47, Dec 1975, b&w 20.00
- ❑48, Jan 1976, b&w 20.00
- ❑49, Mar 1976, b&w 20.00
- ❑50, Apr 1976, b&w 20.00
- ❑51, May 1976, b&w 17.00
- ❑52, Jul 1976, b&w 17.00
- ❑53, Aug 1976, b&w 17.00
- ❑54, Sep 1976, b&w 17.00
- ❑55, Oct 1976, b&w 17.00
- ❑56, Dec 1976, b&w 17.00
- ❑57, Jan 1977, b&w 17.00
- ❑58, Mar 1977, b&w RH (a) 17.00
- ❑59, Apr 1977, b&w 17.00
- ❑60, May 1977, b&w 17.00
- ❑61, Jul 1977, b&w 17.00
- ❑62, Aug 1977, b&w 17.00
- ❑63, Sep 1977, b&w; Reprints from Vampirella (Magazine) #33, 45, 51, 53 and Creepy (Magazine) #79 17.00
- ❑64, Oct 1977, b&w 17.00
- ❑65, Dec 1977, b&w 17.00
- ❑66, Jan 1978, b&w 17.00
- ❑67, Mar 1978, b&w 17.00
- ❑68, Apr 1978, b&w 17.00
- ❑69, May 1978, b&w 17.00
- ❑70, Jul 1978, b&w 17.00
- ❑71, Aug 1978, b&w 16.00
- ❑72, Sep 1978, b&w 16.00
- ❑73, Oct 1978, b&w 16.00
- ❑74, Dec 1978, b&w; Reprints from Vampirella (Magazine) #14, 22 and 23 16.00
- ❑75, Jan 1979, b&w 16.00
- ❑76, Mar 1979, b&w 16.00
- ❑77, Apr 1979, b&w RH (a) 16.00
- ❑78, May 1979, b&w JSn, RH (a) 16.00
- ❑79, Jul 1979, b&w 16.00
- ❑80, Aug 1979, b&w 16.00
- ❑81, Sep 1979, b&w; Reprints from Vampirella (Magazine) #16 and 18 16.00
- ❑82, Oct 1979, b&w 16.00
- ❑83, Dec 1979, b&w; Reprints from Vampirella (Magazine) #30, 32 and 58 16.00
- ❑84, Jan 1980, b&w 16.00
- ❑85, Mar 1980, b&w 16.00
- ❑86, Apr 1980, b&w 16.00
- ❑87, May 1980, b&w; Reprints from Vampirella (Magazine) #60-62, 65 and part of 66 16.00
- ❑88, Jul 1980, b&w 16.00
- ❑89, Aug 1980, b&w 16.00
- ❑90, Sep 1980, b&w 16.00
- ❑91, Oct 1980, b&w; Reprints from Vampirella (Magazine) #53, 56, 57 and 59 16.00
- ❑92, Dec 1980, b&w 16.00
- ❑93, Jan 1981, b&w 16.00
- ❑94, Mar 1981, b&w 16.00
- ❑95, Apr 1981, b&w 16.00
- ❑96, May 1981, b&w 16.00
- ❑97, Jul 1981, b&w 16.00
- ❑98, Aug 1981, b&w 16.00
- ❑99, Sep 1981, b&w 16.00
- ❑100, Oct 1981, b&w; Reprints from Vampirella (Magazine) #19 and 20 30.00
- ❑101, Dec 1981, b&w 16.00
- ❑102, Jan 1982, b&w 16.00
- ❑103, Mar 1982, b&w 16.00
- ❑104, Apr 1982, b&w 16.00
- ❑105, May 1982, b&w 16.00
- ❑106, Jul 1982, b&w 16.00
- ❑107, Aug 1982, b&w; Reprints from Vampirella (Magazine) #26, 34, 39 and 49 16.00
- ❑108, Sep 1982, b&w 16.00
- ❑109, Oct 1982, b&w; Reprints from Vampirella (Magazine) #18, 22, 24, 34, 38, 39, 55, Creepy (Magazine) #45 and 52 16.00
- ❑110, Dec 1982, b&w ATh (a) 16.00
- ❑111, Jan 1983, b&w; Reprints from Vampirella (Magazine) #28, 29, 39, 40, 59, 62 and 68 16.00
- ❑112, Mar 1983, b&w 45.00
- ❑113 1983, b&w; 1st Harris comic; Scarce 195.00
- ❑Ann 1, b&w; O: Vampirella 175.00
- ❑Special 1, Jan 1977, b&w; Special edition; Special edition (Softcover); Large, square-bound, all color; Only available through mail order 30.00

Vampirella
Harris

- ❑0, Dec 1994, contains Vampirella timeline; enhanced cover 5.00
- ❑0/A, Dec 1994, Blue logo 5.00
- ❑0/Silver, Dec 1994, Silver logo 5.00
- ❑0/Gold, Dec 1994, Gold edition, Limited to 500 copies; Contains timeline 15.00
- ❑1, Nov 1992, KB (w); Adam Hughes cover 15.00
- ❑1/2nd, Nov 1996, KB (w); 2nd printing; Commemorative Edition; Alternate cover by Louis Small Jr and Caesar 5.00
- ❑2, Feb 1993, KB (w); A: Dracula. Adam Hughes cover 12.00
- ❑3, Mar 1993, KB (w) 10.00
- ❑4, Jul 1993, KB (w); John K. Snyder III cover 8.00
- ❑5, Nov 1993, Dan Brereton cover 8.00

Vampirella: Ascending Evil
Harris

- ❑1 2.95
- ❑1/AmEnt; American Entertainment variant cover 5.00
- ❑2 2.95
- ❑3 2.95
- ❑4 2.95

Vampirella: Blood Lust
Harris

- ❑1, Jul 1997; cardstock cover 5.00
- ❑2, Aug 1997; cardstock cover 5.00

Vampirella Classic
Harris

- ❑1, Feb 1995; Reprints Vampirella #12 in color 2.95
- ❑2, Apr 1995; Reprints Vampirella #13 in color 2.95
- ❑3, Jun 1995; Reprints Vampirella #14 in color 2.95
- ❑4, Aug 1995; Reprints Vampirella #15 in color 2.95
- ❑5, Oct 1995; Reprints Vampirella #16 in color 2.95

Weird War Tales

Horror comes to the battlefield
©DC

Weird Western Tales

All-Star Western got Weird with Jonah Hex
©DC

Weird Worlds

Burroughs' other series found a home
©DC

Welcome Back, Kotter

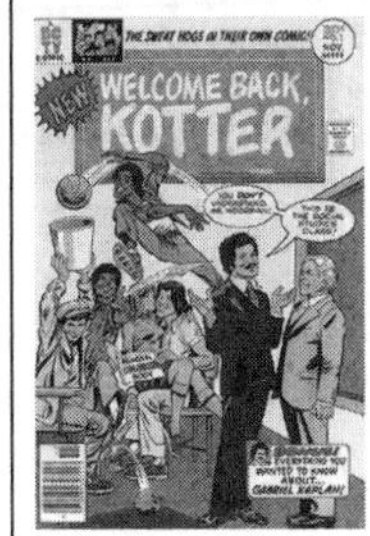

TV writer Mark Evanier also wrote comic
©DC

Wendy, the Good Little Witch

Precocious sorceress does white magic
©Harvey

Vampirella Commemorative Edition
Harris

	N-MINT
❑1, Nov 1996	2.95

Vampirella: Crossover Gallery
Harris

	N-MINT
❑1, Sep 1997; wraparound cover; pin-ups	2.95

Vampirella: Death & Destruction
Harris

	N-MINT
❑1, Jul 1996	2.95
❑1/A, Jul 1996; Vampirella sitting on cover	3.00
❑1/Ltd., Jul 1996; Vampirella logo only on cover	5.00
❑2, Aug 1996	2.95
❑3, Sep 1996	2.95
❑Ashcan 1, Apr 1996; Billy Tucci cover; Red gloved cover; b&w pages and sketches of the Death and Destruction series	3.00

Vampirella/Dracula & Pantha Showcase
Harris

	N-MINT
❑1, Aug 1997; Vampirella on cover; flip-book with previews of Vampirella/ Dracula and Pantha	1.50
❑1/A, Aug 1997; Pantha on cover; flip-book with previews of Vampirella/ Dracula and Pantha	1.50

Vampirella/Dracula: The Centennial
Harris

	N-MINT
❑1, Oct 1997; John Bolton cover; Dracula grasping Vampirella from behind	5.95
❑1/A, Oct 1997; David Mack cover; Head and shoulders of Dracula	5.95
❑1/B, Oct 1997; Gary Frank cover; Blood Red Edition Cavalcade Comics exclusive; Vampirella alone with a silhouette of Dracula's head behind	5.95
❑2, Oct 1997	5.95

Vampirella: Julie Strain Special
Harris

	N-MINT
❑1, Sep 2000; Regular edition photo cover	3.95
❑1/A, Sep 2000; Chrome version	14.95
❑1/B, Sep 2000; Holo-chrome version; 500 copies printed	24.95

Vampirella/Lady Death
Harris

	N-MINT
❑1, Feb 1999	3.50
❑1/A, Feb 1999; Valentine edition; Red foil	5.00
❑1/Ltd., Feb 1999; Signed and numbered	10.00

Vampirella Lives
Harris

	N-MINT
❑1, Dec 1996; white cardstock outer cover with cutout	3.50
❑1/A, Dec 1996; Cover depicts Vampirella leaning forward	4.00
❑1/B, Dec 1996; Cover depicts Vampirella side view	4.00
❑1/C, Dec 1996; Die-cut linen cover	10.00
❑2, Jan 1997; Vampirella bathing in blood	2.95
❑2/A, Jan 1997; Blue background	3.00
❑2/B, Jan 1997; Photo cover	4.00
❑3, Feb 1997; Drawn cover	2.95
❑3/A, Feb 1997; Photo cover	4.00

Vampirella Monthly
Harris

	N-MINT
❑0, Jan 1999; Vampirella standing, two figures in background	4.00
❑0/A, Jan 1999; Vampirella bathing in blood	4.00
❑1, Nov 1997; Gold foil logo on cover	4.00
❑1/A, Nov 1997; Vampirella eating something bloody on cover	5.00
❑1/B, Nov 1997; Vampirella eating something bloody on cover; Gold marking	5.00
❑1/C, Nov 1997; Vampirella standing on cover, demon-eyed figures in background	5.00
❑1/D, Nov 1997; Vampirella standing on cover, black background, blue logo	59.95
❑1/E, Nov 1997; American Entertainment Edition; Vampirella reclining on skull	10.00
❑1/F, Nov 1997; Vampirella standing on cover, black background with foil logo	19.95
❑2, Dec 1997; Vampirella holding a cross dipped in blood	3.00
❑2/A, Dec 1997; Man shooting gun at Vampirella	9.95
❑3, Jan 1998; Vampirella with crossbow beside left-hand column group montage	3.00
❑3/A, Jan 1998; Vampirella on motorcycle (only figure on cover)	9.95
❑4, Feb 1998; Vampirella holding gun beside armor-clad nun with longbow	3.00
❑4/A, Feb 1998; Crimson edition; American Entertainment Linsner cover	4.00
❑4/B, Feb 1998; Vampirella holding gun	3.00
❑5, Mar 1998; Vampirella holding gun, white background	3.00
❑6, Apr 1998; Vampirella reclining on a rug	3.00
❑7, Jun 1998; A: Shi. Vampirella regular cover	3.00
❑7/A, Jun 1998; Vampirella with finger to mouth	10.00
❑7/B, Jun 1998; Shi on cover in foreground, Vampirella in background	4.00
❑7/C, Jun 1998; Shi in background, Vampirella in foreground	4.95
❑7/D, Jun 1998; Vampirella and Shi on checkerboard floor, foil logo	12.00
❑7/E, Jun 1998; Vampirella and Shi on checkerboard floor	10.00
❑8, Jul 1998; A: Shi. Shi and Pantha all on cover; Vampirella	3.00
❑9, Aug 1998 A: Shi	3.00
❑10, Sep 1998; Cover with Vampirella sitting in giant clawed hand; Team-up with Pantha	3.00
❑10/A, Sep 1998; Black-and-white cover	6.00
❑10/B, Sep 1998; Color cover with no words	5.00
❑11, Oct 1998	3.00
❑12, Nov 1998; Vampirella with bat wings costume cover	3.00
❑12/A, Nov 1998; Vampirella in spiky bodysuit	3.00
❑12/B, Nov 1998; Vampirella hurling woman	15.00
❑12/Variant, Nov 1998; Like B cover	6.00
❑13, Mar 1999; Vampirella standing, people in background; Pantha backup story	3.00
❑13/A, Mar 1999; Vampirella holding heart	3.00
❑14, Apr 1999; Close-up of Vampirella in clutches of a monster	2.95
❑14/A, Apr 1999; Vampirella standing, figure in background	3.00
❑15, May 1999; Vampirella facing forward	2.95
❑15/A, May 1999; Vampirella facing away	2.95
❑15/B, May 1999; alternate cover (facing away)	2.95
❑16, Jun 1999; Regular Pantha photo cover; Cover depicts Pantha standing, orange/red background	2.95
❑16/A, Jun 1999; Vampirella ¯ 4 other similarly clad women on cover	3.00
❑16/B, Jun 1999; Cover depicts Pantha standing, orange/red background	4.00
❑16/C, Jun 1999; Vampirella photo cover	5.00
❑16/D, Jun 1999; Pantha drawn cover	3.00
❑16/E, Jun 1999; Cover depicts Pantha crawling, white background	4.00
❑16/F, Jun 1999; Cover depicts Pantha standing, blue background	4.00
❑17, Jul 1999; Photo cover of Pantha standing, blue background	4.00
❑17/A, Jul 1999; Vampirella bound on cover	3.00
❑17/B, Jul 1999; Cover depicts Pantha standiing, blue background	4.00
❑17/C, Jul 1999; Vampirella photo cover	4.00
❑17/D, Jul 1999; Two women with giant serpent in background on cover	3.00
❑17/E, Jul 1999; Cover depicts Pantha sitting with arm outstretched, blue background	4.00
❑18, Aug 1999; JPH (w); Vampirella standing with flame background	2.95
❑18/A, Aug 1999; Vampirella with arms outstretched on cover	5.00
❑18/B, Aug 1999; "Chesty" close-up Vampirella cover	5.00
❑19, Sep 1999; Two Vampirellas on cover	2.95
❑19/A, Sep 1999; Vampirella holding skull on cover	5.00
❑20, Oct 1999; Vampirella with gun	2.95
❑20/A, Oct 1999; Vampirella standing with fangs present	5.00
❑21, Nov 1999; Cover has tinted background	2.95
❑21/A, Nov 1999; Drawn cover	5.00
❑21/B, Nov 1999; Julie Strain Limited Photo cover, white background	4.00
❑22, Dec 1999; Cover has red tinted background	4.00
❑22/A, Dec 1999; Drawn cover	3.00
❑22/B, Dec 1999; Photo cover, white background	4.00
❑23, Jan 2000; Vampirella fighting Lady Death, cover has words	2.95
❑23/A, Jan 2000; Wordless cover with Vampirella on knees	7.00
❑23/B, Jan 2000; Red-logo cover with Vampirella on knees	5.00
❑23/C, Jan 2000; Silver logo cover with Vampirella on knees	19.95
❑23/D, Jan 2000; Wordless cover with Vampirella fighting Lady Death	10.00
❑24, Feb 2000; Vampirella with gun, fishnet stockings in foreground on cover	2.95

Other grades: Multiply price above by 5/6 for VF/NM • 2/3 for VERY FINE • 1/3 for FINE • 1/5 for VERY GOOD • 1/8 for GOOD

N-MINT N-MINT N-MINT

- ❑24/A, Feb 2000; Reflections in sunglasses on cover 3.00
- ❑24/B, Feb 2000; Vampirella on motorcycle, other female figure at top 9.95
- ❑25, Mar 2000; Vampirella in chains with male figure 2.95
- ❑25/A, Mar 2000; Two women on motorcycles 3.00
- ❑26, Apr 2000; Vampirella facing Lady Death on cover 2.95
- ❑26/A, Apr 2000; Vampirella in foreground, Lady Death in background 3.00
- ❑Ashcan 1, Aug 1997; "Ascending Evil" on cover 5.00
- ❑Ashcan 1/A, Aug 1997; "Holy War" on cover 5.00
- ❑Ashcan 2, Jan 1998; Holy War cover; Features b&w art from Vampirella Monthly #4 plus sketches (no speech balloons) 5.00
- ❑Ashcan 3, Apr 1998; Queen's Gambit cover; Features b&w art from Vampirella Monthly #7 plus sketches (no speech balloons) 5.00
- ❑Ashcan 3/A; Leather cover; Convention exclusive limited to 1000 copies........ 15.00
- ❑Ashcan 4, Jul 1998; Hell on Earth cover; Features b&w art from Vampirella Monthly #10 plus sketches........ 3.00
- ❑Ashcan 5, Feb 1999; World's End cover; Features b&w art from Vampirella Monthly #13 (no speech balloons)..... 3.00
- ❑Ashcan 6, Apr 1999; Pantha photo cover, white background; Features b&w art from Vampirella Monthly #17 plus sketches and covers (no speech balloons) 3.00

Vampirella: Morning in America
Harris

- ❑1, b&w; distributed by Dark Horse; squarebound 3.95
- ❑2, Nov 1991, b&w; squarebound 3.95
- ❑3, Jan 1992, b&w; squarebound........ 3.95
- ❑4, Apr 1992, b&w; squarebound........ 3.95

Vampirella of Drakulon
Harris

- ❑0........ 2.95
- ❑1, Jan 1995 .... 2.95
- ❑2, Mar 1995 .... 2.95
- ❑3, May 1995; Poly-bagged........ 2.95

Vampirella/Painkiller Jane
Harris

- ❑1, May 1998; crossover with Event; foil-enhanced cover........ 3.50
- ❑1/A, May 1998; Variant cover, Vampirella and Painkiller Jane on rooftop........ 5.00
- ❑1/B, May 1998; Blue cover, Vampirella and Painkiller posing (in mid-air!)...... 24.95
- ❑1/Gold, May 1998; Gold edition; Gold foil lettering; Vampirella and Painkiller posing in mid-air against blue background 24.95
- ❑Ashcan 1, Jan 1998; no cover price..... 3.00

Vampirella Pin-Up Special
Harris

- ❑1, Oct 1995; Vampirella in front of blue-black stained window; Artbook........ 2.95
- ❑1/A, Oct 1995; White background and snake on cover 2.95

Vampirella: Sad Wings of Destiny
Harris

- ❑1, Sep 1996; gold edition limited to 5000; cardstock cover........ 3.95
- ❑1/Gold, Sep 1996; Gold mark on cover 5.00

Vampirella/ShadowHawk: Creatures of the Night
Harris

- ❑1, Feb 1995; crossover with Image; concludes in Shadowhawk - Vampirella #2 .... 4.95
- ❑2, Feb 1995; "ShadowHawk/Vampirella" 4.95

Vampirella/Shi
Harris

- ❑1, Sep 1997, crossover with Crusade; no cover price........ 2.95

Vampirella: Silver Anniversary Collection
Harris

- ❑1/A, Jan 1997; Good Girl cover........ 2.50
- ❑1/B, Jan 1997; Bad Girl cover 2.50
- ❑2/A, Feb 1997; Good Girl cover........ 2.50
- ❑2/B, Feb 1997; Bad Girl cover........ 2.50
- ❑3/A, Mar 1997; Good Girl cover........ 2.50
- ❑3/B, Mar 1997; Bad Girl cover........ 2.50
- ❑4/A, Apr 1997; Good Girl cover........ 2.50
- ❑4/B, Apr 1997; Bad Girl cover 2.50

Vampirella's Summer Nights
Harris

- ❑1, ca. 1992, b&w; NN........ 3.95

Vampirella Strikes
Harris

- ❑1, Oct 1995; Photo cover........ 3.00
- ❑1/A, Oct 1995; alternate cover; marble background 3.00
- ❑1/B, Oct 1995; Cover has Vampirella with moon in background 3.00
- ❑1/C, Oct 1995; Cover has Vampirella against blue background........ 3.00
- ❑1/Ltd., Oct 1995; Dynamic Forces signed edition; Includes Certificate of Authenticity; Signed by Tom Sniegoski and Ed McGuiness 10.00
- ❑2, Dec 1995 .... 3.00
- ❑3, Feb 1996........ 3.00
- ❑4, Apr 1996........ 3.00
- ❑5, Jun 1996 A: Eudaemon........ 3.00
- ❑6, Aug 1996 .... 3.00
- ❑7, Oct 1996; Reprints Call Me Pantha from Warren magazine; Flip book, covers by David Mack and Rudy Nebres; Final Issue........ 3.00
- ❑Ann 1, Dec 1996; Vampirella surrounded by flames........ 3.00
- ❑Ann 1/A, Dec 1996; Alternate cover; Vampirella with lightning behind........ 3.00
- ❑Ann 1/B, Dec 1996; Dynamic Forces edition signed by Louis Small Jr.; Vampirella with lightning behind........ 3.00

Vampirella 30th Anniversary Celebration
Harris

- ❑1 .... 3.00

Vampirella 25th Anniversary Special
Harris

- ❑1, Oct 1996; prestige format; NN; One-shot 5.95
- ❑1/A, Oct 1996; Silver logo with no words on cover 6.00

Vampirella vs Hemorrhage
Harris

- ❑1, Apr 1997........ 3.50
- ❑1/A, Mar 1997; Vampirella with red hand on cover 3.50
- ❑1/Ashcan, Mar 1997; ashcan; no cover price 1.00
- ❑2, May 1997........ 3.50
- ❑3, Jun 1997........ 3.50

Vampirella vs Pantha
Harris

- ❑1/A, Mar 1997; cardstock cover; Vampirella standing over body in street with police cars in background........ 3.50
- ❑1/B, Mar 1997; cardstock cover........ 3.50
- ❑1/C, Mar 1997; Pantha on cover with black background........ 3.50
- ❑Ashcan 1, Jan 1997; "Special Showcase Edition" on cover; JRo (w); Special Showcase Edition on cover 3.50

Vampirella/Wetworks
Harris

- ❑1, Jun 1997; Regular Mike Bair cover; Vampirella kneeling in foreground...... 3.00

Vampire Miyu
Antarctic

- ❑1, Oct 1995........ 3.50
- ❑2, Nov 1995........ 3.00
- ❑3, Dec 1995 .... 3.00
- ❑4, Jan 1996........ 3.00
- ❑5, Feb 1996........ 3.00
- ❑6, Mar 1996........ 3.00
- ❑Ashcan 1; Ashcan promotional edition from 1995 San Diego Comic-Con; 1: Vampire Miyu........ 0.50

Vampires Lust
CFD / Boneyard

- ❑1, Sep 1996, b&w; Adult........ 2.95
- ❑1/Nude, Sep 1996; nude cover........ 3.95

Vampire's Prank
Acid Rain

- ❑1 .... 2.95

Vampire Tales
Marvel

- ❑1, Aug 1973; ME (w); BEv (a); A: Morbius. 1st full Morbius story...... 35.00
- ❑2, Oct 1973; 1: Satana 18.00
- ❑3, Feb 1974........ 18.00
- ❑4, Apr 1974........ 18.00
- ❑5, Jun 1974........ 18.00
- ❑6, Aug 1974 A: Lilith 18.00
- ❑7, Oct 1974........ 18.00
- ❑8, Dec 1974 A: Blade 20.00
- ❑9, Feb 1975 A: Blade........ 20.00
- ❑10, Apr 1975 A: Blade........ 20.00
- ❑11, Jun 1975; Final Issue........ 25.00
- ❑Ann 1, Oct 1975; Reprints 30.00

Vampire the Masquerade: Toreador
Moonstone

- ❑1, ca. 2003........ 5.95

Vampire Verses
CFD

- ❑1, Aug 1995, b&w........ 2.95
- ❑1/2nd, Dec 2001, b&w; 2nd printing from CFD........ 2.95
- ❑1/3rd, Dec 2001, b&w; 3rd printing from Asylum Press 2.95
- ❑1/Ltd., b&w; limited edition of 1000 copies; alternate nude cover........ 5.00
- ❑2, b&w........ 2.95
- ❑2/2nd, Jul 2002, b&w; 2nd printing from Asylum Press 2.95
- ❑2/3rd, b&w........ 2.95
- ❑2/Ltd., b&w; limited edition of 1000 copies; alternate cover 5.00
- ❑3, Jun 1996, b&w 2.95
- ❑3/2nd, Jun 1996, b&w; 2nd printing from Asylum Press........ 2.95
- ❑3/Ltd., Jun 1996, b&w; limited edition of 1000 copies; alternate nude cover...... 5.00
- ❑4, b&w........ 2.95
- ❑4/2nd, b&w; 2nd printing from Asylum Press........ 2.95
- ❑4/Ltd., b&w; limited edition of 1000 copies; alternate cover 5.00

Vampire Vixens
Acid Rain

- ❑1; Adult 2.75

Vampire World
Acid Rain

- ❑1 .... 2.75

Vampire Yui
Ironcat

- ❑1, Jul 2000........ 2.95

Vampiric Jihad
Apple

- ❑1, b&w; cardstock cover; reprints material from Blood of Dracula #14-19 4.95

Vampornella
Adam Post

- ❑1; Adult 2.95

Vampress Luxura
Brainstorm

- ❑1, Feb 1996; wraparound cover 2.95
- ❑1/Gold, Feb 1996 .... 8.00

Vamps
DC / Vertigo

- ❑1, Aug 1994 .... 2.50
- ❑2, Sep 1994 .... 2.50
- ❑3, Oct 1994 BB (c) 2.50
- ❑4, Nov 1994 BB (c) 2.50
- ❑5, Dec 1994 BB (c) 2.50
- ❑6, Jan 1995........ 2.50

Vamps: Hollywood & Vein
DC / Vertigo

- ❑1, Feb 1996........ 2.50
- ❑2, Mar 1996 .... 2.50
- ❑3, Apr 1996........ 2.50
- ❑4, May 1996........ 2.50
- ❑5, Jun 1996........ 2.50
- ❑6, Jul 1996, Final Issue........ 2.50

Other grades: Multiply price above by 5/6 for VF/NM • 2/3 for VERY FINE • 1/3 for FINE • 1/5 for VERY GOOD • 1/8 for GOOD

Wendy Witch World

Lotta had Foodland, Richie had Money World ...
©Harvey

Werewolf By Night

Main character was named after terrier
©Marvel

West Coast Avengers

Avengers branch out with B-characters
©Marvel

Western Gunfighters

Reprints adventures of Old West's Kids
©Marvel

Wetworks

Suicide mission squad acquires symbiotes
©Image

N-MINT

Vamps: Pumpkin Time
DC / Vertigo

❑1, Dec 1998 ... 2.50
❑2, Jan 1999 ... 2.50
❑3, Feb 1999 ... 2.50

Vampurada
Tavicat

❑1, Jul 1995 ... 1.95

Vampyres
Eternity

❑1, b&w; Reprints ... 2.25
❑2, b&w; Reprints ... 2.25
❑3, Mar 1989, b&w; Reprints ... 2.25
❑4, Jul 1989, b&w; Reprints ... 2.25

Vampyre's Kiss
Aircel

❑1, Jun 1990, b&w; Adult ... 2.50
❑2, Jul 1990, b&w; Adult ... 2.50
❑3, Aug 1990, b&w; Adult ... 2.50
❑4, Sep 1990, b&w; Adult ... 2.50

Vampyre's Kiss, Book II
Aircel

❑1, Dec 1990, b&w; Adult ... 2.50
❑2, Dec 1990, b&w; Adult ... 2.50
❑3, Feb 1991, b&w; Adult ... 2.50
❑4, Mar 1991, b&w; Adult ... 2.50

Vampyre's Kiss, Book III
Aircel

❑1, Aug 1991, b&w; Adult ... 2.50
❑2, ca. 1991, b&w; Adult ... 2.50
❑3, ca. 1991, b&w; Adult ... 2.50
❑4, ca. 1991, b&w; Adult ... 2.50

Vandala
Chaos!

❑1, Aug 2000 ... 2.95

Vanguard
Image

❑1, Oct 1993; EL (w); EL (a); Wraparound and gate-fold cover ... 2.00
❑2, Nov 1993 EL (w); EL (a) ... 2.00
❑3, Dec 1993 EL (w); EL (a); A: Savage Dragon ... 2.00
❑4, Feb 1994 EL (w); EL (a) ... 2.00
❑5, Apr 1994 EL (w); EL (a) ... 2.00
❑6, May 1994 EL (w); EL (a) ... 2.00

Vanguard
Image

❑1, Oct 1996, b&w ... 2.95
❑2, Oct 1996, b&w ... 2.95
❑3, Dec 1996, b&w ... 2.95
❑4, Jan 1997, b&w; cover says Feb, indicia says Jan ... 2.95

Vanguard: Ethereal Warriors
Image

❑1, Aug 2000 ... 5.95

Vanguard Illustrated
Pacific

❑1, Nov 1983 SR, TY (a) ... 1.50
❑2, Jan 1984 DSt (c); SR, BMc, DSt (a) ... 1.50
❑3, Mar 1984 AW (c); SR, TY (a) ... 1.50
❑4, Apr 1984 SR (c) ... 1.50
❑5, May 1984 ... 1.50

N-MINT

❑6, Jun 1984 GP (a) ... 1.50
❑7 1984; GE (a); 1: Mr. Monster. 1: Mr. Monster ... 4.00

Van Helsing One-Shot
Dark Horse

❑1, May 2004 ... 2.99

Vanity
Pacific

❑1, Jun 1984 ... 1.50
❑2, Aug 1984 ... 1.50

Vanity Angel
Antarctic

❑1, Sep 1994, b&w; Adult ... 3.50
❑1/2nd, May 1995; 2nd printing; Adult ... 3.50
❑2, Oct 1994, b&w; Adult ... 3.50
❑2/2nd, Jun 1995; 2nd printing; Adult ... 3.50
❑3, Nov 1994, b&w; Adult ... 3.50
❑4, Dec 1994, b&w; Adult ... 3.50
❑5, Jan 1995, b&w; Adult ... 3.50
❑6, Feb 1995, b&w; Adult ... 3.50

Varcel's Vixens
Caliber

❑1, Feb 1990, b&w ... 2.50
❑2, Mar 1990, b&w ... 2.50
❑3, Apr 1990, b&w ... 2.50

Variations on the Theme
Scarlet Rose

❑1 ... 2.75
❑2 ... 2.75
❑3 ... 2.75
❑4 ... 2.75

Varick: Chronicles of the Dark Prince
Q

❑1, Jul 1999 ... 1.95

Variogenesis
Dagger

❑0, Jun 1994 ... 3.50

Varla Vortex
Boneyard

❑1; Adult ... 2.95

Varmints
Blue Comet

❑1 ... 2.00
❑Special 1; Panda Khan ... 2.50

Vast Knowledge of General Subjects
Fantagraphics

❑1, Sep 1994, b&w ... 4.95

Vault of Doomnation
B-Movie

❑1 1986, b&w ... 1.70

Vault of Evil
Marvel

❑1, Feb 1973 ... 60.00
❑2, Apr 1973 ... 25.00
❑3, Jun 1973 ... 25.00
❑4, Aug 1973, FB (c); GC, JR (a); Reprint from Strange Tales #8, Journey into Mystery (1st Series) #15 and Astonishing #59 ... 25.00
❑5, Sep 1973 ... 15.00
❑6, Oct 1973 ... 15.00
❑7, Nov 1973 ... 15.00

N-MINT

❑8, Dec 1973 ... 15.00
❑9, Feb 1974 ... 15.00
❑10, Apr 1974 ... 15.00
❑11, Jun 1974 ... 12.00
❑12, Aug 1974; Reprints from Meance #11, Spellbound #14, Adventures into Terror #12 and Uncanny Tales #29 ... 12.00
❑13, Sep 1974 ... 12.00
❑14, Oct 1974 ... 12.00
❑15, Nov 1974 ... 12.00
❑16, Dec 1974 ... 12.00
❑17, Feb 1975 ... 12.00
❑18, Apr 1975 ... 12.00
❑19, Jun 1975 ... 12.00
❑20, Aug 1975; Reprints from Tales to Astonish #30, Journey into Mystery (1st Series) #53, Adventures into Terror #30 and Uncanny Tales # 54 ... 12.00
❑21, Sep 1975; Reprints from Uncanny Tales #14, Mystic #6 and Uncanny Tales #37 ... 12.00
❑22, Oct 1975 ... 12.00
❑23, Nov 1975; Final Issue ... 12.00

Vault of Horror
Gladstone

❑1, Aug 1990; Reprints The Vault of Horror #34, The Haunt of Fear #1 ... 2.50
❑2, Oct 1990; Reprints The Vault of Horror #27, The Haunt of Fear #17 ... 2.50
❑3, Dec 1990; Reprints The Vault of Horror #13, The Haunt of Fear #22 ... 2.50
❑4, Feb 1991; Reprints The Vault of Horror #23, The Haunt of Fear #13 ... 2.50
❑5, Apr 1991; AF, JCr, WW, JKa, GI (a); Reprints The Vault of Horror #19, The Haunt of Fear #5 ... 2.50
❑6, Jun 1991; Reprints The Vault of Horror #32, Weird Fantasy #6 ... 2.50
❑7, Aug 1991; Reprints The Vault of Horror #26, Weird Fantasy #7 ... 2.50

Vault of Horror
Cochran

❑1, Sep 1991 ... 2.00
❑2, Nov 1991; Reprints Vault of Horror #33, Weird Science #20 ... 2.00
❑3, Jan 1992; Reprints Vault of Horror #26, Weird Science #7 ... 2.00
❑4, Mar 1992; Reprints Vault of Horror #35, Weird Science #15 ... 2.00
❑5, May 1992 ... 2.00

Vault of Horror (RCP)
Gemstone

❑1, Oct 1992; Reprints The Vault of Horror #12 ... 2.00
❑2, Jan 1993; Reprints The Vault of Horror #13 ... 2.00
❑3, Apr 1993; Reprints The Vault of Horror #14 ... 2.00
❑4, Jul 1993; Reprints The Vault of Horror #15 ... 2.00
❑5, Oct 1993; Reprints The Vault of Horror #16 ... 2.00
❑6, Jan 1994; Reprints The Vault of Horror #17 ... 2.00
❑7, Apr 1994; Reprints The Vault of Horror #18 ... 2.00
❑8, Jul 1994; Reprints The Vault of Horror #19 ... 2.00

Other grades: Multiply price above by 5/6 for VF/NM • 2/3 for VERY FINE • 1/3 for FINE • 1/5 for VERY GOOD • 1/8 for GOOD

N-MINT

- ❑9, Oct 1994; Reprints The Vault of Horror #20 ... 2.00
- ❑10, Jan 1995; Reprints The Vault of Horror #21 ... 2.00
- ❑11, Apr 1995; Reprints The Vault of Horror #22 ... 2.00
- ❑12, Jul 1995; Reprints The Vault of Horror #23 ... 2.00
- ❑13, Oct 1995; Reprints The Vault of Horror #24 ... 2.00
- ❑14, Jan 1996; Reprints The Vault of Horror #25 ... 2.00
- ❑15, Apr 1996; Reprints The Vault of Horror #26 ... 2.00
- ❑16, Jul 1996; Reprints The Vault of Horror #27 ... 2.50
- ❑17, Oct 1996; Reprints The Vault of Horror #28 ... 2.50
- ❑18, Jan 1997; Reprints The Vault of Horror #29 ... 2.50
- ❑19, Apr 1997; Reprints The Vault of Horror #30 ... 2.50
- ❑20, Jul 1997; Reprints The Vault of Horror #31 ... 2.50
- ❑21, Oct 1997; Reprints The Vault of Horror #32 ... 2.50
- ❑22, Jan 1998; Reprints The Vault of Horror #33 ... 2.50
- ❑23, Apr 1998; Reprints The Vault of Horror #34 ... 2.50
- ❑24, Jul 1998; Reprints The Vault of Horror #35 ... 2.50
- ❑25, Oct 1998; Reprints The Vault of Horror #36 ... 2.50
- ❑26, Jan 1999; Reprints The Vault of Horror #37 ... 2.50
- ❑27, Apr 1999; Reprints The Vault of Horror #38 ... 2.50
- ❑28, Jul 1999; Reprints The Vault of Horror #39 ... 2.50
- ❑29, Oct 1999; Reprints The Vault of Horror #40 ... 2.50
- ❑Ann 1; Collects The Vault of Horror #1-5 ... 8.95
- ❑Ann 2; Collects The Vault of Horror #6-10 ... 9.95
- ❑Ann 3; Collects The Vault of Horror #11-15 ... 10.95
- ❑Ann 4 ... 12.95
- ❑Ann 5 ... 13.50

Vault of Screaming Horror
Fantaco

- ❑1 ... 3.50

Vector
Now

- ❑1, Jul 1986 ... 1.50
- ❑2, Sep 1986 ... 1.50
- ❑3, Nov 1986 ... 1.50
- ❑4, Jan 1987 ... 1.50

Vegas Knights
Pioneer

- ❑1 ... 1.95

Vegetable Lover
Fantagraphics / Eros

- ❑1, Jan 1992, b&w; Adult ... 2.75

Vegman
Checker

- ❑1, Spr 1998, b&w; Spring 1998 ... 2.95
- ❑2, Sum 1998, b&w; indicia for #1 repeated inside ... 2.95

Veils
DC / Vertigo

- ❑1, Dec 1999; hardcover; art and photos ... 14.95
- ❑1/HC; hardcover; art and photos ... 19.95

Velocity
Image

- ❑1, Nov 1995 ... 2.50
- ❑2, Dec 1995 ... 2.50
- ❑3, Jan 1996 ... 2.50

Velocity
Eclipse

- ❑5, b&w ... 2.95

Velvet
Adventure

- ❑1, Jan 1993, b&w; 1: Velvet; Garrison G. Garro ... 2.50
- ❑2, Feb 1993, b&w ... 2.50
- ❑3, Mar 1993, b&w ... 2.50
- ❑4, Apr 1993, b&w ... 2.50

N-MINT

Velvet Artichoke Theatre
Velvet Artichoke

- ❑1, Sum 1998, b&w; Summer 1998 ... 2.00

Velvet Touch
Antarctic

- ❑1, Oct 1993; Adult ... 4.00
- ❑1/Platinum, Oct 1993, platinum ... 4.00
- ❑1/2nd, Apr 1995; 2nd printing; Adult ... 4.00
- ❑2, Jan 1994; Adult ... 3.95
- ❑3, Jul 1994; Adult ... 3.95
- ❑4, Aug 1994; Adult ... 3.95
- ❑5, Oct 1994; Adult ... 3.95
- ❑6, Jan 1995; Adult ... 3.95

Vendetta: Holy Vindicator
Red Bullet

- ❑1, b&w; first printing limited to 500 copies ... 2.50
- ❑2, b&w; first printing limited to 500 copies ... 2.50
- ❑3, b&w; first printing limited to 3000 copies ... 2.50
- ❑4, b&w; Final Issue ... 2.50

Vengeance of the Aztecs
Caliber

- ❑1, b&w ... 2.95
- ❑2, b&w ... 2.95
- ❑3, b&w ... 2.95
- ❑4 ... 2.95
- ❑5 ... 2.95

Vengeance of Vampirella
Harris

- ❑0, Nov 1995 ... 2.95
- ❑½ ... 4.00
- ❑½/A; Gold cover ... 19.95
- ❑1, Apr 1994; red foil wraparound cover ... 3.50
- ❑1/A, Apr 1994; Blue foil ... 3.00
- ❑1/Gold, Apr 1994; Gold promotional edition ... 2.95
- ❑1/2nd, ca. 1994; blue foil wraparound cover ... 3.00
- ❑2, May 1994 ... 3.00
- ❑3, Jun 1994 ... 3.00
- ❑4, Jul 1994 ... 3.00
- ❑5, Aug 1994; 1: The Undead ... 3.00
- ❑6, Sep 1994; Adam Hughes cover ... 3.00
- ❑6/A, Sep 1994; Special Limited Edition on cover ... 19.95
- ❑7, Oct 1994 ... 3.00
- ❑8, Nov 1994; Includes trading card ... 3.00
- ❑9, Dec 1994 ... 3.00
- ❑10, Jan 1995 ... 3.00
- ❑11, Feb 1995; polybagged with trading card ... 3.00
- ❑12, Mar 1995; 1: Passion. cover date Feb 95 ... 3.00
- ❑13, Apr 1995 ... 3.00
- ❑14, May 1995 ... 3.00
- ❑14/A, May 1995; Vampirella sitting, man at top ... 3.00
- ❑15, Jun 1995 ... 3.00
- ❑15/A, Jun 1995; Back-to-back with man holding gun ... 3.00
- ❑16, Jul 1995 ... 3.00
- ❑16/A, Jul 1995; Vampirella springing, fingernails outstretched ... 3.00
- ❑17, Aug 1995 ... 3.00
- ❑17/A, Aug 1995; Woman with sword at right swinging at Vampirella ... 3.00
- ❑18, Sep 1995 ... 3.00
- ❑18/A, Sep 1995; Vampirella against purple-red background ... 3.00
- ❑19, Oct 1995 ... 3.00
- ❑19/A, Oct 1995; Vampirella holding heart ... 3.00
- ❑20, Nov 1995 ... 3.00
- ❑21, Dec 1995 ... 3.00
- ❑22, Jan 1996 ... 3.00
- ❑23, Feb 1996 ... 3.00
- ❑24, Mar 1996 ... 3.00
- ❑25, Apr 1996; cardstock cover with red foil ... 3.00
- ❑25/A, ca. 1996; Vampirella with candles on cover ... 3.00
- ❑25/B, ca. 1996; Blue foil on cover ... 5.00
- ❑25/Gold, ca. 1996; Gold logo ... 5.00
- ❑25/Platinum, ca. 1996; Platinum logo ... 6.00
- ❑25/Ashcan, Mar 1995; Preview Ashcan ... 5.00

N-MINT

Vengeance Squad
Charlton

- ❑1, Jul 1975, Vengeance Squad; Michael Mauser Private Eye ... 9.00
- ❑2, Sep 1975 ... 5.00
- ❑3, Nov 1975, JSa, PM (a); Vengeance Squad; Michael Mauser Private Eye ... 5.00
- ❑4, Jan 1976 ... 5.00
- ❑5, Mar 1976, Vengeance Squad; Michael Mauser Private Eye ... 5.00
- ❑6, May 1976 ... 5.00

Vengeful Skye
Davdez

- ❑1, Sum 1998; Summer 1998 ... 2.95

Venger Robo
Viz

- ❑1 ... 2.75
- ❑2 ... 2.75
- ❑3 ... 2.75
- ❑4 ... 2.75
- ❑5 ... 2.75
- ❑6 ... 2.75
- ❑7 ... 2.75

Venom
Marvel

- ❑1, Jun 2003 ... 10.00
- ❑2, Jul 2003 ... 3.00
- ❑3, Aug 2003 ... 2.25
- ❑4, Sep 2003 ... 2.25
- ❑5, Oct 2003 ... 2.25
- ❑6, Nov 2003 ... 2.25
- ❑7, Dec 2003 ... 2.25
- ❑8, Jan 2004 ... 2.99
- ❑9, Feb 2004 ... 4.00
- ❑10, Mar 2004 ... 2.99
- ❑11, Apr 2004 ... 2.99
- ❑12, May 2004 ... 2.99
- ❑13, Jun 2004 ... 2.99
- ❑14, Jul 2004 ... 2.99
- ❑15, Jul 2004 ... 2.99
- ❑16, Aug 2004 ... 2.99
- ❑17, Sep 2004 ... 2.99
- ❑18, Oct 2004, Final Issue ... 2.99

Venom: Along Came a Spider
Marvel

- ❑1, Jan 1996 ... 2.95
- ❑2, Feb 1996 ... 2.95
- ❑3, Mar 1996 ... 2.95
- ❑4, Apr 1996 ... 2.95

Venom: Carnage Unleashed
Marvel

- ❑1, Apr 1995; cardstock cover ... 2.95
- ❑2, May 1995; cardstock cover ... 2.95
- ❑3, Jun 1995; cardstock cover ... 2.95
- ❑4, Jul 1995; cardstock cover ... 2.95

Venom: Deathtrap: The Vault
Marvel

- ❑1; one-shot (also published as Avengers: Deathtrap: The Vault) ... 6.95

Venom: Finale
Marvel

- ❑1, Nov 1997; gatefold summary ... 2.00
- ❑2, Dec 1997; gatefold summary; V: Spider-Man ... 2.00
- ❑3, Jan 1998; gatefold summary; V: Spider-Man ... 2.00

Venom: Funeral Pyre
Marvel

- ❑1, Aug 1993; foil cover ... 2.95
- ❑2, Sep 1993 ... 2.95
- ❑3, Oct 1993 ... 2.95

Venom: Lethal Protector
Marvel

- ❑1, Feb 1993; Metallic ink cover ... 3.00
- ❑1/Black, Feb 1993; Black Cover printing error ... 75.00
- ❑1/Gold, Feb 1993; Gold edition; O: Venom ... 5.00
- ❑2, Mar 1993 A: Spider-Man ... 3.00
- ❑3, Apr 1993 AM (a) ... 3.00
- ❑4, May 1993 A: Spider-Man ... 3.00
- ❑5, Jun 1993 A: Spider-Man ... 3.00
- ❑6, Jul 1993 A: Spider-Man ... 3.00

What If...?

Explores alternate possibilities
©Marvel

What If...?

Updated alternative choices at Marvel
©Marvel

What The-?!

Longer-lived than Not Brand Ecch
©Marvel

Wheel of Worlds

Reversed title sounds like car show
©Tekno

Where Monsters Dwell

Pre-hero tales from Marvel's past
©Marvel

N-MINT

Venom: License to Kill
Marvel
❑1, Jun 1997 ... 2.00
❑2, Jul 1997 ... 2.00
❑3, Aug 1997; gatefold summary ... 2.00

Venom: Nights of Vengeance
Marvel
❑1, Aug 1994, red foil cover ... 2.95
❑2, Sep 1994, cardstock cover ... 2.95
❑3, Oct 1994, cardstock cover ... 2.95
❑4, Nov 1994, cardstock cover ... 2.95

Venom: On Trial
Marvel
❑1, Mar 1997 A: Daredevil. A: Spider-Man 2.00
❑2, Apr 1997 A: Daredevil. A: Spider-Man 2.00
❑3, May 1997 A: Daredevil. A: Carnage. A: Spider-Man ... 2.00

Venom: Seed of Darkness
Marvel
❑-1, Jul 1997; Flashback ... 2.00

Venom: Separation Anxiety
Marvel
❑1, Dec 1994; Embossed cover ... 2.95
❑2, Jan 1995 ... 2.95
❑3, Feb 1995 ... 2.95
❑4, Mar 1995 ... 2.95

Venom: Sign of the Boss
Marvel
❑1, Sep 1997; gatefold summary ... 2.00
❑2, Oct 1997; gatefold summary; A: Ghost Rider ... 2.00

Venom: Sinner Takes All
Marvel
❑1, Aug 1995; 1: Sin-Eater III ... 2.95
❑2, Sep 1995 ... 2.95
❑3, Oct 1995 ... 2.95
❑4, Nov 1995 ... 2.95
❑5, Dec 1995 ... 2.95

Venom Super Special
Marvel
❑1, Aug 1995; Flip-book; two of the stories continue in Spectacular Spider-Man Super Special #1 ... 3.95

Venom: The Enemy Within
Marvel
❑1, Feb 1994; Glow-in-the-dark cover ... 2.95
❑2, Mar 1994 ... 2.95
❑3, Apr 1994 ... 2.95

Venom: The Hunger
Marvel
❑1, Aug 1996 ... 2.00
❑2, Sep 1996 ... 2.00
❑3, Oct 1996 ... 2.00
❑4, Nov 1996 ... 2.00

Venom: The Hunted
Marvel
❑1, May 1996 ... 2.95
❑2, Jun 1996 ... 2.95
❑3, Jul 1996 ... 2.95

N-MINT

Venom: The Mace
Marvel
❑1, May 1994; Embossed cover ... 2.95
❑2, Jun 1994 ... 2.95
❑3, Jul 1994; V: Sunrise Society ... 2.95

Venom: The Madness
Marvel
❑1, Nov 1993; Embossed cover ... 2.95
❑2, Dec 1993; V: Juggernaut; Some ink credits in letters page ... 2.95
❑3, Jan 1994; V: Juggernaut ... 2.95

Venom: Tooth and Claw
Marvel
❑1, Nov 1996, A: Wolverine. V: Wolverine 2.00
❑2, Dec 1996, V: Wolverine ... 2.00
❑3, Jan 1997, V: Wolverine; Final Issue. 2.00

Venom vs. Carnage
Marvel
❑1, Sep 2004 ... 6.00
❑2, Oct 2004 ... 2.99
❑3, Nov 2004 ... 2.99
❑4, Dec 2004 ... 2.99

Venture
AC
❑1, Aug 1986; Bolt; Explorers Ltd.; Astron 1.75
❑2 1986; Bolt; Femforce; Explorers Ltd.. 1.75
❑3 1987; Bolt; Explorers Ltd.; Faze One Fazers ... 1.75

Venture
Image
❑1, Jan 2003 ... 2.95
❑2, Feb 2003 ... 2.95
❑3, Apr 2003 ... 2.95
❑4, Sep 2003 ... 2.95

Venture San Diego Comic-Con Special Edition
Venture
❑1, Jul 1994, b&w ... 2.50

Venumb
Parody
❑1 1993, b&w ... 2.50
❑1/Deluxe 1993, b&w; enhanced cover. 2.95

Venus Domina
Verotik
❑1, ca. 1997 ... 4.95
❑2, ca. 1997 ... 4.95
❑3, Mar 1997 ... 4.95

Venus Interface
HM Communications
❑1 ... 6.00

Venus Wars
Dark Horse
❑1, Apr 1991, b&w; Japanese; trading cards ... 2.50
❑2, May 1991, b&w; Japanese; trading cards ... 2.25
❑3, Jun 1991, b&w; Japanese; trading cards ... 2.25
❑4, Jul 1991 ... 2.25
❑5, Aug 1991 ... 2.25
❑6, Sep 1991 ... 2.25
❑7, Oct 1991 ... 2.25
❑8, Nov 1991 ... 2.25

N-MINT

❑9, Dec 1991 ... 2.25
❑10, Jan 1992 ... 2.25
❑11, Feb 1992 ... 2.25
❑12, Mar 1992 ... 2.25
❑13, Apr 1992 ... 2.25
❑14, May 1992 ... 2.25

Venus Wars II
Dark Horse
❑1, Jun 1992; 48 pages ... 2.50
❑2, Jul 1992 ... 2.50
❑3, Aug 1992 ... 2.50
❑4, Sep 1992 ... 2.50
❑5, Oct 1992, b&w ... 2.50
❑6, Nov 1992, b&w ... 2.50
❑7, Dec 1992, b&w ... 2.50
❑8, Jan 1993, b&w ... 2.50
❑9, Feb 1993, b&w ... 2.50
❑10, Mar 1993, b&w ... 2.50
❑11, Apr 1993, b&w ... 2.95
❑12, May 1993, b&w ... 2.95
❑13, Jun 1993 ... 2.95
❑14, Jul 1993 ... 2.95
❑15, Aug 1993 ... 2.95

Verbatim
Fantagraphics
❑1, Apr 1993, b&w ... 2.75
❑2, ca. 1993, b&w ... 2.75

Verdict
Eternity
❑1, ca. 1998 ... 1.95
❑2, ca. 1998 ... 1.95
❑3, Jun 1988 ... 1.95
❑4, ca. 1988 ... 1.95

Vermillion
DC / Helix
❑1, Oct 1996 ... 2.25
❑2, Nov 1996 ... 2.25
❑3, Dec 1996 ... 2.25
❑4, Jan 1997 ... 2.25
❑5, Feb 1997 ... 2.25
❑6, Mar 1997 ... 2.25
❑7, Apr 1997 ... 2.25
❑8, May 1997 ... 2.25
❑9, Jun 1997 ... 2.25
❑10, Jul 1997 ... 2.25
❑11, Aug 1997 ... 2.25
❑12, Sep 1997 ... 2.25

Veronica
Archie
❑1, Apr 1989 ... 2.00
❑2, Jul 1989 ... 1.50
❑3, Sep 1989 ... 1.50
❑4, Oct 1989 ... 1.50
❑5, Dec 1989 ... 1.50
❑6 1990 ... 1.50
❑7, Apr 1990 ... 1.50
❑8, Jun 1990 ... 1.50
❑9, Jul 1990 ... 1.50
❑10, Sep 1990 ... 1.50
❑11, Oct 1990 ... 1.50
❑12, Dec 1990 ... 1.50
❑13, Feb 1991 ... 1.50
❑14, Apr 1991 ... 1.50
❑15, Jun 1991 ... 1.50

Other grades: Multiply price above by 5/6 for VF/NM • 2/3 for VERY FINE • 1/3 for FINE • 1/5 for VERY GOOD • 1/8 for GOOD

	N-MINT
❑16, Aug 1991	1.50
❑17, Oct 1991	1.50
❑18, Dec 1991	1.50
❑19, Feb 1992	1.50
❑20, Apr 1992	1.50
❑21, Jun 1992	1.25
❑22, Aug 1992	1.25
❑23, Sep 1992	1.25
❑24, Oct 1992	1.25
❑25, Dec 1992	1.25
❑26, Feb 1993	1.25
❑27, Apr 1993	1.25
❑28, Jun 1993	1.25
❑29, Aug 1993	1.25
❑30, Sep 1993	1.25
❑31, Oct 1993	1.25
❑32, Dec 1993	1.25
❑33, Feb 1994	1.25
❑34, Apr 1994	1.25
❑35, Jun 1994	1.25
❑36, Aug 1994	1.50
❑37, Sep 1994	1.50
❑38, Oct 1994	1.50
❑39, Dec 1994	1.50
❑40, Jan 1995	1.50
❑41, Mar 1995	1.50
❑42, Apr 1995	1.50
❑43, Jun 1995	1.50
❑44, Jul 1995	1.50
❑45, Aug 1995	1.50
❑46, Sep 1995	1.50
❑47, Oct 1995	1.50
❑48, Nov 1995	1.50
❑49, Jan 1996	1.50
❑50, Feb 1996	1.50
❑51, Apr 1996	1.50
❑52, Jun 1996	1.50
❑53, Jul 1996	1.50
❑54, Aug 1996	1.50
❑55, Sep 1996	1.50
❑56, Oct 1996	1.50
❑57, Nov 1996	1.50
❑58, Dec 1996	1.50
❑59, Jan 1997	1.50
❑60, Feb 1997	1.50
❑61, Mar 1997	1.50
❑62, Apr 1997	1.50
❑63, May 1997	1.50
❑64, Jun 1997	1.50
❑65, Jul 1997	1.50
❑66, Aug 1997	1.50
❑67, Sep 1997	1.50
❑68, Oct 1997	1.50
❑69, Nov 1997	1.50
❑70, Dec 1997	1.50
❑71, Jan 1998	1.50
❑72, Feb 1998	1.50
❑73, Mar 1998	1.50
❑74, Apr 1998, Veronica markets Jughead's beanie	1.50
❑75, May 1998	1.50
❑76, Jun 1998	1.50
❑77, Jul 1998	1.50
❑78, Aug 1998	1.50
❑79, Sep 1998	1.75
❑80, Oct 1998	1.75
❑81, Nov 1998, Veronica in Oz	1.75
❑82, Dec 1998	1.75
❑83, Jan 1999	1.75
❑84, Feb 1999	1.75
❑85, Mar 1999	1.75
❑86, Apr 1999	1.79
❑87, May 1999	1.79
❑88, Jun 1999	1.79
❑89, Jul 1999	1.79
❑90, Aug 1999	1.79
❑91, Aug 1999	1.79
❑92, Oct 1999	1.79
❑93, Nov 1999	1.79
❑94, Dec 1999	1.79
❑95, Jan 2000	1.79
❑96, Feb 2000	1.79
❑97, Mar 2000	1.79
❑98, Apr 2000	1.79
❑99, May 2000	1.99
❑100, Jun 2000	1.99
❑101, Jul 2000	1.99

	N-MINT
❑102, Aug 2000	1.99
❑103, Sep 2000	1.99
❑104, Oct 2000	1.99
❑105, Nov 2000	1.99
❑106, Dec 2000	1.99
❑107, Jan 2001	1.99
❑108, Feb 2001	1.99
❑109, Mar 2001	1.99
❑110, Apr 2001	1.99
❑111, May 2001	1.99
❑112, Jun 2001	1.99
❑113, Jul 2001	1.99
❑114, Jul 2001	1.99
❑115, Aug 2001	1.99
❑116, Sep 2001	1.99
❑117, Oct 2001	1.99
❑118, Nov 2001	1.99
❑119, Dec 2001	1.99
❑120, Jan 2002	1.99
❑121, Feb 2002	1.99
❑122, Mar 2002	1.99
❑123, Apr 2002	1.99
❑124, May 2002	1.99
❑125, Jun 2002	1.99
❑126, Jul 2002	1.99
❑127, Jul 2002	1.99
❑128, Aug 2002	1.99
❑129, Sep 2002	1.99
❑130, Oct 2002	1.99
❑131, Nov 2002	1.99
❑132, Dec 2002	1.99
❑133, Jan 2003	1.99
❑134, Feb 2003	2.19
❑135, Mar 2003	2.19
❑136, Apr 2003	2.19
❑137, May 2003	2.19
❑138, Jun 2003	2.19
❑139, Jul 2003	2.19
❑140, Jul 2003	2.19
❑141, Aug 2003	2.19
❑142, Sep 2003	2.19
❑143, Oct 2003	2.19
❑144, Nov 2003	2.19
❑145, Dec 2003	2.19
❑146, Jan 2004	2.19
❑147, Feb 2004	2.19
❑148, Mar 2004	2.19
❑149, Apr 2004	2.19
❑150, May 2004	2.19
❑151, Jun 2004	2.19
❑152, Jul 2004	2.19
❑153, Aug 2004	2.19
❑154, Sep 2004	2.19
❑155, Oct 2004	2.19
❑156, Jan 2004	2.19
❑157, Feb 2005	2.19
❑158, Mar 2005	2.19
❑159, Apr 2005	2.19
❑160, May 2005	2.19
❑161, Jun 2005	2.19
❑162, Jul 2005	2.25
❑163, Aug 2005	2.25
❑164, Sep 2005	2.25
❑165, Oct 2005; Includes Bionicle preview comic	2.25
❑166, Dec 2005	2.25
❑167, Jan 2006, Veronicas partial photo cover	2.25
❑168, May 2006	2.25
❑169, May 2006	2.25
❑170, Jul 2006	2.25
❑171, Aug 2006	2.25
❑172, Aug 2006	2.25
❑173, Oct 2006	2.25
❑174, Oct 2006	2.25
❑175, Dec 2006	2.25
❑176, Jan 2007, Includes 3-D Heroscape glasses; Includes Teen Titans: Sparktop mini-comic	2.25
❑177, Mar 2007, Includes The Adventures of Finn & Friends insert comic	2.25
❑178	2.25
❑179	2.25
❑180	2.25
❑181	2.25
❑182	2.25
❑183	2.25
❑184	2.25

	N-MINT
❑185	2.25
❑186	2.25
❑187	2.25
❑188	2.25
❑189	2.25
❑190	2.25
❑191	2.25
❑192	2.25
❑193	2.25

Veronica's Digest Magazine
Archie

❑1, ca. 1992	2.00
❑2, ca. 1993	1.75
❑3, ca. 1994	1.75
❑4, Sep 1995	1.75
❑5, Sep 1996	1.75
❑6, Oct 1997	1.79

Verotika
Verotik

❑1, Oct 1994; Adult	4.00
❑2, Jan 1995; Adult	3.00
❑3, May 1995; FF (c); Frank Frazetta cover; Adult	3.00
❑4, Jun 1995; Adult	3.00
❑5 1995; Adult	3.00
❑6 1995; Adult	3.00
❑7, Dec 1995; Adult	3.00
❑8, Feb 1996; Adult	3.00
❑9, Mar 1996; Adult	3.00
❑10, May 1996; Adult	3.00
❑11; Adult	3.00
❑12; Adult	3.00
❑13; Adult	3.00
❑14; Adult	3.00
❑15; Adult	3.95

Verotik Illustrated
Verotik

❑1, Aug 1997	6.95
❑2, Dec 1997	6.95
❑3, Apr 1998	6.95

Verotik Rogues Gallery of Villains
Verotik

❑1, Nov 1997; pin-ups	3.95

Verotik World
Verotik

❑1, Aug 2002; Regular edition	3.95
❑1/Variant, Aug 2002; Fan Club cover edition; no cover price; solicited with a $5 cost	5.00
❑2, Mar 2004	3.95
❑3	3.95
❑3/Variant	10.00

Version
Dark Horse

❑1.1, ca. 1993	2.50
❑1.2, ca. 1993	2.50
❑1.3, ca. 1993	2.50
❑1.4, ca. 1993	2.50
❑1.5, ca. 1993	2.50
❑1.6, ca. 1993	2.50
❑1.7, ca. 1993	2.50
❑1.8, ca. 1993	2.50
❑2.1, ca. 1993	2.95
❑2.2, ca. 1993	2.95
❑2.3, ca. 1993	2.95
❑2.4, ca. 1993	2.95
❑2.5, ca. 1993	2.95
❑2.6, ca. 1993	2.95
❑2.7, ca. 1993	2.95

Vertical
DC

❑1, Feb 2004	4.95

Vertigo Gallery: Dreams and Nightmares
DC / Vertigo

❑1; MW, BSz, ATh, CV (a); pin-ups	4.00

Vertigo Jam
DC / Vertigo

❑1, Aug 1993	3.95

Vertigo Pop! Bangkok
DC / Vertigo

❑1, Jul 2003	2.95
❑2, Aug 2003	2.95

Other grades: Multiply price above by 5/6 for VF/NM • 2/3 for VERY FINE • 1/3 for FINE • 1/5 for VERY GOOD • 1/8 for GOOD

Whiteout

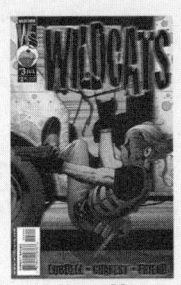

Criminal investigations in the Antarctic

©Oni

Who's Who in the DC Universe

Looseleaf bio pages added filing work

©DC

Wildcards

Based on super-hero prose anthologies

©Marvel

WildC.A.T.s

C.A.T.s are Covert Action Teams

©Image

WildCats

Move to DC lost acronym

©DC

N-MINT

❑3, Sep 2003 .... 2.95
❑4, Oct 2003 .... 2.95

Vertigo Pop! London
DC / Vertigo

❑1, ca. 2002 .... 2.95
❑2, ca. 2002 .... 2.95
❑3, ca. 2002 .... 2.95
❑4, Feb 2003 .... 2.95

Vertigo Pop! Tokyo
DC / Vertigo

❑1, Sep 2002 .... 2.95
❑2, Oct 2002 .... 2.95
❑3, Nov 2002 .... 2.95

Vertigo Preview
DC / Vertigo

❑1; MW, NG (w); Previews DC Vertigo titles 1.50

Vertigo Rave
DC / Vertigo

❑1, Aut 1994 .... 1.50

Vertigo Secret Files & Origins: Swamp Thing
DC / Vertigo

❑1, Nov 2000 .... 4.95

Vertigo Secret Files: Hellblazer
DC / Vertigo

❑1, Aug 2000 PG (a) 4.95

Vertigo Verité: The Unseen Hand
DC / Vertigo

❑1, Sep 1996 .... 2.50
❑2, Oct 1996 .... 2.50
❑3, Nov 1996 .... 2.50
❑4, Dec 1996 .... 2.50

Vertigo Visions: Doctor Occult
DC / Vertigo

❑1, Jul 1994; One-shot 3.95

Vertigo Visions: Dr. Thirteen
DC / Vertigo

❑1, Sep 1998; One-shot 5.95

Vertigo Visions: Prez
DC / Vertigo

❑1, Sep 1995; One-shot 3.95

Vertigo Visions: The Geek
DC / Vertigo

❑1, Jun 1993 .... 3.95

Vertigo Visions: The Phantom Stranger
DC / Vertigo

❑1, Oct 1993 .... 3.50

Vertigo Visions: Tomahawk
DC / Vertigo

❑1, Jul 1998; One-shot 4.95

Vertigo Voices: The Eaters
DC / Vertigo

❑1; ca. 1995 .... 4.95

Vertigo: Winter's Edge
DC / Vertigo

❑1, Jan 1998; prestige format anthology; wraparound cover 7.95

N-MINT

❑2, Jan 1999; wraparound cover 6.95
❑3, Jan 2000 .... 6.95

Vertigo X Preview
DC / Vertigo

❑1, Apr 2003 .... 0.99

Very Best of Dennis the Menace
Marvel

❑1, Apr 1982; reprints 3.00
❑2, Jun 1982; reprints 2.00
❑3, Aug 1982; reprints 2.00

Very Mu Christmas, A
Mu

❑1, Nov 1992; NN; Features stories of Desert Peach, Shanda the Panda and Rhudiprrt 2.95

Very Vicky
Iconografix

❑1, ca. 1993, b&w 2.95
❑1/2nd, ca. 1993; 2nd printing 2.50
❑2, ca. 1993, b&w 2.50
❑3, ca. 1993, b&w 2.50
❑4, ca. 1993, b&w 2.50
❑5, ca. 1993, b&w 2.50
❑6, ca. 1993, b&w 2.50
❑7, ca. 1993, b&w 2.50
❑8, ca. 1993, b&w 2.50

Vespers
Mars Media Group

❑1, Aug 1995 .... 2.50

Vext
DC

❑1, Mar 1999, O: Vext 2.50
❑2, Apr 1999, 1: Road Rage 2.50
❑3, May 1999 .... 2.50
❑4, Jun 1999 .... 2.50
❑5, Jul 1999 .... 2.50
❑6, Aug 1999 .... 2.50

V for Vendetta
DC

❑1, Sep 1988, AMo (w); Wraparound cover 3.00
❑2, Oct 1988, AMo (w) 2.50
❑3, Nov 1988, AMo (w) 2.50
❑4, Dec 1988, AMo (w) 2.50
❑5, Win 1988, AMo (w) 2.50
❑6, Hol 1988, AMo (w) 2.50
❑7, Jan 1989, AMo (w) 2.50
❑8, Feb 1989, AMo (w) 2.50
❑9, Mar 1989, AMo (w) 2.50
❑10, May 1989, AMo (w) 2.50

Vibe
Young Gun

❑1, Mar 1994 .... 1.95

Vic & Blood
Mad Dog

❑1, Oct 1987, b&w; O: Blood; Wraparound cover 2.00
❑2, Feb 1988, b&w 2.00

V.I.C.E.
Image

❑1, Nov 2005 .... 2.99
❑1/Silvestri, Nov 2005 .... 2.99
❑1/Variant, Nov 2005 .... 2.99

N-MINT

❑2, Dec 2005 .... 2.99
❑3, Jan 2006 .... 2.99
❑4, Jan 2006 .... 2.99
❑5, Apr 2006 .... 2.99

Vicious
Brainstorm

❑1, b&w; Adult 2.95

Vicki
Atlas-Seaboard

❑1, Feb 1975; reprints Tippy Teen 28.00
❑2, Apr 1975; reprints Tippy Teen 18.00
❑3, Jun 1975; reprints Tippy Teen 12.00
❑4, Aug 1975; reprints Tippy Teen 12.00

Vicki Valentine
Renegade

❑1, Jul 1985, b&w 1.70
❑2, Nov 1985, b&w 1.70
❑3 1986, b&w 1.70
❑4 1986, b&w 1.70

Victim
Silverwolf

❑1, Feb 1987, b&w 1.50

Victims
Eternity

❑1, Oct 1988, b&w; Reprints 2.00
❑2, Nov 1988, b&w; Reprints 2.00
❑3, Dec 1988, b&w; Reprints 2.00
❑4, Jan 1989, b&w; Reprints 2.00
❑5, Feb 1989, b&w; Reprints 2.00
❑6, Mar 1983 .... 2.00

Victorian
Penny-Farthing

❑½, Aug 1998; preview of upcoming series; Sketches and notes for series 1.00
❑1, Mar 1999 .... 3.00
❑2, Apr 1999 .... 2.95
❑3, May 1999 .... 2.95
❑4, Jun 1999 .... 2.95
❑5, Jul 1999 .... 2.95
❑7, Sep 1999 .... 2.95
❑6, Aug 1999 .... 2.95
❑8, Apr 2001 .... 2.95
❑9, Jun 2001 .... 2.95
❑10, Aug 2001 .... 2.95
❑11, Nov 2001 .... 2.95
❑12, Dec 2001 .... 2.95
❑13, Jan 2002 .... 2.95
❑14, Aug 2002 .... 2.95
❑15, Sep 2002 .... 2.95
❑16, Oct 2002 .... 2.95
❑17, Dec 2002 .... 2.95
❑18, Feb 2003 .... 2.95
❑19, Jul 2003 .... 2.95
❑20, Sep 2003 .... 2.95
❑21, Nov 2003 .... 2.95
❑22 .... 2.95
❑23, Apr 2004 .... 2.95
❑24, Jul 2004 .... 2.95
❑25, Feb 2005 .... 2.95

Victoria's Secret Service
Alias

❑0, Dec 2005 .... 0.75
❑1 .... 2.00

Vic Torry
Avalon

❑1 ... 2.95

Victor Vector & Yondo
Fractal

❑1, Jul 1994 ... 1.95
❑2 1994 ... 1.95
❑3 1994 ... 1.95

Victory
Topps

❑1, Jun 1994, First and final issue (series cancelled); Liefeld cover variant ... 2.50
❑1/Kirby, Jun 1994; First and final issue (series cancelled); Kirby cover variant ... 0.00

Victory
Image

❑1, Jun 2003 ... 2.95
❑1/A, Jul 2003 ... 2.95
❑1/B, Jul 2003 ... 2.95
❑2, Oct 2003 ... 2.95
❑2/A, Oct 2003 ... 2.95
❑3, Dec 2003 ... 2.95
❑3/A, Dec 2003 ... 2.95
❑4, May 2004 ... 2.95

Victory (Vol. 2)
Image

❑1/A, ca. 2004 ... 2.95
❑1/B, ca. 2004 ... 2.95
❑2/A, ca. 2004 ... 2.95
❑2/B, ca. 2004 ... 2.95
❑3/A, ca. 2005 ... 2.95
❑3/B, ca. 2005 ... 2.95
❑4/A, ca. 2005 ... 2.95
❑4/B, ca. 2005 ... 2.95
❑4/C, ca. 2005 ... 2.95

Video Classics
Eternity

❑1, b&w; Mighty Mouse ... 3.50
❑2, b&w; Mighty Mouse ... 3.50

Video Girl AI
Viz

❑1, Jun 2003, b&w ... 15.95
❑2, Aug 2003, b&w ... 15.95
❑3, Dec 2003, b&w ... 15.95
❑4, Feb 2004, b&w ... 15.95
❑5, Apr 2004, b&w ... 15.95
❑6, Apr 2004, b&w ... 12.95
❑7, Jun 2004, b&w ... 12.95
❑8, Aug 2004, b&w ... 12.95
❑9, Oct 2004, b&w ... 9.99
❑10, Jan 2005; b&w ... 9.99
❑11, Apr 2005; b&w ... 9.99
❑12, Jul 2005; Read right to left; b&w ... 9.99
❑13, Oct 2005 ... 9.99

Video Hiroshima
Aeon

❑1, Aug 1995, b&w; NN; One-shot ... 2.50

Video Jack
Marvel / Epic

❑1, Sep 1987 ... 1.25
❑2, Nov 1987 ... 1.25
❑3, Mar 1988 ... 1.25
❑4, May 1988 ... 1.25
❑5, Jul 1988 ... 1.25
❑6, Sep 1988 ... 1.25

Vietnam Journal
Apple

❑1, Nov 1987, b&w ... 2.00
❑1/2nd, ca. 1988; 2nd printing ... 2.00
❑2, Jan 1988 ... 2.00
❑3, Mar 1988 ... 2.00
❑4, May 1988 ... 2.00
❑5, Jul 1988 ... 2.00
❑6, Sep 1988 ... 2.00
❑7, Nov 1988 ... 2.00
❑8, Jan 1989 ... 2.00
❑9, Mar 1989 ... 2.00
❑10, May 1989 ... 2.00
❑11, Jul 1989 ... 2.25
❑12, Sep 1989 ... 2.25
❑13, Nov 1989 ... 2.25
❑14, Jan 1990 ... 2.25
❑15, Mar 1990 ... 2.25
❑16, May 1990; Final Issue ... 2.25

Vietnam Journal: Bloodbath at Khe Sanh
Apple

❑1, b&w ... 2.75
❑2, b&w ... 2.75
❑3, b&w ... 2.75
❑4, b&w ... 2.75

Vietnam Journal: Tet '68
Apple

❑1, b&w ... 2.75
❑2, b&w ... 2.75
❑3, b&w ... 2.75
❑4, b&w ... 2.75
❑5, b&w ... 2.75
❑6, b&w ... 2.75

Vietnam Journal: Valley of Death
Apple

❑1, Jun 1994, b&w ... 2.75

Vigilante
DC

❑1, Nov 1983; 1: Vigilante II ... 2.00
❑2, Jan 1984 ... 1.50
❑3, Feb 1984; V: Cyborg ... 1.50
❑4, Mar 1984 ... 1.25
❑5, Apr 1984; 1: Cannon; 1: Saber ... 1.25
❑6, May 1984; O: Vigilante II ... 1.25
❑7, Jun 1984; O: Vigilante II ... 1.25
❑8, Jul 1984; Vigilante pinup ... 1.25
❑9, Aug 1984; D: J.J. Davis ... 1.25
❑10, Sep 1984 ... 1.25
❑11, Oct 1984; Michael Eury L.O.C. ... 1.25
❑12, Nov 1984 ... 1.25
❑13, Dec 1984 ... 1.25
❑14, Feb 1985 ... 1.25
❑15, Mar 1985 ... 1.25
❑16, Apr 1985; Kevin Dooley L.O.C. ... 1.25
❑17, May 1985 ... 1.25
❑18, Jun 1985 ... 1.25
❑19, Jul 1985 ... 1.25
❑20, Aug 1985 ... 1.25
❑21, Sep 1985 ... 1.25
❑22, Oct 1985; Crisis ... 1.25
❑23, Nov 1985 ... 1.25
❑24, Dec 1985 ... 1.50
❑25, Jan 1986 ... 1.25
❑26, Feb 1986 ... 1.25
❑27, Mar 1986 ... 1.25
❑28, Apr 1986 ... 1.25
❑29, May 1986 ... 1.25
❑30, Jun 1986 ... 1.25
❑31, Jul 1986 ... 1.25
❑32, Aug 1986 ... 1.25
❑33, Sep 1986 ... 1.25
❑34, Oct 1986 ... 1.25
❑35, Nov 1986; O: Mad Bomber; Continued in Vigilante Ann #2 ... 1.25
❑36, Dec 1986; D: Vigilante ... 1.25
❑37, Jan 1987 ... 1.25
❑38, Feb 1987 ... 1.25
❑39, Mar 1987 ... 1.25
❑40, Apr 1987 ... 1.25
❑41, May 1987 ... 1.25
❑42, Jun 1987 ... 1.25
❑43, Jul 1987 ... 1.25
❑44, Aug 1987 ... 1.25
❑45, Sep 1987; 1: Blackthorn ... 1.25
❑46, Oct 1987 ... 1.25
❑47, Nov 1987 ... 1.25
❑48, Dec 1987 ... 1.25
❑49, Jan 1988 ... 1.25
❑50, Feb 1988; Vigilante commits suicide ... 1.25
❑Ann 1, ca. 1985 ... 2.00
❑Ann 2, ca. 1986 ... 2.00

Vigilante: City Lights, Prairie Justice
DC

❑1, Nov 1995 ... 2.50
❑2, Dec 1995 ... 2.50
❑3, Jan 1996 ... 2.50
❑4, Feb 1996 ... 2.50

Vigilante
DC

❑1 2005 ... 2.99
❑2, Jan 2006 ... 2.99
❑3, Jan 2006 ... 2.99
❑4, Feb 2006 ... 2.99
❑5, Mar 2006 ... 2.99
❑6, May 2006 ... 2.99

Vigilante 8: Second Offense
Chaos

❑1, Dec 1999 ... 2.95

Vigil: Bloodline
Duality

❑1, ca. 1998; b&w ... 2.95
❑2, ca. 1998; b&w ... 2.95
❑3, ca. 1998; b&w ... 2.95
❑4, ca. 1998; b&w ... 2.95
❑5, Nov 1998; b&w ... 2.95
❑6, ca. 1999; b&w ... 2.95
❑7, ca. 1999; b&w ... 2.95
❑8, Jul 1999; b&w ... 2.95

Vigil: Desert Foxes
Millennium

❑1, Jul 1995, b&w ... 3.95
❑2, Aug 1995, b&w ... 3.95

Vigil: Eruption
Millennium

❑1, Aug 1996, b&w ... 2.95
❑2, ca. 1996; b&w ... 2.95

Vigil: Fall from Grace
Innovation

❑1, Mar 1992, b&w; 1: Grace Kimble; 1: Greg Tonelli ... 2.95
❑2, ca. 1992, b&w ... 2.95

Vigil: Kukulkan
Innovation

❑1 ... 2.95

Vigil: Rebirth
Millennium

❑1, Nov 1994, b&w; O: Grace Kimble ... 2.95
❑2, Dec 1994, b&w; O: Grace Kimble ... 2.95

Vigil: Scattershots
Duality

❑1, Jul 1997, b&w ... 3.95
❑2, ca. 1997 ... 3.95

Vigil: The Golden Parts
Innovation

❑1, b&w ... 2.95

Vigil: Vamporum Animaturi
Millennium

❑1, May 1994, b&w; NN ... 3.95

Vignette Comics
Harrier

❑1, b&w ... 1.95

Vile
Raging Rhino

❑1 ... 2.95

Villains & Vigilantes
Eclipse

❑1, Dec 1986; 1: Condor; 1: Shadowman (Eclipse) ... 1.50
❑2, Mar 1987 ... 1.50
❑3, Apr 1987 ... 1.50
❑4, Apr 1987 ... 1.50

Villains United
DC

❑1, Jun 2005, D:Fiddler; D: Bug ... 12.00
❑1/2nd, Jun 2005 ... 8.00
❑1/3rd, Jun 2005 ... 3.00
❑2, Jul 2005 ... 5.00
❑3, Aug 2005; D: Hyena; O: Rag Doll ... 2.50
❑4, Sep 2005; O: Cat Man ... 2.50
❑5, Oct 2005 ... 2.50
❑6, Dec 2005; D: Parademon; D: Pariah ... 4.00

Villains United: Infinite Crisis Special
DC

❑1, Jul 2006, D: Jack; D: Amos Fortune. ... 4.99

Villa of the Mysteries
Fantagraphics

❑1, ca. 1998, b&w ... 3.95
❑2, ca. 1998, b&w ... 3.95
❑3, Jul 1998, b&w ... 3.95

Vimanarama!
DC

❑1, Apr 2005 ... 2.95
❑2, May 2005 ... 2.95
❑3, Jun 2005 ... 2.95

Wild Dog

Small-town vigilante saves the day
©DC

Wild Person in the Woods

Orangutan researcher's life story
©G.T. Labs

Wildstar

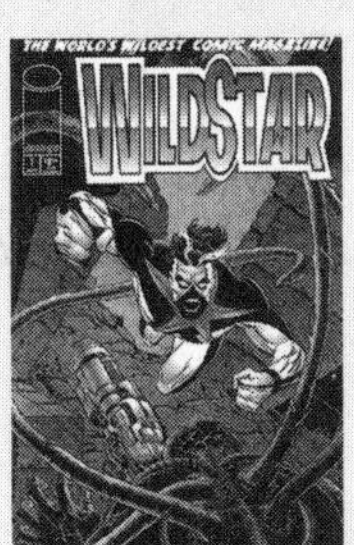

A symbiote-sporting super-hero
©Image

WildStorm Rising

Windsor-Smith's turn at super-heroes
©Image

WildStorms Player's Guide

Short-lived card game's strategy guide
©Image

N-MINT

Vincent J. Mielcarek Jr. Memorial Comic
Cooper Union
- ❑1, Nov 1993, b&w; NN 3.00

Vintage Comic Classics
Recollections
- ❑1, Feb 1990; Red Demon reprint 2.00

Vintage Magnus Robot Fighter
Valiant
- ❑1, Jan 1992; RM (w); RM (a); O: Magnus Robot Fighter. Reprints 5.00
- ❑2, Feb 1992; RM (w); RM (a); Reprints 5.00
- ❑3, Mar 1992; RM (w); RM (a); Reprints 5.00
- ❑4, Apr 1992; RM (w); RM (a); Reprints 5.00

Violator
Image
- ❑1, May 1994, AMo (w); 1: The Admonisher 2.50
- ❑2, Jun 1994, AMo (w) 2.50
- ❑3, Jul 1994, AMo (w) 2.50

Violator vs. Badrock
Image
- ❑1, May 1995 2.50
- ❑1/A, May 1995 2.50
- ❑2, Jun 1995 2.50
- ❑3, Jul 1995 2.50
- ❑4, Aug 1995 2.50

Violent Messiahs
Hurricane
- ❑1, Jul 1997, b&w 2.95
- ❑2, ca. 1997 2.95
- ❑3, ca. 1997 2.95

Violent Messiahs
Image
- ❑½/A, ca. 2000; Two pistols raised on cover 3.00
- ❑½/B, ca. 2000; One pistol up, one down on cover 3.00
- ❑1, Jun 2000 2.95
- ❑2, Aug 2000 2.95
- ❑3, Sep 2000 2.95
- ❑4, Nov 2000 2.95
- ❑5, Jan 2001 2.95
- ❑6, Mar 2001 2.95
- ❑7, Jun 2001 2.95
- ❑8, Sep 2001 2.95

Violent Messiahs: Genesis
Image
- ❑1, Dec 2001, b&w; Collects Violent Messiahs 0.5, Hurricane #1-2, plus sketches 5.95

Violent Messiahs: Lamenting Pain
Image
- ❑1, Sep 2002 2.95
- ❑3, Jan 2003 2.95
- ❑4, Sep 2003 2.95

Violent Tales
Death
- ❑1, Nov 1997, b&w 2.95

Viper
DC
- ❑1, Aug 1994 1.95
- ❑2, Sep 1994 1.95
- ❑3, Oct 1994 1.95
- ❑4, Nov 1994 1.95

Viper Force
Acid Ram
- ❑1, Sep 1995 2.50

Virtex
Oktomica
- ❑0, Oct 1998; Wraparound cover 1.50
- ❑1, Dec 1998 2.50
- ❑2, Jan 1999 2.50
- ❑3 1999 2.50
- ❑Ashcan 1 1999 1.00

Virtua Fighter
Marvel
- ❑1, Aug 1995 2.95

Virtual Bang
Ironcat
- ❑1 2.95
- ❑2 2.95

Virus
Dark Horse
- ❑1, ca. 1993 2.50
- ❑2, ca. 1993 2.50
- ❑3, ca. 1993 2.50
- ❑4, ca. 1994 2.50

Visage Special Edition
Illusion
- ❑1, Aug 1996, b&w 2.00

Vision
Marvel
- ❑1, Nov 1994 1.75
- ❑2, Dec 1994 1.75
- ❑3, Jan 1995 1.75
- ❑4, Feb 1995 1.75

Vision & Scarlet Witch
Marvel
- ❑1, Nov 1982 1.50
- ❑2, Dec 1982, A: Whizzer. D: Whizzer 1.50
- ❑3, Jan 1983, A: Wonder Man 1.50
- ❑4, Feb 1983, A: Magneto 1.50

Vision & Scarlet Witch
Marvel
- ❑1, Oct 1985, RHo (c); RHo (a); Lovers and Zombies; O: the Vision; O: the Scarlet Witch; Continued in West Coast Avengers #2 1.50
- ❑2, Nov 1985, RHo (c); RHo (a); D: Whizzer. D: Whizzer 1.25
- ❑3, Dec 1985, RHo (c); RHo, FH (a) 1.25
- ❑4, Jan 1986, RHo (c); RHo (a) 1.25
- ❑5, Feb 1986, RHo (c); RHo (a) 1.25
- ❑6, Mar 1986, RHo (c); RHo (a) 1.25
- ❑7, Apr 1986, RHo (c); RHo (a) 1.25
- ❑8, May 1986, RHo (c); RHo (a) 1.25
- ❑9, Jun 1986, RHo (c); RHo (a) 1.25
- ❑10, Jul 1986, RHo (c); RHo (a) 1.25
- ❑11, Aug 1986, RHo (a); A: Spider-Man 1.25
- ❑12, Sep 1986, RHo (c); RHo (a) 1.25

Visionaries
Marvel / Star
- ❑1, Jan 1988; Giant sized 1.00
- ❑2, Feb 1988 1.00
- ❑3, Mar 1988 1.00
- ❑4, Apr 1988 1.00
- ❑5, May 1988 1.00
- ❑6, Jun 1988 1.00

Visions
Caliber
- ❑1; b&w 4.95

Visions: David Mack
Caliber
- ❑1 5.95

Visions of Curves
Fantagraphics / Eros
- ❑1, Apr 1994, b&w; Adult 4.95
- ❑2, ca. 1994; Adult 4.95
- ❑3, May 1995; Sketchbook 4.95

Visions: R.G. Taylor
Caliber
- ❑1, b&w; NN 2.50

Visitations
Image
- ❑1, b&w; squarebound 6.95

Visitor
Valiant
- ❑1, Apr 1995 2.00
- ❑2, May 1995; V: Harbinger 2.00
- ❑3, Jun 1995; Acclaim begins publishing 2.00
- ❑4, Jul 1995; Birthquake 2.00
- ❑5, Jul 1995 2.00
- ❑6, Aug 1995; Birthquake 2.00
- ❑7, Aug 1995; Birthquake 2.00
- ❑8, Sep 1995; The Harbinger's identity is revealed 2.00
- ❑9, Sep 1995 2.00
- ❑10, Oct 1995 2.00
- ❑11, Oct 1995 3.00
- ❑12, Nov 1995 3.00
- ❑13, Nov 1995; Final Issue 5.00

Visitor vs. The Valiant Universe
Valiant
- ❑1, Feb 1995; cardstock cover 3.00
- ❑1/$2.50, Feb 1995 10.00
- ❑2, Mar 1995; cardstock cover 3.00
- ❑2/$2.50, Mar 1995 10.00

Visual Assault Omnibus
Visual Assault
- ❑1, b&w 2.50
- ❑2, b&w 2.50
- ❑3, b&w; Flip-book 3.00

Vixen 9
Samson
- ❑1; Flip-book; no indicia 2.50

Vixen Warrior Diaries
Raging Rhino
- ❑1, b&w; Adult 2.95

Vixen Wars
Raging Rhino
- ❑1, b&w; Adult; ca. 1993 2.95
- ❑2, b&w; Adult 2.95
- ❑3, b&w; Adult; ca. 1993 2.95
- ❑4, b&w; Adult 2.95
- ❑5, b&w; Adult 2.95
- ❑6; Adult; b&w; ca. 1993 2.95
- ❑7; Adult 2.95

Other grades: Multiply price above by 5/6 for VF/NM • 2/3 for VERY FINE • 1/3 for FINE • 1/5 for VERY GOOD • 1/8 for GOOD

❑8; Adult 2.95
❑9; Twisted Vixen stories begin........ 2.95
❑10; Title changes to Twisted Vixen 2.95

Vogue
Image

❑1, Oct 1995 .... 2.50
❑1/A, Oct 1995; alternate cover........ 2.50
❑2, Nov 1995 .... 2.50
❑3, Dec 1995........ 2.50
❑4, Jan 1996........ 2.50

Void Indigo
Marvel / Epic

❑1, Nov 1984; VM (a); Continued from Marvel Graphic Novel 2.00
❑2, Mar 1985 VM (a)........ 2.00

Volcanic Nights
Palliard

❑1, b&w; Adult........ 2.95

Volcanic Revolver
Oni

❑1, Jan 1999, b&w........ 2.95
❑2, Jan 1999, b&w........ 2.95
❑3, Mar 1999, b&w 2.95

Voltron
Solson

❑1........ 1.00
❑2........ 1.00
❑3........ 1.00

Voltron: Defender of the Universe
Image

❑0, May 2003........ 2.50
❑1, May 2003........ 2.95
❑2, Jun 2003........ 2.95
❑3, Jul 2003........ 2.95
❑4, Sep 2003........ 2.95
❑5, Oct 2003........ 2.95

Voltron: Defender of the Universe
Devil's Due

❑1, Jan 2004........ 2.95
❑2, Feb 2004........ 2.95
❑3, Mar 2004........ 2.95
❑4, Apr 2004........ 2.95
❑5, May 2004........ 2.95
❑6, Jun 2004........ 2.95
❑7, Jul 2004........ 2.95
❑8, Aug 2004........ 2.95
❑9, Sep 2004........ 2.95
❑10, Oct 2004........ 2.95
❑11, Nov 2005........ 2.95

Volunteer Comics Summer Line-Up '96
Volunteer

❑1, Sum 1996, b&w; previews........ 2.95

Volunteer Comics Winter Line-Up '96
Volunteer

❑1, ca. 1996, b&w; previews........ 2.95

Volunteers Quest for Dreams Lost
Literacy

❑1, b&w; Turtles; Trollords........ 2.00

Von Fange Brothers: Green Hair and Red "S's"
Mikey-Sized Comics

❑1, Jul 1996, b&w........ 1.75

Von Fange Brothers: The Uncommons
Mikey-Sized Comics

❑1, Oct 1996, b&w........ 1.75

VonPyre
Eyeful

❑1........ 2.95

Voodoo
Image

❑1, Nov 1997; Adult........ 2.50
❑2, Dec 1997; Adult........ 2.50
❑3, Jan 1998; Adult........ 2.50
❑4, Mar 1998; Adult........ 2.50

Voodoo Ink
Deja-Vu

❑0, ca. 1989, b&w........ 1.95
❑1, ca. 1990, b&w........ 1.95
❑2, Sum 1990, b&w........ 1.95
❑3, Fal 1990, b&w........ 1.95
❑4, Win 1990, b&w........ 1.95
❑5, ca. 1991, b&w........ 1.95

Voodoom
Oni

❑1, Jun 2000, b&w; smaller than regular comic book........ 4.95

Voodoo•Zealot: Skin Trade
Image

❑1, Aug 1995; NN; One-shot........ 4.95

Vortex
Vortex

❑1, Nov 1982........ 2.00
❑2, ca. 1983........ 2.00
❑3, May 1983........ 2.00
❑4, ca. 1983........ 2.00
❑5, ca. 1983........ 2.00
❑6, ca. 1983........ 2.00
❑7, ca. 1984........ 2.00
❑8, ca. 1984........ 2.00
❑9, ca. 1984........ 2.00
❑10, Sep 1984 GD (w); GD (a)........ 2.00
❑11, ca. 1984........ 1.75
❑12, ca. 1985........ 1.75
❑13, ca. 1985........ 1.75
❑14, ca. 1985........ 1.75
❑15, ca. 1985........ 1.75

Vortex
Comico

❑1, Oct 1991........ 2.50
❑2, ca. 1991........ 2.50
❑3, ca. 1992, Exists?........ 2.50
❑4, ca. 1992, Exists?........ 2.50

Vortex
Hall of Heroes

❑1, Aug 1993, b&w........ 2.50
❑2, Oct 1993........ 2.50
❑3, Dec 1993........ 2.50
❑4, Feb 1994........ 2.50
❑5, Apr 1994........ 2.50
❑6, Dec 1994........ 2.50

Vortex
Entity

❑1, Jan 1996........ 2.95

Vortex the Wonder Mule
Cutting Edge

❑1, b&w........ 2.95
❑2, b&w........ 2.95

Vox
Apple

❑1, Jun 1989, b&w; JBy (c); JBy (a)...... 2.00
❑2, ca. 1989........ 2.25
❑3, ca. 1989........ 2.25
❑4, ca. 1989........ 2.25
❑5, ca. 1989........ 2.25
❑6, ca. 1990........ 2.25
❑7, ca. 1990........ 2.25

Voyage to the Bottom of the Sea
Gold Key

❑1, Dec 1964........ 60.00
❑2, ca. 1965........ 45.00
❑3, Oct 1965........ 35.00
❑4, May 1966........ 35.00
❑5, Aug 1966........ 35.00
❑6, Nov 1966........ 25.00
❑7, Feb 1967........ 25.00
❑8, May 1967........ 25.00
❑9, Aug 1967........ 25.00
❑10, Nov 1967, Richard Baseheart photo in small box on cover........ 25.00
❑11, Feb 1968........ 18.00
❑12, May 1968........ 18.00
❑13, Aug 1968........ 18.00
❑14, Nov 1968........ 18.00
❑15, Feb 1969........ 12.00
❑16, May 1969, Final Issue........ 12.00

Voyeur
Aircel

❑1, Sep 1991, b&w; Adult........ 2.50
❑2, Oct 1991, b&w; Adult........ 2.50
❑3, b&w; Adult........ 2.50
❑4; Adult........ 2.95

Vroom Socko
Slave Labor

❑1, Nov 1993; reprints strips from Deadline U.K........ 2.50

Vulgar Vince
Throb

❑1........ 1.75

Vultures of Whapeton
Conquest

❑1, b&w; ca. 1991........ 2.95

W
Good

❑1, Nov 1996........ 2.95

Wabbit Wampage
Amazing

❑1, Oct 1987........ 1.95

Wacky Adventures of Cracky
Gold Key

❑1, Dec 1972........ 5.00
❑2, Mar 1973........ 3.00
❑3, Jun 1973........ 2.50
❑4, Sep 1973........ 2.50
❑5, Dec 1973........ 2.50
❑6, Mar 1974........ 2.00
❑7, Jun 1974........ 2.00
❑8, Sep 1974........ 2.00
❑9, Dec 1974........ 2.00
❑10, Mar 1975........ 2.00
❑11, Jun 1975........ 2.00
❑12, Sep 1975........ 2.00

Wacky Races
Gold Key

❑1, Aug 1969........ 40.00
❑2, Feb 1971........ 26.00
❑3, May 1971........ 20.00
❑4, Aug 1971........ 20.00
❑5, Nov 1971........ 20.00
❑6, Feb 1972........ 20.00
❑7, May 1972........ 20.00

Wacky Squirrel
Dark Horse

❑1, Oct 1987, b&w; Cover parody of Boris the Bear #1........ 2.00
❑2 1988........ 2.00
❑3, May 1988........ 2.00
❑4, Oct 1988........ 2.00
❑Special 1, Oct 1987; Flip-book; A: Mr. Monster. Halloween Adventure Special 2.00
❑Summer 1, Jul 1987; Summer Fun Special........ 2.00

Wacky Witch
Gold Key

❑1, Jan 1971........ 12.00
❑2, Apr 1971........ 7.00
❑3, Jul 1971........ 5.00
❑4, Oct 1971........ 5.00
❑5, Jan 1972........ 5.00
❑6, Apr 1972........ 4.00
❑7, Jul 1972........ 4.00
❑8, Oct 1972........ 4.00
❑9, Jan 1973........ 4.00
❑10, Apr 1973........ 4.00
❑11, Jul 1973........ 3.00
❑12, Oct 1973........ 3.00
❑13, Jan 1974........ 3.00
❑14, Apr 1974........ 3.00
❑15, Jul 1974........ 3.00
❑16, Oct 1974........ 3.00
❑17, Jan 1975........ 3.00
❑18, Apr 1975........ 3.00
❑19, Jul 1975........ 3.00
❑20, Oct 1975........ 3.00
❑21, Jan 1976........ 3.00

Wagon Train
Gold Key

❑1, Jan 1964........ 38.00
❑2, Apr 1964........ 25.00
❑3, Jul 1964........ 25.00
❑4, Oct 1964........ 25.00

Wahh
Frank & Hank

❑1, b&w; no indicia; cardstock cover..... 2.95
❑2, b&w; cardstock cover........ 2.95

Wild Times: Deathblow

Time-traveling WildStorm adventures
©DC

Wild, Wild West

Show stars featured on photo covers
©Gold Key

Will Eisner's Quarterly

Eisner's Spirit, other work profiled
©Kitchen Sink

Winnie the Pooh

Silly old adventures of silly old bear
©Gold Key

Witchblade

Female cop acquires mystic armor
©Image

N-MINT

Wahoo Morris
Too Hip Gott Go Graphics

❑1, Aug 2005 .... 2.75

Wahoo Morris
Image

❑1, Mar 2000 ....

Wahoo Morris
Too Hip Gott Go Graphics

❑1, Jun 1998, b&w 2.75
❑2, Oct 1988, b&w 2.75
❑3, Mar 1999, b&w 2.75

Waiting for the End of the World
Rodent

❑1 .... 1.00
❑2 .... 1.00
❑3 .... 1.00

Waiting Place
Slave Labor

❑1, Apr 1997 .... 2.95
❑2, May 1997 .... 2.95
❑3, Jun 1997 .... 2.95
❑4, Jul 1997 .... 2.95
❑5, Aug 1997 .... 2.95
❑6, Sep 1997 .... 2.95

Wake
NBM

❑1 .... 9.95
❑2 .... 8.95
❑3 .... 9.95

Waldo World
Fantagraphics

❑1 .... 2.50
❑2 .... 2.50

Walking Dead
Image

❑1, Oct 2003, b&w series 45.00
❑2, Nov 2003, b&w 32.00
❑3, Dec 2003, b&w 15.00
❑4, Jan 2004, b&w 12.00
❑4/A, Jan 2004, b&w 6.00
❑5, Feb 2004, b&w 4.00
❑6, Mar 2004, b&w 2.95
❑7, Apr 2004, b&w 2.95
❑8, May 2004, b&w 2.95
❑9, Jun 2004, b&w 2.95
❑10, Jul 2004, b&w 2.95
❑11, Aug 2004, b&w 2.95
❑12, Sep 2004, b&w 2.95
❑13, Oct 2004, b&w 2.95
❑14, Nov 2004, b&w 2.95
❑15, Dec 2004 .... 2.95
❑16, Jan 2005 .... 2.95
❑17, Feb 2005 .... 2.95
❑18, ca. 2005 .... 2.95
❑19, Jun 2005 .... 2.95
❑20, Aug 2005 .... 2.99
❑21, Oct 2005 .... 2.99
❑22, Nov 2005 .... 2.99
❑23, Dec 2005 .... 2.99
❑24, Jan 2006 .... 2.99
❑25, Jan 2006 .... 2.99
❑26, Apr 2006 .... 2.99
❑27, May 2006 .... 2.99

N-MINT

❑28, Jul 2006 .... 2.99
❑29, Jul 2006 .... 2.99
❑30, Sep 2006 .... 2.99
❑31, Oct 2006; 5-page preview of Rock Bottom upcoming graphic novel; b&w 2.99
❑32, Nov 2006 .... 2.99
❑33, Jan 2007 .... 2.99
❑34 .... 2.99
❑35 .... 2.99
❑36 .... 2.99
❑37 .... 2.99
❑38 .... 2.99
❑39 .... 2.99
❑40 .... 2.99
❑41 .... 2.99
❑42 .... 2.99
❑43 .... 2.99
❑44 .... 2.99
❑45 .... 2.99
❑46 .... 2.99
❑47 .... 2.99
❑48 .... 2.99
❑49 .... 2.99
❑50 .... 2.99
❑51 .... 2.99
❑52 .... 2.99
❑53 .... 2.99
❑54 .... 2.99
❑55 .... 2.99
❑56 .... 2.99
❑57 .... 2.99
❑58 .... 2.99
❑59 .... 2.99
❑60 .... 2.99
❑61 .... 2.99
❑62 .... 2.99

Walking Dead
Aircel

❑1 1989 .... 5.00
❑2 1989 .... 3.00
❑3 1989 .... 3.00
❑4 1989 .... 3.00
❑Special 1 1989, b&w 4.00

Walk Through October
Caliber

❑1, ca. 1995, b&w 2.95

Wally
Gold Key

❑1, Dec 1962 .... 30.00
❑2, Mar 1963 .... 22.00
❑3, Jun 1963 .... 22.00
❑4, Sep 1963 .... 22.00

Wally the Wizard
Marvel / Star

❑1, Apr 1985 .... 1.00
❑2, May 1985 .... 1.00
❑3, Jun 1985 .... 1.00
❑4, Jul 1985 .... 1.00
❑5, Aug 1985 .... 1.00
❑6, Sep 1985 .... 1.00
❑7, Oct 1985 .... 1.00
❑8, Nov 1985 .... 1.00
❑9, Dec 1985 .... 1.00
❑10, Jan 1986 .... 1.00

N-MINT

❑11, Feb 1986 .... 1.00
❑12, Mar 1986, Final Issue 1.00

Walt Disney Comics Digest
Gold Key

❑1, Jun 1968 .... 60.00
❑2, Jul 1968 .... 40.00
❑3, Aug 1968 .... 40.00
❑4, Oct 1968 .... 40.00
❑5, Nov 1968 .... 40.00
❑6, Dec 1968 .... 25.00
❑7, Jan 1969 .... 25.00
❑8, Feb 1969 .... 25.00
❑9, Mar 1969 .... 25.00
❑10, Apr 1969 .... 25.00
❑11, May 1969 .... 25.00
❑12, Jun 1969 .... 25.00
❑13, Jul 1969 .... 25.00
❑14, Aug 1969 .... 20.00
❑15, Sep 1969 .... 20.00
❑16, Oct 1969 .... 20.00
❑17, Nov 1969 .... 20.00
❑18, Dec 1969 .... 20.00
❑19, Jan 1970 .... 20.00
❑20, Feb 1970 .... 20.00
❑21, Apr 1970 .... 15.00
❑22, Jun 1970 .... 15.00
❑23, Jul 1970 .... 15.00
❑24, Aug 1970 .... 15.00
❑25, Oct 1970 .... 15.00
❑26, Dec 1970 .... 15.00
❑27, Feb 1971 .... 15.00
❑28, Apr 1971 .... 15.00
❑29, Jun 1971 .... 15.00
❑30, Aug 1971 .... 15.00
❑31, Oct 1971 .... 15.00
❑32, Dec 1971 .... 15.00
❑33, Feb 1972 .... 15.00
❑34, Apr 1972 .... 15.00
❑35, Jun 1972, Feature on the 1972 film The Biscuit Eater 15.00
❑36, Aug 1972 .... 15.00
❑37, Oct 1972, Feature on the 1972 film Now You See Him, Now You Don't 15.00
❑38, Dec 1972 .... 15.00
❑39, Feb 1973 .... 15.00
❑40, Apr 1973 .... 15.00
❑41, Jun 1973 .... 15.00
❑42, Aug 1973, Mary Poppins cover 15.00
❑43, Oct 1973 .... 15.00
❑44, Dec 1973 .... 40.00
❑45, Feb 1974 .... 15.00
❑46, Apr 1974 .... 15.00
❑47, Jun 1974 .... 15.00
❑48, Aug 1974 .... 15.00
❑49, Oct 1974 .... 15.00
❑50, Dec 1974 .... 15.00
❑51, Feb 1975 .... 10.00
❑52, Apr 1975 .... 10.00
❑53, Jun 1975 .... 10.00
❑54, Aug 1975 .... 10.00
❑55, Oct 1975 .... 10.00
❑56, Dec 1975 .... 10.00
❑57, Feb 1976 .... 10.00

Walt Disney Giant
Gladstone

❑1, Sep 1995; newsprint cover 2.25
❑2, Nov 1995; newsprint cover 2.25
❑3, Jan 1996; newsprint cover 2.25
❑4, Mar 1996; Mickey Mouse; newsprint cover 2.25
❑5, May 1996; Mickey and Donald; newsprint cover 2.25
❑6, Jul 1996; Uncle Scrooge and the Junior Woodchucks; newsprint cover 2.25
❑7, Sep 1996; newsprint cover 2.25

Walt Disney's Autumn Adventures
Disney

❑1, Fal 1991 2.95
❑2, Fal 1992 2.95

Walt Disney's Christmas Parade
Gold Key

❑1, May 1962 75.00
❑2, Jan 1964 50.00
❑3 1965, ca. 1965 50.00
❑4 1966, ca. 1966 50.00
❑5, Feb 1967 50.00
❑6, Feb 1968 50.00
❑7, Jan 1970 50.00
❑8, Jan 1971 50.00
❑9, Jan 1972 20.00

Walt Disney's Christmas Parade (Gladstone)
Gladstone

❑1, Win 1988, cardstock cover; reprints 2.95
❑2, Win 1989, Reprints 2.95

Walt Disney's Christmas Parade
Gemstone

❑1, Nov 2003 8.95
❑3, Dec 2005 8.95

Walt Disney's Comics and Stories
Dell

❑254, Nov 1961, CB (w); CB (a); Vol. 22 #2 60.00
❑255, Dec 1961, CB (w); CB (a); Vol. 22 #3 60.00
❑256, Jan 1962, CB (w); CB (a); Vol. 22 #4 60.00
❑257, Feb 1962, CB (w); CB (a); Vol. 22 #5 60.00
❑258, Mar 1962, CB (w); CB (a); Vol. 22 #6 60.00
❑259, Apr 1962, CB (w); CB (a); Vol. 22 #7 60.00
❑260, May 1962, CB (w); CB (a); Vol. 22 #8 60.00
❑261, Jun 1962, CB (w); CB (a); Vol. 22 #9 50.00
❑262, Jul 1962, CB (w); CB (a); Vol. 22 #10 50.00
❑263, Aug 1962, CB (w); CB (a); Vol. 22 #11 50.00
❑264, Sep 1962, CB (w); CB (a); Vol. 22 #12 50.00
❑265, Oct 1962, CB (w); CB (a); Vol. 23 #1 50.00
❑266, Nov 1962, CB (w); CB (a); Vol. 23 #2 50.00
❑267, Dec 1962, CB (w); CB (a); Vol. 23 #3 50.00
❑268, Jan 1963, CB (w); CB (a); Vol. 23 #4 50.00
❑269, Feb 1963, CB (w); CB (a); Vol. 23 #5 50.00
❑270, Mar 1963, CB (w); CB (a); Vol. 23 #6 50.00
❑271, Apr 1963, CB (w); CB (a); Vol. 23 #7 50.00
❑272, May 1963, CB (w); CB (a); Vol. 23 #8 50.00
❑273, Jun 1963, CB (w); CB (a); Vol. 23 #9 50.00
❑274, Jul 1963, CB (w); CB (a); Vol. 23 #10 50.00
❑275, Aug 1963, CB (w); CB (a); Vol. 23 #11 50.00
❑276, Sep 1963, CB (w); CB (a); Vol. 23 #12 50.00
❑277, Oct 1963, CB (w); CB (a); Vol. 24 #1 50.00
❑278, Nov 1963, CB (w); CB (a); Vol. 24 #2 50.00
❑279, Dec 1963, CB (w); CB (a); Vol. 24 #3 50.00
❑280, Jan 1964, CB (w); CB (a); Vol. 24 #4 50.00
❑281, Feb 1964, CB (w); CB (a); Vol. 24 #5; "Goofy's Mechanical Wizard" reprinted from Four Color #401 50.00
❑282, Mar 1964, CB (w); CB (a); Vol. 24 #6 50.00
❑283, Apr 1964, CB (w); CB (a); Vol. 24 #7; "Cap'n Blight's Mystery Ship" Reprinted in Walt Disney Comics and Stories #440 50.00
❑284, May 1964, Vol. 24 #8 25.00
❑285, Jun 1964, Vol. 24 #9 25.00
❑286, Jul 1964, CB (w); CB (a); Vol. 24 #10 28.00
❑287, Aug 1964, Vol. 24 #11 25.00
❑288, Sep 1964, CB (w); CB (a); Vol. 24 #12 28.00
❑289, Oct 1964, CB (w); CB (a); Vol. 25 #1 28.00
❑290, Nov 1964, Vol. 25 #2 25.00
❑291, Dec 1964, CB (w); CB (a); Vol. 25 #3 28.00
❑292, Jan 1965, CB (w); CB (a); Vol. 25 #4 28.00
❑293, Feb 1965, CB (w); CB (a); Vol. 25 #5 28.00
❑294, Mar 1965, Vol. 25 #6 25.00
❑295, Apr 1965, Vol. 25 #7 25.00
❑296, May 1965, Vol. 25 #8 25.00
❑297, Jun 1965, CB (w); CB (a); Reprints story from Uncle Scrooge #20 28.00
❑298, Jul 1965, CB (w); CB (a); Reprints story from Four Color Comics #1055 (Daisy Duck's Diary) 28.00
❑299, Aug 1965, CB (w); CB (a); Reprints story from Walt Disney's Comics #117 28.00
❑300, Sep 1965, CB (w); CB (a); Reprints story from Walt Disney's Comics #43 28.00
❑301, Oct 1965, CB (w); CB (a); Reprints stories from Four Color Comics #1150 and Walt Disney's Comics #44 28.00
❑302, Nov 1965, CB (w); CB (a); Reprints story from Walt Disney's Comics #47 28.00
❑303, Dec 1965, CB (w); CB (a); Reprints story from Walt Disney's Comics #49 28.00
❑304, Jan 1966, CB (w); CB (a); Reprints stories from Four Color Comics #1150 and Walt Disney's Comics #63 28.00
❑305, Feb 1966, CB (w); CB (a); Reprints stories from Uncle Scrooge #25 andWalt Disney's Comics #70 28.00
❑306, Mar 1966, CB (w); CB (a); Reprints story from Walt Disney's Comics #94 28.00
❑307, Apr 1966, CB (w); CB (a); Reprints story from Walt Disney's Comics #91 28.00
❑308, May 1966, CB (w); CB (a); Vol. 26 #8 28.00
❑309, Jun 1966, Vol. 26 #9 25.00
❑310, Jul 1966, Vol. 26 #10 25.00
❑311, Aug 1966, Vol. 26 #11 25.00
❑312, Sep 1966, CB (w); CB (a); Vol. 26 #12 28.00
❑313, Oct 1966, Vol. 27 #1 14.00
❑314, Nov 1966, Vol. 27 #2 14.00
❑315, Dec 1966, Vol. 27 #3 14.00
❑316, Jan 1967, Vol. 27 #4 14.00
❑317, Feb 1967, Vol. 27 #5 14.00
❑318, Mar 1967, Vol. 27 #6 14.00
❑319, Apr 1967, Vol. 27 #7 14.00
❑320, May 1967, Vol. 27 #8 14.00
❑321, Jun 1967, Vol. 27 #9 14.00
❑322, Jul 1967, Vol. 27 #10 14.00
❑323, Aug 1967, Vol. 27 #11 14.00
❑324, Sep 1967, Vol. 27 #12 14.00
❑325, Oct 1967, Vol. 28 #1 14.00
❑326, Nov 1967, Vol. 28 #2 14.00
❑327, Dec 1967, Vol. 28 #3 14.00
❑328, Jan 1968, CB (w); CB (a); Reprints story from Walt Disney's Comics #148 14.00
❑329, Feb 1968, Vol. 28 #5 14.00
❑330, Mar 1968, Vol. 28 #6 14.00
❑331, Apr 1968, Vol. 28 #7 14.00
❑332, May 1968, Vol. 28 #8 14.00
❑333, Jun 1968, Vol. 28 #9 14.00
❑334, Jul 1968, Vol. 28 #10 14.00
❑335, Aug 1968, CB (w); CB (a); Reprints story from Walt Disney's Comics #129 25.00
❑336, Sep 1968, Vol. 28 #12 14.00
❑337, Oct 1968, Vol. 29 #1 14.00
❑338, Nov 1968, Vol. 29 #2 14.00
❑339, Dec 1968, Vol. 29 #3 14.00
❑340, Jan 1969, Vol. 29 #4 14.00
❑341, Feb 1969, Vol. 29 #5 14.00
❑342, Mar 1969, CB (w); CB (a); Reprints story from Walt Disney's Comics #131 25.00
❑343, Apr 1969, CB (w); CB (a); Reprints story from Walt Disney's Comics #144 25.00
❑344, May 1969, CB (w); CB (a); Reprints story from Walt Disney's Comics #127 25.00
❑345, Jun 1969, CB (w); CB (a); Reprints story from Walt Disney's Comics #139 25.00
❑346, Jul 1969, CB (w); CB (a); Reprints story from Walt Disney's Comics #140 25.00
❑347, Aug 1969, CB (w); CB (a); Reprints story from Walt Disney's Comics #141 25.00
❑348, Sep 1969, CB (w); CB (a); Reprints story from Walt Disney's Comics #155 25.00
❑349, Oct 1969, CB (w); CB (a); Reprints story from Walt Disney's Comics #92 25.00
❑350, Nov 1969, CB (w); CB (a); Reprints story from Walt Disney's Comics #133 25.00
❑351, Dec 1969, CB (w); CB (a); Reprints story from Walt Disney's Comics #147 25.00
❑351/Poster, Dec 1969, CB (w); CB (a); Reprints story from Walt Disney's Comics #147; with poster insert 30.00
❑351/No poster, Dec 1969, CB (w); CB (a); Reprints story from Walt Disney's Comics #147; poster insert removed . 20.00
❑352, Jan 1970, CB (w); CB (a); Reprints story from Walt Disney's Comics #160 25.00
❑352/Poster, Jan 1970, CB (w); CB (a); Reprints story from Walt Disney's Comics #160; with poster insert 30.00
❑352/No poster, Jan 1970, CB (w); CB (a); Reprints story from Walt Disney's Comics #160; poster insert removed . 30.00
❑353, Feb 1970, CB (w); CB (a); Reprints story from Walt Disney's Comics #173 25.00
❑353/Poster, Feb 1970, CB (w); CB (a); Reprints story from Walt Disney's Comics #173; with poster insert 30.00
❑353/No poster, Feb 1970, CB (w); CB (a); Reprints story from Walt Disney's Comics #173; poster insert removed . 20.00
❑354, Mar 1970, CB (w); CB (a); Reprints story from Walt Disney's Comics #197 25.00
❑354/Poster, Mar 1970, CB (w); CB (a); Reprints story from Walt Disney's Comics #197; with poster insert 30.00
❑354/No poster, Mar 1970, CB (w); CB (a); Reprints story from Walt Disney's Comics #197; poster insert removed . 30.00
❑355, Apr 1970, CB (w); CB (a); Reprints story from Walt Disney's Comics #206 25.00
❑355/Poster, Apr 1970, CB (w); CB (a); Reprints story from Walt Disney's Comics #206; with poster insert 30.00
❑355/No poster, Apr 1970, CB (w); CB (a); Reprints story from Walt Disney's Comics #206; poster insert removed . 30.00
❑356, May 1970, CB (w); CB (a); Reprints story from Walt Disney's Comics #103 25.00
❑356/Poster, May 1970, CB (w); CB (a); Reprints story from Walt Disney's Comics #103; with poster insert 30.00
❑356/No poster, May 1970, CB (w); CB (a); Reprints story from Walt Disney's Comics #103; poster insert removed . 20.00
❑357, Jun 1970, CB (w); CB (a); Reprints story from Walt Disney's Comics #145 25.00
❑357/Poster, Jun 1970, CB (w); CB (a); Reprints story from Walt Disney's Comics #145; with poster insert 30.00
❑357/No poster, Jun 1970, CB (w); CB (a); Reprints story from Walt Disney's Comics #145; poster insert removed . 20.00
❑358, Jul 1970, CB (w); CB (a); Reprints story from Walt Disney's Comics #146 25.00
❑358/Poster, Jul 1970, CB (w); CB (a); Reprints story from Walt Disney's Comics #146; with poster insert 30.00
❑358/No poster, Jul 1970, CB (w); CB (a); Reprints story from Walt Disney's Comics #146; poster insert removed . 30.00
❑359, Aug 1970, CB (w); CB (a); Reprints story from Walt Disney's Comics #154 25.00
❑359/Poster, Aug 1970, CB (w); CB (a); Reprints story from Walt Disney's Comics #154; with poster insert 30.00
❑359/No poster, Aug 1970, CB (w); CB (a); Reprints story from Walt Disney's Comics #154; poster insert removed . 20.00
❑360, Sep 1970, CB (w); CB (a); Reprints story from Walt Disney's Comics #200 25.00
❑360/Poster, Sep 1970, CB (w); CB (a); Reprints story from Walt Disney's Comics #200; with poster insert 30.00
❑360/No poster, Sep 1970, CB (w); CB (a); Reprints story from Walt Disney's Comics #200; poster insert removed . 20.00
❑361, Oct 1970, CB (w); CB (a); Reprints story from Walt Disney's Comics #158 25.00
❑362, Nov 1970, CB (w); CB (a); Reprints story from Walt Disney's Comics #180 25.00
❑363, Dec 1970, CB (w); CB (a); Reprints story from Walt Disney's Comics #126 25.00
❑364, Jan 1971, CB (w); CB (a); Reprints story from Walt Disney's Comics #172 25.00
❑365, Feb 1971, CB (w); CB (a); Reprints story from Walt Disney's Comics #149 25.00
❑366, Mar 1971, CB (w); CB (a); Reprints story from Walt Disney's Comics #150 25.00
❑367, Apr 1971, CB (w); CB (a); Reprints story from Walt Disney's Comics #151 25.00
❑368, May 1971, CB (w); CB (a); Reprints story from Walt Disney's Comics #156 25.00
❑369, Jun 1971, CB (w); CB (a); Reprints story from Walt Disney's Comics #143 25.00

Witchfinder

Hunter becomes the hunted
©Image

Witching Hour

Fated to be lesser-known DC horror title
©DC

Wizard's Tale

Pre-Arrowsmith Busiek fantasy tale
©Image

Wolff & Byrd, Counselors of the Macabre

Barristers for beings from beyond
©Exhibit A

Wolverine

Frank Miller sends Logan to Orient
©Marvel

	N-MINT
❑370, Jul 1971, CB (w); CB (a); Reprints story from Walt Disney's Comics #142	25.00
❑371, Aug 1971, CB (w); CB (a); Reprints story from Walt Disney's Comics #153	25.00
❑372, Sep 1971, CB (w); CB (a); Reprints story from Walt Disney's Comics #168	25.00
❑373, Oct 1971, CB (w); CB (a); Reprints story from Walt Disney's Comics #193	25.00
❑374, Nov 1971, CB (w); CB (a); Reprints story from Walt Disney's Comics #203	25.00
❑375, Dec 1971, CB (w); CB (a); Reprints story from Walt Disney's Comics #240	25.00
❑376, Jan 1972, CB (w); CB (a); Reprints story from Walt Disney's Comics #208	25.00
❑377, Feb 1972, CB (w); CB (a); Reprints story from Walt Disney's Comics #185	25.00
❑378, Mar 1972, CB (w); CB (a); Reprints story from Walt Disney's Comics #196	25.00
❑379, Apr 1972, CB (w); CB (a); Reprints story from Walt Disney's Comics #207	25.00
❑380, May 1972, CB (w); CB (a); Reprints story from Walt Disney's Comics #211	25.00
❑381, Jun 1972, CB (w); CB (a); Reprints story from Walt Disney's Comics #202	25.00
❑382, Jul 1972, CB (w); CB (a); Reprints story from Walt Disney's Comics #213	25.00
❑383, Aug 1972, CB (w); CB (a); Reprints story from Walt Disney's Comics #215	25.00
❑384, Sep 1972, CB (w); CB (a); Reprints story from Walt Disney's Comics #177	25.00
❑385, Oct 1972, CB (w); CB (a); Reprints story from Walt Disney's Comics #187	25.00
❑386, Nov 1972, CB (w); CB (a); Reprints story from Walt Disney's Comics #209	25.00
❑387, Dec 1972, CB (w); CB (a); Reprints story from Walt Disney's Comics #205	25.00
❑388, Jan 1973, CB (w); CB (a); Reprints story from Walt Disney's Comics #136	25.00
❑389, Feb 1973, CB (w); CB (a); Reprints story from Walt Disney's Comics #253	25.00
❑390, Mar 1973, CB (w); CB (a); Reprints story from Walt Disney's Comics #239	25.00
❑391, Apr 1973, CB (w); CB (a); Reprints story from Walt Disney's Comics #137	25.00
❑392, May 1973, CB (w); CB (a); Reprints story from Walt Disney's Comics #163	25.00
❑393, Jun 1973, CB (w); CB (a); Reprints story from Walt Disney's Comics #167	25.00
❑394, Jul 1973, CB (w); CB (a); Reprints story from Walt Disney's Comics #176	25.00
❑395, Aug 1973, CB (w); CB (a); Reprints story from Walt Disney's Comics #214	25.00
❑396, Sep 1973, CB (w); CB (a); Reprints story from Walt Disney's Comics #210	25.00
❑397, Oct 1973, CB (w); CB (a); Reprints story from Walt Disney's Comics #218	25.00
❑398, Nov 1973, CB (w); CB (a); Reprints story from Walt Disney's Comics #217	25.00
❑399, Dec 1973, CB (w); CB (a); Reprints story from Walt Disney's Comics #183	25.00
❑400, Jan 1974, CB (w); CB (a); Reprints story from Walt Disney's Comics #171	25.00
❑401, Feb 1974, CB (w); CB (a); Reprints story from Walt Disney's Comics #219	14.00
❑402, Mar 1974, CB (w); CB (a); Reprints story from Walt Disney's Comics #258	14.00
❑403, Apr 1974, CB (w); CB (a); Reprints story from Walt Disney's Comics #255	14.00
❑404, May 1974, CB (w); CB (a); Reprints story from Walt Disney's Comics #223	14.00
❑405, Jun 1974, CB (w); CB (a); Reprints story from Walt Disney's Comics #259	14.00

	N-MINT
❑406, Jul 1974, CB (w); CB (a); Reprints story from Walt Disney's Comics #191	14.00
❑407, Aug 1974, CB (w); CB (a); Reprints story from Walt Disney's Comics #221	14.00
❑408, Sep 1974, CB (w); CB (a); Reprints story from Walt Disney's Comics #229	14.00
❑409, Oct 1974, CB (w); CB (a); Reprints stories from Four Color Comics #1184 (Gyro Gearloose) and Walt Disney's Comics #249	14.00
❑410, Nov 1974, CB (w); CB (a); Reprints story from Walt Disney's Comics #216	14.00
❑411, Dec 1974, CB (w); CB (a); Reprints story from Walt Disney's Comics #254	14.00
❑412, Jan 1975, CB (w); CB (a); Reprints story from Walt Disney's Comics #220	14.00
❑413, Feb 1975, CB (w); CB (a); Reprints story from Walt Disney's Comics #294	14.00
❑414, Mar 1975, CB (w); CB (a); Reprints story from Walt Disney's Comics #269	14.00
❑415, Apr 1975, CB (w); CB (a); Reprints story from Walt Disney's Comics #265	14.00
❑416, May 1975, CB (w); CB (a); Reprints story from Walt Disney's Comics #222	14.00
❑417, Jun 1975, CB (w); CB (a); Reprints story from Walt Disney's Comics #225	14.00
❑418, Jul 1975, CB (w); CB (a); Reprints story from Walt Disney's Comics #236	14.00
❑419, Aug 1975, CB (w); CB (a); Reprints story from Walt Disney's Comics #138	14.00
❑420, Sep 1975, CB (w); CB (a); Reprints story from Walt Disney's Comics #65	14.00
❑421, Oct 1975, CB (w); CB (a); Reprints story from Walt Disney's Comics #152	14.00
❑422, Nov 1975, CB (w); CB (a); Reprints story from Walt Disney's Comics #169	14.00
❑423, Dec 1975, CB (w); CB (a); Reprints story from Walt Disney's Comics #231	14.00
❑424, Jan 1976, CB (w); CB (a); Reprints story from Walt Disney's Comics #256	14.00
❑425, Feb 1976, CB (w); CB (a); Reprints story from Walt Disney's Comics #260	14.00
❑426, Mar 1976, CB (w); CB (a); Reprints story from Walt Disney's Comics #264	14.00
❑427, Apr 1976, CB (w); CB (a); Reprints story from Walt Disney's Comics #273	14.00
❑428, May 1976, CB (w); CB (a); Reprints story from Walt Disney's Comics #275	14.00
❑429, Jun 1976, CB (w); CB (a); Reprints story from Walt Disney's Comics #271	14.00
❑430, Jul 1976, Vol. 36 #10	10.00
❑431, Aug 1976, CB (w); CB (a); Reprints story from Walt Disney's Comics #288	12.00
❑432, Sep 1976, CB (w); CB (a); Reprints story from Walt Disney's Comics #291	12.00
❑433, Oct 1976, Vol. 37 #1	10.00
❑434, Nov 1976, CB (w); CB (a); Reprints story from Walt Disney's Comics #199	12.00
❑435, Dec 1976, CB (w); CB (a); Reprints story from Walt Disney's Comics #201	12.00
❑436, Jan 1977, CB (w); CB (a); Reprints story from Walt Disney's Comics #195	12.00
❑437, Feb 1977, Vol. 37 #5	10.00
❑438, Mar 1977, Vol. 37 #6	10.00
❑439, Apr 1977, CB (w); CB (a); Reprints story from Walt Disney's Comics #292	12.00
❑440, May 1977, CB (w); CB (a); Reprints story from Walt Disney's Comics #283	12.00
❑441, Jun 1977, Vol. 37 #9	10.00
❑442, Jul 1977, CB (w); CB (a); Reprints story from Walt Disney's Comics #312	10.00

	N-MINT
❑443, Aug 1977, CB (w); CB (a); Reprints story from Walt Disney's Comics #297	10.00
❑444, Sep 1977, Vol. 37 #12	6.00
❑445, Oct 1977, Vol. 38 #1	6.00
❑446, Nov 1977, CB (w); SB, CB (a); Reprints story from Walt Disney's Comics #277	10.00
❑447, Dec 1977, CB (w); CB (a); Reprints story from Walt Disney's Comics #212	10.00
❑448, Jan 1978, CB (w); CB (a); Reprints story from Walt Disney's Comics #266	10.00
❑449, Feb 1978, CB (w); CB (a); Reprints story from Walt Disney's Comics #280	10.00
❑450, Mar 1978, CB (w); CB (a); Reprints story from Walt Disney's Comics #270	10.00
❑451, Apr 1978, CB (w); CB (a); Reprints story from Walt Disney's Comics #272	10.00
❑452, May 1978, CB (w); CB (a); Reprints story from Walt Disney's Comics #274	10.00
❑453, Jun 1978, CB (w); CB (a); Reprints story from Walt Disney's Comics #206	10.00
❑454, Jul 1978, CB (w); CB (a); Reprints story from Walt Disney's Comics #262	10.00
❑455, Aug 1978, CB (w); CB (a); Reprints story from Walt Disney's Comics #241	10.00
❑456, Sep 1978, CB (w); CB (a); Reprints story from Walt Disney's Comics #246	10.00
❑457, Oct 1978, CB (w); CB (a); Reprints stories from Walt Disney's Comics #247 and Mickey Mouse #91; has Casper in Hostess ad: "A Real Oddball"	10.00
❑458, Nov 1978, CB (w); CB (a); Reprints story from Walt Disney's Comics #263	10.00
❑459, Dec 1978, CB (w); CB (a); Reprints story from Walt Disney's Comics #242	10.00
❑460, Jan 1979, CB (w); CB (a); Vol. 39 #4	10.00
❑461, Feb 1979, CB (w); CB (a); Vol. 39 #5	10.00
❑462, Mar 1979, CB (w); CB (a); Vol. 39 #6	10.00
❑463, Apr 1979, CB (w); CB (a); Vol. 39 #7	10.00
❑464, May 1979, CB (w); CB (a); Vol. 39 #8	10.00
❑465, Jun 1979, CB (w); CB (a); Vol. 39 #9	10.00
❑466, Jul 1979, Vol. 39 #10	6.00
❑467, Aug 1979, CB (w); CB (a); Vol. 39 #11	10.00
❑468, Sep 1979, CB (w); CB (a); Vol. 39 #12	10.00
❑469, Oct 1979, CB (w); CB (a); Vol. 40 #1	10.00
❑470, Nov 1979, CB (w); CB (a); Vol. 40 #2	10.00
❑471, Dec 1979, CB (w); CB (a); Vol. 40 #3	10.00
❑472, Jan 1980, CB (w); CB (a); Vol. 40 #4	10.00
❑473, Feb 1980, CB (w); CB (a); Vol. 40 #5	10.00
❑474, Mar 1980, CB (w); CB (a); Whitman begins publishing	10.00
❑475, Apr 1980, CB (w); CB (a); Vol. 40 #7	10.00
❑476, May 1980, CB (w); CB (a); Vol. 40 #8	10.00
❑477, Jun 1980, CB (w); CB (a); Vol. 40 #9	10.00
❑478, Jul 1980, CB (w); CB (a); Vol. 40 #10	10.00
❑479, Aug 1980, CB (w); CB (a); Vol. 40 #11	30.00
❑480, Sep 1980, CB (w); CB (a); Vol. 40 #12	125.00
❑481, Oct 1980, CB (w); CB (a); Vol. 41 #1	30.00
❑482, Nov 1980, CB (w); CB (a); Vol. 41 #2	30.00
❑483, Dec 1980, CB (w); CB (a); Vol. 41 #3	30.00
❑484, Jan 1981, CB (w); CB (a); Vol. 41 #4	30.00
❑485, Feb 1981, CB (w); CB (a); Vol. 41 #5	10.00
❑486, Mar 1981, CB (w); CB (a); Vol. 41 #6	10.00

Other grades: Multiply price above by 5/6 for VF/NM • 2/3 for VERY FINE • 1/3 for FINE • 1/5 for VERY GOOD • 1/8 for GOOD

N-MINT N-MINT N-MINT

❑487 1981, CB (w); CB (a); Vol. 41 #7... 10.00
❑488, Jul 1981, CB (w); CB (a); Vol. 41 #8 10.00
❑489, Aug 1981, CB (w); CB (a); Vol. 41 #9 10.00
❑490, Sep 1981, CB (w); CB (a); Vol. 41 #10... 10.00
❑491, Oct 1981, CB (w); CB (a); Vol. 41 #11... 10.00
❑492, Nov 1981, CB (w); CB (a); Vol. 41 #12... 10.00
❑493, Dec 1981, CB (w); CB (a); Reprints story from Walt Disney Comics and Stories #97... 10.00
❑494, Jan 1981, CB (w); CB (a); Reprints story from Walt Disney Comics and Stories #98... 10.00
❑495, Feb 1982, CB (w); CB (a); Vol. 42 #3 10.00
❑496, Feb 1982, CB (w); CB (a); Vol. 42 #4 10.00
❑497, Mar 1982, CB (w); CB (a); Vol. 42 #5 10.00
❑498, Apr 1982, CB (w); CB (a); Vol. 42 #6 10.00
❑499, May 1982, CB (w); CB (a); Vol. 42 #7... 10.00
❑500, ca. 1983, CB (w); CB (a); Vol. 42 #8 10.00
❑501, ca. 1983, CB (w); CB (a); Vol. 42 #9 10.00
❑502, ca. 1983, CB (w); CB (a); Vol. 42 #10 10.00
❑503, ca. 1983, CB (w); CB (a); Vol. 42 #11 10.00
❑504, ca. 1983, CB (w); CB (a); Vol. 42 #12 10.00
❑505, ca. 1983, CB (w); CB (a); Vol. 43 #1 10.00
❑506, ca. 1983, Vol. 43 #2... 10.00
❑507, ca. 1984, CB (w); CB (a); Vol. 43 #3 10.00
❑508, ca. 1984, CB (w); CB (a); Vol. 43 #4 10.00
❑509, ca. 1984, CB (w); CB (a); Vol. 43 #5 10.00
❑510, ca. 1984, CB (w); CB (a); Vol. 43 #6 10.00
❑511, ca. 1986, CB (w); CB (a); Gladstone begins publishing... 15.00
❑512, Nov 1986... 12.00
❑513, Dec 1986... 12.00
❑514, Jan 1987, CB (w); CB (a)... 8.00
❑515, Feb 1987... 8.00
❑516, Mar 1987, CB (w); CB (a)... 8.00
❑517, Apr 1987... 5.00
❑518, May 1987... 5.00
❑519, Jun 1987, CB (w); CB (a)... 14.00
❑520, Jul 1987, CB (w); CB (a)... 10.00
❑521, Aug 1987, CB (w); CB, WK (a)... 10.00
❑522, Sep 1987, CB (w); CB, WK (a); O: Huey, Dewey, Louie... 10.00
❑523, Oct 1987, CB (w); CB, DR (a); 1st Rosa 10-page story... 10.00
❑524, Nov 1987, CB (w); CB (a)... 10.00
❑525, Dec 1987, CB (w); CB (a)... 10.00
❑526, Jan 1988, CB (w); CB (a)... 10.00
❑527, Mar 1988, CB (w); CB (a)... 10.00
❑528, May 1988, CB (w); CB (a)... 10.00
❑529, Jun 1988, CB (w); CB (a); "Funny Fun" reprinted from Uncle Scrooge #39; "The Legend of Loon Lake" reprinted from Walt Disney's Comics and Stories #197... 10.00
❑530, Jul 1988, CB (w); CB (a)... 10.00
❑531, Aug 1988, WK (c); CB, DR (w); CB, DR (a)... 10.00
❑532, Sep 1988, CB (w); CB, DR (a)... 10.00
❑533, Oct 1988, CB (w); CB (a)... 10.00
❑534, Nov 1988, CB (w); CB (a)... 10.00
❑535, Dec 1988, CB (w); CB (a)... 10.00
❑536, Feb 1989, CB (w); CB (a)... 10.00
❑537, Mar 1989, CB (w); CB (a); 1st Wm. Van Horn 10-page story... 10.00
❑538, Apr 1989, WK (c); CB (w); CB (a) 10.00
❑539, Jun 1989, CB (w); CB (a)... 10.00
❑540, Jul 1989, CB (w); CB (a)... 10.00
❑541, Aug 1989, WK (c); CB (w); CB (a); 48 pgs... 10.00
❑542, Sep 1989, CB (w); CB (a); Reprints stories from Walt Disney's Comics & Stories #264, Mickey Mouse Almanac #1, Four Color #703, Picnic Parade #8, and Summer Fun #2... 10.00
❑543, Oct 1989, WK (c); CB (w); CB (a). 10.00
❑544, Nov 1989, WK (c); CB (w); CB (a); Reprints stories from Walt Disney's Comics & Stories #190, 192, and 232; Uncle Scrooge #25; and Walt Disney's Summer Fun #2... 10.00
❑545, Dec 1989, CB (w); CB (a)... 10.00
❑546, Feb 1990, CB (w); CB, WK (a)... 10.00
❑547, Apr 1990, CB (w); CB, DR (a)... 10.00
❑548, Jun 1990, CB (w); CB (a); Disney begins publishing... 10.00
❑549, Jul 1990, CB (w); CB (a)... 10.00
❑550, Aug 1990, CB (w); CB (a); Milkman story... 6.00
❑551, Sep 1990, CB (w); CB (a)... 4.00
❑552, Oct 1990, CB (w); CB (a)... 4.00
❑553, Nov 1990, CB (w); CB (a)... 4.00
❑554, Dec 1990, CB (w); CB (a)... 4.00
❑555, Jan 1991... 3.00
❑556, Feb 1991... 3.00
❑557, Mar 1991, CB (w); CB (a)... 4.00
❑558, Apr 1991, CB (w); CB (a)... 4.00
❑559, May 1991, CB (w); CB (a)... 4.00
❑560, Jun 1991, CB (w); CB (a)... 4.00
❑561, Jul 1991, CB (w); CB (a)... 4.00
❑562, Aug 1991, CB (w); CB (a)... 4.00
❑563, Sep 1991, CB (w); CB (a)... 4.00
❑564, Oct 1991, CB (w); CB (a)... 4.00
❑565, Nov 1991, CB (w); CB (a)... 4.00
❑566, Dec 1991, CB (w); CB (a)... 4.00
❑567, Jan 1992, CB (w); CB, FG (a)... 4.00
❑568, Feb 1992, CB (w); CB, FG (a)... 4.00
❑569, Mar 1992, CB (w); CB, FG (a)... 4.00
❑570, Apr 1992, CB (w); CB (a); Valentine centerfold... 4.00
❑571, May 1992, CB (w); CB, FG (a); 64 pages... 4.00
❑572, Jun 1992, CB (w); CB, FG (a); map piece... 4.00
❑573, Jul 1992, CB (w); CB (a); map piece 4.00
❑574, Aug 1992, CB (w); CB (a); map piece... 5.00
❑575, Sep 1992, CB (w); CB, FG (a)... 5.00
❑576, Oct 1992, CB (w); CB (a)... 5.00
❑577, Nov 1992, CB (w); CB (a); Reprints 5.00
❑578, Dec 1992, CB (w); CB (a); Reprints 3.00
❑579, Jan 1993, CB (w); CB (a)... 3.00
❑580, Feb 1993, CB (w); CB, FG (a); strip reprint... 5.00
❑581, Mar 1993, CB (w); CB (a); Reprints 3.00
❑582, Apr 1993, FG, WK (a)... 3.00
❑583, May 1993, FG, WK (a)... 3.00
❑584, Jun 1993, CB (w); CB (a); Reprints 3.00
❑585, Jul 1993, CB, FG (w); CB, FG (a); Reprints... 5.00
❑586, Aug 1993... 3.00
❑587, Oct 1993... 3.00
❑588, Dec 1993... 3.00
❑589, Feb 1994... 3.00
❑590, Apr 1994... 3.00
❑591, Jun 1994... 3.00
❑592, Aug 1994... 3.00
❑593, Oct 1994... 3.00
❑594, Dec 1994... 3.00
❑595, Feb 1995... 3.00
❑596, Apr 1995... 3.00
❑597, Jun 1995... 3.00
❑598, Aug 1995... 4.00
❑599, Oct 1995... 4.00
❑600, Dec 1995, Giant-size; CB (w); CB, DR (a); reprints first Donald Duck stories by trio... 6.00
❑601, Feb 1996, upgrades to prestige format... 5.95
❑602, Apr 1996... 5.95
❑603, Jun 1996... 5.95
❑604, Aug 1996... 5.95
❑605, Oct 1996... 5.95
❑606, Dec 1996... 5.95
❑607, Jan 1996... 5.95
❑608, Feb 1997... 5.95
❑609, Mar 1997... 5.95
❑610, Mar 1997... 5.95
❑611, Apr 1997... 5.95
❑612, May 1997... 6.95
❑613, Jun 1997... 6.95
❑614, Jul 1997... 6.95
❑615, Aug 1997... 6.95
❑616, Sep 1997... 6.95
❑617, Oct 1997... 6.95
❑618, Nov 1997... 6.95
❑619, Dec 1997, Pinocchio features... 6.95
❑620, Jan 1998... 6.95
❑621, Feb 1998... 6.95
❑622, Mar 1998... 6.95
❑623, Apr 1998... 6.95
❑624, May 1998... 6.95
❑625, Jun 1998... 6.95
❑626, Jul 1998... 6.95
❑627, Aug 1998... 6.95
❑628, Sep 1998... 6.95
❑629, Oct 1998... 6.95
❑630, Nov 1998... 6.95
❑631, Dec 1998... 6.95
❑632, Jan 1999... 6.95
❑633, Feb 1999... 6.95
❑634, Mar 1999... 6.95
❑635, Apr 1999... 6.95
❑636, May 1999... 6.95
❑637, Jun 1999... 6.95
❑638, Jul 1999... 6.95
❑639, Aug 1999... 6.95
❑640, Sep 1999... 6.95
❑641, Oct 1999... 6.95
❑642, Nov 1999... 6.95
❑643, Dec 1999... 6.95
❑644, Jan 2000... 6.95
❑645, Feb 2000... 6.95
❑646, Mar 2000... 6.95
❑647, Apr 2000... 6.95
❑648, May 2000... 6.95

Walt Disney's Comics & Stories
Gemstone

❑634, Jun 2003... 6.95
❑635, Jul 2003... 6.95
❑636, Aug 2003... 6.95
❑637, Sep 2003... 6.95
❑638, Oct 2003... 6.95
❑639, Nov 2003... 6.95
❑640, Dec 2003... 6.95
❑641, Jan 2004... 6.95
❑642, Feb 2004... 6.95
❑643, Mar 2004... 6.95
❑644, Apr 2004... 6.95
❑645, May 2004... 6.95
❑646, Jun 2004... 6.95
❑647, Jul 2004... 6.95
❑648, Aug 2004... 6.95
❑649, Sep 2004... 6.95
❑650, Oct 2004... 6.95
❑651, Nov 2004... 6.95
❑652, Dec 2004... 6.95
❑653, Jan 2005... 6.95
❑654, Feb 2005... 6.95
❑655, Mar 2005... 6.95
❑656, Apr 2005... 6.95
❑657, May 2005... 6.95
❑658, Jun 2005... 6.95
❑659, Jul 2005... 6.95
❑660, Aug 2005... 6.95
❑661, Sep 2005... 6.95

Walt Disney's Comics and Stories Penny Pincher
Gladstone

❑1, May 1997, CB (a); Reprints... 1.00
❑2, Jun 1997, CB (a); reprints Barks' Feud and Far Between... 1.00
❑3, Jul 1997... 1.00
❑4, Aug 1997... 1.00

Walt Disney's Comics Digest
Gladstone

❑1, Dec 1986, CB (c); CB, WK (w); CB, WK (a); Reprints story from Uncle Scrooge #5... 6.00
❑2 1987, CB (a); Reprints story from Uncle Scrooge #29... 4.00
❑3, Mar 1987, CB (a); Reprints story from Uncle Scrooge #31... 4.00
❑4, Apr 1987, CB (a); Reprints stories from Donald Duck #60 and Picnic Party #8... 4.00
❑5, May 1987, CB (a); Reprints story from Uncle Scrooge #23... 4.00
❑6, Jun 1987, CB (a); Reprints story from Uncle Scrooge #24... 4.00
❑7, Jul 1987, CB (a); Reprints stories from Four Color Comics #1025 (Vacation in Disneyland)... 4.00

Walt Disney's Holiday Parade
Disney

❑1, Win 1991; Wraparound cover... 2.95
❑2, Win 1992; Donald Duck: Reprint from Dell Giant #26; Li'l Bad Wolf: Reprint from Christmas Parade #8; Grandma Duck: Reprint from Christmas Parade #3; Chip ěn' Dale: Reprint from Christmas Parade #2; Super Goof; Brer Rabbit: Reprint from Dell Giant #26; Mickey Mouse... 2.95

Other grades: Multiply price above by 5/6 for VF/NM • 2/3 for VERY FINE • 1/3 for FINE • 1/5 for VERY GOOD • 1/8 for GOOD

Wolverine

Ongoing series revealed more origin
©Marvel

Wolverine

Back to basics approach with solo stories
©Marvel

Wolverine Saga

Past stories assembled into timeline
©Marvel

Wolverine: The End

Even nearly ageless mutants die
©Marvel

Wolverine: The Origin

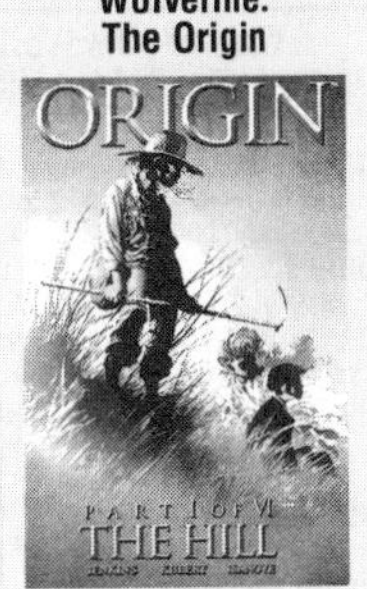

Logan's earliest days revealed
©Marvel

N-MINT

Walt Disney Showcase
Gold Key

- ❑1, Oct 1970, DS (a); Boatniks 16.00
- ❑2, Jan 1971, Moby Duck 10.00
- ❑3, Apr 1971, Bongo & Lumpjaw 9.00
- ❑4, Jul 1971, Pluto 9.00
- ❑5, Oct 1971, DS (a); $1,000,000 Duck 12.00
- ❑6, Jan 1972, DS (a); Bedknobs & Broomsticks 12.00
- ❑7, Apr 1972, Pluto 9.00
- ❑8, Jun 1972, Daisy and Donald; Goofy and Clarabelle 9.00
- ❑9, Aug 1972, 101 Dalmatians 10.00
- ❑10, Sep 1972, DS (a); Napoleon and Samantha movie adaptation 12.00
- ❑11, Oct 1972, Moby Duck 8.00
- ❑12, Dec 1972, Dumbo 8.00
- ❑13, Feb 1973, Pluto 8.00
- ❑14, Apr 1973, DS (a); The World's Greatest Athlete (movie adaptation) 12.00
- ❑15, Jun 1973, Three Little Pigs 8.00
- ❑16, Jul 1973, Aristocats movie adaptation reprint 12.00
- ❑17, Aug 1973, DS (a); Mary Poppins movie adaptation reprint 12.00
- ❑18, Oct 1973, Gyro Gearloose; reprints stories from Four Color Comics #1047 and 1184 (Gyro Gearloose) 12.00
- ❑19, Dec 1973, DS (a); That Darn Cat (move adaptation) 10.00
- ❑20, Feb 1974, Pluto 9.00
- ❑21, Apr 1974, Li'l Bad Wolf and the Three Little Pigs 8.00
- ❑22, Jun 1974, Alice in Wonderland 8.00
- ❑23, Jul 1974, Pluto 8.00
- ❑24, Aug 1974, DS (a); Herbie Rides Again 7.00
- ❑25, Oct 1974, DS (a); Old Yeller 7.00
- ❑26, Dec 1974, DS (a); Lt. Robin Crusoe, USN 7.00
- ❑27, Feb 1975, Island at the Top of the World 7.00
- ❑28, Apr 1975, Brer Rabbit 7.00
- ❑29, Jun 1975, Escape to Witch Mountain 7.00
- ❑30, Jul 1975, Magica De Spell; reprints stories from Uncles Scrooge #36 and Walt Disney's Comics #258 ..... 15.00
- ❑31, Aug 1975, Bambi 9.00
- ❑32, Oct 1975, DS (a); Spin and Marty 9.00
- ❑33, Jan 1976, Pluto 7.00
- ❑34, May 1976, Paul Revere's Ride 7.00
- ❑35, Aug 1976, Goofy 7.00
- ❑36, Sep 1976, Peter Pan 7.00
- ❑37, Nov 1976, Tinker Bell 7.00
- ❑38, Apr 1977, Mickey and The Sleuth 7.00
- ❑39, Jul 1977, Mickey and The Sleuth 7.00
- ❑40, Sep 1977, The Rescuers (movie adaptation) 8.00
- ❑41, Oct 1977, Herbie Goes to Monte Carlo (movie adaptation) 8.00
- ❑42, Jan 1978, Mickey and The Sleuth 7.00
- ❑43, Apr 1978, DS (a); Pete's Dragon (movie adaptation) 9.00
- ❑44, May 1978, DS (a); Return From Witch Mountain (movie adaptation); Castaways 10.00
- ❑45, Aug 1978, The Jungle Book 10.00
- ❑46, Oct 1978, DS (a); The Cat From Outer Space 10.00

N-MINT

- ❑47, Nov 1978, Mickey Mouse Surprise Party 10.00
- ❑48, Jan 1979, The Wonderful Adventures of Pinocchio; The Small One 10.00
- ❑49, Mar 1979, DS (a); The North Avenue Irregulars (Movie adaptation); Zorro double feature 7.00
- ❑50, May 1979, DS (a); Bedknobs & Broomsticks reprint 7.00
- ❑51, Jul 1979, 101 Dalmatians 7.00
- ❑52, Sep 1979, DS (a); Unidentified Flying Oddball 7.00
- ❑53, Nov 1979, The Scarecrow of Romney Marsh 7.00
- ❑54, Jan 1980, DS (a); The Black Hole 7.00

Walt Disney's Spring Fever
Disney

- ❑1, Spr 1991; Wraparound cover 2.95

Walt Disney's Summer Fun
Disney

- ❑1 ..... 2.95

Walt Disney's Three Musketeers
Gemstone

- ❑1 2004 ..... 3.95

Walt Disney's World of Adventure
Gold Key

- ❑1, Apr 1963 ..... 8.00
- ❑2, Jul 1963 ..... 5.00
- ❑3, Oct 1963 ..... 5.00

Walter
Dark Horse

- ❑1, Feb 1996 ..... 2.50
- ❑2, Mar 1996 ..... 2.50
- ❑3, Apr 1996 ..... 2.50
- ❑4, May 1996; Final Issue 2.50

Walter Kitty in...the Hollow Earth
Vision

- ❑1, Jul 1996 ..... 1.95
- ❑2, Jul 1996 ..... 1.95

Walt The Wildcat
MotioN Comics

- ❑1, Sep 1995 ..... 2.50

Wanda Luwand & the Pirate Girls
Fantagraphics / Eros

- ❑1, b&w; Adult 2.50

Wanderers
DC

- ❑1, Jun 1988; 1&O: Aviax. 1&O: The Wanderers. 1&O: The Elvar. 1&O: Re-Animage 1.50
- ❑2, Jul 1988 ..... 1.50
- ❑3, Aug 1988 ..... 1.50
- ❑4, Sep 1988 ..... 1.50
- ❑5, Oct 1988 ..... 1.50
- ❑6, Nov 1988 ..... 1.50
- ❑7, Dec 1988 ..... 1.50
- ❑8, Dec 1988 ..... 1.50
- ❑9, Jan 1989 ..... 1.50
- ❑10, Jan 1989 ..... 1.50
- ❑11, Feb 1989 ..... 1.50
- ❑12, Mar 1989 ..... 1.50
- ❑13, Apr 1989; Final Issue 1.50

N-MINT

Wandering Star
Pen and Ink

- ❑1, ca. 1993, b&w 8.00
- ❑1/2nd, Feb 1994; 2nd printing 4.00
- ❑1/3rd; 3rd printing 3.00
- ❑2, ca. 1993, b&w 5.00
- ❑2/2nd, May 1994; 2nd printing 2.00
- ❑3, ca. 1993, b&w 4.00
- ❑3/2nd, May 1994; 2nd printing 2.00
- ❑4, ca. 1993, b&w; ca. 1993 ..... 4.00
- ❑4/2nd, May 1994; 2nd printing 2.00
- ❑5, Jan 1994, b&w 4.00
- ❑5/2nd, May 1994; 2nd printing 2.00
- ❑6, Mar 1994, b&w 3.00
- ❑7, Jun 1994, b&w 3.00
- ❑8, Oct 1994, b&w; D: Graikor 3.00
- ❑9, Aug 1995, b&w 3.00
- ❑10, Oct 1995, b&w; Extremely small print run 3.00
- ❑11, Jan 1995, b&w 2.50
- ❑12 1996, b&w 2.50
- ❑13, Jun 1996, b&w 2.50
- ❑14 1996, b&w 2.50
- ❑15 1996, b&w 2.50
- ❑16 1996, b&w; Destruction of Earth 2.50
- ❑17 1996, b&w 2.50
- ❑18 1996, b&w 2.50
- ❑19 1996, b&w 2.50
- ❑20 1997, b&w 2.50
- ❑21 1997, b&w 2.50

Wandering Stars
Fantagraphics

- ❑1 ..... 2.00

Wanted
Celebrity

- ❑1 1989 ..... 2.00
- ❑2 1989 ..... 2.00
- ❑3 1989 ..... 2.00
- ❑4 1989 ..... 2.00
- ❑5, Dec 1989; Includes poster 2.00

Wanted
Image

- ❑1, Dec 2003 ..... 12.00
- ❑1/A, Dec 2003 ..... 9.00
- ❑1/B, Dec 2003 ..... 8.00
- ❑1/C, Apr 2004 ..... 2.99
- ❑1/D, Apr 2004; Wizard World 6.00
- ❑1/E, Apr 2004; Death Row Edition 5.00
- ❑2, Jan 2004 ..... 2.99
- ❑2/B, Apr 2004 ..... 4.00
- ❑2/C, May 2004; Death Row Edition 5.00
- ❑3, Apr 2004 ..... 2.99
- ❑3/A, Apr 2004; Death Row Edition 4.00
- ❑4, Aug 2004 ..... 2.99
- ❑4/Variant 2004, Death Row edition 2.99
- ❑5 2004 ..... 2.99
- ❑6, Feb 2005 ..... 2.99

Wanted: Dossier One-Shot
Image

- ❑1, Apr 2004 ..... 2.99

Wanted Dossier One Shot
Image

- ❑1, May 2004 ..... 2.99

Other grades: Multiply price above by 5/6 for VF/NM • 2/3 for VERY FINE • 1/3 for FINE • 1/5 for VERY GOOD • 1/8 for GOOD

Wanted, the World's Most Dangerous Villains
DC

- ❑1, Aug 1972, reprints stories from Batman #112, World's Finest #111, and Green Lantern #1 .... 10.00
- ❑2, Oct 1972, reprints stories from Batman #25 and Flash #121 .... 8.00
- ❑3, Nov 1972, reprints stories from Action #69, More Fun #65, and Flash #100 ... 8.00
- ❑4, Dec 1972, 1: Solomon Grundy. reprints stories from All-American #61 and Kid Eternity #15 .... 6.00
- ❑5, Jan 1973, reprints stories from Green Lantern #33 and Doll Man #15 .... 6.00
- ❑6, Feb 1973, reprints stories from Adventure #77 and Sensation Comics #66 and 71 .... 6.00
- ❑7, Apr 1973, reprints stories from More Fun #76, Flash #90, and Adventure #72 6.00
- ❑8, Jul 1973, reprints stories from Flash #114 and More Fun #73 .... 6.00
- ❑9, Sep 1973, NC (c); CS (a); reprints stories from Action #57 and World's Finest Comics #6 .... 6.00

War
Charlton

- ❑1, Jul 1975, b&w; DP, WW (a); Reprints 8.00
- ❑2, Sep 1975 .... 5.00
- ❑3, Nov 1975 .... 5.00
- ❑4, Jan 1976 .... 5.00
- ❑5, Mar 1976 .... 5.00
- ❑6, May 1976 .... 5.00
- ❑7, Jul 1976 .... 5.00
- ❑8, Sep 1976 .... 5.00
- ❑9, Nov 1976 .... 5.00
- ❑10, Sep 1978 .... 5.00
- ❑11, Jan 1979 .... 3.00
- ❑12, Feb 1979 .... 3.00
- ❑13, Apr 1979 .... 3.00
- ❑14, Jun 1979 .... 3.00
- ❑15, Aug 1979 .... 3.00
- ❑16, Sep 1979 .... 3.00
- ❑17, Nov 1979 .... 3.00
- ❑18, Dec 1979 .... 3.00
- ❑19, Feb 1980 .... 3.00
- ❑20, Apr 1980 .... 3.00
- ❑21, Jun 1980 .... 3.00
- ❑22, Aug 1980 .... 3.00
- ❑23, Oct 1980 .... 2.00
- ❑24, Dec 1980 .... 2.00
- ❑25, Feb 1981 .... 2.00
- ❑26, Apr 1981 .... 2.00
- ❑27, Jun 1981, Reprint from US Air Force Comics #26 .... 2.00
- ❑28, Aug 1981 .... 2.00
- ❑29, Oct 1981 .... 2.00
- ❑30, Dec 1981 .... 2.00
- ❑31, Feb 1982 .... 2.00
- ❑32, Apr 1982 .... 2.00
- ❑33, Jun 1982, Reprints from War #1 and 2 .... 2.00
- ❑34, Aug 1982 .... 2.00
- ❑35, Oct 1982 .... 2.00
- ❑36, Dec 1982 .... 2.00
- ❑37, Feb 1983 .... 2.00
- ❑38, Mar 1983, Reprints from War Heroes #20 and 21 .... 2.00
- ❑39, ca. 1983, Reprint from War at Sea #30 .... 2.00
- ❑40, ca. 1983, Reprint from Fightin' Air Force #31 .... 2.00
- ❑41, Oct 1983 .... 2.00
- ❑42, Dec 1983 .... 2.00
- ❑43, Feb 1984 .... 2.00
- ❑44, Apr 1984 .... 2.00
- ❑45, Jun 1984 .... 2.00
- ❑46, Aug 1984 .... 2.00
- ❑47 1984 .... 2.00
- ❑48 1984 .... 2.00
- ❑49 1984 .... 2.00

War
Marvel

- ❑1, Jun 1989; Series continued from story in "The Draft" 3.50
- ❑2, Jul 1989 .... 3.50
- ❑3, Aug 1989 .... 3.50
- ❑4, Feb 1990 .... 3.50

War Against Crime
Gemstone

- ❑1, Apr 2000, Reprints War Against Crime #1 2.50
- ❑2, May 2000, Reprints War Against Crime #2 .... 2.50
- ❑3, Jun 2000, Reprints War Against Crime #3 .... 2.50
- ❑4, Jul 2000, Reprints War Against Crime #4 2.50
- ❑5, Aug 2000, Reprints War Against Crime #5 .... 2.50
- ❑Ann 1, ca. 2000, Collects issues #1-5.. 13.50

Warblade: Endangered Species
Image

- ❑1, Jan 1995; Tri-fold cover 2.50
- ❑2, Feb 1995 .... 2.50
- ❑3, Mar 1995 .... 2.50
- ❑4, Apr 1995 .... 2.50

Warcat
Coconut

- ❑Ashcan 1, Oct 1997, b&w; preview of issues #1 and 2; no indicia 2.95
- ❑Special 1 .... 2.95

Warchild
Maximum

- ❑1/A, Dec 1994; Warchild charging on cover 2.50
- ❑1/B, Dec 1994; Variant cover with Warchild standing, red background.... 2.50
- ❑2/A, Jan 1995; Warchild and woman on cover 2.50
- ❑2/B, Jan 1995; Warchild alone on cover 2.50
- ❑3/A, Jun 1995; Warchild crouching on cover 2.50
- ❑3/B, Jun 1995; Warchild standing on cover, white background 2.50
- ❑3/C, Jun 1995; Warchild standing on cover, red background 2.50
- ❑4, Aug 1995 .... 2.50

War Criminals
Comic Zone

- ❑1, b&w 2.95

Warcry
Image

- ❑1 .... 2.50

War Dancer
Defiant

- ❑1, Feb 1994; 1: War Dancer. 1: War Dancer (Ahrq Tsolmec) 2.50
- ❑2, Mar 1994 .... 2.50
- ❑3, Apr 1994 .... 2.50
- ❑4, May 1994; Giant-size; O: War Dancer. A: Charlemagne 3.25
- ❑5, Jun 1994 .... 2.50
- ❑6, Jul 1994; Final Issue 2.50

Wargod
Speakeasy Comics

- ❑0, Jul 2005 .... 4.99

Warhawks Comics Module
TSR

- ❑1, ca. 1990 .... 2.95
- ❑2, ca. 1990 .... 2.95
- ❑3, ca. 1990 .... 2.95
- ❑4, ca. 1990 .... 2.95
- ❑5, ca. 1990; Warhawks 2050 .... 2.95
- ❑6, ca. 1990; Warhawks 2050 .... 2.95
- ❑7, ca. 1990; Warhawks 2050 .... 2.95
- ❑8, ca. 1990; Warhawks 2050 .... 2.95
- ❑9, ca. 1990; Warhawks 2050 .... 2.95

Warheads
Marvel

- ❑1, Jun 1992; Wolverine 1.75
- ❑2, Jul 1992 .... 1.75
- ❑3, Aug 1992 .... 1.75
- ❑4, Sep 1992 .... 1.75
- ❑5, Oct 1992 .... 1.75
- ❑6, Nov 1992; Death's Head II cameo.... 1.75
- ❑7, Dec 1992 .... 1.75
- ❑8, Jan 1993 .... 1.75
- ❑9, Feb 1993 .... 1.75
- ❑10, Apr 1993 .... 1.75
- ❑11, May 1993; MyS-TECH Wars Crossover 1.75
- ❑12, Jun 1993 .... 1.75
- ❑13, Jul 1993 .... 1.75
- ❑14, Aug 1993 .... 1.75

Warheads: Black Dawn
Marvel

- ❑1, Jul 1993; foil cover 2.95
- ❑2 1993 .... 2.95

War Heroes Classics
Recollections

- ❑1, Jun 1991, b&w; Reprints 2.00

War Is Hell
Marvel

- ❑1, Jan 1973, AW (a); Reprints 25.00
- ❑2, Mar 1973, Reprints 18.00
- ❑3, May 1973, JSe (c);Reprints 14.00
- ❑4, Jul 1973, Reprints 14.00
- ❑5, Sep 1973, Reprints 14.00
- ❑6, Nov 1973, Reprints 10.00
- ❑7, Jun 1974; SL (w); A: Sgt. Fury. Reprints Sgt. Fury #17 .... 10.00
- ❑8, Aug 1974; A: Sgt. Fury. Reprints 10.00
- ❑9, Oct 1974 .... 8.00
- ❑10, Dec 1974 .... 8.00
- ❑11, Feb 1975; Marvel Value Stamp #5: Dracula 8.00
- ❑12, Apr 1975 .... 8.00
- ❑13, Jun 1975; Marvel Value Stamp #23: Sgt. Fury 8.00
- ❑14, Aug 1975 .... 8.00
- ❑15, Oct 1975; Final Issue 8.00

Warlands
Image

- ❑1, Aug 1999 .... 3.00
- ❑1/A, Aug 1999; alternate cover 3.00
- ❑1/B, Aug 1999; alternate cover 3.00
- ❑2, Sep 1999 .... 2.50
- ❑2/A, Sep 1999; alternate cover 2.50
- ❑3, Nov 1999 .... 2.50
- ❑4 2000 .... 2.50
- ❑5, Mar 2000 .... 2.50
- ❑6, Apr 2000 .... 2.50
- ❑7, Jun 2000 .... 2.50
- ❑8, Jul 2000 .... 2.50
- ❑9, Aug 2000 .... 2.50
- ❑10, Oct 2000 .... 2.50
- ❑11, Nov 2000 .... 2.50
- ❑12, Feb 2001 .... 2.50
- ❑Deluxe 1, Aug 2001; Darklyte 14.95

Warlands: Dark Tide Rising
Dreamwave

- ❑1, Dec 2002; Gatefold summary; Wraparound cover 2.95
- ❑2, Jan 2003 .... 2.95
- ❑3, Feb 2003 .... 2.95
- ❑4, Mar 2003 .... 2.95
- ❑5, Apr 2003 .... 2.95
- ❑6, May 2003 .... 2.95

Warlands Epilogue: Three Stories
Image

- ❑1, Mar 2001 .... 5.95

Warlands: The Age of Ice
Dreamwave

- ❑0, Feb 2002 .... 2.25
- ❑1, Jul 2001 .... 2.95
- ❑2/A, Sep 2001; Brown logo on cover; Flip-book with Warlands: Banished Knights preview 2.95
- ❑2/B, Sep 2001; Blue logo on cover; Flip-book with Warlands: Banished Knights preview 2.95
- ❑3, Oct 2001; Red background 2.95

Warlash
CFD

- ❑1, Apr 1995 .... 2.95

Warlock
Marvel

- ❑1, Aug 1972, GK (c); TS, GK (a); O: Warlock; Reprinted in Warlock (2nd Series) #2 .... 32.00
- ❑2, Oct 1972 .... 15.00
- ❑3, Dec 1972 .... 15.00
- ❑4, Feb 1973, GK (c); TS, GK (a) 8.00
- ❑5, Apr 1973 .... 8.00
- ❑6, Jun 1973 .... 7.00
- ❑7, Aug 1973 .... 7.00
- ❑8, Oct 1973 .... 7.00
- ❑9, Oct 1975, JSn (w); JSn (a); A: Thanos 10.00
- ❑10, Dec 1975, JSn (c); JSn (w); JSn (a); O: Thanos. Part 1 .... 10.00

Other grades: Multiply price above by 5/6 for VF/NM • 2/3 for VERY FINE • 1/3 for FINE • 1/5 for VERY GOOD • 1/8 for GOOD

Wolverine vs. Spider-Man

Collects Marvel Comics Presents arc

©Marvel

Wonderland

Alice, Dorothy, and friends join forces

©Arrow

Wonder Man

Ionically powered hero becomes icon

©Marvel

Wonder Wart-Hog, Hog of Steel

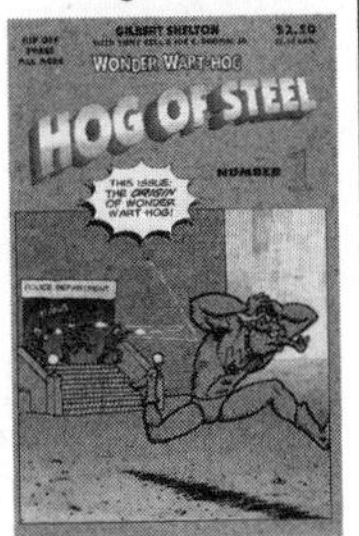

Philbert Desanex's dream becomes reality

©Rip Off

Wonder Woman

Amazonian heroine had feet of clay

©DC

N-MINT

❑11, Feb 1976, JSn (w); JSn (a); A: Thanos. Part 2 … 10.00
❑12, Apr 1976, JSn (w); JSn (a) … 8.00
❑12/30¢, Apr 1976, 30¢ regional price variant … 15.00
❑13, Jun 1976, JSn (w); JSn (a) … 8.00
❑13/30¢, Jun 1976, 30¢ regional price variant … 15.00
❑14, Aug 1976, JSn (w); JSn (a) … 8.00
❑14/30¢, Aug 1976, 30¢ regional price variant … 15.00
❑15, Nov 1976, JSn (w); JSn (a); A: Thanos … 8.00

Warlock
Marvel

❑1, Dec 1982; JSn (c); JSn (w); JSn (a); Reprints … 3.50
❑2, Jan 1983; JSn (c); JSn (w); JSn (a); Reprints Strange Tales #181, Warlock (1st Series) #9 … 3.00
❑3, Feb 1983; JSn (c); JSn (w); JSn (a); Reprints … 3.00
❑4, Mar 1983; JSn (c); JSn (w); JSn (a); Reprints … 3.00
❑5, Apr 1983; JSn (c); JSn (w); JSn, JBy (a); Reprints … 3.00
❑6, May 1983; JSn (c); JSn (w); JSn (a); Reprints … 3.00
❑Special 1, Dec 1982 … 2.00

Warlock
Marvel

❑1, May 1992; Reprints Warlock (2nd Series) #1 … 2.50
❑2, Jun 1992; Reprints Warlock (2nd Series) #2 … 2.50
❑3, Jul 1992; Reprints Warlock (2nd Series) #3 … 2.50
❑4, Aug 1992; Reprints Warlock (2nd Series) #4 … 2.50
❑5, Sep 1992; Reprints Warlock (2nd Series) #5 … 2.50
❑6, Oct 1992; Reprints Warlock (2nd Series) #6 … 2.50

Warlock
Marvel

❑1, Nov 1998; gatefold summary … 3.00
❑2, Dec 1998; gatefold summary; V: Captain Marvel … 3.00
❑3, Jan 1999; gatefold summary; V: Drax … 3.00
❑4, Feb 1999 A: Syphonn. A: Blastaar. A: Annihilus … 3.00

Warlock
Marvel

❑1, Oct 1999; Green background on cover … 2.00
❑2, Nov 1999; Warlock fighting robot on cover … 1.99
❑3, Nov 1999 … 1.99
❑4, Dec 1999 … 1.99

Warlock
Marvel

❑1, Nov 2004 … 2.99
❑2, Dec 2004 … 2.99
❑3, Jan 2004 … 2.99
❑4, Jan 2005 … 2.99

N-MINT

Warlock and the Infinity Watch
Marvel

❑1, Feb 1992; JSn (w); follows events of The Infinity Gauntlet … 2.50
❑2, Mar 1992 JSn (w) … 2.00
❑3, Apr 1992 JSn (w); A: High Evolutionary … 2.00
❑4, May 1992 JSn (w) … 2.00
❑5, Jun 1992 JSn (w) … 2.00
❑6, Jul 1992 JSn (w) … 2.00
❑7, Aug 1992 JSn (w) … 2.00
❑8, Sep 1992 JSn (w) … 2.00
❑9, Oct 1992; JSn (w); O: Gamora. Infinity War … 2.00
❑10, Nov 1992 JSn (w) … 2.00
❑11, Dec 1992 JSn (w) … 1.75
❑12, Jan 1993 … 1.75
❑13, Feb 1993 … 1.75
❑14, Mar 1993 … 1.75
❑15, Apr 1993 … 1.75
❑16, May 1993 … 1.75
❑17, Jun 1993 JSn (w) … 1.75
❑18, Jul 1993 … 1.75
❑19, Aug 1993; JSn (w); Infinity Crusade … 1.75
❑20, Sep 1993; JSn (w); A: Drax the Destroyer. A: Thor. A: Goddess. Infinity Crusade crossover … 1.75
❑21, Oct 1993; JSn (w); A: Drax the Destroyer. A: Thor. A: Goddess. Infinity Crusade crossover … 1.75
❑22, Nov 1993; JSn (w); A: Drax the Destroyer. A: Thor. A: Goddess. Infinity Crusade crossover … 1.75
❑23, Dec 1993 … 1.75
❑24, Jan 1994 … 1.75
❑25, Feb 1994; JSn (w); diecut cover … 2.95
❑26, Mar 1994 … 1.75
❑27, Apr 1994 … 1.75
❑28, May 1994 … 1.75
❑29, Jun 1994 … 1.95
❑30, Jul 1994 JSn (w) … 1.95
❑31, Aug 1994 … 1.95
❑32, Sep 1994 … 1.95
❑33, Oct 1994 … 1.95
❑34, Nov 1994 … 1.95
❑35, Dec 1994 … 1.95
❑36, Jan 1995 … 1.95
❑37, Feb 1995 … 1.95
❑38, Mar 1995 … 1.95
❑39, Apr 1995 … 1.95
❑40, May 1995 … 1.95
❑41, Jun 1995 … 1.95
❑42, Jul 1995; Final Issue … 1.95

Warlock Chronicles
Marvel

❑1, Jul 1993; Prism cover … 2.95
❑2, Aug 1993; Infinity Crusade crossover … 2.00
❑3, Sep 1993; Infinity Crusade crossover … 2.00
❑4, Oct 1993; Infinity Crusade crossover … 2.00
❑5, Nov 1993; Infinity Crusade crossover … 2.00
❑6, Dec 1993 … 2.00
❑7, Jan 1994 … 2.00
❑8, Feb 1994; Final Issue … 2.00

N-MINT

Warlock 5
Aircel

❑1 1986, b&w … 2.00
❑2 1986, b&w … 2.00
❑3, Jan 1987, b&w … 2.00
❑4, Mar 1987, b&w … 2.00
❑5, Apr 1987, b&w; robot skull cover … 2.00
❑6, May 1987, b&w; woman's face on cover; misnumbered #5 … 2.00
❑7, Jun 1987, b&w … 2.00
❑8 1987, b&w … 2.00
❑9 1987, b&w … 2.00
❑10 1987, b&w … 2.00
❑11, Dec 1987, b&w … 2.00
❑12, Jan 1988, b&w … 2.00
❑13, Feb 1988, b&w … 2.00
❑14, Mar 1988, b&w … 2.00
❑15 1988, b&w … 2.00
❑16, Nov 1988, b&w … 2.00
❑17, Dec 1988, b&w … 2.00
❑18, Jan 1989, b&w … 2.00
❑19, Feb 1989, b&w … 2.00
❑20, Mar 1989, b&w … 2.00
❑21 1989, b&w … 2.00
❑22 1989, b&w; final issue … 2.00

Warlock 5
Sirius

❑1, Jan 1998 … 2.50
❑2, Feb 1998 … 2.50
❑3, Mar 1998 … 2.50
❑4, Apr 1998 … 2.50

Warlock 5 Book II
Aircel

❑1, Jun 1989, b&w … 2.00
❑2, Jul 1989, b&w … 2.00
❑3, Aug 1989, b&w … 2.00
❑4, Sep 1989, b&w … 2.00
❑5, Nov 1989, b&w … 2.00
❑6, Dec 1989, b&w … 2.00
❑7, Jan 1990, b&w … 2.00

Warlocks
Aircel

❑1 1988, b&w … 2.00
❑2 1988, b&w … 2.00
❑3 1988, b&w … 2.00
❑4 1988, b&w … 2.00
❑5 1989, b&w … 2.00
❑6 1989, b&w … 2.00
❑7 1989, b&w … 2.00
❑8 1989, b&w … 2.00
❑9 1989, b&w … 2.00
❑10, Nov 1989, b&w … 2.00
❑11, Mar 1990, b&w … 2.00
❑12, Apr 1990, b&w … 2.00
❑Special 1 1989, b&w … 2.25

Warlord
DC

❑1, Feb 1976 MGr (a); O: Warlord. … 10.00
❑2, Apr 1976 MGr (a); 1: Machiste … 4.00
❑3, Nov 1976, MGr (a) … 3.00
❑4, Jan 1977, MGr (a) … 3.00
❑5, Mar 1977, MGr (a); 1: Dragonsword. … 3.00
❑6, May 1977, MGr (a); 1: Mariah Romanola … 3.00

Other grades: Multiply price above by 5/6 for VF/NM • 2/3 for VERY FINE • 1/3 for FINE • 1/5 for VERY GOOD • 1/8 for GOOD

N-MINT | N-MINT | N-MINT

- ❑7, Jul 1977, MGr (a); O: Machiste 2.00
- ❑8, Sep 1977, MGr (a) 2.00
- ❑9, Nov 1977, MGr (a) 2.00
- ❑10, Jan 1978, MGr (a); Deimos 2.00
- ❑11, Mar 1978, MGr (a); reprints 1st Issue Special 1.50
- ❑12, May 1978, MGr (a); 1: Aton 1.50
- ❑13, Jul 1978, MGr (a) 1.50
- ❑14, Sep 1978, MGr (a) 1.50
- ❑15, Nov 1978, MGr (a); 1: Joshua Morgan (Warlord's son). 1.50
- ❑16, Dec 1978, MGr (a) 1.50
- ❑17, Jan 1979, MGr (a) 1.50
- ❑18, Feb 1979, MGr (a) 1.50
- ❑19, Mar 1979, MGr (a) 1.50
- ❑20, Apr 1979, MGr (a) 1.50
- ❑21, May 1979, MGr (a) 1.50
- ❑22, Jun 1979, MGr (a) 1.50
- ❑22/Whitman, Jun 1979, MGr (a); Whitman variant 8.00
- ❑23, Jul 1979, MGr (a) 1.50
- ❑24, Aug 1979, MGr (a) 1.50
- ❑25, Sep 1979, MGr (a) 1.50
- ❑26, Oct 1979, MGr (a) 1.50
- ❑27, Nov 1979, MGr (a) 1.50
- ❑28, Dec 1979, MGr (a); 1: Mongo Ironhand. 1: Wizard World. 1.50
- ❑29, Jan 1980, MGr (a) 1.50
- ❑30, Feb 1980, MGr (a) 1.00
- ❑31, Mar 1980, MGr (a) 1.00
- ❑32, Apr 1980, MGr (a); 1: Shakira 1.00
- ❑33, May 1980, MGr (a) 1.00
- ❑34, Jun 1980, MGr (a) 1.00
- ❑35, Jul 1980, MGr (a) 1.00
- ❑36, Aug 1980, MGr (a) 1.00
- ❑37, Sep 1980, MGr (a); O: Omac (new origin). Omac back-up 1.00
- ❑38, Oct 1980, MGr (a); 1: Jennifer Morgan (Warlord's daughter). Omac back-up 1.00
- ❑39, Nov 1980, MGr (a); Omac back-up 1.00
- ❑40, Dec 1980, MGr (a) 1.00
- ❑41, Jan 1981, MGr (a) 1.00
- ❑42, Feb 1981, MGr (a); A: Omac 1.00
- ❑43, Mar 1981, MGr (a); A: Omac 1.00
- ❑44, Apr 1981, MGr (a) 1.00
- ❑45, May 1981, MGr (a) 1.00
- ❑46, Jun 1981, MGr (a) 1.00
- ❑47, Jul 1981, MGr (a); 1: Rostov. Omac back-up 1.00
- ❑48, Aug 1981, Giant-size MGr, EC (a); 1: Arak. 1: Claw the Unconquered. 1.50
- ❑49, Sep 1981, MGr (a); 1: The Evil One. Claw back-up 1.00
- ❑50, Oct 1981, MGr (a) 1.00
- ❑51, Nov 1981, MGr (a); reprints Warlord #1; Dragonsword back-up 1.00
- ❑52, Dec 1981, MGr (a); Dragonsword back-up 1.00
- ❑53, Jan 1982, Dragonsword back-up 1.00
- ❑54, Feb 1982 .... 1.00
- ❑55, Mar 1982, MGr (c); 1: Lady Chian. 1: Arion. Arion back-up 1.00
- ❑56, Apr 1982, MGr (c);Arion back-up 1.00
- ❑57, May 1982, MGr (c);Arion back-up 1.00
- ❑58, Jun 1982, MGr (c);Arion back-up 1.00
- ❑59, Jul 1982, MGr (c); 1: Garn Daanuth. Arion back-up 1.00
- ❑60, Aug 1982, MGr (c); Arion back-up 1.00
- ❑61, Sep 1982, MGr (c); Arion back-up 1.00
- ❑62, Oct 1982, MGr (c); Arion back-up 1.00
- ❑63, Nov 1982, MGr (c); 1: Conqueror of the Barren Earth. Arion back-up 1.00
- ❑64, Dec 1982, Barren Earth back-up; Masters of the Universe preview 1.00
- ❑65, Jan 1983 .... 1.00
- ❑66, Feb 1983 .... 1.00
- ❑67, Mar 1983 .... 1.00
- ❑68, Apr 1983 .... 1.00
- ❑69, May 1983 .... 1.00
- ❑70, Jun 1983 .... 1.00
- ❑71, Jul 1983 .... 1.00
- ❑72, Aug 1983 .... 1.00
- ❑73, Sep 1983 .... 1.00
- ❑74, Oct 1983 .... 1.00
- ❑75, Nov 1983 .... 1.00
- ❑76, Dec 1983 .... 1.00
- ❑77, Jan 1984 .... 1.00
- ❑78, Feb 1984 .... 1.00
- ❑79, Mar 1984 .... 1.00
- ❑80, Apr 1984 .... 1.00
- ❑81, May 1984 .... 1.00
- ❑82, Jun 1984 .... 1.00
- ❑83, Jul 1984 .... 1.00
- ❑84, Aug 1984 .... 1.00
- ❑85, Sep 1984 .... 1.00
- ❑86, Oct 1984 .... 1.00
- ❑87, Nov 1984 .... 1.00
- ❑88, Dec 1984 .... 1.00
- ❑89, Jan 1985 .... 1.00
- ❑90, Feb 1985 .... 1.00
- ❑91, Mar 1985 O: Travis Morgan. O: Warlord. 1.00
- ❑92, Apr 1985 .... 1.00
- ❑93, May 1985 .... 1.00
- ❑94, Jun 1985 .... 1.00
- ❑95, Jul 1985 .... 1.00
- ❑96, Aug 1985 .... 1.00
- ❑97, Sep 1985 .... 1.00
- ❑98, Oct 1985 .... 1.00
- ❑99, Nov 1985 .... 1.00
- ❑100, Dec 1985; Giant-size MGr (c) 1.00
- ❑101, Jan 1986 MGr (c) 1.00
- ❑102, Feb 1986 MGr (c) 1.00
- ❑103, Mar 1986 MGr (c) 1.00
- ❑104, Apr 1986 MGr (c) 1.00
- ❑105, May 1986 .... 1.00
- ❑106, Jun 1986 .... 1.00
- ❑107, Jul 1986 .... 1.00
- ❑108, Aug 1986 .... 1.00
- ❑109, Sep 1986 .... 1.00
- ❑110, Oct 1986 .... 1.00
- ❑111, Nov 1986 .... 1.00
- ❑112, Dec 1986 MGr (c) 1.00
- ❑113, Jan 1987 .... 1.00
- ❑114, Feb 1987; Legends 1.00
- ❑115, Mar 1987; Legends 1.00
- ❑116, Apr 1987 .... 1.00
- ❑117, May 1987 MGr (c) 1.00
- ❑118, Jun 1987 .... 1.00
- ❑119, Jul 1987 .... 1.00
- ❑120, Aug 1987 .... 1.00
- ❑121, Sep 1987 .... 1.00
- ❑122, Oct 1987 .... 1.00
- ❑123, Nov 1987 .... 1.00
- ❑124, Dec 1987 .... 1.00
- ❑125, Jan 1988 D: Tara 1.00
- ❑126, Feb 1988 .... 1.00
- ❑127, Mar 1988 .... 1.00
- ❑128, Apr 1988 .... 1.00
- ❑129, May 1988 .... 1.00
- ❑130, Jul 1988 .... 1.00
- ❑131, Sep 1988; RL (a); Bonus Book #6; Rob Liefeld's first work at DC 2.00
- ❑132, Nov 1988 .... 1.00
- ❑133, Dec 1988; Giant-size JDu (a) 1.50
- ❑Ann 1, ca. 1982 MGr (a) 3.00
- ❑Ann 2, ca. 1983 .... 1.00
- ❑Ann 3, ca. 1984 .... 1.00
- ❑Ann 4, ca. 1985 .... 1.00
- ❑Ann 5, ca. 1986 .... 1.00
- ❑Ann 6, ca. 1987 .... 1.00

Warlord
DC

- ❑1, Jan 1992 MGr (c); MGr (w) 2.00
- ❑2, Feb 1992 MGr (c); MGr (w) 2.00
- ❑3, Mar 1992 MGr (c); MGr (w) 2.00
- ❑4, Apr 1992 MGr (c); MGr (w) 2.00
- ❑5, May 1992 MGr (c); MGr (w) 2.00
- ❑6, Jun 1992 MGr (c); MGr (w) 2.00

Warlord
DC

- ❑1, May 2006 .... 2.99
- ❑2, Jun 2006 .... 2.99
- ❑3, Jul 2006 .... 2.99
- ❑4, Aug 2006 .... 2.99
- ❑5, Sep 2006 .... 2.99
- ❑6, Oct 2006 .... 2.99
- ❑7, Nov 2006 .... 2.99
- ❑8, Dec 2006 .... 2.99
- ❑9, Jan 2007 .... 2.99
- ❑10, Feb 2007 .... 2.99

War Machine
Marvel

- ❑1, Apr 1994; Giant-size; newsstand 2.00
- ❑1/Variant, Apr 1994; Giant-size; Embossed cover 2.95
- ❑2, May 1994 .... 1.50
- ❑3, Jun 1994 .... 1.50
- ❑4, Jul 1994 .... 1.50
- ❑5, Aug 1994; V: Deathtoll 1.50
- ❑6, Sep 1994; V: Deathtoll 1.50
- ❑7, Oct 1994 .... 1.50
- ❑8, Nov 1994 .... 1.50
- ❑8/CS, Nov 1994; polybagged with 16-page Marvel Action Hour preview, acetate print, coupon, sweepstakes entry form 2.95
- ❑9, Dec 1994; Continues in Iron Man #311 .... 1.50
- ❑10, Jan 1995; Concludes in Iron Man #312 .... 1.50
- ❑11, Feb 1995 .... 1.50
- ❑12, Mar 1995 .... 1.50
- ❑13, Apr 1995 .... 1.50
- ❑14, May 1995 .... 1.50
- ❑15, Jun 1995; flip book with War Machine: Brothers in Arms part 2 .... 2.50
- ❑16, Jul 1995 .... 1.50
- ❑17, Aug 1995 .... 1.50
- ❑18, Sep 1995 .... 1.50
- ❑19, Oct 1995 .... 1.50
- ❑20, Nov 1995 .... 1.50
- ❑21, Dec 1995 .... 1.50
- ❑22, Jan 1996 .... 1.50
- ❑23, Feb 1996 .... 1.50
- ❑24, Mar 1996 .... 1.50
- ❑25, Apr 1996; Final Issue 1.50
- ❑Ashcan 1, ca. 1994; ashcan edition 0.75

War Machine
Marvel / MAX

- ❑1, Nov 2001 .... 1.50
- ❑2, Nov 2001 .... 1.50
- ❑3, Nov 2001 .... 1.50
- ❑4, Nov 2001 .... 1.50
- ❑5, Dec 2001 .... 1.50
- ❑6, Dec 2001 .... 1.50
- ❑7, Dec 2001 .... 1.50
- ❑8, Dec 2001 .... 1.50
- ❑9, Dec 2001 .... 1.50
- ❑10, Jan 2002 .... 1.50
- ❑11, Jan 2002 .... 1.50
- ❑12, Jan 2002 .... 1.50

War Man
Marvel / Epic

- ❑1, Nov 1993; Includes trading cards 2.50
- ❑2, Dec 1993; Includes trading cards 2.50

War of the Gods
DC

- ❑1, Sep 1991; Includes mini-posters; Robin pinup; Wonder Woman pinup; Deathstroke pinup; Circe pinup 1.75
- ❑2, Oct 1991; newsstand cover 1.75
- ❑2/Direct ed., Oct 1991; direct sale cover 1.75
- ❑3, Nov 1991; newsstand cover 1.75
- ❑3/Direct ed., Nov 1991; direct sale cover 1.75
- ❑4, Dec 1991; newsstand cover 1.75
- ❑4/Direct ed., Dec 1991; direct sale cover 1.75

War of the Worlds
Caliber

- ❑1, ca. 1996 .... 2.95
- ❑2, ca. 1996 .... 2.95
- ❑3, ca. 1996 .... 2.95
- ❑4, ca. 1996; ca. 1997 .... 2.95
- ❑5, ca. 1997 .... 2.95

War of the Worlds
Eternity

- ❑1 1990 .... 2.00
- ❑2 1990 .... 2.00
- ❑3 1990 .... 2.00
- ❑4 1990 .... 2.00
- ❑5 1990 .... 2.00
- ❑6 1990 .... 2.00

War of the Worlds: The Memphis Front
Arrow

- ❑1 1998, b&w; wrapraound cover 2.95
- ❑1/A 1998, b&w; expanded page count. 2.95
- ❑2 1998 .... 2.95
- ❑3 1998 .... 2.95

Other grades: Multiply price above by 5/6 for VF/NM • 2/3 for VERY FINE • 1/3 for FINE • 1/5 for VERY GOOD • 1/8 for GOOD

Wonder Woman

Revamped Amazon strives for peace
©DC

Wonder Woman Gallery

Pin-ups celebrate return of heroine
©DC

Wonder Woman: Our Worlds At War

Hippolyta's final fate revealed
©DC

Woodsy Owl

Conservation comic not on recycled paper
©Gold Key

Woody Woodpecker

Birdbrain bashes head in silly situations
©Dell

N-MINT

❑4 1998 ... 2.95
❑5 1998 ... 2.95

Warp
First

❑1, Mar 1983, FB (w); FB (a); 1: Lord Cumulus. 1: Chaos. This is the first comic published by First Comics ... 2.00
❑2, Apr 1983, FB (w); FB (a) ... 1.50
❑3, May 1983, FB (w); FB (a) ... 1.50
❑4, Jun 1983, FB (w); FB (a) ... 1.50
❑5, Aug 1983, FB (w); FB (a) ... 1.50
❑6, Sep 1983, FB (w); FB (a) ... 1.50
❑7, Oct 1983, FB (w); FB (a) ... 1.50
❑8, Nov 1983, FB (w); FB (a); Bill Willingham's first major comics work ... 1.25
❑9, Dec 1983 ... 1.25
❑10, Feb 1984 ... 1.25
❑11, Mar 1984 ... 1.25
❑12, Apr 1984 ... 1.25
❑13, May 1984 ... 1.25
❑14, Jul 1984 ... 1.25
❑15, Aug 1984 ... 1.25
❑16, Sep 1984 ... 1.25
❑17, Oct 1984 ... 1.25
❑18, Dec 1984 ... 1.25
❑19, Feb 1985, Final Issue ... 1.25
❑Special 1, Jul 1983, O: Chaos ... 1.00
❑Special 2, Jan 1984, Lord Cumulus ... 1.00
❑Special 3, Jun 1984, Chaos ... 1.00

Warp-3
Equinox

❑1, Mar 1990, b&w ... 1.50

War Party
Lightning

❑1, Oct 1994 ... 2.95

Warp Graphics Annual
Warp

❑1, WP, PF (w); Elfquest, Panda Khan, Unicorn Isle, Captain Obese, Thunderbunny, MythAdventures ... 3.00

Warpwalking
Caliber

❑1, b&w; ca. 1991 ... 2.50
❑2, b&w ... 2.50
❑3, b&w ... 2.50
❑4, b&w ... 2.50

Warrior
Ultimate Creations

❑1, May 1996 ... 2.95
❑2, Jul 1996 ... 2.95
❑3, Nov 1997 ... 2.95
❑4 1997 ... 2.95

Warrior Bugs
Artcoda

❑1, Mar 2002 ... 2.95

Warrior Nun Areala
Antarctic

❑1, Dec 1994; 1: Shotgun Mary. 1: Warrior Nun Areala ... 5.00
❑1/Ltd., Dec 1994; Limited edition (5000 made); no cover price ... 5.00
❑1/2nd, Mar 1995; 2nd printing ... 3.00
❑2, Feb 1995 ... 4.00
❑3, Apr 1995 ... 4.00

N-MINT

❑3/CS, Apr 1995; Includes CD ... 8.00
❑3/Ltd., Apr 1995; Limited edition (1000 made); no cover price ... 5.00

Warrior Nun Areala
Antarctic

❑1, Jun 1997 ... 3.00
❑1/Variant, Jun 1997; Leather edition; Print run of 700 ... 6.00
❑2, Sep 1997 ... 3.00
❑3, Nov 1997 ... 3.00
❑4, Jan 1998 ... 3.00
❑5, Mar 1998 ... 3.00
❑6, May 1998 ... 3.00

Warrior Nun Areala
Antarctic

❑1, Jul 1999 ... 2.50
❑2, Aug 1999 ... 2.50

Warrior Nun Areala and Avengelyne
Antarctic

❑1/A, Dec 1996; crossover with Maximum Press ... 2.95
❑1/B, Dec 1996; poster edition; logoless cover and poster insert ... 5.95

Warrior Nun Areala and Glory
Antarctic

❑1, Sep 1997; crossover with Awesome ... 2.95
❑1/CS, Sep 1997; limited poster edition; crossover with Awesome ... 5.95

Warrior Nun Areala/Razor: Revenge
Antarctic

❑1, Jan 1999 ... 2.99
❑1/Deluxe, Jan 1999; Deluxe Edition with painted cover ... 5.99

Warrior Nun Areala: Resurrection
Antarctic

❑1, Nov 1998 ... 3.00
❑1/Variant, Sum 1998, alternate logoless cover ... 3.00
❑2, Jan 1999 ... 3.00
❑3, Mar 1999 ... 3.00
❑4 1999 ... 3.00
❑5 1999 ... 3.00
❑6 1999 ... 3.00
❑Ashcan 1, Nov 1998, b&w preview ... 1.00

Warrior Nun Areala: Rheintöchter
Antarctic

❑1, Dec 1997, b&w ... 2.95
❑2, Apr 1998, b&w ... 2.95

Warrior Nun Areala: Rituals
Antarctic

❑1, Aug 1995 ... 2.95
❑1/Variant, Aug 1995; no cover price ... 4.00
❑2, Oct 1995 ... 2.95
❑3, Dec 1995 ... 2.95
❑4, Feb 1996 ... 2.95
❑5, Apr 1996 ... 2.95
❑6, Jun 1996; 40-page special ... 2.95

Warrior Nun: Black & White
Antarctic

❑1, Feb 1997; B&w series ... 3.00
❑2, Apr 1997; cover says Jan, indicia says Apr ... 3.00
❑3, Jun 1997 ... 3.00
❑4, Aug 1997 ... 3.00

N-MINT

❑5, Oct 1997 ... 3.00
❑6, Dec 1997 ... 3.00
❑7, Feb 1998 ... 3.00
❑8, Mar 1998 ... 3.00
❑9, Apr 1998 ... 3.00
❑10, May 1998 ... 3.00
❑11, Jun 1998 ... 3.00
❑12, Jul 1998 ... 3.00
❑13, Sep 1998 ... 3.00
❑14, Oct 1998 ... 3.00
❑15, Nov 1998 ... 2.95
❑16, Jan 1999 ... 2.99
❑17, Feb 1999 ... 2.99
❑18, Mar 1999 ... 2.99
❑19, Apr 1999 ... 2.99
❑20, May 1999 ... 2.99
❑21, Jul 1999 ... 2.50

Warrior Nun Brigantia
Antarctic

❑1, Jun 2000 ... 2.99
❑2 2000 ... 2.99
❑3 2000 ... 2.99

Warrior Nun Dei
Antarctic

❑1; Comics Cavalcade Commemorative Edition ... 5.95

Warrior Nun Dei: Aftertime
Antarctic

❑1, Jan 1997, Montage cover ... 3.00
❑2 1998 ... 3.00
❑3, Mar 1999 ... 3.00

Warrior Nun: Frenzy
Antarctic

❑1, Jan 1998 ... 2.95
❑2, Jun 1998 ... 2.95

Warrior Nun: Scorpio Rose
Antarctic

❑1, Sep 1996; Warrior Nun deflecting green energy ... 2.95
❑2, Nov 1996 ... 2.95
❑3, Jan 1997 ... 2.95
❑4, Mar 1997; Final Issue ... 2.95

Warrior Nun vs Razor
Antarctic

❑1, May 1996; crossover with London Night Studios ... 3.95

Warrior of Waverly Street
Dark Horse

❑1, Nov 1996 ... 2.95
❑2, Dec 1996, Final Issue ... 2.95

Warriors
Adventure

❑1, ca. 1987, b&w ... 2.00
❑2, Dec 1987, b&w ... 2.00
❑3, ca. 1988, b&w ... 2.00
❑4, Jul 1988, b&w ... 2.00
❑5, Nov 1988, b&w ... 2.00

Warriors of Plasm
Defiant

❑1, Aug 1993; 1&O: Warriors of Plasm. 1: Lorca. First Defiant Comic ... 2.95
❑2, Sep 1993 ... 2.95
❑3, Oct 1993 ... 2.95

Other grades: Multiply price above by 5/6 for VF/NM • 2/3 for VERY FINE • 1/3 for FINE • 1/5 for VERY GOOD • 1/8 for GOOD

N-MINT

❑4, Nov 1993 2.95
❑5, Dec 1993 2.50
❑6, Jan 1994; 1: Prudence 2.50
❑7, Feb 1994 2.50
❑8, Mar 1994; 40 pages 2.75
❑9, Apr 1994; 40 pages 2.75
❑10, May 1994 2.50
❑11, Jun 1994 2.50
❑12, Jul 1994 2.50
❑13, Aug 1994; Final issue? 2.50

Warriors of Plasm Graphic Novel
Defiant

❑1, Nov 1993; Home for the Holidays 6.95

Warrior's Way
Bench

❑1 1998 2.99
❑2, Aug 1998 2.99
❑2/A, Aug 1998; alternate cover 2.99
❑3 1998 2.99

War Sirens and Liberty Belles
Recollections

❑1, b&w; cardstock cover 4.95

War Sluts
Pretty Graphic

❑1, b&w; Adult 3.95
❑2, b&w; cardstock cover 3.95

War Story: Archangel
DC / Vertigo

❑1, ca. 2003 4.95

War Story: D-Day Dodgers
DC / Vertigo

❑1, Dec 2001, b&w 4.95

War Story: Johann's Tiger
DC / Vertigo

❑1, Nov 2001, b&w 4.95

War Story: Nightingale
DC / Vertigo

❑1, Feb 2002, b&w 4.95

War Story: Screaming Eagles
DC / Vertigo

❑1, Jan 2002, b&w 4.95

Warstrike
Malibu / Ultraverse

❑1, May 1994, Flip Cover 1.95
❑2, Jun 1994, 1: Backlash (Ultraverse); 1: Domingo; 1: Gaunt; 1: Quixote 1.95
❑3, Jul 1994 1.95
❑4, Aug 1994, 1: Captain U.S.A. 1.95
❑5, Sep 1994, 1: Aeon 1.95
❑6, Oct 1994 1.95
❑7, Nov 1994, Final Issue 1.95
❑GS 1, Dec 1994, Giant-size; Lord Pumpkin reborn 2.50

Warworld!
Dark Horse

❑1, Feb 1989, b&w 1.75

Warzone
Express / Entity

❑1, ca. 1994, b&w; enhanced cardstock cover 2.95
❑2, ca. 1994, b&w; enhanced cardstock cover 2.95
❑3, ca. 1995, b&w; enhanced cardstock cover 2.95

Warzone 3719
Pocket Change

❑1 1.95

Washmen
New York

❑1 1.70

Washouts
Renaissance

❑1, Jul 2002, b&w 2.95

Wash Tubbs Quarterly
Dragon Lady

❑1 4.95
❑2 5.95
❑3 5.95
❑4 5.95
❑5 5.95

N-MINT

Waste L.A.: Descent
John Gaushell

❑1, Jan 1996, b&w; fumetti 2.50
❑2, Mar 1996, b&w; fumetti 2.50
❑3, May 1996, b&w; fumetti 2.50

Wasteland
DC

❑1, Dec 1987 2.00
❑2, Jan 1988 2.00
❑3, Feb 1988 2.00
❑4, Mar 1988 2.00
❑5, Apr 1988; correct cover 2.00
❑5/A, Apr 1988; cover of #6 2.00
❑6, May 1988; correct cover 2.00
❑6/A, May 1988; blank cover 2.00
❑7, Jun 1988 2.00
❑8, Jul 1988 2.00
❑9, Aug 1988 2.00
❑10, Sep 1988 2.00
❑11, Oct 1988 2.00
❑12, Nov 1988 JO (a) 2.00
❑13, Dec 1988 JO (a) 2.00
❑14, Win 1988; JO (a); Winter 1988 2.00
❑15, Hol 1988; JO (a); Hol 1988 2.00
❑16, Feb 1989 JO (a) 2.00
❑17, Apr 1989 JO (a) 2.00
❑18, May 1989; JO (a); Final Issue 2.00

Watchcats
Harrier

❑1; ca. 1987 1.95

Watchmen
DC

❑1, Sep 1986; DaG (c); AMo (w); DaG (a); 1: Rorshach. 1: Doctor Manhattan. 1: Ozymandias. D: The Comedian 8.00
❑2, Oct 1986 DaG (c); AMo (w); DaG (a) 5.00
❑3, Nov 1986 DaG (c); AMo (w); DaG (a) 5.00
❑4, Dec 1986; DaG (c); AMo (w); DaG (a); O: Doctor Manhattan 4.00
❑5, Jan 1987 DaG (c); AMo (w); DaG (a) 4.00
❑6, Feb 1987; AMo (w); DaG (a); O: Rorshach 4.00
❑7, Mar 1987 DaG (c); AMo (w); DaG (a) 4.00
❑8, Apr 1987 DaG (c); AMo (w); DaG (a) 4.00
❑9, May 1987 DaG (c); AMo (w); DaG (a) 4.00
❑10, Jul 1987 DaG (c); AMo (w); DaG (a) 4.00
❑11, Aug 1987; DaG (c); AMo (w); DaG (a); O: Ozymandias 4.00
❑12, Oct 1987; DaG (c); AMo (w); DaG (a); D: Rorshach 4.00

Waterloo Sunset
Image

❑1, Jul 2004 6.95
❑2, Jul 2004 6.95
❑3, Feb 2005 6.95
❑4, Jan 2006 6.99

Waterworld: Children of Leviathan
Acclaim

❑1, Aug 1997; no indicia 2.50
❑2, Sep 1997 2.50
❑3, Oct 1997 2.50
❑4, Nov 1997 2.50

Wavemakers
Blind Bat

❑1, Jan 1990 3.00

Wave Warriors
Astroboys

❑1 2.00

Waxwork
Blackthorne

❑1, b&w; Movie adaptation 2.00
❑3D 1; Movie adaptation 2.50

Way of the Rat
CrossGen

❑1, Jun 2002 2.95
❑2, Jul 2002 2.95
❑3, Aug 2002 2.95
❑4, Sep 2002 2.95
❑5, Oct 2002 2.95
❑6, Nov 2002 2.95
❑7, Dec 2002 2.95
❑8, Jan 2003 2.95
❑9, Feb 2003 2.95
❑10, Mar 2003 2.95
❑11, Apr 2003 2.95

N-MINT

❑12, May 2003 2.95
❑13, Jun 2003 2.95
❑14, May 2003 2.95
❑15, Jul 2003 2.95
❑16, Aug 2003 2.95
❑17, Nov 2003 2.95
❑18, Nov 2003 2.95
❑19, Dec 2003 2.95
❑20, Jan 2004 2.95
❑21, Feb 2004 2.95
❑22, Apr 2004 2.95
❑23, May 2004 2.95
❑23/2nd, Apr 2004 2.95
❑24, May 2004; Final Issue 2.95

Way Out Strips
Fantagraphics

❑1 1994, b&w 2.50
❑2, May 1994, b&w 2.75
❑3, Aug 1994, b&w 2.75

Way Out Strips
Tragedy Strikes

❑1 1992, b&w 2.95
❑2 1992, b&w 2.95
❑3 1992, b&w 2.95

Wayward Warrior
Alpha Productions

❑1 1990, b&w 1.95
❑2 1990, b&w 1.95
❑3 1990, b&w 1.95

WCW World Championship Wrestling
Marvel

❑1, Apr 1992 1.25
❑2, May 1992 1.25
❑3, Jun 1992 1.25
❑4, Jul 1992 1.25
❑5, Aug 1992 1.25
❑6, Sep 1992 1.25
❑7, Oct 1992 1.25
❑8, Nov 1992 1.25
❑9, Dec 1992 1.25
❑10, Jan 1993 1.25
❑11, Feb 1993 1.25
❑12, Mar 1993 1.25

We 3
DC / Vertigo

❑1, Oct 2004 2.95
❑2, Dec 2004 2.95
❑3, Mar 2005 2.95

Weapons File
Antarctic

❑1, Jun 2005 4.95
❑2, Jul 2005 4.95
❑3, ca. 2005 4.95

Weapon X
Marvel

❑1, Mar 1995; Age of Apocalypse 1.95
❑2, Apr 1995; Age of Apocalypse 1.95
❑3, May 1995; Age of Apocalypse 1.95
❑4, Jun 1995; Age of Apocalypse 1.95

Weapon X
Marvel

❑1, Nov 2002 2.25
❑2, Dec 2002 2.25
❑3, Jan 2003 2.25
❑4, Feb 2003 2.25
❑5, Mar 2003 2.25
❑6, Apr 2003 2.25
❑7, May 2003 2.25
❑8, Jun 2003 2.25
❑9, Jul 2003 2.99
❑10, Aug 2003 2.99
❑11, Sep 2004 2.99
❑12, Oct 2003 2.99
❑13, Nov 2003 2.99
❑14, Dec 2003 2.99
❑15, Dec 2003 2.99
❑16, Jan 2004 2.99
❑17, Mar 2004 2.99
❑18, Apr 2004 2.99
❑19, May 2004 2.99
❑20, May 2004 2.99
❑21, Jun 2004 2.99
❑22, Jun 2004 2.99
❑23, Jul 2004 2.99

Other grades: Multiply price above by 5/6 for VF/NM • 2/3 for VERY FINE • 1/3 for FINE • 1/5 for VERY GOOD • 1/8 for GOOD

World Below

Concrete's Chadwick goes spelunking
©Dark Horse

World of Archie

The Riverdale gang strikes again
©Archie

World of Wheels

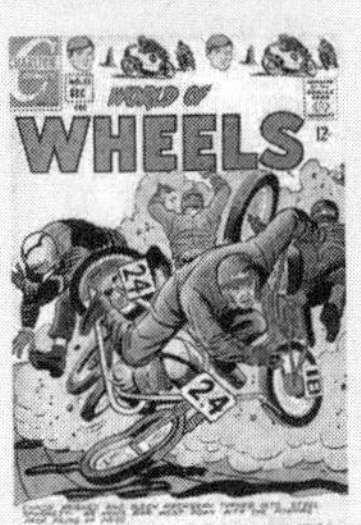

Can't you just hear the echo effect?
©Charlton

World of Wood

No lumber here, just Wally Wood work
©Eclipse

World's Finest Comics

Teamed two of DC's titans
©DC

	N-MINT
❑24, Jul 2004	2.99
❑25, Aug 2004	2.99
❑26, Sep 2004	2.99
❑27, Oct 2004	2.99
❑28, Nov 2004	2.99

Weapon X: Days of Future Now
Marvel

❑1, Aug 2005	2.99
❑2, Sep 2005	2.99
❑3, Oct 2005	2.99
❑4, Dec 2005	2.99
❑5, Jan 2006	2.99

Weapon X: The Draft: Kane
Marvel

❑1, Oct 2002	2.25

Weapon XXX: 0: the Implants
Friendly

❑1, Jul 1992; Adult	2.95
❑2 1992; Adult	2.95
❑3 1992; Adult	2.95

Weapon Zero
Image

❑1, Jun 1995; 1: Weapon Zero. Issue #T-4	3.00
❑1/Gold, Jun 1995; Gold edition; Issue #T-4; 1000 copies produced for Chicago Comicon	2.50
❑2, Aug 1995; Issue #T-3	2.50
❑3, Sep 1995; Issue #T-2	2.50
❑4, Oct 1995; Issue #T-1	2.50
❑5, Dec 1995; Issue #T-0; Issue #T-0	2.50

Weapon Zero
Image

❑1, Mar 1996; indicia gives year of publication as 1995	3.00
❑2, Apr 1996; indicia gives year of publication as 1995	3.00
❑3, May 1996	3.00
❑4, Jun 1996; indicia gives year of publication as 1995	3.00
❑5, Jul 1996; indicia gives year of publication as 1995	3.00
❑6, Aug 1996	2.50
❑7, Sep 1996	2.50
❑8, Nov 1996	2.50
❑9, Dec 1996	2.50
❑10, Feb 1997	2.50
❑11, Apr 1997	2.50
❑12, May 1997	2.50
❑13, Jun 1997	2.50
❑14, Sep 1997	2.50
❑15, Dec 1997	3.50

Weapon Zero/Silver Surfer
Top Cow / Image

❑1, Jan 1997; crossover with Marvel; continues in Cyblade/Ghost Rider	2.95
❑1/A, Jan 1997; alternate cover	2.95

Weasel Guy: Road Trip
Image

❑1, Aug 1999	2.95
❑1/A, Aug 1999; alternate cover	2.95
❑2, Oct 1999	3.50

Weasel Patrol
Eclipse

❑1, b&w	2.00

Weather Woman
CPM Manga

	N-MINT
❑1, Aug 2000, b&w; Adult	2.95
❑1/A, Aug 2000, b&w; alternate cover: Weather Woman smoking	2.95

Weaveworld
Marvel / Epic

❑1, Dec 1991, prestige format	4.95
❑2, Jan 1992, prestige format	4.95
❑3, Feb 1992, prestige format	4.95

Web
DC / Impact

❑1, Sep 1991; 1: The Web (full appearance)	1.25
❑2, Oct 1991; O: The Web	1.00
❑3, Nov 1991; 1: St. James. 1: Meridian	1.00
❑4, Dec 1991; 1: Silver	1.00
❑5, Jan 1992 GK (c)	1.00
❑6, Feb 1992	1.00
❑7, Apr 1992	1.00
❑8, Apr 1992	1.00
❑9, May 1992; GK (c); trading card	1.00
❑10, Jun 1992 GK (c)	1.25
❑11, Jul 1992	1.25
❑12, Aug 1992 GK (c)	1.25
❑13, Sep 1992 GK (c)	1.25
❑14, Oct 1992; GK (c); Final Issue	1.25
❑Ann 1, ca. 1992; MWa (w); trading card	2.50

Webber's World
Allstar

❑1	4.95

Web-Man
Argosy

❑1; gatefold cover	2.50

Web of Horror
Major Magazines

❑1, Dec 1969; Jeff Jones cover; Wrightson, Kaluta art	30.00
❑2, Feb 1970; Jeff Jones cover; Wrightson, Kaluta art	30.00
❑3, Apr 1970; 1st published Wrightson cover; Brunner, Kaluta, Bruce Jones art	30.00

Web of Scarlet Spider
Marvel

❑1, Nov 1995, O: Scarlet Spider; Continued in Amazing Scarlet Spider #1	2.00
❑2, Dec 1995, A: Cyber-Slayers. Continued in Amazing Scarlet Spider #2	2.00
❑3, Jan 1996, A: Firestar. continues in New Warriors #67	2.00
❑4, Feb 1996, Final Issue	2.00

Web of Spider-Man
Marvel

	N-MINT
❑1, Apr 1985, CV (c); Charles Vess cover; Beau Smith LOC	8.00
❑2, May 1985	6.00
❑3, Jun 1985	5.00
❑4, Jul 1985, V: Doctor Octopus	4.00
❑5, Aug 1985, V: Doctor Octopus	4.00
❑6, Sep 1985, Secret Wars II	4.00
❑7, Oct 1985, A: Hulk. V: Hulk	4.00
❑8, Nov 1985	4.00
❑9, Dec 1985	4.00
❑10, Jan 1986, A: Dominic Fortune	4.00
❑11, Feb 1986	3.00
❑12, Mar 1986	3.00
❑13, Apr 1986	3.00
❑14, May 1986	3.00
❑15, Jun 1986; 1: The Foreigner. 1: Chance I (Nicholas Powell)	3.00
❑16, Jul 1986	3.00
❑17, Aug 1986; V: Magma. red suit destroyed	3.00
❑18, Sep 1986; Venom cameo	3.00
❑19, Oct 1986; 1: Solo; 1: Humbug	3.00
❑20, Nov 1986	3.00
❑21, Dec 1986	3.00
❑22, Jan 1987; Credits provided in #24.	3.00
❑23, Feb 1987; O: Slyde	3.00
❑24, Mar 1987	3.00
❑25, Apr 1987	3.00
❑26, May 1987	3.00
❑27, Jun 1987	3.00
❑28, Jul 1987	3.00
❑29, Aug 1987 A: Wolverine. A: Hobgoblin II (Jason Macendale)	5.00
❑30, Sep 1987; O: The Rose	4.00
❑31, Oct 1987; V: Kraven; Continued in Amazing Spider-Man #293	5.00
❑32, Nov 1987; V: Kraven; Continued in Amazing Spider-Man #294	5.00
❑33, Dec 1987 BSz (c)	3.00
❑34, Jan 1988	3.00
❑35, Feb 1988; 1: Tarantula II (Luis Alvarez)	3.00
❑36, Mar 1988; O: Tarantula II (Luis Alvarez)	4.00
❑37, Apr 1988	3.00
❑38, May 1988; A: Hobgoblin II (Jason Macendale). V: Hobgoblin	5.00
❑39, Jun 1988	3.00
❑40, Jul 1988	3.00
❑41, Aug 1988	3.00
❑42, Sep 1988	3.00
❑43, Oct 1988	3.00
❑44, Nov 1988; A: Hulk. Continued in Incredible Hulk #349	2.50
❑45, Dec 1988; V: Vulture	2.50
❑46, Jan 1989	2.50
❑47, Feb 1989; V: Hobgoblin. Inferno	2.50
❑48, Mar 1989; O: Demogoblin. V: Hobgoblin. Inferno	8.00
❑49, Apr 1989	2.00
❑50, May 1989; Giant-sized	2.50
❑51, Jun 1989	2.00
❑52, Jul 1989; V: Chameleon; Spotlight on J. Jonah Jameson	2.00
❑53, Aug 1989; Continued in Spectacular Spider-Man #153	2.00
❑54, Sep 1989; V: Chameleon; Continued in Spectacular Spider-Man #154	2.00
❑55, Oct 1989; V: Chameleon	2.00
❑56, Nov 1989; V: Rocket Racer	2.00
❑57, Nov 1989; V: Skinhead. V: Skinhead	2.00
❑58, Dec 1989; Acts of Vengeance	2.50
❑59, Dec 1989; Acts of Vengeance; Spider-Man with cosmic powers	8.00
❑60, Jan 1990; Acts of Vengeance	2.50
❑61, Feb 1990; Acts of Vengeance	2.50
❑62, Mar 1990	2.00
❑63, Apr 1990	2.00
❑64, May 1990; Acts of Vengeance	2.00
❑65, Jun 1990; Acts of Vengeance	2.00

N-MINT

❑66, Jul 1990 A: Green Goblin 2.00
❑67, Aug 1990 A: Green Goblin 2.00
❑68, Sep 1990 2.00
❑69, Oct 1990; Color credits from #71 2.00
❑70, Nov 1990; Spider-Hulk 2.00
❑71, Dec 1990 2.00
❑72, Jan 1991 2.00
❑73, Feb 1991 2.00
❑74, Mar 1991 2.00
❑75, Apr 1991 2.00
❑76, May 1991 A: Fantastic Four 2.00
❑77, Jun 1991 2.00
❑78, Jul 1991 A: Cloak & Dagger 2.00
❑79, Aug 1991 2.00
❑80, Sep 1991; V: Silvermane 2.00
❑81, Oct 1991 SB (c); KB (w) 2.00
❑82, Nov 1991; KB (w); V: Man-Mountain Marko 2.00
❑83, Dec 1991 KB (w) 2.00
❑84, Jan 1992 A: Hobgoblin 2.00
❑85, Feb 1992 2.00
❑86, Mar 1992 2.00
❑87, Apr 1992 2.00
❑88, May 1992 2.00
❑89, Jun 1992 2.00
❑90, Jul 1992; Double-size; hologram; Poster 5.00
❑90/2nd, Jul 1992; Double-size; hologram; Poster 2.95
❑91, Aug 1992 2.00
❑92, Sep 1992 2.00
❑93, Oct 1992 2.00
❑94, Nov 1992; V: Hobgoblin 2.00
❑95, Dec 1992; A: Ghost Rider. A: Johnny Blaze. V: Venom. V: Venom; Continued in Spirits of Vengeance #5 2.00
❑96, Jan 1993; A: Ghost Rider. A: Johnny Blaze. V: Venom. Painted cover; V: Venom; Continued in Spirits of Vengeance #6 2.00
❑97, Feb 1993 2.00
❑98, Mar 1993 2.00
❑99, Apr 1993; V: New Enforcers 2.00
❑100, May 1993; 1: Spider-Armor. foil cover 4.00
❑101, Jun 1993; Continued in Amazing Spider-Man #378 2.00
❑102, Jul 1993; Continued in Amazing Spider-Man #379 2.00
❑103, Aug 1993; Continued in Amazing Spider-Man #380 2.00
❑104, Sep 1993; Infinity Crusade; Nightwatch story 2.00
❑105, Oct 1993; A: Archangel. Infinity Crusade 2.00
❑106/CS, Nov 1993; Dirtbag special; Infinity Crusade;Polybagged with copy of Dirt Magazine, cassette tape 5.00
❑106, Nov 1993; Infinity Crusade 1.25
❑107, Dec 1993; A: Quicksand. A: Sandman. O: Sandstorm; Cardiac story 2.00
❑108, Jan 1994; A: Quicksand. A: Sandman. Cardiac story 2.00
❑109, Feb 1994 2.00
❑110, Mar 1994 2.00
❑111, Apr 1994; V: Lizard 2.00
❑112, May 1994; Continued in Amazing Spider-Man #389 2.00
❑113, Jun 1994 A: Gambit. A: Black Cat 2.00
❑113/CS, Jun 1994; A: Gambit. A: Black Cat. TV preview; print 4.00
❑114, Jul 1994 2.00
❑115, Aug 1994 2.00
❑116, Sep 1994 2.00
❑117, Oct 1994; Flip-book; A: Ben Reilly. Flip-book; Continued in Amazing Spider-Man #394 3.00
❑117/Variant, Oct 1994; Flip-book; O: Ben Reilly. A: Ben Reilly. foil cover 5.00
❑118, Nov 1994; Continued in Spider-Man #52 3.00
❑118/2nd, Nov 1994; Has blank UPC code 1.50
❑119, Dec 1994; Scarlet Spider vs. Venom 2.00
❑119/CS, Dec 1994; polybagged with Marvel Milestone Edition: Amazing Spider-Man #150 and POP card 6.45
❑120, Jan 1995; Giant-size; A: Morbius. V: Tombstone; Morbius appearance in Flip-book; Web of Life continued Spider-Man #54 4.00
❑121, Feb 1995; V: Kaine; Continued Spider-Man #55 2.00

N-MINT

❑122, Mar 1995; A: Jackal. Continued in Amazing Spider-Man #399 2.00
❑123, Apr 1995 A: Jackal 2.00
❑124, May 1995; Continued in Amazing Spider-Man #401 2.00
❑125, Jun 1995; Giant-size 2.95
❑125/Variant, Jun 1995; Giant-size; Hologram on cover 3.95
❑126, Jul 1995; Continued in Amazing Spider-Man #403 1.50
❑127, Aug 1995; Continued in Amazing Spider-Man #404 1.50
❑128, Sep 1995; Continued in Amazing Spider-Man #405 1.50
❑129, Oct 1995; A: New Warriors. Final Issue; Continued in Web of Scarlet Spider #1 1.50
❑129/CS, Oct 1995; Final Issue; Includes Overpower trading card 5.00
❑Ann 1, ca. 1985; CV (c); A: 4th. Painted cover; 4: Spider-Man's black costume 7.00
❑Ann 2, ca. 1986; A: New Mutants 6.00
❑Ann 3, ca. 1987; pin-ups 3.00
❑Ann 4, ca. 1988; 1: Poison; Poison story; Pinups; Evolutionary War continued in West Coast Avengers Ann #3 3.00
❑Ann 5, ca. 1989; O: Silver Sable. A: Fantastic Four. Atlantis Attacks 2.50
❑Ann 6, ca. 1990; V: Psycho-Man. Tiny Spidey 2.50
❑Ann 7, ca. 1991; O: Hobgoblin. O: Venom. O: Green Goblin. A: Iron Man. A: Black Panther. V: Ultron; Rocket Racer story; Outlaws story 2.50
❑Ann 8, ca. 1992; A: New Warriors. A: Venom. V: Whiplash. V: Beetle. V: Constrictor. V: Rhino; Venom story; Black Cat story; Cloak & Dagger story; Hero Killers continued in New Warriors Ann #2 3.00
❑Ann 9, ca. 1993; 1: The Cadre. trading card 2.95
❑Ann 10, ca. 1994; V: Shriek; Warrant; Black Cat and Black Fox; The Prowler; CA. 1994; Warrant story; Black Cat and Black Fox story; The Prowler story; Pinups; Cardiac pinup; Solo pinup; Puma pinup 2.95
❑SS 1, ca. 1995; Flip-book; Super Special 3.95

Webspinners: Tales of Spider-Man
Marvel

❑1, Jan 1999; gatefold summary; V: Mysterio 2.99
❑1/A, Jan 1999; variant cover: Spider-Man vs. Mysterio with statue against orange background 2.99
❑1/B, Jan 1999; gatefold summary; variant cover 2.99
❑1/Autographed, Jan 1999; Autographed by Michael Zuli 10.00
❑1/Sunburst, Jan 1999 5.00
❑2/A, Feb 1999; Cover A 2.50
❑2/B, Feb 1999; Cover B by Steve Rude 2.50
❑3, Mar 1999; V: Mysterio 2.50
❑4, Apr 1999 2.50
❑5, May 1999 2.50
❑6, Jun 1999 2.50
❑7, Jul 1999; V: Sandman 2.50
❑8, Aug 1999; V: Sandman 2.50
❑9, Sep 1999 2.50
❑10, Oct 1999 2.50
❑11, Nov 1999; V: Chameleon 2.50
❑12, Dec 1999 2.50
❑13, Jan 2000 2.50
❑14, Feb 2000 2.50
❑15, Mar 2000 2.50
❑16, Apr 2000 2.50
❑17, May 2000 2.50
❑18, Jun 2000 2.50

Wedding of Dracula
Marvel

❑1, Jan 1993; Reprints Tomb of Dracula #30, #45, and #46 2.00

Wedding of Popeye and Olive
Ocean

❑1, ca. 1998, b&w; Color interiors 2.75

Weezul
Lightning

❑1/A, Aug 1996; White background cover 2.75
❑1/B, Aug 1996; alternate cover 3.00

N-MINT

Weird
DC

❑1, Apr 1988 1.50
❑2, May 1988 1.50
❑3, Jun 1988 1.50
❑4, Jul 1988 1.50

Weird
DC / Paradox

❑1, Sum 1997, b&w; magazine; reprints material from Big Book of Conspiracies 2.99

Weird
Avalon

❑1 2.99
❑2 2.99
❑3 2.99
❑4 2.99

Weirdfall
Antarctic

❑1, Jul 1995, b&w 2.75
❑2, Sep 1995, b&w 2.75
❑3, Nov 1995, b&w 2.75

Weird Fantasy
Gemstone

❑1, Oct 1992; AF, HK, WW, JKa (a); Reprints 2.50
❑2, Jan 1993; AF, HK, WW, JKa (a); Reprints Weird Fantasy #14 2.00
❑3, Apr 1993; AF, HK, WW, JKa (a); Reprints 2.00
❑4, Jul 1993; AF, HK, WW, JKa (a); Reprints 2.00
❑5, Oct 1993; AF, HK, WW, JKa (w); AF, HK, WW, JKa (a); Reprints 2.00
❑6, Jan 1994; AF, HK, WW, JKa (a); Reprints 2.00
❑7, Apr 1994; AF, WW, JKa (a); Reprints 2.00
❑8, Jul 1994; Reprints 2.00
❑9, Oct 1994; Reprints 2.00
❑10, Jan 1995; Reprints 2.00
❑11, Apr 1995; Reprints 2.50
❑12, Jul 1995; Reprints 2.50
❑13, Oct 1995; Reprints 2.50
❑14, Jan 1996; AW, JO, FF, WW, JKa (a); Reprints 2.50
❑15, Apr 1996; AW, JO, JKa (a); Reprints 2.50
❑16, Jul 1996; AW, JO, JKa (a); Reprints 2.50
❑17, Oct 1996; AW, JO, BE, WW (a); Reprints 2.50
❑18, Jan 1997; Reprints 2.50
❑19, Apr 1997; AW, JO, JSe, BE, JKa (w); AW, JO, JSe, BE, JKa (a); Reprints Weird Fantasy (EC) #19 2.50
❑20, Jul 1997; AW, JO, JSe, BE, JKa (w); AW, JO, JSe, BE, JKa (a); Reprints Weird Fantasy (EC) #20 2.50
❑21, Oct 1997; AW, JO, JSe, BE, JKa (w); AW, JO, JSe, BE, JKa (a); Reprints Weird Fantasy (EC) #21 2.50
❑22, Jan 1998; JO, BK, JKa (w); JO, BK, JKa (a); Reprints Weird Fantasy (EC) #22 2.50
❑Ann 1; Reprints Weird Fantasy #1-5 8.95
❑Ann 2; Reprints Weird Fantasy #6-10 9.95
❑Ann 3 8.95
❑Ann 4 9.95
❑Ann 5; Reprints Weird Fantasy #19-22 10.95

Weird Melvin
Marc Hansen Stuff!

❑1, Feb 1995, b&w; O: Weird Melvin 2.95
❑2, Apr 1995, b&w 2.95
❑3, Jun 1995, b&w 2.95
❑4, Aug 1995, b&w 2.95
❑5, Oct 1995, b&w 2.95

Weird Mystery Tales
DC

❑1, Jul 1972, ME (w); JK (a); 1: Destiny 30.00
❑2, Sep 1972 20.00
❑3, Nov 1972, 3rd story is reprint from House of Mystery #95 15.00
❑4, Jan 1973, JSn (w) 12.00
❑5, Apr 1973 12.00
❑6, Jul 1973 12.00
❑7, Sep 1973 12.00
❑8, Nov 1973 12.00
❑9, Dec 1973 12.00
❑10, Mar 1974 12.00
❑11, Apr 1974 10.00
❑12, Jul 1974, Luis Dominguez (cover) 10.00

Other grades: Multiply price above by 5/6 for VF/NM • 2/3 for VERY FINE • 1/3 for FINE • 1/5 for VERY GOOD • 1/8 for GOOD

World's Worst Comics Awards

Golden Turkeys for the comics industry

©Kitchen Sink

Worst from Mad

Early annuals preceded Super Specials

©E.C.

Wrath

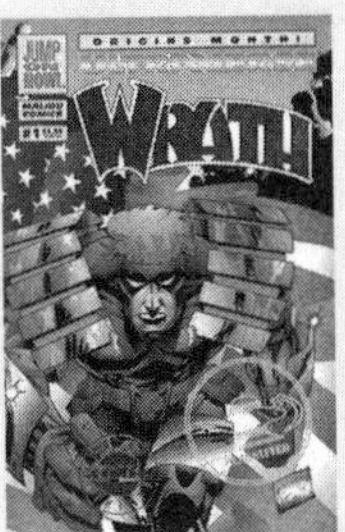

He worked for Aladdin, but was no genie

©Malibu

Wrath of the Spectre

Adventure reprints plus a new story

©DC

Wulf the Barbarian

Conan copy at Atlas/Seaboard

©Atlas-Seaboard

	N-MINT
❑13, Aug 1974, Luis Dominguez (cover)	10.00
❑14, Oct 1974, Luis Dominguez (cover); The Price adopted from John Russell's The Price Of The Head	10.00
❑15, Jan 1975, Luis Dominguez (cover)	10.00
❑16, Mar 1975; Luis Dominguez (cover)	10.00
❑17, Apr 1975	10.00
❑18, May 1975	10.00
❑19, Jun 1975	10.00
❑20, Jul 1975	10.00
❑21, Aug 1975; Wrightson cover	15.00
❑22, Sep 1975	10.00
❑23, Oct 1975	10.00
❑24, Nov 1975; Final Issue	10.00

Weird Romance
Eclipse

❑1, ca. 1988, b&w	2.00

Weird Science
Gladstone

❑1, Sep 1990; WW (c); AF, GE, AW, HK, JO, WW, JKa (w); AF, GE, AW, HK, JO, WW, JKa (a); Reprints Weird Science #22; Weird Fantasy #1	2.00
❑2, Nov 1990; AW, JO, WW, JKa (a); Reprints	2.00
❑3, Jan 1991; WW (c); AF, HK, WW, JKa (a); Reprints Weird Science #9, Weird Fantasy #14	2.00
❑4, Mar 1991; AF, JO, WW, JKa (a); Reprints	2.00

Weird Science
Gemstone

❑1, Sep 1992; AF, HK, WW, JKa (w); AF, HK, WW, JKa (a); Reprints Weird Science #1	2.50
❑2, Dec 1992; Reprints Weird Science #2	2.00
❑3, Mar 1993; Reprints Weird Science #3	2.00
❑4, Jun 1993; AF (c); AF, HK, JKa, GI (a); Reprints Weird Science #4	2.00
❑5, Sep 1993; AF (c); AF, HK, WW, JKa (a); Reprints Weird Science #5	2.00
❑6, Dec 1993; AF (c); AF, HK, WW, JKa (a); Reprints Weird Science #6	2.00
❑7, Mar 1994; AF (c); AF, HK, WW, JKa (a); Reprints Weird Science #7	2.00
❑8, Jun 1994; AF, WW, JKa (a); Reprints Weird Science #8	2.00
❑9, Sep 1994; Reprints Weird Science #9	2.00
❑10, Dec 1994; Reprints Weird Science #10	2.00
❑11, Mar 1995; Reprints Weird Science #11	2.00
❑12, Jun 1995; Reprints Weird Science #12	2.00
❑13, Sep 1995; Reprints Weird Science #13	2.00
❑14, Dec 1995; Reprints Weird Science #14	2.00
❑15, Mar 1996; Reprints Weird Science #15	2.50
❑16, Jun 1996; Reprints Weird Science #16	2.50
❑17, Sep 1996; Reprints Weird Science #17	2.50
❑18, Dec 1996; Reprints Weird Science #18	2.50
❑19, Mar 1997; AW, JO, BE, WW (w); AW, JO, BE, WW (a); Reprints Weird Science #19	2.50
❑20, Jun 1997; AW, JO, WW, JKa (w); AW, JO, WW, JKa (a); Reprints Weird Science #20	2.50
❑21, Sep 1997; AW, JO, WW, JKa (w); AW, JO, FF, WW, JKa (a); Reprints Weird Science #21; EC editors put themselves in story	2.50
❑22, Dec 1997; GE, AW, JO, WW (w); GE, AW, JO, WW (a); Reprints Weird Science #22; Wally Wood puts himself in story	2.50
❑Ann 1; Reprints Weird Science #1-5	8.95
❑Ann 2; Reprints Weird Science #6-10	9.95
❑Ann 3; Reprints Weird Science #11-14	10.95
❑Ann 4; Reprints Weird Science #15-18	9.95
❑Ann 5; Reprints Weird Science #19-22	10.50

Weird Science-Fantasy
Gemstone

❑1, Nov 1992; Reprints Weird Science-Fantasy #23	2.00
❑2, Feb 1993; AF (c); AF, AW, JO, WW, BK (w); AW, JO, WW, BK (a); Reprints Weird Science-Fantasy #24; "Upheaval" by Harlan Ellison (1st professional work by Harlan Ellison)	2.00
❑3, May 1993; AF (c); AW, JO, WW, BK (a); Reprints Weird Science-Fantasy #25	2.00
❑4, Aug 1993; UFO issue; Reprints Weird Science-Fantasy #26; Flying Saucer Report special issue	2.00
❑5, Nov 1993; JO, WW, JKa (a); Reprints Weird Science-Fantasy #27	2.00
❑6, Feb 1994; AF (c); AW, JO, WW, JKa (a); Reprints Weird Science-Fantasy #28	2.00
❑7, May 1994; FF (c); AW, JO, WW (a); Reprints Weird Science-Fantasy #29	2.00
❑8, Aug 1994; Reprints	2.00
❑9, Nov 1994; Reprints	2.00
❑10, Feb 1995; Reprints	2.00
❑11, May 1995; Reprints	2.00
❑Ann 1; Collects Weird Science-Fantasy (RCP) #1-5	8.95
❑Ann 2; Collects Weird Science-Fantasy (RCP) #?	12.95

Weird Secret Origins 80-Page Giant
DC

❑1, Oct 2004	5.95

Weird Sex
Fantagraphics / Eros

❑1, Jan 1999	2.95

Weird Suspense
Atlas-Seaboard

❑1, Feb 1975; 1&O: The Tarantula	12.00
❑2, Apr 1975	8.00
❑3, Jul 1975; Indicia says June 1975	7.00

Weirdsville
Blindwolf

❑1, Feb 1997	2.95
❑2, Apr 1997	2.95
❑3, Jun 1997	2.95
❑4, Aug 1997	2.95
❑5, Sep 1997	2.95
❑6, Dec 1997	2.95
❑7 1998	2.95
❑8, Mar 1998	2.95
❑9, Jun 1998	2.95

Weird Tales Illustrated
Millennium

❑1	2.95
❑1/Deluxe; Deluxe edition with extra stories	4.95
❑2	2.95

Weird Tales of the Macabre
Atlas-Seaboard

❑1, Apr 1975	20.00
❑2, Apr 1975; Scarce. Boris Vallejo cover	30.00

Weird Trips Magazine
Kitchen Sink

❑1	4.00

Weird War Tales
DC

❑1, Sep 1971; JKu (a); 52 pages	125.00
❑2, Nov 1971; JKu (w); MD, JKu (a); 52 pages	75.00
❑3, Jan 1972; 52 pages	45.00
❑4, Mar 1972; JKu (c); MM, JKu (a); 52 pages; Dinosaur story	30.00
❑5, May 1972; 52 pages; N. Adams ghost soldier on cover (reference to Neal Adams?); Includes table-top diorama	30.00
❑6, Jul 1972, JKu (c); ATh, FT, JKu (a)	20.00
❑7, Sep 1972	20.00
❑8, Nov 1972, NA (c); NA, TD (a)	20.00
❑9, Dec 1972, AA (a)	20.00
❑10, Jan 1973, ATh (a)	20.00
❑11, Feb 1973	12.00
❑12, Mar 1973, DP (a)	12.00
❑13, Apr 1973, NR, TD, AN (a)	12.00
❑14, Jun 1973	12.00
❑15, Jul 1973, DP (a)	12.00
❑16, Aug 1973, AA, AN (a)	12.00
❑17, Sep 1973, GE (a)	12.00
❑18, Oct 1973, TD (a)	12.00
❑19, Nov 1973	12.00
❑20, Dec 1973	12.00
❑21, Jan 1974, FR (a)	8.00
❑22, Feb 1974, GE, TD (a)	8.00
❑23, Mar 1974, RB, AA, AN (a)	8.00
❑24, Apr 1974	8.00
❑25, May 1974, AA, AN (a)	8.00
❑26, Jun 1974	8.00
❑27, Jul 1974	8.00
❑28, Aug 1974, AA (a)	8.00
❑29, Sep 1974	8.00
❑30, Oct 1974	8.00
❑31, Nov 1974	8.00
❑32, Dec 1974	6.00
❑33, Jan 1975	6.00
❑34, Feb 1975	6.00
❑35, Mar 1975	6.00
❑36, Apr 1975, Dinosaur & caveman cover	6.00
❑37, May 1975	6.00
❑38, Jun 1975	6.00
❑39, Jul 1975 JKu (c); JKu (a)	6.00
❑40, Aug 1975	6.00
❑41, Sep 1975	6.00
❑42, Oct 1975 JKu, AA (a)	6.00
❑43, Nov 1975	6.00
❑44, Jan 1976 JKu (c)	6.00
❑45, Mar 1976	6.00
❑46, May 1976	6.00
❑47, Jul 1976	6.00
❑48, Sep 1976	6.00
❑49, Nov 1976, SD (a)	6.00
❑50, Jan 1977	6.00
❑51, Mar 1977, JKu (c); MR (a); Kubert cover	5.00

Other grades: Multiply price above by 5/6 for VF/NM • 2/3 for VERY FINE • 1/3 for FINE • 1/5 for VERY GOOD • 1/8 for GOOD

N-MINT | N-MINT | N-MINT

- ❑52, Apr 1977 .... 5.00
- ❑53, May 1977 .... 5.00
- ❑54, Jul 1977 .... 5.00
- ❑55, Sep 1977 .... 5.00
- ❑56, Oct 1977 .... 5.00
- ❑57, Nov 1977 .... 5.00
- ❑58, Dec 1977, JKu (c); A: Hitler 5.00
- ❑59, Jan 1978 .... 5.00
- ❑60, Feb 1978, JKu (c); RE (a); Hindenburg cover/story 5.00
- ❑61, Mar 1978, HC, AN (a) 5.00
- ❑62, Apr 1978, JKu (c); HC (a) 5.00
- ❑63, May 1978 .... 5.00
- ❑64, Jun 1978, JKu (c); FM (a) 5.00
- ❑65, Jul 1978 .... 5.00
- ❑66, Aug 1978, JKu (c); TS (a) 5.00
- ❑67, Sep 1978, JKu (c); HC, MGr, RT (a) 5.00
- ❑68, Oct 1978, JKu (c); FM (a) 5.00
- ❑69, Nov 1978 .... 5.00
- ❑70, Dec 1978 .... 5.00
- ❑71, Jan 1979 .... 5.00
- ❑72, Feb 1979 .... 5.00
- ❑73, Mar 1979, GE (c) 5.00
- ❑74, Apr 1979 .... 5.00
- ❑75, May 1979 .... 5.00
- ❑76, Jun 1979, JKu (c); HC, RT (a) 5.00
- ❑77, Jul 1979 .... 5.00
- ❑78, Aug 1979, JKu (c); RT (a) 5.00
- ❑79, Sep 1979 .... 5.00
- ❑80, Oct 1979, JKu (c); RE, RT (a) 5.00
- ❑81, Nov 1979 .... 5.00
- ❑82, Dec 1979, GE (c); DN, HC (a) 5.00
- ❑83, Jan 1980 .... 5.00
- ❑84, Feb 1980 .... 5.00
- ❑85, Mar 1980 .... 5.00
- ❑86, Apr 1980 .... 5.00
- ❑87, May 1980 .... 5.00
- ❑88, Jun 1980 .... 5.00
- ❑89, Jul 1980 .... 5.00
- ❑90, Aug 1980, JKu (c); RT (a) 5.00
- ❑91, Sep 1980 .... 5.00
- ❑92, Oct 1980, JKu (c) 5.00
- ❑93, Nov 1980, JKu (c); O: Creature Commandos. 1: Creature Commandos 6.00
- ❑94, Dec 1980 .... 5.00
- ❑95, Jan 1981 .... 5.00
- ❑96, Feb 1981, JKu (c); DS (a) 5.00
- ❑97, Mar 1981 .... 5.00
- ❑98, Apr 1981 .... 5.00
- ❑99, May 1981 .... 5.00
- ❑100, Jun 1981, JKu (c); BH (a); Creature Commandos in War That Time Forgot 5.00
- ❑101, Jul 1981, 1: G.I. Robot I 5.00
- ❑102, Aug 1981, A: Creature Commandos. Creature Commandos captured by Hitler 3.50
- ❑103, Sep 1981, JKu (c); BH (a) 3.50
- ❑104, Oct 1981, JKu (c); SD, RT (a) 3.50
- ❑105, Nov 1981, A: Creature Commandos. Creature Commandos 3.50
- ❑106, Dec 1981, JKu (c); SD, JSa (a) 3.50
- ❑107, Jan 1982 .... 3.50
- ❑108, Feb 1982, DN, PB, BH (a); A: G.I. Robot I. A: Creature Commandos. Hitler cover; Creature Commandos, G.I. Robot 3.50
- ❑109, Mar 1982, RB, DS, BH (a); A: Creature Commandos. Creature Commandos 3.50
- ❑110, Apr 1982, 1: Dr. Medusa. A: Creature Commandos 3.50
- ❑111, May 1982, A: G.I. Robot I. A: Creature Commandos. G.I. Robot teams with Creature Commandos 3.50
- ❑112, Jun 1982, A: Creature Commandos. Creature Commandos 3.50
- ❑113, Jul 1982, 1: G.I. Robot II. V: Samurai Robot 3.50
- ❑114, Aug 1982, A: Hitler. A: Creature Commandos. Hitler cover; Creature Commandos 3.50
- ❑115, Sep 1982, A: . A: G.I. Robot II. A: Creature Commandos. G.I. Robot II and Creature Commandos 3.50
- ❑116, Oct 1982, GK (c); CI (a); A: . A: G.I. Robot II. A: Creature Commandos. G.I. Robot II and Creature Commandos 3.50
- ❑117, Nov 1982, A: . A: G.I. Robot II. A: Creature Commandos. G.I. Robot II and Creature Commandos 3.50
- ❑118, Dec 1982, Creature Commandos 3.50
- ❑119, Jan 1983, A: Creature Commandos. Creature Commandos 3.50
- ❑120, Feb 1983, G.I. Robot 3.50
- ❑121, Mar 1983, Creature Commandos 3.50
- ❑122, Apr 1983, A: G.I. Robot II. V: Sumo Robot. V: . G.I. Robot vs. Sumo Robot 3.50
- ❑123, May 1983 .... 3.50
- ❑124, Jun 1983, Final Issue 3.50

Weird War Tales
DC

- ❑1, Jun 1997 .... 2.50
- ❑2, Jul 1997 .... 2.50
- ❑3, Aug 1997 .... 2.50
- ❑4, Sep 1997 .... 2.50
- ❑Special 1, Apr 2000 .... 4.95

Weird West
Fantaco

- ❑1 1992 .... 2.95
- ❑2 1992 .... 2.95
- ❑3 1992 .... 2.95

Weird Western Tales
DC

- ❑12, Jun 1972; JKu (c); BWr, CI, NA, TD (a); Series continued from All-Star Western (2nd series) #11 .... 45.00
- ❑13, Aug 1972, (c); NA, TD (a) 30.00
- ❑14, Oct 1972, (c); ATh, TD (a) 20.00
- ❑15, Dec 1972, NA, (c); NA, GK (a); No Jonah Hex 20.00
- ❑16, Feb 1973, (c); AA, TD (a); Nick Cardy cover 12.00
- ❑17, Apr 1973, (c); AA, TD (a) 12.00
- ❑18, Jul 1973, (c); TD (a); Jonah Hex issue 12.00
- ❑19, Sep 1973, AA, TD (a) 12.00
- ❑20, Nov 1973, SA (w); GK, TD (a) 12.00
- ❑21, Jan 1974, TD (a) 12.00
- ❑22, May 1974, TD (a) 12.00
- ❑23, Jul 1974, TD (a); A: Ulysses S. Grant. Jonah Hex blinded 12.00
- ❑24, Sep 1974, Jonah Hex recovers sight 12.00
- ❑25, Nov 1974 .... 12.00
- ❑26, Jan 1975 .... 12.00
- ❑27, Mar 1975 .... 12.00
- ❑28, May 1975 .... 12.00
- ❑29, Jul 1975; O: Jonah Hex. Jonah Hex's Civil War flashback 16.00
- ❑30, Sep 1975 .... 8.00
- ❑31, Nov 1975 (c) 8.00
- ❑32, Jan 1976 JL (c); JL (a) 8.00
- ❑33, Mar 1976 JKu (c); JL (a) 8.00
- ❑34, May 1976, (c) 8.00
- ❑35, Jul 1976, Bicentennial #3 on cover 8.00
- ❑36, Sep 1976 .... 8.00
- ❑37, Nov 1976, RB, FS (a) 8.00
- ❑38, Jan 1977, JL (c); JL (a); Jonah Hex goes to his own series 8.00
- ❑39, Mar 1977, GE, JL (c); GE (a); 1&O: Scalphunter 8.00
- ❑40, Jun 1977, GE (c); GE (a) 8.00
- ❑41, Aug 1977, GE (c); FS (a) 8.00
- ❑42, Oct 1977, GE (a) 8.00
- ❑43, Dec 1977, GE (c); GE (a) 6.00
- ❑44, Feb 1978, AM, JSn (c); GE (a) 6.00
- ❑45, Apr 1978, JSn (c); GE (a); A: Bat Lash 6.00
- ❑46, Jun 1978, JL (c); GE (a); A: Bat Lash 6.00
- ❑47, Aug 1978, (c); GE (a) 6.00
- ❑48, Oct 1978, DG (c); GE, JAb (a); 1: Cinnamon 6.00
- ❑49, Nov 1978, HC (a) 6.00
- ❑50, Dec 1978, AM, RA (c) 6.00
- ❑51, Jan 1979 .... 5.00
- ❑52, Feb 1979, A: Bat Lash 5.00
- ❑53, Mar 1979, A: . A: Bat Lash. A: Abe Lincoln 5.00
- ❑54, Apr 1979 .... 5.00
- ❑55, May 1979, RT (a) 5.00
- ❑56, Jun 1979 .... 5.00
- ❑57, Jul 1979 .... 5.00
- ❑58, Aug 1979, RT (a) 5.00
- ❑59, Sep 1979, RT (a) 5.00
- ❑60, Oct 1979, RT (a) 5.00
- ❑61, Nov 1979, RT (a) 5.00
- ❑62, Dec 1979, RT (a) 5.00
- ❑63, Jan 1980, RT (a); A: Bat Lash 5.00
- ❑64, Feb 1980, RT (a); A: Bat Lash 5.00
- ❑65, Mar 1980, RT (a) 5.00
- ❑66, Apr 1980, RT (a) 5.00
- ❑67, May 1980, RT (a) 5.00
- ❑68, Jun 1980, RT (a) 5.00
- ❑69, Jul 1980, RT (a) 5.00
- ❑70, Aug 1980, RT (a); Scalphunter moves to back-ups in Jonah Hex 5.00

Weird Western Tales
DC / Vertigo

- ❑1, Apr 2001 .... 2.50
- ❑2, May 2001 .... 2.50
- ❑3, Jun 2001 .... 2.50
- ❑4, Jul 2001 .... 2.50

Weird Wonder Tales
Marvel

- ❑1, Dec 1973, (c); BW (a); Reprints Mystic #6 (Eye of Doom) 14.00
- ❑2, Feb 1974, (c);Reprints 7.00
- ❑3, Apr 1974, (c); BEv (a); Reprints 7.00
- ❑4, Jun 1974, (c); SL (w); SD (a); Reprint from Tales of Suspense #28; Reprint from Tales To Astonish #1; Reprint from Uncanny Tales #44 .... 5.00
- ❑5, Aug 1974, (c); SL (w); SD, JR (a); Reprints 5.00
- ❑6, Oct 1974, (c); JK (a); Reprint from Astonishing #10; Reprint from Astonishing #46; Reprint from Mystic #12; Reprint from Strange Tales #100 .... 5.00
- ❑7, Dec 1974, (c);Reprint from Mystery Tales #21; Reprint from World of Mystery #13; Reprint from World of Fantasy #11; Reprint from Tales of Suspense #9 .... 5.00
- ❑8, Feb 1975, (c); SL (w); Reprint from Adventures Into Weird Worlds #9; Reprint from Tales of Suspense #16; Reprint from Mystery Tales #30; Reprint from Meanace #3 .... 4.00
- ❑9, Apr 1975, (c);Reprint from Marvel Tales #104; Reprint from (Adventures Into Mystery #5); Reprint from Mystery Tales #33; Reprint from Adventures Into Terror #8 .... 4.00
- ❑10, Jun 1975, (c); SD, JK (a); Reprint from Journey into Mystery #99; Reprint from Strange Tales #74; Reprint from Strange Tales #77 .... 4.00
- ❑11, Aug 1975, (c); SL (w); SD, JK (a); Reprint from Tales of Suspense #31; Reprint from Strange Tales #96; Reprint from Strange Tales #76 .... 4.00
- ❑12, Oct 1975, (c); SL (w); SD, MD (a); Reprint from Tales of Suspense #37 .... 4.00
- ❑13, Dec 1975, (c); SL (w); SD, JK, RH (a); Reprint from Strange Tales #75; Reprint from Unknown Worlds #17 .... 4.00
- ❑14, Feb 1976, (c); DH, JAb (a); Reprint from Tower of Shadows #4; Reprint from World of Suspense #3; Reprint from (Astonishing Tales #53); Reprint from Mystic #37 .... 4.00
- ❑15, Apr 1976, TS (w); TS, DH (a); Reprint from Chamber of Darkness #4; Reprint from Strange Tales #95; Reprint from Tales to Astonish #25 .... 4.00
- ❑15/30¢, Apr 1976, 30¢ regional variant 20.00
- ❑16, Jun 1976, (c); BEv, JSt (a); Reprint from Men's Adventure #25; Reprint from Venus #19; Reprint from Tales to Astonish #31 .... 4.00
- ❑16/30¢, Jun 1976, 30¢ regional variant 20.00
- ❑17, Aug 1976, (c); GC, BEv (a); Reprint from Tales to Astonish #25; Reprint from Men's Adventures #24; Reprint from Venus #18 .... 4.00
- ❑17/30¢, Aug 1976, 30¢ regional variant 20.00
- ❑18, Oct 1976, BEv, JK (a); Reprint from Tales to Astonish #14; Reprint from Venus #17 .... 4.00
- ❑19, Dec 1976, (c); SD, JK, BK (a); Doctor Druid; Reprints from Tales to Astonish #13, Astonishing Tales #47 .... 4.00
- ❑20, Jan 1977, SL (w); SD, JK (a); Doctor Druid 4.00
- ❑21, Mar 1977, SL (w); SD (a); Doctor Druid 4.00
- ❑22, May 1977, DC (c); SL (w); JBy, JK, JKu (a); Doctor Druid 4.00

Weird Worlds
DC

- ❑1, Sep 1972, JKu (c); MA (a); continues John Carter of Mars from Tarzan #209 and Pellucidar from Korak 12.00
- ❑2, Nov 1972, JO, CI (c); MA (a); adapts Burroughs' Pellucidar and Martian novels 7.00

Other grades: Multiply price above by 5/6 for VF/NM • 2/3 for VERY FINE • 1/3 for FINE • 1/5 for VERY GOOD • 1/8 for GOOD

X

Dark Horse hero marks the spot

©Dark Horse

X-Calibre

Swashbuckling Nightcrawler seeks mutants

©Marvel

Xena: Warrior Princess

High-pitched screamer comes to comics

©Topps

Xenozoic Tales

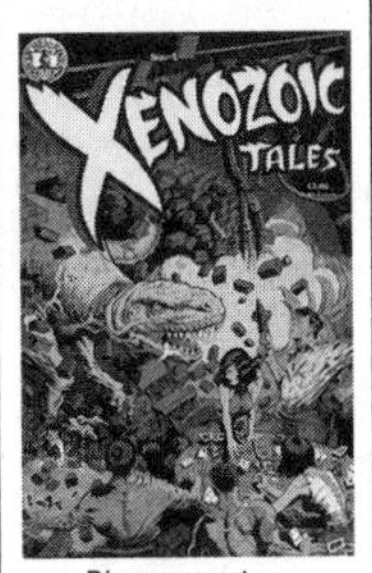

Dinosaurs return after disaster

©Kitchen Sink

X-Factor

Original X-Men return to "hunt" mutants

©Marvel

N-MINT

❑3, Jan 1973, JO (c); MA (a); adapts Burroughs' Pellucidar and Martian novels 7.00
❑4, Mar 1973, (c);adapts Burroughs' Pellucidar and Martian novels 7.00
❑5, May 1973, DGr (a); adapts Burroughs' Pellucidar and Martian novels 7.00
❑6, Aug 1973, (c); DGr (a); adapts Burroughs' Pellucidar and Martian novels 8.00
❑7, Oct 1973, HC (c); DGr (a); adapts Burroughs' Pellucidar and Martian novels; John Carter, Warlord of Mars ends 6.00
❑8, Dec 1973, HC (c); HC (w); HC (a); 1: Iron Wolf 5.00
❑9, Feb 1974, (c); HC (w); HC (a); Iron Wolf 5.00
❑10, Nov 1974, HC (w); HC (a); Iron Wolf 5.00

Welcome Back, Kotter
DC

❑1, Nov 1976, (c); BO (a); based on ABC TV series 10.00
❑2, Jan 1977, BO (c);based on ABC TV series 2.50
❑3, Mar 1977, (c); BO, RE (a); based on ABC TV series 2.50
❑4, May 1977, BO (c); ME (w); BO, RE (a); based on ABC TV series 2.50
❑5, Jul 1977, (c); BO, RE (a); based on ABC TV series 2.50
❑6, Sep 1977, (c); BO, RE (a); based on ABC TV series 2.50
❑7, Nov 1977, RE (c); BO, RE (a); based on ABC TV series 2.50
❑8, Jan 1978, BO (c); BO, RE (a); based on ABC TV series 2.50
❑9, Feb 1978, BO (c); BO, RE (a); based on ABC TV series 2.50
❑10, Mar 1978, BO (c); BO, RE (a); based on ABC TV series 2.50

Welcome Back to the House of Mystery
DC / Vertigo

❑1, Jul 1998, collects stories from House of Mystery and Plop 5.95

Welcome to the Little Shop of Horrors
Roger Corman's Cosmic Comics

❑1, May 1995 .... 2.50
❑2, Jun 1995 .... 2.50
❑3, Jul 1995 .... 2.50

Wendel
Kitchen Sink

❑1, b&w; Adult 2.95

Wendy in 3-D
Blackthorne

❑1 .... 2.50

Wendy Whitebread, Undercover Slut
Fantagraphics / Eros

❑1, b&w; Adult 2.50
❑1/2nd, b&w; 2nd printing; Adult 2.95
❑1/3rd, b&w; 3rd printing; Adult 2.95
❑1/4th, b&w; 4th printing; Adult 2.95
❑1/5th, Nov 1990, b&w; 5th printing; Adult 3.95
❑2, Apr 1992, b&w; Adult 2.50

N-MINT

Wendy Witch World
Harvey

❑1, Oct 1961 .... 90.00
❑2, Sep 1962, Casper cover 50.00
❑3, Dec 1962 .... 50.00
❑4, Mar 1963, Casper cover 50.00
❑5, Jun 1963 .... 50.00
❑6, Sep 1963 .... 35.00
❑7, Dec 1963 .... 35.00
❑8, Mar 1964 .... 35.00
❑9, Jun 1964, Casper cover 35.00
❑10, Sep 1964, ... 35.00
❑11, Dec 1964, Casper cover 26.00
❑12, Mar 1965 .... 26.00
❑13, Jun 1965 .... 26.00
❑14, Sep 1965 .... 26.00
❑15, Dec 1965 .... 26.00
❑16, ca. 1966 .... 26.00
❑17, ca. 1966 .... 26.00
❑18, Nov 1966 .... 26.00
❑19, Jan 1967 .... 26.00
❑20, May 1967 .... 26.00
❑21, Aug 1967 .... 22.00
❑22, Nov 1967 .... 22.00
❑23, Jan 1968 .... 22.00
❑24, May 1968, Casper cover 22.00
❑25, Jul 1968 .... 22.00
❑26, Sep 1968 .... 22.00
❑27, Feb 1969 .... 22.00
❑28, Apr 1969, Casper cover 22.00
❑29, Jun 1969, ... 22.00
❑30, Aug 1969, Casper cover 22.00
❑31, Oct 1969, Casper TV cover 18.00
❑32, Dec 1969 .... 18.00
❑33, Feb 1970 .... 18.00
❑34, Apr 1970, Casper cover 18.00
❑35, ca. 1970, Giant-Size 18.00
❑36, ca. 1970 .... 15.00
❑37, Dec 1970 .... 15.00
❑38, Feb 1971 .... 15.00
❑39, Apr 1971 .... 15.00
❑40, ca. 1971 .... 15.00
❑41, ca. 1971 .... 15.00
❑42, Dec 1971 .... 15.00
❑43, Feb 1972 .... 15.00
❑44, May 1972 .... 15.00
❑45, Sep 1972 .... 12.00
❑46, Dec 1972, Giant-size issues end 12.00
❑47, Feb 1973 .... 12.00
❑48, Apr 1973 .... 12.00
❑49, Jun 1973 .... 12.00
❑50, Aug 1973 .... 8.00
❑51, Oct 1973 .... 8.00
❑52, ca. 1974 .... 8.00
❑53, Sep 1974, Casper cover 8.00

Werewolf
Dell

❑1, Dec 1966, (c);TV show 8.00
❑2, Mar 1967, (c);TV show 5.00
❑3, Apr 1967, (c); O: Werewolf (Major Wiley Wolf). TV show 5.00

Werewolf
Blackthorne

❑1, Sep 1988, b&w 2.00
❑2 1988 .... 2.00

N-MINT

❑3 1988 .... 2.00
❑4, Jan 1989 .... 2.00

Werewolf at Large
Eternity

❑1, Jun 1989, b&w 2.25
❑2, Aug 1989, b&w 2.25
❑3, Oct 1989, b&w 2.25

Werewolf By Night
Marvel

❑1, Sep 1972, MP (c); MP (a) 80.00
❑2, Nov 1972, MP (c); MP (a) 30.00
❑3, Jan 1973, MP (c); MP (a) 15.00
❑4, Mar 1973, MP (c); MP (a) 18.00
❑5, May 1973, MP (c); MP (a) 15.00
❑6, Jun 1973, (c); MP (a) 15.00
❑7, Jul 1973, (c); MP, JM (a) 15.00
❑8, Aug 1973, MP (c) 15.00
❑9, Sep 1973, (c); TS (a) 15.00
❑10, Oct 1973, TS (c); TS (a) 15.00
❑11, Nov 1973, (c); TS, GK (a) 12.00
❑12, Dec 1973, (c); GK, DP (a) 12.00
❑13, Jan 1974, MP (c); MP (a); V: Taboo 12.00
❑14, Feb 1974, MP (c); MP (a) 12.00
❑15, Mar 1974, MP (c); MP (a); Marvel Value Stamp #75: Morbius 15.00
❑16, Apr 1974, (c); MP (a); Marvel Value Stamp #65: Iceman 12.00
❑17, May 1974, (c); DP (a); Marvel Value Stamp #99: Sandman 12.00
❑18, Jun 1974, (c); DP (a) 10.00
❑19, Jul 1974, (c); DP (a); Marvel Value Stamp #61: Red Ghost 10.00
❑20, Aug 1974, (c); DP (a); Marvel Value Stamp #97: Black Knight 10.00
❑21, Sep 1974, (c); DP (a); Marvel Value Stamp #72: Lizard 8.00
❑22, Oct 1974, (c); DP (a); Marvel Value Stamp #51: Bucky Barnes 8.00
❑23, Nov 1974, (c); DP (a); Marvel Value Stamp #93: Silver Surfer 8.00
❑24, Dec 1974, AM, GK (c); DP (a); Marvel Value Stamp #8: Captain America 8.00
❑25, Jan 1975, (c); DP (a); Marvel Value Stamp #63: Sub-Mariner 8.00
❑26, Feb 1975, (c); DP (a); Marvel Value Stamp #28: Hawkeye 8.00
❑27, Mar 1975, (c); DP (a); Marvel Value Stamp #9: Captain Marvel 8.00
❑28, Apr 1975, (c); DP (a) 8.00
❑29, May 1975, (c); DP (a) 8.00
❑30, Jun 1975, (c); DP (a) 8.00
❑31, Jul 1975, (c); DP (w); DP (a) 8.00
❑32, Aug 1975, (c); DP (a); O: Moon Knight. 1: Moon Knight 60.00
❑33, Sep 1975, (c); DP (a); 2: Moon Knight 30.00
❑34, Oct 1975, (c); DP (a) 8.00
❑35, Nov 1975, JSn (c); DP (a); Fred Hembeck LOC 5.00
❑36, Jan 1976, DP (c); DP (a) 5.00
❑37, Mar 1976, DP (a); A: Moon Knight 10.00
❑38, May 1976, DP (c); DP (a) 5.00
❑38/30¢, May 1976, 30¢ regional price variant 15.00
❑39, Jul 1976, RB (c); DP (a) 5.00
❑39/30¢, Jul 1976, 30¢ regional price variant 15.00
❑40, Sep 1976, (c); DP (a) 5.00

Other grades: Multiply price above by 5/6 for VF/NM • 2/3 for VERY FINE • 1/3 for FINE • 1/5 for VERY GOOD • 1/8 for GOOD

N-MINT | N-MINT | N-MINT

❑41, Nov 1976, (c); DP (a); Brother Voodoo ... 5.00
❑42, Jan 1977, DC (c); DP (a) ... 12.00
❑43, Mar 1977, DP (a); Final Issue; Iron Man ... 18.00

Werewolf By Night
Marvel

❑1, Feb 1998, (c) ... 3.00
❑2, Mar 1998, gatefold summary; MP (c) 3.00
❑3, Apr 1998, gatefold summary ... 3.00
❑4, May 1998, gatefold summary; (c) ... 3.00
❑5, Jun 1998, gatefold summary; (c); ... 3.00
❑6, Jul 1998, gatefold summary; A: Ghost Rider ... 3.00

Werewolf in 3-D
Blackthorne

❑1, ca. 1988 ... 2.50

Werewolf the Apocalypse: Black Furies
Moonstone

❑1, ca. 2003 ... 5.95

Werewolf the Apocalypse: Bone Gnawers
Moonstone

❑1, ca. 2003 ... 5.95

West Coast Avengers
Marvel

❑1, Sep 1984, BH (c); BH (a); O: West Coast Avengers. 1: West Coast Avengers ... 2.50
❑2, Oct 1984, BH (c); BH (a) ... 2.00
❑3, Nov 1984, BH (c); BH (a) ... 2.00
❑4, Dec 1984, BH (c); BH (a); V: Graviton 2.00

West Coast Avengers
Marvel

❑1, Oct 1985, AM, JSt (c); AM, JSt (a); Continued in Vision and the Scarlet Witch #1 ... 2.00
❑2, Nov 1985, AM, JSt (c); AM (a); O: Wonder Man; Continued in Vision and the Scarlet Witch #2 ... 1.50
❑3, Dec 1985, AM, JSt (c); AM, JSt (a); V: Kraven; V: Kraven the Hunter ... 1.50
❑4, Jan 1986, AM, JSt (c); AM, JSt (a); 1: Master Pandemonium; O: Firebird. 3.00
❑5, Feb 1986, AM, JSt (c); AM, JSt (a) .. 1.00
❑6, Mar 1986, AM (c); AM (a); O: Tigra; O: Hellcat ... 1.00
❑7, Apr 1986, AM, JSt (c); AM, JSt (a); V: Ultron ... 1.00
❑8, May 1986, AM, JSt (c); AM, JSt (a); V: Rangers ... 1.00
❑9, Jun 1986, AM, JSt (c); AM, JSt (a); O: Master Pandemonium ... 1.00
❑10, Jul 1986, AM, JSt (c); AM, JSt (a) . 1.00
❑11, Aug 1986, AM, JSt (c); AM, JSt (a); O: Mockingbird ... 1.00
❑12, Sep 1986, AM, JSt (c); AM, JSt (a); 1: Halflife. 1: Quantum. V: Zzzax ... 1.00
❑13, Oct 1986, AM, JSt (c); AM, JSt (a); O: Hellstorm; O: Graviton ... 1.00
❑14, Nov 1986, AM, JSt (c); AM, JSt (a); 1: Hellstorm ... 1.00
❑15, Dec 1986, AM, (c); AM, JSt (a); O: Master Pandemonium; Drew Geraci LOC ... 1.00
❑16, Jan 1987, AM, JSt (c); AM, JSt (a) 1.00
❑17, Feb 1987, AM, (c); AM, JSt (a) ... 1.00
❑18, Mar 1987, AM, JSt (c); AM, JSt (a) 1.00
❑19, Apr 1987, AM, (c); AM, JSt (a) ... 1.00
❑20, May 1987, AM, JSt (c); AM, JSt (a) 1.00
❑21, Jun 1987, AM, JSt (c); AM, JSt (a); A: Moon Knight ... 1.00
❑22, Jul 1987, AM, JSt (c); AM (a); A: Doctor Strange ... 1.00
❑23, Aug 1987, AM (c); AM, RT (a); O: Moon Knight ... 1.00
❑24, Sep 1987, AM (c); AM (a) ... 1.00
❑25, Oct 1987, AM (c); AM (a) ... 1.00
❑26, Nov 1987, AM (c); AM (a); V: Zodiac; O: Zodiac ... 1.00
❑27, Dec 1987, AM (c); AM (a); V: Zodiac 1.00
❑28, Jan 1988, AM (c); AM (a); V: Zodiac 1.00
❑29, Feb 1988, AM (c); AM (a) ... 1.00
❑30, Mar 1988, AM (c); AM (w); AM (a) 1.00
❑31, Apr 1988, AM (c); AM (a); V: Arkon 1.00
❑32, May 1988, AM (c); AM, TD (a) ... 1.00
❑33, Jun 1988, AM (c); AM (a); O: Ant-Man; O: Wasp ... 1.00
❑34, Jul 1988, AM (c); AM (a); V: Quicksilver; O: Vision ... 1.00
❑35, Aug 1988, AM (c); AM (a); V: Doctor Doom ... 1.00
❑36, Sep 1988, AM (c); AM (a) ... 1.00
❑37, Oct 1988, AM (c); AM (a) ... 1.00
❑38, Nov 1988 ... 1.00
❑39, Dec 1988, AM, (c); AM (a) ... 1.00
❑40, Jan 1989, AM (c); AM, MGu (a) ... 1.00
❑41, Feb 1989 ... 1.00
❑42, Mar 1989, JBy (c); JBy (w); JBy (a); O: Vision; O: Human Torch ... 1.00
❑43, Apr 1989, JBy (c); JBy (w); JBy (a); O: Vision ... 1.00
❑44, May 1989, JBy (c); JBy (w); JBy (a); 1: U.S.Agent; O: Vision ... 1.00
❑45, Jun 1989, JBy (c); JBy (w); JBy (a); 1: white Vision ... 1.00
❑46, Jul 1989, JBy (c); JBy (w); JBy (a); 1: Great Lakes Avengers. 1: Big Bertha. Title changes to Avengers West Coast 1.00
❑Ann 1, ca. 1986, V: Quicksilver; Concludes story begun in Avengers Ann #15 ... 2.00
❑Ann 2, ca. 1987, AM (c); AM (a); Begins story concluded in Avengers Ann #16;ca. 1987 ... 2.00
❑Ann 3, ca. 1988, AM (c); AM, TD (a); series continues as Avengers West Coast Ann ... 2.00

Western Tales of Terror
Hoarse and Buggy

❑1, Oct 2004; b&w ... 3.50
❑2, Jan 2005; b&w ... 3.50
❑3, Mar 2005; b&w ... 3.50
❑4, Jun 2005; b&w ... 3.50
❑5, Sep 2005 ... 3.50

Western Action
Atlas-Seaboard

❑1, Jun 1975 (c); AM, JAb (a) ... 9.00

Western Gunfighters
Marvel

❑1, Aug 1970, giant ... 28.00
❑2, Oct 1970, O: Nightwind (The Apache Kid's horse). giant ... 15.00
❑3, Dec 1970, giant ... 15.00
❑4, Feb 1971, TS, JR, BS (a); giant ... 18.00
❑5, Jun 1971; giant ... 15.00
❑6, Sep 1971; SL (w); BEv, JR, JSt (a); D: Ghost Rider. giant ... 15.00
❑7, Jan 1972; O: Night Rider (Ghost Rider). 1: Lincoln Slade as Ghost Rider. D: Phantom Rider I (Carter Slade). giant 15.00
❑8, Mar 1972, Reprints from Black Rider #18 and Outlaw Kid #13; Apache Kid; Outlaw Kid; Black Rider ... 7.00
❑9, May 1972, Reprints from Black Rider #18, Outlaw Kid #19 and Apache Kid #11; Outlaw Kid; Apache Kid; Black Rider ... 7.00
❑10, Jul 1972, O: Black Rider; Apache Kid; Matt Slade ... 7.00
❑11, Sep 1972, Black Rider; Apache Kid; Matt Slade ... 7.00
❑12, Nov 1972, O: Matt Slade; Apache Kid; Black Rider ... 7.00
❑13, Jan 1973, Black Rider; Apache Kid; Matt Slade ... 7.00
❑14, Mar 1973, Apache Kid; Black Rider; Matt Slade ... 7.00
❑15, May 1973, Apache Kid; Black Rider; Matt Slade ... 7.00
❑16, Jul 1973, Kid Colt; Black Rider; Apache Kid ... 7.00
❑17, Sep 1973, Kid Colt; Western Kid; Apache Kid ... 5.00
❑18, Oct 1973, Kid Colt; Western Kid; Apache Kid ... 5.00
❑19, Nov 1973, Kid Colt; Western Kid; Apache Kid ... 5.00
❑20, Jan 1974, SL (w); JR (a); New cover; Western Kid; Apache Kid; Kid Colt ... 5.00
❑21, Mar 1974, JK (c); SL (w); JR (a); reprints stories from Kid Colt Outlaw #103, Western Kid #13, and Apache Kid #18 ... 5.00
❑22, May 1974; Kid Colt; Western Kid; Apache Kid ... 5.00
❑23, Jul 1974; Kid Colt; Western Kid; Apache Kid ... 5.00
❑24, Sep 1974; Kid Colt; Western Kid; Apache Kid ... 5.00
❑25, Oct 1974; Kid Colt; Western Kid; Apache Kid ... 5.00
❑26, Nov 1974; Kid Colt; Western Kid; Apache Kid ... 5.00
❑27, Jan 1975; Kid Colt; Western Kid; Apache Kid ... 5.00
❑28, Mar 1975; Kid Colt; Western Kid; Apache Kid ... 5.00
❑29, May 1975; Kid Colt; Western Kid; Apache Kid ... 5.00
❑30, Jul 1975; Kid Colt; Western Kid; Apache Kid ... 5.00
❑31, Sep 1975 (c); SL (w); JR (a); A: Gun-Slinger. A: Apache Kid. A: Kid Colt ... 5.00
❑32, Nov 1975; Kid Colt; Western Kid; Apache Kid ... 5.00
❑33, Jan 1976; Kid Colt; Western Kid; Apache Kid; Final Issue ... 5.00

Western Kid
Marvel

❑1, Dec 1971, Reprints from Western Kid #7 and #12 ... 17.00
❑2, Feb 1972, Reprint from Western Kid #4, 7, 12 and Rawhide Kid #30 ... 8.00
❑3, Apr 1972, Reprints from Western Kid #4, 6 and Rawhide Kid #7 ... 8.00
❑4, Jun 1972, Reprints from Western Kid #6 and #12 ... 8.00
❑5, Aug 1972 ... 8.00

Western Team-Up
Marvel

❑1, Nov 1973, (c); SL (w); 1: The Dakota Kid; Rawhide Kid; Gunsmoke Kid; Reprint from Gunsmoke Western #55 8.00

West of the Dakotas
Comic Book Stories

❑1, Dec 2002 ... 4.99

Westside
Antarctic

❑1, Mar 2000 ... 2.50

West Street Stories
West Street

❑0, Nov 1995, b&w ... 2.50
❑1, Jan 1997, b&w ... 2.50

Wetworks
Image

❑1, Jun 1994, 1&O: Wetworks. 1: Dozer. 1: Dane. 1: Jester ... 2.99
❑1/3D, Jun 1994, 3-D edition; 1&O: Wetworks. 1: Dozer. 1: Dane. 1: Jester. 3-D edition ... 4.95
❑1/Ltd., Jun 1994, Special promotional edition distributed at the 1994 Chicago Comicon; O: Wetworks. 1: Dozer. 1: Jester. 1: Wetworks ... 1.95
❑2, Aug 1994, Standard cover: Beast attacking man ... 1.95
❑2/A, Aug 1994, Variant edition cover with whole team posing; alternate cover ... 1.95
❑3, Sep 1994 ... 1.95
❑4, Nov 1994 ... 2.99
❑5, Jan 1995 ... 2.50
❑6, Mar 1995 ... 2.50
❑7, Apr 1995, The Lone One back-up story 2.50
❑8, May 1995, bound-in trading cards... 2.50
❑8/Variant, May 1995, Includes trading cards ... 2.50
❑9, Aug 1995, The Lone One back-up story; Tim Bradstreet pinup ... 2.50
❑10, Aug 1995, The Lone One back-up story; Tim Bradstreet pinup; Whilce Portacio pinup ... 2.50
❑11, Sep 1995 ... 2.50
❑12, Nov 1995, 1: Pilgrim. indicia says Nov, cover says Dec ... 2.50
❑13, Jan 1996 ... 2.50
❑14, Feb 1996 ... 2.50
❑15, Mar 1996 ... 2.50
❑16, Apr 1996 ... 2.50
❑17, May 1996 ... 2.50
❑18, Jul 1996 ... 2.50
❑19, Aug 1996 ... 2.50
❑20, Aug 1996 ... 2.50
❑21, Sep 1996 ... 2.50
❑22, Oct 1996 ... 2.50
❑23, Nov 1996 ... 2.50
❑24, Dec 1996 ... 2.50
❑25, Jan 1997, Giant-size; wraparound cover ... 3.95
❑25/A, Jan 1997, alternate wraparound cover (previous covers in background) 3.95
❑26, Feb 1997 ... 2.50

Other grades: Multiply price above by 5/6 for VF/NM • 2/3 for VERY FINE • 1/3 for FINE • 1/5 for VERY GOOD • 1/8 for GOOD

X-Factor

Mutant hunting takes nasty turn

©Marvel

X-Farce

Forced parody of Liefeld book

©Eclipse

X-51

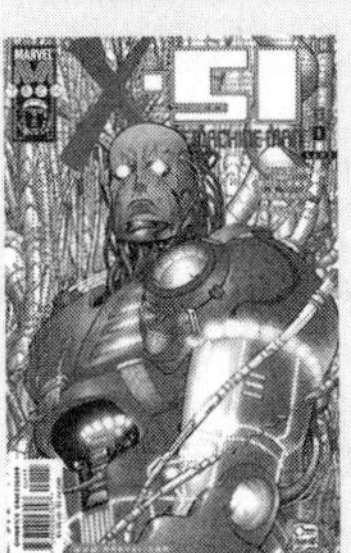

What makes Machine Man tick?

©Marvel

X-Files

Mulder and Scully probe the paranormal

©Topps

X-Files Ground Zero

Adapts Anderson novel

©Topps

N-MINT

❑27, Mar 1997 ... 2.50
❑28, Apr 1997 ... 2.50
❑29, May 1997 ... 2.50
❑30, Jun 1997 ... 2.50
❑31, Jul 1997 ... 2.50
❑32, Aug 1997 ... 2.50
❑32/A, Aug 1997, Voyager pack; alternate cover (mostly b&w) ... 3.50
❑33, Sep 1997 ... 2.50
❑34, Oct 1997 ... 2.50
❑35, Nov 1997 ... 2.50
❑36, Jan 1998 ... 2.50
❑37, Feb 1998 ... 2.50
❑38, Mar 1998 ... 2.50
❑39, Apr 1998 ... 2.50
❑40, May 1998, A: StormWatch ... 2.50
❑41, Jun 1998 ... 2.50
❑42, Jul 1998 ... 2.50
❑43, Aug 1998 ... 2.50
❑3D 1, Feb 1998; with glasses; wraparound cover ... 4.95

Wetworks
DC / Wildstorm

❑1, Nov 2006 ... 2.99
❑2, Jan 2007, Standard cover: Beast attacking man ... 2.99
❑2/Variant, Jan 2007 ... 2.99
❑3, Feb 2007 ... 2.99
❑3/Variant, Feb 2007 ... 2.99
❑4, Mar 2007 ... 2.99
❑4/Variant, Mar 2007 ... 2.99

Wetworks Sourcebook
Image

❑1, Oct 1994; Team History and Arsenal ... 2.50

Wetworks/Vampirella
Image

❑1, Jul 1997; crossover with Harris ... 2.95
❑1/A, Jul 1997; crossover with Harris; alternate cover ... 2.95

Whacked!
River Group

❑1, Mar 1994; Tonya Harding case parody; wraparound cover ... 2.50

Wha... Huh?
Marvel

❑0, Oct 2005 ... 3.99

Wham-O Giant Comics
Wham-O

❑1, Apr 1967, JS, WW (w); JS, WW (a); Wrap-around cover, oversized 14 X 21-inch book ... 100.00

What If...?
Marvel

❑1, Feb 1977, JR, (c); A: Spider-Man. Spider-Man ... 15.00
❑2, Apr 1977, GK (c); TS, HT (a); A: Hulk. Hulk ... 10.00
❑3, Jun 1977, GK, JSt (c); GK (w); GK, KJ (a); A: Avengers. Avengers ... 8.00
❑4, Aug 1977, GK (c); FR, FS (a); A: Invaders. Invaders ... 8.00
❑5, Oct 1977, (c); GT (a); O: Bucky II (Fred Davis). 1: Captain America II (William Nasland). 1: Captain America III (Jeffrey Mace). D: Captain America II (William Nasland). Captain America ... 8.00

N-MINT

❑6, Dec 1977, A: Fantastic 4. Fantastic Four ... 5.00
❑7, Feb 1978, GK, JSt (c); A: Spider-Man. Spider-Man ... 5.00
❑8, Apr 1978, GK, JR (c); JM (a); O: 'Mazing Man-Spider. Daredevil ... 5.00
❑9, Jun 1978, JK, GK, JSt (c); O: Marvel Boy. O: Human Robot. O: 3-D Man. O: Venus. O: Gorilla-Man. Avengers ... 5.00
❑10, Aug 1978, JB, (c); A: Thor. Thor ... 5.00
❑11, Oct 1978, JK, JSt (c); JK (w); JK (a); Marvel Bullpen as Fantastic Four ... 3.50
❑12, Dec 1978, SB, (c); SB (a); Rick Jones as Hulk ... 3.50
❑13, Feb 1979, JB (c); JB (a); A: Conan. Conan ... 5.00
❑14, Apr 1979, HT, (c); HT (a); A: Sgt. Fury. Sgt. Fury ... 3.50
❑15, Jun 1979, JSt (c); CI, JB, GP, RA, JSt (a); A: Nova. Nova ... 3.50
❑16, Aug 1979, A: Fu Manchu. Fu Manchu ... 3.00
❑17, Oct 1979, GC, (c); CI (a); Ghost Rider, Captain Marvel, Spider-Woman ... 3.50
❑18, Dec 1979, GC, (c); TS (a); Doctor Strange ... 3.00
❑19, Feb 1980, (c); PB (a); Spider-Man ... 3.00
❑20, Apr 1980, AM, JSt (c);Avengers ... 3.00
❑21, Jun 1980, GC, (c); GC, BWi (a); Sub-Mariner ... 3.00
❑22, Aug 1980, RB, BMc (c); Doctor Doom ... 3.00
❑23, Oct 1980, AM, JB (c); HT (a); Hulk ... 3.00
❑24, Dec 1980, JR2, BMc (c); RB, GK (a); Spider-Man ... 3.00
❑25, Feb 1981, (c); RB (a); O: Uni-Mind. Thor, Avengers ... 3.00
❑26, Apr 1981, JBy (c); HT (a); Captain America ... 3.00
❑27, Jul 1981, FM (c); FM (a); X-Men ... 5.00
❑28, Aug 1981, FM, (c); FM (w); TS, FM, KJ (a); A: Ghost Rider. Daredevil ... 8.00
❑29, Oct 1981, MG (c); RB, BMc, JSt (a); Avengers ... 3.00
❑30, Dec 1981, BL (c); RB, JM, JSt (a); Spider-Man clone, Inhumans ... 8.00
❑31, Feb 1982, BWi (c);Wolverine ... 8.00
❑32, Apr 1982, BL (c); FM (a); Avengers ... 3.00
❑33, Jun 1982, JR, (c); BL, DP (a); Dazzler ... 3.00
❑34, Aug 1982, BL (c); AM, BSz, FH, BL, JR2, FM, BA (w); AM, BSz, FH, JBy, BL, JR2, FM, BA, BH, JSt, FS, BWi, JAb (a); comedy issue ... 3.00
❑35, Oct 1982, FM (w); SD, FM (a); A: Yellowjacket. Elektra ... 5.00
❑36, Dec 1982, JBy (c); JBy (w); JBy (a); Fantastic Four; Nova ... 3.00
❑37, Feb 1983, JSt (c);Beast; Thing; Silver Surfer ... 3.00
❑38, Apr 1983, Daredevil, Captain America, Vision, Scarlet Witch ... 3.00
❑39, Jun 1983, Thor vs. Conan ... 3.00
❑40, Aug 1983, MG, (c); BG (a); Doctor Strange ... 3.00
❑41, Oct 1983, MG, (c);Sub-Mariner ... 3.00
❑42, Dec 1983, MG (c); JSt (a); Fantastic Four ... 3.00
❑43, Feb 1984, BSz (c); BH, JAb (a); Conan ... 3.00
❑44, Apr 1984, BSz (c); SB (a); Captain America ... 3.00
❑45, Jun 1984, BSz, (c);Hulk ... 3.00

N-MINT

❑46, Aug 1984, BSz (c);Spider-Man ... 3.50
❑47, Oct 1984, BSz (c); Thor, Loki ... 3.00
❑Special 1, Jun 1988, AM, (c); SD (a); Iron Man ... 4.00

What If...?
Marvel

❑-1, Jul 1997, Flashback; Bishop ... 2.00
❑1, Jul 1989, KP (c); MGu (a); Avengers ... 4.00
❑2, Aug 1989, KP (c); Daredevil ... 3.00
❑3, Sep 1989, AM (c); Captain America ... 3.00
❑4, Oct 1989, AM (c); Spider-Man ... 3.00
❑5, Nov 1989, Avengers ... 3.00
❑6, Nov 1989, X-Men ... 3.00
❑7, Dec 1989, RL (c); RL (a); Wolverine ... 3.00
❑8, Dec 1989, AM (c);Iron Man ... 2.50
❑9, Jan 1990, RB (c); RB (a); X-Men ... 2.50
❑10, Feb 1990, MZ, (c); BMc (a); Punisher ... 2.50
❑11, Mar 1990, TMc (c); Fantastic Four ... 2.50
❑12, Apr 1990, X-Men ... 2.50
❑13, May 1990, JLee (c); KB (w); X-Men ... 2.50
❑14, Jun 1990, Captain Marvel ... 2.50
❑15, Jul 1990, Fantastic Four, Galactus ... 2.50
❑16, Aug 1990, Wolverine; Conan ... 3.00
❑17, Sep 1990, JR2 (c); RHo (w); RHo (a); D: Spider-Man. D: Spider-Man ... 2.50
❑18, Oct 1990, LMc (c); LMc (a); Fantastic Four, Doctor Doom ... 2.50
❑19, Nov 1990, Avengers ... 2.50
❑20, Dec 1990, BWi (c);Spider-Man ... 2.50
❑21, Jan 1991, BWi (c); D: Black Cat. Spider-Man ... 2.25
❑22, Feb 1991, Silver Surfer ... 2.25
❑23, Mar 1991, BMc (c); KB (w); X-Men ... 2.25
❑24, Apr 1991, vampire Wolverine ... 3.50
❑25, May 1991, Atlantis Attacks ... 3.25
❑26, Jun 1991, LMc (c); KB (w); LMc (a); Punisher ... 2.00
❑27, Jul 1991, Namor, Fantastic Four ... 2.00
❑28, Aug 1991, (c);Captain America ... 2.00
❑29, Sep 1991, (c);Captain America, Avengers ... 2.00
❑30, Oct 1991, Fantastic Four ... 2.00
❑31, Nov 1991, BMc (c);Spider-Man with cosmic powers ... 2.00
❑32, Dec 1991, Phoenix ... 2.00
❑33, Jan 1992, Phoenix ... 2.00
❑34, Feb 1992, JR (c); parody issue ... 2.00
❑35, Mar 1992, (c); Fantastic Four; Spider-Man; Doctor Doom ... 2.00
❑36, Apr 1992, Avengers vs. Guardians of the Galaxy ... 2.00
❑37, May 1992, Wolverine ... 2.00
❑38, Jun 1992, MR (a); Thor ... 2.00
❑39, Jul 1992, Watcher ... 2.00
❑40, Aug 1992, (c); X-Men ... 2.00
❑41, Sep 1992, Avengers vs. Galactus ... 2.00
❑42, Oct 1992, (c); Spider-Man ... 2.00
❑43, Nov 1992, Wolverine ... 2.00
❑44, Dec 1992, LMc (c); KB (w); LMc (a); Venom, Punisher ... 2.00
❑45, Jan 1993, (c); Ghost Rider ... 2.00
❑46, Feb 1993, (c); KB (w); Cable ... 2.00
❑47, Mar 1993, KB (w); Magneto ... 2.00
❑48, Apr 1993, Daredevil ... 2.00
❑49, May 1993, (c); Silver Surfer ... 2.00
❑50, Jun 1993, silver sculpted cover; Hulk, Wolverine ... 2.95

Other grades: Multiply price above by 5/6 for VF/NM • 2/3 for VERY FINE • 1/3 for FINE • 1/5 for VERY GOOD • 1/8 for GOOD

❑51, Jul 1993, Punisher, Captain America 2.00
❑52, Aug 1993, Doctor Doom 2.00
❑53, Sep 1993, Spider-Man, Hulk, Iron Man 2020 2.00
❑54, Oct 1993, (c); A: Reed Richards. A: Fantastic Four. A: Cage. A: Death's Head II. A: War Machine. A: Captain America. A: Death's Head. A: Charnel. Death's Head 2.00
❑55, Nov 1993, Avengers 2.00
❑56, Dec 1993, Avengers 2.00
❑57, Jan 1994, (c);Punisher 2.00
❑58, Feb 1994, Punisher, Spider-Man 2.00
❑59, Mar 1994, (c); Wolverine/Alpha Flight 2.00
❑60, Apr 1994, KB (w); X-Men wedding 2.00
❑61, May 1994, KB (w); Spider-Man 2.00
❑62, Jun 1994, KB (w); Wolverine 2.00
❑63, Jul 1994, A: War Machine. War Machine 2.00
❑64, Aug 1994, (c);Iron Man 2.00
❑65, Sep 1994, (c); A: Archangel. Archangel 1.75
❑66, Oct 1994, (c);Rogue 1.75
❑67, Nov 1994, Captain America 1.75
❑68, Dec 1994, Captain America 1.75
❑69, Jan 1995, X-Men 1.75
❑70, Feb 1995, Silver Surfer 1.75
❑71, Mar 1995, Hulk 1.50
❑72, Apr 1995, (c);Spider-Man 1.50
❑73, May 1995, Daredevil 1.50
❑74, Jun 1995, (c);Mr. Sinister forms The X-Men 1.50
❑75, Jul 1995, Generation X 1.50
❑76, Aug 1995, Flash Thompson as Spider-Man; last Watcher 1.50
❑77, Sep 1995, (c);Legion 1.50
❑78, Oct 1995, New Fantastic Four remains a team 1.50
❑79, Nov 1995, Storm becomes Phoenix 1.50
❑80, Dec 1995, KGa (a); A: Maestro. Hulk becomes The Maestro 1.50
❑81, Jan 1996, (c); Age of Apocalypse didn't end 1.50
❑82, Feb 1996, J. Jonah Jameson adopts Peter Parker 1.50
❑83, Mar 1996 1.50
❑84, Apr 1996, PS (c); A: Bishop and Shard. Shard lived instead of Bishop 1.50
❑85, May 1996, Magneto ruled all mutants 1.50
❑86, Jun 1996, Scarlet Spider kills Spider-Man 1.50
❑87, Jul 1996, Sabretooth 1.50
❑88, Aug 1996, Spider-Man 1.50
❑89, Sep 1996, Fantastic Four 1.50
❑90, Oct 1996, Cyclops and Havok 1.50
❑91, Nov 1996, Hulk 1.50
❑92, Dec 1996, Joshua Guthrie and a Sentinel 1.50
❑93, Jan 1997, Wolverine 1.50
❑94, Feb 1997, Juggernaut 1.50
❑95, Mar 1997, (c);Ghost Rider 1.95
❑96, Apr 1997, Quicksilver 1.95
❑97, May 1997, A: Doctor Doom. Black Knight 1.95
❑98, Jun 1997, (c);Rogue, Nightcrawler 1.95
❑99, Aug 1997, gatefold summary; Spider-Man 1.99
❑100, Sep 1997, double-sized; (c); KJ (w); KJ (a); A: Fantastic 4; gatefold summary; Gambit 1.99
❑101, Oct 1997, gatefold summary; (c); Archangel 1.99
❑102, Nov 1997, gatefold summary; (c); Daredevil 1.99
❑103, Dec 1997, gatefold summary; (c); Gatefold summary 1.99
❑104, Jan 1998, gatefold summary; Impossible Man with Infinity Gauntlet 1.99
❑105, Feb 1998, gatefold summary; (c); BSz (a); O: Spider-Girl. 1: Spider-Girl. leads into Marvel 2 12.00
❑106, Mar 1998, gatefold summary 1.99
❑107, Apr 1998, gatefold summary; BSz (c); BSz (a); V: Destroyer. Thor as ruler of Asgard 1.99
❑108, May 1998, gatefold summary; Avengers vs. Carnage 1.99
❑109, Jun 1998, gatefold summary; Thing in Liddleville 1.99
❑110, Jul 1998, gatefold summary; X-Men 1.99
❑111, Aug 1998, gatefold summary; Wolverine as War 1.99
❑112, Sep 1998, gatefold summary; (c); Ka-Zar 1.99
❑113, Oct 1998, gatefold summary; (c); Tony Stark as Sorcerer Supreme 1.99
❑114, Nov 1998, gatefold summary; Secret Wars 25 years later 2.50

What If ... Aunt May Had Died Instead of Uncle Ben?
Marvel

❑1, Feb 2005 2.99

What If: Avengers Disassembled
Marvel

❑1, Jan 2007 3.99

What If: Captain America
Marvel

❑1, Feb 2006 2.99

What If: Daredevil
Marvel

❑1, Feb 2006 2.99

What If ... Dr. Doom Had Become The Thing?
Marvel

❑1, Feb 2005 2.99

What If: Fantastic Four
Marvel

❑1, Feb 2006 2.99

What If ... General Ross Had Become The Hulk?
Marvel

❑1, Feb 2005 2.99

What If ... Jessica Jones Had Joined The Avengers?
Marvel

❑1, Feb 2005 2.99

What If ... Karen Page Had Lived?
Marvel

❑1, Feb 2005 2.99

What If ... Magneto Had Formed the X-Men with Professor X?
Marvel

❑1, Feb 2005 2.99

What If: Spider-Man -- The Other
Marvel

❑1, Jan 2007 2.99

What If: Sub-Mariner
Marvel

❑1, Feb 2006 2.99

What If: Thor
Marvel

❑1, Feb 2006 2.99

What If: Wolverine
Marvel

❑1, Feb 2006 2.99

What If: Wolverine — Enemy of the State
Marvel

❑1, Feb 2007 2.99

What If: X-Men — Age of Apocalypse
Marvel

❑1, Mar 2007 2.99

What If: X-Men — Deadly Genesis
Marvel

❑1, Mar 2007 3.99

What Is...THE FACE?
Ace

❑1, Dec 1986 1.75
❑2, May 1987 1.75
❑3, Aug 1987 1.75

What's Michael: A Hard Day's Life
Dark Horse

❑1, Jul 2002 8.95

What's Michael: Fat Cat in the City
Dark Horse

❑1, Feb 2003 8.95

What's Michael: Living Together
Dark Horse

❑1, Jul 1997 5.95

What's Michael: Michael's Album
Dark Horse

❑1, Apr 1997 5.95

What's Michael: Michael's Favorite Spot
Dark Horse

❑1, Jan 2002 8.95

What's Michael: Michael's Mambo
Dark Horse

❑1, Jan 1998 5.95

What's Michael: Off the Deep End
Dark Horse

❑1, Oct 1997 5.95

What's Michael: Show Time
Dark Horse

❑1, Sep 2003 8.95

What's Michael: The Ideal Cat
Dark Horse

❑1, May 2004 8.95

What's New?- The Collected Adventures of Phil & Dixie
Palliard

❑1, Oct 1991, The Collected Adventures of Phil and Dixie 5.95
❑2, ca. 1994, prestige format 7.95

What's New? With Phil and Dixie
Studio Foglio

❑2, Mar 2001, Sex & GamersÕ No, Really. 2nd edition; Reprints articles from Dragon Magazine; Annotations by Kaja Foglio 8.95
❑3, Apr 2000, prestige format; collects strips from The Duelist 10.95

What The-?!
Marvel

❑1, Aug 1988, AM (c); AM, SD, JSe (a); When Titans Tussle! 4.00
❑2, Sep 1988, JBy (c); AM, FH, JBy (w); AW, JBy, JSe, PF (a); Superbman V: Fantastical Four 2.50
❑3, Oct 1988, (c); RHo, FH, KB, PD (w); RHo, FH, TMc, BMc, JSt, KB (a) 3.00
❑4, Nov 1988, BWi (c); FH, KB, PD (w); FH (a) 2.50
❑5, Jul 1989 2.50
❑6, Jan 1990, JBy (c); JBy (w); JBy (a); Acts of Vengeance parody 2.50
❑7, Apr 1990, JBy (c); RHo (w); RHo (a) 2.50
❑8, Jul 1990, JBy (c); KB (w) 2.50
❑9, Oct 1990, JBy (c); PD (w); wraparound cover 1.75
❑10, Jan 1991, prestige format; JBy (c); JBy (a); Holiday special 1.75
❑11, Mar 1991, JBy (c); RL (a); O: Wolverina 1.50
❑12, May 1991 JBy (c) 1.50
❑13, Jul 1991 JBy (c); SL (w); BWi (a) 1.50
❑14, Sep 1991 JBy (c) 1.50
❑15, Nov 1991 1.50
❑16, Jan 1992; EC parody cover 1.50
❑17, Mar 1992 RHo, KB (w) 1.50
❑18, May 1992 1.50
❑19, Jul 1992 1.50
❑20, Aug 1992 1.50
❑21, Sep 1992; JSa (a); Weapon X parody 1.50
❑22, Oct 1992 JSa (a) 1.50
❑23, Nov 1992 1.50
❑24, Dec 1992 1.50
❑25, Sum 1993; Summer Special 2.50
❑26, Fal 1993; Winter Special 2.50
❑27, Win 1993 2.50

Wheelie and the Chopper Bunch
Charlton

❑1, May 1975, JBy (a) 20.00
❑2, Jul 1975, JBy, MZ (a) 12.00
❑3, Sep 1975, JBy (a) 10.00
❑4, Nov 1975 10.00
❑5, Jan 1976 10.00
❑6, Mar 1976 10.00
❑7, May 1976, Final Issue 10.00

Wheel of Worlds
Tekno

❑0, Apr 1995, Direct Market edition; poster 2.95
❑0/CS, Apr 1995, poster 2.95
❑1, May 1996, O: Lady Justice 3.25

Other grades: Multiply price above by 5/6 for VF/NM • 2/3 for VERY FINE • 1/3 for FINE • 1/5 for VERY GOOD • 1/8 for GOOD

X-Force

Once-hot series faded after Liefeld left

©Marvel

X-Force

Less-heralded Liefeld eturn to title

©Marvel

X-Man

Holdover from "Age of Apocalypse"

©Marvel

X-Men

Name for early issues of Uncanny X-Men

©Marvel

X-Men

First issue was all-time best-selling comic book

©Marvel

N-MINT

When Beanies Attack
Blatant

❑1, Mar 1999 ... 2.95
❑1/Variant, Mar 1999; Violent cover ... 4.95

Where Creatures Roam
Marvel

❑1, Jul 1970, SD, DH, JK (a); Reprints from Journey into Mystery (1st Series) #65 ... 25.00
❑2, Sep 1970, SD, DH, JK, JSt (a); Reprints from Tales to Astonish #7-8 ... 10.00
❑3, Nov 1970, SD, JK (a); Reprints from Tales to Astonish #8 and #16 ... 10.00
❑4, Jan 1971, SD, JK (a); Reprints from Tales to Astonish #17 ... 10.00
❑5, Mar 1971, SD, DH, JK (a); Reprints from Tales to Astonish #18 and #24 ... 10.00
❑6, May 1971, SD, DH, JK (a); Reprints from Journey into Mystery (1st Series) #56 and #71 ... 10.00
❑7, Jul 1971, SD, JK (a); Reprints from Journey Into Mystery (1st Series) #72 ... 10.00
❑8, Sep 1971, JK (a) ... 10.00

Where in the World Is Carmen Sandiego?
DC

❑1, Jun 1996, based on computer game series ... 1.75
❑2, Sep 1996 ... 1.75
❑3, Nov 1996 ... 1.75
❑4, Jan 1997, all-alien issue ... 1.75

Where Monsters Dwell
Marvel

❑1, Jan 1970 ... 32.00
❑2, Mar 1970 ... 10.00
❑3, May 1970, JK (a) ... 10.00
❑4, Jul 1970 ... 10.00
❑5, Sep 1970 ... 10.00
❑6, Nov 1970 ... 8.00
❑7, Jan 1971 ... 8.00
❑8, Mar 1971 ... 8.00
❑9, May 1971 ... 8.00
❑10, Jul 1971, SD, SL (w); SD (a) ... 8.00
❑11, Sep 1971 ... 8.00
❑12, Nov 1971, Giant-size ... 10.00
❑13, Jan 1972 ... 8.00
❑14, Mar 1972 ... 8.00
❑15, May 1972 ... 8.00
❑16, Jul 1972 ... 8.00
❑17, Sep 1972 ... 8.00
❑18, Nov 1972 ... 8.00
❑19, Jan 1973 ... 8.00
❑20, Mar 1973 ... 8.00
❑21, May 1973 ... 8.00
❑22, Jul 1973 ... 8.00
❑23, Sep 1973 ... 8.00
❑24, Oct 1973 ... 8.00
❑25, Nov 1973 ... 8.00
❑26, Jan 1974 ... 8.00
❑27, Mar 1974 ... 8.00
❑28, May 1974 ... 8.00
❑29, Jul 1974 ... 8.00
❑30, Sep 1974 ... 8.00
❑31, Oct 1974 ... 8.00
❑32, Nov 1974 ... 7.00
❑33, Jan 1975 ... 7.00
❑34, Mar 1975 ... 7.00

N-MINT

❑35, May 1975 ... 7.00
❑36, Jul 1975 ... 7.00
❑37, Sep 1975 ... 7.00
❑38, Oct 1975; Final Issue ... 7.00

While Fifty Million Died
Tome

❑1, b&w; World War II ... 2.95

Whispers and Shadows
Oasis

❑1 1984, b&w ... 1.50
❑2 1984, b&w ... 1.50
❑3 1984, b&w ... 1.50
❑4 1984, b&w ... 1.50
❑5 1985, b&w ... 1.50
❑6 1985, b&w ... 1.50
❑7 1985, b&w ... 1.50
❑8 1985, b&w ... 1.50

Whisper
Capital

❑1, Dec 1983, O: Whisper ... 2.50
❑2, Mar 1984, Indicia says March 1983. ... 2.00

Whisper
First

❑1, Jun 1986 ... 2.00
❑2, Aug 1986 ... 1.50
❑3, Oct 1986 ... 1.50
❑4, Dec 1986 ... 1.50
❑5, Feb 1987 ... 1.50
❑6, Apr 1987 ... 1.50
❑7, Jun 1987 ... 1.50
❑8, Aug 1987 ... 1.75
❑9, Oct 1987 ... 1.75
❑10, Dec 1987 ... 1.75
❑11, Feb 1988 ... 1.75
❑12, Apr 1988 ... 1.75
❑13, Jun 1988 ... 1.75
❑14, Jul 1988 ... 1.75
❑15, Aug 1988 ... 1.75
❑16, Sep 1988 ... 1.75
❑17, Oct 1988 ... 1.75
❑18, Nov 1988 ... 1.95
❑19, Dec 1988; O: Whisper ... 1.95
❑20, Jan 1989; O: Whisper ... 1.95
❑21, Feb 1989 ... 1.95
❑22, Mar 1989 ... 1.95
❑23, Apr 1989 ... 1.95
❑24, May 1989 ... 1.95
❑25, Jun 1989 ... 1.95
❑26, Jul 1989 ... 1.95
❑27, Aug 1989 ... 1.95
❑28, Sep 1989 ... 1.95
❑29, Oct 1989 ... 1.95
❑30, Nov 1989 ... 1.95
❑31, Dec 1989 ... 1.95
❑32, Jan 1990 ... 1.95
❑33, Feb 1990 ... 1.95
❑34, Mar 1990 ... 1.95
❑35, Apr 1990 ... 1.95
❑36, May 1990 ... 1.95
❑37, Jun 1990 ... 1.95
❑Special 1, Nov 1985; Giant-size ... 2.50

White Devil
Eternity

❑1, Jun 1988, b&w; Adult ... 2.50

N-MINT

❑2, Jul 1988, b&w; Adult ... 2.50
❑3 1988, b&w; Adult ... 2.50
❑4 1988, b&w; Adult ... 2.50
❑5 1989, b&w; Adult ... 2.50
❑6 1989, b&w; Adult ... 2.50
❑7 1989, b&w; Adult ... 2.50
❑8 1989, b&w; Adult ... 2.50

White Fang
Disney

❑1, ca. 1990; newsstand version ... 2.95
❑1/Direct ed., ca. 1990; NN; Movie adaptation ... 5.95

White Like She
Dark Horse

❑1, May 1994, b&w ... 2.95
❑2, Jun 1994, b&w ... 2.95
❑3, Jul 1994, b&w ... 2.95
❑4, Aug 1994, b&w ... 2.95

White Orchid
Atlantis

❑1 ... 2.95

Whiteout
Oni

❑1, Jul 1998; b&w ... 2.95
❑2, Aug 1998; b&w ... 2.95
❑3, Sep 1998; b&w ... 2.95
❑4, Nov 1998; b&w ... 2.95

Whiteout: Melt
Oni

❑1, Sep 1999; b&w ... 2.95
❑2, Oct 1999; b&w ... 2.95
❑3, Nov 1999; b&w ... 2.95
❑4, Dec 1999; b&w ... 2.95

White Raven
Visionary

❑1, ca. 1995, b&w; Adult ... 2.95

White Tiger
Marvel

❑1, Jan 2007 ... 2.99
❑2, Feb 2007 ... 2.99

White Trash
Tundra

❑1; NN ... 3.95
❑2 ... 3.95
❑3 ... 3.95
❑4 ... 3.95

Whiz Kids
Image / Big Bang

❑1, Apr 2003, b&w; one-shot ... 4.95

Whoa, Nellie!
Fantagraphics

❑1, Jul 1996, b&w ... 2.95
❑2, Aug 1996, b&w ... 2.95
❑3, Sep 1996, b&w ... 2.95

Whodunnit?
Eclipse

❑1, Jun 1986 ... 2.00
❑2, Nov 1986 ... 2.00
❑3, Apr 1987 ... 2.00

Who is the Crooked Man
Crusade

❑1, Sep 1996 ... 3.50

Who Really Killed JFK
Revolutionary

❑1, Oct 1993, b&w ... 2.50

Who's Who in Star Trek
DC

❑1, Mar 1987; Wraparound cover; Andorians to McCoy ... 1.50
❑2, Apr 1987; McGivers-Vulcans ... 1.50

Who's Who in the DC Universe
DC

❑1, Aug 1990 ... 4.95
❑2, Sep 1990 ... 4.95
❑3, Oct 1990 ... 4.95
❑4, Nov 1990 ... 4.95
❑5, Dec 1990 ... 4.95
❑6, Jan 1991 ... 4.95
❑7, Feb 1991 ... 4.95
❑8, Apr 1991 ... 4.95
❑9, May 1991 ... 4.95
❑10, Jun 1991 ... 4.95
❑11, Jul 1991 ... 4.95
❑12, Aug 1991 ... 4.95
❑13, Oct 1991 ... 4.95
❑14, Nov 1991; Art Nichols credit in #16 4.95
❑15, Jan 1992 ... 4.95
❑16, Feb 1992; Final issue; Corrects entries for DeSaad, Laurel Gand, Maxwell Lord ... 4.95

Who's Who in the DC Universe Update 1993
DC

❑1, Dec 1992 ... 5.95
❑2, Jan 1993 ... 5.95

Who's Who in the Impact Universe
DC / Impact

❑1, Sep 1991 ... 4.95
❑2, Dec 1991 ... 4.95
❑3, May 1992 ... 4.95

Who's Who in the Legion of Super-Heroes
DC

❑1, Apr 1988; MWa (w); KG, GP, PB, RL, DC, JSa, CS (a); Absorbancy Boy through Doctor Gym'll ... 1.50
❑2, Jun 1988; Doctor Mayavile through High Seer ... 1.50
❑3, Jul 1988; Heroes of Lallor through Legion of Super-Rejects; plus Planets of the 30th Century ... 1.50
❑4, Aug 1988; Wraparound cover; Homeworlds of the Legion of Super-Heroes; Legion of Super-Villians; Lightening Lad through Mon-El ... 1.50
❑5, Sep 1988; Mordru through Science Police Officer Quav; Plus Tour of Legion Headquarters ... 1.50
❑6, Oct 1988; Wraparound cover; Wonders of Metropolis; Seerons Through Timber Wolf ... 1.50
❑7, Nov 1988; Wraparound cover; The Nik Feelds Show; Time Trapper through Zoraz; Index to Who's Who in the Legion ... 1.50

Who's Who: The Definitive Directory of the DC Universe
DC

❑1, Mar 1985, GP (c); JO, CI, KG, JOy, GP, DH, GK, MR (a); Abel through Auron.. 1.50
❑2, Apr 1985, GP (c); DaG, GC, CI, JOy, GP, DG, JK, JKu, BA, GK, CS, MR, JA, JL (a); Automan through Blackhawk Plane ... 1.50
❑3, May 1985, GP, DG (c); BSz, CI, KG, JOy, GP, PB, SR, JK, GK, JSa, CS, JA (a); Black Lightning through Byth ... 1.50
❑4, Jun 1985, GP, DG (c); JO, GM, CI, GP, PB, JBy, JK, BB, BA, GK, DC, DSt, KS, IN (a); The Cadre through Chril KL-99 1.50
❑5, Jul 1985, GP, DG (c); RHo, CI, KG, JOy, GP, PB, DH, JK, BA, GK, CS, DS, MR (a); Chronos through Cyclotron ... 1.50
❑6, Aug 1985, DG (c); MW, DaG, CI, JOy, DH, MGr, JK, GK, CS, MR, JL (a); Daily Planet through Doctor Polaris ... 1.50
❑7, Sep 1985, DG (c); MA, BSz, PB, JBy, JKu, GK, JSa, MR, DSt (a); Doctor Psycho through Fastback ... 1.50
❑8, Oct 1985, DG (c); AM, RB, MA, KG, JOy, GP, LMc, JK, JKu, GK, DS (a); Fatal Five through Garguax ... 1.50
❑9, Nov 1985, DG (c); BSz, CI, JDu, GP, LMc, JK, JKu, GK, RH, JA, IN (a); Garn Daanuth through Guardians of the Universe ... 1.50
❑10, Dec 1985, DG (c); MA, CI, TMc, JOy, GP, FT, PS, SR, JK, JKu, GK, CS, JA (a); Gunner & Sarge through Hyena ... 1.50
❑11, Jan 1986, DG (c); TS, MA, JO, TMc, JOy, GP, LMc, DH, HC, JK, JKu, GK, JSa, CS, MR (a); Icicle through Jonni Thunder ... 1.50
❑12, Feb 1986, DG (c); FMc, AM, MA, TMc, JOy, GP, LMc, JK, MR, JA, JL (a); Johnny Double through Kong ... 1.50
❑13, Mar 1986, GP (c); JSn, KG, JDu, GP, JK, GK, DC, JSa, CS (a); Krona through Losers ... 1.50
❑14, Apr 1986, GP, DG (c); JSn, MA, RHo, BSz, GP, JBy, MGr, JK, GK, CS (a); Luther I through Masters of Disaster . 1.50
❑15, May 1986, GP, DG (c); MA, BSz, CI, KG, GP, JK, TVE, RA, MR, JA (a); Matrix-Prime through Mister Tawky-Tawny ... 1.50
❑16, Jun 1986, GP, DG (c); JSn, BSz, GC, GP, PB, JBy, JK, BB, GK (a); Mr. Terrific through Nightmaster ... 1.50
❑17, Jul 1986, GP (c); GC, CI, KG, JOy, GP, JK, GK, CS, JA, RE (a); Nightshade through Persuader ... 1.50
❑18, Aug 1986, GP, DG (c); DaG, CI, JOy, GP, JBy, DG, SR, JK, JSa, JA, DSt (a); Phantom Girl through Pursuer ... 1.50
❑19, Sep 1986, SD, MA, CI, GP, JBy, DH, JK, JKu, GK, JL (a); Puzzler through Roy Raymond ... 1.50
❑20, Oct 1986, DG (c); GE, DG, JK, CS, RA, RH, JL, KS (a); Rubber Duck through Shining Knight ... 1.50
❑21, Nov 1986, GC, DG (c); SD, MA, BSz, CI, JOy, GK, RA, JA, KS, IN (a); Shrinking Violet through Starfinger ... 1.50
❑22, Dec 1986, JBy (c); SD, JOy, GP, JBy, LMc, GT, JK, GK, JL (a); Starfire I through Syonide ... 1.50
❑23, Jan 1987, JSa (c); MA, RHo, JOy, GP, MGr, GK, JSa, CS, JA, IN (a); Syrene through Time Trapper ... 1.50
❑24, Feb 1987, BSz, CI, GP, JBy, DG, TVE, DS, JM, MR, RT (a); Tim Trench through Universo ... 1.50
❑25, Mar 1987, DG (c); GM, GP, LMc, MGr, JK, JKu, GK, CS, DS (a); Unknown Soldier through Witch Boy ... 1.50
❑26, Apr 1987, DG (c); FH, GM, JDu, GP, MGr, TY, JSa, RA, JL, PF, ME (a); Wizard through The 1000 ... 1.50

Who's Who Update '87
DC

❑1, Aug 1987, DG (c); KG, TMc, GP, PB, JBy, LMc, GK, JSa, JA (a); All-Star Squadron through Calyst ... 1.50
❑2, Sep 1987, DG (c); MA, RHo, TMc, GP, PB, JSa, JA (a); Catwoman II through Goldstar ... 1.50
❑3, Oct 1987, RHo, JDu, TMc, GP, JBy, LMc, BB, JSa (a); Gray Man through Lionmane ... 1.50
❑4, Nov 1987, TMc (c); AM, DaG, TMc, GP, PB, JBy, RA, JA (a); Lois Lane through Ame Starr ... 1.50
❑5, Dec 1987, DaG, JBy, LMc, DG, JSa, KGa, JA (a); Reaper through Robert Campenella ... 1.50

Who's Who Update '88
DC

❑1, Aug 1988, KG, JOy, PB, LMc, MGu, EL (a); Amazing Man through Harlequin II ... 1.50
❑2, Sep 1988, JBy, EL, JA (a); Icemaiden through Nightwing ... 1.50
❑3, Oct 1988, JOy, GP, RL, AA, DS, JM, EL (a); Parliament of Trees through Trident ... 1.50
❑4, Nov 1988, KG, GP, DGr, LMc (a); Ultra-Humanite through Zuggernaut plus Supporting Characters (Abby Cable to Wade Eiling) ... 1.50

Whotnot
Fantagraphics

❑1, b&w ... 2.50
❑2, b&w ... 2.50
❑3, b&w ... 2.50

Wicked
Millennium

❑1, Nov 1994; b&w ... 2.50
❑2 1995 ... 2.50
❑3, Apr 1995, b&w; cover dated Mar ... 2.50

Wicked
Image

❑1, Dec 1999, Man, demon on cover ... 2.95
❑1/A, Dec 1999, Figure against red background on cover ... 2.95
❑1/B, Dec 1999, Girl with glowing book on cover ... 2.95
❑2, Feb 2000 ... 2.95
❑3, Mar 2000 ... 2.95
❑4 2000 ... 2.95
❑5, Jun 2000 ... 2.95
❑6, Jun 2000 ... 2.95
❑7, Aug 2000 ... 2.95
❑Ashcan 1, Jul 1999, Preview edition ... 5.00

Wicked: Medusa's Tale
Image

❑1, Nov 2000 ... 3.95

Widow
Avatar

❑0 ... 3.95
❑0/Nude, Jun 2000, b&w ... 0.00

Widow: Flesh and Blood
Ground Zero

❑1, Oct 1992 ... 2.50
❑2, Dec 1992 ... 2.50
❑3, Mar 1993 ... 2.50

Widow: Metal Gypsies
London Night

❑1, Aug 1995; Adult ... 3.95

Wiindows
Cult

❑1, Mar 1993, b&w; Partial prism cover 3.50
❑2, Apr 1993, b&w ... 3.00
❑3, May 1993, b&w ... 3.00
❑4, Jun 1993, b&w ... 2.50
❑5, Jul 1993, b&w ... 2.50
❑6, Aug 1993, b&w ... 2.50
❑7, Sep 1993, b&w ... 2.50
❑8, Oct 1993, b&w ... 2.50
❑9, Nov 1993, b&w ... 2.50
❑10, Dec 1993, b&w ... 2.50
❑11, Jan 1994, b&w ... 2.50
❑12, Feb 1994, b&w ... 2.50
❑13, Mar 1994, b&w ... 2.50
❑14, Apr 1994, b&w ... 2.50
❑15, May 1994, b&w ... 2.50
❑16, Jun 1994, b&w ... 2.50
❑17, Jun 1994, b&w ... 2.50

Wild!
Mu

❑1 2003 ... 3.75
❑2 ... 3.75
❑3 ... 3.75
❑4 ... 3.75
❑5 ... 3.75
❑6 ... 3.75
❑7 ... 3.75
❑8 ... 3.75
❑9 ... 3.75
❑10 ... 3.75
❑11 ... 3.75
❑12 ... 3.75
❑13, Jul 2005 ... 3.75
❑14, Aug 2005 ... 3.75

Wild Animals
Pacific

❑1, ca. 1982 ... 1.50

Wild Bill Hickok
Super

❑10, Jun 1952 ... 60.00
❑11, ca. 1963, (c) ... 60.00
❑12 ... 60.00

Wild Bill Pecos
AC

❑1, ca. 1989 ... 3.50

WildB.R.A.T.s
Fantagraphics

❑1, Oct 1992 ... 3.25

Wildcards
Marvel / Epic

❑1, Sep 1990, prestige format; based on prose anthology series ... 4.50

Other grades: Multiply price above by 5/6 for VF/NM • 2/3 for VERY FINE • 1/3 for FINE • 1/5 for VERY GOOD • 1/8 for GOOD

X-Men Adventures (Vol. 1)

Based on the TV series' first season

©Marvel

X-Men Adventures (Vol. 2)

Some copies of #4 included notorious catalog

©Marvel

X-Men Adventures (Vol. 3)

Third season of animated series adapted

©Marvel

X-Men Alpha

Kicked off the "Age of Apocalypse"

©Marvel

X-Men Classic

Renamed version of Classic X-Men

©Marvel

N-MINT

❑2, Oct 1990, prestige format; based on prose anthology series 4.50
❑3, Nov 1990, prestige format; based on prose anthology series 4.50
❑4, Dec 1990, prestige format; based on prose anthology series 4.50

WildC.A.T.s
Image

❑0, Jun 1993; Wraparound cover; Packaged with WildC.A.T.S. Book #1.. 3.00
❑1, Aug 1992, JLee (c); JLee (w); JLee (a); 1: Maul. 1: Grifter. 1: Spartan. 1: Gnome. 1: Tri-Ad. 1: Helspont. 1: Pike. 1: WildC.A.T.s. 1: Hightower. Trading cards enclosed........ 4.00
❑1/3D, Aug 1997; 3-D edition; JLee (w); JLee (a); 3-D edition........ 4.95
❑1/Gold, Aug 1992; Gold edition; JLee (c); JLee (w); JLee (a); Gold edition........ 10.00
❑1/Variant, Aug 1992; Wizard Ace edition; JLee (c); JLee (w); JLee (a)........ 5.00
❑2, Sep 1992, JLee (c); JLee (w); JLee (a); 1: Black Razor. 1: Wetworks. Coupon for Image Comics #0 enclosed; Prism cover........ 4.00
❑3, Dec 1992, JLee (c); JLee (w); JLee (a); A: Youngblood........ 3.00
❑4, Mar 1993, JLee (w); JLee (a); Includes card........ 3.00
❑4/A, Mar 1993; (c); JLee (w); JLee (a); bagged; red trading card........ 3.00
❑5, Nov 1993, JLee (c); JLee (w); JLee (a); Quad gatefold pages........ 2.50
❑6, Dec 1993, JLee (c); JLee (w); JLee (a); V: Cyberforce; WildC.A.T.S. #6, Cyber Force #2, WildC.A.T.S. #7, Cyber Force #3; Killer Instinct Crossover...... 2.50
❑6/Gold, Dec 1993; Gold edition........ 3.00
❑7, Jan 1994, JLee (c); JLee (w); JLee (a); V: Cyber Force........ 2.50
❑7/Platinum, Jan 1994; Platinum edition 3.00
❑8, Feb 1994, JLee (c); JLee (w); JLee (a); A: Cyclops and Jean Grey. V: Lord Entropy........ 2.50
❑9, Mar 1994, JLee (c); JLee (w); JLee (a); V: Lord Entropy........ 2.50
❑10, Apr 1994, JLee (c); JLee (a); series becomes WildC.A.T.S........ 2.50
❑11, Jun 1994; JLee (c); JLee (a); Title changes to WildC.A.T.S........ 15.00
❑11/Holofoil, Jun 1994; variant cover.... 22.00
❑12, Aug 1994; 1: Savant. 1: Savant...... 8.00
❑13, Sep 1994; Beavis and Butthead cameo........ 6.00
❑14, Sep 1994; V: Freak Force........ 2.50
❑15, Nov 1994........ 2.50
❑16, Dec 1994........ 2.50
❑17, Jan 1995 A: StormWatch........ 2.50
❑18, Mar 1995........ 2.50
❑19, Apr 1995........ 2.50
❑20, May 1995; with cards........ 2.50
❑21, Jul 1995; JLee (c); AMo (w); JLee (a); 1st Moore-written issue........ 2.50
❑22, Aug 1995 AMo (w)........ 2.50
❑23, Sep 1995 AMo (w)........ 2.50
❑24, Nov 1995 AMo (w)........ 2.50
❑25, Dec 1995; AMo (w); enhanced wraparound cover........ 4.95
❑26, Feb 1996 AMo (w)........ 2.50
❑27, Mar 1996 AMo (w)........ 2.50
❑28, Apr 1996 AMo (w)........ 2.50

N-MINT

❑29, May 1996; AMo (w); cover says Apr, indicia says May........ 2.50
❑30, Jun 1996; AMo (w); V: Overtkill..... 2.50
❑31, Sep 1996; AMo (w); V: Overtkill..... 2.50
❑32, Jan 1997; JLee (c); AMo (w); JLee (a); V: Overtkil; Tao revealed as traitor 2.50
❑33, Feb 1997; AMo (w); V: Tao........ 2.50
❑34, Feb 1997 AMo (w)........ 2.50
❑35, Mar 1997; V: Crusade........ 2.50
❑36, Mar 1997; V: Crusade........ 2.50
❑37, Apr 1997........ 2.50
❑38, May 1997........ 2.50
❑39, Jun 1997........ 2.50
❑40, Jul 1997........ 2.50
❑40/A, Jul 1997; alternate mostly b&w cover........ 2.50
❑40/B, Jul 1997; alternate mostly b&w cover........ 2.50
❑41, Aug 1997........ 2.50
❑42, Sep 1997........ 2.50
❑43, Oct 1997........ 2.50
❑44, Nov 1997........ 2.50
❑45, Jan 1998........ 2.50
❑46, Feb 1998........ 2.50
❑47, Mar 1998........ 2.50
❑47/A, Mar 1998; alternate cover with Grifter........ 2.50
❑47/B, Mar 1998; alternate cover with Grifter........ 2.50
❑48, Apr 1998........ 2.50
❑49, May 1998........ 2.50
❑50, Jun 1998; Giant-size; JRo, AMo (w); JLee (a); Wraparound cover........ 4.00
❑50/Variant, Jun 1998; chromium cover 5.00
❑Ann 1, Feb 1998 JRo (w)........ 2.95
❑Special 1, Nov 1993........ 3.50

WildCats
DC / Wildstorm

❑1, Mar 1999, JLee (c)........ 2.50
❑1/B, Mar 1999........ 2.50
❑1/C, Mar 1999........ 2.50
❑1/D, Mar 1999........ 2.50
❑1/E, Mar 1999, Joe Madureira Cover... 2.50
❑1/F, Mar 1999........ 2.50
❑1/Dynamic, Mar 1999, DFE alternate cover 6.95
❑1/Sketch, Mar 1999, Euro-Edition sketch cover; Euro-Edition sketch cover........ 10.00
❑2, May 1999........ 2.50
❑3, Jul 1999........ 2.50
❑4, Sep 1999........ 2.50
❑5, Nov 1999........ 2.50
❑6, Dec 1999, V: the Kenyan........ 2.50
❑7, Mar 2000, V: Pike........ 2.50
❑8, Apr 2000........ 2.50
❑9, May 2000, D: Kenyan; D: Emp........ 2.50
❑10, Jun 2000, D: Kenyan; D: Emp........ 2.50
❑11, Jul 2000........ 2.50
❑12, Aug 2000........ 2.50
❑13, Sep 2000........ 2.50
❑14, Oct 2000........ 2.50
❑15, Nov 2000........ 2.50
❑16, Dec 2000, V: Slaughterhouse Smith 2.50
❑17, Jan 2001........ 2.50
❑18, Feb 2001, JLee (c); V: Slaughter-house Smith........ 2.50
❑19, Mar 2001, JLee (c);V: Slaughter-house Smith........ 2.50

N-MINT

❑20, Apr 2001........ 2.50
❑21, May 2001........ 2.50
❑22, Jun 2001........ 2.50
❑23, Jul 2001........ 2.50
❑24, Aug 2001........ 2.50
❑25, Sep 2001........ 2.50
❑26, Oct 2001........ 2.50
❑27, Nov 2001........ 2.50
❑28, Dec 2001........ 2.50
❑Ann 2000, Dec 2000........ 3.50

WildC.A.T.S Adventures
Image

❑1, Sep 1994; O: Warblade. O: WildC.A.T.s 2.00
❑2, Nov 1994; V: Troika........ 2.00
❑3, Nov 1994; V: Coda........ 2.00
❑4, Dec 1994........ 2.50
❑5, Jan 1995........ 2.50
❑6, Feb 1995; V: Majestic........ 2.50
❑7, Mar 1995........ 2.50
❑8, Apr 1995........ 2.50
❑9, May 1995........ 2.50
❑10, Jun 1995........ 2.50

WildC.A.T.S Adventures Sourcebook
Image

❑1, Jan 1995........ 2.95

WildC.A.T.S/Aliens
Image

❑1, Aug 1998, crossover with Dark Horse; cardstock cover........ 4.95
❑1/A, Aug 1998; crossover with Dark Horse; alternate cardstock cover (Zealot vs. Alien)........ 4.95

WildCats/Cyberforce: Killer Instinct
DC / Wildstorm

❑1, ca. 2004, collects Wildcats: Covert Action Teams #5-7 and Cyberforce #1-3 14.95

WildC.A.T.S
Image

❑1, Apr 1995, no cover price; informational comic for San Diego Police Dept........ 2.00

WildCats: Ladytron
DC / Wildstorm

❑1, Oct 2000........ 5.95

WildCats: Mosaic
DC / Wildstorm

❑1, Feb 2000........ 3.95

WildCats: Nemesis
DC / Wildstorm

❑1, Oct 2005........ 2.99
❑2, Dec 2005........ 2.99
❑3, Jan 2006........ 2.99
❑4, Feb 2006........ 2.99
❑5, Mar 2006........ 2.99
❑6, Apr 2006........ 2.99
❑7, May 2006........ 2.99
❑8, Jun 2006........ 2.99
❑9, Jul 2006, Final issue........ 2.99

WildC.A.T.S Sourcebook
Image

❑1, Sep 1993, (c); JLee (w); JLee (a); bio information on various WildC.A.T.S characters........ 2.50

Other grades: Multiply price above by 5/6 for VF/NM • 2/3 for VERY FINE • 1/3 for FINE • 1/5 for VERY GOOD • 1/8 for GOOD

N-MINT

❑1/Gold, Sep 1993; Gold edition; JLee (w); JLee (a); bio information on various WildC.A.T.S characters 3.00
❑2, Nov 1994; bio information on various WildC.A.T.S characters 2.50

WildCats
DC / Wildstorm

❑1, Dec 2006 .... 2.99
❑1/Variant, Dec 2006 .... 2.99
❑1/2nd variant, Dec 2006 .... 2.99

WildC.A.T.S Trilogy
Image

❑1, Jun 1993, Foil cover 2.50
❑2, Sep 1993, WildC.A.T.S. Special #1 preview 1.95
❑3, Nov 1993, Zealot pinup 1.95

WildCats Version 3.0
DC / Wildstorm

❑1, Oct 2002; Gray sketch background on cover 2.95
❑2, Nov 2002 .... 2.95
❑3, Dec 2002 .... 2.95
❑4, Jan 2003 .... 2.95
❑5, Feb 2003 .... 2.95
❑6, Mar 2003 .... 2.95
❑7, Apr 2003 .... 2.95
❑8, May 2003 .... 2.95
❑9, Jun 2003 .... 2.95
❑10, Jul 2003 .... 2.95
❑11, Aug 2003 .... 2.95
❑12, Sep 2003 .... 2.95
❑13, Oct 2003 .... 2.95
❑14, Nov 2003 .... 2.95
❑15, Dec 2003 .... 2.95
❑16, Jan 2004 .... 2.95
❑17, Feb 2004 .... 2.95
❑18, Mar 2004 .... 2.95
❑19, May 2004 .... 2.95
❑20, Jun 2004 .... 2.95
❑21, Jul 2004 .... 2.95
❑22, Aug 2004 .... 2.95
❑23, Sep 2004 .... 2.95
❑24, Oct 2004; Final issue 2.95

WildC.A.T.s/X-Men: The Golden Age
Image

❑1, Feb 1997; crossover with Marvel 4.50
❑1/A, Feb 1997; JLee (c);crossover with Marvel; cardstock cover; Autographed by Travis Charest 5.00
❑1/Scroll, Feb 1997; crossover with Marvel; scroll cover; cardstock cover; Autographed by Jim Lee 8.00
❑1/C, Feb 1997; crossover with Marvel; cardstock cover 4.50
❑1/w. glasses, Sep 1997; crossover with Marvel; with glasses 6.50
❑1/Scroll w. gla, Sep 1997; crossover with Marvel; with glasses; scroll cover 9.00
❑1/F, Sep 1997; cardstock cover; crossover with Marvel; Autographed by Jim Lee 4.50

WildC.A.T.s/X-Men: The Modern Age
Image

❑1, Aug 1997; Cardstock cover with Wolverine 4.50
❑1/A, Aug 1997; crossover with Marvel; cardstock cover; Includes certificate of authenticity; Autographed by Adam Hughes 6.00
❑1/Nightcrawler, Aug 1997; crossover with Marvel; cardstock cover; Nightcrawler cover 8.00
❑1/w. glasses, Nov 1997; crossover with Marvel; 3-D glasses bound-in 6.50
❑1/E, Nov 1997; cardstock cover; crossover with Marvel; Includes certificate of authenticity; Autographed by James Robinson 8.00
❑1/D, Nov 1997; crossover with Marvel; Nightcrawler cover; 3-D glasses bound-in 5.00

WildC.A.T.s/X-Men: The Silver Age
Image

❑1, Jun 1997; JLee (c); JLee (a); (Grifter standing center) 4.95
❑1/A, Jun 1997; NA (c); JLee (a); crossover with Marvel; cardstock cover; (Brood attacking) 4.95
❑1/B, Jun 1997; JLee (a); crossover with Marvel; cardstock cover 4.50
❑1/3D, Jun 1997; 3-D edition; JLee (a) .. 6.95
❑1/E, Oct 1997; JLee (c); JLee (a); cardstock cover; crossover with Marvel; (Grifter standing center); Autographed by Jim Lee 4.50
❑1/D, Oct 1997; JLee (a); crossover with Marvel; has indicia for WildC.A.T.S/X-Men: The Modern Age 3-D; 3-D glasses bound-in 6.50

Wildcore
Image

❑1, Nov 1997, Three figures fighting on cover 2.50
❑1/A, Nov 1997, white background 2.50
❑1/B, Nov 1997, alternate cover: white background 5.00
❑2, Dec 1997, Vigor standing on cover .. 2.50
❑2/A, Dec 1997, variant cover 3.00
❑3, Jan 1998 .... 2.50
❑4, Mar 1998 .... 2.50
❑5, Jun 1998 .... 2.50
❑6, Jul 1998 .... 2.50
❑7, Aug 1998 .... 2.50
❑8, Oct 1998 .... 2.50
❑9, Nov 1998 .... 2.50
❑10, Dec 1998 .... 2.50
❑Ashcan 1, Oct 1997, Preview edition ... 3.00

Wild Dog
DC

❑1, Sep 1987, DG (c); DG (a) 1.50
❑2, Oct 1987, DG (c); DG (a) 1.50
❑3, Nov 1987, DG (c); DG (a) 1.50
❑4, Dec 1987, DG (c); DG (a) 1.50
❑Special 1, Nov 1989, (c) 2.50

Wildflower
Sirius

❑1, Feb 1998 .... 2.50
❑2, Apr 1998 .... 2.50
❑3, Jun 1998 .... 2.50
❑4, Aug 1998 .... 2.50
❑5, Oct 1998 .... 2.50

Wild Frontier
Shanda

❑1, Jan 2000, b&w (c) 60.00
❑2, Jan 1956 .... 2.95

Wild Girl
DC / Wildstorm

❑1, Jan 2005 .... 2.95
❑2, Feb 2005 .... 2.95
❑3, Mar 2005 .... 2.95
❑4, Apr 2005 .... 2.95
❑5, May 2005 .... 2.95
❑6, Jun 2005 .... 2.99

Wildguard: Casting Call
Image

❑1/A-2; 2nd printing; Todd Nauck cover 2.95
❑5/A, Jan 2004; Todd Nauck cover 2.95
❑4/B, Dec 2003; Paco Medina cover 2.95
❑4/A, Dec 2003; Todd Nauck cover 2.95
❑3/B, Nov 2003; Arthur Adams cover 2.95
❑3/A, Nov 2003; Todd Nauck cover 2.95
❑1/B, Oct 2003; Ed McGuinness cover .. 2.95
❑1/A, Oct 2003; Todd Nauck cover 2.95
❑1, Sep 2003 .... 2.95
❑2, Oct 2003 .... 2.95
❑3, Nov 2003 .... 2.95
❑4, Dec 2003 .... 2.95
❑5, Jan 2004 .... 2.95
❑6, May 2004 .... 2.99

Wildguard: Fire Power
Image

❑1/A, Dec 2004, Cover A by Todd Nauck 3.50
❑1/B, Dec 2004; Cover B by E-House..... 3.50

WildGuard: Fool's Gold
Image

❑1 2005 .... 3.50
❑2, Sep 2005 .... 3.50

Wild Kingdom
Mu

❑1, Oct 1991, b&w 2.50
❑2, May 1993, b&w 2.95
❑3, Jan 1995, b&w 2.95
❑4, Apr 1995, b&w; Mu Pub #249 .... 2.95
❑5, Aug 1995, b&w 2.95
❑6, Dec 1995, b&w 2.95
❑7 .... 2.95
❑8, Nov 1996, b&w; Mu Pub # 329 .... 3.50
❑9, May 1998, b&w; Mu Pub # 380 .... 3.50
❑10, Sep 1998, b&w; (c);Mu Pub # 385 3.50
❑11 .... 3.50
❑12 .... 3.50
❑13, Apr 2002, b&w; Mu Pub # 408 ...... 3.50
❑14, Aug 2002, b&w; Mu Pub # 409 ..... 3.50

Wild Knights
Eternity

❑1, Mar 1988, b&w 1.95
❑2, Apr 1988 .... 1.95
❑3 1988 .... 1.95
❑4 1988 .... 1.95
❑5 1988 .... 1.95
❑6 1988 .... 1.95
❑7 1988 .... 1.95
❑8, Apr 1989, b&w 1.95
❑9, Dec 1988 .... 1.95
❑10, Feb 1989 .... 1.95

Wild Life
Antarctic

❑1, Feb 1993, b&w 2.50
❑2, May 1993, b&w 2.50
❑3, Jul 1993, b&w 2.50
❑4, Nov 1993, b&w 2.75
❑5, Feb 1994, b&w 2.75
❑6, Apr 1994, b&w 2.75
❑7, Jun 1994, b&w 2.75
❑8, Aug 1994, b&w 2.75
❑9, Oct 1994, b&w 2.75
❑10, Dec 1994, b&w 2.75
❑11, Feb 1995, b&w 2.75
❑12, Apr 1995, b&w; Final Issue 2.75

Wild Life
Fantagraphics

❑1, Aug 1994, b&w 2.75
❑2, Aug 1994, b&w 2.75

Wildlifers
Radio

❑1, Sep 1999, b&w 4.95

Wildman
Megaton

❑1 .... 1.50
❑2 .... 1.50

Wild Person in the Woods
G.T. Labs

❑1 1999 .... 2.50

Wild Side
United

❑1, Jan 1998, b&w; Wrap-around cover 3.95
❑2 .... 3.95
❑3 .... 3.95
❑4, Oct 1998, b&w; Wrap-around cover 3.95
❑5, Mar 1999, b&w; Wrap-around cover 3.95
❑6, Jul 1999, b&w; Wrap-around cover. 3.95

Wildsiderz
DC

❑0, Jul 2005 .... 1.99
❑0/Variant, Jul 2005 .... 3.00
❑1/A cover, Sep 2005 .... 3.50
❑1/B cover, Sep 2005 .... 5.00
❑1/Lenticular, Sep 2005 .... 6.00
❑2, Jan 2006 .... 3.50

Wildstar
Image

❑1, Sep 1995 .... 2.50
❑1/A, Sep 1995; Variant Cover (fighting) 2.50
❑2, Nov 1995 .... 2.50
❑3, Jan 1996 .... 2.50
❑4, Mar 1996 .... 2.50

Wild Stars
Collector's

❑1, Sum 1984, b&w 1.00

Wild Stars
Little Rocket

❑1, Jul 2001, b&w 2.95
❑2, Sep 2001, b&w 2.95
❑3, Nov 2001, b&w 2.95
❑4, Jan 2002, b&w 2.95
❑5, Mar 2002, b&w 2.95
❑6, May 2002, b&w 2.95
❑7, Jul 2002, b&w 2.95

Other grades: Multiply price above by 5/6 for VF/NM • 2/3 for VERY FINE • 1/3 for FINE • 1/5 for VERY GOOD • 1/8 for GOOD

Wildstar: Sky Zero
Image

❑1, Mar 1993, JOy (c); JOy (a); silver foil embossed cover ... 3.00
❑1/Gold, Mar 1993, JOy (c); JOy (a); gold embossed cover ... 4.00
❑2, May 1993, JOy (c); JOy (a) ... 2.00
❑3, Sep 1993, JOy (c); JOy (a); A: Savage Dragon ... 2.50
❑4, Nov 1993, JOy (c); JOy (a); A: Savage Dragon ... 2.50

WildStorm!
Image

❑1, Aug 1995, Gen13, Grifter, Deathblow, Union, Spartan ... 2.50
❑2, Oct 1995, cover says Sep, indicia says Oct ... 2.50
❑3, Nov 1995; Anthology; Union story; Taboo story; Spartan story ... 2.50
❑4, Dec 1995; StormWatch Showcase... 2.50

WildStorm Annual
DC / Wildstorm

❑2000, Dec 2000... 3.50

WildStorm Chamber of Horrors
Image

❑1, Oct 1995; Anthology ... 3.50

WildStorm Fine Art Spotlight: Jim Lee
DC / Wildstorm

❑1, Feb 2007 ... 3.50

WildStorm Fine Arts: The Gallery Collection
Image

❑1, Dec 1998; collects pin-up books and other art... 19.95

WildStorm Halloween '97
Image

❑1, Oct 1997; Anthology ... 2.50

WildStorm Rarities
Image

❑1, Dec 1994; Crusade: Released reprinted from Killer Instinct Tour Book #1; StormWatch: Urban Storm reprinted from The Art Of Homage Studios #1; StormWatch: Deadly Tidings reprinted from Image #0; Gen13: Dangerous Travel reprinted from Gen13 (Mini-Series) #0.5... 4.95

WildStorm Rising
Image

❑1, May 1995; with cards... 2.50
❑2, Jun 1995; bound-in trading cards.... 1.95

WildStorm Sampler
Image

❑1; giveaway; no cover price... 1.00

WildStorms Player's Guide
Image

❑1, Mar 1996; tips on WildStorms card game ... 1.95

WildStorm Spotlight
Image

❑1, Feb 1997; Majestic... 2.50
❑2, Mar 1997; Loner ... 2.50
❑3, Apr 1997; Loner... 2.50
❑4, May 1997; StormWatch; no indicia.. 2.50

Wildstorm Summer Special
DC / Wildstorm

❑1, Oct 2001 ... 5.95

WildStorm Swimsuit Special
Image

❑1, Dec 1994; Pin-ups ... 2.95
❑2, Aug 1995; pin-ups ... 2.50
❑1997, May 1997; pin-ups; WildStorm Swimsuits '97... 2.50

WildStorm Thunderbook
DC / Wildstorm

❑1, Oct 2000 ... 6.95

Wildstorm Ultimate Sports Official Program
Image

❑1, Aug 1997; pin-ups ... 2.50

WildStorm Universe 97
Image

❑1, Dec 1996; information on various Wildstorm characters ... 2.50
❑2, Jan 1997; information on various Wildstorm characters... 2.50
❑3, Feb 1997; information on various Wildstorm characters... 2.50

WildStorm Universe Sourcebook
Image

❑1, May 1995... 2.50
❑2 ... 2.50

Wildstorm Winter Special
DC / Wildstorm

❑1, Jan 2005... 4.95

Wild Thing
Marvel

❑1, Apr 1993, Embossed cover... 2.50
❑2, May 1993... 1.75
❑3, Jun 1993... 1.75
❑4, Jul 1993... 1.75
❑5, Aug 1993... 1.75
❑6, Sep 1993 ... 1.75
❑7, Oct 1993... 1.75

Wild Thing
Marvel

❑1, Oct 1999... 1.99
❑2, Nov 1999... 1.99
❑3, Dec 1999 ... 1.99
❑4, Jan 1999... 1.99
❑5, Feb 2000... 1.99

Wild Things
Metro

❑1, ca. 1986, b&w ... 2.00
❑2, ca. 1987, b&w ... 2.00
❑3, ca. 1987, b&w ... 2.00

Wild Thingz
ABC

❑0/A; ca. 1986 ... 3.00
❑0/B; swimsuit cover... 5.95
❑0/Platinum; Virgin Special Preview; limited to 300 copies... 3.00

Wild Think
Wild Think

❑1, Apr 1987... 2.00

Wild Times: Deathblow
DC / Wildstorm

❑1, Aug 1999; set in 1899... 2.50

Wild Times: DV8
DC / Wildstorm

❑1, Aug 1999; set in 1944... 2.50

Wild Times: Gen13
DC / Wildstorm

❑1, Aug 1999, b&w; set in 1969, 1972, and 1973... 2.50

Wild Times: Grifter
DC / Wildstorm

❑1, Aug 1999; set in 1920s... 2.50

Wild Times: Wetworks
DC / Wildstorm

❑1, Aug 1999... 2.50

Wild West
Charlton

❑58, Nov 1966, Series continued from Black Fury #57 ... 10.00

Wild West C.O.W.-Boys of Moo Mesa
Archie

❑1, Mar 1993... 1.25
❑2, May 1993... 1.25
❑3, Jul 1993... 1.25

Wild, Wild West
Gold Key

❑1, Jun 1966, 10174-606 ... 70.00
❑2, Aug 1966, Photo cover... 45.00
❑3, Jun 1968, Photo cover... 35.00
❑4, Dec 1968, Photo cover ... 35.00
❑5, Apr 1969, Photo cover... 35.00
❑6, Jul 1969, Photo cover... 35.00
❑7, Oct 1969, Photo cover... 35.00

Wild, Wild West
Millennium

❑1, ca. 1990; TV... 2.95
❑2, ca. 1990; TV... 2.95
❑3, ca. 1991; TV... 2.95
❑4, ca. 1991; TV... 2.95

Wild Women
Paragon

❑1 ... 4.95

Wild Zoo
Radio

❑1, Jul 2000, b&w ... 2.95
❑2, Sep 2000 ... 2.95
❑3, Nov 2000, b&w... 2.95
❑4, Jan 2001, b&w ... 2.95
❑5 ... 2.95
❑6, May 2001, b&w ... 2.95
❑7, Jul 2001, b&w ... 2.99
❑8, Sep 2001, b&w... 3.99

Will Eisner Presents
Eclipse

❑1, Dec 1990, b&w; Mr. Mystic ... 2.50
❑2; Mr. Mystic... 2.50
❑3; Mr. Mystic... 2.50

Will Eisner Reader
DC

❑1, Oct 2000, Collects stories from Will Eisner Quarterly #6-8; ca. 1991... 9.95

Will Eisner's 3-D Classics: Spirit
Kitchen Sink

❑1, Dec 1985; 3-D... 2.00

Will Eisner's John Law: Angels and Ashes, Devils and Dust
Idea & Design Works

❑1, May 2006... 3.99

Will Eisner's Quarterly
Kitchen Sink

❑1, Nov 1983; A Life Force; The Spirit; Mr Mystic... 2.95
❑2, Feb 1984; A Life Force; The Spirit; Lady Luck; Mr. Mystic ... 3.50
❑3, Aug 1984; A Life Force; The Spirit; Mr. Mystic ... 2.00
❑4, Jan 1985; A Life Force; The Spirit; Mr. Mystic ... 2.00
❑5, Apr 1985; A Life Force; The Spirit.... 2.00
❑6, Sep 1985 ... 2.00
❑7, Dec 1985 ... 2.00
❑8, Mar 1986 ... 2.00

William Shatner
Celebrity

❑1 ... 5.95

Willow
Marvel

❑1, Aug 1988, BH (c); BH (a); Movie adaptation ... 1.50
❑2, Sep 1988; BH (c); BH (a); Movie adaptation ... 1.50
❑3, Oct 1988; BH (c); BH (a); Movie adaptation ... 1.50

Willow
Angel

❑0, Jun 1996, b&w ... 2.95
❑0/Nude, Jun 1996; nude cardstock cover 10.00

Will to Power
Dark Horse

❑1, Jun 1994... 1.50
❑2, Jun 1994... 1.00
❑3, Jun 1994... 1.00
❑4, Jul 1994; 1: Counterstrike... 1.00
❑5, Jul 1994... 1.00
❑6, Jul 1994... 1.00
❑7, Jul 1994... 1.00
❑8, Aug 1994 ... 1.00
❑9, Aug 1994 ... 1.00
❑10, Aug 1994... 1.00
❑11, Aug 1994... 1.00
❑12, Aug 1994; D: Titan; Final Issue ... 1.00

Wimmen's Comix
Renegade

❑1, ca. 1972, Published by Last Gasp.... 10.00
❑2, ca. 1973, Published by Last Gasp.... 8.00
❑3, ca. 1973, Published by Last Gasp.... 8.00
❑4, ca. 1974; Published by Last Gasp.... 8.00
❑5, ca. 1975; Published by Last Gasp.... 5.00
❑6; Published by Last Gasp ... 5.00
❑7, ca. 1976; Published by Last Gasp.... 5.00
❑8, Mar 1983; Adult; b&w... 5.00
❑9, May 1984; Adult; b&w ... 4.00
❑10, Oct 1985; Adult; b&w ... 4.00

- ❑11, ca. 1987, b&w; Adult 3.00
- ❑12, Apr 1987; 3-D; 3-D; Adult 3.00
- ❑13; Occult issue 3.00
- ❑14, Feb 1989, b&w; Disastrous Relationships 2.50
- ❑15, Aug 1989, b&w; Adult 2.50
- ❑16, Nov 1990, b&w; Adult 2.50
- ❑17, Aug 1992, b&w; Adult 2.50
- ❑18; Adult 2.50

Windburnt Plains of Wonder
Lohman Hills

- ❑1, Fal 1996; b&w Emma Davenport one-shot 11.95

Wind in the Willows
NBM

- ❑1 15.95
- ❑2, Feb 1999 15.95

Windraven
Heroic / Blue Comet

- ❑1, b&w 2.95

Windraven Adventures
Blue Comet

- ❑1, Jan 1993, b&w; Rob Liefeld sketches 3.00

Windsor
Win-Mil

- ❑1 1.95
- ❑2; Flip-cover format 1.95

Wingbird Akuma-She
Verotik

- ❑1, Jan 1998; cardstock cover 3.95

Wingbird Returns
Verotik

- ❑1, Oct 1997; prestige format; NN; Adult 9.95

Wingding Orgy
Fantagraphics / Eros

- ❑1, Jul 1997; Adult 3.95
- ❑2, Jul 1997; Adult; b&w 3.95

Winged Tiger
Cartoonists Across America

- ❑3, Sum 1999 2.95

Winging It
Solo

- ❑1 2.00

Wings
Mu

- ❑1, Sep 1992 2.50

Wings Comics (A-List)
A-List

- ❑1, Spr 1997, b&w; Golden Age reprint 2.50
- ❑2, Fal 1997, b&w; Golden Age reprint 2.50
- ❑3 2.95
- ❑4 2.95

Wings of Anasi
Image

- ❑0, Sep 2005 6.95

Winnie the Pooh (Walt Disney...)
Gold Key / Whitman

- ❑1, Jan 1977 20.00
- ❑2, May 1977, Cracky in Hostess ad ("Time on My Hands") 10.00
- ❑3, Sep 1977 7.00
- ❑4, Nov 1977 7.00
- ❑5, Feb 1978 7.00
- ❑6, May 1978 7.00
- ❑7, Jun 1978 7.00
- ❑8, Aug 1978 7.00
- ❑9, Oct 1978 7.00
- ❑10, Dec 1978 7.00
- ❑11, Feb 1979 7.00
- ❑12, Apr 1979 7.00
- ❑13, Jun 1979 7.00
- ❑14, Aug 1979 7.00
- ❑15, Oct 1979 7.00
- ❑16, Dec 1979 7.00
- ❑17, Feb 1980 7.00
- ❑18, Apr 1980 10.00
- ❑19, May 1980 10.00
- ❑20, Aug 1980 125.00
- ❑21, Oct 1980 10.00
- ❑22, ca. 1980 10.00
- ❑23, Jan 1981 10.00
- ❑24, Feb 1981 10.00
- ❑25, Sep 1981 10.00
- ❑26, Nov 1981, Reprints from Winnie the Pooh (Walt Disney) #8 10.00
- ❑27, Feb 1982 10.00
- ❑28, Apr 1982 10.00
- ❑29, ca. 1982 20.00
- ❑30, ca. 1982; Reprint from Winnie the Pooh (Walt Disney) #3 20.00
- ❑31, ca. 1983; ca. 1983 20.00
- ❑32, Apr 1984 20.00
- ❑33, ca. 1984 20.00

Winning in the Desert
Apple

- ❑1; booklet 2.95
- ❑2; booklet 2.95

Winter Men
DC / Wildstorm

- ❑1, Sep 2005 2.99
- ❑2, Oct 2005 2.99
- ❑3, Jan 2006 2.99
- ❑4, Jun 2006 2.99
- ❑5, Dec 2006 2.99

Winter Soldier: Winter Kills
Marvel

- ❑1, Mar 2007 3.99

Winterstar
Echo

- ❑1, Dec 1996, b&w 2.95

Winterworld
Eclipse

- ❑1, Sep 1987 2.00
- ❑2, Dec 1987 2.00
- ❑3, Mar 1988 2.00

Wisdom
Marvel

- ❑1, Jan 2007 3.99

Wise Son: The White Wolf
DC / Milestone

- ❑1, Nov 1996 2.50
- ❑2, Dec 1996 2.50
- ❑3, Jan 1997 2.50
- ❑4, Feb 1997 2.50

Wish
Tokyopop

- ❑1, Aug 2002, b&w; printed in Japanese format 9.99

Wish Upon a Star
Warp

- ❑1, May 1994; giveaway; no price 1.00

Wisp
Oktomica

- ❑1, Feb 1999 2.50

Witch
Eternity

- ❑1, b&w; Reprints 1.95

Witchblade
Image

- ❑½, Nov 2002, Overstreet Fan promotional edition 15.00
- ❑1, Nov 1995; 2: Witchblade 25.00
- ❑1/B, Nov 1995; Wizard Ace edition 15.00
- ❑2, Jan 1996; Relatively scarce 18.00
- ❑2/A, Jan 1996; Wizard Ace edition 15.00
- ❑2/2nd; Encore edition; 2nd printing 4.00
- ❑3, Mar 1996 10.00
- ❑4, Apr 1996 8.00
- ❑5, May 1996 8.00
- ❑6, Jun 1996; 1: Julie Pezzini 6.00
- ❑7, Jul 1996 6.00
- ❑8, Aug 1996; wraparound cover 5.00
- ❑9, Sep 1996 5.00
- ❑9/A, Sep 1996; Tony Daniel cover 5.00
- ❑10, Nov 1996; 1: The Darkness. A: Darkness; Woman in foreground brandishing witchblade 5.00
- ❑10/Dynamic, Nov 1996; 1: The Darkness. A: Darkness. Alternate cover sold through Dynamic Forces: Shows two characters back-to-back 20.00
- ❑10/AmEnt, Nov 1996; A: Darkness. American Entertainment alternate cover 27.95
- ❑10/Autographed, Nov 1996; 1: The Darkness. Regular cover, signed by creators and sold through Dynamic Forces; limited to 2,500 copies 27.95
- ❑11, Dec 1996 4.00
- ❑12, Mar 1997 4.00
- ❑13, Apr 1997 3.50
- ❑14, May 1997 3.50
- ❑14/Gold, May 1997; Gold logo edition 6.00
- ❑15, Jul 1997 3.50
- ❑16, Aug 1997 3.00
- ❑17, Sep 1997 3.00
- ❑18, Nov 1997; continues in The Darkness #9; Witchblade and Darkness face each other on cover 3.00
- ❑18/A, Nov 1997; variant cover 2.50
- ❑18/AmEnt, Nov 1997; American Entertainment Edition; Green variant cover 5.00
- ❑19, Dec 1997 3.00
- ❑20, Feb 1998 3.00
- ❑21, Mar 1998 2.50
- ❑22, May 1998; Cover by Michael Turner 2.50
- ❑23, Jun 1998 2.50
- ❑24, Jul 1998 2.50
- ❑24/Variant, Jul 1998; Variant cover 5.00
- ❑25, Aug 1998; Yellow background cover 3.00
- ❑25/A, Aug 1998; With Fathom in pool cover 4.00
- ❑25/B, Aug 1998; Holofoil cover 8.00
- ❑25/C, Aug 1998; Printer Error; Holofoil cover 15.00
- ❑26, Oct 1998 2.50
- ❑27, Nov 1998 2.50
- ❑27/Variant, Nov 1998 2.50
- ❑28, Feb 1999 2.50
- ❑28/Variant, Feb 1999; Splitter Chrome Edition 2.50
- ❑29, Mar 1999 2.50
- ❑29/Variant, Mar 1999; Infinity Edition Cardstock Cover 5.00
- ❑30, Apr 1999 2.50
- ❑31, May 1999 2.50
- ❑32, Jul 1999 2.50
- ❑32/Variant, Jul 1999; Sultry Lingerie Foil Edition; Wizard World Chicago 2005; TopCow/Jay Company 15.00
- ❑33, Aug 1999 2.50
- ❑34, Sep 1999 2.50
- ❑35, Oct 1999 2.50
- ❑36, Dec 1999 2.50
- ❑36/Variant, Dec 1999; wraparound variant cover 2.50
- ❑37, Feb 2000 2.50
- ❑38, Mar 2000 2.50
- ❑39, May 2000 2.50
- ❑40, Jun 2000 2.50
- ❑40/A, Jun 2000; alternate cover 2.50
- ❑40/Ashcan, Jun 2000; 5000 printed;Pittsburgh Convention Preview 2.50
- ❑41, Jul 2000 2.50
- ❑41/A, Jul 2000; e-Wanted alternate cover (Pezzini sitting) 9.99
- ❑42, Sep 2000; Regular Cover 2.50
- ❑43, Nov 2000 2.50
- ❑44, Jan 2001 2.50
- ❑45, Mar 2001 2.50
- ❑45/Variant, Mar 2001 2.50
- ❑46, May 2001 2.50
- ❑47, Jun 2001 2.50
- ❑48, Jul 2001 2.50
- ❑49, Aug 2001 2.50
- ❑50, Sep 2001; Giant-size; wraparound cover 4.95
- ❑50/Dynamic, Sep 2001; DFE alternate cover 14.99
- ❑50/Autographed, Sep 2001; DFE Signed alternate cover 29.99
- ❑50/Silvestri, Sep 2001; Silvestri cover 4.95
- ❑50/Keown, Sep 2001; Dale Keown, D-Tron, Steve Firchow cover 4.95
- ❑50/Turner, Sep 2001; Michael Turner, D-Tron, Steve Firchow cover 5.00
- ❑51, Oct 2001 2.50
- ❑52, Nov 2001 2.50
- ❑53, Dec 2001 2.50
- ❑54, Jan 2002; Double cover 2.50
- ❑54/Dynamic, Jan 2002; Virgin cover; Includes certificate of authenticity 2.50
- ❑55, Feb 2002 2.50
- ❑56, Jun 2002; Includes preview of Battle of the Planets #1 2.50
- ❑57, Aug 2002; Cover by Francis Manapull, Jason Gorder, Steve Firchow 2.50
- ❑58, Sep 2002 2.50

❑59, Oct 2002; Endgame Prelude........... 2.50
❑60, Nov 2002 .... 2.99
❑61, Feb 2002 .... 2.99
❑62, Mar 2003 .... 2.99
❑63, May 2003 .... 2.99
❑64, Jun 2003 .... 2.99
❑65, Jun 2003 .... 2.99
❑66, Jun 2003 .... 2.99
❑67, Aug 2003 .... 2.99
❑67/Manga, Aug 2003; Manga-style cover 2.99
❑68, Sep 2003 .... 2.99
❑69, Sep 2003 .... 2.99
❑70, Oct 2003 .... 2.99
❑71, Nov 2003 .... 2.99
❑72, Dec 2003 .... 2.99
❑73, Feb 2004 .... 2.99
❑73/Variant, Feb 2004 .... 2.99
❑74, May 2004 .... 2.99
❑75, Apr 2004 .... 4.99
❑75/Variant, Apr 2004; New Dimension Comics Exclusive cover 4.99
❑76, Jul 2004 .... 2.99
❑77, Aug 2004 .... 2.99
❑78, Sep 2004; Tony Daniel Cover 2.99
❑78/Variant, Sep 2004; Greg Land Cover 2.99
❑79, Oct 2004 .... 2.99
❑80, Nov 2004 .... 2.99
❑80/Holiday, Nov 2004; Offered through Top Cow. Variant cover. A total of 1,000 copies made 5.00
❑80/Cho, Nov 2004; Michael Choi cover 2.99
❑80/Land, Nov 2004; Frank Cho cover... 2.99
❑80/Conv, Nov 2004; Holiday special; Free reader copy.................................. 5.00
❑81, Jan 2005, Indicia misprints publication date as January 2004....... 2.99
❑82, Feb 2005 .... 2.99
❑83, Mar 2005 .... 2.99
❑84, Apr 2005 .... 2.99
❑85, ca. 2005 .... 2.99
❑86, Jul 2005, AH! Cover........................ 2.99
❑87, Aug 2005 .... 2.99
❑87/Variant, Aug 2005 .... 2.99
❑88, Sep 2005 .... 2.99
❑89, Oct 2005 .... 2.99
❑90, Nov 2005 .... 2.99
❑91, Dec 2005 .... 2.99
❑92, Dec 2005, 10th Anniversary Edition; O: Witchblade; Giant-size 4.99
❑93, Jan 2006 .... 2.99
❑94, Feb 2006 .... 2.99
❑95, Mar 2006 .... 2.99
❑96, Apr 2006, Cover by Terry Dodson.. 2.99
❑97, May 2006 .... 2.99
❑98, Jun 2006, Cover by Tyler Kirkham . 2.99
❑99, Jul 2006 .... 2.99
❑100/Turner, Jul 2006 .... 4.99
❑100/Choi, Jul 2006 .... 4.99
❑100/Silvestri, Jul 2006 .... 4.99
❑100/Linsner, Jul 2006 .... 4.99
❑100/Anime, Sep 2006 .... 4.99
❑101, Oct 2006 .... 2.99
❑102, Jan 2007 .... 2.99
❑500, ca. 1998; Limited edition foil cover; Given away as premium for subscription to Wizard 5.00
❑Deluxe 1; Deluxe Collected Edition; Collects Witchblade #1-8.................... 24.95
❑Deluxe 2, Oct 2000; Revelations Collected Edition; Collects Witchblade #9-17 .... 24.95
❑Deluxe 3, Oct 2000; Prevailing; Collects Witchblade #20-25 .... 24.95

Witchblade/Dark Minds: Return of Paradox
Image

❑1, ca. 2004 .... 9.99

Witchblade/Aliens/ The Darkness/Predator
Dark Horse

❑1, Nov 2000 .... 2.99
❑2, Dec 2000 .... 2.99
❑3, Jan 2001 .... 2.99

Witchblade: Animated One Shot
Image

❑1, Aug 2003 .... 2.99

Witchblade: Blood Oath
Image

❑1, Aug 2004 .... 4.99

Witchblade/Darkchylde
Image

❑1, Sep 2000 .... 2.50

Witchblade/Darkness Special
Image

❑½/Platinum, Sep 2000; Promotional giveaway when applying for Wizard credit card; Platinum logo edition 35.00
❑1, Dec 1999 .... 3.95

Witchblade: Destiny's Child
Image

❑1, May 2000 .... 2.95
❑2, Jul 2000 .... 2.95
❑3, Sep 2000 .... 2.95

Witchblade/Elektra
Marvel

❑1, Mar 1997; crossover with Image; continues in Elektra/Cyblade #1 .... 2.95
❑1/AmEnt, Mar 1997; American Entertainment Edition; Cover by Benitez, Aaron Sowd, Team-Tron, JD Smith 5.00

Witchblade Gallery
Image

❑1, Nov 2000 .... 2.95

Witchblade Infinity
Image

❑1, May 1999 .... 3.50

Witchblade/Lady Death
Image

❑1, Nov 2001 .... 4.95

Witchblade/Lady Death Special
Image

❑1, Sep 2003 .... 0.00

Witchblade: Movie Edition
Image

❑1/C, Aug 2000; Witchblade.com Exclusive cover (standing in alley) 2.50
❑1/B, Aug 2000; Witchblade.com Exclusive Holofoil cover (standing in alley, holofoil) 2.50
❑1/A, Aug 2000; Dynamic Forces photo cover (like #1, but with DF logo) 2.50
❑1, Aug 2000 .... 2.50

Witchblade: Nottingham
Image

❑1, Mar 2003 .... 4.99

Witchblade: Obakemono
Image

❑1, Jul 2002 .... 9.95

Witchblade Origin
Image

❑1/AmEnt, Oct 1997; American Entertainment Edition 3.00

Witchblade 10th Anniversary Cover Gallery
Image

❑1, Dec 2005, b&w 2.99

Witchblade/Tomb Raider
Image

❑½, Jul 2000, Women shooting guns to the right on cover 5.00
❑1/A, Dec 1998, Bedroom bikini cover .. 4.00
❑1/B, Dec 1998, alternate cover (white background) 5.00
❑1/C, Dec 1998, Croft standing on top of Pezzini with guns crossed on cover ... 7.00

Witchblade & Tomb Raider
Image

❑1 2005 .... 2.99

Witchblade/Wolverine
Image

❑1, Apr 2004 .... 2.99

Witchcraft
DC / Vertigo

❑1, Jun 1994, covers form triptych........ 2.95
❑2, Jul 1994, Sex, violence-recommended for mature readers...... 2.95
❑3, Aug 1994 .... 2.95

Witchcraft: La Terreur
DC / Vertigo

❑1, Apr 1998; covers form triptych........ 2.50
❑2, May 1998; covers form triptych....... 2.50
❑3, Jun 1998; covers form triptych........ 2.50

Witches
Marvel

❑1, Aug 2004 .... 2.99
❑2, Aug 2004 .... 2.99
❑3, Sep 2004; Stargate: Atlantis poster inserted 2.99
❑4, Sep 2004 .... 2.99

Witches' Cauldron: The Battle of the Cherkassy Pocket
Heritage Collection

❑1, b&w; NN; b&w 3.50

Witchfinder
Image

❑1, Sep 1999; Man with torch on cover facing forward 2.95
❑1/A, Sep 1999; Witchfinder posed before Celtic Knot 2.95
❑1/B, Sep 1999; alternate cover 2.95
❑2, Nov 1999; Witchfinder and woman running in woods 2.95

Witch Hunter
Malibu / Ultraverse

❑1, Apr 1996; 1&O: Witch Hunter.......... 2.50

Witching
DC / Vertigo

❑1, Aug 2004 .... 2.95
❑2, Sep 2004 .... 2.95
❑3, Oct 2004 .... 2.95
❑4, Nov 2004 .... 2.95
❑5, Dec 2004 .... 2.95
❑6, Jan 2005 .... 2.95
❑7, Feb 2005 .... 2.95
❑8, Mar 2005 .... 2.95
❑9, Apr 2005 .... 2.95
❑10, May 2005, Final issue 2.95

Witching Hour
DC

❑1, Mar 1969, NC (c); ATh (a)................ 150.00
❑2, May 1969, NC (c); DG (a) 70.00
❑3, Jul 1969, NC (c); ATh, BWr, DG (a); Prologue by Alex Toth; Epilogue by Mike Sekowsky and Dick Giordano 50.00
❑4, Sep 1969, NC (c); ATh (a)................ 25.00
❑5, Nov 1969, NC (c); ATh, BWr, DG (a) 25.00
❑6, Jan 1970, NC (c); ATh, DH (a) 25.00
❑7, Mar 1970, NA, (c); ATh, JAb (a)....... 18.00
❑8, May 1970, NA, (c); ATh (w); ATh, NA, NC (a) 15.00
❑9, Jul 1970, NA, (c); MA, ATh, JAb (a). 15.00
❑10, Sep 1970, NA, (c); GM (w); ATh, GM (a) 15.00
❑11, Nov 1970, NA, NC (c); ATh, GT (a) 15.00
❑12, Jan 1971, NC (c); ATh, GT, GK (a) . 15.00
❑13, Mar 1971, (c); GM, NA (a); 1: Psions 15.00
❑14, May 1971, NA, (c); AW, JJ (a) 10.00
❑15, Jul 1971, NC (c); GM, WW (a)....... 10.00
❑16, Sep 1971, NC (c); JO, GM, TD (a); 52 pages; The Wondrous Witch's Cauldron reprinted from edited version in House of Mystery #174; The Curse of the Cat reprinted from House of Mystery #177 .... 10.00
❑17, Nov 1971, NC, (c); CI, DH, GT (a); 52 pages; Fingers of Fear reprinted from Sensation Comics #109; The Second Life of Simon Steele reprinted from House of Secrets #46 .... 10.00
❑18, Jan 1972, NC (c); JA (w); GT, JK, NC, JA (a); 52 pages; The Face Behind The Mask reprinted from Tales of the Unexpected #13; I Was A Prisoner of the Supernatural reprinted from Tales of the Unexpected #13 .... 10.00
❑19, Mar 1972, NC (c); GT, NC (a); 52 pages; The Four Threads of Doom reprinted from Tales of the Unexpected #12; The Lamp That Changed People! reprinted from House of Mystery #20 10.00
❑20, Apr 1972, NC (c); NR, DH, GT (a); 52 pages; Beware The 13th Guest reprinted from House of Secrets #59; The Diamond Hands of the Sun God reprinted from House of Secrets #8 ... 10.00

❑21, Jun 1972, NC (c); NR, GT, NC, RMo (a); 52 pages; Prisoner of Sorcerers' City reprinted from House of Secrets #42; Designs for Disaster reprinted from House of Secrets #19 .... 10.00
❑22, Aug 1972, NC (c) 10.00
❑23, Sep 1972, NC (c); NR, TD (a) 10.00
❑24, Oct 1972, NC (c); AA (a) 10.00
❑25, Nov 1972, NC (c); JA (a) 10.00
❑26, Dec 1972, NC (c); DD, JAb (a) 10.00
❑27, Jan 1973, NC (c); AA (a) 10.00
❑28, Feb 1973, NC (c) 10.00
❑29, Mar 1973, NC (c) 10.00
❑30, Apr 1973, NC (c) 10.00
❑31, Jun 1973, NC (c); AN (a) 10.00
❑32, Jul 1973, NC (c) 10.00
❑33, Aug 1973, NC (c); AA (a) 10.00
❑34, Sep 1973, NC (c); NR (a) 10.00
❑35, Oct 1973, NC (c) 10.00
❑36, Nov 1973, NC (c) 10.00
❑37, Dec 1973, NC (c) 10.00
❑38, Jan 1974, NC (c); MA, ATh (a); Save The Last Dance For Me; Eternal Hour; The Perfect Surf; The Man With The Stolen Eyes; Brush With Death; Dream Girl; The Demon In The Mirror; The Phantom Ship; Round Trip To The Past; Trail of the Lucky Coin 10.00
❑39, Feb 1974, NC (c) 10.00
❑40, Mar 1974, NC (c); AN (a) 10.00
❑41, Apr 1974, NC (c); AA (a) 10.00
❑42, May 1974, NC (c) 10.00
❑43, Jun 1974, NC (c); AA (a) 10.00
❑44, Jul 1974, NC (c); DP (a) 10.00
❑45, Aug 1974, NC (c); DP, AN (a) 10.00
❑46, Sep 1974, NC (c) 10.00
❑47, Oct 1974, NC (c); AN (a) 10.00
❑48, Nov 1974, NC (c) 10.00
❑49, Dec 1974, NC (c) 10.00
❑50, Jan 1975, NC (c) 10.00
❑51, Feb 1975, NC (c) 10.00
❑52, Mar 1975, NC (c); DP (a) 8.00
❑53, Apr 1975, NR (c) 8.00
❑54, May 1975, (c) 8.00
❑55, Jun 1975 .... 8.00
❑56, Jul 1975 .... 8.00
❑57, Aug 1975 .... 8.00
❑58, Sep 1975, (c) 8.00
❑59, Oct 1975 .... 8.00
❑60, Nov 1975, NC (c) 8.00
❑61, Jan 1976 .... 8.00
❑62, Mar 1976, (c) 8.00
❑63, May 1976 .... 8.00
❑64, Jun 1976, (c) 8.00
❑65, Aug 1976, (c) 8.00
❑66, Nov 1976, (c) 8.00
❑67, Jan 1977 .... 5.00
❑68, Feb 1977, RB (c) 5.00
❑69, Mar 1977, DP (a) 5.00
❑70, Apr 1977 .... 5.00
❑71, May 1977, DP (a) 5.00
❑72, Jul 1977, (c) 5.00
❑73, Sep 1977 .... 5.00
❑74, Oct 1977, (c) 5.00
❑75, Nov 1977 .... 5.00
❑76, Jan 1978 .... 5.00
❑77, Feb 1978 .... 5.00
❑78, Mar 1978 .... 5.00
❑79, Apr 1978 .... 5.00
❑80, May 1978, AA, CS, JAb (a) 5.00
❑81, Jun 1978, PB (a) 5.00
❑82, Jul 1978 .... 5.00
❑83, Aug 1978 .... 5.00
❑84, Sep 1978 .... 5.00
❑85, Oct 1978, (c);Final Issue 5.00

Witching Hour
DC / Vertigo

❑1, Jan 2000 .... 5.95
❑2, Feb 2000 .... 5.95
❑3, Mar 2000 .... 5.95

Witching Hour
Millennium

❑1, ca. 1992 .... 2.50
❑2, ca. 1993, bound-in Talamasca business card 2.50
❑3, ca. 1993 .... 2.50
❑4, ca. 1993 .... 2.50
❑5, Feb 1996 .... 2.50
❑6 .... 2.50
❑7 .... 2.50
❑8 .... 2.50
❑9 .... 2.50
❑10 .... 2.50
❑11 .... 2.50
❑12 .... 2.50
❑13 .... 2.50

Within Our Reach
Star*Reach

❑1; Spider-Man, Concrete, Gift of the Magi; Christmas benefit comic 7.95

Wizard in Training
Upper Deck

❑0, Jan 2002 .... 2.95

Wizard of 4th Street
Dark Horse

❑1, ca. 1987, b&w 2.00
❑2, ca. 1987, b&w; ca. 1988 .... 2.00
❑3 .... 2.00
❑4 .... 2.00
❑5 .... 2.00
❑6 .... 2.00

Wizard of 4th Street
David P. House

❑1 .... 1.50
❑2 .... 1.50
❑3 .... 1.50

Wizard of Time
DPH

❑1 .... 1.50
❑2, Oct 1986 .... 1.50

Wizards of the Last Resort
Blackthorne

❑1, Feb 1987, b&w 1.75
❑2, Apr 1987 .... 1.75
❑3, Jun 1987 .... 1.75
❑4, Aug 1987 .... 1.75

Wizard's Tale
Image

❑1, ca. 1997 .... 19.95
❑1/HC; Hardcover 29.95

WJHC
Wilson Place

❑1, Dec 1998 .... 1.95

Wogglebug
Arrow

❑1, ca. 1988; Dark Oz tie-in one shot 2.75

Wolf & Red
Dark Horse

❑1, Apr 1995; based on Tex Avery cartoons; Droopy back-up 2.50
❑2, May 1995; based on Tex Avery cartoons; Screwball Squirrel back-up. 2.50
❑3, Jun 1995; based on Tex Avery cartoons; Droopy back-up 2.50

Wolff & Byrd, Counselors of the Macabre
Exhibit A

❑1, May 1994 .... 4.00
❑2, Jul 1994 .... 3.00
❑3, Sep 1994 .... 3.00
❑4, Nov 1994 .... 3.00
❑5, Feb 1995 .... 3.00
❑6, Apr 1995 .... 2.50
❑7, Jun 1995 .... 2.50
❑8, Sep 1995 .... 2.50
❑9, Nov 1995 .... 2.50
❑10, Feb 1996 .... 2.50
❑11, Apr 1996 .... 2.50
❑12, Aug 1996; b&w 2.50
❑13, Oct 1996; cover purposely upside down and backwards 2.50
❑14, Jan 1997; Anne Rice parody 2.50
❑15, Mar 1997 .... 2.50
❑16, Jul 1997 BWr, CV (a) 2.50
❑17, Oct 1997; Halloween issue; reprint strips 2.50
❑18, Mar 1998 .... 2.50
❑19, Apr 1998 .... 2.50
❑20, May 1998 .... 2.50
❑21, Nov 1988 .... 2.50
❑22, Feb 1999 .... 2.50
❑23, Aug 1999, b&w; Title becomes Supernatural Law with #24 .... 2.50

Wolff & Byrd, Counselors of the Macabre's Secretary Mavis
Exhibit A

❑1, Aug 1998 .... 2.95
❑2, Apr 1999 .... 2.95
❑3, Jul 2001; Title changes to Supernatural Law Secretary Mavis 3.50
❑4, Jan 2003 .... 3.50

Wolfpack
Marvel

❑1, Aug 1988, O: Wolfpack. 1: Wolfpack 1.00
❑2, Sep 1988 .... 1.00
❑3, Oct 1988 .... 1.00
❑4, Nov 1988 .... 1.00
❑5, Dec 1988 .... 1.00
❑6, Jan 1989 .... 1.00
❑7, Feb 1989 .... 1.00
❑8, Mar 1989 .... 1.00
❑9, Apr 1989 .... 1.00
❑10, May 1989 .... 1.00
❑11, Jun 1989 .... 1.00
❑12, Jul 1989 .... 1.00

Wolf Run: A Known Associates Mystery
Known Associates

❑1, b&w 2.50

Wolph
Blackthorne

❑1, Jul 1987 .... 2.00

Wolverbroad vs. Hobo
Spoof

❑1, Sep 1992, b&w; parody 2.95

Wolverine
Marvel

❑1, Sep 1982, FM, (c); FM (a); A: Mariko 25.00
❑2, Oct 1982, FM, (c); FM (a); 1: Yukio.. .... 18.00
❑3, Nov 1982, FM, (c); FM (a) 17.00
❑4, Dec 1982, FM, (c); FM (a) 16.00

Wolverine
Marvel

❑-1, Jul 1997, A: Sabretooth. A: Carol Danvers. A: Nick Fury. Flashback; Flashback issue 2.00
❑½, ca. 1997, Wizard mail-away edition; Wizard mail-away edition; Promotion from Wizard #75 .... 3.00
❑½/Ltd., ca. 1997, Blue foil 8.00
❑1, Nov 1988, JB, (c); AW, JB (a); 1st Wolverine as Patch; Wolverine pinup 10.00
❑2, Dec 1988, JB, KJ (c); JB, KJ (a); V: Silver Samurai; Wolverine pin-up... .... 6.00
❑3, Jan 1989, AW, JB (c); AW, JB (a); V: Silver Samurai; Wolverine pinup 5.00
❑4, Feb 1989, AW, JB (c); AW, JB (a); A: Roughhouse. V: Roughouse & Bloodscream; Wolverine pinup 5.00
❑5, Mar 1989, AW, JB (c); AW, JB (a); 1: Shotgun I. 1: Harriers. 1: Battleaxe II. 1: Hardcase; Wolverine pinup 5.00
❑6, Apr 1989, AW, JB (c); AW, JB, TMc (a); A: Roughhouse. V: Roughouse & Bloodscream; Wolverine pinup 4.00
❑7, May 1989, JB, (c); JB (a); A: Hulk. V: Roughouse & Bloodscream 5.00
❑8, Jun 1989, JB, (c); JB, RL (a); A: Hulk. V: Roughouse & Bloodscream; Wolverine pinup 5.00
❑9, Jul 1989, GC, JB (c); PD (w); MW, GC (a); Wolverine pinup 5.00
❑10, Aug 1989, BSz (c); BSz, JB (a); V: Sabretooth 8.00
❑11, Sep 1989, KN (c); PD (w); BSz, JB (a); New Costume 4.00
❑12, Sep 1989, KN (c); PD (w); BSz, JB (a) 4.00
❑13, Oct 1989, KN (c); PD (w); BSz, JB (a) 4.00
❑14, Oct 1989, KN (c); PD (w); BSz, JB (a) 4.00
❑15, Nov 1989, KN (c); PD (w); BSz, JB (a) 5.00
❑16, Nov 1989, KN (c); PD (w); BSz, JB (a) 4.00
❑17, Nov 1989, JBy (c); JBy, KJ (a); V: Roughouse & Bloodscream 4.00
❑18, Dec 1989, JBy (c); JBy, KJ (a); V: Roughouse 4.00
❑19, Dec 1989, JBy (c); JBy, KJ (a); A: Tiger Shark. Acts of Vengeance 4.00
❑20, Jan 1990, JBy (c); JBy, KJ (a); A: Tiger Shark. Acts of Vengeance 5.00
❑21, Feb 1990, JBy, (c); JBy, KJ (a); A: Geist 4.00

Other grades: Multiply price above by 5/6 for VF/NM • 2/3 for VERY FINE • 1/3 for FINE • 1/5 for VERY GOOD • 1/8 for GOOD

N-MINT

❑22, Mar 1990, JBy (c); JBy, KJ (a); A: Geist 4.00
❑23, Apr 1990, JBy (c); JBy (a); A: Geist 4.00
❑24, May 1990, JLee (c); PD (w); GC (a); V: Snow Queen 3.00
❑25, Jun 1990, JLee (c); JB (a) 3.00
❑26, Jul 1990, KJ (c); TP, KJ (a) 3.00
❑27, Jul 1990, JLee (c); JB, DGr (a) 3.00
❑28, Aug 1990 .... 3.00
❑29, Aug 1990, KJ (c); AM (a) 3.00
❑30, Sep 1990, AM (c) 3.00
❑31, Sep 1990, DGr (c); DGr (a); V: Yakuza 2.50
❑32, Oct 1990, DGr (c); DGr (a); A: Jean Grey. V: Yakuza 2.50
❑33, Nov 1990, DGr (c); DGr (a); V: Yakuza 2.50
❑34, Dec 1990, DGr (c); DGr (a) 2.50
❑35, Jan 1991, DGr (c); DGr (a); A: Lady Deathstrike. V: Lady Deathstrike 2.50
❑36, Feb 1991, DGr (a); A: Lady Deathstrike 2.50
❑37, Mar 1991, DGr (c); DGr (a); A: Lady Deathstrike. V: Lady Deathstrike; First appearance of Albert and Elsie Dee 2.50
❑38, Apr 1991, DGr (c); DGr (a); A: Storm 2.50
❑39, May 1991, DGr (c); DGr (a); A: Storm 2.50
❑40, Jun 1991, DGr (a) 2.50
❑41, Jul 1991, DGr (c); DGr (a); A: Sabretooth. A: Cable. V: Sabretooth 4.00
❑41/2nd, Jul 1991, A: Sabretooth. Gold cover 1.75
❑42, Jul 1991, DGr (c); DGr (a); A: Sabretooth. A: Nick Fury. A: Cable. V: Sabretooth 2.00
❑42/2nd, Jul 1991, A: Sabretooth. A: Nick Fury. A: Cable. Gold cover 3.50
❑43, Aug 1991, DGr (a); A: Sabretooth .. 3.00
❑44, Aug 1991, (c); PD (w); AM (a) 2.00
❑45, Sep 1991, DGr (c); DGr (a); V: Sabretooth, Lady Deathstrike, Hunter in Darkness 2.50
❑46, Sep 1991, DGr (a); V: Sabretooth, Lady Deathstrike, Hunter in Darkness; V: Lady Deathstrike 2.50
❑47, Oct 1991 .... 2.50
❑48, Nov 1991, DGr (c); DGr (a); Weapons X sequel: Logan's past 2.50
❑49, Dec 1991, DGr (a); Weapons X sequel: Logan's past 2.50
❑50, Jan 1992, (c); DGr, TP (a); 1: Shiva. diecut cover 4.00
❑51, Feb 1992, DGr (a); A: Mystique 2.00
❑52, Mar 1992, DGr (c); DGr (a); A: Spiral. V: Mojo 2.00
❑53, Apr 1992, DGr (c); DGr, KJ (a); A: Mojo. V: Mojo 2.00
❑54, May 1992, A: Shatterstar 2.00
❑55, Jun 1992, (c); DGr (a); A: Cylla 2.00
❑56, Jul 1992, DGr (c); DGr (a); A: Cylla. V: Cylla, The Hand; V: Cylla; V: The Hand 2.00
❑57, Jul 1992, DGr (c); AM, DGr (a); D: Mariko Yashida; V: Cylla, The Hand; V: Cylla; V: The Hand 3.00
❑58, Aug 1992, A: Terror. V: Monkeywrench 2.00
❑59, Aug 1992, A: Terror 2.00
❑60, Sep 1992, DGr (c); A: Sabretooth. Versus, The Hand, Shiva Vs. Sabretooth; V: The Hand; Shiva V: Sabretooth 2.00
❑61, Sep 1992, A: Sabretooth 2.00
❑62, Oct 1992, A: Sabretooth. Weapon X Project Team Unravels Past 2.00
❑63, Nov 1992, A: Sabretooth. Weapon X Project Team Unravels Past; V: Ferro.. 2.00
❑64, Dec 1992, A: Sabretooth. D: Silver Fox. D: Silver Fox; Weapon X Project Team Unravels Past 2.00
❑65, Jan 1993, Silver Fox Death Aftermath 2.00
❑66, Feb 1993, Silver Fox Death Aftermath 2.00
❑67, Mar 1993 .... 2.00
❑68, Apr 1993 .... 2.00
❑69, May 1993, (c); V: Sauron; V: Mutates; In Savage Land 2.00
❑70, Jun 1993 .... 2.00
❑71, Jul 1993, KJ (c);V: Sauron; V: Mutates; In Savage Land 2.00
❑72, Aug 1993, A: Sentinel 2.00
❑73, Sep 1993, A: Sentinel 2.00
❑74, Oct 1993, A: Jubilee. A: Sentinel 2.00
❑75, Nov 1993, DGr (a); hologram; Wolverine loses adamantium skeleton 4.00

N-MINT

❑76, Dec 1993, AM (a); A: Lady Deathstrike 2.00
❑77, Jan 1994, A: Lady Deathstrike 2.00
❑78, Feb 1994, D: Cylla. D: Bloodscream; V: Cylla; V: Bloodscream 2.00
❑79, Mar 1994 .... 2.00
❑80, Apr 1994, AM (c); AM (a) 8.00
❑81, May 1994 .... 2.00
❑82, Jun 1994, JKu, BMc (a); V: the Hand 2.00
❑83, Jul 1994, V: Hunter in Darkness 2.00
❑84, Aug 1994, AM, TP (a); V: Hunter in Darkness 2.00
❑85, Sep 1994 .... 2.50
❑85/Variant, Sep 1994, enhanced cover 3.50
❑86, Oct 1994, (c) 2.00
❑87, Nov 1994, DGr (a) 1.50
❑87/Deluxe, Nov 1994, Deluxe edition ... 4.00
❑88, Dec 1994, V: Deadpool 1.50
❑88/Deluxe, Dec 1994, Deluxe edition; V: Deadpool 4.00
❑89, Jan 1995 .... 1.50
❑89/Deluxe, Jan 1995, Deluxe edition.... 4.00
❑90, Feb 1995, DGr (a); V: Sabretooth... 1.50
❑90/Deluxe, Feb 1995, Deluxe edition; Wrap around cover; V: Sabretooth 4.00
❑91, Jul 1995 .... 2.00
❑92, Aug 1995, DGr (a) 2.00
❑93, Sep 1995, DGr (a); V: Juggernaut.. 2.00
❑94, Oct 1995, AM (a); A: Generation X. V: Token 2.00
❑95, Nov 1995, DGr (a); A: Vindicator ... 2.00
❑96, Dec 1995, DGr (a); D: Cyber 2.00
❑97, Jan 1996, DGr (a); V: Chimera 2.00
❑98, Feb 1996, (c); AM (a) 2.00
❑99, Mar 1996, DGr (a) 4.00
❑100, Apr 1996, DGr (a) 5.00
❑100/Variant, Apr 1996, enhanced cardstock cover with hologram 7.50
❑101, May 1996, DGr (c) 2.00
❑102, Jun 1996, DGr (c); DGr (a) 2.00
❑103, Jul 1996, A: Elektra. 40 pages 2.00
❑104, Aug 1996, (c); A: Elektra. Beginning of Onslaught Impact 1; 40 pages 2.00
❑105, Sep 1996, A: Stick 2.00
❑106, Oct 1996, AM (a); A: Elektra 2.00
❑107, Nov 1996, DGr (a); 40 pages 2.00
❑108, Dec 1996, DGr (a); V: the Hand ... 2.00
❑109, Jan 1997, DGr (a); 40 pages 2.00
❑110, Feb 1997, A: Shaman. 40 pages .. 2.00
❑111, Mar 1997, DGr (a); 40 pages 2.00
❑112, Apr 1997, DGr (a); 40 pages 2.00
❑113, May 1997, V: Killer Mime; 40 pages 2.00
❑114, Jun 1997, V: Deathstrike 2.00
❑115, Aug 1997, gatefold summary; (c); Operation Zero Tolerance 2.00
❑116, Sep 1997, gatefold summary; (c); Operation Zero Tolerance 2.00
❑117, Oct 1997, gatefold summary; (c); A: Jubilee. Operation Zero Tolerance .. 2.00
❑118, Nov 1997, gatefold summary; (c); A: Jubilee. Operation Zero Tolerance Epilogue 2.00
❑119, Dec 1997, gatefold summary; (c); V: White Ghost 2.00
❑120, Jan 1998, gatefold summary; (c); V: White Ghost 2.00
❑121, Feb 1998, (c); V: White Ghost 2.00
❑122, Mar 1998, gatefold summary; (c);V: White Ghost; Gatefold summary 2.00
❑123, Apr 1998, gatefold summary; (c); BSz (a); V: Roughhouse; V: Bloodscream 2.00
❑124, May 1998, gatefold summary; BSz (a); A: Captain America 2.00
❑125, Jun 1998, gatefold summary; A: Lady Hydra. wraparound cover 3.50
❑125/A, Jun 1998, DFE alternate cover.. 10.00
❑125/B, Jun 1998, DFE alternate cover.. 10.00
❑126, Jul 1998, gatefold summary; V: Lady Hydra. V: Sabretooth 1.99
❑127, Aug 1998, gatefold summary; V: Sabretooth 1.99
❑128, Sep 1998, gatefold summary; A: Shadow Cat. A: Viper. V: Sabretooth 1.99
❑129, Oct 1998, gatefold summary; (c); V: Wendigo 1.99
❑130, Nov 1998, gatefold summary; (c);V: Wendigo; Gatefold summary 1.99

N-MINT

❑131, Nov 1998, gatefold summary; (c); Letterer's error resulted in ethnic slur appearing (out of context, clearly unintentional) on page 6; issue recalled but copies did reach circulation 5.00
❑131/A, Nov 1998, Corrected edition 3.00
❑132, Dec 1998, gatefold summary 1.99
❑133, Jan 1999, gatefold summary; EL (w); A: Warbird. V: Powerhouse 1.99
❑133/Variant, Jan 1999 .... 4.00
❑134, Feb 1999, gatefold summary; EL (w); V: Everybody 1.99
❑135, Feb 1999, EL (w); A: Starjammers. A: Aria 1.99
❑136, Mar 1999, EL (w); V: Collector 1.99
❑137, Apr 1999, EL (w); A: Starjammers. A: Collector 1.99
❑138, May 1999, (c); EL (w); A: Galactus. V: Galactus 1.99
❑139, Jun 1999, EL (w); A: Cable. V: Arnim Zola 1.99
❑140, Jul 1999, EL (w); A: Nightcrawler. V: Solo. V: Cardiac 1.99
❑141, Aug 1999, EL (w); Emma Frost appearance 1.99
❑142, Sep 1999, (c); EL (w) 1.99
❑143, Oct 1999, EL (w); wraparound cover 1.99
❑144, Nov 1999, EL (w); A: The Leader. V: the Leader 1.99
❑145, Dec 1999, EL (w); A: Hulk. V: Incredible Hulk; V: Sabretooth; V: Hulk 4.00
❑145/Gold foil, Dec 1999 .... 25.00
❑145/DF, Dec 1999 .... 50.00
❑145/Silver foil, Dec 1999 .... 30.00
❑145/Nabisco, Dec 1999, Rare Nabisco variant; mail-in offer, fewer than 2,500 in circulation; cover reads "Limited Edition" 400.00
❑146, Jan 2000, EL (w); V: Kitty Pryde .. 5.00
❑147, Feb 2000, EL (w); V: Archangel 2.25
❑148, Mar 2000, EL (c); EL (w); Ages of Apocalypse 2.25
❑149, Apr 2000, EL (w); V: Reanimator . 2.25
❑150, May 2000, Giant-size; A: Nova 2.99
❑150/Dynamic, May 2000, Dynamic Forces chromium variant; no "Revolution" logo 14.00
❑151, Jun 2000 .... 2.25
❑152, Jul 2000 .... 2.25
❑153, Aug 2000 .... 2.25
❑154, Sep 2000, RL (c); RL (w); RL (a). 2.25
❑155, Oct 2000, RL (c); RL (w); RL (a); A: Deadpool. Siryn regains voice 2.25
❑156, Nov 2000, RL (w); A: Spider-Man 2.25
❑157, Dec 2000, RL (c); RL (w); A: Mole Man. V: Carver 2.25
❑158, Jan 2001, polybagged with Marvel Online CD-ROM 2.25
❑159, Feb 2001, V: T & A; V: Blok; Versus 2.25
❑160, Mar 2001, V: Mr. X 2.25
❑161, Apr 2001, V: Mr. X 2.25
❑162, May 2001 .... 2.25
❑163, Jun 2001, V: Shiver 2.25
❑164, Jul 2001 .... 2.25
❑165, Aug 2001, (c); V: Mauvais 2.25
❑166, Sep 2001, Weapon X Origin flashback art by Barry Windsor-Smith 3.00
❑166/A, Sep 2001, DFE Signed, limited edition; DFE Signed 39.99
❑167, Oct 2001 .... 2.25
❑168, Nov 2001, V: Mr. X 2.25
❑169, Dec 2001 .... 2.25
❑170, Jan 2002, V: Mauvais 2.25
❑171, Feb 2002, 'Nuff Said (silent issue) 2.25
❑172, Mar 2002, A: Alpha Flight 2.25
❑173, Apr 2002, A: Lady Deathstrike. wraparound cover 2.25
❑174, May 2002, wraparound cover 2.25
❑175, Jun 2002, A: Sabretooth. wraparound cover 2.25
❑176, Jul 2002, wraparound cover 2.25
❑177, Aug 2002, wraparound cover 2.25
❑178, Aug 2002, wraparound cover 2.25
❑179, Sep 2002, wraparound cover 2.25
❑180, Oct 2002, wraparound cover 2.25
❑181, Nov 2002, TP (a); wraparound cover 2.25
❑182, Dec 2002, TP (a); wraparound cover 2.25
❑183, Jan 2003, TP (a); A: Lady Deathstrike. wraparound cover 2.25

Other grades: Multiply price above by 5/6 for VF/NM • 2/3 for VERY FINE • 1/3 for FINE • 1/5 for VERY GOOD • 1/8 for GOOD

❑184, Feb 2003, TP (a); wraparound cover 2.25
❑185, Mar 2003, TP (a); wraparound cover 2.25
❑186, Apr 2003, A: The Punisher 2.25
❑187, May 2003 2.25
❑188, May 2003 2.25
❑189, Jun 2003, wraparound cover 2.25
❑Ann 1995, Sep 1995 3.95
❑Ann 1996, Oct 1996, (c); JPH (w); V: Red Ronin. wraparound cover 2.95
❑Ann 1997, ca. 1997, gatefold summary; wraparound cover 2.99
❑Ann 1999, ca. 1999, A: Deadpool 3.50
❑Ann 2000, ca. 2000 3.50
❑Ann 2001, ca. 2001 2.99
❑Special 1, Win 1999; Blue Print edition; Winter Special 4.00

Wolverine
Marvel

❑1, Jul 2003 7.00
❑2, Jul 2003 5.00
❑3, Aug 2003 4.00
❑4, Aug 2003 3.00
❑5, Nov 2003 3.00
❑6, Dec 2003, TP (a) 2.99
❑7, Jan 2004 2.99
❑8, Jan 2004 2.99
❑9, Feb 2004 2.99
❑10, Mar 2004 2.25
❑11, Apr 2004 2.99
❑12, May 2004, TP (a) 2.99
❑13, Jun 2004 2.99
❑14, Jun 2004 2.99
❑15, Jul 2004, (c); TP (a) 2.99
❑16, Aug 2004 2.25
❑17, Sep 2004 2.99
❑18, Oct 2004 2.25
❑19, Nov 2004, Sabretooth appearance 2.25
❑20, Dec 2004 2.25
❑20/Variant, Dec 2004, Retailer incentive 90.00
❑20/Texas 2004, Wizard World Texas giveaway 20.00
❑21, Jan 2005 2.25
❑22, Jan 2005 2.25
❑23, Feb 2005 2.25
❑24, Mar 2005 2.25
❑25, Apr 2005; D: Northstar at Wolverine's hands 2.25
❑26, Jan 2005; Greg Land cover 2.25
❑26/Silvestri, Jan 2005; Mark Silvestri cover; supplied to retailers at 1:15 regular copies of #26; Part 1 (of 6) 15.00
❑26/DF, Jan 2005; Signed by John Romita Sr., initially offered at $10, then priced at $49.99 20.00
❑27 2005 2.25
❑27/Quesada 2005 25.00
❑28 2005 2.25
❑29 2005 2.25
❑30, Sep 2005 2.50
❑31, Oct 2005 2.50
❑32 2005 2.50
❑33 2005 2.50
❑34 2.50
❑35, Dec 2005 2.50
❑36, Jan 2006 5.00
❑36/Quesada, Jan 2006 12.00
❑37, Feb 2006 2.50
❑38, Mar 2006 2.99
❑39, May 2006 2.50
❑40, Jun 2006 2.99
❑41, Jul 2006 2.99
❑42, Aug 2006 12.00
❑43, Sep 2006 2.99
❑44, Oct 2006 2.99
❑45, Nov 2006 2.99
❑46, Nov 2006 2.99
❑47, Dec 2006 2.99
❑48, Dec 2006 2.99
❑49, Jan 2007 2.99
❑50, Feb 2007 3.99
❑51 3.99
❑52 3.99
❑53 3.99
❑54 3.99
❑55 3.99
❑56 3.99
❑57 3.99
❑58 3.99
❑59 3.99
❑60 3.99
❑61 3.99
❑62 3.99
❑63 3.99
❑64 3.99
❑65 3.99
❑66 3.99
❑67 3.99
❑68 3.99
❑69 3.99
❑70 3.99
❑71 3.99
❑72 3.99
❑73 3.99
❑74 3.99

Wolverine and the Punisher: Damaging Evidence
Marvel

❑1, Oct 1993 2.00
❑2, Nov 1993 2.00
❑3, Dec 1993 2.00

Wolverine Battles the Incredible Hulk
Marvel

❑1, ca. 1989; reprints Incredible Hulk #180 and #181 4.95

Wolverine: Black Rio
Marvel

❑1, Nov 1998 5.99

Wolverine: Blood Hungry!
Marvel

❑1, ca. 1993; reprint stories 6.95
❑1/2nd, Mar 2002; Reprints from Marvel Comics Presents #85-92 6.95

Wolverine: Bloodlust
Marvel

❑1, Dec 1990; NN 4.95

Wolverine: Bloody Choices
Marvel

❑1, ca. 1993; ca 1991, Large Format Graphic Novel 7.95

Wolverine/Captain America
Marvel

❑1, Apr 2004 4.00
❑2, Apr 2004 2.99
❑3, Apr 2004, (c) 2.99
❑4, Apr 2004 2.99

Wolverine: Days of Future Past
Marvel

❑1, Dec 1997, gatefold summary; Wolverine in early 21st century 2.50
❑2, Jan 1998; gatefold summary; Wolverine in early 21st century 2.50
❑3, Feb 1998; gatefold summary; Wolverine in early 21st century 2.50

Wolverine: Doombringer
Marvel

❑1, Nov 1997 5.99
❑1/Variant; foil cover 14.95

Wolverine/Doop
Marvel

❑1, Jul 2003 2.99
❑2, Jul 2003 2.99

Wolverine/Gambit: Victims
Marvel

❑1, Sep 1995; enhanced cardstock cover 2.95
❑2, Oct 1995; enhanced cardstock cover 2.95
❑3, Nov 1995; enhanced cardstock cover 2.95
❑4, Dec 1995; enhanced cardstock cover 2.95

Wolverine: Global Jeopardy
Marvel

❑1, Dec 1993, Embossed cover 2.95

Wolverine/Hulk
Marvel

❑1, Apr 2002 3.50
❑2, May 2002 3.50
❑3, Jun 2002 3.50
❑4, Jul 2002 3.50

Wolverine: Knight of Terra
Marvel

❑1, Aug 1995, Prestige format 6.95

Wolverine: Netsuke
Marvel

❑1, Nov 2002 3.99
❑2, Dec 2002 3.99
❑3, Jan 2003 3.99
❑4, Feb 2003 3.99

Wolverine and Nick Fury: Scorpio Rising
Marvel

❑1, Oct 1994, Sequel to Wolverine/Nick Fury: The Scorpio Connection; perfect bound 4.95

Wolverine: Origins
Marvel

❑1, Jun 2006, Wolverine and (animal) Wolverine cover 2.99
❑1/Turner, Jun 2006 2.99
❑2, Jul 2006, Joe Quesada cover; V: Nuke 2.99
❑2/Variant, Jul 2006 2.99
❑2/2nd variant, Jul 2006 2.99
❑3, Aug 2006, Joe Quesada cover 2.99
❑3/Variant, Aug 2006 2.99
❑3/2nd variant, Aug 2006 2.99
❑4, Sep 2006, V: Captain America; V: Nuke; Joe Quesada cover 2.99
❑4/Variant, Sep 2006 2.99
❑5, Oct 2006, Joe Quesada cover 2.99
❑5/Variant, Oct 2006 2.99
❑5/Sketch, Oct 2006 2.99
❑6, Nov 2006, Joe Quesada cover 2.99
❑7, Dec 2006, V: Omega Red 2.99
❑8, Jan 2007, Joe Quesada cover 2.99
❑8/Variant, Jan 2007 2.99
❑9, Mar 2007 2.99
❑9/Variant, Mar 2007 2.99
❑10 2.99
❑11 2.99
❑12 2.99
❑13 2.99
❑14 2.99
❑15 2.99
❑16 2.99
❑17 2.99
❑18 2.99
❑19 2.99
❑20 2.99
❑21 2.99
❑22 2.99
❑23 2.99
❑24 2.99
❑25 2.99
❑26 2.99
❑27 2.99
❑28 2.99
❑29 2.99
❑30 2.99
❑31 2.99
❑32 2.99
❑33 2.99
❑34 2.99
❑35 2.99
❑36 2.99
❑37 2.99

Wolverine Poster Magazine
Marvel

❑1, pin-ups 4.95

Wolverine/Punisher
Marvel

❑1, May 2004 2.99
❑2, Jun 2004 2.99
❑3, Jul 2004 2.99
❑4, Aug 2004 2.99
❑5, Oct 2004 2.99

Wolverine/Punisher Revelation
Marvel

❑1, Jun 1999 2.99
❑1/2nd, Apr 2001; 2nd printing 2.99
❑2, Jul 1999 2.99
❑2/2nd, May 2001; 2nd printing 2.99
❑3, Aug 1999 2.99
❑4, Sep 1999 2.99

Wolverine: Rahne of Terra
Marvel

❑1, Aug 1991, prestige format; NN 5.95

Wolverine Saga
Marvel

❑1, Sep 1989 ... 4.00
❑2, Nov 1989 ... 4.00
❑3, Dec 1989 ... 4.00
❑4, Dec 1989 ... 4.00

Wolverine: Save the Tiger!
Marvel

❑1, May 1992, NN; Reprints Wolverine story from Marvel Comics Presents #1-10 ... 2.95

Wolverine: Snikt!
Marvel

❑1, Jul 2003 ... 2.99
❑2, Aug 2003 ... 2.99
❑3, Sep 2003 ... 2.99
❑4, Oct 2003 ... 2.99
❑5, Nov 2003 ... 2.99

Wolverine: Soultaker
Marvel

❑1, May 2005 ... 2.99
❑2, May 2005 ... 2.99
❑3, Jun 2005 ... 2.99
❑4, Jul 2005 ... 2.99
❑5, Aug 2005 ... 2.99

Wolverine: The End
Marvel

❑1, Jan 2004 ... 7.00
❑1/Texas, Jan 2004 ... 15.00
❑2, Mar 2004 ... 6.00
❑3, May 2004 ... 5.00
❑4, Aug 2004 ... 4.00
❑5, Nov 2004 ... 3.00
❑6, Dec 2004 ... 2.99

Wolverine: The Jungle Adventure
Marvel

❑1, ca. 1990, NN ... 4.50

Wolverine: The Origin
Marvel

❑1, Nov 2001; O: Wolverine ... 25.00
❑1/Dynamic, Nov 2001; Dynamic Forces S&N w/ cert ... 50.00
❑2, Dec 2001; O: Wolverine ... 12.00
❑2/Dynamic, Dec 2001; Dynamic Forces S&N w/ cert ... 24.00
❑3, Jan 2002; O: Wolverine ... 8.00
❑3/Dynamic, Jan 2002; Dynamic Forces S&N w/ cert ... 20.00
❑4, Feb 2002; O: Wolverine ... 5.00
❑4/Dynamic, Feb 2002; Dynamic Forces S&N w/ cert ... 20.00
❑5, May 2002; O: Wolverine. O: Sabretooth ... 4.00
❑5/Dynamic, May 2002; Dynamic Forces S&N w/ cert ... 20.00
❑6, Jul 2002; O: Wolverine. O: Sabretooth ... 5.00
❑6/Dynamic, Jul 2002; Dynamic Forces S&N w/ cert ... 20.00
❑Book 1/CS, ca. 2003 ... 14.99
❑Book 1/HC; O: Wolverine. O: Sabretooth; Hardcover (regular) ... 34.95

Wolverine vs. Spider-Man
Marvel

❑1, Mar 1995; collects story arc from Marvel Comics Presents #48-50; cardstock cover ... 3.00

Wolverine/Witchblade
Image

❑1, Mar 1997 ... 4.50
❑1/A, Mar 1997; crossover with Marvel; continues in Witchblade/Elektra ... 2.95

Wolverine: Xisle
Marvel

❑1, Jun 2003 ... 2.50
❑2, Jun 2003 ... 2.50
❑3, Jun 2003 ... 2.50
❑4, Jun 2003 ... 2.50
❑5, Jun 2003 ... 2.50

Women in Fur
Shanda Fantasy Arts

❑2, b&w; Anthology ... 4.50

Women in Rock Special
Revolutionary

❑1, Dec 1993, b&w ... 2.50

Women of Marvel Poster Book
Marvel

❑1, Nov 2006, Book of fold-out pinups.. 4.99

Women on Top
Fantagraphics / Eros

❑1, Jun 1991, b&w; Adult ... 2.25

Wonderland
Arrow

❑1, Sum 1985 ... 2.95
❑2, Feb 1985 ... 2.95
❑3, Apr 1986 ... 2.95

Wonderlanders
Oktomica

❑1, Jan 1999 ... 2.50

Wonder Man
Marvel

❑1, Mar 1986, Poster ... 1.50

Wonder Man
Marvel

❑1, Sep 1991, poster ... 1.50
❑2, Oct 1991, A: West Coast Avengers . 1.25
❑3, Nov 1991, 1: Splice ... 1.25
❑4, Dec 1991 ... 1.25
❑5, Jan 1992, A: Beast ... 1.25
❑6, Feb 1992 ... 1.25
❑7, Mar 1992, A: Rick Jones. Operation Galactic Storm ... 1.25
❑8, Apr 1992, A: Starjammers. Operation Galactic Storm ... 1.25
❑9, May 1992, (c); Operation Galactic Storm ... 1.25
❑10, Jun 1992 ... 1.25
❑11, Jul 1992 ... 1.25
❑12, Aug 1992 ... 1.25
❑13, Sep 1992 ... 1.25
❑14, Oct 1992, Infinity War ... 1.25
❑15, Nov 1992 ... 1.25
❑16, Dec 1992 ... 1.25
❑17, Jan 1993 ... 1.25
❑18, Feb 1993 ... 1.25
❑19, Mar 1993 ... 1.25
❑20, Apr 1993 ... 1.25
❑21, May 1993, A: Splice ... 1.25
❑22, Jun 1993 ... 1.25
❑23, Jul 1993, Covers to Wonder Man #21-24 form quadtych ... 1.25
❑24, Aug 1993 ... 1.25
❑25, Sep 1993, Embossed cover ... 2.95
❑26, Oct 1993, A: Hulk ... 1.25
❑27, Nov 1993, A: Hulk ... 1.25
❑28, Dec 1993, A: Spider-Man ... 1.25
❑29, Jan 1994, A: Spider-Man ... 1.25
❑Ann 1, ca. 1992, KB (w) ... 2.25
❑Ann 2, ca. 1993, trading card ... 2.95

Wonder Man
Marvel

❑1, Feb 2007 ... 2.99

Wonders and Oddities
Dark Horse

❑1, Dec 1988, b&w; NN ... 2.00

Wonder Wart-Hog, Hog of Steel
Rip Off

❑1, b&w; Reprints ... 3.00
❑2, b&w; Reprints ... 2.50
❑3, b&w; Reprints ... 2.50

Wonder Woman
DC

❑126, Nov 1961, RA, (a); 1: Mister Genie ... 70.00
❑127, Jan 1962, (c); RA (a) ... 70.00
❑128, Feb 1962, (c); RA (a); O: Wonder Woman's Invisible Jet ... 70.00
❑129, Apr 1962 ... 70.00
❑130, May 1962, (c); RA (a) ... 70.00
❑131, Jul 1962, (c); RA (a) ... 56.00
❑132, Aug 1962, (c); RA (a); A: Mer-Man ... 56.00
❑133, Oct 1962, (c); RA (a); A: Wonder Family ... 56.00
❑134, Nov 1962, (c); RA (a); A: Wonder Girl ... 56.00
❑135, Jan 1963, (c); RA (a); A: Mer-Boy ... 56.00
❑136, Feb 1963, (c); RA (a) ... 56.00
❑137, Apr 1963, (c); RA (a) ... 56.00
❑138, May 1963, (c); RA (a); A: Wonder Family ... 56.00
❑139, Jul 1963, (c); RA (a) ... 56.00
❑140, Aug 1963, (c); RA (a); A: Mer-Boy ... 56.00
❑141, Oct 1963, (c); RA (a) ... 56.00
❑142, Nov 1963, (c); RA (a); A: Wonder Family ... 56.00
❑143, Jan 1964, (c); RA (a) ... 56.00
❑144, Feb 1964, (c); RA (a) ... 56.00
❑145, Apr 1964, (c); (w); RA (a); A: Wonder Family ... 56.00
❑146, May 1964, (c); RA (a) ... 56.00
❑147, Jul 1964, (c); RA (a) ... 56.00
❑148, Aug 1964, RA, (c); RA (a) ... 56.00
❑149, Oct 1964, (c); RA (a); A: Wonder Family ... 56.00
❑150, Nov 1964, (c); RA (a); A: Bird-Boy ... 50.00
❑151, Jan 1965, RA, (c); RA (a); A: Mer-Boy ... 50.00
❑152, Feb 1965, (c); RA (a); A: Mer-Boy. O: Wonder Woman ... 50.00
❑153, Apr 1965, (c); RA (a); A: Mer-Boy ... 50.00
❑154, May 1965, RA, (c); RA (a); A: Mer-Man ... 50.00
❑155, Jul 1965, (c); RA (a); A: Bird-Man ... 50.00
❑156, Aug 1965, (c); RA (a) ... 50.00
❑157, Oct 1965, (c); RA (a); A: Egg Fu .. 50.00
❑158, Nov 1965, (c); RA (a); A: Egg Fu.. 50.00
❑159, Jan 1966, RA (a); O: Wonder Woman ... 50.00
❑160, Feb 1966, (c); RA (a); A: Cheetah I (Priscilla Rich) ... 30.00
❑161, Apr 1966, (c); RA (a); A: Countess Draska Nishki ... 30.00
❑162, May 1966, (c); RA (a); O: Wonder Woman's Secret Identity ... 40.00
❑163, Jul 1966, (c); RA (a); A: Doctor Psycho ... 30.00
❑164, Aug 1966, (c); RA (a) ... 30.00
❑165, Oct 1966, RA (c); RA (a); A: Doctor Psycho ... 30.00
❑166, Nov 1966, RA (c); RA (a); A: Egg Fu 30.00
❑167, Jan 1967, RA (c); RA (a); Irene Vartanoff L.O.C.; Mark Evanier L.O.C.. 30.00
❑168, Feb 1967, RA (c); RA (a); A: Paula Von Gunta ... 30.00
❑169, Apr 1967, RA (c); RA (a) ... 30.00
❑170, Jun 1967, RA, (c); RA (a) ... 30.00
❑171, Aug 1967, RA (c); RA (a); A: Mouse Man ... 25.00
❑172, Oct 1967, (c) ... 25.00
❑173, Dec 1967, (c) ... 25.00
❑174, Feb 1968, (c) ... 25.00
❑175, Apr 1968, (c) ... 25.00
❑176, Jun 1968, (c) ... 25.00
❑177, Aug 1968, IN (c); JAb (a); A: Supergirl. V: Klamos ... 25.00
❑178, Oct 1968, (c); 1: Mod Diana Prince 25.00
❑179, Dec 1968, (c); 1: Doctor Cyber 25.00
❑180, Feb 1969, (c); D: Steve Trevor 25.00
❑181, Apr 1969, (c); A: Doctor Cyber 33.00
❑182, Jun 1969 ... 33.00
❑183, Aug 1969, (c) ... 33.00
❑184, Oct 1969, (c) ... 33.00
❑185, Dec 1969, (c) ... 33.00
❑186, Feb 1970, (c) ... 33.00
❑187, Apr 1970, (c); A: Doctor Cyber 33.00
❑188, Jun 1970, (c); A: Doctor Cyber 33.00
❑189, Aug 1970, (c) ... 33.00
❑190, Oct 1970, (c) ... 33.00
❑191, Dec 1970, (c) ... 40.00
❑192, Feb 1971, (c); DG (a) ... 40.00
❑193, Apr 1971, (c); DG (a) ... 40.00
❑194, Jun 1971, (c); DG (a) ... 40.00
❑195, Aug 1971 ... 40.00
❑196, Oct 1971, (c); DG (a); A: Cheetah 40.00
❑197, Dec 1971, DG (c); DG (a) ... 40.00
❑198, Feb 1972, DG (c); DG (a); 52 pages 40.00
❑199, Apr 1972, JJ (c); DH, DG (a); A: Jonny Double. Bondage cover; 52 pages ... 40.00
❑200, Jun 1972, JJ (c); DG (a); D: Doctor Cyber. Bondage cover; 52 Pages ... 40.00
❑201, Aug 1972, DG (c); DG (a); A: Catwoman ... 14.00
❑202, Oct 1972, DG (c); DG (a); A: Fafhrd and The Gray Mouser ... 14.00
❑203, Dec 1972, DG (c); DG (a) ... 14.00
❑204, Feb 1973, (c); D: I-Ching ... 14.00
❑205, Apr 1973, (c); BO, DH (a); Suggestive cover ... 14.00
❑206, Jun 1973, (c); DH (a) ... 14.00

❑207, Aug 1973, (c); RE (a) 14.00
❑208, Oct 1973, (c); RE (a); A: Steve Trevor 14.00
❑209, Dec 1973, RE (c); RE (a) 14.00
❑210, Feb 1974, (c); RE (a) 14.00
❑211, Apr 1974, NC (c); RE (a); A: Mer-Boy. 100 pages 25.00
❑212, Jun 1974, (c); CS (a); A: JLA 11.00
❑213, Aug 1974, (c); IN (a); A: Flash 11.00
❑214, Oct 1974, BO (c); CS, RA (a); A: Green Lantern. 100 pages 30.00
❑215, Dec 1974, (c); A: Aquaman 11.00
❑216, Feb 1975, NC (c); A: Black Canary 11.00
❑217, Apr 1975, MGr (c); DD, RA (a); A: Green Arrow 11.00
❑218, Jun 1975, (c); KS (a); A: Red Tornado 11.00
❑219, Aug 1975, DG, (c); CS (a); A: Elongated Man 7.00
❑220, Oct 1975, DG (c); DG (a); A: Atom 7.00
❑221, Dec 1975, CS (a); A: Hawkman 7.00
❑222, Feb 1976, A: Batman 7.00
❑223, Apr 1976, A: Steve Trevor. Return of Steve Trevor 7.00
❑224, Jun 1976, CS (a) 7.00
❑225, Aug 1976 7.00
❑226, Oct 1976, (c) 7.00
❑227, Dec 1976 7.00
❑228, Feb 1977, (c) 7.00
❑229, Mar 1977, JL (c); Begins tales set on Earth Two during World War II 7.00
❑230, Apr 1977, (c); A: Cheetah 7.00
❑231, May 1977, MN (c);Slight crossover with Isis #5 7.00
❑232, Jun 1977, MN (c); MN (a) 7.00
❑233, Jul 1977, GM (c); DH (a) 7.00
❑234, Aug 1977, JL (c); DH (a) 7.00
❑235, Sep 1977, JL (c); A: Doctor Mid-Nite 7.00
❑236, Oct 1977, RB (c) 7.00
❑237, Nov 1977, RB (c); O: Wonder Woman. 1: Kung 6.00
❑238, Dec 1977, RB (c); A: Sandman 6.00
❑239, Jan 1978, RB (c); A: Golden Age Flash 6.00
❑240, Feb 1978, DG, JL (c); A: Golden Age Flash 6.00
❑241, Mar 1978, DG, JSa (c); DG, JSa (a); A: new Spectre. Spectre apperrance 6.00
❑242, Apr 1978, RB (c) 6.00
❑243, May 1978, RB, (c); A: Angle Man 6.00
❑244, Jun 1978, RB (c) 6.00
❑245, Jul 1978, JSa (c) 6.00
❑246, Aug 1978, DG, JSa (c) 6.00
❑247, Sep 1978, RB, DG (c); A: Elongated Man. Tales of the Amazons story 6.00
❑248, Oct 1978, JL (c); D: Steve Trevor; Tales of the Amazons story 6.00
❑249, Nov 1978, RB, DG (c); A: Hawkgirl. Hawkgirl cover/team-up; Tales of the Amazons story 6.00
❑250, Dec 1978, RB, DG (c); 1: Orana (new Wonder Woman) 6.00
❑250/Whitman, Dec 1978, RB, DG (c); 1: Orana (new Wonder Woman). Whitman variant 12.00
❑251, Jan 1979, DG, RA (c); D: Orana (new Wonder Woman) 6.00
❑251/Whitman, Jan 1979, DG, RA (c); Whitman variant 12.00
❑252, Feb 1979, DG, RA (c); 1: Stacy Macklin 6.00
❑252/Whitman, Feb 1979, DG, RA (c); 1: Stacy Macklin. Whitman variant 12.00
❑253, Mar 1979, DG (c) 6.00
❑254, Apr 1979, DG, RA (c); A: Angle Man 6.00
❑255, May 1979, DG (c) 6.00
❑255/Whitman, May 1979, DG (c); Whitman variant 12.00
❑256, Jun 1979, (c) 6.00
❑256/Whitman, Jun 1979, (c); Whitman variant 12.00
❑257, Jul 1979, DG, RA (c); A: Multi-Man 6.00
❑257/Whitman, Jul 1979, DG, RA (c); A: Multi-Man. Whitman variant 12.00
❑258, Aug 1979, DG (c) 6.00
❑258/Whitman, Aug 1979, DG (c); Whitman variant 12.00
❑259, Sep 1979, DG (c); A: Hercules 6.00
❑259/Whitman, Sep 1979, DG (c); A: Hercules. Whitman variant 12.00
❑260, Oct 1979, A: Hercules 6.00
❑260/Whitman, Oct 1979, A: Hercules. Whitman variant 12.00
❑261, Nov 1979, DG (c); A: Hercules 5.00
❑261/Whitman, Nov 1979, DG (c); A: Hercules. Whitman variant 15.00
❑262, Dec 1979, DG (c); RE (a) 5.00
❑262/Whitman, Dec 1979, DG (c); RE (a); Whitman variant 10.00
❑263, Jan 1980, DG (c) 5.00
❑263/Whitman, Jan 1980, DG (c); Whitman variant 15.00
❑264, Feb 1980, DG, RA (c) 5.00
❑264/Whitman, Feb 1980, Whitman variant 10.00
❑265, Mar 1980, DG, RA (c); RE (a); A: Wonder Girl. Wonder Girl backup story 5.00
❑266, Apr 1980, RA, (c); RE (a); Wonder Girl backup story 5.00
❑267, May 1980, DG, RA (c); A: Animal Man. O: Animal Man 5.00
❑268, Jun 1980, DG, RA (c); A: Animal Man 5.00
❑269, Jul 1980, DG, RA (c); WW (a) 4.00
❑270, Aug 1980, RA, (c); A: Steve Trevor 4.00
❑271, Sep 1980, DG, RA (c); JSa (a); A: Huntress. Huntress backup series begins 4.00
❑272, Oct 1980, DG, DC (c); JSa (a); A: Huntress. Huntress story 4.00
❑273, Nov 1980, DG, RA (c); JSa (a); A: Solomon Grundy. Huntress story 4.00
❑274, Dec 1980, RA, (c); JSa (a); 1: Cheetah II (Deborah Domaine); D: Cheetah (Priscilla Rich); Huntress backup story 4.00
❑275, Jan 1981, RB, DG (c); JSa (a); A: Power Girl. Huntress backup story 4.00
❑276, Feb 1981, DG, RA (c); JSa (a); A: Kobra. Huntress backup story 4.00
❑277, Mar 1981, DG, RA (c); JSa (a); A: Kobra. Huntress backup story 4.00
❑278, Apr 1981, DG, RA (c); JSa (a); A: Kobra. Huntress backup story 4.00
❑279, May 1981, DG, RA (c); JSa (a); Huntress backup story 4.00
❑280, Jun 1981, DG, RA (c); JSa (a); A: Etrigan. Huntress backup story 3.00
❑281, Jul 1981, DG, RA (c); JSa (a); A: Joker. Huntress Back-up Story 5.00
❑282, Aug 1981, RB, DG (c); JSa (a); A: Joker. Huntress backup story 5.00
❑283, Sep 1981, GP, DG (c); JSa (a); A: Joker. Huntress backup story 5.00
❑284, Oct 1981, GP, DG (c); JSa (a); A: Earth-2 Robin. Robin and Huntress Back-up Story 2.50
❑285, Nov 1981, GP, (c); JSa (a); A: Earth-2 Robin. Robin and Huntress Back-up Story 2.50
❑286, Dec 1981, DG, RA (c); JSa (a); Huntress backup story 2.50
❑287, Jan 1982, RA, (c); DH, JSa, RT (a); A: New Teen Titans. Huntress backup story 2.50
❑288, Feb 1982, GC, (c); GC, RT (a); 1: The Silver Swan; Continued from DC Comics Presents #41 2.50
❑289, Mar 1982, GC, DG (c); GC, JSa, RT (a); 1: Captain Wonder. O: Dr. Psycho; Huntress backup story 2.50
❑290, Apr 1982, RA, (c); GC, JSa, RT (a); A: Captain Wonder. Huntress backup story 2.50
❑291, May 1982, DG, RA (c); FMc, GC (a); A: Zatanna 2.50
❑292, Jun 1982, DG, RA (c); FMc, GC (a); A: Supergirl 2.50
❑293, Jul 1982,DG, RA (c); FMc, GC (a); A: Raven. A: Starfire 2.50
❑294, Aug 1982, GK (c); FMc, GC, JOy, JSa (a); A: Blockbuster. Huntress backup story 2.50
❑295, Sep 1982, RB (c); FMc, GC, JOy, JSa (a); Huntress backup story 2.50
❑296, Oct 1982, FMc, GC, JOy, JSa (a); Huntress backup story 2.50
❑297, Nov 1982, FMc, GC, JSa, CS (a); 1: Aegeus; Masters of the Universe preview story; Huntress backup story; 1: Blackwing 2.50
❑298, Dec 1982, DG, FM (c); FMc, GC, JSa (a); Huntress backup story 2.50
❑299, Jan 1983, DG (c); FMc, GC, JSa (a); Huntress backup story 2.50
❑300, Feb 1983, Giant-size; DG (c); FMc, RB, GC, KG, JDu, GP, KP, DG, RA (a); A: New Teen Titans. Wrap-around cover; George Perez pinup inside front cover; Mike Kaluta pinup inside back cover; 1: Fury; 300th anniversary issue 6.00
❑301, Mar 1983, DG (c); FMc, GC, DH (a); Huntress backup story 2.50
❑302, Apr 1983, DG (c); FMc, GC (a); Huntress backup story 2.50
❑303, May 1983, GK (c); FMc, GC (a); A: Doctor Polaris. Huntress backup story 2.50
❑304, Jun 1983, GK (c); FMc, GC (a); A: Green Lantern. Huntress backup story 2.50
❑305, Jul 1983, GK (c); FMc, GC (a); 1: Circe (DC); WW pinup by Mike Hernandez and Rick Bryant; Huntress backup story 2.50
❑306, Aug 1983, DG, JL (c); DH (a); A: Aegeus. Huntress backup story 2.50
❑307, Sep 1983, GK (c); DH (a); A: Aegeus. Huntress backup story 2.50
❑308, Oct 1983, DG, RA (c); DH (a); A: Black Canary. Huntress backup story 2.50
❑309, Nov 1983, RA, (c); DH (a); 1: Earthworm; Huntress backup story 2.50
❑310, Dec 1983, DG (c); Huntress backup story 2.50
❑311, Jan 1984, DG, RA (c); DH (a); Huntress backup story; Ad for Superman Peanut Butter (Creamy or Crunchy) 2.50
❑312, Feb 1984, GK (c); DH, DS (a); Huntress backup story 2.50
❑313, Mar 1984, DG (c); DH (a); A: Circe (DC). Huntress backup story 2.50
❑314, Apr 1984, GK (c); DH (a); A: Circe (DC). Huntress backup story 2.50
❑315, May 1984, DG (c); DH (a); A: Tezcatlipoca. Huntress backup story 2.50
❑316, Jun 1984, DH (a); A: Tezcatlipoca. Huntress story 2.50
❑317, Jul 1984, DH (a); Huntress backup story 2.50
❑318, Aug 1984, KB (w); IN (a); Huntress backup story 2.50
❑319, Sep 1984, DH (a); A: Doctor Cyber. Huntress backup story 2.50
❑320, Oct 1984, DH (a); A: Doctor Cyber. Huntress backup story 2.50
❑321, Nov 1984, DH (a); A: Doctor Cyber. Huntress backup story 2.50
❑322, Dec 1984, DH (a); A: Eros 2.50
❑323, Feb 1985, DH (a); A: The Monitor 2.50
❑324, Apr 1985, RT (c); DH (a); A: Atomic Knight 2.50
❑325, May 1985, DH (a); A: Atomic Knight 2.50
❑326, Jul 1985, DH (a) 2.50
❑327, Sep 1985, DH (a); A: Tezcatlipoca. Crisis 2.50
❑328, Dec 1985, DG (c); DH (a); Crisis 2.50
❑329, Feb 1986, Giant-size; JL (c); DH (a); Crisis 2.50

Wonder Woman
DC

❑0, Oct 1994, BB (c); O: The Amazons 6.00
❑1, Feb 1987, GP (c); GP (w); GP (a); O: Wonder Woman (new origin). 1: Ares (DC); Wraparound cover 4.00
❑2, Mar 1987, GP (c); GP (w); GP (a); A: Steve Trevor 3.00
❑3, Apr 1987, GP (c); GP (w); GP (a); 1: Vanessa Kapatelis. 1: Jack Kapatelis. 1: Decay 3.00
❑4, May 1987, GP (c); GP (w); GP (a); 2: Decay 3.00
❑5, Jun 1987, GP, (c); GP (w); GP (a); V: Ares. V: Phobos; V: Deimos 3.00
❑6, Jul 1987, GP (c); GP (w); GP (a); V: Ares 2.50
❑7, Aug 1987, GP (c); GP (w); GP (a); 1: Myndi Mayer; 1: Cheetah (Barbara Minerva) 2.50
❑8, Sep 1987, GP (c); GP (w); GP (a); Legends crossover 2.50
❑9, Oct 1987, GP (c); GP (w); GP (a); 1: Cheetah 2.50
❑10, Nov 1987, GP (c); GP (w); GP (a); gatefold 2.50
❑10/A, Nov 1987, no gatefold; gatefold 2.50
❑11, Dec 1987, GP (c); GP (w); GP (a) 2.00
❑12, Jan 1988, GP (c); GP (w); GP (a); Millennium 2.00

N-MINT

❑13, Feb 1988, GP (c); GP (w); GP (a); Millennium ... 2.00
❑14, Mar 1988, GP (c); GP (w); GP (a); A: Hercules ... 2.00
❑15, Apr 1988, GP (c); GP (w); GP (a); 1: Silver Swan. 1: Ed Indelicato ... 2.00
❑16, May 1988, GP (c); GP (w); GP (a); A: Silver Swan. Continued in Superman #17; Continued in Adventures of Superman #440; Continued in Action Comics #600 ... 2.00
❑17, Jun 1988, GP (c); GP (w); GP, DG (a); 1: Circe ... 2.00
❑18, Jul 1988, GP (c); GP (w); GP, DG (a); A: Circe (DC). Bonus Book ... 2.00
❑19, Aug 1988, GP (c); GP (w); FMc, GP (a); A: Circe (DC). V: Circe ... 2.00
❑20, Sep 1988, GP (c); GP (w); GP, BMc (a); A: Ed Indelicato ... 2.00
❑21, Oct 1988, GP (c); GP (w); GP, BMc (a) 2.00
❑22, Nov 1988, GP (c); GP (w); GP, BMc (a); Continued in Wonder Woman Ann #1; Connected with Who Is Wonder Girl? storyline ... 2.00
❑23, Dec 1988, GP (c); GP (w); GP (a) .. 2.00
❑24, Hol 1988, GP (c); GP (w); GP (a); Hol 1988 ... 2.00
❑25, Jan 1989, GP (c); KG, GP (w); Invasion! ... 2.00
❑26, Jan 1989, GP (c); KG, GP (w); Invasion! ... 2.00
❑27, Feb 1989, GP (c); GP (w) ... 2.00
❑28, Mar 1989, GP (c); GP (w); A: Cheetah. O: Cheetah ... 2.00
❑29, Apr 1989, GP (c); GP (w); O: Cheetah 2.00
❑30, May 1989, GP (c); GP (w); A: Cheetah ... 2.00
❑31, Jun 1989, GP (c); GP (w); A: Cheetah 1.75
❑32, Jul 1989, GP (c); GP (w) ... 1.75
❑33, Aug 1989, GP (c); GP (w) ... 1.75
❑34, Sep 1989, GP (c); GP (w); A: Shim'Tar ... 1.75
❑35, Oct 1989, GP (c); GP (w); A: Shim'Tar ... 1.75
❑36, Nov 1989, GP (c); GP (w) ... 1.75
❑37, Dec 1989, GP (c); GP (w); A: Superman ... 1.75
❑38, Jan 1990, GP (c); GP (w); A: Lois Lane ... 1.75
❑39, Feb 1990, GP (c); GP (w); A: Lois Lane ... 1.75
❑40, Mar 1990, GP (c); GP (w); A: Lois Lane ... 1.75
❑41, Apr 1990, GP (c); GP (w); RT (a) ... 1.75
❑42, May 1990, GP (c); GP (w); RT (a); A: Silver Swan. V: Silver Swan ... 1.75
❑43, Jun 1990, GP (c); GP (w); RT (a); A: Silver Swan. V: Silver Swan ... 1.75
❑44, Jul 1990, GP (c); GP (w); RT (a); A: Silver Swan ... 1.75
❑45, Aug 1990, GP (c); GP (w); RT (a) .. 1.75
❑46, Sep 1990, GP (c); GP (w); RT (a) ... 1.75
❑47, Oct 1990, GP (c); GP (w); RT (a); A: Troia ... 1.75
❑48, Nov 1990, GP (c); GP (w); RT (a) .. 1.75
❑49, Dec 1990, GP (c); GP (w); A: Princess Diana ... 1.75
❑50, Jan 1991, GP (c); GP, RT (w); MW, SA, BB, CR, KN, RT (a); Giant-size; 50th issue ... 1.75
❑51, Feb 1991, GP (c); GP (w); RT (a); A: Lord Hermes ... 1.50
❑52, Mar 1991, GP (c); GP (w); KN (a) .. 1.50
❑53, Apr 1991, GP (c); GP (w); RT (a); A: Pariah ... 1.50
❑54, May 1991, GP (c); GP (w); RT (a); A: Doctor Psycho ... 1.50
❑55, Jun 1991, GP (c); GP (w); RT (a); A: Doctor Psycho ... 1.50
❑56, Jul 1991, GP (c); GP (w); RT (a) ... 1.50
❑57, Aug 1991, (c); GP (w); RT (a) ... 1.50
❑58, Sep 1991, GP (c); GP (w); RT (a); War of Gods ... 1.50
❑59, Oct 1991, GP (c); GP (w); RT (a); A: Batman. War of Gods ... 1.50
❑60, Nov 1991, GP (c); GP (w); A: Lobo. War of Gods ... 1.50
❑61, Jan 1992, GP (w); War of Gods ... 1.50
❑62, Feb 1992, GP (w); RT (a); Hawkwoman ... 1.50
❑63, Jun 1992, BB (c); RT (a); A: Deathstroke. Continued from Wonder Woman Special #1 ... 1.50
❑64, Jul 1992, BB (c); A: . A: Ed Indelicato 1.50

N-MINT

❑65, Aug 1992, BB (c); V: Dr. Psycho ... 1.50
❑66, Sep 1992, BB (c); 1: Natasha Teranova ... 1.50
❑67, Oct 1992, BB (c); A: Natasha Teranova ... 1.50
❑68, Nov 1992, BB (c); FMc (a); A: Natasha Teranova ... 1.50
❑69, Dec 1992, BB (c); A: Natasha Teranova ... 1.50
❑70, Jan 1993, BB (c); RT (a); A: Natasha Teranova ... 1.50
❑71, Feb 1993, BB (c); RT (a); A: Natasha Teranova ... 1.50
❑72, Mar 1993, BB (c) ... 1.50
❑73, Apr 1993, BB (c) ... 1.50
❑74, May 1993, BB (c); A: White Magician 1.50
❑75, Jun 1993, BB (c) ... 1.50
❑76, Jul 1993, BB (c); A: Doctor Fate ... 1.50
❑77, Aug 1993, BB (c); A: JLA ... 1.50
❑78, Sep 1993, BB (c); A: Mayfly ... 1.50
❑79, Oct 1993, BB (c); A: Flash. V: Mayfly. V: Mayfly ... 1.50
❑80, Nov 1993, BB (c); A: Ares ... 1.50
❑81, Dec 1993, BB (c) ... 1.50
❑82, Jan 1994, BB (c); V: Ares ... 1.50
❑83, Feb 1994, BB (c) ... 1.50
❑84, Mar 1994, BB (c) ... 1.50
❑85, Apr 1994, BB (c); Mike Deodato Jr.'s first U.S. work ... 10.00
❑86, May 1994, BB (c) ... 4.00
❑87, Jun 1994, BB (c) ... 3.00
❑88, Jul 1994, BB (c); A: Superman ... 3.00
❑89, Aug 1994, BB (c); RT (a); A: Circe (DC). ... 3.00
❑90, Sep 1994, BB (c); A: Artemis. Issue 0 follow; Issue 0 follow,1: Artemis ... 3.00
❑91, Nov 1994, BB (c); A: Artemis. Follows Issue 0 ... 3.00
❑92, Dec 1994, BB (c); A: Artemis. Issue has no title page denoting story title .. 3.00
❑93, Jan 1995, BB (c); Artemis is new Wonder Woman ... 3.00
❑94, Feb 1995, BB (c); V: Cheshire. V: Poison Ivy ... 2.00
❑95, Mar 1995, BB (c); V: Cheetah. V: Cheshire. V: Poison Ivy ... 2.00
❑96, Apr 1995, BB (c); V: Joker ... 2.00
❑97, May 1995, BB (c); V: Joker ... 2.00
❑98, Jun 1995, BB (c); V: Joker ... 2.00
❑99, Jul 1995, BB (c) ... 2.00
❑100, Jul 1995, Giant-size; D: Athena. Wonder Woman returns to old uniform 2.95
❑100/Variant, Jul 1995, Giant-size; BB, (c); D: Athena. Wonder Woman returns to old uniform; enhanced cover ... 4.00
❑101, Sep 1995, JBy (c); JBy (w); JBy (a); A: Darkseid ... 1.95
❑102, Oct 1995, JBy (c); JBy (w); JBy (a); A: Darkseid. V: Darkseid ... 1.95
❑103, Nov 1995, JBy (c); JBy (w); JBy (a); A: Darkseid. V: Darkseid ... 1.95
❑104, Dec 1995, JBy (c); JBy (w); JBy (a); A: Darkseid. V: Darkseid ... 1.95
❑105, Jan 1996, JBy (c); JBy (w); JBy (a); 1: Cassie Sandsmark (future Wonder Girl); Phantom Stranger cameo ... 1.95
❑106, Feb 1996, JBy (c); JBy (w); JBy (a); A: Phantom Stranger. Demon Etrigan Cameo ... 1.95
❑107, Mar 1996, JBy (c); JBy (w); JBy (a); A: Demon ... 1.95
❑108, Apr 1996, JBy (c); JBy (w); JBy (a); A: Phantom Stranger ... 1.95
❑109, May 1996, JBy (c); JBy (w); JBy (a); V: Flash (fake) ... 1.95
❑110, Jun 1996, JBy (c); JBy (w); JBy (a); V: Sinestro (fake) ... 1.95
❑111, Jul 1996, JBy (c); JBy (w); JBy (a); V: Doomsday (fake). 1: Wonder Girl (Cassie Sandsmark) ... 1.95
❑112, Aug 1996, JBy (c); JBy (w); JBy (a); A: Decay. V: Doomsday (fake) ... 1.95
❑113, Sep 1996, JBy (c); JBy (w); JBy (a); A: Wonder Girl. Tribute to Sheldon Mayer ... 1.95
❑114, Oct 1996, JBy (c); JBy (w); JBy (a); A: Doctor Psycho. V: Dr. Psycho ... 1.95
❑115, Nov 1996, JBy (c); JBy (w); JBy (a); A: Cave Carson ... 1.95
❑116, Dec 1996, JBy (c); JBy (w); JBy (a); A: Cave Carson ... 1.95
❑117, Jan 1997, JBy, (c); JBy (w); JBy (a); 1: Invisible Plane ... 1.95

N-MINT

❑118, Feb 1997, JL (c); JBy (w); JBy (a); V: Cheetah ... 1.95
❑119, Mar 1997, JL (c); JBy (w); JBy (a); V: Cheetah ... 1.95
❑120, Apr 1997, 10th anniversary issue; GP (c); JBy (w); JBy, BB, NC (a); Giant-size; Wonder Woman pin-ups ... 2.95
❑121, May 1997, JBy (c); JBy (w); JBy (a); A: Artemis. D: Terry Long ... 1.95
❑122, Jun 1997, JBy (c); JBy (w); JBy (a); A: Jason Blood. ... 1.95
❑123, Jul 1997, JBy (w); JBy (a); V: Artemis ... 1.95
❑124, Aug 1997, JL (c); JBy (w); JBy (a); V: Artemis ... 1.95
❑125, Sep 1997, JL (c); JBy (w); JBy (a); O: Demon. A: Superman. A: Flash. A: Martian Manhunter. A: Green Lantern. A: Batman. Diana in intensive care ... 1.95
❑126, Oct 1997, JBy (c); JBy (w); JBy (a); Genesis ... 1.95
❑127, Nov 1997, JL (c); JBy (w); JBy (a); Diana is turned into a goddess and goes to Olympus ... 1.95
❑128, Dec 1997, JL (c); JBy (w); JBy (a); A: Egg Fu. Face cover ... 1.95
❑129, Jan 1998, JL (c); JBy (w); JBy (a); A: Demon ... 1.95
❑130, Feb 1998, JBy (c); JBy (w); JBy (a); A: Justice Society of America. A: Jay Garrick ... 1.95
❑131, Mar 1998, JBy (c); JBy (w); JBy (a); A: Justice Society of America. A: Jay Garrick ... 1.95
❑132, Apr 1998, JBy (c); JBy (w); JBy (a); A: Justice Society of America. A: Jay Garrick ... 1.95
❑133, May 1998, JBy (c); JBy (w); JBy (a); A: Justice Society of America. A: Jay Garrick ... 1.95
❑134, Jun 1998, JBy (c); JBy (w); JBy (a); A: Dark Angel ... 1.95
❑135, Jul 1998, JBy (c); JBy (w); JBy (a); O: Donna Troy; V: Dark Angel; V: Morgan Le Fay ... 1.95
❑136, Aug 1998, JBy (c); JBy (w); JBy (a); A: Donna Troy. Diana returns to Earth; Return of Donna Troy ... 1.99
❑137, Sep 1998, RT (a) ... 1.99
❑138, Oct 1998, RT (a) ... 1.99
❑139, Dec 1998, BMc (a); Diana becomes mortal again ... 1.99
❑140, Jan 1999, BMc (a); A: Superman. A: Batman ... 1.99
❑141, Feb 1999, BMc (a); A: Superman. A: Batman. A: Oblivion ... 1.99
❑142, Mar 1999, BMc (a) ... 1.99
❑143, Apr 1999, BMc (a); 1: Devastation 1.99
❑144, May 1999, BMc (a); V: Devastation 1.99
❑145, Jun 1999, BMc (a); V: Devastation 1.99
❑146, Jul 1999, BMc (a); V: Devastation 1.99
❑147, Aug 1999, BMc (a) ... 1.99
❑148, Sep 1999, BMc (a) ... 1.99
❑149, Oct 1999, BMc (a) ... 1.99
❑150, Nov 1999 ... 1.99
❑151, Dec 1999 ... 1.99
❑152, Jan 2000 ... 1.99
❑153, Feb 2000, Wonder Girl spotlight .. 1.99
❑154, Mar 2000 ... 1.99
❑155, Apr 2000 ... 1.99
❑156, May 2000, V: Devastation ... 1.99
❑157, Jun 2000, V: Devastation ... 1.99
❑158, Jul 2000, V: Devastation ... 1.99
❑159, Aug 2000 ... 2.25
❑160, Sep 2000, V: Clayface ... 2.25
❑161, Oct 2000, V: Clayface ... 2.25
❑162, Nov 2000 ... 2.25
❑163, Dec 2000, V: Triton ... 2.25
❑164, Jan 2001 ... 2.25
❑165, Feb 2001 ... 2.25
❑166, Mar 2001, A: Batman ... 2.25
❑167, Apr 2001 ... 2.25
❑168, May 2001, GP (w) ... 2.25
❑169, Jun 2001, GP (w); GP (a); Wraparound cover ... 2.25
❑170, Jul 2001 ... 2.25
❑171, Aug 2001, Our Worlds At War: Prelude To War!; Continued in Superman #172 and JLA: Our Worlds At War #1 ... 2.25
❑172, Sep 2001, D: Hippolyta; Our Worlds At War: All-Out War! ... 2.25

N-MINT

❑173, Oct 2001, Our Worlds At War: Casualties of War! 2.25
❑174, Nov 2001, JLee (c) 2.25
❑175, Dec 2001, JLee (c); Joker: Last Laugh crossover 2.25
❑176, Jan 2002 2.25
❑177, Feb 2002 2.25
❑178, Mar 2002, Troia back-up story; "Lost" story part based on issues #182 and #183 2.25
❑179, Apr 2002, Troia story; "Lost" story part based on issues #182 and #183; 1: Angle Man 2.25
❑180, May 2002, O: Cyborgirl; O: Giganta; O: Jinx; O: Dr. Poison; O: Queen Clea; Troia story 2.25
❑181, Jun 2002, Troia story 2.25
❑182, Aug 2002, Troia story 2.25
❑183, Sep 2002, (c);Troia story 2.25
❑184, Oct 2002 2.25
❑185, Nov 2002, (c) 2.25
❑186, Dec 2002 2.25
❑187, Feb 2003 2.25
❑188, Mar 2003 2.25
❑189, Apr 2003, JOy, CR (a) 2.25
❑190, May 2003, JOy, CR (a); O: Wonder Woman 2.25
❑191, Jun 2003, JOy, CR (a) 2.25
❑192, Jul 2003, JOy, CR (a) 2.25
❑193, Aug 2003, JOy, CR (a) 2.25
❑194, Sep 2003, JOy, CR (a) 2.25
❑195, Oct 2003 2.25
❑196, Nov 2003 2.25
❑197, Dec 2003 2.25
❑198, Jan 2004 2.25
❑199, Feb 2004 2.25
❑200, Mar 2004, Giant-size; Wonder Woman pinups 3.95
❑201, Apr 2004 2.25
❑202, May 2004, O: Veronica Cale 2.25
❑203, Jun 2004 2.25
❑204, Jul 2004 2.25
❑205, Aug 2004 2.25
❑206, Sep 2004 2.25
❑207, Oct 2004 2.25
❑208, Nov 2004 2.25
❑209, Jan 2005, Includes Heroscape #2: Trapped Behind Enemy Minds mini-comic insert 2.25
❑210, Feb 2005 2.25
❑211, Mar 2005 2.25
❑212, Apr 2005 2.25
❑213, May 2005 2.25
❑214, Jun 2005; Continued from Flash v2 #219 25.00
❑215, May 2005 10.00
❑216, Jun 2005 7.00
❑217, Jul 2005 6.00
❑218, Aug 2005 5.00
❑219, Sep 2005; D: Max Lord; OMAC Project tie-In; Continued from Adventures of Superman #642 15.00
❑219/2nd, Sep 2005 3.00
❑220, Oct 2005 12.00
❑220/2nd, Oct 2005 3.00
❑221, Nov 2005; OMAC Project tie-in 2.50
❑222, Dec 2005 2.50
❑223, Jan 2006 2.50
❑224, Feb 2006 2.50
❑225, Mar 2006 2.50
❑226, May 2006, Final issue 2.50
❑1000000, Nov 1998 3.00
❑Ann 1, ca. 1988, GP (c); GP (w); GP, BB, CS, RA, BMc, JL (a); Private Lives story; ca. 1988 2.00
❑Ann 2, Sep 1989, GP (c); GP (w); JDu, GP (a) 2.00
❑Ann 3, ca. 1992, KN (c);Eclipso 2.50
❑Ann 4, ca. 1995, BA, (c); BA (a); Year One 3.50
❑Ann 5, ca. 1996, DC (c); JBy (w); DC (a); Legends of the Dead Earth; 1996 Ann 2.95
❑Ann 6, ca. 1997, JBy (w); JBy, TP (a); A: Artemis. Pulp Heroes 3.95
❑Ann 7, Sep 1998, (c); RT (a); Ghosts 2.95
❑Ann 8, Sep 1999, JLApe 2.95
❑Special 1, ca. 1992, JOy (c); A: Deathstroke. Story continues in Wonder Woman #63 1.75
❑139/Ltd., Dec 1998, Signed edition 14.95

N-MINT

Wonder Woman
Abbeville

❑1, Oct 1995; Front cover: detail of Wonder Woman (2nd) 63; Back cover Wonder Woman (1st) 1; Introduction by Gloria Steinem; A portion of the text by Gloria Steinem appered in Wonder Woman, a Ms. Book published by Holt, Rinehart and Winston, Inc. and Warner Books, Inc. 1972 11.95

Wonder Woman: Amazonia
DC

❑1, Jan 1998; Oversized; Elseworlds 7.95

Wonder Woman Plus
DC

❑1, Jan 1997 2.95

Wonder Woman Secret Files
DC

❑1, Mar 1998, background on Wonder Woman and supporting cast 4.95
❑2, Jul 1999, background on Wonder Woman and supporting cast 4.95
❑3, May 2002, nn; prestige format one-shot; domestic violence 4.95

Wonderworld Express
That Other Comix Co.

❑1 1984, b&w 2.25

Wonderworlds
Innovation

❑1, Jan 1992; Reprints 3.50

Wood Boy
Image

❑1, ca. 2005 2.95

Woodstock: The Comic
Marvel

❑1 5.95

Woodsy Owl
Gold Key

❑1, Nov 1973 8.00
❑2, Feb 1974 5.00
❑3, May 1974 4.00
❑4, Aug 1974 4.00
❑5, Nov 1974 4.00
❑6, Feb 1975 3.00
❑7, May 1975 3.00
❑8, Aug 1975 3.00
❑9, Nov 1975 3.00
❑10, Feb 1976 3.00

Woody Woodpecker
Dell

❑69, Nov 1961 9.00
❑70, Jan 1962 9.00
❑71, Mar 1962 9.00
❑72, Jun 1962 9.00
❑73, Oct 1962; Giant-size; Gold Key begins publishing 25.00
❑74, Dec 1962; Giant-size 25.00
❑75, Mar 1963; Giant-size 25.00
❑76, Jun 1963 15.00
❑77, Sep 1963 15.00
❑78, Dec 1963 15.00
❑79, Mar 1964 15.00
❑80, Jun 1964 15.00
❑81, Sep 1964 15.00
❑82, Dec 1964 15.00
❑83, Mar 1965 15.00
❑84, Apr 1965 15.00
❑85, Jun 1965 15.00
❑86, Aug 1965 15.00
❑87, Oct 1965 15.00
❑88, Dec 1965 15.00
❑89, Feb 1966 15.00
❑90, Apr 1966 15.00
❑91, Jun 1966 15.00
❑92, Aug 1966, reprints 15.00
❑93, Oct 1966 15.00
❑94, Dec 1966 15.00
❑95, Feb 1967 15.00
❑96, Apr 1967 15.00
❑97, Jun 1967 15.00
❑98, Aug 1967 15.00
❑99, Nov 1967 15.00
❑100, Feb 1968 15.00
❑101, May 1968 10.00
❑102, Aug 1968 10.00
❑103, Nov 1968 10.00

N-MINT

❑104, Feb 1969 10.00
❑105, May 1969 10.00
❑106, Aug 1969 10.00
❑107, Sep 1969 10.00
❑108, Nov 1969 10.00
❑109, Jan 1970 10.00
❑110, Mar 1970 10.00
❑111, May 1970 10.00
❑112, Jul 1970 10.00
❑113, Sep 1970 10.00
❑114, Nov 1970 10.00
❑115, Jan 1971 10.00
❑116, Mar 1971 10.00
❑117, May 1971 10.00
❑118, Jul 1971 10.00
❑119, Sep 1971 10.00
❑120, Nov 1971 10.00
❑121, Jan 1972 6.00
❑122, Mar 1972 6.00
❑123, May 1972 6.00
❑124, Jul 1972 6.00
❑125, Sep 1972 6.00
❑126, Nov 1972 6.00
❑127, Jan 1973 6.00
❑128, Mar 1973 6.00
❑129, May 1973 6.00
❑130, Jul 1973 6.00
❑131, Sep 1973 2.50
❑132, Oct 1973 2.50
❑133, Nov 1973 2.50
❑134, Jan 1974 2.50
❑135, Mar 1974 2.50
❑136, May 1974 2.50
❑137, Jul 1974 2.50
❑138, Sep 1974 2.50
❑139, Oct 1974 2.50
❑140, Nov 1974 2.50
❑141, Jan 1975 2.50
❑142, Mar 1975 2.50
❑143, May 1975 2.50
❑144, Jul 1975 2.50
❑145, Sep 1975 2.50
❑146, Oct 1975 2.50
❑147, Nov 1975 2.50
❑148, Jan 1976 2.50
❑149, Mar 1976 2.50
❑150, May 1976 2.50
❑151, Jul 1976 2.50
❑152, Aug 1976 2.50
❑153, Sep 1976 2.50
❑154, Oct 1976 2.50
❑155, Dec 1976 2.50
❑156, Feb 1977 2.50
❑157, Apr 1977 2.50
❑158, Jun 1977 2.50
❑159, Aug 1977 2.50
❑160, Oct 1977 2.50
❑161, Dec 1977 2.50
❑162, Jan 1978 2.50
❑163, Feb 1978 2.50
❑164, Mar 1978 2.50
❑165, Apr 1978 2.50
❑166, May 1978 2.50
❑167, Jun 1978 2.50
❑168, Jul 1978 2.50
❑169, Aug 1978 2.50
❑170, Sep 1978 2.50
❑171, Oct 1978 2.00
❑172, Nov 1978 2.00
❑173, Dec 1978 2.00
❑174, Jan 1979 2.00
❑175, Feb 1979 2.00
❑176, Mar 1979 2.00
❑177, Apr 1979 2.00
❑178, May 1979 2.00
❑179, Jun 1979 2.00
❑180, Jul 1979 2.00
❑181, Aug 1979 2.00
❑182, Sep 1979 2.00
❑183, Oct 1979 2.00
❑184, Nov 1979 2.00
❑185, Dec 1979 2.00
❑186, Jan 1980 2.00
❑187, Feb 1980 2.00
❑188, Mar 1980 10.00
❑189 1980 10.00
❑190 1980 25.00

❑191 1980 ... 25.00
❑193 1981; #192 never printed ... 15.00
❑194, Oct 1981, Published by Whitman; production code 90062-110 ... 15.00
❑195, Dec 1982 ... 15.00
❑196, Feb 1982 ... 15.00
❑197, Apr 1982 ... 15.00
❑198 1982 ... 15.00
❑199 1983 ... 15.00
❑200 1984 ... 15.00
❑201 1984; Final Issue ... 15.00

Woody Woodpecker
Harvey

❑1, Sep 1991 ... 1.50
❑2, Nov 1991 ... 1.25
❑3, Jan 1992 ... 1.25
❑4, Mar 1992 ... 1.25
❑5, Jun 1992 ... 1.25
❑6, Sep 1992 ... 1.25
❑7, Mar 1993; Holiday Special ... 1.25
❑8, Jun 1993 ... 1.25
❑9, Dec 1993 ... 1.50
❑10, Feb 1994 ... 1.50
❑11, Apr 1994 ... 1.50
❑12, Jun 1994 ... 1.50

Woody Woodpecker 50th Anniversary Special
Harvey

❑1, Oct 1991; Reprints ... 2.50

Woody Woodpecker Adventures
Harvey

❑1, May 1992; Reprints ... 1.25
❑2 ... 1.25
❑3 ... 1.25

Woody Woodpecker and Friends
Harvey

❑1, Dec 1991; Reprints ... 1.25
❑2, Feb 1992; Reprints ... 1.25
❑3, Apr 1992; Reprints ... 1.25
❑4, Jun 1992; Reprints ... 1.25

Woody Woodpecker Digest
Harvey

❑1, Jun 1992; Reprints ... 1.75

Woofers and Hooters
Fantagraphics / Eros

❑1, b&w; Adult ... 2.50

Words & Pictures
Maverick

❑1, Fal 1994, b&w ... 3.95
❑2, Spr 1995, b&w ... 3.95

Wordsmith
Renegade

❑1, Aug 1985, b&w ... 1.70
❑2, Oct 1985, b&w ... 1.70
❑3, Dec 1985, b&w ... 1.70
❑4, Dec 1985, b&w ... 1.70
❑5, May 1986, b&w ... 1.70
❑6, Aug 1986, b&w ... 1.70
❑7, Nov 1986, b&w ... 2.00
❑8, Nov 1986, b&w ... 2.00
❑9, May 1987, b&w ... 2.00
❑10, Aug 1987, b&w ... 2.00
❑11, Nov 1987, b&w ... 2.00
❑12, Jan 1988, b&w ... 2.00

Wordsmith
Caliber

❑1 1996 ... 2.95
❑2 1996 ... 2.95
❑3 1996 ... 2.95
❑4 1996 ... 2.95
❑5 1997, b&w ... 2.95
❑6 1997 ... 2.95

Word Warriors
Literacy Volunteers

❑1, b&w; Ms. Tree, Jon Sable ... 1.50

Worgard: Viking Berserkir
Stronghold

❑1, Oct 1997, b&w ... 2.95

Workshop
Blue Comet

❑1 ... 2.95

World Bank
Public Services International

❑1; educational comic; no indicia ... 2.95

World Below
Dark Horse

❑1, Mar 1999 ... 2.50
❑2, Apr 1999 ... 2.50
❑3, May 1999 ... 2.50
❑4, Jun 1999 ... 2.50

World Below: Deeper and Stranger
Dark Horse

❑1, Dec 1999, b&w ... 2.95
❑2, Jan 2000, b&w ... 2.95
❑3, Feb 2000, b&w ... 2.95
❑4, Mar 2000, b&w ... 2.95

World Class Comics
Image

❑1, Aug 2002, b&w; hardcover ... 4.95

World Exists for Me
Tokyopop

❑1, Dec 2005 ... 9.99

World Hardball League
Titus

❑1, Aug 1994, b&w ... 2.75
❑2, Jan 1995, b&w ... 2.75

World of Archie
Archie

❑1, Aug 1992 ... 2.00
❑2, Nov 1992 ... 1.50
❑3, Feb 1993 ... 1.50
❑4, May 1993 ... 1.50
❑5, Aug 1993 ... 1.50
❑6, Nov 1993 ... 1.50
❑7, Feb 1994 ... 1.50
❑8, Apr 1994 ... 1.50
❑9, Jun 1994 ... 1.50
❑10, Aug 1994 ... 1.50
❑11, Sep 1994 ... 1.50
❑12, Nov 1994 ... 1.50
❑13, Jan 1995 ... 1.50
❑14, Mar 1995 ... 1.50
❑15, Jun 1995 ... 1.50
❑16, Sep 1995 ... 1.50
❑17, Dec 1995 ... 1.50
❑18, Mar 1996 ... 1.50
❑19, Jun 1996, DDC (w); DDC (a) ... 1.50
❑20, Sep 1996 ... 1.50
❑21, Dec 1996, Archie and Veronica run for class president ... 1.50
❑22, Mar 1997 ... 1.50

World of Ginger Fox
Comico

❑1 ... 6.95
❑1/HC ... 27.95

World of Hartz
Tokyopop

❑1, May 2004 ... 9.99

World of Krypton
DC

❑1, Jul 1979, RA (c); MA, HC (a); O: Jor-El ... 2.00
❑2, Aug 1979, RA (c); HC (a) ... 2.00
❑3, Sep 1979, RA (c); HC (a) ... 2.00

World of Krypton
DC

❑1, Dec 1987, JBy (c); JBy (w) ... 2.00
❑2, Jan 1988, JBy (c); JBy (w); 1: Black Zero; 1: Sen-M; 1: League of Light ... 2.00
❑3, Feb 1988, JBy (c); JBy (w) ... 2.00
❑4, Mar 1988, JBy (c); JBy (w); Final issue ... 2.00

World of Metropolis
DC

❑1, Aug 1988, (c); JBy (w); FMc, DG (a) ... 1.50
❑2, Sep 1988, (c); JBy (w); DG (a) ... 1.50
❑3, Oct 1988, (c); JBy (w); DG (a) ... 1.50
❑4, Nov 1988, (c); JBy (w); DG (a) ... 1.50

World of Smallville
DC

❑1, Apr 1988, (c); JBy (w); AA, KS (a) ... 1.50
❑2, May 1988, (c); JBy (w); AA, KS (a) ... 1.50
❑3, Jun 1988, (c); JBy (w); AA, KS (a) ... 1.50
❑4, Jul 1988, (c); JBy (w); AA, KS (a) ... 1.50

World of Warcraft
DC

❑1, Jan 2008; Samwise Didier cover ... 2.99
❑1/A, Jan 2008; Jim Lee cover ... 2.99
❑2, Feb 2008 ... 2.99
❑2/A, Feb 2008; Variant cover ... 2.99
❑3, Mar 2008 ... 2.99
❑3/A, Mar 2008 ... 2.99
❑4, Apr 2008 ... 2.99
❑4/A, Apr 2008; Jim Lee cover ... 2.99

World of Wheels
Charlton

❑17, Oct 1967, Previous issues published as Drag-Strip Hotrodders ... 12.00
❑18, Dec 1967 ... 12.00
❑19, Feb 1968 ... 12.00
❑20, Apr 1968 ... 12.00
❑21, Aug 1968 ... 8.00
❑22, Oct 1968 ... 8.00
❑23, Dec 1968 ... 8.00
❑24, Feb 1969 ... 8.00
❑25, Apr 1969 ... 8.00
❑26, Jun 1969 ... 8.00
❑27, Aug 1969 ... 8.00
❑28, Oct 1969 ... 8.00
❑29, Dec 1969 ... 8.00
❑30, Feb 1970 ... 8.00
❑31, Apr 1970 ... 8.00
❑32, Jun 1970 ... 8.00

World of Wood
Eclipse

❑1, May 1986, DSt (c); WW (w); WW, DA (a); Indicia says #2 ... 2.00
❑2, May 1986, WW, DSt (c); WW (w); WW (a); Indicia for #1 corrected ... 2.00
❑3, Jun 1986, AW, WW (c); WW (w); WW (a); centaur ... 2.00
❑4, Jun 1986, WW (c); WW (w); WW (a) 2.00
❑5, Feb 1989, b&w; WW, (c); AW, WW (a); reprints Flying Saucers #1; reprints Forbidden Worlds #3 ... 2.00

World of X-Ray
Pyramid

❑1, b&w ... 1.80

World of Young Master
New Comics

❑1, Mar 1989, b&w; Demonblade ... 1.95

World's Best Comics: Silver Age DC Archive Sampler
DC

❑1, Aug 2004 ... 0.99

Worlds Collide
DC / Milestone

❑1, Jul 1994; 1: Rift ... 2.50
❑1/CS, Jul 1994; 1: Rift. vinyl clings; Include press-apply stick-ons; enhanced cover ... 4.00
❑1/Platinum, Jul 1994; Platinum edition 4.00

World's Finest
DC

❑1, ca. 1990, SR (c); DaG (w); SR (a); V: Lex Luthor; V: Joker ... 5.00
❑2, ca. 1990, SR (c); DaG (w); SR (a); V: Joker; V: Lex Luthor ... 4.50
❑3, ca. 1990, SR (c); DaG (w); SR (a); V: Joker; V: Lex Luthor 4.50

World's Finest Comics
DC

❑121, Nov 1961 (c); MA, JM (a) ... 85.00
❑122, Dec 1961, (c) ... 75.00
❑123, Feb 1962, (c) ... 75.00
❑124, Mar 1962, (c) ... 75.00
❑125, May 1962, (c); NC (a) ... 75.00
❑126, Jun 1962, (c); NC (a); A: Lex Luthor 75.00
❑127, Aug 1962, (c) ... 75.00
❑128, Sep 1962, (c) ... 75.00
❑129, Nov 1962, DD, (c); JM (a); A: Lex Luthor. A: Joker ... 75.00
❑130, Dec 1962, (c); JM (a) ... 75.00
❑131, Feb 1963, (c) ... 75.00
❑132, Mar 1963, (c) ... 75.00
❑133, May 1963, (c); JM (a); Aqua-Girl tryout ... 75.00
❑134, Jun 1963, (c); A: Miss Arrowette. 75.00
❑135, Aug 1963, (c) ... 75.00
❑136, Sep 1963, (c) ... 75.00

	N-MINT
❑137, Nov 1963, (c); A: Lex Luthor	75.00
❑138, Dec 1963, (c); JM (a)	75.00
❑139, Feb 1964, (c)	75.00
❑140, Mar 1964, (c); A: Clayface	75.00
❑141, May 1964, CS, (c); CS (a); Back-up reprint stories begin	75.00
❑142, Jun 1964, (c); CS (a); 1: Composite Superman. A: Legion of Super-Heroes	75.00
❑143, Aug 1964, (c); CS (a); Green Arrow reprint from Adventure Comics #266	52.00
❑144, Sep 1964, CS, (c); CS (a); A: Clayface. A: Brainiac. Aquaman story reprinted from Adventure Comics #267	52.00
❑145, Nov 1964, (c); CS (a)	52.00
❑146, Dec 1964, CS, (c); CS (a); Superman story reprinted from Superman #131	52.00
❑147, Feb 1965, CS, (c); CS (a)	52.00
❑148, Mar 1965, CS, (c); CS (a); A: Lex Luthor. A: Clayface. Congorilla back-ups begin	52.00
❑149, May 1965, CS, (c); CS (a); Congorilla back-up	52.00
❑150, Jun 1965, CS, (c); CS (a); Congorilla back-up	52.00
❑151, Aug 1965, (c); Congorilla back-up	50.00
❑152, Sep 1965, (c)	50.00
❑153, Nov 1965, CS, (c); A: Lex Luthor	45.00
❑154, Dec 1965, CS, (c); A: Super-Sons	45.00
❑155, Feb 1966, CS, (c); RMo (a)	45.00
❑156, Mar 1966, (c); 1: Bizarro Batman. A: Joker. A: Bizarro Superman	55.00
❑157, May 1966, CS, (c); A: Super-Sons. Imaginary story	45.00
❑158, Jun 1966, CS, (c); CS (a); A: Brainiac	45.00
❑159, Aug 1966, (c); CS (a); A: Joker	45.00
❑160, Sep 1966, CS, (c); CS (a); Editors' Round Table reprinted from Tales of the Unexpected #5	45.00
❑161, Nov 1966; Giant-size; (c);aka 80 Page Giant #G-28	45.00
❑162, Nov 1966, CS, (c); CS (a); Irene Vartanoff L.O.C	38.00
❑163, Dec 1966, CS, (c)	38.00
❑164, Feb 1967, CS, (c); CS (a); A: Brainiac	38.00
❑165, Mar 1967, CS, (c)	38.00
❑166, May 1967, CS, (c); RMo (a); A: Joker. V: Joker; Roy Raymond TV Detective back up story	38.00
❑167, Jun 1967, CS, (c); JK, CS (a); Imaginary story	38.00
❑168, Aug 1967, (c); CS (a)	38.00
❑169, Sep 1967, CS, (c); CS (a); Reprint from Tales of the Unexpected #9; Editors' Round Table	38.00
❑170, Nov 1967; Giant-size; CS, (c);aka 80 Page Giant #G-40	38.00
❑171, Nov 1967, CS, (c); CS (a); Irene Vartanoff L.O.C	38.00
❑172, Dec 1967, CS, (c); CS (a); A: Lex Luthor. Imaginary story; Clark and Bruce as brothers	38.00
❑173, Feb 1968, CS, (c); CS (a); reprints from Action #241	38.00
❑174, Mar 1968, NA (c); GK, JAb (a)	38.00
❑175, May 1968, NA, (c); NA (a); O: Martian Manhunter	38.00
❑176, Jun 1968, NA, (c); NA (a); Reprint from Detective Comics #226; Editors' Round Table	38.00
❑177, Aug 1968, RA, (c); CS (a); A: Lex Luthor. A: Joker	38.00
❑178, Sep 1968, NA, (c); CS (a); 2-part story continued in World's Finest Comics #180	30.00
❑179, Nov 1968; NA, (c); aka 80 Page Giant #G-52	30.00
❑180, Nov 1968, (c); RA (a)	30.00
❑181, Dec 1968, (c); RA (a)	25.00
❑182, Feb 1969, (c); RA (a)	25.00
❑183, Mar 1969, NA, (c); RA (a); A: Lex Luthor. A: Brainiac. Reprints story from House of Mystery #80	25.00
❑184, May 1969, (c); CS, JAb (a)	25.00
❑185, Jun 1969, (c); RA (a); Tommy Tomorrow reprinted from Action Comics #223	25.00
❑186, Aug 1969, NA, (c); RA (a)	25.00
❑187, Sep 1969, MA, CS (c); RA (a); O: Green Arrow	25.00
❑188, Oct 1969; Giant-size; CS, (c);aka Giant #G-64	25.00
❑189, Nov 1969, MA, (c); RA, RMo (a); A: Lex Luthor	25.00
❑190, Dec 1969, MA, (c); RA, JM (a); A: Lex Luthor. Robin reprint from Star-Spangled Comics #125	25.00
❑191, Feb 1970, (c); RA (a); Robin reprinted from Star-Spangled Comics #130; Irene Vartanoff L.O.C	20.00
❑192, Mar 1970, CS, (c); RA (a); Robin story reprinted from Star-Spangled Comics #126	20.00
❑193, May 1970, CS (c); RA (a); Robin story reprinted from Star-Spangled Comics #120	20.00
❑194, Jun 1970, CS, (c); RA (a)	20.00
❑195, Aug 1970, CS, (c); RA (a)	20.00
❑196, Sep 1970, CS, (c); CS (a)	20.00
❑197, Nov 1970; Giant-size; CS, (c); JK (a); aka Giant #G-76	20.00
❑198, Nov 1970, CI, (c); DD (a); Superman/Flash race	80.00
❑199, Dec 1970, NA, (c); DD (a); Superman/Flash race	80.00
❑200, Feb 1971, NA, (c); DD (a); A: Robin	16.00
❑201, Mar 1971, NA, (c); DD (a); A: Doctor Fate. A: Green Lantern. Martin Pasko L.O.C	16.00
❑202, May 1971, NA, (c); DD (a); Guy H. Lillian III L.O.C	16.00
❑203, Jun 1971, NA, (c); DD (a); A: Aquaman. Martin Pasko L.O.C	16.00
❑204, Aug 1971; NA, (c); MA, DD (a); A: Wonder Woman. Green Arrow back-up; Captain Comet back-up	16.00
❑205, Sep 1971; NA, (c); MA, FF, DD (a); A: Teen Titans. Superman and Teen Titans; Shining Knight back-up; Fiction Is Stranger Than Truth! story; Marty Pasko LOC; Bob Rozakis LOC; "Secret" reprinted from Strange Adventures #111; Shining Knight reprinted from Adventure Comics #153	16.00
❑206, Nov 1971, Giant-size; DG (c); JM (a); aka Giant #G-88	16.00
❑207, Nov 1971; MA, (c); GC, DD (a); Reprints from Star-Spangled Comics #11 & Strange Adventures #30; Martin Pasko L.O.C.; 48 pages	16.00
❑208, Dec 1971; NA (c); DD (a); A: Doctor Fate. Reprints from Flash Comics #36 & Detective Comics #138; 48 pages; Tom Peyer L.O.C	16.00
❑209, Feb 1972; NA, (c); DD (a); A: Hawkman. 48 pages; Reprint from Detective Comics #74	16.00
❑210, Mar 1972; NA, (c); DD (a); A: Green Arrow. Reprints from Sensation Comics #2 and World's Best Comics #11; Green Arrow Team-Up	16.00
❑211, May 1972; NA, (c); DD (a); Reprints Green lantern story from All-American Comics #89; Batman Team-Up	16.00
❑212, Jun 1972; NC, (c); DD (a); A: Martian Manhunter. Martian Manhunter Team-Up (continued from Superman (1st Series #253); The Grim Ghost: Sensation Comics #8; Air Wave: Detective Comics #88	16.00
❑213, Sep 1972, NC, (c); DD (a); A: Atom	14.00
❑214, Nov 1972, NC, (c); DD (a); A: Vigilante	14.00
❑215, Jan 1973, NC, (c); DD (a); A: Super-Sons	14.00
❑216, Mar 1973, NC, (c); MA, DD (a); A: Super-Sons	14.00
❑217, May 1973, NC, (c); MA, DD (a); A: Metamorpho	14.00
❑218, Aug 1973, NC, (c); DC, DD (a); Bob Rozakis L.O.C	14.00
❑219, Oct 1973, NC, (c); DD (a); Bob Rozakis L.O.C	14.00
❑220, Dec 1973, NC, (c); MA, DD (a)	14.00
❑221, Feb 1974, NC, (c); MA, DD (a); A: Super-Sons	14.00
❑222, Apr 1974, NC, (c); DD (a); A: Super-Sons	14.00
❑223, Jun 1974, Giant-size; NC (c); NA, DD, CS (a); O: Deadman. giant; Reprints from World's Finest Comics #77 and #142	14.00
❑224, Aug 1974, Giant-size	14.00
❑225, Oct 1974, Giant-size	14.00
❑226, Dec 1974, Giant-size; NC (c); ATh, JK, NA, DD (a); A: Metamorpho. giant	14.00
❑227, Feb 1975, Giant-size; A: Deadman. giant	14.00
❑228, Mar 1975, Giant-size; A: Super-Sons	14.00
❑229, Apr 1975; Reprint	6.00
❑230, May 1975, Giant-size	6.00
❑231, Jul 1975 A: Super-Sons	6.00
❑232, Sep 1975	6.00
❑233, Oct 1975	6.00
❑234, Dec 1975	6.00
❑235, Jan 1976	6.00
❑236, Mar 1976	6.00
❑237, Apr 1976	6.00
❑238, Jun 1976, Super-Sons story	6.00
❑239, Jul 1976, Bicentennial #26	6.00
❑240, Sep 1976	6.00
❑241, Oct 1976	6.00
❑242, Dec 1976, A: Super-Sons. Super-Sons story	6.00
❑243, Feb 1977	6.00
❑244, May 1977; Giant-size; NA (c); MN, MA, JL (a)	6.00
❑245, Jul 1977; Giant-size; NA (c); MN, MA, GM, CS (a); A: Martian Manhunter	6.00
❑246, Sep 1977; NA (c); MN, MA, GM, DH, KS (a); 1: Baron Blitzkrieg. A: Justice League of America. Giant-size	6.00
❑247, Nov 1977; Giant-size; DG, JL (c); GM, KS (a); A: Justice League of America	6.00
❑248, Jan 1978; Giant-size; DG, JL (c); GM, DG, TVE, KS (a)	6.00
❑249, Mar 1978; Giant-size; JA (c); SD (w); SD, TVE, KS (a); A: Phantom Stranger	6.00
❑250, May 1978; Giant-size; JA (c); SD (w); SD, GT (a)	6.00
❑251, Jul 1978; Giant-size; JA (c); SD (w); SD, BL, GT, TVE, RE, JAb (a); 1: Count Vertigo. A: Speedy	6.00
❑252, Sep 1978; Giant-size; JA (c); SD (w); SD, GT, TVE, JAb (a); A: Poison Ivy	6.00
❑253, Nov 1978; Giant-size; JA (c); SD (w); DN, SD, TVE, KS (a)e; No ads begins; wraparound cover	6.00
❑254, Jan 1979; Giant-size; JA (c); SD (w); DN, SD, GT, TVE, JA, KS (a)	6.00
❑255, Mar 1979; JA (c); SD (w); DN, SD, TVE, JL, KS, DA (a); A: Bulletman. A: Bulletgirl. Giant-size	6.00
❑256, May 1979; Giant-size; RA, (c); DN, MA, DG, DD, KS (a)	6.00
❑257, Jul 1979; Giant-size; JA (c); DN, FMc, RB, GT, DD, KS, RT (a)	6.00
❑258, Sep 1979; Giant-size; DG, NA (c); DN, RB, DG, JL, KS, RT (a)	6.00
❑259, Nov 1979; RB, DG (c); DN, MN, RB, DG, MR, KS (a); Giant-size; Ads begin again	6.00
❑260, Jan 1980; RB, DG (c); DN, MN, RB, DG (a); Giant-size	6.00
❑261, Mar 1980; DG, RA (c); DN, RB, DG, RT (a); Giant-size	6.00
❑262, May 1980; DG, RA (c); DN, DG, JSa, DA, RT (a); Giant-size	6.00
❑263, Jul 1980; DG, RA (c); DN, RB, DG, TVE (a); A: Super-Sons. Giant-size	6.00
❑264, Sep 1980; DG, RA (c); DN, RB, DG, TVE (a); V: Clayface; V: Dr. Light; V: Monster Society of Evil; Giant-size	6.00
❑265, Nov 1980; JA (c); DN, DG, TVE, RE (a); O: Red Tornado; V: Simon Magus; V: King Kull; V: Mr. Atom; Giant-size	6.00
❑266, Jan 1981; JA (c); DN, RB, TVE (a); 1: Lady Lunar; V: Lady Lunar; V: Dr. Sivana; V: Ibac	6.00
❑267, Mar 1981; RB, DG (c); DN, RB, DG, TVE (a); A: Challengers of the Unknown. V: T.O. Morrow; V: Monster Society of Evil	6.00
❑268, May 1981; DG (c); DN, TVE, RT (a); O: Captain Marvel Jr.; V: T.O. Morrow	6.00
❑269, Jul 1981; RB, DG (c); DN, FMc, RB, TVE, DA (a); 1: Doctor Jymbi Humm; V: Sabbac	6.00
❑270, Aug 1981; RB, (c); DN, RB, TVE, RT (a); V: Metallo; V: Count Vertigo; V: Shadow-Thief	6.00
❑271, Sep 1981; GP, (c); FMc, RB (a); O: Superman/Batman team in World's Finest	4.00
❑272, Oct 1981; DG, RA (c); DN, RB, TVE (a); V: Count Vertigo; V: Chain Lightning	4.00
❑273, Nov 1981; RA, (c); DN, JSa, TVE, DA (a); V: Count Vertigo; V: Dr. Sivana	4.00
❑274, Dec 1981; DG, RA (c); DN, GC, TVE (a); Superman and Batman story	4.00
❑275, Jan 1982; (c); DN, FMc, RB, TVE, DS, DA (a); V: Mr. Freeze; V: Matter Master	4.00

Other grades: Multiply price above by 5/6 for VF/NM • 2/3 for VERY FINE • 1/3 for FINE • 1/5 for VERY GOOD • 1/8 for GOOD

❑276, Feb 1982; GP (c); DN, RB, CI, TVE, DS, DA (a); V: Dr. Double X; V: Slingshot; V: Weather Wizard 4.00
❑277, Mar 1982; GP (c); DN, DH, TVE, DS, RT (a) 4.00
❑278, Apr 1982; GP, (c); DN, RB, TVE, DS (a); A: Hawkman 4.00
❑279, May 1982; (c); DN, KP, TVE (a); A: Kid Eternity. V: Major Disaster 4.00
❑280, Jun 1982; RB (c); DN, RB, TVE (a); A: Kid Eternity. O: Captain Marvel Jr.; O: Kid Eternity; V: Captain Cutlass; V: Trickster; V: Major Disaster 4.00
❑281, Jul 1982; GK (c); DN, TVE, IN (a); A: Kid Eternity. V: Major Disaster; V: Captain Cutlass; V: Mr. Mind 4.00
❑282, Aug 1982; GK (c); FMc, CI, GK, IN (a); A: Kid Eternity. V: Slingshot; V: Her Highness; V: Silk; V: Aunt Minerva 4.00
❑283, Sep 1982, RB (c); FMc, GT, GK, IN (a); V: Composite Superman. V: Slingshot 4.00
❑284, Oct 1982, KG (c); GT, DS (a); A: Legion. V: Composite Superman; V: Clock King 4.00
❑285, Nov 1982, DG, FM (c); RB (a); A: Zatanna. V: Dr. Zodiac 4.00
❑286, Dec 1982, RB, DG (c); RB (a); A: Zatanna. V: Dr. Zodiac; V: Madam Zodiac 4.00
❑287, Jan 1983, RB, RT (c); TVE (a); V: Madam Zodiac 4.00
❑288, Feb 1983, DG (c); V: Madam Zodiac 4.00
❑289, Mar 1983, GK (c) 4.00
❑290, Apr 1983, KJ (c); TD (a) 4.00
❑291, May 1983, TD (a) 4.00
❑292, Jun 1983, KJ (c) 4.00
❑293, Jul 1983, KJ (c); TD (a); A: Null. A: Void. V: Null and Void; Norm Breyfogle LOC 4.00
❑294, Aug 1983, KJ (c); 1: Tonatiuh 4.00
❑295, Sep 1983, KJ (c); FMc (a); V: Moondancers 4.00
❑296, Oct 1983, RA, KJ (c); RA (a); V: Pantheon 4.00
❑297, Nov 1983, GC, KJ (c); GC (a); V: Pantheon 4.00
❑298, Dec 1983; DG (c); V: Pantheon 4.00
❑299, Jan 1984; KJ (c); GC (a); V: Pantheon 4.00
❑300, Feb 1984; Giant-size; DG (c); GP, RA, KJ (a); A: Justice League of America. A: Titans. A: Outsiders 4.00
❑301, Mar 1984; KJ (c); V: Siphon 3.00
❑302, Apr 1984; KJ (c); DG, NA (a); Reprint from World's Finest #176 .... 3.00
❑303, May 1984 KJ (c) 3.00
❑304, Jun 1984; KJ (c); O: Null. O: Void 3.00
❑305, Jul 1984; KJ (c); TVE (a); V: Null and Void 3.00
❑306, Aug 1984; KJ (c); O: Swordfish and Barracuda; Michael Eury LOC 3.00
❑307, Sep 1984 KJ (c); TVE (a) 3.00
❑308, Oct 1984 KJ (c); KB (w); GT (a) ... 3.00
❑309, Nov 1984; KJ (c); KB (w); AA (a); Bonus Book 3.00
❑310, Dec 1984; KJ (c); A: Sonik. 1: Sonik 3.00
❑311, Jan 1985 KJ (c); A: Monitor 3.00
❑312, Feb 1985; (c); AA (a); V: Network 3.00
❑313, Mar 1985; KJ (c); AA (a); V: The Network 3.00
❑314, Apr 1985 KJ (c); AA (a); A: Monitor 3.00
❑315, May 1985; V: Network 3.00
❑316, Jun 1985 .... 3.00
❑317, Jul 1985 .... 3.00
❑318, Aug 1985 RT (c); AA (a); A: Sonik 3.00
❑319, Sep 1985; RT (c); AA (a); Mask special preview 3.00
❑320, Oct 1985 .... 3.00
❑321, Nov 1985; RB (c); AA (a); V: Chronos 3.00
❑322, Dec 1985 KG (c); KG (a) 3.00
❑323, Jan 1986; DG (c); AA (a); Final Issue 3.00

World's Finest: Our Worlds at War
DC

❑1, Oct 2001, hardcover; Our Worlds At War; Casualties of War; Follows Action Comics #782 .... 2.95

World's Funnest Comics
Moordam

❑1, Mar 1998, b&w; Cray-Baby Adventures, Mr. Beat 2.95

Worldstorm
DC

❑1, Dec 2006, Previews upcoming Wildstorm titles; Cover by Arthur Adams 2.99

Worlds Unknown
Marvel

❑1, May 1973, (c); GK (w); GK, AT (a); adapted from Frederik Pohl story 17.00
❑2, Jul 1973, (c); TS, VM, GK (a); adapted from L. Sprague de Camp story; adapted from Keith Laumer story 10.00
❑3, Sep 1973, WH (c); RA, WH (a); adapted from Harry Bates story 7.00
❑4, Nov 1973, (c); JB, DG (a); adapted from Frederic Brown story 5.00
❑5, Feb 1974, (c); JM, DA, JAb (a); adapted from A.E. Van Vogt story 5.00
❑6, Apr 1974, (c); adapted from Theodore Sturgeon story; Marvel Value Stamp #35: Killraven 5.00
❑7, Jun 1974, (c); GT (a); adapted from Brian Clemens screenplay; Marvel Value Stamp #32: Red Skull 5.00
❑8, Aug 1974, (c); GT (a); Final Issue; Marvel Value Stamp #75: Morbius 5.00

World's Worst Comics Awards
Kitchen Sink

❑1, Dec 1990, b&w 2.50
❑2, Jan 1991, b&w 2.50

World War II: 1946
Antarctic

❑1, Jul 1999, Families of Altered Wars #62 ... 2.50
❑2, Aug 1999, Families of Altered Wars #63 ... 2.50
❑3, Sep 1999, Families of Altered Wars #64 ... 2.50
❑4, Oct 1999, Families of Altered Wars #65 ... 2.50
❑5, Nov 1999, Families of Altered Wars #66 ... 2.50
❑6, Dec 1999, Families of Altered Wars #67 ... 2.50
❑7, Jan 2000, Families of Altered Wars #68 ... 2.50
❑8, Feb 2000, Families of Altered Wars #69 ... 2.50
❑9, Mar 2000, Families of Altered Wars #70 ... 2.50
❑10, Apr 2000, Families of Altered Wars #71 ... 2.50
❑11, May 2000, Families of Altered Wars #72 ... 2.50
❑12, Jun 2000, Families of Altered Wars #73 ... 2.50

World War II: 1946/Families of Altered Wars
Antarctic

❑1, Jul 1998, b&w; Compilation Edition. ... 3.95
❑1/2nd, Oct 1998 .... 3.95
❑2, Nov 1998, b&w; has indicia from #1 ... 3.95
❑2/2nd, Aug 1998 .... 3.95

World without End
DC

❑1, ca. 1990 .... 2.50
❑2, ca. 1990 .... 2.50
❑3, ca. 1990 .... 2.50
❑4, ca. 1990 .... 2.50
❑5, ca. 1990 .... 2.50
❑6, ca. 1990 .... 2.50

Wormwood Gentleman Corpse
Idea & Design Works

❑1, Aug 2006 .... 3.99
❑2, Sep 2006 .... 3.99
❑3, Oct 2006 .... 3.99
❑4, Nov 2006 .... 3.99

Wormwood Gentleman Corpse: The Taster
Idea & Design Works

❑1, May 2006 .... 3.99

Woron's Worlds
Illustration

❑1/A; Includes trading card; Adult 2.95
❑1/B; Adults-only cover 2.95
❑1/A/2nd; Includes coupon for disk of images; Adult 3.25
❑1/B/2nd; Includes coupon for disk of images; Adult 3.25
❑2/A; Includes coupon for free print; Adult ... 2.95
❑2/B; Adults-only cover 2.95
❑3/A, Nov 1994; Includes coupon for Woron's Female Fantasy disk; Adult ... 3.25
❑3/B, Nov 1994; Adults-only cover 3.25

W.O.W. The World of Ward
Allied American Artists

❑1, b&w; Reprints 3.95

Wraithborn
DC / Wildstorm

❑1, Jun 2005, Glow in the dark cover ... 2.99
❑2, Jun 2005 .... 2.99
❑3, Jan 2006 .... 2.99
❑4, Feb 2006 .... 2.99
❑5, May 2006 .... 2.99
❑6, Aug 2006 .... 3.99

Wraith
Outlander Comics Group

❑1, Aug 1991, b&w 1.75
❑2, Oct 1991 .... 1.75

Wrath
Malibu / Ultraverse

❑1, Jan 1994, A: Mantra 2.00
❑1/Ltd., Jan 1994; Ultra-limited edition; A: Mantra 3.00
❑2, Feb 1994 .... 2.00
❑3, Mar 1994, 1: Slayer 2.00
❑4, Apr 1994, A: Freex 1.95
❑5, May 1994, A: Freex 1.95
❑6, Jun 1994 .... 1.95
❑7, Jul 1994, 1: Ogre. 1: Pierce. 1: Doc Virtual 1.95
❑8, Oct 1994, 1: Project Patriot. A: Warstrike 1.95
❑9, Dec 1994, D: Project Patriot; Final Issue 2.25
❑GS 1, Aug 1994, Giant-size Wrath #1; 40 pgs 2.50

Wrath of the Spectre
DC

❑1, May 1988, Reprints from Adventure Comics #431-433, 426 .... 2.50
❑2, Jun 1988, Reprints 2.50
❑3, Jul 1988, Reprints 2.50
❑4, Aug 1988, new stories 2.50

Wretch
Caliber

❑1, Jul 1997, b&w 2.95
❑2, Sep 1997, b&w 2.95
❑3, Nov 1997, b&w 2.95
❑4 1998, b&w 2.95

Wretch
Slave Labor / Amaze Ink

❑1, Jul 1997, b&w; Dedicated to Alex Toth and Steve Ditko 2.95
❑2, Sep 1997, b&w; Dedicated to Alex Toth and Steve Ditko 2.95
❑3, Nov 1997, b&w; Dedicated to Frank Miller 2.95
❑4, May 1998, b&w; Dedicated to Jack Curtiss 2.95
❑5, May 1998, b&w; Dedicated to Will Eisner 2.95
❑6, Jul 1998, b&w; Dedicated to Stan, Jack, and Steve 2.95

Writers' Bloc Anthology
Writers' Bloc

❑1; ca. 2002 .... 3.00

Wulf the Barbarian
Atlas-Seaboard

❑1, Feb 1975, (c); O: Wulf. Larry Hama/ Klaus Janson 12.00
❑2, Apr 1975, (c); PB, NA, WW, BMc, KJ, JAb (a); Hama/Janson; art assists by Neal Adams, Wally Wood and Ralph Reese 9.00
❑3, May 1975, (c); indicia says July 8.00
❑4, Sep 1975, (c); Jim Craig art 8.00

Wu Wei
Angus

❑1 .... 2.50
❑2 .... 2.50
❑3 .... 2.50
❑4 .... 2.50
❑5 .... 2.50
❑6 .... 2.50

WW 2
NEC

❑1 .... 3.50
❑2, Nov 2000 .... 3.50

WW2 Rommel
New England

❑1 2005 .... 3.95

N-MINT N-MINT N-MINT

WWF: World Wrestling Foundation
Valiant

❑1, 21841 ... 2.95
❑2, 21842 ... 2.95
❑3, 21843 ... 2.95
❑4, 21844 ... 2.95

Wyatt Earp: Dodge City
Moonstone

❑1 2005 ... 2.95
❑2, Aug 2005 ... 2.95

Wynonna Earp
Image

❑1, Dec 1996; 1: Wynonna Earp ... 2.50
❑2, Jan 1997 ... 2.50
❑3, Feb 1997, cover says Jan, indicia says Feb ... 2.50
❑4, Mar 1997 ... 2.50
❑5, Apr 1997, final issue ... 2.50

Wyoming Territory
Ark

❑1, Jan 1989, b&w ... 1.95

Wyrd the Reluctant Warrior
Slave Labor

❑1, Jul 1999 ... 2.95
❑2, Aug 1999 ... 2.95
❑3, Sep 1999 ... 2.95
❑4, Oct 1999 ... 2.95
❑5, Nov 1999 ... 2.95
❑6, Dec 1999 ... 2.95

X
Dark Horse

❑1, Feb 1994; embossed cardstock cover 2.50
❑2, Mar 1994 ... 2.50
❑3, Apr 1994 ... 2.50
❑4, May 1994 ... 2.00
❑5, Jun 1994 ... 2.00
❑6, Aug 1994 ... 2.00
❑7, Sep 1994 ... 2.00
❑8, Oct 1994 ... 2.50
❑9, Nov 1994 ... 2.50
❑10, Dec 1994 ... 2.50
❑11, Jan 1995 ... 2.50
❑12, Mar 1995 ... 2.50
❑13, Apr 1995 ... 2.50
❑14, May 1995 ... 2.50
❑15, Jun 1995 ... 2.50
❑16, Jul 1995 ... 2.50
❑17, Aug 1995 ... 2.50
❑18, Sep 1995; FM (c); FM (a); V: Predator 2.50
❑19, Oct 1995 FM (c); FM (a) ... 2.50
❑20, Nov 1995 FM (c); FM (a) ... 2.50
❑21, Dec 1995 FM (c); FM (a) ... 2.50
❑22, Jan 1996 FM (c); FM (a) ... 2.50
❑23, Feb 1996 ... 2.50
❑24, Mar 1996 ... 2.50
❑25, Apr 1996; Final Issue; Includes 3 page Heartbreakers preview ... 2.50
❑Hero ed. 1, Jun 1994; Included with Hero Illustrated magazine; Hero Special edition #1; Included with Hero Illustrated magazine ... 1.00

X-Men: Colossus: Bloodline
Marvel

❑1, Oct 2005 ... 2.99
❑2, Dec 2005 ... 2.99
❑3, Jan 2006 ... 2.99
❑4, Feb 2006 ... 2.99
❑5, Mar 2006 ... 2.99

X-Men: Kitty Pryde: Shadow & Flame
Marvel

❑1, Aug 2005 ... 2.99
❑2, Sep 2005 ... 2.99
❑3, Oct 2005 ... 2.99
❑4 2005 ... 2.99
❑5, Jan 2006 ... 2.99

X-Men: The 198
Marvel

❑1, Mar 2006 ... 2.99
❑2, Apr 2006 ... 2.99
❑3, May 2006 ... 2.99
❑4, Jun 2006 ... 2.99
❑5, Jul 2006, D: Mr. M ... 2.99

Xanadu
Thoughts & Images

❑1, May 1988, b&w; 1: Fatima; 1: Tabbe Le Fauve; 1: Jonathan; 1: Reginald Plume; 1: Octavius; 1: Alicia; 1: Scratch 2.00
❑2, Jun 1988, b&w; 1: Firepetal; 1: Gruht;1: Kajiko Firelake;1: Kinomon Firestar ... 2.00
❑3, Jul 1988, b&w; D: Firepetal; 2: Firepetal; 2: Gruht; 2: Kajiko Firelake; 2: Kinomon Firestar ... 2.00
❑4, Aug 1988, b&w; 1: Toad; 1: Typhon; 1: Harold; D: Gruht; Typhon possesses Reginald Plume ... 2.00
❑5, Nov 1988, b&w; cover says Part Three of Five ... 2.00

Xanadu
3-D Zone

❑1 1986, b&w ... 2.00
❑2 1986, b&w ... 2.00
❑3 1986, b&w ... 2.00
❑4 1986, b&w ... 2.00

Xanadu: Across Diamond Seas
Mu

❑1, Jan 1994, b&w ... 2.50
❑2, Feb 1994, b&w; MU PUB #205 ... 2.50
❑3, Mar 1994, b&w ... 2.95
❑4, Apr 1994, b&w ... 2.95
❑5, May 1994, b&w ... 2.95

Xanadu Color Special
Eclipse

❑1, Dec 1988 ... 2.00

Xander in Lost Universe
Tekno

❑0, Nov 1995 ... 2.25
❑1, Dec 1995 ... 2.25
❑2, Dec 1995 ... 2.25
❑3, Jan 1996 ... 2.25
❑4, Jan 1996 ... 2.25
❑5, Feb 1996 ... 2.25
❑6, Mar 1996 ... 2.25
❑7, Apr 1996 ... 2.25
❑8, May 1996, The Big Crossover, Part 5: The Big Bang ... 2.25

Xanth Graphic Novel
Father Tree

❑1, Jul 1990; First part of the adaptation Of Isle of View by Piers Anthony ... 9.95

X-Babies: Murderama
Marvel

❑1, Aug 1998 ... 2.99

X-Babies: Reborn
Marvel

❑1, Jan 2000 ... 3.50

X-Calibre
Marvel

❑1, Mar 1995, (c);The Age of Apocalypse 2.00
❑2, Apr 1995, cover says Jun; The Age of Apocalypse ... 2.00
❑3, May 1995, The Age of Apocalypse ... 2.00
❑4, Jun 1995, The Age of Apocalypse ... 2.00

Xena
Brainstorm

❑1, Jan 1995 ... 2.95

Xena: Warrior Princess
Topps

❑0, Oct 1997 ... 2.95
❑1, Aug 1997, A: Hercules. back-up Tales of Salmoneus ... 2.95
❑1/A, Aug 1997, Photo cover of Xena poised to strike ... 4.00
❑1/AmEnt, Aug 1997, American Entertainment ... 7.00
❑1/Variant, Aug 1997 ... 4.00
❑2, Sep 1997 ... 2.95
❑2/Variant, Sep 1997, Photo cover ... 4.00

Xena: Warrior Princess
Dark Horse

❑1, Sep 1999 ... 3.00
❑1/Variant, Sep 1999, Photo cover ... 3.00
❑2, Oct 1999 ... 3.00
❑2/Variant, Oct 1999, Photo cover ... 3.00
❑3, Nov 1999 ... 3.00
❑3/Variant, Nov 1999, Photo cover ... 3.00
❑4, Dec 1999 ... 3.00
❑4/Variant, Dec 1999, Photo cover ... 3.00
❑5, Jan 2000 ... 3.00
❑5/Variant, Jan 2000, Photo cover ... 3.00
❑6, Feb 2000 ... 2.95
❑6/Variant, Feb 2000, Photo cover ... 2.95
❑7, Mar 2000 ... 2.95
❑7/Variant, Mar 2000, Photo cover ... 2.95
❑8, Apr 2000 ... 2.95
❑8/Variant, Apr 2000, Photo cover ... 2.95
❑9, May 2000 ... 2.95
❑9/Variant, May 2000, Photo cover ... 2.95
❑10, Jun 2000 ... 2.95
❑10/Variant, Jun 2000, Photo cover ... 2.95
❑11, Jul 2000 ... 2.95
❑11/Variant, Jul 2000, Photo cover ... 2.95
❑12, Aug 2000 ... 2.95
❑12/Variant, Aug 2000, Photo cover ... 2.95
❑13, Sep 2000 ... 2.95
❑13/Variant, Sep 2000, Photo cover ... 2.95
❑14, Oct 2000, Final Issue ... 2.99
❑14/Variant, Oct 2000, Photo cover; Final Issue ... 2.99

Xena: Warrior Princess And the Original Olympics
Topps

❑1, Jun 1998 ... 2.95
❑2, Jul 1998 ... 2.95
❑3, Aug 1998 ... 2.95

Xena: Warrior Princess: Bloodlines
Topps

❑1, May 1998 ... 2.95
❑2, Jun 1998 ... 2.95

Xena: Warrior Princess/Joxer: Warrior Prince
Topps

❑1, Nov 1997 ... 2.95
❑1/Variant, Nov 1997, Photo cover ... 2.95
❑2, Dec 1997 ... 2.95
❑2/Variant, Dec 1997, Photo cover ... 2.95
❑3, Jan 1998 ... 2.95
❑3/Variant, Jan 1998, Photo cover ... 2.95

Xena: Warrior Princess: The Dragon's Teeth
Topps

❑1, Dec 1997 ... 2.95
❑1/Variant, Dec 1997 ... 2.95
❑2, Jan 1998 ... 2.95
❑2/Variant, Jan 1998 ... 2.95
❑3, Feb 1998 ... 2.95
❑3/Variant, Feb 1998 ... 2.95

Xena: Warrior Princess: The Orpheus Trilogy
Topps

❑1, Mar 1998, Adam Hughes pinup ... 2.95
❑1/Variant, Mar 1998, Photo cover ... 2.95
❑2, Apr 1998 ... 2.95
❑2/Variant, Apr 1998, Photo cover ... 2.95
❑3, May 1998 ... 2.95
❑3/Variant, May 1998, Photo cover ... 2.95

Xena: Warrior Princess: The Warrior Way Of Death
Dark Horse

❑1, Sep 1999 ... 2.95
❑1/Variant, Sep 1999 ... 2.95
❑2, Oct 1999 ... 2.95
❑2/Variant, Oct 1999 ... 2.95

Xena: Warrior Princess vs. Callisto
Topps

❑1, Feb 1998 ... 2.95
❑1/A, Feb 1998, No cover price ... 5.00
❑1/Variant, Feb 1998, Photo cover ... 2.95
❑2, Mar 1998 ... 2.95
❑2/Variant, Mar 1998, Photo cover ... 2.95
❑3, Mar 1998 ... 2.95
❑3/Variant, Mar 1998, Photo cover ... 2.95

Xena, Warrior Princess: Wrath of Hera
Topps

❑1 1998 ... 2.95
❑1/Variant 1998, Photo cover ... 3.00
❑2 1998 ... 2.95
❑2/Variant 1998, Photo cover ... 3.00

Xena: Warrior Princess, Year One
Topps

❑1 1998, O: Xena; Photo cover of Xena smiling ... 5.00
❑1/Gold 1998, O: Xena. Gold logo cover 10.00

Other grades: Multiply price above by 5/6 for VF/NM • 2/3 for VERY FINE • 1/3 for FINE • 1/5 for VERY GOOD • 1/8 for GOOD

Xene
Eyeball Soup Designs

❑1, Jan 1996; cardstock cover ... 4.95
❑2, Mar 1996; cardstock cover ... 4.95
❑3, May 1996; cardstock cover ... 4.95
❑4, Jul 1996; cardstock cover ... 4.95

Xenobrood
DC

❑0, Oct 1994, 1: Xenobrood; O: Xenobrood ... 1.50
❑1, Nov 1994 ... 1.50
❑2, Dec 1994 ... 1.50
❑3, Jan 1995 ... 1.50
❑4, Feb 1995 ... 1.50
❑5, Mar 1995 ... 1.50
❑6, Apr 1995, Final Issue ... 1.50

Xeno-Men
Blackthorne

❑1, Nov 1987, b&w; 1: Xeno-Men ... 1.75

Xenon
Eclipse / Viz

❑1, Dec 1987, b&w ... 2.00
❑2, Dec 1987, b&w ... 2.00
❑3, Jan 1988, b&w ... 2.00
❑4, Jan 1988, b&w ... 2.00
❑5, Feb 1988, b&w ... 2.00
❑6, Feb 1988, b&w ... 2.00
❑7, Mar 1988, b&w ... 2.00
❑8, Mar 1988, b&w ... 2.00
❑9, Apr 1988, b&w ... 2.00
❑10, Apr 1988, b&w ... 2.00
❑11, May 1988, b&w ... 1.50
❑12, May 1988, b&w ... 1.50
❑13, Jun 1988, b&w ... 1.50
❑14, Jun 1988, b&w ... 1.50
❑15, Jul 1988, b&w ... 1.50
❑16, Jul 1988, b&w ... 1.50
❑17, Aug 1988, b&w ... 1.50
❑18, Aug 1988, b&w ... 1.50
❑19, Sep 1988, b&w ... 1.50
❑20, Sep 1988, b&w ... 1.50
❑21, Oct 1988, b&w ... 1.50
❑22, Oct 1988, b&w ... 1.50
❑23, Nov 1989, b&w; Final Issue ... 1.50

Xeno's Arrow
Cup o' Tea

❑1, Feb 1999, b&w ... 2.50
❑2, Apr 1999 ... 2.50
❑3, Jun 1999 ... 2.50
❑4, Aug 1999 ... 2.50

Xenotech
Mirage / Next

❑1, Aug 1994, Includes trading cards ... 2.75
❑1/A, Aug 1994, Variant cover with monster attacking; Includes trading cards ... 2.75
❑2, Oct 1994, Includes trading cards ... 2.75
❑3, Dec 1994, Includes trading cards ... 2.75

Xenozoic Tales
Kitchen Sink

❑1, Feb 1987, b&w ... 8.00
❑1/2nd, Mar 1987, b&w; 2nd printing ... 3.00
❑2, Apr 1987, b&w ... 6.00
❑3, Jun 1987, b&w ... 6.00
❑4, Nov 1987, b&w ... 6.00
❑5, Feb 1988, b&w ... 6.00
❑6, May 1988, b&w; ca. 1988 ... 5.00
❑7, Oct 1988, b&w; ca. 1988 ... 5.00
❑8, Jan 1989, b&w; ca. 1988 ... 5.00
❑9, Sep 1989, b&w; ca. 1988 ... 5.00
❑10, Apr 1990, b&w; ca. 1989 ... 5.00
❑11, Apr 1991, b&w; ca. 1990 ... 4.00
❑12, Apr 1992, b&w; ca. 1991 ... 4.00
❑13, Dec 1994, b&w; Cardstock cover ... 4.00
❑14, Oct 1996, b&w; cardstock cover ... 4.00

Xenya
Sanctuary

❑1, Jul 1994 ... 2.95
❑2, Sep 1994 ... 2.95
❑3, ca. 1995; no cover price ... 2.95

Xero
DC

❑1, May 1997 ... 2.00
❑2, Jun 1997 ... 1.75
❑3, Jul 1997, (c) ... 1.75
❑4, Aug 1997, (c) ... 1.75
❑5, Sep 1997 ... 1.75
❑6, Oct 1997, (c); V: Polaris. Genesis ... 1.75
❑7, Nov 1997 ... 1.75
❑8, Dec 1997, (c); Face cover ... 1.95
❑9, Jan 1998, (c) ... 1.95
❑10, Feb 1998, (c) ... 1.95
❑11, Mar 1998, (c) ... 1.95
❑12, Apr 1998, Final Issue ... 1.95

X-Factor
Marvel

❑-1, Jul 1997, (c);Flashback ... 2.00
❑1, Feb 1986, Giant-size; (c); BL (w); BG (a); O: X-Factor. 1: Rusty Collins. Giant-size ... 3.00
❑2, Mar 1986, MZ (c); BL (w); BG (a); 1: Artie; 1: Tower ... 2.00
❑3, Apr 1986, BL (w); BG (a) ... 2.00
❑4, May 1986, BL (w); KP (a); 1: Frenzy ... 2.00
❑5, Jun 1986, BL (w); BG (a); 1: Apocalypse (in shadows); Glenn Greenberg LOC ... 3.00
❑6, Jul 1986, (c); BG (a); 1: Apocalypse (full appearance); Apocalypse ... 5.00
❑7, Aug 1986, (c); BG (a); 1: Skids ... 3.00
❑8, Sep 1986, (c) ... 2.00
❑9, Oct 1989, Mutant Massacre ... 2.00
❑10, Nov 1989, Mutant Massacre ... 2.00
❑11, Dec 1989, Mutant Massacre ... 2.00
❑12, Jan 1987, O: Famine. 1: Famine ... 2.00
❑13, Feb 1987, A: Phoenix ... 2.00
❑14, Mar 1987, 1st mention of The Twelve; Angel's wings are amputated ... 2.00
❑15, Apr 1987, 1: Horseman of Apocalypse; Angel attempts suicide ... 2.00
❑16, May 1987, O: Skids ... 2.00
❑17, Jun 1987, 1: Rictor ... 2.00
❑18, Jul 1987, (c) ... 2.00
❑19, Aug 1987 ... 2.00
❑20, Sep 1987 ... 2.00
❑21, Oct 1987 ... 2.00
❑22, Nov 1987, SB (a) ... 2.00
❑23, Dec 1987, 1: Archangel (cameo). registration card ... 5.00
❑24, Jan 1988, O: Apocalypse. 1: Archangel (full appearance); The Fall of the Mutants ... 8.00
❑25, Feb 1988, Fall of Mutants ... 2.00
❑26, Mar 1988, Fall of Mutants ... 2.00
❑27, Apr 1988, BWi (c) ... 2.00
❑28, May 1988 ... 2.00
❑29, Jun 1988, 1: Infectia ... 2.00
❑30, Jul 1988 ... 2.00
❑31, Aug 1988 ... 2.00
❑32, Sep 1988, 1: N'astirh. A: Avengers ... 2.00
❑33, Oct 1988, 1: Orphan Maker ... 2.00
❑34, Nov 1988, D: Candy Southern ... 2.00
❑35, Dec 1988 ... 2.00
❑36, Jan 1989, Inferno ... 2.00
❑37, Feb 1989, Inferno ... 2.00
❑38, Mar 1989, Giant-size; D: Madelyn Pryor. Inferno ... 2.00
❑39, Apr 1989, Inferno ... 2.00
❑40, May 1989, AM, RL (c); RL (a); V: Nanny; V: Orphan-Maker ... 2.00
❑41, Jun 1989, 1: Alchemy; V: trolls ... 2.00
❑42, Jul 1989, V: trolls ... 2.00
❑43, Aug 1989, PS (c); PS (a); Judgement War, Part 1 ... 2.00
❑44, Sep 1989, PS (c); PS (a); Judgement War, Part 2 ... 2.00
❑45, Oct 1989, PS (c); PS (a); Judgement War, Part 3 ... 2.00
❑46, Nov 1989, PS (c); PS (a); Judgement War, Part 4 ... 2.00
❑47, Nov 1989, AM (c); Solo Archangel story ... 2.00
❑48, Dec 1989, PS (c); PS (a); Judgement War, Part 5 ... 2.00
❑49, Dec 1989, AM (c); PS (a); Judgement War, Part 6 ... 2.00
❑50, Jan 1990, Giant-size; TMc, RL (c); RB (a) ... 2.50
❑51, Feb 1990, A: Sabretooth. 1: Opal Tanaka; 1: Charlotte Jones ... 2.50
❑52, Mar 1990, AM, RL (c); A: Sabretooth. Archangel vs. Sabretooth ... 2.50
❑53, Apr 1990, AM (c); A: Sabretooth. Cyclops proposes to Jean Grey; Archangel vs. Caliban ... 2.50
❑54, May 1990, AM (c); 1: Crimson ... 1.50
❑55, Jun 1990, PD (w); Beast vs. Mesmero ... 1.50
❑56, Jul 1990, AM (c) ... 1.50
❑57, Aug 1990, Archangel vs. Crimson ... 1.50
❑58, Sep 1990, AM (c);V: Crimson ... 1.50
❑59, Oct 1990, AM (c) ... 1.50
❑60, Nov 1990, AM (c); Cyclops vs. Havok ... 2.50
❑60/2nd, Nov 1990, AM (c); Gold cover ... 1.50
❑61, Dec 1990, AM (c); Cable vs. Cameron Hodge ... 2.50
❑62, Jan 1991, JLee (c) ... 2.50
❑63, Feb 1991 ... 2.50
❑64, Mar 1991 ... 2.50
❑65, Apr 1991, JLee (w); 1: Dark Riders; 1: Gauntlet; 1: Foxbat; 1: Harddrive; 1: Tusk; 1: Barrage; 1: Psynapse ... 2.50
❑66, May 1991, JLee (w); 1: As'kani ... 2.50
❑67, Jun 1991, JLee (w); 1: Shinobi Shaw ... 2.50
❑68, Jul 1991, JLee (w); Baby Nathan is sent into future ... 2.50
❑69, Aug 1991, Muir Island Saga ... 2.50
❑70, Sep 1991, PD (w); Muir Island Epilogue ... 2.00
❑71, Oct 1991, AM (c); PD (w); AM (a); new team; Havok, Madrox, Polaris & Wolfsbane ... 2.00
❑71/2nd, Oct 1991, AM (c); PD (w); AM (a); Havok, Madrox, Polaris & Wolfsbane ... 1.50
❑72, Nov 1991, AM (c); PD (w); AM (a); 1: Vic Chalker; 1: Ricochet ... 1.50
❑73, Dec 1991, AM (c); PD (w); AM (a); V: Madrox's clones ... 1.50
❑74, Jan 1992, AM (c); PD (w); AM (a); 1: Slab ... 1.50
❑75, Feb 1992, Giant-size; (c); PD (w) ... 2.00
❑76, Mar 1992, AM (c); PD (w); V: Pantheon ... 1.50
❑77, Apr 1992, AM (c); PD (w); AM (a); D: Vic Chalker ... 1.50
❑78, May 1992, PD (w) ... 1.50
❑79, Jun 1992, KN (c); PD (w); 1: Rhapsody ... 1.50
❑80, Jul 1992, AM (c); PD (w); AM (a) ... 1.50
❑81, Aug 1992, (c); PD (w) ... 1.50
❑82, Sep 1992, AM (c); PD (w) ... 1.50
❑83, Oct 1992, AM (c); PD (w) ... 1.50
❑84/CS, Nov 1992, AM (c); PD (w); AM (a); Includes Caliban trading card ... 2.00
❑85/CS, Dec 1992, PD (w); Includes trading card ... 2.00
❑86/CS, Jan 1993, PD (w); Includes Dark Riders trading card ... 2.00
❑87, Feb 1993, AM (c); PD (w) ... 1.50
❑88, Mar 1993, AM (c); PD (w) ... 1.50
❑89, Apr 1993, AM (c); PD (w) ... 1.50
❑90, May 1993 ... 1.50
❑91, Jun 1993, AM (c) ... 1.50
❑92, Jul 1993, AM (c); AM (a); Hologram cover; Fatal Attractions ... 4.00
❑93, Aug 1993, PS (c); AM (a) ... 1.50
❑94, Sep 1993, (c); AM (a) ... 1.50
❑95, Oct 1993, AM (c); A: Polaris. A: Random ... 1.50
❑96, Nov 1993, AM (c); AM (a); 1: Haven ... 1.50
❑97, Dec 1993, (c); AM, JDu (a); Siege of Darkness preview ... 1.50
❑98, Jan 1994, AM (c) ... 1.50
❑99, Feb 1994, AM, JDu (c); AM, JDu (a); 1: Monsoon ... 1.50
❑100, Mar 1994, Giant-size; (c); JDu (a); D: Multiple Man ... 2.00
❑100/Variant, Mar 1994, Giant-size; (c); JDu (a); D: Multiple Man; foil embossed cover ... 3.00
❑101, Apr 1994, AM, JDu (c); JDu (a) ... 1.50
❑102, May 1994, (c); JDu (a); Includes trading cards ... 1.50
❑103, Jun 1994, JDu (c); AM, JDu (a) ... 1.50
❑104, Jul 1994, AM, JDu (c); JDu (a) ... 1.50
❑105, Aug 1994, (c) ... 1.50
❑106, Sep 1994, JDu (a); wraparound cover; Phalanx Covenant ... 2.00
❑106/Variant, Sep 1994, JDu (a); enhanced cover; Phalanx Covenant ... 2.95
❑107, Oct 1994, AM, KGa (c) ... 1.50
❑108, Nov 1994, JDu (a) ... 1.50

N-MINT

❑108/Deluxe, Nov 1994, Deluxe edition; JDu (a) 2.00
❑109, Dec 1994, AM (c); JDu (a) 1.50
❑109/Deluxe, Dec 1994, Deluxe edition; AM (c); JDu (a) 2.00
❑110, Jan 1995, AM (c); JDu (a); A: Lila Cheney 1.50
❑110/Deluxe, Jan 1995, Deluxe edition; AM (c); JDu (a); A: Lila Cheney. Deluxe edition 2.00
❑111, Feb 1995, AM (c); JDu (a) 1.50
❑111/Deluxe, Feb 1995, Deluxe edition; AM (c); JDu (a); Deluxe edition; Bound-in trading cards 2.00
❑112, Jul 1995 1.95
❑113, Aug 1995 1.95
❑114, Sep 1995 1.95
❑115, Oct 1995, AM (a); bound-in trading cards 1.95
❑116, Nov 1995, A: Alpha Flight 1.95
❑117, Dec 1995, A: Cyclops. A: Wild Child. A: Havok. A: Mystique. A: Random 1.95
❑118, Jan 1996, Havok V: Random; Naze V: Adversary; Brotherhood kidnaps Havok 1.95
❑119, Feb 1996, A: Shard. 1.95
❑120, Mar 1996, (c) 1.95
❑121, Apr 1996, V: Adversary 1.95
❑122, May 1996, AM (c) 1.95
❑123, Jun 1996, V: Hound 1.95
❑124, Jul 1996, Onslaught Update 1.95
❑125, Aug 1996, AM (c); AM (a); Onslaught: Impact, Part 1 2.95
❑126, Sep 1996, HT (a); A: real Beast. real Beast returns; Heroes Reborn Update 1.95
❑127, Oct 1996, AW (a); bound-in trading cards; Heroes Reborn Update 1.95
❑128, Nov 1996, AM (a) 1.95
❑129, Dec 1996 1.95
❑130, Jan 1997, D: Graydon Creed 2.50
❑131, Feb 1997, (c); Dark Beast escapes prison 1.95
❑132, Mar 1997, 40 pages 1.95
❑133, Apr 1997, 40 pages 1.95
❑134, May 1997, 40 pages 1.95
❑135, Jun 1997, A: Guido Carosella (Strong Guy). return of Strong Guy 1.95
❑136, Aug 1997, gatefold summary; A: Sabretooth 1.99
❑137, Sep 1997, gatefold summary 1.99
❑138, Oct 1997, gatefold summary; A: Sabretooth. V: Omega Red 1.99
❑139, Nov 1997, gatefold summary 1.99
❑140, Dec 1997, gatefold summary; A: Xavier's Underground Enforcers 1.99
❑141, Jan 1998, gatefold summary 1.99
❑142, Feb 1998, gatefold summary 1.99
❑143, Mar 1998, gatefold summary 1.99
❑144, Apr 1998, gatefold summary; V: Random 1.99
❑145, May 1998, gatefold summary 1.99
❑146, Jun 1998, gatefold summary; A: Multiple Man 1.99
❑147, Jul 1998, gatefold summary 1.99
❑148, Aug 1998, gatefold summary; A: Polaris. V: Mandroids 1.99
❑149, Sep 1998, gatefold summary 1.99
❑Ann 1, ca. 1986, BL (c); BL (w); BL (a) 3.00
❑Ann 2, ca. 1987 3.00
❑Ann 3, ca. 1988, JOy, JBy (a); O: High Evolutionary 3.00
❑Ann 4, ca. 1989, JBy (c); JBy (w); JBy (a) 2.50
❑Ann 5, ca. 1990, PD (w); A: Fantastic Four. A: New Mutants 2.50
❑Ann 6, ca. 1991, PD (w); D: Proteus 2.50
❑Ann 7, ca. 1992, PD (w) 2.25
❑Ann 8, ca. 1993, PD (w); AM (a); A: Guido Carosella (Strong Guy). trading card 2.95
❑Ann 9, ca. 1994, KGa (a); V: Power 2.95

X-Factor
Marvel

❑1, Feb 2006 7.00
❑2, Feb 2006 2.99
❑3, Mar 2006 2.99
❑4, May 2006 2.99
❑5, Jun 2006 2.99
❑6, Jul 2006 2.99
❑7, Aug 2006 2.99
❑8, Sep 2006 8.00
❑9, Sep 2006 2.99
❑10, Nov 2006 2.99
❑11, Nov 2006 2.99
❑12, Dec 2006 2.99
❑14, Feb 2007 2.99
❑15, Mar 2007 2.99
❑16, Apr 2007 2.99
❑17, May 2007 2.99
❑18, Jun 2007 2.99
❑19, Jul 2007 2.99
❑20, Aug 2007 2.99
❑21, Sep 2007 2.99
❑22, Oct 2007 2.99
❑23, Nov 2007 2.99
❑24, Dec 2007 2.99
❑25, Jan 2008 6.00
❑26, Feb 2008 6.00
❑27, Mar 2008 3.00
❑28 2.99
❑29 2.99
❑30 2.99
❑31 2.99
❑32 2.99
❑33 2.99
❑34 2.99
❑35 2.99
❑36 2.99
❑37 2.99
❑38 2.99
❑39 2.99
❑40 2.99
❑41 2.99
❑42 2.99
❑43 2.99

X-Farce
Eclipse

❑1, Jan 1992, b&w; parody 2.50

X-Farce vs. X-Cons: X-tinction
Parody

❑1 1993, b&w 2.75
❑1.5 1993, b&w; w/ trading cards 2.75

X-51
Marvel

❑0, ca. 1999; Wizard Promo 1.00
❑1, Sep 1999 1.99
❑2, Sep 1999 1.99
❑3, Oct 1999 1.99
❑4, Nov 1999 1.99
❑5, Dec 1999; V: Vision; V: Firestar; V: Justice 1.99
❑6, Jan 2000 1.99
❑7, Feb 2000 1.99
❑8, Mar 2000 1.99
❑9, Apr 2000 1.99
❑10, May 2000 1.99
❑11, Jun 2000 1.99
❑12, Jul 2000; Final issue 1.99

X-Files
Topps

❑-2, Sep 1996, no cover price 10.00
❑-1, Sep 1996, no cover price 10.00
❑0/A, adapts pilot episode; forms diptych with Scully cover 4.00
❑0/B, adapts pilot episode; forms diptych with Mulder cover 4.00
❑0/C, adapts pilot episode 4.00
❑½, Wizard promotional edition 10.00
❑1, Jan 1995 8.00
❑1/2nd, Jan 1995 2.50
❑2, Feb 1995 5.00
❑3, Mar 1995, Cover gives storyline as "The Return"; b&w variant 4.00
❑3/2nd, Mar 1995, Cover gives storyline as "The Return"; b&w variant 2.50
❑4, Apr 1995 3.50
❑4/2nd, Apr 1995 2.95
❑5, May 1995 3.00
❑6, Jun 1995 3.00
❑7, Jul 1995 3.00
❑8, Aug 1995 3.00
❑9, Sep 1995 3.00
❑10, Oct 1995 3.00
❑11, Nov 1995 3.00
❑12, Dec 1995 3.00
❑13, Feb 1996 3.00
❑14, Apr 1996 3.00
❑15, May 1996 3.00
❑16, May 1996 3.00
❑17, May 1996 3.00
❑18, Jun 1996 3.00
❑19, Jun 1996 3.00
❑20, Jul 1996 3.00
❑21, Aug 1996, Includes trading card 3.00
❑22, Sep 1996 2.95
❑23, Nov 1996, Donor 2.95
❑24, Dec 1996 2.95
❑25, Jan 1997 2.95
❑26, Feb 1997 2.95
❑27, Mar 1997 2.95
❑28, Apr 1997 2.95
❑29, May 1997 2.95
❑30, Jun 1997 2.95
❑31, Jul 1997 2.95
❑32, Aug 1997 2.95
❑33, Sep 1997 2.95
❑33/Variant, Sep 1997, Variant photo cover 5.00
❑34, Oct 1997 2.95
❑35, Nov 1997 2.95
❑36, Dec 1997 2.95
❑37, Jan 1998 2.95
❑38, Feb 1998 2.95
❑39, Mar 1998 2.95
❑40, Apr 1998 2.95
❑41, May 1998 2.95
❑41/Variant, Jun 1998, Photo cover 2.95
❑Ann 1, Aug 1995 3.95
❑Ann 2, ca. 1996, E.L.F.s 3.95
❑Ashcan 1, Jan 1995, no cover price; polybagged with Star Wars Galaxy #2 4.00
❑Special 1, Jun 1995, reprints issues #1 and 2 4.95
❑Special 2, ca. 1995, Reprints X-Files #4-6 4.95
❑Special 3, ca. 1996, HK (w); MW (a); Reprints X-Files #7-9 4.95
❑Special 4, Nov 1996, reprints Feelings of Unreality 4.95
❑Special 5, ca. 1997, Reprints X-Files #13, Ann #1 4.95

X-Files Comics Digest
Topps

❑1, Dec 1995, Bradbury back-up stories 3.50
❑2, Apr 1996, Bradbury back-up stories 3.50
❑3, Sep 1996, Bradbury back-up stories 3.50

X-Files Ground Zero
Topps

❑1, Dec 1997, adapts Kevin J. Anderson novel 2.95
❑2, Jan 1998, adapts Kevin J. Anderson novel 2.95
❑3, Feb 1998, adapts Kevin J. Anderson novel 2.95
❑4, Mar 1998, adapts Kevin J. Anderson novel 2.95

X-Files: Season One
Topps

❑1, Jul 1997, prestige format; adapts pilot episode 4.95
❑2, ca. 1997, prestige format; Indicia lists as Season One, Vol. 1 4.95
❑2/A, ca. 1997, variant cover 4.95
❑3, Oct 1997 4.95
❑3/A, Oct 1997, variant cover 4.95
❑4, Dec 1997 4.95
❑5, Jan 1998 4.95
❑6, Feb 1998 4.95
❑7, Mar 1998 4.95
❑8, Apr 1998 4.95
❑9, Jul 1998 4.95

X-Files: Afterflight
Topps

❑1 5.95

X-Flies Bug Hunt
Twist and Shout

❑1, Dec 1996 2.95
❑2, Jan 1997; Flip Book; The Complete Wurx of William Shakespeare #0 on back 2.95
❑3, Feb 1997 2.95
❑4, Mar 1997 2.95

X-Flies Conspiracy
Twist and Shout

❑1, Mar 1996 2.95

X-Flies Special
Twist and Shout

❑1, Sep 1995 2.95

X-Force
Marvel

❑-1, Jul 1997, AM (a); Flashback; Proudstars team up 2.00
❑1/A, Aug 1991, RL (c); RL (w); RL (a); 1: G.W. Bridge. with Cable card 2.00
❑1/B, Aug 1991, RL (c); RL (w); RL (a); 1: G.W. Bridge. with Deadpool card 2.00
❑1/C, Aug 1991, RL (c); RL (w); RL (a); 1: G.W. Bridge. with Shatterstar card . 2.00
❑1/D, Aug 1991, RL (c); RL (w); RL (a); 1: G.W. Bridge. with Sunspot & Gideon card 2.00
❑1/E, Aug 1991, RL (c); RL (w); RL (a); 1: G.W. Bridge. with X-Force group card 2.00
❑1/2nd, Aug 1991, RL (c); RL (w); RL (a); 1: G.W. Bridge. Gold cover 1.50
❑2, Sep 1991, RL (c); RL (w); RL (a); 1: Weapon X II (Garrison Kane); Garrison Kane V: Deadpool 2.50
❑3, Oct 1991, RL (c); RL (w); RL (a); V: Juggernaut. Storyline continued in Spider-Man #16; V: Juggernaut; V: Black Tom Cassidy 2.00
❑4, Nov 1991, RL, (c); RL (w); RL (a); A: Spider-Man. Sideways printing 2.00
❑5, Dec 1991, RL, (c); RL (w); RL (a); A: Brotherhood of Evil Mutants. Siryn joins; 1: Phantazia 2.00
❑6, Jan 1992, RL (c); RL (w); RL (a); 1: Thornn; 1: Phantazia; V: Masque; V: Brotherhood of Evil Mutants 2.00
❑7, Feb 1992, RL (c); RL (w); RL (a); Weapon X story; V: Brotherhood of Evil Mutants; V: Masque 2.00
❑8, Mar 1992, RL (c); RL (w); RL (a); 1: Grizzly II; 1: Domino (flashback); 1: Wild Pack 2.00
❑9, Apr 1992, RL (c); RL (a); D: Masque; V: Masque; V: Brotherhood of Evil Mutants; Cannonball revealed as Eternal 2.00
❑10, May 1992, RL (w); 1: Absalom; Weapon X (Garrison Kane) V: Stryfe .. 2.00
❑11, Jun 1992, RL (c); RL (w); 1: Domino 2.00
❑12, Jul 1992, RL (w) 2.00
❑13, Aug 1992 .... 2.00
❑14, Sep 1992 .... 2.00
❑15, Oct 1992, Sunspot joins; Rictor joins 2.00
❑16/CS, Nov 1992, Includes Cable card . 2.00
❑17/CS, Dec 1992, O: Zero. O: Stryfe. Includes trading card 2.00
❑18/CS, Jan 1993, Includes trading card 2.00
❑19, Feb 1993, Boom-Boom becomes Boomer 1.50
❑20, Mar 1993 .... 1.50
❑21, Apr 1993, V: SHIELD; V: War Machine; SHIELD seeks Cable's technology 1.50
❑22, May 1993, V: SHIELD; V: War Machine; SHIELD seeks Cable's technology 1.50
❑23, Jun 1993 .... 1.50
❑24, Jul 1993, X-Men/Avengers promo insert 1.50
❑25, Aug 1993, Hologram cover 3.00
❑26, Sep 1993, 1: Reignfire 1.50
❑27, Oct 1993, A: Mutant Liberation Front. 1: Reignfire 1.50
❑28, Nov 1993, (c); Feral quits 1.50
❑29, Dec 1993, A: Arcade. Shatterstar spotlight; V: Arcade; Versys Adam-X .. 1.50
❑30, Jan 1994, Shatterstar spotlight; V: Arcade; Versys Adam-X 1.50
❑31, Feb 1994, Siryn spotlight 1.25
❑32, Mar 1994, 1: Husk; Continued in New Warriors #45 .... 1.25
❑33, Apr 1994, Continued in New Warriors #46 .... 1.25
❑34, May 1994, (c) 1.50
❑35, Jun 1994, V: Nimrod 1.50
❑36, Jul 1994 .... 1.50
❑37, Aug 1994, AM (c); Continued in X-Factor #106 .... 1.50
❑38, Sep 1994, Phalanx Covenant 2.00
❑38/Variant, Sep 1994, enhanced cover; Phalanx Covenant 3.00
❑39, Oct 1994 .... 1.50
❑40, Nov 1994 .... 1.50
❑40/Deluxe, Nov 1994, Deluxe edition ... 1.95
❑41, Dec 1994 .... 1.50
❑41/Deluxe, Dec 1994, Deluxe edition ... 1.95
❑42, Jan 1995 .... 1.50
❑42/Deluxe, Jan 1995, Deluxe edition 1.95
❑43, Feb 1995 .... 1.50
❑43/Deluxe, Feb 1995, Deluxe edition; bound-in trading cards 1.95
❑44, Jul 1995, (c); JPH (w); A: Cannonball. Cannonball leaves 1.95
❑45, Aug 1995, JPH (w); Caliban vs. Sabretooth 1.95
❑46, Sep 1995, (c); JPH (w); V: Mimic .. 1.95
❑47, Oct 1995, JPH (w); bound-in trading cards 1.95
❑48, Nov 1995, JPH (w); Sabretooth storyline continued Uncanny X-Men #328 .... 1.95
❑49, Dec 1995, JPH (w); A: Holocaust. A: Sebastian Shaw. V: Holocaust; V: Sebastian Shaw 1.50
❑49/Deluxe, Dec 1995, Direct Edition; JPH (w) 1.90
❑50, Jan 1996, Giant-size; (c); JPH (w); wraparound fold-out cover 3.00
❑50/A, Jan 1996, Giant-size; RL (c); JPH (w); Giant-size 4.00
❑50/Variant, Jan 1996, Giant-size; (c); JPH (w); enhanced wraparound fold-out cardstock cover 1.95
❑51, Feb 1996, JPH (w); 1: Meltdown (formerly Boomer/Boom Boom); 1: Risque 1.95
❑52, Mar 1996, JPH (w); D: Gideon. V: Blob. D: Gideon; V: Blob 1.95
❑53, Apr 1996, JPH (w); X-Force, Crule and Absalom V: Selene 1.95
❑54, May 1996, (c); JPH (w); D: Crule; D: Absalom; X-Force, Crule and Absalom V: Selene 1.95
❑55, Jun 1996, JPH (w); V: S.H.I.E.L.D.. V: S.H.I.E.L.D 1.95
❑56, Jul 1996, JPH (w); Onslaught preview 1.95
❑57, Aug 1996, JPH (w); Onslaught: Impact; Part 1; Heroes Reborn preview 1.95
❑58, Sep 1996, JPH (w); Onslaught: Impact, Part 2 .... 1.95
❑59, Oct 1996, JPH (w); bound-in trading cards 1.95
❑60, Nov 1996, JPH (w); O: Shatterstar; Time Slip preview; V: Mojo 1.95
❑61, Dec 1996, JPH (w); O: Shatterstar. 1.95
❑62, Jan 1997 .... 1.95
❑63, Feb 1997, team invades Doom's castle 1.95
❑64, Mar 1997, A: Baron Von Strucker. 40 pages; Ka-Zar preview; SHIELD and X-Force transported to WWII 1.95
❑65, Apr 1997, 40 pages; V: Blob; V: Mimic; Risque kidnaps Warpath 1.95
❑66, May 1997, Hulk preview; 1: Sledge; V: Risque; 40 pages 1.95
❑67, Jun 1997, A: Dani Moonstar. Return of Dani Moonstar; 40 pages 1.99
❑68, Aug 1997, gatefold summary; A: Vanisher 1.99
❑69, Sep 1997, gatefold summary 1.99
❑70, Oct 1997, gatefold summary 1.99
❑71, Nov 1997, gatefold summary 1.99
❑72, Dec 1997, gatefold summary 1.99
❑73, Jan 1998, gatefold summary; D: Warpath 1.99
❑74, Feb 1998, gatefold summary; V: Stryfe 1.99
❑75, Mar 1998, gatefold summary; A: Cannonball 1.99
❑76, Apr 1998, gatefold summary; Domino vs. Shatterstar 1.99
❑77, May 1998, gatefold summary 1.99
❑78, Jun 1998, gatefold summary 1.99
❑79, Jul 1998, gatefold summary; O: Reignfire 1.99
❑80, Aug 1998, gatefold summary 1.99
❑81, Sep 1998, gatefold summary; poster 1.99
❑82, Oct 1998, gatefold summary 1.99
❑83, Nov 1998, gatefold summary 1.99
❑84, Dec 1998, gatefold summary; V: New Deviants 1.99
❑85, Jan 1999, gatefold summary 1.99
❑86, Jan 1999, gatefold summary 1.99
❑87, Feb 1999, A: Hellions. Paradigm appearnace 1.99
❑88, Mar 1999, A: Christopher Bedlam. A: Hellions. V: New Hellions 1.99
❑89, Apr 1999, A: Armageddon Man. A: Hellions. Feral appearanace 1.99
❑90, May 1999 .... 1.99
❑91, Jun 1999, Siryn solo tale 1.99
❑92, Jul 1999, Domino vs. Halloween Jack 1.99
❑93, Aug 1999 .... 1.99
❑94, Sep 1999 .... 1.99
❑95, Oct 1999 .... 1.99
❑96, Nov 1999, Spider-Man: Fast Lane insert 1.99
❑97, Dec 1999 .... 2.25
❑98, Jan 2000, Spider-Man: Fast Lane insert 2.25
❑99, Feb 2000, BSz (c) 2.99
❑100, Mar 2000, Brown/white background; Giant-size; Spider-Man Fast Lane preview 2.25
❑101, Apr 2000, Spider-Man: Fast Lane insert 2.25
❑102, May 2000, Revolution 2.25
❑103, Jun 2000 .... 2.25
❑104, Jul 2000 .... 2.25
❑105, Aug 2000, D: Pete Wisdom 2.25
❑106, Sep 2000 .... 2.25
❑107, Oct 2000 .... 2.25
❑108, Nov 2000, Indicia says November 00 .... 2.25
❑109, Dec 2000, indicia says Nov 2000. 2.25
❑110, Jan 2001, Indicia says January 01 2.25
❑111, Feb 2001 .... 2.25
❑112, Mar 2001 .... 2.25
❑113, Apr 2001, Indicia says April 01 .... 2.25
❑114, May 2001, indicia says March 01 2.25
❑115, Jun 2001, (c); Indicia says June 01 2.25
❑116, Jul 2001, indicia says May 01 .... 2.25
❑117, Aug 2001, indicia says June 01 ... 2.25
❑118, Sep 2001 .... 2.25
❑119, Oct 2001 .... 2.25
❑120, Nov 2001, A: Wolverine 2.25
❑121, Dec 2001 .... 2.25
❑122, Jan 2002 .... 2.25
❑123, Feb 2002, 'Nuff Said (silent issue) 2.25
❑124, Mar 2002 .... 2.25
❑125, Apr 2002 .... 2.25
❑126, May 2002 .... 2.25
❑127, Jun 2002 .... 2.25
❑128, Jul 2002, Amazing Spider-Man story 2.25
❑129, Aug 2002, Final issue 2.25
❑Ann 1, ca. 1992, (c); BSz (a); Wiz Kid; Artie and Leech story 2.50
❑Ann 2, ca. 1993, 1: Neurotap. 1: X-Treme. 1: Stronghold. Polybagged with trading card 2.95
❑Ann 3, ca. 1994, (c); BWi (a) 2.95
❑Ann 1995, Dec 1995, JPH (w); wraparound cover; X-Force and Cable '95 .... 3.95
❑Ann 1996, ca. 1996, wraparound cover; X-Force and Cable '96 .... 2.99
❑Ann 1997, ca. 1997, (c); A: Asgard. wraparound cover; X-Force and Cable '97 .... 2.99
❑Ann 1998, Dec 1998, gatefold summary; (c); wraparound cover; X-Force/ Champions '98 .... 3.50
❑Ann 1999, ca. 1999 .... 3.50

X-Force
Marvel

❑1, Oct 2004 .... 4.00
❑2, Nov 2004 .... 2.99
❑3, Dec 2004 .... 2.99
❑4, Jan 2005 .... 2.99
❑5, Feb 2005 .... 2.99
❑6, Mar 2005 .... 2.99

X-Force/Youngblood
Marvel

❑1, Aug 1996, crossover with Image; prestige format one-shot 4.95

XIII
Alias

❑1, Jul 2005; Includes preview of Imperial Dragons 1.00
❑2, Oct 2005 .... 2.99
❑3, Nov 2005 .... 2.99
❑5, Jan 2006 .... 2.99

Ximos: Violent Past
Triumphant

❑1, Mar 1994 .... 2.50
❑2, Mar 1994 .... 2.50

Xiola
Xero

❑0 1994, b&w ... 1.95

❑1, Oct 1994, b&w ... 1.95

❑2 1995, b&w ... 1.95

❑3, May 1995, b&w ... 1.95

❑Ashcan 1 1994, b&w; no cover price ... 1.00

XL
Blackthorne

❑1, b&w ... 3.50

X-Lax
Thwack! Pow!

❑1, Mini-Comic ... 1.25

X-Man
Marvel

❑-1, Jul 1997, Flashback ... 2.00

❑1, Mar 1995, JPH (w) ... 3.00

❑1/2nd, Mar 1995, JPH (w); 2nd printing ... 2.25

❑2, Apr 1995, JPH (w); After Xavier: Age of Apocalypse ... 2.50

❑3, May 1995, JPH (w); After Xavier: Age of Apocalypse ... 2.50

❑4, Jun 1995, JPH (w); After Xavier: Age of Apocalypse ... 2.50

❑5, Jul 1995, JPH (w) ... 2.00

❑6, Aug 1995, JPH (w) ... 2.00

❑7, Sep 1995, JPH (w) ... 2.00

❑8, Oct 1995, JPH (w); OverPower cards bound in ... 2.00

❑9, Nov 1995, JPH (w) ... 2.00

❑10, Dec 1995, JDu (a); V: Xavier ... 2.00

❑11, Jan 1996, A: Rogue ... 1.95

❑12, Feb 1996, V: Excalibur ... 1.95

❑13, Mar 1996 ... 1.95

❑14, Apr 1996 ... 1.95

❑15, May 1996, A: Onslaught ... 2.50

❑16, Jun 1996, V: Holocaust ... 2.00

❑17, Jul 1996, V: Holocaust; 40 pages ... 2.00

❑18, Aug 1996, Onslaught, Phase 1 ... 1.95

❑19, Sep 1996, A: Mr. Sinister. 40 pages; Onslaught Phase 2 ... 1.95

❑20, Oct 1996, V: Abomination. bound-in trading cards ... 1.95

❑21, Nov 1996, Time Slip preview; 40 pages ... 1.95

❑22, Dec 1996, 40 pages; Deadpool preview ... 1.95

❑23, Jan 1997, 40 pages; Continued in X-Man Ann 1996; Generation X preview ... 1.95

❑24, Feb 1997, A: Spider-Man. A: Morbius. V: Morbius; 40 pages; Thunderbolts preview ... 1.95

❑25, Mar 1997, Giant-size; A: Madelyne Pryor. wraparound cover ... 2.99

❑26, Apr 1997, 40 pages ... 1.95

❑27, May 1997, 40 pages ... 1.95

❑28, Jun 1997, 40 pages ... 1.95

❑29, Aug 1997, gatefold summary ... 1.95

❑30, Sep 1997, gatefold summary ... 1.95

❑31, Oct 1997, gatefold summary ... 1.99

❑32, Nov 1997, gatefold summary ... 1.99

❑33, Dec 1997, gatefold summary ... 1.99

❑34, Jan 1998, gatefold summary ... 1.99

❑35, Feb 1998, gatefold summary ... 1.99

❑36, Mar 1998, gatefold summary ... 1.99

❑37, Apr 1998, gatefold summary; A: Spider-Man ... 1.99

❑38, May 1998, gatefold summary; A: Spider-Man ... 1.99

❑39, Jun 1998, gatefold summary ... 1.99

❑40, Jul 1998, gatefold summary ... 1.99

❑41, Aug 1998, gatefold summary; A: Madelyne Pryory ... 1.99

❑42, Sep 1998, gatefold summary; A: Madelyne Pryor ... 1.99

❑43, Oct 1998, gatefold summary ... 1.99

❑44, Nov 1998, gatefold summary; V: Nemesis ... 1.99

❑45, Dec 1998, gatefold summary ... 1.99

❑46, Dec 1998, gatefold summary ... 1.99

❑47, Jan 1999, gatefold summary ... 1.99

❑48, Feb 1999, gatefold summary ... 1.99

❑49, Mar 1999 ... 1.99

❑50, Apr 1999, A: Dark Beast. A: White Queen. Story continues from Generation X #50 ... 1.99

❑51, May 1999 ... 1.99

❑52, Jun 1999 ... 1.99

❑53, Jul 1999, A: Cyclops. A: Jean Grey ... 1.99

❑54, Aug 1999 ... 1.99

❑55, Sep 1999 ... 1.99

❑56, Oct 1999, A: Spider-Man ... 1.99

❑57, Nov 1999; 40 pages ... 1.99

❑58, Dec 1999 ... 1.99

❑59, Jan 2000; A: Fantastic Four. 40 pages ... 1.99

❑60, Feb 2000 ... 1.99

❑61, Mar 2000, 40 pages ... 1.99

❑62, Apr 2000 ... 1.99

❑63, May 2000, Revolution ... 1.99

❑64, Jun 2000 ... 2.25

❑65, Jul 2000 ... 2.25

❑66, Aug 2000 ... 2.25

❑67, Sep 2000 ... 2.25

❑68, Oct 2000 ... 2.25

❑69, Nov 2000, polybagged with AOL CD-ROM ... 2.25

❑70, Dec 2000 ... 2.25

❑71, Jan 2001 ... 2.25

❑72, Feb 2001 ... 2.25

❑73, Mar 2001 ... 2.25

❑74, Apr 2001 ... 2.25

❑75, May 2001, double-sized; 48 pages ... 2.99

❑Ann 1996, ca. 1996, wraparound cover ... 3.50

❑Ann 1997, ca. 1997, A: Sugar Man. A: Nemesis. A: Dark Beast. wraparound cover ... 3.50

❑Ann 1998, ca. 1998, V: Thanos. wraparound cover; X-Man/Hulk '98 ... 3.50

X-Men
Marvel

❑1, Sep 1963, JK, (c); SL (w); JK (a); 1&O: X-Men. 1: Cyclops. 1: Professor X. 1: Angel II. 1: Marvel Girl. 1: Iceman. 1: Magneto. 1: Beast ... 7000.00

❑2, Nov 1963, (c); SL (w); JK (a); 1: The Vanisher ... 1900.00

❑3, Jan 1964, JK, (c); SL (w); JK (a); 1: The Blob ... 1030.00

❑4, Mar 1964, JK, (c); SL (w); JK (a); 1: Toad. 1: Mastermind. 1: Scarlet Witch. 1: Quicksilver. 1: Brotherhood of Evil Mutants ... 900.00

❑5, May 1964, JK, (c); SL (w); JK (a); A: Evil Mutants; 1: asteroid M ... 550.00

❑6, Jul 1964, (c); SL (w); JK (a); A: Evil Mutants. A: Sub-Mariner ... 500.00

❑7, Sep 1964, (c); SL (w); JK (a); A: Blob. A: Evil Mutants. Cerebro ... 475.00

❑8, Nov 1964, (c); SL (w); JK (a); 1&O: Unus the Untouchable ... 360.00

❑9, Jan 1965, (c); SL (w); JK (a); 1: Lucifer ... 360.00

❑10, Mar 1965, JK (c); SL (w); JK (a); 1: Ka-Zar; 1: Zabu ... 360.00

❑11, May 1965, (c); SL (w); JK (a); 1: The Stranger ... 300.00

❑12, Jul 1965, (c); SL (w); ATh, JK (a); O: Professor X. 1&O: Juggernaut ... 500.00

❑13, Sep 1965, JK, (c); SL (w); JK, JSt (a); V: Juggernaut ... 275.00

❑14, Nov 1965, JK, (c); SL (w); JK (a); 1&O: Sentinels; 1: Dr. Bolivar Trask .. 250.00

❑15, Dec 1965, JK, (c); SL (w); JK (a); O: Beast. 1: Master Mold; 2: Sentinels; 2: Dr. Bolivar Trask ... 190.00

❑16, Jan 1966, JK, (c); SL (w); JK (a); A: Sentinels. A: Master Mold. D: Bolivar Trask ... 190.00

❑17, Feb 1966, JK, (c); SL (w); JK (a); V: Magneto. 1: Dr. John Thomas ... 100.00

❑18, Mar 1966, JK (c); SL (w); JK (a); A: Stranger. V: Magneto ... 100.00

❑19, Apr 1966, JK (c); SL (w); 1&O: Mimic ... 100.00

❑20, May 1966, V: Unus. V: Lucifer. 1: Supreme One; 1: Dominus; V: Blob ... 100.00

❑21, Jun 1966, JK (c); V: Lucifer ... 90.00

❑22, Jul 1966, JK (c); V: Count Nefaria.. 90.00

❑23, Aug 1966, V: Count Nefaria ... 90.00

❑24, Sep 1966, JK (c); 1: Locust; 1: Ted Roberts ... 90.00

❑25, Oct 1966, JK (c); 1: El Tigre; 1: Ramon; 1: Toloc ... 90.00

❑26, Nov 1966, JK, (c); 2: El Tigre; 2: Ramon; 2: Toloc ... 90.00

❑27, Dec 1966, JK, (c); V: Puppet Master. Mimic returns ... 90.00

❑28, Jan 1967, JK, (c); 1: Banshee; 1: Ogre; 1: Factor Three ... 155.00

❑28/2nd, ca. 1993, (c); 1: Banshee. 2nd printing ... 2.00

❑29, Feb 1967, JK, (c); V: Super-Adaptoid ... 90.00

❑30, Mar 1967, JK, (c); 1: Maha Yogi ... 90.00

❑31, Apr 1967, JK, (c); 1: Cobalt Man; 1: Candy Sothern ... 90.00

❑32, May 1967, JK, (c); V: Juggernaut .. 90.00

❑33, Jun 1967, GK, (c); V: Juggernaut. 1: Xorak the Outcast; D: Zorak the Outcast ... 90.00

❑34, Jul 1967, (c); DA (a); V: Tyrannus. V: Mole Man; Ralph Roberts apperance; Ted Roberts appearance ... 90.00

❑35, Aug 1967, JK, (c); DA (a); 1: Changeling. A: Spider-Man. A: Banshee ... 150.00

❑36, Sep 1967, (c); RA (a); 1: Mekano .. 65.00

❑37, Oct 1967, (c); DH, RA (a); V: Factor Three. 1: Mutant Master; Peter Sanderson L.O.C ... 65.00

❑38, Nov 1967, DA (c); DH (a); V: Blob. V: Vanisher. The Origins of the X-Men back-ups begin ... 80.00

❑39, Dec 1967, GT (c); DH (a); D: Mutant-Master. 1: Jack O'Diamonds; V: Factor Three ... 90.00

❑40, Jan 1968, GT (c); DH, GT (a); V: Frankenstein. 2: Jack O'Diamonds . 90.00

❑41, Feb 1968, GT (c); DH, GT (a); 1: Grotesk the Sub-Human; Guy H. Lillian L.O.C.; Fred Hembeck L.O.C ... 65.00

❑42, Mar 1968, JB (c); HT, DH, GT (a); D: Changeling (disguised as Professor X). V: Grotesk ... 65.00

❑43, Apr 1968, JB (c); GT (a); V: Brotherhood of Evil Mutants ... 65.00

❑44, May 1968, DH (c); DH, GT (a); O: Red Raven. O: Iceman. 1: Red Raven (in modern age). A: Magneto. Return of Red Raven ... 65.00

❑45, Jun 1968, JB (c); DH, GT (a); O: Iceman. V: Evil Mutants ... 65.00

❑46, Jul 1968, DH (c); DH, GT (a); O: Iceman. V: Juggernaut ... 65.00

❑47, Aug 1968, DH (c); DH (a); V: Maha Yogi ... 65.00

❑48, Sep 1968, JR (c); DH (a); V: Quasimodo; Tony Isabella L.O.C ... 65.00

❑49, Oct 1968, JSo (c); DH, JSo (a); 1: Mesmero. 1: Polaris; 1: Lorna Dane; 1: Polaris; O: Beast; Tony Isabella L.O.C 75.00

❑50, Nov 1968, JSo (c); JSo (a); V: Mesmero. 1: El Conquistador; 1: Chico; 2: Mesmero; 2: Lorna Dane; 2: Polaris; O: Beast ... 75.00

❑51, Dec 1968, JSo (c); JSo (a); V: Mesmero. 1: Eric the Red; 2: El Conquistador; 2: Chico; O: the Beast.. 75.00

❑52, Jan 1969, DH (a); O: Lorna Dane. 2: Eric the Red; O: Beast ... 65.00

❑53, Feb 1969, V: Blastaar. Barry Windsor-Smith's 1st comic book art.. 72.00

❑54, Mar 1969, DH (a); O: Havok. 1: Alex Summers (Havok). 1: Living Pharaoh. 1: Alex Summers (Havok); 1: Living Pharaoh; O: Havok; O: Angel; Bob Wiacek L.O.C ... 72.00

❑55, Apr 1969, DH (a); O: Havok. 2: Alex Summers (Havok); 2: Living Pharaoh; O: Havok; O: Angel ... 72.00

❑56, May 1969, NA (c); NA, TP (a); 1: Living Monolith. V: Living Monolith. Living Pharaoh becomes Living Monolith ... 72.00

❑57, Jun 1969, NA (c); NA, TP (a); 1: Mark II Sentinels; 1: Larry Trask; 1: Judge Chalmers ... 72.00

❑58, Jul 1969, NA (c); NA, TP (a); 1: Havok (in costume); 2: Mark II Sentinels; 2: Larry Trask; 2: Judge Chalmers ... 100.00

❑59, Aug 1969, NA (c); NA, TP (a); 1: Dr. Karl Lykos ... 70.00

❑60, Sep 1969, NA (c); NA, TP (a); O: Sauron. 1: Sauron; Don McGregor L.O.C ... 70.00

❑61, Oct 1969, NA (c); NA, TP (a); V: Sauron. 2: Sauron ... 70.00

❑62, Nov 1969, NA (c); NA, TP (a); 1: Piper. 1: Lupo. 1: Barbarus. A: Ka-Zar; 1: Amphibius; 1: Equilibrius; 1: Gaza; 1: Brainchild; Lettering above title is white ... 70.00

❑62/2nd, ca. 1994, NA (c); NA (a); 1: Piper. 1: Lupo. 1: Barbarus. A: Ka-Zar. 2nd printing; Lettering above Title is black 1.50

❑63, Dec 1969, NA (c); NA, TP (a); O: Piper. O: Lupo. A: Ka-Zar. V: Magneto. 1: Lorelei; 2: Barbarus; 2: Lupo; 2: Amphibius; 2: Gaza; 2: Brainchild ... 70.00

Other grades: Multiply price above by 5/6 for VF/NM • 2/3 for VERY FINE • 1/3 for FINE • 1/5 for VERY GOOD • 1/8 for GOOD

X-Men: Evolution

Adapts episodes from the animated series
©Marvel

X-Men Forever

Similar concept to Avengers Forever
©Marvel

X-Men Prime

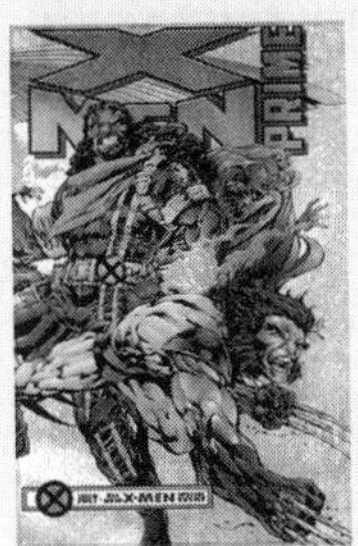

Final stages of "Age of Apocalypse"
©Marvel

X-Men: The Early Years

Reprints stories from the 1960s
©Marvel

X-Men: The Hidden Years

Covers the time that X-Men was in reprints
©Marvel

N-MINT

❑63/2nd, ca. 1994, NA (c); NA (a); O: Piper. O: Lupo. A: Ka-Zar. V: Magneto. 2nd printing 2.00
❑64, Jan 1970, SB (c); DH, TP (a); O: Sunfire. 1: Sunfire 70.00
❑65, Feb 1970, TP (c); NA, TP (a); A: Havok, SHIELD, Fantastic Four. D: Changeling (revealed) 70.00
❑66, Mar 1970, SB (a); A: Havok. A: Hulk. Guy Lillian L.O.C 80.00
❑67, Dec 1970, (c); SL (w); ATh, JK, JSt (a); reprints stories from X-Men #12 and 13 .... 35.00
❑68, Feb 1971, JK, (c); SL (w); JK (a); reprints stories from X-Men #14 and 15 .... 35.00
❑69, Apr 1971, SB (c); SL (w); JK (a); reprints stories from X-Men #16 and 19 .... 35.00
❑70, Jun 1971, JK, (c); SL (w); JK (a); reprints stories from X-Men #17 and 18 .... 35.00
❑71, Aug 1971, JK (c); SL (w); reprints X-Men #20 .... 35.00
❑72, Oct 1971, JK (c); reprints stories from X-Men #21 and 24 .... 35.00
❑73, Dec 1971, BEv, (c); reprints X-Men #25 .... 35.00
❑74, Feb 1972, GK (c); reprints X-Men #26 .... 35.00
❑75, Apr 1972, JR, (c); reprints X-Men #27 .... 35.00
❑76, Jun 1972, GK (c); reprints X-Men #28 .... 35.00
❑77, Aug 1972, GT (c); reprints X-Men #29 .... 35.00
❑78, Oct 1972, GK (c); reprints X-Men #30 .... 35.00
❑79, Dec 1972, GK (c); reprints X-Men #31 .... 35.00
❑80, Feb 1973, GK (c); reprints X-Men #32 .... 35.00
❑81, Apr 1973, GK, (c); reprints X-Men #33 .... 40.00
❑82, Jun 1973, DA, (c); DA (a); reprints X-Men #34 .... 40.00
❑83, Aug 1973, JK, (c); DA (a); reprints X-Men #35 .... 40.00
❑84, Oct 1973, RA, (c); RA (a); reprints X-Men #36 .... 40.00
❑85, Dec 1973, DH, JK, (c); DH, RA (a); reprints X-Men #37 .... 40.00
❑86, Feb 1974, DA (c); SD, SL (w); SD, DH (a); reprints stories from X-Men #38 and Amazing Adult Fantasy #2 .... 35.00
❑87, Apr 1974, GT (c); SL (w); SD, DH (a); reprints stories from X-Men #39 and Amazing Adult Fantasy #10 .... 35.00
❑88, Jun 1974, GT (c); SL, (w); DH, GT (a); reprints X-Men #40 .... 35.00
❑89, Aug 1974, (c); SL (w); SD, DH, GT (a); reprints stories from X-Men #41 and Amazing Adult Fantasy #11 .... 35.00
❑90, Oct 1974, JB (c); SL (w); SD, DH, GT (a); reprints stories from X-Men #42 and Amazing Adult Fantasy #7 .... 35.00
❑91, Dec 1974, JB (c); SL (w); SD, GT (a); reprints stories from X-Men #43 and Amazing Adult Fantasy #7 .... 35.00
❑92, Feb 1975, (c); DH (a); reprints stories from X-Men #44 and Mystery Tales #30 .... 35.00
❑93, Apr 1975, JB (c); SL (w); SD, DH (a); reprints stories from X-Men #45 and Journey Into Mystery #74 .... 35.00
❑94, Aug 1975, New X-Men begin (from Giant-Size X-Men #1); GK, DC (c); DC, BMc (a); 1: New X-Men. Old X-Men leave 500.00

N-MINT

❑95, Oct 1975, DC (c); DC (a); D: Thunderbird 85.00
❑96, Dec 1975, SB, DC (c); DC (a); 1: Moira MacTaggart 55.00
❑97, Feb 1976, RB, DC (c); DC (a); 1: Lilandra Neramani. Cyclops vs. Havok 48.00
❑98, Apr 1976, DC (c); DC (a); A: Nick Fury. A: Matt Murdock. V: Sentinels 48.00
❑98/30¢, Apr 1976, 30¢ regional variant 125.00
❑99, Jun 1976, DC (c); DC (a); 1: Black Tom Cassidy 48.00
❑99/30¢, Jul 1976, 30¢ regional variant 125.00
❑100, Aug 1976, DC (c); DC (a); V: X-Men. Old X-Men vs. New X-Men 60.00
❑100/30¢, Aug 1976, 30¢ regional variant; Old X-Men vs. New X-Men 135.00
❑101, Oct 1976, DC (c); DC (a); 1: Phoenix II (Jean Grey). A: Juggernaut. D: Jean Grey. 1: Phoenix 55.00
❑102, Dec 1976, DC (c); DC (a); O: Storm. V: Juggernaut and Black Tom 28.00
❑103, Feb 1977, DC (c); DC (a); V: Black Tom. V: Juggernaut 28.00
❑104, Apr 1977, DC (c); DC (a); 1: Starjammers (cameo). 1: Muir Island. V: Magneto 28.00
❑105, Jun 1977, DC (c); BL, DC (a); A: Firelord 28.00
❑105/35¢, Jun 1977, 35¢ regional variant 60.00
❑106, Aug 1977, DC (c); TS, DC (a); A: Firelord 28.00
❑106/35¢, Aug 1977, 35¢ regional variant 60.00
❑107, Oct 1977, DC (c); DGr, DC (a); 1: Starjammers; 1: Gladiator II; 1: Fang; 1: Chod; 1: Oracle; 1: Starbolt; 1: Titan; 1: Hepzibah; 1: Raza; 1: Shapeshifter; Reed Richards; Thing (cameos) 28.00
❑107/35¢, Oct 1977, 35¢ regional variant 60.00
❑108, Dec 1977, DC (c); JBy (a); O: Polaris. A: Fantastic Four. 1st Byrne art on X-Men 35.00
❑109, Feb 1978, DC (c); JBy (a); 1: Vindicator (Weapon Alpha); 1: Weapon Alpha 30.00
❑110, Apr 1978, DC (c); DC, TD (a); A: Warhawk 20.00
❑111, Jun 1978, DC (c); JBy (a); A: Beast, Magneto. V: Mesmero 20.00
❑112, Aug 1978, GP, BL (c); JBy (a); V: Magneto 20.00
❑113, Sep 1978, JBy, BL (c); JBy (w); JBy (a); V: Magneto 20.00
❑114, Oct 1978, JBy (c); JBy (w); JBy (a); V: Sauron 20.00
❑115, Nov 1978, JBy (c); JBy (w); JBy (a); 1: Nereel. A: Ka-Zar. V: Sauron 20.00
❑116, Dec 1978, JBy (c); JBy (w); JBy (a); A: Ka-Zar 16.00
❑117, Jan 1979, DC (c); JBy (w); JBy (a); O: Professor X 16.00
❑118, Feb 1979, DC (c); JBy (w); JBy (a); 1: Mariko Yashida. Newsstand edition (distributed by Curtis); issue number in box 16.00
❑118/Whitman, Feb 1979, DC (c); JBy (w); JBy (a); 1: Mariko Yashida. Special markets edition (usually sold in Whitman bagged prepacks); price appears in a diamond; no UPC barcode 16.00
❑119, Mar 1979, DC (c); JBy (w); JBy (a); 1: Proteus (voice only) 16.00

N-MINT

❑120, Apr 1979, JBy (w); JBy (a); 1: Aurora. 1: Alpha Flight (cameo). 1: Snowbird. 1: Northstar. 1: Sasquatch. 1: Vindicator; 1: Aurora 28.00
❑121, May 1979, DC (c); JBy (w); JBy (a); 1: Alpha Flight (full). A: Mastermind 28.00
❑122, Jun 1979, DC (c); JBy (w); JBy (a); 1: Hellfire Club. V: Arcade 12.00
❑123, Jul 1979, JBy (w); JBy (a); O: Colossus. V: Arcade 12.00
❑124, Aug 1979, DC (c); JBy (w); JBy (a); O: Arcade. A: Arcade 12.00
❑125, Sep 1979, DC (c); JBy (w); JBy (a); 1: Proteus (full appearance). Phoenix cover 12.00
❑126, Oct 1979, DC (c); JBy (a) 12.00
❑127, Nov 1979, JBy (c); JBy (w); JBy (a) 12.00
❑128, Dec 1979, GP (c); JBy (w); JBy (a); O: Proteus. D: Proteus 12.00
❑129, Jan 1980, JBy (c); JBy (w); JBy (a); 1: Donald Pierce (the White Bishop). 1: White Queen (Emma Frost). 1: Kitty Pryde. Dark Phoenix Saga starts; Emma Front appearance 20.00
❑130, Feb 1980, JR2 (c); JBy (w); JBy (a); 1: Dazzler 12.00
❑131, Mar 1980, JBy (c); JBy (w); JBy (a); A: Angel, White Queen. A: Dazzler 12.00
❑132, Apr 1980, JBy (c); JBy (w); JBy (a); A: Hugh Hefner. A: Angel 12.00
❑133, May 1980, JBy (c); JBy (w); JBy (a); 1: Dark Phoenix. 1: Senator Edward Kelly. A: Angel 12.00
❑134, Jun 1980, JBy (c); JBy (w); JBy (a); A: Dark Phoenix 12.00
❑135, Jul 1980, JBy (c); JBy (w); JBy (a); A: Dark Phoenix. A: Spider-Man 12.00
❑136, Aug 1980, JBy (c); JBy (w); JBy (a) 11.00
❑137, Sep 1980, Giant-size; JBy (c); JBy (w); JBy (a); 1: Hussar. A: Angel. D: Phoenix II (Jean Grey) 14.00
❑138, Oct 1980, JBy (c); JBy (w); JBy (a); A: Angel. History of the X-Men retold 8.00
❑139, Nov 1980, JBy (c); JBy (w); JBy (a); 1: Stevie Hunter. Kitty Pryde joins X-Men; New costume for Wolverine 11.00
❑140, Dec 1980, JBy (c); JBy (w); JBy (a); A: Alpha Flight 11.00
❑141, Jan 1981, JBy (c); JBy (w); JBy (a); 1: Avalanche. 1: Rachel Summers (Phoenix III). 1: Pyro. series continues as Uncanny X-Men 11.00

X-Men
Marvel

❑-1, Jul 1997, O: Magneto. Flashback 3.00
❑-1/A, Jul 1997, Variant cover: "Magneto's Rage, Xavier's Hope; I had a Dream!" 4.00
❑1/Beast, Oct 1991, JLee (c); JLee (w); JLee (a); Storm cover 5.00
❑1/Colossus, Oct 1991, JLee (c); JLee (w); JLee (a); Colossus cover 3.00
❑1/Cyclops, Oct 1991, JLee (c); JLee (w); JLee (a); Wolverine Cover 4.00
❑1/Magneto, Oct 1991, JLee (c); JLee (w); JLee (a); Magneto Cover 3.00
❑1/Collector's, Oct 1991, JLee (c); JLee (w); JLee (a); Double gatefold cover combining A-D images 5.00
❑2, Nov 1991, JLee (c); JLee (w); JLee (a); V: Magneto 4.00

Other grades: Multiply price above by 5/6 for VF/NM • 2/3 for VERY FINE • 1/3 for FINE • 1/5 for VERY GOOD • 1/8 for GOOD

N-MINT

❑3, Dec 1991, JLee (c); JLee (w); JLee (a); V: Magneto; V: Acolytes 3.00
❑4, Jan 1992, JLee (c); JBy, JLee (w); JLee (a); 1: Omega Red; V: Omega Red 3.00
❑5, Feb 1992, JLee (c); JBy, JLee (w); JLee (a); 1: Maverick; V: Omega Red; V: Fenris; 1: Maverick (David North)... 3.00
❑6, Mar 1992, JLee (c); JLee (w); JLee (a); A: Sabretooth. V: Omega Red; V: Mojo 3.00
❑7, Apr 1992, JLee (c); JLee (w); JLee (a); V: Omega Red; V: Fenris; V: Mojo; 36 pages... 3.00
❑8, May 1992, JLee (c); JLee (w); JLee (a); A: Ghost Rider. Continued in Ghost Rider #26.. 3.00
❑9, Jun 1992, JLee (c); JLee (w); JLee (a); A: Ghost Rider. V: the Brood; Continued from Ghost Rider #26; Continued in Ghost Rider #27 .... 3.00
❑10, Jul 1992, JLee (c); JLee (w); JLee, BWi (a); A: Longshot. V: Mojo; Maverick story.................................... 3.00
❑11, Aug 1992, JLee (c); JLee (w); JLee, BWi (a); V: Mojo; Maverick story........ 3.00
❑12, Sep 1992, V: Hazard...................... 3.00
❑13, Oct 1992, V: Hazard; Continued in Uncanny X-Men #294........................ 3.00
❑14/CS, Nov 1992, Apocalypse trading card 3.00
❑15/CS, Dec 1992, trading card 3.00
❑16/CS, Jan 1993, trading card 3.00
❑17, Feb 1993, indicia says February 1992 2.50
❑18, Mar 1993, D: Colossus' parents..... 2.50
❑19, Apr 1993, BWi (a); V: Skinner of Souls 2.50
❑20, May 1993, BWi (a); V: Revanche.... 2.50
❑21, Jun 1993, V: Revanche 2.00
❑22, Jul 1993, V: Silver Samurai; 48 pages; X-Men-Avengers multi-page insert 2.00
❑23, Aug 1993, V: Dark Riders; V: Shinobi Shaw; 1st mention of a 3rd Summers' brother; Legacy Virus mentioned 2.00
❑24, Sep 1993, Continued in Uncanny X-Men #304...................................... 2.00
❑25, Oct 1993, A: Magneto. Hologram cover; Wolverine loses adamantium skeleton 5.00
❑25/Gold, Oct 1993, Gold limited edition; A: Magneto. Hologram cover; limited Gold Edition.. 25.00
❑25/Ltd., Oct 1993, A: Magneto. Cover black and white w/ hologram............ 30.00
❑26, Nov 1993, V: Cortez; 48 pages; Continued from Avengers #368; Continued in Avengers West Coast #101; Siege of Darkness insert.......... 2.00
❑27, Dec 1993, BWi (a); 1st Appearance Threnody; D: Infectia; V: Mr. Sinister; 48 pages.. 2.00
❑28, Jan 1994, A: Sabretooth. 48 pages; Punisher-New Warriors insert 2.00
❑29, Feb 1994, A: Sabretooth. V: Shinobi Shaw 2.00
❑30, Mar 1994, Double-size; trading cards; wedding of Jean Grey and Scott Summers.. 3.00
❑31, Apr 1994, D: Revanche (Kwannon in Psylockes original body) 1.75
❑32, May 1994, Trading cards............... 1.75
❑33, Jun 1994, A: Sabretooth 1.75
❑34, Jul 1994, V: Riptide....................... 1.75
❑35, Aug 1994, Cyclops and Jean Grey spotlight 1.75
❑36, Sep 1994, V: Phalanx; Phalanx Covenant; Continued from Uncanny X-Men #316; Wraparound cover; Continued in Uncanny X-Men #317.... 1.50
❑36/Variant, Sep 1994, Foil cover 2.00
❑37, Oct 1994, D: Blink; Phalanx Covenant; Wraparound cover; 40 pages; Continued in Generation X #1 . 1.50
❑37/Variant, Oct 1994, enhanced cover . 2.00
❑38, Nov 1994 .... 1.50
❑38/Deluxe, Nov 1994, Deluxe edition ... 2.00
❑39, Dec 1994.. 1.50
❑39/Deluxe, Dec 1994, Deluxe edition ... 2.00
❑40, Jan 1995, Sabretooth continued in Wolverine #90; Continued from Uncanny X-Men #320; Continued in Uncanny X-Men #321 .... 1.50

N-MINT

❑40/Deluxe, Jan 1995, Deluxe edition; Sabretooth continued in Wolverine #90; Continued from Uncanny X-Men #320; Continued in Uncanny X-Men #321.. 2.00
❑41, Feb 1995, D: Professor X; V: Legion; Leads into Age of Apocalypse event... 1.50
❑41/Deluxe, Feb 1995, Deluxe edition; trading cards.................................... 2.00
❑42, Jul 1995, PS (a); D: Rusty Collins; V: Holocaust; Return from Age of Apocalypse event 2.00
❑43, Aug 1995, PS (a); V: Acolytes; V: Holocaust; V: Exodus 2.00
❑44, Sep 1995, Continued in Uncanny X-Men #325 .... 2.00
❑45, Oct 1995, enhanced wraparound gatefold cardstock cover 2.00
❑46, Nov 1995, A: X-babies. 1: Joseph; Return of X-babies; Joseph continued in Uncanny X-Men #327.................... 2.00
❑47, Dec 1995, A: Dazzler. A: X-babies .. 2.00
❑48, Jan 1996, A: Sugar Man. A: alternate Beast 2.00
❑49, Feb 1996, MWa (w); V: Fatale........ 2.00
❑50, Mar 1996, Giant-size; wraparound cover 3.00
❑50/Variant, Mar 1996, Giant-size; foil wraparound cardstock cover............. 4.00
❑51, Apr 1996, MWa (w); V: Mr. Sinister 2.00
❑52, May 1996, MWa (w); V: Mr. Sinister; Bastion appearance (in shadow) 2.00
❑53, Jun 1996, MWa (w); Jean Grey vs. Onslaught... 2.00
❑54, Jul 1996, MWa (w); Identity of Onslaught revealed............................ 2.00
❑54/Silver, Jul 1996............................... 25.00
❑55, Aug 1996, MWa (w); V: Onslaught; Onslaught Phase 1 .... 2.00
❑56, Sep 1996, MWa (w); V: Sentinels; V: Onslaught; Phase 2; Continued in Onslaught: Marvel Universe 2.00
❑57, Oct 1996, 40 pages....................... 2.00
❑58, Nov 1996, Gambit vs. Magneto 2.00
❑59, Dec 1996, A: Hercules. 40 pages... 2.00
❑60, Jan 1997, V: Candra; 40 pages; Storm spotlight 2.00
❑61, Feb 1997, V: Juggernaught; 40 pages 2.00
❑62, Mar 1997, A: Shang-Chi. 40 pages 2.00
❑62/A, Mar 1997, A: Shang-Chi. alternate cover 3.00
❑63, Apr 1997, A: Kingpin. A: Sebastian Shaw. V: Sebastian Shaw; 40 pages... 2.00
❑64, May 1997, 40 pages 2.00
❑65, Jun 1997, 1: Cecilia Reyes; 40 pages; Operation: Zero Tolerance 2.00
❑66, Aug 1997, gatefold summary; 40 pages 2.00
❑67, Sep 1997, gatefold summary; V: Bastion... 2.00
❑68, Oct 1997, gatefold summary; V: Sentinels; 40 pages....................... 2.00
❑69, Nov 1997, gatefold summary; V: Sentinels; V: Bastion; 40 pages...... 2.00
❑70, Dec 1997, gatefold summary; giant-size... 2.00
❑71, Jan 1998, gatefold summary; Cyclops and Phoenix leave................ 2.00
❑72, Feb 1998, gatefold summary......... 2.00
❑73, Mar 1998, gatefold summary 2.00
❑74, Apr 1998, gatefold summary; A: Abomination. V: Abomination 2.00
❑75, May 1998, gatefold summary; wraparound cover; giant size 2.00
❑76, Jun 1998, gatefold summary; O: Maggot 2.00
❑77, Jul 1998, gatefold summary; V: Shadow King 2.00
❑78, Aug 1998, gatefold summary; V: Shadow King................................. 2.00
❑79, Sep 1998, gatefold summary......... 2.00
❑80, Oct 1998, double-sized................. 3.00
❑80/Holofoil, Oct 1998.......................... 10.00
❑80/DF, Oct 1998 .... 7.00
❑81, Nov 1998, gatefold summary; V: Kali 2.00
❑82, Dec 1998, gatefold summary; Continued from Uncanny X-Men #362; Continued in Uncanny X-Men #363; 40 pages 2.00
❑83, Jan 1999, gatefold summary; BWi (a); V: Cerebro; Continued from Uncanny X-Men #363; Continued in Uncanny X-Men #364........................ 2.00
❑84, Feb 1999, gatefold summary; A: Nina. V: Cerebro.......................... 2.00

N-MINT

❑85, Feb 1999, A: Magneto. Continued in X:Men: The Magneto War.................. 2.00
❑86, Mar 1999, O: Joseph. A: Astra. A: Joseph. A: Acolytes. A: Magneto; Continued from X-Men: The Magneto War; Continued in Uncanny X-Men #367... 1.99
❑87, Apr 1999, A: Joseph. A: Magneto. Cover says April, indicia says May 1.99
❑88, May 1999, Continued in Uncanny X-Men #369 .... 1.99
❑89, Jun 1999, V: Skrulls; 40 pages 1.99
❑90, Jul 1999, A: Galactus.................... 1.99
❑91, Aug 1999, V: Red Skull; Dawn of M-Tech; Continued X-Men Ann 1999...... 1.99
❑92, Sep 1999, Continued from Uncanny X-Men #372; Continued in Astonishing X-Men v2 #1....................................... 1.99
❑93, Oct 1999 .... 1.99
❑94, Nov 1999, JBy (w); JBy, TP (a); double-sized.. 1.99
❑95, Dec 1999, Death is revealed to be Wolverine 1.99
❑96, Jan 2000, Spider-Man Fast Lane insert; Apocalypse: The Twelve; 40 pages 2.25
❑97, Feb 2000, V: Apocalypse; V: Deathbird; Red cover with Cyclops; Continued from Uncanny X-Men #377; Apocalypse: The Twelve 2.25
❑98, Mar 2000, Spider-Man Fast Lane insert; Continued from Uncanny X-Men #378.. 2.25
❑99, Apr 2000, PS (c); Continued in Uncanny X-Men #380......................... 2.99
❑100/A, May 2000, White background, team charging 2.99
❑100/B, May 2000, Nightcrawler vs. Villain cover... 2.99
❑100/C, May 2000, JBy (c); Nightcrawler, Wolverine, Colossus, Jean Gray, Storm on cover 2.99
❑100/D, May 2000, DC (c); Rogue vs. Villain on cover................................. 2.99
❑100/E, May 2000, JR2 (c);Team stacked cover 2.99
❑100/F, May 2000, PS (c); Team in chains cover 2.99
❑100/G, May 2000, Rogue, Nightcrawler, Shadowcat, etc. charging 2.99
❑101, Jun 2000, V: Neo 2.25
❑102, Jul 2000, V: Neo 2.25
❑103, Aug 2000 .... 2.25
❑104, Sep 2000, Continued in Uncanny X-Men #385 .... 2.25
❑105, Oct 2000, V: Twisted Sisters 2.99
❑106, Nov 2000, double-sized 2.25
❑107, Dec 2000, V: Blood Brothers; Maximum Security; Continued from Bishop: The Last X-Man #15; Continued in X-Men Unlimited #29 .... 2.25
❑108, Jan 2001, D: Moira MacTaggert; D: Senator Robert Kelly; Continued from Bishop: The Last X-Man #16 ..... 2.25
❑109, Feb 2001, JBy (w); JBy, DC (a); Monster sized; with reprints from X-Men (1st series) #98, 143, Uncanny X-Men #341 .... 2.25
❑110, Mar 2001, Funeral for Colossus... 2.25
❑111, Apr 2001, A: Magneto. Eve of Destruction Prelude; Continued Uncanny X-Men #392........................ 2.25
❑112, May 2001 .... 2.25
❑113, Jun 2001, Title becomes New X-Men 2.25
❑114, Jul 2001....................................... 5.00
❑115, Aug 2001 .... 2.25
❑116, Sep 2001 .... 2.25
❑117, Oct 2001...................................... 2.25
❑118, Nov 2001 .... 2.25
❑119, Dec 2001 .... 2.25
❑120, Jan 2002...................................... 2.25
❑121, Feb 2002, 'Nuff Said month (silent issue) 2.25
❑122, Mar 2002 .... 2.25
❑123, Apr 2002...................................... 2.25
❑124, May 2002..................................... 2.25
❑125, Jun 2002...................................... 2.25
❑126, Jul 2002....................................... 2.25
❑127, Aug 2002, BSz (a)........................ 2.25
❑128, Aug 2002 .... 2.25
❑129, Sep 2002 .... 2.25
❑130, Oct 2002...................................... 2.25
❑131, Oct 2002, BSz (a)........................ 2.25

Other grades: Multiply price above by 5/6 for VF/NM • 2/3 for VERY FINE • 1/3 for FINE • 1/5 for VERY GOOD • 1/8 for GOOD

X-Men: The Search for Cyclops

Followed "The Twelve" storyline in X-Men titles
©Marvel

X-Men 2099

Enclave of outcasts, rebels, and mutants
©Marvel

X-Men Unlimited

Compilation of X-Men short stories
©Marvel

X-O Manowar

Name is most powerful of a line of alien armors
©Valiant

X-O Manowar (Vol. 2)

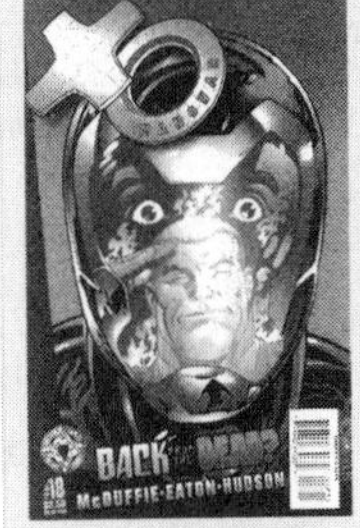

Series restarted under the Acclaim label
©Acclaim

	N-MINT
❑132, Nov 2002	2.25
❑133, Dec 2002	2.25
❑134, Jan 2003	2.25
❑135, Feb 2003	2.25
❑136, Mar 2003	2.25
❑137, Apr 2003	2.25
❑138, May 2003	2.25
❑139, Jun 2003	2.25
❑140, Jun 2003	2.25
❑141, Jul 2003, cardstock cover	2.25
❑142, Aug 2003, cardstock cover	2.25
❑143, Aug 2003	2.25
❑144, Sep 2003	2.25
❑145, Oct 2003	2.99
❑146, Nov 2003	2.99
❑147, Nov 2003	2.99
❑148, Dec 2003	2.25
❑149, Jan 2004	2.99
❑150, Feb 2004	3.50
❑151, Mar 2004	2.99
❑152, Mar 2004	2.25
❑153, Apr 2004	2.99
❑154, May 2004	2.99
❑155, Jun 2004	2.99
❑156, Jun 2004	2.99
❑157, Jul 2004, loses "New" from title, becomes X-Men again	2.99
❑158, Aug 2004	2.25
❑159, Sep 2004	2.99
❑160, Oct 2004	2.25
❑161, Nov 2004, 1: Mammomax	2.25
❑162, Dec 2004, D: Sammy the Squidboy	2.25
❑163, Jan 2005	2.25
❑164, Feb 2005	2.25
❑165, Mar 2005	2.99
❑166, Apr 2005	2.25
❑167, May 2005	2.25
❑168, Jun 2005	2.25
❑169, Jul 2005; 1: Gazer	2.25
❑170, Jul 2005	2.50
❑171, Aug 2005; 1: Foxx (Mystique)	2.50
❑172, Sep 2005	2.50
❑173, Sep 2005; 1: Pulse V	2.50
❑174, Oct 2005	2.50
❑175, Nov 2005; Crossover with Black Panther #8-9; Nick Fury's Howling Commandos preview	2.50
❑176, Dec 2005; Crossover with Black Panther #8-9	2.50
❑177, Jan 2006; Decimation tie-in	2.50
❑178, Jan 2006, Decimation tie-in	2.50
❑179, Feb 2006, Decimation tie-in	2.50
❑180, Feb 2006	2.50
❑181, Mar 2006, Franklin Richard; Son of a Genius story	2.50
❑182, Apr 2006, Horsemen of the Apocalypse story	2.50
❑183, May 2006, Horsemen of the Apocalypse story	2.50
❑184, Jun 2006, Horsemen of the Apocalypse story; 1st Gambit as Death	2.50
❑185, Jun 2006, Horsemen of the Apocalypse story	2.99
❑187, Sep 2006, Masked Marvel Backup Story included	2.99
❑188, Sep 2006	2.99
❑189, Oct 2006, 1: Perro; Masked Marvel story	2.99

	N-MINT
❑190, Nov 2006	2.99
❑191, Dec 2006	2.99
❑192, Jan 2007	2.99
❑193, Feb 2007	2.99
❑194, Mar 2007	2.99
❑195	2.99
❑196	2.99
❑197	2.99
❑198	2.99
❑199	2.99
❑200	2.99
❑201	2.99
❑202	2.99
❑203	2.99
❑204	2.99
❑205	2.99
❑206	2.99
❑207	2.99
❑208	2.99
❑209	2.99
❑210	2.99
❑211	2.99
❑212	2.99
❑213	2.99
❑214	2.99
❑215	2.99
❑216	2.99
❑217	2.99
❑218	2.99
❑219	2.99
❑220	2.99
❑221	2.99
❑222	2.99
❑223	2.99
❑224	2.99
❑225	2.99
❑Ann 1, ca. 1992, JLee (c); CR, JLee (a); Rogue vs. Villain on cover	3.00
❑Ann 2, ca. 1993, (c); AM, BWi (a); 1: Empyrean. Polybagged w/ trading card; Rogue vs. Villain on cover	3.00
❑Ann 3, ca. 1994, TP, BWi (a); Rogue vs. Villain on cover	2.95
❑Ann 1995, Oct 1995, Rogue vs. Villain on cover	3.95
❑Ann 1996, Nov 1996, wraparound cover	2.99
❑Ann 1997, ca. 1997, wraparound cover	2.99
❑Ann 1998, ca. 1998, X-Men/Doctor Doom '98; wraparound cover	2.99
❑Ann 1999, Aug 1999, V: Red Skull	3.50
❑Ann 2001, Sep 2001, (c); Indicia says X-Men 2001	3.50
❑Ashcan 1, ca. 1995, ashcan edition	0.75

X-Men Adventures
Marvel

	N-MINT
❑1, Nov 1992	3.00
❑2, Dec 1992	2.00
❑3, Jan 1993	2.00
❑4, Feb 1993	2.00
❑5, Mar 1993	2.00
❑6, Apr 1993, A: Sabretooth	2.00
❑7, May 1993, Slave Island, Part 1	2.00
❑8, Jun 1993, Slave Island, Part 2	2.00
❑9, Jul 1993	2.00
❑10, Aug 1993, The Muir Island Saga, Part 1	2.00
❑11, Sep 1993, The Muir Island Saga, Part 2	1.50
❑12, Oct 1993, A: Apocalypse. The Muir Island Saga, Part 3	1.50
❑13, Nov 1993, Days of Future Past, Part 1	1.50
❑14, Dec 1993, Days of Future Past, Part 2	1.50
❑15, Jan 1994, Giant-size	1.75

X-Men Adventures
Marvel

	N-MINT
❑1, Feb 1994	2.00
❑2, Mar 1994	1.25
❑3, Apr 1994	1.25
❑4, May 1994, Marvel Mart insert	1.25
❑5, Jun 1994	1.25
❑6, Jul 1994	1.25
❑7, Aug 1994, Time Fugitives, Part 1	1.25
❑8, Sep 1994, Time Fugitives, Part 2	1.25
❑9, Oct 1994, Includes comic insert promoting collecting football cards	1.50
❑10, Nov 1994	1.50
❑11, Dec 1994	1.50
❑12, Jan 1995	1.50
❑13, Feb 1995, Reunion, Part 2	1.50

X-Men Adventures
Marvel

	N-MINT
❑1, Mar 1995, O: Lady Deathstrike	2.00
❑2, Apr 1995	1.50
❑3, May 1995, The Phoenix Saga, Part 1	1.50
❑4, Jun 1995, The Phoenix Saga, Part 2	1.50
❑5, Jul 1995, The Phoenix Saga, Part 3	1.50
❑6, Aug 1995, The Phoenix Saga, Part 4	1.50
❑7, Sep 1995, The Phoenix Saga, Part 5	1.50
❑8, Oct 1995	1.50
❑9, Nov 1995	1.50
❑10, Dec 1995, A: Dazzler. A: Hellfire Club. A: Jason Wyngarde. The Dark Phoenix Saga, Part 1	1.50
❑11, Jan 1996, Dark Phoenix, Part 2	1.50
❑12, Feb 1996, Dark Phoenix, Part 3	1.50
❑13, Mar 1996	1.50

X-Men: Age of Apocalypse
Marvel

	N-MINT
❑0 2005	3.99

X-Men: Age of Apocalypse
Marvel

	N-MINT
❑1, May 2005	4.00
❑2, May 2005	2.99
❑3, May 2005	2.99
❑4, May 2005	2.99
❑5, May 2005	2.99
❑6, May 2005	2.99

X-Men Alpha
Marvel

	N-MINT
❑1, Feb 1995, MWa (w); 1: X-Men (Age of Apocalypse). enhanced cover; one-shot	3.00
❑1/Gold, Feb 1995, Gold edition; MWa (w); 1: X-Men (Age of Apocalypse). gold edition	20.00

X-Men/Alpha Flight
Marvel

	N-MINT
❑1, Dec 1985, PS, BWi (c); PS, BWi (a); 1: The Berserkers.	3.00
❑2, Feb 1986, PS, BWi (c); PS, BWi (a); V: Loki	3.00

Other grades: Multiply price above by 5/6 for VF/NM • 2/3 for VERY FINE • 1/3 for FINE • 1/5 for VERY GOOD • 1/8 for GOOD

N-MINT

X-Men/Alpha Flight
Marvel
❑1, May 1998 ... 2.99
❑2, Jun 1998, V: Baron Strucker ... 2.99

X-Men and Power Pack
Marvel
❑1, Dec 2005 ... 2.99
❑2, Jan 2006 ... 2.99
❑3, Feb 2006 ... 2.99
❑4, Mar 2006 ... 2.99

X-Men & The Micronauts
Marvel
❑1, Jan 1984, BG, BWi (c); BG, BWi (a); Limited Series ... 3.00
❑2, Feb 1984, BG, BWi (c); BG, BWi (a). 2.00
❑3, Mar 1984, BG (c); BG, BWi (a); centaur
❑ ... 2.00
❑4, Apr 1984, BG, BWi (c); BG, BWi (a). 1.00

X-Men: Apocalypse vs. Dracula
Marvel
❑1, Apr 2006 ... 2.99
❑2, May 2006 ... 2.99
❑3, Jun 2006 ... 2.99
❑4, Jul 2006 ... 2.99

X-Men Archives
Marvel
❑1, Jan 1995, BSz (a); A: Legion. Reprints New Mutants #26; cardstock cover ... 2.50
❑2, Jan 1995, BSz (a); A: Legion. Reprints New Mutants #27; cardstock cover ... 2.50
❑3, Jan 1995, BSz (a); A: Legion. Reprints New Mutants #28; cardstock cover ... 2.50
❑4, Jan 1995, DC (a); A: Magneto. Reprints Uncanny X-Men #161; cardstock cover ... 2.50

X-Men Archives Sketchbook
Marvel
❑1, Dec 2000, character sketches ... 2.99

X-Men at the State Fair
Marvel
❑1, JR (c); KGa (a); 1: Eques. Dallas Times-Herald ... 2.00

X-Men: Books of the Askani
Marvel
❑1, ca. 1995, wraparound cardstock cover; background info on Askani'son 2.95

X-Men: Children of the Atom
Marvel
❑1, Nov 1999, SR (c); SR (a); prequel to X-Men (first series) #1; cardstock cover 3.00
❑2, Dec 1999, SR (c); SR (a); prequel to X-Men (first series) #1; cardstock cover 3.00
❑3, Jun 2000, SR (c); SR (a); prequel to X-Men (first series) #1; cardstock cover 3.00
❑4, Jul 2000, SR (c); PS (a); prequel to X-Men (first series) #1; cardstock cover 3.00
❑5, Aug 2000, prequel to X-Men (first series) #1; cardstock cover ... 2.99
❑6, Sep 2000, prequel to X-Men (first series) #1; cardstock cover ... 2.99

X-Men Chronicles
Fantaco
❑1, Jul 1981, b&w; magazine; DC (c); DC (a); Not a magazine, regular comic size; Includes checklist for X-Men #1-151; b&w ... 2.00

X-Men Chronicles
Marvel
❑1, Mar 1995, Age of Apocalypse ... 3.95
❑2, Jun 1995, Age of Apocalypse ... 3.95

X-Men: Clandestine
Marvel
❑1, Oct 1996, wraparound cover ... 2.95
❑2, Nov 1996, wraparound cover ... 2.95

X-Men Classic
Marvel
❑46, Apr 1990, JBy (w); JBy (a); Series continued from Classic X-Men #45 ... 2.00
❑47, May 1990, JBy (w); JBy (a) ... 2.00
❑48, Jun 1990, BA (a) ... 2.00
❑49, Jul 1990, DC (a) ... 2.00
❑50, Aug 1990, DC (a); Reprints Uncanny X-Men #146 ... 2.00
❑51, Sep 1990, DC (a); Reprints Uncanny X-Men #147 ... 2.00

N-MINT

❑52, Oct 1990, DC (a); Reprints Uncanny X-Men #148 ... 2.00
❑53, Nov 1990, DC (a); Reprints Uncanny X-Men #149 ... 2.00
❑54, Dec 1990, DC, BWi (a); Reprints Uncanny X-Men #150 ... 2.00
❑55, Jan 1991, BMc (a); Reprints Uncanny X-Men #151 ... 2.00
❑56, Feb 1991, BMc (a); Reprints Uncanny X-Men #152 ... 2.00
❑57, Mar 1991, DC (a); Reprints Uncanny X-Men #153 ... 2.00
❑58, Apr 1991, DC, BWi (a); Reprints Uncanny X-Men #154 ... 2.00
❑59, May 1991, DC, BWi (a); Reprints Uncanny X-Men #155 ... 2.00
❑60, Jun 1991, DC, BWi (a); Reprints Uncanny X-Men #156 ... 2.00
❑61, Jul 1991, DC, BWi (a); Reprints Uncanny X-Men #157 ... 2.00
❑62, Aug 1991, DC, BWi (a); Reprints Uncanny X-Men #158 ... 1.75
❑63, Sep 1991, Reprints Uncanny X-Men #159 ... 1.75
❑64, Oct 1991, BA (a); Reprints Uncanny X-Men #160 ... 1.75
❑65, Nov 1991, DC, BWi (a); Reprints Uncanny X-Men #161 ... 1.75
❑66, Dec 1991, DC, BWi (a); Reprints Uncanny X-Men #162 ... 1.75
❑67, Jan 1992, DC, BWi (a); Reprints Uncanny X-Men #163 ... 1.75
❑68, Feb 1992, DC (a); Reprints Uncanny X-Men #164 ... 1.75
❑69, Mar 1992, PS, BWi (a); Reprints Uncanny X-Men #165 ... 1.75
❑70, Apr 1992, Giant-size; PS, BWi (a); Reprints Uncanny X-Men #166; Giant-size ... 1.75
❑71, May 1992, (c); PS (a); Reprints Uncanny X-Men #167 ... 1.50
❑72, Jun 1992, (c); PS (a); Reprints Uncanny X-Men #168 ... 1.50
❑73, Jul 1992, (c); PS (a); Reprints Uncanny X-Men #169 ... 1.50
❑74, Aug 1992, PS (a); Reprints Uncanny X-Men #170 ... 1.50
❑75, Sep 1992, Reprints Uncanny X-Men #171 ... 1.50
❑76, Oct 1992, Reprints Uncanny X-Men #172 ... 1.50
❑77, Nov 1992, Reprints Uncanny X-Men #173 ... 1.50
❑78, Dec 1992, Reprints Uncanny X-Men #174 ... 1.50
❑79, Jan 1993, Giant-size; Reprints Uncanny X-Men #175 ... 1.75
❑80, Feb 1993, JR2 (a); 1: Valerie Cooper. Reprints Uncanny X-Men #176 ... 1.50
❑81, Mar 1993, JR2 (a); Reprints Uncanny X-Men #177 ... 1.50
❑82, Apr 1993, JR2 (a); Reprints Uncanny X-Men #178 ... 1.50
❑83, May 1993, JR2 (a); Reprints Uncanny X-Men #179 ... 1.50
❑84, Jun 1993, JR2 (a); Reprints Uncanny X-Men #180 ... 1.50
❑85, Jul 1993, JR2 (a); Reprints Uncanny X-Men #181 ... 1.50
❑86, Aug 1993, JR2 (a); Reprints Uncanny X-Men #182 ... 1.50
❑87, Sep 1993, JR2 (a); Reprints Uncanny X-Men #183 ... 1.50
❑88, Oct 1993, JR2 (a); 1: Forge. A: Rachel. A: Selene. Reprints Uncanny X-Men #184 ... 1.50
❑89, Nov 1993, PS (c); JR2 (a); Reprints Uncanny X-Men #185; Storm loses powers ... 1.50
❑90, Dec 1993, double-sized; Reprints Uncanny X-Men #186 ... 1.50
❑91, Jan 1994, JR2 (a); Reprints Uncanny X-Men #187 ... 1.50
❑92, Feb 1994, JR2 (a); Reprints Uncanny X-Men #188 ... 1.50
❑93, Mar 1994, JR2 (a); reprints Uncanny X-Men #189 ... 1.50
❑94, Apr 1994, JR2 (a); A: Spider-Man. A: Avengers. Reprints Uncanny X-Men #190 ... 1.50
❑95, May 1994, JR2 (a); A: Spider-Man. A: Avengers. Reprints Uncanny X-Men #191 ... 1.50
❑96, Jun 1994, JR2 (a); Reprints Uncanny X-Men #192 ... 1.50

N-MINT

❑97, Jul 1994, double-sized; JR2 (a); giant; Reprints Uncanny X-Men #193; 100th New X-Men ... 1.50
❑98, Aug 1994, JR2 (a); A: Juggernaut. Reprints Uncanny X-Men #194 ... 1.50
❑99, Sep 1994, JR2 (a); A: Power-Pack. Reprints Uncanny X-Men #195 ... 1.50
❑100, Oct 1994, JR2 (a); Reprints Uncanny X-Men #196 ... 1.50
❑101, Nov 1994, JR2 (a); reprints Uncanny X-Men #197 ... 1.50
❑102, Dec 1994, reprints Uncanny X-Men #198 ... 1.50
❑103, Jan 1995, JR2 (a); 1: Phoenix III (Rachel Summers). reprints Uncanny X-Men #199 ... 1.50
❑104, Feb 1995, Double-size; JR2 (a); reprints Uncanny X-Men #200 ... 1.50
❑105, Mar 1995, 1: Cable (as baby). reprints Uncanny X-Men #201; 1st Portacio art in X-Men ... 1.50
❑106, Apr 1995, reprints Uncanny X-Men #202 ... 1.50
❑107, May 1995, reprints Uncanny X-Men #203 ... 1.50
❑108, Jun 1995, reprints Uncanny X-Men #204 ... 1.50
❑109, Jul 1995, reprints Uncanny X-Men #205 ... 1.50
❑110, Aug 1995, reprints Uncanny X-Men #206 ... 1.50

X-Men Classics
Marvel
❑1, Dec 1983, TP, MZ (c); NA (a); Reprints X-Men #56-58 ... 3.50
❑2, Jan 1984, TP, MZ (c); NA (a); Reprints X-Men #59-61
❑ ... 3.50
❑3, Feb 1984, TP, MZ (c); NA (a); Reprints X-Men #62-63 ... 3.50

X-Men Collector's Edition
Marvel
❑2, Pizza Hut giveaway in 1993; contains fold-out poster cover ... 1.00

X-Men: Deadly Genesis
Marvel
❑1, Jan 2006, 1: Vulcan (in shadows); 1: Petra; O: Petra ... 6.00
❑1/Quesada, Jan 2006 ... 14.00
❑1/Hairsine, Jan 2006 ... 7.00
❑2, Feb 2006, 1: Darwin; D: Banshee ... 3.50
❑3, Mar 2006, 1: Sway; O: Sway ... 3.50
❑4, Apr 2006, 1: Vulcan (full) ... 3.50
❑5, Jun 2006, Return Professor X; Squadron Supreme #1 preview; White Queen story ... 3.50
❑6, Jul 2006, D: Petra; D: Sway ... 3.50

X-Men: Evolution
Marvel
❑1, Feb 2002 ... 2.25
❑2, Mar 2002 ... 2.25
❑3, Apr 2002 ... 2.25
❑4, May 2002 ... 2.25
❑5, May 2002 ... 2.25
❑6, Jun 2002 ... 2.25
❑7, Jul 2002 ... 2.25
❑8, Aug 2002 ... 2.25
❑9, Sep 2002 ... 2.25

X-Men/Fantastic Four
Marvel
❑1, Jan 2005, Wraparound cover ... 3.50
❑2, Feb 2005, V: the Brood ... 3.50
❑3, Mar 2005 ... 3.50
❑4, Apr 2005; V: the Brood ... 3.50
❑5, May 2005; V: the Brood ... 3.50

X-Men: First Class
Marvel
❑1, Nov 2006 ... 2.99
❑2, Dec 2006 ... 2.99
❑3, Jan 2007 ... 2.99
❑4, Mar 2007 ... 2.99

X-Men Forever
Marvel
❑1, Jan 2001, cardstock cover ... 3.50
❑2, Feb 2001, cardstock cover ... 3.50
❑3, Mar 2001, cardstock cover ... 3.50
❑4, Apr 2001, cardstock cover ... 3.50
❑5, May 2001, cardstock cover ... 3.50
❑6, Jun 2001, cardstock cover ... 3.50

Other grades: Multiply price above by 5/6 for VF/NM • 2/3 for VERY FINE • 1/3 for FINE • 1/5 for VERY GOOD • 1/8 for GOOD

Xombi

Your average man who can't die

©DC

X-Treme X-Men

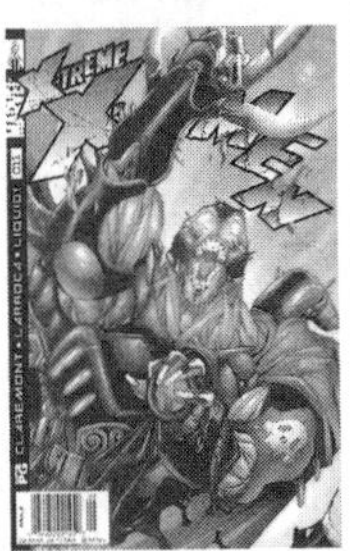

Claremont returns to writing X-Men

©Marvel

X-Universe

Filled in "Age of Apocalypse" background

©Marvel

Yeah!

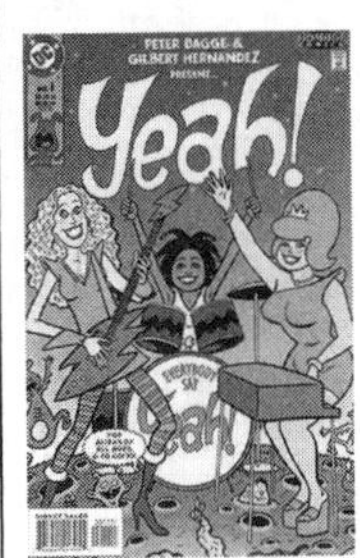

Second issue pulped for adult language

©DC

Yogi Bear

Smarter than your average Charlton title

©Charlton

N-MINT

X-Men: Hellfire Club
Marvel

- ❑1, Jan 2000 ... 2.50
- ❑2, Feb 2000, Irene Merryweather investigates Sebastian Shaw's family during the Revolutionary War ... 2.50
- ❑3, Mar 2000, Irene Merryweather learns of Mister Sinister's alteration of Shaw family DNA during WWI ... 2.50
- ❑4, Apr 2000 ... 2.50

X-Men: Lost Tales
Marvel

- ❑1, Apr 1997, reprints back-up stories from Classic X-Men #3-5 and 12 ... 3.00
- ❑2, Apr 1997, reprints back-up stories from Classic X-Men #10, 17, 21, and 23 ... 3.00

X-Men: Millennial Visions
Marvel

- ❑1, Jul 2000 ... 3.99
- ❑1/A, Jul 2000, Computer-generated cover ... 3.50

X-Men Movie Adaptation
Marvel

- ❑1, Sep 2000 ... 5.95

X-Men Movie Premiere Prequel Edition
Marvel

- ❑1, Jul 2000, Toys "R" Us giveaway ... 2.00

X-Men Movie Prequel: Magneto
Marvel

- ❑1, Aug 2000 ... 5.95

X-Men Movie Prequel: Rogue
Marvel

- ❑1, Aug 2000 ... 5.95
- ❑1/Variant, Aug 2000, Photo cover ... 5.95

X-Men Movie Prequel: Wolverine
Marvel

- ❑1, Aug 2000 ... 5.95
- ❑1/Variant, Aug 2000, Photo cover ... 5.95

X-Men Mutant Search R.U. 1?
Marvel

- ❑1, Aug 1998, no cover price; prototype for children's comic ... 2.00

X-Men Omega
Marvel

- ❑1, Jun 1995, JR2, KJ (c); MWa (w); AM (a); Age of Apocalypse finale; enhanced wraparound cover ... 6.00
- ❑1/Gold, Jun 1995, Gold edition; JR2 (c); MWa (w); AM (a); Age of Apocalypse finale; gold cover ... 25.00

X-Men: Phoenix
Marvel

- ❑1, Dec 1999 ... 4.00
- ❑2, Jan 2000 ... 2.50
- ❑3, Feb 2000 ... 2.50

X-Men: Phoenix — Endsong
Marvel

- ❑1, Jan 2005 ... 8.00
- ❑1/Variant, Jan 2005 ... 6.00
- ❑2, Feb 2005 ... 6.00
- ❑2/Variant, Feb 2005 ... 5.00
- ❑3, Mar 2005 ... 4.00
- ❑4, Apr 2005 ... 5.00
- ❑5, May 2005 ... 5.00

X-Men Prime
Marvel

- ❑1, Jul 1995, AM, TP, CR (a); enhanced wraparound cover with acetate overlay ... 5.00

X-Men Rarities
Marvel

- ❑1, Jul 1995, NN ... 5.95

X-Men: Road to Onslaught
Marvel

- ❑1, Oct 1996, background on Onslaught's origins ... 2.50

X-Men: Ronin
Marvel

- ❑1, May 2003 ... 4.00
- ❑2, May 2003 ... 2.99
- ❑3, Jun 2003 ... 2.99
- ❑4, Jun 2003 ... 2.99
- ❑5, Jul 2003 ... 2.99

X-Men Special Edition
Marvel

- ❑1, Feb 1983, reprints Giant-Size X-Men #1; DC (c); GK, DC (a); O: Storm. O: Nightcrawler. 1: X-Men (new). 1: Thunderbird. 1: Colossus. 1: Storm. 1: Nightcrawler. 1: Illyana Rasputin. reprints Giant-Size X-Men #1 ... 4.50

X-Men Spotlight On... Starjammers
Marvel

- ❑1, May 1990, V: Deathbird ... 4.50
- ❑2, Jun 1990, V: Deathbird; V: Imperial Guard ... 4.50

X-Men: Survival Guide to the Mansion
Marvel

- ❑1, Aug 1993, spiralbound ... 6.95

X-Men: The Early Years
Marvel

- ❑1, May 1994, SL (w); JK (a); O: X-Men. Reprints X-Men (1st Series) #1 ... 2.50
- ❑2, Jun 1994, SL (w); JK (a); Reprints X-Men (1st Series) #2 ... 2.00
- ❑3, Jul 1994, SL (w); JK (a); Reprints X-Men (1st Series) #3 ... 2.00
- ❑4, Aug 1994, SL (w); JK (a); Reprints X-Men (1st Series) #4 ... 2.00
- ❑5, Sep 1994, SL (w); JK (a); Reprints X-Men (1st Series) #5 ... 2.00
- ❑6, Oct 1994, SL (w); JK (a); Reprints X-Men (1st Series) #6 ... 2.00
- ❑7, Nov 1994, SL (w); JK (a); Reprints X-Men (1st Series) #7 ... 2.00
- ❑8, Dec 1994, SL (w); JK (a); Reprints X-Men (1st Series) #8 ... 2.00
- ❑9, Jan 1995, SL (w); JK (a); Reprints X-Men (1st Series) #9 ... 2.00
- ❑10, Feb 1995, SL (w); JK (a); Reprints X-Men (1st Series) #10 ... 2.00
- ❑11, Mar 1995, SL (w); JK (a); Reprints X-Men (1st Series) #11 ... 2.00
- ❑12, Apr 1995, SL (w); ATh, JK (a); Reprints X-Men (1st Series) #12 ... 2.00
- ❑13, May 1995, SL (w); JK (a); Reprints X-Men (1st Series) #13 ... 2.00
- ❑14, Jun 1995, SL (w); JK (a); Reprints X-Men (1st Series) #14 ... 2.00
- ❑15, Jul 1995, SL (w); JK (a); Reprints X-Men (1st Series) #15 ... 2.00
- ❑16, Aug 1995, SL (w); JK (a); Reprints X-Men (1st Series) #16 ... 2.00
- ❑17, Sep 1995, Double-size; SL (w); JK (a); Reprints X-Men (1st Series) #17 and #18 ... 2.50

X-Men: The Hidden Years
Marvel

- ❑1, Dec 1999, Continued from Uncanny X-Men #66 and prevew in X-Men #94 ... 3.50
- ❑2, Jan 2000, Dinosaur charging on cover; Spider-Man Fast Lane insert ... 2.50
- ❑3, Feb 2000 ... 2.50
- ❑4, Mar 2000, V: Magneto; Spider-Man Fast Lane insert; Kurt Busiek LOC ... 2.50
- ❑5, Apr 2000, V: Magneto, Gerry Alanguilan LOC; V: Magneto ... 2.75
- ❑6, May 2000, V: Deluge; Spider-Man Fast Lane insert ... 2.50
- ❑7, Jun 2000, V: Deluge ... 2.50
- ❑8, Jul 2000 ... 2.50
- ❑9, Aug 2000 ... 2.50
- ❑10, Sep 2000 ... 2.50
- ❑11, Oct 2000 ... 2.50
- ❑12, Nov 2000, V: Brotherhood of Evil Mutants; V: Sauron; V: Magneto; Magneto continued in Fantastic Four #102 ... 2.50
- ❑13, Dec 2000, V: Brotherhood of Evil Mutants ... 2.50
- ❑14, Jan 2001, V: Brotherhood of Evil Mutants; V: Dazzler (Burt Worthington) ... 2.50
- ❑15, Feb 2001, V: Dazzler (Burt Worthington) ... 2.50
- ❑16, Mar 2001 ... 2.50
- ❑17, Apr 2001, V: Kraven the Hunter ... 2.50
- ❑18, May 2001 ... 2.50
- ❑19, Jun 2001 ... 2.50
- ❑20, Jul 2001, V: Mole Man ... 2.50
- ❑21, Aug 2001, V: Mole Man ... 2.50
- ❑22, Sep 2001, V: Mole Man; V: Magneto ... 2.50

X-Men: The Manga
Marvel

- ❑1, Mar 1998 ... 3.00
- ❑2, Apr 1998 ... 2.95
- ❑3, Apr 1998 ... 2.95
- ❑4, Apr 1998 ... 2.99
- ❑5, May 1998 ... 2.95
- ❑6, May 1998 ... 2.95
- ❑7, Jun 1998 ... 2.95
- ❑8, Jul 1998, cover says Jun, indicia says Jul ... 2.95
- ❑9, Jul 1998 ... 2.95
- ❑10, Aug 1998 ... 2.95
- ❑11, Aug 1998 ... 2.95
- ❑12, Sep 1998 ... 2.95
- ❑13, Sep 1998, V: Sentinels ... 2.95
- ❑14, Oct 1998 ... 2.95
- ❑15, Oct 1998 ... 2.95
- ❑16, Nov 1998, Colossus vs. Juggernaut ... 3.99
- ❑17, Nov 1998 ... 3.99
- ❑18, Dec 1998 ... 3.99
- ❑19, Dec 1998 ... 3.99
- ❑20, Jan 1999 ... 3.99
- ❑21, Jan 1999 ... 3.99
- ❑22, Feb 1999 ... 3.99
- ❑23, Feb 1999 ... 3.99

N-MINT

❑24, Mar 1999 ... 3.99
❑25, Mar 1999 ... 3.99
❑26, Apr 1999, Mystique apperance ... 3.99

X-Men: The Movie Special
Marvel

❑1, ca. 2000, Giveaway; wraparound cover ... 1.00

X-Men: The 198 Files
Marvel

❑1, Mar 2006, Profiles of mutants ... 3.99

X-Men: The Search for Cyclops
Marvel

❑3/A, Feb 2001; Scott and Jean Grey embracing on cover; V: Gauntlet; Jean Grey embracing on cover ... 2.99
❑1, Oct 2000, Single figure (red against black background) on cover ... 2.99
❑1/A, Oct 2000, Alternate cover: Blue/white split background, man with glowing eyes kneeling at right ... 2.99
❑2, Jan 2001 ... 2.99
❑2/A, Jan 2001 ... 2.99
❑3, Feb 2001 ... 2.99
❑4, Mar 2001 ... 2.99

X-Men: The Ultra Collection
Marvel

❑1, Dec 1994, Pin-ups ... 2.95
❑2, Jan 1995, Pin-ups ... 2.95
❑3, Feb 1995, Pin-ups ... 2.95
❑4, Mar 1995, Pin-ups ... 2.95
❑5, Apr 1995, Pin-ups ... 2.95

X-Men: The Wedding Album
Marvel

❑1 1994, BSz, JBy, (a); One-shot magazine ... 3.00

X-Men: True Friends
Marvel

❑1, Sep 1999 ... 2.99
❑2, Oct 1999 ... 2.99
❑3, Nov 1999 ... 2.99

X-Men 2 Movie
Marvel

❑1, Jun 2003, adapts X2: X-Men United ... 3.50

X-Men 2 Movie Prequel: Nightcrawler
Marvel

❑1, May 2003 ... 3.50

X-Men 2 Movie Prequel: Wolverine
Marvel

❑1, May 2003 ... 3.50

X-Men 2099
Marvel

❑1, Oct 1993, 1: X-Men 2099. foil cover ... 2.00
❑1/Gold, Oct 1993, Gold edition; 1: X-Men 2099. foil cover ... 3.00
❑1/2nd, Oct 1993, 1: X-Men 2099. foil cover ... 1.75
❑2, Nov 1993 ... 1.50
❑3, Dec 1993, D: Serpentina; Punisher and New Warriors multi-page inserts. ... 1.50
❑4, Jan 1994, 1: The Theatre of Pain ... 1.50
❑5, Feb 1994, Story continued from Ravage 2099 #15; Continued in Doom 2099 #14 ... 1.50
❑6, Mar 1994, 1: The Freakshow ... 1.25
❑7, Apr 1994, (c) ... 1.25
❑8, May 1994, (c) ... 1.50
❑9, Jun 1994 ... 1.50
❑10, Jul 1994 ... 1.50
❑11, Aug 1994 ... 1.50
❑12, Sep 1994 ... 1.50
❑13, Oct 1994 ... 1.50
❑14, Nov 1994 ... 1.50
❑15, Dec 1994 ... 1.50
❑16, Jan 1995 ... 1.50
❑17, Feb 1995 ... 1.50
❑18, Mar 1995 ... 1.50
❑19, Apr 1995, (c) ... 1.50
❑20, May 1995 ... 1.95
❑21, Jun 1995 ... 1.95
❑22, Jul 1995 ... 1.95
❑23, Aug 1995 ... 1.95
❑24, Sep 1995 ... 1.95
❑25, Oct 1995, (2.50)-Double sized ... 2.50
❑25/Variant, Oct 1995, enhanced wraparound cardstock cover ... 3.95
❑26, Nov 1995 ... 1.95

N-MINT

❑27, Dec 1995, A: Herod. A: Doom. Story continued from 2099 Apocalypse and Doom 2099 #36 ... 1.95
❑28, Jan 1996 ... 1.95
❑29, Feb 1996 ... 1.95
❑30, Mar 1996, Story continued in X-Nation #1 ... 1.95
❑31, Apr 1996 ... 1.95
❑32, May 1996, JDu (a) ... 1.95
❑33, Jun 1996, JDu (c); JDu (a) ... 1.95
❑34, Jul 1996, JDu (c); JDu (a) ... 1.95
❑35, Aug 1996, (c); JDu (a); A: Nostromo. Final Issue ... 1.95
❑Special 1, Oct 1995 ... 3.95

X-Men 2099: Oasis
Marvel

❑1, Aug 1996, NN ... 5.95

X-Men Ultra III Preview
Marvel

❑1, Nov 1995, enhanced cardstock cover; previews Fleer card art ... 2.95

X-Men Universe
Marvel

❑1, Dec 1999, contains material originally published as Astonishing X-Men #1, Generation X #55, and Uncanny X-Men #373 ... 4.99
❑2, Jan 2000 ... 4.99
❑3, Feb 2000 ... 4.99
❑4, Mar 2000 ... 4.99
❑5, Apr 2000 ... 4.99
❑6, May 2000 ... 4.99
❑7, Jun 2000 ... 4.99
❑8, Jul 2000 ... 4.99
❑9, Aug 2000 ... 4.99
❑10, Sep 2000 ... 4.99
❑11, Oct 2000 ... 4.99
❑12, Nov 2000 ... 3.99
❑13, Dec 2000 ... 3.99
❑14, Jan 2001 ... 3.99
❑15, Feb 2001 ... 3.99
❑16, Mar 2001 ... 3.99
❑17, Apr 2001 ... 3.99

X-Men Universe: Past, Present and Future
Marvel

❑1, Feb 1999, Wraparound cover ... 2.99

X-Men Unlimited
Marvel

❑1, Jun 1993, V: Siena Blaze; X-Men pinups ... 3.00
❑2, Sep 1993, Magneto story ... 3.00
❑3, Dec 1993, Sabretooth pinup ... 3.00
❑4, Mar 1994, O: Rogue; X-Men story; Nightcrawler storyline continued in Excalibur #76; X-Men pin-ups ... 3.00
❑5, Jun 1994, X-Men story; X-Men pinups ... 3.00
❑6, Sep 1994 ... 3.00
❑7, Dec 1994 ... 3.00
❑8, Oct 1995 ... 3.00
❑9, Dec 1995, V: Bloodscream; X-Men story ... 3.00
❑10, Mar 1996, Age of Apocalypse Beast imprisons and replaces real Beast ... 3.00
❑11, Jun 1996, Magneto and Rogue ... 3.00
❑12, Sep 1996, Onslaught: Impact; Juggernaut imprisoned in Cyttorak Gem ... 2.95
❑13, Dec 1996, X-Men story; Juggernaut story ... 2.95
❑14, Mar 1997, Franklin Richards story. ... 2.99
❑15, Jun 1997, Wolverine vs. Maverick. ... 2.99
❑16, Sep 1997, 1: Primal; V: Bastion; Generation X story ... 2.99
❑17, Dec 1997, V: Sabretooth; Wolverine story ... 2.99
❑18, Mar 1998, Gambit story; Marrow story ... 2.99
❑19, Jun 1998, V: Belasco; Nightcrawler story ... 2.99
❑20, Sep 1998, Generation X story ... 2.99
❑21, Dec 1998, X-Factor story ... 2.99
❑22, Mar 1999, V: Flag-Smasher; X-Men story ... 2.99
❑23, Jun 1999, X-Men story ... 2.99
❑24, Sep 1999, Wolverine story; Magneto story ... 2.99
❑25, Dec 1999, Wolverine story ... 2.99
❑26, Mar 2000, Age of Apocalypse ... 2.99

N-MINT

❑27, Jun 2000 ... 2.99
❑28, Sep 2000, Deadpool story ... 2.99
❑29, Dec 2000, Maximum Security ... 2.99
❑30, Mar 2001 ... 2.99
❑31, Jun 2001 ... 2.99
❑32, Sep 2001 ... 3.50
❑33, Dec 2001 ... 3.50
❑34, May 2002 ... 3.50
❑35, Jun 2002 ... 3.50
❑36, Jul 2002 ... 3.50
❑37, Sep 2002, X-Men story ... 3.50
❑38, Nov 2002, Kitty Pryde story ... 3.50
❑39, Jan 2003, Storm stories ... 3.50
❑40, Feb 2003, Sabretooth story; Mystique story; Juggernaut story; Preview of Incredible Hulk #50 ... 3.50
❑41, Mar 2003, Exiles story; Exiles pinup; X-Statix story; Random mutant story. ... 3.50
❑42, Apr 2003, White Queen story; Moonstar story; Professor X story ... 3.50
❑43, May 2003, New Mutants story; Lockheed the Dragon story ... 3.50
❑44, May 2003, Sammy Pare (Fish Boy) story ... 2.50
❑45, Jun 2003, Alpha Flight story ... 2.50
❑46, Jun 2003, Wolverine stories ... 2.50
❑47, Jul 2003, Psylocke story; Cyclops story ... 2.50
❑48, Jul 2003, Wolverine story; Mystique story ... 2.50
❑49, Aug 2003; Nightcrawler story ... 2.50
❑50, Sep 2003; Wolverine story; Wolverine pinup; Rogue pinup; Storm pinup ... 2.50

X-Men Unlimited
Marvel

❑1, Apr 2004, Sage storyline; X-Men story ... 2.99
❑2, Jun 2004, Bishop storyline continued in District X #1; Jubilee story ... 2.99
❑3, Aug 2004, Gambit story; Cannonball story ... 2.99
❑4, Oct 2004, Juggernaut story; White Queen and Wolverine story ... 2.99
❑5, Dec 2005, Wolverine story ... 2.99
❑6, Feb 2005, X-Men storyline; Rogue and Marvel Girl storyline ... 2.99
❑7, Apr 2005 ... 2.99
❑8, Jun 2005 ... 2.99
❑9, Jul 2005; Wolverine; Iceman; Cover by Mark Brooks is "after Byrne" ... 2.99
❑10, Aug 2005 ... 2.99
❑11, Dec 2005 ... 2.99
❑12, Feb 2006 ... 2.99
❑13, Apr 2006 ... 2.99
❑14, Jun 2006 ... 2.99

X-Men vs. the Avengers
Marvel

❑1, Apr 1987, 1: Titanium Man II. A: Magneto ... 4.00
❑2, May 1987, A: Magneto ... 3.00
❑3, Jun 1987, A: Magneto ... 3.00
❑4, Jul 1987, KP (c); KP (a); A: Magneto ... 3.00

X-Men vs. the Brood
Marvel

❑1, Sep 1996, wraparound cover ... 2.95
❑2, Oct 1996, wraparound cover ... 2.95

X-Men/Wildc.A.T.S: The Dark Age
Marvel

❑1/A, May 1998, cardstock cover ... 4.50
❑1/B, May 1998, alternate cardstock cover ... 4.50

X-Men: Wrath of Apocalypse
Marvel

❑1, Feb 1996, reprints X-Factor #65-68; Nathan Summers sent into future (becomes Cable) ... 4.95

X-Nation 2099
Marvel

❑1, Mar 1996, foil cover ... 3.95
❑2, Apr 1996 ... 1.95
❑3, May 1996 ... 1.95
❑4, Jun 1996 ... 1.95
❑5, Jul 1996 ... 1.95
❑6, Aug 1996, Final Issue ... 1.95

X/1999
Viz

❑1 1996, b&w ... 3.00
❑2 1996, b&w ... 2.75

Other grades: Multiply price above by 5/6 for VF/NM • 2/3 for VERY FINE • 1/3 for FINE • 1/5 for VERY GOOD • 1/8 for GOOD

Yosemite Sam

A few pop cultural gags snuck in
©Gold Key

Young All-Stars

Roy Thomas undoes parts of the Crisis
©DC

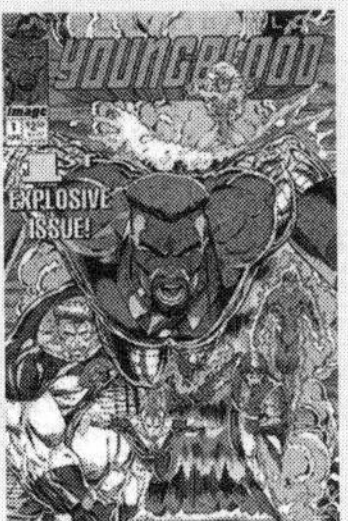

Youngblood

Rob Liefeld's leading title at Image
©Image

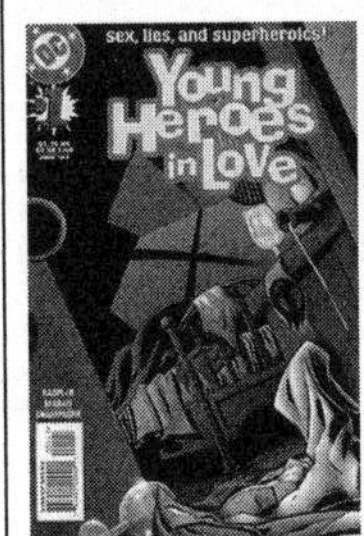

Young Heroes in Love

Goofy people discover super-powers
©DC

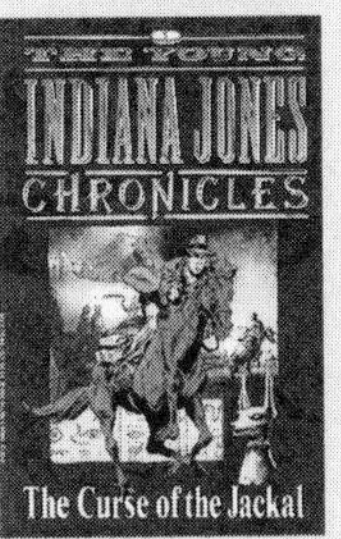

Young Indiana Jones Chronicles

Based on series of television specials
©Dark Horse

	N-MINT
❑3 1996, b&w	2.75
❑4 1996, b&w	2.75
❑5 1996, b&w	2.75
❑6 1996, b&w	2.75

X-O Manowar
Valiant

	N-MINT
❑0, Aug 1993, BL (w); O: X-O Manowar. chromium cover	2.00
❑0/Gold, Aug 1993, Gold logo edition; BL (w); O: X-O Manowar. chromium cover	35.00
❑½, Nov 1994, Mini-comic from Wizard Magazine; Mini-comic from Wizard Magazine; Continued in X-O Manowar #37	8.00
❑½/Gold, Nov 1994	55.00
❑1, Feb 1992, BL (c); BL (a); 1&O: X-O Manowar. 1: Aric Dacia; Pre-Unity	7.00
❑2, Mar 1992, BL (c)	6.00
❑3, Apr 1992, BL (c); A: Solar	6.00
❑4, May 1992, (c); BL (w); 1: Shadowman (cameo, out of costume). A: Harbinger; Pre-Unity	6.00
❑5, Jun 1992	5.00
❑6, Jul 1992, BL (c); BL (w); SD (a)	4.00
❑7, Aug 1992, FM (c); BL (w); FM (a)	3.00
❑8, Sep 1992, BL (w)	3.00
❑9, Oct 1992, (c); BL (w)	2.00
❑10, Nov 1992, BL (w)	1.00
❑11, Dec 1992, BL (w)	1.00
❑12, Jan 1993, BL (w)	1.00
❑13, Feb 1993, BL (w); A: Solar	1.00
❑14, Mar 1993, BL (c); BL (w); (a); A: Turok. V: Raptors	1.00
❑15, Apr 1993, (c); BL (w); A: Turok. V: Raptors	1.00
❑15/Pink, Apr 1993 (c); BL (w)	8.00
❑16, May 1993	1.00
❑17, Jun 1993, BL (c)	1.00
❑18, Jul 1993	1.00
❑19, Aug 1993, Includes serial number coupon for contest	1.00
❑20, Sep 1993, Includes serial number coupon for contest	1.00
❑21, Oct 1993, BL (c); V: Ax; Randy becomes X-O	1.00
❑22, Nov 1993, (c)	1.00
❑23, Dec 1993	1.00
❑24, Jan 1994	1.00
❑25, Feb 1994, with Armorines #0	1.00
❑26, Mar 1994, Ken spotlight	1.00
❑27, Apr 1994, A: Turok	1.00
❑28, May 1994, trading card	2.00
❑29, Jun 1994, A: Turok	1.00
❑30, Aug 1994, A: Solar	1.00
❑31, Sep 1994, (c); New armor	1.00
❑32, Oct 1994, Story continued in The Chaos Effect	1.00
❑33, Nov 1994, BL (c); Chaos Effect Delta 3	1.00
❑34, Dec 1994, (c)	1.00
❑35, Jan 1995	1.00
❑36, Feb 1995, (c); Contains Sneak-Peek Card	2.00
❑37, Mar 1995	1.00
❑38, Mar 1995	1.00
❑39, Mar 1995	1.00
❑40, Mar 1995	1.00
❑41, Apr 1995	1.00
❑42, May 1995, V: Shadowman. contains Birthquake preview	2.00
❑43, Jun 1995	2.00
❑44, Jul 1995, Birthquake	2.00
❑45, Jul 1995, Birthquake	2.00
❑46, Aug 1995	2.00
❑47, Aug 1995, D: Ken Clarkson	2.00
❑48, Sep 1995	2.00
❑49, Sep 1995	2.00
❑50, Oct 1995, cover forms diptych with X-O Manowar #50-O	2.00
❑50/A, Oct 1995, cover forms diptych with X-O Manowar #50-X	2.00
❑51, Nov 1995	2.00
❑52, Nov 1995	2.00
❑53, Dec 1995	2.00
❑54, Dec 1995	2.00
❑55, Jan 1996, (c)	3.00
❑56, Jan 1996	3.00
❑57, Feb 1996	3.00
❑58, Feb 1996, KG (w); V: Hotwire	3.00
❑59, Mar 1996, KG (w); V: Powerhouse	3.00
❑60, Mar 1996, KG, BL (w)	3.00
❑61, Apr 1996, KG (w)	3.00
❑62, Apr 1996, KG (w)	3.00
❑63, May 1996, KG (w); Master Darque acquires X-O armor	4.00
❑64, May 1996, (c); KG (w); PG (a); D: Master Darque	4.00
❑65, Jun 1996, KG (w); X-O armor asserts control over itself	4.00
❑66, Jul 1996, (c); BL (w); D: Ax. D: Gamin. Aric's armor rebels	5.00
❑67, Aug 1996, BG (c); BL (w); BG (a)	7.00
❑68, Sep 1996, BG (c); BL (w); BG (a); Final Issue	12.00
❑YB 1, Apr 1995, 1995 YB; 1995 YB	3.50

X-O Manowar
Acclaim

	N-MINT
❑1, Oct 1996, (c); MWa (w); D: Rand Banion. cover says Feb, indicia says Oct 96	2.50
❑1/Variant, Oct 1996, MWa (w); Painted cover	2.50
❑2, Mar 1997, (c); MWa (w); Donovan Wylie becomes X-O	2.50
❑3, Apr 1997, (c); MWa (w)	2.50
❑4, May 1997, MWa (w)	2.50
❑5, Jun 1997, MWa (w)	2.50
❑6, Jul 1997, MWa (w); V: Magnus	2.50
❑7, Aug 1997, A: New Hard Corps	2.50
❑8, Sep 1997	2.50
❑9, Oct 1997, Return of Hard C.O.R.P.S.	2.50
❑10, Nov 1997, A: Bravado. Avengers #3 homage cover	2.50
❑11, Dec 1997	2.50
❑12, Jan 1998	2.50
❑13, Feb 1998	2.50
❑14, Mar 1998	2.50
❑15, Apr 1998	2.50
❑16, Jan 1998, V: Quantum & Woody. no cover date, indicia says Jan	2.50
❑17, Feb 1998	2.50
❑18, Mar 1998, return of Rand Banion	2.50
❑19, Apr 1998, 1: Master Blaster	2.50
❑20, May 1998	2.50
❑21, Jun 1998, Final Issue	2.50
❑Ashcan 1, Oct 1996, b&w; no cover price; preview of upcoming series	1.00

X-O Database
Valiant

	N-MINT
❑1, Jun 1993, BL (a); no cover price; polybagged with X-O TPB; armor schematics	4.00
❑1/VVSS, Jun 1993	30.00

X-O Manowar/Iron Man: In Heavy Metal
Acclaim / Valiant

	N-MINT
❑1, Sep 1996, crossover with Marvel; concludes in Iron Man/X-O Manowar: In Heavy Metal	2.50

Xombi
DC / Milestone

	N-MINT
❑0, Jan 1994; 1: Xombi. Shadow War	2.50
❑1, Jun 1994, O: Xombi. 1: Catholic Girl. 1: Nun of the Above	2.00
❑1/Platinum, Jun 1994, Platinum cover	3.00
❑2, Jul 1994, 1: Knight of the Spoken Fire	1.75
❑3, Aug 1994	1.75
❑4, Sep 1994	1.75
❑5, Oct 1994	1.75
❑6, Nov 1994	1.75
❑7, Dec 1994	1.75
❑8, Jan 1995	1.75
❑9, Feb 1995	1.75
❑10, Mar 1995	1.75
❑11, Apr 1995	1.75
❑12, May 1995	1.75
❑13, Jun 1995	1.75
❑14, Jul 1995	2.50
❑15, Aug 1995	2.50
❑16, Sep 1995	2.50
❑17, Oct 1995	0.99
❑18, Nov 1995	2.50
❑19, Dec 1995	2.50
❑20, Jan 1996	2.50
❑21, Feb 1996, Giant-size; Final Issue	3.50

X: One Shot to the Head
Dark Horse

	N-MINT
❑1, Aug 1994, b&w; NN; One-shot	2.50

X-Patrol
Marvel / Amalgam

	N-MINT
❑1, Apr 1996, 1: Beastling; 1: Elasti-Girl; 1: Ferro-Man; 1: Niles Cable; 1: Shatterstarfire	1.95

X-Ray Comics
Slave Labor / Amalgam

	N-MINT
❑1, Feb 1998	2.95
❑2, May 1998	2.95
❑3, Apr 1998	2.95

XSE
Marvel

	N-MINT
❑1, Nov 1996, (c); A: Bishop and Shard. Regular cover with Shard getting zapped; Regular cover with Shard and Bishop running	1.95
❑1/A, Nov 1996, A: Bishop and Shard. variant cover	2.50
❑2, Dec 1996, A: Bishop and Shard.	1.95
❑3, Jan 1997, A: Bishop and Shard.	1.95
❑4, Feb 1997, A: Bishop and Shard. final issue	1.95

Other grades: Multiply price above by 5/6 for VF/NM • 2/3 for VERY FINE • 1/3 for FINE • 1/5 for VERY GOOD • 1/8 for GOOD

N-MINT | N-MINT | N-MINT

X-Statix
Marvel

❑1, Sep 2002, 1: Corkscrew 2.99
❑2, Oct 2002 .... 2.25
❑3, Nov 2002 .... 2.25
❑4, Dec 2002 .... 2.25
❑5, Jan 2003, Uncanny X-Men #416 preview 2.25
❑6, Feb 2003, Origin Venus D. Milo 2.25
❑7, Mar 2003 .... 2.25
❑8, Apr 2003 .... 2.99
❑9, May 2003 .... 2.99
❑10, Jun 2003 .... 2.99
❑11, Aug 2003; 1: El Guapo 2.99
❑12, Sep 2003 .... 2.99
❑13, Oct 2003 .... 2.99
❑14, Nov 2003 .... 2.99
❑15, Dec 2003 .... 2.99
❑16, Jan 2004 .... 2.99
❑17, Feb 2004 .... 2.99
❑18, Mar 2004 .... 2.99
❑19, Apr 2004 .... 2.99
❑20, May 2004 .... 2.99
❑21, Jun 2004, vs Avengers 2.99
❑22, Jun 2004, (c); vs. Avengers 2.99
❑23, Jul 2004 .... 2.99
❑24, Aug 2004 .... 2.99
❑25, Sep 2004 .... 2.99
❑26, Oct 2004; Final issue 2.99

X-Statix Presents Dead Girl
Marvel

❑1, Mar 2006 .... 2.99
❑2, Apr 2006 .... 2.99
❑3, Jun 2006 .... 2.99
❑4, Jun 2006 .... 2.99
❑5, Aug 2006 .... 2.99

X-Terminators
Marvel

❑1, Oct 1988, 1: X-Terminators. Inferno. 2.00
❑2, Nov 1988, Inferno 2.00
❑3, Dec 1988, Inferno 2.00
❑4, Jan 1989, Inferno 2.00

X Man With X-Ray Eyes
Gold Key

❑1, Sep 1963 .... 50.00

X-Treme X-Men
Marvel

❑1, Jul 2001 .... 2.99
❑2, Aug 2001, Group Cover 2.99
❑2/A, Aug 2001, Group Cover 2.99
❑2/B, Aug 2001, Psylocke Cover 2.99
❑3, Sep 2001 .... 2.99
❑4, Oct 2001, V: Vargas 2.99
❑5, Nov 2001, 1: Red Lotus 2.99
❑6, Dec 2001, 1: Lifeguard; V: Lady Mastermind; V: Sebastian Shaw 2.99
❑7, Jan 2002, V: Lady Mastermind; V: Sebastian Shaw 2.99
❑8, Feb 2002, V: Sebastian Shaw; V: Lady Mastermind; 'Nuff Said silent issue 2.99
❑9, Mar 2002, V: Lady Mastermind; V: Sebastian Shaw 2.99
❑10, Apr 2002, V: Shaitan 2.99
❑11, May 2002 .... 2.99
❑12, Jun 2002 .... 2.99
❑13, Jul 2002, Call of Duty preview 2.99
❑14, Aug 2002 .... 2.99
❑15, Sep 2002, V: Vargas 2.99
❑16, Sep 2002, V: Vargas 2.99
❑17, Oct 2002, V: Vargas 2.99
❑18, Nov 2002 .... 2.99
❑19, Dec 2002, Continued in X-Treme X-Men X-Pose #1-2 .... 2.99
❑20, Mar 2003, Avengers #65 preview... 2.99
❑21, Apr 2003 .... 2.99
❑22, May 2003 .... 2.99
❑23, May 2003 .... 2.99
❑24, Jun 2003 .... 2.99
❑25, Jul 2003, Ultimate X-Men #34 preview 2.99
❑26, Jul 2003, V: William Stryker; V: Lady Deathstrike; V: Reverend Stryker 2.99
❑27, Aug 2003, V: William Stryker; V: Lady Deathstrike 2.99
❑28, Sep 2003, V: William Stryker; V: Lady Deathstrike 2.99
❑29, Oct 2003, V: William Stryker; V: Lady Deathstrike 2.99
❑30, Oct 2003, V: William Stryker; V: Lady Deathstrike 2.99
❑31, Nov 2003; Rogue returns 2.99
❑32, Dec 2003 .... 2.99
❑33, Dec 2003 .... 2.99
❑34, Jan 2004 .... 2.99
❑35, Jan 2004 .... 2.99
❑36, Feb 2004 .... 3.50
❑37, Feb 2004 .... 3.50
❑38, Feb 2004, V: Masque 3.50
❑39, Feb 2004, V: Masque 3.50
❑40, Mar 2004, V: Manacle; V: Rolling Thunder; V: Bludgeon; V: Cudgel; V: Revenant; V: Bogan 2.99
❑41, Apr 2004, V: Bogan 2.99
❑42, Apr 2004, V: Bogan 2.99
❑43, May 2004 .... 2.99
❑44, May 2004 .... 2.99
❑45, Jun 2004 .... 2.99
❑46, Jun 2004, Final issue; Continued in Uncanny X-Men #444 .... 2.99
❑Ann 2001, Dec 2001, Printed sideways 4.95

X-Treme X-Men: Savage Land
Marvel

❑1, Nov 2001 .... 2.99
❑2, Dec 2001 .... 2.99
❑3, Jan 2001 .... 2.99
❑4, Feb 2001 .... 2.99

X-TV
Comic Zone

❑1, Sep 1998, b&w; Adult 2.95
❑2, Nov 1998, b&w; Adult 2.95

X-23
Marvel

❑1, Jan 2005, White background 7.00
❑1/Variant, Jan 2005 .... 3.00
❑2, Feb 2005 .... 4.00
❑2/Variant, Feb 2005 .... 6.00
❑3, Apr 2005 .... 5.00
❑4, May 2005 .... 4.00
❑5, Jun 2005 .... 2.99

X-Universe
Marvel

❑1, May 1995, After Xavier: The Age of Apocalypse; foil cover 3.50
❑2, Jun 1995, After Xavier: The Age of Apocalypse; foil cover 3.50

XXXenophile
Palliard

❑1, Jun 1989, b&w; PF (c); PF (w); PF (a); It's Not Cheap, But It Is Easy 8.00
❑1/2nd, Jun 1989, b&w; PF (c); PF (w); PF (a); It's Not Cheap, But It Is Easy... 2.50
❑1/3rd, Dec 1989, It's Not Cheap, But It Is Easy 2.50
❑2, Dec 1989, b&w; PF (c); PF (w); PF (a); Tales of One Fisted Adventure 5.00
❑2/2nd, Jun 1991, b&w; PF (c); PF (w); PF (a); Tales of One Fisted Adventure; 2nd Printing 2.50
❑3, Jul 1990, b&w; PF (w); PF (a); Just Plane Sex 4.00
❑3/2nd, Mar 1992, b&w; PF (w); PF (a); Just Plane Sex; 2nd Printing 2.50
❑4, Feb 1991, b&w; PF (w); PF (a); Practicing Safe Sex Until We Get It Right 4.00
❑4/2nd, Mar 1993, b&w; PF (c); PF (w); PF (a); 2nd printing 2.95
❑5, Jul 1991, b&w; PF (c); PF (w); PF (a); Bringing Good Things To Life 2.95
❑6, Feb 1992, b&w; PF (c); PF (w); PF (a); Giving The Public What I Want 2.95
❑7, Jul 1992, b&w; PF (c); PF (w); PF (a); It's Okay, It's Art 2.95
❑8, Feb 1993, b&w; PF (c); PF (w); PF (a); The Comic in the Fancy Brown Paper Wrapper 2.95
❑9, Jan 1994, b&w; PF (c); PF (w); PF (a); The Adventures of Le Petit Mort 2.95
❑10, Jan 1995, b&w; PF (c); PF (w); PF (a); trading-card game cover; led to Xxxenophile card game 2.95
❑11, Sep 1998, b&w; PF (c); PF (w); PF (a); New material from Books 1-5; published by Xxxenophile 3.50

XXXenophile Presents
Palliard

❑1, Apr 1992, b&w; Adult 2.95
❑2, Dec 1993, b&w; Adult 2.95
❑3, Aug 1994, b&w; Adult 2.95
❑4, Jul 1995, b&w; Adult 2.95

XXX Women
Fantagraphics / Eros

❑1, b&w 2.95
❑2, b&w 2.95
❑3, b&w 2.95
❑4, b&w 2.95

XYZ Comics
Kitchen Sink

❑1, Jun 1972, b&w 25.00
❑1/2nd, b&w; 2nd printing 12.00
❑1/3rd, b&w; 3rd printing 8.00
❑1/4th, b&w; 4th printing 6.00
❑1/5th, b&w; 5th printing 6.00
❑1/6th, b&w; sixth printing 5.00
❑1/7th, Jan 1987, b&w; seventh printing 3.00

Y2K: The Comic
NEC

❑1, Oct 1999 .... 3.95

Yahoo
Fantagraphics

❑1, Oct 1988; The Jaded Comix Bistro... 2.50
❑2, Oct 1989; In the Company of Longhair 2.25
❑3, Apr 1990 .... 2.00
❑4, Jan 1991; Airpower Through Victory 2.50
❑5, Dec 1991 .... 2.50
❑6, Aug 1992; Take It Off (Topless cover) 2.50

Yakuza
Eternity

❑1, Sep 1987 .... 1.95
❑2, Nov 1987 .... 1.95
❑3, Jan 1988 .... 1.95
❑4, Apr 1988 .... 1.95

Yang
Charlton

❑1, Nov 1973, 1: Yang. Series begins again (reprints) 9.00
❑2, May 1974, Indicia says Vol. 2 #2 .... 5.00
❑3, Jul 1974 .... 5.00
❑4, Sep 1974 .... 5.00
❑5, Nov 1975 .... 5.00
❑6, Feb 1975, Indicia says Vol. 3 #6 .... 5.00
❑7, Apr 1975 .... 5.00
❑8, Jun 1975 .... 5.00
❑9, Sep 1975 .... 5.00
❑10, Nov 1975 .... 5.00
❑11, Jan 1976 .... 5.00
❑12, Mar 1976 .... 5.00
❑13, May 1976, Final issue of original run 5.00
❑15, Sep 1985, Series begins again (reprints); reprints #1 .... 3.00
❑16, Nov 1985, reprints #2 .... 3.00
❑17, Jan 1986, reprints #3 .... 3.00

Yarn Man
Kitchen Sink

❑1, Oct 1989, b&w 2.00

Yawn
Parody

❑1, Sep 1992, b&w; Spawn parody 2.50
❑1/2nd, b&w; 2nd printing 2.50

Yeah!
DC / Homage

❑1, Oct 1999 .... 2.95
❑2, Nov 1999, all copies destroyed 2.95
❑3, Dec 1999 .... 2.95
❑4, Jan 2000 .... 2.95
❑5, Feb 2000 .... 2.95
❑6, Mar 2000 .... 2.95
❑7, Apr 2000 .... 2.95
❑8, May 2000 .... 2.95

Year in Review: Spider-Man
Marvel

❑1, Feb 2000 .... 2.99

Year of the Monkey
Image / Homage

❑1, ca. 1997 .... 2.95
❑2, Oct 1997 .... 2.95

Year One: Batman/Ra's al Ghul
DC

❑1, Jul 2005 .... 5.99
❑2, Sep 2005 .... 5.99

Other grades: Multiply price above by 5/6 for VF/NM • 2/3 for VERY FINE • 1/3 for FINE • 1/5 for VERY GOOD • 1/8 for GOOD

Young Justice

Sort of a teen-age Justice League
©DC

Young Love (DC)

Romance series lasted far into the 1970s
©DC

Y: The Last Man

Last man alive in world full of women
©DC

Yummy Fur

Odd stories cheese off the establishment
©Vortex

Zatanna

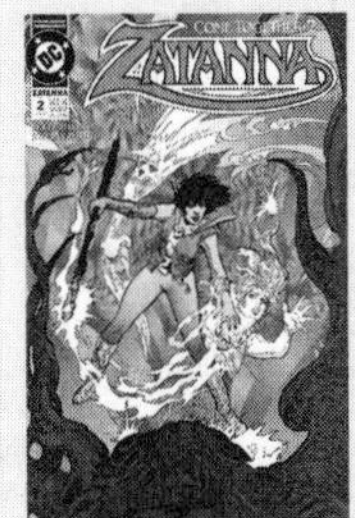

Half-human, half-Atlantean sorceress
©DC

Year One: Batman-Scarecrow
DC

	N-MINT
❑1, Jun 2005	5.99
❑2, Jul 2005	5.99

Yellow Submarine
Gold Key

	N-MINT
❑1, Feb 1969, adapts movie; poster	110.00

Yenny
Alias

	N-MINT
❑1, Dec 2005, b&w	4.99
❑1/Variant, Dec 2005	2.99

Yikes!
Weissman

	N-MINT
❑1, ca. 1995, b&w	2.50
❑2, ca. 1995, b&w	2.50
❑3, ca. 1995, b&w	2.50
❑4, Win 1995, b&w; Winter 1995; b&w	2.50
❑5, ca. 1996; b&w with spot color	2.50

Yikes!
Alternative

	N-MINT
❑1, Nov 1997, b&w; green and white	2.95
❑2, ca. 1998, b&w	2.95

Yogi Bear
Dell / Gold Key

	N-MINT
❑4, Sep 1961	40.00
❑5, Nov 1961	40.00
❑6, Jan 1962	40.00
❑7, Mar 1962	40.00
❑8, May 1962	40.00
❑9, Jul 1962, Last Dell issue	40.00
❑10, Oct 1962, Jellystone Jollies	55.00
❑11, Jan 1963, Jellystone Jollies (Christmas issue)	55.00
❑12, Apr 1963, Jellystone Album	30.00
❑13, Jul 1963, Surprise Party	55.00
❑14, Oct 1963	30.00
❑15, Jan 1964	30.00
❑16, Apr 1964	30.00
❑17, Jul 1964	30.00
❑18, Oct 1964	30.00
❑19, Jan 1965	30.00
❑20, Apr 1965	30.00
❑21, Jul 1965	20.00
❑22, Oct 1965	20.00
❑23, Jan 1966	20.00
❑24, Apr 1966	20.00
❑25, Jul 1966	20.00
❑26, Oct 1966	20.00
❑27, Jan 1967	20.00
❑28, Apr 1967	20.00
❑29, Jul 1967	20.00
❑30, Oct 1967	20.00
❑31, Jan 1968	20.00
❑32, Apr 1968	15.00
❑33, Jul 1968	15.00
❑34, Oct 1968	15.00
❑35, Jan 1969	15.00
❑36, Apr 1969	15.00
❑37, Jul 1969	15.00
❑38, Oct 1969	15.00
❑39, Jan 1970	15.00
❑40, Apr 1970	15.00
❑41, Jul 1970	15.00
❑42, Oct 1970	15.00

Yogi Bear
Charlton

	N-MINT
❑1, Nov 1970	22.00
❑2, ca. 1971	15.00
❑3, ca. 1971	15.00
❑4, May 1971	12.00
❑5, ca. 1971	12.00
❑6, ca. 1971	12.00
❑7, Sum 1971	15.00
❑8, ca. 1971	12.00
❑9, Feb 1972	12.00
❑10, Mar 1972	12.00
❑11, ca. 1972	8.00
❑12, ca. 1972	8.00
❑13, ca. 1972	8.00
❑14, ca. 1972	8.00
❑15, ca. 1972	8.00
❑16, ca. 1973	8.00
❑17, ca. 1973	8.00
❑18, Jun 1973	8.00
❑19, ca. 1973	8.00
❑20, Oct 1973	8.00
❑21, Dec 1973	6.00
❑22, Sep 1974	6.00
❑23, ca. 1974	6.00
❑24, Feb 1975	6.00
❑25, Apr 1975	6.00
❑26, Jun 1975	6.00
❑27, Aug 1975	6.00
❑28, Oct 1975	6.00
❑29, Dec 1975	6.00
❑30, Feb 1976	6.00
❑31, Apr 1976	6.00
❑32, ca. 1976	6.00
❑33, Sep 1976	6.00
❑34, ca. 1976	6.00
❑35, ca. 1977, Final Issue	6.00

Yogi Bear
Marvel

	N-MINT
❑1, Nov 1977	6.00
❑2, Jan 1978	4.00
❑3, Mar 1978	4.00
❑4, May 1978	4.00
❑5, Jul 1978	4.00
❑6, Sep 1978	3.00
❑7, Nov 1978	3.00
❑8, Jan 1979	3.00
❑9, Mar 1979	3.00

Yogi Bear
Harvey

	N-MINT
❑1, Sep 1992	1.50
❑2, Jan 1993	1.25
❑3, Jun 1993	1.25
❑4, Sep 1993	1.25
❑5, Dec 1993	1.25
❑6, Mar 1994	1.25

Yogi Bear
Archie

	N-MINT
❑1, May 1997	1.50

Yosemite Sam
Gold Key / Whitman

	N-MINT
❑1, Dec 1970	35.00
❑2, Mar 1971	20.00
❑3, Jun 1971	20.00
❑4, Sep 1971	20.00
❑5, Nov 1971	20.00
❑6, Mar 1972	15.00
❑7, Apr 1972	15.00
❑8, Jun 1972	15.00
❑9, Aug 1972	15.00
❑10, Oct 1972	15.00
❑11, Dec 1972	10.00
❑12, Feb 1973	10.00
❑13, Mar 1973	10.00
❑14, ca. 1973	10.00
❑15, ca. 1973	10.00
❑16, ca. 1973	10.00
❑17, Oct 1973	10.00
❑18, Dec 1973	10.00
❑19, Feb 1974	10.00
❑20, Apr 1974	10.00
❑21, ca. 1974	4.00
❑22, ca. 1974	4.00
❑23, ca. 1974	4.00
❑24, ca. 1974	4.00
❑25, Dec 1974	4.00
❑26, Feb 1975	4.00
❑27, Apr 1975	4.00
❑28, Jun 1975	4.00
❑29, Jul 1975	4.00
❑30, Aug 1975	4.00
❑31, Sep 1975	4.00
❑32, Oct 1975	4.00
❑33, Dec 1975	4.00
❑34, Feb 1976	4.00
❑35, Apr 1976	4.00
❑36, Jun 1976	4.00
❑37, Jul 1976	4.00
❑38, Aug 1976	4.00
❑39, Sep 1976	4.00
❑40, Oct 1976	4.00
❑41, Dec 1976	4.00
❑42, Feb 1977	4.00
❑43, Apr 1977	4.00
❑44, Jun 1977	4.00
❑45, Jul 1977	4.00
❑46, Aug 1977	4.00
❑47, Sep 1977	4.00
❑48, Oct 1977	4.00
❑49, Dec 1977	4.00
❑50, Feb 1978	4.00
❑51, Apr 1978	2.50
❑52, Jun 1978	2.50
❑53, Jul 1978	2.50
❑54, Aug 1978	2.50
❑55, Sep 1978	2.50
❑56, Oct 1978	2.50
❑57, Dec 1978	2.50
❑58, Feb 1979	2.50
❑59, Apr 1979	2.50
❑60, Jun 1979	2.50
❑61, Jul 1979	2.50
❑62, Aug 1979	2.50
❑63, Sep 1979	2.50
❑64, Oct 1979	2.50
❑65, Dec 1979	2.50
❑66, ca. 1980	8.00
❑67, ca. 1980; Whitman	8.00
❑68, ca. 1980	20.00
❑69, ca. 1980	17.00

Other grades: Multiply price above by 5/6 for VF/NM • 2/3 for VERY FINE • 1/3 for FINE • 1/5 for VERY GOOD • 1/8 for GOOD

N-MINT

❑70, ca. 1980 .... 17.00
❑71, Feb 1981 .... 10.00
❑72, ca. 1981 .... 10.00
❑73, Sep 1981 .... 10.00
❑74, Oct 1981 .... 10.00
❑75, Jan 1982 .... 10.00
❑76, Feb 1982 .... 10.00
❑77, Mar 1982 .... 10.00
❑78, Apr 1982 .... 10.00
❑79, Jul 1983; 90263 .... 17.00
❑80, Aug 1983; 90263 .... 17.00
❑81, Feb 1984; Final Issue; 90263 .... 17.00

Yotsuba!
ADV Manga

❑1, ca. 2005 .... 9.99
❑2, ca. 2005 .... 9.99
❑3, ca. 2005 .... 9.99

You and Your Big Mouth
Fantagraphics

❑1, ca. 1993, b&w 2.50
❑2, ca. 1994, b&w 2.50
❑3, ca. 1994, b&w 2.50
❑4, Aug 1994, b&w; Anthology 2.50

You Can Draw Manga
Antarctic

❑1, Feb 2004 .... 4.95
❑2, Mar 2004 .... 4.95
❑3, Apr 2004 .... 4.95
❑4, May 2004 .... 4.95
❑5, Jun 2004 .... 4.95
❑6, Jun 2004 .... 4.95
❑7, Jul 2004 .... 4.95
❑8, Aug 2004 .... 4.95
❑9, Sep 2004 .... 4.95
❑10, Oct 2004 .... 4.95
❑11, Nov 2004 .... 4.95
❑12, Dec 2005 .... 4.95

Young All-Stars
DC

❑1, Jun 1987, 1: Iron Munroe. 1: Flying Fox. 1: Fury. Iron Munroe cover 3.00
❑2, Jul 1987, Tsunami cover 2.50
❑3, Aug 1987, Flying Fox cover 2.50
❑4, Sep 1987, Neptune Perkins cover 1.75
❑5, Oct 1987, Fury cover 1.75
❑6, Nov 1987, Dan the Dyna-Mite cover 1.75
❑7, Dec 1987 .... 1.50
❑8, Jan 1988, Millennium 1.50
❑9, Feb 1988, Millennium 1.50
❑10, Mar 1988, (c); O: Iron Munro 1.50
❑11, Apr 1988, (c); O: Iron Munro 1.50
❑12, May 1988, V: Deathbolt 1.50
❑13, Jun 1988 .... 1.50
❑14, Jul 1988, (c); V: Deathbolt; V: Ultra Humanite 1.50
❑15, Aug 1988, (c); V: Deathbolt 1.50
❑16, Sep 1988, O: Neptune Perkins 1.50
❑17, Oct 1988, O: Neptune Perkins 1.50
❑18, Nov 1988 .... 1.50
❑19, Dec 1988, (c) 1.75
❑20, Dec 1988, TD (a); O: Flying Fox 1.75
❑21, Jan 1988, (c) 1.75
❑22, Jan 1989, (c); 1: Fireball; 1: The Kuei; 1: Phantasmo; O: Phantasmo; O: Fireball; O: Kuei; O: Squire 1.75
❑23, Mar 1989, V: Axis Amerika 1.75
❑24, Apr 1989, (c); V: Baron Blitzkreig; V: Sumo; V: Axis Amerika 1.75
❑25, May 1989, V: Axis Amerika; V: Baron Blitzkrieg 1.75
❑26, Jun 1989, (c) 1.75
❑27, Jul 1989, Mr. America becomes Americommando 1.75
❑28, Aug 1989, (c); All-Star Squadron pin-up 1.75
❑29, Sep 1989 .... 1.75
❑30, Oct 1989, (c) 1.75
❑31, Nov 1989, Final Issue, Tigress pin-up 1.75
❑Ann 1, ca. 1988, (c); JKu, MGu (a); A: Infinity Inc.. 1988; Private Lives 3.00

Young Avengers
Marvel

❑1, Apr 2005; 1: Iron Lad; 1: Hulkling; 1: Patriot; 1: Asgardian; 1: Kate Bishop 10.00
❑1/DirCut, Apr 2005 .... 6.00
❑1/Conv, Apr 2005; Wizard World Los Angeles 2005 .... 15.00

N-MINT

❑2, May 2005; O: Iron Lad 7.00
❑3, Jun 2005; V: Growing Man 4.00
❑4, Jul 2005; V: Kang; Vision returns 2.99
❑5, Aug 2005; V: Kang 2.99
❑6, Sep 2005; 1: Stature 2.99
❑8, Dec 2005; V: Mr. Hyde; Nick Fury's Howling Commandos preview 2.99
❑9, Jan 2006; V: Super-Skrull 2.99
❑10, Apr 2006, 1: Speed; V: Super-Skrull 2.99
❑11, Jun 2006, V: Kree; V: Skrulls 2.99
❑12, Sep 2006, 1: Kate Bishop as Hawkeye; V: Electro; Masked Marvel story 2.99

Young Avengers Special
Marvel

❑1, Feb 2006 .... 2.99

Youngblood
Image

❑0, Dec 1992, RL (c); RL (w); RL (a); wraparound cover 2.00
❑0/Gold, Dec 1992, RL (c); RL (w); RL (a); gold 4.00
❑1, Apr 1992, Flip-book; RL (w); RL (a); 1: Chapel. 1: Youngblood. 1: The Four. trading card; First comic by Image Comics 2.50
❑1/2nd, May 1992, RL (w); RL (a); 1: Chapel. 1: Youngblood. 1: The Four. gold border; First comic by Image Comics 2.00
❑2, Jul 1992, RL (c); RL (w); RL (a); 1: Kirby. 1: Shadowhawk. 1: Darkthorn. 1: Prophet. 1: Berserkers. red logo; cover says Jun, indicia says Jul 2.50
❑2/A, Jul 1992, RL (c); RL (w); RL (a); 1: Kirby. 1: Shadowhawk. 1: Darkthorn. 1: Prophet. 1: Berserkers. green logo; cover says Jun, indicia says Jul 2.50
❑3, Aug 1992, Flip-book; RL (w); RL (a); 1: Showdown. 1: Supreme; 40 pages; Flip-book 2.50
❑4, Feb 1993, RL (c); RL (w); RL (a); 1: Pitt; 40 pages 2.50
❑5, Jul 1993, backed with Brigade #4 .... 2.00
❑6, Jun 1994, Includes poster 3.50
❑7, Jul 1994, V: Overtkill; Continued in Team Youngblood #11 .... 2.50
❑8, Sep 1994 .... 2.50
❑9, Sep 1994, Image X-Month 2.50
❑9/A, Sep 1994, Image X-Month 2.50
❑10, Dec 1994, A: Spawn. D: Chapel 2.50
❑SS 1, Super Special 4.00
❑YB 1, Jul 1993, YB 1; 1: Kanan; 1: Tyrax; YB 1; Pinups 3.00

Youngblood
Image

❑1, Sep 1995 .... 2.50
❑2, Oct 1995 .... 2.50
❑2/A, Oct 1995, alternate cover 2.50
❑3, Nov 1995, Babewatch 2.50
❑3/A, Nov 1995, Shaft cover 2.50
❑3/B, Nov 1995, Cougar cover 2.50
❑3/C, Nov 1995, Knightsabre cover 2.50
❑4, Jan 1996, polybagged with Riptide card 2.50
❑5, Feb 1996 .... 2.50
❑5/A, Feb 1996, alternate cover 2.50
❑6, Mar 1996 .... 2.50
❑7, Apr 1996, Shadowhunt 2.50
❑8, May 1996 .... 2.50
❑9, Jun 1996 .... 2.50
❑10, Jul 1996, flipbook with Blindside #1 preview 2.50
❑11, ca. 1996 .... 2.50
❑12, ca. 1996 .... 2.50
❑13, ca. 1996 .... 2.50
❑14, ca. 1997 .... 2.50
❑15, ca. 1997, Final Issue 2.50

Youngblood
Awesome

❑1/A, Feb 1998, AMo (w); Blue Awesome logo, Orange Youngblood logo 2.50
❑1/B, Feb 1998, AMo (w); Purple Awesome and Youngblood logos 2.50
❑1/C, Feb 1998, AMo (w); Teal Awesome and Youngblood logos 2.50
❑1/D, Feb 1998, AMo (w); White Awesome logo, Yellow Youngblood logo; Shaft in foreground 2.50
❑1/E, Feb 1998, AMo (w); Blue Awesome logo, White Youngblood logo 2.50

N-MINT

❑1/F, Feb 1998, AMo (w); White Awesome and Youngblood logos 2.50
❑1/G, Feb 1998, AMo (w); White Awesome logo, Yellow Youngblood logo; Suprema in foreground 2.50
❑1/H, Feb 1998, AMo (w); Baby Shaft on cover; Blue Awesome logo 2.50
❑1/I, Feb 1998, AMo (w); Orange Awesome logo, Red Youngblood logo 2.50
❑1/J, Feb 1998, AMo (w); White Awesome logo, Teal Youngblood logo; Suprema in foreground 2.50
❑1/K, Feb 1998, AMo (w); 3 women on cover; White Awesome logo, Teal Youngblood logo 2.50
❑1/L, Feb 1998, AMo (w); Teal Awesome logo, Yellow Youngblood logo 2.50
❑1/M, Feb 1998, AMo (w); A! List exclusive; Foil logo; Three women posing on cover, leaning against wall 3.50
❑1/N, Feb 1998, AMo (w); 1+ issue 2.50
❑2, Aug 1998, AMo (w) 2.50

Youngblood: Strikefile
Image

❑1, Apr 1993, RL (c); RL (w); RL (a); 1: The Allies. 1: Giger. 1: Glory; Flipbook 2.50
❑1/Gold, Apr 1993, Gold edition; RL (c); RL (w); RL (a); 1: Glory; 1: Allies; 1: Giger; Flipbook 2.50
❑2, Jul 1993, RL (c); RL (w); RL (a) 2.50
❑2/Gold, Jul 1993, Gold edition; RL (c); RL (w); RL (a); Diehard V: Super Patriot 2.50
❑3, Sep 1993, RL (w); RL (a) 2.50
❑4, Oct 1993, RL (c); RL (w) 2.50
❑5, Jul 1994 .... 2.50
❑6, Aug 1994, O: Bad Rock; Masada protects anti-semite 2.50
❑7, Sep 1994 .... 2.50
❑8, Nov 1994, KG, KB (w); KG (a); Busiek short story; cover says Oct 2.50
❑9, Nov 1994 .... 2.50
❑10, Dec 1994 .... 2.50
❑11, Feb 1995, RL (w); polybagged with card 2.50

Youngblood/X-Force
Image

❑1/A, Jul 1996, prestige format; crossover with Marvel 4.95
❑1/B, Jul 1996, alternate cover (black background) 4.95
❑1/C, Jul 1996, alternate cover 4.95

Youngbrother
Multicultural

❑1, Apr 1994 .... 2.25

Young Bug
Zoo Arsonist

❑1, ca. 1996 .... 2.95
❑2, ca. 1996 .... 2.95
❑3, ca. 1996 .... 2.95

Young Death
Fleetway-Quality

❑1, ca. 1992 .... 2.95
❑2, ca. 1992 .... 2.95
❑3, ca. 1993 .... 2.95

Young Dracula: Prayer of the Vampire
Boneyard

❑1, ca. 1997 .... 2.95
❑2, Feb 1998 .... 2.95
❑3, ca. 1998 .... 2.95
❑4, ca. 1998 .... 2.95

Young Girl on Girl: Passion and Fashion
Angel

❑1; Adult 3.00
❑1/Nude; Nude edition; Adult 3.95

Young Gun
AC

❑1, b&w; reprints Billy the Kid story 2.95

Young Guns 2004 Sketch Book
Marvel

❑1, Jan 2005 .... 3.99

Young Guns Reloaded Sketchbook
Marvel

❑1, Feb 2007 .... 3.99

Other grades: Multiply price above by 5/6 for VF/NM • 2/3 for VERY FINE • 1/3 for FINE • 1/5 for VERY GOOD • 1/8 for GOOD

Young Hero
AC

- ❑1, Dec 1989, b&w; reprints Daredevil #72 (1950) 2.50
- ❑2, Aug 1990, b&w; reprints Little Wise Guys 2.75

Young Heroes in Love
DC

- ❑1, Jun 1997, 1: Young Heroes 1.75
- ❑1/Ltd., Jun 1997, Wizard "Certified Authentic" edition; Autographed by Dan Raspler 6.00
- ❑2, Jul 1997 .... 1.75
- ❑3, Aug 1997, A: Superman 1.75
- ❑4, Sep 1997 .... 1.75
- ❑5, Oct 1997, Genesis 1.75
- ❑6, Nov 1997 .... 1.75
- ❑7, Dec 1997, Face cover 1.95
- ❑8, Jan 1998, V: Scarecrow 1.95
- ❑9, Feb 1998 .... 1.95
- ❑10, Mar 1998 .... 1.95
- ❑11, Apr 1998 .... 1.95
- ❑12, May 1998 .... 1.95
- ❑13, Jun 1998 .... 1.95
- ❑14, Jul 1998 .... 1.95
- ❑15, Aug 1998, O: Monstergirl 1.95
- ❑16, Sep 1998, D: Lou 1.95
- ❑17, Oct 1998, O: Monstergirl; Smokey revealed as alien; Young Heroes V: Smokey 2.50
- ❑1000000, Nov 1998, Final Issue 3.00

Young Indiana Jones Chronicles
Dark Horse

- ❑1, Feb 1992, KB (w); A: T.E. Lawrence. Egypt May 1908 .... 3.00
- ❑2, Mar 1992, KB (w); A: Pancho Villa. Mexico March 1916 .... 2.50
- ❑3, Apr 1992, KB (w); GM (a); A: Teddy Roosevelt 2.50
- ❑4, May 1992, KB (w); GM (a) 2.50
- ❑5, Jun 1992, KB (w) 2.50
- ❑6, Jul 1992, KB (w) 2.50
- ❑7, Aug 1992, KB (w) 2.50
- ❑8, Sep 1992, KB (w) 2.50
- ❑9, Oct 1992, KB (w) 2.50
- ❑10, Dec 1992, KB (w) 2.50
- ❑11, Jan 1993, KB (w) 2.50
- ❑12, Feb 1993, KB (w) 2.50

Young Indiana Jones Chronicles
Hollywood

- ❑1, ca. 1992, reprints Dark Horse issues #1 and 2 for newsstand distribution 2.50
- ❑2, ca. 1992, reprints Dark Horse issues #3 and 4 for newsstand distribution 2.50
- ❑3, ca. 1992, Reprints 2.50

Young Justice
DC

- ❑1, Sep 1998, PD (w); 1: Supercycle. 1: Mighty Endowed. A: Superboy. A: Martian Manhunter. A: Impulse. A: Robin 4.00
- ❑2, Oct 1998, PD (w); 1: Rip Roar. A: Ali Ben Styn; V: Rip Roar 3.00
- ❑3, Dec 1998, PD (w); A: Mr. Mxyzptlk. V: Mr. Mxyzptlk; Halloween issue 3.00
- ❑4, Jan 1999, PD (w); 1: Harm. 1: Tora. A: Wonder Girl. A: Spirit. A: Arrowette. V: Harm. 1: Harm; 1: Harm (Billy Hayes) 3.00
- ❑5, Feb 1999, PD (w); V: Harm 3.00
- ❑6, Mar 1999, PD (w); A: Wonder Woman. A: Superman. A: Justice League of America. A: Flash III (Wally West). A: Martian Manhunter. A: Green Lantern. A: Batman. A: Aquaman. V: Despero 2.50
- ❑7, Apr 1999, PD (w); A: Nightwing. A: Max Mercury. Parent/Teacher conference 2.50
- ❑8, May 1999, A: Psyba-Rats 2.50
- ❑9, Jun 1999, PD (w) 2.50
- ❑10, Jul 1999, PD (w) 2.50
- ❑11, Aug 1999, PD (w) 2.50
- ❑12, Sep 1999, PD (w); Continued in Supergirl #36 .... 2.50
- ❑13, Oct 1999, PD (w); A: Supergirl. Continued from Supergirl #36; Continued in Supergirl #37 .... 2.50
- ❑14, Nov 1999, PD (w); A: Harm. Day of Judgment 2.50
- ❑15, Dec 1999, PD (w); Arrowette spotlight 2.50
- ❑16, Jan 2000, PD (w); 1: Old Justice 2.50
- ❑17, Feb 2000, PD (w); Arrowette leaves 2.50
- ❑18, Mar 2000, PD (w); 1: Point Men 2.50
- ❑19, Apr 2000, PD (w); 1: Empress; Continued in Young Justice Sins of Youth #1; 1: Empress (Anita Fite); V: Point Men 2.50
- ❑20, Jun 2000, PD (w); A: Li'l Lobo. A: JLA. Continued from Young Justice: Sins of Youth #2 .... 2.50
- ❑21, Jul 2000, (c); PD (w); V: Klarion the Witch Boy 2.50
- ❑22, Aug 2000, PD (w); Robin story; Red Tornado story, Robin story, Wonder Girl story 2.50
- ❑23, Sep 2000, PD (w); at Olympic Games 2.50
- ❑24, Oct 2000, PD (w); Misprinted copies exist with duplicated ad 2.50
- ❑25, Nov 2000, PD (w); at Olympic Games 2.50
- ❑26, Dec 2000, PD (w) 2.50
- ❑27, Jan 2001, PD (w) 2.50
- ❑28, Feb 2001, PD (w); A: Forever People 2.50
- ❑29, Mar 2001, PD (w); A: Forever People. A: Darkseid 2.50
- ❑30, Apr 2001, PD (w) 2.50
- ❑31, May 2001, PD (w); Silent issue 2.50
- ❑32, Jun 2001, PD (w); O: Empress 2.50
- ❑33, Jul 2001, PD (w) 2.50
- ❑34, Aug 2001, PD (w) 2.50
- ❑35, Sep 2001, PD (w); Our Worlds At War; All-Out War 2.50
- ❑36, Oct 2001, PD (w); Our Worlds At War; Casualties of War 2.50
- ❑37, Nov 2001, PD (w); A: Darkseid. A: Granny Goodness. V: Granny Goodness; V: Female Furies; V: Darkseid 2.50
- ❑38, Dec 2001, PD (w); Joker: Last Laugh crossover 2.50
- ❑39, Jan 2002, PD (w) 2.50
- ❑40, Feb 2002, PD (w); Christmas story 2.50
- ❑41, Mar 2002, PD (w); A: The Ray. Lifesaver/Mad insert 2.50
- ❑42, Apr 2002, PD (w); A: Spectre. O: Secret 2.50
- ❑43, May 2002, PD (w) 2.50
- ❑44, Jun 2002, PD (w); Continued in Impulse #85 .... 2.50
- ❑45, Jul 2002, PD (w); V: Bedlam; Continued in Impulse #86 .... 2.50
- ❑46, Aug 2002, PD (w) 2.50
- ❑47, Sep 2002, PD (w) 2.50
- ❑48, Oct 2002, PD (w) 2.50
- ❑49, Nov 2002, PD (w) 2.50
- ❑50, Dec 2002, PD (w); V: Devastation; Giant-size 3.95
- ❑51, Jan 2003, PD (w); Includes preview of Aquaman (6th Series) #1 .... 2.50
- ❑52, Feb 2003, PD (w) 2.50
- ❑53, Mar 2003, PD (w) 2.50
- ❑54, Apr 2003 .... 2.75
- ❑55, May 2003, D: Slo-bo, Final issue; Final issue 2.75
- ❑1000000, Nov 1998, PD (w); 1: Young Justice Legion S; Published between Young Justice #2 and #3 .... 3.50
- ❑GS 1, May 1999, PD (w); 80 pages 4.95

Young Justice Secret Files
DC

- ❑1, Jan 1999, Includes profiles of Young Justice members; Includes timeline 4.95

Young Romance
DC

- ❑125, Sep 1963, Series continued from Young Romance (Prize) #124 .... 42.00
- ❑126, Nov 1963 .... 18.00
- ❑127, Jan 1964 .... 18.00
- ❑128, Mar 1964 .... 18.00
- ❑129, May 1964 .... 18.00
- ❑130, Jul 1964 .... 18.00
- ❑131, Sep 1964 .... 18.00
- ❑132, Nov 1964 .... 18.00
- ❑133, Jan 1965 .... 18.00
- ❑134, Mar 1965 .... 18.00
- ❑135, May 1965 .... 18.00
- ❑136, Jul 1965 .... 18.00
- ❑137, Sep 1965 .... 18.00
- ❑138, Nov 1965 .... 18.00
- ❑139, Jan 1966 .... 18.00
- ❑140, Mar 1966 .... 18.00
- ❑141, May 1966 .... 15.00
- ❑142, Jul 1966 .... 15.00
- ❑143, Sep 1966 .... 15.00
- ❑144, Nov 1966 .... 15.00
- ❑145, Jan 1967 .... 15.00
- ❑146, Mar 1967 .... 15.00
- ❑147, May 1967 .... 15.00
- ❑148, Jul 1967 .... 15.00
- ❑149, Sep 1967 .... 15.00
- ❑150, Nov 1967 .... 15.00
- ❑151, Jan 1968 .... 12.00
- ❑152, Mar 1968 .... 12.00
- ❑153, May 1968 .... 12.00
- ❑154, Jul 1968 .... 12.00
- ❑155, Sep 1968 .... 12.00
- ❑156, Nov 1968 .... 12.00
- ❑157, Jan 1969 .... 12.00
- ❑158, Mar 1969 .... 12.00
- ❑159, May 1969 .... 12.00
- ❑160, Jul 1969 .... 10.00
- ❑161, Sep 1969 .... 10.00
- ❑162, Nov 1969 .... 10.00
- ❑163, Jan 1970 .... 10.00
- ❑164, Mar 1970 .... 10.00
- ❑165, May 1970 .... 10.00
- ❑166, Jul 1970 .... 10.00
- ❑167, Sep 1970 .... 10.00
- ❑168, Nov 1971 .... 10.00
- ❑169, Jan 1971 .... 10.00
- ❑170, Mar 1971, 64 pages 10.00
- ❑171, May 1971, 64 pages 9.00
- ❑172, Jul 1971, 64 pages 9.00
- ❑173, Aug 1971 .... 9.00
- ❑174, Sep 1971 .... 9.00
- ❑175, Oct 1971 .... 9.00
- ❑176, Nov 1971 .... 9.00
- ❑177, Dec 1971 .... 9.00
- ❑178, Jan 1972 .... 9.00
- ❑179, Feb 1972 .... 9.00
- ❑180, Mar 1972 .... 9.00
- ❑181, Apr 1972 .... 9.00
- ❑182, May 1972 .... 9.00
- ❑183, Jun 1972 .... 9.00
- ❑184, Jul 1972 .... 9.00
- ❑185, Aug 1972 .... 9.00
- ❑186, Sep 1972 .... 9.00
- ❑187, Oct 1972 .... 9.00
- ❑188, Nov 1972 .... 9.00
- ❑189, Dec 1972 .... 9.00
- ❑190, Jan 1973 .... 9.00
- ❑191, Feb 1973 .... 9.00
- ❑192, Mar 1973 .... 9.00
- ❑193, May 1973 .... 9.00
- ❑194, Aug 1973 .... 9.00
- ❑195, Oct 1973 .... 9.00
- ❑196, Dec 1973 .... 9.00
- ❑197, Feb 1974 .... 9.00
- ❑198, Apr 1974, 100 pages 20.00
- ❑199, Jun 1974, 100 pages 20.00
- ❑200, Aug 1974, 100 pages 20.00
- ❑201, Oct 1974, 100 pages 20.00
- ❑202, Dec 1974 .... 8.00
- ❑203, Feb 1975 .... 8.00
- ❑204, Apr 1975 .... 8.00
- ❑205, Jun 1975 .... 8.00
- ❑206, Aug 1975 .... 8.00
- ❑207, Oct 1975 .... 8.00
- ❑208, Dec 1975, Final Issue 8.00

Youngspud
Spoof

- ❑1 .... 2.95

Young Witches
Fantagraphics / Eros

- ❑1, May 1991, b&w; 24 pages; Adult 2.50
- ❑2, Jun 1991, b&w; 24 pages; Adult 2.50
- ❑3, Jul 1991, b&w; (c); Adult 2.50
- ❑4, Sep 1991, b&w; Adult 2.50

Young Witches VI: Wrath of Agatha
Fantagraphics

- ❑1 .... 3.95
- ❑2 .... 3.95

Young Witches: London Babylon
Fantagraphics / Eros

❑1, ca. 1992, b&w 3.50
❑2, ca. 1992, b&w 3.50
❑3, ca. 1992, b&w 3.50
❑4, ca. 1992, b&w 3.50
❑5, ca. 1992, b&w 3.50
❑6, ca. 1992, b&w 3.50

You're Under Arrest!
Dark Horse / Manga

❑1, Dec 1995, b&w 2.95
❑2, Jan 1996, b&w 2.95
❑3, Feb 1996, b&w 2.95
❑4, Mar 1996, b&w 2.95
❑5, Apr 1996, b&w 2.95
❑6, May 1996, b&w 2.95
❑7, Jun 1996, b&w 2.95
❑8, Jul 1996, b&w 2.95

Your Hytone Comix
Apex Novelties

❑1, Feb 1971, b&w; underground 8.00

Y's Guys
October

❑1, Jul 1999 .... 2.95

Y: The Last Man
DC / Vertigo

❑1, Sep 2002 .... 30.00
❑2, Oct 2002 .... 15.00
❑3, Nov 2002 .... 5.00
❑4, Dec 2002 .... 4.00
❑5, Jan 2003 .... 4.00
❑6, Feb 2003 .... 2.95
❑7, Mar 2003 .... 2.95
❑8, Apr 2003 .... 2.95
❑9, May 2003 .... 2.95
❑10, Jun 2003 .... 2.95
❑11, Jul 2003 .... 2.95
❑12, Aug 2003 .... 2.95
❑13, Sep 2003 .... 2.95
❑14, Oct 2003 .... 2.95
❑15, Nov 2003 .... 2.95
❑16, Jan 2004 .... 2.95
❑17, Feb 2004 .... 2.95
❑18, Mar 2004 .... 2.95
❑19, Apr 2004 .... 2.95
❑20, May 2004 .... 2.95
❑21, Jun 2004 .... 2.95
❑22, Jul 2004 .... 2.95
❑23, Aug 2004 .... 2.95
❑24, Sep 2004 .... 2.95
❑25, Oct 2004 .... 2.95
❑26, Nov 2004 .... 2.95
❑27, Dec 2004 .... 2.95
❑28, Jan 2005 .... 2.95
❑29, Feb 2005 .... 2.95
❑30, Mar 2005 .... 2.95
❑31, Apr 2005 .... 2.95
❑32, May 2005; Price increase 2.99
❑33, Jun 2005 .... 2.99
❑34, Jul 2005 .... 2.99
❑35, Aug 2005 .... 2.99
❑36, Sep 2005 .... 2.99
❑37, Oct 2005 .... 2.99
❑38, Dec 2005 .... 2.99
❑39, Jan 2006 .... 2.99
❑40, Jan 2006 .... 2.99
❑41, Mar 2006, American Virgin #1 preview pages included 2.99
❑42, Mar 2006 .... 2.99
❑43, May 2006 .... 2.99
❑44, Jun 2006 .... 2.99
❑45, Jul 2006 .... 2.99
❑46, Aug 2006 .... 2.99
❑47, Sep 2006 .... 2.99
❑48, Oct 2006, Includes preview of Vertigo Deadman series 2.99
❑49, Nov 2006 .... 2.99
❑50, Dec 2006 .... 2.99
❑51, Jan 2007 .... 2.99
❑52, Mar 2007 .... 2.99
❑53 .... 2.99
❑54 .... 2.99
❑55 .... 2.99
❑56 .... 2.99
❑57 .... 2.99
❑58 .... 2.99
❑59 .... 2.99
❑60 .... 2.99

Yuggoth Cultures
Avatar

❑1, Oct 2003 .... 3.95
❑2, Nov 2003 .... 3.95
❑3, Dec 2003 .... 3.95

Yu-Gi-Oh!
Viz

❑1 2003 .... 7.95

Yu-Gi-Oh!: Duelist
Viz

❑1, Feb 2005 .... 7.95
❑2, Mar 2005 .... 7.95
❑3, Apr 2005 .... 7.95
❑4, May 2005 .... 7.95
❑5, Jun 2005 .... 7.95
❑6, Jul 2005 .... 7.95
❑7, Aug 2005 .... 7.95
❑8, Sep 2005; D: Maximillion J. Pegasus 7.95
❑9, Oct 2005 .... 7.95

Yummy Fur
Vortex

❑1, Dec 1986, b&w; reprint mini-comics #1-3 .... 6.00
❑2 1986, b&w; reprint mini-comics #4-6; no date of publication; says #4 in indicia 5.00
❑3, Feb 1987, b&w; reprint mini-comic #7 .... 4.00
❑4, Apr 1987, b&w 4.00
❑5, Jun 1987, b&w 4.00
❑6, Aug 1987, b&w 3.00
❑7 1987, b&w 3.00
❑8, Nov 1987, b&w 3.00
❑9 1988, b&w 3.00
❑10, May 1988, b&w 3.00
❑11, Jul 1988, b&w 2.50
❑12 1988, b&w; no date of publication 2.50
❑13, Nov 1988, b&w 2.50
❑14, Jan 1989, b&w 2.50
❑15, Mar 1989, b&w 2.50
❑16, Jun 1989, b&w 2.50
❑17, Aug 1989, b&w 2.50
❑18, Oct 1989, b&w 2.50
❑19, Jan 1990, b&w 2.50
❑20, Apr 1990, b&w 2.50
❑21, Jun 1990, b&w 2.50
❑22, Sep 1990, b&w 2.50
❑23, Dec 1990, b&w 2.50
❑24 1991, b&w 2.50
❑25, Jul 1991, b&w 2.50
❑26, Oct 1991, b&w 2.50
❑27 1992, b&w 2.50
❑28, May 1992, b&w 2.50
❑29, Aug 1992, b&w 2.50
❑30, Apr 1993, b&w 2.50
❑31 1993, b&w 2.50
❑32, Jan 1994, b&w; Drawn & Quarterly Publishes 2.95

Yuppies from Hell
Marvel

❑1, b&w 2.95

Yuppies, Rednecks and Lesbian Bitches From Mars
Fantagraphics / Eros

❑1 1997, b&w; Adult 2.95
❑2 1997, b&w; Adult 2.95
❑3 1997, b&w; Adult 2.95
❑4 1997, b&w; Adult 2.95
❑5 1998, b&w; Adult 2.95
❑6 1998, b&w; Adult 2.95
❑7, May 1998, b&w; Adult 2.95

Yuri Monogatari
-Ism

❑1, ca. 2005; b&w 15.00

YuYu Hakusho
Viz

❑1, Jun 2003 .... 7.95
❑2, Oct 2003 .... 7.95
❑3, Feb 2004 .... 7.95
❑4, Jun 2004 .... 7.95
❑5, Oct 2004 .... 7.95
❑6, Feb 2005 .... 7.95
❑7, Jun 2005 .... 7.95
❑8, Oct 2005 .... 7.95

Z
Keystone Graphics

❑1, Nov 1994, b&w 2.75
❑2, Jul 1995, b&w 2.75
❑3, Nov 1995, b&w 2.75

Zaibatsu Tears
Limelight

❑1, ca. 2000, b&w 2.95
❑2, ca. 2000 .... 2.95
❑3, ca. 2000 .... 2.95

Zatanna
DC

❑1, Jul 1993, (c) 2.00
❑2, Aug 1993, (c); Zatanna gets new costume 2.00
❑3, Sep 1993 .... 2.00
❑4, Oct 1993, (c) 2.00

Zatanna: Everyday Magic
DC / Vertigo

❑1, May 2003 .... 5.95

Zatanna Special
DC

❑1, ca. 1987, V: Allura; ca. 1987 .... 2.00

Zatch Bell!
Viz

❑1, Aug 2005 .... 9.99
❑2, Sep 2005 .... 9.99
❑3, Oct 2005 .... 9.99

Zaza the Mystic
Avalon

❑1 .... 2.95

Zealot
Image

❑1, Aug 1995 .... 2.50
❑2, Oct 1995 .... 2.50
❑3, Nov 1995 .... 2.50

Zell Sworddancer
3-D Zone

❑1, b&w 2.00

Zell, Sworddancer
Thoughts & Images

❑1, Jul 1986, b&w 2.00

Zendra
Penny-Farthing

❑1, Jan 2002 .... 2.95
❑2, Feb 2002 .... 2.95
❑3, Mar 2002 .... 2.95
❑4, Apr 2002 .... 2.95

Zen Illustrated Novella
Entity

❑1 .... 2.95
❑2 .... 2.95

Zen, Intergalactic Ninja
Zen

❑1, Nov 1987, b&w 3.00
❑1/2nd, ca. 1988; 2nd printing 2.00
❑2, ca. 1988, b&w 2.00
❑3, ca. 1988, b&w 2.00
❑3/2nd, ca. 1988, b&w; 2nd printing 2.00
❑4, ca. 1988, b&w 2.00
❑5, ca. 1988, b&w 2.00
❑6, ca. 1988, b&w 2.00

Zen, Intergalactic Ninja
Zen

❑1, ca. 1990, b&w 2.00
❑2, ca. 1990, b&w 2.00
❑3, ca. 1990, b&w 2.00
❑4, ca. 1990, b&w 2.00

Zen, Intergalactic Ninja
Zen

❑1, ca. 1992, b&w 2.25
❑2, ca. 1992, b&w 2.25
❑3, ca. 1992, b&w 2.25
❑4, ca. 1992, b&w 2.25
❑5, ca. 1992, b&w 2.25
❑Holiday 1, ca. 1992, b&w; Flip-book; Christmas Special 2.95

Zen Intergalactic Ninja
Archie

❑1, May 1992 .... 1.25
❑2 1992 .... 1.25
❑3 1992 .... 1.25

Zero Zero

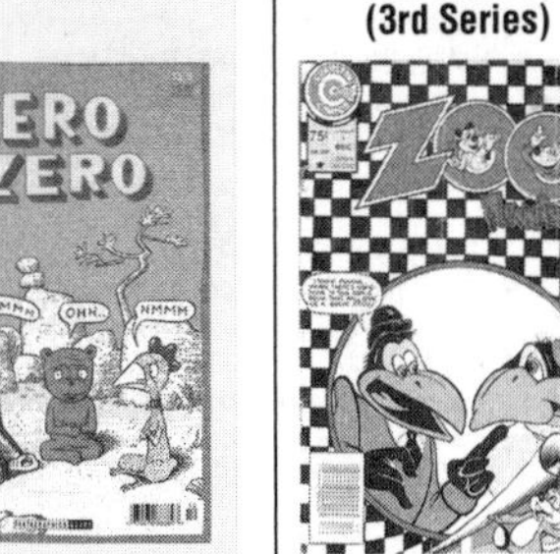

Spotlights experimental cartoonists
©Fantagraphics

Zoo Funnies (3rd Series)

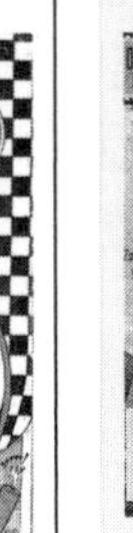

One-shot reprints strips from earlier runs
©Charlton

Zorro (Dell)

Dell issues were based on the Disney TV show
©Dell

Zot!

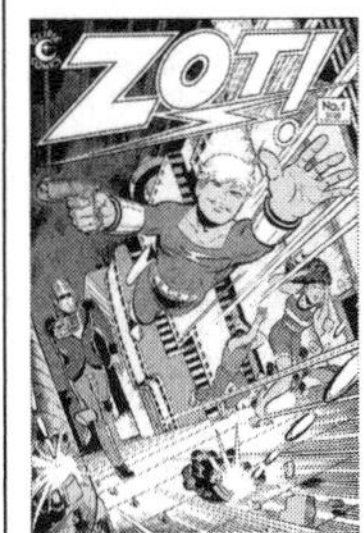

Hero crosses over to our world
©Eclipse

ZZZ

Funny sleepwalker from Alan Bunce
©Alan Bunce

N-MINT

Zen Intergalactic Ninja
Archie

❑1, Sep 1992, O: Zen Intergalactic Ninja ... 1.25
❑2, Oct 1992 ... 1.25
❑3, Dec 1992 ... 1.25
❑4, ca. 1993 ... 1.25
❑5, ca. 1993 ... 1.25
❑6, ca. 1993 ... 1.25
❑7, ca. 1993 ... 1.25

Zen Intergalactic Ninja
Express / Entity

❑0, Jun 1993; 1: Nira X. Gray trim around outside cover ... 3.00
❑0/A, Jun 1993, b&w; 1: Nira X. foil cover ... 2.95
❑0/B, Jun 1993, b&w; 1: Nira X. chromium cover ... 3.50
❑0/Ltd., Jun 1993, b&w; 1: Nira X. Printing limited to 3,000 copies; All-gold trim ... 3.00
❑1, ca. 1993, b&w ... 3.00
❑1/Variant, ca. 1993, b&w; Chromium, die-cut cover ... 3.95
❑2, ca. 1994, b&w ... 3.00
❑3, ca. 1994, b&w ... 3.00
❑4, ca. 1994 ... 3.00
❑Ashcan 1, ca. 1993, b&w; no cover price; contains previews of Zen: Hazardous Duty and Zen: Tour of the Universe ... 1.00
❑Spring 1, ca. 1994; Spring Spectacular ... 2.95

Zen Intergalactic Ninja All-New Color Special
Express / Entity

❑0, ca. 1994, Chronium Cover ... 3.50

Zen Intergalactic Ninja Color
Express / Entity

❑1, ca. 1994, diecut foil cover ... 3.95
❑2, ca. 1994 ... 3.95
❑3, ca. 1994 ... 3.95
❑4, ca. 1994 ... 2.50
❑5, ca. 1994 ... 2.50
❑6, ca. 1995 ... 2.50
❑7, ca. 1995, says #6a on cover, #7 in indicia ... 2.95

Zenith: Phase I
Fleetway-Quality

❑1 ... 2.00
❑2 ... 2.00
❑3 ... 2.00

Zenith: Phase II
Fleetway-Quality

❑1 ... 1.95
❑2 ... 1.95

Zen: The New Adventures
Zen

❑1, ca. 1997 ... 2.50

Zero
Zero Comics

❑1, Mar 1975, b&w; Adult ... 3.00
❑2, Mar 1975, b&w; 36 pages, with print run of 10000 copies; Adult ... 3.00
❑3, May 1976, b&w; 36 pages with print run of 10000 copies; Adult ... 3.00

Zero Girl
Homage

❑1, Feb 2001 ... 2.95
❑2, Mar 2001 ... 2.95
❑3, Apr 2001 ... 2.95
❑4, May 2001 ... 2.95
❑5, Jun 2001 ... 2.95

Zero Girl: Full Circle
DC / Homage

❑1, Jan 2004 ... 2.95
❑2, Feb 2004 ... 2.95
❑3, Mar 2004 ... 2.95
❑4, Apr 2004 ... 2.95
❑5, May 2004 ... 2.95

Zero Hour
Dog Soup

❑1, Apr 1995, b&w; says Pat Leidy's Catfight on cover ... 2.95

Zero Hour: Crisis in Time
DC

❑4, Sep 1994, JOy (a); (#1 in sequence) ... 2.00
❑3, Sep 1994, JOy (a); D: Atom. D: Hourman. remainder of Justice Society of America aged; (#2 in sequence) ... 2.00
❑2, Sep 1994, JOy (a); (#3 in sequence) ... 2.00
❑1, Sep 1994, JOy (a); 1: Parallax. 1: David Knight. 1: Jack Knight. Silver Age Atom de-aged; (#4 in sequence) ... 3.00
❑0, Sep 1994, JOy (a); V: Extant. contains Zero Hour checklist and new DC timeline foldout; (#5 in sequence) ... 2.00
❑Ashcan 1, ca. 1994, Ashcan Preview ... 1.00

Zero Patrol
Continuity

❑1, Nov 1984, NA (c); NA (w); NA (a); O: The Zero Patrol. 1: The Zero Patrol ... 2.00
❑2, Feb 1985, NA (c); NA (w); NA (a) ... 2.00

Zero Patrol
Continuity

❑1, ca. 1987 ... 2.00
❑2, Nov 1987 ... 2.00
❑3, Apr 1988, Includes Shaman back-up story ... 2.00
❑4, Mar 1989 ... 2.00
❑5, May 1989 ... 2.00

Zero Street
Amaze Ink

❑1, Sep 2000 ... 2.95

Zero Tolerance
First

❑1, Oct 1990 ... 2.25
❑2, Nov 1990 ... 2.25
❑3, Dec 1990; Vigil ... 2.25
❑4, Jan 1991 ... 2.25

Zero Zero
Fantagraphics

❑1, Mar 1995, b&w ... 4.00
❑2, May 1995, b&w ... 4.00
❑3, Jul 1995, b&w ... 4.00
❑4, Aug 1995, b&w; issue number determined by back cover cartoon ... 4.00
❑5, Sep 1995, b&w; issue number determined by back cover cartoon ... 4.00
❑6, Nov 1995, b&w ... 4.00
❑7, Jan 1996, b&w ... 4.00
❑8, Mar 1996, b&w; issue number determined by back cover cartoon ... 5.95
❑9, May 1996, b&w; issue number determined by back cover cartoon ... 3.95
❑10, Jul 1996, b&w; cover says Jul 96, indicia says May ... 3.95
❑11, Aug 1996, b&w ... 3.95
❑12, Sep 1996, b&w ... 3.95
❑13, Nov 1996, b&w ... 3.95
❑14, Jan 1997, b&w ... 3.95
❑15, Mar 1997, b&w; Bosnia prequel ... 3.95
❑16, Apr 1997, b&w ... 3.95
❑17, Jun 1997, b&w ... 3.95
❑18, Jul 1997, b&w ... 3.95
❑19, Aug 1997, b&w ... 3.95
❑20, Sep 1997, b&w and color ... 3.95
❑21, Nov 1997, b&w ... 3.95
❑22, Jan 1998, b&w ... 3.95
❑23, Mar 1998, b&w ... 3.95
❑24, Sum 1998, b&w; Summer 1998 ... 3.95
❑25, Fal 1998, b&w; Fall 1998 ... 3.95
❑26, ca. 1998, b&w ... 3.95

Zetraman
Antarctic

❑1, Sep 1991, b&w ... 1.95
❑2, Oct 1991, b&w ... 1.95
❑3, Feb 1992, b&w ... 1.95

Zetraman: Revival
Antarctic

❑1, Oct 1993 ... 2.75
❑2, Dec 1993 ... 2.75
❑3, Aug 1995 ... 2.75

Zillion
Eternity

❑1, Apr 1993, b&w ... 2.50
❑2, May 1993, b&w ... 2.50
❑3, Jun 1993, b&w ... 2.50
❑4, Jul 1993, b&w ... 2.50

Zip Comics
Cozmic

❑1; Adult; ca. 1973 ... 4.00

Zippy Quarterly
Fantagraphics

❑1, ca. 1993, b&w ... 4.95
❑2, ca. 1993, b&w ... 4.95
❑3, ca. 1993, b&w; strip reprint ... 3.50
❑4, ca. 1994, b&w; strip reprint ... 3.50
❑5, ca. 1994, b&w; strip reprint ... 3.50
❑7, Aug 1994, b&w; strip reprint ... 3.50
❑8, Nov 1994, b&w; strip reprint ... 3.50
❑12, Dec 1995, b&w; strip reprint ... 3.95
❑13, Aug 1996, b&w; cardstock cover; strip reprint ... 3.95

Zodiac P.I.
Tokyopop

❑1, Jul 2003, b&w; printed in Japanese format ... 9.99

Zölasträya and the Bard
Twilight Twins

❑1, Jan 1987, b&w ... 1.70
❑2, ca. 1987, b&w ... 1.70
❑3, ca. 1987, b&w ... 1.70
❑4, ca. 1987, b&w ... 1.70
❑5, ca. 1987, b&w ... 1.70

Other grades: Multiply price above by 5/6 for VF/NM • 2/3 for VERY FINE • 1/3 for FINE • 1/5 for VERY GOOD • 1/8 for GOOD

N-MINT

Zombie
Marvel

❑1, Dec 2006 ... 3.99
❑2, Jan 2007 ... 3.99
❑3, Feb 2007 ... 3.99
❑4, Mar 2007 ... 3.99

Zombie 3-D
3-D Zone

❑1; NN ... 3.95

Zombie Boy
Antarctic

❑1, Nov 1996, b&w; wraparound cover ... 2.95
❑2, ca. 1997, b&w ... 2.95
❑3, ca. 1997, b&w ... 2.95

Zombie Boy Rises Again
Timbuktu

❑1, Jan 1994, b&w; Collects Zombie Boy #1 and Zombie Boy's Hoodoo Tales #1; Beverly Hillbillies cameo ... 2.50

Zombie Boy
Timbuktu

❑1, b&w ... 1.50

Zombie King
Image

❑0, Aug 2005 ... 2.95

Zombie Love
ZuZupetal

❑1 ... 2.50
❑2 ... 2.50
❑3 ... 2.50

Zombies!
Idea & Design Works

❑1, Jun 2006 ... 3.99
❑2, Jul 2006 ... 3.99
❑3, Aug 2006 ... 3.99
❑4, Sep 2006 ... 3.99
❑5, Oct 2006 ... 3.99

Zombies: Eclipse of the Undead
Idea & Design Works

❑1, Nov 2006 ... 3.99
❑2, Jan 2007 ... 3.99

Zombies vs. Robots
Idea & Design Works

❑1, Nov 2006 ... 3.99

Zombie War
Tundra

❑1, ca. 1992 ... 3.50

Zombie War
Fantaco

❑1, ca. 1992, b&w ... 3.50
❑2, ca. 1992, b&w; Wraparound cover ... 3.50

Zombie War: Earth Must Be Destroyed
Fantaco

❑1, ca. 1993, b&w ... 2.95
❑1/CS, ca. 1993, b&w; trading card ... 2.95
❑2, ca. 1993, b&w ... 2.95
❑3, ca. 1993, b&w ... 2.95
❑4, ca. 1993, b&w ... 2.95

ZombieWorld: Champion of the Worms
Dark Horse

❑1, Sep 1997, b&w ... 2.95
❑2, Oct 1997, b&w ... 2.95
❑3, Nov 1997, b&w ... 2.95

ZombieWorld: Dead End
Dark Horse

❑1, Jan 1998, b&w ... 2.95
❑2, Feb 1998, b&w ... 2.95

ZombieWorld: Eat Your Heart Out
Dark Horse

❑1, Apr 1998, b&w; NN; One-shot ... 2.95

ZombieWorld: Home for the Holidays
Dark Horse

❑1, Dec 1997, b&w; NN; One-shot ... 2.95

ZombieWorld: Tree of Death
Dark Horse

❑1, Jun 1999, b&w ... 2.95
❑2, Aug 1999, b&w ... 2.95
❑3, Sep 1999, b&w ... 2.95
❑4, Oct 1999, b&w ... 2.95

N-MINT

ZombieWorld: Winter's Dregs
Dark Horse

❑1, May 1998, b&w ... 2.95
❑2, Jun 1998, b&w ... 2.95
❑3, Jul 1998, b&w ... 2.95
❑4, Aug 1998, b&w ... 2.95

Zomboy
Inferno

❑1, Aug 1996, b&w ... 2.95

Zomoid Illustories
3-D Zone

❑1, b&w; not 3-D ... 2.50

Zone
Dark Horse

❑1, b&w ... 2.00

Zone Continuum
Caliber

❑1, b&w ... 2.95
❑2, b&w ... 2.95

Zone Zero
Planet Boy

❑1, b&w ... 2.95

Zoot!
Fantagraphics

❑1, Nov 1992, b&w ... 2.50
❑2, Mar 1993, b&w ... 2.50
❑3, May 1993, b&w ... 2.50
❑4, Jul 1993, b&w ... 2.50
❑5, Sep 1993, b&w ... 2.50
❑6, Nov 1993, b&w ... 2.50

Zorann: Star-Warrior!
Blue Comet

❑0, May 1994, b&w; May-94 ... 2.95
❑1, ca. 1994, b&w ... 2.00

Zori J's 3-D Bubble Bath
3-D Zone

❑1, b&w; NN; b&w ... 3.95

Zori J's Super-Swell Bubble Bath Adventure-Oh Boy!
3-D Zone

❑1, b&w; NN ... 2.95

Zorro
Gold Key

❑1, Jan 1966 ... 70.00
❑2, May 1966 ... 38.00
❑3, Sep 1966 ... 38.00
❑4, Dec 1966, Reprints from Zorro (Dell) #9 ... 38.00
❑5, Mar 1967 ... 34.00
❑6, Jun 1967 ... 34.00
❑7, Sep 1967 ... 34.00
❑8, Dec 1967, Reprints from Four Color Comics (2nd Series) #933 ... 28.00
❑9, Mar 1968 ... 28.00

Zorro
Marvel

❑1, Dec 1990, FM (c); FM (a); O: Zorro ... 3.00
❑2, Jan 1991 ... 2.00
❑3, Feb 1991 ... 2.00
❑4, Mar 1991 ... 2.00
❑5, Apr 1991 ... 2.00
❑6, May 1991 ... 2.00
❑7, Jun 1991 ... 2.00
❑8, Jul 1991 ... 2.00
❑9, Aug 1991 ... 2.00
❑10, Sep 1991, ATh (c) ... 2.00
❑11, Oct 1991, ATh (c) ... 2.00
❑12, Nov 1991, ATh (c); Final Issue ... 2.00

Zorro
Topps

❑0, Nov 1993, 1: Buck Wylde ... 2.50
❑1, Jan 1994, FM (c); 1: Machete ... 3.50
❑2, Feb 1994, 1: Lady Rawhide (out of costume) ... 8.00
❑3, Mar 1994, 1: Lady Rawhide (in costume) ... 3.00
❑4, Apr 1994, MGr (c); 1: Moonstalker ... 3.00
❑5, May 1994, KG, JSt (c); KG (a); A: Lady Rawhide ... 3.00
❑6, Jun 1994 ... 3.00
❑7, Jul 1994, PG (c); A: Lady Rawhide ... 2.50
❑8, Aug 1994, GP (c); GP (a); A: Lady Rawhide ... 2.50

N-MINT

❑9, Sep 1994 ... 2.50
❑10, Oct 1994, A: Lady Rawhide ... 2.95
❑11, Nov 1994, A: Lady Rawhide. Wraparound cover; Final Issue ... 2.50

Zot!
Eclipse

❑1, Apr 1984, (c); 1: Jenny Weaver. 1: Zot!. Color issues begin ... 5.00
❑2, May 1984, 1: Dekko (cameo). 1: 9-Jack-9 ... 2.50
❑3, Jun 1984, 1: Dekko (full) ... 2.50
❑4, Jul 1984, (c); O: Zot! ... 2.50
❑5, Aug 1984, Wordless panels Inside front cover in b&w ... 2.50
❑6, Nov 1984 ... 2.50
❑7, Dec 1984, KB (w); DS (a); The Magic Shop back-up features begin ... 2.50
❑8, Mar 1985, (c) ... 2.50
❑9, May 1985 ... 2.50
❑10, Jul 1985, (c) ... 2.50
❑10½, Mini-comic ... 2.50
❑11, Jan 1987, b&w; Black & white issues begin ... 2.50
❑12, Mar 1987, b&w (c) ... 2.25
❑13, May 1987 ... 2.25
❑14, Jul 1987 ... 2.25
❑14.5; Adventures of Zot! in Dimension 10 1/2, The ... 2.25
❑15, Oct 1987 ... 2.25
❑16, Dec 1987 ... 2.25
❑17, Feb 1988 ... 2.25
❑18, Apr 1988 ... 2.25
❑19, Jun 1988 ... 2.25
❑20, Jun 1988 ... 2.25
❑21, Aug 1988; V: Blotch ... 2.25
❑22, Oct 1988; V: Blotch ... 2.25
❑23, Nov 1988; V: 9-Jack-9 ... 2.25
❑24, Dec 1988 ... 2.25
❑25, Feb 1989 ... 2.25
❑26, Apr 1989; V: 9-Jack-9; V: Dekko; V: Dr. Bellows; V: Devoes; V: Zybox; V: Blotch ... 2.25
❑27, Jun 1989 ... 2.25
❑28, Sep 1989 ... 2.25
❑29, Dec 1989 ... 2.25
❑30, Mar 1990 ... 2.25
❑31, May 1990 ... 2.25
❑32, Jul 1990 ... 2.25
❑33, Oct 1990; Lesbian friend comes out to Jenny ... 2.25
❑34, Dec 1990 ... 2.25
❑35, Mar 1991; Jenny and Zot kiss ... 2.25
❑36, Jul 1991; Final Issue; Zot returns home ... 2.95

Zu
Mu

❑1, Feb 1992; NN; One-shot ... 3.95

Zu
Mu

❑1, Jan 1995, b&w ... 2.95
❑2, Mar 1995, b&w ... 2.95
❑3, May 1995, b&w ... 2.95
❑4, Jul 1995, b&w ... 2.95
❑5, Sep 1995, b&w ... 2.95
❑6, Nov 1995, b&w ... 2.95
❑7, Jan 1996, b&w ... 2.95
❑8, Mar 1996, b&w ... 2.95
❑9, May 1996, b&w ... 2.95
❑10, Jul 1996, b&w ... 2.95
❑11, Sep 1996, b&w ... 2.95
❑12, Nov 1996, b&w ... 2.95
❑13, Jan 1997, b&w ... 2.95
❑14, Mar 1997, b&w ... 2.95
❑15, May 1997, b&w ... 2.95
❑16, Jul 1997, b&w ... 2.95
❑17, Sep 1997, b&w ... 2.95
❑18, Nov 1997, b&w ... 2.95
❑19, Jan 1998, b&w ... 2.95

Zwanna, Son of Zulu
Dark Zulu Lies

❑1 ... 2.00

ZZZ
Alan Bunce

❑1, Mar 2000, b&w ... 2.35

Other grades: Multiply price above by 5/6 for VF/NM • 2/3 for VERY FINE • 1/3 for FINE • 1/5 for VERY GOOD • 1/8 for GOOD